WEBSTER'S NEW WORLD™ DICTIONARY AND THESAURUS

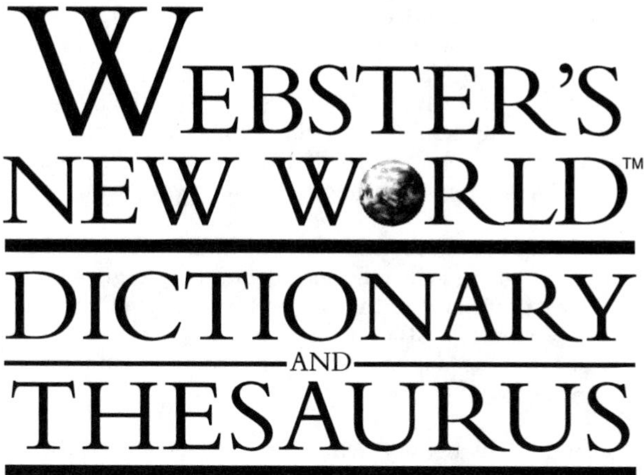

WEBSTER'S NEW WORLD™ DICTIONARY AND THESAURUS

SECOND EDITION

Compiled by the Editors of
Webster's New World Dictionaries

Michael Agnes
Editor in Chief

With Principal Thesaurus Text by
Charlton Laird

Wiley Publishing, Inc.

For general information on our other products and services please contact our Customer Care Department within the U.S. at 800-762-2974, outside the U.S. at 317-572-3993 or fax 317-572-4002.

Wiley also publishes its books in a variety of electronic formats. Some content that appears in print may not be available in electronic books.

Library of Congress Cataloging-in-Publication Data:
Webster's New World dictionary and thesaurus / compiled by the staff of Webster's New World Dictionary ; Michael Agnes, editor in chief ; with principal thesaurus text by Charlton Laird.— 2nd ed.
p. cm.
ISBN 0-7645-6339-4 (hardcover). — ISBN 0-7645-6545-1 (paperback).
1. English language—Dictionaries. 2. English language—Synonyms and antonyms. I. Agnes, Michael. II. Laird, Charlton Grant, 1901-1984.
PE1628 .W56314 2002
423—dc21

00-051364

Manufactured in the United States of America

15 14 13

CONTENTS

WEBSTER'S NEW WORLD

Editor in Chief
Michael Agnes

Project Editors
Andrew N. Sparks
Donald Stewart

Editors
Jonathan L. Goldman
James E. Naso
Katherine Soltis
Stephen P. Teresi
Laura Borovac Walker

Database Administrator
Donald Stewart

Administrative and Data Processing
Cynthia M. Sadonick
Betty Dziedzic Thompson

Citation Readers
Batya Jundef
Joan Komic

Manufacturing Coordinator
Paul Gilchrist

Prepress Production
Kristine Leonardo
Kathie Schutte

Database Service and Principal Typesetting
Thury O'Connor
Lexi-Comp, Inc.

FOREWORD

Webster's New World Dictionary and Thesaurus was first published in 1996 and quickly proved an immensely useful language reference work for people from all walks of life — students, office professionals, in fact, anyone needing a concise, up-to-date dictionary combined with a full-length thesaurus in a single volume.

The dictionary portion of this Second Edition draws on our flagship *Webster's New World College Dictionary*, Fourth Edition, published in 1999. That work, updated annually, provides comprehensive, up-to-date coverage of the newest terms entering our vocabulary. For this derived work, more than 3,000 new entries have been added. Specially commissioned fonts have been used to improve page clarity and readability. The thesaurus section derives from Charlton Laird's *Webster's New World Thesaurus,* first published in 1971 and comprehensively updated several times since then. Thesaurus entries in the previous edition have been thoroughly reviewed and augmented.

Readers who found the previous work a useful reference guide to the English language will appreciate an important innovation in the Second Edition: the inclusion of biographical and geographical entries. These entries fall conveniently within the single alphabetical listing, making it unnecessary for a user to consult separate appendixes to find them. Finally, extensive reference tables are incorporated in the back of the book.

We recommend a careful reading of the two sections of the Guide to the Use of This Book, which begins on the following page. It gives a clear explanation of how to access the wealth of information stored within the dictionary and thesaurus entries.

The Second Edition is the ideal portable reference work for our time. Every entry demonstrates the expertise of Webster's New World's staff of lexicographers, with their combined 150 years of experience in editing dictionaries and thesauruses.

Michael Agnes
Editor in Chief

GUIDE TO THE USE OF THIS BOOK

THE DICTIONARY

I. GUIDE WORDS

The two guide words at the top of each page indicate the alphabetical range of entries on that page. The first and last main entry words in the dictionary portion of a page serve as the guide words.

II. THE MAIN ENTRY WORD

A. Arrangement of Entries—All main entries, including single words, hyphenated and unhyphenated compounds, proper names, prefixes, suffixes, combining forms, and abbreviations, are listed in strict alphabetical order and are set in large boldface type.

a[2] (ə; *stressed,* ā) ***adj.*** ...
a[3] *abbrev.* **1** about **2** ...
a-[2] *prefix* ...
aard·vark (ärd′värk′) ***n.*** ...
Aar·on (er′ən) ***n.*** *Bible* ...
AB[1] (ā′bē′) ***n.*** a blood type
AB[2] *abbrev.* **1** Alberta (Canada) **2** ...
ab- [L] *prefix* ...
a·back (ə bak′) ***adv.*** [Archaic] backward; back —**taken aback** ...

In biographical entries only the last, or family, name is used in alphabetization; but when two or more persons have the same family name, they appear within the entry block in alphabetical order by first names.

John·son (jän′sen) **1 An·drew** ... **2 Lyn·don Baines** ... **3 Samuel** ...

Biographical and geographical names that are spelled the same way are given separate entry blocks.

Idiomatic phrases after a main entry are also listed alphabetically within each group.

fly[1] (flī) ***vi.*** ... **—let fly (at)** ... **—on the fly** ...

B. Alternative Spellings and Variant Forms—When different spellings of a word are some distance apart alphabetically, the definition appears with the spelling most frequently used, and the other spellings are cross-referred to this entry. If two commonly used alternative spellings are alphabetically close to each other, they appear as a joint boldface entry, but the order of entry does not necessarily indicate that the form entered first is "more correct" or is preferred.

the·a·ter or **the·a·tre** (thē′ə tər) ***n.*** ...

If an alternative spelling is alphabetically close to the prevailing spelling, it is given at the end of the entry block in small boldface.

cook′ie ***n.*** ...: also **cook′y,** *pl.* **–ies** ...

C. Cross-references—When an entry is cross-referred to another term that has the same meaning but is more frequently used, the entry cross-referred to is usually set in small capitals.

an·aes·the·sia ... ***n.*** ANESTHESIA ...

D. Homographs—Main entries that are spelled alike but are different in meaning and origin, such as **bat** (a club), **bat** (the animal), and **bat** (to wink), have separate entry blocks and are marked by superscript numbers following the boldface spelling.

bat[1] ... ***n.*** ...
bat[2] ... ***n.*** ...
bat[3] ... ***vt.*** ...

E. Foreign Terms—Foreign words and phrases occurring with some frequency in English, but not completely naturalized, are set in boldface italic type. This is a signal to the user of the dictionary to print these terms in italics or underline them in writing.

bon·jour (bōn zho͞or′) ***interj., n.*** [Fr] ...

F. Prefixes, Suffixes, & Combining Forms—Prefixes and initial combining forms have a hyphen at the end.

hemi- ... *prefix* half ...

Suffixes and terminal combining forms have a hyphen at the beginning.

-a·ble ... *suffix* **1** that can or will ...

The abundance of these forms, whose syllabification and pronunciation can be determined from the words containing them, makes it possible for the reader to understand and pronounce many complex terms not entered in the dictionary but formed with affixes and words that are entered.

G. ***Word Division***—Boldface entry words are divided into syllables that are separated by either a center dot or a stress mark.

gen′er·a′tor
in′ter·me′di·ar′y

For information regarding stress marks, see the GUIDE TO PRONUNCIATION.

III. PRONUNCIATION

The handling of pronunciations in the dictionary is explained in the GUIDE TO PRONUNCIATION, which follows this general guide.

IV. PART-OF-SPEECH LABELS

The dictionary portion of this book gives part-of-speech labels, in boldface italic type, for most main entry words that are solid or hyphenated forms. Labels are not given to prefixes, suffixes, combining forms, trademarks and service marks, abbreviations, and biographical and geographical entries.

Here are the part-of-speech labels used in the dictionary portion of this book:

n.	noun
pl.n.	plural noun
sing.n.	singular noun
fem.n.	feminine noun
masc.n.	masculine noun
pron.	pronoun
v.	verb
vt.	transitive verb
vi.	intransitive verb
v.aux.	auxiliary verb
v.impersonal	impersonal verb
adj.	adjective
adv.	adverb
prep.	preposition
conj.	conjunction
interj.	interjection
definite article	
indefinite article	
possessive pronominal adj.	

When an entry word is used as more than one part of speech, long dashes introduce each separate part-of-speech label.

round ... ***adj.*** ... —***n.*** ... —***vt.*** ... —***vi.*** ... —***adv.*** ... —***prep.*** ...

Sometimes an entry has two or more part-of-speech labels separated by commas, with a definition or cross-reference that is understood to apply to all parts of speech.

des·patch ... ***vt., n.*** DISPATCH

V. INFLECTED FORMS

The dictionary shows three types of inflected forms: plurals of nouns, principal parts of verbs, and comparative and superlative forms of adjectives and adverbs.

Only inflected forms regarded as irregular or offering difficulty in spelling are entered. They appear in boldface immediately after the part-of-speech label. They are shortened where possible, and syllabified and pronounced where necessary.

cit·y ... ***n.,*** *pl.* **-ies** ...
hap·py ... ***adj.*** **-pi·er, -pi·est** ...
an′a·lyze′ ... ***vt.*** **-lyzed′, -lyz′ing** ...

Plurals: This dictionary does not show regular plurals:

1) formed by adding *-s* to the singular (**cats**)
2) formed by adding *-es* to a singular that ends with *s, x, z,* and *sh* (**boxes** or **bushes**)
3) formed by adding *-es* to a singular that ends with *ch* when *ch* is pronounced [ch] (**churches**) and by adding *-s* when *ch* is pronounced [k] (**stomachs)**

Principal Parts: This dictionary does not show principal parts when:

1) the past tense and past participle are formed by simply adding *-ed* to the infinitive (**search/searched, talk/talked**)
2) the present participle is formed by simply adding *-ing* to the infinitive (**search/searching, talk/talking**)

If only two principal parts are shown, as at **love**, the first is both the past tense and the past participle (**loved**) and the second is the present participle (**loving**). If three principal parts are shown, as at **go,** the first is the past tense (**went**), the second is the past participle (**gone**), and the third is the present participle (**going**).

Comparatives & Superlatives: This dictionary does not show comparatives and superlatives formed by the simple addition of *-er* or *-est* to the base form (**tall/taller/tallest**).

VI. ETYMOLOGY

The etymology, or word history, appears inside open double brackets immediately before the definitions. The symbols and abbreviations used in the etymologies are found in the list immediately preceding page 1 of the dictionary proper.

di·shev·el ... ⟦< OFr *des-*, DIS- + *chevel,* hair⟧ ...

If the parts making up an entry word are obvious to the reader, no etymology appears at that entry.

VII. THE DEFINITIONS

A. Order of Senses—In general, each entry lists meanings in historical order; the standard, general senses of a word appear first. Informal, slang, etc. senses come next. Technical senses preceded by field labels, such as *Astron.* or *Chem.,* follow in alphabetical order.

B. Numbering & Grouping of Senses—Senses are numbered consecutively within a part of speech in boldface numerals. Where a primary sense of a word is subdivided into several closely related meanings, those meanings are preceded by italicized letters.

flat[1] ... ***adj.*** ... **1** having ... **2** lying ... **10** *Music a)* lower ... *b)* below **—*adv.*** ... **—*n.* 1** anything ... **2** ... **3** *Music* a) a note ... *b)* the symbol ... **—*vt.*** ... **—*vi.*** ...

C. Capitalization—If a main entry word is capitalized in all its senses, the entry word itself begins with a capital letter. If a capitalized main entry word has a sense or senses that are not capitalized, these are marked with the corresponding small-boldface, lowercase letter followed by a short dash and enclosed in brackets.

Pu·ri·tan ... ***n.*** ... **1** ... **2** [**p-**] ...

If a lowercase main entry word has a meaning or meanings that are capitalized, they are marked with the corresponding small-boldface, uppercase letter followed by a short dash and enclosed in brackets.

left[1] ... **—*n.* 1** ... **2** [*often* **L-**] ...

In some of these usage notes, a self-explanatory qualifying word may be added.

D. Plural Forms—In a singular noun entry, the designation "[*pl.*]" (or "[*often pl.*]," "[*usually pl.*]," etc.) before a definition indicates that it is (or *often, usually,* etc. is) the plural form of the entry word that has the meaning given in the definition.

look ... ***vi.*** ... **—*n.* 1** ... **2** ... **3** [Inf.] *a)* [*usually pl.*] appearance *b)* [*pl.*] personal appearance ...

If a plural is used as a singular with a singular verb, the designation [*with sing. v.*] is added.

E. Verbs Followed by Prepositions or Objects—In many cases, one or more specific prepositions follow a particular verb in general use. This dictionary shows this either by including the preposition in the definition, italicized and usually enclosed in parentheses, or by adding a note after the definition giving the particular prepositions associated with that definition of the verb.

In definitions of transitive verbs, the specific or generalized object of the verb, where given, is enclosed in parentheses, since the object is not grammatically part of the definition of the verb.

F. Illustrative Examples—Phrases or sentences containing the entry word and showing how it is used in context are enclosed in italic brackets. The word being illustrated is set in italics within its phrase or sentence.

a·cross ... ***adv.*** ... **—*prep.* 1**... **2** ... **3** into contact with by chance *[*to come *across* an oldfriend*]*

VIII. USAGE LABELS

People use language in different ways depending on differences in geographic location, age, education, and employment; people's individual language usage varies also according to the situation they are in or their purpose in speaking or writing. The usage labels used in this dictionary are listed below, with an explanation of each.

Informal: The word or meaning is widely used in everyday talk, personal letters, etc., but not in formal speaking or writing. Abbreviated *Inf.*

Slang: The word or meaning is not generally considered standard usage but is used, even by the best speakers and writers, in very informal situations or for creating special effects. People belonging to a certain group often use their own slang terms.

Old Informal, Old Slang: The word or meaning was informal or slang when regularly used in the recent past and is not used much today.

Obsolete: The word or meaning is no longer used but occurs in earlier writings. Abbreviated *Obs.*

Archaic: The word or meaning is not used in ordinary speech or writing today but occurs in certain special situations such as church ritual and in older books.

Old-fashioned: The word or meaning is not yet considered archaic but seems out-of-date.

Rare: The word or meaning has never been in general use.

Now Rare: The word or meaning is not used much today but was in general use in the past.

Historical: The word or meaning refers to something that no longer exists and for which there is not a modern term.

Old Poetic: The word or meaning was often used in the past, especially in poetry, but is used today only in certain kinds of traditional or somewhat old-fashioned poetry. Abbreviated *Old Poet.*

Literary: The word or meaning is regarded as having an elevated, polished, highly formal quality.

Dialect: The word or meaning is used regularly only in certain geographical areas. When a word or meaning is used mainly in some specific area of the U.S., a more specific label, such as *South* or *Northwest,* appears. Abbreviated *Dial.*

British: The word or meaning is used mainly in Great Britain and also, usually, in the other English-speaking regions of the world outside the U.S. Abbreviated *Brit.*

Canadian (or *Irish,* etc.): The word or meaning is used mainly in Canada (or Ireland, etc.). Abbreviated *Cdn.,* etc.

In addition to the above usage labels, supplementary information often appears in a short note after the definition, indicating that a word or meaning is used in an insulting, familiar, ironic, humorous, or other way.

IX. RUN-IN DERIVED ENTRIES

It is possible in English to create an almost infinite number of derived forms simply by adding certain prefixes and suffixes to the base word. The editors have included as many of these common derived words as space permitted, as run-in entries in boldface type—but only when the meaning of such words is immediately clear from the meanings of the base words and the affixes.

Thus, **greatness** and **liveliness** are run in at the end of the entries for **great** and **lively;** the suffix **-ness** is found as a separate entry meaning "state, quality, or instance of being." Many words formed with common suffixes, such as **-able**, **-er**, **-less**, **-like**, **-ly**, and **-tion**, are similarly treated as run-in entries with the base word from which they are derived. All such entries are syllabified and either accented to show stress in pronunciation or, where necessary, pronounced in full or in part.

When a derived word has a meaning or meanings different from those that can be deduced from the sum of its parts, it has been entered separately, pronounced, and fully defined (see **folder**).

THE THESAURUS

I. ARRANGEMENT OF ENTRIES

As in the Dictionary portion of this book, all headwords, including single words, hyphenated and unhyphenated compounds, and phrases, are listed in strict alphabetical order and are set in large, boldface type.

account ***n.*** ...
accountant ***n.*** ...
account for ***v.*** ...
acquaintance ***n.*** ...
acquainted (**with**) ***a.*** ...
acquaint with ***v.*** ...
acting ***a.*** ...

Idiomatic phrases that are listed within an entry have also been alphabetized.

action ***n.*** ... **—bring action** ... **—see action** ... **—take action** ...

II. Part-of-Speech Labels

Part-of-speech labels are given for all headwords, including single words, hyphenated and open compounds, and phrases. Generally, a word having more than one part of speech is given a separate entry block for each part of speech.

abuse ***n.*** misuse, debasement, degradation, ...
abuse ***v.*** insult, injure, hurt, ...

Sometimes, though, its synonyms can be conveniently grouped together in a single entry block.

above *a.*, ***prep.*** **1** [High in position] over, high, higher, superior, ...

III. THE ENTRY BLOCK

*A. **Synonyms***—Every entry block in the Thesaurus lists synonyms (words or phrases that are similar in meaning).

wholly *a.* totally, entirely, fully; see COMPLETELY.
therefore *a.*, ***conj.*** accordingly, consequently, hence, wherefore, for, since, inasmuch as, ...

Since we do not have space to list every synonym at every entry block, we have chosen certain entry blocks or numbered senses to be the primary location of synonyms belonging to a particular family of meanings. These primary locations are "main entries." Main entries always contain more than three synonyms.

dwell *v.* live, inhabit, stay, lodge, stop, settle, remain, live in, live at, continue, ...

Entry blocks or numbered senses containing only three synonyms are "brief entries." Brief entries always refer the user to a primary location of synonyms in the Thesaurus and often refer to two or more main entries.

abide *v.* **1** [To lodge] stay, room, reside; see DWELL. ...
locate *v.* ... **2** [To take up residence] settle down, establish oneself, inhabit; see DWELL, SETTLE 5.

When we wish to call the user's attention to another, closely related, family of synonyms, we have placed a cross-reference from one main entry to another.

settle *v.* ... **5** [To establish residence] locate, lodge, become a citizen, reside, ... establish a home, keep house; see also DWELL.

All cross-references in the Thesaurus portion of the book are to other Thesaurus entries. No cross-references are made from the Thesaurus to the Dictionary.

*B. **Definitions***—Distinct senses located in a single entry block are numbered consecutively in boldface numerals and may be further distinguished by brief definitions or explanatory notes in brackets.

capital *n.* **1** [A seat of government] ... **2** [Money and property] ... **3** [A letter usually used initially] ...
calm *a.* **1** [*Said especially of persons*] ... **2** [*Said often of things*] ...

*C. **Lists of Examples***—Often, a writer or speaker is looking not for other words similar to a word at hand, but for a specific thing in a general category. So, in addition to providing synonyms, the Thesaurus also provides lists of concrete examples.

boat *n.* *Types of small boats include the following:* sailboat, rowboat, shell, scull, kayak, dugout, canoe, scow, raft, ...
verb *n.* *Verbs include the following:* finite, active, passive, transitive, intransitive, modal, auxiliary, linking, ...
writer *n.* ... *Major writers include the following—British:* Daniel Defoe, Jonathan Swift, Henry Fielding, Samuel Johnson, ... ; *Spanish:* Miguel de Cervantes, Jorge Luis Borges; *Yiddish:* I. B. Singer.

*D. **Antonyms***—Antonyms (words that are opposite or nearly opposite in meaning) are listed after the synonyms.

insulted *a.* slandered, libeled, reviled, disgraced, ... shamed; see also HURT.—*Ant.* PRAISED, admired, extolled.
a[2] *a.*, ***indefinite article, prep.*** **1** ... .—*Ant.* THE, this, that.

Antonyms in small capitals are Thesaurus entries that the user will find especially useful.

*E. **The Asterisk***—A headword, a run-on idiomatic phrase, a definition in brackets, a synonym, or an antonym may be marked with an asterisk. An asterisk is intended to alert the user that the word, definition, etc. is slang, informal, dialectal, regional, archaic, etc. The user is thus cautioned to consider whether that term is appropriate for his or her purposes. The Dictionary will usually provide information on a word marked with an asterisk, but remember that not every synonym or antonym in the Thesaurus is entered in the Dictionary.

IV. HOMOGRAPHS AND SUPERSCRIPTS

Superscripts in the Dictionary portion of this book are used to distinguish *homographs*—headwords that are spelled alike but that are different in meaning and origin.

An example of Dictionary homographs:

bat·ter[1] (...) ***vt.*** ... **1** to strike with blow after blow ...

bat·ter[2] (...) ***n.*** ... *Baseball, Cricket* the player at bat

bat·ter[3] (...) ***n.*** ... a flowing mixture of flour, milk, etc. for making pancakes, etc.

Superscripts in the Thesaurus, however, have a different function. They serve to link an entry block in the Thesaurus half of a page to an entry block in the Dictionary half of the same page. In the Thesaurus, homographs may be joined together in a single entry, so long as they share the same part of speech.

The Thesaurus entry that links to the above Dictionary homographs:

batter[2,3] ***n.*** **1** [One who bats] ... **2** [Baking mixture] ...

The superscripts "2,3" link this Thesaurus entry block to both **batter**[2] and **batter**[3] in the Dictionary.

V. SUGGESTIONS FOR USING THE THESAURUS

For convenience, here is a summary of things you may want to have in mind while you use the Thesaurus portion of this book:

1. Look up any word that you have thought of but are, for some reason, not fully satisfied with.
2. Unless you have thought of a rare word, you should find: (a) a main entry, with many alternative terms, some antonyms, and possibly a "see also" cross-reference, or (b) a brief entry, with three synonyms and one or more cross-references.
3. If you have turned to a main entry, check to see whether more than one meaning is recognized, and, if so, pick the one you want. The various meanings will be numbered in boldface numerals.
4. Work through the list, looking for a term that meets your needs. Try the cross-reference at the end if you need it.
5. If you find a word or phrase you may want to use but do not know very well, look it up in the Dictionary. But remember that not every synonym or antonym given in the Thesaurus is necessarily entered in the Dictionary.
6. If you have looked up a brief entry, it will provide a few common synonyms. If you are not satisfied with any of them, turn to the main entry cross-referred there. The entry to which you are referred may have more than one grammatical use—*fast* can be an adjective, adverb, noun, or verb. Choose synonyms having the same part of speech as your original, brief entry.

GUIDE TO PRONUNCIATION

I. PRONUNCIATION STYLE

Pronunciations are provided in the Dictionary as needed. Pronunciations are given in parentheses immediately after the boldface entry word:

mil·len·ni·um (mi len′ē əm)

Pronunciations have sometimes been shortened so as to cover only a particular part of the entry word, generally the part most likely to cause confusion or difficulty. Hyphens are used to indicate which part of the pronunciation is not shown.

home′stead′ (-sted′)

More than one pronunciation is sometimes given. Each variant pronunciation may be regarded as having wide currency in American English unless a qualifying note has been added to a particular variant indicating that it is less common. Variants may be also qualified with respect to particular grammatical usage.

av·o·ca·do (av′ə kä′dō, ä′və-)
ex·cuse (ek skyo͞oz′; *for n.*, -skyo͞os′)

This dictionary does not attempt to cover all pronunciations of a given word and does not indicate differences arising out of various regional dialects.

II. PRONUNCIATION KEY

The Pronunciation Key lists the pronunciation symbols used in this dictionary along with several Key Words. Key Words are short, familiar words that illustrate each of the various sounds represented by the symbols.

PRONUNCIATION KEY

Vowel Sounds

Symbol	*Key Words*
a	at, cap, parrot
ā	ape, play, sail
ä	cot, father, heart
e	ten, wealth, merry
ē	even, feet, money
i	is, stick, mirror
ī	ice, high, sky
ō	go, open, tone
ô	all, law, horn
o͝o	could, look, pull
yo͝o	cure, furious
o͞o	boot, crew, tune
yo͞o	cute, few, use
oi	boy, oil, royal
ou	cow, out, sour
u	mud, ton, blood, trouble
ʉ	her, sir, word
ə	ago, agent, collect, focus
′l	cattle, paddle
′n	sudden, sweeten

Consonant Sounds

Symbol	*Key Words*
b	bed, table, rob
d	dog, middle, sad
f	for, phone, cough
g	get, wiggle, dog
h	hat, hope, ahead
hw	which, white
j	joy, badge, agent
k	kill, cat, quiet
l	let, yellow, ball
m	meet, number, time
n	net, candle, ton
p	put, sample, escape
r	red, wrong, born
s	sit, castle, office
t	top, letter, cat
v	voice, every, love
w	wet, always, quart
y	yes, canyon, onion
z	zoo, misery, rise
ch	chew, nature, punch
sh	shell, machine, bush
th	thin, nothing, truth
th	then, other, bathe
zh	beige, measure, seizure
ŋ	ring, anger, drink

III. FOREIGN SOUNDS

A number of foreign words are entered in the dictionary. An approximation of the native pronunciation—typically French or Spanish in this dictionary—has been provided. Foreign pronunciations use sounds not generally found in English, and, therefore, some additional pronunciation symbols are required. Below is a short explanation of these symbols.

- ȧ Used in French; a sound between [a] as in *cat* and [ä] as in *cot*.
- ë Used in French; round the lips as though to say *oh* while pronouncing [e] as in *get*.
- ö Used chiefly in French; round the lips as though to say *oh* while pronouncing the sound [ā] as in *ate*.
- ô Used in French, German, Spanish, etc.; round the lips loosely as though to say *aw* while pronouncing [u] as in *cut*.
- ü Used in French and German; round the lips as though to say *oh* while pronouncing [ē] as in *meet*.
- kh Used in German and Scots English; pronounce [k] while allowing the breath to escape in a stream, as in saying [h].
- H Used in German; pronounce [sh] while keeping the tip of the tongue pointed downward.
- *n* Used chiefly in French; this symbol indicates that the vowel sound preceding it is pronounced with air expelled through both the mouth and the nose.
- *r* Pronounce [r] with a vibrating of the tip of the tongue in Spanish or Italian, or with a trilling of the uvula in French or German.
- ’ Used in French to indicate that a final consonant is short and unvoiced or that a letter *e* is silent or nearly so.
- y’ Used in Russian; pronounce an unvoiced [y] immediately after pronouncing the preceding consonant.

IV. STRESS MARKS

Stress marks appear in the pronunciations and in boldface entry words that are not given full pronunciation. A heavy mark [ʹ] after a syllable indicates that the syllable is spoken with the most force. A light mark [′] after a syllable indicates that the syllable is spoken with relatively less force. Syllables with no marking are given the least force.

dic·tion·ar·y (dikʹshə ner′ē)

ABBREVIATIONS AND SYMBOLS USED IN THIS BOOK

a.	adjective or adverb (i.e., modifier); used only in the thesaurus section
abbrev.	abbreviated, abbreviation
adj.	adjective
adv.	adverb
Afr	African
Afrik	Afrikaans
alt.	alternative
Am	American
AmInd	American Indian
AmSp	American Spanish
Anat.	Anatomy
Anglo-Fr	Anglo-French
Ar	Arabic
Aram	Aramaic
Archit.	Architecture
Austral.	Australian
Biol.	Biology
Bot.	Botany
Brit	British
C	Celsius
c.	century
c.	circa
cap.	capital city
Cdn	Canadian
Celt	Celtic
cf.	compare
Ch.	Church
Chem.	Chemistry
Chin	Chinese
compar.	comparative
Comput.	Computer Science
conj.	conjunction
contr.	contraction (grammar)
Dan	Danish
Dial., dial.	dialectal
dim.	diminutive
Du	Dutch
E	eastern, English
EC	east central
Eccles.	Ecclesiastical
Educ.	Education
e.g.	for example
Egypt	Egyptian
Elec.	Electricity
Eng	English
Esk	Eskimo
esp.	especially
etc.	and the like
Ex.	example
exc.	except
F	Fahrenheit
fem.	feminine
Fl	Flemish
fol.	following entry
Fr	French
ft.	foot, feet
Gael	Gaelic
Geol.	Geology
Geom.	Geometry
Ger	German
Gmc	Germanic
Gr	Classical Greek
Gram.	Grammar
Haw	Hawaiian
Heb	Hebrew
Hung	Hungarian
IE	Indo-European
i.e.	that is
in.	inch(es)
indic.	indicative
Inf., inf.	informal
infl.	influenced
intens.	intensive
interj.	interjection
Ir	Irish
It	Italian
Jpn	Japanese
km	kilometer(s)
L	Classical Latin
lb.	pound(s)
lit.	literally
LL	Late Latin
LowG	Low German
m	meter(s)
masc.	masculine
Math.	Mathematics
MDu	Middle Dutch
ME	Middle English
Mech.	Mechanics
Med.	Medicine
met.	metropolitan
Mex	Mexican
MHG	Middle High German
mi.	mile(s)
Mil.	Military
ML	Middle Latin
ModGr	Modern Greek
ModL	modern scientific Latin
Myth	Mythology
N	northern
n.	noun
Naut.	nautical usage
NC	north central

NE	northeastern
NormFr	Norman French
Norw	Norwegian
NW	northwestern
Obs., obs.	obsolete
occas.	occasionally
OE	Old English
OFr	Old French
OHG	Old High German
ON	Old Norse
orig.	origin, originally
OS	Old Saxon
OSlav	Old Church Slavonic
oz.	ounce(s)
pers.	person (grammar)
Pers	Persian
Photog.	Photography
pl.	plural
pl.n.	plural noun
Poet.	Poetic
Pol	Polish
pop.	population
Port	Portuguese
poss.	possessive
pp.	past participle
prec.	preceding entry
prep.	preposition
pres.	present tense
prob.	probably
pron.	pronoun
Prov	Provençal
prp.	present participle
pseud.	pseudonym
Psychol.	Psychology
pt.	past tense
R.C.Ch.	Roman Catholic Church
Rom.	Roman
Russ	Russian
S	southern
Sans	Sanskrit
SC	south central
Scand	Scandinavian
Scot	Scottish
SE	southeastern
sing.	singular
sing.n.	singular noun
Sp	Spanish
sp.	spelling, spelled
specif.	specifically
sq.	square
superl.	superlative
SW	southwestern
Swed	Swedish
Theol.	Theology
transl.	translated, translation
Turk	Turkish
ult.	ultimately
v.	verb
var.	variant
v.aux.	auxiliary verb
vi.	intransitive verb
VL	Vulgar Latin
vt.	transitive verb
W	western
WC	west central
WInd	West Indian
WWI	World War I
WWII	World War II

Symbols

<	derived from
?	uncertain or unknown
+	plus
&	and
°	degree
*	slang, informal, dialectal, regional, archaic, etc.; used only in the thesaurus section

a[1] or **A** (ā) ***n.**, pl.* **a's, A's** (āz) the first letter of the English alphabet

a[2] (ə; *stressed,* ā) ***adj., indefinite article*** ⟦< AN⟧ **1** one; one sort of **2** each; any one —***prep.*** per *[once a day]* Before words beginning with a consonant sound, *a* is used *[a child, a home, a uniform]* See AN

a[3] *abbrev.* **1** about **2** adjective **3** alto **4** answer

A[1] (ā) ***n.*** **1** a blood type **2** a grade indicating excellence **3** *Music* the sixth tone in the scale of C major

A[2] *abbrev.* **1** answer **2** April **3** *Baseball, Basketball* assist(s) **4** August

a-[1] ⟦< OE⟧ *prefix* **1** in, into, on, at, to *[ashore]* **2** in the act or state of *[asleep]*

a-[2] *prefix* **1** ⟦< OE⟧ up, out *[arise]* **2** ⟦< OE⟧ off, of *[akin]* **3** ⟦< Gr⟧ not, without *[amoral]*

AA *abbrev.* **1** Alcoholics Anonymous **2** Associate in (or of) Arts

aard·vark (ärd′värk′) ***n.*** ⟦Du, earth pig⟧ a nocturnal, ant-eating S African mammal

Aar·on (er′ən) ***n.*** *Bible* the first high priest of the Hebrews

AB[1] (ā′bē′) ***n.*** a blood type

AB[2] *abbrev.* **1** Alberta (Canada) **2** Bachelor of Arts: also **A.B.**

ab- ⟦L⟧ *prefix* away, from, from off, down *[abdicate]*

ABA *abbrev.* American Bar Association

a·back (ə bak′) ***adv.*** [Archaic] backward; back —**taken aback** startled and confused; surprised

ab·a·cus (ab′ə kəs) ***n.**, pl.* **-cus·es** or **-ci′** (-sī′) ⟦< Gr *abax*⟧ a frame with sliding beads for doing arithmetic

a·baft (ə baft′) ***adv.*** ⟦< OE *on,* on + *be,* by + *æftan,* aft⟧ aft —***prep.*** *Naut.* behind

ab·a·lo·ne (ab′ə lō′nē) ***n.*** ⟦< AmInd⟧ an edible sea mollusk with an oval, somewhat spiral shell

a·ban·don (ə ban′dən) ***vt.*** ⟦< OFr *mettre a bandon,* to put under (another's) ban⟧ **1** to give up completely **2** to desert —***n.*** unrestrained activity; exuberance —**a·ban′don·ment** ***n.***

a·ban′doned ***adj.*** **1** deserted **2** shamefully wicked **3** unrestrained

a·base (ə bās′) ***vt.*** **a·based′, a·bas′ing** ⟦< ML *abassare,* to lower⟧ to humble —**a·base′ment** ***n.***

a·bash (ə bash′) ***vt.*** ⟦< OFr *es-,* intens. + *baer,* gape⟧ to make ashamed and uneasy; disconcert —**a·bash′ed·ly** ***adv.***

a·bate (ə bāt′) ***vt., vi.*** **a·bat′ed, a·bat′ing** ⟦< OFr *abattre,* beat down⟧ **1** to make or become less **2** *Law* to end —**a·bate′ment** ***n.***

ab·at·toir (ab′ə twär′) ***n.*** ⟦Fr: see prec.⟧ a slaughterhouse

ab·bé (a′bā) ***n.*** ⟦Fr: see ABBOT⟧ a French priest's title

ab·bess (ab′əs) ***n.*** ⟦see ABBOT⟧ a woman who heads a convent of nuns

ab·bey (ab′ē) ***n.*** **1** a monastery or convent **2** a church belonging to an abbey

ab·bot (ab′ət) ***n.*** ⟦< Aram *abbā,* father⟧ a man who heads a monastery

abbr or **abbrev** *abbrev.* **1** abbreviated **2** abbreviation

ab·bre·vi·ate (ə brē′vē āt′) ***vt.*** **-at′ed, -at′ing** ⟦< L *ad-,* to + *brevis,* brief⟧ to make shorter; esp., to shorten (a word) by omitting letters

ab·bre′vi·a′tion (-ā′shən) ***n.*** **1** a shortening **2** a shortened form of a word or phrase, as *Mr.* for *Mister*

ABC (ā′bē′sē′) ***n.**, pl.* **ABC's** [*usually pl.*] **1** the alphabet **2** the basic elements (of a subject)

ab·di·cate (ab′di kāt′) ***vt., vi.*** **-cat′ed, -cat′ing** ⟦< L *ab-,* off + *dicare,* to proclaim⟧ **1** to give up formally (a throne, etc.) **2** to surrender (a right, responsibility, etc.) —**ab′di·ca′tion** ***n.***

ab·do·men (ab′də mən, ab dō′-) ***n.*** ⟦L⟧ the part of the body between the diaphragm and the pelvis; belly —**ab·dom′i·nal** (-däm′ə nəl) ***adj.***

ab·duct (ab dukt′) ***vt.*** ⟦< L *ab-,* away + *ducere,* to lead⟧ to kidnap —**ab·duc′tion** ***n.*** —**ab·duc′tor** ***n.***

a·beam (ə bēm′) ***adv., adj.*** at right angles to a ship's length or keel

a·bed (ə bed′) ***adv., adj.*** in bed

A·bel (ā′bəl) ***n.*** *Bible* the second son of Adam and Eve: see CAIN

a·be·li·a (ə bēl′yə, ə bē′lē ə) ***n.*** an ornamental shrub with clusters of fragrant flowers

ab·er·ra·tion (ab′ər ā′shən) ***n.*** ⟦< L *ab-,* from + *errare,* wander⟧ **1** a deviation from what is right, true, normal, etc. **2** mental derangement or lapse **3** *Optics* the failure of light rays from one point to converge at a single focus —**ab·er′rant** (-ənt) ***adj.*** —**ab′er·ra′tion·al** ***adj.***

a·bet (ə bet′) ***vt.*** **a·bet′ted, a·bet′ting** ⟦< OFr *a-,* to + *beter,* to bait⟧ to urge on or help, esp. in crime —**a·bet′tor** or **a·bet′ter** ***n.***

a·bey·ance (ə bā′əns) ***n.*** ⟦< OFr *a-,* to, at + *bayer,* wait expectantly⟧ temporary suspension, as of an activity or ruling

ab·hor (ab hôr′) ***vt.*** **-horred′, -hor′ring** ⟦< L *ab-,* from + *horrere,* to shudder⟧ to shrink from in disgust, hatred, etc.; detest —**ab·hor′rence** ***n.***

ab·hor′rent (-ənt) ***adj.*** causing disgust, hatred, etc.; detestable —**ab·hor′rent·ly** ***adv.***

a·bide (ə bīd′) ***vi.*** **a·bode′** or **a·bid′ed, a·bid′ing** ⟦< OE *ā-,* intens. + *bīdan,* bide⟧ **1** to remain **2** [Archaic] to reside —***vt.*** **1** to await **2** to put up with —**abide by** **1** to live up to (a promise, etc.) **2** to submit to and carry out —**a·bid′ance** ***n.***

a·bid′ing ***adj.*** enduring; lasting

a·bil·i·ty (ə bil′ə tē) ***n.**, pl.* **-ties** ⟦< L *habilitas*⟧ **1** a being able; power to do **2** talent or skill

-a·bil·i·ty (ə bil′ə tē) ⟦L *-abilitas*⟧ *suffix* a (specified) ability, capacity, or tendency

ab·ject (ab′jekt′, ab jekt′) ***adj.*** ⟦< L *ab-,* from + *jacere,* to throw⟧ **1** miserable; wretched **2** lacking self-respect; degraded —**ab′ject′ly** ***adv.*** —**ab·jec′tion** or **ab′ject′ness** ***n.***

ab·jure (ab joor′, əb-) ***vt.*** **-jured′, -jur′ing** ⟦< L *ab-,* away + *jurare,* swear⟧ **1** to give up (rights, allegiance, etc.) on oath; renounce **2** to recant —**ab·ju·ra·tion** (ab′jə rā′shən) ***n.*** —**ab·jur′a·to′ry** (-ə tôr′ē) ***adj.*** —**ab·jur′er** ***n.***

ab·late (ab lāt′) ***vt.*** **-lat′ed, -lat′ing** ⟦see fol.⟧ **1** to remove,

THESAURUS

a[2] ***a., indefinite article, prep.*** **1** [The indefinite article; *before vowels, written "an"*] some, one, any, each, some kind of, some particular, any of, any one of, a certain.—*Ant.* THE, this, that. **2** [An indication of frequency] per, every, at the rate of; see EACH 2.

abandon ***n.*** unrestraint, spontaneity, freedom, exuberance, spirit, enthusiasm, vigor.

abandon ***v.*** **1** [To give up] leave, quit, withdraw, discontinue, break off, go off from, cast away, cast aside, let go, cease, cast off, discard, vacate, give away, part with, evacuate, surrender, yield, desist, concede, renounce, abdicate, lose hope of, go back on, secede, waive, forgo, back down from, lay aside, dispose of, have done with, throw in the towel*, break the habit. **2** [To leave someone or something in trouble] desert, forsake, ostracize, back out on, break with, break up with, run away, defect, reject, disown, cast off, maroon, depart from, throw overboard, jettison, leave behind, slip away from, stand up*, leave in the lurch, turn one's back on, run out on*, walk out on*, doublecross*, let down, drop.

abandoned ***a.*** deserted, desolate, destitute, desperate, empty, unused, vacated, left, neglected, relinquished, lonely, forsaken, solitary, hopeless, cast off, cast aside, cast away, forgotten, shunned, forlorn, avoided, outcast, rejected, helpless, unfortunate, alone, discarded, scorned, lost, doomed, friendless, wretched, thrown overboard*, out on a limb*, waiting at the church*, left in the lurch, in the cold, left holding the bag*.—*Ant.* INHABITED, befriended, in use.

abbreviate ***v.*** shorten, cut, condense; see DECREASE 2.

abbreviation ***n.*** contraction, abridgment, sketch, brief, abstract, synopsis, reduction, abstraction, condensation, digest, résumé, outline, summary, short form; see also SUMMARY.

abdicate ***v.*** relinquish, give up, withdraw; see ABANDON 1.

abdomen ***n.*** midsection, belly, gut*; see STOMACH.

abduct ***v.*** capture, seize, carry off; see KIDNAP.

abide ***v.*** **1** [To lodge] stay, room, reside; see DWELL. **2** [To submit to] put up with, bear, bear with, withstand; see also ENDURE 2. **—abide by** follow, observe, comply with; see FOLLOW 3.

ability ***n.*** aptitude, intelligence, innate qualities, powers, potency, worth, talent, gift, genius, capability, competence, proficiency, adeptness, qualifications, knowledge, self-sufficiency, technique, craft, skill, artistry, cunning, skillfulness, dexterity, facility, flair, finesse, mastery, cleverness, deftness, experience, ingenuity, strength, understanding, faculty, comprehension, makings, sense, what it takes*, brains, knack, the hang of something, know-how*.—*Ant.* IGNORANCE, incompetence, inexperience.

as by surgery **2** to wear away, burn away, or vaporize —*vi.* to be ablated, as a rocket shield in reentry —**ab·la'tion** *n.*
ab·la·tive (ab'lə tiv) *n.* ⟦< L *ab-*, away + *ferre*, to bear⟧ *Gram.* the case expressing removal, cause, agency, etc., as in Latin
a·blaze (ə blāz') *adj.* **1** burning brightly **2** greatly excited
a·ble (ā'bəl) *adj.* **a'bler, a'blest** ⟦< L *habere*, have⟧ **1** having enough power, skill, etc. to do something **2** skilled; talented **3** *Law* competent —**a'bly** *adv.*
-a·ble (ə bəl) ⟦< L⟧ *suffix* **1** that can or will *[perishable]* **2** capable of being ___ed *[manageable]* **3** worthy of being ___ed *[lovable]* **4** having qualities of *[comfortable]* **5** inclined to *[peaceable]*
a'ble-bod'ied *adj.* healthy and strong
able-bodied seaman a trained or skilled seaman: also **able seaman**
a·bloom (ə blo͞om') *adj.* in bloom
ab·lu·tion (ab lo͞o'shən) *n.* ⟦< L *ab-*, off + *luere*, to wash⟧ [*usually pl.*] a washing of the body, esp. as a religious ceremony
-a·bly (ə blē) *suffix* in a way indicating a (specified) ability, tendency, etc.
ABM *abbrev.* anti-ballistic missile
ab·ne·gate (ab'nə gāt') *vt.* **-gat'ed, -gat'ing** ⟦< L *ab-*, from + *negare*, deny⟧ to give up (rights, claims, etc.); renounce —**ab'ne·ga'tion** *n.*
ab·nor·mal (ab nôr'məl) *adj.* not normal, average, or typical; irregular —**ab·nor'mal·ly** *adv.*
ab'nor·mal'i·ty (-mal'ə tē) *n.* **1** an abnormal condition **2** *pl.* **-ties** an abnormal thing
a·board (ə bôrd') *adv.*, *prep.* on or in (a train, ship, etc.)
a·bode (ə bōd') *vi.*, *vt. alt. pt. & pp. of* ABIDE —*n.* a home; residence
a·bol·ish (ə bäl'ish) *vt.* ⟦< L *abolere*, destroy⟧ to do away with; void —**a·bol'ish·ment** *n.*
ab·o·li·tion (ab'ə lish'ən) *n.* **1** complete destruction; annulment **2** [*occas.* **A-**] the abolishing of slavery in the U.S. —**ab'o·li'tion·ist** *n.*
a·bom·i·na·ble (ə bäm'ə nə bəl) *adj.* ⟦see fol.⟧ **1** disgusting; vile **2** very bad —**a·bom'i·na·bly** *adv.*
a·bom'i·nate' (-nāt') *vt.* **-nat'ed, -nat'ing** ⟦< L *abominari*, regard as an ill omen⟧ **1** to hate; loathe **2** to dislike very much —**a·bom'i·na'tion** *n.*
ab·o·rig·i·nal (ab'ə rij'ə nəl) *adj.* **1** existing (in a region) from the beginning; first; indigenous **2** of aborigines —*n.* an aborigine
ab'o·rig'i·ne' (-nē') *n.*, *pl.* **-nes'** ⟦L < *ab-*, from + *origine*, origin⟧ **1** any of the first known inhabitants of a region **2** [**A-**] a member of the aboriginal people of Australia
a·born·ing (ə bôr'niŋ) *adv.* while being born or created *[the plan died aborning]*
a·bort (ə bôrt') *vi.* ⟦< L *aboriri*, miscarry⟧ to have a miscarriage —*vt.* **1** to cause to have an abortion **2** to cut short (a flight, etc.), as because of an equipment failure
a·bor·tion (ə bôr'shən) *n.* any expulsion of a fetus before it is able to survive, esp. if induced on purpose —**a·bor'tion·ist** *n.*
a·bor·tive (ə bôrt'iv) *adj.* **1** unsuccessful; fruitless **2** *Biol.* arrested in development
a·bound (ə bound') *vi.* ⟦< L *ab-*, away + *undare*, rise in waves⟧ **1** to be plentiful **2** to be rich (*in*) or teem (*with*)
a·bout (ə bout') *adv.* ⟦< OE *onbūtan*, around⟧ **1** all around **2** near **3** in an opposite direction **4** approximately **5** [Inf.] nearly *[about ready]* —*adj.* **1** astir *[he is up and about]* **2** likely immediately *[about to leave]* —*prep.* **1** on all sides of **2** near to **3** with **4** concerning
a·bout'-face' *n.* a reversal of position or opinion —*vi.* **-faced', -fac'ing** to turn or face in the opposite direction
a·bove (ə buv') *adv.* ⟦OE *abūfan*⟧ **1** in a higher place; up **2** earlier (in a book, etc.) **3** higher in rank, etc. —*prep.* **1** over; on top of **2** better or more than *[above the average]* —*adj.* mentioned earlier —*n.* something that is above —**above all** most of all; mainly
a·bove'board' *adv.*, *adj.* without dishonesty or concealment
a·bove'ground' *adj.*, *adv.* **1** above or on the surface of the earth **2** not secret(ly); open(ly)
a·brade (ə brād') *vt.*, *vi.* **a·brad'ed, a·brad'ing** ⟦< L *ab-*, away + *radere*, to scrape⟧ to rub off; scrape away
A·bra·ham (ā'brə ham') *n. Bible* the first patriarch of the Hebrews
a·bra·sion (ə brā'zhən) *n.* **1** an abrading **2** an abraded spot
a·bra'sive (-siv) *adj.* **1** causing abrasion **2** aggressively annoying; irritating —*n.* a substance, as sandpaper, used for grinding, polishing, etc.
a·breast (ə brest') *adv.*, *adj.* **1** side by side **2** informed (*of*) recent happenings
a·bridge (ə brij') *vt.* **a·bridged', a·bridg'ing** ⟦< LL *abbreviare*, abbreviate⟧ **1** to shorten, lessen, or curtail **2** to shorten (a piece of writing) while keeping the substance —**a·bridg'ment** or **a·bridge'ment** *n.*
a·broad (ə brôd') *adv.* **1** far and wide **2** in circulation; current **3** outdoors **4** to or in foreign lands —**from abroad** from a foreign land
ab·ro·gate (ab'rə gāt') *vt.* **-gat'ed, -gat'ing** ⟦< L *ab-*, away + *rogare*, ask⟧ to cancel or repeal by authority —**ab'ro·ga'tion** *n.* —**ab'ro·ga'tor** *n.*
a·brupt (ə brupt') *adj.* ⟦< L *ab-*, off + *rumpere*, to break⟧ **1** sudden; unexpected **2** brusque **3** very steep **4** disconnected, as some writing —**a·brupt'ly** *adv.* —**a·brupt'ness** *n.*
ABS *abbrev.* anti-lock braking system
Ab·sa·lom (ab'sə ləm) *n. Bible* David's son who rebelled against him
ab·scess (ab'ses') *n.* ⟦< L *ab(s)-*, from + *cedere*, go⟧ a swollen area in body tissues, containing pus —*vi.* to form an abscess —**ab'scessed'** *adj.*
ab·scis·sa (ab sis'ə) *n.*, *pl.* **-sas** or **-sae** (-ē) ⟦L < *ab-*, from + *scindere*, to cut⟧ *Math.* the horizontal distance of a point from a vertical axis
ab·scond (ab skänd', əb-) *vi.* ⟦< L *ab(s)-*, from + *condere*, hide⟧ to leave hastily and secretly, esp. to escape the law —**ab·scond'er** *n.*

THESAURUS

able *a.* intelligent, ingenious, worthy, talented, gifted, fitted, capable, effective, efficient, qualified, masterful, adequate, competent, expert, experienced, skilled, learned, clever, suitable, smart, crafty, cunning, bright, knowing, dexterous, endowed, deft, apt, agile, adept, alert, adaptable, smooth, ready, versatile, equal to, suited, suited to, well-rounded, mighty, powerful, strong, robust, sturdy, brawny, vigorous, courageous, fit for, sharp, cut out for*.—*Ant.* STUPID, bungling, unadaptable.

able-bodied *a.* fit, powerful, sturdy; see STRONG 1.

abnormal *a.* strange, irregular, unnatural; see UNUSUAL 2.

abnormality *n.* peculiarity, singularity, malformation; see IRREGULARITY.

aboard *a.* on board, on ship, shipped, loaded, on board ship, freight on board, being shipped, en route, consigned, in transit, being transported, embarked, afloat, at sea, on deck, traveling.

abolish *v.* suppress, eradicate, terminate, exterminate, obliterate, annul, remove, revoke, end, finish, nullify, set aside, annihilate, repeal, subvert, reverse, rescind, prohibit, extinguish, cancel, erase, root out, pull up, uproot, demolish, invalidate, overturn, overthrow, declare null and void, do away with, stamp out, undo, throw out, put an end to, inhibit, dispense with, cut out, raze, squelch*, ravage; see also DESTROY.

abort *v.* miscarry, fall short, terminate; see FAIL 1.

about *a.*, *prep.* **1** [Approximately] roughly, nearly, in general; see APPROXIMATELY. **2** [Concerning] regarding, respecting, touching, of, on, in relation to, relative to, relating to, as regards, in regard to, in which, with respect to, in the matter of, with reference to, referring to, so far as something is concerned, in connection with, concerned with, thereby, wherein, as for, dealing with. **3** [Around] surrounding, round about, on all sides; see AROUND.

above *a.*, *prep.* **1** [High in position] over, high, higher, superior, beyond, raised, above one's head, in a higher place, aloft, overhead, toward the sky; see also HIGHER, OVER 1.—*Ant.* BELOW, low, beneath. **2** [Referring to something earlier] before, foregoing, earlier; see PRECEDING. —**above all** in the first place, chiefly, especially; see PRINCIPALLY.

aboveboard *a.* candidly, honestly, frankly; see OPENLY 1.

abrasive *a.* **1** grinding, sharpening, cutting; see ROUGH 1. **2** irritating, annoying, caustic; see DISTURBING.

abreast *a.* in line, equal, side by side; see BESIDE.

abroad *a.* away, at large, adrift, wandering, elsewhere, overseas, traveling, touring, outside, distant, far away, gone, out of the country, removed.

abrupt *a.* **1** [*Said of things, usually landscape*] uneven, jagged, precipitous; see STEEP. **2** [*Said of people or their actions*] blunt, hasty, gruff; see RUDE.

ab·sence (ab′səns) ***n.*** **1** a being absent **2** the time of this **3** a lack

ab·sent (ab′sənt; *for v.*, ab sent′) ***adj.*** ⟦< L *ab-*, away + *esse*, be⟧ **1** not present **2** not existing; lacking **3** not attentive —***vt.*** to keep (oneself) away —***prep.*** in the absence of *[absent* her testimony, our case is weak*]* —**ab′sent·ly** ***adv.***

ab·sen·tee (ab′sən tē′) ***n.*** one who is absent, as from work —***adj.*** designating, of, or from one who is absent —**ab′sen·tee′ism′** ***n.***

absentee ballot a ballot to be marked and sent to a board of elections by a person (**absentee voter**) unable to be at the polls at election time

ab′sent-mind′ed or **ab′sent·mind′ed** ***adj.*** **1** not attentive; preoccupied **2** habitually forgetful —**ab′sent-mind′ed·ly** ***adv.*** —**ab′sent-mind′ed·ness** ***n.***

absent without leave *Mil.* absent from duty without official permission

ab·sinthe or **ab·sinth** (ab′sinth′) ***n.*** ⟦< Gr⟧ a green, bitter, toxic liqueur

ab·so·lute (ab′sə lo͞ot′) ***adj.*** ⟦see ABSOLVE⟧ **1** perfect; complete **2** not mixed; pure **3** not limited *[absolute* power*]* **4** positive **5** not doubted; real *[absolute* truth*]* **6** not relative —**ab′so·lute′ly** ***adv.***

absolute value the value of a real number, disregarding its positive or negative sign *[*the *absolute value* of -4 or +4 is 4*]*

absolute zero the lower limit on physically obtainable temperatures: equal to -273.16°C or -459.69°F

ab·so·lu·tion (ab′sə lo͞o′shən) ***n.*** **1** a freeing (*from* guilt) **2** remission (*of* sin or penalty for it)

ab·so·lut·ism (ab′sə lo͞o tiz′əm) ***n.*** government by absolute rule; despotism —**ab′so·lut′ist** ***n.***, ***adj.***

ab·solve (ab zälv′, əb-) ***vt.*** **-solved′**, **-solv′ing** ⟦< L *ab-*, from + *solvere*, loosen⟧ **1** to free from guilt, a duty, etc. **2** to give religious absolution to

ab·sorb (ab sôrb′, -zôrb′; əb-) ***vt.*** ⟦< L *ab-*, from + *sorbere*, drink in⟧ **1** to suck up **2** to interest greatly; engross **3** to assimilate **4** to pay for (costs, etc.) **5** to take in (a shock, etc.) without recoil **6** to take in and not reflect (light or sound) —**ab·sorb′ing** ***adj.***

ab·sorb′ent ***adj.*** capable of absorbing moisture, etc. —***n.*** a thing that absorbs —**ab·sorb′en·cy** ***n.***

ab·sorp·tion (ab sôrp′shən, -zôrp′-; əb-) ***n.*** **1** an absorbing or being absorbed **2** great interest —**ab·sorp′tive** ***adj.***

ab·stain (ab stān′, əb-) ***vi.*** ⟦< L *ab(s)-*, from + *tenere*, to hold⟧ to voluntarily do without; refrain (*from*) —**ab·stain′er** ***n.*** —**ab·sten′tion** (-sten′shən) ***n.***

ab·ste·mi·ous (ab stē′mē əs, əb-) ***adj.*** ⟦< L *ab(s)-*, from + *temetum*, strong drink⟧ moderate in eating and drinking; temperate

ab·sti·nence (ab′stə nəns) ***n.*** an abstaining from some or all food, liquor, etc. —**ab′sti·nent** ***adj.***

ab·stract (*for adj.*, ab strakt′, ab′strakt′; *for n. & vt. 2*, ab′strakt′; *for vt. 1*, ab strakt′) ***adj.*** ⟦< L *ab(s)-*, from + *trahere*, to draw⟧ **1** thought of apart from material objects **2** expressing a quality so thought of **3** theoretical **4** *Art* not representing things realistically —***n.*** a summary —***vt.*** **1** to take away **2** to summarize —**ab·stract′ly** ***adv.*** —**ab·stract′ness** ***n.***

ab·stract′ed ***adj.*** preoccupied

ab·strac·tion (ab strak′shən) ***n.*** **1** an abstracting; removal **2** an abstract idea, thing, etc. **3** mental withdrawal **4** an abstract painting, sculpture, etc.

ab·struse (ab stro͞os′) ***adj.*** ⟦< L *ab(s)-*, away + *trudere*, to thrust⟧ hard to understand —**ab·struse′ly** ***adv.*** —**ab·struse′ness** ***n.***

ab·surd (ab surd′, -zurd′; əb-) ***adj.*** ⟦< L *ab-*, intens. + *surdus*, dull, insensible⟧ so unreasonable as to be ridiculous —**ab·surd′i·ty** ***n.*** —**ab·surd′ly** ***adv.***

a·bun·dance (ə bun′dəns) ***n.*** ⟦see ABOUND⟧ a great supply; more than enough —**a·bun′dant** ***adj.*** —**a·bun′dant·ly** ***adv.***

a·buse (ə byo͞oz′; *for n.*, ə byo͞os′) ***vt.*** **a·bused′**, **a·bus′ing** ⟦< L *ab-*, away + *uti*, to use⟧ **1** to use wrongly **2** to mistreat, esp. by inflicting physical or sexual harm on **3** to insult; revile —***n.*** **1** wrong use **2** mistreatment, esp. by the infliction of physical or sexual harm **3** a corrupt practice **4** insulting language —**a·bu·sive** (ə byo͞o′siv) ***adj.*** —**a·bu′sive·ly** ***adv.***

a·but (ə but′) ***vi.***, ***vt.*** **a·but′ted**, **a·but′ting** ⟦< OFr *a-*, to + *bout*, end⟧ to border (*on* or *upon*)

a·but′ment ***n.*** **1** an abutting **2** a part supporting an arch, bridge, etc.

THESAURUS

absence ***n.*** **1** [The state of being elsewhere] truancy, nonattendance, nonappearance, loss, vacancy, cut*, hooky*. **2** [The state of lacking something] deficiency, need, inadequacy; see LACK 1.

absent ***a.*** away, missing, elsewhere, vanished, gone, gone out, not at home, not present, out, wanting, lacking, abroad, lost, astray, nowhere to be found, on vacation, AWOL*, playing hooky*.

absent-minded ***a.*** preoccupied, dreamy, listless, lost, absent, thoughtless, oblivious, inattentive, daydreaming, unconscious, unaware, withdrawn, removed, faraway, distracted, remote, forgetful, in the clouds.—*Ant.* OBSERVANT, attentive, alert.

absolute ***a.*** **1** [Without limitation] total, complete, entire, infinite, unqualified, supreme, full, unrestricted, unlimited, unconditional, unbounded, independent, wholehearted, sheer, pure, unmitigated, utter, unabridged, thorough, clean, outright, downright, ideal, simple, perfect, full, blanket, all-out, out-and-out.—*Ant.* RESTRICTED, limited, qualified. **2** [Without limit in authority] supreme, authoritarian, domineering, arbitrary, official, autocratic, tyrannical, fascist, haughty, overbearing, czarist, nazi, totalitarian, oppressive, antidemocratic, imperial, dogmatic, commanding, controlling, compelling, despotic, intimidating, fanatic, dictatorial, arrogant, with an iron hand, high and mighty*.—*Ant.* LENIENT, tolerant, temperate. **3** [Certain] positive, unquestionable, undeniable; see CERTAIN 2.

absolutely ***a.*** **1** [Completely] utterly, unconditionally, thoroughly; see COMPLETELY. **2** [Positively] unquestionably, certainly, definitely; see SURELY.

absolve ***v.*** pardon, set free, clear; see EXCUSE.

absorb ***v.*** digest, take in, ingest, use up, assimilate, blot, imbibe, swallow, consume, incorporate, sop up, soak up, sponge up.

absorbed ***a.*** assimilated, taken in, swallowed up, consumed, drunk, imbibed, dissolved, incorporated, fused, united, digested.—*Ant.* REMOVED, unassimilated, unconsumed.

absorbent ***a.*** porous, spongy, permeable, penetrable, receptive, retentive, thirsty.—*Ant.* impermeable, impervious, solid.

absorbing ***a.*** engaging, exciting, enthralling; see INTERESTING.

absorption ***n.*** assimilation, digestion, osmosis, saturation, penetration, fusion, intake, union, merging, blending, consumption, ingestion, swallowing up, taking in, reception, retention, incorporation, appropriation, drinking in, suction, sopping up, soaking up, sponging up, inhalation.—*Ant.* REMOVAL, ejection, discharge.

abstain ***v.*** refrain, refrain from, renounce, desist, withhold, avoid, stop, deny oneself, refuse, decline, hold back, shun, evade, cease, dispense with, do without, fast, starve oneself, have nothing to do with, let alone, do nothing, keep from, keep one's hands off, swear off, lay off*, turn over a new leaf, have no hand in, take the pledge.—*Ant.* JOIN, indulge, gorge.

abstinence ***n.*** abstaining, temperance, denial, self-denial, self-control, self-restraint, continence, fasting, frugality, renunciation, avoidance, sobriety, austerity, refraining, nonindulgence, chastity, moderation, soberness, asceticism, teetotalism.—*Ant.* INDULGENCE, intemperance, overindulgence.

abstract ***a.*** conceptual, intellectual, ideal; see OBSCURE 1.

absurd ***a.*** preposterous, ridiculous, ludicrous; see STUPID.

absurdity ***n.*** improbability, foolishness, senselessness; see NONSENSE 1, 2.

abundance ***n.*** bounty, more than enough, profusion; see PLENTY.

abundant ***a.*** sufficient, ample, copious; see PLENTIFUL 2.

abundantly ***a.*** plentifully, lavishly, richly, handsomely, in large measure, profusely, amply, sufficiently, generously, affluently, inexhaustibly, many times over, to one's heart's content, off the fat of the land; see also ADEQUATELY.

abuse ***n.*** misuse, debasement, degradation, desecration, injury, damage, harm, hurt, wrong, injustice, insult, mistreatment, violation, malevolence, mishandling, mismanagement, pollution, defilement, perversion, prostitution.—*Ant.* CARE, respect, veneration.

abuse ***v.*** insult, injure, hurt, harm, damage, impair, offend, overwork, ill-treat, misuse, maltreat, mistreat, wrong, persecute, molest, victimize, oppress, ruin, mar, spoil, do wrong to, mishandle, pervert, profane, prostitute, desecrate, pollute, harass, manhandle, do an injustice to, violate, defile, impose upon, deprave, taint, debase, corrupt.—*Ant.* DEFEND, protect, befriend.

abused ***a.*** wronged, injured, harmed; see HURT.

a·bys·mal (ə biz′məl) ***adj.*** **1** of or like an abyss; not measurable **2** very bad; wretched —**a·bys′mal·ly** ***adv.***

a·byss (ə bis′) ***n.*** ⟦< Gr *a-*, without + *byssos*, bottom⟧ **1** a bottomless gulf **2** anything too deep for measurement *[an abyss of shame]*

Ab·ys·sin·i·a (ab′ə sin′ē ə) *former name for* ETHIOPIA — **Ab′ys·sin′i·an** ***adj., n.***

ac *abbrev.* acre(s)

Ac *Chem. symbol for* actinium

AC *abbrev.* **1** air conditioning **2** alternating current

-ac (ak, ək) ⟦< Gr⟧ *suffix* **1** characteristic of *[elegiac]* **2** relating to *[cardiac]* **3** affected by *[maniac]*

a·ca·cia (ə kā′shə) ***n.*** ⟦< Gr *akē*, thorn⟧ **1** a tree or shrub with yellow or white flower clusters **2** the locust tree

ac·a·dem·ic (ak′ə dem′ik) ***adj.*** **1** of colleges, universities, etc.; scholastic **2** having to do with the liberal arts rather than technical education **3** formal; pedantic **4** merely theoretical —**ac′a·dem′i·cal·ly** ***adv.***

a·cad·e·mi·cian (ə kad′ə mish′ən, ak′ə də-) ***n.*** a member of an ACADEMY (sense 3)

a·cad·e·my (ə kad′ə mē) ***n.***, *pl.* **-mies** ⟦< Gr *akadēmeia*, place where Plato taught⟧ **1** a private secondary school **2** a school for special instruction **3** an association of scholars, writers, etc., for advancing an art or science

a·can·thus (ə kan′thəs) ***n.***, *pl.* **-thus·es** or **-thi′** (-thī′, -thē′) ⟦< Gr *akē*, a point⟧ **1** a plant with lobed, often spiny leaves **2** *Archit.* a representation of these leaves

a cap·pel·la (ä′ kə pel′ə) ⟦It, in chapel style⟧ without instrumental accompaniment: said of vocalists or vocal groups: also sp. **a ca·pel′la**

A·ca·pul·co (ä′kə po͝ol′kō, ak′ə-) city & seaport in S Mexico, on the Pacific: a winter resort: pop. 593,000

ac·cede (ak sēd′) ***vi.*** **-ced′ed**, **-ced′ing** ⟦< L *ad-*, to + *cedere*, go, yield⟧ **1** to enter upon the duties (of an office); attain (*to*) **2** to assent; agree (*to*)

ac·cel·er·ate (ak sel′ər āt′, ək-) ***vt.*** **-at′ed**, **-at′ing** ⟦< L *ad-*, to + *celerare*, hasten⟧ **1** to increase the speed of **2** to cause to happen sooner —***vi.*** to go faster —**ac·cel′er·a′tion** ***n.***

ac·cel′er·a′tor ***n.*** that which accelerates something; esp., the foot throttle of a motor vehicle

ac·cent (ak′sent′; *for v., also* ak sent′) ***n.*** ⟦< L *ad-*, to + *canere*, sing⟧ **1** emphasis given a spoken syllable or word **2** a mark showing such emphasis or indicating pronunciation **3** a distinguishing manner of pronunciation *[an Irish accent]* **4** special emphasis or attention **5** *Music, Prosody* rhythmic stress —***vt.*** **1** to mark with an accent **2** to emphasize; stress

ac·cen·tu·ate (ak sen′cho͞o āt′, ək-) ***vt.*** **-at′ed**, **-at′ing** to accent; emphasize —**ac·cen′tu·a′tion** ***n.***

ac·cept (ak sept′, ək-) ***vt.*** ⟦< L *ad-*, to + *capere*, take⟧ **1** to receive, esp. willingly **2** to approve **3** to agree or consent to **4** to believe in **5** to reply "yes" to **6** to agree to pay

ac·cept′a·ble ***adj.*** worth accepting; satisfactory —**ac·cept′a·bil′i·ty** or **ac·cept′a·ble·ness** ***n.*** —**ac·cept′a·bly** ***adv.***

ac·cept′ance ***n.*** **1** an accepting **2** approval **3** belief in; assent **4** a promise to pay

ac·cept′ed ***adj.*** generally regarded as true, proper, etc.; conventional; approved

ac·cess (ak′ses′) ***n.*** ⟦see ACCEDE⟧ **1** approach or means of approach **2** the right to enter, use, etc. **3** an outburst; fit *[an access of anger]* —***vt.*** to get data from, or add data to, a database

ac·ces·si·ble (ak ses′ə bəl, ək-) ***adj.*** **1** that can be approached or entered, esp. easily **2** obtainable **3** easily understood —**ac·ces′si·bil′i·ty** ***n.*** —**ac·ces′si·bly** ***adv.***

ac·ces·sion (ak sesh′ən, ək-) ***n.*** **1** the act of attaining (a throne, power, etc.) **2** assent **3** *a)* increase by addition *b)* an addition

ac·ces·so·ry (ak ses′ər ē, ək-) ***adj.*** ⟦see ACCEDE⟧ **1** additional; extra **2** helping in an unlawful act —***n.***, *pl.* **-ries** **1** something extra or complementary **2** one who, though absent, helps another to break the law

ac·ci·dent (ak′sə dənt) ***n.*** ⟦< L *ad-*, to + *cadere*, to fall⟧ **1** an unexpected or unintended happening, as one resulting in injury, loss, etc. **2** chance

ac′ci·den′tal (-dent′'l) ***adj.*** happening by chance —**ac′ci·den′tal·ly** ***adv.***

ac′ci·dent-prone′ ***adj.*** seemingly inclined to become involved in accidents

ac·claim (ə klām′) ***vt.*** ⟦< L *ad-*, to + *clamare*, to cry out⟧ to greet or announce with loud approval or applause; hail —***n.*** loud approval

ac·cla·ma·tion (ak′lə mā′shən) ***n.*** **1** loud applause or approval **2** an approving vote by voice

ac·cli·mate (ak′lə māt′, ə klī′mət) ***vt.***, ***vi.*** **-mat·ed**, **-mat·ing** ⟦< L *ad-*, to + Gr *klima*, region⟧ to accustom or become accustomed to a new climate or environment —**ac′cli·ma′tion** ***n.***

ac·cli·ma·tize (ə klī′mə tīz′) ***vt.***, ***vi.*** **-tized′**, **-tiz′ing** ACCLIMATE —**ac·cli′ma·ti·za′tion** ***n.***

ac·cliv·i·ty (ə kliv′ə tē) ***n.***, *pl.* **-ties** ⟦< L *ad-*, up + *clivus*, hill⟧ an upward slope

ac·co·lade (ak′ə lād′) ***n.*** ⟦< L *ad*, to + *collum*, neck⟧ anything done or given to show great respect, appreciation, etc.

ac·com·mo·date (ə käm′ə dāt′) ***vt.*** **-dat′ed**, **-dat′ing** ⟦< L *ad-*, to + *commodare*, to fit⟧ **1** to adapt **2** to do a favor for **3** to have space for

ac·com′mo·dat′ing ***adj.*** obliging

ac·com′mo·da′tion ***n.*** **1** adjustment **2** willingness to do favors **3** a help; convenience **4** [*pl.*] *a)* lodgings *b)* traveling space, as in a train

ac·com·pa·ni·ment (ə kum′pə nə mənt, -nē-; *often* ə kump′nə-, -nē-) ***n.*** anything that accompanies something else, as an instrumental part supporting a solo voice, etc.

ac·com·pa·ny (ə kum′pə nē; *often* ə kump′nē) ***vt.*** **-nied**, **-ny·ing** ⟦see AD- & COMPANION⟧ **1** to go with **2** to sup-

THESAURUS

academic ***a.*** scholastic, erudite, scholarly; see LEARNED.

academy ***n.*** preparatory school, boarding school, finishing school, secondary school, prep school; see also SCHOOL 1.

accelerate ***v.*** quicken, speed up, hurry; see HASTEN 2.

acceleration ***n.*** speeding up, hastening, increase of speed, quickening, hurrying, stepping up, picking up speed; see also SPEED.

accent ***n.*** stress, beat, stroke, emphasis, pitch, accentuation, inflection, intonation, rhythm, meter, cadence.

accept ***v.*** receive, get, admit, be resigned, give in to, believe, trust, surrender, suffer, endure, allow, tolerate, take in one's stride, consent, acquiesce; see also AGREE.

acceptable ***a.*** satisfactory, agreeable, pleasing; see PLEASANT 2.

acceptance ***n.*** recognition, assent, approval; see AGREEMENT 1.

accepted ***a.*** taken, received, assumed, approved, adopted, recognized, endorsed, verified, acclaimed, welcomed, engaged, hired, claimed, delivered, used, employed, affirmed, upheld, authorized, preferred, acknowledged, accredited, allowed, settled, established, sanctioned, unopposed, customary, authentic, confirmed, chosen, acceptable, popular, formally admitted, stereotyped, orthodox, standard, conventional, current, taken for granted, credited, OK'd*; see also POPULAR 1, 3.—*Ant.* REFUSED, denied, nullified.

access ***n.*** admittance, entree, introduction; see ENTRANCE 1, 2.

accessible ***a.*** approachable, obtainable, attainable; see AVAILABLE.

accessories ***n.*** frills, ornaments, adornments, decorations, additions, attachments, gimmicks*, doodads*.

accessory ***n.*** **1** [An accomplice] helper, aid, assistant; see ASSOCIATE. **2** [Something added] attachment, consequence, attendant, complement, supplement, addition.

accident ***n.*** luck, fortune, contingency, occurrence, circumstance, event, occasion; see also CHANCE 1.

accidental ***a.*** adventitious, chance, coincidental; see AIMLESS, UNFORTUNATE.

accidentally ***a.*** unintentionally, involuntarily, unwittingly, unexpectedly, inadvertently, casually, by chance, haphazardly, incidentally, randomly, not purposely, by a fluke*.—*Ant.* DELIBERATELY, voluntarily, intentionally.

accommodate ***v.*** **1** [To render a service] help, aid, comfort, make comfortable, oblige, suit, serve, gratify, please, arrange, settle, provide, benefit, tender, supply, furnish, assist, support, sustain, do a favor, indulge, humor, pamper, accept, put oneself out for, do a service for. **2** [To suit one thing to another] fit, adapt, correspond; see ADJUST 1. **3** [To provide lodging] house, lodge, put up; see ENTERTAIN 2.

accommodations ***n.*** quarters, rooms, lodging, housing, apartment, hotel, room and board, roof over one's head; see also HOME 1.

accompanied ***a.*** chaperoned, attended, escorted, shown around, shown about, not alone.

accompaniment ***n.*** harmony, instrumental music, musical background; see MUSIC 1.

accompany ***v.*** escort, attend, be with, follow, keep company with, guard, guide, usher, show in, show around, show the way, conduct, go along, go along with, chaperon, associate with, consort with, look after, go

plement **3** to play or sing an accompaniment for or to —**ac·com'pa·nist** ***n.***
ac·com·plice (ə käm'plis) ***n.*** ⟦< ME *a* (the article) + LL *complex*, a confederate⟧ a partner in crime
ac·com·plish (ə käm'plish) ***vt.*** ⟦< L *ad-*, intens. + *complere*, fill up⟧ to succeed in doing; complete
ac·com'plished ***adj.*** **1** done; completed **2** skilled; expert
ac·com'plish·ment ***n.*** **1** completion **2** work completed; an achievement **3** a social art or skill: *usually used in pl.*
ac·cord (ə kôrd') ***vt.*** ⟦< L *ad-*, to + *cor*, heart⟧ **1** to make agree **2** to grant —***vi.*** to agree; harmonize (*with*) —***n.*** mutual agreement; harmony —**of one's own accord** willingly —**with one accord** all agreeing
ac·cord'ance ***n.*** agreement; conformity —**ac·cord'ant** ***adj.***
ac·cord'ing ***adj.*** in harmony —**according to** **1** in agreement with **2** as stated by
ac·cord'ing·ly ***adv.*** **1** in a fitting and proper way **2** therefore
ac·cor·di·on (ə kôr'dē ən) ***n.*** ⟦prob. < It *accordare*, to be in tune⟧ a musical instrument with keys and a bellows, which is pressed to force air through reeds
ac·cost (ə kôst') ***vt.*** ⟦< L *ad-*, to + *costa*, side⟧ to approach and speak to, esp. in a bold way
ac·count (ə kount') ***vt.*** ⟦< OFr *a-*, to + *conter*, tell⟧ to judge to be —***vi.*** **1** to give a financial reckoning (*to*) **2** to give reasons (*for*) **3** to be the reason (*for*) —***n.*** **1** [*often pl.*] a record of business transactions **2** *a)* BANK ACCOUNT *b)* CHARGE ACCOUNT **3** a credit customer or client **4** worth; importance **5** an explanation **6** a report —**on account** as partial payment —**on account of** because of —**on no account** under no circumstances —**take into account** to consider
ac·count'a·ble ***adj.*** responsible; liable —**ac·count'a·bil'i·ty** ***n.***
ac·count'ant ***n.*** one whose work is accounting
ac·count'ing ***n.*** the figuring and recording of financial accounts
ac·cou·ter (ə ko͞ot'ər) ***vt.*** ⟦prob. < L *consuere*, to sew⟧ to outfit; equip
ac·cou·ter·ments or **ac·cou·tre·ments** (ə ko͞ot'ər mənts, -ko͞o'trə-) ***pl.n.*** **1** clothes **2** equipment
ac·cred·it (ə kred'it) ***vt.*** ⟦see CREDIT⟧ **1** to authorize; certify **2** to believe in **3** to attribute —**ac·cred'i·ta'tion** ***n.***
ac·cre·tion (ə krē'shən) ***n.*** ⟦< L *ad-*, to + *crescere*, to grow⟧ **1** growth in size, esp. by addition **2** accumulated matter **3** a growing together of parts **4** a part added separately; addition
ac·crue (ə kro͞o') ***vi.*** **-crued'**, **-cru'ing** ⟦see prec.⟧ to come as a natural growth or periodic increase, as interest on money —**ac·cru'al** ***n.***
acct *abbrev.* account
ac·cul·tur·ate (ə kul'chər āt') ***vi.***, ***vt.*** **-at'ed**, **-at'ing** to undergo, or change by, acculturation
ac·cul'tur·a'tion ***n.*** **1** adaptation to a culture, esp. a new or different one **2** mutual influence of different cultures
ac·cu·mu·late (ə kyo͞o'myə lāt') ***vt.***, ***vi.*** **-lat'ed**, **-lat'ing** ⟦< L *ad-*, to + *cumulare*, to heap⟧ to pile up or collect —**ac·cu'mu·la'tion** ***n.*** —**ac·cu'mu·la'tive** (-lāt'iv, -lə tiv) ***adj.***
ac·cu·ra·cy (ak'yoor ə sē, -yər-) ***n.*** the quality or state of being accurate; precision
ac'cu·rate (-it) ***adj.*** ⟦< L *ad-*, to + *cura*, care⟧ **1** careful and exact **2** free from errors; precise —**ac'cu·rate·ly** ***adv.*** —**ac'cu·rate·ness** ***n.***
ac·curs·ed (ə kur'sid, -kurst') ***adj.*** **1** under a curse **2** damnable Also **ac·curst'** —**ac·curs'ed·ness** ***n.***
ac·cu·sa·tion (ak'yo͞o zā'shən, -yə-) ***n.*** **1** an accusing or being accused **2** what one is accused of —**ac·cu·sa·to·ry** (ə kyo͞o'zə tôr'ē) ***adj.***
ac·cu·sa·tive (ə kyo͞o'zə tiv) ***n.*** ⟦see fol.⟧ *Gram.* the case of the direct object of a verb; also, the objective case in English
ac·cuse (ə kyo͞oz') ***vt.*** **-cused'**, **-cus'ing** ⟦< L *ad-*, to + *causa*, a cause⟧ **1** to blame **2** to bring charges against —**ac·cus'er** ***n.***
ac·cus·tom (ə kus'təm) ***vt.*** to make familiar with something by custom, habit, or use; habituate (*to*)
ac·cus'tomed ***adj.*** **1** customary; usual **2** habituated (*to*)
AC/DC or **A.C./D.C.** (ā'sē'dē'sē') ***adj.*** ⟦< *a(lternating) c(urrent or) d(irect) c(urrent)*⟧ [Slang] bisexual
ace (ās) ***n.*** ⟦< L *as*, unit⟧ **1** a playing card, etc. with one spot **2** a point, as in tennis, made by a serve one's opponent cannot return **3** an expert, esp. in combat flying —***adj.*** [Inf.] first-rate —***vt.*** **aced**, **ac'ing** **1** [Slang] to defeat completely: often with *out* **2** [Inf.] to earn a grade of A in, on, etc.
Ace bandage ⟦< *Ace*, trademark for such a bandage⟧ an elasticized cloth bandage used to provide support, as for a sprain
ace in the hole [Slang] any advantage held in reserve
a·cer·bi·ty (ə sur'bə tē) ***n.***, *pl.* **-ties** ⟦< L *acerbus*, bitter⟧ **1** sourness **2** sharpness of temper, words, etc. —**a·cer'bic** ***adj.***
a·ce·ta·min·o·phen (ə sēt'ə min'ə fən, as'ə tə-) ***n.*** a crystalline powder used to lessen fever and pain
ac·et·an·i·lide (as'ət an'ə līd') ***n.*** ⟦< ACETIC + ANILINE⟧ a drug used to lessen pain and fever
ac·e·tate (as'i tāt') ***n.*** **1** a salt or ester of acetic acid **2** something, esp. a fabric, made with an acetate of cellulose
a·ce·tic (ə sēt'ik) ***adj.*** ⟦< L *acetum*, vinegar⟧ of the sharp, sour liquid (**acetic acid**) found in vinegar
ac·e·tone (as'i tōn') ***n.*** ⟦see prec.⟧ a colorless, flammable liquid used as a solvent, esp. in making rayon —**ac'e·ton'ic** (-tän'ik) ***adj.***

THESAURUS

hand in hand with, go side by side with, hang around with*.

accomplice ***n.*** confederate, helper, aid; see ASSOCIATE.

accomplish ***v.*** fulfill, perform, finish; see ACHIEVE, SUCCEED 1.

accomplished ***a.*** **1** [Done] completed, consummated, concluded; see FINISHED. **2** [Skilled] proficient, expert, skillful; see ABLE.

accomplishment ***n.*** execution, fulfillment, attainment; see SUCCESS 2.

accordingly ***a.*** in consequence, consequently, equally, respectively, duly, subsequently, in respect to, thus, hence, therefore, as a result, as a consequence, as the case may be, under the circumstances, as things go, to that end, in that event.

according to ***prep.*** in accordance with, as, to the degree that, conforming to, in keeping with, in line with, in agreement with, consistent with, commensurate with.

account ***n.*** statement, record, report; see RECORD 1. —**give a good account of oneself** acquit oneself creditably, do well, do oneself proud*, behave courageously. —**on account** charged, in layaway, on layaway, on call; see also UNPAID 1. —**on account of** because of, by virtue of, since; see BECAUSE. —**on no account** for no reason, no way, under no circumstances; see NEVER. —**on someone's account** because of someone, for someone's sake, in someone's behalf; see BECAUSE. —**take account of** judge, evaluate, investigate; see EXAMINE 1. —**take into account** judge, allow for, weigh; see CONSIDER.

accountant ***n.*** bookkeeper, auditor, CPA; see CLERK.

account for ***v.*** clarify, justify, elucidate; see EXPLAIN.

accumulate ***v.*** hoard, get together, gather, amass, amalgamate, collect, heap, store, assemble, concentrate, compile, pile up, accrue, scrape up, stockpile, store up, acquire, gain, load up, rake up, unite, add to, build up, gain control of, roll in*, bank; see also GET 1.

accuracy ***n.*** efficiency, exactness, precision, correctness, skillfulness, sharpness, incisiveness, mastery, dependability, strictness, certainty, sureness.—*Ant.* ERROR, inaccuracy, mistake.

accurate ***a.*** **1** [Free from error] exact, correct, perfect; see RIGHT 1. **2** [Characterized by precision] deft, reliable, trustworthy, true, correct, exact, specific, dependable, skillful, methodical, systematic, distinct, particular, realistic, authentic, genuine, careful, close, critical, detailed, factual, severe, rigorous, rigid, strict, meticulous, sharp, faithful, punctual, scientific, objective, rational, unmistakable, reasonable, right, explicit, definite, defined, on the button*, on the dot*, on the nose*, solid.—*Ant.* INCOMPETENT, faulty, slipshod.

accurately ***a.*** correctly, precisely, exactly; see CAREFULLY 1.

accusation ***n.*** indictment, allegation, denunciation, slur, complaint, citation, charge, insinuation, imputation, smear*, frame-up*, rap*.

accuse ***v.*** denounce, charge, indict; see BLAME.

accused ***a.*** arraigned, indicted, incriminated, charged with, under suspicion, alleged to be guilty, apprehended, held for questioning, liable, involved, under attack, under fire, implicated.—*Ant.* DISCHARGED, acquitted, cleared.

accuser ***n.*** prosecutor, plaintiff, adversary; see OPPONENT 1.

accustomed ***a.*** usual, customary, habitual; see CONVENTIONAL 1. —**accustomed to** in the habit of, used to, inclined to; see ADDICTED (TO).

ace ***a.*** expert, first-rate, outstanding; see DISTINGUISHED 2, ABLE.

ace ***n.*** expert, master, champion; see SPECIALIST.

a·cet·y·lene (ə set′'l ēn′) ***n.*** a gas used for lighting and, with oxygen, in welding
a·ce·tyl·sal·i·cyl·ic acid (ə sēt′'l sal′ə sil′ik) ASPIRIN
ache (āk) ***vi.*** **ached, ach′ing** ⟦< OE *acan*⟧ **1** to have or give dull, steady pain **2** [Inf.] to yearn —***n.*** a dull, continuous pain
a·chene (ā kēn′, ə-) ***n.*** ⟦< Gr *a-*, not + *chainein*, to gape⟧ any small, dry fruit with one seed
a·chieve (ə chēv′) ***vt.*** **a·chieved′, a·chiev′ing** ⟦< OFr < *a-*, to + L *caput*, head⟧ **1** to do; accomplish **2** to get by effort —**a·chiev′a·ble** ***adj.*** —**a·chiev′er** ***n.***
a·chieve′ment ***n.*** **1** an achieving **2** a thing achieved; feat
achievement test a test for measuring a student's mastery of a given subject or skill
A·chil·les (ə kil′ēz′) ***n.*** a Greek hero killed in the Trojan War
Achilles' heel (one's) vulnerable spot
Achilles tendon the tendon connecting the heel to the calf muscles
a·choo (ä cho͞o′) ***interj.*** used to suggest a sneeze
ach·ro·mat·ic (ak′rə mat′ik; ā′krə-) ***adj.*** ⟦< Gr *a-*, without + *chrōma*, color⟧ refracting white light without breaking it up into its component colors
ach·y (āk′ē) ***adj.*** **-i·er, -i·est** having an ache
ac·id (as′id) ***adj.*** ⟦L *acidus*, sour⟧ **1** sour; sharp; tart **2** of an acid —***n.*** **1** a sour substance **2** [Slang] LSD **3** *Chem.* any compound that reacts with a base to form a salt —**a·cid·i·ty** (ə sid′ə tē), *pl.* **-ties,** ***n.*** —**ac′id·ly** ***adv.***
a·cid·i·fy (ə sid′ə fī′) ***vt., vi.*** **-fied′, -fy′ing** **1** to make or become sour **2** to change into an acid
ac·i·do·sis (as′ə dō′sis) ***n.*** a condition in which there is an abnormal retention of acid or loss of alkali in the body
acid rain rain with a high concentration of acids produced by the gases from burning fossil fuels
acid test a crucial, final test
a·cid·u·lous (ə sij′o͞o ləs) ***adj.*** **1** somewhat acid or sour **2** sarcastic
-a·cious (ā′shəs) ⟦< L⟧ *suffix* inclined to, full of *[tenacious]*
-ac·i·ty (as′ə tē) ⟦< L⟧ *suffix* a (specified) characteristic, quality, or tendency *[tenacity]*
ac·knowl·edge (ak näl′ij, ək-) ***vt.*** **-edged, -edg·ing** ⟦see KNOWLEDGE⟧ **1** to admit as true **2** to recognize the authority or claims of **3** to respond to **4** to express thanks for **5** to state that one has received (a letter, etc.) —**ac·knowl′edg·ment** or **ac·knowl′edge·ment** ***n.***
ACLU *abbrev.* American Civil Liberties Union
ac·me (ak′mē) ***n.*** ⟦Gr *akmē*, a point, top⟧ the highest point; peak
ac·ne (ak′nē) ***n.*** ⟦see prec.⟧ a skin disorder usually causing pimples on the face, etc.
ac·o·lyte (ak′ə līt′) ***n.*** ⟦< Gr *akolouthos*, follower⟧ **1** one who helps a priest at services, esp. at Mass **2** an attendant; helper
ac·o·nite (ak′ə nīt′) ***n.*** ⟦< Gr⟧ a plant with hoodlike flowers
a·corn (ā′kôrn′) ***n.*** ⟦< OE *æcern*, nut⟧ the nut of the oak tree
acorn squash a kind of winter squash, acorn-shaped with dark-green skin and yellow flesh
a·cous·tic (ə ko͞os′tik) ***adj.*** ⟦< Gr *akouein*, to hear⟧ **1** having to do with hearing or acoustics **2** of or using a musical instrument that is not amplified Also **a·cous′ti·cal** —**a·cous′ti·cal·ly** ***adv.***
a·cous′tics (-tiks) ***pl.n.*** the qualities of a room, etc. that determine how clearly sounds can be heard in it —***n.*** the branch of physics dealing with sound
ac·quaint (ə kwānt′) ***vt.*** ⟦< L *ad-*, to + *cognoscere*, know⟧ **1** to inform **2** to make familiar (*with*)
ac·quaint′ance ***n.*** **1** knowledge gotten from personal experience **2** a person whom one knows slightly
ac·qui·esce (ak′wē es′) ***vi.*** **-esced′, -esc′ing** ⟦< L *ad-*, to + *quiescere*, grow quiet⟧ to consent without enthusiasm: often with *in* —**ac′qui·es′cence** ***n.*** —**ac′qui·es′cent** ***adj.***
ac·quire (ə kwīr′) ***vt.*** **-quired′, -quir′ing** ⟦< L *ad-*, to + *quaerere*, to seek⟧ **1** to gain by one's own efforts **2** to get as one's own —**ac·quire′ment** ***n.***
ac·qui·si·tion (ak′wə zish′ən) ***n.*** **1** an acquiring **2** something acquired
ac·quis·i·tive (ə kwiz′ə tiv) ***adj.*** eager to acquire (money, etc.); grasping —**ac·quis′i·tive·ness** ***n.***
ac·quit (ə kwit′) ***vt.*** **-quit′ted, -quit′ting** ⟦< L *ad-*, to + *quietare*, to quiet⟧ **1** to release from an obligation, etc. **2** to clear (a person) of a charge **3** to conduct (oneself); behave —**ac·quit′tal** ***n.***
a·cre (ā′kər) ***n.*** ⟦OE *æcer*, field⟧ a measure of land, 4,840 sq. yards
a′cre·age ***n.*** acres collectively
ac·rid (ak′rid) ***adj.*** ⟦< L *acris*, sharp⟧ **1** sharp or bitter to the taste or smell **2** sharp in speech, etc. —**a·crid·i·ty** (ə krid′ə tē) ***n.*** —**ac′rid·ly** ***adv.***
ac·ri·mo·ny (ak′ri mō′nē) ***n.***, *pl.* **-nies** ⟦< L *acer*, sharp⟧ bitterness or harshness of manner or speech —**ac′ri·mo′ni·ous** ***adj.***
ac·ro·bat (ak′rə bat′) ***n.*** ⟦< Gr *akrobatos*, walking on tiptoe⟧ a performer on the trapeze, tightrope, etc.; gymnast —**ac′ro·bat′ic** ***adj.***
ac′ro·bat′ics ***pl.n.*** [*also with sing. v.*] **1** an acrobat's tricks **2** any tricks requiring great skill
ac·ro·nym (ak′rə nim′) ***n.*** ⟦< Gr *akros*, at the end +

THESAURUS

ache ***n.*** twinge, pang, spasm; see PAIN 2.

ache ***v.*** pain, throb, be sore; see HURT.

achieve ***v.*** complete, end, terminate, conclude, finish, finish up, finish off, do, perform, execute, fulfill, carry out, carry through, bring about, settle, effect, bring to a conclusion, close, stop, produce, realize, actualize, discharge, wind up, work out, adjust, resolve, solve, accomplish, make an end of, enact, manage, contrive, negotiate, sign, seal, bring to pass, see it through, get done, close up, carry to completion, follow through, deliver, knock off*, fill the bill*, round out*, come through, polish off*, clean up*, mop up*, put across*, pull off*, make short work of*, put through, go all the way*, go the limit*, call it a day*, put the finishing touch on*, dispose of.—*Ant.* ABANDON, fail, give up.

achievement ***n.*** fulfillment, feat, exploit, accomplishment, triumph, hit, success, realization, creation, completion, execution, actualization, masterpiece, performance, deed, act, enactment, victory, conquest, attainment, feather in one's cap.—*Ant.* FAILURE, blunder, collapse.

acid ***a.*** sharp, tart, biting; see SOUR.

acid ***n.*** **1** [A sour substance] strong acid, weak acid, corrosive, Lewis acid. *Common acids include the following:* vinegar, lemon juice; citric, ascorbic, lactic, nicotinic, boric, acetic, sulfuric, hydrochloric, formic, stearic, phosphoric, carbolic, nitric, benzoic, amino, fatty. **2** [A drug] lysergic acid, LSD, mescaline; see DRUG.

acidity ***n.*** sourness, bitterness, tartness, sharpness, pungency, harshness, causticity.

acknowledge ***v.*** **1** [To admit] concede, confess, declare; see ADMIT 2. **2** [To recognize the authority of] endorse, certify, confirm, uphold, support, recognize, ratify, approve, defend, subscribe to, accede to, attest to, take an oath by, defer to.

acknowledged ***a.*** admitted, confessed, recognized, unquestioned, accepted, authorized, confirmed, received, sanctioned, accredited, approved, out-and-out.

acknowledgment ***n.*** greeting, reply, answer, response, nod, confession, statement, apology, guarantee, return, support, signature, receipt, letter, card, contract, applause, vote of thanks, IOU.

acquaintance ***n.*** **1** [A person one knows] colleague, associate, neighbor; see FRIEND. **2** [Acquired knowledge] familiarity, awareness, experience; see AWARENESS, EXPERIENCE.

acquainted (with) ***a.*** introduced, on speaking terms, having some connections; see FAMILIAR WITH.

acquaint with ***v.*** introduce, make acquainted, present; see INTRODUCE 3.

acquire ***v.*** take, earn, procure; see GET 1.

acquired ***a.*** reached, inherited, accrued, derived, granted, endowed, bequeathed, handed down, transmitted, allowed, awarded, passed on, willed to, attained, accomplished, learned, adopted, earned, collected, gathered, harvested, secured, procured, obtained, captured, regained, realized, gotten by the sweat of one's brow, dug out*, raked in*, cornered*, netted, salted away*, grabbed; see also WON.

acquisition ***n.*** inheritance, gift, donation, grant, wealth, riches, fortune, profit, gain, earnings, wages, salary, income, winnings, return, returns, proceeds, benefit, prize, reward, award, accomplishment, achievement, premium, bonus, fee, commission, pension, annuity, allowance, gain, dividend.

acquit ***v.*** clear, absolve, vindicate; see EXCUSE.

acquittal ***n.*** absolution, clearance, exoneration, dismissal, deliverance, amnesty, discharge, pardon, reprieve, exemption, liberation, release, freedom.—*Ant.* PUNISHMENT, sentence, imprisonment.

acre ***n.*** plot, acreage, bit of land, estate; see also PROPERTY 2.

acrobat ***n.*** tumbler, clown, trampolinist, aerialist, trapeze artist, trapezist, contortionist, tightrope walker, stuntman, figure skater, circus performer, ballet dancer, gymnast.

onyma, name⟧ a word formed from the first (or first few) letters of several words, as *radar*

ac·ro·pho·bi·a (ak′rō fō′bē ə) ***n.*** ⟦< Gr *akros*, at the top + PHOBIA⟧ an abnormal fear of being in high places

A·crop·o·lis (ə kräp′ə lis) ⟦< Gr *akros*, at the top + *polis*, city⟧ the fortified hill in Athens on which the Parthenon was built

a·cross (ə krôs′) ***adv.*** **1** crosswise **2** from one side to the other —***prep.*** **1** from one side to the other of **2** on or to the other side of **3** into contact with by chance *[to come across an old friend]*

a·cross′-the-board′ ***adj.*** **1** combining win, place, and show, as a bet **2** including or affecting all classes or groups

a·cros·tic (ə krôs′tik) ***n.*** ⟦Gr *akrostichos* < *akros*, at the end + *stichos*, line of verse⟧ a poem, etc. in which certain letters in each line, as the first or last, spell out a word, motto, etc.

a·cryl·ic (ə kril′ik) ***adj.*** **1** designating any of a group of synthetic fibers used to make fabrics **2** designating any of a group of clear, synthetic resins used to make paints, plastics, etc.

act (akt) ***n.*** ⟦< L *agere*, to do⟧ **1** a thing done **2** an action **3** a law **4** a main division of a drama or opera **5** a short performance, as on a variety show **6** something done merely for show —***vt.*** to perform in (a play or part) —***vi.*** **1** to perform in a play, movie, etc. **2** to behave **3** to function **4** to have an effect (*on*) **5** to appear to be —**act up** [Inf.] to misbehave

ACTH ⟦*a*(*dreno*)*c*(*ortico*)*t*(*ropic*) *h*(*ormone*)⟧ a pituitary hormone that acts on the adrenal cortex

act′ing ***adj.*** temporarily doing the duties of another —***n.*** the art of an actor

ac·ti·nide series (ak′tə nīd′) a group of radioactive chemical elements from element 89 (actinium) through element 103 (lawrencium)

ac·tin·i·um (ak tin′ē əm) ***n.*** ⟦< Gr *aktis,* ray⟧ a white, radioactive, metallic chemical element

ac·tion (ak′shən) ***n.*** **1** the doing of something **2** a thing done **3** [*pl.*] behavior **4** the way of working, as of a machine **5** the moving parts, as of a gun **6** the sequence of events, as in a story **7** a lawsuit **8** military combat **9** [Slang] activity

ac·ti·vate (ak′tə vāt′) ***vt.*** **-vat′ed**, **-vat′ing** **1** to make active **2** to put (a military unit) on active status —**ac′ti·va′tion** ***n.*** —**ac′ti·va′tor** ***n.***

activated carbon a form of highly porous carbon that can adsorb gases, vapors, and colloidal particles: also **activated charcoal**

ac·tive (ak′tiv) ***adj.*** **1** acting; working **2** causing motion or change **3** lively; agile **4** *Gram.* indicating the voice of a verb whose subject performs the action —**ac′tive·ly** ***adv.***

ac′tiv·ism′ (-tə viz′əm) ***n.*** the taking of direct action to achieve a political or social end —**ac′tiv·ist** ***adj.***, ***n.***

ac·tiv·i·ty (ak tiv′ə tē) ***n.***, *pl.* **-ties** **1** a being active **2** liveliness **3** a specific action or function *[student activities]*

ac·tor (ak′tər) ***n.*** **1** one who does a thing **2** one who acts in plays, movies, etc. —**ac′tress** (-tris) ***fem.n.***

ac·tu·al (ak′cho͞o əl) ***adj.*** ⟦< L *agere*, to do⟧ **1** existing in reality **2** existing at the time —**ac′tu·al·ly** ***adv.***

ac′tu·al′i·ty (-al′ə tē) ***n.*** **1** reality **2** *pl.* **-ties** an actual thing; fact

ac′tu·al·ize′ (-əl īz′) ***vt.*** **-ized′**, **-iz′ing** **1** to make actual or real **2** to make realistic

ac·tu·ar·y (ak′cho͞o er′ē) ***n.***, *pl.* **-ies** ⟦L *actuarius*, clerk⟧ one who figures insurance risks, premiums, etc. —**ac′tu·ar′i·al** ***adj.***

ac·tu·ate (ak′cho͞o āt′) ***vt.*** **-at′ed**, **-at′ing** **1** to put into action **2** to cause to take action —**ac′tu·a′tor** ***n.***

a·cu·i·ty (ə kyo͞o′ə tē) ***n.*** ⟦< L *acus*, needle⟧ keenness of thought or vision

a·cu·men (ə kyo͞o′mən, ak′yə mən) ***n.*** ⟦< L *acuere*, sharpen⟧ keenness of mind; shrewdness

ac·u·punc·ture (ak′yo͞o puŋk′chər) ***n.*** ⟦< L *acus*, needle + PUNCTURE⟧ the ancient practice, esp. among the Chinese, of piercing parts of the body with needles to treat disease or relieve pain —**ac′u·punc′tur·ist** ***n.***

a·cute (ə kyo͞ot′) ***adj.*** ⟦< L *acuere*, sharpen⟧ **1** sharp-pointed **2** keen of mind **3** sensitive *[acute hearing]* **4** severe, as pain **5** severe but not chronic *[an acute disease]* **6** very serious **7** less than 90° *[an acute angle]* —**a·cute′ly** ***adv.*** —**a·cute′ness** ***n.***

THESAURUS

across ***a.***, ***prep.*** crosswise, crossed, to the opposite side of, over, opposite, on the other side, from side to side of, from one side to another, transversely, in front of, opposite to, beyond.

act ***n.*** **1** [An action] deed, performance, exploit; see ACTION 2. **2** [An official or legal statement] law, proposal, judgment, order, commitment, verdict, amendment, announcement, edict, ordinance, decree, statute, writ, bull, warrant, summons, subpoena, document, bill, code, clause, law of the land*. **3** [A division of a play] scene, prologue, epilogue, introduction; first act, second act, third act, etc. **4** [A pose] falsification, feigning, affectation; see PRETENSE 1.

act ***v.*** **1** [To perform an action] do, execute, carry out, carry on, operate, transact, accomplish, achieve, consummate, carry into effect, perpetrate, persist, labor, work, officiate, function, preside, serve, go ahead, step into, take steps, play a part, begin, move, enforce, maneuver, create, practice, develop, make progress, be active, commit, fight, combat, respond, keep going, answer, pursue, put forth energy, hustle*, get going*.—*Ant.* WAIT, await, rest. **2** [To conduct oneself] behave, seem, appear, carry oneself, give the appearance of, represent oneself as, take on, play one's part, impress one as, put on airs; see also BEHAVE. **3** [To take part in a play] perform, impersonate, represent, act out, simulate, pretend, mimic, burlesque, parody, feign, portray, rehearse, take a part, dramatize, star, play the part of, debut. —**act up** goof off*, be naughty, create a disturbance; see MISBEHAVE. —**act upon** (or **on**) **1** [To act in accordance with] adjust, regulate, behave; see ACT 1, 2. **2** [To influence] affect, sway, impress; see INFLUENCE.

acting ***a.*** substituting, alternate, assistant; see TEMPORARY.

acting ***n.*** pretending, feigning, simulating, gesturing, ranting, dramatizing, performing, behaving, playing, showing off, impersonation, depiction, portrayal, pantomime, rendition, dramatics, theatricals, performance, dramatic action, mime.

action ***n.*** **1** [Any state opposed to rest and quiet] activity, conflict, business, occupation, work, response, reaction, movement, industry, bustle, turmoil, stir, flurry, animation, vivacity, enterprise, energy, liveliness, alertness, vigor, commotion, rush, motion, mobility, haste, speed, go*, life, doings. **2** [An individual deed] feat, exploit, performance, performing, execution, blow, stroke, maneuver, step, stunt, achievement, act, deed, thing, stratagem, something done, accomplishment, commission, effort, enterprise, move, movement, doing, effect, transaction, exertion, operation, handiwork, dealings, procedure. —**bring action** accuse, start a lawsuit, take to court; see SUE. —**see action** do battle, engage in combat, fight; see FIGHT. —**take action** become active, do, initiate activity; see ACT 1.

actions ***n.*** deportment, conduct, manners; see BEHAVIOR.

activate ***v.*** stimulate, initiate, arouse; see BEGIN 1.

active ***a.*** busy, eventful, lively, dynamic, energetic, alive, mobile, hasty, going, rapid, progressive, speedy, walking, traveling, movable, bustling, humming, efficient, functioning, working, moving, restless, swarming, rustling, flowing, in process, in effect, in force, simmering, overflowing, streaming, stirring, effective, at work, operating, operative, agitated, brisk, industrious, enthusiastic, agile, quick, nimble, rapid, dexterous, spry, fresh, sprightly, frisky, wiry, alert, ready, sharp, keen, wide-awake, animated, enlivened, ardent, purposeful, persevering, resolute, aggressive, forceful, intense, determined, diligent, hardworking, assiduous, enterprising, inventive, vigorous, strenuous, eager, zealous, bold, daring, dashing, high-spirited, hopping*, going full blast, in high gear*, snappy*, on the ball*, peppy*.

activity ***n.*** motion, movement, liveliness; see ACTION 1.

actor ***n.*** player, performer, character actor, character actress, star, comedian, impersonator, leading man, leading woman, entertainer, performing artist, television star, villain, motion picture actor, stage player, supporting actor, mimic, mime, clown, ventriloquist, pantomimist, performance artist, understudy, Thespian, protagonist, headliner, bit player*, ham*, extra, matinee idol; see also CAST 2.

actress ***n.*** comedienne, starlet, leading lady; see ACTOR, CAST 2.

actual ***a.*** original, real, exact; see GENUINE 1.

actually ***a.*** truly, in fact, as a matter of fact; see REALLY 1.

acute ***a.*** **1** [Crucial] decisive, important, vital; see CRITICAL. **2** [Sharp] severe, keen, cutting; see INTENSE. **3** [Shrewd] clever, bright, perceptive; see INTELLIGENT.

acutely ***a.*** keenly, severely, sharply; see VERY.

acute accent a mark (´) showing primary stress, the quality of a vowel, etc.
-a·cy (ə sē) ⟦ult. < Gr⟧ *suffix* quality, condition, etc. *[supremacy]*
a·cy·clo·vir (ā sī′klō vir′) ***n.*** a synthetic powder used in the treatment of certain viral infections, as herpes
ad (ad) ***n.*** [Inf.] an advertisement
AD or **A.D.** *abbrev.* ⟦L *Anno Domini,* in the year of the Lord⟧ of the Christian era: used with dates
ad- ⟦L⟧ *prefix* motion toward, addition to, nearness to: becomes *a-, ac-, af-, ag-, al-, an-,* etc. before certain consonants
ad·age (ad′ij) ***n.*** ⟦< L *ad-,* to + *aio,* I say⟧ an old saying; proverb
a·da·gio (ə dä′jō, -zhō) ***adv.*** ⟦It *ad agio,* at ease⟧ *Music* slowly —***adj.*** slow —***n.,*** *pl.* **-gios** **1** a slow movement in music **2** a slow ballet dance Also written ***a·da′gio,*** *pl.* ***-gios***
Ad·am (ad′əm) ***n.*** ⟦Heb < *adam,* a human being⟧ *Bible* the first man
ad·a·mant (ad′ə mənt) ***adj.*** ⟦< Gr *a-,* not + *daman,* subdue⟧ inflexible; unyielding
Ad·ams (ad′əmz) **1 John** 1735-1826; 2d president of the U.S. (1797-1801) **2 John Quin·cy** (kwin′zē, -sē) 1767-1848; 6th president of the U.S. (1825-29): son of John
Adam's apple the projection of cartilage in the front of the throat: seen chiefly in men
a·dapt (ə dapt′) ***vt.*** ⟦< L *ad-,* to + *aptare,* to fit⟧ **1** to make suitable, esp. by changing **2** to adjust (oneself) to new circumstances —***vi.*** to adjust oneself —**ad·ap·ta·tion** (ad′əp tā′shən) ***n.*** —**a·dapt′er** or **a·dap′tor** ***n.***
a·dapt′a·ble ***adj.*** able to adjust or be adjusted —**a·dapt′a·bil′i·ty** ***n.***
add (ad) ***vt.*** ⟦< L *ad-,* to + *dare,* to give⟧ **1** to join (*to*) so as to increase **2** to state further **3** to combine (numbers) into a sum —***vi.*** **1** to cause an increase (*to*) **2** to find a sum —**add up** to seem reasonable —**add up to** to mean; signify
ADD *abbrev.* attention-deficit disorder
ad·dend (ad′end′) ***n.*** ⟦< fol.⟧ *Math.* a number or quantity to be added to another
ad·den·dum (ə den′dəm) ***n.,*** *pl.* **-da** (-də) ⟦L⟧ a thing added, as an appendix
ad·der (ad′ər) ***n.*** ⟦< OE *nædre*⟧ **1** a poisonous snake of Europe **2** any of various other snakes, some harmless
ad·dict (ə dikt′; *for n.,* ad′ikt) ***vt.*** ⟦< L *addicere,* give assent⟧ **1** to give (oneself) up *to* a strong habit: usually in the passive voice *[addicted* to heroin*]* **2** to make an addict of —***n.*** one addicted to a habit, as to using drugs —**ad·dic′tion** ***n.*** —**ad·dic′tive** ***adj.***
Ad·dis A·ba·ba (ad′is ab′ə bə) capital of Ethiopia: pop. 1,700,000
ad·di·tion (ə dish′ən) ***n.*** **1** an adding of numbers to get a sum **2** a joining of one thing to another **3** a part added —**in addition (to)** besides
ad·di′tion·al ***adj.*** added; more; extra —**ad·di′tion·al·ly** ***adv.***
ad·di·tive (ad′ə tiv) ***adj.*** of addition —***n.*** a substance added in small quantities
ad·dle (ad′'l) ***vi., vt.*** **-dled, -dling** ⟦< OE *adela,* mud⟧ to make or become confused
ad·dress (ə dres′; *for n. 2, 3, & 4, also* a′dres′) ***vt.*** ⟦< L *dirigere,* to direct⟧ **1** to direct (words) *to* **2** to speak or write to **3** to write the destination on (a letter, etc.) **4** to apply (oneself) *to* **5** to deal or cope with —***n.*** **1** a speech **2** the place where one lives or receives mail **3** the destination indicated on an envelope, etc. **4** *Comput. a)* a code identifying the location of an item of information *b)* a string of characters serving as an e-mail destination or Web location
ad·dress·ee (a′dres ē′) ***n.*** the person to whom mail, etc. is addressed
ad·duce (ə do͞os′) ***vt.*** **-duced′, -duc′ing** ⟦< L *ad-,* to + *ducere,* to lead⟧ to give as a reason or proof
-ade (ād) ⟦ult. < L⟧ *suffix* **1** the act of ___ing *[blockade]* **2** participant(s) in an action *[brigade]* **3** ⟦after LEMONADE⟧ drink made from *[limeade]*
Ad·e·laide (ad′ə lād′) seaport in S Australia: pop. 1,076,000
A·den (äd′'n, ād′'n), **Gulf of** gulf of the Arabian Sea, south of Arabia
ad·e·nine (ad′ə nēn′) ***n.*** a purine base contained in the DNA, RNA, and ADP of all tissue
ad·e·noids (ad′'n oidz′, ad′noidz′) ***pl.n.*** ⟦< Gr *adēn,* gland + -OID⟧ lymphoid growths in the throat behind the nose: they can obstruct nasal breathing
a·dept (ə dept′; *for n.* ad′ept′) ***adj.*** ⟦< L *ad-,* to + *apisci,* attain⟧ highly skilled —***n.*** **ad′ept′** an expert —**a·dept′ly** ***adv.*** —**a·dept′ness** ***n.***
ad·e·quate (ad′i kwət) ***adj.*** ⟦< L *ad-,* to + *aequus,* equal⟧ enough for what is required; sufficient; suitable —**ad′e·qua·cy** (-kwə sē) ***n.*** —**ad′e·quate·ly** ***adv.***
ad·here (ad hir′, əd-) ***vi.*** **-hered′, -her′ing** ⟦< L *ad-,* to + *haerere,* to stick⟧ **1** to stick fast; stay attached **2** to give allegiance or support (*to*) —**ad·her′ence** ***n.***
ad·her′ent ***n.*** a supporter or follower (*of* a person, cause, etc.)
ad·he·sion (ad hē′zhən, əd-) ***n.*** **1** a being stuck together **2** body tissues abnormally joined
ad·he′sive (-siv) ***adj.*** **1** sticking **2** sticky —***n.*** an adhesive substance
ad hoc (ad häk′) ⟦L, to this⟧ for a specific purpose *[an ad hoc* committee*]*
a·dieu (ə dyo͞o′, -do͞o′; *Fr* à dyö′) ***interj., n.,*** *pl.* **a·dieus′** or **a·dieux** (ə dyo͞oz′, -do͞oz′; *Fr* à dyö′) ⟦Fr⟧ goodbye
ad in·fi·ni·tum (ad in′fə nīt′əm) ⟦L⟧ endlessly; without limit
a·di·os (a′dē ōs′, ä′-; *Sp* ä dyôs′) ***interj.*** ⟦Sp⟧ goodbye

THESAURUS

ad* ***n.*** announcement, display, notice; see ADVERTISEMENT.
AD or **A.D.** *abbrev.* of the Christian era, after Christ, post-Christian, year of our Lord.
adage ***n.*** axiom, saying, maxim; see PROVERB.
adapt ***v.*** modify, revise, adjust; see ALTER 1.
adaptability ***n.*** changeability, flexibility, versatility, adjustability, conformability, pliancy, docility, compliancy, pliability, plasticity.
adaptable ***a.*** adjustable, elastic, pliable; see FLEXIBLE.
add ***v.*** **1** [To bring together, usually by mathematics] total, sum up, sum, figure, figure up, count up, compute, calculate, add up, tally, reckon, enumerate.—*Ant.* DECREASE, subtract, take away. **2** [To make a further remark] append, say further, continue, write further, annex, supplement, affix, add a postscript, reply, tack on. —**add to** augment, amplify, expand; see INCREASE. —**add up** be plausible, be probable, be reasonable, be logical, stand to reason, hold water; see also MAKE SENSE. —**add up to** indicate, signify, imply; see MEAN 1.
addict ***n.*** drug abuser, user, crackhead*, cokehead*, head*, dope fiend*, drug fiend*, mainliner*, junkie*, alcoholic, druggie*, freak*.
addicted (to) ***a.*** disposed to, inclined, in the habit of, prone, accustomed, attached, abandoned, wedded, devoted, predisposed, used to, imbued with, fanatic about, obsessed with, hooked on*.
addiction ***n.*** fixation, inclination, bent; see HABIT 2, OBSESSION.
addition ***n.*** **1** [That which has been added] additive, gain, profit, dividend, bonus, interest, raise, supplement, reinforcement, appendage, appendix, accessory, attachment, extension, increase, annex.—*Ant.* LOSS, reduction, shrinkage. **2** [A real estate development] annex, annexation, subdivision, shopping center, development, tract, extension, expansion, branch, construction.
additional ***a.*** supplementary, new, further; see EXTRA.
address ***n.*** **1** [A formal speech] oration, lecture, sermon; see SPEECH 3. **2** [Place at which one may be reached] residence, legal residence, home, quarters, living quarters, dwelling, headquarters, place of business, box number, Web address, URL, website, home page, Internet address; see also HOME 1.
address ***v.*** **1** [To provide directions for delivery] label, mark, prepare for mailing; see WRITE 2. **2** [To speak formally to an assemblage] lecture, lecture to, discuss, give a talk, give an address, give a speech, take the floor, harangue, rant, sermonize, spout off*, spiel*.
adept ***a.*** skillful, proficient, capable; see ABLE.
adequate ***a.*** sufficient, equal to the need, satisfactory; see ENOUGH 1.
adequately ***a.*** sufficiently, appropriately, suitably, fittingly, satisfactorily, abundantly, copiously, acceptably, tolerably, decently, modestly, fairly well, well enough, capably, good enough, to an acceptable degree, competently; see also WELL 2, 3.—*Ant.* INADEQUATELY, badly, insufficiently.
adhere (to) ***v.*** **1** [To serve] follow, be devoted to, practice; see OBEY. **2** [To stick to] attach, cling, hold fast; see STICK 1.
adhesive ***a.*** gummy, clinging, gluey; see STICKY.
ad infinitum ***a.*** endlessly, forever, ceaselessly; see REGULARLY.

ad·i·pose (ad′ə pōs′) ***adj.*** ⟦ult. < Gr *aleipha*, fat⟧ of animal fat; fatty

Ad·i·ron·dack Mountains (ad′ə rän′dak′) mountain range in NE New York: also **Adirondacks**

adj *abbrev.* **1** adjective **2** adjustment

ad·ja·cent (ə jā′sənt) ***adj.*** ⟦< L *ad-*, to + *jacere*, to lie⟧ near or close (*to*); adjoining —**ad·ja′cen·cy** (-sən sē) ***n.*** —**ad·ja′cent·ly** ***adv.***

ad·jec·tive (aj′ik tiv) ***n.*** ⟦< L *adjacere*, lie near⟧ a word used to modify a noun or other substantive —**ad′jec·ti′val** (-tī′vəl) ***adj.*** —**ad′jec·ti′val·ly** ***adv.***

ad·join (ə join′) ***vt.*** ⟦< L *ad-*, to + *jungere*, to join⟧ to be next to —***vi.*** to be in contact —**ad·join′ing** ***adj.***

ad·journ (ə jurn′) ***vt.*** ⟦< OFr *a*, at + *jorn*, day⟧ to suspend (a meeting, session, etc.) for a time —***vi.*** **1** to close a meeting, etc. for a time **2** [Inf.] to retire (*to* another room, etc.) —**ad·journ′ment** ***n.***

ad·judge (ə juj′) ***vt.*** **-judged′**, **-judg′ing** ⟦< L *ad-*, to + *judicare*, to judge⟧ **1** to decide by law **2** to declare, order, or award by law

ad·ju·di·cate (ə jo͞o′di kāt′) ***vt.*** **-cat′ed**, **-cat′ing** to hear and decide (a case) —***vi.*** to serve as a judge (*in* or *on*) —**ad·ju′di·ca′tion** ***n.*** —**ad·ju′di·ca′tor** ***n.*** —**ad·ju′di·ca·to′ry** (-kə tôr′ē) ***adj.***

ad·junct (a′juŋkt′) ***n.*** ⟦see ADJOIN⟧ a secondary or nonessential addition —***adj.*** in a temporary or part-time position

ad·jure (ə joor′) ***vt.*** **-jured′**, **-jur′ing** ⟦< L *ad-*, to + *jurare*, to swear⟧ **1** to charge solemnly under oath **2** to ask earnestly —**ad·ju·ra·tion** (aj′oo rā′shən) ***n.***

ad·just (ə just′) ***vt.*** ⟦< OFr *a-*, to + *joster*, to tilt⟧ **1** to change so as to fit **2** to regulate or set (a watch, etc.) **3** to settle rightly **4** to decide the amount to be paid in settling (an insurance claim) —***vi.*** to adapt oneself —**ad·just′a·ble** ***adj.*** —**ad·just′er** or **ad·jus′tor** ***n.*** —**ad·just′ment** ***n.***

ad·ju·tant (aj′ə tənt) ***n.*** ⟦< L *ad-*, to + *juvare*, to help⟧ **1** an assistant **2** a military staff officer who assists the commanding officer

ad-lib (ad′lib′) [Inf.] ***vt.***, ***vi.*** **-libbed′**, **-lib′bing** ⟦< L *ad libitum*, at pleasure⟧ to improvise (words, etc. not in a prepared script, etc.) —***n.*** an ad-libbed remark: also **ad lib** —***adj.*** spoken or done extemporaneously —***adv.*** extemporaneously: also **ad lib**

adm or **admin** *abbrev.* **1** administration **2** administrative

Adm *abbrev.* admiral

ad′man′ ***n.***, *pl.* **-men′** a man whose work is advertising

ad·min·is·ter (ad min′is tər, əd-) ***vt.*** ⟦< L *ad-*, to + *ministrare*, to serve⟧ **1** to manage; direct **2** to give out, as punishment **3** to apply (medicine, etc.) **4** to direct the taking of (an oath, etc.)

ad·min′is·trate′ (-trāt′) ***vt.*** **-trat′ed**, **-trat′ing** to administer; manage

ad·min′is·tra′tion (-trā′shən) ***n.*** **1** management **2** [*often* **A-**] the executive officials of a government, etc. and their policies **3** their term of office **4** the administering (*of* punishment, medicine, etc.) —**ad·min′is·tra′tive** (-trāt′iv, -trə tiv) ***adj.***

ad·min′is·tra′tor ***n.*** **1** one who administers **2** *Law* one appointed to settle an estate

ad·mi·ra·ble (ad′mə rə bəl) ***adj.*** deserving admiration; excellent —**ad′mi·ra·bly** ***adv.***

ad·mi·ral (ad′mə rəl) ***n.*** ⟦< Ar *'amīr*, leader + *'ālī*, high⟧ **1** the commanding officer of a fleet **2** a naval officer of the highest rank

ad′mi·ral·ty ***n.***, *pl.* **-ties** [*often* **A-**] the governmental department in charge of naval affairs, as in England

ad·mi·ra·tion (ad′mə rā′shən) ***n.*** **1** an admiring **2** pleased approval

ad·mire (ad mīr′, əd-) ***vt.*** **-mired′**, **-mir′ing** ⟦< L *ad-*, at + *mirari*, to wonder⟧ **1** to regard with wonder and delight **2** to esteem highly —**ad·mir′er** ***n.***

ad·mis·si·ble (ad mis′ə bəl, əd-) ***adj.*** that can be accepted or admitted —**ad·mis′si·bil′i·ty** ***n.***

ad·mis·sion (ad mish′ən, əd-) ***n.*** **1** an admitting or being admitted **2** an entrance fee **3** a conceding, confessing, etc. **4** a thing conceded, confessed, etc.

ad·mit (ad mit′, əd-) ***vt.*** **-mit′ted**, **-mit′ting** ⟦< L *ad-*, to + *mittere*, to send⟧ **1** to permit or entitle to enter or use **2** to allow; leave room for **3** to concede or confess —***vi.*** **1** to allow: with *of* **2** to concede or confess (*to*) —**ad·mit′tance** ***n.***

ad·mit′ted·ly ***adv.*** by admission or general agreement

ad·mix·ture (ad miks′chər) ***n.*** ⟦< L *ad-*, to + *miscere*, to mix⟧ **1** a mixture **2** a thing added in mixing

ad·mon·ish (ad män′ish, əd-) ***vt.*** ⟦< L *ad-*, to + *monere*, to warn⟧ **1** to warn **2** to reprove mildly **3** to exhort —**ad·mo·ni·tion** (ad′mə nish′ən) ***n.*** —**ad·mon′i·to′ry** (-i tôr′ē) ***adj.***

ad nau·se·am (ad nô′zē əm) ⟦L⟧ to the point of disgust

a·do (ə do͞o′) ***n.*** fuss; trouble

THESAURUS

adjacent ***a.*** beside, alongside, bordering; see NEAR 1.

adjective ***n.*** modifier, article, determiner, attribute, attributive, qualifier, descriptive word, limiting word, adjectival construction, identifier, qualifying word.

adjourn ***v.*** leave, postpone, discontinue; see SUSPEND 2.

adjournment ***n.*** intermission, pause, break; see RECESS 1.

adjust ***v.*** **1** [To bring to agreement] settle, arrange, conclude, complete, accord, reconcile, clarify, conform, allocate, regulate, organize, systematize, coordinate, straighten, standardize, clean up. **2** [To place or regulate parts] fix, connect, square, balance, regulate, tighten, fit, repair, focus, fine-tune, readjust, rectify, correct, set, mend, improve, overhaul, grind, sharpen, renovate, polish, bring into line, align, calibrate, put in working order, temper, service.

adjustable ***a.*** adaptable, stretchable, tractable; see FLEXIBLE.

adjustment ***n.*** settlement, arrangement, pay, remuneration, reimbursement, compensation, compromise, reconciliation, agreement, making up, improvement, regulation, fixing, adaptation, correction, calibration.

ad-lib* ***v.*** improvise, make up, devise; see INVENT 1.

administer ***v.*** **1** [To manage] conduct, direct, control; see MANAGE 1. **2** [To furnish] extend, dispense, give; see OFFER 1.

administration ***n.*** **1** [The direction of affairs] government, supervision, command; see MANAGEMENT. **2** [Those who direct affairs] directors, administrators, officers, supervisors, superintendents, advisors, command, executives, strategists, officials, committee, board, board of directors, executive, executive branch, legislature, president, presidency, chief executive, CEO, CFO, cabinet, ministry, commander, chairman, general, admiral, commander in chief, central office, headquarters, management, bureau, consulate, embassy, legation, department, Washington, party in power, brass*, front office*, the powers that be, the man*. **3** [The period in which a political administration is operative] term of office, regime, tenure; see sense 2.

administrative ***a.*** executive, controlling, ruling; see GOVERNING.

administrator ***n.*** manager, director, chairman; see EXECUTIVE.

admirable ***a.*** worthy, attractive, good; see EXCELLENT.

admiration ***n.*** praise, deference, approval, regard, fondness, esteem, respect, appreciation, favor, adoration, applause, glorification, idolatry, honor, recognition, valuing, liking, love, high regard, high opinion, reverence, veneration, homage.—*Ant.* OBJECTION, disregard, distrust.

admire ***v.*** esteem, honor, applaud, praise, extol, respect, approve, revere, venerate, laud, boost, glorify, reverence, hold dear, appreciate, credit, commend, value, treasure, prize, look up to, rate highly, pay homage to, idolize, adore, hail, put a high price on, have a high opinion of, think highly of, show deference to, think well of, take stock in, put stock in, put on a pedestal.—*Ant.* BLAME, censure, deride.

admirer ***n.*** supporter, believer, patron; see FOLLOWER.

admissible ***a.*** proper, suitable, right; see PERMITTED.

admission ***n.*** **1** [The act of granting entrance] acceptance, admittance, permission, reception, welcome, recognition, acknowledgment, confirmation, selection, initiation.—*Ant.* REMOVAL, rejection, expulsion. **2** [The entrance fee] cover charge, fee, price, ticket, charges, toll, tax, minimum, donation, cover*, gate. **3** [Something acknowledged] statement, disclosure, confession, acknowledgment, affirmation, concession, divulgence, declaration, confirmation, assertion, testimony, allegation, deposition, affidavit.—*Ant.* DENIAL, disallowance, repudiation.

admit ***v.*** **1** [To grant entrance] bring in, give access to, allow entrance to; see RECEIVE 4. **2** [To confess] acknowledge, indicate, disclose, unveil, uncover, expose, proclaim, declare, open up, bring to light, go over, go into details, confide to, tell, relate, narrate, enumerate, divulge, reveal, communicate, make known, tell the whole story, plead guilty, own up to, talk, sing*, cough up*, come clean*, spill the beans*.—*Ant.* HIDE, cover up, obscure.

admonish ***v.*** reprove, chide, rebuke; see SCOLD.

admonition ***n.*** advice, caution, exhortation; see WARNING.

a·do·be (ə dō′bē) ***n.*** ⟦Sp⟧ **1** unburnt, sun-dried brick **2** clay for making this brick **3** a building of adobe

ad·o·les·cence (ad′ə les′əns) ***n.*** the time of life between puberty and maturity

ad′o·les′cent ***adj.*** ⟦< L *ad-*, to + *alescere*, grow up⟧ of or in adolescence —***n.*** a person during adolescence

A·don·is (ə dän′is) ***n.*** **1** *Gr. Myth.* a young man loved by Aphrodite **2** a handsome young man

a·dopt (ə däpt′) ***vt.*** ⟦< L *ad-*, to + *optare*, to choose⟧ **1** to take legally into one's own family and raise as one's own child **2** to take as one's own **3** to choose or accept —**a·dop′tion** ***n.***

a·dop·tive (ə däp′tiv) ***adj.*** that has become so by adoption

a·dor·a·ble (ə dôr′ə bəl) ***adj.*** [Inf.] delightful; charming —**a·dor′a·bly** ***adv.***

ad·o·ra·tion (ad′ə rā′shən) ***n.*** **1** a worshiping **2** great love or devotion

a·dore (ə dôr′) ***vt.*** **-dored′**, **-dor′ing** ⟦< L *ad-*, to + *orare*, to speak⟧ **1** to worship as divine **2** to love greatly **3** [Inf.] to like very much

a·dorn (ə dôrn′) ***vt.*** ⟦< L *ad-*, to + *ornare*, fit out⟧ **1** to be an ornament to **2** to put decorations on —**a·dorn′ment** ***n.***

ADP (ā′dē′pē′) ⟦*a*(*denosine*) *d*(*i*)*p*(*hosphate*)⟧ a basic unit of nucleic acids vital to the energy processes of all living cells

a·dre·nal (ə drē′nəl) ***adj.*** ⟦AD- + RENAL⟧ **1** near the kidneys **2** of two ductless glands (**adrenal glands**) just above the kidneys

a·dren·a·line (ə dren′ə lin) ***n.*** ⟦< *Adrenalin*, a trademark⟧ a hormone secreted by the adrenal glands, which increases endurance, strength, etc.

A·dri·at·ic (Sea) (ā′drē at′ik) sea between Italy and the Balkan Peninsula

a·drift (ə drift′) ***adv.***, ***adj.*** floating without mooring or direction

a·droit (ə droit′) ***adj.*** ⟦< Fr *à*, to + L *dirigere*, lay straight⟧ skillful and clever —**a·droit′ly** ***adv.*** —**a·droit′ness** ***n.***

ad·sorb (ad sôrb′, -zôrb′) ***vt.*** ⟦< AD- + L *sorbere*, drink in⟧ to collect (a gas, etc.) in condensed form on a surface —**ad·sorb′ent** ***adj.*** —**ad·sorp′tion** (-sôrp′shən, -zôrp′-) ***n.***

ad·u·late (a′jo͞o lāt′, -jə-) ***vt.*** **-lat′ed**, **-lat′ing** ⟦< L *adulari*, fawn upon⟧ to admire intensely —**ad′u·la′tion** ***n.*** —**ad′u·la·to′ry** (-lə tôr′ē) ***adj.***

a·dult (ə dult′, ad′ult′) ***adj.*** ⟦see ADOLESCENT⟧ **1** grown up; mature **2** for adult people —***n.*** a mature person, animal, or plant —**a·dult′hood** ***n.***

a·dul·ter·ate (ə dul′tər āt′) ***vt.*** **-at′ed**, **-at′ing** ⟦< L *ad-*, to + *alter*, other⟧ to make inferior, impure, etc. by adding an improper substance —**a·dul′ter·a′tion** ***n.***

a·dul·ter·y (ə dul′tər ē) ***n.***, *pl.* **-ies** sexual intercourse between a married person and another who is not that person's spouse —**a·dul′ter·er** ***n.*** —**a·dul′ter·ess** ***fem.n.*** —**a·dul′ter·ous** ***adj.***

ad·um·brate (ad um′brāt′, ad′əm brāt′) ***vt.*** **-brat′ed**, **-brat′ing** ⟦< L *ad-*, to + *umbra*, shade⟧ **1** to outline vaguely **2** to foreshadow —**ad′um·bra′tion** ***n.***

adv *abbrev.* **1** adverb **2** advertisement

ad·vance (ad vans′, əd-) ***vt.*** **-vanced′**, **-vanc′ing** ⟦< L *ab-*, from + *ante*, before⟧ **1** to bring forward **2** to promote **3** to suggest **4** to raise the rate of **5** to lend —***vi.*** **1** to go forward **2** to improve; progress **3** to rise in rank, price, etc. —***n.*** **1** a moving forward **2** an improvement **3** a rise in value **4** [*pl.*] approaches to get favor **5** a payment made before it is due —***adj.*** **1** in front *[advance guard]* **2** beforehand —**in advance** **1** in front **2** ahead of time —**ad·vance′ment** ***n.***

ad·vanced′ ***adj.*** **1** in front **2** far on in life; old **3** ahead or higher in progress, price, etc.

advance man a person hired to travel in advance of a theatrical company, political candidate, etc. to arrange for publicity, appearances, etc.

ad·van·tage (ad vant′ij, əd-) ***n.*** ⟦< L *ab-* + *ante*: see ADVANCE⟧ **1** superiority **2** a favorable circumstance, event, etc. **3** gain or benefit —***vt.*** **-taged**, **-tag·ing** to be a benefit or aid to —**take advantage of** **1** to use for one's own benefit **2** to impose upon —**ad·van·ta·geous** (ad′van tā′jəs) ***adj.***

Ad·vent (ad′vent′) ***n.*** ⟦< L *ad-*, to + *venire*, to come⟧ **1** *Christianity* the period including the four Sundays just before Christmas **2** [**a-**] a coming or arrival

ad·ven·ti·tious (ad′ven tish′əs) ***adj.*** ⟦see prec.⟧ not inherent; accidental

ad·ven·ture (ad ven′chər, əd-) ***n.*** ⟦see ADVENT⟧ **1** a daring, hazardous undertaking **2** an unusual, stirring, often romantic experience —***vi.*** **-tured**, **-tur·ing** to engage in adventure —**ad·ven′tur·ous** or **ad·ven′ture·some** ***adj.*** —**ad·ven′tur·ous·ly** ***adv.***

ad·ven′tur·er ***n.*** **1** one who has or looks for adventures **2** one who seeks to become rich, etc. by dubious schemes —**ad·ven′tur·ess** ***fem.n.***

ad·verb (ad′vurb′) ***n.*** ⟦< L *ad-*, to + *verbum*, word⟧ a word used to modify a verb, an adjective, or another adverb, by expressing time, place, manner, degree, etc. —**ad·ver′bi·al** ***adj.*** —**ad·ver′bi·al·ly** ***adv.***

ad·ver·sar·i·al (ad′vər ser′ē əl) ***adj.*** of or relating to adversaries, as in a lawsuit

ad′ver·sar′y ***n.***, *pl.* **-ies** ⟦see ADVERT⟧ an opponent; foe

ad·verse (ad vurs′, ad′vurs′) ***adj.*** ⟦see ADVERT⟧ **1** opposed **2** unfavorable —**ad·verse′ly** ***adv.***

ad·ver·si·ty (ad vur′sə tē) ***n.*** **1** misfortune; wretched or troubled state **2** *pl.* **-ties** a calamity; disaster

ad·vert (ad vurt′) ***vi.*** ⟦< L *ad*, to + *vertere*, to turn⟧ to call attention (*to*)

THESAURUS

adolescence ***n.*** young adulthood, puberty, teens; see YOUTH 1.

adolescent ***a.*** pubescent, juvenile, youthful; see YOUNG 1.

adolescent ***n.*** youngster, minor, teenager; see YOUTH 3.

adopt ***v.*** **1** [To take as a son or daughter] father, mother, take in, raise, make one's heir, take as one's own, naturalize, foster. **2** [To take as one's own] embrace, appropriate, pick, choose, select, transfer, seize, take up, take over, choose, assume, use, utilize, imitate, borrow, mimic.—*Ant.* DENY, repudiate, reject.

adoption ***n.*** choosing, election, choice; see SELECTION 1.

adorable* ***a.*** delightful, lovable, cute; see CHARMING.

adoration ***n.*** devotion, homage, veneration; see WORSHIP 1.

adore ***v.*** **1** [To worship] venerate, revere, glorify; see WORSHIP. **2** [To love] cherish, treasure, prize; see LOVE 1.

adorn ***v.*** beautify, embellish, ornament; see DECORATE.

adorned ***a.*** trimmed, decked, garnished; see ORNATE.

adult ***a.*** of age, grown, developed; see MATURE.

adult ***n.*** mature person, grown-up, fully developed member of a species; see MAN 2, WOMAN 1.

adulterate ***v.*** dilute, lessen, taint; see POLLUTE, WEAKEN.

adultery ***n.*** promiscuity, infidelity, unfaithfulness; see FORNICATION.

advance ***n.*** **1** [The act of moving forward] impetus, progression, motion; see PROGRESS 1. **2** [Promotion] enrichment, betterment, increase; see IMPROVEMENT 1. —**in advance** ahead of, earlier, in time; see BEFORE.

advance ***v.*** **1** [To move forward physically] progress, proceed, move on, forge ahead, press on, push ahead, go on, go forth, gain ground, make headway, step forward, come to the front, conquer territory, march on, move onward, continue ahead, push on, press on.—*Ant.* STOP, halt, stand still. **2** [To propose] set forth, introduce, suggest; see PROPOSE 1. **3** [To promote] further, encourage, urge; see PROMOTE 1. **4** [To lend] loan, provide with, furnish; see LEND. **5** [To improve] develop, make progress, get better; see IMPROVE 2.

advanced ***a.*** **1** [Superior] precocious, first, exceptional; see EXCELLENT. **2** [Aged] seasoned, venerable, time-honored; see OLD 1, 3. **3** [Progressive] radical, unconventional, ahead of the times; see LIBERAL.

advancement ***n.*** **1** [Promotion in rank] improvement, elevation, raise; see PROMOTION 1. **2** [Progress] gain, headway, progression; see PROGRESS 1.

advantage ***n.*** luck, favor, approval, help, aid, sanction, good, patronage, support, preference, odds, protection, start, leg up*, helping hand, upper hand, leverage, hold, opportunity, dominance, superiority, supremacy, lead, influence, power, mastery, authority, prestige, sway, pull*, edge*, ace in the hole*.—*Ant.* WEAKNESS, handicap, disadvantage. —**take advantage of** exploit, profit by, utilize; see DECEIVE, USE 1.

adventure ***n.*** happening, experience, episode; see EVENT.

adventurer ***n.*** explorer, pirate, soldier of fortune, daredevil, hero, pioneer, mountain climber, big game hunter, romantic; see also PIONEER 2, TRAVELER.

adventurous ***a.*** bold, daring, courageous; see BRAVE.

adverse ***a.*** untimely, improper, unfortunate; see UNFAVORABLE.

adversely ***a.*** negatively, resentfully, unsympathetically; see UNFAVORABLY.

adversity ***n.*** misfortune, distress, trouble; see DIFFICULTY 1, 2.

ad·ver·tise (ad′vər tīz′) ***vt.*** **-tised′**, **-tis′ing** ⟦see prec.⟧ to describe or praise publicly, usually so as to promote sales —***vi.*** **1** to call public attention to things for sale **2** to ask *(for)* by public notice —**ad′ver·tis′er** ***n.*** —**ad′ver·tis′ing** ***n.***

ad·ver·tise·ment (ad′vər tīz′mənt, əd vur′tīz-) ***n.*** a public notice, usually paid for

ad′ver·to′ri·al (-tôr′ē əl) ***n.*** ⟦ADVER(TISE) + (EDI)TORIAL⟧ an advertisement, as in a magazine, made to resemble an article or editorial

ad·vice (ad vīs′, əd-) ***n.*** ⟦< L *ad-*, at + *videre*, to look⟧ opinion given as to what to do; counsel

ad·vis·a·ble (ad vīz′ə bəl, əd-) ***adj.*** wise; sensible —**ad·vis′a·bil′i·ty** ***n.***

ad·vise (ad vīz′, əd-) ***vt.*** **-vised′**, **-vis′ing** ⟦< ML *advisum*, advice⟧ **1** to give advice to; counsel **2** to offer as advice **3** to notify; inform —**ad·vi′sor** or **ad·vis′er** ***n.***

ad·vis′ed·ly (-id lē) ***adv.*** deliberately

ad·vise′ment ***n.*** careful consideration —**take under advisement** to consider carefully

ad·vi·so·ry (ad vī′zə rē, əd-) ***adj.*** advising or empowered to advise —***n.***, *pl.* **-ries** a report, esp. about weather conditions

ad·vo·cate (ad′və kit; *for v.*, -kāt′) ***n.*** ⟦< L *ad-*, to + *vocare*, to call⟧ one who speaks or writes in support of another or a cause —***vt.*** **-cat′ed**, **-cat′ing** to be an advocate of —**ad′vo·ca·cy** (-kə sē) ***n.***

advt. *abbrev.* advertisement

adz or **adze** (adz) ***n.*** ⟦< OE *adesa*⟧ an axlike tool for trimming and smoothing wood

Ae·ge·an (Sea) (ē jē′ən) sea between Greece and Turkey

ae·gis (ē′jis) ***n.*** ⟦< Gr *aigis*, shield of Zeus⟧ **1** protection **2** sponsorship

Ae·ne·as (i nē′əs) ***n.*** *Gr. & Rom. Myth.* a Trojan whose adventures are told in a poem (the **Ae·ne′id**) by Virgil

ae·on (ē′ən, ē′än′) ***n.*** *alt. sp. of* EON

aer·ate (er′āt′, ā′ər āt′) ***vt.*** **-at′ed**, **-at′ing** ⟦AER(O)- + -ATE[1]⟧ **1** to expose to air **2** to charge (liquid) with gas, as to make soda water —**aer·a′tion** ***n.*** —**aer′a′tor** ***n.***

aer·i·al (er′ē əl) ***adj.*** ⟦< Gr *aēr*, air + -AL⟧ **1** of, in, or by air **2** unreal; imaginary **3** of aircraft or flying —***n.*** a radio or TV antenna

aer′i·al·ist ***n.*** an acrobat on a trapeze, high wire, etc.

a·er·ie (ā′ər ē, ē′rē, er′ē, ir′ē) ***n.*** ⟦prob. < L *ager*, field⟧ **1** the high nest of an eagle or other bird of prey **2** a house or stronghold on a high place

aero- ⟦< Gr *aēr*, air⟧ *combining form* **1** air **2** aircraft or flying **3** gas, gases Also **aer-** or **aeri-**

aer·o·bat·ics (er′ō bat′iks) ***pl.n.*** ⟦prec. + (ACRO)BATICS⟧ stunts done while flying an aircraft

aer·o·bic (er ō′bik) ***adj.*** ⟦< Gr *aēr*, air + *bios*, life⟧ **1** able to live or grow only where free oxygen is present **2** of exercise, as running, that conditions the heart and lungs by increasing efficient intake of oxygen by the body —***n.*** [*pl., with sing. or pl. v.*] aerobic exercises

aer·o·dy·nam·ics (er′ō dī nam′iks) ***n.*** the branch of mechanics dealing with forces exerted by air or other gases in motion —***pl.n.*** the characteristics of a vehicle's body that affect its efficient movement through the air —**aer′o·dy·nam′ic** ***adj.*** —**aer′o·dy·nam′i·cal·ly** ***adv.***

aer·o·nau·tics (er′ə nôt′iks) ***n.*** the science of making and flying aircraft —**aer′o·nau′ti·cal** ***adj.***

aer·o·sol (er′ə sôl′, -säl′) ***n.*** ⟦AERO- + SOL(UTION)⟧ a suspension of insoluble particles in a gas —***adj.*** of or from a container in which gas under pressure dispenses liquid spray

aer·o·space (er′ō spās′) ***n.*** the earth's atmosphere and the space outside it —***adj.*** of aerospace, or of missiles, etc. for flight in aerospace

Aes·chy·lus (es′ki ləs) 525?-456 B.C.; Gr. writer of tragedies

Ae·sop (ē′səp, -säp′) Gr. fable writer: supposedly lived 6th c. B.C.

aes·thete (es′thēt′) ***n.*** ⟦Gr *aisthētēs*, one who perceives⟧ a person who is or pretends to be highly sensitive to art and beauty

aes·thet·ic (es thet′ik) ***adj.*** **1** of aesthetics **2** of beauty **3** sensitive to art and beauty

aes·thet′ics ***n.*** the philosophy of art and beauty

a·far (ə fär′) ***adv.*** [Archaic] at or to a distance —**from afar** from a distance

af·fa·ble (af′ə bəl) ***adj.*** ⟦< L *ad-*, to + *fari*, to speak⟧ pleasant; friendly —**af′fa·bil′i·ty** ***n.*** —**af′fa·bly** ***adv.***

af·fair (ə fer′) ***n.*** ⟦< L *ad-*, to + *facere*, to do⟧ **1** any matter, event, etc. **2** [*pl.*] matters of business **3** an event arousing public controversy **4** a social gathering **5** a sexual relationship outside of marriage

af·fect (ə fekt′; *for vt. 3 & 4, usually* a fekt′; *for n.*, af′ekt′) ***vt.*** ⟦< L *ad-*, to + *facere*, to do⟧ **1** to have an effect on; influence **2** to stir the emotions of **3** to like to use, wear, etc. **4** to make a pretense of being, feeling, etc. —***n.*** an emotion or emotional response

af·fec·ta·tion (af′ek tā′shən) ***n.*** **1** a pretending to like, have, etc. **2** artificial behavior meant to impress others

af·fect·ed (ə fekt′id; *for 4 & 5, usually* a-) ***adj.*** **1** afflicted **2** influenced **3** emotionally moved **4** assumed for effect **5** full of affectation

af·fect·ing (ə fekt′iŋ) ***adj.*** emotionally moving

af·fec·tion (ə fek′shən) ***n.*** fond or tender feeling

af·fec′tion·ate ***adj.*** tender and loving —**af·fec′tion·ate·ly** ***adv.***

af·fect·less (af′ekt′lis) ***adj.*** lacking emotion

af·fer·ent (af′ər ənt) ***adj.*** ⟦< L *ad-*, to + *ferre*, to carry⟧ bringing inward to a central part, as nerves

af·fi·da·vit (af′ə dā′vit) ***n.*** ⟦ML, he has made oath⟧ a written statement made under oath

af·fil·i·ate (ə fil′ē āt′; *for n., usually*, -it) ***vt.*** **-at′ed**, **-at′ing** ⟦< ML *affiliare*, adopt as a son⟧ **1** to take in as a mem-

THESAURUS

advertise ***v.*** publicize, proclaim, herald, announce, declare, notify, warn, display, exhibit, show, reveal, expose, disclose, unmask, divulge, uncover, communicate, publish abroad, issue, broadcast, print, circulate, show off, parade, propagate, disseminate, inform, celebrate, spread, call public attention to, promulgate, give out, plug*, play up*; see also DECLARE.

advertised ***a.*** announced, posted, noted, publicized, billed, printed, published, made public, broadcast, emphasized, pointed out, displayed, exhibited, shown, offered, presented, put on sale, flaunted, plugged*, boosted, built up, pushed*.

advertisement ***n.*** announcement, notice, publicity, exhibit, exhibition, display, circular, handbill, placard, poster, public notice, broadcast, bill, proclamation, classified advertisement, sample, endorsement, want ad*, buildup*, plug*, ballyhoo, blurb*, spread*, classified.

advice ***n.*** guidance, instruction, consultation, suggestion, preaching, information, admonition, forewarning, warning, caution, a word to the wise, injunction, lesson, directions, opinion, counsel, advisement, encouragement, persuasion, prescription, recommendation, proposition, proposal, view, help, aid, judgment.

advise ***v.*** recommend, prescribe, guide, exhort, direct, admonish, warn, point out, instruct, counsel, advocate, suggest, urge, prompt, show, tell, inform, caution, charge, encourage, preach, teach, persuade, offer an opinion to, forewarn, prepare, straighten out.—*Ant.* DECEIVE, misdirect, lead astray.

advisor ***n.*** counselor, instructor, consultant.—*Ant.* FRIEND, TEACHER.

advisory ***a.*** consulting, having power to advise, prudential; see HELPING.

advocate ***v.*** bolster, push, further, advance; see also PROMOTE 1.

aerial ***a.*** in the air, atmospheric, flying; see HIGH 2.

aesthetic ***a.*** creative, artistic, tasteful; see BEAUTIFUL.

affair ***n.*** **1** [Business; *often plural*] concern, responsibility, matter, duty, topic, subject, case, circumstance, thing, question, function, private concern, personal business, calling, employment, occupation, profession, pursuit, avocation, obligation, job, province, realm, interest, mission, assignment, task; see also JOB 1. **2** [An illicit love affair] liaison, rendezvous, intimacy, romance, relationship.

affect ***v.*** impress, sway, induce; see INFLUENCE.

affected ***a.*** **1** [Being subject to influence] moved, touched, melted, influenced, awakened, sympathetic, stimulated, stirred, grieved, overwhelmed, moved to tears, hurt, injured, excited, struck, impressed, overwrought, devoured by, concerned, reached, compassionate, tender, sorry, troubled, distressed.—*Ant.* INDIFFERENT, unmoved, untouched. **2** [Insincere or artificial] pretentious, melodramatic, unnatural, stilted, superficial, theatrical, stiff, strained, overdone, ostentatious, hollow, shallow, showy, fake, stuck-up*.—*Ant.* SIMPLE, natural, genuine.

affection ***n.*** love, friendship, liking, attachment, goodwill, partiality, passion, ardor, friendliness, amiability, amicability, concern, regard, desire, closeness, kindness, devotion, tenderness, fondness.—*Ant.* HATRED, dislike, enmity.

affectionate ***a.*** kind, tender, friendly; see LOVING.

affidavit ***n.*** testimony, sworn statement, affirmation; see OATH 1.

ber **2** to associate (oneself) *with* a group, etc. —***vi.*** to join —***n.*** an affiliated person, club, etc. —**af·fil'i·a'tion** ***n.***

af·fin·i·ty (ə fin'i tē) ***n.***, *pl.* **-ties** ⟦< L *affinis*, adjacent⟧ **1** relationship by marriage **2** close relationship **3** a likeness implying common origin **4** a natural liking or sympathy

af·firm (ə furm') ***vt.*** ⟦< L *ad-*, to + *firmare*, make firm⟧ **1** to declare positively; assert **2** to confirm; ratify —***vi.*** *Law* to make a formal statement, but not under oath —**af·fir·ma·tion** (af'ər mā'shən) ***n.***

af·firm·a·tive (ə furm'ə tiv) ***adj.*** affirming; answering "yes" —***n.*** **1** an expression of assent **2** the side upholding the proposition being debated

affirmative action a plan to offset past discrimination in employing or educating women, blacks, etc.

af·fix (ə fiks'; *for n.* af'iks') ***vt.*** ⟦< L *ad-*, to + *figere*, fasten⟧ **1** to fasten; attach **2** to add at the end —***n.*** **1** a thing affixed **2** a prefix or suffix

af·flict (ə flikt') ***vt.*** ⟦< L *ad-*, to + *fligere*, to strike⟧ to cause pain or suffering to; distress greatly

af·flic·tion (ə flik'shən) ***n.*** **1** pain; suffering **2** any cause of suffering

af·flu·ence (af'lo͞o əns) ***n.*** ⟦< L *ad-*, to + *fluere*, to flow⟧ riches; wealth

af'flu·ent ***adj.*** wealthy; rich —**af'flu·ent·ly** ***adv.***

af·ford (ə fôrd') ***vt.*** ⟦< OE *geforthian*, to advance⟧ **1** to spare (money, time, etc.) without much inconvenience **2** to give; yield *[it affords* pleasure*]* —**af·ford'a·bil'i·ty** ***n.*** —**af·ford'a·ble** ***adj.***

af·fray (ə frā') ***n.*** ⟦< OFr *esfraer*, frighten⟧ a noisy brawl

af·front (ə frunt') ***vt.*** ⟦< ML *ad-*, to + *frons*, forehead⟧ to insult openly —***n.*** an open insult

Af·ghan (af'gan', -gən) ***n.*** **1** a native of Afghanistan **2** [a-] a soft blanket or shawl, crocheted or knitted

Af·ghan·i·stan (af gan'i stan') country in SC Asia, east of Iran: 251,773 sq. mi.; pop. 15,551,000

a·fi·cio·na·do (ə fish'ə nä'dō) ***n.*** ⟦Sp⟧ a devotee of some sport, art, etc.

a·field (ə fēld') ***adv.*** **1** in or to the field **2** away (from home); astray

a·fire (ə fīr') ***adv.***, ***adj.*** on fire

a·flame (ə flām') ***adv.***, ***adj.*** **1** in flames **2** glowing

AFL-CIO *abbrev.* American Federation of Labor and Congress of Industrial Organizations

a·float (ə flōt') ***adj.***, ***adv.*** **1** floating **2** at sea **3** flooded **4** current **5** free of debt, etc.

a·flut·ter (ə flut'ər) ***adv.***, ***adj.*** in a flutter

a·foot (ə foot') ***adv.*** **1** on foot **2** in progress

a·fore·men·tioned (ə fôr'men'chənd) ***adj.*** mentioned before

a·fore'said' ***adj.*** spoken of before

a·fore'thought' ***adj.*** thought out beforehand; premeditated

a·foul (ə foul') ***adv.***, ***adj.*** in a collision or a tangle —**run** (or **fall**) **afoul of** to get into trouble with

a·fraid (ə frād') ***adj.*** ⟦see AFFRAY⟧ feeling frightened: followed by *of, that*, or an infinitive: often used informally to indicate regret *[I'm afraid* I must go*]*

Af·ri·ca (af'ri kə) second largest continent, south of Europe: *c.* 11,700,000 sq. mi.; pop. *c.* 705,000,000 —**Af'ri·can** ***adj.***, ***n.***

Af'ri·can-A·mer'i·can ***n.*** a black American of African ancestry —***adj.*** of African-Americans, their culture, etc.

Af·ri·can·ized bee (af'ri kən īzd') a hybrid of African and European bees, known for superior honey production; killer bee

African violet a tropical African plant with violet, white, or pinkish flowers and hairy leaves, often grown as a houseplant

Af·ri·kaans (af'ri käns', -känz') ***n.*** ⟦Afrik < *Afrika*, Africa⟧ an official language of South Africa, based on Dutch

Af·ro (af'rō') ***n.***, *pl.* **-ros'** a full, bushy hair style, as worn by some African-Americans

Afro- ⟦< L *Afer*, an African⟧ *combining form* African, African and

Af'ro-A·mer'i·can ***n.***, ***adj.*** AFRICAN-AMERICAN

aft (aft) ***adv.*** ⟦< OE *æftan*⟧ at, near, or toward the stern of a ship or rear of an aircraft

af·ter (af'tər) ***adv.*** ⟦OE *æfter*⟧ **1** behind **2** later —***prep.*** **1** behind **2** later than **3** in search of **4** as a result of **5** in spite of *[after* all I've said, he's still going*]* **6** lower in rank or order than **7** in imitation of **8** for *[*named *after* Lincoln*]* —***conj.*** following the time when —***adj.*** **1** next; later **2** nearer the rear

af'ter·birth' ***n.*** the placenta and membranes expelled after the birth of offspring

af'ter·burn'er ***n.*** a device attached to some engines for burning or utilizing exhaust gases

af'ter·ef·fect' ***n.*** an effect coming later, or as a secondary result

af'ter·life' ***n.*** a life after death

af'ter·math' (-math') ***n.*** ⟦< AFTER + OE *mæth*, cutting of grass⟧ a result, esp. an unpleasant one

af·ter·noon (af'tər no͞on'; *for adj., also* af'tər no͞on') ***n.*** the time from noon to evening —***adj.*** in the afternoon

af'ter-tax' ***n.*** occurring or remaining after the payment of taxes

af'ter·thought' ***n.*** **1** an idea, explanation, part, etc. coming or added later **2** a thought coming too late to be apt

af'ter·ward ***adv.*** later; subsequently: also **af'ter·wards**

Ag ⟦L *argentum*⟧ *Chem. symbol for* silver

a·gain (ə gen') ***adv.*** ⟦< OE *on-*, up to + *gegn*, direct⟧ **1** back into a former condition **2** once more **3** besides **4** on the other hand —**again and again** often; repeatedly —**as much again** twice as much

a·gainst (ə genst') ***prep.*** ⟦see prec.⟧ **1** in opposition to **2** toward so as to strike *[thrown against* the wall*]* **3** in contact with **4** in preparation for **5** as a charge on

Ag·a·mem·non (ag'ə mem'nän') ***n.*** *Gr. Myth.* commander of the Greek army in the Trojan War

a·gape (ə gāp') ***adv.***, ***adj.*** ⟦A-[1] + GAPE⟧ wide open

a·gar (ä'gər) ***n.*** ⟦Malay⟧ a gelatinous product made from seaweed, used in bacterial cultures: also **a'gar-a'gar**

ag·ate (ag'it) ***n.*** ⟦< Gr *achatēs*⟧ a hard, semiprecious stone with striped or clouded coloring

a·ga·ve (ə gä'vē) ***n.*** ⟦< proper name in Gr. myth⟧ a desert plant with thick, fleshy leaves

agcy *abbrev.* agency

age (āj) ***n.*** ⟦< L *aetas*⟧ **1** the length of time that a person or thing has existed **2** a stage of life **3** old age **4** a

THESAURUS

affinity ***n.*** **1** [Attraction based on affection] fondness, liking, closeness; see AFFECTION. **2** [Similarity] likeness, resemblance, kinship; see SIMILARITY.

affirmative ***a.*** agreeing, consenting, concurring, approving, assenting, supporting.—*Ant.* NEGATIVE, contradictory, noncommittal. —**in the affirmative** favorably, in assent, in agreement, with an affirmative answer; see also YES.

afflict ***v.*** injure, torment, trouble; see HURT.

affliction ***n.*** trouble, hardship, plight; see DIFFICULTY 1, 2.

affluent ***a.*** wealthy, well-off, well-to-do; see RICH 1.

afford ***v.*** have enough for, bear, manage, be able to, have the means for, be financially able, swing*, be in the market for.

afire ***a.*** flaming, on fire, blazing; see BURNING.

afloat ***a.*** adrift, at sea, sailing; see FLOATING.

afoot ***a.*** on foot, hiking, marching; see WALKING.

afraid ***a.*** hesitant, anxious, apprehensive, disturbed, frightened, fearful, nervous, uneasy, fidgety, alarmed, intimidated, discouraged, disheartened, perplexed, worried, perturbed, upset, panic-stricken, cowardly, scared, terrified, terrorized, shocked, frozen, aghast, alarmed, startled, aroused, horrified, petrified, stunned, rattled, struck dumb, trembling, distressed, jittery*, jumpy, leery, shaky.—*Ant.* CONFIDENT, self-assured, poised.

African ***a.*** North African, Saharan, sub-Saharan, East African, West African, Central African, South African.

aft ***a.*** rearward, behind, astern; see BACK.

after ***a.***, ***prep.*** **1** [Behind in space] back of, in the rear, behind; see BACK. **2** [Following] next, later, subsequent; see FOLLOWING.

afternoon ***n.*** PM, siesta time, early afternoon, late afternoon, mid-afternoon.

afterward ***a.*** later, after, subsequently, in a while, a while later, afterwards, by and by, eventually, soon, on the next day, ultimately, another time, then, at a later time.

again ***a.*** anew, afresh, newly, once more, once again, repeatedly, over, from the beginning, on and on, another time, over again, a second time, recurrently, ditto. —**again and again** repeatedly, once again, continuously; see AGAIN. —**as much again** doubled, twice as much, multiplied; see DOUBLE.

against ***prep.*** **1** [Counter to] in the face of, into, toward, opposite to, facing. **2** [In contact with] on, upon, in collision with, touching; see also NEXT 2. **3** [Contrary to] in opposition to, opposed to, counter to, adverse to, in violation of, versus, over against. **4** [Opposite] facing, fronting, corresponding; see OPPOSITE 3.

age ***n.*** **1** [The period of one's exist-

historical or geological period **5** [*often pl.*] [Inf.] a long time —***vi., vt.*** **aged**, **ag′ing** or **age′ing** to grow or make old, ripe, mature, etc. —**of age** having reached the age when one is qualified for full legal rights

-age (ij) ⟦< LL *-aticum*⟧ *suffix* **1** act, state, or result of *[usage]* **2** amount or number of *[acreage]* **3** cost of *[postage]* **4** place of *[steerage]*

a·ged (ā′jid; *for 2* ājd) ***adj.*** **1** old **2** of the age of —**the aged** old people

age·ism (āj′iz′əm) ***n.*** ⟦AGE + (RAC)ISM⟧ discrimination against older people

age′less ***adj.*** **1** seemingly not growing older **2** eternal

a·gen·cy (ā′jən sē) ***n.***, *pl.* **-cies** ⟦< L *agere*, to act⟧ **1** action; power **2** means **3** a firm, etc. empowered to act for another **4** an administrative government division **5** an organization that offers assistance *[a social agency]*

a·gen·da (ə jen′də) ***n.***, *pl.* **-das** ⟦< L *agere*, to do⟧ a list of things to be dealt with, as at a meeting

a·gent (ā′jənt) ***n.*** ⟦< L *agere*, to do⟧ **1** an active force or substance producing an effect **2** a person, firm, etc. empowered to act for another **3** a representative of a government agency

Agent Orange ⟦military code name, from *orange*-colored containers⟧ a highly toxic defoliant

age′-old′ ***adj.*** ancient

ag·er·a·tum (aj′ər āt′əm) ***n.*** ⟦< Gr *agēratos*, not growing old⟧ a plant of the composite family with small, thick heads of bluish flowers

ag·glom·er·ate (ə gläm′ər āt′; *for adj. & n.*, -it) ***vt., vi.*** **-at′ed**, **-at′ing** ⟦< L *ad-*, to + *glomerare*, form into a ball⟧ to gather into a mass or ball —***adj.*** gathered into a mass or ball —***n.*** a jumbled heap, mass, etc.

ag·glu·ti·nate (ə glo͞ot′'n it; *for v.*, -āt′) ***adj.*** ⟦< L *ad-*, to + *gluten*, glue⟧ stuck together —***vt., vi.*** **-nat′ed**, **-nat′ing** to stick together, as with glue —**ag·glu′ti·na′tion** ***n.***

ag·gran·dize (ə gran′dīz′; *also*, ag′rən-) ***vt.*** **-dized′**, **-diz′ing** ⟦< Fr *a-*, to + *grandir*, to increase⟧ to make greater, more powerful, richer, etc. —**ag·gran·dize·ment** (ə gran′diz mənt, ag′rən dīz′-) ***n.***

ag·gra·vate (ag′rə vāt′) ***vt.*** **-vat′ed**, **-vat′ing** ⟦< L *ad-*, to + *gravis*, heavy⟧ **1** to make worse **2** [Inf.] to annoy; vex —**ag′gra·va′tion** ***n.***

ag′gra·vat′ed ***adj.*** *Law* designating a grave form of a specified offense

ag·gre·gate (ag′rə git; *for v.*, -gāt′) ***adj.*** ⟦< L *ad-*, to + *grex*, a herd⟧ total —***n.*** a mass of distinct things gathered into a total or whole —***vt.*** **-gat′ed**, **-gat′ing** **1** to gather into a mass **2** to total —**ag′gre·ga′tion** ***n.***

ag·gres·sion (ə gresh′ən) ***n.*** ⟦< L *aggredi*, to attack⟧ **1** an unprovoked attack or warlike act **2** a being aggressive —**ag·gres′sor** ***n.***

ag·gres·sive (ə gres′iv) ***adj.*** **1** boldly hostile; quarrelsome **2** bold and active; enterprising —**ag·gres′sive·ly** ***adv.*** —**ag·gres′sive·ness** ***n.***

ag·grieve (ə grēv′) ***vt.*** **-grieved′**, **-griev′ing** ⟦see AGGRAVATE⟧ to cause grief or injury to; offend

a·ghast (ə gast′) ***adj.*** ⟦< OE *gast*, ghost⟧ feeling great horror or dismay

ag·ile (aj′əl) ***adj.*** ⟦< L *agere*, to act⟧ quick and easy of movement —**ag′ile·ly** ***adv.*** —**a·gil·i·ty** (ə jil′ə tē) ***n.***

ag·i·tate (aj′i tāt′) ***vt.*** **-tat′ed**, **-tat′ing** ⟦< L *agere*, to act⟧ **1** to stir up or shake up **2** to excite the feelings of —***vi.*** to stir up people so as to produce changes —**ag′i·ta′tion** ***n.*** —**ag′i·ta′tor** ***n.***

a·gleam (ə glēm′) ***adv., adj.*** gleaming

a·glit·ter (ə glit′ər) ***adv., adj.*** glittering

a·glow (ə glō′) ***adv., adj.*** in a glow (of color or emotion)

ag·nos·tic (ag näs′tik) ***n.*** ⟦< Gr *a-*, not + base of *gignōskein*, know⟧ one who believes it impossible to know if God exists —***adj.*** of an agnostic —**ag·nos′ti·cism′** (-ti siz′əm) ***n.***

a·go (ə gō′) ***adj.*** ⟦< OE *agan*, pass away⟧ gone by; past *[years ago]* —***adv.*** in the past *[long ago]*

a·gog (ə gäg′) ***adv., adj.*** ⟦< OFr *en*, in + *gogue*, joke⟧ with eager anticipation or excitement

ag·o·nize (ag′ə nīz′) ***vi.*** **-nized′**, **-niz′ing** **1** to struggle **2** to be in agony —***vt.*** to torture

ag·o·ny (ag′ə nē) ***n.***, *pl.* **-nies** ⟦< Gr *agōn*, a contest⟧ **1** great mental or physical pain **2** death pangs **3** a strong outburst (*of* emotion)

ag·o·ra·pho·bi·a (ag′ər ə fō′bē ə) ***n.*** ⟦< Gr *agora*, marketplace + -PHOBIA⟧ an abnormal fear of being in public places —**ag′o·ra·pho′bic** ***adj., n.***

a·grar·i·an (ə grer′ē ən) ***adj.*** ⟦< L *ager*, field⟧ **1** of land or the ownership of land **2** of agriculture

a·gree (ə grē′) ***vi.*** **-greed′**, **-gree′ing** ⟦< L *ad*, to + *gratus*, pleasing⟧ **1** to consent (*to*) **2** to be in accord **3** to be of the same opinion (*with*) **4** to arrive at an understanding (*about* prices, etc.) **5** to be suitable, healthful, etc.: followed by *with* —***vt.*** to grant *[I agree that it's true]*

a·gree′a·ble ***adj.*** **1** pleasing or pleasant **2** willing to consent **3** conformable **4** acceptable —**a·gree′a·bly** ***adv.***

a·gree′ment ***n.*** **1** an agreeing **2** an understanding between people, countries, etc. **3** a contract

agri- *combining form* agriculture: also **agro-**

ag·ri·busi·ness (ag′rə biz′nis) ***n.*** ⟦see fol. + BUSINESS⟧ farming and associated businesses and industries

THESAURUS

ence] span, lifetime, duration; see LIFE 4. **2** [A particular point or time in one's life] infancy, childhood, girlhood, boyhood, adolescence, adulthood, youth, middle age, old age, senility. **3** [A period of time] epoch, era, period, time, century, millennium, decade, generation, interval, term; see also LIFE 4. —**of age** adult, twenty-one, having attained majority; see MATURE.

age ***v.*** grow feeble, decline, wane, advance in years, wrinkle, waste away, have one foot in the grave, become long in the tooth.

aged ***a.*** gray, elderly, worn; see OLD.

agency ***n.*** **1** [Place where business is transacted] firm, bureau, company; see OFFICE 3, BUSINESS 4. **2** [That by which something is done] power, auspices, action; see MEANS 1.

agenda ***n.*** list, plan, schedule; see PROGRAM 2.

agent ***n.*** broker, promoter, operator, representative, salesman, saleswoman, salesperson, assistant, emissary, intermediary, appointee, servant, executor, attorney, lawyer, go-between, surrogate, mediary, deputy, minister, envoy, middleman, commissioner, delegate, proxy, substitute, steward, functionary, ambassador, proctor, negotiator, advocate, coagent, press agent, booking agent.

aggravate ***v.*** exasperate, annoy, provoke; see BOTHER 2.

aggravation ***n.*** **1** [A cause of aggravation] worry, affliction, distress; see DIFFICULTY 1, 2, TROUBLE 1. **2** [Annoyance] irritation, provocation, exasperation; see ANNOYANCE 1.

aggression ***n.*** offensive, assault, invasion; see ATTACK 1.

aggressive ***a.*** warlike, attacking, combative, threatening, advancing, offensive, firm, strong, assertive, disruptive, disturbing, hostile, intrusive, contentious, destructive, intruding, invading, assailing, barbaric, up in arms, on the warpath.—*Ant.* SERENE, peace-loving, peaceful.

agile ***a.*** nimble, quick, spry, deft, vigorous, athletic, sure-footed, light-footed, frisky, spirited, lithe, sprightly, supple, dexterous, rapid, active, ready, alive, buoyant, energetic, stirring, brisk, lively, swift, alert, bustling.—*Ant.* AWKWARD, slow, clumsy.

agility ***n.*** nimbleness, dexterity, spryness, quickness, briskness, swiftness, deftness, adroitness, fleetness, friskiness, liveliness, alertness.

agitate ***v.*** stir, move, arouse; see EXCITE.

agitated ***a.*** disturbed, upset, aroused; see EXCITED.

ago ***a.*** gone, since, past; see BEFORE.

agony ***n.*** suffering, torture, anguish; see PAIN 1, 2.

agree ***v.*** coincide, get along, side with, harmonize with, match up, concur, stand together, parallel, go along with, fit in, suit, say "yes" to, conform, go hand in hand with, equal, correspond, go together, synchronize, measure up to, square with*, click*, hit it off with, see eye to eye.—*Ant.* DIFFER, disagree, debate. —**agree about** come to terms, see eye to eye, settle; see SETTLE 1. —**agree on** come to terms, make an arrangement, make a bargain; see SETTLE 1. —**agree to** promise, consent, approve; see ACCEPT. —**agree with** coincide, accord, harmonize; see AGREE.

agreeable ***a.*** pleasing, satisfactory, acceptable; see PLEASANT 1, 2.

agreeably ***a.*** kindly, politely, pleasantly, well, wonderfully, satisfactorily, genially, cheerfully, peacefully; see also FAVORABLY.—*Ant.* OPPOSITE, disagreeably, negatively.

agreement ***n.*** **1** [The state of being in accord] conformity, friendship, accordance, accommodation, correspondence, harmony, concord, unison, concert, common view, understanding, brotherhood, affiliation, alliance, fellowship, companionship, goodwill, cooperation, assent, approval, compromise, treaty, pact, contract, bargain, settlement, satisfaction, affinity, closeness, concurrence, reconciliation, uniformity, balance, kinship, peace, love, unity, union, tie.—*Ant.* DISAGREEMENT, enmity, disunity. **2** [An expression of agreement] approval, treaty, contract; see DEAL 1.

ag·ri·cul·ture (ag′ri kul′chər) ***n.*** ⟦< L *ager*, field + *cultura*, cultivation⟧ the work of producing crops and raising livestock; farming —**ag′ri·cul′tur·al** ***adj.*** —**ag′ri·cul′tur·al·ly** ***adv.*** —**ag′ri·cul′tur·ist** ***n.***

a·gron·o·my (ə grän′ə mē) ***n.*** ⟦< Gr *agros*, field + *nemein*, govern⟧ the science and economics of crop production —**a·gron′o·mist** ***n.***

a·ground (ə ground′) ***adv.***, ***adj.*** on or onto the shore, a reef, etc.

a·gue (ā′gyo͞o′) ***n.*** ⟦< ML *(febris) acuta*, violent (fever)⟧ a fever, usually malarial, marked by chills

ah (ä, ô) ***interj.*** used to express delight, surprise, pain, etc.

a·ha (ä hä′) ***interj.*** used to express triumph, surprise, satisfaction, etc.

a·head (ə hed′) ***adv.***, ***adj.*** **1** in or to the front **2** forward; onward **3** in advance **4** winning or profiting —**get ahead** to advance financially, etc.

a·hem (ə hem′) ***interj.*** used to get someone's attention, etc.

-a·hol·ic (ə hôl′ik, -häl′-) *combining form* one preoccupied with (something specified)

a·hoy (ə hoi′) ***interj.*** used in hailing *[ship ahoy!]*

AI *abbrev.* artificial intelligence

aid (ād) ***vt.***, ***vi.*** ⟦< L *ad-*, to + *juvare*, to help⟧ to help; assist —***n.*** **1** help or assistance **2** a helper

aide (ād) ***n.*** ⟦Fr⟧ **1** an assistant **2** an aide-de-camp

aide-de-camp or **aid-de-camp** (ād′də kamp′) ***n.***, *pl.* **aides′-** or **aids′-** ⟦Fr⟧ a military officer serving as an assistant to a superior

AIDS (ādz) ***n.*** ⟦*A(cquired) I(mmune) D(eficiency) S(yndrome)*⟧ a condition of deficiency of certain leukocytes, resulting in infections, cancer, neural degeneration, etc.: see HIV

ai·grette or **ai·gret** (ā gret′, ā′gret′) ***n.*** ⟦see EGRET⟧ a bunch of the long, white, showy plumes of the egret

ail (āl) ***vt.*** ⟦OE *eglian*, to trouble⟧ to cause pain and trouble to —***vi.*** to be in poor health

ai·le·ron (ā′lə rän′) ***n.*** ⟦Fr < L *ala*, wing⟧ a pilot-controlled airfoil at the trailing edge of an airplane wing, for controlling rolling

ail·ment (āl′mənt) ***n.*** a mild illness

aim (ām) ***vi.***, ***vt.*** ⟦< L *ad-*, to + *aestimare*, to estimate⟧ **1** to direct (a weapon, blow, etc.) so as to hit **2** to direct (one's efforts) **3** to intend —***n.*** **1** an aiming **2** the ability to hit a target **3** intention —**take aim** to aim a weapon, etc.

aim′less ***adj.*** having no purpose —**aim′less·ly** ***adv.*** —**aim′less·ness** ***n.***

ain't (ānt) ⟦< *amn't*, contr. of *am not*⟧ *contr.* [Inf.] am not: also a dialectal or nonstandard contraction for *is not, are not, has not*, and *have not*

ai·o·li or **aï·o·li** (ī ō′lē) ***n.*** ⟦ult. < L *allium*, garlic + *oleum*, oil⟧ a mayonnaise containing crushed raw garlic

air (er) ***n.*** ⟦< Gr *aēr*⟧ **1** the invisible mixture of gases surrounding the earth **2** *a)* a breeze; wind *b)* fresh air **3** an outward appearance *[an air of dignity]* **4** general mood **5** [*pl.*] affected, superior manners **6** public expression **7** AIR CONDITIONING **8** a song or tune —***adj.*** of or by aircraft —***vt.*** **1** to let air into **2** to publicize **3** to broadcast —***vi.*** to be broadcast —**in the air** current or prevalent —**on** (or **off**) **the air** that is (or is not) broadcasting —**up in the air** not settled

air bag a bag that inflates instantly within an automobile in a collision, to protect riders from being thrown forward

air base a base for military aircraft

air′borne′ ***adj.*** **1** carried by or through the air **2** aloft or flying

air brake a brake operated by the action of compressed air on a piston

air′brush′ ***n.*** an atomizer worked by compressed air and used for spraying on paint, etc.: also **air brush** —***vt.*** to spray or modify with an airbrush

air′bus′ ***n.*** an extremely large passenger airplane, esp. for short trips

air conditioning a method of keeping air humidity and temperature at desired levels in buildings, cars, etc. —**air′-con·di′tion** ***vt.*** —**air conditioner**

air′-cooled′ ***adj.*** cooled by having air passed over, into, or through it

air′craft′ ***n.***, *pl.* **-craft′** any machine for traveling through the air

aircraft carrier a warship with a large, flat deck, for carrying aircraft

air′drop′ ***n.*** the dropping of supplies, troops, etc. from an aircraft in flight —**air′drop′** ***vt.***

Aire·dale (er′dāl′) ***n.*** ⟦after *Airedale*, valley in England⟧ a large terrier with a wiry coat

air′fare′ ***n.*** fare for transportation on a commercial airplane

air′field′ ***n.*** a field where aircraft can take off and land

air′foil′ ***n.*** a wing, rudder, etc. of an aircraft

air force the aviation branch of a country's armed forces

air′freight′ ***n.*** cargo transported by air —***vt.*** to transport or send by airfreight

air guitar the imagined guitar of someone pretending to play music, using movements typical of actual playing

air gun a gun or gunlike device operated by compressed air

air′head′ ***n.*** [Slang] a silly, ignorant person

air lane a route for travel by air; airway

air′lift′ ***n.*** a system of transporting troops, supplies, etc. by aircraft —***vt.*** to transport by airlift

air′line′ ***n.*** a system or company for moving freight and passengers by aircraft —***adj.*** of or on an airline

air′lin′er ***n.*** a large airline-operated aircraft for carrying passengers

air lock an airtight compartment, with adjustable air pressure, between places of unequal air pressure

air′mail′ ***n.*** mail transported by air; esp., in the U.S., mail going overseas by air: also sp. **air mail** —***adj.*** of or for mail sent by air —***vt.*** to send (mail) by air

air′man (-mən) ***n.***, *pl.* **-men** (-mən) **1** an aviator **2** an enlisted person in the U.S. Air Force

air mass *Meteorol.* a huge, uniform body of air having the properties of its place of origin

air mattress a pad filled with air, used as a mattress for camping, etc.

air′plane′ ***n.*** a motor-driven or jet-propelled aircraft kept aloft by the forces of air upon its wings

THESAURUS

agriculture ***n.*** tillage, cultivation, horticulture; see FARMING.

ahead ***a.*** before, earlier, in advance, ahead of, advanced, preceding, foremost, leading, in the lead, at the head of, in the foreground, to the fore, in the vanguard, first, in front of, preliminary.—*Ant.* behind, back, toward the end. —**get ahead** advance, prosper, progress; see SUCCEED.

aid ***n.*** comfort, benefit, favor; see HELP 1.

ailing ***a.*** ill, feeble, weak; see SICK.

ailment ***n.*** sickness, infirmity, disease; see ILLNESS 1, 2.

aim ***n.*** intention, object, plan; see PURPOSE 1. —**take aim** point, direct, train; see AIM, *v.*

aim ***v.*** train, steer, level, direct, set up, set one's sights, sight, take aim, zero in on, draw a bead on.

aimed ***a.*** proposed, marked, intended for, earmarked, directed, designed, dedicated, calculated, leveled, trained, steered, set, planned, anticipated.

aimless ***a.*** purposeless, pointless, erratic, thoughtless, careless, heedless, nonchalant, rambling, wandering, blind, random, unsettled, flighty, capricious, wayward, without aim, chance, haphazard, to no purpose, drifting, stray, accidental, undirected, casual, indecisive, irresolute, fitful, fanciful, fickle, eccentric, unplanned, helpless, unpredictable, shiftless.—*Ant.* CAREFUL, purposeful, planned.

air ***n.*** **1** [The gaseous envelope of the earth] atmosphere, aerosphere, stratosphere, troposphere, thermosphere, substratosphere, ozonosphere, ozone layer, mesosphere, ionosphere, chemosphere, homosphere, heterosphere, exosphere, mesopause, stratopause, aeropause, tropopause; wind, breeze, draft, the open air, sky, oxygen, the open, ventilation, the out-of-doors. **2** [The apparent quality] look, mien, demeanor; see LOOKS. —**in the air** prevalent, abroad, current; see FASHIONABLE, POPULAR 1. —**off the air** not being broadcast, closed, signed off; see QUIET. —**on the air** broadcasting, going on, televising, telecasting, being telecast, live. —**up in the air** undecided, unsettled, unsure; see UNCERTAIN.

air ***v.*** ventilate, open, freshen, air out, circulate air, air-condition, expose to air, draw in air, fan, refresh, cool, purify.

aired ***a.*** **1** [Exposed to the air] ventilated, opened, freshened, purified, hung out, sunned, dried.—*Ant.* CLOSED, stuffy, dark. **2** [Exposed to public attention] exposed, disclosed, discussed, revealed, told, unveiled; see also EXPOSED.—*Ant.* SECRET, undisclosed, concealed.

air force ***n.*** aviation service, air power, air cover; see ARMY 1.

airline ***n.*** air carrier, commercial airline, air freight carrier; see BUSINESS 4.

airman ***n.*** pilot, copilot, navigator; see PILOT.

airplane ***n.*** aircraft, aeroplane, air-

air′play′ *n.* the playing of a recording over radio or TV
air pocket an atmospheric condition that causes an aircraft to make a sudden, short drop while in flight
air′port′ *n.* a place where aircraft can land and take off, usually with facilities for repair, etc.
air power the total capacity of a nation for air war
air pressure the pressure of the atmosphere or of compressed air
air raid an attack by aircraft, esp. bombers
air rifle a rifle operated by compressed air
air′ship′ *n.* a self-propelled, steerable aircraft that is lighter than air
air′sick′ *adj.* nauseated because of air travel —**air′sick′ness** *n.*
air′space′ *n.* the space above a nation over which it can claim jurisdiction
air′strike′ *n.* an attack made by aircraft
air′strip′ *n.* a temporary airfield
air′tight′ *adj.* **1** too tight for air or gas to enter or escape **2** having no weaknesses *[an airtight alibi]*
air′time′ *n. Radio & TV* the period of time during which a program, commercial, etc. may be broadcast: also **air time**
air′waves′ *pl.n.* the medium through which radio signals are transmitted
air′way′ *n.* AIR LANE
air·y (er′ē) *adj.* **-i·er, -i·est 1** of air **2** open to the air; breezy **3** unsubstantial as air **4** light as air; graceful **5** lighthearted **6** affectedly nonchalant —**air′i·ly** *adv.* —**air′i·ness** *n.*
aisle (īl) *n.* ⟦< L *ala*, wing⟧ a passageway, as between sections of seats in rows
a·jar (ə jär′) *adv., adj.* ⟦OE *cier*, a turn⟧ slightly open, as a door
AK Alaska
aka (ā′kā′ā′) *abbrev.* also known as: used before an alias: also **a.k.a., a k a**
a·kim·bo (ə kim′bō) *adv., adj.* ⟦< ON *keng*, bent + *bogi*, a bow⟧ with hands on hips and elbows bent outward *[with arms akimbo]*
a·kin (ə kin′) *adj.* **1** of one kin; related **2** similar
Ak·ron (ak′rən) city in N Ohio: pop. 223,000
Al *Chem. symbol for* aluminum
-al (əl, ′l) ⟦< L⟧ *suffix* **1** of, like, or suitable for *[theatrical]* **2** the act or process of ___ing *[rehearsal]*
à la or **a la** (ä′lə, -lä) ⟦Fr⟧ in the manner or style of
Al·a·bam·a (al′ə bam′ə) Southern state of the SE U.S.: 50,750 sq. mi.; pop. 4,041,000; cap. Montgomery: abbrev. **AL** —**Al′a·bam′i·an** or **Al′a·bam′an** *adj., n.*
al·a·bas·ter (al′ə bas′tər) *n.* ⟦< Gr *alabastros*, perfume vase⟧ a translucent, whitish variety of gypsum, used for statues, vases, etc.
a la carte (ä′lə kärt′) ⟦Fr⟧ with a separate price for each item on the menu
a·lac·ri·ty (ə lak′rə tē) *n.* ⟦< L *alacer*, lively⟧ eager willingness, often with quick, lively action
A·lad·din (ə lad′′n) *n.* a boy in *The Arabian Nights* who finds a magic lamp
à la king (ä′lə kiŋ′) in a cream sauce containing mushrooms, pimentos, etc.
Al·a·mo (al′ə mō′) Franciscan mission at San Antonio, Texas: scene of a massacre of Texans by Mexican troops (1836)
a la mode (al′ə mōd′) ⟦< Fr⟧ **1** in fashion **2** served in a certain style, as pie with ice cream Also **à la mode**
a·lar (ā′lər) *adj.* ⟦< L *ala*, a wing⟧ **1** of a wing **2** having wings
a·larm (ə lärm′) *n.* ⟦< It *all′arme*, to arms⟧ **1** [Archaic] a sudden call to arms **2** a warning of danger **3** a mechanism that warns of danger, arouses from sleep, etc. **4** fear caused by danger —*vt.* **1** to warn of danger **2** to frighten
alarm clock a clock that can be set to buzz, flash a light, etc. at a given time, as to awaken a person
a·larm′ing *adj.* frightening
a·larm′ist *n.* one who spreads alarming rumors, exaggerated reports of danger, etc. —*adj.* of an alarmist
a·las (ə las′) *interj.* an exclamation of sorrow, pity, etc.
A·las·ka (ə las′kə) state of the U.S. in NW North America: 570,374 sq. mi.; pop. 550,000; cap. Juneau: abbrev. *AK* —**A·las′kan** *adj., n.*
alb (alb) *n.* ⟦< L *albus*, white⟧ a white robe worn by a priest at Mass
al·ba·core (al′bə kôr′) *n.* ⟦< Ar *al*, the + *buko*, young camel⟧ a tuna with unusually long pectoral fins
Al·ba·ni·a (al bā′nē ə) country in the W Balkan Peninsula: 11,101 sq. mi.; pop. 3,185,000 —**Al·ba′ni·an** *adj., n.*
Al·ba·ny (ôl′bə nē) capital of New York, on the Hudson: pop. 101,000
al·ba·tross (al′bə trôs′) *n.* ⟦< Sp < Ar *al qādūs*, a scoop⟧ **1** a large, web-footed sea bird **2** a burden
al·be·it (ôl bē′it) *conj.* ⟦ME *al be it*, al(though) it be⟧ although
Al·ber·ta (al burt′ə) province of SW Canada: 255,285 sq. mi.; pop. 2,697,000; cap. Edmonton: abbrev. *AB*
al·bi·no (al bī′nō) *n., pl.* **-nos** ⟦< L *albus*, white⟧ a person, animal, or plant lacking normal coloration: human albinos have white skin, whitish hair, and pink eyes
al·bum (al′bəm) *n.* ⟦< L *albus*, white⟧ **1** a book with blank pages for mounting pictures, stamps, etc. **2** one or more compact discs, LPs, etc. packaged in a holder
al·bu·men (al byo͞o′mən) *n.* ⟦L < *albus*, white⟧ **1** the white of an egg **2** the nutritive protein in seeds, etc. **3** ALBUMIN
al·bu·min (al byo͞o′min) *n.* ⟦see prec.⟧ a water-soluble protein found in milk, egg, blood, vegetable tissues, etc. —**al·bu′mi·nous** *adj.*
Al·bu·quer·que (al′bə kur′kē) city in central New Mexico: pop. 385,000
al·che·my (al′kə mē) *n.* ⟦< Ar < Gr *chēmeia*; infl. by Gr *cheein*, pour⟧ the chemistry of the Middle Ages, the chief aim of which was to change base metals into gold —**al′che·mist** *n.*
al·co·hol (al′kə hôl′) *n.* ⟦< Ar *alkuḥl*, antimony powder⟧ **1** a colorless, volatile, pungent liquid, used in various forms as a fuel, as an intoxicating ingredient in fermented liquors, etc. **2** any such intoxicating liquor
al′co·hol′ic *adj.* **1** of alcohol **2** suffering from alcoholism —*n.* one who has chronic alcoholism
al′co·hol′ism′ *n.* the habitual excessive drinking of alcoholic liquor, or a resulting diseased condition
al·cove (al′kōv′) *n.* ⟦< Ar *al*, the + *qubba*, an arch⟧ a recessed section of a room
al·der (ôl′dər) *n.* ⟦OE *alor*⟧ a small tree or shrub of the birch family
al·der·man (ôl′dər mən) *n., pl.* **-men** (-mən) ⟦< OE *eald*, old + *man*⟧ in some U.S. cities, a municipal officer representing a certain district or ward —**al′der·man′ic** (-man′ik) *adj.*
ale (āl) *n.* ⟦OE *ealu*⟧ a fermented drink of malt and hops, like beer
a·le·a·to·ry (ā′lē ə tôr′ē) *adj.* ⟦< L *aleatorius*, of gambling < *alea*, chance⟧ depending on chance or luck
a·lem·bic (ə lem′bik) *n.* ⟦< Ar *al-anbīq* < Gr *ambix*, a cup⟧ **1** an apparatus formerly used for distilling **2** anything that purifies
a·lert (ə lurt′) *adj.* ⟦< L *erigere*, to erect⟧ **1** watchful; vigilant **2** active; nimble —*n.* a warning signal; alarm —*vt.* **1** to warn to be ready, etc. **2** to make aware of *[alert them to their duties]* —**on the alert** vigilant —**a·lert′ly** *adv.* —**a·lert′ness** *n.*
A·leu·tian Islands (ə lo͞o′shən) chain of U.S. islands off the SW tip of Alaska —**A·leu′tian** *adj., n.*

THESAURUS

liner; see PLANE 3.
airport *n.* airfield, spaceport, flying field, landing field, airstrip, hangar, heliport, terminal, runway.
airtight *a.* impermeable to air, closed, sealed; see TIGHT 2.
airy *a.* windy, breezy, draughty, exposed, ventilated, open, spacious, lofty, atmospheric, well-ventilated, aerial, out-of-doors, outdoors, in the open.
aisle *n.* passageway, opening, way, walk, path, course, clearing, avenue, corridor, passage, gangway, alley, lane.
alarm *n.* drum, siren, horn, tocsin, signal, foghorn, fire siren, call, SOS, red light, hoot, blast, shout, warning sound, danger signal, cry, yell, scream, air-raid siren.
alarmed *a.* frightened, fearful, aroused; see AFRAID.
alarming *a.* frightening, foreboding, distressing; see DISTURBING.
album *n.* collection, register, index, scrapbook, notebook, photograph album, stamp book, portfolio, commonplace book.
alcohol *n.* spirits, liquor, intoxicant; see DRINK 2.
alcoholic *a.* hard, fermented, distilled; see STRONG 4.
alcoholic *n.* addict, heavy drinker, sot; see DRUNKARD.
alcoholism *n.* intoxication, insobriety, dipsomania; see DRUNKENNESS.
alert *a.* wary, on guard, wide-awake; see OBSERVANT. —**on the alert** watchful, vigilant, on guard; see OBSERVANT.
alert *v.* inform, put on guard, signal; see WARN.

ale·wife (āl′wīf′) ***n.***, *pl.* **-wives′** ⟦< ?⟧ a NW Atlantic fish resembling the herring, used for food and in fertilizers

Al·ex·an·der the Great (al′ig zan′dər) 356-323 B.C.; military conqueror: king of Macedonia (336-323)

Al′ex·an′dri·a (-drē ə) seaport in N Egypt: pop. 2,319,000

al·fal·fa (al fal′fə) ***n.*** ⟦Sp < Ar *al-fisfiṣa*, fodder⟧ a plant of the pea family, used for fodder and pasture and as a cover crop

Al·fred the Great (al′frəd) A.D. 849-899; Anglo-Saxon king (871-899)

al·fres·co (al fres′kō, äl-) ***adv.*** ⟦It < *al*, in the + *fresco*, cool⟧ outdoors —***adj.*** outdoor Also **al fresco**

al·gae (al′jē′) ***pl.n.***, *sing.* **al′ga** (-gə) ⟦pl. of L *alga*, seaweed⟧ a group of simple organisms, one-celled or many-celled, containing chlorophyll and found in water or damp places

al·ge·bra (al′jə brə) ***n.*** ⟦< Ar *al*, the + *jabara*, to reunite⟧ a mathematical system using symbols, esp. letters, to generalize certain arithmetical operations and relationships —**al′ge·bra′ic** (-brā′ik) ***adj.*** —**al′ge·bra′i·cal·ly** ***adv.***

Al·ge·ri·a (al jir′ē ə) country in N Africa: 919,595 sq. mi.; pop. 22,972,000 —**Al·ge′ri·an** ***adj.***, ***n.***

-al·gia (al′jə) ⟦< Gr *algos*⟧ *combining form* pain *[neuralgia]*

Al·giers (al jirz′) seaport & capital of Algeria: pop. 1,688,000

Al·gon·qui·an (al gäŋ′kē ən, -kwē-) ***adj.*** designating or of a widespread family of North American Indian languages —***n.*** this family of languages

al·go·rithm (al′gə rith′əm) ***n.*** ⟦ult. < Ar⟧ **1** any systematic method of solving a certain kind of mathematical problem **2** *Comput.* a set of instructions with a limited number of steps for solving a problem

a·li·as (ā′lē əs) ***n.***, *pl.* **-as·es** ⟦L < *alius*, other⟧ an assumed name —***adv.*** otherwise named *[*Bell *alias* Jones*]*

A·li Ba·ba (ä′lē bä′bə, al′ə bab′ə) in *The Arabian Nights*, a poor man who finds the treasure of forty thieves

al·i·bi (al′ə bī′) ***n.***, *pl.* **-bis′** ⟦L < *alius ibi*, elsewhere⟧ **1** *Law* the plea or fact that an accused person was elsewhere than at the scene of the crime **2** [Inf.] an excuse —***vi.***, ***vt.*** **-bied′**, **-bi′ing** [Inf.] to offer an excuse (for)

al·ien (āl′yən, āl′ē ən) ***adj.*** ⟦< L *alius*, other⟧ **1** foreign **2** not natural; strange **3** opposed or repugnant *[*beliefs *alien* to mine*]* **4** of aliens —***n.*** **1** a foreigner **2** a foreign-born resident who is not naturalized **3** a hypothetical being from outer space

al′ien·a·ble (-ə bəl) ***adj.*** capable of being transferred to a new owner

al′ien·ate′ (-āt′) ***vt.*** **-at′ed**, **-at′ing** **1** to transfer the ownership of (property) to another **2** to make unfriendly or withdrawn **3** to cause a transference of (affection) —**al′ien·a′tion** ***n.***

a·light[1] (ə līt′) ***vi.*** **a·light′ed** or **a·lit′**, **a·light′ing** ⟦ME *alihtan*⟧ **1** to get down or off; dismount **2** to come down after flight

a·light[2] (ə līt′) ***adj.*** lighted up; burning

a·lign (ə līn′) ***vt.*** ⟦< Fr *a-*, to + *ligne*, LINE[1]⟧ **1** to bring into a straight line **2** to bring (components or parts) into adjustment **3** to bring into agreement, etc. —***vi.*** to line up —**a·lign′ment** ***n.***

a·like (ə līk′) ***adj.*** ⟦< OE *gelic*⟧ like one another —***adv.*** **1** similarly **2** equally

al·i·ment (al′ə mənt) ***n.*** ⟦< L *alere*, nourish⟧ nourishment; food

al′i·men′ta·ry (-men′tə rē, -men′trē) ***adj.*** **1** of food or nutrition **2** nourishing

alimentary canal (or **tract**) the passage in the body (from the mouth to the anus) that food goes through

al·i·mo·ny (al′ə mō′nē) ***n.*** ⟦< L *alere*, nourish⟧ money a court orders paid to a person by that person's legally separated or divorced spouse

a·line (ə līn′) ***vt.***, ***vi.*** **a·lined′**, **a·lin′ing** ALIGN —**a·line′ment** ***n.***

a·lit (ə lit′) ***vi.*** *alt. pt. & pp. of* ALIGHT[1]

a·live (ə līv′) ***adj.*** ⟦< OE *on*, in + *līfe*, life⟧ **1** having life; living **2** in existence, operation, etc. **3** lively; alert —**alive to** aware of —**alive with** teeming with

a·li·yah or **a·li·ya** (ä′lē yä′) ***n.*** ⟦< Heb, lit., ascent⟧ immigration by Jews to Israel

al·ka·li (al′kə lī′) ***n.***, *pl.* **-lies′** or **-lis′** ⟦< Ar *al-qili*, the ashes of a certain plant⟧ **1** any base, as soda, that is soluble in water and gives off ions in solution **2** a mineral salt, etc. that can neutralize acids

al′ka·line (-lin, -līn′) ***adj.*** of or like an alkali —**al′ka·lin′i·ty** (-lin′ə tē) ***n.***

al′ka·lize′ (-līz′) ***vt.*** **-lized′**, **-liz′ing** to make alkaline —**al′ka·li·za′tion** ***n.***

al′ka·loid′ (-loid′) ***n.*** a bitter, alkaline substance, such as caffeine, morphine, etc., containing nitrogen

al·kyd (al′kid) ***n.*** ⟦ult. < ALKALI + (ACI)D⟧ a synthetic resin used in paints, varnishes, etc.: also **alkyd resin**

all (ôl) ***adj.*** ⟦OE *eal*⟧ **1** the whole quantity of *[all* the gold*]* **2** every one of *[all* men*]* **3** the greatest possible *[*in *all* sincerity*]* **4** any *[*beyond *all* doubt*]* **5** alone; only *[all* work and no play*]* —***pron.*** **1** [*with pl. v.*] everyone **2** everything **3** every part or bit —***n.*** **1** one's whole property, effort, etc. *[*gave his *all]* **2** a totality; whole —***adv.*** **1** wholly; entirely *[all* worn out*]* **2** apiece *[*a score of two *all]* —**after all** nevertheless —**all in** [Inf.] very tired —**all in all** **1** considering everything **2** as a whole —**all out** completely —**all the better** (or **worse**) so much the better (or worse) —**all the same** **1** nevertheless **2** unimportant —**at all** **1** in the least **2** in any way **3** under any considerations —**in all** altogether

all- *combining form* **1** wholly, entirely *[all*-American*]* **2** for every *[all*-purpose*]* **3** of everything *[all*-inclusive*]*

Al·lah (al′ə, ä′lə) ***n.*** ⟦< Ar *al*, the + *ilāh*, god⟧ *the Muslim name for* God

all′-A·mer′i·can ***adj.*** representative of the U.S. as a whole, or chosen as the best in the U.S. —***n.*** **1** a hypothetical football team, etc. made up of U.S. college players voted the best of the year **2** a player on such a team

all′-a·round′ ***adj.*** having many abilities, talents, or uses; versatile

al·lay (a lā′, ə-) ***vt.*** **-layed′**, **-lay′ing** ⟦< OE *a-*, down + *lecgan*, lay⟧ **1** to calm; quiet **2** to relieve (pain, etc.)

all′-clear′ ***n.*** a siren or other signal that an air raid or alert is over

al·le·ga·tion (al′ə gā′shən) ***n.*** an assertion, esp. one without proof or to be proved

al·lege (ə lej′) ***vt.*** **-leged′**, **-leg′ing** ⟦< L *ex-*, out of + *litigare*, to dispute⟧ **1** to declare or assert, esp. without proof **2** to offer as an excuse

al·leged (ə lejd′, ə lej′id) ***adj.*** **1** declared, but without proof **2** so-called *[alleged* friends*]* —**al·leg′ed·ly** ***adv.***

Al·le·ghe·ny Mountains (al′ə gā′nē) mountain range in

THESAURUS

alibi ***n.*** proof of absence, plea, explanation, declaration, defense, statement, case, allegation, avowal, assurance, profession, excuse, assertion, answer, reply, retort, vindication.

alien ***a.*** exotic, strange, unknown; see FOREIGN.

alien ***n.*** foreigner, stranger, refugee, displaced person, outsider, migrant, colonist, immigrant, guest, visitor, newcomer, barbarian, settler, stateless person, intruder, squatter, interloper, invader, noncitizen, man without a country, extraterrestrial.—*Ant.* INHABITANT, native, citizen.

alienate ***v.*** estrange, turn away, set against, withdraw the affections of, make unfriendly, come between, disunite, separate, divide, part, turn off*.—*Ant.* UNITE, reconcile, acclimate.

align ***v.*** arrange, straighten, regulate; see ADJUST 1, 2.

alike ***a.*** like, same, equal, identical, matching, selfsame, akin, similar, comparable, parallel, resembling, related, approximate, equivalent, allied, of a kind, twin, one, indistinguishable, facsimile, duplicate, matched, mated, one and the same, all one, in the same boat, on all fours with.

alimony ***n.*** upkeep, maintenance, support; see PAYMENT 1.

alive ***a.*** live, animate, living, breathing, existing, existent, vital, not dead, mortal, organic, extant, viable, growing, having life, conscious, alive and kicking*, above ground*, among the living.—*Ant.* DEAD, lifeless, inanimate.

all ***a.*** **1** [Completely] totally, wholly, entirely; see COMPLETELY. **2** [Each] every, any, each and every, any and every, every member of, without exception, barring no one, bar none, beginning and end, alpha and omega, from A to Z.—*Ant.* no, not any, none. **3** [Exclusively] alone, nothing but, solely; see ONLY 1.

all ***n.*** everything, everyone, every person, sum, collection, group, ensemble, total, totality, sum total, quantity, unit, entity, whole kit and caboodle*; lock, stock and barrel*; the works*.—*Ant.* NONE, nobody, nothing. **—after all** nevertheless, in spite of everything, despite; see ALTHOUGH. **—at all** anyhow, ever, in any way, in any case, in any respect, under any condition, under any circumstances, anyway, anywise, in the least, in any manner, to any extent, in the least degree, anyways*. **—in all** all told, collectively, on the whole; see ALTOGETHER.

allegedly ***a.*** assertedly, according to the statement, supposedly; see APPARENTLY.

Pennsylvania, Maryland, West Virginia, & Virginia: also **Al'le·ghe'nies**

al·le·giance (ə lē'jəns) ***n.*** ⟦< OFr *liege*, liege⟧ **1** the duty of being loyal to one's ruler, country, etc. **2** loyalty; devotion, as to a cause

al·le·go·ry (al'ə gôr'ē) ***n.***, *pl.* **-ries** ⟦< Gr *allos*, other + *agoreuein*, speak in assembly⟧ a story in which people, things, and events have a symbolic meaning, often instructive —**al'le·gor'i·cal** ***adj.*** —**al'le·gor'i·cal·ly** ***adv.*** —**al'le·go'rist** ***n.***

al·le·gret·to (al'ə gret'ō) ***adj.***, ***adv.*** ⟦It, dim. of *allegro*⟧ *Music* moderately fast: also written ***al'le·gret'to***

al·le·gro (ə le'grō', -lā'-) ***adj.***, ***adv.*** ⟦It⟧ *Music* fast: also written ***al'le'gro'***

al·lele (ə lēl') ***n.*** ⟦< Gr *allēlōn*, of one another⟧ a gene transferring inherited characteristics

al·le·lu·ia (al'ə lo͞o'yə, ä'lə-) ***interj.***, ***n.*** ⟦LL(Eccles.)⟧ HALLELUJAH

al·ler·gen (al'ər jən) ***n.*** ⟦Ger⟧ a substance inducing an allergic reaction —**al'ler·gen'ic** (-jen'ik) ***adj.***

al·ler·gic (ə lur'jik) ***adj.*** **1** of, caused by, or having an allergy **2** [Inf.] averse (*to*)

al·ler·gist (al'ər jist) ***n.*** a doctor who specializes in treating allergies

al·ler·gy (al'ər jē) ***n.***, *pl.* **-gies** ⟦Ger < Gr *allos*, other + *ergon*, work⟧ **1** a hypersensitivity to a specific substance (as a food, pollen, dust, etc.) or condition (as heat or cold) **2** an aversion

al·le·vi·ate (ə lē'vē āt') ***vt.*** **-at'ed**, **-at'ing** ⟦< L *ad-*, to + *levis*, light⟧ **1** to lessen or relieve (pain, etc.) **2** to decrease (poverty, etc.) —**al·le'vi·a'tion** ***n.***

al·ley (al'ē) ***n.***, *pl.* **-leys** ⟦< OFr *aler*, go⟧ **1** a narrow street between or behind buildings **2** a bowling lane

alley cat a homeless, mongrel cat

al'ley·way' ***n.*** an alley between buildings

all'-fired' ***adj.***, ***adv.*** ⟦< *hell-fired*⟧ [Slang] extreme(ly)

al·li·ance (ə lī'əns) ***n.*** ⟦see ALLY⟧ **1** an allying or close association, as of nations for a common objective, families by marriage, etc. **2** an agreement for this **3** the countries, groups, etc. in such association

al·lied (ə līd', al'īd') ***adj.*** **1** united by kinship, treaty, etc. **2** closely related

al·li·ga·tor (al'ə gāt'ər) ***n.*** ⟦< Sp *el*, the + L *lacerta*, lizard⟧ a large reptile of the U.S. and China, like the crocodile but with a shorter, broader snout

alligator clip a fastening device with spring-loaded jaws for making an electrical connection

alligator pear AVOCADO

all'-im·por'tant ***adj.*** highly important; necessary; essential

all'-in·clu'sive ***adj.*** including everything; comprehensive

al·lit·er·a·tion (ə lit'ər ā'shən) ***n.*** ⟦< L *ad-*, to + *littera*, letter⟧ repetition of an initial sound in two or more words of a phrase —**al·lit'er·a'tive** (-āt'iv, -ə tiv) ***adj.***

al·lo·cate (al'ə kāt') ***vt.*** **-cat'ed**, **-cat'ing** ⟦< L *ad-*, to + *locus*, a place⟧ **1** to set apart for a specific purpose **2** to distribute or allot —**al'lo·ca'tion** ***n.***

al·lot (ə lät') ***vt.*** **-lot'ted**, **-lot'ting** ⟦< OFr *a-*, to + *lot*, lot⟧ **1** to distribute in arbitrary shares; apportion **2** to assign as one's share —**al·lot'ment** ***n.***

all'-out' ***adj.*** complete or wholehearted

all'o'ver ***adj.*** over the whole surface

al·low (ə lou') ***vt.*** ⟦see ALLOCATE⟧ **1** to permit; let *[*I'm not *allowed* to go*]* **2** to let have *[*she *allowed* herself no sweets*]* **3** to acknowledge as valid **4** to provide (a certain amount), as for shrinkage, waste, etc. —**allow for** to leave room, time, etc. for —**al·low'a·ble** ***adj.***

al·low'ance (-əns) ***n.*** **1** an allowing **2** something allowed **3** an amount of money, food, etc. given regularly to a child, soldier, etc. **4** a reduction in price, as for a trade-in —**make allowance(s) for** to excuse because of mitigating factors

al·loy (al'oi; *also, and for v. usually*, ə loi') ***n.*** ⟦< L *ad-*, to + *ligare*, to bind⟧ **1** a substance that is a mixture of two or more metals **2** something that debases another thing when mixed with it —***vt.*** to make into an alloy

all'-pur'pose ***adj.*** useful in many ways

all right **1** satisfactory; adequate **2** unhurt; safe **3** correct **4** yes; very well **5** [Inf.] certainly

all'-round' ***adj.***, ***adv.*** *var. of* ALL-AROUND

all·spice (ôl'spīs') ***n.*** a spice, that seems to combine the flavors of several spices, made from the berry of a West Indian tree of the myrtle family

all'-star' ***adj.*** **1** made up of outstanding or star performers **2** of or characteristic of an all-star event —***n.*** a member of an all-star team

all'-time' ***adj.*** unsurpassed up to the present time

al·lude (ə lo͞od') ***vi.*** **-lud'ed**, **-lud'ing** ⟦L *alludere*, to jest⟧ to refer indirectly (*to*)

al·lure (ə loor') ***vt.***, ***vi.*** **-lured'**, **-lur'ing** ⟦< OFr *a-*, to + *loirer*, to lure⟧ to tempt with something desirable; attract; entice —***n.*** fascination; charm —**al·lure'ment** ***n.*** —**al·lur·ing** (ə loor'iŋ, a-) ***adj.***

al·lu·sion (ə lo͞o'zhən) ***n.*** **1** an alluding **2** an indirect or casual reference

al·lu'sive (-siv) ***adj.*** **1** containing an allusion **2** full of allusions —**al·lu'sive·ly** ***adv.*** —**al·lu'sive·ness** ***n.***

al·lu·vi·um (ə lo͞o'vē əm) ***n.***, *pl.* **-vi·ums** or **-vi·a** (-vē ə) ⟦< L *ad-*, to + *luere*, to wash⟧ sand, clay, etc. deposited by moving water —**al·lu'vi·al** ***adj.***

al·ly (ə lī'; *also, and for n. usually*, al'ī) ***vt.***, ***vi.*** **-lied'**, **-ly'ing** ⟦< L *ad-*, to + *ligare*, to bind⟧ **1** to unite or join for a specific purpose **2** to relate by similarity of structure, etc. —***n.***, *pl.* **-lies** a country or person joined with another for a common purpose

al·ma ma·ter (al'mə mät'ər, äl'-) ⟦L, fostering mother⟧ **1** the college or school that one attended **2** its anthem

al·ma·nac (ôl'mə nak', al'-) ***n.*** ⟦< *c.* 5th-c. Gr *almenichiaka*, calendar⟧ **1** a calendar with astronomical data, weather forecasts, etc. **2** a book published annually, with statistical information

THESAURUS

allegiance ***n.*** fidelity, homage, fealty; see LOYALTY.

allergic to ***a.*** sensitive to, affected by, subject to, susceptible to, repelled by, oversensitive to.—*Ant.* IMMUNE, unaffected by, hardened to.

allergy ***n.*** hypersensitive reaction, hypersensitivity, antipathy to certain substances; see ILLNESS 2.

alley ***n.*** back street, lane, rear way; see ROAD 1. —**up** (or **down**) **one's alley*** suited to one's abilities, in keeping with one's tastes, enjoyable, useful, what the doctor ordered*.

alliance ***n.*** **1** [The state of being allied] connection, membership, affinity, participation, cooperation, support, union, agreement, common understanding, marriage, kinship, relation, collaboration, federation, friendship, partnership, coalition, association, affiliation, confederation, implication, bond, tie. **2** [The act of joining] fusion, combination, coupling; see UNION 1. **3** [A union] league, federation, company; see ORGANIZATION 2.

allied ***a.*** unified, confederated, associated; see UNITED.

allot ***v.*** earmark, allocate, dole; see ASSIGN, DISTRIBUTE.

allotment ***n.*** portion, lot, part; see SHARE.

all-out ***a.*** total, wholehearted, complete; see ABSOLUTE 1.

allow ***v.*** permit, let, sanction, grant, consent to, tolerate, favor, yield, bear, approve of, give leave, endorse, certify, have no objection to, release, pass, authorize, license, warrant, put up with, give the green light to*, give the go-ahead to.—*Ant.* DENY, forbid, prohibit. —**allow for** take into account, take into consideration, provide for; see CONSIDER.

allowable ***a.*** permissible, proper, legal; see ADMISSIBLE.

allowance ***n.*** salary, wage, wages, commission, fee, hire, remittance, stipend, gift, grant, pension, alimony, palimony, annuity, settled rate, endowment, scholarship, fellowship, prize, subsidy, pay, bequest, legacy, inheritance, contribution, aid, handout, pocket money. —**make allowances for** weigh, excuse, rationalize; see CONSIDER.

alloy ***n.*** compound, mixture, combination; see METAL. *Common metal alloys include the following:* amalgam, pewter, brass, bronze, cast iron, Babbitt metal, britannia metal, gunmetal, pinchbeck, wrought iron, steel, vanadium steel, titanium steel, chrome steel, nichrome, tungsten steel, stainless steel, nonmagnetic steel, chromium steel, high tensile steel, cobalt steel, finishing steel, structural steel, carbon steel, sterling silver, white gold, aluminum metals, ferrous metals, nonferrous metals, nickel-silver.

all right ***a.*** **1** [Adequately] tolerably, acceptably, fairly well; see ADEQUATELY. **2** [Yes] agreed, very well, OK*; see YES. **3** [Certainly] without a doubt, definitely, positively; see SURELY. **4** [Uninjured] safe, well, unhurt; see WHOLE. **5** [Correct] exact, precise, right; see RIGHT 1.

all-time ***a.*** unsurpassed, record-breaking, to the greatest extent; see BEST 1.

ally ***n.*** confederate, partner, collaborator; see ASSOCIATE.

almanac ***n.*** calendar, yearbook, annual, register, world almanac, chronicle, journal, record, register of the year.

al·might·y (ôl mīt′ē) ***adj.*** all-powerful —**the Almighty** God

al·mond (ä′mənd, al′-, ôl′-; am′ənd) ***n.*** ⟦< Gr *amygdalē*⟧ **1** the edible, nutlike kernel of a peachlike fruit **2** the tree it grows on **3** the light-tan color of its shell —***adj.*** shaped like an almond; oval and pointed at one or both ends

al·most (ôl′mōst′, ôl mōst′) ***adv.*** very nearly; all but

alms (ämz) ***n.***, *pl.* **alms** ⟦< Gr *eleos*, mercy⟧ money, food, etc. given to poor people —**alms′giv′er** ***n.***

alms′house′ ***n.*** **1** [Archaic] a poorhouse **2** [Brit.] a privately endowed home for the poor

al·oe (al′ō′) ***n.***, *pl.* **-oes′** ⟦< Gr *aloē*⟧ an African plant of the lily family

a·loft (ə lôft′) ***adv.*** ⟦ME < *o*, on+ *loft*, loft⟧ **1** high up **2** in the air; flying **3** high above the deck of a ship

a·lo·ha (ä lō′hə, -hä′; ə lō′ə) ***n.***, ***interj.*** ⟦Haw, love⟧ **1** hello **2** goodbye

a·lone (ə lōn′) ***adj.***, ***adv.*** ⟦ME < *al*, all + *one*, one⟧ **1** apart from anything or anyone else **2** without any other person **3** only **4** without equal —**let alone 1** to refrain from interfering with: also **leave alone 2** not to speak of *[we hadn't a dime, let alone a dollar]*

a·long (ə lôŋ′) ***prep.*** ⟦< OE *and-*, over against + *-lang*, long⟧ **1** on or beside the length of **2** in conformity with —***adv.*** **1** lengthwise **2** progressively forward **3** together (*with*) **4** with one *[take me along]* **5** advanced *[well along in years]* —**all along** from the beginning —**be along** [Inf.] to come or arrive —**get along 1** to advance **2** to manage **3** to survive **4** to be compatible

a·long′shore′ ***adv.*** near or beside the shore

a·long′side′ ***adv.*** at or by the side; side by side —***prep.*** beside —**alongside of** at the side of

a·loof (ə lo͞of′) ***adv.*** ⟦< *a-*, on & Du *loef*, windward side⟧ at a distance but in view —***adj.*** cool and reserved *[an aloof manner]* —**a·loof′ness** ***n.***

a·loud (ə loud′) ***adv.*** **1** loudly **2** with the normal voice; not silently

alp (alp) ***n.*** ⟦after ALPS⟧ a high mountain

al·pac·a (al pak′ə) ***n.*** ⟦< AmInd⟧ **1** a South American llama **2** its silky wool, or cloth woven from it

al·pha (al′fə) ***n.*** **1** the first letter of the Greek alphabet (Α, α) **2** the beginning of anything —***adj.*** of the dominant member of a group

al′pha·bet′ (-bet′) ***n.*** ⟦< Gr *alpha* & *bēta*, first two letters of the Gr alphabet⟧ the letters used in writing a language, esp. as arranged in their usual order —**al′pha·bet′i·cal** ***adj.*** —**al′pha·bet′i·cal·ly** ***adv.***

al·pha·bet·ize (al′fə bə tīz′) ***vt.*** **-ized′**, **-iz′ing** to arrange in the usual order of the alphabet —**al′pha·bet′i·za′tion** ***n.***

al′pha·nu·mer′ic (-no͞o mer′ik) ***adj.*** having both alphabetical and numerical symbols

alpha particle a positively charged particle given off by certain radioactive substances

alpha ray a stream of alpha particles

alpha wave an electrical brain wave indicating relaxation: also **alpha rhythm**

Al·pine (al′pīn′) ***adj.*** **1** of the Alps **2** [**a-**] of or like high mountains

Alps (alps) mountain system in SC Europe

al·read·y (ôl red′ē) ***adv.*** **1** by or before the given or implied time **2** even now or even then

al·right (ôl rīt′) ***adj.***, ***adv.***, ***interj.*** *disputed sp. of* ALL RIGHT

Al·sace (al sās′, al′sas′) historical region of NE France —**Al·sa′tian** (-sā′shən) ***adj.***, ***n.***

al·so (ôl′sō) ***adv.*** ⟦< OE *eall*, all + *swa*, so⟧ in addition; likewise; too; besides

al′so-ran′ ***n.*** [Inf.] a defeated contestant in a race, election, etc.

alt *abbrev.* **1** alternate **2** altitude **3** alto

al·tar (ôl′tər) ***n.*** ⟦< L *altus*, high⟧ **1** a platform where sacrifices are made to a god, etc. **2** a table, etc. for sacred purposes in a place of worship

altar boy a boy or man who helps a priest at religious services, esp. at Mass

al·ter (ôl′tər) ***vt.***, ***vi.*** ⟦< L *alter*, other⟧ to change; make or become different —**al′ter·a′tion** ***n.***

al·ter·ca·tion (ôl′tər kā′shən) ***n.*** ⟦< L *altercari*, to dispute⟧ an angry or heated argument; quarrel

al′ter e′go ⟦L, other I⟧ **1** another aspect of oneself **2** a constant companion

al·ter·nate (ôl′tər nit; *for v.*, -nāt′) ***adj.*** ⟦< L *alternus*, one after the other⟧ **1** succeeding each other **2** every other **3** ALTERNATIVE (*adj.* 1) —***n.*** a substitute —***vt.*** **-nat′ed**, **-nat′ing** to do or use by turns —***vi.*** **1** to act, happen, etc. by turns **2** to take turns regularly —**al′ter·nate·ly** ***adv.*** —**al′ter·na′tion** ***n.***

alternating current an electric current reversing direction periodically: abbrev. *AC*

al·ter·na·tive (ôl tʉr′nə tiv) ***adj.*** **1** providing a choice between things **2** of an institution, etc. appealing to unconventional interests *[an alternative school]* —***n.*** **1** a choice between things **2** one of the things to be chosen **3** something left to choose

al·ter·na·tor (ôl′tər nāt′ər) ***n.*** an electric generator producing alternating current

THESAURUS

almighty ***a.*** **1** [Omnipotent] invincible, all-powerful, mighty; see POWERFUL 1. **2** [Divine] infinite, eternal, godlike, all-knowing, all-seeing, deathless, immortal, celestial, godly, pervading.

almost ***a.*** all but, nearly, approximately, roughly, to all intents, as good as, near to, substantially, essentially, in effect, on the verge of, relatively, for all practical purposes, to that effect, not quite, about to, with some exceptions, in the vicinity of, bordering on, within sight of, with little tolerance, close upon, in the neighborhood of, about, just about*, not quite, most*, around*, within a hair of.

aloft ***a.*** on high, overhead, up; see ABOVE 1, OVER 1.

alone ***a.*** lone, lonely, solitary, deserted, abandoned, individual, forsaken, desolate, detached, friendless, unaccompanied, isolated, lonesome, apart, by oneself, single, widowed, unattached, unconnected.—*Ant.* ACCOMPANIED, attended, escorted. —**let alone 1** [Besides] not to mention, also, in addition to; see BESIDES. **2** [Neglect] ignore, isolate, refrain from disturbing; see NEGLECT 2. —**let well enough alone** forget, ignore, let alone; see NEGLECT 2.

along ***a.***, ***prep.*** **1** [Near] by, at, adjacent; see NEAR 1. **2** [Ahead] on, onward, forward; see AHEAD. **3** [Together with] with, accompanying, in addition to, in company with, along with, side by side, coupled with, at the same time, simultaneously. —**all along** all the time, from the beginning, constantly; see REGULARLY. —**get along 1** [To succeed] prosper, get by, make ends meet; see SUCCEED 1. **2** [To advance] progress, move on, push ahead; see ADVANCE 1. **3** [To agree] accord, stand together, equal; see AGREE.

alongside ***a.***, ***prep.*** parallel to, close by, close at hand, by the side of, at the side of, along the side, side by side, equal with, on the same plane with, almost touching, neck and neck.—*Ant.* BEYOND, ahead, behind.

aloof ***a.*** remote, reserved, distant; see INDIFFERENT.

aloud ***a.*** vociferously, audibly, noisily; see LOUDLY.

alphabet ***n.*** letters, runes, pictographs, ideographs, characters, symbols, signs, hieroglyphs, cryptograms, phonemes, morphemes, phonetic characters; see also LETTER 1.

alphabetical ***a.*** alphabetic, systematic, logical, consecutive, progressive, one after another, step by step, graded, planned, ordered, letter by letter, from A to Z, indexed.

alphabetize ***v.*** arrange alphabetically, index, systematize; see ORDER 3.

alpine ***a.*** mountainous, high, lofty, snowcapped, rocky, soaring, rangy, snow-clad, elevated, towering; see also HIGH 1, 2.

already ***a.*** previously, by now, now, even now, by this time, at present, just now, in the past, up to now, by that time, then.

also ***a.*** too, likewise, besides, as well, in addition, additionally, along with, more than that, over and above, in conjunction with, thereto, together with, ditto, more, moreover, further, furthermore, including, plus, to boot.—*Ant.* WITHOUT, excluding, otherwise.

alter ***v.*** **1** [To change for a purpose] vary, turn, diminish, replace, mutate, warp, alternate, remodel, renovate, evolve, translate, disguise, restyle, revolutionize, reduce, substitute, reorganize, increase, intensify, shape, shift, modify, transform, remake, convert, reform, re-form, tailor, adjust, adapt, invert, reverse, reconstruct. **2** [To become different] convert, develop, decay; see CHANGE 2.

alteration ***n.*** conversion, modification, revision; see CHANGE 1.

altered ***a.*** modified, converted, revised; see CHANGED 2.

alternate ***a.*** alternative, substitute, makeshift; see TEMPORARY.

alternate ***n.*** replacement, equivalent, double; see SUBSTITUTE.

alternate ***v.*** **1** [To take or do by turns] substitute, follow in turn, happen by turns, follow one another, do by turns, do one then the other, relieve, fill in for, exchange. **2** [To fluctuate] vary, rise and fall, shift; see WAVER.

alternative ***n.*** option, discretion, opportunity; see CHOICE.

al·though (ôl *th*ō′) ***conj.*** ⟦ME < *al*, even + THOUGH⟧ in spite of the fact that; though: sometimes sp. **al·tho′**
al·tim·e·ter (al tim′ət ər) ***n.*** ⟦< L *altus*, high + -METER⟧ an instrument for measuring altitude
al·ti·tude (al′tə to͞od′) ***n.*** ⟦< L *altus*, high⟧ **1** the height of a thing, esp. above sea level **2** a high place: *usually used in pl.*
al·to (al′tō) ***n.***, *pl.* **-tos** ⟦It < L *altus*, high⟧ **1** the range of a voice between tenor and mezzo-soprano **2** a voice, singer, or instrument with such a range **3** a part for an alto —***adj.*** of or for an alto
al·to·geth·er (ôl′to͞o ge*th*′ər) ***adv.*** **1** completely **2** in all **3** on the whole
al·tru·ism (al′tro͞o iz′əm) ***n.*** ⟦< L *alter*, other⟧ unselfish concern for the welfare of others —**al′tru·ist** ***n.*** —**al′tru·is′tic** ***adj.*** —**al′tru·is′ti·cal·ly** ***adv.***
al·um (al′əm) ***n.*** ⟦< L *alumen*⟧ any of a group of salts of aluminum, etc., used in manufacturing and medicine
al·u·min·i·um (al′yo͞o min′ē əm) ***n.*** [Brit.] *var. of* ALUMINUM
a·lu·mi·num (ə lo͞o′mə nəm) ***n.*** ⟦< L *alumen*, alum⟧ a silvery, lightweight metallic chemical element
a·lum·nus (ə lum′nəs) ***n.***, *pl.* **-ni′** (-nī′) ⟦L, foster son⟧ a person, esp. a boy or man, who has attended or is a graduate of a particular school, college, etc. —**a·lum′na** (-nə), *pl.* **-nae** (-nē), ***fem.n.***
al·ways (ôl′wāz) ***adv.*** ⟦OE *ealne weg*⟧ **1** at all times **2** all the time **3** at any time **4** in every instance
Alz·hei·mer's disease (älts′hī′mərz) ⟦after A. *Alzheimer*, 20th-c. Ger doctor⟧ a degenerative brain disease
am (am) ***vi.*** ⟦OE *eom*⟧ *1st pers. sing., pres. indic., of* BE
Am *abbrev.* **1** America **2** American
AM[1] (ā′em′) ***n.*** amplitude-modulation broadcasting or sound transmission
AM[2] *abbrev.* **1** amplitude modulation **2** ⟦L *ante meridiem*⟧ before noon: used to designate the time from midnight to noon: also **A.M.**, **am**, or **a.m.** **3** ⟦L *Artium Magister*⟧ master of arts: also **A.M.**
AMA *abbrev.* American Medical Association
a·mal·gam (ə mal′gəm) ***n.*** ⟦< Gr *malagma*, an emollient⟧ **1** any alloy of mercury with another metal *[a dental filling of silver amalgam]* **2** a mixture; blend
a·mal′ga·mate′ (-gə māt′) ***vt.***, ***vi.*** **-mat′ed**, **-mat′ing** to unite; mix; combine —**a·mal′ga·ma′tion** ***n.***
a·man·dine (ä′mən dēn′) ***adj.*** ⟦Fr⟧ prepared with almonds
a·man·u·en·sis (ə man′yo͞o en′sis) ***n.***, *pl.* **-ses′** (-sēz′) ⟦L < *a-*, from + *manus*, hand + *-ensis*, relating to⟧ a secretary: now a jocular usage
am·a·ranth (am′ə ranth′) ***n.*** ⟦< Gr *amarantos*, unfading⟧ **1** any of a large group of similar plants, some bearing showy flowers **2** [Old Poet.] an imaginary flower that never dies
am·a·ret·to (am′ə ret′ō) ***n.*** ⟦It, rather bitter⟧ [*also* **A-**] a liqueur with an almond flavor
Am·a·ril·lo (am′ə ril′ō) city in NW Texas: pop. 158,000
am·a·ryl·lis (am′ə ril′is) ***n.*** ⟦< Gr *Amaryllis*, name for a shepherdess⟧ a lilylike plant with white, purple, pink, or red flowers
a·mass (ə mas′) ***vt.*** ⟦< Fr < L *massa*, a lump⟧ to pile up; accumulate
am·a·teur (am′ə chər, -tər) ***n.*** ⟦Fr < L *amare*, to love⟧ **1** one who does something for pleasure, not for money; nonprofessional **2** one who is somewhat unskillful —***adj.*** of or done by amateurs —**am′a·teur′ish** (-cho͝or′-) ***adj.*** —**am′a·teur·ism′** ***n.***
am·a·to·ry (am′ə tôr′ē) ***adj.*** ⟦< L *amare*, to love⟧ of or showing love, esp. sexual love
a·maze (ə māz′) ***vt.*** **a·mazed′**, **a·maz′ing** ⟦OE *āmasian*⟧ to fill with great surprise or wonder; astonish —**a·maze′ment** ***n.*** —**a·maz′ing** ***adj.*** —**a·maz′ing·ly** ***adv.***
Am·a·zon[1] (am′ə zän′, -zən) ***n.*** **1** *Gr. Myth.* any of a race of female warriors **2** [**a-**] a tall, strong, aggressive woman
Am′a·zon′[2] river in N South America: *c.* 4,000 mi.
am·bas·sa·dor (am bas′ə dər) ***n.*** ⟦< Prov *ambaissador*⟧ the highest-ranking diplomatic representative of one country to another —**am·bas′sa·do′ri·al** (-dôr′ē əl) ***adj.*** —**am·bas′sa·dor·ship′** ***n.***
am·ber (am′bər) ***n.*** ⟦< Ar *'anbar*, ambergris⟧ **1** a brownish-yellow fossil resin used in jewelry, etc. **2** its color —***adj.*** amberlike or amber-colored
am′ber·gris′ (-grēs′, -gris′) ***n.*** ⟦< OFr *ambre gris*, gray amber⟧ a grayish, waxy substance in the intestines of sperm whales, used in perfumes
ambi- ⟦L⟧ *combining form* both *[ambidextrous]*
am·bi·dex·trous (am′bə deks′trəs) ***adj.*** ⟦< earlier *ambidexter* + -OUS⟧ using both hands with equal ease —**am′bi·dex·ter′i·ty** (-deks ter′ə tē) ***n.***
am·bi·ence (am′bē əns, äm′bē äns′) ***n.*** ⟦Fr: see fol.⟧ an environment or its distinct atmosphere: also sp. **am′bi·ance** (-əns)
am·bi·ent (am′bē ənt) ***adj.*** ⟦< L *ambi-*, around + *ire*, to go⟧ surrounding; on all sides
am·bi·gu·i·ty (am′bə gyo͞o′ə tē) ***n.*** **1** a being ambiguous **2** *pl.* **-ties** an ambiguous word, statement, etc.
am·big·u·ous (am big′yo͞o əs) ***adj.*** ⟦< L *ambi-*, around + *agere*, to do⟧ **1** having two or more meanings **2** not clear; vague —**am·big′u·ous·ly** ***adv.***
am·bi·tion (am bish′ən) ***n.*** ⟦< L *ambitio*, a going around (to solicit votes)⟧ **1** a strong desire for fame, power, etc. **2** the thing so desired
am·bi′tious (-əs) ***adj.*** **1** full of or showing ambition **2** demanding great effort —**am·bi′tious·ly** ***adv.***
am·biv·a·lence (am biv′ə ləns) ***n.*** ⟦AMBI- + VALENCE⟧ simultaneous conflicting feelings —**am·biv′a·lent** ***adj.*** —**am·biv′a·lent·ly** ***adv.***
am·ble (am′bəl) ***vi.*** **-bled**, **-bling** ⟦< L *ambulare*, to walk⟧ **1** to move at an easy gait, as a horse **2** to walk in a leisurely way —***n.*** **1** a horse's ambling gait **2** a leisurely walking pace
am·bro·sia (am brō′zhə) ***n.*** ⟦< Gr *a-*, not + *brotos*, mortal⟧ **1** *Gr. & Rom. Myth.* the food of the gods **2** anything that tastes or smells delicious —**am·bro′sial** ***adj.***
am·bu·lance (am′byə ləns) ***n.*** ⟦< L *ambulare*, to walk⟧ a vehicle equipped for carrying the sick or wounded
am·bu·late (am′byo͞o lāt′, -byə-) ***vi.*** **-lat′ed**, **-lat′ing** to move about; walk —**am′bu·lant** (-lənt) ***adj.*** —**am′bu·la′tion** ***n.***
am′bu·la·to′ry (-lə tôr′ē) ***adj.*** **1** of or for walking **2** able to walk
am·bus·cade (am′bəs kād′) ***n.***, ***vt.***, ***vi.*** **-cad′ed**, **-cad′ing** AMBUSH
am·bush (am′bo͝osh′) ***n.*** ⟦< ML *in-*, in + *boscus*, woods⟧ **1** a deployment of persons in hiding to make a surprise attack **2** their hiding place **3** a surprise attack —***vt.***, ***vi.*** to attack from ambush
a·me·ba (ə mē′bə) ***n.***, *pl.* **-bas** or **-bae** (-bē) *alt. sp. of* AMOEBA —**a·me′bic** (-bik) ***adj.***
a·mel·io·rate (ə mēl′yə rāt′) ***vt.***, ***vi.*** **-rat′ed**, **-rat′ing** ⟦< Fr

THESAURUS

although ***conj.*** though, even though, despite, still, despite the fact that, in spite of, even if, while, however, for all that.
altitude ***n.*** elevation, loftiness, eminence; see HEIGHT.
altogether ***a.*** all told, collectively, on the whole, in the aggregate, in sum total, in a mass, all in all, all things considered, by and large, all, taking all things together, as a whole, for the most part.
always ***a.*** **1** [Constantly] periodically, continually, ceaselessly; see REGULARLY. **2** [Forever] perpetually, eternally, evermore; see FOREVER.
AM[2] or **A.M.** *abbrev.* ante meridiem, antemeridian, after midnight, morning, early hours, before noon, forenoon, dawn, sunup.
amass ***v.*** gather, hoard, store up; see ACCUMULATE.
amateur ***n.*** beginner, novice, learner, nonprofessional, dabbler, recruit, dilettante, hopeful, neophyte, initiate, apprentice, freshman, tenderfoot, rookie*, greenhorn, cub.—*Ant.* VETERAN, professional, expert.
amaze ***v.*** astonish, perplex, astound; see SURPRISE.
amazement ***n.*** astonishment, awe, bewilderment; see WONDER 1.
amazing ***a.*** astonishing, astounding, marvelous; see UNUSUAL 1.
ambassador ***n.*** representative, envoy, minister; see DIPLOMAT.
ambiguity ***n.*** doubtfulness, incertitude, vagueness; see UNCERTAINTY 2.
ambiguous ***a.*** equivocal, enigmatic, vague; see OBSCURE 1.
ambition ***n.*** hope, earnestness, aspiration, yearning, eagerness, longing, craving, passion, lust, itch, hunger, thirst, appetite, energy, ardor, zeal, enthusiasm, spirit, vigor, enterprise, get up and go*, what it takes*.—*Ant.* INDIFFERENCE, apathy, laziness.
ambitious ***a.*** aspiring, longing, hopeful, zealous, hungry, thirsty, inspired, industrious, goal-oriented, enthusiastic, energetic, avid, sharp, climbing, ardent, designing, earnest, enterprising, aggressive, Type A, resourceful, pushy*.
ambush ***n.*** pitfall, snare, deception; see TRAP 1.
ambush ***v.*** waylay, ensnare, lay for, bushwhack, set a trap, keep out of sight, decoy, entrap, hook in, lurk, lie in wait for, surround, hem in; see also ATTACK.

< L *melior*, better⟧ to make or become better; improve —**a·mel'io·ra'tion** ***n.***

a·men (ā'men', ä'-) ***interj.*** ⟦< Heb *amen*, truly⟧ may it be so!: used after a prayer or to express approval

a·me·na·ble (ə mē'nə bəl, -men'ə-) ***adj.*** ⟦< OFr < L *minare*, to drive (animals)⟧ **1** responsible or answerable **2** able to be controlled; submissive —**a·me'na·bil'i·ty** ***n.*** —**a·me'na·bly** ***adv.***

a·mend (ə mend') ***vt.*** ⟦< L *emendare*⟧ **1** to correct; emend **2** to improve **3** to change or revise (a law, etc.) —***vi.*** to improve one's conduct —**a·mend'a·ble** ***adj.***

a·mend'ment ***n.*** **1** a correction of errors, faults, etc. **2** improvement **3** a revision or change proposed or made in a bill, law, etc.

a·mends (ə mendz') ***pl.n.*** ⟦see AMEND⟧ [*sometimes with sing. v.*] payment made or satisfaction given for injury, loss, etc.

a·men·i·ty (ə men'ə tē, -mēn'-) ***n.***, *pl.* **-ties** ⟦< L *amoenus*, pleasant⟧ **1** pleasantness **2** an attractive feature or convenience **3** [*pl.*] courteous acts

am·ent (am'ənt, ā'mənt) ***n.*** ⟦< L *amentum*, thong⟧ CATKIN

Am·er·a·sian (am'ər ā'zhən) ***n.*** ⟦AMER(ICAN) + ASIAN⟧ a person of both American and Asian descent —***adj.*** both American and Asian [*an Amerasian child*]

a·merce (ə murs') ***vt.*** **a·merced'**, **a·merc'ing** ⟦< OFr *a merci*, at the mercy of⟧ to punish, esp. by imposing a fine —**a·merce'ment** ***n.***

A·mer·i·ca (ə mer'i kə) ⟦associated with *Amerigo* VESPUCCI⟧ **1** North America, South America, and the West Indies, considered together: also **the Americas** **2** North America **3** the United States of America

A·mer'i·can (-kən) ***adj.*** **1** of or in America **2** of the U.S. or its people —***n.*** **1** a person born or living in North or South America **2** a citizen of the U.S.

A·mer·i·can·a (ə mer'i kan'ə, -kä'nə) ***pl.n.*** books, papers, objects, etc. having to do with the U.S., its people, and its history

American Indian a member of any of the indigenous peoples of North or South America or the West Indies

A·mer'i·can·ism' ***n.*** **1** a custom or belief of or originating in the U.S. **2** a word or idiom originating in American English **3** devotion to the U.S., its customs, etc.

A·mer'i·can·ize' (-īz') ***vt.***, ***vi.*** **-ized'**, **-iz'ing** to make or become American in character, manners, etc. —**A·mer'i·can·i·za'tion** ***n.***

American plan a system of hotel operation in which the price charged covers room, service, and meals

American Revolution the war (1775-83) fought by the American colonies to gain independence from Great Britain

American Samoa group of seven islands in the SW Pacific: an unincorporated territory of the U.S.: 77 sq. mi.; pop. 47,000

Am·er·in·di·an (am'ər in'dē ən) ***n.***, ***adj.*** AMERICAN INDIAN —**Am'er·ind'** ***n.***, ***adj.***

am·e·thyst (am'i thist) ***n.*** ⟦< Gr *amethystos*, not drunken: the Greeks thought the amethyst prevented intoxication⟧ **1** a purple or violet quartz or corundum, used in jewelry **2** purple or violet

a·mi·a·ble (ā'mē ə bəl) ***adj.*** ⟦< L *amicus*, friend⟧ good-natured; friendly —**a'mi·a·bil'i·ty** ***n.*** —**a'mi·a·bly** ***adv.***

am·i·ca·ble (am'i kə bəl) ***adj.*** ⟦see prec.⟧ friendly; peaceable —**am'i·ca·bil'i·ty** ***n.*** —**am'i·ca·bly** ***adv.***

a·mid (ə mid') ***prep.*** in the middle of; among: also **a·midst** (ə midst')

am·ide (am'īd') ***n.*** any of several organic compounds derived from ammonia

a·mid'ships' ***adv.***, ***adj.*** in or toward the middle of a ship

a·mi·go (ə mē'gō) ***n.***, *pl.* **-gos'** (-gōz') ⟦Sp⟧ a friend

a·mi·no acid (ə mē'nō) ⟦< AMMONIA⟧ any of the nitrogenous organic acids that form proteins necessary for all life

Am·ish (äm'ish, am'-) ***pl.n.*** ⟦after Jacob *Ammann* (or *Amen*), the founder⟧ the members of a Christian sect that favors plain living in an agrarian society —***adj.*** of this sect

a·miss (ə mis') ***adv.*** ⟦see A-[1] & MISS[1]⟧ in a wrong way; astray —***adj.*** wrong, faulty, improper, etc. [*what is amiss?*]

am·i·ty (am'i tē) ***n.***, *pl.* **-ties** ⟦< L *amicus*, friend⟧ peaceful relations

am·me·ter (am'mēt'ər) ***n.*** ⟦AM(PERE) + -METER⟧ an instrument for measuring an electric current in amperes

am·mo (am'ō) ***n.*** [Slang] ammunition

am·mo·ni·a (ə mōn'yə) ***n.*** ⟦prob. from a salt found near Egyptian shrine of Jupiter *Ammon*⟧ **1** a colorless, pungent gas, a compound of nitrogen and hydrogen **2** a 10% water solution of this gas

am·mu·ni·tion (am'yoo nish'ən) ***n.*** ⟦< L *munire*, fortify⟧ **1** bullets, gunpowder, bombs, grenades, rockets, etc. **2** any means of attack or defense

am·ne·sia (am nē'zhə) ***n.*** ⟦< Gr *a-*, not + *mnasthai*, to remember⟧ partial or total loss of memory

am·nes·ty (am'nəs tē) ***n.***, *pl.* **-ties** ⟦< Gr *amnēstia*, a forgetting⟧ a pardon, esp. for political offenses —***vt.*** **-tied**, **-ty·ing** to pardon

am·ni·o·cen·te·sis (am'nē ō'sen tē'sis) ***n.*** ⟦< fol. + Gr *kentēsis*, a pricking⟧ the surgical procedure of extracting amniotic fluid from a pregnant woman to determine the sex of the fetus, detect disease, etc.

am·ni·on (am'nē ən, -än') ***n.***, *pl.* **-ni·ons** or **-ni·a** (-ə) ⟦Gr, dim. of *amnos*, lamb⟧ the membrane enclosing the embryo of a mammal, reptile, or bird: it is filled with a watery fluid (**amniotic fluid**) —**am'ni·ot'ic** (-ät'ik) ***adj.***

a·moe·ba (ə mē'bə) ***n.***, *pl.* **-bas** or **-bae** (-bē) ⟦< Gr *ameibein*, to change⟧ a one-celled, microscopic organism reproducing by fission —**a·moe'bic** (-bik) ***adj.***

a·mok (ə muk') ***adj.***, ***adv.*** ⟦< Malay *amuk*, attacking furiously⟧ used chiefly in **run amok**, lose control and behave violently

a·mong (ə muŋ') ***prep.*** ⟦< OE *on*, in + *gemang*, a crowd⟧ **1** surrounded by [*among* friends] **2** in the group of [*best among* books] **3** to or for each or several of [*divide it among* the crowd] **4** by the joint action of Also [Chiefly Brit.] **a·mongst** (ə muŋst')

A·mon-Re (ä'mən rā') ***n.*** the ancient Egyptian sun god: also **A'mon-Ra'** (-rä')

a·mon·til·la·do (ə män'tə lä'dō) ***n.*** ⟦< Sp, after *Montilla*, town in Spain⟧ a pale, dry sherry

a·mor·al (ā môr'əl) ***adj.*** **1** neither moral nor immoral **2** without moral sense —**a'mo·ral'i·ty** ***n.*** —**a·mor'al·ly** ***adv.***

am·o·rous (am'ə rəs) ***adj.*** ⟦< L *amor*, love⟧ **1** fond of making love **2** full of love **3** of sexual love —**am'o·rous·ly** ***adv.***

a·mor·phous (ə môr'fəs) ***adj.*** ⟦< Gr *a-*, without + *morphē*, form⟧ **1** without definite form **2** vague or indefinite **3** *Chem.* not crystalline

am·or·tize (am'ər tīz', ə môr'-) ***vt.*** **-tized'**, **-tiz'ing** ⟦< ME < L *ad*, to + *mors*, death⟧ to put money aside at intervals for gradual payment of (a debt, etc.) —**am'or·ti·za'tion** ***n.***

a·mount (ə mount') ***vi.*** ⟦< OFr *amont*, upward < L *ad*, to + *mons*, mountain⟧ **1** to add up (*to*) **2** to be equal (*to*) in value, etc. —***n.*** **1** a sum total **2** the whole value or effect **3** a quantity

a·mour (ə moor') ***n.*** ⟦< L *amor*, love⟧ a love affair, esp. an illicit one

a·mour-pro·pre (à moor prô'pr') ***n.*** ⟦Fr⟧ self-esteem

THESAURUS

amend ***v.*** correct, mend, revise; see ALTER 1.

amendment ***n.*** bill, measure, act, clause, motion, revision, codicil, supplement, rider.

American ***a.*** **1** [Related to the Western Hemisphere] continental, North American, Latin American, South American, Central American, Pan-American. **2** [Related to the United States of America] republican, constitutional, democratic, patriotic, all-American.

American ***n.*** citizen of the United States, United States national, Yankee, Northerner, Southerner, Native American, Indian, pioneer.

Americanism ***n.*** patriotism, nationalism, isolationism, provincialism, flag waving, fair play, free enterprise, America first, spirit of '76*.

amiable ***a.*** pleasant, genial, charming; see FRIENDLY.

ammunition ***n.*** *Types of ammunition include the following:* projectile, charge, grenade, buckshot, gunpowder, cartridge, bullet, bomb, missile, hand grenade, fuse, fuze, shrapnel, torpedo, shell, ball, cannonball, shot, ammo*; see also BOMB, BULLET, EXPLOSIVE, GAS 3, SHOT 1.

among ***prep.*** between, in between, in the midst of, in the middle of, encompassed by, surrounded by, in connection with, amid, amongst, amidst, in the company of, betwixt*.

amount ***n.*** **1** [The total of several quantities] sum, product, sum total; see WHOLE. **2** [Price] expense, output, outlay; see PRICE. **3** [Quantity] bulk, mass, number; see QUANTITY.

amount to ***v.*** reach, extend to, come to, effect, be equal to, approximate, check with, total up to, be in all, be in the whole, total, tally with, add up to, be tantamount to.

amp[1] (amp) ***n.*** *short for:* **1** AMPERE **2** AMPLIFIER
amp[2] *abbrev.* **1** amperage **2** ampere(s)
am·per·age (am′pər ij) ***n.*** the strength of an electric current in amperes
am·pere (am′pir′) ***n.*** ⟦< A. M. *Ampère*, 19th-c. Fr physicist⟧ the standard unit for measuring an electric current, equal to one coulomb per second
am·per·sand (am′pər sand′) ***n.*** ⟦< *and per se and*, (the sign) & by itself (is) *and*⟧ a sign (&), meaning *and*
am·phet·a·mine (am fet′ə mēn′, -min) ***n.*** a drug used esp. as a stimulant and to lessen appetite
am·phib·i·an (am fib′ē ən) ***n.*** ⟦see fol.⟧ **1** any amphibious animal, as a frog, or plant **2** any aircraft that can take off from or land on water or land —***adj.*** AMPHIBIOUS
am·phib′i·ous ***adj.*** ⟦Gr *amphibios*, living a double life < *amphi-*, around + *bios*, life⟧ that can live or operate on land and in water
am·phi·the·a·ter or **am·phi·the·a·tre** (am′fə thē′ə tər) ***n.*** ⟦< Gr *amphi-*, around + *theatron*, theater⟧ a round or oval building with rising rows of seats around an open space
am·ple (am′pəl) ***adj.*** **-pler, -plest** ⟦< L *amplus*⟧ **1** large in size, scope, etc. **2** more than enough **3** adequate —**am′ply *adv.***
am·pli·fi·er (am′plə fī′ər) ***n.*** one that amplifies; esp., a device for strengthening electrical signals
am′pli·fy′ (-fī′) ***vt.*** **-fied′, -fy′ing** ⟦< L *amplus*, large + *facere*, to make⟧ **1** to make stronger; esp., to strengthen (electrical signals) **2** to develop more fully —**am′pli·fi·ca′tion *n.***
am·pli·tude (am′plə to͞od′) ***n.*** ⟦see AMPLE⟧ **1** scope, extent, breadth, etc. **2** abundance **3** range from mean to extreme of a fluctuating quantity, as of an alternating current
amplitude modulation the changing of the amplitude of the transmitting radio wave in accordance with the signal being broadcast: abbrev. *AM*
am·pul (am′po͞ol′) ***n.*** ⟦< L *ampulla*, bottle⟧ a small, sealed, glass or plastic container for a single dose of a hypodermic medicine: also **am′pule′** (-pyo͞ol′) or **am′poule′** (-po͞ol′)
am·pu·tate (am′pyo͞o tāt′) ***vt., vi.*** **-tat′ed, -tat′ing** ⟦< L *am-*, AMBI- + *putare*, to prune⟧ to cut off (an arm, etc.), esp. by surgery —**am′pu·ta′tion *n.***
am′pu·tee′ (-tē′) ***n.*** one who has had a limb or limbs amputated
Am·ster·dam (am′stər dam′) constitutional capital of the Netherlands: pop. 724,000
amt *abbrev.* amount
Am·trak (am′trak′) *abbrev.* ⟦*Am(erican) tr(avel) (tr)a(c)k*⟧ a national U.S. passenger railroad system
a·muck (ə muk′) ***n.*** *alt. sp. of* AMOK
am·u·let (am′yo͞o lit) ***n.*** ⟦< L⟧ something worn to protect against evil
a·muse (ə myo͞oz′) ***vt.*** **a·mused′, a·mus′ing** ⟦< Fr < *à*, at + OFr *muser*, to gaze⟧ **1** to keep pleasantly occupied; entertain **2** to make laugh, smile, etc. —**a·mus′ed·ly *adv.***
a·muse′ment ***n.*** **1** a being amused **2** something that amuses; entertainment
amusement park an outdoor place with devices for entertainment, as a merry-go-round, roller coaster, etc.
am·yl·ase (am′ə lās′) ***n.*** ⟦< Gr *amylon*, starch⟧ an enzyme that helps change starch into sugar, found in saliva, etc.
an (an; *unstressed*, ən, ′n) ***adj., indefinite article*** ⟦< OE *an*, one⟧ **1** one; one sort of **2** each; any one —***prep.*** per *[two an hour] An* is used before words beginning with a vowel sound *[an eye, an honor]* See also A[2]
-an (ən, in, ′n) ⟦< L *-anus*⟧ *suffix* **1** (one) belonging to *[diocesan]* **2** (one) born in or living in *[Mexican]* **3** (one) believing in *[Lutheran]*
a·nach·ro·nism (ə nak′rə niz′əm) ***n.*** ⟦< Gr *ana-*, against + *chronos*, time⟧ **1** anything out of its proper historical time **2** the representation of this —**a·nach′ro·nis′tic *adj.***
an·a·con·da (an′ə kän′də) ***n.*** ⟦< Sinhalese *henacandāya*, a snake of Sri Lanka⟧ a long, heavy South American boa living in trees and water
an·aer·o·bic (an′ər ō′bik) ***adj.*** ⟦< Gr *an-*, without + *aēr*, air + *bios*, life⟧ able to live and grow without air or free oxygen, as certain bacteria
an·aes·the·sia (an′əs thē′zhə) ***n.*** ANESTHESIA —**an′aes·thet′ic** (-thet′ik) ***adj., n.***
an·a·gram (an′ə gram′) ***n.*** ⟦< Gr *anagrammatizein*, transpose letters⟧ **1** a word, etc. made by rearranging letters (Ex.: *now* — *won*) **2** [*pl., with sing. v.*] a word game based on this
An·a·heim (an′ə hīm′) city in SW California: pop. 266,000
a·nal (ā′nəl) ***adj.*** **1** of or near the anus **2** [Inf.] excessively orderly, stingy, etc.
an·al·ge·si·a (an′əl jē′zē ə) ***n.*** ⟦< Gr *an-*, without + *algēsia*, pain⟧ a fully conscious state in which pain is not felt
an′al·ge′sic (-zik) ***adj.*** of or causing analgesia —***n.*** a drug that produces analgesia
an·a·log (an′ə lôg′) ***adj.*** **1** of electronic devices in which the signal corresponds to a physical change **2** using hands, dials, etc. to show numerical amounts, as on a clock: cf. DIGITAL (sense 2) —***n.*** ANALOGUE
a·nal·o·gize (ə nal′ə jīz′) ***vi., vt.*** **-gized′, -giz′ing** to use, or explain by, analogy
a·nal′o·gous (-gəs) ***adj.*** ⟦see ANALOGY⟧ similar in some way —**a·nal′o·gous·ly *adv.***
an·a·logue (an′ə lôg′) ***n.*** something analogous
a·nal·o·gy (ə nal′ə jē) ***n.***, *pl.* **-gies** ⟦< Gr *ana-*, according to + *logos*, word, reckoning⟧ **1** similarity in some ways **2** the inference that certain resemblances imply further similarity
a·nal·y·sand (ə nal′ə sand′) ***n.*** a person undergoing psychoanalysis
a·nal′y·sis (-sis) ***n.***, *pl.* **-ses′** (-sēz′) ⟦< Gr *ana-*, up + *lysis*, a loosing⟧ **1** *a)* a breaking up of a whole into its parts to find out their nature, etc. *b)* any detailed examination **2** a statement of the results of this **3** PSYCHOANALYSIS **4** *Chem.* an analysis of compounds or mixtures —**an·a·lyt·ic** (an′ə lit′ik) or **an′a·lyt′i·cal *adj.*** —**an′a·lyt′i·cal·ly *adv.***
an·a·lyst (an′ə list) ***n.*** **1** one who analyzes **2** a psychoanalyst
an′a·lyze′ (-līz′) ***vt.*** **-lyzed′, -lyz′ing** **1** to make an analysis of; examine in detail **2** to psychoanalyze —**an′a·lyz′a·ble *adj.*** —**an′a·lyz′er *n.***
an·a·pest (an′ə pest′) ***n.*** ⟦< Gr *ana-*, back + *paiein*, to strike⟧ a metrical foot of two unaccented syllables followed by an accented one
an·ar·chism (an′ər kiz′əm) ***n.*** **1** the theory that all forms of government interfere unjustly with individual liberty **2** resistance to all government —**an′ar·chist′ *n.*** —**an′ar·chis′tic *adj.***
an′ar·chy (-kē) ***n.***, *pl.* **-chies** ⟦< Gr *an-*, without + *archos*, leader⟧ **1** the absence of government **2** political disorder and violence **3** disorder; confusion —**an·ar·chic** (an är′kik) ***adj.*** —**an·ar′chi·cal·ly *adv.***
a·nath·e·ma (ə nath′ə mə) ***n.***, *pl.* **-mas** ⟦Gr, thing devoted to evil⟧ **1** a thing or person accursed or damned **2** a thing or person greatly detested **3** a formal curse, as in excommunication
a·nath′e·ma·tize′ (-tīz′) ***vt., vi.*** **-tized′, -tiz′ing** to utter an anathema (against); curse
a·nat·o·mize (ə nat′ə mīz′) ***vt., vi.*** **-mized′, -miz′ing** ⟦see ANATOMY⟧ **1** to dissect (an animal or plant) in order to examine the structure **2** to analyze —**a·nat′o·mist *n.***
a·nat′o·my (-mē) ***n.***, *pl.* **-mies** ⟦< Gr *ana-*, up + *temnein*, to cut⟧ **1** dissection of an organism to study its structure **2** the science of the structure of animals or plants **3** the structure of an organism **4** any analysis —**an·a·tom·i·cal** (an′ə täm′i kəl) or **an′a·tom′ic *adj.***
-ance (əns) ⟦< L⟧ *suffix* **1** the act or process of ___ing *[discontinuance]* **2** the quality or state of being *[forbearance]* **3** a thing that ___s *[hindrance]* **4** a thing that is ___ed *[utterance]*
an·ces·tor (an′ses′tər) ***n.*** ⟦< L *ante-*, before + *cedere*, go⟧ **1** a person from whom one is descended; forebear **2** a

THESAURUS

ample ***a.*** sufficient, plentiful, adequate; see ENOUGH 1.
amplify ***v.*** expand, augment, elaborate; see INCREASE.
amply ***a.*** enough, sufficiently, copiously; see ADEQUATELY.
amputate ***v.*** cut off, sever, cut away; see REMOVE.
amuse ***v.*** divert, cheer, enliven; see ENTERTAIN 1.
amusement ***n.*** recreation, pastime, play; see ENTERTAINMENT.
amusing ***a.*** engaging, diverting, enchanting; see ENTERTAINING.
analysis ***n.*** study, investigation, interpretation; see EXAMINATION 1.
analyze ***v.*** dissect, examine, investigate, separate, break down, disintegrate, take apart, resolve into elements, determine the essential features of.
anarchy ***n.*** turmoil, chaos, mob rule; see DISORDER.
anatomy ***n.*** physique, form, figure; see BODY 1.
ancestor ***n.*** progenitor, forebear, father, mother, forefather, foremother, parent, sire, forerunner, author, predecessor, originator, precursor, grandfather, grandmother,

precursor or forerunner —**an·ces·tral** (an ses′trəl) ***adj.*** —**an·ces·tress** (an′ses′trəs) ***fem.n.***

an′ces′try (-trē) ***n.***, *pl.* **-tries** **1** family descent **2** ancestors collectively

an·chor (aŋ′kər) ***n.*** ⟦< Gr *ankyra*, an anchor, hook⟧ **1** a heavy object, usually an iron weight with flukes, lowered from a vessel, as by cable, to prevent drifting **2** anything giving stability **3** one who anchors a newscast: also **an′chor·per′son** —***vt.*** **1** to hold secure as by an anchor **2** to be the final contestant on (a relay team, etc.) **3** to serve as coordinator and chief reporter for (a newscast) —***vi.*** **1** to lower an anchor overboard **2** to be or become fixed —**at anchor** kept from drifting by its anchor

an′chor·age (-ij) ***n.*** **1** an anchoring or being anchored **2** a place to anchor

An·chor·age (aŋ′kər ij) seaport in S Alaska: pop. 226,000

an·cho·rite (aŋ′kə rīt′) ***n.*** ⟦< Gr *ana-*, back + *chōrein*, retire⟧ a religious recluse; hermit

an′chor·man′ ***n.***, *pl.* **-men′** a person, often, specif., a man, who anchors a newscast —**an′chor·wom′an**, *pl.* **-wom′en**, ***fem.n.***

an·cho·vy (an′chō′vē) ***n.***, *pl.* **-vies** ⟦< Port *anchova*⟧ a herringlike fish, eaten as a relish

an·cient (ān′chənt) ***adj.*** ⟦< L *ante*, before⟧ **1** of times long past **2** very old —***n.*** an aged person

an·cil·la (an sil′ə) ***n.*** a handbook or manual

an·cil·lar·y (an′sə ler′ē) ***adj.*** ⟦< L *ancilla*, maidservant⟧ **1** subordinate: often with *to* **2** auxiliary

-an·cy (ən sē) *suffix* -ANCE

and (and; *unstressed*, ənd, ən) ***conj.*** ⟦OE⟧ **1** also; in addition **2** plus **3** as a result **4** in contrast; but **5** then; following this **6** [Inf.] to *[try and come today]*

an·dan·te (än dän′tā) ***adj.***, ***adv.*** ⟦It < *andare*, to walk⟧ *Music* moderate in tempo: also written ***an·dan′te***

An·der·sen (an′dər sən), **Hans Christian** (häns, hänz) 1805-75; Dan. writer of fairy tales

An·des (Mountains) (an′dēz′) mountain system of W South America

and·i·ron (and′ī′ərn) ***n.*** ⟦< OFr *andier*⟧ either of a pair of metal supports for logs in a fireplace

and/or (and′ôr′) ***conj.*** either *and* or *or [personal and/or real property]*

An·dor·ra (an dôr′ə) country in the E Pyrenees: 175 sq. mi.; pop. 63,000

an·dro·gen (an′drō jən) ***n.*** ⟦< Gr *andros*, of man + -GEN⟧ a type of steroid that acts as a male sex hormone —**an′dro·gen′ic** (-jen′ik) ***adj.***

an·drog·y·nous (an drä′jə nəs) ***adj.*** ⟦< Gr *andros*, of man + *gynē*, woman⟧ **1** both male and female in one **2** that blends male and female characteristics, roles, etc. **3** not differentiated as to gender *[androgynous clothing]*

an·droid (an′droid′) ***n.*** ⟦< Gr *andros*, of man + -OID⟧ in science fiction, a robot made to resemble a human being

an·ec·dote (an′ik dōt′) ***n.*** ⟦< Gr *anekdotos*, unpublished⟧ a short, entertaining account of some event —**an′ec·dot′al** ***adj.***

a·ne·mi·a (ə nē′mē ə) ***n.*** ⟦< Gr *an-*, without + *haima*, blood⟧ a condition in which the blood is low in red cells or in hemoglobin, resulting in paleness, weakness, etc. —**a·ne′mic** ***adj.***

an·e·mom·e·ter (an′ə mäm′ət ər) ***n.*** ⟦< Gr *anemos*, the wind + -METER⟧ a gauge for determining the force or speed of the wind; wind gauge

a·nem·o·ne (ə nem′ə nē′) ***n.*** ⟦< Gr *anemos*, the wind⟧ **1** a plant with cup-shaped flowers of white, pink, red, or purple **2** SEA ANEMONE

a·nent (ə nent′) ***prep.*** ⟦< OE *on efen*, on even (with)⟧ [Now Rare] concerning; about

aneroid barometer (an′ər oid′) ⟦< Gr *a-*, without + *nēros*, liquid + -OID⟧ a barometer working by the bending of a thin metal disk instead of by the rise or fall of mercury

an·es·the·sia (an′es thē′zhə) ***n.*** ⟦< Gr *an-*, without + *aisthēsis*, feeling⟧ a partial or total loss of the sense of pain, touch, etc., specif. when induced by an anesthetic

an′es·the′si·ol′o·gist (-thē′zē äl′ə jist) ***n.*** a doctor who specializes in giving anesthetics —**an′es·the′si·ol′o·gy** ***n.***

an′es·thet′ic (-thet′ik) ***adj.*** of or producing anesthesia —***n.*** a drug, gas, etc. used to produce anesthesia, as before surgery

an·es·the·tist (ə nes′thə tist′) ***n.*** one trained to give anesthetics

an·es′the·tize′ (-tīz′) ***vt.*** **-tized′**, **-tiz′ing** to cause anesthesia in —**an·es′the·ti·za′tion** ***n.***

an·eu·rysm or **an·eu·rism** (an′yoo riz′əm) ***n.*** ⟦< Gr *ana-*, up + *eurys*, broad⟧ a sac formed by an enlargement in a weakened wall of an artery, a vein, or the heart

a·new (ə noo′) ***adv.*** **1** once more; again **2** in a new manner or form

an·gel (ān′jəl) ***n.*** ⟦< Gr *angelos*, messenger⟧ **1** *Theol. a)* a messenger of God *b)* a supernatural being with greater than human power, etc. **2** an image of a human figure with wings and a halo **3** a person regarded as beautiful, good, innocent, etc. **4** [Inf.] a financial backer, as for a play —**an·gel·ic** (an jel′ik) or **an·gel′i·cal** ***adj.*** —**an·gel′i·cal·ly** ***adv.***

angel dust [Slang] a powerful psychedelic drug

An·ge·le·no (an′jə lē′nō) ***n.***, *pl.* **-nos** ⟦AmSp⟧ a person born or living in Los Angeles

an·gel·fish (ān′jəl fish′) ***n.***, *pl.* **-fish′** or (for different species) **-fish′es** a bright-colored tropical fish with spiny fins

angel (food) cake a light, spongy, white cake made with egg whites

an·ger (aŋ′gər) ***n.*** ⟦< ON *angr*, distress⟧ a feeling of displeasure and hostility that a person has because of being injured, mistreated, opposed, etc. —***vt.***, ***vi.*** to make or become angry

an·gi·na (pec·to·ris) (an jī′nə pek′tər is) ⟦L, lit., squeezing of the breast⟧ a condition marked by chest pain, caused by a sudden decrease of blood to the heart

an·gi·o·gram (an′jē ō gram′) ***n.*** an X-ray photograph of blood vessels

an′gi·o·plas′ty (-plas′tē) ***n.*** any of various surgical techniques for repairing or replacing damaged blood vessels

an′gi·o·sperm′ (-spurm′) ***n.*** ⟦< Gr *angos*, vessel + *sperma*, seed⟧ any of a large division of plants having seeds produced within a closed pod or ovary

an·gle[1] (aŋ′gəl) ***n.*** ⟦< Gr *ankylos*, bent⟧ **1** the shape or space made by two straight lines or plane surfaces that meet **2** the measure of this space, expressed in degrees, etc. **3** a sharp corner **4** a point of view; aspect **5** [Inf.] a tricky method for achieving a purpose —***vt.***, ***vi.*** **-gled**, **-gling** **1** to move or bend at an angle **2** [Inf.] to give a specific point of view to (a story, etc.)

an·gle[2] (aŋ′gəl) ***vi.*** **-gled**, **-gling** ⟦< OE *angul*, fishhook⟧ **1** to fish with a hook and line **2** to use tricks to get something *[to angle for a promotion]* —**an′gler** ***n.***

An·gle (aŋ′gəl) ***n.*** a member of a Germanic people that settled in E England in the 5th c. A.D.

angle iron a piece of iron or steel bent at a right angle, for joining or reinforcing two beams, etc.

an′gle·worm′ ***n.*** an earthworm

An·gli·can (aŋ′gli kən) ***adj.*** ⟦< ML *Anglicus*, of the

THESAURUS

procreator, patriarch, relative, begetter, founder, kinsman.

ancestral ***a.*** inborn, innate, inherited; see INHERENT.

ancestry ***n.*** lineage, heritage, parentage; see FAMILY.

anchor ***n.*** stay, tie, grapnel, mooring, grappling iron, support, mainstay, ballast, safeguard, security, protection, hold, fastener, grip, defense, protection, foothold.

anchor ***v.*** make port, tie up, moor, berth, bring a ship in, drop anchor, cast anchor.

ancient ***a.*** antique, antiquated, aged; see OLD 1, 2, 3.

and ***conj.*** in addition, in addition to, also, plus, together with, as well as, furthermore, moreover.

anecdote ***n.*** tale, incident, episode; see STORY.

anemic ***a.*** pallid, weak, sickly; see PALE 1.

anesthetic ***n.*** sedative, painkiller, opiate; see DRUG.

angel ***n.*** Angel of Death, good angel, dark angel, archangel, guardian angel, spirit, cherub, celestial spirit, saint.—*Ant.* DEVIL, demon, Satan.

angelic ***a.*** saintly, good, humble, heavenly, spiritual, kind, radiant, beautiful, divine, holy, pure, lovely, devout, virtuous, above reproach, righteous, cherubic.—*Ant.* WICKED, demonic, evil.

anger ***n.*** wrath, rage, fury, passion, temper, bad temper, animosity, indignation, hatred, resentment, ire, hot temper, impatience, vexation, annoyance, provocation, violence, turbulence, excitement, frenzy, tantrum, exasperation, huff, irritation, dander*.—*Ant.* PATIENCE, mildness, calm.

anger ***v.*** infuriate, annoy, irritate; see ENRAGE.

angle[1] ***n.*** **1** [Shape formed by intersecting lines or intersecting planes] notch, crotch, elbow, fork, cusp, incline, decline, Y, V, point where two lines meet.—*Ant.* CURVE, arc, oval. **2** [Point of view] standpoint, outlook, perspective; see VIEWPOINT.

angle for ***v.*** plot for, scheme for, maneuver for; see PLAN 1.

angler ***n.*** fisher, fisherwoman, sportsman; see FISHERMAN.

Angles⟧ of or connected with the Church of England —*n.* an Anglican church member

An′gli·cize′ (-glə sīz′) *vt., vi.* **-cized′**, **-ciz′ing** [*also* **a-**] to change to English idiom, pronunciation, customs, etc. —**An′gli·ci·za′tion** *n.*

An·glo (aŋ′glō) *n., pl.* **-glos** ⟦AmSp⟧ [*also* **a-**] a white inhabitant of the U.S. who is of non-Hispanic descent

Anglo- *combining form* **1** English **2** Anglican

An′glo-A·mer′i·can (aŋ′glō-) *adj.* English and American —*n.* an American of English birth or ancestry

An′glo-French′ *adj.* English and French —*n.* the French spoken in England from the Norman Conquest through the Middle Ages

An′glo-Sax′on *n.* **1** a member of the Germanic peoples in England at the time of the Norman Conquest **2** the language of these peoples, OLD ENGLISH **3** an Englishman —*adj.* **1** of the Anglo-Saxons **2** of the English

An·go·la (aŋ gō′lə, an-) country on the SW coast of Africa: 481,354 sq. mi.; pop. 5,646,000

An·go·ra (aŋ gôr′ə, an-) *n.* ⟦former name of ANKARA⟧ **1** a breed of cat, goat, or rabbit with long, silky fur or hair **2** *a*) yarn of Angora rabbit hair *b*) mohair

an·gry (aŋ′grē) *adj.* **-gri·er**, **-gri·est** **1** feeling or showing anger **2** wild and stormy —**an′gri·ly** (-grə lē) *adv.*

ang·strom (aŋ′strəm) *n.* ⟦after A. J. *Angström*, 19th-c. Swed physicist⟧ one hundred-millionth of a centimeter: a unit used in measuring the length of light waves

an·guish (aŋ′gwish) *n.* ⟦< L *angustia*, tightness⟧ great mental or physical pain; agony —*vi., vt.* to feel or cause to feel anguish —**an′guished** *adj.*

an·gu·lar (aŋ′gyə lər) *adj.* **1** having or forming an angle or angles; having sharp corners **2** lean; gaunt **3** without ease or grace; stiff —**an′gu·lar′i·ty** (-lar′ə tē), *pl.* **-ties**, *n.*

an·i·line (an′ə lin) *n.* ⟦< Ar *an-nīl*, the indigo plant⟧ a colorless, poisonous, oily derivative of benzene, used in making dyes, resins, etc.

an·i·mad·vert (an′i məd vurt′, -mad′-) *vi.* ⟦L *animadvertere*, lit., to turn the mind⟧ to comment adversely (*on* or *upon*) —**an′i·mad·ver′sion** *n.*

an·i·mal (an′i məl) *n.* ⟦L < *anima*, breath, soul⟧ **1** any of a group of living organisms, excluding plants, bacteria, and certain other simple organisms, typically able to move about **2** any such organism other than a human being; esp., any four-footed creature **3** a brutish or inhuman person —*adj.* **1** of or like an animal **2** gross, bestial, etc.

an·i·mate (an′i māt′; *for adj.*, -mit) *vt.* **-mat′ed**, **-mat′ing** ⟦see prec.⟧ **1** to give life or motion to **2** to make energetic or spirited **3** to inspire —*adj.* living —**an′i·ma′tion** *n.* —**an′i·ma′tor** *n.*

an′i·mat′ed *adj.* **1** living or lifelike **2** lively **3** designating or of a movie made by photographing a series of drawings so that the figures in them seem to move

an·i·mism (an′i miz′əm) *n.* ⟦< L *anima*, soul⟧ the belief that all life is produced by a spiritual force, or that all natural phenomena have souls —**an′i·mis′tic** *adj.*

an·i·mos·i·ty (an′ə mäs′ə tē) *n., pl.* **-ties** ⟦see fol.⟧ a feeling of strong dislike or hatred; hostility

an·i·mus (an′ə məs) *n.* ⟦L, passion⟧ animosity; hostility

an·i·on (an′ī′ən) *n.* ⟦< Gr *anion*, thing going up⟧ a negatively charged ion: in electrolysis, anions move toward the anode

an·ise (an′is) *n.* ⟦< Gr *anison*⟧ **1** a dicotyledonous plant related to celery and parsley **2** its fragrant seed, used for flavoring: also **an′i·seed′** (-i sēd′)

an·i·sette (an′i zet′, -set′) *n.* ⟦Fr⟧ a sweet, anise-flavored liqueur

An·ka·ra (aŋ′kər ə, äŋ′-) capital of Turkey: pop. 2,235,000

ankh (aŋk) *n.* ⟦Egypt, life, soul⟧ a cross with a loop at the top, an ancient Egyptian symbol of life

an·kle (aŋ′kəl) *n.* ⟦OE *ancleow*⟧ **1** the joint that connects the foot and the leg **2** the area of the leg between the foot and calf

an·klet (aŋk′lit) *n.* **1** an ornament worn around the ankle **2** a short sock

an·nals (an′əlz) *pl.n.* ⟦< L *annus*, year⟧ **1** a written account of events year by year **2** historical records; history **3** a journal containing reports of a society, etc. —**an′nal·ist** *n.*

An·nap·o·lis (ə nap′ə lis) capital of Maryland: pop. 33,000

Ann Ar·bor (an är′bər) city in SE Michigan: pop. 110,000

an·neal (ə nēl′) *vt.* ⟦< OE *an-*, on + *æl*, fire⟧ to heat (glass, metals, etc.) and cool to prevent brittleness

an·ne·lid (an′ə lid′) *n.* ⟦< L dim. of *anulus*, a ring⟧ any of various wormlike animals, including leeches, having long, segmented bodies

an·nex (ə neks′; *for n.*, an′eks′) *vt.* ⟦< L *ad-*, to + *nectere*, to tie⟧ **1** to attach or append, esp. to something larger **2** to incorporate into a country, etc. the territory of (another country, etc.) —*n.* something annexed; esp., an addition to a building —**an·nex·a·tion** (an′eks ā′shən) *n.*

an·ni·hi·late (ə nī′ə lāt′) *vt.* **-lat′ed**, **-lat′ing** ⟦< L *ad*, to + *nihil*, nothing⟧ to destroy completely —**an·ni′hi·la′tion** *n.* —**an·ni′hi·la′tor** *n.*

an·ni·ver·sa·ry (an′ə vur′sə rē) *n., pl.* **-ries** ⟦< L *annus*, year + *vertere*, to turn⟧ the date on which some event occurred in an earlier year

an·no·tate (an′ō tāt′) *vt., vi.* **-tat′ed**, **-tat′ing** ⟦< L *ad-*, to + *nota*, a sign⟧ to provide explanatory notes for (a text, etc.) —**an′no·ta′tion** *n.* —**an′no·ta′tor** *n.*

an·nounce (ə nouns′) *vt.* **-nounced′**, **-nounc′ing** ⟦< L *ad-*, to + *nuntius*, messenger⟧ **1** to declare publicly **2** to make known the arrival of **3** to be an announcer for —*vi.* to serve as announcer —**an·nounce′ment** *n.*

an·nounc′er *n.* one who announces; specif., one who introduces radio or TV programs

THESAURUS

angrily *a.* heatedly, indignantly, irately, grouchily, crisply, sharply, savagely, hotly, fiercely, tartly, bitterly, furiously, wildly, violently.—*Ant.* CALMLY, softly, quietly.

angry *a.* enraged, fierce, fiery, irate, raging, fuming, infuriated, furious, wrathful, stormy, indignant, outraged, cross, vexed, resentful, irritated, bitter, ferocious, offended, sullen, annoyed, provoked, displeased, riled, affronted, huffy, hostile, rabid, mad, hot under the collar*, boiling, steamed up*, at the boiling point, with one's back up*, fit to be tied*, all worked up, up in arms.—*Ant.* CALM, quiet, restrained. **—get angry** become enraged, become furious, lose one's temper, get mad, blow up*, blow one's cool*, lose one's cool*, get hot under the collar*, get steamed up*, fly off the handle*, blow a fuse*.

anguish *n.* wretchedness, pain, agony; see PAIN 1.

angular *a.* sharp-cornered, intersecting, crossing, oblique, with corners, Y-shaped, V-shaped, forked, bent, crooked, pointed, triangular, rectangular, jagged, staggered, zigzag.—*Ant.* ROUND, parallel, side by side.

animal *a.* bestial, beastly, swinish, brutish, wild, beastlike, untamed, mammalian, bovine, canine, feline, reptilian.

animal *n.* living thing, creature, critter*, being, human being, beast, worm, mollusk, jellyfish, fish, crustacean, amphibian, reptile, insect, arachnid, bird, mammal, vertebrate, invertebrate, wild animal, domestic animal; see also BIRD, FISH, INSECT, MAN 1.

animate *v.* activate, vitalize, make alive, arouse, give life to, energize, put life into, breathe new life into.

animated *a.* spirited, vivacious, lively; see HAPPY.

animosity *n.* dislike, enmity, ill will; see HATRED.

ankle *n.* anklebone, joint, tarsus; see BONE, FOOT 2.

annex *n.* extension, additional quarters, new wing; see ADDITION 1, 2.

annex *v.* append, attach, affix; see ADD.

annihilate *v.* demolish, exterminate, obliterate; see DESTROY.

anniversary *n.* holiday, saint's day, birth date, birthday, yearly observance of an event, feast day, ceremony, annual meeting, biennial, triennial, quadrennial, quinquennial, silver anniversary, golden anniversary, diamond jubilee, jubilee, festival, centennial, centenary, red-letter day.

announce *v.* proclaim, publish, state; see DECLARE.

announced *a.* reported, given out, broadcast, issued, circulated, proclaimed, declared, published, disclosed, divulged, released, made known, disseminated, revealed, publicized, made public.—*Ant.* HIDDEN, unannounced, unrevealed.

announcement *n.* declaration, notification, prediction, proclamation, communication, publication, report, statement, advertisement, decision, news, tidings, returns, bulletin, edict, white paper, message, notice, interim report, survey, advice, item, communiqué, speech, release, handbill, poster, pamphlet, circular, billboard, brochure, form letter, fax, e-mail, telegram, cablegram, letter, leaflet; see also ADVERTISEMENT.—*Ant.* SECRET, ban, silence.

announcer *n.* broadcaster, telecaster, commentator, sportscaster, newscaster, anchor, moderator, emcee, weatherman, disc jockey.

an·noy (ə noi′) ***vt.*** ⟦< VL *in odio,* in hate⟧ to irritate or bother, as by a repeated action —**an·noy′ance** ***n.*** —**an·noy′ing** ***adj.*** —**an·noy′ing·ly** ***adv.***

an·nu·al (an′yo͞o əl) ***adj.*** ⟦< L *annus,* year⟧ **1** of or measured by a year **2** yearly **3** living only one year or season —***n.*** **1** a periodical published once a year **2** a plant living only one year or season —**an′nu·al·ly** ***adv.***

an·nu·i·ty (ə no͞o′ə tē) ***n.,*** *pl.* **-ties** ⟦see prec.⟧ **1** an investment yielding periodic payments, esp. yearly **2** such a payment —**an·nu′i·tant** ***n.***

an·nul (ə nul′) ***vt.*** **-nulled′**, **-nul′ling** ⟦< L *ad-,* to + *nullum,* nothing⟧ **1** to do away with **2** to make no longer legally binding; nullify —**an·nul′ment** ***n.***

an·nu·lar (an′yo͞o lər) ***adj.*** ⟦< L *anulus,* a ring⟧ like or forming a ring

an·nun·ci·a·tion (ə nun′sē ā′shən) ***n.*** an announcing —**the Annunciation** **1** *Bible* the angel Gabriel's announcement to Mary that she would bear Jesus **2** the church festival commemorating this

an·ode (an′ōd′) ***n.*** ⟦< Gr *anodos,* a way up⟧ **1** the positive electrode in an electrolytic cell **2** the principal electrode for collecting electrons in an electron tube **3** the negative electrode in a battery

an·o·dize (an′ō dīz′) ***vt.*** **-dized′**, **-diz′ing** to put a protective film on (a metal) by an electrolytic process in which the metal is the anode

an′o·dyne′ (-dīn′) ***adj.*** ⟦< Gr *an-,* without + *odynē,* pain⟧ **1** soothing **2** bland; insipid —***n.*** anything that relieves pain or soothes

a·noint (ə noint′) ***vt.*** ⟦< L *in-,* on + *unguere,* to smear⟧ to put oil on, as in consecrating —**a·noint′ment** ***n.***

a·nom·a·lous (ə näm′ə ləs) ***adj.*** ⟦< Gr *an-,* not + *homos,* the same⟧ **1** abnormal **2** inconsistent or odd

a·nom′a·ly (-lē) ***n.,*** *pl.* **-lies** **1** abnormality **2** anything anomalous

an·o·mie or **an·o·my** (an′ə mē) ***n.*** ⟦Fr < Gr *anomia,* lawlessness⟧ lack of purpose, identity, etc.

a·non (ə nän′) ***adv.*** ⟦< OE *on an,* into one⟧ [Archaic] **1** soon **2** at another time

Anon or **anon** *abbrev.* anonymous

a·non·y·mous (ə nän′ə məs) ***adj.*** ⟦< Gr *an-,* without + *onyma,* name⟧ **1** with no name known **2** given, written, etc. by one whose name is withheld or unknown **3** lacking individuality —**an·o·nym·i·ty** (an′ə nim′ə tē) ***n.*** —**a·non′y·mous·ly** ***adv.***

a·noph·e·les (ə näf′ə lēz′) ***n.*** ⟦< Gr *anōphelēs,* harmful⟧ the mosquito that can transmit malaria

an·o·rex·i·a (an′ə reks′ē ə) ***n.*** ⟦< Gr *an-,* without + *orexis,* desire⟧ an eating disorder characterized by obsession with weight loss: in full **anorexia ner·vo·sa** (nər vō′sə) —**an′o·rex′ic** ***adj., n.***

an·oth·er (ə nuth′ər) ***adj.*** **1** one more; an additional **2** a different —***pron.*** **1** one additional **2** a different one **3** one of the same kind

an·swer (an′sər) ***n.*** ⟦< OE *and-,* against + *swerian,* swear⟧ **1** a reply to a question, letter, etc. **2** any act in response **3** a solution to a problem —***vi.*** **1** to reply **2** to be sufficient **3** to be responsible or liable (*to* a person *for* an action, etc.) **4** to conform (*to*) *[*he *answers* to the description*]* —***vt.*** **1** to reply or respond to **2** to serve or fulfill *[*to *answer* the purpose*]* **3** to defend oneself against (a charge) **4** to conform to *[*she *answers* the description*]* —**answer back** [Inf.] to reply forcefully or insolently —**an′swer·a·ble** ***adj.***

an′swer·ing machine a device for recording telephone messages automatically

answering service a business whose function is to answer telephone calls for its clients

ant (ant) ***n.*** ⟦< OE *æmet(t)e*⟧ any of a family of insects, generally wingless, that live in complex colonies

ant- *prefix* ANTI-

-ant (ənt) ⟦ult. < L⟧ *suffix* **1** that has, shows, or does *[defiant]* **2** one that *[occupant]*

ant·ac·id (ant′as′id) ***adj.*** counteracting acidity, specif. gastric acidity —***n.*** an antacid substance

an·tag·o·nism (an tag′ə niz′əm) ***n.*** ⟦see ANTAGONIZE⟧ opposition or hostility

an·tag′o·nist ***n.*** an adversary; opponent —**an·tag′o·nis′tic** ***adj.*** —**an·tag′o·nis′ti·cal·ly** ***adv.***

an·tag′o·nize′ (-nīz′) ***vt.*** **-nized′**, **-niz′ing** ⟦< Gr *anti-,* against + *agōn,* a contest⟧ to incur the dislike of or make an enemy of

ant·arc·tic (ant ärk′tik, -är′-) ***adj.*** ⟦see ANTI- & ARCTIC⟧ of or near the South Pole or the region around it —**the Antarctic** the region including Antarctica and the Antarctic Ocean

Ant·arc′ti·ca (-ti kə) land area about the South Pole, completely covered by an ice shelf: *c.* 5,400,000 sq. mi.

Antarctic Circle [*also* **a- c-**] an imaginary circle parallel to the equator, *c.* 66°34′ south of it

ant bear a large anteater of Central America and tropical South America

an·te (an′tē) ***n.*** ⟦L, before⟧ *Poker* the stake that each player must put into the pot before receiving cards —***vt., vi.*** **-ted** or **-teed**, **-te·ing** *Poker* to put in (one's ante): also **ante up**

ante- ⟦see prec.⟧ *prefix* before in time or place

ant′eat′er ***n.*** a mammal with a long snout, that feeds mainly on ants

an·te·bel·lum (an′ti bel′əm) ***adj.*** ⟦L⟧ before the war; specif., before the American Civil War

an·te·ced·ent (an′tə sēd′′nt) ***adj.*** ⟦< L *ante-,* before + *cedere,* go⟧ prior; previous —***n.*** **1** any thing prior to another **2** [*pl.*] one's ancestry, past life, etc. **3** *Gram.* the word or phrase to which a pronoun refers

an·te·cham·ber (an′ti chām′bər) ***n.*** a room leading into a larger or main room

an′te·date′ (-dāt′) ***vt.*** **-dat′ed**, **-dat′ing** **1** to put a date on that is earlier than the actual date **2** to come before in time

an′te·di·lu′vi·an (-də lo͞o′vē ən) ***adj.*** ⟦< ANTE- + L *diluvium,* a flood + -AN⟧ **1** of the time before the biblical Flood **2** very old or old-fashioned

an·te·lope (an′tə lōp′) ***n.*** ⟦< Gr *antholops,* deer⟧ a swift, cud-chewing, horned animal resembling the deer

an·te me·ri·di·em (an′tē mə rid′ē əm) ⟦L⟧ before noon

an·ten·na (an ten′ə) ***n.*** ⟦L, sail yard⟧ **1** *pl.* **-nae** (-ē) or **-nas** either of a pair of feelers on the head of an insect, crab, etc. **2** *pl.* **-nas** *Radio, TV* an arrangement of wires, rods, etc. used in sending and receiving electromagnetic waves

THESAURUS

annoy ***v.*** pester, irritate, trouble; see BOTHER 2.

annoyance ***n.*** **1** [A feeling of annoyance] vexation, irritation, pique, uneasiness, disgust, displeasure, provocation, nervousness, exasperation, indignation, touchiness, perturbation, moodiness, mortification, vexation, worry, distress, unhappiness, discontent, heartache, misery, aches and pains, dissatisfaction, impatience, peeve*.—*Ant.* JOY, pleasure, delight. **2** [A source of annoyance] worry, inconvenience, nuisance; see DIFFICULTY 1, 2, TROUBLE 1.

annoying ***a.*** irritating, bothersome, vexatious; see DISTURBING.

annual ***a.*** yearly, each year, every year, once a year, lasting a year, anniversary, seasonal.

annually ***a.*** each year, once a year, periodically; see YEARLY.

annul ***v.*** invalidate, render void, repeal, revoke; see also CANCEL.

annulment ***n.*** invalidation, nullification, dissolution; see CANCELLATION.

anonymous ***a.*** unsigned, nameless, unknown, unnamed, unacknowledged, unclaimed, unidentified, secret, of unknown authorship, without a name, bearing no name, incognito, pseudonymous.—*Ant.* NAMED, signed, acknowledged.

another ***a.*** **1** [Additional] one more, a further, an added; see EXTRA. **2** [Different] a separate, a distinct, some other; see DIFFERENT.

another ***pron.*** someone else, a different person, one more, an additional one, something else.

answer ***n.*** **1** [A reply] response, return, statement, retort, echo, repartee, password, rebuttal, reaction, approval, acknowledgment, sign, rejoinder, comeback.—*Ant.* QUESTION, query, request. **2** [A solution] discovery, find, disclosure, revelation, explanation, interpretation, clue, resolution, key, the why and the wherefore.

answer ***v.*** **1** [To reply] reply, respond, rejoin, retort, acknowledge, give answer, say, echo, return, refute, react, rebut, argue, plead, claim, remark, talk back, shoot back*.—*Ant.* QUESTION, inquire, ask. **2** [To provide a solution] solve, elucidate, clarify; see EXPLAIN. —**answer for** be responsible for, take the blame for, accept the responsibility for, pay for, atone for, be liable for, take upon oneself, sponsor, do at one's own risk, take the rap for*. —**answer to** be responsible to, be ruled by, respect the authority of; see RESPECT 2.

answerable ***a.*** responsible, liable, accountable; see RESPONSIBLE 1.

antagonism ***n.*** enmity, hostility, opposition; see HATRED.

antagonistic ***a.*** opposing, hostile, inimical; see UNFRIENDLY.

antecedent ***a.*** preliminary, previous, prior; see PRECEDING.

antenna ***n.*** aerial, TV antenna, receiving wire; see WIRE.

an·te·ri·or (an tir′ē ər) ***adj.*** ⟦< L *ante*, before⟧ **1** at or toward the front **2** previous; earlier

an·te·room (an′tē ro͞om′) ***n.*** a room leading to a larger or main room

an·them (an′thəm) ***n.*** ⟦< Gr *anti-*, over against + *phōnē*, voice⟧ **1** a religious choral song **2** a song of praise or devotion, as to a nation

an·ther (an′thər) ***n.*** ⟦< Gr *anthēros*, blooming⟧ the part of a stamen that produces pollen

ant′hill′ ***n.*** the soil heaped up by ants around their nest opening

an·thol·o·gize (an thäl′ə jīz′) ***vi.*** **-gized′**, **-giz′ing** to make anthologies —***vt.*** to include in an anthology —**an·thol′o·gist** (-jist) or **an·thol′o·giz′er** ***n.***

an·thol′o·gy (-jē) ***n.***, *pl.* **-gies** ⟦< Gr *anthos*, flower + *legein*, gather⟧ a collection of poems, stories, songs, etc.

An·tho·ny (an′thə nē, -tə-), **Mark** *see* ANTONY, Mark

an·thra·cite (an′thrə sīt′) ***n.*** ⟦< Gr *anthrax*, coal⟧ hard coal, which gives much heat and little smoke

an·thrax (an′thraks′) ***n.*** ⟦< Gr, coal, carbuncle⟧ an infectious disease of cattle, sheep, etc. that can be transmitted to humans

anthropo- ⟦< Gr *anthrōpos*, man⟧ *combining form* man, human

an·thro·po·cen·tric (an′thrə pō′sen′trik) ***adj.*** ⟦see ANTHROPO-⟧ centering one's view of everything around humankind

an·thro·poid (an′thrə poid′) ***adj.*** ⟦see ANTHROPO- & -OID⟧ **1** resembling a human **2** apelike —***n.*** any of certain highly developed primates, as the chimpanzee and gorilla

an·thro·pol·o·gy (an′thrə päl′ə jē) ***n.*** ⟦ANTHROPO- + -LOGY⟧ the study of the characteristics, customs, etc. of humanity —**an′thro·po·log′i·cal** (-pə läj′i kəl) ***adj.*** —**an′thro·pol′o·gist** ***n.***

an′thro·po′mor′phism′ (-pō′môr′fiz′əm) ***n.*** the attributing of human characteristics to gods, objects, etc. —**an′thro·po′mor′phic** ***adj.*** —**an′thro·po′mor′phi·cal·ly** ***adv.*** —**an′thro·po′mor′phize′** (-fīz′), **-phized′**, **-phiz′ing**, ***vt.***, ***vi.***

an·ti (an′tī′, -tē) [Inf.] ***n.***, *pl.* **-tis′** ⟦< fol.⟧ a person opposed to something —***prep.*** opposed to

anti- ⟦< Gr *anti*, against⟧ *prefix* **1** against, hostile to **2** that operates against **3** that prevents, cures, or neutralizes **4** opposite, reverse **5** rivaling

an·ti·air·craft (an′tē er′kraft′) ***adj.*** used against hostile aircraft

an′ti·bal·lis′tic missile (-bə lis′tik) a missile intended to destroy an enemy ballistic missile in flight

an′ti·bi·ot′ic (-bī ät′ik, -bē-) ***n.*** ⟦< ANTI- + Gr *bios*, life⟧ any of certain substances, as penicillin or streptomycin, produced by various microorganisms and capable of destroying or weakening bacteria, etc. —***adj.*** of antibiotics

an·ti·bod·y (an′ti bäd′ē) ***n.***, *pl.* **-bod′ies** a protein produced in the body to neutralize a toxin or other antigen

an·tic (an′tik) ***adj.*** ⟦< L: see ANTIQUE⟧ odd and funny —***n.*** a playful or ludicrous act, trick, etc.: *usually used in pl.*

An·ti·christ (an′ti krīst′) ***n.*** *Bible* the great opponent of Christ: 1 John 2:18

an·tic·i·pate (an tis′ə pāt′) ***vt.*** **-pat′ed**, **-pat′ing** ⟦< L *ante-*, before + *capere*, take⟧ **1** to look forward to **2** to forestall **3** to use or deal with in advance **4** to be ahead of in doing —**an·tic′i·pa′tion** ***n.*** —**an·tic′i·pa·to′ry** (-pə tôr′ē) ***adj.***

an·ti·cli·max (an′ti klī′maks′) ***n.*** **1** a sudden drop from the important to the trivial **2** a descent which is in disappointing contrast to a preceding rise —**an′ti·cli·mac′tic** (-klī mak′tik) ***adj.***

an·ti·cline (an′ti klīn′) ***n.*** ⟦< ANTI- + Gr *klinein*, to lean⟧ *Geol.* a sharply arched fold of stratified rock

an·ti·co·ag·u·lant (an′ti kō ag′yo͞o lənt) ***n.*** a drug or substance that delays or prevents the clotting of blood

an′ti·de·pres′sant (-dē pres′ənt) ***adj.*** lessening emotional depression —***n.*** an antidepressant drug

an·ti·dote (an′tə dōt′) ***n.*** ⟦< Gr *anti-*, against + *dotos*, given⟧ **1** a remedy to counteract a poison **2** anything that works against an evil or unwanted condition

an·ti·freeze (an′ti frēz′) ***n.*** a substance used, as in the radiator of an automobile, to prevent freezing

an·ti·gen (an′tə jən) ***n.*** ⟦ANTI- + -GEN⟧ any substance to which the body reacts by producing antibodies

An·ti·gua and Bar·bu·da (an tē′gwə ′n bär bo͞o′də) country in the E West Indies, consisting of three small islands: 171 sq. mi.; pop. 66,000

an·ti·he·ro (an′tī hir′ō) ***n.***, *pl.* **-roes** the protagonist of a novel, etc. who lacks the virtues of a traditional hero

an·ti·his·ta·mine (an′ti his′tə mēn′, -min) ***n.*** any of several drugs used to block histamine, as in allergic reactions

an·ti·in·flam·ma·to·ry (an′tē in flam′ə tôr′ē) ***adj.*** reducing inflammation —***n.*** an anti-inflammatory medication, as aspirin

an·ti·knock (an′ti näk′) ***n.*** a substance added to the fuel of internal-combustion engines to reduce noise resulting from too rapid combustion

An·til·les (an til′ēz′) group of islands of the West Indies, including Cuba, Jamaica, etc. (**Greater Antilles**) & the Leeward Islands and Windward Islands (**Lesser Antilles**)

an·ti·lock (an′tē läk′) ***adj.*** designating an automotive braking system that prevents the wheels from locking during a sudden stop

an·ti·log·a·rithm (an′ti lôg′ə rith′əm) ***n.*** the number resulting when a base is raised to a power by a logarithm

an·ti·ma·cas·sar (an′ti mə kas′ər) ***n.*** ⟦ANTI- + *macassar*, a hair oil⟧ a small cover on the back or arms of a chair, sofa, etc. to prevent soiling

an·ti·mat·ter (an′ti mat′ər) ***n.*** a form of matter in which the electrical charge or other property of each particle is the reverse of that in the usual matter of our universe

an·ti·mis·sile (an′tī mis′əl) ***adj.*** designed as a defense against ballistic missiles

an·ti·mo·ny (an′tə mō′nē) ***n.*** ⟦< ML⟧ a silvery-white, nonmetallic chemical element used in alloys to harden them

an·ti·pas·to (an′ti päs′tō, -pas′-) ***n.*** ⟦It < *anti-*, before + *pasto*, food⟧ an appetizer of meats, cheeses, marinated vegetables, etc.

an·tip·a·thy (an tip′ə thē) ***n.***, *pl.* **-thies** ⟦< Gr *anti-*, against + *pathein*, to suffer⟧ **1** strong dislike; aversion **2** the object of such dislike

an·ti·per·son·nel (an′ti pur′sə nel′) ***adj.*** intended to destroy people rather than objects *[antipersonnel mines]*

an′ti·per′spi·rant (-pur′spə rənt) ***n.*** a substance applied to the skin to reduce perspiration

an·tiph·o·nal (an tif′ə nəl) ***adj.*** ⟦see ANTHEM⟧ sung or chanted in alternation

an·tip·o·des (an tip′ə dēz′) ***pl.n.*** ⟦< Gr *anti-*, opposite + *pous*, foot⟧ any two places directly opposite each other on the earth —**an·tip′o·dal** ***adj.***

an·ti·quar·i·an (an′ti kwer′ē ən) ***adj.*** **1** of antiques or antiquities **2** of antiquaries **3** dealing in old books —***n.*** an antiquary

an·ti·quar·y (an′ti kwer′ē) ***n.***, *pl.* **-quar′ies** a collector or student of antiquities

an′ti·quate′ (-kwāt′) ***vt.*** **-quat′ed**, **-quat′ing** ⟦see fol.⟧ to make old, out-of-date, or obsolete —**an′ti·quat′ed** ***adj.*** —**an′ti·qua′tion** ***n.***

an·tique (an tēk′) ***adj.*** ⟦< L *antiquus*, ancient⟧ **1** of ancient times **2** out-of-date **3** of, or in the style of, a former period **4** dealing in antiques —***n.*** **1** any ancient relic **2** a piece of furniture, etc. from a former period —***vt.*** **-tiqued′**, **-tiqu′ing** to make look antique —***vi.*** to shop for antique furniture, etc.

an·tiq·ui·ty (an tik′wə tē) ***n.***, *pl.* **-ties** ⟦see prec.⟧ **1** the ancient period of history **2** great age **3** [*pl.*] relics, etc. of the distant past

an·ti-Se·mit·ic (an′tē sə mit′ik) ***adj.*** **1** having or showing

THESAURUS

anthem ***n.*** hymn, song of devotion, song of praise; see SONG.

antibiotic ***n.*** antitoxin, wonder drug, bacteriostat; see MEDICINE 2.

antibody ***n.*** immunizer, neutralizer, immunoglobulin; see PREVENTION.

anticipate ***v.*** expect, forecast, prophesy, predict, hope for, look forward to, wait for, count on, plan on, have a hunch about, bargain for, hold in view, have in prospect, assume, suppose, divine, conjecture, promise oneself, lean upon, entertain the hope of, await, reckon on, count on, have a funny feeling about*, feel it in one's bones.—*Ant.* FEAR, be surprised by, be caught unawares by.

anticipated ***a.*** foreseen, predictable, prepared for; see EXPECTED, LIKELY 1.

anticipation ***n.*** expectancy, outlook, trust, prospect, impatience, preoccupation, hope, prevision, presentiment, intuition, foresight, inkling, premonition, apprehension, foreboding, awareness, forethought, hunch, a feeling in one's bones.—*Ant.* SURPRISE, shock, wonder.

antidote ***n.*** antitoxin, counteractant, remedy; see MEDICINE 2.

antique ***a.*** ancient, archaic, prehistoric; see OLD 3.

antique ***n.*** relic, artifact, heirloom, survival, rarity, monument, vestige, ruin.

prejudice against Jews **2** discriminating against or persecuting Jews Also **an'ti·se·mit'ic** —**an'ti-Sem'ite'** (-sem'īt') ***n.*** —**an'ti-Sem'i·tism'** (-ə tiz'əm) ***n.***
an·ti·sep·sis (an'tə sep'sis) ***n.*** ⟦ANTI- + SEPSIS⟧ **1** a being antiseptic **2** the use of antiseptics
an'ti·sep'tic (-tik) ***adj.*** **1** preventing infection, decay, etc. by acting against bacteria, etc. **2** using antiseptics **3** sterile —***n.*** any antiseptic substance —**an'ti·sep'ti·cal·ly** ***adv.***
an·ti·se·rum (an'ti sir'əm) ***n.***, *pl.* **-rums** or **-ra** a serum containing antibodies
an'ti·slav'er·y (an'tī-) ***adj.*** against slavery
an'ti·so'cial ***adj.*** **1** not sociable; avoiding others **2** harmful to the welfare of people
an'ti·tank' ***adj.*** for use against tanks in war
an·tith·e·sis (an tith'ə sis) ***n.***, *pl.* **-ses'** (-sēz') ⟦< Gr *anti-*, against + *tithenai*, to place⟧ **1** a contrast or opposition, as of ideas **2** the exact opposite —**an·ti·thet·i·cal** (an'tə thet'i kəl) ***adj.*** —**an'ti·thet'i·cal·ly** ***adv.***
an·ti·tox·in (an'ti täks'in) ***n.*** **1** a circulating antibody formed by the body to act against a specific toxin **2** a serum containing an antitoxin, injected into a person to prevent a disease
an·ti·trust (an'tī trust') ***adj.*** opposed to or regulating trusts, or business monopolies
an·ti·vi·ral (an'tī vī'rəl) ***adj.*** capable of checking the growth of a virus
an'ti·viv'i·sec'tion·ist (-viv'ə sek'shən ist) ***n.*** one opposing vivisection
ant·ler (ant'lər) ***n.*** ⟦< OFr *antoillier*⟧ the branched, bony growth on the head of any animal of the deer family —**ant'lered** (-lərd) ***adj.***
An·to·ny (an'tə nē), **Mark** (or **Marc**) 83?-30 B.C.; Rom. general
an·to·nym (an'tə nim') ***n.*** ⟦< Gr *anti-*, opposite + *onyma*, name⟧ a word meaning the opposite of another
Ant·werp (an'twərp') seaport in N Belgium: pop. 459,000
a·nus (ā'nəs) ***n.***, *pl.* **a'nus·es** or **a'ni'** (-nī') ⟦L⟧ the opening at the lower end of the alimentary canal
an·vil (an'vəl) ***n.*** ⟦< OE *anfilt*⟧ **1** an iron or steel block on which metal objects are hammered into shape **2** one of three small bones in the middle ear
anx·i·e·ty (aŋ zī'ə tē) ***n.***, *pl.* **-ties** ⟦see fol.⟧ **1** worry or uneasiness about what may happen **2** an eager but uneasy desire [*anxiety* to do well]
anx·ious (aŋk'shəs) ***adj.*** ⟦< L *angere*, to choke⟧ **1** worried **2** causing anxiety **3** eagerly wishing —**anx'ious·ly** ***adv.***
an·y (en'ē) ***adj.*** ⟦OE *ænig*⟧ **1** one, no matter which, of more than two [*any* boy may go] **2** some [has he *any* pain?] **3** without limit [*any* number can play] **4** even one or the least amount of [I haven't *any* dimes] **5** every [*any* child can do it] —***pron.*** (*sing. & pl.*) any one or ones —***adv.*** to any degree or extent; at all [is he *any* better today?]
an'y·bod'y (-bäd'ē, -bud'ē) ***pron.*** any person —***n.***, *pl.* **-bod'ies** a person of some importance
an'y·how' ***adv.*** ANYWAY
an'y·more' ***adv.*** now; nowadays
an'y·one' ***pron.*** any person; anybody
any one any single (person or thing)
an'y·place' ***adv.*** [Inf.] in, at, or to any place
an'y·thing' ***pron.*** any object, event, fact, etc. —***n.*** a thing, no matter of what kind —***adv.*** in any way —**anything but** not at all
an'y·time' ***adv.*** at any time —***conj.*** WHENEVER
an'y·way' ***adv.*** **1** in any manner **2** nevertheless; anyhow **3** haphazardly
an'y·where' ***adv.*** **1** in, at, or to any place **2** [Inf.] at all
A/o or **a/o** *abbrev.* account of
A-OK (ā'ō kā') ***adj.*** ⟦A(LL) OK⟧ [Inf.] excellent, fine, in working order, etc.: also **A'-O·kay'**
A one (ā' wun') [Inf.] first-class: also **A 1** or **A number 1**
a·or·ta (ā ôr'tə) ***n.***, *pl.* **-tas** or **-tae** (-tē) ⟦< Gr *aeirein*, to raise⟧ the main artery of the body, carrying blood from the heart —**a·or'tic** or **a·or'tal** ***adj.***
AP *abbrev.* Associated Press
a·pace (ə pās') ***adv.*** at a fast pace
A·pach·e (ə pach'ē) ***n.***, *pl.* **-es** or **-e** ⟦AmSp⟧ a member of a group of North American Indians of the SW U.S.
a·part (ə pärt') ***adv.*** ⟦< L *ad*, to, at + *pars*, part⟧ **1** aside **2** away in place or time **3** in or to pieces —***adj.*** separated —**apart from** other than —**tell apart** to distinguish between or among
a·part·heid (ə pär'tāt', -tīt') ***n.*** ⟦Afrik, separateness⟧ the official policy of racial segregation as practiced in South Africa, c. 1950-91
a·part'ment ***n.*** ⟦< It *appartare*, to separate⟧ a room or suite of rooms to live in, esp. one of a number in an **apartment building** (or **house**)
ap·a·thy (ap'ə thē) ***n.***, *pl.* **-thies** ⟦< Gr *a-*, without + *pathos*, emotion⟧ **1** lack of emotion **2** lack of interest; indifference; listlessness —**ap'a·thet'ic** (-thet'ik) ***adj.*** —**ap'a·thet'i·cal·ly** ***adv.***
ap·a·tite (ap'ə tīt') ***n.*** ⟦< Ger < Gr *apatē*, deceit⟧ a mineral incorporating calcium phosphate and found in rocks, bones, and teeth
a·pat·o·saur·us (ə pat'ə sôr'əs) ***n.*** a huge, plant-eating dinosaur
APB (ā'pē'bē') ***n.*** all-points bulletin
ape (āp) ***n.*** ⟦< OE *apa*⟧ **1** any gibbon or great ape **2** loosely, any monkey **3** a mimic **4** a person who is uncouth, clumsy, etc. —***vt.*** **aped**, **ap'ing** to mimic —**ape'like'** ***adj.***
Ap·en·nines (ap'ə nīnz') mountain range of central Italy
a·pe·ri·tif (ə per'ə tēf') ***n.*** ⟦Fr⟧ an alcoholic drink taken before a meal
ap·er·ture (ap'ər chər) ***n.*** ⟦< L *aperire*, to open⟧ an opening; hole
a·pex (ā'peks') ***n.***, *pl.* **a'pex'es** or **ap·i·ces** (ap'ə sēz') ⟦L⟧ **1** the highest point **2** the pointed end; tip **3** the climax
a·pha·sia (ə fā'zhə) ***n.*** ⟦Gr < *a-*, not + *phanai*, to say⟧ loss of the power to use or understand words —**a·pha'sic** (-zik) ***adj.***, ***n.***
a·phe·li·on (ə fē'lē ən) ***n.***, *pl.* **-li·ons** or **-li·a** (-ə) ⟦< Gr *apo-*, from + *hēlios*, sun⟧ the point farthest from the sun in the orbit of a planet or comet, or of a man-made satellite
a·phid (ā'fid, af'id) ***n.*** ⟦< ModL *aphis*⟧ an insect that lives on plants by sucking their juices

THESAURUS

antiseptic ***a.*** clean, germ-free, sterilized; see PURE 2.
antiseptic ***n.*** disinfectant, detergent, prophylactic, preservative, preventive, preventative, counterirritant, sterilizer, immunizing agent, vaccine, germicide, microbicide, fumigant; see also MEDICINE 2.
antitoxin ***n.*** vaccine, antibody, serum; see MEDICINE 2.
antlers ***n.*** horns, prongs, rack; see HORN 2.
anxiety ***n.*** concern, trouble, misgiving; see FEAR.
anxious ***a.*** **1** [Disturbed in mind] apprehensive, concerned, dreading; see TROUBLED. **2** [Eager] desirous, eager, fervent; see ZEALOUS.
any ***a.*** either, whatever, any sort of, any kind of, any one, each, some, several, each and every, all, one and all; see also EACH 1, SOME.
any ***pron.*** any sort, any kind, some number, some amount, any one thing.
anybody ***pron.*** anyone, everyone, everybody, all, the whole world, the public, the rabble, the masses, each and every one, any person, any one of.—*Ant.* NOBODY, no one, somebody.
anyhow ***a.*** in any event, at any rate, nevertheless, at all, in any case, regardless, anyway, in any way, in whatever way, under any circumstances, in one way or the other, in any respect, in either way, whatever happens, irregardless*, somehow or other.
anyone ***pron.*** any person, one, anyone at all; see ANYBODY.
anyplace* ***a.*** everywhere, wherever, in any place; see ANYWHERE.
anything ***pron.*** everything, all, anything at all, any, any one thing, aught, whatever one wants, you name it*.—*Ant.* NOTHING, something, one thing.
anyway ***a.*** in any event, nevertheless, in any manner; see ANYHOW.
anywhere ***a.*** wherever, in any place, all over, everywhere, in whatever place, wherever you go, anyplace*.—*Ant.* NOWHERE, in no place, somewhere. —**get anywhere*** prosper, thrive, advance; see SUCCEED 1.
apart ***a.*** **1** [Separated] disconnected, distant, disassociated; see SEPARATED. **2** [Separately] freely, exclusively, alone; see INDEPENDENTLY. —**take apart** dismember, dissect, reduce to its parts; see ANALYZE, DIVIDE. —**tell apart** characterize, discriminate, differentiate; see DISTINGUISH 1.
apartment ***n.*** rooms, quarters, flat, suite, penthouse, residence, home, duplex, pad*, walk-up.
apartment building ***n.*** tenement, hotel, apartment house, condominium, high-rise apartments.
apathetic ***a.*** unemotional, unresponsive, unconcerned; see INDIFFERENT.
apathy ***n.*** dullness, insensitivity, unconcern; see INDIFFERENCE.
ape ***n.*** great ape, primate, simian, gorilla, orangutan, chimpanzee, baboon, bonobo, gibbon; see also MONKEY.
ape ***v.*** copy, mimic, impersonate; see IMITATE 1.

aph·o·rism (af′ə riz′əm) ***n.*** ⟦< Gr *apo-*, from + *horizein*, to bound⟧ a concise statement of a general truth; maxim; adage —**aph′o·ris′tic** ***adj.*** —**aph′o·ris′ti·cal·ly** ***adv.***

aph·ro·di·si·ac (af′rə dē′zē ak′) ***adj.*** ⟦ult. after fol.⟧ arousing or increasing sexual desire —***n.*** an aphrodisiac drug, etc.

Aph·ro·di·te (af′rə dīt′ē) ***n.*** the Greek goddess of love and beauty

a·pi·ar·y (ā′pē er′ē) ***n.***, *pl.* **-ar′ies** ⟦< L *apis*, bee⟧ a place where bees are kept —**a′pi·a·rist** (-ə rist) ***n.***

a·piece (ə pēs′) ***adv.*** ⟦ME *a pece*⟧ for each one; each

a·plen·ty (ə plen′tē) ***adj.***, ***adv.*** [Inf.] in abundance

a·plomb (ə pläm′, -plum′) ***n.*** ⟦Fr: see PLUMB⟧ self-possession; poise

a·poc·a·lypse (ə päk′ə lips′) ***n.*** ⟦< Gr *apokalyptein*, disclose⟧ **1** a revelation of a violent struggle in which evil will be destroyed **2** a disastrous event, esp. the end of the world **3** [**A-**] *Bible* the book of Revelation —**a·poc′a·lyp′tic** (-lip′tik) ***adj.***

A·poc·ry·pha (ə päk′rə fə) ***pl.n.*** ⟦< Gr *apo-*, away + *kryptein*, to hide⟧ fourteen books of the Septuagint rejected in Judaism and Protestantism: eleven are in the Roman Catholic Bible

a·poc′ry·phal (-fəl) ***adj.*** **1** of doubtful authenticity **2** not genuine; spurious

ap·o·gee (ap′ə jē′) ***n.*** ⟦< Gr *apo-*, from + *gē*, earth⟧ the point farthest from the earth in the orbit of the moon or a satellite

a·po·lit·i·cal (ā′pə lit′i kəl) ***adj.*** not concerned with political matters —**a′po·lit′i·cal·ly** ***adv.***

A·pol·lo (ə päl′ō) ***n.*** **1** the Greek and Roman god of music, poetry, prophecy, and medicine **2** *pl.* **-los** a handsome young man

a·pol·o·get·ic (ə päl′ə jet′ik) ***adj.*** showing regret; making an apology —**a·pol′o·get′i·cal·ly** ***adv.***

a·pol·o·gist (ə päl′ə jist) ***n.*** one who defends or attempts to justify a doctrine, faith, action, etc.

a·pol′o·gize′ (-jīz′) ***vi.*** **-gized′**, **-giz′ing** to make an apology —**a·pol′o·giz′er** ***n.***

a·pol·o·gy (ə päl′ə jē) ***n.***, *pl.* **-gies** ⟦< Gr *apo-*, from + *logos*, speech⟧ **1** a formal defense of some idea, doctrine, etc.: also **ap·o·lo·gi·a** (ap′ə lō′jē ə) **2** an expression of regret for a fault, insult, etc.

ap·o·plex·y (ap′ə plek′sē) ***n.*** ⟦< Gr *apo-*, from + *plēssein*, to strike⟧ [Old-fashioned] STROKE (*n.* 3) —**ap′o·plec′tic** (-plek′tik) ***adj.***

a·pos·ta·sy (ə päs′tə sē) ***n.***, *pl.* **-sies** ⟦< Gr *apo-*, away + *stasis*, a standing⟧ an abandoning of what one has believed in, as a faith or cause

a·pos′tate′ (-tāt′) ***n.*** a person guilty of apostasy

a·pos′ta·tize′ (-tə tīz′) ***vi.*** **-tized′**, **-tiz′ing** to become an apostate

a pos·te·ri·o·ri (ā′ päs tir′ē ôr′ī) ⟦L⟧ **1** from effect to cause **2** based on observation or experience

a·pos·tle (ə päs′əl) ***n.*** ⟦< Gr *apo-*, from + *stellein*, send⟧ **1** [*usually* **A-**] any of the disciples of Jesus, esp. the original twelve **2** the leader of a new movement

ap·os·tol·ic (ap′əs täl′ik) ***adj.*** **1** of the Apostles or their teachings, work, etc. **2** [*often* **A-**] of the pope; papal

a·pos·tro·phe (ə päs′trə fē) ***n.*** ⟦< Gr *apo-*, from + *strephein*, to turn⟧ **1** a mark (’) indicating: *a*) omission of a letter or letters from a word (Ex.: *it's* for *it is*) *b*) the possessive case (Ex.: *Mary's* dress) *c*) certain plural forms (Ex.: five *6's*, dot the *i's*) **2** an exclamatory address to a person or thing

a·poth·e·car·y (ə päth′ə ker′ē) ***n.***, *pl.* **-ies** ⟦< Gr *apothēkē*, storehouse⟧ [Old-fashioned] a pharmacist or druggist

ap·o·thegm (ap′ə them′) ***n.*** ⟦< Gr *apo-*, from + *phthengesthai*, to utter⟧ a short, pithy saying

a·poth·e·o·sis (ə päth′ē ō′sis, ap′ə thē′ə sis) ***n.***, *pl.* **-ses′** (-sēz′) ⟦< Gr *apo-*, from + *theos*, god⟧ **1** the deifying of a person **2** the glorification of a person or thing **3** a glorified ideal

Ap·pa·la·chi·a (ap′ə lā′chə, -chē ə; -lach′ə) the highland region of the E U.S. extending from SW Pennsylvania through N Alabama

Ap′pa·la′chi·an Mountains mountain system extending from S Quebec to N Alabama: also **Appalachians**

ap·pall or **ap·pal** (ə pôl′) ***vt.*** **-palled′**, **-pal′ling** ⟦ult. < L *ad*, to + *pallere*, to be pale⟧ to horrify, dismay, or shock

ap·pa·loo·sa (ap′ə lo͞o′sə) ***n.*** ⟦after *Palouse* Indians of NW U.S.⟧ a Western saddle horse with black and white spots on the rump and loins

ap·pa·ra·tus (ap′ə rat′əs, -rāt′-) ***n.***, *pl.* **-tus** or **-tus·es** ⟦< L *ad-*, to + *parare*, prepare⟧ **1** the instruments, materials, tools, etc. for a specific use **2** any complex device, machine, or system

ap·par·el (ə per′əl) ***n.*** ⟦ult. < L *ad-*, to + *parere*, prepare⟧ clothing; attire —***vt.*** **-eled** or **-elled**, **-el·ing** or **-el·ling** to clothe; dress

ap·par·ent (ə per′ənt) ***adj.*** ⟦see APPEAR⟧ **1** readily seen; visible **2** evident; obvious **3** appearing real or true —**ap·par′ent·ly** ***adv.***

ap·pa·ri·tion (ap′ə rish′ən) ***n.*** ⟦see APPEAR⟧ **1** anything that appears unexpectedly or in a strange way **2** a ghost; phantom

ap·peal (ə pēl′) ***vt.*** ⟦< L *ad-*, to + *pellere*, to drive⟧ to make an appeal of (a case) —***vi.*** **1** to appeal a law case to a higher court **2** to make an urgent request (*to* a person *for* help, etc.) **3** to be attractive or interesting —***n.*** **1** a call upon some authority for a decision **2** a request for the transference of a case to a higher court for rehearing **3** a request for help, etc. **4** a quality that arouses interest, desire, etc. —**ap·peal′ing** ***adj.***

ap·pear (ə pir′) ***vi.*** ⟦< L *ad-*, to + *perere*, be visible⟧ **1** to come into sight **2** to come into being **3** to become understood or obvious **4** to seem; look **5** to present oneself formally in court **6** to come before the public

ap·pear′ance ***n.*** **1** an appearing **2** the look or outward aspect of a person or thing **3** an outward show; pretense —**keep up appearances** to maintain an outward show of being proper, prosperous, etc.

ap·pease (ə pēz′) ***vt.*** **-peased′**, **-peas′ing** ⟦ult. < L *ad*, to + *pax*, peace⟧ to pacify, quiet, or satisfy, esp. by giving in to the demands of —**ap·pease′ment** ***n.*** —**ap·peas′er** ***n.***

THESAURUS

apiece ***a.*** respectively, separately, individually; see EACH.

apologetic ***a.*** regretful, self-incriminating, atoning, rueful, contrite, remorseful, sorry, penitent, down on one's knees*.—*Ant.* STUBBORN, obstinate, unrepentant.

apologize ***v.*** beg pardon, excuse oneself, atone, ask forgiveness, make amends, give satisfaction, clear oneself, make up with someone, confess, admit one's guilt, retract something said, eat crow*, eat one's words.—*Ant.* INSULT, offend, hurt.

apology ***n.*** regrets, plea, justification; see EXPLANATION.

apostle ***n.*** messenger, witness, disciple; see FOLLOWER.

appall ***v.*** amaze, horrify, dismay; see SHOCK 2.

appalling ***a.*** horrifying, shocking, dreadful; see FRIGHTFUL.

apparatus ***n.*** appliance, machinery, outfit; see EQUIPMENT.

apparel ***n.*** clothes, attire, garments; see DRESS 1.

apparent ***a.*** **1** [Open to view] visible, clear, manifest; see OBVIOUS 1. **2** [Seeming, but not actual] seeming, possible, plausible; see LIKELY 1.

apparently ***a.*** obviously, at first sight, in plain sight, unmistakably, at a glance, indubitably, perceptibly, plainly, patently, evidently, clearly, openly, supposedly, overtly, conspicuously, palpably, tangibly, presumably, possibly, manifestly, most likely, reasonably, seemingly, reputedly, as if, as though, to all appearances, in almost every way, allegedly, as it were, on the face of it, to the eye.—*Ant.* SURELY, certainly, undoubtedly.

appeal ***n.*** **1** [A plea] request, bid, claim, suit, petition, motion, question, entreaty, prayer, invocation, supplication, address, demand, overture, application, proposition, proposal.—*Ant.* DENIAL, refusal, renunciation. **2** [Attractiveness] charm, glamour, interest, allure, charisma, seductiveness, sex appeal, class*.

appeal ***v.*** **1** [To ask another seriously] plead, make a request, petition; see BEG. **2** [To be attractive or interesting] be pleasing, draw attention, be tempting; see FASCINATE.

appear ***v.*** **1** [To become visible] emerge, rise, come into view, come forth, come out, come forward, be in sight, become plain, loom, arrive, come to light, enter the picture, recur, materialize, become visible, loom up, break through, show up, crop up, burst forth, turn up, stand out, spring up, bob up, see the light of day, meet the eye, break cover.—*Ant.* DISAPPEAR, depart, vanish. **2** [To seem] look, be likely to be, be apparently; see SEEM.

appearance ***n.*** **1** [Looks] bearing, mien, features; see LOOKS. **2** [That which only seems to be real] impression, idea, image, reflection, air, mirage, vision, facade, dream, illusion, semblance, seeming.—*Ant.* FACT, being, substance. —**keep up appearances** be outwardly proper, hide one's faults, keep up with the Joneses; see DECEIVE. —**make** (or **put in**) **an appearance** appear publicly, be present, come; see ARRIVE.

appease ***v.*** comply with, meet the requirements of, assuage; see SATISFY 1, 3.

appeasement ***n.*** amends, settlement, reparation, conciliation, com-

ap·pel·lant (ə pel′ənt) ***n.*** a person who appeals to a higher court

ap·pel′late (-it) ***adj.*** *Law* having to do with appeals *[an appellate court]*

ap·pel·la·tion (ap′ə lā′shən) ***n.*** ⟦see APPEAL⟧ **1** a naming **2** a name or title

ap·pend (ə pend′) ***vt.*** ⟦< L *ad-*, to + *pendere*, hang⟧ to attach or affix; add as a supplement or appendix

ap·pend′age ***n.*** **1** anything appended **2** any external organ or part, as a tail

ap·pen·dec·to·my (ap′ən dek′tə mē) ***n.***, *pl.* **-mies** ⟦see -ECTOMY⟧ the surgical removal of the appendix

ap·pen·di·ci·tis (ə pen′də sīt′is) ***n.*** ⟦see -ITIS⟧ inflammation of the appendix

ap·pen·dix (ə pen′diks) ***n.***, *pl.* **-dix·es** or **-di·ces′** (-də sēz′) ⟦L, appendage⟧ **1** additional material at the end of a book **2** a small, saclike appendage of the large intestine

ap·per·tain (ap′ər tān′) ***vi.*** ⟦< L *ad-*, to + *pertinere*, to reach⟧ to belong as a function, part, etc.; pertain

ap·pe·ten·cy (ap′ə tən sē) ***n.***, *pl.* **-cies** ⟦see fol.⟧ a craving; appetite

ap·pe·tite (ap′ə tīt′) ***n.*** ⟦< L *ad-*, to + *petere*, to desire⟧ **1** a desire for food **2** any strong desire or craving

ap′pe·tiz′er (-tī′zər) ***n.*** a small portion of a tasty food to stimulate the appetite

ap′pe·tiz′ing (-tī′ziŋ) ***adj.*** **1** stimulating the appetite **2** savory; delicious

ap·plaud (ə plôd′) ***vt.***, ***vi.*** ⟦< L *ad-*, to + *plaudere*, clap hands⟧ **1** to show approval (of) by clapping the hands, etc. **2** to approve —**ap·plaud′er** ***n.***

ap·plause (ə plôz′) ***n.*** approval, esp. as shown by clapping hands

ap·ple (ap′əl) ***n.*** ⟦< OE *æppel*, fruit, apple⟧ **1** a firm, round, edible fruit **2** the tree it grows on

apple butter a thick, sweet spread made from apples stewed with spices

ap′ple·jack′ ***n.*** brandy distilled from fermented cider

ap′ple-pie′ ***adj.*** [Inf.] **1** neat and tidy *[apple-pie order]* **2** suggesting wholesomeness

ap′ple·sauce′ ***n.*** a dessert or relish of apples cooked to a pulp in water and sweetened

ap·pli·ance (ə plī′əns) ***n.*** a device or machine, esp. one for household use

ap·pli·ca·ble (ap′li kə bəl) ***adj.*** that can be applied; appropriate —**ap′pli·ca·bil′i·ty** (-bil′ə tē) ***n.***

ap′pli·cant (-kənt) ***n.*** one who applies, as for employment or help

ap·pli·ca·tion (ap′li kā′shən) ***n.*** **1** an applying **2** anything applied, as a remedy **3** a specific use **4** a request, or a form filled out in making one *[an employment application]* **5** continued effort; diligence **6** relevance or practicality **7** a computer program for performing a specific task

ap·pli·ca·tor (ap′li kāt′ər) ***n.*** any device for applying medicine or paint, polish, etc.

ap·plied (ə plīd′) ***adj.*** used in actual practice *[applied science]*

ap·pli·qué (ap′li kā′) ***n.*** ⟦Fr⟧ a decoration made of one material attached to another —***vt.*** **-quéd′**, **-qué′ing** to decorate with appliqué

ap·ply (ə plī′) ***vt.*** **-plied′**, **-ply′ing** ⟦< L *ad-*, to + *plicare*, to fold⟧ **1** to put or spread on *[apply glue]* **2** to put to practical or specific use *[apply your knowledge]* **3** to devote (oneself or one's faculties) diligently —***vi.*** **1** to make a formal request **2** to be suitable or relevant —**ap·pli′er** ***n.***

ap·point (ə point′) ***vt.*** ⟦< L *ad*, to + *punctum*, a point⟧ **1** to set (a date, place, etc.) **2** to name for an office, position, etc. **3** to furnish *[well-appointed]* —**ap·point′ee′** ***n.***

ap·point′ive ***adj.*** of or filled by appointment *[an appointive office]*

ap·point′ment ***n.*** **1** an appointing or being appointed **2** a position filled by appointing **3** an arrangement to meet someone or be somewhere **4** [*pl.*] furniture; equipment

Ap·po·mat·tox Court House (ap′ə mat′əks) former village in central Virginia, where Lee surrendered to Grant (1865)

ap·por·tion (ə pôr′shən) ***vt.*** ⟦see AD- & PORTION⟧ to distribute in shares according to a plan —**ap·por′tion·ment** ***n.***

ap·pose (ə pōz′) ***vt.*** **-posed′**, **-pos′ing** ⟦< L *ad-*, to + *ponere*, put⟧ to put side by side or opposite

ap·po·site (ap′ə zit) ***adj.*** ⟦see prec.⟧ appropriate; apt —**ap′po·site·ly** ***adv.*** —**ap′po·site·ness** ***n.***

ap·po·si·tion (ap′ə zish′ən) ***n.*** **1** an apposing, or the position resulting from this **2** the placing of a word or phrase beside another in explanation *["my niece" is in apposition with "Jill" in "Jill, my niece, is here"]* —**ap·pos·i·tive** (ə päz′ə tiv) ***adj.***, ***n.***

ap·prais·al (ə prāz′əl) ***n.*** **1** an appraising **2** an appraised value

ap·praise (ə prāz′) ***vt.*** **-praised′**, **-prais′ing** ⟦< L *ad*, to + *pretium*, price⟧ **1** to set a price for; estimate the value of **2** to judge the quality or worth of —**ap·prais′er** ***n.***

ap·pre·ci·a·ble (ə prē′shə bəl, -shē ə-) ***adj.*** ⟦see prec.⟧ enough to be perceived or estimated; noticeable —**ap·pre′ci·a·bly** ***adv.***

ap·pre·ci·ate (ə prē′shē āt′) ***vt.*** **-at′ed**, **-at′ing** ⟦see APPRAISE⟧ **1** to think well of; esteem **2** to recognize gratefully **3** to estimate the quality of **4** to be fully or sensitively aware of —***vi.*** to rise in value —**ap·pre′ci·a′tor** ***n.*** —**ap·pre′ci·a·to′ry** (-shə tôr′ē, -shē ə-) ***adj.***

ap·pre′ci·a′tion ***n.*** **1** grateful recognition, as of a favor **2** sensitive awareness, as of art **3** a rise in value or price

THESAURUS

promise; see also SATISFACTION 2.

appendix ***n.*** supplement, attachment, addendum; see ADDITION 1.

appetite ***n.*** hunger, thirst, craving, longing, urge, need for food, need to drink, starvation, empty stomach, thirstiness, ravenousness, desire; see also HUNGER, THIRST.—*Ant.* INDIFFERENCE, satiety, surfeit.

appetizing ***a.*** savory, tasty, delectable; see DELICIOUS.

applaud ***v.*** clap, cheer, acclaim; see PRAISE 1.

applause ***n.*** ovation, cheers, clapping; see PRAISE 2.

appliance ***n.*** instrument, machine, apparatus; see DEVICE 1. *Common household appliances include the following:* broiler, deep-fryer, coffee maker, can opener, blender, mixer, food processor, electric frying pan, oven, toaster oven, microwave, stove, dishwasher, disposal, refrigerator, freezer, waffle iron, trash compactor, hair dryer, electric toothbrush, shaver, curling iron, clothes dryer, washing machine, iron, water heater, sewing machine, vacuum cleaner, paper shredder, electric fan, air conditioner, space heater.

applicable ***a.*** suitable, appropriate, usable; see FIT.

applicant ***n.*** petitioner, aspirant, appellant; see CANDIDATE.

application ***n.*** **1** [Putting to use] employment, bringing to bear, utilization; see USE 1. **2** [The ability to apply oneself] devotion, zeal, diligence; see ATTENTION. **3** [A request] petition, entreaty, demand; see APPEAL 1. **4** [The instrument by which a request is made] petition, form, blank, paper, letter, credentials, certificate, statement, requisition, draft, check, bill.

applied ***a.*** used, related, enforced, practiced, utilized, brought to bear, adapted, devoted, adjusted, activated.

apply ***v.*** **1** [To make a request] petition, make a demand, appeal; see BEG. **2** [To make use of] utilize, employ, practice, exploit; see also USE 1. **3** [To be relevant (to)] be pertinent, pertain, bear on, bear upon, have a bearing on, relate to, allude to, concern, touch on, touch upon, involve, affect, regard, have reference to, connect, refer, suit, be in relationship, hold true, come into play. —**apply oneself (to)** attend to, dedicate oneself, address oneself, be occupied with, keep one's mind on, direct oneself to, concentrate on, persevere, persist in, be industrious, buckle down.

appoint ***v.*** select, designate, elect; see DELEGATE 1, 2.

appointed ***a.*** selected, chosen, delegated; see NAMED 2.

appointment ***n.*** **1** [The act of appointing] designation, election, selection, nomination, approval, choice, promotion, assignment, authorization, installation, delegation, certification, empowering. **2** [An engagement] interview, meeting, rendezvous, assignation, invitation, errand, something to do, date. —**keep an appointment** show up, be on time, be there; see ARRIVE.

appraisal ***n.*** examination, evaluation, assessment; see ESTIMATE.

appraise ***v.*** assess, evaluate, assay; see PRICE.

appreciable ***a.*** considerable, sizable, measurable; see LARGE 1.

appreciate ***v.*** **1** [To be grateful for] welcome, enjoy, be obliged for, be indebted for, acknowledge, never forget, give thanks for, overflow with gratitude for; see also THANK.—*Ant.* COMPLAIN, find fault with, minimize, object to. **2** [To recognize the worth of] esteem, honor, praise; see ADMIRE.

appreciation ***n.*** **1** [Sense of gratitude] thankfulness, recognition, gratefulness; see GRATITUDE. **2** [Favorable opinion] esteem, enjoyment, love, affection, attraction, commendation, high regard; see also ADMIRATION.

ap·pre'ci·a·tive (-shə tiv, -shē ə-) ***adj.*** feeling or showing appreciation —**ap·pre'ci·a·tive·ly** ***adv.***

ap·pre·hend (ap'rē hend') ***vt.*** ⟦< L *ad-*, to + *prehendere*, take⟧ **1** to capture or arrest **2** to perceive; understand **3** to fear; dread

ap'pre·hen'sion (-hen'shən) ***n.*** **1** capture or arrest **2** perception or understanding **3** fear; anxiety

ap'pre·hen'sive (-siv) ***adj.*** anxious; uneasy —**ap'pre·hen'sive·ly** ***adv.*** —**ap'pre·hen'sive·ness** ***n.***

ap·pren·tice (ə pren'tis) ***n.*** ⟦see APPREHEND⟧ **1** a person being taught a craft or trade, now usually as a member of a labor union **2** any beginner —***vt.*** **-ticed**, **-tic·ing** to place or accept as an apprentice —**ap·pren'tice·ship'** ***n.***

ap·prise or **ap·prize** (ə prīz') ***vt.*** **-prised'** or **-prized'**, **-pris'ing** or **-priz'ing** ⟦see APPREHEND⟧ to inform or notify

ap·proach (ə prōch') ***vi.*** ⟦< L *ad-*, to + *propius*, nearer⟧ to come closer —***vt.*** **1** to come nearer to **2** to approximate **3** to make a proposal or request to **4** to begin dealing with —***n.*** **1** a coming closer **2** an approximation **3** an overture (*to* someone): *usually used in pl.* **4** a means of reaching a person or place; access **5** a means of attaining a goal —**ap·proach'a·ble** ***adj.***

ap·pro·ba·tion (ap'rə bā'shən) ***n.*** ⟦see APPROVE⟧ approval

ap·pro·pri·ate (ə prō'prē āt'; *for adj.*, -it) ***vt.*** **-at'ed**, **-at'ing** ⟦< L *ad-*, to + *proprius*, one's own⟧ **1** to take for one's own use, often improperly **2** to set aside (money, etc.) for a specific use —***adj.*** suitable; fit; proper —**ap·pro'pri·ate·ly** ***adv.*** —**ap·pro'pri·ate·ness** ***n.*** —**ap·pro'pri·a'tor** ***n.***

ap·pro'pri·a'tion ***n.*** **1** an appropriating or being appropriated **2** money set aside for a specific use

ap·prov·al (ə pro͞o'vəl) ***n.*** **1** the act of approving **2** favorable attitude or opinion **3** formal consent —**on approval** for the customer to examine and decide whether to buy or return

ap·prove (ə pro͞ov') ***vt.*** **-proved'**, **-prov'ing** ⟦< L *ad-*, to + *probus*, good⟧ **1** to give one's consent to **2** to consider to be good, satisfactory, etc. —***vi.*** to have a favorable opinion (*of*) —**ap·prov'ing·ly** ***adv.***

ap·prox·i·mate (ə präk'sə mit; *for v.*, -māt') ***adj.*** ⟦< L *ad-*, to + *proximus*, nearest⟧ **1** much like; resembling **2** more or less correct or exact —***vt.*** **-mat'ed**, **-mat'ing** to come near to; be almost the same as —**ap·prox'i·mate·ly** ***adv.***

ap·prox'i·ma'tion ***n.*** an estimate or guess that is approximately correct

ap·pur·te·nance (ə purt''n əns) ***n.*** ⟦see APPERTAIN⟧ **1** anything added to a more important thing **2** [*pl.*] apparatus or equipment **3** *Law* an incidental right attached to some thing

APR *abbrev.* annual percentage rate

ap·ri·cot (ap'ri kät', ā'pri-) ***n.*** ⟦Fr *abricot* < L *praecoquum*, early matured (fruit)⟧ **1** a small, yellowish-orange, peachlike fruit **2** the tree it grows on

A·pril (ā'prəl) ***n.*** ⟦< L⟧ the fourth month of the year, having 30 days: abbrev. **Apr**

a pri·o·ri (ā' prī ôr'ī) ⟦L⟧ **1** from cause to effect; deductive or deductively **2** based on theory, logic, etc. instead of experience

a·pron (ā'prən) ***n.*** ⟦< L *mappa*, napkin⟧ **1** a garment worn over the front part of the body to protect one's clothes **2** any extending or protecting part **3** a paved area, as where a driveway broadens to meet the road **4** the part of a stage in front of the proscenium arch

ap·ro·pos (ap'rə pō') ***adv.*** ⟦Fr *à propos*, to the purpose⟧ at the right time; opportunely —***adj.*** relevant; apt —***prep.*** with regard to —**apropos of** with regard to

apse (aps) ***n.*** ⟦L *apsis*, an arch⟧ a semicircular or polygonal projection of a church, usually domed or vaulted

apt[1] (apt) ***adj.*** ⟦< L *aptus*⟧ **1** appropriate; fitting *[an apt remark]* **2** tending or inclined; likely *[apt to rain]* **3** quick to learn —**apt'ly** ***adv.*** —**apt'ness** ***n.***

apt[2] *abbrev.* apartment

ap·ti·tude (ap'tə to͞od') ***n.*** ⟦see APT[1]⟧ **1** a natural tendency, ability, or talent **2** quickness to learn

aq·ua (ak'wə, äk'-) ***n.***, *pl.* **-uas** or **-uae'** (-wē') ⟦L⟧ water —***adj.*** ⟦< AQUAMARINE⟧ bluish-green

aq'ua·cul'ture ***n.*** ⟦prec. + CULTURE⟧ the cultivation of water plants and animals for human use

aq'ua·ma·rine' ***n.*** ⟦L *aqua marina*, sea water⟧ bluish green —***adj.*** bluish-green

aq'ua·naut' (-nôt') ***n.*** ⟦AQUA + (ASTRO)NAUT⟧ one trained to use a watertight underwater chamber as a base for undersea experiments

aq'ua·plane' ***n.*** ⟦AQUA + PLANE[1]⟧ a board on which one rides standing up as it is pulled by a motorboat —***vi.*** **-planed'**, **-plan'ing** to ride on such a board as a sport

a·quar·i·um (ə kwer'ē əm) ***n.***, *pl.* **-i·ums** or **-i·a** (-ə) ⟦< L *aquarius*, of water⟧ **1** a tank, etc. for keeping live water animals and plants **2** a building where such collections are exhibited

A·quar'i·us (-əs) ***n.*** ⟦L, water carrier⟧ the 11th sign of the zodiac

a·quat·ic (ə kwat'ik, -kwät'-) ***adj.*** **1** growing or living in water **2** done in or upon the water *[aquatic sports]*

aq·ua·vit (ak'wə vēt', äk'-) ***n.*** ⟦< L *aqua vitae*, water of life⟧ a Scandinavian alcoholic liquor distilled from grain or potatoes and flavored with caraway

aq·ue·duct (ak'wə dukt') ***n.*** ⟦< L *aqua*, water + *ductus*, a leading⟧ **1** a large pipe or conduit for bringing water from a distant source **2** an elevated structure supporting this

THESAURUS

appreciative ***a.*** grateful, obliged, satisfied; see THANKFUL.

apprehend ***v.*** **1** [To understand] perceive, comprehend, grasp; see UNDERSTAND 1. **2** [To arrest] seize, place under arrest, take into custody; see ARREST.

apprehension ***n.*** **1** [Foreboding] trepidation, dread, misgiving; see FEAR. **2** [Understanding] comprehension, grasp, perspicacity; see JUDGMENT 1. **3** [Arrest] capture, seizure, detention; see ARREST.

apprehensive ***a.*** fearful, worried, uncertain; see TROUBLED.

apprentice ***n.*** beginner, student, learner; see AMATEUR.

approach ***n.*** **1** [A way] path, entrance, gate; see WAY 1, 2. **2** [Plan of action] method, program, procedure; see PLAN 2.

approach ***v.*** **1** [To approach personally] appeal to, address, speak to, talk to, propose something to, request of, make advances to, make overtures to, take aside, talk to in private, buttonhole, corner, descend on.—*Ant.* AVOID, shun, turn away. **2** [To come near in space] drift toward, loom up, creep up, drive up, near, go near, draw near, close in, surround, come near to, come up to, bear down on, edge up to, ease up to, head into; see also APPEAR 1.—*Ant.* LEAVE, recede, depart. **3** [To come near in time] be imminent, threaten, near, draw near, impend, stare someone in the face.—*Ant.* EXTEND, stretch out, recede. **4** [To approximate] come near, take after, come close to; see RESEMBLE.

approaching ***a.*** nearing, advancing, impending, oncoming, touching, approximating, coming, drawing near, next to come, threatening, rising, moving closer, gaining.

appropriate ***a.*** proper, suitable, suited, fitting; see also FIT.

appropriate ***v.*** **1** [To seize] secure, usurp, take possession of; see GET 1. **2** [To provide money] set aside, set apart, allocate, assign to a particular use, reserve, apportion, devote, allow for, budget, allot.

appropriately ***a.*** fittingly, suitably, justly, aptly, rightly, properly, agreeably, happily, fortunately.—*Ant.* BADLY, inappropriately, improperly.

appropriation ***n.*** stipend, grant, fund, allotment, allowance, allocation, contribution, cash, budget, gift, remuneration, donation, support, pay.

approval ***n.*** **1** [Favorable opinion] regard, esteem, favor; see ADMIRATION. **2** [Sanction] endorsement, support, consent; see PERMISSION.

approve ***v.*** ratify, affirm, encourage, support, endorse, seal, confirm, license, favor, consent to, agree to, sanction, empower, charter, validate, legalize, recognize, accredit, recommend, authorize, second, subscribe to, allow, go along with, maintain, vote for, advocate, establish, pass, OK*, give the green light to*, hold with.—*Ant.* OPPOSE, reject, veto.

approved ***a.*** certified, authorized, validated, passed, affirmed, legalized, ratified, sanctioned, permitted, endorsed, vouched for, praised, recognized, recommended, backed, supported, upheld, made official, agreed to, allowed, proven, ordered, established, OK'd*.—*Ant.* REFUSED, censured, disapproved.

approximate ***a.*** rough, inexact, uncertain, guessed, imprecise, imperfect, close, surmised, unscientific, by means of trial and error, almost, more or less, not quite, coming close, fair, nearly correct.

approximately ***a.*** nearly, closely, roughly, close to, near to, almost, around, about, in general, in round numbers, not quite, not far from, more or less, practically, just about, on the edge of, for all practical purposes, bordering on, generally.

apron ***n.*** cover, smock, bib; see CLOTHES.

apt[1] ***a.*** **1** [Quick to learn] adept, clever, bright; see INTELLIGENT. **2** [Inclined] prone, tending, liable; see LIKELY 4.

aptitude ***n.*** capability, competence, talent; see ABILITY.

a·que·ous (ā′kwē əs, ak′wē-) ***adj.*** of, like, or formed by water

aqueous humor a watery fluid in the space between the cornea and the lens of the eye

aq·ui·fer (ak′wə fər, äk′-) ***n.*** ⟦< L *aqua*, water + *ferre*, carry⟧ an underground layer of porous rock, etc. containing water

aq·ui·line (ak′wə līn′, -lin) ***adj.*** ⟦< L *aquila*, eagle⟧ **1** of or like an eagle **2** curved like an eagle's beak *[an aquiline nose]*

A·qui·nas (ə kwī′nəs), Saint **Thom·as** (täm′əs) (1225?-74); It. theologian & philosopher

Ar *Chem. symbol for* argon

AR Arkansas

Ar·ab (ar′əb, er′-) ***n.*** **1** a person born or living in Arabia **2** a member of a Semitic people orig. living in Arabia, now throughout the Middle East

ar·a·besque (ar′ə besk′, er′-) ***n.*** ⟦< It *Arabo*, Arab⟧ an elaborate design of intertwined lines suggesting flowers, foliage, etc.

A·ra·bi·a (ə rā′bē ə) peninsula in SW Asia —**A·ra′bi·an** ***adj.***, ***n.***

Arabian camel the one-humped camel ranging from N Africa to India

Arabian Nights, The a collection of tales from Arabia, India, Persia, etc.

Arabian Peninsula ARABIA

Ar·a·bic (ar′ə bik, er′-) ***adj.*** **1** of Arabia **2** of the Arabs or their language or culture —***n.*** the Semitic language of the Arabs, spoken in Arabia, Syria, N Africa, etc.

Arabic numerals the figures 1, 2, 3, 4, 5, 6, 7, 8, 9, and the 0 (zero)

ar·a·ble (ar′ə bəl, er′-) ***adj.*** ⟦< L *arare*, to plow⟧ suitable for plowing and farming

a·rach·nid (ə rak′nid) ***n.*** ⟦< Gr *arachnē*, spider⟧ any of a class of arthropods with four pairs of legs, including spiders and scorpions

Ar·a·ma·ic (ar′ə mā′ik, er′-) ***n.*** a Semitic language spoken during biblical times

ar·bi·ter (är′bət ər) ***n.*** ⟦L, a witness or judge⟧ an arbitrator; judge

ar·bi·trage (är′bə träzh′) ***n.*** ⟦see prec.⟧ the simultaneous purchase and sale, as of stock, in two financial markets to profit from a price difference

ar·bit·ra·ment (är bi′trə mənt) ***n.*** **1** arbitration **2** an arbitrator's verdict or award

ar·bi·trar·y (är′bə trer′ē) ***adj.*** ⟦see ARBITER⟧ **1** left to one's judgment **2** based on one's preference or whim; capricious **3** absolute; despotic —**ar′bi·trar′i·ly** ***adv.***

ar′bi·trate′ (-trāt′) ***vt.***, ***vi.*** **-trat′ed**, **-trat′ing** ⟦see ARBITER⟧ **1** to submit (a dispute) to an arbitrator **2** to decide (a dispute) as an arbitrator —**ar′bi·tra′tion** ***n.***

ar′bi·tra′tor ***n.*** a person selected to judge a dispute, as in collective bargaining

ar·bor (är′bər) ***n.*** ⟦< L *herba*, grass, herb⟧ a place shaded by trees or shrubs or by vines on a latticework; bower

ar·bo·re·al (är bôr′ē əl) ***adj.*** ⟦< L *arbor*, tree⟧ **1** of or like a tree **2** living in trees

ar·bo·re·tum (är′bə rēt′əm) ***n.***, *pl.* **-tums** or **-ta** (-ə) ⟦L⟧ a place where many kinds of trees and shrubs are grown for exhibition or study

ar·bor·vi·tae (är′bər vīt′ē) ***n.*** ⟦L, tree of life⟧ any of various cypress trees having sprays of scalelike leaves

ar·bu·tus (är byo͞ot′əs) ***n.*** ⟦L⟧ **1** a tree or shrub with dark-green leaves and strawberrylike fruit **2** a trailing plant with white or pink flower clusters

arc (ärk) ***n.*** ⟦< L *arcus*, a bow, arch⟧ **1** a bowlike curved line or object **2** the band of incandescent light formed when a current leaps a short gap between electrodes **3** any part of a curve, esp. of a circle —***vi.*** **arced** or **arcked**, **arc′ing** or **arck′ing** to move in a curved course or form an arc

ar·cade (är kād′) ***n.*** ⟦see prec.⟧ **1** a covered passageway, esp. one lined with shops **2** a line of arches and their supporting columns **3** a penny arcade or a similar place with coin-operated video games

ar·cane (är kān′) ***adj.*** ⟦< L *arcanus*, hidden⟧ secret or esoteric

arch[1] (ärch) ***n.*** ⟦see ARC⟧ **1** a curved structure used as a support over an open space, as in a doorway **2** the form of an arch **3** anything shaped like an arch —***vt.*** to span with or as an arch —***vi.*** to form an arch

arch[2] (ärch) ***adj.*** ⟦< ARCH-⟧ **1** chief; principal **2** gaily mischievous; pert *[an arch look]*

Arch or **arch** *abbrev.* **1** archaic **2** architecture

arch- ⟦< Gr *archos*, first, ruler⟧ *prefix* main, principal *[archenemy]*

-arch (ärk) ⟦see prec.⟧ *suffix* ruler *[matriarch]*

ar·chae·ol·o·gy (är′kē äl′ə jē) ***n.*** ⟦< Gr *archaios*, ancient + -LOGY⟧ the study of the life of ancient peoples, as by excavation of ancient cities or artifacts: also sp. **ar′che·ol′o·gy** —**ar′chae·o·log′i·cal** (-ə läj′i kəl) ***adj.*** —**ar′chae·o·log′i·cal·ly** ***adv.*** —**ar′chae·ol′o·gist** ***n.***

ar·cha·ic (är kā′ik) ***adj.*** ⟦< Gr *archaios*, ancient⟧ **1** ancient **2** old-fashioned **3** no longer used except in poetry, church ritual, etc.: said as of the word *thou* —**ar·cha′i·cal·ly** ***adv.***

ar·cha·ism (är′kā iz′əm) ***n.*** an archaic word, usage, style, etc. —**ar′cha·is′tic** ***adj.***

arch·an·gel (ärk′ān′jəl) ***n.*** an angel of high rank

arch′bish′op (ärch′-) ***n.*** a bishop of the highest rank

arch′dea′con ***n.*** a church official ranking just below a bishop

arch′di′o·cese ***n.*** the diocese of an archbishop —**arch′di·oc′e·san** ***adj.***

arch′duke′ ***masc.n.*** a sovereign prince, esp. of the former Austrian imperial family —**arch′duch′ess** ***fem.n.***

arch′en′e·my ***n.***, *pl.* **-mies** a chief enemy —**the archenemy** Satan

arch·er (är′chər) ***n.*** ⟦< L *arcus*, bow⟧ one who shoots with bow and arrow

arch′er·y ***n.*** the sport of shooting with bow and arrow

ar·che·type (är′kə tīp′) ***n.*** ⟦< Gr *archos*, first + *typos*, a mark⟧ **1** an original pattern, or model; prototype **2** a perfect example of a type or group —**ar′che·typ′al** (-tīp′əl) or **ar′che·typ′i·cal** (-tip′i kəl) ***adj.***

ar·chi·e·pis·co·pal (är′kē ē pis′kə pəl) ***adj.*** of or related to an archbishop

Ar·chi·me·des (är′kə mē′dēz′) 287?-212 B.C.; Gr. mathematician & inventor

ar·chi·pel·a·go (är′kə pel′ə gō′) ***n.***, *pl.* **-goes′** or **-gos′** ⟦< Gr *archi-*, chief + *pelagos*, sea⟧ **1** a sea with many islands **2** a group of many islands

ar·chi·tect (är′kə tekt′) ***n.*** ⟦< Gr *archi-*, chief + *tektōn*, carpenter⟧ **1** one who designs buildings and supervises their construction **2** any designer or planner

ar·chi·tec·ton·ics (är′kə tek tän′iks) ***pl.n.*** [*usually with sing. v.*] **1** the science of architecture **2** structural design, as of a symphony —**ar′chi·tec·ton′ic** ***adj.***

ar·chi·tec·ture (är′kə tek′chər) ***n.*** **1** the science or profession of designing and constructing buildings **2** a style of construction **3** design and construction —**ar′chi·tec′tur·al** ***adj.*** —**ar′chi·tec′tur·al·ly** ***adv.***

ar·chi·trave (är′kə trāv′) ***n.*** ⟦< L *archi-*, first + *trabs*, a beam⟧ in a classical building, the beam resting directly on the tops of the columns

ar·chive (är′kīv′) ***n.*** ⟦< Gr *archeion*, town hall⟧ [*usually pl.*] **1** a place for keeping public records, documentary material, etc. **2** the records, material, etc. kept there —***vt.*** **-chived′**, **-chiv′ing** to keep in or as in archives —**ar·chi·vist** (är′kə vist, -kī′-) ***n.***

arch·way (ärch′wā′) ***n.*** a passage under an arch, or the arch itself

-ar·chy (är kē) ⟦< Gr *archein*, to rule⟧ *combining form* rule, government *[monarchy]*

THESAURUS

Arabian ***a.*** Arabic, Semitic, from Arabia, Middle Eastern, Near Eastern, Moorish, Levantine.

arbitrary ***a.*** willful, tyrannical, temporary, unpremeditated, irrational, generalized, deceptive, superficial, unscientific, unreasonable, whimsical, fanciful, determined by no principle, optional, uncertain, inconsistent, discretionary, subject to individual will.

arbitrate ***v.*** settle, adjust, reconcile; see NEGOTIATE.

arbitrator ***n.*** arbiter, referee, mediator; see JUDGE.

arc ***n.*** bend, curve, segment of a circle; see ARCH.

arch[1] ***n.*** arc, curve, vault, dome, cupola, bend, arching, archway, curvature, cove.

arch[1] ***v.*** extend, round, stretch, curve, bend, shape, hunch, cover, hump, hook, arch over.—*Ant.* STRAIGHTEN, unbend, flatten.

archaic ***a.*** antiquated, old, ancient; see OLD-FASHIONED.

architect ***n.*** planner, designer, draftsman, artist, engineer, builder, master builder, designer of buildings.

architecture ***n.*** construction, planning, designing, building, structure, architectonics, house-building, shipbuilding, bridge-building.

archives ***n.*** **1** [Place to store documents] repository, vault, library; see MUSEUM. **2** [Documents] chronicles, annals, public papers; see RECORDS.

arc·tic (ärk′tik, är′-) ***adj.*** ⟦< Gr *arktikos*, northern⟧ **1** of or near the North Pole **2** very cold —**the Arctic** the region around the North Pole

Arctic Circle [*also* **a- c-**] an imaginary circle parallel to the equator, *c.* 66°34′ north of it

Arctic Ocean ocean surrounding the North Pole

-ard (ərd) ⟦< MHG *hart*, bold⟧ *suffix* one who does something to excess *[drunkard]*

ar·dent (är′dənt) ***adj.*** ⟦< L *ardere*, to burn⟧ **1** passionate **2** zealous **3** glowing or burning —**ar′dent·ly** ***adv.***

ar·dor (är′dər) ***n.*** ⟦< L *ardor*, a flame⟧ **1** emotional warmth; passion **2** zeal **3** intense heat Also, Brit. sp., **ar′dour**

ar·du·ous (är′jo͞o əs) ***adj.*** ⟦L *arduus*, steep⟧ **1** difficult to do; laborious **2** using much energy; strenuous —**ar′du·ous·ly** ***adv.***

are (är) ***vi.*** ⟦OE *aron*⟧ *pl. & 2d pers. sing., pres. indic., of* BE

ar·e·a (er′ē ə) ***n.*** ⟦L, vacant place⟧ **1** a part of the earth's surface; region **2** the measure, in square units, of a surface **3** a location having a specific use or character *[play area]* **4** scope or extent

area code a three-digit telephone code assigned to a specific area of the U.S., Canada, etc.

a·re·na (ə rē′nə) ***n.*** ⟦L, sandy place⟧ **1** a place or building for contests, shows, etc. **2** any sphere of struggle *[political arena]*

arena theater a theater having a central stage surrounded by seats

aren't (ärnt) *contr.* are not

Ar·es (er′ēz′) ***n.*** *Gr. Myth.* the god of war

ar·gent (är′jənt) ***adj.*** ⟦L *argentum*, silver⟧ [Old Poet.] silvery

Ar·gen·ti·na (är′jən tē′nə) country in S South America: 1,073,518 sq. mi.; pop. 32,616,000 —**Ar′gen·tine′** (-tēn′, -tīn′) or **Ar′gen·tin′i·an** (-tin′ē ən) ***adj., n.***

ar·gon (är′gän′) ***n.*** ⟦Gr, inert⟧ a chemical element, a nonreactive gas found in the air and used in light bulbs, electron tubes, etc.

Ar·go·naut (är′gə nôt′) ***n.*** *Gr. Myth.* any of those who sail with Jason to search for the Golden Fleece

ar·go·sy (är′gə sē) ***n.***, *pl.* **-sies** ⟦after *Ragusa*, It name of Dubrovnik in Croatia⟧ [Old Poet.] a large merchant ship or a fleet of such ships

ar·got (är′gō, -gət) ***n.*** ⟦Fr⟧ the specialized vocabulary of a particular group, as of criminals

ar·gue (är′gyo͞o) ***vi.*** **-gued**, **-gu·ing** ⟦< L *arguere*, prove⟧ **1** to give reasons (*for* or *against*) **2** to quarrel; dispute —***vt.*** **1** to discuss; debate **2** to maintain; contend **3** to persuade by giving reasons —**ar′gu·a·ble** ***adj.***

ar·gu·ment (är′gyo͞o mənt) ***n.*** **1** a reason or reasons offered in arguing **2** an arguing; debate **3** a summary

ar′gu·men·ta′tion (-men tā′shən) ***n.*** the process of arguing; debate

ar′gu·men′ta·tive (-men′tə tiv) ***adj.*** **1** controversial **2** apt to argue; contentious Also **ar′gu·men′tive**

ar·gyle (är′gīl′) ***adj.*** ⟦after *Argyll*, Scotland⟧ knitted or woven in a diamond-shaped pattern *[argyle socks]*

a·ri·a (ä′rē ə) ***n.*** ⟦It < L *aer*, air⟧ a song, as in an opera, for solo voice

-ar·i·an (er′ē ən) ⟦< L⟧ *suffix* **1** (one) characterized by *[octogenarian]* **2** (one) believing in or associated with *[Unitarian]*

ar·id (ar′id) ***adj.*** ⟦< L *arere*, be dry⟧ **1** dry and barren **2** uninteresting; dull —**a·rid·i·ty** (ə rid′ə tē) ***n.***

Ar·i·es (er′ēz′) ***n.*** ⟦L, ram (male sheep)⟧ the first sign of the zodiac

a·right (ə rīt′) ***adv.*** correctly

a·rise (ə rīz′) ***vi.*** **a·rose′** (-rōz′), **a·ris′en** (-riz′ən), **a·ris′ing** ⟦< OE *a-*, out + *risan*, to rise⟧ **1** to get up, as from sleeping **2** to ascend **3** to come into being **4** to result (*from*)

ar·is·toc·ra·cy (ar′i stä′krə sē) ***n.***, *pl.* **-cies** ⟦< Gr *aristos*, best + *kratos*, to rule⟧ **1** government by a privileged minority, usually of inherited wealth **2** a country with such government **3** a privileged ruling class

a·ris·to·crat (ə ris′tə krat′) ***n.*** **1** a member of the aristocracy **2** one with the tastes, manners, etc. of the upper class —**a·ris′to·crat′ic** ***adj.***

Ar·is·toph·a·nes (ar′i stäf′ə nēz′) 450?-388? B.C.; Gr. writer of comedies

Ar·is·tot·le (ar′is tät′l) 384-322 B.C.; Gr. philosopher —**Ar·is·to·te·li·an** (ar′is tə tēl′yən) ***adj., n.***

a·rith·me·tic (ə rith′mə tik) ***n.*** ⟦< Gr *arithmos*, number⟧ the science or art of computing by positive, real numbers —**ar·ith·met·ic** (ar′ith met′ik) or **ar′ith·met′i·cal** ***adj.*** —**ar′ith·me·ti′cian** (-mə tish′ən) ***n.***

arithmetic mean the average obtained by dividing a sum by the number of its addends

Ar·i·zo·na (ar′ə zō′nə) state of the SW U.S.: 113,956 sq. mi.; pop. 3,665,000; cap. Phoenix: abbrev. *AZ* —**Ar′i·zo′nan** or **Ar′i·zo′ni·an** ***adj., n.***

ark (ärk) ***n.*** ⟦< L *arcere*, enclose⟧ **1** ARK OF THE COVENANT **2** an enclosure in a synagogue for the scrolls of the Torah **3** *Bible* the boat in which Noah, his family, and two of every kind of creature survived the Flood

Ar·kan·sas (är′kən sô′) state of the SC U.S.: 53,187 sq. mi.; pop. 2,351,000; cap. Little Rock: abbrev. *AR* —**Ar·kan′san** (-kan′zən) ***adj., n.***

ark of the covenant the chest containing the two stone tablets inscribed with the Ten Commandments

Ar·ling·ton (är′liŋ tən) city in NE Texas: pop. 262,000

arm[1] (ärm) ***n.*** ⟦OE *earm*⟧ **1** an upper limb of the human body **2** anything like this in shape, function, position, etc. **3** anything connected to something larger *[arm of the sea]* —**with open arms** cordially

arm[2] (ärm) ***n.*** ⟦< L *arma*, weapons⟧ **1** a weapon: *usually used in pl.* **2** any branch of the military forces —***vt.*** to provide with weapons, etc. —***vi.*** to prepare for war or any struggle —**under arms** ready for war —**up in arms** **1** prepared to fight **2** indignant

ar·ma·da (är mä′də) ***n.*** ⟦Sp < L *arma*, weapons⟧ **1** a fleet of warships **2** a fleet of military aircraft

ar·ma·dil·lo (är′mə dil′ō) ***n.***, *pl.* **-los** ⟦Sp: see prec.⟧ a burrowing mammal of tropical America, covered with bony plates

Ar·ma·ged·don (är′mə ged′′n) ***n.*** **1** *Bible* the site of the last, decisive battle between the forces of good and evil **2** any great, decisive battle

ar·ma·ment (är′mə mənt) ***n.*** ⟦< L *armare*, to arm⟧ **1** [*often pl.*] all the military forces and equipment of a nation **2** all the military equipment of a warship, tank, etc. **3** an arming or being armed for war

ar·ma·ture (är′mə chər) ***n.*** ⟦< L *armare*, to arm⟧ **1** any

THESAURUS

arctic ***a.*** polar, frozen, icy; see COLD 1.

ardent ***a.*** fervent, impassioned, warm; see ZEALOUS.

arduous ***a.*** hard, severe, laborious; see DIFFICULT 1.

area ***n.*** section, lot, neighborhood, plot, zone, belt, sector, space, spot, patch, square, quarter, block, precinct, ward, field, territory, district, ghetto, town, township, region, tract, enclosure, parcel, division, city, county, parish, diocese, principality, dominion, kingdom, empire, state; see also MEASURE 1.

arena ***n.*** field, pit, ground, park, coliseum, square, stadium, playing field, amphitheater, bowl, stage, platform, course, gymnasium, gym*.

argue ***v.*** plead, appeal, explain, justify, show, reason with, dispute, contend, wrangle, oppose, battle, demonstrate, establish, have it out, put up an argument, bicker, have a brush with.—*Ant.* AGREE, ignore, get along with.

argument ***n.*** **1** [An effort to convince] debate, exchange, contention; see DISCUSSION. **2** [Verbal disagreement] controversy, quarrel, row; see DISPUTE.

argumentative ***a.*** hostile, contentious, factious; see QUARRELSOME.

arid ***a.*** parched, barren, dried; see DRY 1.

arise ***v.*** **1** [To get up] rise, stand up, turn out, get out of bed, get out of a chair, get to one's feet, jump up, roll out, hit the deck*.—*Ant.* FALL, SIT, LIE. **2** [To ascend] mount, go up, climb; see RISE 1.

aristocracy ***n.*** nobility, privileged class, superior group, ruling class, noblemen, the elite, gentry, high society, upper classes, persons of rank, patricians.

aristocrat ***n.*** nobleman, noblewoman, peer, lord, noble, baron, earl, prince, patrician, ruler, gentleman, thoroughbred, duke, viscount, count, king, emperor, empress, queen, princess, duchess, countess, baroness, knight, lady, marquis; see also KING 1, LADY 2.

aristocratic ***a.*** patrician, refined, well-bred; see NOBLE 1, 2, 3.

arithmetic ***n.*** computation, calculation, ciphering*; see MATHEMATICS.

arm[1] ***n.*** **1** [The upper human limb] member, appendage, forelimb, forearm, fin*, flapper*, soupbone*. **2** [Anything resembling an arm] bend, crook, projection, cylinder, sofa-end, branch, limb, rod, bough, offshoot, wing, prong, stump, hook, handle. —**at arm's length** at a distance, not friendly, not intimate, aloof. —**with open arms** warmly, affectionately, joyously; see EAGERLY.

arm[2] ***v.*** furnish with weapons, load, give firearms to, issue weapons to, equip with arms, outfit, fit out.—*Ant.* DISARM, demilitarize, deactivate.

protective covering **2** the iron core wound with wire in which electromotive force is produced in a generator or motor

arm'chair' ***n.*** a chair with supports at the sides for one's arms

armed forces all the military, naval, and air forces of a country

Ar·me·ni·a (är mēn'yə, -mē'nē ə) country in W Asia: 11,490 sq. mi.; pop. 3,305,000 —**Ar·me'ni·an** ***adj., n.***

arm·ful (ärm'fool) ***n.***, *pl.* **-fuls** as much as the arms or one arm can hold

arm'hole' ***n.*** an opening for the arm in a garment

ar·mi·stice (är'mə stis) ***n.*** ⟦< L *arma*, weapons + *stare*, to stand⟧ a truce preliminary to the signing of a peace treaty

Armistice Day Nov. 11, the anniversary of the armistice of WWI in 1918

arm·let (ärm'lət) ***n.*** **1** an ornamental band worn around the upper arm **2** a narrow, deep inlet of the sea

arm'load' ***n.*** an armful

ar·mor (är'mər) ***n.*** ⟦< L *armare*, to arm⟧ any defensive or protective covering —***vt.***, ***vi.*** to put armor on —**ar'mored** ***adj.***

armored car a vehicle covered with armor plate, as a truck for carrying money to or from a bank

ar·mo·ri·al (är môr'ē əl) ***adj.*** of coats of arms

armor plate a protective covering of steel plates

ar·mor·y (är'mər ē) ***n.***, *pl.* **-mor·ies** ⟦see ARMOR⟧ **1** an arsenal **2** a National Guard unit drill hall

arm'pit' ***n.*** the hollow under the arm at the shoulder

arm'rest' ***n.*** a support for the arm, as on the inside of an automobile door

ar·my (är'mē) ***n.***, *pl.* **-mies** ⟦ult. < L *arma*, weapons⟧ **1** a large, organized body of soldiers for waging war, esp. on land **2** a large number of persons, animals, etc. *[an army of ants]*

Ar·nold (är'nəld), **Ben·e·dict** (ben'ə dikt') 1741-1801; Am. Revolutionary general who became a traitor

a·ro·ma (ə rō'mə) ***n.*** ⟦< Gr *arōma*, spice⟧ a pleasant odor; fragrance

a·ro'ma·ther'a·py ***n.*** the therapeutic use of aromatic oils from herbs, etc.

ar·o·mat·ic (ar'ə mat'ik) ***adj.*** of or having an aroma; fragrant or pungent —***n.*** an aromatic plant, chemical, etc. —**ar'o·mat'i·cal·ly** ***adv.***

a·rose (ə rōz') ***vi.*** *pt. of* ARISE

a·round (ə round') ***adv.*** ⟦ME⟧ **1** in a circle **2** in every direction **3** in circumference **4** to the opposite direction **5** [Inf.] nearby *[stay around]* —***prep.*** **1** so as to encircle or envelop **2** on the border of **3** in various places in or on **4** about *[around 1890]*

a·rouse (ə rouz') ***vt.*** **a·roused'**, **a·rous'ing** **1** to awaken, as from sleep **2** to stir, as to action **3** to evoke *[to arouse pity]* —**a·rous'al** ***n.***

ar·peg·gio (är pej'ō) ***n.***, *pl.* **-gios** ⟦It < *arpa*, a harp⟧ a chord whose notes are played in quick succession

ar·raign (ə rān') ***vt.*** ⟦< L *ad*, to + *ratio*, reason⟧ **1** to bring before a law court to answer charges **2** to call to account; accuse —**ar·raign'ment** ***n.***

ar·range (ə rānj') ***vt.*** **-ranged'**, **-rang'ing** ⟦< OFr *a-*, to + *renger*, to range⟧ **1** to put in the correct order **2** to classify **3** to prepare or plan **4** to arrive at an agreement about **5** *Music* to adapt (a composition) to particular instruments or voices —***vi.*** *Music* to write arrangements, esp. as a profession —**ar·rang'er** ***n.***

ar·range'ment ***n.*** **1** an arranging **2** a result or manner of arranging **3** [*usually pl.*] a plan **4** a settlement **5** *Music a*) an arranging of a composition *b*) the composition as thus arranged

ar·rant (ar'ənt) ***adj.*** ⟦var. of ERRANT⟧ that is plainly such; out-and-out; notorious

ar·ras (ar'əs) ***n.*** ⟦after *Arras*, Fr city⟧ a wall hanging, esp. of tapestry

ar·ray (ə rā') ***vt.*** ⟦< OFr *areer*⟧ **1** to place in order **2** to dress in finery —***n.*** **1** an orderly grouping, esp. of troops **2** an impressive display **3** fine clothes

ar·rears (ə rirz') ***pl.n.*** ⟦< L *ad*, to + *retro*, behind⟧ overdue debts —**in arrears** behind in paying a debt, doing one's work, etc.

ar·rest (ə rest') ***vt.*** ⟦< L *ad-*, to + *restare*, to stop⟧ **1** to stop or check **2** to seize by authority of the law **3** to catch and keep (one's attention, etc.) —***n.*** an arresting or being arrested —**under arrest** in legal custody

ar·rest'ing ***adj.*** attracting attention; interesting

ar·rhyth·mi·a (ə rith'mē ə) ***n.*** ⟦< Gr *a-*, without + *rhythmos*, measure⟧ an irregularity in the heart's rhythm —**ar·rhyth'mic** or **ar·rhyth'mi·cal** ***adj.***

ar·riv·al (ə rī'vəl) ***n.*** **1** an arriving **2** a person or thing that arrives

ar·rive (ə rīv') ***vi.*** **-rived'**, **-riv'ing** ⟦< L *ad-*, to + *ripa*, shore⟧ **1** to reach one's destination **2** to come *[the time has arrived]* **3** to attain fame, etc. —**arrive at** to reach by thinking, etc.

ar·ri·ve·der·ci (är rē've der'chē) ***interj.*** ⟦It⟧ goodbye

THESAURUS

armchair ***n.*** easy chair, rocker, recliner; see CHAIR.

armed ***a.*** equipped, outfitted, in battle formation, loaded, provided with arms, fortified, protected, fitted out, in arms, well-armed.—*Ant.* UNARMED, vulnerable, unprotected.

armistice ***n.*** truce, cease-fire, temporary peace; see PEACE.

armor ***n.*** shield, chain mail, armor plate, helmet, bulletproof vest, tank, armored car.

armory ***n.*** ordnance headquarters, training center, drilling place, depot, arsenal, drill center, shooting range, National Guard building, reserve corps headquarters.

arms ***n.*** armament, armor, ammunition, firearms, munitions, guns, small arms, instruments of war, deadly weapons, lethal weapons, pistols, rifles, machine guns, submachine guns, equipment, supplies, ordnance, artillery, materiel, hardware, ammo*; see also WEAPON. —**bear arms** carry weapons, be armed, be militant; see ARM. —**take up arms** go to war, rebel, do battle; see FIGHT. —**up in arms** hostile, indignant, willing to fight; see ANGRY.

army ***n.*** **1** [Military land forces] armed force, standing army, regulars, soldiery, troops, men, cavalry, infantry, artillery, air corps, reserves. **2** [A unit of an army] division, regiment, armored division, airborne division, infantry division, battalion, company, corps, brigade, flight, wing, amphibious force, task force, detail, detachment, squad, troop, patrol, unit, command, formation, point, column, legion, platoon, outfit.

aroma ***n.*** fragrance, perfume, odor; see SMELL 1, 2.

around ***a., prep.*** **1** [Surrounding] about, in this area, on all sides, on every side, in circumference, neighboring, in the vicinity of, all around, round about, encompassing, nearby, in a circle, along a circuit, all about, close to, on various sides, round and round, right and left.—*Ant.* DISTANT, remote, far-off. **2** [Approximately] almost, about, close to; see APPROXIMATELY. —**have been around*** have had wide experience, be worldly, be sophisticated; see EXPERIENCED.

arouse ***v.*** move, stir up, stimulate; see EXCITE.

arrange ***v.*** **1** [To put in order] regulate, systematize, put in order; see ORDER 3. **2** [To make ready] determine, plan, devise, contrive, prepare for, get ready, make ready, draft, scheme, design, provide, make preparations for, set the stage for, prepare, put into shape, make plans for, line up, organize, adjust, manage, direct, establish, decide, resolve.—*Ant.* BOTHER, disorganize, disturb.

arrangement ***n.*** **1** [The result of arranging] method, system, form; see ORDER 3. **2** [An agreement] settlement, adjustment, compromise; see AGREEMENT 1. **3** [A design] pattern, composition, combination; see DESIGN.

arrest ***n.*** appropriation, imprisonment, apprehension, commitment, confinement, incarceration, capture, captivity, protective custody, taking by force, taking into custody, constraint, duress, seizure, detention, bust*.—*Ant.* FREEDOM, acquittal, release. —**under arrest** arrested, caught, apprehended, taken into custody, seized, taken in, handcuffed, confined, jailed, imprisoned, detained, shut up, penned up, put in irons, sent to prison, sent to jail, busted*, pinched*, booked, collared*, nabbed*, sent up the river*.

arrest ***v.*** apprehend, hold, place under arrest, take into custody, capture, imprison, jail, incarcerate, detain, secure, seize, get, catch, take prisoner, nab*, pick up, bust*.—*Ant.* FREE, liberate, parole.

arrival ***n.*** **1** [The act of arriving] entrance, advent, coming, entry, appearance, landing, homecoming, debarkation, approach, return, meeting.—*Ant.* DEPARTURE, leaving, leave-taking. **2** [That which has arrived] passenger, visitor, tourist, guest, newcomer, delegate, traveler, cargo, freight, mail, shipment, package, parcel.

arrive ***v.*** enter, land, disembark, alight, dismount, halt, roll up*, reach one's destination, get in, visit, make shore, drop anchor, reach home, appear, get to, hit*, blow into*, breeze in*, check in*, pull in, hit town*.—*Ant.* LEAVE, go, depart.

ar·ro·gant (ar′ə gənt) ***adj.*** ⟦< L *arrogare*, to claim⟧ full of or due to pride; haughty —**ar′ro·gance** ***n.*** —**ar′ro·gant·ly** ***adv.***

ar′ro·gate′ (-gāt′) ***vt.*** **-gat′ed, -gat′ing** ⟦< L *ad-*, for + *rogare*, to ask⟧ to claim or seize without right —**ar′ro·ga′tion** ***n.***

ar·row (ar′ō) ***n.*** ⟦OE *arwe*⟧ **1** a pointed shaft for shooting from a bow **2** a sign (←), used to indicate direction

ar′row·head′ ***n.*** the separable, pointed tip of an arrow

ar′row·root′ ***n.*** ⟦from use as antidote for poisoned arrows⟧ **1** a tropical plant with starchy roots **2** a starch made from its roots

ar·roy·o (ə roi′ō) ***n.***, *pl.* **-os** ⟦Sp < L *arrugia*, mine shaft⟧ [Southwest] **1** a dry gully **2** a rivulet or stream

ar·se·nal (är′sə nəl) ***n.*** ⟦< Ar *dār aṣṣinā′a*, workshop⟧ **1** a place for making or storing weapons **2** a store or collection

ar·se·nic (är′sə nik′; *for adj.* är sen′ik) ***n.*** ⟦< Gr *arsenikon*⟧ a very poisonous chemical element, compounds of which are used in insecticides, etc. —***adj.*** of or containing arsenic: also **ar·sen′i·cal**

ar·son (är′sən) ***n.*** ⟦< L *ardere*, to burn⟧ the crime of purposely setting fire to a building or property —**ar′son·ist** ***n.***

art[1] (ärt) ***n.*** ⟦< L *ars*⟧ **1** human creativity **2** skill **3** any specific skill or its application **4** any craft or its principles **5** creative work or its principles **6** any branch of creative work, as painting or sculpture **7** products of this, as paintings or statues **8** *a)* a branch of learning *b)* [*pl.*] LIBERAL ARTS **9** cunning **10** sly trick; wile: *usually used in pl.*

art[2] (ärt) ***vi.*** *archaic 2d pers. sing., pres. indic., of* BE: used with *thou*

art[3] *abbrev.* **1** article **2** artificial

art dec·o (dek′ō) a decorative style of the late 1920s and the 1930s, derived from cubism

ar·te·ri·al (är tir′ē əl) ***adj.*** **1** of or in the arteries **2** of a main road

ar·te·ri·ole (är tir′ē ōl′) ***n.*** ⟦see ARTERY⟧ any of the small blood vessels between the arteries and capillaries

ar·te·ri·o·scle·ro·sis (är tir′ē ō′sklə rō′sis) ***n.*** ⟦< Gr *artēria*, artery + SCLEROSIS⟧ an abnormal thickening and hardening of the walls of the arteries

ar·ter·y (ärt′ər ē) ***n.***, *pl.* **-ter·ies** ⟦< Gr *aeirein*, to lift⟧ **1** any of the blood vessels that carry blood away from the heart **2** a main route

ar·te·sian well (är tē′zhən) ⟦Fr *artésien*, of Artois (in France)⟧ a deep well in which water is forced up by pressure of underground water draining from higher ground

art film a film characterized by artistic sophistication, realism, etc.

art·ful (ärt′fəl) ***adj.*** **1** skillful or clever **2** cunning; crafty —**art′ful·ly** ***adv.*** —**art′ful·ness** ***n.***

art house a theater that shows art films, etc.

ar·thri·tis (är thrīt′is) ***n.*** ⟦Gr < *arthron*, joint + -ITIS⟧ inflammation of a joint or joints —**ar·thrit·ic** (är thrit′ik) ***adj.***

arthro- ⟦< Gr *arthron*, joint⟧ *combining form* joint, joints

ar·thro·pod (är′thrə päd′) ***n.*** ⟦prec. + -POD⟧ any of a phylum of invertebrates with jointed legs and a segmented body

ar′thro·scope′ (-skōp′) ***n.*** ⟦ARTHRO- + -SCOPE⟧ an endoscope used inside a joint —**ar′thro·scop′ic** (-skäp′ik) ***adj.***

Ar·thur[1] (är′thər) ***n.*** legendary 6th-c. king of Britain —**Ar·thu·ri·an** (är thoor′ē ən) ***adj.***

Ar·thur[2] (är′thər), **Ches·ter A(lan)** (ches′tər) 1829-86; 21st president of the U.S. (1881-85)

ar·ti·choke (ärt′ə chōk′) ***n.*** ⟦ult. < Ar *al-ḥarshaf*⟧ **1** a thistlelike plant **2** its edible flower head

ar·ti·cle (ärt′i kəl) ***n.*** ⟦< L *artus*, joint⟧ **1** one of the sections of a document **2** a complete piece of writing, as in a newspaper, magazine, etc. **3** a separate item *[an article of luggage]* **4** *Gram.* any one of the words *a, an,* or *the*, used as adjectives

ar·tic·u·late (är tik′yoo lit; *for v.*, -lāt′) ***adj.*** ⟦see prec.⟧ **1** jointed: usually **ar·tic′u·lat′ed** **2** made up of distinct sounds, as speech **3** able to speak **4** expressing oneself clearly —***vt.*** **-lat′ed, -lat′ing** **1** to connect by joints **2** to arrange in connected sequence **3** to utter distinctly **4** to express clearly —***vi.*** **1** to speak distinctly **2** to be jointed or connected —**ar·tic′u·late·ly** ***adv.*** —**ar·tic′u·la′tion** ***n.***

ar·ti·fact (ärt′ə fakt′) ***n.*** any object made by human work

ar·ti·fice (ärt′ə fis) ***n.*** ⟦< L *ars*, art + *facere*, make⟧ **1** skill or ingenuity **2** trickery **3** an artful trick

ar·tif·i·cer (är tif′ə sər) ***n.*** **1** a skilled craftsman **2** an inventor

ar·ti·fi·cial (ärt′ə fish′əl) ***adj.*** ⟦see ARTIFICE⟧ **1** made by human work; not natural **2** simulated *[artificial teeth]* **3** affected *[an artificial smile]* —**ar′ti·fi′ci·al′i·ty** (-fish′ē al′ə tē), *pl.* **-ties**, ***n.*** —**ar′ti·fi′cial·ly** ***adv.***

artificial intelligence **1** the capability of computers to mimic human thought processes **2** the science dealing with this

artificial respiration the maintenance of breathing by artificial means, as by forcing air into the mouth

ar·til·ler·y (är til′ər ē) ***n.*** ⟦< OFr *atillier*, equip⟧ **1** mounted guns, as cannon or missile launchers **2** gunnery —**the artillery** the branch of an army using heavy mounted guns —**ar·til′ler·y·man** (-mən), *pl.* **-men** (-mən), ***n.***

ar·ti·san (ärt′ə zən) ***n.*** ⟦ult. < L *ars*, art⟧ a skilled craftsman

art·ist (ärt′ist) ***n.*** **1** one who is skilled in any of the fine arts **2** one who does anything very well **3** a professional in any of the performing arts

ar·tis·tic (är tis′tik) ***adj.*** **1** of art or artists **2** done skillfully and tastefully **3** sensitive to beauty —**ar·tis′ti·cal·ly** ***adv.***

art·ist·ry (ärt′is trē) ***n.*** artistic quality, ability, or work

art·less (ärt′lis) ***adj.*** **1** lacking skill or art **2** simple; natural **3** without guile; ingenuous; innocent —**art′less·ly** ***adv.***

Arts and Crafts a 19th-c. movement that promoted handwork and craftsmanship

art·y (ärt′ē) ***adj.*** **art′i·er, art′i·est** [Inf.] affectedly artistic —**art′i·ness** ***n.***

ar·um (er′əm) ***n.*** ⟦L⟧ any of a family of plants with flowers enveloped within a hoodlike leaf

Ar·y·an (ar′ē ən) ***n.*** ⟦< Sans *āzya-*, noble⟧ **1** [Obs.] the hypothetical parent language of the Indo-European family **2** a person supposed to be a descendant of the prehistoric peoples that spoke this language: *Aryan* is not a valid ethnological term

as (az) ***adv.*** ⟦< ALSO⟧ **1** equally *[just as happy at home]* **2** for instance *[a card game, as bridge]* **3** when related in

THESAURUS

arrogance ***n.*** insolence, smugness, vanity, audacity, haughtiness; see also PRIDE 2.

arrogant ***a.*** domineering, autocratic, sneering; see EGOTISTIC.

arrogantly ***a.*** proudly, haughtily, insolently, loftily, with one's nose in the air*.

arrow ***n.*** shaft, dart, missile; see WEAPON.

arson ***n.*** setting fire to property, pyromania, deliberate burning of property; see CRIME.

art[1] ***n.*** representation, illustration, abstraction, imitation, modeling, description, portrayal, design, composition, performance, drama, poetry, fiction, singing, dancing, playing an instrument, personification, sketching, molding, shaping, painting, characterization, creating, sculpting, carving; see also ARCHITECTURE, DANCE 1, LITERATURE 1, MUSIC 1, PAINTING, SCULPTURE.

artery ***n.*** **1** [Main channel of communication or travel] highway, thoroughfare, line, supply route, canal; see also ROAD 1, WAY 2. **2** [Blood vessel] aorta, arteriole, arterial passageway; see VEIN 3.

artful ***a.*** clever, adroit, ingenious; see ABLE.

article ***n.*** **1** [An individual thing] object, item, commodity; see THING 1. **2** [Nonfiction appearing in a periodical] essay, editorial, report; see WRITING 2.

articulate ***v.*** **1** [To speak clearly] enunciate, pronounce, verbalize; see SPEAK 1. **2** [To join] fit together, combine, connect, link; see also JOIN 1.

artificial ***a.*** imitation, synthetic, counterfeit; see FALSE 3.

artillery ***n.*** gunnery, ordnance, cannon; see ARMS, CANNON.

artist ***n.*** master, creator, painter, composer, virtuoso, musician, poet, novelist, dramatist, essayist, actress, actor, playwright, writer, performing artist, cartoonist, opera singer, instrumentalist, dancer, ballerina, sculptor, etcher, engraver, designer, architect, photographer.

artistic ***a.*** inventive, skillful, imaginative, discriminating, creative, graceful, talented, accomplished, well-executed, well-wrought, pleasing, sublime, aesthetic, cultured, tasteful, exquisite, sensitive, fine, elegant, harmonious, grand, stimulating, elevated, noble, beautiful.

artistry ***n.*** workmanship, skill, proficiency; see ABILITY.

as ***a., conj., prep.*** **1** [While] in the process of, in the act of, on the point of; see WHILE 1. **2** [Because] since, inasmuch as, for the reason that; see BECAUSE. **3** [To the same degree

a specified way [my view *as* contrasted with yours] —**conj.** 1 to the same amount or degree that [straight *as* an arrow] 2 in the same manner that [do *as* you are told] 3 while [she wept *as* she spoke] 4 because [*as* you object, we won't go] 5 that the consequence is [so obvious *as* to need no reply] 6 though [tall *as* he was, he couldn't reach it] —**pron.** 1 a fact that [we are tired, *as* you can see] 2 that: preceded by *such* or *the same* [such books *as* I own] —**prep.** in the role or function of [he poses *as* a friend] —**as for** (or **to**) concerning —**as if** (or **though**) as it (or one) would if —**as is** [Inf.] just as it is —**as it were** as if it were so

As *Chem. symbol for* arsenic

ASAP *abbrev.* as soon as possible

as·bes·tos (as bes'təs, az-) **n.** ⟦< Gr *a-*, not + *sbennynai*, extinguish⟧ a nonconducting, fireproof mineral used, esp. formerly, in electrical insulation, roofing, etc.

as·cend (ə send') **vi.** ⟦< L *ad-*, to + *scandere*, to climb⟧ to move upward; rise —**vt.** 1 to move upward along; mount 2 to succeed to (a throne)

as·cend·an·cy or **as·cend·en·cy** (ə sen'dən sē) **n.** a position of control; domination

as·cend'ant or **as·cend'ent** (-dənt) **adj.** 1 rising 2 in control; dominant —**in the ascendant** at or approaching the height of power, fame, etc.

as·cen'sion (-shən) **n.** 1 an ascending 2 [**A-**] the 40th day after Easter, celebrating the Ascension —**the Ascension** *Bible* the bodily ascent of Jesus into heaven

as·cent (ə sent') **n.** 1 an ascending 2 an upward slope

as·cer·tain (as'ər tān') **vt.** ⟦see AD- & CERTAIN⟧ to find out with certainty

as·cet·ic (ə set'ik) **adj.** ⟦< Gr *askein*, to train the body⟧ self-denying; austere —**n.** ⟦< Gr *awkētēs*, monk⟧ one who leads a life of strict self-denial, esp. for religious purposes —**as·cet'i·cism'** (-ə siz'əm) **n.**

ASCII (as'kē) **n.** a code that facilitates information exchange among various computers

a·scor·bic acid (ə skôr'bik) ⟦A-[2] + *scorbutic*, of scurvy + -IC⟧ vitamin C

as·cot (as'kət, -kät') **n.** a necktie with very broad ends hanging from the knot

as·cribe (ə skrīb') **vt.** **-cribed'**, **-crib'ing** ⟦< L *ad-*, to + *scribere*, write⟧ 1 to assign (something) *to* a supposed cause 2 to regard (something) as belonging *to* or coming from someone —**as·crip·tion** (ə skrip'shən) **n.**

a·sep·tic (ā sep'tik, ə-) **adj.** free from disease-producing bacteria, etc.

a·sex·u·al (ā sek'sho͞o əl) **adj.** 1 having no sex or sexual organs 2 without the union of male and female germ cells 3 having little or no sexual activity, desire, character, etc. —**a·sex'u·al·ly adv.**

ash[1] (ash) **n.** ⟦< OE *æsce*⟧ 1 the grayish powder left after something has burned 2 fine, volcanic lava 3 the gray color of wood ash See also ASHES

ash[2] (ash) **n.** ⟦< OE *æsc*⟧ 1 a shade tree of the olive family 2 its wood

a·shamed (ə shāmd') **adj.** 1 feeling shame 2 reluctant because fearing shame beforehand —**a·sham·ed·ly** (ə shām'id lē) **adv.**

ash·en (ash'ən) **adj.** 1 of ashes 2 like ashes, esp. in color; pale

ash·es (ash'iz) **pl.n.** 1 the grayish powder and small particles left after a thing has burned 2 human remains, esp. the part left after cremation

a·shore (ə shôr') **adv.**, **adj.** 1 to or on the shore 2 to or on land

ash·ram (äsh'rəm) **n.** ⟦< Sans *ā*, toward + *śrama*, penance⟧ 1 a secluded place for a Hindu religious community 2 such a community

ash'tray' **n.** a container for smokers' tobacco ashes, etc.: also **ash tray**

Ash Wednesday the first day of Lent: from the putting of ashes on the forehead in penitence

ash'y **adj.** **-i·er**, **-i·est** 1 of or covered with ashes 2 ashen; pale

A·sia (ā'zhə) largest continent, in the Eastern Hemisphere: *c.* 17,400,000 sq. mi.; pop. *c.* 3,451,000,000 —**A'sian** or less preferred **A·si·at·ic** (ā'zhē at'ik) **adj.**, **n.**

Asia Minor large peninsula in W Asia, between the Black Sea and the Mediterranean

a·side (ə sīd') **adv.** 1 on or to one side 2 in reserve [put one *aside* for me] 3 apart; notwithstanding [joking *aside*] —**n.** words spoken by an actor but supposedly not heard by the other actors —**aside from** 1 with the exception of 2 apart from

as·i·nine (as'ə nīn') **adj.** ⟦< L *asinus*, ass⟧ like an ass; stupid; silly —**as'i·nine'ly adv.** —**as'i·nin'i·ty** (-nin'ə tē) **n.**

ask (ask) **vt.** ⟦OE *āscian*⟧ 1 to use words in seeking the answer to (a question) 2 to inquire of (a person) 3 to request or demand 4 to invite —**vi.** 1 to make a request (*for*) 2 to inquire (*about* or *after*) —**ask'er n.**

a·skance (ə skans') **adv.** ⟦ME⟧ 1 with a sideways glance 2 with suspicion, disapproval, etc.

a·skew (ə skyo͞o') **adv.** to one side; awry —**adj.** on one side; awry

asking price the price asked by a seller, esp. as a basis for bargaining

a·slant (ə slant') **adv.** on a slant —**prep.** on a slant across —**adj.** slanting

a·sleep (ə slēp') **adj.** 1 sleeping 2 inactive; dull 3 numb 4 dead —**adv.** into a sleeping condition

a·so·cial (ā sō'shəl) **adj.** 1 avoiding contact with others 2 selfish

asp (asp) **n.** ⟦< Gr *aspis*⟧ a poisonous snake of Africa, Arabia, etc.

as·par·a·gus (ə spar'ə gəs, -sper'-) **n.** ⟦< Gr *asparagos*⟧ 1 a plant of the lily family, with edible shoots 2 these shoots

as·par·tame (as'pər tām') **n.** an artificial, low-calorie sweetener, used in soft drinks, candy, etc.

as·pect (as'pekt') **n.** ⟦< L *ad-*, to + *specere*, to look⟧ 1 the way one appears 2 the appearance of something from a specific position or viewpoint 3 a side facing in a given direction

as·pen (as'pən) **n.** ⟦OE *æspe*⟧ a poplar tree whose leaves flutter in the least breeze

as·per·i·ty (ə sper'ə tē) **n.**, *pl.* **-ties** ⟦< L *asper*, rough⟧ 1 roughness or harshness 2 sharpness of temper

as·per·sion (ə spur'zhən) **n.** a damaging or disparaging remark; slander

as·phalt (as'fôlt') **n.** ⟦< Gr *asphaltos*⟧ a brown or black tarlike substance mixed with sand or gravel and used

THESAURUS

that] in the same way that, in the same manner that, equally, comparatively, similarly. 4 [For the purpose, use, etc. of] just for, serving as, functioning as, acting as, being. —**as a matter of fact** truly, actually, indeed; see REALLY 1. —**as if** just as if, just as though, in such a way that, as if it were, supposing, as would be if, as might be if, just like*. —**as is*** as it stands, as usual, just the same, the same way. —**as it were** so to speak, figuratively speaking, in a way, as it seems, as it would seem, in some sort, in a manner, so to say, kind of*, in a manner of speaking, sort of*. —**as though** just as, just as if, just as though; see AS IF.

ascend *v.* go upward, climb, soar; see RISE 1.

ascent *n.* upward path, climbing, ascension; see RISE 1.

ashamed *a.* embarrassed, shamed, regretful, meek, repentant, penitent, apologetic, debased, abashed, conscience-stricken, mortified, uncomfortable, hesitant, perplexed, bewildered, shamefaced, bowed down, disconcerted, sputtering, stammering, stuttering, gasping, floundering, rattled, muddled, confused, blushing, flustered, distraught, humbled, feeling like a jackass, off balance, in the hole*, taken down a peg, red in the face*, looking silly, at a loss.

ashes *n.* cinders, dust, powder, slag, embers, charcoal, soot.

Asian *a.* Asiatic, Eastern, Far Eastern, Oriental, Siberian, Middle Eastern, Mideastern, Near Eastern, South Asian, Southeast Asian.

aside *a.* to the side, to one side, on one side, at rest, out, by oneself, apart, at one side, by itself, alone, alongside, out of the way, aloof, away, in safekeeping, abreast, at a short distance, by. —**aside from** apart from, in addition to, excluding; see BESIDES.

ask *v.* request, query, question, interrogate, examine, cross-examine, demand, raise a question, inquire, frame a question, order, command, put questions to, requisition, bid, charge, petition, call upon, invite, urge to, challenge, pry, investigate, quiz, grill, needle*, sound out, pump*, put through the third degree*.—*Ant.* ANSWER, refute, rejoin.

asleep *a.* sleeping, dreaming, quiet, resting, snoring, in a sound sleep, fast asleep, sound asleep, slumbering, reposing, taking a siesta, hibernating, dozing, wakeless, napping, unconscious, dead to the world*, in the land of Nod, snoozing*, conked out*, out like a light*.—*Ant.* AWAKE, waking, alert. —**fall asleep** go to sleep, doze, drop off*; see SLEEP.

aspect *n.* 1 [Looks] countenance, face, features; see LOOKS. 2 [View] perspective, regard, slant; see VIEWPOINT.

for paving, roofing, etc. —*vt.* to pave, roof, etc. with asphalt

as·pho·del (as′fə del′) ***n.*** ⟦< Gr *asphodelos*⟧ a plant of the lily family, having white or yellow flowers

as·phyx·i·ate (as fik′sē āt′) ***vt.***, ***vi.*** **-at′ed**, **-at′ing** ⟦< Gr *a-*, not + *sphyzein*, to throb⟧ **1** to make or become unconscious from lack of oxygen in the blood **2** to suffocate —**as·phyx′i·a′tion** ***n.***

as·pic (as′pik′) ***n.*** ⟦< OFr *aspe*, asp⟧ a cold jelly of meat juice, tomato juice, etc., served as a garnish or in a mold

as·pi·rant (as′pə rənt, ə spī′-) ***adj.*** aspiring —***n.*** one who aspires

as·pi·rate (as′pə rāt′; *for n.*, -pər it) ***vt.*** **-rat′ed**, **-rat′ing** **1** to begin (a word) with the sound of English (h) **2** to follow (a consonant) with an audible puff of breath **3** to suck in or draw in **4** *Med.* to remove (fluid, etc.) by suction —***n.*** an aspirated sound

as·pi·ra·tion (as′pə rā′shən) ***n.*** **1** *a)* strong desire or ambition, as for advancement *b)* the thing so desired **2** a drawing in by breathing or suction **3** *Med.* removal of fluid, etc. by suction

as′pi·ra′tor ***n.*** an apparatus using suction to remove air, fluids, etc.

as·pire (ə spīr′) ***vi.*** **-pired′**, **-pir′ing** ⟦< L *ad-*, to + *spirare*, breathe⟧ to be ambitious (*to* get or do something); seek (*after*)

as·pi·rin (as′pə rin′, -prin′) ***n.*** ⟦Ger⟧ **1** a white, crystalline powder used for reducing fever, relieving pain, etc. **2** a tablet of this

ass (as) ***n.*** ⟦< L *asinus*⟧ **1** a horselike animal having long ears and a short mane **2** a stupid or silly person

as·sail (ə sāl′) ***vt.*** ⟦< L *ad-*, to + *salire*, to leap⟧ **1** to attack physically and violently **2** to attack with arguments, etc. —**as·sail′a·ble** ***adj.***

as·sail′ant (-ənt) ***n.*** an attacker

as·sas·sin (ə sas′ən) ***n.*** ⟦< Ar *ḥashshāshīn*, hashish users⟧ a murderer who strikes suddenly; now, esp., the murderer of a politically important or prominent person

as·sas′si·nate′ (-āt′) ***vt.*** **-nat′ed**, **-nat′ing** to murder as an assassin does —**as·sas′si·na′tion** ***n.***

as·sault (ə sôlt′) ***n.*** ⟦< L *ad-*, to + *salire*, to leap⟧ **1** a violent attack **2** *euphemism for* RAPE[1] **3** *Law* an unlawful threat or attempt to harm another physically —***vt.***, ***vi.*** to make an assault (upon)

assault and battery *Law* the carrying out of threatened physical harm

as·say (as′ā, a sā′; *for v.* a sā′) ***n.*** ⟦< OFr *essai*, trial⟧ **1** a testing **2** an analysis of the ingredients of an ore, drug, etc. —***vt.*** **1** to make an assay of; test **2** to try; attempt —***vi.*** to be shown by assay to have a specified proportion of something —**as·say′er** ***n.***

as·sem·blage (ə sem′blij; *for 3, also* ä′sem bläzh′) ***n.*** **1** an assembling **2** a group of persons or things gathered together **3** *Art* things assembled in a sculptured collage

as·sem·ble (ə sem′bəl) ***vt.***, ***vi.*** **-bled**, **-bling** ⟦< L *ad-*, to + *simul*, together⟧ **1** to gather into a group; collect **2** to fit or put together the parts of —**as·sem′bler** ***n.***

as·sem′bly (-blē) ***n.***, *pl.* **-blies** **1** an assembling **2** a group of persons gathered together **3** *a)* a legislative body *b)* [**A-**] the lower house of some state legislatures **4** a fitting together of parts to make a whole

assembly line in many factories, a method whereby each worker performs a specific task in assembling the work as it is passed along

as·sem′bly·man (-mən) ***n.***, *pl.* **-men** a member of a legislative assembly —**as·sem′bly·wom′an**, *pl.* **-wom′en**, ***fem.n.***

as·sent (ə sent′) ***vi.*** ⟦< L *ad-*, to + *sentire*, to feel⟧ to express acceptance; agree (*to*) —***n.*** consent or agreement

as·sert (ə surt′) ***vt.*** ⟦< L *ad-*, to + *serere*, join⟧ **1** to declare; affirm **2** to maintain or defend (rights, etc.) —**assert oneself** to insist on one's rights, or on being recognized —**as·sert′er** or **as·ser′tor** ***n.***

as·ser·tion (ə sur′shən) ***n.*** **1** an asserting **2** a positive statement

as·ser·tive (ə surt′iv) ***adj.*** persistently, forcefully, or boldly positive or confident —**as·ser′tive·ly** ***adv.*** —**as·ser′tive·ness** ***n.***

as·sess (ə ses′) ***vt.*** ⟦< L *ad-*, to + *sedere*, sit⟧ **1** to set an estimated value on (property, etc.) for taxation **2** to set the amount of (a tax, fine, etc.) **3** to impose a tax, etc. on **4** to judge the worth or importance of —**as·sess′ment** ***n.*** —**as·ses′sor** ***n.***

as·set (as′et) ***n.*** ⟦< L *ad*, to + *satis*, enough⟧ **1** anything owned that has value **2** a desirable thing *[charm is an asset]* **3** [*pl.*] the accounting entries showing the resources of a person or business **4** [*pl.*] *Law* property available to pay debts

as·sev·er·ate (ə sev′ə rāt′) ***vt.*** **-at′ed**, **-at′ing** ⟦< L *ad-*, to + *severus*, earnest⟧ to state positively; assert —**as·sev′er·a′tion** ***n.***

as·sid·u·ous (ə sij′o͞o əs) ***adj.*** ⟦< L *assidere*, to assist⟧ diligent; persevering; careful —**as·si·du·i·ty** (as′ə dyo͞o′ə tē), *pl.* **-ties**, ***n.*** —**as·sid′u·ous·ly** ***adv.*** —**as·sid′u·ous·ness** ***n.***

as·sign (ə sīn′) ***vt.*** ⟦< L *ad-*, to + *signare*, to sign⟧ **1** to set apart or mark for a specific purpose; designate **2** to appoint, as to a duty **3** to give out as a task; allot **4** to ascribe; attribute **5** *Law* to transfer (a right, etc.) —**as·sign′a·ble** ***adj.*** —**as·sign′er** or *Law* **as·sign·or** (ə sīn′ôr′) ***n.***

as·sig·na·tion (as′ig nā′shən) ***n.*** an appointment to meet, esp. one made secretly by lovers, or the meeting itself

as·sign·ment (ə sīn′mənt) ***n.*** **1** an assigning or being assigned **2** anything assigned

as·sim·i·late (ə sim′ə lāt′) ***vt.*** **-lat′ed**, **-lat′ing** ⟦< L *ad-*, to + *similare*, make similar⟧ **1** to absorb and incorporate **2** to make like or alike: with *to* —***vi.*** **1** to become like or alike **2** to become absorbed and incorporated —**as·sim′i·la′tion** ***n.***

as·sist (ə sist′) ***vt.***, ***vi.*** ⟦< L *ad-*, to + *sistere*, make stand⟧ to help; aid —***n.*** an instance or act of helping —**assist at** to be present at; attend

as·sist·ance (ə sis′təns) ***n.*** help; aid

THESAURUS

aspiration ***n.*** yearning, eagerness, inclination; see AMBITION.

aspire ***v.*** strive, struggle, yearn; see TRY 1.

aspiring ***a.*** ambitious, hopeful, enthusiastic; see ZEALOUS.

ass ***n.*** **1** [A stupid person] dolt, dunce, blockhead; see FOOL. **2** [A donkey] burro, jackass, jennet; see ANIMAL.

assailant ***n.*** antagonist, foe, enemy; see OPPONENT.

assassin ***n.*** murderer, slayer, butcher; see KILLER.

assassinate ***v.*** slay, slaughter, put to death; see KILL 1.

assassination ***n.*** killing, shooting, slaying; see MURDER.

assault ***n.*** **1** [An attack] harm, advance, onslaught; see ATTACK. **2** [A rape] attack, abduction, violation; see RAPE.

assault ***v.*** **1** [To attack] assail, advance, strike; see ATTACK. **2** [To rape] attack, violate, ravish; see RAPE.

assemble ***v.*** **1** [To bring together] rally, call, convoke, muster, round up, group, convene, summon, mobilize, call together, accumulate, amass, invite, gather, collect, hold a meeting, unite, pack them in, throw a party*, herd together, rally round, gather around, gang around*.—*Ant.* SCATTER, break up, send away. **2** [To put together] piece together, set up, erect, construct, join, unite, solder, mold, weld, glue.—*Ant.* BREAK, disassemble, break down.

assembly ***n.*** **1** [A gathering of persons] assemblage, meeting, association; see GATHERING. **2** [The process of bringing parts together] construction, collection, piecing together, fitting in, joining, assembling, modeling, attachment, adjustment, welding, soldering, molding, fixing.—*Ant.* SEPARATION, dismantling, wrecking.

assent ***n.*** approval, authorization, consent; see PERMISSION.

assert ***v.*** state, say, affirm; see DECLARE.

assertion ***n.*** affirmation, statement, report; see DECLARATION.

assess ***v.*** **1** [To tax] charge, exact tribute, exact from; see TAX 1. **2** [To estimate] judge, reckon, guess; see ESTIMATE.

assets ***n.*** holdings, possessions, capital; see PROPERTY.

assign ***v.*** commit, commission, authorize, hand over, earmark, allocate, detail, appoint, allot, prescribe, nominate, name, select, hold responsible, empower, entrust, allow, cast, deputize, attach, charge, accredit, hire, elect, ordain, enroll, relegate, draft.—*Ant.* MAINTAIN, reserve, keep back.

assignment ***n.*** **1** [An appointment] designation, authorization, nomination; see APPOINTMENT 1. **2** [Something assigned] job, responsibility, task; see DUTY 2.

assimilate ***v.*** **1** [To absorb] take up, digest, incorporate; see ABSORB. **2** [To understand] grasp, learn, comprehend; see UNDERSTAND 1.

assist ***v.*** support, aid, serve; see HELP.

assistance ***n.*** support, comfort, compensation; see HELP 1.

as·sist'ant (-tənt) ***adj.*** assisting; helping —***n.*** one who assists; helper; aid

assisted living a living arrangement providing assistance to elderly or disabled persons

as·siz·es (ə sīz'iz) ***pl.n.*** ⟦see ASSESS⟧ **1** court sessions held periodically in each county of England **2** the time or place of these

assn *abbrev.* association

assoc *abbrev.* **1** associate(s) **2** association

as·so·ci·ate (ə sō'shē āt', -sē-; *for n. & adj.*, -it) ***vt.*** **-at'ed, -at'ing** ⟦< L *ad-*, to + *socius*, companion⟧ **1** to connect; combine; join **2** to bring into relationship as partner, etc. **3** to connect in the mind —***vi.*** to join (*with*) as a partner, friend, etc. —***n.*** **1** a friend, partner, co-worker, etc. **2** a degree granted by a junior college —***adj.*** **1** joined with others in work, etc. **2** having less than full status

as·so'ci·a'tion ***n.*** **1** an associating or being associated **2** fellowship; partnership **3** an organization, society, etc. **4** a mental connection between ideas, etc.

association football soccer

as·so'ci·a'tive (-shē āt'iv, -sē-; -shə tiv) ***adj.*** **1** of, by, or causing association **2** *Math.* producing the same result regardless of how the elements are grouped

as·so·nance (as'ə nəns) ***n.*** ⟦< L *ad-*, to + *sonare*, to sound⟧ **1** likeness of sound **2** a partial rhyme made by repetition of a vowel sound —**as'so·nant** ***adj., n.***

as·sort (ə sôrt') ***vt.*** ⟦ult. < L *ad-*, to + *sors*, lot, fate⟧ to sort or classify

as·sort'ed ***adj.*** **1** various; miscellaneous **2** sorted; classified

as·sort'ment ***n.*** **1** an assorting **2** a miscellaneous collection; variety

asst *abbrev.* assistant

as·suage (ə swāj') ***vt.*** **-suaged', -suag'ing** ⟦< L *ad-*, to + *suavis*, sweet⟧ **1** to lessen (pain, distress, etc.) **2** to calm (anger, etc.) **3** to satisfy or slake (thirst, etc.)

as·sume (ə so͞om') ***vt.*** **-sumed', -sum'ing** ⟦< L *ad-*, to + *sumere*, to take⟧ **1** to take on (the appearance, role, etc. of) **2** to seize; usurp **3** to undertake **4** to take for granted; suppose **5** to pretend to have; feign —**as·sum'a·ble** ***adj.***

as·sumed' ***adj.*** **1** pretended; fictitious **2** taken for granted

as·sump·tion (ə sump'shən) ***n.*** **1** [**A-**] *R.C.Ch. a)* the ascent of the Virgin Mary into heaven *b)* a feast on Aug. 15 celebrating this **2** an assuming **3** a supposition —**as·sump'tive** ***adj.***

as·sur·ance (ə sho͝or'əns) ***n.*** **1** an assuring or being assured **2** a promise, guarantee, etc. **3** self-confidence **4** [Chiefly Brit.] insurance

as·sure (ə sho͝or') ***vt.*** **-sured', -sur'ing** ⟦< L *ad-*, to + *securus*, secure⟧ **1** to make (a person) sure of something **2** to give confidence to; reassure **3** to tell or promise confidently **4** to guarantee **5** [Chiefly Brit.] to insure against loss

as·sured' ***adj.*** **1** made sure; certain **2** confident; sure of oneself —**as·sur·ed·ly** (ə sho͝or'id lē) ***adv.***

As·syr·i·a (ə sir'ē ə) ancient empire in SW Asia —**As·syr'i·an** ***adj., n.***

as·ter (as'tər) ***n.*** ⟦< Gr *astēr*, star⟧ any of several plants of the composite family with variously colored daisylike flowers

as·ter·isk (as'tər isk') ***n.*** ⟦< Gr dim. of *astēr*, star⟧ a starlike sign (*) used in printing to mark footnotes, etc.

a·stern (ə sturn') ***adv.*** **1** behind a ship or aircraft **2** AFT **3** backward

as·ter·oid (as'tər oid') ***n.*** ⟦see ASTER & -OID⟧ any of the small planets in orbits mainly between Mars and Jupiter

asth·ma (az'mə) ***n.*** ⟦Gr⟧ a chronic disorder characterized by wheezing, coughing, difficulty in breathing, etc. —**asth·mat·ic** (az mat'ik) ***adj., n.***

a·stig·ma·tism (ə stig'mə tiz'əm) ***n.*** ⟦< Gr *a-*, without + *stigma*, a mark + -ISM⟧ an irregularity in the lens of the eye, that prevents proper focusing of light rays, causing distortion, poor eyesight, etc. —**as·tig·mat·ic** (as'tig mat'ik) ***adj.***

a·stil·be (ə stil'bē) ***n.*** a plant having spikes of white, pink, or red flowers

a·stir (ə stur') ***adv., adj.*** **1** in motion **2** out of bed

as·ton·ish (ə stän'ish) ***vt.*** ⟦< L *ex-*, intens. + *tonare*, to thunder⟧ to fill with sudden wonder; amaze —**as·ton'ish·ing** ***adj.*** —**as·ton'ish·ing·ly** ***adv.*** —**as·ton'ish·ment** ***n.***

as·tound (ə stound') ***vt.*** ⟦see prec.⟧ to astonish greatly —**as·tound'ing** ***adj.*** —**as·tound'ing·ly** ***adv.***

a·strad·dle (ə strad''l) ***adv.*** in a straddling position

as·tra·khan (as'trə kən) ***n.*** ⟦after *Astrakhan,* Russ city⟧ loosely curled fur from young lamb pelts, or a wool fabric resembling this

as·tral (as'trəl) ***adj.*** ⟦< Gr *astron*, star⟧ of, from, or like the stars

a·stray (ə strā') ***adv., adj.*** ⟦ME < pp. of OFr *estraier*, stray⟧ **1** off the right path **2** in error

a·stride (ə strīd') ***adv.*** with a leg on either side —***prep.*** **1** with a leg on either side of **2** extending over or across

as·trin·gent (ə strin'jənt) ***adj.*** ⟦< L *ad-*, to + *stringere*, to draw tight⟧ **1** that contracts body tissue and stops secretions **2** harsh; biting —***n.*** an astringent substance —**as·trin'gen·cy** ***n.***

astro- ⟦< Gr *astron*, star⟧ *combining form* star or stars *[astrophysics]*

as·tro·bi·ol·o·gy (as'trō bī äl'ə jē) ***n.*** the branch of biology that investigates the existence of living organisms on planets other than earth

THESAURUS

assistant ***n.*** aide, deputy, henchman, friend, follower, adherent, auxiliary, lieutenant, associate, companion, colleague, partner, helper, apprentice, fellow-worker, secretary, helping hand, patron, backer, bodyguard, aide-de-camp, ally, accessory, clerk, collaborator, confederate, mate, helpmate, accomplice, copartner, coworker, flunky, man Friday, girl Friday, right arm*, yes man*, right-hand man, friend in need*.—*Ant.* ENEMY, rival, antagonist.

associate ***n.*** comrade, brother-in-arms, peer, colleague, partner, copartner, friend, ally, buddy*, accomplice, assistant, aide, attendant, henchman, confederate, auxiliary, co-worker, helper, collaborator, fellow-worker, helping hand, right-hand man, man Friday, girl Friday, teammate; see also ASSISTANT.—*Ant.* ENEMY, foe, antagonist.

associate ***v.*** **1** [To unite with] work with, join with, get along with, be friendly with; see also GO WITH, JOIN 2. **2** [To relate] correlate, link, connect, join; see also COMPARE.

association ***n.*** **1** [The act of associating] frequenting, fraternization, friendship, acquaintanceship, cooperation, assistance, relationship, affiliation, agreement, participation, companionship, fellowship, familiarity, friendliness, camaraderie, membership, acquaintance, mingling, union, community.—*Ant.* DISAGREEMENT, severance, rupture. **2** [The process of intellectual comparison] connection, comparison, linking, correlation, relation, mental connection, train of thought, connection of ideas in thought, recollection, impression, remembering, combination. **3** [An organization] union, federation, corporation; see ORGANIZATION 2.

assorted ***a.*** varied, miscellaneous, mixed; see VARIOUS.

assortment ***n.*** variety, combination, group; see COLLECTION.

assume ***v.*** suppose, presume, posit, understand, gather, find, theorize, presuppose, ascertain, draw the inference, divine, get the idea, have an idea that, suspect, postulate, regard, consider, infer, hypothesize, guess, conjecture, suppose as fact, deem, imagine, surmise, opine, judge, estimate, speculate, fancy, take the liberty, be of the opinion, dare say, deduce, conclude, put two and two together, be inclined to think, hold the opinion, think, calculate, hope, feel, be afraid, believe, have faith, take it, expect, allow, reckon*.—*Ant.* DOUBT, be surprised, be unaware that.

assumed ***a.*** presumed, understood, presupposed, counted on, inferred, given, granted, taken as known, conjectured, accepted, supposed, hypothetical, hypothesized.

assumption ***n.*** **1** [The act of taking for granted] supposition, presupposition, presumption, conjecture, assuming, suspicion, surmise, theorization, hypothesization.—*Ant.* PROOF, demonstration, establishing. **2** [Something assumed] hypothesis, theory, postulate; see OPINION 1.

assurance ***n.*** **1** [A guarantee] insurance, support, pledge; see PROMISE 1. **2** [Confidence] conviction, trust, certainty; see FAITH 1.

assure ***v.*** **1** [To guarantee] vouch for, aver, attest; see GUARANTEE. **2** [To convince] prove, persuade, reassure; see CONVINCE.

assured ***a.*** **1** [Certain] sure, undoubted, guaranteed; see CERTAIN. **2** [Confident] self-possessed, bold, unhesitating; see CONFIDENT.

astonish ***v.*** shock, amaze, astound; see SURPRISE.

astonishing ***a.*** surprising, startling, extraordinary; see UNUSUAL 1.

astonishment ***n.*** surprise, amazement, bewilderment; see WONDER 1.

astound ***v.*** amaze, shock, startle; see SURPRISE.

astray ***a.*** straying, roaming, adrift; see WANDERING 1.

as'tro·dy·nam'ics *n.* the branch of dynamics dealing with the motion and gravitation of objects in space

as·trol·o·gy (ə sträl'ə jē) *n.* ⟦< Gr *astron*, star + *-logia*, -LOGY⟧ a method or theory based on the assumption that the positions of the moon, sun, and stars affect human affairs and can be used to foretell the future —**as·trol'o·ger** *n.* —**as·tro·log·i·cal** (as'trə läj'i kəl) *adj.*

as·tro·naut (as'trə nôt') *n.* ⟦< Fr < Gr *astron*, star + *nautēs*, sailor⟧ one trained to make flights into outer space —**as'tro·nau'tics** *n.*

as·tro·nom·i·cal (as'trə näm'i kəl) *adj.* **1** of astronomy **2** extremely large: said as of numbers Also **as'tro·nom'ic** —**as'tro·nom'i·cal·ly** *adv.*

astronomical unit a unit of length based on the mean distance of the earth from the sun, *c.* 149.6 million km (*c.* 93 million mi.)

as·tron·o·my (ə strän'ə mē) *n.* ⟦< Gr *astron*, star + *nomos*, law⟧ the science that studies the origin, size, motion, etc. of stars, planets, etc. —**as·tron'o·mer** *n.*

as·tro·phys·ics (as'trō fiz'iks) *n.* the branch of astronomy dealing with the physical properties of the universe —**as'tro·phys'i·cist** (-ə sist) *n.*

As'tro·Turf' (-turf') *trademark for* a grasslike synthetic carpet used in stadiums, etc.

as·tute (ə sto͞ot') *adj.* ⟦< L *astus*, craft, cunning⟧ clever or shrewd; keen —**as·tute'ly** *adv.* —**as·tute'ness** *n.*

a·sun·der (ə sun'dər) *adv.* ⟦< OE *on sundran*⟧ **1** into pieces **2** apart in direction or position

a·sy·lum (ə sī'ləm) *n.* ⟦< Gr *a-*, without + *sylon*, right of seizure⟧ **1** a place of safety; refuge **2** an institution for the care of mentally ill, aged, or poor people: a term now rarely used

a·sym·me·try (ā sim'ə trē) *n.* lack of symmetry —**a·sym·met·ri·cal** (ā'sə me'tri kəl) *adj.* —**a'sym·met'ri·cal·ly** *adv.*

a·symp·to·mat·ic (ā'simp tə ma'tik) *adj.* without symptoms

at (at) *prep.* ⟦< OE *æt*⟧ **1** on; in; near; by *[at the office]* **2** to or toward *[look at her]* **3** from *[visible at one mile]* **4** attending *[at a party]* **5** busy with *[at work]* **6** in the state or manner of *[at war, at a trot]* **7** because of *[sad at his death]* **8** with reference to *[good at tennis]* **9** in the amount, etc. of *[at five cents each]* **10** on or near the time or age of *[at noon, at twenty-one]* **11** attacking, etc. *[they're at him again]*

at·a·vism (at'ə viz'əm) *n.* ⟦< L *at-*, beyond + *avus*, grandfather⟧ resemblance or reversion to a characteristic of a remote ancestor —**at'a·vis'tic** *adj.*

a·tax·i·a (ə tak'sē ə) *n.* ⟦< Gr *a-*, not + *tassein*, arrange⟧ an inability to coordinate one's movements, as in walking —**a·tax'ic** *adj., n.*

ate (āt; *Brit, or U.S. dial.*, et) *vt., vi. pt. of* EAT

-ate[1] (āt; *for 2*, it) *suffix* **1** to become, cause to become, form, provide with *[maturate, ulcerate]* **2** of or characteristic of, characterized by, having *[passionate]*

-ate[2] (āt, it) *suffix* an office, function, agent, or official *[directorate]*

at·el·ier (at'l yā') *n.* ⟦Fr⟧ a studio or workshop, esp. of an artist

Ath·a·bas·kan or **Ath·a·bas·can** (ath'ə bas'kən) *n.* a family of North American Indian languages, including Navajo —*adj.* designating or of these languages or the peoples that speak them

a·the·ism (ā'thē iz'əm) *n.* ⟦< Gr *a-*, without + *theos*, god⟧ the belief that there is no God —**a'the·ist** *n.* —**a'the·is'tic** *adj.*

A·the·na (ə thē'nə) *n.* the Greek goddess of wisdom, skills, and warfare

Ath·ens (ath'ənz) capital of Greece, in the SE part: pop. 772,000 —**A·the·ni·an** (ə thē'nē ən) *adj., n.*

ath·er·o·scle·ro·sis (ath'ər ō'sklə rō'sis) *n.* ⟦< Gr *athērōma*, grainy tumor + SCLEROSIS⟧ formation of fatty nodules on hardening artery walls

a·thirst (ə thurst') *adj.* **1** [Archaic] thirsty **2** eager; longing *(for)*

ath·lete (ath'lēt') *n.* ⟦< Gr *athlon*, a prize⟧ a person trained in exercises or games requiring strength, skill, stamina, etc.

athlete's foot ringworm of the feet

ath·let·ic (ath let'ik) *adj.* **1** of or like athletes or athletics **2** physically strong, active, fit, etc. —**ath·let'i·cal·ly** *adv.* —**ath·let'i·cism'** (-ə siz'əm) *n.*

ath·let'ics *pl.n.* [*sometimes with sing. v.*] athletic sports, games, etc.

-a·thon (ə thän') ⟦< (MAR)ATHON⟧ *suffix* an event marked by length or endurance *[walkathon]*

a·thwart (ə thwôrt') *prep.* **1** across **2** against —*adv.* crosswise

a·tilt (ə tilt') *adj., adv.* tilted

-a·tion (ā'shən) ⟦< Fr or L⟧ *suffix* the act, condition, or result of *[alteration]*

-a·tive (ə tiv, āt'iv) ⟦< Fr or L⟧ *suffix* of or relating to, serving to *[informative]*

At·lan·ta (at lan'tə) capital of Georgia: pop. 394,000

At·lan·tic (at lan'tik) ocean touching the Americas to the west and Europe and Africa to the east

Atlantic City city in SE New Jersey: an ocean resort: pop. 38,000

At·lan·tis (at lan'tis) *n.* ⟦< Gr⟧ legendary sunken continent in the Atlantic

At·las (at'ləs) *n.* **1** *Gr. Myth.* a giant who supports the heavens on his shoulders **2** [a-] a book of maps

ATM (ā'tē em') *n.* ⟦*a(utomated) t(eller) m(achine)*⟧ a computer terminal that allows a bank customer to deposit, withdraw, or transfer funds automatically

at·mos·phere (at'məs fir') *n.* ⟦< Gr *atmos*, vapor + *sphaira*, sphere⟧ **1** the air surrounding the earth **2** a pervading mood or spirit **3** the general tone or effect **4** a unit of pressure equal to 101,325 newtons per sq. m —**at'mos·pher'ic** (-fer'ik, -fir'-) *adj.* —**at'mos·pher'i·cal·ly** *adv.*

at·oll (a'tôl') *n.* ⟦< Malayalam *atolu*⟧ a ring-shaped coral island surrounding a lagoon

at·om (at'əm) *n.* ⟦< Gr *a-*, not + *temnein*, to cut⟧ **1** a tiny particle; jot **2** *Chem., Physics* any of the smallest particles of an element that combine with similar particles of other elements to form molecules —**the atom** nuclear energy

atom bomb ATOMIC BOMB

a·tom·ic (ə täm'ik) *adj.* **1** of an atom or atoms **2** of or using atomic energy or atomic bombs **3** tiny —**a·tom'i·cal·ly** *adv.*

THESAURUS

astronaut *n.* space traveler, cosmonaut, spaceman, spacewoman, space pilot, rocket man, spacewalker.

asunder *a.* apart, in two, in half, to shreds, into bits and pieces, dismantled, dissected, in two parts, divided, into separate parts, separated, disjoined, rent, carved, dismembered, torn apart, split; see also BROKEN 1, TORN.—*Ant.* WHOLE, together, sound.

at *prep.* **1** [Position] on, by, near to, about, occupying the precise position of, in the vicinity of, placed at, situated at, found in, in front of, appearing in; see also IN 1, NEAR 1. **2** [Direction] toward, in the direction of, through; see TO 1.

atheism *n.* heresy, agnosticism, godlessness, ungodliness, impiety, positivism, denial of God, iconoclasm, unbelief, nihilism, irreligion, irreverence, rationalism, infidelity, materialism, skepticism, freethinking, disbelief; see also DOUBT.

athlete *n.* acrobat, gymnast, player, contestant, champion, sportsman, sportswoman, amateur, professional, semiprofessional, contender, challenger, letterman, muscle man*, jock*. *Athletes include the following:* baseball player, football player, basketball player, soccer player, rugby player, boxer, wrestler, swimmer, golfer, tennis player, volleyball player, jockey, trackman, javelin thrower, high-jumper, discus thrower, shot putter, biathlete, decathlete, triathlete, skier, ski jumper, slalom racer, runner, marathon runner, relay runner, long jumper, pole vaulter, hurdler, equestrian, polo player, hockey player, skater, bicyclist, cyclist, fencer, swordsman, cricket player, miler.

athletic *a.* muscular, husky, wiry, springy, slim, fast, solid, strapping, hardy, robust, strong, vigorous, powerful, brawny, sinewy, sturdy, well-proportioned, well-built, manly, Herculean, Amazonian, built like an ox*.—*Ant.* SICK, weak, fat.

athletics *n.* gymnastics, sports, games; see SPORT 3.

atmosphere *n.* **1** [The air] layer of air, gaseous envelope, air pressure; see AIR 1. **2** [A pervading quality] environment, climate, mood; see CHARACTER 1, CHARACTERISTIC.

atmospheric *a.* climatic, meteorological, aerial; see AIRY.

atom *n.* grain, mite, speck, particle, molecule, iota; see also BIT 1, ELEMENT. *Parts of atoms include the following:* electron, proton, neutron, positron, neutrino, quark, antiquark, meson, baryon, nucleon, boson, fermion, muon, photon, lepton, hadron, hyperon.

atom bomb *n.* atomic bomb, nuclear weapon, nuclear device, thermonuclear device, hydrogen bomb, A-bomb, H-bomb.

atomic *a.* microscopic, tiny, diminutive; see MINUTE 1.

atomic bomb an extremely destructive bomb whose power results from a chain reaction of nuclear fission
atomic energy NUCLEAR ENERGY
atomic number *Chem.* a number indicating the number of protons in the nucleus of an atom of an element
atomic weight *Chem.* the weight of one atom of an element based upon the average weight of the element's isotopes
at·om·iz·er (at′əm ī zər) ***n.*** a device used to shoot out a fine spray, as of medicine or perfume
a·to·nal·i·ty (ā′tō nal′ə tē) ***n.*** *Music* the organization of tones without relation to a key —**a·ton·al** (ā tōn′əl) ***adj.*** —**a·ton′al·ly** ***adv.***
a·tone (ə tōn′) ***vi.*** **a·toned′**, **a·ton′ing** ⟦< ME *at one*, in accord⟧ to make amends (*for* wrongdoing, etc.)
a·tone′ment ***n.*** **1** an atoning **2** amends —**the Atonement** *Theol.* the redeeming of humanity by the death of Jesus
a·top (ə täp′) ***adv.*** on or at the top —***prep.*** on the top of
a·top·ic (ā täp′ik) ***adj.*** of allergic reactions, as a type of dermatitis, thought to be inherited
-a·to·ry (ə tôr′ē) ⟦< L⟧ *suffix* -ORY
ATP (ā′tē′pē′) ***n.*** ⟦*a*(*denosine*) *t*(*ri*)*p*(*hosphate*)⟧ an organic compound present in, and vital to, all living cells
a·tri·um (ā′trē əm) ***n.***, *pl.* **a′tri·a** (-ə) or **a′tri·ums** ⟦L⟧ **1** the central court or main room of an ancient Roman house **2** a court or entrance hall, usually of more than one story **3** either of the heart's upper chambers
a·tro·cious (ə trō′shəs) ***adj.*** ⟦< L *atrox*, fierce⟧ **1** very cruel, evil, etc. **2** very bad or unpleasant; offensive —**a·tro′cious·ly** ***adv.*** —**a·tro′cious·ness** ***n.***
a·troc·i·ty (ə träs′ə tē) ***n.***, *pl.* **-ties** **1** atrocious behavior **2** an atrocious act **3** [Inf.] a very displeasing thing
at·ro·phy (a′trə fē) ***n.*** ⟦< Gr *a-*, not + *trephein*, to feed⟧ a wasting away or failure to grow, esp. of body tissue, an organ, etc. —***vi.*** **-phied**, **-phy·ing** to undergo atrophy —***vt.*** to cause atrophy in
at·ro·pine (at′rə pēn′, -pin′) ***n.*** ⟦< Gr *Atropos*, one of the Fates + -INE[3]⟧ an alkaloid obtained from belladonna, used to relieve spasms, etc.
at·tach (ə tach′) ***vt.*** ⟦< OFr *estache*, a post, stake⟧ **1** to fasten by sticking, tying, etc. **2** to join: often used reflexively **3** to connect by ties of affection, etc. **4** to add (a signature, etc.) **5** to ascribe **6** *Law* to take (property) by writ —**at·tach′a·ble** ***adj.***
at·ta·ché (at′ə shā′; *chiefly Brit* ə tash′ā) ***n.*** ⟦Fr: see prec.⟧ a member of an ambassador's diplomatic staff
attaché case a briefcase
at·tach′ment ***n.*** **1** an attaching or being attached **2** anything that attaches; fastening **3** devotion **4** anything attached **5** an accessory for an electrical appliance, etc. **6** *Law* a taking of property into custody
at·tack (ə tak′) ***vt.*** ⟦< It *attaccare*⟧ **1** to use force against in order to harm **2** to speak or write against **3** to undertake vigorously **4** to begin acting upon harmfully —***vi.*** to make an assault —***n.*** **1** an attacking **2** any hostile action, esp. with troops **3** the onset of a disease **4** a beginning of a task, undertaking, etc. —**at·tack′er** ***n.***
at·tain (ə tān′) ***vt.*** ⟦< L *ad-*, to + *tangere*, to touch⟧ **1** to gain; accomplish; achieve **2** to reach; arrive at —**at·tain′a·bil′i·ty** ***n.*** —**at·tain′a·ble** ***adj.***
at·tain′der (-dər) ***n.*** ⟦see prec.⟧ loss of civil rights and property of one sentenced to death or outlawed
at·tar (at′ər) ***n.*** ⟦< Ar *'iṭr*, perfume⟧ a perfume made from flower petals, esp. of roses (**attar of roses**)
at·tempt (ə tempt′) ***vt.*** ⟦< L *ad-*, to + *temptare*, to try⟧ to try to do, get, etc. —***n.*** **1** a try; endeavor **2** an attack, as on a person's life
at·tend (ə tend′) ***vt.*** ⟦< L *ad-*, to + *tendere*, to stretch⟧ **1** [Now Rare] to take care of **2** to go with **3** to accompany as a result **4** to be present at —***vi.*** **1** to pay attention **2** to wait (*on* or *upon*) **3** to apply oneself (*to*) **4** to give the required care (*to*)
at·tend′ance ***n.*** **1** an attending **2** the number of persons attending
at·tend′ant ***adj.*** **1** attending or serving **2** being present **3** accompanying —***n.*** one who attends or serves
at·ten·tion (ə ten′shən) ***n.*** ⟦see ATTEND⟧ **1** mental concentration or readiness **2** notice or observation **3** care or consideration **4** an act of courtesy or devotion: *usually used in pl.* **5** the erect posture of soldiers ready for a command
attention-deficit hyperactivity disorder a mental disorder marked by inability to concentrate, impulsiveness, etc.
at·ten′tive (-tiv) ***adj.*** **1** paying attention **2** courteous, devoted, etc. —**at·ten′tive·ly** ***adv.*** —**at·ten′tive·ness** ***n.***
at·ten·u·ate (ə ten′yo͞o āt′) ***vt.*** **-at′ed**, **-at′ing** ⟦< L *ad-*, to + *tenuis*, thin⟧ **1** to make thin **2** to dilute **3** to lessen or weaken —***vi.*** to become thin, weak, etc. —**at·ten′u·a′tion** ***n.*** —**at·ten′u·a′tor** ***n.***
at·test (ə test′) ***vt.*** ⟦< L *ad-*, to + *testari*, to bear witness⟧ **1** to declare to be true or genuine **2** to certify, as by oath **3** to serve as proof of —***vi.*** to bear witness (*to*) —**at·tes·ta·tion** (at′əs tā′shən) ***n.***
at·tic (at′ik) ***n.*** ⟦< Gr *Attikos*, of Attica (ancient Gr state): with reference to architectural style⟧ the room or space just below the roof; garret
At·ti·la (at′'l ə, ə til′ə) A.D. 406?-453; king of the Huns: called *Attila the Hun*
at·tire (ə tīr′) ***vt.*** **-tired′**, **-tir′ing** ⟦< OFr *a*, to + *tire*, order, row⟧ to dress, esp. in fine garments; clothe —***n.*** clothes, esp. fine or rich apparel
at·ti·tude (at′ə to͞od′) ***n.*** ⟦ult. < L *aptus*, apt⟧ **1** a bodily posture showing mood, action, etc. **2** a manner showing one's feelings or thoughts **3** one's disposition, opinion,

THESAURUS

atone for ***v.*** compensate for, do penance for, make amends for; see PAY FOR.

atrocity ***n.*** **1** [Brutality] inhumanity, wickedness, barbarity; see CRUELTY. **2** [A cruel deed] abomination, outrage, horror; see CRIME.

attach ***v.*** **1** [To join] connect, append, add; see JOIN 1. **2** [To attribute] associate, impute, ascribe; see GIVE 1.

attachment ***n.*** **1** [Affection] fondness, liking, devction; see AFFECTION. **2** [Something attached] accessory, adjunct, annex; see ADDITION 1.

attack ***n.*** **1** [Offensive tactical action] assault, raid, onslaught, advance, charge, thrust, offense, drive, aggression, onset, outbreak, skirmish, encounter, volley, shooting, barrage, siege, firing, trespass, blockade, crossfire, invasion, offensive, intrusion, intervention, onrush, inroad, encroachment, incursion.—*Ant.* WITHDRAWAL, retreat, retirement. **2** [Verbal attack] libel, slander, denunciation; see BLAME.

attack ***v.*** **1** [To fight offensively; *used of an army*] assault, beset, besiege, invade, storm, advance, infiltrate, raid, assail, march against, shell, board, take by surprise, make a push, bombard, bomb, go over the top, lay siege to, open fire, shoot at, snipe at, lay into*, launch an attack, ambush, strafe, waylay, engage, set upon, torpedo, push, combat, attempt violence against, charge, strike the first blow, bayonet, stab, close with, rake, have at, counterattack.—*Ant.* RETREAT, fall back, recoil. **2** [To assault; *used of an individual*] molest, beat, overwhelm; see FIGHT, RAPE. **3** [To assail with words] revile, refute, reprove; see BLAME. **4** [To proceed vigorously with] take up, deal with, start on; see ACT 1.

attacked ***a.*** assaulted, bombed, bombarded, assailed, stoned, torpedoed, fired upon, stormed, under attack, strafed, invaded, besieged; see also RUINED 1.

attacker ***n.*** aggressor, fighter, assailant, antagonist, invader, foe, enemy, criminal, plunderer, intruder, trespasser, violator, ravager, spoiler, felon.—*Ant.* VICTIM, prey, martyr.

attain ***v.*** win, achieve, accomplish; see SUCCEED.

attempt ***n.*** trial, struggle, endeavor; see EFFORT.

attempt ***v.*** endeavor, strive, venture; see TRY 1.

attend ***v.*** be present at, frequent, sit in on, be a guest, revisit, haunt, be a member, be a habitué, make an appearance.—*Ant.* LEAVE, be missing, absent oneself.

attendance ***n.*** **1** [The act of attending] presence, participation, appearance, being present, putting in an appearance, turning up, showing up.—*Ant.* ABSENCE, nonappearance, nonattendance. **2** [The persons attending] audience, spectators, assembly; see GATHERING.

attendant ***n.*** aide, orderly, valet, nurse, usher, bellhop, servant, domestic, secretary, understudy, disciple, pupil, companion, caregiver, escort, flight attendant, steward, stewardess, maid; see also ASSISTANT.

attention ***n.*** observation, observance, regard, vigilance, mindfulness, inspection, heed, heedfulness, watching, listening, consideration, intentness, study, alertness, thought, application, diligence, caution, preoccupation, thoroughness, recognition, concentration, care.

attitude ***n.*** mood, opinion, idea, belief, air, demeanor, condition of mind, state of feeling, position, reaction, bias, set, leaning, bent, inclination, propensity, cast, emotion, temper, temperament, sensibility, disposition, mental state, notion, philosophy, view, orientation, nature, makeup, frame of mind, character; see also VIEWPOINT.

etc. **4** [Slang] a quarrelsome or haughty temperament or manner

at·ti·tu·di·nize (at'ə to͞od''n īz') ***vi.*** **-nized', -niz'ing** to pose for effect

Attn or **attn** *abbrev.* attention

at·tor·ney (ə tur'nē) ***n.***, *pl.* **-neys** ⟦< OFr *a-*, to + *torner*, to turn⟧ any person legally empowered to act for another; esp., a lawyer

attorney at law a lawyer

attorney general *pl.* **attorneys general** or **attorney generals** the chief law officer of a government

at·tract (ə trakt') ***vt.*** ⟦< L *ad-*, to + *trahere*, to draw⟧ **1** to draw to itself or oneself **2** to get the admiration, attention, etc. of; allure —***vi.*** to be attractive —**at·tract'a·ble** ***adj.***

at·trac·tion (ə trak'shən) ***n.*** **1** an attracting or being attracted **2** power to attract; esp., charm **3** anything that attracts **4** *Physics* the mutual tendency of bodies to draw together

at·trac'tive (-tiv) ***adj.*** that attracts; esp., pleasing, charming, pretty, etc. —**at·trac'tive·ly** ***adv.*** —**at·trac'tive·ness** ***n.***

at·trib·ute (ə trib'yo͞ot; *for n.* a'trə byo͞ot') ***vt.*** **-ut·ed, -ut·ing** ⟦< L *ad-*, to + *tribuere*, assign⟧ to think of as belonging *to* a certain person or thing —***n.*** a characteristic or quality of a person or thing —**at·trib'ut·a·ble** ***adj.*** —**at·tri·bu·tion** (a'trə byo͞o'shən) ***n.***

at·trib·u·tive (ə trib'yo͞o tiv) ***adj.*** **1** attributing **2** preceding the noun it modifies: said of an adjective —**at·trib'u·tive·ly** ***adv.***

at·tri·tion (ə trish'ən) ***n.*** ⟦< L *ad-*, to + *terere*, to rub⟧ **1** a wearing away by or as by friction **2** a normal loss of personnel, as by retirement

at·tune (ə to͞on') ***vt.*** **-tuned', -tun'ing** **1** to tune **2** to bring into harmony

atty *abbrev.* attorney

ATV (ā'tē'vē') ***n.***, *pl.* **ATVs** ⟦*A(ll-)T(errain) V(ehicle)*⟧ a small motor vehicle for traveling over rough ground, snow and ice, etc.

a·twit·ter (ə twit'ər) ***adv.***, ***adj.*** twittering

a·typ·i·cal (ā tip'i kəl) ***adj.*** not typical; abnormal —**a·typ'i·cal·ly** ***adv.***

Au ⟦L *aurum*⟧ *Chem. symbol for* gold

au·burn (ô'bərn) ***adj.***, ***n.*** ⟦< L *albus*, white: infl. by ME *brun*, brown⟧ reddish brown

Auck·land (ôk'lənd) seaport in N New Zealand: pop. 910,000

auc·tion (ôk'shən) ***n.*** ⟦< L *augere*, to increase⟧ a public sale of items, one by one, to the highest bidder for each item —***vt.*** to sell at auction —**auction off** to sell at auction —**auc'tion·eer'** ***n.***

au·da·cious (ô dā'shəs) ***adj.*** ⟦< L *audax*, bold⟧ **1** bold; daring **2** too bold; brazen; insolent —**au·da'cious·ly** ***adv.*** —**au·da'cious·ness** ***n.***

au·dac·i·ty (ô das'ə tē) ***n.*** **1** bold courage **2** insolence; impudence **3** *pl.* **-ties** an audacious act or remark

au·di·ble (ô'də bəl) ***adj.*** ⟦< L *audire*, hear⟧ loud enough to be heard —**au'di·bil'i·ty** (-bil'ə tē) ***n.*** —**au'di·bly** ***adv.***

au·di·ence (ô'dē əns) ***n.*** ⟦< L *audire*, hear⟧ **1** those assembled to hear and see something **2** all those reached by a TV or radio program, book, etc. **3** a hearing, esp. a formal interview

au·di·o (ô'dē ō') ***adj.*** ⟦< L *audire*, hear⟧ **1** of frequencies corresponding to audible sound waves **2** of sound reproduction, as of the sound phase of television

au'di·o·book' ***n.*** a recording of a reading of a book, as by the author

au·di·ol·o·gy (ô'dē äl'ə jē) ***n.*** evaluation and treatment of hearing defects —**au'di·ol'o·gist** ***n.***

au'di·om'e·ter (-äm'ət ər) ***n.*** an instrument for measuring the sharpness and range of hearing —**au'di·o·met'ric** (-ō me'trik) ***adj.***

au·di·o·phile (ô'dē ō fīl') ***n.*** a devotee of high-fidelity sound reproduction, as from recordings

au·di·o·vis·u·al (ô'dē ō vizh'o͞o əl) ***adj.*** **1** involving both hearing and sight **2** of teaching aids such as films and recordings

au·dit (ôd'it) ***n.*** ⟦< L *auditus*, a hearing⟧ a formal checking of financial records —***vt.***, ***vi.*** **1** to check (accounts, etc.) **2** to attend (a college class) as a listener receiving no credit

au·di·tion (ô dish'ən) ***n.*** ⟦< L *audire*, hear⟧ a hearing to try out an actor, singer, etc. —***vt.***, ***vi.*** to try out in an audition

au·di·tor (ô'dit ər) ***n.*** **1** a listener **2** one who audits accounts **3** one who audits classes

au·di·to·ri·um (ô'də tôr'ē əm) ***n.*** **1** a room where an audience sits **2** a building or hall for speeches, concerts, etc.

au·di·to·ry (ô'də tôr'ē) ***adj.*** of hearing or the sense of hearing

auf Wie·der·seh·en (ouf vē'dər zā'ən) ⟦Ger⟧ goodbye

au·ger (ô'gər) ***n.*** ⟦< OE *nafu*, hub (of a wheel) + *gar*, a spear⟧ a tool for boring holes in wood

aught (ôt) ***n.*** ⟦< OE *a*, ever + *wiht*, creature⟧ **1** anything whatever **2** ⟦< (N)AUGHT⟧ a zero

aug·ment (ôg ment') ***vt.***, ***vi.*** ⟦< L *augere*, to increase⟧ to make or become greater —**aug'men·ta'tion** ***n.*** —**aug·ment'er** ***n.***

au gra·tin (ō grat''n, -grät'-) ⟦Fr⟧ with a crust of bread crumbs and grated cheese

au·gur (ô'gər) ***n.*** ⟦L, priest at fertility rites⟧ a prophet; soothsayer —***vt.***, ***vi.*** **1** to prophesy **2** to be an omen (of) —**augur ill** (or **well**) to be a bad (or good) omen

au·gu·ry (ô'gyo͞o rē) ***n.*** **1** the practice of divination **2** *pl.* **-ries** an omen; portent

au·gust (ô gust') ***adj.*** ⟦L *augustus*⟧ inspiring awe; imposing —**au·gust'ly** ***adv.*** —**au·gust'ness** ***n.***

Au·gust (ô'gəst) ***n.*** ⟦< L *Augustus*⟧ the eighth month of the year, having 31 days: abbrev. **Aug**

Au·gus·ta (ô gus'tə) capital of Maine: pop. 21,000

Au·gus·tine (ô'gəs tēn', ə gus'tin), Saint (A.D. 354-430); early Christian church father

Au·gus·tus (ô gus'təs) 63 B.C.-A.D. 14; 1st Rom. emperor (27 B.C.-A.D. 14)

au jus (ō zho͞o', ō jo͞os') ⟦Fr⟧ served in its natural juices: said of meat

auk (ôk) ***n.*** ⟦< ON *alka*⟧ a diving bird of northern seas, with webbed feet and short wings used as paddles

auld lang syne (ôld' laŋ' zīn') ⟦Scot, lit., old long since⟧ the good old days

aunt (ant, änt) ***n.*** ⟦< L *amita*⟧ **1** a sister of one's mother or father **2** the wife of one's uncle

au poivre (ō pwäv'rə) ⟦Fr⟧ with crushed black peppercorns and a sauce

au·ra (ô'rə) ***n.***, *pl.* **-ras** or **-rae** (-rē) ⟦< Gr⟧ **1** an invisible emanation **2** a particular quality surrounding a person or thing

au·ral (ô'rəl) ***adj.*** ⟦< L *auris*, ear⟧ of the ear or the sense of hearing

au·re·ole (ô'rē ōl') ***n.*** ⟦< L *aurum*, gold⟧ **1** a halo **2** a corona around the sun

Au·re·o·my·cin (ô'rē ō mī'sin) *trademark for* an antibiotic used to treat infections and viruses

au re·voir (ō'rə vwär') ⟦Fr⟧ goodbye

au·ri·cle (ô'ri kəl) ***n.*** ⟦< L dim. of *auris*, ear⟧ the outer part of the ear

THESAURUS

attorney ***n.*** attorney at law, barrister, counsel; see LAWYER.

attract ***v.*** **1** [To draw] pull, drag, bring; see DRAW 1. **2** [To allure] entice, lure, charm; see FASCINATE.

attraction ***n.*** **1** [The act of drawing toward] magnetism, drawing power, allure, fascination, temptation, pull, gravitation, affinity, inclination, tendency, enticement; see also APPEAL 2. **2** [An event] spectacle, display, demonstration; see EVENT.

attractive ***a.*** good-looking, winning, engaging; see BEAUTIFUL, HANDSOME.

attribute ***n.*** property, quality, trait; see CHARACTERISTIC.

attribute ***v.*** ascribe, impute, connect with; see GIVE 1.

auction ***n.*** disposal, bidding, public sale; see SALE.

auction ***v.*** put on sale, sell at auction, put on the block; see SELL.

audible ***a.*** perceptible, discernible, distinct, loud enough to be heard, capable of being heard, within earshot, within hearing distance, hearable, sounding, resounding, loud, deafening, roaring, aloud, clear, plain, emphatic; see also HEARD.

audience ***n.*** witnesses, spectators, patrons; see GATHERING.

audit ***n.*** checking, scrutiny, inspection; see EXAMINATION 1.

audit ***v.*** examine, check, inspect; see EXAMINE 1.

auditorium ***n.*** hall, lecture room, theater, playhouse, movie house, reception hall, amphitheater, assembly hall, opera house, music hall, concert hall, chapel, assembly room. *Sections of an auditorium include the following:* stage, proscenium, orchestra, parquet, stalls, boxes, pit, orchestra circle, dress circle, balcony, gallery, top gallery, tiers, box office.

auger ***n.*** bit, twist drill, screw auger; see DRILL 2.

augment ***v.*** enlarge, expand, magnify; see INCREASE.

aunt ***n.*** mother's sister, father's sister, uncle's wife, grandaunt, great-aunt, auntie*; see also RELATIVE.

Au·ro·ra[1] (ô rôr′ə) ***n.***, *pl.* for 2 & 3 **-ras** or **-rae** (-ē) **1** the Rom. goddess of dawn **2** [a-] the dawn **3** [a-] a luminous band in the night sky

Au·ro·ra[2] (ô rôr′ə) city in central Colorado: pop. 222,000

aurora aus·tra·lis (ô strā′lis) the aurora in the sky of the S Hemisphere

aurora bo·re·al·is (bôr′ē al′is) the aurora in the sky of the N Hemisphere

aus·cul·ta·tion (ôs′kəl tā′shən) ***n.*** ⟦L *auscultare*, to listen⟧ a listening, often with a stethoscope, to sounds in the chest, abdomen, etc. so as to determine the condition of the heart, lungs, etc. —**aus′cul·tate′**, **-tat′ed**, **-tat′ing**, ***vt.***, ***vi.***

aus·pice (ôs′pis) ***n.***, *pl.* **-pi·ces** (-pə siz, -sēz′) ⟦< L *auspicium*, omen⟧ **1** an omen **2** a favorable omen or sign **3** [*pl.*] sponsorship; patronage

aus·pi·cious (ôs pish′əs) ***adj.*** **1** favorable; propitious **2** successful —**aus·pi′cious·ly** ***adv.*** —**aus·pi′cious·ness** ***n.***

Aus·sie (ôs′ē) ***adj.***, ***n.*** [Inf.] Australian

Aus·ten (ôs′tən), **Jane** 1775-1817; Eng. novelist

aus·tere (ô stir′) ***adj.*** ⟦< Gr *austēros*, dry⟧ **1** stern; severe **2** showing strict self-control; ascetic **3** very plain; lacking ornament —**aus·tere′ly** ***adv.***

aus·ter·i·ty (ô ster′ə tē) ***n.***, *pl.* **-ties** **1** sternness **2** an austere practice, act, or manner **3** tightened economy

Aus·tin (ôs′tən) capital of Texas, in the central part: pop. 466,000

aus·tral (ôs′trəl) ***adj.*** ⟦< L *auster*, the south⟧ southern

Aus·tral·ia (ô strāl′yə) **1** island continent between the S Pacific and Indian oceans **2** country comprising this continent & Tasmania: 2,966,150 sq. mi.; pop. 16,849,000 —**Aus·tral′i·an** ***adj.***, ***n.***

Aus·tri·a (ôs′trē ə) country in central Europe: 32,378 sq. mi.; pop. 7,796,000 —**Aus′tri·an** ***adj.***, ***n.***

au·then·tic (ô then′tik) ***adj.*** ⟦< Gr *authentikos*, genuine⟧ **1** credible, reliable, etc.: said as of a news report **2** genuine; real —**au·then′ti·cal·ly** ***adv.*** —**au·then·tic·i·ty** (ô′ thən tis′ə tē) ***n.***

au·then′ti·cate′ (-ti kāt′) ***vt.*** **-cat′ed**, **-cat′ing** **1** to make authentic or valid **2** to verify **3** to prove to be genuine —**au·then′ti·ca′tion** ***n.***

au·thor (ô′thər) ***n.*** ⟦< L *augere*, to increase⟧ **1** one who makes or creates something **2** a writer of books, etc. —***vt.*** to be the author of

au·thor·i·tar·i·an (ə thôr′ə ter′ē ən) ***adj.*** believing in or characterized by absolute obedience to authority —***n.*** an advocate or enforcer of such obedience —**au·thor′i·tar′i·an·ism′** ***n.***

au·thor′i·ta′tive (-tāt′iv) ***adj.*** **1** having authority; official **2** based on competent authority; reliable —**au·thor′i·ta′tive·ly** ***adv.*** —**au·thor′i·ta′tive·ness** ***n.***

au·thor′i·ty (-tē) ***n.***, *pl.* **-ties** ⟦see AUTHOR⟧ **1** the power or right to command, act, etc. **2** [*pl.*] officials with this power **3** power or influence resulting from knowledge, prestige, etc. **4** a person, writing, etc. cited to support an opinion **5** an expert

au·thor·ize (ô′thər īz′) ***vt.*** **-ized′**, **-iz′ing** **1** to give official approval to **2** to give power or authority to **3** to justify —**au′thor·i·za′tion** ***n.*** —**au′thor·iz′er** ***n.***

Authorized Version the revised English translation of the Bible published in England in 1611 with the authorization of King James I

au′thor·ship′ ***n.*** origin or source with regard to author or originator

au·tism (ô′tiz′əm) ***n.*** ⟦AUT(O)- + -ISM⟧ a developmental disorder marked by impaired social interaction, communication difficulties, etc. —**au·tis′tic** (-tis′tik) ***adj.***

au·to (ôt′ō) ***n.***, *pl.* **-tos** an automobile

auto- ⟦< Gr *autos*, self⟧ *combining form* **1** self **2** by oneself or itself **3** automatic

au·to·bi·og·ra·phy (ôt′ō bī ä′grə fē) ***n.***, *pl.* **-phies** the story of one's own life written by oneself —**au′to·bi′o·graph′i·cal** (-bī′ə graf′i kəl) ***adj.*** —**au′to·bi′o·graph′i·cal·ly** ***adv.***

au·toc·ra·cy (ô tä′krə sē) ***n.*** ⟦see fol.⟧ **1** government in which one person has absolute power **2** *pl.* **-cies** a country with such government

au·to·crat (ôt′ə krat′) ***n.*** ⟦< Gr *autos*, self + *kratos*, power⟧ **1** a ruler with absolute power **2** any domineering person —**au′to·crat′ic** ***adj.*** —**au′to·crat′i·cal·ly** ***adv.***

au·to·di·dact (ôt′ō dī′dakt′) ***n.*** ⟦see AUTO- & DIDACTIC⟧ a person who is self-taught

au·to·graph (ôt′ə graf′) ***n.*** ⟦< Gr *autos*, self + *graphein*, write⟧ a person's own signature or handwriting —***vt.*** to write one's signature on or in

au′to·mate′ (-māt′) ***vt.*** **-mat′ed**, **-mat′ing** ⟦< AUTOMATION⟧ to convert to automation or use automation in

au·to·mat·ic (ôt′ə mat′ik) ***adj.*** ⟦Gr *automatos*, self-moving⟧ **1** done unthinkingly, as from habit or by reflex **2** working by itself **3** using automatic equipment **4** capable of firing continuously until the trigger is released —***n.*** **1** an automatic firearm **2** a motor vehicle with a transmission that shifts gears automatically —**au′to·mat′i·cal·ly** ***adv.***

automatic pilot a gyroscopic instrument that automatically keeps an aircraft, missile, etc. to a predetermined course and position

au′to·ma′tion (-mā′shən) ***n.*** ⟦AUTOMA(TIC) + -TION⟧ a manufacturing system in which many or all of the processes are automatically performed or controlled, as by electronic devices

au·tom·a·tism (ô täm′ə tiz′əm) ***n.*** automatic quality, condition, or action —**au·tom′a·tize′** (-tīz′), **-tized′**, **-tiz′ing**, ***vt.***

au·tom′a·ton′ (-tän′, -tən) ***n.***, *pl.* **-tons′** or **-ta** (-tə) ⟦see AUTOMATIC⟧ **1** any automatic device, esp. a robot **2** a person acting like a robot

au·to·mo·bile (ôt′ə mə bēl′) ***n.*** ⟦Fr: see AUTO- & MOBILE⟧ a four-wheeled passenger car with a built-in engine

THESAURUS

auspices ***n.*** protection, aegis, support, sponsorship, backing.

austere ***a.*** harsh, hard, ascetic; see SEVERE 1, 2.

austerity ***n.*** sternness, severity, strictness, harshness, hardness, grimness, stiffness, seriousness, rigidity, gravity, rigor, formality; see also DETERMINATION.

authentic ***a.*** **1** [Reliable] trustworthy, authoritative, factual; see RELIABLE. **2** [Genuine] real, true, actual; see GENUINE 1.

authenticate ***v.*** verify, confirm, validate; see PROVE.

author ***n.*** writer, journalist, columnist, dramatist, playwright, tragedian, humorist, biographer, poet, novelist, short-story writer, essayist, paperback writer, mystery writer, science-fiction writer, contributor, scriptwriter, screenwriter, correspondent, reporter, copywriter, ghostwriter, encyclopedist, lexicographer, scholar, publicist, critic, annotator, hack writer, freelance writer, adman; see also EDITOR, WRITER.

authoritative ***a.*** **1** [Official] definitive, authentic, well-documented; see RELIABLE. **2** [Authorized] lawful, legal, mandatory; see APPROVED, AUTHORIZED. **3** [Suggestive of authority] dogmatic, autocratic, domineering; see ABSOLUTE 2.

authority ***n.*** **1** [Power based on right] right, authorization, jurisdiction; see POWER 2. **2** [The appearance of having authority] prestige, political influence, esteem; see INFLUENCE. **3** [One who knows] expert, scholar, professional; see SPECIALIST.

authorization ***n.*** sanction, signature, support; see PERMISSION.

authorize ***v.*** **1** [To allow] permit, tolerate, suffer; see ALLOW. **2** [To approve] sanction, ratify, endorse; see APPROVE.

authorized ***a.*** allowed, official, legal, lawful, mandatory, authoritative, decisive, valid, standard, sanctioned, confirmed; see also APPROVED.

auto ***n.*** car, vehicle, wheels*; see AUTOMOBILE.

autobiography ***n.*** memoirs, personal history, self-portrayal, confession, life, experiences, diary, adventures, biography, life story, journal, letters.

autocratic ***a.*** dictatorial, domineering, aggressive; see ABSOLUTE 2.

autograph ***n.*** name, signature, John Hancock*; see SIGNATURE.

automated ***a.*** mechanical, mechanized, motorized, computerized, automatic, electronic, programmed, cybernetic; see also AUTOMATIC.

automatic ***a.*** self-starting, motorized, self-regulating, automated, mechanized, under its own power, electric, cybernetic, computerized, self-moving, self-propelled, programmed, electronic, self-activating, push-button, involuntary, unthinking, mechanical, instinctive, spontaneous, reflex, reflexive, intuitive, unintentional, unforced, unconscious.

automobile ***n.*** motor car, car, vehicle, passenger car, machine, auto, wheels*. *Types of automobiles include the following:* subcompact, squad car, hearse, limousine, sedan, hardtop, compact, sports car, convertible, station wagon, taxicab, hatchback, limo*, van, minivan, conversion van, recreational vehicle, RV, sport utility vehicle, SUV, stretch limo*, jeep, crate*, buggy*, clunker*, jalopy*. *Principal parts of an automobile include the following:* wheels, tires, fenders, chassis, motor, radiator, engine, fan, cylinders, carburetor, exhaust, muffler, throttle, gear shift, clutch, steering wheel, transmission, universal joint, generator, distributor, alternator, windshield, windshield wipers, catalytic converter,

au'to·mo'tive (-mōt'iv) ***adj.*** ⟦AUTO- + -MOTIVE⟧ **1** self-moving **2** having to do with automobiles, trucks, etc.

au'to·nom'ic (-näm'ik) ***adj.*** of or controlled by the part of the nervous system regulating motor functions of the heart, lungs, etc.

au·ton·o·mous (ô tän'ə məs) ***adj.*** ⟦< Gr *autos*, self + *nomos*, law⟧ **1** having self-government **2** existing or functioning independently —**au·ton'o·mous·ly *adv.*** —**au·ton'o·my** (-mē) ***n.***

au·top·sy (ô'täp'sē) ***n.***, *pl.* **-sies** ⟦< Gr *autos*, self + *opsis*, a sight⟧ examination of a dead body to discover the cause of death

au·tumn (ôt'əm) ***n.*** ⟦< L *autumnus*⟧ the season between summer and winter; fall —**au·tum·nal** (ô tum'nəl) ***adj.***

aux·il·ia·ry (ôg zil'yə rē, -ə rē) ***adj.*** ⟦< L *augere*, to increase⟧ **1** helping **2** subsidiary **3** supplementary —***n.***, *pl.* **-ries** an auxiliary person or thing

auxiliary verb *Gram.* a verb that helps form tenses, moods, voices, etc. of other verbs, as *have, be, do, will, must*

aux·in (ôk'sin) ***n.*** ⟦< Gr *auxein*, to increase⟧ a plant hormone that promotes and controls growth

av *abbrev.* **1** average **2** avoirdupois

Av *abbrev.* **1** Avenue **2** avoirdupois

a·vail (ə vāl') ***vi., vt.*** ⟦< L *ad*, to + *valere*, be strong⟧ to be of use, help, or worth (to) —***n.*** use or help; advantage *[to no avail]* —**avail oneself of** to take advantage of; utilize

a·vail'a·ble ***adj.*** **1** that can be used **2** that can be gotten or had; handy —**a·vail'a·bil'i·ty *n.***

av·a·lanche (av'ə lanch') ***n.*** ⟦Fr⟧ **1** a large mass of loosened snow, earth, etc. sliding down a mountain **2** an overwhelming amount coming suddenly

a·vant-garde (ə vänt'gärd', ä'-) ***n.*** ⟦Fr⟧ the leaders in new movements, esp. in the arts; vanguard —***adj.*** of such movements

av·a·rice (av'ə ris) ***n.*** ⟦< L *avere*, to desire⟧ greed for money —**av·a·ri·cious** (av'ə rish'əs) ***adj.*** —**av'a·ri'cious·ly *adv.***

a·vast (ə vast') ***interj.*** ⟦< Du *houd vast*, hold fast⟧ *Naut.* stop! cease!

av·a·tar (av'ə tär') ***n.*** ⟦Sans *avatāra*, descent⟧ **1** *Hinduism* a god's coming to earth in bodily form **2** an embodiment, as of a quality in a person

a·vaunt (ə vônt') ***interj.*** ⟦< L *ab*, from + *ante*, before⟧ [Archaic] go away!

avdp *abbrev.* avoirdupois

Ave *abbrev.* Avenue

A·ve Ma·ri·a (ä'vā mə rē'ə) ⟦L⟧ *R.C.Ch.* the prayer beginning with the words "Hail, Mary"

a·venge (ə venj') ***vt.* a·venged', a·veng'ing** ⟦< L *ad*, to + *vindicare*, to claim⟧ **1** to get revenge for (an injury, etc.) **2** to take vengeance on behalf of —**a·veng'er *n.***

av·e·nue (av'ə no͞o') ***n.*** ⟦< L *ad-*, to + *venire*, come⟧ **1** a street, drive, etc., esp. when broad **2** a way of approach

a·ver (ə vur') ***vt.* a·verred', a·ver'ring** ⟦< L *ad-*, to + *verus*, true⟧ to declare to be true; affirm; assert

av·er·age (av'ər ij, av'rij) ***n.*** ⟦< OFr *avarie*, damage to ship or goods; hence, idea of shared losses⟧ **1** the result of dividing the sum of two or more quantities by the number of quantities **2** the usual kind, amount, etc. —***adj.*** **1** constituting an average **2** ordinary; normal —***vt.* -aged, -ag·ing** **1** to figure out the average of **2** to do, take, etc. on average *[to average six sales a day]* **3** to divide proportionally —**average out** to arrive at an average eventually —**on (the) average** as an average amount, rate, etc.

a·verse (ə vurs') ***adj.*** ⟦see AVERT⟧ unwilling; opposed (*to*)

a·ver·sion (ə vur'zhən) ***n.*** **1** an intense dislike **2** the object arousing this

a·vert (ə vurt') ***vt.*** ⟦< L *a-*, from + *vertere*, to turn⟧ **1** to turn (the eyes, etc.) away **2** to ward off; prevent

avg *abbrev.* average

a·vi·an (ā'vē ən) ***adj.*** ⟦< L *avis*, bird + -AN⟧ of or having to do with birds

a·vi·ar·y (ā'vē er'ē) ***n.***, *pl.* **-ar'ies** ⟦< L *avis*, bird⟧ a large cage or building for keeping many birds

a·vi·a·tion (ā'vē ā'shən) ***n.*** ⟦see prec.⟧ **1** the art or science of flying airplanes **2** the field of aircraft design, construction, etc.

a'vi·a'tor ***n.*** ⟦Fr *aviateur*⟧ an airplane pilot —**a'vi·a'trix** (-triks), *pl.* **-trix·es** or **-tri·ces'** (-tri sēz'), ***fem.n.***

av·id (av'id) ***adj.*** ⟦< L *avere*, to desire⟧ very eager or greedy —**a·vid·i·ty** (ə vid'ə tē) ***n.*** —**av'id·ly *adv.***

a·vi·on·ics (ā'vē än'iks) ***n.*** ⟦AVI(ATION) + (ELECTR)ONICS⟧ electronics as applied in aviation and astronautics

av·o·ca·do (av'ə kä'dō, ä'və-) ***n.***, *pl.* **-dos** ⟦< AmInd⟧ **1** a thick-skinned, pear-shaped tropical fruit with yellow, buttery flesh **2** the tree it grows on **3** a yellowish-green color

av·o·ca·tion (av'ə kā'shən) ***n.*** ⟦< L *a-*, away + *vocare*, to call⟧ something done in addition to one's regular work; hobby —**av'o·ca'tion·al *adj.***

a·void (ə void') ***vt.*** ⟦ME < OFr *esvuidier*, to empty⟧ **1** to keep away from; evade; shun **2** to prevent —**a·void'a·ble *adj.*** —**a·void'a·bly *adv.*** —**a·void'ance *n.***

av·oir·du·pois (av'ər də poiz') ***n.*** ⟦< OFr *aveir de peis*, goods of weight⟧ **1** a system of weights in which 16 oz. = 1 lb.: also **avoirdupois weight** **2** [Inf.] weight, esp. of a person

a·vouch (ə vouch') ***vt.*** ⟦see ADVOCATE⟧ **1** to vouch for **2** to affirm **3** to avow

a·vow (ə vou') ***vt.*** ⟦see ADVOCATE⟧ to declare or acknowledge openly —**a·vow'al *n.*** —**a·vowed' *adj.*** —**a·vow'ed·ly *adv.***

a·vun·cu·lar (ə vuŋ'kyo͞o lər) ***adj.*** ⟦< L *avunculus*⟧ of or like an uncle

aw (ô) ***interj.*** a sound of protest, sympathy, etc.

a·wait (ə wāt') ***vt., vi.*** **1** to wait for or expect **2** to be in store for

THESAURUS

brakes, starter, speedometer, odometer, spark plugs, axles, emergency brake, accelerator, shock absorbers, pistons, intake and exhaust valves, fuel pump, gas tank, control panel, steering column, instrument gauges, water pump, air conditioner, heater, radio, audiocassette player, CD player, belts, hoses, filters, drive shaft, oil pan, computer module, battery, seats, seat belts, headlights, brake lights, turn signals, sun visors.

autonomous ***a.*** self-governing, self-ruling, independent; see FREE 1.

autonomy ***n.*** liberty, independence, sovereignty; see FREEDOM 1.

autopsy ***n.*** post-mortem examination, dissection, investigation; see EXAMINATION 1.

autumn ***n.*** harvest time, Indian summer, fall; see FALL 3.

auxiliary ***a.*** **1** [Subsidiary] secondary, accessory, subservient; see SUBORDINATE. **2** [Supplementary] spare, supplemental, reserve; see EXTRA.

available ***a.*** accessible, usable, ready, convenient, serviceable, prepared, handy, on call, ready for use, open to, derivable from, obtainable, attainable, practicable, achievable, feasible, possible, procurable, realizable, reachable, within reach, at one's disposal, at one's beck and call, at hand, at one's elbow, on tap*, on deck*.—*Ant.* OCCUPIED, unavailable, unobtainable.

avalanche ***n.*** **1** [A mass moving down a slope] mudslide, snowslide, landslide, rockslide, icefall. **2** [Any overwhelming mass] flood, deluge, torrent; see PLENTY.

avenue ***n.*** street, boulevard, drive; see ROAD 1.

average ***a.*** ordinary, medium, mediocre; see COMMON 1.

average ***n.*** midpoint, standard, center, median, norm, middle, mean, typical kind, rule, average person.—*Ant.* EXTREME, highest, lowest. —**on the average** usually, commonly, ordinarily; see REGULARLY.

average ***v.*** **1** [To compute an average] split the difference, find the mean, find the arithmetic average; see BALANCE 2. **2** [To do, etc., on an average] complete, make, receive; see DO 1, EARN 2, PERFORM 1. —**average out** stabilize, balance, make even; see EQUALIZE.

avert ***v.*** turn aside, sidetrack, shove aside, shunt, turn away from, look away, look another way.

aviation ***n.*** flying, flight, aeronautics, theory of flight, aeronautical engineering, piloting, aerodynamics, airmanship.

aviator ***n.*** flier, airman, copilot; see PILOT 1.

avid ***a.*** eager, enthusiastic, desirous; see ZEALOUS.

avoid ***v.*** keep away from, flee from, abstain from, shrink from, escape from, evade, shun, elude, dodge, give someone the slip, draw back from, hold off, turn aside from, recoil from, keep at arm's length, withdraw, back out of, shirk, let alone, keep out of the way of, keep clear of, keep at a respectful distance, let well enough alone, keep in the background, keep one's distance, keep away from, refrain from, steer clear of, lay off*, pass up*, shake off.—*Ant.* FACE, meet, undertake.

avoidance ***n.*** evasion, delay, elusion, escape, retreat, restraint, abstention, nonparticipation, evasive action, temperance, flight, recoil, recession, escape mechanism, dodge.—*Ant.* MEETING, encounter, participation.

await ***v.*** wait for, anticipate, expect; see ANTICIPATE.

a·wake (ə wāk′) ***vt., vi.*** **a·woke′** or **a·waked′**, **a·waked′** or **a·wok′en**, **a·wak′ing** ⟦< OE⟧ **1** to rouse from sleep **2** to rouse from inactivity —***adj.*** **1** not asleep **2** active or alert

a·wak·en (ə wā′kən) ***vt., vi.*** to awake; wake up —**a·wak′en·ing** ***n., adj.***

a·ward (ə wôrd′) ***vt.*** ⟦< ME < Anglo-Fr *eswarder*⟧ **1** to give, as by legal decision **2** to give (a prize, etc.); grant —***n.*** **1** *Law* a decision, as by a judge **2** something awarded; prize

a·ware (ə wer′) ***adj.*** ⟦< OE *wær*, cautious⟧ knowing; realizing; conscious —**a·ware′ness** ***n.***

a·wash (ə wôsh′) ***adv., adj.*** **1** at a level where the water washes over the surface **2** flooded

a·way (ə wā′) ***adv.*** ⟦< OE *on weg*⟧ **1** from a place *[run away]* **2** *a)* in another place or direction *[away from here]* *b)* in the proper place *[put your tools away]* **3** off; aside *[turn away]* **4** far *[away behind]* **5** from one's possession *[give it away]* **6** at once *[fire away]* **7** continuously *[working away all night]* —***adj.*** **1** absent **2** at a distance *[a mile away]* —***interj.*** begone! —**away with** go, come, or take away —**do away with** get rid of or kill

awe (ô) ***n.*** ⟦< ON *agi*⟧ a mixed feeling of reverence, fear, and wonder —***vt.*** **awed**, **aw′ing** to fill with awe —**stand** (or **be**) **in awe of** to respect and fear

a·weigh (ə wā′) ***adj.*** just clear of the bottom: said of an anchor

awe·some (ô′səm) ***adj.*** **1** inspiring awe **2** [Slang] wonderful; impressive —**awe′some·ly** ***adv.*** —**awe′some·ness** ***n.***

awe-struck (ô′struk′) ***adj.*** filled with awe: also **awe′strick′en** (-strik′ən)

aw·ful (ô′fəl) ***adj.*** **1** inspiring awe **2** terrifying **3** very bad —***adv.*** [Inf.] very —**aw′ful·ness** ***n.***

aw·ful·ly (ô′fə lē, ô′flē) ***adv.*** **1** in an awful way **2** [Inf.] very

a·while (ə wīl′, -hwīl′) ***adv.*** for a short time

awk·ward (ôk′wərd) ***adj.*** ⟦< ON *ǫfugr*, turned backward⟧ **1** clumsy; bungling **2** hard to handle; unwieldy **3** uncomfortable *[an awkward pose]* **4** embarrassed or embarrassing —**awk′ward·ly** ***adv.*** —**awk′ward·ness** ***n.***

awl (ôl) ***n.*** ⟦< OE *æl*⟧ a small, pointed tool for making holes in wood, leather, etc.

awn (ôn) ***n.*** ⟦< ON *ǫgn*⟧ the bristly fibers on a head of barley, oats, etc.

awn·ing (ôn′iŋ) ***n.*** ⟦< ? MFr *auvent*, a sloping roof⟧ a structure, as of canvas, extended before a window, door, etc. as a protection from the sun or rain

a·woke (ə wōk′) ***vt., vi. pt. of*** AWAKE

a·wok′en ***vt., vi. alt. pp. of*** AWAKE

A·WOL or **a·wol** (ā′wôl′) ***adj., adv.*** *Mil.* absent without leave

a·wry (ə rī′) ***adv., adj.*** ⟦see A-[1] & WRY⟧ **1** with a twist to a side; askew **2** wrong; amiss *[our plans went awry]*

ax or **axe** (aks) ***n., pl.*** **ax′es** ⟦< OE *æx*⟧ a tool with a long handle and a head with a blade, for chopping wood, etc. —***vt.*** **axed**, **ax′ing** **1** to trim, split, etc. with an ax **2** to get rid of —**give** (or **get**) **the ax** [Inf.] to discharge (or be discharged) from a job —**have an ax to grind** [Inf.] to have an object of one's own to gain or promote

ax·el (ak′səl) ***n.*** ⟦after *Axel* Paulsen (1865-1938), Norw skater⟧ a jump in which a skater turns in the air and lands facing in the opposite direction

ax·i·al (ak′sē əl) ***adj.*** **1** of, like, or forming an axis **2** around, on, or along an axis —**ax′i·al·ly** ***adv.***

ax·i·om (ak′sē əm) ***n.*** ⟦< Gr *axios*, worthy⟧ **1** *a)* a statement universally accepted as true; maxim *b)* a self-evident truth **2** an established principle, scientific law, etc. —**ax′i·o·mat′ic** (-ə mat′ik) ***adj.***

ax·is (ak′sis) ***n., pl.*** **ax′es** (-sēz′) ⟦L⟧ **1** a real or imaginary straight line on which an object rotates **2** a central line around which the parts of a thing, system, etc. are evenly arranged —**the Axis** Germany, Italy, and Japan in WWII

ax·le (ak′səl) ***n.*** ⟦< ON *ǫxull*⟧ **1** a rod on or with which a wheel turns **2** *a)* a bar connecting two opposite wheels, as of an automobile *b)* the spindle at either end of such a bar

Ax·min·ster (aks′min′stər) ***n.*** ⟦< English town where first made⟧ varicolored, patterned carpet with a cut pile

ax·o·lotl (ak′sə lät′'l) ***n.*** ⟦< AmInd⟧ a dark salamander of Mexico and the W U.S.

ax·on (ak′sän′) ***n.*** ⟦< Gr *axōn*, axis⟧ that part of a nerve cell through which impulses travel away from the cell body

a·ya·tol·lah (ī′yə tō′lə) ***n.*** ⟦< Ar *āyat*, sign + *Allah*, Allah⟧ a leader of a Muslim sect, serving as teacher, judge, etc.

aye[1] (ā) ***adv.*** ⟦< ON *ei*⟧ [Old Poet.] always; ever: also **ay**

aye[2] (ī) ***adv.*** ⟦prob. < *I*, pers. pron.⟧ yes —***n.*** an affirmative vote or voter Also **ay**

AZ Arizona

a·za·lea (ə zāl′yə) ***n.*** ⟦< Gr *azaleos*, dry: it thrives in dry soil⟧ **1** a shrub of the heath family, with flowers of various colors **2** the flower

Az·er·bai·jan (äz′ər bī jän′, az′-) country in W Asia: formerly a republic of the U.S.S.R.: 33,430 sq. mi.; pop. 7,021,000

az·i·muth (az′ə məth) ***n.*** ⟦< Ar *al*, the + *samt*, way⟧ *Astronomy, Surveying* distance clockwise in degrees from the north point or, in the Southern Hemisphere, south point

A·zores (ā′zôrz′, ə zôrz′) group of Portuguese islands in the N Atlantic, west of Portugal

AZT (ā′zē′tē′) ***n.*** ⟦*az(ido)t(hymidine)*⟧ an antiviral drug used to treat AIDS

Az·tec (az′tek′) ***n.*** **1** a member of an Amerindian people that had an advanced civilization in Mexico before the Spanish conquest in 1519 **2** the language of this people —***adj.*** of the Aztecs, their language, etc.: also **Az′tec·an**

az·ure (azh′ər) ***adj.*** ⟦< Pers *lāzhuward*, lapis lazuli⟧ sky-blue —***n.*** sky blue or any similar blue color

THESAURUS

awake ***a.*** alert, vigilant, observant; see CONSCIOUS.

awake ***v.*** open one's eyes, become aware, gain consciousness, see the light, stir, get up, come out of sleep, rub one's eyes, rise up, stretch one's limbs, show signs of life, arise, wake up, rise and shine*.—*Ant.* SLEEP, doze off, slumber.

awaken ***v.*** awake, call, play reveille, arouse, rouse, wake up, excite, stir up, stimulate.

awakening ***n.*** rebirth, arousal, renewal; see REVIVAL 1.

award ***n.*** citation, honor, scholarship; see PRIZE.

award ***v.*** grant, confer, bestow; see GIVE 1.

aware ***a.*** knowledgeable, cognizant, informed; see CONSCIOUS.

awareness ***n.*** sensibility, mindfulness, discernment, cognizance, consciousness, alertness, keenness, attentiveness, recognition, comprehension, perception, apprehension, appreciation, experience.

away ***a.*** absent, not present, distant, at a distance, not here, far afield, at arm's length, remote, out of, far off, apart, beyond, off.—*Ant.* HERE, present, at hand. —**do away with** **1** [To eliminate] get rid of, cancel, take away; see ELIMINATE, REMOVE 1. **2** [To kill] slay, execute, put to death; see KILL 1.

awe ***n.*** wonder, fright, admiration; see REVERENCE.

awesome ***a.*** striking, moving, impressive; see GRAND.

awful ***a.*** **1** [Frightful] horrible, terrible, dreadful; see FRIGHTFUL. **2** [Shocking] appalling, disgusting, repulsive; see OFFENSIVE 2. **3** [*Very great] gigantic, colossal, stupendous; see BIG 1.

awfully ***a.*** **1** [Badly] poorly, imperfectly, clumsily; see BADLY 1. **2** [*Very] very much, indeed, truly; see VERY.

awhile ***a.*** for a moment, briefly, momentarily, for a short time, for some time, not for long, temporarily, for a little while, for a spell*.—*Ant.* FOREVER, permanently, for a long time.

awkward ***a.*** clumsy, bungling, ungraceful, gawky, floundering, stumbling, ungainly, unwieldy, unable, fumbling, bumbling, lacking dexterity, without skill, unskilled, inept, unfit, inexperienced, shuffling, uncouth, incompetent, rusty, green, amateurish, butterfingered*, all thumbs, with two left feet.—*Ant.* ABLE, dexterous, smooth.

awkwardly ***a.*** clumsily, unskillfully, lumberingly, ineptly, ponderously, uncouthly, gracelessly, inelegantly, incompetently, artlessly, amateurishly, ungracefully, stiffly, woodenly, rigidly, with difficulty, with embarrassment.—*Ant.* GRACEFULLY, skillfully, adroitly.

awkwardness ***n.*** ineptitude, inability, incompetence, ineptness, artlessness, crudeness, heavy-handedness, ungainliness, oafishness, ungracefulness, gracelessness.—*Ant.* ABILITY, grace, competence.

awning ***n.*** canvas covering, canopy, sunshade; see COVER 1.

ax ***n.*** hatchet, adz, tomahawk, battleax, poleax, pickax, mattock, cleaver, broadax, hand ax. —**have an ax to grind*** want something, have a purpose, complain about something; see WANT 1.

axis ***n.*** shaft, pivot, axle, pole, stem, support, dividing line, spindle, arbor, line of symmetry, line of rotation, line of revolution.

axle ***n.*** shaft, spindle, pin; see AXIS.

B

b[1] or **B** (bē) ***n.**, pl.* **b's, B's** the second letter of the English alphabet

b[2] *abbrev.* born

B[1] (bē) ***n.*** **1** a blood type **2** a grade indicating above-average but not outstanding work **3** *Music* the seventh tone in the scale of C major —***adj.*** inferior to the best *[a B movie]*

B[2] *abbrev.* **1** bachelor **2** *Baseball a)* base *b)* baseman **3** *Music* bass Also **b**

B[3] *Chem. symbol for* boron

Ba *Chem. symbol for* barium

BA or **B.A.** *abbrev.* Bachelor of Arts

baa (bä) ***vi., n.*** ⟦echoic⟧ bleat

Ba·al (bā′əl) ***n.*** ⟦< Heb⟧ an ancient fertility god

bab·ble (bab′əl) ***vi.* -bled, -bling** ⟦echoic⟧ **1** to talk like a small child; prattle **2** to talk foolishly or too much **3** to murmur, as a brook does when flowing over stones —***vt.*** to say incoherently or foolishly —***n.*** **1** incoherent vocal sounds **2** foolish talk **3** a murmuring sound —**bab′bler *n.***

babe (bāb) ***n.*** **1** a baby **2** a naive person: also **babe in the woods** **3** [Slang] a girl or young woman, esp. an attractive one

Ba·bel (bā′bəl, bab′əl) ***n.*** **1** *Bible* a city thwarted in building a tower to heaven when God created a confusion of tongues **2** [*also* **b-**] a confusion of voices, sounds, etc. or the scene of this

ba·boon (ba bo͞on′, bə-) ***n.*** ⟦< OFr *babuin,* ape, fool⟧ a large, fierce, dog-faced, short-tailed monkey of Africa and Arabia

ba·bush·ka (bə bo͝osh′kə) ***n.*** ⟦Russ, grandmother⟧ a woman's scarf worn on the head and tied under the chin

ba·by (bā′bē) ***n.**, pl.* **-bies** ⟦ME *babi*⟧ **1** a very young child; infant **2** one who acts like an infant **3** a very young animal **4** the youngest or smallest in a group **5** [Slang] darling; honey **6** [Slang] any person or thing —***adj.*** **1** of or for an infant **2** very young **3** small of its kind **4** childish —***vt.* -bied, -by·ing** to pamper; coddle —**ba′by·hood′ *n.*** —**ba′by·ish *adj.***

baby beef meat from a prime heifer or steer that is one to two years old

baby boom′er a person born during the birthrate increase (the **baby boom**) after 1945

baby carriage a small vehicle, pushed by hand, for wheeling a baby about: also **baby buggy**

baby grand a small grand piano

Bab·y·lon (bab′ə län′) capital of Babylonia: noted for luxury and wickedness

Bab·y·lo·ni·a (bab′ə lō′nē ə) ancient empire in SW Asia —**Bab′y·lo′ni·an *adj., n.***

baby's breath a plant with small, delicate, white or pink flowers

baby sitter a person hired to take care of a child or children, as when the parents are away for the evening —**ba′by-sit′, -sat′, -sit′ting, *vi., vt.***

baby talk playful talk for amusing a baby or in imitating a baby

bac·ca·lau·re·ate (bak′ə lôr′ē it) ***n.*** ⟦< ML *baccalaris,* young nobleman seeking knighthood⟧ **1** the degree of Bachelor of Arts, Bachelor of Science, etc. **2** a commencement address

bac·cha·nal (bak′ə nal′) ***n.*** a drunken orgy —**bac′cha·na′li·an** (-nā′lē ən) ***adj., n.***

Bac·chus (bak′əs) ***n.*** the Greek and Roman god of wine and revelry

Bach (bäkh), **Jo·hann Se·bas·ti·an** (yō′hän′ zā bäs′tē än′) 1685-1750; Ger. organist & composer

bach·e·lor (bach′ə lər, bach′lər) ***n.*** ⟦< ML *baccalaris:* see BACCALAUREATE⟧ an unmarried man —**bach′e·lor·hood′ *n.***

Bachelor of Arts (or **Science,** etc.) **1** a degree given by a college or university to one who has completed a four-year course in the humanities (or in science, etc.): also **bachelor's degree** **2** one who holds this degree

bachelor's button any of several plants with white, pink, or blue flowers, as the cornflower

ba·cil·lus (bə sil′əs) ***n.**, pl.* **-cil′li′** (-ī′) ⟦< L *bacillum,* little stick⟧ **1** any of a genus of rod-shaped bacteria **2** loosely, any of the bacteria —**bac·il·lar·y** (bas′ə ler′ē, bə sil′ər ē) ***adj.***

back (bak) ***n.*** ⟦< OE *baec*⟧ **1** the rear (or, in some animals, the top) part of the body from the nape of the neck to the end of the spine **2** the backbone **3** a part that supports or fits the back **4** the rear part or reverse of anything **5** *Sports* a player or position behind the front line —***adj.*** **1** at the rear **2** remote **3** of or for the past *[back pay]* **4** backward —***adv.*** **1** at, to, or toward the rear **2** to or toward a former condition, time, etc. **3** in reserve or concealment **4** in return or requital *[pay him back]* —***vt.*** **1** to move backward **2** to support **3** to bet on **4** to provide or be a back for —***vi.*** to go backward —**back and forth** backward and forward —**back down** to withdraw from a position or claim —**(in) back of** behind —**back off** **1** to move back **2** [Inf.] BACK DOWN —**back out (of)** **1** to withdraw from an enterprise **2** to evade keeping a promise, etc. —**back up** **1** to support **2** to move backward: also **back away** **3** to accumulate because of restricted movement *[traffic backed up]* **4** *Comput.* to make a standby copy of (data, etc.) —**go back on** [Inf.] **1** to be disloyal to; betray **2** to fail to keep (one's word, etc.) —**turn one's back on** **1** to turn away from, as in contempt **2** to abandon

back′ache′ *n.* an ache or pain in the back

back′bite′ *vt., vi.* -bit′, -bit′ten or **-bit′, -bit′ing** to slander (someone absent) —**back′bit′er *n.***

back′board′ *n.* **1** a board at or forming the back of something **2** *Basketball* the board behind the basket

back′bone′ *n.* **1** the spine **2** a main support **3** willpower, courage, etc.

back′break′ing *adj.* very tiring

back′coun′try *n.* a remote, thinly populated area

THESAURUS

babble *n.* jabber, chatter, twaddle; see NONSENSE 1.

babble *v.* talk incoherently, talk foolishly, rant, rave, gush, run on, go on*, gossip, murmur, chat, chatter, prattle, tattle, jabber, blurt, run off at the mouth*, talk off the top of one's head*, rattle on, gab*, cackle, blab, sputter, gibber, blabber*, clatter; see also TALK 1.

baby *a.* infantile, babyish, juvenile; see CHILDISH.

baby *n.* suckling, babe, child, toddler, tot, brat, young one, little one, papoose*, bambino, chick, kid*, cherub, little shaver*, bundle of joy*, another mouth to feed*.—*Ant.* MAN, adolescent, grown-up.

baby *v.* pamper, coddle, pet, spoil, fondle, caress, nurse, cherish, foster, cuddle, make much of, humor, indulge; see also PAMPER.

baby-sit *v.* watch, care for, sit; see GUARD.

bachelor *n.* unmarried man, single man, stag, free man*, single, lone wolf*.—*Ant.* HUSBAND, married man, benedict.

back *a.* rear, after, backward, hindmost, behind, astern, hind, rearward, aft, to the rear, in the rear, dorsal, caudal, following, posterior, terminal, in the wake, in the background, final.—*Ant.* FRONT, forward, head.

back *n.* **1** [The rear part or side] hind part, posterior, stern, poop, aft, tailpiece, tail, back end.—*Ant.* FRONT, fore part, fore. **2** [The rear of the torso] posterior, backside, spinal area; see SPINE. **3** [One who plays behind the line, especially in football] linebacker, fullback, halfback, quarterback, cornerback, safety, running back, tailback, wingback, slot back, blocking back. —**behind someone's back** in secret, slyly, hidden; see SECRETIVE. —**(flat) on one's back** ill, bedridden, helpless; see SICK. —**get off someone's back*** let alone, ignore, stop nagging; see NEGLECT 1. —**get one's back up*** become angry, be stubborn, lose one's temper; see RAGE 1. —**go back on** betray, reject, turn against; see DECEIVE. —**in back of** at the rear, behind, coming after; see FOLLOWING. —**turn one's back on** reject, desert, fail; see ABANDON 1. —**with one's back to the wall** desperate, cornered, stopped; see HOPELESS.

back *v.* **1** [To push backward] drive back, repel, repulse; see PUSH 2. **2** [To further] uphold, stand behind, encourage; see SUPPORT 2. **3** [To equip with a back] stiffen, reinforce, line; see LINE 1, STRENGTHEN. —**back down** withdraw, recoil, back out; see RETREAT. —**back off** fall back, withdraw, retire; see RETREAT. —**back out of** withdraw, shrink from, escape; see RETREAT. —**back up** **1** [To move backward] fall back, withdraw, reverse; see RETREAT. **2** [To support] aid, assist, help; see SUPPORT 2.

back and forth *a.* zigzag, in and out, from side to side; see TO AND FRO.

backbone *n.* **1** [Line of bones in the back supporting the body] spinal column, vertebrae, chine; see SPINE 2. **2** [Determination] firmness, fortitude, resolution; see DETERMINATION.

back'drop' ***n.*** **1** a curtain, often scenic, at the back of a stage **2** background or setting
back'er ***n.*** **1** a patron; sponsor **2** one who bets on a contestant
back'field' ***n.*** *Football* the players behind the line
back'fire' ***n.*** **1** the burning out of a small area, as in a forest, to check the spread of a big fire **2** premature ignition or an explosion of gases in an internal-combustion engine **3** reverse explosion in a gun —***vi.*** **-fired', -fir'ing** **1** to explode as a backfire **2** to go awry or boomerang
back'gam'mon (-gam'ən) ***n.*** ⟦BACK + ME *gammen*, game⟧ a game for two, with dice governing moves of pieces on a special board
back'ground' ***n.*** **1** the distant part of a scene **2** surroundings, sounds, etc. behind or subordinate to something **3** one's training and experience **4** events leading up to something
back'ground'er ***n.*** a press briefing at which background information is provided
back'hand' ***n.*** **1** handwriting that slants up to the left **2** a backhand catch, stroke, etc. —***adj.*** **1** done with the back of the hand; specif., done with the back of the hand turned inward, as for a baseball catch, or forward, as for a tennis stroke, and with the arm across the body **2** written in backhand —***adv.*** with a backhand —***vt.*** to hit, catch, swing, etc. backhand
back'hand'ed ***adj.*** **1** BACKHAND **2** indirect or sarcastic —***adv.*** with a backhand
back'hoe' (-hō') ***n.*** an excavating vehicle with a hinged bucket at the end of a long arm
back'ing ***n.*** **1** something forming a back for support **2** support given to a person or cause **3** supporters; backers
back'lash' ***n.*** sharp reaction or recoil
back'log' ***n.*** an accumulation or reserve —***vi., vt.*** **-logged', -log'ging** to accumulate as a backlog
back order an order not yet filled
back'pack' ***n.*** a knapsack, specif. one attached to a frame and worn as by hikers —***vi., vt.*** to hike with, or carry in, a backpack —**back'pack'er** ***n.***
back'ped'al ***vi.*** **-ped'aled** or **-ped'alled, -ped'al·ing** or **-ped'al·ling** **1** to pedal backward, as in braking a bicycle **2** to move backward; retreat **3** to retract an earlier opinion
back'rest' ***n.*** a support for or at the back
back'-scratch'ing ***n.*** [Inf.] a reciprocal exchange of favors, etc.
back'side' ***n.*** **1** the back part **2** the rump
back'slap'per (-slap'ər) ***n.*** [Inf.] an effusively friendly person
back'slash' ***n.*** a short diagonal line (\): a character found esp. on computer keyboards
back'slide' ***vi.*** **-slid', -slid'** or **-slid'den, -slid'ing** to regress in morals, etc. —**back'slid'er** ***n.***
back'space' ***vi.*** **-spaced', -spac'ing** to move a typewriter carriage, cursor, etc. one or more spaces back along the line
back'spin' ***n.*** a backward spin given to a ball, etc., making it reverse direction upon hitting a surface
back'splash' ***n.*** a washable surface behind a sink, etc. to protect a wall from splashes
back'stage' ***adv., adj.*** behind and off the stage, as in the wings or dressing rooms
back'stairs' ***adj.*** involving intrigue or scandal; secret: also **back'stair'**
back'stop' ***n.*** a fence, screen, etc. to keep balls from going too far, as behind the catcher in baseball
back'stretch' ***n.*** the part of a racetrack opposite the homestretch
back'stroke' ***n.*** a swimming stroke made while lying face upward
back'swing' ***n.*** that part of a player's swing in which the golf club, tennis racket, etc. is swung backward before being swung forward
back talk [Inf.] insolent replies
back'-to-back' ***adj.*** [Inf.] one right after another
back'track' ***vi.*** **1** to return by the same path **2** to retreat or recant
back'up' or **back'-up'** ***adj.*** **1** standing by as an alternate or auxiliary **2** supporting —***n.*** a backing up; specif., *a)* an accumulation *b)* a support or help
back'ward ***adv.*** **1** toward the back **2** with the back foremost **3** in reverse order **4** in a way opposite to usual **5** into the past Also **back'wards** —***adj.*** **1** turned toward the rear or in the opposite way **2** shy **3** slow or retarded —**back'ward·ness** ***n.***
back'wash' ***n.*** **1** water or air moved backward, as by a ship, propeller, etc. **2** a reaction caused by some event
back'wa'ter ***n.*** **1** water moved or held back by a dam, tide, etc. **2** stagnant water in an inlet, etc. **3** a backward place or condition
back'woods' ***pl.n.*** [*occas. with sing. v.*] **1** heavily wooded areas far from centers of population **2** any remote, thinly populated area —***adj.*** of or like the backwoods —**back'woods'man** (-mən), *pl.* **-men** (-mən), ***n.***
ba·con (bā'kən) ***n.*** ⟦< OS *baco*, side of bacon⟧ salted and smoked meat from the back or sides of a hog
Ba·con (bā'kən), **Fran·cis** (fran'sis) 1561-1626; Eng. philosopher & writer
bac·te·ri·a (bak tir'ē ə) ***pl.n.***, *sing.* **-ri·um** (-əm) or **-ri·a** ⟦< Gr *baktērion*, small staff⟧ microorganisms which have no chlorophyll and multiply by simple division: some bacteria cause diseases, but others are necessary for fermentation, etc. —**bac·te'ri·al** ***adj.***
bac·te'ri·cide' (-tir'ə sīd') ***n.*** an agent that destroys bacteria —**bac·te'ri·cid'al** ***adj.***
bac·te'ri·ol'o·gy (-tir'ē äl'ə jē) ***n.*** the science that deals with bacteria —**bac·te'ri·o·log'i·cal** (-ə läj'ə kəl) ***adj.*** —**bac·te'ri·ol'o·gist** ***n.***
bad[1] (bad) ***adj.*** **worse, worst** ⟦ME⟧ **1** not good; not as it should be **2** inadequate or unfit **3** unfavorable *[bad news]* **4** rotten or spoiled **5** incorrect or faulty **6** *a)* wicked; immoral *b)* misbehaving; mischievous **7** harm-

THESAURUS

backed ***a.*** **1** [Propelled backward] driven back, shoved, repelled, repulsed, pushed, retracted.—*Ant.* AHEAD, moved forward, impelled. **2** [Supported] upheld, encouraged, approved, heartened, aided, assisted, advanced, promoted, sustained, fostered, favored, championed, advocated, supplied, maintained, asserted, established, helped, bolstered, propped, furthered, seconded, prompted, served, pushed, boosted, primed.—*Ant.* OPPOSED, discouraged, obstructed. **3** [Supplied with a back, or backing] stiffened, built up, strengthened; see REINFORCED.

backer ***n.*** benefactor, supporter, follower; see PATRON.

backfire ***v.*** **1** [To explode] burst, erupt, detonate; see EXPLODE. **2** [To go awry] boomerang, ricochet, have an unwanted result; see FAIL 1.

background ***n.*** **1** [Setting] backdrop, framework, environment; see SETTING. **2** [The total of one's experiences] education, qualifications, preparation, grounding, rearing, credentials, capacities, accomplishments, achievements, attainments, deeds, actions; see also EXPERIENCE, KNOWLEDGE 1. **—in the background** retiring, unseen, out of sight; see OBSCURE 3, UNNOTICED, WITHDRAWN.

backhanded ***a.*** obscure, sarcastic, equivocal; see INDIRECT.

backing ***n.*** **1** [Assistance] subsidy, encouragement, aid; see HELP 1. **2** [Support] reinforcement, buttress, lining; see SUPPORT 2.

backlash ***n.*** response, repercussion, resentment; see REACTION.

backlog ***n.*** reserve, supply, stock; see RESERVE 1.

backslide ***v.*** revert, break faith, fall from grace; see RELAPSE.

backstop ***n.*** screen, net, barrier; see FENCE.

backward ***a.*** **1** [To the rear] rearward, astern, behind, retrograde, regressive.—*Ant.* FORWARD, progressive, onward. **2** [Reversed] turned around, counterclockwise, inverted; see REVERSED. **3** [Behind in development] underdeveloped, slow, slow to develop, retarded, delayed, arrested, checked, late, undeveloped, underprivileged; see also DULL 3. **—bend over backward** try hard to please, conciliate, be fair; see TRY 1.

bacon ***n.*** flitch, Canadian bacon, salt pork; see MEAT. **—bring home the bacon*** provide for, be the breadwinner, achieve; see EARN 2, PROVIDE 1, SUCCEED 1, SUPPORT 3.

bacteria ***n.*** bacilli, microbes, microscopic organisms; see GERM.

bad[1] ***a.*** **1** [Wicked] evil, sinful, immoral, wrong, corrupt, base, foul, gross, profane, naughty, degenerate, decadent, depraved, heartless, degraded, debauched, indecent, mean, scandalous, nasty, vicious, fiendish, devilish, criminal, murderous, sinister, monstrous, dangerous, vile, rotten*, dirty, crooked.—*Ant.* GOOD, honest, pure. **2** [Spoiled] rancid, decayed, putrid; see ROTTEN 1, 2. **3** [Below standard] defective, inferior, imperfect; see POOR 2. **4** [In poor health] ill, diseased, ailing; see SICK. **5** [Injurious] hurtful, damaging, detrimental; see HARMFUL. **6** [*Very good] stylish, effective, sharp*; see FASHIONABLE, EXCELLENT. **—go bad** degenerate, deteriorate, rot; see SPOIL. **—not bad*** all right, pretty good, passable; see FAIR 2.

ful **8** severe **9** ill **10** sorry; distressed [he feels *bad* about it] **11** offensive —***adv.*** [Inf.] badly —***n.*** anything bad —**not bad** [Inf.] fairly good —**bad'ness** ***n.***

bad[2] (bad) ***vt.***, ***vi.*** *archaic pt. of* BID

bad blood (mutual) ill will

bade (bad) ***vt.***, ***vi.*** *alt. pt. of* BID

bad egg [Slang] a mean or dishonest person: also **bad actor**, **bad apple**, or **bad lot**

bad faith insincerity; dishonesty

badge (baj) ***n.*** ⟦ME *bage*⟧ **1** an emblem worn to show rank, membership, etc. **2** any distinctive sign, etc.

badg·er (baj'ər) ***n.*** ⟦< ?⟧ **1** a burrowing animal with a broad back and thick, short legs **2** its fur —***vt.*** to nag or torment

bad·i·nage (bad''n äzh') ***n.*** ⟦Fr⟧ playful talk; banter

bad·lands (bad'landz') ***pl.n.*** **1** an area of barren land with dry soil and soft rocks eroded into odd shapes **2** [**B-**] any of several such W U.S. areas

bad'ly ***adv.*** **worse**, **worst** **1** in a bad manner **2** [Inf.] very much; greatly

bad'man' (-man') ***n.***, *pl.* **-men'** (-men') a cattle thief or desperado of the old West

bad·min·ton (bad'mint''n) ***n.*** ⟦after *Badminton,* Eng estate⟧ a game in which a shuttlecock is batted back and forth with rackets across a net

bad'-mouth' ***vt.*** [Slang] to find fault with; disparage

bad'-tem'pered ***adj.*** irritable

Bae·de·ker (bā'də kər) ***n.*** **1** any of a series of guidebooks to foreign countries, first published in Germany **2** loosely, any guidebook

baf·fle (baf'əl) ***vt.*** **-fled**, **-fling** ⟦< ?⟧ **1** to perplex completely; bewilder **2** to impede; check —***n.*** a wall or screen to deflect air, sound, etc. —**baf'fle·ment** ***n.*** —**baf'fler** ***n.*** —**baf'fling** ***adj.***

bag (bag) ***n.*** ⟦< ON *baggi*⟧ **1** a nonrigid container of paper, plastic, etc., with an open top **2** a satchel; suitcase, etc. **3** a purse **4** game taken in hunting **5** a baglike shape or part **6** a bagful **7** [Slang] an unattractive woman **8** [Slang] one's special interest **9** *Baseball* a base —***vt.*** **bagged**, **bag'ging** **1** to put into a bag **2** to capture **3** to kill in hunting **4** [Slang] to obtain —***vi.*** **1** to swell; bulge **2** to hang loosely —**in the bag** [Slang] having its success assured

bag·a·telle (bag'ə tel') ***n.*** ⟦Fr < L *baca*, berry⟧ a trifle

ba·gel (bā'gəl) ***n.*** ⟦Yiddish⟧ a chewy bread roll shaped like a small doughnut

bag'ful' ***n.***, *pl.* **-fuls'** as much as a bag will hold

bag·gage (bag'ij) ***n.*** ⟦< ML *bagga*, chest, bag⟧ **1** the bags, etc. of a traveler; luggage **2** burdensome beliefs, practices, etc.

bag·gie (bag'ē) ***n.*** ⟦< *Baggies*, a trademark for such bags⟧ a small, clear plastic bag for storing food, etc.

bag·gy (bag'ē) ***adj.*** **-gi·er**, **-gi·est** puffed out or hanging loosely —**bag'gi·ly** ***adv.*** —**bag'gi·ness** ***n.***

Bagh·dad (bag'dad) capital of Iraq: pop. 1,900,000: also sp. **Bag·dad**

bag lady [Slang] a homeless, poor woman who wanders city streets carrying her belongings in shopping bags

bag'pipe' ***n.*** [*often pl.*] a wind instrument, now chiefly Scottish, played by forcing air from a bag into reed pipes and fingering the stops

bah (bä, ba) ***interj.*** used to express contempt, scorn, or disgust

Ba·ha·mas (bə hä'məz) country on a group of islands (**Bahama Islands**) in the West Indies: 5,353 sq. mi.; pop. 264,000

Bah·rain (bä rān') country on a group of islands in the Persian Gulf: 266 sq. mi.; pop. 518,000: also sp. **Bah·rein**

bail[1] (bāl) ***n.*** ⟦< L *bajulare,* bear a burden⟧ **1** money deposited with the court to get a prisoner temporarily released **2** such a release —***vt.*** **1** to have (a prisoner) set free by giving bail **2** to help out of financial or other difficulty Often with *out* —**bail'a·ble** ***adj.***

bail[2] (bāl) ***n.*** ⟦ME *baille*, bucket⟧ a bucket for dipping up water from a boat —***vi.***, ***vt.*** to dip out (water) from (a boat): usually with *out* —**bail out** **1** to parachute from an aircraft **2** [Inf.] to flee a difficult situation

bail[3] (bāl) ***n.*** ⟦ME *beil*⟧ a hoop-shaped handle for a bucket, etc.

bail·iff (bā'lif) ***n.*** ⟦ME *bailif*⟧ **1** a deputy sheriff **2** a court officer who guards the jurors, keeps order in the court, etc. **3** in England, a district official **4** [Chiefly Brit.] a steward of an estate

bail·i·wick (bā'lə wik') ***n.*** ⟦ME < *baili,* bailiff + *wik*, village⟧ **1** a bailiff's district **2** one's particular area of activity, authority, interest, etc.

bails·man (bālz'mən) ***n.***, *pl.* **-men** (-mən) a person who gives bail for another

bairn (bern) ***n.*** [Scot.] a child

bait (bāt) ***vt.*** ⟦< ON *beita*⟧ **1** to set dogs on for sport [to *bait* bears] **2** to torment or harass, esp. by verbal attacks **3** to goad or provoke **4** to put food on (a hook or trap) as a lure for game **5** to lure; entice; tempt —***n.*** **1** food, etc. put on a hook or trap as a lure **2** anything used as a lure

bait'-and-switch' ***adj.*** of or using an unethical sales technique in which a seller lures customers by advertising an often nonexistent bargain item and then tries to switch their attention to more expensive items

baize (bāz) ***n.*** ⟦< L *badius,* brown⟧ a coarse, feltlike woolen cloth

Ba·ja Ca·li·for·nia (bä'hä kä'lē fôr'nyä) state of NW Mexico, south of California: 27,071 sq. mi.; pop. 1,661,000

Baja California Sur state of NW Mexico, south of Baja California: 28,447 sq. mi.; pop. 318,000

bake (bāk) ***vt.*** **baked**, **bak'ing** ⟦< OE *bacan*⟧ **1** to cook (food) by dry heat, esp. in an oven **2** to dry and harden (pottery, etc.) by heat; fire —***vi.*** **1** to bake bread, etc. **2** to become baked —***n.*** **1** a baking **2** a social affair at which baked food is served

baked beans navy beans baked with salt pork, molasses or brown sugar, etc.

bak·er (bā'kər) ***n.*** one whose work or business is baking bread, etc.

baker's dozen thirteen

Bak·ers·field (bā'kərz fēld') city in SC California: pop. 175,000

bak'er·y ***n.*** **1** *pl.* **-er·ies** a place where bread, etc. is baked or sold **2** [Dial.] baked goods

baking powder a leavening agent containing baking soda and an acid-forming substance

baking soda sodium bicarbonate, used as a leavening agent and as an antacid

THESAURUS

badge ***n.*** **1** [Outward evidence] marker, symbol, identification; see EMBLEM. **2** [A device worn as evidence] pin, emblem, seal, medal, insignia, shield, epaulet, ribbon, medallion, marker, feather, rosette, clasp, button, signet, crest, star, chevron, stripe.

badger ***v.*** harass, annoy, pester; see BOTHER 2.

badly ***a.*** **1** [In an ineffectual or incompetent manner] wrongly, imperfectly, ineffectively, inefficiently, poorly, unsatisfactorily, crudely, boorishly, unskillfully, defectively, weakly, haphazardly, clumsily, carelessly, negligently, incompetently, stupidly, blunderingly, mistakenly, awkwardly, faultily, shiftlessly, abominably, awfully, terribly*.—*Ant.* CAREFULLY, competently, adequately. **2** [*To a marked degree] severely, seriously, greatly; see VERY. —**go badly** miscarry, fall short, dissatisfy; see DISAPPOINT, FAIL 1.

baffle ***v.*** perplex, puzzle, bewilder; see CONFUSE.

bag ***n.*** purse, sack, pouch, grip, handbag, tote bag, knapsack, backpack, carpetbag, kit, satchel, saddlebag, gunny sack, suitcase, briefcase, attaché case, duffel bag, pack, container, feedbag, quiver, packet, pocketbook, holster, vanity bag, valise, case, wallet, haversack, holdall, carryall. —**in the bag*** absolute, sure, definite; see CERTAIN 2. —**left holding the bag*** framed*, tricked, deserted; see ABANDONED.

bag ***v.*** trap, seize, get; see CATCH 1.

baggage ***n.*** luggage, gear, bags, trunks, valises, suitcases, overnight cases, parcels, paraphernalia, effects, equipage, equipment, packs, things.

baggy ***a.*** slack, unshapely, bulging; see LOOSE 1.

bail[1] ***n.*** bond, surety, recognizance, pledge, warrant, guaranty, collateral.

bail[2] ***v.*** **1** [To dip] scoop, spoon out, dredge; see DIP 2. **2** [To empty] clear, drain, deplete; see EMPTY.

bail out ***v.*** **1** [Secure the release of] give security for, post bail for, assure, underwrite, guarantee, warrant, insure, deliver, go bail for, spring*. **2** [Run away] desert, blow*, retreat; see ESCAPE.

bait ***n.*** lure, inducement, bribe; see ATTRACTION.

bait ***v.*** **1** [To torment] anger, nag, tease; see BOTHER 2. **2** [To lure] entice, attract, draw; see FASCINATE.

bake ***v.*** roast, toast, warm; see COOK.

baked ***a.*** parched, scorched, dried, toasted, warmed, heated, cooked, grilled, burned, charred, roasted, incinerated.

baker ***n.*** pastry chef, chef, *pâtissier* (French); see COOK.

bakery ***n.*** bake shop, pastry shop, confectionery, bread store, patisserie, cake shop.

bal·a·lai·ka (bal′ə lī′kə) ***n.*** ⟦Russ⟧ a Russian stringed instrument somewhat like a guitar

bal·ance (bal′əns) ***n.*** ⟦< LL *bilanx*, having two scales⟧ **1** an instrument for weighing, esp. one with two matched hanging scales **2** a state of equilibrium in weight, value, etc. **3** bodily equilibrium **4** mental or emotional stability **5** harmonious proportion of elements in a design, etc. **6** a weight, value, etc. that counteracts another **7** equality of debits and credits, or the difference between them **8** a remainder —***vt.*** **-anced, -anc·ing 1** to weigh in or as in a balance **2** to compare as to relative value, etc. **3** to counteract; offset **4** to bring into proportion, harmony, etc. **5** to make or be equal to in weight, value, etc. **6** to find the difference between, or to equalize, the debits and credits of (an account) —***vi.*** **1** to be in equilibrium **2** to be equal in weight, value, etc. **3** to have the credits and debits equal —**in the balance** not yet settled

balance sheet a statement showing the financial status of a business

bal·co·ny (bal′kə nē) ***n.***, *pl.* **-nies** ⟦< It *balcone*⟧ **1** a platform projecting from an upper story and enclosed by a railing **2** an upper floor of seats in a theater, etc., often projecting over the main floor

bald (bôld) ***adj.*** ⟦< ME⟧ **1** having a head with white fur, etc. growing on it **2** lacking hair on the head **3** not covered by natural growth **4** having the tread worn off **5** plain or blunt *[bald* truth*]* —**bald′ly *adv.*** —**bald′ness *n.***

bald eagle a large eagle of North America, with a white-feathered head

bal·der·dash (bôl′dər dash′) ***n.*** ⟦orig. (17th c.), an odd mixture⟧ nonsense

bald·faced (bôld′fāst′) ***adj.*** brazen; shameless *[a bald-faced* lie*]*

bald′ing *adj.* becoming bald

bal·dric (bôl′drik′) ***n.*** ⟦ult. < L *balteus*, belt⟧ a belt worn over one shoulder to support a sword, etc.

bale (bāl) ***n.*** ⟦< OHG *balla*, ball⟧ a large bundle, esp. a standardized quantity of goods, as raw cotton, compressed and bound —***vt.*** **baled, bal′ing** to make into bales —**bal′er *n.***

ba·leen (bə lēn′) ***n.*** ⟦ult. < Gr *phallaina*, whale⟧ the horny, elastic material hanging from the upper jaw of some whales (**baleen whales**)

bale·ful (bāl′fəl) ***adj.*** ⟦< OE *bealu*, evil⟧ deadly; harmful; ominous

Ba·li (bä′lē, bal′ē) island of Indonesia —**Ba′li·nese′**, *pl.* **-nese′**, ***adj.***, ***n.***

balk (bôk) ***n.*** ⟦OE *balca*, ridge⟧ **1** an obstruction, hindrance, etc. **2** *Baseball* an illegal motion by the pitcher entitling base runners to advance one base —***vt.*** to obstruct; foil —***vi.*** **1** to stop and refuse to move or act **2** to hesitate or recoil (*at*)

Balkan Peninsula peninsula in SE Europe, east of Italy

Bal·kans (bôl′kənz) countries of Yugoslavia, Slovenia, Croatia, Bosnia and Herzegovina, Macedonia, Romania, Bulgaria, Albania, Greece, & European Turkey, in SE Europe —**Bal′kan *adj.***

balk·y (bôk′ē) ***adj.*** **-i·er, -i·est** stubbornly resisting

ball[1] (bôl) ***n.*** ⟦ME *bal*⟧ **1** any round object; sphere; globe **2** *a)* a round or egg-shaped object used in various games *b)* any of several such games, esp. baseball **3** a throw or pitch of a ball *[a fast ball]* **4** a missile for a cannon, rifle, etc. **5** a rounded part of the body **6** *Baseball* a pitched ball that is not hit and is not a strike —***vi.***, ***vt.*** to form into a ball —**ball up** [Slang] to muddle or confuse —**be on the ball** [Slang] to be alert; be efficient

ball[2] (bôl) ***n.*** ⟦< Fr < Gr *ballizein*, to dance⟧ **1** a formal social dance **2** [Slang] a good time

bal·lad (bal′əd) ***n.*** ⟦< OFr *ballade*, dancing song⟧ **1** a sentimental song with the same melody for each stanza **2** a narrative song or poem, usually anonymous, with simple words, short stanzas, and a refrain **3** a popular love song —**bal′lad·eer′ *n.*** —**bal′lad·ry *n.***

ball′-and-sock′et joint a joint, as of the hip, formed by a ball in a socket

bal·last (bal′əst) ***n.*** ⟦< MDu *bal*, bad⟧ **1** anything heavy carried in a ship or vehicle to give stability **2** crushed rock or gravel, used in railroad beds, etc. —***vt.*** to furnish with ballast

ball bearing 1 a bearing in which the parts turn on freely rolling metal balls **2** one of these balls

bal·le·ri·na (bal′ə rē′nə) ***n.*** ⟦It⟧ a girl or woman ballet dancer

bal·let (ba lā′, bal′ā) ***n.*** ⟦Fr⟧ **1** an artistic dance form of graceful, precise gestures and movements **2** a play, etc. performed by ballet dancers, or the music for this **3** ballet dancers

ball′game′ *n.* **1** a game played with a ball **2** [Inf.] a set of circumstances *[a different ballgame]*

ballistic missile a long-range guided missile designed to fall free as it approaches its target

bal·lis·tics (bə lis′tiks) ***n.*** the science dealing with the motion and impact of projectiles —**bal·lis′tic *adj.***

ball joint a ball-and-socket joint used in automotive vehicles to connect the tie rods to the turning wheels

bal·loon (bə lo͞on′) ***n.*** ⟦< Fr < It *palla*, ball⟧ **1** a large, airtight bag that rises when filled with hot air or a gas lighter than air **2** an airship with such a bag **3** an inflatable rubber bag, used as a toy **4** the large final payment on certain loans —***vt.*** to inflate —***vi.*** to swell; expand —***adj.*** like a balloon —**bal·loon′ist *n.***

bal·lot (bal′ət) ***n.*** ⟦< It *palla*, ball⟧ **1** a ticket, card, form, etc. by which a vote is registered **2** act or right of voting, as by ballots **3** the total number of votes cast —***vi.*** to vote

ball′park′ *n.* a baseball stadium

ball′-peen′ hammer a hammer with one end of the head rounded and the other end flat

ball′play′er *n.* a baseball player

ball′point′ (pen) a writing pen with a small ball bearing instead of a point: also **ball′-point′ *n.***

ball′room′ *n.* a large hall for dancing

bal·lute (ba lo͞ot′) ***n.*** ⟦BALL(OON) + (PARACH)UTE⟧ a balloonlike device used to slow down a spacecraft reentering the atmosphere

bal·ly·hoo (bal′ē ho͞o′) ***n.*** ⟦< ?⟧ noisy talk, sensational

THESAURUS

balance *n.* **1** [Whatever remains] excess, surplus, residue; see REMAINDER. **2** [An equilibrium] poise, counterpoise, symmetry, offset, equivalence, counterbalance, tension, equalization, equality of weight, parity.—*Ant.* INCONSISTENCY, top-heaviness, imbalance. **3** [An excess of credits over debits] surplus, dividend, credit balance; see PROFIT 2. —**in the balance** undetermined, undecided, critical; see UNCERTAIN.

balance *v.* **1** [To offset] counterbalance, compensate for, allow for; see sense 2. **2** [To place in balance] place in equilibrium, steady, stabilize, neutralize, set, level, equalize, support, poise, oppose, even, weigh, counteract, make equal, compensate, tie, adjust, square, parallel, coordinate, readjust, pair off, equate, match, level off, attune, harmonize, tune, accord, correspond.—*Ant.* UPSET, turn over, topple. **3** [To demonstrate that debits and credits are in balance] estimate, compare, audit; see CHECK 2.

balanced *a.* **1** [Made even] equalized, poised, offset, in equilibrium, evened, counterweighted, equivalent, stabilized, symmetrical, counterpoised, counterbalanced, on an even keel.—*Ant.* UNSTABLE, unbalanced, unequal. **2** [Audited] validated, confirmed, certified; see APPROVED.

balance of power *n.* equilibrium, distribution, apportionment; see BALANCE 2.

balcony *n.* gallery, mezzanine, terrace; see UPSTAIRS.

bald *a.* hairless, shaven, shaved, bare, featherless, glabrous, shiny, smooth, like a billiard ball; see also SMOOTH 3.—*Ant.* HAIRY, covered, hirsute.

balderdash *n.* senseless talk, gibberish, bombast; see NONSENSE 1.

bale *n.* bundle, bunch, parcel; see PACKAGE.

balk *v.* turn down, demur, desist; see REFUSE.

balky *a.* contrary, obstinate, perverse; see STUBBORN.

ball[1,2] ***n.*** **1** [A spherical body] marble, globe, spheroid, sphere, balloon, rounded object, orb, globule, globular object, pellet, pill, drop, knot. **2** [A game played with a ball] baseball, football, catch; see SPORT 3. **3** [A dance] grand ball, promenade, reception; see PARTY 1. —**carry the ball*** assume responsibility, take control, bear the burden; see LEAD 1. —**get the ball rolling*** initiate action, commence, start; see BEGIN 1. —**have something on the ball*** be skilled, have ability, be efficient; see ABLE.

ballad *n.* carol, chant, folk song; see SONG.

ballast *n.* sandbags, counterbalance, counterweight; see WEIGHT 2.

ballet *n.* toe dancing, choreography, dance on *pointe* (French); see DANCE 1.

ballet dancer *n.* ballerina, danseuse, danseur; see DANCER.

balloon *n.* dirigible, aircraft, airship, weather balloon, hot-air balloon, radiosonde, barrage balloon, lighter-than-air craft, toy balloon, zeppelin, observation balloon, blimp*, gasbag.

ballot *n.* tally, ticket, poll; see VOTE 1.

advertising, etc. —*vt., vi.* **-hooed′, -hoo′ing** [Inf.] to promote with ballyhoo

balm (bäm) ***n.*** ⟦< Gr *balsamon*⟧ **1** a fragrant, healing ointment or oil **2** anything healing or soothing

balm′y ***adj.*** **-i·er, -i·est** **1** soothing, mild, etc. **2** [Slang, Chiefly Brit.] crazy

ba·lo·ney (bə lō′nē) ***n.*** ⟦< *bologna*⟧ **1** bologna **2** [Slang] nonsense

bal·sa (bôl′sə) ***n.*** ⟦Sp⟧ **1** the wood, very light in weight, of a tropical American tree **2** the tree

bal·sam (bôl′səm) ***n.*** ⟦see BALM⟧ **1** an aromatic resin obtained from certain trees **2** any of various aromatic, resinous oils or fluids **3** balm **4** any of various trees yielding balsam

bal·sam·ic vinegar (bôl sam′ik) aromatic, dark-brown vinegar used in salad dressings, etc.

Bal·tic Sea (bôl′tik) sea in N Europe, west of Latvia, Lithuania, & Estonia

Bal·ti·more (bôl′tə môr) seaport in N Maryland: pop. 736,000

bal·us·ter (bal′əs tər) ***n.*** ⟦< Gr *balaustion*, wild pomegranate flower: from the shape⟧ any of the small posts of a railing, as on a staircase

bal·us·trade (bal′əs trād′) ***n.*** a railing having an upper rail supported by balusters

Bal·zac (bál zák′; *E* bôl′zak), **Ho·no·ré de** (ô nô rā′də) 1799-1850; Fr. novelist

bam·boo (bam bo͞o′) ***n.*** ⟦Malay *bambu*⟧ a treelike tropical grass with woody, jointed, often hollow stems used for furniture, canes, etc.

bam·boo·zle (bam bo͞o′zəl) ***vt.*** **-zled, -zling** ⟦< ?⟧ **1** to trick; cheat; dupe **2** to confuse; puzzle

ban (ban) ***vt.*** **banned, ban′ning** ⟦< OE *bannan*, summon⟧ to prohibit or forbid, esp. officially —***n.*** **1** a condemnation by church authorities **2** a curse **3** an official prohibition **4** strong public condemnation

ba·nal (bā′nəl, bə nal′) ***adj.*** ⟦Fr: see prec.⟧ trite; hackneyed —**ba·nal′i·ty,** *pl.* **-ties,** ***n.*** —**ba′nal·ly** ***adv.***

ba·nan·a (bə nan′ə) ***n.*** ⟦Sp & Port⟧ **1** a tropical plant with large clusters of edible fruit **2** the narrow, curved fruit, having soft pulp and thick, usually yellow skin

band[1] (band) ***n.*** ⟦ON⟧ **1** something that binds, ties, or encircles, as a strip or ring of wood, rubber, metal, etc. **2** a strip of color or of material **3** a division of an LP phonograph record **4** a range of wavelengths —***vt.*** to put a band on or around

band[2] (band) ***n.*** ⟦< Gothic *bandwa*, a sign⟧ **1** a group of people united for some purpose **2** a group of musicians playing together, esp. upon wind and percussion instruments —***vi., vt.*** to unite for some purpose

band·age (ban′dij) ***n.*** ⟦Fr < *bande*, a strip⟧ a strip of cloth, etc. used to bind or cover an injury —***vt.*** **-aged, -ag·ing** to put a bandage on

Band-Aid (band′ād′) ⟦prec. + AID⟧ *trademark for* a small bandage of gauze and adhesive tape —***n.*** [*also* **band-aid**] such a bandage: also **band′aid′**

ban·dan·na or **ban·dan·a** (ban dan′ə) ***n.*** ⟦Hindi *bāndhnū*, a method of dyeing⟧ a large, colored handkerchief

band′box′ ***n.*** a light, round box to hold hats, etc.

ban·deau (ban dō′) ***n.,*** *pl.* **-deaux′** (-dōz′) ⟦Fr⟧ **1** a narrow ribbon **2** a band of material covering the breasts, as a strapless bikini top

ban·dit (ban′dit) ***n.*** ⟦< It⟧ **1** a robber; brigand **2** one who steals, defrauds, etc. —**ban′dit·ry** ***n.***

ban·do·leer or **ban·do·lier** (ban′də lir′) ***n.*** ⟦< Fr⟧ a broad belt with pockets for bullets, etc., worn over one shoulder and across the chest

band saw an endless toothed steel belt on pulleys, powered for sawing

bands·man (bandz′mən) ***n.,*** *pl.* **-men** (-mən) a member of a band of musicians

band′stand′ ***n.*** a platform for a band, esp. one for outdoor concerts

band′wag′on ***n.*** a wagon for a band to ride on, as in a parade —**on the bandwagon** [Inf.] on the popular or apparently winning side

band′width′ ***n.*** the transmission rate of information along electronic communications lines

ban·dy[1] (ban′dē) ***vt.*** **-died, -dy·ing** ⟦Fr *bander*, bandy at tennis⟧ **1** to toss or hit back and forth **2** to pass (rumors, etc.) freely **3** to exchange (words), esp. angrily

ban·dy[2] (ban′dē) ***adj.*** ⟦Fr *bandé*, bent⟧ curved outward; bowed

ban′dy·leg′ged (-leg′id, -legd′) ***adj.*** bowlegged

bane (bān) ***n.*** ⟦OE *bana*⟧ **1** ruin, death, harm, or their cause **2** [Obs.] poison —**bane′ful** ***adj.***

bang[1] (baŋ) ***vt.*** ⟦ON *banga*, to pound⟧ to hit, shut, etc. hard and noisily —***vi.*** **1** to make a loud noise **2** to hit noisily or sharply —***n.*** **1** a hard, noisy blow or impact **2** a loud, sudden noise **3** [Inf.] a burst of vigor **4** [Slang] a thrill —***adv.*** **1** hard and noisily **2** abruptly —**bang up** to damage

bang[2] (baŋ) ***n.*** ⟦< prec.: see *adv.*, 2⟧ [*usually pl.*] hair cut to hang straight across the forehead

Bang·kok (baŋ′käk′) seaport & capital of Thailand: pop. 4,697,000

Ban·gla·desh (bäŋ′glə desh′, baŋ′-) country in S Asia, on the Bay of Bengal: 57,295 sq. mi.; pop. 109,887,000

ban·gle (baŋ′gəl) ***n.*** ⟦Hindi *bangrī*⟧ a decorative bracelet or anklet

bang-up (baŋ′up′) ***adj.*** [Inf.] very good; excellent

ban·ish (ban′ish) ***vt.*** ⟦< OFr *banir*⟧ **1** to exile **2** to get rid of —**ban′ish·ment** ***n.***

ban·is·ter (ban′is tər) ***n.*** ⟦< BALUSTER⟧ a handrail, specif. one with balusters

ban·jo (ban′jō′) ***n.,*** *pl.* **-jos′** or **-joes′** ⟦of Afr orig.⟧ a musical instrument with a long neck, circular body, and strings that are plucked —**ban′jo·ist** ***n.***

bank[1] (baŋk) ***n.*** ⟦ult. < OHG *bank*, bench⟧ **1** an establishment for receiving or lending money **2** a reserve supply; pool —***vi.*** to do business with a bank —***vt.*** to deposit (money) in a bank —**bank on** [Inf.] to rely on —**bank′a·ble** ***adj.***

bank[2] (baŋk) ***n.*** ⟦< ON *bakki*⟧ **1** a long mound or heap **2** a steep slope **3** a rise of land along a river, etc. **4** a shallow place, as in a sea **5** the lateral, slanting turn of an aircraft —***vt.*** **1** to cover (a fire) with ashes and fuel so that it will burn slowly **2** to pile up so as to form a bank **3** to slope (a curve in a road, etc.) **4** to make (an aircraft) slant laterally on a turn **5** to make (a billiard ball) recoil from a cushion

bank[3] (baŋk) ***n.*** ⟦< OFr *banc*, bench⟧ **1** a row of oars **2** a

THESAURUS

balm ***n.*** **1** [Anything healing and soothing] solace, consolation, comfort, relief, refreshment, remedy, cure. **2** [A healing ointment] salve, lotion, dressing; see MEDICINE 2.

bamboozle ***v.*** swindle, trick, dupe; see DECEIVE.

ban ***n.*** taboo, prohibition, limitation; see REFUSAL.

ban ***v.*** outlaw, prevent, declare illegal; see FORBID, PREVENT.

banal ***a.*** dull, trite, hackneyed; see COMMON 1.

band[1,2] ***n.*** **1** [A beltlike strip] circuit, meridian, latitude, circle, ring, orbit, zodiac, circumference, zone, ribbon, belt, line, strip, stripe, tape, sash, twine, scarf, bandage, girdle, thong, wristband, bond, tie, binding, stay, truss, belt, cord, harness, brace, strap, binding, waistband, collar, hatband, cable, rope, link, chain, line, string, guy wire. **2** [A company of people] group, collection, association; see GATHERING. **3** [A group of musicians] orchestra, company, troupe, ensemble, group, combo. *Kinds of bands include the following:* military, brass, marching, concert, parade, jazz, stage, dance, Dixieland, jug, string, rock, swing.

bandage ***n.*** compress, cast, gauze; see DRESSING 3.

bandage ***v.*** tie, fix, bind up; see BIND 1, FASTEN.

bandit ***n.*** burglar, thief, raider; see ROBBER.

bang[1] ***n.*** **1** [A loud report] blast, roar, detonation; see NOISE 1. **2** [A blow] hit, cuff, whack; see BLOW. **3** [*A thrill] enjoyment, pleasant feeling, kick*; see EXCITEMENT.

bang[1] ***v.*** **1** [To beat] strike, slam, whack; see HIT 1. **2** [To make a noise] crash, clatter, rattle; see SOUND.

banish ***v.*** exile, deport, cast out, expel, expatriate, ostracize, sequester, excommunicate, transport, outlaw, extradite, isolate, dismiss.—*Ant.* RECEIVE, welcome, accept.

banishment ***n.*** expatriation, deportation, expulsion; see EXILE 1.

banister ***n.*** railing, handrail, guardrail; see RAIL 1.

bank[1,2] ***n.*** **1** [Ground rising above adjacent water] ledge, embankment, edge; see SHORE. **2** [A financial establishment] national bank, state bank, commercial bank, savings bank, savings and loan association, thrift, lender, mortgage company, Federal Reserve Bank, private bank, countinghouse, banking house, exchequer, credit union, trust company, treasury.

bank[1,2] ***v.*** **1** [To deposit money] save, put in the bank, enter in an account; see DEPOSIT 2. **2** [To tilt on a curve] lean, bend, slope; see LEAN 1. —**bank on*** depend on, believe in, be sure about; see TRUST 1.

row or tier, as of keys in a keyboard —***vt.*** to arrange in a row or tier
bank account money deposited in a bank and credited to the depositor
bank'book' ***n.*** a book recording a bank depositor's deposits and withdrawals; passbook
bank card an encoded plastic card issued by a bank as for use at an ATM
bank'er ***n.*** a person who owns or manages a bank
bank'ing ***n.*** the business of a bank
bank note a promissory note issued by a bank: a form of paper money
bank'roll' ***n.*** a supply of money —***vt.*** [Inf.] to supply with money; finance
bank·rupt (baŋk'rupt') ***n.*** ⟦< Fr < It *banca,* bench + *rotta,* broken⟧ a person legally declared unable to pay debts —***adj.*** **1** that is a bankrupt; insolvent **2** lacking in some quality [*morally bankrupt*] —***vt.*** to make bankrupt —**bank'rupt'cy,** *pl.* **-cies,** ***n.***
ban·ner (ban'ər) ***n.*** ⟦ME *banere* < OFr *baniere*⟧ **1** a flag **2** a headline running across a newspaper page —***adj.*** foremost
banns (banz) ***pl.n.*** ⟦see BAN⟧ the proclamation made in church of an intended marriage
ban·quet (baŋ'kwət) ***n.*** ⟦ult. < OHG *bank,* bench⟧ **1** a feast **2** a formal dinner —***vt.*** to honor with a banquet
ban·quette (baŋ ket') ***n.*** ⟦Fr⟧ **1** a gunners' platform inside a trench, etc. **2** an upholstered bench
ban·shee or **ban·shie** (ban'shē) ***n.*** ⟦< Ir *bean,* woman + *sith,* fairy⟧ *Celt. Folklore* a female spirit whose wailing warns of impending death
ban·tam (ban'təm) ***n.*** ⟦after *Bantam,* former province in Java⟧ **1** any of various small, domestic fowls **2** a small but aggressive person —***adj.*** like a bantam
ban'tam·weight' ***n.*** a boxer weighing 113 to 118 lb.
ban·ter (ban'tər) ***vt.*** ⟦17th-c. slang⟧ to tease playfully —***vi.*** to exchange banter (*with* someone) —***n.*** playful teasing —**ban'ter·ing·ly** ***adv.***
Ban·tu (ban'to͞o') ***n.*** ⟦Bantu *ba-ntu,* the men⟧ **1** a large group of languages of S Africa, including Swahili and Zulu **2** *pl.* **-tus'** or **-tu'** a member of a Bantu-speaking people
ban·yan (ban'yən) ***n.*** ⟦ult. < Sans⟧ an Indian fig tree whose branches grow shoots that take root and become new trunks over a wide area
ba·o·bab (bā'ō bab', bä'-) ***n.*** ⟦< ? Ethiopian native name⟧ a thick-trunked tree of Africa, with edible, gourdlike fruit
bap·tism (bap'tiz'əm) ***n.*** ⟦see BAPTIZE⟧ **1** the sacrament of admitting a person into a Christian church by immersing the individual in water or by sprinkling water on the individual **2** an initiating experience —**bap·tis'mal** (-tiz'məl) ***adj.***
Bap'tist (-tist) ***n.*** a member of a Protestant denomination practicing baptism of believers by immersion
bap'tis·ter·y (-tis tər ē, -tis trē) ***n.,*** *pl.* **-ies** a place, esp. in a church, used for baptizing: also **bap'tis·try,** *pl.* **-tries**
bap·tize (bap tīz', bap'tīz) ***vt.*** **-tized', -tiz'ing** ⟦< Gr *baptizein,* to immerse⟧ **1** to administer baptism to **2** to initiate **3** to christen
bar (bär) ***n.*** ⟦< ML *barra*⟧ **1** any long, narrow piece of wood, metal, etc., often used as a barrier, lever, etc. **2** an oblong piece, as of soap **3** anything that obstructs or hinders **4** a band or strip **5** a law court, esp. that part, enclosed by a railing, where the lawyers sit **6** lawyers collectively **7** the legal profession **8** a counter, as for serving alcoholic drinks **9** a place with such a counter **10** *Music a*) a vertical line dividing a staff into measures *b*) a measure —***vt.*** **barred, bar'ring** **1** to fasten with a bar **2** to obstruct; close **3** to oppose **4** to exclude —***prep.*** excluding [*the best, bar none*] —**cross the bar** to die
barb (bärb) ***n.*** ⟦< L *barba,* beard⟧ **1** a beardlike growth **2** a sharp point projecting backward from the main point of a fishhook, etc. **3** a cutting remark —***vt.*** to provide with a barb —**barbed** ***adj.***
Bar·ba·dos (bär bā'dōs, -dōz) country on an island in the West Indies: 166 sq. mi.; pop. 263,000
bar·bar·i·an (bär ber'ē ən) ***n.*** ⟦see BARBAROUS⟧ **1** a member of a people considered primitive, savage, etc. **2** a cruel person —***adj.*** uncivilized, cruel, etc. —**bar·bar'i·an·ism'** ***n.***
bar·bar'ic (-ber'ik) ***adj.*** **1** uncivilized; primitive **2** wild, crude, etc.
bar·ba·rism (bär'bə riz'əm) ***n.*** **1** a nonstandard word or expression **2** the state of being primitive or uncivilized **3** a barbarous act or custom
bar·bar·i·ty (bär ber'ə tē) ***n.,*** *pl.* **-ties** **1** cruelty; brutality **2** a barbaric taste, manner, etc.
bar·ba·rize (bär'bə rīz') ***vt.*** **-rized', -riz'ing** to make or become barbarous —**bar'ba·ri·za'tion** ***n.***
bar·ba·rous (bär'bə rəs) ***adj.*** ⟦< Gr *barbaros,* foreign⟧ **1** uncivilized; primitive **2** crude, coarse, etc. **3** cruel; brutal —**bar'ba·rous·ly** ***adv.***
bar·be·cue (bär'bə kyo͞o') ***n.*** ⟦AmSp *barbacoa*⟧ **1** *a*) a hog, steer, etc. roasted whole over an open fire *b*) any meat broiled over an open fire **2** a party, picnic, etc. featuring this —***vt.*** **-cued', -cu'ing** to roast or broil over an open fire, often with a highly seasoned sauce (**barbecue sauce**)
barbed wire wire with barbs at close intervals
bar·bel (bär'bəl) ***n.*** ⟦< L *barba,* beard⟧ a threadlike growth from the lips or jaws of certain fishes
bar·bell (bär'bel') ***n.*** ⟦BAR + (DUMB)BELL⟧ a metal bar with weights attached at each end, used for weight lifting: also **bar bell**
bar·ber (bär'bər) ***n.*** ⟦see BARB⟧ one whose work is cutting hair, shaving beards, etc. —***vt.*** to cut the hair of, shave, etc. —***vi.*** to work as a barber
bar·ber·ry (bär'ber'ē, -bə rē) ***n.,*** *pl.* **-ries** ⟦< ML *barberis*⟧ **1** a spiny shrub with sour, red berries **2** the berry
bar·bi·tu·rate (bär bich'ər it, -bich'ə wit) ***n.*** ⟦< Ger⟧ a salt or ester of a crystalline acid (**bar'bi·tu'ric acid**), used as a sedative
barb'wire' ***n.*** BARBED WIRE
bar·ca·role or **bar·ca·rolle** (bär'kə rōl') ***n.*** ⟦< Fr < It⟧ a Venetian gondolier song, or music like this
Bar·ce·lo·na (bär'sə lō'nə) seaport in NE Spain: pop. 1,753,000
bar code UNIVERSAL PRODUCT CODE
bard (bärd) ***n.*** ⟦Gael & Ir⟧ **1** an ancient Celtic poet **2** a poet
bare (ber) ***adj.*** **bar'er, bar'est** ⟦OE *bær*⟧ **1** not covered or clothed; naked **2** without furnishings; empty **3** simple;

THESAURUS

banker ***n.*** treasurer, teller, officer of the bank, broker, financier, capitalist, investment banker, moneylender.
banking ***n.*** investment, funding, moneylending; see BUSINESS 1.
bankrupt ***a.*** failed, out of business, broke*; see RUINED 3.
bankruptcy ***n.*** insolvency, destitution, distress; see FAILURE 1.
banner ***n.*** colors, pennant, flag; see EMBLEM.
banquet ***n.*** repast, fete, feast; see DINNER.
baptism ***n.*** dedication, christening, initiation; see CEREMONY 2.
baptize ***v.*** immerse, purify, regenerate, sprinkle, dip, christen, name.
bar ***n.*** **1** [A relatively long, narrow object] strip, stake, stick, crossbar, boom, rib, crosspiece, pole, spar, rail, yard, yardarm, lever, rod, crowbar, shaft, slab. **2** [A counter serving refreshments, especially drinks] barroom, tavern, cocktail lounge, saloon, public house, counter, hotel, inn, canteen, beer parlor, cabaret, restaurant, cafeteria, roadhouse, brass rail, snack bar, beer garden, watering hole*, dive*, pub*, grill. **3** [The legal profession] lawyers, counselors, barristers, solicitors, jurists, attorneys, bar association, advocates, judiciary. **4** [An obstruction] hindrance, obstacle, hurdle; see BARRIER. **5** [A relatively long, narrow area] strip, stripe, ribbon; see BAND 1.
bar ***v.*** **1** [To raise a physical obstruction] barricade, dam, dike, fence, wall, erect a barrier, brick up, blockade, clog, exclude, shut out, lock out, keep out, bolt, cork, plug, seal, stop, impede, roadblock.—*Ant.* OPEN, free, clear. **2** [To obstruct by refusal] ban, forbid, deny, refuse, prevent, stop, boycott, ostracize, preclude, shut out, keep out, exclude, exile, reject, outlaw, condemn, discourage, interfere with, restrain, frustrate, circumvent, override, segregate, interdict, veto, blackball, freeze out*.—*Ant.* ALLOW, admit, welcome. **3** [To close] shut, lock, seal; see CLOSE 4.
barbarian ***n.*** savage, brute, cannibal, rascal, ruffian, monster, yahoo, Philistine, Hun, Vandal, troglodyte, clod; see also BEAST 2.
barbaric ***a.*** inhuman, brutal, fierce; see CRUEL.
barbarity ***n.*** savageness, cruelty, brutality; see CRUELTY.
barbecue ***n.*** **1** [A grill] roaster, grill, broiler; see APPLIANCE. **2** [A picnic] cookout, wiener roast, picnic; see MEAL 2.
barbecue ***v.*** grill, sear, broil; see COOK.
bare ***a.*** **1** [Without covering] uncovered, bald, stripped; see NAKED 1, OPEN 4. **2** [Plain] unadorned, simple, unornamented; see MODEST 2. **3**

plain **4** mere *[bare* needs*]* —***vt.* bared, bar′ing** to make bare; uncover —**lay bare** to uncover; expose —**bare′ness** ***n.***

bare′back′ ***adv., adj.*** on a horse with no saddle

bare′-bones′ ***adj.*** simple; basic

bare′faced′ ***adj.*** **1** with the face uncovered **2** open; shameless

bare′foot′ ***adj., adv.*** without shoes and stockings: also **bare′foot′ed**

bare′hand′ed ***adj., adv.*** **1** with hands uncovered or unprotected **2** without weapons, etc.

bare′head′ed ***adj., adv.*** wearing no hat or other covering on the head

bare′leg′ged (-leg′id, -legd′) ***adj., adv.*** with the legs bare

bare·ly (ber′lē) ***adv.*** **1** plainly **2** only just; scarcely **3** scantily

bar·gain (bär′gən) ***n.*** ⟦< OFr *bargaignier,* haggle⟧ **1** a mutual agreement or contract **2** such an agreement with regard to worth *[*a bad *bargain]* **3** something sold at a price favorable to the buyer —***vi.*** **1** to haggle **2** to make a bargain —**bargain for** (or **on**) to expect; count on —**into** (or **in**) **the bargain** besides —**bar′gain·er** ***n.***

bargain counter a store counter for displaying goods at reduced prices

barge (bärj) ***n.*** ⟦< ML *barga*⟧ **1** a large, flat-bottomed boat for freight on rivers, etc. **2** a large pleasure boat —***vi.* barged, barg′ing** **1** to move slowly and clumsily **2** to come or go (*in* or *into*) rudely or abruptly

bar graph a graph in which the lengths of parallel bars are used to compare quantities, etc.

Bar Harbor resort town on an island off E Maine: pop. 4,400

bar·i·tone (bar′ə tōn′) ***n.*** ⟦< Gr *barys,* deep + *tonos,* tone⟧ **1** the range of a male voice between tenor and bass **2** a voice, singer, or instrument with such a range

bar·i·um (ber′ē əm) ***n.*** ⟦< Gr *barys,* heavy⟧ a metallic chemical element

bark[1] (bärk) ***n.*** ⟦< ON *bǫrkr*⟧ the outside covering of trees and woody plants —***vt.*** **1** to remove bark from **2** [Inf.] to scrape; skin (the knees, etc.)

bark[2] (bärk) ***vi.*** ⟦OE *beorcan*⟧ **1** to make the sharp, abrupt cry of a dog or a similar sound **2** to speak sharply; snap —***n.*** the characteristic cry of a dog, or any noise like this —**bark up the wrong tree** to misdirect one's attack, energies, etc.

bark[3] (bärk) ***n.*** ⟦< LL *barca*⟧ **1** [Old Poet.] a boat **2** a sailing vessel with two square-rigged masts forward and a fore-and-aft mast aft

bar′keep′er ***n.*** **1** an owner of a barroom **2** a bartender Also **bar′keep′**

bark′er ***n.*** one who talks loud to attract customers to a sideshow, etc.

bar·ley (bär′lē) ***n.*** ⟦OE *bærlic*⟧ **1** a cereal grass **2** its grain, used in making malt, in soups, etc.

bar′maid′ ***n.*** a waitress who serves alcoholic drinks in a bar

bar mitz·vah (bär mits′və) ⟦< Yiddish < Aram *bar,* son of + Heb *mitsva,* commandment⟧ [*also* **B- M-**] **1** a Jewish boy who has arrived at the age of religious responsibility, thirteen years **2** the ceremony celebrating this event

barn (bärn) ***n.*** ⟦OE *bern*⟧ a farm building for sheltering harvested crops, livestock, machines, etc.

bar·na·cle (bär′nə kəl) ***n.*** ⟦ME *bernacle*⟧ a saltwater shellfish that attaches itself to rocks, ship bottoms, etc.

barn′burn′er ***n.*** [Slang] something dramatic and exciting, as a close contest

barn′storm′ ***vi., vt.*** to tour (the country, esp. rural areas) giving speeches or lectures, performing exhibitions, etc. —**barn′storm′er** ***n.***

barn′yard′ ***n.*** the ground near a barn —***adj.*** of, like, or fit for a barnyard; specif., earthy or crude

ba·rom·e·ter (bə räm′ət ər) ***n.*** ⟦< Gr *baros,* weight + -METER⟧ **1** an instrument for measuring atmospheric pressure and thus forecasting weather **2** anything that marks change —**bar·o·met·ric** (bar′ə me′trik) ***adj.***

bar·on (bar′ən) ***n.*** ⟦ME⟧ **1** a member of the lowest rank of British nobility **2** a magnate —**bar′on·age** ***n.*** —**bar′on·ess** ***fem.n.*** —**ba·ro·ni·al** (bə rō′nē əl) ***adj.***

bar′on·et (-ət) ***n.*** a man holding the lowest hereditary British title, below a baron —**bar′on·et·cy,** *pl.* **-cies,** ***n.***

ba·roque (bə rōk′) ***adj.*** ⟦Fr < Port *barroco,* imperfect pearl⟧ **1** [*often* **B-**] *a)* very ornate and full of curved lines, as much art and architecture of about 1600-1750 *b)* full of highly embellished melodies, fugues, etc., as much music of that time **2** gaudily ornate

bar·racks (bar′əks) ***pl.n.*** ⟦< Sp *barro,* clay⟧ [*often with sing. v.*] a building or group of buildings for housing soldiers, etc.

bar·ra·cu·da (bar′ə ko͞o′də) ***n.,*** *pl.* **-da** or **-das** ⟦AmSp⟧ a fierce, pikelike fish of tropical seas

bar·rage (bə räzh′, -räj′) ***n.*** ⟦Fr < *barrer,* to stop⟧ **1** artillery fire that holds down the enemy while one's army attacks **2** any prolonged attack —***vi., vt.* -raged′, -rag′ing** to subject to a barrage

barred (bärd) ***adj.*** **1** having bars or stripes **2** closed off with bars **3** not allowed

bar·rel (bar′əl) ***n.*** ⟦< ML *barillus*⟧ **1** a large, cylindrical container with slightly bulging sides and flat ends **2** a similar cylindrical container **3** the capacity of a standard barrel, used as a measure **4** the straight tube of a gun —***vt.* -reled** or **-relled, -rel·ing** or **-rel·ling** to put in barrels —***vi.*** [Slang] to go at high speed

bar′rel·ful′ (-fo͝ol′) ***n.*** **1** as much as a barrel will hold **2** [Inf.] a great amount

bar′rel·head′ ***n.*** the flat end of a barrel —**on the barrelhead** when delivered *[*to pay cash *on the barrelhead]*

barrel organ a mechanical musical instrument played by turning a crank

bar·ren (bar′ən) ***adj.*** ⟦< OFr⟧ **1** that cannot bear offspring; sterile **2** without vegetation **3** unproductive **4** boring; dull **5** devoid (*of*) —**bar′ren·ness** ***n.***

bar·rette (bə ret′) ***n.*** ⟦Fr⟧ a bar or clasp for holding a woman's hair in place

bar·ri·cade (bar′i kād′; *also, esp. for v.,* bar′ə kād′) ***n.*** ⟦Fr < It *barricare,* fortify⟧ a barrier, esp. one put up hastily for defense —***vt.* -cad′ed, -cad′ing** to block with a barricade

bar·ri·er (bar′ē ər) ***n.*** ⟦< ML *barra*⟧ **1** an obstruction, as a fence **2** anything that blocks or hinders

bar·ring (bär′iŋ) ***prep.*** excepting

bar·ris·ter (bar′is tər) ***n.*** ⟦< *bar* (law court)⟧ in England, a lawyer who pleads cases in court

bar′room′ ***n.*** a room with a bar where alcoholic drinks are sold

THESAURUS

[Without content] barren, void, unfurnished; see EMPTY.

barefaced ***a.*** **1** [Open] unconcealed, clear, apparent; see OBVIOUS 1, 2. **2** [Impudent] shameless, audacious, bold; see RUDE 2.

barefoot ***a.*** shoeless, barefooted, unshod; see NAKED 1.

barely ***a.*** almost, scarcely, just; see HARDLY.

bargain ***n.*** **1** [An agreement] pact, compact, contract; see DEAL 1. **2** [An advantageous purchase] good value, good deal, discount, reduction, sale price, marked-down price, buy*, steal*, giveaway*, deal. —**into the bargain** in addition, too, additionally; see ALSO.

bargain ***v.*** **1** [To trade] barter, do business, merchandise; see BUY, SELL. **2** [To negotiate] make terms, arrange, confer; see NEGOTIATE 1. —**bargain for** expect, plan on, foresee; see ANTICIPATE.

bargaining ***n.*** trade, transaction, haggling; see BUSINESS 1.

bark[1,2] ***n.*** **1** [An outer covering, especially of trees] peel, cork, husk; see COVER 1, SHELL 1. **2** [A short, explosive sound] yelp, yap, grunt; see NOISE 1.

bark[2] ***v.*** yelp, yap, bay, howl, cry, growl, snarl, yip*, woof, arf. —**bark up the wrong tree** miscalculate, misdirect one's effort, make a mistake; see MISJUDGE 2.

barn ***n.*** outbuilding, shed, outhouse, shelter, lean-to, coop, hutch, sty, pen, kennel, stable.

barnyard ***n.*** feedyard, pen, corral, stableyard, lot, feedlot, run.

barred ***a.*** **1** [Equipped or marked with bars] striped, banded, streaked, pleated, pied, motley, calico, mottled, dappled, crosshatched, veined, ribbed, ridged, marked, piped, lined. **2** [Prohibited] banned, outlawed, unlawful; see ILLEGAL.

barrel ***n.*** cask, keg, vat, tub, receptacle, container, vessel.

barren ***a.*** **1** [Incapable of producing young] impotent, infertile, childless; see STERILE 1. **2** [Incapable of producing vegetation] fallow, unproductive, fruitless; see STERILE 2.

barricade ***n.*** obstacle, bar, obstruction; see BARRIER.

barricade ***v.*** obstruct, block, fortify; see BAR 1.

barrier ***n.*** bar, obstruction, difficulty, hindrance, obstacle, hurdle, stumbling block, fence, sound barrier, restriction, restraint, impediment, drawback, check, stop, stay, bulwark, barricade, rampart, wall, earthwork, embankment, blockade, barbed wire, bamboo curtain, iron curtain.—*Ant.* WAY, path, trail.

barroom ***n.*** tavern, saloon, pub*;

bar·row[1] (bar′ō) ***n.*** ⟦< OE *beran,* to bear⟧ a handbarrow or wheelbarrow

bar·row[2] (bar′ō) ***n.*** ⟦< OE *beorg,* hill⟧ a heap of earth or rocks covering a grave

bar′tend′er ***n.*** one who serves alcoholic drinks at a bar

bar·ter (bärt′ər) ***vi., vt.*** ⟦< OFr *barater*⟧ to trade by exchanging (goods) without money —***n.*** **1** a bartering **2** anything bartered —**bar′ter·er** ***n.***

Bar·tók (bär′tôk′), **Bé·la** (bā′lä) 1881-1945; Hung. composer

bar·y·on (bar′ē än′) ***n.*** ⟦< Gr *barys,* heavy + (ELECTR)ON⟧ any of certain subatomic particles including the proton and neutron

ba·sal (bā′səl) ***adj.*** **1** of or at the base **2** basic; fundamental

basal metabolism the minimum quantity of energy used by an organism at rest to sustain its life

ba·salt (bə sôlt′, bā′sôlt′) ***n.*** ⟦L *basaltes*⟧ a hard, dark volcanic rock

base[1] (bās) ***n.*** ⟦< Gr *basis*⟧ **1** the thing or part on which something rests **2** the most important element or principal ingredient **3** the part of a word to which affixes are attached **4** a basis **5** any of the four markers a baseball player must consecutively touch to score a run **6** a headquarters or a source of supply **7** *Chem.* a substance that forms a salt when it reacts with an acid —***adj.*** forming a base —***vt.*** **based**, **bas′ing** **1** to make a base for **2** to establish

base[2] (bās) ***adj.*** **bas′er**, **bas′est** ⟦< VL *bassus,* low⟧ **1** mean; ignoble **2** menial **3** poor in quality **4** of comparatively low worth *[base* metal*]* —**base′ly** ***adv.*** —**base′ness** ***n.***

base′ball′ ***n.*** **1** a game played with a ball and bat by two opposing teams on a field with four bases forming a diamond **2** the ball used in this game

base′board′ ***n.*** a board or molding at the base of a wall

base hit *Baseball* a play in which the batter hits a fair ball and gets on base without an error or without forcing out a teammate

base′less ***adj.*** having no basis in fact; unfounded —**base′less·ness** ***n.***

base line **1** a line serving as a base **2** *Baseball* the lane between any two consecutive bases **3** *Basketball, Tennis* the line at either end of the court Also **base′line′**

base′man (-mən) ***n.,*** *pl.* **-men** (-mən) *Baseball* an infielder stationed at first, second, or third base

base′ment ***n.*** the story below the main floor

base on balls *Baseball* WALK

base pay the basic rate of pay not counting overtime pay, etc.

base runner *Baseball* a player who is on base or is trying to reach a base

bash (bash) ***vt.*** ⟦echoic⟧ [Inf.] to hit hard —***n.*** [Slang] a party

bash′ful (-fəl) ***adj.*** ⟦(A)BASH + -FUL⟧ easily embarrassed; shy —**bash′ful·ly** ***adv.*** —**bash′ful·ness** ***n.***

bas·ic (bā′sik) ***adj.*** **1** fundamental **2** *Chem.* alkaline —***n.*** a basic principle, factor, etc. —**bas′i·cal·ly** ***adv.***

BASIC (bā′sik) ***n.*** ⟦*B(eginner's) A(ll-purpose) S(ymbolic) I(nstruction) C(ode)*⟧ a simple computer language that uses common words and algebra

bas·il (bā′zəl, baz′əl) ***n.*** ⟦< Gr *basilikon*⟧ a fragrant herb of the mint family, used in cooking

ba·sil·i·ca (bə sil′i kə) ***n.*** ⟦< Gr *basilikē (stoa),* royal (portico)⟧ **1** a church with a broad nave, side aisles, and an apse **2** *R.C.Ch.* a church with certain ceremonial rights

ba·sin (bā′sin) ***n.*** ⟦< VL *bacca,* water vessel⟧ **1** a wide, shallow container for liquid **2** its contents **3** a sink **4** any shallow, rounded hollow, often containing water **5** RIVER BASIN

ba·sis (bā′sis) ***n.,*** *pl.* **-ses′** (-sēz′) ⟦< Gr, a base⟧ **1** a base or foundation **2** a principal constituent **3** a fundamental principle or theory

bask (bask) ***vi.*** ⟦ME *basken,* to wallow⟧ **1** to warm oneself pleasantly **2** to enjoy a warm feeling from being in a certain situation

bas·ket (bas′kit) ***n.*** ⟦ME⟧ **1** a container made of interwoven cane, wood strips, etc. **2** its contents **3** *Basketball a)* the goal, a round, open, hanging net *b)* a goal made by shooting the ball through this net

bas′ket·ball′ ***n.*** ⟦invented & named (1891) by James A. Naismith (1861-1939)⟧ **1** a team game played with a bouncy, round ball on a court having a raised basket at each end **2** this ball

basket weave a weave of fabrics resembling the weave used in making baskets

bas′ket·work′ ***n.*** work that is woven like a basket; wickerwork

bas mitz·vah (bäs mits′və) BAT MITZVAH

Basque (bask) ***n.*** **1** a member of a people living in the W Pyrenees **2** the language of this people —***adj.*** of the Basques

bas-re·lief (bä′ri lēf′, bas′-) ***n.*** ⟦Fr < It: see BASS[1] & RELIEF⟧ sculpture in which figures project slightly from a flat background

bass[1] (bās) ***n.*** ⟦< VL *bassus,* low⟧ **1** the range of the lowest male voice **2** a voice, singer, or instrument with such a range; specif., a double bass **3** a part for a bass **4** a low, deep sound —***adj.*** of or for a bass

bass[2] (bas) ***n.,*** *pl.* **bass** or **bass′es** ⟦OE *baers*⟧ a spiny-finned food and game fish of fresh or salt water

bas·set (bas′it) ***n.*** ⟦< OFr *bas,* low⟧ a hunting hound with a long body, short forelegs, and long, drooping ears

bas·si·net (bas′ə net′) ***n.*** ⟦< Fr dim. of *berceau,* a cradle⟧ a basketlike bed for an infant, often hooded and on wheels

bas·so (bas′ō, bäs′-) ***n.,*** *pl.* **-sos** or **-si** (-sē) ⟦< VL *bassus,* low⟧ a bass voice or singer

bas·soon (ba so͞on′, bə-) ***n.*** ⟦< VL *bassus,* low⟧ a double-reed bass woodwind instrument

bast (bast) ***n.*** ⟦OE *bæst*⟧ plant fiber used in ropes, mats, etc.

bas·tard (bas′tərd) ***n.*** ⟦< OFr⟧ an illegitimate child —***adj.*** **1** of illegitimate birth **2** inferior, sham, etc. —**bas′tar·dy** (-tər dē) ***n.***

bas·tard·ize (bas′tər dīz′) ***vt.*** **-ized′**, **-iz′ing** **1** to make, declare, or show to be a bastard **2** to make corrupt; debase —**bas′tard·i·za′tion** ***n.***

baste[1] (bāst) ***vt.*** **bast′ed**, **bast′ing** ⟦< Gmc *bastjan,* make with bast⟧ to sew temporarily with long, loose stitches until properly sewed

baste[2] (bāst) ***vt.*** **bast′ed**, **bast′ing** ⟦< OFr *bassin,* basin⟧ to moisten (meat) with melted butter, drippings, etc. while roasting —**bast′er** ***n.***

THESAURUS

see BAR 2.

barter ***n.*** trade, exchange, traffic; see BUSINESS 1.

barter ***v.*** trade, bargain, swap*; see BUY, SELL.

base[1] ***n.*** **1** [A point from which action is initiated] camp, field, landing field, airport, airfield, airstrip, port, headquarters, terminal, base camp, home base, firebase, base of operations, center, depot, supply base, dock, harbor, station. **2** [The bottom, thought of as a support] root, foot, footing; see FOUNDATION 2. **3** [Foundation of a belief or statement] principle, authority, evidence; see BASIS. **4** [A goal, especially in baseball] mark, bound, station, plate, post, goal; first base, second base, third base, home plate. —**off base*** erring, mistaken, incorrect; see WRONG 2.

base[2] ***a.*** low, foul, sordid; see VULGAR.

baseball ***n.*** ball, little league, the national pastime; see SPORT 3.

baseball player ***n.*** pitcher, catcher, infielder, batter, shortstop, left fielder, right fielder, center fielder, first baseman, second baseman, third baseman, designated hitter, ballplayer, slugger*.

based ***a.*** confirmed, planted, founded; see ESTABLISHED 2.

basement ***n.*** cellar, excavation, storage room, wine cellar, furnace room, vault, crypt.

bashful ***a.*** retiring, reserved, timid; see HUMBLE 1, MODEST 2, SHY.

basic ***a.*** essential, central, primary; see FUNDAMENTAL, NECESSARY.

basically ***a.*** fundamentally, primarily, radically; see ESSENTIALLY.

basin ***n.*** pan, tub, bowl; see CONTAINER.

basis ***n.*** support, foundation, justification, reason, explanation, background, source, authority, principle, groundwork, assumption, premise, backing, sanction, proof, evidence, nucleus, center.

bask ***v.*** relax, enjoy, indulge oneself; see WALLOW.

basket ***n.*** bushel, crate, bin; see CONTAINER.

basketball ***n.*** hoops*, cage meet, roundball*; see SPORT 3.

bastard ***a.*** illegitimate, natural, false, mongrel, baseborn, misbegotten.—*Ant.* TRUE, legitimate, wellborn.

bastard ***n.*** **1** [An illegitimate child] out-of-wedlock birth, whoreson*, love child, woods colt*, Sunday's child*. **2** [*A rascal] scoundrel, cheat, SOB*; see RASCAL.

baste[1,2] ***v.*** **1** [To sew temporarily] stitch, catch, tack; see SEW. **2** [To dress cooking meat with fat or sauce] moisten, grease, season; see COOK.

baste[3] (bāst) ***vt.* bast'ed, bast'ing** ⟦ON *beysta*⟧ **1** to beat soundly **2** to attack with words

bas·tille or **bas·tile** (bas tēl') ***n.*** ⟦< OFr *bastir,* to build⟧ a prison —**the Bastille** a state prison in Paris destroyed (1789) in the French Revolution

bas·tion (bas'chən, -tē ən) ***n.*** ⟦see BASTILLE⟧ **1** a projection from a fortification **2** any strong defense

bat[1] (bat) ***n.*** ⟦OE *batt*⟧ **1** a stout club **2** a club to hit the ball in baseball, etc. **3** a turn at batting **4** [Inf.] a blow —***vt.* bat'ted, bat'ting** to hit, as with a bat —***vi.*** to take a turn at batting

bat[2] (bat) ***n.*** ⟦< Scand⟧ a furry, nocturnal flying mammal with membranous wings

bat[3] (bat) ***vt.* bat'ted, bat'ting** ⟦< OFr *battre,* to batter⟧ [Inf.] to wink —**not bat an eye** [Inf.] not show surprise

batch (bach) ***n.*** ⟦OE *bacan,* to bake⟧ **1** the amount (of bread, etc.) in one baking **2** one set, lot, group, etc. **3** an amount of work for processing by a computer in a single run

bate (bāt) ***vt.* bat'ed, bat'ing** ⟦< OFr *abattre,* beat down⟧ to abate or lessen —**with bated breath** holding the breath, as in fear

bath (bath) ***n.***, *pl.* **baths** (ba*th*z, baths) ⟦OE *bæth*⟧ **1** a washing, esp. of the body, in water **2** water, etc. for bathing or for soaking or treating something **3** a bathtub **4** a bathroom **5** a BATHHOUSE (sense 1)

bathe (bā*th*) ***vt.* bathed, bath'ing** ⟦OE *bæth*⟧ **1** to put into a liquid **2** to give a bath to **3** to cover as with liquid —***vi.*** **1** to take a bath **2** to soak oneself in something —**bath·er** (bā'*th*ər) ***n.***

bath'house' ***n.*** **1** a public building for taking baths **2** a building used by bathers for changing clothes

bathing suit a swimsuit

bath'mat' ***n.*** a mat used in or next to a bathtub

ba·thos (bā'thäs') ***n.*** ⟦< Gr *bathys,* deep⟧ **1** ANTICLIMAX (sense 1) **2** excessive sentimentality **3** triteness —**ba·thet·ic** (bə thet'ik) ***adj.***

bath'robe' ***n.*** a loose robe worn to and from the bath, etc.

bath'room' ***n.*** **1** a room with a bathtub, toilet, etc. **2** a lavatory

bath'tub' ***n.*** a tub to bathe in

bath·y·scaph (bath'ə skaf') ***n.*** ⟦< Gr *bathys,* deep + *skaphē,* boat⟧ a deep-sea diving apparatus for reaching great depths without a cable: also **bath'y·scaphe'** (-skaf', -skāf')

ba·tik (bə tēk') ***n.*** ⟦Malay⟧ cloth with a design made by dyeing only the parts not coated with wax

ba·tiste (bə tēst', ba-) ***n.*** ⟦Fr: after supposed orig. maker, *Baptiste*⟧ a fine, thin cloth of cotton, rayon, etc.

bat mitz·vah (bät mits'və) [*also* **B- M-**] **1** a Jewish girl who has arrived at the age of religious responsibility, 13 years **2** the ceremony celebrating this event

ba·ton (bə tän', ba-) ***n.*** ⟦Fr⟧ **1** a staff serving as a symbol of office **2** a slender stick used in directing music **3** a metal rod twirled by a drum major **4** a short, light rod used in relay races

Bat·on Rouge (bat''n ro͞ozh') capital of Louisiana: pop. 220,000

bat·tal·ion (bə tal'yən) ***n.*** ⟦< VL *battalia,* battle⟧ a tactical military unit forming part of a division

bat·ten[1] (bat''n) ***n.*** ⟦var. of *baton*⟧ **1** a sawed strip of wood **2** a strip of wood put over a seam between boards as a fastening or covering —***vt.*** to fasten or supply with battens

bat·ten[2] (bat''n) ***vi.*, *vt.*** ⟦ON *batna,* improve⟧ to fatten; thrive

bat·ten[3] (bat''n) ***n.*** ⟦< OFr *battre,* to batter⟧ in a loom, the movable frame that presses into place the threads of a woof

bat·ter[1] (bat'ər) ***vt.*** ⟦< L *battuere,* to beat⟧ **1** to strike with blow after blow **2** to injure by pounding, hard wear, or use —***vi.*** to pound noisily and repeatedly

bat·ter[2] (bat'ər) ***n.*** *Baseball, Cricket* the player at bat

bat·ter[3] (bat'ər) ***n.*** ⟦OFr *bature*⟧ a flowing mixture of flour, milk, etc. for making pancakes, etc.

battering ram a heavy beam, etc. for battering down gates, etc.

bat·ter·y (bat'ər ē) ***n.***, *pl.* **-ies** ⟦< OFr *battre,* to batter⟧ **1** a battering **2** a set of things used together **3** *Baseball* the pitcher and the catcher **4** *Elec.* a cell or group of cells storing an electrical charge and able to furnish a current **5** *Law* any illegal beating of another person: see ASSAULT AND BATTERY **6** *Mil.* a set of heavy guns, rockets, etc.

bat·ting (bat''n, -iŋ) ***n.*** ⟦OE *batt,* BAT[1]⟧ cotton, wool, or synthetic fiber wadded into sheets

bat·tle (bat''l) ***n.*** ⟦< L *battuere,* to beat⟧ **1** a large-scale fight between armed forces **2** armed fighting **3** any fight or conflict —***vt.*, *vi.* -tled, -tling** to fight —**give** (or **do**) **battle** to fight

bat'tle-ax' or **bat'tle-axe'** ***n.*** **1** a heavy ax formerly used as a weapon **2** [Slang] a harsh, domineering woman

bat'tle·field' ***n.*** the site of a battle: also **bat'tle·ground'**

bat'tle·ment (-mənt) ***n.*** ⟦< OFr *batailler,* fortify⟧ a parapet with spaces for shooting, built atop a tower, etc.

battle royal *pl.* **battles royal** **1** a free-for-all **2** a heated dispute

bat'tle·ship' ***n.*** a large warship with big guns and very heavy armor

bat·ty (bat'ē) ***adj.* -ti·er, -ti·est** ⟦< BAT[2]⟧ [Slang] crazy or eccentric

bau·ble (bô'bəl) ***n.*** ⟦< L *bellus,* pretty⟧ a showy trifle; trinket

baud (bôd) ***n.*** ⟦after J. M. E. *Baudot* (1845-1903), Fr inventor⟧ the number of bits per second transmitted in a computer system

baux·ite (bôks'īt') ***n.*** ⟦Fr, after (*Les*) *Baux,* town in S France⟧ a claylike sedimentary rock, the chief ore of aluminum

Ba·var·i·a (bə ver'ē ə) state of SW Germany —**Ba·var'i·an** ***adj.*, *n.***

bawd (bôd) ***n.*** ⟦< ? OFr *baud,* licentious⟧ [Literary] a person, esp. a woman, who keeps a brothel

bawd·y (bô'dē) ***adj.* -i·er, -i·est** indecent; lewd —**bawd'i·ness** ***n.***

bawl (bôl) ***vi.*, *vt.*** ⟦< ML *baulare,* to bark⟧ **1** to shout **2** to weep loudly —***n.*** **1** an outcry **2** a noisy weeping —**bawl out** [Slang] to scold angrily

bay[1] (bā) ***n.*** ⟦< ML *baia*⟧ a wide inlet of a sea or lake, along the shoreline

bay[2] (bā) ***n.*** ⟦< VL *batare,* to gape⟧ **1** an alcove or recess **2** BAY WINDOW

bay[3] (bā) ***vi.*** ⟦< OFr *baiier*⟧ to bark or howl in long, deep tones —***n.*** **1** the sound of baying **2** the situation of a

THESAURUS

bat[1] ***v.*** strike, whack, sock*; see HIT 1.

bat[1,2,3] ***n.*** club, racket, stick; see STICK. —**blind as a bat** sightless, unseeing, blinded; see BLIND 1. —**go to bat for*** intervene for, support, back up; see DEFEND 2. —**have bats in one's belfry*** be mad, be eccentric, be peculiar; see INSANE. —**not bat an eye*** not be surprised, not be shocked, not be amazed, ignore, remain unruffled; see also NEGLECT 1. —**(right) off the bat*** at once, without delay, instantly; see IMMEDIATELY.

batch ***n.*** stack, group, shipment; see BUNCH.

bath ***n.*** **1** [The act of cleansing the body] washing, sponge bath, shower, tub, bath, steam bath, sauna, soak*, dip, soaking*. **2** [An enclosure prepared for bathing] bathroom, toilet, shower, washroom, powder room, lavatory, steam room, sauna, Turkish bath, sitz bath, hot tub, whirlpool, spa, Jacuzzi (trademark), mikvah (Jewish), public baths, shower room.

bathe ***v.*** soap, cleanse, scrub; see WASH 1.

bathrobe ***n.*** robe, dressing gown, kimono; see CLOTHES.

bathroom ***n.*** shower, toilet, lavatory; see BATH 2, TOILET.

battalion ***n.*** unit, force, corps; see ARMY 2.

batter[2,3] ***n.*** **1** [One who bats] hitter, pinch hitter, switch-hitter; see BASEBALL PLAYER. **2** [Baking mixture] dough, mix, paste, recipe, concoction, mush; see also MIXTURE 1.

battery ***n.*** **1** [Cells which generate or store electricity] dry cell, storage cells, storage battery, energy unit, flashlight battery, solar battery, atomic battery, electric cell. **2** [The act of beating] assault, attack, thumping, beating, physical violence, mugging.

battle ***n.*** strife, contention, struggle, combat, bombing, fighting, bloodshed, clash, onslaught, onset, barrage, conflict, warfare, fray, assault, crusade, military campaign, hostilities, havoc, carnage; see also FIGHT. —**give** (or **do**) **battle** fight back, struggle, engage in battle; see ATTACK, FIGHT.

battlefield ***n.*** field of battle, battleground, front, theater of war, disputed territory, no man's land.

battleship ***n.*** man of war, floating fortress, battlewagon*; see SHIP.

bawl ***v.*** weep, shed tears, sob; see CRY 1. —**bawl out*** chide, berate, admonish; see SCOLD.

bay[1] ***n.*** inlet, gulf, bayou, loch, bight, sound, fiord, firth, estuary, strait, narrows, road, arm of the sea, mouth, lagoon, cove, harbor.

hunted animal forced to turn and fight —**at bay** **1** cornered **2** held off —**bring to bay** to corner

bay[4] (bā) ***n.*** ⟦< L *baca,* berry⟧ **1** LAUREL (*n.* 1) **2** [*pl.*] a laurel wreath

bay[5] (bā) ***adj.*** ⟦< L *badius*⟧ reddish-brown —***n.*** **1** a reddish-brown horse, etc. **2** reddish brown

bay'ber'ry ***n.***, *pl.* **-ries** **1** a shrub with small, wax-coated, berrylike fruit **2** the fruit

bay leaf the dried, aromatic leaf of certain laurel plants, used as a seasoning

bay·o·net (bā'ə net', bā'ə nət) ***n.*** ⟦< Fr: after *Bayonne,* city in France⟧ a detachable blade put on a rifle muzzle, for stabbing —***vt.***, ***vi.*** **-net'ed** or **-net'ted**, **-net'ing** or **-net'ting** to stab with a bayonet

bay·ou (bī'o͞o') ***n.*** ⟦< AmInd *bayuk,* small stream⟧ in S U.S., a marshy inlet or outlet of a lake, river, etc.

bay window **1** a window or set of windows jutting out from a wall **2** [Slang] a large protruding belly

ba·zaar (bə zär') ***n.*** ⟦Pers *bāzār*⟧ **1** a marketplace, esp. in the Middle East **2** a benefit sale for a church, etc.

ba·zoo·ka (bə zo͞o'kə) ***n.*** ⟦< name of a comic horn⟧ a portable weapon for launching armor-piercing rockets

BB (bē'bē') ***n.***, *pl.* **BB's** ⟦designation of size⟧ a pellet of shot (diameter, .18 in.) fired from an air rifle (**BB gun**) or shotgun

bbl *abbrev.* barrel

BC *abbrev.* **1** before Christ: also **B.C.** **2** British Columbia

B cell any of the lymphatic leukocytes not derived from the thymus, that build antibodies: cf. T CELL

be (bē) ***vi.*** **was** or **were**, **been**, **being** ⟦OE *beon*⟧ **1** to exist; live **2** to happen; occur **3** to remain or continue *Note: be* is used to link its subject to a predicate complement *[she is nice]* or as an auxiliary: (1) with a past participle: *a)* to form the passive voice *[he will be sued] b)* [Archaic] to form the perfect tense *[Christ is risen]* (2) with a present participle to express continuation *[he is running]* (3) with a present participle or infinitive to express futurity, possibility, obligation, intention, etc. *[she is going soon, he is to cut it] Be* is conjugated in the present indicative: (I) *am,* (he, she, it) *is,* (we, you, they) *are*; in the past indicative: (I, he, she, it) *was,* (we, you, they) *were*

Be *Chem. symbol for* beryllium

be- ⟦< OE *bi-, be-,* at⟧ *prefix* **1** around *[beset]* **2** completely *[bedeck]* **3** away *[betake]* **4** about *[bemoan]* **5** to make *[besot]* **6** to furnish with, affect by *[becloud]*

beach (bēch) ***n.*** ⟦E dial., pebbles⟧ a sandy shore —***vt.***, ***vi.*** to ground (a boat) on a beach

beach'comb'er (-kōm'ər) ***n.*** **1** COMBER (sense 2) **2** one who lives on items found on beaches —**beach'comb'ing** ***n.***

beach'head' ***n.*** a position gained, specif. by invading an enemy shore

beach'wear' ***n.*** garments worn at the beach, as swimsuits

bea·con (bē'kən) ***n.*** ⟦< OE *beacen,* a signal⟧ **1** a light for warning or guiding **2** a radio transmitter sending guiding signals for aircraft

bead (bēd) ***n.*** ⟦< OE *bed,* prayer bead⟧ **1** a small ball of glass, etc., pierced for stringing **2** [*pl.*] a rosary **3** [*pl.*] a string of beads **4** any small, round object, as the front sight of a rifle **5** a drop or bubble **6** the rim edge of a rubber tire —***vt.*** to decorate with beads —**draw a bead on** to take careful aim at —**say one's beads** to pray with a rosary —**bead'y**, **-i·er**, **-i·est**, ***adj.***

bea·dle (bēd''l) ***n.*** ⟦ME *bidel*⟧ [Historical] a minor officer in the Church of England, who kept order in church

bea·gle (bē'gəl) ***n.*** ⟦< ? Fr *bee gueule,* wide throat⟧ a small hound with short legs and drooping ears

beak (bēk) ***n.*** ⟦< L *beccus*⟧ **1** a bird's bill **2** a beaklike part, as the snout of various insects

beak·er (bēk'ər) ***n.*** ⟦< ? Gr *bikos,* vessel with handles⟧ **1** a goblet **2** *Chem.* a glass or metal container with a beaklike lip for pouring

beam (bēm) ***n.*** ⟦ME⟧ **1** a long, thick piece of wood, metal, etc. **2** the crossbar of a balance **3** a ship's breadth at its widest point **4** a shaft of light, etc. **5** a radiant look, smile, etc. **6** a steady radio or radar signal for guiding aircraft or ships —***vt.*** **1** to give out (shafts of light) **2** to direct (a radio signal, etc.) —***vi.*** **1** to shine brightly **2** to smile warmly —**on the beam** [Inf.] working well

bean (bēn) ***n.*** ⟦OE *bean*⟧ **1** a plant of the pea family, bearing kidney-shaped seeds **2** the edible, smooth seed of this plant **3** any beanlike seed *[coffee bean]* **4** [Slang] the head or brain —***vt.*** [Slang] to hit on the head —**full of beans** [Slang] lively —**spill the beans** [Inf.] to tell a secret

bear[1] (ber) ***vt.*** **bore**, **borne** or **born**, **bear'ing** ⟦OE *beran*⟧ **1** to carry **2** to have or show **3** to give birth to **4** to produce or yield **5** to support or sustain **6** to withstand or endure **7** to need *[this bears watching]* **8** to carry or conduct (oneself) **9** to give *[to bear witness]* —***vi.*** **1** to be productive **2** to lie, point, or move in a given direction **3** to have bearing *(on)* **4** to tolerate —**bear down (on)** **1** to exert pressure or effort (on) **2** to approach —**bear out** to confirm —**bear up** to endure —**bear'a·ble** ***adj.*** —**bear'er** ***n.***

bear[2] (ber) ***n.***, *pl.* **bears** or **bear** ⟦OE *bera*⟧ **1** a large, heavy mammal with shaggy fur and a short tail **2** one who is clumsy, rude, etc. **3** one who sells stocks, etc. hoping to buy them back later at a lower price **4** [Slang] a difficult task —***adj.*** falling in price —**bear'like'** ***adj.***

beard (bird) ***n.*** ⟦OE⟧ **1** the hair on the chin and cheeks of a man **2** any beardlike part **3** an awn —***vt.*** **1** to defy **2** to provide with a beard —**beard'ed** ***adj.*** —**beard'less** ***adj.***

bear·ing (ber'iŋ) ***n.*** **1** way of carrying and conducting oneself **2** a supporting part **3** a producing or ability to

THESAURUS

bayonet ***n.*** spike, lance, pike; see KNIFE.

BC or **B.C.** *abbrev.* before Christ, pre-Christian, Old-Testament; see OLD 3.

be ***v.*** **1** [To have being] live, stay, be alive, exist, remain, continue, endure, go on, stand, subsist, breathe, last, prevail, abide, survive, move, act, do, hold, have place.—*Ant.* DIE, disappear, stop. **2** [To mean] signify, denote, imply; see MEAN 1.

beach ***n.*** seaside, sand, the coast; see SHORE.

beached ***a.*** stranded, marooned, aground; see ABANDONED.

beacon ***n.*** flare, lantern, guide, signal fire, lighthouse, lamp, beam, radar, sonar, airline beacon, radio beacon, air control beacon.

bead ***n.*** drop, droplet, pellet, grain, particle, speck, dot, dab, pea, shot, pill, driblet.

beads ***n.*** necklace, pendant, string of jewels; see NECKLACE.

beak ***n.*** nose, prow, bill, mandible, projection, proboscis, snout, nozzle.

beam ***n.*** **1** [A relatively long, stout bar] timber, brace, scantling, rafter, stringer, stud, two-by-four, strut, joist, bolster, axle, girder, sleeper, stay, crosspiece, prop, support, trestle, spar, pole, crossbar, T-beam, I-beam, steel beam, boom, post, column, pillar, sill, jamb, cantilever, shaft, scaffolding; see also BAR 1. **2** [Radio waves intended as a guide] direction finder, unidirectional radio signal, radar; see BEACON. —**off the beam*** faulty, incorrect, inaccurate; see WRONG 2. —**on the beam*** alert, on target, efficient; see ABLE.

beam ***v.*** **1** [To emit] transmit, broadcast, give out; see SEND 1. **2** [To shine] radiate, glitter, glare; see SHINE 1. **3** [To smile] grin, laugh, smirk; see SMILE.

beaming ***a.*** **1** [Giving forth beams] radiant, glowing, gleaming; see BRIGHT 1. **2** [In very genial humor] grinning, animated, sunny; see HAPPY.

bean ***n.*** *Varieties include the following:* kidney, navy, lima, soy, castor, black, pinto, string, black-eyed, black-eye, garbanzo, green, wax; see also VEGETABLE. —**full of beans*** **1** lively, vital, energetic; see ACTIVE. **2** mistaken, erring, incorrect; see WRONG 2. —**spill the beans*** divulge information, tell secrets, talk; see TELL 1.

bear[1] ***v.*** **1** [To suffer] tolerate, support, undergo; see ENDURE 2. **2** [To support weight] sustain, hold up, shoulder; see SUPPORT 1. **3** [To give birth to] deliver, bring to birth, bring forth; see PRODUCE 1. —**bear down on** (or **upon**) **1** [To press] squeeze, compress, push; see PRESS 1. **2** [To try] endeavor, strive, attempt; see TRY 1. —**bear out** confirm, substantiate, support; see PROVE. —**bear up** persist, persevere, carry on; see ENDURE 2. —**bear upon** pertain to, refer to, relate to, regard; see also CONCERN 1. —**bear with** tolerate, be patient with, suffer, put up with; see also ENDURE 2.

bear[2] ***n.*** grizzly, polar bear, brown bear, black bear, cinnamon bear, kodiak bear, sloth bear, koala, Bruin, *ursus* (Latin); see also ANIMAL.

bearable ***a.*** endurable, tolerable, passable, admissible, supportable, sufferable.

beard ***n.*** whiskers, brush, Van Dyke, chin whiskers, imperial, muttonchops, goatee, spade beard, forked beard, side whiskers.

bearded ***a.*** bewhiskered, bushy, unshaven; see HAIRY.

bearing ***n.*** **1** [A point of support] frame, ball bearing, roller bearing; see SUPPORT 2. **2** [Manner of carriage] mien, deportment, manner; see BEHAVIOR, POSTURE 1.

produce **4** endurance **5** [*often pl.*] relative direction or position **6** [*pl.*] awareness of one's situation **7** relevance; relation **8** a part of a machine on which another part revolves, slides, etc.

bear′ish *adj.* **1** bearlike; rude, rough, etc. **2** falling, or causing, expecting, etc. a fall, in prices on the stock exchange —**bear′ish·ly** *adv.*

bé·ar·naise sauce (bā′är nāz′) a creamy sauce, esp. for meat or fish

bear′skin′ *n.* **1** the fur or hide of a bear **2** a rug, coat, etc. made from this

beast (bēst) *n.* ⟦< L *bestia*⟧ **1** any large, four-footed animal **2** one who is gross, brutal, etc.

beast′ly *adj.* **-li·er, -li·est** **1** of or like a beast; brutal, etc. **2** [Inf.] disagreeable; unpleasant —**beast′li·ness** *n.*

beast of burden any animal used for carrying things

beast of prey any animal that hunts and kills other animals for food

beat (bēt) *vt.* **beat, beat′en, beat′ing** ⟦OE *beatan*⟧ **1** to hit repeatedly; pound **2** to punish by so hitting; whip, spank, etc. **3** to dash repeatedly against **4** *a)* to form (a path, etc.) by repeated treading or riding *b)* to keep walking on **5** to mix (eggs, etc.) by hard stirring **6** to move (esp. wings) up and down **7** to search through (a forest, etc.) **8** to defeat or outdo **9** to mark (time or rhythm) by tapping, etc. **10** [Inf.] to baffle **11** [Inf.] to cheat or trick **12** [Slang] to escape the penalties of (an indictment, rap, etc.) —*vi.* **1** to hit or dash repeatedly **2** to throb, vibrate, etc. —*n.* **1** a beating, as of the heart **2** any of a series of movements, blows, etc. **3** a throb **4** a habitual route **5** the unit of musical rhythm **6** BEATNIK —*adj.* **1** [Inf.] tired out **2** of a group of young persons, esp. of the 1950s, expressing social disillusionment by unconventional dress, actions, etc. —**beat down** to put or force down —**beat it!** [Slang] go away! —**beat off** to drive back —**beat up (on)** [Slang] to give a beating to —**beat′er** *n.*

beat′en *adj.* **1** shaped by hammering **2** much traveled [a *beaten* path] **3** crushed in spirit; defeated **4** tired out

be·a·tif·ic (bē′ə tif′ik) *adj.* **1** making blessed **2** showing happiness or delight

be·at·i·fy (bē at′ə fī′) *vt.* **-fied′, -fy′ing** ⟦< L *beatus*, happy + *facere*, to make⟧ **1** to make blissfully happy **2** *R.C.Ch.* to declare (a deceased person) to be in heaven —**be·at′i·fi·ca′tion** *n.*

beat′ing *n.* **1** the act of one that beats **2** a whipping **3** a throbbing **4** a defeat

be·at·i·tude (bē at′ə to͞od′) *n.* ⟦< L *beatus*, happy⟧ perfect blessedness or happiness —**the Beatitudes** the pronouncements in the Sermon on the Mount

beat·nik (bēt′nik) *n.* a member of the beat group

beat′-up′ *adj.* [Slang] worn-out, dilapidated, etc.

beau (bō) *n., pl.* **beaus** or **beaux** (bōz) ⟦Fr < L *bellus*, pretty⟧ [Old-fashioned] a woman's sweetheart

beau·te·ous (byo͞ot′ē əs) *adj.* ⟦ME⟧ beautiful —**beau′te·ous·ly** *adv.*

beau·ti·cian (byo͞o tish′ən) *n.* one who works in a beauty shop

beau·ti·ful (byo͞ot′ə fəl) *adj.* having beauty —**beau′ti·ful·ly** *adv.*

beau′ti·fy′ (-fī′) *vt., vi.* **-fied′, -fy′ing** to make or become beautiful —**beau′ti·fi·ca′tion** *n.* —**beau′ti·fi′er** *n.*

beau·ty (byo͞ot′ē) *n., pl.* **-ties** ⟦< L *bellus*, pretty⟧ **1** the quality of being very pleasing, as in form, color, etc. **2** a thing with this quality **3** good looks **4** a very attractive person, feature, etc.

beauty salon (or **shop, parlor,** etc.) a place where people, esp. women, go for hair styling, manicuring, etc.

bea·ver (bē′vər) *n.* ⟦< OE *beofor*⟧ **1** a large amphibious rodent with soft, brown fur, webbed hind feet, and a flat, broad tail **2** its fur

be·calm (bē käm′, bi-) *vt.* **1** to make calm **2** to make (a ship) motionless from lack of wind

be·cause (bē kôz′, -kuz′; bi-) *conj.* ⟦ME *bi*, by + *cause*⟧ for the reason or cause that —**because of** by reason of

beck (bek) *n.* a beckoning gesture —**at the beck and call of** at the service of

beck·on (bek′′n) *vi., vt.* ⟦OE *beacnian*⟧ **1** to summon by a gesture **2** to lure; entice

be·cloud (bē kloud′, bi-) *vt.* **1** to cloud over **2** to confuse; muddle

be·come (bē kum′, bi kum′) *vi.* **-came′, -come′, -com′ing** ⟦OE *becuman*⟧ to come or grow to be —*vt.* to befit; suit [modesty *becomes* her] —**become of** to happen to

be·com′ing *adj.* **1** appropriate; fit **2** suitable to the wearer

bed (bed) *n.* ⟦OE⟧ **1** a piece of furniture for sleeping or resting on **2** a plot of soil where plants are raised **3** the

THESAURUS

beast *n.* **1** [A large animal] brute, creature, lower animal; see ANIMAL. **2** [A person of brutish nature] monster, brute, degenerate, animal, fiend, swine, pervert, lout, savage, barbarian, monstrosity, Bluebeard; see also PERVERT.

beastly *a.* brutal, savage, coarse, repulsive, gluttonous, obscene, unclean, piggish, hoggish, irrational, boorish, brutish, depraved, abominable, loathsome, vile, low, degraded, sensual, foul, base, disgusting, inhuman, gross, vulgar.—*Ant.* REFINED, sweet, nice.

beat* *a.* weary, fatigued, worn-out; see TIRED.

beat *n.* **1** [A throb] thump, pound, quake, flutter, pulse, pulsation, cadence, flow, vibration, turn, ripple, pressure, impulse, quiver, shake, surge, swell, palpitation, undulation, rhythm. **2** [A unit of music] accent, vibration, division, stress, measure, rhythm.

beat *v.* **1** [To thrash] hit, punish, whip, pistol-whip, flog, trounce, spank, scourge, switch, lash, slap, cuff, box, strap, birch, cane, horsewhip, buffet, pommel, tap, rap, strike, bump, pat, knock, pound, club, punch, bat, flail, batter, maul, whack, hammer, clout, smack, bang, swat, slug*, beat black and blue*, whale*, belt*, whack, beat the tar out of*, beat the daylights out of*, beat the hell out of*, knock the stuffing out of*, wallop*, lick*, paste*, bash*, work over*, thwack. **2** [To pulsate] pound, thump, pulse; see THROB. **3** [To worst] overcome, surpass, conquer; see DEFEAT 2, 3. **4** [To mix] stir, whip, knead; see MIX 1.

beaten *a.* **1** [Defeated] worsted, humbled, thwarted, bested, disappointed, frustrated, baffled, conquered, overthrown, subjugated, ruined, mastered, trounced, undone, vanquished, crushed, overwhelmed, overpowered, licked*, done in*, done for*, kayoed*, mugged, skinned*, trimmed*, had it*, washed up*, sunk*.—*Ant.* SUCCESSFUL, victorious, triumphant. **2** [Made firm and hard] hammered, tramped, stamped, rolled, milled, forged, trod, pounded, tramped down, tamped.—*Ant.* SOFT, spongy, loose. **3** [Made light by beating] whipped, frothy, foamy, mixed, churned, creamy, bubbly, meringued.

beater *n.* whipper, mixer, eggbeater; see APPLIANCE.

beating *n.* thrashing, whipping, drubbing; see DEFEAT.

beatnik *n.* bohemian, hippie, nonconformist; see RADICAL.

beautiful *a.* lovely, attractive, appealing, comely, pleasing, pretty, fair, fine, nice, dainty, good-looking, delightful, charming, enticing, fascinating, admirable, rich, graceful, ideal, delicate, refined, elegant, symmetrical, well-formed, shapely, well-made, splendid, gorgeous, brilliant, radiant, exquisite, dazzling, resplendent, magnificent, superb, marvelous, wonderful, grand, awe-inspiring, imposing, majestic, excellent, impressive, handsome, divine, blooming, rosy, beauteous, statuesque, well-favored, bewitching, personable, taking, alluring, slender, svelte, lissome, lithe, bright-eyed, easy on the eyes*.—*Ant.* UGLY, deformed, hideous.

beautifully *a.* gracefully, exquisitely, charmingly, attractively, prettily, delightfully, appealingly, seductively, alluringly, elegantly, gorgeously, splendidly, magnificently, ideally, tastefully, sublimely, handsomely, superbly, divinely.

beauty *n.* **1** [A pleasing physical quality] grace, comeliness, fairness, pulchritude, charm, delicacy, elegance, attraction, fascination, allurement, shapeliness, majesty, attractiveness, good looks, glamour, loveliness, bloom.—*Ant.* UGLINESS, homeliness, deformity. **2** [A beautiful woman] goddess, belle, siren, enchantress, seductress, Venus, *femme fatale* (French), vision, knockout*, looker*, charmer*.—*Ant.* WITCH, blemish, fright.

because *conj.* on account of, in consequence of, in view of, by reason of, for the reason that, for the sake of, in behalf of, on the grounds that, in the interest of, as a result of, as things go, by virtue of, in that, since, by the agency of, due to*, being as how*, owing to.

beckon *v.* signal, motion, sign; see SUMMON.

become *v.* develop into, change into, turn into, grow into, eventually be, emerge as, turn out to be, come to be, shift, assume the form of, be reformed, be converted to, convert, mature, shift toward, incline to, melt into; see also GROW 2.

becoming *a.* attractive, beautiful, neat, agreeable, handsome, seemly, comely, tasteful, well-chosen, fair, trim, graceful, flattering, effective, excellent, acceptable, welcome, nice.

bed *n.* **1** [A place of rest] mattress, cot, couch, bedstead, berth, bunk,

bottom of a river, lake, etc. **4** any flat surface used as a foundation **5** a geologic layer; stratum **6** the flat surface of a truck —***vt.*** **bed'ded, bed'ding 1** to put to bed **2** to provide with a sleeping place **3** to embed **4** to plant in a bed of earth **5** to arrange in layers —***vi.*** **1** to go to bed; rest; sleep **2** to stratify

bed'-and-break'fast ***adj., n.*** (of) a hotel, etc. that provides breakfast as part of the price: also **bed and breakfast**

be·daz·zle (bē daz'əl, bi-) ***vt.*** **-zled, -zling** to dazzle thoroughly; bewilder

bed'bug' ***n.*** a small, wingless, biting insect that infests beds, etc.

bed'clothes' ***pl.n.*** sheets, blankets, etc. for a bed

bed'cov'er ***n.*** a cover for a bed; bedspread

bed'ding ***n.*** **1** mattresses and bedclothes **2** a bottom layer; base **3** straw, etc. for animals to sleep on

be·deck (bē dek', bi-) ***vt.*** to adorn

be·dev·il (bē dev'əl, bi-) ***vt.*** **-iled** or **-illed, -il·ing** or **-il·ling** to plague or bewilder —**be·dev'il·ment** ***n.***

bed'fel'low ***n.*** **1** a person who shares one's bed **2** an associate, ally, etc.

be·dim (bē dim', bi-) ***vt.*** **-dimmed', -dim'ming** to make (the eyes or the vision) dim

bed·lam (bed'ləm) ***n.*** ⟦after (the old London mental hospital of St. Mary of) *Bethlehem*⟧ any place or condition of noise and confusion

bed of roses [Inf.] a situation or position of ease and luxury

Bed·ou·in (bed'o͞o in') ***n., pl.*** **-ins** or **-in** ⟦< Ar *badāwīn,* desert dwellers⟧ [*also* **b-**] an Arab of the desert tribes of Arabia, Syria, or N Africa

bed'pan' ***n.*** a shallow pan for use as a toilet by one confined to bed

be·drag·gle (bē drag'əl, bi-) ***vt.*** **-gled, -gling** to make wet, limp, and dirty, as by dragging through mire

bed'rid'den (-rid''n) ***adj.*** confined to bed by illness, infirmity, etc.

bed'rock' ***n.*** **1** solid rock beneath the soil, etc. **2** a foundation or bottom

bed'roll' ***n.*** a portable roll of bedding, as for sleeping outdoors

bed'room' ***n.*** a room for sleeping

bed'side' ***n.*** the space beside a bed —***adj.*** near a bed

bed'sore' ***n.*** a sore on the body of a bedridden person, caused by chafing

bed'spread' ***n.*** an ornamental spread covering the blanket on a bed

bed'stead' (-sted') ***n.*** a framework for supporting the mattress, etc. of a bed

bed'time' ***n.*** one's usual time for going to bed

bee[1] (bē) ***n.*** ⟦OE *beo*⟧ a broad-bodied, four-winged, hairy insect that gathers pollen and nectar and that can sting

bee[2] (bē) ***n.*** ⟦OE *ben,* compulsory service⟧ a meeting of people to work together or to compete *[*a spelling *bee]*

beech (bēch) ***n.*** ⟦OE *bece*⟧ **1** a tree with smooth, gray bark, hard wood, and edible nuts **2** its wood

beech'nut' ***n.*** the small, three-cornered, edible nut of the beech tree

beef (bēf) ***n., pl.*** for 1 & 5, **beefs**; for 1, also **beeves** ⟦< L *bos,* ox⟧ **1** a full-grown ox, cow, bull, or steer, esp. one bred for meat **2** such animals collectively **3** their meat **4** [Inf.] *a)* human flesh *b)* strength **5** [Slang] a complaint —***vi.*** [Slang] to complain —**beef up** [Inf.] to reinforce

beef'cake' ***n.*** ⟦BEEF (*n.* 4*a*) + (CHEESE)CAKE⟧ [Inf.] display of the figure of a nude or partly nude, muscular man, as in a photograph

beef'steak' ***n.*** a thick slice of beef for broiling or frying

beef'y ***adj.*** **-i·er, -i·est** brawny —**beef'i·ness** ***n.***

bee'hive' ***n.*** **1** a shelter for a colony of bees **2** a place of great activity

bee'keep'er ***n.*** one who keeps bees for producing honey —**bee'keep'ing** ***n.***

bee'line' ***n.*** a straight line or direct route

Be·el·ze·bub (bē el'zə bub') ***n.*** *Bible* the chief devil; Satan

been (bin; *often* ben) ***vi. pp. of*** BE

beep (bēp) ***n.*** ⟦echoic⟧ the brief, high-pitched sound of a horn or electronic signal —***vi., vt.*** to make or cause to make this sound

beer (bir) ***n.*** ⟦OE *beor*⟧ **1** an alcoholic, fermented drink made from malt and hops **2** a soft drink made from extracts of roots, etc. *[*root *beer]*

bees'wax' ***n.*** wax secreted by honeybees, used to make their honeycombs: it is used in candles, etc.

beet (bēt) ***n.*** ⟦< L *beta*⟧ **1** a plant with edible leaves and a thick, fleshy, white or red root **2** the edible root, also a source of sugar

Bee·tho·ven (bā'tō'vən), **Lud·wig van** (lo͞ot'viH vän) 1770-1827; Ger. composer

bee·tle[1] (bēt''l) ***n.*** ⟦OE *bītan,* to bite⟧ an insect with hard front wings that cover the membranous hind wings when these are folded

bee·tle[2] (bēt''l) ***vi.*** **-tled, -tling** ⟦prob. < fol.⟧ to overhang —***adj.*** overhanging: also **bee'tling**

bee'tle-browed' (-broud') ***adj.*** ⟦< ME < ? *bitel,* sharp + *brouwe,* brow⟧ **1** having overhanging or bushy eyebrows **2** frowning

be·fall (bē fôl', bi-) ***vi., vt.*** **-fell', -fall'en, -fall'ing** ⟦< OE *be-,* BE- + *feallan,* to fall⟧ to happen or occur (to)

be·fit (bē fit', bi-) ***vt.*** **-fit'ted, -fit'ting** to be suitable or proper for; be suited to —**be·fit'ting** ***adj.***

be·fog (bē fôg', -fäg'; bi-) ***vt.*** **-fogged', -fog'ging 1** to envelop in fog; make foggy **2** to obscure; confuse

be·fore (bē fôr', bi-) ***adv.*** ⟦OE *be-,* by + *foran,* fore⟧ **1** ahead; in front **2** previously **3** earlier; sooner —***prep.*** **1** ahead of in time, space, order, etc. **2** located in front of **3** in or into the sight, presence, etc. of **4** earlier than; prior to **5** in preference to **6** being considered, judged, or decided by *[*a case *before* the court*]* —***conj.*** **1** earlier than the time that *[*call *before* you go*]* **2** rather than *[*I'd die *before* I'd tell*]*

be·fore'hand' ***adv., adj.*** ahead of time; in anticipation

be·foul (bē foul', bi-) ***vt.*** **1** to make filthy **2** to slander

be·friend (bē frend', bi-) ***vt.*** to act as a friend to

be·fud·dle (bē fud''l, bi-) ***vt.*** **-dled, -dling** to confuse or stupefy

beg (beg) ***vt., vi.*** **begged, beg'ging** ⟦< Du *beggaert,* religious mendicant⟧ **1** to ask for (alms) **2** to ask earnestly; entreat —**beg off** to ask to be released from —**go begging** to be available but unwanted

be·gan (bē gan', bi-) ***vi., vt. pt. of*** BEGIN

be·get (bē get', bi-) ***vt.*** **-got'** or [Archaic] **-gat'** (-gat'), **-got'ten** or **-got', -get'ting** ⟦< OE *begietan,* acquire⟧ **1** to be the father of **2** to produce; cause

THESAURUS

hay*, sack*. *Beds include the following:* single bed, double bed, davenport, cot, four-poster, trundle bed, twin bed, fold-away bed, Murphy bed, hammock, futon, feather bed, stretcher, folding bed, bunk bed, litter, cradle, crib, bassinet, king-size bed, queen-size bed, water bed, hospital bed, sofa bed, day bed. **2** [A foundation] base, bottom, groundwork; see FOUNDATION 2. **3** [A seed plot] patch, row, planting; see GARDEN.

bedding ***n.*** bedclothes, bed linen, thermal blankets, covers, bedcovers, pillows, coverlets, sheets, quilts, spreads, comforters.

bed down ***v.*** turn in, retire, hit the hay*; see SLEEP.

bedlam ***n.*** confusion, pandemonium, clamor; see CONFUSION, NOISE 2.

bedridden ***a.*** incapacitated, confined to bed, laid up; see DISABLED.

bedroom ***n.*** sleeping room, guest room, master bedroom; see ROOM 2.

bedspread ***n.*** spread, quilt, comforter; see BEDDING.

bedtime ***n.*** slumbertime, time to retire, sack time*; see NIGHT.

beef ***n.*** **1** [Bovine flesh used as food] cow's flesh, beefsteak, red meat; see MEAT. **2** [A grown animal of the genus *Bos*] bovine, bull, steer; see COW. **3** [*A complaint] dispute, protestation, gripe*; see OBJECTION.

beef up* ***v.*** intensify, augment, increase; see STRENGTHEN.

beer ***n.*** malt beverage, malt liquor, brew, suds*. *Varieties include the following:* lager, bock beer, ale, stout, porter, pale ale, pilsener, bitter, light beer, dark beer.

before ***a.*** previously, earlier, in the past, since, gone by, in old days, heretofore, former, formerly, back, sooner, up to now, ahead, in front, in the forefront, in advance, facing.—*Ant.* AFTERWARD, in the future, to come.

before ***prep.*** prior to, previous to, in front of, ahead of, under jurisdiction of, antecedent to.—*Ant.* BEHIND, following, at the rear.

beforehand ***a.*** previously, already, in anticipation; see BEFORE.

befriend ***v.*** encourage, advise, stand by; see HELP.

beg ***v.*** entreat, implore, beseech, supplicate, crave, solicit, pray for, urge, plead, sue, importune, petition, apply to, request, press, appeal to, requisition, conjure, adjure, apostrophize, dun, canvass; see also ASK.—*Ant.* ADMIT, concede, accede.

beg·gar (beg′ər) ***n.*** **1** one who begs **2** a pauper —***vt.*** **1** to make poor **2** to make (a description, etc.) seem inadequate —**beg′gar·y,** *pl.* **-ies,** ***n.***

beg′gar·ly ***adj.*** very poor, worthless, inadequate, etc.

be·gin (bē gin′, bi-) ***vi., vt.*** **-gan′, -gun′, -gin′ning** ⟦< OE *beginnan*⟧ **1** to start doing, acting, etc. **2** to originate **3** to have a first part or be the first part of

be·gin′ner ***n.*** one just beginning to do or learn something; novice

be·gin′ning ***n.*** **1** a starting **2** the time or place of starting; origin **3** the first part **4** [*usually pl.*] an early stage or example

be·gone (bē gôn′, bi-) ***interj., vi.*** (to) be gone; go away; get out

be·gon·ia (bi gōn′yə) ***n.*** ⟦after M. *Bégon* (1638-1710), Fr patron of science⟧ a tropical plant with showy flowers and ornamental leaves

be·got (bē gät′, bi-) ***vt.*** *pt. & alt. pp. of* BEGET

be·got′ten ***vt.*** *alt. pp. of* BEGET

be·grime (bē grīm′, bi-) ***vt.*** **-grimed′, -grim′ing** to cover with grime; soil

be·grudge (bē gruj′, bi gruj′) ***vt.*** **-grudged′, -grudg′ing** **1** to resent another's possession of (something) **2** to give with reluctance —**be·grudg′ing·ly** ***adv.***

be·guile (bē gīl′, bi-) ***vt.*** **-guiled′, -guil′ing** **1** to mislead by tricking, etc.; deceive **2** to deprive *of* or cheat *out of* by deceit **3** to pass (time) pleasantly **4** to charm or delight —**be·guile′ment** ***n.*** —**be·guil′er** ***n.***

be·gun (bē gun′, bi-) ***vi., vt.*** *pp. of* BEGIN

be·half (bē haf′, bi-) ***n.*** ⟦OE *be,* by + *healf,* side⟧ support —**in** (or **on**) **behalf of** in the interest of; for

be·have (bē hāv′, bi-) ***vt., vi.*** **-haved′, -hav′ing** ⟦see BE- & HAVE⟧ **1** to conduct (oneself) in a specified way; act **2** to conduct (oneself) properly

be·hav′ior (-yər) ***n.*** way of behaving; conduct or action —**be·hav′ior·al** ***adj.***

behavioral science any of the sciences, as sociology, that study human behavior

be·head (bē hed′, bi-) ***vt.*** to cut off the head of

be·held (bē held′, bi-) ***vt.*** *pt. & pp. of* BEHOLD

be·he·moth (bə hē′məth) ***n.*** ⟦< Heb *behema,* beast⟧ **1** *Bible* some huge animal **2** any huge or powerful animal or thing

be·hest (bē hest′, bi-) ***n.*** ⟦< OE *behæs,* a vow⟧ an order, command, or request

be·hind (bē hīnd′, bi-) ***adv.*** ⟦< OE *behindan*⟧ **1** in or to the rear **2** in a former time, place, etc. **3** in or into arrears **4** slow; late —***prep.*** **1** remaining after **2** in or to the rear of **3** inferior to in position, achievement, etc. **4** later than *[behind* schedule*]* **5** beyond **6** gone by or ended for *[*school was *behind* him now*]* **7** supporting *[behind* their team*]* **8** prompting or instigating *[behind* the plot*]* **9** hidden by *[*what's *behind* this news*]* —***n.*** [Inf.] the buttocks

be·hind′hand′ ***adv., adj.*** behind in payment, time, or progress

be·hold (bē hōld′, bi-) ***vt.*** **-held′, -hold′ing** ⟦< OE *bihealdan*⟧ to look at; see —***interj.*** look! see! —**be·hold′er** ***n.***

be·hold′en ***adj.*** obliged to feel grateful; indebted

be·hoove (bē ho͞ov′, bi-) ***vt.*** **-hooved′, -hoov′ing** ⟦< OE *behofian,* to need⟧ to be incumbent upon or proper for *[*it *behooves* you to drive carefully*]*

beige (bāzh) ***n., adj.*** ⟦Fr⟧ grayish tan

Bei·jing (bā′jiŋ′, -zhiŋ′) capital of China, in the NE part: pop. 5,531,000

be·ing (bē′iŋ) ***n.*** ⟦see BE⟧ **1** existence; life **2** fundamental nature **3** one that lives or exists **4** personality —**being as** (or **that**) [Inf. or Dial.] since; because —**for the time being** for now

Bei·rut (bā ro͞ot′) seaport & capital of Lebanon: pop. *c.* 1,500,000

be·jew·el (bē jo͞o′əl, bi-) ***vt.*** **-eled** or **-elled, -el·ing** or **-el·ling** to decorate with or as with jewels

be·la·bor (bē lā′bər, bi-) ***vt.*** **1** to beat severely **2** to scold **3** to spend too much time on

Bel·a·rus (bel′ə ro͞os′) country in central Europe: formerly part of the U.S.S.R.: 80,134 sq. mi.; pop. 10,152,000

be·lat·ed (bē lāt′id, bi-) ***adj.*** late or too late —**be·lat′ed·ly** ***adv.***

be·lay (bi lā′) ***vt., vi.*** **-layed′, -lay′ing** ⟦< OE *belecgan,* make fast⟧ **1** to make (a rope) secure by winding around a cleat, etc. **2** [Inf.] *Naut.* to hold; stop **3** to secure by a rope

bel can·to (bel′kän′tō) ⟦It⟧ a style of singing with brilliant vocal display

belch (belch) ***vi., vt.*** ⟦OE *bealcian*⟧ **1** to expel (gas) through the mouth from the stomach **2** to throw forth (its contents) violently —***n.*** a belching

be·lea·guer (bē lē′gər, bi-) ***vt.*** ⟦< Du < *be-,* around + *leger,* a camp⟧ **1** to besiege by encircling **2** to beset or harass

Bel·fast (bel′fast) seaport & capital of Northern Ireland: pop. 284,000

bel·fry (bel′frē) ***n.,*** *pl.* **-fries** ⟦ult. < OHG⟧ **1** a bell tower **2** the part of a tower that holds the bells

Belg Belgium

Bel·gium (bel′jəm) kingdom in W Europe: 11,778 sq. mi.; pop. 9,979,000 —**Bel′gian** ***adj., n.***

Bel·grade (bel′grād′, -gräd′) capital of Yugoslavia: pop. 1,470,000

be·lie (bē lī′, bi-) ***vt.*** **-lied′, -ly′ing** **1** to disguise or misrepresent **2** to leave unfulfilled; disappoint **3** to prove false

be·lief (bə lēf′, bē-) ***n.*** ⟦< OE *geleafa*⟧ **1** conviction that certain things are true **2** religious faith **3** trust or confi-

THESAURUS

beggar ***n.*** pauper, poor person, hobo, tramp, indigent, vagrant, poverty-stricken person, destitute person, dependent, bankrupt, panhandler*, moocher*, bum*.

begging ***a.*** anxious, in need, imploring, supplicating; see also WANTING 1.

begin ***v.*** **1** [To initiate] start, cause, inaugurate, make, occasion, impel, produce, effect, set in motion, launch, mount, start in, start on, start up, start off, induce, do, create, bring about, get going, set about, institute, lead up to, undertake, enter upon, open, animate, motivate, go ahead, lead the way, bring on, bring to pass, act on, generate, drive, actualize, introduce, originate, found, establish, set up, trigger, give birth to, take the lead, plunge into, lay the foundation for, break ground.—*Ant.* END, finish, terminate. **2** [To come into being, or start functioning] commence, get under way, set out, start in, start out, come out, arise, rise, dawn, sprout, originate, crop up, come to birth, come into the world, be born, emanate, come into existence, occur, burst forth, issue forth, come forth, bud, grow, flower, blossom, break out, set to work, kick off, jump off*, go to it*, dig in*, take off*, see the light of day.—*Ant.* STOP, cease, subside.

beginner ***n.*** novice, apprentice, rookie*; see AMATEUR.

beginning ***n.*** **1** [The origin in point of time or place] source, outset, root; see ORIGIN 2. **2** [The origin, thought of as the cause] germ, heart, antecedent; see ORIGIN 3.

begun ***a.*** started, initiated, instituted, under way, in motion, in progress, on foot, inaugurated, happening, proceeding, going, active, underway, existing, operative, working, in force.

behalf ***n.*** interest, benefit, sake; see WELFARE.

behave ***v.*** act with decorum, follow the golden rule, do unto others as you would have others do unto you, be nice, be good, be civil, mind one's p's and q's, be orderly, play one's part, live up to, observe the law, reform, mind one's manners, comport oneself, deport oneself, behave oneself, be on one's best behavior, act one's age, avoid offense, toe the line, play fair.

behavior ***n.*** bearing, deportment, comportment, demeanor, air, presence, carriage, conduct, manners, actions, attitudes, way of life, speech, talk, tone, morals, habits, tact, social graces, correctness, decorum, form, convention, propriety, taste, management, routine, practice, what's done, style, expression, performance, code, role, observance, course, guise, act, deed, ethics, way, front.

behind ***a., prep.*** **1** [To the rear in space] back of, following, after; see BACK. **2** [Late in time] tardy, dilatory, behind time; see LATE 1, SLOW 2. **3** [Slow in progress] sluggish, slow-moving, delayed, backward, underdeveloped, retarded, behind schedule, belated; see also SLOW 2.—*Ant.* FAST, rapid, on time.

being ***n.*** **1** [Existence] presence, actuality, animation; see LIFE 1. **2** [The essential part] nature, core, marrow; see ESSENCE 1. **3** [A living thing] creature, conscious agent, beast; see ANIMAL. —**for the time being** temporarily, tentatively, for now, for the present; see also BRIEFLY, NOW.

belated ***a.*** remiss, tardy, overdue; see LATE 1, SLOW 3.

belief ***n.*** idea, opinion, faith, creed, tenet, doctrine, principle, feeling, hope, intuition, view, expectation, acceptance, trust, notion, persuasion, position, understanding, conviction, confidence, suspicion, knowledge, conclusion, presumption, surmise, hypothesis, thinking, judgment, certainty, impression, assumption, conjecture, fancy, theory, guess, conception, inference.

dence **4** creed or doctrine **5** an opinion; expectation; judgment

be·lieve (bə lēv′, bē-) ***vt.* -lieved′, -liev′ing** ⟦< OE *geliefan*⟧ **1** to take as true, real, etc. **2** to trust a statement or promise of (a person) **3** to suppose or think —***vi.*** to have trust, faith, or confidence (*in*) —**be·liev′a·ble *adj.*** —**be·liev′er *n.***

be·lit·tle (bē lit′'l, bi-) ***vt.* -tled, -tling** to make seem little, less important, etc. —**be·lit′tle·ment *n.***

Be·lize (bə lēz′) country in Central America, on the Caribbean: 8,866 sq. mi.; pop. 184,000

bell (bel) ***n.*** ⟦OE *belle*⟧ **1** a hollow, cuplike object, as of metal, which rings when struck **2** the sound of a bell **3** anything shaped like a bell **4** *Naut.* a bell rung to mark the periods of the watch —***vt.*** to attach a bell to —***vi.*** to flare out like a bell

Bell (bel), **Al·ex·an·der Gra·ham** (al′ig zan′dər grā′əm) 1847-1922; U.S. inventor of the telephone, born in Scotland

bel·la·don·na (bel′ə dän′ə) ***n.*** ⟦< It, beautiful lady⟧ **1** a poisonous plant with purplish flowers and black berries **2** ATROPINE

bell′-bot′tom *adj.* flared at the ankles, as trousers or slacks: also **bell′-bot′tomed** —***n.*** [*pl.*] bell-bottom trousers

bell′boy′ *n.* BELLHOP

belle (bel) ***n.*** ⟦Fr, fem. of *beau*⟧ a pretty woman or girl

belles-let·tres (bel le′tr′, -trə) ***pl.n.*** ⟦Fr⟧ literature as distinguished from technical writings

bell′hop′ *n.* one employed by a hotel, club, etc. to carry luggage and do errands

bel·li·cose (bel′i kōs′) ***adj.*** ⟦< L *bellicus*, of war⟧ quarrelsome; warlike —**bel′li·cos′i·ty** (-käs′ə tē) ***n.***

bel·lig·er·ent (bə lij′ər ənt) ***adj.*** ⟦< L *bellum,* war + *gerere*, carry on⟧ **1** at war **2** of war **3** warlike **4** ready to fight or quarrel —***n.*** a belligerent person, group, or nation —**bel·lig′er·ence *n.*** —**bel·lig′er·en·cy *n.*** —**bel·lig′er·ent·ly *adv.***

bell jar a bell-shaped container made of glass, used to keep air, moisture, etc. in or out: also **bell glass**

bel·low (bel′ō) ***vi.*** ⟦< OE *bylgan*⟧ **1** to roar with a reverberating sound, as a bull **2** to cry out loudly, as in anger —***vt.*** to utter loudly or powerfully —***n.*** a bellowing sound

bel·lows (bel′ōz′) ***n.*** ⟦< ME *beli*, belly⟧ [*with sing. or pl. v.*] **1** a device that forces air out when its sides are pressed together: used in pipe organs, for blowing fires, etc. **2** anything like a bellows

bell pepper a large, sweet red pepper

Bell's palsy ⟦after C. *Bell* (1774-1842), Scot anatomist⟧ a sudden, usually temporary paralysis of the muscles on one side of the face

bell·weth·er (bel′weth′ər) ***n.*** ⟦ME⟧ **1** a male sheep, usually wearing a bell, that leads the flock **2** a leader

bel·ly (bel′ē) ***n.***, *pl.* **-lies** ⟦< OE *belg,* leather bag⟧ **1** the part of the body between the chest and thighs; abdomen **2** the underside of an animal's body **3** the stomach **4** the deep interior, as of a ship —***vt.***, ***vi.* -lied, -ly·ing** to swell out

bel′ly·ache′ *n.* pain in the abdomen —***vi.* -ached′, -ach′ing** [Slang] to complain

bel′ly·but′ton *n.* [Inf.] the navel

bel′ly·ful′ (-fool′) ***n.*** **1** enough or more than enough to eat **2** [Slang] all that one can bear

belly laugh [Inf.] a hearty laugh

be·long (bē lôŋ′, bi-) ***vi.*** ⟦< ME⟧ **1** to have a proper place *[it belongs here]* **2** to be related (*to*) **3** to be a member: with *to* **4** to be owned: with *to*

be·long′ings *pl.n.* possessions

be·lov·ed (bi luv′id, -luvd′) ***adj.*** ⟦ME *biloven*⟧ dearly loved —***n.*** a dearly loved person

be·low (bi lō′) ***adv.***, ***adj.*** ⟦see BE- & LOW[1]⟧ **1** in or to a lower place; beneath **2** later (in a book, etc.) **3** in or to hell **4** on earth **5** under in rank, amount, etc. —***prep.*** **1** lower than **2** unworthy of

Bel·shaz·zar (bel shaz′ər) ***n.*** *Bible* the last king of Babylon

belt (belt) ***n.*** ⟦ult. < L *balteus*⟧ **1** a band of leather, etc. worn around the waist **2** any encircling thing like this **3** an endless band for transferring motion, as with pulleys, or conveying things **4** a distinctive area *[the Corn Belt]* **5** [Inf.] a hard blow; punch **6** [Slang] *a)* a gulp, esp. of liquor *b)* a thrill —***vt.*** **1** to encircle or fasten with a belt **2** [Inf.] to hit hard **3** [Inf.] to sing loudly: usually with *out* **4** [Slang] to gulp (liquor): often with *down* —**below the belt** unfair(ly) —**tighten one's belt** to live more thriftily —**under one's belt** [Inf.] as part of one's experience

belt′-tight′en·ing *n.* an economizing —***adj.*** involving the cutting of expenses

belt′way′ *n.* an expressway passing around an urban area

be·moan (bē mōn′, bi-) ***vt.***, ***vi.*** to lament

be·muse (bē myo͞oz′, bi-) ***vt.* -mused′, -mus′ing** ⟦BE- + MUSE⟧ **1** to confuse or stupefy **2** to preoccupy —**be·muse′ment *n.***

bench (bench) ***n.*** ⟦OE *benc*⟧ **1** a long, hard seat **2** the place where judges sit in a court **3** [*sometimes* **B-**] *a)* the status of a judge *b)* judges collectively *c)* a law court **4** WORKBENCH **5** a seat on which members of a sports team sit when they are not playing —***vt.*** *Sports* to take (a player) out of a game —**on the bench 1** serving as a judge **2** *Sports* not playing

bench mark a standard in measuring, judging quality, etc.: also **bench′mark′ *n.***

bench press a weight-lifting exercise, done while one is lying on a bench with the feet on the floor, in which a barbell is pushed upward from the chest —**bench′-press′ *vt.***

bench warrant an order issued by a judge or court for the arrest of a person

bend[1] (bend) ***vt.* bent, bend′ing** ⟦< OE *bendan*, confine with a string⟧ **1** to make curved or crooked **2** to turn, esp. from a straight line **3** to make submit —***vi.* 1** to

THESAURUS

believable *a.* trustworthy, credible, acceptable; see CONVINCING.

believe *v.* accept, hold, think, understand, consider, swear by, conceive, affirm, conclude, be of the opinion, have faith, have no doubt, take at one's word, take someone's word for, be convinced, be certain of, give credence to, rest assured.—*Ant.* DENY, doubt, suspect. —**believe in** swear by, look to, have faith in; see TRUST 1.

believer *n.* convert, devotee, adherent, apostle, disciple, prophet, confirmed believer; see also FOLLOWER.

believing *a.* maintaining, trusting, presuming, assuming, holding, accepting, under the impression.

belittle *v.* lower, disparage, decry; see ABUSE.

bell *n.* chimes, siren, signal, gong, buzzer; see also ALARM.

belligerent *a.* warlike, pugnacious, hostile; see AGGRESSIVE.

bellow *n.* howl, cry, roar; see CRY 1.

bellow *v.* howl, call, shout; see CRY 2, YELL.

belly *n.* paunch, abdomen, gut*; see STOMACH.

bellyache* *v.* whine, grumble, protest; see COMPLAIN.

belong *v.* **1** [To be properly placed] fit in, have a place, relate; see FIT 1. **2** [To be acceptable in a group; *said of persons*] fit in, have a place, have its place, be born so, be a member, take one's place with, be one of, be counted among, be included in, owe allegiance to, be a part of, be one of the family.—*Ant.* DIFFER, fight, not fit in. —**belong to** pertain to, relate to, be occupied by, be enjoyed by, be owned by, be in the possession of, be at the disposal of, be the property of, concern, come with, go with, fall under.—*Ant.* ESCAPE, be free, have no owner.

belongings *n.* possessions, goods, things*; see PROPERTY 1.

beloved *a.* loved, adored, worshiped, cherished, dear, favorite, idolized, precious, prized, dearest, yearned for, revered, treasured, favored, doted on, nearest to someone's heart, dearly beloved, after someone's own heart, darling, admired, popular, well-liked, cared for, respected, pleasing.—*Ant.* HATED, abhorred, disliked.

beloved *n.* fiancé, sweetheart, object of someone's affection; see LOVER 1.

below *a.*, ***prep.*** **1** [Lower in position] beneath, underneath, down from; see UNDER 1. **2** [Lower in rank or importance] inferior, subject, under; see SUBORDINATE. **3** [Farther along in written material] later, on a following page, in a statement to be made, hereafter, subsequently.—*Ant.* ABOVE, earlier, on a former page. **4** [On earth] existing, in this world, here below, under the sun, on the face of the earth, in this our life, here. **5** [In hell] in the underworld, damned, condemned; see DAMNED 1.

belt *n.* girdle, ribbon, string; see BAND 1. —**below the belt** unjust, foul, unsporting; see UNFAIR. —**tighten one's belt** endure hunger, suffer, bear misfortune; see ENDURE 2. —**under one's belt** past, finished, completed; see DONE 1.

bench *n.* **1** [A long seat] pew, seat, stall; see CHAIR 1. **2** [A long table] workbench, desk, counter; see TABLE 1.

bend[1] ***n.*** crook, bow, arch; see

turn, esp. from a straight line **2** to yield by curving, as from pressure **3** to curve the body; stoop (*over* or *down*) **4** to give in; yield —***n.*** **1** a bending or being bent **2** a bent part —**bend′a·ble** ***adj.***

bend[2] (bend) ***n.*** ⟦ME < prec.⟧ any of various knots for tying rope

be·neath (bē nēth′, bi-) ***adv.***, ***adj.*** ⟦OE *beneothan*⟧ in a lower place; underneath —***prep.*** **1** below **2** under; underneath **3** unworthy of *[it is beneath him to cheat]*

ben·e·dic·tion (ben′ə dik′shən) ***n.*** ⟦< L *bene*, well + *dicere*, speak⟧ **1** a blessing **2** an invocation of blessing, esp. at the end of a religious service

ben·e·fac·tion (ben′ə fak′shen) ***n.*** ⟦< L *bene*, well + *facere*, do⟧ **1** the act of helping, esp. by charitable gifts **2** the money or help given

ben·e·fac·tor (ben′ə fak′tər) ***n.*** one who has given help, esp. financially; patron —**ben′e·fac′tress** (-tris) ***fem.n.***

ben·e·fice (ben′ə fis) ***n.*** ⟦< L *beneficium*, a kindness⟧ an endowed church office providing a living for a vicar, rector, etc.

be·nef·i·cence (bə nef′ə səns) ***n.*** ⟦see BENEFACTION⟧ **1** a being kind **2** a charitable act or gift

be·nef′i·cent (-sənt) ***adj.*** showing beneficence; doing or resulting in good —**be·nef′i·cent·ly** ***adv.***

ben·e·fi·cial (ben′ə fish′əl) ***adj.*** producing benefits; advantageous; favorable —**ben′e·fi′cial·ly** ***adv.***

ben′e·fi′ci·ar′y (-fish′ē er′ē, -fish′ər ē) ***n.***, *pl.* **-ar′ies** anyone receiving or to receive benefits, as funds from a will or insurance policy

ben·e·fit (ben′ə fit) ***n.*** ⟦see BENEFACTION⟧ **1** anything contributing to improvement; advantage **2** [*often pl.*] payments made by an insurance company, public agency, etc. as during sickness or retirement, or for death **3** a public performance, bazaar, etc. the proceeds of which are to help some person or cause —***vt.*** **-fit·ed, -fit·ing** to help; aid —***vi.*** to receive advantage; profit

be·nev·o·lence (bə nev′ə ləns) ***n.*** ⟦< L *bene*, well + *volens*, wishing⟧ **1** an inclination to do good; kindliness **2** a kindly, charitable act —**be·nev′o·lent** ***adj.*** —**be·nev′o·lent·ly** ***adv.***

Ben·gal (ben gôl′), **Bay of** part of the Indian Ocean, east of India

be·night·ed (bē nīt′id, bi-) ***adj.*** **1** surrounded by darkness **2** not enlightened; ignorant

be·nign (bi nīn′) ***adj.*** ⟦< L *benignus*, good, lit., well-born⟧ **1** good-natured; kindly **2** favorable; beneficial **3** *Med.* not malignant; specif., not cancerous —**be·nign′ly** ***adv.***

be·nig·nant (bi nig′nənt) ***adj.*** ⟦< prec.⟧ **1** kindly or gracious **2** BENIGN (senses 2 & 3)

be·nig′ni·ty (-nə tē) ***n.*** **1** kindliness **2** *pl.* **-ties** a kind act

Be·nin (be nēn′) country in WC Africa: 43,484 sq. mi.; pop. 4,855,000

ben·i·son (ben′ə zən, -sən) ***n.*** ⟦OFr < L: see BENEDICTION⟧ [Archaic] a blessing

bent[1] (bent) ***vt.***, ***vi.*** *pt. & pp. of* BEND[1] —***adj.*** **1** curved or crooked **2** strongly determined: with *on* **3** [Slang] *a)* dishonest *b)* eccentric; odd —***n.*** a natural leaning; propensity

bent[2] (bent) ***n.*** ⟦OE *beonot*⟧ a dense, low-growing grass that spreads by runners, used for lawns: also **bent′grass′**

bent′wood′ ***adj.*** of furniture made of wood permanently bent into various forms

be·numb (bē num′, bi-) ***vt.*** **1** to make numb **2** to deaden the mind, will, etc. of

ben·zene (ben′zēn, ben zēn′) ***n.*** ⟦ult. < Ar *lubān jāwi*, incense of Java⟧ a clear, flammable, poisonous, aromatic liquid used as a solvent, in plastics, etc.

ben·zo·caine (ben′zō kān′, -zə-) ***n.*** ⟦< BENZENE & COCAINE⟧ a white, odorless powder used in ointments as a local anesthetic and for protection against sunburn

be·queath (bē kwēth′, -kwēth′; bi-) ***vt.*** ⟦< OE *be-*, BE- + *cwethan*, say⟧ **1** to leave (property) to another by one's will **2** to hand down; pass on

be·quest′ (-kwest′) ***n.*** **1** a bequeathing **2** anything bequeathed

be·rate (bē rāt′, bi-) ***vt.*** **-rat′ed, -rat′ing** ⟦BE- + RATE[2]⟧ to scold severely

Ber·ber (bur′bər) ***n.*** **1** a member of a Muslim people of N Africa **2** the language of this people —***adj.*** of the Berbers

be·reave (bē rēv′, bi-) ***vt.*** **-reaved′** or **-reft′** (-reft′), **-reav′ing** ⟦< OE *be-*, BE- + *reafian*, rob⟧ **1** to deprive: now usually in the pp. *bereft [bereft of hope]* **2** to leave forlorn, as by death —**be·reave′ment** ***n.***

be·ret (bə rā′) ***n.*** ⟦< Fr < L *birrus*, a hood⟧ a flat, round cap of felt, wool, etc.

berg (burg) ***n.*** ICEBERG

ber·i·ber·i (ber′ē ber′ē) ***n.*** ⟦Sinhalese, intens. of *beri*, weakness⟧ a disease caused by lack of vitamin B_1 and characterized by nerve disorders, etc.

Ber·ing Sea (ber′iŋ) part of the N Pacific, between Siberia & Alaska

Bering Strait strait joining the Bering Sea with the Arctic Ocean

Berke·ley (burk′lē) city in California, near San Francisco: pop. 103,000

Ber·lin (bər lin′) city & state of E Germany; capital of Germany (1871-1945; 1990-): formerly divided into four sectors of occupation, the eastern sector (*East Berlin*), capital of East Germany, and three western sectors (*West Berlin*), a state of West Germany: pop. 3,305,000

berm (burm) ***n.*** ⟦< MDu *baerm*⟧ **1** a ledge **2** [Dial.] a shoulder, as along the edge of a paved road

Ber·mu·da (bər myōō′də) group of British islands in the W Atlantic

Bermuda shorts knee-length pants: also **ber·mu′das** ***pl.n.***

Bern or **Berne** (burn) capital of Switzerland: pop. 134,000

ber·ry (ber′ē) ***n.***, *pl.* **-ries** ⟦OE *berie*⟧ **1** any small, juicy, fleshy fruit, as a strawberry **2** the dry seed of various plants, as a coffee bean —***vi.*** **-ried, -ry·ing** **1** to produce berries **2** to pick berries —**ber′ry·like′** ***adj.***

ber·serk (bər surk′, -zurk′; bə-) ***adj.***, ***adv.*** ⟦ON *berserkr*, warrior⟧ in or into a violent rage or frenzy

berth (burth) ***n.*** ⟦< BEAR[1] + -TH[1]⟧ **1** a place where a ship anchors or moors **2** a position, job, etc. **3** a built-in bed, as on a ship or train —***vt.*** to put into or furnish with a berth —***vi.*** to occupy a berth —**give (a) wide berth to** to keep well clear of

ber·yl (ber′əl) ***n.*** ⟦< Gr *bēryllos*⟧ a very hard mineral of which emerald and aquamarine are two varieties

be·ryl·li·um (bə ril′ē əm) ***n.*** ⟦< L *beryllus*, beryl⟧ a hard, silver-white, metallic chemical element used in forming alloys

be·seech (bē sēch′, bi-) ***vt.*** **-sought′** or **-seeched′**, **-seech′ing** ⟦< OE *be-* + *secan*, seek⟧ **1** to ask (someone) earnestly; entreat **2** to beg for —**be·seech′ing·ly** ***adv.***

be·seem (bē sēm′, bi-) ***vi.*** [Archaic] to be suitable or appropriate (to)

be·set (bē set′, bi-) ***vt.*** **-set′, -set′ting** ⟦< OE *be-* + *settan*, set⟧ **1** to attack from all sides; harass **2** to surround or hem in

be·set′ting ***adj.*** constantly harassing

be·side (bē sīd′, bi-) ***prep.*** ⟦OE *bi sidan*⟧ **1** at the side of; near **2** in comparison with *[beside yours my share*

THESAURUS

CURVE.

bend[1] ***v.*** twist, contort, deform, round, crimp, flex, spiral, coil, crinkle, detour, curl, buckle, crook, bow, incline, deflect, double, loop, twine, curve, arch, wind, stoop, lean, waver, zigzag, reel, crumple, meander, circle, swerve, diverge, droop.—*Ant.* STRAIGHTEN, extend, stretch.

bending ***a.*** twisting, veering, curving, buckling, twining, spiraling, looping, doubling, drooping, leaning, inclining, bowing, arching, curling, winding, stooping, crumpling, waving, wavering.

beneath ***a.***, ***prep.*** **1** [Under] below, underneath, in a lower place; see UNDER 1. **2** [Lower in rank or importance] subject to, inferior to, under; see SUBORDINATE.

benefactor ***n.*** helper, protector, angel*; see PATRON.

beneficiary ***n.*** recipient, receiver, inheritor; see HEIR.

benefit ***n.*** gain, profit, good; see ADVANTAGE.

benefit ***v.*** serve, profit, avail; see HELP.

bent[1] ***a.*** curved, warped, hooked, beaked, looped, sinuous, twined, crooked, bowed, contorted, stooped, doubled over, limp, wilted, drooping, humped, slumped, hunched, humpbacked, bowlegged, inclined; see also TWISTED 1.—*Ant.* STRAIGHT, rigid, erect.

bent[1] ***n.*** leaning, tendency, propensity; see INCLINATION 1.

bequeath ***v.*** grant, hand down, pass on; see GIVE 1.

berry ***n.*** *Common berries include the following:* raspberry, blackberry, blueberry, loganberry, boysenberry, cranberry, huckleberry, gooseberry, currant, strawberry, mulberry.

berth ***n.*** place, situation, employment; see JOB 1, PROFESSION 1. —**give a wide berth** keep clear of, evade, stay away from; see AVOID.

beside ***prep.*** at the side of, at the edge of, adjacent to, next to, adjoining, alongside, near, close at hand, by, with, abreast, side by side, bordering on, neighboring, overlooking, next

seems small*]* **3** in addition to **4** other than **5** not relevant to *[*that's *beside* the point*]* —**beside oneself** wild or upset, as with fear or rage

be·sides' (-sīdz') ***adv.*** **1** in addition **2** except for that mentioned **3** moreover —***prep.*** **1** in addition to **2** other than

be·siege (bē sēj', bi-) ***vt.* -sieged', -sieg'ing** **1** to hem in with armed forces **2** to crowd around **3** to overwhelm, harass, etc. *[*she was *besieged* with queries*]*

be·smear (bē smir', bi-) ***vt.*** ⟦OE *bismerian*⟧ to smear over; soil

be·smirch (bē smurch', bi-) ***vt.*** to soil

be·som (bē'zəm) ***n.*** ⟦OE *besma*⟧ a broom, esp. one made of twigs tied to a handle

be·sot (bē sät', bi-) ***vt.* -sot'ted, -sot'ting** to stupefy, as with liquor —**be·sot'ted** ***adj.***

be·sought (bē sôt', bi-) ***vt.*** *alt. pt. & alt. pp. of* BESEECH

be·span·gle (bē spaŋ'gəl, bi-) ***vt.* -gled, -gling** to cover with or as with spangles

be·spat·ter (bē spat'ər, bi-) ***vt.*** to spatter, as with mud or slander

be·speak (bē spēk', bi-) ***vt.* -spoke'** (-spōk'), **-spo'ken** or **-spoke', -speak'ing** **1** to speak for in advance; reserve **2** to be indicative of; show

best (best) ***adj.*** ⟦OE *betst*⟧ **1** *superl. of* GOOD **2** most excellent **3** most suitable, desirable, etc. **4** largest *[*the *best* part of a day*]* —***adv.*** **1** *superl. of* WELL² **2** in the most excellent manner **3** in the highest degree —***n.*** **1** the most excellent person, thing, etc. **2** the utmost *[*she did her *best]* —***vt.*** to defeat or outdo —**all for the best** turning out to be good after all —**at best** under the most favorable conditions —**get the best of** **1** to defeat **2** to outwit —**make the best of** to do as well as one can with

bes·tial (bes'chəl, -tyəl; *often* bēs'-) ***adj.*** ⟦< L *bestia,* beast⟧ like a beast; savage, brutal, etc. —**bes·ti·al·i·ty** (bes'chē al'ə tē, -tē-; *often* bēs'-), *pl.* **-ties,** ***n.***

bes·tial·ize (bes'chəl īz', -tyəl-; *often* bēs'-) ***vt.* -ized', -iz'ing** to make bestial

bes·ti·ar·y (bes'tē er'ē) ***n., pl.* -ies** ⟦< L *bestia,* beast⟧ a medieval book with fables about real or mythical animals

be·stir (bē stur', bi-) ***vt.* -stirred', -stir'ring** to stir to action; busy (oneself)

best man the principal attendant of the bridegroom at a wedding

be·stow (bē stō', bi-) ***vt.*** ⟦see BE- & STOW⟧ to present as a gift: often with *on* or *upon* —**be·stow'al** ***n.***

be·strew (bē strōō', bi-) ***vt.* -strewed', -strewed'** or **-strewn', -strew'ing** **1** to cover (a surface) *with* something **2** to strew or scatter about a surface

be·stride (bē strīd', bi-) ***vt.* -strode'** (-strōd'), **-strid'den** (-strid''n), **-strid'ing** to sit on, mount, or stand over with a leg on each side

bet (bet) ***n.*** ⟦prob. < ABET⟧ **1** an agreement in which the person proved wrong about the outcome of something will do or pay what is stipulated **2** the thing or sum thus staked **3** a person or thing with regard to its likelihood of bringing about some result *[*a good *bet* to win the election*]* —***vt., vi.* bet** or **bet'ted, bet'ting** **1** to declare as in a bet **2** to stake (money, etc.) in a bet with (someone)

be·ta (bāt'ə) ***n.*** the second letter of the Greek alphabet (Β, β)

beta blocker a drug used to control heartbeat, treat hypertension, etc.

beta car·o·tene (kar'ə tēn') a hydrocarbon found in butter, carrots, etc. and converted by the liver into vitamin A

be·take (bē tāk', bi-) ***vt.* -took'** (-to͝ok'), **-tak'en, -tak'ing** ⟦ME *bitaken*⟧ to go (used reflexively) *[*he *betook* himself to his castle*]*

beta particle an electron or positron ejected from the nucleus of an atom during radioactive disintegration

beta ray a stream of beta particles

be·tel nut (bēt''l) ⟦Port < Malayalam *veṭṭilai*⟧ the fruit of a palm (**betel palm**), chewed together with lime and the leaves of a pepper plant (**betel pepper**) by some Asians as a mild stimulant

be·think (bē thiŋk', bi-) [Archaic] ***vt.* -thought'** (-thôt'), **-think'ing** ⟦OE *bethencan*⟧ to remind (oneself)

Beth·le·hem (beth'lə hem') ancient town in Judea: traditionally regarded as Jesus' birthplace

be·tide (bē tīd', bi-) ***vi., vt.* -tid'ed, -tid'ing** ⟦< ME *be-*, BE- + *tiden*, happen⟧ to happen (to); befall

be·times (bē tīmz', bi-) ***adv.*** [Archaic] **1** early or early enough **2** promptly

be·to·ken (bē tō'kən, bi-) ***vt.*** ⟦ME *betocnen*⟧ **1** to be a token or sign of **2** to show beforehand; presage

be·tray (bē trā', bi-) ***vt.*** ⟦< L *tradere,* hand over⟧ **1** to help the enemy of (one's country, etc.) **2** to expose treacherously **3** to fail to uphold *[*to *betray* a trust*]* **4** to deceive; specif., to seduce and then desert **5** to reveal unknowingly **6** to disclose (secrets, etc.) —**be·tray'al** ***n.*** —**be·tray'er** ***n.***

be·troth (bē trōth', -trôth', bi-) ***vt.*** ⟦< ME: see BE- & TRUTH⟧ to promise in marriage —**be·troth'al** ***n.***

be·trothed' (-trōthd', -trôtht') ***adj.*** engaged to be married —***n.*** the person to whom one is engaged

bet·ta (bet'ə) ***n.*** ⟦ModL⟧ a brightly colored gourami of SE Asia: often an aquarium fish

bet·ter (bet'ər) ***adj.*** ⟦OE *betera*⟧ **1** *compar. of* GOOD **2** more excellent **3** more suitable, desirable, etc. **4** larger *[*the *better* part of a day*]* **5** improved in health —***adv.*** **1** *compar. of* WELL² **2** in a more excellent manner **3** in a higher degree **4** more —***n.*** **1** a person superior in authority, etc. **2** a more excellent thing, condition, etc. —***vt.*** **1** to outdo; surpass **2** to improve —**better off** in a better situation —**get** (or **have**) **the better of** **1** to outdo **2** to outwit —**had better** ought to

bet'ter·ment (-mənt) ***n.*** a bettering; improvement

bet·tor (bet'ər) ***n.*** one who bets: also **bet'ter**

be·tween (bē twēn', bi-) ***prep.*** ⟦OE *betweonum*⟧ **1** in the space, time, etc. that separates (two things) **2** connecting *[*a bond *between* friends*]* **3** by the joint action of **4** possessed jointly by **5** from one or the other of *[*choose *between* us*]* **6** involving *Between* is sometimes used of

THESAURUS

door to, to one side, nearby, connected with.

besides ***a.*** in addition to, additionally, moreover, over and above, added to, likewise, further, furthermore, beyond, exceeding, secondly, more than, apart from, extra, in excess of, plus, also, in other respects, exclusive of, with the exception of, as well as, not counting, other than, too, to boot, on top of that, aside from, else.

best ***a.*** **1** [Generally excellent] first, greatest, finest, highest, transcendent, prime, premium, supreme, incomparable, crowning, paramount, matchless, unrivaled, unparalleled, second to none, unequaled, inimitable, beyond compare, superlative, foremost, peerless, first-rate; see also EXCELLENT.—*Ant.* WORST, poorest, lowest. **2** [Applied especially to actions and persons] noblest, sincerest, most praiseworthy; see NOBLE.

best ***n.*** first, favorite, choice, finest, top, pick, prime, flower, cream, cream of the crop. —**all for the best** favorable, fortunate, advantageous; see HELPFUL 1, HOPEFUL 2. —**as best one can** skillfully, ably, capably; see ABLE. —**at best** good, highest, most favorable; see BEST. —**at one's best** well, in one's prime, capable; see ABLE, STRONG 1. —**get** (or **have**) **the best of** outdo, surpass, defeat; see EXCEED. —**make the best of** suffer, tolerate, get by; see ENDURE 2. —**with the best** excellently, well, ably; see ABLE.

best ***v.*** worst, get the better of, overcome; see DEFEAT 3.

bestow ***v.*** bequeath, present, offer; see GIVE 1.

bet ***n.*** gamble, wager, venture, pot, hazard, tossup, stake, speculation, betting, raffle, uncertainty, chance, lottery, game of chance, sweepstakes, risk, ante, long shot*, shot in the dark*.

bet ***v.*** wager, gamble, stake, bet on, bet against, venture, hazard, trust, play against, speculate, play for, put money down, put money on, risk, chance, make a bet, take a chance, lay down, buy in on*, lay odds, lay even money*. —**you bet*** certainly, by all means, yes indeed; see SURELY, YES.

betray ***v.*** **1** [To deliver into the hands of an enemy] delude, trick, double-cross*; see DECEIVE. **2** [To reveal] divulge, disclose, make known; see REVEAL.

betrayal ***n.*** treason, treachery, disloyalty; see DECEPTION, DISHONESTY.

betrayer ***n.*** renegade, deceiver, conspirator; see TRAITOR.

better ***a.*** **1** [Superior] greater, finer, preferred, bigger, stronger, higher; see also BEST. **2** [Recovering health] convalescent, improved in health, improving, on the road to recovery, on the mend.—*Ant.* SICK, failing, wasting away. —**for the better** favorable, fortunate, helpful; see HOPEFUL 2. —**get** (or **have**) **the better of** outdo, overcome, defeat; see EXCEED.

better ***v.*** ameliorate, revamp, refine; see IMPROVE 1.

between ***prep.*** separating, within, bounded by, amidst, amid, among, in, in between, mid, intervening, in the midst of, in the middle, centrally located, surrounded by, midway, halfway, in the thick; see also AMONG. —**between you and me** confidentially, privately, personally; see SECRETLY.

more than two if each part is seen as individually related to each of the others *[peace between nations]* —**adv.** in an intermediate space, time, etc. —**between ourselves** as a secret: also **between you and me**

be·twixt (bē twikst′, bi-) **prep., adv.** ⟦< OE *be,* by + *twegen,* twain⟧ between: archaic except in **betwixt and between,** in an intermediate position

BeV or **bev** (bev) *abbrev.* one billion (10^9) electron-volts

bev·el (bev′əl) **n.** ⟦< ?⟧ **1** a tool for measuring or marking angles, etc. **2** an angle other than a right angle **3** sloping part or surface —**adj.** beveled —**vt.** **-eled** or **-elled, -el·ing** or **-el·ling** to cut to an angle other than a right angle —**vi.** to slope at an angle; slant

bevel gear a gearwheel meshed with another at an angle

bev·er·age (bev′ər ij′, bev′rij) **n.** ⟦< L *bibere,* to drink⟧ any liquid for drinking, esp. one other than water

bev·y (bev′ē) **n.,** *pl.* **-ies** ⟦ME *bevey*⟧ **1** a group, esp. of girls or women **2** a flock: now used chiefly of quail

be·wail (bē wāl′, bi-) **vt.** to wail over; lament; mourn

be·ware (bē wer′, bi-) **vi., vt.** **-wared′, -war′ing** ⟦prob. < OE *bewarian,* keep watch⟧ to be wary or careful (of)

be·wigged (bē wigd′, bi-) **adj.** wearing a wig

be·wil·der (bē wil′dər, bi-) **vt.** ⟦ult. < OE *wilde,* wild⟧ to confuse hopelessly; puzzle —**be·wil′der·ing·ly adv.** —**be·wil′der·ment n.**

be·witch (bē wich′, bi-) **vt.** ⟦< OE *wicca,* sorcerer⟧ **1** to cast a spell over **2** to attract and delight greatly —**be·witch′ing adj.**

bey (bā) **n.** ⟦Turk⟧ a Turkish title of respect and former title of rank

be·yond (bē änd′) **prep.** ⟦< OE *be,* by + *geond,* yonder⟧ **1** farther on than; past **2** later than **3** outside the reach of *[beyond help]* **4** more than —**adv.** farther away —**the (great) beyond** whatever follows death

bez·el (bez′əl) **n.** ⟦< ?⟧ **1** a sloping surface, as the cutting edge of a chisel **2** the slanting faces of the upper part of a cut gem **3** the groove and flange holding a gem, watch crystal, etc. in place

Bhu·tan (bo͞o tän′) kingdom in the Himalayas, SC Asia: 18,000 sq. mi.; pop. 600,000

Bi *Chem. symbol for* bismuth

bi- ⟦L⟧ *prefix* **1** having two **2** doubly **3** happening every two (specified periods) **4** happening twice during every (specified period) **5** using two or both **6** joining or involving two

bi·an·nu·al (bī an′yo͞o əl) **adj.** coming twice a year; semiannual —**bi·an′nu·al·ly adv.**

bi·as (bī′əs) **n.,** *pl.* **-as·es** ⟦MFr *biais,* a slant⟧ **1** a slanting or diagonal line, cut or sewn in cloth **2** partiality; prejudice —**adj.** slanting; diagonal —**adv.** diagonally —**vt.** **-ased** or **-assed, -as·ing** or **-as·sing** to prejudice —**on the bias** diagonally

bi·ath·lon (bī ath′län′) **n.** ⟦BI- + Gr *athlon,* contest⟧ a winter sports event combining cross-country skiing and rifle marksmanship

bib (bib) **n.** ⟦< L *bibere,* to drink⟧ **1** a cloth or plastic cover tied under a child's chin at meals **2** the upper front part of an apron

Bib *abbrev.* **1** Bible **2** Biblical

bibb lettuce (bib) ⟦after J. *Bibb* (1789-1884), who developed it⟧ a type of lettuce with loose heads of crisp, dark-green leaves

Bi·ble (bī′bəl) **n.** ⟦< Gr *biblos,* papyrus < *Byblos,* Phoenician city that exported papyrus⟧ **1** the sacred book of Christianity; Old Testament and New Testament **2** the Holy Scriptures of Judaism; Old Testament **3** [**b-**] any book regarded as authoritative or official —**bib·li·cal** or **Bib·li·cal** (bib′li kəl) **adj.**

biblio- ⟦< Gr *biblion,* book⟧ *combining form* book, books *[bibliophile]*

bib·li·og·ra·phy (bib′lē äg′rə fē) **n.,** *pl.* **-phies** a list of writings on a given subject or by a given author, or of those used by the author of a given work —**bib′li·og′ra·pher n.** —**bib′li·o·graph′ic** (-ə graf′ik) **adj.**

bib′li·o·phile′ (-ə fīl′) **n.** a person who loves or collects books

bib·u·lous (bib′yo͞o ləs) **adj.** ⟦< L *bibere,* to drink⟧ addicted to or fond of alcoholic beverages

bi·cam·er·al (bī kam′ər əl) **adj.** ⟦< BI- + L *camera,* chamber⟧ having two legislative chambers

bi·car·bon·ate of soda (bī kär′bən it) SODIUM BICARBONATE

bi·cen·ten·ni·al (bī′sen ten′ē əl) **adj.** happening once in every 200 years —**n.** a 200th anniversary

bi·ceps (bī′seps′) **n.,** *pl.* **-ceps** or **-ceps′es** ⟦< L < *bis,* two + *caput,* head⟧ a muscle with two points of origin; esp., the large muscle in the front of the upper arm

bick·er (bik′ər) **vi.** ⟦ME *bikeren*⟧ to squabble; quarrel —**bick′er·er n.**

bi·con·cave (bī kän′kāv′) **adj.** concave on both surfaces *[a biconcave lens]*

bi·con′vex′ (-veks′) **adj.** convex on both surfaces *[a biconvex lens]*

bi·cus·pid (bī kus′pid) **adj.** ⟦< BI- + L *cuspis,* pointed end⟧ having two points —**n.** any of eight adult teeth with two-pointed crowns

bi·cy·cle (bī′sik′əl, -si kəl) **n.** ⟦Fr: see BI- & CYCLE⟧ a vehicle consisting of a metal frame on two large wheels, with handlebars, foot pedals, and a seat —**vi.** **-cled, -cling** to ride or travel on a bicycle —**vt.** **1** to carry on or as on a bicycle **2** to travel over by bicycle —**bi′cy′clist n.**

bid (bid) **vt.** **bade** or **bid, bid′den** or **bid, bid′ding** ⟦< OE *biddan,* to urge & *beodan,* to command⟧ **1** to command, ask, or tell **2** to state (an amount) as the price one will pay or accept **3** to express *[to bid farewell]* **4** *Card Games* to state (a number of tricks) and declare (trump) —**vi.** to make a bid —**n.** **1** a bidding **2** an amount bid **3** a chance to bid **4** an attempt or try *(for)* **5** [Inf.] an invitation —**bid fair** to seem likely —**bid′der n.**

bid·dy (bid′ē) **n.,** *pl.* **-dies** ⟦< ?⟧ **1** a hen **2** [Inf.] an elderly woman regarded as annoying, gossipy, etc.: usually **old biddy**

bide (bīd) **vi.** **bode** or **bid′ed, bid′ed, bid′ing** ⟦OE *bidan*⟧ [Now Chiefly Dial.] **1** to stay; continue **2** to dwell **3** to wait —**vt.** [Now Chiefly Dial.] to endure or tolerate —**bide one's time** to wait patiently for an opportunity *[she bided her time]*

bi·det (bē dā′) **n.** ⟦Fr⟧ a low, bowl-shaped bathroom fixture, with running water, for bathing the crotch

bi·en·ni·al (bī en′ē əl) **adj.** ⟦< L *bi-,* BI- + *annus,* year⟧ **1** happening every two years **2** lasting for two years —**n.** **1** a biennial event **2** *Bot.* a plant that lasts two years —**bi·en′ni·al·ly adv.**

bier (bir) **n.** ⟦OE *bær*⟧ a portable framework on which a coffin is placed

bi·fo·cals (bī′fō′kəlz) **pl.n.** eyeglasses with lenses having one part ground for close focus and the other for distant focus

bi·fur·cate (bī′fər kāt′) **vt., vi.** **-cat′ed, -cat′ing** ⟦< L *bi-,* BI- + *furca,* a fork⟧ to divide into two parts or branches —**bi′fur·ca′tion n.**

big (big) **adj.** **big′ger, big′gest** ⟦ME⟧ **1** of great size; large **2** great in amount or force **3** full-grown **4** elder *[his big*

THESAURUS

beverage *n.* liquor, refreshment, draft; see DRINK 2.

bewilder *v.* confound, disconcert, puzzle; see CONFUSE.

bewildered *a.* confused, amazed, misguided, lost, astonished, thunderstruck, shocked, muddled, upset, dazed, giddy, dizzy, reeling, puzzled, misled, uncertain, surprised, baffled, disconcerted, appalled, aghast, adrift, at sea, off the track, awed, stupefied, astounded, struck speechless, breathless, befuddled, startled, struck dumb, dumbfounded, dazzled, stunned, electrified, confounded, staggered, petrified, awe-struck, flabbergasted, flustered, rattled, up in the air*, stumped*.

beyond *a., prep.* on the other side, on the far side, over there, in advance of, away, out of range, a long way off, yonder, past, free of, clear of, farther off, ahead, behind, more remote.—*Ant.* HERE, on this side, nearer.

bias *n.* bent, preference, leaning; see INCLINATION 1.

bias *v.* influence, prejudice, sway; see INFLUENCE.

Bible *n.* the Good Book, God's word, the Word, Scripture, the Scriptures, the Canon, the Testaments, Sacred History, Holy Writ, the Holy Bible, the Word of God, Testament, the Old Testament, the New Testament.

bibliography *n.* catalog, compilation, list of books; see LIST.

bicker *v.* wrangle, squabble, dispute; see QUARREL.

bicycle *n.* cycle, bike*, two-wheeler; see VEHICLE.

bid *n.* proposal, proposition, declaration; see SUGGESTION 1.

bid *v.* **1** [To propose a price for purchase] venture, bid for, submit a bid; see OFFER 1. **2** [To order] tell, charge, direct; see COMMAND 1.

big *a.* **1** [Of great size] huge, great, swollen, fat, obese, bloated, overgrown, gross, mammoth, wide, grand, vast, immense, considerable, substantial, massive, extensive, spacious, colossal, gigantic, titanic, monstrous, towering, mighty, magnificent, enormous, giant, tremendous, whopping*.—*Ant.* LITTLE, tiny, small. **2** [Grown, or partially grown] grown-up, full-grown, adult; see MATURE. **3** [Important] prominent, significant, influential; see IMPORTANT 1, 2. **4** [Pompous] presumptuous, preten-

sister] **5** noticeably pregnant (*with*) **6** loud **7** important [*big* plans] **8** famous **9** extravagant [*big* talk] **10** noble [a *big* heart] —*adv.* [Inf.] **1** boastfully **2** impressively —**big'ness** *n.*

big·a·my (big'ə mē) *n.* ⟦< L *bi-*, BI- + Gr *gamos,* marriage⟧ the crime of marrying a second time when one is already legally married —**big'a·mist** *n.* —**big'a·mous** *adj.* —**big'a·mous·ly** *adv.*

big'-bang' theory a theory that the expansion of the universe began with a gigantic explosion (**big bang**) between 12 and 20 billion years ago

Big Dipper, the a dipper-shaped group of bright stars in the northern sky

big game 1 large wild animals hunted for sport, as lions, tigers, moose, etc. **2** the object of any important or dangerous undertaking

big'heart'ed (-här'tid) *adj.* quick to give or forgive; generous —**big'heart'ed·ly** *adv.*

big'horn' *n., pl.* **-horns'** or **-horn'** a Rocky Mountain wild sheep with large horns

bight (bīt) *n.* ⟦OE *byht,* a bend⟧ **1** a slack part in a rope **2** a curve in a coastline **3** a bay formed by such a curve

big'mouth' *n.* [Slang] a person who talks too much, esp. in an opinionated way

big·ot (big'ət) *n.* ⟦Fr < ?⟧ **1** one who holds blindly and intolerantly to a particular creed, opinion, etc. **2** a prejudiced person —**big'ot·ed** *adj.* —**big'ot·ry** *n.*

big shot [Slang] an important or influential person: also **big wheel**

big'-time' *adj., adv.* [Slang] at, of, or to a very great degree, extent, etc.

bike (bīk) *n.* [Inf.] **1** a bicycle **2** a motorcycle —**bik'er** *n.*

bi·ki·ni (bi kē'nē) *n.* ⟦Fr after *Bikini,* Pacific atoll⟧ **1** a very brief two-piece swimsuit for women **2** very brief, legless underpants or swimming trunks

bi·lat·er·al (bī lat'ər əl) *adj.* **1** of, having, or involving two sides, factions, etc. **2** affecting both sides equally; reciprocal [a *bilateral* pact] —**bi·lat'er·al·ly** *adv.*

bile (bīl) *n.* ⟦Fr < L *bilis*⟧ **1** the bitter, greenish fluid secreted by the liver: it aids digestion **2** bad temper; anger

bilge (bilj) *n.* ⟦var. of BULGE⟧ **1** the rounded lower part of a ship's hold **2** stagnant water that collects there: also **bilge water 3** [Slang] nonsense

bi·lin·gual (bī liŋ'gwəl) *adj.* ⟦< L *bi-*, BI- + *lingua,* tongue⟧ of, in, or able to use two languages —**bi·lin'gual·ism'** *n.*

bil·ious (bil'yəs) *adj.* ⟦< L *bilis,* bile⟧ **1** having or appearing to have some ailment of the bile or liver **2** bad-tempered

bilk (bilk) *vt.* ⟦? < BALK⟧ to cheat or swindle; defraud —**bilk'er** *n.*

bill[1] (bil) *n.* ⟦< ML *bulla,* sealed document⟧ **1** a statement of charges for goods or services; invoice **2** a list, as a menu or theater program **3** a poster or handbill **4** a draft of a proposed law **5** a bill of exchange **6** a piece of paper money **7** *Law* a written declaration of charges or complaints filed —*vt.* **1** to make out a bill of (items) **2** to present a statement of charges to **3** *a*) to advertise by bills *b*) to book (a performer) —**fill the bill** [Inf.] to meet the requirements —**bill'a·ble** *adj.*

bill[2] (bil) *n.* ⟦OE *bile*⟧ **1** the projecting jaws of a bird, usually pointed; beak **2** a beaklike part of the mouth, as that of a turtle —*vi.* to touch bills together —**bill and coo** to kiss, talk softly, etc. in a loving way

bill'board' *n.* a signboard, usually outdoors, for advertising posters

bil·let (bil'it) *n.* ⟦see BILL[1]⟧ **1** *a*) a written order to provide lodging for military personnel *b*) the lodging **2** a position, job, or situation —*vt.* to assign to lodging by billet

bil·let-doux (bē'yā do͞o') *n., pl.* **bil·lets-doux** (bē'yā do͞o') ⟦Fr, sweet letter⟧ a love letter

bill·fold (bil'fōld') *n.* a wallet

bil·liard (bil'yərd) *adj.* of or for billiards

bil'liards (-yərdz) *n.* ⟦< Fr *billard,* orig., a cue⟧ a game played with a cue and three hard balls on a table with raised, cushioned edges

bill·ing (bil'iŋ) *n.* **1** the listing of actors' names on a theater marquee, etc. **2** the order in which the names are listed

bil·lings·gate (bil'iŋz gāt') *n.* ⟦after a London fish market⟧ foul, vulgar, abusive talk

bil·lion (bil'yən) *n.* ⟦Fr < *bi-*, two + (*mi*)*llion*⟧ **1** a thousand millions (1,000,000,000) **2** *former Brit. term for* TRILLION (a million millions) —**bil'lionth** *adj., n.*

bil'lion·aire' (-yə ner') *n.* a person whose wealth comes to at least a billion dollars, pounds, francs, etc.

bill of exchange a written order to pay a certain sum of money to the person named

bill of fare a menu

bill of lading a receipt issued to a shipper by a carrier, describing the goods to be shipped

Bill of Rights the first ten amendments to the U.S. Constitution, which guarantee civil liberties

bill of sale a written statement transferring ownership of something by sale

bil·low (bil'ō) *n.* ⟦ON *bylgja*⟧ **1** a large wave **2** any large swelling mass or surge, as of smoke —*vi.* to surge or swell in a billow —**bil'low·y, -i·er, -i·est,** *adj.*

bil·ly (bil'ē) *n., pl.* **-lies** ⟦ult. < OFr *bille,* tree trunk⟧ a club, esp. a policeman's heavy stick: in full **billy club**

billy goat a male goat

Bi·lox·i (bə luk'sē, -läk'sē) city in SE Mississippi, on the Gulf of Mexico: pop. 46,000

bi·me·tal·lic (bī'mə tal'ik) *adj.* ⟦< Fr *bi-*, BI- + *métallique,* metallic⟧ **1** of, containing, or using two metals **2** of or based on bimetallism

bi·met·al·lism (bī met''l iz'əm) *n.* the use of two metals, esp. gold and silver, as the monetary standard, with fixed values in relation to each other

bi·month·ly (bī munth'lē) *adj., adv.* **1** once every two months **2** [Now Rare] twice a month

bin (bin) *n.* ⟦OE, crib⟧ a box or enclosed space used for storage

bi·na·ry (bī'nə rē) *adj.* ⟦< L *bis,* double⟧ **1** made up of two parts; double **2** designating or of a number system in which the base used is two, each number being expressed by using only two digits, specif. 0 and 1 —*n., pl.* **-ries** something with two parts

bi·na·tion·al (bī nash'ə nəl) *adj.* involving two nations or two nationalities

bin·au·ral (bī nôr'əl) *adj.* **1** of or involving both ears **2** of or using two sources of sound

bind (bīnd) *vt.* **bound, bind'ing** ⟦< OE *bindan*⟧ **1** to tie together, as with rope **2** to hold or restrain **3** to encircle with a belt, etc. **4** to bandage: often with *up* **5** to constipate **6** to reinforce or ornament the edges of by a band, as of tape **7** to fasten together the pages of (a book) and enclose in a cover **8** to obligate by duty, love, etc. **9** to compel, as by oath, legal restraint, or contract —*vi.* **1** to do the act of binding **2** to be or become tight or stiff **3** to stick together **4** to be obligatory or binding in force —*n.* **1** anything that binds **2** [Inf.] a difficult or restrictive situation

bind'er *n.* **1** one that binds **2** a substance that binds, as tar **3** a cover for holding sheets of paper together

THESAURUS

tious, imperious; see EGOTISTIC. **5** [Generous] magnanimous, liberal, unselfish; see GENEROUS, KIND.

bigot *n.* narrow-minded person, opinionated person, racist, chauvinist, xenophobe, jingoist, hatemonger, dogmatist, redneck*; see also RADICAL.

bigoted *a.* biased, dogmatic, opinionated; see PREJUDICED.

bigotry *n.* intolerance, narrowmindedness, injustice; see FANATICISM, PREJUDICE.

big shot* *n.* big wheel*, bigwig*, VIP*; see EXECUTIVE.

bill[1] *v.* dun, solicit, render account of indebtedness, draw upon.

bill[1,2] *n.* **1** [A statement of account] invoice, statement of indebtedness, request for payment; see STATEMENT 2. **2** [A piece of paper money] Federal Reserve note, bank note, greenback; see MONEY 1. **3** [A statement prepared for enactment into law] measure, proposal, piece of legislation; see LAW 3. **4** [A beak] nib, mandible, projection; see BEAK. —**fill the bill*** meet requirements, be satisfactory, serve the purpose; see SATISFY 3.

billboard *n.* outdoor advertisement, display panel, poster board; see ADVERTISEMENT, ANNOUNCEMENT.

billfold *n.* card case, pocketbook, purse; see WALLET.

bin *n.* storeroom, granary, silo; see CONTAINER.

binary *a.* double, twofold, digital; see DOUBLE.

bind* *n.* dilemma, tight situation, quandary; see PREDICAMENT.

bind *v.* **1** [To constrain with bonds] truss up, tie up, shackle, fetter, cinch, clamp, chain, leash, constrict, manacle, enchain, lace, pin, restrict, hamper, handcuff, muzzle, hitch, secure, yoke, pin down, fix, strap, tether, bind up, lash down, clamp down on, hogtie. **2** [To hold together or in place] secure, attach, adhere; see FASTEN. **3** [To obligate] oblige, necessitate, compel; see FORCE. **4** [To dress] treat, dress, bandage; see HEAL. **5** [To join] unite, put together, connect; see JOIN 1.

bind'er·y *n.*, *pl.* **-er·ies** a place where books are bound
bind'ing *n.* a thing that binds, as a band, a tape, the covers and backing of a book, or a cohesive substance —*adj.* that binds, obligates, etc.
binge (binj) [Inf.] *n.* unrestrained activity; spree —*vi.* **binged, binge'ing** to indulge without restraint
bin·go (biŋ'gō) *n.* a game played with cards having rows of numbered squares: the first player with an entire row drawn by lot wins —*interj.* used to signify sudden success, etc.
bin·na·cle (bin'ə kəl) *n.* ⟦ult. < L *habitaculum,* dwelling place⟧ the case holding a ship's compass
bin·oc·u·lar (bī näk'yə lər; *for n.*, bi-) *adj.* ⟦< L *bini,* double + *oculus,* eye⟧ using, or for, both eyes —*n.* [*pl.*] field glasses
bi·no·mi·al (bī nō'mē əl) *n.* ⟦< L *bi-*, BI- + Gr *nomos,* law⟧ **1** *Math.* an expression consisting of two terms connected by a plus or minus sign **2** a two-word scientific name of a plant or animal, indicating the genus and species
bi·o (bī'ō) *n.*, *pl.* **bios** [Inf.] a biography
bio- ⟦Gr < *bios,* life⟧ *combining form* life, of living things
bi·o·chem·is·try (bī'ō kem'is trē) *n.* the study of the chemistry of life processes in plants and animals —**bi'o·chem'ist** *n.*
bi·o·cide (bī'ō sīd') *n.* ⟦BIO- + -CIDE⟧ a substance that kills microorganisms
bi·o·de·grad·a·ble (bī'ō di grā'də bəl) *adj.* ⟦BIO- + *degrad(e),* decompose + -ABLE⟧ capable of being readily decomposed by the action of microbes, as some detergents
bi'o·di·ver'si·ty *n.* variety in the living things of a particular area
bi'o·feed'back' *n.* a technique of seeking to control certain emotional states by training oneself, using electronic devices, to modify autonomic body functions, such as heartbeat
biog *abbrev.* **1** biographical **2** biography
bi·og·ra·phy (bī äg'rə fē) *n.*, *pl.* **-phies** ⟦< Gr: see BIO- & -GRAPHY⟧ a person's life story written by another —**bi·og'ra·pher** *n.* —**bi·o·graph·i·cal** (bī'ə graf'i kəl) *adj.*
biol *abbrev.* **1** biological **2** biology
biological warfare the use of toxic microorganisms, etc. in war
bi·ol·o·gy (bī äl'ə jē) *n.* ⟦see BIO- & -LOGY⟧ the science that deals with the origin, history, characteristics, etc. of plants and animals —**bi·o·log·i·cal** (bī'ə läj'i kəl) *adj.* —**bi'o·log'i·cal·ly** *adv.* —**bi·ol'o·gist** *n.*
bi·on·ic (bī än'ik) *adj.* ⟦see fol.⟧ **1** of bionics **2** having an artificial body part or parts, as in science fiction, so as to enhance strength, etc.
bi·on'ics *n.* ⟦BI(O)- + (ELECTR)ONICS⟧ the science of designing instruments or systems modeled after living organisms
bi·o·phys·ics (bī'ō fiz'iks) *n.* the study of biological phenomena in relation to physics —**bi'o·phys'i·cal** *adj.* —**bi'o·phys'i·cist** *n.*
bi·o·pic (bī'ō pik') *n.* [Inf.] a film dramatizing the life of a famous person
bi·op·sy (bī'äp'sē) *n.*, *pl.* **-sies** ⟦< BI(O)- + Gr *opsis,* a sight⟧ *Med.* the removal of bits of living tissue for diagnosis
bi·o·rhythm (bī'ō rith'əm) *n.* any biological cycle that involves periodic changes in blood pressure, body temperature, etc.
bi·o·tin (bī'ə tin) *n.* ⟦< Gr *bios,* life⟧ a factor of the vitamin B group
bi·par·ti·san (bī pär'tə zən) *adj.* of, representing, or supported by two parties —**bi·par'ti·san·ship'** *n.*
bi·par·tite (bī pär'tīt') *adj.* ⟦< L *bi-*, BI- + *partire,* to divide⟧ **1** having two parts **2** involving two
bi·ped (bī'ped') *n.* ⟦< L *bi-*, BI- + *pes,* foot⟧ any two-footed animal —**bi·ped'al** *adj.*
bi·plane (bī'plān') *n.* an airplane with two sets of wings, one above the other
bi·po·lar (bī pō'lər) *adj.* **1** of or involving poles or polarity **2** having alternating periods of mania and mental depression
bi·ra·cial (bī rā'shəl) *adj.* consisting of or involving two races
birch (burch) *n.* ⟦OE *beorc*⟧ **1** a tree having smooth bark in thin layers, and hard, closegrained wood **2** its wood **3** a bunch of birch twigs used for whipping —*vt.* to flog
bird (burd) *n.* ⟦< OE *bridd,* young bird⟧ a warmblooded vertebrate with feathers and wings —*vi.* to observe wild birds in their habitat —**birds of a feather** people with the same traits or tastes —**for the birds** [Slang] ridiculous, foolish, etc.
bird'er *n.* a bird-watcher
bird'ie *n.* *Golf* a score of one stroke under par for a hole
bird'ing *n.* bird-watching
bird's'-eye' *adj.* having marks resembling birds' eyes *[bird's-eye* maple*]*
bird's-eye view **1** a view from high above **2** an overall, but cursory, view
bird'-watch'ing *n.* a hobby involving observation of wild birds in their habitat —**bird'-watch'er** *n.*
bi·ret·ta (bə ret'ə) *n.* ⟦< LL *birrettum,* small cloak⟧ a square ceremonial hat with three or four vertical projections, worn by Roman Catholic clergy
Bir·ming·ham (bur'miŋ əm; *for 2,* -ham') **1** city in central England: county district pop. 961,000 **2** city in N Alabama: pop. 265,000
birth (burth) *n.* ⟦< ON *byrth*⟧ **1** the act of bringing forth offspring **2** a being born **3** origin or descent **4** the beginning of anything —*vi.*, *vt.* to give birth (to) —**give birth (to)** **1** to bring forth (offspring) **2** to create
birth'day' *n.* the anniversary of the day of a person's birth
birth'ing *adj.*, *n.* (of or for) giving birth
birth'mark' *n.* a skin blemish or mark present at birth
birth'place' *n.* the place of one's birth or of a thing's origin
birth'rate' *n.* the number of births per year per thousand people in a given area, group, etc.: also **birth rate**
birth'right' *n.* any right that a person has by birth
birth'stone' *n.* a gem symbolizing the month of a person's birth
bis·cot·ti (bi skät'ē) *pl.n.*, *sing.* **-to** or **-ti** ⟦It, cognate with fol.⟧ hard, bar-shaped cookie made with almonds, etc.
bis·cuit (bis'kit) *n.*, *pl.* **-cuits** or **-cuit** ⟦< L *bis,* twice + *coquere,* to cook⟧ **1** [Chiefly Brit.] a cracker or cookie **2** *a)* a quick bread baked in small pieces *b)* any of these pieces
bi·sect (bī sekt') *vt.* ⟦< L *bi-*, BI- + *secare,* to cut⟧ **1** to cut in two **2** *Geom.* to divide into two equal parts —*vi.* to divide; fork —**bi·sec'tor** (-sekt'ər) *n.*
bi·sex·u·al (bī sek'shoo əl) *adj.* of, or sexually attracted to, both sexes —*n.* one who is bisexual
bish·op (bish'əp) *n.* ⟦< Gr *episkopos,* overseer⟧ **1** a high-ranking member of the Christian clergy, governing a diocese or church district **2** a chess piece that can move in a diagonal direction only
bish·op·ric (bish'əp rik) *n.* the district, office, or rank of a bishop
Bis·marck[1] (biz'märk'), Prince **Ot·to von** (ät'ō vän) 1815-98; Prussian chancellor (1871-90) who unified Germany
Bis·marck[2] (biz'märk') capital of North Dakota: pop. 49,000
bis·muth (biz'məth) *n.* ⟦< Ger *wismut*⟧ a brittle, grayish-

THESAURUS

binding *a.* obligatory, requisite, required; see NECESSARY.
binding *n.* **1** [The act of joining] merging, coupling, junction; see UNION 1. **2** [Anything used to bind] tie, adhesive, binder; see FASTENER. **3** [A cover] wrapper, jacket, book cover; see COVER 1.
biography *n.* life story, saga, memoir, journal, experiences, autobiography, life, adventures, life history, confessions, profile, sketch, biographical account; see also RECORD 1, STORY.
biological *a.* organic, life, living, zoological, botanical, concerning life.
biology *n.* science of organisms, ecology, natural science, natural history, nature study, life science; see also SCIENCE 1.
bird *n.* *Types of birds include the following:* sparrow, starling, robin, blue jay, hawk, meadowlark, owl, vulture, buzzard, woodpecker, cardinal, kingfisher, chickadee, swallow, skylark, nightingale, nuthatch, whippoorwill, thrush, finch, warbler, bluebird, cuckoo, bobolink, wren, gull, eagle, osprey, blackbird, dove, duck, goose, pheasant, chicken, parakeet, parrot, canary, penguin, dodo, crane, heron, egret, mockingbird, ostrich. —**eat like a bird** fast, starve, nibble; see DIET. —**for the birds*** ridiculous, absurd, useless; see STUPID, WORTHLESS.
birth *n.* delivery, parturition, nativity, beginning, blessed event, visit from the stork.—*Ant.* DEATH, decease, demise. —**give birth** bring forth, have a child, reproduce; see PRODUCE 1.
birthday *n.* natal day, name day, celebration; see ANNIVERSARY.
biscuit *n.* cracker, wafer, roll; see BREAD.
bishop *n.* father, archbishop, primate; see MINISTER 1, PRIEST.

white metallic chemical element used in alloys of low melting point

bi·son (bī′sən) ***n.***, *pl.* **bi′son** ⟦< L, wild ox⟧ a bovine ruminant having a shaggy mane and a humped back, as the American buffalo

bisque (bisk) ***n.*** ⟦Fr⟧ a thick, creamy soup made as from shellfish or vegetables

bis·tro (bē′strō′) ***n.*** ⟦Fr⟧ a small cafe

bit[1] (bit) ***n.*** ⟦< OE *bite,* a bite⟧ **1** the part of a bridle in the horse's mouth, used as a control **2** anything that curbs or controls **3** a drilling or boring tool for use in a brace, drill press, etc.

bit[2] (bit) ***n.*** ⟦< OE *bita,* a piece⟧ **1** *a)* a small piece or quantity *b)* small extent *[a bit bored] c)* a short time **2** [Inf.] 12$\frac{1}{2}$ cents: now usually in *two bits* —***adj.*** very small *[a bit role]* —**bit by bit** gradually —**do one's bit** to do one's share

bit[3] (bit) ***n.*** ⟦*b(inary) (dig)it*⟧ **1** a single digit in a binary number system **2** a unit of information

bitch (bich) ***n.*** ⟦OE *bicce*⟧ **1** the female of the dog, fox, etc. **2** a woman regarded as bad-tempered, malicious, etc. **3** [Slang] anything especially difficult —***vi.*** [Slang] to complain

bitch′y ***adj.*** **-i·er, -i·est** [Slang] bad-tempered or malicious: used esp. of a woman

bite (bīt) ***vt.*** **bit** (bit), **bit·ten** (bit′'n) or **bit, bit′ing** ⟦OE *bītan*⟧ **1** to seize or pierce with or as with the teeth **2** to cut into, as with a sharp weapon **3** to sting, as an insect **4** to cause to smart **5** to eat into; corrode —***vi.*** **1** to press or snap the teeth (*into, at,* etc.) **2** to cause a biting sensation **3** to grip **4** to seize a bait **5** to be caught, as by a trick —***n.*** **1** a biting **2** biting quality; sting **3** a wound or sting from biting **4** *a)* a mouthful *b)* a snack **5** [Inf.] a sum deducted, as by a tax —**bite the bullet** to confront a painful situation bravely: from the patient's biting a bullet during battlefield surgery without an anesthetic

bit·ing (bīt′iŋ) ***adj.*** **1** cutting; sharp **2** sarcastic —**bit′ing·ly** ***adv.***

bit·ter (bit′ər) ***adj.*** ⟦OE *biter,* akin to *bītan,* to bite⟧ **1** having a sharp, often unpleasant taste **2** causing or showing sorrow, pain, etc. **3** sharp and disagreeable; harsh *[a bitter wind]* **4** resentful or cynical —**bit′ter·ly** ***adv.*** —**bit′ter·ness** ***n.***

bit·tern (bit′ərn) ***n.*** ⟦< OFr *butor*⟧ a wading bird with a thumping cry

bit′ters ***pl.n.*** a liquor containing bitter herbs, etc. and usually alcohol, used as in some cocktails

bit′ter·sweet′ ***n.*** **1** a woody vine bearing small orange fruits with bright-red fleshy seeds **2** a poisonous vine with purple flowers and red berries **3** pleasure mixed with sadness —***adj.*** **1** both bitter and sweet **2** pleasant and sad

bi·tu·men (bi to͞o′mən) ***n.*** ⟦L < Celt⟧ any of various black mixtures of hydrocarbons obtained in the distillation of petroleum, used for paints, roofing, etc. —**bi·tu′mi·nous** (-mə nəs) ***adj.***

bituminous coal coal that yields pitch or tar when it burns; soft coal

bi·va·lent (bī vā′lənt) ***adj.*** *Chem.* DIVALENT

bi·valve (bī′valv′) ***n.*** any mollusk having a shell made of two valves hinged together, as a clam

biv·ou·ac (biv′wak′) ***n.*** ⟦Fr < OHG *bi-,* by + *wahta,* watchman⟧ a temporary encampment (esp. of soldiers) in the open —***vi.*** **-acked′, -ack′ing** to encamp in the open

bi·week·ly (bī wēk′lē) ***adj., adv.*** **1** once every two weeks **2** [Now Rare] semiweekly

bi·zarre (bi zär′) ***adj.*** ⟦Fr < Basque *bizar,* beard⟧ **1** odd; grotesque **2** unexpected; fantastic

bk *abbrev.* **1** bank **2** book

bl *abbrev.* **1** bale(s) **2** barrel(s)

B/L or **b/l** *abbrev.* bill of lading

blab (blab) ***vt., vi.*** **blabbed, blab′bing** ⟦ME *blabben*⟧ **1** to reveal (a secret) **2** to chatter; prattle Also **blab′ber** —***n.*** gossip

blab′ber·mouth′ ***n.*** [Inf.] one who blabs

black (blak) ***adj.*** ⟦OE *blæc*⟧ **1** opposite to white; of the color of coal **2** [*sometimes* **B-**] of or for the dark-skinned peoples of Africa, etc. or their descendants elsewhere, specif. African-Americans in the U.S. *[black studies]* **3** without light; dark **4** dirty **5** evil; wicked **6** sad; dismal **7** sullen —***n.*** **1** black color or pigment **2** black clothes, esp. when worn in mourning **3** [*sometimes* **B-**] a member of a black people **4** darkness —***vt., vi.*** to blacken —**black out** to lose consciousness —**in the black** operating at a profit —**black′ish** ***adj.*** —**black′ly** ***adv.*** —**black′ness** ***n.***

black′-and-blue′ ***adj.*** discolored, as by a bruise

black′ball′ ***n.*** a vote against —***vt.*** **1** to vote against **2** to ostracize

black belt a black belt or sash awarded to an expert of the highest skill in judo or karate

black′ber′ry (-ber′ē, -bər ē) ***n.***, *pl.* **-ries** **1** the fleshy, purple or black, edible fruit of various brambles of the rose family **2** a bush or vine bearing this fruit

black′bird′ ***n.*** any of various birds the male of which is almost entirely black

black′board′ ***n.*** a smooth, usually dark surface on which to write with chalk

black′en (-ən) ***vi.*** to become black or dark —***vt.*** **1** to make black; darken **2** to slander; defame

black eye **1** a discoloration of the skin around an eye, resulting from a blow or contusion **2** [Inf.] dishonor, or its cause

black′-eyed′ Su′san (-so͞o′zən) a yellow, daisylike wildflower with a dark center

black·guard (blag′ərd) ***n.*** a scoundrel; villain

black′head′ ***n.*** a dark plug of dried fatty matter in a pore of the skin

black hole **1** an object or region in space with intense gravitation from which light, etc. cannot escape **2** *a)* an emptiness or void *b)* anything endlessly devouring resources, etc.

black′jack′ ***n.*** **1** a small, leather-covered bludgeon with a flexible handle **2** a gambling card game in which a player getting closer to 21 points than the dealer, without exceeding it, wins —***vt.*** to hit with a blackjack

black light ultraviolet or infrared radiation used for fluorescent effects

black′list′ ***n.*** a list of those who are censured, refused employment, etc. —***vt.*** to put on a blacklist

THESAURUS

bit[2] ***n.*** **1** [A small quantity] piece, fragment, crumb, dot, particle, jot, trifle, mite, iota, whit, splinter, parcel, portion, droplet, trickle, driblet, morsel, pinch, snip, shred, atom, speck, molecule, shard, chip, fraction, sliver, segment, section, lump, slice, shaving, sample, specimen, scale, flake, excerpt, scrap, part, division, share, trace, item, chunk, paring, taste, mouthful, stub, butt, stump, a drop in the bucket*, peanuts*, chicken feed*, gob, hunk*. **2** [A small degree] jot, minimum, inch, hairbreadth, trifle, iota, mite, fraction, tolerance, margin, whisker, hair, skin of one's teeth. —**do one's bit** participate, share, do one's share; see JOIN 2. —**every bit** wholly, altogether, entirely; see COMPLETELY.

bite ***n.*** **1** [What one takes in the mouth at one time] mouthful, chew, taste, spoonful, forkful, morsel, nibble. **2** [The result of being bitten] wound, sting, laceration; see INJURY. **3** [A quick meal] snack, nibble, brunch; see FOOD.

bite ***v.*** **1** [To seize or sever with the teeth] snap, gnaw, sink one's teeth into, nip, nibble, chew, mouth, gulp, worry, taste, masticate, clamp, champ, munch, bite into, crunch, mangle, chaw*; see also EAT 1, TASTE 1. **2** [To be given to biting] snap, be vicious, attack; see HURT. **3** [To cut or corrode] rot, decay, decompose; see RUST.

biting ***a.*** **1** [Acidulous] sharp, keen, tangy; see SOUR. **2** [Sarcastic] caustic, acrimonious, bitter; see SARCASTIC.

bitten ***a.*** chewed, torn, lacerated, slashed, gulped, gnawed, nibbled, tasted, devoured, eaten, stung, pierced, mangled, punctured, cut, ripped.

bitter ***a.*** **1** [Acrid] astringent, acid, tart; see SOUR. **2** [Intense] sharp, harsh, severe; see INTENSE. **3** [Sarcastic] acrimonious, caustic, biting; see SARCASTIC.

bitterness ***n.*** tartness, piquancy, pungency, acidity, sourness, acridity, brackishness, brininess.

bizarre ***a.*** odd, fantastic, grotesque; see UNUSUAL 2.

blab ***v.*** disclose, tell, divulge; see REVEAL.

black ***a.*** **1** [Opposite to white] dark, blackish, raven, coal-black, dusky, dingy, murky, inklike, somber, swarthy, swart, jet, inky, ebony, pitch-black, black as coal, sooty, gunmetal, flat black, jet black, black as night*.—*Ant.* WHITE, colored, colorful. **2** [Without light] gloomy, shadowy, clouded; see DARK 1.

black ***n.*** **1** [A chromatic color least resembling white] carbon, darkest gray, jet, sable, ebony, blackness.—*Ant.* WHITE, blond, brightness. **2** [A Negro] colored person*, Negro, African, Afro-American, African-American. —**in the black** successful, lucrative, gainful; see PROFITABLY.

blacken ***v.*** darken, deepen, make black; see SHADE 2.

black lung (disease) a disease of the lungs caused by the inhalation of coal dust
black magic sorcery
black'mail' ***n.*** ⟦lit., black rent < ME *male,* rent⟧ **1** payment extorted to prevent disclosure of information that could bring disgrace **2** extortion of such payment —***vt.*** to get or try to get blackmail from —**black'mail'er** ***n.***
black mark an unfavorable item in one's record
black market a system for selling goods illegally —**black marketeer** (or **marketer**)
black'out' ***n.*** **1** an extinguishing of stage lights to end a scene **2** a concealing of lights that might be visible to enemy aircraft at night **3** a temporary loss of electric power **4** temporary unconsciousness **5** suppression, as of news by censorship
black power political and economic power as sought by black Americans in the struggle for civil rights
Black Sea sea between Asia & SE Europe, north of Turkey
black sheep a family or group member regarded as not so respectable as the others
black'smith' ***n.*** a smith who works in iron and makes and fits horseshoes
black'thorn' ***n.*** a thorny shrub with purple or black, plumlike fruit; sloe
black'top' ***n.*** a bituminous mixture, usually asphalt, used as a surface for roads, etc. —***vt.*** **-topped'**, **-top'ping** to cover with blacktop
black widow a black spider with a red mark underneath: the female has a poisonous bite and sometimes eats its mate
blad·der (blad'ər) ***n.*** ⟦OE *blædre*⟧ **1** a sac that fills with fluid or gas, esp. one that holds urine flowing from the kidneys **2** a thing like this
blade (blād) ***n.*** ⟦OE *blæd,* leaf⟧ **1** *a)* the leaf of a plant, esp. of grass *b)* the flat part of a leaf **2** a broad, flat surface or part, as of an oar or snowplow **3** the cutting part of a tool, knife, etc. **4** a sword or swordsman
Blair (bler), **To·ny** (tō'nē) 1953- ; Brit. prime minister (1997-)
blam·a·ble or **blame·a·ble** (blām'ə bəl) ***adj.*** that deserves blame —**blam'a·bly** ***adv.***
blame (blām) ***vt.*** **blamed, blam'ing** ⟦see BLASPHEME⟧ **1** to accuse of being at fault; condemn (*for*) **2** to put the responsibility of (an error, etc.) *on* —***n.*** **1** a blaming **2** responsibility for a fault —**be to blame** to be at fault —**blame'less** ***adj.*** —**blame'less·ly** ***adv.*** —**blame'less·ness** ***n.***
blame'wor'thy ***adj.*** deserving to be blamed
blanch (blanch) ***vt.*** ⟦< OFr *blanc,* white⟧ **1** to whiten or bleach **2** to make pale **3** to scald (vegetables, almonds, etc.) —***vi.*** to turn pale
bland (bland) ***adj.*** ⟦L *blandus,* mild⟧ **1** gently agreeable **2** mild; not harsh **3** insipid —**bland'ly** ***adv.*** —**bland'ness** ***n.***
blan·dish (blan'dish) ***vt., vi.*** ⟦< L *blandiri,* to flatter⟧ to flatter; coax; cajole —**blan'dish·ment** ***n.***
blank (blaŋk) ***adj.*** ⟦< OFr *blanc,* white⟧ **1** not written on **2** empty; vacant; plain **3** dazed or vacant *[a blank look]* **4** utter; complete *[a blank denial]* —***n.*** **1** an empty space, esp. one to be filled out in a printed form **2** such a printed form **3** an empty place or time **4** a powder-filled cartridge without a bullet —***vt.*** to hold (an opponent) scoreless —**blank out** to conceal by covering over —**draw a blank** [Inf.] **1** to be unsuccessful **2** to be unable to remember a particular thing —**blank'ly** ***adv.*** —**blank'ness** ***n.***
blank check **1** a bank check not yet filled in **2** a signed check with no amount filled in **3** permission to use an unlimited amount of money, authority, etc.
blan·ket (blaŋk'it) ***n.*** ⟦< OFr dim. of *blanc,* white⟧ **1** a large piece of cloth used for warmth, esp. as a bed cover **2** any covering like this *[a blanket of leaves]* —***adj.*** including many or all items *[blanket insurance]* —***vt.*** **1** to cover; overlie **2** to obscure
blank verse unrhymed verse having five iambic feet per line
blan·quette (blän ket') ***n.*** ⟦Fr⟧ a stew, as of chicken or veal, in cream sauce
blare (bler) ***vt., vi.*** **blared, blar'ing** ⟦ME *bleren,* to wail⟧ to sound or exclaim loudly —***n.*** a loud, harsh sound
blar·ney (blär'nē) ***n.*** ⟦< *Blarney* stone in Ireland, traditionally kissed to gain skill in flattery⟧ smooth or flattering talk
bla·sé (blä zā') ***adj.*** ⟦Fr⟧ unexcited or jaded
blas·pheme (blas fēm') ***vt.*** **-phemed'**, **-phem'ing** ⟦< Gr *blasphēmein,* to speak evil of⟧ **1** to speak profanely of or to (God or sacred things) **2** to curse —***vi.*** to utter blasphemy —**blas·phem'er** ***n.***
blas'phe·my (-fə mē) ***n.***, *pl.* **-mies** profane speech, writing, or action concerning God or sacred things —**blas'phe·mous** ***adj.***
blast (blast) ***n.*** ⟦OE *blæst,* puff of wind⟧ **1** a strong rush of air or gas **2** the sound of a sudden rush of air, as through a horn **3** a blight **4** an explosion, as of dynamite **5** an outburst, as of criticism **6** [Slang] an exciting, enjoyable experience —***vi.*** **1** to make a loud, harsh sound **2** to set off explosives, etc. —***vt.*** **1** to wither; ruin **2** to blow up; explode **3** to criticize sharply —**blast off** to take off: said of a rocket, etc. —(**at**) **full blast** at full speed or capacity
blast furnace a smelting furnace in which a blast of air forced in from below produces the intense heat
blast'off' or **blast'-off'** ***n.*** the launching of a rocket, spacecraft, etc.
bla·tant (blāt''nt) ***adj.*** ⟦prob. < L *blaterare,* to babble⟧ **1** disagreeably loud; noisy **2** boldly conspicuous or obtrusive —**bla'tan·cy** ***n.***
blaze[1] (blāz) ***n.*** ⟦OE *blæse*⟧ **1** a bright burst of flame; fire **2** a very bright light **3** a spectacular outburst or display —***vi.*** **blazed, blaz'ing** **1** to burn rapidly or shine brightly **2** to be excited, as with anger
blaze[2] (blāz) ***n.*** ⟦< ON *blesi*⟧ **1** a light-colored spot on an animal's face **2** a mark made on a tree by cutting off bark —***vt.*** **blazed, blaz'ing** to mark (a tree or trail) with blazes
blaze[3] (blāz) ***vt.*** **blazed, blaz'ing** ⟦ME *blasen,* to blow < OE or ON⟧ to proclaim
blaz·er (blā'zər) ***n.*** a light sport coat usually in a solid color and with metal buttons
bla·zon (blā'zən) ***n.*** ⟦OFr *blason,* a shield⟧ a coat of arms —***vt.*** **1** to proclaim **2** to adorn

THESAURUS

black magic ***n.*** sorcery, witchcraft, necromancy; see MAGIC 1, 2.

blackmail ***n.*** hush money, tribute, protection*; see BRIBE.

blackmail ***v.*** extort, coerce, shake down*; see BRIBE, FORCE.

blackness ***n.*** gloom, duskiness, murkiness; see DARKNESS 1.

black out ***v.*** **1** [To delete] rub out, eradicate, blot out; see CANCEL, ERASE. **2** [To faint] pass out, lose consciousness, swoon; see FAINT. **3** [To darken] put out the lights, make dark, cause a blackout in; see SHADE 2.

blade ***n.*** **1** [A cutting instrument] edge, sword, saber; see KNIFE. **2** [A relatively long leaf] frond, spear, shoot; see LEAF.

blame ***n.*** disapproval, condemnation, denunciation, disparagement, depreciation, opposition, abuse, disfavor, objection, reproach, criticism, repudiation, reprimand, invective, slur, accusation, reproof, attack, chiding, rebuke, impeachment, complaint, diatribe, tirade, charge, indictment, recrimination, arraignment, implication, calumny, frowning upon.—*Ant.* PRAISE, commendation, appreciation.

blame ***v.*** charge, condemn, criticize, arraign, challenge, involve, attack, brand, implicate, arrest, sue, prosecute, slander, impeach, bring to trial, connect with, indict, impute, put the finger on*, smear, point the finger at*, bring home to, dis*. —**be to blame** guilty, at fault, culpable; see WRONG 2.

blameless ***a.*** faultless, not guilty, inculpable; see INNOCENT 1.

bland ***a.*** flat, dull, insipid; see TASTELESS 1.

blank ***a.*** white, clear, virgin, fresh, plain, empty, untouched, pale, new, spotless, vacant, hollow, meaningless.

blank ***n.*** **1** [An empty space] void, hollow, hole, cavity, vacancy, womb, gulf, nothingness, hollowness, abyss, opening, vacuum, gap, interval; see also EMPTINESS. **2** [A form] questionnaire, data sheet, information blank; see FORM 5. —**draw a blank** be unable to remember, lose one's memory, disremember*; see FORGET.

blanket ***n.*** quilt, comforter, throw, electric blanket, thermal blanket, afghan, stadium blanket.

blanket ***v.*** envelop, conceal, bury; see COVER 1.

blank out ***v.*** delete, black out, cross out; see CANCEL, ERASE.

blast ***n.*** **1** [An explosion] burst, eruption, detonation; see EXPLOSION. **2** [A loud sound] roar, din, bang; see NOISE 1. **3** [An explosive charge] gunpowder, TNT, dynamite; see EXPLOSIVE. —(**at**) **full blast** at full speed, rapidly, quickly; see FAST 1.

blast ***v.*** blow up, dynamite, detonate; see EXPLODE. —**blast off** rocket, climb, soar up; see RISE 1.

blaze[1] ***n.*** conflagration, combustion, burning; see FIRE.

blaze[1] ***v.*** flame, flash, flare up; see BURN.

bldg *abbrev.* building
bleach (blēch) ***vt., vi.*** ⟦OE *blæcan*⟧ to make or become white or colorless —***n.*** a substance for bleaching
bleach'ers ***pl.n.*** benches in tiers, for spectators as at sporting events
bleak (blēk) ***adj.*** ⟦ON *bleikr,* pale⟧ **1** exposed to wind and cold; bare **2** cold; harsh **3** gloomy **4** not hopeful —**bleak'ly** ***adv.*** —**bleak'ness** ***n.***
blear·y (blir'ē) ***adj.*** **-i·er, -i·est** ⟦< ME *blere*⟧ dim or blurred, as the eyes by tears, fatigue, etc.: also **blear**
bleat (blēt) ***vi.*** ⟦OE *blætan*⟧ to make the cry of a sheep, goat, or calf —***n.*** a bleating cry or sound
bleed (blēd) ***vi.*** **bled** (bled), **bleed'ing** ⟦< OE *blod,* blood⟧ **1** to emit or lose blood **2** to feel pain, grief, or sympathy **3** to ooze sap, juice, etc. **4** to show through or run together: said of dyes, stains, etc. —***vt.*** **1** to draw blood from **2** to ooze (sap, juice, etc.) **3** to draw off (liquid, etc.) slowly —**bleed'er** ***n.***
bleep (blēp) ***n., vi.*** ⟦echoic⟧ beep —***vt.*** to censor (something said) in a telecast, etc., as with a beep
blem·ish (blem'ish) ***vt.*** ⟦< OFr *blesmir,* injure⟧ to mar; spoil —***n.*** a flaw, defect, etc., as a spot or scar
blench (blench) ***vt., vi.*** to blanch
blend (blend) ***vt.*** **blend'ed** or **blent**, **blend'ing** ⟦OE *blendan*⟧ **1** to mix or mingle (varieties of tea, etc.) **2** to mix thoroughly —***vi.*** **1** to mix or merge **2** to pass gradually into each other, as colors **3** to harmonize —***n.*** **1** a blending **2** a mixture of varieties
blend'er ***n.*** an electrical appliance that can chop, whip, mix, or liquefy foods
bless (bles) ***vt.*** **blessed** or **blest**, **bless'ing** ⟦< OE *bletsian,* consecrate with blood⟧ **1** to make holy **2** to ask divine favor for **3** to endow (*with*) **4** to make happy **5** to glorify **6** to make the sign of the cross over
bless·ed (bles'id, blest) ***adj.*** **1** holy; sacred **2** blissful **3** beatified **4** bringing comfort or joy —**bless'ed·ly** ***adv.*** —**bless'ed·ness** ***n.***
bless'ing ***n.*** **1** an invocation or benediction **2** a grace said before or after eating **3** good wishes or approval **4** anything that gives happiness
blew (blo͞o) ***vi., vt.*** *pt. of* BLOW[1] & BLOW[3]
blight (blīt) ***n.*** ⟦? < ON *blikja,* turn pale⟧ **1** any insect, disease, etc. that destroys plants **2** anything that destroys, frustrates, etc. —***vt.*** **1** to wither **2** to destroy
blimp (blimp) ***n.*** [Inf.] a nonrigid or semirigid airship
blind (blīnd) ***adj.*** ⟦OE⟧ **1** without the power of sight **2** of or for sightless persons **3** lacking insight **4** hard to see; hidden **5** closed at one end *[a blind alley]* **6** not controlled by intelligence *[blind destiny]* **7** guided only by instruments *[a blind landing]* —***vt.*** **1** to make sightless **2** to dazzle **3** to deprive of insight —***n.*** **1** anything that obscures sight or keeps out light, as a window shade **2** a place of concealment **3** a decoy —***adv.*** **1** blindly **2** guided only by instruments *[to fly blind]* —**blind'ly** ***adv.*** —**blind'ness** ***n.***
blind date [Inf.] **1** a date with a stranger, arranged by a third person **2** either person involved
blind'ers ***pl.n.*** bridle flaps for preventing a horse from seeing to the side
blind'fold' ***vt.*** ⟦< ME *blindfeld,* struck blind⟧ to cover the eyes of, as with a cloth —***n.*** a cloth used to cover the eyes —***adj., adv.*** **1** with the eyes covered **2** reckless(ly)
blind'side' ***vt.*** **-sid'ed, -sid'ing** to attack (someone) from an unexpected direction
blink (bliŋk) ***vi.*** ⟦ME *blenken*⟧ **1** to wink one or more times **2** to flash on and off **3** to ignore (with *at*) —***vt.*** **1** to cause (eyes, light, etc.) to blink **2** to evade or avoid —***n.*** **1** a blinking **2** a glimmer —**on the blink** [Slang] not working right
blink'er ***n.*** a flashing warning light
blintz (blints) ***n.*** ⟦Yiddish *blintze* < Russ *blin,* pancake⟧ a thin pancake rolled with a filling of cottage cheese, fruit, etc.
blip (blip) ***n.*** ⟦echoic of a brief sound⟧ a luminous image on an oscilloscope
bliss (blis) ***n.*** ⟦< OE *blithe,* blithe⟧ **1** great happiness **2** spiritual joy —**bliss'ful** ***adj.*** —**bliss'ful·ly** ***adv.*** —**bliss'ful·ness** ***n.***
blis·ter (blis'tər) ***n.*** ⟦< ?⟧ **1** a raised patch of skin, filled with watery matter and caused as by a burn **2** anything like a blister —***vt.*** **1** to raise blisters on **2** to lash with words —***vi.*** to form blisters
blis'ter·ing ***adj.*** very hot, intense, etc.
blithe (blīth, blīth) ***adj.*** ⟦OE⟧ cheerful; carefree; lighthearted: also **blithe'some** (-səm) —**blithe'ly** ***adv.*** —**blithe'ness** ***n.***
blitz (blits) ***n.*** ⟦< Ger *blitz,* lightning⟧ a sudden destructive or overwhelming attack —***vt.*** to subject to a blitz
bliz·zard (bliz'ərd) ***n.*** ⟦? < dial. *bliz,* violent blow⟧ a violent snowstorm with very cold winds
bloat (blōt) ***vt., vi.*** ⟦< ON *blautr,* soft⟧ **1** to swell, as with water or air **2** to puff up, as with pride
blob (bläb) ***n.*** ⟦echoic⟧ **1** a drop or a small lump or spot **2** something of indefinite shape —***vt.*** **blobbed, blob'bing** to splash, as with blobs
bloc (bläk) ***n.*** ⟦Fr < MDu *block,* log⟧ an alliance of persons, nations, etc.
block (bläk) ***n.*** ⟦< OFr *bloc* & MDu *block*⟧ **1** a large, solid piece of wood, stone, metal, etc. **2** a heavy stand on which chopping, etc. is done **3** an auctioneer's platform

THESAURUS

bleach ***v.*** blanch, wash out, whiten; see FADE.
bleak ***a.*** dreary, desolate, bare, cheerless, wild, exposed, barren, windswept, blank, disheartening, weary, melancholy, lonely, flat, somber, distressing, depressing, comfortless, joyless, uninviting, dull, sad, mournful, monotonous, waste, gloomy, dismal, unsheltered, unpopulated, desert, deserted, scorched, stony, burned over, bulldozed, cleared, frozen.—*Ant.* GREEN, verdant, fruitful.
bleed ***v.*** lose blood, shed blood, be bleeding, hemorrhage, gush, spurt, be bled, open a vein, draw blood; see also FLOW.
blemish ***n.*** flaw, defect, stain, spot, smudge, imperfection, disfigurement, defacement, blot, blur, chip, taint, tarnish, smirch, stigma, brand, deformity, dent, discoloration, mole, pock, blister, birthmark, wart, scar, impurity, speckle, bruise, freckle, pimple, patch, lump, zit*.—*Ant.* PERFECTION, flawlessness, consummation.
blend ***n.*** combination, compound, amalgam; see MIXTURE 1.
blend ***v.*** combine, mingle, compound; see MIX 1.
bless ***v.*** baptize, canonize, glorify, honor, dedicate, make holy, pronounce holy, exalt, give benediction to, absolve, anoint, ordain, hallow, consecrate, beatify, sanctify, enshrine, offer, render acceptable to, sacrifice, commend.
blessed ***a.*** **1** [Marked by God's favor, especially in heaven] saved, redeemed, glorified, translated, exalted, rewarded, resurrected, sanctified, glorious, beatified, holy, spiritual, religious.—*Ant.* DOOMED, lost, accursed. **2** [Consecrated] sacred, dedicated, sanctified; see DIVINE.
blessing ***n.*** **1** [Benediction] commendation, sanctification, laying on of hands, absolution, baptism, unction, consecration, Eucharist.—*Ant.* CURSE, damnation, anathema. **2** [Anything that is very welcome] boon, benefit, good, advantage, help, asset, good fortune, stroke of luck, godsend, windfall, miracle, manna from heaven, lucky break.—*Ant.* NUISANCE, obstacle, disadvantage.
blight ***n.*** disease, withering, mildew; see DECAY.
blight ***v.*** decay, spoil, ruin; see SPOIL.
blind ***a.*** **1** [Without sight] sightless, unseeing, eyeless, blinded, visionless, in darkness, dim-sighted, groping, deprived of sight, sun-blind, undiscerning, stone-blind, moon-blind, blind as a bat.—*Ant.* OBSERVANT, perceptive, discerning. **2** [Without looking] obtuse, unseeing, by guesswork, by calculation, with instruments; see also BLINDLY, UNAWARE. **3** [Without passage] obstructed, blocked, without egress; see TIGHT 2, 3. **4** [Random] chance, accidental, unplanned; see AIMLESS.
blind ***v.*** darken, shadow, dim; see SHADE 2.
blindly ***a.*** at random, wildly, in all directions, frantically, heedlessly, carelessly, recklessly, passionately, thoughtlessly, impulsively, inconsiderately, unreasonably, without rhyme or reason, senselessly, instinctively, madly, pell-mell, purposelessly, aimlessly, indiscriminately.—*Ant.* CAREFULLY, deliberately, considerately.
blindness ***n.*** sightlessness, purblindness, myopia, astigmatism, night blindness, snow blindness, color blindness.—*Ant.* SIGHT, vision, seeing.
blink ***v.*** **1** [To wink rapidly] flicker, bat one's eyes, flutter one's eyelids; see WINK. **2** [To twinkle] glimmer, flash on and off, shimmer; see SHINE 1.
bliss ***n.*** joy, rapture, ecstasy; see HAPPINESS.
blister ***n.*** vesicle, sac, weal, welt, blood blister, water blister, second-degree burn; see also SORE.
blister ***v.*** scald, irritate, mark; see HURT.
blizzard ***n.*** snowstorm, williwaw, snow squall; see STORM.
bloc ***n.*** cabal, group, ring; see FACTION.
block ***n.*** **1** [A mass, usually with flat surfaces] slab, chunk, piece, square, cake, cube, slice, segment, loaf, clod, bar, hunk. **2** [The area between streets] vicinity, square, lots;

4 an obstruction or hindrance 5 a pulley in a frame 6 [Now Brit.] a group or row of buildings 7 an area with streets or buildings on four sides 8 a number of things regarded as a unit 9 a toy brick, typically a cube of wood, etc. 10 *Printing* a piece of wood, etc. engraved with a design —*vt.* 1 to obstruct; hinder 2 to mount or mold on a block 3 to sketch roughly: often with *out* —**block'er** *n.*

block·ade (blä kād') *n.* ⟦prec. + -ADE⟧ 1 a shutting off of a place by troops or ships to prevent passage 2 any strategic barrier —*vt.* **-ad'ed, -ad'ing** to subject to a blockade

block and tackle an arrangement of pulley blocks and ropes, used for lifting heavy objects

block'bust'er *n.* a particularly effective person or thing; specif., an expensive film, etc. generating widespread appeal

block'bust'ing *n.* [Inf.] the inducing of owners to sell their homes out of fear that a minority group may move into the neighborhood

block grant a grant of federal funds to a state or local government to fund a block of programs

block'head' *n.* a stupid person

block'house' *n.* 1 [Historical] a wooden, two-story fortified building 2 a reinforced structure for observers, as of missile launchings

blond (bländ) *adj.* ⟦OFr < ? Gmc⟧ 1 having light-colored hair and, often, fair skin 2 light in color Also **blonde** —*n.* a blond person —**blonde** *fem.n.* —**blond'ness** *n.*

blood (blud) *n.* ⟦OE *blod*⟧ 1 the red fluid circulating in the arteries and veins of animals 2 bloodshed 3 the essence of life; life 4 the sap of a plant 5 passion, temperament, etc. 6 parental heritage; lineage 7 kinship 8 people, esp. youthful people *[new blood in a group]* —**bad blood** anger; hatred —**in cold blood** 1 with cruelty 2 deliberately

blood bank a supply of blood stored for future use in transfusion

blood count the number of red or white cells in a given volume of blood

blood'cur'dling (-kurd'liŋ) *adj.* frightening; terrifying

blood'ed *adj.* 1 having (a specified kind of) blood *[hot-blooded]* 2 of fine breed

blood'hound' *n.* any of a breed of large tracking dogs with a keen sense of smell

blood'less *adj.* 1 without bloodshed 2 anemic or pale 3 having little energy —**blood'less·ly** *adv.* —**blood'less·ness** *n.*

blood'line' *n.* line of descent

blood'mo·bile' (-mō bēl') *n.* a traveling unit for collecting blood from donors for blood banks

blood poisoning *nontechnical term for* SEPTICEMIA

blood pressure the pressure of the blood against the blood-vessel walls

blood relation (or **relative**) a person related by birth

blood'shed' *n.* the shedding of blood; killing

blood'shot' *adj.* tinged with red because small blood vessels are broken: said of eyes

blood'suck'er *n.* an animal that sucks blood, esp. a leech

blood'thirst'y *adj.* murderous; very cruel —**blood'thirst'i·ness** *n.*

blood vessel an artery, vein, or capillary

blood'y *adj.* **-i·er, -i·est** 1 of, like, containing, or covered with blood 2 involving bloodshed 3 bloodthirsty 4 [Brit. Slang] cursed; damned —*adv.* [Brit. Slang] very —*vt.* **-ied, -y·ing** to stain with blood —**blood'i·ly** *adv.* —**blood'i·ness** *n.*

bloody mar·y (mer'ē) *pl.* **bloody mar'ys** a drink made of vodka and tomato juice

bloom (blo͞om) *n.* ⟦< ON *blomi*, flowers⟧ 1 a flower; blossom 2 the state or time of flowering 3 a period of greatest health, vigor, etc. 4 a youthful, healthy glow 5 the powdery coating on some fruits and leaves —*vi.* 1 to blossom 2 to be in one's prime 3 to glow with health, etc.

bloom'ers *pl.n.* ⟦after Amelia *Bloomer* (1818-94), U.S. feminist⟧ baggy trousers gathered at the knee, once worn by women for athletics

bloom'ing *adj.* 1 blossoming 2 flourishing 3 [Inf.] complete *[a blooming idiot]*

bloop·er (blo͞op'ər) *n.* ⟦*bloop*, echoic + -ER⟧ 1 a stupid mistake 2 *Baseball* a fly that falls just beyond the infield for a hit

blos·som (bläs'əm) *n.* ⟦OE *blostma*⟧ 1 a flower, esp. of a fruit-bearing plant 2 a state or time of flowering —*vi.* 1 to have or open into blossoms 2 to begin to flourish —**blos'som·y** *adj.*

blot (blät) *n.* ⟦ME < ?⟧ 1 a spot or stain, esp. of ink 2 anything that spoils or mars 3 disgrace —*vt.* **blot'ted, blot'ting** 1 to spot; stain 2 to disgrace 3 to erase, obscure, or get rid of: often with *out* 4 to dry, as with blotting paper —*vi.* 1 to make blots 2 to become blotted 3 to be absorbent

blotch (bläch) *n.* ⟦? < prec.⟧ 1 a discoloration on the skin 2 any large blot or stain —*vt.* to mark with blotches —**blotch'y, -i·er, -i·est,** *adj.*

blot·ter (blät'ər) *n.* 1 a piece of blotting paper 2 a book for recording events as they occur *[a police blotter]*

blotting paper a thick, soft, absorbent paper used to dry a surface freshly written on in ink

blouse (blous) *n.* ⟦Fr, workman's smock⟧ 1 a garment like a shirt, worn by women and girls 2 a uniform coat worn by soldiers, etc. —*vi., vt.* **bloused, blous'ing** to gather in and drape over loosely

blow[1] (blō) *vi.* **blew, blown, blow'ing** ⟦OE *blawan*⟧ 1 to move with some force, as the wind 2 to send forth air,

THESAURUS

see NEIGHBORHOOD. 3 [The distance of the side of a city block] street, city block, intersection; see DISTANCE 3. 4 [An obstruction] hindrance, bar, obstacle; see BARRIER. —**knock someone's block off*** thrash, hit, beat up*; see BEAT 1.

block *v.* 1 [To impede] interfere with, prevent, close off; see HINDER. 2 [In sports, to impede a play] throw a block, tackle, check; see STOP 1. —**block out** 1 [To obscure] conceal, screen, cover; see HIDE 1. 2 [To plan] outline, sketch, chart; see PLAN 2.

blockade *n.* barricade, encirclement, strategic barrier; see BARRIER.

blockhead *n.* nitwit, fool, imbecile; see FOOL.

blond *a.* fair, fair-skinned, pale, light, light-skinned, lily-white, white-skinned, creamy, whitish, milky, albino, pearly, platinum, gray-white, towheaded, snowy, light-haired, golden-haired, fair-haired, yellow-haired, sandy-haired, ash-blond, bleached, strawberry-blond, bleached-blond.

blood *n.* lifeblood, plasma, serum, vital fluid, vital juices, gore, sanguine fluid. —**bad blood** malice, rancor, feud; see ANGER, HATRED. —**in cold blood** 1 heartlessly, ruthlessly, unmercifully; see BRUTALLY. 2 cruelly, intentionally, indifferently; see DELIBERATELY. —**make someone's blood boil** disturb, infuriate, agitate; see ENRAGE. —**make someone's blood run cold** terrify, horrify, scare; see FRIGHTEN.

bloodless *a.* pallid, wan, anemic; see PALE 1.

bloodshed *n.* slaughter, butchery, gore; see BATTLE, MURDER.

bloodshot *a.* inflamed, streaked, red; see BLOODY 1.

bloody *a.* 1 [Showing blood] bleeding, bloodstained, blood-spattered, gaping, unstaunched, grisly, crimson, open, wounded, dripping blood, raw, blood-soaked.—*Ant.* WHOLE, unhurt, uninjured. 2 [Fiercely fought] savage, heavy, murderous; see CRUEL.

bloom *n.* blossom, floweret, efflorescence; see FLOWER.

bloom *v.* flower, burst into bloom, open, bud, prosper, grow, wax, bear fruit, thrive, germinate, flourish, mature, be in peak condition, blossom, come out in flower, be in flower.

blooming *a.* flowering, blossoming, in flower; see BUDDING, GROWING.

blossom *n.* bloom, floweret, bud; see FLOWER.

blossom *v.* flower, blow*, burst into blossom; see BLOOM.

blossoming *n.* blooming, flowering, budding; see BUDDING, GROWING.

blot *n.* spot, stain, smudge; see BLEMISH.

blot *v.* smudge, blotch, soil; see DIRTY. —**blot out** 1 [To mark out] deface, cross out, scratch out, delete; see also CANCEL. 2 [To obscure] darken, blur, shroud; see SHADE 2.

blouse *n.* pullover, overblouse, jersey; see CLOTHES, SHIRT.

blow[1] *v.* 1 [To send forth air rapidly] puff, blast, pant, fan, whiff, whisk, whisper, puff away, exhale, waft, breathe, whistle. 2 [To carry on the wind] waft, flutter, bear, whisk, drive, fling, whirl, flap, flip, wave, buffet, sweep. 3 [To play a wind instrument] pipe, toot, mouth; see PLAY 3. 4 [To sound when blown] trumpet, vibrate, blare; see SOUND. 5 [To give form by inflation] inflate, swell, puff up, pump up; see also FILL 1. 6 [*To fail] miss, flounder, miscarry; see FAIL 1. 7 [*To spend] lay out, pay out, waste, squander; see also SPEND. —**blow up** 1 [To fill] pump up, puff up, swell, inflate; see also FILL 1. 2 [To explode] erupt, rupture, go off; see EXPLODE. 3 [To destroy with explosives] bomb, dynamite, detonate; see ATTACK, DESTROY. 4 [*To lose one's temper] become enraged, rave, lose self-control; see RAGE 1.

as with the mouth **3** to pant **4** to give sound by blowing or being blown **5** to spout water and air, as whales do **6** to be carried by the wind **7** to be stormy **8** to burst suddenly: often with *out* **9** [Slang] to leave —***vt.*** **1** to force air from, into, onto, or through **2** to drive or expel by blowing **3** to sound by blowing **4** to form by blown air or gas **5** to burst by an explosion: often with *up* **6** to melt (a fuse, etc.) **7** [Inf.] to spend (money) freely **8** [Slang] to leave **9** [Slang] to bungle **10** [Slang] to reveal *[to blow one's cover]* —***n.*** **1** a blowing **2** a blast of air or a gale —**blow over** to pass over or by —**blow up** **1** to enlarge or exaggerate **2** [Inf.] to lose one's temper —**blow'er** ***n.***

blow[2] (blō) ***n.*** ⟦ME *blowe*⟧ **1** a hard hit, as with the fist **2** a sudden attack **3** a sudden calamity; shock —**come to blows** to begin fighting one another

blow[3] (blō) ***vi.*** **blew, blown, blow'ing** ⟦OE *blowan*⟧ [Archaic] to bloom

blow'-by-blow' ***adj.*** told in great detail

blow'-dry' ***vt.*** **-dried', -dry'ing** to dry (wet hair) with hot air blown from an electric device (**blow'-dry'er**)

blow'fly' ***n.***, *pl.* **-flies'** a fly that lays its eggs on meat, in wounds, etc.

blow'gun' ***n.*** a long tube through which darts, etc. are blown

blow'hard' ***n.*** [Slang] a loudly boastful person

blow'out' ***n.*** **1** the bursting of a tire **2** [Slang] a party, banquet, etc.

blow'torch' ***n.*** a small torch that shoots out a hot flame

blow'up' ***n.*** **1** an explosion **2** an enlarged photograph **3** [Inf.] an angry outburst

blow'y ***adj.*** **-i·er, -i·est** windy

blowz·y (blou'zē) ***adj.*** **-i·er, -i·est** ⟦< obs. *blouze,* wench⟧ slovenly: also **blows'y**

BLT (bē'el'tē') ***n.*** a bacon, lettuce, and tomato sandwich

blub·ber[1] (blub'ər) ***n.*** ⟦ME *blober,* a bubble⟧ the fat of the whale —**blub'ber·y** ***adj.***

blub·ber[2] (blub'ər) ***vi.*** ⟦ME *bloberen,* to bubble⟧ to weep loudly, like a child

bludg·eon (bluj'ən) ***n.*** ⟦? < earlier Fr *bouge,* club⟧ a short club with a heavy end —***vt., vi.*** **1** to strike with a bludgeon **2** to bully or coerce

blue (blo͞o) ***adj.*** ⟦< ?⟧ **1** of the color of the clear sky **2** livid: said of the skin **3** sad and gloomy **4** puritanical **5** [Inf.] indecent; risqué —***n.*** **1** the color of the clear sky **2** any blue pigment —**out of the blue** unexpectedly —**the blue** **1** the sky **2** the sea

blue baby a baby born with bluish skin, esp. because of a heart defect

blue'bell' ***n.*** any of various plants with blue, bell-shaped flowers

blue'ber'ry (-ber'ē, -bər ē) ***n.***, *pl.* **-ries** **1** a shrub bearing small, edible, blue-black berries **2** any of the berries

blue'bird' ***n.*** a small North American songbird with a bluish back

blue blood an aristocrat: also **blue'blood'** ***n.*** —**blue'-blood'ed** ***adj.***

blue cheese a strong cheese containing bluish mold

blue'-chip' ***adj.*** ⟦< high-value *blue chips* of poker⟧ **1** of any high-priced stock with good earnings and a stable price **2** [Inf.] valuable

blue'-col'lar ***adj.*** ⟦< color of work shirts⟧ designating or of industrial workers

blue flu ⟦< *blue* police uniforms⟧ a sickout, esp. by police officers

blue'gill' ***n.*** a freshwater sunfish of a bluish color

blue'grass' ***n.*** **1** a type of grass with bluish-green horizontal stems **2** fast, bluesy country music

blue'jack'et ***n.*** an enlisted person in the navy

blue jay a common crested bird with a blue upper body and head: sometimes **blue'jay'** ***n.***

blue'jeans' (-jēnz') ***pl.n.*** jeans made of blue denim: also **blue jeans**

blue law a puritanical law, esp. one prohibiting certain activities on Sunday

blue'nose' ***n.*** [Inf.] a puritanical person

blue'-pen'cil ***vt.*** **-ciled** or **-cilled, -cil·ing** or **-cil·ling** to edit or correct with or as with a blue pencil

blue'-plate' special an inexpensive restaurant meal served at a fixed price

blue'point' ***n.*** ⟦after *Blue Point*, Long Island, New York⟧ a small oyster, usually eaten raw

blue'print' ***n.*** **1** a photographic reproduction in white on a blue background, as of architectural plans **2** any detailed plan or outline —***vt.*** to make a blueprint of

blues (blo͞oz) ***pl.n.*** [*with sing. or pl. v.*] **1** [Inf.] a depressed feeling: with *the* **2** black folk music having, usually, slow tempo, melancholy words, etc.: often with *the* —**blues'y, -i·er, -i·est,** ***adj.***

blue'stock'ing ***n.*** a learned or bookish woman

blu·et (blo͞o'it) ***n.*** ⟦< Fr dim. of *bleu,* blue⟧ a small plant having little, pale-blue flowers

blue whale a baleen whale with a blue-gray back: the largest animal

bluff[1] (bluf) ***vt., vi.*** ⟦prob. < Du *bluffen,* to brag, or *verbluffen,* to baffle⟧ to mislead (a person) by a false, bold front —***n.*** **1** a bluffing **2** one who bluffs: also **bluff'er**

bluff[2] (bluf) ***adj.*** ⟦? < Du *blaf,* flat⟧ **1** having a flat, steep front **2** having a rough, frank manner —***n.*** a high, steep bank or cliff

blu·ing (blo͞o'iŋ) ***n.*** a blue rinse used on white fabrics to prevent yellowing

blu'ish (-ish) ***adj.*** somewhat blue: also **blue'ish**

blun·der (blun'dər) ***vi.*** ⟦< ON *blunda,* shut the eyes⟧ **1** to move clumsily **2** to make a foolish mistake —***n.*** a foolish mistake —**blun'der·er** ***n.***

blun'der·buss' (-bus') ***n.*** ⟦< Du *donderbus*, thunder box⟧ [Historical] a short gun with a broad muzzle

blunt (blunt) ***adj.*** ⟦< ?⟧ **1** having a dull edge, etc. **2** plainspoken —***vt., vi.*** to make or become dull —**blunt'ly** ***adv.*** —**blunt'ness** ***n.***

blur (blur) ***vt., vi.*** **blurred, blur'ring** ⟦< ?⟧ **1** to smear or smudge **2** to make or become indistinct in shape, etc. **3** to dim —***n.*** anything indistinct or hazy —**blur'ry, -ri·er, -ri·est,** ***adj.*** —**blur'ri·ness** ***n.***

blurb (blurb) ***n.*** ⟦a coinage⟧ an advertisement, as on a book jacket, esp. a laudatory one

blurt (blurt) ***vt.*** ⟦prob. echoic⟧ to say impulsively: often with *out*

blush (blush) ***vi.*** ⟦< OE *blyscan*, to shine⟧ **1** to become red in the face, as from embarrassment **2** to be ashamed: usually with *at* or *for* **3** to become rosy —***n.*** **1** a reddening of the face, as from shame **2** a rosy color **3** BLUSHER (sense 2) —***adj.*** rosy —**at first blush** at first sight

blush'er ***n.*** **1** one who blushes readily **2** a red or reddish cosmetic powder, cream, etc. for the cheeks

blush wine a dry, pale-pink wine

THESAURUS

blow[2] ***n.*** hit, strike, swing, bump, wallop, rap, bang, whack, thwack, cuff, smack, uppercut, knock, clout, slam, bruise, swipe*, kick, stroke, punch, jab, gouge, lunge, thrust, swat, poke, prod, slap, the old one-two*, belt*, lick*, crack, kayo*, K.O.*.

blowing ***a.*** blasting, puffing, fanning, panting, whisking, breathing, gasping, fluttering, flapping, waving, streaming, whipping, drifting, tumbling, gliding, straining; see also FLYING.—*Ant.* MOTIONLESS, standing still, hovering.

blown ***a.*** buffeted, fluttered, fanned; see BLOWING.

blowout ***n.*** eruption, blast, detonation, tear, break, puncture, rupture, leak, flat tire, flat.

blue ***a., n.*** **1** [One of the primary colors] *Tints and shades of blue include the following:* indigo, sapphire, turquoise, lapis lazuli, aquamarine, blue-black, azure, sky-blue, blue-green; royal, Prussian, navy, powder, baby, cobalt, peacock, robin's egg, pale, light, dark, deep, electric, etc., blue; see also COLOR. **2** [Despondent] depressed, moody, melancholy; see SAD 1. —**once in a blue moon** rarely, infrequently, once in a while; see SELDOM. —**out of the blue** without warning, unpredicted, unforeseen; see UNEXPECTED.

blues ***n.*** **1** [A state of despondency; *often with "the"*] depressed spirits, melancholy, dejection; see GLOOM. **2** [Rhythmic lamentation in a minor key] dirge, lament, torch song; see MUSIC 1.

bluff[1] ***v.*** fool, mislead, trick; see DECEIVE.

bluff[1,2] ***n.*** **1** [A bank] cliff, precipice, promontory; see HILL, MOUNTAIN 1. **2** [A trick] ruse, deception, delusion; see TRICK 1.

blunder ***n.*** mistake, lapse, oversight; see ERROR.

blunt ***a.*** **1** [Dull] unsharpened, unpointed, round; see DULL 1. **2** [Abrupt] brusque, curt, bluff; see RUDE 2.

blur ***v.*** obscure, cloud, smear; see SHADE 2.

blurt out ***v.*** speak unthinkingly, jabber, utter; see TALK 1.

blush ***v.*** change color, flush, redden, turn red, glow, have rosy cheeks, turn scarlet.

blushing ***a.*** coloring, dyeing, staining, reddening, turning red, flushing, glowing, changing color, burning, red as a rose, rosy-red, with burning cheeks*.

blus·ter (blus′tər) ***vi.*** ⟦? < LowG *blüstern*⟧ **1** to blow stormily: said of wind **2** to speak in a noisy, swaggering manner —***n.*** **1** stormy blowing or noisy commotion **2** noisy or swaggering talk —**blus′ter·er** ***n.*** —**blus′ter·y** ***adj.***

Blvd *abbrev.* Boulevard

BM *abbrev.* [Inf.] bowel movement

BO *abbrev.* body odor

bo·a (bō′ə) ***n.*** ⟦L⟧ **1** a tropical snake that suffocates its prey in its coils, as the anaconda **2** a woman's long scarf, as of fur or feathers

boar (bôr) ***n.***, *pl.* **boars** or **boar** ⟦OE *bar*⟧ **1** a mature, uncastrated male pig **2** a wild hog

board (bôrd) ***n.*** ⟦OE *bord*, plank⟧ **1** a long, flat piece of sawed wood **2** a flat piece of wood, etc. for some special use *[bulletin board]* **3** pasteboard **4** meals, esp. as provided regularly for pay **5** a group of administrators; council **6** [*also* **B-**] [*pl.*] *Educ.* a qualifying examination for admission to an academic program —***vt.*** **1** to cover (*up*) with boards **2** to provide with meals, or room and meals, regularly for pay **3** to get on (a ship, train, etc.) —***vi.*** to receive meals, or room and meals, regularly for pay —**on board** **1** on a ship, aircraft, etc. **2** in a group as a member, etc. —**the boards** the stage (of a theater) —**board′er** ***n.***

board′ing·house′ ***n.*** a house where meals, or room and meals, can be had for pay: also **boarding house**

board′walk′ ***n.*** a walk made of thick boards, esp. one along a beach

boast (bōst) ***vi.*** ⟦< Anglo-Fr⟧ to talk, esp. about oneself, with too much pride; brag —***vt.*** **1** to brag about **2** glory in having or doing (something) —***n.*** **1** a boasting **2** anything boasted of —**boast′er** ***n.*** —**boast′ful** ***adj.*** —**boast′ful·ly** ***adv.***

boat (bōt) ***n.*** ⟦OE *bat*⟧ **1** a small, open vehicle for traveling on water **2** loosely, a ship **3** a boat-shaped dish —**in the same boat** in the same unfavorable situation —**rock the boat** [Inf.] to disturb the status quo —**boat′man** (-mən), *pl.* **-men** (-mən), ***n.***

boat′er ***n.*** a stiff straw hat with a flat crown and brim

boat′ing ***n.*** rowing, sailing, etc.

boat·swain (bō′sən) ***n.*** a ship's petty officer in charge of the deck crew, the rigging, anchors, boats, etc.

bob (bäb) ***n.*** ⟦ME *bobbe*, hanging cluster; 3 & 4 < the *v.*⟧ **1** any knoblike hanging weight **2** a woman's or child's short haircut **3** a quick, jerky motion **4** a float on a fishing line —***vt.*** **bobbed**, **bob′bing** ⟦ME *bobben*, knock against⟧ **1** to make move with a jerky motion **2** to cut (hair, etc.) short —***vi.*** to move with a jerky motion —**bob up** to appear suddenly

bob·bin (bäb′in) ***n.*** ⟦Fr *bobine* < ?⟧ a spool for thread or yarn, used in spinning, machine sewing, etc.

bob·ble (bäb′əl) ***n.*** [Inf.] *Sports* an awkward fumbling of the ball —***vt.*** **-bled**, **-bling** [Inf.] to make a bobble with (a ball)

bob·by (bäb′ē) ***n.***, *pl.* **-bies** ⟦after Sir Robert (*Bobby*) Peel (1788-1850), who reorganized the London police force⟧ [Inf., Chiefly Brit.] a British policeman

bobby pin ⟦from use with *bobbed* hair⟧ a small metal hairpin with the sides pressing close together

bobby socks (or **sox**) ⟦< BOB (*vt.* 2)⟧ [Inf.] esp. in the 1940s and 1950s, girls' ankle-length socks

bob′by-sox′er or **bob′by·sox′er** (-säks′ər) ***n.*** [Inf.] esp. in the 1940s, a girl in her early teens

bob′cat′ ***n.*** a small North American lynx

bob′sled′ ***n.*** a long racing sled with a protective shell —***vi.*** **-sled′ded**, **-sled′ding** to ride or race on a bobsled

Boc·cac·ci·o (bō käch′ē ō; *It* bô kä′chô), **Gio·van·ni** (jô vän′nē) 1313-75; It. writer

boc·cie, boc·ce, or **boc·ci** (bäch′ē) ***n.*** ⟦It *bocce,* (wooden) balls⟧ an Italian game similar to lawn bowling

bode[1] (bōd) ***vt.*** **bod′ed**, **bod′ing** ⟦< OE *boda,* messenger⟧ to be an omen of —**bode ill** (or **well**) to be a bad (or good) omen

bode[2] (bōd) ***vi.*** *alt. pt. of* BIDE

bod·ice (bäd′is) ***n.*** ⟦altered < *bodies,* pl. of *body*⟧ the upper part of a dress

bod·i·ly (bäd′'l ē) ***adj.*** **1** physical **2** of, in, by, or to the body —***adv.*** **1** in person **2** as a single group

bod·kin (bäd′kin) ***n.*** ⟦ME *bodekin* < ?⟧ [Obs.] a dagger

bod·y (bäd′ē) ***n.***, *pl.* **-ies** ⟦OE *bodig,* cask⟧ **1** the whole physical substance of a human being, animal, or plant **2** the trunk of a human being or animal **3** a corpse **4** [Inf.] a person **5** a distinct group of people or things **6** the main part **7** a distinct mass *[a body of water]* **8** density or consistency, as of paint or fabric **9** richness of flavor

bod′y·guard′ ***n.*** a person or persons assigned to guard someone

body language gestures, unconscious bodily movements, etc. that serve as nonverbal communication

body politic the people who collectively constitute a political unit under a government

body stocking a tightfitting garment, usually of one piece, that covers the torso and, sometimes, the legs

bod′y·suit′ ***n.*** a one-piece, tightfitting garment that covers the torso, usually worn with slacks, a skirt, etc.: also **body shirt**

Boer (bôr, boor, bō′ər) ***n.*** ⟦Du *boer,* peasant⟧ a South African of Dutch descent

bog (bäg, bôg) ***n.*** ⟦< Gael & Ir *bog,* soft, moist⟧ wet, spongy ground; a small marsh —***vt.***, ***vi.*** **bogged**, **bog′ging** to sink in or as in a bog: often with *down* —**bog′gy** ***adj.***

bo·gey (bō′gē; *for 1, usually* boog′ē) ***n.*** **1** BOGY **2** ⟦after an imaginary Col. *Bogey*⟧ *Golf* one stroke more than par on a hole: also **bo′gie**

bog·gle (bäg′əl) ***vi.*** **-gled**, **-gling** ⟦< Scot *bogle,* specter⟧ **1** to be startled (*at*) **2** to hesitate (*at*) —***vt.*** to confuse (the mind, imagination, etc.)

Bo·go·tá (bō′gə tä′) capital of Colombia: pop. 3,975,000

bo·gus (bō′gəs) ***adj.*** ⟦< ?⟧ not genuine; false

bo·gy (boog′ē, bō′gē) ***n.***, *pl.* **-gies** ⟦< Scot *bogle,* specter⟧ an imaginary evil spirit; goblin: also **bo′gie**

bo·gy·man or **bo·gey·man** (boog′ē man′, bō′gē-) ***n.***, *pl.* **-men′** (-men′) BOOGEYMAN

Bo·he·mi·a (bō hē′mē ə) region of Czech Republic: a former kingdom

Bo·he′mi·an (-ən) ***n.*** **1** CZECH (*n.* 2) **2** a person born or living in Bohemia **3** [*usually* **b-**] one who lives unconventionally —***adj.*** **1** of Bohemia or its people, etc. **2** [*usually* **b-**] like a bohemian —**Bo·he′mi·an·ism′** ***n.***

THESAURUS

bluster ***v.*** brag, swagger, strut; see BOAST.

board ***n.*** **1** [A piece of thin lumber] plank, lath, strip; see LUMBER. **2** [Meals] food, fare, provisions; see FOOD, MEAL 2. **3** [A body of persons having specific responsibilities] jury, council, cabinet; see COMMITTEE. —**across the board** general, universal, common; see UNIVERSAL 2. —**go by the board** be lost, be ruined, vanish; see FAIL 1. —**on board** present, in transit, en route; see ABOARD.

board ***v.*** **1** [Cover] cover up, close up, batten down; see COVER 1. **2** [Go aboard] embark, cast off, go on board ship; see LEAVE 1. **3** [Take care of] lodge, room, house; see FEED.

boast ***n.*** brag, vaunt, source of pride, pretension, self-satisfaction, bravado.

boast ***v.*** gloat, triumph, swagger, bully, exult, show off, vaunt, swell, brag, strut, bluff, flaunt, bluster, flourish, blow*, sound off*, crow, pat oneself on the back, blow one's own horn*, attract attention.—*Ant.* APOLOGIZE, humble oneself, admit defeat.

boastful ***a.*** bragging, pretentious, bombastic; see EGOTISTIC.

boat ***n.*** *Types of small boats include the following:* sailboat, rowboat, shell, scull, kayak, dugout, canoe, scow, raft, launch, motorboat, dory, catboat, tartan, hydrofoil, speedboat, yawl, sloop, cutter, ketch, schooner, lifeboat, barge, punt, outrigger, dinghy, racer, hydroplane, catamaran, skiff, gondola, longboat, war canoe, flatboat, riverboat, canal boat. —**in the same boat** in the same situation, in a similar situation, in the same condition, concurrently; see also TOGETHER 2. —**miss the boat*** miss, fall short, neglect; see FAIL 1. —**rock the boat*** upset, disturb, distort; see CONFUSE.

bobsled ***n.*** sleigh, toboggan, coaster; see SLED.

bodily ***a.*** carnal, fleshly, gross, somatic, solid, physical, corporeal, unspiritual, tangible, material, substantial, human, natural, normal, organic; see also BIOLOGICAL, PHYSICAL 1.

body ***n.*** **1** [The human organism] frame, physique, form, figure, shape, make, carcass*, build, makeup. **2** [A corpse] cadaver, corpus delecti (Latin), dust, clay, carcass*, dead body, relics, the dead, the deceased, mummy, skeleton, ashes, carrion, bones, remains, stiff*, goner. **3** [The central portion of an object] chassis, basis, groundwork, frame, fuselage, assembly, trunk, hull, bed, box, skeleton, scaffold, anatomy, bones, guts*. **4** [Individuals having an organization] society, group, party; see ORGANIZATION 2. **5** [A unified or organized mass] reservoir, supply, variety; see COLLECTION. —**keep body and soul together** stay alive, endure, earn a living; see SURVIVE 1.

bo·ho (bō′hō′) [Slang] ***n.*** BOHEMIAN (*n.* 3) —***adj.*** BOHEMIAN (*adj.* 2)

boil[1] (boil) ***vi.*** ⟦< L *bulla,* a bubble⟧ **1** to bubble up and vaporize over direct heat **2** to seethe like a boiling liquid **3** to be agitated, as with rage **4** to cook in boiling liquid —***vt.*** **1** to heat to the boiling point **2** to cook in boiling liquid —***n.*** the act or state of boiling —**boil down 1** to lessen in quantity by boiling **2** to condense

boil[2] (boil) ***n.*** ⟦OE *byle*⟧ an inflamed, painful, pus-filled swelling on the skin

boil′er ***n.*** **1** a container in which things are boiled or heated **2** a tank in which water is turned to steam **3** a tank for heating water and storing it

boiling point 1 the temperature at which a specified liquid boils **2** the point at which one loses one's temper

Boi·se (boi′zē, -sē) capital of Idaho: pop. 126,000: also **Boise City**

bois·ter·ous (bois′tər əs) ***adj.*** ⟦ME *boistreous,* crude⟧ **1** rough and stormy; turbulent **2** loud and exuberant; rowdy —**bois′ter·ous·ly *adv.***

bok choy (bäk′ choi′) ⟦Chin⟧ a variety of Chinese cabbage

bo·la (bō′lə) ***n.*** ⟦< Sp, a ball⟧ a set of cords with heavy balls at the ends, thrown to entangle cattle

bold (bōld) ***adj.*** ⟦OE *beald*⟧ **1** daring; fearless **2** too free in manner; impudent **3** steep **4** prominent and clear —**bold′ly *adv.*** —**bold′ness *n.***

bold′face′ ***n.*** a heavy, dark printing type

bold′faced′ ***adj.*** impudent

bole (bōl) ***n.*** ⟦ON *bolr*⟧ a tree trunk

bo·le·ro (bō ler′ō) ***n.,*** *pl.* **-ros** ⟦Sp < L *bulla,* a bubble⟧ **1** a lively Spanish dance, or the music for it **2** a short, open vest

Bol·í·var (bäl′ə vər), **Si·món** (sī′mən) 1783-1830; South American revolutionary leader

Bo·liv·i·a (bə liv′ē ə) inland country in WC South America: 424,165 sq. mi.; pop. 7,610,000 —**Bo·liv′i·an *adj., n.***

boll (bōl) ***n.*** ⟦ME *bolle,* BOWL[1]⟧ the roundish seed pod of a plant, esp. of cotton or flax

boll weevil a small weevil whose larvae destroy cotton bolls

bo·lo·gna (bə lō′nē) ***n.*** ⟦after *Bologna,* It city⟧ a large smoked sausage of beef, pork, or veal

Bol·she·vik (bōl′shə vik′) ***n.,*** *pl.* **-viks′** or **-vi′ki** (-vē′kē) ⟦Russ < *ból′she,* larger⟧ [*also* **b-**] **1** a member of a faction that seized power in Russia in 1917 **2** a Communist, esp. of the Soviet Union —**Bol′she·vism′** ***n.*** —**Bol′she·vist *n., adj.***

bol·ster (bōl′stər) ***n.*** ⟦OE⟧ **1** a long, narrow pillow **2** any bolsterlike object or support —***vt.*** to prop up as with a bolster: often with *up*

bolt[1] (bōlt) ***n.*** ⟦OE⟧ **1** a short, blunt arrow shot from a crossbow **2** a flash of lightning **3** a sudden dash **4** a sliding bar for locking a door, etc. **5** a threaded metal rod used with a nut for joining parts **6** a roll (*of* cloth, paper, etc.) —***vt.*** **1** to say suddenly; blurt (*out*) **2** to swallow (food) hurriedly **3** to fasten as with a bolt **4** to abandon (a party, group, etc.) —***vi.*** **1** to start suddenly; spring away **2** to withdraw support from one's party, etc. —**bolt upright** erect or erectly

bolt[2] (bōlt) ***vt.*** ⟦< OFr *buleter*⟧ to sift (flour, grain, etc.)

bo·lus (bō′ləs) ***n.*** ⟦< Gr *bōlos*⟧ **1** a small, round lump **2** a mass injected into a blood vessel, as a radioactive tracer **3** a large pill

bomb (bäm) ***n.*** ⟦prob. < Gr *bombos,* hollow sound⟧ **1** a container filled as with an explosive or incendiary chemical, for dropping, hurling, etc. **2** a small container with compressed gas in it *[an aerosol bomb]* **3** [Inf.] a complete failure —***vt.*** to attack with bombs —***vi.*** [Inf.] to be a complete failure

bom·bard (bäm bärd′) ***vt.*** ⟦< Fr *bombarde,* mortar⟧ **1** to attack with artillery or bombs **2** to attack with questions, etc. **3** to direct a stream of particles at (atomic nuclei) —**bom·bard′ment *n.***

bom′bar·dier′ (-bər dir′) ***n.*** one who releases the bombs in a bomber

bom·bast (bäm′bast′) ***n.*** ⟦< Pers *pambak,* cotton⟧ grand, pompous language with little real meaning —**bom·bas′tic *adj.*** —**bom·bas′ti·cal·ly *adv.***

Bom·bay (bäm′bā′) seaport in W India: pop. 8,243,000: now officially *Mumbai*

bomb·er (bäm′ər) ***n.*** **1** an airplane for dropping bombs **2** one who bombs

bomb′shell′ ***n.*** **1** a bomb **2** any sudden, shocking surprise

bo·na fi·de (bō′nə fīd′, bō′nə fī′dē) ⟦L⟧ **1** in good faith; without fraud *[a bona fide offer]* **2** genuine; real *[a bona fide movie star]*

bo·nan·za (bə nan′zə) ***n.*** ⟦Sp, prosperity⟧ **1** a rich vein of ore **2** any source of wealth

Bo·na·parte (bō′nə pärt′), **Na·po·le·on** (nə pō′lē ən) 1769-1821; Fr. military leader & emperor (1804-15)

bon·bon (bän′bän′; *Fr* bōn bōn′) ***n.*** ⟦< Fr *bon,* good⟧ a small piece of candy

bond (bänd) ***n.*** ⟦ult. < Gothic *bindan,* bind⟧ **1** anything that binds, fastens, or unites **2** [*pl.*] shackles **3** a binding agreement **4** an obligation imposed by a contract, promise, etc. **5** the status of goods kept in a warehouse until taxes or duties are paid **6** an interest-bearing certificate issued by a government or business, redeemable on a specified date **7** surety provided against theft, embezzlement, etc. **8** an amount paid for bail, etc. —***vt.*** **1** to join; bind **2** to furnish surety for (someone) **3** to place or hold (goods) in bond

bond·age (bän′dij) ***n.*** ⟦ult. < ON *bua,* inhabit⟧ **1** serfdom or slavery **2** subjection to some force, influence, etc.

bond′ing ***n.*** the development of a close relationship, esp. between family members

bond′man (-mən) ***n.,*** *pl.* **-men** (-mən) **1** a serf **2** a slave —**bond′wom′an,** *pl.* **-wom′en, *fem.n.***

bond paper ⟦orig. used for bonds, etc.⟧ high-quality writing paper

bonds·man (bändz′mən) ***n.,*** *pl.* **-men** (-mən) **1** BONDMAN **2** one who furnishes bail, etc.

bone (bōn) ***n.*** ⟦< OE *ban*⟧ **1** any of the parts of hard tissue forming the skeleton of most vertebrates **2** this

THESAURUS

boil[1] ***v.*** steep, seethe, stew, bubble, simmer, steam, parboil, boil over, evaporate, sterilize; see also COOK. —**boil down** condense, summarize, sum up; see DECREASE 2, SUMMARIZE.

boiling *a.* stewing, steeping, percolating, steaming, bubbling, seething, simmering, evaporating, boiling over; see also COOKING.

boisterous *a.* tumultuous, uproarious, noisy; see LOUD 2, RUDE 2.

bold *a.* **1** [Courageous] intrepid, fearless, daring; see BRAVE. **2** [Impertinent] presumptuous, impudent, brazen; see RUDE 2. **3** [Prominent] strong, clear, plain; see DEFINITE 2.

boldly *a.* **1** [*Said of animate beings*] impetuously, headlong, intrepidly, fearlessly, recklessly, courageously, dauntlessly, daringly, valiantly, stoutly, resolutely, brazenly, firmly.—*Ant.* COWARDLY, fearfully, cravenly. **2** [*Said of inanimate objects*] prominently, conspicuously, saliently, sharply, clearly, plainly, openly, abruptly, steeply, eminently, vividly, strongly, palpably, commandingly, compellingly, showily.—*Ant.* VAGUELY, inconspicuously, unobtrusively.

boldness *n.* audacity, impudence, daring; see COURAGE.

bolster *v.* prop, hold up, reinforce, sustain; see also SUPPORT 1, 2.

bolt[1] ***n.*** staple, brad, nut, skewer, peg, rivet, pin, spike, stud, coupling, key; see also NAIL, SCREW.

bomb *n.* weapon, high explosive, charge; see EXPLOSIVE. *Types of bombs include the following:* incendiary, multiple warhead, high explosive, demolition glider, time, smoke, delayed action, antipersonnel, smart, etc. bomb; atom bomb, atomic bomb, A-bomb, cobalt bomb, hydrogen bomb, H-bomb; torpedo, depth charge, cherry bomb, hand grenade, Molotov cocktail*, stink bomb.

bomb *v.* shell, bombard, torpedo, napalm, blow up, wipe out, blast, attack from the air, zero in on, raid, dive-bomb.

bombing *n.* bombardment, shelling, attack; see ATTACK.

bond *n.* **1** [A link] attachment, union, obligation, connection, relation, affinity, affiliation, bond of union, restraint; see also FRIENDSHIP, MARRIAGE, RELATIONSHIP. **2** [A secured debenture] security, warranty, debenture, certificate, registered bond, government bond, municipal bond, long-term bond, short-term bond, junk bond*. **3** [Bail] surety, guaranty, warrant; see BAIL.

bondage *n.* servitude, serfdom, subjugation; see SLAVERY 1.

bone *n.* *Bones of the human body include the following:* cranium, skull, frontal bone, temporal bone, parietal bone, occipital bone, cheekbone, mandible, jawbone, spinal column, vertebrae, backbone, rib cage, clavicle, collarbone, shoulder blade, humerus, radius, ulna, carpal, metacarpal, phalanges, pelvis, illium, hipbone, femur, thighbone, patella, kneecap, tibia, shinbone, fibula, tarsal, metatarsal. —**feel in one's bones** be convinced, expect, be sure; see TRUST 1. —**have a bone to pick*** have a complaint, be angry, express an objection; see COMPLAIN. —**make no bones about*** confess, reveal, expose; see ADMIT 2.

hard tissue **3** a bonelike substance or thing —***vt.* boned, bon'ing** to remove the bones from —***vi.*** [Slang] to study hard: usually with *up* —**have a bone to pick** [Inf.] to have cause to quarrel —**make no bones about** [Inf.] admit freely —**boneless *adj.***

bone china translucent china made of white clay to which the ash of burned bones has been added

bone'-dry' ***adj.*** [Inf.] very dry

bone meal crushed or ground bones, used as feed, fertilizer, or a nutritional supplement

bon·er (bōn'ər) ***n.*** [Slang] a blunder

bon·fire (bän'fīr') ***n.*** ⟦ME *banefyre,* bone fire, pyre⟧ an outdoor fire

bong (bôŋ, bäŋ) ***n.*** ⟦echoic⟧ a deep ringing sound, as of a large bell —***vi.*** to make this sound

bon·go (bäŋ'gō) ***n.***, *pl.* **-gos** ⟦AmSp < ?⟧ either of a pair of small drums of different pitch struck with the fingers: in full **bongo drum**

bo·ni·to (bō nēt'ō, bə-) ***n.***, *pl.* **-tos** or **-toes** ⟦Sp⟧ a saltwater food fish similar to a tuna

bon·jour (bōn zhōōr') ***interj.***, ***n.*** ⟦Fr⟧ good day; hello

bonk·ers (bäŋ'kərz) ***adj.*** [Slang] crazy

bon mot (bōn' mō'; *Fr* bōn mō') *pl.* **bons mots** (bōn' mōz'; *Fr*, -mō') ⟦Fr, lit., good word⟧ a clever or witty remark

Bonn (bän) city in W Germany: capital of West Germany (1949-90): pop. 298,000

bon·net (bän'it) ***n.*** ⟦< OFr *bonet*⟧ [Inf.] any hat worn by a woman or girl

bon·ny or **bon·nie** (bän'ē) ***adj.*** **-ni·er, -ni·est** ⟦< L *bonus*, good⟧ [Now Chiefly Brit.] **1** handsome or pretty, with a healthy glow **2** pleasant

bo·no·bo (bə nō'bō) ***n.***, *pl.* **-bos** a kind of chimpanzee, small with long limbs

bon·sai (bän'sī') ***n.***, *pl.* **-sai'** ⟦Jpn⟧ a tree or shrub grown in a pot and dwarfed by pruning, etc.

bo·nus (bō'nəs) ***n.***, *pl.* **-nus·es** ⟦L, good⟧ anything given in addition to the customary or required amount

bon voy·age (bän' voi äzh') ⟦Fr⟧ pleasant journey

bon·y (bō'nē) ***adj.*** **-i·er, -i·est** **1** of, like, or having bones **2** thin; emaciated

bony fish any fish with an air bladder, covered gills, and a bony skeleton

boo (bōō) ***interj.***, ***n.***, *pl.* **boos** a sound made to express disapproval, etc., or to startle someone —***vi.***, ***vt.*** **booed, boo'ing** to shout "boo" (at)

boo-boo or **boo·boo** (bōō'bōō') ***n.***, *pl.* **-boos'** [Slang] a stupid mistake

boob tube [Slang] TV or a TV set

boo·by (bōō'bē) ***n.***, *pl.* **-bies** ⟦prob. < Sp *bobo*⟧ a fool; nitwit: also **boob** (bōōb)

booby trap any scheme or device for tricking a person unexpectedly

boo·dle (bōōd''l) ***n.*** ⟦< Du *boedel,* property⟧ [Old Slang] **1** something given as a bribe; graft **2** the loot taken in a robbery

boo·gey·man (boog'ē man', bō'gē-) ***n.***, *pl.* **-men'** (-men') a frightening imaginary being

book (book) ***n.*** ⟦OE *boc*⟧ **1** a printed work on sheets of paper bound together, usually between protective covers **2** a main division of a literary work **3** [*usually pl.*] the records or accounts as of a business **4** [*pl.*] studies; lessons **5** *a*) a libretto *b*) the script of a play **6** a booklike package, as of matches —***vt.*** **1** to record in a book; list **2** to engage (rooms, etc.) ahead of time **3** to record charges against on a police record —**by the book** according to the rules —**the (Good) Book** the Bible

book'bind'ing ***n.*** the art, trade, or business of binding books —**book'bind'er *n.***

book'case' ***n.*** a set of shelves or a cabinet for holding books

book'end' ***n.*** a support, usually one of a pair, used to keep a row of books upright

book'ie (-ē) ***n.*** [Slang] a bookmaker

book'ing ***n.*** an engagement, as for a concert

book'ish (-ish) ***adj.*** **1** inclined to read and study **2** pedantic

book'keep'ing ***n.*** the work of keeping a record of business transactions —**book'keep'er *n.***

book'let (-lit) ***n.*** a small book

book'mak'er ***n.*** a person in the business of taking bets, as on horses

book'mark' ***n.*** a thing put between the pages of a book to mark a place

book matches safety matches made of paper and fastened into a cardboard holder

book'mo·bile' (-mō bēl') ***n.*** a lending library in a van that visits rural schools, etc.

book'plate' ***n.*** a label pasted in a book to identify its owner

book'shelf ***n.***, *pl.* **-shelves'** a shelf on which books are kept

book'store' ***n.*** a store where books are sold: also **book'shop'**

book'worm' ***n.*** **1** an insect larva that feeds on the binding, paste, etc. of books **2** one who reads or studies frequently

boom[1] (bōōm) ***vi.***, ***vt.*** ⟦echoic⟧ to make, or say with, a deep, hollow, resonant sound —***n.*** this sound

boom[2] (bōōm) ***n.*** ⟦Du, a beam⟧ **1** a spar extending from a mast to hold the bottom of a sail outstretched **2** a long beam extending as from an upright for supporting and guiding anything lifted */*the *boom* of a derrick*/* **3** a barrier, as of logs, to prevent floating logs from dispersing —***vi.*** to go rapidly along

boom[3] (bōōm) ***vi.*** ⟦< ? prec. *vi.*⟧ to increase or grow rapidly —***n.*** a period of prosperity

boom'box' ***n.*** [Slang] a large portable radio and tape player

boom'er ***n.*** *short for* BABY BOOMER

boom·er·ang (bōōm'ər aŋ') ***n.*** ⟦< Australian native name⟧ **1** a flat, curved stick that can be thrown so that it returns to the thrower **2** a scheme gone awry, to the schemer's harm —***vi.*** to act as a boomerang

boom'town' ***n.*** a town that has grown very rapidly: also **boom town**

boon[1] (bōōn) ***n.*** ⟦ON *bon,* a petition⟧ a welcome benefit; blessing

boon[2] (bōōn) ***adj.*** ⟦< L *bonus,* good⟧ merry; convivial: now only in **boon companion**, a close friend

boon·docks (bōōn'däks') ***pl.n.*** ⟦< native Philippine name⟧ [Inf.] **1** a jungle or wilderness **2** any remote rural region Used with *the*

boon·dog·gle (bōōn'dôg'əl, -däg'-) ***n.*** a trifling, pointless project —***vi.*** **-gled, -gling** to engage in a boondoggle —**boon'dog'gler *n.***

boor (boor) ***n.*** ⟦Du *boer*, a peasant⟧ a rude, awkward, or ill-mannered person —**boor'ish *adj.*** —**boor'ish·ly *adv.***

boost (bōōst) ***vt.*** ⟦< ?⟧ **1** to raise as by a push from below **2** to urge others to support **3** to increase —***n.*** **1** a push upward or forward **2** an increase —**boost'er *n.***

THESAURUS

bonus *n.* gratuity, reward, additional compensation; see GIFT 1, TIP 2.

bony *a.* emaciated, skinny, scrawny; see THIN 2.

book *n.* publication, work, volume, booklet, pamphlet, reprint, preprint, offprint, hardcover, softcover, text, edition, brochure, folio, copy, monograph, writing, scroll, periodical, magazine, paperback. *Kinds of books include the following:* manual, handbook, reference book, children's book, atlas, cookbook, guidebook, story book, song book, trade book, textbook, workbook, hymnbook, Bible, treatise, tract. —**by the book** strictly, according to rule, rigidly; see LEGALLY, OFFICIALLY 1. —**in one's book** in one's opinion, for oneself, to one's mind; see PERSONALLY 2. —**in the book** practiced, done, established, prevalent; see also KNOWN 2. —**know like a book** understand, comprehend, be aware of; see KNOW 1. —**one for the books*** source of amazement, shock, novelty; see SURPRISE 2. —**on the books** listed, noted, set down; see RECORDED. —**throw the book at*** accuse, charge with every possible offense, be overzealous with; see BLAME.

bookkeeper *n.* controller, comptroller, accountant, auditor; see also CLERK.

boom[1,3] ***n.*** **1** [A loud noise] roar, blast, blare; see NOISE 1. **2** [Sudden increase, especially sudden prosperity] rush, growth, inflation; see INCREASE.

boom[1,3] ***v.*** **1** [To make a loud sound] roar, reverberate, thunder; see SOUND. **2** [To increase rapidly] prosper, expand, swell; see GROW 1. —**lower the boom on*** take action against, move against, beat, overcome; see also ATTACK.

boon[1] ***n.*** benefit, good fortune, help; see BLESSING 2.

boor *n.* peasant, yokel, rustic, lout, clown, bumpkin, churl, oaf, lubber, bear, plowman, lumpkin, gaffer, yahoo, hick*, rube*, hayseed*, clod, clodhopper.

boorish *a.* awkward, clumsy, churlish; see RUDE 1, 2.

boost *n.* **1** [Aid] assistance, aid, helping hand; see HELP 1. **2** [An increase] addition, advance, hike*; see INCREASE.

boost *v.* **1** [To raise] shove, hoist, advance; see RAISE 1. **2** [To promote] encourage, support, advertise; see PROMOTE 1, 2. **3** [To increase] raise,

booster shot a later injection of a vaccine, for maintaining immunity

boot[1] (bo͞ot) ***n.*** ⟦OFr *bote*⟧ **1** a covering of leather, rubber, etc. for the foot and part of the leg **2** a kick —***vt.*** **1** to put boots on **2** to kick **3** [Inf.] to dismiss (a person) **4** to start (a computer): often with *up* —***vi.*** to start a computer: usually with *up* —**the boot** [Slang] dismissal

boot[2] (bo͞ot) ***n.***, ***vt.***, ***vi.*** ⟦OE *bot,* advantage⟧ [Archaic] profit —**to boot** besides; in addition

boot′black′ ***n.*** one whose work is shining shoes or boots

boot·ee or **boot·ie** (bo͞o tē′; *for 2* bo͞ot′ē) ***n.*** **1** a short boot for women or children **2** a baby's knitted or cloth shoe

booth (bo͞oth) ***n.***, *pl.* **booths** (bo͞oths, bo͞o*th*z) ⟦< ON *bua,* dwell⟧ **1** a stall for selling goods **2** a small enclosure for voting **3** a small structure to house a public telephone, etc. **4** an eating area in a restaurant with a table and benchlike seats

boot′leg′ ***vt.***, ***vi.*** **-legged′**, **-leg′ging** ⟦< hiding liquor in a boot⟧ to make or sell (liquor, etc.) illegally —***adj.*** bootlegged; illegal —***n.*** bootlegged liquor, etc. —**boot′leg′ger** ***n.***

boot′less ***adj.*** ⟦BOOT[2] + -LESS⟧ useless

boo·ty (bo͞ot′ē) ***n.***, *pl.* **-ties** ⟦LowG *bute*⟧ **1** spoils of war **2** plunder

booze (bo͞oz) ***vi.*** **boozed**, **booz′ing** ⟦< MDu *busen*⟧ [Inf.] to drink too much liquor —***n.*** [Inf.] liquor —[Slang] **booz′er** ***n.***

bop[1] (bäp) ***vt.*** **bopped**, **bop′ping** [Inf.] to hit; punch

bop[2] (bäp) ***n.*** a style of jazz (*c.* 1945-55) marked by complex rhythms, harmonic experimentation, etc. —***vi.*** **bopped**, **bop′ping** [Slang] to walk, esp. in an easy, strutting way

bo·rax (bôr′aks′) ***n.*** ⟦< Pers *būrah*⟧ a white crystalline salt used in the manufacture of glass, soaps, etc.

Bor·deaux (bôr dō′) ***n.*** ⟦after *Bordeaux*, city and region in SW France⟧ [*also* **b-**] **1** a red or white wine from the Bordeaux region **2** a similar wine made elsewhere

bor·der (bôr′dər) ***n.*** ⟦< OFr *border*, to border⟧ **1** an edge or part near an edge; margin **2** a dividing line between two countries, etc. **3** a narrow strip along an edge —***vt.*** **1** to provide with a border **2** to extend along the edge of —***adj.*** of or near a border —**border on** (or **upon**) **1** to be next to **2** to be like; almost be

bor′der·land′ ***n.*** **1** land near a border **2** a vague condition

bor′der·line′ ***n.*** a boundary —***adj.*** **1** on a boundary **2** indefinite

bore[1] (bôr) ***vt.*** **bored**, **bor′ing** ⟦< OE *bor,* auger⟧ **1** to make a hole in with a drill, etc. **2** to make (a well, etc.) as by drilling **3** to weary by being dull —***vi.*** to bore a hole or passage —***n.*** **1** a hole made as by boring **2** *a*) the hollow part of a tube or gun barrel *b*) its inside diameter **3** a tiresome, dull person or thing

bore[2] (bôr) ***vt.***, ***vi.*** *pt. of* BEAR[1]

bore·dom (bôr′dəm) ***n.*** the condition of being bored or uninterested

bo·ric acid (bôr′ik) a white crystalline compound, used as an antiseptic, in making glass, etc.

born (bôrn) ***vt.***, ***vi.*** *alt. pp. of* BEAR[1] —***adj.*** **1** brought into life **2** natural, as if from birth [*a born athlete*]

born-a·gain (bôrn′ə gen′) ***adj.*** having a new, strong faith or belief

borne (bôrn) ***vt.***, ***vi.*** *alt. pp. of* BEAR[1]

Bor·ne·o (bôr′nē ō′) large island in the Malay Archipelago

bo·ron (bôr′än′) ***n.*** ⟦< BORAX⟧ a nonmetallic chemical element

bor·ough (bʉr′ō) ***n.*** ⟦OE *burg,* town⟧ **1** a self-governing, incorporated town **2** any of the five administrative units of New York City

bor·row (bär′ō, bôr′-) ***vt.***, ***vi.*** ⟦OE *borgian*⟧ **1** to take or receive (something) with the intention of returning it **2** to adopt (an idea, etc.) as one's own —**bor′row·er** ***n.***

borscht or **borsch** (bôrsh) ***n.*** ⟦Russ *borshch*⟧ a beet soup, served usually with sour cream

bor·zoi (bôr′zoi′) ***n.*** ⟦Russ *borzój*, swift⟧ a large dog with a narrow head, long legs, and silky coat

bosh (bäsh) ***n.***, ***interj.*** ⟦Turk, empty⟧ [Inf.] nonsense

Bos·ni·a and Her·ze·go·vi·na (bäz′nē ə and hert′sə gō vē′nə) country in SE Europe: 19,741 sq. mi.; pop. 4,366,000 —**Bos′ni·an** ***adj.***, ***n.***

bos·om (booz′əm; *also* bo͞o′zəm) ***n.*** ⟦OE *bosm*⟧ **1** the human breast **2** the breast regarded as the source of feelings **3** the inside; midst [*in the bosom of one's family*] **4** the part of a garment that covers the breast —***adj.*** close; intimate [*a bosom friend*]

bos′om·y ***adj.*** having large breasts

bos·on (bō′sän) ***n.*** ⟦after S. N. *Bose* (1894-1974), Indian physicist + -ON⟧ any of certain subatomic particles, including photons and mesons

boss[1] (bôs, bäs) ***n.*** ⟦Du *baas*, a master⟧ **1** an employer or manager **2** one who controls a political organization —***vt.*** **1** to act as boss of **2** [Inf.] to order (a person) about —***adj.*** [Slang] excellent

boss[2] (bôs, bäs) ***n.*** ⟦OFr *boce*, a swelling⟧ a protruding ornament or projecting knob

boss′y ***adj.*** **-i·er**, **-i·est** [Inf.] domineering —**boss′i·ness** ***n.***

Bos·ton (bôs′tən, bäs′-) seaport & capital of Massachusetts: pop. 574,000 —**Bos·to′ni·an** (-tō′nē ən) ***adj.***, ***n.***

bo·sun (bō′sən) ***n.*** *phonetic sp. of* BOATSWAIN

bot·a·ny (bät′'n ē) ***n.*** ⟦< Gr *botanē*, a plant⟧ the science that deals with plants and plant life —**bo·tan·i·cal** (bə tan′i kəl) or **bo·tan′ic** ***adj.*** —**bot′a·nist** ***n.***

botch (bäch) ***vt.*** ⟦ME *bocchen,* to repair < ?⟧ to bungle —***n.*** a bungled piece of work —**botch′er** ***n.***

bot·fly (bät′flī′) ***n.***, *pl.* **-flies′** a fly resembling a small bumblebee

both (bōth) ***adj.***, ***pron.*** ⟦OE *ba tha,* both these⟧ the two [*both birds sang loudly*] —***conj.***, ***adv.*** together; equally [*both tired and hungry*]

THESAURUS

heighten, expand; see INCREASE.

boot[1] ***n.*** hip boot, bootee, wader, galosh, jackboot, chukka boot, combat boot, hiking boot, ski boot, cowboy boot, riding boot. —**bet your boots*** be certain, rely on it, trust in it; see DEPEND ON.

booth ***n.*** stall, counter, nook, kiosk, pew, berth, compartment, shed, manger, cubbyhole, coop, pen, hut, enclosure, stand, cubicle, box.

bootleg ***a.*** illegal, unlawful, contraband; see ILLEGAL.

booty ***n.*** plunder, spoils, winnings, stolen goods, ill-gotten gains, seizure, prize, haul*, pickings, loot, take*.

booze* ***n.*** liquor, alcohol, whiskey; see DRINK 2.

border ***n.*** **1** [Edge] hem, end, trim; see DECORATION 2, FRINGE. **2** [Boundary] frontier, outpost, perimeter; see BOUNDARY, EDGE 1.

border ***v.*** be adjacent to, adjoin, abut on; see JOIN 3. —**border on** lie next to, abut, touch; see JOIN 3.

bordering ***a.*** rimming, bounding, neighboring, fringing, edging, lining, verging, connecting, on the edge of, flanking; see also NEAR 1.

bore[1] ***n.*** nuisance, pest, tiresome person; see TROUBLE.

bore[1] ***v.*** **1** [To pierce by rotary motion] drill, ream, perforate; see PENETRATE. **2** [To weary] fatigue, tire, put to sleep; see TIRE 2.

bored ***a.*** wearied, fatigued, jaded, dull, irked, annoyed, bored to death*, in a rut, sick and tired, bored stiff*, bored silly*, fed up*; see also TIRED.—*Ant.* EXCITED, thrilled, exhilarated.

boredom ***n.*** lack of interest, tiresomeness, apathy, doldrums, listlessness, monotony, indifference, tedium, the blahs*.

boring ***a.*** tedious, stupid, monotonous; see DULL 3, 4.

born ***a.*** intrinsic, innate, inherent; see NATURAL 1.

borrow ***v.*** accept the loan of, obtain the use of, take a loan, go into debt, get temporary use of, use, rent, hire, obtain, give a note for, sponge*, hit up for*, bum*, beg, chisel*, mooch*.—*Ant.* LEND, loan, give back.

borrowed ***a.*** appropriated, taken, acquired, assumed, adopted, hired, plagiarized, imported, cultivated, imitated.—*Ant.* owned, possessed, purchased.

boss[1] ***n.*** supervisor, manager, administrator; see EXECUTIVE.

botanical ***a.*** concerning plants, vegetable, floral, arboreal, herbaceous, horticultural, agricultural; see also BIOLOGICAL.

botany ***n.*** phytology, natural history, horticulture; see BIOLOGY, SCIENCE.

botch ***v.*** bungle, spoil, mar, ruin, wreck, mutilate, fumble, distort, blunder, mishandle, do clumsily, muddle, make a mess of, trip, flounder, err, fall down, be mistaken, misjudge, mismanage, miscalculate, misconstrue, misestimate, execute clumsily, do unskillfully, stumble, put one's foot in it*, goof up*, butcher, screw up*, mess up, put out of whack*; see also FAIL 1.—*Ant.* SUCCEED, fix, do well.

both ***a.*** the two, both together, the one and the other, the pair, the couple, one as well as the other.

both·er (bäth′ər) ***vt., vi.*** ⟦prob. < *pother*⟧ **1** to worry; harass **2** to concern (oneself) —***n.*** **1** worry; trouble **2** one who gives trouble —**both′er·some** (-səm) ***adj.***

Bot·swa·na (bät swä′nə) country in S Africa: 224,607 sq. mi.; pop. 1,327,000

Bot·ti·cel·li (bät′ə chel′ē; *It* bôt′tē chel′ē), **San·dro** (sän′ drô) 1445?-1510; It. painter

bot·tle (bät′'l) ***n.*** ⟦< LL *buttis,* a cask⟧ **1** a narrow-necked container for liquids, usually of glass **2** its contents —***vt.*** **-tled, -tling** to put into a bottle —**bottle up** to restrain —**hit the bottle** [Slang] to drink much alcoholic liquor —**bot′tler** ***n.***

bot′tle·neck′ ***n.*** **1** a narrow passage or road where traffic is slowed or stopped **2** any similar hindrance to movement or progress

bot·tom (bät′əm) ***n.*** ⟦OE *botm,* ground⟧ **1** the lowest part or place **2** the part on which something rests **3** the side underneath **4** the seat of a chair **5** the ground beneath a body of water **6** basis; cause; source **7** [Inf.] the buttocks —***adj.*** lowest; last; basic —**at bottom** fundamentally —**bot′tom·less** ***adj.***

bottom line **1** [Inf.] profits or losses, as of a business **2** [Slang] *a*) the basic factor, etc. *b*) the final statement, decision, etc.

bot·u·lism (bäch′ə liz′əm) ***n.*** ⟦< L *botulus,* sausage⟧ poisoning, often fatal, by the toxin produced by a bacterium sometimes found in foods improperly canned or preserved

bou·doir (bōō dwär′, bōō′dwär′) ***n.*** ⟦< Fr, lit., pouting room⟧ a woman's private room

bouf·fant (bōō fänt′) ***adj.*** ⟦< Fr *bouffer,* puff out⟧ puffed out; full

bou·gain·vil·le·a or **bou·gain·vil·lae·a** (bōō′gən vil′ē ə, -vil′yə, -vē′yə) ***n.*** ⟦ModL⟧ a woody tropical vine having large, showy purple or red bracts

bough (bou) ***n.*** ⟦OE *bog,* shoulder or arm⟧ a main branch of a tree

bought (bôt) ***vt.*** *pt. & pp. of* BUY

bouil·lon (bool′yän′, -yən) ***n.*** ⟦< Fr *bouillir,* to boil⟧ a clear broth

boul·der (bōl′dər) ***n.*** ⟦< ME *bulderston,* noisy stone⟧ a large rock worn by weather and water

bou·le·vard (bool′ə värd′) ***n.*** ⟦Fr < MDu *bolwerc,* bulwark⟧ a broad street lined with trees, etc.

bounce (bouns) ***vi.*** **bounced, bounc′ing** ⟦ME *bounsen,* to thump⟧ **1** to spring back, as upon impact; rebound **2** to spring; leap **3** [Slang] to be returned: said of a worthless check —***vt.*** **1** to cause (a ball, etc.) to bounce **2** [Slang] to put (a person) out by force **3** [Slang] to fire from a job —***n.*** **1** *a*) a bouncing; rebound *b*) a leap or jump **2** capacity for bouncing **3** [Inf.] energy, zest, etc. —**the bounce** [Slang] dismissal —**bounc′y** ***adj.***

bounc′er ***n.*** [Slang] a person hired to remove disorderly people from a nightclub, restaurant, etc.

bounc′ing ***adj.*** big, healthy, etc.

bound[1] (bound) ***vi.*** ⟦< OFr *bondir,* to leap⟧ **1** to move with a leap or leaps **2** to bounce; rebound —***vt.*** to cause to bound or bounce —***n.*** **1** a jump; leap **2** a bounce; rebound

bound[2] (bound) ***vt., vi.*** *pt. & pp. of* BIND —***adj.*** **1** tied **2** closely connected **3** certain; sure *[bound to lose]* **4** obliged **5** having a binding: said as of a book **6** [Inf.] determined; resolved

bound[3] (bound) ***adj.*** ⟦< ON *bua,* prepare⟧ going; headed *[bound for home]*

bound[4] (bound) ***n.*** ⟦< ML *butina,* boundary⟧ **1** a boundary **2** [*pl.*] an area near a boundary —***vt.*** **1** to limit **2** to be a limit or boundary to **3** to name the boundaries of —**out of bounds** **1** beyond the boundaries **2** forbidden

bound·a·ry (boun′drē, -də rē) ***n., pl.*** **-ries** anything marking a limit; bound

bound′en ***adj.*** ⟦old pp. of BIND⟧ **1** [Archaic] obligated; indebted **2** obligatory *[one's bounden duty]*

bound′er ***n.*** ⟦< BOUND[1]⟧ [Inf., Chiefly Brit.] a cad

bound′less ***adj.*** unlimited; vast

boun·te·ous (boun′tē əs) ***adj.*** ⟦see BOUNTY⟧ **1** generous **2** plentiful —**boun′te·ous·ly** ***adv.***

boun′ti·ful (-tə fəl) ***adj.*** BOUNTEOUS

boun′ty (-tē) ***n., pl.*** **-ties** ⟦< L *bonus,* good⟧ **1** generosity **2** a generous gift **3** a reward or premium

bou·quet (bō kā′; *for 2, usually* bōō-) ***n.*** ⟦Fr⟧ **1** a bunch of flowers **2** aroma, as of wine

bour·bon (bur′bən) ***n.*** ⟦after *Bourbon* County, KY⟧ [*sometimes* **B-**] a whiskey distilled from corn mash

bour·geois (boor zhwä′) ***n., pl.*** **-geois′** ⟦Fr < OFr *borc,* town⟧ a member of the bourgeoisie —***adj.*** of the bourgeoisie: used variously to mean conventional, smug, materialistic, etc.

bour·geoi·sie (boor′zhwä zē′) ***n.*** [*with sing. or pl. v.*] the social class between the very wealthy and the working class; middle class

bout (bout) ***n.*** ⟦ME *bught*⟧ **1** a struggle or contest **2** a period of some activity, as a spell of illness

bou·tique (bōō tēk′; *occas.,* bō-) ***n.*** ⟦Fr < L *apotheca,* storehouse⟧ a small shop where fashionable articles are sold

bou·ton·niere or **bou·ton·nière** (bōō′tə nir′, -tən yer′) ***n.*** ⟦Fr, buttonhole⟧ a flower worn in a buttonhole

bo·vine (bō′vīn′, -vēn′) ***adj.*** ⟦< L *bos,* ox⟧ **1** of an ox, cow, etc. **2** slow, dull, stupid, etc.

bow[1] (bou) ***vi.*** ⟦< OE *bugan,* to bend⟧ **1** to bend down the head or body in respect, agreement, etc. **2** to give in —

THESAURUS

bother ***n.*** **1** [Worry] vexation, distress, anxiety; see CARE 2. **2** [A cause of worry] problem, concern, care; see DIFFICULTY 1, 2, TROUBLE.

bother ***v.*** **1** [To take trouble] put oneself out, fret, go out of one's way, make a fuss about, fuss over, take pains, make an effort, exert oneself, concern oneself, be concerned about, worry about. **2** [To give trouble] plague, vex, annoy, perplex, pester, molest, irritate, irk, provoke, insult, harass, heckle, aggravate, badger, discommode, disturb, discompose, mortify, goad, intrude upon, disquiet, pursue, hinder, impede, carp at, scare, exasperate, bore, afflict, taunt, torment, torture, bedevil, browbeat, tease, tantalize, ride, rub the wrong way, pick on, nag, needle*, bug*, get under someone's skin*.—*Ant.* HELP, please, delight.

bothered ***a.*** annoyed, agitated, disturbed; see TROUBLED.

bothersome ***a.*** annoying, irksome, troublesome; see DISTURBING.

bottle ***n.*** flask, flagon, decanter, cruet, jug, urn, canteen, cruse, jar, gourd, carafe, hip flask, vial, vacuum bottle, container. —**hit the bottle*** get drunk, imbibe, booze*; see DRINK 2.

bottom ***n.*** underside, base, nadir, foot, depths, bed, floor, underpart, deepest part, sole, ground.—*Ant.* TOP, peak, pinnacle. —**at bottom** fundamentally, basically, actually; see REALLY 1. —**be at the bottom of** originate, be the reason for, activate; see CAUSE. —**bet one's bottom dollar*** bet, risk, wager; see GAMBLE.

bottomless ***a.*** deep, unfathomable, boundless; see INFINITE.

bottom line* ***n.*** **1** [Profits or losses] net income, net loss, net profits; see INCOME, PROFIT 2, LOSS 3. **2** [Final decision] conclusion, determination, last word; see END 2.

bottoms ***n.*** low land, marsh, bottomland; see SWAMP.

bough ***n.*** limb, arm, fork; see BRANCH 2.

bought ***a.*** purchased, procured, budgeted for, requisitioned, paid for, on order, to be delivered, contracted for, acquired; see also ORDERED 1.—*Ant.* STOLEN, sold, given away.

boulder ***n.*** stone, slab, crag; see ROCK 2.

boulevard ***n.*** street, avenue, highway; see ROAD 1.

bounce ***v.*** ricochet, recoil, carom, rebound, glance off, spring back, leap, hop, bolt, vault, skip, bob, buck, jump, bound, jerk up and down, snap back, boomerang, backlash.

bound[1,4] ***v.*** **1** [To move in leaps] leap, spring, vault; see JUMP 1. **2** [To rebound] bounce, ricochet, recoil; see BOUNCE. **3** [To set limits] restrict, confine, circumscribe; see DEFINE 1. —**out of bounds** off limits, not permitted, restricted; see ILLEGAL.

bound[2] ***a.*** **1** [Literally confined in bonds] fettered, shackled, trussed up, manacled, chained, enchained, handcuffed, hobbled, captive, pinioned, muzzled, in leash, tied up, harnessed, bound hand and foot, pinned down, tethered, picketed, secured, roped, gagged.—*Ant.* FREE, unrestrained, loose. **2** [Figuratively constrained] impelled, compelled, obliged, obligated, restrained, under compulsion, constrained, forced, coerced, driven, pressed, urged, necessitated, under necessity, made, having no alternative, required, duty-bound. —**bound to** certain to, sure to, destined to; see INEVITABLE.

boundary ***n.*** outline, border, verge, rim, beginning, end, confine, bounds, radius, terminus, landmark, march, extremity, fence, compass, side, hem, frame, skirt, termination, margin, line, barrier, frontier, outpost, perimeter, parameter, extent, circumference, horizon, periphery, fringe, mark, confines, limit, borderland.

bounded ***a.*** limited, enclosed, bordered; see SURROUNDED.

bounty ***n.*** prize, premium, bonus; see PAY 1, 2.

bouquet ***n.*** nosegay, garland, corsage, boutonniere, flower arrangement, wreath, spray.

bow[1] ***v.*** **1** [To bend] curtsey, stoop, dip; see BEND. **2** [To submit] surren-

vt. **1** to bend (the head or body) down in respect, etc. **2** to weigh (*down*) **—*n.*** a bending down of the head or body, as in respect or greeting **—take a bow** to acknowledge applause, etc.

bow[2] (bō) ***n.*** ⟦OE *boga*⟧ **1** anything curved *[a rainbow]* **2** a curve; bend **3** a flexible, curved strip of wood with a cord connecting the two ends, for shooting arrows **4** a slender stick strung with horsehairs, as for playing a violin **5** a decorative knot, as a bowknot **—*adj.*** curved **—*vt.*, *vi.*** **1** to bend; curve **2** to play (a violin, etc.) with a bow

bow[3] (bou) ***n.*** ⟦< LowG *būg*⟧ the front part of a ship, etc.

bowd·ler·ize (boud′lər īz′) ***vt.* -ized′, -iz′ing** ⟦after T. *Bowdler* (1754-1825), Eng editor⟧ to expurgate **—bowd′ler·ism′ *n.* —bowd′ler·i·za′tion *n.***

bow·el (bou′əl) ***n.*** ⟦< L *botulus,* sausage⟧ **1** an intestine, esp. of a human being **2** [*pl.*] the inner part **—move one's bowels** to defecate

bow·er (bou′ər) ***n.*** ⟦< OE *bur,* dwelling⟧ a place enclosed by boughs or vines; arbor

bow·ie knife (bo͞o′ē, bō′-) ⟦after Col. J. *Bowie* (1799?-1836)⟧ a long single-edged hunting knife

bow·knot (bō′nät′) ***n.*** a decorative knot, usually with two loops and two ends

bowl[1] (bōl) ***n.*** ⟦OE *bolla*⟧ **1** a deep, rounded dish **2** the contents of a bowl **3** a bowllike thing or part **4** an amphitheater or stadium **—bowl′like′ *adj.***

bowl[2] (bōl) ***n.*** ⟦< L *bulla,* bubble⟧ **1** the wooden ball used in the game of lawn bowling **2** a roll of the ball in bowling **—*vi.*** **1** to roll a ball or participate in bowling **2** to move swiftly and smoothly **—bowl over 1** to knock over **2** [Inf.] to astonish **—bowl′er *n.***

bowl·der (bōl′dər) ***n.*** *alt. sp. of* BOULDER

bow·leg (bō′leg′) ***n.*** a leg with outward curvature **—bow′leg′ged** (-leg′id, -legd′) ***adj.***

bowl′ing ***n.*** **1** a game in which a heavy ball is rolled along a wooden lane (**bowling alley**) at ten wooden pins **2** LAWN BOWLING

bowling green a lawn for lawn bowling

bowls (bōlz) ***n.*** LAWN BOWLING

bow·man (bō′mən) ***n.*, *pl.* -men** (-mən) an archer

bow·sprit (bou′sprit′, bō′-) ***n.*** ⟦prob. < Du⟧ a tapered spar extending forward from the bow of a sailing ship

bow tie (bō) a necktie tied in a bow

box[1] (bäks) ***n.*** ⟦< Gr *pyxos,* BOX[3]⟧ **1** a container, usually rectangular and lidded; case **2** the contents of a box **3** a boxlike thing or space *[a jury box]* **4** a small, enclosed group of seats, as in a theater **5** a booth *[a sentry box]* **6** *Baseball* an area designated for the batter, catcher, etc. **—*vt.*** to put into a box **—box in** (or **up**) to shut in or keep in; surround or confine **—in a box** [Inf.] in difficulty **—box′like′ *adj.* —box′y, -i·er, -i·est, *adj.***

box[2] (bäks) ***n.*** ⟦< ?⟧ a blow struck with the hand **—*vt.*** **1** to strike with such a blow **2** to engage in boxing with **—*vi.*** to fight with the fists

box[3] (bäks) ***n.*** ⟦< Gr *pyxos*⟧ an evergreen shrub with small leathery leaves: also **box′wood′**

box′car′ ***n.*** a fully enclosed railroad freight car

box′er ***n.*** **1** one who boxes; prizefighter **2** a medium-sized dog with a sturdy body and a smooth coat

box′ing ***n.*** the skill or sport of fighting with the fists, esp. in padded leather mittens (**boxing gloves**)

box office 1 a place where admission tickets are sold, as in a theater **2** [Inf.] the power of a show or performer to attract a paying audience

box wrench a wrench with an enclosed head

boy (boi) ***n.*** ⟦ME *boie*⟧ **1** a male child **2** any man: familiar term **3** a male servant: a patronizing term **—*interj.*** [Slang] used to express pleasure, surprise, etc.: often **oh, boy! —boy′hood′ *n.* —boy′ish *adj.***

boy·cott (boi′kät′) ***vt.*** ⟦after Capt. *Boycott,* Irish land agent so treated in 1880⟧ to join together in refusing to deal with, buy, etc. so as to punish or coerce **—*n.*** a boycotting

boy′friend′ ***n.*** [Inf.] **1** a sweetheart or escort of a girl or woman **2** a boy who is someone's friend

Boy Scout a member of the **Boy Scouts**, a boys' organization that stresses outdoor life and service to others

boy·sen·ber·ry (boi′zən ber′ē) ***n.*, *pl.* -ries** ⟦after R. *Boysen,* U.S. horticulturist, developer (*c.* 1935)⟧ a berry that is a cross of the raspberry, loganberry, and blackberry

Br[1] *abbrev.* **1** Branch **2** British **3** Brother

Br[2] *Chem. symbol for* bromine

bra (brä) ***n.*** ⟦< BRASSIERE⟧ a woman's undergarment for supporting the breasts

brace (brās) ***vt.* braced, brac′ing** ⟦< Gr *brachiōn,* arm⟧ **1** to bind **2** to strengthen by supporting the weight of, etc. **3** to make ready for an impact, shock, etc. **4** to stimulate; invigorate **—*n.*** **1** a couple; pair **2** a thing that clasps or connects **3** [*pl.*] [Brit.] suspenders **4** a device for setting up or maintaining tension **5** either of the signs { }, used to connect words, lines, etc. **6** any propping device **7** *a)* a device for supporting a weak part of the body *b)* [*often pl.*] a device worn for straightening teeth **8** a tool for holding a drilling bit **—brace up** to call forth one's courage, etc.

brace and bit a tool for boring, consisting of a removable drill (*bit*) in a rotating handle (*brace*)

brace·let (brās′lit) ***n.*** ⟦< Gr *brachiōn,* arm⟧ an ornamental band or chain worn around the wrist or arm **—brace′let·ed *adj.***

brack·en (brak′ən) ***n.*** ⟦ME *braken*⟧ a large, weedy fern found in meadows, woods, etc.

brack·et (brak′it) ***n.*** ⟦< Fr *brague,* knee pants⟧ **1** a support projecting from a wall, etc. **2** any angle-shaped support **3** either of the signs [ ], used to enclose a word, etc. **4** the part of a classified grouping within certain limits *[high income bracket]* **—*vt.*** **1** to support with brackets **2** to enclose within brackets **3** to classify together

brack·ish (brak′ish) ***adj.*** ⟦< MDu *brak*⟧ **1** salty **2** nauseating **—brack′ish·ness *n.***

bract (brakt) ***n.*** ⟦L *bractea,* thin metal plate⟧ a modified leaf growing at the base of a flower or on its stalk

brad (brad) ***n.*** ⟦ON *broddr,* arrow⟧ a thin wire nail with a small head

brae (brā, brē) ***n.*** ⟦ON *bra,* brow⟧ [Scot.] a sloping bank; hillside

brag (brag) ***vt.*, *vi.* bragged, brag′ging** ⟦ME *braggen* < ?⟧ to boast **—*n.*** boastful talk **—brag′ger *n.***

brag′gart (-ərt) ***n.*** an offensively boastful person **—*adj.*** boastful

Brah·ma (brä′mə) ***n.*** Hindu god regarded as the creator of the universe

Brah·man (brä′mən) ***n.*, *pl.* -mans** ⟦Hindi < Sans, worship⟧ **1** a member of the Hindu priestly caste **2** a breed of domestic cattle developed from the zebu of India and having a large hump

THESAURUS

der, acquiesce, capitualate; see YIELD 1.

bow[1,3] ***n.*** **1** [Front of a boat] forepart, bowsprit, prow, head, nose, stem, fore; see also FRONT 1. **2** [A bend from the waist] nod, curtsey, bowing and scraping; see ACKNOWLEDGMENT. **—take a bow** accept praise, be congratulated, feel honored; see BEND.

bow[2] ***n.*** longbow, crossbow, single-piece bow; see WEAPON.

bowels ***n.*** viscera, entrails, guts; see INSIDES.

bowl[1] ***n.*** vessel, tureen, pot, saucer, crock, jar, urn, pitcher, basin, casserole, boat; see also CONTAINER, DISH.

bowling ***n.*** lawn bowling, tenpins, boccie; see SPORT 3.

box[1] ***n.*** receptacle, crate, carton; see CONTAINER.

box[1,2] ***v.*** **1** [To enclose in a box] confine, package, crate; see PACK 2. **2** [To fight for sport] spar, punch, slug; see FIGHT.

boxer ***n.*** pugilist, fighter, prizefighter; see FIGHTER 1.

boxing ***n.*** pugilism, prizefighting, fisticuffs*; see SPORT 3.

boy ***n.*** lad, youth, stripling, fellow, schoolboy, youngster, whippersnapper, kid*, junior, little gentleman; see also CHILD.

boycott ***v.*** withhold patronage, hold aloof from, ostracize; see AVOID, STRIKE 2.

boyfriend ***n.*** young man, beau*, companion, steady*, lover, sweetheart, flame, suitor, paramour, main man*, old man*.

boyhood ***n.*** school days, formative period, adolescence; see CHILDHOOD, YOUTH 1.

boyish ***a.*** juvenile, youthful, adolescent; see CHILDISH, YOUNG 1.

Boy Scout ***n.*** Cub Scout, Explorer, Eagle Scout; see SCOUT 2.

brace ***n.*** prop, bolster, stay, support, lever, beam, girder, block, rib, buttress, reinforcement, bearing, truss, bracket, strengthener, band, bracer, stirrup, arm, splint, boom, bar, staff, rafter, jack, crutch.

brace ***v.*** prop, bolster, hold up; see SUPPORT 1.

bracelet ***n.*** charm bracelet, wristlet, bangle; see JEWELRY.

brag ***v.*** swagger, exult, gloat; see BOAST.

braggart ***n.*** boaster, blowhard*, windbag*, showoff, swaggerer, strutter, hot dog*, blusterer, bragger, know-it-all*, big talker.

Brahms (brämz), **Jo·han·nes** (yō hän′əs) 1833-97; Ger. composer

braid (brād) ***vt.*** ⟦< OE *bregdan,* to move quickly⟧ **1** to interweave three or more strands of (hair, straw, etc.) **2** to make by such interweaving —***n.*** **1** a length of hair, etc. formed by braiding **2** a woven band of cloth, etc., used to bind or decorate clothing

Braille (brāl) ***n.*** ⟦after L. *Braille* (1809-52), its Fr inventor⟧ [*also* **b-**] a system of printing for the blind, using raised dots felt with the fingers

brain (brān) ***n.*** ⟦OE *brægen*⟧ **1** the mass of nerve tissue in the cranium of vertebrates **2** [*often pl.*] intelligence **3** [Inf.] an intelligent person —***vt.*** [Slang] to hit hard on the head

brain′child′ ***n.*** [Inf.] an idea, plan, etc. produced by a person's own mental labor

brain drain [Inf.] an exhausting of the intellectual or professional resources of a country, region, etc., esp. through emigration

brain′less ***adj.*** foolish or stupid

brain′storm′ ***n.*** [Inf.] a sudden inspiration, idea, or plan —***vi.*** to engage in brainstorming

brain′storm′ing ***n.*** the unrestrained offering of ideas by all members of a group to seek solutions to problems

brain′wash′ ***vt.*** [Inf.] to indoctrinate so thoroughly as to effect a radical change of beliefs and attitudes

brain wave a series of rhythmic electric impulses from the nerve centers in the brain

brain′y ***adj.*** **-i·er, -i·est** [Inf.] having a good mind; intelligent

braise (brāz) ***vt.*** **braised, brais′ing** ⟦< Fr *braise,* live coals⟧ to brown (meat, etc.) and then simmer slowly

brake (brāk) ***n.*** ⟦< ODu *breken,* to break⟧ any device for slowing or stopping a vehicle or machine, as by causing a block, band, etc. (**brake shoe**) to press against a moving part —***vt.,*** ***vi.*** **braked, brak′ing** to slow down or stop with or as with a brake —**brake′less** ***adj.***

brake′man (-mən) ***n.,*** *pl.* **-men** (-mən) a railroad worker who operated the brakes on a train, but is now chiefly an assistant to the conductor

bram·ble (bram′bəl) ***n.*** ⟦< OE *brom,* broom (the plant)⟧ a prickly shrub of the rose family, as the raspberry or blackberry —**bram′bly** ***adj.***

Bramp·ton (bramp′tən) city in SE Ontario, Canada: pop. 268,000

bran (bran) ***n.*** ⟦OFr *bren*⟧ the husk of grains of wheat, rye, etc. separated from the flour

branch (branch) ***n.*** ⟦< LL *branca,* a claw⟧ **1** any woody extension from a tree or shrub; limb **2** a tributary stream **3** any part or extension of a main body or system, as a division of a family or a separately located unit of a business, library, etc. —***vi.*** **1** to put forth branches **2** to come out (*from* the main part) as a branch —**branch off 1** to separate into branches **2** to diverge —**branch out** to extend one's interests, activities, etc. —**branched** (brancht) ***adj.*** —**branch′like′** ***adj.***

brand (brand) ***n.*** ⟦OE < *biernan,* to burn⟧ **1** a burning or partially burned stick **2** a mark burned on the skin, formerly used to punish criminals, now used on cattle to show ownership **3** the iron used in branding **4** a stigma **5** *a)* an identifying mark or label on a company's products *b)* the make of a commodity *[*a *brand* of coffee*]* *c)* a special kind —***vt.*** **1** to mark with a brand **2** to put a stigma on —**brand′er** ***n.***

brand′ing ***n.*** the marketing of products by connecting them with a popular brand name

bran·dish (bran′dish) ***vt.*** ⟦< OFr *brandir*⟧ to wave menacingly or as a challenge; flourish

brand name the name by which a certain brand or make of commodity is known —**brand′-name′** ***adj.***

brand′-new′ ***adj.*** ⟦orig., fresh from the fire: see BRAND⟧ entirely new

bran·dy (bran′dē) ***n.,*** *pl.* **-dies** ⟦< Du *brandewijn,* distilled wine⟧ an alcoholic liquor distilled from wine or from fermented fruit juice —***vt.*** **-died, -dy·ing** to flavor or preserve with brandy

brant (brant) ***n.*** ⟦< ?⟧ a wild goose of Europe and North America

brash (brash) ***adj.*** ⟦orig. Brit dial.; < ?⟧ **1** hasty and reckless **2** insolent; impudent

Bra·sí·lia (brä zē′lyä; *E* brə zil′yə) capital of Brazil, in the central part: pop. 1,596,000

brass (bras) ***n.,*** *pl.* **brass′es** ⟦OE *bræs*⟧ **1** a yellowish metal, an alloy of copper and zinc **2** [*often with pl. v.*] musical instruments made of brass **3** [Inf.] bold impudence **4** [*often with pl. v.*] [Slang] officers or officials of high rank —***adj.*** of brass —**brass′y, -i·er, -i·est,** ***adj.***

bras·siere or **bras·sière** (brə zir′) ***n.*** ⟦Fr < *bras,* an arm⟧ a bra

brass tacks [Inf.] basic facts: used chiefly in **get** (or **come**) **down to brass tacks**

brat (brat) ***n.*** ⟦< Gael *bratt,* cloth, rag, ? child's bib⟧ a child, esp. an impudent, unruly child: scornful or playful term

Bra·ti·sla·va (brä′ti slä′və) capital of Slovakia, on the Danube: pop. 448,000

brat·wurst (brät′wurst′) ***n.*** ⟦Ger < OHG, *brato,* lean meat + *wurst,* sausage⟧ highly seasoned, fresh sausage of veal and pork

braun·schwei·ger (broun′shwī′gər) ***n.*** ⟦after *Braunschweig*, Germany, where orig. made⟧ smoked liver sausage

bra·va·do (brə vä′dō) ***n.*** ⟦< Sp < *bravo,* brave⟧ pretended courage or feigned defiant confidence

brave (brāv) ***adj.*** **brav′er, brav′est** ⟦Fr < It *bravo*⟧ **1** not afraid; having courage **2** having a fine appearance —***n.*** **1** any brave man **2** a North American Indian warrior —***vt.*** **braved, brav′ing 1** to face with courage **2** to defy; dare —**brave′ly** ***adv.*** —**brave′ness** ***n.***

brav·er·y (brāv′ər ē) ***n.*** courage; valor

bra·vo (brä′vō) ***interj.*** ⟦It⟧ well done! excellent! —***n.,*** *pl.* **-vos** a shout of "bravo!"

bra·vu·ra (brə vyoor′ə) ***n.*** ⟦It < *bravo,* brave⟧ **1** bold daring; dash **2** a brilliant musical passage or brilliant technique

brawl (brôl) ***vi.*** ⟦ME *braulen,* to cry out⟧ to quarrel or fight noisily —***n.*** a noisy quarrel or fight

brawn (brôn) ***n.*** ⟦< OFr *braon,* muscle⟧ **1** strong, well-developed muscles **2** muscular strength —**brawn′y, -i·er, -i·est,** ***adj.*** —**brawn′i·ness** ***n.***

bray (brā) ***vi.*** ⟦< OFr *braire*⟧ to make the loud, harsh cry

THESAURUS

brain ***n.*** **1** [The organ of intelligence] cerebrum, gray matter, brain cells; see HEAD 1. **2** [The intelligence] intellect, genius, mentality; see MIND 1. **3** [*A very intelligent person] academician, scholar, egghead*; see INTELLECTUAL. —**have on the brain** be obsessed with, be involved with, fuss over, stew about; see also BOTHER 2.

brainwash* ***v.*** indoctrinate, instill, mold; see CONVINCE, INFLUENCE, TEACH.

brake ***n.*** check, hamper, curb, deterrent, obstacle, damper, hindrance, restraint, governor.

bramble ***n.*** brier, thorn, burr, stinging nettle, prickly shrub, thistle, bramble bush, hedge.

branch ***n.*** **1** [A part, usually of secondary importance] subsidiary, outpost, subdivision; see DIVISION 2. **2** [A secondary shoot] bough, limb, offshoot, sprig, twig, bud, arm, fork, growth.

branch off ***v.*** diverge, separate, part; see DIVIDE.

branch out ***v.*** expand, extend, add to; see GROW 1, INCREASE.

brand ***n.*** **1** [A trademark] brand name, make, kind, label, seal, name. **2** [A mark on the body] stigma, scar, sear, welt, range brand, earmark.

brand ***v.*** blaze, stamp, imprint; see MARK 1.

brandish ***v.*** flourish, gesture, warn; see THREATEN.

brass ***n.*** **1** [An alloy of copper and zinc] copper alloy, pinchbeck, brassware, yellow metal. **2** [*High-ranking officials] officers, front office, brass hats*; see OFFICER 3. **3** [*Impudence] effrontery, impertinence, audacity; see RUDENESS.

brat ***n.*** impudent child, unruly child, youngster, kid*; see also CHILD.

brave ***a.*** fearless, daring, dauntless, valiant, intrepid, undaunted, undismayed, confident, unabashed, chivalrous, valorous, heroic, bold, imprudent, adventurous, reckless, foolhardy, dashing, forward, audacious, gallant, resolute, militant, defiant, hardy, unafraid, stout, stouthearted, lionhearted, manly, firm, plucky, high-spirited, unshrinking, strong, stalwart, unflinching, unyielding, indomitable, game, unconquerable, spunky*, nervy*, gutsy*.—*Ant.* COWARDLY, timid, craven.

bravely ***a.*** courageously, fearlessly, valiantly, boldly, daringly, dauntlessly, intrepidly, heroically, gallantly, hardily, stoutly, manfully, staunchly, with courage, with fortitude, resolutely, valorously, spiritedly, audaciously, chivalrously, firmly, indomitably, with guts*, like a man*.—*Ant.* COWARDLY, fearfully, timidly.

bravery ***n.*** valor, guts*, fearlessness; see COURAGE, STRENGTH.

brawl ***n.*** fracas, squabble, riot; see FIGHT 1.

of a donkey —*n.* the harsh cry of a donkey, or a sound like this

braze (brāz) *vt.* **brazed, braz′ing** ⟦Fr *braser*⟧ to solder with a metal having a high melting point

bra·zen (brā′zən) *adj.* ⟦< OE *bræsen*, brass⟧ **1** of brass **2** like brass in color, etc. **3** shameless; bold; impudent **4** harsh and piercing —**brazen it out** to act in a bold, unashamed way —**bra′zen·ly** *adv.* —**bra′zen·ness** *n.*

bra·zier[1] (brā′zhər) *n.* ⟦see BRAISE⟧ a metal container to hold burning coals

bra·zier[2] (brā′zhər) *n.* ⟦see BRASS⟧ a person who works in brass

Bra·zil (brə zil′) country in South America, on the Atlantic: 3,286,485 sq. mi.; pop. 146,155,000 —**Bra·zil′ian** *adj.*, *n.*

Brazil nut the edible, three-sided seed of a tree of South America

breach (brēch) *n.* ⟦< OE *brecan*, to break⟧ **1** a failure to observe a law, promise, etc. **2** an opening made by a breakthrough **3** a break in friendly relations —*vt.* **1** to make a breach in **2** to violate (a contract, etc.) —**breach of promise** a breaking of a promise, esp. to marry

bread (bred) *n.* ⟦OE, crumb⟧ **1** a baked food made of flour or meal mixed with water, etc. **2** livelihood *[to earn one's bread]* —*vt.* to coat with bread crumbs before cooking —**break bread** to eat

breadth (bredth) *n.* ⟦< OE *brad*, broad⟧ **1** width **2** scope; extent **3** lack of restriction

bread·win·ner (bred′win′ər) *n.* one who supports dependents by his or her earnings

break (brāk) *vt.* **broke, bro′ken, break′ing** ⟦OE *brecan*⟧ **1** to split or crack into pieces; smash **2** to cut open the surface of (soil, the skin, etc.) **3** to make unusable by cracking, disrupting, etc. **4** to tame as with force **5** to get rid of (a habit) **6** to demote **7** to make poor, ill, bankrupt, etc. **8** to surpass (a record) **9** to violate (a law, promise, etc.) **10** to disrupt the order of *[break ranks]* **11** to interrupt (a journey, electric circuit, etc.) **12** to reduce the force of by interrupting (a fall, etc.) **13** to bring to an end suddenly or by force **14** to penetrate (silence, darkness, etc.) **15** to disclose **16** to decipher or solve *[break a code]* —*vi.* **1** to split into pieces; come apart **2** to force one's way (*through* obstacles, etc.) **3** to stop associating (*with*) **4** to become unusable **5** to change suddenly *[his voice broke]* **6** to begin suddenly *[to break into song]* **7** to come suddenly into being, notice, etc. *[the story broke]* **8** to stop activity temporarily **9** to suffer a collapse as of spirit —*n.* **1** a breaking **2** a broken place **3** a beginning or appearance *[the break of day]* **4** an interruption of regularity **5** a gap, interval, or rest **6** a sudden change **7** an escape **8** a chance piece of luck —**break down 1** to go out of working order **2** to have a physical or nervous collapse **3** to analyze —**break in 1** to enter forcibly **2** to interrupt **3** to train (a beginner) **4** to prepare (something new) by use or wear —**break off** to stop abruptly —**break out 1** to become covered with pimples, etc. **2** to escape suddenly —**break up 1** to separate; disperse **2** to stop **3** [Inf.] to laugh or make laugh —**give someone a break** [Inf.] to stop treating someone harshly, critically, etc. —**break′a·ble** *adj.*, *n.*

break′age *n.* **1** a breaking **2** things broken **3** loss due to breaking or the sum allowed for it

break′down′ *n.* **1** a breaking down **2** a failure of health **3** an analysis

break′er *n.* **1** a person or thing that breaks **2** a wave that breaks into foam

break·fast (brek′fəst) *n.* the first meal of the day —*vi.* to eat breakfast

break·front (brāk′frunt′) *adj.* having a projecting center section in front —*n.* a breakfront cabinet

break′-in′ *n.* the act of forcibly entering a building, esp. in order to rob

break′neck′ *adj.* very fast, reckless, or dangerous *[breakneck speed]*

break′through′ *n.* **1** the act of forcing a way through against resistance, as in warfare **2** a very important advance or discovery

break′up′ *n.* **1** a dispersion **2** a disintegration **3** a collapse

break′wa′ter *n.* a barrier to break the impact of waves, as before a harbor

breast (brest) *n.* ⟦OE *breost*⟧ **1** either of two milk-secreting glands on a woman's body **2** the upper front part of the body **3** the part of a garment, etc. over the breast **4** the breast regarded as the center of emotions —*vt.* to face firmly; oppose

breast′bone′ *n.* STERNUM

breast′-feed′ *vt.* **-fed′, -feed′ing** to feed (a baby) milk from the breast

breast′plate′ *n.* a piece of armor for the breast

breast stroke a swimming stroke in which both arms are brought out sideways from the chest

breast′work′ *n.* a low wall put up quickly as a defense in battle

breath (breth) *n.* ⟦< OE *bræth*, odor⟧ **1** air taken into the lungs and then let out **2** respiration **3** the power to breathe easily **4** life; spirit **5** a fragrant odor **6** a slight

THESAURUS

breach *n.* violation, infringement, transgression; see CRIME, VIOLATION.

bread *n.* loaf, baked goods, the staff of life. *Types of bread include the following:* whole wheat, rye, salt-rising, leavened, unleavened, yeast, quick, corn, sourdough, raisin, French, Italian, white, black, Boston brown, potato; hardtack, flatbread, pita, matzo, pumpernickel, bun, roll, bagel, biscuit, muffin. *Breadlike foods include the following:* spoon bread, cake, dumpling, turnover, cookie, English muffin, scone, shortbread, Indian bread. —**break bread** partake, have a meal, indulge; see EAT 1. —**know which side one's bread is buttered on** be prudent, save, look out for number one*; see UNDERSTAND 1.

breadth *n.* largeness, extent, vastness, compass, magnitude, greatness, extensiveness, scope, broadness, width, comprehensiveness, amplitude; see also SIZE 2.

break *n.* **1** [The act of breaking] fracture, rift, split, schism, cleavage, breach, rupture, eruption, bursting, failure, division, parting, collapse.—*Ant.* REPAIR, mending, restoration. **2** [A pause] intermission, interim, lapse; see PAUSE. **3** [Fortunate change or event] good luck, advantage, favorable circumstances; see LUCK 1.

break *v.* **1** [To start a rupture] burst, split, crack, rend, sunder, sever, fracture, tear, cleave, break into, break through, force open, puncture, split, snap, slash, gash, dissect, slice, disjoin, separate; see also CUT. **2** [To shatter] smash, shiver, crash, break up, crush, splinter, pull to pieces, burst, break into pieces, break into smithereens*, fall apart, fall to pieces, collapse, break down, come apart, come unglued, go to wrack and ruin, get wrecked, bust*, split up; see also DISINTEGRATE and sense 1. **3** [To bring to ruin or to an end] demolish, annihilate, eradicate; see DESTROY. **4** [To happen] come to pass, occur, develop; see HAPPEN 2. —**break down 1** [To analyze] examine, investigate, dissect; see ANALYZE. **2** [To malfunction] fail, stop, falter, misfire, give out, go down, crack up*, cease, backfire, conk out*, peter out*, fizzle out*, collapse, go kaput*, come unglued*, run out of gas*. —**break in 1** [Train] educate, instruct, prepare; see TEACH. **2** [Intrude] rob, burglarize, trespass; see MEDDLE 2, STEAL. —**break off** end, cease, discontinue; see STOP 2. —**break out 1** [To start] begin, commence, occur; see BEGIN 2. **2** [To escape] burst out, flee, depart; see LEAVE 1. **3** [To erupt] get blemishes, have acne, get a rash, get hives, get pimples. —**break through** penetrate, force a way, intrude; see PENETRATE. —**break up 1** [To scatter] disperse, disband, separate; see DISINTEGRATE, DIVIDE. **2** [To stop] put an end to, halt, terminate; see STOP 2. **3** [*To distress] hurt, sadden, wound; see HURT. **4** [*To end relations] discontinue, break off, stop; see END 1.

breakable *a.* fragile, delicate, frail; see WEAK 2.

breakage *n.* harm, wreckage, ruined goods; see DAMAGE 2.

breakdown *n.* collapse, stoppage, disruption; see FAILURE 1.

breakfast *n.* morning meal, first meal of the day, early meal, brunch, continental breakfast; see also MEAL 2.

breaking *a.* bursting, splitting, cracking, rending, sundering, parting, severing, exploding, erupting, shattering, splintering, fracturing, tearing, cleaving, snapping, breaking up, dispersing, separating, smashing, shivering, crashing, splintering, disintegrating, collapsing, caving in, falling, busting*, going to pot.—*Ant.* STRONG, stable, enduring.

breakthrough *n.* discovery, finding, invention; see DISCOVERY.

breakwater *n.* pier, wharf, jetty; see DOCK.

breast *n.* **1** [The forepart of the body above the abdomen] thorax, heart, bosom; see CHEST 2. **2** [An enlarged mammary gland or glands] bosom, chest, teat, tit*, nipple, bust, udder, boob*, jug*, knocker*. —**beat one's breast** repent, humble oneself, be sorry; see APOLOGIZE, REGRET 1. —**make a clean breast of** confess, reveal, expose; see ADMIT 2.

breath *n.* inspiration, expiration,

breeze **7** a whisper; murmur —**catch one's breath 1** to gasp **2** [Inf.] to rest or pause —**in the same breath** almost simultaneously —**out of breath** breathless, as from exertion —**take someone's breath away** to thrill someone —**under** (or **below**) **one's breath** in a whisper

breathe (brēth) ***vi., vt.* breathed, breath'ing 1** to take (air) into the lungs and let it out again; inhale and exhale **2** to live **3** to rest —**breathe again** to have a feeling of relief —**breath'a·ble** ***adj.***

breath·er (brē'thər) ***n.* 1** one who breathes **2** [Inf.] a pause for rest

breath·less (breth'lis) ***adj.* 1** without breath **2** panting; gasping **3** unable to breathe easily because of emotion —**breath'less·ly** ***adv.***

breath'tak'ing ***adj.*** very exciting

breath'y ***adj.* -i·er, -i·est** marked by an audible emission of breath

bred (bred) ***vt., vi.*** *pt. & pp. of* BREED

breech (brēch) ***n.*** ⟦OE *brec*⟧ **1** the buttocks **2** the part of a gun behind the barrel

breech'cloth' ***n.*** LOINCLOTH

breech·es (brich'iz) ***pl.n.*** ⟦see BREECH⟧ **1** trousers reaching to the knees **2** [Inf.] any trousers

breed (brēd) ***vt.* bred, breed'ing** ⟦< OE *brod*, fetus⟧ **1** to bring forth (offspring) **2** to be the source of; produce **3** to raise (animals) **4** to rear; train —***vi.* 1** to be produced; originate **2** to reproduce —***n.* 1** a stock; strain **2** a sort; type —**breed'er** ***n.***

breed'ing ***n.* 1** the producing of young **2** good upbringing **3** the producing of plants and animals, esp. for improving the stock

breeze (brēz) ***n.*** ⟦16th-c. nautical term *brise*, prob. < Du⟧ **1** a gentle wind **2** [Inf.] a thing easy to do —***vi.* breezed, breez'ing** [Inf.] to move or go quickly

breeze'way' ***n.*** a covered passageway, as between a house and garage

breez'y ***adj.* -i·er, -i·est 1** slightly windy **2** light and lively —**breez'i·ly** ***adv.*** —**breez'i·ness** ***n.***

Bre·men (brem'ən) seaport in NW Germany: pop. 553,000

breth·ren (breth'rən) ***pl.n.*** ⟦ME *bretheren*⟧ brothers: now chiefly religious

bre·vet (brə vet') ***n.*** ⟦< L *brevis*, brief⟧ [Historical] *Mil.* a commission of higher honorary rank without extra pay —***vt.* -vet'ted** or **-vet'ed, -vet'ting** or **-vet'ing** to give a brevet to

bre·vi·ar·y (brē'vē er'ē) ***n., pl.* -ar'ies** ⟦< L *brevis*, brief⟧ a book of Psalms, prayers, etc. to be recited daily by priests, nuns, etc.

brev·i·ty (brev'ə tē) ***n.*** ⟦< L *brevis*, brief⟧ **1** briefness **2** conciseness

brew (brōō) ***vt.*** ⟦OE *breowan*⟧ **1** to make (beer, etc.) from malt and hops by boiling and fermenting **2** to steep (tea, etc.) **3** to plot —***vi.*** to begin to form —***n.*** a brewed beverage —**brew'er** ***n.***

brew·er·y (brōō'ər ē) ***n., pl.* -er·ies** a place where beer, etc. is brewed

bri·ar[1] (brī'ər) ***n.*** BRIER[1]

bri·ar[2] (brī'ər) ***n.*** a tobacco pipe made from the root of the BRIER[2]

bribe (brīb) ***n.*** ⟦< OFr *briber*, to beg⟧ anything given or promised as an inducement, esp. to do something illegal or wrong —***vt.* bribed, brib'ing** to offer or give a bribe to —**brib'er·y** ***n.***

bric-a-brac (brik'ə brak') ***n.*** ⟦< Fr *de bric et de brac*, by hook or by crook⟧ **1** small artistic objects used to ornament a room **2** knickknacks

brick (brik) ***n.*** ⟦MDu < *breken*, piece of baked clay⟧ **1** an oblong block of baked clay, used in building, etc. **2** anything shaped like a brick **3** bricks collectively —***adj.*** built or paved with brick —***vt.*** to build or cover with brick

brick'bat' ***n.* 1** a piece of brick used as a missile **2** an unfavorable remark

brick'lay'er ***n.*** one whose work is building with bricks —**brick'lay'ing** ***n.***

brid·al (brīd''l) ***adj.*** ⟦< OE *bryd ealu*, marriage feast⟧ **1** of a bride **2** of a wedding

bride (brīd) ***n.*** ⟦OE *bryd*⟧ a woman just married or about to be married

bride'groom' ***n.*** ⟦< OE *bryd*, bride + *guma*, man⟧ a man just married or about to be married

brides·maid (brīdz'mād') ***n.*** one of the women who attend the bride at a wedding

bridge[1] (brij) ***n.*** ⟦OE *brycge*⟧ **1** a structure built over a river, etc. to provide a way across **2** a thing that provides connection, contact, etc. **3** the bony upper part of the nose **4** a raised platform on a ship **5** a mounting for false teeth **6** *Music* a connecting passage —***vt.* bridged, bridg'ing** to build or be a bridge over —**burn one's bridges** (**behind one**) to follow a course from which there is no retreat —**bridge'a·ble** ***adj.***

bridge[2] (brij) ***n.*** ⟦< ? Russ⟧ a card game, for two pairs of players, in which they bid for the right to name the trump suit or declare no-trump

bridge'head' ***n.*** a fortified position established by an attacking force on the enemy's side of a bridge, river, etc.

Bridge·port (brij'pôrt') seaport in SW Connecticut: pop. 142,000

bridge'work' ***n.*** a dental bridge or bridges

bri·dle (brīd''l) ***n.*** ⟦< OE *bregdan*, move quickly⟧ **1** a head harness for guiding a horse: it has a bit for the mouth to which the reins are fastened **2** anything that controls or restrains —***vt.* bri'dled, bri'dling 1** to put a bridle on **2** to curb or control —***vi.* 1** to pull one's head back quickly as an expression of anger, scorn, etc. **2** to take offense (*at*)

bridle path a path for horseback riding

brief (brēf) ***adj.*** ⟦< L *brevis*⟧ **1** short **2** concise —***n.* 1** a summary, specif. of the main points of a law case **2** [*pl.*] legless undershorts —***vt.* 1** to summarize **2** to supply with all pertinent information —**brief'ly** ***adv.*** —**brief'ness** ***n.***

brief'case' ***n.*** a flat, flexible case for carrying papers, books, etc.

brief'ing ***n.*** a supplying of pertinent information

THESAURUS

inhalation, exhalation, breathing, gasp, sigh, pant, wheeze. —**catch one's breath*** rest, stop, slow down; see PAUSE. —**in the same breath** simultaneously, concurrently, at the same time; see TOGETHER 2. —**out of breath** gasping, choking, out of wind; see BREATHLESS. —**save one's breath*** be quiet, stop talking, never mind; see SHUT UP 1. —**take someone's breath away** thrill, stimulate, invigorate; see EXCITE. —**under one's breath** quietly, in a whisper, murmuring; see WHISPERING.

breathe ***v.*** respire, inhale, exhale, draw in, breathe in, breathe out, gasp, pant, wheeze, snort, sigh, huff, puff, scent, sniff.

breathless ***a.*** out of breath, winded, spent, exhausted, tired, used up, gasping, choking, wheezing, short-winded, puffing, panting, asthmatic, short of breath, out of wind.

breed ***n.*** strain, variety, kind; see RACE 1.

breed ***v.* 1** [To produce] give birth to, deliver, bring forth; see PRODUCE 1. **2** [To cause] bring about, effect, produce; see BEGIN 1.

breeze ***n.*** draft, gust, blast; see WIND. —**in a breeze*** effortlessly, readily, simply; see EASILY. —**shoot the breeze*** converse, chat, chatter; see TALK 1.

brew ***n.*** concoction, preparation, distillation, compound, broth, liquor, blend, beer, ale; see also DRINK 1, 2.

brew ***v.*** concoct, ferment, plot; see COOK.

bribe ***n.*** fee, reward, hush money, lure, gift, graft, compensation, remuneration, protection, bait, tip, blackmail, price, present, gratuity.

bribe ***v.*** corrupt, get to, reward, tip, coax, hire, entice, tempt, pervert, lure, buy, influence, buy off, fix*.

brick ***n.*** cube, chunk, section, block, slab, cinder block, glass block, adobe brick, building brick, paving stone, floor tile; see also STONE.

bridal ***a.*** nuptial, marriage, wedding, matrimonial, marital, conjugal, wedded.

bride ***n.*** spouse, mate, partner; see WIFE.

bridegroom ***n.*** groom, mate, spouse; see HUSBAND.

bridge[1] ***v.*** connect, span, link; see JOIN 1.

bridge[1,2] ***n.* 1** [An elevated structure] viaduct, platform, catwalk, gangplank, drawbridge, trestle, aqueduct, scaffold. *Types of bridges include the following:* arch, pier, girder, concrete arch, suspension, cantilever, bascule, pontoon, swing, floating, covered, cable-stayed, steel arch, lift, truss. **2** [A game at cards] contract bridge, auction bridge, duplicate bridge; see GAME 1. **3** [A link] connection, bond, tie; see JOINT 1, LINK.

brief ***a.* 1** [Abrupt] hasty, curt, blunt; see RUDE 2. **2** [Short in time] short-term, fleeting, concise; see SHORT 2. —**in brief** concisely, to the point, cut short, abbreviated; see also BRIEFLY.

briefing ***n.*** instruction, training session, orientation; see INTRODUCTION 4, PREPARATION 1.

briefly ***a.*** shortly, curtly, abruptly, tersely, quickly, hastily, hurriedly,

bri·er[1] (brī′ər) ***n.*** ⟦OE *brer*⟧ any thorny bush, as a bramble

bri·er[2] (brī′ər) ***n.*** ⟦Fr *bruyère*⟧ a variety of heath, whose root is used for making tobacco pipes

brig[1] (brig) ***n.*** ⟦< BRIGANTINE⟧ a two-masted ship with square sails

brig[2] ***n.*** ⟦< ?⟧ a prison, as on a warship

bri·gade (bri gād′) ***n.*** ⟦< OIt *briga,* strife⟧ **1** a military unit composed of two or more battalions with service and administrative units **2** a group of people organized to function as a unit in some work *[a fire brigade]*

brig·a·dier general (brig′ə dir′) *U.S. Mil.* a military officer ranking just above a colonel

brig·and (brig′ənd) ***n.*** ⟦see BRIGADE⟧ a bandit, esp. one of a roving band

brig′and·age ***n.*** plundering by brigands

brig·an·tine (brig′ən tēn′) ***n.*** ⟦< OIt *brigantino,* pirate vessel⟧ a ship with a square-rigged foremast and a square-rigged topsail on the mainmast

bright (brīt) ***adj.*** ⟦OE *bryht*⟧ **1** shining with light **2** brilliant in color or sound; vivid **3** lively; cheerful **4** mentally quick; smart **5** favorable or hopeful **6** illustrious —***bright′ly adv.*** —***bright′ness n.***

bright′en ***vt., vi.*** to make or become bright or brighter

Brigh·ton (brīt′′n) resort city in S England: county district pop. 144,000

bril·liant (bril′yənt) ***adj.*** ⟦< Fr < It *brillare,* to sparkle⟧ **1** shining brightly **2** vivid; intense **3** very splendid **4** very intelligent, talented, etc. —**bril′liance** or ***bril′lian·cy n.*** —***bril′liant·ly adv.***

bril·lian·tine (bril′yən tēn′) ***n.*** ⟦< Fr⟧ an oily substance for grooming the hair

brim (brim) ***n.*** ⟦ME *brimme*⟧ **1** the topmost edge of a cup, glass, etc. **2** a projecting rim, as of a hat —***vt., vi.*** **brimmed, brim′ming** to fill or be full to the brim —***brim′less adj.***

brim′ful′ (-fool′) ***adj.*** full to the brim

brim′stone′ ***n.*** ⟦< OE *bærnan,* to kindle + *stan,* stone⟧ sulfur

brin·dle (brin′dəl) ***adj.*** BRINDLED —***n.*** **1** a brindled color **2** a brindled animal

brin′dled (-dəld) ***adj.*** ⟦prob. < ME *brennen,* to burn⟧ having a gray or tawny coat streaked or spotted with a darker color

brine (brīn) ***n.*** ⟦OE⟧ **1** water full of salt **2** the ocean —**brin′y, -i·er, -i·est,** ***adj.***

bring (briŋ) ***vt.*** **brought, bring′ing** ⟦OE *bringan*⟧ **1** to carry or lead "here" or to a place where the speaker will be **2** to cause to be, happen, appear, have, etc. **3** to lead to an action or belief **4** to sell for —**bring about** to cause —**bring forth** to give birth to; produce —**bring off** to accomplish —**bring out 1** to reveal **2** to offer (a play, book, etc.) to the public —**bring up 1** to rear (children) **2** to introduce, as into discussion

brink (briŋk) ***n.*** ⟦< MLowG or Dan, shore⟧ the edge, esp. at the top of a steep place; verge

brink′man·ship′ (-mən ship′) ***n.*** the policy of pursuing a risky course of action to the brink of disaster: also **brinks′man·ship′**

bri·oche (brē ōsh′) ***n.*** ⟦Fr⟧ a light, rich roll made with flour, butter, eggs, and yeast

bri·quette or **bri·quet** (bri ket′) ***n.*** ⟦Fr < *brique,* brick⟧ a small block of charcoal, coal dust, etc., used for fuel or kindling

Bris·bane (briz′bān′, -bən) seaport in E Australia: pop. 1,455,000

brisk (brisk) ***adj.*** ⟦< ? Fr *brusque,* brusque⟧ **1** quick in manner; energetic **2** keen, bracing, etc. —***brisk′ly adv.*** —***brisk′ness n.***

bris·ket (bris′kit) ***n.*** ⟦ME *brusket*⟧ meat cut from the breast of an animal

bris·ling (bris′liŋ) ***n.*** ⟦< Dan *bretling*⟧ SPRAT

bris·tle (bris′əl) ***n.*** ⟦< OE *byrst*⟧ **1** any short, stiff hair **2** such a hair, or a piece like it, in a brush —***vi.*** **-tled, -tling 1** to be stiff and erect **2** to have the bristles become erect **3** to stiffen with anger **4** to be thickly covered (*with*) —**bris′tly** (-lē), **-tli·er, -tli·est,** ***adj.***

bris′tle·cone′ pine a Rocky Mountain pine tree of the W U.S.

Bris·tol (bris′təl) seaport in SW England: county district pop. 376,000

Brit *abbrev.* British

Brit·ain (brit′′n) GREAT BRITAIN

britch·es (brich′iz) ***pl.n.*** [Inf.] BREECHES (sense 2)

Brit·i·cism (brit′ə siz′əm) ***n.*** a word or idiom peculiar to British English

Brit·ish (brit′ish) ***adj.*** of Great Britain or its people, language, etc. —**the British** the people of Great Britain

British Columbia province of SW Canada: 367,671 sq. mi.; pop. 3,725,000; cap. Victoria: abbrev. *BC*

British Commonwealth (of Nations) *former name for* THE COMMONWEALTH

British Isles group of islands including Great Britain, Ireland, etc.

British thermal unit a unit of heat equal to about 252 calories

Brit·on (brit′′n) ***n.*** **1** a member of an early Celtic people of S Britain **2** a person born or living in Great Britain, esp. in England

brit·tle (brit′′l) ***adj.*** ⟦< OE *breotan,* to break⟧ easily broken or shattered —***n.*** a brittle, crunchy candy with nuts in it —***brit′tle·ness n.***

broach (brōch) ***n.*** ⟦< ML *brocca,* a spike⟧ a tapering bit for boring holes —***vt.*** **1** to make a hole in so as to let out liquid **2** to ream with a broach **3** to start a discussion of

THESAURUS

momentarily, fleetingly, suddenly, temporarily, in passing, casually, lightly, briskly, in brief, in outline, in a few words, in a capsule, in a nutshell.

bright ***a.*** **1** [Shining or vivid] gleaming, shiny, glittering, luminous, lustrous, burnished, polished, sparkling, mirrorlike, glowing, flashing, scintillating, shimmering, incandescent, twinkling, illumined, light, golden, silvery, illuminated, shining, irradiated, glistening, radiant, burning, glaring, beaming, glimmering, splendid, resplendent, brilliant, dazzling, alight, aglow, lighted up, full of light, ablaze, flamelike, moonlit, sunlit, on fire, phosphorescent, blazing, glossy, colored, colorful, tinted, intense, deep, sharp, rich, tinged, hued, touched with color, fresh, clear, ruddy, psychedelic.—*Ant.* DULL, clouded, dark. **2** [Intelligent] clever, quick, alert; see INTELLIGENT. **3** [Not rainy] clear, sunny, mild; see FAIR 3. **4** [Cheerful] lively, vivacious, joyful; see HAPPY.

brighten ***v.*** **1** [To become brighter] clear up, lighten, grow calm, improve, grow sunny, glow. **2** [To make brighter] polish, intensify, lighten; see SHINE 3.

brightly ***a.*** lustrously, radiantly, splendidly, brilliantly, dazzlingly, sparklingly, glowingly, gleamingly, shinily, gaily, freshly, vividly, colorfully, cleverly, sunnily.—*Ant.* dully, dingily, darkly.

brightness ***n.*** shine, luster, illumination; see LIGHT 1.

brilliant ***a.*** **1** [Shining] dazzling, gleaming, sparkling; see BRIGHT 1. **2** [Showing remarkable ability] ingenious, profound, smart; see INTELLIGENT.

brilliantly ***a.*** **1** [Very brightly] shiningly, radiantly, blazingly; see BRIGHTLY. **2** [With superior intelligence] cleverly, shrewdly, knowledgeably; see INTELLIGENTLY.

brim ***n.*** margin, rim, border; see EDGE 1.

bring ***v.*** **1** [To transport] convey, take along, bear; see CARRY 1, PICK UP 6. **2** [To be worth in sale] sell for, earn, bring in; see PAY 2. **3** [To cause] produce, effect, make; see BEGIN 1. —**bring about 1** [To achieve] do, accomplish, realize; see ACHIEVE, SUCCEED 1. **2** [To cause] produce, effect, do; see BEGIN 1, MANAGE 1. —**bring forth** deliver, bear, yield; see PRODUCE 1, 2. —**bring off** accomplish, realize, execute; see ACHIEVE, SUCCEED 1. —**bring out 1** [To excite] elicit, arouse, evoke; see EXCITE. **2** [To publish] print, issue, put out; see PUBLISH 1. **3** [To produce a play] present, put on the stage, exhibit; see PERFORM 2. **4** [To intensify] heighten, sharpen, magnify; see EMPHASIZE, INCREASE. —**bring up 1** [To rear] educate, teach, train; see RAISE 2, SUPPORT 3. **2** [To discuss] tender, submit, advance; see DISCUSS, PROPOSE 1.

bringing ***n.*** fetching, carrying, transporting, accompanying, introducing, shipping, bearing, hauling, bringing in, getting, providing, procuring.

brink ***n.*** limit, brim, rim; see EDGE 1.

brisk ***a.*** lively, refreshing, invigorating; see STIMULATING.

briskly ***a.*** energetically, quickly, brusquely, rapidly, impulsively, nimbly, agilely, dexterously, decisively, firmly, actively, promptly, readily, vigorously, in a lively manner; see also EMPHATICALLY.—*Ant.* SLOWLY, listlessly, sluggishly.

bristle ***n.*** hair, fiber, quill; see POINT 2.

British ***a.*** Anglo-Saxon, Celtic, Brit*; see ENGLISH.

brittle ***a.*** fragile, crisp, inelastic; see WEAK 2.

broad (brôd) ***adj.*** ⟦OE *brad*⟧ **1** of large extent from side to side; wide **2** extending about; full *[broad* daylight*]* **3** obvious *[a broad* hint*]* **4** tolerant; liberal *[a broad* view*]* **5** wide in range *[a broad* variety*]* **6** not detailed; general *[in broad* outline*]* —**broad'ly *adv.*** —**broad'ness *n.***
broad'band' ***adj.*** designating cable, communication devices, etc. allowing the transmission of much data at high speeds
broad'-based' ***adj.*** comprehensive or extensive
broad'cast' (-kast') ***vt., vi.*** **-cast'** or **-cast'ed, -cast'ing** **1** to scatter or spread widely **2** to transmit by radio or TV —***adj.*** of or for radio or TV broadcasting —***n.*** a radio or TV program —***adv.*** far and wide —**broad'cast'er *n.***
broad'cloth' ***n.*** a fine, smooth woolen, cotton, or silk cloth
broad'en ***vt., vi.*** to widen
broad jump *former name for* LONG JUMP
broad'loom' ***adj.*** woven on a wide loom
broad'-mind'ed ***adj.*** tolerant of unconventional opinions and behavior; liberal —**broad'-mind'ed·ly *adv.*** —**broad'-mind'ed·ness *n.***
broad'side' ***n.*** **1** the firing of all guns on one side of a warship **2** a vigorous attack in words —***adv.*** **1** with the side facing **2** in the side *[hit broadside]* **3** indiscriminately
broad'-spec'trum ***adj.*** effective against a wide range of germs
broad'sword' ***n.*** a broad-bladed sword for slashing
Broad·way (brôd'wā') street in New York City, with many theaters, etc.
bro·cade (brō kād') ***n.*** ⟦< Sp < It *broccare,* embroider⟧ a rich cloth with a raised design woven into it —***vt.*** **-cad'ed, -cad'ing** to weave a raised design into (cloth)
broc·co·li (bräk'ə lē) ***n.*** ⟦It < ML *brocca,* a spike⟧ a plant related to the cauliflower but bearing tender shoots with greenish buds
bro·chette (brō shet') ***n.*** ⟦Fr⟧ a skewer for broiling chunks of meat, etc.
bro·chure (brō shoor') ***n.*** ⟦Fr < *brocher,* to stitch⟧ a pamphlet
bro·gan (brō'gən) ***n.*** ⟦Ir⟧ a heavy work shoe, fitting high on the ankle
brogue[1] (brōg) ***n.*** ⟦< ?⟧ a dialectal pronunciation, esp. that of English by the Irish
brogue[2] (brōg) ***n.*** ⟦< Ir *brōg,* a shoe⟧ a man's heavy oxford shoe
broil (broil) ***vt., vi.*** ⟦< OFr *bruillir*⟧ to cook by exposure to direct heat
broil'er ***n.*** **1** a pan, grill, etc. for broiling **2** a chicken suitable for broiling
broke (brōk) ***vt., vi.*** *pt. of* BREAK —***adj.*** [Inf.] without money; bankrupt
bro·ken (brō'kən) ***vt., vi.*** *pp. of* BREAK —***adj.*** **1** splintered, fractured, etc. **2** not in working order **3** violated *[a broken* promise*]* **4** ruined **5** interrupted; discontinuous **6** imperfectly spoken **7** tamed —**bro'ken·ly *adv.*** —**bro'ken·ness *n.***
bro'ken-down' ***adj.*** **1** sick or worn out **2** out of order; useless
bro'ken·heart'ed ***adj.*** crushed by sorrow, grief, etc.
bro·ker (brō'kər) ***n.*** ⟦< OFr *brokier,* to tap; orig. sense "wine dealer"⟧ **1** a person hired as an agent in negotiating contracts, buying and selling, etc. **2** STOCKBROKER —***vt., vi.*** **1** to act as a broker (for) **2** to negotiate
bro'ker·age ***n.*** **1** the business or office of a broker **2** a broker's fee
bro·mide (brō'mīd') ***n.*** **1** a compound of bromine with another element or a radical **2** potassium bromide, used as a sedative **3** a trite saying
bro·mid'ic (-mid'ik) ***adj.*** trite or dull
bro·mine (brō'mēn') ***n.*** ⟦< Gr *brōmos,* stench⟧ a chemical element, a reddish-brown, corrosive liquid
bron·chi (bräŋ'kī) ***pl.n., sing.*** **-chus** (-kəs) ⟦< Gr *bronchos,* windpipe⟧ the two main branches of the windpipe —**bron'chi·al** (-kē əl) ***adj.***
bron·chi'tis (-kīt'is) ***n.*** an inflammation of the bronchial tubes
bron·co (bräŋ'kō) ***n., pl.*** **-cos** ⟦Sp, rough⟧ a wild or only partly tamed horse or pony of the W U.S.: also **bron'cho** ***n., pl.*** **-chos**
bron'co·bust'er ***n.*** [Inf.] a tamer of broncos —**bron'co·bust'ing *n.***
Bron·të (brän'tē) **1 Char·lotte** (shär'lət) 1816-55; Eng. novelist **2 Em·i·ly** (em'ə lē) 1818-48; Eng. novelist: sister of Charlotte
bron·to·saur (brän'tō sôr', -tə-) ***n.*** ⟦< Gr *brontē,* thunder + *sauros,* lizard⟧ APATOSAURUS: also **bron'to·saur'us**
Bronx (bräŋks) borough of New York City: pop. 1,204,000: used with *the*
bronze (bränz) ***n.*** ⟦Fr, prob. ult. < Pers *birinğ,* copper⟧ **1** an alloy of copper and tin **2** a reddish-brown color —***adj.*** of or like bronze —***vt.*** **bronzed, bronz'ing** ⟦Fr *bronzer* < the *n.*⟧ to make bronze in color
brooch (brōch, brooch) ***n.*** ⟦see BROACH⟧ a large ornamental pin with a clasp
brood (brood) ***n.*** ⟦OE *brod*⟧ **1** a group of birds hatched at one time **2** the children in a family —***vi.*** **1** to sit on and hatch eggs **2** to worry: often with *on, over,* or *about*
brood'er ***n.*** **1** one that broods **2** a heated shelter for raising fowl
brood'mare' ***n.*** a mare kept for breeding
brook[1] (brook) ***n.*** ⟦< OE *broc*⟧ a small stream
brook[2] (brook) ***vt.*** ⟦OE *brucan,* to use⟧ to put up with; endure
Brook·lyn (brook'lən) borough of New York City: pop. 2,301,000
broom (broom, broom) ***n.*** ⟦OE *brom,* brushwood⟧ **1** a flowering shrub of the pea family **2** a bundle of fibers or straws fastened to a long handle (**broom'stick'**), used for sweeping
Bros or **bros** *abbrev.* brothers
broth (brôth) ***n.*** ⟦OE⟧ a thin soup made by boiling meat, etc. in water
broth·el (bräth'əl) ***n.*** ⟦< OE *broethan,* go to ruin⟧ a house of prostitution
broth·er (bruth'ər) ***n., pl.*** **-ers** or **breth'ren** ⟦OE *brothor*⟧ **1** a male related to one by having the same parents **2** a friend who is like a brother **3** a fellow member of the

THESAURUS

broad ***a.*** **1** [Physically wide] deep, extended, large, extensive, ample, spacious, expansive, immense, wide, roomy, outstretched, thick, widespread, full, stocky.—*Ant.* NARROW, thin, slender. **2** [Wide in range] cultivated, experienced, cosmopolitan; see CULTURED. **3** [Tolerant] progressive, open-minded, unbiased; see LIBERAL.

broadcast ***n.*** program, newscast, telecast; see PERFORMANCE.

broadcast ***v.*** announce, relay, telephone, send out, telegraph, radio, transmit, televise, telecast, air, put on the air, go on the air, be on the air; see also SEND 2.

broadcasting ***n.*** radio, announcing, television, airing, telecasting, newscasting, transmitting, reporting, cable television, cable, TV, direct TV, digital television.

broaden ***v.*** widen, expand, increase; see GROW 1, INCREASE.

broad-minded ***a.*** tolerant, progressive, unprejudiced; see LIBERAL.

brochure ***n.*** handout, circular, pamphlet; see ADVERTISEMENT.

broil ***v.*** sear, bake, roast; see COOK.

broiler ***n.*** oven, grill, barbecue; see APPLIANCE.

broke* ***a.*** bankrupt, out of money, indebted; see RUINED 3. —**go for broke*** gamble, wager, risk everything; see RISK. —**go broke*** become bankrupt, lose everything, be reduced to poverty; see FAIL 4, LOSE 2.

broken ***a.*** **1** [Fractured] shattered, hurt, ruptured, burst, splintered, smashed, in pieces, collapsed, destroyed, pulverized, crumbled, mutilated, bruised, injured, damaged, rent, split, cracked, mangled, dismembered, fragmentary, disintegrated, crippled, shredded, crushed, gashed, defective, busted*.—*Ant.* WHOLE, intact, sound. **2** [Not functioning properly] defective, inoperable, in need of repair, in disrepair, out of order, busted*, gone to pot*, screwed up*, shot*, gone haywire*, on the fritz*, on the blink*, gone to pieces, out of whack*, out of commission; see also FAULTY. **3** [Discontinuous] spasmodic, erratic, intermittent; see IRREGULAR 1, 4. **4** [Incoherent; *said of speech*] muttered, unintelligible, mumbled; see INCOHERENT.

broken-down ***a.*** shattered, dilapidated, battered; see OLD 2.

brokenhearted ***a.*** despondent, crushed, grieved; see SAD 1.

brood ***n.*** flock, offspring, young; see FAMILY, HERD.

brood ***v.*** **1** [To hatch] set, cover, incubate, warm, sit; see also PRODUCE 1. **2** [To nurse one's troubles] think, meditate, grieve, fret, sulk, mope, ponder, consider, muse, deliberate, dwell upon, speculate, daydream, reflect, dream, agonize, ruminate, chafe inwardly, give oneself over to reflections, mull over, eat one's heart out; see also WORRY 2.

brook[1] ***n.*** creek, stream, streamlet; see RIVER.

broom ***n.*** sweeper, carpet sweeper, whisk broom, mop, feather duster.

broth ***n.*** brew, concoction, soup, consommé, purée, bouillon, stock, chowder, gumbo, porridge, borscht, vichyssoise; see also FOOD, SOUP.

same race, church, profession, etc. 4 [*often* **B-**] a lay member of a men's religious order

broth'er·hood' *n.* 1 the state of being brothers 2 an association of men united in some interest, work, etc. 3 a feeling of unity among all people

broth'er-in-law' *n., pl.* **broth'ers-in-law'** 1 the brother of one's spouse 2 the husband of one's sister 3 the husband of the sister of one's spouse

broth'er·ly *adj.* 1 of or like a brother 2 friendly, kind, loyal, etc.

brought (brôt) *vt. pt. & pp. of* BRING

brou·ha·ha (bro͞o'hä hä') *n.* [Fr] an uproar or commotion

brow (brou) *n.* [OE *bru*] 1 the eyebrow 2 the forehead 3 the edge of a cliff

brow'beat' *vt.* **-beat', -beat'en, -beat'ing** to intimidate with harsh, stern looks and talk; bully

brown (broun) *adj.* [OE *brun*] 1 having the color of chocolate, a mixture of red, black, and yellow 2 tanned; dark-skinned —*n.* brown color —*vt., vi.* to make or become brown —**brown'ish** *adj.*

brown'-bag' *vt., vi.* **-bagged', -bag'ging** to carry (one's lunch) to work or school, as in a brown paper bag

brown·ie (broun'ē) *n.* 1 a small, helpful elf 2 a small square cut from a flat chocolate cake

Brown·ing (broun'iŋ), **Rob·ert** (räb'ərt) 1812-89; Eng. poet

brown'out' *n.* a dimming of lights in a city, as during an electric power shortage

brown rice rice that has not had its brown outer coating removed

brown'stone' *n.* a reddish-brown sandstone, used for building

brown study deep thought; reverie

brown sugar sugar whose crystals retain a brown coating of syrup

browse (brouz) *n.* [< OS *brustian,* to sprout] leaves, shoots, etc. which animals feed on —*vt., vi.* **browsed, brows'ing** 1 to nibble at (leaves, shoots, etc.) 2 to examine (a book, articles for sale, etc.) in a casual way

brows'er *n.* 1 one that browses 2 software for gaining access to the World Wide Web

bru·in (bro͞o'in) *n.* [Du, brown] a bear

bruise (bro͞oz) *vt.* **bruised, bruis'ing** [< OE *brysan,* crush] 1 to injure and discolor (body tissue) without breaking the skin 2 to injure the surface of, causing spoilage, denting, etc. 3 to hurt (the feelings, spirit, etc.) —*vi.* to be or become bruised —*n.* a bruised area, as of tissue

bruis'er *n.* [Inf.] a strong, pugnacious man

bruit (bro͞ot) *vt.* [< OFr, noise, rumor] to spread (*about*) by rumor

brunch (brunch) *n.* a combined breakfast and lunch —*vi.* to eat brunch

Bru·nei (bro͞o nī') country on the N coast of Borneo: 2,226 sq. mi.; pop. 261,000

bru·net (bro͞o net') *adj.* [< OFr, dim. of *brun,* brown] having black or dark-brown hair, often with dark eyes and complexion —*n.* a brunet person

bru·nette' (-net') *adj.* BRUNET —*n.* a brunette woman or girl

Bruns·wick (brunz'wik) city in NC Germany: pop. 258,000

brunt (brunt) *n.* [ME *bront*] 1 the shock (of an attack) or impact (of a blow) 2 the hardest part

brush[1] (brush) *n.* [< OFr *broce,* bush] 1 BRUSHWOOD 2 sparsely settled country 3 a device for cleaning, painting, etc., having bristles, wires, etc. fastened into a back 4 a brushing 5 a light, grazing stroke 6 a bushy tail, as of a fox —*vt.* 1 to clean, paint, etc. with a brush 2 to apply, remove, etc. as with a brush 3 to touch or graze in passing —*vi.* to graze past something —**brush up** to refresh one's memory

brush[2] (brush) *n.* [< ME *bruschen,* to rush] a short, quick fight

brush'off' *n.* [Slang] a curt dismissal, esp. in the phrase **give** (or **get**) **the brushoff**

brush'wood' *n.* 1 chopped-off tree branches 2 underbrush

brusque (brusk) *adj.* [Fr < ML *bruscus,* brushwood] rough and abrupt in manner or speech; curt: also **brusk** —**brusque'ly** *adv.* —**brusque'ness** *n.*

Brus·sels (brus'əlz) capital of Belgium: pop. 952,000

Brussels sprout 1 *often* **Brussels sprouts** a plant that bears small cabbagelike heads on an erect stem 2 one of its edible heads

bru·tal (bro͞ot''l) *adj.* 1 like a brute; very savage, cruel, etc. 2 very harsh —**bru'tal·ly** *adv.*

bru·tal·i·ty (bro͞o tal'ə tē) *n.* 1 a being brutal 2 *pl.* **-ties** a brutal act

bru·tal·ize (bro͞ot''l īz') *vt.* **-ized', -iz'ing** 1 to make brutal 2 to treat in a brutal way —**bru'tal·i·za'tion** *n.*

brute (bro͞ot) *adj.* [< L *brutus,* irrational] of or like an animal; specif., savage, stupid, etc. —*n.* 1 an animal 2 a brutal person —**brut'ish** *adj.* —**brut'ish·ly** *adv.*

bs *abbrev.* bill of sale

BS *abbrev.* Bachelor of Science: also **B.S.**

Btu *abbrev.* British thermal unit(s): also **BTU** or **btu**

bu *abbrev.* bushel(s)

bub·ble (bub'əl) *n.* [echoic] 1 a film of liquid forming a ball around air or gas 2 a tiny ball of air or gas in a liquid or solid 3 a transparent dome 4 a plausible scheme that proves worthless —*vi.* **-bled, -bling** 1 to rise in bubbles; boil 2 to make a gurgling sound —**on the bubble** with the outcome uncertain but already being determined —**bub'bly, -bli·er, -bli·est,** *adj.*

bubble gum a kind of chewing gum that can be blown into large bubbles

bub'ble·head' *n.* a person who is silly, ignorant, etc.

Bubble Wrap *trademark for* plastic packaging material with air bubbles —[**b- w-**] such packaging material

bu·bo (byo͞o'bō') *n., pl.* **-boes'** [< Gr *boubōn,* groin] an inflamed swelling of a lymph node, esp. in the armpit or groin

bu·bon'ic plague (-bän'ik) a contagious disease characterized by buboes, fever, and delirium

buc·ca·neer (buk'ə nir') *n.* [< Fr *boucanier*] a pirate

Bu·chan·an (byo͞o kan'ən), **James** (jāmz) 1791-1868; 15th president of the U.S. (1857-61)

Bu·cha·rest (bo͞o'kə rest') capital of Romania: pop. 1,990,000

buck[1] (buk) *n.* [OE *bucca,* male goat] 1 a male deer, goat, etc.: see DOE 2 the act of bucking 3 BUCKSKIN 4

THESAURUS

brotherhood *n.* fellowship, equality, kinship, intimacy, relationship, affiliation, association, society, fraternity, family, race, comradeship, camaraderie, friendship, amity.

brotherly *a.* kindly, humane, sympathetic; see FRIENDLY, KIND, LOVING.

browbeat *v.* bully, intimidate, frighten; see THREATEN.

brown *n.* *Shades and tints of brown include the following:* tan, bay, chestnut, nutbrown, russet, copper-colored, mahogany, bronze, russet, chocolate, cinnamon, hazel, reddish-brown, sorrel, sepia, tawny, ochre, rust-colored, rust, brownish, puce, fawn, liver-colored, beige, dust, drab, coffee, khaki, maroon, cocoa, umber, brick, ginger, light brown, dark brown, auburn, buff; see also COLOR.

brown *v.* toast, scorch, sauté; see COOK, FRY.

browse *v.* skim, peruse, scan, glance at, look through, run through, flip through, look over, survey, inspect loosely, examine cursorily, glance over, check over, run over, go through carelessly, dip into, leaf through, thumb through.

bruise *n.* abrasion, wound, swelling; see BLEMISH.

bruise *v.* beat, injure, wound; see DAMAGE, HURT.

brunet *a.* dark, tawny, dusky, brown, tanned, swarthy, dark-complexioned, dark-haired, dark-skinned, Latin, Mediterranean.—*Ant.* FAIR, light-skinned, light-complexioned.

brush[1] *n.* 1 [A brushing instrument] *Varieties include the following:* bristle, nail, clothes, rotary, paint, tooth, scrubbing, floor, toilet, hair, wire, scrub. 2 [A touch] rub, tap, stroke; see TOUCH 2. 3 [Underbrush] bush, thicket, undergrowth, secondary growth, chaparral, cover, brushwood, shrubbery, canebrake, hedge, fern, underwood, scrub, brake, sedge.

brush[1] *v.* 1 [To cleanse by brushing] sweep, whisk, wipe; see CLEAN. 2 [To touch lightly] stroke, smooth, graze; see TOUCH 1.

brush up on *v.* reread, look over again, review; see STUDY.

brutal *a.* pitiless, harsh, unmerciful; see CRUEL.

brutality *n.* savageness, ruthlessness, harshness; see CRUELTY.

brutally *a.* ruthlessly, cruelly, callously, relentlessly, mercilessly, heartlessly, grimly, viciously, meanly, inhumanly, inhumanely, brutishly, savagely, pitilessly, barbarously, remorselessly, unkindly, wildly, fiercely, hardheartedly, murderously, ferociously, animalistically, demoniacally, diabolically, barbarically, in cold blood.—*Ant.* NICELY, kindly, gently.

bubble *n.* sac, air bubble, balloon, foam, froth, spume, effervescence, lather.

bubble *v.* froth, gurgle, gush, well, trickle, effervesce, boil, percolate, simmer, seep, eddy, ferment, erupt, issue, fester.

[Inf.] a bold, vigorous young man —***vi.*** **1** to rear upward quickly, as to throw off a rider: said of a horse **2** [Inf.] to resist something as if plunging against it —***vt.*** **1** to dislodge or throw by bucking **2** [Inf.] to resist stubbornly —**buck for** [Slang] to work eagerly for (a promotion, etc.) —**buck up** [Inf.] to cheer up

buck[2] (buk) ***n.*** ⟦< ?⟧ [Slang] a dollar —**pass the buck** [Inf.] to try to shift blame or responsibility onto another person

buck'board' ***n.*** ⟦BUCK[1], *vi.* + BOARD⟧ an open carriage whose floorboards rest directly on the axles

buck·et (buk'it) ***n.*** ⟦< OE *buc,* pitcher⟧ **1** a cylindrical container with a curved handle, for carrying water, etc.; pail **2** the amount held by a bucket: also **buck'et·ful'**, *pl.* **-fuls'** **3** a thing like a bucket, as a scoop on a steam shovel —**kick the bucket** [Slang] to die

bucket seat a single contoured seat with a movable back, as in sports cars

buck·eye (buk'ī') ***n.*** ⟦BUCK[1] + EYE < the appearance of the seed⟧ **1** a horse chestnut with large capsules enclosing shiny brown seeds **2** the seed

buck·le[1] (buk'əl) ***n.*** ⟦< L *buccula,* cheek strap of a helmet⟧ a clasp for fastening a strap, belt, etc. —***vt., vi.*** **-led, -ling** to fasten with a buckle —**buckle down** to apply oneself energetically

buck·le[2] (buk'əl) ***vt., vi.*** **-led, -ling** ⟦prob. infl. by OFr *bocler,* to bulge: see prec.⟧ to bend or crumple —***n.*** a bend, bulge, etc.

buck·ler (buk'lər) ***n.*** ⟦< OFr *bocler*⟧ a small, round shield

buck'-pass'er ***n.*** [Inf.] one who regularly tries to shift blame or responsibility to someone else —**buck'-pass'ing** ***n.***

buck·ram (buk'rəm) ***n.*** ⟦? < *Bukhara,* city in central Asia⟧ a coarse, stiff cloth used in bookbinding, etc.

buck'saw' ***n.*** a wood-cutting saw set in a frame

buck'shot' ***n.*** a large lead shot for shooting deer and other large game

buck'skin' ***n.*** **1** a soft leather made from the skins of deer or sheep **2** [*pl.*] clothes made of buckskin

buck'tooth' ***n.***, *pl.* **-teeth'** a projecting front tooth —**buck'toothed'** ***adj.***

buck'wheat' ***n.*** ⟦< OE *boc-,* beech + WHEAT⟧ **1** a plant with beechnut-shaped seeds **2** a dark flour made from the seeds

bu·col·ic (byoo̅ käl'ik) ***adj.*** ⟦< Gr *boukolos,* herdsman⟧ **1** of shepherds; pastoral **2** of country life; rustic —**bu·col'i·cal·ly** ***adv.***

bud (bud) ***n.*** ⟦ME *budde*⟧ **1** a small swelling on a plant, from which a shoot, leaf, or flower develops **2** an early stage of development —***vi.*** **bud'ded, bud'ding** **1** to put forth buds **2** to begin to develop —**in (the) bud** **1** in a budding condition **2** in an early stage —**bud'like'** ***adj.***

Bu·da·pest (boo̅'də pest') capital of Hungary: pop. 2,104,000

Bud·dha (boo̅'də) religious leader who lived in India 563?-483? B.C.: founder of Buddhism

Bud·dhism (boo̅'diz'əm) ***n.*** a religion of Asia teaching that by right thinking and self-denial one achieves nirvana, a state of blessedness —**Bud'dhist** ***n., adj.***

bud·dy (bud'ē) ***n.***, *pl.* **-dies** ⟦< ?⟧ [Inf.] a close friend; comrade

budge (buj) ***vt., vi.*** **budged, budg'ing** ⟦< OFr *bouger,* to move⟧ to move even a little

budg·er·i·gar (buj'ər i gär') ***n.*** ⟦native name⟧ a greenish-yellow Australian parakeet: also [Inf.] **budg'ie**

budg·et (buj'it) ***n.*** ⟦< L *bulga,* bag⟧ **1** a plan adjusting expenses to income **2** estimated cost of living, operating, etc. **3** amount allotted for a specific use —***vt.*** **1** to put on a budget **2** to plan *[budget* your time*]* —**budg'et·ar'y** ***adj.***

Bue·nos Ai·res (bwā'nəs er'ēz) seaport & capital of Argentina: pop. 2,908,000

buff (buf) ***n.*** ⟦< Fr < It *bufalo,* buffalo⟧ **1** a soft, brownish-yellow leather **2** a dull brownish yellow **3** [Inf.] a devotee; fan —***adj.*** of the color buff —***vt.*** to polish or shine, as with soft leather —**in the buff** naked

buf·fa·lo (buf'ə lō') ***n.***, *pl.* **-loes', -lo',** or **-los'** ⟦It *bufalo* < Gr *bous,* ox⟧ **1** any of various wild oxen, as the water buffalo of India **2** popularly, the American bison —***vt.*** **-loed', -lo'ing** [Slang] to baffle, bluff, etc.

Buf·fa·lo (buf'ə lō') city in W New York, on Lake Erie: pop. 328,000

Buffalo wings ⟦after prec.⟧ [*also* **b- w-**] spicy fried segments of chicken wings

buff·er[1] (buf'ər) ***n.*** ⟦BUFF, *v.* + -ER⟧ **1** one who buffs **2** something used for buffing

buff·er[2] (buf'ər) ***n.*** ⟦< OFr *buffe,* a blow⟧ **1** anything that lessens shock, as of collision **2** a temporary storage area in a computer, for data being transferred to another device

buf·fet[1] (buf'it) ***n.*** ⟦OFr < *buffe,* a blow⟧ a blow or shock —***vt.*** **1** to punch; hit **2** to thrust about

buf·fet[2] (bə fā', boo-) ***n.*** ⟦Fr⟧ **1** a sideboard **2** a counter or table at which guests, etc. serve themselves food **3** a meal served on such a table, etc.

buf·foon (bə foo̅n') ***n.*** ⟦< Fr < It *buffare,* to jest⟧ one who is always clowning and trying to be funny; clown —**buf·foon'er·y** ***n.*** —**buf·foon'ish** ***adj.***

bug (bug) ***n.*** ⟦prob. < ME *bugge*: see fol.⟧ **1** an insect with sucking mouthparts **2** any small arthropod, as a cockroach **3** a defect, as in a machine **4** [Inf.] a germ or virus **5** [Inf.] a hidden microphone —***vt.*** **bugged, bug'ging** **1** [Inf.] to hide a microphone in (a room, etc.) **2** [Slang] to annoy, anger, etc.

bug'bear' ***n.*** ⟦ME *bugge,* a hobgoblin + BEAR[2]⟧ **1** an imaginary evil being **2** a cause of needless fear Also **bug'a·boo'** (-ə boo̅') ***n.***, *pl.* **-boos'**

bug'-eyed' ***adj.*** [Slang] with bulging eyes

bug·gy[1] (bug'ē) ***n.***, *pl.* **-gies** ⟦< ?⟧ **1** a light one-horse carriage with one seat **2** BABY CARRIAGE

bug·gy[2] (bug'ē) ***adj.*** **-gi·er, -gi·est** infested with bugs

bu·gle (byoo̅'gəl) ***n.*** ⟦< L *buculus,* young ox⟧ a brass instrument like a small trumpet, usually without valves —***vi., vt.*** **-gled, -gling** to signal by blowing a bugle —**bu'gler** ***n.***

build (bild) ***vt.*** **built, build'ing** ⟦< OE *bold,* house⟧ **1** to make by putting together materials, parts, etc.; construct **2** to establish; base *[build* a theory on facts*]* **3** to create or develop: often with *up* —***vi.*** **1** to put up buildings **2** to grow or intensify: often with *up* —***n.*** the way a thing is built or shaped *[*a stocky *build]* —**build up** to make more attractive, healthy, etc. —**build'er** ***n.***

build'ing ***n.*** **1** anything that is built; structure **2** the work or business of making houses, etc.

build'up' or **build'-up'** ***n.*** [Inf.] **1** praise or favorable publicity **2** a gradual increase or expansion

THESAURUS

bucket ***n.*** pail, canister, can; see CONTAINER, POT 1. —**kick the bucket*** expire, lose one's life, pass away; see DIE 1.

buckle[1] ***n.*** clasp, harness, fastening; see FASTENER.

buckle down ***v.*** apply oneself, attend to, keep one's mind on; see CONCENTRATE 2.

buck up* ***v.*** comfort, hearten, cheer; see ENCOURAGE.

bud ***n.*** shoot, embryo, germ; see FLOWER. —**nip in the bud** check, halt, stop; see PREVENT.

budding ***a.*** maturing, developing, opening, blossoming, bursting forth, putting forth shoots, burgeoning, flowering, fresh, pubescent, blooming, promising, young, sprouting, germinating, aspiring, latent, embryonic, in bud; see also GROWING.

buddy* ***n.*** peer, companion, pal*; see ASSOCIATE, FRIEND.

budge ***v.*** stir, change position, shift; see MOVE 1.

budget ***n.*** estimates, estimated expenses, allocations, accounts, financial statement, financial plan, cost of operation, funds; see also ESTIMATE.

budget ***v.*** allocate expenditures, balance income and expenses, forecast, allow for, figure in, plan, estimate necessary expenditures; see also ESTIMATE.

bug ***n.*** **1** [An insect] beetle, pest, gnat; see INSECT. **2** [*A microbe] pathogen, microorganism, virus; see GERM. **3** [*A defect] flaw, fault, imperfection; see BLEMISH, DEFECT. **4** [*An enthusiast] devotee, zealot, fanatic; see FOLLOWER.

bug* ***v.*** **1** [To annoy] irritate, plague, pester; see BOTHER 2, DISTURB. **2** [To install hidden microphones] spy, overhear, listen in on, wiretap, tap; see also EAVESDROP.

build ***v.*** create, form, erect, frame, raise, make, construct, manufacture, put together, fit together, fabricate, contrive, assemble, put up, model, hammer together, set up, reconstruct, mold, sculpture, fashion, compose, evolve, compile, cast, produce, forge, bring about, devise, carve, weave.—*Ant.* DESTROY, demolish, wreck. —**build up** **1** [To increase] strengthen, add to, expand; see INCREASE. **2** [To construct] make, erect, establish; see BUILD.

building ***n.*** edifice, construction, fabrication, house, framework, superstructure, structure, palace, mansion, apartment house, barn, castle, church, factory, home, hotel, motel, skyscraper, temple, office building, mosque, mall, store, school, stadium, arena; see also ARCHITECTURE.

built (bilt) ***vt.***, ***vi.*** *pt. & pp. of* BUILD
built'-in' ***adj.*** **1** made as part of the structure **2** inherent
built'-up' ***adj.*** **1** made higher, stronger, etc. with added parts **2** having many buildings on it
bulb (bulb) ***n.*** ⟦< Gr *bolbos*⟧ **1** an underground bud with roots and a short, scaly stem, as in a lily or onion **2** a tuber or tuberous root resembling a bulb, as in a crocus **3** anything shaped like a bulb *[an electric light bulb]* —**bul'bous** ***adj.***
Bul·gar·i·a (bəl ger'ē ə, bool-) country in SE Europe: 42,855 sq. mi.; pop. 8,473,000 —**Bul·gar'i·an** ***adj.***, ***n.***
bulge (bulj) ***n.*** ⟦< L *bulga*, leather bag⟧ an outward swelling; protuberance —***vi.***, ***vt.*** **bulged**, **bulg'ing** to swell or bend outward —**bulg'y**, **-i·er**, **-i·est**, ***adj.***
bu·lim·i·a (byoo lē'mē ə) ***n.*** ⟦< Gr *bous*, ox + *limos*, hunger⟧ **1** *Med.* a continuous, abnormal hunger **2** a disorder characterized by eating large quantities of food followed by self-induced vomiting, etc.: also **bulimia nervosa** —**bu·lim'ic** ***adj.***
bulk (bulk) ***n.*** ⟦< ON *bulki*, a heap⟧ **1** size, mass, or volume, esp. if great **2** the main mass; largest part —***vi.*** to have, or to increase in, size or importance —***adj.*** **1** total; aggregate **2** not put up in individual packages —**bulk'y**, **-i·er**, **-i·est**, ***adj.***
bulk·head (bulk'hed') ***n.*** ⟦< ON *balkr*, partition + HEAD⟧ **1** an upright partition, as in a ship, that is watertight, fireproof, etc. **2** a retaining wall **3** a boxlike structure over an opening
bull[1] (bool) ***n.*** ⟦< OE *bula*, a steer⟧ **1** the adult male of any bovine animal, as the ox, or of certain other large animals, as the elephant or whale **2** a speculator who buys stocks expecting their prices to rise, or who seeks to bring about such a rise **3** [Slang] insincere talk; nonsense —***adj.*** **1** male **2** rising in price
bull[2] (bool) ***n.*** ⟦< LL *bulla*, a seal⟧ an official document from the pope
bull'dog' ***n.*** a short-haired, heavily built dog with a strong stubborn grip —***adj.*** like a bulldog; stubborn —***vt.*** **-dogged'**, **-dog'ging** to throw (a steer) by holding its horns and twisting its neck
bull'doze' (-dōz') ***vt.*** **-dozed'**, **-doz'ing** ⟦< *bull*, a flogging + DOSE⟧ **1** [Inf.] to force or frighten by threatening; bully **2** to move, make level, etc. with a bulldozer
bull'doz'er ***n.*** a tractor with a large, shovel-like blade, for pushing earth, debris, etc.
bul·let (bool'it) ***n.*** ⟦< L *bulla*, a knob⟧ a small, shaped piece of lead, steel, etc., to be shot from a firearm
bul·le·tin (bool'ə tin) ***n.*** ⟦< LL *bulla*, a seal⟧ **1** a brief statement of the latest news **2** a regular publication, as of an organization
bulletin board a board or wall area on which bulletins, notices, etc. are put up
bul'let·proof' ***adj.*** that bullets cannot pierce —***vt.*** to make bulletproof
bull'fight' ***n.*** a spectacle in which a bull is first provoked in various ways and then killed with the thrust of a sword by a matador —**bull'fight'er** ***n.*** —**bull'fight'ing** ***n.***
bull'frog' ***n.*** a large North American frog with a deep, loud croak
bull'head'ed ***adj.*** blindly stubborn; headstrong —**bull'head'ed·ness** ***n.***
bull'horn' ***n.*** a portable electronic voice amplifier
bul·lion (bool'yən) ***n.*** ⟦< OFr *billon*, small coin⟧ ingots, bars, etc. of gold or silver
bull·ish (bool'ish) ***adj.*** **1** of or like a bull **2** rising, or causing a rise, in prices on the stock exchange **3** optimistic
bull'ock (-ək) ***n.*** ⟦< OE dim. of *bula*, steer⟧ a castrated bull; steer
bull'pen' ***n.*** **1** [Inf.] a temporary detention room in a jail **2** *Baseball a)* a practice area for relief pitchers *b)* the relief pitchers of one team
bull's'-eye' ***n.*** **1** the central mark of a target **2** a direct hit
bul·ly (bool'ē) ***n.***, *pl.* **-lies** ⟦< MHG *buole*, lover; later infl. by BULL[1]⟧ a person who hurts or browbeats those who are weaker —***vt.*** **-lied**, **-ly·ing** to behave as a bully toward —***adj.***, ***interj.*** [Inf.] fine; good
bul·rush (bool'rush') ***n.*** ⟦< ME *bol*, stem + *rusche*, a rush⟧ a tall plant of the sedge family, found in wet places
bul·wark (bool'wərk) ***n.*** ⟦MDu *bolwerc*⟧ **1** a defensive wall; rampart **2** a defense; protection **3** [*usually pl.*] a ship's side above the deck
bum (bum) ***n.*** ⟦prob. < Ger *bummeln*, go slowly⟧ [Inf.] **1** a vagrant **2** a loafer **3** a devotee, as of golf or skiing —***vi.*** **bummed**, **bum'ming** [Inf.] to live as a bum or by begging —***vt.*** [Slang] to get by begging *[to bum a cigarette]* —***adj.*** **bum'mer**, **bum'mest** [Slang] **1** poor in quality **2** false **3** lame —**bum someone out** [Slang] to annoy, depress, bore, etc. someone —**on the bum** [Inf.] **1** living as a vagrant **2** out of repair
bum·ble (bum'bəl) ***vi.*** **-bled**, **-bling** to blunder —***vt.*** to bungle or botch —**bum'bler** ***n.***
bum'ble·bee' ***n.*** ⟦< ME *bomben*, to buzz⟧ a large, hairy, yellow-and-black bee
bummed ***adj.*** ⟦< BUM⟧ [Slang] depressed, upset, annoyed, etc.: usually with *out*
bum·mer (bum'ər) ***n.*** [Slang] an unpleasant experience
bump (bump) ***vt.***, ***vi.*** ⟦echoic⟧ to collide (with) or hit (against) with a jolt —***n.*** **1** a knock; light jolt **2** a swelling, esp. one caused by a blow —**bump into** [Inf.] to meet unexpectedly —**bump off** [Slang] to murder —**bump'y**, **-i·er**, **-i·est**, ***adj.***
bump'er[1] ***n.*** a device to absorb the shock of a collision; esp., either of the bars at the front and rear of a motor vehicle
bump'er[2] ***adj.*** ⟦prob. < obs. *bombard*, liquor jug⟧ unusually abundant *[a bumper crop]*
bumper sticker a gummed paper with a printed slogan, witticism, etc., for sticking on a vehicle's bumper
bump·kin (bump'kin) ***n.*** ⟦prob. < MDu *bommekijn*, small cask⟧ an awkward or simple person from the country
bump'tious (-shəs) ***adj.*** ⟦prob. < BUMP⟧ disagreeably conceited or forward —**bump'tious·ly** ***adv.*** —**bump'tious·ness** ***n.***
bun (bun) ***n.*** ⟦prob. < OFr *buigne*, a swelling⟧ **1** a small roll made of bread dough, sometimes sweetened **2** hair worn in a roll or knot
bunch (bunch) ***n.*** ⟦< Fl *boudje*, little bundle⟧ **1** a cluster of similar things growing or grouped together **2** [Inf.] a group of people —***vt.***, ***vi.*** to collect into a bunch —**bunch'y**, **-i·er**, **-i·est**, ***adj.***
bun·combe (buŋ'kəm) ***n.*** ⟦after *Buncombe* county, NC⟧ [Inf.] BUNKUM
bun·dle (bun'dəl) ***n.*** ⟦MDu *bondel*⟧ **1** a number of things bound together **2** a package **3** a bunch; collection —***vt.***

THESAURUS

built ***a.*** constructed, fabricated, manufactured, made, put together, produced, assembled, contrived, remodeled, completed, established, perfected, finished, realized, created; see also FORMED.
bulb ***n.*** globe, globule, light bulb, ball, knob, corn, tuber, protuberance, head, bunch, swelling, tumor, nodule.
bulge ***n.*** swelling, bunch, lump, protuberance, hump, bump, bulb, outgrowth, protrusion, nodule, sagging, growth, prominence, excess, bagginess, appendage, projection, tumor, egg, sac, knob, horn, ridge, wart, promontory.
bulge ***v.*** puff out, distend, protrude; see SWELL.
bulk ***n.*** greater part, main part, predominant part, better part, most, majority, plurality, biggest share, greater number, nearly all, body, more than half, best, gross, lion's share.—*Ant.* BIT, remnant, fraction.
bulky ***a.*** massive, big, huge; see HIGH 1, LARGE 1, LONG 1.
bull[1] ***n.*** **1** [The male of various cattle] steer, ox, bullock; see COW. **2** [*Nonsense] balderdash, rubbish, trash; see NONSENSE 1.
bullet ***n.*** shell, cartridge, ball, projectile, missile, piece of ammunition, dumdum, slug, ammo*; see also SHOT 1.
bulletin ***n.*** release, notice, communiqué; see ANNOUNCEMENT.
bully ***n.*** ruffian, rowdy, tough; see RASCAL.
bully ***v.*** tease, domineer, harass; see THREATEN.
bum ***n.*** hobo, tramp, vagrant; see BEGGAR.
bump ***n.*** **1** [A jarring collision] knock, bang, bounce, jar, box, smash, pat, crack, jolt, crash, sideswipe, punch, hit, clap, push, shove, thrust, boost, shock, clash, impact, stroke, rap, tap, slap, clout, jab, jerk, crash, prod, slam, nudge, buffet, swat, bash*, wallop*, belt*, bat*, swipe*, thump, whack, poke*, clunk*, sock*, whop*, lick*, smack, cuff, slug*. **2** [A swelling] projection, protuberance, knob; see BULGE, LUMP.
bump ***v.*** **1** [To collide with] collide, run against, strike; see CRASH 4, HIT 1. **2** [To make a bumping sound] thud, whack, smack; see SOUND.
bumper[1] ***n.*** cover, guard, protector; see DEFENSE 2, FENDER.
bun ***n.*** muffin, biscuit, roll; see BREAD, ROLL 4, PASTRY.
bunch ***n.*** clump, group, batch, spray, sheaf, tuft, shock, stack, thicket, group, gathering, host, galaxy, bundle, knot, accumulation, collection, mess, bouquet, oodles*.
bundle ***n.*** packet, parcel, pack; see PACKAGE.

-dled, -dling 1 to make into a bundle **2** to hustle (*away, off, out,* or *into*) —**bundle up** to dress warmly

Bundt (bunt, boont) *trademark for* a deep cake pan with a tube in the center and grooved sides —***adj.*** [*often* **b-**] designating or baked in such a pan

bung (buŋ) ***n.*** ⟦< MDu *bonge*⟧ a stopper for a bunghole

bun·ga·low (buŋ′gə lō′) ***n.*** ⟦< Hindi *bānglā,* thatched house⟧ a small house or cottage, usually of one story and an attic

bun·gee cord (bun′jē) elasticized cord used as to secure luggage or to hold persons leaping for sport from great heights

bung·hole (buŋ′hōl′) ***n.*** a hole in a barrel or keg for pouring in or drawing out liquid

bun·gle (buŋ′gəl) ***vt., vi.*** **-gled, -gling** ⟦< ?⟧ to do or make (something) badly or clumsily —***n.*** **1** a bungling **2** a bungled piece of work —**bun′gler *n.*** —**bung′ling·ly *adv.***

bun·ion (bun′yən) ***n.*** ⟦< OFr: see BUN⟧ an inflamed swelling at the base of the big toe

bunk[1] (buŋk) ***n.*** ⟦prob. < Scand cognate of BENCH⟧ **1** a shelflike bed built against a wall, as in a ship **2** [Inf.] any sleeping place —***vi.*** to sleep in a bunk —***vt.*** to provide a sleeping place for

bunk[2] (buŋk) ***n.*** [Slang] *short for* BUNKUM

bunk′er *n.* ⟦Scot < ?⟧ **1** a large bin, as for a ship's fuel **2** an underground fortification **3** a sand trap or other area serving as a hazard on a golf course

bunk′house′ *n.* a barracks for ranch hands

bun·kum (buŋ′kəm) ***n.*** ⟦respelling of BUNCOMBE⟧ [Inf.] empty, insincere talk

bun·ny (bun′ē) ***n.,*** *pl.* **-nies** ⟦dim. of dial. *bun*⟧ a rabbit: a child's term

buns (bunz) ***pl.n.*** [Slang] the human buttocks

Bun·sen burner (bun′sən) ⟦after R. W. *Bunsen,* 19th-c. Ger chemist⟧ a small tubular gas burner that produces a hot, blue flame

bunt (bunt) ***vt., vi.*** ⟦< ? ME *bounten,* to return⟧ *Baseball* to bat (a pitch) lightly without swinging so that it rolls within the infield —***n.*** a bunted ball

bun·ting[1] (bun′tiŋ) ***n.*** ⟦< ? ME *bonten,* sift⟧ **1** a thin cloth for making flags, etc. **2** decorative flags

bun·ting[2] (bun′tiŋ) ***n.*** ⟦ME⟧ a small, brightly colored, short-billed bird

buoy (bo͞o′ē, boi) ***n.*** ⟦< L *boia,* fetter⟧ **1** a floating object anchored in water to warn of a hazard, etc. **2** a ring-shaped life preserver —***vt.*** ⟦< Sp *boyar,* to float⟧ **1** to mark with a buoy **2** to keep afloat **3** to lift up in spirits

buoy·ant (boi′ənt; *also* bo͞o′yənt) ***adj.*** ⟦< ? Sp *boyar,* to float⟧ **1** having the ability or tendency to float **2** cheerful —**buoy′an·cy *n.***

bur (bʉr) ***n.*** ⟦< Scand⟧ **1** a rough, prickly seed capsule of certain plants **2** a plant with burs **3** BURR[1] & BURR[2]

Bur *abbrev.* Bureau

bur·den[1] (bʉrd′′n) ***n.*** ⟦< OE *byrthen*⟧ **1** anything that is carried; load **2** heavy load, as of work, care, or duty **3** the carrying capacity of a ship —***vt.*** to put a burden on; oppress —**bur′den·some *adj.***

bur·den[2] (bʉrd′′n) ***n.*** ⟦< OFr *bourdon,* a humming⟧ **1** a chorus or refrain of a song **2** a repeated, central idea; theme

bur·dock (bʉr′däk′) ***n.*** ⟦BUR + DOCK[3]⟧ a plant with large leaves and purple-flowered heads with prickles

bu·reau (byoor′ō) ***n.,*** *pl.* **-reaus** or **-reaux** (-ōz) ⟦Fr, desk⟧ **1** a chest of drawers, as for clothing **2** an agency **3** a government department

bu·reauc·ra·cy (byoo rä′krə sē) ***n.,*** *pl.* **-cies 1** government by departmental officials following an inflexible routine **2** the officials collectively **3** inflexible governmental routine **4** the concentration of authority in administrative bureaus —**bu·reau·crat** (byoor′ə krat′) ***n.*** —**bu′reau·crat′ic *adj.*** —**bu′reau·crat′i·cal·ly *adv.***

bu·reauc′ra·tize′ (-tīz′) ***vt., vi.*** **-tized′, -tiz′ing** to develop into a bureaucracy —**bu·reauc′ra·ti·za′tion *n.***

burg (bʉrg) ***n.*** [Inf.] a quiet or dull town

bur·geon (bʉr′jən) ***vi.*** ⟦< OFr *burjon,* a bud⟧ **1** to put forth buds, etc. **2** to grow or develop rapidly

bur·ger (bʉr′gər) ***n.*** [Inf.] a hamburger, cheeseburger, etc.

-bur·ger (bʉr′gər) *combining form* sandwich of ground meat, etc. *[hamburger]*

burgh (bʉrg; *Scot* bu′rə) ***n.*** ⟦Scot var. of BOROUGH⟧ **1** [Brit.] a borough **2** in Scotland, a chartered town

burgh·er (bʉr′gər) ***n.*** a citizen of a town

bur·glar (bʉr′glər) ***n.*** ⟦< OFr *burgeor*⟧ one who commits burglary

bur′glar·ize′ *vt.* **-ized′, -iz′ing** to commit burglary in

bur′gla·ry (-glə rē) ***n.,*** *pl.* **-ries** the act of breaking into a building to commit a felony, as theft, or a misdemeanor

bur·gle (bʉr′gəl) ***vt., vi.*** **-gled, -gling** [Inf.] to burglarize or commit burglary

bur·go·mas·ter (bʉr′gō mas′tər, -gə-) ***n.*** ⟦< MDu *burg,* town + *meester,* master⟧ the mayor of a town in the Netherlands, Flanders, Austria, or Germany

Bur·gun·dy (bʉr′gən dē) ***n.,*** *pl.* **-dies** [*often* **b-**] a red or white wine, typically dry, orig. made in Burgundy, a region in E France —**Bur·gun·di·an** (bər gun′dē ən) ***adj., n.***

bur·i·al (ber′ē əl) ***n.*** the burying of a dead body in a grave, tomb, etc.

Bur·ki·na Fa·so (boor kē′nə fä′sō) country in W Africa: 105,839 sq. mi.; pop. 7,967,000

burl (bʉrl) ***n.*** ⟦< OFr *bourle,* ends of threads⟧ **1** a knot in thread or yarn that makes cloth look nubby **2** a knot on some tree trunks **3** veneer from wood with burls —**burled *adj.***

bur·lap (bʉr′lap′) ***n.*** ⟦< ? ME *borel*⟧ a coarse cloth of jute or hemp

bur·lesque (bər lesk′) ***n.*** ⟦Fr < It *burla,* a jest⟧ **1** any broadly comic or satirical imitation; parody **2** a sort of vaudeville with low comedy, striptease acts, etc. —***vt., vi.*** **-lesqued′, -lesqu′ing** to imitate comically

bur·ley (bʉr′lē) ***n.*** ⟦< ?⟧ [*also* **B-**] a thin-leaved, light-colored tobacco grown in Kentucky, etc.

bur·ly (bʉr′lē) ***adj.*** **-li·er, -li·est** ⟦ME *borlich,* excellent⟧ **1** big and strong **2** hearty in manner

Bur·ma (bʉr′mə) *former name for* MYANMAR —**Bur·mese** (bər mēz′), *pl.* **-mese′, *adj., n.***

burn (bʉrn) ***vt.*** **burned** or **burnt, burn′ing** ⟦< OE *beornan,* to be on fire⟧ **1** to set on fire, as in order to produce heat, light, or power **2** to destroy by fire **3** to injure or damage by fire, acid, etc. **4** to consume as fuel **5** to sunburn **6** to cause (a hole, etc.) as by fire **7** to cause a sensation of heat in **8** to transform (body fat, etc.) into energy **9**

THESAURUS

bungle *v.* blunder, fumble, mishandle; see BOTCH, FAIL 1.

bungler *n.* fumbler, lout, blunderer, flounderer, muddler, numskull, featherbrain, dolt, scatterbrain, dunce, clod, ignoramus, idiot, duffer, addlebrain, butterfingers, bonehead*, blockhead, goof-off*, clumsy oaf, bull in a china shop*, harebrain*, klutz*, knucklehead*, dork*, airhead*.

bungling *a.* clumsy, unskillful, inept; see AWKWARD, INCOMPETENT.

bunk[1,2] ***n.*** **1** [A bed] berth, cot, mattress; see BED 1. **2** [*Anything untrue, silly, or unreliable] rubbish, rot, hogwash; see NONSENSE 1.

buoy *n.* pontoon, channel marker, life preserver; see FLOAT.

burden[1] ***n.*** **1** [Something carried] cargo, freight, pack; see LOAD 1. **2** [Anything hard to support or endure] encumbrance, punishment, misery; see DIFFICULTY 2, MISFORTUNE.

burden[1] ***v.*** weigh down, force, hinder, encumber, overwhelm, hamper, strain, load with, lade, saddle with, handicap, obligate, tax, afflict, vex, try, trouble, pile, bog down, crush, depress, impede, overload, oppress, make heavy, press down.—*Ant.* LIGHTEN, relieve, unload.

burdensome *a.* heavy, oppressive, troublesome; see DIFFICULT 1, 2, DISTURBING.

bureau *n.* **1** [Committee] commission, authority, board; see COMMITTEE. **2** [Chest of drawers] highboy, dresser, cabinet; see CHEST 1, FURNITURE.

bureaucracy *n.* the Establishment, the authorities, the system; see GOVERNMENT 1, 2.

burglar *n.* thief, housebreaker, robber; see CRIMINAL.

burglary *n.* housebreaking, stealing, robbery; see CRIME, THEFT.

burial *n.* last rites, interment, entombment; see FUNERAL.

burn *n.* scorch, singe, scald; see BLISTER.

burn *v.* ignite, kindle, incinerate, burn up, burn down, blaze, flame, flare, burst into flame, rage, consume, enkindle, cremate, consume with flames, set a match to, set on fire, set ablaze, set afire, sear, singe, scorch, brand, fire, light, torch, char, roast, toast, heat, bake; see also COOK.—*Ant.* EXTINGUISH, put out, quench.

burned *a.* scorched, charred, seared, burnt, singed, branded, cauterized, marked, blistered, scalded. —**burned up*** angered, enraged, infuriated; see ANGRY.

burning *a.* fiery, blazing, glowing, ablaze, afire, on fire, smoking, in flames, aflame, inflamed, kindled, enkindled, ignited, scorching, turning to ashes, searing, in a blaze, blistering, red-hot, white-hot, roasting; see also PASSIONATE 2.—*Ant.* COLD, frozen, out.

[Slang] to cheat or trick *[I got burned in that deal]* —*vi.* **1** to be on fire **2** to give out light or heat **3** to be destroyed or injured by fire or heat **4** to feel hot **5** to be excited —*n.* **1** an injury or damage caused by fire, heat, etc. **2** the process or result of burning —**burn down** to burn to the ground —**burn out** to exhaust or become exhausted from overwork, etc. —**burn up** [Slang] to make or become angry —**burn'a·ble** *adj., n.*

burn'er *n.* the part of a stove, furnace, etc. from which the flame comes

bur·nish (bʉr'nish) *vt., vi.* ⟦< OFr *brunir*, make brown⟧ to make or become shiny by rubbing —*n.* a gloss or polish —**bur'nish·er** *n.*

bur·noose (bər no͞os') *n.* ⟦< Ar *burnus*⟧ a hooded cloak worn by Arabs

burn·out (bʉrn'out') *n.* **1** the point at which a rocket's fuel is burned up and the rocket enters free flight or is jettisoned **2** a state of emotional exhaustion from mental stress

Burns (bʉrnz), **Rob·ert** (rä'bərt) 1759-96; Scot. poet

burnt (bʉrnt) *vt., vi. alt. pt. & pp. of* BURN

burp (bʉrp) *n., vi.* ⟦echoic⟧ belch —*vt.* to cause (a baby) to belch

burr[1] (bʉr) *n.* ⟦var. of BUR⟧ **1** a bur **2** a rough edge left on metal, etc. by cutting or drilling —*vt.* to form a rough edge on

burr[2] (bʉr) *n.* ⟦prob. echoic⟧ **1** the trilling of *r*, as in Scottish speech **2** a whir

bur·ri·to (bə rē'tō) *n., pl.* **-tos** ⟦MexSp < Sp, little burro⟧ a Mexican dish consisting of a flour tortilla wrapped around a filling of meat, cheese, fried beans, etc.

bur·ro (bʉr'ō) *n., pl.* **-ros** ⟦Sp < LL *burricus,* small horse⟧ a donkey

bur·row (bʉr'ō) *n.* ⟦see BOROUGH⟧ **1** a hole dug in the ground by an animal **2** any similar hole —*vi.* **1** to make a burrow **2** to live or hide in a burrow **3** to search, as if by digging —*vt.* **1** to make burrows in **2** to make by burrowing

bur·sa (bʉr'sə) *n., pl.* **-sae** (-sē) or **-sas** ⟦< Gr *byrsa*, a hide⟧ *Anat.* a sac or cavity with a lubricating fluid, as between a tendon and bone

bur·sar (bʉr'sər) *n.* ⟦< ML *bursa*, a purse⟧ a treasurer, as of a college

bur·si·tis (bər sīt'is) *n.* ⟦< BURSA + -ITIS⟧ inflammation of a bursa

burst (bʉrst) *vi.* **burst, burst'ing** ⟦OE *berstan*⟧ **1** to come apart suddenly and violently; explode **2** to give sudden vent; break (*into* tears, etc.) **3** to appear, start, etc. suddenly **4** *a)* to be as full or crowded as possible *b)* to be filled (*with* pride, etc.) —*vt.* to cause to burst —*n.* **1** a bursting **2** a break or rupture **3** a sudden action or effort; spurt **4** a volley of shots

Bu·run·di (bo͞o ro͞on'dē, -run'-) country in EC Africa, east of Democratic Republic of the Congo: 10,759 sq. mi.; pop. 5,293,000

bur·y (ber'ē) *vt.* **-ied, -y·ing** ⟦OE *byrgan*⟧ **1** to put (a dead body) into the earth, a tomb, etc. **2** to hide or cover **3** to put away **4** to immerse *[to bury oneself in work]*

bus (bus) *n., pl.* **bus'es** or **bus'ses** ⟦< (OMNI)BUS⟧ a large motor coach for many passengers, usually following a regular route —*vt.* **bused** or **bussed, bus'ing** or **bus'sing** **1** to transport by bus **2** to clear dirty dishes from —*vi.* **1** to go by bus **2** to do the work of a busboy

bus'boy' *n.* a restaurant worker who clears tables, brings water, etc.

bus·by (buz'bē) *n., pl.* **-bies** ⟦prob. < name *Busby*⟧ a tall fur hat worn with a full-dress uniform

bush (bo͝osh) *n.* ⟦OE *busc*⟧ **1** a low woody plant with spreading branches; shrub **2** anything like a bush **3** uncleared land —*vi.* to grow thickly —**beat around the bush** to talk around a subject without getting to the point

Bush (bo͝osh) **1 George** (**Herbert Walker**) 1924- ; 41st president of the U.S. (1989-93) **2 George W**(**alker**) 1946- ; 43d president of the U.S. (2001-): son of George

bushed (bo͝osht) *adj.* [Inf.] very tired; exhausted

bush·el (bo͝osh'əl) *n.* ⟦< OFr *boisse*, grain measure⟧ a dry measure equal to 4 pecks or 32 quarts

bush·ing (bo͝osh'iŋ) *n.* ⟦< MDu *busse*, box⟧ a removable metal lining for reducing friction on moving parts

bush league [Slang] a small or second-rate minor league, etc. —**bush'-league'** *adj.* —**bush leaguer**

bush'man (-mən) *n., pl.* **-men** (-mən) one who lives in the Australian bush

bush'mas'ter *n.* a large poisonous snake of Central and South America

bush'whack' *vt., vi.* to ambush —**bush'whack'er** *n.*

bush'y *adj.* **-i·er, -i·est** thick and spreading out like a bush

bush'y-tailed' *adj.* used mainly in **bright-eyed and bushy-tailed**, alert, eager, etc.

bus·i·ly (biz'ə lē) *adv.* in a busy manner

busi·ness (biz'nis) *n.* ⟦OE *bisignes*: see BUSY⟧ **1** one's work; occupation **2** a special task, duty, etc. **3** rightful concern *[no one's business but his own]* **4** a matter or activity **5** commerce; trade **6** a commercial or industrial establishment —*adj.* of or for business —**mean business** [Inf.] to be in earnest

business administration college studies covering finance, management, etc. to prepare for a business career

business agent a representative of a labor union local

business card a small card identifying one's business connection, given to clients, etc.

business college a school of typing, bookkeeping, etc.

busi'ness·like' *adj.* efficient, methodical, systematic, etc.

busi'ness·man' *n., pl.* **-men'** (-men') a man in business, esp. as an owner —**busi'ness·wom'an**, *pl.* **-wom'en**, *fem.n.*

business school a school offering graduate courses in business administration

bus·ing or **bus·sing** (bus'iŋ) *n.* the transporting of chil-

THESAURUS

burnt *a.* scorched, singed, charred; see BURNED.

burst *n.* **1** [An explosion] blowout, blast, blowup; see EXPLOSION. **2** [A sudden spurt] rush, outburst, torrent; see FIT 2.

burst *v.* **1** [To explode] blow up, erupt, rupture; see BREAK 2, DISINTEGRATE, EXPLODE. **2** [To break] crack, split, fracture; see BREAK 1, DESTROY. —**burst into tears** weep, start crying, sob; see CRY 1.

bury *v.* **1** [To inter] lay in the grave, entomb, enshrine, deposit in the earth, to give burial to, embalm, hold funeral services for, hold last rites for, lay out. **2** [To cover] conceal, mask, stow away; see HIDE 1. **3** [To defeat] overcome, win over, conquer; see DEFEAT 2, 3.

bus *n.* coach, minibus, school bus, shuttle bus, sightseeing bus, common carrier, public conveyance, Greyhound (trademark).

bus *v.* transport, ship, convey; see CARRY.

bush *n.* shrub, bramble, thicket, hedge, shrubbery, briar bush, rose bush; see also PLANT. —**beat around the bush** speak evasively, avoid the subject, be deceptive; see EVADE.

bushy *a.* fuzzy, disordered, thick, shaggy, rough, full, tufted, fringed, woolly, nappy, fluffy, furry, crinkly, stiff, wiry, rumpled, prickly, feathery, leafy, bristly, heavy, hairy.—*Ant.* THIN, sleek, smooth.

busily *a.* diligently, actively, energetically, strenuously, eagerly, earnestly, seriously, intently, rapidly, dexterously, industriously, carefully, intently, studiously, hurriedly, briskly, purposefully, ardently, arduously, fervently, nimbly, zealously, vigorously, restlessly, enthusiastically, speedily, hastily, persistently, like hell*.—*Ant.* SLOWLY, listlessly, idly.

business *n.* **1** [Industry and trade] commerce, exchange, trade, traffic, barter, commercial enterprise, gainful occupation, buying and selling, negotiation, production and distribution, dealings, affairs, sales, contracts, transaction, bargaining, trading, banking, marketing, undertaking, speculation, market, mercantilism, wholesale and retail, capital and labor, free enterprise, game*, racket*, wheeling and dealing*. **2** [Occupation] trade, profession, vocation; see JOB 1. **3** [A person's proper concerns] affair, concern, interest; see AFFAIR 1. **4** [A commercial enterprise] firm, factory, mill, store, company, shop, corporation, concern, combine, conglomerate, cooperative, establishment, enterprise, partnership, institution, house, market, syndicate, cartel, trust, monopoly, holding company, consortium. —**do business with** deal with, trade with, patronize; see BUY, SELL, TREAT 1. —**get the business*** be mistreated, be abused, endure; see SUFFER 1. —**give the business*** mistreat, bother, victimize; see ABUSE. —**mean business*** be serious, stress, impress; see EMPHASIZE.

businesslike *a.* purposeful, systematic, methodical; see PRACTICAL.

businessman *n.* businesswoman, industrialist, capitalist, employer, tycoon, broker, retailer, stockbroker, manager, buyer, operator, backer, financier, systems expert, comptroller, accountant, investor, speculator, entrepreneur, purchasing agent, storekeeper, tradesman; see also EXECUTIVE.

dren by bus to a school outside of their neighborhood, esp. so as to desegregate the school

bus·kin (bus′kin) ***n.*** ⟦? < MDu *brosekin,* small boot⟧ **1** a high, laced boot worn in ancient tragedy **2** tragic drama

buss (bus) ***n., vt., vi.*** ⟦prob. of echoic orig.⟧ [Now Chiefly Dial.] kiss

bust[1] (bust) ***n.*** ⟦< It *busto*⟧ **1** a sculpture of a person's head and shoulders **2** a woman's bosom

bust[2] (bust) [Inf.] ***vt., vi.*** ⟦< BURST⟧ **1** to burst or break **2** to make or become bankrupt or demoted **3** to hit **4** to arrest —***n.*** **1** a failure **2** financial collapse **3** a punch **4** a spree **5** an arrest —**bust′ed** ***adj.***

bus·tle[1] (bus′əl) ***vi., vt.*** **-tled, -tling** ⟦< ME *busken,* prepare⟧ to hurry busily —***n.*** busy and noisy activity

bus·tle[2] (bus′əl) ***n.*** ⟦< ?⟧ a padding formerly worn to fill out the upper back of a woman's skirt

bus·y (biz′ē) ***adj.*** **-i·er, -i·est** ⟦OE *bisig*⟧ **1** active; at work **2** full of activity **3** in use, as a telephone **4** too detailed —***vt.*** **bus′ied, bus′y·ing** to make or keep busy —**bus′y·ness** ***n.***

bus′y·bod′y ***n., pl.*** **-ies** a meddler in the affairs of others

but (but) ***prep.*** ⟦OE *butan,* without⟧ except; save *[*nobody went *but* me*]* —***conj.*** **1** yet; still *[*it's good, *but* not great*]* **2** on the contrary *[*I am old, *but* you are young*]* **3** unless *[*it never rains *but* it pours*]* **4** that *[*I don't doubt *but* you're right*]* **5** that . . . not *[*I never gamble *but* I lose*]* —***adv.*** **1** only *[*if I had *but* known*]* **2** merely *[*he is *but* a child*]* —***pron.*** who . . . not; which . . . not *[*not a man *but* felt it*]* —**but for** if it were not for

bu·tane (byoo′tān′) ***n.*** ⟦ult. < L *butyrum,* butter⟧ a hydrocarbon used as a fuel, etc.

butch (booch) ***adj.*** ⟦< ? fol.⟧ [Slang] masculine: sometimes said of a lesbian —***n.*** [Inf.] BUZZ CUT

butch·er (booch′ər) ***n.*** ⟦< OFr *bouc,* he-goat⟧ **1** one whose work is killing and dressing animals for meat **2** one who cuts meat for sale **3** a brutal killer —***vt.*** **1** to kill or dress (animals) for meat **2** to kill brutally or senselessly **3** to botch —**butch′er·y,** *pl.* **-ies,** ***n.***

but·ler (but′lər) ***n.*** ⟦< OFr *bouteille,* bottle⟧ a manservant, usually the head servant of a household

butt[1] (but) ***n.*** ⟦< ?⟧ **1** the thick end of anything **2** a stub or stump, as of a cigar **3** a target **4** an object of ridicule **5** [Slang] a cigarette —***vt., vi.*** to join end to end

butt[2] (but) ***vt., vi.*** ⟦< OFr *buter,* thrust against⟧ **1** to ram with the head **2** to project —***n.*** a butting —**butt in** (or **into**) [Inf.] to mix into (another's business, etc.)

butt[3] (but) ***n.*** ⟦< LL *buttis,* cask⟧ a large cask for wine or beer

butte (byoot) ***n.*** ⟦Fr, mound⟧ a steep hill with a flat top, surrounded by a plain

but·ter (but′ər) ***n.*** ⟦< Gr *bous,* cow + *tyros,* cheese⟧ **1** the solid, yellowish, edible fat that results from churning cream **2** any substance somewhat like butter —***vt.*** **1** to spread with butter **2** [Inf.] to flatter: often with *up* —**but′ter·y** ***adj.***

butter bean a light-colored bean, as a lima bean or wax bean

but′ter·cup′ ***n.*** a plant with yellow, cup-shaped flowers

but′ter·fat′ ***n.*** the fatty part of milk, from which butter is made

but′ter·fin′gers ***n.*** [Inf.] one who often fumbles and drops things

but′ter·fly′ ***n., pl.*** **-flies′** ⟦OE *buttorfleoge*⟧ an insect with a slender body and four broad, usually brightly colored wings

but′ter·milk′ ***n.*** **1** the liquid left after churning butter from milk **2** a drink made from skim milk

but′ter·nut′ ***n.*** **1** a walnut tree of E North America **2** its edible, oily nut

but′ter·scotch′ ***n.*** **1** a hard, sticky candy made with brown sugar, butter, etc. **2** the flavor of this candy **3** a syrup with this flavor

but·tock (but′ək) ***n.*** ⟦< OE *buttuc,* end⟧ **1** either of the fleshy, rounded parts behind the hips **2** [*pl.*] the rump

but·ton (but′'n) ***n.*** ⟦< OFr *boton*⟧ **1** any small disk or knob used as a fastening, ornament, etc., as on a garment **2** anything small and shaped like a button —***vt., vi.*** to fasten with a button or buttons

but′ton-down′ ***adj.*** **1** designating a collar, as on a shirt, fastened down by small buttons **2** conservative, unimaginative, etc.

but′ton·hole′ ***n.*** a slit or loop through which a button is inserted —***vt.*** **-holed′, -hol′ing** **1** to make buttonholes in **2** to detain and talk to

but·tress (bu′tris) ***n.*** ⟦see BUTT[2]⟧ **1** a structure built against a wall to support or reinforce it **2** a support or prop —***vt.*** to prop up; bolster

bux·om (buk′səm) ***adj.*** ⟦ME, humble⟧ having a shapely, full-bosomed figure: said of a woman

buy (bī) ***vt.*** **bought, buy′ing** ⟦OE *bycgan*⟧ **1** to get by paying money; purchase **2** to get by an exchange *[buy* victory with human lives*]* **3** to bribe **4** [Slang] to accept as true *[*I can't *buy* this excuse*]* —***n.*** **1** anything bought **2** [Inf.] something worth its price —**buy in** [Slang] to pay money so as to participate —**buy into** [Slang] BUY (*vt.* 4) —**buy off** to bribe —**buy out** to buy all the stock, rights, etc. of —**buy up** to buy all that is available of

buy′back′ ***n.*** *Finance* the buying by a corporation of its own stock to reduce the outstanding shares

buy′er ***n.*** **1** one who buys; consumer **2** one whose work is to buy merchandise for a retail store

buy′out′ ***n.*** the outright purchase of a business, as by the employees or management

buzz (buz) ***vi.*** ⟦echoic⟧ **1** to hum like a bee **2** to gossip **3** to be filled with noisy activity or talk —***vt.*** **1** to fly an airplane low over (a building, etc.) **2** to signal with a buzzer —***n.*** **1** a sound like a bee's hum **2** [Inf.] BUZZ CUT

buz·zard (buz′ərd) ***n.*** ⟦< L *buteo,* kind of hawk⟧ **1** a kind of hawk that is slow and heavy in flight **2** TURKEY VULTURE

buzz cut [Inf.] a man's very short haircut

buzz′er ***n.*** an electrical device that makes a buzzing sound as a signal

buzz saw a saw with teeth around the edge of a large disk fixed on a motor-driven shaft

bx *abbrev.* box

THESAURUS

busy ***a.*** **1** [Engaged] occupied, diligent, industrious, employed, working, in conference, in a meeting, in the field, in the laboratory, on an assignment, on duty, on the job, at work, busy with, on the run, on the road, hard-working, busy as a bee*, hustling*, up to one's ears*, hard at it*.—*Ant.* IDLE, unemployed, unoccupied. **2** [In use] employed, occupied, taken; see RENTED.

busybody ***n.*** meddler, tattletale, troublemaker; see GOSSIP 2.

but ***conj., prep.*** **1** [Indicating contrast] however, on the other hand, in contrast, nevertheless, still, yet, though, on the contrary, but then, but as you see; see also ALTHOUGH. **2** [Indicating an exception] save, disregarding, without, not including, not taking into account, let alone, aside from, with the exception of, not to mention, passing over, barring, setting aside, forgetting; see also EXCEPT. **3** [Indicating a limitation] only, merely, simply, barely, solely, purely, just, no more, exactly, no other than, without; see also ONLY 1.

butcher ***v.*** **1** [To slaughter for human consumption] carve, pack, dress, clean, cure, smoke, salt, cut, trim. **2** [To kill inhumanly] slaughter, slay, massacre; see KILL 1. **3** [To ruin] mess up, spoil, wreck; see BOTCH, DESTROY.

butt[1] ***n.*** base, tail end, bottom, hilt, extremity, tail, tip, fundament, stump, rump, bottom, seat, posterior; see also BOTTOM.

butt[2] ***v.*** hit, ram, push headfirst, bump, batter, knock, collide with, run into, smack, strike, gore, buck, toss, crash into.

butter ***n.*** *Varieties of butter include the following:* creamery, sweet, dairy, cube, tub, vegetable, salted, unsalted.

button ***n.*** knob, catch, disk; see FASTENER. —**on the button*** correctly, precisely, accurately; see RIGHT 1.

button ***v.*** close, clasp, snap; see FASTEN.

buy* ***n.*** value, good deal, steal*; see BARGAIN 2.

buy ***v.*** purchase, get, bargain for, procure, gain, contract for, sign for, get in exchange, go marketing, buy and sell, order, invest in, make an investment, shop for, acquire ownership of, procure title to, pay for, redeem, pay a price for, buy into, score*. —**buy off** corrupt, influence, fix*; see BRIBE.

buyer ***n.*** purchasing agent, purchaser, customer, client, prospect, consumer, representative, patron, user, shopper.—*Ant.* SELLER, vendor, dealer.

buying ***n.*** purchasing, getting, obtaining, acquiring, paying, investing, exchange, bartering, bargaining, procuring, trafficking.—*Ant.* SELLING, vending, auctioning.

buzz ***n.*** murmur, buzzing, hum; see NOISE 1.

buzz ***v.*** drone, hum, whir; see SOUND.

buzzer ***n.*** siren, signal, bell; see ALARM, WARNING, WHISTLE 1.

by (bī) ***prep.*** ⟦OE *be, bi*⟧ **1** near; at *[sit by the fire]* **2** *a)* in or during *[to travel by day]* *b)* not later than *[be back by noon]* **3** *a)* through; via *[to Boston by Route 6]* *b)* past; beyond *[he walked right by me]* **4** toward *[east by northeast]* **5** within a distance of *[missed by a foot]* **6** in behalf of *[she did well by me]* **7** through the agency of *[gained by fraud]* **8** according to *[to go by the book]* **9** at the rate of *[getting dark by degrees]* **10** following in series *[marching two by two]* **11** *a)* in or to the amount of *[apples by the peck]* *b)* and in another dimension *[two by four]* *c)* using (the given number) as multiplier or divisor —***adv.*** **1** close at hand *[stand by]* **2** away; aside *[to put money by]* **3** past *[she sped by]* **4** at the place specified *[stop by on your way]* —**by and by** soon or eventually —**by and large** considering everything —**by the by** incidentally

by- *prefix* **1** near **2** secondary *[byproduct]*

by-and-by (bī'ən bī') ***n.*** a future time

bye (bī) ***n.*** ⟦var. of BY⟧ the privilege, granted a contestant in a tournament with an uneven number of participants, of not being paired with another contestant in the first round

bye-bye (bī'bī') ***n., interj.*** [Inf.] goodbye

by·gone (bī'gôn') ***adj.*** past; former —***n.*** anything gone or past

by'law' ***n.*** ⟦< ME *bi*, village + *laue*, law⟧ any of a set of rules adopted by an organization or assembly for its own meetings or affairs

by'line' ***n.*** a line identifying the writer of a newspaper or magazine article

by'pass' ***n.*** **1** a way, pipe, channel, etc. between two points that avoids or is auxiliary to the main way **2** a surgical operation to allow fluid to pass around a diseased or blocked part or organ —***vt.*** **1** to detour **2** to furnish with a bypass **3** to ignore

by'path' or **by'-path'** ***n.*** a byway

by'play' ***n.*** action, gestures, etc. going on aside from the main action or conversation

by'prod'uct or **by'-prod'uct** ***n.*** anything produced in the course of making another thing

By·ron (bī'rən), **George Gor·don** (jôrj gôrd''n) 1788-1824; Eng. poet

by'stand'er ***n.*** a person who stands near but does not participate

byte (bīt) ***n.*** ⟦arbitrary formation⟧ a string of binary digits (*bits*), usually eight, operated on as a basic unit by a digital computer

by'way' ***n.*** a secondary road or path, esp. one not much used

by'word' ***n.*** **1** a proverb **2** one well-known for some quality **3** an object of scorn or ridicule **4** a favorite word or phrase

THESAURUS

by ***prep.*** **1** [Near] close to, next to, nigh; see NEAR 1, NEXT 2. **2** [By stated means] over, with, through, by means of, in the name of, at the hand of, along with, through the medium of, with the assistance of, with the aid of, on, supported by.

bylaw ***n.*** ordinance, local law, regulation; see LAW 3.

bypass ***n.*** detour, temporary route, side road; see ROAD 1.

bypass ***v.*** miss, evade, detour around; see AVOID.

bystander ***n.*** onlooker, watcher, spectator; see OBSERVER.

C

c or **C** (sē) ***n.***, *pl.* **c's, C's** the third letter of the English alphabet

C¹ (sē) ***n.*** **1** a Roman numeral for 100 **2** *Educ.* a grade for average work **3** *Music* the first tone in the scale of C major

C² *abbrev.* **1** carat(s) **2** *Baseball* catcher **3** Catholic **4** Celsius (or centigrade) **5** cent(s) **6** *Sports* center **7** centimeter(s) **8** Central **9** century **10** chapter **11** circa: also **ca 12** College **13** copyright **14** cup(s) **15** cycle(s) Also, except 3, 4, 8, & 12, **c**

C³ *Chem. symbol for* carbon

Ca *Chem. symbol for* calcium

CA California

cab (kab) ***n.*** ⟦< Fr *cabriole*, a leap⟧ **1** a carriage, esp. one for public hire **2** TAXICAB **3** the place in a truck, crane, etc. where the operator sits —***vi.*** **cabbed, cab'bing** [Inf.] to take or drive a taxicab

ca·bal (kə bäl′) ***n.*** ⟦Fr, intrigue⟧ **1** a small group joined in a secret intrigue **2** an intrigue; plot

cab·a·la (kab′ə lə, kə bä′lə) ***n.*** ⟦< Heb *kabala*, tradition⟧ **1** a Jewish mystical movement **2** any esoteric or secret doctrine

ca·bal·le·ro (kab′ə ler′ō, -əl yer′ō) ***n.***, *pl.* **-ros** ⟦Sp⟧ **1** a Spanish gentleman **2** [Southwest] *a)* a horseman *b)* a lady's escort

ca·ban·a (kə ban′ə, -bä′nə) ***n.*** ⟦Sp < LL *capanna*⟧ **1** a cabin or hut **2** a small bathhouse

cab·a·ret (kab′ə rā′) ***n.*** ⟦Fr, tavern⟧ a cafe with musical entertainment

cab·bage (kab′ij) ***n.*** ⟦OFr *caboche* < ?⟧ a vegetable with thick leaves formed into a round head

cab·by or **cab·bie** (kab′ē) ***n.***, *pl.* **-bies** [Inf.] one who drives a cab

ca·ber·net (kab′ər nā′) ***n.*** [*also* **C-**] a dry red wine; esp., CABERNET SAUVIGNON

cabernet sau·vi·gnon (sō vē nyōn′) [*also* **C- S-**] a fragrant, dry red wine

cab·in (kab′in) ***n.*** ⟦< LL *capanna*, hut⟧ **1** a small, crudely or simply built house; hut **2** a room on a ship or boat **3** the space for passengers, crew, or cargo in an aircraft

cab·i·net (kab′ə nit) ***n.*** ⟦Fr, prob. ult. < L *cavea*, cage⟧ **1** a case with drawers or shelves **2** a case holding a TV, radio, etc. **3** [*often* **C-**] a body of official advisors to a chief executive

cab′i·net·mak′er ***n.*** a maker of fine furniture

cab′i·net·work′ ***n.*** articles made by a cabinetmaker: also **cab′i·net·ry**

cabin fever a condition of increased anxiety caused by being confined or isolated

ca·ble (kā′bəl) ***n.*** ⟦< L *capere*, to take hold⟧ **1** a thick, heavy rope, often of wire strands **2** a bundle of insulated wires to carry an electric current **3** a cablegram **4** CABLE TV —***vt.*** **-bled, -bling 1** to fasten with a cable **2** to send a cablegram to —***vi.*** to send a cablegram

cable car a car drawn by a moving cable, as up a steep incline

ca′ble·cast′ ***vt.*** **-cast′, -cast′ing** to transmit to receivers by coaxial cable —***n.*** a program that is cablecast

ca′ble·gram′ ***n.*** a message sent by undersea cable

cable TV a TV system in which various antennas receive local and distant signals and transmit them by cable to subscribers' receivers

cab·o·chon (kab′ə shän′) ***n.*** ⟦Fr < *caboche*, head⟧ any precious stone cut in convex shape

ca·bood·le (kə bo͞od′'l) ***n.*** ⟦< BOODLE⟧ [Inf.] lot; group *[the whole caboodle]*

ca·boose (kə bo͞os′) ***n.*** ⟦MDu *kambuis*, cabin house⟧ the car at the rear of a freight train, used by the crew when eating, sleeping, etc.

ca·ca·o (kə kā′ō, -kä′-) ***n.***, *pl.* **-os** ⟦Sp < AmInd (Mexico)⟧ **1** the seed of a tropical American tree from which cocoa and chocolate are made: also **cacao bean 2** this tree

cache (kash) ***n.*** ⟦Fr < L *cogere*, to collect⟧ **1** a safe place in which stores of food, supplies, etc. are hidden **2** anything so hidden —***vt.*** **cached, cach′ing** to place in a cache

cache·pot (kash′pät, -pō′) ***n.*** ⟦Fr < *cacher*, to hide⟧ a decorative jar for holding potted plants: also **cache pot**

ca·chet (ka shā′) ***n.*** ⟦Fr⟧ **1** a stamp or official seal, as on a document **2** any sign of official approval, authenticity, superior quality, etc. **3** distinction; prestige

cack·le (kak′əl) ***vi.*** **-led, -ling** ⟦echoic⟧ **1** to make the shrill, broken vocal sounds of a hen **2** to laugh or chatter with similar sounds —***n.*** a cackling

ca·coph·o·ny (kə käf′ə nē) ***n.***, *pl.* **-nies** ⟦< Gr *kakos*, bad + *phōnē*, voice⟧ harsh, jarring sound; discord —**ca·coph′o·nous** ***adj.***

cac·tus (kak′təs) ***n.***, *pl.* **-tus·es** or **-ti′** (-tī′) ⟦< Gr *kaktos*, kind of thistle⟧ any of various desert plants with fleshy stems and spinelike leaves

cad (kad) ***n.*** ⟦< CADET⟧ a man whose behavior is not gentlemanly —**cad′dish** ***adj.*** —**cad′dish·ly** ***adv.*** —**cad′dish·ness** ***n.***

ca·dav·er (kə dav′ər) ***n.*** ⟦L, prob. < *cadere*, to fall⟧ a corpse, as for dissection

ca·dav′er·ous ***adj.*** ⟦< L⟧ of or like a cadaver; esp., pale, ghastly, etc.

CAD/CAM (kad′kam′) ***n.*** ⟦*C(omputer-)A(ided) D(esign)/C(omputer-)A(ided) M(anufacturing)*⟧ design and manufacturing by means of a computer system, as for complex wiring diagrams

cad·die (kad′ē) ***n.*** ⟦Scot form of Fr *cadet*: see CADET⟧ one who attends a golfer, carrying the clubs, etc. —***vi.*** **-died, -dy·ing** to act as a caddie

cad·dy¹ (kad′ē) ***n.***, *pl.* **-dies** ⟦< Malay *kātī*, unit of weight⟧ a small container for holding or storing

cad·dy² (kad′ē) ***n.***, ***vi.*** CADDIE

-cade (kād) ⟦< (CAVAL)CADE⟧ *suffix* procession, parade *[motorcade]*

ca·dence (kād′'ns) ***n.*** ⟦< L *cadere*, to fall⟧ **1** fall of the voice in speaking **2** any rhythmic flow of sound **3** measured movement, as in marching

ca·den·za (kə den′zə) ***n.*** ⟦It: see prec.⟧ an elaborate passage for the solo instrument in a concerto

ca·det (kə det′) ***n.*** ⟦Fr < L dim. of *caput*, head⟧ **1** a student in training at an armed forces academy **2** any trainee, as a practice teacher

cadge (kaj) ***vt.***, ***vi.*** **cadged, cadg′ing** ⟦< ?⟧ to beg or get by begging; sponge —**cadg′er** ***n.***

cad·mi·um (kad′mē əm) ***n.*** ⟦< L *cadmia*, zinc ore (with which it occurs)⟧ a silver-white, metallic chemical element used in alloys, pigments, etc.

ca·dre (ka′drē, -drā; kä′-) ***n.*** ⟦< Fr < L *quadrum*, a square⟧ a nucleus around which an expanded organization, as a military unit, can be built

ca·du·ce·us (kə do͞o′sē əs) ***n.***, *pl.* **-ce·i′** (-sē ī′) ⟦L⟧ the winged staff of Mercury: now a symbol of the medical profession

Cae·sar¹ (sē′zər) ***n.*** ⟦after fol.⟧ **1** the title of the Roman emperors from 27 B.C. to A.D. 138 **2** [*often* **c-**] any emperor or dictator

Cae·sar² (sē′zər), **Jul·ius** (jo͞ol′yəs) 100?-44 B.C.; Rom. general & dictator (49-44)

Cae·sar·e·an section (sə zer′ē ən) CESAREAN (SECTION)

cae·su·ra (si zyo͞or′ə, -zho͞or′ə) ***n.***, *pl.* **-ras** or **-rae** (-ē) ⟦L < *caedere*, to cut down⟧ a break or pause in a line of verse, usually in the middle

ca·fe or **ca·fé** (kə fā′, ka-) ***n.*** ⟦Fr, coffeehouse⟧ a small restaurant or a barroom, nightclub, etc.

caf·e·te·ri·a (kaf′ə tir′ē ə) ***n.*** ⟦AmSp, coffee store⟧ a self-service restaurant

caf·feine or **caf·fein** (ka fēn′, kaf′ēn′) ***n.*** ⟦Ger *kaffein*⟧ the alkaloid present in coffee, tea, cola nuts, etc.: it is a stimulant

caf·tan (kaf′tən, -tan′) ***n.*** ⟦Turk *qaftān*⟧ **1** a long-sleeved robe, worn in eastern Mediterranean countries **2** a long, loose dress with wide sleeves

THESAURUS

cab ***n.*** taxi, taxicab, hack*; see AUTOMOBILE, VEHICLE.

cabin ***n.*** log house, cottage, hut; see HOME 1, SHELTER.

cabinet ***n.*** council, advisory council, authority, bureaucracy, committee, bureau, governing body, administrators, assembly, assistants, department heads, advisors, United States Cabinet, ministry, shadow cabinet, backstairs cabinet, brain trust; see also GOVERNMENT 2.

cable ***n.*** cord, preformed cable, wire twist; see CHAIN, WIRE 1.

cackle ***v.*** chuckle, snicker, giggle; see LAUGH.

cactus ***n.*** *Cactuses include the following:* giant, saguaro, barrel, cholla, hedgehog, cochineal, nipple, night-blooming cereus, century plant, prickly pear, mescal; see also PLANT.

cad ***n.*** rogue, scoundrel, rake; see RASCAL.

cadence ***n.*** rhythm, meter, flow; see BEAT 2, MEASURE 3.

cafe ***n.*** cafeteria, lunchroom, coffee shop; see RESTAURANT.

cage (kāj) *n.* ⟦< L *cavea*, hollow place⟧ **1** a structure of wires, bars, etc., for confining animals **2** any openwork structure or frame —*vt.* **caged, cag′ing** to put or confine, as in a cage

cag·er (kāj′ər) *n.* [Slang] a basketball player

ca·gey or **ca·gy** (kā′jē) *adj.* **-gi·er, -gi·est** ⟦< ?⟧ [Inf.] **1** sly; tricky; cunning **2** cautious —**ca′gi·ly** *adv.* —**ca′gi·ness** *n.*

ca·hoots (kə ho͞ots′) *pl.n.* ⟦< ?⟧ [Slang] used chiefly in **in cahoots (with)**, in league (with): usually applied to questionable dealing, etc.

Cain (kān) *n. Bible* oldest son of Adam and Eve: he killed his brother Abel —**raise Cain** [Slang] to create a great commotion, cause trouble, etc.

cairn (kern) *n.* ⟦Scot⟧ a conical heap of stones built as a monument

Cai·ro (kī′rō) capital of Egypt: pop. 5,084,000

cais·son (kā′sən) *n.* ⟦Fr < L *capsa*, box⟧ **1** a two-wheeled wagon with a chest for ammunition **2** a watertight box for underwater construction work

cai·tiff (kāt′if) *n.* ⟦< L *captivus*, CAPTIVE⟧ a mean or cowardly person —*adj.* mean or cowardly

ca·jole (kə jōl′) *vt., vi.* **-joled′, -jol′ing** ⟦< Fr⟧ to coax with flattery and insincere talk —**ca·jol′er** *n.* —**ca·jol′er·y** *n.*

Ca·jun or **Ca·jan** (kā′jən) *n.* **1** a native of Louisiana of Canadian French ancestry **2** the dialect of Cajuns —*adj.* of spicy cooking

cake (kāk) *n.* ⟦< ON⟧ **1** a small, flat mass of baked or fried dough, batter, hashed food, etc. **2** a mixture of flour, eggs, sugar, etc. baked as in a loaf and often covered with icing **3** a shaped, solid mass, as of soap —*vt., vi.* **caked, cak′ing** to form into a hard mass or crust —**take the cake** [Inf.] to be the prime example of something: usually used ironically —**cak′y** or **cak′ey, -i·er, -i·est,** *adj.*

cal *abbrev.* **1** caliber **2** calorie(s)

cal·a·bash (kal′ə bash′) *n.* ⟦< Sp *calabaza*⟧ **1** the gourdlike fruit of a tropical American tree **2** *a)* the bottle-shaped, gourdlike fruit of a tropical vine *b)* a large smoking pipe made from it **3** a gourd

cal·a·boose (kal′ə bo͞os′) *n.* ⟦Sp *calabozo*⟧ [Dial. or Old Slang] a prison; jail

ca·la·ma·ri (kä′lə mä′rē) *n.* squid cooked as food, esp. as an Italian dish

cal·a·mine (kal′ə mīn′) *n.* ⟦Fr < L *cadmia*, zinc ore⟧ a zinc oxide powder used in skin lotions

ca·lam·i·ty (kə lam′ə tē) *n., pl.* **-ties** ⟦< L *calamitas*⟧ a great misfortune; disaster —**ca·lam′i·tous** *adj.*

cal·car·e·ous (kal ker′ē əs) *adj.* ⟦< L *calx*, lime⟧ of or like limestone, calcium, or lime

cal·ci·fy (kal′sə fī′) *vt., vi.* **-fied′, -fy′ing** ⟦< L *calx*, lime + -FY⟧ to change into a hard, stony substance by the deposit of lime or calcium salts —**cal′ci·fi·ca′tion** *n.*

cal′ci·mine′ (-mīn′) *n.* ⟦< L *calx*, lime⟧ a white liquid, used as a wash for plastered surfaces —*vt.* **-mined′, -min′ing** to coat with calcimine

cal·cine (kal′sīn′) *vt., vi.* **-cined′, -cin′ing** ⟦< L *calx*, lime⟧ to change to an ashy powder by heat

cal·cite (kal′sīt′) *n.* CALCIUM CARBONATE

cal·ci·um (kal′sē əm) *n.* ⟦< L *calx*, lime⟧ a soft, silver-white, metallic chemical element found combined in limestone, chalk, etc.

calcium carbonate a white powder or crystalline compound found in limestone, chalk, marble, bones, shells, etc.

cal·cu·late (kal′kyə lāt′) *vt.* **-lat′ed, -lat′ing** ⟦< L *calculare*, reckon⟧ **1** to determine by using mathematics; compute **2** to determine by reasoning; estimate **3** to plan or intend for a purpose —*vi.* **1** to compute **2** to rely (*on*) —**cal′cu·la·ble** (-lə bəl) *adj.*

cal′cu·lat′ed *adj.* deliberately planned or carefully considered —**cal′cu·lat′ed·ly** *adv.*

cal′cu·lat′ing *adj.* shrewd or scheming

cal′cu·la′tion *n.* **1** a calculating **2** something deduced by calculating **3** careful planning or forethought —**cal′cu·la′tive** *adj.*

cal′cu·la′tor *n.* **1** one who calculates **2** a device for the automatic performance of mathematical operations

cal′cu·lus (-ləs) *n., pl.* **-li′** (-lī′) or **-lus·es** ⟦L, pebble used in counting⟧ **1** an abnormal stony mass in the body **2** *Math.* a system of calculation or analysis using special symbolic notation

Cal·cut·ta (kal kut′ə) seaport in NE India: pop. 9,194,000

cal·de·ra (kal der′ə) *n.* ⟦Sp < L *caldarium*, room for hot baths⟧ a broad, craterlike basin of a volcano

cal·dron (kôl′drən) *n.* ⟦< L *calidus*, warm, hot⟧ **1** a large kettle or boiler **2** a state of violent agitation

cal·en·dar (kal′ən dər) *n.* ⟦< L *kalendarium*, account book⟧ **1** a system of determining the length and divisions of a year **2** a table that shows the days, weeks, and months of a given year **3** a schedule, as of programs

cal·en·der (kal′ən dər) *n.* ⟦< Gr *kylindros*, cylinder⟧ a machine with rollers for giving paper, cloth, etc. a smooth or glossy finish

calf[1] (kaf) *n., pl.* **calves** ⟦< OE *cealf*⟧ **1** a young cow or bull **2** the young of some other large animals, as the elephant or seal **3** CALFSKIN

calf[2] (kaf) *n., pl.* **calves** ⟦ON *kalfi*⟧ the fleshy back part of the leg below the knee

calf′skin′ *n.* soft leather made from the skin of a calf

Cal·ga·ry (kal′gə rē) city in S Alberta, Canada: pop. 768,000

cal·i·ber (kal′ə bər) *n.* ⟦Fr & Sp, ult. < Gr *kalopodion*, shoemaker's last⟧ **1** the diameter of a cylindrical body, esp. of a bullet or shell **2** the diameter of the bore of a gun **3** quality or ability Also, esp. Brit., **cal′i·bre**

cal·i·brate (kal′ə brāt′) *vt.* **-brat′ed, -brat′ing** **1** to determine the caliber of **2** to fix or correct the graduations of (a measuring instrument) —**cal′i·bra′tion** *n.* —**cal′i·bra′tor** *n.*

cal·i·co (kal′i kō′) *n., pl.* **-coes′** or **-cos′** ⟦after *Calicut*, city in India⟧ a printed cotton fabric —*adj.* spotted like calico *[a calico cat]*

Cal·i·for·nia (kal′ə fôr′nyə) state of the SW U.S., on the Pacific: 155,973 sq. mi.; pop. 29,760,000; cap. Sacramento: abbrev. *CA* —**Cal′i·for′nian** *adj., n.*

cal·i·per (kal′ə pər) *n.* ⟦var. of CALIBER⟧ **1** [*usually pl.*] an instrument consisting of a pair of hinged legs, for measuring thickness or diameter **2** a part of a braking system on a bicycle or motor vehicle

ca·liph (kā′lif; *also*, kal′if) *n.* ⟦Ar *khalīfa*⟧ supreme ruler: the title taken by Mohammed's successors as heads of Islam —**ca′liph·ate** (-ət, -āt′) *n.*

cal·is·then·ics (kal′is then′iks) *pl.n.* ⟦< Gr *kallos*, beauty + *sthenos*, strength⟧ athletic exercises —**cal′is·then′ic** *adj.*

calk (kôk) *vt.* CAULK —**calk′er** *n.*

call (kôl) *vt.* ⟦< ON *kalla*⟧ **1** to say in a loud tone; shout **2** to summon **3** to give or apply a name to **4** to describe as

THESAURUS

cage *n.* coop, jail, crate; see ENCLOSURE 1, PEN 1.

cake *n.* **1** [A flattish, compact mass] cube, bar, loaf; see BLOCK 1. **2** [Sweet baked goods] *Kinds of cake include the following:* wedding, birthday, angel food, devil's-food, corn, caramel, German chocolate, upside-down, Martha Washington, maple, orange, white, yellow, chocolate, carrot, Bundt (trademark), lemon, walnut, almond, layer, spice, marble, Lady Baltimore cake; spongecake, fruitcake, poundcake, torte, cheesecake, cupcake, Boston cream pie, coffeecake, jellyroll, gingerbread, shortbread; see also BREAD, PASTRY. —**take the cake*** excel, outdo, win the prize; see EXCEED.

cake *v.* crust, solidify, pack; see FREEZE 1, HARDEN, THICKEN.

calamity *n.* cataclysm, distress, trial; see CATASTROPHE, DISASTER, MISFORTUNE, TRAGEDY 1.

calculate *v.* count, measure, reckon, enumerate, determine, rate, forecast, weigh, gauge, number, figure, figure up, account, compute, sum up, divide, multiply, subtract, add, work out, cipher, tally, dope out*; see also ESTIMATE.

calculation *n.* **1** [The act of calculating] adding, totaling, count; see ESTIMATE. **2** [A forecast] prediction, divination, prognostication; see FORECAST.

calendar *n.* list, program, record, timetable, schedule, annals, journal, diary, daybook, chronology, log, logbook, table, register, almanac, agenda, itinerary, docket; see also ALMANAC.

calf[1] *n.* young cow, young bull, yearling; see COW.

calisthenics *n.* exercises, workout, aerobics; see EXERCISE 1, GYMNASTICS.

call *n.* **1** [A shout] yell, whoop, hail; see ALARM, CRY 1. **2** [Characteristic sound] twitter, tweet, shriek; see CRY 2. **3** [A brief visit] visiting, a few words, stop; see VISIT. **4** [Word of command] summons, battle cry, reveille; see ALARM, COMMAND, CRY 1. **5** [An invitation] bidding, solicitation, proposal; see INVITATION, REQUEST. —**on call** usable, ready, prepared; see AVAILABLE. —**within call** close by, approximate, not far away; see NEAR 1.

call *v.* **1** [To raise the voice] shout, call out, exclaim; see YELL. **2** [To bring a body of people together] collect, convene, muster; see ASSEMBLE 2. **3** [To address or label as] denomi-

specified **5** to awaken **6** to telephone **7** to give orders for (a strike, etc.) **8** to stop (a game, etc.) **9** to demand payment of (a loan, etc.) **10** to expose (someone's bluff) by challenging it **11** *Poker* to equal (the preceding bet) or to equal the bet of (the last previous bettor) —***vi.*** **1** to shout **2** to visit for a short while: often with *on* **3** to telephone —***n.*** **1** a calling **2** a loud utterance **3** the distinctive cry of an animal or bird **4** a summons; invitation **5** an act of telephoning **6** CALLING (sense 3) **7** an economic demand, as for a product **8** need *[no call for tears]* **9** a demand for payment **10** a brief visit **11** an option to buy a stock, commodity, etc. at a specified price and time **12** a referee's decision —**call down** [Inf.] to scold —**call for** **1** to demand **2** to come and get —**call off** to cancel (a scheduled event) —**call up** **1** to recall **2** to summon for duty **3** to telephone —**on call** available when summoned —**call'er** ***n.***

cal·la (kal'ə) ***n.*** ⟦< L, a plant (of uncert. kind)⟧ a plant with a large, white leaf around a yellow flower spike: also **calla lily**

call forwarding a telephone service that allows incoming calls to be transferred automatically to another number

call girl a prostitute who is called by telephone to assignations

cal·lig·ra·phy (kə lig'rə fē) ***n.*** ⟦< Gr *kallos*, beauty + *graphein*, write⟧ artistic handwriting —**cal·lig'ra·pher** ***n.*** —**cal·li·graph·ic** (kal'ə graf'ik) ***adj.***

call'-in' ***adj.*** of a radio or TV program whose audience members telephone to comment, ask questions, etc.

call'ing ***n.*** **1** the act of one that calls **2** one's work or profession **3** an inner urging toward some vocation

calling card **1** a small card with one's name and address on it **2** a credit card for long-distance telephone calls

cal·li·o·pe (kə lī'ə pē', kal'ē ōp') ***n.*** ⟦< Gr *kallos*, beauty + *ops*, voice⟧ a keyboard instrument like an organ, having a series of steam whistles

call letters the letters, and sometimes numbers, that identify a radio or TV station

cal·lous (kal'əs) ***adj.*** ⟦< L *callum*, hard skin⟧ **1** hardened: usually **cal'loused** **2** unfeeling —**cal·los·i·ty** (kə läs'ə tē) ***n.*** —**cal'lous·ly** ***adv.*** —**cal'lous·ness** ***n.***

cal·low (kal'ō) ***adj.*** ⟦OE *calu*, bare⟧ immature; inexperienced —**cal'low·ness** ***n.***

cal·lus (kal'əs) ***n.***, *pl.* **-lus·es** ⟦L, var. of *callum*, hard skin⟧ a hardened, thickened place on the skin

call waiting a telephone service that signals an incoming call to a person already talking and allows that person to take that call by putting the first call on hold

calm (käm) ***n.*** ⟦< Gr *kauma*, heat⟧ **1** lack of motion; stillness **2** lack of excitement; tranquillity —***adj.*** **1** still; quiet **2** not excited; tranquil —***vt.***, ***vi.*** to make or become calm: often with *down* —**calm'ly** ***adv.*** —**calm'ness** ***n.***

ca·lor·ic (kə lôr'ik) ***adj.*** of calories —**ca·lor'i·cal·ly** ***adv.***

cal·o·rie (kal'ə rē) ***n.*** ⟦Fr < L *calor*, heat⟧ a unit for measuring heat, esp. for measuring the energy produced by food when oxidized in the body

cal·o·rif·ic (kal'ə rif'ik) ***adj.*** ⟦< L *calor*, heat + *facere*, make⟧ producing heat

cal·u·met (kal'yə met') ***n.*** ⟦CdnFr < L *calamus*, reed⟧ a long-stemmed ceremonial pipe, smoked by North American Indians as a token of peace

ca·lum·ni·ate (kə lum'nē āt') ***vt.***, ***vi.*** **-at'ed**, **-at'ing** ⟦see fol.⟧ to slander

cal·um·ny (kal'əm nē) ***n.***, *pl.* **-nies** ⟦< L *calumnia*, slander⟧ a false and malicious statement; slander

Cal·va·ry (kal'və rē) ***n.*** *Bible* the place where Jesus was crucified

calve (kav) ***vi.***, ***vt.*** **calved**, **calv'ing** to give birth to (a calf)

calves (kavz) ***n.*** *pl. of* CALF[1] & CALF[2]

Cal·vin (kal'vin), **John** 1509-64; Fr. Protestant reformer

Cal'vin·ism' ***n.*** the Christian doctrines of John Calvin and his followers, esp. predestination —**Cal'vin·ist** ***n.***, ***adj.*** —**Cal'vin·is'tic** ***adj.***

ca·lyp·so (kə lip'sō) ***n.*** ⟦< ?⟧ a kind of lively, topical folk song that originated in Trinidad

ca·lyx (kā'liks'; *also* kal'iks') ***n.***, *pl.* **-lyx'es** or **-ly·ces'** ⟦L, pod⟧ the outer whorl of protective leaves, or sepals, of a flower

cam (kam) ***n.*** ⟦Du *cam*, orig., a comb⟧ a wheel, projection on a wheel, etc. that gives irregular motion, as to a wheel or shaft, or receives such motion from it

ca·ma·ra·de·rie (kam'ə räd'ə rē, käm'-) ***n.*** ⟦Fr⟧ loyalty and warm, friendly feeling among comrades

cam·ber (kam'bər) ***n.*** ⟦OFr < L *camur*, arched⟧ a slight convex curve of a surface, as of a road —***vt.***, ***vi.*** to arch slightly

cam·bi·um (kam'bē əm) ***n.*** ⟦< LL *cambiare*, to change⟧ a layer of cells between the wood and bark in woody plants, which will eventually become more wood and bark —**cam'bi·al** ***adj.***

Cam·bo·di·a (kam bō'dē ə) country in S Indochina: 69,898 sq. mi.; pop. 5,756,000; cap. Phnom Penh —**Cam·bo'di·an** ***adj.***, ***n.***

cam·bric (kām'brik) ***n.*** ⟦after *Cambrai*, Fr city⟧ a fine linen or cotton cloth

Cam·bridge (kām'brij') **1** city in EC England: county district pop. 92,000 **2** city in E Massachusetts: pop. 96,000

cam·cord·er (kam'kôrd'ər) ***n.*** a small, portable videotape recorder and TV camera

came (kām) ***vi.*** *pt. of* COME

cam·el (kam'əl) ***n.*** ⟦ult. < Heb *gāmāl*⟧ a large, domesticated mammal with a humped back and long neck: because it can store water in its body, it is used in Asian and African deserts

ca·mel·lia (kə mēl'yə, -mē'lē ə) ***n.*** ⟦after G. J. *Kamel* (1661-1706), missionary to the Far East⟧ **1** an Asiatic evergreen tree or shrub with glossy leaves and roselike flowers **2** the flower

Cam·em·bert (cheese) (kam'əm ber', -bərt) ⟦after *Camembert*, Fr village⟧ a soft, rich, creamy cheese

cam·e·o (kam'ē ō') ***n.***, *pl.* **-os'** ⟦< It < ML *camaeus*⟧ **1** a gem carved with a figure raised in relief **2** a choice minor role, esp. one played by a notable actor

cam·er·a (kam'ər ə, kam'rə) ***n.*** ⟦L, vault⟧ **1** a device for taking photographs: a closed box containing a sensitized

THESAURUS

nate, designate, term; see NAME 1. **4** [To invite] summon, request, ask; see INVITE. —**call down*** rebuke, chide, admonish; see SCOLD. —**call for** **1** [To ask] ask for, request, make inquiry about; see ASK. **2** [To need] require, want, demand; see NEED. **3** [To come to get] come for, collect, fetch; see GET 1, PICK UP 6. —**call in** [To collect] collect, remove, receive; see WITHDRAW. —**call off** cancel, postpone, cease; see HALT, STOP 2. —**call on** (or **upon**) stop in, have an appointment with, go to see; see VISIT. —**call up** **1** [To remember] recollect, recall, summon up; see REMEMBER 1. **2** [To summon] send for, bid, order; see INVITE, SUMMON. **3** [To telephone] phone, call, ring; see TELEPHONE.

called ***a.*** christened, termed, labeled; see NAMED 1.

calling ***n.*** occupation, vocation, work; see JOB 1, PROFESSION 1, TRADE 2.

callous ***a.*** unfeeling, hardened, insensitive; see INDIFFERENT.

calm ***a.*** **1** [*Said especially of persons*] dignified, reserved, cool, composed, collected, unmoved, levelheaded, coolheaded, impassive, detached, aloof, unconcerned, disinterested, unhurried, neutral, gentle, sedate, serene, unanxious, unexcited, contented, meek, satisfied, pleased, amiable, temperate, placid, civil, kind, moderate, confident, poised, tranquil, self-possessed, restful, relaxed, dispassionate, mild, still, patient, self-controlled, untroubled, cool as a cucumber, unflappable*; see also RESERVED 3, PATIENT 1.—*Ant.* VIOLENT, excited, furious. **2** [*Said often of things*] quiet, undisturbed, unruffled, comfortable, moderate, in order, soothing, at peace, placid, smooth, still, restful, harmonious, peaceful, pacific, balmy, waveless, windless, serene, motionless, slow; see also QUIET.—*Ant.* ROUGH, agitated, aroused. —**keep calm** take one's time, keep cool, be patient; see CALM DOWN, RELAX.

calm ***n.*** **1** [Peace] stillness, peacefulness, quiet; see PEACE 2, REST 1, SILENCE 1. **2** [Composure] serenity, tranquillity, peace of mind; see COMPOSURE, PATIENCE 1, RESTRAINT 1.

calm ***v.*** tranquilize, soothe, pacify; see QUIET 1. —**calm down** compose oneself, control oneself, calm oneself, keep oneself under control, keep cool, take it easy*, get organized, rest, get hold of oneself, cool it*, cool off, cool down, simmer down, keep one's shirt on*; see also RELAX.

calmly ***a.*** quietly, unexcitedly, tranquilly, unconcernedly, serenely, confidently, sedately, collectedly, composedly, placidly, smoothly, restfully, motionlessly, peacefully, naturally, comfortably, unhurried, without anxiety, without fuss, dully; see also EASILY, EVENLY.—*Ant.* EXCITEDLY, agitatedly, disturbedly.

calmness ***n.*** quietness, tranquillity, calm; see COMPOSURE, PATIENCE 1, PEACE 2.

calumny ***n.*** slander, defamation, detraction; see LIE.

camera ***n.*** *Kinds of cameras include the following:* cinecamera, X-ray machine, microcamera, photomicroscope, photostat, spectrograph, motion-picture, television, TV, mini-

plate or film on which an image is formed when light enters through a lens **2** *TV* the device that receives the image and transforms it into a flow of electrical impulses for transmission —**in camera** in privacy or secrecy

cam′er·a·man′ (-man′) ***n.***, *pl.* **-men′** (-men′) an operator of a film or TV camera

Cam·e·roon (kam′ə ro͞on′) country in WC Africa, on the Atlantic: 183,569 sq. mi.; pop. 10,494,000 —**Cam′e·roon′i·an** ***adj.***, ***n.***

cam·i·sole (kam′i sōl′) ***n.*** ⟦Fr < LL *camisia*, shirt⟧ a woman's sleeveless undergarment for the upper body

cam·o·mile (kam′ə mīl′, -mēl′) ***n.*** ⟦< Gr *chamaimēlon*, earth apple⟧ a plant whose dried, daisylike flower heads are used in a medicinal tea

cam·ou·flage (kam′ə fläzh′, -fläj′) ***n.*** ⟦Fr < *camoufler*, to disguise⟧ **1** a disguising, as of ships or guns, to conceal them from the enemy **2** a disguise; deception —***vt.***, ***vi.*** **-flaged′**, **-flag′ing** to disguise (a thing or person) for concealment —**cam′ou·flag′er** ***n.***

camp (kamp) ***n.*** ⟦< L *campus*, field⟧ **1** *a)* a place where temporary tents, huts, etc. are put up, as for soldiers *b)* a group of such tents, etc. **2** the supporters of a particular cause **3** a recreational place in the country for vacationers, esp. children **4** the people living in a camp **5** [Slang] banality, artifice, etc. so extreme as to amuse or have a perversely sophisticated appeal —***vi.*** **1** to set up a camp **2** to live or stay in a camp: often with *out* —**break camp** to dismantle a camp and depart

cam·paign (kam pān′) ***n.*** ⟦Fr < L *campus*, field⟧ **1** a series of military operations with a particular objective **2** a series of planned actions, as to elect a candidate —***vi.*** to participate in a campaign —**cam·paign′er** ***n.***

cam·pa·ni·le (kam′pə nē′lē) ***n.***, *pl.* **-les** or **-li** (-lē) ⟦It < LL *campana*, a bell⟧ a bell tower

camp·er (kam′pər) ***n.*** **1** a vacationer at a camp **2** a motor vehicle or trailer equipped for camping out

camp′fire′ ***n.*** **1** an outdoor fire at a camp **2** a social gathering around such a fire

cam·phor (kam′fər) ***n.*** ⟦< Sans *karpuraḥ*, camphor tree⟧ a crystalline substance with a strong odor, derived from the wood of an E Asian evergreen tree (**camphor tree**): used to repel moths, in medicine as a stimulant, etc. —**cam′phor·at′ed** ***adj.***

camp meeting a religious meeting held outdoors or in a tent, etc.

camp′site′ ***n.*** **1** any site for a camp **2** an area in a park set aside for camping

cam·pus (kam′pəs) ***n.***, *pl.* **-pus·es** ⟦L, a field⟧ the grounds, and sometimes buildings, of a school or college —***adj.*** of a school or college *[campus* politics*]*

camp′y ***adj.*** **-i·er**, **-i·est** [Slang] characterized by CAMP (*n.* 5)

cam′shaft′ ***n.*** a shaft having a cam, or to which a cam is fastened

can[1] (kan; *unstressed* kən) ***vi.***, ***v.aux.*** *pt.* **could** ⟦< OE *cunnan*, to know⟧ **1** know(s) how (to) **2** am, are, or is able (to) **3** am, are, or is likely (to) *[can* that be true?*]* **4** have or has the right (to) **5** [Inf.] am, are, or is permitted (to); may —**can but** can only

can[2] (kan) ***n.*** ⟦OE *canne*, a cup⟧ **1** a container, usually metal, with a separate cover *[*a garbage *can]* **2** a tinned metal container in which foods, etc. are sealed for preservation **3** the amount a can holds —***vt.*** **canned**, **can′ning** **1** to put up in cans or jars for preservation **2** [Slang] to dismiss

Ca·naan (kā′nən) ancient region at the SE end of the Mediterranean: the Biblical Promised Land

Can·a·da (kan′ə də) country in N North America: 3,849,671 sq. mi.; pop. 28,847,000; cap. Ottawa —**Ca·na·di·an** (kə nā′dē ən) ***adj.***, ***n.***

Canadian bacon cured, smoked pork taken from the loin

Canadian English English as spoken and written in Canada

Ca·na′di·an·ism′ ***n.*** **1** a custom or belief originating in Canada **2** a word or phrase originating in Canadian English

ca·nal (kə nal′) ***n.*** ⟦< L *canalis*, channel⟧ **1** an artificial waterway for transportation or irrigation **2** *Anat.* a tubular passage or duct

Canal Zone *former name for* a strip of land on either side of the Panama Canal: leased by the U.S. (1904-79)

ca·na·pé (kan′ə pā′, kan′ə pē) ***n.*** ⟦Fr⟧ a small piece of bread or a cracker, spread with spiced meat, cheese, etc., served as an appetizer

ca·nard (kə närd′) ***n.*** ⟦Fr, a duck⟧ a false, esp. malicious, report

ca·nar·y (kə ner′ē) ***n.***, *pl.* **-ies** ⟦after *Canary* Islands⟧ **1** a small, yellow finch **2** a light yellow

Canary Islands group of Spanish islands off NW Africa

ca·nas·ta (kə nas′tə) ***n.*** ⟦Sp, basket⟧ a card game using a double deck

Can·ber·ra (kan′ber′ə, -bə rə) capital of Australia: pop. 328,000

can·can (kan′kan′) ***n.*** ⟦Fr⟧ a lively dance with much high kicking

can·cel (kan′səl) ***vt.*** **-celed** or **-celled**, **-cel·ing** or **-cel·ling** ⟦< L *cancellus*, lattice⟧ **1** to mark over with lines, etc., as in deleting written matter or marking a postage stamp, check, etc. as used **2** to make invalid **3** to do away with; abolish **4** to neutralize or balance: often with *out* **5** *Math.* to remove (a common factor, equivalents, etc.) —**can′cel·la′tion** ***n.***

can·cer (kan′sər) ***n.*** ⟦L, crab⟧ **1** [**C-**] the fourth sign of the zodiac **2** a malignant tumor that can spread **3** anything bad or harmful that spreads —**can′cer·ous** ***adj.***

can·de·la·brum (kan′də lä′brəm, -lā′-) ***n.***, *pl.* **-bra** (-brə) or **-brums** ⟦L: see CHANDELIER⟧ a large branched candlestick: also **can′de·la′bra**, *pl.* **-bras**

can·did (kan′did) ***adj.*** ⟦L *candidus*, white, pure, sincere⟧ **1** very honest or frank **2** unposed and informal *[*a *candid* photo*]* —**can′did·ly** ***adv.***

can·di·date (kan′də dāt′, -dət) ***n.*** ⟦L *candidatus*, white-robed, as were Roman office seekers⟧ **1** one seeking an office, award, etc. **2** one seemingly destined to come to a certain end

can·died (kan′dēd′) ***adj.*** cooked in sugar or syrup until glazed or encrusted

THESAURUS

cam, video, camcorder, press, movie, film, flash, still, electron-diffraction, box, stereo, zoom-lens, Polaroid (trademark), single-lens reflex, double-lens reflex, spectroscopic, telescopic.

camouflage ***n.*** dissimulation, deceit, masquerade, simulation, cloak, shade, shroud, veil, blackout, masking, paint, netting; see also DISGUISE, SCREEN 1.

camouflage ***v.*** cover, conceal, veil; see DECEIVE, DISGUISE, HIDE 1.

camp ***n.*** **1** [A temporary living place] camping ground, campground, campsite, encampment, tents, bivouac, tent city, wigwams, tepees, wickiups. **2** [Temporary living quarters] tent, lean-to, cottage, tilt, shack, hut, lodge, cabin, chalet, shed, log house, summer home, cottage. —**break camp** dismantle, depart, pack up; see LEAVE 1.

camp ***v.*** bivouac, stop over, make camp, encamp, dwell, nest, locate, pitch camp, pitch a tent, tent, quarter, lodge, sleep out, station, put up for the night, camp out, rough it, sleep under the stars.

campaign ***n.*** operations, crusade, warfare; see ATTACK, FIGHT.

campaign ***v.*** crusade, electioneer, run, agitate, contend for, contest, canvass for, solicit votes, lobby, barnstorm, mend fences, go to the grass roots, stump, beat the bushes*, whistle-stop; see also COMPETE.

campus ***n.*** seat of learning, buildings and grounds, school grounds, physical plant, alma mater, academia, quad; see also COLLEGE, UNIVERSITY.

can[1,2] ***v.*** **1** [To preserve] bottle, put up, keep; see PRESERVE 3. **2** [To be able] could, may, be capable of, be equal to, be up to, have in one's power to, have within one's control, manage, can do, take care of, make it*, make the grade.

can[2] ***n.*** **1** [A container] tin can, tin (British), canister, receptacle, package, jar, bottle, quart can, bucket, gallon can, vessel; see also CONTAINER. **2** [*Jail] prison, penitentiary, stir*; see JAIL. **3** [*A toilet] lavatory, restroom, washroom; see TOILET.

canal ***n.*** waterway, trench, ditch; see CHANNEL, WATER 2.

cancel ***v.*** repudiate, nullify, ignore, invalidate, suppress, countermand, call off, set aside, rule out, refute, rescind, remove, repeal, counteract, recall, retract, abrogate, discharge, void, make void, put an end to, abort, offset, revoke, overthrow, scratch, drop; see also ABOLISH.—*Ant.* SUSTAIN, approve, uphold.

cancellation ***n.*** cancelling, annulment, nullification, abrogation, dissolution, invalidation, revocation, repudiation, repeal, abolition, retraction, reversal, voiding, recall, overruling, withdrawing, abandoning, undoing; see also REMOVAL.

cancer ***n.*** growth, tumor, malignancy; see GROWTH 3, ILLNESS 2.

cancerous ***a.*** carcinogenic, virulent, mortal; see HARMFUL.

candid ***a.*** straightforward, sincere, open; see FRANK, HONEST 1.

candidate ***n.*** aspirant, possible choice, nominee, applicant, political contestant, office-seeker, successor, competitor, bidder, solicitor, petitioner; see also CONTESTANT.

can·dle (kan′dəl) ***n.*** ⟦< L *candela*⟧ a cylinder of tallow or wax with a wick through it, which gives light when burned —***vt.*** **-dled**, **-dling** to examine (eggs) for freshness by placing in front of a light —**can′dler** ***n.***

can′dle·stick′ ***n.*** a cupped or spiked holder for a candle or candles

can′-do′ ***adj.*** [Inf.] confident of one's ability to accomplish something

can·dor (kan′dər) ***n.*** ⟦L, openness⟧ unreserved honesty or frankness in expressing oneself: Brit. sp. **can′dour**

can·dy (kan′dē) ***n.***, *pl.* **-dies** ⟦< Pers *qand*, cane sugar⟧ a solid confection of sugar or syrup with flavoring, fruit, nuts, etc. —***vt.*** **-died**, **-dy·ing** **1** to cook in sugar, esp. so as to preserve **2** to crystallize into sugar

cane (kān) ***n.*** ⟦< Gr *kanna*⟧ **1** the slender, jointed stem of certain plants, as bamboo **2** a plant with such a stem, as sugar cane **3** WALKING STICK **4** split rattan —***vt.*** **caned**, **can′ing** **1** to flog with a cane **2** to make (chair seats, etc.) with cane —**can′er** ***n.***

cane·brake (kān′brāk′) ***n.*** a dense growth of cane plants

ca·nine (kā′nīn′) ***adj.*** ⟦< L *canis*, dog⟧ **1** of or like a dog **2** of the family of carnivores that includes dogs, wolves, and foxes —***n.*** **1** a dog or other canine animal **2** any of the sharp-pointed teeth next to the incisors: in full **canine tooth**

can·is·ter (kan′is tər) ***n.*** ⟦< Gr *kanastron*, wicker basket⟧ a small box or can for coffee, tea, etc.

can·ker (kaŋ′kər) ***n.*** ⟦< L *cancer*, a crab⟧ an ulcerlike sore, esp. in the mouth —**can′ker·ous** ***adj.***

can·na·bis (kan′ə bis) ***n.*** ⟦L, hemp⟧ **1** HEMP **2** marijuana or any other substance made from the flowering tops of the hemp

canned (kand) ***adj.*** **1** preserved, as in cans **2** [Slang] recorded for reproduction, as on radio or TV

can·nel (coal) (kan′əl) a dense bituminous coal that burns with a steady, bright flame

can·ner·y (kan′ər ē) ***n.***, *pl.* **-ies** a factory where foods are canned

can·ni·bal (kan′ə bəl) ***n.*** ⟦Sp *canibal*⟧ **1** a person who eats human flesh **2** an animal that eats its own kind —***adj.*** of or like cannibals —**can′ni·bal·ism′** ***n.*** —**can′ni·bal·is′tic** ***adj.***

can′ni·bal·ize′ (-īz′) ***vt.***, ***vi.*** **-ized′**, **-iz′ing** to strip (old or worn equipment) of parts for use in other units

can·non (kan′ən) ***n.***, *pl.* **-nons** or **-non** ⟦< L *canna*, cane⟧ **1** a large, mounted piece of artillery **2** an automatic gun on an aircraft

can′non·ade′ (-ād′) ***n.*** a continuous firing of artillery —***vt.***, ***vi.*** **-ad′ed**, **-ad′ing** to fire artillery (at)

can·not (kan′ät′, kə nät′) can not —**cannot but** have or has no choice but to

can·ny (kan′ē) ***adj.*** **-ni·er**, **-ni·est** ⟦< CAN[1]⟧ cautious and shrewd —**can′ni·ly** ***adv.*** —**can′ni·ness** ***n.***

ca·noe (kə no͞o′) ***n.*** ⟦< Sp *canoa* < WInd⟧ a light, narrow boat moved by paddles —***vi.*** **-noed′**, **-noe′ing** to paddle, or go in, a canoe —**ca·noe′ist** ***n.***

ca·no·la (oil) (kə nō′lə) an oil from the seed of the rape plant, used in cooking

can·on (kan′ən) ***n.*** ⟦OE, a rule < L⟧ **1** a law or body of laws of a church **2** *a*) a basic rule or principle *b*) a criterion **3** an official list, as of books of the Bible **4** the complete works, as of an author **5** *Music* a round **6** a clergyman serving in a cathedral

ca·ñon (kan′yən) ***n.*** *alt. sp. of* CANYON

ca·non·i·cal (kə nän′i kəl) ***adj.*** **1** of or according to church law **2** of or belonging to a canon

can·on·ize (kan′ən īz′) ***vt.*** **-ized′**, **-iz′ing** **1** to declare (a deceased person) a saint **2** to glorify —**can′on·i·za′tion** ***n.***

can·o·py (kan′ə pē) ***n.***, *pl.* **-pies** ⟦< Gr *kōnōpeion*, couch with mosquito nets⟧ **1** a drapery, etc. fastened above a bed, throne, etc., or held over a person **2** a rooflike projection —***vt.*** **-pied**, **-py·ing** to place or form a canopy over; cover

cant[1] (kant) ***n.*** ⟦< L *cantus*, song⟧ **1** the secret slang of beggars, thieves, etc.; argot **2** the special vocabulary of those in a certain occupation; jargon **3** insincere talk, esp. when pious —***vi.*** to use cant

cant[2] (kant) ***n.*** ⟦L *cantus*, tire of a wheel⟧ **1** an outside angle **2** a beveled edge **3** a tilt, turn, slant, etc. —***vt.***, ***vi.*** to slant; tilt

can't (kant, känt) *contr.* cannot

can·ta·loupe or **can·ta·loup** (kant′ə lōp′) ***n.*** ⟦Fr < It *Cantalupo*, estate near Rome, where first grown in Europe⟧ a muskmelon with a rough rind and juicy, orange flesh

can·tan·ker·ous (kan taŋ′kər əs) ***adj.*** ⟦prob. < ME *contakour*, troublemaker⟧ bad-tempered; quarrelsome —**can·tan′ker·ous·ly** ***adv.*** —**can·tan′ker·ous·ness** ***n.***

can·ta·ta (kän tät′ə, kən-) ***n.*** ⟦It < *cantare*, to sing⟧ a choral composition that sets to music the words of a story to be sung but not acted

can·teen (kan tēn′) ***n.*** ⟦< Fr < It *cantina*, wine cellar⟧ **1** a recreation center for military personnel, teenagers, etc. **2** a place where food is dispensed, as in a disaster area **3** a small flask for carrying water

can·ter (kant′ər) ***n.*** ⟦< *Canterbury gallop*, a riding pace⟧ a moderate gallop —***vi.***, ***vt.*** to ride at a canter

can·ti·cle (kan′ti kəl) ***n.*** ⟦< L *cantus*, song⟧ a hymn with words taken from the Bible

can·ti·le·ver (kant′'l ē′vər, -ev′ər) ***n.*** ⟦< ?⟧ a bracket or block projecting as a support; esp., a projecting structure anchored at one end to a pier or wall —***vt.*** to support by means of cantilevers —**can′ti·le′vered** ***adj.***

can·to (kan′tō) ***n.***, *pl.* **-tos** ⟦It < L *cantus*, song⟧ any of the main divisions of certain long poems

can·ton (kan′tən, -tän′) ***n.*** ⟦Fr < LL *cantus*, corner⟧ any of the states in the Swiss Republic

Can·ton (kan tän′) *a former transliteration of* GUANGZHOU

Can·ton·ese (kan′tə nēz′) ***n.*** **1** *pl.* **-ese′** a person born or living in Canton, China **2** the variety of Chinese spoken in Canton —***adj.*** of Canton

can·ton·ment (kan tän′mənt, -tōn′-) ***n.*** ⟦Fr: see CANTON⟧ temporary quarters for troops

can·tor (kan′tər) ***n.*** ⟦L, singer⟧ a singer of liturgical solos in a synagogue

can·vas (kan′vəs) ***n.*** ⟦< L *cannabis*, hemp⟧ **1** a coarse cloth of hemp, cotton, etc., used for tents, sails, etc. **2** a sail, tent, etc. **3** an oil painting on canvas

can′vas·back′ ***n.*** a North American wild duck with a grayish back

can·vass (kan′vəs) ***vt.***, ***vi.*** ⟦< *canvas* < ? use of canvas for sifting⟧ to go through (places) or among (people) asking for (votes, opinions, orders, etc.) —***n.*** a canvassing —**can′vass·er** ***n.***

can·yon (kan′yən) ***n.*** ⟦Sp *cañón*, tube < L *canna*, a reed⟧ a long, narrow valley between high cliffs

cap[1] (kap) ***n.*** ⟦< LL *cappa*, hooded cloak⟧ **1** any closefitting head covering, with or without a visor or brim **2** a caplike part or thing; cover or top —***vt.*** **capped**, **cap′ping** **1** to put a cap on **2** to cover the top or end of **3** to equal or excel

THESAURUS

candle ***n.*** taper, rush, torch; see LIGHT 3. —**burn the candle at both ends** dissipate, squander, use up; see WASTE 1, 2. —**not hold a candle to** be unequal to, not measure up to, be inferior to; see FAIL 1.

candlestick ***n.*** candelabrum, candelabra, taper holder, flat candlestick, menorah, candleholder.

candy ***n.*** confection, confectionery, sweetmeat, bonbon. *Varieties of candy include the following:* caramel, taffy, saltwater taffy, licorice, fondant, jelly bean, chocolate bar, fudge, cream, lemon drop, cotton candy, nougat, peanut brittle, praline, fruit roll, marshmallow, Turkish delight, lollipop, halvah, marzipan, gumdrop, divinity, toffee, after-dinner mint, butterscotch, peppermint stick, hard candy, sucker, rock candy, sourball, jawbreaker; bubble gum.

cane ***n.*** walking stick, staff, pole; see STICK.

canned ***a.*** bottled, conserved, sealed; see PRESERVED 2.

cannon ***n.*** *Types of cannon include the following:* self-propelled, muzzle-loading, breech-loading, tank destroyer, turret, mountain, siege, coast defense, field, antiaircraft, railway, antitank gun, knee mortar, recoilless rifle, howitzer.

canoe ***n.*** kayak, dugout, outrigger; see BOAT.

canon ***n.*** decree, rule, church law; see COMMAND, DECLARATION, LAW 3.

canonize ***v.*** sanctify, saint, beatify; see BLESS, LOVE 1, WORSHIP.

canopy ***n.*** awning, sunshade, umbrella; see COVER 1.

canteen ***n.*** jug, flask, water supply; see BOTTLE, CONTAINER.

canvas ***n.*** **1** [A coarse cloth] tenting, awning cloth, sailcloth, duck, coarse cloth; see also CLOTH. **2** [Anything made of canvas] sail, awning, tarpaulin; see COVER 1, TENT. **3** [A painting on canvas] portrait, still life, oil; see ART, PAINTING 1.

canyon ***n.*** gulch, gorge, gully; see RAVINE, VALLEY.

cap[1] ***n.*** beret, skullcap, tam-o'-shanter; see HAT.

cap[2] *abbrev.* **1** capacity **2** capital

ca·pa·ble (kā′pə bəl) ***adj.*** ⟦< L *capere*, to take⟧ having ability; skilled; competent —**capable of** **1** having the qualities necessary for **2** able or ready to —**ca′pa·bil′i·ty,** *pl.* **-ties, *n.*** —**ca′pa·bly *adv.***

ca·pa·cious (kə pā′shəs) ***adj.*** ⟦< L *capere*, to take⟧ roomy; spacious —**ca·pa′cious·ly *adv.*** —**ca·pa′cious·ness *n.***

ca·pac·i·tor (kə pas′ə tər) ***n.*** a device for storing an electric charge

ca·pac′i·ty (-tē) ***n.***, *pl.* **-ties** ⟦< L *capere*, take⟧ **1** the ability to contain, absorb, or receive **2** all that can be contained; volume **3** ability **4** maximum output **5** position; function

ca·par·i·son (kə par′i sən, -zən) ***n.*** ⟦< LL *cappa*, cloak⟧ trappings for a horse —***vt.*** to cover (a horse) with trappings

cape[1] (kāp) ***n.*** ⟦see prec.⟧ a sleeveless garment fastened at the neck and hanging over the back and shoulders

cape[2] (kāp) ***n.*** ⟦< L *caput*, head⟧ a piece of land projecting into a body of water

ca·per[1] (kā′pər) ***vi.*** ⟦? < Fr *capriole*, a leap⟧ to skip about in a playful manner —***n.*** **1** a playful leap **2** a prank **3** [Slang] a criminal act, esp. a robbery —**cut a caper** (or **cut capers**) to caper

ca·per[2] (kā′pər) ***n.*** ⟦< Gr *kapparis*⟧ the green flower bud of a Mediterranean bush, pickled and used as a seasoning

cape′skin′ *n.* ⟦orig. made from the skin of goats from the *Cape* of Good Hope⟧ fine leather made from sheepskin

Cape Town seaport in South Africa: seat of the legislature: pop. 855,000

Cape Verde (vurd) country on a group of islands in the Atlantic, west of Senegal: 1,557 sq. mi.; pop. 337,000

cap·il·lar·y (kap′ə ler′ē) ***adj.*** ⟦< L *capillus*, hair⟧ very slender —***n.***, *pl.* **-ies** **1** a tube with a very small bore: also **capillary tube** **2** any of the tiny blood vessels connecting the arteries with the veins

capillary attraction the action by which liquids in contact with solids, as in a capillary tube, rise or fall: also **capillary action**

cap·i·tal (kap′ət ′l) ***adj.*** ⟦< L *caput*, head⟧ **1** punishable by death **2** principal; chief **3** of, or being, the seat of government **4** of capital, or wealth **5** excellent —***n.*** **1** CAPITAL LETTER **2** a city that is the seat of government of a state or nation **3** money or property owned or used in business **4** [*often* **C-**] capitalists collectively **5** the top part of a column

capital gain profit resulting from the sale of capital investments such as stocks

cap′i·tal·ism′ *n.* an economic system in which the means of production and distribution are privately owned and operated for profit

cap′i·tal·ist *n.* **1** an owner of wealth used in business **2** an upholder of capitalism **3** a wealthy person —**cap′i·tal·is′tic *adj.***

cap′i·tal·ize′ (-īz′) ***vt.*** **-ized′, -iz′ing** **1** to use as or convert into capital **2** to supply capital to or for **3** to begin (a word) with a capital letter —**capitalize on something** to use something to one's advantage —**cap′i·tal·i·za′tion *n.***

capital letter the form of an alphabetical letter used to begin a sentence or proper name, as *A*, *B*, or *C*

cap′i·tal·ly *adv.* very well

capital punishment the penalty of death for a crime

Cap·i·tol (kap′ət ′l) ***n.*** ⟦< L *Capitolium*, temple of Jupiter in Rome⟧ **1** the building in which the U.S. Congress meets in Washington, DC **2** [*usually* **c-**] the building in which a state legislature meets

ca·pit·u·late (kə pich′yoo lāt′, -pich′ə lāt′) ***vi.*** **-lat′ed, -lat′ing** ⟦< LL *capitulare*, arrange conditions⟧ **1** to give up (*to* an enemy) on prearranged conditions **2** to stop resisting —**ca·pit′u·la′tion *n.***

cap·let (kap′lit) ***n.*** a solid, elongated medicine tablet, coated for easy swallowing

ca·pon (kā′pän′, -pən) ***n.*** ⟦< L *capo*⟧ a castrated rooster fattened for eating

cap·puc·ci·no (kä′pə chē′nō, kap′ə-) ***n.*** ⟦It⟧ espresso coffee mixed with steamed milk and topped with cinnamon, etc.

ca·price (kə prēs′) ***n.*** ⟦Fr < It⟧ **1** a sudden, impulsive change in thinking or acting **2** a capricious quality

ca·pri·cious (kə prish′əs) ***adj.*** subject to caprices; erratic —**ca·pri′cious·ly *adv.*** —**ca·pri′cious·ness *n.***

Cap·ri·corn (kap′ri kôrn′) ***n.*** ⟦< L *caper*, goat + *cornu*, horn⟧ the tenth sign of the zodiac

cap·size (kap′sīz′, kap sīz′) ***vt., vi.*** **-sized′, -siz′ing** ⟦< ?⟧ to overturn or upset: said esp. of a boat

cap·stan (kap′stən) ***n.*** ⟦? < L *capere*, take⟧ an upright cylinder, as on ships, around which cables are wound for hoisting anchors, etc.

cap·sule (kap′səl, -syool′) ***n.*** ⟦Fr < L *capsa*, box⟧ **1** a soluble gelatin container enclosing a dose of medicine **2** a detachable compartment to hold people, instruments, etc. in a rocket: in full **space capsule** **3** *Bot.* a seed vessel —***adj.*** in a concise form —**cap′su·lar *adj.***

cap′sul·ize′ (-īz′) ***vt.*** **-ized′, -iz′ing** **1** to enclose in a capsule **2** to condense

Capt *abbrev.* Captain

cap·tain (kap′tən) ***n.*** ⟦< L *caput*, head⟧ **1** a chief; leader **2** *U.S. Mil.* an officer ranking just above first lieutenant **3** *U.S. Navy* an officer ranking just above commander **4** *a*) the person in command of a ship *b*) the pilot of an airplane **5** the leader of a team, as in sports —***vt.*** to be captain of —**cap′tain·cy,** *pl.* **-cies, *n.***

cap·tion (kap′shən) ***n.*** ⟦< L *capere*, to take⟧ **1** a heading or title, as of a newspaper article or illustration **2** *Film, TV* a subtitle —***vt.*** to supply a caption for

cap′tious (-shəs) ***adj.*** ⟦see prec.⟧ **1** made only for the sake of argument or faultfinding *[a captious remark]* **2** quick to find fault —**cap′tious·ly *adv.*** —**cap′tious·ness *n.***

cap·ti·vate (kap′tə vāt′) ***vt.*** **-vat′ed, -vat′ing** to capture the attention or affection of —**cap′ti·vat′ing·ly *adv.*** —**cap′ti·va′tion *n.*** —**cap′ti·va′tor *n.***

cap·tive (kap′tiv) ***n.*** ⟦< L *capere*, to take⟧ a prisoner —***adj.*** **1** taken or held prisoner **2** obliged to listen *[a captive audience]* —**cap·tiv′i·ty,** *pl.* **-ties, *n.***

cap′tor (-tər) ***n.*** one who captures

cap′ture (-chər) ***vt.*** **-tured, -tur·ing** ⟦< L *capere*, to take⟧ **1** to take or seize by force, surprise, etc. **2** to represent in a more permanent form *[to capture her charm on canvas]* —***n.*** a capturing or being captured

THESAURUS

capability *n.* capacity, skill, aptitude; see ABILITY, INCLINATION 1.

capable *a.* proficient, competent, fitted; see ABLE, INTELLIGENT.

capacity *n.* contents, limit, space, room, size, volume, holding power, extent, compass, magnitude, spread, expanse, scope, latitude, bulk, dimensions, measure, range, quantity, size, reach, holding ability, sweep, proportions, mass, sufficiency.

cape[1,2] ***n.*** **1** [Land jutting into the water] headland, peninsula, foreland, point, promontory, jetty, head, tongue, neck of land, ness, mole, finger, arm. **2** [An overgarment] cloak, wrapper, mantilla, mantle, shawl, wrap, overdress, poncho; see also COAT 1.

caper[1] ***n.*** prank, trick, escapade; see JOKE.

caper[1] ***v.*** frolic, gambol, cavort; see PLAY 1, 2.

capital *n.* **1** [A seat of government] metropolis, principal city, capitol; see CENTER 2, CITY. **2** [Money and property] cash, assets, interests; see ESTATE, PROPERTY 1, WEALTH. **3** [A letter usually used initially] initial, uppercase, majuscule; see LETTER 1.

capitalism *n.* capitalistic system, free enterprise, private ownership; see DEMOCRACY, ECONOMICS, GOVERNMENT 2.

capitalist *n.* entrepreneur, investor, landowner; see BANKER, BUSINESSMAN, FINANCIER.

capitol *n.* statehouse, state capitol, seat of government; see CENTER 2.

capitulate *v.* surrender, submit, give up; see YIELD 1.

capsize *v.* overturn, invert, tip over; see UPSET 1.

caption *n.* inscription, title, subtitle; see HEADING.

captive *a.* restrained, incarcerated, jailed; see BOUND 1, 2, RESTRICTED.

captive *n.* hostage, convict, POW; see PRISONER.

captivity *n.* imprisonment, jail, restraint, slavery, bondage, subjection, servitude, duress, detention, incarceration, enslavement, constraint, the guardhouse, custody; see also CONFINEMENT.—*Ant.* FREEDOM, liberty, independence.

capture *n.* capturing, arrest, recovery, seizing, taking, seizure, acquisition, obtaining, securing, gaining, winning, occupation, appropriation, ensnaring, abduction, laying hold of, grasping, catching, trapping, commandeering, apprehending, confiscation, apprehension, taking into custody, fall.—*Ant.* RESCUE, liberation, setting free.

capture *v.* seize, take, apprehend; see ARREST, SEIZE 2.

captured *a.* taken, seized, arrested, apprehended, detained, grasped, overtaken, grabbed, snatched, kidnapped, abducted, netted, hooked, secured, collared*, nabbed*, bagged; see also UNDER ARREST.—*Ant.* RELEASED, unbound, loosed.

car (kär) ***n.*** ⟦< L *carrus*, chariot⟧ **1** any vehicle on wheels **2** a vehicle that moves on rails, as a streetcar **3** an automobile **4** an elevator cage

Ca·ra·cas (kə räk′əs, -rak′-) capital of Venezuela: pop. 1,825,000

car·a·cul (kar′ə kul′, -kəl) ***n.*** *alt. sp. of* KARAKUL (esp. sense 2)

ca·rafe (kə raf′, -räf′) ***n.*** ⟦Fr⟧ a glass bottle for serving wine, water, or coffee

car·a·mel (kär′məl, kar′ə məl) ***n.*** ⟦Fr⟧ **1** burnt sugar used to color or flavor food **2** a chewy candy made from sugar, milk, etc.

car′a·mel·ize′ (-īz′) ***vt., vi.*** **-ized′**, **-iz′ing** to turn into CARAMEL (sense 1)

car·a·pace (kar′ə pās′) ***n.*** ⟦Fr < Sp⟧ the upper shell of the turtle, crab, etc.

car·at (kar′ət) ***n.*** ⟦Fr < Gr *keration*, little horn⟧ **1** a unit of weight for precious stones, equal to 200 milligrams **2** KARAT

car·a·van (kar′ə van′) ***n.*** ⟦< Pers *kārwān*⟧ **1** a company of people traveling together for safety, as through a desert **2** VAN[2]

car·a·van·sa·ry (kar′ə van′sə rē) ***n.***, *pl.* **-ries** ⟦< Pers *kārwān*, caravan + *sarāi*, palace⟧ in the Middle East, an inn for caravans

car·a·way (kar′ə wā′) ***n.*** ⟦< Ar *al-karawiyā′*⟧ the spicy seeds of an herb, used to flavor bread, etc.

car·bide (kär′bīd′) ***n.*** a solid compound of a metal with carbon

car·bine (kär′bīn′, -bēn′) ***n.*** ⟦< Fr *scarabée*, beetle⟧ **1** a short-barreled rifle **2** a light, semiautomatic or automatic rifle of relatively limited range

carbo- *combining form* carbon: also **carb-**

car·bo·hy·drate (kär′bō hī′drāt, -bə-) ***n.*** ⟦prec. + HYDRATE⟧ an organic compound composed of carbon, hydrogen, and oxygen, as a sugar or starch

car·bol·ic acid (kär bäl′ik) *see* PHENOL

car·bon (kär′bən) ***n.*** ⟦< L *carbo*, coal⟧ **1** a nonmetallic chemical element found esp. in all organic compounds: diamond and graphite are pure carbon: a radioactive isotope of carbon (**carbon-14**) is used in dating fossils, etc. **2** CARBON PAPER **3** a copy made with carbon paper —***adj.*** of or like carbon

car′bon·ate (-bə nit; *also, and for v. always*, -nāt′) ***n.*** a salt or ester of carbonic acid —***vt.*** **-at′ed**, **-at′ing** to charge with carbon dioxide —**car′bon·a′tion** ***n.***

carbon black carbon produced by the incomplete burning of oil or gas

carbon copy **1** a copy made with carbon paper **2** anything very much like another

carbon dating a method of establishing the approximate age of fossils, etc. by measuring the amount of carbon-14 in them —**car′bon-date′**, **-dat′ed**, **-dat′ing**, ***vt.***

carbon di·ox·ide (dī äks′īd′) a heavy, colorless, odorless gas: it passes out of the lungs in respiration

car·bon·ic acid (kär bän′ik) a weak acid formed by carbon dioxide in water

car·bon·if·er·ous (kär′bə nif′ər əs) ***adj.*** containing carbon or coal

carbon mon·ox·ide (mə näks′īd′) a colorless, odorless, highly poisonous gas

carbon paper thin paper coated on one side, as with a carbon preparation, used to make copies of letters, etc.

carbon tet·ra·chlo·ride (te′trə klôr′īd′) a nonflammable liquid, used as a solvent for fats and oils, etc.

Car·bo·run·dum (kär′bə run′dəm) ⟦CARB(ON) + (c)*orundum*⟧ *trademark for* a hard abrasive, esp. of carbon and silicon —***n.*** [**c-**] such a substance

car·boy (kär′boi′) ***n.*** ⟦< Pers *qarābah*⟧ a large bottle enclosed in a protective container, for holding corrosive liquids

car·bun·cle (kär′buŋ′kəl) ***n.*** ⟦< L dim. of *carbo*, coal⟧ a painful bacterial infection deep beneath the skin —**car·bun′cu·lar** (-kyoo lər) ***adj.***

car·bu·ret·or (kär′bə rāt′ər) ***n.*** a device for mixing air with gasoline spray to make an explosive mixture in an internal-combustion engine

car·cass (kär′kəs) ***n.*** ⟦< Fr *carcasse*⟧ **1** the dead body of an animal **2** a framework or shell

car·cin·o·gen (kär sin′ə jən) ***n.*** ⟦< fol. + -GEN⟧ any substance that produces cancer —**car·ci·no·gen·ic** (kär′sə nō jen′ik) ***adj.***

car·ci·no·ma (kär′sə nō′mə) ***n.***, *pl.* **-mas** or **-ma·ta** (-mə tə) ⟦L < Gr *karkinos*, crab⟧ any of several kinds of epithelial cancer

car coat a short overcoat

card[1] (kärd) ***n.*** ⟦< Gr *chartēs*, layer of papyrus⟧ **1** a flat, stiff piece of paper or pasteboard; specif., *a*) any of a pack of playing cards *b*) a card identifying a person, esp. as a member, agent, etc. *c*) a postcard *d*) an illustrated, usually folded card bearing a greeting *e*) any of a series of cards on which information is recorded **2** a small, plug-in circuit board **3** [Inf.] a witty or clowning person —**put** (or **lay**) **one's cards on the table** to reveal something frankly

card[2] (kärd) ***n.*** ⟦< L *carrere*, to card⟧ a metal comb or a machine with wire teeth for combing fibers of wool, cotton, etc. —***vt.*** to use a card on

card′board′ ***n.*** stiff, thick paper or pasteboard, used for cards, boxes, etc.

car·di·ac (kär′dē ak′) ***adj.*** ⟦< Gr *kardia*, heart⟧ of or near the heart

cardiac arrest the complete failure of the heart to pump blood

car·di·gan (kär′di gən) ***n.*** ⟦after 7th Earl of *Cardigan*⟧ a sweater or jacket, usually knitted and collarless, that opens down the front

car·di·nal (kärd′'n əl) ***adj.*** ⟦< L *cardo*, pivot⟧ **1** principal; chief **2** bright-red —***n.*** **1** an official appointed by the pope to his council **2** a bright-red American songbird **3** CARDINAL NUMBER

cardinal number any number used in counting or in showing how many (e.g., two, 40, 627, etc.)

cardio- ⟦< Gr *kardia*, heart⟧ *combining form* of the heart

car·di·o·gram (kär′dē ō gram′, -dē ə-) ***n.*** ELECTROCARDIOGRAM

car′di·o·graph′ (-graf′) ***n.*** ELECTROCARDIOGRAPH

car′di·ol′o·gy (-äl′ə jē) ***n.*** the branch of medicine dealing with the heart —**car′di·ol′o·gist** ***n.***

car·di·o·pul·mo·nar·y (kär′dē ō pool′ mə ner′ē) ***adj.*** of or involving the heart and lungs

car′di·o·vas′cu·lar (-vas′kyə lər) ***adj.*** of the heart and the blood vessels as a unified body system

cards ***pl.n.*** any game played with a deck of playing cards, as poker

card′sharp′ ***n.*** [Inf.] a professional cheater at cards: also **card shark**

care (ker) ***n.*** ⟦< OE *caru*, sorrow⟧ **1** *a*) a troubled state of mind; worry *b*) a cause of such a mental state **2** close attention; heed **3** a liking or regard (*for*) **4** custody; protection **5** a responsibility —***vi.*** **cared**, **car′ing** **1** to feel

THESAURUS

car ***n.*** auto, motorcar, wheels*; see AUTOMOBILE, VEHICLE. *Types of cars include the following:* passenger car, limousine, sedan, hardtop, compact, subcompact, sports car, coupe, roadster, convertible, ragtop*, town car, ranch wagon, station wagon, taxicab, squad car, prowl car, staff car, saloon (British), SUV.

carcass ***n.*** corpse, cadaver, remains; see BODY 2.

card[1] ***n.*** cardboard, ticket, sheet, square, Bristol board, fiberboard. *Varieties of cards include the following:* poster, window card, show card, ticket, label, badge, tally, check, billet, voucher, pass; calling card, playing card, fortunetelling cards, tarot cards, address card, visiting card, credit card, bank card, greeting card, registration card, filing card, index card, check-cashing card, FOP card, social security card, identification card, ID card; see also PAPER 1. —**in the cards** probable, predicted, possible; see LIKELY 1. —**put one's cards on the table** reveal, tell the truth, expose; see ADMIT 2.

care ***n.*** **1** [Careful conduct] heed, concern, caution, consideration, regard, thoughtfulness, forethought, attention, precaution, wariness, vigilance, watchfulness, watching, diligence, nicety, pains, application, conscientiousness, thought, discrimination, exactness, exactitude, watch, concentration; see also ATTENTION, PRUDENCE.—*Ant.* CARELESSNESS, neglect, negligence. **2** [Worry] concern, anxiety, distress; see WORRY 2. **3** [Custody] supervision, administration, keeping; see CUSTODY. **4** [A cause of worry] problem, care, concern; see DISASTER, MISFORTUNE. —**take care** be careful, be cautious, beware, heed; see also MIND 3, WATCH OUT. —**take care of** protect, attend to, be responsible for; see GUARD.

care ***v.*** **1** [To be concerned] attend, take pains, regard; see CONSIDER. **2** [To be careful] look out for, be on guard, watch out; see MIND 3. —**care about** cherish, be fond of, hold dear; see LIKE 2, LOVE 1. —**care for** **1** [To look after] provide for, attend to, nurse; see RAISE 2, SUPPORT 3. **2** [To like] be fond of, hold dear, prize; see LIKE 2, LOVE 1. —**care to** prefer, desire, wish; see LIKE 1, WANT 1.

concern **2** to feel love or a liking *(for)* **3** to look after; provide *(for)* **4** to wish *(for)*; want —*vt.* **1** to feel concern about or interest in **2** to wish —**(in) care of** at the address of —**take care of 1** to attend to **2** to provide for

ca·reen (kə rēn′) *vt., vi.* ⟦< L *carina*, keel⟧ to lean or cause to lean sideways; tip; tilt; lurch

ca·reer (kə rir′) *n.* ⟦< L *carrus*, car⟧ **1** [Archaic] a swift course **2** one's progress through life **3** a profession or occupation —*vi.* to rush wildly

care′free′ *adj.* free from worry

care′ful *adj.* **1** cautious; wary **2** accurate; thorough; painstaking —**care′ful·ly** *adv.* —**care′ful·ness** *n.*

care′giv′er *n.* one who takes care of a child, invalid, etc.

care′less *adj.* **1** carefree; untroubled **2** not paying enough heed; neglectful **3** done or made without enough attention, precision, etc. —**care′less·ly** *adv.* —**care′less·ness** *n.*

ca·ress (kə res′) *vt.* ⟦ult. < L *carus*, dear⟧ to touch lovingly or gently —*n.* an affectionate touch

car·et (kar′it, ker′-) *n.* ⟦L, there is lacking⟧ a mark (∧) used to show where something is to be inserted in a written or printed line

care′tak′er *n.* **1** a person hired to take care of something or someone **2** one acting as temporary replacement

care′worn′ *adj.* worn out by, or showing the effects of, troubles and worry; haggard

car·fare (kär′fer′) *n.* the price of a ride on a subway, bus, etc.

car·go (kär′gō) *n., pl.* **-goes** or **-gos** ⟦< Sp *cargar*, to load⟧ the load carried by a ship, truck, etc.; freight

car′hop′ *n.* ⟦CAR + (BELL)HOP⟧ one who serves food at a drive-in restaurant

Car·ib·be·an (Sea) (kar′ə bē′ən, kə rib′ē ən) part of the Atlantic, bounded by the West Indies, Central America, and N South America

car·i·bou (kar′ə bo͞o′) *n.* ⟦CdnFr⟧ a large North American reindeer

car·i·ca·ture (kar′i kə chər) *n.* ⟦Fr < It *caricare*, exaggerate⟧ **1** the exaggerated imitation of a person, literary style, etc. for satirical effect **2** a picture, etc. in which this is done —*vt.* **-tured, -tur·ing** to depict as in a caricature —**car′i·ca·tur·ist** *n.*

car·ies (ker′ēz′) *n.* ⟦L, decay⟧ decay of bones or, esp., of teeth

car·il·lon (kar′ə län′) *n.* ⟦Fr, chime of four bells < L *quattuor*, four⟧ a set of bells tuned to the chromatic scale

ca·ri·tas (kär′ē täs′) *n.* love for all people

car·jack·ing (kär′jak′iŋ) *n.* the taking of a car and its passengers by force —**car′jack′** *vt.* —**car′jack′er** *n.*

car·mine (kär′min, -mīn′) *n.* ⟦ult. < Ar *qirmiz*, crimson⟧ a red or purplish-red color —*adj.* red or purplish-red

car·nage (kär′nij) *n.* ⟦Fr < L caro, flesh⟧ extensive slaughter, esp. in battle

car′nal (-nəl) *adj.* ⟦< L *caro*, flesh⟧ **1** of the flesh; material; worldly **2** sensual or sexual —**car·nal′i·ty** (-nal′i tē), *pl.* **-ties**, *n.* —**car′nal·ly** *adv.*

car·na·tion (kär nā′shən) *n.* ⟦< L *caro*, flesh⟧ **1** a plant of the pink family, widely cultivated for its white, pink, or red flowers **2** its flower

car·nel·ian (kär nēl′yən) *n.* ⟦< L *carnis*, of flesh (color)⟧ a red variety of chalcedony, used in jewelry

car·ni·val (kär′nə vəl) *n.* ⟦< Fr *carnaval* (or It *carnevale*)⟧ **1** the period of feasting and revelry just before Lent **2** a reveling; festivity **3** an entertainment with sideshows, rides, etc.

car·ni·vore (kär′nə vôr′) *n.* a carnivorous animal or plant

car·niv·o·rous (kär niv′ə rəs) *adj.* ⟦< L *caro*, flesh + *vorare*, to devour⟧ **1** flesh-eating **2** of the carnivores —**car·niv′o·rous·ness** *n.*

car·ob (kar′əb) *n.* a tree of the E Mediterranean region with sweet pods used in making candy, etc.

car·ol (kar′əl) *n.* ⟦< OFr *carole*, kind of dance⟧ a song of joy or praise; esp., a Christmas song —*vi., vt.* **-oled** or **-olled, -ol·ing** or **-ol·ling** to sing; esp., to sing Christmas carols —**car′ol·er** or **car′ol·ler** *n.*

car·om (kar′əm) *n.* ⟦< Sp *carambola*⟧ **1** *Billiards* a shot in which the cue ball successively hits two balls **2** a hitting and rebounding —*vi.* **1** to make a carom **2** to hit and rebound

ca·rot·id (kə rät′id) *adj.* ⟦Gr *karōtis*⟧ designating or of either of the two main arteries, one on each side of the neck, which convey blood to the head —*n.* a carotid artery

ca·rouse (kə rouz′) *vi.* **-roused′, -rous′ing** ⟦< Ger *gar austrinken*, to drink⟧ to engage in a noisy drinking party —*n.* a noisy drinking party

car·ou·sel (kar′ə sel′) *n.* ⟦Fr < It dial. (Naples) *carusiello*, kind of tournament⟧ **1** a merry-go-round **2** a circular baggage conveyor in an airport

carp[1] (kärp) *n., pl.* **carp** or **carps** ⟦< VL *carpa*⟧ an edible freshwater fish widely cultivated for food

carp[2] (kärp) *vi.* ⟦< ON *karpa*, to brag⟧ to find fault in a petty or nagging way —**carp′er** *n.*

car·pal (kär′pəl) *adj.* of the carpus —*n.* a bone of the carpus

carpal tunnel syndrome a condition of a pinched nerve in the wrist, often caused by repetitive movement

car·pel (kär′pəl) *n.* ⟦< Gr *karpos*, fruit⟧ a simple pistil, regarded as a modified leaflike structure

car·pen·ter (kär′pən tər) *n.* ⟦< L *carpentum*, a cart⟧ one who builds and repairs wooden things, esp. buildings, ships, etc. —**car′pen·try** (-trē) *n.*

carpenter ant a large ant that gnaws holes in trees, wooden buildings, etc. for its nest

car·pet (kär′pət) *n.* ⟦< L *carpere*, to card⟧ **1** a heavy fabric for covering a floor **2** anything that covers like a carpet —*vt.* to cover as with a carpet —**on the carpet** being reprimanded

car′pet·bag′ *n.* an old-fashioned traveling bag, made of carpeting

car′pet·bag′ger *n.* a politician, promoter, etc. from the outside whose influence is resented

car′pet·ing *n.* carpets or carpet fabric

THESAURUS

career *n.* occupation, vocation, work; see JOB 1, PROFESSION 1.

carefree *a.* lighthearted, cheerful, jovial; see HAPPY, CALM 1.

careful *a.* thorough, concerned, deliberate, conservative, prudent, meticulous, particular, rigorous, fussy, finicky, prim, exacting, wary, sober, vigilant, watchful, suspicious, alert, wide-awake, scrupulous, religious, hard to please, discriminating, sure-footed, precise, painstaking, exact, on one's guard, on the alert, conscientious, attentive, calculating, mindful, cautious, guarded, considerate, shy, circumspect, discreet, noncommittal, self-possessed, cool, calm, self-disciplined, solid, farsighted, frugal, thrifty, stealthy, observant, on guard, apprehensive, leery, choosy*, picky*, feeling one's way, seeing how the land lies, going to great lengths.—*Ant.* CARELESS, heedless, haphazard.

carefully *a.* **1** [Scrupulously] conscientiously, exactly, rigidly, correctly, strictly, precisely, minutely, painstakingly, faithfully, honorably, attentively, rigorously, providently, deliberately, reliably, particularly, solicitously, concernedly, meticulously, laboriously, thoroughly, dependably, in detail.—*Ant.* haphazardly, neglectfully, indifferently. **2** [Cautiously] prudently, discreetly, watchfully; see CAUTIOUSLY.

careless *a.* loose, lax, remiss, unguarded, incautious, forgetful, unthinking, unobservant, reckless, unheeding, indiscreet, inadvertent, unconcerned, wasteful, regardless, imprudent, unconsidered, hasty, inconsiderate, heedless, mindless, untroubled, negligent, neglectful, thoughtless, indifferent, casual, oblivious, absent-minded, listless, abstracted, nonchalant, blasé, undiscerning, offhand, slack, blundering; see also RASH.—*Ant.* THOUGHTFUL, attentive, careful.

carelessly *a.* heedlessly, negligently, neglectfully, thoughtlessly, nonchalantly, offhandedly, rashly, unconcernedly, at random, happen what may, incautiously, improvidently, wastefully, without caution, without care, without concern, with no attention, like crazy*.

carelessness *n.* unconcern, nonchalance, heedlessness, rashness, omission, slackness, delinquency, indolence, procrastination, dereliction, neglect, negligence, disregard, imprudence, haphazardness; see also INDIFFERENCE.—*Ant.* CARE, consideration, caution.

caress *n.* embrace, stroke, fondling; see HUG, KISS, TOUCH 2.

caress *v.* embrace, cuddle, pet; see LOVE 2, TOUCH 1.

caretaker *n.* porter, keeper, janitor; see CUSTODIAN, WATCHMAN.

cargo *n.* shipload, baggage, lading; see FREIGHT, LOAD 1.

carnal *a.* fleshly, bodily, sensuous; see LEWD 2, SENSUAL 2.

carnival *n.* sideshow, circus, fair; see ENTERTAINMENT, SHOW 1.

carol *n.* hymn, Christmas song, ballad; see SONG.

carpenter *n.* cabinetmaker, woodworker, craftsman; see LABORER, WORKMAN.

carpet *n.* wall-to-wall carpet, carpeting, linoleum, floor covering, matting; see also RUG. —**(called) on the carpet** reprimanded, censured, interrogated; see IN TROUBLE.

car pool a plan by a group to rotate the use of their cars, as for going to work —**car'pool'** ***vi., vt.***

car·port (kär'pôrt') ***n.*** an automobile shelter built as a roof extending from the side of a building

car·pus (kär'pəs) ***n., pl.*** **-pi'** (-pī') ⟦< Gr *karpos,* wrist⟧ *Anat.* the wrist, or the wrist bones

car·rel or **car·rell** (kar'əl) ***n.*** ⟦< ML *carula*⟧ a small enclosure in a library, for privacy in studying or reading

car·riage (kar'ij) ***n.*** ⟦ult. < L *carrus,* chariot⟧ **1** a carrying; transportation **2** the manner of carrying oneself; bearing **3** *a)* a horse-drawn passenger vehicle, esp. one with four wheels *b)* a baby carriage **4** a moving part, as on a typewriter, that supports and shifts something

car·ri·er (kar'ē ər) ***n.*** **1** one that carries **2** one in the business of transporting **3** one that transmits disease germs **4** AIRCRAFT CARRIER **5** *a)* a telephone-service company *b)* an insurance company

carrier pigeon *former name for* HOMING PIGEON

car·ri·on (kar'ē ən) ***n.*** ⟦< L *caro,* flesh⟧ the decaying flesh of a dead body

Car·roll (kar'əl), **Lew·is** (lo͞o'is) (pseud. of *C. L. Dodgson*) 1832-98; Eng. writer

car·rot (kar'ət) ***n.*** ⟦< Gr *karōton*⟧ **1** a plant with an edible, fleshy, orange-red root **2** the root

car·rou·sel (kar'ə sel') ***n.*** *alt. sp. of* CAROUSEL

car·ry (kar'ē) ***vt.*** **-ried, -ry·ing** ⟦< L *carrus,* chariot⟧ **1** to hold or support **2** to take from one place to another **3** to keep with one *[to carry an ID]* **4** to transmit *[air carries sounds]* **5** to transfer or extend **6** to have as a quality, consequence, etc. *[to carry a guarantee]* **7** to bear (oneself) in a specified way **8** to win (an election, argument, etc.) **9** *a)* to keep in stock *b)* to keep on one's account books, etc. **10** to publish or broadcast *[to carry a syndicated column, a TV show, etc.]* —***vi.*** to cover a range or distance: said of a voice, missile, etc. —***n., pl.*** **-ries** the distance covered by a gun, ball, etc. —**be** (or **get**) **carried away** to become very emotional or enthusiastic —**carry on 1** to engage in **2** to go on (*with*) **3** [Inf.] to behave wildly or childishly —**carry out** (or **through**) **1** to put (plans, etc.) into practice **2** to accomplish —**carry over** to postpone

carrying charge interest paid on the balance owed in installment buying

car'ry-on' ***adj.*** small enough to fit under an airplane seat or in an overhead compartment —***n.*** a piece of carry-on luggage

car'ry·out' ***adj.*** designating or of prepared food sold as by a restaurant to be consumed elsewhere

car'ry-o'ver ***n.*** something carried over or left over

car seat a seat in an automobile, specif., a portable seat for securing a small child

car'sick' ***adj.*** nauseated from riding in an automobile, bus, etc.

Car·son City (kär'sən) capital of Nevada, in the W part: pop. 40,000

cart (kärt) ***n.*** ⟦< ON *kartr*⟧ **1** a small wagon, carriage, etc. **2** a handcart —***vt., vi.*** to carry as in a cart, truck, etc.; transport

cart·age (kärt'ij) ***n.*** **1** the work of carting **2** the charge for this

carte blanche (kärt' blänsh') ⟦Fr, lit., white card⟧ full authority or freedom

car·tel (kär tel') ***n.*** ⟦< Ger < Fr⟧ an association of businesses in an international monopoly; trust

Car·ter (kärt'ər), **Jim·my** (jim'ē) (legal name *James Earl Carter, Jr.*) 1924- ; 39th president of the U.S. (1977-81)

car·ti·lage (kärt''l ij) ***n.*** ⟦< L *cartilago*⟧ tough, elastic tissue forming parts of the skeleton; gristle —**car'ti·lag'i·nous** (-aj'ə nəs) ***adj.***

car·tog·ra·phy (kär täg'rə fē) ***n.*** ⟦see CARD[1] & -GRAPHY⟧ the art of making maps or charts —**car·tog'ra·pher** ***n.***

car·ton (kärt''n) ***n.*** ⟦Fr < It *carta,* card⟧ a cardboard box or container

car·toon (kär to͞on') ***n.*** ⟦< Fr: see prec.⟧ **1** a drawing caricaturing a person or event **2** *a)* COMIC STRIP *b)* an animated cartoon —***vi.*** to draw a cartoon —**car·toon'ist** ***n.***

car·tridge (kär'trij) ***n.*** ⟦< Fr < It *carta,* card⟧ **1** a cylindrical case containing the charge and primer, and usually the projectile, for a firearm **2** a small container, as for camera film or ink for a pen

cart'wheel' ***n.*** a handspring performed sideways

carve (kärv) ***vt.*** **carved, carv'ing** ⟦OE *ceorfan*⟧ **1** to make or shape by or as by cutting **2** to decorate the surface of with cut designs **3** to divide by cutting; slice —***vi.*** **1** to carve statues or designs **2** to carve meat —**carv'er** ***n.*** —**carv'ing** ***n.***

car'wash' ***n.*** an establishment at which automobiles are washed

car·y·at·id (kar'ē at'id) ***n., pl.*** **-ids** or **-i·des'** (-ə dēz') ⟦< Gr *karyatides,* priestesses at Karyai, in ancient Greece⟧ a supporting column having the form of a draped female figure

ca·sa·ba (kə sä'bə) ***n.*** ⟦after *Kasaba,* town in Asia Minor⟧ a kind of cultivated melon with a hard, yellow rind

Ca·sa·blan·ca (kas'ə blaŋ'kə, kä'sə bläŋ'kə) seaport in NW Morocco: pop. 1,506,000

Ca·sa·no·va (kaz'ə nō'və, kas'ə-) ***n.*** ⟦after G. *Casanova* (1725-98), It adventurer⟧ a man who has many love affairs

cas·cade (kas kād') ***n.*** ⟦Fr < L *cadere,* to fall⟧ **1** a small, steep waterfall **2** anything resembling this, as a shower of sparks —***vt., vi.*** **-cad'ed, -cad'ing** to fall or drop in a cascade

cas·car·a (kas ker'ə) ***n.*** ⟦Sp *cáscara,* bark⟧ a thorny tree growing on the Pacific coast of the U.S.

case[1] (kās) ***n.*** ⟦< L *casus,* a chance < *cadere,* to fall⟧ **1** an example or instance *[a case of flu]* **2** a person being helped, as by a doctor **3** any matter requiring study or investigation **4** *a)* the argument of one side, as in a law court *b)* convincing arguments *[he has no case]* **5** a lawsuit **6** *Gram.* the syntactic function of a noun or pronoun *[nominative, objective, or possessive case]* —***vt.*** **cased, cas'ing** [Slang] to look over carefully —**in any**

THESAURUS

carriage ***n.*** **1** [The manner of carrying the body] walk, pace, step, attitude, aspect, presence, look, cast, gait, bearing, posture, pose, mien, demeanor, poise, air; see also BEHAVIOR. **2** [A horse-drawn passenger vehicle] buggy, surrey, coach, coach-and-four, buckboard, cart, dogcart, two-wheeler, trap, gig, sulky, hansom, coupe, four-wheeler, stagecoach, chariot, hack, hackney coach; see also WAGON.

carrier ***n.*** aircraft carrier, escort carrier, flattop*; see SHIP.

carry ***v.*** **1** [To transport] convey, move, transplant, transfer, cart, import, transmit, freight, remove, conduct, bear, take, bring, shift, haul, change, convoy, relocate, relay, lug, tote, fetch; see also SEND 1. **2** [To transmit] pass on, transfer, relay; see SEND 1. **3** [To support weight] bear, sustain, shoulder; see SUPPORT 1. **4** [To give support] corroborate, back up, confirm; see APPROVE, SUPPORT 2, STRENGTHEN. —**carried away** zealous, aroused, exuberant; see EXCITED. —**carry on 1** [To continue] keep going, proceed, persist; see ACHIEVE, CONTINUE 1, 2, ENDURE 1. **2** [To manage] conduct, engage in, administer; see MANAGE 1. **3** [To behave badly] blunder, be indecorous, raise Cain*; see MISBEHAVE. —**carry out** complete, accomplish, fulfill; see ACHIEVE, COMPLETE, SUCCEED 1. —**carry over** continue, persist, survive; see ENDURE 1.

carry (oneself) ***v.*** appear, seem, behave; see ACT 2, WALK 1.

carry-over ***n.*** holdover, vestige, remains; see REMAINDER.

cart ***n.*** truck, wheelbarrow, little wagon, tip cart, handcart, gig, dray, two-wheeler, pushcart, go-cart, two-wheeled cart; see also CARRIAGE 2, WAGON. —**put the cart before the horse** reverse, be illogical, err; see MISTAKE.

cartoon ***n.*** animation, animated film, anime; comic, comics, comic strip, funnies*.

carve ***v.*** create, form, hew, chisel, engrave, etch, sculpt, incise, mold, fashion, cut, shape, model, tool, block out, scrape, pattern, trim; see also CUT 1, ENGRAVE.

carved ***a.*** incised, graven, cut, chiseled, chased, furrowed, formed, hewn, hewed, etched, sculptured, scratched, slashed, done in relief, scrolled, grooved, sliced, scissored; see also ENGRAVED.—*Ant.* PLAIN, molded, cast.

case[1,2] ***n.*** **1** [An example] instance, illustration, sample; see EXAMPLE 1. **2** [Actual conditions] incident, occurrence, fact; see CIRCUMSTANCE 1, EVENT, FACT 2, STATE. **3** [A legal action] suit, litigation, lawsuit; see TRIAL 2. **4** [An organized argument] argument, petition, evidence; see CLAIM, PROOF 1. **5** [A container or its contents] carton, canister, crate, crating, box, baggage, trunk, casing, chest, drawer, holder, tray, receptacle, coffer, crib, chamber, bin, bag, grip, cabinet, sheath, scabbard, wallet, safe, basket, casket; see also CONTAINER. —**in any case** in any event, anyway, however; see ANYHOW. —**in case** in the event that, provided, if it should happen that; see IF. —**in case of** in the event of, in order to be prepared for, as a provision against; see IF.

case anyhow —**in case** in the event that; if —**in case of** in the event of —**in no case** never

case[2] (kās) ***n.*** ⟦< L *capsa*, box⟧ **1** a container, as a box **2** a protective cover *[*a watch *case]* **3** a full box or its contents *[*a *case* of beer*]* **4** a frame, as for a window —***vt.*** **cased, cas′ing 1** to put in a container **2** to enclose; encase

case′hard′en (-härd′'n) ***vt.*** *Metallurgy* to form a hard surface on (an iron alloy)

ca·se·in (kā′sē in, -sēn′) ***n.*** ⟦< L *caseus*, cheese⟧ a protein that is one of the chief constituents of milk

case′load′ ***n.*** the number of cases handled by a court, social agency, etc.

case′ment (-mənt) ***n.*** ⟦ult. < OFr *enchassement*⟧ a window frame that opens on hinges along the side

case′work′ ***n.*** social work in which guidance is given in cases of personal or family maladjustment —**case′work′er** ***n.***

cash (kash) ***n.*** ⟦< L *capsa*, box⟧ **1** money that a person actually has; esp., ready money **2** bills and coins **3** money, a check, etc. paid at the time of purchase —***vt.*** to give or get cash for —***adj.*** of or for cash —**cash in** to exchange for cash

cash·ew (kash′o͞o; *also*, kə sho͞o′) ***n.*** ⟦< AmInd (Brazil) *acajú*⟧ **1** a tropical tree bearing kidney-shaped nuts **2** the nut

cash·ier[1] (ka shir′) ***n.*** ⟦Fr⟧ a person handling the cash transactions of a bank or store

cash·ier[2] (ka shir′) ***vt.*** ⟦< LL *cassare*, destroy⟧ to dismiss in dishonor

cash·mere (kash′mir′, kazh′-) ***n.*** ⟦after *Kashmir*, region in India⟧ **1** a fine carded wool from goats of N India and Tibet **2** a soft, twilled cloth as of this wool

cash register a device, usually with a money drawer, used for registering visibly the amount of a sale

cas·ing (kās′iŋ) ***n.*** **1** the skin of a sausage **2** the outer covering of a pneumatic tire **3** a frame, as for a door

ca·si·no (kə sē′nō) ***n.***, *pl.* **-nos** ⟦It < *casa*, house⟧ **1** a room or building for dancing, gambling, etc. **2** a card game for two to four players

cask (kask) ***n.*** ⟦ult. < L *quassare*, shatter⟧ **1** a barrel of any size, esp. one for liquids **2** its contents

cas·ket (kas′kit) ***n.*** ⟦< NormFr *casse*, box⟧ **1** a small box or chest, as for valuables **2** a coffin

Cas·pi·an (Sea) (kas′pē ən) inland salt sea between Asia and extreme SE Europe

Cas·san·dra (kə san′drə) ***n.*** *Gr. Myth.* a Trojan prophetess of doom whose prophecies are never believed

cas·sa·va (kə sä′və) ***n.*** ⟦< Fr < WInd *casávi*⟧ **1** a tropical American plant with starchy roots **2** a starch made from these roots, used in tapioca

cas·se·role (kas′ə rōl′) ***n.*** ⟦Fr < Gr *kyathos*, a bowl⟧ **1** a baking dish in which food can be cooked and served **2** the food baked in such a dish

cas·sette (kə set′, ka-) ***n.*** ⟦< NormFr *casse*, box⟧ a case with magnetic tape or film in it, for loading a tape recorder, VCR, camera, etc. quickly

cas·sia (kash′ə, kas′ē ə) ***n.*** ⟦ult. < Heb *qeṣīʿāh*, lit., something scraped off⟧ **1** *a)* the bark of a tree of SE Asia: a source of cinnamon *b)* the tree **2** any of various tropical plants whose leaves yield senna

cas·si·no (kə sē′nō) ***n.*** *alt. sp. of* CASINO

cas·sock (kas′ək) ***n.*** ⟦prob. < Turk *qazaq*, nomad⟧ a long, closefitting vestment worn by clergymen, etc.

cast (kast) ***vt.*** **cast, cast′ing** ⟦< ON *kasta*⟧ **1** to throw with force; hurl **2** to deposit (a ballot or vote) **3** to direct *[*to *cast* one's eyes*]* **4** to project *[*to *cast* light*]* **5** to throw off or shed (a skin) **6** to shape (molten metal, etc.) by pouring into a mold **7** to select (an actor) for (a role or play) **8** to calculate —***vi.*** to throw —***n.*** **1** a casting; throw **2** *a)* something formed in a mold *b)* a mold or impression **3** a plaster form for immobilizing a broken limb **4** the set of actors in a play, movie, etc. **5** an appearance, as of features **6** a kind; quality **7** a tinge; shade —**cast about** to look *(for)* —**cast aside** (or **away** or **off**) to discard

cas·ta·nets (kas′tə nets′) ***pl.n.*** ⟦< Sp < L *castanea*, chestnut: from the shape⟧ a pair of small, hollowed pieces of hard wood or ivory, clicked together in the hand in time to music

cast′a·way′ ***n.*** a shipwrecked person —***adj.*** **1** discarded **2** shipwrecked

caste (kast) ***n.*** ⟦Fr < L *castus*, pure⟧ **1** any of the hereditary Hindu social classes of a formerly segregated system of India **2** any exclusive group **3** rigid class distinction based on birth, wealth, etc. —**lose caste** to lose social status

cast′er ***n.*** **1** a container for vinegar, oil, etc. at the table **2** any of a set of small wheels for supporting and moving furniture

cas·ti·gate (kas′ti gāt′) ***vt.*** **-gat′ed, -gat′ing** ⟦< L *castigare*⟧ to rebuke severely, esp. by public criticism —**cas′ti·ga′tion** ***n.*** —**cas′ti·ga′tor** ***n.***

cast′ing ***n.*** a thing, esp. of metal, cast in a mold

cast iron a hard, brittle alloy of iron used for casting —**cast′-i′ron** ***adj.***

cas·tle (kas′əl) ***n.*** ⟦< L *castrum*, fort⟧ **1** a large, fortified building or group of buildings **2** any massive dwelling like this **3** *Chess* ROOK[2]

cast′off′ ***adj.*** discarded; abandoned —***n.*** a person or thing cast off

cas·tor-oil plant (kas′tər oil′) a tropical plant with large seeds that yield an oil (**castor oil**) used as a cathartic

cas·trate (kas′trāt′) ***vt.*** **-trat′ed, -trat′ing** ⟦< L *castrare*⟧ to remove the testicles of; emasculate —**cas·tra′tion** ***n.***

cas·u·al (kazh′o͞o əl) ***adj.*** ⟦< L *casus*, chance⟧ **1** happening by chance; not planned; incidental **2** occasional **3** careless or cursory **4** nonchalant **5** *a)* informal *b)* for informal use —**cas′u·al·ly** ***adv.*** —**cas′u·al·ness** ***n.***

cas·u·al·ty (kazh′o͞o əl tē) ***n.***, *pl.* **-ties** **1** an accident, esp. a fatal one **2** a member of the armed forces killed, wounded, captured, etc. **3** anyone hurt or killed in an accident **4** anything lost, destroyed, etc.

cas·u·ist·ry (kazh′o͞o is trē) ***n.***, *pl.* **-ries** ⟦< L *casus*, CASE[1]⟧ subtle but false reasoning, esp. about moral issues; sophistry —**cas′u·ist** ***n.***

cat (kat) ***n.*** ⟦OE⟧ **1** a small, soft-furred animal, often kept as a pet or for killing mice **2** any flesh-eating mammal related to this, as the lion, tiger, leopard, etc. **3** a spiteful woman —**let the cat out of the bag** to let a secret be found out

cat·a·clysm (kat′ə kliz′əm) ***n.*** ⟦< Gr *kata-*, down + *klyzein*, to wash⟧ any sudden, violent change, as in war —**cat′a·clys′mic** (-kliz′mik) ***adj.***

cat·a·comb (kat′ə kōm′) ***n.*** ⟦< ? L *cata*, by + *tumba*, tomb⟧

THESAURUS

cash ***n.*** money in hand, ready money, liquid assets, currency, legal tender, principal, available means, working assets, funds, payment, capital, finances, stock, resources, wherewithal, investments, savings, riches, reserve, treasure, moneys, security; ready cash, cold cash, hard cash, cash on the barrelhead; see also MONEY 1, WEALTH.

cash ***v.*** cash in, change, draw; see PAY 1. —**cash in** realize, change, exchange, turn into money, discharge, draw, pay.

cashier[1] ***n.*** purser, treasurer, receiver; see CLERK.

cast ***n.*** **1** [A plaster reproduction] facsimile, duplicate, replica; see COPY, SCULPTURE. **2** [Those in a play] persons in the play, cast of characters, players, roles, parts, dramatis personae, company, troupe, producers, dramatic artists. **3** [Aspect] complexion, face, appearance; see LOOKS. **4** [A surgical dressing] plaster-of-Paris dressing, plaster cast, arm cast, leg cast, knee cast, body cast, traction, splints; see also DRESSING 3. **5** [A tinge] hue, shade, tint; see COLOR.

cast ***v.*** **1** [To throw] pitch, fling, hurl; see THROW 1. **2** [To form in a mold] shape, roughcast, wetcast; see FORM 1. **3** [To select actors for a play] appoint, designate, decide upon, determine, pick, give parts, detail, name; see also ASSIGN, CHOOSE. —**cast away** dispose of, reject, throw out; see ABANDON 1. —**cast off** reject, jettison, throw away; see ABANDON 1.

castle ***n.*** stronghold, manor, seat, villa, fortress, château, citadel, keep, fort, hold, safehold; see also FORTIFICATION.

castrate ***v.*** emasculate, sterilize, asexualize, mutilate, cut, spay, geld, unman, steer, caponize, effeminize, deprive of manhood; see also MAIM.

casual ***a.*** **1** [Accidental] chance, unexpected, unplanned; see SPONTANEOUS. **2** [Nonchalant] blasé, apathetic, unconcerned; see CARELESS, INDIFFERENT.

casually ***a.*** **1** [Accidentally] unintentionally, by chance, inadvertently; see ACCIDENTALLY. **2** [Nonchalantly] indifferently, coolly, unemotionally; see CARELESSLY, EASILY.

casualty ***n.*** fatality, loss, death toll; see LOSS 3.

cat ***n.*** **1** [A domestic animal] tomcat, kitten, kit, tabby, puss*, pussy*, mouser, kitty*. *House cats include the following:* Maltese, Persian, Siamese, Angora, shorthair, tortoise shell, alley, tiger, calico; see also ANIMAL. **2** [A member of the cat family] feline, lion, tiger, leopard, puma, wildcat, cheetah, lynx, bobcat, mountain lion, caracal, serval, panther, ocelot, cougar, jaguar; see also ANIMAL. —**let the cat out of the bag** expose, tell a secret, let slip; see REVEAL.

a gallery in an underground burial place: *usually used in pl.*

cat′a·falque′ (-falk′, -fôlk′) ***n.*** ⟦Fr < It *catafalco*, funeral canopy⟧ a wooden framework on which a body in a coffin lies in state

cat′a·lep′sy (-lep′sē) ***n.*** ⟦< Gr *katalēpsis*, a seizing⟧ a condition of muscle rigidity and sudden, temporary loss of consciousness, as in epilepsy —**cat′a·lep′tic *adj.*, *n.***

cat·a·log or **cat·a·logue** (kat′ə lôg′) ***n.*** ⟦< Gr *kata-*, down + *legein*, to count⟧ a complete list, as a card file of the books in a library, a list of articles for sale, etc. —***vt.*, *vi.*** **-loged′** or **-logued′**, **-log′ing** or **-logu′ing** to arrange (an item or items) in a catalog —**cat′a·log′er** or **cat′a·logu′er *n.***

ca·tal·pa (kə tal′pə) ***n.*** ⟦< AmInd⟧ a tree with heart-shaped leaves and slender, beanlike pods

ca·tal·y·sis (kə tal′ə sis) ***n.***, *pl.* **-ses′** (-sēz′) ⟦< Gr *katalysis*, dissolution⟧ the speeding up or, sometimes, slowing down of a chemical reaction by adding a substance which itself is not changed thereby

cat·a·lyst (kat′ə list) ***n.*** **1** a substance serving as the agent in catalysis **2** anything bringing about or hastening a result —**cat′a·lyt′ic** (-lit′ik) ***adj.***

catalytic converter a chemical filter connected to the exhaust system of an automotive vehicle, to reduce air pollution

cat·a·ma·ran (kat′ə mə ran′) ***n.*** ⟦Tamil *kaṭṭumaram*⟧ **1** a narrow log raft propelled by sails or paddles **2** a boat like this with two parallel hulls

cat·a·mount (kat′ə mount′) ***n.*** a wildcat, esp. a cougar or lynx

cat·a·pult (kat′ə pult′) ***n.*** ⟦< Gr *kata-*, down + *pallein*, to hurl⟧ **1** an ancient military contrivance for throwing large stones, etc. **2** a device for launching an airplane, missile, etc. as from a deck or ramp —***vt.*** to shoot or launch as from a catapult —***vi.*** to leap

cat·a·ract (kat′ə rakt′) ***n.*** ⟦< Gr *kata-*, down + *rhassein*, to strike or ? *arassein*, to smite⟧ **1** a large waterfall **2** *a*) an eye disease in which the lens becomes opaque, causing partial or total blindness *b*) the opaque area

ca·tas·tro·phe (kə tas′trə fē) ***n.*** ⟦< Gr *kata-*, down + *strephein*, to turn⟧ any great and sudden disaster —**cat·a·stroph·ic** (kat′ə sträf′ik) ***adj.***

cat·a·ton·ic (kat′ə tän′ik) ***adj.*** ⟦< Gr *kata-*, down + *tonos*, tension⟧ of or having a psychiatric condition involving catalepsy —***n.*** a catatonic person

cat′bird′ ***n.*** a slate-gray North American songbird with a call like a cat's

cat′boat′ ***n.*** a sailboat with a single sail on a mast set well forward

cat′call′ ***n.*** a shrill shout or whistle expressing derision, etc. —***vi.*** to make catcalls

catch (kach, kech) ***vt.*** **caught**, **catch′ing** ⟦< L *capere*, to take hold⟧ **1** to seize and hold; capture **2** to take by a trap **3** to deceive **4** to surprise in some act **5** *a*) to get to in time *[to catch a train]* *b*) to overtake **6** to lay hold of; grab *[to catch a ball]* **7** to become infected with *[he caught a cold]* **8** to understand **9** to cause to be entangled or snagged **10** [Inf.] to see, hear, etc. —***vi.*** **1** to become held, fastened, etc. **2** to take hold, as fire **3** to keep hold, as a lock —***n.*** **1** a catching **2** a thing that catches **3** something caught **4** one worth catching, esp. as a spouse **5** a break in the voice **6** [Inf.] a tricky qualification or condition —**catch at** to seize desperately —**catch on** **1** to understand **2** to become popular —**catch up** **1** to seize; snatch **2** to overtake

catch′all′ ***n.*** a container or place for holding all sorts of things

catch′er ***n.*** *Baseball* the player behind home plate, who catches pitched balls

catch′ing ***adj.*** **1** contagious; infectious **2** attractive

catch′phrase′ ***n.*** a phrase that has become popular

catch′up′ (-up′) ***n.*** KETCHUP

catch′y ***adj.*** **-i·er**, **-i·est** **1** attracting attention and easily remembered *[a catchy tune]* **2** tricky

cat·e·chism (kat′ə kiz′əm) ***n.*** ⟦< Gr *kata-*, thoroughly + *ēchein*, to sound⟧ **1** a handbook of questions and answers for teaching the principles of a religion **2** a close questioning

cat·e·gor·i·cal (kat′ə gôr′i kəl) ***adj.*** **1** positive; explicit: said of a statement, etc. **2** of, as, or in a category —**cat′e·gor′i·cal·ly *adv.***

cat·e·go·rize (kat′ə gə rīz′) ***vt.*** **-rized′**, **-riz′ing** to place in a category; classify

cat′e·go′ry (-gôr′ē) ***n.***, *pl.* **-ries** ⟦< Gr *katēgorein*, to assert⟧ a division in a scheme of classification

ca·ter (kāt′ər) ***vi.*** ⟦< L *ad-*, to + *capere*, take hold⟧ **1** to provide food and service, as for parties **2** to seek to gratify another's needs or desires: with *to* —***vt.*** to serve as caterer for (a banquet, etc.) —**ca′ter·er *n.***

cat·er-cor·nered (kat′ə kôr′nərd, kat′ē-) ***adj.*** ⟦< OFr *catre*, four + CORNERED⟧ diagonal —***adv.*** diagonally Also **cat′er-cor′ner**

cat·er·pil·lar (kat′ər pil′ər, kat′ə-) ***n.*** ⟦< L *catta pilosus*, hairy cat⟧ the wormlike larva of a butterfly, moth, etc. —[**C-**] *trademark for* a kind of tractor for rough or muddy ground

cat·er·waul (kat′ər wôl′) ***vi.*** ⟦prob. echoic⟧ to make a shrill sound like that of a cat; wail —***n.*** such a sound

cat′fight′ ***n.*** [Inf.] a fight between two women

cat′fish′ ***n.***, *pl.* **-fish′** or (for different species) **-fish′es** a fish with long, whiskerlike feelers about the mouth

cat′gut′ ***n.*** a tough thread made from dried intestines, as of sheep, and used for surgical sutures, etc.

ca·thar·sis (kə thär′sis) ***n.*** ⟦< Gr *katharos*, pure⟧ a relieving of emotional tensions, as through the arts or psychotherapy

ca·thar′tic (-tik) ***adj.*** purging —***n.*** a medicine for purging the bowels; purgative

ca·the·dral (kə thē′drəl) ***n.*** ⟦< Gr *kata-*, down + *hedra*, a seat⟧ **1** the main church of a bishop's see **2** any large, imposing church

cath·e·ter (kath′ət ər) ***n.*** ⟦< Gr *kata-*, down + *hienai*, to send⟧ a slender tube inserted into a body passage, as into the bladder for drawing off urine —**cath′e·ter·ize′** (-īz′), **-ized′**, **-iz′ing**, ***vt.*** —**cath′e·ter·i·za′tion *n.***

cath·ode (kath′ōd′) ***n.*** ⟦< Gr < *kata-*, down + -ODE⟧ **1** the negative electrode in an electrolytic cell **2** the electron emitter in an electron tube **3** the positive terminal of a battery

cathode rays streams of electrons projected from a cathode: they produce X-rays when they strike solids

cath′ode-ray′ tube a vacuum tube in which a stream of electrons can be focused on a fluorescent screen: such tubes are used as picture tubes, etc.

cath·o·lic (kath′ ə lik, kath′lik) ***adj.*** ⟦< Gr *kata-*, com-

THESAURUS

catalog ***n.*** register, file, directory, schedule, inventory, index, bulletin, syllabus, brief, slate, table, calendar, list, docket, classification, record, draft, roll, timetable, table of contents, prospectus, program, *catalogue raisonné* (French); see also LIST.

catalog ***v.*** classify, record, index; see LIST 1.

catastrophe ***n.*** calamity, mishap, mischance, misadventure, misery, accident, trouble, casualty, infliction, affliction, stroke, havoc, ravage, wreck, fatality, grief, crash, devastation, desolation, hardship, blow, ruin, reverse, emergency, scourge, convulsion, tragedy, adversity, bad luck, upheaval; see also DISASTER.

catch ***n.*** **1** [A desirable mate] match, sweetheart, fiancé; see LOVER 1. **2** [*A trick] puzzle, trick, trap; see JOKE. **3** [A hook] clasp, clamp, snap; see FASTENER.

catch ***v.*** **1** [To seize hold of] snatch, take, take hold of, snag, grab, pick, pounce on, fasten upon, snare, pluck, hook, claw, clench, clasp, grasp, clutch, grip, nab, net, bag*; see also SEIZE. **2** [To bring into captivity] trap, apprehend, capture; see ARREST, SEIZE 2. **3** [To come to from behind] overtake, reach, come upon; see PASS 1. **4** [To contract a disease] get, fall ill with, become infected with, incur, become subject to, be liable to, fall victim to, take, succumb to, break out with, receive, come down with.—*Ant.* ESCAPE, ward off, get over. —**catch on** **1** [To understand] grasp, comprehend, perceive; see UNDERSTAND 1. **2** [To become popular] become fashionable, become prevalent, become common, become widespread, become acceptable, grow in popularity, find favor; see also SUCCEED 1. —**catch up** catch, join, equal; see REACH 1.

catching ***a.*** contagious, communicable, transmittable, infectious, epidemic, endemic, pestilential, noxious, dangerous, pandemic; see also CONTAGIOUS.

category ***n.*** level, section, classification; see CLASS 1, DIVISION 2, KIND.

cathedral ***n.*** temple, house of God, house of prayer, holy place, basilica, minster; see also CHURCH 1. *Parts of a cathedral include the following:* altar, sanctuary, holy of holies, sacristy, sacrarium, holy table, baptistery, chancel, apse, choir, nave, aisle, transept, crypt, pew, seat, pulpit, confessional. *Famous cathedrals include the following:* St. Peter's (Rome), St. Paul's (London), Notre Dame (Paris), St. Matthew's, Washington National (Washington, D.C.), St. John the Divine, St. Patrick's (New York).

pletely + *holos*, whole] **1** all-inclusive; universal **2** broad in sympathies, tastes, etc. **3** [C-] ROMAN CATHOLIC —*n.* [C-] ROMAN CATHOLIC —**Ca·thol·i·cism** (kə thäl'ə siz'əm) *n.* —**cath·o·lic·i·ty** (kath'ə lis'i tē) *n.*

cat·i·on (kat'ī'ən) *n.* [< Gr *kata*, down + *ienai*, to go] a positively charged ion: in electrolysis, cations move toward the cathode

cat·kin (kat'kin) *n.* [< Du *katte*, cat] a drooping, scaly spike of small flowers without petals, as on poplars, walnuts, etc.

cat'nap' *n.* a short nap; doze —*vi.* **-napped'**, **-nap'ping** to doze briefly

cat'nip' *n.* [CAT + dial. *nep*, catnip] an herb of the mint family: cats like its odor

cat-o'-nine-tails (kat'ə nīn'tālz') *n.*, *pl.* **-tails'** a whip made of nine knotted cords attached to a handle

CAT scan (kat) [*c(omputerized) a(xial) t(omography)*] CT SCAN —**CAT scanner** —**CAT scanning**

cat's cradle a game in which a string looped over the fingers is transferred back and forth on the hands of the players so as to form designs

Cats·kill Mountains (kats'kil') mountain range in SE New York: also **Cats'kills'**

cat's-paw (kats'pô') *n.* a person used to do distasteful or unlawful work

cat·sup (kat'səp) *n.* KETCHUP

cat'tail' *n.* a tall marsh plant with long, brown, fuzzy spikes

cat·tle (kat''l) *pl.n.* [ult. < L *caput*, head] **1** [Archaic] farm animals **2** cows, bulls, steers, or oxen —**cat'tle·man** (-mən), *pl.* **-men** (-mən), *n.*

cat·ty (kat'ē) *adj.* **-ti·er**, **-ti·est** **1** of or like a cat **2** spiteful, mean, malicious, etc. —**cat'ti·ness** *n.*

cat'ty-cor'nered *adj.*, *adv.* CATER-CORNERED: also **cat'ty-cor'ner**

cat'walk' *n.* a narrow, elevated walk

Cau·ca·sian (kô kā'zhən) *adj.* **1** of the Caucasus or its people, etc. **2** CAUCASOID —*n.* **1** a person born or living in the Caucasus **2** CAUCASOID

Cau·ca·soid (kô'kə soid') *adj.* designating or of one of the major geographical varieties of human beings, loosely called the *white race* —*n.* a member of the Caucasoid population

Cau·ca·sus (kô'kə səs) **1** border region between SE Europe & W Asia, between the Black and Caspian seas: often called **the Caucasus** **2** mountain range in this region

cau·cus (kô'kəs) *n.* [< ?] **1** a meeting of a party or faction to decide on policy, pick candidates, etc. **2** the group attending such a meeting **3** a faction of politicians —*vi.* **-cused** or **-cussed**, **-cus·ing** or **-cus·sing** to hold a caucus

cau·dal (kôd''l) *adj.* [< L *cauda*, tail + -AL] of, like, at, or near the tail

caught (kôt) *vt.*, *vi. pt. & pp. of* CATCH

caul (kôl) *n.* the membrane enveloping the head of a child at birth

caul·dron (kôl'drən) *n. alt. sp. of* CALDRON

cau·li·flow·er (kô'lə flou'ər) *n.* [< It *cavolo*, cabbage + *fiore*, flower] **1** a variety of cabbage with a dense white head of fleshy flower stalks **2** the head, eaten as a vegetable

caulk (kôk) *vt.* [< L *calx*, a heel] to stop up (cracks, etc.) of (a boat, etc.) as with a puttylike sealant or oakum —*n.* a soft, puttylike compound used in caulking: also **caulking compound** —**caulk'er** *n.*

caus·al (kôz'əl) *adj.* **1** of, being, or expressing a cause **2** relating to cause and effect —**cau·sal·i·ty** (kô zal'i tē), *pl.* **-ties**, *n.* —**caus'al·ly** *adv.*

cau·sa·tion (kô zā'shən) *n.* **1** a causing **2** a causal agency; anything producing an effect

cause (kôz) *n.* [< L *causa*] **1** anything producing an effect or result **2** a reason or motive for producing an effect **3** any objective or movement that people are interested in and support **4** *Law* a case to be resolved by a court —*vt.* **caused**, **caus'ing** to be the cause of; bring about —**caus'a·tive** *adj.* —**cause'less** *adj.* —**caus'er** *n.*

cau·se·rie (kō'zə rē') *n.* [Fr] **1** a chat **2** a short, informal piece of writing

cause·way (kôz'wā') *n.* [ult. < L *calx*, lime + WAY] a raised path or road, as across wet ground or shallow water

caus·tic (kôs'tik) *adj.* [< Gr *kaiein*, to burn] **1** that can burn tissue by chemical action; corrosive **2** sarcastic; biting —*n.* a caustic substance —**caus'ti·cal·ly** *adv.* —**caus·tic'i·ty** (-tis'i tē) *n.*

cau·ter·ize (kôt'ər īz') *vt.* **-ized'**, **-iz'ing** [see prec.] to burn with a hot needle, a laser, a caustic substance, etc. so as to destroy dead tissue, etc. —**cau'ter·i·za'tion** *n.*

cau·tion (kô'shən) *n.* [< L *cautio*] **1** a warning **2** wariness; prudence —*vt.* to warn —**cau'tion·ar'y** *adj.*

cau·tious (kô'shəs) *adj.* full of caution; careful to avoid danger —**cau'tious·ly** *adv.* —**cau'tious·ness** *n.*

cav·al·cade (kav'əl kād', kav'əl kād') *n.* [Fr < L *caballus*, horse] a procession, as of horsemen, carriages, etc.

cav·a·lier (kav'ə lir') *n.* [Fr: see prec.] **1** an armed horseman; knight **2** a gallant gentleman, esp. a lady's escort —*adj.* **1** casual or indifferent toward important matters **2** arrogant —**cav'a·lier'ly** *adv.*

cav·al·ry (kav'əl rē) *n.*, *pl.* **-ries** [< Fr: see CAVALCADE] combat troops mounted originally on horses but now often riding in motorized armored vehicles —**cav'al·ry·man** (-mən), *pl.* **-men** (-mən), *n.*

cave (kāv) *n.* [< L *cavus*, hollow] a hollow place inside the earth; cavern —*vi.* **caved**, **cav'ing** to cave in —**cave in** **1** to collapse **2** [Inf.] to give in; yield

ca·ve·at emp·tor (kā'vē at' emp'tôr') [L] let the buyer beware

cave'-in' *n.* **1** a caving in **2** a place where the ground, etc. has caved in

cave man a prehistoric human being of the Stone Age who lived in caves

cav·ern (kav'ərn) *n.* a cave, esp. a large cave —**cav'ern·ous** *adj.*

cav·i·ar or **cav·i·are** (kav'ē är') *n.* [Fr < Pers *khāya*, egg + *-dār*, bearing] the salted eggs of sturgeon, etc. eaten as an appetizer

cav·il (kav'əl) *vi.* **-iled** or **-illed**, **-il·ing** or **-il·ling** [< L *cavilla*, jeering] to object unnecessarily; quibble —*n.* a trivial objection; quibble —**cav'il·er** or **cav'il·ler** *n.*

cav·i·ty (kav'i tē) *n.*, *pl.* **-ties** [see CAVE] **1** a natural hollow place within the body **2** a hollow place, as one caused by decay in a tooth

ca·vort (kə vôrt') *vi.* [< ?] **1** to prance or caper **2** to romp; frolic

caw (kô) *n.* [echoic] the harsh cry of a crow —*vi.* to make this sound

cay·enne (pepper) (kī en', kā-) [< AmInd (Brazil) *kynnha*] very hot red pepper made from the dried fruit of a pepper plant

cay·use (kī'yo͞os', kī yo͞os') *n.*, *pl.* **-us'es** or **-use'** [< AmInd tribal name] a small Western horse used by cowboys

CB (sē'bē') *adj.* [*c(itizens') b(and)*] designating or of shortwave radio frequencies set aside by the FCC for local use by private persons or businesses

cc *abbrev.* **1** carbon copy **2** cubic centimeter(s)

CD (sē'dē') *n.* a compact disc

Cd *Chem. symbol for* cadmium

CDC *abbrev.* Centers for Disease Control and Prevention

Cdn *abbrev.* Canadian

CD-ROM (sē'dē'räm') *n.* a compact disc on which stored data can be accessed

THESAURUS

cattle *n.* stock, cows, steers, calves, herd, beef cattle, dairy cattle; see also COW.

caucus *n.* assembly, meeting, council; see GATHERING.

caught *a.* taken, seized, arrested; see CAPTURED, UNDER ARREST.

cause *n.* **1** [Purpose] motive, causation, object, end, explanation, inducement, incitement, prime mover, motive power, mainspring, ultimate cause, ground, matter, element, stimulation, instigation, foundation, the why and wherefore; see also BASIS, REASON 3.—*Ant.* RESULT, effect, outcome. **2** [Moving force] agent, case, condition; see CIRCUMSTANCES. **3** [A belief] principles, conviction, creed; see BELIEF, FAITH 2.

cause *v.* originate, provoke, generate, occasion, let, kindle, give rise to, lie at the root of, be at the bottom of, bring to pass, bring into effect, sow the seeds of; see also BEGIN.

caution *n.* care, heed, discretion; see ATTENTION, PRUDENCE.

caution *v.* forewarn, alert, advise; see WARN.

cautious *a.* circumspect, watchful, wary; see CAREFUL.

cautiously *a.* tentatively, prudently, discreetly, watchfully, wisely, sparingly, thoughtfully, heedfully, delicately, mindfully, anxiously, with care, with caution, gingerly, with forethought, slowly.

cave *n.* rock shelter, cavern, grotto; see HOLE.

cavern *n.* cave, hollow, grotto; see HOLE.

cavity *n.* **1** [Sunken area] pit, depression, basin; see HOLE. **2** [Hollow place in a tooth] caries, distal pit, gingival pit; see DECAY.

cease (sēs) ***vt., vi.*** **ceased, ceas′ing** ⟦see CEDE⟧ to end; stop

cease′-fire′ ***n.*** a temporary cessation of warfare; truce

cease′less ***adj.*** unceasing; continual

ce·cum (sē′kəm) ***n.***, *pl.* **-ca** (-kə) ⟦< L *caecus*, blind⟧ the pouch at the beginning of the large intestine

ce·dar (sē′dər) ***n.*** ⟦< Gr *kedros*⟧ **1** a pine tree having fragrant, durable wood **2** its wood —***adj.*** of cedar

cede (sēd) ***vt.*** **ced′ed, ced′ing** ⟦< L *cedere*, to yield⟧ **1** to surrender formally **2** to transfer the title of

ce·dil·la (sə dil′ə) ***n.*** ⟦Sp dim. of *zeda*, a zeta or *z*⟧ a hooklike mark put under *c*, as in some French words (Ex.: *façade*) to show that it has an *s* sound

ceil·ing (sēl′iŋ) ***n.*** ⟦< L *caelum*, heaven⟧ **1** the inside top part of a room, opposite the floor **2** an upper limit *[a price ceiling]* **3** *Aeronautics* cloud cover affecting visibility, or the height of this —**hit the ceiling** [Slang] to lose one's temper

cel·an·dine (sel′ən dīn′, -dēn′) ***n.*** **1** a plant related to the poppy, with yellow flowers **2** a plant of the buttercup family, with yellow flowers

cel·e·brate (sel′ə brāt′) ***vt.*** **-brat′ed, -brat′ing** ⟦< L *celebrare*, to honor⟧ **1** to perform (a ritual, etc.) **2** to commemorate (an anniversary, holiday, etc.) with festivity **3** to honor publicly —***vi.*** to mark a happy occasion with festive activities —**cel′e·brant** (-brənt) ***n.*** —**cel·e·bra′tion** ***n.*** —**cel′e·bra′tor** ***n.***

cel′e·brat′ed ***adj.*** famous; renowned

ce·leb·ri·ty (sə leb′rə tē) ***n.*** **1** fame **2** *pl.* **-ties** a famous person

ce·ler·i·ty (sə ler′i tē) ***n.*** ⟦< L *celer*, swift⟧ swiftness; speed

cel·er·y (sel′ər ē, sel′rē) ***n.*** ⟦< Gr *selinon*, parsley⟧ a plant whose crisp leafstalks are eaten as a vegetable

ce·les·tial (sə les′chəl) ***adj.*** ⟦< L *caelum*, heaven⟧ **1** of or in the sky or universe **2** of heaven; divine **3** of the finest kind

cel·i·ba·cy (sel′ə bə sē) ***n.*** **1** the state of being unmarried **2** sexual abstinence

cel·i·bate (sel′ə bət) ***n.*** ⟦< L *caelebs*⟧ **1** an unmarried person **2** one who abstains from sexual intercourse —***adj.*** of or in a state of celibacy

cell (sel) ***n.*** ⟦< L *cella*⟧ **1** a small room, as in a prison **2** a small hollow, as in a honeycomb **3** a small unit of protoplasm: all plants and animals are made up of one or more cells **4** a container holding an electrolyte, used to generate electricity **5** a small unit of an organization —**celled** ***adj.***

cel·lar (sel′ər) ***n.*** ⟦see prec.⟧ a room or rooms below ground and usually under a building

cel·lo (chel′ō) ***n.***, *pl.* **-los** or **-li** (-ē) ⟦< VIOLONCELLO⟧ an instrument of the violin family, between the viola and double bass in size and pitch —**cel′list** ***n.***

cel·lo·phane (sel′ə fān′) ***n.*** ⟦< CELLULOSE⟧ a thin, clear material made from cellulose, used as a wrapping

cell′phone′ ***n.*** *short for* CELLULAR PHONE

cel·lu·lar (sel′yo͞o lər) ***adj.*** of, like, or containing a cell or cells

cellular phone a mobile radio phone used in a communications system of geographically distributed transmitters: also **cellular telephone**

cel·lu·lite (sel′yo͞o līt′) ***n.*** ⟦Fr⟧ fatty deposits on the hips and thighs: a nonmedical term

cel·lu·loid (sel′yo͞o loid′) ***n.*** ⟦fol. + -OID⟧ a tough, flammable plastic substance used, esp. formerly, for making various articles, photographic film, etc.

cel·lu·lose (sel′yo͞o lōs′) ***n.*** ⟦Fr < L *cella*, cell + -OSE[1]⟧ the chief substance in the cell walls of plants, used in making paper, textiles, etc.

cellulose acetate any of several nonflammable thermoplastics, used in making lacquers, etc.

ce·lo·sia (sə lō′shə, -sē ə) ***n.*** an annual garden plant with large clusters of tiny, brilliant red or yellow flowers

Cel·si·us (sel′sē əs) ***adj.*** ⟦after A. *Celsius* (1701-44), Swed astronomer, the inventor⟧ designating or of a thermometer on which 0° is the freezing point and 100° is the boiling point of water

Celt (kelt; *also* selt) ***n.*** ⟦< L⟧ a Celtic-speaking person

Celt′ic ***adj.*** of the Celts, their languages, etc. —***n.*** a subfamily of languages including Gaelic and Welsh

ce·ment (sə ment′) ***n.*** ⟦< L *caementum*, rough stone⟧ **1** a powdered substance of lime and clay, mixed with water and sand to make mortar or with water, sand, and gravel to make concrete: it hardens upon drying **2** CONCRETE **3** anything that bonds —***vt.*** **1** to unite as with cement **2** to cover with cement

cem·e·ter·y (sem′ə ter′ē) ***n.***, *pl.* **-ies** ⟦< Gr < *koiman*, to put to sleep⟧ a place for the burial of the dead

cen·o·bite (sen′ə bīt′) ***n.*** ⟦< Gr < *koinos*, common + *bios*, life⟧ a member of a religious order living in a monastery or convent

cen·o·taph (sen′ə taf′) ***n.*** ⟦< Gr *kenos*, empty + *taphos*, tomb⟧ a monument honoring a dead person whose remains are elsewhere

Ce·no·zo·ic (sē′nə zō′ik, sen′ə-) ***adj.*** ⟦*ceno-* (< Gr *kainos*, recent) + ZO(O)- + -IC⟧ designating the geologic era that includes the present, during which the various mammals have developed

cen·ser (sen′sər) ***n.*** a container in which incense is burned

cen·sor (sen′sər) ***n.*** ⟦L < *censere*, to judge⟧ an official with the power to examine literature, mail, etc. and remove or prohibit anything considered obscene, objectionable, etc. —***vt.*** to subject (a book, etc.) to a censor's examination —**cen′sor·ship′** ***n.***

cen·so·ri·ous (sen sôr′ē əs) ***adj.*** inclined to find fault; harshly critical

cen·sure (sen′shər) ***n.*** ⟦< L *censor*, censor⟧ strong disapproval; condemnation —***vt.*** **-sured, -sur·ing** to condemn as wrong —**cen′sur·a·ble** ***adj.***

cen·sus (sen′səs) ***n.*** ⟦L < *censere*, enroll⟧ an official count of population and gathering of demographic data

THESAURUS

cease ***v.*** desist, terminate, discontinue; see HALT, STOP 1, 2.

ceaseless ***a.*** continual, endless, unending; see CONSTANT, ETERNAL.

celebrate ***v.*** **1** [To recognize an occasion] keep, observe, consecrate, hallow, dedicate, commemorate, honor, proclaim, ritualize.—*Ant.* FORGET, overlook, neglect. **2** [To indulge in celebration] feast, give a party, carouse, rejoice, kill the fatted calf, revel, go on a spree, make whoopee*, blow off steam*, let off steam*, have a party, have a ball*, kick up one's heels*, let loose*, let go, live it up*, whoop it up*, make merry, kick up a row*, party*.

celebrated ***a.*** renowned, well-known, noted; see FAMOUS, IMPORTANT 2.

celebration ***n.*** commemoration, holiday, anniversary, jubilee, inauguration, installation, coronation, presentation, carnival, revelry, spree, festivity, festival, feast, merrymaking, gaiety, frolic, hilarity, joviality, merriment, remembrance, ceremonial, observance, fete, Mardi Gras, birthday.

celebrity ***n.*** famous man, famous woman, hero, heroine, leader, notable, magnate, dignitary, worthy, figure, personage, famous person, person of note, someone, somebody, VIP*, luminary, lion, lioness, star, superstar, bigwig*, big gun*, big shot*, big name.

cell ***n.*** **1** [A unit of a living organism] corpuscle, cellule, microorganism, vacuole, spore, plastid, organism, egg, ectoplasm, protoplasm, cytoplasm, embryo, germ, follicle. **2** [A room] vault, hold, pen, cage, tower, hole, coop, keep, bastille, chamber, den, recess, retreat, alcove, manger, crypt, crib, nook, burrow, stall, closet, booth, cloister, compartment, lockup; see also ROOM 2.

cellar ***n.*** half basement, underground room, basement apartment; see BASEMENT.

cement ***n.*** glue, putty, tar, gum, mortar, paste, adhesive, rubber cement, epoxy, bond.

cement ***v.*** mortar, plaster, connect; see FASTEN, JOIN 1.

cemetery ***n.*** burial ground, memorial park, funerary grounds, churchyard, necropolis, potter's field, catacomb, mausoleum, tomb, vault, crypt, charnel house, sepulcher, graveyard, mortuary, last resting place, Golgotha, boneyard*.

censor ***n.*** inspector, judge, expurgator, bowdlerizer, guardian of morals; see also EXAMINER.

censor ***v.*** control, restrict, strike out, forbid, suppress, ban, withhold, inspect, oversee, abridge, expurgate, bowdlerize, bleep, review, criticize, exert pressure, conceal, prevent publication, blacklist, blue-pencil, cut, black out; see also RESTRICT.

censorship ***n.*** licensing, restriction, forbidding, controlling the press, infringing the right of freedom of speech, governmental control, security blackout, news blackout, thought control, thought police*; see also RESTRAINT.

censure ***n.*** criticism, reproof, admonition; see BLAME, OBJECTION.

censure ***v.*** **1** [To blame] criticize, judge, disapprove; see BLAME. **2** [To scold] rebuke, reprove, attack; see SCOLD.

census ***n.*** statistics, enumeration, valuation, account, registration, listing, evaluation, demography, figures, statement, numbering, registering, roll call, tabulation, tally, poll, count,

cent[1] (sent) ***n.*** ⟦< L *centum*, hundred⟧ a 100th part of a dollar, or a coin of this value; penny
cent[2] *abbrev.* century; centuries
cen·taur (sen′tôr′) ***n.*** ⟦< Gr *Kentauros*⟧ *Gr. Myth.* a monster with a man's head, trunk, and arms, and a horse's body and legs
cen·ta·vo (sen tä′vō) ***n.***, *pl.* **-vos** ⟦Sp, a hundredth < L *centum*, hundred⟧ a 100th part of the monetary unit of various countries
cen·te·nar·i·an (sen′tə ner′ē ən) ***n.*** ⟦< fol.⟧ a person at least 100 years old
cen·te·nar·y (sen′tə ner′ē, sen ten′ər ē) ***adj.*** ⟦< L < *centum*, hundred⟧ **1** of a century **2** of a centennial —***n.***, *pl.* **-ies** CENTENNIAL
cen·ten·ni·al (sen ten′ē əl) ***adj.*** ⟦< L *centum*, hundred + *annus*, year + -AL⟧ of or lasting 100 years —***n.*** a 100th anniversary or its commemoration
cen·ter (sent′ər) ***n.*** ⟦< Gr *kentron*, sharp point⟧ **1** a point equally distant from all points on the circumference of a circle or surface of a sphere **2** a pivot **3** the approximate middle point or part of anything **4** a focal point of activity **5** [*often* **C-**] a group or position between the left (liberals) and right (conservatives) **6** *Sports* a player whose position is at the center of the line or playing area —***vt.*** **1** to place in or near the center **2** to gather to one place —***vi.*** to be focused
cen′ter·board′ ***n.*** a movable board or plate that, when lowered through a slot in the floor of a sailboat, functions like a keel
cen′ter·fold′ ***n.*** the center facing pages of a magazine, often with an extra fold, showing a photograph, as of a nude woman or man
center of gravity that point in a body or system around which its weight is evenly balanced
cen′ter·piece′ ***n.*** an ornament for the center of a table
centi- ⟦L⟧ *combining form* **1** one hundred **2** a 100th part of
cen·ti·grade (sen′tə grād′) ***adj.*** ⟦Fr: see prec. & GRADE⟧ CELSIUS
cen·time (sän′tēm′; *Fr* sän tēm′) ***n.*** ⟦Fr⟧ a 100th part of a franc
cen·ti·me·ter (sen′tə mēt′ər) ***n.*** ⟦Fr: see CENTI- & METER[1]⟧ a unit of measure, $\frac{1}{100}$ meter: Brit. sp. **cen′ti·me′tre**
cen·ti·pede (sen′tə pēd′) ***n.*** ⟦Fr < L *centi-*, CENTI- + *pes*, FOOT⟧ an elongated arthropod with a pair of legs for each body segment
cen·tral (sen′trəl) ***adj.*** ⟦L *centralis*⟧ **1** in, near, or of the center **2** equally accessible from various points **3** main; basic **4** of a controlling source in a system —**cen·tral′i·ty** (-tral′i tē) ***n.*** —**cen′tral·ly** ***adv.***
Central African Republic country in central Africa: 240,324 sq. mi.; pop. 2,568,000
Central America part of North America between Mexico and South America —**Central American**
central city the crowded, industrial, central area of a large city
cen′tral·ize′ (-īz′) ***vt.*** **-ized′**, **-iz′ing** **1** to make central; bring to a center **2** to organize under one control —***vi.*** to become centralized —**cen′tral·i·za′tion** ***n.*** —**cen′tral·iz′er** ***n.***
cen·tre (sent′ər) ***n.***, ***vt.***, ***vi.*** **-tred**, **-tring** *Brit. sp. of* CENTER
centri- *combining form* CENTRO-
cen·trif·u·gal (sen trif′ə gəl) ***adj.*** ⟦< prec. + L *fugere*, to flee + -AL⟧ using or acted on by a force (**centrifugal force**) that tends to make rotating bodies move away from the center of rotation
cen·tri·fuge (sen′trə fyo͞oj′) ***n.*** a machine using centrifugal force to separate particles of varying density
cen·trip·e·tal (sen trip′ət′l) ***adj.*** ⟦< CENTRI- + L *petere*, rush at⟧ using or acted on by a force (**centripetal force**) that tends to make rotating bodies move toward the center of rotation
cen·trist (sen′trist) ***n.*** a person with moderate political opinions —**cen′trism′** ***n.***
centro- ⟦< L *centrum*, center⟧ *combining form* center
cen·tu·ri·on (sen to͝or′ē ən) ***n.*** ⟦see fol.⟧ the commanding officer of an ancient Roman military unit, originally of 100 men
cen·tu·ry (sen′chə rē) ***n.***, *pl.* **-ries** ⟦L < *centum*, hundred⟧ a period of 100 years, esp. as reckoned from A.D.1
CEO *abbrev.* chief executive officer
ce·phal·ic (sə fal′ik) ***adj.*** ⟦< Gr < *kephalē*, head⟧ **1** of the head or skull **2** in, on, near, or toward the head
cephalo- ⟦see prec.⟧ *combining form* the head, skull, or brain
ce·ram·ic (sə ram′ik) ***adj.*** ⟦Gr < *keramos*, potter's clay⟧ **1** of pottery, porcelain, etc. **2** of ceramics —***n.*** **1** [*pl., with sing v.*] the art or work of making pottery, etc. of baked clay **2** an object made of baked clay: *often used in pl.*
ce·ram·ist (ser′ə mist, sə ram′ist) ***n.*** one who works in ceramics; ceramic artist: also **ce·ram·i·cist** (sə ram′ə sist)
ce·re·al (sir′ē əl) ***adj.*** ⟦< L *Cerealis*, of Ceres, Rom goddess of agriculture⟧ of grain —***n.*** **1** any grain used for food, as wheat, rice, etc. **2** any grass producing such grain **3** food made from grain, as oatmeal
cer·e·bel·lum (ser′ə bel′əm) ***n.***, *pl.* **-lums** or **-la** (-ə) ⟦L, dim. of *cerebrum*⟧ the section of the brain behind and below the cerebrum
cer·e·bral (ser′ə brəl, sə rē′-) ***adj.*** **1** of the brain or cerebrum **2** of, by, or for the intellect
cerebral palsy a muscular disorder resulting from damage to the nervous system, esp. at birth
cer·e·brate (ser′ə brāt′) ***vi.*** **-brat′ed**, **-brat′ing** ⟦< L *cerebrum*, the brain + -ATE[1]⟧ to think —**cer′e·bra′tion** ***n.***
cer·e·brum (ser′ə brəm, sə rē′brəm) ***n.***, *pl.* **-brums** or **-bra** (-brə) ⟦L⟧ the upper, main part of the brain of vertebrates
cer·e·ment (ser′ə mənt, sir′mənt) ***n.*** ⟦< Gr *kēros*, wax⟧ [*usually pl.*] a shroud for a dead person
cer·e·mo·ni·al (ser′ə mō′nē əl) ***adj.*** of or consisting of ceremony; formal —***n.*** **1** a system of rites **2** a rite or ceremony —**cer′e·mo′ni·al·ly** ***adv.***
cer′e·mo′ni·ous (-nē əs) ***adj.*** **1** full of ceremony **2** very polite or formal —**cer′e·mo′ni·ous·ly** ***adv.***
cer·e·mo·ny (ser′ə mō′nē) ***n.***, *pl.* **-nies** ⟦< L *caerimonia*⟧ **1** a set of formal acts proper to a special occasion, as a religious rite **2** behavior that follows rigid etiquette **3** *a*) formality *b*) empty or meaningless formality —**stand on ceremony** to insist on formality
ce·rise (sə rēz′, -rēs′) ***n.***, ***adj.*** ⟦< OFr *cerise*, cherry⟧ cherry red
cer·met (sur′met′) ***n.*** ⟦CER(AMIC) + MET(AL)⟧ a bonded mixture of ceramic material and a metal
cert *abbrev.* **1** certificate **2** certified
cer·tain (surt′'n) ***adj.*** ⟦< L *certus*, determined⟧ **1** fixed; settled **2** inevitable **3** reliable; dependable **4** sure; posi-

THESAURUS

counting, head count, nose count; see also COUNT.
cent[1] ***n.*** penny, 100th part of a dollar, red cent*; see MONEY 1.
center ***a.*** mid, middle, inmost, inner, midway, medial, dead-center, deepest, at the inmost, innermost, internal, interior, at the halfway point; see also CENTRAL, MIDDLE.—*Ant.* OUTSIDE, outer, exterior.
center ***n.*** **1** [A central point] point, middle, focus, nucleus, core, place, heart, hub, navel, point of convergence, point of concentration, focal point, midst, middle point, centrality, marrow, kernel, bull's-eye, pivot, axis, pith, dead center; see also MIDDLE. **2** [A point that attracts people] city, town, metropolis, plaza, capital, shopping center, trading center, station, hub, mart, market, crossroads, mall, social center, meeting place, club, market place. **3** [Essence] core, gist, kernel; see CHARACTER 1.
center ***v.*** concentrate, centralize, focus, intensify, unify, unite, combine, converge upon, join, meet, gather, close on, consolidate, bring to a focus, center round, center in, zero in, gather together, flock together, collect, draw together, bring together, focus attention, attract; see also MEET 1.—*Ant.* SPREAD, decentralize, branch off.
central ***a.*** middle, midway, equidistant, medial, focal, nuclear, midmost, mean, inner, median, inmost, middlemost, intermediate, interior, in the center of; see also MIDDLE.—*Ant.* OUTER, peripheral, verging on.
centrally ***a.*** in the middle, focal, middlemost, in the center, in the heart of; see also CENTRAL.
century ***n.*** 100 years, centenary, era; see AGE 3, TIME 1.
ceramics ***n.*** earthenware, crockery, porcelain; see POTTERY, SCULPTURE.
cereal ***n.*** corn, breakfast food, seed; see GRAIN 1.
ceremonial ***a.*** ritual, formal, stately; see CONVENTIONAL 3.
ceremony ***n.*** **1** [A public event] function, commemoration, services; see CELEBRATION. **2** [A rite] observance, ritual, rite, service, solemnity, formality, custom, tradition, liturgy, ordinance, sacrament, liturgical practice, conformity, etiquette, politeness, propriety, preciseness, decorum, strictness, nicety, formalism, conventionality.
certain ***a.*** **1** [Confident] calm, assured, sure, positive, satisfied, self-confident, undoubting, believing, secure, untroubled, unconcerned, undisturbed, unperturbed, fully con-

tive **5** definite, but unnamed *[a certain person]* **6** some *[to a certain extent]* —**for certain** without doubt

cer'tain·ly ***adv.*** undoubtedly; surely

cer'tain·ty ***n.*** **1** the state or fact of being certain **2** *pl.* **-ties** anything certain

cer·tif·i·cate (sər tif'i kit; *for v.*, -kāt') ***n.*** ⟦see CERTIFY⟧ a document attesting to a fact, qualification, etc. —***vt.*** **-cat'ed, -cat'ing** to issue a certificate to

certificate of deposit a bank certificate issued for a specified deposit of money that draws interest and requires written notice for withdrawal

certified public accountant a public accountant certified as having passed a state examination

cer·ti·fy (surt'ə fī') ***vt.*** **-fied', -fy'ing** ⟦< L *certus*, certain + -FY⟧ **1** to declare (a thing) true, accurate, etc. by formal statement **2** to declare officially insane **3** to guarantee (a check, document, etc.) **4** to issue a certificate or license to —**cer'ti·fi'a·ble** ***adj.*** —**cer'ti·fi·ca'tion** ***n.***

cer·ti·tude (surt'ə to͞od') ***n.*** sureness; inevitability

ce·ru·le·an (sə ro͞o'lē ən) ***adj.*** ⟦< L < *caelum*, heaven⟧ sky-blue; azure

Cer·van·tes (sər van'tēz', -vän'-), **Mi·guel de** (mē gel' *th*e) 1547-1616; Sp. writer

cer·vix (sur'viks) ***n.***, *pl.* **cer·vi·ces** (sər vī'sēz', sur'və-) or **-vix·es** ⟦L, neck⟧ a necklike part, esp. of the uterus —**cer'vi·cal** (-vi kəl) ***adj.***

ce·sar·e·an (section) (sə zer'ē ən) ⟦from the ancient story that Julius CAESAR was born this way⟧ surgery to deliver a baby by cutting through the mother's abdominal and uterine walls

ce·si·um (sē'zē əm) ***n.*** ⟦ult. < L *caesius*, bluish-gray⟧ a metallic chemical element, used in photoelectric cells, radiation therapy, etc.

ces·sa·tion (se sā'shən) ***n.*** ⟦< L *cessare*, cease⟧ a ceasing or stopping

ces·sion (sesh'ən) ***n.*** ⟦< L *cedere*, to yield⟧ a ceding (of rights, property, etc.) to another

cess·pool (ses'po͞ol') ***n.*** ⟦< ? It *cesso*, privy⟧ a deep hole in the ground to receive drainage or sewage from the sinks, toilets, etc. of a house

ce·ta·cean (sə tā'shən) ***n.*** ⟦< L *cetus*, whale⟧ any of certain fishlike water mammals, including whales, porpoises, etc. —***adj.*** of the cetaceans

Cey·lon (sə län', sā-, sē-) *former name for* SRI LANKA —**Cey·lo·nese** (sel'ə nēz', sā'lə-), *pl.* **-nese',** ***adj.***, ***n.***

Cé·zanne (sā zán'), **Paul** 1839-1906; Fr. painter

cf ⟦L *confer*⟧ *abbrev.* compare

CFO *abbrev.* chief financial officer

cg or **cgm** *abbrev.* centigram(s)

Ch or **ch** *abbrev.* **1** chapter **2** church

Cha·blis (sha blē') ***n.*** [*occas.* **c-**] a dry white Burgundy wine, orig. from Chablis, France

Chad (chad) country in NC Africa: 495,755 sq. mi.; pop. 6,288,000

chafe (chāf) ***vt.*** **chafed, chaf'ing** ⟦< L *calefacere*, make warm⟧ **1** to rub so as to make warm **2** to wear away or make sore by rubbing **3** to annoy; irritate —***vi.*** **1** to rub (*on* or *against*) **2** to be annoyed or impatient

chaff (chaf) ***n.*** ⟦OE *ceaf*⟧ **1** threshed or winnowed husks of grain **2** anything worthless **3** teasing; banter —***vt.***, ***vi.*** to tease in a good-natured way

chaf·ing dish (chāf'iŋ) a pan with a heating apparatus beneath it, as to cook food at the table

cha·grin (shə grin') ***n.*** ⟦Fr⟧ embarrassment and annoyance due to failure, disappointment, etc. —***vt.*** **-grined', -grin'ing** to cause to feel chagrin

chain (chān) ***n.*** ⟦< L *catena*⟧ **1** a flexible series of joined links **2** [*pl.*] *a)* bonds; shackles *b)* captivity **3** a chainlike measuring instrument, as for surveying **4** a series of things connected causally, logically, physically, etc. **5** a number of stores, etc. owned by one company —***vt.*** **1** to fasten with chains **2** to restrain, etc.

chain gang a gang of prisoners chained together, as when working

chain reaction **1** a self-sustaining series of chemical or nuclear reactions in which the reaction products keep the process going **2** a series of events, each of which results in the following one

chain saw a portable power saw with an endless chain that carries the cutting teeth

chair (cher) ***n.*** ⟦< L *cathedra*: see CATHEDRAL⟧ **1** a piece of furniture with a back, for one person to sit on **2** an important or official position **3** a chairman —***vt.*** to preside over as chairman

chair'lift' ***n.*** seats suspended from a power-driven endless cable, used to carry skiers up a slope

chair'man (-mən) ***n.***, *pl.* **-men** (-mən) a person in charge of a meeting, etc.: also **chair'per'son** —**chair'man·ship'** ***n.*** —**chair'wom'an**, *pl.* **-wom'en**, ***fem.n.***

chaise (shāz) ***n.*** ⟦Fr⟧ a lightweight carriage, having two or four wheels

chaise longue (lôŋ; *also* lounj) ⟦Fr, lit., long chair⟧ a couchlike chair with a long seat: also **chaise lounge** (lounj)

chal·ced·o·ny (kal sed''n ē) ***n.*** quartz having a waxy luster and, often, colored bands

cha·let (shal ā', shal'ā) ***n.*** ⟦Swiss-Fr⟧ **1** a Swiss house with overhanging eaves **2** any similar building

chal·ice (chal'is) ***n.*** ⟦< L *calix*, cup⟧ **1** a cup; goblet **2** the cup for Communion wine

chalk (chôk) ***n.*** ⟦< L *calx*, limestone⟧ **1** a soft, whitish limestone **2** a piece of chalk or chalklike substance used for writing on a blackboard —***adj.*** made with chalk —***vt.*** to mark or rub with chalk —**chalk up** **1** to score, get, or achieve **2** to ascribe —**chalk'i·ness** ***n.*** —**chalk'y, -i·er, -i·est,** ***adj.***

chalk'board' ***n.*** BLACKBOARD

chal·lenge (chal'ənj) ***n.*** ⟦< L *calumnia*, calumny⟧ **1** a demand for identification **2** a calling into question **3** a call to a duel, contest, etc. **4** anything that calls for special effort —***vt.*** **-lenged, -leng·ing** to subject to a challenge —***vi.*** to make a challenge —**chal'leng·er** ***n.***

chal'lenged ***adj.*** disabled or handicapped

chal·lis (shal'ē) ***n.*** ⟦< ?⟧ a soft, lightweight fabric of wool, etc.

cham·ber (chām'bər) ***n.*** ⟦< LL *camera*, a chamber, room⟧ **1** a room, esp. a bedroom **2** [*pl.*] a judge's office near the courtroom **3** an assembly hall **4** a legislative or judicial body **5** a council *[chamber of commerce]* **6** an enclosed space; compartment; specif. the part of a gun holding a cartridge —**cham'bered** ***adj.***

cham'ber·lain (-lin) ***n.*** ⟦< OHG *chamarlinc*⟧ **1** an officer in charge of the household of a ruler or lord; steward **2** [Brit.] a treasurer

cham'ber·maid' ***n.*** a woman whose work is taking care of bedrooms, as in a hotel

THESAURUS

vinced, assertive, cocksure; see also CONFIDENT. **2** [Beyond doubt] indisputable, unquestionable, assured, positive, real, true, genuine, plain, clear, undoubted, guaranteed, unmistakable, sure, incontrovertible, undeniable, definite, unqualified, infallible, undisputed, unerring, sound, reliable, trustworthy, evident, conclusive, authoritative, irrefutable, unconditional, incontestable, unquestioned, absolute, unequivocal, inescapable, conclusive, in the bag*; see also TRUE 1, 3. **3** [Fixed] settled, concluded, set; see DEFINITE 1, DETERMINED 1. **4** [Specific but not named] special, definite, individual, marked, one, some, a few, a couple, several, upwards of, regular, particular, singular, precise, specific, express; see also SOME. —**for certain** without doubt, absolutely, certainly; see SURELY.

certainly ***a.*** positively, absolutely, unquestionably; see SURELY.

certificate ***n.*** declaration, warrant, voucher, testimonial, credentials, license, testament, endorsement, affidavit, certification, diploma, coupon, document, pass, ticket, warranty, guarantee, testimony, receipt, affirmation; see also RECORD 1.

certify ***v.*** swear, attest, state; see DECLARE, TESTIFY 2.

chain ***n.*** **1** [A series of links] series, train, set, string, connection, cable, link, charm bracelet, atomic ring, shackle, manacle; see also SERIES. **2** [A sequence] succession, progression, continuity; see SERIES.

chain ***v.*** connect, attach, secure; see FASTEN, HOLD 1.

chair ***n.*** **1** [A single seat] seat, place, room, space; see also FURNITURE. *Chairs include the following:* stool, throne, footstool, rocker, wing chair, armchair, easy chair, wheelchair, highchair, occasional chair, dining-room chair, desk chair, kitchen chair, deck chair, lawn chair, swivel chair, folding chair, recliner. **2** [A position of authority] throne, professorship, fellowship; see INFLUENCE.

chairman ***n.*** chairperson, chairwoman, chair, president, administrator, director, toastmaster, speaker, moderator, monitor, leader, principal, captain, master of ceremonies, MC, emcee; see also LEADER 2.

chalk up ***v.*** credit, enter, register; see ADD 1, RECORD 1, SCORE 1.

challenge ***n.*** dare, provocation, threat; see OBJECTION.

challenge ***v.*** **1** [To call to a contest, etc.] defy, confront, throw down the gauntlet; see DARE 2, THREATEN. **2** [To question] dispute, inquire, search out; see ASK, DOUBT, QUESTION.

chamber music music for performance by a small group, as a string quartet
chamber of commerce an association established to further the business interests of its community
cham·bray (sham′brā′) ***n.*** ⟦var. of *cambric*⟧ a smooth fabric of cotton, etc. with white threads woven across a colored warp
cha·me·le·on (kə mē′lē ən, -mēl′yən) ***n.*** ⟦< Gr *chamai*, on the ground + *leōn*, LION⟧ any of various lizards that can change the color of their skin
cham·ois (sham′ē) ***n.***, *pl.* **-ois** ⟦Fr⟧ **1** a small, goatlike antelope of the mountains of Europe and the Caucasus **2** a soft leather made from the skin of chamois, sheep, deer, etc.: also **cham·my** (sham′ē), *pl.* **-mies**
cham·o·mile (kam′ə mīl′, -mēl′) ***n.*** *alt. sp. of* CAMOMILE
champ[1] (champ) ***vt.*** ⟦prob. echoic⟧ to chew hard and noisily; munch —**champ at the bit** to be impatient when held back
champ[2] (champ) ***n.*** [Inf.] CHAMPION (sense 2)
cham·pagne (sham pān′) ***n.*** an effervescent white wine, orig. from Champagne, region in NE France
cham·paign (sham pān′) ***n.*** ⟦< L *campus*, field⟧ flat, open country
cham·pi·on (cham′pē ən) ***n.*** ⟦< LL *campio*, gladiator⟧ **1** one who fights for another or for a cause; defender **2** a winner of first place in a competition —***adj.*** excelling all others —***vt.*** to fight for; defend; support —**cham′pi·on·ship′** ***n.***
chance (chans) ***n.*** ⟦< L *cadere*, to fall⟧ **1** the happening of events without apparent cause; luck **2** an unpredictable event **3** a risk or gamble **4** a ticket in a lottery **5** an opportunity **6** [*often pl.*] a possibility or probability —***adj.*** accidental —***vi.*** **chanced**, **chanc′ing** to have the fortune, good or bad —***vt.*** to risk —**by chance** accidentally —**chance on** (or **upon**) to find or meet by chance —(**the**) **chances are** the likelihood is —**on the** (**off**) **chance** relying on the (remote) possibility
chan·cel (chan′səl) ***n.*** ⟦< L *cancelli*, lattices⟧ the part of a church around the altar, for the clergy and the choir
chan′cel·ler·y (-sə lər ē) ***n.***, *pl.* **-ies** ⟦< ML *cancellaria*⟧ the rank or position of a chancellor
chan′cel·lor (-sə lər) ***n.*** ⟦< LL *cancellarius*, secretary⟧ **1** a high government official, as, in certain countries, a prime minister **2** in some universities, the president or other executive officer
chan·cer·y (chan′sər ē) ***n.***, *pl.* **-ies** ⟦< ML *cancellaria*⟧ **1** a court of equity **2** an office of public archives **3** *R.C.Ch.* the diocesan office performing secretarial services for the bishop
chan·cre (shaŋ′kər) ***n.*** ⟦Fr: see CANCER⟧ a sore or ulcer of syphilis
chanc·y (chan′sē) ***adj.*** **-i·er**, **-i·est** risky; uncertain —**chanc′i·ness** ***n.***
chan·de·lier (shan′də lir′) ***n.*** ⟦Fr < L *candela*, candle⟧ a lighting fixture hung from a ceiling, with branches for candles, light bulbs, etc.
chan·dler (chand′lər) ***n.*** ⟦< L *candela*, candle⟧ **1** a maker of candles **2** a retailer of supplies, as for ships
Chang (chäŋ) river in central China, flowing into the East China Sea: former transliteration YANGTZE
change (chānj) ***vt.*** **changed**, **chang′ing** ⟦< L *cambire*, to barter⟧ **1** to put or take (a thing) in place of something else *[to change jobs]* **2** to exchange *[to change seats]* **3** to make different; alter —***vi.*** **1** to alter; vary **2** to leave one train, plane, etc. and board another **3** to put on other clothes —***n.*** **1** a substitution, alteration, or variation **2** variety **3** another set of clothes **4** *a*) money returned as the difference between the price and the greater sum presented *b*) coins or bills that together equal a single larger coin or bill *c*) small coins —**change off** to take turns —**ring the changes** to ring a set of bells with all possible variations —**change′a·ble** ***adj.*** —**change′less** ***adj.***
change′ling (-liŋ) ***n.*** a child secretly put in the place of another, as, in folk tales, by fairies
change of life MENOPAUSE: also [Inf.] **the change**
change′o′ver ***n.*** a complete change, as in goods produced
chan·nel (chan′əl) ***n.*** ⟦see CANAL⟧ **1** the bed or deeper part of a river, harbor, etc. **2** a body of water joining two larger ones **3** any means of passage **4** [*pl.*] the official course of transmission of communications **5** a groove or furrow **6** a frequency band assigned to a radio or television station —***vt.*** **-neled** or **-nelled**, **-nel·ing** or **-nel·ling** **1** to make a channel in **2** to send through a channel
Channel Islands group of British islands in the English Channel
chan′nel·ize′ (-īz′) ***vt.*** **-ized′**, **-iz′ing** to provide a channel for
chan·son (shän sôn′) ***n.***, *pl.* ***-sons′*** (-sôn′) ⟦Fr⟧ a song
chant (chant) ***n.*** ⟦< L *cantare*, to sing⟧ **1** a song; esp., a liturgical song with a series of syllables or words sung to each tone **2** a singsong way of speaking —***vi.***, ***vt.*** to sing or say in a chant —**chant′er** ***n.***
chan·teuse (shän to͞oz′) ***n.*** ⟦Fr⟧ a woman singer, esp. of popular ballads
chan·tey (shan′tē, chan′tē) ***n.***, *pl.* **-teys** a song formerly sung by sailors while working: also **chan′ty**, *pl.* **-ties**
chan·ti·cleer (chan′ti klir′) ***n.*** ⟦< OFr *chante-cler*, lit., sing loud⟧ a rooster
Cha·nu·kah (khä′noo kä′) ***n.*** HANUKKAH
cha·os (kā′äs′) ***n.*** ⟦< Gr, space⟧ extreme confusion or disorder —**cha·ot·ic** (kā ät′ik) ***adj.***
chap[1] (chap) ***n.*** ⟦< Brit *chapman*, peddler⟧ [Inf.] a man; fellow

THESAURUS

champion ***n.*** vanquisher, conqueror, victor; see HERO 1, WINNER.
chance ***a.*** accidental, unintentional, haphazard; see AIMLESS, INCIDENTAL.
chance ***n.*** **1** [The powers of uncertainty] fate, fortune, hazard, casualty, lot, accident, luck, good luck, bad luck, destiny, outcome, cast, lottery, gamble, adventure, contingency, happening, future, doom, destination, occurrence, Lady Luck*, turn of the cards, heads or tails.—*Ant.* PURPOSE, aim, design. **2** [A possibility] opening, occasion, prospect; see OPPORTUNITY 1, POSSIBILITY 2. **3** [Probability; *often plural*] likelihood, feasibility, indications; see ODDS. —**by chance** by accident, as it happens, unexpectedly; see ACCIDENTALLY. —**on the off chance** in case, in the event that, supposing; see IF.
chance ***v.*** venture, stake, hazard, wager, jeopardize, speculate, tempt fate, tempt fortune, play with fire, take a shot*, take a leap in the dark, buy a pig in a poke, go out on a limb*, chance it, take a fling at*, put all one's eggs in one basket, skate on thin ice*, run the risk; see also RISK.
change ***n.*** **1** [An alteration] modification, correction, remodeling, switch, reformation, reconstruction, shift, reform, conversion, transformation, revolution, rearrangement, adjustment, readjustment, reorganization, reshaping, renovation, realignment, redirection, reprogramming, variation, addition, refinement, advance, development, diversification, turn, turnover, enlargement, revision, qualification, distortion, compression, contraction, widening, narrowing, lengthening, flattening, shortening, fitting, setting, adjusting, rounding, mutation, evolution. **2** [Substitution] switch, replacement, exchange; see SHIFT 1. **3** [Variety] diversity, novelty, variance; see DIFFERENCE 1, VARIETY 1.
change ***v.*** **1** [To make different] vary, turn, alternate; see ALTER 1. **2** [To become different] alter, vary, modify, evolve, be converted, turn into, resolve into, grow, ripen, mellow, mature, transform, reform, moderate, adapt, adjust, mutate, evolve; see also BECOME. **3** [To put in place of another] displace, supplant, transpose; see EXCHANGE 1, REPLACE 1, SUBSTITUTE. **4** [To change clothing] switch outfits, slip into something comfortable, undress; see DRESS 1.
changeable ***a.*** **1** [*Said of persons*] fickle, flighty, unreliable; see UNSTABLE 2. **2** [*Said of conditions*] variable, unsteady, unsettled; see UNCERTAIN.
changed ***a.*** **1** [Exchanged] substituted, replaced, traded; see RETURNED. **2** [Altered] reconditioned, modified, limited, reformed, shifted, moved, mutated, deteriorated, aged, run down, rewritten, qualified, conditioned, modernized, remodeled, reprogrammed, rescheduled, redone, done over, brought up to date, edited, censored, moderated, innovated, deviated, diverted, fluctuated, chopped, warped, passed to, re-created, converted, transfigured, metamorphosed, transmuted.—*Ant.* UNCHANGED, PERMANENT, final.
changing ***a.*** changeful, changeable, mobile, dynamic, alternative, unstable, inconstant, uncertain, mutable, fluid, mercurial, declining, deteriorating, degenerating, unsteady, irresolute, wavering; see also UNCERTAIN.—*Ant.* FIXED, stable, unchanging.
channel ***n.*** conduit, tube, canal, duct, course, gutter, furrow, trough, runway, tunnel, strait, sound, race, sewer, main, artery, vein, ditch, aqueduct, canyon; see also WAY 2.
channel ***v.*** route, send, direct; see SEND 1.
chant ***n.*** religious song, chorus, incantation; see SONG.
chant ***v.*** intone, chorus, carol; see SING.
chaos ***n.*** turmoil, anarchy, discord; see CONFUSION, DISORDER.
chaotic ***a.*** disorganized, disordered, uncontrolled; see CONFUSED 2.

chap[2] (chap) ***vt.***, ***vi.*** **chapped** or **chapt**, **chap′ping** ⟦ME *chappen*, cut⟧ to crack open; split; roughen, as skin —***n.*** a chapped place in the skin

chap[3] *abbrev.* **1** chaplain **2** chapter

chap·ar·ral (shap′ə ral′, chap′-) ***n.*** ⟦Sp < *chaparro*, evergreen oak⟧ [Southwest] a thicket of shrubs, etc.

cha·peau (sha pō′) ***n.***, *pl.* **-peaus′** or **-peaux′** (-pōz′) ⟦Fr⟧ a hat

chap·el (chap′əl) ***n.*** ⟦< ML *cappella*, dim. of *cappa*, cape⟧ **1** a small church **2** a private place of worship, as in a hospital **3** a religious service

chap·er·on or **chap·er·one** (shap′ər ōn′, shap′ər ōn′) ***n.*** ⟦< OFr, hood⟧ one who accompanies young, unmarried people to supervise their behavior, as at dances —***vt.***, ***vi.*** **-oned′**, **-on′ing** to act as chaperon (to)

chap·lain (chap′lən) ***n.*** ⟦see CHAPEL⟧ **1** a clergyman attached to a chapel **2** a clergyman serving in a religious capacity with the armed forces, or in a prison, hospital, etc.

chap·let (chap′lit) ***n.*** ⟦< LL *cappa*, cape⟧ **1** a garland for the head **2** a string of beads, esp. prayer beads

chaps (chaps, shaps) ***pl.n.*** ⟦< MexSp *chaparreras*⟧ leather trousers without a seat, worn over ordinary trousers by cowboys to protect their legs

chap·ter (chap′tər) ***n.*** ⟦< L *caput*, head⟧ **1** a main division, as of a book **2** a local branch of an organization

chapter book a book divided into chapters, intended for very young readers

char (chär) ***vt.***, ***vi.*** **charred**, **char′ring** ⟦< CHARCOAL⟧ **1** to reduce to charcoal by burning **2** to burn slightly; scorch

char·ac·ter (kar′ik tər) ***n.*** ⟦< Gr *charassein*, engrave⟧ **1** any letter, figure, or symbol used in writing and printing **2** a distinctive trait, quality, etc.; characteristic **3** kind or sort **4** behavior typical of a person or group **5** moral strength **6** reputation **7** status; position **8** a person in a play, novel, etc. **9** [Inf.] an eccentric person

char′ac·ter·is′tic (-is′tik) ***adj.*** typical; distinctive —***n.*** a distinguishing trait or quality —**char′ac·ter·is′ti·cal·ly *adv.***

char′ac·ter·ize′ (-īz′) ***vt.*** **-ized′**, **-iz′ing** **1** to describe the particular traits of **2** to be a characteristic of —**char′ac·ter·i·za′tion *n.***

cha·rade (shə rād′) ***n.*** ⟦Fr < Prov *charrar*, to gossip⟧ **1** [*pl.*] a game in which words to be guessed are pantomimed, often syllable by syllable **2** an obvious pretense or fiction

char·broil or **char-broil** (chär′broil′) ***vt.*** to broil over a charcoal fire

char·coal (chär′kōl′) ***n.*** ⟦ME *char cole*⟧ **1** a dark, porous form of carbon made by partially burning wood or other organic matter in an airless kiln or retort: used for fuel, etc. **2** a very dark gray or brown

chard (chärd) ***n.*** ⟦< L *carduus*, thistle⟧ a kind of beet with edible leaves and stalks

char·don·nay (shär′də nā′) ***n.*** [*also* **C-**] a dry white wine

charge (chärj) ***vt.*** **charged**, **charg′ing** ⟦ult. < L *carrus*, wagon⟧ **1** to load or fill (*with* something) **2** to add an electrical charge to (a battery, etc.) **3** to give as a duty, command, etc. to **4** to accuse **5** to make liable for (an error, etc.) **6** to ask as a price **7** to record as a debt **8** to pay for by using a credit card **9** to attack vigorously —***vi.*** **1** to ask payment (*for*) **2** to attack vigorously —***n.*** **1** a load or burden **2** the necessary quantity, as of fuel, for a container or device **3** the amount of chemical energy stored in a battery **4** a cartridge or shell, or the amount of gunpowder needed to discharge a gun, etc. **5** responsibility or care (*of*) **6** a person or thing entrusted to someone's care **7** instruction; command **8** accusation; indictment **9** cost **10** a debt, debit, or expense **11** an onslaught **12** the signal for an attack **13** [Slang] a thrill —**in charge (of)** having the responsibility, control, or supervision (of) —**charge′a·ble *adj.***

charge account an arrangement by which a customer may pay for purchases within a specified future period

charge card a thin, flat, plastic card embossed with the owner's name, account number, etc., used when charging purchases

charg′er *n.* **1** a person or thing that charges **2** a horse ridden in battle **3** a device used to charge storage batteries

char·grill (chär′gril′) ***vt.*** to grill (meat) over a charcoal fire, etc.

char·i·ly (cher′ə lē, char′-) ***adv.*** cautiously —**char′i·ness *n.***

char·i·ot (char′ē ət) ***n.*** ⟦see CAR⟧ a horse-drawn, two-wheeled cart used in ancient times for war, racing, etc. —**char′i·ot·eer′** (-ə tir′) ***n.***

cha·ris·ma (kə riz′mə) ***n.*** ⟦< Gr, favor, grace⟧ a special quality in one that inspires devotion or fascination

char·is·mat·ic (kar′iz mat′ik) ***adj.*** **1** of or having charisma **2** designating or of a religious group that stresses direct divine inspiration, manifested as in glossolalia, etc. —***n.*** a member of a charismatic group

char·i·ta·ble (char′i tə bəl) ***adj.*** **1** generous to the needy **2** of or for charity **3** kind and forgiving; lenient —**char′i·ta·bly *adv.***

char·i·ty (char′i tē) ***n.***, *pl.* **-ties** ⟦< L *caritas*, affection⟧ **1** *Christian Theol.* love for one's fellow human beings **2** leniency in judging others **3** *a)* generosity toward the needy *b)* help so given **4** a welfare institution, fund, etc.

char·la·tan (shär′lə tən) ***n.*** ⟦ult. < VL *cerretanus*, seller of papal indulgences⟧ a fraud; quack

Char·le·magne (shär′lə mān′) A.D. 742-814; king of the Franks (768-814): emperor of the Holy Roman Empire (800-814)

Charles·ton[1] (chärls′tən) ***n.*** ⟦< name of the seaport⟧ a lively dance of the 1920s, in 4/4 time

Charles·ton[2] (chärls′tən) capital of West Virginia, in the W part: pop. 57,000

char·ley horse (chär′lē) [Inf.] a cramp in a muscle, esp. a thigh muscle

Char·lotte (shär′lət) city in S North Carolina: pop. 396,000

THESAURUS

chapel *n.* nondenominational place of worship, small church, shrine; see CHURCH 1.

chapter *n.* part, section, book; see DIVISION 2.

character *n.* **1** [The dominant quality] temper, temperament, attitude, nature, sense, complex, mood, streak, attribute, badge, tone, style, aspect, complexion, spirit, genius, humor, frame, grain, vein; see also CHARACTERISTIC. **2** [The sum of a person's characteristics] personality, reputation, constitution, repute, individuality, estimation, record, caliber, standing, type, shape, quality, habit, appearance; see also KIND 2. **3** [A symbol, especially in writing] sign, figure, emblem; see LETTER 1, MARK 1. **4** [An odd or striking person] personality, figure, personage, original, eccentric, crank*, nut*, oddball*, weirdo*, freak*, piece of work. —**in character** consistent, usual, predictable; see CONVENTIONAL 1. —**out of character** inconsistent, unpredictable, unusual; see UNEXPECTED.

characteristic *a.* innate, fixed, essential, distinctive, distinguishing, marked, discriminative, symbolic, individualizing, representative, specific, personal, original, peculiar, individualistic, individual, idiosyncratic, unique, special, particular, symptomatic, private, exclusive, inherent, inborn, inbred, ingrained, native, indicative, inseparable, genetic; see also NATURAL 2, TYPICAL.—*Ant.* IRREGULAR, erratic, aberrant.

characteristic *n.* flavor, attribute, quality, faculty, peculiarity, individuality, style, aspect, tone, tinge, feature, distinction, manner, bearing, inclination, nature, personality, temperament, frame, originality, singularity, qualification, virtue, mark, essence, caliber, complexion, particularity, idiosyncrasy, trick, earmark, mannerism, trademark, badge, symptom, disposition, specialty, mood, character, bent, tendency, component, thing*.

characterize *v.* delineate, designate, portray; see DEFINE 2, DESCRIBE.

charge *n.* **1** [A charged sale] entry, debit, credit; see PRICE. **2** [An attack] assault, invasion, outbreak; see ATTACK. —**in charge** responsible, controlling, managing; see RESPONSIBLE 1.

charge *v.* **1** [To ask a price] require, sell for, fix the price at; see PRICE. **2** [To enter on a charge account] debit, put to account, charge to, run up an account, take on account, put on one's account, incur a debt, put down, credit, encumber, sell on credit, buy on credit, chalk up, put on the books, carry, put on the cuff*, take plastic*; see also BUY, SELL. **3** [To attack] assail, assault, invade; see ATTACK. **4** [To accuse] indict, censure, impute; see BLAME.

charged *a.* **1** [Bought but not paid for] debited, outstanding, unpaid, on credit, on time, owing, owed, on the cuff*, on the tab*; see also BOUGHT, DUE. **2** [Accused] taxed, confronted with, arraigned; see ACCUSED.

charitable *a.* openhanded, liberal, philanthropic; see GENEROUS, KIND.

charity *n.* **1** [Kindness] benevolence, magnanimity, compassion; see KINDNESS 1, TOLERANCE 1. **2** [An organization to aid the needy] charitable institution, welfare organization, foundation; see FOUNDATION 3.

Char·lotte·town (shär′lət toun′) capital of Prince Edward Island, Canada: pop. 33,000

charm (chärm) ***n.*** ⟦< L *carmen*⟧ **1** an action, object, or words assumed to have magic power **2** a trinket worn on a bracelet, etc. **3** a quality that attracts or delights **4** *Particle Physics* a property of certain quarks —***vt., vi.*** **1** to act on as if by magic **2** to fascinate; delight —**charm′er *n.*** —**charm′ing *adj.*** —**charm′ing·ly *adv.***

char·meuse (shär mo͞oz′, -mo͞os′) ***n.*** ⟦Fr < *charmer*, to bewitch⟧ a smooth fabric of silk or polyester

char·nel (house) (chär′nəl) ⟦< LL *carnale*, graveyard⟧ a building or place where corpses or bones are deposited

Cha·ron (ker′ən) ***n.*** *Gr. Myth.* the ferryman on the river Styx

chart (chärt) ***n.*** ⟦< Gr *chartēs*, layer of papyrus⟧ **1** a map, esp. for use in navigation **2** an information sheet with tables, graphs, etc. **3** a table, graph, etc. —***vt.*** **1** to make a chart of **2** to plan (a course of action)

char·ter (chärt′ər) ***n.*** ⟦see prec.⟧ **1** a franchise granted by a government **2** a written statement of basic laws or principles; constitution **3** written permission to form a local chapter or lodge of a society **4** the hire or lease of an airplane, bus, etc. —***vt.*** **1** to grant a charter to **2** to hire for exclusive use

charter member a founder or original member

charter school a publicly-funded alternative school founded on a charter with the government

char·treuse (shär tro͞oz′, -tro͞os′) ***n.*** ⟦Fr⟧ pale, yellowish green

char·wom·an (chär′wo͝om′ən) ***n.***, *pl.* **-wom′en** ⟦see CHORE⟧ a cleaning woman

char·y (cher′ē, char′ē) ***adj.*** **-i·er**, **-i·est** ⟦< OE *cearig*, sorrowful⟧ **1** careful; cautious **2** sparing

chase[1] (chās) ***vt.*** **chased**, **chas′ing** ⟦ult. < L *capere*, to take⟧ **1** to follow so as to catch **2** to run after; pursue **3** to drive away **4** to hunt —***vi.*** **1** to go in pursuit **2** [Inf.] to rush —***n.*** **1** a chasing; pursuit **2** the hunting of game —**give chase** to pursue

chase[2] (chās) ***vt.*** **chased**, **chas′ing** ⟦< OFr *enchasser*⟧ to ornament (metal) as by engraving

chas′er *n.* **1** one that chases or hunts; pursuer **2** a mild drink, as water, taken after whiskey, etc.

chasm (kaz′əm) ***n.*** ⟦< Gr *chasma*⟧ **1** a deep crack in the earth's surface; abyss **2** any break or gap

chas·sis (chas′ē, shas′ē) ***n.***, *pl.* **-sis′** (-ēz′) ⟦Fr⟧ **1** the frame, wheels, engine, etc. of a motor vehicle, but not the body **2** *a*) a frame, as for the parts of a TV set *b*) the assembled frame and parts

chaste (chāst) ***adj.*** ⟦< L *castus*, pure⟧ **1** not indulging in unlawful sexual activity; virtuous **2** decent; modest **3** simple in style; not ornate —**chaste′ly *adv.***

chas·ten (chās′ən) ***vt.*** ⟦< L *castigare*, punish⟧ **1** to punish so as to correct **2** to restrain or subdue

chas·tise (chas tīz′, chas′tīz′) ***vt.*** **-tised′**, **-tis′ing** ⟦see prec.⟧ **1** to punish, esp. by beating **2** to scold sharply —**chas·tise′ment *n.*** —**chas·tis′er *n.***

chas·ti·ty (chas′tə tē) ***n.*** a being chaste; specif., *a*) virtuousness *b*) sexual abstinence; celibacy *c*) decency or modesty

chas·u·ble (chaz′ə bəl, chas′-) ***n.*** ⟦< ML *casula*⟧ a sleeveless outer vestment worn by priests at Mass

chat (chat) ***vi.*** **chat′ted**, **chat′ting** ⟦< CHATTER⟧ **1** to talk in a light, informal manner **2** to hold an electronic conversation by exchanging typed messages on computers —***n.*** light, informal talk

châ·teau (sha tō′) ***n.***, *pl.* **-teaux′** (-tōz′, -tō′) or **-teaus′** ⟦Fr < L *castellum*, castle⟧ **1** a French feudal castle **2** a large country house and estate, esp. in France Also **cha·teau′**

chat·e·laine (shat′'l ān′) ***n.*** ⟦Fr⟧ **1** the mistress of a château **2** a woman's ornamental chain or clasp

Chat·ta·noo·ga (chat′ə no͞o′gə) city in SE Tennessee: pop. 152,000

chat·tel (chat′'l) ***n.*** ⟦see CATTLE⟧ a movable item of personal property, as furniture

chat·ter (chat′ər) ***vi.*** ⟦echoic⟧ **1** to make short, rapid, indistinct sounds, as squirrels do **2** to talk much and foolishly **3** to click together rapidly, as teeth do from cold —***n.*** **1** a chattering **2** foolish talk —**chat′ter·er *n.***

chat′ter·box′ *n.* an incessant talker

chat·ty (chat′ē) ***adj.*** **-ti·er**, **-ti·est** fond of chatting —**chat′ti·ness *n.***

Chau·cer (chô′sər), **Geof·frey** (jef′rē) 1340?-1400; Eng. poet

chauf·feur (shō′fər, shō fur′) ***n.*** ⟦Fr, lit., stoker⟧ one hired to drive a private automobile for someone else —***vt.*** to act as chauffeur to

chau·vin·ism (shō′vin iz′əm) ***n.*** ⟦after N. *Chauvin*, fanatical Fr patriot⟧ **1** militant and boastful patriotism; jingoism **2** unreasoning and boastful devotion to one's race, sex, etc. —**chau′vin·ist *n., adj.*** —**chau′vin·is′tic *adj.*** —**chau′vin·is′ti·cal·ly *adv.***

cheap (chēp) ***adj.*** ⟦ult. < L *caupo*, tradesman⟧ **1** low in price **2** worth more than the price **3** easily gotten [a *cheap* victory] **4** of little value **5** contemptible **6** [Inf.] stingy —***adv.*** at a low cost —**cheap′ly *adv.*** —**cheap′ness *n.***

cheap′en *vt., vi.* to make or become cheap or cheaper

cheap shot [Slang] an unnecessarily rough or mean action or remark

cheap′skate′ *n.* [Slang] a stingy person

cheat (chēt) ***n.*** ⟦< L *ex-*, out + *cadere*, to fall⟧ **1** a fraud; swindle **2** a swindler —***vt.*** **1** to defraud; swindle **2** to foil, deprive, or elude [to *cheat* death] —***vi.*** **1** to be dis-

THESAURUS

charm *n.* **1** [An object thought to possess power] amulet, talisman, mojo, fetish, mascot, good-luck piece, lucky piece, rabbit's foot. **2** [The quality of being charming] grace, attractiveness, attraction; see BEAUTY 1.

charm *v.* enchant, captivate, possess, enrapture, enthrall, transport, delight, please, entrance, bewitch, mesmerize; see also FASCINATE.

charmed *a.* enchanted, bewitched, enraptured, entranced, captivated, attracted, lured, tempted, enticed, bedazzled, hypnotized, mesmerized, under a spell, in a trance, spellbound, moonstruck, possessed, obsessed, infatuated, starstruck; see also FASCINATED.

charming *a.* enchanting, bewitching, entrancing, captivating, cute, fascinating, delightful, lovable, sweet, winning, irresistible, attractive, amiable, appealing, alluring, charismatic, pleasing, nice, graceful, winsome, seducing, seductive, desirable, enticing, tempting, inviting, ravishing, enrapturing, glamorous, elegant, infatuating, dainty, delicate, absorbing, tantalizing, engrossing, titillating, engaging, enthralling, rapturous, electrifying, lovely, intriguing, thrilling, fair, exquisite, likable, diverting, fetching, provocative, delectable, sexy*.—*Ant.* OFFENSIVE, disgusting, unpleasant.

chart *n.* graph, outline, diagram; see MAP, PLAN 1.

chart *v.* map, outline, plot; see PLAN 2.

charter *n.* contract, settlement, pact; see AGREEMENT 2, TREATY.

chase[1] ***v.*** trail, track, seek; see HUNT 1, PURSUE 1.

chaste *a.* immaculate, unstained, clean, innocent, virginal, unblemished, unsullied, moral, modest, proper, decent, demure, virgin, celibate, platonic, controlled, unmarried, unwed, spotless, infallible, strong; see also INNOCENT 2.—*Ant.* WEAK, corruptible, frail.

chastise *v.* scold, discipline, spank; see PUNISH.

chastity *n.* innocence, purity, virtue, uprightness, honor, celibacy, integrity, decency, delicacy, cleanness, goodness, demureness, abstinence, morality, chasteness, modesty, sinlessness, continence, coldness, reserve, restraint, virginity, spotlessness.—*Ant.* LEWDNESS, adultery, licentiousness.

chat *v.* converse, prattle, chatter; see TALK 1.

chatter *v.* gossip, chat, prattle; see BABBLE.

cheap *a.* **1** [Low in price] inexpensive, low-priced, moderate, family-size, economy-size, budget, depreciated, slashed, cut-rate, on sale, competitive, lowered, thrifty, bargain, irregular, reduced, cut-priced, low-cost, at a bargain, reasonable, marked down, closed-out, half-priced, popular-priced, worth the money, dime-a-dozen*, dirt-cheap*, for peanuts*, for a song*, second, bargain-basement; see also ECONOMICAL.—*Ant.* EXPENSIVE, dear, costly. **2** [Low in quality] inferior, ordinary, shoddy; see COMMON 1, POOR 2. **3** [Dishonest or base] dirty, tawdry, low; see DISHONEST, MEAN 3, VULGAR.

cheapen *v.* spoil, depreciate, demean; see CORRUPT, DAMAGE.

cheaply *a.* economically, inexpensively, advantageously, at a bargain price, at a good price, on sale, at cost, below cost, discounted, at a discount, reduced, at a reduced price, sacrificed, dirt-cheap*, given away*.

cheat *n.* rogue, cheater, confidence man, quack, charlatan, conniver, fraud, swindler, chiseler*, beguiler, fake, bluff, deceiver, inveigler, hypocrite, trickster, pretender, dodger, humbug, crook*, wolf in sheep's clothing, con artist*, shark*, fourflusher*, shill*; see also CRIMINAL.

cheat *v.* defraud, swindle, beguile; see DECEIVE.

cheated *a.* defrauded, swindled, duped, tricked, imposed upon, victimized, beguiled, trapped, foiled, lured, taken in*, bamboozled, hoodwinked;

honest or deceitful **2** [Slang] to be sexually unfaithful: often with *on* —**cheat'er** *n.*

check (chek) *n.* ⟦< OFr *eschec*, a check in chess⟧ **1** a sudden stop **2** any restraint **3** one that restrains **4** a supervision or test of accuracy, etc. **5** a mark (✓) to show verification **6** an identification ticket, token, etc. *[a hat check]* **7** one's bill at a restaurant or bar **8** a written order to a bank to pay a sum of money **9** a pattern of squares, or one of the squares **10** *Chess* the state of a king that is in danger **11** *Hockey* a bumping of an opponent —*interj.* [Inf.] agreed! right! —*vt.* **1** to stop suddenly **2** to restrain; curb; block **3** to test, verify, etc. by examination or comparison: often with *out* **4** to mark with a check (✓): often with *off* **5** to mark with a pattern of squares **6** to deposit temporarily, as in a checkroom **7** to clear (esp. luggage) for shipment **8** *Chess* to place (the opponent's king) in check **9** *Hockey* to bump (an opponent) —*vi.* **1** to agree with one another, item for item: often with *out* **2** to investigate or verify: often with *on, up on* —**check in 1** to register at a hotel, etc. **2** [Inf.] to present oneself, as at work —**check out 1** to pay and leave a hotel, etc. **2** to add up the prices of (items selected) for payment **3** to prove to be accurate, in good condition, etc. —**in check** under control —**check'er** *n.*

check'book' *n.* a book of detachable forms for writing bank checks

checked (chekt) *adj.* having a pattern of squares

check'er·board' *n.* a square board with 64 squares of two alternating colors, used in checkers and chess

check·ered (chek'ərd) *adj.* **1** having a pattern of squares **2** varied *[a checkered career]*

check'ers (-ərz) *n.* **1** a game for two played with flat disks on a checkerboard **2** the disks

checking account a bank account against which the depositor can draw checks

check'list' *n.* a list of things, names, etc. to be referred to: also **check list**

check'mate' *n.* ⟦ult. < Pers *šāh māt*, the king is dead⟧ **1** *Chess a)* the move that wins the game by checking the opponent's king so that it cannot be protected *b)* the condition of the king after this move **2** total defeat, frustration, etc. —*vt.* **-mat'ed, -mat'ing 1** *Chess* to place in checkmate **2** to defeat; thwart

check'off' *n.* the withholding of members' dues for the union by the employer

check'out' *n.* **1** the act or place of checking out purchases **2** the time by which one must check out of a hotel, etc.

check'point' *n.* a place on a road, etc. where traffic is inspected

check'room' *n.* a room in which hats, coats, etc. may be left until called for

check'up' *n.* an examination, esp. a medical one

ched·dar (cheese) (ched'ər) ⟦after *Cheddar*, England⟧ [*often* **C-**] a hard, smooth cheese

cheek (chēk) *n.* ⟦OE *ceoke*, jaw⟧ **1** either side of the face below the eye **2** either of two sides of anything **3** [Inf.] sauciness; impudence

cheek'bone' *n.* the bone across the upper cheek, just below the eye

cheek'y *adj.* **-i·er, -i·est** [Inf.] saucy; impudent —**cheek'i·ness** *n.*

cheep (chēp) *n.* ⟦echoic⟧ the short, shrill sound made by a young bird —*vt., vi.* to make, or utter with, this sound —**cheep'er** *n.*

cheer (chir) *n.* ⟦< Gr *kara*, the head⟧ **1** state of mind or of feeling; spirit *[be of good cheer]* **2** gladness; joy **3** festive entertainment **4** encouragement **5** *a)* a glad, excited shout to urge on, greet, etc. *b)* a rallying cry, etc. —*vt.* **1** to gladden; comfort: often with *up* **2** to urge on, greet, or applaud with cheers —*vi.* **1** to become cheerful: usually with *up* **2** to shout cheers

cheer'ful *adj.* **1** full of cheer; joyful **2** bright and attractive **3** willing; ready *[a cheerful helper]* —**cheer'ful·ly** *adv.* —**cheer'ful·ness** *n.*

cheer'i·o' (-ē ō') *interj.* [Brit. Inf.] **1** goodbye **2** good health: used as a toast

cheer'lead' (-lēd') *vi., vt.* to act as a cheerleader (for) —**cheer'lead'ing** *n.*

cheer'lead'er *n.* a leader of cheers, as at football games

cheer'less *adj.* not cheerful; dismal; dreary —**cheer'less·ly** *adv.* —**cheer'less·ness** *n.*

cheers (chirz) *interj.* good health: used as a toast

cheer'y *adj.* **-i·er, -i·est** cheerful; lively; bright —**cheer'i·ly** *adv.* —**cheer'i·ness** *n.*

cheese (chēz) *n.* ⟦OE *cyse*⟧ a solid food made from milk curds

cheese'burg'er *n.* a hamburger topped with melted cheese

cheese'cake' *n.* **1** a cake made with cottage cheese or cream cheese **2** [Inf.] photographic display of the figure, esp. the legs, of a pretty woman

cheese'cloth' *n.* ⟦from its use for wrapping cheese⟧ a thin cotton cloth with a very loose weave

chees'y *adj.* **-i·er, -i·est 1** like cheese **2** [Slang] inferior; poor

chee·tah (chēt'ə) *n.* ⟦Hindi < Sans *chitraka*, spotted⟧ a swift cat of Africa and S Asia, with long legs and a spotted coat

chef (shef) *n.* ⟦Fr, head, chief⟧ **1** a head cook **2** any cook

Che·khov (chek'ôf), **An·ton** (än tôn') 1860-1904; Russ. writer

chem *abbrev.* **1** chemical(s) **2** chemistry

chem·i·cal (kem'i kəl) *adj.* **1** of, made by, or used in chemistry **2** made with or operated by chemicals **3** of or involving a drug, alcohol, etc. *[chemical dependency]* —*n.* **1** any substance used in or obtained by a chemical process **2** [Slang] a drug, alcoholic beverage, etc. —**chem'i·cal·ly** *adv.*

chemical abuse the habitual use of a mood-altering drug, alcohol, etc. —**chemical abuser**

chemical engineering the science or profession of applying chemistry to industrial uses

THESAURUS

see also DECEIVED.

cheating *n.* lying, defrauding, deceiving; see DECEPTION, DISHONESTY.

check *n.* **1** [An order on a bank] money order, letter of credit, traveler's check, bank check, cashier's check, note, remittance; see also MONEY 1. **2** [A control] limit, curb, rein; see RESTRAINT 2. **3** [An examination] investigation, analysis, inquiry; see EXAMINATION 1, 3. **4** [A pattern in squares] patchwork, checkered design, checkerboard; see DESIGN. —**in check** controlled, under control, checked; see HELD.

check *v.* **1** [To bring under control] bridle, repress, inhibit, control, checkmate, counteract, discourage, repulse, neutralize, squelch*; see also RESTRAIN.—*Ant.* FREE, liberate, loose. **2** [To determine accuracy] review, monitor, inspect, test, balance the books, keep account of, correct, compare, find out, investigate, vet*, count, tell, call the roll, take account of, take stock, go through, go over with a fine-toothed comb*, keep tabs on*, keep track of; see also EXAMINE. **3** [To halt] hold, terminate, cut short; see HALT, STOP 1. —**check in** appear, sign in, come; see ARRIVE, REGISTER 4. —**check off** mark off, notice, correct; see MARK 2. —**check out** depart, pay one's bill, settle up; see LEAVE 1, PAY 1. —**check up on** watch, investigate, control; see EXAMINE.

cheek *n.* jowl, gill, chop; see FACE 1.

cheer *n.* **1** [An agreeable mental state] delight, mirth, glee; see JOY. **2** [An encouraging shout] roar, applause, ovation, hurrah, hurray, college yell, approval; see also YELL.

cheer *v.* **1** [To hearten] console, inspirit, brighten; see COMFORT 1, ENCOURAGE, HELP. **2** [To support with cheers] applaud, shout, salute; see SUPPORT 2, YELL. —**cheer up** enliven, inspirit, exhilarate, inspire, brighten, rally, restore, perk up, boost, buck up*, pat on the back; see also IMPROVE 1.

cheerful *a.* **1** [*Said especially of persons*] gay, merry, joyful; see HAPPY. **2** [*Said especially of things*] bright, sunny, sparkling; see COMFORTABLE 2, PLEASANT 2.

cheerfully *a.* cheerily, gladly, willingly, happily, merrily, joyfully, lightheartedly, pleasantly, blithely, brightly, vivaciously, airily, genially, jovially, sportively, elatedly, winsomely, gleefully, gaily, mirthfully, playfully, hopefully, breezily, briskly, with good cheer.—*Ant.* SADLY, unwillingly, reluctantly.

cheers *interj.* here's to you, to your health, skoal; see TOAST 1.

cheese *n.* *Varieties of cheese include the following:* mild, sharp, hard, soft, semisoft, aged, ripened, fresh, blue-veined, blue, bleu, cow's-milk, sheep's-milk, goat, process, smoked cheese; American, cheddar, Monterey Jack, Edam, Roquefort (trademark), brie, mozzarella, provolone, Gorgonzola, Swiss, Camembert, Liederkranz (trademark), Neufchâtel, Gruyère, Parmesan, Stilton, Gouda, Limburger, Muenster, Port du Salut, ricotta, feta, Romano, Colby, longhorn, chèvre, havarti; cottage, pot, cream, brick cheese; see also FOOD.

chemical *a.* synthetic, artificial, ersatz; see FALSE 3.

chemical *n.* substance, synthetic, compound; see DRUG, MEDICINE 2.

chemical warfare warfare by means of poisonous gases, etc.

che·mise (shə mēz′) ***n.*** ⟦< LL *camisia*, tunic⟧ **1** a woman's loose, short slip **2** a straight, loose dress

chem·ist (kem′ist) ***n.*** ⟦ult. < Ar < ? Gr *cheein*, to pour⟧ **1** a specialist in chemistry **2** [Brit.] a pharmacist, or druggist

chem·is·try (kem′is trē) ***n.*** ⟦< prec.⟧ **1** the science dealing with the composition and properties of substances, and with the reactions by which substances are produced from or converted into other substances **2** [Inf.] rapport

che·mo (kē′mō) ***n.*** [Inf.] *short for* CHEMOTHERAPY

chemo- *combining form* of, with, or by chemicals: also, before a vowel, **chem-**

che′mo·ther′a·py (kē′mō-) ***n.*** the use of drugs to prevent or treat a disease

chem·ur·gy (kem′ər jē) ***n.*** chemistry dealing with the use of organic, esp. farm, products in industrial manufacture

che·nille (shə nēl′) ***n.*** ⟦Fr, lit., caterpillar⟧ **1** a tufted, velvety yarn **2** a fabric filled or woven with this

cheque (chek) ***n.*** *Brit. sp. of* CHECK (*n.* 8)

cher·ish (cher′ish) ***vt.*** ⟦< L *carus*, dear⟧ **1** to feel or show love for **2** to protect; foster **3** to cling to the idea or feeling of

Cher·o·kee (cher′ə kē′) ***n.***, *pl.* **-kees′** or **-kee′** a member of a North American Indian people now chiefly of Oklahoma and North Carolina

che·root (shə ro͞ot′) ***n.*** ⟦< Tamil⟧ a cigar with both ends cut square

cher·ry (cher′ē) ***n.***, *pl.* **-ries** ⟦< Gr *kerasion*⟧ **1** a small, fleshy fruit with a smooth, hard pit **2** the tree that bears this fruit **3** the wood of this tree **4** a bright red color —***adj.*** bright-red

chert (churt) ***n.*** a very dense type of quartz, including jasper and flint

cher·ub (cher′əb) ***n.***, *pl.* **-ubs**; for 1 usually **-u·bim′** (-yo͞o bim′, -ə bim′) *or* **-u·bims** ⟦< Heb *kerūbh*⟧ **1** any of a kind of angel, often represented as a chubby, rosy-faced child with wings **2** a child, etc. having a sweet, innocent face —**che·ru·bic** (chə ro͞o′bik) ***adj.*** —**che·ru′bi·cal·ly** ***adv.***

cher·vil (chur′vəl) ***n.*** ⟦< Gr *chairephyllon*⟧ an herb like parsley, with leaves used to flavor salads, soups, etc.

Ches·a·peake Bay (ches′ə pēk′) arm of the Atlantic, extending into Virginia and Maryland

chess (ches) ***n.*** ⟦< OFr *eschec*, a check in chess⟧ a game played on a chessboard by two players, using a variety of pieces (**chess′men**)

chess′board′ ***n.*** a checkerboard used for chess

chest (chest) ***n.*** ⟦< Gr *kistē*, a box⟧ **1** a box with a lid **2** a cabinet with drawers, as for clothes **3** a cabinet with shelves, as for medicines **4** the part of the body enclosed by the ribs, breastbone, and diaphragm

ches·ter·field (ches′tər fēld′) ***n.*** ⟦after a 19th-c. Earl of *Chesterfield*⟧ a single-breasted topcoat, usually with a velvet collar

chest·nut (ches′nut′) ***n.*** ⟦< Gr *kastaneia*⟧ **1** the edible nut of various trees of the beech family **2** such a tree, or its wood **3** reddish brown **4** a reddish-brown horse **5** [Inf.] an old, stale joke, story, etc. —***adj.*** reddish-brown

chev·i·ot (shev′ē ət; *also* chev′ē ət) ***n.*** ⟦after *Cheviot* Hills, on the Scottish-English border⟧ [*sometimes* **C-**] a rough, twilled wool fabric

chèvre or **che·vre** (shev′rə) ***n.*** a soft cheese made from goat's milk

chev·ron (shev′rən) ***n.*** ⟦< OFr, rafter⟧ a V-shaped bar on the sleeve of a uniform, showing rank

chew (cho͞o) ***vt.***, ***vi.*** ⟦ OE *ceowan*⟧ to bite and crush with the teeth —***n.*** **1** a chewing **2** something chewed or for chewing —**chew′er** ***n.*** —**chew′y**, **-i·er**, **-i·est**, ***adj.***

chew′ing gum a gummy substance, as chicle, flavored for chewing

Chey·enne[1] (shī an′, -en′) ***n.***, *pl.* **-ennes′** or **-enne′** a member of a North American Indian people now chiefly of Oklahoma

Chey·enne[2] (shī an′, -en′) capital of Wyoming, in the SE part: pop. 50,000

chg(d) *abbrev.* charge(d)

chi (kī, kē) ***n.*** the 22d letter of the Greek alphabet (X, χ)

Chi·an·ti (kē än′tē, -an′-) ***n.*** ⟦It⟧ [*also* **c-**] a dry red wine

chi·a·ro·scu·ro (kē är′ə sko͝or′ō) ***n.***, *pl.* **-ros** ⟦It < L *clarus*, clear + *obscurus*, dark⟧ **1** light and shade in a painting, etc. treated to suggest depth or for effect **2** a style of painting, etc. emphasizing this **3** a painting in which this is used

chic (shēk) ***n.*** ⟦Fr < medieval LowG *schick*, skill⟧ smart elegance of style —***adj.*** pleasingly stylish

Chi·ca·go (shə kä′gō, -kô′-) city and port in NE Illinois: pop. 2,784,000 (met. area, 6,070,000)

chi·can·er·y (shi kān′ər ē) ***n.***, *pl.* **-ies** ⟦< Fr⟧ **1** trickery **2** a trick

Chi·ca·no (chi kä′nō) ***n.***, *pl.* **-nos** ⟦< AmSp⟧ a U.S. citizen or inhabitant of Mexican descent —***adj.*** of Chicanos —**Chi·ca′na** (-nə), *pl.* **-nas**, ***fem.n.***

chi·chi or **chi-chi** (shē′shē) ***adj.*** ⟦Fr⟧ extremely chic, specif. in a showy way

chick (chik) ***n.*** ⟦ME *chike*⟧ **1** a young chicken or bird **2** [Slang] a young woman

chick·a·dee (chik′ə dē′) ***n.*** ⟦echoic⟧ any of various titmice

chick·en (chik′ən) ***n.*** ⟦< OE *cycen*⟧ **1** a common farm bird raised for its edible eggs or flesh; hen or rooster, esp. a young one **2** its flesh **3** [Slang] a cowardly person —***adj.*** [Slang] cowardly —***vi.*** [Slang] to quit from fear: usually with *out*

chicken feed [Slang] a small sum of money

chick′en-fried′ ***adj.*** coated with seasoned flour or batter and fried

chick′en-heart′ed ***adj.*** cowardly; timid: also **chick′en-liv′ered**

chick′en·pox′ ***n.*** an acute, contagious viral disease, esp. of children, characterized by skin eruptions

chicken wire light, pliable wire fencing

chick′pea′ ***n.*** **1** a bushy annual plant with short, hairy pods **2** its edible seed

chick′weed′ ***n.*** a low-growing plant often found as a weed in lawns, etc.

chic·le (chik′əl) ***n.*** ⟦AmSp⟧ a gumlike substance from a tropical American tree, used in chewing gum

chic·ly (shek′lē) ***adv.*** in a chic way —**chic′ness** ***n.***

chic·o·ry (chik′ə rē) ***n.***, *pl.* **-ries** ⟦< Gr *kichora*⟧ **1** a plant usually with blue flowers: the leaves are used for salad **2** its root, ground for mixing with coffee or for use as a coffee substitute

chide (chīd) ***vt.***, ***vi.*** **chid′ed** or **chid** (chid), **chid′ed** or **chid** or **chid·den** (chid′'n), **chid′ing** ⟦OE *cidan*⟧ to reprove mildly —**chid′ing·ly** ***adv.***

chief (chēf) ***n.*** ⟦< L *caput*, head⟧ a leader; head —***adj.*** main; principal

chief′ly ***adv.*** **1** most of all **2** mainly —***adj.*** of or like a chief

chief′tain (-tən) ***n.*** ⟦< L *caput*, head⟧ a chief, esp. of a clan or tribe

chif·fon (shi fän′) ***n.*** ⟦Fr⟧ a sheer, silky fabric —***adj.*** **1** of chiffon **2** made fluffy as with beaten egg whites [*lemon chiffon* pie]

chif·fo·nier or **chif·fon·nier** (shif′ə nir′) ***n.*** ⟦Fr⟧ a narrow, high chest of drawers, often with a mirror

THESAURUS

chemistry ***n.*** *Branches of chemistry include the following:* pure, quantitative, qualitative, organic, inorganic, theoretical, physical, physiological, pathological, metallurgical, mineralogical, geological, applied, agricultural, pharmaceutical, sanitary, industrial, technical, engineering chemistry; biochemistry, electrochemistry, zoochemistry; see also MEDICINE 3, SCIENCE 1.

cherish ***v.*** treasure, value, adore; see LOVE 1, 2.

cherry ***a.*** ruddy, reddish, rosy; see RED, PINK.

chest ***n.*** **1** [A boxlike container] case, box, coffer, cabinet, strongbox, receptacle, crate, locker, bureau, coffin, casket, treasury; see also CONTAINER. **2** [The ribbed portion of the body] breast, thorax, bosom, rib cage, heart, upper trunk, pulmonary cavity, peritoneum, ribs.

chew ***v.*** bite, champ, munch, crunch, masticate, nibble, feast upon, gnaw, gulp, grind, rend, scrunch, ruminate; see also EAT 1.

chicken ***n.*** **1** [A barnyard fowl] chick, hen, rooster; see FOWL. **2** [Flesh of the chicken] white meat, dark meat, giblets; see MEAT. **3** [*A coward] recreant, dastard, craven; see COWARD. —**count one's chickens before they are hatched** rely on, depend on, put trust in; see ANTICIPATE.

chief ***a.*** leading, first, foremost; see MAIN, PRINCIPAL.

chief ***n.*** principal, manager, overseer, governor, president, foreman, proprietor, supervisor, director, chairman, ringleader, general, master, dictator, superintendent, head, prince, emperor, duke, majesty, monarch, overlord, lord, potentate, sovereign, chieftain, ruler, captain, commander, bigwig*, prima donna*, boss, it*; see also LEADER.

chiefly ***a.*** mainly, particularly, in the first place; see PRINCIPALLY.

chig·ger (chig′ər) ***n.*** ⟦of Afr orig.⟧ the tiny, red larva of certain mites, whose bite causes severe itching

chi·gnon (shēn′yän′) ***n.*** ⟦Fr < L *catena*, chain⟧ a coil of hair worn at the back of the neck

Chi·hua·hua[1] (chi wä′wä) ***n.*** ⟦after fol.⟧ a Mexican breed of very small dog with large, pointed ears

Chi·hua·hua[2] (chi wä′wä) state of N Mexico, on the U.S. border: 95,401 sq. mi.; pop. 2,442,000

chil·blain (chil′blān′) ***n.*** ⟦CHIL(L) + *blain* < OE *blegen*, a sore⟧ a painful swelling or sore, esp. on the fingers or toes, caused by exposure to cold

child (chīld) ***n.***, *pl.* **chil′dren** ⟦OE *cild*⟧ **1** an infant **2** a boy or girl before puberty **3** a son or daughter; offspring —**with child** pregnant —**child′hood′** ***n.*** —**child′less** ***adj.***

child′birth′ ***n.*** the act of giving birth to a child

child′ish ***adj.*** of or like a child; specif., immature, silly, etc. —**child′ish·ly** ***adv.*** —**child′ish·ness** ***n.***

child′like′ ***adj.*** of or like a child; specif., innocent, trusting etc.

chil·dren (chil′drən) ***n.*** *pl. of* CHILD

child's play any very simple task

Chi·le (chil′ē) country on the SW coast of South America: 284,520 sq. mi.; pop. 13,232,000 —**Chil·e·an** (chi lā′ən, chil′ē ən) ***adj.***, ***n.***

chi·le re·lle·no (chē′le re yā′nō) *pl.* **chi·les re·lle·nos** (chē′les re yā′nōs) a hot, green pepper stuffed with cheese, meat, etc. and fried

chil·i (chil′ē) ***n.***, *pl.* **-ies** or **-is** ⟦MexSp⟧ **1** the very hot, dried pod of red pepper, often ground as a seasoning (**chili powder**) **2** any of certain other peppers used in Mexican cooking **3** a highly spiced dish of beef, chilies or chili powder, and often beans and tomatoes: in full **chil′i con car′ne** (-kän kär′nē) Also **chil′e**

chili dog a hot dog served with chili con carne

chili sauce a spiced sauce of chopped tomatoes, sweet peppers, onions, etc.

chill (chil) ***n.*** ⟦< OE *ciele*⟧ **1** coldness or coolness causing shivers **2** a moderate coldness **3** a sudden fear, etc. **4** unfriendliness —***adj.*** CHILLY —***vi.*** **1** to become cold **2** to shake or shiver **3** [Slang] to relax or calm down: usually with *out* —***vt.*** **1** to make cool or cold **2** to cause a chill in **3** to check (enthusiasm, etc.)

chill factor WINDCHILL FACTOR

chill′y ***adj.*** **-i·er**, **-i·est** **1** moderately cold **2** unfriendly —**chill′i·ness** ***n.***

chime (chīm) ***n.*** ⟦< Gr *kymbalon*, cymbal⟧ **1** [*usually pl.*] *a*) a set of tuned bells or metal tubes *b*) the musical sounds made by these **2** a single bell, as in a clock —***vi.*** **chimed**, **chim′ing** **1** to sound as a chime or bells **2** to agree —***vt.*** to give (the time) by chiming —**chime in** **1** to join in **2** to agree —**chim′er** ***n.***

Chi·me·ra (kī mir′ə, ki-) ***n.*** ⟦< Gr *chimaira*, orig., she-goat⟧ **1** *Gr. Myth.* a monster, with a lion's head, goat's body, and serpent's tail **2** [**c-**] an impossible fancy

chi·mer′i·cal (-mer′i kəl) ***adj.*** **1** imaginary; unreal **2** fanciful

chim·ney (chim′nē) ***n.***, *pl.* **-neys** ⟦ult. < Gr *kaminos*, oven⟧ **1** the passage or structure through which smoke escapes from a fire, usually extending above the roof **2** a glass tube around the flame of a lamp **3** a narrow column of rock

chim·pan·zee (chim′pan zē′, chim pan′zē) ***n.*** ⟦< Bantu⟧ a medium-sized great ape of Africa: also [Inf.] **chimp** (chimp)

chin (chin) ***n.*** ⟦OE *cin*⟧ the part of the face below the lower lip —***vt.*** **chinned**, **chin′ning** to pull (oneself) up, while hanging by the hands from a bar, until the chin is just above the bar

Chin *abbrev.* Chinese

chi·na (chī′nə) ***n.*** ⟦orig. made in China⟧ **1** porcelain or any ceramic ware like porcelain **2** dishes, etc. made of china **3** any earthenware Also **chi′na·ware′**

Chi·na (chī′nə) country in E Asia: 3,696,100 sq. mi.; pop. 1,130,511,000

chin·chil·la (chin chil′ə) ***n.*** ⟦prob. dim. of Sp *chinche*, a small bug⟧ **1** a small rodent of South America **2** its soft, gray fur

chine (chīn) ***n.*** ⟦< OFr *eschine*, spine⟧ a cut of meat from the backbone

Chi·nese (chī nēz′, -nēs′) ***n.*** **1** *pl.* **-nese′** a person born or living in China **2** the standard language of China, any related language of China, or the group consisting of these languages —***adj.*** of China or its people, language, etc.

Chinese checkers a game in which marbles are moved as checkers, on a board with holes arranged in the shape of a six-pointed star

Chinese lantern a paper lantern that can be folded up

chink[1] (chiŋk) ***n.*** ⟦OE *chine*⟧ a crack —***vt.*** to close up the chinks in

chink[2] (chiŋk) ***n.*** ⟦echoic⟧ a sharp, clinking sound —***vi.***, ***vt.*** to make or cause to make this sound

chi·no (chē′nō, shē′-) ***n.***, *pl.* **-nos** ⟦< ?⟧ **1** a strong, twilled cotton, khaki cloth **2** [*pl.*] pants of chino for casual wear

Chi·nook (shə no͝ok′, -no͞ok′; chə-) ***n.***, *pl.* **-nooks′** or **-nook′** ⟦< AmInd name⟧ a member of a North American Indian people of Washington and Oregon

chintz (chints) ***n.*** ⟦< Hindi *chhīnt*⟧ a cotton cloth printed in colored designs and usually glazed

chintz′y (-ē) ***adj.*** **-i·er**, **-i·est** ⟦prec. + -Y[3]⟧ **1** like chintz **2** [Inf.] cheap, stingy, etc.

chin-up ***n.*** PULL-UP

chip (chip) ***vt.*** **chipped**, **chip′ping** ⟦< OE⟧ to break or cut off small pieces from —***vi.*** **1** to break off in small pieces **2** *Golf* to make a short, lofted shot (**chip shot**) —***n.*** **1** a small piece of wood, etc. cut or broken off **2** a place where a small piece has been chipped off **3** a small disk used in gambling games as a counter **4** a thin slice of food *[a potato chip]* **5** INTEGRATED CIRCUIT —**chip in** [Inf.] to contribute (money, etc.) —**chip on one's shoulder** [Inf.] an inclination to fight or quarrel

chip′munk′ (-muŋk′) ***n.*** ⟦< AmInd⟧ a small, striped North American squirrel

chipped beef dried or smoked beef sliced into shavings

chip·per (chip′ər) ***adj.*** ⟦< N Brit Dial.⟧ [Inf.] sprightly; in good spirits

chiro- ⟦< Gr *cheir*, hand⟧ *combining form* hand

chi·rog·ra·phy (kī räg′rə fē) ***n.*** ⟦prec. + -GRAPHY⟧ handwriting

chi·rop·o·dy (kī räp′ə dē) ***n.*** ⟦CHIRO- + -POD + -Y[4]⟧ PODIATRY —**chi·rop′o·dist** ***n.***

chi·ro·prac·tic (kī′rō prak′tik) ***n.*** ⟦< CHIRO- + Gr *praktikos*, practical⟧ a method of treating disease by manipulation of the body joints, esp. of the spine —**chi′ro·prac′tor** ***n.***

chirp (churp) ***vi.***, ***vt.*** ⟦echoic⟧ to make, or utter in, short, shrill tones, as some birds do —***n.*** this sound

THESAURUS

child ***n.*** newborn, infant, youth, adolescent, youngster, daughter, son, grandchild, stepchild, offspring, innocent, minor, juvenile, tot, cherub, papoose, moppet*, kid*, kiddie*, kiddy*, whelp*, brat*, imp, small fry; see also BOY, GIRL.—*Ant.* PARENT, forefather, adult. —**with child** carrying a child, going to have a baby, expecting*; see PREGNANT.

childbirth ***n.*** delivery, childbearing, parturition, childbed, labor, nativity, delivering, accouchement, lying in, confinement, reproduction, giving birth, blessed event; see also BIRTH.

childhood ***n.*** infancy, youth, minority, school days, adolescence, nursery days, babyhood, boyhood, girlhood, teens, puberty, immaturity, tender age.—*Ant.* AGE, maturity, senility.

childish ***a.*** childlike, foolish, stupid, baby, infantile, juvenile, youthful, babyish, boyish, girlish, adolescent, green, soft, immature; see also NAIVE, SIMPLE 1, YOUNG 2.—*Ant.* MATURE, adult, grown.

chill ***n.*** crispness, coolness, coldness; see COLD 1.

chill ***v.*** **1** [To reduce temperature] refrigerate, frost, make cold; see COOL, FREEZE 1. **2** [To check] dispirit, dishearten, dampen; see DEPRESS 2, DISCOURAGE.

chilly ***a.*** brisk, fresh, crisp; see COLD 1, COOL 1.

chime ***v.*** tinkle, clang, toll; see RING 2, SOUND.

chimney ***n.*** smokestack, fireplace, furnace, hearth, flue, vent, pipe, funnel, chimney pot, stack.

chin ***n.*** mentum, mandible, jawbone; see JAW.

china ***n.*** porcelain, pottery, crockery; see DISH.

Chinese ***a.*** Sinitic, Asian, Asiatic; see ORIENTAL.

chip ***n.*** **1** [A fragment] fragment, slice, wedge; see BIT 1, FLAKE, PART 1. **2** [A microcircuit] integrated circuit, semiconductor, microprocessor, microchip. —**having a chip on one's shoulder** ready to fight, disturbed, agitated; see ANGRY. —**when the chips are down** in a crisis, having trouble, in a difficult position; see IN TROUBLE.

chip ***v.*** slash, hew, hack, crumble, snip, fragment, incise, whittle, crack off, splinter, notch, sliver, cut off, chop, split, slice, chisel, clip, break, crack, flake, cut away, nick, shiver, reduce, shear; see also BREAK.

chip in* ***v.*** contribute, pay, pitch in*; see SHARE 1.

chirp ***v.*** twitter, warble, cheep; see

chir·rup (chir′əp) ***vi.*** ⟦< prec.⟧ to chirp repeatedly —***n.*** a chirruping sound

chis·el (chiz′əl) ***n.*** ⟦< L *caedere,* to cut⟧ a sharp-edged hand tool for cutting or shaping wood, stone, etc. —***vi., vt.*** **-eled** or **-elled, -el·ing** or **-el·ling** **1** to cut or shape with a chisel **2** [Inf.] to swindle or get by swindling —**chis′el·er** or **chis′el·ler** ***n.***

chit (chit) ***n.*** ⟦< Hindi⟧ a voucher of a small sum owed for drink, food, etc.

chit·chat (chit′chat′) ***n.*** ⟦< CHAT⟧ **1** light, informal talk **2** gossip

chi·tin (kī′tin) ***n.*** ⟦< Gr *chitōn,* tunic⟧ the tough, horny outer covering of insects, crustaceans, etc.

chi·ton (kī′tən) ***n.*** ⟦Gr *chitōn,* tunic⟧ a small marine mollusk with a dorsal shell of eight plates

chit·ter·lings, chit·lins, or **chit·lings** (chit′linz) ***pl.n.*** ⟦< Gmc base⟧ small intestines of pigs, used for food

chiv·al·rous (shiv′əl rəs) ***adj.*** **1** gallant, courteous, etc. like an ideal knight **2** of chivalry Also **chiv′al·ric′** (-rik′, shi val′rik) —**chiv′al·rous·ly** ***adv.***

chiv′al·ry (-rē) ***n.*** ⟦< OFr *chevaler,* knight < *cheval,* horse⟧ **1** medieval knighthood **2** the qualities of an ideal knight, as courage, honor, etc.

chives (chīvz) ***pl.n.*** ⟦< L *cepa,* onion⟧ [*sometimes with sing. v.*] an herb with slender, hollow leaves and a mild onion odor, used for flavoring

chla·myd·i·a (klə mid′ē ə) ***n.*** a widespread venereal disease

chlo·ral (hydrate) (klôr′əl) a colorless, crystalline compound used as a sedative

chlo′ride′ (-īd′) ***n.*** a compound of chlorine with another element or radical

chlo′ri·nate′ (-ə nāt′) ***vt.*** **-nat′ed, -nat′ing** to combine (a substance) with chlorine; esp., to treat (water or sewage) with chlorine for purification —**chlo′ri·na′tion** ***n.***

chlo′rine′ (-ēn′) ***n.*** ⟦< Gr *chlōros,* pale green⟧ a greenish-yellow, poisonous, gaseous chemical element with a disagreeable odor, used in bleaching, water purification, etc.

chloro- ⟦< Gr *chlōros,* pale green⟧ *combining form* **1** green **2** having chlorine in the molecule

chlo·ro·form (klôr′ə fôrm′) ***n.*** ⟦< Fr: see prec. & FORMIC⟧ a colorless, volatile liquid used as a solvent and, formerly, as an anesthetic —***vt.*** to anesthetize or kill with chloroform

chlo′ro·phyll′ or **chlo′ro·phyl′** (-fil′) ***n.*** ⟦< Fr, ult. < Gr *chlōros,* green + *phyllon,* leaf⟧ the green pigment found in plant cells, essential to photosynthesis

chock (chäk) ***n.*** ⟦NormFr *choque,* a block⟧ a block or wedge placed under a wheel, etc. to prevent motion —***vt.*** to wedge fast as with a chock —***adv.*** as close or tight as can be

chock′-full′ ***adj.*** as full as possible

choc·o·late (chôk′lət, chäk′-; chôk′ə lət, chäk′ə-) ***n.*** ⟦ult. < AmInd (Mexico)⟧ **1** a substance made from roasted and ground cacao seeds **2** a drink or candy made with chocolate **3** reddish brown —***adj.*** **1** made of or flavored with chocolate **2** reddish-brown —**choc′o·lat·y** or **choc′o·lat·ey** ***adj.***

choice (chois) ***n.*** ⟦< OFr < Gothic *kausjan,* to test⟧ **1** a choosing; selection **2** the right or power to choose **3** a person or thing chosen **4** the best part **5** a variety from which to choose **6** an alternative —***adj.*** **choic′er, choic′est** **1** of special excellence **2** carefully chosen —**of choice** that is preferred

choir (kwīr) ***n.*** ⟦< L < Gr *choros*⟧ **1** a group of singers, esp. in a church **2** the part of a church they occupy

choke (chōk) ***vt.*** **choked, chok′ing** ⟦< OE *aceocian*⟧ **1** to prevent from breathing by blocking the windpipe; strangle; suffocate **2** to obstruct by clogging **3** to hinder the growth or action of **4** to cut off some air from the carburetor of (a gasoline engine) so as to make a richer gasoline mixture —***vi.*** **1** to be suffocated **2** [Inf.] to be unable to perform because of fear, tension, etc. —***n.*** **1** a choking **2** a sound of choking **3** the valve that chokes a carburetor —**choke back** to hold back (feelings, sobs, etc.) —**choke down** to swallow with difficulty —**choke off** to bring to an end

choke collar a training collar for a dog, that tightens when the dog strains at the leash: also **choke chain**

choke′hold′ ***n.*** **1** a locking one's arms around another's neck **2** absolute control

chok′er ***n.*** a closefitting necklace

chol·er (käl′ər) ***n.*** ⟦< L *cholera*: see fol.⟧ [Now Rare] anger or ill humor

chol·er·a (käl′ər ə) ***n.*** ⟦< Gr *cholē,* bile⟧ any of several severe intestinal diseases

chol′er·ic ***adj.*** easily angered

cho·les·ter·ol (kə les′tər ôl′, -ōl′) ***n.*** ⟦< Gr *cholē,* bile + *stereos,* solid⟧ a crystalline alcohol found esp. in animal fats, blood, nerve tissue, and bile

chomp (chämp) ***vt., vi.*** ⟦var. of CHAMP[1]⟧ **1** to chew hard and noisily **2** to bite down (*on*) repeatedly —**chomp at the bit** to be impatient when held back

Chong·qing (choonŋ′chiŋ′) city in SC China: pop. 2,673,000

choose (cho͞oz) ***vt., vi.*** **chose, cho′sen, choos′ing** ⟦OE *ceosan*⟧ **1** to take as a choice; select **2** to decide or prefer [*to choose* to go] —**cannot choose but** cannot do otherwise than —**choos′er** ***n.***

choos′y or **choos′ey** ***adj.*** **-i·er, -i·est** [Inf.] careful or fussy in choosing

chop (chäp) ***vt.*** **chopped, chop′ping** ⟦ME *choppen*⟧ **1** to cut by blows with a sharp tool **2** to cut into small bits; mince —***vi.*** to make quick, cutting strokes —***n.*** **1** a short, sharp stroke **2** a cut of meat and bone from the rib, loin, or shoulder **3** a short, broken movement of waves

Cho·pin (shō′pan; *Fr* shô pan′), **Fré·dé·ric** (fred′rik; *Fr* frā dā rēk′) 1810-49; Pol. composer, in France after 1831

chop·per (chäp′ər) ***n.*** **1** one that chops **2** [*pl.*] [Slang] teeth **3** [Inf.] a helicopter

chop′py ***adj.*** **-pi′er, -pi·est** **1** rough with short, broken waves, as the sea **2** making abrupt starts and stops —**chop′pi·ness** ***n.***

chops (chäps) ***pl.n.*** **1** the jaws **2** the mouth and lower cheeks

chop′sticks′ ***pl.n.*** ⟦Pidgin English⟧ two small sticks held together in one hand and used, mainly in parts of Asia, as an eating utensil

chop su·ey (chäp′ so͞o′ē) ⟦< Chin *tsa-sui,* various pieces⟧ a Chinese-American dish of meat, bean sprouts, etc., served with rice

cho·ral (kôr′əl) ***adj.*** of, for, or sung by a choir or chorus —**cho′ral·ly** ***adv.***

cho·rale or **cho·ral** (kə ral′, -räl′) ***n.*** **1** a hymn tune **2** a choir or chorus

chord[1] (kôrd) ***n.*** ⟦altered (infl. by L *chorda*) < CORD⟧ **1** [Archaic] the string of a musical instrument **2** *Geom.* a straight line joining any two points on an arc

chord[2] (kôrd) ***n.*** ⟦< ME *accord,* accord⟧ *Music* a combination of three or more tones sounded together in harmony

chor·date (kôr′dāt′) ***n.*** ⟦L *chorda,* CORD + -ATE[1]⟧ any of a

THESAURUS

SOUND.

chisel ***n.*** gouge, blade, edge; see KNIFE, TOOL 1.

chisel ***v.*** **1** [To work with a chisel] carve, hew, incise; see CUT 1. **2** [*To get by imposition] impose upon, defraud, gyp*; see DECEIVE, STEAL.

chivalrous ***a.*** courteous, heroic, valiant; see BRAVE, NOBLE 1, 2, POLITE.

chivalry ***n.*** valor, gallantry, honor; see COURTESY 1.

chock-full ***a.*** packed, crammed, stuffed; see FULL 1.

choice ***a.*** superior, fine, exceptional; see BEST 1.

choice ***n.*** selection, preference, alternative, election, substitute, favorite, pick, a good bet; see also OPTION 1.

choke ***v.*** asphyxiate, strangle, strangulate, stifle, throttle, garrote, drown, noose, smother, grab by the throat, wring the neck of, stop the breath of, gag, gasp, suffocate, choke off, be choked, die out, die by asphyxiation; see also DIE. —**choke up*** give way to one's feelings, weep, break down; see CRY 1.

choose ***v.*** take, pick out, draw lots, cull, prefer, make a choice of, accept, weigh, judge, sort, appoint, embrace, will, call for, fancy, take up, separate, favor, determine, resolve, discriminate, make a decision, adopt, collect, mark out for, cut out, arrange, keep, make one's choice, pick and choose, settle on, use one's discretion, determine upon, fix on, place one's trust in, glean, single out, espouse, exercise one's option, make up one's mind, set aside, set apart, commit oneself, separate the wheat from the chaff, incline toward, opt for, burn one's bridges; see also DECIDE.—*Ant.* DISCARD, reject, refuse.

choosing ***n.*** selecting, picking, judging; see JUDGMENT 2.

chop ***v.*** fell, cut with an ax, whack; see CUT 1.

chord[2] ***n.*** harmonizing tones, triad, octave; major chord, minor chord, diminished chord, augmented chord, inverted chord, broken chord; tonic chord, dominant chord, subdominant chord; tetrachord, perfect fourth, arpeggio, common chord; see also HARMONY 1, MUSIC 1.

phylum of animals having a dorsal nerve cord, including the vertebrates

chore (chôr) *n.* ⟦< OE *cierr*, job⟧ **1** a routine task **2** a hard task

chor·e·o·graph (kôr′ē ə graf′) *vt.*, *vi.* ⟦< fol.⟧ **1** to design or plan the movements of (a dance) **2** to plan (something) in careful detail —**chor′e·og′ra·pher** (-äg′rə fər) *n.*

chor·e·og·ra·phy (kôr′ē äg′rə fē) *n.* ⟦Gr *choreia*, dance + -GRAPHY⟧ **1** dancing, esp. ballet dancing **2** the devising of dances, esp. ballets —**chor′e·o·graph′ic** (-ə graf′ik) *adj.*

chor·is·ter (kôr′is tər) *n.* ⟦see CHORUS⟧ a member of a choir

cho·roid (kôr′oid′) *n.* ⟦Gr < *chorion*, fetal membrane + *-eidēs*, -OID⟧ the dark, middle membrane of the eye

chor·tle (chôrt′'l) *vi.* **-tled**, **-tling** ⟦prob. < CHUCKLE + SNORT⟧ to make a gleeful chuckling or snorting sound —*n.* such a sound —**chor′tler** *n.*

cho·rus (kôr′əs) *n.* ⟦< Gr *choros*⟧ **1** a group of dancers and singers performing together **2** the part of a drama, song, etc. performed by a chorus **3** a group singing or speaking something together **4** music written for group singing **5** the refrain of a song —*vt.*, *vi.* to sing, speak, or say in unison —**in chorus** in unison

chose (chōz) *vt.*, *vi. pt. & obs. pp. of* CHOOSE

cho·sen (chō′zən) *vt.*, *vi. pp. of* CHOOSE —*adj.* selected

Chou En-lai (jō′en′lī′) 1898-1976; Chin. premier (1949-76): Pinyin *Zhou En-lai*

chow (chou) *n.* ⟦< Chin⟧ **1** any of a breed of medium-sized dog, originally from China: also **chow chow** **2** [Slang] food

chow·der (chou′dər) *n.* ⟦Fr *chaudière*, a pot⟧ a thick soup usually of onions and potatoes and, often, clams and milk

chow′hound′ *n.* [Slang] a glutton

chow mein (chou′ mān′) ⟦Chin *ch'ao*, fry + *mien*, flour⟧ a Chinese-American dish of meat, bean sprouts, etc., served with fried noodles

Chré·tien (krā tyan′), **Jean** (zhän) 1934- ; prime minister of Canada (1993-)

chrism (kriz′əm) *n.* ⟦< Gr *chrisma*, oil⟧ holy oil used as in baptism

Christ (krīst) ⟦< Gr *christos*, the anointed⟧ Jesus of Nazareth, regarded by Christians as the prophesied Messiah

chris·ten (kris′ən) *vt.* **1** to baptize **2** to give a name to, as at baptism **3** [Inf.] to use for the first time —**chris′ten·ing** *n.*

Chris′ten·dom (-dəm) *n.* **1** Christians collectively **2** those parts of the world where most of the inhabitants profess Christianity

Chris·tian (kris′chən) *n.* a believer in Jesus as the prophesied Messiah, or in the religion based on the teachings of Jesus —*adj.* **1** of Jesus Christ **2** of or professing the religion based on his teachings **3** having the qualities taught by Jesus Christ, as love, kindness, humility, etc. **4** of Christians or Christianity

Chris·ti·an·i·ty (kris′chē an′ə tē) *n.* **1** Christians collectively **2** the Christian religion **3** the state of being a Christian

Chris·tian·ize (kris′chən īz′) *vt.* **-ized′**, **-iz′ing** to make Christian

Christian name the baptismal name or given name, as distinguished from the surname or family name

Christian Science a religion and system of healing: official name **Church of Christ, Scientist**

Chris·tie (kris′tē) *n.*, *pl.* **-ties** ⟦after *Christiania*, former name of Oslo, Norway⟧ *Skiing* a high-speed turn with the skis parallel

Christ·mas (kris′məs) *n.* ⟦see CHRIST & MASS⟧ a holiday on Dec. 25 celebrating the birth of Jesus Christ

chro·mat·ic (krō mat′ik) *adj.* ⟦< Gr *chrōma*, color⟧ **1** of or having color or colors **2** *Music* progressing by semitones —**chro·mat′i·cal·ly** *adv.*

chro·ma·tin (krō′mə tin) *n.* ⟦< Gr *chrōma*, color⟧ a substance in cell nuclei containing the genes: it readily absorbs a coloring agent, as for observation under a microscope

chrome (krōm) *n.* ⟦Fr: see CHROMIUM⟧ chromium or chromium alloy —*adj.* designating any of various pigments (**chrome red**, **chrome yellow**) made from chromium compounds —*vt.* **chromed**, **chrom′ing** to plate with chromium

-chrome (krōm) ⟦< Gr *chrōma*, color⟧ *combining form* **1** color or coloring agent **2** chromium

chro·mi·um (krō′mē əm) *n.* ⟦< Gr *chrōma*, color⟧ a hard, metallic chemical element resistant to corrosion

chromo- ⟦< Gr *chrōma*, color⟧ *combining form* color or pigment *[chromosome]* Also **chrom-**

chro·mo·some (krō′mə sōm′) *n.* ⟦< prec.⟧ any of the microscopic rod-shaped bodies carrying the genes

chron·ic (krän′ik) *adj.* ⟦< Gr *chronos*, time⟧ **1** lasting a long time or recurring: said of a disease **2** having had an ailment for a long time **3** habitual —**chron′i·cal·ly** *adv.*

chron·i·cle (krän′i kəl) *n.* ⟦< Gr *chronika*, annals⟧ a historical record of events in the order in which they happened —*vt.* **-cled**, **-cling** to tell the history of; recount; record —**chron′i·cler** *n.*

chrono- ⟦< Gr *chronos*, time⟧ *combining form* time: also **chron-**

chro·nol·o·gy (krə näl′ə jē) *n.*, *pl.* **-gies** ⟦prec. + -LOGY⟧ **1** the science of measuring time and of dating events **2** the arrangement of events in the order of occurrence —**chron·o·log·i·cal** (krän′ə läj′i kəl) *adj.* —**chron′o·log′i·cal·ly** *adv.*

chro·nom′e·ter (-näm′ət ər) *n.* ⟦CHRONO- + -METER⟧ a highly accurate kind of clock or watch

chrys·a·lis (kris′ə lis) *n.*, *pl.* **chry·sal·i·des** (kri sal′ə dēz′) or **chrys′a·lis·es** ⟦< Gr *chrysallis*⟧ **1** the pupa of a butterfly, encased in a cocoon **2** the cocoon

chrys·an·the·mum (kri san′thə məm) *n.* ⟦< Gr *chrysos*, gold + *anthemon*, flower⟧ **1** a late-blooming plant of the composite family, with showy flowers **2** the flower

chub (chub) *n.*, *pl.* **chub** or **chubs** a small freshwater fish often used as bait

chub·by (chub′ē) *adj.* **-bi·er**, **-bi·est** round and plump —**chub′bi·ness** *n.*

chuck[1] (chuk) *vt.* ⟦< ? Fr *choquer*, strike against⟧ **1** to tap playfully, esp. under the chin **2** to throw; toss **3** [Slang] to get rid of —*n.* a chucking

chuck[2] (chuk) *n.* ⟦prob. var. of CHOCK⟧ **1** a cut of beef from around the neck and shoulder blade **2** a clamplike holding device, as on a lathe

chuck′-full′ *adj. var. of* CHOCK-FULL

chuck′hole′ *n.* ⟦see CHOCK & HOLE⟧ a rough hole in pavement

THESAURUS

chore *n.* task, work, errand; see JOB 2.

chorus *n.* **1** [A body of singers] choir, singing group, choristers, voices, glee club, singing society, church singers, male chorus, female chorus, mixed chorus, chorale; see also MUSIC 1. **2** [A refrain] melody, strain, tune; see SONG.

chosen *a.* picked, elected, preferred; see NAMED 2.

Christ *n.* the Saviour, Jesus, Jesus Christ, Jesus of Nazareth, the Redeemer, the Messiah, Immanuel, Emmanuel, the Anointed, the Word, the Son, the Son of Man, the Son of God, God the Son, the Son of David, the Son of Mary, the Risen, the King of Glory, the Prince of Peace, the Good Shepherd, King of the Jews, the Lamb of God, the Only Begotten, King of Kings, Lord of Lords, Christ Our Lord, the Way, the Door, the Truth, the Life, the Light of the World, Alpha and Omega, the Incarnate Word, the Word made Flesh; see also GOD 2.

christen *v.* immerse, sprinkle, name; see BAPTIZE, BLESS.

Christian *a.* pious, reverent, gentile; see HUMBLE 1, RELIGIOUS 1, 2.

Christian *n.* Protestant, Catholic, gentile; see CHURCH 3, SAINT.

Christianity *n.* **1** [A religion based upon the divinity of Christ] teachings of Christ, the Gospel, the Faith; see FAITH 2, RELIGION 2. **2** [The body of Christian people] Christendom, Christians, followers of Christ; see CHURCH 3. **3** [An attitude associated with Christianity] Christian spirit, forgiving disposition, mercy; see KINDNESS 1, TOLERANCE 1.

Christmas *n.* Xmas*, the Nativity, Yule; see HOLIDAY, WINTER.

chronic *a.* inveterate, confirmed, settled, rooted, deep-seated, continuing, persistent, stubborn, incurable, lasting, lingering, deep-rooted, perennial, fixed, continual, incessant, long-standing, recurring, continuous, of long duration, long-lived, protracted, ceaseless, sustained, lifelong, prolonged, recurrent, obstinate, inborn, inbred, ingrained, ever-present; see also CONSTANT, HABITUAL, PERMANENT.—*Ant.* TEMPORARY, acute, casual.

chronicle *n.* narrative, annals, account; see HISTORY, RECORD 1.

chronological *a.* temporal, historical, classified according to chronology, in the order of time, sequential, consecutive, properly dated, measured in time, in sequence, progressive in time, ordered, in order, in due course.

chubby *a.* plump, round, pudgy; see FAT.

chuck·le (chuk′əl) ***vi.* -led, -ling** ⟦? < var. of CLUCK⟧ to laugh softly in a low tone —***n.*** a soft, low-toned laugh
chuck wagon a wagon equipped as a kitchen for feeding cowboys, etc.
chuck·wal·la (chuk′wäl′ə) ***n.*** ⟦< AmInd (Mexico)⟧ a large, edible iguana of Mexico and SW U.S.
chug (chug) ***n.*** ⟦echoic⟧ any of a series of puffing or explosive sounds, as of a locomotive —***vi.* chugged, chug′ging** to make, or move with, such sounds —***vt.*** [Slang] to drink in gulps
chuk·ka (boot) (chuk′ə) an ankle-high bootlike shoe
chum (chum) [Inf.] ***n.*** ⟦prob. < *chamber* (*mate*)⟧ a close friend —***vi.* chummed, chum′ming** to be close friends —**chum′my, -mi·er, -mi·est, *adj.*** —**chum′mi·ness *n.***
chump (chump) ***n.*** ⟦akin to MHG *kumpf,* dull⟧ [Inf.] a fool or dupe
Chung·king (choonˈkiŋ′) *a former transliteration of* CHONGQING
chunk (chuŋk) ***n.*** ⟦< ? CHUCK[2]⟧ a short, thick piece
chunk′y *adj.* -i·er, -i·est 1 short and thick **2** stocky **3** containing chunks —**chunk′i·ness *n.***
church (church) ***n.*** ⟦< Gr *kyriakē* (*oikia*), Lord's (house)⟧ **1** a building for public worship, esp. Christian worship **2** religious service **3** [*usually* **C-**] *a*) all Christians *b*) a particular Christian denomination **4** a religious congregation **5** ecclesiastical, as opposed to secular, government
church′go′er (-gō′ər) ***n.*** a person who attends church, esp. regularly
Church·ill (chur′chil), Sir **Win·ston** (win′stən) 1874-1965; Brit. prime minister (1940-45; 1951-55)
church′man (-mən) ***n.**, pl.* -men** (-mən) **1** a clergyman **2** a church member
Church of England the episcopal church of England; Anglican Church: it is an established church headed by the sovereign
church′war′den (-wôrd′'n) ***n.*** a lay officer handling certain secular matters in a church
church′yard′ *n.* the ground adjoining a church, often used as a cemetery
churl (churl) ***n.*** ⟦OE *ceorl,* peasant⟧ **1** a peasant **2** a surly person; boor —**churl′ish *adj.*** —**churl′ish·ness *n.***
churn (churn) ***n.*** ⟦OE *cyrne*⟧ a container in which milk or cream is stirred or shaken to form butter —***vt., vi.* 1** to stir or shake (milk or cream) in a churn **2** to make (butter) thus **3** to stir up or move vigorously —**churn out** to produce in abundance
chute[1] (shōōt) ***n.*** ⟦Fr, a fall⟧ an inclined or vertical trough or passage down which things slide or drop
chute[2] (shōōt) ***n.*** [Inf.] *short for* PARACHUTE
chut·ney (chut′nē) ***n.**, pl.* -neys** ⟦Hindi *chatnī*⟧ a relish of fruits, spices, herbs, and vinegar
chutz·pah or **chutz·pa** (hoots′pə, khoots′-) ***n.*** ⟦Yiddish < Heb⟧ [Inf.] impudence; brass
chyme (kīm) ***n.*** ⟦< Gr *chymos,* juice⟧ the semifluid mass formed as the stomach digests food: it passes into the small intestine
CIA *abbrev.* Central Intelligence Agency
ci·ca·da (si kā′də) ***n.**, pl.* -das** or **-dae** (-dē) ⟦L⟧ a large, flylike insect with transparent wings: the male makes a loud, shrill sound
cic·a·trix (sik′ə triks′) ***n.**, pl.* cic·a·tri·ces** (sik′ə trī′sēz′) or **cic′a·trix′es** ⟦L⟧ a scar
Cic·e·ro (sis′ə rō′) 106-43 B.C.; Rom. statesman & orator
-cide (sīd) ⟦< L *caedere,* to kill⟧ *suffix* **1** a killer **2** a killing
ci·der (sī′dər) ***n.*** ⟦< Gr *sikera,* an intoxicant⟧ juice pressed from apples, used as a drink or for making vinegar
ci·gar (si gär′) ***n.*** ⟦Sp *cigarro*⟧ a roll of cut tobacco wrapped in a tobacco leaf for smoking
cig·a·rette or **cig·a·ret** (sig′ə ret′, sig′ə ret′) ***n.*** ⟦Fr⟧ a small roll of finely cut tobacco wrapped in thin paper for smoking
cig·a·ril·lo (sig′ə ril′ō) ***n.**, pl.* -los** ⟦Sp, dim. of *cigarro,* cigar⟧ a small, thin cigar
ci·lan·tro (si lan′trō, -län′-) ***n.*** coriander leaves used as an herb
cil·i·a (sil′ē ə) ***pl.n.**, sing.* -i·um** (-ē əm) ⟦< L⟧ small hairlike projections, as those extending from certain plant cells or from around protozoa
ci·met·i·dine (sə met′ə dēn′) ***n.*** a drug that reduces gastric secretion: used to treat peptic ulcers
cinch (sinch) ***n.*** ⟦< Sp < L *cingulum,* girdle⟧ **1** a saddle or pack girth **2** [Slang] a thing easy to do —***vt.* 1** to fasten (a saddle) on (a horse, etc.) with a cinch **2** [Slang] to make sure of
cin·cho·na (sin kō′nə) ***n.*** ⟦after 17th-c. Peruvian Countess del *Chinchón*⟧ **1** a tropical tree with a bitter bark from which quinine is made **2** this bark
Cin·cin·nat·i (sin′sə nat′ē, -ə) city in SW Ohio: pop. 364,000
cinc·ture (siŋk′chər) ***n.*** ⟦L *cinctura*⟧ a belt or girdle
cin·der (sin′dər) ***n.*** ⟦OE *sinder,* slag⟧ **1** a tiny piece of partly burned coal, wood, etc. **2** [*pl.*] ashes from coal or wood
Cin·der·el·la (sin′dər el′ə) ***n.*** in a fairy tale, a household drudge who eventually marries a prince
cin·e·ma (sin′ə mə) ***n.*** ⟦< Gr *kinēma,* motion⟧ [Chiefly Brit.] a film theater —**the cinema 1** the making of films **2** films collectively —**cin′e·mat′ic *adj.***
cin·e·ma·tog·ra·phy (sin′ə mə täg′rə fē) ***n.*** the art, science, and work of photography in making films —**cin′e·ma·tog′ra·pher *n.*** —**cin′e·mat′o·graph′ic** (-mat′ə graf′ik) ***adj.***
cin·na·bar (sin′ə bär′) ***n.*** ⟦< Gr *kinnabari*⟧ mercuric sulfide, a heavy, bright-red mineral
cin·na·mon (sin′ə mən) ***n.*** ⟦< Heb *qinnāmōn*⟧ **1** the yellowish-brown spice made from the dried inner bark of a laurel tree of the East Indies **2** this bark
ci·pher (sī′fər) ***n.*** ⟦< Ar *ṣifr*⟧ **1** the symbol 0; zero **2** a nonentity **3** secret writing based on a key; code **4** the key to such a code
cir·ca (sur′kə) ***prep.*** ⟦L⟧ about: used before an approximate date or figure: also written ***cir′ca***
cir·ca·di·an (sər kā′dē ən) ***adj.*** ⟦coined < L *circa,* about + *dies,* day⟧ of the behavioral or physiological rhythms associated with the 24-hour cycle of the earth's rotation
Cir·ce (sur′sē) ***n.*** in the *Odyssey*, an enchantress who turns men into swine
cir·cle (sur′kəl) ***n.*** ⟦< Gr *kirkos*⟧ **1** a plane figure bounded by a single curved line every point of which is equally distant from the center **2** this curved line **3** anything like a circle, as a ring **4** a complete or recurring series; cycle **5** a group of people with common interests **6** extent, as of influence; scope —***vt.* -cled, -cling 1** to form a circle around **2** to move around, as in a circle —***vi.*** to go around in a circle —**cir′cler *n.***

THESAURUS

chuckle *n.* chortle, snicker, giggle; see LAUGH.

chuckle *v.* giggle, chortle, snicker; see LAUGH.

chummy* ***a.*** affectionate, sociable, palsy-walsy*; see FRIENDLY.

chunk *n.* piece, mass, lump; see PART 1.

chunky *a.* stocky, thickset, stout; see FAT.

church *n.* 1 [A building consecrated to worship] cathedral, house of God, Lord's house, temple, synagogue, mosque, house of worship, meetinghouse, chapel, basilica, tabernacle, abbey, sanctuary, house of prayer, mission, shrine, pagoda. **2** [A divine service] rite, prayers, prayer meeting, Sunday school, worship, Mass, liturgy, Lord's Supper, sacrament, the holy sacrament, rosary, ritual, religious rite, morning service, evening service, congregational worship, fellowship, devotion, office, revival meeting, chapel service, sermon, communion; see also CEREMONY. **3** [An organized religious body] congregation, gathering, denomination, sect, chapter, body, order, communion, faith, religion, religious order, affiliation, persuasion, belief, faction, doctrine, creed, cult. *Christian churches include the following:* Methodist, Presbyterian, Episcopal, Baptist, Christian Science, Mormon, Congregational, Lutheran, Roman Catholic, Eastern Orthodox, Greek Catholic, Pentecostal, Church of England, Church of the Nazarene, Society of Friends.

churn *v.* stir, beat, agitate; see MIX 1.

cigarette *n.* fag*, smoke*, coffin nail*, weed*.

cinema *n.* film, motion pictures, the movies; see MOVIE.

circle *n.* 1 [A round closed plane figure] ring, loop, wheel, sphere, globe, orb, orbit, zodiac, bowl, vortex, hoop, horizon, perimeter, periphery, circumference, full turn, circuit, disk, meridian, equator, ecliptic, cycle, bracelet, belt, wreath. **2** [An endless sequence of events] cycle, course, succession; see PROGRESS 1, SERIES, SEQUENCE 1. —**come full circle** go through a cycle, come back, revert; see RETURN 1.

circle *v.* round, encircle, loop, tour, circumnavigate, ring, belt, embrace, encompass, wind about, revolve around, circumscribe, curve around, circuit, enclose, spiral, coil, circulate, detour, wind, roll, wheel, swing past, go round about, evade; see also SURROUND 1.—*Ant.* DIVIDE, bisect, cut across.

cir′clet (-klit) ***n.*** **1** a small circle **2** a circular ornament, as for the head

cir·cuit (sʉr′kit) ***n.*** ⟦< L *circum,* around + *ire,* go⟧ **1** a boundary line or its length **2** a going around something **3** the regular journey through a district of a person at work, as a preacher **4** the district of a U.S. Court of Appeals **5** a chain or association, as of theaters or resorts **6** the path or line of an electric current —***vi.*** to go in a circuit —***vt.*** to make a circuit about —**cir′cuit·al** ***adj.***

circuit breaker a device that automatically interrupts the flow of an electric current

circuit court a court that holds sessions in various places within its district

cir·cu·i·tous (sər kyo͞o′ət əs) ***adj.*** roundabout; indirect —**cir·cu′i·tous·ly** ***adv.*** —**cir·cu′i·tous·ness** ***n.***

cir·cuit·ry (sʉr′kə trē) ***n.*** the system or the elements of an electric circuit

cir·cu·lar (sʉr′kyə lər) ***adj.*** **1** in the shape of a circle; round **2** moving in a circle **3** circuitous —***n.*** an advertisement, etc., intended for many readers —**cir′cu·lar′i·ty** (-ler′ə tē) ***n.***

cir′cu·lar·ize′ (-īz′) ***vt.*** **-ized′, -iz′ing** **1** to make circular **2** to send circulars to **3** to canvass —**cir′cu·lar·i·za′tion** ***n.*** —**cir′cu·lar·iz′er** ***n.***

cir·cu·late (sʉr′kyə lāt′) ***vi.*** **-lat′ed, -lat′ing** ⟦< L *circulari,* form a circle⟧ **1** to move in a circle or circuit and return, as the blood **2** to go from person to person or from place to place —***vt.*** to make circulate —**cir′cu·lat′or** ***n.*** —**cir′cu·la·to′ry** (-lə tôr′ē) ***adj.***

cir·cu·la·tion (sʉr′kyə lā′shən) ***n.*** **1** a circulating **2** the movement of blood through the arteries and veins **3** the distribution of newspapers, magazines, etc. **4** the average number of copies of a periodical sold in a given period

circum- ⟦< L *circum*⟧ *prefix* around, about, surrounding

cir·cum·cise (sʉr′kəm sīz′) ***vt.*** **-cised′, -cis′ing** ⟦< L < *circum,* around + *caedere,* to cut⟧ to cut off all or part of the foreskin of —**cir′cum·ci′sion** (-sizh′ən) ***n.***

cir·cum·fer·ence (sər kum′fər əns, -frəns) ***n.*** ⟦< L *circum,* around + *ferre,* to carry⟧ **1** the line bounding a circle, ball, etc. **2** the length of this line

cir·cum·flex (sʉr′kəm fleks′) ***n.*** ⟦< L *circum,* around + *flectere,* to bend⟧ a mark (^ or ~) used over a vowel to indicate pronunciation

cir′cum·lo·cu′tion (-lō kyo͞o′shən) ***n.*** ⟦< L: see CIRCUM- & LOCUTION⟧ a roundabout way of saying something

cir′cum·nav′i·gate′ (-nav′ə-) ***vt.*** **-gat′ed, -gat′ing** ⟦< L: see CIRCUM- & NAVIGATE⟧ to sail or fly around (the earth, etc.) —**cir′cum·nav′i·ga′tion** ***n.***

cir′cum·scribe′ (-skrīb′) ***vt.*** **-scribed′, -scrib′ing** ⟦< L: see CIRCUM- & SCRIBE⟧ **1** to trace a line around; encircle **2** to limit; confine —**cir′cum·scrip′tion** (-skrip′shən) ***n.***

cir′cum·spect′ (-spekt′) ***adj.*** ⟦< L *circumspicere,* look about⟧ cautious; discreet —**cir′cum·spec′tion** ***n.*** —**cir′cum·spect′ly** ***adv.***

cir′cum·stance′ (-stans′) ***n.*** ⟦< L *circum,* around + *stare,* to stand⟧ **1** a fact or event, specif. one accompanying another **2** [*pl.*] conditions affecting a person, esp. financial conditions **3** chance; luck **4** ceremony; show —***vt.*** **-stanced′, -stanc′ing** to place in certain circumstances —**under no circumstances** never —**cir′cum·stanced′** ***adj.***

cir′cum·stan′tial (-stan′shəl) ***adj.*** **1** having to do with, or depending on, circumstances **2** incidental **3** complete in detail —**cir′cum·stan′tial·ly** ***adv.***

circumstantial evidence *Law* indirect evidence of a fact at issue, based on attendant circumstances

cir′cum·vent′ (-vent′) ***vt.*** ⟦< L *circum,* around + *venire,* come⟧ to get the better of or prevent by craft or ingenuity —**cir′cum·ven′tion** ***n.***

cir·cus (sʉr′kəs) ***n.*** ⟦L, a circle⟧ **1** in ancient Rome, an amphitheater **2** a traveling show of acrobats, trained animals, clowns, etc. **3** [Inf.] a place or event regarded as being frenzied, wildly entertaining, etc.

ci·ré (sē rā′) ***adj.*** ⟦< Fr *cire,* wax⟧ having a smooth, glossy finish

cir·rho·sis (sə rō′sis) ***n.*** ⟦< Gr *kirrhos,* tawny + -OSIS⟧ a degenerative disease, esp. of the liver, marked by excess formation of connective tissue —**cir·rhot′ic** (-rät′ik) ***adj.***

cir·rus (sir′əs) ***n.,*** *pl.* **cir′rus** ⟦L, a curl⟧ the type of cloud resembling a wispy filament and found at high altitudes

CIS *abbrev.* Commonwealth of Independent States

cis- ⟦< L *cis,* on this side⟧ *prefix* on this side of

cis·tern (sis′tərn) ***n.*** ⟦< L *cista,* chest⟧ a large tank for storing water, esp. rainwater

cit·a·del (sit′ə del′) ***n.*** ⟦< L *civitas,* city⟧ a fortress

cite (sīt) ***vt.*** **cit′ed, cit′ing** ⟦< L *citare,* summon⟧ **1** to summon before a court of law **2** to quote **3** to mention by way of example, proof, etc. **4** to mention in an official report as meritorious —**ci·ta′tion** ***n.***

cit·i·fied (sit′i fīd′) ***adj.*** having the manners, dress, etc. of city people

cit·i·zen (sit′ə zən) ***n.*** ⟦< L *civis,* townsman⟧ a member of a state or nation who owes allegiance to it by birth or naturalization and is entitled to full civil rights —**cit′i·zen·ship′** ***n.***

cit′i·zen·ry ***n.*** citizens as a group

cit·ric (si′trik) ***adj.*** designating or of an acid obtained from citrus fruits

cit′ron (-trən) ***n.*** ⟦< Fr, lemon⟧ **1** a yellow, thick-skinned, lemonlike fruit **2** its candied rind

cit·ron·el·la (si′trə nel′ə) ***n.*** ⟦see prec.⟧ a sharp-smelling oil used in soap, insect repellents, etc.

cit′rus (-trəs) ***n.*** ⟦L⟧ **1** any of the trees that bear oranges, lemons, limes, etc. **2** any such fruit —***adj.*** of these trees: also **cit′rous**

cit·y (sit′ē) ***n.,*** *pl.* **-ies** ⟦< L *civis,* townsman⟧ **1** a population center larger or more important than a town **2** in the U.S., an incorporated municipality with boundaries and powers defined by state charter **3** the people of a city —***adj.*** of, in, or for a city —**cit′y·wide′** ***adj.***

city hall (a building that houses) a municipal government

civ·et (siv′it) ***n.*** ⟦< Ar *zabād*⟧ **1** the musky secretion of a

THESAURUS

circuit ***n.*** circumference, course, circle; see ORBIT 1, REVOLUTION 1.

circular ***a.*** annular, spherical, cyclical; see ROUND 1.

circular ***n.*** handbill, flier, leaflet; see ADVERTISEMENT, PAMPHLET.

circulate ***v.*** **1** [To go about] move around, go about, wander; see TRAVEL, WALK 1. **2** [To send about] diffuse, report, broadcast; see DISTRIBUTE.

circulation ***n.*** **1** [Motion in a circle] rotation, passage, flow; see FLOW, REVOLUTION 1. **2** [Number of copies distributed] volume, apportionment, dissemination; see DISTRIBUTION.

circumference ***n.*** perimeter, periphery, border; see CIRCLE 1.

circumscribe ***v.*** encircle, encompass, girdle; see SURROUND 1.

circumstance ***n.*** **1** [An attendant condition] situation, condition, contingency, phase, factor, detail, item, fact, case, place, time, cause, status, element, feature, point, incident, article, stipulation, concern, matter, event, occurrence, crisis, coincidence, fate, chance, happenstance*. **2** [An occurrence] episode, happening, incident; see EVENT.

circumstances ***n.*** **1** [Condition in life] worldly goods, outlook, prospects, chances, means, assets, prosperity, financial condition, resources, standing, property, net worth, financial standing, credit rating, terms, way of life, rank, class, degree, capital, position, financial responsibility, footing, income, sphere, substance, stock in trade, lot, prestige, what one is worth, place on the ladder; see also STATE 2, WEALTH. **2** [Attendant conditions] situation, environment, surroundings, facts, particulars, factors, features, motives, controlling factors, governing factors, the times, occasion, basis, grounds, setting, background, needs, requirements, necessities, course of events, legal status, change, life, fluctuation, phase, case, condition, state of affairs, surrounding facts, the score*, the scene*, the story*, where it's at*, how the land lies, the lay of the land, current regime, ups and downs. —**under no circumstances** under no conditions, by no means, absolutely not; see NEVER. —**under the circumstances** conditions being what they are, for this reason, because of this; see BECAUSE.

circumstantial ***a.*** presumptive, inferential, inconclusive; see UNCERTAIN.

circumvent ***v.*** **1** [To go around] encircle, encompass, entrap; see SURROUND 1. **2** [To avoid] dodge, elude, bypass; see AVOID, EVADE.

circus ***n.*** carnival, spectacle, fair; see ENTERTAINMENT.

citation ***n.*** subpoena, charge, summons; see COMMAND.

citizen ***n.*** inhabitant, denizen, national, subject, cosmopolite, commoner, civilian, urbanite, taxpayer, member of the community, householder, native, occupant, settler, voter, dweller, immigrant, naturalized person, townsman, the man in the street, villager, John Q. Public; see also RESIDENT.

city ***a.*** metropolitan, urban, civic; see MUNICIPAL.

city ***n.*** town, place, municipality, capital, megalopolis, metropolis, suburb, county seat, trading center, inner city, downtown, shopping district, business district, financial district, incorporated town, village, metropolitan area, township, borough, port; see also CENTER 2.

catlike carnivore (**civet cat**) of Africa and S Asia: used in some perfumes **2** the animal, or its fur

civ·ic (siv′ik) ***adj.*** ⟦< L *civis,* townsman⟧ of a city, citizens, or citizenship

civ′ic-mind′ed ***adj.*** having or showing concern for the welfare of one's community

civ′ics (-iks) ***n.*** the study of civic affairs and the duties and rights of citizenship

civ·il (siv′əl) ***adj.*** ⟦see CIVIC⟧ **1** of a citizen or citizens **2** polite **3** of citizens in matters not military or religious **4** having to do with the private rights of individuals —**civ′il·ly** ***adv.***

civil disobedience nonviolent opposition to a law through refusal to comply with it, on grounds of conscience

civil engineering engineering dealing with the construction of highways, bridges, harbors, etc. —**civil engineer**

ci·vil·ian (sə vil′yən) ***n.*** ⟦see CIVIC⟧ a person not in military or naval service —***adj.*** of or for civilians; nonmilitary

ci·vil′i·ty (-ə tē) ***n.*** **1** politeness **2** *pl.* **-ties** a civil, or polite, act

civ·i·li·za·tion (siv′ə lə zā′shən) ***n.*** **1** a civilizing or being civilized **2** the total culture of a people, period, etc. **3** the peoples considered to have attained a high social development

civ′i·lize′ (-līz′) ***vt.*** **-lized′**, **-liz′ing** ⟦see CIVIC⟧ **1** to bring out of a primitive or savage condition to a higher level of social organization and of cultural and technological development **2** to make refined, sophisticated, etc. —**civ′i·lized′** ***adj.***

civil law the body of law having to do with private rights

civil liberties liberties guaranteed to all individuals by law, custom, court decisions, etc.; rights, as of speaking or acting as one likes, granted without hindrance except in the interests of the public welfare

civil rights those rights guaranteed to all individuals by the 13th, 14th, 15th, and 19th Amendments to the U.S. Constitution, as the right to vote and the right to equal treatment under the law

civil servant a civil service employee

civil service all those employed in government administration, esp. through competitive public examination

civil war war between different factions of the same nation —**the Civil War** the war between the North (the Union) and the South (the Confederacy) in the U.S. (1861-65)

civ·vies (siv′ēz) ***pl.n.*** [Inf.] civilian clothes: also **civ′ies**

ck *abbrev.* check

cl *abbrev.* centiliter(s)

Cl *Chem. symbol for* chlorine

clack (klak) ***vi.***, ***vt.*** ⟦prob. echoic < ON⟧ to make or cause to make a sudden, sharp sound —***n.*** this sound

clad (klad) ***vt.*** *alt. pt. & pp. of* CLOTHE —***adj.*** **1** clothed; dressed **2** having a bonded outer layer of another metal or an alloy *[clad* steel*]*

clad′ding ***n.*** a layer of some metal or alloy bonded to another metal

claim (klām) ***vt.*** ⟦< L *clamare,* cry out⟧ **1** to demand as rightfully belonging to one **2** to require; deserve *[to claim* attention*]* **3** to assert —***n.*** **1** a claiming **2** a right to something **3** something claimed **4** an assertion —**claim′a·ble** ***adj.*** —**claim′ant** or **claim′er** ***n.***

clair·voy·ance (kler voi′əns) ***n.*** ⟦Fr < *clair,* clear + *voyant,* seeing⟧ the supposed ability to perceive things that are not in sight —**clair·voy′ant** ***n.***, ***adj.***

clam (klam) ***n.*** ⟦< obs. *clam,* a clamp⟧ any of various hard-shelled, usually edible, bivalve mollusks —***vi.*** **clammed**, **clam′ming** to dig for clams —**clam up** [Inf.] to keep silent —**clam′mer** ***n.***

clam′bake′ ***n.*** **1** a picnic at which steamed or baked clams are served **2** [Inf.] any large, noisy party

clam·ber (klam′bər) ***vi.*** ⟦ME *clambren*⟧ to climb clumsily, esp. by using both the hands and the feet

clam·my (klam′ē) ***adj.*** **-mi·er**, **-mi·est** ⟦ME, prob. < OE *clam,* mud⟧ unpleasantly moist, cold, and sticky —**clam′mi·ly** ***adv.*** —**clam′mi·ness** ***n.***

clam·or (klam′ər) ***n.*** ⟦< L *clamare,* cry out⟧ **1** a loud outcry; uproar **2** a loud demand or complaint, as by the public —***vi.*** to make a clamor —**clam′or·ous** ***adj.***

clamp (klamp) ***n.*** ⟦< MDu *klampe*⟧ a device for clasping or fastening things together —***vt.*** to fasten or brace, as with a clamp —**clamp down (on)** to become more strict (with)

clan (klan) ***n.*** ⟦< Gael < L *planta,* offshoot⟧ **1** a group of families claiming descent from a common ancestor **2** a group of people with interests in common —**clans·man** (klanz′mən), *pl.* **-men** (-mən), ***n.***

clan·des·tine (klan des′tin) ***adj.*** ⟦< L *clam,* secret⟧ secret or hidden; furtive —**clan·des′tine·ly** ***adv.***

clang (klaŋ) ***vi.***, ***vt.*** ⟦echoic⟧ to make or cause to make a loud, ringing sound, as by striking metal —***n.*** this sound

clang′or (-ər) ***n.*** ⟦L < *clangere,* to sound⟧ a continuous clanging sound

clank (klaŋk) ***n.*** ⟦echoic⟧ a sharp, metallic sound —***vi.***, ***vt.*** to make or cause to make this sound

clan·nish (klan′ish) ***adj.*** **1** of a clan **2** tending to associate closely with one's own group only —**clan′nish·ly** ***adv.*** —**clan′nish·ness** ***n.***

clap (klap) ***vi.*** **clapped**, **clap′ping** ⟦OE *clæppan,* to beat⟧ **1** to make a sudden, explosive sound, as of two flat surfaces struck together **2** to strike the hands together, as in applauding —***vt.*** **1** to strike together briskly **2** to strike with an open hand **3** to put, move, etc. swiftly *[he was clapped into jail]* —***n.*** **1** the sound or act of clapping **2** a sharp slap

clap·board (klab′ərd) ***n.*** ⟦transl. of MDu *klapholt* < *klappen,* to fit + *holt,* wood⟧ a thin board with one thicker edge, used as siding —***vt.*** to cover with clapboards

clap′per ***n.*** **1** a person who claps **2** the moving part of a bell, that strikes the side of the bell

clap′trap′ ***n.*** ⟦CLAP + TRAP⟧ insincere, empty talk intended to get applause

claque (klak) ***n.*** ⟦Fr < *claquer,* to clap⟧ **1** a group of people paid to applaud at a play, etc. **2** a group of fawning admirers

clar·et (klar′it) ***n.*** ⟦< OFr (*vin*) *claret,* clear (wine)⟧ a dry red wine

clar·i·fy (klar′ə fī′) ***vt.***, ***vi.*** **-fied′**, **-fy′ing** ⟦< L *clarus,* clear + *facere,* to make⟧ to make or become clear —**clar′i·fi·ca′tion** ***n.***

clar·i·net (klar′ə net′) ***n.*** ⟦< Fr < L *clarus,* clear⟧ a single-reed woodwind instrument played by means of holes and keys —**clar′i·net′ist** or **clar′i·net′tist** ***n.***

clar·i·on (klar′ē ən) ***adj.*** ⟦< L *clarus,* clear⟧ clear, sharp, and ringing *[a clarion* call*]*

clar·i·ty (klar′ə tē) ***n.*** ⟦< L *clarus,* clear⟧ the quality of being clear; clearness

THESAURUS

civic ***a.*** civil, urban, municipal; see PUBLIC 1, 2.

civil ***a.*** **1** [Civic] local, civic, public; see MUNICIPAL. **2** [Polite] formal, courteous, refined; see POLITE.

civilian ***n.*** private citizen, noncombatant, nonmilitary person; see CITIZEN.

civilization ***n.*** cultivation, polish, enlightenment, refinement, civility, illumination, advancement of knowledge, elevation, edification, culture, advancement, social well-being, sophistication, literacy, material well-being, education, breeding; see also CULTURE 1, PROGRESS 1.—*Ant.* barbarism, savagery, degeneration.

civilize ***v.*** enlighten, cultivate, enrich, reclaim, refine, acculturate, spiritualize, humanize, edify, uplift, tame, foster, instruct, indoctrinate, idealize, elevate, educate, advance, ennoble; see also DEVELOP 1, TEACH.

civilized ***a.*** enlightened, refined, humanized; see CULTURED, EDUCATED.

civil rights ***n.*** civil liberties, equality, human rights; see CHOICE, FREEDOM 1.

claim ***n.*** demand, declaration, profession, entreaty, petition, suit, ultimatum, call, request, requirement, application, case, assertion, plea, right, interest, title, stake, part; see also APPEAL 1. —**lay claim to** demand, appropriate, stake out a claim to; see OWN 1.

claim ***v.*** **1** [To assert a claim to] demand, attach, lay claim to; see OWN 1. **2** [To assert] insist, maintain, allege; see BELIEVE, DECLARE.

clam ***n.*** bivalve, mollusk, shellfish; see FISH.

clammy ***a.*** moist, damp, sweaty; see COLD 1, WET 1.

clamor ***n.*** din, outcry, discord; see NOISE 2, UPROAR.

clamp ***n.*** vise, clasp, clip; see FASTENER, LOCK 1.

clan ***n.*** group, clique, tribe; see ORGANIZATION 2, RACE 2.

clang ***n.*** clank, clash, jangle; see NOISE 1.

clank ***n.*** chink, clang, clink; see NOISE 1.

clap ***v.*** **1** [To applaud] cheer, acclaim, applaud; see PRAISE 1. **2** [To strike] bang, slap, slam; see HIT 1.

clarification ***n.*** exposition, elucidation, description; see DEFINITION, EXPLANATION, INTERPRETATION.

clarify ***v.*** interpret, define, elucidate; see EXPLAIN.

clarity ***n.*** transparency, clearness, purity, limpidity, brightness, precision, explicitness, exactness, distinct-

clash (klash) ***vi.*** ⟦echoic⟧ **1** to collide with a loud, harsh, metallic noise **2** to conflict; disagree —***vt.*** to strike with a clashing noise —***n.*** **1** the sound of clashing **2** conflict

clasp (klasp) ***n.*** ⟦ME *claspe*⟧ **1** a fastening, as a hook, to hold things together **2** a holding or grasping; embrace **3** a grip of the hand —***vt.*** **1** to fasten with a clasp **2** to hold or embrace tightly **3** to grip with the hand

class (klas) ***n.*** ⟦< L *classis*⟧ **1** a number of people or things grouped together because of certain likenesses; kind; sort **2** a social or economic rank *[the working class]* **3** *a)* a group of students taught together *b)* a meeting of such a group *c)* a group graduating together **4** grade or quality **5** [Inf.] excellence, as of style or appearance —***vt.*** to classify —**class'less** ***adj.***

class action (suit) a legal action brought by one or more persons on behalf of themselves and a much larger group

clas·sic (klas'ik) ***adj.*** ⟦< L *classis*, class⟧ **1** being an excellent model of its kind **2** CLASSICAL (senses 2 & 3) **3** balanced, formal, regular, simple, etc. **4** famous as traditional or typical —***n.*** **1** a literary or artistic work of the highest excellence **2** a creator of such a work **3** [*pl.*] the works of outstanding ancient Greek and Roman authors: usually with *the* **4** a famous traditional or typical event

clas·si·cal (klas'i kəl) ***adj.*** **1** CLASSIC (*adj.* 1 & 3) **2** of the art, literature, etc. of the ancient Greeks and Romans **3** typical of or derived from the artistic standards of the ancient Greeks and Romans **4** well versed in Greek and Roman culture **5** standard and traditional *[classical economics]* **6** designating, of, or like music conforming to certain standards of form, complexity, etc. —**clas'si·cal·ly** ***adv.*** —**class'i·cal'i·ty** (-kal'ə tē) ***n.***

clas'si·cism' (-ə siz'əm) ***n.*** **1** the aesthetic principles of ancient Greece and Rome **2** adherence to these principles **3** knowledge of classical literature and art —**clas'si·cist** ***n.***

class·i·fied (klas'ə fīd') ***adj.*** **1** confidential and available only to authorized persons **2** of classified advertising —***n.*** [*pl.*] a section of classified advertisements

classified advertising advertising arranged according to subject, under such listings as *help wanted* —**classified advertisement**

clas·si·fy (klas'ə fī') ***vt.*** **-fied', -fy'ing** **1** to arrange in classes according to a system **2** to designate (government documents) to be secret or restricted to use by authorized persons only —**clas'si·fi'a·ble** ***adj.*** —**clas'si·fi·ca'tion** ***n.*** —**clas'si·fi'er** ***n.***

class'mate' ***n.*** a member of the same class at a school or college

class'room' ***n.*** a room in a school or college in which classes are taught

class'y ***adj.*** **-i·er, -i·est** [Inf.] first-class, esp. in style; elegant —**class'i·ness** ***n.***

clat·ter (klat'ər) ***vi., vt.*** ⟦ME *clateren*⟧ to make or cause to make a clatter —***n.*** **1** a rapid succession of loud, sharp noises **2** a tumult; hubbub

clause (klôz) ***n.*** ⟦< L *claudere*, to close⟧ **1** a group of words containing a subject and a finite verb: see DEPENDENT CLAUSE, INDEPENDENT CLAUSE **2** a provision in a document —**claus'al** ***adj.***

claus·tro·pho·bi·a (klôs'trə fō'bē ə) ***n.*** ⟦< L *claustrum*, enclosed place + -PHOBIA⟧ an abnormal fear of being in an enclosed or confined place —**claus'tro·pho'bic** ***adj.***

clav·i·chord (klav'i kôrd') ***n.*** ⟦< L *clavis*, key + *chorda*, string⟧ a stringed musical instrument with a keyboard, predecessor of the piano

clav·i·cle (klav'i kəl) ***n.*** ⟦< L *clavis*, key⟧ a bone connecting the breastbone with the shoulder blade

cla·vier (klə vir'; *for 1, also* klā'vē ər) ***n.*** ⟦Fr < L *clavis*, key⟧ **1** the keyboard of an organ, piano, etc. **2** any stringed keyboard instrument

claw (klô) ***n.*** ⟦OE *clawu*⟧ **1** a sharp, hooked nail on an animal's or bird's foot **2** the pincers of a lobster, etc. —***vt., vi.*** to scratch, clutch, tear, etc. with or as with claws

clay (klā) ***n.*** ⟦OE *clæg*⟧ **1** a firm, plastic earth, used in making bricks, etc. **2** *a)* earth *b)* the human body —**clay'ey, clay'i·er, clay'i·est,** ***adj.***

clean (klēn) ***adj.*** ⟦OE *clæne*⟧ **1** *a)* free from dirt and impurities; unsoiled *b)* free from disease, radioactivity, pollutants, etc. **2** morally pure **3** fair; sportsmanlike **4** neat and tidy **5** well-formed **6** clear **7** thorough —***adv.*** [Inf.] completely —***vt., vi.*** to make or be made clean —**clean up** **1** to make neat **2** [Inf.] to finish **3** [Slang] to make much profit —**come clean** [Slang] to confess —**clean'ly** ***adv.*** —**clean'ness** ***n.***

clean'-cut' ***adj.*** **1** with a sharp edge or outline **2** well-formed **3** trim, neat, etc.

THESAURUS

ness, plain speech, openness, directness, prominence, salience, conspicuousness, certainty, lucidity.—*Ant.* DARKNESS, haze, obscurity.

clash ***n.*** **1** [Collision] crash, jolt, impact; see COLLISION. **2** [Disagreement] opposition, conflict, argument; see DISAGREEMENT 1, DISPUTE.

clash ***v.*** be dissimilar, mismatch, conflict; see CONTRAST, DIFFER 1.

clasp ***n.*** buckle, pin, catch; see FASTENER.

clasp ***v.*** clamp, pin, secure; see FASTEN.

class ***n.*** **1** [A classification] degree, order, rank, grade, standing, genus, division, distinction, breed, type, kingdom, subdivision, phylum, subphylum, superorder, family, sect, category, rate, collection, denomination, department, sort, species, variety, branch, group, genre, range, brand, set, kind, section, domain, color, origin, character, temperament, school, designation, sphere, spirit, vein, persuasion, province, make, grain, source, name, form, selection, stamp, status, range, property, aspect, tone; see also CLASSIFICATION. **2** [A group organized for study] lecture, seminar, study session; see SCHOOL 1. **3** [A division of society] set, caste, social level; see FAMILY. —**in a class by itself** unusual, different, one of a kind; see UNIQUE.

class ***v.*** identify, rank, grade; see CLASSIFY, MARK 2.

classic ***n.*** opus, masterwork, exemplar; see MASTERPIECE.

classical ***a.*** **1** [Of recognized importance] standard, first-rate, established, ideal, flawless, distinguished, paramount, aesthetic, superior, artistic, well-known; see also EXCELLENT.—*Ant.* POPULAR, modern, transitory. **2** [Concerning ancient Greece or Rome] humanistic, academic, classic; see OLD 3.

classification ***n.*** arrangement, assortment, grouping, ordering, allotment, organization, gradation, coordination, disposition, categorizing, apportionment, analysis, division, assignment, designation, assorting, distribution, allocation, categorization; see also CLASS 1, ORDER 3.

classified ***a.*** sorted, assorted, grouped, classed, indexed, filed, orderly, recorded, listed, registered, detailed, arranged, regulated, compiled, coordinated, ranked, distributed, cataloged, separated, labeled, numbered, systematized, tabulated, alphabetized, typed, on file, rated.—*Ant.* MIXED, confused, jumbled.

classify ***v.*** arrange, order, pigeonhole, tabulate, organize, distribute, categorize, systematize, coordinate, correlate, incorporate, label, alphabetize, place in a category, range, form into classes, divide, allocate, number, rate, class, rank, catalog, segregate, distinguish, allot, analyze, regiment, name, group, tag, type, put in order, break down, assort, sort, index, grade, match, size, reduce to order; see also FILE 1, LIST 1.—*Ant.* DISORGANIZE, disorder, disarrange.

clatter ***v.*** rattle, clash, crash; see SOUND.

clause ***n.*** **1** [A provision] condition, codicil, stipulation; see LIMITATION 2, REQUIREMENT 1. **2** [A grammatical structure] construction, sentence, word group; see GRAMMAR.

claw ***n.*** talon, hook, spur, paw, grappling iron, grappling hook, forked end, clutching hand, grapnel, crook, barb, pincers, fingernail.

claw ***v.*** tear, scratch, rip open; see BREAK 1, HURT, RIP.

clay ***n.*** earth, till, marl, kaolin, potter's clay, clayware, green pottery, terra cotta, green brick, china clay, porcelain clay, adobe; see also MUD.

clean ***a.*** **1** [Not soiled] spotless, washed, stainless, laundered, untarnished, unstained, neat, tidy, clear, fresh, pure, blank, white, unblemished, unspotted, snowy, well-kept, dustless, cleansed, immaculate, unsoiled, unpolluted, spick-and-span, clean as a whistle*.—*Ant.* DIRTY, soiled, stained. **2** [Not contaminated] unadulterated, antiseptic, sanitary; see PURE 2. **3** [Having sharp outlines] clear-cut, sharp, distinct; see DEFINITE 2. **4** [Thorough] complete, entire, total; see ABSOLUTE 1, WHOLE 1. **5** [Fair] reliable, decent, lawful; see FAIR 1, HONEST 1. —**come clean*** confess, tell the truth, own up; see ADMIT 2.

clean ***v.*** cleanse, clean up, clear up, clear out, purify, soak, shake out, wash down, scrub off, disinfect, tidy up, deodorize, swab, polish, sterilize, scrape, sweep out, scour, launder, vacuum, scald, dust, mop, cauterize, rinse, sponge, brush, comb, whisk, scrub, sweep, wipe up, clarify, rake, clean away, make clear, bathe, soap, bleach, erase, neaten, shampoo, refine, flush, blot, do up*, spruce up, slick up*; see also WASH 1, 2.—*Ant.* DIRTY, soil, smear.

clean'er *n.* a person or thing that cleans; specif., one who dry-cleans clothing
clean·ly (klen'lē) *adj.* **-li·er, -li·est 1** keeping oneself or one's surroundings clean **2** always kept clean —**clean'li·ness** *n.*
clean room a room designed to be nearly 100% free of dust, pollen, etc.
cleanse (klenz) *vt.* **cleansed, cleans'ing** ⟦OE *clænsian*⟧ to make clean, pure, etc. —**cleans'er** *n.*
clean'up' *n.* **1** a cleaning up **2** elimination of crime
clear (klir) *adj.* ⟦< L *clarus*⟧ **1** free from clouds; bright **2** transparent **3** easily seen or heard; distinct **4** keen or logical *[a clear mind]* **5** not obscure; obvious **6** certain; positive **7** free from guilt **8** free from deductions; net **9** free from debt **10** free from obstruction; open —*adv.* **1** in a clear way **2** completely —*vt.* **1** to make clear **2** to free from impurities, blemishes, etc. **3** to make lucid; clarify **4** to open *[to clear a path]* **5** to get rid of **6** to prove the innocence of **7** to pass or leap over, by, etc., esp. without touching **8** to be passed or approved by **9** to make as profit **10** *Banking* to pass (a check, etc.) through a clearinghouse —*vi.* **1** to become clear **2** *Banking* to pass through a clearinghouse: said as of a check —**clear away** (or **off**) to remove so as to leave a cleared space —**clear out** [Inf.] to depart —**clear up** to make or become clear —**in the clear 1** free from obstructions **2** [Inf.] guiltless —**clear'ly** *adv.* —**clear'ness** *n.*
clear'ance (-əns) *n.* the clear space between a moving object and that which it is passing
clear'-cut' *adj.* **1** clearly outlined **2** distinct; definite **3** with all its trees cut down
clear'ing *n.* an area of land cleared of trees
clear'ing·house' *n.* **1** an office maintained by several banks for exchanging checks, balancing accounts, etc. **2** a central office, as for exchanging information
cleat (klēt) *n.* ⟦ME *clete*⟧ a piece of wood or metal fastened to something to strengthen it or give secure footing
cleav·age (klēv'ij) *n.* **1** a cleaving; dividing **2** a cleft; fissure; division
cleave[1] (klēv) *vt., vi.* **cleaved** or **cleft** or **clove, cleaved** or **cleft** or **clo'ven, cleav'ing** ⟦OE *cleofan*⟧ to divide by a blow; split; sever —**cleav'a·ble** *adj.*
cleave[2] (klēv) *vi.* **cleaved, cleav'ing** ⟦OE *cleofian*⟧ **1** to adhere; cling (*to*) **2** to be faithful (*to*)
cleav·er (klēv'ər) *n.* a heavy cutting tool with a broad blade, used by butchers
clef (klef) *n.* ⟦Fr < L *clavis,* key⟧ a symbol used at the beginning of a musical staff to indicate the pitch of the notes
cleft[1] (kleft) *n.* ⟦< OE *cleofan*: see CLEAVE[1]⟧ an opening or hollow made by or as if by cleaving; crack; crevice
cleft[2] (kleft) *vt., vi. alt. pt. & pp. of* CLEAVE[1] —*adj.* split; divided
cleft lip a vertical cleft in the upper lip, often accompanying a CLEFT PALATE
cleft palate a cleft from front to back along the middle of the roof of the mouth, due to incomplete prenatal development
clem·a·tis (klem'ə tis) *n.* ⟦< Gr *klēma,* vine⟧ a vine of the buttercup family, with bright-colored flowers
clem·en·cy (klem'ən sē) *n.* mercy; forbearance
Clem·ens (klem'ənz), **Sam·u·el Lang·horne** (sam'yo͞o əl laŋ'hôrn) (pseud. *Mark Twain*) 1835-1910; U.S. writer & humorist
clem'ent (-ənt) *adj.* ⟦L *clemens*⟧ **1** lenient **2** mild: said as of weather
clench (klench) *vt.* ⟦< OE (*be*)*clencan,* to make cling⟧ **1** to close (the teeth or fist) firmly **2** to grip tightly —*n.* a firm grip
Cle·o·pa·tra (klē'ō pa'trə, klē' ə-) 69?-30 B.C.; queen of Egypt (51-49; 48-30)
clere·sto·ry (klir'stôr'ē) *n., pl.* **-ries** ⟦< ME *cler,* clear + *storie,* story (of a building)⟧ the upper part of a wall, as of a church, having windows for lighting the central space
cler·gy (klʉr'jē) *n., pl.* **-gies** ⟦see CLERK⟧ ministers, priests, rabbis, etc., collectively
cler'gy·man (-mən) *n., pl.* **-men** (-mən) a member of the clergy; minister, priest, rabbi, etc. —**cler'gy·wom'an,** *pl.* **-wom'en,** *fem.n.*
cler·ic (kler'ik) *n.* a member of the clergy
cler·i·cal (kler'i kəl) *adj.* **1** of the clergy or one of its members **2** of office clerks or their work
cler'i·cal·ism' (-iz'əm) *n.* political power of the clergy —**cler'i·cal·ist** *n.*
clerk (klʉrk) *n.* ⟦< Gr *klērikos,* a cleric⟧ **1** a lay member of a church with minor duties **2** an office worker who

THESAURUS

cleaner *n.* detergent, disinfectant, cleaning agent; see CLEANSER, SOAP.
cleaning *a.* cleansing, purgative, detergent, washing, delousing, dusting, sweeping, scouring, soaking, sterilizing, laundering, vacuuming, scalding, purifying.
cleaning *n.* cleansing, purge, scrubbing, scouring, purification, sweeping, prophylaxis, sterilization, dry cleaning, ablution, sanitizing, shampooing, disinfection, washing, brushing, purifying, deodorizing, catharsis.
cleanliness *n.* cleanness, neatness, pureness, purity, tidiness, trimness, immaculateness, spotlessness, orderliness, whiteness, disinfection, sanitation.—*Ant.* FILTH, dirtiness, griminess.
cleanse *v.* **1** [To remove dirt from the surface of] launder, wash, scrub; see CLEAN. **2** [To remove impurities from within] refine, disinfect, purge; see CLEAN, PURIFY.
cleanser *n.* cleansing agent, cleaning agent, abrasive, lather, solvent, purgative, deodorant, fumigant, soap flakes, polish, disinfectant, antiseptic, purifier, scouring powder, spray cleaner, cleaner, detergent, soap powder, cleaning fluid, suds; see also SOAP. *Cleansers include the following:* water, soap and water, soap, detergent, washing soda, scouring powder, oven cleaner, naphtha, furniture polish, borax, lye, household ammonia, solvent, bluing, carbon tetrachloride, toilet-bowl cleaner, baking soda, chlorine compound, silver polish, kerosene, gasoline, vinegar, rug shampoo.
clear *a.* **1** [Open to the sight or understanding] explicit, plain, manifest; see OBVIOUS 1, 2. **2** [Offering little impediment to the vision] lucid, pure, transparent, apparent, limpid, translucent, crystal, crystalline, crystal clear.—*Ant.* OPAQUE, dark, muddy. **3** [Unclouded] sunny, bright, rainless; see FAIR 3. **4** [Freed from legal charges] free, guiltless, cleared, exonerated, blameless, innocent, dismissed, discharged, absolved; see also INNOCENT 1.—*Ant.* GUILTY, accused, blamed. **5** [Audible] loud enough to be heard, distinct, definite; see AUDIBLE. —**in the clear** guiltless, not suspected, cleared; see FREE 2, INNOCENT 1.
clear *v.* **1** [To free from uncertainty] clear up, relieve, clarify; see EXPLAIN. **2** [To free from obstacles] disentangle, unblock, unloose; see FREE, REMOVE 1. **3** [To profit] realize, net, make; see RECEIVE 1. —**clear out 1** [To remove] clean out, dispose of, get rid of; see ELIMINATE. **2** [*To leave] depart, go, remove oneself; see LEAVE 1. —**clear up 1** [To become clear; *said especially of weather*] improve, blow over, stop raining, stop snowing, run its course, die away, die down, show improvement, pick up, lift, become fair, have fair weather. **2** [To make clear] explicate, clarify, make plausible, make understandable, resolve, settle, make reasonable; see also EXPLAIN.
clear-cut *a.* precise, plain, evident; see OBVIOUS 1, 2.
cleared *a.* **1** [Emptied] cleaned, unloaded, cleared out; see EMPTY. **2** [Freed of charges] vindicated, absolved, set right; see DISCHARGED, FREE 2.
clearing *n.* **1** [The act of clearing] clearance, freeing, removing; see REMOVAL. **2** [A cleared space] open space, clearing, glade; see AREA, COURT, EXPANSE, YARD 1.
clearly *a.* **1** [Distinctly; *said of sight*] plainly, precisely, lucidly, purely, brightly, perceptibly, unmistakably, in full view, in focus, discernibly, decidedly, incontestably, undoubtedly, noticeably, before one's eyes, beyond doubt, prominently, obviously, openly, overtly, observably, certainly, apparently, manifestly, recognizably, conspicuously, in plain sight, definitely, markedly, surely, visibly, positively, seemingly, evidently, at first sight, to all appearances, on the face of it.—*Ant.* hazily, dully, cloudily. **2** [Distinctly; *said of sounds*] sharply, acutely, penetratingly, audibly, bell-like.—*Ant.* indistinctly, mutteringly, unclearly.
clearness *n.* brightness, distinctness, lucidity; see CLARITY.
clench *v.* grip, grasp, double up; see HOLD 1.
clergy *n.* priesthood, prelacy, pastorate; see MINISTRY 2.
clergyman *n.* cleric, pastor, preacher; see MINISTER 1, PRIEST, RABBI.
clerical *a.* **1** [Concerning clerks] stenographic, accounting, bookkeeping, secretarial, typing, written, assistant, subordinate. **2** [Concerning the clergy] ministerial, priestly, apostolic, monastic, monkish, churchly, papal, episcopal, canonical, pontifical, ecclesiastic, rabbinical, sacred, holy, ecclesiastical, in God's service, devoted to the Lord, in the Lord's work.
clerk *n.* salesgirl, saleswoman,

types, files, etc. **3** an official who keeps the records of a court, town, etc. **4** a salesclerk —*vi.* to work as a salesclerk

Cleve·land[1] (klēv′lənd), (**Stephen**) **Gro·ver** (grō′vər) 1837-1908; 22d and 24th president of the U.S. (1885-89; 1893-97)

Cleve·land[2] (klēv′lənd) city and port in NE Ohio: pop. 506,000

clev·er (klev′ər) ***adj.*** ⟦? < Norw *klöver*⟧ **1** skillful; adroit **2** intelligent; ingenious; smart —**clev′er·ly *adv.*** —**clev′er·ness *n.***

clev·is (klev′is) ***n.*** ⟦see CLEAVE[2]⟧ a U-shaped piece of iron with holes for a pin, for attaching one thing to another

clew (klo͞o) ***n.*** ⟦OE *cliwen*⟧ **1** a ball of thread or yarn **2** *archaic sp. of* CLUE

cli·ché (klē shā′) ***n.*** ⟦Fr < pp. of *clicher,* to stereotype⟧ a trite expression or idea

cli·chéd (klē shād′) ***adj.*** trite; stereotyped

click (klik) ***n.*** ⟦echoic⟧ a slight, sharp sound like that of a door latch snapping into place —***vi., vt.*** to make or cause to make a click

cli·ent (klī′ənt) ***n.*** ⟦< L *cliens,* follower⟧ **1** a person or company for whom a lawyer, accountant, etc. is acting **2** a customer

cli·en·tele (klī′ən tel′) ***n.*** ⟦< Fr < L *clientela,* patronage⟧ all one's clients or customers, collectively

cliff (klif) ***n.*** ⟦OE *clif*⟧ a high, steep face of rock

cliff′hang′er or **cliff′-hang′er *n.*** a suspenseful film, story, situation, etc.

cli·mac·ter·ic (klī mak′tər ik, klī′mak ter′ik) ***n.*** ⟦< Gr *klimax,* ladder⟧ a crucial period in life; esp., menopause —***adj.*** crucial

cli·mate (klī′mət) ***n.*** ⟦< Gr *klima,* region⟧ **1** the prevailing weather conditions of a place **2** a region with reference to its prevailing weather —**cli·mat′ic** (-mat′ik) ***adj.***

cli·max (klī′maks′) ***n.*** ⟦L < Gr *klimax,* ladder⟧ **1** the final, culminating element in a series; highest point of interest, excitement, etc. **2** the turning point of action in a drama, etc. **3** an orgasm —***vi., vt.*** to reach, or bring to, a climax —**cli·mac′tic** (-mak′tik) ***adj.***

climb (klīm) ***vi., vt.*** **climbed**, **climb′ing** ⟦OE *climban*⟧ **1** to move up by using the feet and, often, the hands **2** to ascend gradually **3** to move (*down, over, along,* etc.) using the hands and feet **4** to grow upward on (a wall, etc.) —***n.*** **1** a climbing **2** a thing or place to be climbed —**climb′a·ble *adj.*** —**climb′er *n.***

clime (klīm) ***n.*** ⟦see CLIMATE⟧ [Old Poet.] a region, esp. with regard to climate

clinch (klinch) ***vt.*** ⟦var. of CLENCH⟧ **1** to fasten (a driven nail, etc.) by bending the projecting end **2** to settle (an argument, bargain, etc.) definitely —***vi.*** **1** *Boxing* to grip the opponent with the arms so as to hinder punching effectiveness **2** [Slang] to embrace —***n.*** a clinching

clinch′er *n.* **1** one that clinches **2** a decisive point, argument, act, etc.

cling (kliŋ) ***vi.*** **clung**, **cling′ing** ⟦OE *clingan*⟧ **1** to adhere; hold fast, as by embracing **2** to be or stay near **3** to be emotionally attached —**cling′er *n.*** —**cling′y, -i·er, -i·est, *adj.***

clin·ic (klin′ik) ***n.*** ⟦< Gr *klinē,* bed⟧ **1** the teaching of medicine by treatment of patients in the presence of students **2** a place where medical specialists practice as a group **3** an outpatient department, as in a hospital **4** an intensive session of group instruction, as in a certain skill

clin′i·cal (-i kəl) ***adj.*** **1** of or connected with a clinic or sickbed **2** having to do with the treatment and observation of patients, as distinguished from theoretical study **3** purely scientific —**clin′i·cal·ly *adv.***

cli·ni·cian (kli nish′ən) ***n.*** one who practices clinical medicine, psychology, etc.

clink (kliŋk) ***vi., vt.*** ⟦echoic⟧ to make or cause to make a slight, sharp sound, as of glasses striking together —***n.*** **1** such a sound **2** [Inf.] a jail

clink·er (kliŋ′kər) ***n.*** ⟦Du *klinker*⟧ **1** a hard mass of fused stony matter, formed as from burned coal **2** [Slang] a mistake

Clin·ton (klint′'n), **Bill** (bil) (legal name *William Jefferson Clinton;* born *William Jefferson Blythe IV*) 1946- ; 42d president of the U.S. (1993-2001)

clip[1] (klip) ***vt.*** **clipped**, **clip′ping** ⟦< ON *klippa*⟧ **1** to cut, as with shears **2** to cut short **3** to cut the hair of **4** [Inf.] to hit sharply **5** [Slang] to swindle —***vi.*** to move rapidly —***n.*** **1** a clipping **2** an excerpt from a film, videotape, etc. **3** a rapid pace **4** [Inf.] a quick, sharp blow

clip[2] (klip) ***vi., vt.*** **clipped**, **clip′ping** ⟦OE *clyppan,* to embrace⟧ to grip tightly; fasten —***n.*** any of various devices that clip, fasten, hold, etc.

clip′board′ *n.* a writing board with a hinged clip at the top to hold papers

clip joint [Slang] a nightclub, store, etc. that charges excessive prices

clipped form a shortened form of a word, as *pike* (for *turnpike*) or *fan* (for *fanatic*)

clip·per (klip′ər) ***n.*** **1** [*usually pl.*] a tool for cutting or trimming **2** a sailing ship built for great speed

clip′ping *n.* a piece cut out or off, as an item clipped from a newspaper

clique (klik, klēk) ***n.*** ⟦Fr < OFr *cliquer,* make a noise⟧ a small, exclusive circle of people; coterie —**cliqu′ish *adj.*** —**cliqu′ish·ly *adv.***

clit·o·ris (klit′ər is) ***n.,*** *pl.* **clit′o·ris·es** (-is iz) or **cli·tor·i·des** (kli tôr′i dēz′) ⟦< Gr⟧ a small, sensitive, erectile organ of the vulva

clo·a·ca (klō ā′kə) ***n.,*** *pl.* **-cae** (-sē′, -kē′) or **-cas** ⟦L < *cluere,* to cleanse⟧ a cavity, as in reptiles and birds, into which both the intestinal and the genitourinary tracts empty

cloak (klōk) ***n.*** ⟦< ML *clocca,* bell: from its shape⟧ **1** a loose, usually sleeveless outer garment **2** something that covers or conceals; disguise —***vt.*** **1** to cover with a cloak **2** to conceal

clob·ber (kläb′ər) ***vt.*** ⟦< ?⟧ [Slang] **1** to beat or hit repeatedly **2** to defeat decisively

cloche (klōsh) ***n.*** ⟦Fr, a bell⟧ a woman's closefitting, bell-shaped hat

clock[1] (kläk) ***n.*** ⟦ME *clokke,* orig., clock with bells < ML *clocca,* bell⟧ a device for measuring and indicating time,

THESAURUS

saleslady, shopgirl, shop assistant, shopkeeper, salesclerk, salesman, salesperson, counterman, seller, auditor, bookkeeper, recorder, registrar, stenographer, timekeeper, cashier, teller, office worker, notary, controller, copyist, typist, inputter, file clerk, law clerk, switchboard operator; see also SECRETARY 2.

clever *a.* **1** [Apt, particularly with one's hands] skillful, expert, adroit; see ABLE. **2** [Mentally quick] smart, bright, shrewd; see INTELLIGENT, SLY.

cleverly *a.* neatly, skillfully, tactfully, dexterously, ingeniously, resourcefully, deftly, nimbly, agilely, adroitly, proficiently, expertly, smoothly, quickly, speedily; see also EASILY.—*Ant.* AWKWARDLY, clumsily, unskillfully.

cleverness *n.* skill, adroitness, ingenuity; see ABILITY.

cliché *n.* commonplace, platitude, stereotype, proverb, saying, slogan, trite phrase, vapid expression, triteness, banality, triviality, hackneyed phrase, trite idea; see also MOTTO.

click *n.* tick, snap, crack; see NOISE 1.

click *v.* **1** [To make a clicking sound] tick, snap, bang; see SOUND. **2** [*To be successful] match, go off well, meet with approval; see SUCCEED 1.

client *n.* customer, patient, patron; see BUYER.

cliff *n.* bluff, crag, steep rock; see HILL, MOUNTAIN 1, WALL 1.

climate *n.* characteristic weather, atmospheric conditions, aridity, humidity, temperature, weather conditions; see also COLD 1, HEAT 1, WEATHER.

climax *n.* peak, apex, highest point, culmination, acme, pinnacle, crest, zenith, summit, apogee, extremity, limit, utmost extent, highest degree, turning point, crowning point; see also MAXIMUM, TOP 1.—*Ant.* DEPRESSION, anticlimax, nadir.

climax *v.* culminate, tower, end, conclude, reach a peak, come to a head, reach the zenith, break the record; see also ACHIEVE.

climb *n.* **1** [The act of climbing] ascent, clamber, mounting; see RISE. **2** [An ascending place] slope, incline, dune; see GRADE 1, HILL.

climb *v.* scale, work one's way up, ascend gradually, scramble up, clamber up, swarm up, start up, go up, ascend, struggle up, get on, climb on, progress upward, rise, rise hand over hand, come up, creep up, escalate, surmount, shinny up, shoot up. —**climb down** step off, come down, dismount; see DESCEND.

cling *v.* adhere, clasp, hold fast; see STICK 1.

clip[1] ***v.*** snip, crop, clip off; see CUT 1, DECREASE 2.

clippers *n.* shears, trimmers, barber's tools; see SCISSORS.

clique *n.* coterie, inner circle, club; see FACTION, ORGANIZATION 2.

clock[1] ***n.*** timepiece, timekeeper, chronometer, timer, alarm clock, cuckoo clock, electric clock, grandfather clock, pendulum clock, atomic clock, digital clock, clock radio, hourglass, stopwatch, sundial, wristwatch; see also WATCH 1. —**around the clock** continuously, continually, twenty-four hours a day; see REGULARLY.

clock[1] ***v.*** time, measure time, regis-

usually by means of pointers moving over a dial: clocks are not meant to be worn or carried about —*vt.* to record the time of (a race, etc.) with a stopwatch

clock[2] (kläk) *n.* ⟦< ? prec., because of original bell shape⟧ a woven or embroidered ornament on a sock, going up from the ankle

clock radio a radio with a built-in clock that can turn it on or off

clock'wise' *adv.*, *adj.* in the direction in which the hands of a clock rotate

clock'work' *n.* **1** the mechanism of a clock **2** any similar mechanism, with springs and gears —**like clockwork** very regularly

clod (kläd) *n.* ⟦OE⟧ **1** a lump, esp. of earth or clay **2** a dull, stupid person —**clod'dish** *adj.*

clod'hop'per *n.* ⟦prec. + HOPPER⟧ **1** a plowman **2** a clumsy, stupid person **3** a coarse, heavy shoe

clog (kläg) *n.* ⟦ME *clogge,* lump of wood⟧ **1** anything that hinders or obstructs; hindrance **2** a shoe with a thick, usually wooden, sole —*vt.* **clogged**, **clog'ging** **1** to hinder **2** to obstruct (a passage); jam —*vi.* to become clogged

cloi·son·né (kloi'zə nā') *adj.* ⟦Fr, lit., partitioned⟧ designating enamel work in which the surface decoration is set in hollows formed by thin strips of wire

clois·ter (klois'tər) *n.* ⟦< L *claudere,* to close⟧ **1** a monastery or convent **2** monastic life **3** a covered walk along a courtyard wall in a monastery, etc., with an open colonnade —*vt.* to confine as in a cloister —**clois'tered** *adj.*

clomp (klämp) *vi.* to walk heavily or noisily

clone (klōn) *n.* ⟦< Gr *klōn,* a twig⟧ **1** all the descendants derived asexually from a single organism **2** a genetically identical duplicate of an organism, produced by replacing the nucleus of an unfertilized ovum with the nucleus of a body cell from the organism **3** [Inf.] a person or thing very much like another —*vt.* **cloned**, **clon'ing** to produce a clone of —**clon'al** *adj.*

clop (kläp) *n.* ⟦echoic⟧ a clattering sound, like hoofbeats —*vi.* **clopped**, **clop'ping** to make, or move with, such a sound

close[1] (klōs) *adj.* **clos'er**, **clos'est** ⟦see fol.⟧ **1** confined or confining *[close* quarters*]* **2** secretive; reserved **3** miserly; stingy **4** warm and stuffy **5** with little space between; near together **6** compact; dense *[close* weave*]* **7** near to the surface *[a close* shave*]* **8** intimate; familiar *[a close* friend*]* **9** strict; careful *[close* attention*]* **10** nearly alike *[a close* resemblance*]* **11** nearly equal or even *[a close* contest*]* —*adv.* in a close manner —**close'ly** *adv.* —**close'ness** *n.*

close[2] (klōz) *vt.* **closed**, **clos'ing** ⟦< L *claudere,* to close⟧ **1** to shut **2** to fill up or stop (an opening) **3** to finish —*vi.* **1** to undergo shutting **2** to come to an end **3** to come close or together —*n.* an end or conclusion —**close down** (or **up**) to shut or stop entirely —**close in** to draw near from all directions —**close out** to dispose of (goods) by sale

close call (klōs) [Inf.] a narrow escape from danger: also **close shave**

close-cropped (klōs'kräpt') *adj.* clipped very short *[close-cropped* hair*]*

closed circuit a system for telecasting by cable, etc. only to receivers connected in the circuit —**closed'-cir'cuit** *adj.*

close·fist·ed (klōs'fis'tid) *adj.* stingy

close'fit'ting (-fit'iŋ) *adj.* fitting tightly

close'-knit' (-nit') *adj.* closely united or joined

close·mouthed (klōz'mouthd', -moutht') *adj.* not talking much; taciturn

close'out' (-out') *n.* a discounted sale of goods no longer carried, or of those of a business being closed down through liquidation

clos·er (klō'zər) *n.* a person adept at completing a deal, an assignment, etc. successfully

clos·et (kläz'it) *n.* ⟦< L *claudere,* to close⟧ **1** a small room or cupboard for clothes, supplies, etc. **2** a small, private room **3** a state of secrecy —*vt.* to shut up in a private room for confidential talk

close-up (klōs'up') *n.* a photograph, etc. taken at very close range

clo·sure (klō'zhər) *n.* ⟦< L *claudere,* to close⟧ **1** a closing or being closed **2** a finish; end **3** anything that closes **4** CLOTURE

clot (klät) *n.* ⟦OE⟧ a soft lump or thickened mass *[a blood clot]* —*vt.*, *vi.* **clot'ted**, **clot'ting** to form into a clot or clots; coagulate

cloth (klôth) *n.*, *pl.* **cloths** (klôthz, klôths) ⟦OE *clath*⟧ **1** a woven, knitted, or pressed fabric of fibrous material, as cotton, wool, silk, or synthetic fibers **2** a tablecloth, washcloth, etc. —*adj.* made of cloth —**the cloth** the clergy collectively

clothe (klōth) *vt.* **clothed** or **clad**, **cloth'ing** ⟦see prec.⟧ **1** to provide with or dress in clothes **2** to cover

clothes (klōthz, klōz) *pl.n.* ⟦OE *clathas*⟧ articles, usually of cloth, for covering, protecting, or adorning the body

clothes'pin' *n.* a small clip for fastening clothes on a line, as for drying

cloth·ier (klōth'yər) *n.* a dealer in clothes or cloth

cloth·ing (klō'thiŋ) *n.* **1** clothes; garments **2** a covering

clo·ture (klō'chər) *n.* ⟦see CLOSURE⟧ the ending of legislative debate by having the bill put to an immediate vote

THESAURUS

ter speed; see MEASURE 1.

clog *v.* stop up, jam, obstruct; see CLOSE 2, HINDER.

close[1] *a.* **1** [Nearby] neighboring, across the street, around the corner; see NEAR 1. **2** [Intimate] confidential, intimate, familiar; see PRIVATE. **3** [Compact] dense, solid, compressed; see THICK 1. **4** [Stingy] narrow, parsimonious, miserly; see STINGY. **5** [Stifling] sticky, stuffy, unventilated, heavy, motionless, uncomfortable, stale-smelling, musty, stagnant, confined, suffocating, sweltering, tight, stale, oppressive, breathless; see also UNCOMFORTABLE 2.—*Ant.* FRESH, refreshing, brisk. **6** [Similar] resembling, having common qualities, much the same; see ALIKE, LIKE.

close[2] *n.* termination, adjournment, ending; see END 2.

close[2] *v.* **1** [To put a stop to] conclude, finish, terminate; see END 1. **2** [To put a stopper into] shut, stop, choke off, stuff, clog, prevent passage, shut off, turn off, lock, block, bar, dam, cork, seal; see also CLOSE 2.—*Ant.* OPEN, uncork, unseal. **3** [To come together] meet, unite, agree; see JOIN 1. **4** [To shut] slam, close down, shut, shut down, shut up, seal, fasten, bolt, bar, shutter, lock, bring to.

closed *a.* **1** [Terminated] ended, concluded, final; see FINISHED 1. **2** [Not in operation] shut down, out of order, out of service, bankrupt, closed up, padlocked, having folded up*; see also BROKEN 2. **3** [Not open] shut, fastened, sealed; see TIGHT 2.

closely *a.* approximately, similarly, exactly, nearly, strictly, intimately, jointly, in conjunction with; see also ALMOST.—*Ant.* INDIVIDUALLY, separately, one by one.

closet *n.* cabinet, recess, cupboard, buffet, locker, wardrobe, receptacle, safe, bin, vault, cold storage, armoire, cloakroom, storeroom.

clot *n.* lump, bulk, clotting, curdling, coagulation, mass, clump, coagulum, thickness, coalescence, curd.

clot *v.* coagulate, curdle, lump; see THICKEN.

cloth *n.* fabric, material, textiles; see GOODS.

clothe *v.* attire, dress up, costume; see DRESS 1.

clothed *a.* clad, invested, costumed, robed, shod, dressed, attired, decked, disguised, covered, draped, veiled.—*Ant.* NAKED, exposed, stripped.

clothes *n.* wearing apparel, raiment, clothing, garments, garb, vestments, attire, array, casual wear, informal wear, formal wear, evening clothes, work clothes, suit of clothes, costume, wardrobe, trappings, gear, underclothes, outfit, get-up*, rags*, togs*, duds*, threads*, things; see also COAT 1, DRESS 1, 2, HAT, PANTS 1, SHIRT. *Men's clothes include the following:* business suit, sport jacket, sport coat, trousers, breeches, knickers*, tuxedo, tux*, dress suit, dinner jacket, uniform, shirt, tie, necktie, bow tie, ascot, bolo tie, long underwear, long johns*, undershirt, T-shirt, briefs, undershorts. *Women's clothes include the following:* dress, evening gown, frock, shirtwaist, blouse, skirt, housecoat, negligee, nightgown, nightie*, underwear, lingerie, bra, brassiere, panties, underpants, camisole, pantyhose, nylons, stockings, tights, girdle, slip, kimono, suit, housedress, smock, miniskirt, shift, muumuu, jumper, petticoat, bonnet. *Clothes worn by both men and women include the following:* blue jeans, Levi's (trademark), shirt, turtleneck, sweat shirt, sweat pants, tank top, pajamas, pj's*, slacks, pants, sweater, cardigan, pullover, coat, raincoat, hat, gloves, socks, shoes, robe, bathrobe, slippers, shorts, cutoffs, bell-bottoms, hat, cap, beret, uniform, scarf. *Children's clothes include the following:* rompers, playsuit, coveralls, snowsuit. *Work clothes include the following:* overalls, windbreaker, blue jeans, coveralls.

clothing *n.* attire, apparel, garb; see CLOTHES, DRESS 1.

cloud (kloud) ***n.*** ⟦OE *clud*, mass of rock⟧ **1** a visible mass of condensed water droplets or ice crystals in the sky **2** a mass of smoke, dust, etc. **3** a crowd; swarm *[a cloud of locusts]* **4** anything that darkens, obscures, etc. —***vt.*** **1** to darken or obscure as with clouds **2** to make gloomy **3** to sully (a reputation, etc.) —***vi.*** to become cloudy, gloomy, etc. —**under a cloud** under suspicion —**cloud'less** ***adj.*** —**cloud'y, -i·er, -i·est,** ***adj.*** —**cloud'i·ness** ***n.***
cloud'burst' ***n.*** a sudden, heavy rain
clout (klout) ***n.*** ⟦< OE *clut*, a patch⟧ **1** a blow, as with the hand **2** [Inf.] power, esp. political power —***vt.*** **1** [Inf.] to strike, as with the hand **2** to hit (a ball) hard
clove[1] (klōv) ***n.*** ⟦< L *clavus*, nail: from its shape⟧ **1** the dried flower bud of a tropical evergreen tree, used as a spice **2** the tree
clove[2] (klōv) ***n.*** ⟦OE *clufu*⟧ a segment of a bulb, as of garlic
clove[3] (klōv) ***vt., vi.*** *alt. pt. of* CLEAVE[1]
clo·ven (klō'vən) ***vt., vi.*** *alt. pp. of* CLEAVE[1] —***adj.*** divided; split *[a cloven foot]*
clo·ver (klō'vər) ***n.*** ⟦OE *clafre*⟧ any of various low-growing plants of the pea family, with leaves of three leaflets and small flowers in dense heads
clo'ver·leaf' ***n.***, *pl.* **-leafs'** a highway interchange with an overpass and curving ramps, allowing traffic to move unhindered in any of four directions
clown (kloun) ***n.*** ⟦< ? Scand⟧ **1** a clumsy or boorish person **2** one who entertains, as in a circus, by antics, jokes, etc. **3** a buffoon —***vi.*** to act as a clown does —**clown'ish** ***adj.***
cloy (kloi) ***vt.*** ⟦< OFr *encloyer*, nail up < L *clavus*, nail⟧ to surfeit with too much of something that is sweet, rich, etc.
cloy'ing ***adj.*** **1** displeasing because of excess *[cloying sweetness]* **2** overly sweet or sentimental
club (klub) ***n.*** ⟦< ON *klubba*, cudgel⟧ **1** a heavy stick used as a weapon **2** an implement used to hit the ball in golf **3** *a)* a group of people united for a common purpose *b)* its meeting place **4** *a)* any of a suit of playing cards marked with black figures shaped like leaves of clover (♣) *b)* [*pl.*] this suit —***vt.*** **clubbed, club'bing** to strike as with a club —***vi.*** to unite for a common purpose
club'foot' ***n.***, *pl.* **-feet'** a congenitally misshapen, often clublike, foot
club'house' ***n.*** **1** a building used by a club **2** a locker room used by an athletic team
club soda SODA WATER
cluck (kluk) ***vi.*** ⟦echoic⟧ to make a low, sharp, clicking sound, as of a hen calling her chicks —***n.*** this sound
clue (kloo) ***n.*** a fact, object, etc. that helps to solve a problem or mystery —***vt.*** **clued, clu'ing** [Inf.] to provide with clues or needed facts: often with *in*
clue'less ***adj.*** [Inf.] **1** stupid **2** uninformed, esp. about a given situation
clump (klump) ***n.*** ⟦< LowG *klump*⟧ **1** a lump; mass **2** a cluster, as of trees **3** the sound of heavy footsteps —***vi.*** **1** to walk heavily **2** to form clumps —**clump'y, -i·er, -i·est,** ***adj.***
clum·sy (klum'zē) ***adj.*** **-si·er, -si·est** ⟦ME *clumsid*, numb with cold⟧ **1** lacking grace or skill; awkward **2** awkwardly shaped or made —**clum'si·ly** ***adv.*** —**clum'si·ness** ***n.***
clung (kluŋ) ***vi.*** *pt. & pp. of* CLING
clunk (kluŋk) ***n.*** ⟦echoic⟧ a dull, heavy, hollow sound —***vi.*** to move with a clunk or clunks
clunk'er ***n.*** [Slang] an old machine or automobile in poor repair
clus·ter (klus'tər) ***n.*** ⟦OE *clyster*⟧ a number of persons or things grouped together —***vi., vt.*** to gather or grow in a cluster
cluster bomb a bomb that explodes in midair and scatters smaller bombs widely
clutch[1] (kluch) ***vt.*** ⟦OE *clyccan*, to clench⟧ to grasp or hold eagerly or tightly —***vi.*** to snatch or seize (*at*) —***n.*** **1** [*usually pl.*] power; control **2** a grasp; grip **3** a device for engaging and disengaging a motor or engine **4** a woman's small purse
clutch[2] (kluch) ***n.*** ⟦< ON *klekja*, to hatch⟧ **1** a nest of eggs **2** a brood of chicks **3** a cluster
clut·ter (klut'ər) ***n.*** ⟦< CLOT⟧ a number of things scattered in disorder; jumble —***vt.*** to put into disorder; jumble: often with *up*
cm *abbrev.* centimeter(s)
Cmdr *abbrev.* Commander
cni·dar·i·an (ni der'ē ən) ***n.*** any of a phylum of invertebrates, as jellyfishes, having stinging cells and a saclike body with only one opening
Co[1] or **co** *abbrev.* **1** company **2** county
Co[2] *Chem. symbol for* cobalt
CO *abbrev.* **1** Colorado **2** Commanding Officer
co- ⟦var. of COM-⟧ *prefix* **1** together **2** equally *[coextensive]* **3** joint or jointly *[copilot]*
C/O or **c/o** *abbrev.* care of
coach (kōch) ***n.*** ⟦after *Kócs*, village in Hungary⟧ **1** a large, covered, four-wheeled carriage **2** a railroad passenger car **3** the lowest-priced class of airline accommodations **4** a bus **5** an instructor or trainer, as of athletes, actors, or singers —***vt., vi.*** to instruct and train (athletes, actors, etc.)
coach'man (-mən) ***n.***, *pl.* **-men** (-mən) the driver of a coach, or carriage
co·ad·ju·tor (kō aj'ə tər) ***n.*** ⟦< L *co-*, together + *adjuvare*, to help⟧ an assistant, esp. to a bishop
co·ag·u·late (kō ag'yoo lāt') ***vt.*** **-lat'ed, -lat'ing** ⟦< L *co-*, together + *agere*, to drive⟧ to cause (a liquid) to become somewhat firm; clot —***vi.*** to become coagulated —**co·ag'u·lant** (-lənt) ***n.*** —**co·ag'u·la'tion** ***n.***
coal (kōl) ***n.*** ⟦OE *col*⟧ **1** a black, combustible mineral solid used as fuel **2** a piece (or pieces) of this **3** an ember —***vt., vi.*** to supply or be supplied with coal —**haul** (or **rake, drag,** or **call**) **over the coals** to criticize sharply
co·a·lesce (kō'ə les') ***vi.*** **-lesced', -lesc'ing** ⟦< L *co-*, together + *alescere*, grow up⟧ to unite into a single body or group —**co'a·les'cence** (-əns) ***n.***
co'a·li'tion (-lish'ən) ***n.*** ⟦see prec.⟧ a combination or alliance, as of factions, esp. a temporary one
coal oil **1** kerosene **2** oil produced from coal, used as a lamp fuel
coal tar a thick, black liquid obtained from the distillation of bituminous coal: used in dyes, medicines, etc.
co-an·chor (kō'aŋ'kər) ***n.*** one of the usually two anchors of a TV or radio newscast
coarse (kôrs) ***adj.*** **coars'er, coars'est** ⟦< COURSE in the sense "ordinary or usual order"⟧ **1** of poor quality; common **2** consisting of rather large particles *[coarse sand]* **3** rough; harsh **4** unrefined; vulgar; crude —**coarse'ly** ***adv.*** —**coarse'ness** ***n.***
coars·en (kôr'sən) ***vt., vi.*** to make or become coarse

THESAURUS

cloud ***n.*** haze, mist, fogginess, haziness, film, puff, billow, smoke, veil, cloud cover, overcast. *Types of clouds include the following:* cirrus, cumulus, stratus, nimbus, cirrocumulus, cirrostratus. —**in the clouds** fanciful, fantastic, romantic; see IMPRACTICAL. —**under a cloud** suspect, dubious, uncertain; see SUSPICIOUS 2.

cloudy ***a.*** **1** [Hazy] overcast, foggy, sunless; see DARK 1. **2** [Not clear] dense, nontransparent, murky, textiles; see also OPAQUE.

clown ***n.*** buffoon, fool, joker, harlequin, Punch, funnyman, humorist, jester, comedian, cutup*; see also ACTOR.

clown (around) ***v.*** fool around, kid around, cut up*; see JOKE.

club ***n.*** **1** [A social organization] association, order, society; see FACTION, ORGANIZATION 2. **2** [A heavy stick] bat, baton, blackjack; see STICK.

club ***v.*** batter, whack, pound; see BEAT 1, HIT 1.

clue ***n.*** evidence, trace, mark; see PROOF 1, SIGN 1.

clump ***n.*** cluster, bundle, knot; see BUNCH.

clumsily ***a.*** crudely, gawkily, stumblingly; see AWKWARDLY.

clumsiness ***n.*** crudity, ineptitude, boorishness; see AWKWARDNESS.

clumsy ***a.*** ungainly, gawky, inexpert; see AWKWARD.

cluster ***n.*** group, batch, clump; see BUNCH.

clutch[1] ***v.*** grab, grasp, grip; see HOLD 1, SEIZE 1.

clutches ***n.*** control, grasp, keeping; see POWER 2.

clutter ***n.*** disarray, jumble, mess; see CONFUSION.

coach ***n.*** **1** [A carriage] stagecoach, chaise, victoria; see CARRIAGE 2, VEHICLE. **2** [An instructor] physical education instructor, drillmaster, mentor; see TEACHER, TRAINER.

coach ***v.*** train, drill, instruct; see TEACH.

coagulate ***v.*** curdle, clot, congeal; see THICKEN.

coal ***n.*** anthracite, bituminous coal, peat; see FUEL. —**haul** (or **rake** or **drag**) **over the coals*** reprimand, criticize, castigate; see BLAME.

coalition ***n.*** compact, alliance, association; see FACTION.

coarse ***a.*** **1** [Not fine] rough, granular, harsh; see CRUDE. **2** [Vulgar] low, common, rude; see RUDE 1, VULGAR.

coast (kōst) ***n.*** ⟦< L *costa*, rib, side⟧ **1** land alongside the sea; seashore **2** a slide down an incline, as on a sled —***vi.*** **1** to sail near or along a coast **2** to go down an incline, as on a sled **3** to continue in motion on momentum —**coast·al** (kōs′təl) ***adj.***

coast′er ***n.*** **1** a person or thing that coasts **2** a small mat, disk, etc. placed under a glass to protect a table

coaster brake a brake on a bicycle operated by reverse pressure on the pedals

coast guard **1** a governmental force employed to defend a nation's coasts, aid vessels in distress, etc. **2** [**C- G-**] such a branch of the U.S. armed forces

coast′line′ ***n.*** the outline of a coast

coat (kōt) ***n.*** ⟦OFr *cote*, a coat⟧ **1** a sleeved outer garment opening down the front **2** the natural covering of an animal or plant **3** a layer of some substance, as paint, over a surface —***vt.*** to cover with a coat or layer

coat′ing ***n.*** a surface coat or layer

coat of arms *pl.* **coats of arms** a group of heraldic emblems, as on a shield, used as the insignia of a family or group

coat′tail′ ***n.*** either half of the divided lower back part of a coat

co·au·thor (kō′ô′thər) ***n.*** a joint author; collaborator

coax (kōks) ***vt.***, ***vi.*** ⟦< obs. slang *cokes*, a fool⟧ to urge with or use soft words, flattery, etc. —**coax′er** ***n.*** —**coax′ing·ly** ***adv.***

co·ax·i·al (kō ak′sē əl) ***adj.*** **1** having a common axis **2** designating a double-conductor high-frequency transmission line, as for television

cob (käb) ***n.*** ⟦prob. < LowG⟧ **1** a corncob **2** a short-legged, thickset horse

co·balt (kō′bôlt′) ***n.*** ⟦< Ger *kobold*, lit., goblin⟧ a hard, steel-gray, metallic chemical element

cob·ble (käb′əl) ***vt.*** **-bled**, **-bling** ⟦ME < *cobelere*, cobbler⟧ **1** to mend (shoes, etc.) **2** to put together clumsily: often with *up*

cob·bler[1] (käb′lər) ***n.*** ⟦< ?⟧ a kind of deep-dish fruit pie

cob·bler[2] (käb′lər) ***n.*** ⟦ME *cobelere* < ?⟧ one who makes or mends shoes

cob′ble·stone′ ***n.*** a rounded stone formerly much used for paving streets

CO·BOL (kō′bôl′) ***n.*** ⟦*co*(*mmon*) *b*(*usiness*) *o*(*riented*) *l*(*anguage*)⟧ a computer language using English words, for business applications

co·bra (kō′brə) ***n.*** ⟦< Port⟧ a very poisonous snake of Asia and Africa

cob·web (käb′web′) ***n.*** ⟦ME *coppe*, spider + WEB⟧ **1** a web spun by a spider **2** anything flimsy, gauzy, or ensnaring like this —**cob′web′by** ***adj.***

co·caine (kō kān′) ***n.*** ⟦< *coca*, tropical shrub from whose leaves it is extracted⟧ a crystalline alkaloid that is habit-forming when used as a stimulant

coc·cus (käk′əs) ***n.***, *pl.* **coc′ci′** (-sī′) ⟦< Gr *kokkos*, kernel⟧ a spherical bacterium

coc·cyx (käk′siks′) ***n.***, *pl.* **coc·cy·ges** (käk sī′jēz′) ⟦< Gr *kokkyx*, cuckoo: it is shaped like a cuckoo's beak⟧ a small bone at the base of the spine

co-chair (kō cher′, kō′cher′) ***n.*** one who presides over a meeting, etc. jointly with another —***vt.*** to preside over as co-chair

coch·le·a (käk′lē ə) ***n.***, *pl.* **-ae′** (-ē′) or **-as** ⟦< Gr *kochlias*, snail⟧ the spiral-shaped part of the inner ear —**coch′le·ar** ***adj.***

cock[1] (käk) ***n.*** ⟦OE *coc*⟧ **1** a rooster or other male bird **2** a faucet or valve **3** *a*) the hammer of a gun *b*) its firing position **4** a jaunty tilt, as of a hat —***vt.*** **1** to tilt jauntily **2** to raise erectly **3** to turn toward **4** to set (a gun) to fire

cock[2] (käk) ***n.*** ⟦ME *cokke*⟧ a small, cone-shaped pile, as of hay

cock·ade (käk ād′) ***n.*** ⟦< OFr *coq*, COCK[1] (*n.* 1)⟧ a rosette, knot of ribbon, etc. worn on the hat as a badge

cock·a·ma·mie (käk′ə mā′mē) ***adj.*** ⟦< *decalcomania*: see DECAL⟧ [Slang] **1** inferior **2** ridiculous

cock′-and-bull′ story an absurd, improbable story

cock·a·too (käk′ə to͞o′) ***n.***, *pl.* **-toos′** ⟦< Malay *kakatua*⟧ a crested parrot of Australia and the East Indies

cock′a·trice′ (-tris′) ***n.*** ⟦< L *calcare*, to tread⟧ a mythical serpent supposedly able to kill by a look

cocked hat a three-cornered hat with a turned-up brim

cock·er (käk′ər) ***n.*** [Slang] an old man

cock′er·el (-əl) ***n.*** a young rooster, less than a year old

cocker spaniel ⟦< use in hunting woodcock⟧ a small spaniel with long, silky hair and drooping ears

cock′eyed′ ***adj.*** ⟦< COCK[1], *v.* + EYE⟧ **1** cross-eyed **2** [Slang] *a*) awry *b*) silly; foolish *c*) drunk

cock′fight′ ***n.*** a fight between gamecocks, usually wearing metal spurs —**cock′fight′ing** ***n.***

cock·le (käk′əl) ***n.*** ⟦< Gr *konchē*, mussel⟧ an edible mollusk having two heart-shaped shells —**warm the cockles of someone's heart** to make someone pleased or cheerful

cock·ney (käk′nē) ***n.***, *pl.* **-neys** ⟦ME *cokenei*, spoiled child, milksop⟧ [*often* **C-**] **1** one born in the East End of London, England, speaking a characteristic dialect **2** this dialect

cock′pit′ ***n.*** **1** an enclosed area for cockfights **2** the space in a small airplane for the crew and passengers, or in a large one for the crew

cock′roach′ ***n.*** ⟦Sp *cucaracha*⟧ an insect with long feelers and a flat, soft body: a household pest

cocks·comb (käks′kōm′) ***n.*** the red, fleshy growth on a rooster's head

cock′sure′ ***adj.*** ⟦COCK[1] + SURE⟧ absolutely sure or self-confident, esp. stubbornly or overbearingly

cock′tail′ ***n.*** ⟦< ?⟧ **1** a mixed alcoholic drink, usually iced **2** an appetizer, as of shrimp or juice

cock′y ***adj.*** **-i·er**, **-i·est** ⟦< COCK[1] + -Y[2]⟧ [Inf.] jauntily conceited; aggressively self-confident —**cock′i·ly** ***adv.*** —**cock′i·ness** ***n.***

co·co (kō′kō′) ***n.***, *pl.* **-cos′** ⟦Sp < Gr *kokkos*, berry⟧ **1** the coconut palm tree **2** its fruit; coconut

co·coa (kō′kō′) ***n.*** ⟦var. of CACAO⟧ **1** powder made from roasted cacao seeds **2** a drink made of this and sugar, hot milk, etc. **3** a reddish-yellow brown

cocoa butter a yellowish-white fat prepared from cacao seeds

co·co·nut or **co·coa·nut** (kō′kə nut′) ***n.*** the oval fruit of a tropical tree (**coconut palm**), with a hard, brown husk, edible white meat, and a sweet, milky fluid (**coconut milk**) inside

co·coon (kə ko͞on′) ***n.*** ⟦< Fr < ML *coco*, shell⟧ the silky or fibrous case which the larva of certain insects spins about itself for shelter during the pupa stage

cod (käd) ***n.***, *pl.* **cod** or **cods** ⟦ME⟧ a food fish of northern seas

Cod (käd), **Cape** hook-shaped peninsula in E Massachusetts: 64 mi. long

COD or **cod** *abbrev.* cash, or collect, on delivery

co·da (kō′də) ***n.*** ⟦It < L *cauda*, tail⟧ an added concluding passage, as in music

cod·dle (käd′'l) ***vt.*** **-dled**, **-dling** ⟦< ?⟧ **1** to cook (esp. eggs in shells) in water not quite boiling **2** to pamper

code (kōd) ***n.*** ⟦< L *codex*, wooden tablet⟧ **1** a systematized body of laws **2** a set of principles, as of ethics **3** a set of signals for sending messages **4** a system of symbols for secret writing, etc. —***vt.*** **cod′ed**, **cod′ing** to put into code —**cod′er** ***n.***

co·deine (kō′dēn′) ***n.*** ⟦< Gr *kōdeia*, poppy head⟧ an alkaloid derived from opium: used for pain relief and in cough medicines: also **co′dein′**

co·de·pend·ent or **co-de·pend·ent** (kō′dē pen′dənt) ***adj.*** psychologically influenced by or needing another who is addicted to alcohol, etc. —***n.*** one who is

THESAURUS

coast ***n.*** shoreline, beach, seaboard; see SHORE.

coast ***v.*** glide, float, ride on the current; see DRIFT, RIDE 1.

coat ***n.*** **1** [An outer garment] topcoat, overcoat, cloak, suit coat, tuxedo, dinner jacket, sport coat, blazer, dress coat, fur coat, ski jacket, parka, mackintosh, raincoat, trench coat, jacket, windbreaker, peacoat, three-quarter-length coat, wrap, leather jacket, southwester, slicker, waterproof*; see also CLOTHES. **2** [The covering of an animal] protective covering, shell, scales, fleece, epidermis, pelt, membrane; see also FUR, HIDE, SKIN. **3** [An applied covering] coating, layer, wash, primer, finish, glaze, crust, painting, overlay, whitewashing, varnish, lacquer, gloss, tinge, prime coat, plaster; see also FINISH 2.

coat ***v.*** cover, glaze, enamel; see PAINT 2, VARNISH.

coating ***n.*** crust, covering, layer; see COAT 3.

coax ***v.*** persuade, cajole, inveigle; see INFLUENCE, URGE 2.

cocktail ***n.*** mixed drink, aperitif, highball. *Cocktails include the following:* Manhattan, martini, old-fashioned, champagne, margarita, pink lady, whiskey sour, screwdriver, bloody mary, daiquiri, Alexander, piña colada, mint julep; see also DRINK 2.

code ***n.*** body of laws, regulations, digest; see LAW 2, SYSTEM.

codependent —**co′de·pend′ence** or **co′-de·pend′ence** ***n.*** —**co′de·pend′en·cy** or **co′-de·pend′en·cy**, *pl.* **-cies**, ***n.***
co·dex (kō′deks′) ***n.***, *pl.* **co·di·ces** (kō′də sēz′, käd′ə-) ⟦L: see CODE⟧ a manuscript volume, esp. of the Scriptures or of a classic text
cod′fish′ ***n.***, *pl.* **-fish′** or (for different species) **-fish′es** a cod
codg·er (käj′ər) ***n.*** ⟦prob. var. of CADGER⟧ [Inf.] an elderly fellow, sometimes one who is eccentric
cod·i·cil (käd′i səl) ***n.*** ⟦see CODE⟧ an addition to a will
cod·i·fy (käd′ə fī′) ***vt.*** **-fied′**, **-fy′ing** to arrange (laws, rules, etc.) systematically —**cod′i·fi·ca′tion** ***n.*** —**cod′i·fi′er** ***n.***
cod′-liv′er oil oil from the liver of the cod: it is rich in vitamins A & D
co·ed or **co-ed** (kō′ed′) [Inf.] ***n.*** a young woman attending a coeducational college —***adj.*** **1** coeducational **2** of a coed
co·ed·u·ca·tion (kō′ej′ə kā′shən) ***n.*** an educational system in which students of both sexes attend classes together —**co′ed′u·ca′tion·al** ***adj.***
co·ef·fi·cient (kō′ə fish′ənt) ***n.*** ⟦CO- + EFFICIENT⟧ **1** a factor that contributes to a result **2** a multiplier of a variable or unknown quantity (Ex.: *6* in *6ab*) **3** a number used as a multiplier in measuring some property
coe·len·ter·ate (si len′tər it) ***n.*** ⟦< Gr *koilos*, hollow + *enteron*, intestine⟧ CNIDARIAN
co·e·qual (kō ē′kwəl) ***adj.***, ***n.*** equal —**co′e·qual′i·ty** (-ē kwäl′ə tē) ***n.*** —**co·e′qual·ly** ***adv.***
co·erce (kō ʉrs′) ***vt.*** **-erced′**, **-erc′ing** ⟦< L *co-*, together + *arcere*, confine⟧ **1** to restrain by force **2** to compel **3** to enforce —**co·er′cion** (-ʉr′shən) ***n.*** —**co·er′cive** (-siv) ***adj.***
co·e·val (kō ē′vəl) ***adj.***, ***n.*** ⟦< L *co-*, together + *aevum*, age⟧ contemporary
co′ex·ist′ (-ig zist′) ***vi.*** **1** to exist together at the same time or in the same place **2** to live together peacefully, despite differences —**co′ex·ist′ence** ***n.*** —**co′ex·ist′ent** ***adj.***
co′ex·ten′sive (-ik sten′siv) ***adj.*** extending equally in time or space
C of E *abbrev.* Church of England
cof·fee (kôf′ē) ***n.*** ⟦< Ar *qahwa*⟧ **1** a drink made from the roasted, ground, beanlike seeds of a tall tropical shrub of the madder family **2** the seeds, whole or ground, or the shrub **3** light brown
coffee break a brief respite from work when coffee, etc. is taken
cof′fee·cake′ ***n.*** a kind of cake or roll to be eaten as with coffee
cof′fee·house′ ***n.*** a place where coffee is served and people gather for talk, entertainment, etc.
cof′fee·pot′ ***n.*** a container with a spout, for making or serving coffee
coffee shop a small, informal restaurant serving coffee and light refreshments or meals
coffee table a low table, usually in front of a sofa
cof·fer (kôf′ər) ***n.*** ⟦see fol.⟧ **1** a chest for holding money or valuables **2** [*pl.*] a treasury; funds
cof·fin (kôf′in) ***n.*** ⟦< Gr *kophinos*, basket⟧ the case or box in which a dead body is buried
cog (käg) ***n.*** ⟦ME⟧ **1** one of the teeth on the rim of a cogwheel **2** a cogwheel
co·gent (kō′jənt) ***adj.*** ⟦< L *co-*, together + *agere*, to drive⟧ convincingly to the point —**co′gen·cy** ***n.***
cog·i·tate (käj′ə tāt′) ***vi.***, ***vt.*** **-tat′ed**, **-tat′ing** ⟦< L⟧ to think deeply (about); ponder —**cog′i·ta′tion** ***n.*** —**cog′i·ta′tive** ***adj.*** —**cog′i·ta′tor** ***n.***
co·gnac (kōn′yak′, kôn′-) ***n.*** ⟦Fr⟧ **1** a brandy from Cognac, France **2** loosely, any brandy
cog·nate (käg′nāt′) ***adj.*** ⟦< L *co-*, together + *gnasci*, to be born⟧ **1** related by family **2** from a common original form, as two words **3** related or similar —***n.*** a cognate person or thing
cog·ni·tion (käg nish′ən) ***n.*** ⟦< L *co-*, together + *gnoscere*, know⟧ **1** the process of knowing, perceiving, etc. **2** an idea, perception, etc. —**cog′ni·tive** (-nə tiv) ***adj.***
cognitive science the study of cognition
cog·ni·za·ble (käg′ni zə bəl) ***adj.*** **1** that can be known or perceived **2** *Law* within the jurisdiction of a court
cog′ni·zance (-zəns) ***n.*** **1** perception or knowledge **2** notice; heed —**cog′ni·zant** ***adj.***
cog·no·men (käg nō′mən) ***n.*** ⟦< L *co-*, with + *nomen*, name⟧ **1** surname **2** any name; esp., a nickname
cog′wheel′ ***n.*** a wheel rimmed with teeth that mesh with those of another wheel, etc., to transmit or receive motion
co·hab·it (kō hab′it) ***vi.*** ⟦< L *co-*, together + *habitare*, dwell⟧ to live together, esp. as if legally married —**co·hab′i·ta′tion** ***n.***
co·heir (kō′er′, kō er′) ***n.*** one who inherits jointly with another or others
co·here (kō hir′) ***vi.*** **-hered′**, **-her′ing** ⟦< L *co-*, together + *haerere*, to stick⟧ **1** to stick together **2** to be connected naturally or logically
co·her′ent (-hir′ənt, -her′-) ***adj.*** **1** sticking together; cohering **2** logically connected and intelligible **3** capable of logical, intelligible speech, thought, etc. —**co·her′ence** ***n.*** —**co·her′ent·ly** ***adv.***
co·he′sion (-hē′zhən) ***n.*** a cohering; tendency to stick together —**co·he′sive** (-hēs′iv) ***adj.***
co·ho (kō′hō′) ***n.***, *pl.* **-ho′** or **-hos′** a small Pacific salmon now fished in N U.S. waters
co·hort (kō′hôrt′) ***n.*** ⟦< L *cohors*, enclosure⟧ **1** a band of soldiers **2** any group or band **3** an associate
coif (koif; *for 2 usually* kwäf) ***n.*** **1** ⟦< LL *cofea*, a cap⟧ a closefitting cap **2** ⟦< fol.⟧ a hairstyle
coif·fure (kwä fyoor′) ***n.*** ⟦Fr⟧ **1** a headdress **2** a hairstyle
coil (koil) ***vt.***, ***vi.*** ⟦< L *com-*, together + *legere*, gather⟧ to wind into circular or spiral form —***n.*** **1** a series of rings or a spiral, or anything in this form **2** a single turn of a coil **3** *Elec.* a spiral of wire
coin (koin) ***n.*** ⟦< L *cuneus*, a wedge⟧ **1** a piece of stamped metal, issued by a government as money **2** such pieces collectively —***vt.*** **1** to make (coins) by stamping metal **2** to invent (a new word, phrase, etc.) —**coin′age** ***n.***
co·in·cide (kō′in sīd′) ***vi.*** **-cid′ed**, **-cid′ing** ⟦< L *co-*, together + *incidere*, fall upon⟧ **1** to take up the same place in space **2** to occur at the same time **3** to agree exactly
co·in·ci·dence (kō in′sə dəns) ***n.*** **1** a coinciding **2** an accidental, but seemingly planned, occurrence of events, ideas, etc. at the same time —**co·in′ci·dent** or **co·in′ci·den′tal** ***adj.*** —**co·in′ci·den′tal·ly** ***adv.***
co·i·tus (kō′it əs) ***n.*** ⟦< L < *co-*, together + *ire*, go⟧ sexual intercourse: also **co·i·tion** (kō ish′ən)
coke[1] (kōk) ***n.*** ⟦< ME *colke*, core⟧ coal from which most of the gases have been removed by heating: used as an industrial fuel
coke[2] (kōk) ***n.*** [Slang] COCAINE
col *abbrev.* column
COL *abbrev.* **1** Colonel **2** cost of living
col- *prefix* COM-: used before *l*

THESAURUS

coerce ***v.*** impel, compel, constrain; see FORCE.
coercion ***n.*** compulsion, persuasion, constraint; see PRESSURE 2, RESTRAINT 2.
coexist ***v.*** exist together, coincide, be contemporary; see ACCOMPANY.
coexistence ***n.*** order, détente, accord; see PEACE 1, 2.
coffee ***n.*** caffeinated beverage, decaf*, java*; see DRINK 2. *Prepared coffee includes the following:* Turkish, Armenian, drip, percolated, vacuum, instant, French roast, coffee with cream, demitasse, espresso, café au lait, latte, cappuccino, black coffee.
coffin ***n.*** box, casket, sarcophagus, burial urn, funerary urn, pine box, mummy case; see also CONTAINER.
cohabit ***v.*** shack up with*, play house with*, be roommates; see ACCOMPANY.
coherence ***n.*** stickiness, viscosity, gumminess, cementation, adhesiveness, sticking together, coagulation, viscidity, adherence, fusion, sticking, union, adhesion, cohesiveness, consistency.
coherent ***a.*** comprehensible, sound, intelligible; see LOGICAL, UNDERSTANDABLE.
coil ***n.*** curl, turn, ring, wind, convolution, twist, twirl, lap, loop, curlicue, corkscrew, roll, spiral, helix, scroll; see also CIRCLE 1.
coil ***v.*** scroll, wind, loop, twist, fold, twine, intertwine, entwine, convolute, lap, twirl, wreathe; see also CURL.—*Ant.* UNFOLD, unwind, ravel.
coin ***n.*** legal tender, silver, copper; see MONEY 1.
coin ***v.*** **1** [To mint money] mint, strike, stamp; see MANUFACTURE. **2** [To invent a word, etc.] create, originate, make up; see INVENT 1.
coincide ***v.*** correspond, agree, concur, match, accord, harmonize; see also AGREE.
coincidence ***n.*** luck, fortune, circumstance; see ACCIDENT, CHANCE 1.
coincidental ***a.*** **1** [Occurring simultaneously] concurrent, concomitant, contemporaneous; see SIMULTANEOUS. **2** [Apparently accidental] chance, unpredictable, unplanned; see RANDOM.

co·la (kō′lə) ***n.*** ⟦< Afr name⟧ **1** an African tree with nuts that yield an extract used in soft drinks and medicine **2** a carbonated soft drink flavored with this extract

col·an·der (kul′ən dər, käl′-) ***n.*** ⟦prob. ult. < L *colum,* strainer⟧ a perforated pan for draining off liquids

cold (kōld) ***adj.*** ⟦OE *cald*⟧ **1** of a temperature much lower than normal, expected, or comfortable **2** not warmed or warmed up **3** unfriendly, indifferent, or depressing **4** devoid of feeling; emotionless **5** *a)* not fresh (said of a hunting scent) *b)* off the track **6** [Inf.] unconscious *[knocked cold]* **7** [Inf.] unlucky or ineffective *[a cold streak in shooting a basketball]* —***adv.*** [Inf.] **1** completely *[she was stopped cold]* **2** without preparation —***n.*** **1** lack of heat or warmth **2** cold weather **3** a viral infection of the respiratory tract, causing sneezing, coughing, etc. —**catch** (or **take**) **cold** to become ill with a cold —**have** (or **get**) **cold feet** [Inf.] to be (or become) timid —**in the cold** neglected —**cold′ly** ***adv.*** —**cold′ness** ***n.***

cold′blood′ed ***adj.*** **1** having a body temperature that varies with the surrounding air, water, etc., as fish and reptiles **2** cruel or callous

cold cream a creamy preparation for softening and cleansing the skin

cold cuts sliced cold meats and, usually, cheeses

cold front the forward edge of a cold air mass advancing under a warmer mass

cold shoulder [Inf.] a slight; rebuff; snub —**cold′-shoul′der** ***vt.***

cold sore a sore, caused by a viral infection, consisting of little blisters in or around the mouth during a cold or fever; herpes simplex

cold turkey [Slang] **1** totally and abruptly: said of withdrawal from drugs or tobacco by an addict or user **2** without preparation

cold war an extended period of conflict between nations that does not include direct warfare

cole (kōl) ***n.*** ⟦< L *caulis,* cabbage⟧ any of various plants related to the cabbage; esp., rape

cole′slaw′ (-slô′) ***n.*** ⟦< Du: see prec. & SLAW⟧ a salad of shredded raw cabbage: also **cole slaw**

co·le·us (kō′lē əs) ***n.*** ⟦< Gr *koleos,* a sheath⟧ any of various plants of the mint family with bright-colored leaves

col·ic (käl′ik) ***n.*** ⟦< Gr *kōlon,* colon⟧ **1** acute abdominal pain **2** a condition of infants with frequent crying from discomfort —**col′ick·y** ***adj.***

col·i·se·um (käl′ə sē′əm) ***n.*** ⟦< L *colosseum*⟧ a large stadium

co·li·tis (kō līt′is) ***n.*** ⟦< COLON² + -ITIS⟧ inflammation of the large intestine

coll *abbrev.* **1** collect **2** college

col·lab·o·rate (kə lab′ə rāt′) ***vi.*** **-rat′ed, -rat′ing** ⟦< L *com-,* with + *laborare,* to work⟧ **1** to work together, esp. in some literary or scientific undertaking **2** to cooperate with the enemy —**col·lab′o·ra′tion** ***n.*** —**col·lab′o·ra′tor** ***n.***

col·lage (kə läzh′) ***n.*** ⟦Fr, a pasting⟧ an art form in which bits of objects are pasted together on a surface

col·la·gen (käl′ə jən) ***n.*** a fibrous protein in bone and cartilage

col·lapse (kə laps′) ***vi.*** **-lapsed′, -laps′ing** ⟦< L *com-,* together + *labi,* to fall⟧ **1** to fall down or cave in **2** to break down suddenly **3** to fail suddenly in health **4** to fold together compactly —***vt.*** to make collapse —***n.*** a collapsing —**col·laps′i·ble** ***adj.***

col·lar (käl′ər) ***n.*** ⟦< L *collum,* neck⟧ **1** the part of a garment that encircles the neck **2** a band of leather, etc. for an animal's neck **3** anything like a collar —***vt.*** **1** to put a collar on **2** [Inf.] to seize, as by the collar

col′lar·bone′ ***n.*** CLAVICLE

col·lard (käl′ərd) ***n.*** ⟦< ME⟧ a kind of kale with coarse leaves

col·late (kō′lāt′, kä′-) ***vt.*** **-lat′ed, -lat′ing** ⟦< L *com-,* together + *latus,* brought⟧ **1** to compare (texts, etc.) carefully **2** to put (pages) in proper order —**col·la′tor** ***n.***

col·lat·er·al (kə lat′ər əl) ***adj.*** ⟦< L *com-,* together + *lateralis,* lateral⟧ **1** parallel or corresponding **2** accompanying or supporting *[collateral evidence]* **3** having the same ancestors but in a different line **4** designating or of security given as a pledge for the repayment of a loan, etc. —***n.*** **1** a collateral relative **2** collateral security

col·la·tion (kə lā′shən) ***n.*** **1** the act or result of collating **2** a light meal

col·league (käl′ēg′) ***n.*** ⟦< Fr < L *com-,* with + *legare,* appoint as deputy⟧ a fellow worker in the same profession

col·lect (kə lekt′) ***vt.*** ⟦< L *com-,* together + *legere,* gather⟧ **1** to gather together **2** to gather (stamps, etc.) as a hobby **3** to call for and receive (money) for (bills, etc.) **4** to regain control of (oneself) —***vi.*** to assemble or accumulate —***adj.***, ***adv.*** with payment to be made by the receiver *[to telephone someone collect]* —**col·lect′i·ble** or **col·lect′a·ble** ***adj.***, ***n.*** —**col·lec′tor** ***n.***

col·lect′ed ***adj.*** **1** gathered together **2** in control of oneself; calm

col·lec′tion ***n.*** **1** a collecting **2** things collected **3** a mass or pile; accumulation **4** money collected

col·lec′tive ***adj.*** **1** formed by collecting **2** of, as, or by a group *[collective effort]* **3** designating a singular noun, as *tribe*, denoting a collection of individuals —***n.*** **1** any collective enterprise; specif., a collective farm **2** the people who work together in it **3** a collective noun —**col·lec′tive·ly** ***adv.***

collective bargaining negotiation between organized workers and their employer concerning wages, hours, etc.

col·lec′tiv·ism′ ***n.*** collective ownership and control —**col·lec′tiv·ist** ***n.***, ***adj.*** —**col·lec′tiv·ize′, -ized′, -iz′ing,** ***vt.*** —**col·lec′ti·vi·za′tion** ***n.***

col·leen (kä lēn′) ***n.*** ⟦< Ir *caile,* girl⟧ [Irish] a girl

col·lege (käl′ij) ***n.*** ⟦see COLLEAGUE⟧ **1** a group of individuals with certain powers and duties *[the electoral col-*

THESAURUS

cold ***a.*** **1** [*Said of the weather*] crisp, cool, icy, freezing, frosty, frigid, wintry, bleak, nippy, brisk, keen, penetrating, snowy, frozen, cutting, snappy, piercing, chill, bitter, numbing, severe, stinging, glacial, intense, Siberian, chilly, sharp, raw, nipping, arctic, polar, below zero, biting.—*Ant.* HOT, warm, heated. **2** [*Said of persons, animals, etc.*] coldblooded, frozen, clammy, stiff, chilled, frostbitten, shivering, blue from cold.—*Ant.* HOT, perspiring, thawed. **3** [*Said of temperament*] unconcerned, apathetic, distant; see INDIFFERENT, RESERVED 3. —**have** (or **get**) **cold feet** go back on one's word, hold back, back down; see FEAR, STOP 2. —**throw cold water on** dishearten, squelch, dampen; see DISCOURAGE.

cold ***n.*** **1** [Conditions having a cold temperature] coldness, frozenness, chilliness, frostiness, draft, frostbite, absence of warmth, want of heat, chill, shivers, coolness, goose flesh, numbness, iciness, frigidity, freeze, glaciation, refrigeration; see also WEATHER.—*Ant.* HEAT, warmth, heat wave. **2** [Head or respiratory congestion] cough, sore throat, sickness, head cold, sinus trouble, chest cold, bronchial irritation, common cold, laryngitis, hay fever, whooping cough, influenza, flu, asthma, bronchitis, strep throat, strep, sniffles*, frog in one's throat; see also ILLNESS 2. —**catch cold** come down with a cold, become ill, get a cold; see SICKEN 1. —**leave out in the cold** ignore, slight, neglect; see ABANDON 2. —**(out) in the cold** forgotten, ignored, rejected; see NEGLECTED.

coldblooded ***a.*** relentless, callous, unfeeling; see CRUEL.

collaborate ***v.*** work together, conspire, work with; see COOPERATE.

collapse ***n.*** breakdown, downfall, destruction; see FAILURE 1, WRECK.

collapse ***v.*** break down, cave in, give way; see FAIL 1, FALL 1, 2.

collar ***n.*** neckband, neckpiece, dickey; see CLOTHES.

collateral ***n.*** security, guarantee, pledge; see INSURANCE, MONEY 1, WEALTH.

colleague ***n.*** partner, collaborator, teammate; see ASSOCIATE.

collect ***v.*** **1** [To bring into one place] amass, consolidate, convoke; see ACCUMULATE, ASSEMBLE 2, CONCENTRATE 1. **2** [To come together] congregate, assemble, flock; see GATHER. **3** [To obtain funds] solicit, raise, secure; see GET 1.

collected ***a.*** **1** [Composed] self-possessed, poised, cool; see CALM 1. **2** [Assembled] accumulated, amassed, compiled; see GATHERED.

collection ***n.*** specimens, samples, examples, extracts, gems, models, assortment, medley, accumulation, pile, stack, group, assemblage, compilation, mass, quantity, selection, treasury, anthology, miscellany, aggregation, combination, number, store, stock, digest, arrangement, concentration, finds, batch, mess, lot, heap, bunch; see also ORDER 3.

collector ***n.*** authority, hobbyist, fancier, serious amateur, gatherer, discoverer, curator, compiler, finder, assembler, hoarder, librarian, archivist; see also SCIENTIST, SPECIALIST.

college ***n.*** institute, institution, community college, liberal arts college, teachers college, junior college, state college, denominational college, nondenominational college, private college, business school, technical

lege] **2** an institution of higher education that grants degrees **3** any of the schools of a university **4** a school offering specialized instruction *[a business college]* **5** the building or buildings of a college

col·le·gial (kə lē′jəl) ***adj.*** **1** collegiate **2** characterized by consideration and respect among colleagues —**col·le′gi·al′i·ty** (-jē al′ə tē) ***n.***

col·le·gian (kə lē′jən) ***n.*** a college student

col·le′giate (-jit) ***adj.*** of or like a college or college students

col·lide (kə līd′) ***vi.*** **-lid′ed, -lid′ing** ⟦< L *com-,* together + *laedere,* to strike⟧ **1** to come into violent contact; crash **2** to conflict; clash

col·lid′er ***n.*** a research device for directing beams of subatomic particles at each other

col·lie (käl′ē) ***n.*** ⟦< ?⟧ a large, long-haired dog, orig. bred as a sheepdog

col·lier (käl′yər) ***n.*** ⟦< ME: see COAL & -IER⟧ [Chiefly Brit.] **1** a coal miner **2** a coal freighter

col′lier·y ***n.***, *pl.* **-ies** [Chiefly Brit.] a coal mine and its buildings, etc.

col·li·sion (kə lizh′ən) ***n.*** **1** a colliding **2** a clash or conflict

col·lo·cate (käl′ə kāt′) ***vt.*** **-cat′ed, -cat′ing** ⟦< L *com-,* together + *locare,* to place⟧ to arrange; esp., to set side by side —**col′lo·ca′tion** ***n.***

col·lo·di·on (kə lō′dē ən) ***n.*** a nitrocellulose solution that dries into a tough, elastic film

col·loid (käl′oid′) ***n.*** ⟦< Gr *kolla,* glue + -OID⟧ a substance made up of tiny particles that remain suspended in a medium of different matter —**col·loi′dal** ***adj.***

col·lo·qui·al (kə lō′kwē əl) ***adj.*** ⟦see COLLOQUY⟧ **1** conversational **2** INFORMAL (sense *d*) —**col·lo′qui·al·ism′** ***n.*** —**col·lo′qui·al·ly** ***adv.***

col·lo′qui·um (-əm) ***n.***, *pl.* **-qui·a** (-ə) or **-qui·ums** ⟦L: see fol.⟧ an organized conference or seminar on some subject

col·lo·quy (käl′ə kwē) ***n.***, *pl.* **-quies** ⟦< L *com-,* together + *loqui,* speak⟧ a conversation or conference

col·lude (kə lo͞od′) ***vi.*** **-lud′ed, -lud′ing** to act in collusion; conspire

col·lu·sion (kə lo͞o′zhən) ***n.*** ⟦< L *com-,* with + *ludere,* to play⟧ a secret agreement for fraudulent or illegal purpose; conspiracy —**col·lu′sive** (-siv) ***adj.*** —**col·lu′sive·ly** ***adv.***

co·logne (kə lōn′) ***n.*** ⟦< Fr *eau de cologne,* lit., water of Cologne, city in Germany⟧ a perfumed toilet water made of alcohol and aromatic oils

Co·logne (kə lōn′) city in W Germany, on the Rhine: pop. 962,000

Co·lom·bi·a (kə lum′bē ə) country in NW South America: 440,829 sq. mi.; pop. 29,482,000 —**Co·lom′bi·an** ***adj.***, ***n.***

co·lon[1] (kō′lən) ***n.*** ⟦< Gr *kōlon,* verse part⟧ a mark of punctuation (:) used before a long quotation, explanation, example, series, etc. and after the salutation of a formal letter

co·lon[2] (kō′lən) ***n.***, *pl.* **-lons** or **-la** (-lə) ⟦< Gr *kolon*⟧ that part of the large intestine extending from the cecum to the rectum

colo·nel (kur′nəl) ***n.*** ⟦< It *colonna,* (military) column⟧ a military officer ranking just above a lieutenant colonel

co·lo·ni·al (kə lō′nē əl) ***adj.*** **1** of, in, or having a colony **2** [*often* **C-**] of the thirteen British colonies that became the U.S. —***n.*** an inhabitant of a colony

co·lo′ni·al·ism′ ***n.*** the system by which a country maintains foreign colonies, esp. for economic exploitation —**co·lo′ni·al·ist** ***n.***, ***adj.***

col·o·nist (käl′ə nist) ***n.*** a settler or inhabitant of a colony

col′o·nize′ (-nīz′) ***vt.***, ***vi.*** **-nized′, -niz′ing** **1** to found a colony (in) **2** to settle in a colony —**col′o·ni·za′tion** ***n.*** —**col′o·niz′er** ***n.***

col·on·nade (käl′ə nād′) ***n.*** ⟦< L *columna,* column⟧ *Archit.* a row of columns, as along the side of a building

co·lon·os·co·py (kō′lən äs′kə pē) ***n.*** an examination of the inside of the colon using a fiber-optic device

col·o·ny (käl′ə nē) ***n.***, *pl.* **-nies** ⟦< L *colere,* cultivate⟧ **1** *a)* a group of settlers in a distant land, under the jurisdiction of their native land *b)* the region settled **2** any territory ruled over by a distant state **3** a community of the same nationality or pursuits, as within a city **4** *Biol.* a group living or growing together

col·o·phon (käl′ə fən, -fän′) ***n.*** ⟦LL < Gr *kolophōn,* top⟧ a publisher's emblem

col·or (kul′ər) ***n.*** ⟦L⟧ **1** the property of reflecting light of a particular visible wavelength: the *colors* of the spectrum are red, orange, yellow, green, blue, indigo, and violet **2** any coloring matter; dye; pigment **3** color of the face or skin **4** [*pl.*] a colored badge, etc. to identify the wearer **5** [*pl.*] a flag **6** outward appearance **7** vivid quality —***vt.*** **1** to give color to; paint, dye, etc. **2** to change the color of **3** to alter, as by distorting *[to color a story]* —***vi.*** **1** to become colored **2** to change color **3** to blush or flush **4** to draw or color pictures with wax crayons —**show one's** (**true**) **colors** to reveal one's true self

Col·o·rad·o (käl′ə rad′ō, -rä′dō) Mountain State of the W U.S.: 103,729 sq. mi.; pop. 3,294,000; cap. Denver: abbrev. *CO* —**Col′o·rad′an** ***adj.***, ***n.***

Colorado Springs city in central Colorado: site of the U.S. Air Force Academy: pop. 280,000

col·or·ant (kul′ər ənt) ***n.*** a coloring agent

col′or·a′tion (-ā′shən) ***n.*** a coloring

col·o·ra·tu·ra (kul′ə rə to͝or′ə) ***n.*** ⟦It⟧ **1** brilliant runs, trills, etc., used to display a singer's skill **2** a soprano capable of singing such music: also **coloratura soprano**

col′or·blind′ ***adj.*** **1** unable to distinguish certain colors or any colors **2** not influenced by considerations of race —**col′or·blind′ness** ***n.***

co·lo·rec·tal (kō′lə rek′təl) ***adj.*** of the colon and rectum

col·ored (kul′ərd) ***adj.*** **1** having color **2** *a)* non-Caucasoid *b)* [Old-fashioned] BLACK (*adj.* 2)

col′or·fast′ ***adj.*** with color not subject to fading or running

col′or·ful ***adj.*** **1** full of color **2** picturesque, vivid, etc. —**col′or·ful·ly** ***adv.*** —**col′or·ful·ness** ***n.***

col′or·ing ***n.*** **1** anything applied to impart color; pigment, etc. **2** the way a thing is colored **3** false appearance

col′or·less ***adj.*** **1** without color **2** lacking interest; dull —**col′or·less·ly** ***adv.*** —**col′or·less·ness** ***n.***

color line the barrier of social, political, and economic restrictions imposed on blacks or other nonwhites: also **color bar**

co·los·sal (kə läs′əl) ***adj.*** enormous in size, degree, etc.; astonishingly great —**co·los′sal·ly** ***adv.***

co·los·sus (kə läs′əs) ***n.***, *pl.* **-si′** (-ī′) or **-sus·es** ⟦< Gr⟧ **1** a gigantic statue **2** anything huge or important

THESAURUS

school, higher education, graduate school, medical school, law school, seminary; see also UNIVERSITY.

collide ***v.*** **1** [To come into violent contact] hit, strike, smash; see CRASH 4. **2** [To come into conflict] clash, conflict, disagree; see OPPOSE 1.

collision ***n.*** impact, contact, shock, accident, crash, colliding, bump, jar, jolt, sideswipe, strike, hit, slam, blow, thud, thump, knock, smash, head-on crash, fender bender*; see also DISASTER.

colonial ***a.*** **1** [Concerning a colony] pioneer, isolated, dependent, settled, provincial, frontier, Pilgrim, emigrant, immigrant, territorial, outland, distant, remote, early American, overseas, established. **2** [Having qualities suggestive of colonial life] hard, raw, crude, harsh, wild, unsettled, limited, uncultured, new, unsophisticated.

colonization ***n.*** immigration, settlement, expansion; see FOUNDATION 2.

colonize ***v.*** found, people, pioneer; see ESTABLISH 2, SETTLE 5.

colony ***n.*** settlement, dependency, subject state, colonial state, dominion, offshoot, political possession, province, group, new land, protectorate, hive, daughter country, satellite state, community, group migration; see also NATION 1.

color ***n.*** hue, tone, tint, shade, tinge, dye, complexion, brilliance, undertone, value, iridescence, intensity, coloration, discoloration, pigmentation, coloring, cast, glow, blush, wash, tincture. *Colors include the following—colors in the solar spectrum:* red, orange, yellow, green, blue, violet; *primary colors of the spectrum:* red, green, blue; *psychological primary colors:* red, yellow, green, blue, black, white; *primary colors of paints or pigments:* red, blue, yellow; see also BLACK 1, BLUE 1, PURPLE, BROWN, GREEN 1, ORANGE 1, PINK, RED, YELLOW. —**change color** flush, redden, become red in the face; see BLUSH. —**lose color** become pale, blanch, faint; see WHITEN 1.

color ***v.*** chalk, daub, gild, enamel, lacquer, suffuse, stipple, pigment, glaze, tinge, tint, stain, tone, shade, dye, wash, crayon, enliven, embellish, give color to, adorn, imbue, emblazon, illuminate, rouge; see also DECORATE, PAINT 1, 2.

colored ***a.*** hued, tinted, tinged, shaded, flushed, reddened, glowing, stained, dyed, washed, rouged; see also PAINTED 2.

colorful ***a.*** vivid, glowing, realistic; see BRIGHT 1.

colorless ***a.*** drab, pale, neutral; see DULL 2, TRANSPARENT 1.

colossal ***a.*** huge, enormous, immense; see LARGE 1.

co·los·to·my (kə läs′tə mē) ***n.***, *pl.* **-mies** a surgical construction of an artificial anal opening from the colon
co·los·trum (kə läs′trəm) ***n.*** ⟦L⟧ fluid secreted by the mammary glands just after a birth
col·our (kul′ər) ***n., vt., vi.*** *Brit. sp. of* COLOR
colt (kōlt) ***n.*** ⟦OE⟧ a young male horse, etc.
colt′ish ***adj.*** of or like a colt; esp., frisky, frolicsome, etc. —**colt′ish·ly** ***adv.***
Co·lum·bi·a (kə lum′bē ə, -byə) **1** capital of South Carolina: pop. 98,000 **2** river flowing from Canada through Washington, & along the Washington-Oregon border into the Pacific
col·um·bine (käl′əm bīn′) ***n.*** ⟦< L *columbinus,* dovelike⟧ a plant of the buttercup family, having dainty, spurred flowers of various colors
Co·lum·bus[1] (kə lum′bəs), **Chris·to·pher** (kris′tə fər) 1451?-1506; It. explorer: discovered America (1492)
Columbus[2] **1** capital of Ohio, in the central part: pop. 633,000 **2** city in W Georgia: pop. 179,000
col·umn (käl′əm) ***n.*** ⟦< L *columna*⟧ **1** a slender upright structure, usually a supporting member in a building **2** anything like a column *[*the spinal *column]* **3** a file formation of troops, etc. **4** any of the vertical sections of printed matter on a page **5** a feature article appearing regularly in a newspaper, etc. —**co·lum·nar** (kə lum′nər) ***adj.***
col·um·nist (käl′əm nist′) ***n.*** a writer of a COLUMN (sense 5)
Com *abbrev.* **1** Commissioner **2** Committee
com- ⟦< L *com-,* with⟧ *prefix* with, together: also used as an intensive
co·ma (kō′mə) ***n.*** ⟦< Gr *kōma,* deep sleep⟧ a period of deep, prolonged unconsciousness caused by injury or disease
co·ma·tose (kō′mə tōs′, käm′ə-) ***adj.*** **1** of, like, or in a coma **2** lethargic
comb (kōm) ***n.*** ⟦< OE *camb*⟧ **1** a thin strip of hard rubber, plastic, etc., with teeth, used to arrange or clean the hair **2** any similar tool, as for cleaning and straightening wool, flax, etc. **3** a red, fleshy outgrowth on the head, as of a rooster **4** a honeycomb —***vt.*** **1** to arrange, etc. with a comb **2** to search thoroughly
com·bat (kəm bat′; *for n. & adj.,* käm′bat′) ***vi.*** **-bat′ed** or **-bat′ted, -bat′ing** or **-bat′ting** ⟦< Fr < L *com-,* with + *battuere,* to fight⟧ to fight, contend, or struggle —***vt.*** to fight or actively oppose —***n.*** **1** armed fighting; battle **2** any struggle or conflict —***adj.*** of or for military combat —**com·bat′ant** ***adj., n.***
combat fatigue a psychiatric condition involving anxiety, depression, etc., as after prolonged combat in warfare
com·bat′ive ***adj.*** ready or eager to fight
comb′er ***n.*** **1** one that combs **2** a large wave that breaks on a beach, etc.
com·bi·na·tion (käm′bə nā′shən) ***n.*** **1** a combining or being combined **2** a thing formed by combining **3** an association of persons, firms, etc. for a common purpose **4** the series of numbers to which a dial is turned on a lock (**combination lock**) to open it
com·bine (kəm bīn′; *for n.* käm′bīn′) ***vt., vi.*** **-bined′, -bin′ing** ⟦< L *com-,* together + *bini,* two by two⟧ to join into one, as by blending; unite —***n.*** **1** a machine for harvesting and threshing grain **2** an association of persons, corporations, etc. for commercial or political purposes —**com·bin′er** ***n.***
comb′ings ***pl.n.*** loose hair, wool, etc. removed in combing
combining form a word form occurring only in compounds and derivatives (Ex.: *cardio-* in *cardiograph*)
com·bo (käm′bō′) ***n.***, *pl.* **-bos′** **1** [Inf.] a combination **2** a small jazz ensemble
com·bust (kəm bust′) ***vi.*** to burn
com·bus·ti·ble (kəm bus′tə bəl) ***adj.*** that can burn; flammable —**com·bus′ti·bil′i·ty** ***n.*** —**com·bus′ti·bly** ***adv.***
com·bus′tion (-chən) ***n.*** ⟦< L *com-,* intens. + *urere,* to burn⟧ the act or process of burning
come (kum) ***vi.*** **came, come, com′ing** ⟦< OE *cuman*⟧ **1** to move from "there" to "here" **2** to arrive or appear **3** to extend; reach **4** to happen **5** to occur mentally *[*the answer *came* to me*]* **6** to occur in a certain order *[*after 8 *comes* 9*]* **7** to be derived or descended **8** to be a native or resident: with *from [*to *come* from Ohio*]* **9** to be caused; result **10** to proceed or progress (*along*) **11** to become *[*to *come* loose*]* **12** to be available *[*it *comes* in four sizes*]* **13** to amount (*to*) —***interj.*** used to express irritation, impatience, etc. —**come about** **1** to happen **2** to turn about —**come across** (or **upon**) to meet or find by chance —**come along** **1** to appear or arrive **2** to proceed or succeed —**come around** (or **round**) **1** to recover **2** to yield —**come by** to get; gain —**come down with** to contract (a flu, etc.) —**come into** **1** to enter into **2** to inherit —**come off** **1** to become detached **2** to end up **3** [Inf.] to prove effective, etc. —**come out** **1** to be disclosed **2** to make a debut **3** to end up **4** to reveal that one is homosexual —**come out for** to announce endorsement of —**come through** **1** to complete something successfully **2** [Inf.] to do or give what is wanted —**come to** to recover consciousness —**come up** to arise, as a point in a discussion —**how come?** [Inf.] why?
come′back′ ***n.*** **1** a return to a previous state or position, as of power **2** a witty answer; retort

THESAURUS

colt ***n.*** foal, filly, yearling; see HORSE.

column ***n.*** **1** [A pillar] support, prop, shaft, monument, totem, pylon, obelisk, tower, minaret, cylinder, mast, monolith, upright, pedestal; see also POST. **2** [Journalistic commentary] article, editorial, Op-Ed; see NEWS 1.

columnist ***n.*** feature writer, journalist, correspondent; see REPORTER, WRITER.

coma ***n.*** unconsciousness, insensibility, stupor; see SLEEP.

comb ***n.*** pocket comb, pick, currycomb; see BRUSH 1.

comb ***v.*** untangle, disentangle, cleanse, scrape, arrange, straighten, part, tease, smooth.

combat ***n.*** struggle, warfare, conflict; see BATTLE, FIGHT.

combat ***v.*** battle, oppose, resist; see FIGHT.

combination ***n.*** **1** [The act of combining] uniting, joining, unification; see UNION 1. **2** [An association] union, alliance, federation; see ORGANIZATION 2. **3** [Something formed by combining] compound, aggregate, blend; see MIXTURE 1.

combine ***v.*** **1** [To bring together] connect, mix, link; see JOIN 1. **2** [To become one] fuse, merge, blend; see MIX 1, UNITE.

combined ***a.*** linked, mingled, connected; see JOINED.

combustion ***n.*** flaming, burning, oxidization; see FIRE 1.

come ***v.*** **1** [To move toward] close in, advance, draw near; see APPROACH 2. **2** [To arrive] appear at, reach, attain; see ARRIVE. **3** [To be available] appear, be at someone's disposal, be ready, be obtainable, be handy, be accessible, be able to be reached, show up, turn up; see also APPEAR 1. **4** [*To have an orgasm] reach sexual fulfillment, ejaculate, climax; see ACHIEVE, COPULATE. —**as good as they come** excellent, superior, fine; see BEST. —**come about** occur, take place, result; see HAPPEN 2. —**come across** **1** [To find] uncover, stumble upon, notice; see DISCOVER, FIND. **2** [*To give] deliver, pay, hand over; see GIVE 1. —**come along** **1** [To accompany] accompany, go with, attend; see ARRIVE, ADVANCE 1. **2** [To progress] show improvement, do well, prosper; see IMPROVE 2. —**come around** **1** [To recover] improve, recuperate, rally; see RECOVER 3, REVIVE 2. **2** [*To visit] call on, stop by, drop in on; see VISIT. —**come by** **1** [To pass] go by, overtake, move past; see PASS 1. **2** [To acquire] get, win, procure; see GET 1. —**come into** **1** [To inherit] fall heir to, succeed to, acquire; see INHERIT, RECEIVE 1. **2** [To join] enter into, associate with, align; see JOIN 2. —**come off** **1** [To become separated] be disconnected, be disengaged, be severed, be parted, be disjoined, be detached, be disunited; see also DIVIDE. **2** [To happen] occur, turn out, come about; see HAPPEN 2. —**come out** **1** [To be made public] be published, be made known, be announced, be issued, be brought out, be reported, be revealed, be divulged, be disclosed, be exposed; see also APPEAR 1. **2** [To result] end, conclude, terminate; see SUCCEED 1. —**come out for** announce, state, affirm; see DECLARE, SUPPORT 1. —**come through** **1** [To be successful] accomplish, score, triumph; see ACHIEVE, SUCCEED 1. **2** [To survive] live through, persist, withstand; see ENDURE 2. **3** [To do] accomplish, achieve, carry out; see PERFORM 1. —**come to** **1** [To recover] rally, come around, recuperate; see RECOVER 3, REVIVE 2. **2** [To result in] end in, terminate by, conclude; see HAPPEN 2, RESULT. —**come up** appear, arise, move to a higher place; see RISE 1. —**how come?*** for what reason?, how so?, what is the cause of that?; see WHY.

comeback* ***n.*** **1** [Improvement] revival, progress, betterment; see IMPROVEMENT 1, RECOVERY 1, 2. **2** [Witty answer] retort, reply, rejoinder; see ANSWER 1.

co·me·di·an (kə mē′dē ən) ***n.*** **1** an actor who plays comic parts **2** an entertainer who tells jokes —**co·me′di·enne′** (-en′) ***fem.n.***
co·me′dic (-dik) ***adj.*** having to do with comedy
come′down′ ***n.*** a loss of status
com·e·dy (käm′ə dē) ***n.***, *pl.* **-dies** ⟦< Gr *kōmos*, revel + *aeidein*, sing⟧ **1** a humorous play, etc. with a nontragic ending **2** an amusing event
come·ly (kum′lē) ***adj.*** **-li·er, -li·est** ⟦< OE *cymlic*⟧ attractive; fair —**come′li·ness** ***n.***
come′-on′ ***n.*** [Slang] an inducement
co·mes·ti·ble (kə mes′tə bəl) ***n.*** ⟦< L *com-*, intens. + *edere*, to eat⟧ [*usually pl.*] food
com·et (käm′it) ***n.*** ⟦< Gr *komē*, hair⟧ a small, frozen mass of dust and gas revolving around the sun: as it nears the sun it vaporizes, usually forming a long, luminous tail
come·up·pance (kum′up′əns) ***n.*** [Inf.] deserved punishment
com·fit (kum′fit, käm′-) ***n.*** ⟦< L *com-*, with + *facere*, do⟧ a candied fruit, nut, etc.
com·fort (kum′fərt) ***vt.*** ⟦< L *com-*, intens. + *fortis*, strong⟧ to soothe in distress or sorrow; console —***n.*** **1** relief from distress, etc. **2** one that comforts **3** a state of, or thing that provides, ease and quiet enjoyment —**com′fort·ing** ***adj.*** —**com′fort·less** ***adj.***
com·fort·a·ble (kumf′tər bəl, kum′fərt ə bəl) ***adj.*** **1** providing comfort **2** at ease in body or mind **3** [Inf.] sufficient to satisfy *[a comfortable salary]* —**com′fort·a·bly** ***adv.***
com′fort·er ***n.*** **1** one that comforts **2** a quilted bed covering
comfort station a public toilet or restroom
com·fy (kum′fē) ***adj.*** **-fi·er, -fi·est** [Inf.] comfortable
com·ic (käm′ik) ***adj.*** **1** of comedy **2** amusing; funny —***n.*** **1** a comedian **2** the humorous element in art or life **3** *a)* COMIC STRIP *b)* [*pl.*] a section of comic strips *c)* a comic book
com′i·cal (-i kəl) ***adj.*** causing amusement; humorous; funny —**com′i·cal′i·ty** (-kal′ə tē) ***n.*** —**com′i·cal·ly** ***adv.***
comic strip a series of cartoons telling a humorous or adventurous story, as in a newspaper or in a booklet (**comic book**)
com·ing (kum′iŋ) ***adj.*** **1** approaching; next **2** showing promise of being successful, etc. —***n.*** arrival or approach
com·i·ty (käm′ə tē) ***n.*** ⟦< L *comis*, polite⟧ civility
comm *abbrev.* **1** commission **2** committee
com·ma (käm′ə) ***n.*** ⟦< Gr *komma*, clause⟧ a mark of punctuation (,) used to indicate a slight separation of sentence elements
com·mand (kə mand′) ***vt.*** ⟦< L *com-*, intens. + *mandare*, entrust⟧ **1** to give an order to; direct **2** to have authority over; control **3** to have for use *[to command a fortune]* **4** to deserve and get *[to command respect]* **5** to control (a position); overlook —***vi.*** to have authority —***n.*** **1** an order; direction **2** controlling power or position **3** mastery **4** military or naval force, or district, under a specified authority
com·man·dant (käm′ən dant′, -dänt′) ***n.*** a commanding officer, as of a fort
com′man·deer′ (-dir′) ***vt.*** ⟦see COMMAND⟧ **1** to seize (property) for military or government use **2** [Inf.] to take forcibly
com·mand′er ***n.*** **1** one who commands **2** *U.S. Navy* an officer ranking just above a lieutenant commander
commander in chief *pl.* **commanders in chief** the supreme commander of the armed forces of a nation
com·mand′ing ***adj.*** **1** having authority **2** impressive **3** very large
com·mand′ment ***n.*** a command; specif., any of the TEN COMMANDMENTS
com·man·do (kə man′dō) ***n.***, *pl.* **-dos** or **-does** ⟦Afrik < Port⟧ a member of a small military force trained to operate within enemy territory
command post the field headquarters of a military unit, from which operations are directed
com·mem·o·rate (kə mem′ə rāt′) ***vt.*** **-rat′ed, -rat′ing** ⟦< L *com-*, intens. + *memorare*, remind⟧ **1** to honor the memory of, as by a ceremony **2** to serve as a memorial to —**com·mem′o·ra′tion** ***n.*** —**com·mem′o·ra′tor** ***n.***

THESAURUS

comedian ***n.*** comic, humorist, entertainer; see ACTOR, CLOWN.
comedown ***n.*** reversal, blow, defeat; see FAILURE 1.
comedy ***n.*** comic drama, tragicomedy, stand-up comedy, situation comedy, sitcom, musical comedy, farce, satire, burlesque, parody, cartoon, skit, slapstick, light entertainment; see also DRAMA.
comfort ***n.*** rest, quiet, relaxation, repose, relief, poise, well-being, cheer, abundance, sufficiency, gratification, luxury, warmth, plenty, prosperity, pleasure, happiness, contentment, convenience, restfulness, peacefulness, cheerfulness, coziness, exhilaration, complacency, bed of roses*; see also EASE 1, ENJOYMENT, SATISFACTION 2.—*Ant.* WEAKNESS, discomfort, uneasiness.
comfort ***v.*** **1** [To console] share with, commiserate, solace, grieve with, cheer, gladden, uphold, hearten, pat on the back, put someone in a good humor, sustain, support, help, aid, confirm, reassure, refresh; see also ENCOURAGE, PITY 1.—*Ant.* DISCOURAGE, be indifferent to, depress. **2** [To make easy physically] alleviate, relieve, make comfortable, assuage, soothe, mitigate, gladden, quiet someone's fears, help someone in need, lighten someone's burden, encourage, calm, revive, sustain, aid, assist, nourish, support, compose oneself, delight, divert, bolster up, invigorate, refresh, put at ease, reassure, warm, lighten, soften, remedy, release, restore, free, make well, revitalize; see also EASE 1, HELP, STRENGTHEN.—*Ant.* WEAKEN, make uneasy, worsen.
comfortable ***a.*** **1** [In physical ease] contented, cheerful, easy, at rest, relaxed, at ease, untroubled, healthy, rested, pleased, complacent, soothed, relieved, strengthened, restored, in comfort, at home with, without care, snug as a bug in a rug*; see also HAPPY, SATISFIED.—*Ant.* UNEASY, ill, disturbed. **2** [Conducive to physical ease] satisfactory, snug, cozy, warm, sheltered, convenient, protected, cared for, appropriate, useful, roomy, spacious, luxurious, rich, satisfying, restful, in comfort, well-off, well-to-do; see also PLEASANT 2.—*Ant.* SHABBY, run-down, uncomfortable.
comfortably ***a.*** luxuriously, in comfort, restfully, snugly, cozily, pleasantly, warmly, conveniently, adequately, with ease, competently, amply; see also EASILY.—*Ant.* INADEQUATELY, insufficiently, poorly.
comforting ***a.*** sympathetic, cheering, encouraging, invigorating, health-giving, warming, consoling, sustaining, reassuring, inspiring, refreshing, relieving, soothing, lightening, mitigating, alleviating, softening, curing, restoring, releasing, freeing, revitalizing, tranquilizing.—*Ant.* DISTURBING, distressing, upsetting.
comic ***a.*** humorous, ridiculous, ironic; see FUNNY 1.
comical ***a.*** witty, amusing, humorous; see FUNNY 1.
coming ***a.*** **1** [Approaching] advancing, drawing near, progressing, nearing, in the offing, arriving, gaining upon, pursuing, getting near, converging, coming in, close at hand, coming on, near at hand, almost upon, immediate, future, in view, preparing, to come, eventual, fated, written, hereafter, at hand, in store, due, about to happen, hoped for, deserved, close, imminent, prospective, anticipated, forthcoming, looming, threatening, certain, ordained, impending, to be, expected, near, pending, foreseen, in the cards, in the wind; see also EXPECTED, LIKELY 1.—*Ant.* DISTANT, going, leaving. **2** [Having a promising future] promising, advancing, probable; see ABLE, AMBITIOUS. **3** [Future] lying ahead, pending, impending; see EXPECTED, FUTURE.
coming ***n.*** approach, landing, homecoming; see ARRIVAL 1.
command ***n.*** order, injunction, direction, demand, decree, prohibition, interdiction, canon, rule, call, summons, imposition, precept, mandate, charge, behest, edict, proclamation, instruction, proscription, ban, requirement, dictate, subpoena, commandment, dictum, word of command, writ, citation, notification, will, regulation, ordinance, act, fiat, bidding, word, requisition, ultimatum, exaction, enactment, caveat, prescript, warrant; see also LAW 3, POWER 2, REQUEST.
command ***v.*** **1** [To issue an order] charge, tell, demand; see ORDER 1. **2** [To have control] rule, dominate, master; see CONTROL.
commandeer ***v.*** appropriate, take, confiscate; see SEIZE 2.
commander ***n.*** commandant, officer, head; see ADMINISTRATION 2, ADMINISTRATOR, CHIEF, LEADER 2.
commanding ***n.*** **1** [Ruling] leading, directing, determining, ordering, instructing, dictating, dominating, compelling, managing, checking, curbing, forcing, coercing, requiring, restraining, in command, in authority, in charge, regulating. **2** [Important] decisive, impressive, significant; see IMPORTANT 1.
commemorate ***v.*** solemnize, honor, memorialize; see ADMIRE, CELEBRATE 1.
commemoration ***n.*** recognition,

com·mem'o·ra·tive (-rə tiv, -rāt'iv) ***adj.*** commemorating —***n.*** a stamp or coin marking an event, honoring a person, etc.

com·mence (kə mens') ***vi., vt.*** **-menced', -menc'ing** ⟦< L *com-,* together + *initiare,* begin⟧ to begin; start

com·mence'ment ***n.*** **1** a beginning; start **2** the ceremony of conferring degrees or diplomas at a school

com·mend (kə mend') ***vt.*** ⟦see COMMAND⟧ **1** to put in the care of another; entrust **2** to recommend **3** to praise —**com·mend'a·ble** ***adj.*** —**com·mend'a·bly** ***adv.*** —**com·men·da·tion** (käm'ən dā'shən) ***n.***

com·mend·a·to·ry (kə men'də tôr'ē) ***adj.*** praising or recommending

com·men·su·ra·ble (kə men'shoor ə bəl, -sər-) ***adj.*** ⟦< L *com-,* together + *mensura,* measurement⟧ measurable by the same standard or measure

com·men'su·rate (-shoor it, -sər-) ***adj.*** ⟦see prec.⟧ **1** equal in measure or size; coextensive **2** proportionate **3** commensurable

com·ment (käm'ent') ***n.*** ⟦< L *com-,* intens. + *meminisse,* remember⟧ **1** an explanatory or critical note **2** a remark or observation **3** talk; gossip —***vi.*** to make a comment or comments

com·men·tar·y (käm'ən ter'ē) ***n.,*** *pl.* **-ies** a series of explanatory notes or remarks

com'men·tate' (-tāt') ***vi.*** **-tat'ed, -tat'ing** to perform as a commentator

com'men·ta'tor (-tāt'ər) ***n.*** one who reports and analyzes events, trends, etc., as on television

com·merce (käm'ərs) ***n.*** ⟦< L *com-,* together + *merx,* merchandise⟧ trade on a large scale, as between countries

com·mer·cial (kə mur'shəl) ***adj.*** **1** of commerce or business **2** made or done for profit —***n.*** *Radio, TV* a paid advertisement —**com·mer'cial·ism'** ***n.*** —**com·mer'cial·ly** ***adv.***

com·mer'cial·ize' (-īz') ***vt.*** **-ized', -iz'ing** to make use of mainly for profit —**com·mer'cial·i·za'tion** ***n.***

com·min·gle (kə miŋ'gəl) ***vt., vi.*** **-gled, -gling** to mingle together

com·mis·er·ate (kə miz'ər āt') ***vi.*** **-at'ed, -at'ing** ⟦< L *com-,* intens. + *miserari,* to pity⟧ to sympathize (*with*) —**com·mis'er·a'tion** ***n.***

com·mis·sar (käm'ə sär') ***n.*** ⟦Russ *komissar*⟧ the head of any former U.S.S.R. COMMISSARIAT (sense 2): now called *minister*

com'mis·sar'i·at (-ser'ē ət) ***n.*** ⟦Fr < L: see COMMIT⟧ **1** an army branch providing food and supplies **2** a government department in the U.S.S.R.: now called *ministry*

com'mis·sar'y (-ser'ē) ***n.,*** *pl.* **-ies** ⟦see COMMIT⟧ **1** a store, as in an army camp, where food and supplies are sold **2** a restaurant in a movie or TV studio

com·mis·sion (kə mish'ən) ***n.*** ⟦see COMMIT⟧ **1** *a)* an authorization to perform certain duties or tasks *b)* a document giving such authorization *c)* the authority so granted **2** that which one is authorized to do **3** a group of people appointed to perform specified duties **4** a committing; doing **5** a percentage of money from sales, allotted to an agent, etc. **6** *Mil. a)* an official certificate conferring rank *b)* the rank conferred —***vt.*** **1** to give a commission to **2** to authorize **3** to put (a ship or boat) into service —**in** (or **out of**) **commission** in (or not in) working order

commissioned officer an officer in the armed forces holding a commission

com·mis'sion·er ***n.*** **1** a person authorized to do certain things by a commission or warrant **2** a member of a COMMISSION (*n.* 3) **3** an official in charge of a government bureau, etc. **4** a person selected to regulate and control a professional sport, an amateur league, etc.

com·mit (kə mit') ***vt.*** **-mit'ted, -mit'ting** ⟦< L *com-,* together + *mittere,* send⟧ **1** to deliver for safekeeping; entrust; consign **2** to put in custody or confinement *[committed* to prison*]* **3** to do or perpetrate (a crime) **4** to bind, as by a promise; pledge —***vi.*** [Inf.] to make a pledge: often with *to* —**com·mit'ment** ***n.*** —**com·mit'tal** ***n.***

com·mit·tee (kə mit'ē) ***n.*** ⟦see prec.⟧ a group of people chosen to report or act upon a certain matter —**com·mit'tee·man** (-mən), *pl.* **-men,** ***n.*** —**com·mit'tee·wom'an,** *pl.* **-wom'en,** ***fem.n.***

com·mode (kə mōd') ***n.*** ⟦Fr < L: see COM- & MODE⟧ **1** a chest of drawers **2** a toilet

com·mod·i·fy (kə mäd'ə fī') ***vt.*** **-fied', -fy'ing** to treat like or make into a mere commodity —**com·mod'i·fi·ca'tion** ***n.***

com·mo·di·ous (kə mō'dē əs) ***adj.*** ⟦see COMMODE⟧ spacious; roomy

com·mod·i·ty (kə mäd'ə tē) ***n.,*** *pl.* **-ties** ⟦see COMMODE⟧ **1** any useful thing **2** anything bought and sold **3** [*pl.*] basic products, as of agriculture

com·mo·dore (käm'ə dôr') ***n.*** ⟦see COMMAND⟧ *U.S. Navy* [Historical] an officer ranking just above a captain

com·mon (käm'ən) ***adj.*** ⟦< L *communis*⟧ **1** belonging to or shared by each or all **2** general; widespread **3** famil-

THESAURUS

remembrance, observance; see CELEBRATION, CEREMONY, CUSTOM.

commemorative ***a.*** dedicated to the memory of, in remembrance of, in honor of; see MEMORABLE 1.

commence ***v.*** start, initiate, set in motion; see BEGIN 2.

commend ***v.*** laud, support, acclaim; see APPROVE, PRAISE 1.

commendable ***a.*** praiseworthy, laudable, deserving; see EXCELLENT.

commendation ***n.*** tribute, approval, approbation; see HONOR, PRAISE 1.

comment ***n.*** report, commentary, editorial; see DISCUSSION, EXPLANATION, REMARK.

comment ***v.*** observe, remark, criticize, notice, state, express, pronounce, assert, affirm, mention, interject, say, note, touch upon, disclose, bring out, point out, conclude; see also MENTION, TALK 1.

commentary ***n.*** criticism, analysis, description; see EXPLANATION, INTERPRETATION.

commerce ***n.*** buying and selling, trading, marketing; see BUSINESS 1, ECONOMICS.

commercial ***a.*** trading, business, financial, economic, materialistic, practical, profitable, mercantile, merchandising, bartering, exchange, fiscal, monetary, trade, market, retail, wholesale, marketable, in the market, for sale, profit-making, money-making, across the counter; see also INDUSTRIAL, PROFITABLE.

commercial ***n.*** message from the sponsor, commercial announcement, plug*; see ADVERTISEMENT.

commercialize ***v.*** lower the quality of, degrade, cheapen; see ABUSE.

commission ***n.*** **1** [An authorization] order, license, command; see PERMISSION. **2** [A committee] commissioners, representatives, board; see COMMITTEE. **3** [A payment] percentage, fee, rake-off*; see PAY 2, PAYMENT 1. —**out of commission** damaged, not working, out of order; see BROKEN 2.

commission ***v.*** send, appoint, authorize, charge, empower, constitute, ordain, commit, entrust, send out, dispatch, deputize, assign, engage, employ, inaugurate, invest, name, nominate, hire, enable, license, command, elect, select; see also DELEGATE 1.

commissioner ***n.*** administrator, magistrate, government official; see EXECUTIVE.

commit ***v.*** **1** [To perpetrate] do, be guilty of, carry out; see PERFORM 1. **2** [To entrust] confide, delegate, relegate to, leave to, give to do, promise, assign, turn over to, put in the hands of, charge, invest, rely upon, depend upon, confer a trust, bind over, make responsible for, put an obligation upon, employ, dispatch, send, vest in, engage, commission; see also ASSIGN.—*Ant.* DISMISS, relieve of, discharge.

commitment ***n.*** pledge, responsibility, agreement; see DUTY 1, PROMISE 1, GUARANTY.

committee ***n.*** consultants, board, bureau, council, cabinet, investigators, trustees, appointed group, board of inquiry, representatives, investigating committee, executive committee, standing committee, planning board, ad hoc committee, special committee, referees, task force, study group, subcommittee; see also REPRESENTATIVE 2.

commodity ***n.*** goods, articles, stocks, merchandise, wares, materials, possessions, property, assets, belongings, things, stock in trade, consumers' goods, line, what one handles, what one is showing.

common ***a.*** **1** [Ordinary] universal, familiar, natural, normal, everyday, accepted, commonplace, characteristic, customary, bourgeois, conventional, passable, general, informal, wearisome, unassuming, pedestrian, lower-level, habitual, prevalent, probable, typical, prosaic, simple, current, prevailing, trite, household, second-rate, banal, unvaried, homely, colloquial, trivial, stock, oft-repeated, indiscriminate, tedious, worn-out, hackneyed, monotonous, stale, casual, undistinguished, uneducated, artless, workaday, provincial, unsophisticated, unrefined, untutored, plain, uncultured, vulgar, unadorned, ugly, obvious, average, orthodox, mediocre, humdrum, well-known, insipid, stereotyped, patent, moderate, middling, abiding, indifferent, tolerable, temperate, innocuous, undistinguished, run-of-the-mill, not too bad*, garden-variety, fair to middling*, so-so, nothing to write home about*; see

iar; usual **4** not of the upper classes *[the common people]* **5** vulgar; coarse **6** designating a noun (as *book*) that refers to any of a group —*n.* [*sometimes pl.*] land owned or used by all the inhabitants of a place —**in common** shared by each or all —**com'mon·ly** *adv.*

com'mon·al·ty (-əl tē) *n.* the common people; public: also **com'mon·al'i·ty** (-al'ə tē)

common carrier a person or company that transports people or goods for a fee

common denominator **1** a common multiple of the denominators of two or more fractions **2** a characteristic, etc. held in common

com'mon·er *n.* a person not of the nobility; one of the common people

common law the law based on custom, usage, and judicial decisions

com'mon-law' marriage *Law* a marriage not solemnized by religious or civil ceremony

common market an association of countries for closer economic union

common multiple *Math.* a multiple of each of two or more quantities

com'mon·place' *n.* **1** a platitude **2** anything common or ordinary —*adj.* trite or ordinary

common pleas *Law* in some States, a court having jurisdiction over civil and criminal trials

com'mons *pl.n.* **1** the common people **2** [C-] HOUSE OF COMMONS **3** [*often with sing. v.*] a room, building, etc. for dining, as at a college

common sense good sense or practical judgment —**com'mon-sense'** *adj.*

common stock stock in a company without the privileges of preferred stock, but usually giving its owner a vote

com'mon·weal' (-wēl') *n.* the public good; general welfare

com'mon·wealth' (-welth') *n.* **1** the people of a nation or state **2** a democracy or republic **3** a federation of states —**the Commonwealth** association of independent nations united under the British crown for purposes of consultation and mutual assistance

Commonwealth of Independent States a loose confederation of countries that were part of the U.S.S.R.

com·mo·tion (kə mō'shən) *n.* ⟦< L *com-*, together + *movere*, to move⟧ **1** violent motion **2** confusion; bustle

com·mu·nal (kə myōōn'əl, käm'yə nəl) *adj.* **1** of a commune **2** of the community; public **3** marked by common ownership of property —**com·mu'nal·ize'**, **-ized'**, **-iz'ing**, *vt.* —**com·mu'nal·ly** *adv.*

com·mune[1] (kə myōōn') *vi.* **-muned'**, **-mun'ing** ⟦< OFr *comuner*, to share⟧ **1** to talk together intimately **2** to be in close rapport

com·mune[2] (käm'yōōn') *n.* ⟦< L *communis*, common⟧ **1** the smallest administrative district of local government in some European countries **2** a small group of people living communally

com·mu·ni·ca·ble (kə myōō'ni kə bəl) *adj.* that can be communicated, as an idea, or transmitted, as a disease —**com·mu'ni·ca·bil'i·ty** *n.*

com·mu'ni·cant (-kənt) *n.* one who receives Holy Communion

com·mu·ni·cate (kə myōō'ni kāt') *vt.* **-cat'ed**, **-cat'ing** ⟦< L *communicare*⟧ **1** to impart; transmit **2** to give (information, etc.) —*vi.* **1** to give or exchange information **2** to have a meaningful relationship **3** to be connected, as rooms —**com·mu'ni·ca'tor** *n.*

com·mu'ni·ca'tion *n.* **1** a transmitting **2** *a*) a giving or exchanging of information, etc. *b*) a message, letter, etc. **3** a means of communicating —**com·mu'ni·ca'tive** (-kāt'iv, -kə tiv) *adj.*

com·mun·ion (kə myōōn'yən) *n.* ⟦see COMMON⟧ **1** possession in common **2** a communing **3** a Christian denomination **4** [C-] HOLY COMMUNION

com·mu·ni·qué (kə myōō'ni kā', kə myōō'ni kā') *n.* ⟦Fr⟧ an official communication

com·mu·nism (käm'yōō niz'əm, -yə-) *n.* ⟦see COMMON⟧ **1** any theory or system of common ownership of property **2** [*often* C-] *a*) socialism as formulated by Marx, Lenin, etc. *b*) any government or political movement supporting this

com'mu·nist (-nist) *n.* **1** an advocate or supporter of communism **2** [C-] a member of a Communist Party —*adj.* of, like, or supporting communism or communists —**com'mu·nis'tic** *adj.*

com·mu·ni·ty (kə myōō'nə tē) *n.*, *pl.* **-ties** ⟦see COMMON⟧ **1** *a*) any group living in the same area or having interests, work, etc. in common *b*) such an area **2** the general public **3** a sharing in common

community college a junior college serving a certain community

community service unpaid work for the community

com·mu·ta·tive (kə myōōt'ə tiv, käm'yə tāt'iv) *adj.* **1** involving exchange or replacement **2** *Math.* of an operation in which the order of the elements does not affect the result, as, in addition, 3 + 2 = 2 + 3

com·mute (kə myōōt') *vt.* **-mut'ed**, **-mut'ing** ⟦< L *com-*, intens. + *mutare*, to change⟧ **1** to exchange; substitute **2** to change (an obligation, punishment, etc.) to a less severe one —*vi.* to travel as a commuter —*n.* [Inf.] the trip of a commuter —**com·mu·ta·tion** (käm'yə tā'shən) *n.*

com·mut'er *n.* a person who travels regularly by train, bus, etc. between two locations that are some distance apart

Com·o·ros (käm'ə rōz') country on a group of islands in the W Indian Ocean: 719 sq. mi.; pop. 347,000

comp *abbrev.* **1** comparative **2** compound

THESAURUS

also CONVENTIONAL 1, DULL 4, POPULAR 1, 3, TRADITIONAL.—*Ant.* UNIQUE, extraordinary, unnatural. **2** [Of frequent occurrence] customary, constant, usual; see FREQUENT 1, HABITUAL, REGULAR 3. **3** [Generally known] general, prevalent, well-known; see FAMILIAR, TRADITIONAL. **4** [Low] cheap, inferior, shoddy; see POOR 2, SUBORDINATE. **5** [Held or enjoyed in common] shared, joint, mutual; see COOPERATIVE, PUBLIC 2. —**in common** shared, communal, mutually held; see PUBLIC 2.

commonly *a.* usually, ordinarily, generally; see REGULARLY.

commonplace *a.* usual, hackneyed, mundane; see COMMON 1, CONVENTIONAL 1, 3.

common sense *n.* good sense, judgment, horse sense*; see SENSE 2, WISDOM.

commotion *n.* violence, tumult, uproar; see DISTURBANCE 2, FIGHT.

communal *a.* shared, cooperative, mutual; see PUBLIC 2.

commune[2] *n.* community, collective, co-op*; see COOPERATIVE.

communicate *v.* **1** [To impart information] convey, inform, advise; see TEACH, TELL 1. **2** [To be in communication] correspond, be in touch, have access to, contact, reach, hear from, be within reach, be in correspondence with, be near, be close to, have the confidence of, associate with, establish contact with, be in agreement with, be in agreement about, confer, talk, converse, chat, speak together, deal with, write to, telephone, e-mail, wire, cable, fax, network, reply, answer, have a meeting of minds, find a common denominator; see also AGREE.—*Ant.* AVOID, withdraw, elude.

communication *n.* talk, utterance, announcing, extrasensory perception, telepathy, ESP, publication, writing, drawing, painting, broadcasting, televising, correspondence, disclosure, speaking, disclosing, conference, faxing, telephoning, wiring, e-mailing, cabling, networking, description, mention, announcement, presentation, interchange, expression, narration, relation, declaration, assertion, elucidation, transmission, reception, reading, translating, interpreting, news, ideas, statement, speech, language, warning, communiqué, briefing, bulletin, summary, information, report, account, publicity, translation, printed work, advice, tidings, conversation. *Means of communication include the following:* book, letter, newspaper, magazine, radio, TV, e-mail, proclamation, broadcast, dispatch, press-release, fax, wire, printout, telecast, telephone call, telegram, cable, broadside, circular, flier, brochure, notes, memorandum, postcard, poster, billboard; see also MAIL, NEWS 1, 2, RADIO 2, TELEPHONE, TELEVISION.

communications *n.* mail, mass media, telephone; see COMMUNICATION.

communism *n.* state socialism, Marxism, dictatorship of the proletariat, collectivism, state ownership of production; see also GOVERNMENT 2.

communist *n.* Marxist, commie*, red*; see RADICAL.

community *n.* **1** [A town] village, colony, hamlet; see CITY, TOWN 1. **2** [Society] the public, the people, the nation; see SOCIETY 2.

commute *v.* **1** [To exchange for something less severe] reduce, lessen, mitigate; see DECREASE 2. **2** [Travel] go back and forth, drive, take the train; see TRAVEL.

commuter *n.* suburbanite, city worker, daily traveler; see DRIVER, TRAVELER.

com·pact (kəm pakt′, käm′pakt; *for n.* käm′pakt) ***adj.*** ⟦< L *com-,* with, together + *pangere,* to fix⟧ **1** closely and firmly packed **2** taking little space **3** terse; concise —***vt.*** **1** to pack or join firmly together **2** to make by putting together —***n.*** **1** a small cosmetic case, usually containing face powder and a mirror **2** a relatively small car **3** an agreement; covenant —**com·pact′ly** ***adv.*** —**com·pact′ness** ***n.***

compact disc (or **disk**) a digital disc on which music, data, etc. has been encoded for playing on a device using a laser beam to read the encoded matter

com·pac·tor (kəm pak′tər, käm′pak′tər) ***n.*** a device that compresses trash into small bundles

com·pan·ion (kəm pan′yən) ***n.*** ⟦< L *com-,* with + *panis,* bread⟧ **1** an associate; comrade **2** a person paid to live or travel with another **3** one of a pair or set —**com·pan′ion·a·ble** ***adj.*** —**com·pan′ion·ship′** ***n.***

com·pan′ion·way′ ***n.*** a stairway leading from one deck of a ship to another

com·pa·ny (kum′pə nē) ***n.,*** *pl.* **-nies** ⟦see COMPANION⟧ **1** companionship; society **2** a group of people gathered or associated for some purpose **3** a guest or guests **4** a body of troops **5** a ship's crew —**keep company** **1** to associate (*with*) **2** to go together, as a couple intending to marry —**part company** to stop associating (*with*)

com·pa·ra·ble (käm′pə rə bəl, kəm par′ə bəl) ***adj.*** **1** that can be compared **2** worthy of comparison —**com′pa·ra·bly** ***adv.***

com·par·a·tive (kəm par′ə tiv) ***adj.*** **1** involving comparison **2** not absolute; relative **3** *Gram.* designating the second degree of comparison of adjectives and adverbs —***n.*** *Gram.* the comparative degree [*"finer" is the comparative of "fine"*] —**com·par′a·tive·ly** ***adv.***

com·pare (kəm per′) ***vt.*** **-pared′, -par′ing** ⟦< L *com-,* with + *parare,* make equal⟧ **1** to liken (*to*) **2** to examine for similarities or differences **3** *Gram.* to form the degrees of comparison of —***vi.*** **1** to be worth comparing (*with*) **2** to make comparisons —**beyond** (or **past** or **without**) **compare** incomparably good, great, etc.

com·par·i·son (kəm par′ə sən) ***n.*** **1** a comparing or being compared **2** likeness; similarity **3** *Gram.* change in an adjective or adverb to show the positive, comparative, and superlative degrees —**in comparison with** compared with

com·part·ment (kəm pärt′mənt) ***n.*** ⟦< L *com-,* intens. + *partire,* divide⟧ **1** any of the divisions into which a space is partitioned off **2** a separate section or category —**com·part·men·tal·ize** (käm′pärt ment′′l īz′), **-ized′, -iz′ing,** ***vt.***

com·pass (kum′pəs; *also* käm′-) ***vt.*** ⟦< L *com-,* together + *passus,* a step⟧ **1** [Archaic] to go around **2** to surround **3** to understand **4** to achieve or contrive —***n.*** **1** [*often pl.*] an instrument with two adjustable legs, for drawing circles, for measuring, etc. **2** a boundary **3** an enclosed area **4** range; scope **5** an instrument for showing direction, esp. one with a swinging magnetic needle pointing north

com·pas·sion (kəm pash′ən) ***n.*** ⟦< L *com-,* together + *pati,* suffer⟧ deep sympathy; pity —**com·pas′sion·ate** ***adj.*** —**com·pas′sion·ate·ly** ***adv.***

com·pat·i·ble (kəm pat′ə bəl) ***adj.*** ⟦see prec.⟧ **1** getting along or going well together **2** that can be mixed, used, etc. together effectively —**com·pat′i·bil′i·ty** ***n.*** —**com·pat′i·bly** ***adv.***

com·pa·tri·ot (kəm pā′trē ət) ***n.*** ⟦see COM- & PATRIOT⟧ a person of one's own country

com·peer (käm′pir′, käm pir′) ***n.*** ⟦see COM- & PAR⟧ **1** an equal; peer **2** a comrade

com·pel (kəm pel′) ***vt.*** **-pelled′, -pel′ling** ⟦< L *com-,* together + *pellere,* to drive⟧ to force or get by force —**com·pel′ling·ly** ***adv.***

com·pen·di·um (kəm pen′dē əm) ***n.,*** *pl.* **-ums** or **-a** (-ə) ⟦< L *com-,* together + *pendere,* weigh⟧ a concise but comprehensive summary

com·pen·sate (käm′pən sāt′) ***vt.*** **-sat′ed, -sat′ing** ⟦< L *com-,* with + *pendere,* weigh⟧ **1** [Now Rare] to make up for; counterbalance **2** to make suitable payment to —***vi.*** to make or serve as amends (*for*) —**com′pen·sa′tion** ***n.*** —**com·pen·sa·to·ry** (kəm pen′sə tôr′ē) ***adj.***

com·pete (kəm pēt′) ***vi.*** **-pet′ed, -pet′ing** ⟦< L *com-,* together + *petere,* to desire⟧ to be in rivalry; contend; vie (*in* a contest, etc.)

com·pe·tence (käm′pə təns) ***n.*** **1** sufficient means for one's needs **2** ability; fitness **3** legal power, jurisdiction, etc. Also **com′pe·ten·cy** (-tən sē)

com′pe·tent (-tənt) ***adj.*** ⟦see COMPETE⟧ **1** capable; fit **2** sufficient; adequate **3** having legal competence —**com′pe·tent·ly** ***adv.***

com·pe·ti·tion (käm′pə tish′ən) ***n.*** ⟦L *competitio*⟧ **1** a competing; rivalry **2** a contest; match **3** rivalry in business **4** those against whom one competes —**com·pet·i·tive** (kəm pet′ə tiv) ***adj.***

com·pet·i·tor (kəm pet′ət ər) ***n.*** ⟦L⟧ one who competes, as a business rival

com·pile (kəm pīl′) ***vt.*** **-piled′, -pil′ing** ⟦< L *com-,* together + *pilare,* to compress⟧ **1** to collect and assemble (statis-

THESAURUS

companion ***n.*** attendant, comrade, associate, partner, escort, chaperon, protector, guide, friend, bodyguard.

companionship ***n.*** fraternity, rapport, association; see BROTHERHOOD, FELLOWSHIP 1, FRIENDSHIP.

company ***n.*** **1** [A group of people] assembly, throng, band; see GATHERING. **2** [People organized for business] partnership, firm, corporation; see BUSINESS 4. **3** [A guest or guests] visitors, callers, overnight guests; see GUEST. —**keep (a person) company** stay with, visit, amuse; see ENTERTAIN 1. —**keep company (with)** fraternize, accompany, associate, go together, date, go with*, take up with*, hang around with*, pal around with*. —**part company** separate, part, stop associating with; see LEAVE 1.

comparable ***a.*** **1** [Worthy of comparison] as good as, equivalent, tantamount; see EQUAL. **2** [Capable of comparison] similar, akin, relative; see ALIKE, LIKE.

comparatively ***a.*** relatively, similarly, analogously; see APPROXIMATELY.

compare ***v.*** **1** [To liken] relate, connect, make like, notice the similarities, associate, link, distinguish between, bring near, put alongside, reduce to a common denominator, declare similar, equate, match, express by metaphor, correlate, parallel, show to be analogous, identify with, bring into meaningful relation with, collate, balance, bring into comparison, estimate relatively, set over against, compare notes, exchange observations, weigh one thing against another, set side by side, measure, place in juxtaposition, note the similarities and differences of, juxtapose, draw a parallel between, tie up, come up to, stack up with; see also DISTINGUISH 1. **2** [To examine on a comparative basis] contrast, set against, weigh; see ANALYZE, EXAMINE. **3** [To stand in relationship to another] match, vie, rival; see EQUAL, MATCH 3. —**beyond** (or **past** or **without**) **compare** incomparable, without equal, distinctive; see UNIQUE. —**compare to** (or **with**) put side by side, relate to, equate; see COMPARE 1.

comparison ***n.*** likening, metaphor, simile, resemblance, analogy, illustration, correspondence, relation, correlation, parable, allegory, similarity, identification, equation, measurement, example, contrast, parallel, connection, paralleling; see also ASSOCIATION 2.

compartment ***n.*** section, portion, subdivision; see PART 1.

compassion ***n.*** sympathy, consideration, clemency; see KINDNESS 1, PITY.

compassionate ***a.*** kind, humane, sympathetic; see MERCIFUL.

compatible ***a.*** agreeable, congruous, cooperative; see HARMONIOUS 2.

compel ***v.*** enforce, constrain, coerce; see FORCE.

compensate ***v.*** recompense, remunerate, requite; see PAY 1, REPAY 1.

compensation ***n.*** remuneration, recompense, indemnity, satisfaction, reparation, restitution, remittal, return for services, commission, gratuity, reimbursement, allowance, deserts, remittance, salary, stipend, wages, hire, earnings, settlement, honorarium, coverage, consideration, damages, repayment, fee, reckoning, bonus, premium, amends, reward, advantage, profit, benefit, gain, kickback*; see also PAY 2, PAYMENT 1.—*Ant.* LOSS, deprivation, confiscation.

compete ***v.*** enter competition, take part, strive, struggle, vie with, be in the running, become a competitor, enter the lists, run for, participate in, engage in a contest, oppose, wrestle, be rivals, battle, bid, spar, fence, face, clash, encounter, match wits, play, grapple, take on all comers, go in for*, lock horns, go out for; see also FIGHT.

competence ***n.*** capability, skill, fitness; see ABILITY.

competent ***a.*** fit, qualified, skilled; see ABLE.

competition ***n.*** race, match, contest, meet, fight, bout, boxing match, game of skill, trial, athletic event, wrestling; see also GAME 1, SPORT 1, 3. —**in competition with** opposed to, competing against, in a rivalry with; see AGAINST 1.

competitive ***a.*** competing, aggressive, ambitious; see RIVAL.

competitor ***n.*** foe, rival, antagonist; see CONTESTANT, OPPONENT 1.

compile ***v.*** collect, arrange, assemble; see ACCUMULATE, EDIT.

tics, facts, etc.) **2** to compose (a book, etc.) of materials from various sources —**com·pi·la·tion** (käm′pə lā′shən) ***n.***

com·pla·cen·cy (kəm plā′sən sē) ***n.*** ⟦< L *com-*, intens. + *placere*, to please⟧ contentment; often, specif., self-satisfaction, or smugness: also **com·pla′cence** —**com·pla′cent** ***adj.***

com·plain (kəm plān′) ***vi.*** ⟦< L *com-*, intens. + *plangere*, to strike⟧ **1** to express pain, displeasure, etc. **2** to find fault **3** to make an accusation —**com·plain′er** ***n.***

com·plain′ant (-ənt) ***n.*** *Law* a plaintiff

com·plaint′ (-plānt′) ***n.*** **1** a complaining **2** a cause for complaining **3** an ailment **4** *Law* a formal charge or accusation

com·plai·sant (kəm plā′zənt, -sənt) ***adj.*** ⟦see COMPLACENCY⟧ willing to please; obliging —**com·plai′sant·ly** ***adv.*** —**com·plai′sance** ***n.***

com·plect′ed (-plek′tid) ***adj.*** COMPLEXIONED

com·ple·ment (käm′plə mənt; *for v.*, -ment′) ***n.*** ⟦see fol.⟧ **1** that which completes or perfects **2** the amount needed to fill or complete **3** *Math.* the number of degrees that must be added to a given angle to make it equal 90 degrees —***vt.*** to make complete —**com′ple·men′ta·ry** (-men′tə rē) ***adj.***

com·plete (kəm plēt′) ***adj.*** ⟦< L *com-*, intens. + *plere*, fill⟧ **1** whole; entire **2** finished **3** thorough; absolute —***vt.*** **-plet′ed, -plet′ing** **1** to finish **2** to make whole or perfect **3** to successfully execute —**com·plete′ly** ***adv.*** —**com·plete′ness** ***n.*** —**com·ple′tion** (-plē′shən) ***n.***

com·plex (käm pleks′, käm′pleks′ *for n.* käm′pleks′) ***adj.*** ⟦< L *com-*, with + *plectere*, to weave⟧ **1** consisting of two or more related parts **2** complicated —***n.*** **1** a complex whole **2** an assemblage of units, as buildings **3** *Psychoanalysis a)* a group of mainly unconscious impulses, etc. strongly influencing behavior *b)* popularly, an exaggerated dislike or fear —**com·plex′i·ty** ***n.***

complex fraction a fraction with a fraction in its numerator or denominator, or in both

com·plex·ion (kəm plek′shən) ***n.*** ⟦see COMPLEX⟧ **1** the color, texture, etc. of the skin, esp. of the face **2** nature; character; aspect

com·plex′ioned ***adj.*** having a (specified) complexion *[light-complexioned]*

complex sentence a sentence consisting of an independent clause and one or more dependent clauses

com·pli·ance (kəm plī′əns) ***n.*** **1** a complying; acquiescence **2** a tendency to give in readily to others Also **com·pli′an·cy** —**com·pli′ant** ***adj.***

com·pli·cate (käm′pli kāt′) ***vt.***, ***vi.*** **-cat′ed, -cat′ing** ⟦< L *com-*, together + *plicare*, to fold⟧ to make or become intricate, difficult, or involved —**com′pli·ca′tion** ***n.***

com′pli·cat′ed ***adj.*** intricately involved; hard to solve, analyze, etc.

com·plic·i·tous (kəm plis′ə təs) ***adj.*** having complicity; implicated: also **com·plic′it** (-it)

com·plic′i·ty (-tē) ***n.***, *pl.* **-ties** ⟦see COMPLICATE⟧ partnership in wrongdoing

com·pli·ment (käm′plə mənt; *for v.*, -ment′) ***n.*** ⟦Fr < L: see COMPLETE⟧ **1** a formal act of courtesy **2** something said in praise **3** [*pl.*] respects —***vt.*** to pay a compliment to

com′pli·men′ta·ry (-men′tə rē) ***adj.*** **1** paying or containing a compliment **2** given free as a courtesy

com·ply (kəm plī′) ***vi.*** **-plied′, -ply′ing** ⟦see COMPLETE⟧ to act in accordance (*with* a request, order, etc.)

com·po·nent (kəm pō′nənt) ***adj.*** ⟦see COMPOSITE⟧ serving as one of the parts of a whole —***n.*** a part, element, or ingredient

com·port (kəm pôrt′) ***vt.*** ⟦< L *com-*, together + *portare*,

THESAURUS

complacent ***a.*** self-satisfied, contented, self-righteous; see EGOTISTIC, HAPPY, SATISFIED, SMUG.

complain ***v.*** disapprove, accuse, deplore, criticize, denounce, differ, disagree, dissent, charge, report adversely, reproach, oppose, grumble, whine, whimper, remonstrate, fret, protest, fuss, moan, make a fuss, take exception to, object to, deprecate, enter a demurrer, demur, defy, carp, impute, indict, attack, refute, grouse*, kick*, bitch*, grouch, gripe*, grunt, beef*, bellyache*, kick up a fuss*.—*Ant.* APPROVE, sanction, countenance.

complaining ***a.*** objecting, lamenting, murmuring, mourning, regretting, bewailing, deploring, weeping, moaning, protesting, charging, accusing, disapproving, grumbling, fretting, whining, imputing, resenting, dissenting, registering a protest, filing a complaint, making an adverse report, kicking.—*Ant.* enjoying, appreciating, praising.

complaint ***n.*** **1** [An objection] charge, criticism, reproach; see ACCUSATION, OBJECTION. **2** [An illness] ailment, disease, infirmity; see ILLNESS 1.

complementary ***a.*** paired, mated, corresponding; see ALIKE, MATCHED.

complete ***a.*** **1** [Not lacking in any part] total, intact, entire; see FULL 1, WHOLE 1. **2** [Finished] concluded, terminated, ended; see FINISHED 1. **3** [Perfect] flawless, unblemished, impeccable; see PERFECT, WHOLE 2.

complete ***v.*** execute, consummate, perfect, accomplish, realize, perform, achieve, fill out, fulfill, equip, actualize, furnish, make up, elaborate, make good, make complete, develop, fill in, refine, effect, carry out, crown, get through, round out; see also CREATE.—*Ant.* BEGIN, start, commence.

completed ***a.*** achieved, ended, concluded; see BUILT, DONE 2, FINISHED 1.

completely ***a.*** entirely, fully, totally, utterly, wholly, perfectly, exclusively, simply, effectively, competently, solidly, absolutely, unanimously, thoroughly, en masse, exhaustively, minutely, painstakingly, extensively, conclusively, unconditionally, finally, to the utmost, ultimately, altogether, comprehensively, to the end, from beginning to end, on all counts, in all, in full measure, to the limit, to the full, in full, to completion, to the nth degree, to a frazzle*, downright, through thick and thin, down to the ground, through and through, rain or shine, in one lump, from A to Z, from head to foot; hook, line, and sinker*.—*Ant.* PARTLY, somewhat, partially.

completion ***n.*** finish, conclusion, fulfillment; see END 2.

complex ***a.*** **1** [Composed of several parts] composite, heterogeneous, conglomerate, multiple, mosaic, manifold, multiform, compound, complicated, aggregated, involved, combined, compact, compounded, miscellaneous, multiplex, multifarious, variegated; see also MIXED 1. **2** [Difficult to understand] entangled, tangled, circuitous, convoluted, puzzling, mixed, mingled, muddled, jumbled, impenetrable, inscrutable, unfathomable, indecipherable, bewildering, intricate, perplexing, complicated, involved, enigmatic, hermetic, Byzantine, hidden, knotted, meandering, winding, tortuous, snarled, rambling, twisted, disordered, devious, discursive, cryptic, inextricable, knotty, roundabout; see also CONFUSED 2, DIFFICULT 2.—*Ant.* UNDERSTANDABLE, plain, apparent.

complex ***n.*** **1** [An obsession] phobia, mania, neurosis, obsessive-compulsive disorder, repressed emotions, repressed desires; see also FEAR, INSANITY. **2** [A composite] conglomerate, syndrome, ecosystem, aggregation, association, totality; see also COLLECTION.

complexion ***n.*** tone, glow, color, coloration, general coloring, tinge, cast, flush, skin texture, tint, hue, pigmentation; see also SKIN. *Descriptions of complexions include the following:* blond, blonde, fair, pale, sallow, sickly, dark, brunet, olive, bronze, sandy, rosy, red, ruddy, brown, yellow, tan, black, peaches-and-cream*.

compliant ***a.*** obedient, pliant, acquiescent; see DOCILE.

complicate ***v.*** involve, obscure, confound, muddle, clog, jumble, interrelate, elaborate, embellish, implicate, tangle, conceal, mix up, snarl up, encumber, impede, perplex, hinder, hamper, handicap, tie up with, ball up*; see also CONFUSE, ENTANGLE.—*Ant.* SIMPLIFY, clear up, unfold.

complicated ***a.*** intricate, various, mixed; see COMPLEX 2, CONFUSED 2, DIFFICULT 2.

complication ***n.*** complexity, dilemma, development; see CONFUSION, DIFFICULTY 1, 2.

compliment ***n.*** felicitation, tribute, approval, commendation, endorsement, confirmation, sanction, applause, flattery, acclaim, adulation, notice, puff, blurb, regards, honor, appreciation, respects, blessing, ovation, veneration, admiration, congratulations, homage, good word, sentiment; see also PRAISE 2.—*Ant.* ABUSE, censure, disapproval.

compliment ***v.*** wish joy to, remember, commemorate, pay one's respects, honor, cheer, salute, hail, toast, applaud, extol, celebrate, felicitate, pay tribute to, be in favor of, commend, endorse, sanction, confirm, acclaim, pay a compliment to, sing the praises of, speak highly of, exalt, applaud, worship, eulogize, glorify, magnify, flatter, fawn upon, butter up*, puff, hand it to*; see also PRAISE 1.—*Ant.* DENOUNCE, disapprove of, censure.

complimentary ***a.*** flattering, laudatory, approving, celebrating, honoring, respectful, congratulatory, well-wishing, highly favorable, praising, singing the praises of, with highest recommendations, with high praise; see also POLITE.

carry] to behave (oneself) in a specified manner —*vi.* to accord (*with*) —**com·port'ment** *n.*

com·pose (kəm pōz') *vt.* **-posed'**, **-pos'ing** [< OFr *com-*, with + *poser*, to place] **1** to make up; constitute **2** to put in proper form **3** to create (a musical or literary work) **4** to make calm **5** *a*) to set (type) *b*) to produce (printed matter) as by computer, etc. —*vi.* to create musical works, etc. —**com·pos'er** *n.*

com·posed' *adj.* calm; self-possessed

com·pos·ite (kəm päz'it) *adj.* [< L *com-*, together + *ponere*, to place] **1** compound **2** *Bot.* designating a large family of plants with flower heads composed of dense clusters of small flowers, including the daisy and the chrysanthemum —*n.* a thing of distinct parts —**com·pos'ite·ly** *adv.*

com·po·si·tion (käm'pə zish'ən) *n.* **1** a composing, esp. of literary or musical works **2** the makeup of a person or thing **3** something composed

com·pos·i·tor (kəm päz'ət ər) *n.* one who sets matter for printing, esp. a typesetter

com·post (käm'pōst') *n.* [see COMPOSITE] a mixture of decomposing vegetable refuse for fertilizing soil —*vt.* to convert (vegetable matter) into compost

com·po·sure (kəm pō'zhər) *n.* [see COMPOSE] calmness; self-possession

com·pote (käm'pōt') *n.* [Fr: see COMPOSITE] **1** a dish of stewed fruits **2** a long-stemmed dish, as for candy

com·pound[1] (käm pound', käm'pound'; *for adj. usually & for n. always*, käm'pound') *vt.* [see COMPOSITE] **1** to mix or combine **2** to make by combining parts **3** to compute (compound interest) **4** to increase or intensify by adding something new —*adj.* made up of two or more parts —*n.* **1** a thing formed by combining parts **2** a substance containing two or more elements chemically combined —**compound a felony** (or **crime**) to agree, for payment, not to inform about or prosecute a felony (or crime)

com·pound[2] (käm'pound') *n.* [Malay *kampong*] an enclosed area with a building or buildings in it

compound eye an eye made up of numerous simple eyes functioning collectively, as in insects

compound fracture a fracture in which the broken bone pierces the skin

compound interest interest paid on both the principal and the accumulated unpaid interest

compound sentence a sentence consisting of two or more independent, coordinate clauses

com·pre·hend (käm'prē hend', -pri-) *vt.* [< L *com-*, with + *prehendere*, seize] **1** to grasp mentally; understand **2** to include; take in; comprise —**com'pre·hen'si·ble** (-hen'sə bəl) *adj.* —**com'pre·hen'sion** *n.*

com'pre·hen'sive (-hen'siv) *adj.* wide in scope; inclusive —**com'pre·hen'sive·ly** *adv.* —**com'pre·hen'sive·ness** *n.*

com·press (kəm pres'; *for n.* käm'pres') *vt.* [< L *com-*, together + *premere*, to press] to press together and make more compact —*n.* a pad of folded cloth, often wet or medicated, applied to the skin —**com·pressed'** *adj.* —**com·pres'sion** *n.*

com·pres'sor (-pres'ər) *n.* a machine, esp. a pump, for compressing air, gas, etc.

com·prise' (-prīz') *vt.* **-prised'**, **-pris'ing** [see COMPREHEND] **1** to consist of **2** to make up; form

com·pro·mise (käm'prə mīz') *n.* [< L *com-*, together + *promittere*, to promise] **1** a settlement in which each side makes concessions **2** something midway —*vt.*, *vi.* **-mised'**, **-mis'ing** **1** to adjust by compromise **2** to lay open to suspicion, disrepute, etc. **3** to weaken

comp·trol·ler (kən trō'lər) *n.* [altered (infl. by Fr *compte*, an account) < CONTROLLER] CONTROLLER (sense 1, esp. in government usage)

com·pul·sion (kəm pul'shən) *n.* **1** a compelling or being compelled **2** a driving force **3** an irresistible impulse to perform some act —**com·pul'sive** (-siv) *adj.* —**com·pul'sive·ly** *adv.*

com·pul'so·ry (-sə rē) *adj.* **1** obligatory; required **2** compelling

com·punc·tion (kəm puŋk'shən) *n.* [< L *com-*, intens. + *pungere*, to prick] an uneasy feeling prompted by guilt; remorse

com·pute (kəm pyo͞ot') *vt.* **-put'ed**, **-put'ing** [< L *com-*, with + *putare*, reckon] to calculate (an amount, etc.) —*vi.* **1** to calculate an amount, etc. **2** [Inf.] to make sense —**com·pu·ta·tion** (käm'pyo͞o tā'shən) *n.*

com·put'er *n.* an electronic machine that performs rapid, complex calculations or compiles and correlates data —**com·put'er·ize'**, **-ized'**, **-iz'ing**, *vt.* —**com·put'er·i·za'tion** *n.*

com·rade (käm'rad', -rəd) *n.* [< Sp *camarada*, chamber mate < L *camera*, room] **1** a friend; close companion **2** an associate —**com'rade·ship'** *n.*

con[1] (kän) *adv.* [< L *contra*] against —*n.* an opposing reason, vote, etc.

con[2] (kän) *vt.* **conned**, **con'ning** [< OE *cunnan*, know] to study carefully

THESAURUS

compose *v.* **1** [To be the parts or the ingredients of] constitute, comprise*, go into the making of, make up, merge into, be a component of, be an element of, belong to, consist of, be made of; see also COMPRISE, INCLUDE 1. **2** [To create] fabricate, produce, write music, score, arrange, orchestrate, forge, discover, design, conceive, imagine, make up, turn out, draw up; see also CREATE, INVENT 1.

composed *a.* **1** [Made] created, made up, fashioned; see FORMED. **2** [Calm] poised, confident, cool; see CALM 1, CONFIDENT.

composer *n.* arranger, songwriter, musical author; see AUTHOR, MUSICIAN, POET, WRITER. *Major composers include the following—Baroque period:* Antonio Vivaldi, Henry Purcell, J.S. Bach, George Frideric Handel; *Classical period:* Joseph Haydn, Wolfgang Amadeus Mozart, Ludwig van Beethoven, Franz Schubert, Gioacchino Rossini; *Romantic period;* Hector Berlioz, Felix Mendelssohn, Frédéric Chopin, Franz Liszt, Giuseppe Verdi, Richard Wagner, Anton Bruckner, Johann Strauss, Johannes Brahms, Peter Tchaikovsky, Antonín Dvořák, Giacomo Puccini, Gustav Mahler, Claude Debussy, Sergei Rachmaninoff, Maurice Ravel; *Modern period:* Igor Stravinsky, Béla Bartók, Richard Strauss, Arnold Schönberg, Sergey Prokofiev, Jean Sibelius, Dmitri Shostakovich, Aaron Copland.

composition *n.* creation, making, fashioning, formation, conception, presentation, invention; novel, tale, essay, play, drama, poem, verse, stanza, symphony, concerto, quartet, song, rhapsody, melody; see also BIOGRAPHY, LITERATURE 2, MUSIC 1, POETRY, WRITING 2.

composure *n.* serenity, peace of mind, calm, calmness, self-possession, nonchalance, coolheadedness, control, self-control, balance, contentment, tranquillity, stability, harmony, assurance, self-assurance, poise, composed state of mind, even temper, equanimity, coolness, levelheadedness, fortitude, moderation, gravity, sobriety, a cool head, presence of mind, equilibrium, aplomb, self-restraint, ease, evenness, complacence, tolerance, content, quiet, command, forbearance, cool*; see also PATIENCE 1, PEACE.—*Ant.* EXUBERANCE, passion, wildness.

compound[1] *n.* composite, union, aggregate; see MIXTURE 1.

comprehend *v.* grasp, discern, perceive; see KNOW 1, UNDERSTAND 1.

comprehension *n.* understanding, perception, cognizance; see AWARENESS, KNOWLEDGE 1.

comprehensive *a.* extensive, sweeping, complete; see ABSOLUTE 1, GENERAL 1, INFINITE, LARGE 1.

compress *v.* condense, compact, press together, consolidate, squeeze together, tighten, cramp, contract, crowd, constrict, abbreviate, shrivel, make brief, reduce, dehydrate, pack, shorten, shrink, narrow, abridge, bind tightly, wrap closely, wedge, boil down, cram; see also PRESS 1, TIGHTEN 1.—*Ant.* SPREAD, stretch, expand.

comprise *v.* comprehend, contain, embrace, include, involve, enclose, embody, encircle, encompass, sum up, cover, consist of, be composed of, be made up of, constitute, incorporate, span, hold, engross, take into account, be contained in, add up to, amount to, take in; see also COMPOSE 1, INCLUDE 1.—*Ant.* BAR, lack, exclude.

compromise *n.* covenant, bargain, give-and-take; see AGREEMENT.

compromise *v.* agree, conciliate, find a middle ground; see NEGOTIATE 1.

compulsion *n.* **1** [Force] drive, necessity, need; see REQUIREMENT 2. **2** [An obsession] preoccupation, obsession, engrossment; see REQUIREMENT 2.

compulsive *a.* driving, impelling, besetting; see PASSIONATE 2.

compulsory *a.* obligatory, required, requisite; see NECESSARY.

compute *v.* count, figure, measure; see CALCULATE.

computer *n.* electronic brain, thinking machine, calculator, data processor, word processor, electronic circuit, cybernetic device, analog computer, digital computer, workstation, terminal, console, personal computer, PC, microcomputer, minicomputer, server, mainframe, laptop, palmtop, desktop; see also MACHINE.

comrade *n.* companion, confidante, intimate; see ASSOCIATE, FRIEND.

con[1] *a.* conversely, opposed to, in opposition; see AGAINST 1.

con[3] (kän) ***adj.*** [Slang] CONFIDENCE *[a con man]* —***vt.*** **conned, con'ning** [Slang] to swindle or trick

con[4] (kän) ***n.*** [Slang] *short for* CONVICT

con- *prefix* COM-: used before *c, d, g, j, n, q, s, t, v,* and sometimes *f*

con·cat·e·na·tion (kən kat′'n ā′shən, kän-) ***n.*** ⟦< L *com-*, together + *catena*, a chain⟧ a connected series, as of events

con·cave (kän kāv′, kän′kāv′) ***adj.*** ⟦< L *com-*, intens. + *cavus*, hollow⟧ hollow and curved like the inside half of a bowl —**con·cav′i·ty** (-kav′ə tē), *pl.* **-ties**, ***n.***

con·ceal (kən sēl′) ***vt.*** ⟦< L *com-*, together + *celare*, to hide⟧ **1** to hide **2** to keep secret —**con·ceal′ment** ***n.***

con·cede (kən sēd′) ***vt.*** **-ced′ed, -ced′ing** ⟦< L *com-*, with + *cedere*, cede⟧ **1** to admit as true, valid, certain, etc. **2** to grant as a right

con·ceit (kən sēt′) ***n.*** ⟦see CONCEIVE⟧ **1** an exaggerated opinion of oneself, one's merits, etc.; vanity **2** a fanciful expression or notion

con·ceit′ed ***adj.*** vain

con·ceiv·a·ble (kən sēv′ə bəl) ***adj.*** that can be understood, imagined, or believed —**con·ceiv′a·bil′i·ty** ***n.*** —**con·ceiv′a·bly** ***adv.***

con·ceive (kən sēv′) ***vt.*** **-ceived′, -ceiv′ing** ⟦< L *com-*, together + *capere*, take⟧ **1** to become pregnant with **2** to form in the mind; imagine **3** to understand —***vi.*** **1** to become pregnant **2** to form an idea (*of*)

con·cen·trate (kän′sən trāt′) ***vt.*** **-trat′ed, -trat′ing** ⟦< L *com-*, together + *centrum*, center + -ATE[1]⟧ **1** to focus (one's thoughts, efforts, etc.) **2** to increase the strength, density, etc. of —***vi.*** to fix one's attention (*on* or *upon*) —***n.*** a concentrated substance —**con′cen·tra′tion** ***n.***

concentration camp a prison camp for political dissidents, ethnic minorities, etc.

con·cen·tric (kən sen′trik) ***adj.*** ⟦< L *com-*, together + *centrum*, center⟧ having a common center: said of circles —**con·cen′tri·cal·ly** ***adv.***

con·cept (kän′sept′) ***n.*** ⟦see CONCEIVE⟧ an idea or thought; abstract notion

con·cep·tion (kən sep′shən) ***n.*** **1** a conceiving or being conceived in the womb **2** the beginning, as of a process **3** the formulation of ideas **4** a concept **5** an original idea or design

con·cep′tu·al (-cho͞o əl) ***adj.*** of conception or concepts —**con·cep′tu·al·ly** ***adv.***

con·cep′tu·al·ize′ (-īz′) ***vt.*** **-ized′, -iz′ing** to form a concept of —**con·cep′tu·al·i·za′tion** ***n.***

con·cern (kən surn′) ***vt.*** ⟦< L *com-*, with + *cernere*, sift⟧ **1** to have a relation to **2** to engage or involve **3** to cause to feel uneasy —***n.*** **1** a matter of interest to one **2** interest in or regard for a person or thing **3** worry; anxiety **4** a business firm —**as concerns** in regard to —**concern oneself** **1** to busy oneself **2** to be worried

con·cerned′ ***adj.*** **1** involved or interested (*in*) **2** uneasy or anxious

con·cern′ing ***prep.*** relating to; about

con·cert (kän′sərt) ***n.*** ⟦< L *com-*, with + *certare*, strive⟧ **1** mutual agreement; concord **2** a performance of music —**in concert** in unison

con·cert·ed (kən surt′id) ***adj.*** mutually arranged or agreed upon; combined —**con·cert′ed·ly** ***adv.***

con·cer·ti·na (kän′sər tē′nə) ***n.*** ⟦< CONCERT⟧ a small accordion

con·cert·ize (kän′sər tīz′) ***vi.*** **-ized′, -iz′ing** to perform as a soloist in concerts, esp. while touring

con′cert·mas′ter ***n.*** the leader of the first violin section of a symphony orchestra, and often the assistant to the conductor

con·cer·to (kən cher′tō) ***n.***, *pl.* **-tos** or **-ti** (-tē) ⟦It⟧ a musical composition for one or more solo instruments and an orchestra

con·ces·sion (kən sesh′ən) ***n.*** **1** a conceding **2** a thing conceded; acknowledgment **3** a privilege granted by a government, company, etc., as the right to sell food at a park

con·ces′sion·aire′ (-ə ner′) ***n.*** ⟦< Fr⟧ the holder of a CONCESSION (sense 3)

conch (käŋk, känch) ***n.***, *pl.* **conchs** (käŋks) or **conch·es** (kän′chiz) ⟦< Gr *konchē*⟧ the spiral, one-piece shell of various sea mollusks

con·ci·erge (kän′sē erzh′; *Fr* kōn syerzh′) ***n.*** ⟦Fr < L *conservus*, fellow slave⟧ a custodian or head porter, as of an apartment house or hotel

con·cil·i·ar (kən sil′ē ər) ***adj.*** of, from, or by means of a council

con·cil′i·ate′ (-āt′) ***vt.*** **-at′ed, -at′ing** ⟦see COUNCIL⟧ to win over; make friendly; placate —**con·cil′i·a′tion** ***n.*** —**con·cil′i·a′tor** ***n.*** —**con·cil′i·a·to′ry** (-ə tôr′ē) ***adj.***

con·cise (kən sīs′) ***adj.*** ⟦< L *com-*, intens. + *caedere*, to cut⟧ brief and to the point; short and clear —**con·cise′ly** ***adv.*** —**con·cise′ness** ***n.*** —**con·ci′sion** (-sizh′ən) ***n.***

con·clave (kän′klāv′) ***n.*** ⟦< L *com-*, with + *clavis*, a key⟧ **1** a private meeting; specif., one held by cardinals to elect a pope **2** any large convention

con·clude (kən klo͞od′) ***vt.***, ***vi.*** **-clud′ed, -clud′ing** ⟦< L *com-*, together + *claudere*, to shut⟧ **1** to end; finish **2** to deduce **3** to decide; determine **4** to arrange (a treaty, etc.)

THESAURUS

con[3]* ***n.*** deception, swindle, fraud; see TRICK 1.

con[3]* ***v.*** cheat, dupe, mislead; see DECEIVE.

concave ***a.*** curved, sunken, cupped; see ROUND 2.

conceal ***v.*** screen, secrete, cover; see HIDE 1.

concealed ***a.*** covered, obscured, unseen; see HIDDEN.

concealment ***n.*** hiding, covering, camouflage; see DISGUISE.

concede ***v.*** yield, grant, acknowledge; see ADMIT 2, ALLOW.

conceit ***n.*** arrogance, self-admiration, narcissism; see VANITY.

conceited ***a.*** vain, arrogant, stuck-up*; see EGOTISTIC.

conceivable ***a.*** understandable, credible, believable; see CONVINCING, IMAGINABLE, LIKELY 1.

conceive ***v.*** **1** [To form a concept or image of] consider, formulate, speculate; see IMAGINE, THINK 1. **2** [To become pregnant] be with child, get pregnant, be impregnated, be in the family way*.

concentrate ***v.*** **1** [To bring or come together] amass, mass, assemble, combine, consolidate, compact, condense, reduce, hoard, garner, centralize, store, bring into a small compass, bring toward a central point, embody, localize, strengthen, direct toward one object, constrict, fix, cramp, focus, reduce, intensify, crowd together, flock together, contract, muster, bunch, heap up, swarm, conglomerate, stow away, congest, narrow, compress, converge, center, collect, cluster, congregate, huddle; see also ACCUMULATE, GATHER 2, PACK 2. **2** [To employ all one's mental powers] think intensely, give attention to, meditate upon, ponder, focus attention on, direct attention, weigh, consider closely, scrutinize, regard carefully, contemplate, study deeply, examine closely, brood over, put one's mind to, be engrossed in, be absorbed in, attend, give exclusive attention to, occupy the thoughts with, fix one's attention, apply the mind, give heed, focus one's thought, give the mind to, direct the mind upon, center, think hard, rack one's brains, be on the beam*, keep one's eye on the ball*, knuckle down, buckle down; see also ANALYZE, EXAMINE, THINK 1.—*Ant.* DRIFT, be inattentive, ignore.

concentrated ***a.*** **1** [Undiluted] rich, unmixed, unadulterated, straight; see also STRONG 4, THICK 1. **2** [Intense] intensive, deep, hard; see INTENSE.

concentration ***n.*** **1** [Attention] close attention, concern, application; see THOUGHT 1. **2** [Density] solidity, consistency, frequency; see CONGESTION, DENSITY.

concept ***n.*** idea, theory, notion; see THOUGHT 2.

conception ***n.*** **1** [The act of conceiving mentally] perception, apprehension, comprehension, imagining, speculating, meditation, dreaming, cogitating, deliberating, concentrating, meditating, realization, consideration, speculation, understanding, cognition, mental grasp, apperception, forming an idea, formulation of a principle; see also THOUGHT 1. **2** [The act of conceiving physically] inception, impregnation, insemination; see FERTILIZATION 2.

concern ***n.*** **1** [Affair] business, matter, interest; see AFFAIR 1. **2** [Regard] care, interest, solicitude; see ATTENTION.

concern ***v.*** **1** [To have reference to] refer to, pertain to, relate to, be related to, have significance for, bear on, regard, be connected with, be about, have to do with, be a matter of concern to, have a bearing on, have connections with, be applicable to, depend upon, be dependent upon, answer to, deal with, belong to, touch upon, figure in; see also INFLUENCE, TREAT 1. **2** [Concern oneself] be concerned, become involved, take pains; see BOTHER 1, CARE, WORRY 2.

concerning ***prep.*** respecting, touching, regarding; see ABOUT 2.

concert ***n.*** musicale, recital, serenade; see PERFORMANCE.

concise ***a.*** succinct, brief, condensed; see SHORT 1.

conclude ***v.*** **1** [To finish] terminate, bring to an end, complete; see ACHIEVE. **2** [To deduce] presume, reason, gather; see ASSUME.

con·clu′sion (-klo͞o′zhən) ***n.*** **1** the end **2** a judgment or opinion formed after thought **3** an outcome **4** a concluding (*of* a treaty, etc.) —**in conclusion** lastly; in closing

con·clu′sive (-siv) ***adj.*** final; decisive —**con·clu′sive·ly** ***adv.*** —**con·clu′sive·ness** ***n.***

con·coct (kən käkt′) ***vt.*** ⟦< L *com-*, together + *coquere*, to cook⟧ **1** to make by combining ingredients **2** to devise; plan —**con·coc′tion** ***n.***

con·com′i·tant (-käm′ə tənt) ***adj.*** ⟦< L *com-*, together + *comes*, companion⟧ accompanying; attendant —***n.*** a concomitant thing —**con·com′i·tant·ly** ***adv.***

con·cord (kän′kôrd′, käŋ′-) ***n.*** ⟦< L *com-*, together + *cor*, heart⟧ **1** agreement; harmony **2** peaceful relations, as between nations

Con·cord (kän′kôrd; *for 2* käŋ′kərd) **1** city in W California: pop. 111,000 **2** capital of New Hampshire: pop. 36,000

con·cord·ance (kən kôrd′′ns) ***n.*** **1** agreement **2** an alphabetical list of the words used in a book, with references to the passages in which they occur

con·cord′ant ***adj.*** agreeing

con·cor·dat (kən kôr′dat′) ***n.*** ⟦Fr < L: see CONCORD⟧ a formal agreement

Con·cord (grape) (käŋ′kərd) a large, dark-blue grape used esp. for juice and jelly

con·course (kän′kôrs′) ***n.*** ⟦see CONCUR⟧ **1** a crowd; throng **2** an open space for crowds, as in a park **3** a broad thoroughfare

con·crete (kän′krēt′, kän krēt′) ***adj.*** ⟦< L *com-*, together + *crescere*, grow⟧ **1** having a material existence; real; actual **2** specific, not general **3** made of concrete —***n.*** **1** anything concrete **2** a hard building material made of sand and gravel, bonded together with cement —***vt.***, ***vi.*** **-cret′ed**, **-cret′ing** **1** to solidify **2** to cover with concrete —**con·crete′ly** ***adv.*** —**con·crete′ness** ***n.***

con·cre·tion (kən krē′shən) ***n.*** **1** a solidifying **2** a solidified mass

con·cu·bine (kän′kyo͞o bīn′, käŋ′-) ***n.*** ⟦< L *com-*, with + *cubare*, lie down⟧ in some societies, a secondary wife, of inferior social and legal status

con·cu·pis·cence (kən kyo͞op′ə səns) ***n.*** ⟦< L *com-*, intens. + *cupiscere*, to desire⟧ strong desire, esp. sexual desire; lust —**con·cu′pis·cent** ***adj.***

con·cur (kən kur′) ***vi.*** **-curred′**, **-cur′ring** ⟦< L *com-*, together + *currere*, to run⟧ **1** to occur at the same time **2** to act together **3** to agree (*with*) —**con·cur′rence** ***n.***

con·cur′rent ***adj.*** **1** occurring at the same time **2** acting together **3** *Law* having equal authority —**con·cur′rent·ly** ***adv.***

con·cus·sion (kən kush′ən) ***n.*** ⟦< L *com-*, together + *quatere*, to shake⟧ **1** a violent shaking; shock, as from impact **2** a condition of impaired functioning, esp. of the brain, caused by a violent blow —**con·cus′sive** (-kus′iv) ***adj.***

con·demn (kən dem′) ***vt.*** ⟦< L *com-*, intens. + *damnare*, to harm⟧ **1** to disapprove of strongly **2** to declare guilty **3** to inflict a penalty upon **4** to doom **5** to appropriate (property) for public use **6** to declare unfit for use —**con·dem·na·tion** (kän′dem nā′shən) ***n.*** —**con·dem·na·to·ry** (kən dem′nə tôr′ē) ***adj.*** —**con·demn′er** ***n.***

con·dense (kən dens′) ***vt.*** **-densed′**, **-dens′ing** ⟦< L *com-*, intens. + *densus*, dense⟧ **1** to make more dense or compact **2** to express in fewer words **3** to change to a denser form, as from gas to liquid —***vi.*** to become condensed —**con·den·sa·tion** (kän′dən sā′shən) ***n.***

condensed milk milk made very thick by evaporation, sweetened with sugar, and then canned

con·dens′er ***n.*** one that condenses; specif., *a*) an apparatus for liquefying gases *b*) a lens for concentrating light rays *c*) *Elec.* CAPACITOR

con·de·scend (kän′di send′) ***vi.*** ⟦< L *com-*, together + *descendere*, descend⟧ **1** to be gracious about doing a thing regarded as beneath one's dignity **2** to deal with others in a proud or haughty way —**con′de·scend′ing·ly** ***adv.*** —**con′de·scen′sion** (-sen′shən) ***n.***

con·dign (kən dīn′, kän′dīn′) ***adj.*** ⟦< L *com-*, intens. + *dignus*, worthy⟧ deserved; suitable: said esp. of punishment

con·di·ment (kän′də mənt) ***n.*** ⟦< L *condire*, to pickle⟧ a seasoning or relish, as pepper, mustard, or a sauce

con·di·tion (kən dish′ən) ***n.*** ⟦< L *com-*, together + *dicere*, to speak⟧ **1** anything required for the performance, completion, or existence of something else; provision or prerequisite **2** *a*) state of being *b*) an illness *c*) a healthy state **3** social position; rank —***vt.*** **1** to stipulate **2** to impose a condition on **3** to bring into fit condition **4** to make accustomed (*to*) —**on condition that** provided that; if —**con·di′tion·er** ***n.***

con·di′tion·al ***adj.*** containing, expressing, or dependent on a condition; qualified —***n.*** *Gram.* a word, clause, tense, etc. expressing a condition —**con·di′tion·al·ly** ***adv.***

con·di′tioned ***adj.*** **1** subject to conditions **2** in a desired condition **3** affected by conditioning **4** accustomed (*to*)

con·do (kän′dō) ***n.***, *pl.* **-dos** or **-does** *short for* CONDOMINIUM (sense 3)

con·dole (kən dōl′) ***vi.*** **-doled′**, **-dol′ing** ⟦< L *com-*, with + *dolere*, grieve⟧ to express sympathy; commiserate —**con·do′lence** ***n.***

con·dom (kän′dəm, kun′-) ***n.*** ⟦< It *guanto*, a glove⟧ a thin, latex sheath for the penis, used as a prophylactic or contraceptive

con·do·min·i·um (kän′də min′ē əm) ***n.*** ⟦ult. < L *com-*, with + *dominium*, ownership⟧ **1** joint rule by two or more states **2** the territory ruled **3** one of the units in a multiunit dwelling, each separately owned; also, the dwelling as a whole

con·done (kən dōn′) ***vt.*** **-doned′**, **-don′ing** ⟦< L *com-*, intens. + *donare*, give⟧ to forgive or overlook (an offense) —**con·don′a·ble** ***adj.***

con·dor (kän′dər, -dôr) ***n.*** ⟦< Sp < AmInd (Peru)⟧ **1** a large vulture of the South American Andes, with a bare head and neck **2** a similar vulture of S California

con·duce (kən do͞os′) ***vi.*** **-duced′**, **-duc′ing** ⟦< L *com-*,

THESAURUS

conclusion ***n.*** **1** [An end] finish, termination, completion; see END 2. **2** [A decision] determination, resolve, resolution; see JUDGMENT 3. —**in conclusion** lastly, in closing, in the end; see FINALLY 1.

conclusive ***a.*** final, decisive, absolute; see CERTAIN 2.

concord ***n.*** harmony, consensus, accord; see AGREEMENT, UNITY 1.

concrete ***a.*** **1** [Specific] particular, solid, precise; see DEFINITE 1, DETAILED, REAL 2. **2** [Made of concrete] cement, poured, prefabricated, precast, concrete and steel, unyielding; see also FIRM 2.

concrete ***n.*** cement, ferroconcrete, reinforced concrete; see CEMENT, PAVEMENT.

concur ***v.*** accord with, be consonant with, be in harmony with; see AGREE, APPROVE, EQUAL.

concurrent ***a.*** synchronous, parallel, coexisting; see SIMULTANEOUS.

concussion ***n.*** jolt, shock, head trauma; see FRACTURE, INJURY.

condemn ***v.*** doom, sentence, damn, pass sentence on, find guilty, seal the doom of, pronounce judgment, prescribe punishment; see also CONVICT, PUNISH.—*Ant.* EXCUSE, acquit, exonerate.

condemnation ***n.*** denunciation, disapprobation, reproach; see ACCUSATION, BLAME, OBJECTION.

condense ***v.*** **1** [To compress] press together, constrict, consolidate; see COMPRESS, CONTRACT 1, DECREASE 1, 2. **2** [To abridge] abbreviate, summarize, digest; see DECREASE 2.

condensed ***a.*** **1** [Shortened] concise, brief, succinct; see SHORT 2. **2** [Concentrated] undiluted, rich, evaporated; see THICK 3.

condescend ***v.*** stoop, lower oneself, agree, humble oneself, demean oneself, submit with good grace, assume a patronizing air, lower one's tone, descend, comply, oblige, favor, concede, grant, accord, accommodate to, come down a peg, come down off one's high horse*; see also PATRONIZE 2.

condescending ***a.*** patronizing, disdainful, superior; see EGOTISTIC.

condition ***n.*** **1** [A state] situation, position, status; see STATE 2. **2** [A requisite] stipulation, contingency, provision; see REQUIREMENT 1. **3** [A limitation] restriction, qualification, prohibition; see LIMITATION 2, RESTRAINT 2. **4** [State of health] fitness, tone, trim, shape; see also HEALTH. **5** [Illness] ailment, infirmity, temper; see ILLNESS 1, 2. —**in condition** physically fit, conditioned, in the pink*; see HEALTHY, STRONG 1.

condition ***v.*** adapt, modify, customize; see PRACTICE 1, TRAIN 1.

conditional ***a.*** provisional, subject, contingent, limited, restricted, relying on, subject to, restrictive, guarded, not absolute, granted on certain terms; see also DEPENDENT 3.

conditionally ***a.*** hypothetically, subject to a condition, with reservations, with limitations, tentatively, possibly; see also TEMPORARILY.

conditioned ***a.*** altered, disciplined, modified; see TRAINED.

condominium ***n.*** cooperative apartment dwelling, condo, commonly owned apartment house, town house, co-op*; see also APARTMENT, HOME 1.

condone ***v.*** pardon, excuse, overlook; see APPROVE.

together + *ducere,* to lead⟧ to tend or lead (*to* an effect) —**con·du′cive** ***adj.***

con·duct (kän′dukt′; *for v.* kən dukt′) ***n.*** ⟦< L *com-,* together + *ducere,* to lead⟧ **1** management **2** behavior —***vt.*** **1** to lead **2** to manage **3** to direct (an orchestra, etc.) **4** to behave (oneself) **5** to transmit or convey —**con·duc′tion** (-duk′shən) ***n.*** —**con·duc′tive** ***adj.*** —**con′duc·tiv′i·ty** (-duk tiv′ə tē) ***n.***

con·duct·ance (kən duk′təns) ***n.*** the ability to conduct electricity

con·duc′tor ***n.*** **1** the leader of an orchestra, etc. **2** one in charge of the passengers on a train **3** a thing that conducts electricity, heat, etc.

con·du·it (kän′do͞o it) ***n.*** ⟦see CONDUCE⟧ **1** a channel for conveying fluids **2** a tube for electric wires

cone (kōn) ***n.*** ⟦< Gr *kōnos*⟧ **1** a solid with a circle for its base and a curved surface tapering to a point **2** any cone-shaped object **3** the scaly fruit of evergreen trees **4** a light-sensitive cell in the retina

Co·ney Island (kō′nē) beach & amusement park in Brooklyn, New York

con·fab (kän′fab′) ***n.*** ⟦ult. < L *com-,* together + *fabulari,* to converse⟧ [Inf.] a chat

con·fec·tion (kən fek′shən) ***n.*** ⟦< L *com-,* with + *facere,* make⟧ a candy or other sweet, as ice cream

con·fec′tion·er ***n.*** one who makes or sells candy and other confections

con·fec′tion·er′y (-er′ē) ***n.,*** *pl.* **-ies** a confectioner's shop; candy store

con·fed·er·a·cy (kən fed′ər ə sē) ***n.,*** *pl.* **-cies** a league or alliance —**the Confederacy** the 11 Southern states that seceded from the U.S. in 1860 & 1861: official name, **Confederate States of America**

con·fed′er·ate (-it; *for v.,* -āt′) ***adj.*** ⟦< L *com-,* together + *foedus,* a league⟧ **1** united in an alliance **2** [**C-**] of the Confederacy —***n.*** **1** an ally; associate **2** an accomplice **3** [**C-**] a Southern supporter of the Confederacy —***vt., vi.*** **-at′ed, -at′ing** to unite in a confederacy; ally

con·fed′er·a′tion ***n.*** a league or federation

con·fer (kən fʉr′) ***vt.*** **-ferred′, -fer′ring** ⟦< L *com-,* together + *ferre,* to bear⟧ to give or bestow —***vi.*** to have a conference —**con·fer·ee** (kän′fər ē′) ***n.*** —**con·fer′rer** ***n.***

con·fer·ence (kän′fər əns) ***n.*** **1** a formal meeting for discussion **2** an association of schools, churches, etc.

con·fer·ral (kən fʉr′əl) ***n.*** the bestowing of an honor, degree, or favor: also **con·fer′ment** ***n.***

con·fess (kən fes′) ***vt., vi.*** ⟦< L *com-,* together + *fateri,* acknowledge⟧ **1** to admit or acknowledge (a fault, crime, belief, etc.) **2** *a)* to tell (one's sins) to God or a priest *b)* to hear the confession of (a person) (said of a priest) —**confess to** to acknowledge

con·fess′ed·ly (-id lē) ***adv.*** admittedly

con·fes·sion (kən fesh′ən) ***n.*** **1** a confessing **2** something confessed **3** *a)* a creed *b)* a church having a creed

con·fes′sion·al ***n.*** an enclosure in a church, where a priest hears confessions

con·fes′sor ***n.*** **1** one who confesses **2** a priest who hears confessions

con·fet·ti (kən fet′ē) ***n.*** ⟦< It, sweetmeats⟧ bits of colored paper scattered about at celebrations

con·fi·dant (kän′fə dant′, -dänt′) ***n.*** a close, trusted friend —**con′fi·dante′** (-dant′, -dänt′) ***fem.n.***

con·fide (kən fīd′) ***vi.*** **-fid′ed, -fid′ing** ⟦< L *com-,* intens. + *fidere,* to trust⟧ to trust (*in* someone), esp. by sharing secrets —***vt.*** **1** to tell about as a secret **2** to entrust

con·fi·dence (kän′fə dəns) ***n.*** **1** trust; reliance **2** assurance **3** belief in one's own abilities **4** the belief that another will keep a secret **5** something told as a secret —***adj.*** swindling or used so as to swindle

confidence game a swindle effected by one (**confidence man**) who first gains the confidence of the victim

con′fi·dent (-dənt) ***adj.*** full of confidence; specif., *a)* certain *b)* sure of oneself —**con′fi·dent·ly** ***adv.***

con′fi·den′tial (-den′shəl) ***adj.*** **1** secret **2** of or showing trust **3** entrusted with private matters —**con′fi·den′ti·al′i·ty** (-shē al′ə tē) ***n.*** —**con′fi·den′tial·ly** ***adv.***

con·fig·u·ra·tion (kən fig′yə rā′shən) ***n.*** ⟦< L *com-,* together + *figurare,* to form⟧ **1** arrangement of parts **2** contour; outline

con·fig′ure (-yər) ***vt.*** **-ured, -ur·ing** to arrange in a certain way

con·fine (kän′fīn′; *for v.* kən fīn′) ***n.*** ⟦< L *com-,* with + *finis,* an end⟧ [*usually pl.*] a boundary or bounded region —***vt.*** **-fined′, -fin′ing** **1** to keep within limits; restrict **2** to keep shut up, as in prison or a sickbed —**con·fine′ment** ***n.***

con·firm (kən fʉrm′) ***vt.*** ⟦< L *com-,* intens. + *firmare,* strengthen⟧ **1** to make firm **2** to give formal approval to **3** to prove the truth of **4** to cause to undergo religious confirmation

con·fir·ma·tion (kän′fər mā′shən) ***n.*** **1** a confirming **2** something that confirms **3** a Christian ceremony admitting a person to full church membership, etc. **4** a Jewish ceremony reaffirming basic beliefs

con·firmed′ ***adj.*** **1** firmly established; habitual **2** corroborated

THESAURUS

conduct ***n.*** deportment, demeanor, manner; see BEHAVIOR.

conduct ***v.*** **1** [To guide] escort, convoy, attend; see ACCOMPANY, LEAD 1. **2** [To manage] administer, handle, carry on; see MANAGE 1. **—conduct oneself** comport oneself, act properly, acquit oneself well; see BEHAVE.

conductor ***n.*** **1** [That which conducts] conduit, conveyor, transmitter; see CHANNEL, WIRE 1, WIRING. **2** [One who conducts] orchestra leader, pilot, head; see ADMINISTRATOR, GUIDE, LEADER 2. **3** [One in charge of a car or train] trainman, railroad man, ticket taker, brakeman, streetcar conductor, motorman, bus driver; see also DRIVER.

Confederacy ***n.*** Confederate States of America, CSA, rebel states, the South, Dixie; see also SOUTH.

confer ***v.*** converse, deliberate, parley; see DISCUSS.

conference ***n.*** convention, consultation, meeting; see GATHERING.

conferring ***a.*** discussing, conversing, in conference; see TALKING.

confess ***v.*** acknowledge, own, concede; see ADMIT 2.

confession ***n.*** **1** [The act of confessing] concession, allowance, owning to, owning up, revelation, disclosure, publication, affirmation, assertion, admission, declaration, telling, exposure, narration, exposé, proclamation, making public; see also ACKNOWLEDGMENT.—*Ant.* DENIAL, concealment, disclaimer. **2** [A sacrament] absolution, contrition, penance; see SACRAMENT.

confidant ***n.*** comrade, intimate, associate, companion; see also FRIEND.

confide ***v.*** disclose, admit, divulge; see REVEAL, TELL 1.

confidence ***n.*** self-confidence, self-reliance, morale, fearlessness, boldness, resolution, firmness, sureness, faith in oneself, tenacity, fortitude, certainty, daring, spirit, reliance, grit, cool*, heart, backbone, nerve, moxie*, spunk*; see also COURAGE, DETERMINATION.

confident ***a.*** self-confident, assured, being certain, fearless, assertive, positive, sure, convinced, self-reliant, sure of oneself, dauntless, self-sufficient, bold; see also CERTAIN 1.

confidential ***a.*** classified, intimate, privy; see PRIVATE, SECRET 1, 3.

confidentially ***a.*** privately, personally, in confidence; see SECRETLY.

confidently ***a.*** in an assured way, with conviction, assuredly; see BOLDLY 1, POSITIVELY 1.

confine ***v.*** **1** [To restrain] repress, hold back, keep within limits; see HINDER, RESTRAIN. **2** [To imprison] cage, incarcerate, shut up; see ENSLAVE, IMPRISON.

confined ***a.*** **1** [Restricted] limited, hampered, compassed; see BOUND 1, 2, RESTRICTED. **2** [Bedridden] on one's back, ill, laid up; see SICK. **3** [In prison] behind bars, locked up, in bonds, in irons, in chains, in jail, imprisoned, jailed, immured, incarcerated, detained, under lock and key.—*Ant.* FREE, released, at liberty.

confinement ***n.*** restriction, limitation, constraint, repression, control, coercion, keeping, safekeeping, custody, curb, bounds, check, bonds, bondage, detention, imprisonment, incarceration; see also JAIL.—*Ant.* FREEDOM, release, independence.

confines ***n.*** bounds, limits, periphery; see BOUNDARY.

confining ***a.*** limiting, restricting, bounding, prescribing, restraining, hampering, repressing, checking, enclosing, imprisoning, incarcerating, detaining, keeping locked up, keeping behind bars.

confirm ***v.*** **1** [To ratify] sanction, affirm, settle; see APPROVE, ENDORSE 2. **2** [To prove] verify, authenticate, validate; see EXPLAIN, PROVE.

confirmation ***n.*** ratification, proving, authentication, corroboration, support, endorsement, sanction, authorization, verification, affirmation, acceptance, passage, validation, approval, attestation, assent, admission, recognition, witness, consent, testimony, agreement, evidence; see also AGREEMENT, PROOF 1.—*Ant.* CANCELLATION, annulment, disapproval.

confirmed ***a.*** **1** [Firmly established] proved, valid, accepted; see CERTAIN 2, ESTABLISHED 2, GUARANTEED. **2** [Inveterate] ingrained, seasoned, regular; see CHRONIC, HABITUAL.

con·fis·cate (kän′fis kāt′) ***vt.*** **-cat′ed, -cat′ing** ⟦< L *com-,* together + *fiscus,* treasury⟧ **1** to seize (private property) for the public treasury as a penalty **2** to seize by or as by authority; appropriate —**con′fis·ca′tion** ***n.*** —**con′fis·ca′tor** ***n.***
con·fis·ca·to·ry (kən fis′kə tôr′ē) ***adj.*** of or effecting confiscation
con·fla·gra·tion (kän′flə grā′shən) ***n.*** ⟦< L *com-,* intens. + *flagrare,* to burn⟧ a big, destructive fire
con·flict (kən flikt′; *for n.* kän′flikt′) ***vi.*** ⟦< L *com-,* together + *fligere,* to strike⟧ to be antagonistic, incompatible, etc. —***n.*** **1** a fight or war **2** sharp disagreement, as of interests or ideas **3** emotional disturbance due to conflicting impulses, ideas, etc.
con·flict′ed ***adj.*** in emotional conflict
conflict of interest a conflict between one's obligation to the public, as that of a public officeholder, and one's self-interest
con·flic·tu·al (kən flik′cho͞o əl) ***adj.*** characterized by or having to do with conflict
con·flu·ence (kän′flo͞o əns) ***n.*** ⟦< L *com-,* together + *fluere,* to flow⟧ **1** a flowing together, esp. of streams **2** the place of this **3** a crowd —**con′flu·ent** ***adj.***
con·form (kən fôrm′) ***vt.*** ⟦< L *com-,* together + *formare,* to form⟧ **1** to make similar **2** to bring into agreement —***vi.*** **1** to be or become similar **2** to be in agreement **3** to act in accordance with accepted rules, customs, etc. —**con·form′ism′** ***n.*** —**con·form′ist** ***n.***
con·for·ma·tion (kän′fôr mā′shən) ***n.*** **1** a symmetrical arrangement of the parts of a thing **2** the shape or outline, as of an animal
con·form·i·ty (kən fôr′mə tē) ***n.,*** *pl.* **-ties** **1** agreement; correspondence; similarity **2** conventional behavior
con·found (kən found′; *for 2* kän′-) ***vt.*** ⟦< L *com-,* together + *fundere,* pour⟧ **1** to confuse or bewilder **2** to damn: a mild oath —**con·found′ed** ***adj.***
con·fra·ter·ni·ty (kän′frə tur′nə tē) ***n.,*** *pl.* **-ties** ⟦see CON- & FRATERNAL⟧ **1** brotherhood **2** a religious society, usually of laymen
con·frere (kän′frer′, kän frer′) ***n.*** ⟦OFr⟧ a colleague or associate
con·front (kən frunt′) ***vt.*** ⟦< L *com-,* together + *frons,* forehead⟧ **1** to face, esp. boldly or defiantly **2** to bring face to face (*with*) —**con·fron·ta·tion** (kän′frən tā′shən) ***n.*** —**con′fron·ta′tion·al** ***adj.***
Con·fu·cius (kən fyo͞o′shəs) 551?-479? B.C.; Chin. philosopher —**Con·fu′cian** (-shən) ***adj., n.***
con·fuse (kən fyo͞oz′) ***vt.*** **-fused′, -fus′ing** ⟦see CONFOUND⟧ **1** to put into disorder **2** to bewilder or embarrass **3** to mistake the identity of —**con·fus′ed·ly** ***adv.***
con·fu′sion (-fyo͞o′zhən) ***n.*** a confusing or being confused; specif., disorder, bewilderment, etc.
con·fute (kən fyo͞ot′) ***vt.*** **-fut′ed, -fut′ing** ⟦L *confutare*⟧ to prove to be in error or false —**con·fu·ta·tion** (kän′fyo͞o tā′shən) ***n.***
Cong *abbrev.* **1** Congregational **2** Congress
con·geal (kən jēl′) ***vt., vi.*** ⟦< L *com-,* together + *gelare,* freeze⟧ **1** to freeze **2** to thicken; coagulate; jell —**con·geal′ment** ***n.***
con·ge·nial (kən jēn′yəl) ***adj.*** ⟦see CON- & GENIAL⟧ **1** kindred; compatible **2** like-minded; friendly **3** suited to one's needs; agreeable —**con·ge′ni·al′i·ty** (-jē′nē al′ə tē) ***n.*** —**con·ge′nial·ly** ***adv.***
con·gen·i·tal (kən jen′ə təl) ***adj.*** ⟦< L *congenitus,* born together with⟧ existing as such at birth —**con·gen′i·tal·ly** ***adv.***
con·ger (eel) (käŋ′gər) ⟦< Gr *gongros*⟧ a large, edible saltwater eel
con·ge·ries (kän′jə rēz′) ***n.,*** *pl.* **-ries′** ⟦L: see fol.⟧ a heap or pile of things
con·gest (kən jest′) ***vt.*** ⟦< L *com-,* together + *gerere,* carry⟧ **1** to cause too much blood, mucus, etc. to accumulate in (a part of the body) **2** to fill to excess; overcrowd —**con·ges′tion** ***n.*** —**con·ges′tive** ***adj.***
con·glom·er·ate (kən gläm′ər āt′; *for adj. & n.,* -it) ***vt., vi.*** **-at′ed, -at′ing** ⟦< L *com-,* together + *glomus,* ball⟧ to form into a rounded mass —***adj.*** **1** formed into a rounded mass **2** formed of substances collected into a single mass, esp. of rock fragments or pebbles cemented together by clay, silica, etc. —***n.*** **1** a conglomerate mass **2** a large corporation formed by merging many diverse companies **3** a conglomerate rock —**con·glom′er·a′tion** ***n.***
Con·go (käŋ′gō) **1** river in central Africa, flowing into the Atlantic **2** **Democratic Republic of the Congo** country in central Africa: 905,365 sq. mi.; pop. 29,671,000: formerly *Belgian Congo* (1908-60), *Zaire* (1971-97) **3** **Republic of the Congo** country in WC Africa, west of Democratic Republic of the Congo: 131,978 sq. mi.; pop. 1,909,000: formerly *People's Republic of the Congo* —**Con·go·lese** (käŋ′gə lēz′) ***adj., n.***
con·grat·u·late (kən grach′ə lāt′) ***vt.*** **-lat′ed, -lat′ing** ⟦< L *com-,* together + *gratulari,* to wish joy⟧ to express to (another) one's pleasure at that person's good fortune, etc.; felicitate *[congratulate* the winner*]* —**con·grat′u·la·to′ry** (-lə tôr′ē) ***adj.***

THESAURUS

confiscate ***v.*** appropriate, impound, usurp; see SEIZE 2, STEAL.
conflict ***n.*** struggle, strife, engagement; see BATTLE, FIGHT.
conflict ***v.*** clash, contrast, contend; see DIFFER 1, FIGHT, OPPOSE 1, 2.
conform ***v.*** comply, accord, submit, accommodate, live up to, fit, suit, acclimate, accustom, be regular, harmonize, adapt, be guided by, fit the pattern, be in fashion, reconcile, obey, grow used to, do as others do, get in line, fall in with, go by, adhere to, adjust to, keep to, keep up, keep up with the Joneses*, chime in with, join the parade, play the game, follow the beaten path, toe the line, follow suit, run with the pack, follow the crowd, adhere to the status quo, when in Rome do as the Romans do; see also AGREE, FOLLOW 2, OBEY.—*Ant.* DIFFER, CONFLICT, disagree.
conforming ***a.*** agreeing, in line with, in agreement; see HARMONIOUS 2.
conformist ***n.*** conformer, philistine, advocate; see FOLLOWER.
conformity ***n.*** **1** [Similarity] congruity, correspondence, resemblance; see SIMILARITY. **2** [Obedience] willingness, submission, compliance; see AGREEMENT.
confound ***v.*** puzzle, perplex, bewilder; see CONFUSE.
confounded ***a.*** confused, bewildered, disconcerted; see DOUBTFUL.
confront ***v.*** brave, defy, repel; see DARE 2, FACE 1.
confrontation ***n.*** meeting, battle, strife; see DISPUTE, FIGHT 1.
confuse ***v.*** upset, befuddle, mislead, misinform, puzzle, perplex, confound, fluster, bewilder, embarrass, daze, dazzle, astonish, disarrange, disorder, jumble, blend, mix, mingle, cloud, fog, stir up, disconcert, abash, agitate, amaze, worry, trouble, snarl, unsettle, muddle, clutter, complicate, involve, rattle, derange, baffle, nonplus, frustrate, perturb, dismay, distract, entangle, encumber, befog, obscure, mystify, make a mess of, throw off the scent, cross up, foul up, mix up, ball up*, lead astray, stump, rattle, make one's head swim; see also DISTURB, TANGLE.—*Ant.* CLEAR UP, clarify, untangle.
confused ***a.*** **1** [Puzzled in mind] disconcerted, abashed, perplexed; see DOUBTFUL. **2** [Not properly distinguished] mistaken, jumbled, snarled, deranged, bewildered, out of order, disarrayed, confounded, mixed, mixed up, chaotic, disordered, muddled, fuddled, befuddled, slovenly, untidy, messy, involved, misunderstood, blurred, obscured, topsy-turvy, balled up*, fouled up*, screwed up*, in a mess, haywire*, snafu*; see also OBSCURE 1, TANGLED.—*Ant.* DISTINGUISHED, discriminated, ordered.
confusing ***a.*** disconcerting, confounding, baffling, puzzling, disturbing, unsettling, upsetting, embarrassing, obscuring, blurring, befuddling, tangling, snarling, cluttering, muddling, disarranging; see also DIFFICULT 2, OBSCURE 1.—*Ant.* ORDERLY, reassuring, clear.
confusion ***n.*** complication, intricacy, muss, untidiness, complexity, difficulty, mistake, bewilderment, turmoil, tumult, pandemonium, commotion, stir, ferment, disarray, jumble, convulsion, bustle, trouble, row, riot, uproar, fracas, distraction, agitation, emotional upset, daze, astonishment, surprise, fog, haze, consternation, racket, excitement, chaos, turbulence, dismay, uncertainty, irregularity, maze, interruption, stoppage, clutter, entanglement, backlash, clog, break, breakdown, knot, trauma, congestion, obstruction, interference, nervousness, disorganization, muddle, mass, snarl, to-do*, hubbub, tie-up, botch, rumpus, scramble, shuffle, mess, hodgepodge, stew, going round and round, jam*, fix*, bull in a china shop; see also DISORDER.—*Ant.* ORDER, quiet, calm.
confute ***v.*** confound, refute, invalidate; see DENY, OPPOSE 1.
congenial ***a.*** kindred, agreeable, genial; see FRIENDLY, HARMONIOUS 2.
congestion ***n.*** profusion, crowdedness, overpopulation, press, traffic jam, gridlock, overcrowding, overdevelopment, too many, too much, concentration, surplus; see also EXCESS 1.
congratulate ***v.*** felicitate, wish joy to, toast; see COMPLIMENT, PRAISE 1.

con·grat'u·la'tion (-lā'shən) ***n.*** **1** a congratulating **2** [*pl.*] expressions of pleasure in another's good fortune, etc.

con·gre·gate (käŋ'grə gāt') ***vt., vi.*** **-gat'ed, -gat'ing** ⟦< L *com-*, together + *grex*, a flock⟧ to gather into a crowd; assemble

con'gre·ga'tion (-gā'shən) ***n.*** **1** a gathering; assemblage **2** an assembly of people for religious worship **3** its members

con'gre·ga'tion·al ***adj.*** **1** of or like a congregation **2** [**C-**] of a Protestant denomination in which each member church is self-governing

con·gress (käŋ'grəs) ***n.*** ⟦< L *com-*, together + *gradi*, to walk⟧ **1** an association or society **2** an assembly or conference **3** a legislature, esp. of a republic **4** [**C-**] the legislature of the U.S.; the Senate and the House of Representatives —**con·gres·sion·al** (kən gresh'ə nəl) ***adj.*** —**con·gres'sion·al·ly** ***adv.***

con'gress·man (-mən) ***n.***, *pl.* **-men** (-mən) [*often* **C-**] a member of Congress, esp. of the House of Representatives: also **con'gress·per'son** (-pur'sən) —**con'gress·wom'an**, *pl.* **-wom'en**, ***fem.n.***

con·gru·ent (käŋ'groo͞ ənt, kən groo͞'ənt) ***adj.*** ⟦< L *congruere*, agree⟧ **1** corresponding; harmonious **2** of geometric figures of the same shape and size —**con'gru·ence** ***n.***

con·gru·ous (käŋ'groo͞ əs) ***adj.*** **1** congruent **2** fitting; suitable; appropriate —**con·gru·i·ty** (kän groo͞'ə tē), *pl.* **-ties**, ***n.*** —**con'gru·ous·ly** ***adv.*** —**con'gru·ous·ness** ***n.***

con·i·cal (kän'i kəl) ***adj.*** **1** of a cone **2** shaped like a cone Also **con'ic** —**con'i·cal·ly** ***adv.***

con·i·fer (kän'ə fər, kō'nə-) ***n.*** ⟦L < *conus*, cone + *ferre*, to bear⟧ any of a class of cone-bearing trees and shrubs, mostly evergreens —**co·nif·er·ous** (kō nif'ər əs, kə-) ***adj.***

conj *abbrev.* **1** conjugation **2** conjunction

con·jec·ture (kən jek'chər) ***n.*** ⟦< L *com-*, together + *jacere*, to throw⟧ **1** an inferring, theorizing, or predicting from incomplete evidence; guesswork **2** a guess —***vt., vi.*** **-tured, -tur·ing** to guess —**con·jec'tur·al** ***adj.*** —**con·jec'tur·al·ly** ***adv.***

con·join (kən join') ***vt., vi.*** ⟦< L *com-*, together + *jungere*, join⟧ to join together —**con·joint'** ***adj.***

con·ju·gal (kän'jə gəl) ***adj.*** ⟦< L *conjunx*, spouse⟧ of marriage or the relation between husband and wife —**con'ju·gal·ly** ***adv.***

con·ju·gate (kän'jə gət; *also, and for v. always*, -gāt') ***adj.*** ⟦< L *com-*, together + *jugare*, join⟧ joined together; coupled —***vt.*** **-gat'ed, -gat'ing** *Gram.* to give in order the inflectional forms of (a verb) —**con'ju·ga'tion** ***n.***

con·junc·tion (kən juŋk'shən) ***n.*** ⟦see CONJOIN⟧ **1** a joining together; union; combination **2** coincidence **3** a word used to connect words, phrases, or clauses (Ex.: *and, but, or, if*) —**con·junc'tive** ***adj.***

con·junc·ti·va (kän'jəŋk tī'və) ***n.***, *pl.* **-vas** or **-vae** (-vē) ⟦see CONJOIN⟧ the mucous membrane covering the inner eyelids and the front of the eyeball

con·junc·ti·vi·tis (kən juŋk'tə vīt'is) ***n.*** inflammation of the conjunctiva

con·junc·ture (kən juŋk'chər) ***n.*** ⟦see CONJOIN⟧ a combination of events creating a crisis

con·jure (kun'jər, kän'-; *for vt.* kən joor') ***vi.*** **-jured, -jur·ing** ⟦< L *com-*, together + *jurare*, swear⟧ **1** to summon a demon or spirit by magic **2** to practice magic —***vt.*** to entreat solemnly —**conjure up** to cause to appear as by magic —**con'ju·ra'tion** (-jə rā'shən) ***n.*** —**con'jur·er** or **con'ju·ror** ***n.***

conk (käŋk, kôŋk) ***n., vt.*** ⟦< CONCH⟧ [Slang] hit on the head —**conk out** [Slang] **1** to fail suddenly: said as of a motor **2** to fall asleep from fatigue

con man [Slang] a confidence man; swindler

con·nect (kə nekt') ***vt.*** ⟦< L *com-*, together + *nectere*, fasten⟧ **1** to join (two things together, or one thing *with* or *to* another) **2** to show or think of as related —***vi.*** to join —**con·nec'tor** or **con·nect'er** ***n.***

Con·nect·i·cut (kə net'ə kət) New England state of the U.S.: 4,844 sq. mi.; pop. 3,287,000; cap. Hartford: abbrev. *CT*

con·nec·tion (kə nek'shən) ***n.*** **1** a connecting or being connected **2** a thing that connects **3** a relationship; association **4** *a*) a relative, as by marriage *b*) an influential associate, etc.: *usually used in pl.* **5** [*often pl.*] a transferring from one bus, plane, etc. to another

con·nec'tive (-tiv) ***adj.*** connecting —***n.*** that which connects, esp. a connecting word, as a conjunction

connective tissue body tissue, as cartilage, serving to connect and support other tissues

con·nip·tion (kə nip'shən) ***n.*** ⟦pseudo-L⟧ [*often pl.*] [Inf.] a fit of anger, hysteria, etc.; tantrum: also **conniption fit**

con·nive (kə nīv') ***vi.*** **-nived', -niv'ing** ⟦< L *conivere*, to wink, connive⟧ **1** to pretend not to look (*at* crime, etc.), thus giving tacit consent **2** to cooperate secretly (*with* someone), esp. in wrongdoing; scheme —**con·niv'ance** ***n.*** —**con·niv'er** ***n.***

con·nois·seur (kän'ə sur') ***n.*** ⟦< Fr < L *cognoscere*, know⟧ one who has expert knowledge and keen discrimination, esp. in the fine arts —**con'nois·seur'ship** ***n.***

con·note (kə nōt') ***vt.*** **-not'ed, -not'ing** ⟦< L *com-*, together + *notare*, to mark⟧ to suggest or convey (associations, etc.) in addition to the explicit, or denoted, meaning —**con·no·ta·tion** (kän'ə tā'shən) ***n.*** —**con'no·ta'tive** or **con'no·ta'tion·al** ***adj.***

con·nu·bi·al (kə noo͞'bē əl) ***adj.*** ⟦< L *com-*, together + *nubere*, marry⟧ of marriage; conjugal —**con·nu'bi·al·ly** ***adv.***

con·quer (käŋ'kər) ***vt.*** ⟦< L *com-*, intens. + *quaerere*, seek⟧ **1** to get control of as by winning a war **2** to overcome; defeat —***vi.*** to win —**con'quer·a·ble** ***adj.*** —**con'quer·or** ***n.***

con·quest (käŋ'kwest') ***n.*** **1** a conquering **2** something conquered **3** a winning of someone's affection

con·quis·ta·dor (kän kwis'tə dôr', -kēs'-) ***n.***, *pl.* **-dors'** or **con·quis'ta·do'res'** (-dôr'ēz') ⟦Sp, conqueror⟧ any of the 16th-cent. Spanish conquerors of Mexico, Peru, etc.

con·san·guin·e·ous (kän'saŋ gwin'ē əs) ***adj.*** ⟦see CON- & SANGUINE⟧ having the same ancestor —**con'san·guin'i·ty** ***n.***

con·science (kän'shəns) ***n.*** ⟦< L *com-*, with + *scire*, know⟧ a sense of right and wrong, with an urge to do right —**con'science·less** ***adj.***

con·sci·en·tious (kän'shē en'shəs) ***adj.*** ⟦see prec. & -OUS⟧ **1** governed by one's conscience; scrupulous **2** painstaking —**con'sci·en'tious·ly** ***adv.*** —**con'sci·en'tious·ness** ***n.***

THESAURUS

congratulations ***interj.*** best wishes, compliments, congrats*; see COMPLIMENT.

congregate ***v.*** convene, meet, converge; see GATHER 1.

congregation ***n.*** meeting, group, assemblage; see GATHERING.

congress ***n.*** [*often capital C*] parliament, assembly, legislative body; see COMMITTEE, GOVERNMENT, LEGISLATURE.

congruent ***a.*** in agreement, harmonious, corresponding; see HARMONIOUS 2.

congruous ***a.*** suitable, appropriate, fitting; see HARMONIOUS 2.

conjunction ***n.*** **1** [Act of joining together] combination, connection, association; see UNION 1. **2** [A syntactic connecting word] *Conjunctions include the following:* and, but, if, for, or, nor, so, yet, only, that, than, before, since, then, though, when, whenever, provided, where, why, both, either, while, as, neither, although, because, unless, until.

conjure up ***v.*** call, invoke, materialize; see SUMMON, URGE 2.

connect ***v.*** **1** [To join] combine, unite, attach; see JOIN 1. **2** [To associate] relate, equate, correlate; see COMPARE 1.

connected ***a.*** **1** [Joined together] united, combined, coupled; see JOINED. **2** [Related] associated, applicable, pertinent; see RELATED 2, RELEVANT.

connecting ***a.*** joining, linking, combining, uniting, associating, relating, tying, cementing, knitting, fusing, hooking, bringing together, clinching, fastening, mixing, mingling, intertwining, welding, pairing, coupling; see also JOINED.

connection ***n.*** **1** [Relationship] kinship, association, reciprocity; see ASSOCIATION 2, RELATIONSHIP. **2** [A junction] combination, juncture, consolidation; see UNION 1. **3** [A link] attachment, fastening, bond; see LINK. —**in connection with** in conjunction with, associated with, together with; see WITH.

connotation ***n.*** implication, intention, essence; see MEANING.

conquer ***v.*** subdue, overcome, crush; see DEFEAT 2.

conqueror ***n.*** vanquisher, victor, conquistador; see HERO 1, WINNER.

conquest ***n.*** triumph, success, conquering; see VICTORY.

conscience ***n.*** moral sense, inner voice, the still small voice; see DUTY 1, MORALS, SHAME 2. —**have on one's conscience** be culpable for, be responsible for, feel guilty about; see GUILTY. —**in (all) conscience** rightly, fairly, properly; see JUSTLY 1.

conscientious ***a.*** fastidious, meticulous, scrupulous; see CAREFUL, RELIABLE.

conscientiousness ***n.*** exactness, care, honor; see CARE 1, DUTY 1, HON-

conscientious objector one who for reasons of conscience refuses to take part in warfare

con·scious (kän′shəs) ***adj.*** ⟦< L: see CONSCIENCE⟧ **1** having an awareness (*of* or *that*) **2** able to feel and think; awake **3** aware of oneself as a thinking being **4** intentional *[conscious humor]* **5** known to oneself —**con′scious·ly *adv.***

con′scious·ness *n.* **1** the state of being conscious; awareness **2** the totality of one's thoughts and feelings

con·script (kən skript′; *for n.* kän′skript′) ***vt.*** ⟦ult. < L *com-*, with + *scribere*, write⟧ to enroll for compulsory service in the armed forces; draft —***n.*** a draftee —**con·scrip′tion *n.***

con·se·crate (kän′si krāt′) ***vt.* -crat′ed, -crat′ing** ⟦< L *com-*, together + *sacrare*, make holy⟧ **1** to set apart as holy **2** to devote to sacred or serious use —**con′se·cra′tion *n.***

con·sec·u·tive (kən sek′yoo tiv) ***adj.*** ⟦see CONSEQUENCE⟧ following in order, without interruption; successive —**con·sec′u·tive·ly *adv.*** —**con·sec′u·tive·ness *n.***

con·sen·sus (kən sen′səs) ***n.*** ⟦see fol.⟧ **1** an opinion held by all or most **2** general agreement, esp. in opinion

con·sent (kən sent′) ***vi.*** ⟦< L *com-*, with + *sentire*, feel⟧ to agree, permit, or assent —***n.*** **1** permission; approval **2** agreement *[by common consent]* —**con·sen′su·al** (-sen′shoo əl) ***adj.***

con·se·quence (kän′si kwens′, -kwəns) ***n.*** ⟦< L *com-*, with + *sequi*, follow⟧ **1** a result; effect **2** importance —**take the consequences** to accept the results of one's actions

con′se·quent′ (-kwent′, -kwənt) ***adj.*** following as a result; resulting —**con′se·quent′ly *adv.***

con′se·quen′tial (-kwen′shəl) ***adj.*** **1** consequent **2** important

con·ser·va·tion (kän′sər vā′shən) ***n.*** **1** a conserving; preservation **2** the official care or management of natural resources —**con′ser·va′tion·ist *n.***

con·serv·a·tive (kən sur′və tiv) ***adj.*** **1** tending to conserve **2** tending to preserve established institutions, etc.; opposed to change **3** moderate; cautious —***n.*** a conservative person —**con·serv′a·tism′ *n.*** —**con·serv′a·tive·ly *adv.***

con·serv′a·to′ry (-tôr′ē) ***n.***, *pl.* **-ries** **1** a greenhouse **2** a music school

con·serve (kən surv′; *for n., usually* kän′surv′) ***vt.* -served′, -serv′ing** ⟦< L *com-*, with + *servare*, keep⟧ to keep from being damaged, lost, or wasted; save —***n.*** [*often pl.*] a jam made of two or more fruits

con·sid·er (kən sid′ər) ***vt.*** ⟦< L *considerare*, observe⟧ **1** to think about in order to understand or decide **2** to keep in mind **3** to be thoughtful of (others) **4** to regard as

con·sid′er·a·ble *adj.* **1** worth considering; important **2** much or large —**con·sid′er·a·bly *adv.***

con·sid′er·ate (-it) ***adj.*** having regard for others and their feelings —**con·sid′er·ate·ly *adv.*** —**con·sid′er·ate·ness *n.***

con·sid′er·a′tion (-ā′shən) ***n.*** **1** the act of considering; deliberation **2** thoughtful regard for others **3** something considered in making a decision **4** a recompense; fee **5** something given, as to make a binding contract —**take into consideration** to keep in mind —**under consideration** being thought over or discussed

con·sid′ered *adj.* arrived at after careful thought

con·sid′er·ing *prep.* in view of; taking into account

con·sign (kən sīn′) ***vt.*** ⟦< L *consignare*, to seal⟧ **1** to hand over; deliver **2** to entrust **3** to assign to an inferior place **4** to send (goods to be sold)

con·sign′ment *n.* **1** a consigning or being consigned **2** a shipment of goods sent to a dealer for sale —**on consignment** with payment due after sale of the consignment

con·sist (kən sist′) ***vi.*** ⟦< L *com-*, together + *sistere*, to stand⟧ **1** to be formed or composed (*of*) **2** to be contained or inherent (*in*)

con·sis′ten·cy (-sis′tən sē) ***n.***, *pl.* **-cies** **1** firmness or thickness, as of a liquid **2** agreement; harmony **3** conformity with previous practice

con·sis′tent (-tənt) ***adj.*** **1** in agreement or harmony; compatible **2** holding to the same principles or practice —**con·sis′tent·ly *adv.***

con·sis′to·ry (-tə rē) ***n.***, *pl.* **-ries** ⟦see CONSIST⟧ **1** a church council or court **2** its session

con·so·la·tion (kän′sə lā′shən) ***n.*** **1** comfort; solace **2** one that consoles

con·sole[1] (kən sōl′) ***vt.* -soled′, -sol′ing** ⟦< L *com-*, with + *solari*, to comfort, solace⟧ to make feel less sad or disap-

THESAURUS

ESTY, RESPONSIBILITY 1.

conscious *a.* cognizant, aware, informed, sure, certain, assured, discerning, knowing, sensible, sensitive, acquainted, attentive, watchful, mindful, vigilant, understanding, keen, alert, alert to, alive to, sensitive to, conscious of, mindful of, cognizant of, hip to*, on to*; see also INTELLIGENT.—*Ant.* UNAWARE, insensitive, inattentive.

consciousness *n.* alertness, cognizance, mindfulness; see AWARENESS, KNOWLEDGE 1.

consecrate *v.* hallow, sanctify, anoint; see BLESS.

consecrated *a.* blessed, sanctified, hallowed; see DIVINE.

consecration *n.* making holy, sanctification, exalting; see CELEBRATION.

consecutive *a.* continuous, chronological, serial, in turn, progressive, connected, in order, in sequence, sequential, going on, continuing, one after another, one after the other, serialized, seriatim, numerical; see also CONSTANT, REGULAR 3.

consecutively *a.* following, successively, continuously; see GRADUALLY.

consensus *n.* consent, unison, accord; see AGREEMENT.

consent *n.* assent, approval, acquiescence; see PERMISSION.

consent *v.* accede, assent, acquiesce; see AGREE, ALLOW, APPROVE.

consequence *n.* **1** [Effect] outgrowth, end, outcome; see RESULT. **2** [Importance] moment, value, weight; see IMPORTANCE. —**in consequence of** because of, owing to, consequently; see BECAUSE. —**take the consequences** accept the results of one's actions, suffer, bear the burden; see ENDURE 2.

conservation *n.* maintenance, keeping, preservation, preserving, conserving, guarding, protecting, stewardship, husbandry, saving, safekeeping, storage, upkeep, economy, keeping in trust; see also PRESERVATION.—*Ant.* WASTE, misuse, destruction.

conservative *a.* conserving, preserving, unchanging, unchangeable, stable, constant, steady, traditional, reactionary, conventional, moderate, unprogressive, firm, obstinate, inflexible, opposed to change, cautious, sober, Tory, taking no chances, timid, fearful, unimaginative, right-wing, in a rut*; see also CAREFUL, MODERATE 3.—*Ant.* RADICAL, risky, changing.

conservative *n.* reactionary, right-winger, die-hard, Tory, Whig, Federalist, champion of the status quo, opponent of change, classicist, traditionalist, unprogressive, conventionalist, mossback*, old fogy, fossil*.—*Ant.* RADICAL, progressive, liberal.

consider *v.* allow for, provide for, grant, take up, concede, acknowledge, recognize, favor, value, take under advisement, deal with, regard, make allowance for, take into consideration, keep in mind, reckon with, play around with*, toss around, see about; see also RECONSIDER, THINK 1.—*Ant.* REFUSE, deny, reject.

considerable *a.* **1** [Important] noteworthy, significant, essential; see IMPORTANT 1. **2** [Much] abundant, lavish, bountiful; see MUCH 2, PLENTIFUL 1.

considerate *a.* charitable, kind, solicitous; see POLITE, THOUGHTFUL 2.

consideration *n.* **1** [The state of being considerate] kindliness, thoughtfulness, attentiveness; see COURTESY 1, KINDNESS 1, TOLERANCE 1. **2** [Payment] remuneration, salary, fee; see PAYMENT 1. **3** [Something to be considered] situation, problem, judgment, notion, fancy, puzzle, proposal, difficulty, incident, evidence, new development, occurrence, taste, pass, occasion, emergency, idea, thought, trouble, plan, particulars, items, scope, extent, magnitude; see also IDEA 1, PLAN 2. —**in consideration of** because of, on account of, for; see CONSIDERING. —**take into consideration** take into account, weigh, keep in mind; see CONSIDER. —**under consideration** thought over, discussed, evaluated; see CONSIDERED.

considered *a.* carefully thought about, treated, gone into, contemplated, weighed, meditated, examined, investigated; see also DETERMINED 1.

considering *prep.*, *conj.* in light of, in view of, in consideration of, pending, taking into account, everything being equal, inasmuch as, insomuch as, with something in view.

consign *v.* convey, dispatch, transfer; see GIVE 1, SEND 1.

consistency *n.* **1** [Harmony] union, compatibility, accord; see AGREEMENT, SYMMETRY. **2** [The degree of firmness or thickness] hardness, softness, firmness; see DENSITY, TEXTURE 1.

consistent *a.* compatible, equable, expected; see LOGICAL, RATIONAL 1, REGULAR 3.

consist of *v.* embody, contain, involve; see COMPRISE, INCLUDE 1.

consolation *n.* sympathy, compassion, support; see PITY, RELIEF 1, 4.

console[1] *v.* solace, sympathize with, hearten; see COMFORT 1,

pointed; comfort —**con·sol'a·ble** *adj.* —**con·sol'ing·ly** *adv.*

con·sole[2] (kän'sōl') ***n.*** ⟦Fr⟧ **1** the desklike frame containing the keys, stops, etc. of an organ **2** a radio, television, or phonograph cabinet designed to stand on the floor **3** a control panel for operating aircraft, computers, electronic systems, etc. **4** a raised portion between automobile bucket seats

con·sol·i·date (kən säl'ə dāt') ***vt., vi.*** **-dat'ed, -dat'ing** ⟦< L *com-,* together + *solidus,* solid⟧ **1** to combine into a single whole; unite **2** to make or become strong or stable *[to consolidate one's power]* —**con·sol'i·da'tion** ***n.*** —**con·sol'i·da'tor** ***n.***

con·som·mé (kän'sə mā') ***n.*** ⟦Fr⟧ a clear, strained meat soup

con·so·nance (kän'sə nəns) ***n.*** ⟦< L *com-,* with + *sonus,* sound⟧ **1** harmony of parts or elements **2** musical harmony **3** repetition of consonants

con'so·nant (-nənt) ***adj.*** in harmony or accord —***n.*** **1** a speech sound made by obstructing the air stream **2** a letter representing such a sound, as *p, t, l,* or *f*

con·sort (kän'sôrt'; *for v.* kən sôrt') ***n.*** ⟦< L *com-,* with + *sors,* a share⟧ a wife or husband, esp. of a reigning king or queen —***vt., vi.*** to associate

con·sor·ti·um (kən sôrt'ē əm, -sôr'shē əm) ***n.,*** *pl.* **-ti·a** (-ə) ⟦see prec.⟧ an international alliance, as of business firms or banks

con·spec·tus (kən spek'təs) ***n.*** ⟦L: see fol.⟧ **1** a general view **2** a summary; digest

con·spic·u·ous (kən spik'yōō əs) ***adj.*** ⟦< L *com-,* intens. + *specere,* see⟧ **1** easy to see **2** outstanding; striking —**con·spic'u·ous·ly** ***adv.*** —**con·spic'u·ous·ness** ***n.***

con·spir·a·cy (kən spir'ə sē) ***n.,*** *pl.* **-cies** **1** a conspiring **2** an unlawful plot **3** a conspiring group

con·spire (kən spīr') ***vi.*** **-spired', -spir'ing** ⟦< L *com-,* together + *spirare,* breathe⟧ **1** to plan together secretly, esp. to commit a crime **2** to work together for any purpose or effect —**con·spir'a·tor** (-spir'ət ər) ***n.*** —**con·spir'a·to'ri·al** (-spir'ə tôr'ē əl) ***adj.***

con·sta·ble (kän'stə bəl) ***n.*** ⟦< LL *comes stabuli,* lit., count of the stable⟧ **1** a peace officer in a small town **2** [Chiefly Brit.] a police officer

con·stab·u·lar·y (kən stab'yə ler'ē) ***n.,*** *pl.* **-ies** **1** constables, collectively **2** militarized police

con·stant (kän'stənt) ***adj.*** ⟦< L *com-,* together + *stare,* to stand⟧ **1** not changing; faithful, regular, stable, etc. **2** continual; persistent —***n.*** anything that does not change or vary —**con'stan·cy** ***n.*** —**con'stant·ly** ***adv.***

Con·stan·tine I (kän'stən tēn', -tīn') A.D. 280?-337; first Christian emperor of Rome (306-337)

Con·stan·ti·no·ple (kän'stan tə nō'pəl) *former name* (A.D. 330-1930) *for* ISTANBUL

con·stel·la·tion (kän'stə lā'shən) ***n.*** ⟦< L *com-,* with + *stella,* star⟧ **1** a visible grouping of stars in the sky, usually named for some object, animal, etc. suggested by its outline **2** any brilliant group or gathering

con·ster·na·tion (kän'stər nā'shən) ***n.*** ⟦< L *consternare,* terrify⟧ great fear or shock

con·sti·pate (kän'stə pāt') ***vt.*** **-pat'ed, -pat'ing** ⟦< L *com-,* together + *stipare,* cram⟧ to cause constipation in

con'sti·pa'tion (-pā'shən) ***n.*** infrequent and difficult movement of the bowels

con·stit·u·en·cy (kən stich'ōō ən sē) ***n.,*** *pl.* **-cies** the voters in a district

con·stit'u·ent (-ənt) ***adj.*** ⟦see fol.⟧ **1** necessary to the whole; component *[a constituent part]* **2** that elects —***n.*** **1** a voter in a district **2** a component

con·sti·tute (kän'stə tōōt') ***vt.*** **-tut'ed, -tut'ing** ⟦< L *com-,* together + *statuere,* to set⟧ **1** to establish (a law, government, etc.) **2** to set up (an assembly, etc.) in a legal form **3** to appoint **4** to make up; form —**con'sti·tu'tive** ***adj.***

con'sti·tu'tion (-tōō'shən) ***n.*** **1** a constituting **2** structure; organization **3** *a)* the system of basic laws and principles of a government, society, etc. *b)* a document stating these laws and principles *c)* [**C-**] such a document of the U.S.

con'sti·tu'tion·al (-shə nəl) ***adj.*** **1** of or in one's constitution or structure; basic **2** of or in accordance with the constitution of a government, society, etc. —***n.*** a walk taken for one's health —**con'sti·tu'tion·al'i·ty** (-shə nal'ə tē) ***n.*** —**con'sti·tu'tion·al·ly** ***adv.***

con·strain (kən strān') ***vt.*** ⟦< L *com-,* together + *stringere,* draw tight⟧ **1** to confine **2** to restrain **3** to compel

con·straint' (-strānt') ***n.*** **1** confinement or restriction **2** force; compulsion **3** forced, unnatural manner **4** something that constrains

con·strict (kən strikt') ***vt.*** ⟦see CONSTRAIN⟧ to make smaller or narrower by squeezing, etc. —**con·stric'tion** ***n.***

con·stric'tor (-strik'tər) ***n.*** a snake that kills its prey by squeezing

con·struct (kən strukt'; *for n.* kän'strukt') ***vt.*** ⟦< L *com-,* together + *struere,* pile up⟧ to build, devise, etc. —***n.*** **1** something put together systematically **2** a concept or theory —**con·struc'tor** ***n.***

con·struc'tion (-struk'shən) ***n.*** **1** a constructing or manner of being constructed **2** a structure **3** an interpretation, as of a statement **4** the arrangement of words in a sentence

construction paper sturdy, colored paper for children's art projects, etc.

con·struc'tive ***adj.*** leading to improvement; positive

con·strue (kən strōō') ***vt., vi.*** **-strued', -stru'ing** ⟦see CONSTRUCT⟧ **1** to analyze the construction of (a sentence) **2** to explain; interpret

con·sul (kän'səl) ***n.*** ⟦< L *consulere,* to deliberate⟧ **1** a chief magistrate of ancient Rome **2** a government official appointed to live in a foreign city and look after his or her country's citizens and business there —**con'sul·ar** (-ər) ***adj.***

con'sul·ate (-it) ***n.*** **1** the position, powers, etc. of a consul **2** the office or residence of a consul

THESAURUS

ENCOURAGE.

consolidate ***v.*** connect, mix, unify; see COMPRESS, PACK 2.

consolidation ***n.*** alliance, association, federation; see UNION 1.

consonant ***n.*** *Linguistic terms referring to consonant sounds include the following:* voiceless, voiced, stop, fricative, semivowel, affricate, bilabial, glottal, sibilant, implosive, plosive, nasal, click, glide, continuant, trill. *In English spelling, consonants are represented as follows:* b,c,d,f, g,h,j,k,l,m,n,p,q,r,s,t,v,w,x,y,z; see also LETTER, SOUND 2, VOWEL.

conspicuous ***a.*** outstanding, eminent, distinguished, celebrated, noted, renowned, famed, notorious, important, influential, notable, illustrious, striking, prominent, well-known, arresting, remarkable, noticeable, flagrant, glaring, like a sore thumb*; see also PROMINENT 1.—*Ant.* UNKNOWN, inconspicuous, unsung.

conspiracy ***n.*** intrigue, collusion, connivance; see TRICK 1.

conspirator ***n.*** betrayer, schemer, cabalist; see TRAITOR.

conspire ***v.*** plot, scheme, contrive; see PLAN 1.

constant ***a.*** steady, uniform, perpetual, unchanging, continual, continuous, uninterrupted, unvarying, connected, even, incessant, unbroken, nonstop, monotonous, standardized, regularized; see also REGULAR 3.

constantly ***a.*** uniformly, steadily, invariably; see REGULARLY.

constituency ***n.*** the voters, constituents, electorate, body politic, electors, voting public, balloters, the people; see also VOTER.

constituent ***n.*** component, element, ingredient; see PART 1.

constitute ***v.*** **1** [To found] establish, develop, create; see ESTABLISH 2. **2** [To make up] frame, compound, aggregate; see COMPOSE 1.

constitution ***n.*** **1** [Health] vitality, physique, build; see HEALTH. **2** [A basic political document] legal code, written law, doctrines; see LAW 2.

constitutional ***a.*** lawful, safeguarding liberty, democratic; see LEGAL, DEMOCRATIC.

constrain ***v.*** necessitate, compel, stifle; see FORCE, URGE 2.

constraint ***n.*** **1** [The use of force] coercion, force, compulsion; see PRESSURE 2. **2** [Shyness] bashfulness, restraint, humility; see RESERVE 2. **3** [Confinement] captivity, detention, restriction; see ARREST, CONFINEMENT.

constrict ***v.*** contract, cramp, choke; see TIGHTEN 1.

construct ***v.*** make, erect, fabricate; see BUILD, CREATE.

construction ***n.*** **1** [The act of constructing] formation, manufacture, building; see ARCHITECTURE, BUILDING, PRODUCTION 1. **2** [A method of constructing] structure, arrangement, organization, system, plan, development, steel and concrete, contour, format, mold, cast, outline, type, shape, build, cut, fabric, formation, turn, framework, configuration, brick and mortar, prefab*. —**under construction** in production, in preparation, being built, going up.

constructive ***a.*** useful, valuable, effective; see HELPFUL 1.

construe ***v.*** infer, deduce, interpret; see EXPLAIN.

con·sult (kən sult′) *vi.* ⟦< L *consulere,* consider⟧ to talk things over; confer —*vt.* **1** to seek advice or information from **2** to consider —**con·sul·ta·tion** (kän′səl tā′shən) *n.*

con·sult′ant *n.* an expert who gives professional or technical advice —**con·sult′an·cy,** *pl.* **-cies,** *n.*

con·sume′ (-so͞om′) *vt.* **-sumed′, -sum′ing** ⟦< L *com-,* together + *sumere,* to take⟧ **1** to destroy, as by fire **2** to use up or waste (time, money, etc.) **3** to eat or drink up; devour **4** to engross

con·sum′er *n.* one that consumes; specif., one who buys goods or services for personal needs only rather than to produce other goods

con·sum′er·ism′ *n.* a movement for protecting the consumer against defective products, misleading business practices, etc.

con·sum·mate (kän′sə mit, kən sum′it; *for v.* kän′sə māt′) *adj.* ⟦< L *com-,* together + *summa,* a sum⟧ perfect; supreme —*vt.* **-mat′ed, -mat′ing 1** to complete **2** to complete (a marriage) by sexual intercourse —**con′sum·mate·ly** *adv.* —**con·sum·ma·tion** (kän′sə mā′shən) *n.*

con·sump·tion (kən sump′shən) *n.* **1** a consuming or being consumed **2** the using up of goods or services **3** the amount consumed **4** [Old-fashioned] tuberculosis of the lungs

cont *abbrev.* continued

con·tact (kän′takt′) *n.* ⟦< L *com-,* together + *tangere,* to touch⟧ **1** a touching or meeting **2** the state of being in association (*with*) **3** a connection **4** an influential acquaintance **5** *short for* CONTACT LENS —*vt.* **1** to come into contact with **2** to get in touch with —*vi.* to come into contact

contact lens a tiny, thin correctional lens worn directly over the cornea of the eye

con·ta·gion (kən tā′jən) *n.* ⟦see CONTACT⟧ **1** the spreading of disease by contact **2** a contagious disease **3** the spreading of an emotion, idea, etc.

con·ta′gious (-jəs) *adj.* **1** spread by contact: said of diseases **2** carrying the causative agent of a contagious disease **3** spreading from person to person —**con·ta′gious·ness** *n.*

con·tain (kən tān′) *vt.* ⟦< L *com-,* together + *tenere,* to hold⟧ **1** to have in it; hold **2** to have the capacity for holding **3** to hold back or restrain within fixed limits —**con·tain′ment** *n.*

con·tain′er *n.* a thing for containing something; box, can, etc.

con·tain′er·ize′ *vt.* **-ized′, -iz′ing** to pack (cargo) into huge, standardized containers for shipment

con·tam·i·nant (kən tam′ə nənt) *n.* a contaminating substance

con·tam′i·nate′ (-nāt′) *vt.* **-nat′ed, -nat′ing** ⟦< L *com-,* together + *tangere,* to touch⟧ to make impure, corrupt, etc. by contact; pollute; taint —**con·tam′i·na′tion** *n.*

contd *abbrev.* continued

con·tem·plate (kän′təm plāt′) *vt.* **-plat′ed, -plat′ing** ⟦< L *contemplari,* observe⟧ **1** to look at or think about intently **2** to expect or intend —*vi.* to muse —**con′tem·pla′tion** (-plā′shən) *n.* —**con·tem·pla·tive** (kən tem′plə tiv, kän′təm plāt′iv) *adj.*

con·tem·po·ra·ne·ous (kən tem′pə rā′nē əs) *adj.* ⟦see fol.⟧ happening in the same period —**con·tem′po·ra·ne′i·ty** (-rə nē′ə tē; -nā′-) *n.* —**con·tem′po·ra′ne·ous·ly** *adv.*

con·tem′po·rar′y (-rer′ē) *adj.* ⟦< L *com-,* with + *tempus,* time⟧ **1** living or happening in the same period **2** of about the same age **3** of the present time; modern —*n., pl.* **-ies** one living in the same period as another or others

con·tempt (kən tempt′) *n.* ⟦< L *com-,* intens. + *temnere,* to scorn⟧ **1** the feeling one has toward somebody or something one considers low, worthless, etc. **2** the condition of being despised **3** a showing disrespect for the dignity of a court (or legislature)

con·tempt′i·ble *adj.* deserving of contempt or scorn; despicable —**con·tempt′i·bly** *adv.*

con·temp·tu·ous (kən temp′cho͞o əs) *adj.* full of contempt; scornful —**con·temp′tu·ous·ly** *adv.* —**con·temp′tu·ous·ness** *n.*

con·tend (kən tend′) *vi.* ⟦< L *com-,* together + *tendere,* to stretch⟧ **1** to fight or argue **2** to compete —*vt.* to assert —**con·tend′er** *n.*

con·tent[1] (kən tent′) *adj.* ⟦see CONTAIN⟧ happy with one's lot; satisfied —*vt.* to satisfy —*n.* contentment

con·tent[2] (kän′tent′) *n.* ⟦see CONTAIN⟧ **1** [*usually pl.*] *a)* what is in a container *b)* what is dealt with in a book, speech, etc. **2** substance or meaning **3** amount contained

con·tent′ed *adj.* satisfied —**con·tent′ed·ly** *adv.* —**con·tent′ed·ness** *n.*

con·ten·tion (kən ten′shən) *n.* ⟦see CONTEND⟧ **1** strife, dispute, etc. **2** a point argued for —**in** (or **out of**) **contention** having a (or no) chance to win —**con·ten′tious** *adj.* —**con·ten′tious·ly** *adv.* —**con·ten′tious·ness** *n.*

con·tent′ment *n.* the state or fact of being contented

con·ter·mi·nous (kən tʉr′mə nəs) *adj.* ⟦< L *com-,* together + *terminus,* an end⟧ **1** having a common boundary **2** contained within the same boundaries —**con·ter′mi·nous·ly** *adv.*

con·test (kən test′; *for n.* kän′test′) *vt.* ⟦< L *com-,* together + *testis,* a witness⟧ **1** to dispute (a point, etc.) **2** to fight for (a position, etc.) —*vi.* to struggle (*with* or *against*) —*n.* **1** a fight; struggle **2** a competitive game, race, etc. —**con·test′a·ble** *adj.*

con·test′ant *n.* ⟦Fr⟧ a competitor in a game, etc.

con·text (kän′tekst′) *n.* ⟦< L *com-,* together + *texere,* to weave⟧ **1** the parts just before and after a passage, that determine its meaning **2** the whole background or environment, as of an event —**con·tex·tu·al** (kən teks′cho͞o əl) *adj.*

con·tex·tu·al·ize (kən teks′cho͞o əl īz′) *vt.* **-ized′, -iz′ing** to put in a context, as for analysis

con·tig·u·ous (kən tig′yo͞o əs) *adj.* ⟦see CONTACT⟧ **1** in

THESAURUS

consult *v.* take counsel, deliberate, confer, parley, conspire with, be closeted with, compare notes about, put heads together, commune, treat, negotiate, debate, argue, talk over, call in, ask advice of, turn to, seek advice; see also ASK, DISCUSS.

consultation *n.* interview, conference, deliberation; see DISCUSSION.

consume *v.* **1** [To use] use, buy, wear out; see SPEND, USE 1. **2** [To eat or drink] absorb, feed, devour; see EAT 1.

consumer *n.* user, customer, shopper; see BUYER.

consumption *n.* using, spending, expending; see DESTRUCTION 1, USE 1, WASTE 1.

contact *n.* touch, junction, connection; see MEETING 1. —**in contact with 1** [Contiguous] meeting, joining, connecting, bordering, adjacent, close; see also NEAR 1.—*Ant.* DISTANT, out of contact, far. **2** [Communicating with] in touch with, writing to, corresponding with, in communication with.

contact *v.* speak to, reach, make contact with; see COMMUNICATE 2, TALK 1, MEET.

contagion *n.* poison, virus, illness; see ILLNESS 1.

contagious *a.* communicable, infectious, transmittable, spreading, poisonous, epidemic, deadly, endemic, tending to spread; see also CATCHING.

contain *v.* **1** [Include] comprehend, embrace, be composed of; see INCLUDE 1. **2** [Restrict] hold, keep back, stop; see RESTRAIN.

container *n.* receptacle, basket, bin, bowl, dish, tub, holder, caldron, vessel, capsule, package, packet, chest, purse, pod, pouch, cask, sack, pot, pottery, jug, bucket, canteen, pit, box, carton, canister, crate, pail, kettle; see also BAG, CAN 1, CASE 5, JAR 1, VASE.

contaminate *v.* pollute, infect, defile; see CORRUPT, DIRTY.

contamination *n.* impurity, taint, infection; see POLLUTION.

contemplate *v.* ponder, muse, speculate on; see STUDY, THINK 1.

contemporary *a.* present, fashionable, current; see MODERN 1, 3.

contempt *n.* scorn, derision, disdain; see HATRED.

contend *v.* contest, battle, dispute; see FIGHT.

content[1] *a.* appeased, gratified, comfortable; see HAPPY, SATISFIED.

contented *a.* happy, pleased, thankful; see HAPPY, SATISFIED.

contention *n.* **1** [A quarrel] struggle, belligerency, combat; see COMPETITION, DISPUTE, FIGHT. **2** [An assertion supported by argument] explanation, stand, charge; see ATTITUDE, DECLARATION.

contentment *n.* peace, pleasure, happiness; see COMFORT, EASE 1, SATISFACTION 2.

contents *n.* constituents, components, elements, filling, content, aspects, gist, essence, meaning, significance, intent, implication, connotation, text, subject matter, sum, substance, sum and substance, details; see also INGREDIENTS, MATTER 1.

contest *n.* trial, match, challenge; see GAME 1, SPORT 1.

contest *v.* oppose, battle, quarrel; see DARE, FIGHT.

contestant *n.* competitor, opponent, participant, rival, challenger, contester, disputant, antagonist, adversary, combatant, player, team member; see also PLAYER 1.

context *n.* connection, text, frame of reference; see MEANING.

contact; touching **2** near or next —**con·ti·gu·i·ty** (kän′tə gyōō′ə tē) ***n.***

con·ti·nence (känt′'n əns) ***n.*** ⟦see CONTAIN⟧ self-restraint; specif., a refraining from all sexual activity

con′ti·nent (-ənt) ***adj.*** ⟦see CONTAIN⟧ characterized by continence —***n.*** any of the main large land areas of the earth

con′ti·nen′tal (-ent′'l) ***adj.*** **1** of a continent **2** [*sometimes* **C-**] European **3** [**C-**] of the American colonies at the time of the American Revolution

continental breakfast a light breakfast, as of rolls and coffee

continental drift the theory that continents slowly shift position

continental shelf submerged land sloping out gradually from the edge of a continent

con·tin·gen·cy (kən tin′jən sē) ***n.***, *pl.* **-cies** **1** dependence on chance **2** a possible or chance event

con·tin′gent ***adj.*** ⟦see CONTACT⟧ **1** possible **2** accidental **3** dependent (*on* or *upon* an uncertainty) —***n.*** **1** a quota, as of troops **2** a part of a larger group

con·tin·u·al (kən tin′yōō əl) ***adj.*** **1** repeated often **2** continuous —**con·tin′u·al·ly** ***adv.***

con·tin′u·ance ***n.*** **1** a continuing **2** duration **3** *Law* postponement or adjournment

con·tin′u·a′tion (-ā′shən) ***n.*** **1** a continuing **2** a beginning again; resumption **3** a part added; sequel

con·tin·ue (kən tin′yōō) ***vi.*** **-ued**, **-u·ing** ⟦< L *continuare*, join⟧ **1** to last; endure **2** to go on in a specified course of action or condition **3** to extend **4** to stay **5** to go on again after an interruption —***vt.*** **1** to go on with **2** to extend **3** to cause to remain, as in office **4** *Law* to postpone

con·ti·nu·i·ty (kän′tə nōō′ə tē, -nyōō′-) ***n.***, *pl.* **-ties** ⟦OFr < L *continuitas*⟧ **1** a continuous state or quality **2** an unbroken, coherent whole **3** the script for a film, radio or TV program, etc.

con·tin·u·ous (kən tin′yōō əs) ***adj.*** going on without interruption; unbroken —**con·tin′u·ous·ly** ***adv.***

con·tin′u·um (-yōō əm) ***n.***, *pl.* **-u·a** (-yōō ə) or **-u·ums** ⟦L⟧ a continuous whole, quantity, or series

con·tort (kən tôrt′) ***vt.***, ***vi.*** ⟦< L *com-*, together + *torquere*, to twist⟧ to twist or wrench out of shape; distort —**con·tor′tion** ***n.***

con·tor′tion·ist ***n.*** one who can contort his or her body into unnatural positions

con·tour (kän′toor′) ***n.*** ⟦Fr < L *com-*, intens. + *tornare*, to turn⟧ the outline of a figure, land, etc. —***vt.*** to shape to the contour of something —***adj.*** conforming to the shape or contour of something

con·tra (kän′trə) ***prep.*** against

contra- ⟦< L *contra*⟧ *prefix* against, opposite, opposed to

con·tra·band (kän′trə band′) ***n.*** ⟦< Sp < It⟧ smuggled goods —***adj.*** illegal to import or export

con·tra·cep·tion (kän′trə sep′shən) ***n.*** ⟦CONTRA- + (CON)CEPTION⟧ prevention of the fertilization of an ovum, as by special devices or drugs —**con′tra·cep′tive** ***adj.***, ***n.***

con·tract (kän′trakt′ *for n. & usually for vt. 1 & vi. 1*; kən trakt′ *for v. generally*) ***n.*** ⟦< L *com-*, together + *trahere*, draw⟧ an agreement between two or more people, esp. a written one enforceable by law —***vt.*** **1** to undertake by contract **2** to get or incur (a disease, debt, etc.) **3** to reduce in size; shrink —***vi.*** **1** to make a contract **2** to become smaller

con·trac·tile (kən trak′til) ***adj.*** having the power of contracting

con·trac·tion (kən trak′shən) ***n.*** **1** a contracting or being contracted **2** the shortening of a muscle of the uterus during labor **3** the shortened form of a word or phrase (Ex.: *aren't* for *are not*)

con·trac·tor (kän′trak′tər) ***n.*** a builder, etc. who contracts to do work or supply materials

con·trac·tu·al (kən trak′chōō əl) ***adj.*** of, or having the nature of, a contract —**con·trac′tu·al·ly** ***adv.***

con·tra·dict (kän′trə dikt′) ***vt.*** ⟦< L *contra-*, against + *dicere*, speak⟧ **1** to assert the opposite of (something said) **2** to deny the statement of (someone) **3** to be contrary to —**con′tra·dic′tion** ***n.*** —**con′tra·dic′to·ry** ***adj.***

con′tra·dis·tinc′tion (-dis tiŋk′shən) ***n.*** distinction by contrast

con·trail (kän′trāl′) ***n.*** ⟦CON(DENSATION) + TRAIL⟧ a white trail of water vapor in an aircraft's wake

con·tra·in·di·cate (kän′trə in′di kāt′) ***vt.*** **-cat′ed**, **-cat′ing** to make (as an indicated medical treatment) inadvisable

con·tral·to (kən tral′tō) ***n.***, *pl.* **-tos** ⟦It: see CONTRA- & ALTO⟧ **1** the range of the lowest female voice; alto **2** a voice or singer with such a range

con·trap·tion (kən trap′shən) ***n.*** ⟦< ?⟧ a contrivance or gadget

con·tra·pun·tal (kän′trə punt′'l) ***adj.*** ⟦< It *contrappunto*, counterpoint⟧ of or characterized by counterpoint

con·trar·i·an (kän trer′ē ən) ***n.***, ***adj.*** (one) characterized by thought or action that is contrary to accepted opinion

con·trar·i·wise (kän′trer′ē wīz′) ***adv.*** **1** on the contrary **2** in the opposite way, order, etc.

con·trar·y (kän′trer′ē; *for adj. 4, often* kən trer′ē) ***adj.*** ⟦< L *contra*, against⟧ **1** opposed **2** opposite in nature,

THESAURUS

continent ***n.*** mainland, continental landmass, body of land; see LAND.

continual ***a.*** repeated, constant, connected; see CONSECUTIVE, REGULAR 3.

continually ***a.*** steadily, continuously, constantly; see FREQUENTLY, REGULARLY.

continuation ***n.*** succession, line, extension, increase, endurance, prolongation, protraction, elongation, sustaining, preservation, perseverance, supplement, complement, new version; see also ADDITION 1, SEQUENCE 1.—*Ant.* END, pause, delay.

continue ***interj.*** keep on, carry on; keep going, keep talking, keep reading, etc.; keep it up.

continue ***v.*** **1** [To persist] persevere, carry forward, maintain, carry on, keep on, go on, run on, live on, never stop, sustain, promote, progress, uphold, forge ahead, remain, press onward, make headway, move ahead, keep the ball rolling*, leave no stone unturned, chip away at*; see also ADVANCE 1, ENDURE 1.—*Ant.* END, cease, give up. **2** [To resume] begin again, renew, begin over, return to, take up again, begin where one left off, be reestablished, be restored; see also RESUME.—*Ant.* HALT, discontinue, postpone.

continuing ***a.*** persevering, carrying on, progressing; see CONSTANT, REGULAR 3.

continuity ***n.*** continuousness, constancy, continuance, flow, succession, unity, sequence, chain, linking, train, progression, dovetailing, extension; see also CONTINUATION.—*Ant.* INTERRUPTION, stop, break.

continuous ***a.*** uninterrupted, unbroken, perpetual; see CONSECUTIVE, CONSTANT, REGULAR 3.

contort ***v.*** deform, misshape, twist; see DISTORT 2.

contortion ***n.*** deformity, distortion, grimace, twist, ugliness, pout, crookedness.

contour ***n.*** profile, silhouette, shape; see FORM 1.

contraband ***n.*** plunder, smuggling, illegal goods; see BOOTY.

contract ***n.*** agreement, compact, stipulation, contractual statement, contractual obligation, understanding, promise, pledge, covenant, obligation, guarantee, settlement, gentlemen's agreement, commitment, bargain, pact, arrangement, the papers, deal; see also AGREEMENT, TREATY.

contract ***v.*** **1** [To diminish] draw in, draw back, shrivel, weaken, shrink, become smaller, decline, fall away, subside, grow less, ebb, wane, lessen, lose, dwindle, recede, fall off, wither, waste, condense, constrict, deflate, evaporate; see also DECREASE 1.—*Ant.* STRETCH, strengthen, expand. **2** [To cause to diminish] abbreviate, narrow, condense; see COMPRESS, DECREASE 2. **3** [To enter into an agreement by contract] pledge, undertake, come to terms, make terms, adjust, dicker, make a bargain, agree on, limit, establish by agreement, engage, stipulate, consent, enter into a contractual obligation, sign the papers, negotiate a contract, accept an offer, obligate oneself, put something in writing, swear to, sign for, give one's word, sign on the dotted line, shake hands on it, initial, close; see also AGREE. **4** [To catch; *said of diseases*] get, incur, become infected with; see CATCH 4.

contraction ***n.*** shrinkage, shrinking, recession, reduction, withdrawal, consumption, condensation, omission, deflation, evaporation, constriction, shortening, compression, decrease, confinement, curtailment, omitting, abridgment, cutting down, consolidating, consolidation, lowering; see also ABBREVIATION, REDUCTION 1, SHRINKAGE.—*Ant.* INCREASE, expansion, extension.

contractor ***n.*** builder, jobber, subcontractor; see ARCHITECT.

contradict ***v.*** differ, call in question, repudiate; see DARE 2, OPPOSE 1.

contradiction ***n.*** incongruity, inconsistency, opposition; see DIFFERENCE 1, OPPOSITE.

contrary ***a.*** **1** [Opposed] antagonistic to, hostile, counter; see AGAINST 1, OPPOSED. **2** [Unfavorable] untimely, bad, unpropitious; see UNFAVORABLE. **3** [Obstinate] willful, contradictory, headstrong; see STUBBORN. **—on the**

order, etc.; altogether different **3** unfavorable **4** always resisting or disagreeing —*n., pl.* **-ies** the opposite —**on the contrary** as opposed to what has been said —**to the contrary** to the opposite effect —**con'tra·ri'e·ty** (-trə rī'ə tē) *n.* —**con'trar'i·ly** *adv.* —**con'trar'i·ness** *n.*

con·trast (kən trast'; *for n.* kän'trast') *vt.* ⟦< L *contra,* against + *stare,* to stand⟧ to compare so as to point out the differences —*vi.* to show differences when compared —*n.* **1** a contrasting or being contrasted **2** a striking difference between things being compared **3** a person or thing showing differences when compared with another

con·tra·vene (kän'trə vēn') *vt.* **-vened', -ven'ing** ⟦< L *contra,* against + *venire,* come⟧ **1** to go against; violate **2** to contradict —**con'tra·ven'tion** (-ven'shən) *n.*

con·tre·temps (kän'trə tän') *n., pl.* **-temps'** (-tän') ⟦Fr⟧ a confusing, embarrassing, or awkward occurrence

con·trib·ute (kən trib'yo͞ot) *vt., vi.* **-ut·ed, -ut·ing** ⟦< L: see CON- & TRIBUTE⟧ **1** to give jointly with others **2** to write (an article, etc.) as for a magazine **3** to furnish (ideas, etc.) —**contribute to** to be partly responsible for (a result) —**con·trib'u·tor** *n.* —**con·trib'u·to'ry** *adj.*

con·tri·bu·tion (kän'trə byo͞o'shən) *n.* **1** a contributing **2** something contributed, as money

con·trite (kən trīt') *adj.* ⟦< L *com-,* together + *terere,* to rub⟧ having or showing deep sorrow for having done wrong; repentant —**con·trite'ly** *adv.* —**con·trite'ness** *n.* —**con·tri'tion** (-trish'ən) *n.*

con·triv·ance (kən trī'vəns) *n.* **1** the act, way, or power of contriving **2** something contrived; device, invention, etc.

con·trive (kən trīv') *vt.* **-trived', -triv'ing** ⟦ult. < VL *contropare,* compare⟧ **1** to think up; devise **2** to make inventively **3** to bring about; manage —**con·triv'er** *n.*

con·trol (kən trōl') *vt.* **-trolled', -trol'ling** ⟦< ML *contrarotulus,* a register⟧ **1** to regulate **2** to verify (an experiment) by comparison **3** to exercise authority over; direct **4** to restrain —*n.* **1** power to direct or regulate **2** a means of controlling; check **3** an apparatus to regulate a mechanism: *usually used in pl.* —**con·trol'la·ble** *adj.*

control group the group, in an experiment, that is not given the drug, etc. being tested

controlled substance a drug whose sale is regulated by law

con·trol'ler *n.* **1** the person in charge of auditing accounts, as in a business **2** a person or device that controls

control tower an airport tower from which air traffic is directed

con·tro·ver·sial (kän'trə vur'shəl) *adj.* subject to or stirring up controversy

con'tro·ver'sy (-sē) *n., pl.* **-sies** ⟦< L *contra,* against + *vertere,* to turn⟧ a conflict of opinion; dispute

con·tro·vert (kän'trə vurt', kän'trə vurt') *vt.* **1** to argue against; dispute **2** to argue about; debate —**con'tro·vert'i·ble** *adj.*

con·tu·ma·cy (kän'tyo͞o mə sē) *n., pl.* **-cies** ⟦< L *com-,* intens. + *tumere,* swell up⟧ stubborn resistance to authority —**con'tu·ma'cious** (-mā'shəs) *adj.*

con·tu·me·ly (kän'to͞o mə lē, -to͞om lē; kən to͞o'mə lē) *n., pl.* **-lies** ⟦< L *contumelia,* abuse⟧ **1** humiliating treatment **2** a scornful insult —**con'tu·me'li·ous** (-mē'lē əs) *adj.*

con·tu·sion (kən tyo͞o'zhən, -to͞o'-) *n.* ⟦< L *com-,* intens. + *tundere,* to beat⟧ a bruise

co·nun·drum (kə nun'drəm) *n.* ⟦pseudo-L⟧ **1** a riddle whose answer contains a pun **2** any puzzling problem

con·ur·ba·tion (kän'ər bā'shən) *n.* ⟦< CON- + L *urbs,* city + -ATION⟧ a vast urban area around and including a large city

con·va·lesce (kän'və les') *vi.* **-lesced', -lesc'ing** ⟦< L *com-,* intens. + *valere,* be strong⟧ to regain strength and health —**con'va·les'cence** *n.* —**con'va·les'cent** *adj., n.*

con·vec·tion (kən vek'shən) *n.* ⟦< L *com-,* together + *vehere,* carry⟧ **1** a transmitting **2** *a*) movement of parts of a fluid within the fluid because of differences in heat, etc. *b*) heat transference by such movement —**con·vec'tion·al** *adj.* —**con·vec'tive** *adj.*

con·vene (kən vēn') *vi., vt.* **-vened', -ven'ing** ⟦< L *com-,* together + *venire,* come⟧ to assemble for a meeting —**con·ven'er** *n.*

con·ven·ience (kən vēn'yəns) *n.* ⟦see prec.⟧ **1** the quality of being convenient **2** comfort **3** anything that adds to one's comfort or saves work —**at someone's convenience** at a time or place suitable to someone

con·ven'ient (-yənt) *adj.* easy to do, use, or get to; handy —**con·ven'ient·ly** *adv.*

con·vent (kän'vənt, -vent') *n.* ⟦see CONVENE⟧ **1** the residence of a religious community, esp. of women **2** the community itself

con·ven·ti·cle (kən ven'ti kəl) *n.* ⟦see CONVENE⟧ a religious assembly held illegally and secretly

con·ven·tion (kən ven'shən) *n.* ⟦see CONVENE⟧ **1** *a*) an assembly, often periodical, of members or delegates *b*) such members or delegates **2** an agreement, as between nations **3** a customary practice **4** customary practices collectively —**con·ven'tion·eer'** *n.*

THESAURUS

contrary conversely, antithetically, inversely, contrastingly, on the other hand, at the opposite pole, on the other side; see also NOT. —**to the contrary** in disagreement with, in opposition to, in contradiction to; see AGAINST 1, ON THE CONTRARY.

contrast *n.* divergence, incompatibility, variation, variance, dissimilarity, inequality, distinction, oppositeness, contradiction, diversity, disagreement, opposition; see also DIFFERENCE 1.—*Ant.* AGREEMENT, similarity, uniformity. —**in contrast to** (or **with**) as against, opposed to, contrasting; see AGAINST 3, OPPOSED.

contrast *v.* contradict, disagree, conflict, set off, be contrary to, diverge from, depart from, deviate from, differ from, vary, show difference, stand out; see also DIFFER 1, OPPOSE 1.—*Ant.* AGREE, concur, be identical.

contribute *v.* add, share, endow, supply, furnish, bestow, present, confer, commit, dispense, settle upon, grant, afford, donate, dispense, assign, give away, subscribe, devote, will, bequeath, subsidize, hand out, ante up*, chip in*, kick in*, have a hand in, get in the act*, go Dutch*; see also GIVE 1, OFFER 1, PROVIDE 1.—*Ant.* RECEIVE, accept, take.

contributing *a.* aiding, helpful, supporting, ancillary, secondary, subordinate, valuable, sharing, causative, forming a part of, not to be overlooked, to be considered, coming into the picture; see also HELPFUL.

contribution *n.* donation, present, bestowal; see GIFT 1, GRANT.

contributor *n.* subscriber, giver, grantor; see DONOR, PATRON.

contrive *v.* make, improvise, devise; see CREATE, INVENT 1.

control *n.* **1** [The power to direct] dominion, reign, direction; see POWER 2. **2** [A device that regulates; *often plural*] instrument, switch, dial, knob, button, key, lever, handle, toggle switch, valve, regulator, governor, instrument panel, dashboard, keyboard, keypad, remote control.

control *v.* **1** [To hold in check] constrain, master, repress; see CHECK 1, RESTRAIN. **2** [To direct] lead, rule, dominate, determine, master, conquer, conduct, administer, supervise, run, coach, head, dictate, manage, influence, prevail, domineer, constrain, charge, subdue, push, coerce, oblige, train, limit, officiate, drive, move, regulate, take over, rule the roost, crack the whip, call the shots*; see also GOVERN.

controlling *a.* ruling, supervising, regulating; see GOVERNING.

controversial *a.* disputable, debatable, suspect; see UNCERTAIN.

controversy *n.* contention, debate, quarrel; see DIFFERENCE 1, DISCUSSION.

convene *v.* unite, congregate, collect; see ASSEMBLE 2, GATHER 1.

convenience *n.* **1** [The quality of being convenient] fitness, availability, accessibility, suitability, appropriateness, decency, acceptability, receptiveness, openness, accord, consonance, adaptability, usefulness. **2** [An aid to ease or comfort] ease, comfort, accommodation, help, aid, assistance, means, support, luxury, personal service, relief, cooperation, promotion, advancement, satisfaction, service, benefit, contribution, advantage, utility, labor saver, labor-saving device, modern convenience, time saver, lift; see also ADVANTAGE, APPLIANCE. —**at one's convenience** at one's leisure, conveniently, when convenient; see APPROPRIATELY.

convenient *a.* **1** [Serving one's convenience] ready, favorable, suitable, adapted, available, fitted, suited, adaptable, roomy, well-arranged, appropriate, well-planned, decent, agreeable, acceptable, useful, serviceable, assisting, aiding, beneficial, accommodating, advantageous, conducive, comfortable, opportune, timesaving, labor-saving; see also HELPFUL.—*Ant.* DISTURBING, disadvantageous, unserviceable. **2** [Near] handy, close by, easy to reach; see NEAR 1.

convention *n.* **1** [An occasion at which delegates assemble] assembly, convocation, meeting; see GATHERING. **2** [Custom] practice, habit, fashion; see CUSTOM.

con·ven'tion·al ***adj.*** **1** having to do with a convention **2** sanctioned by or following custom or usage; customary **3** formal **4** nonnuclear *[conventional* weapons*]* **—con·ven'tion·al'i·ty** (-nal'ə tē) ***n.*** **—con·ven'tion·al·ly** ***adv.***

con·ven'tion·al·ize' ***vt.*** **-ized', -iz'ing** to make conventional

con·verge (kən vʉrj') ***vi.*** **-verged', -verg'ing** ⟦< L *com-,* together + *vergere,* to bend⟧ to come together at a point **—con·ver'gence** ***n.*** **—con·ver'gent** ***adj.***

con·ver·sant (kən vʉr'sənt, kän'vər-) ***adj.*** familiar or acquainted (*with*)

con·ver·sa·tion (kän'vər sā'shən) ***n.*** a conversing; informal talk **—con'ver·sa'tion·al** ***adj.*** **—con'ver·sa'tion·al·ist** ***n.*** **—con'ver·sa'tion·al·ly** ***adv.***

conversation piece something, as an unusual article of furniture, that invites comment

con·verse[1] (kən vʉrs'; *for n.* kän'vʉrs') ***vi.*** **-versed', -vers'ing** ⟦< L *conversari,* live with⟧ to hold a conversation; talk **—*n.*** conversation

con·verse[2] (kän'vʉrs'; *also, for adj.,* kən vʉrs') ***adj.*** ⟦see CONVERT⟧ reversed in position, order, etc.; opposite; contrary **—*n.*** a thing related in a converse way; the opposite **—con·verse'ly** ***adv.***

con·ver·sion (kən vʉr'zhən) ***n.*** a converting or being converted

con·vert (kən vʉrt'; *for n.* kän'vʉrt') ***vt.*** ⟦< L *com-,* together + *vertere,* to turn⟧ **1** to change; transform **2** to change from one religion, doctrine, etc. to another **3** to exchange for something equal in value **—*vi.*** to be converted **—*n.*** a person converted, as to a religion **—con·vert'er** ***n.***

con·vert·i·ble (kən vʉrt'ə bəl) ***adj.*** that can be converted **—*n.*** an automobile with a folding or removable top

con·vex (kän veks', kän'veks') ***adj.*** ⟦< L *com-,* together + *vehere,* bring⟧ curving outward like the surface of a sphere **—con·vex'i·ty** ***n.***

con·vey (kən vā') ***vt.*** ⟦< L *com-,* together + *via,* way⟧ **1** to take from one place to another; transport; carry **2** to transmit **3** *Law* to transfer (property, etc.) **—con·vey'a·ble** ***adj.***

con·vey'ance ***n.*** **1** a conveying **2** a means of conveying; esp., a vehicle

con·vey'or (belt) a device, consisting of a continuous moving belt, for conveying things: also **con·vey'er (belt)**

con·vict (kən vikt'; *for n.* kän'vikt') ***vt.*** ⟦see CONVINCE⟧ to prove or find (a person) guilty **—*n.*** a convicted person serving a prison sentence

con·vic·tion (kən vik'shən) ***n.*** **1** a convicting or being convicted **2** a being convinced; strong belief

con·vince (kən vins') ***vt.*** **-vinced', -vinc'ing** ⟦< L *com-,* intens. + *vincere,* conquer⟧ to persuade by argument or evidence; make feel sure **—con·vinc'ing** ***adj.*** **—con·vinc'ing·ly** ***adv.***

con·viv·i·al (kən viv'ē əl) ***adj.*** ⟦< L *com-,* together + *vivere,* to live⟧ **1** festive **2** fond of eating, drinking, and good company; sociable **—con·viv'i·al'i·ty** (-al'ə tē) ***n.***

con·vo·ca·tion (kän'vō kā'shən) ***n.*** **1** a convoking **2** an ecclesiastical or academic assembly

con·voke (kən vōk') ***vt.*** **-voked', -vok'ing** ⟦< L *com-,* together + *vocare,* to call⟧ to call together; convene

con·vo·lut·ed (kän'və lo͞ot'id) ***adj.*** **1** having convolutions; coiled **2** involved; complicated

con'vo·lu'tion (-lo͞o'shən) ***n.*** ⟦< L *com-,* together + *volvere,* to roll⟧ **1** a twisting, coiling, or winding together **2** a fold, twist, or coil

con·voy (kän'voi') ***vt.*** ⟦see CONVEY⟧ to escort in order to protect **—*n.*** **1** a convoying **2** a protecting escort **3** a group of ships, vehicles, etc. traveling together

con·vulse (kən vuls') ***vt.*** **-vulsed', -vuls'ing** ⟦< L *com-,* together + *vellere,* to pluck⟧ **1** to shake violently; agitate **2** to cause to shake with laughter, rage, etc. **—con·vul'sive** ***adj.*** **—con·vul'sive·ly** ***adv.***

con·vul'sion (-vul'shən) ***n.*** **1** a violent, involuntary spasm of the muscles: *often used in pl.* **2** a fit of laughter **3** a violent disturbance

coo (ko͞o) ***vi.*** ⟦echoic⟧ to make the soft, murmuring sound of pigeons or doves **—*n.*** this sound

COO *abbrev.* chief operating officer

cook (ko͝ok) ***n.*** ⟦< L *coquere,* to cook⟧ one who prepares food **—*vt.*** to prepare (food) by boiling, baking, frying, etc. **—*vi.*** **1** to be a cook **2** to undergo cooking **—cook up** [Inf.] to devise; invent **—cook'er** ***n.***

cook'book' ***n.*** a book containing recipes and other food-preparation information

cook'er·y ***n.*** [Chiefly Brit.] the art or practice of cooking

cook'ie ***n.*** ⟦prob. < Du *koek,* cake⟧ a small, sweet cake, usually flat and either crisp or chewy: also **cook'y**, *pl.* **-ies**

cook'out' ***n.*** a meal cooked and eaten outdoors

cook'top' ***n.*** a stove top, with burners, or such a unit installed as on a kitchen counter

cool (ko͞ol) ***adj.*** ⟦OE *col*⟧ **1** moderately cold **2** tending to reduce the effects of heat *[cool* clothes*]* **3** not excited;

THESAURUS

conventional *a.* **1** [Established by convention] accustomed, prevailing, accepted, customary, traditional, regular, standard, orthodox, normal, typical, expected, usual, routine, general, everyday, commonplace, ordinary, plain, current, popular, prevalent, predominant, expected, in established usage, well-known, stereotypical; see also COMMON 1, FAMILIAR, HABITUAL.—*Ant.* UNUSUAL, atypical, unpopular. **2** [In accordance with convention] established, sanctioned, correct; see POPULAR 3. **3** [Devoted to or bound by convention] formal, stereotyped, orthodox, narrow, narrow-minded, dogmatic, parochial, strict, rigid, puritanical, inflexible, hidebound, conservative, conforming, believing, not heretical, literal, bigoted, obstinate, straight*, straight-laced; see also PREJUDICED.—*Ant.* LIBERAL, broad-minded, unconventional.

conversation *n.* talk, discussion, communion, consultation, hearing, conference, gossip, chat, rap*, dialogue, discourse, expression of views, mutual exchange, questions and answers, traffic in ideas, getting to know one another, general conversation, talking it out, heart-to-heart talk, powwow*, bull session*, chitchat; see also COMMUNICATION, SPEECH 3.

converse[2] *n.* inverse, antithesis, reverse; see OPPOSITE.

conversion *n.* changeover, transformation, metamorphosis; see CHANGE 1.

convert *n.* proselyte, neophyte, disciple; see FOLLOWER.

convert *v.* **1** [To alter the form or use] turn, transform, alter; see CHANGE 2. **2** [To alter convictions] persuade, proselytize, bring around; see CONVINCE, REFORM 1.

convertible *n.* open car, sports car, ragtop*; see AUTOMOBILE.

convey *v.* pass on, communicate, conduct; see SEND 1, 2.

convict *n.* captive, malefactor, felon; see CRIMINAL, PRISONER.

convict *v.* find guilty, sentence, pass sentence on, doom, declare guilty, bring to justice, send up; see also CONDEMN.—*Ant.* FREE, acquit, find not guilty.

conviction *n.* persuasion, confidence, reliance; see BELIEF, FAITH 2.

convince *v.* prove to, persuade, establish, refute, satisfy, assure, demonstrate, argue into, change, effect, overcome, turn, win over, bring around, put across, bring to one's senses, bring to reason, gain the confidence of, sell a bill of goods; see also PROVE, TEACH. **—convince oneself** be convinced, be converted, persuade oneself, make up one's mind; see also BELIEVE, PROVE.

convinced *a.* converted, indoctrinated, talked into something; see CHANGED 2.

convincing *a.* trustworthy, credible, acceptable, reasonable, creditable, plausible, probable, likely, presumable, possible, dependable, hopeful, worthy of confidence, to be depended on; see also RELIABLE.

convulsion *n.* paroxysm, epilepsy, attack; see FIT 1.

cook *n.* short-order cook, chef, caterer; see SERVANT.

cook *v.* prepare, fix, warm up, warm over, stew, simmer, sear, braise, scald, broil, parch, scorch, poach, dry, chafe, fricassee, percolate, steam, bake, microwave, sauté, shirr, charbroil, griddle, brew, boil, seethe, barbecue, grill, roast, pan-fry, panbroil, deep-fry, French fry, brown; see also FRY, HEAT 1. **—cook up*** make up, concoct, falsify; see ARRANGE 2, PLAN 1, 2.

cookie *n.* small cake, sweet wafer, biscuit (British); see BREAD, CAKE 2, PASTRY. *Common varieties of cookies include the following:* cream, lemon, icebox, oatmeal, vanilla, chocolate, sugar, molasses, ginger, etc., cookie; gingersnap, fig bar, raisin bar, Scotch shortbread, macaroon, tart, fruit bar, brownie, wafer.

cooking *a.* simmering, heating, scalding, brewing, stewing, steeping, frying, broiling, griddling, grilling, browning, roasting, baking; see also BOILING.

cooking *n.* cookery, dish, cuisine; see FOOD.

cool *a.* **1** [Having a low temperature] cooling, frigid, frosty, wintry, somewhat cold, chilly, shivery, chill, chilling, refrigerated, air-conditioned, snappy, nippy, biting; see also COLD 1.—*Ant.* WARM, tepid, heated. **2** [Calm] unruffled, imperturbable, composed; see CALM 1. **3** [Somewhat angry or disapproving] disapproving,

composed **4** showing dislike or indifference **5** calmly bold **6** [Inf.] without exaggeration *[a cool $1,000]* **7** [Slang] very good —***n.*** **1** a cool place, time, etc. *[the cool of the evening]* **2** [Slang] cool, dispassionate manner —***vt.***, ***vi.*** to make or become cool or colder —**cool'ly** ***adv.*** —**cool'ness** ***n.***

cool'ant ***n.*** a fluid or other substance for cooling engines, etc.

cool'er ***n.*** **1** a container or room for keeping things cool **2** a cold, refreshing drink **3** [Slang] jail: with *the*

Coo·lidge (ko͞o'lij), **(John) Calvin** 1872-1933; 30th president of the U.S. (1923-29)

coo·lie (ko͞o'lē) ***n.*** ⟦Hindi *qulī,* servant⟧ an unskilled native laborer, esp. formerly, in India, China, etc.

coon (ko͞on) ***n.*** *short for* RACCOON

coon'skin' ***n.*** the skin of a raccoon, used as a fur

coop (ko͞op) ***n.*** ⟦< L *cupa,* cask⟧ a small pen as for poultry —***vt.*** to confine as in a coop: usually with *up*

co-op (kō'äp') ***n.*** [Inf.] a cooperative

coop·er (ko͞op'ər) ***n.*** ⟦see COOP⟧ one whose work is making or repairing barrels and casks

co·op·er·ate or **co-op·er·ate** (kō äp'ər āt') ***vi.*** **-at'ed**, **-at'ing** ⟦< L *co-,* with + *opus,* work⟧ to act or work together with another or others —**co·op'er·a'tion** or **co-op'er·a'tion** ***n.***

co·op'er·a·tive or **co-op'er·a·tive** (-ər ə tiv, -ər āt'iv) ***adj.*** **1** cooperating **2** owned collectively by members who share in its benefits —***n.*** a cooperative store, etc.

co-opt (kō äpt', kō'äpt') ***vt.*** ⟦< L < *co-,* with + *optare,* choose⟧ **1** to get (an opponent) to join one's side **2** to take over for one's own purposes

co·or·di·nate or **co-or·di·nate** (kō ôrd''n it; *for v.*, -āt') ***adj.*** ⟦< L *co-,* with + *ordo,* order⟧ **1** of the same order, importance, etc. *[coordinate clauses in a sentence]* **2** of coordination or coordinates —***n.*** **1** a coordinate person or thing **2** [*pl.*] items of clothing, luggage, etc. that form a pleasing ensemble —***vt.*** **-nat'ed**, **-nat'ing** **1** to make coordinate **2** to bring into proper order or relation; adjust —**co·or'di·na'tor** or **co-or'di·na'tor** ***n.***

coordinating conjunction a conjunction connecting coordinate words, clauses, etc. (Ex.: *and, but, nor*)

co·or'di·na'tion or **co-or'di·na'tion** ***n.*** **1** a coordinating or being coordinated **2** harmonious action, as of muscles

coot (ko͞ot) ***n.*** ⟦ME *cote*⟧ **1** a ducklike water bird **2** [Inf.] an eccentric old man

coot·ie (ko͞ot'ē) ***n.*** [Slang] a louse

cop (käp) ***vt.*** **copped**, **cop'ping** ⟦prob. < L *capere,* take⟧ [Slang] to seize, steal, etc. —***n.*** [Slang] a policeman —**cop out** [Slang] **1** to renege **2** to give up; quit

co·part·ner (kō pärt'nər, kō'pärt'-) ***n.*** an associate

co·pay·ment (kō'pā'mənt) ***n.*** the part of a medical bill, often a fixed fee, not covered by insurance

cope[1] (kōp) ***vi.*** **coped**, **cop'ing** ⟦< OFr *coper,* to strike⟧ **1** to fight or contend (*with*) successfully **2** to deal with problems, etc.

cope[2] (kōp) ***n.*** ⟦< LL *cappa*⟧ **1** a large, capelike vestment worn by priests **2** any cover like this

Co·pen·hag·en (kō'pən hā'gən, -hä'-) capital of Denmark: pop. 626,000

Co·per·ni·cus (kō pur'ni kəs), **Nic·o·la·us** (nik'ə lā'əs) 1473-1543; Pol. astronomer —**Co·per'ni·can** ***adj.***

cop·i·er (käp'ē ər) ***n.*** **1** one who copies **2** a duplicating machine

co·pi·lot (kō'pī'lət) ***n.*** the assistant pilot of an airplane

cop·ing (kō'piŋ) ***n.*** ⟦< COPE[2]⟧ the top layer of a masonry wall

co·pi·ous (kō'pē əs) ***adj.*** ⟦< L *copia,* abundance⟧ plentiful; abundant —**co'pi·ous·ly** ***adv.*** —**co'pi·ous·ness** ***n.***

cop'-out' ***n.*** [Slang] a copping out, as by reneging or quitting

cop·per (käp'ər) ***n.*** ⟦< LL *cuprum*⟧ **1** a reddish-brown, ductile, metallic chemical element **2** a reddish brown —***adj.*** **1** of copper **2** reddish-brown —**cop'per·y** ***adj.***

cop'per·head' ***n.*** a poisonous North American snake

co·pra (kä'prə, kō'-) ***n.*** ⟦Port < Hindi *khoprā*⟧ dried coconut meat, the source of coconut oil

copse (käps) ***n.*** ⟦< OFr *coper,* to strike⟧ a thicket of small trees or shrubs: also **cop·pice** (käp'is)

cop·ter (käp'tər) ***n.*** *short for* HELICOPTER

cop·u·la (käp'yo͞o lə) ***n.***, *pl.* **-las** ⟦L, a link⟧ LINKING VERB —**cop'u·la'tive** (-lāt'iv) ***adj.***

cop·u·late (käp'yo͞o lāt') ***vi.*** **-lat'ed**, **-lat'ing** ⟦< L *co-,* together + *apere,* to join⟧ to have sexual intercourse —**cop'u·la'tion** ***n.***

cop·y (käp'ē) ***n.***, *pl.* **-ies** ⟦< L *copia,* plenty⟧ **1** a thing made just like another; imitation or reproduction **2** any of a number of books, magazines, etc. having the same contents **3** matter to be typeset **4** the words of an advertisement —***vt.***, ***vi.*** **cop'ied**, **cop'y·ing** **1** to make a copy of **2** to imitate **3** [Inf.] to provide (with) a copy —**cop'y·ist** ***n.***

cop'y·cat' ***n.*** an imitator: chiefly a child's term —***adj.*** done in imitation *[a copycat crime]*

cop'y·right' ***n.*** the exclusive right to the publication, sale, etc. of a literary or artistic work —***vt.*** to protect (a book, etc.) by copyright

cop'y·writ'er ***n.*** a writer of copy, esp. for advertisements

co·quette (kō ket') ***n.*** ⟦Fr⟧ a girl or woman who flirts —**co·quet'tish** ***adj.***

cor- *prefix* COM-: used before *r*

cor·al (kôr'əl) ***n.*** ⟦< Gr *korallion*⟧ **1** the hard skeleton secreted by certain marine polyps: reefs and atolls of coral occur in tropical seas **2** a piece of coral **3** a yellowish red —***adj.*** of coral

coral snake a small, poisonous snake marked with coral, yellow, and black bands

cor·bel (kôr'bəl) ***n.*** ⟦< L *corvus,* raven⟧ a piece of stone, wood, etc. projecting from a wall and supporting a cornice, arch, etc.

cord (kôrd) ***n.*** ⟦< Gr *chordē*⟧ **1** a thick string **2** a measure of wood cut for fuel (128 cubic feet) **3** a rib on the surface of a fabric **4** ribbed cloth **5** [*pl.*] corduroy trousers **6** *Anat.* any part like a cord **7** *Elec.* a slender cable

THESAURUS

distant, offended; see ANGRY, INDIFFERENT. **4** [*Excellent] neat*, splendid, great*; see EXCELLENT. —**play it cool*** hold back, underplay, exercise restraint; see RESTRAIN.

cool ***v.*** lose heat, lessen, freeze, reduce, calm, chill, cool off, become cold, be chilled to the bone, become chilly, moderate, refrigerate, air-cool, air-condition, pre-cool, frost, freeze, quick-freeze; see also FREEZE 1.—*Ant.* BURN, warm, defrost.

cool it* ***v.*** quiet down, hold back, be sensible; see CALM DOWN.

cooperate ***v.*** unite, combine, concur, conspire, pool, join forces, act in concert, hold together, stick together, comply with, join in, go along, make common cause, unite efforts, share in, second, take part, work in unison, participate, work side by side, side with, join hands, play along, play fair, throw in with*, fall in with, be in cahoots*, chip in*, stand shoulder to shoulder, pull together; see also AGREE.—*Ant.* DIFFER, act independently, diverge.

cooperation ***n.*** collaboration, participation, combination, concert, union, confederacy, confederation, conspiracy, alliance, society, company, partnership, coalition, federation, clanship, unanimity, concord, harmony; see also AGREEMENT, UNITY 2.—*Ant.* DISAGREEMENT, discord, separation.

cooperative ***a.*** cooperating, agreeing, joining, combining, collaborating, coactive, allying, uniting, concurring, participating, in joint operation; see also HELPFUL, UNITED.

cooperative ***n.*** marketing cooperative, consumer's cooperative, communal society, kibbutz, commune, collective, co-op*; see also UNITY 2.

coordinate ***v.*** harmonize, regulate, organize; see ADJUST 1, AGREE.

coordinator ***n.*** superintendent, supervisor, organizer; see EXECUTIVE.

cope (with) ***v.*** manage, deal with, handle; see ENDURE 2, FACE 1.

copulate ***v.*** sleep with, make love, go to bed, unite, couple, cover, lie with, know*, have relations, have sexual relations, have marital relations, have extramarital relations, be carnal, have carnal knowledge of someone, unite sexually, have sexual intercourse, have intercourse, have sex, breed, cohabit, fornicate, fool around*, do it*, make it*, get it on*.—*Ant.* ABSTAIN, be continent, be celibate.

copulation ***n.*** coitus, intercourse, sex, sex act, sexual union, sexual congress, coupling, mating, coition, carnal knowledge, making love; see also SEX 1, 4.

copy ***n.*** imitation, facsimile, photostat, likeness, print, similarity, mimeograph sheet, fax, simulation, mirror image, spitting image, spit and image, impersonation, offprint, xerox, semblance, forgery, counterfeit, reprint, rubbing, transcript, carbon, replica, typescript, cast, tracing, counterpart, likeness, portrait, model, reflection, representation, study, photograph, carbon copy, certified copy, office copy, typed copy, pencil copy, fair copy, ditto; see also DUPLICATE, REPRODUCTION 2.

copy ***v.*** **1** [To imitate] follow, mimic, ape; see IMITATE 1. **2** [To reproduce] duplicate, counterfeit, forge, depict, portray, picture, draw, sketch, paint, sculpt, mold, engrave; see also REPRODUCE 2.

cord ***n.*** string, cordage, fiber; see ROPE.

cord′age ***n.*** cords and ropes

cor·dial (kôr′jəl) ***adj.*** ⟦< L *cor,* heart⟧ warm; hearty; sincere —***n.*** a liqueur —**cor′di·al′i·ty** (-jē al′ə tē) ***n.*** —**cor′dial·ly** ***adv.***

cor·dil·le·ra (kôr′dil yer′ə, -də ler′ə) ***n.*** ⟦Sp < L *chorda,* a cord⟧ a system or chain of mountains

cord·ite (kôr′dīt′) ***n.*** ⟦< CORD: it is stringy⟧ a smokeless explosive made of nitroglycerin, etc.

cord·less (kôrd′lis) ***adj.*** operated by batteries, as an electric shaver

cor·don (kôr′dən) ***n.*** ⟦see CORD⟧ a line or circle of police, troops, etc. guarding an area —***vt.*** to encircle with a cordon

cor·do·van (kôr′də vən) ***n.*** ⟦after *Córdoba,* Spain⟧ a soft, colored leather

cor·du·roy (kôr′də roi′) ***n.*** ⟦prob. < CORD + obs. *duroy,* a coarse fabric⟧ a heavy, ribbed cotton fabric

core (kôr) ***n.*** ⟦prob. < L *cor,* heart⟧ **1** the central part of an apple, pear, etc. **2** the central part of anything **3** the most important part —***vt.*** **cored**, **cor′ing** to remove the core of

co·re·spond·ent (kō′ri spän′dənt) ***n.*** ⟦CO- + RESPONDENT⟧ *Law* a person charged with having committed adultery with the wife or husband from whom a divorce is being sought

co·ri·an·der (kôr′ē an′dər) ***n.*** ⟦< Gr *koriandron*⟧ an annual herb with strong-smelling, seedlike fruit used as a flavoring

cork (kôrk) ***n.*** ⟦ult. < L *quercus,* oak⟧ **1** the light, thick, elastic outer bark of an oak tree (**cork oak**) **2** a stopper made of cork, for a bottle, etc. **3** any stopper —***adj.*** of cork —***vt.*** to stop with a cork

cork′board′ ***n.*** a bulletin board made of granulated cork

cork′screw′ ***n.*** a spiral-shaped device for pulling corks out of bottles —***adj.*** spiral —***vi.***, ***vt.*** to move in a spiral; twist

corm (kôrm) ***n.*** ⟦< Gr *kormos,* a log⟧ a fleshy, underground stem, as that of the gladiolus

cor·mo·rant (kôr′mə rənt) ***n.*** ⟦< L *corvus,* raven + *marinus,* marine⟧ a large, voracious sea bird

corn[1] (kôrn) ***n.*** ⟦OE⟧ **1** a small, hard seed, esp. of a cereal grass; kernel **2** *a)* an American cereal plant with kernels growing in rows along a woody husk-enclosed core (**corncob**) *b)* the kernels **3** [Brit.] grain, esp. wheat **4** the leading cereal crop in a place **5** [Inf.] ideas, humor, etc. regarded as old-fashioned, trite, etc. —***vt.*** to pickle (meat, etc.) in brine

corn[2] (kôrn) ***n.*** ⟦< L *cornu,* horn⟧ a hard, thick, painful growth of skin, esp. on a toe

corn′ball′ ***adj.*** ⟦CORN[1], *n.* 5 + (SCREW)BALL⟧ [Slang] corny

corn bread bread made with cornmeal

cor·ne·a (kôr′nē ə) ***n.*** ⟦< L *cornu,* horn⟧ the transparent outer coat of the eyeball —**cor′ne·al** ***adj.***

cor·ner (kôr′nər) ***n.*** ⟦< L *cornu,* horn⟧ **1** the point or place where lines or surfaces join and form an angle **2** the angle formed **3** any of the angles formed at a street intersection **4** a remote, secluded place **5** a region; quarter **6** a position hard to escape from **7** a monopoly acquired on a stock or commodity so as to raise the price —***vt.*** **1** to force into a CORNER (*n.*6) **2** to get a monopoly on (a stock, etc.) —***vi.*** to turn corners: said of a vehicle —***adj.*** at, on, or for a corner —**cut corners** to cut down expenses, time, etc. —**cor′nered** ***adj.***

cor′ner·back′ ***n.*** *Football* either of two defensive backs positioned outside the linebackers

cor′ner·stone′ ***n.*** **1** a stone laid at a corner of a building, esp. at a ceremony for the beginning of construction **2** the basic part; foundation

cor·net (kôr net′) ***n.*** ⟦< L *cornu,* horn⟧ a brass instrument similar to the trumpet but more compact

corn′flow′er ***n.*** an annual plant with tiny, white, pink, or blue flowers that form a round head

cor·nice (kôr′nis) ***n.*** ⟦< Gr *korōnis,* wreath⟧ **1** a horizontal molding projecting along the top of a wall, etc. **2** a decorative cover for a curtain rod

corn′meal′ ***n.*** meal made from corn

corn′starch′ ***n.*** a powdery starch made from corn, used in cooking

corn syrup a syrup made from cornstarch

cor·nu·co·pi·a (kôr′nə kō′pē ə) ***n.*** ⟦L *cornu copiae,* horn of plenty⟧ **1** a horn-shaped container overflowing with fruits, flowers, etc. **2** an abundance

corn·y (kôr′nē) ***adj.*** **-i·er**, **-i·est** [Inf.] trite, sentimental, etc.

co·rol·la (kə rōl′ə, -räl′ə) ***n.*** ⟦< L, dim. of *corona,* crown⟧ the petals of a flower

cor·ol·lar·y (kôr′ə ler′ē) ***n.***, *pl.* **-ies** ⟦see prec.⟧ **1** a proposition that follows from one already proved **2** a normal result

co·ro·na (kə rō′nə) ***n.***, *pl.* **-nas** or **-nae** (-nē) ⟦L⟧ **1** the layer of ionized gas surrounding the sun **2** a ring of colored light seen around a luminous body, as the sun or moon

cor·o·nar·y (kôr′ə ner′ē) ***adj.*** **1** of or like a crown **2** of the arteries supplying blood to the heart muscle —***n.***, *pl.* **-ies** a thrombosis in a coronary artery: in full **coronary thrombosis**

cor·o·na·tion (kôr′ə nā′shən) ***n.*** the crowning of a sovereign

cor·o·ner (kôr′ə nər) ***n.*** ⟦ME, officer of the crown⟧ a public officer who must determine the cause of any death not obviously due to natural causes

cor·o·net (kôr′ə net′, kôr′ə net′) ***n.*** ⟦< OFr *corone,* crown⟧ **1** a small crown worn by nobility **2** a band of jewels, flowers, etc. for the head

Corp *abbrev.* **1** Corporal **2** Corporation: also **corp**

cor·po·ral[1] (kôr′pə rəl, -prəl) ***n.*** ⟦< L *caput,* head⟧ the lowest-ranking noncommissioned officer, just below a sergeant

cor·po·ral[2] (kôr′pə rəl, -prəl) ***adj.*** ⟦< L *corpus,* body⟧ of the body; bodily

corporal punishment bodily punishment, as flogging

cor·po·rate (kôr′pə rit, -prit) ***adj.*** ⟦< L *corpus,* body⟧ **1** of, like, or being a corporation **2** shared; joint

cor′po·ra′tion (-pə rā′shən) ***n.*** a legal entity, usually a group of people, that has a charter granting it certain legal powers generally given to individuals, as to buy and sell property or to enter into contracts

cor·po·re·al (kôr pôr′ē əl) ***adj.*** ⟦< L *corpus,* body⟧ **1** of or for the body; physical **2** of a material nature; tangible

corps (kôr) ***n.***, *pl.* **corps** (kôrz) ⟦< L *corpus,* body⟧ **1** a body of people associated under common direction **2** *Mil. a)* a specialized branch of the armed forces *b)* a tactical subdivision of an army

corpse (kôrps) ***n.*** ⟦var. of prec.⟧ a dead body, esp. of a person

cor·pu·lence (kôr′pyo͞o ləns, -pyə-) ***n.*** ⟦< L *corpus,* body⟧ fatness; obesity —**cor′pu·lent** ***adj.***

cor·pus (kôr′pəs) ***n.***, *pl.* **cor′po·ra** (-pə rə) ⟦L⟧ **1** a body, esp. a dead one **2** a complete collection, as of laws

Cor·pus Chris·ti (kôr′pəs kris′tē) city in SE Texas: pop. 257,000

cor·pus·cle (kôr′pus′əl) ***n.*** ⟦< L dim. of *corpus,* body⟧ an unattached body cell, esp. a red or white blood cell —**cor·pus′cu·lar** (-kyo͞o lər) ***adj.***

corpus de·lic·ti (də lik′tī′) ⟦ModL, lit., body of the crime⟧ **1** the facts constituting a crime **2** loosely, the body of a murder victim

cor·ral (kə ral′) ***n.*** ⟦Sp < L *currere,* to run⟧ an enclosure for horses, cattle, etc.; pen —***vt.*** **-ralled′**, **-ral′ling** **1** to drive into or confine in a corral **2** to surround or capture

cor·rect (kə rekt′) ***vt.*** ⟦< L *com-,* together + *regere,* to rule⟧ **1** to make right **2** to point out or mark the errors of **3** to scold or punish **4** to cure or remove (a fault, etc.)

THESAURUS

cordial ***a.*** genial, hearty, warm-hearted; see FRIENDLY.

core ***n.*** **1** [Essence] gist, kernel, heart; see ESSENCE 1. **2** [Center] hub, focus, pivot; see CENTER 1.

cork ***n.*** stopper, tap, spike; see PLUG 1.

corn[1] ***n.*** oats, millet, maize; see FOOD, GRAIN 1.

corn bread ***n.*** corn pone, hoecake, corndodger*, corncake, hot bread, johnnycake, hush puppy, spoon bread, corn tortilla; see also BREAD, CAKE 2.

corner ***n.*** **1** [A projecting edge] ridge, sharp edge, projection; see EDGE 1, RIM. **2** [A recess] niche, nook, indentation; see HOLE 1. **3** [A sharp turn] bend, veer, shift; see CURVE, TURN 2. **4** [The angle made where ways intersect] V, Y, intersection; see ANGLE 1. **5** [*Difficulty] impediment, distress, knot; see DIFFICULTY 2. —**around the corner** immediate, imminent, next; see NEAR 1, SOON. —**cut corners** cut down, shorten, reduce; see DECREASE 2.

corner ***v.*** trap, trick, fool; see CATCH 1, DECEIVE.

corny* ***a.*** old-fashioned, trite, sentimental; see DULL 4, STUPID.

corporation ***n.*** partnership, enterprise, company; see BUSINESS 4.

corps ***n.*** troops, brigade, regiment; see ARMY 2, ORGANIZATION 2.

corpse ***n.*** carcass, remains, cadaver; see BODY 2.

correct ***a.*** **1** [Accurate] exact, true, right; see ACCURATE 2. **2** [Proper] suitable, becoming, fitting; see FIT.

correct ***v.*** better, help, remove the errors of, remove the faults of, remedy, alter, rectify, accommodate for,

—*adj.* **1** conforming to an established standard **2** true; accurate; right —**cor·rect'a·ble** *adj.* —**cor·rec'tive** *adj.*, *n.* —**cor·rect'ly** *adv.* —**cor·rect'ness** *n.*

cor·rec'tion (-rek'shən) *n.* **1** a correcting or being corrected **2** a change that corrects a mistake **3** punishment to correct faults **4** *Finance* a temporary reversal in rising stock prices, etc. —**cor·rec'tion·al** *adj.*

cor·re·late (kôr'ə lāt') *vi.*, *vt.* -**lat'ed**, -**lat'ing** ⟦see COM- & RELATE⟧ to be in or bring into mutual relation —**cor're·la'tion** *n.*

cor·rel·a·tive (kə rel'ə tiv) *adj.* **1** having a mutual relationship **2** *Gram.* expressing mutual relation and used in pairs, as the conjunctions *neither* and *nor* —*n.* a correlative word, etc.

cor·re·spond (kôr'ə spänd') *vi.* ⟦< L *com-*, together + *respondere*, respond⟧ **1** to be in agreement (*with* something) **2** to be similar or equal (*to* something) **3** to communicate by letters —**cor're·spond'ing·ly** *adv.*

cor're·spond'ence *n.* **1** agreement; conformity **2** similarity **3** *a*) communication by letters *b*) the letters

cor're·spond'ent *adj.* corresponding; agreeing; analogous —*n.* **1** a thing that corresponds **2** one who exchanges letters with another **3** one hired by a newspaper, radio network, etc. to furnish news, etc. from a distant place

cor·ri·dor (kôr'ə dər, -dôr') *n.* ⟦Fr < L *currere*, to run⟧ a long hall

cor·rob·o·rate (kə räb'ə rāt') *vt.* -**rat'ed**, -**rat'ing** ⟦< L *com-*, intens. + *robur*, strength⟧ to confirm; support —**cor·rob'o·ra'tion** *n.* —**cor·rob'o·ra'tive** (-ə rāt'iv, -ər ə tiv) *adj.* —**cor·rob'o·ra'tor** *n.*

cor·rode (kə rōd') *vt.*, *vi.* -**rod'ed**, -**rod'ing** ⟦< L *com-*, intens. + *rodere*, gnaw⟧ to eat into or wear away gradually, as by rusting or the action of chemicals —**cor·ro'sion** (-rō'zhən) *n.* —**cor·ro'sive** (-rō'siv) *adj.*, *n.* —**cor·ro'sive·ly** *adv.*

cor·ru·gate (kôr'ə gāt') *vt.*, *vi.* -**gat'ed**, -**gat'ing** ⟦< L *com-*, intens. + *rugare*, to wrinkle⟧ to shape into parallel grooves and ridges —**cor'ru·ga'tion** *n.*

cor·rupt (kə rupt') *adj.* ⟦< L *com-*, together + *rumpere*, to break⟧ **1** evil; depraved **2** taking bribes **3** containing alterations, errors, etc. —*vt.*, *vi.* to make or become corrupt —**cor·rupt'i·ble** *adj.* —**cor·rup'tion** *n.* —**cor·rupt'ly** *adv.*

cor·sage (kôr säzh') *n.* ⟦see CORPS & -AGE⟧ a small bouquet for a woman to wear, as at the waist or shoulder

cor·sair (kôr'ser') *n.* ⟦< Fr < L *cursus*, course⟧ a pirate or a pirate ship

cor·set (kôr'sit) *n.* ⟦see CORPS⟧ a closefitting undergarment worn, chiefly by women, to give support to or shape the body

cor·tege or **cor·tège** (kôr tezh', -tāzh') *n.* ⟦Fr < L *cohors*⟧ **1** a retinue **2** a ceremonial procession

cor·tex (kôr'teks') *n.*, *pl.* -**ti·ces'** (-tə sēz') ⟦L, bark of a tree⟧ **1** the outer part of an internal organ; esp., the outer layer of gray matter over most of the brain **2** an outer layer of plant tissue —**cor'ti·cal** (-ti kəl) *adj.*

cor·ti·sone (kôrt'ə sōn', -zōn') *n.* ⟦so named by E. C. Kendall (1886-1972), U.S. physician⟧ a hormone used to treat adrenal insufficiency, inflammatory diseases, etc.

co·run·dum (kə run'dəm) *n.* ⟦< Sans *kuruvinda*, ruby⟧ a very hard mineral used for grinding and polishing

cor·us·cate (kôr'ə skāt') *vi.* -**cat'ed**, -**cat'ing** ⟦< L *coruscus*, vibrating⟧ to glitter; sparkle —**cor'us·ca'tion** *n.*

cor·vette (kôr vet') *n.* ⟦Fr⟧ a fast warship smaller than a destroyer and used chiefly for convoy duty

Co·sa Nos·tra (kō'sə nō'strə) *name for* MAFIA, esp. in U.S.

co·sign (kō'sīn') *vt.*, *vi.* **1** to sign (a promissory note) in addition to the maker, thus becoming responsible if the maker defaults **2** to sign jointly —**co'sign'er** *n.*

co·sig'na·to'ry (-sig'nə tôr'ē) *n.*, *pl.* -**ries** one of two or more joint signers, as of a treaty

cos·met·ic (käz met'ik) *adj.* ⟦< Gr *kosmos*, order⟧ beautifying, or correcting faults in, the face, hair, etc. —*n.* a cosmetic preparation, as lipstick —**cos·met'i·cal·ly** *adv.*

cos'me·tol'o·gy (-mə täl'ə jē) *n.* the work of a beautician —**cos'me·tol'o·gist** *n.*

cos·mic (käz'mik) *adj.* ⟦< Gr *kosmos*, universe⟧ **1** of the cosmos **2** vast

cosmic rays streams of high-energy charged particles from outer space

cos·mog·o·ny (käz mäg'ə nē) *n.* ⟦< Gr *kosmos*, universe + *-gonos*, generation⟧ **1** the study of the origin of the universe **2** *pl.* -**nies** a theory of this

cos·mol'o·gy (-mäl'ə jē) *n.* ⟦< ML⟧ **1** the scientific study of the form, evolution, etc. of the universe **2** the branch of metaphysics dealing with the origin and structure of the universe —**cos'mo·log'i·cal** (-mə läj'ə kəl) *adj.*

cos·mo·naut (käz'mə nôt') *n.* ⟦Russ *kosmonavt*⟧ a Soviet or Russian astronaut

cos·mo·pol·i·tan (käz'mə päl'ə tən) *adj.* ⟦< Gr *kosmos*, universe + *polis*, city-state⟧ **1** common to or representative of all or many parts of the world **2** not bound by local or national habits or prejudices; at home in all places —*n.* a cosmopolitan person or thing: also **cos·mop'o·lite'** (-mäp'ə līt')

cos·mos (käz'məs, -mōs') *n.* ⟦< Gr *kosmos*, universe⟧ **1** the universe considered as an orderly system **2** any complete and orderly system

co·spon·sor (kō'spän'sər) *n.* a joint sponsor, as of a proposed piece of legislation —*vt.* to be a cosponsor of —**co'spon'sor·ship'** *n.*

Cos·sack (käs'ak', -ək) *n.* a member of any of several groups of peasants that lived in autonomous communal settlements, esp. in the Ukraine, until the late 19th c.

cost (kôst) *vt.* **cost**, **cost'ing** ⟦< L *com-*, together + *stare*, to stand⟧ **1** to be obtained for (a certain price) **2** to require the expenditure, loss, etc. of —*n.* **1** the amount of

THESAURUS

make right, mend, amend, fix up, do over, reform, remodel, review, reconstruct, reorganize, edit, revise, make corrections, put to rights, put in order, doctor*, touch up, polish; see also REPAIR.

corrected *a.* rectified, amended, reformed; see CHANGED 2.

correction *n.* revision, reexamination, rereading, remodeling, rectification, editing, righting, reparation, mending, fixing, amending, changing; see also REPAIR.

corrective *a.* restorative, curative, healing; see MEDICAL.

correctly *a.* rightly, precisely, perfectly; see RIGHT 1.

correctness *n.* **1** [Accuracy] precision, exactness, rightness; see ACCURACY, TRUTH. **2** [Propriety] decency, decorum, fitness; see PROPRIETY.

correlate *v.* connect, equate, associate; see COMPARE 1.

correlation *n.* interdependence, alternation, equivalence; see RELATIONSHIP.

correspond *v.* **1** [To be alike] compare, match, be identical; see RESEMBLE. **2** [To communicate with, usually by letter] write to, reply to, drop a line to; see ANSWER 1, COMMUNICATE 2. —**correspond to** be in accord with, mesh with, harmonize with; see AGREE, FIT.

correspondence *n.* **1** [The quality of being like] conformity, equivalence, accord; see AGREEMENT, SIMILARITY. **2** [Communication, usually by letter] messages, reports, exchange of letters; see COMMUNICATION.

corresponding *a.* identical, similar, coterminous; see LIKE.

corrode *v.* rot, degenerate, deteriorate; see RUST.

corrupt *a.* exploiting, underhanded, mercenary, fraudulent, crooked, nefarious, profiteering, unscrupulous, shady*, fixed*, on the take*; see also DISHONEST.

corrupt *v.* pervert, degrade, demean, lower, pull down, reduce, adulterate, depreciate, deprave, debauch, defile, demoralize, pollute, taint, contaminate, infect, stain, spoil, blight, blemish, undermine, impair, mar, injure, harm, hurt, damage, deface, disfigure, deform, abuse, maltreat, ill-treat, outrage, mistreat, misuse, dishonor, disgrace, violate, waste, ravage, cause to degenerate; see also RAPE, WEAKEN 2.—*Ant.* CLEAN, purify, restore.

corrupted *a.* debased, perverted, depraved; see WICKED.

corruption *n.* **1** [Vice] baseness, depravity, degradation; see CRIME, EVIL 1. **2** [Conduct involving graft] extortion, exploitation, fraudulence, misrepresentation, dishonesty, bribery, racketeering; see also CRIME.

cosmetic *n.* beauty preparation, makeup, beauty-care product, cosmetics; see also MAKEUP 1. *Cosmetics include the following:* hair, body, suntan, etc., oil; hair, eye, cold, cleansing, hormone, complexion, skin, hand, etc., cream; after-shave, hand, suntan, etc., lotion; talcum, face, bath, tooth, etc., powder; eyebrow pencil, mascara, eye shadow, eyeliner, lipstick, nail polish, moisturizer, blush, blusher, rouge, foundation, powder, perfume, toilet water, cologne, hair tonic, hair dye, hair bleach, mouthwash, toothpaste, shampoo, shaving soap, shaving cream, shaving foam, depilatory, deodorant, antiperspirant; see also LOTION, PERFUME, SOAP.

cosmic *a.* vast, empyrean, grandiose; see UNIVERSAL 1.

cosmopolitan *a.* metropolitan, worldly, fashionable; see INTERNATIONAL, PUBLIC 2.

cosmos *n.* solar system, galaxy, star system; see UNIVERSE.

cost *n.* payment, value, charge; see PRICE, VALUE 1. —**at all costs** by any

money, etc. asked or paid for a thing; price **2** the time, effort, etc. needed to do something **3** loss; sacrifice **—at all costs** by any means required
co·star (kō′stär′; *for v., usually* kō′stär′) ***n.*** any featured actor or actress given equal billing with another in a movie, play, etc. —***vt., vi.*** **-starred′, -star′ring** to present as or be a costar
Cos·ta Ri·ca (käs′tə rē′kə, kôs′-, kōs′-) country in Central America: 19,730 sq. mi.; pop. 2,417,000 **—Cos′ta Ri′can**
cost-ef·fec·tive (kôst′ə fek′tiv) ***adj.*** producing good results for the amount of money spent; efficient or economical **—cost′-ef·fec′tive·ness *n.***
cos·tive (käs′tiv, kôs′-) ***adj.*** ⟦< L *constipare,* to press together⟧ constipated or constipating
cost′ly *adj.* **-li·er, -li·est** ⟦ME⟧ **1** costing much; expensive **2** magnificent **—cost′li·ness *n.***
cost of living the average cost of the necessities of life, as food, shelter, and clothes
cos·tume (käs′tōōm′, -tyōōm′) ***n.*** ⟦< L *consuetudo,* custom⟧ **1** *a)* the style of dress typical of a certain country, period, etc. *b)* a set of such clothes, as worn in a play **2** a set of outer clothes —***vt.*** **-tumed′, -tum′ing** to provide with a costume
co·sy (kō′zē) ***adj.*** **-si·er, -si·est,** ***n.,*** *pl.* **-sies** *chiefly Brit. sp. of* COZY **—co′si·ly *adv.*** **—co′si·ness *n.***
cot[1] (kät) ***n.*** ⟦< Sans *khāṭvā*⟧ a narrow, collapsible bed, as one made of canvas on a folding frame
cot[2] (kät) ***n.*** ⟦OE⟧ a small shelter
cote (kōt) ***n.*** ⟦ME⟧ a small shelter for doves, sheep, etc.
co·te·rie (kōt′ər ē) ***n.*** ⟦Fr⟧ a close circle of friends; clique
co·ter·mi·nous (kō tʉr′mə nəs) ***adj.*** CONTERMINOUS
co·til·lion (kō til′yən) ***n.*** ⟦< OFr *cote,* coat⟧ **1** an intricate, formal group dance **2** a formal ball Also sp. **co·til′lon**
cot·tage (kät′ij) ***n.*** ⟦ME⟧ **1** a small house **2** a house used for vacations **—cot′tag·er *n.***
cottage cheese a soft, white cheese made from the curds of sour milk
cot·ter pin (kät′ər) a pin with two stems that can be spread apart to fasten the pin in place
cot·ton (kät′'n) ***n.*** ⟦< Ar *quṭun*⟧ **1** the soft, white hairs around the seeds of certain plants of the mallow family **2** such a plant or plants **3** thread or cloth made of cotton **—cotton to** [Inf.] to take a liking to **—cot′ton·y *adj.***
cotton gin ⟦see GIN[2]⟧ a machine for separating cotton from the seeds
cot′ton·mouth′ *n.* WATER MOCCASIN
cot′ton·seed′ *n.* the seed of the cotton plant, yielding an oil (**cottonseed oil**) used in margarine, cooking oil, soap, etc.
cot′ton·tail′ *n.* a common American rabbit with a short, fluffy tail
cot′ton·wood′ *n.* a poplar that has seeds thickly covered with cottony or silky hairs
cot·y·le·don (kät′ə lēd′'n) ***n.*** ⟦< Gr *kotylē,* cavity⟧ the first leaf or one of the first pair of leaves produced by the embryo of a flowering plant
couch (kouch) ***n.*** ⟦< OFr *coucher,* lie down⟧ an article of furniture on which one may sit or lie down; sofa —***vt.*** **1** to place as on a couch **2** to word in a certain way; phrase; express
cou·gar (kōō′gər) ***n.*** ⟦< AmInd (Brazil)⟧ a large, powerful, tawny cat; mountain lion; puma
cough (kôf) ***vi.*** ⟦ME *coughen*⟧ to expel air suddenly and noisily from the lungs —***vt.*** to expel by coughing —***n.*** **1** the act of coughing **2** a condition causing frequent coughing **—cough up** [Slang] to hand over (money, etc.)
cough drop a small medicated tablet for the relief of coughs, etc.
could (kood) ***v.aux.*** **1** *pt. of* CAN[1] **2** an auxiliary verb generally equivalent to CAN[1], expressing esp. a shade of doubt *[it could be so]*
cou·lomb (kōō′läm′, -lōm′) ***n.*** ⟦after C. A. de *Coulomb* (1736-1806), Fr physicist⟧ a unit of electric charge equal to the charge of 6.281×10^{18} electrons
coun·cil (koun′səl) ***n.*** ⟦< L *com-,* together + *calere,* to call⟧ **1** a group of people called together for discussion, advice, etc. **2** an administrative, advisory, or legislative body **—coun′cil·man** (-mən), *pl.* **-men** (-mən), ***n.*** **— coun′cil·per′son *n.*** **—coun′cil·wom′an,** *pl.* **-wom′en, *fem.n.***
coun′ci·lor (-sə lər) ***n.*** a member of a council
coun·sel (koun′səl) ***n.*** ⟦< L *consilium*⟧ **1** advice **2** a lawyer or group of lawyers **3** a consultant —***vt.*** **-seled** or **-selled, -sel·ing** or **-sel·ling** **1** to give advice to **2** to recommend (an action, etc.)
coun′se·lor or **coun′sel·lor** (-sə lər) ***n.*** **1** an advisor **2** a lawyer **3** one in charge of children at a camp
count[1] (kount) ***vt.*** ⟦< L *computare,* compute⟧ **1** to name or add up, unit by unit, to get a total **2** to take account of; include **3** to believe to be; consider —***vi.*** **1** to name numbers or add up items in order **2** to be taken into account; have importance **3** to have a specified value: often with *for* **4** to rely or depend (*on* or *upon*) —***n.*** **1** a counting **2** the total number **3** a reckoning **4** *Law* any of the charges in an indictment
count[2] (kount) ***n.*** ⟦< L *comes,* companion⟧ a European nobleman with a rank equal to that of an English earl
count′down′ *n.* **1** the schedule of operations just before the firing of a rocket, etc. **2** the counting off, in reverse order, of time units in this schedule
coun·te·nance (koun′tə nəns, kount′'n əns) ***n.*** ⟦< L *continentia,* bearing⟧ **1** facial expression **2** the face **3** approval; support —***vt.*** **-nanced, -nanc·ing** to approve or tolerate
count·er[1] (kount′ər) ***n.*** **1** a person, device, etc. that counts something **2** a small disk for keeping count in games **3** an imitation coin or token **4** a long table, cabinet top, etc. for the displaying of goods, serving of food, etc. **—under the counter** in a secret manner: said of sales, etc. made illegally
coun·ter[2] (kount′ər) ***adv.*** ⟦< L *contra,* against⟧ in opposition; opposite **—*adj.*** contrary; opposed **—*n.*** the opposite; contrary —***vt., vi.*** to act, do, etc. counter to; oppose
counter- ⟦< L *contra-,* against⟧ *combining form* **1** contrary to *[counterclockwise]* **2** in retaliation *[counterattack]* **3** complementary *[counterpart]*
coun′ter·act′ *vt.* to act against; neutralize **—coun′ter·ac′tion *n.***
coun′ter·at·tack′ *n.* an attack made in opposition to another attack —***vt., vi.*** to attack so as to offset the enemy's attack
coun′ter·bal′ance *n.* a weight, force, etc. that balances another —***vt.*** **-anced, -anc·ing** to be a counterbalance to; offset
coun′ter·claim′ *n.* an opposing claim —***vt., vi.*** to present as, or make, a counterclaim

THESAURUS

means, in spite of difficulties, without fail; see REGARDLESS 2.
cost *v.* require, take, be priced at, be marked at, be valued at, be worth, amount to, be for sale at, command a price of, bring in, sell for, set one back*, go for.
costing *a.* as much as, to the amount of, priced at, no less than, estimated at, selling for, on sale at, reduced to, a bargain at, a steal at*.
costly *a.* high-priced, dear, precious; see EXPENSIVE.
costume *n.* attire, apparel, garb; see CLOTHES, DRESS 1.
cottage *n.* cabin, shack, small house; see HOME 1.
cotton *n.* *Cotton cloth includes the following:* chintz, organdy, dotted swiss, voile, cambric, calico, flannel, denim, ticking, net, muslin, crinoline, flannelette, gingham, jersey, lace, monk's cloth, poplin, velveteen, gabardine, crepe, twill, canvas, percale, terry cloth, sailcloth, cheesecloth, theatrical gauze.
couch *n.* sofa, lounge, davenport; see CHAIR 1, FURNITURE.
cough *n.* hem, hack, frog in one's throat; see COLD 2, ILLNESS 2.
cough *v.* hack, convulse, bark*; see CHOKE.
council *n.* advisory board, cabinet, directorate; see COMMITTEE.
counsel *n.* **1** [Advice] guidance, instruction, information; see ADVICE, SUGGESTION 1. **2** [A lawyer] attorney, legal adviser, barrister; see LAWYER. **—keep one's own counsel** be secretive, conceal oneself, keep quiet; see HIDE 1.
counsel *v.* give advice to, direct, inform; see ADVISE, TEACH.
counselor *n.* guide, instructor, mentor; see TEACHER.
count[1] ***n.*** total, number, enumeration, account, listing, statistics, returns, figures, tabulation, tally, poll, sum, outcome; see also RESULT, WHOLE.
count[1] ***v.*** compute, reckon, enumerate, number, add up, figure, count off, count up, foot up, count heads, count noses; see also ADD, TOTAL. **—count on** rely on, depend on, depend upon, lean upon, expect from, take for granted, believe in, swear by; see also TRUST 1.
counter[1] ***n.*** board, shelf, ledge; see BENCH 2, TABLE 1. **—under the counter** unofficial, black-market, underhanded; see ILLEGAL.
counteract *v.* offset, check, invalidate; see HALT, HINDER, PREVENT.

coun′ter·clock′wise′ *adj.*, *adv.* in a direction opposite to that in which the hands of a clock move
coun′ter·cul′ture *n.* a culture with a lifestyle that is opposed to the prevailing culture
coun′ter·es′pi·o·nage′ *n.* actions to prevent or thwart enemy espionage
coun′ter·feit′ (-fit′) *adj.* ⟦< OFr *contre-*, counter- + *faire*, to make⟧ **1** made in imitation of something genuine so as to deceive; forged **2** sham; pretended —*n.* an imitation made to deceive; forgery —*vt.*, *vi.* **1** to make an imitation of (money, etc.), usually to deceive **2** to pretend —**coun′ter·feit′er** *n.*
count′er·man′ (-man′) *n.*, *pl.* **-men′** (-men′) a man who serves customers at a counter, as of a lunchroom
coun′ter·mand′ (-mand′) *vt.* ⟦< L *contra*, against + *mandare*, to command⟧ to cancel or revoke by a contrary order
coun′ter·mel′o·dy *n.* a melody distinct from the principal melody
coun′ter·pane′ (-pān′) *n.* ⟦ult. < L *culcita puncta*, embroidered quilt⟧ a bedspread
coun′ter·part′ *n.* **1** one that closely resembles another **2** a copy or duplicate
coun′ter·point′ *n.* ⟦< It: see COUNTER- & POINT⟧ **1** the technique of combining two or more distinct lines of music that sound simultaneously **2** any melody played or sung against a basic melody **3** a thing set up in contrast with another
coun′ter·poise′ *n.* ⟦see COUNTER² & POISE⟧ **1** a counterbalance **2** equilibrium —*vt.* **-poised′**, **-pois′ing** to counterbalance
coun′ter·pro·duc′tive *adj.* having results contrary to those intended
coun′ter·rev′o·lu′tion *n.* a political movement against a government set up by a previous revolution —**coun′ter·rev′o·lu′tion·ar′y**, *pl.* **-ies**, *n.*, *adj.*
coun′ter·sign′ *n.* **1** a signature added to a previously signed document, as for confirmation **2** a secret signal to another, as a password —*vt.* to confirm with one's own signature
coun′ter·sink′ *vt.* **-sunk′**, **-sink′ing** **1** to enlarge the top part of (a hole) so that the head of a bolt, etc. will fit flush with the surface **2** to sink (a bolt, etc.) into such a hole
coun′ter·ten′or *n.* **1** the range of the highest male voice, above tenor **2** a voice or singer with such a range
count′er·top′ *n.* the upper surface of a COUNTER¹ (sense 4)
coun′ter·weight′ *n.* a counterbalance
count·ess (kount′is) *n.* **1** the wife or widow of a count or earl **2** a woman of nobility with a rank equal to that of a count or earl
count·less (kount′lis) *adj.* too many to count; innumerable; myriad
coun·try (kun′trē) *n.*, *pl.* **-tries** ⟦< L *contra*, against⟧ **1** an area of land; region **2** the whole land, or the people, of a nation **3** the land of one's birth or citizenship **4** land with farms and small towns **5** *short for* COUNTRY MUSIC
country club a social club with a clubhouse, golf course, etc.
coun′try·man (-mən) *n.*, *pl.* **-men** (-mən) a person of one's own country
country music popular music that derives from the rural folk music of the S U.S.
coun′try·side′ *n.* a rural region
coun′try·wide′ *adj.*, *adv.* throughout the entire nation
coun·ty (kount′ē) *n.*, *pl.* **-ties** ⟦< ML *comitatus*, jurisdiction of a count⟧ a small administrative district of a country, U.S. state, etc.
coup (ko͞o) *n.*, *pl.* **coups** (ko͞oz) ⟦Fr < L *colaphus*, a blow⟧ **1** a sudden, successful action **2** COUP D'ÉTAT
coup de grâce (ko͞o′ də gräs′) ⟦Fr, stroke of mercy⟧ **1** the blow, shot, etc. that brings death to a sufferer **2** a finishing stroke
coup d'é·tat (ko͞o′ dā tä′) ⟦Fr, stroke of state⟧ the sudden, forcible overthrow as of a ruler or government
coupe (ko͞op) *n.* ⟦< Fr *couper*, to cut⟧ a closed, two-door automobile
cou·ple (kup′əl) *n.* ⟦< L *copula*⟧ **1** a link **2** a pair of things or persons, as a man and woman who are engaged, married, etc. **3** [Inf.] a few —*vt.*, *vi.* **-pled**, **-pling** to link or unite
cou·plet (kup′lit) *n.* two successive lines of poetry, esp. two that rhyme
cou·pling (kup′liŋ) *n.* **1** a joining together **2** a mechanical device for joining parts together
cou·pon (ko͞o′pän′, kyo͞o′-) *n.* ⟦Fr < *couper*, to cut⟧ **1** a detachable printed statement on a bond, specifying the interest due at a given time **2** a certificate entitling one to a specified right, as a discount or gift
cour·age (kur′ij) *n.* ⟦< L *cor*, heart⟧ the quality of being brave; valor
cou·ra·geous (kə rā′jəs) *adj.* having or showing courage; brave —**cou·ra′geous·ly** *adv.*
cou·ri·er (koor′ē ər, kur′-) *n.* ⟦< L *currere*, to run⟧ a messenger
course (kôrs) *n.* ⟦< L *currere*, to run⟧ **1** an onward movement; progress **2** a way, path, or channel **3** the direction taken **4** a regular manner of procedure or conduct [our wisest *course*] **5** a series of like things in order **6** a part of a meal served at one time **7** *Educ.* *a*) a complete series of studies, as for a degree *b*) any of the separate units of such a series —*vi.* **coursed**, **cours′ing** to run or race —**in due course** in the usual sequence (of events) —**in the course of** during —**of course** **1** naturally **2** certainly
cours·er (kôr′sər) *n.* a graceful, spirited, or swift horse
court (kôrt) *n.* ⟦< L *cohors*, enclosure⟧ **1** a courtyard **2** a short street **3** a space for playing a game, as basketball **4** *a*) the palace, or the family, etc., of a sovereign *b*) a

THESAURUS

counterfeit *a.* sham, spurious, fictitious; see FALSE 3.
counterfeit *v.* make counterfeit money, coin (British), make funny money*, circulate bad money; see also FORGE.
counterfeiter *n.* forger, paperhanger*, plagiarist; see CRIMINAL.
countless *a.* innumerable, incalculable, numberless; see INFINITE, MANY.
country *a.* **1** [*Said of people*] rural, homey, unpolished; see IGNORANT 2, RUDE 1. **2** [*Said of areas*] rustic, agrarian, provincial; see RURAL.
country *n.* **1** [Rural areas] farms, farmland, farming district, rural region, rural area, range, country district, backcountry, bush, forests, woodlands, backwoods, sparsely settled areas, sticks*, the boondocks*, boonies*; see also FARM, FOREST.—*Ant.* CITY, borough, municipality. **2** [A nation] government, a people, a sovereign state; see NATION 1. **3** [Land and all that is associated with it] homeland, native land, fatherland; see LAND 2.
countryside *n.* rural district, farmland, woods; see COUNTRY 1.
county *n.* province, constituency, shire; see AREA, REGION 1.
couple *n.* **1** [A pair] two, set, brace; see PAIR. **2** [*A few] two, several, a handful; see FEW.
couple *v.* unite, come together, link; see COPULATE, JOIN 1.
coupon *n.* token, box top, order blank, detachable portion, premium certificate, ticket; see also CARD, TICKET 1.
courage *n.* bravery, valor, boldness, fearlessness, spirit, audacity, audaciousness, temerity, manliness, pluck, mettle, enterprise, stoutheartedness, firmness, self-reliance, hardihood, heroism, gallantry, daring, prowess, power, resolution, dash, recklessness, defiance, the courage of one's convictions, spunk*, grit, backbone, guts*, what it takes*, moxie*, nerve; see also STRENGTH.—*Ant.* FEAR, cowardice, timidity.
courageous *a.* daring, gallant, intrepid; see BRAVE.
course *n.* **1** [A route] passage, path, way; see ROUTE 1. **2** [A prepared way, especially for racing] lap, cinder path, track; see ROAD 1. **3** [A plan of study] subject, studies, curriculum; see EDUCATION 1. **4** [A series of lessons] classes, lectures, seminar; see EDUCATION 1. —**in due course** in due time, properly, conveniently; see APPROPRIATELY. —**in the course of** during, in the process of, when; see WHILE 1. —**of course** certainly, by all means, indeed; see SURELY. —**off course** misdirected, erratic, going the wrong way; see WRONG 2. —**on course** on target, correct, going in the right direction; see ACCURATE 2.
court *n.* **1** [An enclosed, roofless area] square, courtyard, patio; see YARD 1. **2** [An instrument for administering justice] tribunal, bench, magistrate, bar, session. *Types of courts include the following:* the Supreme Court of the United States, appellate court of the United States, federal court, state supreme court, district court, county court, justice's court, magistrate's court, mayor's court, police court. **3** [A sovereign's family, attendants, etc.] lords and ladies, attendants, royal household; see GOVERNMENT 2, ROYALTY, RULER 1. **4** [An area for playing certain games] arena, rink, ring; see FIELD 2.
court *v.* attract, allure, solicit, beseech, entice, pursue, accompany, follow, plead, make love, pay court, pay attentions to, pay court to, make

sovereign and councilors, etc. as a governing body *c)* a formal gathering held by a sovereign **5** attention paid to someone in order to get something **6** *Law a)* a judge or judges *b)* a place where trials are held —***vt.*** **1** to pay attention to (a person) so as to get something **2** to seek as a mate; woo **3** to try to get *[to court favor]* —***vi.*** to carry on a courtship

cour·te·ous (kurt′ē əs) ***adj.*** ⟦see prec. & -EOUS⟧ polite and gracious —**cour′te·ous·ly** ***adv.***

cour·te·san (kôrt′ə zən) ***n.*** ⟦see COURT⟧ a prostitute: also **cour′te·zan**

cour·te·sy (kurt′ə sē) ***n.***, *pl.* **-sies** **1** courteous behavior **2** a polite or considerate act or remark —***adj.*** provided free; complimentary

court′house′ ***n.*** **1** a building housing law courts **2** a building housing offices of a county government

cour·ti·er (kôrt′ē ər, -yər) ***n.*** an attendant at a royal court

court′ly ***adj.*** **-li·er, -li·est** suitable for a king's court; dignified; elegant —**court′li·ness** ***n.***

court′-mar′tial ***n.***, *pl.* **courts′-mar′tial**; for 2, now often **court′-mar′tials** **1** a court in the armed forces for the trial of persons accused of breaking military law **2** a trial by a court-martial **3** a conviction by a court-martial —***vt.*** **-tialed** or **-tialled**, **-tial·ing** or **-tial·ling** to try or convict by a court-martial

court reporter one who records exactly what is said in a courtroom during a trial

court′room′ ***n.*** *Law* a room in which trials are held

court′ship′ ***n.*** the act, process, or period of wooing

court′side′ ***n.*** *Sports* the area immediately around a basketball court, tennis court, etc.

court′yard′ ***n.*** a space enclosed by walls, adjoining or within a large building

cous·cous (ko͞os′ko͞os′) ***n.*** ⟦Fr < Ar *kaskasa,* to grind⟧ a N African dish made with crushed grain, served as with lamb in a spicy sauce

cous·in (kuz′ən) ***n.*** ⟦ult. < L *com-,* with + *soror,* sister⟧ **1** the son or daughter of one's uncle or aunt **2** loosely, any relative by blood or marriage

cous′in·age (-ij) ***n.*** **1** the relationship between cousins **2** a group of cousins or relatives

cou·tu·ri·er (ko͞o′to͝or ē ā′) ***n.*** ⟦Fr⟧ a designer of women's fashions —**cou′tu·ri·ère′** (-ē er′) ***fem.n.***

cove (kōv) ***n.*** ⟦OE *cofa,* cave⟧ a small bay or inlet

cov·en (kuv′ən) ***n.*** ⟦see CONVENE⟧ a gathering or meeting, esp. of witches

cov·e·nant (kuv′ə nənt) ***n.*** ⟦see CONVENE⟧ an agreement; compact —***vt.*** to promise by a covenant —***vi.*** to make a covenant

cov·er (kuv′ər) ***vt.*** ⟦< L *co-,* intens. + *operire,* to hide⟧ **1** to place something on or over **2** to extend over **3** to clothe **4** to conceal; hide **5** to shield, protect, or watch (someone or something) **6** to include; deal with *[to cover a subject]* **7** to protect financially *[to cover a loss]* **8** to accept (a bet) **9** to travel over **10** to point a firearm at **11** *Journalism* to gather the details of (a news story) —***vi.*** **1** to spread over a surface, as a liquid does **2** to provide an alibi *(for)* —***n.*** **1** anything that covers, as a lid, top, etc. **2** a shelter for protection **3** a tablecloth and setting **4** COVER CHARGE **5** something used to hide one's real actions, etc. —**cover up** to keep blunders, crimes, etc. from being known —**take cover** to seek shelter —**under cover** in secrecy or concealment

cov′er·age (-ij) ***n.*** **1** the amount, extent, etc. covered by something **2** *Insurance* the risks covered by a policy

cov′er·all′ ***n.*** *[usually pl.]* a one-piece outer garment, often worn over regular clothing while working, etc.

cover charge a fixed charge in addition to the cost of food and drink, as at a nightclub or restaurant

cover crop a crop, as clover, grown to prevent erosion and restore soil fertility

covered wagon a large wagon with an arched cover of canvas

cov′er·ing ***n.*** anything that covers

cov′er·let (-lit) ***n.*** ⟦< OFr *covrir,* to cover + *lit,* bed⟧ a bedspread

cover letter an explanatory letter sent with an enclosure or package: also **covering letter**

cover story the article in a magazine that deals with the subject depicted on the cover

cov·ert (kō′vərt, kuv′ərt) ***adj.*** ⟦see COVER⟧ hidden or disguised —***n.*** a protected place, as for game —**cov′ert·ly** ***adv.***

cov′er-up′ ***n.*** an attempt to hide blunders, crimes, etc.

cov·et (kuv′it) ***vt., vi.*** ⟦< L *cupiditas,* cupidity⟧ to want intensely (esp., something that another person has)

cov′et·ous ***adj.*** tending to covet; greedy —**cov′et·ous·ly** ***adv.*** —**cov′et·ous·ness** ***n.***

cov·ey (kuv′ē) ***n.***, *pl.* **-eys** ⟦< OFr *cover,* to hatch⟧ a small flock of birds, esp. partridges or quail

cow[1] (kou) ***n.*** ⟦OE *cu*⟧ **1** the mature female of domestic cattle, valued for its milk **2** the mature female of certain other mammals, as the whale

cow[2] (kou) ***vt.*** ⟦< ON *kūga,* subdue⟧ to make timid; intimidate

cow·ard (kou′ərd) ***n.*** ⟦ult. < L *cauda,* tail⟧ a person who lacks courage, esp. one who is shamefully afraid

cow′ard·ice′ (-ər dis′) ***n.*** lack of courage

cow′ard·ly ***adj.*** of or like a coward —***adv.*** in the manner of a coward —**cow′ard·li·ness** ***n.***

THESAURUS

overtures, go courting, woo, propose, ask in marriage, set one's cap for*, pop the question*, go steady*, go together*, go with*, make a play for*; see also DATE 2.

courteous ***a.*** courtly, affable, cultivated; see POLITE.

courteously ***a.*** civilly, affably, obligingly; see POLITELY.

courtesy ***n.*** **1** [Courteous conduct] kindness, friendliness, affability, courteousness, gentleness, consideration, thoughtfulness, sympathy, geniality, cordiality, graciousness, tact, good manners, politeness, refinement, chivalry, gallantry, respect, deference, polished manners, good breeding; see also GENEROSITY, KINDNESS 1. **2** [Courteous act] favor, polite gesture, charitable act; see KINDNESS 2.

cousin ***n.*** kin, an aunt's child, an uncle's child; see RELATIVE.

cove ***n.*** inlet, sound, lagoon; see BAY.

cover ***n.*** **1** [A covering object] covering, ceiling, canopy, hood, sheath, sheet, awning, tent, umbrella, dome, stopper, lid, canvas, tarpaulin, book cover, folder, wrapper, wrapping paper, jacket, case, spread, tarp*; see also BLANKET, ENVELOPE, FOLDER, ROOF. **2** [A covering substance] paint, varnish, polish; see COAT 3, SHEET 2. **3** [Shelter] harbor, asylum, refuge; see RETREAT 2, SHELTER. **—take cover** conceal oneself, take shelter, go indoors; see HIDE 1. **—under cover** secretive, hiding, concealed; see HIDDEN.

cover ***v.*** **1** [To place as a covering] carpet, put on, overlay, surface, board up, superimpose, black in, black out; see also SPREAD 3. **2** [To wrap] envelop, enshroud, encase; see WRAP. **3** [To protect] shield, screen, house; see DEFEND 1, 2, SHELTER. **4** [To hide] screen, camouflage, mask; see DISGUISE, HIDE 1. **5** [To include] embrace, comprise, incorporate; see INCLUDE 1. **6** [To travel] traverse, journey over, cross; see TRAVEL. **7** [To send down in plenty] drench, engulf, overcome; see FLOOD. **8** [To report upon, especially for a newspaper] recount, narrate, relate; see BROADCAST, RECORD 3. **—cover up** lie about, keep secret, keep the lid on*; see DEFEND 1, 2, SHELTER.

covered ***a.*** **1** [Provided with cover] topped, lidded, roofed, wrapped, enveloped, bound, painted, varnished, coated, camouflaged, sheltered, shielded, disguised, masked, secreted, protected, concealed; see also HIDDEN.—*Ant.* OBVIOUS, revealed, exposed. **2** [Plentifully bestrewn] scattered with, sprinkled over, spattered, spangled, dotted, strewn with, starred, starry with, flowered, spotted with, sown, dusted over, powdered, spread with.—*Ant.* EMPTY, bare, unfurnished. **3** [Attended to] noted, taken note of, reported, recorded, written, included, marked, explored, regarded, scrutinized, examined, surveyed, investigated, observed, looked to, hurdled, cared for; see also DONE 1, RECOGNIZED.—*Ant.* unheeded, unnoticed, passed over.

covering ***n.*** concealment, top, spread; see COVER 1.

covet ***v.*** desire, envy, wish for; see WANT 1.

cow[1] ***n.*** heifer, milk cow, dairy cow, bovine, bossy*; see also CATTLE.

coward ***n.*** sneak, milksop, shirker, deserter, weakling, alarmist, slacker*, quitter*, chicken*, lily-liver*, scaredy-cat*, chicken-heart*, fraidy-cat*, yellow-belly*.

cowardice ***n.*** cowardliness, timidity, faintheartedness, fear, weakness, quailing, lack of courage, apprehension, shyness, dread, fearfulness, yellow streak*, cold feet*; see also FEAR.—*Ant.* bravery, valor, fearlessness.

cowardly ***a.*** timid, frightened, afraid, fearful, shy, backward, cowering, apprehensive, nervous, anxious, dismayed, fainthearted, panicky, scared, scary*, jittery*, craven, mean-spirited, weak, soft, chicken-livered*, lily-livered*, yellow*, skulking, sneaking, cringing, trembling, shaken, crouching, running, quaking, afraid of one's own shadow, shaking like a leaf, shaking in one's boots*; see also AFRAID, WEAK 3.—*Ant.* BRAVE, fear-

cow'boy' *n.* a ranch worker who herds cattle: also **cow'hand'** —**cow'girl'** *fem.n.*
cow·er (kou'ər) *vi.* ⟦ME *couren*⟧ to crouch or huddle up, as from fear or cold; shrink; cringe
cow'hide' *n.* **1** the hide of a cow **2** leather from it
cowl (koul) *n.* ⟦< L *cucullus,* hood⟧ **1** a monk's hood or a monk's cloak with a hood **2** a hood-shaped part or structure
cow·lick (kou'lik') *n.* ⟦< its looking as if licked by a cow⟧ a tuft of hair that cannot easily be combed flat
cowl·ing (koul'iŋ) *n.* ⟦see COWL⟧ a metal covering for an airplane engine, etc.
co-work·er (kō'wur'kər) *n.* a fellow worker
cow'poke' *n.* [Inf.] COWBOY
cow pony a horse for herding cattle
cow'pox' *n.* a disease of cows: a vaccine with its virus gives temporary immunity to smallpox
cox·comb (käks'kōm') *n.* ⟦for *cock's comb*⟧ a silly, vain fellow; dandy
cox·swain (käk'sən, -swān') *n.* ⟦< *cock*, small boat + SWAIN⟧ one who steers a boat or racing shell
coy (koi) *adj.* ⟦ME, quiet⟧ **1** bashful; shy **2** pretending to be shy —**coy'ly** *adv.* —**coy'ness** *n.*
coy·o·te (kī ōt'ē, kī'ōt') *n.* ⟦< AmInd (Mex)⟧ a small, wolf-like animal of North America
coz·en (kuz'ən) *vt., vi.* ⟦< ME *cosin,* fraud⟧ to cheat; deceive —**coz'en·age** *n.*
co·zy (kō'zē) *adj.* **-zi·er, -zi·est** ⟦Scot⟧ warm and comfortable; snug —*n., pl.* **-zies** a padded cover for a teapot, to keep the tea hot —**cozy up to** [Inf.] to try to ingratiate oneself with —**co'zi·ly** *adv.* —**co'zi·ness** *n.*
CPA *abbrev.* Certified Public Accountant
CPI *abbrev.* consumer price index
CPO *abbrev.* Chief Petty Officer
CPR *abbrev.* cardiopulmonary resuscitation
CPU (sē'pē'yoo') *n.* central processing unit: also **cpu**
Cr *Chem. symbol for* chromium
crab (krab) *n.* ⟦OE *crabba*⟧ **1** a crustacean with four pairs of legs and a pair of pincers **2** a peevish person —*vi.* **crabbed, crab'bing** [Inf.] to complain
crab apple **1** a small, very sour apple **2** a tree bearing crab apples: also **crab tree**
crab·bed (krab'id) *adj.* ⟦< CRAB (APPLE)⟧ **1** peevish **2** hard to read or understand, as handwriting —**crab'bed·ness** *n.*
crab'by *adj.* **-bi·er, -bi·est** ⟦see prec.⟧ cross and complaining —**crab'bi·ly** *adv.* —**crab'bi·ness** *n.*
crab grass a weedy grass, with freely rooting stems, that spreads rapidly
crack[1] (krak) *vi.* ⟦< OE *cracian,* resound⟧ **1** to make a sudden, sharp noise, as in breaking **2** to break or split, usually without separation of parts **3** to rasp or shift erratically in register: said of the voice **4** [Inf.] to break down as from strain —*vt.* **1** to cause to make a sharp, sudden noise **2** to cause to break or split **3** to break down (petroleum) into the lighter hydrocarbons of gasoline, etc. **4** to hit hard **5** to solve **6** [Inf.] to break into or force open **7** [Slang] to make (a joke) —*n.* **1** a sudden, sharp noise **2** a partial break; fracture **3** a chink; crevice **4** a cracking of the voice **5** a sudden, sharp blow **6** [Inf.] an attempt or try **7** [Slang] a joke or gibe —*adj.* [Inf.] excellent; first-rate —**crack down** (**on**) to become strict (with) —**cracked up to be** [Inf.] believed to be — **crack up** **1** to crash **2** [Inf.] *a*) to break down physically or mentally *b*) to laugh or cry
crack[2] (krak) *n.* [Slang] a highly potent and purified form of cocaine for smoking
crack'down' *n.* a resorting to strict or stricter discipline or punishment
cracked *adj.* **1** having a crack or cracks **2** sounding harsh or strident **3** [Inf.] crazy
crack'er *n.* **1** a firecracker **2** a thin, crisp wafer
crack'er·jack' *adj.* [Slang] outstanding; excellent —*n.* [Slang] an excellent person or thing
crack'head' *n.* [Slang] a habitual user of CRACK[2]
crack·le (krak'əl) *vi.* **-led, -ling** ⟦ME *crakelen,* to crack⟧ to make a series of slight, sharp, popping sounds —*n.* **1** a series of such sounds **2** the fine, irregular surface cracks on some pottery, etc.
crack'pot' *n.* [Inf.] a crazy or eccentric person —*adj.* [Inf.] crazy or eccentric
crack'up' *n.* **1** a crash **2** [Inf.] a physical or mental breakdown
-cra·cy (krə sē) ⟦< Gr *kratos,* rule⟧ *combining form* a (specified) type of government; rule by *[autocracy]*
cra·dle (krād''l) *n.* ⟦OE *cradol*⟧ **1** a baby's small bed, usually on rockers **2** infancy **3** the place of a thing's beginning **4** anything like a cradle —*vt.* **-dled, -dling** **1** to place, rock, or hold in or as in a cradle **2** to take care of in infancy
cra'dle·song' *n.* a lullaby
craft (kraft) *n.* ⟦OE *cræft,* power⟧ **1** a special skill or art **2** an occupation requiring special skill **3** the members of a skilled trade **4** guile; slyness **5** *pl.* **craft** a boat, ship, or aircraft
crafts·man (krafts'mən) *n., pl.* **-men** (-mən) a skilled worker; artisan —**crafts'man·ship'** *n.*
craft'y *adj.* **-i·er, -i·est** ⟦ME *crafti,* sly⟧ subtly deceitful; sly —**craft'i·ly** *adv.* —**craft'i·ness** *n.*
crag (krag) *n.* ⟦< Celt⟧ a steep, rugged rock rising from a rock mass —**crag'gy, -gi·er, -gi·est,** *adj.*
cram (kram) *vt.* **crammed, cram'ming** ⟦OE *crammian*⟧ **1** to pack full or too full **2** to stuff; force **3** to feed to excess —*vi.* **1** to eat too much or too quickly **2** to study a subject in a hurried, intensive way, as for an examination
cramp (kramp) *n.* ⟦< OFr *crampe,* bent⟧ **1** a sudden, painful, involuntary contraction of a muscle from chill, strain, etc. **2** [*usually pl.*] abdominal or uterine spasms and pain —*vt.* **1** to cause a cramp or cramps in **2** ⟦< MDu *krampe,* bent in⟧ to hamper; restrain
cramped *adj.* **1** confined or restricted **2** irregular and crowded, as some handwriting
cran·ber·ry (kran'ber'ē, -bər ē) *n., pl.* **-ries** ⟦< Du *kranebere*⟧ **1** a firm, sour, edible, red berry, the fruit of an evergreen shrub **2** the shrub
crane (krān) *n.* ⟦OE *cran*⟧ **1** a large wading bird with very long legs and neck **2** a machine for lifting or moving heavy weights, using a movable projecting arm or a

THESAURUS

less, open.
cowboy *n.* cowhand, hand, wrangler, rider, herder, cattle-herder, drover, gaucho, cowpuncher*, cowpoke*, buckaroo; see also RANCHER.
cower *v.* cringe, shrink, fear, run, quake, shiver, tremble, shake, snivel, flinch, quail; see also GROVEL.
coy *a.* bashful, shy, demure; see HUMBLE 1.
cozy *a.* secure, sheltered, snug; see COMFORTABLE 2, SAFE 1.
crab *n.* crayfish, crustacean, seafood; see SHELLFISH.
crack[1]* *a.* first-rate, first-class, skilled; see ABLE, EXCELLENT.
crack[1] *n.* **1** [An incomplete break] chink, split, cut; see HOLE 1. **2** [A crevice] cleft, fissure, rift; see HOLE 1. **3** [A blow] hit, thwack, stroke; see BLOW. **4** [*A witty or brazen comment] return, witticism, jest; see JOKE, REMARK.
crack[1] *v.* **1** [To become cracked] cleave, burst, split; see BREAK. **2** [To cause to crack] cleave, split, sever; see BREAK. **3** [To damage] injure, hurt, impair; see DAMAGE. **4** [*To become mentally deranged] become insane, go crazy, have a nervous breakdown; see CRACK UP 2. **5** [To solve] figure out, answer, decode; see SOLVE. —**crack a joke** quip, jest, jape; see JOKE. —**crack up** **1** [*To crash a vehicle] collide, be in an accident, smash up; see CRASH 4. **2** [*To fail suddenly in health, mind, or strength] go to pieces, fail, deteriorate, sicken, go insane, go crazy, become demented, freak out*, have a nervous breakdown, go out of one's mind, go off one's rocker*, blow a fuse*, go off the deep end*; see also WEAKEN 1. **3** [*To laugh] roar, howl, roll in the aisles*; see LAUGH. —**get cracking*** get going, get a move on*, start; see BEGIN 2, MOVE 1.
cracked *a.* shattered, split, fractured; see BROKEN 1.
cracker *n.* wafer, cookie, soda cracker, oyster cracker, biscuit, saltine, hardtack, sea biscuit, wheat biscuit; see also BREAD.
cradle *n.* trundle bed, crib, bassinet; see BED 1, FURNITURE.
craft *n.* **1** [Skill] proficiency, competence, aptitude; see ABILITY. **2** [Trade] occupation, career, work; see JOB 1, PROFESSION 1. **3** [Ship] vessel, aircraft, spacecraft; see BOAT, SHIP.
craftsman *n.* artisan, skilled worker, journeyman, maker, technician, manufacturer, machinist, handcraftsman, mechanic; see also ARTIST, LABORER, SPECIALIST.
crafty *a.* clever, sharp, shrewd; see INTELLIGENT.
cram *v.* **1** [To stuff] crush, jam, press; see COMPRESS, PACK. **2** [To study hurriedly] review, bone up*, burn the midnight oil; see STUDY.
cramp *n.* spasm, crick, pang; see PAIN 2.
cramped *a.* narrow, confined, restraining; see RESTRICTED, UNCOMFORTABLE 1.

horizontal traveling beam —*vt.*, *vi.* **craned, cran'ing** to stretch (the neck)
cra·ni·um (krā'nē əm) *n.*, *pl.* **-ni·ums** or **-ni·a** (-ə) ⟦< Gr *kranion*⟧ the skull, esp. the part containing the brain —**cra'ni·al** *adj.*
crank (kraŋk) *n.* ⟦OE *cranc-*, something twisted⟧ **1** a handle or arm bent at right angles and connected to a machine shaft to transmit motion **2** [Inf.] an eccentric or irritable person —*vt.* to start or operate by a crank —**crank out** [Inf.] to produce steadily and prolifically
crank'case' *n.* the metal casing that encloses the crankshaft of an internal-combustion engine
crank'shaft' *n.* a shaft with one or more cranks for transmitting motion
crank'y *adj.* **-i·er, -i·est** **1** apt to operate poorly **2** irritable **3** eccentric —**crank'i·ly** *adv.* —**crank'i·ness** *n.*
cran·ny (kran'ē) *n.*, *pl.* **-nies** ⟦< VL *crena*, a notch⟧ a crevice; crack
crap (krap) *n.* ⟦< ML *crappa*, chaff⟧ [Slang] **1** nonsense **2** junk; trash **3** excrement: somewhat vulgar —**crap'py, -pi·er, -pi·est,** *adj.*
crape (krāp) *n.* **1** CREPE (sense 1) **2** a piece of black crepe as a sign of mourning
crap·pie (krap'ē) *n.* a small North American sunfish
craps (kraps) *n.* ⟦Fr *crabs*⟧ a gambling game played with two dice
crap'shoot' *n.* [Inf.] a very risky undertaking
crap·shoot·er (krap'sho͞ot'ər) *n.* a gambler at craps
crash (krash) *vi.* ⟦ME⟧ **1** to fall, collide, or break with a loud noise **2** to collapse; fail **3** [Slang] to sleep or get a temporary place to sleep —*vt.* **1** to cause (a car, airplane, etc.) to crash **2** to force with or as with a crashing noise: with *in, out, through*, etc. **3** [Inf.] to get into (a party, etc.) without an invitation, etc. —*n.* **1** a loud, sudden noise **2** a crashing **3** a sudden collapse, as of business —*adj.* [Inf.] using all possible resources, effort, and speed [a *crash* program to build roads]
crash'-land' *vt.*, *vi.* to bring (an airplane) down in a forced landing, esp. without use of the landing gear —**crash landing**
crash pad [Slang] a place to live or sleep temporarily
crass (kras) *adj.* ⟦L *crassus*, thick⟧ **1** tasteless, insensitive, etc. **2** materialistic —**crass'ly** *adv.* —**crass'ness** *n.*
-crat (krat) ⟦< Gr *kratos*, rule⟧ *combining form* member or supporter of (a specified kind of) government
crate (krāt) *n.* ⟦L *cratis*, wickerwork⟧ a packing case made of slats of wood —*vt.* **crat'ed, crat'ing** to pack in a crate
cra·ter (krāt'ər) *n.* ⟦< Gr *kratēr*, mixing bowl⟧ **1** a bowl-shaped cavity, as at the mouth of a volcano **2** a pit made by an exploding bomb, etc. —*vt.* to make craters in —*vi.* to form craters
cra·vat (krə vat') *n.* ⟦< Fr⟧ a necktie
crave (krāv) *vt.* **craved, crav'ing** ⟦OE *crafian*⟧ **1** to ask for earnestly; beg **2** to desire strongly
cra·ven (krā'vən) *adj.* ⟦< L *crepare*, to rattle⟧ cowardly —*n.* a coward —**cra'ven·ly** *adv.* —**cra'ven·ness** *n.*
crav'ing *n.* an intense and prolonged desire, as for affection or for a food or drug
craw (krô) *n.* ⟦ME *craue*⟧ **1** the crop of a bird **2** the stomach
craw·fish (krô'fish') *n.*, *pl.* **-fish'** or (for different species) **-fish'es** crayfish
crawl (krôl) *vi.* ⟦< ON *krafla*⟧ **1** to move slowly by dragging the body along the ground **2** to go on hands and knees; creep **3** to move slowly **4** to move or act in a servile manner **5** to swarm (*with* crawling things) —*n.* **1** a slow movement **2** an overarm swimming stroke
crawl space an unfinished space, as under a floor, allowing access to wiring, plumbing, etc.
crawl'y *adj.* **-i·er, -i·est** CREEPY
cray·fish (krā'fish') *n.*, *pl.* **-fish'** or (for different species) **-fish'es** ⟦< OHG *krebiz*⟧ a freshwater crustacean somewhat like a little lobster
cray·on (krā'ən, -än') *n.* ⟦Fr, pencil < L *creta*, chalk⟧ **1** a small stick of chalk, charcoal, or colored wax, used for drawing, coloring, or writing **2** a drawing made with crayons —*vt.* to draw or color with crayons
craze (krāz) *vt.*, *vi.* **crazed, craz'ing** ⟦ME *crasen*, to crack⟧ to make or become insane —*n.* a fad
cra·zy (krā'zē) *adj.* **-zi·er, -zi·est** ⟦< CRAZE⟧ **1** unsound of mind; insane **2** [Inf.] foolish; not sensible **3** [Inf.] very enthusiastic or eager —*n.*, *pl.* **-zies** [Slang] a crazy person —**like crazy** [Inf.] with great energy, intensity, etc. —**cra'zi·ly** *adv.* —**cra'zi·ness** *n.*
crazy bone FUNNY BONE
crazy quilt **1** a patchwork quilt with no regular design **2** a hodgepodge
creak (krēk) *vi.*, *vt.* ⟦echoic⟧ to make, cause to make, or move with a harsh, squeaking sound —*n.* such a sound —**creak'y, -i·er, -i·est,** *adj.* —**creak'i·ly** *adv.* —**creak'i·ness** *n.*
cream (krēm) *n.* ⟦< OFr⟧ **1** the oily, yellowish part of milk **2** a cosmetic, emulsion, or food with a creamy consistency **3** the best part **4** yellowish white —*adj.* made of or with cream —*vt.* **1** to add cream to **2** to beat into a creamy consistency **3** [Slang] *a*) to beat or defeat soundly *b*) to hurt, damage, etc., as by striking with great force —**cream of** creamed purée of —**cream'y, -i·er, -i·est,** *adj.* —**cream'·i·ness** *n.*
cream cheese a soft, white cheese made of cream or of milk and cream
cream'er *n.* **1** a pitcher for cream **2** a nondairy substance used in place of cream
cream'·er·y *n.*, *pl.* **-ies** a place where dairy products are processed or sold
cream of tartar a white substance used in baking powder, etc.
crease (krēs) *n.* ⟦< ME *creste*, crest⟧ **1** a line made by folding and pressing **2** a fold or wrinkle —*vt.* **creased, creas'ing** **1** to make a crease in **2** to wrinkle —*vi.* to become creased
cre·ate (krē āt') *vt.* **-at'ed, -at'ing** ⟦< L *creare*⟧ **1** to cause to come into existence; make; originate **2** to bring about; give rise to; cause

THESAURUS

cranium *n.* brain, cerebrum, cerebellum, brainpan, braincase, skull; see also HEAD 1.
crank *n.* **1** [A device for revolving a shaft] bracket, lever, handle; see ARM 2, HANDLE 1. **2** [*A person with an obsession] eccentric, fanatic, monomaniac; see CHARACTER 4. **3** [*An ill-natured person] curmudgeon, misanthrope, complainer; see GROUCH.
cranky *a.* disagreeable, cross, testy; see IRRITABLE.
crash *n.* **1** [A crashing sound] clatter, clash, din; see NOISE 1, SOUND 2. **2** [A collision] wreck, accident, shock; see COLLISION.
crash *v.* **1** [To fall with a crash] overturn, upset, break down, plunge, be hurled, pitch, smash, dive, hurtle, lurch, sprawl, tumble, fall headlong, fall flat, drop, slip, collapse; see also FALL 1. **2** [To break into pieces] shatter, shiver, splinter; see BREAK, SMASH. **3** [To make a crashing sound] clatter, bang, smash; see SOUND. **4** [To have a collision] collide, run together, run into, smash into, bang into, meet, jostle, bump, butt, knock, punch, jar, jolt, crack up; see also HIT 1. **5** [To collapse] fail, come to ruin, collapse; see FAIL 1, FALL 1, 2. **6** [*To go uninvited] disturb, gate-crash*, intrude; see INTERRUPT, MEDDLE 1.
crash program* *n.* crash project*, accelerated program, crash course*, intensive program, around-the-clock endeavor, marathon, speedup; see also EMERGENCY.
crass *a.* gross, tasteless, coarse; see IGNORANT 1, 2, VULGAR.
crate *n.* carton, box, cage; see CONTAINER, PACKAGE.
crater *n.* hollow, opening, abyss; see HOLE 1.
craving *n.* need, longing, yearning; see DESIRE 1.
crawl *v.* creep, worm along, wriggle, squirm, slither, move on hands and knees, writhe, go on all fours, worm one's way, go on one's belly; see also GROVEL, SNEAK.
crayon *n.* chalk, pastel, colored wax; see PENCIL.
craze *n.* fad, rage, fashion; see FAD.
crazily *a.* furiously, irrationally, hastily, madly, rashly, insanely, psychotically, maniacally; see also VIOLENTLY, WILDLY.
crazy *a.* crazed, demented, mad; see INSANE 1. —**go crazy** become insane, lose one's wits, get angry; see RAGE 1.
cream *n.* **1** [The fatty portion of milk] heavy cream, light cream, crème, coffee cream, whipping cream, ice cream, half-and-half, butterfat, sour cream, crème fraîche; see also MILK. **2** [A creamy substance] emulsion, salve, jelly; see COSMETIC, LOTION.
creamy *a.* smooth, buttery, creamed; see RICH 2, SOFT 1.
crease *n.* tuck, overlap, pleat; see FOLD, WRINKLE.
crease *v.* double, rumple, crimp; see FOLD 1, WRINKLE.
create *v.* make, produce, form, perform, bring into being, bring into existence, build, fashion, constitute, originate, generate, construct, discover, shape, forge, design, plan, fabricate, cause to be, conceive, give birth to; see also COMPOSE 2, INVENT 1, PRODUCE 2.

cre·a'tion (-ā'shən) ***n.*** **1** a creating or being created **2** the universe **3** anything created —**the Creation** God's creating of the world
cre·a'tive (-āt'iv) ***adj.*** **1** creating or able to create **2** inventive **3** stimulating the imagination —**cre·a'tive·ly** ***adv.*** —**cre·a'tive·ness** ***n.*** —**cre'a·tiv'i·ty** (-ā tiv'ə tē) ***n.***
cre·a'tor (-āt'ər) ***n.*** ⟦L⟧ one who creates —**the Creator** God
crea·ture (krē'chər) ***n.*** ⟦< L *creatura*⟧ a living being, animal or human
crèche (kresh, krāsh) ***n.*** ⟦Fr⟧ a display of the stable scene of Jesus' birth
cre·dence (krēd''ns) ***n.*** ⟦< L *credere*, believe⟧ belief, esp. in the reports or testimony of another
cre·den·tial (kri den'shəl) ***n.*** ⟦see prec.⟧ [*usually pl.*] a letter or certificate showing one's right to a certain position or authority
cre·den·za (kri den'zə) ***n.*** ⟦It⟧ **1** a type of buffet or sideboard **2** a low office cabinet
credibility gap **1** a disparity between what is said and the facts **2** the inability to have one's truthfulness or honesty accepted
cred·i·ble (kred'ə bəl) ***adj.*** ⟦< L *credere*, believe⟧ that can be believed; reliable —**cred'i·bil'i·ty** ***n.*** —**cred'i·bly** ***adv.***
cred·it (kred'it) ***n.*** ⟦< L *credere*, believe⟧ **1** belief; confidence **2** favorable reputation **3** praise or approval **4** a person or thing bringing approval or honor **5** *a)* acknowledgment of work done *b)* [*pl.*] a list of such acknowledgments in a film, book, etc. **6** a sum available to one, as in a bank account **7** the entry, in an account, of payment on a debt **8** trust in one's ability to meet payments when due **9** the time allowed for payment **10** a completed unit of study in a school —***vt.*** **1** to believe; trust **2** to give credit to or commendation for **3** to give credit in a bank account, etc. —**do credit to** to bring honor to —**on credit** with an agreement to pay later
cred'it·a·ble ***adj.*** deserving some credit or praise —**cred'it·a·bly** ***adv.***
credit card a card entitling one to charge purchases, etc. at certain businesses
cred'i·tor (-it ər) ***n.*** one to whom money is owed
credit union a cooperative association for pooling savings of members and making low-interest loans to them
cred'it·wor'thy ***adj.*** sufficiently sound financially to be granted credit —**cred'it·wor'thi·ness** ***n.***
cre·do (krē'dō', krā'-) ***n.***, *pl.* **-dos'** ⟦L, I believe⟧ a creed
cred·u·lous (krej'oo ləs, -ə ləs) ***adj.*** ⟦< L *credere*, believe⟧ tending to believe too readily —**cre·du·li·ty** (krə dōō'lə tē, -dyōō-) ***n.*** —**cred'u·lous·ly** ***adv.***
creed (krēd) ***n.*** ⟦< L *credo*, I believe⟧ **1** a brief statement of religious belief, esp. one accepted as authoritative by a church **2** any statement of belief, principles, etc.
creek (krēk, krik) ***n.*** ⟦< ON *kriki*, a bend, winding⟧ a small stream —**up the creek** [Slang] in trouble
creel (krēl) ***n.*** ⟦< L *cratis*, wickerwork⟧ a wicker basket for holding fish
creep (krēp) ***vi.*** **crept**, **creep'ing** ⟦OE *creopan*⟧ **1** to move with the body close to the ground, as on hands and knees **2** to move slowly or stealthily **3** to grow along the ground or a wall, as ivy —***n.*** **1** the act of creeping **2** [Slang] an annoying or disgusting person —**make one's flesh creep** to give one a feeling of fear, disgust, etc. —**the creeps** [Inf.] a feeling of fear, disgust, etc. —**creep'er** ***n.***
creep'y ***adj.*** **-i·er**, **-i·est** having or causing a feeling of fear or disgust —**creep'i·ly** ***adv.*** —**creep'i·ness** ***n.***
cre·mains (krē mānz') ***pl.n.*** the ashes remaining after cremation
cre·mate (krē'māt', kri māt') ***vt.*** **-mat'ed**, **-mat'ing** ⟦< L *cremare*⟧ to burn (a dead body) to ashes —**cre·ma'tion** ***n.***
cre·ma·to·ry (krē'mə tôr'ē, krem'ə-) ***n.***, *pl.* **-ries** a furnace for cremating: also **cre'ma·to'ri·um** (-ē əm), *pl.* **-ri·ums**, **-ri·a** (-ē ə), or **-ries** —***adj.*** of or for cremation
crème de menthe (krem' də mänt', menth', mint') ⟦Fr, cream of mint⟧ a sweet, mint-flavored liqueur
crème fraîche (krem' fresh') ⟦Fr, fresh cream⟧ slightly fermented high-fat cream, used in sauces, desserts, etc.
cren·el·ate or **cren·el·late** (kren'əl āt') ***vt.*** **-el·at'ed** or **-el·lat'ed**, **-el·at'ing** or **-el·lat'ing** ⟦< VL *crena*, a notch⟧ to furnish with battlements or with squared notches —**cren'el·a'tion** or **cren'el·la'tion** ***n.***
Cre·ole (krē'ōl') ***n.*** ⟦< Fr < Port *crioulo*, native⟧ **1** a person descended from the original French settlers of Louisiana **2** a person of mixed Creole and black descent **3** [**c-**] a language that develops when different languages remain in contact with each other —***adj.*** [*usually* **c-**] prepared with sautéed tomatoes, green peppers, onions, spices, etc.
cre·o·sote (krē'ə sōt') ***n.*** ⟦< Gr *kreas*, flesh + *sōzein*, to save⟧ an oily liquid distilled from tar and used as a wood preservative, etc.
crepe or **crêpe** (krāp; *for 5, also* krep) ***n.*** ⟦< Fr < L *crispus*, curly⟧ **1** a thin, crinkled cloth of silk, rayon, wool, etc. **2** CRAPE (sense 2) **3** wrinkled soft rubber used for shoe soles: also **crepe rubber** **4** thin, crinkled paper: also **crepe paper** **5** a thin pancake, rolled and filled
crêpes su·zette (krāp' sōō zet') ⟦Fr⟧ crêpes rolled in a hot, orange-flavored sauce and served in flaming brandy
crept (krept) ***vi.*** *pt. & pp. of* CREEP
cre·scen·do (kri shen'dō') ***adj.***, ***adv.*** ⟦It < L *crescere*, grow⟧ *Music* with a gradual increase in loudness: also written ***cre·scen'do*** —***n.***, *pl.* **-dos'** a gradual increase in loudness, force, etc.
cres·cent (kres'ənt) ***n.*** ⟦< L *crescere*, grow⟧ **1** a phase of a planet or a moon, when it appears to have one concave edge and one convex edge **2** anything shaped like this —***adj.*** shaped like a crescent
crescent wrench ⟦< *Crescent*, a trademark⟧ a wrench with a crescent-shaped head and an adjustable jaw
cress (kres) ***n.*** ⟦OE *cressa*⟧ a plant with pungent leaves, as watercress, used in salads, etc.
crest (krest) ***n.*** ⟦< L *crista*⟧ **1** any growth on the head of an animal, as a comb or tuft **2** a heraldic device placed on seals, silverware, etc. **3** the top line or surface; summit **4** the highest point, level, degree, etc. —***vi.*** to form or reach a crest —**crest'ed** ***adj.***
crest'fall'en ***adj.*** dejected, disheartened, etc.
Cre·ta·ceous (kri tā'shəs, krē-) ***adj.*** ⟦< L *creta*, chalk⟧ of the latest period of the Mesozoic Era, marked by the dying out of dinosaurs, the rise of mammals and flowering plants, and the formation of oil deposits
Crete (krēt) Greek island in the E Mediterranean —**Cre·tan** (krēt''n) ***adj.***, ***n.***
cre·tonne (krē tän', krē'tän') ***n.*** ⟦Fr, after *Creton*, village in Normandy⟧ a heavy, printed cotton or linen cloth, used for curtains, slipcovers, etc.
cre·vasse (krə vas') ***n.*** ⟦Fr⟧ a deep crack, esp. in a glacier
crev·ice (krev'is) ***n.*** ⟦< L *crepare*, to rattle⟧ a narrow opening caused by a crack or split; fissure

THESAURUS

creation ***n.*** **1** [The process of creating] imagination, production, formulation; see CONCEPTION 1, MAKING. **2** [All that has been created] cosmos, nature, totality; see EARTH 1, UNIVERSE. **3** [A work of art] creative work, masterpiece, brainchild*; see PRODUCTION 1.
creative ***a.*** formative, inventive, productive; see ARTISTIC, ORIGINAL 2.
Creator ***n.*** First Cause, Deity, Maker; see GOD.
creature ***n.*** creation, being, beast; see ANIMAL, HUMAN BEING.
credential ***n.*** declaration, document, voucher; see CERTIFICATE, RECORD 1.
credibility ***n.*** likelihood, probability, trustworthiness; see POSSIBILITY 2.
credible ***a.*** trustworthy, dependable, sincere; see RELIABLE.
credit ***n.*** **1** [Belief] credence, reliance, confidence; see FAITH 1. **2** [Unencumbered funds] assets, capital, stocks, bonds, paper credit, bank account, mortgages, liens, securities, debentures, cash; see also WEALTH. **3** [Permission to defer payment] extension, borrowing power, line of credit, trust; see also LOAN. —**do credit to** bring approval to, reflect well on, do honor to; see SATISFY 1. —**give credit to** believe in, rely on, have confidence in; see TRUST 1. —**give one credit for** believe in, rely on, have confidence in; see TRUST 1. —**on credit** on loan, on a charge, charged; see UNPAID 1. —**to one's credit** good, honorable, beneficial; see WORTHWHILE.
credit card ***n.*** charge card, smart card, gold card, plastic*, plastic money*.
creditor ***n.*** lessor, lender, mortgager; see BANKER.
creed ***n.*** belief, doctrine, dogma; see FAITH 2.
creek ***n.*** stream, spring, brook; see RIVER. —**up the creek*** in difficulty, desperate, lost; see IN TROUBLE.
creep ***v.*** slither, writhe, worm along; see CRAWL.
creeping ***a.*** crawling, squirming, writhing, wriggling, crouching, cowering, slinking, skulking, inching, dragging, lagging, limping, faltering, shuffling, hobbling, sneaking, moving slowly, going at a snail's place, worming along.
crevice ***n.*** chasm, cleft, slit; see GAP 3.

crew[1] (kro͞o) ***n.*** ⟦< L *crescere*, grow⟧ **1** a group of people working together *[a road crew]* **2** a ship's personnel, excluding the officers —**crew'man**, *pl.* **-men** (-mən), ***n.***

crew[2] (kro͞o) ***vi.*** [Chiefly Brit.] *alt. pt. of* CROW[2] (sense 1)

crew cut a man's haircut in which the hair is cropped close to the head

crew·el (kro͞o'əl) ***n.*** ⟦ME *crule*⟧ a loosely twisted, worsted yarn —**crew'el·work'** ***n.***

crib (krib) ***n.*** ⟦OE, ox stall⟧ **1** a rack or box for fodder **2** a small bed with high sides, for a baby **3** an enclosure for storing grain **4** an underwater structure serving as a pier, water intake, etc. **5** [Inf.] a translation or other aid used dishonestly in doing schoolwork —***vt.*** **cribbed, crib'bing 1** to confine **2** to furnish with a crib **3** [Inf.] to plagiarize —***vi.*** [Inf.] to do schoolwork dishonestly

crib·bage (krib'ij) ***n.*** a card game in which the object is to form combinations for points

crib death SUDDEN INFANT DEATH SYNDROME

crick[1] (krik) ***n.*** ⟦< ON *kriki*, bend⟧ a painful cramp in the neck, back, etc.

crick[2] (krik) ***n.*** [Dial.] CREEK

crick·et[1] (krik'it) ***n.*** ⟦< OFr *criquer*, to creak⟧ a leaping insect similar to a grasshopper

crick·et[2] (krik'it) ***n.*** ⟦OFr *criquet*, a bat⟧ an outdoor game played by two teams of eleven players each, using a ball, bats, and wickets

cried (krīd) ***vi.***, ***vt.*** *pt. & pp. of* CRY

cri·er (krī'ər) ***n.*** **1** one who cries **2** one who shouts out announcements, news, etc.

crime (krīm) ***n.*** ⟦< L *crimen*, offense⟧ **1** an act in violation of a law; specif., a serious violation, as a felony **2** a sin

Cri·me·a (krī mē'ə) peninsula in SW Ukraine, extending into the Black Sea —**Cri·me'an** ***adj.***

crim·i·nal (krim'ə nəl) ***adj.*** **1** having the nature of crime **2** relating to or guilty of crime —***n.*** a person guilty of a crime —**crim'i·nal'i·ty** (-nal'ə tə) ***n.*** —**crim'i·nal·ly** ***adv.***

crim'i·nal·ist (-nəl ist) ***n.*** an expert in the scientific analysis of criminal evidence

crim'i·nol'o·gy (-näl'ə jē) ***n.*** the scientific study of crime and criminals —**crim'i·nol'o·gist** ***n.***

crimp (krimp) ***vt.*** ⟦< MDu *crimpen*, to wrinkle⟧ **1** to press into narrow folds; pleat **2** to curl (hair) **3** to pinch together —***n.*** **1** a crimping **2** anything crimped —**put a crimp in** [Inf.] to hinder

crim·son (krim'zən, -sən) ***n.*** ⟦< Ar *qirmiz*⟧ deep red —***adj.*** deep-red —***vt.***, ***vi.*** to make or become crimson

cringe (krinj) ***vi.*** **cringed, cring'ing** ⟦< OE *cringan*, to fall (in battle)⟧ **1** to draw back, crouch, etc., as when afraid; cower **2** to act timidly servile

crin·kle (kriŋ'kəl) ***vi.***, ***vt.*** **-kled, -kling** ⟦see prec.⟧ **1** to wrinkle **2** to rustle or crackle, as crushed paper —**crin'kly, -kli·er, -kli·est,** ***adj.***

crin·o·line (krin'ə lin) ***n.*** ⟦Fr < It < *crino*, horsehair + *lino*, linen⟧ **1** a coarse, stiff cloth used as a lining in garments **2** HOOP SKIRT

crip·ple (krip'əl) ***n.*** ⟦< OE *creopan*, to creep⟧ a disabled person: now somewhat offensive —***vt.*** **-pled, -pling 1** to lame **2** to disable; impair

cri·sis (krī'sis) ***n.***, *pl.* **-ses'** (-sēz') ⟦L < Gr *krinein*, to separate⟧ **1** the turning point of a disease for better or worse **2** a decisive or crucial time, etc. **3** a time of great danger, etc.

crisp (krisp) ***adj.*** ⟦< L *crispus*, curly⟧ **1** easily crumbled **2** fresh and firm **3** sharp and clear **4** fresh and invigorating **5** curled and wiry Also **crisp'y, -i·er, -i·est** —**crisp'ly** ***adv.*** —**crisp'ness** ***n.***

criss·cross (kris'krôs') ***n.*** ⟦ME *Christcros*, Christ's cross⟧ a mark or pattern made of crossed lines —***adj.*** marked by crossing lines —***vt.*** to mark with crossing lines —***vi.*** to move to and fro —***adv.*** **1** crosswise **2** awry

cri·te·ri·on (krī tir'ē ən) ***n.***, *pl.* **-ri·a** (-ē ə) or **-ri·ons** ⟦< Gr *kritēs*, judge⟧ a standard, test, etc. by which a thing can be judged

crit·ic (krit'ik) ***n.*** ⟦< Gr *krinein*, discern⟧ **1** one who judges books, music, plays, etc., as for a newspaper **2** one who finds fault

crit'i·cal (-i kəl) ***adj.*** **1** tending to find fault **2** of critics or criticism **3** of or forming a crisis; decisive or dangerous —**crit'i·cal·ly** ***adv.***

crit'i·cism' (-ə siz'əm) ***n.*** **1** the act of making judgments, esp. of literary or artistic work **2** a review, article, etc. expressing such judgment **3** censure **4** the principles or methods of critics

crit'i·cize' (-ə sīz') ***vi.***, ***vt.*** **-cized', -ciz'ing 1** to analyze and judge as a critic **2** to find fault (with) —**crit'i·ciz'a·ble** ***adj.*** —**crit'i·ciz'er** ***n.***

cri·tique (kri tēk') ***n.*** ⟦Fr⟧ a critical analysis or review —***vt.***, ***vi.*** **-tiqued', -tiqu'ing** to criticize (a subject, art work, etc.)

crit·ter (krit'ər) ***n.*** *dial. var. of* CREATURE

croak (krōk) ***vi.*** ⟦echoic⟧ **1** to make a deep, hoarse sound, as a frog does **2** [Slang] to die —***vt.*** to utter in deep, hoarse tones —***n.*** a croaking sound

Cro·at (krō'at', -ət) ***n.*** a person born or living in Croatia

Cro·a·tia (krō ā'shə) country in SE Europe: 21,829 sq. mi.; pop. 4,784,000 —**Cro·a'tian** ***adj.***, ***n.***

THESAURUS

crew[1] ***n.*** **1** [Company of sailors] seafarers, sailors, hands, able seamen, ship's company, mariners, sea dogs, gobs*. **2** [A group of people organized to do a particular job] company, troupe, squad; see ORGANIZATION 2, TEAM 1.

crime ***n.*** transgression, misdemeanor, vice, outrage, wickedness, immorality, infringement, depravity, evil behavior, wrongdoing, misconduct, corruption, delinquency, wrong, trespass, malefaction, dereliction, lawlessness, domestic violence, hate crime, discrimination, harassment, arson, bigamy, killing, forgery, atrocity, felony, capital crime, offense, white-collar crime, scandal, infraction, violation, mortal sin, homicide, voluntary manslaughter, involuntary manslaughter, simple assault, aggravated assault, battery, larceny, robbery, burglary, holdup, kidnapping, swindling, fraud, defrauding, embezzlement, smuggling, extortion, bribery, mugging, date rape, statutory rape, attack, sexual molestation, breach of promise, malicious mischief, breach of the peace, libel, perjury, conspiracy, counterfeiting, inciting to revolt, sedition, mayhem, crime of passion, war crime, crime against humanity; see also CORRUPTION, EVIL 2, MURDER, RAPE, SIN, THEFT, TREASON.

criminal ***a.*** unlawful, felonious, illegal; see BAD 1.

criminal ***n.*** lawbreaker, felon, crook*. *Criminals include the following:* murderer, killer, rapist, perjurer, arsonist, mugger, desperado, thug, gangster, gang leader, burglar, safecracker, swindler, clip artist*, confidence man, con man*, thief, bandit, second-story man*, cattle rustler, horse thief, car thief, pickpocket, counterfeiter, forger, smuggler, extortionist, kidnapper, gunman, triggerman*, accomplice, informer, stool pigeon*, stoolie*, squealer*, con*, dope peddler*, pusher*.

crimson ***a.*** blood-red, bright red, scarlet; see COLOR *n.*, RED *n.*

cringe ***v.*** flinch, quail, wince; see COWER, CRAWL.

crinkle ***v.*** coil, wind, crease; see WRINKLE.

cripple ***v.*** disable, mangle, injure; see HURT.

crippled ***a.*** maimed, mutilated, mangled; see DEFORMED, DISABLED.

crisis ***n.*** straits, urgency, necessity, dilemma, puzzle, pressure, embarrassment, pinch, juncture, pass, change, contingency, situation, condition, plight, impasse, deadlock, predicament, corner, trauma, quandary, extremity, trial, crux, moment of truth, turning point, critical situation, pickle*, stew*, fix*, mess, hot water*.—*Ant.* STABILITY, normality, regularity.

crisp ***a.*** **1** [Fresh and firm] green, plump, firm; see FRESH 1, RIPE 1. **2** [Brisk] fresh, invigorating, bracing; see STIMULATING.

criterion ***n.*** basis, foundation, test, standard, rule, proof, scale, prototype, pattern, example, standard of judgment, standard of criticism, archetype, norm, precedent, fact, law, principle; see also MEASURE 2, MODEL 2.

critic ***n.*** **1** [One who makes adverse comments] faultfinder, censor, quibbler, detractor, slanderer, complainer, doubter, nagger, fretter, scolder, worrier, mudslinger*.—*Ant.* BELIEVER, praiser, supporter. **2** [One who endeavors to interpret and judge] commentator, reviewer, analyst, connoisseur, writer of reviews, cartoonist, caricaturist, expert; see also EXAMINER, WRITER.

critical ***a.*** **1** [Disapproving] faultfinding, trenchant, derogatory, disapproving, hypercritical, demanding, satirical, cynical, nagging, scolding, condemning, censuring, reproachful, disapproving, disparaging, exacting, sharp, cutting, biting; see also SARCASTIC. **2** [Capable of observing and judging] penetrating, perceptive, discerning; see DISCREET, OBSERVANT. **3** [Crucial] decisive, significant, deciding; see IMPORTANT 1.

criticism ***n.*** **1** [A serious estimate or interpretation] study, analysis, critique; see JUDGMENT 2, REVIEW 1. **2** [An adverse comment] blame, carping, faultfinding; see OBJECTION.

criticize ***v.*** **1** [To make a considered analysis] study, probe, scrutinize; see ANALYZE, EXAMINE. **2** [To make adverse comments] chastise, reprove, reprimand; see BLAME.

cro·chet (krō shā′) ***n.*** ⟦Fr, small hook⟧ needlework done with one hooked needle —***vi.***, ***vt.*** **-cheted′** (-shād′), **-chet′ing** to do, or make by, crochet —**cro·chet′er** ***n.***
crock (kräk) ***n.*** ⟦OE *crocca*⟧ an earthenware pot or jar —**crock′er·y** ***n.***
crocked (kräkt) ***adj.*** ⟦< *crock*, to disable⟧ [Slang] drunk
croc·o·dile (kräk′ə dīl′) ***n.*** ⟦< Gr *krokodilos*, lizard⟧ a large, lizardlike reptile of tropical streams, having a long, narrow head with massive jaws
cro·cus (krō′kəs) ***n.***, *pl.* **-cus·es** or **-ci′** (-sī′) ⟦< Gr *krokos*, saffron⟧ a spring-blooming plant of the iris family, with a yellow, purple, or white flower
Croe·sus (krē′səs) flourished 6th c. B.C.; king noted for his great wealth
crois·sant (krə sänt′; *Fr* krwȧ sän′) ***n.*** ⟦Fr, crescent⟧ a crescent-shaped, flaky bread roll
Cro-Mag·non (krō mag′nən) ***adj.*** ⟦after *Cro-Magnon* cave in France⟧ of a Stone Age type of tall human of the European continent
Crom·well (kräm′wel), **Ol·i·ver** (äl′ə vər) 1599-1658; Eng. revolutionary leader & head (Lord Protector) of England (1653-58)
crone (krōn) ***n.*** ⟦< MDu *kronje*, old ewe⟧ an ugly, withered old woman
cro·ny (krō′nē) ***n.***, *pl.* **-nies** ⟦< Gr *chronos*, time⟧ a close companion
crook (kro͝ok) ***n.*** ⟦< ON *krōkr*, hook⟧ **1** a hooked or curved staff, etc.; hook **2** a bend or curve **3** [Inf.] a swindler or thief —***vt.***, ***vi.*** **crooked** (kro͝okt), **crook′ing** to bend or curve
crook·ed (kro͝okt; *for 2 & 3* kro͝ok′id) ***adj.*** **1** having a crook **2** not straight; bent **3** dishonest —**crook′ed·ly** ***adv.*** —**crook′ed·ness** ***n.***
crook′neck′ ***n.*** a squash with a long, curved neck
croon (kro͞on) ***vi.***, ***vt.*** ⟦ME *cronen*⟧ **1** to sing or hum in a low, gentle tone **2** to sing (popular songs) softly and sentimentally —***n.*** a low, gentle singing or humming —**croon′er** ***n.***
crop (kräp) ***n.*** ⟦OE *croppa*, a cluster⟧ **1** a saclike part of a bird's gullet, in which food is stored before digestion **2** any agricultural product, growing or harvested **3** the yield of any product in one season or place **4** a group **5** the handle of a whip **6** a riding whip **7** hair cut close to the head —***vt.*** **cropped**, **crop′ping** **1** to cut or bite off the tops or ends of **2** to cut (the hair, etc.) short —**crop out** (or **up**) to appear unexpectedly
crop′-dust′ing ***n.*** the spraying of crops with pesticides from an airplane —**crop′-dust′** ***vi.***, ***vt.***
crop′per ***n.*** **1** one that crops **2** a sharecropper —**come a cropper** [Inf.] to come to ruin; fail
cro·quet (krō kā′) ***n.*** ⟦Fr, dial. form of *crochet*, small hook⟧ an outdoor game in which the players use mallets to drive a ball through hoops in the ground
cro·quette (krō ket′) ***n.*** ⟦Fr < *croquer*, to crunch⟧ a small mass of meat, fish, etc. fried in deep fat
cro·sier (krō′zhər) ***n.*** ⟦< OFr *croce*⟧ the staff carried by a bishop or abbot
cross (krôs) ***n.*** ⟦< L *crux*⟧ **1** an upright post with a bar across it, on which the ancient Romans executed people **2** a representation of this as a symbol of the crucifixion of Jesus, hence of Christianity **3** any trouble or affliction **4** any design or mark made by two intersecting lines, bars, etc. **5** a crossing of varieties or breeds —***vt.***, ***vi.*** **1** to make the sign of the cross (upon) **2** to place or lie across or crosswise **3** to intersect **4** to draw a line or lines across **5** to go or extend across **6** to meet and pass (each other) **7** to oppose **8** to interbreed (animals or plants) —***adj.*** **1** lying or passing across **2** contrary; opposed **3** cranky; irritable **4** of mixed variety or breed —**cross off** (or **out**) to cancel as by drawing lines across —**cross someone's mind** to come suddenly to someone's mind —**cross someone's path** to meet someone —**cross′ly** ***adv.***
cross′bar′ ***n.*** a bar, line, or stripe placed crosswise
cross′beam′ ***n.*** any transverse beam in a structure
cross′bones′ ***n.*** a representation of two bones placed across each other, under that of a skull, used to symbolize death or danger
cross′bow′ (-bō′) ***n.*** a weapon consisting of a bow set transversely on a grooved wooden stock —**cross′bow′man** (-mən), *pl.* **-men** (-mən), ***n.***
cross′breed′ ***vt.***, ***vi.*** **-bred′**, **-breed′ing** HYBRIDIZE —***n.*** HYBRID (sense 1)
cross′-coun′try ***adj.***, ***adv.*** across open country or fields *[a cross-country race]*
cross′cut′ saw a saw designed to cut across the grain of wood
cross′-dress′ing ***n.*** the wearing of clothing worn by the opposite sex
cross′-ex·am′ine ***vt.***, ***vi.*** **-ined**, **-in·ing** *Law* to question (a witness called by the opposing side) in order to challenge the witness's previous testimony —**cross′-ex·am′i·na′tion** ***n.***
cross′-eye′ ***n.*** an abnormal condition in which the eyes are turned toward each other —**cross′-eyed′** ***adj.***
cross′fire′ ***n.*** **1** lines of fire from two or more positions that cross **2** an energetic exchange, as by opposing forces or of opposing opinions
cross′hatch′ (-hach′) ***vt.***, ***vi.*** to shade (a drawing) with two sets of parallel lines that cross each other
cross′ing ***n.*** **1** the act of passing across, interbreeding, etc. **2** an intersection, as of streets **3** a place where a street, etc. may be crossed
cross′piece′ ***n.*** a piece lying across another
cross′-pol′li·nate′ ***vt.***, ***vi.*** **-nat′ed**, **-nat′ing** to transfer pollen from the anther of (a flower) to the stigma of (a genetically different flower) —**cross′-pol′li·na′tion** ***n.***
cross′-pur′pose ***n.*** a contrary purpose —**at cross-purposes** having a misunderstanding as to each other's purposes
cross′-ref′er·ence ***n.*** a reference from one part of a book, etc. to another —***vt.*** **-enced**, **-enc·ing** to provide (an index, etc.) with cross-references —**cross′-re·fer′** ***vt.***, ***vi.***
cross′road′ ***n.*** **1** a road that crosses another **2** [*usually pl., often with sing. v.*] *a*) the place where roads intersect *b*) any center of activity, etc. *c*) a time of important changes or major decisions
cross section **1** *a*) a cutting through something *b*) a piece so cut off *c*) a representation of this **2** a representative part of a whole —**cross′-sec′tion** ***vt.***
cross′town′ ***adj.*** **1** going across a city *[a crosstown bus]* **2** on the other side of a city *[a crosstown rival]*
cross′walk′ ***n.*** a lane marked off for pedestrians to use in crossing a street
cross′wise′ ***adv.*** so as to cross: also **cross′ways′**
cross′word′ puzzle an arrangement of numbered squares to be filled in with the letters of words, arranged vertically and horizontally, whose synonyms and definitions are given as clues
crotch (kräch) ***n.*** ⟦ME *crucche*, crutch⟧ **1** a forked place, as on a tree **2** the place where the legs fork from the human body or from the upper part of a pair of trousers
crotch·et (kräch′it) ***n.*** ⟦ult. < OFr *croc*, a hook⟧ a peculiar whim or stubborn notion —**crotch′et·y** ***adj.***
crouch (krouch) ***vi.*** ⟦< OFr *croc*, a hook⟧ to stoop low with legs bent —***n.*** a crouching position

THESAURUS

crook* ***n.*** **1** [A criminal] swindler, thief, rogue; see CRIMINAL. **2** [A bend] fork, bend, hook; see ANGLE 1.
crooked ***a.*** **1** [Having a crook] curved, curving, hooked, winding, bowed, spiral, serpentine, not straight, zigzag, twisted, meandering, tortuous, sinuous; see also ANGULAR, BENT, OBLIQUE.—*Ant.* STRAIGHT, unbent, direct. **2** [Dishonest] iniquitous, corrupt, nefarious; see DISHONEST.
crop ***n.*** harvest, yield, product, reaping, hay, fodder, grains, vintage, fruits; see also PRODUCE.
cross ***a.*** ill-tempered, easily annoyed, pettish; see CRITICAL, IRRITABLE.
cross ***n.*** **1** [Religious symbol, especially of Christianity] crucifix, Greek cross, papal cross, Maltese cross, Latin cross. **2** [A tribulation] affliction, trial, misfortune; see DIFFICULTY 2. **3** [A mixed offspring] mongrel, crossbreed, half-breed; see HYBRID, MIXTURE 1.
cross ***v.*** **1** [To pass over] traverse, go across, go over, pass, ford, cut across, span. **2** [To lie across] intersect, lean on, extend across; see DIVIDE. **3** [To mix breeds] hybridize, interbreed, cross-pollinate; see MIX 1.
cross-examine ***v.*** investigate, check, interrogate; see EXAMINE, QUESTION.
crossing ***n.*** **1** [A place to cross] intersection, overpass, crosswalk; see BRIDGE 1. **2** [A mixing of breeds] hybridization, interbreeding, cross-pollination; see MIXTURE 1.
crossroad ***n.*** intersecting road, intersection, junction; see ROAD 1.
crosswise ***a.*** across, cross, perpendicular, transversely, vertically, horizontally, at right angles, over, sideways, crisscross, askew, crossways; see also ANGULAR.
crotch ***n.*** **1** [Angle] fork, corner, elbow; see ANGLE 1, CURVE. **2** [Loins] pubic area, groin, pelvic girdle; see BODY 1.
crouch ***v.*** **1** [To stoop] dip, duck, bow; see BEND. **2** [To cower] cringe, flinch, quail; see COWER, CRAWL.

croup (kro͞op) ***n.*** ⟦< obs. or dial. *croup,* speak hoarsely⟧ an inflammation of the respiratory passages, with labored breathing, hoarse coughing, etc.

crou·pi·er (kro͞o′pē ā′, -ər) ***n.*** ⟦Fr⟧ one in charge of a gambling table

crou·ton (kro͞o′tän′, kro͞o tän′) ***n.*** ⟦Fr < *croûte,* a crust⟧ a small, crisp piece of toasted bread served in soup or salads

crow[1] (krō) ***n.*** ⟦OE *crawa*⟧ a large, glossy-black bird with a harsh call —**as the crow flies** in a straight, direct line —**eat crow** [Inf.] to admit an error

crow[2] (krō) ***vi.*** **crowed** or, for 1, [Chiefly Brit.] **crew** (kro͞o), **crowed, crow′ing** ⟦OE *crawan*⟧ **1** to make the shrill cry of a rooster **2** to boast in triumph **3** to make a sound of pleasure —***n.*** a crowing sound

crow′bar′ ***n.*** a long metal bar used as a lever for prying, etc.

crowd (kroud) ***vi.*** ⟦< OE *crudan*⟧ **1** to push one's way (*into*) **2** to throng —***vt.*** **1** to press or push **2** to fill too full; cram —***n.*** **1** a large number of people or things grouped closely **2** the common people; the masses **3** [Inf.] a set; clique —**crowd′ed** ***adj.***

crow′foot′ ***n.***, *pl.* **-foots′** or **-feet′** a plant of the buttercup family, with leaves resembling a crow's foot

crown (kroun) ***n.*** ⟦< Gr *korōnē,* wreath⟧ **1** a wreath worn on the head in victory **2** a reward; honor **3** a monarch's headdress **4** [*often* **C-**] *a*) the power of a monarch *b*) the monarch **5** a British coin equal to 25 (new) pence: no longer minted **6** the top part, as of the head **7** the highest quality, state, etc. of anything **8** *a*) the part of a tooth outside the gum *b*) an artificial substitute for this —***vt.*** **1** to put a crown on **2** to make (a person) a monarch **3** to honor **4** to be the highest part of **5** to complete successfully

crown prince the male heir apparent to a throne —**crown princess**

crow's-foot (krōz′foot′) ***n.***, *pl.* **-feet′** any of the wrinkles that often develop at the outer corners of the eyes of adults

crow's′-nest′ (-nest′) ***n.*** a lookout's platform high on a ship's mast

cro·zier (krō′zhər) ***n.*** CROSIER

CRT (sē′är′tē′) ***n.*** a cathode-ray tube

cru·cial (kro͞o′shəl) ***adj.*** ⟦< L *crux,* a cross⟧ decisive; critical —**cru′cial·ly** ***adv.***

cru·ci·ble (kro͞o′sə bəl) ***n.*** ⟦ML *crucibulum,* lamp⟧ **1** a heat-resistant container for melting ores, metals, etc. **2** a severe trial

cru·ci·fix (kro͞o′sə fiks′) ***n.*** ⟦see CRUCIFY⟧ a cross with the figure of the crucified Jesus Christ on it

cru′ci·fix′ion (-fik′shən) ***n.*** **1** a crucifying **2** [**C-**] the crucifying of Jesus, or a representation of this

cru′ci·form′ (-fôrm′) ***adj.*** cross-shaped

cru′ci·fy′ (-fī′) ***vt.*** **-fied′, -fy′ing** ⟦< L *crux,* a cross + *figere,* fasten⟧ **1** to execute by nailing or binding to a cross and leaving to die **2** to be very cruel to; torment

crude (kro͞od) ***adj.*** **crud′er, crud′est** ⟦< L *crudus,* raw⟧ **1** in a raw or natural condition **2** lacking grace, tact, taste, etc. **3** roughly made —**crude′ly** ***adv.*** —**crude′ness** ***n.*** —**cru·di·ty** (kro͞o′də tē) ***n.***

cru·di·tés (kro͞o′də tā′) ***pl.n.*** ⟦Fr, raw things⟧ raw vegetables cut up and served as hors d'oeuvres, usually with a dip or sauce

cru·el (kro͞o′əl) ***adj.*** ⟦see CRUDE⟧ causing pain and suffering; pitiless —**cru′el·ly** ***adv.*** —**cru′el·ness** ***n.*** —**cru′el·ty,** *pl.* **-ties,** ***n.***

cru·et (kro͞o′it) ***n.*** ⟦< OFr *crue,* earthen pot⟧ a small glass bottle, as for holding vinegar or oil for the table

cruise (kro͞oz) ***vi.*** **cruised, cruis′ing** ⟦< Du *kruisen,* to cross⟧ **1** to sail or ride about from place to place, as for pleasure or in search of something **2** to move at the most efficient speed for sustained travel **3** to operate at a predetermined speed by use of a regulating mechanism (**cruise control**) —***vt.*** to sail or journey over or about —***n.*** a cruising voyage

cruise missile a long-range, jet-propelled winged missile that can be launched from an airplane, submarine, ship, etc. and guided to its target by remote control

cruis′er ***n.*** **1** anything that cruises, as a police car **2** a fast warship smaller than a battleship

crul·ler (krul′ər) ***n.*** ⟦Du < *krullen,* to curl⟧ a kind of twisted doughnut

crumb (krum) ***n.*** ⟦< OE *cruma,* a bit scraped from bread crust⟧ **1** a small piece broken off, as of bread **2** any bit or scrap *[crumbs* of knowledge*]* —**crumb·y** (krum′ē), **-i·er, -i·est,** ***adj.***

crum·ble (krum′bəl) ***vt.*** **-bled, -bling** ⟦< prec.⟧ to break into crumbs —***vi.*** to fall to pieces; disintegrate —**crum′bly** (-blē), **-bli·er, -bli·est,** ***adj.***

crum·my (krum′ē) ***adj.*** **-mi·er, -mi·est** [Slang] **1** dirty, cheap, etc. **2** inferior, worthless, etc.

crum·pet (krum′pit) ***n.*** ⟦< OE *crump,* twisted⟧ an unsweetened batter cake baked on a griddle

crum·ple (krum′pəl) ***vt.*** **-pled, -pling** ⟦ult. < MDu *crimpen,* to wrinkle⟧ to crush together into wrinkles

crunch (krunch) ***vi., vt.*** ⟦echoic⟧ **1** to chew, press, grind, etc. with a noisy, crackling sound **2** [Inf.] to process (a large quantity of data) rapidly *[crunching* numbers on a computer*]* —***n.*** **1** the act or sound of crunching **2** [Slang] a showdown or tight situation —**crunch′y, -i·er, -i·est,** ***adj.***

crunch′time′ ***n.*** [Slang] the tense, crucial phase of some activity

crup·per (krup′ər, kroop′-) ***n.*** ⟦< OFr *crope,* rump⟧ a leather strap attached to a saddle or harness and passed under a horse's tail

cru·sade (kro͞o sād′) ***n.*** ⟦ult. < L *crux,* a cross⟧ **1** [*sometimes* **C-**] any of the Christian military expeditions (11th-13th c.) to recover the Holy Land from the Muslims **2** a vigorous, concerted action for some cause, or against some abuse —***vi.*** **-sad′ed, -sad′ing** to engage in a crusade —**cru·sad′er** ***n.***

cruse (kro͞os, kro͞oz) ***n.*** ⟦OE⟧ a small container for water, oil, etc.

crush (krush) ***vt.*** ⟦< OFr *croisir,* to crash, break⟧ **1** to press with force so as to break or put out of shape **2** to grind or pound into small bits **3** to subdue; overwhelm —***vi.*** to become crushed —***n.*** **1** a crushing; severe pres-

THESAURUS

crowd ***n.*** host, horde, flock, mob, company, swarm, press, crush, surge, legion, group, body, pack, army, drove, party, flood, throng, troupe, deluge, multitude, congregation, cluster, assembly, crew, herd, bunch, gang; see also GATHERING.

crowd ***v.*** stuff, jam, squeeze; see PACK 2, PUSH 1.

crowded ***a.*** packed, huddled, crushed; see FULL 1.

crown ***n.*** diadem, headdress, tiara, coronet, circlet.

crown ***v.*** commission, authorize, invest, enable, sanction, inaugurate, exalt, raise, heighten, set up, ennoble, establish; see also DELEGATE 1.

crucial ***a.*** decisive, climactic, deciding; see IMPORTANT 1.

crude ***a.*** rude, rough, unpolished, in a raw state, homemade, thick, coarse, harsh, rudimentary, homespun, rough-hewn, unfashioned, unformed, undeveloped, in the rough, raw, immature, sketchy; see also UNFINISHED 1.—*Ant.* FINISHED, polished, refined.

crudely ***a.*** clumsily, coarsely, impudently; see RUDELY.

cruel ***a.*** malevolent, spiteful, depraved, wicked, vengeful, evil, sinful, degenerate, brutish, demonic, outrageous, tyrannical, gross, demoralized, evil-minded, vicious, brutal, rough, wild, bestial, ferocious, monstrous, demoniac, debased, destructive, harmful, mischievous, callous, unnatural, merciless, sadistic, unpitying, unmerciful, unyielding, remorseless, pitiless, unfeeling, inflexible, bloodthirsty, unrelenting, relentless, grim, inhuman, inhumane, atrocious, harsh, heartless, stony, unconcerned, showing no mercy, turning a deaf ear, hard as nails*.—*Ant.* MERCIFUL, kindly, compassionate.

cruelly ***a.*** savagely, inhumanly, viciously; see BRUTALLY.

cruelty ***n.*** brutality, barbarity, sadism, inhumanity, barbarism, mercilessness, wickedness, coarseness, ruthlessness, severity, malice, rancor, venom, coldness, unfeelingness, insensibility, indifference, fierceness, bestiality, ferocity, savagery, grimness, monstrousness, inflexibility, fiendishness, hardness of heart, bloodthirstiness, torture, relentlessness, persecution, harshness, heartlessness, atrocity; see also EVIL 1, 2, TYRANNY.—*Ant.* KINDNESS, benevolence, humanity.

cruise ***n.*** voyage, sail, jaunt; see JOURNEY.

cruise ***v.*** voyage, navigate, coast; see SAIL 1, TRAVEL.

cruiser ***n.*** cabin cruiser, boat, privateer; see SHIP.

crumb ***n.*** particle, scrap, morsel; see BIT 1.

crumble ***v.*** fall apart, decay, break up; see DISINTEGRATE.

crumbly ***a.*** breaking up, breaking down, falling to pieces, decayed, perishing, deteriorating, soft, corroded, rusted, rotted, worn away, fragile, brittle, friable, crisp, frail, rotten, breakable, eroded, disintegrated; see also DECAYING, GRITTY.—*Ant.* FIRM, sound, undecayed.

crumple ***v.*** rumple, crush, crease; see WRINKLE.

crush ***v.*** **1** [To break into small pieces] smash, pulverize, powder; see

sure **2** a crowded mass of people **3** [Inf.] an infatuation —**crush'er** ***n.***

crush'ing ***adj.*** **1** overwhelming **2** hurtful

crust (krust) ***n.*** ⟦< L *crusta*⟧ **1** the hard, outer part of bread **2** any dry, hard piece of bread **3** the pastry shell of a pie **4** any hard surface layer **5** [Slang] insolence **6** *Geol.* the solid outer layer of the earth —***vt.***, ***vi.*** to cover or become covered with a crust —**crust'y**, **-i·er**, **-i·est**, ***adj.***

crus·ta·cean (krus tā'shən) ***n.*** ⟦see prec.⟧ any of a class of arthropods, including shrimps, crabs, and lobsters, that have a hard outer shell

crutch (kruch) ***n.*** ⟦< OE *crycce*, staff⟧ **1** a device used by lame people as an aid in walking, typically a staff with a crosspiece on top that fits under the armpit **2** any prop or support

crux (kruks) ***n.***, *pl.* **crux'es** or **cru·ces** (kro͞o'sēz') ⟦L, a cross⟧ **1** a difficult problem **2** the essential or deciding point

cry (krī) ***vi.*** **cried**, **cry'ing** ⟦< L *quiritare*, to wail⟧ **1** to utter a loud sound, as in pain or fright **2** to sob and shed tears; weep **3** to plead or clamor *(for)* **4** to show a great need *(for)* **5** to utter its characteristic call: said of an animal —***vt.*** to utter loudly; shout —***n.***, *pl.* **cries** **1** a shout **2** a plea **3** a fit of weeping **4** the characteristic call of an animal —**a far cry** a great distance or difference

cry'ba'by ***n.***, *pl.* **-bies** one who complains when failing to get his or her own way

cry·o·gen·ics (krī'ō jen'iks, -ə-) ***n.*** ⟦< Gr *kryos*, cold + -GEN + -ICS⟧ the science that deals with the production of very low temperatures and their effect on the properties of matter —**cry'o·gen'ic** ***adj.***

cry'o·sur'ger·y ***n.*** ⟦< Gr *kryos*, cold + SURGERY⟧ surgery that destroys tissues by freezing them

crypt (kript) ***n.*** ⟦< Gr *kryptein*, to hide⟧ an underground vault, esp. one under a church, used for burial

cryp·tic (krip'tik) ***adj.*** **1** hidden or mysterious; baffling **2** obscure and curt in expression —**cryp'ti·cal·ly** ***adv.***

crypto- ⟦see CRYPT⟧ *combining form* **1** secret or hidden *[cryptogram]* **2** being such secretly and not publicly *[a crypto-*Fascist*]*

cryp·to·gram (krip'tō gram', -tə-) ***n.*** ⟦prec. + -GRAM⟧ a message in code or cipher

cryp·tog·ra·phy (krip täg'rə fē) ***n.*** ⟦CRYPTO- + -GRAPHY⟧ the art of writing or deciphering messages in code —**cryp·tog'ra·pher** ***n.***

crys·tal (kris'təl) ***n.*** ⟦< Gr *krystallos*, crystal, ice < *kryos*, frost⟧ **1** pure quartz **2** *a)* a very clear, brilliant glass *b)* articles of such glass, as goblets **3** anything clear like crystal, as the cover on a watch face **4** a solidified form of a substance having plane faces arranged in a symmetrical, three-dimensional pattern —***adj.*** **1** of or made of crystal **2** like crystal; clear

crys'tal·line (-tə lin) ***adj.*** **1** made of crystal **2** like crystal; clear and transparent

crys'tal·lize' (-tə līz') ***vi.***, ***vt.*** **-lized'**, **-liz'ing** **1** to become or cause to become crystalline **2** to take on or cause to take on a definite form —**crys'tal·li·za'tion** ***n.***

cs *abbrev.* case(s)

Cs *Chem. symbol for* cesium

C-sec·tion (sē'sek'shən) ***n.*** [Inf.] CESAREAN (SECTION)

CST *abbrev.* Central Standard Time

ct *abbrev.* **1** cent **2** court

CT *abbrev.* **1** Central Time **2** Connecticut

CT scan ⟦*c(omputerized) t(omography)*⟧ **1** a diagnostic X-raying of soft tissues, using many single-plane X-rays (*tomograms*) to form the image **2** such an image —**CT scanner** —**CT scanning**

cu *abbrev.* cubic

Cu ⟦L *cuprum*⟧ *Chem. symbol for* copper

cub (kub) ***n.*** ⟦< ? Old Ir *cuib*, a whelp⟧ **1** a young fox, bear, lion, whale, etc. **2** an inexperienced or immature person

Cu·ba (kyo͞o'bə) country on an island in the West Indies, south of Florida: 42,803 sq. mi.; pop. 9,724,000 —**Cu'ban** ***adj.***, ***n.***

cub·by·hole (kub'ē hōl') ***n.*** ⟦< Brit dial. *cub*, little shed + HOLE⟧ a small, enclosed space: also **cub'by**

cube (kyo͞ob) ***n.*** ⟦< Gr *kybos*⟧ **1** a solid with six equal, square sides **2** the product obtained by multiplying a given number by its square *[*the *cube* of 3 is 27*]* —***vt.*** **cubed**, **cub'ing** **1** to obtain the cube of (a number) **2** to cut or shape into cubes —**cub'er** ***n.***

cube root the number of which a given number is the cube *[*the *cube root* of 8 is 2*]*

cu·bic (kyo͞o'bik) ***adj.*** **1** having the shape of a cube: also **cu'bi·cal** (-bi kəl) **2** having the volume of a cube whose length, width, and depth each measure the given unit *[*a *cubic* foot*]*

cu·bi·cle (kyo͞o'bi kəl) ***n.*** ⟦< L *cubare*, lie down⟧ a small compartment

cub·ism (kyo͞ob'iz'əm) ***n.*** a school of modern art characterized by the use of cubes and other geometric forms in abstract arrangements —**cub'ist** ***n.***, ***adj.*** —**cu·bis'tic** ***adj.***

cu·bit (kyo͞o'bit) ***n.*** ⟦< L *cubitum*, elbow⟧ an ancient measure of length, about 18 to 22 inches

cuck·old (kuk'əld) ***n.*** ⟦see fol.⟧ a man whose wife has committed adultery —***vt.*** to make a cuckold of —**cuck'old·ry** (-rē) ***n.***

cuck·oo (ko͞o'ko͞o') ***n.*** ⟦< OFr *cucu*, echoic⟧ **1** a gray-brown bird with a long, slender body: many species lay eggs in the nests of other birds **2** its call —***adj.*** [Slang] crazy; foolish

cu·cum·ber (kyo͞o'kum'bər) ***n.*** ⟦< L *cucumis*⟧ a long, green-skinned fruit with firm, white flesh, used in salads or preserved as pickles

cud (kud) ***n.*** ⟦OE *cudu*⟧ a mouthful of swallowed food regurgitated from the first two parts of the stomach of cattle and other ruminants and chewed again

cud·dle (kud''l) ***vt.*** **-dled**, **-dling** ⟦early Modern Eng, make comfortable⟧ to hold lovingly in one's arms —***vi.*** to lie close and snug; nestle —***n.*** an embrace; hug

cud'dly (-lē) ***adj.*** **-dli·er**, **-dli·est** that invites cuddling: also **cud'dle·some**

cudg·el (kuj'əl) ***n.*** ⟦< OE *cycgel*⟧ a short, thick stick or club —***vt.*** **-eled** or **-elled**, **-el·ing** or **-el·ling** to beat with a cudgel

cue[1] (kyo͞o) ***n.*** ⟦< *q*, *Q* (? for L *quando*, when) found in 16th-c. plays⟧ **1** a signal in dialogue, etc. for an actor's entrance or speech **2** any signal to do something **3** a hint —***vt.*** **cued**, **cu'ing** or **cue'ing** to give a cue to

cue[2] (kyo͞o) ***n.*** ⟦var. of QUEUE⟧ a long, tapering rod used in billiards and pool to strike the white ball (**cue ball**)

Cuer·na·va·ca (kwer'nə vä'kə) city in SC Mexico: pop. 281,000

cuff (kuf) ***n.*** ⟦< ME *cuffe*, glove⟧ **1** a band or fold at the end of a sleeve **2** a turned-up fold at the bottom of a

THESAURUS

GRIND. **2** [To bruise severely] press, mash, bruise; see BEAT 1, BREAK 1. **3** [To defeat utterly] overwhelm, force down, annihilate; see DEFEAT 2.

crust ***n.*** hull, rind, pie crust; see SHELL 1.

cry ***n.*** **1** [A loud utterance] outcry, exclamation, clamor, shout, call, battle cry, halloo, hurrah, cheer, scream, shriek, yell, whoop, squall, groan, bellow, howl, bawl, holler, uproar, acclamation, roar; see also sense 2 and NOISE 2.—*Ant.* WHISPER, murmur, silence. **2** [A characteristic call] howl, hoot, wail, bawl, screech, bark, squawk, squeak, yelp, meow, whinny, moo, chatter, bay, cluck, crow, whine, trill, quack, cackle, caw, bellow, croak, coo, whistle, gobble, hiss, growl; see also YELL. **3** [A fit of weeping] sobbing, wailing, shedding tears, sorrowing, mourning, whimpering; see also TEARS. —**a far cry (from)** unlike, dissimilar, remote; see DIFFERENT.

cry ***v.*** **1** [To weep] weep, sob, wail, shed tears, snivel, sniffle, squall, lament, mourn, bewail, bemoan, moan, howl, keen, whimper, whine, weep over, complain, deplore, sorrow, grieve, fret, groan, burst into tears, choke up, cry one's eyes out, break down, break up*, blubber, bawl.—*Ant.* LAUGH, rejoice, exult. **2** [To call; *said of other than human creatures*] howl, bark, hoot, scream, screech, squawk, squeak, yelp, grunt, roar, shriek, meow, whinny, moo, bawl, snarl, chatter, bay, cluck, crow, whine, pipe, trill, coo, whistle, caw, bellow, quack, gabble, hiss, growl, croak, cackle, twitter, tweet; see also YELL.

crying ***n.*** shrieking, sorrow, sobbing; see TEARS. —**for crying out loud*** for God's sake; for heaven's sake; oh, no; see CURSE, NO.

crystallize ***v.*** become definite, take shape, be outlined; see FORM 4.

cub ***n.*** young, offspring, whelp; see ANIMAL.

cube ***n.*** six-sided solid, hexahedron, die; see SOLID.

cuddle ***v.*** snuggle, huddle, curl up; see NESTLE.

cue[1] ***n.*** prompt, warning signal, opening bars*; see SIGN 1.

cuff ***n.*** **1** [Edge of a sleeve or pants leg] French cuff, fold, wristband; see BAND 1. **2** [A blow] slap, punch, hit; see BLOW. —**off the cuff*** extemporaneous, extemporaneously, offhand; see INFORMAL. —**on the cuff*** on credit, charged, delayed; see UNPAID 1.

trouser leg **3** a slap —***vt.*** to slap —**off the cuff** [Slang] in an offhand manner; extemporaneously —**on the cuff** [Slang] on credit

cuff link a pair of linked buttons or any similar small device for fastening a shirt cuff

cui·sine (kwi zēn′, kwē-) ***n.*** ⟦Fr < L *coquere*, to cook⟧ **1** a style of cooking or preparing food **2** the food prepared, as at a restaurant

cuke (kyo͞ok) ***n.*** [Inf.] *short for* CUCUMBER

cul-de-sac (kul′də sak′) ***n.***, *pl.* **-sacs′** ⟦Fr, bottom of a sack⟧ a dead-end street

cu·li·nar·y (kyo͞o′lə ner′ē, kul′ə-) ***adj.*** ⟦< L *culina*, kitchen⟧ of cooking

cull (kul) ***vt.*** ⟦< L *colligere*, collect⟧ **1** to pick out and discard **2** to select and gather —***n.*** something rejected as not being up to standard

cul·mi·nate (kul′mə nāt′) ***vi.*** **-nat′ed**, **-nat′ing** ⟦< L *culmen*, peak⟧ to reach its highest point or climax —**cul′mi·na′tion *n.***

cu·lotte (ko͞o′lät′) ***n.*** ⟦Fr < L *culus*, posterior⟧ [*often pl.*] a woman's garment consisting of trousers made full in the legs to resemble a skirt

cul·pa·ble (kul′pə bəl) ***adj.*** ⟦< L *culpa*, fault⟧ deserving blame —**cul′pa·bil′i·ty *n.*** —**cul′pa·bly *adv.***

cul·prit (kul′prit) ***n.*** ⟦< Anglo-Fr *culpable*, guilty + *prit*, ready (to prove)⟧ a person guilty of a crime or offense

cult (kult) ***n.*** ⟦< L *cultus*, care, cultivation⟧ **1** a system of religious worship or ritual **2** devoted attachment to a person, principle, etc. **3** a sect —**cult′ism′ *n.*** —**cult′ist *n.***

cul·ti·vate (kul′tə vāt′) ***vt.*** **-vat′ed**, **-vat′ing** ⟦< L *colere*, to till⟧ **1** to prepare (land) for growing crops; till **2** to loosen the soil and kill weeds around (plants) **3** to grow (plants) **4** to develop or improve *[cultivate* your mind*]* **5** to seek to become familiar with —**cul′ti·va·ble** (-və bəl) or **cul′ti·vat′a·ble *adj.*** —**cul′ti·va′tor *n.***

cul′ti·va′tion *n.* **1** the act of cultivating **2** refinement, or culture

cul·ture (kul′chər) ***n.*** ⟦see CULT⟧ **1** cultivation of the soil **2** a growth of bacteria, etc. in a prepared substance **3** improvement of the mind, manners, etc. **4** development by special training or care **5** the skills, arts, etc. of a given people in a given period; civilization —***vt.*** **-tured**, **-tur·ing** to cultivate —**cul′tur·al *adj.*** —**cul′tur·al·ly *adv.***

culture shock the alienation, confusion, etc. that may be experienced by someone encountering new surroundings, a different culture, etc.

cul·vert (kul′vərt) ***n.*** ⟦< ?⟧ a drain or conduit under a road or embankment

cum (kum, ko͝om) ***prep.*** ⟦L⟧ with

cum·ber (kum′bər) ***vt.*** ⟦< OFr *combre*, a barrier⟧ to hinder; hamper

cum′ber·some *adj.* burdensome; unwieldy: also **cum′brous** (-brəs)

cum·in (kum′in, ko͞o′min) ***n.*** ⟦< Gr *kyminon*⟧ **1** an herb related to parsley and celery **2** its aromatic fruits, used as a seasoning

cum·mer·bund (kum′ər bund′) ***n.*** ⟦< Ar-Pers *kamar*, loins + Pers *band*, band⟧ a wide sash worn as a waistband, esp. with men's formal dress

cu·mu·la·tive (kyo͞o′myə lə tiv′, -lāt′iv) ***adj.*** ⟦< L *cumulus*, a heap⟧ increasing in effect, size, etc. by successive additions

cu·mu·lus (kyo͞o′myə ləs) ***n.***, *pl.* **-li′** (-lī′) ⟦L, a heap⟧ a bright, billowy type of cloud with a dark, flat base

cu·ne·i·form (kyo͞o nē′ə fôrm′) ***adj.*** ⟦< L *cuneus*, a wedge + -FORM⟧ **1** wedge-shaped **2** designating the characters in ancient Assyrian and Babylonian inscriptions —***n.*** cuneiform writing

cun·ning (kun′iŋ) ***adj.*** ⟦< ME *cunnen*, know⟧ **1** sly; crafty **2** made with skill **3** pretty and delicate; cute —***n.*** slyness; craftiness —**cun′ning·ly *adv.***

cup (kup) ***n.*** ⟦< L *cupa*, tub⟧ **1** a small, open container for beverages, usually bowl-shaped and with a handle **2** a cup and its contents **3** a cupful **4** anything shaped like a cup —***vt.*** **cupped**, **cup′ping** to shape like a cup

cup·board (kub′ərd) ***n.*** a closet or cabinet with shelves for cups, plates, food, etc.

cup′cake′ *n.* a small, round cake, often iced

cup′ful′ *n.*, *pl.* **-fuls′** as much as a cup will hold; specif., eight ounces

Cu·pid (kyo͞o′pid) ***n.*** **1** *Rom. Myth.* the god of love **2** [**c-**] a representation of Cupid as a naked, winged boy with bow and arrow

cu·pid·i·ty (kyo͞o pid′ə tē) ***n.*** ⟦< L *cupere*, to desire⟧ strong desire for wealth; avarice

cu·po·la (kyo͞o′pə lə) ***n.*** ⟦It < L *cupa*, a tub⟧ a small dome, etc. on a roof

cu·pro·nick·el (kyo͞o′prō nik′əl) ***n.*** an alloy of copper and nickel, used as in coins

cur (kʉr) ***n.*** ⟦prob. < ON *kurra*, to growl⟧ **1** a dog of mixed breed; mongrel **2** a contemptible person

cu·rate (kyoor′it) ***n.*** ⟦< L *cura*, care⟧ a member of the clergy who assists a vicar or rector —**cu′ra·cy** (-ə sē), *pl.* **-cies**, ***n.***

cu·ra·tive (kyoor′ət iv) ***adj.*** having the power to cure —***n.*** a remedy

cu·ra·tor (kyo͞o rāt′ər, kyoor′āt′ər) ***n.*** ⟦< L *curare*, take care of⟧ a person in charge of a department or collection in a museum, etc. —**cu·ra·to·ri·al** (kyoor′ə tôr′ē əl) ***adj.*** —**cu·ra′tor·ship *n.***

curb (kʉrb) ***n.*** ⟦< L *curvus*, bent⟧ **1** a chain or strap attached to a horse's bit, used to check the horse **2** anything that checks or restrains **3** a stone or concrete edging along a street —***vt.*** to restrain; control

curb service service offered to customers in parked cars, as at some restaurants

curb′side′ *adj.* at the curb or on the sidewalk adjacent to the street

curb′stone′ *n.* any of the stones or a row of stones, making up a curb

curd (kʉrd) ***n.*** ⟦< ME *crud*, coagulated substance⟧ [*often pl.*] the coagulated part of soured milk, from which cheese is made

cur·dle (kʉrd′'l) ***vt.***, ***vi.*** **-dled**, **-dling** to form into curd; coagulate

cure (kyoor) ***n.*** ⟦< L *cura*, care⟧ **1** a healing or being healed **2** a remedy **3** a method of medical treatment —***vt.*** **cured**, **cur′ing** **1** to restore to health **2** to get rid of (an ailment, evil, etc.) **3** *a*) to preserve (meat), as by

THESAURUS

culminate *v.* finish, close, end up*; see END 1.

culprit *n.* offender, felon, accused; see CRIMINAL.

cult *n.* clique, sect, followers; see FACTION, RELIGION 2.

cultivate *v.* **1** [Plant] till, garden, seed; see HARVEST, PLANT. **2** [Educate] nurture, refine, improve; see TEACH.

cultivation *n.* horticulture, agriculture, gardening; see FARMING.

cultural *a.* educational, socializing, refining, refined, constructive, influential, nurturing, disciplining, enlightening, civilizing, instructive, humanizing, beneficial, learned, artistic, aesthetic, educative, polishing, enriching, elevating, uplifting, ennobling, broadening, developmental.—*Ant.* PRIMITIVE, barbaric, crude.

culture *n.* **1** [Civilizing tradition] folklore, folkways, instruction, education, study, society, family, convention, habit, inheritance, learning, arts, sciences, custom, mores, knowledge, letters, literature, poetry, painting, music, lore, architecture, history, religion, humanism, the arts and sciences; see also CIVILIZATION.—*Ant.* DISORDER, barbarism, chaos. **2** [Refinement and education] breeding, gentility, enlightenment, learning, capacity, ability, skill, science, lore, education, training, art, perception, discrimination, finish, taste, grace, dignity, politeness, savoir-faire, manners, urbanity, dress, fashion, address, tact, nobility, kindness, polish; see also COURTESY 1, ELEGANCE, EXPERIENCE.—*Ant.* IGNORANCE, crudeness, vulgarity.

cultured *a.* cultivated, educated, informed, advanced, accomplished, enlightened, polished, well-bred, genteel, elegant, courteous, intellectual, sophisticated, sensitive, intelligent, au courant, able, well-read, up-to-date, well-informed, traveled, experienced, tolerant, understanding, appreciative, civilized, literary, urbane, mannerly, gently bred, chivalrous, erudite, gallant, lettered, highbrow, high-class*; see also LIBERAL, POLITE, REFINED 2.—*Ant.* PREJUDICED, narrow, backward.

cunning *a.* clever, skillful, ingenious; see INTELLIGENT.

cup *n.* vessel, bowl, goblet, mug, tumbler, beaker, stein, bumper, teacup, coffee cup, measuring cup, chalice; see also CAN 1, CONTAINER.

cupboard *n.* closet, locker, storeroom; see FURNITURE.

curable *a.* improvable, subject to cure, not hopeless, correctable, capable of improvement, healable, restorable, mendable.

curb *n.* **1** [Restraint] hindrance, chain, check; see BARRIER, RESTRAINT 2. **2** [Edge] border, ledge, lip; see EDGE 1, RIM.

curb *v.* retard, impede, subdue; see HINDER, RESTRAIN, RESTRICT.

curdle *v.* coagulate, condense, clot; see THICKEN.

cure *n.* restorative, remedy, antidote; see MEDICINE 2.

cure *v.* make healthy, restore, make whole; see HEAL.

salting or smoking *b*) to process (tobacco, leather, etc.), as by drying or aging —**cur'a·ble** *adj.* —**cur'er** *n.*
cu·ré (kyōō rā') *n.* ⟦Fr < L *cura*, care⟧ in France, a parish priest
cure'-all' *n.* something supposed to cure all ailments or evils
cu·ret·tage (kyōō ret'ij, kyōō'rə täzh') *n.* ⟦Fr⟧ the process of cleaning or scraping the walls of a body cavity with a spoonlike instrument
cur·few (kʉr'fyōō') *n.* ⟦< OFr *covrefeu*, lit., cover fire: orig. a nightly signal to cover fires and retire⟧ a time in the evening beyond which children, etc. may not appear on the streets or in public places
Cu·ri·a (kyoor'ē ə) *n.*, *pl.* **-ri·ae'** (-ē') ⟦L⟧ the official body governing the Roman Catholic Church under the authority of the pope
Cu·rie (kyoo rē', kyoor'ē), **Ma·rie** (mə rē') 1867-1934; Pol. chemist in France
cu·ri·o (kyoor'ē ō') *n.*, *pl.* **-os'** ⟦contr. of fol.⟧ an unusual or rare article
cu·ri·os·i·ty (kyoor'ē äs'ə tē) *n.*, *pl.* **-ties** **1** a desire to learn or know **2** inquisitiveness **3** anything curious, rare, etc.
cu·ri·ous (kyoor'ē əs) *adj.* ⟦< L *curiosus*, careful⟧ **1** eager to learn or know **2** prying or inquisitive **3** unusual; strange —**cu'ri·ous·ly** *adv.*
curl (kʉrl) *vt.* ⟦< ME *crul*, curly⟧ **1** to twist (esp. hair) into ringlets **2** to cause to bend around —*vi.* **1** to form curls **2** to form a spiral or curve —*n.* **1** a ringlet of hair **2** anything with a curled shape —**curl'er** *n.* —**curl'y**, **-i·er**, **-i·est**, *adj.* —**curl'i·ness** *n.*
cur·lew (kʉr'lōō', kʉrl'yōō') *n.* ⟦echoic⟧ a large, brownish wading bird with long legs
curl·i·cue (kʉr'li kyōō') *n.* ⟦< CURLY + CUE[2]⟧ a fancy curve, flourish, etc.
curl·ing (kʉr'liŋ) *n.* a game played on ice by two teams, in which a heavy disk of stone or iron is slid toward a target
cur·rant (kʉr'ənt) *n.* ⟦ult. < *Corinth*, ancient Gr city⟧ **1** a small, seedless raisin from the Mediterranean region **2** *a*) the sour berry of several species of hardy shrubs, made into jelly or jam *b*) any such shrub
cur·ren·cy (kʉr'ən sē) *n.*, *pl.* **-cies** ⟦see fol.⟧ **1** circulation **2** the money in circulation in any country; often, specif., paper money **3** general use or acceptance
cur·rent (kʉr'ənt) *adj.* ⟦< L *currere*, to run⟧ **1** now going on; of the present time **2** circulating **3** commonly accepted; prevalent —*n.* **1** a flow of water or air in a definite direction **2** a general tendency or drift, as of opinion **3** the flow or rate of flow of electricity in a conductor —**cur'rent·ly** *adv.*
cur·ric·u·lum (kə rik'yōō ləm, -yə-) *n.*, *pl.* **-la** (-lə) or **-lums** ⟦L, course for racing⟧ a course of study in a school —**cur·ric'u·lar** *adj.*
cur·ry[1] (kʉr'ē) *vt.* **-ried**, **-ry·ing** ⟦< OFr *correier*, to put in order⟧ **1** to use a currycomb on **2** to prepare (tanned leather) —**curry favor** to try to win favor as by flattery
cur·ry[2] (kʉr'ē) *n.*, *pl.* **-ries** ⟦Tamil *kari*, sauce⟧ **1** a powder prepared from various spices, or a sauce made with this **2** a stew made with curry —*vt.* **-ried**, **-ry·ing** to prepare with curry
cur'ry·comb' *n.* a circular comb with teeth or ridges, for rubbing down and cleaning a horse's coat —*vt.* to use a currycomb on
curse (kʉrs) *n.* ⟦OE *curs*⟧ **1** a calling on God or the gods to bring evil on some person or thing **2** a profane or obscene oath **3** evil or injury that seems to come in answer to a curse —*vt.* **cursed**, **curs'ing** **1** to call evil down on **2** to swear at **3** to afflict —*vi.* to swear; blaspheme —**be cursed with** to suffer from
curs·ed (kʉr'sid, kʉrst) *adj.* **1** under a curse **2** deserving to be cursed; evil; hateful
cur·sive (kʉr'siv) *adj.* ⟦ult. < L *currere*, to run⟧ designating writing in which the letters are joined
cur·sor (kʉr'sər) *n.* ⟦L, runner⟧ a movable indicator light on a computer video screen, marking the current position at which a character may be entered, changed, etc.
cur·so·ry (kʉr'sə rē) *adj.* ⟦ult. < L *currere*, to run⟧ hastily, often superficially, done —**cur'so·ri·ly** *adv.* —**cur'so·ri·ness** *n.*
curt (kʉrt) *adj.* ⟦L *curtus*, short⟧ brief, esp. to the point of rudeness —**curt'ly** *adv.* —**curt'ness** *n.*
cur·tail (kər tāl') *vt.* ⟦< L *curtus*, short⟧ to cut short; reduce —**cur·tail'ment** *n.*
cur·tain (kʉrt''n) *n.* ⟦< LL *cortina*⟧ a piece of cloth, etc. hung at a window, in front of a stage, etc. to decorate or conceal —*vt.* to provide with or shut off as with a curtain
curtain call **1** a call, usually by applause, for performers to return to the stage **2** such a return
curt·sy (kʉrt'sē) *n.*, *pl.* **-sies** ⟦var. of COURTESY⟧ a woman's gesture of greeting, respect, etc. made by bending the knees and lowering the body slightly —*vi.* **-sied**, **-sy·ing** to make a curtsy Also sp. **curt'sey**
cur·va·ceous (kər vā'shəs) *adj.* ⟦< CURVE⟧ having a full, shapely figure: said of a woman
cur·va·ture (kʉr'və chər) *n.* **1** a curving or being curved **2** a curve
curve (kʉrv) *n.* ⟦< L *curvus*, bent⟧ **1** a line having no straight part; bend with no angles **2** something shaped like, or moving in, a curve —*vt.*, *vi.* **curved**, **curv'ing** **1** to form a curve by bending **2** to move in a curve —**curv'y**, **-i·er**, **-i·est**, *adj.*
cush·ion (koosh'ən) *n.* ⟦< ML *coxinum*⟧ **1** a pillow or pad **2** a thing like this in shape or use **3** anything that absorbs shock —*vt.* to provide with a cushion
cush·y (koosh'ē) *adj.* **-i·er**, **-i·est** ⟦< Pers *khūsh*, pleasant⟧ [Slang] easy; comfortable
cusp (kusp) *n.* ⟦L *cuspis*⟧ a point or pointed end, as on the chewing surface of a tooth —**on the cusp** at a time of transition
cus·pid (kus'pid) *n.* ⟦see prec.⟧ a tooth with one cusp; canine tooth
cus·pi·dor (kus'pə dôr') *n.* ⟦< Port *cuspir*, to spit⟧ a spittoon
cuss (kus) *n.*, *vt.*, *vi.* [Inf.] CURSE
cus·tard (kus'tərd) *n.* ⟦< L *crusta*, crust⟧ a mixture of eggs, milk, sugar, etc., boiled or baked

THESAURUS

curfew *n.* late hour, time limit, check-in time; see LIMITATION 2.

curiosity *n.* **1** [Interest] concern, regard, inquiring mind, inquisitiveness, thirst for knowledge, a questing mind, questioning, interest, desire to know, interest in learning, scientific interest, healthy curiosity. **2** [An unusual object] oddity, rarity, marvel; see WONDER 2.

curious *a.* **1** [Strange or odd] rare, odd, unique; see UNUSUAL 2. **2** [Interested] inquiring, inquisitive, questioning; see INTERESTED 1.

curl *n.* coil, spiral, wave; see HAIR 1.

curl *v.* curve, coil, bend, spiral, crinkle, wind, twine, loop, crimp, lap, fold, roll, contort, form into a spiral, form into a curved shape, meander, ripple, buckle, zigzag, wrinkle, twirl.—*Ant.* STRAIGHTEN, uncurl, unbend.

curly *a.* curled, kinky, wavy, coiled, crinkly, looped, winding, wound; see also ROLLED 1.

currency *n.* coin, bank notes, cash; see MONEY 1.

current *a.* prevailing, contemporary, in fashion; see FASHIONABLE, MODERN 1, POPULAR 3.

current *n.* drift, tidal motion, ebb and flow; see FLOW, TIDE.

curse *n.* oath, blasphemy, obscenity, sacrilege, anathema, ban, cursing, profanity, denunciation, damning, cuss word*, cussing*, swearword, four-letter word. *Common exclamations and curses include the following (many of which are old-fashioned):* Lord, oh God, the Devil, bless my soul, bless me, mercy, gracious, goodness, in Heaven's name, gee*, sakes alive*, darn*, hang it all*, dang*, blast*, damn it*, damn*, by golly*, for crying out loud*, Judas Priest*, hell's bells*, geez*, jeez*, shoot*, hell*, good grief, nuts*, wow.

curse *v.* blaspheme, profane, swear, use foul language, be foulmouthed, be obscene, take the Lord's name in vain, damn, turn the air blue*, abuse, revile, swear at, insult, call down curses on the head of, blast, doom, fulminate, denounce, call names, cuss*, cuss out*.

cursed *a.* blighted, doomed, confounded; see DAMNED 1.

curt *a.* brief, concise, terse; see SHORT 2.

curtain *n.* hanging, screen, shade, drape, drapery, window covering, window treatment, blind. *Kinds of curtains include the following:* draw curtain, roller shade, valance, sheer, portiere, cafe curtains, vertical blinds, Venetian blinds.

curve *n.* sweep, bow, arch, circuit, curvature, crook. *Types of curves include the following:* bell curve, bell-shaped curve, hairpin curve, S-curve, sine curve, extrapolated curve, hyperbola, parabola, normal curve, logarithmic curve, French curve, circle, ellipse, arc.

curve *v.* bow, crook, twist; see BEND.

curved *a.* bowed, arched, rounded; see BENT.

cushion *n.* mat, seat, pad; see PILLOW.

cus·to·di·an (kəs tō′dē ən) ***n.*** ⟦< fol.⟧ **1** one who is responsible for the custody or care of something; caretaker **2** a person responsible for the maintenance of a building

cus·to·dy (kus′tə dē) ***n.***, *pl.* **-dies** ⟦< L *custos*, a guard⟧ a guarding or keeping safe; care; guardianship —**in custody** under arrest —**cus·to′di·al** (-tō′dē əl) ***adj.***

cus·tom (kus′təm) ***n.*** ⟦< L *com-*, intens. + *suere*, be accustomed⟧ **1** a usual practice; habit **2** *a)* a social practice carried on by tradition *b)* such practices collectively **3** [*pl.*] duties or taxes imposed on imported goods **4** the regular patronage of a business —***adj.*** **1** made or done to order **2** making things to order

cus′tom·ar′y ***adj.*** in keeping with custom; usual; habitual —**cus′tom·ar′i·ly** ***adv.***

cus′tom-built′ ***adj.*** built to order, to the customer's specifications

cus′tom·er ***n.*** a person who buys, esp. one who buys regularly

cus′tom·house′ ***n.*** an office where customs or duties are paid

cus′tom·ize′ ***vt.*** **-ized′**, **-iz′ing** to make according to individual specifications

cus′tom-made′ ***adj.*** made to order, to the customer's specifications

cut (kut) ***vt.*** **cut**, **cut′ting** ⟦ME *cutten*⟧ **1** to make an opening in with a sharp-edged instrument; gash **2** to pierce sharply so as to hurt **3** to have (a new tooth) grow through the gum **4** to divide into parts with a sharp-edged instrument; sever **5** to intersect; divide **6** to hew **7** to mow or reap **8** to reduce; curtail **9** to trim; pare **10** to divide (a pack of cards) **11** to make or do as by cutting **12** to hit (a ball) so that it spins **13** [Inf.] to pretend not to recognize (a person) **14** [Inf.] to stay away from (a school class, etc.) without being excused **15** [Slang] to stop —***vi.*** **1** to pierce, sever, gash, etc. **2** to take cutting *[pine cuts easily]* **3** to go (*across* or *through*) **4** to change direction suddenly **5** to make a sudden shift, as from one scene to another in a film **6** [Inf.] to swing a bat, etc. at a ball —***adj.*** **1** that has been cut **2** made or formed by cutting —***n.*** **1** a cutting or being cut **2** a stroke or opening made by a sharp-edged instrument **3** a piece cut off, as of meat **4** a reduction **5** a passage or channel cut out **6** the style in which a thing is cut **7** an act, remark, etc. that hurts one's feelings **8** a block or plate engraved for printing, or the impression from this **9** [Inf.] an unauthorized absence from school, etc. **10** [Inf.] a share, as of profits —**cut and dried** **1** arranged beforehand **2** lifeless; dull —**cut down** to reduce; lessen —**cut it out** [Inf.] to stop doing what one is doing —**cut off** **1** to sever **2** to stop abruptly; shut off —**cut out** [Inf.] fit or suited —**cut up** **1** to cut into pieces **2** [Slang] to clown, joke, etc.

cu·ta·ne·ous (kyo͞o tā′nē əs) ***adj.*** ⟦< L *cutis*, skin⟧ of or on the skin

cut′a·way′ ***n.*** a man's formal coat cut so as to curve back to the tails

cut′back′ ***n.*** a reduction or discontinuance, as of production

cute (kyo͞ot) ***adj.*** **cut′er**, **cut′est** ⟦< ACUTE⟧ [Inf.] **1** clever; shrewd **2** pretty or attractive, esp. in a dainty way —**cute′ly** ***adv.*** —**cute′ness** ***n.***

cute·sy or **cute·sie** (kyo͞ot′sē) ***adj.*** **-si·er**, **-si·est** [Inf.] cute in an affected way

cut·i·cle (kyo͞ot′i kəl) ***n.*** ⟦< L *cutis*, skin⟧ **1** the outer layer of the skin **2** hardened skin, as at the base and sides of a fingernail

cut·lass (kut′ləs) ***n.*** ⟦< L *culter*, plowshare⟧ a short, thick, curved sword

cut·ler·y (kut′lər ē) ***n.*** ⟦< L *culter*, plowshare⟧ **1** cutting implements, as knives and scissors **2** implements used in preparing and eating food

cut·let (kut′lit) ***n.*** ⟦< L *costa*, rib⟧ **1** a small slice of meat from the ribs or leg **2** a small, flat croquette of chopped meat or fish

cut′off′ ***n.*** a road, etc. that is a shortcut

cut′-rate′ ***adj.*** selling at a lower price

cut·ter (kut′ər) ***n.*** **1** a person or thing that cuts **2** a small, swift boat or ship

cut′throat′ ***n.*** a murderer —***adj.*** **1** murderous **2** merciless; ruthless

cut·ting (kut′iŋ) ***n.*** a shoot cut away from a plant for rooting or grafting —***adj.*** **1** that cuts; sharp **2** chilling or piercing **3** sarcastic; wounding —**cut′ting·ly** ***adv.***

cutting edge the leading or most advanced position; vanguard

cut·tle·fish (kut′'l fish′) ***n.***, *pl.* **-fish′** or (for different species) **-fish′es** ⟦OE *cudele*⟧ a sea mollusk with eight arms and two tentacles and a hard internal shell (**cut′tle·bone′**)

cwt *abbrev.* hundredweight

-cy (sē) ⟦< Gr *-kia*⟧ *suffix* **1** quality, condition, or fact of being *[idiocy]* **2** position, rank, or office of *[captaincy]*

cy·a·nide (sī′ə nīd′) ***n.*** a white, crystalline compound that is extremely poisonous

cy·ber·net·ics (sī′bər net′iks) ***n.*** ⟦< Gr *kybernan*, to steer + -ICS⟧ the comparative study of human control systems, as the brain, and complex electronic systems —**cy′ber·net′ic** ***adj.***

cy·ber·punk (sī′bər puŋk′) ***n.*** ⟦*cyber-* (see prec.) + PUNK[2] (*n.* 2)⟧ science fiction describing a future filled with violence, computers, and drugs

cy′ber·space′ (-spās′) ***n.*** the electronic system of linked computer networks, etc., thought of as an unlimited environment for accessing information, communicating, etc.

cy·cla·men (sī′klə mən) ***n.*** ⟦< Gr⟧ a plant of the primrose family with heart-shaped leaves

cy·cle (sī′kəl) ***n.*** ⟦< Gr *kyklos*, a circle⟧ **1** *a)* a period within which a round of regularly recurring events is completed *b)* a complete set of such events **2** a series of poems or songs on one theme **3** a bicycle, motorcycle,

THESAURUS

custodian ***n.*** superintendent, janitor, porter, cleaner, cleaning man, cleaning woman, attendant, caretaker, building superintendent, keeper, gatekeeper, night watchman; see also WATCHMAN.

custody ***n.*** care, guardianship, supervision, keeping, safekeeping, watch, superintendence, safeguarding; see also MANAGEMENT. —**take into custody** capture, apprehend, seize; see ARREST.

custom ***n.*** habit, practice, usage, wont, fashion, routine, precedent, use, form, addiction, rule, procedure, observance, characteristic, second nature, matter of course, beaten path, rut, manner, way, mode, method, system, style, vogue, convention, formality, mold, pattern, design, type, taste, character, ritual, rite, attitude, mores, dictate of society, unwritten law, etiquette, conventionality.—*Ant.* DEPARTURE, deviation, shift.

customarily ***a.*** usually, commonly, generally; see REGULARLY.

customary ***a.*** usual, wonted, habitual; see COMMON 1, CONVENTIONAL 1, 2.

customer ***n.*** client, patron, consumer; see BUYER.

cut ***a.*** **1** [Formed] shaped, modeled, arranged; see FORMED. **2** [Reduced] lowered, debased, marked down; see REDUCED 1, 2. **3** [Severed] split, divided, sliced through; see CARVED.

cut ***n.*** **1** [The using of a sharp instrument] slash, thrust, dig, prick, gouge, penetrating, dividing, separation, severance, slitting, hacking, slice, carving, chop, stroke, incision, cleavage, penetration, gash, cleft, mark, nick, notch, opening, groove, furrow, slit, wound, fissure; see also HOLE 1, INJURY. **2** [A reduction] decrease, diminution, lessening; see REDUCTION 1. **3** [The shape] fashion, figure, construction; see FORM 1. **4** [A section] segment, slice, portion; see PART 1, PIECE 1. **5** [A piece of butchered meat] piece, slice, chunk; see MEAT. **6** [*An insult] indignity, offense, abuse; see INSULT. —**a cut above*** superior, higher, more capable; see BETTER 1.

cut ***v.*** **1** [To sever] slice, separate, slice through, cut into, cleave, mow, prune, reap, shear, dice, chop down, chop, slit, split, cut apart, hew, fell, rip, saw through, chisel, cut away, snip, chip, quarter, clip, behead, scissor, bite, shave, dissect, bisect, amputate, gash, incise, truncate, lacerate, slash, notch, nick, indent, score, mark, scratch, rake, furrow, wound, gouge; see also CARVE. **2** [To cross] intersect, pass, move across; see CROSS 1. **3** [To shorten] curtail, delete, lessen; see DECREASE 2. **4** [To divide] split, break apart, separate; see DIVIDE. **5** [*To absent oneself from] shirk, avoid, stay away; see EVADE. **6** [To record electronically] make a record, make a recording, tape; see RECORD 3. —**cut back** reduce, curtail, shorten; see DECREASE 2. —**cut off** **1** [To remove] eliminate, sever, cut out; see REMOVE 1. **2** [To interrupt] intrude, break in on, cut in on; see INTERRUPT. —**cut out for** suited to, adequate, good for; see FIT. —**cut up** **1** [To chop] chop up, slice, dice; see CUT 1. **2** [*To clown] show off, play jokes, fool around*; see JOKE, PLAY 2.

cute* ***a.*** dainty, attractive, delightful; see CHARMING, PLEASANT 1, 2.

cycle ***n.*** revolution of time, period, recurrence; see AGE 3, SEQUENCE 1, SERIES.

etc. **4** *Elec.* one complete period of the reversal of an alternating current from positive to negative and back again —***vi.* -cled, -cling** to ride a bicycle, etc.

cy·cli·cal (sik′li kəl) ***adj.*** of, or having the nature of, a cycle; occurring in cycles

cy·clist (sīk′list, sī′kə list) ***n.*** one who rides a bicycle, motorcycle, etc.

cyclo- ⟦< Gr *kyklos*, a circle⟧ *combining form* of a circle or wheel; circular

cy·clom·e·ter (sī kläm′ət ər) ***n.*** ⟦prec. + -METER⟧ an instrument that records the revolutions of a wheel for measuring distance traveled

cy·clone (sī′klōn′) ***n.*** ⟦< Gr *kyklōma*, wheel⟧ a storm with strong winds rotating about a center of low pressure

cyclone fence a heavy-duty fence of interwoven steel links

Cy·clops (sī′kläps′) ***n.**, pl.* **Cy·clo·pes** (sī klō′pēz′) *Gr. Myth.* any of a race of one-eyed giants

cy·clo·tron (sī′klō trän′, -klə-) ***n.*** a circular apparatus for giving high energy to positive ions, as protons, used in atomic research

cyg·net (sig′net, -nit) ***n.*** ⟦< Gr *kyknos*, swan⟧ a young swan

cyl·in·der (sil′ən dər) ***n.*** ⟦< Gr *kylindein*, to roll⟧ **1** a solid, tubular figure consisting of two equal, parallel, circular bases joined by a smooth, continuous surface **2** anything with this shape; specif., *a)* the turning part of a revolver *b)* the piston chamber of an engine —**cy·lin·dri·cal** (sə lin′dri kəl) ***adj.***

cym·bal (sim′bəl) ***n.*** ⟦< Gr *kymbē*, hollow of a vessel⟧ *Music* a circular brass plate that makes a sharp, ringing sound when hit —**cym′bal·ist *n.***

cyn·ic (sin′ik) ***n.*** ⟦< Gr *kynikos*, doglike⟧ a cynical person

cyn′i·cal (-i kəl) ***adj.*** **1** denying the sincerity of people's motives and actions **2** sarcastic, sneering, etc. —**cyn′i·cal·ly *adv.***

cyn′i·cism′ (-ə siz′əm) ***n.*** **1** the attitude or beliefs of a cynic **2** a cynical remark, idea, etc.

cy·no·sure (sī′nə shoor′, sin′ə-) ***n.*** ⟦< Gr *kynosoura*, dog's tail⟧ a center of attention or interest

cy·pher (sī′fər) ***n.**, **vi.*** *Brit. sp. of* CIPHER

cy·press (sī′prəs) ***n.*** ⟦< Gr *kyparissos*⟧ **1** an evergreen tree with cones and dark foliage **2** its wood

Cy·prus (sī′prəs) country on an island at the E end of the Mediterranean: 3,572 sq. mi.; pop. 714,000 —**Cyp·ri·ot** (sip′rē ət) ***adj.**, **n.***

cyst (sist) ***n.*** ⟦< Gr *kystis*, sac⟧ a saclike structure in plants or animals, esp. one filled with diseased matter —**cyst′ic *adj.***

cystic fibrosis a children's disease marked by fibrosis of the pancreas and by frequent respiratory infections

cy·tol·o·gy (sī täl′ə jē) ***n.*** ⟦< Gr *kytos*, a hollow + -LOGY⟧ the branch of biology dealing with cells —**cy·tol′o·gist *n.***

cy·to·plasm (sīt′ō plaz′əm) ***n.*** ⟦< Gr *kytos*, a hollow + *plasma*, something molded⟧ the protoplasm of a cell, outside the nucleus

cy·to·sine (sīt′ō sēn′) ***n.*** ⟦Ger *zytosin*⟧ one of the four bases that combine to form DNA

czar (zär) ***n.*** ⟦Russ < L *Caesar*⟧ **1** the title of any of the former emperors of Russia **2** a person with wide-ranging power —**cza·ri·na** (zä rē′nə) ***fem.n.***

Czech (chek) ***n.*** **1** a member of a Slavic people of central Europe **2** the West Slavic language of the Czechs **3** loosely, a person born or living in Czechoslovakia **4** a person born or living in the Czech Republic —***adj.*** of the Czech Republic, its people, or their language

Czech·o·slo·va·ki·a (chek′ə slō vä′kē ə) former country in central Europe: divided (1993) into Czech Republic and Slovakia —**Czech′o·slo′vak** or **Czech′o·slo·vak′i·an *adj.**, **n.***

Czech Republic country in central Europe: formerly the W republic of Czechoslovakia: 30,450 sq. mi.; pop. 10,324,000

THESAURUS

cylinder ***n.*** **1** [An automobile part] compression chamber, combustion chamber, cylinder block; see AUTOMOBILE. **2** [A geometric form] circular cylinder, circular solid, barrel; see CIRCLE 1.

cynic ***n.*** misanthrope, misogynist, mocker, satirist, scoffer, pessimist, sarcastic person, caviler, carper, sneerer, unbeliever, egotist, man-hater, skeptic, doubter, questioner, detractor, doubting Thomas; see also CRITIC 1.—*Ant.* BELIEVER, optimist, idealist.

cynical ***a.*** scornful, skeptical, sneering; see SARCASTIC.

cynicism ***n.*** criticism, ridicule, contempt; see SARCASM.

czar ***n.*** emperor, autocrat, despot; see DICTATOR, KING, LEADER 2.

D

d[1] or **D** (dē) ***n.***, *pl.* **d's, D's** the fourth letter of the English alphabet

d[2] *abbrev.* **1** day(s) **2** degree **3** diameter **4** died **5** ⟦L *denarii*⟧ penny; pence

D[1] (dē) ***n.*** **1** a Roman numeral for 500 **2** a grade for below-average work **3** *Music* the second tone in the scale of C major

D[2] *abbrev.* **1** December **2** Democrat

-'d *contr.* **1** had or would: a shortened form used in contractions *[I'd seen; they'd see]* **2** *old sp. of* -ED *[foster'd]*

DA or **D.A.** *abbrev.* District Attorney

dab (dab) ***vt.***, ***vi.*** **dabbed, dab'bing** ⟦ME *dabben*, to strike⟧ **1** to touch lightly and quickly; pat **2** to put on (paint, etc.) with light, quick strokes —***n.*** **1** a tap; pat **2** a soft or moist bit of something

dab·ble (dab'əl) ***vi.*** **-bled, -bling** ⟦Du *dabbelen*, freq. of MDu *dabben*, to strike, dab⟧ **1** to play, dip, or paddle in water **2** to do something superficially: with *in* or *at*

Dac·ca (dä'kä) *former sp. of* DHAKA

dace (dās) ***n.***, *pl.* **dace** or **daces** a small freshwater fish related to the carp

dachs·hund (däks'hoont') ***n.*** ⟦Ger < *dachs*, badger + *hund*, dog⟧ a small dog with a long body, short legs, and drooping ears

Da·cron (dā'krän', dak'rän') *trademark for* a synthetic wrinkle-resistant fabric —***n.*** [*also* **d-**] this fabric

dac·tyl (dak'təl) ***n.*** ⟦< Gr *daktylos*, finger⟧ a metrical foot consisting of one accented syllable followed by two unaccented ones —**dac·tyl'ic** (-til'ik) ***adj.***

dad (dad) ***n.*** ⟦< child's cry *dada*⟧ [Inf.] father: also **dad·dy** (dad'ē), *pl.* **-dies**

daddy long'legs' an arachnid with long legs

da·do (dā'dō) ***n.***, *pl.* **-does** ⟦< L *datum*, a die⟧ **1** the part of a pedestal between the cap and the base **2** the lower part of a wall if decorated differently from the upper part **3** a rectangular groove cut in a board, used in forming a joint

daf·fo·dil (daf'ə dil') ***n.*** ⟦< Gr *asphodelos*⟧ a narcissus with long leaves and yellow flowers

daf·fy (daf'ē) ***adj.*** **-fi·er, -fi·est** ⟦< ME *dafte*, daft⟧ [Inf.] crazy; silly —**daf'fi·ness** ***n.***

daft (daft) ***adj.*** ⟦< OE *(ge)dæfte*, mild⟧ **1** silly **2** insane

dag·ger (dag'ər) ***n.*** ⟦< Prov *daga*⟧ **1** a weapon with a short, pointed blade, used for stabbing **2** *Printing* a reference mark (†)

da·guerre·o·type (də ger'ō tīp') ***n.*** ⟦after L. J. M. *Daguerre*, 19th-c. Fr inventor⟧ an early kind of photograph made on a chemically treated plate —***vt.*** **-typed'**, **-typ'ing** to photograph by this method

dahl·ia (dal'yə, däl'-) ***n.*** ⟦after A. *Dahl*, 18th-c. Swed botanist⟧ a perennial plant with large, showy flowers

dai·li·ness (dā'lē nəs) ***n.*** the ordinary, routine aspects of a way of life

dai·ly (dā'lē) ***adj.*** done, happening, or published every (week)day —***n.***, *pl.* **-lies** a daily newspaper —***adv.*** every day

daily double a bet or betting procedure in which winning depends on choosing both winners in two specified races

dain·ty (dān'tē) ***n.***, *pl.* **-ties** ⟦< OFr *deinté*⟧ a delicacy —***adj.*** **-ti·er, -ti·est** **1** delicious and choice **2** delicately pretty **3** *a)* of refined taste; fastidious *b)* squeamish —**dain'ti·ly** ***adv.*** —**dain'ti·ness** ***n.***

dai·qui·ri (dak'ər ē) ***n.*** ⟦after *Daiquirí*, Cuban village⟧ a cocktail made of rum, sugar, and lime or lemon juice

dair·y (der'ē) ***n.***, *pl.* **-ies** ⟦ME *daie*, dairymaid⟧ **1** a building or room where milk and cream are made into butter and cheese, etc. **2** a farm that produces, or a store that sells, milk and milk products —***adj.*** of milk and milk products —**dair'y·man** (-mən), *pl.* **-men**, ***n.***

dair'y·ing ***n.*** the business of producing or selling dairy products

da·is (dā'is) ***n.***, *pl.* **da'is·es** ⟦< ML *discus*, table⟧ a raised platform, as for a speaker

dai·sy (dā'zē) ***n.***, *pl.* **-sies** ⟦< OE *dæges eage*, day's eye⟧ a plant of the composite family, bearing flowers with white rays around a yellow disk

Da·lai La·ma (dä'lī lä'mə) the high priest of Lamaism

dale (dāl) ***n.*** ⟦OE *dæl*⟧ a valley

Dal·las (dal'əs) city in NE Texas: pop. 1,008,000

dal·ly (dal'ē) ***vi.*** **-lied, -ly·ing** ⟦< OFr *dalier*, to trifle⟧ **1** to flirt **2** to deal carelessly (*with*); toy **3** to waste time; loiter —**dal·liance** (dal'yəns, -ē əns) ***n.***

Dal·ma·tian (dal mā'shən) ***n.*** a large, short-haired dog with dark spots on a white coat

dam[1] (dam) ***n.*** ⟦ME⟧ a barrier built to hold back flowing water —***vt.*** **dammed, dam'ming** **1** to build a dam in **2** to keep back or confine

dam[2] (dam) ***n.*** ⟦see DAME⟧ the female parent of any four-legged animal

dam·age (dam'ij) ***n.*** ⟦< L *damnum*⟧ **1** injury or harm resulting in a loss **2** [*pl.*] *Law* money compensating for injury, loss, etc. —***vt.*** **-aged, -ag·ing** to do damage to —**dam'age·a·ble** ***adj.***

Da·mas·cus (də mas'kəs) capital of Syria: pop. 1,497,000

dam·ask (dam'əsk) ***n.*** ⟦after prec.⟧ **1** a reversible fabric in figured weave, used for table linen, etc. **2** deep pink or rose —***adj.*** **1** of or like damask **2** deep-pink or rose

dame (dām) ***n.*** ⟦< L *domina*, lady⟧ **1** [**D-**] in Great Britain, a woman's title of honor **2** [Slang] any woman

damn (dam) ***vt.*** **damned, damn'ing** ⟦< L *damnare*, condemn⟧ **1** to condemn to an unhappy fate **2** *Theol.* to condemn to hell **3** to condemn as bad, inferior, etc. **4** to swear at by saying "damn" —***n.*** the saying of "damn" as

THESAURUS

dab ***n.*** small quantity, fragment, lump; see BIT 1.

dab ***v.*** tap, pat, nudge; see TOUCH 1.

dabble ***v.*** trifle with, trifle, engage in superficially, amuse oneself with, dally, be an amateur, be a dilettante, have sport with, fiddle with, flirt with, toy with, putter, idle away time, work superficially, putter around, fool with*, fool around*, dip into.—*Ant.* STUDY, work at, become an expert.

dad* ***n.*** daddy*, male parent, pop*; see FATHER, PARENT.

dagger ***n.*** stiletto, short sword, blade; see KNIFE. **—look daggers at** glower at, look at with anger, scowl at; see DISLIKE.

daily ***a.*** diurnal, per diem, every day, occurring every day, issued every day, periodic, cyclic, day after day, once daily, by day, once a day, during the day, day by day, from day to day; see also REGULAR 3.

dainty ***a.*** delicate, fragile, petite, frail, thin, light, pretty, beautiful, lovely, attractive, trim, graceful, fine, neat, elegant, exquisite, precious, rare, soft, tender, airy, lacy, nice, darling*, cute*, sweet; see also CHARMING, WEAK.—*Ant.* ROUGH, coarse, gross.

dairy ***n.*** creamery, dairy farm, ice-cream plant, cheese factory, buttery, milk station, pasteurizing plant, cooperative; see also FARM.

dally with ***v.*** flirt with, trifle with, toy with; see DABBLE.

dam[1] ***n.*** dike, wall, bank, embankment, gate, levee, irrigation dam, beaver dam, cofferdam; see also BARRIER.

dam[1] ***v.*** hold back, check, obstruct, bar, slow, retard, restrict, stop up, close, clog, choke, block up, impede, hold, stop, block, confine; see also HINDER, RESTRAIN.—*Ant.* FREE, release, open up.

damage ***n.*** **1** [Injury] harm, hurt, wound, bruise, wrong, casualty, suffering, illness, stroke, affliction, accident, catastrophe, adversity, outrage, hardship, disturbance, mutilation, impairment, mishap, evil, blow, devastation, mischief, reverse, disablement, loss, collapse, vandalism; see also DISASTER, INJURY, MISFORTUNE.—*Ant.* BLESSING, benefit, boon. **2** [Loss occasioned by injury] ruin, breakage, ruined goods, wreckage, deprivation, waste, shrinkage, depreciation, pollution, corruption, blemish, contamination, defacement, degeneration, deterioration, ravage, havoc, erosion, disrepair, debasement, corrosion, atrophy, scratch, scar, erosion, decay, wear and tear, foul play; see also DESTRUCTION 2, LOSS 1.—*Ant.* IMPROVEMENT, betterment, growth.

damage ***v.*** ruin, wreck, tarnish, burn, scorch, dirty, rot, smash, bleach, drench, batter, discolor, mutilate, scratch, smudge, crack, bang up, abuse, maltreat, mar, deface, disfigure, mangle, contaminate, crumple, dismantle, cheapen, blight, disintegrate, pollute, ravage, sap, stain, tear, undermine, gnaw, corrode, break, split, stab, pierce, lacerate, cripple, rust, warp, maim, wound, taint, despoil, incapacitate, pervert, bruise, spoil, wear away, defile, wrong, corrupt, infect; see also BREAK, DESTROY.

damaged ***a.*** **1** [Injured] marred, in need of repair, in poor condition; see BROKEN 1, 2. **2** [Reduced in value because of damage] secondhand, used, faded; see CHEAP 1.

damages ***n.*** reparations, costs, reimbursement; see COMPENSATION, EXPENSE, EXPENSES.

damn ***v.*** curse, ban, doom, banish, excommunicate, sentence, convict, excoriate, cast into hell, torment, condemn to hell, condemn to eternal punishment, call down curses on; see also CONDEMN.—*Ant.* FORGIVE, bless,

a curse —***adj.***, ***adv.*** [Inf.] *short for* DAMNED —***interj.*** used to express anger, etc.
dam·na·ble (dam′nə bəl) ***adj.*** **1** deserving damnation **2** deserving to be sworn at —**dam′na·bly** ***adv.***
dam·na′tion (-nā′shən) ***n.*** a damning or being damned —***interj.*** used to express anger, etc.
damned (damd) ***adj.*** **1** condemned, as to hell **2** [Inf.] deserving cursing; outrageous —***adv.*** [Inf.] very
Dam·o·cles (dam′ə klēz′) ***n.*** *Classical Legend* a man whose king seated him under a sword hanging by a hair to show him the perils of a ruler's life
damp (damp) ***n.*** ⟦MDu, vapor⟧ a slight wetness —***adj.*** somewhat moist or wet; humid —***vt.*** **1** to bank (a fire): usually with *down* **2** to check or reduce —**damp′ness** ***n.***
damp′-dry′ ***vt.*** **-dried′**, **-dry′ing** to dry (laundry) so that some moisture is retained —***adj.*** designating or of laundry so treated
damp·en (dam′pən) ***vt.*** **1** to make damp; moisten **2** to deaden, depress, or reduce —**damp′en·er** ***n.***
damp·er (dam′pər) ***n.*** ⟦see DAMP⟧ **1** anything that deadens or depresses **2** a valve in a flue to control the draft **3** a device to check vibration in piano strings
dam·sel (dam′zəl) ***n.*** ⟦see DAME⟧ [Old-fashioned] a girl; maiden
dam′sel·fly′ ***n.***, *pl.* **-flies′** a slow-flying, brightly colored dragonfly
dam·son (dam′zən) ***n.*** ⟦ult. < *Damascenus*, of DAMASCUS⟧ a small, purple plum
Dan *abbrev.* Danish
dance (dans) ***vi.*** **danced**, **danc′ing** ⟦< OFr *danser*⟧ **1** to move the body and feet in rhythm, ordinarily to music **2** to move lightly, rapidly, gaily, etc. —***vt.*** **1** to perform (a dance) **2** to cause to dance —***n.*** **1** rhythmic movement, ordinarily to music **2** a particular kind of dance **3** the art of dancing **4** a party for dancing **5** a piece of music for dancing **6** rapid movement —**danc′er** ***n.***
D and C dilation (of the cervix) and curettage (of the uterus)
dan·de·li·on (dan′də lī′ən) ***n.*** ⟦< OFr *dent*, tooth + *de*, of + *lion*, lion⟧ a common weed with yellow flowers
dan·der (dan′dər) ***n.*** ⟦< ?⟧ **1** tiny, allergenic particles from fur, etc. **2** [Inf.] anger or temper
dan·dle (dan′dəl) ***vt.*** **-dled**, **-dling** ⟦< ?⟧ to move (a child) up and down on the knee or in the arms
dan·druff (dan′drəf) ***n.*** ⟦< earlier *dandro* + dial. *hurf*, scab⟧ little scales of dead skin on the scalp
dan·dy (dan′dē) ***n.***, *pl.* **-dies** ⟦< ?⟧ **1** a man overly attentive to his clothes and appearance **2** [Inf.] something very good —***adj.*** **-di·er**, **-di·est** [Inf.] very good; fine
Dane (dān) ***n.*** a person born or living in Denmark
dan·ger (dān′jər) ***n.*** ⟦ult. < L *dominus*, a master⟧ **1** liability to injury, damage, loss, etc.; peril **2** a thing that may cause injury, pain, etc.
dan′ger·ous ***adj.*** full of danger; unsafe; perilous —**dan′ger·ous·ly** ***adv.***
dan·gle (daŋ′gəl) ***vi.*** **-gled**, **-gling** ⟦< Scand⟧ to hang loosely so as to swing back and forth —***vt.*** to cause to dangle —**dan′gler** ***n.***
Dan·iel (dan′yəl) ***n.*** *Bible* a Hebrew prophet whose faith saved him in the lions' den
Dan·ish (dān′ish) ***adj.*** of Denmark or its people, language, etc. —***n.*** **1** the language of the Danes **2** [*also* **d-**] (a) rich, flaky pastry filled with fruit, cheese, etc.: in full **Danish pastry**
dank (daŋk) ***adj.*** ⟦ME⟧ disagreeably damp —**dank′ly** ***adv.*** —**dank′ness** ***n.***
dan·seuse (dän so͞oz′) ***fem.n.*** ⟦Fr⟧ a female ballet dancer —**dan·seur′** (-sʉr′) ***masc.n.***
Dan·te (Alighieri) (dän′tā, dan′tē) 1265-1321; It. poet
Dan·ube (dan′yo͞ob) river in S Europe, flowing from S Germany into the Black Sea
dap·per (dap′ər) ***adj.*** ⟦MDu, nimble⟧ **1** small and active **2** trim, neat, or dressed stylishly
dap·ple (dap′əl) ***adj.*** ⟦< ON *depill*, a spot⟧ marked with spots; mottled: also **dap′pled** —***vt.*** **-pled**, **-pling** to cover with spots
Dar·da·nelles (där′də nelz′) strait separating the Balkan Peninsula from Asia Minor
dare (der) ***vt.***, ***vi.*** **dared**, **dar′ing** ⟦OE *durran*⟧ **1** to have enough courage for (some act) **2** to challenge (someone) to do something —***n.*** a challenge —**dare say** to think probable —**dar′er** ***n.***
dare′dev′il (-dev′əl) ***adj.*** bold and reckless —***n.*** **1** a bold, reckless person **2** one who performs dangerous stunts
dar′ing ***adj.*** fearless; bold —***n.*** bold courage —**dar′ing·ly** ***adv.***
dark (därk) ***adj.*** ⟦< OE *deorc*⟧ **1** entirely or partly without light **2** *a)* almost black *b)* not light in color **3** hidden; secret **4** gloomy **5** evil; sinister **6** ignorant —***n.*** **1** the state of being dark **2** night or nightfall —**in the dark** uninformed; ignorant —**dark′ly** ***adv.*** —**dark′ness** ***n.***
Dark Ages the Middle Ages, esp. the earlier part
dark·en (där′kən) ***vt.***, ***vi.*** to make or become dark or darker —**dark′en·er** ***n.***

THESAURUS

elevate. —**not give a damn*** not care, be indifferent, reject; see NEGLECT 1. —**not worth a damn*** useless, unproductive, valueless; see WORTHLESS.

damnation ***n.*** damning, condemnation, doom; see BLAME, CURSE.

damned ***a.*** **1** [Consigned to hell] cursed, condemned, accursed, lost, infernal, gone to blazes*; see also UNFORTUNATE.—*Ant.* BLESSED, saved, holy. **2** [*Disapproved of] bad, unwelcome, blankety-blank*, blasted*, bloody*, danged*, darned*, doggone*, lousy*; see also BAD 1, UNDESIRABLE.—*Ant.* WELCOMED, desirable, favorite. —**do** (or **try**) **one's damnedest*** endeavor, do one's best, give one's all; see TRY 1.

damp ***a.*** moist, soaked, soggy; see WET 1.

dampen ***v.*** sprinkle, water, rinse; see MOISTEN.

dance ***n.*** **1** [Rhythmic movement] dancing, choreography, caper, hop, skip. *Types of dances include the following—social:* waltz, rumba, fox trot, polka, tango, cha-cha, disco, mambo, samba, twist, jitterbug, two-step, box-step, line dance, lambada, break dancing, slam dancing, Charleston, bunny hop, hokey-pokey; *theatrical:* ballet, modern dance, tap dance, soft-shoe; *traditional:* cotillion, polonaise, quadrille, pavane, mazurka, bolero, fandango, minuet; *folk and ethnic:* sun dance, ghost dance, rain dance, sword dance, snake dance, fertility dance, Highland fling, flamenco, Irish jig, square dance, Virginia reel, tarantella, hornpipe, clog, hora, hula. **2** [A dancing party] grand ball, dress ball, reception, ball, sock hop*, hoedown, shindig*, prom; see also PARTY 1.

dance ***v.*** waltz, shimmy, samba, jitterbug, twist, disco, fox-trot, cha-cha, mambo, tango, polka, hop, skip, jump, leap, bob, scamper, bounce, sway, swirl, sweep, swing, cut a rug*, rock*; see also MOVE 1.

dancer ***n.*** ballerina, danseur, danseuse, chorus girl, showgirl, stripper*, hoofer*; ballet, tap, toe, hula, belly, go-go, folk, square, modern, flamenco, break, etc. dancer.

dandy* ***n.*** very good, fine, first-rate; see EXCELLENT.

danger ***n.*** uncertainty, risk, peril, emergency, crisis, jeopardy, threat, hazard, insecurity, instability, exposure, menace, vulnerability; see also CHANCE 1.—*Ant.* SAFETY, security, certainty.

dangerous ***a.*** perilous, critical, serious, pressing, vulnerable, exposed, full of risk, threatening, alarming, urgent, hazardous, risky, menacing, ugly, nasty, formidable, terrible, deadly, insecure, precarious, ticklish, delicate, unstable, touchy, treacherous, bad, thorny, breakneck, shaky, on a collision course*, hairy*, under fire*, unhealthy, hot*; see also ENDANGERED, UNCERTAIN, UNSAFE.—*Ant.* CERTAIN, sure, secure.

dangerously ***a.*** desperately, precariously, severely; see SERIOUSLY 1.

dangle ***v.*** hover, swing, suspend; see HANG 1, 2.

dare ***v.*** **1** [To be courageous] take a chance, venture, adventure, undertake, try, attempt, endeavor, try one's hand, hazard, have the courage of one's convictions, take the bull by the horns*, go ahead, go for it*; see also CHANCE, RISK, TRY 1.—*Ant.* AVOID, dread, fear. **2** [To defy] meet, confront, oppose, disregard, brave, scorn, insult, resist, threaten, spurn, denounce, bully, mock, laugh at, challenge, have the nerve, face the music*, face up to, call someone's bluff; see also FACE 1.—*Ant.* AVOID, shun, evade.

daredevil ***n.*** stuntman, stuntwoman, gambler; see ADVENTURER.

daring ***a.*** bold, courageous, fearless; see BRAVE.

dark ***a.*** **1** [Lacking illumination] unlighted, unlit, dim, shadowy, somber, cloudy, foggy, sunless, lightless, indistinct, dull, faint, vague, dusky, dingy, murky, gloomy, obscure, pitch-dark, pitch-black, shady, shaded, clouded, darkened, overcast, opaque, without light, inky; see also BLACK 1, HAZY.—*Ant.* BRIGHT, lighted, illuminated. **2** [Dark in complexion] tan, swarthy, dark-complexioned; see BLACK 1. **3** [Evil] wicked, immoral, corrupt; see BAD 1.

dark ***n.*** gloom, evening, dusk; see DARKNESS 1. —**in the dark** uninformed, unaware, naive; see IGNORANT 1.

darken ***v.*** **1** [To grow darker] cloud up, cloud over, become dark; see SHADE 3. **2** [To make darker] cloud, shadow, blacken; see SHADE 2.

dark horse a little-known contestant thought unlikely to win
dark'room' ***n.*** a darkened room for developing photographs
dar·ling (där'liŋ) ***n.*** ⟦OE *deorling*⟧ a person much loved by another —***adj.*** **1** very dear; beloved **2** [Inf.] cute or attractive
darn[1] (därn) ***vt., vi.*** ⟦< Fr dial. *darner*⟧ to mend (cloth) by sewing a network of stitches across the gap —***n.*** a darned place in fabric
darn[2] (därn) ***vt., n., adj., adv., interj.*** [Inf.] damn: a euphemism —**darned** ***adj., adv.***
dart (därt) ***n.*** ⟦< OFr⟧ **1** a small, pointed missile for throwing or shooting **2** a sudden movement **3** a short, tapered seam **4** [*pl., with sing. v.*] a game in which darts (see sense 1) are thrown at a target (**dart'board'**) —***vt., vi.*** to send out or move suddenly and fast
Dar·von (där'vän') *trademark for* an analgesic drug containing a narcotic painkiller
Dar·win (där'win), **Charles** (**Robert**) (chärlz) 1809-82; Eng. naturalist: originated theory of evolution —**Dar·win'i·an** ***adj., n.*** —**Dar'win·ism'** ***n.***
dash (dash) ***vt.*** ⟦< Scand⟧ **1** to throw so as to break; smash **2** to throw or thrust (*away, down*, etc.) **3** to splash **4** to destroy, frustrate —***vi.*** **1** to strike violently (*against*) **2** to rush —***n.*** **1** a splash **2** a bit of something added *[*a *dash* of salt*]* **3** a rush **4** a short, fast race **5** spirit; vigor **6** the mark of punctuation (— or –) used to indicate a break, omission, etc. —**dash off** to do, write, etc. hastily —**dash'er** ***n.***
dash'board' ***n.*** a panel with controls and gauges, as in an automobile
da·shi·ki (dä shē'kē) ***n.*** a loosefitting, brightly colored robe or tunic, modeled after an African tribal garment
dash'ing ***adj.*** **1** full of dash or spirit; lively **2** showy; striking; stylish —**dash'ing·ly** ***adv.***
das·tard·ly (das'tərd lē) ***adj.*** ⟦< ME *dastard*, a craven⟧ mean, cowardly, etc.
dat *abbrev.* dative
da·ta (dāt'ə, dat'ə) ***pl.n.*** [*now usually with sing. v.*] **1** facts or figures from which conclusions can be drawn **2** information in a form suitable for computer storage, etc.
da'ta·base' ***n.*** a mass of data, as in a computer, arranged for rapid expansion, updating, and retrieval: also **data base**
data processing the handling of large amounts of information, esp. by a computer —**data processor**
date[1] (dāt) ***n.*** ⟦< L *dare*, give⟧ **1** the time at which a thing happens, was made, etc. **2** the day of the month **3** [*pl.*] a person's birth and death dates **4** *a)* an appointment *b)* a romantic social engagement with a person *c)* this person —***vt.*** **dat'ed, dat'ing** **1** to mark (a letter, etc.) with a date **2** to find out or give the date of **3** to make seem old-fashioned **4** to have romantic social engagements with —***vi.*** **1** to belong to a definite period in the past: usually with *from* **2** to have romantic social engagements —**to date** up to now —**dat'er** ***n.***
date[2] (dāt) ***n.*** ⟦< Gr *daktylos*, a date⟧ the sweet, fleshy fruit of a desert palm tree (**date palm**)
date'book' ***n.*** a notebook for entering appointments, etc.
date'line' ***n.*** the date and place of writing or issue, as given in a line in a newspaper story, etc.
da·tive (dāt'iv) ***n.*** ⟦< L *dativus*, relating to giving⟧ *Gram.* the case of the indirect object of a verb
da·tum (dāt'əm, dat'-) ***n.*** ⟦L, what is given⟧ *sing. of* DATA
daub (dôb) ***vt., vi.*** ⟦< L *de-*, intens. + *albus*, white⟧ **1** to cover or smear with sticky, soft matter **2** to paint badly —***n.*** **1** anything daubed on **2** a daubing stroke —**daub'er** ***n.***
daugh·ter (dôt'ər) ***n.*** ⟦< OE *dohtor*⟧ **1** a girl or woman as she is related to either or both parents **2** a female descendant —**daugh'ter·ly** ***adj.***
daugh'ter-in-law' ***n., pl.*** **daugh'ters-in-law'** the wife of one's son
Dau·mier (dō myā'), **Ho·no·ré** (ô nô rā') 1808-79; Fr. painter
daunt (dônt) ***vt.*** ⟦< L *domare*, to tame⟧ to intimidate or dishearten
daunt'less ***adj.*** that cannot be daunted; fearless —**daunt'less·ly** ***adv.*** —**daunt'less·ness** ***n.***
dau·phin (dô'fin) ***n.*** ⟦Fr, dolphin⟧ the eldest son of the king of France: a title used from 1349 to 1830
dav·en·port (dav'ən pôrt') ***n.*** ⟦< ?⟧ a large couch or sofa
Da·vid (dā'vid) ***n.*** *Bible* the second king of Israel and Judah
da Vin·ci (də vin'chē), **Le·o·nar·do** (lē'ə när'dō) 1452-1519; It. painter, sculptor, architect, & scientist
Da·vis (dā'vis), **Jefferson** 1808-89; president of the Confederacy (1861-65)
da·vit (dā'vit, dav'it) ***n.*** ⟦OFr dim. of *David*⟧ either of a pair of uprights on a ship for lowering or raising a small boat
daw·dle (dôd''l) ***vi., vt.*** **-dled, -dling** ⟦< ?⟧ to waste (time) in trifling or by being slow —**daw'dler** ***n.***
dawn (dôn) ***vi.*** ⟦< OE *dagian*⟧ **1** to begin to be day **2** to begin to appear, develop, etc. **3** to begin to be understood or felt —***n.*** **1** daybreak **2** the beginning (*of* something)
day (dā) ***n.*** ⟦OE *dæg*⟧ **1** the period of light between sunrise and sunset **2** the time (24 hours) that it takes the earth to rotate once on its axis **3** [*also pl.*] a period; era **4** a time of power, glory, etc. **5** daily work period *[*an 8-hour *day]* —**day after day** every day: also **day in, day out**
day'bed' ***n.*** a couch that can also be used as a bed
day'break' ***n.*** the time in the morning when light first appears
day care daytime care given to children, as at a day-care

THESAURUS

darkness ***n.*** **1** [Gloom] dark, dusk, murkiness, dimness, shade, blackness, pitchdarkness, twilight, eclipse, nightfall, obscurity, cloudiness; see also NIGHT 1. **2** [Evil] wickedness, sin, corruption; see EVIL 1. **3** [Secrecy] concealment, isolation, seclusion; see PRIVACY, SECRECY.

darling ***n.*** lover, sweetheart, dear one, beloved, dear heart, heart's desire, dearest, pet, angel, love, sweetie pie*, sugar*, honey, precious*, sweetie*, hon*, light of my life*, baby*, one and only*.

darn[1] ***v.*** mend, sew, patch; see REPAIR.

dart ***n.*** missile, barb, arrow; see WEAPON.

dart ***v.*** shoot, shoot out, speed, plunge, launch, thrust, hurtle, fling, heave, pitch, dash, spurt, spring, spring up, fly, fire off, scoot*; see also MOVE 1.—*Ant.* STOP, amble, loiter.

dash ***n.*** **1** [A short, swift movement] spurt, charge, rush; see RUN 1. **2** [Punctuation marking a break in thought] em, em dash, en dash, hyphen; see also MARK 1, PUNCTUATION. **3** [A little of something] a few drops, hint, sprinkle, seasoning, touch, grain, trace, suspicion, suggestion, taste; see also BIT 1, PART 1.—*Ant.* TOO MUCH, quantity, excess.

dash ***v.*** **1** [To discourage] dampen, dismay, dispirit; see DISCOURAGE. **2** [To sprint] race, speed, hurry; see RUN 1.

data ***n.*** evidence, reports, details, results, notes, documents, abstracts, testimony, facts, raw data, memorandums, memos, records, findings, numbers, statistics, figures, measurements, conclusions, information, experiments, info*, dope*; see also DECLARATION, KNOWLEDGE 1, PROOF 1.

date[1] ***n.*** **1** [A specified time or period of time] epoch, period, era, generation, day, term, course, spell, duration, span, moment, minute, reign, hour, century; see also AGE 3, TIME 2, YEAR. **2** [An appointment] meeting, rendezvous, engagement, interview, call, visit; see also APPOINTMENT 2. **3** [Person with whom one has a date] partner, companion, associate; see FRIEND, LOVER 1. —**out of date** obsolete, passé, antiquated; see OLD-FASHIONED. —**to date** until now, as yet, so far; see NOW 1. —**up-to-date** modern, contemporary, current; see FASHIONABLE.

date[1] ***v.*** **1** [To indicate historical time] ascertain the time of, determine, assign a time to, mark with a date, fix the date of, chronicle, isolate, carbon-date; see also DEFINE 1, MEASURE 1, RECORD 1. **2** [To court or be courted] escort, associate with, take out*, keep company with, go out with*, go together*, make a date with, go steady*; see also ACCOMPANY.

daughter ***n.*** female child, female offspring, descendant, stepdaughter, infant; see also CHILD, GIRL.

dawn ***n.*** dawning, sunrise, daybreak; see MORNING 1.

day ***n.*** **1** [The time of light or work] daylight, daytime, full day, working day, daylight hours, eight-hour day, sizzler*, scorcher*; good day, bad day, hot day, rainy day. **2** [A special day] feast day, celebration, festival; see HOLIDAY. **3** [A period of time] era, age, time; see AGE 3. —**call it a day*** finish, quit working, end; see STOP 1. —**day after day** continuously, daily, steadily; see REGULARLY. —**day in and day out** consistently, steadily, every day; see DAILY, REGULARLY. —**from day to day** without thought for the future, sporadically, heedlessly; see IRREGULARLY.

center, or to the elderly, as at a social agency —**day'-care'** *adj.*
day'dream' *n.* **1** a pleasant, dreamy series of thoughts **2** a visionary scheme —*vi.* to have daydreams
day'light' *n.* **1** the light of day **2** dawn **3** understanding
daylight saving time [*often* **D- S- T-**] time that is one hour later than standard time: also **daylight savings time**
Day of Atonement Yom Kippur
day'time' *n.* the time between dawn and sunset
day'-to-day' *adj.* daily; routine
Day·ton (dāt′'n) city in SW Ohio: pop. 182,000
Day·to·na Beach (dā tō′nə) resort city in NE Florida, on the Atlantic: pop. 62,000
day trading rapid buying and selling of stocks on the Internet —**day trader**
daze (dāz) *vt.* **dazed, daz'ing** ⟦< ON *dasi*, tired⟧ to stun or bewilder —*n.* a dazed condition —**daz'ed·ly** *adv.*
daz·zle (daz′əl) *vt., vi.* **-zled, -zling** ⟦freq. of DAZE⟧ **1** to overpower or be overpowered by bright light **2** to surprise or arouse admiration with brilliant qualities, display, etc. —*n.* a dazzling —**daz'zler** *n.*
db or **dB** *abbrev.* decibel(s)
DC *abbrev.* **1** direct current: also **dc** **2** District of Columbia
DD or **D.D.** *abbrev.* Doctor of Divinity
DDS or **D.D.S.** *abbrev.* Doctor of Dental Surgery
DDT (dē′dē′tē′) *n.* ⟦< its chemical name⟧ a powerful insecticide
de- ⟦< Fr *dé-* or L *de*⟧ *prefix* **1** away from, off *[derail]* **2** down *[degrade]* **3** entirely *[defunct]* **4** reverse the action of *[decode]*
DE Delaware
DEA *abbrev.* Drug Enforcement Administration
dea·con (dē′kən) *n.* ⟦< Gr *diakonos*, servant⟧ **1** a cleric ranking just below a priest **2** a church officer who helps the minister —**dea'con·ess** *fem.n.*
de·ac·ti·vate (dē ak′tə vāt′) *vt.* **-vat'ed, -vat'ing** **1** to make (an explosive, chemical, etc.) inactive **2** *Mil.* to demobilize
dead (ded) *adj.* ⟦OE⟧ **1** no longer living **2** without life **3** deathlike **4** lacking warmth, interest, brightness, etc. **5** without feeling, motion, or power **6** extinguished or extinct **7** no longer used; obsolete **8** unerring *[a dead shot]* **9** complete *[a dead stop]* **10** precise *[dead center]* **11** [Inf.] very tired —*n.* the time of most darkness, most cold, etc. *[the dead of night]* —*adv.* **1** completely **2** directly *[dead ahead]* —**the dead** those who have died
dead'beat' *n.* [Slang] one who tries to evade paying debts
dead'bolt' *n.* a lock for a door, with a bolt that can be moved only by turning the key
dead·en (ded′'n) *vt.* **1** to lessen the vigor or intensity of; dull **2** to numb
dead end **1** a street, alley, etc. closed at one end **2** an impasse —**dead'-end'** *adj.*
dead heat a race in which two or more contestants finish even; tie
dead letter **1** a rule, law, etc. no longer enforced **2** an unclaimed postal letter
dead'line' *n.* the latest time by which something must be done
dead'lock' *n.* a standstill resulting from the action of equal and opposed forces —*vt., vi.* to bring or come to a deadlock
dead'ly *adj.* **-li·er, -li·est** **1** causing or likely to cause death **2** implacable *[deadly enemies]* **3** typical of death *[deadly pallor]* **4** extreme **5** very boring **6** very accurate *[deadly aim]* —*adv.* extremely —**dead'li·ness** *n.*
dead'-on' *adj.* [Inf.] completely accurate
dead'pan' *adj., adv.* without expression; blank(ly)
Dead Sea inland body of salt water on the Israeli-Jordanian border
dead'wood' *n.* anything useless or burdensome
deaf (def) *adj.* ⟦OE⟧ **1** unable to hear **2** unwilling to respond, as to a plea —**deaf'ness** *n.*
deaf'en (-ən) *vt.* **1** to make deaf **2** to overwhelm with noise —**deaf'en·ing** *adj.*
deaf'-mute' *n.* a person who is deaf and therefore has not learned to speak
deal[1] (dēl) *vt.* **dealt** (delt), **deal'ing** ⟦< OE *dǣlan*⟧ **1** to portion out or distribute **2** to give; administer (a blow, etc.) **3** [Slang] to sell (illegal drugs) —*vi.* **1** to have to do (*with*) *[science deals with facts]* **2** to conduct oneself *[deal fairly with others]* **3** to do business (*with* or *in*) **4** to distribute playing cards to the players —*n.* **1** the distributing of playing cards **2** a business transaction **3** a bargain or agreement, esp. when secret **4** [Inf.] treatment *[a fair deal]* —**deal'er** *n.*
deal[2] (dēl) *n.* ⟦OE *dǣl*, a part⟧ an indefinite amount —**a good** (or **great**) **deal** **1** a large amount **2** very much
deal'er·ship' *n.* a franchise to sell a product in a specified area
deal'ing *n.* **1** way of acting **2** [*usually pl.*] transactions or relations
dean (dēn) *n.* ⟦< LL *decanus*, chief of ten (monks, etc.)⟧ **1** the presiding official of a cathedral **2** a college official in charge of students or faculty **3** the senior or preeminent member of a group
dean's list a list of students at a college who have earned high grades
dear (dir) *adj.* ⟦OE *deore*⟧ **1** much loved **2** esteemed: a polite form of address *[Dear Sir]* **3** high-priced; costly **4** earnest *[our dearest wish]* —*n.* a loved person; darling —**dear'ly** *adv.* —**dear'ness** *n.*
Dear John (letter) [Inf.] a letter, as to a fiancé, breaking off a close relationship
dearth (durth) *n.* ⟦ME *derth*⟧ scarcity or lack
death (deth) *n.* ⟦OE⟧ **1** the act or fact of dying **2** the state of being dead **3** end or destruction **4** the cause of death —**death'like'** *adj.*

THESAURUS

daydream *n.* trance, vision, fantasy; see DREAM.
daylight *n.* daytime, daylight hours, broad daylight; see DAY 1. —**scare** (or **beat** or **knock**) **the daylights out of*** frighten, scare, beat; see THREATEN.
daze *n.* stupor, trance, bewilderment; see CONFUSION.
dazed *a.* confused, bewildered, disoriented; see DOUBTFUL.
dead *a.* **1** [Without life] not existing, expired, deceased, perished, lifeless, inanimate, late, defunct, breathless, no longer living, devoid of life, departed, brain-dead, clinically dead, gone, no more*, done for*, gone the way of all flesh*, gone to one's reward*, gone to meet one's Maker, at rest with God*, out of one's misery*, snuffed out*, pushing up daisies*, rubbed out*, wasted*, liquidated*, erased*, gone by the board, resting in peace*.—*Ant.* ALIVE, animate, enduring. **2** [Without the appearance of life] inert, still, stagnant; see DULL 2. **3** [Numb] insensible, deadened, anesthetized; see NUMB 1, UNCONSCIOUS. **4** [*Exhausted] wearied, worn, spent; see TIRED.
deaden *v.* blunt, impair, dull, repress, slow, paralyze, freeze, anesthetize, put to sleep, numb, knock out, incapacitate, depress, stifle, benumb, smother, retard, KO*; see also HURT, WEAKEN 2.—*Ant.* EXCITE, revitalize, invigorate.
deadlock *n.* standstill, stalemate, impasse; see PAUSE.
deadly *a.* fatal, lethal, murderous, mortal, homicidal, virulent, poisonous, bloody, destructive, venomous, life-threatening, deathly, toxic, terminal, malignant, injurious, carcinogenic, suicidal, bloodthirsty, cannibalistic, harmful, violent; see also DANGEROUS.
deaf *a.* unable to hear, hearing-impaired, without hearing, deaf and dumb, deafened, stunned, hard of hearing.
deafening *a.* thunderous, overpowering, shrieking; see LOUD 1, 2.
deal[1] *v.* trade, bargain, barter; see BUY, SELL. —**deal with** handle, manage, have to do with; see TREAT 1.
deal[1,2] *n.* **1** [An agreement] pledge, compromise, pact; see AGREEMENT, CONTRACT. **2** [A secret or dishonest agreement] swindle, robbery, graft; see CRIME, THEFT. **3** [A lot] much, abundance, superabundance; see PLENTY. —**a good** (or **great**) **deal** a lot, quite a bit, a considerable amount; see MUCH. —**make a big deal out of*** expand, magnify, blow up; see EXAGGERATE.
dealer *n.* retailer, trader, vendor; see BUSINESSMAN, MERCHANT.
dealings *n.* business, trade, transactions; see BUSINESS 1, 4.
dear *a.* precious, respected, cherished; see BELOVED.
dear *n.* loved one, sweetheart, love; see DARLING, LOVER 1.
dearly *a.* **1** [In an affectionate manner] fondly, affectionately, yearningly; see LOVINGLY. **2** [To a great extent] greatly, extremely, profoundly; see VERY.
death *n.* decease, dying, demise, passing, loss of life, departure, release, parting, end of life, afterlife, other world, grave, tomb, paradise, heaven, hell, extinction, mortality, exit, end, finish, the way of all flesh*, the Grim Reaper*, eternal rest, last rest*; see also DESTRUCTION 1.—*Ant.* LIFE, birth, beginning. —**at death's door** failing, wasting away, nearly dead; see DYING 1, 2. —**to death** very much, extremely, to the extreme; see MUCH 1. —**to the death** to the end,

death'bed' *n.* used chiefly in the phrase **on one's deathbed**, during the last hours of one's life

death'blow' *n.* **1** a blow that kills **2** a thing fatal (*to* something)

death'less *adj.* that cannot die; immortal —**death'less·ly** *adv.*

death'ly *adj.* like or characteristic of death —*adv.* extremely *[deathly* ill*]*

death'trap' *n.* an unsafe building, vehicle, etc.

Death Valley dry, hot desert basin in E California & S Nevada

deb (deb) *n.* [Inf.] *short for* DEBUTANTE

de·ba·cle (di bä'kəl) *n.* ⟦Fr *débâcler*, break up⟧ **1** a crushing defeat **2** a ruinous collapse

de·bar (dē bär') *vt.* **-barred'**, **-bar'ring** ⟦< Anglo-Fr: see DE- & BAR⟧ to keep (a person) *from* some right, etc. —**de·bar'ment** *n.*

de·bark (dē bärk') *vt.*, *vi.* ⟦< Fr: see DE- & BARK[3]⟧ to unload from or leave a ship or aircraft —**de·bar·ka·tion** (dē'bär kā'shən) *n.*

de·base (dē bās') *vt.* **-based'**, **-bas'ing** ⟦DE- + BASE[2]⟧ to make lower in value, dignity, etc. —**de·base'ment** *n.*

de·bate (dē bāt') *vi.*, *vt.* **-bat'ed**, **-bat'ing** ⟦< OFr: see DE- & BATTER[1]⟧ **1** to discuss reasons for and against (something) **2** to take part in a debate with (a person) or about (a question) —*n.* **1** a discussion of opposing reasons **2** a formal contest of skill in reasoned argument —**de·bat'a·ble** *adj.* —**de·bat'er** *n.*

de·bauch (dē bôch') *vt.* ⟦< OFr *desbaucher*, seduce⟧ to lead astray morally; corrupt; deprave —*n.* an orgy —**de·bauch'er·y**, *pl.* **-ies**, *n.*

deb·au·chee (deb'ô shē', di bôch'ē') *n.* a dissipated person

de·ben·ture (di ben'chər) *n.* ⟦< L: see DEBT⟧ **1** a voucher acknowledging a debt **2** an interest-bearing bond issued without specified security

de·bil·i·tate (dē bil'ə tāt') *vt.* **-tat'ed**, **-tat'ing** ⟦< L *debilis*, weak⟧ to make weak

de·bil·i·ty (də bil'ə tē) *n.*, *pl.* **-ties** ⟦see prec.⟧ weakness; feebleness

deb·it (deb'it) *n.* ⟦< L *debere*, owe⟧ **1** an entry in an account of money owed **2** the total of such entries —*vt.* to enter as a debit

debit card a bank card that allows the cost of purchases to be deducted from a bank account

deb·o·nair (deb'ə ner') *adj.* ⟦< OFr *de bon aire*, lit., of good breed⟧ **1** carefree; jaunty **2** urbane Also sp. **deb'o·naire'** —**deb'o·nair'ly** *adv.*

de·brief (dē brēf') *vt.* ⟦DE- + BRIEF⟧ to receive information from (a pilot, emissary, etc.) about a recent mission

de·bris or **dé·bris** (də brē') *n.* ⟦Fr < OFr *desbrisier*, break apart⟧ bits and pieces of stone, rubbish, etc.

debt (det) *n.* ⟦< L *debere*, owe⟧ **1** something owed to another **2** the condition of owing *[*to be in *debt]*

debt'or (-ər) *n.* one who owes a debt

de·bug (dē bug') *vt.* **-bugged'**, **-bug'ging** ⟦DE- + BUG⟧ **1** to correct defects in **2** [Inf.] to find and remove hidden electronic listening devices from

de·bunk (dē buŋk') *vt.* ⟦DE- + BUNK[2]⟧ to expose the exaggerated or false claims, etc. of

De·bus·sy (də bü sē'; *E* deb'yoo sē'), **Claude** (klōd; *E* klôd) 1862-1918; Fr. composer

de·but or **dé·but** (dā byoo', dā'byoo') *n.* ⟦Fr < *débuter*, to lead off⟧ **1** a first public appearance **2** the formal introduction of a young woman into society —*vi.* to make a debut

deb·u·tante (deb'yoo tänt') *n.* ⟦Fr⟧ a young woman making a debut into society

dec *abbrev.* deceased

Dec *abbrev.* December

deca- ⟦< Gr *deka*, ten⟧ *combining form* ten: also **dec-**

dec·ade (dek'ād') *n.* ⟦< Gr *deka*, ten⟧ a period of ten years

dec·a·dence (dek'ə dəns, di kād''ns) *n.* ⟦< L *de-*, from + *cadere*, to fall⟧ a decline, as in morals, art, etc.; deterioration —**dec'a·dent** *adj.*, *n.*

de·caf (dē'kaf') *n.* [Inf.] decaffeinated coffee

de·caf·fein·at·ed (dē kaf'ə nāt'id) *adj.* with caffeine removed

de·cal (dē'kal, di kal') *n.* ⟦< *decalcomania* < Fr < L *calcare*, to tread + Gr *mania*, madness⟧ a picture or design transferred from prepared paper to glass, wood, etc.

Dec·a·logue or **Dec·a·log** (dek'ə lôg') *n.* ⟦see DECA- & -LOGUE⟧ [*sometimes* **d-**] TEN COMMANDMENTS

de·camp (dē kamp') *vi.* ⟦< Fr⟧ **1** to break camp **2** to go away suddenly and secretly

de·cant (dē kant') *vt.* ⟦< Fr < L *de-*, from + *canthus*, tire of a wheel⟧ to pour gently from one container into another

de·cant'er *n.* a decorative glass bottle for serving wine, etc.

de·cap·i·tate (dē kap'ə tāt') *vt.* **-tat'ed**, **-tat'ing** ⟦< L *de-*, off + *caput*, head⟧ to behead —**de·cap'i·ta'tion** *n.*

de·cath·lon (di kath'län') *n.* ⟦DEC(A)- + Gr *athlon*, a prize⟧ an athletic contest in which each contestant takes part in ten TRACK (sense 6*b*) events

de·cay (dē kā') *vi.* ⟦see DECADENCE⟧ **1** to lose strength, prosperity, etc. gradually; deteriorate **2** to rot **3** to undergo radioactive disintegration —*vt.* to cause to decay —*n.* **1** deterioration **2** a rotting or rottenness

de·cease (dē sēs') *n.* ⟦< L *de-*, from + *cedere*, go⟧ death

de·ceased (dē sēst') *adj.* dead —**the deceased** the dead person or persons

de·ce·dent (dē sēd''nt) *n.* ⟦see DECEASE⟧ *Law* a deceased person

de·ceit (dē sēt') *n.* **1** a deceiving or lying **2** a dishonest action **3** deceitful quality

de·ceit'ful *adj.* **1** apt to lie or cheat **2** deceptive; false —**de·ceit'ful·ly** *adv.*

de·ceive (dē sēv') *vt.*, *vi.* **-ceived'**, **-ceiv'ing** ⟦< L *de-*, from + *capere*, take⟧ to make (a person) believe what is not true; mislead —**de·ceiv'er** *n.* —**de·ceiv'ing·ly** *adv.*

de·cel·er·ate (dē sel'ər āt') *vt.*, *vi.* **-at'ed**, **-at'ing** ⟦DE- + (AC)CELERATE⟧ to reduce the speed (of); slow down —**de·cel'er·a'tion** *n.*

De·cem·ber (dē sem'bər) *n.* ⟦< L *decem*, ten: tenth month

THESAURUS

constantly, faithfully; see LOYALLY.

debatable *a.* disputable, unsettled, up for discussion; see CONTROVERSIAL, QUESTIONABLE 1.

debate *n.* contest, argumentation, dispute; see DISCUSSION.

debate *v.* refute, oppose, question, contend, contest, reason with, wrangle, answer, differ, dispute, quarrel, bandy words with, argue the pros and cons of; see also ARGUE, DISCUSS.—*Ant.* AGREE, concur, concede.

debauched *a.* corrupted, debased, depraved; see WICKED.

debit *n.* deficit, obligation, liability; see DEBT.

debris *n.* rubbish, litter, wreckage; see TRASH 1.

debt *n.* liability, obligation, mortgage, duty, arrears, deficit, note, bill, account payable, indebtedness; see also OBLIGATION.—*Ant.* CASH, asset, capital.

debtor *n.* one that owes, borrower, mortgagor; see BUYER.

debunk *v.* uncover, disclose, demystify; see EXPOSE 1.

decadence *n.* decline, deterioration, degeneration; see DECAY, EVIL 1.

decadent *a.* immoral, wicked, degenerate; see BAD 1.

decay *n.* decline, decrease, consumption, decomposition, collapse, downfall, decadence, depreciation, corruption, spoilage, wasting away, degeneration, dry rot, putrefaction, corruption, dissolution, rottenness, spoiling, breakup, breakdown, mold, rust, atrophy, blight, mildew, deterioration, extinction, disintegration, ruin, crumbling, waste, corrosion, wear and tear.

decay *v.* corrode, rot, wither; see SPOIL 1.

decayed *a.* decomposed, putrid, spoiled; see ROTTEN 1.

decaying *a.* rotting, crumbling, spoiling, breaking down, breaking up, wasting away, deteriorating, wearing away, disintegrating, worsening, tumbling down; see also ROTTEN 1.

deceased *a.* late, lifeless, departed; see DEAD 1.

deceit *n.* fraud, trickery, duplicity; see DECEPTION, DISHONESTY.

deceitful *a.* tricky, cunning, insincere; see DISHONEST.

deceive *v.* mislead, swindle, outwit, fool, delude, rob, defraud, not play fair, play a practical joke on, victimize, betray, beguile, take advantage of, entrap, ensnare, hoodwink, dupe, fleece, con*, skin*, sucker*, string along*, screw out of*, lead astray, bamboozle*, cross up, bilk*, gouge*, clip*, fake, gyp*, put on*, burn*, sell out*, chisel*, double-cross*, shake down*, make a sucker out of*, take to the cleaners*, take for a ride*, snow*, put one over on*, take in*, pull the wool over someone's eyes*, flimflam*, give someone the runaround*, do a snow job on*, play upon*, make a monkey of*, stack the cards*; see also TRICK.

deceived *a.* duped, fooled, humbugged, hoaxed, snared, trapped, decoyed, baited, deluded, defrauded, hoodwinked, betrayed, bamboozled*, sucked in*, conned*; see also CHEATED.—*Ant.* dealt with openly, informed, freed from illusion.

deceiver *n.* conniver, swindler, impostor; see CHEAT.

in Roman calendar] the twelfth and last month of the year, having 31 days

de·cen·cy (dē′sən sē) ***n.***, *pl.* **-cies** a being decent; propriety, courtesy, etc.

de·cen·ni·al (dē sen′ē əl) ***adj.*** [< L *decem*, ten + *annus*, year] **1** happening every ten years **2** lasting ten years

de·cent (dē′sənt) ***adj.*** [< L *decere*, befit] **1** proper and fitting **2** not obscene **3** respectable **4** adequate *[decent* wages*]* **5** fair and kind —**de′cent·ly** ***adv.***

de·cen·tral·ize (dē sen′trə līz′) ***vt.*** **-ized′**, **-iz′ing** to break up a concentration of (governmental authority, industry, etc.) and distribute more widely —**de·cen′tral·i·za′tion** ***n.***

de·cep·tion (dē sep′shən) ***n.*** **1** a deceiving or being deceived **2** an illusion or fraud —**de·cep′tive** ***adj.***

deci- [< L *decem*, ten] *combining form* one tenth part of

dec·i·bel (des′ə bəl) ***n.*** [prec. + *bel*, after BELL] a unit for measuring relative loudness of a sound

de·cide (dē sīd′) ***vt.*** **-cid′ed**, **-cid′ing** [< L *de-*, off + *caedere*, to cut] **1** to end (a contest, dispute, etc.) by giving one side the victory **2** to reach a decision about; resolve —***vi.*** to reach a decision —**de·cid′a·ble** ***adj.***

de·cid′ed ***adj.*** **1** definite; clear-cut **2** determined —**de·cid′ed·ly** ***adv.***

de·cid·u·ous (dē sij′oo əs) ***adj.*** [< L *de-*, off, down + *cadere*, to fall] **1** falling off or out at a certain season or stage of growth, as some leaves or antlers do **2** shedding leaves annually

dec·i·mal (des′ə məl) ***adj.*** [< L *decem*, ten] of or based on the number 10 —***n.*** a fraction with a denominator of 10 or some power of 10, shown by a point (**decimal point**) before the numerator (Ex.: .5 = $\frac{5}{10}$)

dec·i·mate (des′ə māt′) ***vt.*** **-mat′ed**, **-mat′ing** [< L *decem*, ten] to destroy or kill a large part of (lit., a tenth part of) —**dec′i·ma′tion** ***n.***

de·ci·pher (dē sī′fər) ***vt.*** [DE- + CIPHER] **1** DECODE **2** to make out the meaning of (illegible writing, etc.)

de·ci·sion (dē sizh′ən) ***n.*** **1** the act of deciding or settling a dispute or question **2** the act of making up one's mind **3** a judgment or conclusion **4** determination; firmness of mind

de·ci·sive (dē sī′siv) ***adj.*** **1** that settles a dispute, question, etc.; conclusive **2** critically important; crucial **3** showing firmness —**de·ci′sive·ly** ***adv.***

deck[1] (dek) ***n.*** [prob. < earlier LowG *verdeck*] **1** a floor of a ship **2** any platform, floor, etc., like a ship's deck **3** a pack of playing cards **4** TAPE DECK

deck[2] (dek) ***vt.*** [MDu *decken*, to cover] to array or adorn: often with *out*

de·claim (dē klām′) ***vi.***, ***vt.*** [< L *de-*, intens. + *clamare*, to cry] to recite or speak in a studied, dramatic, or impassioned way —**dec·la·ma·tion** (dek′lə mā′shən) ***n.*** —**de·clam·a·to·ry** (dē klam′ə tôr′ē) ***adj.***

dec·la·ra·tion (dek′lə rā′shən) ***n.*** **1** a declaring; announcement **2** a formal statement

de·clar·a·tive (dē kler′ə tiv) ***adj.*** making a statement or assertion

de·clare (dē kler′) ***vt.*** **-clared′**, **-clar′ing** [< L *de-*, intens. + *clarus*, clear] **1** to announce openly or formally **2** to show or reveal **3** to say emphatically —**de·clar′er** ***n.***

de·clas·si·fy (dē klas′ə fī′) ***vt.*** **-fied′**, **-fy′ing** to make (secret documents, etc.) available to the public —**de·clas′si·fi·ca′tion** ***n.***

de·clen·sion (dē klen′shən) ***n.*** [see fol.] **1** a descent **2** a decline **3** *Gram.* the inflection of nouns, pronouns, or adjectives

de·cline (dē klīn′) ***vi.*** **-clined′**, **-clin′ing** [< L *de-*, from + *clinare*, to bend] **1** to bend or slope downward **2** to deteriorate; decay **3** to refuse something —***vt.*** **1** to cause to bend or slope downward **2** to refuse politely **3** *Gram.* to give the inflected forms of (a noun, pronoun, or adjective) —***n.*** **1** a declining; dropping, failing, decay, etc. **2** a period of decline **3** a downward slope —**dec·li·na·tion** (dek′lə nā′shən) ***n.*** —**de·clin′er** ***n.***

de·cliv·i·ty (dē kliv′ə tē) ***n.***, *pl.* **-ties** [< L *de-*, down + *clivus*, a slope] a downward slope

de·code (dē kōd′) ***vt.*** **-cod′ed**, **-cod′ing** to decipher (a coded message)

dé·col·le·té (dā käl′ə tā′) ***adj.*** [Fr < L *de*, from + *collum*, neck] cut low so as to bare the neck and shoulders

de·col·o·ni·za·tion (dē käl′ə nə zā′shən) ***n.*** a freeing or being freed from colonial status —**de·col′o·nize′** (-ə nīz′), **-nized′**, **-niz′ing**, ***vt.***, ***vi.***

de·com·pose (dē′kəm pōz′) ***vt.***, ***vi.*** **-posed′**, **-pos′ing** [< Fr: see DE- & COMPOSE] **1** to break up into basic parts **2** to rot —**de·com·po·si·tion** (dē käm pə zish′ən) ***n.***

de·com·press (dē′kəm pres′) ***vt.*** to free from pressure, esp. from air pressure —**de′com·pres′sion** ***n.***

de·con·gest·ant (dē′kən jes′tənt) ***n.*** a medication that relieves congestion, as in the nasal passages

de·con·struct (dē′kən strukt′) ***vt.*** [Fr] **1** to analyze rigorously **2** to take apart; disassemble —**de′con·struc′tion** ***n.***

de·con·tam·i·nate (dē′kən tam′ə nāt′) ***vt.*** **-nat′ed**, **-nat′ing** to rid of a harmful substance, as radioactive material

dé·cor or **de·cor** (dā kôr′) ***n.*** [Fr] a decorative scheme, as of a room

dec·o·rate (dek′ə rāt′) ***vt.*** **-rat′ed**, **-rat′ing** [< L *decus*, an ornament] **1** to adorn; ornament **2** to paint or wallpaper **3** to give a medal or similar honor to —**dec·o·ra·tive** (dek′ə rə tiv, -ə rāt′iv) ***adj.*** —**dec′o·ra′tor** ***n.***

THESAURUS

decency ***n.*** propriety, righteousness, respectability; see HONESTY, VIRTUE 1.

decent ***a.*** **1** [In accordance with common standards] accepted, standard, approved; see CONVENTIONAL 3. **2** [In accordance with the moral code] proper, moral, honest, honorable, chaste, modest, pure, ethical, spotless, respectable, prudent, mannerly, virtuous, immaculate, delicate, stainless, clean, trustworthy, upright, worthy, untarnished, unblemished, straight; see also GOOD 1.

deception ***n.*** trickery, double-dealing, untruth, insincerity, craftiness, treachery, treason, betrayal, mendacity, disinformation, falsehood, trickiness, lying, deceitfulness, deceit, duplicity, cunning, fast one*, snow job*, hokum*; see also DISHONESTY.—*Ant.* HONESTY, frankness, sincerity.

deceptive ***a.*** misleading, ambiguous, deceitful; see FALSE 2, 3.

decide ***v.*** settle, determine, judge, conclude, compromise, choose, terminate, vote, poll, make a decision, come to a conclusion, form an opinion, form a judgment, make up one's mind, make a selection, select, pick, make one's choice, commit oneself, come to an agreement, have the final word; see also AGREE, RESOLVE.—*Ant.* DELAY, hesitate, hedge.

decided ***a.*** **1** [Determined] settled, decided upon, arranged for; see DETERMINED 1. **2** [Certain] clear, emphatic, determined; see DEFINITE 1.

deciding ***a.*** determining, crucial, conclusive; see IMPORTANT 1, NECESSARY.

decipher ***v.*** interpret, translate, explain; see SOLVE.

decision ***n.*** resolution, result, declaration; see JUDGMENT 3, OPINION 1.

decisive ***a.*** final, definitive, absolute; see DEFINITE 1, DETERMINED 1.

deck[1] ***n.*** **1** [The floor of a ship] level, flight, story, layer, tier, topside; see also FLOOR 1, 2. **2** [Cards sufficient for a game] pack, set, pinochle deck, playing cards, the cards; see also CARD. —**on deck*** prepared, available, on hand; see READY 2.

declaration ***n.*** statement, assertion, utterance, information, affirmation, profession, manifesto, document, bulletin, denunciation, proclamation, confirmation, ultimatum, notice, notification, resolution, affidavit, testimony, charge, indictment, allegation, bill of rights, constitution, creed, article of faith, presentation, exposition, communication, disclosure, explanation, revelation, publication, answer, advertisement, saying, report, oath, admission; see also ACKNOWLEDGMENT, ANNOUNCEMENT.

declare ***v.*** assert oneself, announce, pronounce, claim, tell, state, point out, affirm, maintain, attest to, testify to, confess, reveal, swear, disclose, impart, represent, indicate, notify, repeat, insist, contend, advance, allege, argue, demonstrate, propound, bring forward, put forward, set forth, stress, cite, advocate, pass, proclaim, acknowledge, profess, give out, certify, swear; see also REPORT 1, SAY.—*Ant.* HIDE, equivocate, withhold.

decline ***n.*** deterioration, dissolution, lessening; see DECAY.

decline ***v.*** **1** [To refuse] desist, beg to be excused, send regrets; see REFUSE. **2** [To decrease] degenerate, deteriorate, backslide; see DECREASE 1.

decompose ***v.*** rot, crumble, break up; see DISINTEGRATE.

decomposition ***n.*** dissolution, breakdown, disintegration; see DECAY.

decontaminate ***v.*** disinfect, purify, sterilize; see CLEAN.

decor ***n.*** decoration, ornamentation, adornment; see DECORATION 1.

decorate ***v.*** adorn, beautify, ornament, deck, paint, color, renovate, enrich, brighten, enhance, festoon, embellish, illuminate, spangle, elaborate, enamel, bead, polish, varnish, grace, garnish, finish, tile, redecorate, add the finishing touches, perfect, dress up, fix up, deck out, pretty up.

decorated ***a.*** adorned, ornamented, embellished; see ORNATE.

dec'o·ra'tion *n.* **1** a decorating **2** an ornament **3** a medal, etc.

Decoration Day MEMORIAL DAY

dec·o·rous (dek'ə rəs, di kôr'əs) *adj.* having or showing decorum, good taste, etc. —**dec'o·rous·ly** *adv.*

de·co·rum (di kôr'əm) *n.* ⟦< L *decorus*, proper⟧ propriety and good taste in behavior, speech, etc.

de·cou·page or **dé·cou·page** (dā'ko͞o päzh') *n.* ⟦< Fr *dé-*, DE- + *couper*, to cut⟧ the art of decorating a surface with varnished paper cutouts

de·coy (dē koi'; *for n., usually* dē'koi') *n.* ⟦< Du *de kooi*, the cage⟧ **1** an artificial or trained bird, etc. used to lure game within gun range **2** a thing or person used to lure into danger —*vt.* to lure into danger

de·crease (dē krēs'; *for n., usually* dē'krēs') *vi., vt.* **-creased', -creas'ing** ⟦< L *de-*, from + *crescere*, grow⟧ to become or make less, smaller, etc.; diminish —*n.* **1** a decreasing **2** amount of decreasing

de·cree (dē krē') *n.* ⟦< L *de-*, from + *cernere*, to judge⟧ an official order or decision —*vt.* **-creed', -cree'ing** to order or decide by decree

de·crep·it (dē krep'it) *adj.* ⟦< L *de-*, intens. + *crepare*, to creak⟧ broken down or worn out by old age or long use —**de·crep'i·tude'** (-ə to͞od') *n.*

de·cre·scen·do (dā'krə shen'dō, dē'-) [*also in italics*] *Music adj., adv.* ⟦It < L, DECREASE⟧ gradually decreasing in loudness —*n., pl.* **-dos** a gradual decrease in loudness

de·crim·i·nal·ize (dē krim'ə nəl īz') *vt.* **-ized', -iz'ing** to eliminate or reduce the penalties for (a crime)

de·cry (dē krī') *vt.* **-cried', -cry'ing** ⟦< Fr: see DE- & CRY⟧ to speak out against openly; denounce

ded·i·cate (ded'i kāt') *vt.* **-cat'ed, -cat'ing** ⟦< L *de-*, intens. + *dicare*, proclaim⟧ **1** to set apart for, or devote to, a special purpose **2** to address (a book, etc.) to someone as a sign of honor —**ded'i·ca'tion** *n.*

ded'i·cat'ed *adj.* **1** devoted; faithful **2** designating a device, etc. to be used only for a particular purpose

de·duce (dē do͞os') *vt.* **-duced', -duc'ing** ⟦< L *de-*, down + *ducere*, to lead⟧ to infer or decide by reasoning —**de·duc'i·ble** *adj.*

de·duct (dē dukt') *vt.* ⟦see prec.⟧ to take away or subtract (a quantity)

de·duct'i·ble (-duk'tə bəl) *adj.* that can be deducted —*n.* an amount stipulated in an insurance policy to be paid by the person insured in the event of a loss, etc., with the insurer paying the remainder

de·duc'tion (-duk'shən) *n.* **1** a deducting; subtraction **2** an amount deducted **3** *a)* reasoning from the general to the specific *b)* a conclusion reached by such reasoning —**de·duc'tive** *adj.*

deed (dēd) *n.* ⟦< OE *ded*⟧ **1** a thing done; act **2** a feat of courage, skill, etc. **3** a legal document which transfers a property —*vt.* to transfer (property) by deed

deem (dēm) *vt., vi.* ⟦< OE *deman*, to judge⟧ to think, believe, or judge

de·em·pha·size (dē em'fə sīz') *vt.* **-sized', -siz'ing** to lessen the importance of —**de·em'pha·sis** (-sis) *n.*

deep (dēp) *adj.* ⟦OE *deop*⟧ **1** extending far downward, inward, backward, etc. **2** hard to understand; abstruse **3** serious; profound **4** dark and rich *[a deep red]* **5** absorbed by: with *in [deep in thought]* **6** great in degree; intense **7** of low pitch *[a deep voice]* **8** large; big —*n.* a deep place —*adv.* far down, far back, etc. —**the deep** [Old Poet.] the ocean —**deep'ly** *adv.* —**deep'ness** *n.*

deep'en *vt., vi.* to make or become deep or deeper

deep'freeze' *n.* a condition of suspended activity, etc. —*vt.* **-froze', -fro'zen, -freez'ing** to subject (foods) to sudden freezing so as to preserve and store

deep'-fry' *vt.* **-fried', -fry'ing** to fry in a deep pan of boiling fat or oil

deep'-root'ed *adj.* **1** having deep roots **2** firmly fixed

deep'-seat'ed *adj.* **1** buried deep **2** firmly fixed

deep'-six' *vt.* ⟦< six fathoms⟧ [Slang] to get rid of, as by throwing overboard

deep space OUTER SPACE

deer (dir) *n., pl.* **deer** or **deers** ⟦OE *deor*, wild animal⟧ any of various ruminants, including the elk, moose, and reindeer, the male of which grows and sheds antlers annually

de·es·ca·late (dē es'kə lāt') *vi., vt.* **-lat'ed, -lat'ing** to reduce in scope, magnitude, etc. —**de·es'ca·la'tion** *n.*

de·face (dē fās') *vt.* **-faced', -fac'ing** ⟦see DE- & FACE⟧ to spoil the look of; mar —**de·face'ment** *n.*

de fac·to (dē fak'tō) ⟦L⟧ actually existing but not officially approved

de·fal·cate (dē fal'kāt') *vi.* **-cat'ed, -cat'ing** ⟦< L *de-*, from + *falx*, a sickle⟧ to steal or misuse funds entrusted to one's care; embezzle —**de'fal·ca'tion** *n.*

de·fame (dē fām') *vt.* **-famed', -fam'ing** ⟦< L *dis-*, from + *fama*, fame⟧ to attack the reputation of; slander or libel —**def·a·ma·tion** (def'ə mā'shən) *n.* —**de·fam·a·to·ry** (dē fam'ə tôr'ē) *adj.* —**de·fam'er** *n.*

de·fang (dē faŋ') *vt.* **1** to remove the fangs of **2** to make harmless —**de·fanged'** *adj.*

THESAURUS

decoration *n.* **1** [The act of decorating] adornment, ornamentation, embellishment; see DESIGN, IMPROVEMENT 1. **2** [Something used for decorating] tinsel, thread work, lace, ribbon, braid, gilt, color, appliqué, scroll, wreath, glass, flourish, tooling, inlay, figure work, spangle, finery, filigree, design, ornament, extravagance; see also JEWELRY, PAINT 1. **3** [An insignia of honor] citation, medal, ribbon; see EMBLEM.

decorative *a.* embellishing, beautifying, florid; see ORNATE.

decoy *n.* imitation, bait, lure; see CAMOUFLAGE, TRICK 1.

decrease *n.* shrinkage, lessening, contraction; see DISCOUNT, REDUCTION 1.

decrease *v.* **1** [To grow less] lessen, diminish, decline, wane, deteriorate, degenerate, dwindle, sink, settle, lighten, slacken, ebb, melt, lower, moderate, subside, shrink, shrivel up, depreciate, soften, quiet, narrow, waste away, fade, run low, weaken, crumble, let up, dry up, slow down, calm down, burn away, burn down, die away, die down, decay, evaporate, slack off, wear off, wear away, wear out, wear down, slump; see also CONTRACT 1.—*Ant.* GROW, increase, multiply. **2** [To make less] cut, reduce, check, curb, restrain, quell, tame, hush, still, sober, pacify, blunt, curtail, lessen, lower, subtract, abridge, abbreviate, condense, shorten, minimize, diminish, slash, dilute, shave, pare, prune, digest, limit, level, deflate, compress, strip, thin, make smaller, curtail, clip, lighten, trim, level off, take from, take off, roll back, hold down, step down, scale down, boil down, cut off, cut down, cut short, cut back, chisel*, wind down, knock off*; see also COMPRESS.—*Ant.* INCREASE, expand, augment.

decree *n.* edict, pronouncement, proclamation; see DECLARATION, JUDGMENT 3.

dedicate *v.* devote, apply, give, appropriate, set aside, surrender, apportion, assign, give over to, donate; see also GIVE 1.

dedication *n.* sanctification, devotion, glorification; see CONSECRATION.

deduct *v.* take away, diminish by, subtract; see DECREASE 2.

deduction *n.* **1** [The act of deducing] deducing, concluding, reasoning; see THOUGHT 1. **2** [A conclusion] result, answer, conclusion; see JUDGMENT 3, OPINION 1. **3** [A reduction] subtraction, abatement, decrease; see DISCOUNT, REDUCTION 1.

deed *n.* **1** [An action] act, feat, accomplishment; see ACTION 2. **2** [Legal title to real property] document, release, agreement, charter, title deed, record, certificate, voucher, indenture, warranty, lease; see also PROOF 1, RECORD 1, SECURITY 2. —**in deed** in fact, actually, really; see SURELY.

deep *a.* **1** [Situated or extending far down] low, below, beneath, bottomless, submerged, subterranean, submarine, inmost, deep-seated, immersed, dark, dim, impenetrable, buried, inward, underground, downreaching, of great depth, depthless, immeasurable; see also UNDER 1.—*Ant.* SHALLOW, near the surface, surface. **2** [Extending laterally or vertically] extensive, far, wide, yawning, penetrating, distant, thick, fat, spread out, to the bone*, to the hilt; see also BROAD, LONG 1.—*Ant.* NARROW, thin, shallow. **3** [Showing evidence of thought and understanding] penetrating, acute, incisive; see PROFOUND. —**go off the deep end*** **1** [To act rashly] go to extremes, go too far, rant; see EXAGGERATE, RAGE 1. **2** [To break down] collapse, lose control of oneself, become insane; see CRACK UP 2.

deepen *v.* intensify, expand, extend; see DEVELOP 1, GROW 1, INCREASE.

deeply *a.* surely, profoundly, genuinely; see SINCERELY, TRULY.

deer *n.* doe, buck, fawn, roe, stag, venison, member of the deer family, cervine animal, cervid animal. *Creatures popularly called deer include the following:* spotted, white-tailed, mule, red, musk deer; antelope, American elk, wapiti, moose, caribou, reindeer, roebuck.

deface *v.* disfigure, scratch, mutilate; see DESTROY.

de·fault (dē fôlt′) ***n.*** ⟦< L *de-*, away + *fallere*, fail⟧ failure to do or appear as required; specif., failure to pay money due —***vi.***, ***vt.*** **1** to fail to do or pay when required **2** to lose (a contest) by default —**de·fault′er** ***n.***

de·feat (dē fēt′) ***vt.*** ⟦< L *dis-*, from + *facere*, do⟧ **1** to win victory over **2** to bring to nothing; frustrate —***n.*** a defeating or being defeated

de·feat′ist ***n.*** one who too readily accepts or expects defeat —**de·feat′ism′** ***n.***

def·e·cate (def′i kāt′) ***vi.*** **-cat′ed, -cat′ing** ⟦< L *de-*, from + *faex*, dregs⟧ to excrete waste matter from the bowels —**def′e·ca′tion** ***n.***

de·fect (dē′fekt′; *for v.* dē fekt′) ***n.*** ⟦< L *de-*, from + *facere*, do⟧ **1** lack of something necessary for completeness **2** an imperfection or weakness; fault —***vi.*** to forsake a party, cause, etc., esp. so as to join the opposition —**de·fec′tion** ***n.*** —**de·fec′tor** ***n.***

de·fec·tive (dē fek′tiv) ***adj.*** having defects; imperfect; faulty

de·fend (dē fend′) ***vt.*** ⟦< L *de-*, away + *fendere*, to strike⟧ **1** to guard from attack; protect **2** to support or justify **3** *Law a)* to oppose (an action) *b)* to act as lawyer for (an accused) —**de·fend′er** ***n.***

de·fend·ant (dē fen′dənt, -dant′) ***n.*** *Law* the person sued or accused

de·fense (dē fens′, dē′fens′) ***n.*** **1** a defending against attack **2** something that defends **3** justification by speech or writing **4** *a)* the arguments of a defendant *b)* the defendant and his or her counsel Brit. sp. **defence** —**de·fense′less** ***adj.*** —**de·fen′si·ble** ***adj.***

defense mechanism any thought process used unconsciously to protect oneself against painful feelings

de·fen′sive ***adj.*** **1** defending **2** of or for defense —***n.*** a position of defense —**de·fen′sive·ly** ***adv.***

de·fer[1] (dē fʉr′) ***vt.***, ***vi.*** **-ferred′, -fer′ring** ⟦see DIFFER⟧ **1** to postpone; delay **2** to postpone the induction of (a person) into compulsory military service —**de·fer′ment** or **de·fer′ral** ***n.***

de·fer[2] (dē fʉr′) ***vi.*** **-ferred′, -fer′ring** ⟦< L *de-*, down + *ferre*, to BEAR[1]⟧ to yield with courtesy (*to*)

def·er·ence (def′ər əns) ***n.*** **1** a yielding in opinion, judgment, etc. **2** courteous respect

def′er·en′tial (-en′shəl) ***adj.*** showing deference; very respectful

de·fi·ance (dē fī′əns) ***n.*** a defying; open, bold resistance to authority —**de·fi′ant** ***adj.*** —**de·fi′ant·ly** ***adv.***

de·fi·cien·cy (dē fish′ən sē) ***n.*** ⟦< L *de-*, from + *facere*, do⟧ **1** a being deficient **2** *pl.* **-cies** a shortage

deficiency disease a disease caused by a lack of vitamins, minerals, etc. in the diet

de·fi·cient (dē fish′ənt) ***adj.*** ⟦see DEFICIENCY⟧ **1** lacking in some essential; incomplete **2** inadequate in amount

def·i·cit (def′ə sit) ***n.*** ⟦L < *deficere*, to lack⟧ the amount by which a sum of money is less than the required amount, as when there are more expenditures than income

de·file[1] (dē fīl′) ***vt.*** **-filed′, -fil′ing** ⟦< OFr *defouler*, tread underfoot⟧ **1** to make filthy **2** to profane; sully —**de·file′ment** ***n.*** —**de·fil′er** ***n.***

de·file[2] (dē fīl′, dē′fīl′) ***vi.*** **-filed′, -fil′ing** ⟦< Fr *dé-*, from + *fil*, thread⟧ to march in single file —***n.*** a narrow passage, valley, etc.

de·fine (dē fīn′) ***vt.*** **-fined′, -fin′ing** ⟦< L *de-*, from + *finis*, boundary⟧ **1** to determine the limits or nature of; describe exactly **2** to state the meaning of (a word, etc.) —**de·fin′er** ***n.***

def·i·nite (def′ə nit) ***adj.*** ⟦see prec.⟧ **1** having exact limits **2** precise in meaning; explicit **3** certain; positive **4**

THESAURUS

default ***n.*** failure, lack, error, offense, failure to act, wrongdoing, transgression, imperfection, oversight, neglect, shortcoming, inadequacy, insufficiency, failure to appear, failure to pay, lapse, weakness, vice, blunder; see also FAILURE 1. —**in default of** lacking, absent, in the absence of; see WANTING.

defeat ***n.*** repulse, reverse, rebuff, conquest, rout, overthrow, subjugation, destruction, breakdown, collapse, extermination, annihilation, check, trap, ambush, breakthrough, withdrawal, setback, stalemate, ruin, blow, loss, butchery, massacre, Waterloo, beating, whipping, thrashing, fall, comedown, upset, battering*, pasting*, walloping*, whaling*, slaughter*, KO*, the old one-two*; see also LOSS 1.—*Ant.* VICTORY, triumph, conquest.

defeat ***v.*** **1** [To get the better of] master, subjugate, overwhelm; see OVERCOME. **2** [To worst in war] overcome, vanquish, conquer, rout, entrap, subdue, overrun, best, overthrow, crush, smash, drive off, annihilate, overwhelm, scatter, repulse, halt, reduce, outflank, finish off, encircle, slaughter, butcher, outmaneuver, ambush, demolish, sack, torpedo, sink, swamp, wipe out, decimate, obliterate, roll back, mop up*, chew up*, mow down*; see also DESTROY, RAVAGE.—*Ant.* YIELD, give up, surrender. **3** [To worst in sport or in personal combat] overpower, outplay, trounce, knock out, throw, floor, pummel, pound, flog, outhit, outrun, outjump, thrash, edge out*, clobber*, lay low, skin alive*, lick*, wallop*, clean up on*, beat up*, take*, KO*, put down*, beat the pants off*, pulverize*, steamroll*, take to the cleaners*, plow under*, smear*, cream*; see also BEAT 1.—*Ant.* FAIL, suffer, be defeated.

defeated ***a.*** crushed, overcome, conquered; see BEATEN 1.

defect ***n.*** imperfection, flaw, drawback; see FAULT 1.

defect ***v.*** change sides, run away, forsake; see ABANDON 2, DESERT, LEAVE 1.

defective ***a.*** imperfect, incomplete, inadequate; see FAULTY, POOR 2, UNFINISHED 1.

defend ***v.*** **1** [To keep safe from an enemy; *often used figuratively*] shield, shelter, screen; see PROTECT. **2** [To support an accused person or thing] plead for, justify, uphold, second, exonerate, back, vindicate, aid, espouse the cause of, befriend, say in defense of, guarantee, endorse, warrant, maintain, recommend, rationalize, plead someone's cause, say a good word for, speak for, stand up for, put in a good word for, apologize for, go to bat for*, cover for*, back up, stick up for*; see also SUPPORT 2.—*Ant.* CONVICT, accuse, charge.

defendant ***n.*** the accused, defense, offender; see PRISONER.

defended ***a.*** protected, guarded, safeguarded; see SAFE 1.

defender ***n.*** champion, patron, sponsor; see GUARDIAN 1, PROTECTOR.

defense ***n.*** **1** [The act of defending] resistance, protection, safeguard, preservation, security, custody, stand, front, backing, guardianship, the defensive, precaution, inoculation, excusing, apologizing, explaining, justifying, exoneration, explanation.—*Ant.* OFFENSE, retaliation, aggression. **2** [A means or system for defending] bulwark, dike, stockade, machine-gun nest, bastion, fort, chemical or biological warfare, barricade, garrison, rampart, fence, wall, embankment, citadel, fortress, armor, antiaircraft gun, camouflage, gas mask, shield, screen, stronghold, parapet, buttress, guard; see also FORTIFICATION, TRENCH.—*Ant.* ATTACK, siege, blitzkrieg. **3** [In law, the reply of the accused] denial, plea, answer; see DECLARATION, PROOF 1, STATEMENT 1.

defensible ***a.*** justfiable, proper, permissible; see FIT 1, 2, LOGICAL.

defensive ***a.*** protecting, guarding, watchful, protective, vigilant; see also CAREFUL.

defensively ***a.*** protectively, guardedly, suspiciously; see CAREFULLY 1.

defer[1,2] ***v.*** **1** [To postpone] put off, postpone, shelve; see DELAY, SUSPEND 2. **2** [To yield] submit, accede, concede; see AGREE.

deference ***n.*** veneration, acclaim, homage; see REVERENCE.

deferred ***a.*** delayed, prolonged, held up; see POSTPONED.

defiance ***n.*** insubordination, rebellion, insurgence; see DISOBEDIENCE.

defiant ***a.*** resistant, obstinate, disobedient; see REBELLIOUS.

deficiency ***n.*** want, need, absence; see LACK 2.

deficient ***a.*** insufficient, skimpy, meager; see INADEQUATE.

deficit ***n.*** shortage, paucity, deficiency; see LACK 2.

defile[1] ***v.*** ravish, violate, molest; see HURT, RAPE.

define ***v.*** **1** [To set limits for] bound, confine, limit, outline, fix, settle, circumscribe, mark, set, distinguish, establish, encompass, mark the limits of, determine the boundaries of, fix the limits of, curb, edge, border, enclose, set bounds to, fence in, rim, encircle, wall in, envelop, flank, stake out; see also LIMIT.—*Ant.* CONFUSE, distort, mix. **2** [To provide a name or description for] paraphrase, give the meaning of, differentiate, gloss, determine, entitle, label, designate, characterize, elucidate, interpret, illustrate, represent, individuate, find out, clarify, construe, denote, spell out, translate, exemplify, specify, prescribe, dub; see also DESCRIBE, EXPLAIN, NAME 1.—*Ant.* MISUNDERSTAND, misconceive, mistitle.

definite ***a.*** **1** [Determined with exactness] fixed, exact, precise, positive, accurate, correct, decisive, absolute, clearly defined, well-defined, limited, strict, explicit, specific, settled, decided, prescribed, restricted, assigned, unequivocal, special, conclusive, categorical, particular, unerring, to the point, beyond doubt; see also CERTAIN 2, DETERMINED.—*Ant.* OBSCURE, indefinite, inexact. **2**

Gram. limiting or specifying [“the” is the *definite* article] —**def'i·nite·ly** *adv.* —**def'i·nite·ness** *n.*

def'i·ni'tion (-nish'ən) *n.* **1** a defining or being defined **2** a statement of the meaning of a word **3** clarity of outline, sound, etc.

de·fin·i·tive (dē fin'ə tiv) *adj.* **1** conclusive; final **2** most nearly complete **3** serving to define

de·flate (dē flāt') *vt., vi.* **-flat'ed, -flat'ing** ⟦DE- + (IN)FLATE⟧ **1** to collapse by letting out air or gas **2** to lessen in size, importance, etc. **3** to cause deflation of (currency, etc.)

de·fla'tion *n.* **1** a deflating **2** a reduction in prices resulting from severe economic decline

de·flect (dē flekt') *vt., vi.* ⟦< L *de-*, from + *flectere*, to bend⟧ to turn or make go to one side —**de·flec'tion** *n.* —**de·flec'tive** *adj.* —**de·flec'tor** *n.*

De·foe (di fō'), **Daniel** 1660-1731; Eng. writer

de·fog·ger (dē fôg'ər) *n.* an apparatus for clearing condensed moisture, as from a car window

de·fo·li·ant (dē fō'lē ənt) *n.* a chemical substance that causes leaves to fall from growing plants

de·fo'li·ate' (-āt') *vt.* **-at'ed, -at'ing** ⟦< L *de-*, from + *folium*, leaf⟧ to strip (trees, etc.) of leaves —**de·fo'li·a'tion** *n.*

de·form (dē fôrm') *vt.* ⟦< L *de-*, from + *forma*, form⟧ **1** to impair the form of **2** to make ugly —**de·for·ma·tion** (dē' fôr mā'shən, def'ər-) *n.*

de·formed' *adj.* misshapen

de·form'i·ty *n., pl.* **-ties** **1** a deformed part, as of the body **2** ugliness or depravity

de·fraud (dē frôd') *vt.* to take property, rights, etc. from by fraud; cheat —**de·fraud'er** *n.*

de·fray (dē frā') *vt.* ⟦Fr *défrayer*⟧ to pay (the cost or expenses) —**de·fray'a·ble** *adj.* —**de·fray'al** *n.*

de·frost (dē frôst') *vt., vi.* to rid or get rid of frost or ice —**de·frost'er** *n.*

deft (deft) *adj.* ⟦see DAFT⟧ skillful; dexterous —**deft'ly** *adv.*

de·funct (dē fuŋkt') *adj.* ⟦< L *defungi*, to finish⟧ no longer existing; dead or extinct

de·fuse (dē fyo͞oz') *vt.* **-fused', -fus'ing** **1** to remove the fuse from (a bomb, etc.) **2** to make harmless, less tense, etc.

de·fy (dē fī') *vt.* **-fied', -fy'ing** ⟦< LL *dis-*, from + *fidus*, faithful⟧ **1** to resist or oppose boldly or openly **2** to dare to do or prove something

de·gen·er·ate (dē jen'ər it; *for v.*, -āt') *adj.* ⟦< L *de-*, from + *genus*, race⟧ **1** having sunk below a former or normal condition, etc.; deteriorated **2** depraved —*n.* a degenerate person —*vi.* **-at'ed, -at'ing** to lose former normal or higher qualities —**de·gen'er·a·cy** (-ə sē) *n.* —**de·gen'er·a'tion** *n.* —**de·gen'er·a·tive** (-ə tiv, -āt'iv) *adj.*

de·grad·a·ble (dē grād'ə bəl) *adj.* capable of being degraded, esp. of being readily decomposed by chemicals, as some plastics

de·grade (dē grād') *vt.* **-grad'ed, -grad'ing** ⟦< L *de-*, down + *gradus*, a step⟧ **1** to demote **2** to lower in quality, moral character, dignity, etc.; debase, dishonor, etc. —**deg·ra·da·tion** (deg'rə dā'shən) *n.*

de·gree (di grē') *n.* ⟦see prec.⟧ **1** any of the successive steps in a process **2** social or official rank **3** extent, amount, or intensity **4** a rank given by a college or university to one who has completed a course of study, or to a distinguished person as an honor **5** a grade of comparison of adjectives and adverbs [the superlative *degree*] **6** *Law* the seriousness of a crime [murder in the first *degree*] **7** *Math.* a unit of measure for angles or arcs, one 360th of the circumference of a circle **8** *Physics* a unit of measure for temperature —**to a degree** somewhat

de·greed' (-grēd') *adj.* having a college or university degree

de·hu·man·ize (dē hyo͞o'mə nīz') *vt.* **-ized', -iz'ing** to deprive of human qualities; make machinelike —**de·hu'man·i·za'tion** *n.*

de·hu·mid·i·fy (dē'hyo͞o mid'ə fī') *vt.* **-fied', -fy'ing** to remove moisture from (air, etc.) —**de'hu·mid'i·fi'er** *n.*

de·hy·drate (dē hī'drāt') *vt.* **-drat'ed, -drat'ing** to remove water from (a substance, etc.); dry —*vi.* to lose water —**de'hy·dra'tion** *n.* —**de·hy'dra'tor** *n.*

de·ice (dē īs') *vt.* **-iced', -ic'ing** to melt ice from —**de-ic'er** *n.*

de·i·fy (dē'ə fī') *vt.* **-fied', -fy'ing** ⟦< L *deus*, god + *facere*, make⟧ **1** to make a god of **2** to look upon as a god —**de'i·fi·ca'tion** (-fi kā'shən) *n.*

deign (dān) *vi., vt.* ⟦< L *dignus*, worthy⟧ to condescend (to do or give)

de·ism (dē'iz'əm) *n.* ⟦< L *deus*, god⟧ the belief that God exists and created the world but takes no part in its functioning —**de'ist** *n.*

de·i·ty (dē'ə tē) *n.* ⟦< L *deus*, god⟧ **1** the state of being a god **2** *pl.* **-ties** a god or goddess —**the Deity** God

dé·jà vu (dā'zhə vo͞o') ⟦Fr, already seen⟧ a feeling of having been in a place or experienced something before

de·ject (dē jekt') *vt.* ⟦< L *de-*, down + *jacere*, throw⟧ to dishearten; depress —**de·ject'ed** *adj.* —**de·jec'tion** *n.*

Del·a·ware (del'ə wer', -war') state of the E U.S.: 1,955 sq. mi.; pop. 666,000; cap. Dover: abbrev. *DE* —**Del'a·war'e·an** *adj., n.*

de·lay (dē lā') *vt.* ⟦< OFr *de-*, intens. + *laier*, to leave⟧ **1** to put off; postpone **2** to make late; detain —*vi.* to linger

THESAURUS

[Clear in detail] sharp, visible, audible, tangible, distinct, vivid, unmistakable in meaning, straightforward, unambiguous, palpable, obvious, marked, plain, not vague, well-drawn, clearly defined, well-marked, well-defined, clear-cut, explicit, unmistakable, distinguishable, undistorted, crisp, bold, graphic, downright, undisguised, in plain sight, clear as day, standing out like a sore thumb*.—*Ant.* CONFUSED, vague, hazy. **3** [Positive] sure, beyond doubt, convinced; see CERTAIN 1.

definitely *a.* clearly, unmistakably, unquestionably; see SURELY.

definition *n.* meaning, terminology, sense, gloss, paraphrase, denotation, exemplification, signification, diagnosis, synonym, exposition, interpretation, explication, clue, key, translation, comment, rationale, commentary, representation, characterization, solution, answer; see also DESCRIPTION, EXPLANATION.

definitive *a.* final, ultimate, conclusive; see ABSOLUTE 1.

deflate *v.* exhaust, flatten, void; see EMPTY 1, 2.

deflect *v.* swerve, divert, curve; see TURN 3, 6.

deform *v.* disfigure, deface, injure; see DAMAGE.

deformed *a.* damaged, distorted, misshapen, disfigured, crippled, misproportioned, malformed, cramped, badly made, disjointed, unseemly, ill-favored, dwarfed, hunchbacked, clubfooted, unshapely, mangled, crushed, warped, curved, contorted, gnarled, crooked, grotesque, lame, irregular; see also TWISTED 1, UGLY 1.—*Ant.* REGULAR, shapely, well-formed.

deformity *n.* malformation, deformation, disfigurement; see CONTORTION, DAMAGE 1.

defraud *v.* hoax, dupe, cheat; see DECEIVE.

defy *v.* insult, resist, confront; see DARE 2, OPPOSE 1, 2.

degenerate *a.* depraved, immoral, corrupt; see BAD.

degradation *n.* depravity, corruption, degeneration; see EVIL 1.

degrade *v.* demote, discredit, diminish; see HUMBLE.

degraded *a.* disgraced, debased, depraved; see BAD.

degree *n.* **1** [One in a series used for measurement] measure, grade, step, unit, mark, interval, space, measurement, gradation, size, dimension, shade, point, line, plane, step in a series, gauge, rung, term, tier, ratio, period, level; see also DIVISION 2. **2** [An expression of relative excellence, attainment, or the like] extent, station, order, quality, development, height, expanse, length, potency, range, proportion, compass, quantity, standing, strength, reach, intensity, scope, caliber, pitch, stage, sort, status, rate; see also RANK 3. **3** [Recognition of academic achievement] title, distinction, testimonial, honor, qualification, eminence, credit, credentials, baccalaureate, bachelor's degree, master's degree, doctorate, sheepskin*; see also DIPLOMA, GRADUATION. —**by degrees** step by step, slowly but surely, inch by inch; see GRADUALLY. —**to a degree** somewhat, partially, to an extent; see PARTLY.

dehydrate *v.* dessicate, parch, drain; see DRY 1.

dejected *a.* depressed, dispirited, cast down; see SAD 1.

delay *n.* deferment, adjournment, putting off, procrastination, suspension, moratorium, reprieve, setback, stay, stop, discontinuation, cooling-off period*, holdup*; see also PAUSE.

delay *v.* postpone, defer, retard, hold up, deter, clog, choke, slacken, keep, hold, keep back, impede, discourage, interfere with, detain, stay, stop, withhold, arrest, check, prevent, repress, curb, obstruct, inhibit, restrict, prolong, encumber, procrastinate, adjourn, block, bar, suspend, table, slow, put aside, hold back, hold off, hold everything*, bide one's time, slow up, slow down, stall, put off, restrain, put on ice*, shelve, pigeonhole; see also HINDER, INTERRUPT.—*Ant.* SPEED, accelerate, encourage.

delayed *a.* held up, slowed, put off;

—*n.* 1 a delaying or being delayed 2 the time one is delayed

de·lec·ta·ble (dē lek′tə bəl) *adj.* ⟦see DELIGHT⟧ delightful or delicious

de·lec·ta·tion (dē′lek tā′shən) *n.* ⟦see DELIGHT⟧ delight; enjoyment

del·e·gate (del′ə git; *for v.*, -gāt′) *n.* ⟦< L *de-*, from + *legare*, send⟧ a person authorized to act for others; representative —*vt.* **-gat′ed, -gat′ing** 1 to appoint as a delegate 2 to entrust (authority, etc.) to another

del′e·ga′tion (-gā′shən) *n.* 1 a delegating or being delegated 2 a body of delegates

de·lete (dē lēt′) *vt.* **-let′ed, -let′ing** ⟦< L *delere*, destroy⟧ to take out (a word, etc.); cross out —**de·le′tion** *n.*

del·e·te·ri·ous (del′ə tir′ē əs) *adj.* ⟦< Gr *dēleisthai*, injure⟧ harmful to health or well-being

delft·ware (delft′wer′) *n.* ⟦after *Delft*, city in the Netherlands⟧ glazed earthenware, usually blue and white: also **delft**

Del·hi (del′ē) city in N India: pop. 4,884,000: see also NEW DELHI

del·i (del′ē) *n. short for* DELICATESSEN

de·lib·er·ate (di lib′ər it; *for v.*, -āt′) *adj.* ⟦< L *de-*, intens. + *librare*, weigh⟧ 1 carefully thought out; premeditated 2 not rash or hasty 3 unhurried —*vi.*, *vt.* **-at′ed, -at′ing** to consider carefully —**de·lib′er·ate·ly** *adv.* —**de·lib′er·a′tive** (-āt′iv, -ə tiv) *adj.*

de·lib′er·a′tion (-ā′shən) *n.* 1 a deliberating 2 [*often pl.*] consideration of alternatives 3 carefulness; slowness

del·i·ca·cy (del′i kə sē) *n.*, *pl.* **-cies** 1 the quality of being delicate; fineness, weakness, sensitivity, etc. 2 a choice food

del′i·cate (-kit) *adj.* ⟦< L *delicatus*, delightful⟧ 1 pleasing in its lightness, mildness, etc. 2 beautifully fine in texture, workmanship, etc. 3 slight and subtle 4 easily damaged 5 frail in health 6 *a*) needing careful handling *b*) showing tact, consideration, etc. 7 finely sensitive —**del′i·cate·ly** *adv.* —**del′i·cate·ness** *n.*

del·i·ca·tes·sen (del′i kə tes′ən) *n.* ⟦< Ger pl. < Fr *délicatesse*, delicacy⟧ 1 prepared cooked meats, fish, cheeses, salads, etc., collectively 2 a shop where such foods are sold

de·li·cious (di lish′əs) *adj.* ⟦see fol.⟧ 1 delightful 2 very pleasing to taste or smell —**de·li′cious·ly** *adv.* —**de·li′cious·ness** *n.*

de·light (di līt′) *vt.* ⟦< L *de-*, from + *lacere*, entice⟧ to give great pleasure to —*vi.* 1 to give great pleasure 2 to be highly pleased; rejoice —*n.* 1 great pleasure 2 something giving great pleasure —**de·light′ed** *adj.*

de·light′ful *adj.* giving delight; very pleasing —**de·light′ful·ly** *adv.*

De·li·lah (di lī′lə) *n. Bible* the mistress and betrayer of Samson

de·lim·it (dē lim′it) *vt.* to fix the limits of —**de·lim′i·ta′tion** *n.*

de·lin·e·ate (di lin′ē āt′) *vt.* **-at′ed, -at′ing** ⟦< L *de-*, from + *linea*, a line⟧ 1 to draw; sketch 2 to depict in words —**de·lin′e·a′tion** *n.*

de·lin·quent (di liŋ′kwənt) *adj.* ⟦< L *de-*, from + *linquere*, leave⟧ 1 failing to do what duty or law requires 2 overdue, as taxes —*n.* a delinquent person; esp., a juvenile delinquent —**de·lin′quen·cy**, *pl.* **-cies**, *n.* —**de·lin′quent·ly** *adv.*

del·i·quesce (del′i kwes′) *vi.* **-quesced′, -quesc′ing** ⟦< L < *de-*, from + *liquere*, be liquid⟧ to become liquid by absorbing moisture from the air —**del′i·ques′cent** *adj.*

de·lir·i·ous (di lir′ē əs) *adj.* 1 in a state of delirium 2 of or caused by delirium 3 wildly excited —**de·lir′i·ous·ly** *adv.* —**de·lir′i·ous·ness** *n.*

de·lir′i·um (-əm) *n.* ⟦< L *de-*, from + *lira*, a line⟧ 1 a temporary mental disturbance, as during a fever, marked by confused speech and hallucinations 2 uncontrollably wild excitement

de·liv·er (di liv′ər) *vt.* ⟦< L *de-*, intens. + *liber*, free⟧ 1 to set free or rescue 2 to assist at the birth of 3 to make (a speech, etc.) 4 to hand over 5 to distribute (mail, etc.) 6 to strike (a blow) 7 to throw (a ball, etc.) —*vi.* 1 to make deliveries 2 to produce, etc. something promised

de·liv′er·ance *n.* a freeing or being freed; rescue

de·liv′er·y *n.*, *pl.* **-er·ies** 1 a handing over 2 a distributing, as of mail 3 a giving birth 4 any giving forth 5 the

THESAURUS

see LATE 1, POSTPONED.

delegate *n.* legate, emissary, proxy, deputy, substitute, consul, appointee, minister, alternate, nominee, ambassador, stand-in*, sub*, pinch hitter*; see also AGENT, REPRESENTATIVE 2.

delegate *v.* 1 [To give authority to] authorize, commission, appoint, name, nominate, select, choose, assign, license, empower, deputize, swear in, ordain, invest, elect, give someone the green light*, give someone the go-ahead*; see also APPROVE.—*Ant.* DISMISS, repudiate, reject. 2 [To give duties to another] entrust, parcel out, hold responsible for; see ASSIGN.

delegation *n.* 1 [The act of assigning to another] assignment, giving over, nomination, trust, commissioning, ordination, authorization, charge, deputation, referring, transferring; see also APPOINTMENT 1. 2 [A group with a specific mission] representatives, deputation, commission; see COMMITTEE, ORGANIZATION 2.

deliberate *a.* thought out, predetermined, conscious, advised, prearranged, fixed, with forethought, well-considered, cautious, studied, intentional, planned in advance, done on purpose, willful, considered, thoughtful, planned, reasoned, calculated, intended, purposeful, premeditated, voluntary, designed, cold-blooded, cut-and-dried; see also CAREFUL.

deliberately *a.* resolutely, determinedly, emphatically, knowingly, meaningfully, voluntarily, consciously, on purpose, willfully, premeditatedly, in cold blood, with malice aforethought, advisedly, freely, independently, without any qualms, by design, intentionally, purposely, all things considered, pointedly, to that end, with eyes wide open*; see also CAREFULLY 1.

delicacy *n.* 1 [Fineness of texture] airiness, daintiness, transparency, flimsiness, softness, smoothness, subtlety, tenderness; see also LIGHTNESS 2. 2 [A rare commodity, especially for the table] tidbit, luxury, gourmet dish, gourmet food, dessert, sweet, delight, party dish, imported food, delicatessen, chef's special*; see also FOOD.

delicate *a.* 1 [Sickly] susceptible, in delicate health, feeble; see SICK, WEAK 1. 2 [Dainty] fragile, frail, fine; see DAINTY.

delicately *a.* deftly, skillfully, cautiously; see CAREFULLY 1.

delicatessen *n.* 1 [Ready-to-serve-foods] *Varieties of delicatessen include the following:* cold meats, luncheon meats, salads, dairy products, salami, pastrami, bologna, wurst, sausage, frankfurters, olives, lox, corned beef, pickled peppers, pickled fish, dill pickles, sweet pickles, caviar, anchovies, pâté; see also BREAD, CHEESE, DESSERT, FISH, FRUIT, MEAT, WINE. 2 [A place that sells delicatessen] food store, butcher shop, grocery; see MARKET 1.

delicious *a.* tasty, savory, good, appetizing, choice, well-seasoned, well-done, spicy, sweet, delectable, exquisite, dainty, luscious, tempting, yummy*, fit for a king*; see also EXCELLENT, RICH 4.—*Ant.* ROTTEN, flat, stale.

delight *n.* enjoyment, joy, pleasure; see HAPPINESS.

delight *v.* fascinate, amuse, please; see ENTERTAIN 1.

delighted *a.* 1 [Greatly pleased] entranced, excited, pleasantly surprised; see HAPPY. 2 [An expression of acceptance or pleasure] thank you, by all means, to be sure, splendid, excellent, overwhelmed, charmed, so glad.

delightful *a.* charming, amusing, engaging; see PLEASANT 1.

delinquent *a.* 1 [Lax in duty] slack, behindhand, tardy, procrastinating, criminal, neglectful, faulty, blamable, negligent, derelict, remiss; see also CARELESS.—*Ant.* PUNCTUAL, punctilious, scrupulous. 2 [Not paid on time; *said especially of taxes*] owed, back, overdue; see DUE, UNPAID 1.

delinquent *n.* defaulter, tax evader, offender, dropout, reprobate, loafer, derelict, bad debtor, poor risk, felon, lawbreaker, wrongdoer, sinner, juvenile offender, juvenile delinquent, JD*, punk*, outlaw, black sheep*; see also CRIMINAL.

delirious *a.* demented, crazy, irrational; see INSANE.

deliver *v.* 1 [To free] set free, liberate, save; see FREE. 2 [To transfer] pass, remit, hand over; see GIVE 1. 3 [To speak formally] present, read, give; see ADDRESS 2. 4 [To bring to birth] bring forth, be delivered of, give birth to; see PRODUCE 2. 5 [To distribute] allot, dispense, give out; see DISTRIBUTE.

delivered *a.* brought, deposited, transported, checked in, forwarded, expressed, hand-delivered, dispatched, at the door, sent out by truck, trucked; see also MAILED.

delivery *n.* 1 [Bringing goods into another's possession] consignment, carting, shipment, transfer, portage, freighting, dispatch, conveyance, mailing, special delivery, parcel post, giving over, handing over, cash on delivery, COD, free on board, FOB; see also TRANSPORTATION. 2 [Deliv-

act or manner of delivering a speech, ball, etc. **6** something delivered

dell (del) ***n.*** ⟦OE *del*⟧ a small, secluded valley or glen, usually wooded

del·phin·i·um (del fin′ē əm) ***n.*** ⟦< Gr *delphin*, dolphin⟧ a tall plant bearing spikes of flowers, usually blue

del·ta (del′tə) ***n.*** **1** the fourth letter of the Greek alphabet (Δ, δ) **2** a deposit of soil, usually triangular, formed at the mouth of a large river

de·lude (di lo͞od′) ***vt.*** **-lud′ed, -lud′ing** ⟦< L *de-*, from + *ludere*, to play⟧ to mislead; deceive

del·uge (del′yo͞oj′) ***n.*** ⟦< L *dis*, off + *luere*, to wash⟧ **1** a great flood **2** a heavy rainfall **3** an overwhelming rush of anything —***vt.*** **-uged′, -ug′ing** **1** to flood **2** to overwhelm

de·lu·sion (di lo͞o′zhən) ***n.*** **1** a deluding or being deluded **2** a false belief, specif. one that persists psychotically —**de·lu′sive** or **de·lu′sion·al** ***adj.***

de·luxe (di luks′, -lo͝oks′) ***adj.*** ⟦Fr, of luxury⟧ of extra fine quality —***adv.*** in a deluxe manner

delve (delv) ***vi.*** **delved, delv′ing** ⟦OE *delfan*⟧ **1** [Now Dial., Chiefly Brit.] to dig **2** to search (*into*) —**delv′er** ***n.***

Dem *abbrev.* **1** Democrat **2** Democratic

de·mag·net·ize (dē mag′nə tīz′) ***vt.*** **-ized′, -iz′ing** to remove magnetism or magnetic properties from —**de·mag′net·i·za′tion** ***n.***

dem·a·gogue or **dem·a·gog** (dem′ə gäg′) ***n.*** ⟦< Gr *dēmos*, the people + *agōgos*, leader⟧ one who tries to stir up people's emotions in order to win them over and so gain power —**dem′a·gog′y** (-gä′jē, -gäg′ē) or **dem′a·gogu′er·y** (-gäg′ər ē) ***n.***

de·mand (di mand′) ***vt.*** ⟦< L *de-*, from + *mandare*, entrust⟧ **1** to ask for boldly or urgently **2** to ask for as a right **3** to require; need —***vi.*** to make a demand —***n.*** **1** a demanding **2** a thing demanded **3** a strong request **4** an urgent requirement **5** *Economics* the desire for a commodity together with ability to pay for it; also, the amount people are ready to buy at a certain price —**in demand** wanted or sought —**on demand** when presented for payment

de·mand′ing ***adj.*** making difficult demands on one's patience, energy, etc.

de·mar·ca·tion (dē′mär kā′shən) ***n.*** ⟦< Sp *de-*, from + *marcar*, to mark⟧ **1** the act of setting and marking limits or boundaries **2** a limit or boundary

de·mean[1] (dē mēn′) ***vt.*** ⟦DE- + MEAN[2]⟧ to degrade; humble

de·mean[2] (dē mēn′) ***vt.*** ⟦see fol.⟧ to behave or conduct (oneself)

de·mean·or (di mēn′ər) ***n.*** ⟦< OFr *demener*, to lead⟧ outward behavior; conduct; deportment: Brit. sp. **demeanour**

de·ment·ed (dē ment′id) ***adj.*** ⟦see fol.⟧ mentally deranged; insane

de·men·tia (di men′shə) ***n.*** ⟦< L *de-*, out from + *mens*, the mind⟧ a disorder of the mind impairing perception, memory, etc.

de·mer·it (dē mer′it) ***n.*** ⟦< L *de-*, intens. + *merere*, to deserve, with *de-* taken as negative⟧ **1** a fault; defect **2** a mark recorded against a student, etc. for poor conduct or work

de·mesne (di mān′, -mēn′) ***n.*** ⟦see DOMAIN⟧ a region or domain

De·me·ter (di mēt′ər) ***n.*** *Gr. Myth.* the goddess of agriculture

demi- ⟦< L *dimidius*, half⟧ *prefix* **1** half **2** less than usual in size, power, etc. *[demigod]*

dem·i·god (dem′i gäd′) ***n.*** **1** a minor deity **2** a godlike person

dem′i·john′ (-jän′) ***n.*** ⟦Fr *dame-jeanne*⟧ a large bottle of glass or earthenware in a wicker casing

de·mil·i·ta·rize (dē mil′ə tə rīz′) ***vt.*** **-rized′, -riz′ing** to free from organized military control

dem·i·monde (dem′i mänd′) ***n.*** ⟦Fr < *demi-* + *monde*, world⟧ the class of women who have lost social standing because of sexual promiscuity

de·mise (dē mīz′) ***n.*** ⟦< L *de-*, down + *mittere*, send⟧ **1** *Law* a transfer of an estate by lease **2** death —***vt.*** **-mised′, -mis′ing** to transfer (an estate) by lease

dem·i·tasse (dem′i täs′, -tas′) ***n.*** ⟦Fr < *demi-* + *tasse*, cup⟧ a small cup of or for after-dinner coffee

dem·o (dem′ō) ***n.***, *pl.* **-os** **1** a recording made to demonstrate a song, the talent of a performer, etc. **2** a product used in demonstrations

de·mo·bi·lize (dē mō′bə līz′) ***vt.*** **-lized′, -liz′ing** to disband (troops) —**de·mo′bi·li·za′tion** ***n.***

de·moc·ra·cy (di mäk′rə sē) ***n.***, *pl.* **-cies** ⟦< Gr *dēmos*, the people + *kratein*, to rule⟧ **1** government by the people, directly or through representatives **2** a country, etc. with such government **3** equality of rights, opportunity, and treatment

dem·o·crat (dem′ə krat′) ***n.*** **1** one who supports or practices democracy **2** [**D-**] a Democratic Party member

dem′o·crat′ic ***adj.*** **1** of or for democracy **2** of or for all the people **3** not snobbish **4** [**D-**] of the Democratic Party —**dem′o·crat′i·cal·ly** ***adv.***

Democratic Party one of the two major political parties in the U.S.

de·mod·u·la·tion (dē mä′jə lā′shən) ***n.*** *Radio* the recovery, at the receiver, of a signal that has been modulated on a carrier wave

dem·o·graph·ics (dem′ə graf′iks) ***pl.n.*** demographic characteristics of a population, as age, sex, or income, used for research, etc.

de·mog·ra·phy (di mä′grə fē) ***n.*** ⟦< Gr *dēmos*, the people + -GRAPHY⟧ the statistical study of human populations —**de·mog′ra·pher** ***n.*** —**dem·o·graph·ic** (dem′ə graf′ik) ***adj.*** —**dem′o·graph′i·cal·ly** ***adv.***

de·mol·ish (di mäl′ish) ***vt.*** ⟦< L *de-*, down + *moliri*, build⟧ **1** to pull down or smash **2** to destroy; ruin —**dem·o·li·tion** (dem′ə lish′ən) ***n.***

de·mon (dē′mən) ***n.*** ⟦< L *daemon*⟧ **1** a devil; evil spirit **2** one regarded as evil, cruel, etc. **3** one with great energy, skill, etc. —**de·mon·ic** (di män′ik) ***adj.*** —**de·mon′i·cal·ly** ***adv.***

de·mon·e·tize (dē män′ə tīz′) ***vt.*** **-tized′, -tiz′ing** to deprive (esp. currency) of its standard value

de·mon·ize (dē′mən īz′) ***vt.*** **-ized′, -iz′ing** **1** to make into a demon **2** to characterize as evil, cruel, etc. —**de′mon·i·za′tion** ***n.***

de·mon·stra·ble (di män′strə bəl) ***adj.*** that can be demonstrated, or proved —**de·mon′stra·bly** ***adv.***

dem·on·strate (dem′ən strāt′) ***vt.*** **-strat′ed, -strat′ing** ⟦< L *de-*, from + *monstrare*, to show⟧ **1** to show by reason-

THESAURUS

ery of a child] parturition, confinement, childbirth, labor, bringing forth, midwifery, obstetrics, cesarean section; see also BIRTH. **3** [The manner of a speaker] articulation, enunciation, accent, utterance, pronunciation, emphasis, elocution; see also ELOQUENCE.

delusion ***n.*** phantasm, hallucination, fancy; see ILLUSION.

deluxe ***a.*** elegant, expensive, grand; see LUXURIOUS.

demand ***n.*** **1** [A peremptory communication] order, call, charge; see COMMAND. **2** [Willingness to purchase] trade, request, sale, bid, need, requirement, interest, call for, rush, search, inquiry, desire to buy, market; see also DESIRE 1.—*Ant.* INDIFFERENCE, lack of interest, sales resistance. —**in demand** sought, needed, requested; see WANTED. —**on demand** ready, prepared, usable; see AVAILABLE.

demand ***v.*** charge, direct, command; see ASK.

demanding ***a.*** fussy, imperious, exacting; see CRITICAL.

demented ***a.*** crazy, bemused, unbalanced; see INSANE.

demerit ***n.*** bad mark, loss of points, poor grade; see FAULT 1, PUNISHMENT.

demobilize ***v.*** disband, disperse, withdraw; see DISARM.

democracy ***n.*** justice, the greatest good for the greatest number, egalitarianism, popular suffrage, individual enterprise, capitalism, laissez faire, rugged individualism, freedom of religion, freedom of speech, freedom of the press, the right to work, private ownership, emancipation, political equality, representative government, democratic spirit, the American Way*; see also EQUALITY, FREEDOM 2.—*Ant.* dictatorship, feudalism, tyranny.

democrat ***n.*** republican, Social Democrat, populist, civil libertarian, advocate of democracy, constitutionalist, individualist.—*Ant.* DICTATOR, Nazi, autocrat.

Democrat ***n.*** Southern Democrat, Jeffersonian Democrat, Dixiecrat*, Great Society Democrat*, New Dealer*, liberal, progressive; see also REPUBLICAN.—*Ant.* REPUBLICAN, Tory, Socialist.

democratic ***a.*** popular, constitutional, representative, free, equal, just, common, bourgeois, individualistic, communal, laissez-faire.

demolish ***v.*** wreck, devastate, obliterate; see DESTROY.

demolition ***n.*** extermination, annihilation, wrecking; see DESTRUCTION 1, EXPLOSION.

demon ***n.*** imp, vampire, incubus; see DEVIL.

demonstrate ***v.*** **1** [To prove] show, make evident, confirm; see PROVE. **2** [To present for effect] exhibit, mani-

ing; prove **2** to explain by using examples, etc. **3** to show how something works —*vi.* to show feelings or views publicly by meetings, etc. —**dem′on·stra′tion** *n.* —**dem′on·stra′tor** *n.*

de·mon·stra·tive (di män′strə tiv) *adj.* **1** illustrative **2** giving proof *(of)* **3** showing feelings openly **4** *Gram.* pointing out *[*"this" is a *demonstrative* pronoun*]* —*n. Gram.* a demonstrative pronoun or adjective —**de·mon′stra·tive·ly** *adv.*

de·mor·al·ize (dē môr′ə līz′) *vt.* **-ized′**, **-iz′ing** **1** to lower the morale of **2** to throw into confusion —**de·mor′al·i·za′tion** *n.*

De·mos·the·nes (di mäs′thə nēz′) 384-322 B.C.; Athenian orator

de·mote (dē mōt′) *vt.* **-mot′ed**, **-mot′ing** ⟦DE- + (PRO)MOTE⟧ to reduce to a lower rank —**de·mo′tion** *n.*

de·mul·cent (dē mul′sənt) *adj.* ⟦< L *de-*, down + *mulcere*, to stroke⟧ soothing —*n.* a soothing ointment

de·mur (dē mʉr′, di-) *vi.* **-murred′**, **-mur′ring** ⟦< L *de-*, from + *mora*, a delay⟧ to hesitate, as because of doubts; have scruples; object —*n.* a demurring: also **de·mur′ral**

de·mure (di myoor′) *adj.* ⟦< ME *de-* (prob. intens.) + OFr *mëur*, mature⟧ **1** modest or reserved **2** affectedly modest; coy —**de·mure′ly** *adv.*

de·mur·rage (di mʉr′ij) *n.* **1** the compensation payable for delaying a vehicle or vessel carrying freight, as by failure to load or unload **2** the delay itself

de·mur·rer (di mʉr′ər) *n.* ⟦see DEMUR⟧ **1** a plea for dismissal of a lawsuit because statements supporting a claim are defective **2** an objection

den (den) *n.* ⟦OE *denn*⟧ **1** the lair of a wild animal **2** a haunt, as of thieves **3** a small, cozy room where a person can be alone to read, work, etc.

de·na·ture (dē nā′chər) *vt.* **-tured**, **-tur·ing** **1** to change the nature of **2** to make (alcohol) unfit to drink

den·drite (den′drīt′) *n.* ⟦< Gr *dendron*, tree⟧ the part of a nerve cell that carries impulses toward the cell body

Deng Xiao·ping (duŋ′ shou′piŋ′) 1904-97; Chin. Communist leader; held various official titles (1967-89); China's de facto ruler (*c.* 1981-97)

de·ni·al (dē nī′əl) *n.* **1** a denying; saying "no" (to a request, etc.) **2** a contradiction **3** a refusal to believe or accept (a doctrine, etc.) **4** SELF-DENIAL

de·nier[1] (den′yər) *n.* ⟦< L *deni*, by tens⟧ a unit of weight for measuring the fineness of threads of silk, nylon, etc.

de·ni·er[2] (dē nī′ər) *n.* one who denies

den·i·grate (den′ə grāt′) *vt.* **-grat′ed**, **-grat′ing** ⟦< L < *de-*, entirely + *nigrare*, blacken⟧ to belittle the character of; defame —**den′i·gra′tion** *n.*

den·im (den′im) *n.* ⟦< Fr *(serge) de Nîmes*, (serge) of Nîmes, town in France⟧ a coarse, twilled cotton cloth

den·i·zen (den′ə zən) *n.* ⟦< L *de intus*, from within⟧ an inhabitant or frequenter of a particular place

Den·mark (den′märk′) country in Europe, on a peninsula & several islands in the North & Baltic seas: 16,631 sq. mi.; pop. 4,938,000

de·nom·i·nate (dē näm′ə nāt′) *vt.* **-nat′ed**, **-nat′ing** ⟦< L *de-*, intens. + *nominare*, to name⟧ to name; call

de·nom′i·na′tion (-nā′shən) *n.* **1** the act of naming **2** a name **3** a class or kind, as of coins, having a specific name or value **4** a particular religious body

de·nom′i·na′tion·al *adj.* of, or under the control of, a religious denomination

de·nom′i·na′tor (-nāt′ər) *n.* **1** a shared characteristic **2** *Math.* the term below the line in a fraction

de·note (dē nōt′) *vt.* **-not′ed**, **-not′ing** ⟦< L *de-*, down + *notare*, to mark⟧ **1** to indicate **2** to signify; mean —**de·no·ta·tion** (dē′nō tā′shən) *n.*

de·noue·ment or **dé·noue·ment** (dā′noo män′) *n.* ⟦Fr⟧ the outcome or unraveling of a plot in a drama, story, etc.

de·nounce (dē nouns′) *vt.* **-nounced′**, **-nounc′ing** ⟦see DENUNCIATION⟧ **1** to accuse publicly; inform against **2** to condemn strongly and usually publicly —**de·nounce′ment** *n.*

dense (dens) *adj.* **dens′er**, **dens′est** ⟦< L *densus*, compact⟧ **1** packed tightly together **2** difficult to get through, penetrate, etc. **3** stupid —**dense′ly** *adv.* —**dense′ness** *n.*

den·si·ty (den′sə tē) *n.*, *pl.* **-ties** **1** a dense condition **2** stupidity **3** number per unit, as of area *[*population *density]* **4** ratio of the mass of an object to its volume

dent (dent) *n.* ⟦ME, var. of DINT⟧ **1** a slight hollow made in a surface by a blow **2** a noticeable effect —*vt.*, *vi.* to make or receive a dent (in)

den·tal (dent′'l) *adj.* ⟦< L *dens*, tooth⟧ of or for the teeth or dentistry

dental floss thread for removing food particles from between the teeth

den·ti·frice (den′tə fris) *n.* ⟦< L *dens*, tooth + *fricare*, rub⟧ any preparation for cleaning teeth

den·tin (den′tin) *n.* ⟦see DENTAL⟧ the hard tissue under the enamel of a tooth: also **den′tine′** (-tēn′, -tin)

den·tist (den′tist) *n.* one whose profession is the care and repair of teeth —**den′tist·ry** *n.*

den·ti·tion (den tish′ən) *n.* the arrangement of teeth in the mouth

den·ture (den′chər) *n.* ⟦see DENTAL⟧ [*often pl.*] a set of artificial teeth

de·nu·cle·ar·ize (dē noo′klē ər īz′) *vt.* **-ized′**, **-iz′ing** to prohibit the possession of nuclear weapons in

de·nude (dē nood′) *vt.* **-nud′ed**, **-nud′ing** ⟦< L *de-*, off + *nudare*, to strip⟧ to make bare or naked; strip

de·nun·ci·a·tion (dē nun′sē ā′shən) *n.* ⟦< L *de-*, intens. + *nuntiare*, announce⟧ the act of denouncing

Den·ver (den′vər) capital of Colorado: pop. 468,000

de·ny (dē nī′) *vt.* **-nied′**, **-ny′ing** ⟦< L *de-*, intens. + *negare*, to deny⟧ **1** to declare (a statement) untrue **2** to refuse to accept as true or right **3** to repudiate **4** to refuse to grant or give **5** to refuse the request of

de·o·dor·ant (dē ō′dər ənt) *adj.* that can counteract undesired odors —*n.* any deodorant preparation, esp. one for use on the body

de·o′dor·ize′ (-dər īz′) *vt.* **-ized′**, **-iz′ing** to counteract the odor of —**de·o′dor·iz′er** *n.*

de·part (dē pärt′) *vi.* ⟦< L *dis-*, apart + *partire*, divide⟧ **1** to go away; leave or set out **2** to die **3** to deviate *(from)* —*vt.* to leave

de·part′ed *adj.* **1** gone away **2** dead —**the departed** the dead

THESAURUS

fest, parade; see DISPLAY.

demonstration *n.* **1** [An exhibition] showing, presentation, exhibit; see DISPLAY, SHOW 1. **2** [A mass rally] picket line, march, sit-in; see PROTEST.

demoralize *v.* weaken, unman, enfeeble; see DISCOURAGE.

demoralized *a.* unnerved, weakened, depressed; see SAD 1.

demote *v.* downgrade, lower, bust*; see DECREASE 2, DISMISS.

den *n.* **1** [The home of an animal] cavern, lair, cave; see HOLE 1. **2** [A private or secluded room] study, recreation room, workroom; see RETREAT 2, ROOM 2.

denial *n.* repudiation, disclaimer, rejection, refutation, rejecting, retraction, dismissal, renunciation, refusal to recognize, the cold shoulder*, the brushoff*; see also OPPOSITION 2.—*Ant.* ACKNOWLEDGMENT, avowal, confession.

denomination *n.* **1** [A class] category, classification, group; see CLASS 1. **2** [A religious group] creed, sect, persuasion; see CHURCH 3.

denounce *v.* condemn, threaten, charge, blame, accuse, indict, arraign, implicate, incriminate, upbraid, impugn, prosecute, revile, stigmatize, ostracize, reproach, castigate, brand, boycott, rebuke, dress down, take to task, damn, impeach, scold, reprimand, reprove, condemn openly, charge with, blacklist, expose, knock*, rip into*, blackball; see also DENY.—*Ant.* PRAISE, laud, commend.

dense *a.* **1** [Close together] solid, compact, impenetrable; see THICK 1. **2** [Slow-witted] stupid, dumb*, imbecilic; see DULL 3, IGNORANT 2.

density *n.* solidity, thickness, impenetrability, consistency, quantity, bulk, heaviness, body, compactness, denseness; see also MASS 1, WEIGHT 1.—*Ant.* LIGHTNESS, rarity, thinness.

dent *n.* indentation, depression, impression, dimple, nick, notch, dip, cavity, cut, incision, sinkhole, pit, trough, furrow, scratch; see also HOLE 1.

dent *v.* hollow, depress, indent, gouge, sink, dig, imprint, mark, dimple, pit, notch, scratch, nick, make a dent in, perforate, furrow.—*Ant.* STRAIGHTEN, bulge, make protrude.

dentist *n.* DDS, dental practitioner, orthodontist; see DOCTOR.

deny *v.* contradict, disagree with, disprove, disallow, gainsay, disavow, disclaim, negate, repudiate, controvert, revoke, rebuff, reject, renounce, discard, not admit, take exception to, disbelieve, spurn, doubt, veto, discredit, nullify, say "no" to; see also DENOUNCE, REFUSE.—*Ant.* ADMIT, accept, affirm.

deodorant *n.* disinfectant, deodorizer, fumigator; see CLEANSER, COSMETIC.

depart *v.* go, quit, withdraw; see LEAVE 1.

departed *a.* **1** [Dead] defunct, expired, deceased; see DEAD 1. **2**

de·part·ment (dē pärt′mənt) ***n.*** **1** a separate part or division, as of a business **2** a field of activity —**de′part·men′tal** (-ment′'l) ***adj.***

de′part·men′tal·ize′ (-men′t'l īz′) ***vt.*** **-ized′**, **-iz′ing** to organize into departments —**de′part·men′tal·i·za′tion** ***n.***

department store a large retail store for the sale of many kinds of goods arranged in departments

de·par·ture (dē pär′chər) ***n.*** **1** a departing **2** a starting out, as on a trip **3** a deviation (*from*)

de·pend (dē pend′) ***vi.*** ⟦< L *de-*, down + *pendere*, to hang⟧ **1** to be determined by something else; be contingent (*on*) **2** to have trust; rely (*on*) **3** to rely (*on*) for support or aid

de·pend′a·ble ***adj.*** trustworthy; reliable —**de·pend′a·bil′i·ty** ***n.*** —**de·pend′a·bly** ***adv.***

de·pend′ence ***n.*** **1** a being dependent **2** reliance (*on*) for support or aid **3** reliance; trust **4** DEPENDENCY (sense 4)

de·pend′en·cy ***n.***, *pl.* **-cies** **1** dependence **2** something dependent **3** a territory, as a possession, subordinate to its governing country **4** addiction to alcohol or drugs

de·pend′ent ***adj.*** **1** hanging down **2** determined by something else **3** relying (*on*) for support, etc. **4** subordinate **5** addicted —***n.*** one relying on another for support, etc. Also **de·pend′ant** —**de·pend′ent·ly** ***adv.***

dependent clause *Gram.* a clause that cannot function as a complete sentence by itself

de·pict (dē pikt′) ***vt.*** ⟦< L *de-*, intens. + *pingere*, to paint⟧ **1** to represent by drawing, painting, etc. **2** to describe —**de·pic′tion** ***n.***

de·pil·a·to·ry (di pil′ə tôr′ē) ***adj.*** ⟦< L *de-*, from + *pilus*, hair⟧ serving to remove unwanted hair —***n.***, *pl.* **-ries** a depilatory substance or device

de·plane (dē plān′) ***vi.*** **-planed′**, **-plan′ing** to get out of an airplane after it lands

de·plete (dē plēt′) ***vt.*** **-plet′ed**, **-plet′ing** ⟦< L *de-*, from + *plere*, fill⟧ **1** to use up (funds, etc.) **2** to use up the resources, etc. of —**de·ple′tion** ***n.***

de·plor·a·ble (dē plôr′ə bəl) ***adj.*** regrettable, very bad, wretched, etc.

de·plore (dē plôr′) ***vt.*** **-plored′**, **-plor′ing** ⟦< L *de-*, intens. + *plorare*, weep⟧ **1** to be sorry about **2** to disapprove of

de·ploy (dē ploi′) ***vt.*** ⟦< L *dis-*, apart + *plicare*, to fold⟧ to spread out or position (troops, equipment, etc.) according to a plan —***vi.*** to be deployed —**de·ploy′ment** ***n.***

de·po·lar·ize (dē pō′lər īz′) ***vt.*** **-ized′**, **-iz′ing** to destroy or counteract the polarization of —**de·po′lar·i·za′tion** ***n.***

de·po·lit·i·cize (dē′pə lit′ə sīz′) ***vt.*** **-cized′**, **-ciz′ing** to remove from political influence

de·pon·ent (dē pōn′ənt) ***n.*** ⟦< L *de-*, down + *ponere*, put⟧ *Law* one who makes a deposition

de·pop·u·late (dē päp′yə lāt′) ***vt.*** **-lat′ed**, **-lat′ing** to reduce the population of —**de·pop′u·la′tion** ***n.***

de·port (dē pôrt′) ***vt.*** ⟦< L *de-*, from + *portare*, carry⟧ **1** to conduct (oneself) in a specified way **2** to expel (an alien) —**de′por·ta′tion** ***n.***

de·port′ment ***n.*** conduct; behavior

de·pose (dē pōz′) ***vt.*** **-posed′**, **-pos′ing** ⟦< OFr *de-*, from + *poser*, cease⟧ **1** to remove from office **2** *Law* to take the deposition of

de·pos·it (dē päz′it) ***vt.*** ⟦< L *de-*, down + *ponere*, put⟧ **1** to place (money, etc.) for safekeeping, as in a bank **2** to give as a pledge or partial payment **3** to put or set down **4** to cause (sediment, etc.) to settle —***n.*** **1** something placed for safekeeping, as money in a bank **2** a pledge or partial payment **3** a natural accumulation, as of minerals —**de·pos′i·tor** ***n.***

dep·o·si·tion (dep′ə zish′ən) ***n.*** **1** a deposing or being deposed, as from office **2** something deposited **3** *Law* testimony made under oath that is written down for later use

de·pos·i·to·ry (dē päz′ə tôr′ē) ***n.***, *pl.* **-ries** a place where things are put for safekeeping

de·pot (dē′pō; *military & Brit* dep′ō) ***n.*** ⟦< Fr: see DEPOSIT⟧ **1** a warehouse **2** a railroad or bus station **3** a storage place for military supplies

de·prave (dē prāv′) ***vt.*** **-praved′**, **-prav′ing** ⟦< L *de-*, intens. + *pravus*, crooked⟧ to make morally bad; corrupt —**de·praved′** ***adj.*** —**de·prav′i·ty** (-prav′ə tē), *pl.* **-ties**, ***n.***

dep·re·cate (dep′rə kāt′) ***vt.*** **-cat′ed**, **-cat′ing** ⟦< L *de-*, off + *precari*, pray⟧ **1** to express disapproval of **2** to belittle —**dep′re·ca′tion** ***n.*** —**dep′re·ca·to′ry** (-kə tôr′ē) ***adj.***

de·pre·ci·ate (dē prē′shē āt′) ***vt.***, ***vi.*** **-at′ed**, **-at′ing** ⟦< L *de-*, from + *pretium*, price⟧ **1** to lessen in value or price **2** to belittle —**de·pre′ci·a′tion** ***n.***

dep·re·da·tion (dep′rə dā′shən) ***n.*** ⟦< L *de-*, intens. + *praedari*, to plunder⟧ a robbing or plundering

de·press (dē pres′) ***vt.*** ⟦< L *de-*, down + *premere*, to press⟧ **1** to press down **2** to sadden or discourage **3** to weaken or make less active **4** to lower in value, price, etc. —**de·pressed′** ***adj.***

de·pres′sant ***n.*** a medicine, drug, etc. that lessens nervous activity

de·pres·sion (dē presh′ən) ***n.*** **1** a depressing or being depressed **2** a hollow or low place **3** low spirits; dejec-

THESAURUS

[Gone away] absent, disappeared, moved; see GONE 1.

department ***n.*** **1** [The field of one's activity] jurisdiction, activity, interest, occupation, province, bureau, business, capacity, dominion, administration, station, function, office, walk of life, vocation, specialty, field, duty, assignment, bailiwick; see also JOB 1. **2** [An organized subdivision] section, office, bureau, precinct, tract, range, quarter, area, arena, corps, agency, board, administration, circuit, territory, ward, state office, district office, force, staff, beat; see also DIVISION 2.

department store ***n.*** variety store, shopping center, shopper's square, mall, drygoods store, mail-order house, five-and-dime, bargain store; see also MARKET 1.

departure ***n.*** going, departing, separation, embarkation, taking leave, sailing, withdrawal, hegira, evacuation, passage, setting out, setting forth, parting, takeoff, taking off, becoming airborne, starting, leaving, flight, exodus, exit, walkout, getaway; see also RETREAT 1.—*Ant.* ARRIVAL, landing, invasion.

dependable ***a.*** trustworthy, steady, sure; see RELIABLE.

dependence ***n.*** reliance, servility, inability to act independently, subordination to the direction of another, subjection to control, subservience; see also NECESSITY 3.

dependent ***a.*** **1** [Subordinate] inferior, secondary, lesser; see SUBORDINATE. **2** [Needing outside support] helpless, poor, immature, clinging, not able to sustain itself, on a string; see also WEAK 5. **3** [Contingent] liable to, subject to, incidental to, conditioned, sustained by, unable to exist without, subordinate, accessory to, controlled by, regulated by, determined by; see also CONDITIONAL.

dependent ***n.*** ward, foster child, charge, orphan, minor, delinquent, protégé, hanger-on.

depending (on) ***a.*** contingent upon, regulated by, controlled by, determined by, in the event of, on the condition that, subject to, providing, provided, secondary to, growing from; see also CONDITIONAL.

depend on ***v.*** **1** [To be contingent upon] be determined by, rest with, rest on, be subordinate to, be dependent on, be based on, be subject to, hinge on, turn on, turn upon, be in the power of, be conditioned by, revolve on, trust to, be at the mercy of. **2** [To rely on] put faith in, confide in, believe in; see TRUST 1.

depleted ***a.*** emptied, exhausted, spent; see WASTED.

depletion ***n.*** exhaustion, consumption, deficiency; see EMPTINESS.

deport ***v.*** exile, ship out, ship away, expel; see also BANISH, DISMISS.

deposit ***v.*** **1** [To lay down] drop, place, put; see INSTALL. **2** [To present money for safekeeping] invest, amass, store, keep, stock up, bank, hoard, collect, treasure, lay away, put in the bank, entrust, transfer, put for safekeeping, put aside for a rainy day, salt away*; see also ACCUMULATE, SAVE 2.—*Ant.* SPEND, withdraw, put out. —**on deposit** in safekeeping, stored, saved; see KEPT 2.

depot ***n.*** station, base, lot, freight depot, passenger depot, railway depot, railroad depot, terminal, railway station, railroad yards, stockyards, sidetrack, siding, loading track, ammunition dump, ticket office, waiting room, junction, central station, airport, harbor, stopping place, destination.

deprave ***v.*** pervert, debase, degrade; see CORRUPT.

depraved ***a.*** low, mean, base; see BAD.

depreciate ***v.*** deteriorate, lessen, worsen; see DECREASE 1.

depreciation ***n.*** harm, reduction, shrinkage; see LOSS 3.

depress ***v.*** **1** [To bring to a lower level] press down, squash, settle; see FLATTEN, PRESS 1. **2** [To bring to a lower state] reduce, dampen, dishearten, debase, degrade, abase, dismay, sadden, mock, darken, scorn, reduce to tears, deject, weigh down, keep down, cast down, beat down, chill, dull, oppress, lower in spirits, throw cold water on*; see also DISCOURAGE, DISGRACE, HUMBLE, HUMILIATE.—*Ant.* URGE, animate, stimulate.

depressed ***a.*** discouraged, dejected, cast down; see SAD 1.

depressing ***a.*** discouraging, disheartening, saddening; see DISMAL, SAD 1.

depression ***n.*** **1** [Something lower than its surroundings] cavity, dent, sinkhole; see HOLE 1. **2** [Low spirits]

tion **4** a condition marked by hopelessness, self-doubt, lethargy, etc. **5** a decrease in force, activity, etc. **6** a period of reduced business, much unemployment, etc.

de·pres·sive (dē pres′iv) ***adj.*** **1** tending to depress **2** characterized by psychological depression —***n.*** one suffering from psychological depression

de·pres·sur·ize (dē presh′ər īz′) ***vt.*** **-ized′**, **-iz′ing** to reduce pressure in

de·prive (dē prīv′) ***vt.*** **-prived′**, **-priv′ing** ⟦< L *de-*, intens. + *privare*, to separate⟧ **1** to take away from forcibly **2** to keep from having, etc. —**dep·ri·va·tion** (dep′rə vā′shən) ***n.***

de·pro·gram (dē prō′gram′, -grəm) ***vt.*** **-grammed′** or **-gramed′**, **-gram′ming** or **-gram′ing** to cause to abandon rigidly held beliefs, etc. by undoing the effects of indoctrination

dept *abbrev.* **1** department **2** deputy

depth (depth) ***n.*** ⟦< ME *dep*, deep + -TH[1]⟧ **1** the distance from the top downward, or from front to back **2** deepness **3** intensity **4** profundity of thought **5** [*usually pl.*] the deepest or inmost part —**in depth** comprehensively

dep·u·ta·tion (dep′yoo tā′shən) ***n.*** **1** a deputing **2** a delegation

de·pute (dē pyoot′) ***vt.*** **-put′ed**, **-put′ing** ⟦< L *de-*, from + *putare*, cleanse⟧ **1** to give (authority, etc.) to a deputy **2** to appoint as one's substitute, etc.

dep·u·tize (dep′yoo tīz′) ***vt.*** **-tized′**, **-tiz′ing** to appoint as deputy

dep·u·ty (dep′yoo tē) ***n.***, *pl.* **-ties** a person appointed to act as a substitute or assistant

de·rail (dē rāl′) ***vt.***, ***vi.*** to run off the rails, as a train —**de·rail′ment** ***n.***

de·rail·leur (də rāl′ər) ***n.*** ⟦Fr⟧ a gear-shifting mechanism on a bicycle for shifting the sprocket chain from one size of sprocket wheel to another

de·range (dē rānj′) ***vt.*** **-ranged′**, **-rang′ing** ⟦< OFr *des-*, apart + *rengier*, to range⟧ **1** to upset or disturb **2** to make insane —**de·range′ment** ***n.***

Der·by (dur′bē; *Brit* där′-) ***n.***, *pl.* **-bies** **1** ⟦after an Earl of *Derby*, who founded the race held in England⟧ any of various horse races, as ones held annually in England, Kentucky, etc. **2** [**d-**] any of various contests or races, open to anyone **3** [**d-**] a stiff felt hat with a round crown

de·reg·u·late (dē reg′yə lāt′) ***vt.*** **-lat′ed**, **-lat′ing** to remove regulations governing —**de·reg′u·la′tion** ***n.***

der·e·lict (der′ə likt′) ***adj.*** ⟦< L *de-*, intens. + *relinquere*: see RELINQUISH⟧ **1** deserted by the owner; abandoned **2** negligent —***n.*** **1** an abandoned ship on the open sea **2** a destitute and rejected person

der′e·lic′tion (-lik′shən) ***n.*** **1** a forsaking or being forsaken **2** a neglect of, or failure in, duty

de·ride (di rīd′) ***vt.*** **-rid′ed**, **-rid′ing** ⟦< L *de-*, down + *ridere*, to laugh⟧ to laugh at in scorn; ridicule —**de·ri′sion** (-rizh′ən) ***n.*** —**de·ri′sive** (-rī′siv) ***adj.*** —**de·ri′sive·ly** ***adv.***

der·i·va·tion (der′ə vā′shən) ***n.*** **1** a deriving or being derived **2** the source or origin of something, specif. of a word

de·riv·a·tive (də riv′ə tiv) ***adj.*** derived; specif., not original or novel —***n.*** something derived

de·rive (di rīv′) ***vt.*** **-rived′**, **-riv′ing** ⟦< L *de-*, from + *rivus*, a stream⟧ **1** to get or receive (something) *from* a source **2** to deduce or infer **3** to trace from or to a source —***vi.*** to come (*from*)

der·ma·bra·sion (dur′mə brā′zhən) ***n.*** ⟦DERM(IS) + ABRASION⟧ the surgical procedure of scraping off upper layers of the skin with an abrasive device, to remove acne scars, blemishes, etc.

der·ma·ti·tis (dur′mə tīt′is) ***n.*** ⟦< Gr *derma*, skin + -ITIS⟧ inflammation of the skin

der·ma·tol·o·gy (dur′mə täl′ə jē) ***n.*** ⟦< Gr *derma*, skin + -LOGY⟧ the branch of medicine dealing with the skin —**der′ma·tol′o·gist** ***n.***

der·mis (dur′mis) ***n.*** ⟦see EPIDERMIS⟧ the layer of skin just below the epidermis

der·o·gate (der′ə gāt′) ***vi.***, ***vt.*** **-gat′ed**, **-gat′ing** ⟦< L *de-*, from + *rogare*, ask⟧ to detract (*from*) or disparage —**der′o·ga′tion** ***n.***

de·rog·a·to·ry (di räg′ə tôr′ē) ***adj.*** ⟦see prec.⟧ disparaging; belittling —**de·rog′a·to′ri·ly** ***adv.***

der·rick (der′ik) ***n.*** ⟦after Thos. *Derrick*, London hangman of the early 17th c.: orig. applied to a gallows⟧ **1** a pivoted beam for lifting and moving heavy objects **2** a tall framework, as over an oil well, to support drilling machinery, etc.

der·ri·ère (der′ē er′) ***n.*** ⟦Fr, back part⟧ the buttocks

der·rin·ger (der′in jər) ***n.*** ⟦after H. *Deringer*, 19th-c. U.S. gunsmith⟧ a small, short-barreled pistol

der·vish (dur′vish) ***n.*** ⟦< Pers *darvēsh*, beggar⟧ a member of any of various Muslim ascetic religious groups

de·sal·i·na·tion (dē′sal′ə nā′shən) ***n.*** ⟦DE- + SALIN(E) + -ATION⟧ the removal of salt, esp. from sea water to make it drinkable —**de′sal′i·nate′**, **-nat′ed**, **-nat′ing**, ***vt.***

Des·cartes (dā kärt′), **Re·né** (rə nā′) 1596-1650; Fr. philosopher

de·scend (dē send′) ***vi.*** ⟦< L *de-*, down + *scandere*, climb⟧ **1** to move down to a lower place **2** to pass from an earlier to a later time, from greater to less, etc. **3** to slope downward **4** to come down (*from* a source) **5** to lower oneself or stoop (*to*) **6** to make a sudden raid (*on* or *upon*) —***vt.*** to move down along

de·scend′ant (-sen′dənt) ***n.*** an offspring of a certain ancestor, family, group, etc.

de·scent′ (-sent′) ***n.*** **1** a coming down or going down **2** ancestry **3** a downward slope **4** a way down **5** a sudden attack (*on* or *upon*) **6** a decline

de·scribe (di skrīb′) ***vt.*** **-scribed′**, **-scrib′ing** ⟦< L *de-*, from + *scribere*, write⟧ **1** to tell or write about **2** to trace the outline of —**de·scrib′er** ***n.***

de·scrip·tion (di skrip′shən) ***n.*** **1** the act or technique of describing **2** a statement or passage that describes **3** sort; kind [*books of every description*] **4** a tracing or outlining —**de·scrip′tive** ***adj.***

THESAURUS

despair, despondency, sorrow, unhappiness, gloom, dejection, melancholy, misery, trouble, worry, discouragement, hopelessness, distress, desperation, desolation, dreariness, dullness, cheerlessness, darkness, bleakness, oppression, gloominess, the dumps*, blues*, doldrums; see also GRIEF, SADNESS.—*Ant.* JOY, cheer, satisfaction. **3** [Period of economic stress] decline, unemployment, slack times, hard times, bad times, inflation, crisis, economic decline, overproduction, economic stagnation, recession, panic, crash, slump; see also FAILURE 1.

deprive ***v.*** strip, despoil, divest; see SEIZE 2.

depth ***n.*** **1** [Vertical or lateral distance] lowness, deepness, drop, distance inward, downward measure; see also EXPANSE.—*Ant.* HEIGHT, shallowness, flatness. **2** [Deepness] profundity, intensity, abyss, pit, base, bottom of the sea; see also BOTTOM. **3** [Intellectual power] profundity, weightiness, acumen; see WISDOM. —**in depth** extensive, broad, thorough, thoroughly.

deputy ***n.*** lieutenant, appointee, aide; see ASSISTANT, DELEGATE.

derail ***v.*** run off the rails, be wrecked, fall off; see CRASH 1, WRECK.

derange ***v.*** madden, craze, unbalance; see CONFUSE, DISTURB.

deranged ***a.*** demented, crazy, mad; see INSANE.

deride ***v.*** scorn, jeer, mock; see RIDICULE.

derision ***n.*** scorn, mockery, disdain; see RIDICULE.

derivation ***n.*** root, source, etymology; see ORIGIN 3.

derive ***v.*** draw a conclusion, work out, conclude; see ASSUME.

derogatory ***a.*** belittling, faultfinding, detracting; see CRITICAL, SARCASTIC.

descend ***v.*** slide, settle, gravitate, slip, dismount, topple, plunge, sink, dip, pass downward, pitch, light, deplane, tumble, move downward, come down upon, slump, trip, stumble, flutter down, plummet, submerge, step down, climb down, go down, swoop down, get off; see also DIVE, DROP 1, FALL 1.—*Ant.* CLIMB, ascend, mount.

descendant ***n.*** offspring, kin, child; see FAMILY.

descent ***n.*** **1** [A downward incline] declivity, slant, slide; see HILL, INCLINATION 2. **2** [The act of descending] slump, downfall, drop, lapse, subsiding, falling, coming down, sinking, reduction, landslide, tumble, decline; see also FALL 1.—*Ant.* RISE, mounting, growth. **3** [Lineal relationship] extraction, origin, lineage; see FAMILY, RELATIONSHIP.

describe ***v.*** delineate, characterize, portray, depict, picture, illuminate, make clear, make apparent, make vivid, give the details of, specify, give meaning to, elucidate, report, draw, paint, illustrate, limn, detail, make sense of, relate, express, narrate, label, name, call, term, write up, give the dope on*, spell out*; see also DEFINE, EXPLAIN.

description ***n.*** narration, story, portrayal, word picture, account, report, delineation, sketch, specifications, characterization, declaration, rehearsal, information, definition, brief, summary, depiction, explanation, write-up*; see also RECORD 1.

descriptive ***a.*** designating, identifying, definitive, photographic,

de·scry (di skrī′) ***vt.*** **-scried′, -scry′ing** ⟦< OFr *descrier*, proclaim⟧ **1** to catch sight of; discern **2** to detect

des·e·crate (des′i krāt′) ***vt.*** **-crat′ed, -crat′ing** ⟦DE- (sense 4) + (CON)SECRATE⟧ to violate the sacredness of; profane —**des′e·cra′tion** ***n.***

de·seg·re·gate (dē seg′rə gāt′) ***vt., vi.*** **-gat′ed, -gat′ing** to abolish racial segregation in (public schools, etc.) —**de·seg′re·ga′tion** ***n.***

de·sen·si·tize (dē sen′sə tīz′) ***vt.*** **-tized′, -tiz′ing** to make less sensitive, as to an allergen

de·sert[1] (di zurt′) ***vt., vi.*** ⟦< L *de-*, from + *serere*, join⟧ **1** to abandon; forsake **2** to leave (one's military post, etc.) without permission and with no intent to return —**de·sert′er** ***n.*** —**de·ser′tion** (-zur′shən) ***n.***

des·ert[2] (dez′ərt) ***n.*** ⟦see prec.⟧ **1** an uninhabited region; wilderness **2** a dry, barren, sandy region, often one that is hot —***adj.*** wild and uninhabited *[a desert island]*

de·sert[3] (di zurt′) ***n.*** ⟦see DESERVE⟧ [*often pl.*] deserved reward or punishment *[one's just deserts]*

de·serve (di zurv′) ***vt., vi.*** **-served′, -serv′ing** ⟦< L *de-*, intens. + *servire*, serve⟧ to be worthy (of); merit —**de·serv′ed·ly** (-zur′vid lē) ***adv.***

des·ic·cate (des′i kāt′) ***vt., vi.*** **-cat′ed, -cat′ing** ⟦< L *de-*, intens. + *siccus*, dry⟧ to dry out completely —**des′ic·ca′tion** ***n.***

de·sid·er·a·tum (di sid′ə rät′əm) ***n., pl.*** **-ta** (-ə) ⟦see DESIRE⟧ something needed and wanted

de·sign (di zīn′) ***vt.*** ⟦< L *de-*, out + *signum*, a mark⟧ **1** to sketch an outline for; plan **2** to contrive **3** to intend —***vi.*** to make original plans, etc. —***n.*** **1** a plan; scheme **2** purpose; aim **3** a working plan; pattern **4** arrangement of parts, form, color, etc. —**by design** purposely —**de·sign′er** ***n.***

des·ig·nate (dez′ig nāt′) ***vt.*** **-nat′ed, -nat′ing** ⟦see prec.⟧ **1** to point out; specify **2** to name **3** to appoint —**des′ig·na′tion** ***n.***

designated driver the one in a group who refrains from drinking alcoholic beverages so as to be able to safely transport the others in a motor vehicle

de·sign′ing ***adj.*** scheming; crafty —***n.*** the art of creating designs, etc.

de·sir·a·ble (di zīr′ə bəl) ***adj.*** **1** worth having **2** arousing desire —**de·sir′a·bil′i·ty** ***n.*** —**de·sir′a·bly** ***adv.***

de·sire (di zīr′) ***vt.*** **-sired′, -sir′ing** ⟦< L *desiderare*⟧ **1** to long for; crave **2** to ask for —***vi.*** to have a desire —***n.*** **1** a wish; craving **2** sexual appetite **3** a request **4** a thing desired —**de·sir′ous** ***adj.***

de·sist (di zist′, -sist′) ***vi.*** ⟦< L *de-*, from + *stare*, to stand⟧ to cease; stop

desk (desk) ***n.*** ⟦< ML *desca*, table⟧ a piece of furniture with a flat surface for writing, etc. —***adj.*** of, for, or at a desk *[a desk job]*

desk′top′ ***n., adj.*** (equipment, as a microcomputer) for use on a desk or table

desk·top publishing the production of printed matter by means of a microcomputer and special software for laying out text and illustrations

Des Moines (də moin′) capital of Iowa: pop. 193,000

des·o·late (des′ə lit; *for v.*, -lāt′) ***adj.*** ⟦< L *de-*, intens. + *solus*, alone⟧ **1** lonely; solitary **2** uninhabited **3** laid waste **4** forlorn —***vt.*** **-lat′ed, -lat′ing** **1** to rid of inhabitants **2** to lay waste **3** to make forlorn

des′o·la′tion ***n.*** **1** a making desolate **2** a desolate condition or place **3** misery **4** loneliness

de·spair (di sper′) ***vi.*** ⟦< L *de-*, without + *sperare*, to hope⟧ to lose hope —***n.*** **1** loss of hope **2** a person or thing causing despair

des·patch (di spach′) ***vt., n.*** DISPATCH

des·per·a·do (des′pər ä′dō, -ā′-) ***n., pl.*** **-does** or **-dos** ⟦< 17th-c. Sp < L *desperare*: see DESPAIR⟧ a dangerous criminal; bold outlaw

des·per·ate (des′pər it) ***adj.*** **1** rash or violent because of despair **2** having a very great need **3** very serious, dangerous, etc. **4** drastic —**des′per·ate·ly** ***adv.***

des·per·a·tion (des′pər ā′shən) ***n.*** **1** the state of being desperate **2** recklessness resulting from despair

des·pi·ca·ble (di spik′ə bəl) ***adj.*** deserving scorn; contemptible

de·spise (di spīz′) ***vt.*** **-spised′, -spis′ing** ⟦< L *de*, down + *specere*, look at⟧ **1** to scorn **2** to loathe

THESAURUS

describing, interpretive, narrative, characterizing, expressive, clear, true to life, illustrative, lifelike, vivid, picturesque, circumstantial, eloquent, detailed, pictorial, indicative, revealing; see also CHARACTERISTIC, EXPLANATORY, GRAPHIC 1, 2.—*Ant.* DULL, analytical, expository.

desert[1] ***v.*** defect, be absent without leave, abandon one's post, sneak off, run away from duty, violate one's oath, leave unlawfully, go AWOL, go over the hill*; see also ABANDON 2.—*Ant.* OBEY, stay, do one's duty.

desert[2] ***n.*** waste, sand, wastelands, wilds, barren plains, arid region, deserted region, sand dunes, lava beds, salt flats, abandoned land; see also WILDERNESS.

deserted ***a.*** left, forsaken, relinquished; see ABANDONED, EMPTY.

deserter ***n.*** runaway, fugitive, refugee, truant, defector, derelict, delinquent, lawbreaker, betrayer, backslider, slacker; see also CRIMINAL, TRAITOR.

desertion ***n.*** abandonment, flight, departure, leaving, defection, defecting, renunciation, withdrawal, avoidance, evasion, elusion, truancy, retirement, resignation, divorce, backsliding, running out on*, going back on*; see also ESCAPE.—*Ant.* LOYALTY, cooperation, union.

deserve ***v.*** merit, be worthy of, earn, be deserving, lay claim to, have the right to, be given one's due, be entitled to, warrant, rate*, have it coming*.—*Ant.* FAIL, be unworthy, usurp.

deserved ***a.*** merited, earned, justified, appropriate, suitable, equitable, right, rightful, proper, fitting, just, due, well-deserved; see also FIT.

deserving ***a.*** meriting, meritorious, exemplary; see WORTHY.

design ***n.*** pattern, layout, conception, diagram, drawing, preliminary sketch, draft, blueprint, picture, tracing, outline, depiction, chart, map, plan, perspective, treatment, idea, study; see also COMPOSITION, FORM 1, PURPOSE 1.—*Ant.* CONFUSION, jumble, mess. —**by design** on purpose, with intent, purposely; see DELIBERATELY.

design ***v.*** block out, outline, sketch; see PLAN 2.

designate ***v.*** indicate, point out, name; see CHOOSE.

designation ***n.*** classification, label, appellation; see CLASS 1, NAME 1.

designer ***n.*** planner, draftsman, creator; see ARCHITECT, ARTIST, SCULPTOR.

desirable ***a.*** **1** [Stimulating erotic desires] seductive, fascinating, alluring; see CHARMING. **2** [Having many good qualities] good, welcome, acceptable; see EXCELLENT.

desire ***n.*** **1** [The wish to enjoy] aspiration, wish, motive, will, urge, eagerness, propensity, fancy, frenzy, craze, mania, hunger, thirst, attraction, longing, yearning, fondness, liking, inclination, proclivity, craving, relish, hankering, itch*, yen*; see also AMBITION, GREED.—*Ant.* INDIFFERENCE, unconcern, apathy. **2** [Erotic wish to possess] lust, passion, hunger, appetite, fascination, infatuation, fervor, excitement, sexual love, nymphomania, libido, sensual appetite, carnal passion, eroticism, biological urge, rut, heat.—*Ant.* ABSTINENCE, coldness, frigidity.

desire ***v.*** **1** [To wish for] long for, crave, wish for; see NEED, WANT 1. **2** [To request] ask for, seek, solicit; see BEG. **3** [To want sexually] lust after, hunger for, have the hots for*, be turned on by*; see also WANT 1.

desk ***n.*** **1** [A piece of furniture] secretary, roll-top, bureau, box, lectern, frame, case, pulpit; see also FURNITURE, TABLE 1. **2** [A department of an editorial office] division, section, bureau; see DEPARTMENT.

desolate ***a.*** deserted, forsaken, uninhabited; see ABANDONED, ISOLATED, ALONE.

desolation ***n.*** bareness, barrenness, devastation, havoc, ruin, dissolution, wreck, demolition, annihilation, extinction; see also DESERT.

despair ***n.*** hopelessness, depression, discouragement; see DESPERATION, GLOOM.

despair ***v.*** lose hope, lose faith, lose heart, give up hope, abandon hope, have no hope, have a heavy heart, abandon oneself to fate; see also ABANDON 1.

despairing ***a.*** hopeless, despondent, miserable; see SAD 1.

desperado ***n.*** outlaw, bandit, ruffian; see CRIMINAL.

desperate ***a.*** **1** [Hopeless] despairing, despondent, downcast; see HOPELESS, SAD 1. **2** [Reckless] incautious, frenzied, wild; see CARELESS, RASH.

desperately ***a.*** severely, harmfully, perilously; see CARELESSLY, SERIOUSLY 1.

desperation ***n.*** despondency, despair, depression, discomfort, dejection, distraction, distress, desolation, anxiety, anguish, agony, melancholy, grief, sorrow, worry, trouble, pain, hopelessness, torture, pang, heartache, concern, misery, unhappiness; see also FEAR, FUTILITY, GLOOM.—*Ant.* HOPE, hopefulness, confidence.

despicable ***a.*** contemptible, abject, base; see MEAN 3.

despise ***v.*** scorn, disdain, condemn; see HATE 1.

de·spite (di spīt′) ***prep.*** ⟦see prec.⟧ in spite of; notwithstanding

de·spoil (dē spoil′) ***vt.*** ⟦< L *de-*, intens. + *spoliare*, to strip⟧ to rob; plunder —**de·spo·li·a·tion** (di spō′lē ā′shən) ***n.***

de·spond·en·cy (di spän′dən sē) ***n.*** ⟦< L *de-*, from + *spondere*, to promise⟧ loss of hope; dejection: also **de·spond′ence** —**de·spond′ent** ***adj.***

des·pot (des′pət) ***n.*** ⟦< Gr *despotēs*, a master⟧ **1** an absolute ruler **2** anyone like a tyrant —**des·pot′ic** (-pät′ik) ***adj.*** —**des′pot·ism′** (-pə tiz′əm) ***n.***

des·sert (di zʉrt′) ***n.*** ⟦< L *de*, from + *servire*, serve⟧ the final course of a meal, typically cake, pie, etc.

des·ti·na·tion (des′tə nā′shən) ***n.*** the place toward which one is going or sent

des·tine (des′tin) ***vt.*** **-tined**, **-tin·ing** ⟦< L *de-*, intens. + *stare*, to stand⟧ **1** to predetermine, as by fate **2** to intend —**destined for** **1** headed for **2** intended for

des·ti·ny (des′tə nē) ***n.***, *pl.* **-nies** **1** the seemingly inevitable succession of events **2** (one's) fate

des·ti·tute (des′tə to͞ot′) ***adj.*** ⟦< L *de-*, down + *statuere*, to set⟧ **1** lacking: with *of* **2** totally impoverished —**des′ti·tu′tion** ***n.***

de·stroy (di stroi′) ***vt.*** ⟦< L *de-*, down + *struere*, to build⟧ **1** to tear down; demolish **2** to ruin **3** to do away with **4** to kill

de·stroy′er ***n.*** **1** one that destroys **2** a small, fast warship

de·struct (di strukt′, dē′strukt′) ***vi.*** ⟦< fol.⟧ to be automatically destroyed

de·struc·tion (di struk′shən) ***n.*** **1** a destroying or being destroyed **2** the cause or means of destroying —**de·struc′tive** ***adj.*** —**de·struc′tive·ly** ***adv.*** —**de·struc′tive·ness** ***n.***

des·ue·tude (des′wi to͞od′) ***n.*** ⟦< L *de-*, from + *suescere*, be accustomed⟧ disuse

des·ul·to·ry (des′əl tôr′ē) ***adj.*** ⟦< L *de-*, from + *salire*, to leap⟧ **1** aimless; disconnected **2** random

de·tach (dē tach′) ***vt.*** ⟦< Fr: see DE- & ATTACH⟧ **1** to unfasten and remove; disconnect; disengage **2** to send (troops, etc.) on a special mission —**de·tach′a·ble** ***adj.***

de·tached′ ***adj.*** **1** not connected **2** aloof; disinterested; impartial

de·tach′ment ***n.*** **1** a detaching **2** a unit of troops, etc. on a special mission **3** impartiality or aloofness

de·tail (di tāl′, dē′tāl′) ***n.*** ⟦< Fr < *dé-*, from + *tailler*, to cut⟧ **1** a dealing with things item by item **2** a minute account *[to go into detail]* **3** a small part; item **4** *a)* one or more soldiers, etc. on special duty *b)* the duty —***vt.*** **1** to tell, item by item **2** to assign to special duty —**in detail** with particulars

de·tain (dē tān′) ***vt.*** ⟦< L *de-*, off + *tenere*, to hold⟧ **1** to keep in custody; confine **2** to keep from going on —**de′tain·ee′** (-ē′) ***n.*** —**de·tain′ment** ***n.***

de·tect (dē tekt′) ***vt.*** ⟦< L *de-*, from + *tegere*, to cover⟧ to discover (something hidden, not clear, etc.) —**de·tect′a·ble** or **de·tect′i·ble** ***adj.*** —**de·tec′tion** ***n.*** —**de·tec′tor** ***n.***

de·tec′tive (-tek′tiv) ***n.*** one whose work is to investigate crimes, uncover evidence, etc.

dé·tente or **de·tente** (dā tänt′) ***n.*** ⟦Fr⟧ a lessening of tension, esp. between nations

de·ten·tion (dē ten′shən) ***n.*** **1** a detaining or being detained **2** the punishment of having to stay after school

detention home a place where juvenile offenders are held in custody

de·ter (dē tʉr′) ***vt.*** **-terred′**, **-ter′ring** ⟦< L *de-*, from + *terrere*, frighten⟧ to keep or discourage (a person or group) from doing something through fear, doubt, etc. —**de·ter′ment** ***n.*** —**de·ter′rence** ***n.***

THESAURUS

despite ***prep.*** in spite of, in defiance of, regardless of, even with.

despondent ***a.*** dejected, discouraged, depressed; see SAD 1.

dessert ***n.*** sweet, tart, cobbler, pastry, torte, custard, sherbet, mousse, cookie, trifle, soufflé, sundae, compote, fruit salad, pudding, ice cream; see also CAKE 2, CANDY, CHEESE, DELICACY 2, FRUIT, PASTRY, PIE.

destination ***n.*** objective, goal, aim; see PURPOSE 1.

destined ***a.*** fated, compulsory, foreordained, menacing, near, forthcoming, threatening, in prospect, predestined, predetermined, compelled, condemned, at hand, impending, inexorable, that is to be, in store, to come, directed, ordained, settled, sealed, closed, predesigned, in the wind, in the cards; see also DOOMED, INEVITABLE.—*Ant.* INVOLUNTARY, at will, by chance.

destiny ***n.*** fate, lot, fortune; see DOOM.

destitute ***a.*** impoverished, poverty-stricken, penniless; see POOR 1.

destroy ***v.*** ruin, demolish, exterminate, raze, tear down, plunder, ransack, eradicate, overthrow, root up, root out, devastate, butcher, consume, liquidate, break up, dissolve, blot out, quash, quell, level, abort, stamp out, suppress, squelch, scuttle, undo, annihilate, lay waste, overturn, impair, damage, ravish, deface, shatter, split up, crush, obliterate, knock to pieces, abolish, crash, extinguish, wreck, dismantle, upset, bomb, mutilate, smash, trample, overturn, maim, mar, end, nullify, blast, neutralize, gut, snuff out, erase, sabotage, repeal, pull down, terminate, conclude, finish, bring to ruin, put a stop to, wipe out, do in*, do away with, finish off, make short work of, total*, cream*, destruct, self-destruct, put an end to; see also DEFEAT, RAVAGE, STOP 1.—*Ant.* BUILD, construct, establish.

destroyed ***a.*** wrecked, annihilated, killed, lost, devastated, wasted, demolished, overturned, overwhelmed, upset, nullified, undone, put to an end, shattered, smashed, scuttled, ravished, engulfed, submerged, overrun, extinguished, eradicated, devoured, consumed, burned up, burned down, gone to pieces, razed, lying in ruins, sacked; see also BROKEN 1, DEAD 1, RUINED 1.—*Ant.* SAVED, protected, restored.

destroyer ***n.*** **1** [An agent of destruction] assassin, terrorist, slayer; see CRIMINAL, KILLER, WEAPON. **2** [A swift, armed surface vessel] armed ship, battleship, fighting vessel; see SHIP, WARSHIP.

destruction ***n.*** **1** [The act of destroying] demolition, annihilation, eradication, slaughter, liquidation, overthrow, extermination, elimination, abolition, murder, assassination, killing, disintegration, bombardment, disruption, extinction, annihilating, wreckage, dissolution, butchery, sabotage, sacking, extinguishing, eliminating, crashing, falling, felling, tearing down; see also DAMAGE 1, DISASTER.—*Ant.* PRODUCTION, formation, erection. **2** [The result of destroying] waste, ashes, annihilation, remnants, devastation, vestiges, desolation, ruins, catastrophe, overthrow, decay, loss, remains, havoc, prostration, injury, downfall, end, dissolution, disorganization; see also DAMAGE 2, WRECK.

destructive ***a.*** **1** [Harmful] hurtful, injurious, troublesome; see HARMFUL. **2** [Deadly] fatal, ruinous, devastating; see DEADLY, VICIOUS.

detach ***v.*** separate, withdraw, disengage; see DIVIDE.

detached ***a.*** **1** [Cut off or removed] loosened, divided, disjoined; see SEPARATED. **2** [Indifferent] apathetic, uninvolved, unconcerned; see INDIFFERENT.

detail ***n.*** item, portion, particular, trait, specialty, feature, aspect, article, peculiarity, fraction, specification, technicality; see also CIRCUMSTANCE, PART 1.—*Ant.* WHOLE, entirety, synthesis. —**in detail** minutely, item by item, part by part, step by step, inch by inch, systematically, intimately.—*Ant.* VAGUELY, generally, indefinitely.

detail ***v.*** itemize, exhibit, show, report, relate, narrate, tell, designate, catalogue, recite, specialize, depict, enumerate, mention, uncover, reveal, recount, recapitulate, analyze, set forth, produce, go into the particulars, get down to cases*; see also DESCRIBE.—*Ant.* DABBLE, summarize, generalize.

detailed ***a.*** enumerated, specified, explicit, specific, particularized, individual, individualized, developed, itemized, definite, minute, described, precise, full, narrow, complete, exact, fussy, particular, meticulous, point by point, circumstantial, accurate, unfolded, disclosed, elaborated, complicated, comprehensive, at length, gone into; see also ELABORATE 2.—*Ant.* GENERAL, brief, hazy.

details ***n.*** analysis, trivia, minutiae, particulars, itemized account, trivialities, factoids, statistics, fine points, items; see also DETAIL.

detain ***v.*** hold, keep, inhibit; see DELAY, RESTRAIN.

detect ***v.*** distinguish, recognize, identify; see DISCOVER.

detection ***n.*** apprehension, investigation, disclosure; see DISCOVERY, EXPOSURE.

detective ***n.*** agent, plainclothes man, private eye*, narcotics agent, police sergeant, police officer, FBI agent, wiretapper, investigator, criminologist, patrolman, sleuth, shadow, eavesdropper, spy, shamus*, flatfoot*, dick*, G-man*, copper*, cop*, fed, narc*; see also POLICE OFFICER.

detention ***n.*** custody, internment, quarantine; see ARREST, CONFINEMENT, RESTRAINT 2.

deter ***v.*** caution, stop, dissuade; see PREVENT, WARN.

de·ter·gent (dē tʉr′jənt) ***adj.*** ⟦< L *de-*, off + *tergere*, wipe⟧ cleansing —***n.*** cleansing substance that emulsifies dirt and oil

de·te·ri·o·rate (dē tir′ē ə rāt′) ***vt., vi.*** **-rat′ed, -rat′ing** ⟦< L *deterior*, worse⟧ to make or become worse —**de·te′ri·o·ra′tion** ***n.***

de·ter·mi·nant (dē tʉr′mi nənt) ***n.*** a thing or factor that determines

de·ter′mi·nate (-nit) ***adj.*** clearly determined; fixed; settled

de·ter′mi·na′tion (-nā′shən) ***n.*** **1** a determining or being determined **2** a firm intention **3** firmness of purpose

de·ter′mine (-mən) ***vt.*** **-mined, -min·ing** ⟦< L *de-*, from + *terminus*, a limit⟧ **1** to set limits to **2** to settle conclusively **3** to decide or decide upon **4** to affect the nature or quality of **5** to find out exactly —***vi.*** to decide —**de·ter′mi·na·ble** ***adj.***

de·ter′mined (-mənd) ***adj.*** **1** having one's mind made up **2** resolute; firm

de·ter′rent ***adj.*** deterring —***n.*** something that deters

de·test (dē test′) ***vt.*** ⟦< L *detestari*, to curse by the gods⟧ to dislike intensely; hate —**de·test′a·ble** ***adj.*** —**de′tes·ta′tion** (-tes tā′shən) ***n.***

de·thatch (dē thach′) ***vt.*** to remove the thatch from (a lawn)

de·throne (dē thrōn′) ***vt.*** **-throned′, -thron′ing** to depose (a monarch)

det·o·nate (det′′n āt′) ***vi., vt.*** **-nat′ed, -nat′ing** ⟦< L *de-*, intens. + *tonare*, to thunder⟧ to explode violently —**det′o·na′tion** ***n.*** —**det′o·na′tor** ***n.***

de·tour (dē′toor′) ***n.*** ⟦< Fr: see DE- & TURN⟧ **1** a roundabout way **2** a substitute route —***vi., vt.*** to go or route on a detour

de·tox (dē täks′; *for n.* dē′täks′) [Inf.] ***vt.*** *short for* DETOXIFY —***n.*** *short for* DETOXIFICATION

de·tox·i·fy (dē täk′si fī′) ***vt.*** **-fied′, -fy′ing** ⟦DE- + TOXI(N) + -FY⟧ **1** to remove a poison or poisonous effect from **2** to treat for drug or alcohol addiction —**de·tox′i·fi·ca′tion** ***n.***

de·tract (dē trakt′) ***vt.*** ⟦< L *de-*, from + *trahere*, to draw⟧ to take away —***vi.*** to take something desirable (*from*) —**de·trac′tion** ***n.***

de·trac′tor (-trak′tər) ***n.*** one who disparages

det·ri·ment (de′trə mənt) ***n.*** ⟦< L *de-*, off + *terere*, to rub⟧ **1** damage; injury **2** anything that causes this —**det′ri·men′tal** (-ment′′l) ***adj.***

de·tri·tus (dē trīt′əs) ***n.*** ⟦L, a rubbing away: see prec.⟧ debris, specif. rock fragments

De·troit (di troit′) city & port in SE Michigan: pop. 1,028,000

deuce (do͞os) ***n.*** ⟦< L *duo*, two⟧ **1** a playing card or side of a die with two spots **2** *Tennis, Badminton, etc.* a tie score after which one side must score twice in a row to win

deu·te·ri·um (do͞o tir′ē əm) ***n.*** ⟦< Gr *deuteros*, second⟧ a hydrogen isotope used in nuclear reactors

Deu·ter·on·o·my (do͞ot′ər än′ə mē) ***n.*** ⟦< Gr *deuteros*, second + *nomos*, law⟧ the fifth book of the Pentateuch

deutsche mark (doich′ märk′) the monetary unit of Germany

de·val·ue (dē val′yo͞o) ***vt.*** **-ued, -u·ing** **1** to lessen the value of **2** to lower the exchange value of (a currency) —**de·val′u·a′tion** ***n.***

dev·as·tate (dev′ə stāt′) ***vt.*** **-tat′ed, -tat′ing** ⟦< L *de-*, intens. + *vastus*, empty⟧ **1** to lay waste; ravage; destroy **2** to make helpless; overwhelm —**dev′as·ta′tion** ***n.*** —**dev′as·ta′tor** ***n.***

de·vel·op (di vel′əp) ***vt.*** ⟦< OFr *des-*, apart + *voloper*, to wrap⟧ **1** to make fuller, bigger, better, etc. **2** to show or work out by degrees **3** to enlarge upon **4** *Photog.* to put (film, etc.) into chemicals to make the picture visible —***vi.*** **1** to come into being or activity; occur **2** to become developed —**de·vel′op·er** ***n.*** —**de·vel′op·ment** ***n.*** —**de·vel′op·men′tal** (-ment′′l) ***adj.***

de·vi·ant (dē′vē ənt) ***adj.*** deviating, esp. from what is considered normal —***n.*** one whose behavior is deviant —**de′vi·ance** or **de′vi·an·cy** ***n.***

de·vi·ate (dē′vē āt′; *for adj. & n.*, -it) ***vi.*** **-at′ed, -at′ing** ⟦< L *de-*, from + *via*, road⟧ to turn aside (*from* a course, standard, etc.); diverge —***adj.*** DEVIANT —***n.*** a deviant, esp. in sexual behavior —**de′vi·a′tion** ***n.*** —**de′vi·a′tor** ***n.***

de·vice (di vīs′) ***n.*** ⟦see DEVISE⟧ **1** a thing devised; plan, scheme, or trick **2** a mechanical contrivance **3** an ornamental figure or design **4** an emblem, as on a coat of arms —**leave to one's own devices** to allow to do as one wishes

dev·il (dev′əl) ***n.*** ⟦ult. < Gr *diabolos*, slanderous⟧ **1** *Theol.* *a)* [*often* **D-**] the chief evil spirit; Satan (with *the*) *b)* any evil spirit; demon **2** a very wicked person **3** a person

THESAURUS

detergent ***n.*** cleansing agent, disinfectant, washing substance; see CLEANSER, SOAP.

deteriorate ***v.*** depreciate, lessen, degenerate; see DECREASE 1.

deterioration ***n.*** decadence, rotting, degeneration; see DECAY.

determinable ***a.*** definable, discoverable, capable of being determined; see DEFINITE 2.

determination ***n.*** resolution, certainty, persistence, stubbornness, obstinacy, resolve, certitude, decision, assurance, conviction, boldness, fixity of purpose, hardihood, tenacity, courage, independence, self-confidence, purposefulness, fortitude, self-assurance, firmness, self-reliance, nerve, heart, bravery, fearlessness, will, energy, vigor, stamina, perseverance, strength of will, a brave front, a bold front, a stout heart, enterprise, guts*, spunk*, a stiff upper lip*; see also CONFIDENCE, FAITH 1, PURPOSE 1.

determine ***v.*** **1** [To define] limit, circumscribe, delimit; see DEFINE 1, RESTRICT. **2** [To find out the facts] ascertain, find out, learn; see DISCOVER. **3** [To resolve] fix upon, settle, conclude; see DECIDE, RESOLVE.

determined ***a.*** **1** [Already fixed or settled] decided, agreed, acted upon, agreed upon, concluded, contracted, set, ended, resolved, closed, terminated, achieved, finished, over, at an end, checked, measured, tested, budgeted, passed, given approval, given the green light*, given the go-ahead, over and done with; see also APPROVED.—*Ant.* UNFINISHED, suspended, moot. **2** [Having a fixed attitude] resolute, firm, strong-minded; see STUBBORN.

deterrent ***n.*** hindrance, impediment, obstacle; see RESTRAINT 2.

detest ***v.*** abhor, loathe, despise; see HATE.

detonate ***v.*** touch off, discharge, blast; see EXPLODE, SHOOT 1.

detour ***n.*** temporary route, alternate route, byway, back road, service road, alternate highway, secondary highway, bypass, circuit, roundabout course.

detract ***v.*** decrease, take away a part, subtract, draw away, diminish, lessen, withdraw, derogate, depreciate, discredit; see also SLANDER.

devalue ***v.*** devaluate, depreciate, mark down; see DECREASE 2.

devastate ***v.*** ravage, demolish, pillage; see DESTROY.

devastation ***n.*** destruction, ruin, waste; see DESOLATION.

develop ***v.*** **1** [To improve] enlarge, expand, extend, promote, advance, magnify, build up, refine, enrich, cultivate, elaborate, polish, finish, perfect, hone, sharpen, deepen, lengthen, heighten, widen, intensify, fix up, shape up*; see also GROW 1, IMPROVE 1, 2, STRENGTHEN.—*Ant.* DAMAGE, disfigure, spoil. **2** [To grow] mature, evolve, advance; see GROW 1. **3** [To reveal slowly] unfold, disclose, exhibit, unravel, uncover, make known, explain, unroll, explicate, produce, detail, tell, state, recount, account for, give an account of; see also REVEAL.—*Ant.* HIDE, conceal, blurt out. **4** [To work out] enlarge upon, elaborate upon, go into detail; see EXPLAIN, INCREASE.

developed ***a.*** grown, refined, advanced; see MATURED, PERFECTED.

development ***n.*** growth, elaboration, unfolding, maturing, ripening, maturation, enlargement, addition, spread, gradual evolution, evolving, advancement, growing, increasing, spreading, adding to, making progress, advancing; see also IMPROVEMENT 1, INCREASE, PROGRESS 1.—*Ant.* REDUCTION, decrease, lessening.

deviate ***v.*** deflect, digress, swerve, detour, vary, wander, stray, turn aside, keep aside, stay aside, go out of control, shy away, depart, break the pattern, not conform, go out of the way, take a wrong turn, veer, go off on a tangent, go haywire*, swim against the stream; see also DIFFER 1.—*Ant.* CONFORM, keep on, keep in line.

deviation ***n.*** change, deflection, alteration; see DIFFERENCE 1, VARIATION 2.

device ***n.*** **1** [An instrument] invention, contrivance, mechanism, gear, equipment, appliance, contraption, means, agent, material, implement, utensil, construction, apparatus, outfit, article, accessory, gadget, thing, whatnot, whatsit*, whatchamacallit*; see also MACHINE, TOOL 1. **2** [A shrewd method] artifice, scheme, design, trap, dodge, pattern, loophole, wile, craft, ruse, expedient, subterfuge, plan, project, plot, racket*, game, finesse, catch*; see also DISCOVERY, METHOD, TRICK 1.

devil ***n.*** Satan, fiend, the Adversary, error, sin, imp, mischief-maker, Beelzebub, fallen angel, hellhound, Mammon, Molech, Hades, Lucifer, Mephistopheles, diabolical force, the Tempter, Prince of Darkness, Lord of the Flies, Evil One; see also EVIL 1.—*Ant.* GOD, angel, Christ. —**give the**

who is mischievous, reckless, unlucky, etc. **4** anything hard to operate, control, etc. —***vt.*** **-iled** or **-illed**, **-il·ing** or **-il·ling** **1** to prepare (food) with hot seasoning **2** to annoy; tease —**dev′il·ish** ***adj.***

dev′il·fish′ ***n.***, *pl.* **-fish′** or (for different species) **-fish′es** MANTA

dev′il-may-care′ ***adj.*** careless or reckless

dev′il·ment ***n.*** mischievous action

devil's advocate a person upholding the wrong side for argument's sake

dev′il's-food′ cake a rich chocolate cake

dev′il·try (-trē) ***n.***, *pl.* **-tries** reckless mischief

de·vi·ous (dē′vē əs) ***adj.*** ⟦< L *de-*, off + *via*, road⟧ **1** not direct; roundabout or deviating **2** not straightforward; dishonest —**de′vi·ous·ness** ***n.***

de·vise (di vīz′) ***vt.***, ***vi.*** **-vised′**, **-vis′ing** ⟦< L *dividere*, to divide⟧ **1** to work out or create (a plan, device, etc.) **2** *Law* to bequeath (real property) by a will —***n.*** *Law* a bequest of property

de·vi·tal·ize (dē vīt′'l īz′) ***vt.*** **-ized′**, **-iz′ing** to deprive of vitality

de·void (di void′) ***adj.*** ⟦see DE- & VOID⟧ completely without; empty (*of*)

de·volve (di välv′, -vôlv′) ***vt.***, ***vi.*** **-volved′**, **-volv′ing** ⟦< L *de-*, down + *volvere*, to roll⟧ **1** to pass (*on*) to another: said of duties, responsibilities, etc. **2** to degenerate —**dev·o·lu·tion** (dev′ə lo͞o′shən) ***n.***

de·vote (di vōt′) ***vt.*** **-vot′ed**, **-vot′ing** ⟦< L *de-*, from + *vovere*, to vow⟧ to set apart for or give up to some purpose, activity, or person; dedicate

de·vot′ed (-id) ***adj.*** very loving, loyal, or faithful —**de·vot′ed·ly** ***adv.***

dev·o·tee (dev′ə tē′, -tā′) ***n.*** one who is strongly devoted to something

de·vo·tion (di vō′shən) ***n.*** **1** a devoting or being devoted **2** piety **3** religious worship **4** [*often pl.*] one or more prayers, etc. **5** loyalty or deep affection —**de·vo′tion·al** ***adj.***

de·vour (di vour′) ***vt.*** ⟦< L *de-*, intens. + *vorare*, swallow whole⟧ **1** to eat hungrily **2** to swallow up **3** to take in greedily, as with the eyes

de·vout (di vout′) ***adj.*** ⟦see DEVOTE⟧ **1** very religious; pious **2** earnest; sincere —**de·vout′ly** ***adv.***

dew (do͞o) ***n.*** ⟦OE *deaw*⟧ **1** atmospheric moisture condensed in drops on cool surfaces at night **2** anything refreshing, pure, etc., like dew —**dew′y**, **-i·er**, **-i·est**, ***adj.***

dew′ber′ry ***n.***, *pl.* **-ries** **1** a trailing blackberry plant **2** its fruit

dew′drop′ ***n.*** a drop of dew

dew′lap′ ***n.*** ⟦see DEW & LAP[1]⟧ loose skin under the throat of cattle, etc.

dew point the temperature at which water vapor in the air starts to condense into liquid

dex·ter·i·ty (deks ter′ə tē) ***n.*** ⟦see fol.⟧ skill in using one's hands, body, or mind

dex·ter·ous (deks′tər əs, -trəs) ***adj.*** ⟦< L *dexter*, right⟧ having or showing dexterity: also **dex′trous**

dex·trose (deks′trōs′) ***n.*** a glucose found in plants and animals

Dhak·a (däk′ə, dak′ə) capital of Bangladesh: pop. 3,459,000

dho·ti (dō′tē) ***n.*** ⟦Hindi *dhotī*⟧ a loincloth worn by Hindu men

dhur·rie or **dur·rie** (dur′ē, du′rē) ***n.*** a coarse rug woven in India

di-[1] ⟦Gr *di-* < *dis-*, twice⟧ *prefix* twice, double, twofold

di-[2] *prefix* DIS-

di·a·be·tes (dī′ə bēt′ēz′, -is) ***n.*** ⟦< Gr *diabainein*, to pass through⟧ a disease caused by an insulin deficiency and characterized by excess sugar in the blood and urine: also **sugar diabetes** —**di′a·bet′ic** (-bet′ik) ***adj.***, ***n.***

di·a·bol·ic (dī′ə bäl′ik) ***adj.*** ⟦see DEVIL⟧ very wicked or cruel; fiendish: also **di′a·bol′i·cal**

di·a·crit·i·cal mark (dī′ə krit′i kəl) ⟦< Gr *dia-*, across + *krinein*, discern⟧ a mark, as a macron, put on a letter or symbol to show pronunciation, etc.: also **di′a·crit′ic** ***n.***

di·a·dem (dī′ə dem′) ***n.*** ⟦< Gr *diadēma*, a band, fillet⟧ **1** a crown **2** an ornamental headband

di·ag·nose (dī′əg nōs′) ***vt.***, ***vi.*** **-nosed′**, **-nos′ing** to make a diagnosis (of)

di′ag·no′sis (-nō′sis) ***n.***, *pl.* **-ses′** (-sēz′) ⟦< Gr *dia-*, through + *gignoskein*, to know⟧ **1** the act of deciding the nature of a disease, situation, problem, etc. by examination and analysis **2** the resulting decision —**di′ag·nos′tic** (-näs′tik) ***adj.*** —**di′ag·nos·ti′cian** (-tish′ən) ***n.***

di·ag·o·nal (dī ag′ə nəl, -ag′nəl) ***adj.*** ⟦< Gr *dia-*, through + *gōnia*, an angle⟧ **1** extending slantingly between opposite corners **2** slanting; oblique —***n.*** a diagonal line, plane, course, part, etc. —**di·ag′o·nal·ly** ***adv.***

di·a·gram (dī′ə gram′) ***n.*** ⟦< Gr *dia-*, across + *graphein*, write⟧ a sketch, plan, graph, etc. that explains something, as by outlining its parts —***vt.*** **-gramed′** or **-grammed′**, **-gram′ing** or **-gram′ming** to make a diagram of

di·al[1] (dī′əl) ***n.*** ⟦< L *dies*, day⟧ **1** the face of a clock, etc. **2** the face of a meter, etc., for indicating, as by a pointer, an amount, direction, etc. **3** a graduated disk, strip, knob, etc., as on a radio or TV for tuning in stations, etc. **4** a rotating disk, or set of numbered push buttons, on a telephone, used to make automatic connections —***vt.***, ***vi.*** **-aled** or **-alled**, **-al·ing** or **-al·ling** **1** to tune in (a radio station, etc.) **2** to call by using a telephone dial

dial[2] *abbrev.* **1** dialect(al) **2** dialectic(al)

di·a·lect (dī′ə lekt′) ***n.*** ⟦< Gr *dia*, between + *legein*, to talk⟧ the form of a spoken language peculiar to a region, social group, etc. —**di′a·lec′tal** ***adj.***

di·a·lec·tic (dī′ə lek′tik) ***n.*** **1** [*often pl.*] the practice of examining ideas logically **2** logical argumentation —***adj.*** DIALECTICAL

di′a·lec′ti·cal (-ti kəl) ***adj.*** **1** of or using dialectic **2** of a dialect

di·a·logue (dī′ə lôg′, -läg′) ***n.*** ⟦see DIALECT⟧ **1** interchange of ideas by open discussion **2** the passages of talk in a play, story, etc. Also sp. **di′a·log′**

di·al·y·sis (dī al′ə sis) ***n.***, *pl.* **-ses′** (-sēz′) ⟦< Gr *dia-*, apart + *lyein*, dissolve⟧ the separation of smaller dissolved molecules from the larger molecules in a solution by diffusion through a membrane: used in purifying the blood of those with impaired kidney function

di·am·e·ter (dī am′ət ər) ***n.*** ⟦< Gr *dia-*, through + *metron*, a measure⟧ **1** a line segment passing through the center of a circle, sphere, etc. from one side to the other **2** its length

di·a·met·ri·cal (dī′ə me′tri kəl) ***adj.*** designating an opposite, a difference, etc. that is wholly so; complete

di·a·mond (dī′mənd, dī′ə mənd) ***n.*** ⟦< Gr *adamas*⟧ **1** nearly pure, colorless, crystalline carbon, the hardest mineral known, used for gems or cutting tools **2** a gem or other piece cut from this **3** *a*) a conventionalized figure of a diamond (◇) *b*) any of a suit of playing cards marked with such figures in red **4** *Baseball* the infield

THESAURUS

devil his due give someone credit, give credit where credit is due, recognize; see ACKNOWLEDGE 2. —**go to the devil** **1** [To decay] degenerate, fall into bad habits, go to pot; see FAIL 1. **2** [A curse] go to hell, damn you, be damned; see CURSE. —**raise the devil*** cause trouble, riot, be unruly; see DISTURB, FIGHT.

devious ***a.*** underhanded, insidious, shrewd; see DISHONEST, SLY.

devote ***v.*** apply, consecrate, give; see BLESS, DEDICATE.

devoted ***a.*** dutiful, loyal, constant; see FAITHFUL.

devotion ***n.*** allegiance, service, consecration, devotedness, adoration, piety, zeal, ardor, earnestness, faithfulness, fidelity, deference, sincerity, adherence, observance; see also LOYALTY, WORSHIP 1.—*Ant.* INDIFFERENCE, apathy, carelessness.

devotions ***n.*** religious worship, church services, prayers; see CHURCH 2, WORSHIP 1.

devour ***v.*** gulp, swallow, gorge; see EAT 1.

devout ***a.*** devoted, pious, reverent; see FAITHFUL, HOLY, RELIGIOUS 2.

diagnosis ***n.*** analysis, determination, investigation; see SUMMARY.

diagonal ***a.*** slanting, inclining, askew; see OBLIQUE.

diagram ***n.*** sketch, layout, picture; see DESCRIPTION, DESIGN, PLAN 1.

dial[1] ***n.*** face, gauge, indicator, meter, register, measuring device, compass; see also CONTROL 2.

dialect ***n.*** idiom, accent, local speech, regional speech, social dialect, pidgin, creole, argot, standard dialect, pidgin English, brogue, lingo*, trade language, lingua franca, usage level, jargon, cant, vernacular, patois; see also LANGUAGE 1.

dialogue ***n.*** talk, exchange, remarks; see CONVERSATION.

diameter ***n.*** breadth, measurement across, broadness; see WIDTH.

diametrical ***a.*** contrary, adverse, facing; see OPPOSITE 3.

diamond ***n.*** **1** [A crystalline jewel] precious stone, solitaire, engagement ring, brilliant, crystal, ring, stone, rock*, sparkler*, glass*, ice*; see also JEWEL. **2** [Shape or figure] lozenge, quadrilateral, rhombus; see FORM 1. **3** [A baseball playing field, particularly the infield] lot, ballpark, sandlot; see FIELD 2, PARK 1.

or the whole field —***adj.*** **1** of a diamond **2** marking the 60th, or sometimes 75th, year

di′a·mond·back′ ***n.*** a large, poisonous rattlesnake of the S U.S.

Di·an·a (dī an′ə) ***n.*** *Rom. Myth.* the goddess of the moon and of hunting

di·a·pa·son (dī′ə pā′zən) ***n.*** ⟦< Gr *dia*, through + *pas*, all⟧ an organ stop covering the instrument's entire range

di·a·per (dī′pər, dī′ə pər) ***n.*** ⟦< ML *diasprum*, flowered cloth⟧ a soft, absorbent cloth folded and arranged between the legs and around the waist of a baby —***vt.*** to put a diaper on (a baby)

di·aph·a·nous (dī af′ə nəs) ***adj.*** ⟦< Gr *dia-*, through + *phainein*, to show⟧ transparent or translucent

di·a·phragm (dī′ə fram′) ***n.*** ⟦< Gr *dia-*, through + *phragma*, fence⟧ **1** the muscular partition between the chest cavity and abdominal cavity **2** a vibrating disk producing sound waves **3** a vaginal contraceptive device

di·ar·rhe·a (dī′ə rē′ə) ***n.*** ⟦< Gr *dia-*, through + *rhein*, to flow⟧ too frequent and loose bowel movements: chiefly Brit. sp. **di′ar·rhoe′a**

di·a·ry (dī′ə rē) ***n.***, *pl.* **-ries** ⟦< L *dies*, day⟧ a daily written record of the writer's experiences, etc. —**di′a·rist** ***n.***

di·a·stase (dī′ə stās′) ***n.*** ⟦< Gr *dia*, apart + *histanai*, stand⟧ an enzyme in the seed of grains and malt capable of changing starches into dextrose

di·as·to·le (dī as′tə lē′) ***n.*** ⟦< Gr *dia-*, apart + *stellein*, put⟧ the usual rhythmic expansion of the heart —**di·a·stol·ic** (dī′ə stäl′ik) ***adj.***

di·a·ther·my (dī′ə thur′mē) ***n.*** ⟦< Gr *dia-*, through + *thermē*, heat⟧ medical treatment by means of heat produced under the skin, as by radiation

di·a·tom (dī′ə täm′) ***n.*** ⟦< Gr *diatomos*, cut in two⟧ any of various microscopic algae that are an important source of food for marine life

di·a·tom·ic (dī′ə täm′ik) ***adj.*** ⟦DI-[1] + ATOMIC⟧ having two atoms or radicals in the molecule

di·a·ton·ic (dī′ə tän′ik) ***adj.*** ⟦< Gr *dia-*, through + *teinein*, to stretch⟧ *Music* designating or of a scale of eight tones that is either a MAJOR SCALE or a MINOR SCALE

di·a·tribe (dī′ə trīb′) ***n.*** ⟦< Gr *dia-*, through + *tribein*, to rub⟧ a bitter, abusive denunciation

dib·ble (dib′əl) ***n.*** ⟦ME *dibbel*⟧ a pointed tool used for making holes in the soil for seeds, bulbs, etc.

dice (dīs) ***pl.n.***, *sing.* **die** or **dice** ⟦see DIE[2]⟧ small cubes marked on each side with a different number of spots (from one to six), used in games of chance —***vi.*** **diced, dic′ing** to play or gamble with dice —***vt.*** to cut (vegetables, etc.) into small cubes —**no dice** [Inf.] **1** no: used in refusing a request **2** no luck

di·chot·o·my (dī kät′ə mē) ***n.***, *pl.* **-mies** ⟦< Gr *dicha*, in two + *temnein*, to cut⟧ division into two parts or groups

dick (dik) ***n.*** [Slang] a detective

Dick·ens (dik′ənz), **Charles** (chärlz) (pseud. *Boz*) 1812-70; Eng. novelist

dick·er (dik′ər) ***vi.*** ⟦ult. < L *decem*, ten⟧ to bargain or haggle

dick·ey (dik′ē) ***n.***, *pl.* **-eys** ⟦< nickname *Dick*⟧ **1** a detachable shirt front **2** a small bird: also **dickey bird** Also **dick′y**, *pl.* **-ies**

Dick·in·son (dik′in sən), **Em·i·ly** (em′ə lē) 1830-86; U.S. poet

di·cot·y·le·don (dī′kät′ə lēd′'n) ***n.*** a plant with two seed leaves (*cotyledons*): also **di′cot′** —**di′cot′y·le′don·ous** ***adj.***

Dic·ta·phone (dik′tə fōn′) ⟦fol. + -PHONE⟧ *trademark for* a machine that records and plays back speech for typed transcripts, etc. —***n.*** [*sometimes* **d-**] any such machine

dic·tate (dik′tāt′) ***vt.***, ***vi.*** **-tat′ed, -tat′ing** ⟦< L *dicere*, speak⟧ **1** to speak (something) aloud for someone else to write down **2** to command forcefully **3** to give (orders) with authority —***n.*** an authoritative order —**dic·ta′tion** ***n.***

dic′ta′tor ***n.*** one who dictates; esp., a ruler or tyrant with absolute power —**dic′ta·to′ri·al** (-tə tôr′ē əl) ***adj.*** —**dic·ta′tor·ship′** ***n.***

dic·tion (dik′shən) ***n.*** ⟦< L *dicere*, say⟧ **1** manner of expression in words; wording **2** enunciation

dic·tion·ar·y (dik′shə ner′ē) ***n.***, *pl.* **-ar′ies** ⟦see prec.⟧ a book of alphabetically listed words in a language, with definitions, pronunciations, etc.

dic·tum (dik′təm) ***n.***, *pl.* **-tums** or **-ta** (-tə) ⟦< L *dicere*, say⟧ a formal statement of opinion; pronouncement

did (did) ***vt.***, ***vi.*** *pt. of* DO[1]

di·dac·tic (dī dak′tik) ***adj.*** ⟦< Gr *didaskein*, teach⟧ **1** intended for instruction **2** morally instructive

did·dle (did′'l) ***vt.***, ***vi.*** **-dled, -dling** ⟦< ?⟧ [Inf.] **1** to cheat **2** to waste (time) in trifling —**did′dler** ***n.***

di·do (dī′dō) ***n.***, *pl.* **-does** or **-dos** ⟦< ?⟧ [Inf.] a mischievous or foolish action

die[1] (dī) ***vi.*** **died, dy′ing** ⟦< ON *deyja*⟧ **1** to stop living **2** to stop functioning; end **3** to lose force or activity **4** [Inf.] to wish very much *[*I'm *dying* to go*]* —**die away** (or **down**) to cease gradually —**die off** to die one by one until all are gone —**die out** to stop existing

die[2] (dī) ***n.***, *pl.* for 2, **dies** (dīz) ⟦< L *dare*, give⟧ **1** *sing. of* DICE **2** a tool for shaping, punching, etc. metal or other material

die′-hard′ or **die′hard′** ***n.*** a person stubbornly resistant to new ideas, reform, etc.

di·e·lec·tric (dī′i lek′trik) ***n.*** ⟦< *dia-*, across + ELECTRIC⟧ a material that does not conduct electricity

di·er·e·sis (dī er′ə sis) ***n.***, *pl.* **-ses′** (-sēz′) ⟦< Gr *dia-*, apart + *hairein*, to take⟧ a mark (¨) placed over the second of two consecutive vowels to show that it is pronounced separately

die·sel (dē′zəl, -səl) ***n.*** ⟦after R. *Diesel* (1858-1913), Ger inventor⟧ [*often* **D-**] an internal-combustion engine that burns oil ignited by heat from air compression: also **diesel engine** (or **motor**) —***vi.*** to continue to run after the ignition is turned off: said of an internal-combustion engine

di·et[1] (dī′ət) ***n.*** ⟦< Gr *diaita*, way of life⟧ **1** what a person or animal usually eats or drinks **2** a special or limited selection of food and drink, chosen or prescribed as to bring about weight loss —***vi.***, ***vt.*** to adhere to or place on a diet —**di′et·er** ***n.*** —**di′e·tar′y** (-ə ter′ē) ***adj.***

di·et[2] (dī′ət) ***n.*** ⟦< ML *dieta*⟧ **1** a formal assembly **2** in some countries, a legislative assembly

di′e·tet′ic (-ə tet′ik) ***adj.*** of or for a particular diet of food and drink

di′e·tet′ics (-iks) ***n.*** the study of the kinds and quantities of food needed for health

di·e·ti·tian (dī′ə tish′ən) ***n.*** an expert in dietetics

dif- *prefix* DIS-: used before *f*

THESAURUS

diary ***n.*** chronicle, journal, log; see RECORD 1.

dicker ***v.*** trade, barter, bargain; see ARGUE, BUY, SELL.

dictate ***v.*** speak, deliver, give forth, compose, formulate, verbalize, record, orate, give an account; see also TALK 1.

dictator ***n.*** autocrat, despot, tyrant, czar, fascist, absolute ruler, oppressor, terrorist, master, leader, ringleader, magnate, lord, commander, chief, advisor, overlord, taskmaster, disciplinarian, headman, cock of the walk*, martinet, slave driver; see also LEADER 2, RULER 1.

dictatorial ***a.*** despotic, authoritarian, tyrannical; see ABSOLUTE 2.

dictatorship ***n.*** despotism, unlimited rule, totalitarianism; see GOVERNMENT 2, TYRANNY.

diction ***n.*** style, enunciation, expression, wording, usage, choice of words, command of language, locution, rhetoric, fluency, oratory, articulation, vocabulary, language, line*, gift of gab*; see also ELOQUENCE, SPEECH 2.

dictionary ***n.*** wordbook, word list, lexicon, thesaurus, reference work, glossary, encyclopedia, Webster*, Webster's*, vocabulary, dictionary of synonyms.

die[1] ***v.*** **1** [To cease living] expire, pass away, pass on, depart, perish, succumb, go, commit suicide, suffocate, lose one's life, cease to exist, drown, hang, fall, meet one's death, be no more, drop dead, be done for*, rest in peace, go to one's final resting place, pass over to the great beyond, give up the ghost*, go the way of all flesh, return to dust*, be a goner*, cash in one's chips*, push up daisies*, buy the farm*, kick the bucket*, bite the dust*, lay down one's life, breathe one's last, croak*, check out*, kick off*, go by the board.—*Ant.* LIVE, thrive, exist. **2** [To cease existing] disappear, vanish, become extinct; see STOP 2. **3** [To decline as though death were inevitable] fade, ebb, wither; see DECAY, WEAKEN 2. —**die away** decline, go away, sink; see STOP 2. —**die down** decline, disappear, recede; see DIE 2, 3, DECREASE 1. —**die off** (or **out**) go, cease to exist, disappear; see VANISH.

die-hard ***n.*** zealot, reactionary, extremist; see CONSERVATIVE.

diet[1] ***n.*** **1** [What one eats] menu, fare, daily bread*; see FOOD. **2** [Restricted intake of food] weight-reduction plan, fast, abstinence from food, starvation diet, bread and water*.

diet[1] ***v.*** lose weight, go without, starve oneself, slim down, go on a diet, reduce, tighten one's belt*.

dif·fer (dif′ər) ***vi.*** ⟦< L *dis-*, apart + *ferre*, to bring⟧ **1** to be unlike or not the same **2** to be of opposite or unlike opinions; disagree

dif·fer·ence (dif′ər əns, dif′rəns) ***n.*** **1** a being different **2** the way in which people or things are different **3** a differing in opinion; disagreement **4** a dispute **5** *Math.* the amount by which one quantity is less than another

dif′fer·ent ***adj.*** **1** not alike **2** not the same **3** various **4** unusual —**dif′fer·ent·ly** ***adv.***

dif·fer·en·tial (dif′ər en′shəl) ***adj.*** of, showing, or constituting a difference —***n.*** **1** a differentiating amount, degree, etc. **2** a differential gear

differential gear (or **gearing**) a gear arrangement allowing one axle of an automobile to turn faster than the other

dif′fer·en′ti·ate′ (-shē āt′) ***vt.*** **-at′ed, -at′ing** **1** to constitute a difference in or between **2** to make unlike **3** to distinguish between —***vi.*** **1** to become different or differentiated **2** to note a difference —**dif′fer·en′ti·a′tion** ***n.***

dif·fi·cult (dif′i kult′, -kəlt) ***adj.*** **1** hard to do, understand, etc. **2** hard to satisfy, deal with, etc.

dif′fi·cul′ty ***n.***, *pl.* **-ties** ⟦< L *dis-*, not + *facilis*, easy⟧ **1** a being difficult **2** something difficult, as a problem, obstacle, or objection **3** trouble

dif′fi·dent (-dənt) ***adj.*** ⟦< L *dis-*, not + *fidere*, to trust⟧ lacking self-confidence; shy —**dif′fi·dence** ***n.***

dif·frac·tion (di frak′shən) ***n.*** ⟦< L *dis-*, apart + *frangere*, to break⟧ **1** the breaking up of light waves as into the colors of the spectrum **2** a similar breaking up as of sound waves

dif·fuse (di fyo͞os′; *for v.*, -fyo͞oz′) ***adj.*** ⟦< L *dis-*, apart + *fundere*, to pour⟧ **1** spread out; not concentrated **2** using more words than are needed —***vt.***, ***vi.*** **-fused′, -fus′ing** to pour in every direction; spread widely —**dif·fuse′ly** ***adv.*** —**dif·fuse′ness** ***n.*** —**dif·fu′sion** ***n.*** —**dif·fu′sive** ***adj.***

dig (dig) ***vt.*** **dug, dig′ging** ⟦< OFr < Du *dijk*, dike⟧ **1** to turn up or remove (ground, etc.) with a spade, the hands, etc. **2** to make (a hole, etc.) by digging **3** to get out by digging **4** to find out, as by careful study **5** to jab **6** [Slang] *a)* to understand *b)* to like —***vi.*** **1** to dig the ground **2** to make a way by digging —***n.*** **1** [Inf.] *a)* a poke, nudge, etc. *b)* a taunt **2** an archaeological excavation —**dig′ger** ***n.***

di·gest (dī′jest′; *for v.* di jest′, dī-) ***n.*** ⟦< L *di-*, apart + *gerere*, to carry⟧ an organized collection of condensed information; summary —***vt.*** **1** to summarize **2** to change (food taken into the body) into an absorbable form **3** to absorb mentally —***vi.*** to undergo digestion —**di·gest′i·ble** ***adj.***

di·ges′tion ***n.*** **1** a digesting or being digested **2** the ability to digest —**di·ges′tive** ***adj.***

dig·it (dij′it) ***n.*** ⟦< L *digitus*, a finger⟧ **1** a finger or toe **2** any number from 0 to 9

dig·i·tal (dij′i təl, -it′l) ***adj.*** **1** of or like a digit **2** using a row of digits, rather than numbers on a dial *[a digital watch]* **3** designating, of, or used by a computer that processes data represented by groups of electronic bits **4** designating a recording technique in which sounds or images are converted into electronic bits: the bits are read electronically, as by a laser beam, for reproduction

dig·i·tal·is (dij′i tal′is) ***n.*** ⟦ModL, foxglove: see DIGIT⟧ **1** a plant with long spikes of thimblelike flowers; foxglove **2** a medicine made from the leaves of the purple foxglove, used as a heart stimulant

dig·i·tize (dij′i tīz′) ***vt.*** **-tized′, -tiz′ing** to translate (analog data) into digital data

dig·ni·fied (dig′nə fīd′) ***adj.*** having or showing dignity

THESAURUS

differ ***v.*** **1** [To be unlike] vary, modify, not conform, digress, take exception, turn, reverse, qualify, alter, change, diverge from, contrast with, bear no resemblance, not look like, jar with, clash with, conflict with, be distinguished from, diversify, stand apart, depart from, go off on a tangent; see also CONTRAST.—*Ant.* RESEMBLE, parallel, take after. **2** [To oppose] disagree, object, fight; see OPPOSE 1.

difference ***n.*** **1** [The quality of being different] disagreement, divergence, nonconformity, contrariness, deviation, opposition, antithesis, dissimilarity, inequality, diversity, departure, variance, discrepancy, separation, differentiation, distinctness, separateness, asymmetry; see also CONTRAST, VARIETY 1.—*Ant.* AGREEMENT, similarity, resemblance. **2** [That which is unlike in comparable things] deviation, departure, exception; see VARIATION 2. **3** [Personal dissension] discord, estrangement, dissent; see DISPUTE. —**make a difference** change, have an effect, affect; see MATTER. —**split the difference** compromise, go halfway, come to an agreement; see AGREE. —**what's the difference?*** what does it matter?, what difference does it make?, so what?*; see WHY.

different ***a.*** **1** [Unlike in nature] distinct, separate, not the same; see UNLIKE. **2** [Composed of unlike things] diverse, miscellaneous, assorted; see VARIOUS. **3** [Unusual] unconventional, strange, startling; see UNUSUAL 1, 2.

differentiate ***v.*** contrast, set apart, discriminate; see DISTINGUISH 1.

differently ***a.*** variously, divergently, individually, distinctively, creatively, uniquely, separately, each in his or her own way, severally, diversely, incongruously, abnormally, not normally, unusually, asymmetrically, in a different manner, with a difference, otherwise.—*Ant.* EVENLY, uniformly, invariably.

difficult ***a.*** **1** [Hard to achieve] laborious, hard, unyielding, strenuous, exacting, stiff, heavy, arduous, painful, labored, trying, bothersome, troublesome, demanding, burdensome, backbreaking, not easy, wearisome, onerous, rigid, crucial, uphill, challenging, exacting, formidable, ambitious, immense, tough, heavy*, no picnic*, stiff; see also SEVERE 1.—*Ant.* EASY, manageable, light. **2** [Hard to understand] intricate, involved, perplexing, abstruse, abstract, delicate, hard, knotty, thorny, troublesome, ticklish, obstinate, puzzling, mysterious, mystifying, subtle, confusing, bewildering, confounding, esoteric, unclear, mystical*, tangled, hard to explain, hard to solve, profound, rambling, loose, meandering, inexplicable, awkward, complex, complicated, deep, stubborn, hidden, formidable, enigmatic, paradoxical, incomprehensible, unintelligible, inscrutable, inexplicable, unanswerable, not understandable, unsolvable, unfathomable, concealed, unaccountable, ambiguous, equivocal, metaphysical, inconceivable, unknown, over someone's head, not making sense, too deep for someone, Greek to someone*; see also OBSCURE 1, 3.—*Ant.* CLEAR, obvious, simple.

difficulty ***n.*** **1** [Something in one's way] obstacle, obstruction, stumbling block, impediment, complication, hardship, adversity, misfortune, distress, deadlock, dilemma, hard job, maze, stone wall, barricade, impasse, knot, opposition, quandary, struggle, crisis, trouble, embarrassment, entanglement, mess, paradox, muddle, emergency, matter, standstill, hindrance, perplexity, bar, trial, check, predicament, hot water*, pickle*, fix*, stew*, scrape, hard nut to crack*, hitch*, dead end*, snag, monkey wrench in the works*, pinch, deep water*, jam*, the devil to pay*, hang-up*; see also sense 2 and BARRIER.—*Ant.* HELP, aid, assistance. **2** [Something mentally disturbing] trouble, annoyance, to-do*, ado, worry, weight, complication, distress, oppression, depression, aggravation, anxiety, discouragement, touchy situation, embarrassment, burden, grievance, irritation, strife, puzzle, responsibility, frustration, harassment, misery, predicament, setback, pressure, stress, strain, charge, struggle, maze, hang-up*, mess*, pickle*, pinch, scrape; see also sense 1 and CRISIS, EMERGENCY.—*Ant.* EASE, comfort, happiness.

dig* ***n.*** **1** [Insult] slur, innuendo, cut; see INSULT. **2** [Excavation] digging, archaeological expedition, exploration; see EXPEDITION.

dig ***v.*** **1** [To stir the earth] delve, spade, mine, excavate, channel, deepen, till, drive a shaft, clean, undermine, burrow, root, dig out, gouge, dredge, scoop out, tunnel out, hollow out, clean out, grub, bulldoze; see also SHOVEL.—*Ant.* BURY, embed, fill. **2** [To remove by digging] dig up, uncover, turn up; see HARVEST. **3** [*To like] enjoy, love, appreciate; see LIKE 1, 2. **4** [*To understand] comprehend, recognize, appreciate; see UNDERSTAND 1. —**dig into** investigate, research, probe; see EXAMINE. —**dig up** find, uncover, excavate; see DIG 2, DISCOVER.

digest ***n.*** epitome, précis, condensation; see SUMMARY.

digest ***v.*** transform food, consume, absorb; see EAT 1.

digestible ***a.*** eatable, absorbable, good to eat; see EDIBLE.

digit ***n.*** figure, Arabic notation, numeral; see NUMBER.

dignified ***a.*** stately, somber, solemn, courtly, reserved, ornate, elegant, classic, lordly, aristocratic, majestic, formal, noble, regal, superior, magnificent, grand, eminent, sublime, august, grave, distinguished, magisterial, imposing, portly, haughty, honorable, decorous, lofty, proud, classy*, snazzy*, sober as a judge*, highbrow; see also CULTURED, REFINED 2.—*Ant.* RUDE, undignified, boorish.

dig·ni·fy (dig′nə fī′) ***vt.*** **-fied′, -fy′ing** ⟦< L *dignus*, worthy + *facere*, make⟧ to give dignity to; exalt

dig′ni·tar′y (-ter′ē) ***n.***, *pl.* **-tar′ies** ⟦< L *dignitas*, dignity⟧ a person holding a high position or office

dig′ni·ty (-tē) ***n.***, *pl.* **-ties** ⟦< L *dignus*, worthy⟧ **1** honorable quality; worthiness **2** high repute or honor, or the degree of this **3** a high position, rank, or title **4** stately appearance or manner **5** self-respect

di·graph (dī′graf′) ***n.*** a combination of two letters to represent one sound (Ex.: r*ea*d, gra*ph*ic)

di·gress (di gres′, dī-) ***vi.*** ⟦< L *dis-*, apart + *gradi*, to go⟧ to wander temporarily from the subject, in talking or writing —**di·gres′sion** (-gresh′ən) ***n.*** —**di·gres′sive** ***adj.***

Di·jon mustard (dē zhän′, dē′zhän′) ⟦after *Dijon*, city in France⟧ a mild mustard paste blended with white wine

dike (dīk) ***n.*** ⟦OE *dic*, ditch⟧ an embankment or dam made to prevent flooding as by the sea

di·lap·i·dat·ed (də lap′ə dāt′id) ***adj.*** ⟦< L *dis-*, apart + *lapidare*, throw stones at⟧ falling to pieces; broken down —**di·lap′i·da′tion** ***n.***

di·late (dī′lāt′, dī lāt′) ***vt.*** **-lat′ed, -lat′ing** ⟦< L *dis-*, apart + *latus*, wide⟧ to make wider or larger —***vi.*** **1** to become wider or larger **2** to speak or write in detail (*on* or *upon* a subject) —**di·la′tion** or **dil·a·ta·tion** (dil′ə tā′shən) ***n.***

dil·a·to·ry (dil′ə tôr′ē) ***adj.*** ⟦see prec.⟧ **1** causing delay **2** inclined to delay; slow; tardy —**dil′a·to′ri·ness** ***n.***

di·lem·ma (di lem′ə) ***n.*** ⟦< LGr *di-*, two + *lēmma*, proposition⟧ **1** any situation requiring a choice between unpleasant alternatives **2** any serious problem

dil·et·tante (dil′ə tänt′, dil′ə tänt′) ***n.***, *pl.* **-tantes′** or **-tan′ti′** (-tī′, -tē) ⟦It < L *delectare*, to delight⟧ one who dabbles in an art, science, etc. in a superficial way —**dil′et·tant′ish** ***adj.*** —**dil′et·tant′ism′** ***n.***

dil·i·gent (dil′ə jənt) ***adj.*** ⟦< L *di-*, apart + *legere*, choose⟧ **1** persevering and careful in work; hard-working **2** done carefully —**dil′i·gence** ***n.*** —**dil′i·gent·ly** ***adv.***

dill (dil) ***n.*** ⟦OE *dile*⟧ an herb related to parsley, with bitter seeds and aromatic leaves, used to flavor pickles, soups, etc.

dil·ly (dil′ē) ***n.***, *pl.* **-lies** ⟦? < DEL(IGHTFUL) + -Y[2]⟧ [Slang] a remarkable person or thing

dil·ly·dal·ly (dil′ē dal′ē) ***vi.*** **-lied, -ly·ing** ⟦< DALLY⟧ to waste time by hesitating; loiter or dawdle

di·lute (di lo͞ot′, dī-) ***vt.*** **-lut′ed, -lut′ing** ⟦< L *dis-*, off + *lavare*, to wash⟧ to thin down or weaken as by mixing with water —***adj.*** diluted —**di·lu′tion** ***n.***

dim[1] (dim) ***adj.*** **dim′mer, dim′mest** ⟦OE⟧ **1** not bright, clear, or distinct; dull, obscure, etc. **2** not seeing, hearing, or understanding clearly **3** [Inf.] stupid —***vt., vi.*** **dimmed, dim′ming** to make or grow dim —**dim′ly** ***adv.*** —**dim′ness** ***n.***

dim[2] *abbrev.* diminutive

dime (dīm) ***n.*** ⟦< L *decem*, ten⟧ a U.S. or Canadian 10-cent coin

di·men·sion (də men′shən) ***n.*** ⟦< L *dis-*, off, from + *metiri*, to measure⟧ **1** any measurable extent, as length, width, or depth **2** [*pl.*] measurements in length, width, and often depth **3** [*often pl.*] extent; scope —**di·men′sion·al** ***adj.***

dime store FIVE-AND-TEN-CENT STORE

di·min·ish (də min′ish) ***vt., vi.*** ⟦< L *diminuere*, reduce⟧ to make or become smaller in size, degree, importance, etc.; lessen —**dim·i·nu·tion** (dim′ə no͞o′shən, -nyo͞o′-) ***n.***

di·min·u·en·do (də min′yo͞o en′dō) ***adj., adv.*** ⟦It: see prec.⟧ *Music* with gradually diminishing volume: also written ***di·min′u·en′do***

di·min·u·tive (də min′yo͞o tiv) ***adj.*** ⟦see DIMINISH⟧ very small; tiny —***n.*** a word having a suffix that expresses smallness, endearment, etc. (Ex.: *piglet*)

dim·i·ty (dim′ə tē) ***n.***, *pl.* **-ties** ⟦< Gr *dis-*, two + *mitos*, a thread⟧ a thin, corded or patterned cotton cloth

dim′mer ***n.*** a device, as a rheostat, for dimming electric lights

dim·ple (dim′pəl) ***n.*** ⟦ME *dimpel*⟧ a small, natural hollow, as on the cheek or chin —***vi., vt.*** **-pled, -pling** to form dimples (in) —**dim′ply** (-plē) ***adj.***

dim sum (dim′ sum′, -so͝om′) ⟦Chin⟧ small dumplings filled with meat, vegetables, etc.; also, a light meal of these together with other foods

dim′wit′ ***n.*** [Slang] a stupid person; simpleton —**dim′wit′ted** ***adj.***

din (din) ***n.*** ⟦OE *dyne*⟧ a loud, continuous noise; confused uproar —***vt.*** **dinned, din′ning** to repeat insistently or noisily —***vi.*** to make a din

din-din (din′din′) ***n.*** [Inf.] dinner

dine (dīn) ***vi.*** **dined, din′ing** ⟦ult. < L *dis-*, away + *jejunus*, hungry⟧ to eat dinner —***vt.*** to provide a dinner for

din·er (dīn′ər) ***n.*** **1** a person eating dinner **2** a railroad car equipped to serve meals **3** a small restaurant built to look like such a car

di·nette (dī net′) ***n.*** an alcove or small space used as a dining room

ding (diŋ) ***n.*** ⟦< Scand⟧ the sound of a bell: also **ding′-dong′** (-dôŋ′)

din·ghy (diŋ′gē) ***n.***, *pl.* **-ghies** ⟦Hindi *ḍiṅgī*⟧ any of various small boats, as one carried on a ship

din·gle (diŋ′gəl) ***n.*** ⟦ME *dingel*, abyss⟧ a small, deep, wooded valley

din·go (diŋ′gō) ***n.***, *pl.* **-goes** ⟦native name⟧ the Australian wild dog, usually tawny in color

ding·us (diŋ′əs) ***n.*** ⟦< Du *ding*, thing⟧ [Inf.] any device; gadget

din·gy (din′jē) ***adj.*** **-gi·er, -gi·est** ⟦orig. dial. var. < DUNG⟧ **1** not bright or clean; grimy **2** dismal; shabby —**din′gi·ness** ***n.***

dining room a room where meals are eaten

dink·y (diŋ′kē) ***adj.*** **-i·er, -i·est** ⟦< Scot *dink*, trim⟧ [Inf.] small and unimportant

din·ner (din′ər) ***n.*** ⟦see DINE⟧ **1** the main meal of the day **2** a banquet in honor of a person or event

dinner jacket a tuxedo jacket

din′ner·ware′ ***n.*** plates, cups, saucers, etc., collectively

di·no·saur (dī′nə sôr′) ***n.*** ⟦< Gr *deinos*, terrible + *sauros*, lizard⟧ an extinct prehistoric reptile, often huge

dint (dint) ***n.*** ⟦OE *dynt*⟧ force; exertion: now chiefly in **by dint of**

di·o·cese (dī′ə sis, -sēz′) ***n.*** ⟦< Gr *dioikein*, to keep house⟧ the district under a bishop's jurisdiction —**di·oc′e·san** (-äs′ə sən) ***adj.***

di·ode (dī′ōd′) ***n.*** ⟦DI-[1] + -ODE⟧ an electron tube used esp. to convert alternating current into direct current

Di·og·e·nes (dī äj′ə nēz′) 412?-323? B.C.; Gr. philosopher

Di·o·ny·sus or **Di·o·ny·sos** (dī′ə nī′səs) ***n.*** *Gr. Myth.* the god of wine and revelry

di·o·ram·a (dī′ə ram′ə) ***n.*** ⟦< Gr *dia-*, through + *horama*, a view⟧ a scenic display, as of three-dimensional figures against a painted background

di·ox·in (dī äk′sin) ***n.*** a highly toxic chemical contaminant found in some herbicides

dip (dip) ***vt.*** **dipped, dip′ping** ⟦OE *dyppan*⟧ **1** to immerse briefly **2** to scoop (liquid) up or out **3** to lower (a flag, etc.) and immediately raise again —***vi.*** **1** to plunge into

THESAURUS

dignify ***v.*** exalt, elevate, ennoble; see PRAISE 1.

dignity ***n.*** nobility, self-respect, lofty bearing, grandeur, quality, culture, distinction, stateliness, elevation, worth, worthiness, character, importance, renown, splendor, majesty, class*; see also HONOR, PRIDE 1.—*Ant.* HUMILITY, lowness, meekness.

dilemma ***n.*** quandary, perplexity, predicament; see DIFFICULTY 1.

diligence ***n.*** alertness, earnestness, quickness, perseverance, industry, vigor, carefulness, heed, intent, intensity, assiduity; see also ATTENTION, CARE 1.—*Ant.* CARELESSNESS, sloth, laziness.

dilute ***v.*** mix, reduce, thin; see WEAKEN 2.

dim[1] ***a.*** faint, dusky, shadowy; see DARK 1.

dimensions ***n.*** size, measurements, extent; see HEIGHT, LENGTH 1, 2, WIDTH.

diminish ***v.*** lessen, depreciate, abbreviate; see DECREASE.

din ***n.*** clamor, commotion, hubbub; see CONFUSION, NOISE 2.

dine ***v.*** lunch, feast, sup; see EAT 1.

dingy ***a.*** grimy, muddy, soiled; see DIRTY 1.

dining room ***n.*** *Varieties include the following:* dining hall, breakfast nook, dinette, tea shop, lunch counter, lunchroom, luncheonette, cafeteria, cafe, ice-cream parlor, drugstore, grill, coffee shop, fast-food outlet, soda fountain, steakhouse, buffet, inn, tavern, deli, eatery, pizza shop, pizzeria, bistro, sandwich shop, diner, mess hall, galley, automat, greasy spoon*; see also RESTAURANT.

dinner ***n.*** feast, banquet, main meal, supper, repast; see also MEAL 2.

dip ***n.*** **1** [The action of dipping] plunge, immersion, soaking, ducking, drenching, sinking; see also BATH 1. **2** [Material into which something is dipped] preparation, solution, suspension, dilution, concoction, saturation, mixture; see also LIQUID. **3** [A low place] depression, slope, inclination; see HOLE 1. **4** [A swim] plunge, bath, dive; see SWIM.

dip ***v.*** **1** [To put into a liquid] plunge, lower, wet, slosh, submerge, irrigate, steep, drench, douse, souse, moisten, splash, slop, water, duck, bathe, rinse, baptize, dunk; see also

a liquid and quickly come out **2** to sink suddenly **3** to decline slightly **4** to slope down **5** to lower a container, the hand, etc. as into water **6** to read or inquire superficially: with *into* —***n.*** **1** a dipping or being dipped **2** a brief plunge into water, etc. **3** a liquid, sauce, etc. into which something is dipped **4** a portion removed by dipping **5** a downward slope or plunge

diph·the·ri·a (dif thir′ē ə, dip-) ***n.*** ⟦< Gr *diphthera*, leather⟧ an acute infectious disease marked by high fever and difficult breathing

diph·thong (dif′thôŋ; *often* dip′-) ***n.*** ⟦< Gr *di-*, two + *phthongos*, a sound⟧ a sound made by gliding from one vowel to another within one syllable, as the sound (oi) in *oil*

di·plo·ma (də plō′mə) ***n.*** ⟦< Gr *diplōma*, folded letter⟧ a certificate issued by a school, college, etc. indicating graduation or the conferring of a degree

di·plo′ma·cy (-sē) ***n.*** **1** the conducting of relations between nations **2** tact

dip·lo·mat (dip′lə mat′) ***n.*** **1** a representative of a government who conducts relations with another government **2** a tactful person

dip′lo·mat′ic ***adj.*** **1** of diplomacy **2** tactful —**dip′lo·mat′i·cal·ly** ***adv.***

di·pole (dī′pōl′) ***n.*** a kind of radio or TV antenna with a single line separated at the center for connection to the receiver

dip·per (dip′ər) ***n.*** a long-handled cup, etc. for dipping

dip·so·ma·ni·a (dip′sə mā′nē ə) ***n.*** ⟦< Gr *dipsa*, thirst + *mania*, madness⟧ an abnormal craving for alcoholic drink —**dip′so·ma′ni·ac′** (-ak′) ***n.***

dip′stick′ ***n.*** a graduated rod for measuring quantity or depth

dir *abbrev.* director

dire (dīr) ***adj.*** **dir′er, dir′est** ⟦L *dirus*⟧ **1** dreadful; terrible: also **dire′ful** **2** urgent *[a dire need]*

di·rect (də rekt′; *also* dī-) ***adj.*** ⟦< L *di-*, apart + *regere*, to rule⟧ **1** not roundabout or interrupted; straight **2** honest; frank *[a direct answer]* **3** with nothing between; immediate **4** in an unbroken line of descent; lineal **5** exact; complete *[the direct opposite]* **6** in the exact words *[a direct quote]* —***vt.*** **1** to manage; guide **2** to order; command **3** to turn or point; aim; head **4** to tell (a person) the way to a place **5** to address (a letter, etc.) **6** *a)* to plan and supervise the action and effects of (a play, film, etc.) *b)* to conduct the performance of (a choir, band, etc.) —***adv.*** directly —**di·rect′ness** ***n.***

direct current an electric current flowing in one direction

di·rec·tion (də rek′shən; *also* dī-) ***n.*** **1** a directing **2** [*usually pl.*] instructions for doing, using, etc. **3** a command **4** the point toward which something faces or the line along which it moves or lies —**di·rec′tion·al** ***adj.***

di·rec′tive (-rek′tiv) ***adj.*** directing —***n.*** a general order issued authoritatively

di·rect′ly ***adv.*** **1** in a direct way or line; straight **2** with nothing or no one between *[directly responsible]* **3** exactly *[directly opposite]* **4** instantly; right away

direct object *Gram.* the word or words denoting the receiver of the action of a transitive verb (Ex.: *me* in "he saw me")

di·rec′tor (-rek′tər) ***n.*** one who directs a school, corporation, etc. or a play, choir, etc. —**di·rec′tor·ship′** ***n.***

di·rec′tor·ate (-it) ***n.*** **1** the position of director **2** a board of directors

di·rec′to·ry (-tə rē) ***n.***, *pl.* **-ries** a book listing the names, addresses, etc. of a specific group of persons

dirge (durj) ***n.*** ⟦< L *dirige* (direct), first word of a prayer⟧ a song, poem, etc. of grief or mourning

dir·i·gi·ble (dir′ə jə bəl, də rij′ə-) ***n.*** ⟦see DIRECT & -IBLE⟧ AIRSHIP

dirk (durk) ***n.*** ⟦< ?⟧ a long dagger

dirn·dl (durn′dəl) ***n.*** ⟦< Ger *dirne*, girl⟧ a full skirt gathered at the waist

dirt (durt) ***n.*** ⟦< ON *drita*, excrement⟧ **1** any unclean matter, as mud or trash; filth **2** earth; soil **3** dirtiness, corruption, etc. **4** obscenity **5** malicious gossip

dirt′-cheap′ ***adj.***, ***adv.*** [Inf.] very inexpensive(ly)

dirt′-poor′ ***adj.*** extremely poor

dirt′y ***adj.*** **-i·er, -i·est** **1** not clean **2** obscene **3** contemptible or nasty **4** unfair; dishonest **5** showing anger *[a dirty look]* **6** rough *[dirty weather]* —***vt.***, ***vi.*** **dirt′ied, dirt′y·ing** to make or become dirty —**dirt′i·ly** ***adv.*** —**dirt′i·ness** ***n.***

dis (dis) ***vt.*** **dissed, dis′sing** [Slang] to insult

dis- ⟦< L⟧ *prefix* separation, negation, reversal *[disbar, disable, disintegrate]*

dis·a·bil·i·ty (dis′ə bil′ə tē) ***n.***, *pl.* **-ties** **1** a disabled condition **2** that which disables, as an illness or physical limitation

dis·a·ble (dis ā′bəl) ***vt.*** **-bled, -bling** to make unable or unfit; cripple; incapacitate

dis·a′bled ***adj.*** having a physical or mental disability

THESAURUS

IMMERSE, SOAK 1, WASH 2. **2** [To transfer by scooping] scoop, shovel, ladle, bale, spoon, dredge, lift, draw, dish, dip up, dip out, offer; see also SERVE.—*Ant.* EMPTY, pour, let stand. **3** [To fall] slope, decline, recede, tilt, swoop, slip, spiral, sink, plunge, bend, verge, veer, slant, settle, slump, slide, go down; see also DIVE, DROP 2, FALL 1.

diploma ***n.*** degree, graduation certificate, credentials, honor, award, recognition, commission, warrant, voucher, confirmation, sheepskin*; see also GRADUATION.

diplomacy ***n.*** artfulness, statesmanship, discretion; see TACT.

diplomat ***n.*** ambassador, consul, minister, legate, emissary, envoy, agent; see also REPRESENTATIVE 2, STATESMAN.

diplomatic ***a.*** tactful, suave, gracious, calculating, shrewd, opportunistic, smooth, capable, conciliatory, conniving, sly, artful, wily, subtle, crafty, sharp, cunning, contriving, scheming, discreet, deft, intriguing, politic, strategic, astute, clever; see also POLITE.

dipped ***a.*** immersed, plunged, bathed, ducked, doused, drenched, soused, covered, dunked; see also SOAKED, WET 1.

dire ***a.*** dreadful, terrible, horrible; see FRIGHTFUL 1.

direct ***a.*** **1** [Without divergence] in a straight line, straight ahead, undeviating, uninterrupted, unswerving, shortest, nonstop, as the crow flies, straight as an arrow, in a beeline, point-blank; see also STRAIGHT 1.—*Ant.* ZIGZAG, roundabout, crooked. **2** [Frank] straightforward, outspoken, candid; see FRANK, HONEST. **3** [Immediate] firsthand, close, primary; see IMMEDIATE.

direct ***v.*** **1** [To show the way] conduct, show, guide; see LEAD 1. **2** [To decide the course of affairs] regulate, govern, influence; see MANAGE 1. **3** [To aim a weapon] sight, train, level; see AIM. **4** [To command] command, bid, charge; see ORDER 1.

directed ***a.*** supervised, controlled, conducted, sponsored, under supervision, assisted, counseled, guided, serviced, managed, orderly, purposeful, functioning; see also AIMED, ORGANIZED.

direction ***n.*** **1** [A position] point of the compass, objective, bearing, region, area, place, spot; see also WAY 2. **2** [Supervision] management, superintendence, control; see ADMINISTRATION 2. **3** [A tendency] bias, bent, proclivity; see INCLINATION 1.

directions ***n.*** instructions, advice, notification, specification, indication, orders, assignment, recommendations, summons, directive, regulation, prescription, plans.

directly ***a.*** instantly, at once, quickly; see IMMEDIATELY.

director ***n.*** manager, supervisor, executive; see LEADER 2.

directory ***n.*** list, syllabus, register, record, almanac, roster, dictionary, gazetteer, telephone book, Yellow Pages, city directory, social register, who's who, blue book; see also CATALOG, INDEX.

dirt ***n.*** **1** [Earth] soil, loam, clay; see EARTH 2. **2** [Filth] rottenness, filthiness, smut; see FILTH.

dirty ***a.*** **1** [Containing dirt] soiled, unclean, unsanitary, unhygienic, filthy, polluted, nasty, slovenly, dusty, messy, squalid, sloppy, disheveled, uncombed, unkempt, unsightly, untidy, straggly, unwashed, stained, tarnished, spotted, smudged, foul, fouled, grimy, greasy, muddy, mucky, sooty, smoked, slimy, rusty, unlaundered, unswept, crummy*, grubby, scuzzy*, scummy.—*Ant.* PURE, unspotted, sanitary. **2** [Obscene] pornographic, smutty, ribald; see LEWD 1, 2, SENSUAL. **3** [Nasty] mean, contemptible, disagreeable; see RUTHLESS.

dirty ***v.*** soil, sully, defile, pollute, foul, tarnish, spot, smear, blot, blur, smudge, smoke, spoil, sweat up, blotch, spatter, splash, stain, debase, corrupt, taint, contaminate.—*Ant.* CLEAN, cleanse, rinse.

disability ***n.*** feebleness, inability, incapacity; see INJURY, WEAKNESS 1.

disable ***v.*** incapacitate, impair, put out of action; see DAMAGE, WEAKEN 2.

disabled ***a.*** handicapped, incapacitated, physically challenged, injured, crippled, helpless, wrecked, stalled, maimed, wounded, mangled, lame, mutilated, run-down, worn-out, weakened, impotent, castrated, paralyzed, senile, decrepit, laid up*, done for*, done in*, cracked up*, out of action*; see also HURT, USELESS 1, WEAK 1.—*Ant.* HEALTHY, strong, capable.

dis·a·buse (dis′ə byo͞oz′) ***vt.*** **-bused′**, **-bus′ing** to rid of false ideas

dis·ad·van·tage (dis′əd vant′ij) ***n.*** **1** an unfavorable situation or circumstance **2** detriment —**dis′ad′van·ta′geous** (-ad′vən tā′jəs) ***adj.***

dis′ad·van′taged ***adj.*** underprivileged

dis·af·fect (dis′ə fekt′) ***vt.*** to make unfriendly, discontented, or disloyal —**dis′af·fect′ed** ***adj.*** —**dis′af·fec′tion** ***n.***

dis′af·fil′i·ate′ (-ə fil′ē āt′) ***vt., vi.*** **-at′ed**, **-at′ing** to end an affiliation (with) —**dis′af·fil′i·a′tion** ***n.***

dis′a·gree′ (-ə grē′) ***vi.*** **-greed′**, **-gree′ing** **1** to fail to agree; differ **2** to differ in opinion **3** to give distress: with *with* [plums *disagree* with me] —**dis′a·gree′ment** ***n.***

dis′a·gree′a·ble ***adj.*** **1** unpleasant; offensive **2** quarrelsome —**dis′a·gree′a·bly** ***adv.***

dis·al·low (dis′ə lou′) ***vt.*** to refuse to allow (a claim, etc.); reject

dis′ap·pear′ (-ə pir′) ***vi.*** **1** to cease to be seen; vanish **2** to cease existing —**dis′ap·pear′ance** ***n.***

dis′ap·point′ (-ə point′) ***vt.*** to fail to satisfy the hopes or expectations of —**dis′ap·point′ment** ***n.***

dis·ap·pro·ba·tion (dis′ap′rə bā′shən) ***n.*** disapproval

dis·ap·prove (dis′ə pro͞ov′) ***vt., vi.*** **-proved′**, **-prov′ing** **1** to have or express an unfavorable opinion (of) **2** to refuse to approve —**dis′ap·prov′al** ***n.*** —**dis′ap·prov′ing·ly** ***adv.***

dis·arm (dis ärm′) ***vt.*** **1** to take away weapons from **2** to make harmless **3** to make friendly —***vi.*** to reduce armed forces and armaments —**dis·ar′ma·ment** (-är′mə mənt) ***n.***

dis·ar·range (dis′ə rānj′) ***vt.*** **-ranged′**, **-rang′ing** to undo the order of; make less neat

dis′ar·ray′ (-ə rā′) ***n.*** disorder

dis′as·sem′ble (-ə sem′bəl) ***vt.*** **-bled**, **-bling** to take apart

dis′as·so′ci·ate′ (-ə sō′shē āt′, -sē-) ***vt.*** **-at′ed**, **-at′ing** to disconnect or separate; dissociate

dis·as·ter (di zas′tər) ***n.*** ⟦< L *dis-*, away + *astrum*, a star⟧ any happening that causes great harm or damage; calamity —**dis·as′trous** (-trəs) ***adj.***

dis·a·vow (dis′ə vou′) ***vt.*** to deny any knowledge of or responsibility for; disclaim —**dis′a·vow′al** ***n.***

dis·band (dis band′) ***vt., vi.*** to break up: said as of an organization or its members

dis·bar′ (-bär′) ***vt.*** **-barred′**, **-bar′ring** to deprive (a lawyer) of the right to practice law —**dis·bar′ment** ***n.***

dis·be·lieve (dis′bə lēv′) ***vt., vi.*** **-lieved′**, **-liev′ing** to refuse to believe —**dis′be·lief′** (-lēf′) ***n.***

dis·burse (dis burs′) ***vt.*** **-bursed′**, **-burs′ing** ⟦< OFr *desbourser*⟧ to pay out; expend —**dis·burse′ment** ***n.*** —**dis·burs′er** ***n.***

disc (disk) ***n.*** **1** DISK **2** a phonograph record

dis·card (dis kärd′; *for n.* dis′kärd′) ***vt.*** ⟦< OFr: see DIS- & CARD[1]⟧ **1** *Card Games* to remove (a card or cards) from one's hand **2** to get rid of as no longer useful —***n.*** **1** a discarding or being discarded **2** something discarded

disc brake a brake, as on a car, with two friction pads that press on a disc rotating with the wheel

dis·cern (di surn′, -zurn′) ***vt.*** ⟦< L *dis-*, apart + *cernere*, to separate⟧ to perceive or recognize clearly —**dis·cern′i·ble** ***adj.*** —**dis·cern′ment** ***n.***

dis·cern′ing ***adj.*** having good judgment; astute

THESAURUS

disadvantage ***n.*** **1** [Loss] damage, harm, deprivation; see LOSS 3. **2** [A position involving difficulties] bar, obstacle, handicap, inconvenience, obstacle, drawbacks; see also RESTRAINT 2, WEAKNESS 1.

disagree ***v.*** **1** [To differ] dissent, object, oppose; see DIFFER 1. **2** [To have uncomfortable effect] nauseate, make ill, be hard on the stomach*; see BOTHER 2.

disagreeable ***a.*** **1** [Having an unpleasant disposition] difficult, obnoxious, offensive; see IRRITABLE, RUDE 2. **2** [Irritating; *said of things and conditions*] bothersome, unpleasant, upsetting; see DISTURBING, OFFENSIVE 2.

disagreement ***n.*** **1** [Discord] contention, strife, conflict, controversy, wrangle, dissension, animosity, ill feeling, ill will, misunderstanding, division, opposition, hostility, breach, discord, feud, clashing, antagonism, bickering, squabble, tension, split, quarreling, falling-out, break, rupture, quarrel, clash, opposition, contest, friction; see also BATTLE, COMPETITION, FIGHT. **2** [Inconsistency] discrepancy, dissimilarity, disparity; see DIFFERENCE 1. **3** [A quarrel] fight, argument, feud; see DISPUTE.

disappear ***v.*** cease, fade, die; see ESCAPE, EVAPORATE, VANISH.

disappearance ***n.*** vanishing, fading, departure, ebbing away, removal, dissipation, ceasing to exist, ceasing to appear, desertion, flight, retirement, escape, exodus, vanishing point, going, disintegration, exit, withdrawal, decline and fall, eclipse; see also ESCAPE, EVAPORATION.

disappoint ***v.*** fail, delude, deceive, dissatisfy, disillusion, harass, embitter, chagrin, dumbfound, fall short, cast down, frustrate, torment, tease, miscarry, abort, thwart, foil, baffle, balk, mislead, bungle, let down, leave in the lurch*, fizzle out*.

disappointed ***a.*** dissatisified, discouraged, unsatisfied, despondent, depressed, objecting, complaining, distressed, hopeless, balked, disconcerted, aghast, disgruntled, disillusioned; see also SAD.—*Ant.* SATISFIED, pleased, content.

disappointing ***a.*** unsatisfactory, ineffective, uninteresting, discouraging, unpleasant, inferior, lame, insufficient, failing, at fault, limited, second-rate, mediocre, ordinary, unexpected, unhappy, depressing, disconcerting, disagreeable, irritating, annoying, troublesome, disheartening, unlucky, uncomfortable, bitter, distasteful, disgusting, deplorable, short of expectations; see also INADEQUATE.

disappointment ***n.*** **1** [The state of being disappointed] dissatisfaction, frustration, chagrin, lack of success, despondency, displeasure, distress, discouragement, disillusionment, check, disillusion, setback, adversity; see also DEFEAT, FAILURE 1, REGRET 1.—*Ant.* SUCCESS, fulfillment, realization. **2** [A person or thing that disappoints] miscarriage, misfortune, calamity, blunder, bad luck, setback, downfall, slip, defeat, mishap, error, mistake, discouragement, obstacle, miscalculation, fiasco, no go*, blind alley, washout*, lemon*, dud*, letdown, bust*; see also sense 1 and FAILURE 2.—*Ant.* ACHIEVEMENT, successful venture, success.

disapproval ***n.*** criticism, censure, disparagement; see OBJECTION.

disapprove ***v.*** blame, chastise, reprove; see DENOUNCE. —**disapprove of** object to, dislike, deplore; see COMPLAIN, OPPOSE 1.

disarm ***v.*** demobilize, disable, unarm, weaken, debilitate, incapacitate, muzzle, deprive of weapons, deprive of means of defense, subdue, strip, tie the hands of, clip the wings of; see also DEFEAT 2, 3.—*Ant.* ARM, outfit, equip.

disarmament ***n.*** arms reduction, cease-fire, de-escalation; see PEACE 1.

disaster ***n.*** accident, calamity, mishap, debacle, casualty, emergency, adversity, harm, misadventure, collapse, slip, fall, collision, crash, hazard, setback, defeat, failure, woe, trouble, scourge, grief, undoing, curse, tragedy, blight, cataclysm, downfall, rainy day, bankruptcy, upset, blast, blow, wreck, bad luck, comedown, crackup, pileup*, smashup, washout*, flop*, bust*; see also CATASTROPHE, MISFORTUNE.

disastrous ***a.*** calamitous, ruinous, unfortunate; see HARMFUL, UNFAVORABLE.

disband ***v.*** scatter, disperse, dismiss; see LEAVE 1.

disbelief ***n.*** unbelief, skepticism, mistrust; see DOUBT.

disbeliever ***n.*** doubter, skeptic, agnostic; see CRITIC 1.

disburse ***v.*** expend, distribute, dispense; see PAY 1, SPEND.

discard ***v.*** reject, expel, repudiate, protest, cast aside, cast away, cast out, cast off, throw away, throw aside, throw overboard, throw out, get rid of, give up, renounce, have done with, dump, make away with, dismantle, discharge, write off, banish, eject, divorce, dispossess, dispense with, shake off, pass up, free oneself from, be free of, give away, part with, dispose of, do away with, shed, relinquish, thrust aside, sweep away, cancel, forsake, desert, cut, have nothing to do with, brush away, scotch, chuck*, drop, wash one's hands of*, junk*; see also ABANDON 1, DISMISS.—*Ant.* SAVE, retain, preserve.

discarded ***a.*** rejected, repudiated, cast off, thrown away, dismantled, dismissed, useless, damaged, outworn, worn-out, done with, run-down, not worth saving, abandoned, obsolete, shelved, neglected, deserted, forsaken, outmoded, out of date, out of style, out of fashion, old-fashioned, old hat*.—*Ant.* KEPT, worthwhile, modern.

discern ***v.*** find out, determine, discriminate; see DISCOVER.

discerning ***a.*** discriminating, perceptive, penetrating; see DISCREET.

dis·charge (dis chärj′; *also, and for n.usually,* dis′chärj′) ***vt.*** **-charged′, -charg′ing** ⟦< L *dis-*, from + *carrus*, wagon⟧ **1** to release or dismiss **2** to unload (a cargo) **3** to shoot (a gun or projectile) **4** to emit [*to discharge* pus] **5** to pay (a debt) or perform (a duty) **6** *Elec.* to remove stored energy from (a battery, etc.) —***vi.*** **1** to get rid of a load, etc. **2** to go off, as a gun —***n.*** **1** a discharging or being discharged **2** that which discharges or is discharged

dis·ci·ple (di sī′pəl) ***n.*** ⟦< L *dis-*, apart + *capere*, to hold⟧ **1** a pupil or follower of any teacher or school **2** an early follower of Jesus, esp. one of the Apostles —**dis·ci′ple·ship′** ***n.***

dis·ci·pli·nar·i·an (dis′ə pli ner′ē ən) ***n.*** a person who believes in or enforces strict discipline

dis·ci·pline (dis′ə plin′) ***n.*** ⟦see DISCIPLE⟧ **1** a branch of learning **2** training that develops self-control, efficiency, etc. **3** strict control to enforce obedience **4** self-control **5** a system of rules, as for a church **6** treatment that corrects or punishes —***vt.*** **-plined′, -plin′ing** **1** to train; control **2** to punish —**dis′ci·pli·nar′y** (-pli ner′ē) ***adj.***

disc jockey one who conducts a radio program of recorded music

dis·claim (dis klām′) ***vt.*** **1** to give up any claim to **2** to repudiate; deny

dis·claim′er ***n.*** a denial or renunciation, as of responsibility

dis·close (dis klōz′) ***vt.*** **-closed′, -clos′ing** to reveal —**dis·clo′sure** (-klō′zhər) ***n.***

dis·co (dis′kō) ***n.*** **1** *pl.* **-cos** a place for dancing to recorded music **2** a kind of popular dance music with a strong beat

dis·col·or (dis kul′ər) ***vt., vi.*** to change in color as by fading, streaking, or staining: Brit. sp. **dis·col′our** —**dis′col·or·a′tion** ***n.***

dis·com·fit (dis kum′fit) ***vt.*** ⟦< L *dis-*, away + *conficere*, prepare⟧ to frustrate or disconcert —**dis·com′fi·ture** (-fi chər) ***n.***

dis·com·fort (dis kum′fərt) ***n.*** **1** lack of comfort; uneasiness **2** anything causing this —***vt.*** to cause discomfort to

dis·com·mode (dis′kə mōd′) ***vt.*** **-mod′ed, -mod′ing** ⟦< DIS- + L *commodare*, to make suitable⟧ to cause bother to; inconvenience

dis′com·pose′ (-kəm pōz′) ***vt.*** **-posed′, -pos′ing** to disturb; fluster —**dis′com·po′sure** (-pō′zhər) ***n.***

dis′con·cert′ (-kən surt′) ***vt.*** to upset; embarrass

dis′con·nect′ (-kə nekt′) ***vt.*** to break the connection of; separate —**dis′con·nec′tion** ***n.***

dis′con·nect′ed ***adj.*** **1** separated **2** incoherent

dis·con·so·late (dis kän′sə lit) ***adj.*** ⟦see DIS- & CONSOLE[1]⟧ inconsolable; dejected —**dis·con′so·late·ly** ***adv.***

dis·con·tent (dis′kən tent′) ***adj.*** ⟦ME⟧ DISCONTENTED —***n.*** dissatisfaction with one's situation: also **dis′con·tent′ment** —***vt.*** to make discontented

dis′con·tent′ed ***adj.*** not contented; wanting something more or different

dis·con·tin·ue (dis′kən tin′yōō) ***vt., vi.*** **-ued, -u·ing** to stop; cease; give up —**dis′con·tin′u·ance** or **dis′con·tin′u·a′tion** ***n.***

dis′con·tin′u·ous (-yōō əs) ***adj.*** not continuous; having interruptions or gaps

dis·cord (dis′kôrd′) ***n.*** ⟦< L *dis-*, apart + *cor*, heart⟧ **1** disagreement **2** harsh noise **3** a lack of musical harmony —**dis·cord′ant** ***adj.***

dis·co·thèque (dis′kə tek′) ***n.*** ⟦Fr⟧ DISCO (sense 1)

dis·count (dis′kount′; *for v., also* dis kount′) ***n.*** ⟦see DIS- & COMPUTE⟧ **1** a reduction from a usual or list price **2** the rate of interest charged on a discounted bill, note, etc.: also called **discount rate** —***vt.*** **1** to pay or receive the value of (a bill, promissory note, etc.), minus a deduction for interest **2** to deduct an amount from (a bill, price, etc.) **3** to sell at less than the regular price **4** *a*) to allow for exaggeration, bias, etc. in (a story, etc.) *b*) to disregard **5** to lessen the effect of by anticipating

dis·coun·te·nance (dis kount′'n əns) ***vt.*** **-nanced, -nanc·ing** **1** to make ashamed or embarrassed **2** to refuse approval or support

discount house (or **store**) a retail store that sells goods for less than regular prices

dis·cour·age (di skur′ij) ***vt.*** **-aged, -ag·ing** **1** to deprive of courage or confidence **2** to persuade (a person) to refrain **3** to try to prevent by disapproving —**dis·cour′age·ment** ***n.***

dis·course (dis′kôrs′; *also, and for v. usually,* dis kôrs′) ***n.*** ⟦< L *dis-*, from + *currere*, to run⟧ **1** talk; conversation **2** a formal treatment of a subject, in speech or writing —***vi.*** **-coursed′, -cours′ing** to talk; confer

dis·cour·te·ous (dis kur′tē əs) ***adj.*** impolite; rude; ill-mannered

dis·cour′te·sy (-kurt′ə sē) ***n.*** **1** lack of courtesy **2** *pl.* **-sies** a rude or impolite act or remark

dis·cov·er (di skuv′ər) ***vt.*** ⟦see DIS- & COVER⟧ **1** to be the first to find out, see, etc. **2** to learn of the existence of —**dis·cov′er·er** ***n.***

THESAURUS

discharge ***v.*** **1** [To unload] unpack, release, remove cargo; see EMPTY, UNLOAD. **2** [To remove] take off, send, carry away; see REMOVE 1. **3** [To cause to fire] blast, shoot off, fire; see SHOOT 1. **4** [To release] emancipate, liberate, let go; see FREE.

discharged ***a.*** mustered out, sent home, recalled, freed, liberated, released, let go, sent away, emancipated, expelled, ejected, dismissed, fired, ousted, canned*, axed*; see also FREE 2, 3.

disciple ***n.*** adherent, pupil, believer, apostle; see also FOLLOWER. *Christ's disciples mentioned in the New Testament include:* Matthew, John, Peter, Bartholomew, Nathaniel, James, Philip, Andrew, Thaddaeus, Thomas, James the son of Alphaeus, Judas Iscariot, Jude, Simon the Canaanite.

discipline ***n.*** **1** [Mental self-training] preparation, development, exercise, drilling, training, regulation, self-disciplining; see also DRILL 3, EDUCATION 1. **2** [A system of obedience] conduct, regulation, drill, orderliness, restraint, limitation, curb, indoctrination, brainwashing*; see also TRAINING.

discipline ***v.*** chastise, correct, limit; see PUNISH.

disc jockey ***n.*** radio announcer, commentator, DJ; see ANNOUNCER, REPORTER.

disclose ***v.*** make known, confess, publish; see REVEAL.

disclosure ***n.*** exposé, acknowledgment, confession; see ADMISSION 3, DECLARATION.

discolor ***v.*** stain, rust, tarnish; see COLOR, DIRTY.

discoloration ***n.*** blot, blotch, splotch; see BLEMISH, STAIN.

discomfort ***n.*** trouble, displeasure, uneasiness; see ANNOYANCE, EMBARRASSMENT.

disconnect ***v.*** separate, detach, disengage; see CUT 1, DIVIDE.

disconnected ***a.*** broken off, detached, switched off; see SEPARATED.

discontent ***n.*** dissatisfaction, unease, restlessness; see REGRET 1.

discontented ***a.*** unhappy, disgruntled, malcontented; see SAD 1.

discontinue ***v.*** finish, close, cease; see END 1, STOP 2.

discontinued ***a.*** ended, terminated, given up; see ABANDONED.

discord ***n.*** **1** [Conflict] strife, contention, dissension; see DISAGREEMENT 1. **2** [Noise] din, dissonance, disharmony; see NOISE 2.

discount ***n.*** deduction, allowance, rebate, decrease, markdown, concession, percentage, premium, subtraction, commission, exemption, modification, qualification, drawback, depreciation, cut rate; see also REDUCTION 1.—*Ant.* INCREASE, markup, surcharge. **—at a discount** discounted, cheap, below face value; see REDUCED 2.

discount ***v.*** reduce, remove, redeem, diminish, depreciate, deduct from, lower, make allowance for, allow, take off, charge off, rebate, mark down, discredit, rake off*; see also DECREASE 2.—*Ant.* RAISE, mark up, advance.

discourage ***v.*** repress, appall, intimidate, break someone's heart, deject, unnerve, scare, confuse, dampen, dismay, daunt, bully, demoralize, throw a wet blanket on*, throw cold water on*, dampen the spirits of, dash someone's hopes; see also DEPRESS 2, FRIGHTEN.—*Ant.* ENCOURAGE, cheer, inspire.

discouraged ***a.*** downcast, demoralized, depressed; see SAD 1.

discouragement ***n.*** **1** [Dejection] melancholy, despair, the blues*; see DEPRESSION 2, SADNESS. **2** [A restriction] constraint, hindrance, deterrent; see IMPEDIMENT 1.

discouraging ***a.*** **1** [Acting to discourage] depressing, disheartening, demoralizing; see DISMAL. **2** [Suggesting an unwelcome future] inopportune, disadvantageous, dissuading; see UNFAVORABLE.

discourteous ***a.*** boorish, crude, impolite; see RUDE 2.

discourtesy ***n.*** impudence, impoliteness, vulgarity; see RUDENESS.

discover ***v.*** invent, find out, ascertain, detect, discern, recognize, distinguish, determine, observe, explore, hear of, hear about, awake to, bring to light, uncover, ferret out, root out, trace out, unearth, look up, stumble on, stumble upon, come on, come upon, run across, fall upon, strike upon, think of, perceive, glimpse,

dis·cov·er·y (di skuv′ər ē) ***n.***, *pl.* **-er·ies** **1** a discovering **2** anything discovered
dis·cred·it (dis kred′it) ***vt.*** **1** to disbelieve **2** to cast doubt on **3** to disgrace —***n.*** **1** loss of belief; doubt **2** disgrace —**dis·cred′it·a·ble** ***adj.***
dis·creet (di skrēt′) ***adj.*** ⟦see DISCERN⟧ careful about what one says or does; prudent —**dis·creet′ly** ***adv.***
dis·crep·an·cy (di skrep′ən sē) ***n.***, *pl.* **-cies** ⟦< L *dis-*, from + *crepare*, to rattle⟧ (a) lack of agreement; inconsistency
dis·crete (di skrēt′) ***adj.*** ⟦see DISCERN⟧ separate and distinct; unrelated
dis·cre·tion (di skresh′ən) ***n.*** **1** the freedom to make decisions **2** the quality of being discreet; prudence —**dis·cre′tion·ar′y** ***adj.***
dis·crim·i·nate (di skrim′i nāt′) ***vi.*** **-nat′ed, -nat′ing** ⟦see DISCERN⟧ **1** to distinguish **2** to make distinctions in treatment; show partiality or prejudice —**dis·crim′i·nat′ing** ***adj.*** —**dis·crim′i·na′tion** ***n.***
dis·crim′i·na·to′ry (-nə tôr′ē) ***adj.*** showing discrimination or bias
dis·cur·sive (di skur′siv) ***adj.*** ⟦see DISCOURSE⟧ wandering from one topic to another; rambling
dis·cus (dis′kəs) ***n.*** ⟦< Gr *diskos*⟧ a heavy disk, usually of metal and wood, thrown for distance at a track meet
dis·cuss (di skus′) ***vt.*** ⟦< L *dis-*, apart + *quatere*, to shake⟧ to talk or write about; consider the pros and cons of —**dis·cus′sion** (-skush′ən) ***n.***
dis·cuss′ant (-ənt) ***n.*** a participant in an organized discussion
dis·dain (dis dān′) ***vt.*** ⟦< L *dis-*, DIS- + *dignari*, deign⟧ to regard as beneath one's dignity; scorn —***n.*** aloof contempt —**dis·dain′ful** ***adj.***
dis·ease (di zēz′) ***n.*** ⟦< OFr *des-*, DIS- + *aise*, ease⟧ **1** illness in general **2** a particular destructive process in an organism; specif., an illness **3** any harmful condition, as of society —**dis·eased′** ***adj.***
dis·em·bark (dis′im bärk′) ***vi.***, ***vt.*** to leave, or unload from, a ship, aircraft, etc. —**dis′em·bar·ka′tion** ***n.***
dis′em·bod′y (-im bäd′ē) ***vt.*** **-bod′ied, -bod′y·ing** to free from bodily existence —**dis′em·bod′i·ment** ***n.***
dis′em·bow′el (-im bou′əl) ***vt.*** **-eled** or **-elled, -el·ing** or **-el·ling** to take out the entrails of
dis′en·chant′ (-in chant′) ***vt.*** **1** to free from an enchantment or illusion **2** DISILLUSION (sense 2) —**dis′en·chant′ment** ***n.***
dis′en·cum′ber (-in kum′bər) ***vt.*** to relieve of a burden
dis·en·fran·chise (dis′in fran′chīz′) ***vt.*** **-chised′, -chis′ing** to deprive of a right, privilege, etc., esp. the right to vote
dis′en·gage′ (-in gāj′) ***vt.***, ***vi.*** **-gaged′, -gag′ing** to release or get loose from something that engages, holds, entangles, etc.; unfasten —**dis′en·gage′ment** ***n.***
dis′en·tan′gle (-in taŋ′gəl) ***vt.*** **-gled, -gling** to free from something that entangles, confuses, etc.; extricate; untangle
dis′es·teem′ (-i stēm′) ***n.*** lack of esteem; disfavor
dis·fa·vor (dis fā′vər) ***n.*** **1** an unfavorable opinion; dislike; disapproval **2** the state of being disliked, etc.
dis·fig′ure (-fig′yər) ***vt.*** **-ured, -ur·ing** to hurt the appearance of; deface —**dis·fig′ure·ment** ***n.***
dis·gorge′ (-gôrj′) ***vt.***, ***vi.*** **-gorged′, -gorg′ing** ⟦< OFr: see DIS- & GORGE⟧ **1** to vomit **2** to pour forth (its contents); empty (itself)
dis·grace′ (-grās′) ***n.*** ⟦< It *dis-*, not + *grazia*, favor⟧ **1** loss of favor or respect; shame; disrepute **2** a person or thing bringing shame —***vt.*** **-graced′, -grac′ing** to bring shame or dishonor upon —**dis·grace′ful** ***adj.***
dis·grun′tle (-grunt′'l) ***vt.*** **-tled, -tling** ⟦ult. < DIS- + GRUNT⟧ to make peevishly discontented; make sullen
dis·guise′ (-gīz′) ***vt.*** **-guised′, -guis′ing** ⟦< OFr: see DIS- & GUISE⟧ **1** to make appear, sound, etc. so different as to

THESAURUS

identify, devise, catch, spot, create, make out, sense, feel, sight, smell, hear, spy, bring out, find a clue, put one's finger on, get wise to*, dig out, dig up, turn up, sniff out, come up with, happen upon, get wind of, hit upon, lay one's hands on; see also FIND, LEARN.—*Ant.* MISS, pass by, omit.

discovered ***a.*** found, searched out, come upon, happened on, happened upon, unearthed, ascertained, detected, revealed, disclosed, unveiled, observed, sighted, shown, exposed, traced out, made out, met with, come across, recognized, identified, laid bare, opened, presented, spotted, perceived, learned; see also REAL 2.—*Ant.* HIDDEN, unfound, lost.

discovery ***n.*** invention, detection, exploration, identification, discernment, distinction, determination, calculation, experimentation, feeling, hearing, sighting, strike, results, findings, formula, device, find, contrivance, design, machine, invention, process, breakthrough, data, principle, law, theorem, innovation, conclusion, method, way; see also RESULT.

discredit ***v.*** question, disbelieve, distrust; see DOUBT.

discreet ***a.*** cautious, prudent, discerning, discriminating, not rash, strategic, noncommittal, heedful, vigilant, civil, sensible, reserved, alert, awake, wary, watchful, wise, circumspect, attentive, considerate, intelligent, guarded, politic, diplomatic, tight-lipped, cagey*; see also CAREFUL, THOUGHTFUL 2.—*Ant.* RASH, indiscreet, imprudent.

discretion ***n.*** caution, foresight, carefulness, wariness, sound judgment, thoughtfulness, attention, heed, concern, consideration, observation, watchfulness, precaution, good sense, providence, maturity, discernment, forethought, calculation, deliberation, vigilance, discrimination, responsibility, presence of mind; see also CARE 1, PRUDENCE, TACT.—*Ant.* CARELESSNESS, thoughtlessness, rashness. —**at one's discretion** as one wishes, whenever appropriate, at one's option; see APPROPRIATELY.

discriminate ***v.*** **1** [To differentiate] specify, separate, tell apart; see DISTINGUISH 1. **2** [To be (racially) prejudiced] be a bigot, show prejudice, set apart, segregate; see also HATE, SEPARATE 1.

discrimination ***n.*** **1** [The power to make distinctions] perception, acuteness, understanding; see INTELLIGENCE 1. **2** [The act of drawing a distinction] separation, differentiation, difference; see JUDGMENT 2. **3** [Partiality] unfairness, bias, bigotry; see HATRED, PREJUDICE.

discuss ***v.*** argue, debate, dispute, talk of, talk about, explain, contest, confer, deal with, reason with, take up, look over, consider, talk over, talk out, take up in conference, engage in conversation, go into, think over, telephone about, have a conference on, discourse about, argue for and against, canvass, consider, handle, present, review, recite, treat of, speak of, converse, discourse, take under advisement, comment upon, have out, speak on, kick around*, toss around*, chew the fat*, jaw*, air out*, knock around*, compare notes*, chew the rag*; see also TALK 1.—*Ant.* DELAY, table, postpone.

discussed ***a.*** talked over, debated, argued; see CONSIDERED.

discussion ***n.*** exchange, consultation, interview, deliberation, argumentation, contention, dialogue, talk, conference, argument, debate, panel discussion, summit meeting, dealing with the agenda, controversy, altercation, review, reasons, rap session*, symposium, quarrel, powwow*, bull session*; see also CONVERSATION, DISPUTE.—*Ant.* AGREEMENT, decision, conclusion.

disease ***n.*** **1** [A bodily infirmity] sickness, malady, ailment; see ILLNESS 1. **2** [Any ailment] condition, disorder, infirmity; see ILLNESS 2.

diseased ***a.*** unhealthy, unsound, ailing; see SICK.

disengage ***v.*** loose, undo, disentangle; see FREE.

disengaged ***a.*** detached, unattached, disjoined; see SEPARATED.

disentangle ***v.*** disengage, untangle, untwist; see FREE.

disfavor ***n.*** displeasure, disapproval, disrespect; see DISAPPOINTMENT 1.

disfigure ***v.*** deface, mar, mutilate; see DAMAGE, HURT.

disgrace ***n.*** scandal, shame, stain, slur, slight, stigma, brand, spot, slander, dishonor, infamy, reproach, disrepute, humiliation, degradation, taint, tarnish, mark of Cain*, scarlet letter; see also INSULT.—*Ant.* PRIDE, praise, credit.

disgrace ***v.*** debase, shame, degrade, abase, dishonor, disparage, discredit, deride, disregard, strip of honors, dismiss from favor, disrespect, mock, humble, reduce, put to shame, tarnish, stain, blot, sully, taint, defile, stigmatize, brand, tar and feather, put down, snub, derogate, belittle, take down a peg*; see also HUMILIATE, RIDICULE, SLANDER.—*Ant.* PRAISE, honor, exalt.

disgraced ***a.*** discredited, in disgrace, dishonored; see ASHAMED.

disgraceful ***a.*** dishonorable, disreputable, shocking; see OFFENSIVE, SHAMEFUL 1, 2.

disguise ***n.*** mask, deceptive covering, makeup, faking, false front, deception, smoke screen, blind, concealment, counterfeit, pseudonym, costume, masquerade, veil, cover, facade, put-on*; see also CAMOUFLAGE.

disguise ***v.*** mask, conceal, camouflage, pretend, screen, cloak, shroud, cover, veil, alter, obscure, feign, counterfeit, varnish, age, redo, make up, simulate, muffle, dress up, touch up, doctor up*; see also CHANGE 2, DECEIVE, HIDE.—*Ant.* REVEAL, open, strip.

disguised ***a.*** cloaked, masked, camouflaged; see CHANGED 2, COVERED 1,

be unrecognizable **2** to hide the real nature of —*n.* **1** anything that disguises **2** a being disguised
dis·gust′ (-gust′) *n.* ⟦< DIS- + L *gustus*, a taste⟧ a sickening dislike —*vt.* to cause to feel disgust —**dis·gust′ed** *adj.* —**dis·gust′ing** *adj.*
dish (dish) *n.* ⟦see DISCUS⟧ **1** a container, generally shallow and concave, for holding food **2** as much as a dish holds **3** a particular kind of food **4** any dishlike object —*vt.* to serve in a dish: with *up* or *out* —**dish it out** [Slang] to subject others to criticism, etc.
dis·ha·bille (dis′ə bēl′) *n.* ⟦< Fr *dés-*, DIS- + *habiller*, to dress⟧ the state of being dressed only partially or in night clothes
dish antenna a radio or TV antenna with a dish-shaped reflector
dis·har·mo·ny (dis här′mə nē) *n.* absence of harmony; discord —**dis′har·mo′ni·ous** (-mō′nē əs) *adj.*
dish′cloth′ *n.* a cloth for washing dishes, etc.
dis·heart·en (dis härt′'n) *vt.* to discourage; depress —**dis·heart′en·ing** *adj.*
di·shev·el (di shev′əl) *vt.* **-eled** or **-elled**, **-el·ing** or **-el·ling** ⟦< OFr *des-*, DIS- + *chevel*, hair⟧ to cause (hair, clothing, etc.) to become disarranged; rumple —**di·shev′el·ment** *n.*
dis·hon·est (dis än′ist) *adj.* not honest; lying, cheating, etc. —**dis·hon′est·ly** *adv.*
dis·hon′es·ty *n.* **1** a being dishonest **2** *pl.* **-ties** a dishonest act
dis·hon·or (dis än′ər) *n.* **1** loss of honor or respect; shame; disgrace **2** a cause of dishonor —*vt.* **1** to insult or disgrace **2** to refuse to pay (a check, etc.) —**dis·hon′or·a·ble** *adj.*
dish′pan′ *n.* a pan in which dishes, cups, etc. are washed
dish′rag′ *n.* DISHCLOTH
dish′wash′er *n.* a person or machine that washes dishes, cups, etc.
dis·il·lu·sion (dis′i lo͞o′zhən) *vt.* **1** to free from illusion **2** to take away the idealism of and make bitter, etc. —**dis′il·lu′sion·ment** *n.*
dis·in·clined (dis′in klīnd′) *adj.* unwilling; reluctant
dis·in·fect (dis′in fekt′) *vt.* to destroy the harmful bacteria, viruses, etc. in —**dis′in·fect′ant** *n.*
dis′in′for·ma′tion (-in′fər mā′shən) *n.* deliberately false information leaked so as to confuse another nation's intelligence operations
dis·in·gen·u·ous (dis′in jen′yo͞o əs) *adj.* not candid or frank; insincere
dis·in·her·it (dis′in her′it) *vt.* to deprive of an inheritance
dis·in·te·grate (dis in′tə grāt′) *vt.*, *vi.* **-grat′ed**, **-grat′ing** **1** to separate into parts or fragments; break up **2** to undergo nuclear transformation —**dis·in′te·gra′tion** *n.*
dis·in·ter (dis′in tʉr′) *vt.* **-terred′**, **-ter′ring** to remove from a grave, etc.; exhume
dis·in·ter·est·ed (dis in′trəs tid, -int′ər əs tid) *adj.* **1** impartial; unbiased **2** uninterested; indifferent
dis′in′ter·me′di·a′tion (-in′tər mē′dē ā′shən) *n.* the withdrawal of funds from banks to invest them at higher rates of interest, as in government securities
dis·joint′ (-jɔint′) *vt.* **1** to put out of joint; dislocate **2** to dismember **3** to destroy the unity, connections, etc. of —**dis·joint′ed** *adj.*
disk (disk) *n.* ⟦L *discus*: see DISCUS⟧ **1** any thin, flat, circular thing **2** DISC **3** a thin, flat, circular plate coated with magnetic particles, for storing computer data **4** a layer of fibrous cartilage between adjacent vertebrae
disk·ette (di sket′) *n.* FLOPPY DISK
dis·like (dis līk′) *vt.* **-liked′**, **-lik′ing** to have a feeling of not liking —*n.* a feeling of not liking
dis·lo·cate (dis′lō kāt′) *vt.* **-cat′ed**, **-cat′ing** **1** to displace (a bone) from its proper position **2** to disarrange; disrupt —**dis′lo·ca′tion** *n.*
dis·lodge (dis läj′) *vt.* **-lodged′**, **-lodg′ing** to force from a place
dis·loy′al (-lɔi′əl) *adj.* not loyal or faithful —**dis·loy′al·ty** *n.*
dis·mal (diz′məl) *adj.* ⟦< ML *dies mali*, evil days⟧ **1** causing gloom or misery **2** dark and gloomy
dis·man·tle (dis mant′'l) *vt.* **-tled**, **-tling** ⟦see DIS- & MANTLE⟧ **1** to strip (a ship, etc.), as of equipment **2** to take apart —**dis·man′tle·ment** *n.*

THESAURUS

HIDDEN.
disgust *n.* loathing, abhorrence, aversion; see HATRED, OBJECTION.
disgust *v.* repel, revolt, offend, displease, nauseate, sicken, make someone sick, fill with loathing, cause aversion, be repulsive, irk, scandalize, shock, upset, turn someone's stomach*; see also DISTURB, INSULT.
disgusted *a.* offended, sickened, displeased, repelled, unhappy, revolted, appalled, overwrought, outraged, having had a bellyful*, fed up*, having had it*, having had enough*; see also INSULTED, SHOCKED. —**disgusted with** repelled by, sick of*, fed up with*; see INSULTED, SHOCKED.
disgusting *a.* repugnant, revolting, sickening; see OFFENSIVE 2.
dish *n.* **1** [Plate] vessel, china, ceramic; see PLATE 3. *Table dishes include the following:* dinner plate, luncheon plate, salad plate, bread and butter plate, platter, casserole, cake plate, coffee cup, coffee mug, espresso cup, demitasse, teacup, egg cup, saucer, cereal bowl, soup bowl, gravy boat, relish tray, cruet, teapot, coffeepot, cream pitcher, water pitcher, lemonade pitcher, sugar bowl, butter dish, saltcellar; saltshaker, pepper shaker, pepper mill see also CONTAINER, CUP, POTTERY. **2** [Meal] course, serving, helping; see MEAL 2.
dishonest *a.* deceiving, fraudulent, double-dealing, backbiting, treacherous, deceitful, cunning, sneaky, tricky, wily, deceptive, misleading, elusive, slippery, shady*, swindling, cheating, sneaking, traitorous, villainous, sinister, underhanded, two-timing*, two-faced, double-crossing*, unprincipled, shiftless, unscrupulous, undependable, disreputable, questionable, dishonorable, counterfeit, infamous, corrupt, immoral, discredited, unworthy, shabby, mean, low, venial, self-serving, contemptible, rotten, fishy*, crooked; see also FALSE 1, LYING 1.—*Ant.* HONEST, irreproachable, scrupulous.
dishonesty *n.* infidelity, faithlessness, falsity, falsehood, deceit, trickery, duplicity, insidiousness, cunning, guile, slyness, double-dealing, trickiness, treachery, crookedness, corruption, cheating, stealing, lying, swindle, fraud, fraudulence, forgery, perjury, treason, flimflam, hocus-pocus*, hanky-panky*; see also DECEPTION, HYPOCRISY, LIE.—*Ant.* HONESTY, virtue, integrity.
dishonor *n.* shame, ignominy, abasement; see DISGRACE.
dish towel *n.* tea towel, kitchen towel, drying towel; see TOWEL.
disillusion *v.* disenchant, disabuse, embitter; see DISAPPOINT.
disinfect *v.* purify, fumigate, use disinfectant on; see CLEAN.
disinherit *v.* disown, evict, dispossess; see DISMISS, NEGLECT 2.
disintegrate *v.* break down, separate, divide, dismantle, break into pieces, disunite, disperse, crumble, disband, take apart, disorganize, detach, break apart, come apart, fall apart, sever, disconnect, fall to pieces, fade away, reduce to ashes; see also DISSOLVE.—*Ant.* UNITE, put together, combine.
disinterested *a.* impartial, not involved, unconcerned; see INDIFFERENT, UNMOVED 2.
disjoint *v.* dismember, cut up, carve; see CUT 1, DIVIDE, SEPARATE 1.
disjointed *a.* disconnected, divided, unattached; see SEPARATED.
dislike *n.* opposition, aversion, distaste; see HATE, HATRED, OBJECTION.
dislike *v.* detest, condemn, deplore, regret, lose interest in, speak down to, have hard feelings toward, not take kindly to, not be able to say much for, not have the stomach for, not speak well of, not want any part of, not care for, bear a grudge, have nothing to do with, keep one's distance from, care nothing for, resent, not appreciate, not endure, be averse to, abhor, abominate, disapprove, loathe, despise, object to, shun, shrink from, mind, shudder at, scorn, avoid, be displeased by, turn up the nose at, look on with aversion, not be able to stomach, regard with displeasure, not like, take a dim view of, have it in for*, be down on*, look down one's nose at*, have a bone to pick with*; see also HATE.
dislocate *v.* disjoint, disunite, disengage; see BREAK 1, DIVIDE, SEPARATE 1.
dislocation *n.* displacement, discontinuity, luxation; see BREAK 1, DIVISION 1.
dislodge *v.* eject, evict, uproot; see OUST, REMOVE 1.
disloyalty *n.* infidelity, betrayal, bad faith; see DISHONESTY, TREASON.
dismal *a.* gloomy, monotonous, dim, melancholy, desolate, dreary, sorrowful, morbid, troublesome, horrid, shadowy, overcast, cloudy, unhappy, discouraging, hopeless, black, unfortunate, ghastly, horrible, boring, gruesome, tedious, mournful, lugubrious, dull, disheartening, regrettable, cheerless, dusky, dingy, sepulchral, joyless, funereal, comfortless, murky, wan, bleak, somber, disagreeable, creepy, spooky*, blue; see also DARK 1.—*Ant.* HAPPY, joyful, cheerful.
dismantle *v.* take apart, disassemble, break down, take down, tear down, knock down, undo, demolish, level, ruin, unrig, subvert, raze, take to pieces, fell, take apart; see also DESTROY.

dis·may′ (-mā′) ***vt.*** ⟦< Anglo-Fr⟧ to make startled and discouraged by some problem, etc. difficult to resolve —***n.*** upset and discouragement caused by a problem, etc. difficult to resolve

dis·mem′ber (-mem′bər) ***vt.*** ⟦see DIS- & MEMBER⟧ **1** to cut or tear the limbs from **2** to pull or cut to pieces —**dis·mem′ber·ment *n.***

dis·miss′ (-mis′) ***vt.*** ⟦< L *dis-*, from + *mittere*, send⟧ **1** to cause or allow to leave **2** to discharge from employment, etc. **3** to put aside mentally **4** *Law* to reject (a claim, etc.) —**dis·miss′al *n.***

dis·mis′sive (-mis′iv) ***adj.*** condescending in dismissing from consideration

dis·mount′ (-mount′) ***vi.*** to get off, as from a horse —***vt.*** **1** to remove (a thing) from its mounting **2** to take apart; dismantle

dis·o·be·di·ence (dis′ō bē′dē əns) ***n.*** refusal to obey; insubordination —**dis′o·be′di·ent *adj.***

dis′o·bey′ (-ō bā′) ***vt.***, ***vi.*** to refuse to obey

dis′o·blige′ (-ə blīj′) ***vt.*** **-bliged′**, **-blig′ing** **1** to refuse to oblige **2** to offend

dis·or′der (-ôr′dər) ***n.*** **1** a lack of order; confusion **2** a breach of public peace; riot **3** an ailment —***vt.*** **1** to throw into disorder **2** to upset the normal functions of

dis·or′der·ly ***adj.*** **1** untidy **2** violating public peace, safety, etc. —**dis·or′der·li·ness *n.***

dis·or·gan·ize (dis ôr′gə nīz′) ***vt.*** **-ized′**, **-iz′ing** to break up the order or system of; throw into confusion —**dis·or′gan·i·za′tion *n.***

dis·o′ri·ent′ (-ôr′ē ent′) ***vt.*** ⟦see DIS- & ORIENT, *v.*⟧ **1** to cause to lose one's bearings **2** to confuse mentally —**dis·o′ri·en·ta′tion *n.***

dis·own′ (-ōn′) ***vt.*** to refuse to acknowledge as one's own; repudiate

dis·par·age (di spar′ij) ***vt.*** **-aged**, **-ag·ing** ⟦< OFr *des-* (see DIS-) + *parage*, rank⟧ **1** to discredit **2** to belittle —**dis·par′age·ment *n.***

dis·pa·rate (dis′pə rət) ***adj.*** ⟦< L *dis-*, not + *par*, equal⟧ distinct or different in kind; unequal —**dis·par·i·ty** (di spar′ə tē), *pl.* **-ties**, ***n.***

dis·pas·sion·ate (dis pash′ə nət) ***adj.*** free from passion or bias; impartial —**dis·pas′sion·ate·ly *adv.***

dis·patch (di spach′; *for n., also* dis′pach′) ***vt.*** ⟦< L *dis-*, away + *pes*, foot⟧ **1** to send promptly, as on an errand **2** to kill **3** to finish quickly —***n.*** **1** a sending off **2** a killing **3** speed; promptness **4** a message **5** a news story sent by a reporter —**dis·patch′er *n.***

dis·pel (di spel′) ***vt.*** **-pelled′**, **-pel′ling** ⟦< L *dis-*, apart + *pellere*, to drive⟧ to scatter and drive away

dis·pen·sa·ble (di spen′sə bəl) ***adj.*** **1** that can be dealt out **2** that can be dispensed with; not important

dis·pen′sa·ry (-sə rē) ***n.***, *pl.* **-ries** a room or place where medicines and first-aid treatment are available

dis·pen·sa·tion (dis′pən sā′shən) ***n.*** **1** a dispensing **2** something dispensed **3** an administrative system **4** a release from an obligation **5** *Theol.* the ordering of events under divine authority

dis·pense (di spens′) ***vt.*** **-pensed′**, **-pens′ing** ⟦< L *dis-*, out + *pendere*, weigh⟧ **1** to give out; distribute **2** to prepare and give out (medicines) **3** to administer (the law or justice) —**dispense with** **1** to get rid of **2** to do without —**dis·pens′er *n.***

dis·perse′ (-spurs′) ***vt.*** **-persed′**, **-pers′ing** ⟦< L *dis-*, out + *spargere*, scatter⟧ **1** to break up and scatter **2** to dispel (mist, etc.) —***vi.*** to scatter —**dis·per′sal *n.*** —**dis·per′sion *n.***

dis·pir·it (di spir′it) ***vt.*** to depress; discourage —**dis·pir′it·ed *adj.***

dis·place (dis plās′) ***vt.*** **-placed′**, **-plac′ing** **1** to move from its usual place **2** to remove from office; discharge **3** to replace

displaced person one forced from one's country, esp. as a result of war

dis·place′ment ***n.*** **1** a displacing or being displaced **2** the weight or volume of air, water, or other fluid displaced by a floating object

dis·play (di splā′) ***vt.*** ⟦< L *dis-*, apart + *plicare*, to fold⟧ **1** [Obs.] to spread out; unfold **2** to exhibit —***n.*** **1** an exhibition **2** anything displayed

dis·please (dis plēz′) ***vt.***, ***vi.*** **-pleased′**, **-pleas′ing** to fail to please; offend

dis·pleas′ure (-plezh′ər) ***n.*** a being displeased

THESAURUS

dismay ***n.*** consternation, dread, anxiety; see FEAR.

dismember ***v.*** dissect, disjoint, amputate; see CUT 1, DIVIDE.

dismiss ***v.*** send away, discard, reject, decline, repel, let out, repudiate, disband, detach, lay off, pack off, cast off, cast out, relinquish, dispense with, disperse, remove, expel, abolish, relegate, push aside, shed, do without, have done with, dispose of, sweep away, clear, rid, chase, dispossess, boycott, exile, expatriate, banish, outlaw, deport, excommunicate, get rid of, send packing, drop, brush off*, kick out*, blackball, write off; see also OUST, REFUSE.—*Ant.* MAINTAIN, retain, keep.

dismissal ***n.*** deposition, displacement, expulsion; see REMOVAL.

dismissed ***a.*** sent away, ousted, removed; see DISCHARGED, FREE 2, 3.

disobedience ***n.*** insubordination, defiance, insurgence, disregard, violation, neglect, mutiny, revolt, nonobservance, strike, stubbornness, noncompliance, infraction of the rules, unruliness, sedition, rebellion, sabotage, riot; see also REVOLUTION 2.

disobedient ***a.*** insubordinate, refractory, defiant; see REBELLIOUS, UNRULY.

disobey ***v.*** balk, decline, neglect, desert, be remiss, ignore the commands of, refuse submission to, disagree, differ, evade, disregard the authority of, break rules, object, defy, resist, revolt, strike, violate, infringe, transgress, shirk, misbehave, withstand, counteract, take the law into one's own hands, not mind, pay no attention to, go counter to, not listen to; see also DARE 2, OPPOSE 1, REBEL.—*Ant.* OBEY, follow, fulfill.

disorder ***n.*** tumult, discord, turmoil, complication, chaos, mayhem, terrorism, rioting, mob rule, anarchy, anarchism, lawlessness, entanglement, commotion, agitation, insurrection, revolution, rebellion, strike, disorganization, riot, reign of terror, uproar, dither, static*; see also DISTURBANCE 2, TROUBLE 1.—*Ant.* ORDER, peace, tranquillity.

disorder ***v.*** disarrange, clutter, scatter; see CONFUSE, DISORGANIZE.

disordered ***a.*** displaced, misplaced, dislocated, mislaid, out of place, deranged, in disorder, out of kilter, out of hand, in confusion, in a mess, all over the place, in a jumble, upset, unsettled, disorganized, disarranged, moved, removed, shifted, tampered with, tumbled, ruffled, rumpled, jumbled, jarred, tossed, stirred up, roiled, jolted, muddled; see also CONFUSED 2, TANGLED.—*Ant.* ORDERED, arranged, settled.

disorderly ***a.*** **1** [Lacking orderly arrangement] confused, jumbled, undisciplined, unrestrained, scattered, dislocated, unsystematic, messy, slovenly, untidy, cluttered, unkempt, scrambled, badly managed, in confusion, untrained, disorganized, out of control, topsy-turvy, all over the place*, mixed-up; see also DISORDERED.—*Ant.* REGULAR, neat, trim. **2** [Creating a disturbance] intemperate, disruptive, rowdy; see UNRULY.

disorganization ***n.*** disunion, dissolution, derangement; see CONFUSION.

disorganize ***v.*** break up, disperse, destroy, scatter, litter, clutter, break down, put out of order, disarrange, disorder, upset, disrupt, derange, dislocate, disband, jumble, muddle, unsettle, disturb, perturb, shuffle, toss, complicate, confound, overthrow, overturn, scramble; see also CONFUSE.—*Ant.* SYSTEMATIZE, order, distribute.

disown ***v.*** repudiate, deny, disavow; see DISCARD.

dispatch ***v.*** **1** [To send something on its way] transmit, express, forward; see SEND 1. **2** [To make an end] finish, conclude, perform; see ACHIEVE.

dispel ***v.*** disperse, deploy, dissipate; see DISTRIBUTE, SCATTER.

dispensable ***a.*** removable, excessive, unnecessary; see TRIVIAL, USELESS 1.

dispense ***v.*** apportion, assign, allocate; see DISTRIBUTE, GIVE 1. —**dispense with** ignore, pass over, brush aside; see DISREGARD, NEGLECT 2.

dispenser ***n.*** vendor, tap, vending machine, spray can, spray gun, cigarette machine, Coke machine (trademark), automat, squeeze bottle.

disperse ***v.*** break up, separate, disband; see SCATTER.

displace ***v.*** **1** [To remove] replace, transpose, dislodge; see REMOVE 1. **2** [To put in the wrong place] mislay, misplace, disarrange; see LOSE 2.

display ***n.*** exhibition, exhibit, presentation, representation, exposition, arrangement, demonstration, performance, revelation, unveiling, procession, parade, pageant, example, appearance, waxworks, fireworks, carnival, fair, pomp, splendor, unfolding; see also SHOW 1.

display ***v.*** show, show off, exhibit, uncover, open up, unfold, reveal, spread, parade, unmask, present, represent, perform, flaunt, lay out, put out, set out, disclose, unveil, arrange, make known; see also EXPOSE.—*Ant.* HIDE, conceal, veil.

displayed ***a.*** presented, visible, on display; see ADVERTISED, SHOWN 1.

displease ***v.*** vex, provoke, enrage; see ANGER.

displeasure ***n.*** disapproval, annoy-

dis·port (di spôrt′) *vi.* ⟦< OFr *des-* (see DIS-) + *porter*, carry⟧ to play; frolic —*vt.* to amuse (oneself)
dis·pos·al (di spō′zəl) *n.* **1** a disposing **2** a device in the drain of a kitchen sink to grind up garbage
dis·pose′ (-spōz′) *vt.* **-posed′**, **-pos′ing** ⟦see DIS- & POSITION⟧ **1** to arrange **2** to settle (affairs) **3** to make willing; incline —**dispose of 1** to settle **2** to give away or sell **3** to get rid of —**dis·pos′a·ble** *adj.*
dis·po·si·tion (dis′pə zish′ən) *n.* **1** arrangement **2** management of affairs **3** a selling or giving away **4** the authority to settle, etc.; control **5** a tendency **6** one's temperament
dis′pos·sess′ (-pə zes′) *vt.* to deprive of the possession of land, a house, etc.; oust
dis·praise′ (-prāz′) *vt.* **-praised′**, **-prais′ing** ⟦< OFr *despreisier*⟧ to blame; censure —*n.* blame
dis′pro·por′tion (-prə pôr′shən) *n.* a lack of proportion —**dis′pro·por′tion·al** or **dis′pro·por′tion·ate** *adj.*
dis·prove′ (-pro͞ov′) *vt.* **-proved′**, **-proved′** or **-prov′en**, **-prov′ing** to prove to be false
dis·pu·ta·tion (dis′pyo͞o tā′shən) *n.* **1** a disputing **2** debate
dis′pu·ta′tious (-pyo͞o tā′shəs) *adj.* inclined to dispute; contentious —**dis′pu·ta′tious·ly** *adv.*
dis·pute (di spyo͞ot′) *vi.* **-put′ed**, **-put′ing** ⟦< L *dis-*, apart + *putare*, to think⟧ **1** to argue; debate **2** to quarrel —*vt.* **1** to argue (a question) **2** to doubt **3** to oppose in any way —*n.* **1** a disputing; debate **2** a quarrel —**in dispute** not settled —**dis·put′a·ble** *adj.* —**dis·pu′tant** *adj.*, *n.*
dis·qual·i·fy (dis kwôl′ə fī′) *vt.* **-fied′**, **-fy′ing** to make or declare unqualified, unfit, or ineligible —**dis·qual′i·fi·ca′tion** *n.*
dis·qui·et (dis kwī′ət) *vt.* to make uneasy; disturb —*n.* restlessness: also **dis·qui′e·tude′** (-ə to͞od′)
dis·qui·si·tion (dis′kwi zish′ən) *n.* ⟦< L *dis-*, apart + *quaerere*, to seek⟧ a formal discussion; treatise
dis·re·gard (dis′ri gärd′) *vt.* **1** to pay little or no attention to **2** to treat without due respect —*n.* **1** lack of attention **2** lack of due regard or respect
dis′re·pair′ (-ri per′) *n.* the condition of needing repairs; state of neglect
dis·rep′u·ta·ble (-rep′yo͞o tə bəl) *adj.* **1** not reputable **2** not fit to be seen
dis′re·pute′ (-ri pyo͞ot′) *n.* lack or loss of repute; bad reputation; disgrace
dis′re·spect′ (-ri spekt′) *n.* lack of respect; discourtesy —**dis′re·spect′ful** *adj.*
dis·robe (dis rōb′) *vt.*, *vi.* **-robed′**, **-rob′ing** to undress
dis·rupt (dis rupt′) *vt.*, *vi.* ⟦< L *dis-*, apart + *rumpere*, to break⟧ **1** to break apart **2** to disturb or interrupt —**dis·rup′tion** *n.* —**dis·rup′tive** *adj.*
dis·sat′is·fy′ (-sat′is fī′) *vt.* **-fied′**, **-fy′ing** to fail to satisfy; displease —**dis·sat′is·fac′tion** *n.*
dis·sect (di sekt′) *vt.* ⟦< L *dis-*, apart + *secare*, to cut⟧ **1** to cut apart piece by piece, as a body for purposes of study **2** to examine or analyze closely —**dis·sec′tion** *n.* —**dis·sec′tor** *n.*
dis·sem·ble (di sem′bəl) *vt.*, *vi.* **-bled**, **-bling** ⟦< OFr *dessembler*⟧ to conceal (the truth, one's feelings, motives, etc.) under a false appearance —**dis·sem′blance** *n.* —**dis·sem′bler** *n.*
dis·sem·i·nate (di sem′ə nāt′) *vt.* **-nat′ed**, **-nat′ing** ⟦< L *dis-*, apart + *seminare*, to sow⟧ to scatter about; spread widely —**dis·sem′i·na′tion** *n.*
dis·sen·sion (di sen′shən) *n.* a dissenting; disagreement or quarreling
dis·sent (di sent′) *vi.* ⟦< L *dis-*, apart + *sentire*, feel⟧ **1** to disagree **2** to reject doctrines of an established church —*n.* a dissenting —**dis·sent′er** *n.*
dis·ser·ta·tion (dis′ər tā′shən) *n.* ⟦< L *dis-*, apart + *serere*, join⟧ a formal discourse or treatise, esp. one written to fulfill the requirements for a doctorate from a university
dis·serv·ice (dis sur′vis) *n.* harm
dis·sev·er (di sev′ər) *vt.* **1** to sever; separate **2** to divide into parts —*vi.* to separate; disunite
dis·si·dence (dis′ə dəns) *n.* ⟦< L *dis-*, apart + *sidere*, sit⟧ disagreement; dissent —**dis′si·dent** (-dənt) *adj.*, *n.*
dis·sim·i·lar (dis sim′ə lər) *adj.* not similar; different —**dis′sim′i·lar′i·ty** (-lar′ə tē), *pl.* **-ties**, *n.*
dis·si·mil·i·tude (dis′si mil′ə to͞od′) *n.* difference
dis·sim·u·late (di sim′yo͞o lāt′) *vt.*, *vi.* **-lat′ed**, **-lat′ing** ⟦see DIS- & SIMULATE⟧ to dissemble —**dis·sim′u·la′tion** *n.* —**dis·sim′u·la′tor** *n.*
dis·si·pate (dis′ə pāt′) *vt.* **-pat′ed**, **-pat′ing** ⟦< L *dis-*, apart + *supare*, to throw⟧ **1** to scatter; disperse **2** to make disappear **3** to waste or squander —*vi.* **1** to vanish **2** to indulge in pleasure to the point of harming oneself —**dis′si·pa′tion** *n.*
dis·so·ci·ate (di sō′shē āt′) *vt.* **-at′ed**, **-at′ing** ⟦< L *dis-*, apart + *sociare*, join⟧ to break the connection between; disunite —**dis·so′ci·a′tion** *n.*
dis·so·lute (dis′ə lo͞ot′) *adj.* ⟦see DISSOLVE⟧ dissipated and immoral; profligate —**dis′so·lute′ly** *adv.* —**dis′so·lute′ness** *n.*
dis·so·lu·tion (dis′ə lo͞o′shən) *n.* a dissolving or being dissolved; specif., *a*) a breaking up or into parts *b*) a termination *c*) death
dis·solve (di zälv′, -zôlv′) *vt.*, *vi.* **-solved′**, **-solv′ing** ⟦< L *dis-*, apart + *solvere*, loosen⟧ **1** to make or become liquid; melt **2** to pass or make pass into solution **3** to break up **4** to end as by breaking up; terminate **5** to disappear or make disappear
dis·so·nance (dis′ə nəns) *n.* ⟦< L *dis-*, apart + *sonus*, a sound⟧ **1** an inharmonious combination of sounds; dis-

THESAURUS

ance, resentment; see ANGER.
disposal *n.* action, provision, determination, disposition, distribution, arrangement, conclusion, settlement, control, winding up; see also RESULT. **—at someone's disposal** ready, prepared, usable; see AVAILABLE.
dispose *v.* settle, adapt, arrange; see ADJUST 1, PREPARE 1. **—dispose of** relinquish, throw away, part with; see DISCARD, SELL.
disposed *a.* inclined, prone, apt; see LIKELY 4.
disposition *n.* **1** [Arrangement] decision, method, distribution; see ORGANIZATION 1, PLAN 2. **2** [Temperament] character, nature, temper; see MOOD, TEMPERAMENT.
disproportionate *a.* unbalanced, incommensurate, excessive; see IRREGULAR 4.
disprove *v.* prove false, throw out, set aside, find fault in, invalidate, weaken, overthrow, tear down, confound, expose, cut the ground from under, poke holes in; see also DENY.
disputable *a.* debatable, doubtful, dubious; see QUESTIONABLE 1, UNCERTAIN.
dispute *n.* argument, quarrel, debate, misunderstanding, conflict, strife, discussion, polemic, bickering, squabble, disturbance, feud, commotion, tiff, fracas, controversy, altercation, dissension, squall, difference of opinion, rumpus*, row, flare-up, fuss, fireworks; see also DISAGREEMENT 1.
dispute *v.* debate, contradict, quarrel; see ARGUE, DISCUSS.
disqualify *v.* preclude, disentitle, disbar; see BAR 2.
disquieting *a.* distressing, troubling, disconcerting; see DISTURBING.
disregard *v.* ignore, pass over, let pass, make light of, have no use for, laugh off, take no account of, brush aside, turn a deaf ear to, be blind to, shut one's eyes to; see also NEGLECT 1.
disrepair *n.* decrepitude, deterioration, dilapidation; see DECAY.
disreputable *a.* low, objectionable, discreditable; see OFFENSIVE 2, SHAMEFUL 1, 2.
disrespect *n.* discourtesy, insolence, irreverence; see RUDENESS.
disrespectful *a.* discourteous, impolite, impudent; see RUDE 2.
disrobe *v.* strip, divest, unclothe; see UNDRESS.
disrupt *v.* disturb, intrude, obstruct; see BREAK 1, INTERRUPT.
disruption *n.* debacle, disturbance, agitation; see CONFUSION.
dissatisfaction *n.* dislike, displeasure, disapproval; see OBJECTION.
dissatisfied *a.* displeased, unsatisfied, fed up*; see DISAPPOINTED.
dissect *v.* dismember, quarter, operate; see CUT 1, DIVIDE.
disseminate *v.* sow, propagate, broadcast; see DISTRIBUTE.
dissension *n.* difference, quarrel, trouble; see DISAGREEMENT 1, DISPUTE.
dissent *n.* nonconformity, difference, heresy; see DISAGREEMENT 1, OBJECTION, PROTEST.
dissent *v.* disagree, refuse, contradict; see DIFFER 1, OPPOSE 1.
dissenter *n.* dissident, protester, demonstrator; see NONCONFORMIST, RADICAL, REBEL.
disservice *n.* wrong, injury, outrage; see DAMAGE 1, INJUSTICE, INSULT.
dissipate *v.* **1** [To dispel] disperse, diffuse, disseminate; see SCATTER 2. **2** [To squander] use up, consume, misuse; see SPEND, WASTE 2.
dissipated *a.* **1** [Scattered] dispersed, strewn, disseminated; see SCATTERED. **2** [Wasted] squandered, spent, consumed; see EMPTY, WASTED.
dissipation *n.* **1** [Dispersion] scattering, dispersal, spread; see DISTRIBUTION. **2** [Debauchery] indulgence, intemperance, dissolution; see EVIL 1.
dissolve *v.* liquefy, melt, thaw, soften, run, defrost, waste away, cause to become liquid; see also EVAPORATE, MELT 1.—*Ant.* HARDEN, freeze, solidify.

cord **2** any lack of harmony or agreement —**dis'so·nant** ***adj.***

dis·suade (di swād') ***vt.*** **-suad'ed, -suad'ing** ⟦< L *dis-*, away + *suadere*, to persuade⟧ to turn (a person) aside (*from* a course, etc.) by persuasion or advice —**dis·sua'sion** (-swā'zhən) ***n.***

dist *abbrev.* **1** distance **2** district

dis·taff (dis'taf') ***n.*** ⟦< OE *dis-*, flax + *stæf*, staff⟧ a staff on which flax, wool, etc. is wound for use in spinning —***adj.*** female; specif., of the maternal side of a family

dis·tal (dis'təl) ***adj.*** ⟦DIST(ANT) + -AL⟧ *Anat.* farthest from the point of attachment or origin; terminal —**dis'tal·ly** ***adv.***

dis·tance (dis'təns) ***n.*** ⟦< L *dis-*, apart + *stare*, to stand⟧ **1** a being separated in space or time; remoteness **2** a gap, space, or interval between two points in space or time **3** a remoteness in behavior; reserve **4** a faraway place —***vt.*** **-tanced, -tanc·ing** to place at an emotional distance (*from*)

dis'tant (-tənt) ***adj.*** **1** far away in space or time **2** away *[100 miles distant]* **3** far apart in relationship **4** aloof; reserved **5** from or at a distance —**dis'tant·ly** ***adv.***

dis·taste (dis tāst') ***n.*** dislike —**dis·taste'ful** ***adj.***

dis·tem·per (dis tem'pər) ***n.*** ⟦< ML *distemperare*, to disorder⟧ an infectious viral disease of young dogs, horses, etc.

dis·tend (di stend') ***vt., vi.*** ⟦< L *dis-*, apart + *tendere*, to stretch⟧ **1** to stretch out **2** to expand, as by pressure from within; make or become swollen —**dis·ten'tion** or **dis·ten'sion** ***n.***

dis·till or **dis·til** (di stil') ***vi., vt.*** **-tilled', -till'ing** ⟦< L *de-*, down + *stillare*, to drop⟧ **1** to fall or let fall in drops **2** to undergo, subject to, or produce by distillation —**dis·till'er** ***n.***

dis·til·late (dis'tə lāt', -lit) ***n.*** a liquid obtained by distilling

dis·til·la·tion (dis'tə lā'shən) ***n.*** **1** the process of heating a mixture and condensing the resulting vapor to produce a more nearly pure substance **2** anything distilled; distillate

dis·till·er·y (di stil'ər ē) ***n., pl.*** **-ies** a place where alcoholic liquors are distilled

dis·tinct (di stiŋkt') ***adj.*** ⟦see DISTINGUISH⟧ **1** not alike **2** separate **3** clearly perceived or marked off **4** unmistakable; definite —**dis·tinct'ly** ***adv.***

dis·tinc'tion (-stiŋk'shən) ***n.*** **1** the act of making or keeping distinct **2** difference **3** a quality or feature that differentiates **4** fame; eminence **5** the quality that makes one seem superior **6** a mark of special recognition or honor

dis·tinc'tive ***adj.*** making distinct; characteristic —**dis·tinc'tive·ly** ***adv.*** —**dis·tinc'tive·ness** ***n.***

dis·tin·guish (di stiŋ'gwish) ***vt.*** ⟦< L *dis-*, apart + *-stinguere*, to prick⟧ **1** to perceive or show the difference in **2** to characterize **3** to perceive clearly **4** to classify **5** to make famous —***vi.*** to make a distinction (*between* or *among*) —**dis·tin'guish·a·ble** ***adj.***

dis·tin'guished ***adj.*** celebrated; famous

dis·tort (di stôrt') ***vt.*** ⟦< L *dis-*, intens. + *torquere*, to twist⟧ **1** to twist out of shape **2** to misrepresent (facts, etc.) **3** to modify so as to reproduce unfaithfully —**dis·tor'tion** ***n.***

dis·tract (di strakt') ***vt.*** ⟦< L *dis-*, apart + *trahere*, draw⟧ **1** to draw (the mind, etc.) away in another direction; divert **2** to confuse; bewilder —**dis·tract'ed** ***adj.*** —**dis·tract'ing** ***adj.***

dis·trac'tion ***n.*** **1** a distracting or being distracted **2** anything that distracts confusingly or amusingly; diversion **3** great mental distress

dis·trait (di strā') ***adj.*** ⟦see DISTRACT⟧ absent-minded; inattentive

dis·traught' (-strôt') ***adj.*** ⟦var. of prec.⟧ **1** mentally confused; distracted **2** driven mad; crazed

dis·tress (di stres') ***vt.*** ⟦ult. < L *dis-*, apart + *stringere*, to stretch⟧ to cause misery or suffering to —***n.*** **1** pain, suffering, etc. **2** an affliction **3** a state of danger or trouble —**dis·tressed'** ***adj.***

dis·trib·ute (di strib'yo͞ot) ***vt.*** **-ut·ed, -ut·ing** ⟦< L *dis-*, apart + *tribuere*, allot⟧ **1** to give out in shares **2** to

THESAURUS

distance ***n.*** **1** [A degree or quantity of space] reach, span, range; see EXPANSE, EXTENT, LENGTH 1, 2. **2** [A place or places far away] background, horizon, as far as the eye can see, sky, heavens, outskirts, foreign countries, different worlds, strange places, distant terrain, outer space, far-off lands, the ends of the earth, the country, beyond the horizon.—*Ant.* NEIGHBORHOOD, surroundings, neighbors. **3** [A measure of space] statute mile, mile, inch, rod, yard, foot, kilometer, meter, centimeter, millimeter, league, fathom, span, hand, cubit, furlong, a stone's throw. —**go the distance** finish, bring to an end, see something through; see COMPLETE. —**keep at a distance** ignore, reject, shun; see AVOID. —**keep one's distance** be aloof, ignore, shun; see AVOID.

distant ***a.*** afar, far off, abroad, faraway, yonder, removed, abstracted, inaccessible, unapproachable, out-of-the-way, at arm's length, stretching to, out of range, out of reach, out of earshot, out of sight, in the background, in the distance, separate, far, farther, further, far away, at a distance; see also SEPARATED.—*Ant.* CLOSE, near, next.

distaste ***n.*** aversion, dislike, abhorrence; see HATRED.

distasteful ***a.*** disagreeable, repugnant, undesirable; see OFFENSIVE 2.

distend ***v.*** enlarge, widen, inflate; see DISTORT 2, INCREASE, STRETCH 1, 2.

distended ***a.*** swollen, bloated, tumescent; see ENLARGED, INFLATED.

distill ***v.*** vaporize and condense, steam, precipitate; see CONCENTRATE 1, EVAPORATE.

distinct ***a.*** **1** [Having sharp outlines] lucid, plain, obvious; see CLEAR 2, DEFINITE 2. **2** [Not connected with another] discrete, separate, disunited; see SEPARATED. **3** [Clearly heard] clear, sharp, enunciated; see AUDIBLE.

distinction ***n.*** **1** [The act or quality of noticing differences] separation, differentiation, refinement; see DEFINITION. **2** [That which makes a thing distinct] distinctive feature, particular, qualification; see CHARACTERISTIC, DETAIL. **3** [A mark of personal achievement] repute, renown, prominence; see FAME.

distinctive ***a.*** peculiar, unique, distinguishing; see CHARACTERISTIC.

distinctly ***a.*** precisely, sharply, plainly; see CLEARLY 1, 2, SURELY.

distinguish ***v.*** **1** [To make distinctions] discriminate, differentiate, classify, specify, identify, individualize, characterize, separate, divide, collate, sort out, sort into, set apart, mark off, select, draw the line, tell from, pick and choose, separate the wheat from the chaff, separate the sheep from the goats; see also DEFINE 2. **2** [To discern] detect, discriminate, notice; see DISCOVER, SEE 1. **3** [To bestow honor upon] pay tribute to, honor, celebrate; see ACKNOWLEDGE 2, ADMIRE, PRAISE 1.

distinguishable ***a.*** separable, perceptible, discernible; see AUDIBLE, OBVIOUS, TANGIBLE.

distinguished ***a.*** **1** [Made recognizable by markings] characterized, labeled, marked, stamped, signed, signified, identified, made certain, obvious, set apart, branded, earmarked, separate, unique, differentiated, observed, distinct, conspicuous; see also SEPARATED.—*Ant.* TYPICAL, unidentified, indistinct. **2** [Notable for excellence] eminent, illustrious, venerable, renowned, honored, memorable, celebrated, well-known, noted, noteworthy, highly regarded, well-thought-of, esteemed, prominent, reputable, superior, outstanding, brilliant, glorious, extraordinary, singular, great, special, striking, unforgettable, shining, foremost, dignified, famed, talked of, first-rate, big-name*, headline*; see also FAMOUS.—*Ant.* OBSCURE, insignificant, unimportant.

distort ***v.*** **1** [To alter the meaning] pervert, misinterpret, misconstrue; see DECEIVE. **2** [To change shape] contort, sag, twist, slump, knot, get out of shape, buckle, writhe, melt, warp, deform, collapse; see also CHANGE 2.

distortion ***n.*** **1** [Deformity] twist, malformation, mutilation; see CONTORTION. **2** [Misrepresentation] perversion, misinterpretation, misuse; see LIE.

distract ***v.*** divert, sidetrack, occupy, amuse, entertain, draw away, call away, draw someone's attention from, lead astray, attract from; see also MISLEAD.

distracted ***a.*** preoccupied, inattentive, unable to concentrate; see ABSENT-MINDED.

distraction ***n.*** **1** [Confusion] perplexity, abstraction, complication; see CONFUSION. **2** [Diversion] amusement, pastime, preoccupation; see ENTERTAINMENT, GAME 1.

distress ***n.*** worry, anxiety, misery, sorrow, wretchedness, pain, dejection, irritation, suffering, heartache, ordeal, desolation, anguish, affliction, woe, torment, shame, embarrassment, disappointment, tribulation, pang; see also GRIEF, TROUBLE 1.—*Ant.* JOY, happiness, jollity.

distress ***v.*** irritate, disturb, upset; see BOTHER 1, 2.

distribute ***v.*** dispense, divide, share, deal, bestow, issue, dispose, disperse, disburse, mete out, pass out,

spread out 3 to classify 4 to put (things) in various distinct places —**dis'tri·bu'tion** ***n.***

dis·trib'u·tor ***n.*** one that distributes; specif., *a)* a dealer who distributes goods to consumers *b)* a device for distributing electric current to the spark plugs of a gasoline engine

dis·trict (dis'trikt) ***n.*** ⟦< L *dis-*, apart + *stringere*, to stretch⟧ **1** a division of a state, city, etc. made for a specific purpose **2** any region

district attorney the prosecuting attorney for the state or the federal government in a specified district

District of Columbia federal district of the U.S., on the Potomac: 61 sq. mi.; pop. 607,000; coextensive with the city of Washington: abbrev. *DC*

dis·trust (dis trust') ***n.*** a lack of trust; doubt —***vt.*** to have no trust in; doubt —**dis·trust'ful** ***adj.***

dis·turb (di sturb') ***vt.*** ⟦< L *dis-*, intens. + *turbare*, to disorder⟧ **1** to break up the quiet or settled order of **2** to make uneasy; upset **3** to interrupt —**dis·turb'er** ***n.***

dis·turb'ance ***n.*** **1** a disturbing or being disturbed **2** anything that disturbs **3** commotion; disorder

dis·u·nite (dis'yoo nīt') ***vt., vi.*** **-nit'ed, -nit'ing** to divide or separate into parts, factions, etc. —**dis·u'ni·ty** ***n.***

dis·use' (-yoos') ***n.*** lack of use

ditch (dich) ***n.*** ⟦OE *dic*⟧ a long, narrow channel dug into the earth, as for drainage —***vt.*** **1** to make a ditch in **2** [Slang] to get rid of

dith·er (dith'ər) ***vi.*** ⟦ME *dideren*⟧ **1** to be nervously excited or confused **2** to be indecisive —***n.*** a nervously excited or confused state

dit·sy (dit'sē) ***adj.*** **-si·er, -si·est** ⟦? < DIZZY⟧ [Slang] silly, flighty, eccentric, etc.: also sp. **dit'zy**

dit·to (dit'ō) ***n., pl.*** **-tos** ⟦It < L *dicere*, to say⟧ **1** the same (as above or before) **2** DITTO MARK

ditto mark a mark (") used in lists or tables to show that the item above is to be repeated

dit·ty (dit'ē) ***n., pl.*** **-ties** ⟦< L *dicere*, to say⟧ a short, simple song

di·u·ret·ic (dī'yoo ret'ik) ***adj.*** ⟦< Gr *dia-*, through + *ourein*, urinate⟧ increasing the flow of urine —***n.*** a diuretic drug or substance

di·ur·nal (dī ur'nəl) ***adj.*** ⟦< L *dies*, day⟧ **1** daily **2** of the daytime —**di·ur'nal·ly** ***adv.***

div *abbrev.* **1** dividend **2** division

di·va (dē'və) ***n., pl.*** **-vas** or **-ve** (-ve) ⟦It < L, goddess⟧ a leading woman singer

di·va·lent (dī'vā'lənt, dī vā'-) ***adj.*** *Chem.* having two valences or a valence of two

di·van (di van', dī'van') ***n.*** ⟦< Pers *dīwān*⟧ a large, low couch or sofa

dive (dīv) ***vi.*** **dived** or **dove, dived, div'ing** ⟦OE *dyfan*⟧ **1** to plunge headfirst into water **2** to submerge **3** to plunge suddenly into something **4** to make a steep descent, as an airplane —***n.*** **1** a diving **2** any sudden plunge **3** a sharp descent **4** [Inf.] a cheap, disreputable saloon, etc. —**div'er** ***n.***

di·verge (dī vurj', di-) ***vi.*** **-verged', -verg'ing** ⟦< L *dis-*, apart + *vergere*, to turn⟧ **1** to go or move in different directions; branch off **2** to differ, as in opinion —**di·ver'gence** ***n.*** —**di·ver'gent** ***adj.***

di·vers (dī'vərz) ***adj.*** ⟦see fol.⟧ various

di·verse (də vurs', dī-) ***adj.*** ⟦< L *dis-*, apart + *vertere*, to turn⟧ **1** different **2** varied —**di·verse'ly** ***adv.***

di·ver·si·fy (də vur'sə fī') ***vt.*** **-fied', -fy'ing** **1** to make diverse; vary **2** to divide up (investments, etc.) among different companies, etc. —***vi.*** to expand product lines, etc. —**di·ver'si·fi·ca'tion** ***n.***

di·ver·sion (də vur'zhən, dī-) ***n.*** **1** a diverting or turning aside **2** distraction of attention **3** a pastime

di·ver'sion·ar'y ***adj.*** serving to divert or distract *[diversionary* tactics*]*

di·ver·si·ty (də vur'sə tē, dī-) ***n., pl.*** **-ties** **1** difference **2** variety

di·vert (də vurt', dī-) ***vt.*** ⟦see DIVERSE⟧ **1** to turn (a person or thing) aside from a course, etc. **2** to distract **3** to amuse

di·ver·tic·u·li·tis (dī'vər tik'yoo līt'is) ***n.*** ⟦< L *de-*, from + *vertere*, to turn + -ITIS⟧ inflammation of a sac (**di'ver·tic'u·lum**) opening out from a tubular organ or main cavity

di·vest (də vest', dī-) ***vt.*** ⟦< L *dis-*, from + *vestire*, to dress⟧ **1** to strip *of* clothing, etc. **2** to deprive *of* rank, rights, etc. **3** to rid *of* something unwanted

di·vide (də vīd') ***vt.*** **-vid'ed, -vid'ing** ⟦< L *dividere*⟧ **1** to separate into parts; sever **2** to classify **3** to make or

THESAURUS

parcel out, dole out, hand out, give away, assign, allocate, ration, appropriate, pay dividends, dish out, divvy up*; see also GIVE 1.—*Ant.* HOLD, keep, preserve.

distributed ***a.*** delivered, scattered, shared, dealt, divided, apportioned, assigned, awarded, sown, dispensed, dispersed, appropriated, budgeted, disbursed, disseminated, returned, rationed, given away, handed out, parceled out, spread.

distribution ***n.*** dispersal, allotment, partitioning, partition, dividing up, deal, circulation, disposal, apportioning, prorating, arrangement, scattering, dissemination, sorting, spreading, parceling out, handing out, peddling, assorting, occurrence, frequency, ordering, pattern, combination, relationship, appearance, configuration, scarcity, number, plenty, saturation, population, demographics, spread, concentration; see also DIVISION 1, 2, ORDER 3.—*Ant.* COLLECTION, retention, storage.

distributor ***n.*** wholesaler, jobber, merchant; see BUSINESSMAN.

district ***a.*** community, provincial, territorial; see LOCAL 1.

district ***n.*** neighborhood, community, vicinity; see AREA.

distrust ***v.*** mistrust, suspect, disbelieve; see DOUBT.

distrustful ***a.*** distrusting, doubting, fearful; see SUSPICIOUS 1.

disturb ***v.*** trouble, worry, agitate, perplex, rattle, startle, shake, amaze, astound, alarm, excite, arouse, badger, plague, fuss, perturb, vex, upset, outrage, molest, grieve, depress, distress, irk, ail, tire, provoke, afflict, irritate, pain, make uneasy, harass, exasperate, pique, gall, displease, complicate, involve, astonish, fluster, ruffle, burn up*; see also BOTHER 2, CONFUSE.—*Ant.* QUIET, calm, soothe.

disturbance ***n.*** **1** [Interpersonal disruption] quarrel, brawl, fisticuffs; see FIGHT 1. **2** [Physical disruption] turmoil, rampage, tumult, clamor, violence, restlessness, uproar, riot, disruption, agitation, turbulence, change, bother, stir, racket, ferment, spasm, convulsion, tremor, shock, explosion, eruption, earthquake, flood, shock wave, storm, whirl; see also TROUBLE. **3** [A political or social uprising] revolt, insurrection, riot; see REVOLUTION 2.

disturbed ***a.*** **1** [Disturbed physically] upset, disorganized, confused; see DISORDERED. **2** [Disturbed mentally] agitated, disquieted, upset; see TROUBLED.

disturbing ***a.*** disquieting, upsetting, tiresome, perturbing, bothersome, unpleasant, provoking, annoying, alarming, painful, discomforting, inauspicious, foreboding, aggravating, disagreeable, troublesome, worrisome, burdensome, trying, distressing, perplexing, frightening, startling, threatening, galling, difficult, severe, hard, inconvenient, discouraging, pessimistic, gloomy, depressing, irritating, harassing, unpropitious, dismaying, troubling, irksome, sinister, embarrassing, ruffling, agitating; see also OMINOUS.

disunite ***v.*** dissociate, disjoin, separate; see DIVIDE.

ditch ***n.*** canal, moat, furrow; see CHANNEL, TRENCH.

ditch* ***v.*** desert, forsake, leave; see ABANDON 2, DISCARD.

dive ***n.*** **1** [A sudden motion downward] plunge, leap, spring, nose dive, headlong leap, pitch, ducking, swim, swoop, dip; see also FALL 1, JUMP 1. **2** [*A cheap saloon, etc.] saloon, tavern, dump*; see BAR 2, RESTAURANT.

dive ***v.*** plunge, spring, jump, vault, leap, go headfirst, plummet, sink, dip, duck, dabble, submerge, nose-dive; see also FALL 1, JUMP 1.

diver ***n.*** high diver, fancy diver, submarine diver, deep-sea diver, aquanaut, pearl diver, skin diver, scuba diver, swimmer, frogman; see also ATHLETE.

diverge ***v.*** radiate, veer, swerve; see DEVIATE.

diverse ***a.*** different, assorted, distinct; see VARIOUS.

diversify ***v.*** vary, expand, alter; see CHANGE 2, INCREASE.

diversion ***n.*** **1** [The act of changing a course] detour, alteration, deviation; see CHANGE 1. **2** [Entertainment] amusement, recreation, pastime; see ENTERTAINMENT, SPORT 1.

divert ***v.*** **1** [To deflect] turn aside, redirect, avert; see TURN 3. **2** [To distract] attract the attention of, lead away from, disturb; see DISTRACT.

diverted ***a.*** deflected, turned aside, redirected, perverted, averted, turned into other channels, rechanneled, taken away, made use of, taken over; see also CHANGED 2.—*Ant.* UNTOUCHED, undiverted, left.

divide ***v.*** part, cut up, fence off, detach, disengage, dissolve, sever, rupture, dismember, sunder, split, unravel, carve, cleave, intersect, cross, bisect, rend, tear, segment, halve, quarter, break down, divorce, dissociate, isolate, count off, pull away, chop, slash, gash, carve, splinter, pull to pieces, tear apart, break

keep separate **4** to apportion **5** to cause to disagree **6** *Math.* to separate into equal parts by a divisor —***vi.*** **1** to be or become separate **2** to disagree **3** to share **4** *Math.* to do division —***n.*** a boundary; specif., a ridge that divides two drainage areas —**di·vid′er** ***n.***

div·i·dend (div′ə dend′) ***n.*** **1** the number or quantity to be divided **2** *a)* a sum to be divided among stockholders, etc. *b)* a single share of this **3** a bonus

div·i·na·tion (div′ə nā′shən) ***n.*** ⟦see fol.⟧ **1** the practice of trying to foretell the future **2** a prophecy

di·vine (də vīn′) ***adj.*** ⟦< L *divus*, god⟧ **1** of, like, or from God or a god; holy **2** devoted to God; religious **3** [Inf.] very pleasing, etc. —***n.*** a member of the clergy —***vt.*** **-vined′**, **-vin′ing** **1** to prophesy **2** to guess **3** to find out by intuition —**di·vine′ly** ***adv.***

divining rod a forked stick believed to dip downward when held over an underground supply of water, etc.

di·vin·i·ty (də vin′ə tē) ***n.*** **1** a being divine **2** *pl.* **-ties** a god **3** theology —**the Divinity** God

di·vis·i·ble (də viz′ə bəl) ***adj.*** that can be divided, esp. without leaving a remainder —**di·vis′i·bil′i·ty** ***n.***

di·vi·sion (də vizh′ən) ***n.*** **1** a dividing or being divided **2** an apportioning **3** a difference of opinion **4** anything that divides **5** a segment, section, department, class, etc. **6** the process of finding how many times a number (the *divisor*) is contained in another (the *dividend*) **7** a major military unit

di·vi·sive (də vī′siv) ***adj.*** causing disagreement or dissension —**di·vi′sive·ly** ***adv.*** —**di·vi′sive·ness** ***n.***

di·vi·sor (də vī′zər) ***n.*** the number by which the dividend is divided

di·vorce (də vôrs′) ***n.*** ⟦< L *dis-*, apart + *vertere*, to turn⟧ **1** legal dissolution of a marriage **2** any complete separation —***vt.*** **-vorced′**, **-vorc′ing** **1** to dissolve legally a marriage between **2** to dissolve the marriage with (one's spouse) **3** to separate —**di·vorce′ment** ***n.***

di·vor·cée or **di·vor·cee** (di vôr′sā′, -sē′) ***fem.n.*** ⟦Fr⟧ a divorced woman —**di·vor′cé′** (-sā′, -sē′) ***masc.n.***

div·ot (div′ət) ***n.*** ⟦Scot⟧ *Golf* a lump of turf dislodged in making a stroke

di·vulge (də vulj′) ***vt.*** **-vulged′**, **-vulg′ing** ⟦< L *dis-*, apart + *vulgare*, make public⟧ to make known; reveal

div·vy (div′ē) ***vt.***, ***vi.*** **-vied**, **-vy·ing** [Slang] to share; divide (*up*)

Dix·ie (dik′sē) ⟦< *Dixie*, the minstrel song⟧ the Southern states of the U.S.

Dix′ie·land′ ***adj.*** in, of, or like a style of jazz with a ragtime tempo

DIY (dē′ī′wī′) ***n.*** DO-IT-YOURSELF

diz·zy (diz′ē) ***adj.*** **-zi·er**, **-zi·est** ⟦OE *dysig*, foolish⟧ **1** feeling giddy or unsteady **2** causing giddiness **3** confused **4** [Inf.] silly; harebrained —**diz′zi·ly** ***adv.*** —**diz′zi·ness** ***n.***

DJ (dē′jā′) *abbrev.* ***n.*** DISC JOCKEY

djel·la·ba or **djel·la·bah** (jə lä′bə) ***n.*** ⟦< Ar⟧ a long, loose outer garment worn in Arabic countries

Dji·bou·ti (ji bo͞ot′ē) country in E Africa: 8,958 sq. mi.; pop. 695,000

DMZ *abbrev.* demilitarized zone

DNA (dē′en′ā′) ***n.*** ⟦< *d(eoxyribo)n(ucleic) a(cid)*⟧ the basic chromosome material, containing and transmitting the hereditary pattern

Dne·pr (nē′pər) river in W Russia, Belarus, & Ukraine, flowing into the Black Sea

do[1] (do͞o) ***vt.*** **did**, **done**, **do′ing** ⟦OE *don*⟧ **1** to perform (an action, etc.) **2** to complete; finish **3** to cause */it does* no harm*/* **4** to exert */do* your best*/* **5** to deal with as is required */do* the ironing*/* **6** to have as one's occupation; work at **7** to move at a speed of */to do* 65 mph*/* **8** [Inf.] to serve (a jail term) **9** [Slang] to ingest */to do* drugs*/* —***vi.*** **1** to behave or perform */do* as you please*/* **2** to be active */up and doing/* **3** to get along; fare */he is doing* well after surgery*/* **4** to be adequate */casual dress will do/* **5** to take place */anything doing* tonight?*/* —***v.aux.*** **1** used to give emphasis */do* stay a while*/* **2** used to ask a question */did* you go?*/* **3** used as a substitute verb */act* as I *do* (act)*/* **4** used in a negative construction */do* not go*/* —**do in** **1** [Slang] to kill **2** [Inf.] to tire out —**do over** [Inf.] to redecorate —**do up** to wrap up —**do with** to make use of —**do without** to get along without —**have to do with** to be related to

do[2] (dō) ***n.*** ⟦It⟧ *Music* the first or last tone of the diatonic scale

DOA *abbrev.* dead on arrival

do·a·ble (do͞o′ə bəl) ***adj.*** that can be done

Do·ber·man (pin·scher) (dō′bər mən pin′chər) ⟦< Ger after L. *Dobermann*, 19th-c. breeder + *pinscher*, terrier⟧ a large dog with a short, dark coat

doc (däk) ***n.*** [Slang] doctor

do·cent (dō′sənt) ***n.*** ⟦< L *docere*, to teach⟧ a lecturer or tour guide, as at a museum

doc·ile (däs′əl) ***adj.*** ⟦see prec.⟧ easy to discipline; submissive —**do·cil·i·ty** (dō sil′ə tē, dä-) ***n.***

dock[1] (däk) ***n.*** ⟦< It *doccia*, canal⟧ **1** an excavated basin for receiving ships **2** a wharf; pier **3** the water between two piers **4** a platform for loading and unloading trucks, etc. —***vt.***, ***vi.*** to bring or come to or into a dock: said of a ship

THESAURUS

apart, segregate, fork, branch, tear limb from limb*, split off, split up; see also BREAK 1, CUT 1, SEPARATE 1.—*Ant.* UNITE, combine, connect.

dividend ***n.*** pay, check, coupon, proceeds, returns, quarterly dividend, annual dividend, share, allotment, appropriation, remittance, allowance, cut*, rakeoff*; see also PROFIT 2.

divine ***a.*** sacred, hallowed, spiritual, sacramental, ceremonial, ritualistic, consecrated, dedicated, devoted, venerable, pious, religious, anointed, sanctified, ordained, sanctioned, set apart, sacrosanct, scriptural, blessed, worshiped, revered, venerated, mystical, adored, solemn, faithful; see also HOLY.

divine ***v.*** predict, prophesy, prognosticate; see FORETELL.

divinity ***n.*** deity, godhead, higher power; see GOD, GOD.

divisible ***a.*** separable, distinguishable, distinct, divided, fractional, fragmentary, detachable; see also SEPARATED.—*Ant.* INSEPARABLE, indivisible, fast.

division ***n.*** **1** [The act or result of dividing] separation, detachment, apportionment, partition, parting, distribution, severance, cutting, subdivision, dismemberment, distinction, distinguishing, selection, reduction, splitting, breakdown, fracture, disjuncture.—*Ant.* UNION, joining, gluing. **2** [A part produced by dividing] section, kind, sort, portion, compartment, share, split, member, subdivision, parcel, segment, fragment, department, category, branch, fraction, cross-section, dividend, degree, piece, slice, lump, wedge, cut, book, chapter, verse, class, race, clan, tribe, caste; see also PART 1. **3** [Discord or disunion] trouble, dissension, schism; see DISAGREEMENT 1, DISPUTE. **4** [A military unit] armored division, airborne division, infantry division; see ARMY 2. **5** [An organized area] state, district, province; see NATION.

divorce ***n.*** separation, partition, divorcement, bill of divorcement, annulment, separate maintenance, parting of the ways, dissolution, split-up.—*Ant.* MARRIAGE, betrothal, wedding.

divorce ***v.*** separate, annul, nullify, put away, split up; see also CANCEL.

divorced ***a.*** dissolved, parted, disunited, divided, split, washed-up*; see also SEPARATED.—*Ant.* MARRIED, joined, mated.

divulge ***v.*** disclose, impart, confess; see ADMIT 2, EXPOSE 1.

dizzy ***a.*** confused, lightheaded, giddy, bemused, staggering, upset, dazzled, dazed, dumb, faint, with spots before one's eyes, out of control, weak-kneed, wobbly; see also UNSTABLE 1.

DNA ***n.*** genetic alphabet, double helix, chromosome, gene, hereditary information, deoxyribonucleic acid, nucleic acids, genetic code.

do[1] ***v.*** **1** [To discharge one's responsibilities] effect, execute, act, finish, complete, work, labor, produce, create, effect, accomplish; see also ACHIEVE, PERFORM 1, SUCCEED 1. **2** [To execute commands or instructions] carry out, complete, fulfill; see OBEY. **3** [To suffice] serve, be sufficient, give satisfaction; see SATISFY 3. **4** [To solve] figure out, work out, decipher, decode; see also SOLVE. **5** [To present a play, etc.] give, put on, produce; see PERFORM 2. **6** [To act] perform, portray, take on the role of; see ACT 3. **7** [To conduct oneself] behave oneself, comport oneself, acquit oneself, seem, appear; see also BEHAVE. —**do in*** eliminate, slay, murder; see DESTROY, KILL 1. —**do without** dispense with, get along without, forgo; see ENDURE 1, 2, NEED. —**have to do with** be related to, be connected with, bear on; see CONCERN 1. —**make do** get by, get along, manage, survive; see also ENDURE 2.

docile ***a.*** meek, mild, tractable, pliant, submissive, accommodating, adaptable, resigned, agreeable, willing, obliging, well-behaved, manageable, tame, yielding, teachable, easily influenced, easygoing, usable, soft, childlike; see also GENTLE 3, HUMBLE 1, OBEDIENT 1.

docility ***n.*** obedience, gentleness, adaptability; see HUMILITY, SHYNESS.

dock[1] ***n.*** pier, wharf, lock, boat landing, marina, dry dock, embarcadero, waterfront.

dock[2] (däk) ***n.*** ⟦< Fl *dok*, a cage⟧ the place where the accused stands or sits in court

dock[3] (däk) ***n.*** ⟦OE *docce*⟧ a tall, coarse weed of the buckwheat family

dock[4] (däk) ***vt.*** ⟦ME *dok*, tail⟧ **1** to cut off the end of (a tail, etc.); bob **2** to deduct from (wages, etc.)

dock·et (däk′it) ***n.*** ⟦< ?⟧ **1** a list of cases to be tried by a law court **2** an agenda —***vt.*** to enter in a docket

dock′yard′ ***n.*** SHIPYARD

doc·tor (däk′tər) ***n.*** ⟦< L, teacher⟧ **1** one who holds a doctorate **2** a physician or surgeon **3** one licensed to practice any of the healing arts —***vt.*** [Inf.] **1** to try to heal **2** to tamper with

doc′tor·ate (-it) ***n.*** the highest degree awarded by universities —**doc′tor·al** ***adj.***

Doctor of Philosophy the highest doctorate awarded for original research

doc·tri·naire (däk′tri ner′) ***adj.*** ⟦Fr⟧ adhering to a doctrine dogmatically —**doc′tri·nair′ism′** ***n.***

doc·trine (däk′trin) ***n.*** ⟦see DOCTOR⟧ something taught, esp. as the principles of a religion, political party, etc.; tenet or tenets; dogma —**doc′tri·nal** (-tri nəl) ***adj.***

doc·u·dra·ma (däk′yo͞o drä′mə) ***n.*** a TV dramatization of real events

doc·u·ment (däk′yo͞o mənt, -yə-; *for v.*, -ment′) ***n.*** ⟦< L *documentum*, proof⟧ anything printed, written, etc. that contains information or is relied upon to record or prove something —***vt.*** to provide with or support by documents

doc′u·men′ta·ry (-ment′ə rē) ***adj.*** **1** of or supported by documents **2** depicting news events, social conditions, etc. in nonfictional but dramatic form —***n.***, *pl.* **-ries** a documentary film, etc.

doc′u·men·ta′tion (-mən tā′shən, -men-) ***n.*** **1** the supplying of documents **2** the documents thus supplied **3** instructions for using computer hardware or software

dod·der (däd′ər) ***vi.*** ⟦ME *daderen*⟧ **1** to shake or tremble, as from old age **2** to totter —**dod′der·ing** ***adj.***

dodge (däj) ***vi.***, ***vt.*** **dodged**, **dodg′ing** ⟦< ?⟧ **1** to move quickly aside, or avoid by so moving **2** to use tricks or evasions, or evade by so doing —***n.*** **1** a dodging **2** a trick used in evading or cheating —**dodg′er** ***n.***

do·do (dō′dō) ***n.***, *pl.* **-dos** or **-does** ⟦Port *doudo*, lit., stupid⟧ **1** a large, flightless bird, now extinct **2** [Slang] a stupid person

doe (dō) ***n.*** ⟦OE *da*⟧ the female deer, antelope, rabbit, etc.

do·er (do͞o′ər) ***n.*** **1** one who does something **2** one who gets things done

does (duz) ***vt.***, ***vi.*** *3d pers. sing., pres. indic., of* DO[1]

doe′skin′ ***n.*** **1** leather from the skin of a female deer **2** a soft woolen cloth

doff (däf, dôf) ***vt.*** ⟦see DO[1] & OFF⟧ to take off (one's hat, clothes, etc.)

dog (dôg) ***n.*** ⟦OE *docga*⟧ **1** any of various canines, esp. one of a domesticated breed kept as a pet, for hunting, etc. **2** a mean, contemptible fellow **3** [*pl.*] [Slang] feet **4** [Slang] an unattractive person or unsatisfactory thing **5** *Mech.* a device for holding or grappling —***vt.*** **dogged**, **dog′ging** to follow or hunt doggedly —**go to the dogs** [Inf.] to deteriorate

dog days the hot, uncomfortable days in July and August

dog′-ear′ ***n.*** a turned-down corner of a page —**dog′-eared′** ***adj.***

dog′fight′ ***n.*** a violent fight; specif., combat between fighter planes

dog′fish′ ***n.***, *pl.* **-fish′** or (for different species) **-fish′es** any of various small sharks

dog·ged (dôg′id) ***adj.*** persistent; stubborn —**dog′ged·ly** ***adv.***

dog·ger·el (dôg′ər əl) ***n.*** ⟦ME *dogerel*⟧ trivial poetry with a monotonous rhythm

dog·gie bag (dôg′ē) a bag supplied by a restaurant for carrying leftovers, as for one's dog

dog′gone′ ***interj.*** damn! darn! —***adj.*** [Inf.] damned

dog′house′ ***n.*** a structure for sheltering a dog —**in the doghouse** [Slang] in disfavor

do·gie (dō′gē) ***n.*** ⟦< ?⟧ [West] a stray calf

dog·ma (dôg′mə) ***n.*** ⟦< Gr, opinion⟧ a doctrine; tenet, esp. a theological doctrine strictly adhered to

dog·mat′ic (-mat′ik) ***adj.*** **1** of or like dogma **2** asserted without proof **3** stating opinion positively or arrogantly —**dog·mat′i·cal·ly** ***adv.***

dog′ma·tism′ (-mə tiz′əm) ***n.*** dogmatic assertion of opinion —**dog′ma·tist** ***n.***

do′-good′er ***n.*** [Inf.] an idealistic, but impractical person who seeks to correct social ills

dog′-tired′ ***adj.*** very tired; exhausted

dog′trot′ ***n.*** a slow, easy trot

dog′wood′ ***n.*** a small, flowering tree of the E U.S.

doi·ly (doi′lē) ***n.***, *pl.* **-lies** ⟦after a 17th-c. London draper⟧ a small mat, as of lace, put under a vase, etc. as a decoration or to protect a surface

do·ings (do͞o′iŋz) ***pl.n.*** actions or events

do′-it-your·self′ ***n.*** the practice of making or repairing things oneself, instead of hiring another —**do′-it-your·self′er** ***n.***

Dol·by (dōl′bē) ⟦after R. *Dolby*, U.S. recording engineer⟧ *trademark for* an electronic system used to reduce unwanted noise

dol·drums (dōl′drəmz, däl′-) ***pl.n.*** ⟦< ? DULL⟧ **1** *a)* low spirits *b)* sluggishness **2** equatorial ocean regions having little wind

dole (dōl) ***n.*** ⟦OE *dal*, a share⟧ **1** money or food given in charity **2** money paid by a government to the unemployed —***vt.*** **doled**, **dol′ing** to give (*out*) sparingly or as a dole

dole′ful (-fəl) ***adj.*** ⟦< L *dolere*, suffer⟧ sad; mournful —**dole′ful·ly** ***adv.***

THESAURUS

dock[4] ***v.*** lessen, withhold, deduct; see DECREASE 2.

doctor ***n.*** Doctor of Medicine, MD, physician, general practitioner, GP, surgeon, consultant, specialist, intern, house physician, resident, veterinarian, chiropractor, homeopath, osteopath, acupuncturist, faith healer, witch doctor, shaman, medicine man, quack, doc*, sawbones*. *Types of doctors include the following:* heart specialist; ear, nose, and throat specialist; inhalation therapist, anesthetist, dentist, pediatrician, gynecologist, oculist, obstetrician, psychiatrist, psychoanalyst, orthopedist, neurologist, cardiologist, pathologist, dermatologist, endocrinologist, ophthalmologist, urologist, hematologist; see also MEDICINE 3.

doctor* ***v.*** tamper with, change, adulterate; see ALTER 1.

doctrine ***n.*** principle, proposition, precept, article, concept, conviction, opinion, convention, attitude, tradition, unwritten law, natural law, common law, teachings, accepted belief, article of faith, canon, regulation, rule, pronouncement, declaration; see also LAW 2, 4.

document ***n.*** paper, diary, report; see RECORD 1.

dodge ***n.*** trick, strategy, scheme; see METHOD, PLAN 1.

dodge ***v.*** duck, elude, evade; see AVOID.

doer ***n.*** actor, performer, activist; see MEANS 1.

dog ***n.*** hound, bitch, puppy, pup, mongrel, stray, canine, cur, guide dog, watchdog, pooch*, mutt*. *Types and breeds of dogs include the following:* hunting dog, racing dog, boxer, shepherd, bloodhound, wolfhound, greyhound, whippet, Saint Bernard, Great Dane, German shepherd, Doberman pinscher, bulldog, Afghan, Irish wolfhound, Labrador retriever, Rottweiler, malamute, husky, collie, Old English sheep dog, Irish setter, pointer, spaniel, cocker spaniel, basset, beagle, dachshund, Dalmatian, poodle, French poodle, Pekingese, Pomeranian, Chihuahua, Airedale, schnauzer, fox terrier, wirehaired terrier, Scottie, Scottish terrier, bull terrier, Boston terrier. —**a dog's life** wretched existence, bad luck, trouble; see POVERTY 1. —**go to the dogs*** deteriorate, degenerate, weaken; see WEAKEN 1, 2. —**let sleeping dogs lie** ignore, leave well enough alone, pass over; see NEGLECT 1. —**put on the dog*** show off, entertain lavishly, put on airs; see DISPLAY. —**teach an old dog new tricks** influence, convince, change; see PERSUADE.

dogged ***a.*** stubborn, tenacious, firm; see STUBBORN.

dogmatic ***a.*** **1** [Based on an assumption of absolute truth] authoritarian, on faith, by nature; see ABSOLUTE 1. **2** [Acting as though possessed of absolute truth] dictatorial, stubborn, egotistical, bigoted, fanatical, intolerant, opinionated, overbearing, magisterial, arrogant, domineering, tyrannical, obstinate, confident, sure, downright, arbitrary, unequivocal, definite, formal, stubborn, determined, emphatic, narrow-minded, one-sided, hidebound, high and mighty*, pigheaded, bullheaded, stubborn as a mule*; see also ABSOLUTE 2.—*Ant.* LIBERAL, tolerant, dubious.

doing ***n.*** performing, accomplishing, achieving; see PERFORMANCE.

doings ***n.*** activities, conduct, dealings; see ACTION 1.

dole out ***v.*** share, assign, parcel out; see DISTRIBUTE.

doll (däl) ***n.*** ⟦< nickname for *Dorothy*⟧ **1** a child's toy made to resemble a human being **2** [Slang] any attractive or lovable person —***vt.***, ***vi.*** [Inf.] to dress stylishly or showily: with *up*

dol·lar (däl'ər) ***n.*** ⟦< Ger *thaler*, a coin⟧ **1** the monetary unit of the U.S., equal to 100 cents **2** the monetary unit of various other countries, as of Canada **3** a piece of money worth one dollar

dol·lop (däl'əp) ***n.*** ⟦< ?⟧ **1** a soft mass **2** a quantity, often a small one

dol·ly (däl'ē) ***n.***, *pl.* **-lies** **1** a doll: child's word **2** a low, flat, wheeled frame for moving heavy objects

dol·men (dōl'mən, däl'-) ***n.*** ⟦Fr⟧ a prehistoric monument consisting of a large, flat stone laid across upright stones

do·lo·mite (dō'lə mīt', däl'ə-) ***n.*** ⟦after D. *Dolomieu*, 18th-c. Fr geologist⟧ **1** a mineral used in making cement, etc. **2** a sedimentary rock used as a building stone

do·lor·ous (dō'lər əs, däl'ər-) ***adj.*** ⟦< L *dolere*, suffer⟧ sorrowful; sad —**do'lor·ous·ly** ***adv.***

dol·phin (däl'fin, dôl'-) ***n.*** ⟦< Gr *delphis*⟧ a highly intelligent toothed whale with a beaklike snout

dolt (dōlt) ***n.*** ⟦prob. < ME *dolte*⟧ a stupid person —**dolt'ish** ***adj.***

-dom (dəm) ⟦OE *dom*, state⟧ *suffix* **1** rank or domain of *[kingdom]* **2** fact or state of being *[martyrdom]* **3** all who are *[officialdom]*

do·main (dō mān') ***n.*** ⟦< L *dominus*, a lord⟧ **1** territory under one government or ruler **2** field of activity or influence

dome (dōm) ***n.*** ⟦< Gr *dōma*, housetop⟧ **1** a rounded roof or ceiling **2** any dome-shaped structure or object; specif., a sports stadium covered with a dome

do·mes·tic (dō mes'tik, də-) ***adj.*** ⟦< L *domus*, house⟧ **1** of the home or family **2** of or made in one's country **3** tame: said of animals **4** enjoying family life —***n.*** a maid, cook, etc. in the home —**do·mes'ti·cal·ly** ***adv.***

do·mes'ti·cate' (-ti kāt') ***vt.*** **-cat'ed**, **-cat'ing** **1** to accustom to home life **2** to tame or cultivate for human use —**do·mes'ti·ca'tion** ***n.***

do·mes·tic·i·ty (dō'mes tis'ə tē) ***n.*** home life or devotion to it

dom·i·cile (däm'ə sīl', -sil; *also* dō'mə-) ***n.*** ⟦< L *domus*, home⟧ a home; residence —***vt.*** **-ciled'**, **-cil'ing** to establish in a domicile

dom·i·nant (däm'ə nənt) ***adj.*** dominating; ruling; prevailing —**dom'i·nance** ***n.*** —**dom'i·nant·ly** ***adv.***

dom'i·nate' (-nāt') ***vt.***, ***vi.*** **-nat'ed**, **-nat'ing** ⟦< L *dominus*, a master⟧ **1** to rule or control by superior power **2** to rise above (the surroundings) —**dom'i·na'tion** ***n.***

dom·i·neer (däm'ə nir') ***vi.***, ***vt.*** ⟦< Du: see prec.⟧ to rule (*over*) in a harsh or arrogant way; tyrannize

dom'i·neer'ing ***adj.*** overbearing

Do·min·i·can Republic (dō min'i kən, də-) country in the E part of Hispaniola, in the West Indies: 18,700 sq. mi.; pop. 5,648,000 —**Do·min'i·can** ***adj.***, ***n.***

do·min·ion (də min'yən) ***n.*** ⟦see DOMINATE⟧ **1** rule or power to rule **2** a governed territory or country **3** [**D-**] [Historical] a self-governing nation of the Commonwealth

dom·i·no (däm'ə nō') ***n.***, *pl.* **-noes'** or **-nos'** ⟦Fr & It⟧ **1** a hooded cloak and a mask, worn at masquerades **2** a small mask that covers the area around the eyes **3** *a)* a small, oblong tile marked with dots *b)* [*pl.*, *with sing. v.*] a game played with such tiles

don[1] (dän) ***n.*** ⟦Sp < L *dominus*, master⟧ **1** [**D-**] Sir; Mr.: a Spanish title of respect **2** a Spanish gentleman **3** [Chiefly Brit.] a teacher at a British university **4** a Mafia leader

don[2] (dän) ***vt.*** **donned**, **don'ning** ⟦contr. of *do on*⟧ to put on (clothes)

Don (dän) river in SC European Russia, flowing into the Black Sea

Do·ña (dô'nyä) ***n.*** ⟦Sp⟧ Lady; Madam: a Spanish title of respect

do·nate (dō'nāt') ***vt.***, ***vi.*** **-nat'ed**, **-nat'ing** ⟦< L *donum*, gift⟧ to give or contribute —**do·na'tion** ***n.*** —**do'nat'or** (-ər) ***n.***

done (dun) ***vt.***, ***vi.*** *pp. of* DO[1] —***adj.*** **1** completed **2** cooked —**done (for)** [Inf.] dead, ruined, etc.

Don Juan (dän' wän') *Sp. Legend* a dissolute nobleman and seducer of women

don·key (däŋ'kē, dôŋ'-, duŋ'-) ***n.***, *pl.* **-keys** ⟦< ?⟧ **1** a domesticated ass **2** a stupid or foolish person

don·ny·brook (dän'ē brook') ***n.*** ⟦after a fair formerly held near Dublin⟧ [Inf.] a rowdy fight or free-for-all

do·nor (dō'nər, -nôr') ***n.*** one who donates

Don Qui·xo·te (dän'kē hōt'ē, dän' kwik'sət) **1** a satirical novel by Cervantes **2** its chivalrous but unrealistic hero

don't (dōnt) *contr.* do not

do·nut (dō'nut') ***n.*** *inf. sp. of* DOUGHNUT

doo·dle (do͞od''l) ***vi.*** **-dled**, **-dling** ⟦Ger *dudeln*, to trifle⟧ to scribble aimlessly —***n.*** a mark made in doodling —**doo'dler** ***n.***

doo-doo (do͞o'do͞o') ***n.*** **1** [Inf.] excrement **2** [Slang] trouble

doom (do͞om) ***n.*** ⟦OE *dom*⟧ **1** a judgment; sentence **2** fate **3** ruin or death —***vt.*** **1** to pass judgment on; condemn **2** to destine to a tragic fate

dooms'day' ***n.*** Judgment Day

doom'y ***adj.*** filled with a sense of doom or disaster

door (dôr) ***n.*** ⟦OE *duru*⟧ **1** a movable structure for opening or closing an entrance **2** a doorway **3** a means of access —**out of doors** outdoors

door'bell' ***n.*** a bell, etc. at the entrance of a building or room, sounded to alert the occupants of a visitor

door'man' (-man', -mən) ***n.***, *pl.* **-men'** (-men', -mən) one whose work is opening the door of a building, hailing taxicabs, etc.

door'mat' ***n.*** a mat to wipe the shoes on before entering a house, etc.

door'step' ***n.*** a step that leads from an outer door to a path, lawn, etc.

door'-to-door' ***adj.***, ***adv.*** from one home to the next, calling on each in turn

door'way' ***n.*** **1** an opening in a wall that can be closed by a door **2** any means of access

THESAURUS

doll ***n.*** manikin, model, dolly, rag doll, paper doll, kewpie doll, Barbie (trademark); see also TOY 1.

dollar ***n.*** coin, legal tender, dollar bill, silver dollar, currency, bank note, greenback, folding money*, buck*; see also MONEY 1.

dollop ***n.*** blob, touch, dab; see DASH 3, BIT 1.

doll up ***v.*** fix up, put on one's best clothes, primp; see DRESS 1.

dolt ***n.*** simpleton, nitwit, blockhead; see FOOL.

domain ***n.*** dominion, field, specialty; see AREA.

dome ***n.*** ceiling, top, vault; see ROOF.

domestic ***a.*** **1** [Home-loving] house-loving, domesticated, stay-at-home, settled, household, family, quiet, private, sedentary, indoor, tame; see also CALM 1, 2, TRANQUIL.—*Ant.* UNRULY, roving, restless. **2** [Homegrown] indigenous, handcrafted, native; see HOMEMADE.

domesticate ***v.*** tame, breed, housebreak; see TEACH, TRAIN 2.

domesticated ***a.*** tamed, trained, housebroken; see TAME 1.

dominant ***a.*** commanding, authoritative, assertive; see AGGRESSIVE, POWERFUL 1.

dominate ***v.*** rule, manage, control, dictate to, subject, subjugate, tyrannize, have one's own way, have influence over, domineer, bully, walk all over*, boss*, keep under one's thumb; see also GOVERN.

domination ***n.*** rule, control, mastery; see COMMAND, POWER 2.

domineering ***a.*** despotic, imperious, oppressive; see EGOTISTIC.

dominion ***n.*** region, district, state; see AREA, NATION 1.

donate ***v.*** grant, bestow, bequeath; see DISTRIBUTE, GIVE 1, PROVIDE 1.

donation ***n.*** contribution, offering, present; see GIFT 1.

done ***a.*** **1** [Accomplished] over, through, completed, realized, effected, actualized, executed, performed, fulfilled, brought to pass, brought about, perfected; see also FINISHED 1.—*Ant.* UNFINISHED, unrealized, failed. **2** [Cooked] brewed, stewed, broiled, boiled, crisped, crusted, fried, browned, roasted, grilled; see also BAKED.—*Ant.* RAW, fresh, uncooked. **—done for*** defeated, conquered, vanquished; see BEATEN 1.

Don Juan ***n.*** Lothario, womanizer, Romeo, libertine, philanderer, rake, seducer, lecher, wolf*.

donkey ***n.*** burro, mule, jackass; see HORSE.

donor ***n.*** benefactor, contributor, patron, humanitarian, philanthropist, giver, subscriber, altruist, good Samaritan, fairy godmother*, angel*, sugar daddy*; see also PATRON.

doom ***n.*** fate, lot, destiny, downfall, future, fortune, ruin, goal.

doomed ***a.*** ruined, cursed, sentenced, lost, condemned, unfortunate, ill-fated, foreordained, predestined, threatened, menaced, suppressed, wrecked; see also DESTROYED, FATED.

door ***n.*** entry, portal, hatchway, doorway, gateway, opening; see also ENTRANCE 2, GATE. **—out of doors** outside, in the air, out; see OUTDOORS. **—show someone the door** show out, ask to leave, dismiss; see OUST.

door'yard' *n.* a yard onto which a door of a house opens
do·pa (dō'pə) *n.* ⟦< chemical name⟧ an amino acid that is converted by an enzyme in the blood into certain biological chemicals: one isomer (*L-dopa*) is used in treating Parkinson's disease
dope (dōp) *n.* ⟦Du *doop*, sauce⟧ **1** any thick liquid used as a lubricant, varnish, filler, etc. **2** [Inf.] a drug or narcotic **3** [Inf.] a stupid person **4** [Slang] information —*vt.* **doped, dop'ing** to drug
dop'er *n.* [Slang] a drug addict
dop·ey or **dop·y** (dō'pē) *adj.* **-i·er, -i·est** [Inf.] **1** lethargic **2** stupid
Dor·ic (dôr'ik) *adj.* designating or of a classical style of architecture marked by fluted columns with plain capitals
dorm (dôrm) *n.* [Inf.] DORMITORY
dor·mant (dôr'mənt) *adj.* ⟦< L *dormire*, to sleep⟧ **1** inactive **2** *Biol.* in a resting or torpid state —**dor'man·cy** *n.*
dor·mer (dôr'mər) *n.* ⟦see prec.⟧ **1** a window set upright in a structure projecting from a sloping roof: also **dormer window 2** such a structure
dor·mi·to·ry (dôr'mə tôr'ē) *n., pl.* **-ries** ⟦see DORMANT⟧ **1** a room with beds for a number of people **2** a building with rooms for many people to sleep and live in, as at a college
dor·mouse (dôr'mous') *n., pl.* **-mice'** (-mīs') ⟦ME *dormous*⟧ a small, furry-tailed Old World rodent
dor·sal (dôr'səl) *adj.* ⟦< L *dorsum*, the back⟧ of, on, or near the back
do·ry (dôr'ē) *n., pl.* **-ries** ⟦< ? AmInd (Central America) *dori*, dugout⟧ a flat-bottomed fishing boat with high sides
dose (dōs) *n.* ⟦< Gr *dosis*, a giving⟧ an amount of a medicine to be taken at one time —*vt.* **dosed, dos'ing** to give doses to —**dos'age** *n.*
do·sim·e·ter (dō sim'ət ər) *n.* a device for measuring exposure to ionizing radiation
dos·si·er (dä'sē ā') *n.* ⟦Fr⟧ a collection of documents about some person or matter
dost (dust) *vt., vi. archaic 2d pers. sing., pres. indic., of* DO[1]: used with *thou*
Dos·to·ev·ski or **Dos·to·yev·sky** (dôs'tô yef'skē), **Feo·dor** (fyô'dôr) 1821-81; Russ. novelist
dot (dät) *n.* ⟦OE *dott*, head of boil⟧ **1** a tiny speck or mark **2** a small, round spot —*vt.* **dot'ted, dot'ting** to mark with or as with a dot or dots —**on the dot** [Inf.] at the exact time
dot·age (dōt'ij) *n.* ⟦ME < *doten*, DOTE⟧ childish state due to old age
dot'ard (-ərd) *n.* one in his or her dotage
dot.com (dät'käm') *adj.* [Inf.] designating or of a company doing business mostly on the Web: also **dot-com**
dote (dōt) *vi.* **dot'ed, dot'ing** ⟦ME *doten*⟧ to be excessively fond: with *on* or *upon*
doth (duth) *vt., vi. archaic 3d pers. sing., pres. indic., of* DO[1]
dot·ing (dōt'iŋ) *adj.* foolishly or excessively fond —**dot'ing·ly** *adv.*
dot'-ma'trix *adj.* of or by printing in which characters are formed of closely spaced dots
Dou·ay Bible (do͞o ā') an English version of the Bible for Roman Catholics: after Douai, France, where the Old Testament was published
dou·ble (dub'əl) *adj.* ⟦< L *duplus*⟧ **1** twofold **2** having two layers **3** paired or repeated *[a double consonant]* **4** being of two kinds *[a double standard]* **5** twice as much, as many, etc. **6** made for two —*adv.* **1** twofold or twice **2** two together —*n.* **1** anything twice as much, as many, etc. as normal **2** a duplicate; counterpart **3** a fold **4** [*pl.*] a game of tennis, etc. with two players on each side **5** *Baseball* a hit on which the batter reaches second base **6** *Bridge* the doubling of an opponent's bid —*vt.* **-bled, -bling 1** to make twice as much or as many **2** to fold **3** to repeat or duplicate **4** *Bridge* to increase the point value or penalty of (an opponent's bid) —*vi.* **1** to become double **2** to turn sharply backward **3** to serve as a double **4** to serve an additional purpose **5** *Baseball* to hit a double —**double back** to turn back in the direction from which one came —**double up 1** to clench (one's fist) **2** to bend over, as in pain **3** to share a room, etc. with someone —**on the double** [Inf.] quickly
double agent a spy employed by two rival espionage organizations
dou'ble-bar'reled *adj.* **1** having two barrels, as a kind of shotgun **2** having a double purpose or meaning
double bass (bās) the largest, deepest-toned instrument of the violin family
dou'ble-blind' *adj.* designating or of a test of the effects of a drug, treatment, etc. in which neither the subjects nor the researchers know who is receiving the drug, treatment, etc.
double boiler a cooking utensil in which one pan, for food, fits over another, for boiling water
dou'ble-breast'ed *adj.* overlapping across the breast, as a coat
dou'ble-cross' *vt.* [Inf.] to betray —**dou'ble-cross'er** *n.*
double date [Inf.] a social engagement shared by two couples —**dou'ble-date', -dat'ed, -dat'ing,** *vi., vt.*
dou'ble-deal'ing *n.* duplicity
dou'ble-deck'er *n.* **1** any structure or vehicle with an upper deck **2** [Inf.] a sandwich with two layers of filling and three slices of bread
dou'ble-dig'it *adj.* amounting to ten percent or more *[double-digit inflation]*
double dipping an unethical receiving of pay from two or more sources
dou·ble-en·ten·dre (dub'əl än tän'drə, do͞o'blôn tôn'drə) *n.* ⟦< Fr⟧ a term with two meanings, esp. when one is risqué
dou'ble-head'er *n.* two games played in succession on the same day
dou'ble-joint'ed *adj.* having joints that permit limbs, fingers, etc. to bend at other than the usual angles
dou'ble-knit' *adj.* knit with a double stitch that makes the fabric extra thick
double play *Baseball* a play in which two players are put out
dou'ble-reed' *adj.* designating or of a woodwind instrument, as the oboe, having two reeds separated by a narrow opening
double standard a system, code, etc. applied unequally; specif., a moral code stricter for women than for men
dou·blet (dub'lit) *n.* ⟦< OFr *double*, orig., something folded⟧ **1** a man's closefitting jacket of the 14th-16th c. **2** a pair, or one of a pair
double take a delayed reaction, as a second glance, following unthinking acceptance
double talk 1 ambiguous and deceptive talk **2** meaningless syllables made to sound like talk
dou·bloon (də blo͞on') *n.* ⟦< Fr < Sp < L *duplus*, double⟧ an obsolete Spanish gold coin
dou·bly (dub'lē) *adv.* **1** twice **2** two at a time
doubt (dout) *vi.* ⟦< L *dubius*, uncertain⟧ to be uncertain or undecided —*vt.* **1** to be uncertain about **2** to tend to

THESAURUS

dope *n.* **1** [*A drug] narcotic, stimulant, opiate; see DRUG. **2** [*Pertinent information] details, account, developments; see INFORMATION 1, KNOWLEDGE 1, NEWS 1. **3** [*A dull-witted person] dunce, dolt, simpleton; see FOOL.

dope *v.* anesthetize, drug, put to sleep; see DEADEN.

dormitory *n.* barracks, residence hall, dorm*; see HOTEL.

dose *n.* prescription, dosage, treatment, spoonful, portion; see also QUANTITY, SHARE.

dot *n.* point, spot, speck; see MARK 1. —**on the dot*** precisely, accurately, punctually; see PUNCTUAL.

dote *v.* adore, pet, admire; see LOVE 1.

double *a.* twofold, two times, paired, coupled, binary, doubled, redoubled, duplex, renewed, dual, both one and the other, repeated, second, increased, as much again, duplicated; see also TWICE, TWIN.—*Ant.* ALONE, single, apart. —**on the double*** hastily, rapidly, hurriedly; see QUICKLY.

double *v.* **1** [To make or become double] make twice as much, duplicate, multiply; see GROW 1, INCREASE. **2** [To replace] substitute, stand in, fill in; see SUBSTITUTE. —**double back** backtrack, reverse, circle; see RETURN 1, TURN 2, 6. —**double up** combine, join, share; see JOIN 1, 2, UNITE.

double-cross *v.* cheat, defraud, trick; see DECEIVE.

double-dealing *n.* deceit, cheating, trickery; see DISHONESTY, HYPOCRISY.

doubly *a.* twofold, redoubled, increased; see AGAIN, DOUBLE, TWICE.

doubt *n.* distrust, mistrust, disbelief, suspicion, misgiving, skepticism, apprehension, agnosticism, incredulity, lack of faith, lack of confidence, jealousy, rejection, scruple, reservation, misgiving, indecision, lack of conviction, ambiguity, dilemma, reluctance, quandary, feeling of inferiority; see also UNCERTAINTY 1, 2.—*Ant.* BELIEF, conviction, certainty. —**beyond** (or **without**) **doubt** doubtless, certainly, without a doubt; see SURELY. —**no doubt** doubtless, in all likelihood, certainly; see PROBABLY, SURELY.

disbelieve —*n.* 1 *a)* a wavering of opinion or belief *b)* lack of trust 2 a condition of uncertainty —**beyond** (or **without**) **doubt** certainly —**no doubt** 1 certainly 2 probably —**doubt'er** *n.* —**doubt'ing·ly** *adv.*

doubt'ful *adj.* 1 uncertain 2 causing doubt or suspicion 3 feeling doubt —**doubt'ful·ly** *adv.*

doubt'less *adv.* 1 without doubt; certainly 2 probably —**doubt'less·ly** *adv.*

douche (do͞osh) *n.* ⟦Fr < It *doccia*⟧ 1 a jet of liquid applied externally or internally to the body 2 a device for douching —*vt.*, *vi.* **douched, douch'ing** to apply a douche (to)

dough (dō) *n.* ⟦OE *dag*⟧ 1 a mixture of flour, liquid, etc. worked into a soft mass for baking 2 [Slang] money

dough'nut' *n.* a small, usually ring-shaped cake, fried in deep fat

dough·ty (dout'ē) *adj.* **-ti·er, -ti·est** ⟦OE *dohtig*⟧ [Now Rare] valiant; brave

dough·y (dō'ē) *adj.* **-i·er, -i·est** of or like dough; soft, pasty, etc.

Doug·las fir (dug'ləs) ⟦after D. *Douglas*, 19th-c. Scot botanist in U.S.⟧ a giant North American evergreen tree valued for its wood

dour (door, dour) *adj.* ⟦< L *durus*, hard⟧ 1 [Scot.] stern; severe 2 sullen; gloomy

douse (dous) *vt.* **doused, dous'ing** ⟦< ?⟧ 1 to thrust suddenly into liquid 2 to drench 3 [Inf.] to put out (a light or fire) quickly

dove[1] (duv) *n.* ⟦ME *douve*⟧ 1 any of the smaller species of pigeon: often used as a symbol of peace 2 an advocate of measures which avoid or end wars

dove[2] (dōv) *vi. alt. pt. of* DIVE

dove'cote' *n.* a cote with compartments for nesting pigeons

Do·ver (dō'vər) capital of Delaware: pop. 28,000

dove·tail (duv'tāl') *n.* a projecting part that fits into a corresponding cut-out space to form a joint —*vt.* to fasten or piece together, as by means of dovetails —*vi.* to fit together closely or logically

dow·a·ger (dou'ə jər) *n.* ⟦< L *dotare*, endow⟧ 1 a widow with a title or property derived from her dead husband 2 an elderly, wealthy woman

dow·dy (dou'dē) *adj.* **-di·er, -di·est** ⟦< ME *doude*, plain woman⟧ not neat or smart in dress —**dow'di·ness** *n.*

dow·el (dou'əl) *n.* ⟦ME *doule*⟧ a peg of wood, etc., usually fitted into corresponding holes in two pieces to fasten them together —*vt.* **-eled** or **-elled, -el·ing** or **-el·ling** to fasten with dowels

dow·er (dou'ər) *n.* ⟦< L *dare*, give⟧ that part of a man's property which his widow inherits for life

down[1] (doun) *adv.* ⟦OE *adune*, from the hill⟧ 1 to, in, or on a lower place or level 2 in or to a low or lower condition, amount, etc. 3 southward *[down* to Mexico*]* 4 from an earlier to a later period 5 out of one's hands *[*put it *down]* 6 in a serious manner *[*get *down* to work*]* 7 completely *[*loaded *down]* 8 when purchased *[*$5 *down* and $5 a week*]* 9 in writing *[*take *down* notes*]* —*adj.* 1 descending 2 in a lower place 3 gone, brought, etc. down 4 dejected; discouraged 5 ill 6 finished *[*four *down*, six to go*]* 7 inoperative *[*the computer is *down]* —*prep.* down toward, along, through, into, or upon —*vt.* 1 to put or throw down 2 to swallow quickly —*n.* 1 a misfortune *[*ups and *downs]* 2 *Football* one of a series of plays in which a team tries to advance the ball —**down and out** penniless, ill, etc. —**down on** [Inf.] angry or annoyed with —**down with!** do away with!

down[2] (doun) *n.* ⟦< ON *dūnn*⟧ 1 soft, fine feathers 2 soft, fine hair

down[3] (doun) *n.* ⟦OE *dun*, hill⟧ an expanse of open, high, grassy land: *usually used in pl.*

down'-and-dirt'y *adj.* [Slang] 1 coarse; vulgar 2 unscrupulous 3 fiercely competitive

down'beat' *n. Music* the first beat of each measure

down'cast' *adj.* 1 directed downward 2 unhappy; dejected

Down East [*also* **d- e-**] [Inf.] in or into New England, esp. Maine

down'er *n.* [Slang] any depressant or sedative

down'fall' *n.* 1 a sudden fall, as from power 2 the cause of this

down'grade' *n.* a downward slope —*vt.* **-grad'ed, -grad'ing** 1 to demote 2 to belittle

down'heart'ed *adj.* discouraged

down'hill' *adv.* toward the bottom of a hill —*adj.* 1 going downward 2 without difficulty

Down·ing Street (doun'iŋ) street in London, location of some of the principal government offices of the United Kingdom

down'load' *vt.*, *vi.* to transfer (information) as from a network or main computer to another computer

down payment a partial payment at the time of purchase

down'play' *vt.* to play down; minimize

down'pour' *n.* a heavy rain

down'right' *adv.* utterly —*adj.* 1 absolute; utter 2 plain; frank

down'scale' *adj.* of or for people who are unstylish, not affluent, etc. —*vt.*, *vi.* **-scaled', -scal'ing** to make smaller, less, cheaper, etc.

down'size' *vt.*, *vi.* **-sized', -siz'ing** to make or become smaller, as by eliminating employees

down'stage' *adj.*, *adv.* of or toward the front of the stage

down'stairs' *adv.* 1 down the stairs 2 on or to a lower floor —*adj.* on a lower floor —*n.* a lower floor

down'state' *adj.*, *adv.* in, to, or from the southerly part of a U.S. state

down'stream' *adv.*, *adj.* in the direction of the current of a stream

down'swing' *n.* 1 a downward swing, as of a golf club 2 a downward trend: also **down'turn'**

Down (or **Down's**) **syndrome** ⟦after J. *Down*, 19th-c. Brit physician⟧ a congenital condition characterized by mental deficiency, a broad face, etc.

down'time' *n.* the time a machine, factory, etc. is not working or functioning

THESAURUS

doubt *v.* wonder, question, query, ponder, dispute, be dubious, be uncertain, be doubtful, refuse to believe, demur, have doubts about, have one's doubts, stop to consider, have qualms, call in question, give no credit to, throw doubt upon, have no conception, not know which way to turn, not know what to make of, close one's mind, not admit, not believe, refuse to believe, not buy*, smell a rat, put no stock in; see also ASK, DENY, QUESTION 1.—*Ant.* TRUST, believe, confide.

doubter *n.* questioner, unbeliever, agnostic; see CYNIC.

doubtful *a.* 1 [Uncertain in mind] dubious, doubting, questioning, undecided, unsure, wavering, hesitant, undetermined, uncertain, unsettled, confused, disturbed, lost, puzzled, perplexed, flustered, baffled, distracted, unresolved, in a quandary, of two minds, unable to make up one's mind, troubled with doubt, having little faith, of little faith, in question, not knowing what's what, not following, up a tree*, not able to make head or tail of, going around in circles*, out of focus, up in the air, wishy-washy*, iffy*; see also SUSPICIOUS 1. 2 [Improbable] probably wrong, questionable, unconvincing; see OBSCURE 1, UNCERTAIN.

doubtless *a.* positively, certainly, unquestionably; see SURELY.

dough *n.* 1 [A soft mixture] paste, pulp, mash; see BATTER 2, MIXTURE 1. 2 [*Money] dollars, change, silver; see MONEY 1, WEALTH.

doughnut *n.* friedcake, cruller, sinker*; see CAKE 2, PASTRY.

douse *v.* submerge, splash, drench; see IMMERSE, SOAK 1.

dove[1] *n.* peacemaker, activist, pacifier; see PACIFIST.

dowdy *a.* untidy, slovenly, frumpy; see SHABBY.

down[1] *a.*, *prep.* forward, headlong, bottomward, downhill, on a downward course, from higher to lower, to the bottom, to a lower position, declining, falling, descending, gravitating, slipping, sliding, sagging, slumping, dropping, sinking, earthward, groundward, downward; see also BACKWARD 1.—*Ant.* UP, upward, rising. —**down and out** ruined, defeated, finished; see BEATEN. —**down on*** against, disillusioned about, furious with; see OPPOSED.

down[1] *v.* put down, throw down, knock down, conquer, topple, fell, subdue, tackle, trip, overthrow, overpower, upset, overturn; see also DEFEAT 3, HIT 1.—*Ant.* RAISE, lift, elevate.

down[2] *n.* feathers, fluff, fur; see HAIR 1.

downcast *a.* discouraged, dejected, unhappy; see SAD 1.

downfall *n.* defeat, comedown, ruin; see DESTRUCTION 2.

downgrade *v.* minimize, deprecate, lower; see DECREASE 2.

downhearted *a.* dejected, downcast, despondent; see SAD 1.

downpour *n.* rain, deluge, flood, monsoon; see also STORM.

downright *a.* total, complete, utter; see ABSOLUTE 1, WHOLE 1.

downstairs *a.* down below, below decks, on the floor below; see BELOW 4, UNDER 1.

downstairs *n.* first floor, ground floor, cellar; see BASEMENT.

down′-to-earth′ *adj.* **1** realistic or practical **2** without affectation

down′town′ *adj., adv.* in or toward the main business section of a city —*n.* the downtown section of a city

down′trod′den *adj.* oppressed

down′ward (-wərd) *adv., adj.* toward a lower place, position, etc.: also **down′wards** *adv.*

down′y *adj.* **-i·er, -i·est 1** covered with soft, fine feathers or hair **2** soft and fluffy, like down

dow·ry (dou′rē) *n., pl.* **-ries** ⟦see DOWER⟧ property a woman brings to her husband at marriage

dowse (douz) *vi.* **dowsed, dows′ing** ⟦< ?⟧ to use a divining rod —**dows′er** *n.*

dox·ol·o·gy (däks äl′ə jē) *n., pl.* **-gies** ⟦< Gr *doxa*, praise + *-logia*, -LOGY⟧ a hymn of praise to God

doz *abbrev.* dozen(s)

doze (dōz) *vi.* **dozed, doz′ing** ⟦prob. < Scand⟧ to sleep lightly; nap —*n.* a light sleep —**doz′er** *n.*

doz·en (duz′ən) *n., pl.* **-ens** or **-en** ⟦< L *duo*, two + *decem*, ten⟧ a set of twelve —**doz′enth** *adj.*

dpt *abbrev.* **1** department **2** deponent

Dr or **Dr.** *abbrev.* **1** Doctor **2** Drive

drab (drab) *n.* ⟦< VL *drappus*, cloth⟧ a dull yellowish brown —*adj.* **drab′ber, drab′best 1** dull yellowish-brown **2** dull; dreary —**drab′ness** *n.*

drach·ma (drak′mə) *n.* ⟦< Gr *drachmē*⟧ **1** an ancient Greek coin **2** the monetary unit of modern Greece

Drac·u·la (drak′yə lə) *n.* the title character in a novel (1897): a Romanian VAMPIRE (sense 1)

draft (draft) *n.* ⟦OE *dragan*, to draw⟧ **1** a drawing or pulling, as of a vehicle or load **2** *a)* a drawing in of a fish net *b)* the amount of fish caught in one draw **3** *a)* a drinking or the amount taken at one drink *b)* [Inf.] a portion of beer, etc. drawn from a cask **4** an inhalation **5** a preliminary or tentative piece of writing **6** a plan or drawing of a work to be done **7** a current of air **8** a device for regulating the current of air in a heating system **9** a written order for payment of money; check **10** *a)* the choosing or taking of persons, esp. for compulsory military service *b)* those so taken **11** the depth of water that a ship needs in order to float —*vt.* **1** to take, as for military service, by drawing from a group **2** to make a sketch of or plans for —*adj.* **1** used for pulling loads **2** drawn from a cask *[draft* beer*]* —**draft′er** *n.*

draft·ee (draf tē′) *n.* a person drafted, esp. for military service

drafts·man (drafts′mən) *n., pl.* **-men** (-mən) **1** one who draws plans, as of machinery **2** an artist skillful in drawing —**drafts′man·ship′** *n.*

draft′y *adj.* **-i·er, -i·est** open to drafts of air

drag (drag) *vt., vi.* **dragged, drag′ging** ⟦see DRAW⟧ **1** to pull or be pulled with effort, esp. along the ground **2** to search (a lake bottom, etc.) with a dragnet or the like **3** to draw (something) out over a period of time; move or pass too slowly: often with *on* or *out* —*n.* **1** a dragging **2** a dragnet, grapnel, etc. **3** anything that hinders **4** [Slang] influence **5** [Slang] clothing of the opposite sex, esp. as worn by a male homosexual **6** [Slang] a puff of a cigarette, etc. **7** [Slang] street *[*the main *drag]* **8** [Slang] a dull person, situation, etc.

drag′gy (-ē) *adj.* **-gi·er, -gi·est** dragging; slow-moving, dull, etc.

drag′net′ *n.* **1** a net dragged along a lake bottom, etc., as for catching fish **2** an organized system or network for catching criminals, etc.

drag·on (drag′ən) *n.* ⟦< Gr *drakōn*⟧ a mythical monster, usually shown as a large, winged reptile breathing out fire

drag′on·fly′ *n., pl.* **-flies′** a large, long-bodied insect with transparent, net-veined wings

dra·goon (drə go͞on′) *n.* ⟦< Fr *dragon*, DRAGON⟧ a heavily armed cavalryman —*vt.* to force *into* doing something; coerce

drag race a race between cars accelerating from a standstill on a short, straight course (**drag strip**) —**drag′-race′, -raced′, -rac′ing,** *vi.*

drain (drān) *vt.* ⟦OE *dryge*, dry⟧ **1** to draw off (liquid) gradually **2** to draw liquid from gradually **3** to drink all the liquid from (a cup, etc.) **4** to exhaust (strength, resources, etc.) gradually —*vi.* **1** to flow off or trickle through gradually **2** to become dry by draining **3** to disappear gradually; fade —*n.* **1** a channel or pipe for draining **2** a draining **3** that which gradually exhausts strength, etc. —**drain′er** *n.*

drain′age *n.* **1** a draining **2** a system of drains **3** that which is drained off **4** an area drained

drain′pipe′ *n.* a pipe used to carry off water, sewage, etc.

drake (drāk) *n.* ⟦ME⟧ a male duck

dram (dram) *n.* ⟦< Gr *drachmē*, handful⟧ **1** a unit of apothecaries' weight equal to 3.89 grams **2** a unit of avoirdupois weight equal to 1.77 grams **3** a small drink of alcoholic liquor

dra·ma (drä′mə, dram′ə) *n.* ⟦< Gr⟧ **1** a literary composition to be performed by actors; play, esp. one that is not a comedy **2** the art of writing, acting, or producing plays **3** a series of events suggestive of those of a play **4** dramatic quality

Dram·a·mine (dram′ə mēn′) *trademark for* a drug to relieve motion sickness

dra·mat·ic (drə mat′ik) *adj.* **1** of drama **2** like a play **3** vivid, striking, etc. —**dra·mat′i·cal·ly** *adv.*

dra·mat′ics *pl.n.* **1** [*usually with sing. v.*] the performing or producing of plays **2** exaggerated emotionalism

dram·a·tist (dram′ə tist, drä′mə-) *n.* a playwright

THESAURUS

down-to-earth *a.* sensible, mundane, practicable; see COMMON 1, PRACTICAL, RATIONAL 1.

downtown *a.* city, central, inner-city, main, midtown, in the business district, on the main street, metropolitan, business; see also URBAN.—*Ant.* RURAL, suburban, residential.

downtown *n.* hub, crossroads, business district; see CENTER 2, CITY.

downtrodden *a.* tyrannized, subjugated, mistreated; see OPPRESSED.

downward *a.* earthward, descending, downwards; see DOWN.

downy *a.* woolly, fuzzy, fluffy; see LIGHT 5, SOFT 2.

doze *v.* nap, drowse, slumber; see SLEEP.

dozen *a.* twelve, baker's dozen, long dozen, handful, pocketful.

drab *a.* **1** [Dismal] dingy, colorless, dreary; see DULL 2, 4. **2** [Dun-colored] yellowish-brown, dull brown, dull gray; see BROWN, GRAY.

draft *n.* **1** [A preliminary sketch] plans, blueprint, sketch; see DESIGN. **2** [A breeze] current of air, gust, puff; see WIND. **3** [An order for payment] cashier's check, bank draft, money order; see CHECK 1. **4** [The selection of troops] conscription, induction, recruiting; see SELECTION 1.

draft *v.* **1** [Make a rough plan] outline, delineate, sketch; see PLAN 1, 2. **2** [Select for military service] select, conscript, choose; see RECRUIT 1.

draftsman *n.* sketcher, designer, drawer; see ARCHITECT, ARTIST.

drag *n.* **1** [A restraint] hindrance, burden, impediment; see BARRIER. **2** [*An annoying person, thing, or situation] bother, annoyance, bore; see NUISANCE 3.

drag *v.* **1** [To go slowly; *said of animate beings*] lag, straggle, dawdle; see LOITER, PAUSE. **2** [To go slowly; *said of an activity*] creep, crawl, be prolonged tediously, pass slowly; see also DELAY.—*Ant.* IMPROVE, progress, pick up. **3** [To pull an object] haul, move, transport; see DRAW 1. —**drag on** go on slowly, keep going, persist; see CONTINUE 1, ENDURE 1.

dragon *n.* mythical beast, serpent, hydra; see MONSTER 1, SNAKE.

drain *n.* duct, channel, sewer; see CHANNEL, PIPE 1. —**down the drain** wasted, ruined, gone; see LOST 1.

drain *v.* **1** [To withdraw fluid] tap, draw off, remove; see EMPTY 2. **2** [To withdraw strength] exhaust, weary, tire out; see SPEND, WEAKEN 2. **3** [To seep away] run off, run out, flow away, seep out, exude, trickle out, filter off, ooze, find an opening, percolate, diminish, leave dry; see also FLOW.

drama *n.* play, theatrical piece, theatrical production, dramatization, stage show, skit, sketch, theatre. *Types of drama include the following:* melodrama, tragicomedy, comedy of manners, burlesque, pantomime, mime, grand opera, operetta, light opera, musical comedy, musical, mystery, murder mystery, farce, classical drama, historical drama, theatre of the absurd, epic, pageant, miracle play, revival; see also ACTING, COMEDY, PERFORMANCE.

dramatic *a.* tense, climactic, moving; see EXCITING.

dramatist *n.* playwright, scriptwriter, scenario writer, screenwriter; see also AUTHOR, WRITER. *Major dramatists include the following—Great Britain:* Christopher Marlowe, Ben Jonson, William Shakespeare, William Congreve, Oscar Wilde, George Bernard Shaw, John Millington Synge, Sean O'Casey, Harold Pinter; *United States:* Eugene O'Neill, Thornton Wilder, Tennessee Williams, Arthur Miller, Edward Albee; *Greece:* Aeschylus, Sophocles, Euripides, Aristophanes; *France:* Moliere, Pierre Corneille, Jean Racine, Jean Anouilh, Eugene Ionesco, Jean Genet, Jean Cocteau; *Germany:* Wolf-

dram'a·tize' (-tīz') *vt.* **-tized', -tiz'ing 1** to make into a drama **2** to regard or show in a dramatic manner —**dram'a·ti·za'tion** *n.*
drank (draŋk) *vt., vi. pt. of* DRINK
drape (drāp) *vt.* **draped, drap'ing** ⟦< VL *drappus*, cloth⟧ **1** to cover or hang as with cloth in loose folds **2** to arrange (a garment, etc.) in folds or hangings —*n.* **1** cloth hanging in loose folds **2** a heavy curtain hanging in loose folds
drap·er (drā'pər) *n.* [Brit.] a dealer in cloth and dry goods
drap'er·y *n., pl.* **-er·ies 1** [Brit.] DRY GOODS **2** hangings or clothing arranged in loose folds **3** [*pl.*] curtains of heavy material
dras·tic (dras'tik) *adj.* ⟦Gr *drastikos*, active⟧ having a strong effect; extreme —**dras'ti·cal·ly** *adv.*
draught (draft) *n., vt., adj. now chiefly Brit. sp. of* DRAFT
draughts (drafts) *n.* [Brit.] the game of checkers
draw (drô) *vt.* **drew, drawn, draw'ing** ⟦OE *dragan*⟧ **1** to make move toward one; pull **2** to pull up, down, back, in, or out **3** to need (a specified depth of water) to float in: said of a ship **4** to attract **5** to breathe in **6** to elicit (a reply, etc.) **7** to bring on; provoke **8** to receive *[to draw a salary]* **9** to withdraw (money) held in an account **10** to write (a check or draft) **11** to reach (a conclusion, etc.); deduce **12** to take or get (a playing card, etc.) **13** to stretch **14** to make (lines, pictures, etc.), as with a pencil **15** to make (comparisons, etc.) **16** to cause to flow —*vi.* **1** to draw something **2** to be drawn **3** to come; move **4** to shrink **5** to allow a draft of air, smoke, etc. to move through **6** to make a demand (*on*) —*n.* **1** a drawing or being drawn **2** the result of drawing **3** a thing drawn **4** a tie; stalemate **5** a thing that attracts **6** a shallow ravine —**draw out 1** to extend **2** to take out; extract **3** to get (a person) to talk —**draw up 1** to arrange in order **2** to draft (a document) **3** to stop
draw'back' *n.* anything that prevents or lessens satisfaction; shortcoming
draw'bridge' *n.* a bridge that can be raised or drawn aside, as to permit passage of ships
draw·er (drô'ər; *for 2* drôr) *n.* **1** one that draws **2** a sliding box in a table, chest, etc.
drawers (drôrz) *pl.n.* UNDERPANTS
draw'ing *n.* **1** the act of one that draws; specif., the art of making pictures, etc., as with a pencil **2** a picture, etc. thus made **3** a lottery
drawing board a flat board to hold paper, etc. for making drawings —**back to the drawing board** [Inf.] back to the beginning, as to see what went wrong
drawing card an entertainer, show, etc. that draws a large audience
drawing room ⟦< *withdrawing room*: guests withdrew there after dinner⟧ a room where guests are received or entertained; living room
drawl (drôl) *vt., vi.* ⟦prob. < DRAW, *v.*⟧ to speak slowly, prolonging the vowels —*n.* such a way of speaking
drawn (drôn) *vt., vi. pp. of* DRAW —*adj.* **1** pulled out **2** disemboweled **3** tense; haggard
drawn butter melted butter
draw'string' *n.* a string drawn through a hem, as to tighten a garment
dray (drā) *n.* ⟦OE *dragan*, to draw⟧ a low cart for carrying heavy loads
dread (dred) *vt.* ⟦OE *ondrædan*⟧ to anticipate with fear or distaste —*n.* **1** intense fear **2** fear mixed with awe **3** reluctance and uneasiness —*adj.* inspiring dread
dread'ful (-fəl) *adj.* **1** awesome or terrible **2** [Inf.] very bad, offensive, etc. —**dread'ful·ly** *adv.*
dread'locks' *pl.n.* hair worn in long, thin braids or uncombed, twisted locks
dread'nought' or **dread'naught'** (-nôt') *n.* a large, heavily armored battleship
dream (drēm) *n.* ⟦OE, joy, music⟧ **1** a sequence of images, etc. passing through a sleeping person's mind **2** a daydream; reverie **3** a fond hope **4** anything dreamlike —*vi., vt.* **dreamed** or **dreamt** (dremt), **dream'ing** to have a dream or remote idea (*of*) —**dream up** [Inf.] to devise (a fanciful plan, etc.) —**dream'er** *n.* —**dream'less** *adj.* —**dream'like'** *adj.*
dream'land' *n.* **1** any lovely but imaginary place **2** sleep
dream world 1 DREAMLAND **2** the realm of fantasy
dream'y *adj.* **-i·er, -i·est 1** filled with dreams **2** fond of daydreaming **3** like something in a dream **4** soothing **5** [Slang] wonderful —**dream'i·ly** *adv.*
drear·y (drir'ē) *adj.* **-i·er, -i·est** ⟦OE *dreorig*, sad⟧ dismal: also [Old Poet.] **drear** —**drear'i·ly** *adv.* —**drear'i·ness** *n.*
dredge[1] (drej) *n.* ⟦prob. < MDu⟧ an apparatus for scooping up mud, etc., as in deepening channels —*vt., vi.* **dredged, dredg'ing 1** to search for or gather (*up*) as with a dredge **2** to enlarge or clean out with a dredge
dredge[2] (drej) *vt.* **dredged, dredg'ing** ⟦ME *dragge*, sweetmeat⟧ to coat (food) with flour, etc.
dregs (dregz) *pl.n.* ⟦< ON *dreggj*⟧ **1** particles settling at the bottom in a liquid **2** the most worthless part
Drei·ser (drī'sər, -zər), **The·o·dore** (**Herman Albert**) (thē'ə dôr') 1871-1945; U.S. novelist
drench (drench) *vt.* ⟦OE *drincan*, to drink⟧ to make wet all over; soak
Dres·den (drez'dən) city in E Germany: pop. 481,000
dress (dres) *vt.* **dressed** or **drest, dress'ing** ⟦< L *dirigere*, lay straight⟧ **1** to put clothes on; clothe **2** to trim; adorn **3** to arrange (the hair) in a certain way **4** to align

THESAURUS

gang von Goethe, Friedrich Schiller, Bertolt Brecht; *other:* Anton Chekov, Henrik Ibsen, August Strindberg, Karel Capek, Luigi Pirandello.

dramatize *v.* enact, produce, execute; see PERFORM 2.

drape *v.* clothe, wrap, model; see DRESS.

drapes *n.* window covering, drapery, hanging; see CURTAIN.

drastic *a.* extravagant, exorbitant, radical; see EXTREME.

draw *v.* **1** [To move an object] pull, drag, attract, move, bring, tug, lug, tow, carry, jerk, wrench, yank, haul, extract.—*Ant.* REPEL, repulse, reject. **2** [To make a likeness by drawing] sketch, describe, etch, pencil, outline, trace, make a picture of, depict, model, portray, engrave, chart, map; see also PAINT 1. —**beat to the draw** be quicker than another, forestall, stop; see ANTICIPATE, PREVENT. —**draw away** pull away from, gain on, increase a lead; see ADVANCE 1, DEFEAT 1, LEAVE 1. —**draw back** withdraw, recede, draw in; see RETREAT. —**draw on** take from, extract from, employ; see USE 1. —**draw out 1** [To induce to talk] make talk, lead on, interrogate; see INTERVIEW. **2** [To pull] drag, tug, attract; see DRAW 1. **3** [To extend] prolong, stretch, lengthen; see INCREASE. —**draw up** draft, execute, prepare; see WRITE 1.

drawback *n.* detriment, hindrance, check; see LACK 1.

drawing *n.* sketching, designing, illustrating, tracing, etching, design, illustration, rendering, graphic art; see also PICTURE 3, REPRESENTATION.

dread *n.* awe, horror, terror; see FEAR.

dreadful *a.* hideous, fearful, shameful; see FRIGHTFUL 1.

dream *n.* nightmare, apparition, hallucination, image, trance, idea, impression, emotion, reverie, daydream, castle in the air, mirage, chimera, pipe dream*; see also FANTASY, ILLUSION, THOUGHT 2, VISION 3, 4.—*Ant.* REALITY, actuality, truth.

dream *v.* **1** [To have visions, usually during sleep or fever] hallucinate, fancy, visualize; see IMAGINE. **2** [To entertain or delude oneself with imagined things] fancy, imagine, conceive, have notions, conjure up, create, picture, idealize, daydream, fantasize, be in the clouds, pipe dream*; see also INVENT 1. —**dream up*** devise, contrive, concoct; see IMAGINE.

dreamer *n.* visionary, idealist, romantic; see RADICAL.

dreaming *a.* thinking, daydreaming, musing; see THOUGHTFUL 1.

dreamy *a.* whimsical, fanciful, daydreaming, visionary, given to reverie, illusory, introspective, otherworldly, idealistic, mythical, utopian, romantic, starry-eyed; see also IMAGINARY, IMPRACTICAL.—*Ant.* PRACTICAL, ACTIVE, REAL.

dreary *a.* damp, raw, windy; see COLD 1, DISMAL.

dregs *n.* scum, grounds, remains; see RESIDUE.

drench *v.* wet, saturate, flood; see IMMERSE, SOAK 1.

dress *n.* **1** [Clothing] ensemble, attire, garments, outfit, garb, apparel, array, costume, wardrobe, uniform, habit, formal dress, evening clothes, trappings, things, get-up*, threads*, rags*, duds*; see also CLOTHES, COAT 1, PANTS 1, SHIRT, SUIT 3, UNDERWEAR. **2** [A woman's outer garment] frock, gown, wedding dress, evening gown, formal, cocktail dress, suit, skirt, robe, shift, sundress, shirtdress, housedress, smock; see also CLOTHES.

dress *v.* **1** [To put on clothes] don, wear, garb, clothe, robe, attire, drape, array, cover, spruce up, dress up, bundle up, get into*, doll up*, dress to the nines*, slip into, dress down; see also WEAR 1. **2** [To provide with clothes] costume, outfit, clothe; see SUPPORT 3. **3** [To give medical treatment] treat, bandage, give first aid; see HEAL. —**dressed up** dressed formally, dressed to kill*, dolled up*; see FANCY, FASHIONABLE, ORNATE. —**dress up** spiff up*, spruce up, put on the dog*; see DRESS 1.

(troops) **5** to apply medicines and bandages to (a wound, etc.) **6** to prepare for use, esp. for cooking *[to dress* a fowl*]* **7** to smooth or finish (stone, wood, etc.) —***vi.*** **1** to put on clothes **2** to dress formally **3** to line up in rank —***n.*** **1** clothing **2** the usual outer garment of women, generally of one piece with a skirt —***adj.*** **1** of or for dresses **2** for formal wear —**dress down** **1** to scold **2** to wear casual clothes to work, etc. —**dress up** to dress formally, elegantly, etc.

dres·sage (dre säzh′) ***n.*** ⟦Fr, training⟧ horsemanship using slight movements to control the horse

dress circle a semicircle of seats in a theater, etc., usually behind and above the orchestra seats

dress code a set of rules governing clothing to be worn, as in a given school or business

dress′er ***n.*** **1** one who dresses (in various senses) **2** a chest of drawers for clothes, usually with a mirror

dress′ing ***n.*** **1** the act of one that dresses **2** bandages, etc. applied to wounds **3** a sauce for salads, etc. **4** a stuffing for roast fowl, etc.

dress′ing-down′ ***n.*** a sound scolding

dressing gown a loose robe for one not fully clothed, as when lounging

dress′mak′er ***n.*** one who makes dresses, etc. —**dress′mak′ing** ***n.***

dress rehearsal a final rehearsal, as of a play, with costumes, etc.

dress′y ***adj.*** **-i·er, -i·est** **1** showy or elaborate in dress or appearance **2** stylish, elegant, etc. —**dress′i·ness** ***n.***

drew (dro͞o) ***vt., vi.*** *pt. of* DRAW

drib·ble (drib′əl) ***vi., vt.*** **-bled, -bling** ⟦< DRIP⟧ **1** to flow, or let flow, in drops **2** to drool **3** *Sports* to move (a ball or puck) along by repeated bouncing, kicking, or tapping —***n.*** **1** a dribbling **2** a tiny amount: also **drib′let** (-lit) —**drib′bler** ***n.***

dried (drīd) ***vt., vi.*** *pt. & pp. of* DRY

dri·er (drī′ər) ***n.*** **1** a substance added to paint, etc. to make it dry fast **2** DRYER —***adj.*** *compar. of* DRY

dri′est (-ist) ***adj.*** *superl. of* DRY

drift (drift) ***n.*** ⟦OE *drifan,* to drive⟧ **1** *a)* a being carried along, as by a current *b)* the course of this **2** a trend; tendency **3** general meaning; intent **4** a heap of snow, sand, etc. piled up by wind —***vi.*** **1** to be carried along, as by a current **2** to go along aimlessly **3** to pile up in drifts —***vt.*** to cause to drift —**drift′er** ***n.***

drift′wood′ ***n.*** wood drifting in the water or washed ashore

drill[1] (dril) ***n.*** ⟦< Du *drillen,* to bore⟧ **1** a tool for boring holes **2** *a)* systematic military or physical training *b)* the method or practice of teaching by repeated exercises —***vt., vi.*** **1** to bore with a drill (the tool) **2** to train in, or teach by means of, a drill —**drill′er** ***n.***

drill[2] (dril) ***n.*** ⟦< ?⟧ a planting machine for making holes or furrows and dropping seeds into them

drill[3] (dril) ***n.*** ⟦< L *trilix,* three-threaded⟧ a coarse, twilled cotton cloth, used for uniforms, etc.

drill′mas′ter ***n.*** **1** an instructor in military drill **2** one who teaches by drilling

drill press a power-driven machine for drilling holes in metal, etc.

dri·ly (drī′lē) ***adv.*** DRYLY

drink (driŋk) ***vt.*** **drank, drunk, drink′ing** ⟦OE *drincan*⟧ **1** to swallow (liquid) **2** to absorb (liquid) **3** to swallow the contents of —***vi.*** **1** to swallow liquid **2** to drink alcoholic liquor, esp. to excess —***n.*** **1** any liquid for drinking **2** alcoholic liquor —**drink in** to take in eagerly with the senses or mind —**drink to** to drink a toast to —**drink′a·ble** ***adj.*** —**drink′er** ***n.***

drip (drip) ***vi., vt.*** **dripped** or **dript, drip′ping** ⟦OE *dryppan*⟧ to fall, or let fall, in drops —***n.*** **1** a dripping **2** the sound of falling drops of a liquid **3** [Slang] a dull person —**drip′per** ***n.***

drip′-dry′ ***adj.*** designating garments that dry quickly when hung wet and require little or no ironing

drive (drīv) ***vt.*** **drove, driv·en** (driv′ən), **driv′ing** ⟦OE *drifan*⟧ **1** to force to go; push forward **2** to force into or from a state or act **3** to force to work, esp. to excess **4** to hit (a ball, etc.) hard **5** to make penetrate **6** *a)* to control the movement of; operate (a car, bus, etc.) *b)* to transport in a car, etc. **7** to push (a bargain, etc.) through **8** to motivate, influence, etc. —***vi.*** **1** to advance violently **2** to try hard, as to reach a goal **3** to drive a blow, ball, etc. **4** to be driven: said of a car, bus, etc. **5** to operate, or go in, a car, etc. —***n.*** **1** a driving **2** a trip in a car, etc. **3** *a)* a road for cars, etc. *b)* a driveway **4** a rounding up of animals **5** an organized effort to gain an objective **6** energy and initiative **7** a strong impulse or urge **8** the propelling mechanism of a machine, etc. **9** a computer device that reads and writes data —**drive at** to mean;

THESAURUS

dresser ***n.*** dressing table, chest of drawers, bureau; see FURNITURE, TABLE 1.

dressing ***n.*** **1** [A food mixture] stuffing, filling, forcemeat. *Dressings include the following:* bread, giblet, oyster, chestnut, potato, prune, plum, apple, duck, turkey, chicken, fish, clam, wild rice, sage. **2** [A flavoring sauce] *Salad dressings include the following:* ranch, French, Russian, Thousand Island, blue cheese, Roquefort (trademark), Italian, Caesar, oil and vinegar; see also SAUCE. **3** [An external medical application] bandage, plaster cast, adhesive tape, Band-Aid (trademark), compress, gauze, tourniquet, pack; see also CAST 4.

dressmaker ***n.*** seamstress, garment worker, designer; see TAILOR.

dressy ***a.*** dressed up, elegant, elaborate; see FANCY, FASHIONABLE, ORNATE.

dribble ***v.*** trickle, spout, squirt; see DROP 1.

dried ***a.*** drained, dehydrated, desiccated; see DRY 1, PRESERVED 2.

drift ***n.*** **1** [The tendency in movement] bent, trend, tendency, end, inclination, impulse, propulsion, aim, scope, goal, push, bias, set, impetus, leaning, progress, disposition, bearing, line; see also DIRECTION 1, WAY 2. **2** [The measure or character of movement] current, deviation, flux; see FLOW.

drift ***v.*** float, ride, sail, wander, stray, sweep, move with the current, gravitate, tend, be carried along by the current, move toward, go with the tide, be caught in the current, move without effort, move slowly; see also FLOW, MOVE 1.—*Ant.* LEAD, steer, guide.

drill[1] ***v.*** **1** [To bore] pierce, sink in, puncture; see DIG 1, PENETRATE. **2** [To train] practice, rehearse, discipline; see TEACH.

drill[1,2] ***n.*** **1** [Practice] preparation, repetition, learning by doing; see PRACTICE 3. **2** [A tool for boring holes] borer, pneumatic drill, electric drill, steam drill, diamond drill, compressed-air drill, drill press, auger, corkscrew, awl, riveter, jackhammer; see also TOOL 1. **3** [Exercise, especially in military formation] training, maneuvers, marching, close-order drill, open-order drill, conditioning, survival training, guerrilla training; see also PARADE 1. **4** [Device for planting seed in holes] planter, seeder, dibble; see TOOL 1.

drink ***n.*** **1** [A draft] gulp, sip, potion, drop, bottle, glass, refreshment, shot, stiff one*, slug*, belt*, nip, swig*, spot*, nightcap*, hair of the dog*, one for the road*. **2** [Something drunk] champagne, rye, bourbon, Scotch, Irish whiskey, ale, stout, rum, liqueur, tequila, vodka, wine cooler, distilled water, mineral water, carbonated water, mixer, tonic, seltzer, iced tea, cocoa, hot chocolate, chocolate milk, milkshake, cola, float, frappé, lemonade, punch, soft drink, soda water, pop, soda, soda pop, ginger ale, ice-cream soda; orange juice, tomato juice, grapefruit juice, etc.; see also BEER, COFFEE, MILK, WATER 1, WHISKEY, WINE.

drink ***v.*** **1** [To swallow liquid] gulp down, take in, sip, down, guzzle, imbibe, wash down, slurp; see also SWALLOW. **2** [To consume alcoholic liquor] tipple, swill, swig, guzzle, belt*, carouse, take a nip, wet one's whistle*, booze*, hit the bottle*, go on a binge*.

drinker ***n.*** tippler, alcoholic, lush*; see DRUNKARD.

drip ***v.*** dribble, trickle, plop; see DROP 1.

drive ***n.*** **1** [A ride in a vehicle] ride, trip, outing, expedition, tour, excursion, jaunt, spin, Sunday drive*; see also JOURNEY. **2** [A road] approach, avenue, boulevard, entrance, street, roadway, parkway, lane, track, path, pavement; see also ROAD 1. **3** [Impelling force] energy, effort, impulse; see FORCE 2.

drive ***v.*** **1** [To urge on] impel, propel, instigate, incite, animate, hasten, egg on, urge on, compel, coerce, induce, force, press, stimulate, hurry, provoke, arouse, make, put up to*, motivate, inspire, prompt, rouse, work on, act upon; see also sense 2 and ENCOURAGE, PUSH 2.—*Ant.* STOP, hinder, drag. **2** [To manage a propelled vehicle] direct, operate, steer, handle, run, wheel, bicycle, bike*, cycle, transport, float, drift, dash, put in motion, start, set going, speed, roll, coast, get under way, keep going, back up, burn up the road*, go like hell*, step on it*, floor it*, gun it*, burn rubber*, give it the gas*; see also RIDE 1. —**drive a bargain** deal, close a deal, bargain; see BUY, SELL. —**drive at** allude to, indicate, signify; see MEAN 1. —**drive away** drive off, disperse, banish; see SCATTER 2.

intend —**drive in** **1** to force in, as by a blow **2** *Baseball* to cause (a runner) to score or (a run) to be scored

drive′-by′ *n., pl.* **-bys′** a shooting in which the shots are fired from a passing car, etc.

drive′-in′ *n.* a restaurant, movie theater, bank, etc. designed to serve people seated in their cars

driv·el (driv′əl) *vi., vt.* **-eled** or **-elled**, **-el·ing** or **-el·ling** ⟦OE *dreflian*⟧ **1** to let (saliva) drool **2** to speak or say in a silly, stupid way —*n.* silly, stupid talk —**driv′el·er** or **driv′el·ler** *n.*

driv′en (-ən) *adj.* acting because of urgency or compulsion

driv·er (drī′vər) *n.* a person or thing that drives, as *a)* one who drives a car, etc. *b)* one who herds cattle *c)* a golf club for hitting from the tee

drive shaft a shaft that transmits motion, as to the rear axle of a car

drive′-through′ *n.* a restaurant, bank, etc. that provides service through a window to a person in a car, etc.: also sp. **drive′-thru′**

drive′train′ *n.* the system that transmits an engine's power to wheels, a propeller, etc.

drive′way′ *n.* a path for cars, from a street to a garage, house, etc.

driz·zle (driz′əl) *vi., vt.* **-zled**, **-zling** ⟦prob. < ME⟧ to rain in fine, misty drops —*n.* a fine, misty rain —**driz′zly** *adj.*

drogue (drōg) *n.* ⟦prob. < Scot *drug*, drag⟧ a funnel-shaped device towed behind an aircraft, etc., as for its drag effect or as a target

droll (drōl) *adj.* ⟦< Fr < MDu *drol*, stout fellow⟧ amusing in an odd or wry way —**droll′er·y** (-ər ē), *pl.* **-ies**, *n.* —**droll′ness** *n.* —**drol′ly** *adv.*

drom·e·dar·y (dräm′ə der′ē) *n., pl.* **-ies** ⟦< LL *dromedarius* (*camelus*), running (camel)⟧ an Arabian camel, esp. one for riding

drone[1] (drōn) *n.* ⟦OE *dran*⟧ **1** a male bee or ant that does no work **2** an idler; loafer **3** a drudge **4** a pilotless airplane

drone[2] (drōn) *vi.* **droned**, **dron′ing** ⟦< prec.⟧ **1** to make a continuous humming sound **2** to talk in a monotonous way —*vt.* to utter in a monotonous tone —*n.* a droning sound

drool (dro͞ol) *vi.* ⟦< DRIVEL⟧ **1** to let saliva flow from one's mouth **2** to flow from the mouth, as saliva —*n.* saliva running from the mouth

droop (dro͞op) *vi.* ⟦< ON *drūpa*⟧ **1** to sink, hang, or bend down **2** to lose strength or vitality **3** to become dejected —*vt.* to let hang down —*n.* a drooping —**droop′y**, **-i·er**, **-i·est**, *adj.* —**droop′i·ness** *n.*

drop (dräp) *n.* ⟦OE *dropa*⟧ **1** a bit of liquid rounded in shape by falling, etc. **2** anything like this in shape, etc. **3** a very small quantity **4** a sudden fall, descent, slump, etc. **5** something that drops, as a curtain or trapdoor **6** the distance between a higher and lower level —*vi.* **dropped**, **drop′ping** **1** to fall in drops **2** to fall; come down **3** to fall exhausted, wounded, or dead **4** to pass into a specified state *[to drop off to sleep]* **5** to come to an end *[let the matter drop]* **6** to become lower —*vt.* **1** to let or make fall **2** to utter (a hint, etc.) casually **3** to send (a letter) **4** to stop, end, or dismiss **5** to lower or lessen **6** [Inf.] to leave at a specified place: often with *off* **7** to omit or remove **8** [Slang] to lose (money, etc.) —**drop in** (or **over** or **by**) to pay a casual visit —**drop off** [Inf.] to fall asleep —**drop out** to stop participating —**drop′let** (-lit) *n.*

drop′-dead′ [Slang] *adj.* spectacular; striking —*adv.* extremely *[drop-dead handsome]*

drop kick *Rugby, etc.* a kick of a dropped ball just as it hits the ground —**drop′-kick′** *vt., vi.* —**drop′-kick′er** *n.*

drop′-off′ *n.* **1** a very steep drop **2** a decline, as in sales or prices

drop′out′ *n.* one who withdraws from school before graduating

drop′per *n.* a small tube with a hollow rubber bulb at one end, used to measure out a liquid in drops

drop·sy (dräp′sē) *n.* ⟦< Gr *hydrōps* < *hydōr*, water⟧ *former term for* EDEMA

dross (drôs) *n.* ⟦OE *dros*⟧ **1** scum on molten metal **2** refuse; rubbish

drought (drout) *n.* ⟦< OE *drugoth*, dryness⟧ **1** prolonged dry weather **2** a prolonged shortage

drove[1] (drōv) *n.* ⟦OE *draf*⟧ **1** a number of cattle, sheep, etc. driven or moving along as a group; flock; herd **2** a moving crowd of people: *usually used in pl.*

drove[2] (drōv) *vt., vi. pt. of* DRIVE

dro·ver (drō′vər) *n.* one who herds droves of animals, esp. to market

drown (droun) *vi.* ⟦ME *drounen*⟧ to die by suffocation in water —*vt.* **1** to kill by such suffocation **2** to flood **3** to be so loud as to overcome (another sound): usually with *out*

drowse (drouz) *vi.* **drowsed**, **drows′ing** ⟦< OE *drusian*, become sluggish⟧ to be half asleep; doze —*n.* a doze

drows·y (drou′zē) *adj.* **-i·er**, **-i·est** being or making sleepy or half asleep —**drows′i·ly** *adv.* —**drows′i·ness** *n.*

drub (drub) *vt.* **drubbed**, **drub′bing** ⟦< Ar *daraba*, to cudgel⟧ **1** to beat as with a stick **2** to defeat soundly —**drub′ber** *n.* —**drub′bing** *n.*

drudge (druj) *n.* ⟦ME *druggen*⟧ one who does hard or tedious work —*vi.* **drudged**, **drudg′ing** to do such work —**drudg′er·y**, *pl.* **-ies**, *n.*

drug (drug) *n.* ⟦< OFr *drogue*⟧ **1** any substance used as or in a medicine **2** a narcotic, hallucinogen, etc. —*vt.*

THESAURUS

driven *a.* blown, drifted, herded, pushed, pounded, washed, guided, steered, directed, urged on, compelled, forced, shoved, sent, hard pressed, impelled, unable to help oneself, with one's back to the wall.

driver *n.* chauffeur, motorist, licensed operator, bus driver, truck driver, cab driver, cabbie*, cabby*, trucker, designated driver.

driveway *n.* drive, entrance, approach; see DRIVE 2, ROAD 1.

drizzle *v.* spray, shower, sprinkle; see DROP 1, RAIN.

drone[1,2] *n.* **1** [A continuous sound] hum, buzz, vibration; see NOISE 1. **2** [An idle person] idler, loafer, parasite; see LOAFER.

drone[2] *v.* hum, buzz, vibrate; see SOUND.

drool *v.* drivel, slaver, slobber, drip, salivate, spit, dribble, trickle, ooze, run; see also DROP 1.

droop *v.* settle, sink, hang down; see LEAN 1.

drop *n.* **1** [Enough fluid to fall] drip, trickle, droplet, bead, teardrop, dewdrop, raindrop; see also TEAR. **2** [A lowering or falling] fall, tumble, reduction, decrease, slide, descent, slump, lapse, slip, decline, downfall, downturn, plunge, dip; see also FALL 1. **3** [A small quantity] speck, dash, dab; see BIT 1. —**at the drop of a hat** without warning, at the slightest provocation, quickly; see IMMEDIATELY.

drop *v.* **1** [To fall in drops] drip, fall, dribble, trickle, descend, leak, ooze, seep, drain, filter, sink, bleed, bead, splash, hail; see also RAIN.—*Ant.* RISE, spurt, squirt. **2** [To cause or to permit to fall] let go, give up, release, shed, relinquish, abandon, loosen, lower, floor, ground, shoot out, knock down, fell, topple; see also DUMP.—*Ant.* RAISE, elevate, send up. **3** [To discontinue] give up, quit, leave; see STOP 2. **4** [To break off an acquaintance] break with, part from, cast off; see ABANDON 1. —**drop a hint** suggest, intimate, imply; see HINT, PROPOSE 1. —**drop a line** write to, post, communicate with; see COMMUNICATE, WRITE 1. —**drop behind** slow down, worsen, decline; see FAIL 1, LOSE 3. —**drop dead*** expire, collapse, succumb; see DIE. —**drop in** call, stop, look in on; see VISIT. —**drop off** **1** [*To sleep] fall asleep, doze, drowse; see SLEEP. **2** [*To deliver] leave, hand over, present; see GIVE 1. —**drop out** withdraw, cease, quit; see ABANDON 1, RETREAT.

dropout *n.* failing student, truant, quitter; see FAILURE 1.

drought *n.* dry season, hot spell, dry spell; see WEATHER.

drove[1] *n.* flock, pack, throng; see CROWD, HERD.

drown *v.* **1** [To cover with liquid] swamp, inundate, overflow; see FLOOD. **2** [To lower into a liquid] dip, plunge, submerge; see IMMERSE, SINK 2. **3** [To kill or die by drowning] go under, suffocate, sink; see DIE, KILL 1. —**drown out** silence, hush, muffle; see QUIET 2.

drowned *a.* suffocated, sunk, submerged; see DEAD 1, GONE 2.

drowsy *a.* sleepy, languid, tired; see LAZY 1.

drudge *n.* slave, drone, hard worker; see LABORER, WORKMAN.

drug *n.* sedative, potion, painkiller*, smelling salts, powder, tonic, opiate, pills, hard drug*, designer drug, uppers*, downers*. *Kinds of drugs include the following—general:* caffeine, alcohol, adrenalin, amphetamine, nicotine, dope*; *hallucinogens:* marijuana, pot*, grass*, weed*; peyote, mescaline, psilocybin; *D*-lysergic acid diethylamide, LSD, acid*; *stimulants:* cocaine, coke*, snow*, crack*; benzedrine, bennies*, pep pills*; dexedrine, dexies*; methedrine, meth*, speed*; Ecstasy*, poppers*; *narcotics:* opium; morphine; heroin, H*, horse*, junk*, smack*; codeine; see also MEDICINE 2.

drug *v.* anesthetize, desensitize, dope*; see DEADEN.

drugged, **drug'ging** 1 to put a harmful drug in (a drink, etc.) 2 to stupefy as with a drug —**drug on the market** a thing in plentiful supply for which there is little or no demand

drug'gie (-ē) ***n.*** [Slang] a habitual user of drugs: also **drug'gy**, *pl.* **-gies**

drug'gist (-ist) ***n.*** 1 a dealer in drugs, medical supplies, etc. 2 a pharmacist 3 a drugstore owner or manager

drug'store' ***n.*** a store where drugs, medical supplies, and various items are sold and prescriptions are filled

dru·id (drōō'id) ***n.*** ⟦< Celt⟧ [*often* **D-**] a member of a Celtic religious order in ancient Britain, Ireland, and France —**dru'id·ism'** ***n.***

drum (drum) ***n.*** ⟦< Du *trom*⟧ 1 a percussion instrument consisting of a hollow cylinder with a membrane stretched over the end or ends 2 the sound produced by beating a drum 3 any drumlike cylindrical object 4 the eardrum —***vi.*** **drummed**, **drum'ming** 1 to beat a drum 2 to tap continually —***vt.*** 1 to play (a rhythm, etc.) as on a drum 2 to instill (ideas, facts, etc.) *into* by continued repetition —**drum out of** to expel from in disgrace —**drum up** to get (business, etc.) by soliciting

drum·lin (drum'lin) ***n.*** ⟦< Ir⟧ a low, flattened, oval mound or hill formed by a glacier

drum major one who leads a marching band, keeping time with a baton —**drum ma'jor·ette'** (-et') ***fem.***

drum'mer ***n.*** 1 a drum player 2 [Old Inf.] a traveling salesman

drum'stick' ***n.*** 1 a stick for beating a drum 2 the lower half of the leg of a cooked fowl

drunk (druŋk) ***vt.***, ***vi.*** *pp. of* DRINK —***adj.*** 1 overcome by alcoholic liquor; intoxicated 2 overcome by any powerful emotion 3 [Inf.] DRUNKEN (sense 2) Usually used in the predicate —***n.*** 1 [Inf.] a drunken person 2 [Slang] a drinking spree

drunk'ard ***n.*** a person who often gets drunk

drunk'en ***adj.*** 1 intoxicated 2 caused by or occurring during intoxication Used before a noun —**drunk'en·ly** ***adv.*** —**drunk'en·ness** ***n.***

drupe (drōōp) ***n.*** ⟦< Gr *druppa* (*elaa*), olive⟧ any fleshy fruit with an inner stone, as a peach

dry (drī) ***adj.*** **dri'er**, **dri'est** ⟦OE *dryge*⟧ 1 not under water *[dry* land*]* 2 not wet or damp 3 lacking rain or water; arid 4 thirsty 5 not yielding milk 6 solid; not liquid 7 not sweet *[dry* wine*]* 8 prohibiting alcoholic beverages *[*a *dry* town*]* 9 funny in a quiet but sharp way *[dry* wit*]* 10 unproductive 11 boring; dull —***n.***, *pl.* **drys** [Inf.] a prohibitionist —***vt.***, ***vi.*** **dried**, **dry'ing** to make or become dry —**dry up** 1 to make or become thoroughly dry 2 to make or become unproductive 3 [Slang] to stop talking —**dry'ly** ***adv.*** —**dry'ness** ***n.***

dry·ad (drī'ad') ***n.*** ⟦< Gr *drys*, tree⟧ [*also* **D-**] *Gr. & Rom. Myth.* a tree nymph

dry cell a voltaic cell containing a moist, pastelike electrolyte which cannot spill

dry'-clean' ***vt.*** to clean (garments, etc.) with a solvent other than water, as naphtha —**dry cleaner**

dry dock a dock from which the water can be emptied, used for building and repairing ships

dry'er ***n.*** 1 one that dries; specif., an appliance for drying clothes with heat 2 DRIER

dry farming farming without irrigation, by conserving the soil's moisture, etc.

dry goods cloth, cloth products, etc.

dry ice solidified carbon dioxide: used as a refrigerant

dry run [Inf.] a simulated or practice performance; rehearsal

dry'wall' ***n.*** PLASTERBOARD —***vt.***, ***vi.*** to cover (a wall, etc.) with plasterboard

DSL *abbrev.* digital subscriber line

DST *abbrev.* daylight saving time

Du *abbrev.* Dutch

du·al (dōō'əl) ***adj.*** ⟦< L *duo*, two⟧ 1 of two 2 double; twofold —**du'al·ism'** ***n.*** —**du·al'i·ty** (-al'ə tē) ***n.***

dub[1] (dub) ***vt.*** **dubbed**, **dub'bing** ⟦< OE *dubbian*, to strike⟧ 1 *a)* to confer a title or rank upon *b)* to name or nickname 2 to smooth by hammering, scraping, etc. —**dub'ber** ***n.***

dub[2] (dub) ***vt.*** **dubbed**, **dub'bing** ⟦< DOUBLE⟧ to provide with a soundtrack, esp. one with dialogue in another language —**dub in** to insert (dialogue, music, etc.) in the soundtrack —**dub'ber** ***n.***

dub·bin (dub'in) ***n.*** ⟦< DUB[1]⟧ a greasy preparation for waterproofing leather

du·bi·e·ty (dōō bī'ə tē) ***n.*** 1 a being dubious 2 *pl.* **-ties** a doubtful thing

du·bi·ous (dōō'bē əs) ***adj.*** ⟦< L *dubius*, uncertain⟧ 1 causing doubt 2 skeptical 3 questionable —**du'bi·ous·ly** ***adv.***

Dub·lin (dub'lən) capital of Ireland: pop. 478,000

du·cal (dōō'kəl) ***adj.*** ⟦< LL *ducalis*, of a leader⟧ of a duke or dukedom

duc·at (duk'ət) ***n.*** ⟦see DUCHY⟧ any of several former European coins

duch·ess (duch'is) ***n.*** 1 a duke's wife or widow 2 a woman ruling a duchy

duch'y (-ē) ***n.***, *pl.* **-ies** ⟦< L *dux*, leader⟧ the territory ruled by a duke or duchess

duck[1] (duk) ***n.*** ⟦< OE *duce*, diver⟧ 1 a small waterfowl with a flat bill, a short neck, and webbed feet 2 the flesh of a duck as food

duck[2] (duk) ***vt.***, ***vi.*** ⟦ME *douken*⟧ 1 to plunge or dip under water for a moment 2 to lower or bend (the head, body, etc.) suddenly, as to avoid a blow 3 [Inf.] to avoid (an issue, etc.) —***n.*** a ducking

duck[3] (duk) ***n.*** ⟦Du *doek*⟧ a cotton or linen cloth like canvas but lighter in weight

duck'bill' ***n.*** PLATYPUS

duck'ling ***n.*** a young duck

duck'pins' ***n.*** a game like bowling, played with smaller pins and balls

duck'y ***adj.*** **-i·er**, **-i·est** [Old Slang] pleasing, delightful, etc.

duct (dukt) ***n.*** ⟦< L *ducere*, to lead⟧ a tube, channel, or pipe, as for passage of a liquid —**duct'less** ***adj.***

duc·tile (duk'til) ***adj.*** ⟦see prec.⟧ 1 that can be drawn or hammered thin without breaking: said of metals 2 easily led; tractable —**duc·til'i·ty** (-til'ə tē) ***n.***

ductless gland an endocrine gland

duct tape a very strong, waterproof tape, used to seal ducts, hoses, etc.

THESAURUS

drugged ***a.*** comatose, doped, stupefied; see UNCONSCIOUS.

druggist ***n.*** apothecary, chemist, registered pharmacist, licensed pharmacist, pharmacologist, proprietor, drugstore owner, merchant; see also DOCTOR.

drum ***n.*** snare drum, skins*, traps; see MUSICAL INSTRUMENT.

drum up ***v.*** attract, provide, succeed in finding; see DISCOVER, FIND.

drunk ***a.*** intoxicated, inebriated, befuddled, tipsy, overcome, sottish, drunken, stoned*, feeling no pain*, out of it*, seeing double*, smashed*, blotto*, gassed*, plowed*, under the table*, tanked*, wiped out*, soused*, high*, pickled*, stewed*, boozed up*, tight*, plastered*, higher than a kite*; see also DIZZY.—*Ant.* SOBER, steady, temperate.

drunkard ***n.*** sot, inebriate, heavy drinker, tippler, alcoholic, drunken sot, drunk*, carouser, boozer*, barfly*, souse*, wino*, lush*, alky*; see also ADDICT.

drunkenness ***n.*** inebriety, intoxication, intemperance, insobriety, alcoholism, jag*.—*Ant.* ABSTINENCE, sobriety, temperance.

dry ***a.*** 1 [Having little or no moisture] arid, parched, waterless, hard, dried up, evaporated, desiccated, barren, dehydrated, drained, rainless, not irrigated, bare, thirsty, waterproof, rainproof, baked, shriveled, desert, dusty, depleted, dry as a bone*, bone-dry*; see also STERILE 2.—*Ant.* WET, moist, damp. 2 [Thirsty] parched, dehydrated, athirst*; see THIRSTY. 3 [Lacking in interest] boring, uninteresting, tedious; see DULL 4. 4 [Possessed of intellectual humor] sarcastic, cynical, biting; see FUNNY 1.

dry ***v.*** 1 [To become dry] dry up, shrivel, wilt; see EVAPORATE, WITHER. 2 [To cause to become dry] air-dry, condense, concentrate, dehydrate, freeze-dry, blot, sponge, parch, scorch, dry up, exhaust; see also DRAIN 1, EMPTY 2. —**dry out** (or **up**) drain, dehydrate, undergo evaporation; see DRY 1, 2.

dry goods ***n.*** cloth, yard goods, yardage; see COTTON, LINEN, WOOL.

dryness ***n.*** aridity, lack of moisture, dehydration; see THIRST.

dual ***a.*** binary, twofold, coupled; see DOUBLE, TWIN.

dubious ***a.*** 1 [Doubtful] indecisive, perplexed, hesitant; see DOUBTFUL, UNCERTAIN. 2 [Vague] ambiguous, indefinite, unclear; see OBSCURE 1.

dubiously ***a.*** doubtfully, doubtingly, indecisively; see SUSPICIOUSLY.

duck[1] ***n.*** teal, mallard, fresh water duck, sea duck; see also BIRD. —**like water off a duck's back** ineffective, ineffectual, weak; see USELESS 1.

duck[2] ***v.*** 1 [To immerse quickly] plunge, submerge, drop; see DIP 1, IMMERSE. 2 [*To avoid] dodge, escape, elude; see AVOID, EVADE.

duct ***n.*** tube, canal, channel; see PIPE 1.

duct'work' ***n.*** a system of ducts used to circulate air for heating, cooling, etc.

dud (dud) ***n.*** ⟦prob. < Du *dood*, dead⟧ [Inf.] **1** a bomb, etc. that fails to explode **2** a failure

dude (do͞od) ***n.*** ⟦< ?⟧ **1** a dandy; fop **2** [West Slang] a tourist at a ranch **3** [Slang] any man or boy —***vt.***, ***vi.*** **dud'ed**, **dud'ing** [Slang] to dress up, esp. in showy clothes: usually with *up*

dude ranch a vacation resort on a ranch, with horseback riding, etc.

dud·geon (duj'ən) ***n.*** now chiefly in **in high dudgeon**, very angry, offended, etc.

duds (dudz) ***pl.n.*** ⟦ME *dudde*, cloth, cloak < ?⟧ [Inf.] **1** clothes **2** belongings

due (do͞o, dyo͞o) ***adj.*** ⟦< L *debere*, owe⟧ **1** owed or owing as a debt; payable **2** suitable; proper **3** enough *[due care]* **4** expected or scheduled to arrive —***adv.*** exactly; directly *[due west]* —***n.*** **1** deserved recognition **2** [*pl.*] fees or other charges *[union dues]* —**due to 1** caused by **2** [Inf.] because of —**pay one's dues** [Slang] to earn a right, etc., as by having suffered in struggle

due bill a receipt for money paid, exchangeable for goods or services only

du·el (do͞o'əl) ***n.*** ⟦< medieval L *duellum*⟧ **1** a prearranged fight between two persons armed with deadly weapons **2** any contest like this —***vi.***, ***vt.*** **-eled** or **-elled**, **-el·ing** or **-el·ling** to fight a duel with —**du'el·ist** or **du'el·list**, **du'el·er** or **du'el·ler** ***n.***

due process (of law) legal proceedings established to protect individual rights and liberties

du·et (do͞o et') ***n.*** ⟦< L *duo*, two⟧ **1** a composition for two voices or instruments **2** the two performers of this

duf·fel (or **duf·fle**) **bag** (duf'əl) ⟦after *Duffel*, town in Belgium⟧ a large cloth bag for carrying clothing, etc.

duff·er (duf'ər) ***n.*** ⟦< thieves' slang *duff*, to fake⟧ [Inf.] **1** a slow-witted or dawdling elderly person **2** a relatively unskilled golfer

dug (dug) ***vt.***, ***vi.*** *pt. & pp. of* DIG

dug'out' ***n.*** **1** a boat hollowed out of a log **2** a shelter, as in warfare, dug in the ground **3** *Baseball* a covered shelter, one for each team

DUI (dē'yo͞o'ī') ***n.*** a citation for driving while under the influence of alcohol, drugs, etc.

du jour (do͞o zhoor') offered on this day *[soup du jour]*

duke[1] (do͝ok) ***n.*** ⟦< L *dux*, leader⟧ **1** a prince ruling an independent duchy **2** a nobleman next in rank to a prince —**duke'dom** ***n.***

duke[2] (do͝ok) ***n.*** [*pl.*] [Slang] the fists or hands —**duke it out** to fight, esp. with the fists

dul·cet (dul'sit) ***adj.*** ⟦< L *dulcis*, sweet⟧ soothing or pleasant to hear

dul·ci·mer (dul'sə mər) ***n.*** ⟦< L *dulce*, sweet + *melos*, song⟧ a musical instrument with metal strings, which are struck with two small hammers or plucked with a plectrum or quill

dull (dul) ***adj.*** ⟦OE *dol*⟧ **1** mentally slow; stupid **2** physically slow; sluggish **3** boring; tedious **4** not sharp; blunt **5** not feeling or felt keenly **6** not vivid or bright *[a dull color]* **7** not distinct; muffled *[a dull thud]* —***vt.***, ***vi.*** to make or become dull —**dull'ness** ***n.*** —**dul'ly** ***adv.***

dull'ard (-ərd) ***n.*** a stupid person

Du·luth (də lo͞oth') city & port in NE Minnesota, on Lake Superior: pop. 85,000

du·ly (do͞o'lē) ***adv.*** in due manner; in the proper way, at the right time, etc.

Du·mas (do͞o mä'), **Alexandre** 1802-70; Fr. novelist & playwright

dumb (dum) ***adj.*** ⟦OE⟧ **1** lacking the power of speech; mute **2** silent **3** ⟦Ger *dumm*⟧ [Inf.] stupid —**dumb down** [Inf.] to make or become less intellectually demanding —**dumb'ly** ***adv.*** —**dumb'ness** ***n.***

dumb'bell' ***n.*** **1** a device consisting of round weights joined by a short bar, lifted for muscular exercise **2** [Slang] a stupid person

dumb'found' or **dum'found'** ***vt.*** ⟦DUMB + (CON)FOUND⟧ to make speechless by shocking; amaze

dumb'wait'er ***n.*** a small elevator for sending food, etc. between floors

dum·dum (bullet) (dum'dum') ⟦after *Dumdum*, arsenal in India⟧ a soft-nosed bullet that expands when it hits, causing a large wound

dum·my (dum'ē) ***n.***, *pl.* **-mies 1** a figure made in human form, as for displaying clothing **2** an imitation; sham **3** [Slang] a stupid person **4** *Bridge* the declarer's partner, whose hand is exposed on the table and played by the declarer —***adj.*** sham

dump (dump) ***vt.*** ⟦prob. < ON⟧ **1** to unload in a heap or mass **2** to throw away (rubbish, etc.) **3** to sell (a commodity) in a large quantity at a low price **4** *Comput. a)* to transfer (data) to another section of storage *b)* to make a printout of (data) —***n.*** **1** a place for dumping rubbish, etc. **2** *Mil.* a temporary storage center in the field **3** an ugly, run-down place —**(down) in the dumps** [Inf.] in low spirits —**dump on** [Slang] to treat with contempt

dump'er ***n.*** [Slang] a container for refuse

dump·ling (dump'liŋ) ***n.*** ⟦< ?⟧ **1** a small piece of steamed or boiled dough served with meat or soup **2** a crust of baked dough filled with fruit

Dump·ster (dump'stər) *trademark for* a large metal trash bin, often one emptied by a special truck —***n.*** [*usually* **d-**] such a trash bin

dump'y ***adj.*** **-i·er**, **-i·est 1** short and thick; squat **2** [Inf.] ugly, run-down, etc.

dun[1] (dun) ***adj.***, ***n.*** ⟦OE⟧ dull grayish-brown

dun[2] (dun) ***vt.***, ***vi.*** **dunned**, **dun'ning** ⟦? dial. var. of DIN⟧ to ask (a debtor) repeatedly for payment —***n.*** an insistent demand for payment

THESAURUS

dud* ***n.*** failure, flop, debacle; see FAILURE 1.

duds* ***n.*** garb, garments, clothing; see CLOTHES.

due ***a.*** payable, owed, owing, overdue, collectible, unsatisfied, unsettled, not met, receivable, to be paid, chargeable, outstanding, in arrears; see also UNPAID 1, 2. —**become** (or **fall**) **due** be owed, payable, remain unsatisfied, mature. —**due to** because of, resulting from, accordingly; see BECAUSE.

duel ***n.*** combat, engagement, contest; see FIGHT 1.

dues ***n.*** contribution, obligation, toll, duty, levy, collection, fee, assessment, tax, rates; see also PAY 1, TAX 1.

dull ***a.*** **1** [Without point or edge] blunt, blunted, unsharpened, pointless, unpointed, round, square, flat, nicked, broken, toothless.—*Ant.* SHARP, sharpened, keen. **2** [Lacking brightness or color] gloomy, sober, somber, drab, dismal, dark, dingy, dim, dusky, colorless, plain, obscure, tarnished, opaque, leaden, grave, grimy, faded, sooty, inky, dead, black, coal-black, unlighted, sordid, dirty, muddy, gray, lifeless, rusty, flat.—*Ant.* BRIGHT, colorful, gleaming. **3** [Lacking intelligence; *said usually of living beings*] slow, retarded, witless; see STUPID. **4** [Lacking interest; *said usually of writing, speaking, or inanimate things*] heavy, prosaic, trite, hackneyed, monotonous, humdrum, tedious, dreary, dismal, dry, arid, colorless, insipid, boring, vapid, flat, senseless, long-winded, stupid, commonplace, ordinary, common, usual, old, ancient, stale, moth-eaten, out-of-date, archaic, worn-out, tiring, banal, tired, uninteresting, wooden, pointless, uninspiring, piddling, senile, proverbial, tame, routine, familiar, known, well-known, conventional, depressing, sluggish, repetitious, repetitive, soporific, tiresome, lifeless, wearying, unexciting, flat, stereotyped, stock, the usual thing, the same old thing, the same thing day after day, slow, dry as a bone*, cut and dried, dead as a doornail.—*Ant.* EXCITING, fascinating, exhilarating. **5** [Not loud or distinct] low, soft, softened; see FAINT 3. **6** [Showing little activity] still, routine, regular; see SLOW 1. **7** [Gloomy] cloudy, dim, unlit; see DARK 1.

dullness ***n.*** **1** [Quality of being boring] flatness, sameness, routine, evenness, tedium, aridity, depression, dreariness, commonplaceness, mediocrity, tameness, familiarity; see also BOREDOM, MONOTONY.—*Ant.* ACTION, liveliness, interest. **2** [Stupidity] nonsense, lunacy, slow-wittedness; see STUPIDITY 1.

duly ***a.*** rightfully, properly, appropriately; see JUSTLY 1.

dumb ***a.*** **1** [Unable to speak] silent, inarticulate, deaf and dumb, voiceless, speechless, having a speech impediment; see also MUTE 1, QUIET. **2** [Slow of wit] simple-minded, feeble-minded, moronic; see DULL 3, STUPID.

dumbbell* ***n.*** blockhead, fool, dunce; see FOOL.

dummy ***n.*** **1** [*Fool] dolt, blockhead, oaf; see FOOL. **2** [Imitation] sham, counterfeit, duplicate; see COPY, IMITATION 2.

dump ***n.*** refuse heap, junk pile, garbage dump, city dump, dumping ground, junkyard, scrapheap, landfill.

dump ***v.*** empty, unload, deposit, unpack, discharge, evacuate, drain, eject, exude, expel, throw out, throw over, throw overboard; see also DISCARD.—*Ant.* LOAD, fill, pack.

dumps ***n.*** despondency, dejection, despair; see DESPERATION, GLOOM.

dunce (duns) ***n.*** ⟦after John *Duns* Scotus, 13th-c. Scot scholar⟧ a dull, ignorant person
dune (do͞on) ***n.*** ⟦Fr < MDu⟧ a rounded hill or ridge of drifted sand
dung (duŋ) ***n.*** ⟦OE⟧ animal excrement; manure
dun·ga·ree (duŋ′gə rē′) ***n.*** ⟦Hindi *dungrī*⟧ **1** a coarse cotton cloth **2** [*pl.*] work trousers or overalls made of this
dun·geon (dun′jən) ***n.*** ⟦< OFr *donjon*⟧ a dark underground cell or prison
dung′hill′ ***n.*** a heap of dung
dunk (duŋk) ***vt.*** ⟦Ger *tunken*⟧ **1** to dip (bread, etc.) into coffee, etc. before eating it **2** to immerse briefly
Dun·kirk (dun′kurk′) seaport in N France: scene of the evacuation of Allied troops under fire (1940)
du·o (do͞o′ō) ***n.***, *pl.* **du′os** ⟦It⟧ **1** DUET (esp. sense 2) **2** a pair; couple
du·o·de·num (do͞o′ō dē′nəm, do͞o äd′′n əm) ***n.***, *pl.* **-na** (-nə) or **-nums** ⟦< L *duodeni*, twelve each: its length is about twelve fingers' breadth⟧ the first section of the small intestine, below the stomach —**du′o·de′nal** ***adj.***
dup *abbrev.* duplicate
dupe (do͞op) ***n.*** ⟦< L *upupa*, stupid bird⟧ a person easily tricked —***vt.*** **duped, dup′ing** to deceive; fool; trick —**dup′er** ***n.***
du·plex (do͞o′pleks′) ***adj.*** ⟦L < *duo*, TWO + *-plex*, -fold⟧ double —***n.*** **1** an apartment with rooms on two floors **2** a house consisting of two separate family units
du·pli·cate (do͞o′pli kit; *for v.*, -kāt′) ***adj.*** ⟦< L *duplicare*, to double⟧ **1** double **2** corresponding exactly —***n.*** an exact copy —***vt.*** **-cat′ed, -cat′ing** **1** to make an exact copy of **2** to make or do again —**du′pli·ca′tion** ***n.***
duplicating machine a machine for making copies of a letter, drawing, etc.
du·plic·i·ty (do͞o plis′ə tē) ***n.***, *pl.* **-ties** ⟦< LL *duplicitas*⟧ hypocritical cunning or deception
du·ra·ble (door′ə bəl) ***adj.*** ⟦< L *durare*, to last⟧ **1** lasting in spite of hard wear or frequent use **2** stable —**du′ra·bil′i·ty** ***n.*** —**du′ra·bly** ***adv.***
du·ra ma·ter (door′ə māt′ər) ⟦< ML, lit., hard mother, transl. of Ar term⟧ the tough, outermost membrane covering the brain and spinal cord
dur·ance (door′əns) ***n.*** ⟦see DURABLE⟧ long imprisonment: mainly in **in durance vile**
du·ra·tion (do͞o rā′shən) ***n.*** ⟦see DURABLE⟧ the time that a thing continues or lasts
du·ress (doo res′) ***n.*** ⟦< L *durus*, hard⟧ coercion
Dur·ham (dur′əm) city in NC North Carolina: pop. 137,000
dur·ing (door′iŋ) ***prep.*** ⟦see DURABLE⟧ **1** throughout the entire time of **2** in the course of
durst (durst) ***vt.***, ***vi.*** *now chiefly dial. pt. of* DARE
du·rum (door′əm) ***n.*** ⟦< L *durus*, hard⟧ a hard wheat that yields flour for macaroni, spaghetti, etc.
dusk (dusk) ***n.*** ⟦< OE *dox*, dark-colored⟧ **1** the dim part of twilight **2** dusky quality —**dusk′y, -i·er, -i·est,** ***adj.***
dust (dust) ***n.*** ⟦OE⟧ **1** powdery earth or any finely powdered matter **2** earth **3** disintegrated mortal remains **4** anything worthless —***vt.*** **1** to sprinkle with dust, powder, etc. **2** to rid of dust, as by wiping: often with *off* —***vi.*** to remove dust, as from furniture —**bite the dust** [Inf.] to die, esp. in battle —**dust′less** ***adj.***
dust bowl an arid region with eroded topsoil easily blown off by winds
dust′er ***n.*** **1** a person or thing that dusts **2** a lightweight housecoat
dust′pan′ ***n.*** a shovel-like pan into which floor dust is swept
dust′y ***adj.*** **-i·er, -i·est** **1** covered with or full of dust **2** powdery **3** muted with gray: said of a color —**dust′i·ness** ***n.***
Dutch (duch) ***n.*** the language of the Netherlands —***adj.*** of the Netherlands or its people, language, or culture —**go Dutch** [Inf.] to have each pay his or her own expenses —**in Dutch** [Inf.] in trouble or disfavor —**the Dutch** Dutch people
Dutch door a door with upper and lower halves that can be opened separately
Dutch oven a heavy pot with an arched lid, for pot roasts, etc.
Dutch treat [Inf.] any date, etc. on which each pays his or her own expenses
Dutch uncle [Inf.] one who bluntly and sternly lectures another, often with benevolent intent
du·te·ous (do͞ot′ē əs) ***adj.*** dutiful; obedient —**du′te·ous·ly** ***adv.***
du·ti·a·ble (do͞ot′ē ə bəl) ***adj.*** necessitating payment of a duty or tax
du·ti·ful (do͞ot′i fəl) ***adj.*** showing, or resulting from, a sense of duty; obedient —**du′ti·ful·ly** ***adv.***
du·ty (do͞ot′ē) ***n.***, *pl.* **-ties** ⟦see DUE & -TY⟧ **1** obedience or respect to be shown to one's parents, elders, etc. **2** any action required by one's position or by moral or legal considerations, etc. **3** service, esp. military service *[overseas duty]* **4** a tax, as on imports —**on** (or **off**) **duty** at (or temporarily relieved from) one's work
du·vet (do͞o vā′, dyo͞o-) ***n.*** a comforter, often down-filled, within a slipcover
DVD ***n.*** ⟦< *d(igital) v(ideo) d(isc)*⟧ a digital optical disc for recording images, sounds, or data for reproduction, specif. one on which a film has been recorded
dwarf (dwôrf) ***n.***, *pl.* **dwarfs** or **dwarves** (dwôrvz) ⟦< OE *dweorg*⟧ **1** any abnormally small person, animal, or plant **2** *Folklore* a little being in human form, with magic powers —***vt.*** **1** to stunt the growth of **2** to make seem small in comparison —***vi.*** to become dwarfed —***adj.*** undersized —**dwarf′ish** ***adj.*** —**dwarf′ism′** ***n.***
dweeb (dwēb) ***n.*** [Slang] a person regarded as dull, awkward, unsophisticated, etc.

THESAURUS

dunce ***n.*** dolt, lout, moron; see FOOL.
dune ***n.*** rise, knoll, ridge; see HILL.
dung ***n.*** offal, defecation, compost, manure, guano, fertilizer, excreta; horse dung, cow dung, etc.; chips, pellets, leavings, muck, feces, filth, garbage, sludge, slop, sewage; see also EXCREMENT, FERTILIZER.
duo ***n.*** couple, two, twosome; see PAIR.
duplicate ***n.*** double, second, mate, facsimile, replica, carbon copy, likeness, counterpart, analogue, parallel, correlate, repetition, duplication, recurrence, match, twin, Xerox (trademark), chip off the old block, clone*; see also COPY, IMITATION. —**in duplicate** duplicated, doubled, copied; see REPRODUCED.
duplicate ***v.*** **1** [To copy] reproduce, counterfeit, make a replica of; see COPY. **2** [To double] make twofold, multiply, make twice as much; see INCREASE. **3** [To repeat] redo, remake, rework; see REPEAT 1.
durability ***n.*** durableness, stamina, persistence; see ENDURANCE.
durable ***a.*** strong, firm, enduring; see PERMANENT.
duration ***n.*** span, continuation, continuance; see TERM 2.
duress ***n.*** compulsion, discipline, control; see PRESSURE 2, RESTRAINT 2.
during ***prep.*** as, at the time, at the same time as, the whole time, the time between, in the course of, in the middle of, when, all along, pending, throughout, in the meanwhile, in the interim, all the while, for the time being; see also MEANWHILE, WHILE 1.
dusk ***n.*** gloom, twilight, nightfall; see NIGHT 1.
dust ***n.*** dirt, lint, soil, sand, flakes, ashes, cinders, grime, soot, grit, filings, sawdust; see also EARTH 2, FILTH. —**bite the dust*** be killed, fall in battle, succumb; see DIE. —**make the dust fly** move swiftly, work hard, be active; see ACT 1, MOVE 1.
dust ***v.*** **1** [To put a powder on] sprinkle, sift, powder; see SCATTER 2. **2** [To remove dust] wipe, whisk, brush; see CLEAN.
dusty ***a.*** undusted, untouched, unused; see DIRTY 1.
dutiful ***a.*** devoted, respectful, conscientious; see FAITHFUL, OBEDIENT 1.
duty ***n.*** **1** [A personal sense of what one should do] moral obligation, conscience, liability, charge, accountability, faithfulness, pledge, burden, good faith, honesty, integrity, sense of duty, call of duty; see also RESPONSIBILITY 1, 2.—*Ant.* DISHONESTY, irresponsibility, disloyalty. **2** [Whatever one has to do] work, task, occupation, function, business, province, part, calling, charge, office, service, mission, obligation, contract, station, trust, burden, undertaking, commission, engagement, assignment, routine, chore, pains, responsibility; see also JOB 2.—*Ant.* ENTERTAINMENT, amusement, sport. **3** [A levy, especially on goods] charge, revenue, custom; see TAX 1. —**off duty** at leisure, off work, inactive; see FREE 2. —**on duty** working, on the job, at work; see BUSY 1.
dwarf ***a.*** dwarfed, low, diminutive; see LITTLE 1.
dwarf ***v.*** minimize, overshadow, dominate, predominate over, tower over, detract from, belittle, rise over, rise above, look down upon.—*Ant.* INCREASE, magnify, enhance.

dwell (dwel) ***vi.*** **dwelt** or **dwelled, dwell'ing** ⟦< OE *dwellan*, to hinder⟧ to make one's home; reside —**dwell on** (or **upon**) to think or talk about at length —**dwell'er** ***n.***
dwell'ing (place) ⟦ME: see prec.⟧ a residence; abode
DWI (dē'dub'əl yoo͞'ī') ***n.*** a citation for driving while intoxicated
dwin·dle (dwin'dəl) ***vi.*** **-dled, -dling** ⟦< OE *dwīnan*, waste away⟧ to keep on becoming smaller or less; diminish; shrink
dyb·buk (dib'ək) ***n.*** ⟦Heb *dibbūq*⟧ *Jewish Folklore* the spirit of a dead person that enters the body of a living person
dye (dī) ***n.*** ⟦< OE *deag*⟧ a substance or solution for coloring fabric, hair, etc.; also, the color produced —***vt.*** **dyed, dye'ing** to color with dye —**dy'er** ***n.***
dyed'-in-the-wool' ***adj.*** not changing, as in beliefs
dye'stuff' ***n.*** any substance constituting or yielding a dye
dy·ing (dī'iŋ) ***vi.*** *prp. of* DIE[1] —***adj.*** **1** about to die or end **2** at death —***n.*** death
dy·nam·ic (dī nam'ik) ***adj.*** ⟦< Gr *dynasthai*, be able⟧ **1** relating to bodies in motion **2** energetic; vigorous —**dy·nam'i·cal·ly** ***adv.***
dy·nam'ics ***n.*** the science dealing with motions produced by given forces —***pl.n.*** the forces operative in any field
dy·na·mite (dī'nə mīt') ***n.*** ⟦see DYNAMIC⟧ a powerful explosive made with nitroglycerin —***vt.*** **-mit'ed, -mit'ing** to blow up with dynamite
dy·na·mo (dī'nə mō') ***n.***, *pl.* **-mos'** ⟦see DYNAMIC⟧ **1** *former term for* GENERATOR **2** a dynamic person
dy·nas·ty (dī'nəs tē) ***n.***, *pl.* **-ties** ⟦< Gr *dynasteia*, rule⟧ a succession of rulers who are members of the same family —**dy·nas'tic** (-nas'tik) ***adj.***
dys- ⟦Gr⟧ *prefix* bad, ill, difficult, etc.
dys·en·ter·y (dis'ən ter'ē) ***n.*** ⟦< Gr *dys-*, bad + *entera*, bowels⟧ an intestinal inflammation characterized by abdominal pain and bloody diarrhea
dys·func·tion (dis fuŋk'shən) ***n.*** abnormal or impaired functioning —**dys·func'tion·al** ***adj.***
dys·lex·i·a (dis lek'sē ə) ***n.*** ⟦< DYS- + L *lexis*, speech⟧ impairment of the ability to read —**dys·lex'ic** or **dys·lec'tic** ***adj.***, ***n.***
dys·pep·si·a (dis pep'sē ə, -shə) ***n.*** ⟦< Gr *dys-*, bad + *pepsis*, digestion⟧ indigestion —**dys·pep'tic** ***adj.***, ***n.***
dz *abbrev.* dozen(s)

THESAURUS

dwell ***v.*** live, inhabit, stay, lodge, stop, settle, remain, live in, live at, continue, go on living, rent, tenant, have a lease on, make one's home at, have one's address at, keep house, be at home, room, bunk*, crash*; see also OCCUPY 2. —**dwell on** involve oneself in, think about, be engrossed in; see CONSIDER, EMPHASIZE.

dweller ***n.*** tenant, inhabitant, occupant; see RESIDENT.

dwelling ***n.*** house, establishment, lodging; see HOME 1.

dye ***n.*** tinge, stain, tint; see COLOR.

dye ***v.*** tint, stain, impregnate with color; see COLOR.

dying ***a.*** **1** [Losing life] sinking, terminal, passing away, fated, going, perishing, failing, expiring, moribund, withering away, at death's door, done for*, cashing in one's chips*, with one foot in the grave; see also WEAK 2. **2** [Becoming worse or less] declining, going down, receding, retarding, decreasing, disappearing, dissolving, disintegrating, vanishing, failing, fading, ebbing, decaying, overripe, decadent, passé, doomed, neglected; see also SICK, WEAK 2.

dynamic ***a.*** energetic, potent, compelling, forceful, changing, progressive, productive, vigorous, magnetic, electric, effective, influential, charismatic, high-powered, peppy*, hopped up; see also ACTIVE, POWERFUL 1.

dynamite ***n.*** nitroglycerin, TNT, blasting powder; see EXPLOSIVE.

dynasty ***n.*** line, house, lineage; see FAMILY.

E

e or **E** (ē) ***n.***, *pl.* **e's, E's** the fifth letter of the English alphabet

E[1] (ē) ***n.*** **1** *Educ.* a grade for below-average work or, sometimes, excellence **2** *Music* the third tone in the scale of C major

E[2] *abbrev.* **1** east(ern) **2** *Baseball* error(s) **3** *Physics* energy

e- *prefix* EX-

E- or **e-** *prefix* done, etc. electronically on the Internet *[E-commerce]*

each (ēch) ***adj., pron.*** ⟦OE *ælc*⟧ every one of two or more considered separately —***adv.*** apiece Abbrev. **ea.** —**each other** each one the other or others; one another

ea·ger (ē′gər) ***adj.*** ⟦< L *acer*⟧ keenly desiring; impatient or anxious —**ea′ger·ly** ***adv.*** —**ea′ger·ness** ***n.***

ea·gle (ē′gəl) ***n.*** ⟦< L *aquila*⟧ **1** a large bird of prey, with sharp vision and powerful wings **2** a representation of the eagle, as the U.S. emblem **3** *Golf* a score of two under par on a hole

ea′gle-eyed′ ***adj.*** having keen vision

ea·glet (ē′glit) ***n.*** a young eagle

ear[1] (ir) ***n.*** ⟦OE *ēare*⟧ **1** the part of the body that perceives sound **2** the visible, external part of the ear **3** one's sense of hearing or hearing ability **4** anything like an ear —**be all ears** to listen attentively —**give** (or **lend**) **ear** to give attention; heed —**play by ear** to play (music) without using notation —**play it by ear** [Inf.] to improvise

ear[2] (ir) ***n.*** ⟦< OE *ēar*⟧ the grain-bearing spike of a cereal plant, esp. of corn —***vi.*** to sprout ears

ear′ache′ ***n.*** an ache in the ear

ear′drum′ ***n.*** TYMPANIC MEMBRANE

earl (url) ***n.*** ⟦< OE *eorl*, warrior⟧ a British nobleman ranking above a viscount —**earl′dom** ***n.***

ear′lobe′ ***n.*** the fleshy lower part of the external ear

ear·ly (ur′lē) ***adv., adj.*** **-li·er, -li·est** ⟦< OE *ær*, before + *-lice*, -ly⟧ **1** near the beginning **2** before the expected or usual time **3** in the distant past **4** in the near future —**early on** at an early stage —**ear′li·ness** ***n.***

ear′mark′ ***n.*** **1** a mark put on the ear of livestock **2** an identifying mark or feature —***vt.*** **1** to put such a mark on **2** to reserve for a special purpose

ear′muffs′ (-mufs′) ***pl.n.*** coverings worn over the ears in cold weather

earn (urn) ***vt.*** ⟦OE *earnian*⟧ **1** to receive (wages, etc.) for one's work **2** to get as deserved **3** to receive (interest, etc.) as from a bank account —**earn′er** ***n.***

ear·nest[1] (ur′nist) ***adj.*** ⟦OE *eornoste*⟧ serious and intense; not joking —**in earnest** **1** serious **2** in a determined manner —**ear′nest·ly** ***adv.*** —**ear′nest·ness** ***n.***

ear·nest[2] (ur′nist) ***n.*** ⟦ult. < Heb *eravon*⟧ money, etc. given as a pledge in binding a bargain

earn′ings ***pl.n.*** **1** wages or other recompense **2** profits, interest, etc.

ear′phone′ ***n.*** a receiver for radio, etc., held to, or put into, the ear

ear′ring′ ***n.*** a ring or other small ornament for the lobe of the ear

ear′shot′ ***n.*** the distance within which a sound can be heard

ear′split′ting ***adj.*** so loud as to hurt the ears; deafening

earth (urth) ***n.*** ⟦OE *eorthe*⟧ **1** [*often* **E-**] the planet we live on, the third planet from the sun: see PLANET **2** this world, as distinguished from heaven and hell **3** land, as distinguished from sea or sky **4** soil; ground —**down to earth** **1** practical; realistic **2** sincere; without affectation

Earth Day April 22, a day on which environmentalist concerns are acknowledged

earth′en ***adj.*** made of earth or clay

earth′en·ware′ ***n.*** clay pottery

earth′ling ***n.*** a human being: now mainly in science fiction

earth′ly ***adj.*** **1** *a*) terrestrial *b*) worldly **2** conceivable *[no earthly reason]*

earth′quake′ ***n.*** a trembling of the earth's crust, caused by underground volcanic forces or shifting of rock

earth′ward ***adv., adj.*** toward the earth: also **earth′wards** ***adv.***

earth′work′ ***n.*** an embankment made by piling up earth, esp. as a fortification

earth′worm′ ***n.*** a round, segmented worm that burrows in the soil

THESAURUS

each ***a.*** **1** [Every] all, any, one by one, separate, particular, specific, private, several, respective, various, piece by piece, individual, personal, without exception. **2** [For each time, person, or the like] individually, proportionately, respectively, for one, per unit, singly, per capita, apiece, separately, every, without exception, by the, per, a whack*, a throw*, a shot*.

each ***pron.*** each one, one, each for himself or herself, each in his or her own way, every last one, one another, each other.

eager ***a.*** anxious, keen, fervent; see ZEALOUS.

eagerly ***a.*** zealously, intently, anxiously, sincerely, vigorously, readily, earnestly, willingly, heartily, strenuously, fiercely, rapidly, hungrily, thirstily, fervently, actively, enthusiastically, gladly, lovingly, with zeal, with open arms, with all the heart, from the bottom of one's heart, with delight, full tilt.—*Ant.* SLOWLY, unwillingly, grudgingly.

eagerness ***n.*** zest, anticipation, excitement; see ZEAL.

eagle ***n.*** hawk, falcon, bird of prey; see BIRD.

eagle-eyed ***a.*** discerning, keen-sighted, clear-sighted; see OBSERVANT.

ear[1] ***n.*** outer ear, middle ear, inner ear, eardrum, labyrinth, acoustic organ, auditory apparatus. —**all ears** attentive, hearing, paying attention; see LISTENING. —**bend someone's ear*** jabber, chatter, gossip; see TALK 1. —**fall on deaf ears** be ignored, fail to attract notice, be received with indifference; see FAIL 1, WAIT 1. —**have** (or **keep**) **an ear to the ground** be aware of, observe, keep one's eyes open; see LISTEN, MIND 3. —**in one ear and out the other** ignored, forgotten, received with indifference; see NEGLECTED. —**play it by ear*** improvise, concoct, go along; see INVENT 1. —**set on its ear*** stir up, agitate, arouse; see EXCITE. —**turn a deaf ear (to)** disregard, ignore, shun; see NEGLECT 1.

earlier ***a.*** former, previous, prior; see PRECEDING.

early ***a.*** **1** [Near the beginning] recent, primitive, prime, new, brand-new, fresh, budding.—*Ant.* LATE, old, tardy. **2** [Sooner than might have been expected] quick, premature, in advance, far ahead, in the bud, preceding, advanced, immediate, unexpected, speedy, ahead of time, direct, prompt, punctual, briefly, shortly, presently, beforehand, on short notice, on the dot*, with time to spare.—*Ant.* SLOW, late, tardy.

earmark ***n.*** characteristic, attribute, quality; see CHARACTERISTIC.

earmark ***v.*** reserve, set aside, keep back; see MAINTAIN 3.

earn ***v.*** **1** [To deserve as reward] win, merit, gain; see DESERVE. **2** [To receive in payment] obtain, attain, get, procure, realize, obtain a return, make money by, acquire, profit, net, clear, score, draw, gather, secure, derive, make money, bring home, bring in, collect, pick up, scrape together.—*Ant.* SPEND, consume, exhaust.

earnest[1] ***a.*** ardent, zealous, warm; see ENTHUSIASTIC.

earnestly ***a.*** solemnly, soberly, thoughtfully; see SERIOUSLY 2.

earnings ***n.*** net proceeds, balance, receipts; see PAY 2.

earring ***n.*** pendant, ornament, jewel; see JEWELRY.

earth ***n.*** **1** [The world] globe, sphere, planet, *terra* (Latin), mundane world, creation, terrestrial sphere, orb, cosmos, universe, biosphere. **2** [The earthly crust] dirt, turf, loam, humus, clay, gravel, sand, land, dry land, terrain, mud, muck, soil, ground, fill, compost, topsoil, alluvium, subsoil, surface, shore, coast, deposit. —**come back** (or **down**) **to earth** be practical, be sensible, return to one's senses, quit dreaming; see also CALM DOWN, WORK 1. —**down to earth** earthly, realistic, mundane; see PRACTICAL. —**on earth** of all things, of everything, what; see WHATEVER.

earthen ***a.*** clay, stone, mud, dirt, rock, fictile, made of earth, made of baked clay.

earthenware ***n.*** crockery, ceramics, china; see POTTERY.

earthly ***a.*** human, mortal, global, mundane, worldly, under the sun, in all creation.—*Ant.* UNNATURAL, alien, superhuman.

earthquake ***n.*** tremor, temblor, aftershock, seismic activity, shock, quake, fault, slip, movement of the earth's crust, earth tremor, volcanic quake.

earth'y ***adj.*** **-i·er, -i·est** **1** of or like earth **2** *a)* coarse; unrefined *b)* simple and natural

ease (ēz) ***n.*** ⟦< L *adjacens,* lying nearby⟧ **1** freedom from pain or trouble; comfort **2** natural manner; poise **3** freedom from difficulty; facility **4** affluence —***vt.*** **eased, eas'ing** **1** to free from pain or trouble; comfort **2** to lessen (pain, anxiety, etc.) **3** to facilitate **4** to reduce the strain or pressure of **5** to move by careful shifting, etc. —***vi.*** to become less tense, severe, etc.

ea·sel (ē'zəl) ***n.*** ⟦ult. < L *asinus,* ass⟧ an upright frame or tripod to hold an artist's canvas, etc.

ease·ment (ēz'mənt) ***n.*** *Law* a right that one may have in another's land, as the right to pass through

eas·i·ly (ē'zə lē) ***adv.*** **1** with ease **2** certainly **3** very likely

east (ēst) ***n.*** ⟦OE⟧ **1** the direction in which sunrise occurs (90° on the compass) **2** a region in or toward this direction —***adj.*** **1** in, of, toward, or facing the east **2** from the east *[an east wind]* —***adv.*** in or toward the east —**the East** **1** the eastern part of the U.S. **2** Asia and the nearby islands

East Asia countries of E Asia, including China, Japan, North & South Korea, and Mongolia —**East Asian**

East Berlin *see* BERLIN

East China Sea part of the Pacific Ocean, between China & Japan

Eas·ter (ēs'tər) ***n.*** ⟦< OE *Eastre,* dawn goddess⟧ an annual Christian festival in the spring, celebrating the resurrection of Jesus

east'er·ly ***adj., adv.*** **1** in or toward the east **2** from the east

east'ern ***adj.*** **1** in, of, or toward the east **2** from the east **3** [E-] of the East

east'ern·er ***n.*** a person born or living in the east

Eastern Hemisphere that half of the earth which includes Europe, Africa, Asia, and Australia

Eastern Orthodox Church the Christian church dominant in E Europe, W Asia, and N Africa

East Germany *see* GERMANY

East In·dies (in'dēz') Malay Archipelago; esp., the islands of Indonesia —**East Indian**

east'ward ***adv., adj.*** toward the east *[moving slowly eastward]*: also **east'wards** ***adv.***

eas·y (ē'zē) ***adj.*** **-i·er, -i·est** ⟦see EASE⟧ **1** not difficult **2** free from anxiety, pain, etc. **3** comfortable; restful **4** free from constraint; not stiff **5** not strict or severe **6** *a)* unhurried *b)* gradual —***adv.*** [Inf.] easily —**take it easy** [Inf.] **1** to refrain from anger, haste, etc. **2** to relax; rest —**eas'i·ness** ***n.***

easy chair a stuffed armchair

eas'y·go'ing ***adj.*** **1** acting in a relaxed manner **2** not strict; lenient

eat (ēt) ***vt.*** **ate, eat'en, eat'ing** ⟦OE *etan*⟧ **1** to chew and swallow (food) **2** to consume or ravage: with *away* or *up* **3** to destroy, as acid does; corrode **4** to make by or as by eating *[acid eats holes in cloth]* **5** [Slang] to worry or bother —***vi.*** to eat food; have a meal —**eat'a·ble** ***adj.*** —**eat'er** ***n.***

eat·er·y (ēt'ər ē) ***n., pl.*** **-ies** [Inf.] a restaurant

eats ***pl.n.*** [Inf.] food

eaves (ēvz) ***pl.n., sing.*** **eave** ⟦< OE *efes,* edge⟧ the projecting lower edge or edges of a roof

eaves'drop' ***vi.*** **-dropped', -drop'ping** ⟦prob. < *eavesdropper,* one who stands under eaves to listen⟧ to listen secretly to a private conversation —**eaves'drop'per** ***n.***

ebb (eb) ***n.*** ⟦OE *ebba*⟧ **1** the flow of the tide back toward the sea **2** a lessening —***vi.*** **1** to recede, as the tide **2** to lessen; decline

eb·on·y (eb'ə nē) ***n., pl.*** **-ies** ⟦< Gr *ebenos*⟧ the hard, heavy, dark wood of certain tropical trees —***adj.*** **1** of ebony **2** like ebony; specif., dark or black

e·bul·lient (i bo͝ol'yənt, -bul'-) ***adj.*** ⟦< L *e-,* out + *bullire,* to boil⟧ **1** bubbling; boiling **2** enthusiastic; exuberant —**e·bul'lience** ***n.***

EC European Community

THESAURUS

earthy ***a.*** **1** [Characteristic of earth] dusty, made of earth, muddy; see EARTHEN. **2** [Unrefined] coarse, dull, unrefined; see CRUDE.

ease ***n.*** **1** [Freedom from pain] comfort, rest, quietness, peace, leisure, repose, satisfaction, calm, calmness, restfulness, serenity, tranquillity, solace, consolation.—*Ant.* PAIN, discomfort, unrest. **2** [Freedom from difficulty] expertness, facility, efficiency, knack, readiness, quickness, skillfulness, dexterity, cleverness, smoothness, child's play, clear sailing*, snap*, breeze*, cinch*, pushover*.—*Ant.* DIFFICULTY, trouble, clumsiness. **—at ease** relaxed, collected, resting; see CALM 1.

ease ***v.*** **1** [To relieve of pain] alleviate, allay, drug, keep under sedation, tranquilize, sedate, anesthetize, reduce, mitigate, assuage, ameliorate, comfort, relieve pressure, cure, attend to, doctor, nurse, soothe.—*Ant.* HURT, injure, aggravate. **2** [To lessen pressure or tension] cheer, lift, bear, hold up, make comfortable, raise, unburden, release, soften, relieve one's mind, lighten, let up on, give rest to, relax, quiet, calm, pacify. **3** [To move carefully] induce, remove, extricate, set right, right, insert, join, slide, maneuver, handle.—*Ant.* HURRY, rush, blunder.

easily ***a.*** readily, with ease, in an easy manner, effortlessly, simply, with no effort, without trouble, handily, regularly, steadily, efficiently, smoothly, plainly, comfortably, calmly, coolly, surely, just like that*, with one hand tied behind one's back*.

easiness ***n.*** carelessness, nonchalance, facility; see ABILITY.

east ***a.*** **1** [Situated to the east] eastward, in the east, on the east side of, toward the sunrise, east side, eastern, easterly, easternmost. **2** [Going toward the east] eastbound, eastward, to the east, headed east, in an easterly direction, out of the west. **3** [Coming from the east] westbound, westward, to the west, headed west, in a westerly direction, out of the east.

East ***n.*** **1** [The eastern part of the United States] East Coast, the eastern states, the Atlantic seaboard, the Eastern seaboard, land east of the Alleghenies, east of the Appalachians, land east of the Mississippi. **2** [The eastern part of Eurasia] Asia, Asia Minor, Near East, Far East, Middle East, Siberia, Mongolia, southeast Asia, Arabia, Orient, Levant.

eastern ***a.*** **1** [Concerning the direction to the east] easterly, eastward, on the east side of; see EAST 1. **2** [Concerning the eastern part of the United States] East, Atlantic, Atlantic Seaboard, East Coast, Northeastern, Southeastern, New England, Middle Atlantic, South Atlantic. **3** [Concerning the Near East or Middle East] Palestinian, Egyptian, of the Holy Land, Arab, Arabic, Israeli, Hellenic, Hebraic, in Asia Minor. **4** [Concerning the Orient] Far Eastern, East Asian, Asian; see ORIENTAL.

easy ***a.*** **1** [Free from constraint] secure, at ease, prosperous, leisurely, unembarrassed, spontaneous, calm, peaceful, tranquil, careless, contented, carefree, untroubled, moderate, hospitable, soft.—*Ant.* DIFFICULT, demanding, hard. **2** [Providing no difficulty] simple, facile, obvious, apparent, yielding, easily done, smooth, manageable, accessible, wieldy, slight, little, paltry, inconsiderable, nothing to it*, simple as ABC*, easy as pie*, like taking candy from a baby*.—*Ant.* HARD, difficult, complicated. **3** [Lax] lenient, indulgent, easygoing; see KIND. **—take it easy*** relax, rest, slow down; see CALM DOWN.

easygoing ***a.*** tranquil, carefree, patient; see CALM 1.

eat ***v.*** **1** [To take as food] consume, bite, chew, devour, swallow, feast on, dine out, gulp, peck at, gorge, gobble up, eat up, digest, masticate, feed on, breakfast, dine, eat out, sup, lunch, feed, feast, banquet, fall to, live on, feed on, wolf down, enjoy a meal, have a bite, put away*, make a pig of oneself*, eat out of house and home*.—*Ant.* FAST, starve, diet. **2** [To reduce gradually] eat up, eat away, liquefy, melt, disappear, vanish, waste, rust away, spill, dissipate, squander, drain, gnaw, run through.—*Ant.* INCREASE, swell, build. **3** [To bother] worry, vex, disturb; see BOTHER 2.

eatable ***a.*** digestible, nutritious, delicious; see EDIBLE.

eating ***n.*** consuming, consumption, devouring, feasting on, gorging on, feeding on, biting, chewing, dining, breakfasting, lunching, eating out, overeating, dining out, eating up, having a coffee break, having a lunch break, having a bite, having a snack, breaking bread, making a pig of oneself*, stuffing oneself, swallowing, gulping down, gobbling up, gobbling down, putting on the feed bag*, eating out of house and home*.

eats* ***n.*** food, victuals*, meal; see FOOD.

eavesdrop ***v.*** overhear, wiretap, listen, listen in on, try to overhear, monitor, bug*, tap.

ebb ***n.*** recession, decline, outward flow, outward sweep, shrinkage, wane, waste, depreciation, reduction, lessening, ebb tide, regression, withdrawal, decrease, depreciation.—*Ant.* INCREASE, flow, rise.

ebb ***v.*** recede, subside, retire, flow back, sink, decline, decrease, drop off, melt, fall away, peter out*, wane, fall off, decay, abate.—*Ant.* INCREASE, flow, rise.

ec·cen·tric (ək sen′trik) ***adj.*** ⟦< Gr *ek-*, out of + *kentron*, center⟧ **1** not concentric: said of two circles, one inside the other **2** with its axis off center *[an eccentric wheel]* **3** not exactly circular **4** odd, as in conduct; unconventional —***n.*** **1** a disk set off center on a shaft, for converting circular motion into back-and-forth motion **2** an eccentric person —**ec·cen′tri·cal·ly** ***adv.*** —**ec·cen·tric·i·ty** (ek′sen tris′ə tē), *pl.* **-ties,** ***n.***

Ec·cle·si·as·tes (e klē′zē as′tēz′) ***n.*** ⟦< Gr *ek-*, out + *kalein*, to call⟧ a book of the Old Testament

ec·cle′si·as′tic (-tik) ***adj.*** ⟦see prec.⟧ ECCLESIASTICAL —***n.*** a member of the clergy

ec·cle′si·as′ti·cal (-ti kəl) ***adj.*** of the church or the clergy

ech·e·lon (esh′ə län′) ***n.*** ⟦< Fr < L *scala*, ladder⟧ **1** a steplike formation of ships, troops, or aircraft **2** a subdivision of a military force **3** any of the levels of responsibility in an organization

e·chi·no·derm (ē kī′nō durm′) ***n.*** ⟦< ModL⟧ a marine animal with a hard, spiny skeleton and radial body, as the starfish

ech·o (ek′ō) ***n.***, *pl.* **-oes** ⟦< Gr *ēchō*⟧ **1** the repetition of a sound by reflection of sound waves from a surface **2** a sound so produced **3** any repetition or imitation of the words, ideas, etc. of another —***vi.*** **-oed, -o·ing** **1** to reverberate **2** to make an echo —***vt.*** to repeat (another's words, ideas, etc.)

e·cho·ic (e kō′ik) ***adj.*** imitative in sound, as the word *tinkle*

é·clair (ā kler′, i-, ē-) ***n.*** ⟦Fr, lit., lightning⟧ an oblong pastry shell filled with custard, etc.

é·clat (ā klä′, i-, ē-) ***n.*** ⟦Fr < *éclater*, burst (out)⟧ **1** brilliant success **2** striking effect **3** acclaim; fame

ec·lec·tic (ek lek′tik) ***adj.*** ⟦< Gr *ek-*, out + *legein*, choose⟧ selecting or selected from various sources —***n.*** one who uses eclectic methods —**ec·lec′ti·cal·ly** ***adv.*** —**ec·lec′ti·cism′** (-tə siz′əm) ***n.***

e·clipse (i klips′, ē-) ***n.*** ⟦< Gr *ek-*, out + *leipein*, leave⟧ **1** the obscuring of the sun when the moon comes between it and the earth (**solar eclipse**), or of the moon when the earth's shadow is cast upon it (**lunar eclipse**) **2** any obscuring of light, or of fame, glory, etc. —***vt.*** **e·clipsed′, e·clips′ing** **1** to cause an eclipse of **2** to surpass

e·clip·tic (i klip′tik) ***n.*** the sun's apparent annual path, as seen from the orbiting earth

ec·logue (ek′lôg′) ***n.*** ⟦see ECLECTIC⟧ a short pastoral poem

eco- ⟦< Gr *oikos*, house⟧ *combining form* **1** environment or habitat **2** ecology

ec·o·cide (ē′kō sīd′) ***n.*** ⟦prec. + -CIDE⟧ the destruction of the environment, as by pollutants

e·col·o·gy (ē käl′ə jē) ***n.*** ⟦< Gr *oikos*, house + *-logia*, -LOGY⟧ the branch of biology that deals with the relations between living organisms and their environment —**ec′o·log′i·cal** ***adj.*** —**ec′o·log′i·cal·ly** ***adv.*** —**e·col′o·gist** ***n.***

econ *abbrev.* economic(s)

ec·o·nom·ic (ek′ə näm′ik, ē′kə-) ***adj.*** **1** of the management of income, expenditures, etc. **2** of economics **3** of the satisfaction of the material needs of people

ec′o·nom′i·cal ***adj.*** **1** not wasting money, time, etc.; thrifty **2** that uses no more of something than is necessary —**ec′o·nom′i·cal·ly** ***adv.***

ec′o·nom′ics ***n.*** **1** the science that deals with the production, distribution, and consumption of wealth **2** economic factors

e·con·o·mist (i kän′ə mist, ē-) ***n.*** a specialist in economics

e·con′o·mize′ (-mīz′) ***vi.*** **-mized′, -miz′ing** to reduce waste or expenses —**e·con′o·miz′er** ***n.***

e·con′o·my (-mē) ***n.***, *pl.* **-mies** ⟦< Gr *oikos*, house + *nomos*, law⟧ **1** the management of the income, expenditures, etc. of a household, government, etc. **2** careful management of wealth, etc.; thrift **3** efficient use of one's materials **4** an instance of thrift **5** a system of producing and distributing wealth —***adj.*** costing less or less per unit than the standard kind

ec·o·sys·tem (ē′kō sis′təm) ***n.*** ⟦< Gr *oikos*, house + SYSTEM⟧ a community of animals and plants, together with its environment

ec·sta·sy (ek′stə sē) ***n.***, *pl.* **-sies** ⟦< Gr *ek-*, out + *histanai*, to set⟧ a state or feeling of overpowering joy; rapture —**ec·stat·ic** (ek stat′ik) ***adj.*** —**ec·stat′i·cal·ly** ***adv.***

-ec·to·my (ek′tə mē) ⟦< Gr *ek-*, out + *temnein*, to cut⟧ *combining form* a surgical excision of

Ec·ua·dor (ek′wə dôr′) country on the NW coast of South America: 104,506 sq. mi.; pop. 9,648,000 —**Ec′ua·do′re·an, Ec′ua·do′ri·an,** or **Ec′ua·dor′an** ***adj.***, ***n.***

ec·u·men·i·cal (ek′yoo men′i kəl) ***adj.*** ⟦< Gr *oikoumenē* (*gē*), the inhabited (world)⟧ **1** general, or universal; esp., of the Christian church as a whole **2** furthering religious unity, esp. among Christian churches —**ec′u·men′i·cal·ly** ***adv.***

ec·u·men·ism (ek′yoo mə niz′əm, e kyoo′-) ***n.*** the ecumenical movement, esp. among Christian churches —**ec′u·men·ist** ***n.***

ec·ze·ma (ek′zə mə, eg′zə-) ***n.*** ⟦< Gr *ek-*, out + *zein*, to boil⟧ a skin disorder characterized by inflammation, itching, and scaliness

ed *abbrev.* **1** edited (by) **2** *a)* edition *b)* editor *c)* education

-ed ⟦OE⟧ *suffix* **1** forming the past tense or past participle of certain verbs **2** forming adjectives from nouns or verbs *[cultured, bearded]*

E·dam (cheese) (ē′dəm, -dam′) ⟦after *Edam*, Netherlands⟧ a mild, yellow cheese

ed·dy (ed′ē) ***n.***, *pl.* **-dies** ⟦prob. < ON *itha*⟧ a little whirlpool or whirlwind —***vi.*** **-died, -dy·ing** to move in an eddy

e·del·weiss (ā′dəl vīs′) ***n.*** ⟦Ger < *edel*, noble + *weiss*, white⟧ a small, flowering plant, esp. of the Alps, with white and woolly leaves

e·de·ma (ē dē′mə) ***n.***, *pl.* **-mas** or **-ma·ta** (-mə tə) ⟦< Gr *oidēma*, swelling⟧ an abnormal accumulation of fluid in body tissues or cavities

E·den (ēd′'n) ***n.*** **1** *Bible* the garden where Adam and Eve first lived; Paradise **2** any delightful place —**E·den′ic** or **e·den·ic** (ē den′ik) ***adj.***

edge (ej) ***n.*** ⟦OE *ecg*⟧ **1** the sharp, cutting part of a blade **2** sharpness; keenness **3** the projecting ledge of a cliff,

THESAURUS

eccentric ***a.*** odd, queer, strange; see UNUSUAL 2.

eccentricity ***n.*** peculiarity, abnormality, idiosyncrasy; see CHARACTERISTIC.

echo ***n.*** repetition, imitation, reply; see ANSWER 1.

echo ***v.*** repeat, mimic, impersonate; see IMITATE 1.

eclipse ***n.*** solar eclipse, lunar eclipse, total eclipse; see DARKNESS 1.

ecologist ***n.*** environmentalist, conservationist, naturalist, ecological engineer, oceanographer, biologist, botanist; see also SCIENTIST.

ecology ***n.*** ecological engineering, environmental science, antipollution projects, pollution control, survival studies, study of ecosystems, conservation of natural resources; see also SCIENCE 1, ZOOLOGY.

economic ***a.*** industrial, business, financial; see COMMERCIAL.

economical ***a.*** **1** [Careful of expenditures] saving, sparing, careful, economizing, thrifty, prudent, frugal, miserly, stingy, mean, parsimonious, close, watchful, tight*, close-fisted, penny-pinching; see also STINGY.—*Ant.* GENEROUS, liberal, wasteful. **2** [Advantageously priced] cheap, low-cost, low, reasonable, fair, moderate, inexpensive, marked down, on sale. **3** [Making good use of materials] practical, efficient, methodical; see EFFICIENT 1.

economics ***n.*** commerce, finance, business, political economy, science of wealth, economic theory, business theory, macroeconomics, microeconomics, fiscal policy, monetary policy; see also LAW 4, SCIENCE 1.

economist ***n.*** statistician, business analyst, efficiency expert; see SCIENTIST.

economize ***v.*** husband, manage, retrench, stint, conserve, scrimp, skimp, be frugal, be prudent, pinch, cut costs, cut corners, meet expenses, keep within one's means, cut down, meet a budget, make both ends meet, tighten one's belt, save for a rainy day*, pinch pennies; see also ACCUMULATE, MAINTAIN 3, SAVE 3.—*Ant.* SPEND, waste, splurge.

economy ***n.*** curtailment, cutback, business recession, retrenchment, rollback, reduction, layoff, wage decrease, cut in wages, moratorium.—*Ant.* INCREASE, outlay, raise.

ecstasy ***n.*** joy, rapture, delight; see HAPPINESS.

edge ***n.*** **1** [The outer portion] border, frontier, extremity, threshold, brink, boundary, end, limit, brim, rim, margin, ring, frame, side, corner, point, bend, peak, turn, crust, verge, perimeter, ledge, skirt, outskirt, lip, limb, hem, seam, fringe, frill, mouth, shore, strand, bank, beach, curb, periphery, circumference.—*Ant.* CENTER, middle, interior. **2** [Anything linear and sharp] blade, cutting edge, razor edge; see KNIFE. **3** [*Advantage] upper hand, handicap, head start; see ADVANTAGE. **—on edge** nervous, tense, uptight*; see IRRITABLE. **—set someone's teeth on edge** irritate, annoy, provoke; see BOTHER 2. **—take the edge off** weaken, subdue, dull; see SOFTEN.

etc.; brink **4** the part farthest from the middle; border; margin **5** [Inf.] advantage *[he has the edge on me]* —***vt.***, ***vi.*** **edged**, **edg'ing** **1** to form an edge (on) **2** to make (one's way) sideways **3** to move gradually —**on edge** **1** very tense; irritable **2** impatient —**edg'er** ***n.***

edge'ways' (-wāz') ***adv.*** with the edge foremost: also **edge'wise'** (-wīz')

edg'ing ***n.*** a fringe, trimming, etc. for a border

edg·y (ej'ē) ***adj.*** **-i·er, -i·est** **1** irritable; on edge **2** [Inf.] innovative, daring, etc. —**edg'i·ness** ***n.***

ed·i·ble (ed'ə bəl) ***adj.*** ⟦< L *edere*, eat⟧ fit to be eaten —***n.*** anything fit to be eaten: *usually used in pl.* —**ed'i·bil'i·ty** (-bil'ə tē) ***n.***

e·dict (ē'dikt') ***n.*** ⟦< L *e-*, out + *dicere*, speak⟧ a public order; decree

ed·i·fice (ed'i fis) ***n.*** ⟦see fol.⟧ a building, esp. a large, imposing one

ed·i·fy (ed'i fī') ***vt.*** **-fied', -fy'ing** ⟦< L *aedificare*, build⟧ to instruct so as to improve or uplift morally —**ed'i·fi·ca'tion** ***n.*** —**ed'i·fi'er** ***n.***

Ed·in·burgh (ed''n bur'ə, -ō) capital of Scotland: district pop. 419,000

Ed·i·son (ed'i sən), **Thom·as Alva** (täm'əs al'və) 1847-1931; U.S. inventor

ed·it[1] (ed'it) ***vt.*** ⟦< EDITOR⟧ **1** to prepare (a manuscript) for publication by arranging, revising, etc. **2** to control the policy and publication of (a newspaper, etc.) **3** to prepare (a film, tape, etc.) for presentation by cutting, dubbing, etc. **4** to make changes in (a computer file)

edit[2] *abbrev.* **1** edited (by) **2** edition **3** editor

e·di·tion (i dish'ən) ***n.*** ⟦see fol.⟧ **1** the size or form in which a book is published **2** the total number of copies of a book, etc. published at one time **3** any particular issue of a newspaper

ed·i·tor (ed'it ər) ***n.*** ⟦L < *e-*, out + *dare*, give⟧ **1** one that edits **2** a department head of a newspaper, etc.

ed·i·to·ri·al (ed'i tôr'ē əl) ***adj.*** of or by an editor —***n.*** a statement of opinion in a newspaper, etc., as by an editor, publisher, or owner —**ed'i·to'ri·al·ly** ***adv.***

ed'i·to'ri·al·ize' (-īz') ***vi.*** **-ized', -iz'ing** to express editorial opinions

editor in chief *pl.* **editors in chief** the editor who heads the editorial staff of a publication

Ed·mon·ton (ed'mən tən) capital of Alberta, Canada: pop. 616,000

educ *abbrev.* **1** education **2** educational

ed·u·ca·ble (ej'oo kə bəl, ej'ə-) ***adj.*** that can be educated or trained —**ed'u·ca·bil'i·ty** ***n.***

ed'u·cate' (-kāt') ***vt.*** **-cat'ed, -cat'ing** ⟦< L *e-*, out + *ducere*, to lead⟧ **1** to develop the knowledge, skill, or character of, esp. by formal schooling; teach **2** to pay for the schooling of —**ed'u·ca'tor** ***n.***

ed'u·cat'ed ***adj.*** **1** having much education **2** based on experience

ed'u·ca'tion (-kā'shən) ***n.*** **1** the process of educating; teaching **2** knowledge, etc. thus developed **3** formal schooling —**ed'u·ca'tion·al** ***adj.***

e·duce (ē do͞os') ***vt.*** **e·duced', e·duc'ing** ⟦see EDUCATE⟧ **1** to draw out; elicit **2** to deduce

-ee (ē) ⟦< Anglo-Fr pp. ending⟧ *suffix* **1** the recipient of a (specified) action *[appointee]* **2** one in a (specified) condition *[absentee]*

EEG *abbrev.* electroencephalogram

eel (ēl) ***n.*** ⟦OE *æl*⟧ a long, slippery, snakelike fish

EEOC *abbrev.* Equal Employment Opportunity Commission

e'er (er, ar) ***adv.*** [Old Poet.] EVER

-eer (ir) ⟦< L *-arius*⟧ *suffix* **1** *a)* one having to do with *[auctioneer]* *b)* one who writes, makes, etc. *[profiteer]* **2** to have to do with *[electioneer]*

ee·rie or **ee·ry** (ir'ē) ***adj.*** **-ri·er, -ri·est** ⟦< OE *earg*, timid⟧ mysterious, uncanny, or weird —**ee'ri·ly** ***adv.*** —**ee'ri·ness** ***n.***

ef- *prefix* EX-: used before *f [efface]*

ef·face (ə fās', i-) ***vt.*** **-faced', -fac'ing** ⟦< L *ex-*, out + *facies*, face⟧ **1** to rub out; erase **2** to make (oneself) inconspicuous —**ef·face'ment** ***n.***

ef·fect (e fekt', i-) ***n.*** ⟦< L *ex-*, out + *facere*, do⟧ **1** anything brought about by a cause; result **2** the power to cause results **3** influence **4** meaning *[spoke to this effect]* **5** an impression made on the mind, or its cause **6** a being operative or in force **7** [*pl.*] belongings; property —***vt.*** to bring about; accomplish —**in effect** **1** actually **2** virtually **3** in operation —**take effect** to become operative

ef·fec'tive ***adj.*** **1** producing a desired effect; efficient **2** in effect; operative **3** impressive —**ef·fec'tive·ly** ***adv.*** —**ef·fec'tive·ness** ***n.***

ef·fec·tu·al (e fek'cho͞o əl, i-) ***adj.*** **1** producing, or able to produce, the desired effect **2** having legal force; valid —**ef·fec'tu·al·ly** ***adv.***

ef·fec'tu·ate' (-āt') ***vt.*** **-at'ed, -at'ing** to bring about; effect

ef·fem·i·nate (e fem'ə nit, i-) ***adj.*** ⟦< L *ex-*, out + *femina*, woman⟧ having qualities attributed to women, as weakness, delicacy, etc.; unmanly —**ef·fem'i·na·cy** ***n.***

ef·fer·ent (ef'ər ənt) ***adj.*** ⟦< L *ex-*, out + *ferre*, to bear⟧ carrying away from a central part, as nerves

ef·fer·vesce (ef'ər ves') ***vi.*** **-vesced', -vesc'ing** ⟦< L *ex-*, out + *fervere*, to boil⟧ **1** to give off gas bubbles; bubble **2** to be lively —**ef'fer·ves'cence** ***n.*** —**ef'fer·ves'cent** ***adj.***

ef·fete (e fēt', i-) ***adj.*** ⟦< L *ex-*, out + *fetus*, productive⟧ **1** no longer able to produce; sterile **2** decadent, soft, too refined, etc. —**ef·fete'ly** ***adv.*** —**ef·fete'ness** ***n.***

ef·fi·ca·cious (ef'i kā'shəs) ***adj.*** ⟦see EFFECT⟧ that produces the desired effect —**ef'fi·ca'cious·ly** ***adv.*** —**ef'fi·ca·cy** (-kə sē) ***n.***

ef·fi'cien·cy ***n.*** **1** a being efficient **2** a small, usually one-room, apartment: in full **efficiency apartment**

THESAURUS

edge ***v.*** **1** [To trim] embellish, beautify, perfect; see TRIM 2, DECORATE. **2** [*To defeat narrowly] nose out, slip past, squeeze by; see DEFEAT 3.

edgy ***a.*** irritable, touchy, excitable; see NERVOUS.

edible ***a.*** palatable, good, delicious, satisfying, fit to eat, savory, tasty, culinary, yummy*, nutritious, digestible; see also DELICIOUS.

edifice ***n.*** structure, architectural monument, pile; see BUILDING.

edit[1] ***v.*** revise, alter, rewrite, rephrase, annotate, abridge, compose, compile, select, arrange, set up, censor, polish, finish, analyze, revise and correct, delete, condense, discard, strike out, write, proofread, cut, trim, blue-pencil, doctor up*.

edition ***n.*** printing, reprint, revision; see BOOK.

editor ***n.*** reviser, copyreader, supervisor, director, manager, editor-in-chief, proofreader, reader, editorial writer, deskman, newspaperman, newspaperwoman; see also AUTHOR, WRITER.

editorial ***n.*** essay, article, column; see COMPOSITION.

educate ***v.*** tutor, instruct, train; see TEACH.

educated ***a.*** trained, accomplished, skilled, well-taught, scientific, scholarly, intelligent, learned, well-informed, well-read, well-versed, well-grounded, disciplined, prepared, instructed, developed, well-trained, fitted, versed in, informed in, acquainted with, professional, expert, polished, cultured, finished, initiated, enlightened, literate, lettered, tutored, schooled.—*Ant.* IGNORANT, illiterate, unlettered.

education ***n.*** **1** [The process of directing learning] schooling, study, training, direction, instruction, guidance, apprenticeship, teaching, coaching, tutelage, learning, reading, discipline, preparation, adult education, book learning, information, indoctrination, brainwashing, cultivation, background, rearing. **2** [Knowledge acquired through education] learning, wisdom, scholarship; see KNOWLEDGE 1. **3** [The teaching profession] teaching, tutoring, pedagogy, instruction, training, the field of education, the educational profession, progressive education, lecturing.

educational ***a.*** enlightening, instructive, enriching; see CULTURAL.

educator ***n.*** pedagogue, instructor, tutor; see TEACHER.

eerie ***a.*** strange, ghostly, weird; see FRIGHTFUL 1.

effect ***n.*** conclusion, consequence, outcome; see RESULT. —**in effect** as a result, in fact, actually; see REALLY 1. —**take effect** work, produce results, become operative; see ACT 1. —**to the effect (that)** as a result, so that, therefore; see FOR.

effect ***v.*** produce, cause, make; see BEGIN 1, CAUSE.

effective ***a.*** efficient, serviceable, useful, operative, effectual, sufficient, adequate, productive, capable, competent, yielding, practical, valid, forceful.—*Ant.* USELESS, inoperative, inefficient.

effectively ***a.*** efficiently, completely, finally, expertly, conclusively, definitely, persuasively, adequately, capably, productively; see also WELL 2, 3.

effects ***n.*** personal property, baggage, possessions; see PROPERTY 1.

effectual ***a.*** adequate, efficient, qualified; see EFFECTIVE.

efficiency ***n.*** productivity, capability, capableness; see ABILITY.

ef·fi·cient (e fish′ənt, i-) ***adj.*** ⟦see EFFECT⟧ producing the desired result with a minimum of effort, expense, or waste —**ef·fi′cient·ly** ***adv.***

ef·fi·gy (ef′i jē) ***n.***, *pl.* **-gies** ⟦< L *ex-*, out + *fingere*, to form⟧ a statue or other image; often, a crude representation of a despised person that is hanged or burned to show protest

ef·flu·ent (ef′lo͞o ənt) ***adj.*** ⟦< L *effluere*, flow out⟧ flowing out —***n.*** the outflow of a sewer, septic tank, etc. —**ef′flu·ence** ***n.***

ef·flu·vi·um (e flo͞o′vē əm) ***n.***, *pl.* **-vi·a** (-ə) or **-vi·ums** ⟦see prec.⟧ a disagreeable vapor or odor

ef·fort (ef′ərt) ***n.*** ⟦< L *ex-*, intens. + *fortis*, strong⟧ **1** the use of energy to do something **2** a try; attempt **3** a result of working or trying —**ef′fort·less** ***adj.*** —**ef′fort·less·ly** ***adv.***

ef·fron·ter·y (e frunt′ər ē, i-) ***n.*** ⟦< L *ex-*, from + *frons*, forehead⟧ impudence; audacity

ef·ful·gence (e ful′jəns, i-) ***n.*** ⟦< L *ex-*, forth + *fulgere*, shine⟧ radiance; brilliance —**ef·ful′gent** ***adj.***

ef·fuse (e fyo͞oz′, i-) ***vt.***, ***vi.*** **-fused′**, **-fus′ing** ⟦< L *ex-*, out + *fundere*, pour⟧ **1** to pour out or forth **2** to spread out; diffuse

ef·fu′sion (-fyo͞o′zhən) ***n.*** **1** a pouring forth **2** unrestrained expression in speaking or writing —**ef·fu′sive** ***adj.*** —**ef·fu′sive·ly** ***adv.*** —**ef·fu′sive·ness** ***n.***

e.g. *abbrev.* ⟦L *exempli gratia*⟧ for example

e·gad (ē gad′) ***interj.*** ⟦prob. < *oh God*⟧ [Archaic] used as a softened oath

e·gal·i·tar·i·an (ē gal′ə ter′ē ən) ***adj.*** ⟦< Fr *égalité*, equality⟧ advocating full political, social, and economic equality for all people —***n.*** a person advocating this

egg[1] (eg) ***n.*** ⟦ON⟧ **1** the oval or round body laid by a female bird, fish, etc., containing the germ of a new individual **2** a reproductive cell produced by a female; ovum **3** a hen's egg, raw or cooked

egg[2] (eg) ***vt.*** ⟦< ON *eggja*, give edge to⟧ to urge or incite: with *on*

egg′beat′er ***n.*** a kitchen utensil for beating eggs, whipping cream, etc.

egg foo yong (or **young** or **yung**) (eg′fo͞o yuŋ′) a Chinese-American dish of beaten eggs cooked with bean sprouts, onions, minced pork or shrimp, etc.

egg′head′ ***n.*** [Slang] an intellectual

egg′nog′ (-näg′) ***n.*** ⟦EGG[1] + *nog*, strong ale⟧ a drink made of beaten eggs, milk, sugar, nutmeg, and, often, whiskey or rum

egg′plant′ ***n.*** **1** a plant with a large, ovoid, purple-skinned fruit eaten as a vegetable **2** the fruit

egg roll a Chinese-American dish, a thin egg pancake wrapped around minced vegetables, meat, etc. and deep-fried

eg·lan·tine (eg′lən tīn′, -tēn′) ***n.*** ⟦< L *aculeus*, a sting⟧ a European rose with sweet-scented leaves and pink flowers

e·go (ē′gō) ***n.***, *pl.* **-gos** ⟦L, I[2]⟧ **1** the self; the individual as self-aware **2** egotism **3** *Psychoanalysis* the part of the psyche that organizes thoughts rationally and governs action

e′go·cen′tric (-sen′trik) ***adj.*** viewing everything in relation to oneself —**e′go·cen′tri·cal·ly** ***adv.*** —**e′go·cen′trism′** ***n.***

e′go·ism′ ***n.*** **1** selfishness; self-interest **2** egotism; conceit —**e′go·ist** ***n.*** —**e′go·is′tic** or **e′go·is′ti·cal** ***adj.***

e′go·tism′ ***n.*** **1** excessive reference to oneself in speaking or writing **2** conceit; vanity —**e′go·tist** ***n.*** —**e′go·tis′tic** or **e′go·tis′ti·cal** ***adj.*** —**e′go·tis′ti·cal·ly** ***adv.***

ego trip [Slang] an experience that gratifies or indulges the ego

e·gre·gious (ē grē′jəs, i-) ***adj.*** ⟦< L *e-*, out + *grex*, a herd⟧ remarkably bad; flagrant —**e·gre′gious·ly** ***adv.*** —**e·gre′gious·ness** ***n.***

e·gress (ē′gres′) ***n.*** ⟦< L *e-*, out + *gradi*, go⟧ a way out; exit

e·gret (ē′gret′, -grit) ***n.*** ⟦< OFr *aigrette*⟧ **1** a kind of heron with long, white plumes **2** AIGRETTE

E·gypt (ē′jipt) country in NE Africa, on the Mediterranean: 386,662 sq. mi.; pop. 48,205,000

E·gyp·tian (ē jip′shən, i-) ***n.*** **1** the language of the ancient Egyptians **2** a person born or living in Egypt —***adj.*** of Egypt or its people, language, etc.

eh (ā, e) ***interj.*** **1** used to express doubt or surprise **2** used to make an inquiry

ei·der (ī′dər) ***n.*** ⟦ult. < ON *æthr*⟧ **1** a large sea duck of northern regions **2** EIDERDOWN

ei′der·down′ ***n.*** the fine, soft down of the eider, used as a stuffing for quilts, pillows, etc.

eight (āt) ***adj.***, ***n.*** ⟦< OE *eahta*⟧ one more than seven; 8; VIII —**eighth** (ātth) ***adj.***, ***n.***

eight ball a black ball with the number eight on it, used in playing pool —**behind the eight ball** [Slang] in a very unfavorable position

eight·een (ā′tēn′) ***adj.***, ***n.*** eight more than ten; 18; XVIII —**eight′eenth′** ***adj.***, ***n.***

eight′y ***adj.***, ***n.***, *pl.* **-ies** eight times ten; 80; LXXX —**the eighties** the numbers or years, as of a century, from 80 through 89 —**eight′i·eth** ***adj.***, ***n.***

Ein·stein (īn′stīn′), **Al·bert** (al′bərt) 1879-1955; U.S. physicist, born in Germany: formulated theory of relativity

Eir·e (er′ə) *Ir. name for* IRELAND

Ei·sen·how·er (ī′zen hou′ər), **Dwight David** (dwīt) 1890-1969; U.S. general & 34th president of the U.S. (1953-61)

ei·ther (ē′*th*ər, ī′-) ***adj.*** ⟦OE *æghwæther*⟧ **1** one or the other (of two) **2** each (of two) —***pron.*** one or the other (of two) —***conj.*** a correlative used with *or* to imply a choice of alternatives *[either go or stay]* —***adv.*** any more than the other; also *[if you don't go, I won't either]*

e·jac·u·late (ē jak′yo͞o lāt′, i-) ***vt.***, ***vi.*** **-lat′ed**, **-lat′ing** ⟦see fol.⟧ **1** to eject (esp. semen) **2** to utter suddenly; exclaim —**e·jac′u·la′tion** ***n.***

e·ject (ē jekt′, i-) ***vt.*** ⟦< L *e-*, out + *jacere*, to throw⟧ to throw or force out; expel —**e·jec′tion** ***n.***

THESAURUS

efficient ***a.*** **1** [*Said of persons*] competent, businesslike, good at, apt, adequate, fitted, able, capable, qualified, skillful, clever, talented, energetic, skilled, adapted, familiar with, deft, adept, expert, experienced, equal to, practiced, practical, proficient, accomplished, active, productive, dynamic, decisive, tough, shrewd.—*Ant.* INCOMPETENT, inefficient, incapable. **2** [*Said of things*] economical, fitting, suitable, suited, effectual, effective, adequate, serviceable, useful, saving, profitable, valuable, expedient, handy, conducive, well-designed, streamlined, cost-effective.—*Ant.* INADEQUATE, unsuitable, ineffectual.

effluent ***a.*** emanating, issuing forth, seeping; see FLOWING.

effort ***n.*** attempt, enterprise, undertaking, struggle, battle, try, trial, work, venture, aim, aspiration, purpose, intention, resolution, exercise, discipline, bid, endeavor, crack*, go*, whirl*; see also ACTION 1, 2.

effortless ***a.*** simple, offhand, smooth; see EASY 2.

egg[1] ***n.*** ovum, seed, germ, spawn, bud, embryo, nucleus, cell. *Prepared eggs include the following:* fried, scrambled, poached, deviled, hard-boiled, soft-boiled, shirred, soufflé, raw, buttered, on toast, egg salad, ham or bacon and eggs, over easy, sunny side up. —**lay an egg*** be unsuccessful, err, make a mistake; see FAIL 1. —**put** (or **have**) **all one's eggs in one basket** chance, gamble, bet; see RISK.

egg on ***v.*** encourage, goad, incite; see DRIVE 1, 2, URGE 2, 3.

ego ***n.*** personality, individuality, self; see CHARACTER 1, 2.

egotism ***n.*** egoism, conceit, vanity, pride, assurance, self-love, self-confidence, self-glorification, self-worship, arrogance, insolence, overconfidence, haughtiness.—*Ant.* MODESTY, humility, meekness.

egotist ***n.*** conceited person, boaster, egoist; see BRAGGART.

egotistic ***a.*** conceited, vain, boastful, inflated, pompous, arrogant, insolent, puffed up, affected, self-centered, self-glorifying, presumptuous, blustering, showy, boisterous, haughty, snobbish, contemptuous, proud, bullying, sneering, aloof, pretentious, assuming, cocky*, brazen, impertinent, selfish, bragging, insulting, theatrical, garish, gaudy, spectacular, reckless, impudent, inflated, stiff, overbearing, domineering, bold, rash, overconfident, self-satisfied, stuck-up*, looking down one's nose*, snooty*, uppity*, wrapped up in oneself*, on one's high horse*, high and mighty*, too big for one's breeches*.—*Ant.* HUMBLE, meek, modest.

egotistically ***a.*** vainly, boastfully, arrogantly, haughtily, pretentiously, loftily, selfishly.

either ***a.***, ***conj.*** on the one hand, whether or not, unless, it could be that, it might be that.

either ***pron.*** one, one or the other, this one, either/or, each of two, as soon one as the other, one of two.

eject ***v.*** dislodge, discard, reject, run out, kick out, throw out, put out, force out, spit out, turn out, squeeze out, oust, do away with, evict, banish, throw off, vomit, excrete, dump, get rid of, send packing, give the boot*, ditch*, bounce*.

ejection ***n.*** eviction, expulsion, dismissal; see REMOVAL.

eke (ēk) ***vt.*** **eked, ek′ing** ⟦< OE *eacan*, to increase⟧ to manage to make (a living) with difficulty: with *out*

EKG *abbrev.* electrocardiogram

e·lab·o·rate (ē lab′ə rit, i-; *for v.*, -rāt′) ***adj.*** ⟦< L *e-*, out + *labor*, work⟧ developed in great detail; complicated —***vt.*** **-rat′ed, -rat′ing** to work out in great detail —***vi.*** to add more details: usually with *on* or *upon* —**e·lab′o·rate·ly** ***adv.*** —**e·lab′o·rate·ness** ***n.*** —**e·lab′o·ra′tion** ***n.***

é·lan (ā län′, -län′) ***n.*** ⟦Fr < *élancer*, to dart⟧ spirited self-assurance; dash

e·lapse (ē laps′, i-) ***vi.*** **e·lapsed′, e·laps′ing** ⟦< L *e-*, out + *labi*, to glide⟧ to slip by; pass: said of time

e·las·tic (ē las′tik, i-) ***adj.*** ⟦< Gr *elaunein*, set in motion⟧ **1** able to spring back to its original size, shape, etc. after being stretched, squeezed, etc.; flexible **2** able to recover easily, as from dejection; buoyant **3** adaptable —***n.*** an elastic band or fabric —**e′las·tic′i·ty** (-tis′ə tē) ***n.***

e·las′ti·cize′ (-tə sīz′) ***vt.*** **-cized′, -ciz′ing** to make (fabric) elastic

e·late (ē lāt′, i-) ***vt.*** **-lat′ed, -lat′ing** ⟦< L *ex-*, out + *ferre*, to bear⟧ to raise the spirits of; make very proud, happy, etc. —**e·la′tion** ***n.***

el·bow (el′bō′) ***n.*** ⟦see ELL[2] & BOW[2]⟧ **1** the joint between the upper and lower arm; esp., the outer angle made by a bent arm **2** anything bent like an elbow —***vt., vi.*** to shove as with the elbows

elbow grease [Inf.] vigorous physical effort

el′bow·room′ ***n.*** ample space or room

eld·er[1] (el′dər) ***adj.*** ⟦< OE *eald*, old⟧ older —***n.*** **1** an older or aged person **2** an older person with some authority, as in a tribe **3** any of certain church officers

el·der[2] (el′dər) ***n.*** ⟦OE *ellern*⟧ a shrub or tree of the honeysuckle family, with red or purple berries

el′der·ber′ry (-ber′ē) ***n., pl.*** **-ries 1** ELDER[2] **2** its berry, used for making wine, jelly, etc.

eld′er·ly ***adj.*** **1** somewhat old **2** in old age; aged

eld·est (el′dist) ***adj.*** oldest; esp., firstborn

El Do·ra·do or **El·do·ra·do** (el′də rä′dō) ***n., pl.*** **-dos** ⟦Sp, the gilded⟧ any place supposed to be rich in gold, opportunity, etc.

e·lect (ē lekt′, i-) ***adj.*** ⟦< L *e-*, out + *legere*, choose⟧ **1** chosen **2** elected but not yet installed in office: usually used in combination *[mayor-elect]* —***vt., vi.*** **1** to select for an office by voting **2** to choose; select —**e·lect′a·ble** ***adj.*** —**e·lect′a·bil′i·ty** ***n.***

e·lec·tion (ē lek′shən, i-) ***n.*** **1** a choosing or choice **2** a choosing or being chosen by vote

e·lec′tion·eer′ ***vi.*** to canvass votes in an election

e·lec′tive (-tiv) ***adj.*** **1** *a)* filled by election *[an elective office] b)* chosen by election **2** having the power to choose **3** optional —***n.*** an optional course or subject in a school curriculum

e·lec′tor (-tər) ***n.*** **1** one who elects; specif., a qualified voter **2** a member of the electoral college —**e·lec′tor·al** ***adj.***

electoral college an assembly elected by the voters to perform the formal duty of electing the president and vice president of the U.S.

e·lec′tor·ate (-it) ***n.*** all those qualified to vote in an election

E·lec·tra (ē lek′trə, i-) ***n.*** *Gr. Myth.* a daughter of Agamemnon: she plots the death of her mother

e·lec·tric (ē lek′trik, i-) ***adj.*** ⟦< Gr *ēlektron*, amber: from the effect of friction upon amber⟧ **1** of, charged with, or conducting electricity **2** producing, or produced by, electricity **3** operated by electricity **4** using electronic amplification *[an electric guitar]* **5** very tense or exciting Also **e·lec′tri·cal** —**e·lec′tri·cal·ly** ***adv.***

electric chair a chair equipped for use in electrocuting persons sentenced to death

e·lec·tri·cian (ē′lek trish′ən, ē lek′-) ***n.*** one whose work is the construction and repair of electric apparatus

e′lec·tric′i·ty (-tris′i tē) ***n.*** **1** a property of certain fundamental particles of all matter, as electrons (negative charges) and protons or positrons (positive charges): electrical charge is generated by friction, induction, or chemical change **2** an electric current **3** electric current as a public utility for lighting, heating, etc.

e·lec·tri·fy (ē lek′trə fī′, i-) ***vt.*** **-fied′, -fy′ing 1** to charge with electricity **2** to excite; thrill **3** to equip for the use of electricity —**e·lec′tri·fi·ca′tion** ***n.*** —**e·lec′tri·fi′er** ***n.***

electro- *combining form* electric, electricity

e·lec·tro·car·di·o·gram (ē lek′trō kär′dē ə gram′, i-) ***n.*** a tracing showing the variations in electric force which trigger heart contractions

e·lec′tro·car′di·o·graph′ (-graf′) ***n.*** an instrument for making electrocardiograms

e·lec′tro·cute′ (-trə kyo͞ot′) ***vt.*** **-cut′ed, -cut′ing** ⟦ELECTRO- + (EXE)CUTE⟧ to kill or execute with electricity —**e·lec′tro·cu′tion** ***n.***

e·lec′trode′ (-trōd′) ***n.*** ⟦ELECTR(O)- + -ODE⟧ any terminal by which electricity enters or leaves a battery, etc.

e·lec′tro·en·ceph′a·lo·gram′ (-trō en sef′ə lō gram′) ***n.*** ⟦see ENCEPHALITIS & -GRAM⟧ a tracing of the variations in electric force in the brain

e·lec′tro·en·ceph′a·lo·graph′ (-graf′) ***n.*** an instrument for making electroencephalograms

e′lec·trol′y·sis (-i sis) ***n.*** ⟦ELECTRO- + -LYSIS⟧ **1** the decomposition of an electrolyte by the action of an electric current passing through it **2** the eradication of unwanted hair with an electrified needle

e·lec·tro·lyte (ē lek′trō līt′, i-) ***n.*** ⟦ELECTRO- + -LYTE⟧ any chemical compound that ionizes when molten or in solution and becomes capable of conducting electricity —**e·lec′tro·lyt′ic** (-lit′ik) ***adj.***

e·lec′tro·mag′net (-mag′nit) ***n.*** a soft iron core that becomes a magnet when an electric current flows through a surrounding coil —**e·lec′tro·mag·net′ic** (-net′ik) ***adj.***

electromagnetic wave a wave generated by an oscillating electric charge

e·lec′tro·mo′tive (-mōt′iv) ***adj.*** producing an electric current through differences in potential

e·lec·tron (ē lek′trän′, i-) ***n.*** ⟦see ELECTRIC⟧ a stable, negatively charged elementary particle that forms a part of all atoms

e·lec·tron·ic (ē′lek trän′ik) ***adj.*** **1** of electrons **2** operating, produced, or done by the action of electrons —**e·lec′tron′i·cal·ly** ***adv.***

THESAURUS

elaborate ***a.*** **1** [Ornamented] gaudy, decorated, garnished, showy, fussy, dressy, refined, flowery, flashy; see also ORNATE.—*Ant.* COMMON, ordinary, unpolished. **2** [Detailed] complicated, extensive, laborious, minute, intricate, involved, many-faceted, complex, a great many, painstaking, studied, convoluted.—*Ant.* GENERAL, usual, simple.

elaborate ***v.*** embellish, bedeck, deck; see DECORATE. —**elaborate upon** expand, discuss, comment upon; see EXPLAIN.

elapse ***v.*** transpire, pass away, slip by; see PASS 2.

elastic ***a.*** plastic, tempered, pliant; see FLEXIBLE.

elasticity ***n.*** resiliency, buoyancy, pliability; see FLEXIBILITY.

elbow ***n.*** joint, angle, funny bone; see BONE. —**rub elbows with** mingle with, associate with, be friends with; see JOIN 2. —**up to the elbows (in)** engaged, employed, working at; see BUSY 1.

elbowroom ***n.*** sweep, range, margin; see SPACE 2.

elder[1] ***n.*** veteran, old lady, old man, old woman, superior, old timer, senior, gramps*, granny*, patriarch, matriarch, chief, tribal head, dignitary, counselor, father, mother, uncle, aunt, grandfather, grandmother, ancestor.

elderly ***a.*** declining, retired, venerable; see OLD 1.

elect ***v.*** choose, name, select; see CHOOSE.

elected ***a.*** chosen, duly elected, picked; see NAMED 2.

election ***n.*** poll, polls, ballot, balloting, ticket, vote, voting, vote-casting, primaries, suffrage, referendum, plebiscite, voice vote.

elective ***a.*** voluntary, selective, not compulsory; see OPTIONAL.

electric ***a.*** **1** [Electrical] magnetic, galvanic, electronic, power-driven, telegraphic, electrified, cordless, battery-operated, photoelectric, solar-powered. **2** [Thrilling] vibrating, energetic, dynamic, pulsing, electrifying.

electricity ***n.*** power, current, service, heat, light, ignition, spark, utilities, alternating current (AC), direct current (DC), voltage, 110 volts, 220 volts, high voltage, high tension, kilowatts, kilowatt hours, juice*.

electrify ***v.*** wire, charge, power, heat, light, equip, lay cables, provide service, magnetize, galvanize, energize, subject to electricity, pass an electric current through, give an electric shock to, charge with electricity.

electrocute ***v.*** execute, put to death, kill by electric shock, put in the electric chair, send to the hot seat*, fry*, burn*.

electron ***n.*** negative particle, subatomic particle, elementary particle; see ATOM.

electronic ***a.*** cathodic, anodic, voltaic, photoelectric, photoelectronic, thermionic, computerized, digital, automatic, automated; see also ELECTRIC.

electronic mail E-MAIL
electronic music music in which the sounds are originated or altered by electronic devices
e'lec·tron'ics *n.* the science dealing with the action of electrons, and with the use of electron tubes, transistors, etc.
electron microscope a device that focuses a beam of electrons on a fluorescent screen, etc. to form a greatly enlarged image of an object
electron tube a sealed glass tube with gas or a vacuum inside, used to control the flow of electrons
e·lec·tro·plate (ē lek'trō plāt', i-) *vt.* **-plat'ed, -plat'ing** to deposit a coating of metal on by electrolysis
e·lec'tro·scope' (-skōp') *n.* a device for detecting very small charges of electricity or radiation —**e·lec'tro·scop'ic** (-skäp'ik) *adj.*
e·lec'tro·shock' therapy shock therapy using electricity
e·lec'tro·type' *n. Printing* a plate made by electroplating a wax or plastic impression of the surface to be reproduced
el·ee·mos·y·nar·y (el'i mäs'ə ner'ē, el'ē ə-) *adj.* ⟦< Gr *eleēmosynē*, pity⟧ of, for, or supported by charity
el·e·gant (el'ə gənt) *adj.* ⟦< L *e-*, out + *legere*, choose⟧ **1** having dignified richness and grace, as of manner, design, or dress; tastefully luxurious **2** cleverly apt and simple *[an elegant solution]* **3** [Inf.] excellent —**el'e·gance** *n.* —**el'e·gant·ly** *adv.*
el·e·gi·ac (el ē'jē ak', el'ə jī'ak') *adj.* **1** of, like, or fit for an elegy **2** sad; mournful
el·e·gy (el'ə jē) *n., pl.* **-gies** ⟦< Gr *elegos*, a lament⟧ a mournful poem, esp. of lament and praise for the dead
el·e·ment (el'ə mənt) *n.* ⟦< L *elementum*⟧ **1** the natural or suitable environment for a person or thing **2** a component part or quality, often one that is basic or essential **3** *Chem.* any substance that cannot be separated into different substances by ordinary chemical methods, but only by radioactive decay or by nuclear reactions: all matter is composed of such substances —**the elements** **1** the first principles; rudiments **2** wind, rain, etc.; forces of the atmosphere
el·e·men·tal (el'ə ment''l) *adj.* **1** of or like basic, natural forces; primal **2** ELEMENTARY (sense 2*a*) **3** being an essential part or parts
el'e·men'ta·ry (-ə rē) *adj.* **1** ELEMENTAL **2** *a*) of first principles or fundamentals; basic; simple *b*) of the formal instruction of children in basic subjects
elementary particle a subatomic particle that cannot be divided
elementary school a school of the first six (sometimes eight) grades, where basic subjects are taught
el·e·phant (el'ə fənt) *n.* ⟦< Gr *elephas*⟧ a huge, thick-skinned mammal with a long, flexible snout, or trunk, and, usually, two ivory tusks
el·e·phan·ti·a·sis (el'ə fən tī'ə sis) *n.* a chronic disease causing the enlargement of certain body parts and hardening of the surrounding skin
el·e·phan·tine (el'ə fan'tēn') *adj.* like an elephant; huge, clumsy, etc.
el·e·vate (el'ə vāt') *vt.* **-vat'ed, -vat'ing** ⟦< L *e-*, out + *levare*, to lift⟧ **1** to lift up; raise **2** to raise in rank **3** to raise to a higher intellectual or moral level **4** to elate; exhilarate
el'e·va'tion (-vā'shən) *n.* **1** an elevating or being elevated **2** a high place or position **3** height above the surface of the earth or above sea level
el'e·va'tor (-vāt'ər) *n.* **1** one that elevates, or lifts up **2** a suspended cage for hoisting or lowering people or things **3** a tall warehouse for storing and discharging grain: in full **grain elevator**
e·lev·en (ē lev'ən, i-) *adj., n.* ⟦OE *endleofan*⟧ one more than ten; 11; XI —**e·lev'enth** (-ənth) *adj., n.*
elf (elf) *n., pl.* **elves** (elvz) ⟦OE *ælf*⟧ *Folklore* a tiny, often mischievous fairy —**elf'in** or **elf'ish** *adj.*
El Gre·co (el grek'ō) 1541?-1614?; painter in Italy & Spain, born in Crete
e·lic·it (ē lis'it, i-) *vt.* ⟦< L *e-*, out + *lacere*, entice⟧ to draw forth; evoke (a response, etc.) —**e·lic'i·ta'tion** *n.*
e·lide (ē līd', i-) *vt.* **e·lid'ed, e·lid'ing** ⟦< L *e-*, out + *laedere*, to hurt⟧ to leave out; esp., to slur over (a vowel, etc.) in pronunciation —**e·li'sion** (-lizh'ən) *n.*
el·i·gi·ble (el'i jə bəl) *adj.* ⟦see ELECT⟧ fit to be chosen; qualified —**el'i·gi·bil'i·ty** *n.*
E·li·jah (ē lī'jə, i-) *n. Bible* a prophet of Israel in the 9th c. B.C.
e·lim·i·nate (ē lim'ə nāt', i-) *vt.* **-nat'ed, -nat'ing** ⟦< L *e-*, out + *limen*, threshold⟧ **1** to remove; get rid of **2** to leave out of consideration; omit **3** to excrete —**e·lim'i·na'tion** *n.*
El·i·ot (el'ē ət) **1 George** (pseud. of *Mary Ann Evans*)

THESAURUS

electronics *n.* radar, photoelectronics, cybernetics, computer electronics, thermionics, microelectronics; see also SCIENCE 1.

elegance *n.* culture, tastefulness, taste, cultivation, politeness, polish, grace, delicacy, splendor, beauty, balance, purity, grace, gracefulness, delicacy, magnificence, courtliness, nobility, charm, sophistication, propriety, style.

elegant *a.* ornate, polished, perfected, elaborate, finished, ornamented, adorned, embellished, embroidered, flowing, artistic, fancy, rich, pure, fluent, neat.—*Ant.* DULL, ill-chosen, inarticulate.

element *n.* **1** [A constitution] portion, particle, detail, component, constituent, ingredient, factor; see also PART 1. **2** [A form of matter] *The older sciences determined the following elements:* earth, air, fire, water; *modern chemistry and physics identify the following elements:* actinium (Ac), aluminum (Al), americium (Am), antimony (Sb), argon (Ar), arsenic (As), astatine (At), barium (Ba), berkelium (Bk), beryllium (Be), bismuth (Bi), bohrium (Bh), boron (B), bromine (Br), cadmium (Cd), calcium (Ca), californium (Cf) carbon (C), cerium (Ce), cesium (Cs), chlorine (Cl), chromium (Cr), cobalt (Co), copper (Cu), curium (Cm), dubnium (Db), dysprosium (Dy), einsteinium (Es), erbium (Er), europium (Eu), fermium (Fm), fluorine (F), francium (Fr), gadolinium (Gd), gallium (Ga), germanium (Ge), gold (Au), hafnium (Hf), hassium (Hs), helium (He), holmium (Ho), hydrogen (H), indium (In), iodine (I), iridium (Ir), iron (Fe), krypton (Kr), lanthanum (La), lawrencium (Lr), lead (Pb), lithium (Li), lutetium (Lu), magnesium (Mg), manganese (Mn), meitnerium (Mt), mendelevium (Md), mercury (Hg), molybdenum (Mo), neodymium (Nd), neon (Ne), neptunium (Np), nickel (Ni), niobium (Nb), nitrogen (N), nobelium (No), osmium (Os), oxygen (O), palladium (Pd), phosphorus (P), platinum (Pt), plutonium (Pu), polonium (Po), potassium (K), praseodymium (Pr), promethium (Pm), protactinium (Pa), radium (Ra), radon (Rn), rhenium (Re), rhodium (Rh), rubidium (Rb), ruthenium (Ru), rutherfordium (Rf), samarium (Sm), scandium (Sc), seaborgium (Sg), selenium (Se), silicon (Si), silver (Ag), sodium (Na), strontium (Sr), sulfur (S), tantalum (Ta), technetium (Tc), tellurium (Te), terbium (Tb), thallium (Tl), thorium (Th), thulium (Tm), tin (Sn), titanium (Ti), tungsten (W), uranium (U), vanadium (V), xenon (Xe), ytterbium (Yb), yttrium (Y), zinc (Zn), zirconium (Zr).

elementary *a.* **1** [Suited to beginners] primary, rudimentary, introductory; see EASY 2. **2** [Fundamental] foundational, essential, basic; see FUNDAMENTAL.

elements *n.* basic material, fundamentals, grammar, ABC's, initial stage, basis, beginning, first step, principles, rudiments, groundwork, brass tacks*.

elevate *v.* **1** [To lift bodily] hoist, heave, tilt; see RAISE 1. **2** [To promote] advance, appoint, further; see PROMOTE 1.

elevated *a.* aerial, towering, tall; see HIGH 2, RAISED 1.

elevation *n.* altitude, tallness, loftiness; see HEIGHT.

elevator *n.* **1** [Machine for lifting] lift, escalator, conveyor, elevator shaft, chair lift, passenger elevator, freight elevator, dumbwaiter, hoist, chute. **2** [A building handling grain] bin, storage plant, silo; see BARN.

elf *n.* brownie, sprite, leprechaun; see FAIRY.

eligibility *n.* fitness, acceptability, capability; see ABILITY.

eligible *a.* qualified, fit, suitable, suited, equal to, worthy of being chosen, capable of, fitted for, satisfactory, trained, employable, usable, likely, in the running, in line for, desirable, available.—*Ant.* UNFIT, ineligible, disqualified.

eliminate *v.* take out, wipe out, clean out, throw out, stamp out, blot out, cut out, phase out, drive out, dispose of, get rid of, do away with, put aside, set aside, exclude, eject, cast off, disqualify, oust, depose, evict, cancel, eradicate, erase, expel, discharge, dislodge, reduce, invalidate, abolish, repeal, abrogate, exterminate, annihilate, kill, murder, throw overboard, be done with, discard, dismiss, obliterate, discount, exile, banish, deport, expatriate, maroon, blackball, ostracize, fire, dump, can*, ditch*, scrap, bounce*, sack*, drop.—*Ant.* INCLUDE, accept, welcome.

elimination *n.* **1** [The act of removing] dismissal, expulsion, exclusion; see REMOVAL. **2** [The act of declining to consider] rejection, repudiation, denial, disqualification, avoidance.

1819-80; Eng. novelist **2 T(homas) S(tearns)** 1885-1965; Brit. poet, born in the U.S.

e·lite (i lēt′, ā-) ***n.*** ⟦Fr < L: see ELECT⟧ [*also with pl. v.*] the group or part of a group regarded as the best, most powerful, etc.

e·lit′ism′ ***n.*** government or control by an elite **—e·lit′ist** ***adj., n.***

e·lix·ir (i liks′ir) ***n.*** ⟦< Ar *al-iksīr*⟧ **1** a hypothetical substance sought by medieval alchemists to change base metals into gold or (in full **elixir of life**) to prolong life indefinitely **2** *Pharmacy* a sweetened solution used for medicines, etc.

E·liz·a·beth (ē liz′ə bəth, i-) **1 Elizabeth I** 1533-1603; queen of England (1558-1603) **2 Elizabeth II** 1926- ; queen of Great Britain & Northern Ireland (1952-)

E·liz·a·be·than (ē liz′ə bē′thən) ***adj.*** of or characteristic of the time of Elizabeth I's reign **—*n.*** an English person, esp. a writer, of that time

elk (elk) ***n.*** ⟦< OE *eolh*⟧ **1** MOOSE: the common term in Europe **2** WAPITI

ell[1] (el) ***n.*** **1** an extension or wing at right angles to the main structure **2** an L-shaped pipe, etc.

ell[2] (el) ***n.*** ⟦< OE *eln*⟧ a former English unit of measure, equal to 45 inches

el·lipse (e lips′, i-) ***n.***, *pl.* **-lip′ses′** (-sēz′) ⟦< Gr *elleipein*, fall short⟧ *Geom.* a closed curve in the form of a symmetrical oval

el·lip′sis (-lip′sis) ***n.***, *pl.* **-ses′** (-sēz′) ⟦see prec.⟧ **1** *Gram.* the omission of a word or words understood in the context (Ex.: "if possible" for "if it is possible") **2** a mark (...) indicating an omission of words: in full **ellipsis points**

el·lip′ti·cal (-ti kəl) ***adj.*** **1** of, or having the form of, an ellipse **2** of or characterized by ellipsis Also **el·lip′tic —el·lip′ti·cal·ly** ***adv.***

elm (elm) ***n.*** ⟦OE⟧ **1** a tall, deciduous shade tree **2** its hard, heavy wood

El Ni·ño (el nēn′yō) a warm inshore current annually flowing south along the coast of Ecuador

el·o·cu·tion (el′ə kyōō′shən) ***n.*** ⟦see ELOQUENT⟧ the art of public speaking **—el′o·cu′tion·ar′y** ***adj.*** **—el′o·cu′tion·ist** ***n.***

e·lo·de·a (ē lō′dē ə, el′ə dē′ə) ***n.*** ⟦< Gr *helōdēs*, swampy⟧ a submerged water plant with whorls of short, grasslike leaves

e·lon·gate (ē lôŋ′gāt′, i-) ***vt.***, ***vi.*** **-gat′ed, -gat′ing** ⟦< L *e-*, out + *longus*, long⟧ to make or become longer; stretch **—e′lon·ga′tion** ***n.***

e·lope (ē lōp′, i-) ***vi.*** **e·loped′, e·lop′ing** ⟦prob. < OE *a-*, away + *hleapan*, to run⟧ to run away secretly, esp. in order to get married **—e·lope′ment** ***n.***

el·o·quent (el′ə kwənt) ***adj.*** ⟦< L *e-*, out + *loqui*, speak⟧ vivid, forceful, fluent, etc. in speech or writing **—el′o·quence** ***n.*** **—el′o·quent·ly** ***adv.***

El Pas·o (el pas′ō) city in westernmost Texas.: pop. 515,000

El Sal·va·dor (el sal′və dôr′) country in Central America, on the Pacific: 8,124 sq. mi.; pop. 5,048,000

else (els) ***adj.*** ⟦OE *elles*⟧ **1** different; other [*somebody else*] **2** in addition [*is there anything else?*] **—*adv.*** **1** differently; otherwise [*where else can I go?*] **2** if not [*study, (or) else you will fail*]

else′where′ ***adv.*** in or to some other place; somewhere else

e·lu·ci·date (ə lōō′sə dāt′) ***vt., vi.*** **-dat′ed, -dat′ing** ⟦< L *e-*, out + *lucidus*, clear⟧ to make (something) clear; explain **—e·lu′ci·da′tion** ***n.***

e·lude (ē lōōd′, i-) ***vt.*** **e·lud′ed, e·lud′ing** ⟦< L *e-*, out + *ludere*, to play⟧ **1** to avoid or escape from by quickness, cunning, etc.; evade **2** to escape the mental grasp of [*his name eludes me*]

e·lu′sive (-lōō′siv) ***adj.*** tending to elude; evasive **—e·lu′sive·ly** ***adv.*** **—e·lu′sive·ness** ***n.***

elves (elvz) ***n.*** *pl. of* ELF

E·ly·si·um (ē lizh′əm, -liz′ē əm; i-) ***n.*** **1** *Gr. Myth.* the dwelling place of virtuous people after death **2** any state of ideal bliss; paradise **—E·ly′si·an** (-lizh′ən, -liz′ē ən) ***adj.***

em (em) ***n.*** ⟦< the letter *M*⟧ *Printing* a unit of measure, as of column width

'em (əm) ***pron.*** [Inf.] them

em- *prefix* EN-: used before *b, m,* or *p*

e·ma·ci·ate (ē mā′shē āt′, -sē-; i-) ***vt.*** **-at′ed, -at′ing** ⟦< L *e-*, out + *macies*, leanness⟧ to cause to become abnormally lean **—e·ma′ci·a′tion** ***n.***

e-mail (ē′māl′) ***n.*** [*also* **E-**] messages sent from one computer terminal to another, as by telephone line

em·a·nate (em′ə nāt′) ***vi.*** **-nat′ed, -nat′ing** ⟦< L *e-*, out + *manare*, to flow⟧ to come forth; issue, as from a source **—em′a·na′tion** ***n.***

e·man·ci·pate (ē man′sə pāt′, i-) ***vt.*** **-pat′ed, -pat′ing** ⟦< L *e-*, out + *manus*, the hand + *capere*, to take⟧ **1** to set free (a slave, etc.) **2** to free from restraint **—e·man′ci·pa′tion** ***n.*** **—e·man′ci·pa′tor** ***n.***

e·mas·cu·late (ē mas′kyōō lāt′) ***vt.*** **-lat′ed, -lat′ing** ⟦< L *e-*, out + *masculus*, male⟧ **1** to castrate **2** to weaken **—e·mas′cu·la′tion** ***n.***

em·balm (em bäm′, im-) ***vt.*** ⟦see EN- & BALM⟧ to preserve (a dead body) with various chemicals **—em·balm′er** ***n.***

em·bank (em baŋk′, im-) ***vt.*** to protect, support, or enclose with a bank of earth, etc. **—em·bank′ment** ***n.***

em·bar·go (em bär′gō, im-) ***n.***, *pl.* **-goes** ⟦Sp < L *in-*, in + ML *barra*, a bar⟧ **1** a government order prohibiting the entry or departure of commercial ships at its ports **2** any legal restriction of commerce **—*vt.*** **-goed, -go·ing** to put an embargo upon

em·bark (em bärk′, im-) ***vt.*** ⟦ult. < L *in-*, in + *barca*, small boat⟧ to put or take (passengers or goods) aboard a ship, aircraft, etc. **—*vi.*** **1** to go aboard a ship, aircraft, etc. **2** to begin; start **—em′bar·ka′tion** (-bär kā′shən) ***n.***

em·bar·rass (em bar′əs, im-) ***vt.*** ⟦< It *in-*, in + ML *barra*, a bar⟧ **1** to cause to feel self-conscious **2** to hinder **3** to cause to be in debt **—em·bar′rass·ing** ***adj.*** **—em·bar′rass·ment** ***n.***

em·bas·sy (em′bə sē) ***n.***, *pl.* **-sies** ⟦see AMBASSADOR⟧ **1** the residence or offices of an ambassador **2** an ambassa-

THESAURUS

elite ***n.*** society, nobility, celebrities; see ARISTOCRACY.

ellipse ***n.*** oval, conic section, closed curve; see CIRCLE 1.

elongate ***v.*** prolong, lengthen, extend; see STRETCH.

eloquence ***n.*** fluency, wit, wittiness, expression, expressiveness, appeal, ability, diction, articulation, delivery, power, force, vigor, facility, style, poise, expressiveness, flow, command of language, gift of gab*.

eloquent ***a.*** vocal, articulate, outspoken; see FLUENT.

elsewhere ***a.*** gone, somewhere else, not here, in another place, in some other place, to some other place, away, absent, abroad, hence, removed, remote, outside, formerly, subsequently.—*Ant.* HERE, at this point, in this spot.

elude ***v.*** dodge, shun, escape; see AVOID.

elusive ***a.*** slippery, fleeting, evasive; see TEMPORARY.

emaciated ***a.*** gaunt, famished, wasted; see THIN 2.

emanate ***v.*** exude, radiate, exhale; see EMIT.

emancipate ***v.*** release, liberate, deliver; see FREE.

emancipation ***n.*** liberty, release, liberation; see FREEDOM.

emasculate ***v.*** geld, unman, sterilize; see CASTRATE.

embalm ***v.*** preserve, process, freeze, anoint, wrap, mummify, prepare for burial, lay out.

embankment ***n.*** dike, breakwater, pier; see DAM.

embargo ***n.*** restriction, prohibition, impediment; see RESTRAINT 2.

embark ***v.*** set out, leave port, set sail; see LEAVE 1.

embarrass ***v.*** perplex, annoy, puzzle, vex, distress, disconcert, agitate, bewilder, confuse, chagrin, confound, upset, bother, plague, tease, worry, trouble, distract, discomfort, disturb, let down, perturb, fluster, irk, shame, stun, rattle, put on the spot*, make a monkey out of.—*Ant.* ENCOURAGE, cheer, please.

embarrassed ***a.*** abashed, perplexed, disconcerted; see ASHAMED.

embarrassing ***a.*** difficult, disturbing, confusing, distracting, bewildering, puzzling, rattling, perplexing, delicate, unbearable, distressing, disconcerting, upsetting, discomforting, ticklish, flustering, troublesome, worrisome, uncomfortable, awkward, disagreeable, helpless, unseemly, impossible, uneasy, mortifying, shameful, inconvenient, annoying, irksome, exasperating, sticky*, unmanageable.—*Ant.* COMFORTABLE, easy, agreeable.

embarrassment ***n.*** confusion, chagrin, mortification, discomfiture, shame, humiliation, shyness, timidity, inhibition, dilemma, puzzle, perplexity, tangle, strait, pinch, quandary, mistake, blunder, clumsiness, indebtedness, uncertainty, hindrance, poverty, destitution, distress, difficulties, involvement, obligation, indiscretion, awkward situation, predicament, plight, fix*, snag, hitch, hot seat*, hot water*, pickle*, stew.

embassy ***n.*** commission, mission, delegation; see COMMITTEE, DIPLOMAT.

dor and his or her staff **3** a group sent on an official mission

em·bat·tled (em bat′'ld) ***adj.*** ⟦< OFr⟧ engaged in battle or conflict

em·bed (em bed′, im-) ***vt.*** **-bed′ded, -bed′ding** to set or fix firmly in earth, in the mind or memory, etc. —**em·bed′ment** ***n.***

em·bel·lish (em bel′ish, im-) ***vt.*** ⟦< OFr *em-*, in + *bel*, beautiful⟧ **1** to adorn **2** to improve (a story, etc.) by adding details, often fictitious —**em·bel′lish·ment** ***n.***

em·ber (em′bər) ***n.*** ⟦OE *æmerge*⟧ **1** a glowing piece of coal, wood, etc. **2** [*pl.*] the smoldering remains of a fire

em·bez·zle (em bez′əl, im-) ***vt.*** **-zled, -zling** ⟦< OFr *en-*, in + *besillier*, destroy⟧ to steal (money, etc. entrusted to one) —**em·bez′zle·ment** ***n.*** —**em·bez′zler** ***n.***

em·bit′ter (-bit′ər) ***vt.*** to make bitter —**em·bit′ter·ment** ***n.***

em·bla′zon (-blā′zən) ***vt.*** ⟦EM- (see EN-) + BLAZON⟧ **1** to decorate (*with* coats of arms, etc.) **2** to display brilliantly **3** to extol —**em·bla′zon·ment** ***n.***

em·blem (em′bləm) ***n.*** ⟦< Gr *en-*, in + *ballein*, throw⟧ a visible symbol of a thing, idea, etc.; sign; badge —**em′blem·at′ic** (-blə mat′ik) ***adj.***

em·bod·y (em bäd′ē, im-) ***vt.*** **-ied, -y·ing** **1** to give bodily form to **2** to give definite form to **3** to bring together into an organized whole; incorporate —**em·bod′i·ment** ***n.***

em·bold′en (-bōl′dən) ***vt.*** to give courage to

em·bo·lism (em′bə liz′əm) ***n.*** ⟦< Gr *en-*, in + *ballein*, to throw⟧ the obstruction of a blood vessel as by a blood clot or air bubble

em·boss (em bôs′, -bäs′; im-) ***vt.*** ⟦see EN- & BOSS²⟧ **1** to decorate with raised designs, patterns, etc. **2** to raise (a design, etc.) in relief —**em·boss′er** ***n.***

em·bou·chure (äm′boo shoor′) ***n.*** ⟦Fr < L *in*, in + *bucca*, cheek⟧ the method of applying the lips and tongue to the mouthpiece of a wind instrument

em·brace (em brās′, im-) ***vt.*** **-braced′, -brac′ing** ⟦< L *im-*, in + *brachium*, an arm⟧ **1** to clasp in the arms lovingly; hug **2** to accept readily **3** to take up or adopt **4** to encircle **5** to include —***vi.*** to clasp each other in the arms —***n.*** an embracing; hug —**em·brace′a·ble** ***adj.***

em·bra·sure (em brā′zhər, im-) ***n.*** ⟦Fr < obs. *embraser*, widen an opening⟧ **1** an opening (for a door, window, etc.) wider on the inside than on the outside **2** an opening in a wall or parapet for a gun, with the sides slanting outward

em·broi·der (em broi′dər, im-) ***vt.***, ***vi.*** ⟦< OFr *en-*, on + *brosder*, embroider⟧ **1** to make (a design, etc.) on (fabric) with needlework **2** to embellish (a story); exaggerate

em·broi′der·y ***n.***, *pl.* **-ies** **1** the art of embroidering **2** embroidered work or fabric **3** embellishment

em·broil (em broil′, im-) ***vt.*** ⟦< OFr *en-*, in + *brouillier*, to dirty⟧ **1** to confuse; muddle **2** to involve in conflict or trouble —**em·broil′ment** ***n.***

em·bry·o (em′brē ō′) ***n.***, *pl.* **-os′** ⟦< Gr *en-*, in + *bryein*, to swell⟧ **1** an animal in the earliest stages of its development in the uterus or egg **2** the rudimentary plant contained in a seed **3** an early stage of something —**em′bry·on′ic** (-än′ik) ***adj.***

em′bry·ol′o·gy (-äl′ə jē) ***n.*** ⟦prec. + -LOGY⟧ the branch of biology dealing with the formation and development of embryos —**em′bry·ol′o·gist** ***n.***

em·cee (em′sē′) ***vi.***, ***vt.*** **-ceed′, -cee′ing** ⟦< MC, sense 1⟧ [Inf.] to act as master of ceremonies (for) —***n.*** [Inf.] a master of ceremonies

e·mend (ē mend′, i-) ***vt.*** ⟦< L *emendare*, to correct⟧ to make scholarly corrections in (a text) —**e·men·da·tion** (ē′men dā′shən, em′ən-) ***n.***

em·er·ald (em′ər əld) ***n.*** ⟦< Gr *smaragdos*⟧ **1** a transparent, bright-green precious stone **2** bright green

e·merge (ē murj′, i-) ***vi.*** **e·merged′, e·merg′ing** ⟦< L *e-*, out + *mergere*, to dip⟧ **1** to rise as from a fluid **2** to become visible or apparent **3** to evolve —**e·mer′gence** ***n.*** —**e·mer′gent** ***adj.***

e·mer·gen·cy (ē mur′jən sē, i-) ***n.***, *pl.* **-cies** ⟦orig. sense, emergence⟧ a sudden, generally unexpected occurrence demanding immediate action —***adj.*** for use in an emergency

emergency room a hospital unit for accident victims and others needing immediate treatment

e·mer·i·tus (ē mer′i təs, i-) ***adj.*** ⟦< L *e-*, out + *mereri*, to serve⟧ retired from active service, usually for age, but retaining one's title [professor *emeritus*]

Em·er·son (em′ər sən), **Ralph Wal·do** (ralf wôl′dō) 1803-82; U.S. writer & philosopher

em·er·y (em′ər ē) ***n.*** ⟦< Gr *smyris*⟧ a dark, coarse variety of corundum used for grinding, polishing, etc.

emery board a small, flat stick coated with powdered emery, used to shape the fingernails

e·met·ic (ē met′ik, i-) ***adj.*** ⟦< Gr *emein*, to vomit⟧ causing vomiting —***n.*** an emetic substance

-e·mi·a (ē′mē ə) ⟦< Gr *haima*, blood⟧ *combining form* a (specified) condition of the blood [*leukemia*]

em·i·grate (em′i grāt′) ***vi.*** **-grat′ed, -grat′ing** ⟦< L *e-*, out + *migrare*, to move⟧ to leave one country or region to settle in another —**em′i·grant** (-grənt) ***adj.***, ***n.*** —**em′i·gra′tion** ***n.***

é·mi·gré or **e·mi·gré** (em′i grā′) ***n.*** ⟦Fr⟧ **1** one who emigrates **2** one forced to flee his or her country for political reasons

em·i·nence (em′i nəns) ***n.*** ⟦< L *eminere*, stand out⟧ **1** a high place, thing, etc. **2** superiority in rank, position, etc. **3** [**E-**] a title of a cardinal: preceded by *Your* or *His*

em′i·nent (-nənt) ***adj.*** ⟦< L *eminens*⟧ **1** high; lofty **2** projecting; prominent **3** renowned; distinguished **4** outstanding —**em′i·nent·ly** ***adv.***

eminent domain the right of a government to take or purchase private property for public use, with just compensation to the owner

e·mir (e mir′, ə-) ***n.*** ⟦< Ar *amara*, to command⟧ in Muslim countries, a ruler or prince

em·is·sar·y (em′i ser′ē) ***n.***, *pl.* **-ies** ⟦see EMIT⟧ a person or agent sent on a specific mission

e·mis·sion (ē mish′ən, i-) ***n.*** **1** an emitting **2** something emitted; discharge

e·mit (ē mit′, i-) ***vt.*** **e·mit′ted, e·mit′ting** ⟦< L *e-*, out + *mittere*, send⟧ **1** to send out; give forth; discharge **2** to utter (words, etc.) —**e·mit′ter** ***n.***

THESAURUS

embed ***v.*** plant, implant, secure; see FASTEN.

embezzle ***v.*** thieve, forge, pilfer; see STEAL.

embezzlement ***n.*** fraud, misappropriation, stealing; see THEFT.

embezzler ***n.*** thief, robber, defaulter; see CRIMINAL.

embitter ***v.*** irritate, aggravate, annoy; see BOTHER 2.

emblem ***n.*** symbol, figure, image, design, token, sign, insignia, banner, seal, colors, crest, coat of arms, representation, effigy, reminder, mark, badge, souvenir, keepsake, medal, memento, character, motto, hallmark, flag, pennant, banner, standard, logo, monogram, colophon.

embodiment ***n.*** incarnation, matter, structure; see CHARACTERISTIC, ESSENCE 1, IMAGE 2.

emboss ***v.*** raise, design, enchase; see DECORATE.

embrace ***v.*** enfold, squeeze, clasp; see HUG.

embroider ***v.*** stitch, knit, weave; see SEW.

embryo ***n.*** fetus, blastula, blastocyst; see EGG.

embryonic ***a.*** incipient, immature, undeveloped; see EARLY 1.

emerald ***n.*** green beryl, valuable gem, precious stone; see JEWEL.

emerge ***v.*** rise, arrive, come out; see APPEAR 1.

emergence ***n.*** rise, evolution, appearance; see VIEW.

emergency ***n.*** accident, unforeseen occurrence, misadventure, strait, urgency, necessity, pressure, tension, distress, turn of events, obligation, plight, crisis, predicament, turning point, impasse, dilemma, quandary, pinch, fix*, hole*; see also DIFFICULTY 1, 2.

emigrant ***n.*** exile, expatriate, émigré, colonist, migrant, displaced person, D.P., traveler, foreigner, pilgrim, refugee, fugitive, wayfarer, wanderer, immigrant, alien, outcast, man without a country.

emigrate ***v.*** migrate, immigrate, quit; see LEAVE 1.

emigration ***n.*** migration, relocation, uprooting, colonization, departure, removal, leaving, expatriation, displacement, moving away, crossing, migrating, exodus, exile, trek, journey, movement, trend, march, travel, voyage, wayfaring, wandering, shift, settling, homesteading.—*Ant.* immigration, arriving, remaining.

émigré ***n.*** exile, emigrant, refugee; see REFUGEE.

eminence ***n.*** standing, prominence, distinction; see FAME.

eminent ***a.*** renowned, celebrated, prominent; see DIGNIFIED, DISTINGUISHED 2.

emissary ***n.*** intermediary, ambassador, consul; see AGENT.

emission ***n.*** ejection, effusion, eruption; see RADIATION 1.

emit ***v.*** give off, let off, give out, let out, send forth, send out, broadcast, throw up, throw out, spill out, pour out, give forth, eject, blow, hurl, gush, secrete, spurt, shoot, erupt, squirt, shed, expel, expend, vomit, belch, excrete, issue, perspire, spew, spit,

e·mol·li·ent (ē mäl′yənt, i-) ***adj.*** ⟦< L *e-*, out + *mollire*, soften⟧ softening; soothing —***n.*** something that softens or soothes, as a preparation applied to the skin
e·mol′u·ment (-yo͞o mənt) ***n.*** ⟦< L *e-*, out + *molere*, to grind⟧ payment received for work; salary, fees, etc.
e·mote (ē mōt′, i-) ***vi.*** **e·mot′ed, e·mot′ing** [Inf.] to act in an emotional or theatrical manner
e·mo·tion (ē mō′shən, i-) ***n.*** ⟦< L *e-*, out + *movere*, to move⟧ **1** strong feeling **2** any specific feeling, as love, hate, fear, or anger
e·mo′tion·al ***adj.*** **1** of or showing emotion **2** easily aroused to emotion **3** appealing to the emotions; moving —**e·mo′tion·al·ism′** ***n.*** —**e·mo′tion·al·ly** ***adv.***
e·mo′tion·al·ize′ ***vt.*** **-ized′, -iz′ing** to treat in an emotional way
em·pa·thet·ic (em′pə thet′ik) ***adj.*** of or showing empathy: also **em·path′ic** (-path′ik)
em·pa·thize (em′pə thīz′) ***vt.*** **-thized′, -thiz′ing** to feel empathy (*with*)
em′pa·thy (-thē) ***n.*** ⟦< Gr *en-*, in + *pathos*, feeling⟧ the ability to share in another's emotions, thoughts, or feelings
em·per·or (em′pər ər) ***n.*** ⟦< L *in-*, in + *parare*, to set in order⟧ the supreme ruler of an empire
em·pha·sis (em′fə sis) ***n.***, *pl.* **-ses′** (-sēz′) ⟦< Gr *en-*, in + *phainein*, to show⟧ **1** force of expression, action, etc. **2** special stress given to a word or phrase in speaking **3** importance; stress
em′pha·size′ (-sīz′) ***vt.*** **-sized′, -siz′ing** to give emphasis to; stress
em·phat·ic (em fat′ik, im-) ***adj.*** **1** felt or done with emphasis **2** using emphasis in speaking, etc. **3** forcible; striking —**em·phat′i·cal·ly** ***adv.***
em·phy·se·ma (em′fə sē′mə, -zē′-) ***n.*** ⟦< Gr *en-*, in + *physaein*, to blow⟧ a condition of the lungs in which the air sacs become distended and lose elasticity
em·pire (em′pīr′) ***n.*** ⟦see EMPEROR⟧ **1** supreme rule **2** government by an emperor or empress **3** a group of states or territories under one ruler **4** an extensive organization under the control of a single person, corporation, etc.
em·pir·i·cal (em pir′i kəl) ***adj.*** ⟦< Gr *en-*, in + *peira*, trial⟧ relying or based on experiment or experience —**em·pir′i·cal·ly** ***adv.*** —**em·pir′i·cism′** (-siz′əm) ***n.***
em·place·ment (em plās′ mənt, im-) ***n.*** the prepared position from which a heavy gun or guns are fired
em·ploy (em ploi′, im-) ***vt.*** ⟦< L *in-*, in + *plicare*, to fold⟧ **1** to use **2** to keep busy or occupied **3** to engage the services of; hire —***n.*** employment
em·ploy′a·ble ***adj.*** that can be employed; specif., physically or mentally fit to be hired for work
em·ploy′ee or **em·ploy′e** (-ē) ***n.*** one hired by another for wages or salary
em·ploy′er ***n.*** one who employs others for wages or salary
em·ploy′ment ***n.*** **1** an employing or being employed **2** work; occupation **3** the number or percentage of persons gainfully employed
em·po·ri·um (em pôr′ē əm) ***n.***, *pl.* **-ri·ums** or **-ri·a** (-ə) ⟦< Gr *en-*, in + *poros*, way⟧ a large store with a wide variety of things for sale
em·pow·er (em pou′ər, im-) ***vt.*** **1** to give power to; authorize **2** to enable —**em·pow′er·ment** ***n.***
em·press (em′pris) ***n.*** **1** an emperor's wife **2** a woman ruler of an empire
emp·ty (emp′tē) ***adj.*** **-ti·er, -ti·est** ⟦OE *æmettig*⟧ **1** having nothing or no one in it; unoccupied **2** worthless *[empty pleasure]* **3** insincere *[empty promises]* —***vt.*** **-tied, -ty·ing** **1** to make empty **2** to remove (the contents) of something —***vi.*** **1** to become empty **2** to pour out; discharge —***n.***, *pl.* **-ties** an empty truck, bottle, etc. —**emp′ti·ly** ***adv.*** —**emp′ti·ness** ***n.***
emp′ty-hand′ed ***adj.*** bringing or carrying away nothing
em·py·re·an (em pir′ē ən, em′pī rē′ən) ***n.*** ⟦< Gr *en-*, in + *pyr*, fire⟧ **1** the highest heaven **2** the sky; firmament
EMT *abbrev.* emergency medical technician
e·mu (ē′myo͞o′) ***n.*** ⟦< Port *ema*, a crane⟧ a large, flightless Australian bird, somewhat like the ostrich but smaller
em·u·late (em′yo͞o lāt′, -yə-) ***vt.*** **-lat′ed, -lat′ing** ⟦< L *aemulus*, trying to equal or excel⟧ **1** to try to equal or surpass **2** to imitate (a person or thing admired) **3** to rival successfully —**em′u·la′tion** ***n.*** —**em′u·la′tive** ***adj.*** —**em′u·la′tor** ***n.***
e·mul·si·fy (ē mul′sə fī′, i-) ***vt.***, ***vi.*** **-fied′, -fy′ing** to form into an emulsion —**e·mul′si·fi·ca′tion** ***n.***
e·mul′sion (-shən) ***n.*** ⟦< L *e-*, out + *mulgere*, to milk⟧ a colloidal suspension of one liquid in another, as photographic film coatings, some medications, etc.
en- ⟦< L *in-*, in⟧ *prefix* **1** to put or get into or on *[enthrone]* **2** to make, cause to be *[endanger]* **3** in or into *[encase]*
-en (ən, ′n) ⟦OE⟧ *suffix* **1** *a)* to become or cause to be *[darken]* *b)* to cause to have *[heighten]* **2** made of *[wooden]* **3** forming plurals *[children]*
en·a·ble (en ā′bəl, in-) ***vt.*** **-bled, -bling** **1** to make able; provide with means, power, etc. (*to* do something) **2** to

THESAURUS

ooze, exhale, emanate; see also EMPTY 2.

emotion ***n.*** feelings, passion, agitation, tremor, commotion, excitement, disturbance, sentiment, feeling, tumult, turmoil, sensation. *Emotions include the following:* love, passion, ecstasy, warmth, glow, fervor, ardor, zeal, thrill, elation, joy, satisfaction, happiness, sympathy, tenderness, concern, grief, remorse, sorrow, sadness, melancholy, despondency, despair, depression, worry, disquiet, uneasiness, dread, fear, apprehension, hate, malice, resentment, conflict, jealousy, greed, anger, rage, ire, shame, pride, sensuality, lust, desire.

emotional ***a.*** hysterical, demonstrative, fiery, warm, zealous, sensuous, fervent, ardent, enthusiastic, passionate, excitable, impulsive, spontaneous, ecstatic, impetuous, nervous, wrought-up, overwrought, temperamental, irrational, sensitive, oversensitive, hypersensitive, sentimental, melodramatic, maudlin, overflowing, affectionate, loving, neurotic, fickle, wearing one's heart on one's sleeve, high-strung, mushy*.—*Ant.* COLD, rational, hard.

emotionalism ***n.*** hysteria, sentimentality, excitement; see EMOTION.

empathy ***n.*** vicarious emotion, insight, understanding; see PITY.

emperor ***n.*** monarch, sovereign, dictator; see RULER 1.

emphasis ***n.*** stress, accent, weight; see IMPORTANCE.

emphasize ***v.*** make clear, make emphatic, underline, underscore, highlight, dramatize, pronounce, enunciate, articulate, accentuate, accent, stress, point up, point out, strike, call to the attention of, reiterate, repeat, insist, maintain, impress, affirm, indicate, rub in*, pound into one's head*, drum into one's head*, labor the point, make a fuss about.

emphatic ***a.*** assured, strong, determined, forceful, forcible, earnest, positive, energetic, potent, powerful, dynamic, stressed, pointed, flat, definitive, categorical, dogmatic, explicit.

emphatically ***a.*** definitely, certainly, of course, undoubtedly, decidely, decisively, absolutely, entirely, flatly, distinctly.—*Ant.* SLOWLY, hesitantly, indistinctly.

empire ***n.*** union, people, federation; see NATION 1.

employ ***v.*** **1** [To make use of] operate, manipulate, apply; see USE 1. **2** [To obtain services for pay] engage, contract, procure; see HIRE.

employed ***a.*** working, occupied, busy, laboring, gainfully employed, not out of work, in one's employ, on the job, hired, operating, active, engaged, on duty, on the payroll.—*Ant.* UNEMPLOYED, out of work, jobless.

employee ***n.*** worker, laborer, servant, domestic, agent, representative, hired hand, salesman, salesperson, assistant, associate, attendant, apprentice, operator, workman, workingman, breadwinner, craftsman, wage earner, hireling, lackey, underling, flunky.

employer ***n.*** owner, manager, proprietor, management, head, director, executive, superintendent, supervisor, president, chief, businessman, manufacturer, corporation, company, boss, front office, big shot*.

employment ***n.*** job, profession, vocation; see BUSINESS 1, TRADE 2, WORK 2.

emptiness ***n.*** void, vacuum, vacancy, gap, chasm, blankness, blank, exhaustion, hollowness.

empty ***a.*** hollow, bare, clear, blank, unfilled, unfurnished, unoccupied, vacated, vacant, void, vacuous, void of, devoid, lacking, wanting, barren, emptied, abandoned, exhausted, depleted, deserted, stark, deprived of, dry, destitute, negative, deflated, evacuated.—*Ant.* FULL, filled, occupied.

empty ***v.*** **1** [To become empty] discharge, leave, pour, flow out, ebb, run out, open into, be discharged, void, release, exhaust, leak, drain off, drain, rush out, escape.—*Ant.* ABSORB, flow in, enter. **2** [To cause to become empty] dump, dip, ladle, tap, void, pour, spill out, let out, deplete, exhaust, deflate, drain, bail out, clean out, clear out, evacuate, eject, expel, draw off, draw out, disgorge, suck dry, drink.—*Ant.* FILL, pack, stuff.

emulate ***v.*** challenge, contend, imitate; see COMPETE, FOLLOW 2.

enable ***v.*** make possible, sanction, give power to, give authority to,

support the dysfunctional behavior of, as by compensating for it —**en·a'bler** ***n.***

en·act (en akt′, in-) ***vt.*** **1** to pass (a bill, law, etc.) **2** to represent as in a play —**en·act'ment** ***n.***

en·am·el (e nam′əl, i-) ***n.*** ⟦< OFr *esmail*⟧ **1** a glassy, opaque substance fused to metal, pottery, etc. as an ornamental or protective coating **2** the hard, white coating of teeth **3** paint that dries to a smooth, glossy surface —***vt.*** **-eled** or **-elled**, **-el·ing** or **-el·ling** to coat with enamel —**en·am'el·er** or **en·am'el·ler** ***n.***

en·am·or (en am′ər, in-) ***vt.*** ⟦ult. < L *in-*, in + *amor*, love⟧ to fill with love; charm: now mainly in the passive voice, with *of [enamored* of her*]*

en bloc (en bläk′) ⟦Fr, lit., in a block⟧ in a mass; all together

en bro·chette (än brô shet′) ⟦Fr⟧ broiled on small skewers

en·camp (en kamp′, in-) ***vi.***, ***vt.*** to set up, or put in, a camp —**en·camp'ment** ***n.***

en·cap·su·late (en kap′sə lāt′) ***vt.*** **-lat'ed**, **-lat'ing** **1** to enclose in a capsule **2** to make concise; condense Also **en·cap'sule** (-səl, -syo͞ol′), **-suled**, **-sul·ing** —**en·cap'su·la'tion** ***n.***

en·case (en kās′, in-) ***vt.*** **-cased'**, **-cas'ing** to enclose, as in a case

en cas·se·role (en kas′ə rōl′) ⟦Fr⟧ (baked and served) in a casserole

-ence (əns, ′ns) ⟦< L⟧ *suffix* act, state, or result *[conference]*

en·ceph·a·li·tis (en sef′ə līt′is) ***n.*** ⟦< Gr *en-*, in + *kephalē*, the head + -ITIS⟧ inflammation of the brain

en·chain (en chān′) ***vt.*** to bind with chains; fetter

en·chant (en chant′, in-) ***vt.*** ⟦< L *in-*, intens. + *cantare*, sing⟧ **1** to cast a spell over **2** to charm greatly; delight —**en·chant'er** ***n.*** —**en·chant'ing** ***adj.*** —**en·chant'ment** ***n.***

en·chi·la·da (en′chi lä′də) ***n.*** ⟦AmSp⟧ a tortilla rolled with meat inside, served with a chili-flavored sauce

en·cir·cle (en sur′kəl, in-) ***vt.*** **-cled**, **-cling** **1** to surround **2** to move in a circle around —**en·cir'cle·ment** ***n.***

encl *abbrev.* enclosure

en·clave (en′klāv′, än′-) ***n.*** ⟦< L *in*, in + *clavis*, a key⟧ a territory surrounded by another country's territory

en·close (en klōz′, in-) ***vt.*** **-closed'**, **-clos'ing** **1** to shut in all around; surround **2** to insert in an envelope, etc., often along with something else

en·clo'sure (-klō′zhər) ***n.*** **1** an enclosing or being enclosed **2** something that encloses, as a fence **3** something enclosed, as in an envelope or by a wall

en·code (en kōd′, in-) ***vt.*** **-cod'ed**, **-cod'ing** to put (a message, etc.) into code

en·co·mi·um (en kō′mē əm) ***n.***, *pl.* **-ums** or **-a** (-ə) ⟦< Gr *en-*, in + *kōmos*, a revel⟧ high praise; eulogy

en·com·pass (en kum′pəs, in-) ***vt.*** **1** to surround **2** to contain; include

en·core (än′kôr′) ***interj.*** ⟦Fr⟧ again; once more —***n.*** a further performance, etc. in answer to an audience's applause

en·coun·ter (en koun′tər, in-) ***vt.*** ⟦< L *in*, in + *contra*, against⟧ **1** to meet unexpectedly **2** to meet in conflict **3** to meet with (difficulties, etc.) —***n.*** **1** a direct meeting, as in battle **2** a meeting, esp. when unexpected

en·cour·age (en kur′ij, in-) ***vt.*** **-aged**, **-ag·ing** **1** to give courage, hope, or confidence to **2** to give support to; help —**en·cour'age·ment** ***n.***

en·croach (en krōch′, in-) ***vi.*** ⟦< OFr *en-*, in + *croc*, a hook⟧ to trespass or intrude (*on* or *upon*) —**en·croach'ment** ***n.***

en croûte (än kro͞ot′) ⟦Fr⟧ wrapped in pastry and baked: said esp. of meats

en·crust (en krust′) ***vt.*** to cover as with a crust —***vi.*** to form a crust —**en'crus·ta'tion** (-krus tā′shən) ***n.***

en·cum·ber (en kum′bər, in-) ***vt.*** ⟦see EN- & CUMBER⟧ **1** to hold back the motion or action of; hinder **2** to burden —**en·cum'brance** ***n.***

-en·cy (ən sē) ⟦L *-entia*⟧ *suffix* -ENCE *[dependency]*

en·cyc·li·cal (en sik′li kəl, in-) ***n.*** ⟦< Gr *en-*, in + *kyklos*, a circle⟧ a papal document addressed to the bishops

en·cy·clo·pe·di·a or **en·cy·clo·pae·di·a** (en sī′klə pē′dē ə) ***n.*** ⟦< Gr *enkyklios*, general + *paideia*, education⟧ a book or set of books with alphabetically arranged articles on all branches, or on one field, of knowledge —**en·cy'clo·pe'dic** or **en·cy'clo·pae'dic** ***adj.***

en·cyst (en sist′) ***vt.***, ***vi.*** to enclose or become enclosed in a cyst, sac, etc. —**en·cyst'ment** ***n.***

end (end) ***n.*** ⟦OE *ende*⟧ **1** a limit; boundary **2** the last part of anything; finish; conclusion **3** a ceasing to exist; death or destruction **4** the part at or near an extremity;

THESAURUS

invest, endow, authorize, allow, let, permit, license; see also APPROVE.

enact ***v.*** decree, sanction, ordain, order, dictate, make into law, legislate, pass, establish, ratify, vote in, proclaim, vote favorably, determine, authorize, appoint, institute, railroad through*, get the floor, put in force, make laws, put through, constitute, fix, set, formulate.

enactment ***n.*** edict, decree, statute; see LAW 3.

enamel ***n.*** lacquer, coating, finish, polish, gloss, top coat, varnish, glaze, veneer.

enamel ***v.*** lacquer, glaze, gloss, paint, veneer, coat, varnish, finish, paint.

encampment ***n.*** village, campsite, bivouac; see CAMP 1.

enchant ***v.*** entrance, entice, allure; see FASCINATE.

enchanted ***a.*** charmed, enraptured, entranced; see FASCINATED.

encircle ***v.*** encompass, circle, cordon off; see SURROUND 1.

enclose ***v.*** insert, jail, pen, corral, impound, confine, blockade, imprison, block off, fence off, set apart, lock up, lock in, keep in, box in, close in, shut in, wall in, box off, seal up, wrap.—*Ant.* FREE, liberate, open.

enclosed ***a.*** locked in, penned in, jailed, packed up, wrapped up, shut up, buried, encased, walled in, fenced in.

enclosure ***n.*** **1** [A space enclosed] pen, sty, yard, jail, garden, corral, cage, asylum, pound, park, zone, precinct, plot, court, patch, coop, den, cell, dungeon, vault, paddock, stockade, concentration camp, prison; see also BUILDING, PLACE 2, ROOM 2. **2** [Something inserted] information, check, money, circular, copy, questionnaire, forms, documents, printed matter.

encompass ***v.*** encircle, compass, gird; see SURROUND 1.

encounter ***n.*** **1** [A coming together] interview, rendezvous, appointment; see MEETING 1. **2** [Physical violence] conflict, clash, collision; see FIGHT 1.

encounter ***v.*** **1** [To meet unexpectedly] meet, confront, come across; see FIND. **2** [To meet in conflict] battle, attack, struggle; see FIGHT.

encourage ***v.*** cheer, refresh, enliven, exhilarate, inspire, cheer up, praise, restore, revitalize, gladden, fortify, console, ease, relieve, help, aid, comfort, approve, reassure, assist, befriend, uphold, reinforce, back, bolster, brace, further, favor, strengthen, side with, cheer on, back up, egg on, buck up*, root for*, pat on the back.—*Ant.* RESTRAIN, discourage, caution.

encouraged ***a.*** inspired, enlivened, renewed, aided, supported, hopeful, confident, enthusiastic, roused, cheered; see also HELPED.—*Ant.* SAD, discouraged, disheartened.

encouragement ***n.*** aid, faith, help, assistance, support, cheer, confidence, trust, advance, promotion, reward, reassurance, incentive, backing, optimism, comfort, consolation, hope, relief, pat on the back, lift, shot in the arm, vote of confidence.

encouraging ***a.*** bright, good, promising; see HOPEFUL 1, 2.

encyclopedia ***n.*** book of facts, book of knowledge, compilation, general reference work, encyclopedic reference work, cyclopedia.

encyclopedic ***a.*** exhaustive, broad, all-encompassing; see COMPREHENSIVE, GENERAL 1, WIDESPREAD.

end ***n.*** **1** [Purpose] aim, object, intention; see PURPOSE 1. **2** [The close of an action] expiration, completion, target date, termination, adjournment, final event, ending, close, finish, conclusion, finis, finale, retirement, accomplishment, attainment, determination, achievement, fulfillment, realization, period, consummation, culmination, execution, performance, last line, curtain, terminus, payoff*, last word*, wrap-up*, windup, cutoff, end of the line*.—*Ant.* ORIGIN, beginning, opening. **3** [A result] conclusion, effect, outcome; see RESULT. **4** [The extremity] terminal, termination, terminus, boundary, limit, borderline, point, stub, stump, tail end, edge, tip, top, head, butt end.—*Ant.* CENTER, middle, hub. **5** [The close of life] demise, passing, doom; see DEATH. —**in the end** at length, in conclusion, as a result; see FINALLY 2. —**keep one's end up*** do one's share, join, participate; see SHARE 1. —**make ends meet** manage, get by, survive; see ENDURE 2. —**no end*** very much, extremely, greatly; see MUCH, VERY. —**on end** **1** [Endless] ceaseless, without interruption, constant; see ENDLESS. **2** [Upright] erect, vertical, standing up; see STRAIGHT 1. —**put an end to** stop, finish, cease; see END 1.

end ***v.*** **1** [To bring to a halt] stop, finish, quit, close, halt, shut down, ban, curtail, settle, bring to an end, make an end of, break off, break up,

tip **5** an object; purpose **6** an outcome; result **7** *Football* a player at either end of the line —***vt.***, ***vi.*** to bring or come to an end; finish; stop —***adj.*** at the end; final —**make (both) ends meet** to manage to keep one's expenses within one's income —**put an end to 1** to stop **2** to do away with

en·dan·ger (en dān′jər, in-) ***vt.*** to expose to danger, harm, etc.; imperil —**en·dan′ger·ment** ***n.***

endangered species a species of animal or plant in danger of becoming extinct

en·dear (en dir′, in-) ***vt.*** to make dear or beloved —**en·dear′ing** ***adj.***

en·dear′ment ***n.*** **1** an endearing **2** a word or act expressing affection

en·deav·or (en dev′ər, in-) ***vi.*** ⟦< EN- + OFr *deveir*, duty⟧ to make an earnest attempt; try: usually with an infinitive —***n.*** an earnest attempt or effort Brit. sp. **en·deav′our**

en·dem·ic (en dem′ik) ***adj.*** ⟦< Gr *en-*, in + *dēmos*, people⟧ native to or constantly present in, a particular place, as a plant or disease —**en·dem′i·cal·ly** ***adv.***

end′ing ***n.*** **1** the last part; finish **2** death

en·dive (en′dīv′, än′dēv′) ***n.*** ⟦< Gr *entybon*⟧ a cultivated plant with curled, narrow leaves used in salads

end′less ***adj.*** **1** having no end; eternal; infinite **2** lasting too long *[an endless speech]* **3** continual *[endless problems]* **4** with the ends joined to form a closed unit *[an endless chain]* —**end′less·ly** ***adv.*** —**end′less·ness** ***n.***

end′most′ ***adj.*** at the end; farthest

endo- ⟦< Gr *endon*⟧ *combining form* within, inner

en·do·crine (en′dō krin′, -krīn′; -də-) ***adj.*** ⟦prec. + Gr *krinein*, to separate⟧ designating or of any gland producing a hormone

en·dorse (en dôrs′, in-) ***vt.*** **-dorsed′**, **-dors′ing** ⟦< L *in*, on + *dorsum*, the back⟧ **1** to write on the back of (a title, check, etc.) to transfer ownership, make a deposit, etc. **2** to sanction, approve, or support **3** to recommend (an advertised product) for a fee —**en·dorse′ment** ***n.*** —**en·dors′er** ***n.***

en·do·scope (en′dō skōp′, -də-) ***n.*** an instrument for examining visually the inside of a hollow organ or cavity of the body, as the rectum

en·dow (en dou′, in-) ***vt.*** ⟦< OFr *en-*, in + *dotare*, to endow⟧ **1** to provide with some talent, quality, etc. *[endowed with courage]* **2** to give money or property to (a college, etc.) —**en·dow′ment** ***n.***

end′point′ ***n.*** a point of completion or furthest progress

end product the final result of a series of changes, processes, etc.

end table a small table placed at the end of a sofa, etc.

en·due (en do͞o′, in-) ***vt.*** **-dued′**, **-du′ing** ⟦< L *in-*, in + *ducere*, to lead⟧ to provide (*with* qualities)

en·dur·ance (en door′əns, in-) ***n.*** the ability to last, stand pain, etc.

en·dure (en door′, in-) ***vt.*** **-dured′**, **-dur′ing** ⟦< L *durus*, hard⟧ **1** to hold up under (pain, etc.) **2** to tolerate —***vi.*** **1** to continue; last **2** to bear pain, etc. without flinching —**en·dur′a·ble** ***adj.***

end′ways′ (-wāz′) ***adv.*** **1** upright **2** with the end foremost **3** lengthwise Also **end′wise′** (-wīz′)

-ene (ēn) ⟦after Gr *-enos*, adj. suffix⟧ *Chem. suffix* a certain type of hydrocarbon *[benzene]*

en·e·ma (en′ə mə) ***n.*** ⟦< Gr *en-*, in + *hienai*, send⟧ the forcing of a liquid, as a purgative, medicine, etc., into the colon through the anus

en·e·my (en′ə mē) ***n.***, *pl.* **-mies** ⟦< L *in-*, not + *amicus*, friend⟧ **1** one who hates and wishes to injure another **2** *a)* a nation or force hostile to another *b)* troops, ship, etc. of a hostile nation **3** one hostile to an idea, cause, etc. **4** anything injurious or harmful

en·er·get·ic (en′ər jet′ik) ***adj.*** having or showing energy; vigorous —**en′er·get′i·cal·ly** ***adv.***

en·er·gize (en′ər jīz′) ***vt.*** **-gized′**, **-giz′ing** to give energy to; activate —**en′er·giz′er** ***n.***

en·er·gy (en′ər jē) ***n.***, *pl.* **-gies** ⟦< Gr *en-*, in + *ergon*, work⟧ **1** force of expression **2** *a)* inherent power; capacity for action *b)* [*often pl.*] such power, esp. in action **3** a resource, as oil or gas, from which usable energy can be produced **4** *Physics* the capacity for doing work

en·er·vate (en′ər vāt′) ***vt.*** **-vat′ed**, **-vat′ing** ⟦< L *e-*, out + *nervus*, nerve⟧ to deprive of strength, force, vigor, etc.; devitalize —**en′er·va′tion** ***n.***

en·fee·ble (en fē′bəl, in-) ***vt.*** **-bled**, **-bling** to make feeble

en·fi·lade (en′fə lād′, en′fə lād′) ***n.*** ⟦Fr⟧ gunfire directed along a line of troops

en·fold (en fōld′, in-) ***vt.*** **1** to wrap in folds; wrap up **2** to embrace

en·force (en fôrs′, in-) ***vt.*** **-forced′**, **-forc′ing** **1** to impose by force *[to enforce one's will]* **2** to compel observance of

THESAURUS

put an end to, discontinue, postpone, delay, conclude, interrupt, dispose of, drop, call it a day*, cut short, wind up, get done, call off, give up, wrap up*.—*Ant.* BEGIN, initiate, start. **2** [To bring to a conclusion] settle, conclude, terminate; see ACHIEVE. **3** [To come to an end] desist, cease, die; see STOP 2. **4** [To die] expire, depart, pass away; see DIE.

endanger ***v.*** imperil, jeopardize, expose to danger, expose to peril, be careless with, lay open, put on the spot*, leave in the middle, leave in the lurch.—*Ant.* SAVE, protect, preserve.

endangered ***a.*** exposed, imperiled, in a dilemma, in a predicament, jeopardized, in danger, in jeopardy, in a bad way*, on thin ice*, hanging by a thread*.

endeavor ***n.*** effort, try, attempt; see EFFORT.

endeavor ***v.*** attempt, aim, essay; see TRY 1.

ending ***n.*** finish, closing, terminus; see END 2.

endless ***a.*** infinite, interminable, untold, without end, unbounded, unlimited, immeasurable, limitless, boundless, incalculable, unfathomable.

endorse ***v.*** **1** [To inscribe one's name] sign, put one's signature to, put one's signature on, countersign, underwrite, sign one's name on, subscribe, notarize, add one's name to, put one's John Hancock on*, sign on the dotted line*. **2** [To indicate one's active support of] approve, confirm, sanction, ratify, guarantee, underwrite, support, stand up for, stand behind, be behind, vouch for, uphold, recommend, praise, give one's word for, OK*, back up, go to bat for*.—*Ant.* BLAME, censure, condemn.

endorsed ***a.*** signed, notarized, legalized, ratified, sealed, settled, approved, upheld, supported, recommended, sanctioned, advocated, backed, OK'd*.

endorsement ***n.*** support, sanction, permission; see SIGNATURE.

endow ***v.*** enrich, provide, supply; see GIVE 1.

endowment ***n.*** benefit, provision, bequest, gratuity, grant, pension, stipend, legacy, inheritance, subsidy, revenue, trust, nest egg.

endurable ***a.*** sustainable, tolerable, supportable; see BEARABLE.

endurance ***n.*** sufferance, fortitude, capacity to endure, long suffering, resignation, patience, tolerance, courage, perseverance, stamina, restraint, resistance, will, backbone, guts*, spunk*.—*Ant.* WEAKNESS, feebleness, infirmity.

endure ***v.*** **1** [To continue] persist, remain, last, continue, exist, be, stay, prevail, wear, sustain, survive, outlast, carry on, live on, go on, hold on, hang on, keep on, linger, outlive, hold out, never say die*, stick to*, ride out.—*Ant.* DIE, cease, end. **2** [To sustain adversity] suffer, tolerate, bear with, bear up, allow, permit, support, undergo, sit through, take, withstand, bear up under, stand, accustom oneself to, submit to, sustain, go through, get through, encounter, be patient with, keep up, resign oneself, weather, brave, face, put up with, live through, stand for*, swallow, stomach, never say die*, grin and bear it, take it*, brace oneself, like it or lump it*, hang on, keep one's chin up.—*Ant.* AVOID, resist, refuse.

enduring ***a.*** lasting, abiding, surviving; see PERMANENT.

enemy ***n.*** foe, rival, assailant, competitor, attacker, antagonist, opponent, adversary, public enemy, criminal, opposition, guerrilla, guerrilla force, fifth column, saboteur, spy, foreign agent, assassin, murderer, betrayer, traitor, terrorist, revolutionary, rebel, invader.—*Ant.* FRIEND, ally, supporter.

energetic ***a.*** industrious, vigorous, forcible; see ACTIVE.

energy ***n.*** **1** [One's internal powers] force, power, virility; see STRENGTH. **2** [Power developed or released by a device] horsepower, motive power, pressure, potential energy, kinetic energy, atomic energy, solar energy, high pressure, foot-pounds, magnetism, friction, voltage, kilowatt-hours, current, electricity, gravity, heat, suction, radioactivity, potential, fuel consumption.

enfold ***v.*** envelope, encase, enclose; see SURROUND 1, WRAP.

enforce ***v.*** urge, compel, impose, exert, drive, demand, carry out vigorously, put in force, dictate, exact, require, execute, coerce, oblige, insist upon, emphasize, necessitate, press, impel, make, sanction, force upon, goad, stress, spur, hound, crack down.—*Ant.* ABANDON, neglect, evade.

enforced ***a.*** compelled, established, exacted, required, executed, pressed, sanctioned, imposed, kept, dictated, admonished, advocated, charged,

(a law, etc.) —**en·force'a·ble** *adj.* —**en·force'ment** *n.* —**en·forc'er** *n.*

en·fran·chise (en fran'chīz', in-) *vt.* **-chised'**, **-chis'ing** **1** to free from slavery **2** to give the right to vote —**en·fran'chise·ment** (-chiz mənt) *n.*

Eng *abbrev.* **1** England **2** English

en·gage (en gāj', in-) *vt.* **-gaged'**, **-gag'ing** ⟦see EN- & GAGE[1]⟧ **1** to pledge (oneself) **2** to bind by a promise of marriage **3** to hire **4** to involve or occupy **5** to attract and hold (the attention, etc.) **6** to enter into conflict with (the enemy) **7** to mesh (gears, etc.) —*vi.* **1** to pledge oneself **2** to occupy or involve oneself [to *engage* in dramatics] **3** to enter into conflict **4** to mesh

en·gaged' *adj.* **1** betrothed **2** occupied; employed **3** involved in combat, as troops **4** in gear; meshed

en·gage'ment *n.* an engaging or being engaged; specif., *a*) a betrothal *b*) an appointment *c*) employment *d*) a conflict; battle

en·gag'ing *adj.* attractive; pleasant; charming —**en·gag'ing·ly** *adv.*

en·gen·der (en jen'dər, in-) *vt.* ⟦< L *in-*, in + *generare*, beget⟧ to bring into being; cause; produce

en·gine (en'jən) *n.* ⟦< L *in-*, in + base of *gignere*, beget⟧ **1** any machine that uses energy to develop mechanical power **2** a railroad locomotive **3** any machine

en·gi·neer (en'jə nir') *n.* **1** one skilled in some branch of engineering **2** one who operates or supervises the operation of engines or technical equipment [a locomotive *engineer*] —*vt.* **1** to plan, construct, etc. as an engineer **2** to manage skillfully

en'gi·neer'ing *n.* **1** the science concerned with putting scientific knowledge to practical uses **2** the planning, designing, construction, or management of machinery, roads, bridges, etc.

Eng·land (iŋ'glənd) division of the United Kingdom in S Great Britain: 50,357 sq. mi.; pop. 46,382,000

Eng·lish (iŋ'glish) *adj.* **1** of England, its people, etc. **2** of the language of England and the U.S. —*n.* **1** the Germanic language of England and the U.S., also spoken in the Commonwealth, etc. **2** [*sometimes* **e-**] a spinning motion given to a ball —**the English** the people of England

English Channel arm of the Atlantic, between England & France

English horn a double-reed woodwind instrument

Eng'lish·man (-mən) *n.*, *pl.* **-men** (-mən) a person born or living in England —**Eng'lish·wom'an**, *pl.* **-wom'en**, *fem.n.*

en·gorge (en gôrj', in-) *vt.* **-gorged'**, **-gorg'ing** ⟦< OFr *en-*, in + *gorge*, gorge⟧ **1** to devour greedily **2** *Med.* to congest (tissue, etc.) with fluid, as blood

en·grave (en grāv', in-) *vt.* **-graved'**, **-grav'ing** ⟦< Fr *en-*, in + *graver*, to incise⟧ **1** to cut or etch letters, designs, etc. in or on (a metal plate, etc.) **2** to print with such a plate **3** to impress deeply —**en·grav'er** *n.*

en·grav'ing *n.* **1** the act or art of one who engraves **2** an engraved plate, drawing, etc. **3** a print made from an engraved surface

en·gross (en grōs', in-) *vt.* ⟦< OFr *engroissier*, become thick⟧ to take the entire attention of; occupy wholly —**en·gross'ing** *adj.*

en·gulf (en gulf', in-) *vt.* to swallow up

en·hance (en hans', in-) *vt.* **-hanced'**, **-hanc'ing** ⟦< L *in-*, in + *altus*, high⟧ to make greater, better, etc.; heighten —**en·hance'ment** *n.*

e·nig·ma (i nig'mə, e-) *n.* ⟦< Gr *ainos*, story⟧ **1** a riddle **2** a perplexing or baffling matter, person, etc. —**en·ig·mat·ic** (en'ig mat'ik) *adj.*

en·jamb·ment or **en·jambe·ment** (en jam'mənt) *n.* ⟦< Fr *enjamber*, to encroach⟧ in poetry, the movement from one line to the next without a pause

en·join (en join', in-) *vt.* ⟦< L *in-*, in + *jungere*, join⟧ **1** to command; order; impose **2** to prohibit, esp. by legal injunction

en·joy (en joi', in-) *vt.* ⟦< OFr *en-*, in + *joir*, rejoice⟧ **1** to get pleasure from; relish **2** to have the use or benefit of —**enjoy oneself** to have a good time —**en·joy'a·ble** *adj.* —**en·joy'ment** *n.*

en·large (en lärj', in-) *vt.* **-larged'**, **-larg'ing** to make larger; expand —*vi.* **1** to become larger; expand **2** to speak or write at greater length: with *on* or *upon* —**en·large'ment** *n.*

en·light·en (en līt''n, in-) *vt.* **1** to free from ignorance, prejudice, etc. **2** to inform —**en·light'en·ment** *n.*

en·list (en list', in-) *vt.*, *vi.* **1** to enroll in some branch of the armed forces **2** to engage in support of a cause or movement —**en·list'ment** *n.*

THESAURUS

meted out.

enforcement *n.* requirement, enforcing, prescription, compulsion, constraint, coercion, pressure, duress, obligation, necessity, insistence, carrying out, fulfilling.

engage *v.* **1** [To hire] employ, contract, retain; see HIRE. **2** [To engross] absorb, captivate, bewitch; see FASCINATE. **3** [To enmesh, especially gears] interlock, mesh, connect; see FASTEN. —**engage in** take part in, participate in, undertake; see PERFORM 1.

engaged *a.* **1** [Promised in marriage] bound, pledged, betrothed, matched, spoken for.—*Ant.* FREE, unpledged, unbetrothed. **2** [Not at liberty] working, occupied, employed; see BUSY 1. **3** [In a profession, business, or the like] employed, practicing, performing, dealing in, doing, interested, absorbed in, pursuing, at work, working at, involved with, involved in, connected with; see also EMPLOYED.—*Ant.* UNEMPLOYED, out of a job, without connection.

engagement *n.* **1** [A predetermined action] meeting, rendezvous, errand; see APPOINTMENT 2. **2** [The state of being betrothed] contract, promise, match, betrothal, espousal, betrothing.

engine *n.* motor, power plant, dynamo, generator, turbine; diesel, rotary, internal-combustion, external-combustion, compound, jet, Wankel, high-compression, low-compression, piston, radial, etc. engine.

engineer *n.* **1** [A professional engineer] surveyor, designer, planner, builder. *Types of engineers include the following:* mining, civil, metallurgical, geological, electrical, architectural, chemical, construction, military, naval, flight, industrial. **2** [The operator of a locomotive] motorman, brakeman, stoker; see DRIVER.

engineering *n.* design, planning, blueprinting, structure, structures, surveying, metallurgy, architecture, shipbuilding, installations, stresses, communications.

English *a.* British, Britannic, Anglian, Anglican, Anglo-, England's, His Majesty's, Her Majesty's, Commonwealth, anglicized, English-speaking, Norman.

engrave *v.* etch, bite, stipple, lithograph, cut, burn, incise, grave, chisel, crosshatch.

engraved *a.* carved, decorated, etched, scratched, bitten into, embossed, furrowed, incised, deepened, marked deeply, lithographed.

engraving *n.* print, wood engraving, etching, aquatint, rotogravure, lithograph, cut, woodcut, illustration, impression, copy, proof.

engross *v.* absorb, busy, fill; see OCCUPY 3.

engulf *v.* swallow up, submerge, inundate; see SINK 2.

enhance *v.* heighten, magnify, amplify; see INCREASE.

enigma *n.* problem, riddle, parable; see PUZZLE 3.

enjoy *v.* **1** [To get pleasure from] relish, luxuriate in, delight in; see LIKE 1. **2** [To have the use or benefit of] experience, partake of, share, undergo, make use of, use. —**enjoy oneself** take pleasure, celebrate, have a good time, revel in, delight in, luxuriate in, be pleased with; see also PLAY 1.

enjoyable *a.* agreeable, welcome, genial; see PLEASANT 1, 2.

enjoyment *n.* pleasure, delight, satisfaction, gratification, triumph, loving, enjoying, rejoicing, having, using, occupation, use, diversion, entertainment, luxury, sensuality, indulgence, self-indulgence, hedonism.—*Ant.* ABUSE, dislike, displeasure.

enlarge *v.* **1** [To increase] expand, spread, swell; see GROW 1. **2** [To cause to increase] extend, augment, expand; see INCREASE.

enlarged *a.* increased, augmented, expanded, enhanced, developed, exaggerated, extended, amplified, spread, added to, lengthened, broadened, widened, thickened, magnified, filled-out, inflated, swelled, swollen, stretched, heightened, intensified, blown up.

enlargement *n.* **1** [Growth or extension] augmentation, amplification, expansion; see INCREASE. **2** [An enlarged photograph] view, 8 x 10, blowup; see PHOTOGRAPH, PICTURE 2.

enlighten *v.* inform, divulge, acquaint; see TEACH, TELL 1.

enlightened *a.* instructed, learned, informed; see EDUCATED.

enlightenment *n.* wisdom, culture, education; see KNOWLEDGE 1.

enlist *v.* **1** [To enroll others] sign up, press into service, hire, retain, call up, recruit, mobilize, induct, register, list, initiate, employ, place, admit, draft, conscript, muster, call to arms.—*Ant.* REFUSE, neglect, turn away. **2** [To enroll oneself] enter, sign up, serve; see JOIN 2, REGISTER 4.

enlisted *a.* recruited, commissioned, registered; see ENROLLED.

enlistment *n.* conscription, levy,

en·list'ed *adj.* of a person in the armed forces who is not a commissioned officer or warrant officer

en·liv·en (en lī'vən, in-) *vt.* to make active, cheerful, etc.; liven up

en masse (en mas') ⟦Fr, lit., in mass⟧ in a group; as a whole

en·mesh (en mesh', in-) *vt.* to catch as in the meshes of a net; entangle

en·mi·ty (en'mə tē) *n., pl.* **-ties** ⟦see ENEMY⟧ the bitter attitude or feelings of an enemy or enemies; hostility

en·no·ble (e nō'bəl, i-) *vt.* **-bled, -bling** to give a noble quality to; dignify —**en·no'ble·ment** *n.*

en·nui (än'wē') *n.* ⟦Fr⟧ weariness and dissatisfaction from lack of interest; boredom

e·nor·mi·ty (ē nôr'mə tē, i-) *n., pl.* **-ties** ⟦< L *enormis*, immense⟧ **1** great wickedness **2** an outrageous act **3** enormous size or extent

e·nor·mous (ē nôr'məs, i-) *adj.* ⟦see prec.⟧ of great size, number, etc.; huge; vast; immense —**e·nor'mous·ly** *adv.*

e·nough (ē nuf', i-) *adj.* ⟦OE *genoh*⟧ as much or as many as necessary; sufficient —*n.* the amount needed —*adv.* **1** sufficiently **2** fully; quite *[oddly enough]* **3** tolerably

e·now (ē nou', i-) *adj., n., adv.* [Archaic] enough

en·plane (en plān', in-) *vi.* **-planed', -plan'ing** to board an airplane

en·quire (en kwīr', in-) *vt., vi.* **-quired', -quir'ing** INQUIRE —**en·quir'y** (-ē), *pl.* **-ies**, *n.*

en·rage (en rāj', in-) *vt.* **-raged', -rag'ing** to put into a rage; infuriate

en·rap·ture (en rap'chər, in-) *vt.* **-tured, -tur·ing** to fill with delight

en·rich (en rich', in-) *vt.* to make rich or richer; give greater value, better quality, etc. to —**en·rich'ment** *n.*

en·roll or **en·rol** (en rōl', in-) *vt., vi.* **-rolled', -roll'ing** **1** to record or be recorded in a roll or list **2** to enlist **3** to make or become a member —**en·roll'ment** or **en·rol'ment** *n.*

en route (än ro͞ot', en-) ⟦Fr⟧ on the way

en·sconce (en skäns', in-) *vt.* **-sconced', -sconc'ing** ⟦< Du *schans*, small fort⟧ to place or settle snugly or securely

en·sem·ble (än säm'bəl) *n.* ⟦Fr < L *in-*, in + *simul*, at the same time⟧ **1** total effect **2** a whole costume of matching parts **3** *a)* a small group of musicians, actors, etc. *b)* the performance of such a group

en·shrine (en shrīn', in-) *vt.* **-shrined', -shrin'ing** **1** to enclose in a shrine **2** to hold as sacred; cherish —**en·shrine'ment** *n.*

en·shroud (en shroud', in-) *vt.* to cover as if with a shroud; hide; obscure

en·sign (en'sīn'; *also, & for 2 always*, -sən) *n.* ⟦see INSIGNIA⟧ **1** a flag or banner **2** *U.S. Navy* a commissioned officer of the lowest rank

en·si·lage (en'sə lij) *n.* ⟦ult. < L *in-*, in + Gr *siros*, silo⟧ the preserving of green fodder in a silo

en·slave (en slāv', in-) *vt.* **-slaved', -slav'ing** **1** to make a slave of **2** to subjugate —**en·slave'ment** *n.*

en·snare (en sner', in-) *vt.* **-snared', -snar'ing** to catch in or as in a snare

en·sue (en so͞o', in-) *vi.* **-sued', -su'ing** ⟦< L *in-*, in + *sequi*, follow⟧ **1** to come afterward **2** to result

en·sure (en shoor', in-) *vt.* **-sured', -sur'ing** **1** to make sure **2** to protect

-ent (ənt) ⟦< OFr *-ent*, L *-ens*, prp. ending⟧ *suffix* **1** that has, shows, or does *[insistent]* **2** a person or thing that *[superintendent, solvent]*

en·tail (en tāl', in-) *vt.* ⟦< OFr *taillier*, to cut⟧ **1** *Law* to limit the inheritance of (real property) to a specific line of heirs **2** to make necessary; require

en·tan·gle (en taŋ'gəl, in-) *vt.* **-gled, -gling** **1** to involve in a tangle **2** to involve in difficulty **3** to confuse **4** to complicate —**en·tan'gle·ment** *n.*

en·tente (än tänt') *n.* ⟦Fr < OFr *entendre*, understand⟧ **1** an understanding or agreement, as between nations **2** the parties to this

en·ter (ent'ər) *vt.* ⟦< L *intra*, within⟧ **1** to come or go into **2** to penetrate **3** to insert **4** to write down in a list, etc. **5** to become a member of or participant in **6** to get (a person, etc.) admitted **7** to begin **8** to put on record, formally or before a law court **9** to input (data, etc.) into a computer —*vi.* **1** to come or go into some place **2** to penetrate —**enter into** **1** to take part in **2** to form a part of —**enter on** (or **upon**) to begin; start

en·ter·i·tis (ent'ər īt'is) *n.* ⟦< Gr *enteron*, intestine + -ITIS⟧ inflammation of the intestine

en·ter·prise (ent'ər prīz') *n.* ⟦ult. < L *inter*, in + *prehendere*, take⟧ **1** an undertaking, esp. a big, bold, or difficult one **2** energy and initiative

en'ter·pris'ing *adj.* showing enterprise; full of energy and initiative

en·ter·tain (ent'ər tān') *vt.* ⟦ult. < L *inter*, between + *tenere*, to hold⟧ **1** to amuse; divert **2** to have as a guest **3** to have in mind; consider —*vi.* to give hospitality to guests

en'ter·tain'er *n.* one who entertains; esp., a popular singer, comedian, etc.

THESAURUS

recruitment; see ENROLLMENT 1, INDUCTION 3.

en masse *a.* bodily, as one, together; see TOGETHER 2, UNIFIED.

enmity *n.* animosity, malice, rancor; see HATRED.

enormous *a.* monstrous, immense, huge; see LARGE 1.

enough *a.* **1** [Sufficient] plenty, abundant, adequate, acceptable, ample, satisfactory, complete, copious, plentiful, satisfying, unlimited, suitable.—*Ant.* INADEQUATE, deficient, insufficient. **2** [Sufficiently] satisfactorily, amply, abundantly; see ADEQUATELY. **3** [Fully] quite, rather, just; see VERY. **4** [Just adequately] tolerably, fairly, barely; see ADEQUATELY.

enough *n.* abundance, sufficiency, adequacy; see PLENTY.

enrage *v.* anger, incite, outrage, provoke, irk, bother, annoy, tease, pester, agitate, arouse, stir, goad, bait, inflame, incense, infuriate, madden; see also INCITE.

enrich *v.* adorn, better, decorate; see IMPROVE 1.

enriched *a.* improved, bettered, embellished; see IMPROVED.

enrichment *n.* advancement, promotion, endowment; see IMPROVEMENT 1.

enroll *v.* **1** [To obtain for service] recruit, obtain, employ; see HIRE. **2** [To register oneself] enter, sign up, enlist; see JOIN 2, REGISTER 4.

enrolled *a.* joined, inducted, registered, installed, pledged, enlisted, commissioned, employed, recruited, on the roll, signed up.—*Ant.* SEPARATED, mustered out, discharged.

enrollment *n.* **1** [The act of enrolling] registering, listing, inducting, recording, enlistment, matriculation, induction, entry, enlisting, selecting, registration. **2** [The persons enrolled] group, students, student body, conscripts, volunteers, number enrolled, response, registration, entrants, subscription.

en route *a.* on the way, in transit, flying, driving, traveling, midway, in passage, on the road, making headway toward, bound, heading toward.—*Ant.* MOTIONLESS, delayed, stalled.

enslave *v.* bind, imprison, incarcerate, shut in, enclose, confine, hold under, hold, subjugate, restrain, oppress, restrict, fetter, coerce, check, subdue, capture, suppress, make a slave of, hold in bondage, compel, chain, jail, deprive, tie, shackle.

enslavement *n.* oppression, subjection, servitude; see SLAVERY 1.

ensnare *v.* entrap, trap, snare; see CATCH 1.

ensure *v.* secure, assure, warrant; see GUARANTEE.

entail *v.* require, necessitate, evoke; see NEED.

entangle *v.* ensnare, entrap, trap, implicate, complicate, involve, snarl, corner, catch, embroil, tangle, ravel, unsettle, foul up*, mess up*, goof up*.—*Ant.* FREE, liberate, disentangle.

entanglement *n.* complexity, intricacy, complication; see DIFFICULTY 1, 2.

enter *v.* invade, make an entrance, set foot in, pass into, come in, drive in, burst in, rush in, go in, break into, get in, barge in, penetrate, intrude, reenter, slip in, sneak in, infiltrate, insert, move in, fall into*, crowd in, worm oneself into.—*Ant.* LEAVE, depart, exit. —**enter into** engage in, take part in, become part of; see JOIN 2. —**enter on** (or **upon**) start, take up, make a beginning; see BEGIN 2.

entered *a.* filed, listed, posted; see RECORDED.

enterprise *n.* affair, undertaking, endeavor; see BUSINESS.

entertain *v.* **1** [To keep others amused] amuse, cheer, please, interest, enliven, delight, divert, beguile, charm, captivate, inspire, stimulate, satisfy, humor, enthrall, elate, tickle, distract, indulge, flatter, relax, comfort.—*Ant.* TIRE, bore, weary. **2** [To act as host or hostess] receive, host, invite, treat, charm, feed, dine, wine and dine, give a party, throw a party*, do the honors, welcome, give a warm reception to, receive with open arms.—*Ant.* NEGLECT, ignore, bore.

entertained *a.* amused, diverted, pleased, occupied, charmed, cheered, interested, relaxed, delighted, engrossed, enjoying oneself, happy, in good humor, in good company.—*Ant.* BORED, depressed, irritated.

entertainer *n.* performer, player,

en'ter·tain'ing *adj.* interesting and pleasurable; amusing

en'ter·tain'ment *n.* **1** an entertaining or being entertained **2** something that entertains; esp., a show or performance

en·thrall or **en·thral** (en thrôl', in-) *vt.* **-thralled', -thrall'ing** ⟦see EN- & THRALL⟧ to captivate; fascinate

en·throne (en thrōn', in-) *vt.* **-throned', -thron'ing** **1** to place on a throne **2** to exalt

en·thuse (en tho͞oz', in-) [Inf.] *vi.* **-thused', -thus'ing** to express enthusiasm —*vt.* to make enthusiastic

en·thu·si·asm (en tho͞o'zē az'əm, in-) *n.* ⟦< Gr *en-*, in + *theos*, god⟧ intense or eager interest; zeal —**en·thu'si·ast'** (-ast', -əst) *n.* —**en·thu'si·as'tic** *adj.* —**en·thu'si·as'ti·cal·ly** *adv.*

en·tice (en tīs', in-) *vt.* **-ticed', -tic'ing** ⟦< L *in*, in + *titio*, a burning brand⟧ to tempt with hope of reward or pleasure —**en·tice'ment** *n.*

en·tire (en tīr', in-) *adj.* ⟦< L *integer*, whole⟧ not lacking any parts; whole; complete; intact —**en·tire'ly** *adv.*

en·tire'ty (-tē) *n.*, *pl.* **-ties** **1** the state or fact of being entire; wholeness **2** an entire thing; whole

en·ti·tle (en tīt''l, in-) *vt.* **-tled, -tling** **1** to give a title or name to **2** to give a right or claim to

en·ti'tle·ment *n.* something to which one is entitled, esp. a benefit, as Medicare, provided by certain government programs

en·ti·ty (en'tə tē) *n.*, *pl.* **-ties** ⟦ult. < L *esse*, to be⟧ **1** existence **2** a thing that has definite existence

en·tomb (en to͞om', in-) *vt.* to place in a tomb; bury —**en·tomb'ment** *n.*

en·to·mol·o·gy (en'tə mäl'ə jē) *n.* ⟦< Gr *entomon*, insect + -LOGY⟧ the branch of zoology that deals with insects —**en'to·mo·log'i·cal** (-mə läj'i kəl) *adj.* —**en'to·mol'o·gist** *n.*

en·tou·rage (än'too räzh') *n.* ⟦Fr < *entourer*, surround⟧ a group of accompanying attendants, etc.; retinue

en·trails (en'trālz, -trəlz) *pl.n.* ⟦< L *interaneus*, internal⟧ the inner organs; specif., the intestines

en·trance[1] (en'trəns) *n.* **1** the act of entering **2** a place for entering; door, etc. **3** permission or right to enter; admission

en·trance[2] (en trans', in-) *vt.* **-tranced', -tranc'ing** ⟦see EN- & TRANCE⟧ to fill with delight; enchant

en·trant (en'trənt) *n.* one who enters

en·trap (en trap', in-) *vt.* **-trapped', -trap'ping** to catch in or as in a trap —**en·trap'ment** *n.*

en·treat (en trēt', in-) *vt., vi.* ⟦< OFr *en-*, in + *traiter*, to treat⟧ to ask earnestly; beg; implore

en·treat'y *n.*, *pl.* **-ies** an earnest request; prayer

en·tree or **en·trée** (än'trā') *n.* ⟦Fr < OFr *entrer*, enter⟧ **1** right to enter, use, etc.; access **2** the main course of a meal

en·trench (en trench', in-) *vt.* **1** to surround or fortify with trenches **2** to establish securely

en·tre·pre·neur (än'trə prə nur') *n.* ⟦Fr: see ENTERPRISE⟧ one who organizes a business undertaking, assuming the risk for the sake of the profit —**en'tre·pre·neur'i·al** *adj.*

en·tro·py (en'trə pē) *n.* ⟦< Gr *entropē*, a turning toward⟧ **1** a thermodynamic measure of the energy unavailable for useful work in a changing system **2** a process of degeneration with increasing uncertainty, chaos, etc., specif., when regarded as the final stage of a social system

en·trust (en trust', in-) *vt.* **1** to charge with a trust or duty **2** to turn over for safekeeping

en·try (en'trē) *n.*, *pl.* **-tries** ⟦< OFr: see ENTER⟧ **1** an entering; entrance **2** a way by which to enter **3** an item or note in a list, journal, etc. **4** one entered in a race, etc.

en'try-lev'el *adj.* **1** designating a job with low pay but possible advancement **2** basic; introductory

en·twine (en twīn', in-) *vt., vi.* **-twined', -twin'ing** to twine together or around

e·nu·mer·ate (ē no͞o'mər āt', i-) *vt.* **-at'ed, -at'ing** ⟦< L *e-*, out + *numerare*, to count⟧ **1** to count **2** to name one by one —**e·nu'mer·a'tion** *n.*

e·nun·ci·ate (ē nun'sē āt', i-) *vt., vi.* **-at'ed, -at'ing** ⟦< L *e-*, out + *nuntiare*, announce⟧ **1** to state definitely **2** to announce **3** to pronounce (words), esp. clearly —**e·nun'ci·a'tion** *n.*

en·u·re·sis (en'yo͞o rē'sis) *n.* ⟦ult. < L *in*, in + Gr *ouron*, urine⟧ inability to control urination

en·vel·op (en vel'əp, in-) *vt.* ⟦< OFr: see EN- & DEVELOP⟧ **1** to wrap up; cover completely **2** to surround **3** to conceal; hide —**en·vel'op·ment** *n.*

en·ve·lope (än'və lōp', en'-) *n.* **1** a thing that envelops; covering **2** a folded paper container for a letter, etc., usually with a gummed flap

en·ven·om (en ven'əm, in-) *vt.* **1** to put venom into **2** to fill with hate

en·vi·a·ble (en'vē ə bəl) *adj.* good enough to be envied or desired —**en'vi·a·bly** *adv.*

en·vi·ous (en'vē əs) *adj.* feeling or showing envy —**en'vi·ous·ly** *adv.*

en·vi·ron·ment (en vī'rən mənt, in-) *n.* ⟦see ENVIRONS⟧ **1** surroundings **2** all the conditions, etc. surrounding, and

THESAURUS

artist; see ACTOR.

entertaining *a.* diverting, amusing, engaging, enchanting, sprightly, lively, witty, clever, interesting, gay, charming, enjoyable, delightful, funny, pleasing, edifying, engrossing, compelling, rousing, cheerful, relaxing, moving, inspiring, captivating, thrilling, entrancing, stirring, poignant, impressive, soul-stirring, stimulating, absorbing, riveting, exciting, provocative, fascinating, ravishing, satisfying, seductive; see also FUNNY 1.—*Ant.* BORING, irritating, dull.

entertainment *n.* amusement, enjoyment, merriment, fun, pleasure, sport, recreation, pastime, diversion, relaxation, distraction, play, feast, banquet, picnic, show, television, the movies, treat, game, party, reception, spree.

enthused* *a.* excited, approving, eager; see ENTHUSIASTIC.

enthusiasm *n.* fervor, ardor, eagerness; see ZEAL.

enthusiast *n.* **1** [A zealous person] zealot, fanatic, partisan; see BELIEVER. **2** [One who has strong interest in something] hobbyist, supporter, freak*; see FOLLOWER.

enthusiastic *a.* interested, fascinated, willing, thrilled, feverish, concerned, passionate, raging, excited, attracted, exhilarated, anxious, eager, yearning, dying to*, inflamed, absorbed, devoted, diligent, ardent, fiery, longing, desiring, spirited, zestful, fervent, ecstatic, impatient, delighted, enraptured, avid, wild about*, crazy about*, mad about*, hot for*, gung-ho*, aching to*.—*Ant.* OPPOSED, reluctant, apathetic.

entice *v.* lure, allure, attract; see FASCINATE.

enticement *n.* lure, bait, promise; see ATTRACTION.

entire *a.* complete, untouched, undamaged; see WHOLE 1, 2.

entirely *a.* **1** [Completely] totally, fully, wholly; see COMPLETELY. **2** [Exclusively] uniquely, solely, undividedly; see ONLY 1.

entirety *n.* total, aggregate, sum; see WHOLE.

entitle *v.* authorize, empower, qualify; see ALLOW.

entity *n.* item, article, something; see THING 1.

entourage *n.* retinue, associates, followers; see FOLLOWING.

entrails *n.* viscera, guts, insides; see INTESTINES.

entrance[1] *n.* **1** [The act of coming in] arrival, entry, passage, approach, induction, initiation, admission, admittance, appearance, introduction, penetration, trespass, debut, enrollment, baptism, invasion, immigration.—*Ant.* ESCAPE, exit, issue. **2** [The opening that permits entry] gate, door, doorway, vestibule, entry, gateway, portal, port, inlet, opening, passage, staircase, porch, hall, hallway, path, way, entry way, passageway, threshold, lobby, corridor, approach, way in.

entrance[2] *v.* charm, captivate, hypnotize; see FASCINATE.

entrap *v.* catch, ensnare, decoy; see CATCH 1.

entrapment *n.* snare, ambush, ruse; see TRAP 1.

entree *n.* main course, main dish, meat dish; see MEAL.

entrepreneur *n.* owner, capitalist, employer; see BUSINESSMAN.

entrust *v.* deposit with, trust to, leave with; see TRUST 4.

entry *n.* approach, hall, lobby, foyer, door, gate; see also ENTRANCE 2.

enumerate *v.* list, mention, identify; see RECORD 1.

enumeration *n.* inventory, catalog, register; see RECORD 1.

envelop *v.* encompass, contain, hide; see SURROUND 1, WRAP.

envelope *n.* receptacle, pouch, pocket, bag, container, box, covering, case, wrapper, enclosure, cover, sheath, casing.

enviable *a.* welcome, good, superior; see EXCELLENT.

envious *a.* covetous, desirous, resentful, desiring, wishful, longing for, aspiring, greedy, grasping, craving, begrudging, green-eyed, hankering, green with envy; see also JEALOUS.—*Ant.* GENEROUS, trustful, charitable.

environment *n.* conditions, living conditions, circumstances, surroundings, scene, external conditions, background, milieu, setting, habitat, eco-

affecting the development of, an organism, food chain, etc. —**en·vi′ron·men′tal** ***adj.***

en·vi′ron·men′tal·ist ***n.*** one working to solve environmental problems, as air and water pollution

en·vi·rons (en vī′rənz, in-) ***pl.n.*** ⟦< OFr *en-*, in + *viron*, a circuit⟧ **1** the districts surrounding a city; suburbs **2** surrounding area; vicinity

en·vis·age (en viz′ij, in-) ***vt.*** **-aged**, **-ag·ing** ⟦see EN- & VISAGE⟧ to form an image of in the mind; visualize

en·vi·sion (en vizh′ən, in-) ***vt.*** ⟦EN- + VISION⟧ to imagine (something not yet in existence)

en·voy (än′voi′, en′-) ***n.*** ⟦< Fr < L *in*, in + *via*, way⟧ **1** a messenger **2** a diplomatic agent just below an ambassador

en·vy (en′vē) ***n.***, *pl.* **-vies** ⟦< L *in-*, in + *videre*, to look⟧ **1** discontent and ill will over another's advantages, possessions, etc. **2** desire for something that another has **3** an object of such feeling —***vt.*** **-vied**, **-vy·ing** to feel envy toward or because of —**en′vy·ing·ly** ***adv.***

en·zyme (en′zīm′) ***n.*** ⟦< Gr *en-*, in + *zymē*, leaven⟧ a protein, formed in plant and animal cells or made synthetically, acting as a catalyst in chemical reactions

e·on (ē′ən, ē′än′) ***n.*** ⟦< Gr *aiōn*, an age⟧ an extremely long, indefinite period of time

-e·ous (ē əs) ⟦< L *-eus* + -OUS⟧ *suffix var. of* -OUS *[gaseous]*

EPA *abbrev.* Environmental Protection Agency

ep·au·let or **ep·au·lette** (ep′ə let′, ep′ə let′) ***n.*** ⟦< Fr dim. of *épaule*, shoulder⟧ a shoulder ornament, esp. on military uniforms

e·pee or **é·pée** (ā pā′) ***n.*** ⟦Fr⟧ a fencing sword like a foil, but heavier and more rigid

e·phed·rine (e fe′drin) ***n.*** ⟦< L *ephedra*, the plant horsetail⟧ an alkaloid used to relieve nasal congestion and asthma

e·phem·er·al (e fem′ər əl, i-) ***adj.*** ⟦< Gr *epi-*, upon + *hēmera*, day⟧ **1** lasting one day **2** short-lived; transitory

epi- ⟦< Gr *epi*, at, on⟧ *prefix* on, upon, over, among *[epiglottis]*

ep·ic (ep′ik) ***n.*** ⟦< Gr *epos*, a word, song, epic⟧ a long narrative poem in a dignified style about the deeds of a hero or heroes —***adj.*** of or like an epic; heroic; grand

ep·i·cen·ter (ep′i sent′ər) ***n.*** **1** the area of the earth's surface directly above the place of origin of an earthquake **2** a focal or central point

ep·i·cure (ep′i kyoor′) ***n.*** ⟦after *Epicurus*, ancient Gr philosopher⟧ one who enjoys and has a discriminating taste for fine foods and drinks

ep·i·cu·re·an (ep′i kyoo rē′ən, ep′i kyoor′ē ən) ***adj.*** fond of sensuous pleasure, esp. that of eating and drinking —***n.*** an epicure

ep·i·dem·ic (ep′ə dem′ik) ***adj.*** ⟦< Fr < Gr *epi-*, among + *dēmos*, people⟧ spreading rapidly among many people in a community, as a disease —***n.*** **1** an epidemic disease **2** the spreading of such a disease **3** a rapid, widespread growth —**ep′i·dem′i·cal·ly** ***adv.***

ep·i·de·mi·ol·o·gy (ep′ə dē′mē äl′ə jē) ***n.*** ⟦prec. + -LOGY⟧ the branch of medicine that studies epidemics

ep·i·der·mis (ep′ə dur′mis) ***n.*** ⟦< Gr *epi-*, upon + *derma*, the skin⟧ the outermost layer of the skin —**ep′i·der′mal** or **ep′i·der′mic** ***adj.***

ep·i·du·ral (ep′ə door′əl) ***adj.*** on or outside the dura mater —***n.*** local anesthesia of the lower body by epidural injection

ep·i·glot·tis (ep′ə glät′is) ***n.*** ⟦see EPI- & GLOTTIS⟧ the thin, lidlike piece of cartilage that covers the windpipe during swallowing

ep·i·gram (ep′ə gram′) ***n.*** ⟦< Gr *epi-*, upon + *graphein*, write⟧ a terse, witty, pointed statement —**ep′i·gram·mat′ic** (-grə mat′ik) ***adj.***

e·pig·ra·phy (ē pig′rə fē, i-) ***n.*** the study of inscriptions, esp. ancient ones

ep·i·lep·sy (ep′ə lep′sē) ***n.*** ⟦< Gr *epi-*, upon + *lambanein*, seize⟧ a recurrent disorder of the nervous system, characterized by seizures that cause convulsions, unconsciousness, etc.

ep′i·lep′tic (-tik) ***adj.*** of or having epilepsy —***n.*** one who has epilepsy

ep·i·logue or **ep·i·log** (ep′ə lôg′) ***n.*** ⟦< Gr *epi-*, upon + *legein*, speak⟧ a closing section added to a novel, play, etc., providing further comment, as a speech by an actor to the audience

E·piph·a·ny (ē pif′ə nē, i-) ***n.***, *pl.* **-nies** ⟦< Gr *epiphainein*, show forth⟧ **1** a Christian feast day (Jan. 6) commemorating the revealing of Jesus as the Christ to the Gentiles **2** [**e-**] *a)* a flash of insight *b)* an experience that brings this about

e·pis·co·pa·cy (ē pis′kə pə sē, i-) ***n.***, *pl.* **-cies** ⟦< Gr *epi-*, upon + *skopein*, to look⟧ **1** church government by bishops **2** EPISCOPATE

e·pis′co·pal (-pəl) ***adj.*** **1** of or governed by bishops **2** [**E-**] designating or of any of various churches governed by bishops

E·pis′co·pa′lian (-pāl′yən) ***adj.*** Episcopal —***n.*** a member of the Protestant Episcopal Church

e·pis′co·pate (-pit, -pāt′) ***n.*** **1** the position, rank, etc. of a bishop **2** bishops collectively

ep·i·sode (ep′ə sōd′) ***n.*** ⟦< Gr *epi-*, upon + *eisodos*, entrance⟧ **1** any part of a novel, poem, etc. that is complete in itself **2** an event or series of events complete in itself —**ep′i·sod′ic** (-säd′ik) ***adj.*** —**ep′i·sod′i·cal·ly** ***adv.***

e·pis·tle (ē pis′əl) ***n.*** ⟦< Gr *epi-*, to + *stellein*, send⟧ **1** a letter **2** [**E-**] any of the letters in the New Testament —**e·pis′to·lar′y** (-tə ler′ē) ***adj.***

ep·i·taph (ep′ə taf′) ***n.*** ⟦< Gr *epi-*, upon + *taphos*, tomb⟧ an inscription on a tomb, etc. in memory of a dead person

ep·i·the·li·um (ep′i thē′lē əm) ***n.***, *pl.* **-li·ums** or **-li·a** (-ə) ⟦< Gr *epi-*, upon + *thēlē*, nipple⟧ cellular tissue covering external body surfaces or lining internal surfaces —**ep′i·the′li·al** (-əl) ***adj.***

ep·i·thet (ep′ə thet′) ***n.*** ⟦< Gr *epi-*, on + *tithenai*, put⟧ a word or phrase characterizing some person or thing

e·pit·o·me (ē pit′ə mē′, i-) ***n.***, *pl.* **-mes′** (-mēz′) ⟦< Gr *epi-*, upon + *temnein*, to cut⟧ **1** an abstract; summary **2** a person or thing that shows the typical qualities of something

e·pit′o·mize′ (-mīz′) ***vt.*** **-mized′**, **-miz′ing** to make or be an epitome of

e plu·ri·bus u·num (ē′ ploor′ē boos′ oo′noom) ⟦L⟧ out of many, one: a motto of the U.S.

ep·och (ep′ək) ***n.*** ⟦< Gr *epi-*, upon + *echein*, to hold⟧ **1** the start of a new period in the history of anything **2** a period of time in terms of noteworthy events, persons, etc. —**ep′och·al** ***adj.***

ep·ox·y (ē päk′sē, i-) ***adj.*** ⟦EP(I)- + OXY(GEN)⟧ designating a resin used in strong, resistant glues, enamels, etc. —***n.***, *pl.* **-ies** an epoxy resin

ep·si·lon (ep′sə län′) ***n.*** ⟦Gr *e psilon*, plain *e*⟧ the fifth letter of the Greek alphabet (Ε, ϵ)

Ep·som salts (or **salt**) (ep′səm) ⟦after *Epsom*, town in England⟧ a white, crystalline salt, magnesium sulfate, used as a cathartic

Ep·stein-Barr virus (ep′stīn bär′) a herpes-like virus that causes infectious mononucleosis and may cause various forms of cancer

eq·ua·ble (ek′wə bəl) ***adj.*** ⟦see fol.⟧ steady; uniform; even; tranquil —**eq′ua·bil′i·ty** ***n.*** —**eq′ua·bly** ***adv.***

e·qual (ē′kwəl) ***adj.*** ⟦< L *aequus*, even⟧ **1** of the same quantity, size, value, etc. **2** having the same rights, abil-

THESAURUS

system, situation.

envoy ***n.*** emissary, ambassador, intermediary; see AGENT.

envy ***n.*** jealousy, ill will, spite, rivalry, opposition, grudge, malice, prejudice, malevolence, covetousness, enviousness, backbiting, maliciousness, the green-eyed monster.

envy ***v.*** begrudge, covet, lust after, crave, be envious of, feel ill toward, have hard feelings toward, feel resentful toward, have a grudge against, object to.

eon ***n.*** eternity, cycle, time; see AGE 3.

epic ***a.*** heroic, classic, grand; see IMPORTANT 1.

epic ***n.*** narrative poem, saga, legend; see POEM, STORY.

epidemic ***n.*** plague, scourge, pestilence; see ILLNESS 1.

epidermis ***n.*** cuticle, dermis, hide; see SKIN.

episode ***n.*** happening, occurrence, incident; see EVENT.

epoch ***n.*** era, period, time; see AGE 3.

equal ***a.*** even, regular, like, same, identical, similar, uniform, invariable, fair, unvarying, commensurate, just, impartial, unbiased, to the same degree, on a footing with, without distinction, equitable, one and the same, level, parallel, corresponding, equivalent, proportionate, comparable, tantamount.—*Ant.* IRREGULAR, unequal, uneven. —**equal to** adequate, capable, qualified; see ABLE.

equal ***n.*** parallel, match, counterpart, complement, peer, fellow, twin, double, likeness, companion, copy, duplicate, rival, competitor, opposite number.

equal ***v.*** match, equalize, rank with, be the same, rival, equate, approach, live up to, come up to, amount to, consist of, comprise, be composed of, be made of, measure up to, even off, break even, come to, compare, square with, tally with, agree,

ity, rank, etc. **3** evenly proportioned **4** having the necessary ability, strength, etc.: with *to* —***n.*** any person or thing that is equal —***vt.*** **e'qualed** or **e'qualled, e'qual·ing** or **e'qual·ling** **1** to be equal to **2** to do or make something equal to —**e·qual·i·ty** (ē kwôl'ə tē, -kwäl'-), *pl.* **-ties,** ***n.*** —**e'qual·ly** ***adv.***

e·qual·ize (ē'kwəl īz') ***vt.*** **-ized', -iz'ing** to make equal or uniform —**e'qual·i·za'tion** ***n.*** —**e'qual·iz'er** ***n.***

e'qual-op'por·tu'ni·ty ***adj.*** treating all employees and job applicants equally, without regard to race, sex, etc.

equal sign the sign (=), indicating that the terms on either side of it are equal or equivalent

e·qua·nim·i·ty (ek'wə nim'ə tē, ē'kwə-) ***n.*** ⟦< L *aequus*, even + *animus*, mind⟧ evenness of temper; composure

e·quate (ē kwāt', i-) ***vt.*** **e·quat'ed, e·quat'ing** **1** to make equal **2** to treat, regard, or express as equal —**e·quat'a·ble** ***adj.***

e·qua·tion (ē kwā'zhən, i-) ***n.*** **1** an equating or being equated **2** a statement of equality between two quantities, as shown by the equal sign (=)

e·qua·tor (ē kwāt'ər, i-) ***n.*** an imaginary circle around the earth, equally distant from the North Pole and the South Pole —**e·qua·to·ri·al** (ē'kwə tôr'ē əl, ek'wə-) ***adj.***

Equatorial Guinea country in WC Africa: 10,831 sq. mi.; pop. 304,000

eq·uer·ry (ek'wər ē, ē kwer'ē) ***n.***, *pl.* **-ries** ⟦< Fr⟧ **1** [Historical] an officer in charge of royal horses **2** an officer who attends a person of royalty

e·ques·tri·an (ē kwes'trē ən, i-) ***adj.*** ⟦< L *equus*, horse⟧ **1** of horses or horsemanship **2** on horseback —***n.*** a rider or circus performer on horseback —**e·ques'tri·enne'** (-trē en') ***fem.n.***

equi- *combining form* equal, equally *[equidistant]*

e·qui·dis·tant (ē'kwi dis'tənt) ***adj.*** equally distant

e'qui·lat'er·al (-lat'ər əl) ***adj.*** ⟦< L *aequus*, even + *latus*, side⟧ having all sides equal

e'qui·lib'ri·um (-lib'rē əm) ***n.***, *pl.* **-ri·ums** or **-ri·a** (-ə) ⟦< L *aequus*, even + *libra*, a balance⟧ a state of balance between opposing forces

e·quine (ē'kwīn') ***adj.*** ⟦< L *equus*, horse⟧ of or like a horse

e·qui·nox (ē'kwi näks', ek'wə näks') ***n.*** ⟦< L *aequus*, even + *nox*, night⟧ the time when the sun crosses the equator, making night and day of equal length in all parts of the earth —**e'qui·noc'tial** (-näk'shəl) ***adj.***

e·quip (ē kwip', i-) ***vt.*** **e·quipped', e·quip'ping** ⟦< OFr *esquiper*, embark⟧ to provide with what is needed

eq·ui·page (ek'wi pij) ***n.*** a carriage with horses and liveried servants

e·quip·ment (ē kwip'mənt, i-) ***n.*** **1** an equipping or being equipped **2** whatever one is equipped with; supplies, furnishings, etc.

eq·ui·poise (ek'wi poiz', ē'kwi-) ***n.*** ⟦EQUI- + POISE⟧ **1** state of equilibrium **2** a counterbalance

eq·ui·ta·ble (ek'wit ə bəl) ***adj.*** ⟦see EQUITY⟧ fair; just —**eq'ui·ta·bly** ***adv.***

eq·ui·ta·tion (ek'wi tā'shən) ***n.*** ⟦< L *equitare*, to ride⟧ the art of riding on horseback

eq·ui·ty (ek'wit ē) ***n.***, *pl.* **-ties** ⟦< L *aequus*, even⟧ **1** fairness; impartiality; justice **2** the value of property beyond the amount owed on it **3** *Finance a)* assets minus liabilities; net worth *b)* [*pl.*] shares of stock **4** *Law* a system of doctrines supplementing common and statute law

e·quiv·a·lent (ē kwiv'ə lənt, i-) ***adj.*** ⟦< L *aequus*, equal + *valere*, be worth⟧ equal in quantity, value, force, meaning, etc. —***n.*** an equivalent thing —**e·quiv'a·lence** ***n.***

e·quiv·o·cal (ē kwiv'ə kəl, i-) ***adj.*** ⟦< L *aequus*, even + *vox*, voice⟧ **1** having two or more meanings; purposely ambiguous **2** uncertain; doubtful **3** suspicious *[equivocal conduct]* —**e·quiv'o·cal·ly** ***adv.*** —**e·quiv'o·cal·ness** ***n.***

e·quiv'o·cate' (-kāt') ***vi.*** **-cat'ed, -cat'ing** to use equivocal terms in order to deceive, hedge, etc. —**e·quiv'o·ca'tion** ***n.*** —**e·quiv'o·ca'tor** ***n.***

ER *abbrev.* emergency room

-er (ər) ⟦ME⟧ *suffix* **1** *a)* a person or thing having to do with *[hatter]* *b)* a person living in *[New Yorker]* *c)* one that ____s *[roller]* **2** forming the comparative degree *[later]* **3** repeatedly: added to verbs *[flicker]*

e·ra (ir'ə, er'ə) ***n.*** ⟦LL *aera*⟧ **1** a period of time measured from some important event **2** a period of time having some special characteristic

ERA *abbrev.* **1** *Baseball* earned run average: also **era** **2** Equal Rights Amendment

e·rad·i·cate (ē rad'i kāt', i-) ***vt.*** **-cat'ed, -cat'ing** ⟦< L *e-*, out + *radix*, root⟧ to uproot; wipe out; destroy —**e·rad'i·ca'tion** ***n.*** —**e·rad'i·ca'tor** ***n.***

e·rase (ē rās', i-) ***vt.*** **e·rased', e·ras'ing** ⟦< L *e-*, out + *radere*, scrape⟧ **1** to rub, scrape, or wipe out (esp. writing) **2** to remove (something recorded) from (magnetic tape) **3** to obliterate, as from the mind —**e·ras'a·ble** ***adj.***

e·ras'er ***n.*** a thing that erases; specif., a rubber device for erasing ink or pencil marks, or a pad for removing chalk marks from a blackboard

E·ras·mus (i raz'məs), **Des·i·der·i·us** (des'ə dir'ē əs) 1466?-1536; Du. humanist & theologian

e·ra·sure (ē rā'shər, i-) ***n.*** **1** an erasing **2** an erased word, mark, etc.

ere (er) [Old Poet.] ***prep.*** ⟦OE *ær*⟧ before (in time) —***conj.*** **1** before **2** rather than

e·rect (ē rekt', i-) ***adj.*** ⟦< L *e-*, up + *regere*, make straight⟧ upright —***vt.*** **1** to construct (a building, etc.) **2** to set in an upright position; raise **3** to set up; assemble —**e·rec'tion** ***n.*** —**e·rect'ly** ***adv.*** —**e·rect'ness** ***n.*** —**e·rec'tor** ***n.***

e·rec·tile (ē rek'til, i-) ***adj.*** that can become erect: used esp. of tissue that becomes rigid when filled with blood

erg (ʉrg) ***n.*** ⟦< Gr *ergon*, work⟧ *Physics* a unit of work or energy

er·go (er'gō) ***adv.*** ⟦L⟧ therefore

er·go·nom·ics (ʉr'gō näm'iks) ***n.*** ⟦ult. < Gr *ergon*, work + (EC)ONOMICS⟧ the science of adapting working conditions to the needs of the worker

Er·ie (ir'ē), **Lake** one of the Great Lakes, between Lake Huron & Lake Ontario

Er·in (er'in) *old poet. name for* IRELAND

Er·i·tre·a (er'ə trē'ə) country in E Africa: 36,171 sq. mi.; pop. 3,525,000 —**Er'i·tre'an** ***adj., n.***

er·mine (ʉr'min) ***n.*** ⟦prob. < OHG *harmo*, weasel⟧ **1** a weasel whose fur is white in winter **2** its white fur

THESAURUS

correspond, be tantamount to, be identical, keep pace with, be commensurate, meet, rise to.

equality ***n.*** balance, parity, uniformity, sameness, likeness, identity, evenness, equalization, equilibrium, impartiality, fairness, civil rights, equivalence, tolerance, all for one and one for all*, even-steven*, fair shake.—*Ant.* INJUSTICE, inequality, unfairness.

equalize ***v.*** make even, make equal, balance, equate, match, level, adjust, establish equilibrium, even up.

equally ***a.*** evenly, symmetrically, proportionately, coordinately, equivalently, on a level, both, impartially, justly, fairly, across the board, on even terms, as well as, the same for one as for another.

equate ***v.*** **1** [To equalize] make equal, average, balance; see EQUALIZE. **2** [To compare] match, link, relate; see COMPARE 1.

equation ***n.*** mathematical statement, formal statement of equivalence, chemical statement. *Kinds of equations include the following:* linear, quadratic, cubic, quartic, polynomial, balanced, unbalanced, chemical.

equator ***n.*** middle, circumference of the earth, tropics; see JUNGLE.

equatorial ***a.*** tropical, in the Torrid Zone, central; see HOT 1.

equilibrium ***n.*** stability, center of gravity, steadiness; see BALANCE 2.

equip ***v.*** furnish, outfit, supply; see PROVIDE 1.

equipment ***n.*** material, materiel, tools, facilities, implements, utensils, apparatus, furnishings, appliances, paraphernalia, belongings, devices, outfit, accessories, attachments, extras, conveniences, articles, tackle, rig, machinery, fittings, trappings, fixtures, contraptions, supplies, accompaniments, gear, fixings, stuff, gadgets, things; see also MACHINE, PART 3.

equipped ***a.*** outfitted, furnished, supplied, rigged up, fitted out, arrayed, dressed, accoutered, assembled, readied, provided, implemented, decked, bedecked, appareled, completed, supplemented, set up.

equitable ***a.*** impartial, just, moral; see FAIR 1.

equity ***n.*** investment, owner's interest, capital; see PROPERTY 1.

equivalent ***a.*** commensurate, comparable, similar; see EQUAL.

era ***n.*** epoch, period, date; see AGE 3, TIME 2.

eradicate ***v.*** eliminate, exterminate, annihilate; see DESTROY.

eradication ***n.*** extermination, annihilation, elimination; see DESTRUCTION 1.

erase ***v.*** delete, expunge, omit, obliterate, cut, clean, nullify, eradicate; see also CANCEL.

erect ***a.*** upright, vertical, perpendicular; see STRAIGHT 1.

erect ***v.*** construct, raise, fabricate; see BUILD.

erected ***a.*** constructed, completed, raised; see BUILT.

erection ***n.*** building, erecting, constructing; see CONSTRUCTION 2.

e·rode (ē rōd′, i-) ***vt.*** **e·rod′ed, e·rod′ing** ⟦< L *e-*, out + *rodere*, gnaw⟧ **1** to wear away **2** to form by wearing away gradually —***vi.*** to become eroded

e·rog·e·nous (ē räj′ə nəs, i-) ***adj.*** ⟦< Gr *erōs*, love + -GEN + -OUS⟧ sensitive to sexual stimulation: also **e·ro·to·gen·ic** (er′ə tō′jen′ik)

E·ros (er′äs′, ir′-) ***n.*** **1** *Gr. Myth.* the god of love **2** [**e-**] sexual love or desire

e·ro·sion (ē rō′zhən, i-) ***n.*** an eroding or being eroded —**e·ro′sive** (-siv) ***adj.***

e·rot·ic (ē rät′ik, i-) ***adj.*** ⟦< Gr *erōs*, love⟧ of or arousing sexual feelings or desires; amatory —**e·rot′i·cal·ly** ***adv.***

e·rot′i·ca (-i kə) ***pl.n.*** [*often with sing. v.*] erotic books, pictures, etc.

err (ʉr, er) ***vi.*** ⟦< L *errare*, wander⟧ **1** to be wrong or mistaken **2** to deviate from the established moral code

er·rand (er′ənd) ***n.*** ⟦OE *ærende*, mission⟧ **1** a trip to do a thing, often esp. for someone else **2** the thing to be done

er·rant (er′ənt) ***adj.*** ⟦see ERR⟧ **1** roving or wandering, esp. in search of adventure *[a medieval knight-errant]* **2** erring **3** shifting about *[an errant wind]*

er·rat·ic (i rat′ik) ***adj.*** ⟦< L *errare*, wander⟧ **1** irregular; random **2** eccentric; queer —**er·rat′i·cal·ly** ***adv.***

er·ra·tum (e rät′əm, -rāt′-) ***n.***, *pl.* **-ta** (-ə) ⟦see ERR⟧ an error in a work already printed

er·ro·ne·ous (e rō′nē əs) ***adj.*** containing error; mistaken; wrong —**er·ro′ne·ous·ly** ***adv.***

er·ror (er′ər) ***n.*** ⟦see ERR⟧ **1** the state of believing what is untrue **2** a wrong belief **3** something incorrectly done; mistake **4** a transgression **5** *Baseball* any misplay in fielding

er·satz (er′zäts′, er zäts′) ***n.***, ***adj.*** ⟦Ger⟧ substitute or synthetic, and usually inferior

Erse (ʉrs) ***adj.***, ***n.*** ⟦ME *Erish*, var. of *Irisc*, Irish⟧ (of) GAELIC and, sometimes, IRISH (*n.* 1)

erst·while (ʉrst′hwīl′) ***adv.*** [Archaic] formerly —***adj.*** former

e·ruct (ē rukt′) ***vt.***, ***vi.*** ⟦< L *e-*, out + *ructare*, to belch⟧ to belch —**e′ruc·ta′tion** ***n.***

er·u·dite (er′yōō dīt′, -ōō-) ***adj.*** ⟦< L *e-*, out + *rudis*, rude⟧ learned; scholarly —**er′u·dite′ly** ***adv.***

er·u·di·tion (er′yōō dish′ən) ***n.*** learning acquired by reading and study

e·rupt (ē rupt′, i-) ***vi.*** ⟦< L *e-*, out + *rumpere*, to break⟧ **1** to burst forth or out *[lava erupting]* **2** to throw forth lava, water, etc. **3** to break out in a rash —***vt.*** to cause to burst forth

e·rup·tion (ē rup′shən, i-) ***n.*** **1** a bursting forth or out **2** *a*) a breaking out in a rash *b*) a rash

-er·y (ər ē, er′ē) ⟦< LL *-aria*⟧ *suffix* **1** a place to *[tannery]* **2** a place for *[nunnery]* **3** the practice or act of *[midwifery]* **4** the product of *[pottery]* **5** a collection of *[greenery]* **6** the condition of *[drudgery]*

er·y·sip·e·las (er′i sip′ə ləs) ***n.*** ⟦ult. < Gr *erythros*, red + *-pelas*, skin⟧ a bacterial infection of the skin or mucous membranes

e·ryth·ro·cyte (e rith′rō sīt′) ***n.*** ⟦< Gr *erythros*, red + *kytos*, a hollow⟧ a mature red blood cell that contains hemoglobin, which carries oxygen to the body tissues

-es (iz, əz, z) ⟦< OE⟧ *suffix* **1** forming plurals *[glasses]* **2** forming the 3d person sing., pres. indic., of verbs *[he kisses]*

E·sau (ē′sô′) ***n.*** *Bible* Isaac's son who sold his birthright to his brother, Jacob

es·ca·late (es′kə lāt′) ***vi.*** **-lat′ed, -lat′ing** **1** to rise as on an escalator **2** to expand step by step **3** to increase rapidly —**es′ca·la′tion** ***n.***

es′ca·la′tor (-ər) ***n.*** ⟦ult. < L *scala*, ladder⟧ a moving stairway on an endless belt

es·ca·pade (es′kə pād′) ***n.*** ⟦Fr: see fol.⟧ a reckless adventure or prank

es·cape (e skāp′, i-) ***vi.*** **-caped′, -cap′ing** ⟦< L *ex-*, out of + LL *cappa*, cloak⟧ **1** to get free **2** to avoid an illness, accident, etc. **3** to leak away —***vt.*** **1** to get away from **2** to avoid *[to escape death]* **3** to come from involuntarily *[a scream escaped her lips]* **4** to be missed or forgotten by —***n.*** **1** an escaping **2** a means of escape **3** a leakage **4** a temporary mental release from reality —***adj.*** providing an escape

es·cap·ee (e skāp′ē′, es′kā pē′) ***n.*** one who has escaped, as from prison

es·cape′ment ***n.*** a notched wheel with a detaining catch that controls the action of a mechanical clock or watch

escape velocity the minimum speed required for a particle, space vehicle, etc. to escape permanently from the gravitational field of a planet, star, etc.

es·cap′ism′ ***n.*** a tendency to escape from reality, responsibilities, etc. through the imagination —**es·cap′ist** ***adj.***, ***n.***

es·car·got (es′kär gō′) ***n.*** ⟦Fr⟧ an edible snail

es·ca·role (es′kə rōl′) ***n.*** ⟦Fr⟧ ENDIVE

es·carp·ment (e skärp′mənt) ***n.*** ⟦< Fr⟧ a steep slope or cliff

-es·cence (es′əns) ⟦see fol.⟧ *suffix* the process of becoming *[obsolescence]*

-es·cent (es′ənt) ⟦L *-escens*⟧ *suffix* **1** starting to be, being, or becoming *[obsolescent]* **2** giving off light (as specified) *[phosphorescent]*

es·chew (es chōō′) ***vt.*** ⟦< OHG *sciuhan*, to fear⟧ to shun; avoid —**es·chew′al** ***n.***

es·cort (es′kôrt′; *for v.* i skôrt′) ***n.*** ⟦< L *ex-*, out + *corrigere*, set right⟧ **1** one or more persons, cars, etc. accompanying another or others to give protection or show honor **2** a man accompanying a woman —***vt.*** to go with as an escort

es·cri·toire (es′kri twär′) ***n.*** ⟦OFr < L *scribere*, write⟧ a writing desk

es·crow (es′krō′) ***n.*** ⟦see SCROLL⟧ used chiefly in **in escrow**, put in the care of a third party until certain conditions are fulfilled

es·cutch·eon (e skuch′ən, i-) ***n.*** ⟦< L *scutum*, shield⟧ a shield on which a coat of arms is displayed

-ese (ēz, ēs) ⟦< L *-ensis*⟧ *suffix* **1** of a country or place *[Javanese]* **2** (in) the language of *[Cantonese]* **3** a person born or living in *[Portuguese]*

Es·ki·mo (es′kə mō′) ***n.*** ⟦prob. < Fr < AmInd⟧ **1** *pl.* **-mos′** or **-mo′** a member of a group of North American peoples in Greenland, N Canada, and Alaska **2** any of the languages of the Eskimos —***adj.*** of the Eskimos or their languages, etc.

Eskimo dog any of several large, strong dogs used by the Eskimos to pull sleds

ESL *abbrev.* English as a second language

e·soph·a·gus (i säf′ə gəs) ***n.***, *pl.* **-gi′** (-jī′) ⟦< Gr *oisophagos*⟧ the tube through which food passes from the pharynx to the stomach

THESAURUS

erode ***v.*** decay, corrode, consume; see DISINTEGRATE.

erosion ***n.*** wearing away, decrease, carrying away; see DESTRUCTION 1, 2.

erotic ***a.*** amorous, stimulating, carnal; see SENSUAL 1, 2.

err ***v.*** misjudge, blunder, be mistaken; see FAIL 1.

errand ***n.*** mission, task, commission; see DUTY 2.

erratic ***a.*** **1** [Wandering] nomadic, rambling, roving; see WANDERING 1. **2** [Strange] eccentric, queer, irregular; see UNUSUAL 2. **3** [Variable] inconsistent, unpredictable, variable; see IRREGULAR 1.

erring ***a.*** mistaken, faulty, blundering; see WRONG 1.

erroneous ***a.*** untrue, inaccurate, incorrect; see FALSE 2.

error ***n.*** blunder, mistake, fault, oversight, inaccuracy, omission, deviation, faux pas, solecism, typo*, fall, slip, wrong, lapse, miss, failure, slight, misunderstanding, misstatement, misstep, flaw, boner*, bad job, blooper*, muff, boo-boo*, botch. —**in error** mistakenly, inaccurately, by mistake; see BADLY 1, WRONG 2, WRONGLY.

ersatz ***a.*** artificial, synthetic, imitation; see FALSE 3.

erupt ***v.*** go off, eject, emit; see EXPLODE.

eruption ***n.*** burst, outburst, flow; see EXPLOSION.

escalate ***v.*** heighten, intensify, make worse; see INCREASE.

escalation ***n.*** intensification, growth, acceleration; see INCREASE, RISE 2.

escapade ***n.*** caper, adventure, prank; see JOKE.

escape ***n.*** flight, retreat, disappearance, evasion, avoidance, leave, departure, withdrawal, liberation, deliverance, desertion, abdication, break, rescue, freedom, release.—*Ant.* IMPRISONMENT, retention, bondage.

escape ***v.*** flee, fly, leave, depart, elude, avoid, evade, shun, run off, run away, make off, disappear, vanish, steal off, steal away, flow out, get away, break out, break away, wriggle out, desert, slip away, run out, go scot-free, take flight, elope, duck out*, get clear of, break loose, cut and run, worm out of, clear out*, bail out, crawl out of, save one's neck, scram*, make a break*.—*Ant.* RETURN, come back, remain.

escaped ***a.*** out, at liberty, liberated; see FREE 2.

escort ***n.*** guide, attendant, guard; see COMPANION.

escort ***v.*** go with, attend, take out*; see ACCOMPANY, DATE 2.

esophagus ***n.*** gullet, food tube, neck; see THROAT.

es·o·ter·ic (es′ə ter′ik) ***adj.*** ⟦< Gr *esōteros*, inner⟧ intended for or understood by only a chosen few
ESP (ē′es′pē′) ***n.*** extrasensory perception
esp. *abbrev.* especially
es·pa·drille (es′pə dril′) ***n.*** ⟦Fr < Sp *esparto*, coarse grass⟧ a casual shoe with a canvas upper and a sole of twisted rope
es·pal·ier (es pal′yər) ***n.*** ⟦Fr < It *spalla*, shoulder⟧ **1** a lattice on which trees or shrubs are trained to grow flat **2** a plant trained in this way —***vt.*** to provide with an espalier
es·pe·cial (e spesh′əl, i-) ***adj.*** special; particular —**es·pe′cial·ly** ***adv.***
Es·pe·ran·to (es′pə rän′tō, -ran′-) ***n.*** an invented international language based on European word roots
es·pi·o·nage (es′pē ə näzh′) ***n.*** ⟦< Fr < It *spia*, spy⟧ the act or practice of spying
es·pla·nade (es′plə nād′, -näd′) ***n.*** ⟦< Fr < It < L *explanare*, to level⟧ a level, open stretch of ground, esp. one serving as a public walk
es·pous·al (e spou′zəl, i-) ***n.*** an espousing (of some cause, idea, etc.); advocacy
es·pouse (e spouz′, i-) ***vt.*** **-poused′**, **-pous′ing** ⟦see SPOUSE⟧ **1** to marry **2** to advocate (some cause, idea, etc.)
es·pres·so (e spres′ō) ***n.***, *pl.* **-sos** ⟦It⟧ coffee made by forcing steam through finely ground coffee beans
es·prit de corps (e sprē′ də kôr′) ⟦Fr⟧ group spirit; pride, etc. shared by those in the same group
es·py (e spī′, i-) ***vt.*** **-pied′**, **-py′ing** ⟦see SPY⟧ to catch sight of; spy
-esque (esk) ⟦Fr < It *-esco*⟧ *suffix* **1** in the manner or style of *[Romanesque]* **2** like *[statuesque]*
es·quire (es′kwīr′) ***n.*** ⟦< L *scutum*, a shield⟧ **1** [Historical] a candidate for knighthood; squire **2** in England, a member of the gentry ranking just below a knight **3** [**E-**] a title of courtesy: in the U.S., now specif. used by lawyers: usually abbrev. **Esq** or **Esqr**
-ess (es, is, əs) ⟦< LL *-issa*⟧ *suffix* female *[lioness]*
es·say (e sā′; *for n. 1 usually, & for n. 2 always*, es′ā) ***vt.*** ⟦< LL *ex-*, out of + *agere*, to do⟧ to try; attempt —***n.*** **1** a trying or testing **2** a short literary composition in which the author analyzes or interprets something in a personal way —**es·say′er** ***n.*** —**es′say·ist** ***n.***
es·sence (es′əns) ***n.*** ⟦< L *esse*, to be⟧ **1** the basic nature (of something) **2** *a)* a concentrated substance that keeps the flavor, etc. of that from which it is extracted *b)* perfume
Es·sene (es′ēn′, e sēn′) ***n.*** a member of an ancient Jewish ascetic sect that existed to the middle of the 1st c. A.D.
es·sen·tial (ə sen′shəl, i-) ***adj.*** **1** of or constituting the essence of something; basic **2** absolutely necessary; indispensable —***n.*** something necessary or fundamental —**es·sen′tial·ly** ***adv.***
est *abbrev.* **1** established: also **estab** **2** estimate **3** estimated
EST *abbrev.* Eastern Standard Time
-est (est, ist, əst) ⟦OE⟧ *suffix* forming the superlative degree *[greatest]*
es·tab·lish (ə stab′lish, i-) ***vt.*** ⟦< L *stabilis*, stable⟧ **1** to order, ordain, or enact (a law, etc.) permanently **2** to set up (a nation, business, etc.) **3** to cause to be; bring about **4** to set up in a business, etc. **5** to cause to be accepted **6** to prove; demonstrate
es·tab′lish·ment ***n.*** **1** an establishing or being established **2** a thing established, as a business —**the Establishment** an inner circle thought of as holding decisive power in a nation, institution, etc.
es·tate (ə stāt′, i-) ***n.*** ⟦< OFr *estat*⟧ **1** a condition or stage of life **2** property; possessions **3** a large, individually owned piece of land containing a residence
es·teem (ə stēm′, i-) ***vt.*** ⟦< L *aestimare*, to value⟧ **1** to value highly; respect **2** to consider —***n.*** favorable opinion
es·ter (es′tər) ***n.*** ⟦Ger < *essig*, vinegar + *äther*, ether⟧ an organic compound formed by the reaction of an acid and an alcohol
Es·ther (es′tər) ***n.*** *Bible* the Jewish wife of a Persian king: she saved her people from slaughter
es·thete (es′thēt′) ***n.*** AESTHETE —**es·thet′ics** (-thet′iks) ***pl.n.***
es·ti·ma·ble (es′tə mə bəl) ***adj.*** worthy of esteem
es·ti·mate (es′tə māt′; *for n.*, -mit) ***vt.*** **-mat′ed**, **-mat′ing** ⟦see ESTEEM⟧ **1** to form an opinion about **2** to calculate approximately (size, cost, etc.) —***n.*** **1** a general calculation; esp., an approximate computation of probable cost **2** an opinion or judgment —**es′ti·ma′tor** ***n.***
es′ti·ma′tion ***n.*** **1** an estimate or judgment **2** esteem; regard
Es·to·ni·a (e stō′nē ə, -stōn′yə) country in N Europe: formerly a republic of the U.S.S.R.: 17,413 sq. mi.; pop. 1,566,000 —**Es·to′ni·an** ***adj.***, ***n.***
es·trange (e strānj′, i-) ***vt.*** **-tranged′**, **-trang′ing** ⟦< L *extraneus*, strange⟧ to turn (a person) from an affectionate attitude to an indifferent or unfriendly one —**es·trange′ment** ***n.***
es·tro·gen (es′trə jən) ***n.*** ⟦< Gr *oistros*, frenzy + -GEN⟧ any of several female sex hormones or synthetic compounds
es·trous cycle (es′trəs) the regular female reproductive cycle of most placental mammals
es·tu·ar·y (es′tyoo er′ē, -choo-) ***n.***, *pl.* **-ies** ⟦< L *aestus*, the

THESAURUS

especially ***a.*** **1** [To an unusual degree] particularly, unusually, abnormally, extraordinarily, uncommonly, peculiarly, unexpectedly, preeminently, eminently, supremely, remarkably, strangely, curiously, notably, uniquely, singularly, to a marked degree, above all. **2** [For one more than for others] chiefly, mainly, primarily; see PRINCIPALLY.
espionage ***n.*** undercover work, reconnaissance, spying; see INFORMATION 1.
espouse ***v.*** advocate, adopt, uphold; see SUPPORT 2.
essay ***n.*** dissertation, treatise, article; see WRITING 2.
essence ***n.*** **1** [Basic material] pith, core, kernel, spirit, gist, root, nature, basis, being, essential quality, reality, constitution, substance, nucleus, vital part, base, quintessence, primary element, germ, heart, marrow, backbone, soul, bottom, life, grain, structure, principle, character, fundamentals. **2** [Distinctive quality] principle, nature, essential quality; see CHARACTERISTIC. —**in essence** ultimately, fundamentally, basically; see ESSENTIALLY.
essential ***a.*** **1** [Necessary] imperative, required, indispensable; see NECESSARY. **2** [Rooted in the basis or essence] basic, primary, quintessential; see FUNDAMENTAL.
essentially ***a.*** basically, fundamentally, radically, at bottom, at heart, centrally, originally, intimately, chiefly, naturally, inherently, permanently, necessarily, primarily, significantly, importantly, at the heart of, in effect, in essence, materially, in the main, at first, characteristically, intrinsically, substantially, typically, approximately, precisely, exactly, actually, truly, really; see also PRINCIPALLY.
establish ***v.*** **1** [To set up in a formal manner] institute, found, authorize; see ORGANIZE 2. **2** [To work or settle in a permanent place] build up, set up, install, build, erect, plant, root, place, settle, practice, live, stay, start.—*Ant.* LEAVE, break up, depart. **3** [To prove] verify, authenticate, confirm; see PROVE.
established ***a.*** **1** [Set up to endure] endowed, founded, organized, instituted, set up, originated, chartered, incorporated, settled, begun, initiated, realized, codified, produced, completed, finished; see also FINISHED 1, CERTAIN.—*Ant.* TEMPORARY, insolvent, unsound. **2** [Conclusively proved] approved, verified, guaranteed, endorsed, demonstrated, determined, confirmed, substantiated, assured, concluded, authenticated, ascertained, achieved, upheld, certain, validated, identified, proved, undeniable.—*Ant.* FALSE, invalidated, untrue.
establishment ***n.*** **1** [A business, organization, or the like] company, corporation, enterprise; see BUSINESS 4. **2** [The act of proving] verification, substantiation, demonstration; see PROOF 1.
estate ***n.*** property, bequest, inheritance, fortune, endowment, wealth, legacy, heritage, belongings, effects, earthly possessions, personal property, private property.
esteem ***n.*** regard, respect, appreciation; see ADMIRATION.
esteem ***v.*** prize, respect, appreciate; see ADMIRE.
estimate ***n.*** evaluation, assessment, valuation, guess, appraisal, estimation, calculation, gauging, rating, survey, measure, reckoning; see also JUDGMENT 2.
estimate ***v.*** rate, value, measure, calculate, appraise, assess, account, compute, evaluate, count, number, reckon, guess, guesstimate*, expect, judge, figure, plan, outline, run over, rank, furnish an estimate, set a value on, set a figure, appraise, assay, consider, predict, suppose, suspect, reason, think through, surmise, determine, decide, budget.
estimated ***a.*** supposed, approximated, guessed at; see LIKELY 1.
estimation ***n.*** opinion, appraisal, valuation; see JUDGMENT 2.

tide]] the wide mouth of a river into which the tide flows from the sea

ET *abbrev.* Eastern Time

-et (et, it, ət) [[< LL *-itus*]] *suffix* little *[islet]*

e·ta (āt′ə, ēt′ə) ***n.*** the seventh letter of the Greek alphabet (Η, η)

ETA *abbrev.* estimated time of arrival

é·ta·gère (ā′tä zher′) ***n.*** [[Fr]] a stand with open shelves, for displaying art objects, ornaments, etc.

et al. *abbrev.* [[L *et alii*]] and others

et cet·er·a (et set′ər ə, se′trə) [[L]] and others; and the like: abbrev. **etc.**

etch (ech) ***vt.*** [[< MHG *ezzen*, eat]] to make (a drawing, design, etc.) on metal, glass, etc. by the action of an acid **—etch′er** ***n.***

etch′ing ***n.*** **1** the art of an etcher **2** a print made from an etched plate

e·ter·nal (ē tur′nəl, i-) ***adj.*** [[< L *aeturnus*]] **1** without beginning or end; everlasting **2** always the same; unchanging **3** seeming never to stop **—e·ter′nal·ly** ***adv.*** **—e·ter′nal·ness** ***n.***

e·ter·ni·ty (ē tur′nə tē, i-) ***n.***, *pl.* **-ties** **1** the state or fact of being eternal **2** infinite or endless time **3** a long period of time that seems endless **4** the endless time after death

eth·ane (eth′ān′) ***n.*** [[< fol.]] an odorless, colorless, gaseous hydrocarbon, found in natural gas and used as a fuel

e·ther (ē′thər) ***n.*** [[< Gr *aithein*, to burn]] **1** an imaginary substance once thought to pervade space **2** the upper regions of space **3** a volatile, colorless, highly flammable liquid used as an anesthetic and a solvent

e·the·re·al (ē thir′ē əl, i-) ***adj.*** **1** very light; airy; delicate **2** not earthly; heavenly; celestial **—e·the′re·al·ly** ***adv.***

eth·ic (eth′ik) ***n.*** [[see fol.]] a system of moral standards

eth·i·cal (eth′i kəl) ***adj.*** [[< Gr *ēthos*, character]] **1** having to do with ethics; of or conforming to moral standards **2** conforming to professional standards of conduct **—eth′i·cal·ly** ***adv.***

eth·ics (eth′iks) ***n.*** **1** the study of standards of conduct and moral judgment **2** [*with sing. or pl. verb*] the system of morals of a particular person, religion, group, etc.

E·thi·o·pi·a (ē′thē ō′pē ə) country in E Africa: 423,940 sq. mi.; pop. 42,019,000 **—E′thi·o′pi·an** ***adj.***, ***n.***

eth·nic (eth′nik) ***adj.*** [[< Gr *ethnos*, nation]] designating or of a group of people having common customs, characteristics, language, etc. **—*n.*** a member of an ethnic group, esp. a minority or nationality group **—eth′ni·cal·ly** ***adv.***

eth·nic·i·ty (eth nis′ə tē) ***n.*** ethnic classification or affiliation

eth·nol·o·gy (eth näl′ə jē) ***n.*** [[< Gr *ethnos*, nation + -LOGY]] the branch of anthropology that studies comparatively the cultures of contemporary, or recent, societies or language groups **—eth′no·log′i·cal** (-nə läj′i kəl) ***adj.*** **—eth·nol′o·gist** ***n.***

e·thos (ē′thäs′) ***n.*** [[Gr *ēthos*, character]] the characteristic attitudes, habits, etc. of an individual or group

eth·yl (eth′əl) ***n.*** [[< ETHER]] the hydrocarbon radical that forms the base of ethyl alcohol, ether, etc.

ethyl alcohol ALCOHOL (sense 1)

eth·yl·ene (eth′əl ēn′) ***n.*** [[ETHYL + -ENE]] a colorless, flammable, gaseous hydrocarbon used to synthesize organic chemicals, esp. polyethylene

ethylene gly·col (glī′kôl′) a colorless, viscous liquid used as an antifreeze, solvent, etc.

e·ti·ol·o·gy (ēt′ē äl′ə jē) ***n.***, *pl.* **-gies** [[< Gr *aitia*, cause + *logia*, description]] **1** the cause assigned, as for a disease **2** the science of causes or origins **—e′ti·o·log′ic** (-ə läj′ik) ***adj.***

et·i·quette (et′i kit) ***n.*** [[Fr *étiquette*, lit., ticket]] the forms, manners, etc. conventionally acceptable or required in society, a profession, etc.

Et·na (et′nə), **Mount** volcanic mountain in E Sicily

E·to·bi·coke (i tō′bi kō′) city within metropolitan Toronto, Canada: pop. 329,000

E·trus·can (i trus′kən) ***adj.*** of an ancient country (*Etruria*) in what is now central Italy

et seq. *abbrev.* [[L *et sequens*]] and the following

-ette (et) [[Fr: see -ET]] *suffix* **1** little *[statuette]* **2** female *[majorette]*

é·tude (ā′to͞od′) ***n.*** [[Fr, a study]] a musical composition for a solo instrument, designed to give practice in some point of technique

et·y·mol·o·gy (et′ə mäl′ə jē) ***n.***, *pl.* **-gies** [[< Gr *etymos*, true + *logos*, word]] **1** the origin and development of a word **2** the linguistic study of word origins **—et′y·mo·log′i·cal** (-mə läj′i kəl) ***adj.*** **—et′y·mol′o·gist** ***n.***

EU *abbrev.* European Union

eu- [[Fr < Gr]] *prefix* good, well *[eulogy, euphony]*

eu·ca·lyp·tus (yo͞o′kə lip′təs) ***n.***, *pl.* **-tus·es** or **-ti′** (-tī′) [[< Gr *eu-*, well + *kalyptos*, covered]] a tall, aromatic, chiefly Australian evergreen tree of the myrtle family

Eu·cha·rist (yo͞o′kə rist) ***n.*** [[< Gr *eucharistia*, gratitude]] **1** HOLY COMMUNION **2** the consecrated bread and wine used in this **—Eu′cha·ris′tic** ***adj.***

eu·chre (yo͞o′kər) ***n.*** [[< ?]] a card game played with thirty-two cards

Eu·clid (yo͞o′klid) flourished 4th c. B.C.; Gr. mathematician: author of a basic work in geometry **—Eu·clid′e·an** (-ē ən) or **Eu·clid′i·an** ***adj.***

Eu·gene (yo͞o jēn′, yo͞o′jēn) city in W Oregon: pop. 113,000

eu·gen·ics (yo͞o jen′iks) ***n.*** [[see EU- & GENESIS]] the movement devoted to improving the human species by controlling heredity **—eu·gen′ic** ***adj.*** **—eu·gen′i·cal·ly** ***adv.*** **—eu·gen′i·cist** (-ə sist) ***n.***

eu·lo·gize (yo͞o′lə jīz′) ***vt.*** **-gized′**, **-giz′ing** [[see fol.]] to praise highly **—eu′lo·gist** or **eu′lo·giz′er** ***n.***

eu′lo·gy (-jē) ***n.***, *pl.* **-gies** [[< Gr *eulegein*, speak well of]] **1** speech or writing praising a person or thing; esp., a funeral oration **2** high praise **—eu′lo·gis′tic** (-jis′tik) ***adj.***

eu·nuch (yo͞o′nək) ***n.*** [[< Gr *eunouchos*, guardian of the bed]] a castrated man

eu·phe·mism (yo͞o′fə miz′əm) ***n.*** [[< Gr *eu-*, good + *phēmē*, speech]] **1** the use of a less direct word or phrase for one considered offensive **2** a word or phrase so substituted **—eu′phe·mis′tic** ***adj.*** **—eu′phe·mis′ti·cal·ly** ***adv.***

eu·pho·ni·ous (yo͞o fō′nē əs) ***adj.*** having a pleasant sound; harmonious **—eu·pho′ni·ous·ly** ***adv.***

eu·pho·ny (yo͞o′fə nē) ***n.***, *pl.* **-nies** [[< Gr *eu-*, good + *phōnē*, voice]] a pleasant combination of agreeable sounds, as in speech

eu·pho·ri·a (yo͞o fôr′ē ə) ***n.*** [[< Gr *eu-*, well + *pherein*, to bear]] a feeling of well-being **—eu·phor′ic** ***adj.***

Eu·phra·tes (yo͞o frāt′ēz) river flowing from EC Turkey through Syria & Iraq into the Persian Gulf: cf. TIGRIS

Eur·a·sia (yoor ā′zhə) land mass made up of Europe & Asia

Eur·a′sian (-zhən) ***adj.*** **1** of Eurasia **2** of mixed European and Asian descent **—*n.*** a person of Eurasian descent

eu·re·ka (yoo rē′kə) ***interj.*** [[< Gr *heurēka*, I have found]] used to express triumphant achievement

Eu·rip·i·des (yoo rip′ə dēz′) 480-406 B.C.; Gr. writer of tragedies

eu·ro (yoor′ō) ***n.*** the basic monetary unit of the European Union: introduced for business use beginning in 1999

Eu·rope (yoor′əp) continent between Asia & the Atlantic: *c.* 3,800,000 sq. mi.; pop. *c.* 710,000,000 **—Eu·ro·pe·an** (yoor′ə pē′ən) ***adj.***, ***n.***

European Community an organization of European

THESAURUS

et cetera (etc.) ***a.*** and so forth, and so on, and others; see AND.

etching ***n.*** print, cut, work of art; see ENGRAVING.

eternal ***a.*** endless, interminable, continual, unbroken, continuous, continued, unceasing, ceaseless, constant, unending, enduring, incessant, relentless, undying, enduring, persistent, always, uninterrupted, everlasting, perpetual, indestructible, unconquerable, never-ending, indefinite, permanent, ageless, boundless, timeless, immortal, forever, indeterminable, immeasurable, having no limit, imperishable, to one's dying day, for ever and ever.—*Ant.* TEMPORARY, finite, ending.

eternally ***a.*** endlessly, continually, perpetually; see REGULARLY.

eternity ***n.*** endlessness, forever, infinite, duration, timelessness, world without end, the future, infinity, all eternity, other world, afterlife, life after death, for ever and ever.—*Ant.* INSTANT, moment, second.

ethical ***a.*** humane, moral, respectable; see DECENT 2, HONEST, NOBLE 1, 2.

ethics ***n.*** conduct, morality, mores, decency, integrity, moral conduct, social values, moral code, principles, right and wrong, natural law, honesty, goodness, honor, social laws, human nature, the Golden Rule.

etiquette ***n.*** conduct, manners, social graces; see BEHAVIOR.

Eucharist ***n.*** sacrament, Host, Communion; see SACRAMENT.

eulogize ***v.*** laud, extol, applaud; see PRAISE 1.

eulogy ***n.*** tribute, glorification, commendation; see PRAISE 2.

euphoria ***n.*** joy, delight, glee; see HAPPINESS.

European ***a.*** Continental, old-coun-

countries established in 1967 to bring about the political and economic unification of W Europe
European plan a system of hotel operation in which guests are charged for rooms and pay for meals separately
European Union a union of European nations created in 1993 to bring about the gradual unification of Europe
eu·ryth·mics (yoo rith'miks) ***n.*** ⟦< Gr *eu-*, good + *rhythmos*, rhythm⟧ the art of performing bodily movements in rhythm, usually to music
eu·sta·chian tube (yoo stā'shən) ⟦after B. *Eustachio*, 16th-c. It anatomist⟧ [*also* **E- t-**] a slender tube between the middle ear and the pharynx
eu·tha·na·si·a (yoo'thə nā'zhə) ***n.*** ⟦< Gr *eu-*, good + *thanatos*, death⟧ the act of causing death painlessly, so as to end suffering
eu·tha·nize (yoo'thə nīz') ***vt.*** **-nized', -niz'ing** to put to death by euthanasia
e·vac·u·ate (ē vak'yoo āt') ***vt.*** **-at'ed, -at'ing** ⟦< L *e-*, out + *vacuus*, empty⟧ **1** to make empty **2** to discharge (bodily waste, esp. feces) **3** to withdraw from —***vi.*** to withdraw —**e·vac'u·a'tion** ***n.*** —**e·vac'u·ee'** (-ē') ***n.***
e·vade (ē vād', i-) ***vi., vt.*** **e·vad'ed, e·vad'ing** ⟦< L *e-*, out, from + *vadere*, go⟧ **1** to avoid or escape (from) by deceit or cleverness **2** to avoid doing or answering directly —**e·vad'er** ***n.***
e·val·u·ate (ē val'yoo āt', i-) ***vt.*** **-at'ed, -at'ing** ⟦ult. < L *valere*, be worth⟧ **1** to find the value or amount of **2** to judge the worth of —**e·val'u·a'tion** ***n.***
ev·a·nes·cent (ev'ə nes'ənt) ***adj.*** ⟦< L *e-*, out + *vanescere*, vanish⟧ tending to fade from sight; fleeting; ephemeral —**ev'a·nes'cence** ***n.***
e·van·gel·i·cal (ē'van jel'i kəl, ev'ən-) ***adj.*** ⟦< Gr *euangelos*, bringing good news⟧ **1** of or according to the Gospels or the New Testament **2** of those Protestant churches that emphasize salvation by faith in Jesus
e·van·ge·list (ē van'jə list) ***n.*** **1** [**E-**] any of the four writers of the Gospels: Matthew, Mark, Luke, or John **2** a revivalist or a preacher who holds large public services in various cities, now often televised —**e·van'ge·lism'** ***n.***
e·van'ge·lize' (-līz') ***vt.*** **-lized', -liz'ing** to convert to Christianity —***vi.*** to preach the gospel
e·vap·o·rate (ē vap'ə rāt') ***vt.*** **-rat'ed, -rat'ing** ⟦< L *e-*, out, from + *vaporare*, emit vapor⟧ **1** to change (a liquid or solid) into vapor **2** to remove moisture from (milk, etc.), as by heating, so as to get a concentrated product —***vi.*** **1** to become vapor **2** to give off vapor **3** to disappear like vapor; vanish —**e·vap'o·ra'tion** ***n.*** —**e·vap'o·ra'tor** ***n.***
e·va·sion (ē vā'zhən, i-) ***n.*** **1** an evading; specif., an avoiding of a duty, question, etc. by deceit or cleverness **2** a way of doing this; subterfuge
e·va'sive (-siv) ***adj.*** **1** tending or seeking to evade **2** elusive —**e·va'sive·ly** ***adv.*** —**e·va'sive·ness** ***n.***
eve (ēv) ***n.*** ⟦< OE *æfen*, evening⟧ **1** [Old Poet.] evening **2** [*often* **E-**] the evening or day before a holiday **3** the period just prior to some event
Eve (ēv) ***n.*** *Bible* the first woman, Adam's wife
e·ven (ē'vən) ***adj.*** ⟦OE *efne*⟧ **1** flat; level; smooth **2** not varying; constant [*an even tempo*] **3** calm; tranquil [*an even temper*] **4** in the same plane or line [*even with the rim*] **5** owing and being owed nothing **6** equal in number, quantity, etc. **7** exactly divisible by two **8** exact [*an even mile*] **9** revenged for a wrong, etc. —***adv.*** **1** however improbable; indeed **2** exactly; just [*it happened even as I expected*] **3** still; yet [*he's even better*] —***vt., vi.*** to make or become even —**even if** though —**e'ven·ly** ***adv.*** —**e'ven·ness** ***n.***
e'ven·hand'ed ***adj.*** impartial; fair
eve·ning (ēv'niŋ) ***n.*** ⟦< OE *æfnung*⟧ **1** the last part of the day and early part of night **2** [Dial.] afternoon
even money equal stakes in betting, with no odds
e·vent (ē vent') ***n.*** ⟦< L *e-*, out + *venire*, come⟧ **1** an occurrence, esp. when important **2** a particular contest in a program of sports **3** any organized activity, celebration, etc. —**in any event** no matter what happens; anyway —**in the event of** in case of —**in the event that** if it should happen that
e'ven-tem'pered ***adj.*** not quickly angered; calm
e·vent'ful ***adj.*** **1** full of outstanding events **2** having an important outcome —**e·vent'ful·ly** ***adv.***
e·ven·tide (ē'vən tīd') ***n.*** [Archaic] evening
e·ven·tu·al (ē ven'choo əl) ***adj.*** ultimate; final —**e·ven'tu·al·ly** ***adv.***
e·ven'tu·al'i·ty (-al'ə tē) ***n.***, *pl.* **-ties** a possible event or outcome
e·ven'tu·ate' (-āt') ***vi.*** **-at'ed, -at'ing** to happen in the end; result
ev·er (ev'ər) ***adv.*** ⟦< OE *æfre*⟧ **1** always [*ever the same*] **2** at any time [*do you ever see her?*] **3** at all; by any chance [*how can I ever repay you?*] —**ever so** [Inf.] very
Ev·er·est (ev'ər ist, ev'rist), **Mount** peak of the Himalayas: highest known mountain in the world: 29,035 ft.
ev'er·glade' ***n.*** marshy land
ev'er·green' ***adj.*** having green leaves all year long, as most conifers —***n.*** an evergreen plant or tree
ev'er·last'ing ***adj.*** lasting forever; eternal —***n.*** eternity
ev'er·more' ***adv.*** [Archaic] forever; constantly
ev·er·y (ev'rē) ***adj.*** ⟦OE *æfre ælc*, lit., ever each⟧ **1** each, individually and separately **2** the greatest possible [to

THESAURUS

try, old-world, Eurasian, Indo-European, West European, East European.
evacuate ***v.*** **1** [To empty] void, exhaust, deplete; see REMOVE 1. **2** [To abandon] vacate, desert, leave; see ABANDON 1.
evacuation ***n.*** **1** [Removal] draining, depletion, exhaustion; see REMOVAL. **2** [Withdrawal] abandonment, removal, retreat; see DEPARTURE.
evade ***v.*** lie, prevaricate, dodge, shun, put off, avoid, elude, trick, baffle, quibble, shift, mystify, cloak, cover, conceal, deceive, screen, veil, hide, drop the subject, pretend, confuse, equivocate, hedge, dodge the issue, beat around the bush, give someone the runaround*, throw off the scent*, lead on a merry chase, pass up, put off, get around, lie out of, take the Fifth*; see also AVOID.—*Ant.* EXPLAIN, make clear, elucidate.
evaluate ***v.*** appraise, judge, assess; see DECIDE, ESTIMATE.
evangelical ***a.*** pious, fervent, spiritual; see RELIGIOUS 2.
evangelist ***n.*** preacher, missionary, revivalist; see MINISTER 1.
evangelize ***v.*** proselytize, instruct, convert; see PREACH.
evaporate ***v.*** diffuse, vanish, fade, dissolve, dissipate, steam, steam away, boil away, burn off, fume, distill, turn to steam, rise in a mist.
evaporation ***n.*** drying, dehydration, vanishing, steaming away, boiling away, vaporization, distillation, dissipation, disappearance, vanishing into thin air.
evasion ***n.*** quibble, subterfuge, equivocation; see LIE, TRICK 1.
evasive ***a.*** elusive, fugitive, shifty; see SLY.
eve ***n.*** evening before, night preceding, evening; see NIGHT 1.
even ***a.*** **1** [Lying in a smooth plane] smooth, level, surfaced; see FLAT 1. **2** [Similar] uniform, unbroken, homogeneous; see ALIKE, REGULAR 3. **3** [Equal] commensurate, equivalent, tied; see EQUAL. **4** [In addition] also, too, as well; see AND. —**break even** make nothing, tie, neither win nor lose; see BALANCE 2.
evening ***n.*** twilight, dusk, gloaming; see NIGHT 1.
evenly ***a.*** **1** [On an even plane] smoothly, regularly, without bumps, without lumps, uniformly, placidly, unvaryingly, steadily, constantly, fluently, on an even keel, without variation, neither up nor down. **2** [Equally proportioned or distributed] exactly, justly, fairly, precisely, equally, impartially, identically, equitably, symmetrically, proportionately, synonymously, analogously, correspondingly, tied, alike, fifty-fifty*, squarely.—*Ant.* WRONGLY, unfairly.
evenness ***n.*** smoothness, similarity, likeness; see REGULARITY.
event ***n.*** occurrence, happening, episode, incident, circumstance, affair, phenomenon, development, function, transaction, experience, appearance, turn, tide, shift, phase, accident, chance, pass, situation, story, case, matter, occasion, catastrophe, mishap, mistake, experience, parade, triumph, coincidence, miracle, adventure, holiday, wonder, marvel, celebration, crisis, predicament, misfortune, situation, calamity, emergency, something to write home about*; see also DISASTER, HOLIDAY, WONDER 2. —**in any event** anyway, no matter what happens, however; see ANYHOW. —**in the event of** (or **that**) in case of, if it should happen that, if there should happen to be; see IF.
eventful ***a.*** momentous, memorable, signal; see IMPORTANT 1.
eventual ***a.*** inevitable, ultimate, consequent; see LAST 1.
eventually ***a.*** in the end, at last, ultimately; see FINALLY 2.
ever ***a.*** eternally, always, at all times; see REGULARLY. —**for ever and a day** always, for ever and ever, perpetually; see FOREVER.
evergreen ***n.*** coniferous tree, ornamental shrub, fir; see PINE, TREE.
everlasting ***a.*** permanent, unending, perpetual; see ETERNAL.
every ***a.*** each one, all, without exception; see EACH 1. —**every now and then** sometimes, occasionally, once in a while; see FREQUENTLY: also **every so often***.

make *every* effort*]* **3** each interval *[*take a pill *every* three hours*]* —**every now and then** occasionally: also [Inf.] **every so often** —**every other** each alternate, as the first, third, fifth, etc. —**every which way** [Inf.] in complete disorder

ev'er·y·bod'y (-bäd'ē, -bud'ē) ***pron.*** every person; everyone

ev'er·y·day' ***adj.*** **1** daily **2** suitable for ordinary days *[everyday* shoes*]* **3** usual; common

ev'er·y·one' ***pron.*** every person

every one every person or thing of those named *[every one* of the boys*]*

ev'er·y·thing' ***pron.*** every thing; all

ev'er·y·where' ***adv.*** in or to every place

e·vict (ē vikt') ***vt.*** ⟦< L *e-*, intens. + *vincere*, conquer⟧ to remove (a tenant) by legal procedure —**e·vic'tion** ***n.***

ev·i·dence (ev'ə dəns) ***n.*** **1** something that makes another thing evident; sign **2** a statement of a witness, an object, etc. bearing on or establishing the point in question in a court of law —***vt.*** **-denced**, **-denc·ing** to make evident —**in evidence** plainly seen

ev·i·dent (ev'ə dənt) ***adj.*** ⟦< L *e-*, from + *videre*, see⟧ easy to see or perceive; clear —**ev'i·dent·ly** ***adv.***

e·vil (ē'vəl) ***adj.*** ⟦OE *yfel*⟧ **1** morally bad or wrong; wicked **2** harmful; injurious **3** unlucky; disastrous —***n.*** **1** wickedness; sin **2** anything that causes harm, pain, etc. —**e'vil·ly** ***adv.***

e'vil·do'er ***n.*** one who does evil —**e'vil·do'ing** ***n.***

e·vince (ē vins') ***vt.*** **e·vinced'**, **e·vinc'ing** ⟦< L *e-*, intens. + *vincere*, conquer⟧ to show plainly; make clear

e·vis·cer·ate (ē vis'ər āt') ***vt.*** **-at'ed**, **-at'ing** ⟦< L *e-*, out + *viscera*, viscera⟧ **1** to remove the entrails from **2** to deprive of an essential part —**e·vis'cer·a'tion** ***n.***

e·voke (ē vōk') ***vt.*** **e·voked'**, **e·vok'ing** ⟦< L *e-*, out, from + *vox*, voice⟧ **1** to call forth **2** to elicit (a reaction, etc.) —**ev·o·ca·tion** (ev'ə kā'shən, ē'vō-) ***n.***

ev·o·lu·tion (ev'ə lo͞o'shən) ***n.*** ⟦see fol.⟧ **1** an unfolding; process of development or change **2** a thing evolved **3** a movement that is part of a series **4** *Biol.* *a)* the development of a species, organism, etc. from its original to its present state *b)* the theory that all species developed from earlier forms —**ev'o·lu'tion·ar'y** ***adj.*** —**ev'o·lu'tion·ist** ***n.***

e·volve (ē välv', -vôlv') ***vt.***, ***vi.*** **e·volved'**, **e·volv'ing** ⟦< L *e-*, out + *volvere*, to roll⟧ **1** to develop gradually **2** to develop by evolution

ewe (yo͞o) ***n.*** ⟦OE *eowu*⟧ a female sheep

ew·er (yo͞o'ər) ***n.*** ⟦< L *aqua*, water⟧ a large, wide-mouthed water pitcher

ex *abbrev.* **1** example **2** exchange

ex- ⟦< OFr or L⟧ *prefix* **1** *a)* from, out *[expel]* *b)* beyond *c)* thoroughly *d)* upward **2** former, previous *[ex-*president*]*

ex·ac·er·bate (eg zas'ər bāt') ***vt.*** **-bat'ed**, **-bat'ing** ⟦< L *ex-*, intens. + *acerbus*, bitter⟧ **1** to aggravate (pain, annoyance, etc.) **2** to exasperate; annoy; irritate —**ex·ac'er·ba'tion** ***n.***

ex·act (eg zakt') ***adj.*** ⟦< L *ex-*, out + *agere*, to do⟧ **1** characterized by or requiring accuracy; methodical; correct **2** without variation; precise —***vt.*** **1** to extort **2** to demand; require —**ex·act'ly** ***adv.*** —**ex·act'ness** ***n.***

ex·act'ing ***adj.*** **1** making severe demands; strict **2** demanding great care, effort, etc.; arduous —**ex·act'ing·ly** ***adv.***

ex·ac·tion (eg zak'shən) ***n.*** **1** an exacting **2** an extortion **3** an exacted fee, tax, etc.

ex·ac'ti·tude' (-tə to͞od') ***n.*** ⟦Fr⟧ the quality of being exact; accuracy

ex·ag·ger·ate (eg zaj'ər āt') ***vt.***, ***vi.*** **-at'ed**, **-at'ing** ⟦< L *ex-*, out + *agger*, a heap⟧ to think or tell of (something) as greater than it is; overstate —**ex·ag'ger·a'tion** ***n.*** —**ex·ag'ger·a'tive** ***adj.*** —**ex·ag'ger·a'tor** ***n.***

ex·alt (eg zôlt') ***vt.*** ⟦< L *ex-*, up + *altus*, high⟧ **1** to raise in status, dignity, etc. **2** to praise; glorify **3** to fill with joy, pride, etc.; elate —**ex·al·ta·tion** (eg'zôl tā'shən) ***n.***

ex·am·i·na·tion (eg zam'ə nā'shən) ***n.*** **1** an examining or being examined **2** a set of questions asked in testing: also **ex·am'**

THESAURUS

everybody ***n.*** each one, every one, all, the public, old and young; men, women, and children; the people, the populace, the voters; the buying public, the voting public; generality, anybody, all sorts, the masses, the man in the street, you and I; see also MAN 1.—*Ant.* NOBODY, no one, not a one.

everyday ***a.*** commonplace, normal, plain; see COMMON 1.

everyone ***pron.*** all, each person, whoever; see EVERYBODY.

everything ***pron.*** all, all things, the universe, the whole complex, the whole, many things, all that, every little thing, the whole kit and caboodle*; lock, stock, and barrel, the whole shebang*, the works*, the lot*.

everywhere ***a.*** everyplace, here and there, at all points, wherever one turns, at each point, without exception, universally, ubiquitously, pervasively, at all times and places; here, there and everywhere; in every direction, on all hands, all over the place, throughout, to the four winds, in all creation, to hell and back*, inside and out, from beginning to end, high and low, all around, the world over.

evict ***v.*** remove, expel, oust; see DISMISS.

eviction ***n.*** ouster, ejection, dispossession; see REMOVAL.

evidence ***n.*** testimony, data, confirmation; see PROOF 1. —**in evidence** evident, visible, manifest; see OBVIOUS 1, 2.

evident ***a.*** apparent, visible, manifest; see OBVIOUS 1.

evidently ***a.*** seemingly, obviously, so far as one can see; see APPARENTLY.

evil ***a.*** immoral, sinful, corrupt; see BAD.

evil ***n.*** **1** [The quality of being evil] sin, wickedness, depravity, crime, sinfulness, corruption, vice, immorality, iniquity, perversity, badness, vileness, baseness, meanness, malevolence, indecency, hatred, viciousness, wrong, debauchery, lewdness, wantonness, grossness, foulness, degradation, obscenity.—*Ant.* VIRTUE, good, goodness. **2** [A harmful or malicious action] ill, harm, mischief, misfortune, scandal, calamity, pollution, contamination, catastrophe, blow, disaster, plague, outrage, foul play, ill wind*, crying shame*, double cross*, raw deal*.

evildoer ***n.*** malefactor, sinner, wrongdoer; see CRIMINAL.

evoke ***v.*** summon forth, call out, invoke; see SUMMON.

evolution ***n.*** growth, unfolding, natural process; see DEVELOPMENT.

evolve ***v.*** result, unfold, emerge; see DEVELOP 3, GROW 2.

exact ***a.*** **1** [Accurate] precise, correct, perfect; see ACCURATE 2, DEFINITE 1. **2** [Clear] sharp, distinct, clear-cut; see DEFINITE 2.

exacting ***a.*** precise, careful, critical; see DIFFICULT 1, 2.

exactly ***a.*** precisely, specifically, correctly; see DETAILED.

exactness ***n.*** precision, nicety, scrupulousness; see ACCURACY.

exaggerate ***v.*** overestimate, overstate, misrepresent, falsify, magnify, expand, amplify, pile up, heighten, intensify, distort, enlarge on, stretch, overdo, misquote, go to extremes, give color to, misjudge, elaborate, romance, embroider, color, make too much of, lie, fabricate, corrupt, paint in glowing colors, carry too far*, lay it on thick*, make a mountain out of a molehill, build up, make much of, make the most of.—*Ant.* UNDERESTIMATE, tell the truth, minimize.

exaggerated ***a.*** colored, magnified, overwrought, extravagant, preposterous, impossible, fabulous, sensational, spectacular, melodramatic, out of proportion, fantastic, high-flown, farfetched, false, distorted, fabricated, strained, artificial, glaring, pronounced, unrealistic, whopping*, too much.—*Ant.* ACCURATE, exact, precise.

exaggeration ***n.*** overestimation, misrepresentation, extravagance, elaboration, coloring, flight of fancy, fantasy, fancy, stretch of the imagination, figure of speech, yarn, making a mountain out of a molehill, tall story*, whopper*.—*Ant.* TRUTH, accuracy, understatement.

exalt ***v.*** commend, glorify, laud; see PRAISE 1.

exaltation ***n.*** rapture, elation, rhapsody; see HAPPINESS.

examination ***n.*** **1** [The act of seeking evidence] search, research, survey, scrutiny, investigation, inquiry into, inspection, observation, checking, exploration, analysis, audit, study, questioning, testing program, inquest, test, trial, cross-examination, the third degree*. **2** [A formal test] experiment, review, questionnaire, battery, quiz, exam, makeup*, midterm*, final, blue book, orals, writtens*; see also TEST. **3** [A medical checkup] checkup, physical examination, physical; see TEST.

ex·am·ine (eg zam′ən) ***vt.*** **-ined, -in·ing** ⟦< L *examinare*, weigh⟧ **1** to look at critically or methodically; investigate; inspect **2** to test by questioning —**ex·am′in·er** ***n.***

ex·am·ple (eg zam′pəl) ***n.*** ⟦< L *eximere*, take out⟧ **1** something selected to show the character of the rest; sample **2** a case that serves as a warning **3** a model; pattern **4** an instance that illustrates a principle

ex·as·per·ate (eg zas′pər āt′) ***vt.*** **-at′ed, -at′ing** ⟦< L *ex-*, out + *asper*, rough⟧ to irritate; anger; vex —**ex·as′per·a′tion** ***n.***

ex·ca·vate (eks′kə vāt′) ***vt.*** **-vat′ed, -vat′ing** ⟦< L *ex-*, out + *cavus*, hollow⟧ **1** to make a hole or cavity in **2** to form (a tunnel, etc.) by hollowing out **3** to unearth **4** to dig out (earth, soil, etc.) —**ex′ca·va′tion** ***n.*** —**ex′ca·va′tor** ***n.***

ex·ceed (ek sēd′) ***vt.*** ⟦< L *ex-*, out + *cedere*, to go⟧ **1** to go or be beyond (a limit, etc.) **2** to surpass

ex·ceed′ing ***adj.*** surpassing; extreme —**ex·ceed′ing·ly** ***adv.***

ex·cel (ek sel′) ***vi.***, ***vt.*** **-celled′, -cel′ling** ⟦< L *ex-*, out of + *-cellere*, to rise⟧ to be better or greater than (another or others)

ex·cel·lence (ek′sə ləns) ***n.*** **1** the fact or state of excelling; superiority **2** a particular virtue

ex′cel·len·cy (-lən sē) ***n.***, *pl.* **-cies** **1** [**E-**] a title of honor for certain dignitaries **2** EXCELLENCE

ex·cel·lent (ek′sə lənt) ***adj.*** ⟦see EXCEL⟧ outstandingly good of its kind; of exceptional merit —**ex′cel·lent·ly** ***adv.***

ex·cel·si·or (eks sel′sē ôr′; *for n.* ek sel′sē ər) ***interj.*** ⟦see EXCEL⟧ always upward! —***n.*** long, thin wood shavings used for packing

ex·cept (ek sept′) ***vt.*** ⟦< L *ex-*, out + *capere*, to take⟧ to leave out or take out; exclude —***prep.*** leaving out; but —***conj.*** [Inf.] were it not that; only —**except for** if it were not for

ex·cept′ing ***prep.***, ***conj.*** EXCEPT

ex·cep′tion ***n.*** **1** an excepting **2** *a*) a case to which a rule does not apply *b*) a person or thing different from others of the same class **3** an objection —**take exception** **1** to object **2** feel offended

ex·cep′tion·a·ble ***adj.*** liable to exception; open to objection

ex·cep′tion·al ***adj.*** **1** unusual; esp., unusually good **2** needing special education, as because mentally gifted or mentally handicapped —**ex·cep′tion·al·ly** ***adv.***

ex·cerpt (ek surpt′; *for n.* ek′surpt′) ***vt.*** ⟦< L *ex-*, out + *carpere*, to pick⟧ to select or quote (passages from a book, etc.); extract —***n.*** a passage selected or quoted; extract

ex·cess (ek ses′; *also, esp. for adj.*, ek′ses′) ***n.*** ⟦see EXCEED⟧ **1** action that goes beyond a reasonable limit **2** an amount greater than is necessary **3** the amount by which one thing exceeds another —***adj.*** extra; surplus —**in excess of** more than

ex·ces′sive ***adj.*** being too much; immoderate —**ex·ces′sive·ly** ***adv.***

ex·change (eks chānj′) ***vt.***, ***vi.*** **-changed′, -chang′ing** ⟦see EX- & CHANGE⟧ **1** to give or receive (something) *for* another thing; barter; trade **2** to interchange (similar things) —***n.*** **1** an exchanging; interchange **2** a thing exchanged **3** a place for exchanging *[*a stock *exchange]* **4** a central office providing telephone service **5** the value of one currency in terms of another —**ex·change′a·ble** ***adj.***

exchange rate the rate at which one currency can be exchanged for another

ex·cheq·uer (eks chek′ər) ***n.*** ⟦ME *escheker*, lit., chessboard < OFr *eschekier*: accounts of revenue were kept on a squared board⟧ **1** a national treasury **2** funds; finances

ex·cise[1] (ek′sīz′) ***n.*** ⟦ult. < L *assidere*, assist (in office)⟧ a tax on various commodities, as liquor or tobacco, within a country: also **excise tax**

ex·cise[2] (ek sīz′) ***vt.*** **-cised′, -cis′ing** ⟦< L *ex-*, out +

THESAURUS

examine ***v.*** **1** [To inspect with care] inspect, analyze, criticize, scrutinize, investigate, go into, inquire into, scan, probe, sift, explore, reconnoiter, audit, take stock of, take note of, make an inventory of, consider, canvass, find out, search out, review, assay, check, check out, check up on, reexamine, go back over, concentrate on, give one's attention to, look at, look into, look over, conduct research on, run checks on, put to the test, sound out, feel out, subject to scrutiny, peer into, look into, pry into, hold up to the light, finger, pick over, sample, experiment with, give the once-over*, size up*, smell around, see about, see into, poke into, nose around, look up and down, go over with a fine-toothed comb, dig into*. **2** [To test] question, interrogate, cross-examine; see TEST.

examined ***a.*** checked, tested, inspected; see INVESTIGATED.

examiner ***n.*** tester, questioner, observer; see INSPECTOR.

example ***n.*** **1** [A representative] illustration, representation, warning, sample, citation, case in point, concrete example, case, prototype, archetype, stereotype, original, copy, instance, quotation. **2** [Something to be imitated] standard, pattern, sample; see MODEL 2. —**for example** for instance, as a model, as an example, to illustrate, to cite an instance, to give an illustration, a case in point, like. —**set an example** instruct, behave as a model, set a pattern; see TEACH.

excavate ***v.*** shovel, empty, hollow out; see DIG 1.

excavation ***n.*** cavity, hollow, pit; see HOLE 1, TUNNEL.

exceed ***v.*** excel, outdo, overdo, outdistance, pass, outrun, beat, get the better of, go beyond, surpass, transcend, eclipse, rise above, pass over, run circles around*, get the edge on*, excel in, have it all over someone*, get the drop on*, beat to the draw*, break the record, have the best of, have the jump on*, be ahead of the game, have the advantage, gain the upper hand.

exceedingly ***a.*** greatly, remarkably, in a marked degree; see VERY.

excel ***v.*** surpass, transcend, improve upon; see EXCEED.

excellence ***n.*** superiority, worth, distinction; see PERFECTION.

excellent ***a.*** first-class, premium, choice, first, choicest, prime, high, the best obtainable, select, exquisite, high-grade, very fine, finest, good, desirable, admirable, distinctive, attractive, great, highest, superior, exceptional, unique, striking, superb, supreme, custom-made, incomparable, surprising, transcendent, priceless, rare, invaluable, highest priced, magnificent, wonderful, skillful, above par, superlative, worthy, refined, well-done, cultivated, competent, skilled, notable, first-rate, terrific*, sensational*, sharp*, groovy*, all right, A-1*, grade A*, classy*, topnotch*, tops*.—*Ant.* POOR, inferior, imperfect.

excellently ***a.*** perfectly, exquisitely, splendidly; see WELL 2.

except ***prep.*** excepting, excluding, rejecting, omitting, barring, save, but, with the exception of, other than, if not, not for, without, outside of, aside from, leaving out, exempting, minus*.

except ***v.*** exclude, reject, leave out; see BAR 1.

exception ***n.*** exclusion, omission, making an exception of, rejection, barring, reservation, leaving out, segregation, limitation, exemption, elimination, expulsion, excusing. —**take exception (to)** **1** [To differ] object, disagree, demur; see DIFFER 1. **2** [To dislike] resent, be offended, take offense; see DISLIKE.

exceptional ***a.*** uncommon, extraordinary, rare; see UNUSUAL 1, 2.

exceptionally ***a.*** unusually, particularly, abnormally; see ESPECIALLY 1.

excerpt ***n.*** selection, extract, citation; see QUOTATION.

excess ***n.*** **1** [More than is needed] profusion, abundance, surplus, remainder, too much, too many, exorbitance, waste, wastefulness, luxuriance, lavishness, oversupply, overstock, surfeit, plenty, bellyful*, too much of a good thing*.—*Ant.* LACK, dearth, deficiency. **2** [Conduct that is not temperate] prodigality, dissipation, intemperance; see GREED, WASTE 1. —**in excess of** additional, surplus, more than; see EXTRA. —**to excess** too much, excessively, extravagantly; see EXTREME.

excessive ***a.*** immoderate, extravagant, exorbitant; see EXTREME.

excessively ***a.*** extravagantly, extremely, unreasonably; see VERY.

exchange ***n.*** **1** [The act of replacing one thing with another] transfer, substitution, replacement, change, rearrangement, shift, revision, sleight-of-hand. **2** [The act of giving and receiving reciprocally] reciprocity, barter, correspondence, interdependence, buying and selling, negotiation, transaction, commerce, trade, give and take. **3** [A substitution] change, shift, swap*, trade, interchange, replacing, shuffle, reciprocation, replacement, switch.

exchange ***v.*** **1** [To replace one thing with another] substitute, transfer, replace, go over to, give in exchange, remove, pass to, reverse, provide a replacement, shuffle, shift, revise, rearrange, change, interchange, transact, reset, change hands, rob Peter to pay Paul, swap*. **2** [To give and receive reciprocally] reciprocate, barter, trade with, buy and sell, deal with, do business with, correspond, swap*.

exchanged ***a.*** restored, traded, brought back; see RETURNED.

caedere, to cut] to remove by cutting out —**ex·ci'sion** (-sizh'ən) ***n.***

ex·cit·a·ble (ek sīt'ə bəl) ***adj.*** easily excited —**ex·cit'a·bil'i·ty** ***n.***

ex·cite (ek sīt') ***vt.*** **-cit'ed, -cit'ing** [< L *ex-*, out + *ciere*, to call] **1** to make active; stir up **2** to arouse; provoke **3** to arouse the feelings of —**ex·ci·ta·tion** (ek'sī tā'shən) ***n.*** —**ex·cit'ed·ly** ***adv.*** —**ex·cit'er** ***n.***

ex·cite'ment ***n.*** **1** an exciting or being excited; agitation **2** that which excites

ex·cit'ing ***adj.*** causing excitement; stirring, thrilling, etc.

ex·claim (ek sklām') ***vi.***, ***vt.*** [< L *ex-*, out + *clamare*, to shout] to cry out; say suddenly and vehemently

ex·cla·ma·tion (ek'sklə mā'shən) ***n.*** **1** an exclaiming **2** something exclaimed; interjection —**ex·clam·a·to·ry** (ek sklam'ə tôr'ē) ***adj.***

exclamation point (or **mark**) a mark (!) used in punctuating to show surprise, strong emotion, etc.

ex·clude (eks klo͞od') ***vt.*** **-clud'ed, -clud'ing** [< L *ex-*, out + *claudere*, to close] **1** to refuse to admit, consider, etc.; reject **2** to put or force out —**ex·clu'sion** (-klo͞o'zhən) ***n.***

ex·clu'sive (-klo͞o'siv) ***adj.*** **1** excluding all others **2** not shared or divided; sole [an *exclusive* right] **3** excluding certain people, as for social or economic reasons —***n.*** something exclusive; specif., a news item distributed by only one news organization —**exclusive of** not including —**ex·clu'sive·ly** ***adv.*** —**ex·clu'sive·ness** ***n.***

ex·com·mu·ni·cate (eks'kə myo͞o'ni kāt') ***vt.*** **-cat'ed, -cat'ing** to exclude from the rights, privileges, etc. of a church —**ex'com·mu'ni·ca'tion** ***n.***

ex·co·ri·ate (eks kôr'ē āt') ***vt.*** **-at'ed, -at'ing** [< L *ex-*, off + *corium*, the skin] to denounce harshly —**ex·co'ri·a'tion** ***n.***

ex·cre·ment (eks'krə mənt) ***n.*** waste matter excreted from the bowels

ex·cres·cence (eks kres'əns) ***n.*** [< L *ex-*, out + *crescere*, grow] an abnormal outgrowth or addition

ex·cre·ta (eks krēt'ə) ***pl.n.*** waste matter excreted from the body

ex·crete (eks krēt') ***vt.***, ***vi.*** **-cret'ed, -cret'ing** [< L *ex-*, out of + *cernere*, sift] to eliminate (waste matter) from the body —**ex·cre'tion** ***n.*** —**ex·cre·to·ry** (eks'krə tôr'ē) ***adj.***

ex·cru·ci·at·ing (eks kro͞o'shē āt'iŋ) ***adj.*** **1** intensely painful; agonizing **2** intense or extreme

ex·cul·pate (eks'kəl pāt') ***vt.*** **-pat'ed, -pat'ing** [< L *ex*, out + *culpa*, fault] to free from blame; prove guiltless —**ex'cul·pa'tion** ***n.*** —**ex·cul'pa·to'ry** ***adj.***

ex·cur·sion (eks kur'zhən) ***n.*** [< L *ex-*, out + *currere*, to run] **1** a short trip; jaunt **2** a round trip at reduced rates —***adj.*** for an excursion

ex·cur·sive (eks kur'siv) ***adj.*** rambling; digressive —**ex·cur'sive·ly** ***adv.*** —**ex·cur'sive·ness** ***n.***

ex·cuse (ek skyo͞oz'; *for n.*, -skyo͞os') ***vt.*** **-cused', -cus'ing** [< L *ex-*, from + *causa*, a charge] **1** to apologize or give reasons for **2** to overlook (an offense or fault) **3** to release from an obligation, etc. **4** to permit to leave **5** to justify —***n.*** **1** a defense of some action; apology **2** something that excuses **3** a pretext —**excuse oneself** **1** to apologize **2** to ask for permission to leave —**ex·cus'a·ble** ***adj.***

exec *abbrev.* **1** executive **2** executor

ex·e·cra·ble (ek'si krə bəl) ***adj.*** [see fol.] **1** detestable **2** very inferior

ex'e·crate' (-krāt') ***vt.*** **-crat'ed, -crat'ing** [< L *execrare*, to curse] **1** to denounce scathingly **2** to loathe; abhor —**ex'e·cra'tion** ***n.***

ex·e·cute (ek'si kyo͞ot') ***vt.*** **-cut'ed, -cut'ing** [see EXECUTOR] **1** to carry out; do **2** to administer (laws, etc.) **3** to put to death by a legal sentence **4** to create in accordance with a plan, etc. **5** to make valid (a deed, will, etc.)

ex'e·cu'tion ***n.*** **1** an executing; specif., *a*) a carrying out, performing, etc. *b*) a putting to death by a legal sentence **2** the manner of performing

ex'e·cu'tion·er ***n.*** one who carries out a court-imposed death penalty

ex·ec·u·tive (eg zek'yo͞o tiv) ***adj.*** [see fol.] **1** of or capable of carrying out duties, functions, etc. **2** empowered to

THESAURUS

excitable ***a.*** sensitive, high-strung, impatient; see NERVOUS.

excite ***v.*** stimulate, inflame, arouse, anger, delight, move, tease, worry, infuriate, madden, stir up, fire up, work up, goad, taunt, mock, provoke, incite, astound, amaze, annoy, jolt, fan the flames, carry away, warm, irritate, offend, bother.

excited ***a.*** aroused, stimulated, inflamed, agitated, hot, annoyed, seething, wrought up, frantic, flushed, overwrought, restless, feverish, apprehensive, roused, disturbed, perturbed, flustered, upset, angry, tense, discomposed, embarrassed, hurt, angered, distracted, distraught, edgy, furious, beside oneself, delighted, eager, enthusiastic, frenzied, troubled, ruffled, moved, avid, hysterical, passionate, provoked, quickened, inspired, wild, nervous, animated, ill at ease, jumpy, jittery*, turned on*, hyped up*, hopped up*, worked up, in a tizzy*, uptight*, all nerves*, blue in the face*, on fire*.—*Ant.* CALM, reserved, self-confident.

excitedly ***a.*** tensely, apprehensively, hysterically; see EXCITED.

excitement ***n.*** confusion, disturbance, tumult, enthusiasm, rage, turmoil, stir, excitation, agitation, movement, feeling, exhilaration, emotion, stimulation, drama, melodrama, activity, commotion, fuss, hullabaloo, bother, dither, hubbub, bustle, to-do*.—*Ant.* PEACE, calm, quiet.

exciting ***a.*** stimulating, moving, animating, provocative, arousing, arresting, stirring, thrilling, dangerous, breathtaking, overwhelming, interesting, new, mysterious, overpowering, inspiring, impressive, soul-stirring, sensational, astonishing, bracing, appealing, bloodcurdling, racy, hair-raising, mindblowing*.—*Ant.* DULL, pacifying, tranquilizing.

exclaim ***v.*** cry out, call out, burst out, assert, shout, call aloud, say loudly; see also YELL.

exclamation ***n.*** yell, clamor, vociferation; see CRY 1.

exclude ***v.*** shut out, reject, ban; see BAR 1, 2.

exclusion ***n.*** keeping out, rejection, elimination, prohibition, nonadmission, omission, segregation, isolation, blockade, repudiation, separation, eviction, dismissal, suspension, refusal, expulsion, barring.—*Ant.* WELCOME, invitation, inclusion.

exclusive ***a.*** restricted, restrictive, fashionable, aristocratic, preferential, privileged, particular, licensed, select, private, segregated, prohibitive, clannish, independent, swank*.—*Ant.* FREE, inclusive, unrestricted.

exclusively ***a.*** particularly, solely, completely; see ONLY 1.

excommunicate ***v.*** expel, curse, oust; see DISMISS.

excommunication ***n.*** expulsion, dismissal, suspension; see REMOVAL.

excrement ***n.*** excretion, stool, fecal matter, offal, droppings, discharge, dung, manure, urine, effluvium, feces, sweat, perspiration, excreta, poop*.

excrete ***v.*** remove, eliminate, eject, defecate, urinate, discharge, secrete, go to the bathroom, go to the toilet, answer a call of nature, pass, expel, exude, perspire, sweat, squeeze out, give off, dump*, poop*.

excretion ***n.*** eliminating, elimination, urinating, discharging, secreting, secretion, defecation, ejecting, ejection, passing off.

excruciating ***a.*** torturing, intense, agonizing; see PAINFUL 1.

excursion ***n.*** jaunt, ramble, tour; see JOURNEY.

excusable ***a.*** pardonable, forgivable, understandable, justifiable, reasonable, defensible, permissible, trivial, passable, slight, plausible, allowable, explainable, not excessive, not fatal, not too bad, not inexcusable, not injurious, moderate, temperate, all right, fair, within limits, OK*.

excuse ***n.*** apology, reason, defense; see EXPLANATION. —**a poor excuse for** inferior, poor, unsatisfactory; see INADEQUATE. —**make one's excuses** regret, apologize, offer an explanation; see APOLOGIZE, EXPLAIN.

excuse ***v.*** pardon, forgive, justify, discharge, vindicate, apologize for, release from, dispense with, free, set free, overlook, purge, exempt, rationalize, acquit, condone, appease, reprieve, absolve, exonerate, clear, give absolution to, pass over, give as an excuse, make excuses for, make allowances for, make apologies for, grant amnesty to, provide with an alibi, plead ignorance, whitewash, let off easy, let go scot-free, wink at*, wipe the slate clean, shrug off, take the rap for*. —**excuse me** pardon me, forgive me, begging your pardon, I'm sorry.

excused ***a.*** forgiven, freed, permitted; see PARDONED.

execute ***v.*** **1** [To carry out instructions] act, do, effect; see PERFORM 1. **2** [To put to death] electrocute, hang, behead; see KILL 1.

executed ***a.*** **1** [Performed] completed, done, carried out; see FINISHED 1. **2** [Formally put to death] killed, hanged, sent to the gallows, electrocuted, gassed, shot at sunrise, sent before a firing squad, beheaded, guillotined, crucified, sent to the chair*, fried*, lethally injected.

execution ***n.*** punishment, capital punishment, killing, electrocution, hanging, gassing, beheading, decapitation, guillotining, crucifixion, martyrdom.

executive ***a.*** administrative, governing, ruling; see MANAGING.

executive ***n.*** businessman, businesswoman, president, vice-president,

administer (laws, government affairs, etc.) —*n.* **1** the branch of government administering the laws and matters of business of a nation **2** one who administers or manages matters of business of a corporation, etc.

ex·ec·u·tor (eg zek′yoo tər) *n.* ⟦< L *ex-*, intens. + *sequi*, to follow⟧ a person appointed to carry out the provisions of a will

ex·e·ge·sis (ek′sə jē′sis) *n., pl.* **-ses′** (-sēz′) ⟦< Gr *ex-*, out + *hēgeisthai*, to lead⟧ interpretation of a word, passage, etc., esp. in the Bible

ex·em·plar (eg zem′plər, -plär′) *n.* ⟦< L *exemplum*, a pattern⟧ **1** a model; pattern **2** a typical specimen

ex·em·pla·ry (eg zem′plə rē) *adj.* ⟦< L *exemplum*, a pattern⟧ serving as a model or example [an *exemplary* life]

ex·em·pli·fy (eg zem′plə fī′) *vt.* **-fied′**, **-fy′ing** ⟦< L *exemplum*, example + *facere*, to make⟧ to show by example —**ex·em′pli·fi·ca′tion** *n.*

ex·empt (eg zempt′) *vt.* ⟦< L *ex-*, out + *emere*, to buy⟧ to free from a rule or obligation which applies to others —*adj.* freed from a usual rule, duty, etc. —**ex·emp′tion** *n.*

ex·er·cise (ek′sər sīz′) *n.* ⟦< L *exercere*, put to work⟧ **1** active use or operation **2** performance (of duties, etc.) **3** activity for developing the body or mind **4** a task to be practiced for developing some skill **5** [*pl.*] a program of speeches, etc. —*vt.* **-cised′**, **-cis′ing** **1** to put into action; use **2** to carry out (duties, etc.); perform **3** to put into use so as to develop or train **4** to exert (influence, etc.) **5** to engage so as to worry, harass, etc. —*vi.* to do exercises

ex·ert (eg zurt′) *vt.* ⟦< L *exserere*, stretch out⟧ **1** to put into action **2** to apply (oneself) with great effort

ex·er′tion *n.* **1** active use of strength, power, etc. **2** effort

ex·hale (eks hāl′) *vt., vi.* **-haled′**, **-hal′ing** ⟦< L *ex-*, out + *halare*, breathe⟧ **1** to breathe out (air) **2** to give off (vapor, etc.) —**ex·ha·la·tion** (eks′hə lā′shən) *n.*

ex·haust (eg zôst′) *vt.* ⟦< L *ex-*, out + *haurire*, to draw⟧ **1** to use up **2** to empty completely; drain **3** to tire out **4** to deal with thoroughly —*n.* **1** the discharge of used steam, gas, etc. from an engine **2** the pipes through which it is released **3** fumes, etc. given off —**ex·haust′i·ble** *adj.*

ex·haus·tion (eg zôs′chən) *n.* **1** an exhausting **2** great fatigue

ex·haus′tive *adj.* leaving nothing out —**ex·haus′tive·ly** *adv.*

ex·hib·it (eg zib′it) *vt.* ⟦< L *ex-*, out + *habere*, to hold⟧ **1** to show; display **2** to present to public view —*vi.* to put art objects, etc. on public display —*n.* **1** a display **2** a thing exhibited **3** *Law* an object produced as evidence in a court —**ex·hib′i·tor** *n.*

ex·hi·bi·tion (ek′sə bish′ən) *n.* **1** an exhibiting **2** that which is exhibited **3** a public showing, as of art

ex′hi·bi′tion·ism′ *n.* **1** a tendency to call attention to oneself or show off **2** a tendency to expose oneself sexually —**ex′hi·bi′tion·ist** *n.*

ex·hil·a·rate (eg zil′ə rāt′) *vt.* **-rat′ed**, **-rat′ing** ⟦< L *ex-*, intens. + *hilaris*, glad⟧ **1** to make cheerful or lively **2** to stimulate —**ex·hil′a·ra′tion** *n.* —**ex·hil′a·ra′tive** *adj.*

ex·hort (eg zôrt′) *vt., vi.* ⟦< L *ex-*, out + *hortari*, to urge⟧ to urge earnestly; advise strongly —**ex′hor·ta′tion** *n.*

ex·hume (eks hyoom′, eg zyoom′) *vt.* **-humed′**, **-hum′ing** ⟦< L *ex-*, out + *humus*, the ground⟧ **1** to dig out of the earth; disinter **2** to bring to light; reveal —**ex′hu·ma′tion** *n.*

ex·i·gen·cy (eks′ə jən sē) *n., pl.* **-cies** ⟦< L *exigere*, drive out⟧ **1** urgency **2** a situation calling for immediate attention **3** [*pl.*] pressing needs —**ex′i·gent** *adj.*

ex·ig·u·ous (eg zig′yoo əs) *adj.* ⟦see prec.⟧ scanty; meager

ex·ile (ek′sīl′, eg′zīl′) *n.* ⟦< L *exul*, an exile⟧ **1** a prolonged living away from one's country, usually enforced **2** a person in exile —*vt.* **-iled′**, **-il′ing** to force (a person) into exile; banish

ex·ist (eg zist′) *vi.* ⟦< L *ex-*, out + *sistere*, to set, place⟧ **1** to have reality or being; be **2** to occur or be present **3** to continue being; live

ex·ist′ence *n.* **1** the act or fact of being **2** life; living **3** occurrence —**ex·ist′ent** *adj.*

ex·is·ten·tial (eg′zis ten′shəl) *adj.* **1** of existence **2** of existentialism

ex′is·ten′tial·ism′ *n.* a philosophical movement stressing individual existence and holding that human beings are totally free and responsible for their acts —**ex′is·ten′tial·ist** *adj., n.*

ex·it (ek′sit, eg′zit) *n.* ⟦< L *ex-*, out + *ire*, to go⟧ **1** an actor's departure from the stage **2** a going out; departure **3** a way out **4** a road leading from an expressway —*vi.* to leave a place —*vt.* to leave (a building, expressway, etc.)

exo- ⟦< Gr *exō*⟧ *prefix* outside, outer, outer part

ex·o·bi·ol·o·gy (eks′ō bī äl′ə jē) *n.* the branch of biology investigating the possibility of extraterrestrial life

ex·o·dus (eks′ə dəs) *n.* ⟦< Gr *ex-*, out + *hodos*, way⟧ **1** [**E-**] the departure of the Israelites from Egypt: with *the* **2** [**E-**] the second book of the Bible, describing this **3** a going out or forth

ex of·fi·ci·o (eks′ ə fish′ē ō′) ⟦L, lit., from office⟧ by virtue of one's position

ex·on·er·ate (eg zän′ər āt′) *vt.* **-at′ed**, **-at′ing** ⟦< L *ex-*, out + *onerare*, to load⟧ to declare or prove blameless —**ex·on′er·a′tion** *n.*

ex·or·bi·tant (eg zôr′bi tənt) *adj.* ⟦< L *ex-*, out + *orbita*, a track⟧ going beyond what is reasonable, just, etc.; excessive —**ex·or′bi·tance** *n.*

ex·or·cise or **ex·or·cize** (eks′ôr sīz′) *vt.* **-cised′** or **-cized′**, **-cis′ing** or **-ciz′ing** ⟦< Gr *ex-*, out + *horkos*, an oath⟧ **1** to drive (an evil spirit) out or away by ritual prayers, etc. **2** to free from such a spirit —**ex′or·cism′** (-siz′əm) *n.* —**ex′or·cist** *n.*

THESAURUS

secretary, treasurer, supervisor, chairman, chairwoman, chairperson, chair, CEO, dean, head, chief, superintendent, bureaucrat, leader, governor, controller, organizer, commander, director, boss, big shot*, official, manager; see also BUSINESSMAN, LEADER 2.

exemplify *v.* illustrate, give an example, represent; see EXPLAIN.

exempt *a.* freed, cleared, liberated, privileged, excused, absolved, not subject to, released from, not responsible to, not responsible for, set apart, excluded, released, not liable, unrestrained, unbound, uncontrolled, unrestricted, not restricted by, not restricted to, outside.—*Ant.* RESPONSIBLE, liable, subject.

exempt *v.* free, liberate, pass by; see EXCUSE.

exemption *n.* exception, immunity, privilege; see FREEDOM.

exercise *n.* **1** [Action undertaken for training] practice, exertion, drill, drilling, gymnastics, sports, calisthenics, workout. **2** [The means by which training is promoted] performance, action, activity; see ACTION. **3** [Use] application, employment, operation; see USE 1.

exercise *v.* **1** [To move the body] stretch, bend, pull, tug, hike, work, promote muscle tone, labor, strain, loosen up, discipline, drill, execute, perform exercises, practice, take a walk, work out, limber up, warm up; see also TRAIN 1. **2** [To use] employ, practice, exert, apply, operate, execute, handle, utilize, devote, put in practice; see also USE 1. **3** [To train] drill, discipline, give training to; see TEACH, TRAIN 1.

exert *v.* put forth, bring to bear, exercise; see USE 1. **—exert oneself** strive, attempt, endeavor; see TRY 1.

exertion *n.* struggle, attempt, endeavor; see EFFORT.

exhalation *n.* emanation, vapor, air; see BREATH.

exhaust *v.* **1** [To consume strength] debilitate, tire, wear out, wear down; see also WEAKEN 1, 2, WEARY 1, 2. **2** [To use entirely] use up, take the last of, deplete; see WEAR 3.

exhausted *a.* **1** [Without further physical resources] debilitated, wearied, worn; see TIRED, WEAK 1. **2** [Having nothing remaining] all gone, consumed, used; see EMPTY.

exhaustion *n.* weariness, fatigue, depletion; see FATIGUE.

exhibit *n.* show, performance, presentation; see DISPLAY.

exhibit *v.* show, present, manifest; see DISPLAY.

exhibited *a.* shown, presented, advertised; see SHOWN 1.

exhibition *n.* exposition, fair, carnival; see SHOW 1.

exile *n.* **1** [Banishment] expulsion, deportation, expatriation, ostracism, displacement, separation. **2** [An outcast] fugitive, outlaw, man without a country; see REFUGEE.

exile *v.* ostracize, outlaw, cast out; see BANISH.

exist *v.* **1** [To have being] breathe, live, survive; see BE 1. **2** [To carry on life] be alive, endure, go on; see SURVIVE 1.

existence *n.* **1** [The carrying on of life] being, actuality, reality; see LIFE 1. **2** [The state of being] presence, actuality, permanence; see REALITY.

existing *a.* for the time being, temporary, just now; see PRESENT 1.

exit *n.* **1** [A means of egress] way out, outlet, opening; see DOOR. **2** [The act of leaving] going, farewell, exodus; see DEPARTURE.

exorbitant *a.* excessive, extravagant, too much; see WASTEFUL.

ex·o·skel·e·ton (eks′ō skel′ə tən) ***n.*** any hard, external supporting structure, as the shell of an oyster

ex′o·ther′mic (-thur′mik) ***adj.*** designating or of a chemical change in which heat is liberated

ex·ot·ic (eg zät′ik) ***adj.*** ⟦< Gr *exō*, outside⟧ **1** foreign **2** strangely beautiful, enticing, etc. —**ex·ot′i·cal·ly** ***adv.***

exp *abbrev.* experience(d)

ex·pand (ek spand′) ***vt.***, ***vi.*** ⟦< L *ex-*, out + *pandere*, to spread⟧ **1** to spread out; unfold **2** to increase in size, scope, etc.; enlarge; develop

ex·panse (ek spans′) ***n.*** a large area or unbroken surface; wide extent

ex·pan′si·ble ***adj.*** that can be expanded: also **ex·pand′a·ble**

ex·pan′sion ***n.*** **1** an expanding or being expanded; enlargement **2** an expanded thing or part **3** the degree or extent of expansion

expansion bolt a bolt with an attachment that expands as the bolt is turned

ex·pan′sive ***adj.*** **1** that can expand **2** broad; extensive **3** effusive; demonstrative —**ex·pan′sive·ly** ***adv.***

ex·pa·ti·ate (eks pā′shē āt′) ***vi.*** **-at′ed**, **-at′ing** ⟦< L *ex(s)patiari*, wander⟧ to speak or write at length (*on* or *upon*) —**ex·pa′ti·a′tion** ***n.***

ex·pa·tri·ate (eks pā′trē āt′; *for n.*, -it) ***vt.***, ***vi.*** **-at′ed**, **-at′ing** ⟦< L *ex*, out of + *patria*, fatherland⟧ to exile (a person or oneself) —***n.*** an expatriated person —**ex·pa′tri·a′tion** ***n.***

ex·pect (ek spekt′) ***vt.*** ⟦< L *ex-*, out + *spectare*, to look⟧ **1** to look for as likely to occur or appear **2** to look for as proper or necessary **3** [Inf.] to suppose; guess —**be expecting** [Inf.] to be pregnant

ex·pect′an·cy ***n.***, *pl.* **-cies** **1** EXPECTATION **2** that which is expected, esp. on a statistical basis

ex·pect′ant ***adj.*** that expects; expecting —**ex·pect′ant·ly** ***adv.***

ex·pec·ta·tion (ek′spek tā′shən) ***n.*** **1** an expecting; anticipation **2** a thing looked forward to **3** [*also pl.*] a reason for expecting something

ex·pec·to·rant (ek spek′tə rənt) ***n.*** ⟦see fol.⟧ a medicine that helps to bring up phlegm

ex·pec′to·rate′ (-tə rāt′) ***vt.***, ***vi.*** **-rat′ed**, **-rat′ing** ⟦< L *ex-*, out + *pectus*, breast⟧ to spit —**ex·pec′to·ra′tion** ***n.***

ex·pe·di·en·cy (ek spē′dē ən sē) ***n.***, *pl.* **-cies** **1** a being expedient; suitability for a given purpose **2** the doing of what is selfish rather than of what is right or just; self-interest **3** an expedient Also **ex·pe′di·ence**

ex·pe′di·ent ***adj.*** ⟦see fol.⟧ **1** useful for effecting a desired result; convenient **2** based on or guided by self-interest —***n.*** an expedient thing; means to an end

ex·pe·dite (eks′pə dīt′) ***vt.*** **-dit′ed**, **-dit′ing** ⟦< L *expedire*, lit., to free the foot⟧ **1** to speed up the progress of; facilitate **2** to do quickly

ex′pe·dit′er ***n.*** one employed to expedite urgent or involved projects: also sp. **ex′pe·di′tor**

ex·pe·di·tion (eks′pə dish′ən) ***n.*** ⟦see EXPEDITE⟧ **1** *a)* a voyage, march, etc., as for exploration or battle *b)* those on such a journey **2** efficient speed —**ex′pe·di′tion·ar′y** ***adj.***

ex′pe·di′tious (-dish′əs) ***adj.*** efficient and speedy; prompt —**ex′pe·di′tious·ly** ***adv.***

ex·pel (ek spel′) ***vt.*** **-pelled′**, **-pel′ling** ⟦< L *ex-*, out + *pellere*, to thrust⟧ **1** to drive out by force **2** to dismiss by authority *[expelled* from college*]* —**ex·pel′la·ble** ***adj.*** —**ex·pel′ler** ***n.***

ex·pend (ek spend′) ***vt.*** ⟦< L *ex-*, out + *pendere*, to weigh⟧ **1** to spend **2** to use up

ex·pend′a·ble ***adj.*** **1** that can be expended **2** *Mil.* designating equipment (or personnel) expected to be used up (or sacrificed) in service

ex·pend·i·ture (ek spen′di chər) ***n.*** **1** an expending of money, time, etc. **2** the amount of money, time, etc. expended

ex·pense (ek spens′) ***n.*** ⟦see EXPEND⟧ **1** financial cost; charge **2** any cost or sacrifice **3** [*pl.*] charges met with in doing one's work, etc.

ex·pen′sive ***adj.*** costly; high-priced

ex·pe·ri·ence (ek spir′ē əns) ***n.*** ⟦< L *experiri*, to try⟧ **1** the act of living through an event **2** anything or everything observed or lived through **3** *a)* training and personal participation *b)* knowledge, skill, etc. resulting from this —***vt.*** **-enced**, **-enc·ing** to have experience of; undergo

ex·pe′ri·enced ***adj.*** having had or having learned from experience

ex·per·i·ment (ek sper′ə mənt; *also, and for v. usually*, -ment′) ***n.*** ⟦< L *experimentum*, a trial⟧ a test, trial, action, etc. undertaken to discover or demonstrate something —***vi.*** to make, perform, conduct, etc. experiments —**ex·per′i·men·ta′tion** (-mən tā′shən) ***n.*** —**ex·per′i·ment′er** ***n.***

THESAURUS

exotic ***a.*** **1** [Foreign] imported, not native, extrinsic; see FOREIGN. **2** [Peculiar] strange, fascinating, different; see FOREIGN, UNUSUAL 2.

expand ***v.*** extend, augment, dilate; see GROW 1.

expanse ***n.*** breadth, width, length, extent, reach, stretch, distance, area, belt, space, field, territory, span, spread, room, scope, range, compass, sphere, margin, sweep, radius, wilderness, region, immensity.

expansion ***n.*** enlargement, augmentation, extension; see INCREASE.

expatriate ***n.*** exile, emigrant, outcast; see REFUGEE.

expatriate ***v.*** exile, ostracize, deport; see BANISH.

expect ***v.*** **1** [To anticipate] await, look for, look forward to, count on, plan on, assume, suppose, lean on, feel it in one's bones*, wait for, hope for; see also ANTICIPATE. **2** [To require] demand, insist upon, exact; see REQUIRE 2. **3** [To assume] presume, suppose, suspect; see ASSUME.

expectancy ***n.*** hope, prospect, likelihood; see ANTICIPATION.

expectant ***a.*** **1** [Characterized by anticipation] expecting, hoping, hopeful, waiting, awaiting, in anticipation, watchful, vigilant, eager, ready, prepared, in suspense, gaping, wide-eyed, on edge, itching.—*Ant.* INDIFFERENT, UNPREPARED, nonchalant. **2** [Anticipating birth] pregnant, parturient, expecting; see PREGNANT.

expectation ***n.*** hope, belief, prospect; see ANTICIPATION.

expected ***a.*** looked for, counted upon, contemplated, looked forward to, hoped for, relied upon, foreseen, predictable, predetermined, foretold, prophesied, planned for, prepared for, budgeted, within normal expectations, in the works, in the cards, coming up, in the bag*; see also LIKELY.

expecting ***a.*** expectant, due, about to become a mother; see PREGNANT.

expediency ***n.*** advantageousness, efficiency, profitableness; see USEFULNESS.

expedient ***a.*** profitable, useful, convenient; see PRACTICAL.

expedition ***n.*** **1** [Travel undertaken] excursion, voyage, campaign; see JOURNEY. **2** [That which undertakes travel] party, hunters, explorers, pioneers, traders, soldiers, scouts, archaeologists, tourists, sightseers, caravan, posse; see also CROWD.

expel ***v.*** **1** [To eject] get rid of, cast out, dislodge; see EJECT. **2** [To dismiss] suspend, discharge, oust; see DISMISS.

expend ***v.*** pay out, write checks for, lay out; see SPEND.

expenditure ***n.*** outgo, investment, payment; see EXPENSE.

expense ***n.*** expenditure, responsibility, obligation, loan, mortgage, lien, debt, liability, investment, insurance, upkeep, alimony, debit, account, cost, price, outlay, charge, payment, outgo, value, worth, sum, amount, risk, capital, rate, tax, carrying charges, budgeted items, cost of materials, overhead, time, payroll, investment.—*Ant.* PROFIT, income, receipts. **—at the expense of** paid by, at the cost of, charged to; see OWED.

expenses ***n.*** living expenses, costs, lodging, room and board, incidentals, carrying charges.

expensive ***a.*** dear, precious, valuable, invaluable, rare, high-priced, pricey*, costly, prized, choice, rich, priceless, high, too high, unreasonable, exorbitant, extravagant, at a premium, out of sight*, at great cost, sky-high, steep*, stiff*.—*Ant.* CHEAP, inexpensive, low.

experience ***n.*** background, skill, knowledge, wisdom, practice, maturity, judgment, practical knowledge, sense, patience, caution, know-how*, savvy*; see also BACKGROUND 2.

experience ***v.*** undergo, feel, live through; see ENDURE 2, FEEL 2.

experienced ***a.*** skilled, practiced, instructed, accomplished, versed, qualified, able, skillful, knowing, savvy*, trained, wise, expert, veteran, mature, with a good background, rounded, knowing the score*, knowing the ropes*, having all the answers, having been around*, having been through the mill*, broken in*.—*Ant.* NEW, apprentice, beginning.

experiment ***n.*** analysis, essay, examination, trial, inspection, search, organized observation, research, scrutiny, speculation, check, proof, operation, test, exercise, quiz, investigation.

experiment ***v.*** analyze, investigate, probe, search, venture, explore, test, rehearse, try out, sample, subject to discipline, prove, conduct an experiment, research, study, examine, scrutinize, weigh, play around with, fool with*.

ex·per'i·men'tal *adj.* 1 based on or used for experiments 2 designed to test 3 tentative —**ex·per'i·men'tal·ly** *adv.*
ex·pert (eks'pərt) *adj.* ⟦see EXPERIENCE⟧ very skillful —*n.* one who is very skillful or well-informed in some special field —**ex'pert·ly** *adv.* —**ex'pert·ness** *n.*
ex·per·tise (ek'spər tēz') *n.* ⟦Fr⟧ the skill or knowledge of an expert
ex·pi·ate (eks'pē āt') *vt.* **-at'ed, -at'ing** ⟦< L *ex-*, out + *piare*, to appease⟧ to make amends for (wrongdoing or guilt); atone for —**ex'pi·a'tion** *n.* —**ex'pi·a·to'ry** (-ə tôr'ē) *adj.*
ex·pire (ek spīr') *vi.* **-pired', -pir'ing** ⟦< L *ex-*, out + *spirare*, breathe⟧ 1 to exhale 2 to die 3 to come to an end —**ex·pi·ra·tion** (ek'spə rā'shən) *n.*
ex·plain (ek splān') *vt.* ⟦< L *ex-*, out + *planus*, level⟧ 1 to make plain or understandable 2 to give the meaning of; expound 3 to account for —*vi.* to give an explanation —**ex·plain'a·ble** *adj.*
ex·pla·na·tion (eks'plə nā'shən) *n.* 1 an explaining 2 something that explains; interpretation, meaning, etc.
ex·plan·a·to·ry (ek splan'ə tôr'ē) *adj.* explaining or intended to explain
ex·ple·tive (eks'plə tiv) *n.* ⟦< L *ex-*, out, up + *plere*, to fill⟧ an oath or exclamation
ex·pli·ca·ble (eks'pli kə bəl, ik splik'ə bəl) *adj.* ⟦see fol.⟧ that can be explained
ex·pli·cate (eks'pli kāt') *vt.* **-cat'ed, -cat'ing** ⟦< L *ex-*, out + *plicare*, to fold⟧ to make clear; explain fully
ex·plic·it (eks plis'it) *adj.* ⟦see prec.⟧ 1 clearly stated or shown; definite 2 outspoken —**ex·plic'it·ly** *adv.*
ex·plode (ek splōd') *vt.* **-plod'ed, -plod'ing** ⟦orig., to drive off the stage < L *ex-*, off + *plaudere*, applaud⟧ 1 to expose as false 2 to make burst with a loud noise 3 to cause to change suddenly and violently, as from a solid to an expanding gas —*vi.* to burst forth noisily —**ex·plod'a·ble** *adj.*
ex·ploit (eks'ploit'; *also, and for v. usually*, ek sploit') *n.* ⟦see EXPLICATE⟧ a daring act; bold deed —*vt.* 1 to make use of 2 to make unethical use of for one's own profit —**ex'ploi·ta'tion** *n.* —**ex·ploit'a·tive** *adj.* —**ex·ploit'er** *n.*
ex·plore (ek splôr') *vt., vi.* **-plored', -plor'ing** ⟦< L *ex-*, out + *plorare*, cry out⟧ 1 to examine (something) carefully; investigate 2 to travel in (a little-known region) to learn about it —**ex·plo·ra·tion** (eks'plə rā'shən) *n.* —**ex·plor'a·to'ry** (-ə tôr'ē) *adj.* —**ex·plor'er** *n.*
ex·plo·sion (ek splō'zhən) *n.* 1 an exploding 2 the noise made by exploding 3 a noisy outburst 4 a sudden, widespread increase
ex·plo'sive (-siv) *adj.* 1 of, causing, or like an explosion 2 tending to explode —*n.* a substance that can explode, as gunpowder —**ex·plo'sive·ly** *adv.* —**ex·plo'sive·ness** *n.*
ex·po·nent (ek spōn'ənt; *also, esp. for 3,* eks'pōn'-) *n.* ⟦see EXPOUND⟧ 1 one who expounds or promotes (principles, etc.) 2 a person or thing that is an example or symbol (*of* something) 3 *Algebra* a symbol placed at the upper right of another to show how many times the latter is to be multiplied by itself (Ex.: $b^2 = b \times b$)
ex·po·nen·tial (eks'pō nen'shəl) *adj.* 1 *Math.* of an exponent 2 of or increasing by very large amounts, etc.
ex·port (ek spôrt'; *also, and for n. always*, eks'pôrt') *vt.* ⟦< L *ex-*, out + *portare*, to carry⟧ 1 to send (goods) to another country, esp. for sale 2 to send (ideas, culture, etc.) from one place to another —*n.* 1 something exported 2 an exporting —**ex'por·ta'tion** *n.* —**ex·port'er** *n.*
ex·pose (ek spōz') *vt.* **-posed', -pos'ing** ⟦see EXPOUND⟧ 1 to lay open (*to* danger, attack, etc.) 2 to reveal; exhibit 3 to make (a crime, etc.) known 4 *Photog.* to subject (a sensitized film or plate) to light, etc.
ex·po·sé (eks'pō zā') *n.* ⟦Fr⟧ a public disclosure of a scandal, crime, etc.
ex·po·si·tion (eks'pə zish'ən) *n.* ⟦see EXPOUND⟧ 1 a detailed explanation 2 writing or speaking that explains 3 a large public exhibition or show
ex·pos·i·tor (ek späz'ət ər) *n.* one who expounds or explains
ex·pos'i·to'ry (-ə tôr'ē) *adj.* of or containing exposition; explanatory
ex post fac·to (eks' pōst fak'tō) ⟦L, from (the thing) done afterward⟧ done afterward, but retroactive
ex·pos·tu·late (ek späs'chə lāt') *vi.* **-lat'ed, -lat'ing** ⟦< L *ex-*, intens. + *postulare*, to demand⟧ to reason with a person earnestly, objecting to that person's actions —**ex·pos'tu·la'tion** *n.*
ex·po·sure (ek spō'zhər) *n.* 1 an exposing or being exposed 2 a location, as of a house, in relation to the sun, etc. *[an eastern exposure]* 3 frequent appearance

THESAURUS

experimental *a.* tentative, trial, temporary, test, provisional, preliminary, preparatory, under probation, on approval, on trial, pending verification, hypothetical, momentary, primary, beginning, in its first stage.—*Ant.* PERMANENT, tried, tested.
expert *a.* skillful, practiced, proficient; see ABLE.
expert *n.* authority, professional, master; see SPECIALIST.
expiration *n.* close, closing, finish; see END 2.
expire *v.* stop, finish, quit; see END 1.
explain *v.* interpret, explicate, account for, elucidate, illustrate, clarify, illuminate, make clear, describe, expound, teach, reveal, point out, demonstrate, tell, read, translate, paraphrase, put in other words, define, justify, untangle, unravel, make plain, come to the point, put across, throw light upon, comment on, remark upon, remark on, offer an explanation of, resolve, clear up, get right, set right, put someone on the right track, spell out, go into detail, get to the bottom of, figure out, cast light upon, get across, get through, bring out, work out, solve, put in plain English*.—*Ant.* CONFUSE, puzzle, confound.
explainable *a.* explicable, accountable, intelligible; see UNDERSTANDABLE.
explained *a.* made clear, interpreted, elucidated; see KNOWN 2, OBVIOUS 2.
explanation *n.* information, answer, account, reason, illustration, description, comment, justification, narrative, story, tale, footnote, anecdote, example, analysis, criticism, exegesis, key, commentary, note, summary, report, brief, the details, budget, breakdown; see also PROOF 1.
explanatory *a.* expository, illustrative, informative, allegorical, interpretative, instructive, guiding, descriptive, analytical, graphic, critical.
explicit *a.* express, sure, plain; see DEFINITE 1, UNDERSTANDABLE.
explode *v.* blow up, blow out, break out, erupt, go off, detonate, discharge, backfire, shatter, fracture, split, collapse, blow off, blast, blow to smithereens*; see also RAGE 1.
exploit *n.* deed, venture, escapade; see ACHIEVEMENT.
exploit *v.* utilize, take advantage of, employ; see USE 1.
exploited *a.* taken advantage of, utilized, worked; see USED.
exploration *n.* investigation, research, search; see EXAMINATION 1.
explore *v.* search, investigate, seek; see EXAMINE.
explorer *n.* adventurer, traveler, pioneer, wayfarer, pilgrim, voyager, space traveler, astronaut, cosmonaut, seafarer, mountaineer, mountain climber, scientist, navigator, colonist.
explosion *n.* detonation, blast, burst, discharge, blowout, blowup, eruption, combustion, outburst, firing, ignition, backfire.
explosive *a.* stormy, fiery, incendiary, forceful, raging, wild, violent, uncontrollable, vehement, sharp, hysterical, frenzied, savage.—*Ant.* MILD, gentle, uneventful.
explosive *n.* mine, gunpowder, ammunition, TNT, plastic explosive, dynamite, nitroglycerine, bomb, missile, blockbuster*, warhead, grenade, charge, shell, Molotov cocktail, firecracker; see also AMMUNITION, WEAPON.
export *n.* shipping, trading, overseas shipment, commodity, international trade, foreign trade.
export *v.* send out, sell abroad, trade abroad, ship, transport, consign, dump.
expose *v.* 1 [To uncover] disclose, smoke out, show up, present, prove, reveal, air, exhibit, unmask, lay open, lay bare, bring to light, open, dig up, give away, bring into view, unfold, let the cat out of the bag, drag through the mud, put the finger on*. 2 [To endeavor to attract attention] show, show off, bare; see DISPLAY. 3 [To open to danger] lay open to, subject to, imperil; see ENDANGER.
exposed *a.* disclosed, defined, revealed, divulged, made public, laid bare, dug up, brought to light, solved, resolved, discovered, found out, seen through.—*Ant.* HIDDEN, concealed, disguised.
exposition *n.* 1 [The process of making clear] elucidation, delineation, explication; see EXPLANATION. 2 [A popular exhibition] exhibit, showing, performance; see DISPLAY.
ex post facto *a.* subsequently, retroactively, retrospectively; see FINALLY 2.
exposure *n.* disclosure, betrayal, display, exhibition, publication, showing, revelation, confession, unveiling, acknowledgment, exposé, giveaway, bombshell, stink*.—*Ant.* SECRECY, protection, concealment.

before the public **4** *Photog. a)* the subjection of a sensitized film or plate to light, X-rays, etc. *b)* a section of a film for one picture *c)* the time during which such a section is exposed

ex·pound (ek spound′) ***vt.*** ⟦< L *ex-*, out + *ponere*, to put⟧ **1** to set forth; state in detail **2** to explain

ex·press (ek spres′) ***vt.*** ⟦< L *ex-*, out + *premere*, to press⟧ **1** to squeeze out (juice, etc.) **2** to put into words; state **3** to reveal; show **4** to symbolize; signify **5** to send by express —***adj.*** **1** expressed; stated; explicit **2** specific **3** fast, direct, and making few stops *[*an *express* bus*]* **4** marked by speed *[*an *express* highway*]* **5** having to do with an express train, bus, service, etc. —***adv.*** by express —***n.*** **1** an express train, bus, etc. **2** *a)* a service for transporting things rapidly *b)* the things sent by express

ex·pres·sion (ek spresh′ən) ***n.*** **1** a putting into words; stating **2** a manner of expressing, esp. with eloquence **3** a particular word or phrase **4** a showing of feeling, character, etc. **5** a look, intonation, etc. that conveys meaning **6** a mathematical symbol or set of symbols —**ex·pres′sion·less *adj.***

ex·pres′sion·ism′ *n.* [*often* **E-**] a 20th-c. movement in art, literature, etc. seeking to give symbolic, objective expression to inner experience —**ex·pres′sion·ist *adj.*, *n.*** —**ex·pres′sion·is′tic *adj.***

ex·pres′sive *adj.* **1** that expresses **2** full of meaning or feeling —**ex·pres′sive·ly *adv.*** —**ex·pres′sive·ness *n.***

ex·press′ly *adv.* **1** plainly; definitely **2** especially; particularly

ex·press′way′ *n.* a divided highway for high-speed, through traffic, with grade separations at intersections

ex·pro·pri·ate (eks prō′prē āt′) ***vt.* -at′ed, -at′ing** ⟦< L *ex-*, out + *proprius*, one's own⟧ to take (land, etc.) from its owner, esp. for public use —**ex·pro′pri·a′tion *n.***

ex·pul·sion (ek spul′shən) ***n.*** an expelling or being expelled

ex·punge (ek spunj′) ***vt.* -punged′, -pung′ing** ⟦< L *ex-*, out + *pungere*, to prick⟧ to blot or strike out; erase

ex·pur·gate (eks′pər gāt′) ***vt.* -gat′ed, -gat′ing** ⟦< L *ex-*, out + *purgare*, cleanse⟧ to remove (passages considered obscene, etc.) from (a book, etc.) —**ex′pur·ga′tion *n.***

ex·qui·site (eks′kwi zit, ek skwiz′it) ***adj.*** ⟦< L *ex-*, out + *quaerere*, to ask⟧ **1** carefully or elaborately done **2** very beautiful, delicate, etc. **3** of highest quality **4** very intense; keen

ext *abbrev.* extension

ex·tant (eks′tənt, ek stant′) ***adj.*** ⟦< L *ex-*, out + *stare*, to stand⟧ still existing; not extinct

ex·tem·po·ra·ne·ous (eks′tem′pə rā′nē əs) ***adj.*** ⟦see fol.⟧ done or spoken with little preparation; offhand —**ex′tem′po·ra′ne·ous·ly *adv.***

ex·tem·po·re (ek stem′pə rē) ***adv.*, *adj.*** ⟦< L *ex-*, out of + *tempus*, time⟧ with little preparation; offhand

ex·tem′po·rize′ (-rīz′) ***vi.*, *vt.* -rized′, -riz′ing** to speak, perform, etc. extempore; improvise

ex·tend (ek stend′) ***vt.*** ⟦< L *ex-*, out + *tendere*, to stretch⟧ **1** to make longer; stretch out; prolong **2** to enlarge in area, scope, etc.; expand **3** to stretch forth **4** to offer; grant **5** to make (oneself) work very hard —***vi.*** to be extended —**ex·tend′ed *adj.*** —**ex·tend′er *n.*** —**ex·ten′si·ble** (-sten′sə bəl) or **ex·tend′i·ble *adj.***

extended care nursing care for a limited time after hospitalization

extended family a nuclear family together with other relatives living with them or nearby

ex·ten′sion (-sten′shən) ***n.*** **1** an extending or being extended **2** range; extent **3** a part forming a continuation or addition **4** an extra telephone connected to the main line

ex·ten′sive (-siv) ***adj.*** having great extent; vast; far-reaching; comprehensive —**ex·ten′sive·ly *adv.*** —**ex·ten′sive·ness *n.***

ex·tent (ek stent′) ***n.*** **1** the space, amount, or degree to which a thing extends; size **2** scope; limits **3** an extended space; vast area

ex·ten·u·ate (ek sten′yo͞o āt′) ***vt.* -at′ed, -at′ing** ⟦< L *ex-*, out + *tenuis*, thin⟧ to make (an offense, etc.) seem less serious —**ex·ten′u·a′tion *n.***

ex·te·ri·or (ek stir′ē ər) ***adj.*** ⟦see EXTERNAL⟧ **1** *a)* on the outside; outer *b)* to be used on the outside *[exterior* paint*]* **2** coming from without —***n.*** an outside or outside surface

ex·ter·mi·nate (ek stur′mə nāt′) ***vt.* -nat′ed, -nat′ing** ⟦< L *ex-*, out + *terminus*, boundary⟧ to destroy entirely; wipe out —**ex·ter′mi·na′tion *n.***

ex·ter′mi·na′tor (-nāt′ər) ***n.*** one that exterminates; specif., one whose work is exterminating vermin

ex·ter·nal (ek stur′nəl) ***adj.*** ⟦< L *externus*⟧ **1** on or of the outside **2** existing apart from the mind; material **3** coming from without **4** superficial **5** foreign —***n.*** an outside surface or part —**ex·ter′nal·ly *adv.***

ex·tinct (ek stiŋkt′) ***adj.*** ⟦see EXTINGUISH⟧ **1** having died down; extinguished **2** no longer in existence

ex·tinc′tion *n.* **1** an extinguishing **2** a destroying or being destroyed **3** a dying out: said as of a species

ex·tin·guish (ek stiŋ′gwish) ***vt.*** ⟦< L *ex-*, out + *stinguere*, extinguish⟧ **1** to put out (a fire, etc.) **2** to destroy —**ex·tin′guish·er *n.***

ex·tir·pate (eks′tər pāt′) ***vt.* -pat′ed, -pat′ing** ⟦< L *ex-*, out + *stirps*, root⟧ to destroy completely —**ex′tir·pa′tion *n.***

ex·tol or **ex·toll** (ek stōl′) ***vt.* -tolled′, -tol′ling** ⟦< L *ex-*, up + *tollere*, to raise⟧ to praise highly; laud

ex·tort (ek stôrt′) ***vt.*** ⟦< L *ex-*, out + *torquere*, to twist⟧ to get (money, etc.) from someone by force or threats

ex·tor′tion *n.* **1** an extorting **2** something extorted —**ex·tor′tion·ate *adj.*** —**ex·tor′tion·ist** or **ex·tor′tion·er *n.***

ex·tra (eks′trə) ***adj.*** ⟦< L *extra*, more than⟧ more or better than normal, expected, etc.; additional or superior —***n.***

THESAURUS

express *a.* **1** [Explicit] definite, specific, exact; see DEFINITE 1. **2** [Nonstop] fast, direct, high-speed; see FAST 1.

express *v.* declare, tell, signify; see UTTER.

expression *n.* **1** [Significant appearance] look, cast, character; see LOOKS. **2** [Putting into understandable form] representation, art product, interpretation, invention, narration, creation, utterance, declaration, commentary, diagnosis, definition, explanation, illustration; see also COMPOSITION, WRITING 1. **3** [A traditional form of speech] locution, idiom, speech pattern; see PHRASE, WORD 1. **4** [Facial cast] grimace, smile, smirk, sneer, pout, grin; see also SMILE.

expressionless *a.* wooden, dull, vacuous; see BLANK.

expressive *a.* eloquent, demonstrative, revealing, indicative, representative, dramatic, stirring, sympathetic, articulate, touching, significant, meaningful, pathetic, spirited, emphatic, strong, forcible, energetic, lively, tender, passionate, warm, colorful, vivid, picturesque, brilliant, stimulating.—*Ant.* INDIFFERENT, impassive, dead.

expulsion *n.* ejection, suspension, purge; see REMOVAL.

exquisite *a.* fine, scrupulous, precise; see DAINTY.

extemporaneous *a.* spontaneous, impromptu, unprepared; see AUTOMATIC, IMMEDIATE, IMMEDIATELY.

extend *v.* **1** [To make larger] lengthen, enlarge, prolong; see INCREASE. **2** [To occupy space to a given point] continue, go as far as, spread; see REACH 1.

extended *a.* **1** [Outspread] spread, widespread, expansive; see WIDESPREAD. **2** [Very long] elongated, drawn-out, lengthened; see LONG 1.

extending *a.* reaching, continuing, continual, perpetual, ranging, stretching, spreading, spanning, going on, running to, drawn out to, lengthening; see also ENDLESS.

extension *n.* section, branch, extra time; see ADDITION 2.

extensive *a.* wide, broad, long; see LARGE 1.

extensively *a.* widely, broadly, greatly; see WIDELY.

extent *n.* degree, limit, span, space, area, measure, size, bulk, length, compass, scope, reach, sweep, wideness, width, range, amount, expanse, magnitude, intensity; see also EXPANSE.

exterior *a.* outer, outlying, outermost; see OUTSIDE.

exterior *n.* surface, covering, visible portion; see OUTSIDE 1.

exterminate *v.* annihilate, eradicate, abolish; see DESTROY.

external *a.* surface, visible, outside; see OBVIOUS 1.

extinct *a.* dead, ended, terminated, exterminated, deceased, lost, unknown, no longer known.

extinction *n.* abolition, extermination, extirpation; see DESTRUCTION 1, MURDER.

extinguish *v.* smother, choke, quench, douse, put out, snuff out, drown out, blow out, stifle, suffocate.

extort *v.* extract, wrench, force; see STEAL.

extortion *n.* fraud, stealing, blackmail; see THEFT.

extortionist *n.* thief, blackmailer, oppressor; see CRIMINAL.

extra *a.* additional, in addition, other, one more, spare, reserve, supplemental, increased, another, new, auxiliary, added, adjunct, besides, also, further, more, beyond, over and above, plus, supplementary, accessory, unused.—*Ant.* LESS, short, subtracted.

an extra person or thing; specif., *a*) a special edition of a newspaper *b*) an extra benefit *c*) an actor hired by the day to play a minor part —***adv.*** more than usually; esp., exceptionally

extra- ⟦see EXTERNAL⟧ *prefix* outside, beyond, besides

ex·tract (ek strakt′; *for n.* eks′trakt′) ***vt.*** ⟦< L *ex-*, out + *trahere*, to draw⟧ **1** to draw out by effort **2** to obtain by pressing, distilling, etc. **3** to deduce, derive, or elicit **4** to select or quote (a passage, etc.) —***n.*** something extracted; specif., *a*) a concentrate *[*beef *extract] b*) an excerpt

ex·trac′tion ***n.*** **1** the act or process of extracting **2** origin; descent

ex·tra·cur·ric·u·lar (eks′trə kə rik′yoo lər) ***adj.*** not part of the required curriculum

ex·tra·dite (eks′trə dīt′) ***vt.*** **-dit′ed, -dit′ing** ⟦< L *ex*, out + *traditio*, a surrender⟧ to turn over (an alleged criminal, etc.) to the jurisdiction of another country, U.S. state, etc. —**ex′tra·di′tion** (-dish′ən) ***n.***

ex·tra·le·gal (eks′trə lē′gəl) ***adj.*** outside of legal control

ex′tra·mar′i·tal (-mar′ət′l) ***adj.*** having to do with sexual intercourse with someone other that one's spouse

ex·tra·ne·ous (ek strā′nē əs) ***adj.*** ⟦L *extraneus*, foreign⟧ **1** coming from outside; foreign **2** not pertinent; irrelevant —**ex·tra′ne·ous·ly** ***adv.***

ex·tra·or·di·nar·y (ek strôrd′′n er′ē) ***adj.*** ⟦< L *extra ordinem*, out of order⟧ **1** not ordinary **2** going far beyond the ordinary; unusual; remarkable

ex·trap·o·late (ek strap′ə lāt′) ***vt., vi.*** **-lat′ed, -lat′ing** ⟦see EXTRA- & INTERPOLATE⟧ to estimate (something unknown) on the basis of known facts —**ex·trap′o·la′tion** ***n.***

ex·tra·sen·so·ry (eks′trə sen′sə rē) ***adj.*** apart from, or in addition to, normal sense perception

ex′tra·ter·res′tri·al (-tə res′trē əl) ***adj.*** being, of, or from outside the earth's limits —***n.*** an extraterrestrial being, as in science fiction

ex·trav·a·gant (ek strav′ə gənt) ***adj.*** ⟦< L *extra*, beyond + *vagari*, to wander⟧ **1** going beyond reasonable limits; excessive **2** costing or spending too much; wasteful —**ex·trav′a·gance** ***n.***

ex·trav·a·gan·za (ek strav′ə gan′zə) ***n.*** ⟦< It *estravaganza*, extravagance⟧ a spectacular theatrical production

ex·treme (ek strēm′) ***adj.*** ⟦< L *exterus*, outer⟧ **1** farthest away; utmost **2** *a*) very great *b*) excessive **3** unconventional or radical, as in politics **4** harsh; drastic —***n.*** **1** either of two things that are as different or far as possible from each other **2** an extreme act, state, etc. **3** *Math.* the first or last term of a proportion —**ex·treme′ly** ***adv.*** —**ex·treme′ness** ***n.***

ex·trem′ism ***n.*** a going to extremes, esp. in politics —**ex·trem′ist** ***adj., n.***

ex·trem·i·ty (ek strem′ə tē) ***n., pl.*** **-ties** **1** the outermost part; end **2** the greatest degree **3** great need, danger, etc. **4** an extreme measure: *usually used in pl.* **5** [*pl.*] the hands and feet

ex·tri·cate (eks′tri kāt′) ***vt.*** **-cat′ed, -cat′ing** ⟦< L *ex-*, out + *tricae*, vexations⟧ to set free (*from* a net, difficulty, etc.) —**ex′tri·ca′tion** ***n.***

ex·trin·sic (eks trin′sik, -zik) ***adj.*** ⟦< L *exter*, without + *secus*, otherwise⟧ not inherent —**ex·trin′si·cal·ly** ***adv.***

ex·tro·vert (eks′trə vurt′) ***n.*** ⟦< L *extra-*, outside + *vertere*, to turn⟧ one who is active and expressive rather than introspective —**ex′tro·ver′sion** (-vur′zhən) ***n.*** —**ex′tro·vert′ed** ***adj.***

ex·trude (ek strood′) ***vt.*** **-trud′ed, -trud′ing** ⟦< L *ex-*, out + *trudere*, to thrust⟧ to force out, as through a small opening —***vi.*** to be extruded —**ex·tru′sion** ***n.***

ex·u·ber·ant (eg zoo′bər ənt) ***adj.*** ⟦< L *ex-*, intens. + *uberare*, bear abundantly⟧ **1** growing profusely; luxuriant **2** characterized by good health and high spirits —**ex·u′ber·ance** ***n.*** —**ex·u′ber·ant·ly** ***adv.***

ex·ude (eg zood′) ***vt., vi.*** **-ud′ed, -ud′ing** ⟦< L *ex-*, out + *sudare*, to sweat⟧ **1** to ooze **2** to seem to radiate *[*to *exude* joy*]* —**ex·u·da·tion** (eks′yoo dā′shən, egz′-) ***n.***

ex·ult (eg zult′) ***vi.*** ⟦< L *ex-*, intens. + *saltare*, to leap⟧ to rejoice greatly; glory —**ex·ult′ant** ***adj.*** —**ex·ul·ta·tion** (eg′zəl tā′shən, eks′əl-) ***n.***

ex·ur·bi·a (eks ur′bē ə) ***n.*** ⟦EX- + (SUB)URBIA⟧ the semi-rural communities beyond the suburbs, typically lived in by upper-income families —**ex·ur′ban** ***adj.*** —**ex·ur′ban·ite′** ***adj., n.***

eye (ī) ***n.*** ⟦OE *eage*⟧ **1** the organ of sight in humans and animals **2** *a*) the eyeball *b*) the iris *[*brown *eyes]* **3** the area around the eye *[*a black *eye]* **4** [*often pl.*] sight; vision **5** a look; glance **6** attention; observation **7** the power of judging, etc. by eyesight *[*a good *eye* for detail*]* **8** [*often pl.*] judgment; opinion *[*in the *eyes* of the law*]* **9** a thing like an eye in appearance or function —***vt.*** **eyed, eye′ing** or **ey′ing** to look at; observe —**have an eye for** to have a keen appreciation of —**keep an eye on** to look after —**lay** (or **set** or **clap**) **eyes on** to look at —**make eyes at** to look at amorously —**see eye to eye** to agree completely —**with an eye to** paying attention to; considering

eye′ball′ ***n.*** the ball-shaped part of the eye —***vt.*** [Inf.] to examine or measure visually

eye′brow′ ***n.*** the bony arch over each eye, or the hair growing on this

eye′-catch′er ***n.*** something that especially attracts one's attention —**eye′-catch′ing** ***adj.***

eye′drops′ ***pl.n.*** liquid medicine for the eyes, applied as with a dropper

eye′ful′ (-fool′) ***n.*** [Slang] a person or thing that looks striking or unusual

eye′glass′ ***n.*** **1** a lens to help faulty vision **2** [*pl.*] a pair of such lenses in a frame; glasses

eye′lash′ ***n.*** any of the hairs on the edge of the eyelid

eye′let (-lit) ***n.*** **1** a small hole for receiving a cord, hook, etc. **2** a metal ring for reinforcing such a hole **3** a small hole edged by stitching in embroidery

THESAURUS

extract ***n.*** distillation, infusion, concentration; see ESSENCE 1.

extract ***v.*** evoke, derive, secure; see OBTAIN 1.

extradite ***v.*** obtain, apprehend, bring to justice; see ARREST.

extraordinarily ***a.*** remarkably, notably, peculiarly; see VERY.

extraordinary ***a.*** remarkable, curious, amazing; see UNUSUAL 1.

extravagance ***n.*** lavishness, improvidence, conspicuous consumption; see WASTE 1.

extravagant ***a.*** lavish, prodigal, immoderate; see WASTEFUL.

extravagantly ***a.*** expensively, beyond one's means, without restraint; see RASHLY, WASTEFULLY.

extreme ***a.*** radical, intemperate, immoderate, imprudent, excessive, inordinate, extravagant, flagrant, outrageous, unreasonable, irrational, improper, preposterous, thorough, far, fanatical, desperate, severe, intense, drastic, sheer, total, advanced, violent, sharp, acute, unseemly, beyond control, fantastic, to the extreme, exaggerated, monstrous, absurd, foolish.—*Ant.* RESTRAINED, cautious, moderate.

extreme ***n.*** height, apogee, apex; see END 4, LIMIT 2. —**go to extremes** be excessive, overreact, act rashly; see EXCEED. —**in the extreme** extremely, to the highest degree, inordinately; see MUCH.

extremely ***a.*** greatly, remarkably, notably; see MUCH.

extremist ***n.*** zealot, fanatic, die-hard; see RADICAL.

exuberance ***n.*** fervor, eagerness, exhilaration; see ZEAL.

exuberant ***a.*** ardent, vivacious, passionate; see ZEALOUS.

eye ***n.*** **1** [The organ of sight] instrument of vision, eyeball, compound eye, simple eye, naked eye, optic, orb, peeper*, lamp*. *Parts of the eye include the following:* eyeball, pupil, retina, iris, cornea, eye muscles, optic nerve, white, lens, conjunctiva, aqueous humor, vitreous humor. **2** [Appreciation] perception, taste, discrimination; see TASTE 1, 3. **3** [A center] focus, core, heart; see CENTER 1. —**private eye*** detective, investigator, gumshoe*; see POLICE OFFICER. —**all eyes*** attentive, aware, perceptive; see OBSERVANT. —**an eye for an eye** punishment, retaliation, vengeance; see REVENGE 1. —**catch one's eye** attract one's attention, cause notice, stand out; see FASCINATE. —**easy on the eyes*** attractive, appealing, pleasant to look at; see BEAUTIFUL. —**give someone the eye*** attract, charm, invite; see SEDUCE. —**have an eye for** appreciate, be interested in, desire; see WANT 1. —**have an eye to** watch out for, be mindful of, attend to; see WATCH OUT. —**have eyes for*** appreciate, be interested in, desire; see WANT 1. —**in a pig's eye*** under no circumstances, impossible, no way; see NEVER. —**in the public eye** well-known, renowned, celebrated; see FAMOUS. —**keep an eye on** look after, watch over, protect; see GUARD. —**keep an eye out for** watch for, be mindful of, attend to; see WATCH OUT. —**keep one's eyes open** (or **peeled**) be aware, be watchful, look out; see WATCH. —**lay eyes on** look at, stare, survey; see SEE 1. —**make eyes at** attract, charm, invite; see SEDUCE. —**open someone's eyes** make aware, inform, apprise; see TELL 1. —**shut one's eyes to** refuse, reject, ignore; see REFUSE. —**with an eye to** considering, mindful of, aware of; see OBSERVANT.

eye′lid′ ***n.*** either of the two folds of flesh that cover and uncover the eyeball

eye′-o′pen·er (-ō′pə nər) ***n.*** a surprising piece of news, sudden realization, etc. —**eye′-o′pen·ing** ***adj.***

eye′piece′ ***n.*** in a telescope, microscope, etc., the lens or lenses nearest the viewer's eye

eye′sight′ ***n.*** **1** the power of seeing; sight **2** the range of vision

eye′sore′ ***n.*** an unpleasant sight

eye′strain′ ***n.*** a tired or strained condition of the eye muscles

eye′tooth′ ***n.***, *pl.* **-teeth′** a canine tooth of the upper jaw

eye′wear′ ***n.*** eyeglasses, sunglasses, etc.

eye′wit′ness ***n.*** one who sees or has seen something happen, as an accident, etc.

ey·rie or **ey·ry** (er′ē, ir′ē) ***n.***, *pl.* **-ries** AERIE

THESAURUS

eyesight ***n.*** vision, sense of seeing, visual perception; see SIGHT 1.

eyesore ***n.*** ugly thing, distortion, blot; see UGLINESS.

eyewitness ***n.*** onlooker, passerby, observer; see WITNESS.

F

f[1] or **F** (ef) ***n.***, *pl.* **f's, F's** the sixth letter of the English alphabet
f[2] *abbrev.* ⟦It⟧ *Music* FORTE[2]
F[1] (ef) ***n.*** **1** *Educ.* a grade for failing work or, sometimes, fair or average work **2** *Music* the fourth tone in the scale of C major
F[2] *abbrev.* **1** Fahrenheit **2** female or feminine **3** folio(s) **4** following **5** franc(s) **6** Friday
F[3] *Chem. symbol for* fluorine
fa (fä) ***n.*** ⟦< ML⟧ *Music* the fourth tone of the diatonic scale
FAA *abbrev.* Federal Aviation Administration
fa·ble (fā′bəl) ***n.*** ⟦< L *fabula*, a story⟧ **1** a fictitious story, usually about animals, meant to teach a moral lesson **2** a myth or legend **3** a falsehood
fa′bled ***adj.*** **1** mythical; legendary **2** unreal; fictitious
fab·ric (fab′rik) ***n.*** ⟦< L *fabrica*, workshop⟧ **1** a framework; structure **2** a material, as cloth, made from fibers, etc. by weaving, felting, etc.
fab·ri·cate (fab′ri kāt′) ***vt.*** **-cat′ed, -cat′ing** ⟦see prec.⟧ **1** to make, build, construct, etc.; manufacture **2** to make up (a story, lie, etc.); invent —**fab′ri·ca′tion** ***n.*** —**fab′ri·ca′tor** ***n.***
fab·u·lous (fab′yoo ləs) ***adj.*** ⟦see FABLE⟧ **1** of or like a fable; fictitious **2** incredible; astounding **3** [Inf.] wonderful —**fab′u·lous·ly** ***adv.***
fa·cade or **fa·çade** (fə säd′) ***n.*** ⟦Fr: see fol.⟧ **1** the front or main face of a building **2** an imposing appearance concealing something inferior
face (fās) ***n.*** ⟦< L *facies*⟧ **1** the front of the head **2** the expression of the countenance **3** the main or front surface **4** the surface that is marked, as of a clock, etc., or that is finished, as of fabric, etc. **5** the appearance; outward aspect **6** dignity; self-respect: usually in **lose** (or **save**) **face** —***vt.*** **faced, fac′ing** **1** to turn, or have the face turned, toward **2** to confront with boldness, etc. **3** to cover with a new surface —***vi.*** to turn, or have the face turned, in a specified direction —**face to face** **1** confronting each other **2** very near to: with *with* —**face up to** to face with courage —**in the face of** **1** in the presence of **2** in spite of —**make a face** to grimace —**on the face of it** apparently
-faced (fāst) *combining form* having a (specified kind of) face *[round-faced]*
face′less ***adj.*** without individuality; anonymous
face′-lift′ ***n.*** **1** plastic surgery to remove wrinkles, etc. from the face **2** an altering, cleaning, etc., as of a building's exterior Also **face lift** —***vt.*** to perform a face-lift on
face′-off′ ***n.*** **1** *Hockey* the start or resumption of play when the referee drops the puck between two opposing players **2** [Inf.] a confrontation
face′-sav′ing ***adj.*** preserving one's dignity or self-respect
fac·et (fas′it) ***n.*** ⟦see FACE⟧ **1** any of the polished plane surfaces of a cut gem **2** any of a number of sides or aspects, as of a personality —***vt.*** **-et·ed** or **-et·ted, -et·ing** or **-et·ting** to cut or make facets on
fa·ce·tious (fə sē′shəs) ***adj.*** ⟦< L *facetus*, witty⟧ joking, esp. at an inappropriate time —**fa·ce′tious·ly** ***adv.***
face value **1** the value printed on a bill, bond, etc. **2** the seeming value
fa·cial (fā′shəl) ***adj.*** of or for the face —***n.*** a cosmetic treatment, massage, etc. for the skin of the face
facial tissue a sheet of soft tissue paper used as a handkerchief, etc.
fac·ile (fas′il) ***adj.*** ⟦Fr < L *facere*, do⟧ **1** not hard to do **2** working or done easily **3** superficial
fa·cil·i·tate (fə sil′ə tāt′) ***vt.*** **-tat′ed, -tat′ing** ⟦see prec.⟧ to make easy or easier —**fa·cil′i·ta′tion** ***n.*** —**fa·cil′i·ta′tor** ***n.***
fa·cil′i·ty (-tē) ***n.***, *pl.* **-ties** **1** ease of doing **2** skill; dexterity **3** [*usually pl.*] the means by which something can be done **4** a building, room, etc. for some activity
fac·ing (fās′iŋ) ***n.*** **1** a lining on the edge of a garment **2** a covering of contrasting material on a building
fac·sim·i·le (fak sim′ə lē) ***n.*** ⟦< L *facere*, make + *simile*, like⟧ an exact reproduction or copy
fact (fakt) ***n.*** ⟦< L *facere*, do⟧ **1** a deed, esp. a criminal deed *[an accessory before (or after) the fact]* **2** a thing that has actually happened or is really true **3** reality; truth **4** something stated to be true —**as a matter of fact** in reality: also **in fact**
fac·tion (fak′shən) ***n.*** ⟦see prec.⟧ **1** a group of people in an organization working in a common cause against the main body **2** dissension —**fac′tion·al** ***adj.*** —**fac′tion·al·ism′** ***n.***
fac′tious (-shəs) ***adj.*** causing dissension or faction
fac·ti·tious (fak tish′əs) ***adj.*** ⟦see FACT⟧ forced or artificial
fac·toid (fak′toid) ***n.*** ⟦FACT + -OID⟧ a trivial or useless fact or statistic
fac·tor (fak′tər) ***n.*** ⟦< L *facere*, do⟧ **1** one who transacts business for another **2** any of the conditions, etc. that bring about a result **3** *Math.* any of the quantities which form a product when multiplied together —***vt.*** *Math.* to resolve into factors —**factor in** (or **into**) to include as a factor
fac·to·ry (fak′tə rē; *often* fak′trē) ***n.***, *pl.* **-ries** ⟦see prec.⟧ a building or buildings in which things are manufactured
fac·to·tum (fak tōt′əm) ***n.*** ⟦< L *facere*, do + *totum*, all⟧ a handyman

THESAURUS

fable ***n.*** allegory, tale, parable; see STORY.
fabled ***a.*** mythical, fanciful, unreal; see LEGENDARY.
fabric ***n.*** textile, cloth, material; see GOODS.
fabricate ***v.*** **1** [To construct] erect, make, form; see BUILD, MANUFACTURE. **2** [To misrepresent] make up, contrive, prevaricate; see LIE 1.
fabulous ***a.*** remarkable, amazing, immense; see UNUSUAL 1.
facade ***n.*** face, appearance, look; see FRONT 3.
face ***n.*** **1** [The front of the head] visage, countenance, appearance, features, silhouette, profile, front, mug*. **2** [An outer or front surface] front, surface, finish; see PLANE 1. **3** [Prestige] status, standing, social position; see REPUTATION 2. —**face to face** eye to eye, cheek by jowl, facing; see OPPOSITE 3. —**make a face** distort one's face, grimace, scowl; see FROWN. —**on the face of it** to all appearances, seemingly, according to the evidence; see APPARENTLY. —**pull** (or **wear**) **a long face** look sad, scowl, pout; see FROWN. —**show one's face** be seen, show up, come; see APPEAR 1. —**to one's face** candidly, openly, frankly; see BOLDLY 1.
face ***v.*** **1** [To confront conflict or trouble] confront, oppose, defy, meet, dare, brave, challenge, withstand, encounter, risk, tolerate, endure, sustain, suffer, bear, tell to someone's face, make a stand, meet face to face, cope with, allow, stand, submit, abide, go up against, swallow, stomach, take, take it.—*Ant.* EVADE, elude, shun. **2** [To put a face on a building] refinish, front, redecorate; see COVER 1, PAINT 2. **3** [To look out on] front, border, be turned toward; see LIE 2.
facet ***n.*** aspect, face, side; see PLANE 1.
facetious ***a.*** humorous, whimsical, ridiculous; see FUNNY 1.
facile ***a.*** simple, obvious, apparent; see EASY 2.
facilitate ***v.*** promote, aid, make easy; see HELP.
facility ***n.*** **1** [Material means; *usually plural*] tools, plant, buildings; see EQUIPMENT. **2** [Administrative agency] department, bureau, agency; see OFFICE 3.
facsimile ***n.*** duplicate, reproduction, likeness; see COPY.
fact ***n.*** **1** [A reliable generality] certainty, truth, appearance, experience, matter, the very thing, not an illusion, what has really happened, something concrete, what is the case, matter of fact, hard evidence, actuality, naked truth, gospel, reality, law, basis, state of being, hard facts*.—*Ant.* FANCY, fiction, imagination. **2** [An individual reality] circumstance, detail, factor, case, evidence, event, action, deed, happening, occurrence, creation, conception, manifestation, being, entity, experience, affair, episode, performance, proceeding, phenomenon, incident, thing done, act, plain fact, accomplishment, accomplished fact, *fait accompli* (French).—*Ant.* error, illusion, untruth. —**in** (or **as a matter of**) **fact** in reality, in fact, actually; see REALLY 1.
faction ***n.*** cabal, combine, party, conspiracy, plot, gang, crew, wing, block, junta, clique, splinter group, set, clan, club, lobby, camp, inner circle, sect, coterie, partnership, cell, unit, mob, side, machine, band, team, knot, circle, concern, guild, schism, outfit, crowd*, bunch*.
factor ***n.*** portion, constituent, determinant; see PART 1, 3.
factory ***n.*** manufactory, plant, shop, industry, workshop, machine shop, mill, laboratory, assembly plant, foundry, forge, loom, mint, carpenter shop, brewery, sawmill, supply house, processing plant, works, workroom, firm, packing plant.

fac·tu·al (fak′cho͞o əl) ***adj.*** **1** of or containing facts **2** real; actual

fac·ul·ty (fak′əl tē) ***n.***, *pl.* **-ties** ⟦see FACILE⟧ **1** any natural or specialized power of a living organism **2** special aptitude or skill **3** all the teachers of a school or of one of its departments

fad (fad) ***n.*** ⟦< Brit dial.⟧ a style, etc. that interests many people for a short time; passing fashion —**fad′dish** ***adj.***

fade (fād) ***vi.*** **fad′ed**, **fad′ing** ⟦< OFr *fade*, pale⟧ **1** to lose color, brilliance, etc. **2** to lose freshness or strength **3** to disappear slowly; die out —***vt.*** to cause to fade —**fade in** (or **out**) *Film, Radio, TV* to appear (or disappear) gradually

fa·er·ie or **fa·er·y** (fā′ər ē, fer′ē) ***n.*** [Archaic] **1** fairyland **2** *pl.* **-ies** a fairy

fag (fag) ***vi.***, ***vt.*** **fagged**, **fag′ging** ⟦< ?⟧ to make or become very tired by hard work

fag·ot or **fag·got** (fag′ət) ***n.*** ⟦ult. < Gr *phakelos*, a bundle⟧ a bundle of sticks or twigs, esp. for use as fuel

fag·ot·ing or **fag·got·ing** (fag′ət iŋ) ***n.*** **1** a hemstitch with wide spaces **2** openwork with crisscross or barlike stitches across the open seam

Fahr·en·heit (fer′ən hīt′) ***adj.*** ⟦after G. D. *Fahrenheit* (1686-1736), Ger physicist⟧ designating or of a thermometer on which 32° is the freezing point and 212° is the boiling point of water

fail (fāl) ***vi.*** ⟦< L *fallere*, deceive⟧ **1** to be insufficient; fall short **2** to weaken; die away **3** to stop operating **4** to be negligent in a duty, expectation, etc. **5** to be unsuccessful **6** to become bankrupt **7** *Educ.* to get a grade of failure —***vt.*** **1** to be of no help to; disappoint **2** to leave; abandon **3** to neglect: used with an infinitive **4** *Educ.* to give a grade of failure to or get such a grade in —**without fail** without failing (to occur, do, etc.)

fail′ing ***n.*** **1** a failure **2** a fault —***prep.*** without; lacking

faille (fīl, fāl) ***n.*** ⟦Fr⟧ a soft, ribbed fabric of silk or rayon

fail′-safe′ ***adj.*** of an intricate procedure for preventing a malfunction or accidental operation, as of nuclear weapons

fail·ure (fāl′yər) ***n.*** **1** *a)* a falling short *b)* a weakening *c)* a breakdown in operation *d)* neglect *e)* a not succeeding *f)* a becoming bankrupt **2** one that does not succeed **3** *Educ.* a failing to pass, or a grade showing this

fain (fān) ***adj.***, ***adv.*** ⟦< OE *fægen*, glad⟧ [Archaic] glad(ly); willing(ly)

faint (fānt) ***adj.*** ⟦see FEIGN⟧ **1** weak; feeble **2** timid **3** feeling weak and dizzy **4** dim; indistinct —***n.*** a state of temporary unconsciousness —***vi.*** to fall into a faint —**faint′ly** ***adv.*** —**faint′ness** ***n.***

fair[1] (fer) ***adj.*** ⟦< OE *fæger*⟧ **1** attractive; beautiful **2** unblemished; clean **3** blond *[fair hair]* **4** clear and sunny **5** easy to read *[a fair hand]* **6** just and honest **7** according to the rules **8** moderately large **9** average *[in fair condition]* **10** *Baseball* that is not foul —***adv.*** in a fair manner —**fair′ness** ***n.***

fair[2] (fer) ***n.*** ⟦< L *feriae*, festivals⟧ **1** [Historical] a regular gathering for barter and sale of goods **2** a carnival or bazaar, often for charity **3** a competitive exhibition of farm, household, and manufactured products, with various amusements and educational displays **4** a show or convention with exhibits, vendors, etc. *[a science fair]*

Fair·banks (fer′baŋks′) city in EC Alaska: pop. 31,000

fair game a legitimate object of attack or pursuit

fair′-haired′ ***adj.*** **1** having blond hair **2** [Inf.] favorite

fair′ly ***adv.*** **1** justly; honestly **2** somewhat; moderately

fair shake [Inf.] fair or just treatment

fair′way′ ***n.*** the mowed part of a golf course between a tee and a green

THESAURUS

factual ***a.*** exact, specific, true; see ACCURATE 1.

faculty ***n.*** **1** [A peculiar aptitude] ability, strength, forte; see ABILITY. **2** [A group of specialists, usually engaged in instruction or research] staff, teachers, research workers, personnel, instructors, university, college, institute, teaching staff, research staff, teaching assistants, professoriate, society, body, organization, mentors, professors, assistant professors, associate professors, docents, tutors, foundation, department, pedagogues, lecturers, advisors, masters, scholars, fellows, profs*.

fad ***n.*** fancy, style, craze, fashion, humor, prank, quirk, kink, eccentricity, popular innovation, vogue, fantasy, whimsy, passing fancy, latest word, all the rage, the latest thing, the last word*; see also FASHION 2.—*Ant.* CUSTOM, convention, practice.

fade ***v.*** **1** [To lose color or light] bleach, tone down, wash out, blanch, tarnish, dim, discolor, pale, grow dim, neutralize, become dull, lose brightness, lose luster, lose color.—*Ant.* COLOR, brighten, glow. **2** [To diminish in sound] hush, quiet, sink; see DECREASE 1.

faded ***a.*** used, washed-out, shopworn; see DULL 2.

fail ***v.*** **1** [To be unsuccessful] fall short, miss, back out, abandon, desert, neglect, slip, lose ground, come to naught, come to nothing, falter, flounder, blunder, break down, get into trouble, abort, fault*, come down, fall flat, go amiss, go astray, fall down, get left, be found lacking, go down, go under, not hold a candle to, fold up, go on the rocks*, not have it in one, miss the boat*, not measure up, lose out, give out, fall short of, not make the grade*, miss the mark, lose control, fall down on the job*, go wrong, be out of it*, blow it*, fizzle out*, hit rock bottom, go up in smoke, bomb*, not get to first base*, get hung up*, get bogged down*, flunk out*, flop*, conk out*, peter out*.—*Ant.* WIN, succeed, triumph. **2** [To prove unsatisfactory] lose out, come short of, displease; see DISAPPOINT. **3** [To grow less] lessen, worsen, sink; see DECREASE 1. **4** [To become insolvent] go bankrupt, go out of business, go broke*; see sense 1. —**without fail** constantly, dependably, reliably; see REGULARLY.

failing ***a.*** declining, feeble, faint; see WEAK 1.

failure ***n.*** **1** [An unsuccessful attempt] fiasco, misadventure, abortion, bankruptcy, miscarriage, frustration, misstep, faux pas, breakdown, checkmate, stoppage, collapse, defeat, overthrow, downfall, total loss, stalemate, flop*, bust*, dud*, washout*, sinking ship*, mess.—*Ant.* SUCCESS, accomplishment, triumph. **2** [An unsuccessful person] incompetent, underachiever, bankrupt, derelict, dropout, loser*, lemon*, bum*, dud*.—*Ant.* SUCCESS, winner, star.

faint ***a.*** **1** [Having little physical strength] shaky, faltering, dizzy; see WEAK 1. **2** [Having little light or color] vague, thin, hazy; see DULL 2. **3** [Having little volume of sound] whispered, breathless, murmuring, inaudible, indistinct, low, stifled, dull, hoarse, soft, heard in the distance, quiet, low-pitched, muffled, hushed, distant, subdued, gentle, softened, from afar, deep, rumbling, far-off, out of earshot.—*Ant.* LOUD, audible, raucous.

faint ***v.*** lose consciousness, become unconscious, fall, go into a coma, drop, collapse, succumb, pass out, go out like a light*, keel over*, black out.—*Ant.* RECOVER, awaken, come to.

fair[1] ***a.*** **1** [Just] forthright, impartial, plain, scrupulous, upright, candid, generous, frank, open, sincere, straightforward, honest, lawful, clean, legitimate, decent, honorable, virtuous, righteous, temperate, unbiased, reasonable, civil, courteous, blameless, uncorrupted, square, equitable, fair-minded, dispassionate, uncolored, objective, unprejudiced, evenhanded, good, principled, moderate, praiseworthy, aboveboard, trustworthy, due, fit, appropriate, on the level*, on the up-and-up*, fair and square*, straight*.—*Ant.* UNFAIR, unjust, biased. **2** [Moderately satisfactory] average, pretty good, not bad, up to standard, ordinary, mediocre, usual, common, all right, commonplace, fair to middling*, so-so, OK*; see also COMMON 1.—*Ant.* POOR, bad, unsatisfactory. **3** [Not stormy or likely to storm] clear, pleasant, sunny, bright, calm, placid, tranquil, favorable, balmy, mild.—*Ant.* STORMY, threatening, overcast. **4** [Of light complexion] blond, blonde, light-colored, light-complexioned, pale, white, white-skinned, flaxen, fair-haired, snow-white, snowy, whitish, light, lily-white, faded, neutral, platinum blonde, peroxide blonde, bleached blond*, pale-faced, white as a sheet, white as a ghost.—*Ant.* DARK, brunet, black.

fair[2] ***n.*** exposition, county fair, state fair, world's fair, carnival, bazaar, exhibition, display, festival, market, exchange, centennial, observance, celebration.

fairly ***a.*** **1** [In a just manner] honestly, reasonably, honorably; see JUSTLY 1. **2** [A qualifying word] somewhat, moderately, reasonably; see ADEQUATELY.

fairness ***n.*** decency, honesty, uprightness, truth, integrity, charity, impartiality, justice, tolerance, honor, moderation, consideration, good faith, decorum, propriety, courtesy, reasonableness, rationality, humanity, equity, justness, goodness, measure for measure, give-and-take, fair-mindedness, open-mindedness, just dealing, good sense, fair treatment, evenhanded justice, due, accuracy, scrupulousness, correctness, virtue, duty, dutifulness, legality, rightfulness, lawfulness, square deal*, fair play, fair shake*.—*Ant.* INJUSTICE, unfairness, partiality.

fair·y (fer′ē) ***n.***, *pl.* **-ies** ⟦< OFr *fée*⟧ a tiny, graceful imaginary being in human form, with magic powers —***adj.*** **1** of fairies **2** graceful; delicate

fair′y·land′ ***n.*** **1** the imaginary land where the fairies live **2** a lovely, enchanting place

fairy tale **1** a story about fairies, magic deeds, etc. **2** an unbelievable or untrue story

fait ac·com·pli (fe tȧ kōn plē′; *E* fāt′ə käm′plē′) ⟦Fr⟧ something done or in effect, making opposition useless

faith (fāth) ***n.*** ⟦< L *fidere*, to trust⟧ **1** unquestioning belief, specif. in God, a religion, etc. **2** a particular religion **3** complete trust or confidence **4** loyalty

faith′ful (-fəl) ***adj.*** **1** loyal **2** conscientious **3** accurate; reliable —**faith′ful·ly** ***adv.*** —**faith′ful·ness** ***n.***

faith′less (-lis) ***adj.*** **1** dishonest or disloyal **2** unreliable —**faith′less·ly** ***adv.*** —**faith′less·ness** ***n.***

fa·ji·ta (fä hē′tä) ***n.*** ⟦AmSp⟧ a dish of grilled strips of beef or chicken, often wrapped in a soft tortilla

fake (fāk) ***vt.***, ***vi.*** **faked**, **fak′ing** ⟦< ?⟧ to make (something) seem real, etc. by deception —***n.*** a fraud; counterfeit —***adj.*** **1** sham; false **2** artificial —**fak′er** ***n.*** —**fak′er·y** ***n.***

fa·kir (fə kir′) ***n.*** ⟦Ar *faqīr*, lit., poor⟧ a Muslim or Hindu itinerant beggar, often one reputed to perform marvels

fa·la·fel (fə läf′əl) ***n.*** ⟦< Ar⟧ a deep-fried patty of ground chickpeas

fal·con (fal′kən, fôl′-, fäl′-) ***n.*** ⟦ult. < L *falx*, sickle⟧ any bird of prey trained to hunt small game —**fal′con·er** ***n.*** —**fal′con·ry** ***n.***

fall (fôl) ***vi.*** **fell**, **fall′en**, **fall′ing** ⟦OE *feallan*⟧ **1** to come down by gravity; drop; descend **2** to come down suddenly from an upright position; tumble or collapse **3** to be wounded or killed in battle **4** to take a downward direction **5** to become lower, less, weaker, etc. **6** to lose power, status, etc. **7** to do wrong; sin **8** to be captured **9** to take on a sad look *[my face fell]* **10** to take place; occur **11** to come by lot, inheritance, etc. **12** to pass into a specified condition *[to fall ill]* **13** to be directed by chance **14** to be divided *(into)* —***n.*** **1** a dropping; descending **2** a coming down suddenly from an upright position **3** a downward direction or slope **4** a becoming lower or less **5** an overthrow; ruin **6** a loss of status, reputation, etc. **7** a yielding to temptation **8** autumn **9** the amount of what has fallen *[a six-inch fall of snow]* **10** the distance that something falls **11** [*usually pl., often with sing. v.*] water falling over a cliff, etc. **12** a long tress of hair, added to a woman's hairdo —***adj.*** of, in, for, or like autumn —**fall back** to withdraw; retreat —**fall for** [Inf.] **1** to fall in love with **2** to be tricked by —**fall in** to line up in formation —**fall off** to become smaller, worse, etc. —**fall on** (or **upon**) to attack —**fall out** **1** to quarrel **2** to leave one's place in a formation —**fall short** to fail to reach, suffice, etc. —**fall through** to fail —**fall to** **1** to begin **2** to start eating

fal·la·cious (fə lā′shəs) ***adj.*** ⟦see fol.⟧ **1** erroneous **2** misleading or deceptive —**fal·la′cious·ly** ***adv.***

fal·la·cy (fal′ə sē) ***n.***, *pl.* **-cies** ⟦< L *fallere*, deceive⟧ **1** a mistaken idea; error **2** a flaw in reasoning

fall·en (fôl′ən) ***adj.*** that fell; dropped, prostrate, ruined, dead, etc.

fall guy [Slang] one put in a position to take the blame, etc. for a scheme that has miscarried

fal·li·ble (fal′ə bəl) ***adj.*** ⟦< L *fallere*, deceive⟧ liable to be mistaken, deceived, or erroneous —**fal′li·bil′i·ty** or **fal′li·ble·ness** ***n.*** —**fal′li·bly** ***adv.***

fall′ing-out′ ***n.*** a quarrel

falling star METEOR (sense 1)

fall′off′ ***n.*** a decline

fal·lo·pi·an tube (fə lō′pē ən) ⟦after G. *Fallopius*, 16th-c. It anatomist⟧ [*also* **F- t-**] either of two tubes that carry ova to the uterus

fall′out′ ***n.*** **1** the descent to earth of radioactive particles, as after a nuclear explosion **2** these particles **3** an incidental consequence

fal·low (fal′ō) ***adj.*** ⟦< OE *fealh*⟧ **1** left unplanted **2** inactive

false (fôls) ***adj.*** **fals′er**, **fals′est** ⟦< L *fallere*, deceive⟧ **1** not true; incorrect; wrong **2** untruthful; lying **3** unfaithful

THESAURUS

fairy ***n.*** spirit, sprite, good fairy, elf, goblin, hobgoblin, nymph, pixie, brownie, gremlin, Puck, fay, dryad, will-o'-the-wisp, mermaid, siren, bogy, genie, imp, enchantress, witch, warlock, banshee, werewolf, ogre, demon, succubus, devil, ghoul, Harpy, poltergeist, troll, gnome, leprechaun, satyr, fiend, Fate, Weird Sister.

fairy tale ***n.*** folk tale, children's story, romance; see STORY.

faith ***n.*** **1** [Complete trust] confidence, trust, credence, credit, assurance, acceptance, troth, dependence, conviction, sureness, fidelity, loyalty, certainty, allegiance, reliance.—*Ant.* DOUBT, suspicion, distrust. **2** [A formal system of beliefs] creed, doctrine, dogma, tenet, revelation, credo, gospel, profession, conviction, canon, principle, church, worship, teaching, theology, denomination, cult, sect. —**bad faith** insincerity, duplicity, infidelity; see DISHONESTY. —**break faith** be disloyal, abandon, fail; see DECEIVE. —**good faith** sincerity, honor, trustworthiness; see HONESTY. —**in faith** indeed, in fact, in reality; see REALLY 1. —**keep faith** be loyal, adhere, follow; see SUPPORT 2.

faithful ***a.*** reliable, genuine, dependable, incorruptible, straight, honest, upright, honorable, scrupulous, firm, sure, unswerving, conscientious, enduring, unchanging, steady, staunch, attached, obedient, steadfast, sincere, resolute, on the level*, devoted, true, dutiful; see also LOYAL.—*Ant.* FALSE, fickle, faithless.

faithfully ***a.*** trustingly, conscientiously, truly; see LOYALLY.

faithfulness ***n.*** trustworthiness, care, duty; see DEVOTION.

fake ***a.*** pretended, fraudulent, bogus; see FALSE 3.

fake ***n.*** deception, counterfeit, sham, copy, cheat, imitation, charlatan, fraud, make-believe, pretense, fabrication, forgery, cheat, humbug, trick, swindle, phony*, gyp*, put-on*, flimflam.—*Ant.* FACT, original, reality.

fake ***v.*** feign, simulate, disguise; see PRETEND 1.

fall ***n.*** **1** [The act of falling] drop, decline, lapse, collapse, breakdown, tumble, spill, downfall, overthrow, defeat, degradation, humiliation, descent, plunge, slump, recession, ebb.—*Ant.* RISE, elevation, ascent. **2** [That which falls] rainfall, snowfall, precipitation; see RAIN 1, SNOW. **3** [The season after summer] autumn, harvest, September, October, November, harvest time. —**ride for a fall** endanger oneself, take chances, act indiscreetly; see RISK.

fall ***v.*** **1** [To pass quickly downward] sink, topple, drop, settle, droop, stumble, trip, plunge, tumble, descend, totter, break down, cave in, make a forced landing, decline, subside, collapse, drop down, pitch, be precipitated, fall down, fall flat, fall in, fold up, keel over, tip over, slip, recede, ebb, diminish, flop.—*Ant.* RISE, ascend, climb. **2** [To be overthrown] submit, yield, surrender, succumb, be destroyed, be taken, bend, defer to, obey, resign, capitulate, back down, fall to pieces, break up.—*Ant.* ENDURE, prevail, resist. —**fall for*** become infatuated with, desire, flip over*; see FALL IN LOVE (WITH) at LOVE. —**fall in** get into line, form ranks, take a place; see LINE UP. —**fall off** decline, lessen, wane; see DECREASE 1. —**fall out** argue, disagree, fight; see QUARREL. —**fall short** fail, be deficient, be lacking; see NEED.

fallacy ***n.*** inconsistency, quibbling, evasion, fallacious reasoning, illogical reasoning, mistake, deceit, deception, subterfuge, inexactness, perversion, bias, prejudice, preconception, ambiguity, paradox, miscalculation, quirk, flaw, irrelevancy, erratum, heresy; see also ERROR.—*Ant.* LAW, theory, reason.

fallible ***a.*** liable to err, faulty, deceptive, frail, imperfect, ignorant, uncertain, erring, unpredictable, unreliable, in question, prone to error, untrustworthy, questionable; see also WRONG 2.

falling ***a.*** dropping, sinking, descending, plunging, slipping, sliding, declining, settling, toppling, tumbling, tottering, diminishing, weakening, decreasing, ebbing, subsiding, collapsing, crumbling, dying.—*Ant.* INCREASING, improving, mounting.

fallow ***a.*** unplowed, unplanted, unproductive; see VACANT 2.

false ***a.*** **1** [*Said of persons*] faithless, treacherous, unfaithful, disloyal, dishonest, lying, foul, hypocritical, double-dealing, malevolent, mean, malicious, deceitful, underhanded, corrupt, wicked, unscrupulous, untrustworthy, dishonorable, two-faced.—*Ant.* FAITHFUL, true, honorable. **2** [*Said of statements or supposed facts*] untrue, spurious, fanciful, lying, untruthful, fictitious, deceptive, fallacious, incorrect, misleading, delusive, imaginary, illusive, erroneous, invalid, inaccurate, deceiving, fraudulent, trumped up.—*Ant.* ACCURATE, correct, established. **3** [*Said of things*] sham, counterfeit, fabricated, manufactured, synthetic, bogus, spurious, make-believe, assumed, unreal, copied, forged, pretended, faked, made-up, simulated, pseudo, hollow, mock, feigned, bastard, alloyed, artificial, contrived, colored, disguised, deceptive, adulterated, so-called, fake, phony*, shoddy, not what it's cracked up to be*.—*Ant.* REAL, genuine, authentic.

4 misleading **5** not real; artificial —*adv.* in a false manner —**false'ly** *adv.* —**false'ness** *n.*
false'hood' *n.* **1** falsity **2** a lie
fal·set·to (fôl set'ō) *n., pl.* **-tos** ⟦It, dim. of *falso*, false⟧ an artificial way of singing in which the voice is much higher pitched than normal
fal·si·fy (fôl'sə fī') *vt.* **-fied', -fy'ing** **1** to misrepresent **2** to alter (a record, etc.) fraudulently —**fal'si·fi·ca'tion** *n.* —**fal'si·fi'er** *n.*
fal'si·ty (-tē) *n.* **1** the quality of being false **2** *pl.* **-ties** a lie
Fal·staff (fôl'staf'), Sir **John** in Shakespeare's plays, a fat, witty, boastful knight
fal·ter (fôl'tər) *vi.* ⟦prob. < ON⟧ **1** to move unsteadily; stumble **2** to stammer **3** to act hesitantly; waver —**fal'ter·ing·ly** *adv.*
fame (fām) *n.* ⟦< L *fama*⟧ **1** reputation, esp. for good **2** the state of being well known —**famed** *adj.*
fa·mil·ial (fə mil'yəl) *adj.* of or common to a family
fa·mil·iar (fə mil'yər) *adj.* ⟦see FAMILY⟧ **1** friendly or intimate **2** too friendly; unduly intimate **3** closely acquainted (*with*) **4** common; ordinary —**fa·mil'iar·ly** *adv.*
fa·mil'i·ar'i·ty (-ē er'ə tē) *n., pl.* **-ties** **1** intimacy **2** informal behavior **3** undue intimacy **4** close acquaintance (*with* something)
fa·mil'iar·ize' (-yər īz') *vt.* **-ized', -iz'ing** **1** to make commonly known **2** to make (another or oneself) fully acquainted —**fa·mil'iar·i·za'tion** *n.*
fam·i·ly (fam'ə lē, fam'lē) *n., pl.* **-lies** ⟦< L *familia*⟧ **1** parents and their children **2** relatives **3** all those descended from a common ancestor; lineage **4** a group of similar or related things —*adj.* suitable for a family; specif., wholesome
family planning the regulation, as by birth control methods, of the size, etc. of a family
family practitioner a doctor specializing in the general medical needs of the family
family room a room in a home set apart for relaxation and recreation
family tree a genealogical chart for a given family
fam·ine (fam'in) *n.* ⟦< L *fames*, hunger⟧ **1** an acute and general shortage of food **2** any acute shortage
fam'ish (-ish) *vt., vi.* ⟦see prec.⟧ to make or be very hungry
fa·mous (fā'məs) *adj.* **1** having fame; renowned **2** [Inf.] excellent; very good
fa'mous·ly *adv.* **1** in a way, statement, etc. that has become famous **2** very well
fan[1] (fan) *n.* ⟦< L *vannus*, basket for winnowing grain⟧ any device used to set up a current of air for ventilating or cooling —*vt.* **fanned, fan'ning** **1** to move (air) as with a fan **2** to direct air toward as with a fan **3** to stir up; excite **4** to strike (a batter) out —*vi. Baseball* to strike out —**fan out** to spread out
fan[2] (fan) *n.* ⟦< FAN(ATIC)⟧ a person enthusiastic about a specified sport, performer, etc.
fa·nat·ic (fə nat'ik) *n.* ⟦< L *fanum*, temple⟧ a fanatic person —*adj.* fanatical —**fa·nat'i·cism'** *n.*
fa·nat'i·cal *adj.* unreasonably enthusiastic; overly zealous —**fa·nat'i·cal·ly** *adv.*
fan·ci·er (fan'sē ər) *n.* a person with a special interest in something, specif. in plant or animal breeding
fan·ci·ful (fan'sə fəl) *adj.* **1** full of fancy; imaginative **2** imaginary; not real —**fan'ci·ful·ly** *adv.*
fan·cy (fan'sē) *n., pl.* **-cies** ⟦contr. < ME *fantasie*, fantasy⟧ **1** imagination when light, playful, etc. **2** a mental image **3** a notion; caprice; whim **4** a liking or fondness —*adj.* **-ci·er, -ci·est** **1** extravagant *[a fancy price]* **2** ornamental; elaborate *[a fancy necktie]* **3** of superior skill or quality —*vt.* **-cied, -cy·ing** **1** to imagine **2** to be fond of **3** to suppose —**fan'ci·ly** *adv.* —**fan'ci·ness** *n.*
fan'cy-free' *adj.* carefree
fan'cy·work' *n.* embroidery, crocheting, and other ornamental needlework
fan·dom (fan'dəm) *n.* fans collectively, as of a sport or entertainer
fan·fare (fan'fer') ⟦Fr, prob. < *fanfaron*, braggart⟧ *n.* **1** a loud flourish of trumpets **2** noisy or showy display
fang (faŋ) *n.* ⟦OE < *fon*, seize⟧ **1** one of the long, pointed teeth of meat-eating mammals **2** one of the long, hollow teeth through which poisonous snakes inject venom
fan·ta·sia (fan tā'zhə) *n.* a musical composition having no fixed form
fan·ta·size (fant'ə sīz') *vt., vi.* **-sized', -siz'ing** to indulge in fantasies or have daydreams (about)
fan·tas·tic (fan tas'tik) *adj.* ⟦see fol.⟧ **1** imaginary; unreal **2** grotesque; odd **3** extravagant **4** incredible —**fan·tas'ti·cal·ly** *adv.*

THESAURUS

falsehood *n.* deception, prevarication, story*; see LIE.
falsely *a.* traitorously, treacherously, deceitfully, foully, faithlessly, behind one's back, disloyally, underhandedly, maliciously, malevolently, unfaithfully, dishonestly, unscrupulously, dishonorably.—*Ant.* TRULY, justly, honorably.
falsify *v.* adulterate, counterfeit, misrepresent; see DECEIVE.
falter *v.* waver, fluctuate, be undecided; see HESITATE.
fame *n.* renown, glory, distinction, eminence, honor, celebrity, esteem, name, estimation, public esteem, credit, note, greatness, dignity, rank, splendor, position, standing, preeminence, superiority, regard, character, station, place, degree, popularity.
familiar *a.* everyday, well-known, customary, frequent, homely, humble, usual, intimate, habitual, accustomed, common, ordinary, informal, unceremonious, plain, simple, matter-of-fact, workaday, prosaic, commonplace, homespun, natural, native, unsophisticated, old hat*, garden-variety.—*Ant.* UNUSUAL, exotic, strange. —**familiar with** well-acquainted with, acquainted with, aware of, informed of, on speaking terms with, having some connections with, cognizant of, attuned to.—*Ant.* UNAWARE, UNKNOWN, unacquainted with.
familiarity *n.* **1** [Acquaintance with people] friendliness, acquaintanceship, fellowship; see FRIENDSHIP. **2** [Acquaintance with things] the feel of, being at home with, comprehension; see AWARENESS, EXPERIENCE.
familiarize (oneself with) *v.* acquaint, accustom, habituate, make the acquaintance of, get acquainted with, gain the friendship of, make friends with, awaken to, come to know, become aware of.
family *n.* kin, folk, clan, relationship, relations, tribe, dynasty, breed, house, kith and kin, blood, blood tie, progeny, offspring, descendants, forebears, heirs, race, ancestry, parents, ancestors, relatives, pedigree, genealogy, descent, parentage, extraction, paternity, inheritance, kinship, lineage, line, one's own flesh and blood, strain, siblings, in-laws, people.
famine *n.* starvation, want, misery; see HUNGER.
famished *a.* starving, hungering, starved; see HUNGRY.
famous *a.* eminent, foremost, famed, preeminent, acclaimed, illustrious, celebrated, noted, conspicuous, prominent, honored, reputable, renowned, recognized, notable, important, well-known, of note, notorious, exalted, remarkable, extraordinary, great, powerful, noble, grand, mighty, imposing, towering, influential, leading, noteworthy, talked of, outstanding, distinguished, excellent, memorable, elevated, in the spotlight, in the limelight.—*Ant.* UNKNOWN, obscure, humble.
fan[1,2] *n.* **1** [An instrument for creating currents of air] ventilator, agitator, blower, forced draft, vane, air conditioner, propeller, electric fan, Japanese fan, windmill. **2** [*Supporter] supporter, enthusiast, devotee; see FOLLOWER.
fanatic *n.* devotee, bigot, enthusiast; see ZEALOT.
fanatical *a.* obsessed, passionate, devoted; see ZEALOUS.
fanaticism *n.* bigotry, intolerance, obsession, prejudice, hatred, superstition, narrow-mindedness, injustice, obstinacy, stubbornness, bias, unfairness, partiality, devotion, violence, immoderation, zeal, willfulness, single-mindedness, infatuation, dogma, arbitrariness, unruliness, enthusiasm, frenzy, passion, rage.—*Ant.* INDIFFERENCE, tolerance, moderation.
fanciful *a.* unreal, incredible, whimsical; see FANTASTIC.
fancy *a.* elegant, embellished, rich, adorned, ostentatious, gaudy, showy, intricate, baroque, lavish; see also ELABORATE, ORNATE.
fancy *n.* **1** [The mind at play] whimsy, frolic, caprice, banter, sport, diversion, whim, notion, quip, prank, wit, buffoonery, fooling, facetiousness, merriment, levity, humor. **2** [The product of a playful mind] whim, notion, impulse; see IDEA. **3** [Inclination] wishes, will, preference; see DESIRE 1.
fang *n.* tusk, prong, venom duct; see TOOTH.
fantastic *a.* whimsical, capricious, extravagant, freakish, strange, odd, queer, quaint, peculiar, outlandish, far-fetched, wonderful, comical, humorous, foreign, exotic, extreme, ludicrous, ridiculous, preposterous, grotesque, absurd, vague, hallucinatory, high-flown, affected, artificial, out of sight*.—*Ant.* COMMON, conventional, routine.

fan·ta·sy (fant′ə sē) ***n.***, *pl.* **-sies** ⟦< Gr *phainein,* to show⟧ **1** imagination or fancy **2** an illusion or reverie **3** fiction portraying highly IMAGINATIVE (sense 2) characters or settings

fan′ta·sy·land′ ***n.*** any imaginary or unreal place

far (fär) ***adj.*** **far′ther, far′thest** ⟦OE *feorr*⟧ **1** distant in space or time **2** more distant *[*the *far* side*]* **3** very different in quality or nature *[far* from poor*]* —***adv.*** **1** very distant in space, time, or degree **2** to or from a distance in time or position **3** very much *[far* better*]* —**as far as** to the distance or degree that —**by far** very much; considerably: also **far and away** —**(in) so far as** to the extent that —**so far** up to this place, time, or degree

far′a·way′ ***adj.*** **1** distant in time, place, etc. **2** dreamy

farce (färs) ***n.*** ⟦Fr < L *farcire,* to stuff⟧ **1** (an) exaggerated comedy based on broadly humorous situations **2** an absurd or ridiculous action, pretense, etc. —**far·ci·cal** (fär′si kəl) ***adj.***

fare (fer) ***vi.*** **fared, far′ing** ⟦< OE *faran,* go⟧ **1** to happen; result **2** to be in a specified condition *[*to *fare* well*]* —***n.*** **1** money paid for transportation **2** a passenger who pays a fare **3** food

Far East EAST ASIA

fare·well (fer wel′; *for adj.* fer′wel′) ***interj.*** goodbye —***n.*** good wishes at parting —***adj.*** parting; final *[*a *farewell* gesture*]*

far-fetched (fär′fecht′) ***adj.*** barely believable; strained; unlikely

far′-flung′ (-fluŋ′) ***adj.*** extending over a wide area

fa·ri·na (fə rē′nə) ***n.*** ⟦< L, meal⟧ flour or meal made from cereal grains, potatoes, etc. and eaten as a cooked cereal

far·i·na·ceous (far′ə nā′shəs) ***adj.*** ⟦see prec.⟧ **1** consisting of or made from flour or meal **2** like meal

farm (färm) ***n.*** ⟦< ML *firma,* fixed payment⟧ **1** a piece of land (with house, barns, etc.) on which crops or animals are raised: orig., such land let out to tenants **2** any place where certain things are raised *[*a fish *farm]* —***vt.*** to cultivate (land) —***vi.*** to work on or operate a farm —**farm out** to send (work) from an office, etc. to workers outside the office

farm′er ***n.*** a person who manages or operates a farm

farm′hand′ ***n.*** a hired farm worker

farm′house′ ***n.*** a house on a farm

farm′ing ***n.*** the business of operating a farm; agriculture

farm′yard′ ***n.*** the yard surrounding or enclosed by farm buildings

far·o (fer′ō) ***n.*** ⟦Fr *pharaon,* pharaoh: from the picture of a Pharaoh on early French faro cards⟧ a gambling game played with cards

far′-off′ ***adj.*** distant; remote

far′-out′ ***adj.*** [Inf.] nonconformist; esp., avant-garde

far·ra·go (fə rā′gō, -rä′-) ***n.***, *pl.* **-goes** ⟦< L *far,* kind of grain⟧ a jumble

far′-reach′ing ***adj.*** having a wide range, extent, influence, or effect

far·ri·er (far′ē ər) ***n.*** ⟦< L *ferrum,* iron⟧ [Chiefly Brit.] a blacksmith

far·row (far′ō) ***n.*** ⟦< OE *fearh,* young pig⟧ a litter of pigs —***vt., vi.*** to give birth to (a litter of pigs)

far·sight·ed (fär′sīt′id; *for 2,* -sīt′əd) ***adj.*** **1** planning ahead; provident: also **far′see′ing** **2** seeing distant objects more clearly than near ones —**far′sight′ed·ness** ***n.***

far·ther (fär′*th*ər) ***adj.*** **1** *compar. of* FAR **2** more distant **3** additional; further —***adv.*** **1** *compar. of* FAR **2** at or to a greater distance **3** to a greater degree; further Cf. FURTHER

far·thest (fär′*th*ist) ***adj.*** **1** *superl. of* FAR **2** most distant —***adv.*** **1** *superl. of* FAR **2** at or to the greatest distance or degree

far·thing (fär′*th*iŋ) ***n.*** ⟦OE *feorthing*⟧ a former British coin worth ¼ penny

fas·ci·nate (fas′ə nāt′) ***vt.*** **-nat′ed, -nat′ing** ⟦< L *fascinum,* a charm⟧ to hold the attention of, as by being very interesting or delightful; charm; captivate —**fas′ci·na′tion** ***n.***

fas·cism (fash′iz′əm) ***n.*** ⟦< It < L *fasces,* rods bound about an ax, ancient Roman symbol of authority⟧ *[sometimes* **F-***]* a system of government characterized by dictatorship, belligerent nationalism and racism, militarism, etc. —**fas′cist** ***n., adj.***

fash·ion (fash′ən) ***n.*** ⟦< L *factio,* a making⟧ **1** the form or shape of a thing **2** way; manner **3** the current style of dress, conduct, etc. —***vt.*** **1** to make; form **2** to fit; accommodate *(to)* —**after** (or **in**) **a fashion** to some extent —**fash′ion·er** ***n.***

fash′ion·a·ble ***adj.*** **1** stylish **2** of or used by people who follow fashion —**fash′ion·a·bly** ***adv.***

THESAURUS

fantasy ***n.*** vision, appearance, illusion, flight, figment, fiction, romance, mirage, nightmare, fairyland.

far ***a.*** **1** [Distant from the speaker] removed, faraway, remote; see DISTANT. **2** [To a considerable degree] extremely, incomparably, notably; see VERY. —**as far as** to the extent that, to the degree that, up to the time that, insofar as. —**by far** very much, considerably, to a great degree; see MUCH 1, VERY. —**few and far between** scarce, sparse, in short supply; see RARE 2. —**(in) so far as** to the extent that, to the degree that, to the point that; see CONSIDERING. —**so far** thus far, until now, up to this point; see NOW 1. —**so far, so good** all right, favorable, going well; see SUCCESSFUL.

farce ***n.*** travesty, burlesque, horseplay; see FUN.

fare ***n.*** **1** [A fee paid, usually for transportation] ticket, charge, passage, passage money, toll, tariff, expenses, transportation, check, token. **2** [Served food] menu, rations, meals; see FOOD.

fare ***v.*** prosper, prove, turn out; see HAPPEN 2.

farewell ***n.*** goodbye, valediction, parting; see DEPARTURE.

far-fetched ***a.*** forced, strained, unbelievable; see FANTASTIC.

farm ***n.*** plantation, ranch, homestead, claim, holding, field, kibbutz, pasture, meadow, grassland, truck farm, estate, land, acres, freehold, cropland, soil, acreage, garden, patch, vegetable garden, orchard, nursery, vineyard.

farm ***v.*** cultivate land, produce crops, cultivate, till, garden, work, run, ranch, crop, graze, homestead, produce, pasture, till the soil. —**farm out** lease, rent, allot; see DISTRIBUTE, RENT 1.

farmer ***n.*** planter, grower, livestock breeder, stockman, tenant farmer, husbandman, cultivator, sower, hydroponist, feeder, agriculturist, rancher, dirt farmer, lessee, homesteader, producer, tiller of the soil, peasant, peon, herdsman, plowman, sharecropper, hired man, cropper, grazer, cattleman, sheepman, harvester, truck gardener, gardener, nurseryman, horticulturist, settler, sodbuster*, farm hand, hired hand.

farming ***n.*** agriculture, tillage, cultivation, husbandry, farm management, soil culture, ranching, sharecropping, homesteading, horticulture, agronomy, grazing, livestock raising, taking up a claim, hydroponics, growing, crop-raising.

farmyard ***n.*** barnyard, yard, farmstead; see FARM.

far-off ***a.*** far, remote, strange; see DISTANT.

farsighted ***a.*** aware, perceptive, sagacious; see INTELLIGENT.

farther ***a.*** at a greater distance, more distant, beyond, further, more remote, remoter, longer.

farthest ***a.*** remotest, ultimate, last; see FURTHEST.

fascinate ***v.*** charm, entrance, captivate, enchant, bewitch, ravish, enrapture, delight, overpower, please, attract, compel, lure, seduce, entice, tempt, draw, engage, excite, stimulate, overwhelm, provoke, arouse, intoxicate, thrill, stir, kindle, absorb, tantalize, win, interest, enthrall, influence, capture, coax, tease, lead on, knock dead*, cast a spell over, catch one's eye, carry away, invite attention.—*Ant.* DISGUST, repel, horrify.

fascinated ***a.*** enchanted, captivated, bewitched, dazzled, attracted, seduced, enraptured, charmed, hypnotized, delighted, infatuated, thrilled, spellbound; see also CHARMED.—*Ant.* DISGUSTED, repelled, disenchanted.

fascinating ***a.*** engaging, attractive, delightful; see CHARMING.

fascination ***n.*** charm, power, enchantment; see ATTRACTION.

fascism ***n.*** dictatorship, totalitarianism, Nazism; see GOVERNMENT 2.—*Ant.* DEMOCRACY, self-government, socialism.

fascist ***n.*** reactionary, Nazi, rightist; see RADICAL.

fashion ***n.*** **1** [The manner of behavior] way, custom, convention, style, vogue, mode, tendency, trend, formality, formula, procedure, practice, device, usage, observance, new look. **2** [Whatever is temporarily in vogue] craze, sport, caprice, whim, hobby, innovation, custom, amusement, eccentricity, rage. —**after** (or **in**) **a fashion** somewhat, to some extent, in a way; see MODERATELY. —**in fashion** stylish, modish, chic; see FASHIONABLE, POPULAR 1.

fashion ***v.*** model, shape, form; see CREATE.

fashionable ***a.*** in fashion, in style, in vogue, being done, well-liked, favored, smart, stylish, chic, hot*, in*, trendy*, up to the minute.

fashioned ***a.*** molded, shaped, intended; see FORMED.

fast[1] (fast) ***adj.*** ⟦OE *fæst*⟧ **1** firm; firmly fastened **2** loyal; devoted **3** nonfading *[fast* colors*]* **4** swift; quick **5** ahead of time *[a fast* watch*]* **6** wild, promiscuous, or reckless **7** [Inf.] glib **8** *Photog.* allowing very short exposure time —***adv.*** **1** firmly; fixedly **2** thoroughly *[fast* asleep*]* **3** rapidly

fast[2] (fast) ***vi.*** ⟦OE *fæstan*⟧ to abstain from all or certain foods —***n.*** **1** a fasting **2** a period of fasting

fas·ten (fas′ən) ***vt.*** ⟦see FAST[1]⟧ **1** to attach; connect **2** to make secure, as by locking, buttoning, etc. **3** to fix (the attention, etc.) *on* something —***vi.*** to become fastened —**fas′ten·er** ***n.***

fas′ten·ing ***n.*** anything used to fasten; bolt, clasp, hook, etc.

fast′-food′ ***adj.*** designating a business that offers food, as hamburgers, prepared and served quickly

fast forward **1** the setting on a VCR, etc. that allows the user to advance the tape or disc rapidly **2** the act or condition of speeding up and advancing —**fast′-for′ward** ***vi., vt.***

fas·tid·i·ous (fa stid′ē əs) ***adj.*** ⟦< L *fastus*, disdain⟧ **1** not easy to please **2** daintily refined; oversensitive —**fas·tid′i·ous·ly** ***adv.*** —**fas·tid′i·ous·ness** ***n.***

fast′ness ***n.*** **1** a being fast **2** a stronghold

fast′-talk′ ***vt.*** [Inf.] to persuade with smooth, but often deceitful talk

fat (fat) ***adj.*** **fat′ter, fat′test** ⟦< OE *fætt*⟧ **1** containing fat; oily **2** *a)* fleshy; plump *b)* too plump **3** thick; broad **4** fertile *[fat* land*]* **5** profitable *[a fat* job*]* **6** plentiful —***n.*** **1** an oily or greasy material found in animal tissue and plant seeds **2** the richest part of anything **3** superfluous part —**chew the fat** [Slang] to chat —**fat′ly** ***adv.*** —**fat′ness** ***n.***

fa·tal (fāt′'l) ***adj.*** **1** fateful; decisive **2** resulting in death **3** destructive; disastrous —**fa′tal·ly** ***adv.***

fa′tal·ism′ ***n.*** the belief that all events are determined by fate and are hence inevitable —**fa′tal·ist** ***n.*** —**fa′tal·is′tic** ***adj.*** —**fa′tal·is′ti·cal·ly** ***adv.***

fa·tal·i·ty (fā tal′ə tē, fə-) ***n.***, *pl.* **-ties** **1** a deadly effect; deadliness **2** a death caused by a disaster or accident

fat′back′ ***n.*** fat from a hog's back, usually dried and salted in strips

fat cat [Slang] a wealthy, influential donor, esp. to a political campaign

fate (fāt) ***n.*** ⟦< L *fatum*, oracle⟧ **1** the power supposed to determine the outcome of events; destiny **2** one's lot or fortune **3** final outcome **4** death; destruction

fat·ed (fāt′id) ***adj.*** **1** destined **2** doomed

fate′ful (-fəl) ***adj.*** **1** prophetic **2** significant; decisive **3** controlled as if by fate —**fate′ful·ly** ***adv.***

Fates (fāts) ***pl.n.*** *Gr. & Rom. Myth.* the three goddesses who control human destiny and life

fa·ther (fä′*th*ər) ***n.*** ⟦OE *fæder*⟧ **1** a male parent **2** an ancestor **3** an originator, founder, or inventor **4** [*often* **F-**] a Christian priest: used esp. as a title **5** [**F-**] God —***vt.*** to be the father of —**fa′ther·hood′** ***n.*** —**fa′ther·less** ***adj.***

fa′ther-in-law′ ***n.***, *pl.* **fa′thers-in-law′** the father of one's spouse

fa′ther·land′ ***n.*** one's native land

fa′ther·ly ***adj.*** of or like a father; kind, protective, etc. —**fa′ther·li·ness** ***n.***

fath·om (fa*th*′əm) ***n.*** ⟦< OE *fæthm*, the two arms outstretched⟧ a length of 6 feet, used as a nautical unit of depth or length —***vt.*** **1** to measure the depth of **2** to understand thoroughly —**fath′om·a·ble** ***adj.*** —**fath′om·less** ***adj.***

fa·tigue (fə tēg′) ***n.*** ⟦Fr < L *fatigare*, to weary⟧ **1** exhaustion; weariness **2** [*pl.*] soldiers' work clothing **3** the tendency of a metal, etc. to crack under continued stress —***vt., vi.*** **-tigued′**, **-tigu′ing** to tire out

fat·so (fat′sō) ***n.***, *pl.* **-sos** or **-soes** [Slang] a fat person

fat·ten (fat′'n) ***vt., vi.*** to make or become fat (in various senses)

fat′ty ***adj.*** **-ti·er, -ti·est** **1** of or containing fat **2** like fat; greasy

fatty acid any of a group of organic acids in animal or vegetable fats and oils

fat·u·ous (fach′o͞o əs) ***adj.*** ⟦L *fatuus*⟧ complacently stupid; foolish —**fa·tu·i·ty** (fə to͞o′ə tē) ***n.*** —**fat′u·ous·ly** ***adv.*** —**fat′u·ous·ness** ***n.***

fau·cet (fô′sit) ***n.*** ⟦prob. < OFr *faulser*, to breach⟧ a device with a valve for regulating the flow of a liquid from a pipe, etc.; tap

Faulk·ner (fôk′nər), **Wil·liam** (wil′yəm) 1897-1962; U.S. novelist

fault (fôlt) ***n.*** ⟦< L *fallere*, deceive⟧ **1** something that mars; defect or failing **2** a misdeed or mistake **3** blame for something wrong **4** a fracture in rock strata **5** *Tennis, etc.* an improper serve —**at fault** deserving blame —**find fault** (**with**) to criticize

fault′find′ing ***n., adj.*** criticizing

fault′less ***adj.*** perfect

fault′y ***adj.*** **fault′i·er, fault′i·est** having a fault or faults; defective —**fault′i·ly** ***adv.*** —**fault′i·ness** ***n.***

THESAURUS

fast[1] ***a.*** **1** [Rapid] swift, fleet, quick, speedy, brisk, accelerated, hasty, nimble, active, electric, agile, ready, quick as lightning, like a flash, racing, like a bat out of hell*, like a house afire*.—*Ant.* SLOW, sluggish, tardy. **2** [Firmly fixed] secure, attached, immovable; see FIRM 1.

fast[2] ***n.*** abstinence, day of fasting, Lent; see ABSTINENCE.

fast[2] ***v.*** not eat, go hungry, observe a fast; see ABSTAIN.

fasten ***v.*** lock, fix, tie, lace, close, bind, tighten, make firm, attach, secure, anchor, grip, zip up, hold, screw up, screw down, clasp, clamp, pin, nail, tack, bolt, rivet, set, weld, cement, glue, hold fast, make secure, make fast, cinch, catch, buckle, bolt, bar, seal up.—*Ant.* RELEASE, loosen, unfasten.

fastened ***a.*** locked, fixed, tied; see TIGHT 2.

fastener ***n.*** buckle, hook, hasp, lock, clamp, tie, stud, vise, grappling iron, clasp, snap, bolt, bar, lace, cinch, pin, safety pin, nail, rivet, tack, thumbtack, screw, dowel, binder, binding, button, padlock, catch, bond, band, mooring, rope, cable, anchor, chain, harness, strap, thong, girdle, latch, staple, zipper.

fastening ***n.*** catch, clasp, hook; see FASTENER.

fat ***a.*** portly, stout, obese, corpulent, fleshy, potbellied, beefy, brawny, solid, plumpish, plump, burly, bulky, unwieldy, heavy, husky, puffy, on the heavy side, in need of reducing, swollen, inflated, ponderous, lumpish, fat as a pig, tubby.—*Ant.* THIN, lean, skinny.

fat ***n.*** blubber, lard, oil; see GREASE. —**chew the fat*** chat, gossip, confer; see TALK 1.

fatal ***a.*** inevitable, mortal, lethal; see DEADLY.

fatality ***n.*** casualty, dying, accident; see DEATH.

fate ***n.*** fortune, destiny, luck; see DOOM.

fated ***a.*** condemned, destined, elected; see DOOMED.

fateful ***a.*** **1** [Momentous] portentous, critical, decisive; see CRUCIAL 0. **2** [Fatal] destructive, ruinous, lethal; see DEADLY.

father ***n.*** **1** [A male parent] sire, progenitor, procreator, forebear, ancestor, head of the household, papa, dad*, daddy*, pa*, the old man*, pappy*, pop*. **2** [An originator] founder, inventor, promoter; see AUTHOR. **3** [A priest, especially a Catholic priest] pastor, clergyman, parson; see PRIEST.

Father ***n.*** Supreme Being, Creator, Author; see GOD 1.

father-in-law ***n.*** spouse's father, parent, in-law*; see RELATIVE.

fatherland ***n.*** mother country, homeland, native land; see NATION 1.

fatherly ***a.*** paternal, patriarchal, benevolent; see KIND.

fatigue ***n.*** weariness, lassitude, exhaustion, weakness, feebleness, faintness, battle fatigue, nervous exhaustion, dullness, heaviness, listlessness, tiredness.

fatness ***n.*** plumpness, obesity, weight, flesh, heaviness, grossness, corpulence, bulkiness, girth, breadth, largeness, protuberance, flabbiness, chubbiness, portliness, fleshiness, stoutness, heftiness*.

fatten ***v.*** feed, stuff, prepare for market, plump, cram, fill, round out.—*Ant.* STARVE, reduce, constrict.

fatty ***a.*** greasy, blubbery, containing fat; see OILY 1.

faucet ***n.*** tap, fixture, petcock, drain, spigot, plumbing, hot-water faucet, cold-water faucet.

fault ***n.*** **1** [A moral delinquency] misdemeanor, weakness, offense, wrongdoing, transgression, crime, sin, impropriety, juvenile delinquency, misconduct, malpractice, failing; see also MISTAKE. **2** [An error] blunder, mistake, misdeed; see ERROR. **3** [Responsibility] liability, accountability, blame; see RESPONSIBILITY 2. —**at fault** culpable, blamable, in the wrong; see GUILTY. —**find fault** (**with**) complain about, carp at, criticize; see BLAME.

faulty ***a.*** imperfect, flawed, blemished, deficient, distorted, weak, tainted, leaky, defective, damaged, unsound, spotted, cracked, warped, injured, broken, wounded, hurt, impaired, worn, battered, frail, crude, botched, insufficient, inadequate, incomplete, out of order, below par, incorrect, unfit; see also UNSATISFACTORY.—*Ant.* WHOLE, perfect, com-

faun (fôn) ***n.*** ⟦< L *faunus*⟧ any of a class of minor Roman deities, half man and half goat

fau·na (fô′nə) ***n.*** ⟦< LL *Fauna*, Roman goddess⟧ the animals of a specified region or time

Faust (foust) ***n.*** a man in legend and literature who sells his soul to the devil for knowledge and power —**Faus′ti·an** ***adj.***

faux pas (fō pä′) *pl.* **faux pas** (fō päz′) ⟦Fr, lit., false step⟧ a social blunder

fa·vor (fā′vər) ***n.*** ⟦< L *favere*, to favor⟧ **1** friendly regard; approval **2** partiality **3** a kind or obliging act **4** a small gift or token —***vt.*** **1** to approve or like **2** to be partial to **3** to support; advocate **4** to make easier; help **5** to do a kindness for **6** to resemble *[to favor one's mother]* **7** to use gently *[to favor a sore leg]* Brit. sp. **fa′vour** —**in favor of** **1** approving **2** to the advantage of —**fa′vor·er** ***n.***

fa′vor·a·ble ***adj.*** **1** approving **2** helpful **3** pleasing —**fa′vor·a·bly** ***adv.***

fa·vor·ite (fā′vər it) ***n.*** **1** a person or thing regarded with special liking **2** a contestant regarded as most likely to win —***adj.*** highly regarded; preferred

fa′vor·it·ism′ ***n.*** partiality; bias

fawn[1] (fôn) ***vi.*** ⟦< OE *fægen*, glad⟧ **1** to show friendliness by licking hands, etc.: said of a dog **2** to try to gain favor by acting humble, flattering, etc. —**fawn′er** ***n.*** —**fawn′ing·ly** ***adv.***

fawn[2] (fôn) ***n.*** ⟦< L *fetus*, progeny⟧ **1** a deer less than one year old **2** a pale, yellowish brown —***adj.*** of this color

fax (faks) ***n.*** ⟦< FACSIMILE⟧ **1** the electronic sending (as over a telephone line) and reproduction of pictures, print, etc. **2** a reproduction made in this way —***vt.*** to send by fax

fay (fā) ***n.*** ⟦see FATE⟧ a fairy

faze (fāz) ***vt.*** **fazed**, **faz′ing** ⟦< OE *fesian*, to drive⟧ to disturb; disconcert

FBI *abbrev.* Federal Bureau of Investigation

FCC *abbrev.* Federal Communications Commission

FDA *abbrev.* Food and Drug Administration

FDIC *abbrev.* Federal Deposit Insurance Corporation

Fe ⟦L *ferrum*⟧ *Chem. symbol for* iron

fe·al·ty (fē′əl tē) ***n.***, *pl.* **-ties** ⟦< L *fidelitas*, fidelity⟧ loyalty, esp. as owed to a feudal lord

fear (fir) ***n.*** ⟦< OE *fær*, sudden attack⟧ **1** anxiety caused by real or possible danger, pain, etc.; fright **2** awe; reverence **3** apprehension; concern **4** a cause for fear —***vt.***, ***vi.*** **1** to be afraid (of) **2** to be in awe (of) **3** to expect with misgiving *[I fear it will rain]* —**fear′less** ***adj.*** —**fear′less·ly** ***adv.***

fear′ful (-fəl) ***adj.*** **1** causing, feeling, or showing fear **2** [Inf.] very bad, great, etc. —**fear′ful·ly** ***adv.*** —**fear′ful·ness** ***n.***

fear′some ***adj.*** causing fear; frightful

fea·si·ble (fē′zə bəl) ***adj.*** ⟦< OFr *faire*, to do⟧ **1** capable of being done; possible **2** likely; probable **3** suitable —**fea′si·bil′i·ty** ***n.*** —**fea′si·bly** ***adv.***

feast (fēst) ***n.*** ⟦< L *festus*, festal⟧ **1** a religious festival **2** a rich and elaborate meal; banquet —***vi.*** to have a feast —***vt.*** **1** to entertain at a feast **2** to delight *[to feast one's eyes on a sight]*

feat (fēt) ***n.*** ⟦< L *factum*, a deed⟧ a deed of unusual daring or skill; exploit

feath·er (feth′ər) ***n.*** ⟦OE *fether*⟧ any of the soft, light growths covering the body of a bird —***vt.*** **1** to provide or adorn with feathers **2** to turn (an oar or propeller blade) so that the edge is foremost —**feather in one's cap** a distinctive achievement —**feath′er·y** ***adj.***

feath′er·bed′ding ***n.*** the practice of limiting output or requiring extra, standby workers

feath′er·weight′ ***n.*** **1** a boxer with a maximum weight of 126 pounds **2** any person or thing of light weight or small size

fea·ture (fē′chər) ***n.*** ⟦< L *facere*, to make⟧ **1** *a)* [*pl.*] facial form or appearance *b)* any of the parts of the face **2** a distinct or outstanding part or quality of something **3** a special attraction, sale item, newspaper article, etc. **4** a film running more than 34 minutes —***vt.*** **-tured**, **-tur·ing** to make a feature of —***vi.*** to have a prominent part —**fea′ture·less** ***adj.***

fe·brile (fē′brəl, feb′rəl) ***adj.*** ⟦< L *febris*, FEVER⟧ feverish

Feb·ru·ar·y (feb′roo er′ē, feb′yoo-) ***n.***, *pl.* **-ies** or **-ys** ⟦< L *Februarius* (*mensis*), orig. month of expiation⟧ the second month of the year, having 28 days (or 29 days in leap years): abbrev. **Feb.**

fe·ces (fē′sēz′) ***pl.n.*** ⟦< L *faeces*, dregs⟧ excrement —**fe′cal** (-kəl) ***adj.***

feck·less (fek′lis) ***adj.*** ⟦Scot < *feck*, effect + -LESS⟧ **1** weak; ineffective **2** irresponsible —**feck′less·ly** ***adv.***

fe·cund (fē′kənd, fek′ənd) ***adj.*** ⟦< L *fecundus*⟧ fertile; productive —**fe·cun·di·ty** (fē kun′də tē) ***n.***

fe·cun·date (fē′kən dāt′, fek′ən-) ***vt.*** **-dat′ed**, **-dat′ing** **1** to make fecund **2** to fertilize

fed (fed) ***vt.***, ***vi.*** *pt. & pp. of* FEED —**fed up** [Inf.] having had enough to become disgusted, bored, etc.

Fed *abbrev.* **1** Federal **2** Federation

fed·a·yeen (fed′ä yēn′) ***pl.n.*** ⟦Ar *fidā′iyīn*, sacrificers⟧ Arab guerrillas

THESAURUS

plete.

favor ***n.*** **1** [Preference] help, support, partiality; see ENCOURAGEMENT. **2** [A kindness] service, courtesy, boon; see KINDNESS 2. —**find favor** please, suit, become welcome; see SATISFY 1. —**in favor** liked, esteemed, wanted; see FAVORITE. —**in favor of** approving, endorsing, condoning; see FOR. —**in one's favor** to one's advantage, on one's side, creditable; see FAVORABLE 3.

favor ***v.*** prefer, like, approve, sanction, praise, regard favorably, be in favor of, pick, choose, lean toward, incline toward, value, prize, esteem, think well of, set great store by, look up to, think the world of, be partial to, grant favors to, promote, play favorites, show consideration for, spare, make an exception for, pull strings for; see also PROMOTE 1.—*Ant.* HATE, dislike, disesteem.

favorable ***a.*** **1** [Friendly] well-disposed, kind, well-intentioned; see FRIENDLY. **2** [Displaying suitable or promising qualities] propitious, convenient, beneficial; see HOPEFUL 2. **3** [Commendatory] approving, commending, assenting, complimentary, well-disposed toward, in favor of, agreeable, in one's favor.

favorably ***a.*** approvingly, agreeably, kindly, helpfully, fairly, willingly, heartily, cordially, genially, graciously, courteously, receptively, in an approving manner, positively, without prejudice.—*Ant.* UNFAVORABLY, adversely, discouragingly.

favorite ***a.*** liked, beloved, favored, intimate, to one's taste, to one's liking, choice, pet, desired, wished-for, preferred, adored.—*Ant.* UNPOPULAR, unwanted, unwelcome.

favorite ***n.*** darling, pet, idol, ideal, favored one, mistress, love, favorite son, favorite child, fair-haired boy*, teacher's pet, odds-on favorite, apple of one's eye.

favoritism ***n.*** bias, partiality, inequity; see INCLINATION 1.

fawn[2] ***n.*** baby deer, baby doe, baby buck; see DEER.

faze ***v.*** bother, intimidate, worry; see DISTURB.

fear ***n.*** fright, terror, horror, panic, dread, dismay, awe, scare, revulsion, aversion, tremor, mortal terror, cowardice, timidity, misgiving, trembling, anxiety, phobia, foreboding, despair, agitation, hesitation, worry, concern, suspicion, doubt, qualm, funk*, cold feet*, cold sweat.—*Ant.* COURAGE, intrepidity, dash. —**for fear of** avoiding, lest, in order to prevent, out of apprehension concerning.

fear ***v.*** be afraid, shun, avoid, falter, lose courage, be alarmed, be frightened, be scared, live in terror, dare not, have qualms about, cower, flinch, shrink, quail, cringe, turn pale, tremble, break out in a sweat*.—*Ant.* DARE, outface, withstand.

fearful ***a.*** timid, shy, apprehensive; see COWARDLY.

fearfully ***a.*** apprehensively, shyly, with fear and trembling, for fear of, in fear.

fearless ***a.*** bold, daring, courageous; see BRAVE.

feasible ***a.*** **1** [Suitable] fit, expedient, worthwhile; see CONVENIENT 1. **2** [Likely] probable, practicable, attainable; see LIKELY 1.

feast ***n.*** banquet, entertainment, festival, treat, merrymaking, fiesta, barbecue, picnic; see also DINNER.

feat ***n.*** act, effort, deed; see ACHIEVEMENT.

feather ***n.*** quill, plume, plumage, down, tuft, crest, fringe. —**in fine** (or **high** or **good**) **feather** well, in good humor, in good health; see HAPPY.

feature ***n.*** **1** [Anything calculated to attract interest] innovation, highlight, prominent part, drawing card, main bout, specialty, special attraction, featured attraction. **2** [Matter other than news published in a newspaper] article, editorial, feature story; see STORY. **3** [A salient quality] point, peculiarity, trait; see CHARACTERISTIC.

features ***n.*** lineaments, looks, appearance; see FACE 1.

featuring ***a.*** presenting, showing, recommending, calling attention to, giving prominence to, emphasizing, making much of, pointing up, drawing attention to, turning the spotlight on, centering attention on, starring.

feces ***n.*** excretion, waste, dung; see EXCREMENT.

fed·er·al (fed′ər əl) ***adj.*** ⟦< L *foedus*, a league⟧ **1** designating or of a union of states, etc. in which each member subordinates its power to a central authority **2** *a*) designating or of a central government in such a union *b*) [*often* **F-**] designating or of the central government of the U.S. **3** [**F-**] of or supporting a former U.S. political party (**Federalist Party**) which favored a strong centralized government **4** [**F-**] of or supporting the Union in the Civil War —***n.*** [**F-**] a supporter or soldier of the Union in the Civil War —**fed′er·al·ism′** ***n.*** —**fed′er·al·ist** ***adj.***, ***n.*** —**fed′er·al·ly** ***adv.***

fed′er·al·ize′ (-īz′) ***vt.*** **-ized′**, **-iz′ing** **1** to unite (states, etc.) in a federal union **2** to put under federal authority —**fed′er·al·i·za′tion** ***n.***

fed·er·ate (fed′ər āt′) ***vt.***, ***vi.*** **-at′ed**, **-at′ing** to unite in a federation

fed·er·a·tion (fed′ər ā′shən) ***n.*** ⟦see FEDERAL⟧ **1** a union of states, groups, etc. in which each subordinates its power to that of the central authority **2** a federated organization

fe·do·ra (fə dôr′ə) ***n.*** ⟦Fr⟧ a soft felt hat worn by men

fee (fē) ***n.*** ⟦ult < Gmc⟧ a charge for professional services, licenses, etc.

fee·ble (fē′bəl) ***adj.*** **-bler**, **-blest** ⟦< L *flere*, weep⟧ **1** weak; infirm *[a feeble old man]* **2** without force or effectiveness *[a feeble attempt]* —**fee′ble·ness** ***n.*** —**fee′bly** ***adv.***

feed (fēd) ***vt.*** **fed**, **feed′ing** ⟦< OE *foda*, food⟧ **1** to give food to **2** to provide something necessary for the growth, operation, etc. of **3** to gratify *[to feed one's vanity]* —***vi.*** to eat: said esp. of animals —***n.*** **1** food for animals; fodder **2** *a*) the material fed into a machine *b*) the part of the machine supplying this material **3** *Radio, TV* a transmission sent by a network, etc. to individual stations for broadcast —**feed′er** ***n.***

feed′back′ ***n.*** **1** the transfer of part of the output back to the input, as of electricity or information **2** a response

feed′stock′ ***n.*** raw material for industrial processing

feel (fēl) ***vt.*** **felt**, **feel′ing** ⟦OE *felan*⟧ **1** to touch; examine by handling **2** to be aware of through physical sensation **3** to experience (an emotion or condition); be affected by **4** to be aware of **5** to think or believe —***vi.*** **1** to have physical sensation **2** to appear to be to the senses *[it feels warm]* **3** to grope **4** to be aware of being *[I feel sad]* **5** to be moved to sympathy, pity, etc. (*for*) —***n.*** **1** the act of feeling **2** the sense of touch **3** the nature of a thing as perceived through touch **4** an instinctive ability or appreciation *[a feel for politics]* —**feel like** [Inf.] to have a desire for —**feel one's way** to advance cautiously —**feel out** to try cautiously to find out the opinions of (someone) —**feel up to** [Inf.] to feel capable of

feel′er ***n.*** **1** a specialized organ of touch in an animal or insect, as an antenna **2** a cautious remark, offer, etc. made to learn more about something

feel′ing ***n.*** **1** the sense of touch **2** the ability to experience physical sensation **3** an awareness; sensation **4** an emotion **5** [*pl.*] sensibilities *[hurt feelings]* **6** sympathy; pity **7** an opinion or sentiment

fee simple absolute and unrestricted ownership of real property

feet (fēt) ***n.*** *pl. of* FOOT

feign (fān) ***vt.***, ***vi.*** ⟦< L *fingere*, to shape⟧ **1** to make up (an excuse, etc.) **2** to pretend; dissemble

feint (fānt) ***n.*** ⟦see prec.⟧ a pretended attack intended to take the opponent off guard, as in boxing —***vi.***, ***vt.*** to deliver (such an attack)

feist·y (fīs′tē) ***adj.*** **-i·er**, **-i·est** ⟦< Norw *fisa,* to puff + -Y[2]⟧ [Inf. or Dial.] full of spirit; specif., quarrelsome, lively, spunky, etc. —**feist′i·ly** ***adv.*** —**feist′i·ness** ***n.***

feld·spar (feld′spär′) ***n.*** ⟦< Ger *feld*, field + *spath*, a mineral⟧ any of several hard, glassy minerals

fe·lic·i·tate (fə lis′i tāt′) ***vt.*** **-tat′ed**, **-tat′ing** ⟦< L *felix*, happy⟧ to wish happiness to; congratulate —**fe·lic′i·ta′tion** ***n.*** —**fe·lic′i·ta′tor** ***n.***

fe·lic′i·tous (-təs) ***adj.*** ⟦< fol.⟧ used or expressed in a way suitable to the occasion; appropriate

fe·lic′i·ty (-tē) ***n.***, *pl.* **-ties** ⟦< L *felix*, happy⟧ **1** happiness; bliss **2** anything producing happiness **3** apt and pleasing expression in writing, etc.

fe·line (fē′līn) ***adj.*** ⟦< L *feles*, cat⟧ **1** of a cat or the cat family **2** catlike; sly —***n.*** any animal of the cat family

fell[1] (fel) ***vi.***, ***vt.*** *pt. of* FALL

fell[2] (fel) ***vt.*** ⟦OE *fellan*⟧ **1** to knock down **2** to cut down (a tree)

fell[3] (fel) ***adj.*** ⟦< ML *fello*⟧ fierce; cruel

fel·low (fel′ō, -ə) ***n.*** ⟦Late OE *feolaga*, partner⟧ **1** an associate **2** one of the same rank; equal **3** one of a pair; mate **4** one holding a fellowship in a college, etc. **5** a member of a learned society **6** [Inf.] a man or boy —***adj.*** **1** having the same position, work, etc. **2** associated *[fellow workers]*

fel′low·ship′ ***n.*** **1** companionship **2** a mutual sharing **3** a group of people with the same interests **4** an endowment for the support of a student or scholar doing advanced work

fellow traveler a nonmember who supports the cause of a party

fel·on[1] (fel′ən) ***n.*** ⟦< ML *felo*, villain⟧ a person guilty of a felony; criminal

fel·on[2] (fel′ən) ***n.*** ⟦ME⟧ a painful infection at the end of a finger or toe

fel·o·ny (fel′ə nē) ***n.***, *pl.* **-nies** ⟦< ML *felonia*, treachery⟧ a major crime, as murder, arson, etc. —**fe·lo·ni·ous** (fə lō′nē əs) ***adj.***

felt[1] (felt) ***n.*** ⟦< OE⟧ a fabric of wool, often mixed with fur, hair, cotton, etc., worked together by pressure, etc. —***adj.*** made of felt —***vt.*** to make into felt

felt[2] (felt) ***vt.***, ***vi.*** *pt. and pp. of* FEEL

fem *abbrev.* **1** female **2** feminine

THESAURUS

federal ***a.*** general, central, governmental; see NATIONAL 1.

federation ***n.*** confederacy, alliance, combination; see ORGANIZATION 2.

fee ***n.*** remuneration, salary, charge; see PAY 2.

feeble ***a.*** fragile, puny, strengthless; see WEAK 1, 2.

feed ***n.*** provisions, supplies, fodder, food for animals, pasture, forage, roughage. *Common feeds include the following:* grain, small grain, corn, oats, barley, rye, wheat, peanuts, hay, clover, sweet clover, alfalfa, sorghum, kale, soybeans, beets, straw, grass, bran.

feed ***v.*** feast, give food to, satisfy the hunger of, nourish, supply, support, satisfy, fill, stuff, cram, gorge, banquet, dine, nurse, maintain, fatten, provide food for, cater to, stock, furnish, nurture, sustain, encourage, serve.—*Ant.* STARVE, deprive, quench.

feel ***n.*** touch, quality, air; see FEELING 2.

feel ***v.*** **1** [To examine by touch] finger, explore, stroke, palm, caress, handle, manipulate, press, squeeze, fondle, tickle, paw, feel for, fumble, grope, grasp, grapple, grip, clutch, clasp, run the fingers over, pinch, poke, contact. **2** [To experience] sense, perceive, receive, be aware of, observe, be moved by, respond, know, acknowledge, appreciate, accept, be affected, be impressed, be excited by, have the experience of, take to heart.—*Ant.* IGNORE, be insensitive to, be unaware of. **3** [To believe] consider, hold, know; see THINK 1. **4** [To give an impression through touch] appear, exhibit, suggest; see SEEM.

feeler ***n.*** hint, tentative proposal, trial balloon; see TEST.

feeling ***n.*** **1** [The sense of touch] tactile sensation, tactility, power of perceiving by touch, touch. **2** [State of the body, or of a part of it] sense, sensation, sensibility, feel, sensitiveness, sensory response, perception, perceptivity, susceptibility, activity, consciousness, receptivity, responsiveness, excitability, excitement, awareness, enjoyment, sensuality, pain, pleasure, reaction, motor response, reflex, excitation.—*Ant.* INDIFFERENCE, apathy, numbness. **3** [A personal reaction] opinion, thought, outlook; see ATTITUDE. **4** [Sensitivity] taste, emotion, passion, tenderness, discrimination, delicacy, discernment, sentiment, sentimentality, refinement, culture, cultivation, capacity, faculty, judgment, affection, sympathy, imagination, intelligence, intuition, spirit, soul, appreciation, response.—*Ant.* RUDENESS, crudeness, coldness.

feign ***v.*** simulate, imagine, fabricate; see PRETEND 1.

feigned ***a.*** imagined, fictitious, simulated; see IMAGINARY.

fell[2] ***v.*** pull down, knock down, cause to fall; see CUT 1.

fellow ***n.*** **1** [A young man] youth, lad, boy, person, teenager, stripling, novice, cadet, apprentice, adolescent, juvenile, youngster, guy*, kid*, squirt*. **2** [An associate] peer, associate, colleague; see FRIEND.

fellowship ***n.*** **1** [Congenial social feeling] comradeship, conviviality, sociability, intimacy, acquaintance, friendliness, familiarity, good-fellowship, amity, affability, camaraderie, togetherness.—*Ant.* RUDENESS, unsociability, surliness. **2** [Subsistence payment to encourage study] stipend, scholarship, honorarium, subsidy, teaching fellowship, assistantship.

felon[1] ***n.*** outlaw, delinquent, convict; see CRIMINAL.

felony ***n.*** major crime, offense, transgression; see CRIME.

fe·male (fē′māl′) ***adj.*** ⟦< L *femina*, woman⟧ **1** designating or of the sex that bears offspring **2** of, like, or suitable to women or girls; feminine **3** consisting of women or girls **4** having a hollow part for receiving an inserted part (called *male*): said of electric sockets, etc. —***n.*** a female person, animal, or plant

fem·i·nine (fem′ə nin) ***adj.*** ⟦< L *femina*, woman⟧ **1** of women or girls **2** having qualities characteristic of or suitable to women; gentle, delicate, etc. **3** *Gram.* designating or of the gender of words referring to females or other words with no distinction of sex —**fem′i·nin′i·ty** ***n.***

fem′i·nism′ (-niz′əm) ***n.*** the movement to win political, economic, and social equality for women —**fem′i·nist** ***n.***, ***adj.*** —**fem′i·nis′tic** ***adj.***

fe·mur (fē′mər) ***n.***, *pl.* **fe′murs** or **fem·o·ra** (fem′ə rə) ⟦< L, thigh⟧ the bone extending from the hip to the knee —**fem′o·ral** ***adj.***

fen (fen) ***n.*** ⟦OE⟧ an area of low, flat, marshy land; swamp; bog

fence (fens) ***n.*** ⟦< ME *defens*, defense⟧ **1** a protective or confining barrier of posts, wire mesh, etc. **2** one who deals in stolen goods —***vt.*** **fenced, fenc′ing** **1** to enclose, as with a fence: with *in*, *off*, etc. **2** to keep (*out*) as by a fence **3** to sell (stolen property) to a fence —***vi.*** **1** to practice the art of fencing **2** to avoid giving a direct reply —**on the fence** uncommitted or undecided —**fenc′er** ***n.***

fenc′ing ***n.*** **1** the art of fighting with a foil or other sword **2** material for making fences **3** a system of fences

fend (fend) ***vt.*** ⟦ME *fenden*, defend⟧ to turn aside; ward (*off*) —***vi.*** —**fend for oneself** to manage by oneself

fend′er ***n.*** anything that fends off or protects something else, as the part of an automobile body over the wheel

fen·nel (fen′əl) ***n.*** ⟦< L *fenum*, hay⟧ a tall herb with aromatic seeds used to flavor foods and medicines

fe·ral (fir′əl, fer′-) ***adj.*** ⟦< L *ferus*, wild⟧ **1** untamed; wild **2** savage; fierce

fer·ment (fʉr′ment′; *for v.* fər ment′) ***n.*** ⟦< L *fervere*, to boil⟧ **1** a substance causing fermentation, as yeast **2** excitement or agitation —***vt.*** **1** to cause fermentation in **2** to excite; agitate —***vi.*** **1** to be in the process of fermentation **2** to be excited or agitated; seethe

fer·men·ta·tion (fʉr′mən tā′shən) ***n.*** **1** the breakdown of complex molecules in organic compounds, caused by the influence of a ferment *[bacteria cause milk to curdle by fermentation]* **2** excitement; agitation

fer·mi·on (fer′mē än′, fʉr′-) ***n.*** ⟦after E. *Fermi*, 20th-c. U.S. nuclear physicist⟧ any of a major subdivision of subatomic particles, including leptons and baryons

fern (fʉrn) ***n.*** ⟦< OE *fearn*⟧ any of a large group of nonflowering plants having roots, stems, and fronds, and reproducing by spores

fe·ro·cious (fə rō′shəs) ***adj.*** ⟦< L *ferus*, wild⟧ **1** fierce; savage; violently cruel **2** [Inf.] very great *[a ferocious appetite]* —**fe·ro′cious·ly** ***adv.*** —**fe·roc·i·ty** (fə räs′ə tē) ***n.***

-fer·ous (fər əs) ⟦< L *ferre*, to bear⟧ *suffix* bearing, yielding

fer·ret (fer′ət) ***n.*** ⟦< L *fur*, thief⟧ a small European polecat, easily tamed for hunting rats, etc. —***vt.*** **1** to force out of hiding with or as if with a ferret **2** to find out by investigation: with *out*

fer·ric (fer′ik) ***adj.*** ⟦< L *ferrum*, iron⟧ of, containing, or derived from iron

Fer·ris wheel (fer′is) ⟦after G. *Ferris* (1859-96), U.S. engineer⟧ a large, upright wheel revolving on a fixed axle and having suspended seats: used as an amusement ride

ferro- ⟦< L *ferrum*, iron⟧ *combining form* **1** iron **2** iron and

fer·rous (fer′əs) ***adj.*** ⟦< L *ferrum*, iron⟧ of, containing, or derived from iron

fer·rule (fer′əl, -o͞ol′) ***n.*** ⟦< L *viriae*, bracelets⟧ a metal ring or cap put around the end of a cane, tool handle, etc. to give added strength

fer·ry (fer′ē) ***vt.*** **-ried, -ry·ing** ⟦OE *ferian*⟧ **1** to take (people, cars, etc.) across a river, etc. **2** to deliver (airplanes) by flying them **3** to transport by airplane —***n.***, *pl.* **-ries** **1** a system for carrying people, goods, etc. across a river, etc. by boat **2** a boat used for this: also **fer′ry·boat′**

fer·tile (fʉrt′'l) ***adj.*** ⟦< L *ferre*, to bear⟧ **1** producing abundantly; fruitful; prolific **2** able to produce young, seeds, fruit, pollen, spores, etc. **3** fertilized *[a fertile egg]* —**fer·til·i·ty** (fər til′ə tē) ***n.***

fer′til·ize′ (-īz′) ***vt.*** **-ized′, -iz′ing** **1** to make fertile **2** to spread fertilizer on **3** to make (the female cell or female) fruitful by pollinating, or impregnating, with the male gamete —**fer′til·iz′a·ble** ***adj.*** —**fer′til·i·za′tion** ***n.***

fer′til·iz′er ***n.*** manure, chemicals, etc., used to enrich the soil

fer·ule (fer′əl, -o͞ol′) ***n.*** ⟦< L *ferula*, a whip, rod⟧ a flat stick or ruler used for punishing children

fer·vent (fʉr′vənt) ***adj.*** ⟦< L *fervere*, to glow⟧ showing great warmth of feeling; intensely devoted or earnest —**fer′ven·cy** ***n.*** —**fer′vent·ly** ***adv.***

fer·vid (fʉr′vid) ***adj.*** ⟦see prec.⟧ impassioned; fervent —**fer′vid·ly** ***adv.***

fer·vor (fʉr′vər) ***n.*** ⟦see FERVENT⟧ great warmth of emotion; ardor; zeal

-fest (fest) ⟦< Ger *fest*, a feast⟧ *combining form* an occasion of much or many *[songfest]*

fes·tal (fes′təl) ***adj.*** ⟦< L *festum*, feast⟧ of or like a joyous celebration; festive

fes·ter (fes′tər) ***n.*** ⟦< L *fistula*, ulcer⟧ a small sore filled with pus —***vi.*** **1** to form pus **2** to grow more bitter, virulent, etc.

fes·ti·val (fes′tə vəl) ***n.*** ⟦see fol.⟧ **1** a time or day of feasting or celebration **2** a celebration or series of performances

fes·tive (fes′tiv) ***adj.*** ⟦< L *festum*, feast⟧ **1** of or for a feast or festival **2** merry; joyous —**fes′tive·ly** ***adv.*** —**fes′tive·ness** ***n.***

fes·tiv·i·ty (fes tiv′ə tē) ***n.***, *pl.* **-ties** **1** merrymaking; gaiety **2** a festival **3** [*pl.*] things done in celebration

THESAURUS

female ***a.*** womanly, sensitive, childbearing, of the female gender.—*Ant.* MALE, masculine, of the male gender.

feminine ***a.*** female, distaff, soft, womanly, delicate, gentle, ladylike, matronly, maidenly, tender, fair; see also WOMANLY.—*Ant.* MALE, masculine, virile.

fence ***n.*** **1** [That which surrounds an enclosure] picket fence, wire fence, board fence, barbed-wire fence, rail fence, chain-link fence, iron fence, hedge, backstop, rail, railing, barricade, net, barrier, wall, dike. **2** [A receiver of stolen goods] accomplice, front*, uncle*; see CRIMINAL. **—mend one's fences** renew contacts, look after one's political interests, solicit votes; see CAMPAIGN. **—on the fence** undecided, uncommitted, indifferent; see UNCERTAIN.

fender ***n.*** guard, mudguard, shield, apron, buffer, mask, cover, frame, protector, bumper.

fend for oneself ***v.*** take care of oneself, stay alive, eke out an existence; see SURVIVE 1.

fend off ***v.*** keep off, ward off, repel; see DEFEND 1.

ferment ***v.*** effervesce, sour, foam, froth, bubble, seethe, fizz, sparkle, boil, work, ripen, dissolve, evaporate, rise.

fermentation ***n.*** souring, foaming, seething; see FROTH.

fern ***n.*** greenery, bracken, lacy plant; see PLANT.

ferocious ***a.*** fierce, savage, wild; see FIERCE.—*Ant.* GENTLE, meek, mild.

ferocity ***n.*** fierceness, brutality, barbarity; see CRUELTY.

ferry ***n.*** boat, barge, packet; see BOAT.

fertile ***a.*** fruitful, rich, productive, fat, teeming, yielding, arable, flowering.—*Ant.* STERILE, barren, desert.

fertility ***n.*** fecundity, richness, fruitfulness, potency, virility, pregnancy, productiveness, productivity, generative capacity.

fertilization ***n.*** **1** [The enrichment of land] manuring, dressing, mulching; see PREPARATION 1. **2** [Impregnation of the ovum] insemination, impregnation, pollination, implantation, breeding, propagation, generation, procreation.

fertilize ***v.*** **1** [To enrich land] manure, dress, lime, mulch, cover, treat, enrich. **2** [To impregnate] breed, make pregnant, generate, germinate, pollinate, inseminate, propagate, procreate, get with child, beget, knock up*.

fertilizer ***n.*** manure, chemical fertilizer, plant food, compost, humus, mulch. *Common fertilizers include the following:* barnyard manure, guano, sphagnum, peat moss, phosphate, dung, crushed limestone, bone dust, kelp, bone meal, nitrogen, ammonium sulfate, legumes, potash.

fervent ***a.*** zealous, eager, ardent; see ENTHUSIASTIC.

fervor ***n.*** fervency, ardor, enthusiasm; see ZEAL.

fester ***v.*** rankle, putrefy, rot; see SPOIL.

festival ***n.*** festivity, feast, entertainment; see CELEBRATION.

festive ***a.*** merry, gay, joyful; see HAPPY.

festivity ***n.*** revelry, pleasure, amusement; see ENTERTAINMENT.

fes·toon (fes to͞on′) ***n.*** ⟦< It *festa*, feast⟧ a wreath or garland of flowers, etc. hanging in a loop or curve —***vt.*** to adorn with festoons

fet·a (**cheese**) (fet′ə) ⟦< ModGr < It *fetta*, a slice⟧ a soft, white cheese, first made in Greece

fe·tal (fēt′'l) ***adj.*** of a fetus

fetch (fech) ***vt.*** ⟦OE *feccan*⟧ **1** to go after and bring back; get **2** to cause to come **3** to sell for

fetch′ing ***adj.*** attractive; charming

fete or **fête** (fāt, fet) ***n.*** ⟦Fr *fête*: see FEAST⟧ a festival; entertainment, esp. outdoors —***vt.*** **fet′ed** or **fêt′ed**, **fet′ing** or **fêt′ing** to honor with a fete

fet·id (fet′id) ***adj.*** ⟦< L *foetere*, to stink⟧ having a bad smell; stinking; putrid —**fet′id·ness** ***n.***

fet·ish (fet′ish) ***n.*** ⟦< Port *feitiço*⟧ **1** any object believed to have magic power **2** anything to which one is irrationally devoted **3** any nonsexual object that abnormally excites erotic feelings Also **fet′ich** —**fet′ish·ism′** ***n.*** —**fet′ish·ist** ***n.***

fet·lock (fet′läk′) ***n.*** ⟦< ME *fet*, feet⟧ **1** a tuft of hair on the back of a horse's leg above the hoof **2** the joint bearing this tuft

fe·to·scope (fē′tə skōp′) ***n.*** **1** an endoscope used to examine a fetus in the womb **2** a special stethoscope used to listen to the fetal heartbeat

fet·ter (fet′ər) ***n.*** ⟦< OE *fot*, foot⟧ **1** a shackle or chain for the feet **2** any check or restraint —***vt.*** **1** to bind with fetters **2** to restrain

fet·tle (fet′'l) ***n.*** ⟦ME *fetlen*, make ready⟧ condition; state *[in fine fettle]*

fe·tus (fēt′əs) ***n.***, *pl.* **-tus·es** ⟦L, a bringing forth⟧ the unborn young of an animal, esp. in its later stages and specif., in humans, from about the eighth week after conception until birth

feud (fyo͞od) ***n.*** ⟦< OFr *faide*⟧ a deadly quarrel, esp. between clans or families —***vi.*** to carry on a feud; quarrel

feu·dal (fyo͞od′'l) ***adj.*** ⟦ML *feudalis*⟧ of or like feudalism

feu′dal·ism′ ***n.*** the economic, political, and social system in medieval Europe, in which land, worked by serfs, was held by vassals in exchange for military and other services they give to overlords —**feu′dal·is′tic** ***adj.***

fe·ver (fē′vər) ***n.*** ⟦< L *febris*⟧ **1** an abnormally increased body temperature **2** any disease marked by a high fever **3** a restless excitement —**fe′ver·ish** ***adj.*** —**fe′ver·ish·ly** ***adv.***

fever blister (or **sore**) COLD SORE

few (fyo͞o) ***adj.*** ⟦OE *feawe*⟧ not many; a small number of —***pron.*** not many; a small number —**few and far between** scarce; rare —**the few** the minority

fey (fā) ***adj.*** ⟦OE *fæge*, fated⟧ strange or unusual; specif., eccentric, whimsical, etc. —**fey′ness** ***n.***

fez (fez) ***n.***, *pl.* **fez′zes** ⟦after *Fez*, city in Morocco⟧ a red, brimless felt hat, shaped like a truncated cone, worn formerly by Turkish men

ff *abbrev.* **1** folios **2** following (pages, etc.)

fi·an·cé (fē′än sā′) ***n.*** ⟦Fr < OFr *fiance*, a promise⟧ a man who is engaged to be married

fi·an·cée (fē′än sā′) ***n.*** ⟦Fr: see prec.⟧ a woman who is engaged to be married

fi·as·co (fē as′kō) ***n.***, *pl.* **-coes** or **-cos** ⟦Fr < It⟧ a complete, ridiculous failure

fi·at (fē′ät, fī′at′) ***n.*** ⟦L, let it be done⟧ **1** a decree; order **2** a sanction; authorization **3** any arbitrary order

fib (fib) ***n.*** ⟦< ? FABLE⟧ a small or trivial lie —***vi.*** **fibbed**, **fib′bing** to tell such a lie —**fib′ber** ***n.***

fi·ber (fī′bər) ***n.*** ⟦< L *fibra*⟧ **1** a threadlike structure that combines with others to form animal or vegetable tissue **2** any substance that can be separated into threadlike parts for weaving, etc. **3** texture **4** character or nature **5** ROUGHAGE —**fi′brous** (-brəs) ***adj.***

fi′ber·board′ ***n.*** a building material consisting of fibers of wood, etc. pressed into stiff sheets

Fi′ber·glas′ (-glas′) *trademark for* finespun filaments of glass made into textiles, insulating material, or molded plastic —***n.*** this substance

fi′ber·glass′ (-glas′) ***n.*** finespun filaments of glass like Fiberglas

fiber optics **1** the science of transmitting light and images, as around curves, through transparent fibers **2** such fibers —**fi′ber-op′tic** or **fiber optic** ***adj.***

fi·bril·la·tion (fib′ri lā′shən) ***n.*** ⟦< L *fibra*, fiber + -ATION⟧ very rapid contractions of part of the heart muscle, causing irregular heartbeats

fi·brin (fī′brin) ***n.*** a fibrous, insoluble blood protein formed in blood clots

fi·brin·o·gen (fī brin′ə jən) ***n.*** ⟦prec. + -GEN⟧ a protein in the blood from which fibrin is formed

fi·broid (fī′broid′) ***adj.*** like or composed of fibrous tissue: said as of a tumor

fi·bro·sis (fī brō′sis) ***n.*** an excessive growth of fibrous connective tissue in an organ, part, etc.

fib·u·la (fib′yo͞o lə) ***n.***, *pl.* **-lae′** (-lē′) or **-las** ⟦L, a clasp⟧ the long, thin outer bone of the lower leg —**fib′u·lar** ***adj.***

-fic (fik) ⟦< L *facere*, make⟧ *suffix* making *[terrific]*

FICA (fī′kə) *abbrev.* Federal Insurance Contributions Act

-fi·ca·tion (fi kā′shən) ⟦see -FIC⟧ *suffix* a making *[glorification]*

fich·u (fish′o͞o) ***n.*** ⟦Fr⟧ a triangular lace or muslin cape for women, worn tied in front

fick·le (fik′əl) ***adj.*** ⟦< OE *ficol*, tricky⟧ changeable or unstable; capricious

fic·tion (fik′shən) ***n.*** ⟦< L *fingere*, to form⟧ **1** an imaginary statement, story, etc. **2** *a)* literary narratives, collectively, with imaginary characters or events, specif. novels and short stories *b)* a narrative of this kind —**fic′tion·al** ***adj.***

fic′tion·al·ize′ (-shə nəl īz′) ***vt.*** **-ized′**, **-iz′ing** to deal with (historical events) in fictional form —**fic′tion·al·i·za′tion** ***n.***

fic·ti·tious (fik tish′əs) ***adj.*** **1** of or like fiction; imaginary **2** false **3** assumed for disguise *[a fictitious name]*

fic·tive (fik′tiv) ***adj.*** **1** of fiction **2** imaginary —**fic′tive·ly** ***adv.***

fi·cus (fī′kəs) ***n.***, *pl.* **fi′cus** ⟦< L, fig tree⟧ any of a genus of tropical shrubs, trees, etc. with glossy, leathery leaves

fid·dle (fid′'l) [Inf.] ***n.*** ⟦OE *fithele*⟧ a violin —***vi.*** **-dled**, **-dling** **1** to play a fiddle **2** to tinker (*with*) nervously —**fid′dler** ***n.***

fid′dle·sticks′ ***interj.*** nonsense!

fi·del·i·ty (fə del′ə tē) ***n.***, *pl.* **-ties** ⟦< L *fides*, faith⟧ **1** faithful devotion to duty; loyalty **2** accuracy of description, sound reproduction, etc.

fidg·et (fij′it) ***n.*** ⟦< ME < ?⟧ a restless or nervous state: esp. in phrase **the fidgets** —***vi.*** to move about restlessly or nervously —**fidg′et·y** ***adj.***

fi·du·ci·ar·y (fi do͞o′shē er′ē) ***adj.*** ⟦< L *fiducia*, trust⟧ holding or held in trust —***n.***, *pl.* **-ies** TRUSTEE (sense 1)

fie (fī) ***interj.*** [Archaic] for shame!

fief (fēf) ***n.*** ⟦Fr: see FEE⟧ in feudalism, heritable land held by a vassal

THESAURUS

fetch ***v.*** bring, get, retrieve; see CARRY 1.

fete ***n.*** festival, entertainment, ball; see CELEBRATION, PARTY 1.

fetish ***n.*** fixation, craze, mania; see OBSESSION.

fetus ***n.*** developing organism, embryo, the young of an animal in the uterus.

feud ***n.*** quarrel, strife, bickering; see FIGHT.

fever ***n.*** abnormal temperature and pulse, febrile disease, high body temperature; see ILLNESS 1.

feverish ***a.*** burning, above normal, running a temperature; see HOT 1.

few ***a.*** not many, scarcely any, less, sparse, scanty, thin, widely spaced, inconsiderable, negligible, infrequent, not too many, some, any, scarce, rare, few and far between.—*Ant.* MANY, numerous, innumerable.

few ***pron.*** not many, a small number, a handful, scarcely any, not too many, several, a scattering, three or four, a sprinkling.—*Ant.* MANY, a multitude, a great many. —**quite a few** several, some, a large number; see MANY.

fiancé ***n.*** intended, betrothed, person engaged to be married; see LOVER.

fib ***n.*** prevarication, fabrication, misrepresentation; see LIE.

fiber ***n.*** thread, cord, string, strand, tissue, filament, vein, hair, strip, shred. *Some common fibers include the following:* vegetable fiber, animal fiber, synthetic fiber, silk, linen, hemp, cotton, wool, jute, rayon, nylon, orlon, polyester, acetate.

fibrous ***a.*** veined, hairy, coarse; see STRINGY.

fickle ***a.*** capricious, whimsical, mercurial; see CHANGING.

fiction ***n.*** novel, tale, romance; see STORY.

fictitious ***a.*** made-up, untrue, counterfeit; see FALSE 1, 2.

fiddle* ***n.*** violin, stringed instrument, cornstalk fiddle*; see MUSICAL INSTRUMENT. —**fit as a fiddle** healthy, strong, sound; see WELL 1. —**play second fiddle** (**to**) defer to, be inferior to, be less successful than; see FAIL 1.

fidelity ***n.*** fealty, constancy, devotion; see LOYALTY.

fidget ***v.*** stir, twitch, worry; see WIGGLE.

fidgety ***a.*** nervous, uneasy, apprehensive; see RESTLESS.

fief'dom (-dəm) ***n.*** **1** FIEF **2** anything under a person's complete control
field (fēld) ***n.*** ⟦OE *feld*⟧ **1** a stretch of open land **2** a piece of cleared land for crops or pasture **3** a piece of land used for a particular purpose *[a landing field]* **4** any wide, unbroken expanse *[a field of ice]* **5** *a)* a battlefield *b)* a battle **6** a realm of knowledge or work **7** the background, as on a flag **8** *a)* an area for athletics or games *b)* all the entrants in a contest **9** *Physics* a physical quantity specified at points throughout a region of space —***vt.*** **1** to stop or catch and throw (a baseball, etc.) **2** to put (a player or team) into active play **3** [Inf.] to answer (a question) extemporaneously —**play the field** to not confine one's activities to one object —**field'er** ***n.***
field day an occasion of extraordinary opportunity or highly successful activity
field glasses a small, portable binocular telescope
field goal **1** *Basketball* a shot, made from play, scoring two points or, if from a certain distance, three points **2** *Football* a goal kicked from the field, scoring three points
field guide a handbook for identifying plants, etc., as while hiking
field hand a hired farm laborer
field hockey HOCKEY (sense 2)
field marshal in some armies, an officer of the highest rank
field'-test' ***vt.*** to test (a device, method, etc.) under operating conditions
fiend (fēnd) ***n.*** ⟦OE *feond*, the one hating⟧ **1** an evil spirit; devil **2** an inhumanly wicked person **3** [Inf.] an addict *[a dope fiend]* —**fiend'ish** ***adj.***
fierce (firs) ***adj.*** **fierc'er, fierc'est** ⟦< L *ferus*, wild⟧ **1** savage **2** violent **3** intense *[a fierce embrace]* —**fierce'ly** ***adv.*** —**fierce'ness** ***n.***
fi·er·y (fī'ər ē) ***adj.*** **-er·i·er, -er·i·est** **1** like fire; glaring, hot, etc. **2** ardent; spirited **3** excitable **4** inflamed
fi·es·ta (fē es'tə) ***n.*** ⟦Sp < L *festus*, festal⟧ **1** a religious festival **2** any gala celebration; holiday
fife (fīf) ***n.*** ⟦Ger *pfeife*⟧ a small flute used mainly with drums in playing marches
fif·teen (fif'tēn') ***adj., n.*** ⟦OE *fiftene*⟧ five more than ten; 15; XV —**fif'teenth'** (-tēnth') ***adj., n., adv.***
fifth (fifth) ***adj.*** ⟦< OE *fif*, five⟧ preceded by four others in a series; 5th —***n.*** **1** the one following the fourth **2** any of the five equal parts of something; $\frac{1}{5}$ **3** a fifth of a gallon —***adv.*** in the fifth place, rank, etc.
Fifth Amendment an amendment to the U.S. Constitution mainly guaranteeing certain protections in criminal cases; specif., the clause protecting persons from being compelled to testify against themselves
fifth column a group of people aiding an enemy from within their own country
fifth wheel a superfluous person or thing
fif·ty (fif'tē) ***adj., n., pl.*** **-ties** ⟦OE *fiftig*⟧ five times ten; 50; L —**the fifties** the numbers or years, as of a century, from 50 through 59 —**fif'ti·eth** (-ith) ***adj., n.***
fif'ty-fif'ty [Inf.] ***adj.*** equal; even —***adv.*** equally
fig[1] (fig) ***n.*** ⟦< L *ficus*⟧ **1** *a)* a small, sweet, pear-shaped fruit that grows on a tree related to the mulberry *b)* the tree **2** a trifle *[not worth a fig]*
fig[2] *abbrev.* **1** figurative(ly) **2** figure(s)
fight (fīt) ***vi.*** **fought, fight'ing** ⟦OE *feohtan*⟧ to take part in a struggle, contest, etc., esp. against a foe or for a cause —***vt.*** **1** to oppose physically or in battle **2** to struggle against **3** to engage in (a war, etc.) **4** to gain (one's way) by struggle —***n.*** **1** any struggle, contest, or quarrel **2** power or readiness to fight
fight'er ***n.*** **1** one that fights **2** a prizefighter **3** a fast, highly maneuverable combat airplane
fig·ment (fig'mənt) ***n.*** ⟦< L *fingere*, to form⟧ something merely imagined
fig·ur·a·tive (fig'yoor ə tiv') ***adj.*** **1** representing by means of a figure or symbol **2** not in its literal sense; metaphorical **3** using figures of speech —**fig'ur·a·tive'ly** ***adv.***
fig·ure (fig'yər) ***n.*** ⟦< L *fingere*, to form⟧ **1** an outline or shape; form **2** the human form **3** a person thought of in a specified way *[a historical figure]* **4** a likeness of a person or thing **5** an illustration; diagram **6** a design; pattern **7** the symbol for a number **8** [*pl.*] arithmetic **9**

THESAURUS

field ***n.*** **1** [Open land] grainfield, hayfield, meadow, pasture, range, acreage, plot, patch, garden, cultivated ground, grassland, green, ranchland, arable land, plowed land, cleared land, cropland, tract, vineyard. **2** [An area devoted to sport] diamond, gridiron, track, rink, court, course, racecourse, golf course, racetrack, arena, stadium, theater, amphitheater, playground, park, turf, green, fairground. **3** [An area devoted to a specialized activity] airfield, airport, flying field, battlefield, battleground, sector, field of fire, terrain, no man's land, theater of war, field of battle, field of honor, parade ground, range. —**play the field** experiment, explore, look elsewhere; see DISCOVER, EXAMINE, TRY 1.

fielder ***n.*** infielder, outfielder, center fielder; see BASEBALL PLAYER.

fiend ***n.*** **1** [A wicked or cruel person] monster, barbarian, brute; see BEAST. **2** [*An addict] fan, aficionado, monomaniac; see ADDICT.

fiendish ***a.*** diabolical, demoniac, infernal; see BAD.

fierce ***a.*** ferocious, wild, furious, enraged, raging, impetuous, untamed, angry, passionate, savage, primitive, brutish, animal, raving, outrageous, terrible, vehement, frightening, awful, horrible, venomous, bold, malevolent, malign, brutal, uncivilized, feral, menacing, fearsome, cruel, hostile, rabid, merciless, monstrous, severe, rough, rude, vicious, dangerous, frenzied, mad, insane, desperate, ravening, frantic, wrathful, irate, fanatical, bestial, boisterous, violent, threatening, stormy, thunderous, howling, tumultuous, turbulent, uncontrolled, storming, blustering, cyclonic, torrential, frightful, fearful, devastating, hellish, rip-roaring*.—*Ant.* MILD, moderate, calm.

fiercely ***a.*** ferociously, violently, wildly, terribly, vehemently, angrily, threateningly, frighteningly, awfully, horribly, mightily, passionately, impetuously, boldly, irresistibly, furiously, riotously, brutally, monstrously, forcibly, forcefully, convulsively, hysterically, severely, roughly, rudely, viciously, dangerously, madly, insanely, desperately, outrageously, savagely, frantically, wrathfully, irately, virulently, relentlessly, turbulently, overpoweringly, strongly, deliriously, fanatically, with rage, in a frenzy, tooth and nail.—*Ant.* PEACEFULLY, mildly, reasonably.

fiesta ***n.*** festival, holiday, feast; see CELEBRATION.

fifty ***a.*** half a hundred, half a century, two score and ten, many, five times ten, a considerable number.

fight ***n.*** **1** [A violent physical struggle] strife, contention, feud, quarrel, contest, encounter, row, dispute, disagreement, battle, confrontation, controversy, brawl, bout, match, fisticuffs, round, fracas, difficulty, altercation, bickering, wrangling, riot, argument, debate, competition, rivalry, conflict, skirmish, clash, scuffle, collision, brush, action, engagement, combat, blow, exchange of blows, wrestling match, squabble, game, discord, estrangement, fuss, tussle, scrap*, free-for-all, ruckus*, run-in*, tiff, flare-up, go*, set-to*, difference of opinion. **2** [Willingness or eagerness to fight] mettle, hardihood, boldness; see COURAGE.

fight ***v.*** strive, war, struggle, resist, assert oneself, challenge, meet, contend, attack, carry on war, withstand, give blow for blow, do battle, war against, persevere, force, go to war, exchange blows, encounter, oppose, tussle, grapple, flare up, engage with, combat, wrestle, box, spar, skirmish, quarrel, bicker, dispute, have it out, squabble, come to grips with, row, light into*, tear into*, mix it up with*.—*Ant.* RETREAT, submit, yield. —**fight back** defend oneself, resist, retaliate; see OPPOSE 2. —**fight off** defend from, hold back, resist; see DEFEND 1.

fighter ***n.*** **1** [One who fights] contestant, disputant, contender, party to a quarrel, warrior, soldier, combatant, belligerent, assailant, aggressor, antagonist, rival, opponent, champion, bully, competitor, controversialist, scrapper*. **2** [A professional pugilist] boxer, prizefighter, pug*, bruiser*.

fighting ***a.*** combative, battling, brawling, unbeatable, argumentative, angry, ferocious, quarrelsome, ready to fight, belligerent, boxing, wrestling, warlike, contending, up in arms.

fighting ***n.*** combat, struggle, strife; see FIGHT.

figurative ***a.*** not literal, metaphorical, allegorical; see ILLUSTRATIVE.

figure ***n.*** **1** [A form] shape, mass, structure; see FORM 1. **2** [The human torso] body, frame, torso, shape, form, configuration, build, appearance, outline, posture, attitude, pose, carriage. **3** [A representation of quantity] sum, total, symbol; see NUMBER. **4** [Price] value, worth, terms; see PRICE.

figure ***v.*** **1** [To compute] reckon, number, count; see CALCULATE. **2** [To estimate] set a figure, guess, fix a price; see ESTIMATE. **3** [*To come to a conclusion] suppose, think, opine; see DECIDE. **4** [To figure out] solve, master, reason; see DISCOVER.

a sum of money **10** *Geom.* a surface or space bounded by lines or planes —***vt.* -ured, -ur·ing 1** to represent in definite form **2** to imagine **3** to ornament with a design **4** to compute with figures **5** [Inf.] to believe; consider —***vi.* 1** to appear prominently **2** to do arithmetic —**figure in** to include —**figure on** to rely on —**figure out 1** to solve **2** to understand —**figure up** to add; total

fig′ure·head′ ***n.* 1** a carved figure on the bow of a ship **2** one put in a position of leadership, but having no real power or authority

figure of speech an expression, as a metaphor or simile, using words in a nonliteral sense or unusual way

figure skating ice skating with emphasis on tracing patterns on the ice or, now, performing leaps and spins —**figure skater**

fig·u·rine (fig′yoo rēn′) ***n.*** ⟦Fr⟧ a small sculptured or molded figure

Fi·ji (fē′jē) country on a group of islands (**Fiji Islands**) in the SW Pacific: 7,078 sq. mi.; pop. 715,000

fil·a·ment (fil′ə mənt) ***n.*** ⟦< L *filum*, thread⟧ a very slender thread or threadlike part; specif., the fine wire in a light bulb or electron tube

fil·bert (fil′bərt) ***n.*** ⟦ME *filberde*⟧ the edible nut of a hazel tree

filch (filch) ***vt.*** ⟦ME *filchen*⟧ to steal (usually something small or petty)

file[1] (fīl) ***vt.* filed, fil′ing** ⟦< L *filum*, thread⟧ **1** to put (papers, etc.) in order for future reference **2** to dispatch or register (a news story, application, etc.) **3** to put on public record —***vi.* 1** to move in a line **2** to make application (*for* divorce, etc.) —***n.* 1** a container for keeping papers in order **2** an orderly arrangement of papers, etc. **3** a line of persons or things **4** *Comput.* a collection of data stored as a single unit —**file′a·ble *adj.*** —**fil′er *n.***

file[2] (fīl) ***n.*** ⟦OE *feol*⟧ a steel tool with a rough, ridged surface for smoothing or grinding —***vt.* filed, fil′ing** to smooth or grind, as with a file

fi·let (fi lā′, fil′ā′) ***n.*** ⟦< OFr: see FILLET⟧ FILLET (*n.* 2) —***vt.*** FILLET

fi·let mi·gnon (fi lā′min yōn′, -yän′) ⟦Fr, lit., tiny fillet⟧ a thick, round cut of lean beef tenderloin

fil·i·al (fil′ē əl, fil′yəl) ***adj.*** ⟦< L *filius*, son⟧ of, suitable to, or due from a son or daughter

fil·i·bus·ter (fil′i bus′tər) ***n.*** ⟦< Sp < MDu *vrijbuiter*, freebooter⟧ **1** the making of long speeches, etc. to obstruct a bill's passage in the Senate **2** a Senator who does this —***vt., vi.*** to obstruct (a bill) by a filibuster

fil·i·gree (fil′i grē′) ***n.*** ⟦< L *filum*, thread + *granum*, grain⟧ lacelike ornamental work of intertwined wire of gold, silver, etc. —***vt.* -greed′, -gree′ing** to ornament with filigree

fil·ing (fīl′iŋ) ***n.*** a small piece scraped off with a file: *usually used in pl.*

Fil·i·pi·no (fil′i pē′nō) ***n., pl.* -nos** ⟦Sp⟧ a person born or living in the Philippines —***adj.*** of the Philippines or its people, etc. —**Fil′i·pi′na** (-nə), *pl.* **-nas, *fem.n., adj.***

fill (fil) ***vt.*** ⟦OE *fyllan*⟧ **1** to put as much as possible into **2** to occupy wholly **3** to put a person into or to occupy (a position, etc.) **4** to supply the things called for in (an order, etc.) **5** to close or plug (holes, etc.) —***vi.*** to become full —***n.* 1** enough to make full or to satisfy **2** anything that fills —**fill in 1** to complete by supplying something **2** to supply for completion **3** to be a substitute —**fill out 1** to make or become larger, etc. **2** to make (a document, etc.) complete by supplying information —**fill up** to make or become completely full —**fill′er *n.***

fil·let (fil′it; *for n. 2 & vt., usually* fi lā′, fil′ā′) ***n.*** ⟦OFr *filet* < L *filum*, thread⟧ **1** a thin strip or band **2** a lean, boneless piece of meat or fish —***vt.*** to bone and slice (meat or fish)

fill′-in′ ***n.*** one that fills a vacancy or gap, often temporarily

fill′ing ***n.*** a substance used to fill something, as gold in a tooth cavity

filling station SERVICE STATION

fil·lip (fil′ip) ***n.*** ⟦< FLIP[1]⟧ **1** an outward snap of a finger from the thumb **2** something that stimulates —***vt.*** to strike or toss with a fillip

Fill·more (fil′môr), **Mill·ard** (mil′ərd) 1800-74; 13th president of the U.S. (1850-53)

fil·ly (fil′ē) ***n., pl.* -lies** ⟦< ON *fylja*⟧ a young female horse

film (film) ***n.*** ⟦OE *filmen*⟧ **1** a fine, thin skin, coating, etc. **2** a flexible cellulose material coated with an emulsion sensitive to light and used in photography **3** a haze or blur **4** a series of still pictures projected on a screen in such rapid succession as to create the illusion of moving persons and objects **5** a play, story, etc. in this form —***vt., vi.* 1** to cover or be covered as with a film **2** to photograph or make a film (of)

film′strip′ ***n.*** a length of film with still photographs, often of illustrations, charts, etc., for projection separately

film′y ***adj.* -i·er, -i·est 1** gauzy; sheer; thin **2** blurred; hazy —**film′i·ness *n.***

fil·ter (fil′tər) ***n.*** ⟦< ML *filtrum*, FELT[1]⟧ **1** a device for straining out solid particles, impurities, etc. from a liquid or gas **2** a device or substance for screening out electric oscillations, light waves, etc. of certain frequencies —***vt., vi.* 1** to pass through or as through a filter **2** to remove with a filter —**fil′ter·a·ble** or **fil′tra·ble** (-trə bəl) ***adj.***

filter tip 1 a cigarette tip of cellulose, charcoal, etc. for filtering the smoke **2** a cigarette with such a tip

filth (filth) ***n.*** ⟦OE *fylthe*⟧ **1** foul dirt **2** obscenity —**filth′y, -i·er, -i·est, *adj.*** —**filth′i·ness *n.***

fil·trate (fil′trāt′) ***vt.* -trat′ed, -trat′ing** to filter —***n.*** a filtered liquid —**fil·tra′tion *n.***

fin (fin) ***n.*** ⟦OE *finn*⟧ **1** any of several winglike organs on the body of a fish, dolphin, etc., used in swimming **2** anything like a fin in shape or use

fi·na·gle (fə nā′gəl) ***vt., vi.* -gled, -gling** ⟦< ?⟧ [Inf.] to get by, or use, craftiness, trickery, etc. —**fi·na′gler *n.***

fi·nal (fī′nəl) ***adj.*** ⟦< L *finis*, end⟧ **1** of or coming at the end; last **2** deciding; conclusive —***n.* 1** anything final **2** [*pl.*] the last of a series of contests **3** a final examination —**fi·nal′i·ty** (-nal′ə tē) ***n.*** —**fi′nal·ly *adv.***

THESAURUS

figure of speech ***n.*** *Varieties include the following:* image, comparison, metaphor, simile, trope, metonymy, synecdoche, personification, hyperbole, litotes, allegory, parable, allusion, euphemism, analogue, parallel, irony, satire, understatement, paradox.

file[1,2] ***n.* 1** [An orderly collection of papers] card index, card file, portfolio, record, classified index, list, register, dossier, notebook. **2** [Steel abrasive] rasp, steel, sharpener. *Types of files include the following:* flat, rat-tail, triangular, fingernail, wood. **3** [A line] rank, row, column; see LINE 1. —**on file** filed, cataloged, registered; see RECORDED.

file[1,2] ***v.* 1** [To arrange in order] classify, index, deposit, categorize, catalog, record, register, list, arrange. **2** [To use an abrasive] abrade, rasp, scrape, smooth, rub down, level off, finish, sharpen.

fill ***n.*** enough, capacity, satiety; see PLENTY.

fill ***v.* 1** [To pour to the capacity of the container] pack, stuff, replenish, furnish, supply, satisfy, blow up, fill up, pump up, fill to capacity, fill to overflowing, brim over, swell, charge, inflate.—*Ant.* EMPTY, exhaust, drain. **2** [To occupy available space] take up, pervade, overflow, stretch, bulge out, distend, brim over, stretch, swell, blow up, run over at the top, permeate, take over. —**fill in 1** [To insert] write in, answer, sign; see ANSWER. **2** [To substitute] replace, act for, represent; see SUBSTITUTE. —**fill out 1** [To enlarge] swell out, expand, round out; see GROW 1. **2** [To insert] fill in, sign, apply; see ANSWER. —**fill up** saturate, pack, stuff; see FILL 1.

filled ***a.*** finished, completed, done; see FULL 1.

filling ***n.*** stuffing, dressing, contents, mixture, center, layer, filler, fill, sauce, insides, lining, wadding, padding, cement, innards*, guts*.

film ***n.* 1** [Thin, membranous matter] gauze, tissue, fabric, sheet, membrane, layer, transparency, foil, fold, skin, coat, coating, scum, veil, cobweb, web, mist, cloud. **2** [A preparation containing a light-sensitive emulsion] negative, positive, microfilm, color film. **3** [A moving picture] motion picture, cinema, photoplay; see MOVIE.

film ***v.*** record, take, shoot; see PHOTOGRAPH.

filter ***v.* 1** [To soak slowly] seep, penetrate, percolate; see SOAK 1. **2** [To clean by filtering] strain, purify, sift, sieve, refine, clarify, clean, separate.

filth ***n.*** dirt, dung, feces, contamination, corruption, pollution, foul matter, sewage, muck, manure, slop, squalor, trash, grime, mud, smudge, silt, garbage, carrion, slush, slime, sludge, foulness, filthiness, excrement, dregs, lees, sediment, rottenness, impurity.—*Ant.* CLEANLINESS, purity, spotlessness.

filthy ***a.*** foul, squalid, nasty; see DIRTY 1.

fin ***n.*** membrane, paddle, propeller, balance, guide, blade, ridge, organ, spine, pectoral fin, ventral fin, dorsal fin, caudal fin, pelvic fin, fish's tail, flipper.

final ***a.*** terminal, concluding, ultimate; see LAST 1.

fi·na·le (fə nal′ē) ***n.*** ⟦It⟧ the concluding part of a musical work, etc.

fi′nal·ist ***n.*** a contestant in the final, deciding contest of a series

fi′nal·ize′ ***vt.*** **-ized′, -iz′ing** ⟦FINAL + -IZE⟧ to make final; complete —**fi′nal·i·za′tion** ***n.***

fi·nance (fī′nans′, fə nans′) ***n.*** ⟦< L *finis*, end⟧ **1** [*pl.*] money resources, income, etc. **2** the science of managing money —***vt.*** **-nanced′, -nanc′ing** to supply or get money for —**fi·nan′cial** (-nan′shəl) ***adj.*** —**fi·nan′cial·ly** ***adv.***

fin·an·cier (fin′ən sir′, fī′nən-) ***n.*** ⟦Fr⟧ one skilled in finance

finch (finch) ***n.*** ⟦OE *finc*⟧ any of various small, seed-eating birds, including canaries, goldfinches, etc.

find (fīnd) ***vt.*** **found, find′ing** ⟦OE *findan*⟧ **1** to discover by chance; come upon **2** to get by searching **3** to perceive; learn **4** to recover (something lost) **5** to reach; attain **6** to decide and declare to be —***vi.*** to reach a decision [the jury *found* for the accused] —***n.*** **1** a finding **2** something found —**find out** to discover; learn —**find′er** ***n.***

find′ing ***n.*** **1** discovery **2** something found **3** [*often pl.*] the verdict of a judge, scholar, etc.

fine[1] (fīn) ***adj.*** ⟦< L *finis*, end⟧ **1** very good; excellent **2** with no impurities; refined **3** in good health **4** clear and bright [*fine* weather] **5** not heavy or coarse [*fine* sand] **6** very thin or small [*fine* print] **7** sharp [a *fine* edge] **8** subtle; delicate [a *fine* distinction] **9** elegant —***adv.*** in a fine manner —**fine′ly** ***adv.*** —**fine′ness** ***n.***

fine[2] (fīn) ***n.*** ⟦see prec.⟧ a sum of money paid as a penalty —***vt.*** **fined, fin′ing** to order to pay a fine

fine art any of the art forms that include drawing, painting, sculpture, etc.: *usually used in pl.*

fin·er·y (fīn′ər ē) ***n., pl.*** **-ies** elaborate clothes, jewelry, etc.

fines herbes (fēn zerb′) ⟦Fr⟧ a seasoning of chopped herbs, traditionally parsley, chives, tarragon, and chervil

fi·nesse (fə nes′) ***n.*** ⟦see FINE[1]⟧ **1** adroitness; skill **2** the ability to handle difficult situations diplomatically **3** cunning; artfulness —***vt.*** **-nessed′, -ness′ing** **1** to manage or bring about by finesse **2** to evade (a problem, etc.)

fin·ger (fiŋ′gər) ***n.*** ⟦OE⟧ **1** any of the five jointed parts extending from the palm of the hand, esp. any one other than the thumb **2** anything like a finger in shape or use —***vt.*** **1** to touch with the fingers; handle **2** *Music* to play by using the fingers in a certain way —**have** (or **keep**) **one's fingers crossed** to hope for or against something —**put one's finger on** to ascertain exactly

fin′ger·board′ ***n.*** the part of a stringed instrument against which the strings are pressed to produce the desired tones

fin′ger·ling (-liŋ) ***n.*** a small fish

fin′ger·nail′ ***n.*** the horny substance at the upper end of a finger

finger painting a painting done by using the fingers, hand, or arm to spread, on wet paper, paints (**finger paints**) made of starch, glycerin, and pigments —**fin′ger-paint′** ***vi., vt.***

fin′ger-point′ing ***n.*** the act of assigning blame to others, often so as to deflect blame from oneself

fin′ger·print′ ***n.*** an impression of the lines and whorls on a finger tip, used to identify a person —***vt.*** to take the fingerprints of

fin′ger·tip′ ***n.*** the tip of a finger —**have at one's fingertips** to have available for instant use

fin·i·al (fin′ē əl) ***n.*** ⟦ult. < L *finis*, end⟧ a decorative terminal part at the tip of a spire, lamp, etc.

fin·ick·y (fin′ik ē) ***adj.*** ⟦< FINE[1]⟧ too particular; fussy: also **fin′i·cal** (-i kəl) or **fin′ick·ing**

fin·is (fin′is; *also, as if Fr,* fē nē′) ***n., pl.*** **-nis·es** the end; finish

fin·ish (fin′ish) ***vt.*** ⟦< L *finis*, an end⟧ **1** *a)* to bring to an end *b)* to come to the end of **2** to consume all of **3** to give final touches to; perfect **4** to give (wood, etc.) a desired surface effect —***vi.*** to come to an end —***n.*** **1** the last part; end **2** *a)* anything used to finish a surface *b)* the finished effect **3** means or manner of completing or perfecting **4** polished manners, speech, etc. —**finish off** **1** to end **2** to kill or ruin —**finish with** to bring to an end —**fin′ished** ***adj.*** —**fin′ish·er** ***n.***

fi·nite (fī′nīt′) ***adj.*** ⟦< L *finis*, end⟧ having definable limits; not infinite

fink (fiŋk) ***n.*** ⟦Ger, lit., finch⟧ [Slang] **1** an informer **2** a strikebreaker —***vi.*** [Slang] to inform (*on*)

Fin·land (fin′lənd) country in N Europe: 130,547 sq. mi.; pop. 5,078,000

Finn (fin) ***n.*** a person born or living in Finland

fin·nan had·die (fin′ən had′ē) ⟦prob. < *Findhorn* (Scotland) *haddock*⟧ smoked haddock

Finn·ish (fin′ish) ***n.*** the language spoken in Finland —***adj.*** of Finland or its people, language, etc.

fin·ny (fin′ē) ***adj.*** **1** having fins **2** like a fin **3** of or being fish

fiord (fyôrd) ***n.*** ⟦Norw < ON *fjörthr*⟧ a narrow inlet of the sea bordered by steep cliffs

fir (fʉr) ***n.*** ⟦OE *fyrh*⟧ **1** a cone-bearing evergreen tree of the pine family **2** its wood

fire (fīr) ***n.*** ⟦OE *fyr*⟧ **1** the flame, heat, and light of combustion **2** something burning **3** a destructive burning [a

THESAURUS

finalized ***a.*** concluded, decided, completed; see FINISHED 1.

finally ***a.*** **1** [As though a matter were settled] with finality, with conviction, settled, in a final manner, certainly, officially, irrevocably, decisively, definitely, beyond recall, permanently, for all time, conclusively, assuredly, done with, once and for all, for good, beyond the shadow of a doubt.—*Ant.* TEMPORARILY, momentarily, for the time being. **2** [After a long period] at length, at last, in the end, subsequently, in conclusion, lastly, after all, after a while, eventually, ultimately, at long last, at the final point, at the last moment, at the end, tardily, belatedly, when all is said and done, in spite of all, at the eleventh hour.

finance ***n.*** business, commerce, financial affairs; see ECONOMICS.

finance ***v.*** fund, support, provide funds for; see PAY FOR.

finances ***n.*** revenue, capital, funds; see WEALTH.

financial ***a.*** economic, business, monetary; see COMMERCIAL.

financier ***n.*** capitalist, banker, investor; see EXECUTIVE.

find ***n.*** fortunate discovery, findings, acquisition; see DISCOVERY.

find ***v.*** discover, detect, notice, observe, perceive, arrive at, discern, hit upon, encounter, uncover, recover, expose, stumble on, happen upon, come across, track down, dig up, turn up, scare up*, run across, run into, lay one's hands on, bring to light, spot; see also SEE 1.—*Ant.* LOSE, mislay, miss. —**find out** recognize, learn, identify; see DISCOVER.

finder ***n.*** acquirer, discoverer, search party; see OWNER.—*Ant.* LOSER, seeker, failure.

finding ***n.*** verdict, decision, sentence; see JUDGMENT 3.

findings ***n.*** data, discoveries, conclusions; see SUMMARY.

fine[1] ***a.*** **1** [Not coarse] light, powdery, granular; see LITTLE 1. **2** [Of superior quality] well-made, supreme, fashionable; see EXCELLENT. **3** [Exact] precise, distinct, strict; see ACCURATE 2, DEFINITE 2.

fine[2] ***n.*** penalty, damage, forfeit; see PUNISHMENT.

fine[2] ***v.*** penalize, exact, tax, confiscate, levy, seize, extort, alienate, make pay; see also PUNISH.

finger ***n.*** digit, organ of touch, tactile member, forefinger, thumb, index finger, extremity, pointer, feeler, tentacle, middle finger, ring finger, little finger, pinkie. —**have** (or **keep**) **one's fingers crossed*** wish, aspire to, pray for; see HOPE. —**lift a finger** make an effort, attempt, endeavor; see TRY 1. —**put one's finger on** indicate, ascertain, detect; see DISCOVER. —**put the finger on*** inform on, turn in, fink on*; see TELL 1.

finger ***v.*** **1** [To feel] handle, touch, manipulate; see FEEL 1. **2** [To choose or specify] appoint, point out, name; see CHOOSE.

fingernail ***n.*** nail, talon, matrix; see CLAW.

finish ***n.*** **1** [The end] close, termination, ending; see END 2. **2** [An applied surface] shine, polish, glaze, surface. *Finishes include the following:* shellac, oil, plastic, turpentine, lacquer, stain, varnish, polish, wallpaper, wash, whitewash, paint, casein paint, enamel, gold leaf, wax, veneer, cement, stucco, luster.

finish ***v.*** **1** [To bring to an end] complete, end, perfect; see ACHIEVE. **2** [To develop a surface] polish, wax, stain; see COVER 1, PAINT 2. **3** [To come to an end] cease, close, end; see STOP.

finished ***a.*** **1** [Completed] done, accomplished, perfected, achieved, ended, performed, executed, dispatched, concluded, complete, through, fulfilled, closed, over, decided, brought about, ceased, stopped, resolved, settled, made, worked out, rounded out, discharged, satisfied, disposed of, realized, finalized, effected, put into effect, all over with, attained, done with, made an end of, brought to a close, said and done, sewed up*, wound up.—*Ant.* UNFINISHED, imperfect, incomplete. **2** [Given a finish] polished, coated, varnished; see PAINTED 2.

fire ***n.*** **1** [Burning] flame, conflagra-

forest *fire]* **4** strong feeling **5** a discharge of firearms —**vt.**, **vi. fired, fir'ing** **1** to start burning; ignite **2** to supply with fuel **3** to bake (bricks, etc.) in a kiln **4** to excite or become excited **5** to shoot (a gun, bullet, etc.) **6** to hurl or direct with force **7** to dismiss from a position; discharge —**catch (on) fire** to ignite —**on fire** **1** burning **2** greatly excited —**under fire** under attack —**fir'er n.**

fire'arm' n. any hand weapon from which a shot is fired by explosive force, as a rifle or pistol

fire'base' n. a military base in a combat zone, from which artillery, rockets, etc. are fired

fire'bomb' n. an incendiary bomb —**vt.** to attack or damage with a firebomb

fire'brand' n. **1** a piece of burning wood **2** one who stirs up others to rebellion or strife

fire'break' n. a strip of forest or prairie land cleared or plowed to stop the spread of fire

fire·brick (fīr'brik') **n.** a highly heat-resistant brick for lining fireplaces, furnaces, etc.

fire'bug' n. [Inf.] one who deliberately starts destructive fires; pyromaniac

fire'crack'er n. a roll of paper containing an explosive, set off as a noisemaker at celebrations, etc.

fire'damp' n. an explosive gas, largely methane, formed in coal mines

fire engine a motor truck with equipment for fighting fires

fire escape an outside stairway for escaping from a burning building

fire'fight' n. a short, intense exchange of gunfire between small units of soldiers

fire'fight'er n. a person whose work is putting out fires —**fire'fight'ing n.**

fire'fly' n., *pl.* **-flies'** a winged beetle whose abdomen glows with a luminescent light

fire'man (-mən) **n.**, *pl.* **-men** (-mən) **1** FIREFIGHTER **2** a person who tends a fire in a furnace, etc.

fire'place' n. a place for a fire, esp. an open place built in a wall under a chimney

fire'plug' n. a street hydrant supplying water for fighting fires

fire'proof' adj. not easily destroyed by fire —**vt.** to make fireproof

fire'side' n. **1** the space around a fireplace **2** home or home life

fire'storm' n. **1** an intense fire over a large area, as one caused by an atomic explosion with its high winds **2** a strong, often violent, outburst or upheaval

fire tower a tower used as a lookout for forest fires

fire'trap' n. a building easily set on fire or hard to get out of if on fire

fire'truck' n. FIRE ENGINE

fire'wa'ter n. alcoholic beverage: now humorous

fire'wood' n. wood used as fuel

fire'works' pl.n. **1** firecrackers, rockets, etc., for noisy effects or brilliant displays: *sometimes used in sing.* **2** a noisy quarrel or display of anger

firing line **1** the line from which gunfire is directed at the enemy **2** the forefront in any kind of activity

firm[1] (furm) **adj.** ⟦< L *firmus*⟧ **1** solid; hard **2** not moved easily; fixed **3** unchanging; steady **4** resolute; constant **5** showing determination; strong **6** definite *[a firm contract]* —**vt.**, **vi.** to make or become firm —**firm'ly adv.** —**firm'ness n.**

firm[2] (furm) **n.** ⟦< It < L *firmus*: see prec.⟧ a business company

fir·ma·ment (fur'mə mənt) **n.** ⟦< L *firmare*, strengthen⟧ the sky, viewed poetically as a solid arch or vault

first (furst) **adj.** ⟦OE *fyrst*⟧ **1** before all others in a series; 1st **2** earliest **3** foremost, as in rank or quality —**adv.** **1** before any other person or thing **2** for the first time **3** sooner; preferably —**n.** **1** any person or thing that is first **2** the beginning **3** a first happening or thing of its kind **4** the winning place, as in a race **5** the slowest forward gear ratio of a motor vehicle transmission

first aid emergency treatment for injury or sudden illness, before regular medical care is available —**first'-aid' adj.**

first'born' adj. born first in a family; oldest —**n.** the firstborn child

first'-class' adj. **1** of the highest class, quality, etc. **2** designating the most expensive accommodations **3** designating or of the most expensive class of ordinary mail —**adv.** **1** with first-class accommodations **2** as or by first-class mail

first family [*often* **F- F-**] the family of the U.S. president

first'hand' adj., **adv.** from the original producer or source; direct

first lady [*often* **F- L-**] the wife of the U.S. president

first lieutenant a military officer ranking just above a second lieutenant

first'ly adv. in the first place; first

first person the form of a pronoun or verb that refers to the speaker or writer

first'-rate' adj. highest in rank, quality, etc. —**adv.** [Inf.] very well

first'-string' adj. [Inf.] *Sports* that is the first choice for regular play at a specified position

firth (furth) **n.** ⟦< ON *fjörthr*⟧ a narrow inlet or arm of the sea

THESAURUS

tion, blaze, campfire, coals, flame and smoke, blazing fire, hearth, burning coals, tinder, bonfire, bed of coals, embers, source of heat, sparks, heat, glow, warmth, luminosity, combustion, pyre, signal fire, flare, inferno. **2** [The discharge of ordnance] artillery attack, bombardment, rounds, barrage, explosions, bombings, curtain of fire, volley, sniping, mortar attack, salvos, shells, pattern of fire, fire superiority, crossfire, machine-gun fire, rifle fire, small-arms fire, antiaircraft fire; see also ATTACK. —**catch (on) fire** begin burning, ignite, flare up; see BURN. —**on fire** **1** [Burning] flaming, fiery, hot; see BURNING. **2** [Excited] full of ardor, enthusiastic, zealous; see EXCITED. —**open fire** start shooting, shoot, attack; see SHOOT 1. —**play with fire** gamble, endanger one's interests, do something dangerous; see RISK. —**set fire to** ignite, oxidize, make burn; see BURN. —**set the world on fire** achieve, become famous, excel; see SUCCEED 1. —**under fire** criticized, censured, under attack; see ATTACKED.

fire v. **1** [To set on fire] kindle, enkindle, ignite, inflame, light, burn, set fire to, put a match to, start a fire, set burning, touch off, rekindle, relight.—*Ant.* EXTINGUISH, smother, quench. **2** [To shoot] discharge, shoot off, blast; see SHOOT 1. **3** [To dismiss] discharge, let go, eject; see DISMISS.

fired a. **1** [Subjected to fire] set on fire, burned, baked, ablaze, afire, on fire, aflame, burning, incandescent, scorched, glowing, kindled, enkindled, smoking, smoldering, heated. **2** [Discharged] dropped, let go, given one's walking papers*; see DISCHARGED.

fireman n. **1** [One who extinguishes fires] firefighter, engineman, ladderman, fire chief. **2** [One who fuels engines or furnaces] stoker, engineer's helper, railroad man, trainman, attendant.

fireplace n. hearth, chimney, hearthside, stove, furnace, blaze, bed of coals, grate.

fireproof a. flameproof, fire-retardant, noncombustible, nonflammable, fire-resistant, incombustible, concrete and steel, asbestos.

fireworks n. rockets, Roman candles, sparklers; see EXPLOSIVE.

firm[1] **a.** **1** [Stable] fixed, solid, rooted, immovable, fastened, motionless, secured, steady, substantial, durable, rigid, bolted, welded, riveted, soldered, embedded, nailed, tightened, fast, secure, sound, immobile, unmovable, mounted, stationary, set, settled.—*Ant.* LOOSE, movable, mobile. **2** [Firm in texture] solid, dense, compact, hard, stiff, impenetrable, impervious, rigid, hardened, inflexible, unyielding, thick, compressed, substantial, heavy, close, condensed, impermeable.—*Ant.* SOFT, porous, flabby. **3** [Settled in purpose] determined, steadfast, resolute; see CONSTANT. —**stand** (or **hold**) **firm** be steadfast, endure, maintain one's resolution; see FIGHT, RESOLVE.

firmly a. **1** [Not easily moved] immovably, solidly, rigidly, stably, durably, enduringly, substantially, securely, heavily, stiffly, inflexibly, soundly, strongly, thoroughly.—*Ant.* LIGHTLY, tenuously, insecurely. **2** [Showing determination] resolutely, steadfastly, doggedly, stolidly, stubbornly, tenaciously, determinedly, staunchly, constantly, intently, purposefully, persistently, obstinately, unwaveringly, through thick and thin.

firmness n. stiffness, hardness, toughness, solidity, impenetrability, durability, imperviousness, temper, impermeability, inflexibility.

first a. beginning, original, primary, prime, primal, antecedent, initial, virgin, earliest, opening, introductory, primeval, leading, in the beginning, front, head, rudimentary.—*Ant.* LAST, ultimate, final. —**in the first place** firstly, initially, to begin with; see FIRST.

first aid n. emergency medical aid, emergency relief, field dressing; see MEDICINE 2, TREATMENT 2.

first-class a. superior, supreme, choice; see EXCELLENT.

first-rate a. prime, very good, choice; see EXCELLENT.

fis·cal (fis′kəl) ***adj.*** ⟦< L *fiscus*, public chest⟧ **1** relating to the public treasury or revenues **2** financial **3** designating or of government policies of spending and taxation —**fis′cal·ly *adv.***

fish (fish) ***n.***, *pl.* **fish** or (for different species) **fish′es** ⟦OE *fisc*⟧ **1** any of a large group of coldblooded vertebrate animals living in water and having fins, gills for breathing, and, usually, scales **2** the flesh of a fish used as food —***vi.*** **1** to catch or try to catch fish **2** to try to get something indirectly: often with *for* —***vt.*** to grope for, find, and bring to view: often with *out*

fish′er *n.* **1** the largest marten, having very dark fur **2** this fur

fish′er·man (-mən) ***n.***, *pl.* **-men** (-mən) **1** a person who fishes for sport or for a living **2** a commercial fishing vessel

fish′er·y *n.*, *pl.* **-ies** **1** the business of catching, selling, etc. fish **2** a place where fish, etc. are caught or bred

fish′hook′ *n.* a hook, usually barbed, for catching fish

fish′ing *n.* the catching of fish for sport or for a living

fish meal ground, dried fish, used as fertilizer or fodder

fish′wife′ *n.*, *pl.* **-wives′** a coarse, scolding woman

fish′y *adj.* **-i·er, -i·est** **1** like a fish in odor, taste, etc. **2** dull or expressionless [*fishy* eyes] **3** [Inf.] questionable; odd —**fish′i·ly *adv.*** —**fish′i·ness *n.***

fis·sion (fish′ən, fizh′-) ***n.*** ⟦< L *findere*, to split⟧ **1** a splitting apart; cleavage **2** NUCLEAR FISSION —**fis′sion·a·ble *adj.***

fis·sure (fish′ər) ***n.*** ⟦see prec.⟧ a cleft or crack

fist (fist) ***n.*** ⟦OE *fyst*⟧ a hand with the fingers closed tightly into the palm

fist·i·cuffs (fis′ti kufs′) ***pl.n.*** [Old-fashioned] a fight with the fists

fis·tu·la (fis′tyo͞o lə, -chə lə) ***n.***, *pl.* **-las** or **-lae′** (-lē′) ⟦L, a pipe, ulcer⟧ an abnormal passage, as from an abscess to the skin

fit[1] (fit) ***vt.*** **fit′ted** or **fit, fit′ting** ⟦ME *fitten*⟧ **1** to be suitable to **2** to be the proper size, shape, etc. for **3** to adjust so as to fit **4** to equip; outfit —***vi.*** **1** [Archaic] to be suitable or proper **2** to have the proper size or shape —***adj.*** **fit′ter, fit′test** **1** suited to some purpose, function, etc. **2** proper; right **3** healthy **4** [Inf.] inclined [she was *fit* to scream] —***n.*** the manner of fitting [a tight *fit*] —**fit′ly *adv.*** —**fit′ness *n.*** —**fit′ter *n.***

fit[2] (fit) ***n.*** ⟦OE *fitt*, conflict⟧ **1** any sudden, uncontrollable attack, as of coughing **2** an outburst, as of anger **3** a seizure involving convulsions, loss of consciousness, etc. —**by fits** (**and starts**) in an irregular way —**have** (or **throw**) **a fit** [Inf.] to become very angry or upset

fit′ful (-fəl) ***adj.*** characterized by intermittent activity; spasmodic —**fit′ful·ly *adv.*** —**fit′ful·ness *n.***

fit′ting *adj.* suitable; proper —***n.*** **1** an adjustment or trying on of clothes, etc. **2** a small part used to join or adapt other parts **3** [*pl.*] fixtures

five (fīv) ***adj.***, ***n.*** ⟦OE *fif*⟧ one more than four; 5; V

five′-and-ten′-cent′ store a store that sells a wide variety of inexpensive merchandise: also **five′-and-ten′ *n.***

five′-star′ *adj.* having the highest rating, based on a given set of criteria for excellence

fix (fiks) ***vt.*** **fixed, fix′ing** ⟦< L *figere*, fasten⟧ **1** to fasten firmly **2** to set firmly in the mind **3** to direct (one's eyes) steadily at something **4** to make rigid **5** to make permanent **6** to establish (a date, etc.) definitely **7** to set in order; adjust **8** to repair **9** to prepare (food or meals) **10** [Inf.] to influence the result or action of (a race, jury, etc.), as by bribery **11** [Inf.] to punish —***vi.*** **1** to become fixed **2** [Inf. or Dial.] to prepare or intend —***n.*** **1** the position of a ship, etc. determined from the bearings of two known positions **2** [Inf.] a predicament **3** [Slang] a contest, etc. that has been fixed **4** [Slang] an injection of a narcotic by an addict —**fix up** [Inf.] **1** to repair **2** to arrange; set in order —**fix′a·ble *adj.*** —**fix′er *n.***

fix·a·tion (fik sā′shən) ***n.*** **1** a fixing or being fixed **2** an obsession **3** a remaining at an early stage of psychosexual development

fix·a·tive (fik′sə tiv) ***adj.*** that is able or tends to make permanent, prevent fading, etc. —***n.*** a fixative substance

fixed (fikst) ***adj.*** **1** firmly in place **2** established; settled **3** resolute; unchanging **4** persistent [a *fixed* idea] —**fix·ed·ly** (fiks′id lē) ***adv.***

fix·ings (fik′siŋz′) ***pl.n.*** [Inf.] accessories or trimmings [turkey and all the *fixings*]

fix·i·ty (fik′si tē) ***n.*** the quality or state of being fixed or steady

fix·ture (fiks′chər) ***n.*** ⟦see FIX⟧ **1** anything firmly in place **2** any attached piece of equipment in a house, etc. **3** a person long established in a job, etc.

fizz (fiz) ***n.*** ⟦? akin to fol.⟧ **1** a hissing, sputtering sound **2** an effervescent drink —***vi.*** **1** to make a hissing sound **2** to effervesce

fiz·zle (fiz′əl) ***vi.*** **-zled, -zling** ⟦< ME⟧ **1** FIZZ (*vi.* 1) **2** [Inf.] to fail, esp. after a good start —***n.*** **1** a hissing sound **2** [Inf.] a failure

fl *abbrev.* **1** floor **2** ⟦L *floruit*⟧ (he or she) flourished **3** fluid

FL *abbrev.* Florida

flab (flab) ***n.*** ⟦< FLABBY⟧ [Inf.] sagging flesh

THESAURUS

fiscal *a.* monetary, economic, financial; see COMMERCIAL.

fish *n.* seafood, panfish, denizen of the deep. *Types of fish include the following:* shark, skate, ray, manta, catfish, pickerel, pike, perch, trout, flounder, sucker, sunfish, bass, crappy, mackerel, cod, salmon, carp, minnow, eel, bullhead, herring, shad, barracuda, swordfish, marlin, grouper, piranha, goldfish, gar, dogfish, flyingfish, whitefish, tuna, pompano, haddock, hake, halibut, mullet, loach, muskellunge, muskie, sardine, smelt, anchovy, angelfish, neon tetra, swordtail, molly; see also SHELLFISH. —**drink like a fish** drink heavily, get drunk, become inebriated; see DRINK 2. —**like a fish out of water** out of place, alien, displaced; see UNFAMILIAR 1.

fish *v.* go fishing, troll for, net, shrimp, bait the hook, trawl, angle, cast one's net. —**fish for** hint at, elicit, try to evoke; see HINT.

fisherman *n.* angler, fisher, harpooner, sailor, seaman, whaler, fish catcher.

fishing *n.* angling, casting, trawling; see SPORT 1.

fishy* ***a.*** improbable, dubious, implausible; see UNLIKELY.

fist *n.* clenched hand, clenched fist, hand, clutch, clasp, grasp, grip, hold.

fit[1] ***a.*** **1** [Appropriate by nature] suitable, proper, fitting, likely, expedient, appropriate, convenient, timely, opportune, feasible, practicable, wise, advantageous, favorable, preferable, beneficial, desirable, adequate, tasteful, becoming, agreeable, seasonable, due, rightful, decent, equitable, legitimate, harmonious, pertinent, according, relevant, in keeping, consistent, applicable, compatible, admissible, concurrent, to the point, adapted, fitted, suited, calculated, prepared, qualified, competent, matched, ready-made, accommodated, right, happy, lucky, cut out for*.—*Ant.* unfit, unseemly, inappropriate. **2** [In good physical condition] trim, in good health, robust; see HEALTHY.

fit[1] ***v.*** **1** [To be suitable in character] agree, suit, accord, harmonize, apply, belong, conform, consist, fit right in, be in keeping, parallel, relate, concur, match, correspond, be comfortable, respond, have its place, answer the purpose, meet, click*.—*Ant.* OPPOSE, disagree, clash. **2** [To make suitable] arrange, alter, adapt; see ADJUST 1.

fit[2] ***n.*** **1** [Sudden attack of disease] muscular convulsion, spasm, seizure, stroke, epileptic attack, paroxysm, spell*; see also ILLNESS 1. **2** [Transitory spell of action or feeling] impulsive action, burst, rush, outbreak, torrent, tantrum, mood, outburst, whimsy, huff, rage, spell. —**have** (or **throw**) **a fit*** become angry, lose one's temper, give vent to emotion; see RAGE 1.

fitness *n.* appropriateness, suitability, propriety, expediency, convenience, adequacy, correspondence, decency, decorum, harmony, keeping, consistency, applicability, compatibility, rightness, timeliness, adaptation, qualification, accommodation, competence.

fix *v.* **1** [To make firm] plant, implant, secure; see FASTEN. **2** [To prepare a meal] prepare, heat, get ready; see COOK. **3** [To put in order] correct, improve, settle, put into shape, reform, patch, rejuvenate, touch up, revive, refresh, renew, renovate, rebuild, make compatible, clean, align, adapt, mend, adjust. —**fix up*** fix, mend, rehabilitate; see REPAIR.

fixed *a.* **1** [Firm] solid, rigid, immovable; see FIRM 1. **2** [Repaired] rebuilt, in order, timed, synchronized, adjusted, settled, mended, rearranged, adapted, corrected, restored, renewed, improved, patched up, put together, in working order. **3** [*Prearranged] predesigned, put-up*, set up*; see PLANNED.

fixings *n.* parts, components, constituents; see INGREDIENTS.

fixture *n.* convenience, gas appliance, electric appliance; see APPLIANCE.

fizz *n.* hissing, sputtering, bubbling; see NOISE 1.

fizzle* ***n.*** disappointment, fiasco, defeat; see FAILURE 1.

flab·ber·gast (flab′ər gast′) ***vt.*** ⟦18th-c. slang < ?⟧ to dumbfound

flab·by (flab′ē) ***adj.*** **-bi·er, -bi·est** ⟦< FLAP⟧ **1** limp and soft **2** weak —**flab′bi·ly *adv.*** —**flab′bi·ness *n.***

flac·cid (flak′sid, flas′id) ***adj.*** ⟦< L *flaccus*⟧ soft and limp; flabby

flack (flak) ***n.*** ⟦< ?⟧ [Slang] PRESS AGENT —**flack′er·y *n.***

fla·con (flak′ən; *Fr* flȧ kōn′) ***n.***, *pl.* **-cons** (-enz; -kōn′) ⟦Fr⟧ a small flask with a stopper, as for perfume

flag[1] (flag) ***n.*** ⟦< FLAG[4], in obs. sense "to flutter"⟧ a cloth with colors, patterns, etc., used as a symbol of a nation, state, etc., or as a signal —***vt.*** **flagged, flag′ging 1** to signal with or as with a flag; esp., to signal to stop: often with *down* **2** to mark with a symbol

flag[2] (flag) ***n.*** ⟦< ON *flaga*, slab of stone⟧ FLAGSTONE

flag[3] (flag) ***n.*** ⟦ME *flagge*⟧ any of various irises, or a flower or leaf of one

flag[4] (flag) ***vi.*** **flagged, flag′ging** ⟦prob. < ON *flǫgra*, to flutter⟧ **1** to become limp; droop **2** to grow weak or tired

flag·el·late (flaj′ə lāt′) ***vt.*** **-lat′ed, -lat′ing** ⟦< L *flagellum*, a whip⟧ to whip; flog —**flag′el·la′tion *n.***

fla·gel·lum (flə jel′əm) ***n.***, *pl.* **-la** (-ə) or **-lums** ⟦L, a whip⟧ a whiplike part of some cells, as of bacteria or protozoans, used as for moving about

flag·on (flag′ən) ***n.*** ⟦< LL *flasco*⟧ a container for liquids, with a handle, a narrow neck, a spout, and, often, a lid

flag′pole′ *n.* a pole on which a flag is raised and flown: also **flag′staff′**

fla·grant (flā′grənt) ***adj.*** ⟦< L *flagrare*, to blaze⟧ glaringly bad; outrageous —**fla′gran·cy** (-grən sē) or **fla′grance *n.*** —**fla′grant·ly *adv.***

flag′ship′ *n.* **1** the ship that carries the commander of a fleet or other large naval unit **2** the largest or most important member or part, as of a group

flag′stone′ *n.* a flat paving stone

flail (flāl) ***n.*** ⟦< L *flagellum*, a whip⟧ a farm tool for threshing grain by hand —***vt.***, ***vi.*** **1** to thresh with a flail **2** to beat **3** to move (one's arms) like flails

flair (fler) ***n.*** ⟦< L *fragrare*, to smell⟧ **1** a natural talent; aptitude **2** a sense of style; dash

flak (flak) ***n.*** ⟦Ger acronym⟧ **1** the fire of antiaircraft guns **2** [Inf.] strong criticism Also sp. **flack**

flake (flāk) ***n.*** ⟦< Scand⟧ **1** a small, thin mass **2** a piece split off; chip —***vt.***, ***vi.*** **flaked, flak′ing 1** to form into flakes **2** to peel off in flakes

flak′y *adj.* **-i·er, -i·est 1** of or producing flakes **2** [Slang] eccentric

flam·bé (fläm bā′) ***adj.*** ⟦Fr⟧ served with a sauce of flaming brandy, rum, etc. —***n.*** a dessert so served

flam·boy·ant (flam boi′ənt) ***adj.*** ⟦Fr < L *flamma*, a flame⟧ **1** flamelike or brilliant **2** too showy or ornate —**flam·boy′ance** or **flam·boy′an·cy *n.*** —**flam·boy′ant·ly *adv.***

flame (flām) ***n.*** ⟦< L *flamma*⟧ **1** the burning gas of a fire, appearing as a tongue of light **2** the state of burning with a blaze **3** a thing like a flame **4** an intense emotion **5** a sweetheart —***vi.*** **flamed, flam′ing 1** to burst into flame **2** to grow red or hot **3** to become excited —***vt.*** [Inf.] to attack, as by e-mail

fla·men·co (flə meŋ′kō) ***n.*** ⟦Sp⟧ a Spanish gypsy style of dance or music

flame′out′ *n.* **1** a failure of combustion in a jet's engine during flight **2** a sudden and complete failure

flame′throw′er *n.* a weapon that shoots flaming oil, napalm, etc.

fla·min·go (flə miŋ′gō′) ***n.***, *pl.* **-gos′** or **-goes′** ⟦Port⟧ a tropical wading bird with long legs and pink or red feathers

flam·ma·ble (flam′ə bəl) ***adj.*** easily set on fire; that will burn readily or quickly —**flam′ma·bil′i·ty *n.***

Flan·ders (flan′dərz) region in NW Europe, in France & Belgium

flange (flanj) ***n.*** ⟦< ? ME⟧ a projecting rim on a wheel, etc., that serves to hold it in place, give it strength, etc.

flank (flaŋk) ***n.*** ⟦< OFr *flanc*⟧ **1** the side of an animal between the ribs and the hip **2** the side of anything **3** *Mil.* the right or left side of a formation or force —***vt.*** **1** to be at the side of **2** *Mil.* to attack, or pass around, the side of (enemy troops)

flan·nel (flan′əl) ***n.*** ⟦prob. < Welsh *gwlan*, wool⟧ **1** a loosely woven cloth of wool or cotton **2** [*pl.*] trousers, etc. made of this

flan·nel·ette or **flan·nel·et** (flan′əl et′) ***n.*** a soft, napped cotton cloth

flap (flap) ***n.*** ⟦ME *flappe*⟧ **1** anything flat and broad hanging loose at one end **2** the motion or sound of a swinging flap **3** [Inf.] a commotion; stir —***vt.*** **flapped, flap′ping 1** to slap **2** to move back and forth or up and down

flap′jack′ *n.* a pancake

flap′per *n.* [Inf.] in the 1920s, a bold, unconventional young woman

flare (fler) ***vi.*** **flared, flar′ing** ⟦ME *fleare* < ?⟧ **1** *a)* to blaze brightly *b)* to burn unsteadily **2** to burst out suddenly, as in anger: often with *up* or *out* **3** to curve outward, as a bell's rim —***n.*** **1** a bright, unsteady blaze **2** a brightly flaming light for signaling, etc. **3** an outburst, as of emotion **4** a curving outward

flare′-up′ *n.* a sudden outburst of flame or of anger, trouble, etc.

flash (flash) ***vi.*** ⟦ME *flashen*, to splash⟧ **1** to send out a sudden, brief light **2** to sparkle **3** to come or pass suddenly —***vt.*** **1** to cause to flash **2** to send (news, etc.) swiftly **3** [Inf.] to display or expose briefly —***n.*** **1** a sudden, brief light **2** a brief moment **3** a sudden, brief display **4** a brief item of late news **5** a gaudy display —***adj.*** happening swiftly or suddenly —**flash′er *n.***

flash′back′ *n.* **1** an interruption in the continuity of a story, etc. by the telling or showing of an earlier episode **2** a sudden, vivid recollection of a past event

flash′bulb′ *n.* a bulb giving a brief, bright light, for taking photographs

flash′cube′ *n.* a rotating cube with flashbulbs in four sides

flash′-for′ward *n.* an interruption in the continuity of a story, etc. by the telling or showing of a future episode

flash′ing *n.* sheets of metal used to weatherproof roof joints or edges

flash′light′ *n.* a portable electric light

flash point the lowest temperature at which vapor, as of an oil, will ignite with a flash

flash′y *adj.* **-i·er, -i·est 1** dazzling **2** gaudy; showy —**flash′i·ness *n.***

flask (flask) ***n.*** ⟦< L *flasca*, bottle⟧ **1** any bottle-shaped container used in laboratories, etc. **2** a small, flat container for liquor, etc., to be carried in the pocket

flat[1] (flat) ***adj.*** **flat′ter, flat′test** ⟦< ON *flatr*⟧ **1** having a smooth, level surface **2** lying spread out **3** broad, even,

THESAURUS

flabby ***a.*** flaccid, slack, soft; see FAT.

flag[1] ***n.*** banner, standard, colors; see EMBLEM.

flag[1] ***v.*** signal, wave, give a sign to; see SIGNAL.

flagrant ***a.*** notorious, disgraceful, infamous; see OUTRAGEOUS.

flair ***n.*** talent, aptitude, gift; see ABILITY.

flake ***n.*** scale, cell, sheet, wafer, peel, skin, slice, sliver, layer, leaf, shaving, plate, section, scab.

flake ***v.*** scale, peel, sliver, shed, drop, chip, slice, pare, trim, wear away.

flamboyant ***a.*** baroque, bombastic, ostentatious; see ORNATE.

flame ***n.*** blaze, flare, flash; see FIRE 1.

flame ***v.*** blaze, oxidize, flare up; see BURN.

flaming ***a.*** blazing, ablaze, fiery; see BURNING.

flannel ***n.*** light woolen cloth, cotton flannel, flannelette; see WOOL.

flap ***n.*** fold, tab, lapel, fly, cover, pendant, drop, tail, appendage, tag, accessory, apron, strip.

flap ***v.*** flutter, flash, swing; see WAVE 1.

flare ***n.*** glare, brief blaze, spark; see FLASH.

flare ***v.*** blaze, glow, burn; see FLASH. —**flare up 1** [*Said of persons*] lose one's temper, rant, seethe; see RAGE 1. **2** [*Said of fire*] glow, burst into flame, blaze; see BURN.

flash ***n.*** glimmer, sparkle, glitter, glisten, gleam, beam, blaze, flicker, flame, glare, burst, impulse, vision, dazzle, shimmer, shine, glow, twinkle, twinkling, phosphorescence, reflection, radiation, ray, luster, spark, streak, stream, illumination, incandescence.

flash ***v.*** glimmer, sparkle, glitter, glisten, gleam, beam, blaze, flame, glare, dazzle, shimmer, shine, glow, twinkle, reflect, radiate, shoot out beams, flicker; see also SHINE 1, 2.

flashlight ***n.*** electric lantern, spotlight, torch (British); see LIGHT 1.

flashy ***a.*** gaudy, showy, ostentatious; see ORNATE.

flask ***n.*** decanter, jug, canteen; see BOTTLE.

flat[1] ***a.*** **1** [Lying in a smooth plane] level, even, smooth, spread out, extended, prostrate, horizontal, low, on a level, fallen, level with the ground, prone.—*Ant.* ROUGH, raised, uneven. **2** [Lacking savor] unseasoned, insipid, flavorless; see TASTELESS 1.

and thin **4** absolute *[a flat denial]* **5** not fluctuating *[a flat rate]* **6** tasteless; insipid **7** not interesting **8** emptied of air *[a flat tire]* **9** without gloss *[flat paint]* **10** *Music a)* lower in pitch by a half step *b)* below true pitch —***adv.*** **1** in a flat manner or position **2** exactly **3** *Music* below true pitch —***n.*** **1** anything flat, esp. a surface, part, or expanse **2** a deflated tire **3** *Music a)* a note one half step below another *b)* the symbol (♭) for this —***vt.*** **flat'ted, flat'ting** *Music* to make flat —***vi.*** to sing or play below true pitch —**fall flat** to fail in the desired effect —**flat'ly** ***adv.*** —**flat'ness** ***n.*** —**flat'tish** ***adj.***

flat[2] (flat) ***n.*** ⟦< Scot dial. *flet,* floor⟧ [Chiefly Brit.] an apartment or suite of rooms

flat'bed' ***n.*** a truck, trailer, etc. having a bed or platform without sides or stakes

flat'boat' ***n.*** a flat-bottomed boat for carrying freight in shallow bodies of water or on rivers

flat'car' ***n.*** a railroad freight car without sides or a roof

flat'fish' ***n.***, *pl.* **-fish'** or (for different species) **-fish'es** a fish having both eyes and mouth on the upper side of a very flat body

flat'foot' ***n.*** **1** a condition of the foot in which the instep arch is flattened **2** *pl.* **-foots'** or **-feet'** [Slang] a policeman —**flat'-foot'ed** ***adj.***

flat'i'ron ***n.*** an iron for clothes

flat'-out' ***adj.*** [Inf.] **1** at full speed, with maximum effort, etc. **2** absolute; thorough

flat·ten (flat''n) ***vt., vi.*** to make or become flat or flatter

flat·ter (flat'ər) ***vt.*** ⟦< OFr *flater,* to smooth⟧ **1** to praise insincerely **2** to try to please, as by praise **3** to make seem more attractive than is so **4** to gratify the vanity of —**flat'ter·er** ***n.*** —**flat'ter·ing·ly** ***adv.*** —**flat'ter·y** ***n.***

flat'top' ***n.*** [Slang] **1** an aircraft carrier **2** a haircut in which the hair on top of the head is cut so as to form a flat surface

flat·u·lent (flach'ə lənt) ***adj.*** ⟦see fol.⟧ **1** having or producing gas in the stomach or intestines **2** pompous —**flat'u·lence** ***n.***

fla·tus (flāt'əs) ***n.*** ⟦L < *flare,* to blow⟧ intestinal gas

flat'ware' ***n.*** knives, forks, and spoons

flat'worm' ***n.*** any of various worms with flat bodies, as the tapeworm

Flau·bert (flō ber'), **Gus·tave** (güs tàv') 1821-80; Fr. novelist

flaunt (flônt) ***vi.*** ⟦? < dial. *flant,* to strut⟧ to make a gaudy or defiant display —***vt.*** **1** to show off proudly or defiantly **2** FLOUT: usage objected to by many —**flaunt'ing·ly** ***adv.***

flau·tist (flôt'ist, flout'-) ***n.*** ⟦< It⟧ *var. of* FLUTIST

fla·vor (flā'vər) ***n.*** ⟦ult. < L *flare,* to blow⟧ **1** that quality of a substance that is a mixing of its characteristic taste and smell **2** flavoring **3** characteristic quality —***vt.*** to give flavor to Brit. sp. **fla'vour** —**fla'vor·ful** ***adj.*** —**fla'vor·less** ***adj.***

fla'vor·ing ***n.*** an essence, extract, etc. that adds flavor to food or drink

flaw (flô) ***n.*** ⟦ME, a flake, splinter⟧ **1** a crack, etc. as in a gem **2** a fault, as in reasoning —**flaw'less** ***adj.*** —**flaw'less·ly** ***adv.*** —**flaw'less·ness** ***n.***

flax (flaks) ***n.*** ⟦< OE *fleax*⟧ **1** a slender, erect plant with delicate blue flowers: its seed (**flax'seed'**) is used to make linseed oil **2** the fibers of this plant, which are spun into linen thread

flax·en (flak'sən) ***adj.*** **1** of or made of flax **2** pale-yellow

flay (flā) ***vt.*** ⟦OE *flean*⟧ **1** to strip off the skin of, as by whipping **2** to criticize harshly

flea (flē) ***n.*** ⟦OE *fleah*⟧ a small, wingless jumping insect that is a bloodsucking parasite as an adult

flea market an outdoor bazaar dealing mainly in cheap, secondhand goods

fleck (flek) ***n.*** ⟦ON *flekkr*⟧ a spot, speck, or flake —***vt.*** to spot; speckle

fled (fled) ***vi., vt.*** *pt. & pp. of* FLEE

fledg·ling (flej'liŋ) ***n.*** ⟦< ME *flegge,* ready to fly⟧ **1** a young bird just able to fly **2** a young, inexperienced person Also, chiefly Brit., **fledge'ling**

flee (flē) ***vi.*** **fled, flee'ing** ⟦OE *fleon*⟧ **1** to go swiftly or escape, as from danger **2** to pass away swiftly —***vt.*** to run away or try to escape from

fleece (flēs) ***n.*** ⟦OE *fleos*⟧ **1** the wool covering a sheep or similar animal **2** a soft, warm, napped fabric —***vt.*** **fleeced, fleec'ing** **1** to shear the fleece from **2** to swindle —**fleec'er** ***n.***

fleec·y (flēs'ē) ***adj.*** **-i·er, -i·est** of or like fleece; soft and light —**fleec'i·ness** ***n.***

fleet[1] (flēt) ***n.*** ⟦OE *fleot*⟧ **1** a number of warships under one command **2** any group of ships, trucks, etc. under one control

fleet[2] (flēt) ***adj.*** ⟦< OE *fleotan,* to float⟧ swift; rapid —**fleet'ness** ***n.***

fleet'ing ***adj.*** passing swiftly —**fleet'ing·ly** ***adv.*** —**fleet'ing·ness** ***n.***

Flem·ish (flem'ish) ***adj.*** of Flanders or its people, language, etc. —***n.*** the West Germanic language of Flanders

flesh (flesh) ***n.*** ⟦OE *flæsc*⟧ **1** the soft substance of the body; esp., the muscular tissue **2** meat **3** the pulpy part of fruits and vegetables **4** the body as distinct from the soul **5** all humankind **6** yellowish pink —**in the flesh** **1** alive **2** in person —**one's (own) flesh and blood** one's close relatives —**flesh'y, -i·er, -i·est,** ***adj.***

flesh'-and-blood' ***adj.*** **1** alive **2** actual **3** present; in person

flesh'ly ***adj.*** **-li·er, -li·est** **1** of the body; corporeal **2** sensual

fleur-de-lis (flur'də lē') ***n.***, *pl.* **fleurs-de-lis** (flur' də lē', -lēz') ⟦< OFr *flor de lis,* lit., flower of the lily⟧ a lilylike emblem: the coat of arms of the former French royal family

flew (flo͞o) ***vi., vt.*** *pt. of* FLY[1]

flex (fleks) ***vt., vi.*** ⟦< L *flectere,* to bend⟧ **1** to bend (an arm, knee, etc.) **2** to shorten and thicken (a muscle) in action

flex·i·ble (flek'sə bəl) ***adj.*** **1** able to bend without breaking; pliant **2** easily influenced **3** adjustable to change —**flex'i·bil'i·ty** ***n.***

flex'time' ***n.*** a system allowing individual employees some flexibility in choosing when they work

flib·ber·ti·gib·bet (flib'ər tē jib'it) ***n.*** ⟦< ?⟧ a frivolous, flighty person

flick[1] (flik) ***n.*** ⟦echoic⟧ a light, quick stroke —***vt.*** to strike, remove, etc. with a light, quick stroke

THESAURUS

flatten ***v.*** level off, even out, smooth, spread out, depress, squash, smash, level, even, knock down, wear down, beat down, fell, floor, ground, roll out, straighten, deflate.—*Ant.* RAISE, elevate, inflate.

flattened ***a.*** leveled, depressed, smoothed; see FLAT 1.

flatter ***v.*** overpraise, adulate, glorify; see PRAISE 1.

flatterer ***n.*** parasite, toady, sycophant, flunky, slave, puppet, groveler, sniveler, yes man*, bootlicker*, apple polisher*, doormat*.

flattering ***a.*** pleasing, favorable, unduly favorable; see COMPLIMENTARY.

flattery ***n.*** adulation, compliments, blandishment, sycophancy, applause, false praise, commendation, tribute, gratification, pretty speeches, soft words, fawning, blarney, soft soap*, hokum*, mush*.—*Ant.* HATRED, criticism, censure.

flaunt ***v.*** vaunt, display, brandish; see BOAST.

flaunting ***a.*** gaudy, ostentatious, pretentious; see ORNATE.

flavor ***n.*** taste, savor, tang, relish, smack, twang, gusto, piquancy, zest, aftertaste. *Individual flavors include the following:* tartness, sweetness, acidity, saltiness, spiciness, pungency, piquancy, astringency, bitterness, sourness, pepperiness, hotness, gaminess, greasiness, fishy taste.

flavor ***v.*** season, salt, pepper, spice, give a tang to, make tasty, bring out a flavor in, put in flavoring.

flavoring ***n.*** essence, extract, seasoning, spice, additive, condiment, sauce, relish; see also HERB, SPICE.

flavorless ***a.*** insipid, flat, bland; see TASTELESS 1.

flaw ***n.*** defect, imperfection, stain; see BLEMISH.

flawless ***a.*** faultless, sound, impeccable; see PERFECT.

flea ***n.*** dog flea, sand flea, flea beetle; see INSECT.

fleck ***n.*** mite, speck, dot; see BIT 1.

flee ***v.*** desert, escape, run; see RETREAT.

fleet[1] ***n.*** armada, naval force, task force; see NAVY.

flesh ***n.*** meat, fat, muscle, brawn, tissue, cells, flesh and blood, protoplasm, body parts, heart, insides*. —**one's (own) flesh and blood** family, kindred, kin; see RELATIVE.

fleshy ***a.*** obese, plump, corpulent; see FAT.

flexibility ***n.*** pliancy, plasticity, flexibleness, pliableness, suppleness, elasticity, extensibility, limberness, litheness.

flexible ***a.*** limber, lithe, supple, plastic, elastic, bending, malleable, pliable, soft, spongy, tractable, moldable, yielding, formable, bendable, impressionable, like putty, like wax, adjustable, stretchable, resilient, rubbery, springy.—*Ant.* STIFF, hard, rigid.

flick[2] (flik) ***n.*** ⟦< fol.⟧ [Slang] a film —**the flicks** [Slang] a showing of a film

flick·er (flik′ər) ***vi.*** ⟦OE *flicorian*⟧ **1** to move with a quick, light, wavering motion **2** to burn or shine unsteadily —***n.*** **1** a flickering **2** a dart of flame or light

fli·er (flī′ər) ***n.*** **1** a thing that flies **2** an aviator **3** a bus, train, etc. with a fast schedule **4** a widely distributed handbill **5** [Inf.] a reckless gamble

flight[1] (flīt) ***n.*** ⟦OE *flyht*⟧ **1** the act, manner, or power of flying **2** the distance flown **3** a group of things flying together **4** an airplane scheduled to fly a certain trip **5** a trip by airplane **6** a soaring above the ordinary *[a flight of fancy]* **7** a set of stairs, as between landings

flight[2] (flīt) ***n.*** ⟦< OE *fleon*, flee⟧ a fleeing from or as from danger

flight attendant an airplane attendant who sees to passengers' comfort and safety

flight′less ***adj.*** not able to fly

flight′y ***adj.*** **-i·er, -i·est** **1** given to sudden whims; frivolous **2** easily excited, upset, etc. —**flight′i·ness** ***n.***

flim·sy (flim′zē) ***adj.*** **-si·er, -si·est** ⟦< ?⟧ **1** easily broken or damaged; frail **2** ineffectual *[a flimsy excuse]* —**flim′si·ly** ***adv.*** —**flim′si·ness** ***n.***

flinch (flinch) ***vi.*** ⟦< OFr *flenchir*⟧ to draw back from a blow or anything difficult or painful —***n.*** a flinching

fling (fliŋ) ***vt.*** **flung, fling′ing** ⟦< ON *flengja*, to whip⟧ **1** to throw, esp. with force; hurl **2** to put abruptly or violently **3** to move (one's limbs, head, etc.) suddenly —***n.*** **1** a flinging **2** a brief time of wild pleasures **3** a spirited dance **4** [Inf.] a try **5** [Inf.] a brief love affair

flint (flint) ***n.*** ⟦OE⟧ a very hard, siliceous rock, usually gray, that produces sparks when struck against steel —**flint′y, -i·er, -i·est,** ***adj.***

flip[1] (flip) ***vt.*** **flipped, flip′ping** ⟦echoic⟧ **1** to toss with a quick jerk; flick **2** to snap (a coin) into the air with the thumb **3** to turn or turn over —***vi.*** **1** to move jerkily **2** [Slang] to lose self-control —***n.*** a flipping —**flip one's lid** (or **wig**) [Slang] to go berserk

flip[2] (flip) ***adj.*** **flip′per, flip′pest** [Inf.] flippant

flip chart a series of large paper sheets containing information, charts, etc., fastened loosely for sequential display

flip′pant (-ənt) ***adj.*** ⟦prob. < FLIP[1]⟧ frivolous and disrespectful; saucy —**flip′pan·cy,** *pl.* **-cies,** ***n.*** —**flip′pant·ly** ***adv.***

flip′per (-ər) ***n.*** ⟦< FLIP[1]⟧ **1** a broad, flat limb adapted for swimming, as in seals **2** a paddlelike rubber device worn on each foot by skin divers, etc.

flirt (flurt) ***vt.*** ⟦< ?⟧ to move jerkily *[the bird flirted its tail]* —***vi.*** **1** to pay amorous attention to someone, without serious intentions **2** to trifle or toy *[to flirt with an idea]* —***n.*** **1** a quick, jerky movement **2** one who flirts with others

flir·ta·tion (flər tā′shən) ***n.*** a frivolous love affair —**flir·ta′tious** ***adj.***

flit (flit) ***vi.*** **flit′ted, flit′ting** ⟦< ON *flytja*⟧ to pass or fly lightly and rapidly

float (flōt) ***n.*** ⟦< OE *flota*, a ship⟧ **1** anything that stays on the surface of a liquid, as a raftlike platform for swimmers, a cork on a fishing line, etc. **2** a floating ball, etc. that regulates a valve, as in a water tank **3** a low, flat vehicle decorated for exhibit in a parade **4** a beverage with ice cream floating in it —***vi.*** **1** to stay on the surface of a liquid **2** to drift easily on water, in air, etc. **3** to move about aimlessly **4** to fluctuate freely: said of exchange rates —***vt.*** **1** to cause to float **2** to put into circulation *[to float a bond issue]* **3** to arrange for (a loan) —**float′er** ***n.***

flock (fläk) ***n.*** ⟦OE *flocc*⟧ **1** a group of certain animals, as sheep, birds, etc., living or feeding together **2** any group, esp. a large one —***vi.*** to assemble or travel in a flock or crowd

flock·ing (fläk′iŋ) ***n.*** ⟦< L *floccus*, tuft of wool⟧ **1** tiny fibers of wool, rayon, etc. applied to a fabric, wallpaper, etc. as a velvetlike surface: also **flock** **2** such a fabric, etc.

floe (flō) ***n.*** ⟦? < Norw *flo*, layer⟧ ICE FLOE

flog (fläg, flôg) ***vt.*** **flogged, flog′ging** ⟦? < L *flagellare*, to whip⟧ to beat with a stick, whip, etc. —**flog′ger** ***n.***

flood (flud) ***n.*** ⟦OE *flod*⟧ **1** an overflowing of water on an area normally dry **2** the rising of the tide **3** a great outpouring, as of words —***vt.*** **1** to cover or fill, as with a flood **2** to put too much water, fuel, etc. on or in —***vi.*** **1** to gush out in a flood **2** to become flooded —**the Flood** *Bible* the great flood in Noah's time

flood′light′ ***n.*** **1** a lamp that casts a broad beam of bright light **2** such a beam of light —***vt.*** **-light′ed** or **-lit′, -light′ing** to illuminate by a floodlight

flood tide the rising tide

floor (flôr) ***n.*** ⟦OE *flor*⟧ **1** the inside bottom surface of a room **2** the bottom surface of anything *[the ocean floor]* **3** a story in a building **4** the right to speak in an assembly —***vt.*** **1** to furnish with a floor **2** to knock down **3** [Inf.] *a)* to defeat *b)* to flabbergast; astound

floor′board′ ***n.*** **1** a board in a floor **2** the floor of an automobile, etc.

floor exercise any gymnastic exercise done without apparatus

floor′ing ***n.*** **1** a floor or floors **2** material for making a floor

floor show a show presenting singers, dancers, etc., as in a nightclub

flop (fläp) ***vt.*** **flopped, flop′ping** ⟦var. of FLAP⟧ to flap or throw noisily and clumsily —***vi.*** **1** to move, drop, or flap around loosely or clumsily **2** [Inf.] to fail —***n.*** **1** the act or sound of flopping **2** [Inf.] a failure —**flop′py, -pi·er, -pi·est,** ***adj.***

flop′house′ ***n.*** [Inf.] a cheap hotel for indigents

floppy disk a small, flexible computer disk for storing data

flo·ra (flôr′ə) ***n.*** ⟦L < *flos*, a flower⟧ the plants of a specified region or time

flo′ral (-əl) ***adj.*** of or like flowers

Flor·ence (flôr′əns) city in central Italy: pop. 403,000 —**Flor′en·tine′** (-ən tēn′) ***adj.***, ***n.***

flo·res·cence (flō res′əns) ***n.*** ⟦< L *flos*, a flower⟧ a blooming or flowering —**flo·res′cent** ***adj.***

flor·id (flôr′id) ***adj.*** ⟦< L *flos*, a flower⟧ **1** ruddy: said of the complexion **2** gaudy; showy; ornate

Flor·i·da (flôr′ə də, flär′-) Southern state of the SE U.S.: 53,937 sq. mi.; pop. 12,938,000; cap. Tallahassee: abbrev. *FL* —**Flo·rid·i·an** (flō rid′ē ən) or **Flor′i·dan** ***adj.***, ***n.***

THESAURUS

flicker ***v.*** sparkle, twinkle, glitter; see FLASH, SHINE 1.

flight[1,2] ***n.*** **1** [Act of remaining aloft] soaring, winging, flying, journey by air. **2** [Travel by air] aerial navigation, aeronautics, flying, gliding, space flight, air transport, aviation. **3** [Act of fleeing] fleeing, running away, retreating; see RETREAT 1. **4** [Stairs] steps, staircase, stairway; see STAIRS.

flighty ***a.*** capricious, fickle, whimsical; see CHANGING.

flimsy ***a.*** slight, infirm, frail, weak, unsubstantial, inadequate, defective, wobbly, fragile, makeshift, decrepit; see also POOR 2.

flinch ***v.*** start, shrink back, blench; see COWER.

fling ***n.*** indulgence, party, good time; see CELEBRATION.

fling ***v.*** toss, sling, dump; see THROW 1.

flippancy ***n.*** impertinence, impudence, sauciness; see RUDENESS.

flippant ***a.*** impudent, saucy, smart*; see RUDE 2.

flirt ***n.*** coquette, tease, wolf*; see LOVER.

flirt ***v.*** coquet, make advances, make eyes at; see SEDUCE.

float ***n.*** buoy, air cell, air cushion, pontoon, bobber, cork, raft, diving platform, life preserver.

float ***v.*** waft, stay afloat, swim; see DRIFT.

floating ***a.*** buoyant, hollow, unsinkable, lighter-than-water, light, swimming, inflated, sailing, soaring, volatile, loose, free.—*Ant.* HEAVY, submerged, sunk.

flock ***n.*** group, pack, drove; see HERD.

flock ***v.*** throng, congregate, crowd; see GATHER 1.

flood ***n.*** deluge, surge, tide, high tide, flash flood, overflow, torrent, wave, flood tide, tidal flood, tidal flow, inundation.

flood ***v.*** inundate, swamp, overflow, deluge, submerge, immerse, brim over.

floor ***n.*** **1** [The lower limit of a room] floorboards, deck, flagstones, tiles, planking, ground, carpet, rug, linoleum. **2** [The space in a building between two floors] story, stage, landing, level, basement, cellar, ground floor, ground story, lower story, first floor, mezzanine, upper story, downstairs, upstairs, loft, attic, garret, penthouse.

flooring ***n.*** floors, woodwork, oak flooring, hardwood flooring, tile, flagstones, boards, cement, floor covering, linoleum.

flop ***v.*** **1** [To move with little control] wobble, teeter, stagger, flounder, wriggle, squirm, stumble, tumble, totter, flounce, quiver, flap. **2** [To fall without restraint] tumble, slump, drop; see FALL 1. **3** [*To be a complete failure] founder, fall short, bomb*; see FAIL 1.

flor·in (flôr′in) ***n.*** ⟦< L *flos*, a flower⟧ any of various European or South African silver or gold coins

flo·rist (flôr′ist) ***n.*** ⟦< L *flos*, a flower⟧ one who grows or sells flowers

floss (flôs, fläs) ***n.*** ⟦ult. < L *floccus*, tuft of wool⟧ **1** the short, downy waste fibers of silk **2** a soft, loosely twisted thread or yarn, as of silk, for embroidery **3** a substance like this **4** DENTAL FLOSS —***vt., vi.*** to clean (the teeth) with dental floss —**floss′y, -i·er, -i·est, *adj.***

flo·ta·tion (flō tā′shən) ***n.*** the act or condition of floating

flo·til·la (flō til′ə) ***n.*** ⟦Sp, dim. of *flota*, a fleet⟧ **1** a small fleet **2** a fleet of boats or small ships

flot·sam (flät′səm) ***n.*** ⟦< MDu *vloten*, to float⟧ the wreckage of a ship or its cargo floating at sea: used in the phrase **flotsam and jetsam**

flounce[1] (flouns) ***vi.*** **flounced, flounc′ing** ⟦< ? Scand⟧ to move with quick, flinging motions of the body, as in anger —***n.*** a flouncing

flounce[2] (flouns) ***n.*** ⟦< OFr *froncir*, to wrinkle⟧ a wide ruffle sewn to a skirt, sleeve, etc. —**flounc′y, -i·er, -i·est, *adj.***

floun·der[1] (floun′dər) ***vi.*** ⟦< ? FOUNDER⟧ **1** to struggle awkwardly, as in deep mud **2** to speak or act in an awkward, confused manner

floun·der[2] (floun′dər) ***n.*** ⟦< Scand⟧ any of various flatfishes caught for food, as the halibut

flour (flour) ***n.*** ⟦orig., flower (i.e., best) of meal⟧ **1** a fine, powdery substance produced by grinding and sifting grain, esp. wheat **2** any finely powdered substance —**flour′y *adj.***

flour·ish (flur′ish) ***vi.*** ⟦< L *flos*, a flower⟧ **1** to grow vigorously; thrive **2** to be at the peak of development, etc. —***vt.*** to brandish (a sword, etc.) —***n.*** **1** anything done in a showy way **2** a brandishing **3** decorative lines in handwriting **4** a musical fanfare

flout (flout) ***vt., vi.*** ⟦< ? ME *flouten*, play the flute⟧ to mock or scoff —***n.*** a scornful act or remark —**flout′er *n.***

flow (flō) ***vi.*** ⟦OE *flowan*⟧ **1** to move as a liquid does **2** to move gently and smoothly **3** to pour out **4** to issue; proceed **5** to hang loose *[flowing* hair*]* **6** to be plentiful —***n.*** **1** a flowing **2** the rate of flow **3** anything that flows **4** the rising of the tide

flow′chart′ *n.* a diagram showing steps in a sequence of operations, as in manufacturing

flow·er (flou′ər) ***n.*** ⟦< L *flos*⟧ **1** the seed-producing structure of a flowering plant; blossom **2** a plant cultivated for its blossoms **3** the best or finest part —***vi.*** **1** to produce blossoms **2** to reach the best stage —**in flower** flowering

flow′er·pot′ *n.* a container in which to grow plants

flow′er·y *adj.* -i·er, -i·est **1** covered or decorated with flowers **2** full of ornate expressions and fine words —**flow′er·i·ness *n.***

flown (flōn) ***vi., vt. pp. of*** FLY[1]

flu (flo͞o) ***n.*** **1** *short for* INFLUENZA **2** a respiratory or intestinal infection caused by a virus

flub (flub) [Inf.] ***vt., vi.*** **flubbed, flub′bing** ⟦< ? FL(OP) + (D)UB[1]⟧ to bungle (a job, stroke, etc.) —***n.*** a blunder

fluc·tu·ate (fluk′cho͞o āt′) ***vi.*** **-at′ed, -at′ing** ⟦< L *fluctus*, a wave⟧ to be continually varying in an irregular way —**fluc′tu·a′tion *n.***

flue (flo͞o) ***n.*** ⟦< ? OFr *fluie*, a flowing⟧ a tube or shaft for the passage of smoke, hot air, etc., esp. in a chimney

flu·ent (flo͞o′ənt) ***adj.*** ⟦< L *fluere*, to flow⟧ **1** flowing or moving smoothly **2** able to write or speak easily, expressively, etc. —**flu′en·cy *n.*** —**flu′ent·ly *adv.***

fluff (fluf) ***n.*** ⟦? blend of *flue*, soft mass + PUFF⟧ **1** soft, light down **2** a loose, soft mass, as of hair **3** something trivial —***vt.*** **1** to shake or pat until loose or fluffy **2** to bungle (one's lines), as in acting

fluff′y *adj.* -i·er, -i·est soft and light like fluff; feathery

flu·id (flo͞o′id) ***adj.*** ⟦< L *fluere*, to flow⟧ **1** that can flow as a liquid or gas does **2** that can change rapidly or easily **3** available for investment or as cash —***n.*** a liquid or gas —**flu·id′i·ty *n.*** —**flu′id·ly *adv.***

fluke[1] (flo͝ok) ***n.*** ⟦OE *floc*, a flatfish⟧ TREMATODE

fluke[2] (flo͝ok) ***n.*** ⟦< ?⟧ **1** a pointed end of an anchor, which catches in the ground **2** a barb of a harpoon, etc. **3** a lobe of a whale's tail **4** [Inf.] a stroke of luck

flung (fluŋ) ***vt. pt. & pp. of*** FLING

flunk (fluŋk) ***vt., vi.*** ⟦< ?⟧ [Inf.] to fail, as in a school assignment

flunk·y (fluŋ′kē) ***n., pl.*** **-ies** ⟦orig. Scot⟧ **1** a toady **2** a person with menial tasks Also **flunk′ey**

fluo·resce (flô res′) ***vi.*** **-resced′, -resc′ing** to produce, show, or undergo fluorescence

fluo·res′cence (-res′əns) ***n.*** ⟦ult. < L *fluor*, flux⟧ **1** the property of producing light when acted upon by radiant energy **2** the production of such light **3** light so produced —**fluo·res′cent *adj.***

fluorescent lamp (or **tube**) a glass tube coated on the inside with a fluorescent substance that gives off light (**fluorescent light**) when mercury vapor in the tube is acted upon by a stream of electrons

fluo·ri·date (flôr′ə dāt′, flo͝or′-) ***vt.*** **-dat′ed, -dat′ing** to add fluorides to (a supply of drinking water) in order to reduce tooth decay —**fluo′ri·da′tion *n.***

fluo·ride (flôr′īd′, flo͝or′īd′) ***n.*** any of various compounds of fluorine, esp. one put in toothpaste, etc. to prevent tooth decay

fluo′rine′ (-ēn′) ***n.*** ⟦< L *fluor*, flux⟧ a greenish-yellow, gaseous chemical element

fluo′rite′ (-īt′) ***n.*** ⟦< L *fluor*, flux⟧ calcium fluoride, a transparent, crystalline mineral: the principal source of fluorine

fluo′ro·car′bon (-kär′bən) ***n.*** any of certain compounds containing carbon, fluorine, and, sometimes, hydrogen

fluo′ro·scope′ (-skōp′) ***n.*** a machine for examining internal structures by viewing the shadows cast on a fluorescent screen by objects through which X-rays are directed

flur·ry (flur′ē) ***n., pl.*** **-ries** ⟦< ?⟧ **1** a sudden gust of wind, rain, or snow **2** a sudden commotion —***vt.*** **-ried, -ry·ing** to confuse; agitate

flush[1] (flush) ***vi.*** ⟦blend of FLASH & ME *flusshen*, fly up suddenly⟧ **1** to flow rapidly **2** to blush or glow **3** to be washed out with a sudden flow of water **4** to start up from cover: said of birds —***vt.*** **1** to wash out with a sudden flow of water **2** to make blush or glow **3** to excite *[flushed* with victory*]* **4** to drive (birds) from cover —***n.*** **1** a rapid flow, as of water **2** a sudden, vigorous

THESAURUS

flounder[1] ***v.*** struggle, wallow, blunder; see FLOP 1, TOSS 2.

flour *n.* meal, pulp, powder, grit, bran, starch, wheat germ, white flour, wheat flour, rye flour, potato flour, barley meal, cornmeal, oatmeal, cake flour, pancake flour, soy flour, unbleached flour, semolina, rice flour, all-purpose flour.

flourish *v.* thrive, increase, wax; see SUCCEED 1.

flourishing *a.* thriving, doing well, growing; see RICH 1, SUCCESSFUL.

flow *n.* current, movement, progress, stream, tide, run, river, flood, ebb, surge, influx, outpouring, effusion, gush, spurt, spout, leakage, dribble, oozing, flux, overflow, issue, discharge, drift, course, draft, downdraft, up-current, wind, breeze.

flow *v.* stream, course, slide, slip, glide, move, progress, run, pass, float, sweep, rush, whirl, surge, roll, swell, ebb, pour out, spurt, squirt, flood, spout, rush, gush, well up, drop, drip, seep, trickle, overflow, spill, spew, brim, leak, run out, ooze, splash, pour forth, bubble.

flower *n.* blossom, bud, spray, cluster, shoot, posy*, herb, vine, annual, perennial, flowering shrub, potted plant; see also FRUIT. *Common flowers include the following:* daisy, violet, cowslip, jack-in-the-pulpit, goldenrod, orchid, primrose, bluebell, salvia, geranium, begonia, pansy, calendula, forsythia, daffodil, jonquil, crocus, dahlia, zinnia, tulip, iris, lily, petunia, gladiolus, gladiola, aster, rose, peony, nasturtium, chrysanthemum, poppy, morning-glory, lily of the valley, clematis, buttercup, bougainvillea, dandelion, fuchsia, bridal wreath, lilac, stock, sweet william, bachelor's button, tuberose, bleeding heart, phlox.

flower *v.* open, blossom, bud; see BLOOM.

flowery *a.* elaborate, ornamented, rococo; see ORNATE.

flowing *a.* sweeping, sinuous, spouting, running, gushing, pouring out, rippling, issuing, fluid, tidal, liquid.

fluctuate *v.* vacillate, waver, falter; see HESITATE.

fluctuation *n.* vacillation, variation, rise and fall; see CHANGE 1.

fluency *n.* facility of speech, volubility, command of language; see ELOQUENCE.

fluent *a.* eloquent, voluble, glib, wordy, smooth, talkative, smooth-spoken, garrulous, verbose, chatty, argumentative, articulate, vocal, cogent, persuasive, silver-tongued, having the gift of gab*.—*Ant.* DUMB, tongue-tied, stammering.

fluffy *a.* fleecy, fuzzy, lacy; see SOFT 1.

fluid *a.* liquid, fluent, flowing, running, watery, molten, liquefied, juicy.—*Ant.* STIFF, solid, frozen.

fluid *n.* water, vapor, solution; see LIQUID.

flunk* ***v.*** miss, drop, have to repeat; see FAIL 1.

growth **3** sudden excitement **4** a blush; glow **5** a sudden feeling of heat, as in a fever —*adj.* **1** well supplied, esp. with money **2** abundant **3** level or even (*with*) **4** direct; full —*adv.* **1** so as to be level **2** directly

flush[2] (flush) *n.* ⟦< L *fluere*, to flow⟧ a hand of cards all in the same suit

flus·ter (flus′tər) *vt.*, *vi.* ⟦prob. < Scand⟧ to make or become confused —*n.* a being flustered

flute (flo͞ot) *n.* ⟦< Prov *fläut*⟧ **1** a high-pitched wind instrument consisting of a long, slender tube with finger holes and keys **2** a groove in the shaft of a column, etc. —**flut′ed** *adj.* —**flut′ing** *n.* —**flut′ist** *n.*

flut·ter (flut′ər) *vi.* ⟦< OE *fleotan*, to float⟧ **1** to flap the wings rapidly, without flying **2** to wave, move, or beat rapidly and irregularly —*vt.* to cause to flutter —*n.* **1** a fluttering movement **2** an excited or confused state —**flut′ter·y** *adj.*

flux (fluks) *n.* ⟦< L *fluere*, to flow⟧ **1** a flowing **2** a continual change **3** a substance used to help metals fuse together, as in soldering

fly[1] (flī) *vi.* **flew**, **flown**, **fly′ing** ⟦OE *fleogan*⟧ **1** to move through the air in an aircraft or by using wings, as a bird does **2** to wave or float in the air **3** to move or pass swiftly **4** to flee **5 flied**, **fly′ing** *Baseball* to hit a fly —*vt.* **1** to cause to float in the air **2** to operate (an aircraft) **3** to flee from —*n.*, *pl.* **flies** **1** a flap that conceals the zipper, etc. in a garment **2** a flap serving as the door of a tent **3** *Baseball* a ball batted high in the air **4** [*pl.*] *Theater* the space above a stage —**let fly (at)** **1** to throw (at) **2** to direct a verbal attack (at) —**on the fly** [Inf.] while in a hurry

fly[2] (flī) *n.*, *pl.* **flies** ⟦OE *fleoge*⟧ **1** any of a large group of insects with two or four wings **2** an artificial fly used as a lure in fishing

fly′a·ble *adj.* suitable for flying

fly′by′ or **fly′-by′** *n.*, *pl.* **-bys′** a flight past a designated point or place by an aircraft or spacecraft

fly′-by-night′ *adj.* financially irresponsible —*n.* an absconding debtor

fly′-by-wire′ *adj.* of a system for controlling an airplane or spacecraft electronically, as by computer

fly′-cast′ *vt.* **-cast′**, **-cast′ing** to fish by casting artificial flies

fly′catch′er *n.* a small bird that catches insects in flight

fly′er *n. alt. sp. of* FLIER

flying buttress a buttress connected with a wall by an arch, serving to resist outward pressure

flying colors used in **with flying colors**, with notable success

fly′ing·fish′ *n.*, *pl.* **-fish′** or (for different species) **-fish′es** a fish with winglike fins used in gliding through the air: also **flying fish**

flying saucer a UFO

fly′leaf′ *n.*, *pl.* **-leaves′** a blank leaf at the beginning or end of a book

fly′pa′per *n.* a sticky or poisonous paper set out to catch flies

fly′speck′ *n.* **1** a speck of fly excrement **2** any tiny spot or petty flaw

fly′way′ *n.* a route taken regularly by birds migrating to and from breeding grounds

fly′weight′ *n.* a boxer who weighs 112 pounds or less

fly′wheel′ *n.* a heavy wheel on a machine, for regulating its speed

FM[1] (ef′em′) *n.* frequency-modulation broadcasting or sound transmission

FM[2] *abbrev.* frequency modulation

f-num·ber (ef′num′bər) *n. Photog.* a number indicating the relative aperture of a lens: a higher number means a smaller opening

foal (fōl) *n.* ⟦OE *fola*⟧ a young horse, mule, etc.; colt or filly —*vt.*, *vi.* to give birth to (a foal)

foam (fōm) *n.* ⟦OE *fam*⟧ **1** the whitish mass of bubbles formed on or in liquids by agitation, fermentation, etc. **2** something like foam, as frothy saliva **3** a rigid or spongy cellular mass, made from liquid rubber, plastic, etc. —*vi.* to produce foam —**foam′y**, **-i·er**, **-i·est**, *adj.*

fob (fäb) *n.* ⟦prob. < dial. Ger *fuppe*, a pocket⟧ **1** a short ribbon or chain attached to a pocket watch **2** any ornament worn on such a chain, etc.

fo·cal (fō′kəl) *adj.* of or at a focus

focal length the distance from the optical center of a lens to the point where the light rays converge

fo′c′sle or **fo′c′s′le** (fōk′səl) *contr. n. phonetic sp. of* FORECASTLE

fo·cus (fō′kəs) *n.*, *pl.* **-cus·es** or **-ci′** (-sī′) ⟦L, hearth⟧ **1** the point where rays of light, heat, etc. come together; specif., the point where rays of reflected or refracted light meet **2** FOCAL LENGTH **3** an adjustment of this to make a clear image [*bring a lens into focus*] **4** any center of activity, attention, etc. —*vt.* **-cused** or **-cussed**, **-cus·ing** or **-cus·sing** **1** to bring into focus **2** to adjust the focal length of (the eye, a lens, etc.) so as to produce a clear image **3** to concentrate —**in focus** clear and sharp —**out of focus** blurred

fod·der (fäd′ər) *n.* ⟦OE *fodor*⟧ coarse food for cattle, horses, etc., as hay

foe (fō) *n.* ⟦OE *fah*, hostile⟧ an enemy

foe·tus (fēt′əs) *n. alt. sp. of* FETUS

fog (fôg, fäg) *n.* ⟦prob. < Scand⟧ **1** a large mass of water vapor condensed to fine particles, at or just above the earth's surface **2** a state of mental confusion —*vt.*, *vi.* **fogged**, **fog′ging** to make or become foggy

fog′gy *adj.* **-gi·er**, **-gi·est** **1** full of fog **2** dim; blurred **3** confused —**fog′gi·ness** *n.*

fog′horn′ *n.* a horn blown to warn ships in a fog

fo·gy (fō′gē) *n.*, *pl.* **-gies** ⟦< ?⟧ one who is old-fashioned: usually with *old*: also **fo′gey**, *pl.* **-geys**

foi·ble (foi′bəl) *n.* ⟦< Fr *faible*, feeble⟧ a small weakness in character

foil[1] (foil) *vt.* ⟦< OFr *fuler*, trample⟧ to keep from being successful; thwart

foil[2] (foil) *n.* ⟦< L *folium*, leaf⟧ **1** a very thin sheet of metal **2** a person or thing that sets off another by contrast **3** ⟦< ?⟧ a long, thin, blunted fencing sword

foist (foist) *vt.* ⟦prob. < dial. Du *vuisten*, to hide in the hand⟧ to get (a thing) accepted, sold, etc. by fraud, deception, etc.; palm off: with *on* or *upon*

fol *abbrev.* **1** folio(s) **2** following

fold[1] (fōld) *vt.* ⟦OE *faldan*⟧ **1** to double (material) up on itself **2** to draw together and intertwine [*to fold the arms*] **3** to embrace **4** to wrap up; envelop —*vi.* **1** to be or become folded **2** [Inf.] *a*) to fail, as a business, play, etc. *b*) to fail suddenly; collapse —*n.* a folded part

fold[2] (fōld) *n.* ⟦OE *fald*⟧ **1** a pen for sheep **2** a flock of sheep **3** a group sharing a common faith, goal, etc.

-fold (fōld) ⟦< OE *-feald*⟧ *suffix* **1** having (a specified number of) parts **2** (a specified number of) times as many or as much [*to profit tenfold*]

fold′a·way′ *adj.* that can be folded together for easy storage

THESAURUS

flute *n.* pipe, piccolo, wind instrument, fife, panpipe, recorder; see also MUSICAL INSTRUMENT.

flutter *v.* flap, ripple, tremble; see WAVE 1, 3.

fly[1] *v.* **1** [To pass through the air] wing, soar, float, glide, remain aloft, take flight, take wing, hover, sail, swoop, dart, drift, flutter, circle. **2** [To move swiftly] rush, dart, flee; see SPEED. **3** [To flee from danger] retreat, hide, withdraw; see ESCAPE. **4** [To manage a plane in the air] pilot, navigate, control, take off, operate, glide, climb, dive, manipulate, maneuver.

fly[1,2] *n.* **1** [An insect] housefly, bluebottle, bug, winged insect, gnat, horsefly, fruit fly, tsetse fly. **2** [A ball batted into the air] infield fly, high fly, fly ball, fungo, pop fly. **3** [A hook baited artificially] lure, fish lure, dry fly, wet fly, spinner, trout fly, bass fly, minnow.

flyer *n.* aviator, navigator, airman; see PILOT 1.

flying *a.* floating, passing through the air, on the wing, soaring, gliding, winging, swooping, darting, plummeting, drifting, rising, airborne, in midair.

foam *n.* fluff, bubbles, lather; see FROTH.

focus *n.* focal point, locus, point of convergence; see CENTER 1. —**in focus** distinct, obvious, sharply defined; see CLEAR 2. —**out of focus** indistinct, unclear, blurred; see OBSCURE 1.

focus *v.* **1** [To draw toward a center] concentrate, converge, convene; see CENTER. **2** [To make an image clear] adjust, bring out, get detail; see SHARPEN 2.

foe *n.* opponent, antagonist, adversary; see ENEMY.

fog *n.* mist, haze, cloud, film, steam, wisp, smoke, smog, soup*, pea soup*.

foggy *a.* dull, misty, gray; see HAZY.

fold[1] *n.* lap, pleat, lapel, tuck, folded portion, part turned over, part turned back, doubled material, crease, turn, folded edge, crimp, wrinkle.

fold[1] *v.* **1** [To place together, or lay in folds] double, crease, curl, crimp, wrinkle, ruffle, pucker, gather, lap, overlap, overlay.—*Ant.* UNFOLD, straighten, expand. **2** [*To fail] become insolvent, declare itself bankrupt, close; see FAIL 4.

fold'er *n.* **1** a sheet of heavy paper folded for holding loose papers **2** a pamphlet or circular of one or more folded, unstitched sheets

fo·li·age (fō'lē ij) *n.* ⟦< L *folia*⟧ leaves, as of a plant or tree

fo·lic acid (fō'lik) ⟦< L *folium*, leaf⟧ a substance belonging to the vitamin B complex, used in treating anemia

fo·li·o (fō'lē ō') *n.*, *pl.* **-os'** ⟦< L *folium*, leaf⟧ **1** a large sheet of paper folded once **2** a large size of book, about 12 by 15 inches, made of sheets so folded **3** the number of a page in a book

folk (fōk) *n.*, *pl.* **folks** or **folk** ⟦OE *folc*⟧ **1** a people or nation **2** [*pl.*] people; persons —*adj.* of or originating among the common people —**one's** (or **the**) **folks** [Inf.] one's family, esp. one's parents

folk'lore' *n.* ⟦prec. + LORE⟧ the traditional beliefs, legends, etc. of a culture

folk song **1** a song made and handed down among the common people **2** a song composed in imitation of this —**folk singer**

folk'sy (-sē) *adj.* **-si·er**, **-si·est** [Inf.] friendly or sociable

fol·li·cle (fäl'i kəl) *n.* ⟦< L *follis*, bellows⟧ any small sac, cavity, or gland for excretion or secretion *[a hair follicle]*

fol·low (fäl'ō) *vt.* ⟦< OE *folgian*⟧ **1** to come or go after **2** to pursue **3** to go along *[follow the road]* **4** to take up (a trade, etc.) **5** to result from **6** to take as a model; imitate **7** to obey **8** to watch or listen to closely **9** to be interested in developments in *[to follow local politics]* **10** to understand —*vi.* **1** to come or go after something else in place, time, etc. **2** to result —**follow out** (or **up**) to carry out fully —**follow through** to continue and complete a stroke or action

fol'low·er *n.* one that follows; specif., *a*) one who follows another's teachings; disciple *b*) an attendant

fol'low·ing *adj.* that follows; next after —*n.* a group of followers —*prep.* after *[following dinner they left]*

fol'low-up' *n.* a letter, visit, etc. that follows as a review, addition, etc.

fol·ly (fäl'ē) *n.*, *pl.* **-lies** ⟦see FOOL⟧ **1** a lack of sense; foolishness **2** a foolish action or belief **3** a foolish and useless but expensive undertaking

fo·ment (fō ment') *vt.* ⟦< L *fovere*, keep warm⟧ to stir up (trouble); incite —**fo'men·ta'tion** *n.*

fond (fänd) *adj.* ⟦< ME *fonnen*, be foolish⟧ **1** tender and affectionate; loving or doting **2** cherished *[a fond hope]* —**fond of** having a liking for —**fond'ly** *adv.* —**fond'ness** *n.*

fon·dle (fän'dəl) *vt.* **-dled**, **-dling** ⟦< prec.⟧ to caress or handle lovingly

fon·due or **fon·du** (fän do͞o', fän'do͞o') *n.* ⟦Fr < *fondre*, melt⟧ melted cheese, etc. used as a dip for cubes of bread

font[1] (fänt) *n.* ⟦< L *fons*, spring⟧ **1** a basin to hold baptismal water **2** a container for holy water **3** a source

font[2] (fänt) *n.* ⟦see FOUND[2]⟧ *Printing* a complete assortment of type in one size and style

fon·ta·nel or **fon·ta·nelle** (fänt''n el') *n.* ⟦ME *fontinel*, a hollow⟧ a soft, boneless area in the skull of a baby or young animal, that gradually closes up as bone is formed

food (fo͞od) *n.* ⟦OE *foda*⟧ **1** any substance, esp. a solid, taken in by a plant or animal to enable it to live and grow **2** anything that nourishes

food chain *Ecology* a sequence (as grass, rabbit, fox) of organisms in a community in which each member feeds on the one below it

food poisoning sickness caused by contaminants, as bacteria, in food, or by naturally poisonous foods

food processor an electrical appliance that can blend, purée, slice, grate, chop, etc. foods rapidly

food stamp any of the federal coupons given to qualifying low-income persons for use in buying food

food'stuff' *n.* any substance used as food

fool (fo͞ol) *n.* ⟦< L *follis*, windbag⟧ **1** a silly or stupid person **2** a jester **3** a victim of a trick, etc.; dupe —*vi.* **1** to act like a fool **2** to joke **3** [Inf.] to meddle (*with*) —*vt.* to trick; deceive —**fool around** [Inf.] to trifle —**fool'er·y** *n.*

fool'har'dy *adj.* **-di·er**, **-di·est** foolishly daring; reckless —**fool'har'di·ly** *adv.* —**fool'har'di·ness** *n.*

fool'ish *adj.* **1** silly; unwise **2** ridiculous **3** embarrassed —**fool'ish·ly** *adv.* —**fool'ish·ness** *n.*

fool'proof' *adj.* so simple, well-designed, etc. as not to be mishandled, damaged, misunderstood, etc. even by a fool

fools·cap (fo͞olz'kap') *n.* ⟦from a watermark of a jester's cap⟧ a size of writing paper, 13 by 16 in. in the U.S.

foot (fo͝ot) *n.*, *pl.* **feet** ⟦OE *fot*⟧ **1** the end part of the leg, on which one stands **2** the base or bottom *[the foot of a*

THESAURUS

folder *n.* **1** [A folded sheet of printed matter] circular, pamphlet, paper, bulletin, advertisement, enclosure, brochure, throwaway, insert. **2** [A light, flexible case] envelope, binder, portfolio, Manila folder.

folk *n.* race, nation, community, tribe, society, nationality, population, state, culture group, people, culture, ethnic group, clan, confederation.

folklore *n.* traditions, lore, fables, folk tales, oral tradition, folk wisdom, oral literature, ballad lore, customs, superstitions, legends, folkways, folk wisdom, traditional lore; see also MYTH.

folks* *n.* relatives, relations, kin; see FAMILY.

follow *v.* **1** [To be later in time] come next, ensue, postdate; see SUCCEED 2. **2** [To regulate one's action] conform, observe, imitate, copy, take after, match, mirror, reflect, follow the example of, do as, mimic, follow suit, do like, tag along, obey, abide by, adhere to, comply, be in keeping, be consistent with.—*Ant.* NEGLECT, disregard, depart from. **3** [To observe] heed, regard, keep an eye on; see WATCH. **4** [To understand] comprehend, catch, grasp; see UNDERSTAND 1. **5** [To result] proceed from, happen, ensue; see RESULT. —**as follows** as explained below, as stated in what follows, thus; see FOLLOWING.

follower *n.* henchman, attendant, hanger-on, companion, lackey, helper, partisan, recruit, disciple, pupil, protégé, imitator, apostle, adherent, supporter, zealot, backer, participant, sponsor, witness, devotee, believer, advocate, member, admirer, patron, promoter, upholder, copycat*, yes man*, groupie*.—*Ant.* OPPONENT, deserter, heretic.

following *a.* succeeding, next, ensuing, subsequent, later, after a while, by and by, later on, a while later, then, henceforth, afterwards, presently, afterward, coming after, directly after, in the wake of, pursuing, in pursuit of, in search of, resulting, latter, rear, back.—*Ant.* PRECEDING, former, earlier.

following *n.* group, clientele, public, audience, train, adherents, supporters, hangers-on, patrons.

fond *a.* enamored, attached, affectionate; see LOVING.

fondness *n.* partiality, attachment, kindness; see AFFECTION.

food *n.* victuals, foodstuffs, meat and drink, meat, drink, nutriment, refreshment, edibles, table, comestibles, provisions, stores, sustenance, subsistence, rations, board, cooking, cookery, cuisine, nourishment, fare, grub*, vittles*, eats*, chow*; see also MEAL 2. For food in the menu, see also BREAD, BUTTER, CAKE 2, CANDY, CHEESE, COFFEE, COOKIE, DELICATESSEN 1, DESSERT, DRESSING 1, 2, DRINK 2, EGG, FISH, FLAVORING, FOWL, FRUIT, HERB, JAM 1, JELLY, MEAT, MILK, NUT 1, PASTRY, PICKLE 1, PIE, RELISH 1, ROLL 4, SALAD, SANDWICH, SOUP, SPICE, STEW, TEA, VEAL, VEGETABLE, WINE.

fool *n.* nitwit, simpleton, dunce, oaf, ninny, cretin, nincompoop, dolt, idiot, jackass, ass, buffoon, blockhead, numskull, boob*, goose, ignoramus, imbecile, moron, clown, loon, dullard, fathead*, half-wit, bonehead*, dope*, sap*, birdbrain*, meathead*, lamebrain*, airhead*, ditz*, knucklehead*, dimwit*.—*Ant.* PHILOSOPHER, sage, scholar. —**no** (or **nobody's**) **fool** shrewd, calculating, capable; see ABLE, INTELLIGENT. —**play the fool** be silly, show off, clown; see JOKE.

fool *v.* trick, dupe, mislead; see DECEIVE. —**fool around*** waste time, idle, dawdle; see PLAY 1, 2, WASTE 1, 2.

fooled *a.* tricked, duped, deluded; see DECEIVED.

fooling *a.* joking, jesting, humorous, deceitful, gay, witty, smart, frivolous, flippant, laughable, insincere, misleading, absurd, clever, playful, merry, kidding*, spoofing*.—*Ant.* SERIOUS, grave, earnest.

foolish *a.* silly, simple, half-witted; see STUPID.

foolishly *a.* stupidly, irrationally, idiotically, insanely, imprudently, ineptly, mistakenly, illogically, unwisely, ill-advisedly, crazily, thoughtlessly, carelessly, senselessly, irresponsibly, absurdly, preposterously, ridiculously, with bad judgment, without good sense.

foolishness *n.* folly, weakness, silliness; see STUPIDITY 1.

foot *n.* **1** [A unit of measurement] twelve inches, running foot, front foot, board foot, square foot, cubic foot. **2** [End of the leg] pedal extremity, hoof, paw, pad, dog*, tootsy*. **3** [A foundation] footing, base, pier; see FOUNDATION 2. **4** [A metrical unit in verse] measure, accent, interval, meter, duple meter, triple meter. *Metrical feet include the following:* iamb, dactyl, spondee, trochee, anapest, pyrrhic. —**on foot** running, hiking, moving; see WALKING. —**on one's feet** **1** [Upright] standing, erect, vertical; see STRAIGHT. **2** [Established]

page*]* **3** the muscular part of a mollusk used in burrowing, moving, etc. **4** a measure of length equal to 12 inches: symbol ′ **5** [*with pl. v.*] [Brit.] infantry **6** a group of syllables serving as a unit of meter in verse —***vt.*** **1** to add (a column of figures): often with *up* **2** [Inf.] to pay (costs, etc.) —**foot it** [Inf.] to dance, walk, etc. —**on foot** walking —**under foot** in the way

foot′age (-ij) ***n.*** **1** measurement in feet, as of film **2** a length of film that has been shot

foot′-and-mouth′ disease a contagious disease of cloven-footed animals, causing blisters in the mouth and around the hoofs

foot′ball′ ***n.*** **1** a game played on a rectangular field with an inflated, oval leather ball by two teams that try to score touchdowns **2** [Brit.] *a*) soccer *b*) rugby **3** the ball used in any of these games

foot′bridge′ ***n.*** a bridge for pedestrians

foot′-can′dle ***n.*** a unit for measuring illumination

foot′ed ***adj.*** having feet of a specified number or kind *[four-footed]*

foot′fall′ ***n.*** the sound of a footstep

foot′hill′ ***n.*** a low hill at or near the foot of a mountain or mountain range

foot′hold′ ***n.*** **1** a secure place for a foot, as in climbing **2** a secure position

foot′ing ***n.*** **1** a secure placing of the feet **2** the condition of a surface, as for walking **3** a foothold **4** a secure position **5** a basis for relationship

foot′less (-lis) ***adj.*** **1** without a foot or feet **2** without basis **3** [Inf.] clumsy; inept

foot′lights′ ***pl.n.*** a row of lights along the front of a stage floor —**the footlights** the theater or the profession of acting

foot′lock′er ***n.*** a small trunk, usually kept at the foot of a bed

foot′loose′ ***adj.*** free to go wherever, or do whatever, one likes

foot′man (-mən) ***n.***, *pl.* **-men** (-mən) a male servant who assists the butler

foot′note′ ***n.*** **1** a note of comment or reference at the bottom of a page **2** such a note at the end of a chapter or a book **3** an additional comment, etc. —***vt.*** **-not′ed, -not′ing** to add a footnote or footnotes to

foot′path′ ***n.*** a narrow path for use by pedestrians only

foot′-pound′ ***n.*** a unit of energy or work, the amount required to raise one pound a distance of one foot

foot′print′ ***n.*** **1** a mark made by a foot **2** an area, or its shape, which something affects, occupies, etc.

foot′sore′ ***adj.*** having sore or tender feet, as from much walking

foot′step′ ***n.*** **1** the distance covered in a step **2** the sound of a step **3** FOOTPRINT (sense 1) —**follow in someone's footsteps** to follow someone's example, etc.

foot′stool′ ***n.*** a low stool for supporting the feet of a seated person

foot′wear′ ***n.*** shoes, boots, etc.

foot′work′ ***n.*** the act or manner of using the feet, as in boxing or dancing

fop (fäp) ***n.*** ⟦ME *foppe*, a fool⟧ DANDY (*n.* 1) —**fop′per·y**, *pl.* **-ies**, ***n.*** —**fop′pish** ***adj.*** —**fop′pish·ly** ***adv.***

for (fôr, fʉr) ***prep.*** ⟦OE⟧ **1** in place of *[*use a rope *for* a belt*]* **2** in the interest of *[*to act *for* another*]* **3** in favor of *[*vote *for* the levy*]* **4** in honor of *[*a party *for* her*]* **5** in order to be, get, have, keep, find, etc. *[*walk *for* exercise, start *for* home*]* **6** meant to be received by *[*flowers *for* a friend*]* **7** suitable to *[*a room *for* sleeping*]* **8** with regard to; concerning *[*an ear *for* music*]* **9** as being *[*to know *for* a fact*]* **10** considering the nature of *[*cool *for* July*]* **11** because of *[*a cry *for* pain*]* **12** at the price of *[*sold *for* $20,000*]* **13** to the length, amount, or duration of —***conj.*** because; since —**for all** in spite of

for- ⟦OE⟧ *prefix* away, apart, off *[forbid, forgo]*

for·age (fôr′ij, fär′-) ***n.*** ⟦< OFr *forre*, fodder⟧ **1** food for domestic animals **2** a search for food —***vi.*** **-aged, -ag·ing** **1** to search for food **2** to search for something one wants —***vt.*** to take food from; raid —**for′ag·er** ***n.***

for·ay (fôr′ā) ***vt., vi.*** ⟦< OFr *forrer*, to forage⟧ to plunder —***n.*** a raid in order to seize things

for·bear[1] (fôr ber′) ***vt.*** **-bore′, -borne′, -bear′ing** ⟦see FOR- & BEAR[1]⟧ to refrain from (doing, saying, etc.) —***vi.*** **1** to refrain **2** to control oneself under provocation

for′bear′[2] ***n.*** *alt. sp. of* FOREBEAR

for·bear′ance ***n.*** **1** the act of forbearing **2** self-restraint

for·bid (fər bid′, fôr-) ***vt.*** **-bade′** (-bad′) or **-bad′, -bid′den, -bid′ding** ⟦see FOR- & BID⟧ **1** to order (a person) not to do (something); prohibit **2** to prevent

for·bid′ding ***adj.*** looking dangerous or disagreeable; repellent —**for·bid′ding·ly** ***adv.***

force (fôrs) ***n.*** ⟦< L *fortis*, strong⟧ **1** strength; power **2** physical coercion against a person or thing **3** the power to control, persuade, etc.; effectiveness **4** military power **5** any group of people organized for some activity *[*a sales *force]* **6** energy that causes or alters motion **7** *Law* binding power; validity —***vt.*** **forced, forc′ing** **1** to make do something by force; compel **2** to break open, into, or through by force **3** to take by force; extort **4** to impose by force: with *on* or *upon* **5** to produce as by force *[*to *force* a smile*]* **6** to cause (plants, etc.) to develop faster by artificial means —**in force** **1** in full strength **2** in effect; valid —**force′less** ***adj.***

forced (fôrst) ***adj.*** **1** compulsory *[forced* labor*]* **2** not natural; strained *[*a *forced* smile*]* **3** due to necessity *[*a *forced* landing*]* **4** at a faster pace *[*a *forced* march*]* —**forc·ed·ly** (fôrs′id lē) ***adv.***

force′-feed′ ***vt.*** **-fed′, -feed′ing** to feed as by a tube through the throat to the stomach

force′ful (-fəl) ***adj.*** full of force; powerful, vigorous, effective, etc. —**force′ful·ly** ***adv.*** —**force′ful·ness** ***n.***

for·ceps (fôr′seps′) ***n.***, *pl.* **-ceps′** ⟦L < *formus*, warm + *capere*, to take⟧ small tongs or pincers for grasping, pulling, etc.

THESAURUS

sound, settled, secure; see ESTABLISHED 1. —**on the wrong foot** unfavorably, ineptly, incapably; see WRONGLY. —**put one's best foot forward*** do one's best, appear at one's best, try hard; see DISPLAY. —**put one's foot down*** be firm, act decisively, determine; see RESOLVE. —**under foot** on the ground, at one's feet, in the way; see UNDER 1.

football ***n.*** American football, Canadian football, association football, soccer, gridiron pastime.

football player ***n.*** *In the United States, football players include the following:* end, flanker, tight end, split end, wide receiver, wideout, tackle, guard, center, quarterback, halfback, fullback, running back, blocking back, tailback, H-back, wingback, slotback, linebacker, cornerback, nose guard, free safety, strong safety, punter, place kicker.

foothold ***n.*** ledge, footing, niche; see STEP 2.

footing ***n.*** basis, substructure, support; see FOUNDATION 2.

footprint ***n.*** trace, trail, spoor; see TRACK 2.

footstep ***n.*** trace, trail, evidence; see TRACK 2. —**follow in someone's footsteps** emulate, succeed, resemble a predecessor; see IMITATE 1.

for ***conj.*** as, since, seeing that; see BECAUSE.

for ***prep.*** toward, to, in favor of, intended to be given to, in order to get, under the authority of, in the interest of, during, in order to, in the direction of, to go to, to the amount of, in place of, in exchange for, as, in spite of, supposing, concerning, with respect to, with regard to, notwithstanding, with a view to, for the sake of, in consideration of, in the name of, on the part of.

forbid ***v.*** prohibit, debar, embargo, restrain, inhibit, preclude, oppose, cancel, hinder, obstruct, bar, prevent, censor, outlaw, declare illegal, withhold, restrict, deny, block, check, disallow, deprive, exclude, ban, taboo, say no to, put under an injunction.—*Ant.* APPROVE, recommend, authorize.

forbidden ***a.*** denied, taboo, kept back; see REFUSED.

forbidding ***a.*** unpleasant, offensive, repulsive; see GRIM 1.

force ***n.*** **1** [Force conceived as a physical property] power, might, energy; see STRENGTH. **2** [Force conceived as part of one's personality] forcefulness, dominance, competence, energy, persistence, willpower, drive, determination, effectiveness, efficiency, authority, impressiveness, ability, capability, potency, sapience, guts*.—*Ant.* INDIFFERENCE, impotence, incompetence. **3** [An organization] group, band, army; see ORGANIZATION 2, POLICE. —**in force** **1** [Powerfully] in full strength, totally, all together; see ALL 2. **2** [In operation] operative, valid, in effect; see WORKING.

force ***v.*** compel, coerce, press, drive, make, impel, constrain, oblige, obligate, necessitate, require, enforce, demand, order, command, inflict, burden, impose, insist, exact, put under obligation, contract, charge, restrict, limit, pin down, pressure, bring pressure to bear upon, bear down, ram down someone's throat*, high-pressure*, strong-arm*, put the squeeze on*.

forced ***a.*** compelled, coerced, constrained; see BOUND 2.

forceful ***a.*** commanding, dominant, electric; see POWERFUL 1.

forcefully ***a.*** forcibly, stubbornly, willfully; see VIGOROUSLY.

for·ci·ble (fôr′sə bəl) ***adj.*** **1** done by force **2** having force —**for′ci·bly** ***adv.***

ford (fôrd) ***n.*** ⟦OE⟧ a shallow place in a stream, etc. where one can cross by wading —***vt.*** to cross at a ford —**ford′a·ble** ***adj.***

Ford (fôrd) **1 Ger·ald R(udolph), Jr.** (jer′əld) 1913- ; 38th president of the U.S. (1974-77) **2 Henry** 1863-1947; U.S. automobile manufacturer

fore (fôr) ***adv., adj.*** ⟦OE⟧ at, in, or toward the front part, as of a ship —***n.*** the front —***interj.*** *Golf* a shout warning that one is about to hit the ball

fore- ⟦OE⟧ *prefix* **1** before in time, place, etc. *[forenoon]* **2** the front part of *[forehead]*

fore-and-aft (fôr′ən aft′) ***adj.*** *Naut.* from the bow to the stern; set lengthwise, as sails

fore′arm′[1] ***n.*** the part of the arm between the elbow and the wrist

fore·arm′[2] ***vt.*** to arm in advance

fore′bear′ (-ber′) ***n.*** ⟦< FORE + BE + -ER⟧ an ancestor

fore·bode′ (-bōd′) ***vt., vi.*** **-bod′ed, -bod′ing** ⟦< OE⟧ **1** to foretell; predict **2** to have a presentiment of (something bad) —**fore·bod′ing** ***n.***

fore′cast′ ***vt.*** **-cast′** or **-cast′ed, -cast′ing** **1** to predict **2** to serve as a prediction of —***n.*** a prediction —**fore′cast′er** ***n.***

fore·cas·tle (fōk′səl, fôr′kas′əl) ***n.*** **1** the upper deck of a ship in front of the foremast **2** the front part of a merchant ship, where the crew's quarters are located

fore·close (fôr klōz′) ***vt., vi.*** **-closed′, -clos′ing** ⟦< OFr *fors*, outside + *clore*, CLOSE[2]⟧ to take away the right to redeem (a mortgage) —**fore·clo′sure** (-klō′zhər) ***n.***

fore·doom′ ***vt.*** to doom in advance

fore′fa′ther ***n.*** an ancestor

fore′fin′ger ***n.*** the finger nearest the thumb

fore′foot′ ***n., pl.*** **-feet′** either of the front feet of an animal

fore′front′ ***n.*** **1** the extreme front **2** the position of most importance, activity, etc.

fore·go′[1] ***vt., vi.*** **-went′, -gone′, -go′ing** to go before in place, time, etc.; precede

fore·go′[2] ***vt.*** *alt. sp. of* FORGO

fore′go′ing ***adj.*** previously said, written, etc.; preceding

fore·gone′ ***adj.*** **1** previous **2** previously determined; inevitable

fore′ground′ ***n.*** **1** the part of a scene, etc. nearest to the viewer **2** the most noticeable position —***vt.*** to place in the foreground; emphasize

fore′hand′ ***n.*** a stroke, as in tennis, made with the palm of the hand turned forward —***adj.*** done as with a forehand

fore·head (fôr′ed′, -hed′; fär′-) ***n.*** the part of the face between the eyebrows and the line where the hair normally begins

for·eign (fôr′in, fär′-) ***adj.*** ⟦< L *foras*, out-of-doors⟧ **1** situated outside one's own country, locality, etc. **2** of, from, or having to do with other countries **3** not belonging; not characteristic

for′eign-born′ ***adj.*** born in some other country; not native

for′eign·er ***n.*** a person from another country; alien

foreign minister a member of a governmental cabinet in charge of foreign affairs for the country

fore·know (fôr nō′) ***vt.*** **-knew′, -known′, -know′ing** to have knowledge of beforehand —**fore′knowl′edge** (-näl′ ij) ***n.***

fore′leg′ ***n.*** either of the front legs of an animal

fore′lock′ ***n.*** a lock of hair growing just above the forehead

fore′man (-mən) ***n., pl.*** **-men** (-mən) **1** the chairman of a jury **2** the head of a group of workers

fore′mast′ ***n.*** the mast nearest the bow of a ship

fore′most′ ***adj.*** first in place, time, etc. —***adv.*** first

fore′noon′ ***n.*** the time from sunrise to noon; morning

fo·ren·sic (fə ren′sik, -zik) ***adj.*** ⟦< L *forum*, marketplace⟧ **1** of or suitable for public debate **2** involving the application of scientific, esp. medical, knowledge to legal matters —***n.*** [*pl.*] debate or formal argumentation —**fo·ren′si·cal·ly** ***adv.***

forensic medicine MEDICAL JURISPRUDENCE

fore′or·dain′ ***vt.*** to ordain beforehand; predestine —**fore′or′di·na′tion** ***n.***

fore′run′ner ***n.*** **1** a herald **2** a sign that tells or warns of something to follow **3** a predecessor; ancestor

fore′sail′ (-sāl′, -səl) ***n.*** the lowest sail on the foremast of a square-rigged ship or a schooner

fore·see′ ***vt.*** **-saw′, -seen′, -see′ing** to see or know beforehand —**fore·see′a·ble** ***adj.*** —**fore·se′er** ***n.***

fore·shad′ow ***vt.*** to indicate or suggest beforehand; prefigure

fore·short′en ***vt.*** in drawing, etc., to shorten some lines of (an object) to give the illusion of proper relative size

fore′sight′ ***n.*** **1** *a)* the act of foreseeing *b)* the power to foresee **2** prudent regard or provision for the future

fore′skin′ ***n.*** the fold of skin that covers the end of the penis

for·est (fôr′ist) ***n.*** ⟦< L *foris*, out-of-doors⟧ a thick growth of trees, etc. covering a large tract of land —***vt.*** to plant with trees

fore·stall′ ***vt.*** ⟦< OE *foresteall*, ambush⟧ **1** to prevent by doing something ahead of time **2** to act in advance of; anticipate

for·est·a·tion (fôr′is tā′shən, fär′-) ***n.*** the planting or care of forests

for′est·ed ***adj.*** covered with trees and underbrush

for′est·er ***n.*** one trained in forestry

for′est·ry ***n.*** the science of planting and taking care of forests

fore·taste (fôr′tāst′) ***n.*** a taste or sample of what can be expected

fore·tell′ ***vt.*** **-told′, -tell′ing** to tell or indicate beforehand; predict

fore′thought′ ***n.*** **1** a thinking or planning beforehand **2** foresight

for·ev·er (fôr ev′ər, fər-) ***adv.*** **1** for always; endlessly **2** at all times; always Also **for·ev′er·more′**

fore·warn (fôr wôrn′) ***vt.*** to warn beforehand

THESAURUS

foreboding ***n.*** premonition, dread, presentiment; see ANTICIPATION.

forecast ***n.*** prediction, guess, estimate, prognosis, divination, forethought, foresight, prescience, foreknowledge, conjecture, prophecy, calculation, foreseeing.

forecast ***v.*** predetermine, predict, guess; see FORETELL.

forefather ***n.*** ancestor, progenitor, forebear; see ANCESTOR.

foregoing ***a.*** prior, former, previous; see PRECEDING.

foreground ***n.*** face, forefront, frontage, facade, neighborhood, proximity, nearness, adjacency, range, reach, view.—*Ant.* BACKGROUND, shadow, perspective.

forehead ***n.*** brow, countenance, temples; see FACE 1.

foreign ***a.*** remote, exotic, strange, far, distant, inaccessible, unaccustomed, different, unknown, alien, imported, borrowed, immigrant, outside, expatriate, exiled, from abroad, overseas, coming from another land, not native, not domestic, nonresident, alienated, faraway, far-off, outlandish.—*Ant.* LOCAL, national, indigenous.

foreigner ***n.*** stranger, immigrant, newcomer; see ALIEN.

foreknowledge ***n.*** foresight, prescience, premonition; see FEELING 4, FORECAST.

foreman ***n.*** overseer, manager, supervisor, superintendent, head, head man, shop foreman, boss.

foremost ***a.*** fore, original, primary; see FIRST.

forerunner ***n.*** herald, harbinger, precursor; see ANCESTOR, MESSENGER.

foresee ***v.*** prophesy, understand, predict; see FORETELL.

foreseen ***a.*** anticipated, predictable, prepared for; see EXPECTED, LIKELY 1.

foreshadow ***v.*** imply, presage, suggest; see FORETELL.

foresight ***n.*** economy, carefulness, preparedness; see PRUDENCE.

forest ***n.*** wood, woods, jungle, timber, growth, stand of trees, grove, woodland, park, greenwood, cover, clump, forested area, shelter, brake, backwoods, tall timber; see also TREE.

forestall ***v.*** thwart, prevent, preclude; see HINDER.

forestry ***n.*** forest management, horticulture, dendrology, woodcraft, forestation, reclamation, woodmanship; see also CONSERVATION.

foretell ***v.*** predict, prophesy, divine, foresee, announce in advance, prognosticate, augur, portend, foreshadow.—*Ant.* RECORD, confirm, recount.

forethought ***n.*** judgment, planning, foresight; see PRUDENCE.

forever ***a.*** everlastingly, permanently, immortally, on and on, ever, perpetually, always, in perpetuity, *in perpetuum* (Latin), world without end, eternally, interminably, infinitely, enduringly, unchangingly, durably, ever and again, indestructibly, endlessly, forevermore, for good, till hell freezes over*, for keeps*, for always, now and forever, for life, till death do us part.—*Ant.* TEMPORARILY, for a time, at present.

forewarn ***v.*** alert, advise, caution; see WARN.

fore'wom'an ***n.***, *pl.* **-wom'en** a woman serving as a foreman

fore'word ***n.*** an introductory statement in a book

for·feit (fôr'fit) ***n.*** ⟦< OFr *forfaire*, transgress⟧ **1** a fine or penalty for some crime, fault, or neglect **2** the act of forfeiting —***adj.*** lost or taken away as a forfeit —***vt.*** to lose or be deprived of as a forfeit

for'fei·ture (-fə chər) ***n.*** **1** the act of forfeiting **2** anything forfeited

for·gath·er (fôr gath'ər) ***vi.*** to come together; meet; assemble

for·gave (fər gāv', fôr-) ***vt.***, ***vi.*** *pt. of* FORGIVE

forge[1] (fôrj) ***n.*** ⟦< L *faber*, workman⟧ **1** a furnace for heating metal to be wrought **2** a place where metal is heated and wrought; smithy —***vt.*** **forged, forg'ing** **1** to form or shape (metal) by heating and hammering **2** to form; shape **3** to imitate (a signature) fraudulently, counterfeit (a check), etc. —***vi.*** **1** to work at a forge **2** to commit forgery —**forg'er** ***n.***

forge[2] (fôrj) ***vi.*** **forged, forg'ing** ⟦prob. < FORCE⟧ to move forward steadily: often with *ahead*

for'ger·y ***n.***, *pl.* **-ies** **1** the act or crime of imitating or counterfeiting documents, signatures, etc. to deceive **2** anything forged

for·get (fər get', fôr-) ***vt.***, ***vi.*** **-got', -got'ten** or **-got', -get'ting** ⟦OE *forgietan*⟧ **1** to be unable to remember **2** to overlook or neglect (something) —**forget oneself** to act in an improper manner —**for·get'ta·ble** ***adj.***

for·get'ful ***adj.*** **1** apt to forget **2** heedless or negligent —**for·get'ful·ly** ***adv.*** —**for·get'ful·ness** ***n.***

for·get'-me-not' ***n.*** a marsh plant with small blue, white, or pink flowers

for·give (fər giv', fôr-) ***vt.***, ***vi.*** **-gave', -giv'en, -giv'ing** ⟦OE *forgiefan*⟧ **1** to give up resentment against or the desire to punish; pardon (an offense or offender) **2** to cancel (a debt) —**for·giv'a·ble** ***adj.*** —**for·give'ness** ***n.*** —**for·giv'er** ***n.***

for·giv'ing ***adj.*** inclined to forgive —**for·giv'ing·ly** ***adv.***

for·go (fôr gō') ***vt.*** **-went', -gone', -go'ing** ⟦OE *forgan*⟧ to do without; abstain from; give up —**for·go'er** ***n.***

for·got (fər gät') ***vt.***, ***vi.*** *pt. & alt. pp. of* FORGET

for·got'ten ***vt.***, ***vi.*** *alt. pp. of* FORGET

fork (fôrk) ***n.*** ⟦< L *furca*⟧ **1** an instrument of varying size with prongs at one end, as for eating food, pitching hay, etc. **2** something like a fork in shape, etc. **3** the place where a road, etc. divides into branches **4** any of these branches —***vi.*** to divide into branches —***vt.*** to pick up or pitch with a fork —**fork over** (or **out** or **up**) [Inf.] to pay out; hand over —**fork'ful'**, *pl.* **-fuls'**, ***n.***

fork'lift' ***n.*** **1** a device for lifting heavy objects by means of projecting prongs that are slid under the load **2** a small truck with such a device

for·lorn (fôr lôrn') ***adj.*** ⟦< OE *forleosan*, lose utterly⟧ **1** abandoned **2** wretched; miserable **3** without hope —**for·lorn'ly** ***adv.***

form (fôrm) ***n.*** ⟦< L *forma*⟧ **1** shape; general structure **2** the figure of a person or animal **3** a mold **4** a particular mode, kind, type, etc. *[*ice is a *form* of water, the *forms* of poetry*]* **5** arrangement; style **6** a way of doing something requiring skill **7** a customary or conventional way of acting; ceremony; ritual **8** a printed document with blanks to be filled in **9** condition of mind or body **10** RACING FORM **11** a changed appearance of a word to show inflection, etc. **12** type, etc. locked in a frame for printing **13** what is expected, based on past performances *[*according to *form]* —***vt.*** **1** to shape; fashion **2** to train; instruct **3** to develop (habits) **4** to make up; constitute **5** to organize into *[*to *form* a club*]* —***vi.*** to be formed

-form (fôrm) ⟦< L⟧ *combining form* having the form of *[cuneiform]*

for·mal (fôr'məl) ***adj.*** ⟦< L *formalis*⟧ **1** according to fixed customs, rules, etc. **2** stiff in manner **3** *a)* designed for wear at ceremonies, etc. *b)* requiring clothes of this kind **4** done or made in explicit, definite form *[*a *formal* contract*]* **5** designating language usage characterized by expanded vocabulary, complex syntax, etc. **6** designating education in schools, etc. —***n.*** **1** a formal dance **2** a woman's evening dress —**for'mal·ly** ***adv.***

form·al·de·hyde (fôr mal'də hīd') ***n.*** ⟦FORM(IC) + *aldehyde*⟧ a pungent gas used in solution as a disinfectant and preservative

for'mal·ism' ***n.*** strict attention to outward forms and traditions

for·mal·i·ty (fôr mal'ə tē) ***n.***, *pl.* **-ties** **1** *a)* an observing of customs, rules, etc.; propriety *b)* excessive attention to convention; stiffness **2** a formal act; ceremony

for·mal·ize (fôr'mə līz') ***vt.*** **-ized', -iz'ing** **1** to shape **2** to make formal —**for'mal·i·za'tion** ***n.***

for'mal·wear' ***n.*** formal clothes, as tuxedos

for·mat (fôr'mat') ***n.*** ⟦< L *formatus*, formed⟧ **1** the shape, size, and arrangement of a book, etc. **2** the arrangement or plan, as of a TV program **3** a specific way in which computer data is stored, processed, etc. **4** a particular type of audio or video recording and playback system —***vt.*** **-mat'ted, -mat'ting** to arrange according to a format

for·ma·tion (fôr mā'shən) ***n.*** **1** a forming or being formed **2** a thing formed **3** the way in which something

THESAURUS

forfeit ***v.*** sacrifice, give up, relinquish; see ABANDON 1.

forge[1] ***v.*** falsify, counterfeit, fabricate, trump up, invent, feign, make, fashion, design, imitate, copy, duplicate, reproduce, trace.

forger ***n.*** falsifier, counterfeiter, con man*; see CRIMINAL.

forgery ***n.*** imitation, copy, counterfeit, fake, fabrication, sham, phony*.—*Ant.* ORIGINAL, real thing, real article.

forget ***v.*** lose consciousness of, put out of one's head, fail to remember, be forgetful, have a short memory, overlook, ignore, omit, neglect, slight, disregard, lose sight of, pass over, skip, think no more of, close one's eyes to, not give another thought to, draw a blank*, dismiss from the mind; see also NEGLECT 2.—*Ant.* REMEMBER, recall, recollect. **—forget oneself** offend, go astray, lose control; see MISBEHAVE.

forgetful ***a.*** inattentive, neglectful, heedless; see CARELESS.

forgetfulness ***n.*** negligence, neglect, inattention; see CARELESSNESS.

forgivable ***a.*** venial, trivial, pardonable; see EXCUSABLE.

forgive ***v.*** pardon, forgive and forget, let pass, excuse, condone, remit, forget, relent, bear no malice, exonerate, exculpate, let bygones be bygones, let it go, kiss and make up, bury the hatchet, turn the other cheek, make allowance, write off.—*Ant.* HATE, resent, retaliate.

forgiven ***a.*** absolved, taken back, excused; see PARDONED.

forgiveness ***n.*** absolution, pardon, acquittal, exoneration, remission, dispensation, reprieve, justification, amnesty, respite.

forgiving ***a.*** charitable, openhearted, generous; see KIND.

forgo ***v.*** quit, relinquish, waive; see ABANDON 1.

forgotten ***a.*** not remembered, not recalled, not recollected, lost, out of one's mind, erased from one's consciousness, beyond recollection, relegated to oblivion, past recall, not recoverable, blanked out, lapsed; see also ABANDONED.

fork ***n.*** **1** [A forked implement] table fork, hayfork, pitchfork, salad fork, cooking fork, trident, prong. **2** [A branch of a road or river] bend, turn, crossroad, tributary, byway, junction, branch, stream, confluence.

form ***n.*** **1** [Shape] figure, appearance, plan, arrangement, design, outline, configuration, formation, structure, style, construction, fashion, mode, scheme, framework, contour, stance, profile, silhouette, skeleton, anatomy. **2** [The human form] body, frame, torso; see FIGURE 2. **3** [The approved procedure] manner, mode, custom; see METHOD. **4** [Anything intended to give form] pattern, model, die; see MOLD 1. **5** [A standard letter or blank] duplicate, form letter, data sheet, information blank, chart, card, reference form, order form, questionnaire, application; see also COPY.

form ***v.*** **1** [To give shape to a thing] mold, pattern, model, arrange, make, block out, fashion, construct, devise, plan, design, contrive, produce, invent, frame, scheme, plot, compose, erect, build, cast, cut, carve, chisel, hammer out, put together, whittle, assemble, conceive, create, outline, trace, develop, cultivate, work, complete, finish, perfect, fix, regulate, establish, sculpt, sculpture, bend, twist, knead, set, determine, arrive at, reach.—*Ant.* DESTROY, demolish, shatter. **2** [To give character to a person] instruct, rear, breed; see TEACH. **3** [To comprise] constitute, figure in, act as; see COMPOSE 1. **4** [To take form] accumulate, condense, harden, set, congeal, accrete, settle, rise, appear, take shape, grow, develop, unfold, mature, materialize, become a reality, take on character, become visible, shape up*, fall into place, get into shape*.—*Ant.* DISAPPEAR, dissolve, waste away.

formal ***a.*** **1** [Notable for arrangement] orderly, precise, set; see REGULAR 3. **2** [Concerned with etiquette and behavior] reserved, distant, stiff; see CONVENTIONAL 3, POLITE. **3** [Official] prescribed, directed, lawful; see APPROVED, LEGAL. **4** [In evening clothes] full dress, black-tie, dressed up; see SOCIAL.

formation ***n.*** arrangement, compo-

is formed; structure **4** an arrangement or positioning, as of troops

form·a·tive (fôr′mə tiv) ***adj.*** helping or involving formation or development

for·mer (fôr′mər) ***adj.*** ⟦ME *formere*⟧ **1** earlier; past *[in former times]* **2** being the first mentioned of two

for′mer·ly *adv.* in the past

form′-fit′ting *adj.* fitting the body closely: also **form′fit′ting**

for·mic (fôr′mik) ***adj.*** ⟦< L *formica*, ant⟧ designating a colorless acid found in ants, spiders, etc.

For·mi·ca (fôr mī′kə) *trademark for* a laminated, heat-resistant plastic used for counter tops, etc.

for·mi·da·ble (fôr′mə də bəl, fôr mid′ə bəl) ***adj.*** ⟦< L *formidare*, to dread⟧ **1** causing fear, dread, or awe **2** hard to handle

form′less *adj.* shapeless; amorphous

form letter a standardized letter, usually one of many, with the date, address, etc. added separately

for·mu·la (fôr′myoo lə, -myə-) ***n.***, *pl.* **-las** or **-lae′** (-lē′, -lī′) ⟦L < *forma*, form⟧ **1** a fixed form of words, esp. a conventional expression **2** a conventional rule for doing something **3** a prescription or recipe **4** fortified milk for a baby **5** a set of symbols expressing a mathematical rule, fact, etc. **6** *Chem.* an expression of the composition, as of a compound, using symbols and figures

for′mu·late′ (-lāt′) ***vt.*** **-lat′ed**, **-lat′ing** **1** to express in a formula **2** to express in a definite way **3** to work out in one's mind; devise —**for′mu·la′tion *n.*** —**for′mu·la′tor *n.***

for·ni·cate (fôr′ni kāt′) ***vi.*** **-cat′ed**, **-cat′ing** ⟦< L *fornix*, a brothel⟧ to commit fornication —**for′ni·ca′tor *n.***

for′ni·ca′tion *n.* sexual intercourse between unmarried persons

for·sake (fôr sāk′) ***vt.*** **-sook′** (-sook′), **-sak′en**, **-sak′ing** ⟦< OE *for-*, FOR- + *sacan*, to strive⟧ **1** to give up (a habit, etc.) **2** to leave; abandon

for·sooth (fôr sooth′) ***adv.*** ⟦ME *forsoth*⟧ [Archaic] indeed

for·swear (fôr swer′) ***vt.*** **-swore′**, **-sworn′**, **-swear′ing** to deny or renounce on oath —***vi.*** to commit perjury

for·syth·i·a (fôr sith′ē ə, fər-) ***n.*** ⟦after W. *Forsyth* (1737-1804), Eng botanist⟧ a shrub with yellow, bell-shaped flowers that bloom in early spring

fort (fôrt) ***n.*** ⟦< L *fortis*, strong⟧ **1** a fortified place for military defense **2** a permanent army post

forte[1] (fôrt; *often* fôr′tā′) ***n.*** ⟦< OFr: see prec.⟧ that which one does particularly well

for·te[2] (fôr′tā′) ***adj.***, ***adv.*** ⟦It < L *fortis*, strong⟧ [*also in italics*] *Music* loud

forth (fôrth) ***adv.*** ⟦OE⟧ **1** forward; onward **2** out into view

Forth (fôrth), **Firth of** long estuary of the Forth River in SE Scotland

forth′com′ing *adj.* **1** about to appear; approaching **2** ready when needed **3** friendly, outgoing, etc. **4** open; frank

forth′right′ *adj.* direct and frank

forth′with′ (-with′, -with′) ***adv.*** at once

for·ti·fy (fôrt′ə fī′) ***vt.*** **-fied′**, **-fy′ing** ⟦< L *fortis*, strong + *facere*, to make⟧ **1** to strengthen physically, emotionally, etc. **2** to strengthen against attack, as with forts **3** to support **4** to add alcohol to (wine, etc.) **5** to add vitamins, etc. to (milk, etc.) —**for′ti·fi·ca′tion *n.*** —**for′ti·fi′er *n.***

for·tis·si·mo (fôr tis′ə mō′) ***adj.***, ***adv.*** ⟦It, superl. of *forte*, strong⟧ [*also in italics*] *Music* very loud

for·ti·tude (fôrt′ə tood′) ***n.*** ⟦< L *fortis*, strong⟧ patient endurance of trouble, pain, etc.; courage

Fort Knox (näks) military reservation in N Kentucky: site of U.S. gold bullion depository

Fort Lau·der·dale (lô′dər dāl′) city on the SE coast of Florida: pop. 149,000

fort·night (fôrt′nīt′) ***n.*** ⟦< OE *feowertyn niht*, lit., fourteen nights⟧ [Chiefly Brit.] a period of two weeks —**fort′night′ly *adj.***, ***adv.***

for·tress (fôr′tris) ***n.*** ⟦< L *fortis*, strong⟧ a fortified place; fort

for·tu·i·tous (fôr too′ə təs) ***adj.*** ⟦< L *fors*, luck⟧ **1** happening by chance **2** lucky —**for·tu′i·tous·ly *adv.***

for·tu·nate (fôr′chə nət) ***adj.*** **1** having good luck **2** coming by good luck; favorable —**for′tu·nate·ly *adv.***

for·tune (fôr′chən) ***n.*** ⟦< L *fors*, luck⟧ **1** luck; chance; fate **2** [*also pl.*] one's future lot, good or bad **3** good luck; success **4** wealth; riches

for′tune·tell′er *n.* one who professes to foretell the future of others —**for′tune·tell′ing *n.***, ***adj.***

Fort Wayne (wān) city in NE Indiana: pop. 173,000

Fort Worth (wurth) city in N Texas: pop. 448,000

for·ty (fôrt′ē) ***adj.***, ***n.***, *pl.* **-ties** ⟦OE *feowertig*⟧ four times ten; 40; XL —**the forties** the numbers or years, as of a century, from 40 through 49 —**for′ti·eth** (-ith) ***adj.***

fo·rum (fôr′əm) ***n.*** ⟦L⟧ **1** the public square of an ancient Roman city **2** an assembly, program, etc. for the discussion of public matters

for·ward (fôr′wərd) ***adj.*** ⟦OE *foreweard*⟧ **1** at, toward, or of the front **2** advanced **3** onward; advancing **4** prompt; ready **5** bold; presumptuous **6** of or for the future —***adv.*** toward the front; ahead —***n.*** *Basketball, Hockey, etc.* a player positioned ahead of the rest of the team, esp. when on the offense —***vt.*** **1** to promote **2** to send on

for′wards *adv.* FORWARD

THESAURUS

sition, constitution, crystallization, deposit, accumulation, development, fabrication, generation, production, creation, genesis.—*Ant.* DESTRUCTION, dissolution, annihilation.

formed *a.* shaped, molded, patterned, modeled, carved, outlined, developed, cultivated, completed, finished, built, forged, created, invented, concocted, designed, accomplished, manufactured, produced, born, perfected, fixed, established, arrived at, solidified, hardened, set, determined.—*Ant.* SHAPELESS, formless, nebulous.

former *a.* earlier, previous, past; see PRECEDING.

formerly *a.* before now, some time ago, once, once upon a time, already, in former times, previously, earlier, in the early days, eons ago, centuries ago, in the past, in the olden days, used to be, long ago, before this, in time past, heretofore, a while back.—*Ant.* RECENTLY, immediately, subsequently.

formula *n.* specifications, prescription, recipe; see METHOD.

formulate *v.* express, give form to, set down; see FORM 1.

fornication *n.* adultery, incontinence, carnality, lechery, illicit sex, lewdness, licentiousness, unfaithfulness, fooling around*, promiscuity, debauchery, libertinism, prostitution.

forsake *v.* desert, leave, quit; see ABANDON 2.

forsaken *a.* destitute, deserted, rejected; see ABANDONED.

fort *n.* fortress, citadel, stockade; see FORTIFICATION.

forth *a.* first, out, into; see AHEAD. —**and so forth** and so on, similarly, and the like; see OTHER.

forthcoming *a.* expected, inevitable, anticipated, future, impending, pending, resulting, awaited, destined, fated, predestined, approaching, in store, at hand, inescapable, imminent, in prospect, prospective, in the wind, in preparation, in the cards.

forthright *a.* at once, straightaway, directly; see IMMEDIATELY.

fortification *n.* fort, fortress, defense, dugout, trench, entrenchment, gun emplacement, barricade, battlement, stockade, outpost, citadel, support, wall, barrier, earthwork, castle, pillbox, bastion, bulwark, breastwork, blockhouse, fortalice*.

fortified *a.* defended, guarded, safeguarded, protected, manned, garrisoned, barricaded, armed, barbed, secured, entrenched, strong, covered, strengthened, supported, surrounded, fortressed, walled, enclosed, stockaded, armored, dug in, hidden, camouflaged.—*Ant.* OPEN, unprotected, unguarded.

fortify *v.* **1** [To strengthen against attack] barricade, entrench, buttress; see DEFEND 1, SUPPORT 1. **2** [To strengthen physically or emotionally] sustain, invigorate, toughen; see STRENGTHEN, SUPPORT 2.

fortitude *n.* firmness, resolution, persistence; see DETERMINATION.

fortunate *a.* lucky, blessed, prosperous, successful, having a charmed life, in luck, favored, well-to-do, happy, triumphant, victorious, overcoming, affluent, thriving, flourishing, healthy, wealthy, well-fixed*, well-heeled*, born with a silver spoon in one's mouth.—*Ant.* UNFORTUNATE, unlucky, cursed.

fortunately *a.* luckily, happily, in good time, auspiciously, favorably, prosperously, in the nick of time.—*Ant.* UNFORTUNATELY, unluckily, unhappily.

fortune *n.* **1** [Chance] luck, fate, uncertainty; see CHANCE 1. **2** [Great riches] possessions, inheritance, estate; see WEALTH. —**a small fortune** a high price, a great expense, a large amount of money; see PRICE.

forward *a.* **1** [Going forward] advancing, progressing, ahead, leading, progressive, onward, propulsive, in advance.—*Ant.* BACKWARD, retreating, regressive. **2** [Bold] presumptuous, impertinent, fresh; see RUDE 2.

forwarded *a.* shipped, expressed, dispatched; see DELIVERED.

fos·sil (fäs′əl) ***n.*** ⟦< L *fossilis*, dug up⟧ **1** any hardened remains of a plant or animal of a previous geologic period, preserved in the earth's crust **2** a person with outmoded ideas or ways —***adj.*** **1** of or like a fossil **2** dug from the earth *[coal is a fossil fuel]* **3** antiquated

fos′sil·ize′ (-īz′) ***vt., vi.*** **-ized′**, **-iz′ing** **1** to change into a fossil **2** to make or become out of date, rigid, etc. —**fos′sil·i·za′tion** ***n.***

fos·ter (fôs′tər) ***vt.*** ⟦OE *fostrian*, to nourish⟧ **1** to bring up; rear **2** to help to develop; promote —***adj.*** having a specified standing in a family but not by birth or adoption *[a foster brother]*

fought (fôt) ***vi., vt.*** *pt. & pp. of* FIGHT

foul (foul) ***adj.*** ⟦OE *ful*⟧ **1** stinking; loathsome **2** extremely dirty **3** indecent; profane **4** wicked; abominable **5** stormy *[foul weather]* **6** tangled *[a foul rope]* **7** not within the limits or rules set **8** designating lines setting limits on a playing area **9** dishonest **10** [Inf.] unpleasant, disagreeable, etc. —***adv.*** in a foul manner —***n.*** *Sports* a hit, blow, move, etc. that is FOUL (*adj.* 7) —***vt.*** **1** to make filthy **2** to dishonor **3** to obstruct *[grease fouls drains]* **4** to entangle (a rope, etc.) **5** to make a foul against, as in a game **6** *Baseball* to bat (the ball) foul —***vi.*** to be or become fouled —**foul up** [Inf.] to bungle —**foul′ly** ***adv.*** —**foul′ness** ***n.***

fou·lard (fo͞o lärd′) ***n.*** ⟦Fr⟧ a lightweight printed fabric of silk, etc.

foul′-up′ ***n.*** [Inf.] a mix-up; botch

found[1] (found) ⟦OE *funden*⟧ ***vt., vi.*** *pp. & pt. of* FIND

found[2] (found) ***vt.*** ⟦< L *fundus*, bottom⟧ **1** to set for support; base **2** to bring into being; set up; establish —**found′er** ***n.***

found[3] (found) ***vt.*** ⟦< L *fundere*, pour⟧ **1** to melt and pour (metal) into a mold **2** to make by founding metal

foun·da·tion (foun dā′shən) ***n.*** **1** a founding or being founded; establishment **2** *a)* an endowment for an institution *b)* such an institution **3** basis **4** the base of a wall, house, etc. **5** cosmetic over which other makeup is applied

foun·der (foun′dər) ***vi.*** ⟦< L *fundus*, bottom⟧ **1** to stumble, fall, or go lame **2** to fill with water and sink: said of a ship **3** to break down

found·ling (found′liŋ′) ***n.*** an infant of unknown parents, found abandoned

found·ry (foun′drē) ***n., pl.*** **-ries** a place where metal is cast

fount (fount) ***n.*** ⟦< L *fons*⟧ **1** [Old Poet.] a fountain or spring **2** a source

foun·tain (fount′'n) ***n.*** ⟦< L *fons*⟧ **1** a natural spring of water **2** a source **3** *a)* an artificial jet or flow of water *[a drinking fountain]* *b)* the basin where this flows **4** a reservoir, as for ink

foun′tain·head′ ***n.*** the source, as of a stream

fountain pen a pen which is fed ink from its own reservoir or cartridge

four (fôr) ***adj., n.*** ⟦OE *feower*⟧ one more than three; 4; IV

four′-flush′er (-flush′ər) ***n.*** ⟦< FLUSH[2]⟧ [Inf.] one who bluffs in an effort to deceive

four′-in-hand′ ***n.*** a necktie tied in a slipknot with the ends left hanging

four′score′ ***adj., n.*** four times twenty; eighty

four′some (-səm) ***n.*** four people

four·square (fôr′skwer′) ***adj.*** **1** square **2** unyielding; firm **3** frank; forthright —***adv.*** in a square form or manner

four·teen (fôr′tēn′) ***adj., n.*** ⟦OE *feowertyne*⟧ four more than ten; 14; XIV —**four′teenth′** ***adj., n.***

fourth (fôrth) ***adj.*** ⟦OE *feortha*⟧ preceded by three others in a series; 4th —***n.*** **1** the one following the third **2** any of the four equal parts of something; $\frac{1}{4}$ **3** the fourth forward gear

fourth′-class′ ***adj., adv.*** of or in a class of mail consisting of merchandise, printed matter, etc. not included in first-class, second-class, or third-class; parcel post

fourth dimension in the theory of relativity, time added as a dimension to those of length, width, and depth

fourth estate [*often* **F- E-**] journalism or journalists

Fourth of July *see* INDEPENDENCE DAY

4WD *abbrev.* four-wheel-drive (vehicle)

four′-wheel′ ***adj.*** **1** having four wheels **2** affecting four wheels *[a four-wheel drive]*

fowl (foul) ***n.*** ⟦OE *fugol*⟧ **1** any bird **2** any of the domestic birds used as food, as the chicken, duck, etc. **3** the flesh of these birds used for food

fox (fäks) ***n.*** ⟦OE⟧ **1** a small, wild animal of the dog family, considered sly and crafty **2** its fur **3** a sly, crafty person —***vt.*** to trick by slyness

fox′glove′ ***n.*** DIGITALIS

fox′hole′ ***n.*** a hole dug in the ground as a protection against enemy gunfire

fox′hound′ ***n.*** a sturdy breed of hound that is trained to hunt foxes

fox terrier a small terrier with a smooth or wiry coat, formerly trained to drive foxes from hiding

fox trot a dance for couples in 4/4 time, or music for it —**fox′-trot′**, **-trot′ted**, **-trot′ting**, ***vi.***

fox′y ***adj.*** **-i·er**, **-i·est** **1** foxlike; crafty; sly **2** [Slang] attractive or sexy: used esp. of women

foy·er (foi′ər; *also* foi′ā′, -yā′) ***n.*** ⟦Fr < L *focus*, hearth⟧ an entrance hall or lobby, as in a theater or hotel

Fr *abbrev.* **1** Father **2** French

frab·jous (frab′jəs) ***adj.*** ⟦coined by Lewis CARROLL⟧ [Inf.] splendid; fine

fra·cas (frā′kəs) ***n.*** ⟦Fr < It *fracassare*, to smash⟧ a noisy fight; brawl

frac·tion (frak′shən) ***n.*** ⟦< L *frangere*, to break⟧ **1** a small part, amount, etc. **2** *Math. a)* a quotient of two whole numbers, as $\frac{13}{4}$, $\frac{2}{5}$ *b)* any quantity expressed in terms of a numerator and denominator —**frac′tion·al** ***adj.*** —**frac′tion·al·ly** ***adv.***

frac·tious (frak′shəs) ***adj.*** ⟦< ?⟧ **1** hard to manage; unruly; rebellious **2** peevish; irritable; cross —**frac′tious·ly** ***adv.*** —**frac′tious·ness** ***n.***

frac·ture (frak′chər) ***n.*** ⟦< L *frangere*, to break⟧ a breaking or break, esp. in a bone —***vt., vi.*** **-tured**, **-tur·ing** to break, crack, or split

frag·ile (fraj′əl) ***adj.*** ⟦< L *frangere*, to break⟧ easily broken or damaged; delicate —**fra·gil·i·ty** (frə jil′ə tē) ***n.***

frag·ment (frag′mənt; *for v., also,* -ment′) ***n.*** ⟦< L *frangere*, to break⟧ **1** a part broken away **2** an incomplete part, as of a novel —***vt., vi.*** to break up —**frag′men·ta′tion** (-mən tā′shən) ***n.***

frag′men·tar′y (-mən ter′ē) ***adj.*** consisting of fragments; not complete

THESAURUS

fossil ***n.*** remains, reconstruction, specimen, skeleton, relic, find, impression, trace, petrified deposit; see also RELIC.

foster ***v.*** cherish, nurse, nourish; see RAISE 2.

foul ***a.*** **1** [Disgusting] nasty, vulgar, coarse; see OFFENSIVE 2. **2** [Unfair] vicious, inequitable, unjust; see DISHONEST.

foul ***v.*** **1** [To make dirty] defile, pollute, sully; see DIRTY. **2** [To become dirty] soil, spot, stain; see DIRTY.

found[1] ***a.*** unearthed, revealed, detected; see DISCOVERED.

found[2] ***v.*** establish, endow, set up; see ESTABLISH 2.

foundation ***n.*** **1** [An intellectual basis] reason, justification, authority; see BASIS. **2** [A physical basis] footing, base, foot, basement, pier, groundwork, bed, ground, bottom, substructure, wall, underpinning, solid rock, infrastructure, pile, roadbed, support, prop, stand, shore, post, pillar, skeleton, column, shaft, pedestal, buttress, framework, scaffold, beam. **3** [That which has been founded] institution, organization, endowment, institute, society, establishment, company, guild, corporation, association, charity, scholarship fund, trust.

founded ***a.*** organized, endowed, set up; see ESTABLISHED 1.

founder ***n.*** originator, sponsor, prime mover; see ANCESTOR, AUTHOR.

fountain ***n.*** **1** [A jet of water] jet, stream, gush, spout, geyser, spurt, spring, pond, basin, pool; see also WATER 1, 2. **2** [A source] origin, font, wellspring; see ORIGIN 2.

fowl ***n.*** barnyard fowl, wild fowl, poultry, chicken, duck, goose, turkey, cock, hen, Cornish hen, pheasant, partridge, prairie chicken, grouse, capon, ptarmigan, swan; see also BIRD.

fox ***n.*** **1** [A clever person] cheat, trickster, con man*; see RASCAL. **2** [An animal] red fox, gray fox, silver fox; see DOG.

fraction ***n.*** section, portion, part; see DIVISION 2.

fractional ***a.*** partial, sectional, fragmentary; see UNFINISHED 1.

fracture ***n.*** rupture, wound, crack, cleavage, shattering, breach, fragmentation, displacement, dislocation, broken bone, shearing, severing, separating, dismembering.

fragile ***a.*** brittle, frail, delicate; see DAINTY, WEAK 1, 2.

fragment ***n.*** piece, scrap, remnant; see BIT 1.

fra·grant (frā′grənt) ***adj.*** ⟦< L *fragrare*, to emit a (sweet) smell⟧ having a pleasant odor; sweet-smelling —**fra′grance** ***n.*** —**fra′grant·ly** ***adv.***

frail (frāl) ***adj.*** ⟦see FRAGILE⟧ **1** easily broken; delicate **2** not robust; weak **3** easily tempted; morally weak —**frail′ly** ***adv.***

frail′ty (-tē) ***n.*** **1** a being frail; esp., moral weakness **2** *pl.* **-ties** a fault arising from such weakness

frame (frām) ***vt.*** **framed, fram′ing** ⟦prob. < ON *frami*, profit or benefit⟧ **1** to form according to a pattern; design *[to frame laws]* **2** to construct **3** to put into words *[to frame an excuse]* **4** to enclose (a picture, etc.) in a border **5** [Inf.] to falsify evidence in order to make (an innocent person) appear guilty —***n.*** **1** body structure **2** the framework, as of a house **3** the structural case enclosing a window, door, etc. **4** an ornamental border, as around a picture **5** the way anything is put together; form **6** condition; state *[a good frame of mind]* **7** one exposure in a strip of film **8** *Bowling, etc.* a division of a game —***adj.*** having a wooden framework *[a frame house]* —**fram′er** ***n.***

frame′-up′ ***n.*** [Inf.] a secret, deceitful scheme, as a falsifying of evidence to make a person seem guilty

frame′work′ ***n.*** **1** a structure to hold together or support something **2** the basic structure, system, etc.

franc (fraŋk) ***n.*** ⟦Fr < L *Francorum rex*, king of the French, phrase on the coin in 1360⟧ the monetary unit of Belgium, France, Switzerland, Chad, etc.

France (frans, fräns) country in W Europe: 210,033 sq. mi.; pop. 56,615,000

fran·chise (fran′chīz′) ***n.*** ⟦< OFr *franc*, free⟧ **1** any special right or privilege granted by a government **2** the right to vote; suffrage **3** the right to sell a product or service —***vt.*** **-chised′, -chis′ing** to grant a franchise to

Franco- *combining form* French, French and

fran·gi·ble (fran′jə bəl) ***adj.*** ⟦< L *frangere*, to break⟧ breakable; fragile

frank (fraŋk) ***adj.*** ⟦< OFr *franc*, free⟧ free in expressing oneself; candid —***vt.*** to send (mail) free of postage —***n.*** **1** the right to send mail free **2** a mark indicating this right —**frank′ly** ***adv.*** —**frank′ness** ***n.***

Frank (fraŋk) ***n.*** a member of the Germanic peoples whose 9th-c. empire extended over what is now France, Germany, and Italy

Frank·en·stein (fraŋ′kən stīn′) ***n.*** **1** the title character in a novel (1818), creator of a monster that destroys him **2** popularly, the monster **3** anything that becomes dangerous to its creator

Frank·fort (fraŋk′fərt) capital of Kentucky: pop. 26,000

Frank·furt (fraŋk′fərt; *Ger* fräŋk′foort) city in W Germany: pop. 656,000

frank·furt·er (fraŋk′fər tər) ***n.*** ⟦Ger: after prec.⟧ a smoked sausage of beef, beef and pork, etc.; wiener: also [Inf.] **frank**

frank·in·cense (fraŋ′kin sens′) ***n.*** ⟦see FRANK & INCENSE[1]⟧ a gum resin burned as incense

Frank·ish (fraŋ′kish) ***n.*** the West Germanic language of the Franks —***adj.*** of the Franks or their language, etc.

Frank·lin (fraŋk′lin), **Ben·ja·min** (ben′jə mən) 1706-90; Am. statesman, scientist, inventor, & writer

fran·tic (fran′tik) ***adj.*** ⟦< Gr *phrenitis*, delirium⟧ wild with anger, pain, worry, etc. —**fran′ti·cal·ly** ***adv.***

frap·pé (fra pā′) ***n.*** ⟦Fr < *frapper*, to strike⟧ **1** a dessert made of partly frozen fruit juices, etc. **2** a beverage poured over shaved ice **3** [New England] a milkshake Also, esp. for 3, **frappe** (frap)

fra·ter·nal (frə tur′nəl) ***adj.*** ⟦< L *frater*, brother⟧ **1** of brothers; brotherly **2** designating or of a society organized for fellowship **3** designating twins developed from separate ova and thus not identical —**fra·ter′nal·ly** ***adv.***

fra·ter·ni·ty (frə tur′nə tē) ***n.***, *pl.* **-ties** **1** brotherliness **2** a group of men joined together for fellowship, etc., as in college **3** a group of people with the same beliefs, work, etc.

frat·er·nize (frat′ər nīz′) ***vi.*** **-nized′, -niz′ing** to associate in a friendly way —**frat′er·ni·za′tion** ***n.***

frat·ri·cide (fra′trə sīd′) ***n.*** ⟦< L *frater*, brother + *caedere*, to kill⟧ **1** the killing of one's own brother or sister **2** one who commits fratricide —**frat′ri·ci′dal** ***adj.***

Frau (frou) ***n.***, *pl.* ***Frau′en*** (-ən) ⟦Ger⟧ **1** Mrs.; Madam: a German title of respect, used to address a married woman and now also a single woman **2** a wife

fraud (frôd) ***n.*** ⟦< L *fraus*⟧ **1** deceit; trickery **2** *Law* intentional deception **3** a trick **4** an impostor or cheat

fraud·u·lent (frô′jə lənt) ***adj.*** **1** based on or using fraud **2** done or obtained by fraud —**fraud′u·lence** ***n.*** —**fraud′u·lent·ly** ***adv.***

fraught (frôt) ***adj.*** ⟦< MDu *vracht*, a load⟧ **1** filled or loaded (*with*) *[a life fraught with hardship]* **2** tense, anxious, etc.

Fräu·lein (froi′līn′; *E* froi′-) ***n.***, *pl.* ***-lein′*** or Eng. **-leins′** ⟦Ger⟧ **1** Miss: a German title of respect **2** an unmarried woman: see note at FRAU

fray[1] (frā) ***n.*** ⟦< AFFRAY⟧ a noisy quarrel or fight; brawl

fray[2] (frā) ***vt.***, ***vi.*** ⟦< L *fricare*, to rub⟧ **1** to make or become worn or ragged **2** to make or become weakened or strained

fraz·zle (fraz′əl) [Inf.] ***vt.***, ***vi.*** **-zled, -zling** ⟦< dial. *fazle*⟧ **1** to wear to tatters; fray **2** to make or become exhausted —***n.*** the state of being frazzled

freak (frēk) ***n.*** ⟦< ?⟧ **1** an odd notion; whim **2** an unusual happening **3** any abnormal animal, person, or plant **4** [Slang] *a)* a user of a specified drug *b)* a devotee; buff *[a chess freak]* —***adj.*** oddly different; abnormal —**freak out** [Slang] **1** to have hallucinations, etc., as from a psychedelic drug **2** to make or become very excited, distressed, etc. —**freak′ish** or **freak′y, -i·er, -i·est,** ***adj.*** —**freak′ish·ly** ***adv.***

freak′out′ ***n.*** [Slang] the act or an instance of freaking out

freck·le (frek′əl) ***n.*** ⟦< Scand⟧ a small, brownish spot on the skin —***vt.***, ***vi.*** **-led, -ling** to make or become spotted with freckles —**freck′led** ***adj.***

Fred·er·ick the Great (fred′rik, -ər ik) 1712-86; king of Prussia (1740-86)

Fred·er·ic·ton (fred′ə rik tən) capital of New Brunswick, Canada: pop. 47,000

free (frē) ***adj.*** **fre′er, fre′est** ⟦< OE *freo*⟧ **1** not under the control or power of another; having liberty; independent

THESAURUS

fragrance ***n.*** perfume, aroma, odor; see SMELL 1.

fragrant ***a.*** aromatic, sweet, perfumed; see SWEET 3.

frail ***a.*** feeble, breakable, tender; see DAINTY.

frailty ***n.*** brittleness, delicacy, feebleness; see WEAKNESS 1.

frame ***n.*** **1** [The structural portion] skeleton, scaffold, framework, scaffolding, casing, framing, support, substructure, infrastructure, stage, groundwork, organization, anatomy, fabric, architecture, enclosure, span, block, window frame, doorjamb. **2** [A border intended as an ornament] margin, fringe, hem, flounce, trim, trimming, outline, mounting, molding.

frame ***v.*** **1** [To make] construct, erect, raise; see BUILD. **2** [To enclose in a frame] mount, border, enclose; see SUPPORT 1. **3** [To act as a frame] encircle, confine, enclose; see SURROUND 1. **4** [*To cause a miscarriage of justice] set up*, double-cross, entrap; see DECEIVE.

framed ***a.*** mounted, enclosed, bordered, encircled, fringed, enveloped, outlined, confined, enclosed, wrapped, clasped.

frame-up* ***n.*** deception, fraud, conspiracy; see TRICK 1.

framework ***n.*** skeleton, structure, core; see FRAME.

frank ***a.*** candid, sincere, free, easy, familiar, open, direct, unreserved, uninhibited, downright, ingenuous, unsophisticated, unaffected, plain, aboveboard, forthright, outspoken, tactless, guileless, straightforward, plain-spoken, natural, blunt, matter-of-fact.—*Ant.* DISHONEST, insincere, secretive.

frankfurter ***n.*** wiener, wiener sausage, weenie*, hot dog*, frank*, dog*, link.

frankly ***a.*** freely, honestly, candidly; see OPENLY 1.

frankness ***n.*** openness, sincerity, candidness; see HONESTY.

frantic ***a.*** distracted, mad, wild, frenetic, furious, raging, raving, frenzied, violent, agitated, deranged, crazy, delirious, insane, angry; see also EXCITED.—*Ant.* CALM, composed, subdued.

fraternity ***n.*** brotherhood, club, fellowship; see ORGANIZATION 2.

fraud ***n.*** **1** [Deceit] trickery, duplicity, guile; see DECEPTION. **2** [An impostor] pretender, charlatan, fake; see CHEAT.

fraudulent ***a.*** deceitful, tricky, swindling; see DISHONEST.

freak ***n.*** monstrosity, monster, rarity, malformation, freak of nature, oddity, aberration, curiosity, hybrid, anomaly, mutation; see also MONSTER.

freckle ***n.*** mole, patch, blotch; see BLEMISH.

free ***a.*** **1** [Not restricted politically] sovereign, independent, autonomous, democratic, self-ruling, self-governing, released, unconstrained, liberated, at liberty, freed.—*Ant.* RESTRICTED, enslaved, subject. **2** [Not restricted in space; *said of persons*] unconfined, at large, cast loose, escaped, let out, scot-free, free as air, free to come and go, unfettered, foot-

2 having civil and political liberty **3** able to move in any direction; loose **4** not burdened by obligations, debts, discomforts, etc. **5** not confined to the usual rules *[free verse]* **6** not exact *[a free translation]* **7** generous; profuse *[a free spender]* **8** frank **9** with no charge or cost **10** exempt from taxes, duties, etc. **11** clear of obstructions *[a free road ahead]* **12** not fastened *[a rope's free end]* —***adv.*** **1** without cost **2** in a free manner —***vt.*** **freed, free'ing** to make free; specif., *a)* to release from bondage or arbitrary power, obligation, etc. *b)* to clear of obstruction, etc. —**free from** (or **of**) without —**free up** to make available for use *[he freed up funds]* —**make free with** to use freely —**free'ly** ***adv.*** —**free'ness** ***n.***

-free (frē) *combining form* free of or from, exempt from, without

free'base' ***n.*** a concentrated form of cocaine for smoking —***vt., vi.*** **-based', -bas'ing** to prepare or use such a form of (cocaine)

free·bie or **free·bee** (frē'bē) ***n.*** [Slang] something given or gotten free of charge, as a theater ticket

free'boot'er (-bo͞ot'ər) ***n.*** ⟦< Du *vrij*, free + *buit*, plunder⟧ a pirate

freed·man (frēd'mən) ***n., pl.*** **-men** (-mən) a man legally freed from slavery

free·dom (frē'dəm) ***n.*** **1** a being free; esp., *a)* independence *b)* civil or political liberty *c)* exemption from an obligation, discomfort, etc. *d)* a being able to act, use, etc. freely *e)* ease of movement *f)* frankness **2** a right or privilege

free fall any unchecked fall, as of a parachutist before the parachute opens

free flight any flight or part of a flight, as of a rocket, occurring without propulsion —**free'-flight'** ***adj.***

free'-for-all' ***n.*** a disorganized, general fight; brawl —***adj.*** open to anyone

free'-form' ***adj.*** **1** irregular in shape **2** spontaneous, unrestrained, etc.

free'hand' ***adj.*** drawn by hand without the use of instruments, etc.

free'hold' ***n.*** an estate in land held for life or with the right to pass it on to heirs —**free'hold'er** ***n.***

free·lance or **free-lance** (frē'lans') ***n.*** a writer, artist, etc. who sells his or her services to individual buyers: also **free'lanc'er** or **free'-lanc'er** —***adj.*** of or working as a freelance —***vi.*** **-lanced', -lanc'ing** to work as a freelance

free'load'er (-lōd'ər) ***n.*** [Inf.] a person who habitually imposes on others for free food, etc. —**free'load'** ***vi.***

free·man (frē'mən) ***n., pl.*** **-men** (-mən) **1** a person not in slavery **2** a citizen

Free·ma·son (frē'mā'sən) ***n.*** a member of an international secret society based on brotherliness and mutual aid —**Free'ma'son·ry** ***n.***

free on board delivered (by the seller) aboard the train, ship, etc. at no extra charge to the buyer

free'stone' ***n.*** a peach, etc. in which the pit does not cling to the pulp

free'think'er ***n.*** one who forms opinions about religion, morals, etc. independently

Free'town' seaport & capital of Sierra Leone: pop. 470,000

free trade trade carried on without protective tariffs, quotas, etc.

free verse poetry without regular meter, rhyme, etc.

free'way' ***n.*** a multiple-lane divided highway with fully controlled access

free'will' ***adj.*** voluntary

freeze (frēz) ***vi.*** **froze, fro'zen, freez'ing** ⟦OE *freosan*⟧ **1** to be formed into, or become covered with, ice; be solidified by cold **2** to become very cold **3** to be damaged or killed by cold **4** to become motionless **5** to be made speechless by strong emotion **6** to become formal or unfriendly —***vt.*** **1** to form into, or cover with, ice; solidify by cold **2** to make very cold **3** to preserve (food) by rapid refrigeration **4** to kill or damage by cold **5** to make motionless **6** to make formal or unfriendly **7** *a)* to fix (prices, etc.) at a given level by authority *b)* to make (funds, etc.) unavailable to the owners —***n.*** **1** a freezing or being frozen **2** a period of freezing weather —**freeze out 1** to die out through freezing, as plants do **2** [Inf.] to keep out by a cold manner, competition, etc. —**freeze over** to become covered with ice —**freez'a·ble** ***adj.***

freeze'-dry' ***vt.*** **-dried', -dry'ing** to quick-freeze (food, etc.) and then dry under high vacuum

freez'er ***n.*** **1** a refrigerator, compartment, etc. for freezing and storing perishable foods **2** a machine for making ice cream

freezing point the temperature at which a liquid freezes: the freezing point of water is 32°F or 0°C

freight (frāt) ***n.*** ⟦< MDu *vracht*, a load⟧ **1** the transporting of goods by water, land, or air **2** the cost for this **3** the goods transported **4** a railroad train for transporting goods: in full **freight train** —***vt.*** **1** to load; burden **2** to send by freight

freight'er ***n.*** a ship for freight

Fre·mont (frē'mänt) city in W California, on San Francisco Bay: pop. 173,000

French (french) ***adj.*** of France or its people, language, etc. —***n.*** the language of France —**the French** the people of France —**French'man** (-mən), *pl.* **-men** (-mən), ***n.***

French bread bread with a crisp crust made with white flour in a long, slender loaf

French cuff a shirt-sleeve cuff turned back on itself and fastened with a cuff link

French doors a pair of doors hinged at the sides to open in the middle

French dressing a creamy, orange-colored salad dressing

French fries [*often* **f- f-**] strips of potato that have been French fried

French fry [*often* **f- f-**] to fry in hot deep fat

French Gui·a·na (gē an'ə, -ä'nə) French administrative division in NE South America

French horn a mellow-toned brass instrument with a long, spiral tube and a flaring bell: in classical music, now usually *horn*

French leave an unauthorized departure

French toast sliced bread dipped in a batter of egg and milk and then fried

fre·net·ic (frə net'ik) ***adj.*** ⟦see PHRENETIC⟧ frantic; frenzied —**fre·net'i·cal·ly** ***adv.***

fren·zy (fren'zē) ***n., pl.*** **-zies** ⟦< Gr *phrenitis*, madness⟧ wild excitement; delirium

Fre·on (frē'än') *trademark for* any of a series of gaseous

THESAURUS

loose and fancy-free, freewheeling*, on the loose.—*Ant.* CONFINED, imprisoned, restrained. **3** [Not restricted in space; *said of things*] unimpeded, unobstructed, unhampered, unattached, loose, not attached, clear, unentangled, unengaged, disengaged, unfastened.—*Ant.* FIXED, fastened, rooted. **4** [Given without charge] gratuitous, gratis, for nothing, without charge, free of cost, complimentary, for free*, on the house.—*Ant.* PAID, charged, costly. —**set free** release, liberate, emancipate; see FREE.

free ***v.*** release, discharge, deliver, save, emancipate, manumit, rescue, extricate, loose, loosen, unbind, disengage, undo, set free, let out, let loose, bail out, cut loose, relieve, absolve, acquit, dismiss, pardon, clear, ransom, redeem, unbind, unchain, disentangle, untie, let go, unlock, unhand, let out of prison, open the cage, turn loose, unfetter, unshackle.—*Ant.* SEIZE, capture, incarcerate.

freedom ***n.*** **1** [Political liberty] independence, sovereignty, self-government, autonomy, democracy, citizenship, representative government, self-determination; see also LIBERTY 4.—*Ant.* SLAVERY, bondage, regimentation. **2** [Exemption from necessity] privilege, immunity, license, indulgence, facility, range, latitude, scope, play, own accord, free rein, leeway, plenty of rope*.—*Ant.* RESTRAINT, constraint, hindrance. **3** [Natural ease and facility] readiness, forthrightness, spontaneity; see EASE 2.

freeing ***n.*** emancipation, releasing, salvation; see RESCUE.

freely ***a.*** **1** [Without physical restriction] loosely, without encumbrance, without restraint, unhindered, as one pleases, easily, smoothly.—*Ant.* with difficulty, uneasily, stressfully. **2** [Without mental restriction] voluntarily, willingly, fancy-free, of one's own accord, at will, at pleasure, of one's own free will, purposely, deliberately, intentionally, advisedly, spontaneously, frankly, openly.—*Ant.* UNWILLINGLY, under compulsion, hesitantly.

freeway ***n.*** turnpike, superhighway, toll road; see HIGHWAY, ROAD 1.

freeze ***v.*** **1** [To change to a solid state] congeal, harden, solidify, ice, quick-freeze, glaciate, chill, benumb, cool, ice up.—*Ant.* MELT, thaw, liquefy. **2** [To suspend] seal, terminate, immobilize; see HALT, SUSPEND 2.

freezing ***a.*** frosty, wintry, frigid; see COLD 1.

freight ***n.*** burden, load, contents, weight, bulk, encumbrance, bales, shipment, cargo, shipping, consignment, goods, tonnage, packages, ware.

freighter ***n.*** tanker, transport, cargo ship; see SHIP.

French ***a.*** Gallic, Latin, Frenchified, Parisian.

frenzy ***n.*** rage, craze, furor; see EXCITEMENT, INSANITY.

compounds of fluorine, carbon, etc.: used as refrigerants, aerosol propellants, etc.

fre·quen·cy (frē′kwən sē) ***n.***, *pl.* **-cies** **1** frequent occurrence **2** the number of times any event recurs in a given period **3** *Physics* the number of oscillations or cycles per unit of time

frequency modulation the variation of the frequency of a carrier wave in accordance with the signal being broadcast: abbrev. *FM*

fre·quent (frē′kwənt; *for v.* frē kwent′) ***adj.*** ⟦< L *frequens*, crowded⟧ **1** occurring often **2** constant; habitual —***vt.*** to go to or be at often —**fre′quent·ly *adv.***

fres·co (fres′kō) ***n.***, *pl.* **-coes** or **-cos** ⟦It, fresh⟧ a painting made with watercolors on wet plaster

fresh[1] (fresh) ***adj.*** ⟦OE *fersc*⟧ **1** recently made, grown, etc. *[fresh coffee]* **2** not salted, pickled, frozen, etc. **3** not spoiled **4** not tired; lively **5** not worn, soiled, faded, etc. **6** new; recent **7** inexperienced **8** cool and refreshing *[a fresh spring day]* **9** brisk: said of wind **10** not salt: said of water —**fresh′ly *adv.*** —**fresh′ness *n.***

fresh[2] (fresh) ***adj.*** ⟦< Ger *frech*, bold⟧ [Slang] bold; saucy; impertinent

fresh′en *vt.*, ***vi.*** to make or become fresh —**freshen up** to bathe, change into fresh clothes, etc. —**fresh′en·er *n.***

fresh′man (-mən) ***n.***, *pl.* **-men** (-mən) ⟦FRESH[1] + MAN⟧ **1** a beginner **2** a person in his or her first year in college, Congress, etc.

fresh′wa′ter *adj.* **1** of or living in water that is not salty **2** sailing only on inland waters

Fres·no (frez′nō) city in central California: pop. 354,000

fret[1] (fret) ***vt.***, ***vi.*** **fret′ted, fret′ting** ⟦OE *fretan*, to devour⟧ **1** to gnaw, wear away, rub, etc. **2** to make or become rough or disturbed *[wind fretting the water]* **3** to irritate or be irritated; worry —***n.*** irritation; worry —**fret′ter *n.***

fret[2] (fret) ***n.*** ⟦ME *frette*⟧ a running design of interlacing small bars

fret[3] (fret) ***n.*** ⟦OFr *frette*, a band⟧ any of the ridges on the fingerboard of a banjo, guitar, etc.

fret′ful (-fəl) ***adj.*** irritable; peevish —**fret′ful·ly *adv.*** —**fret′ful·ness *n.***

fret′work′ *n.* decorative carving or openwork, as of interlacing lines

Freud (froid), **Sig·mund** (sig′mənd) 1856-1939; Austrian physician: founder of psychoanalysis —**Freud′i·an *adj.***, ***n.***

Freudian slip a mistake made in speaking that, it is thought, inadvertently reveals unconscious motives, desires, etc.

Fri *abbrev.* Friday

fri·a·ble (frī′ə bəl) ***adj.*** ⟦Fr < L *friare*, to rub⟧ easily crumbled

fri·ar (frī′ər) ***n.*** ⟦< L *frater*, brother⟧ *R.C.Ch.* a member of certain religious orders

fric·as·see (frik′ə sē′, frik′ə sē′) ***n.*** ⟦< Fr *fricasser*, cut up and fry⟧ a dish consisting of meat cut into pieces, stewed or fried, and served in a sauce of its own gravy —***vt.*** **-seed′, -see′ing** to prepare in this way

fric·tion (frik′shən) ***n.*** ⟦< L *fricare*, to rub⟧ **1** a rubbing of one object against another **2** conflict, as because of differing opinions **3** *Mech.* the resistance to motion of moving surfaces that touch —**fric′tion·al *adj.*** —**fric′tion·less *adj.***

Fri·day (frī′dā) ***n.*** ⟦after *Frigg*, Germanic goddess⟧ **1** the sixth day of the week **2** ⟦after the devoted servant of ROBINSON CRUSOE⟧ a faithful helper: usually **man** (or **girl**) **Friday**

fridge (frij) ***n.*** [Inf.] a refrigerator

fried (frīd) ***vt.***, ***vi.*** *pt. & pp. of* FRY[1]

fried′cake′ *n.* a small cake fried in deep fat; doughnut or cruller

friend (frend) ***n.*** ⟦OE *freond*⟧ **1** a person whom one knows well and is fond of **2** an ally, supporter, or sympathizer **3** **[F-]** a member of the Society of Friends; Quaker —**make** (or **be**) **friends with** to become (or be) a friend of —**friend′less *adj.***

friend′ly *adj.* **-li·er, -li·est** **1** of or like a friend; kindly **2** not hostile; amicable **3** supporting; helping —**friend′li·ly *adv.*** —**friend′li·ness *n.***

friend′ship′ *n.* **1** the state of being friends **2** friendly feeling

fries (frīz) ***pl.n.*** [Inf.] *short for* FRENCH FRIES

frieze (frēz) ***n.*** ⟦< ML *frisium*⟧ an ornamental band with designs or carvings, positioned along a wall, around a room, etc.

frig·ate (frig′it) ***n.*** ⟦< It *fregata*⟧ a fast, medium-sized sailing warship of the 18th and early 19th c.

fright (frīt) ***n.*** ⟦OE *fyrhto*⟧ **1** sudden fear; alarm **2** an ugly, startling, etc. person or thing

fright′en *vt.* **1** to make suddenly afraid; scare **2** to force (*away, out,* or *off*) by scaring —**fright′en·ing·ly *adv.***

fright′ful (-fəl) ***adj.*** **1** causing fright; alarming **2** shocking; terrible **3** [Inf.] *a)* unpleasant; annoying *b)* great

THESAURUS

frequency *n.* recurrence, number, reiteration; see REGULARITY.

frequent *a.* **1** [Happening often] repeated, numerous, common, habitual, monotonous, profuse, incessant, continual, customary, intermittent, familiar, commonplace, expected, various.—*Ant.* RARE, infrequent, occasional. **2** [Happening regularly] recurrent, usual, periodic; see REGULAR 3.

frequent *v.* visit often, go to, be seen at daily, attend regularly, be at home in, be often in, be accustomed to, hang around*, hang out at*; see also VISIT.

frequently *a.* often, regularly, usually, commonly, successively, many times, in many instances, all the time, notably, repeatedly, intermittently, generally, at times, not infrequently, often enough, not seldom, periodically, at regular intervals; see also REGULARLY.—*Ant.* SELDOM, infrequently, rarely.

fresh[1] ***a.*** **1** [Newly produced] new, green, crisp, raw, recent, current, late, this season's, factory-fresh, garden-fresh, farm-fresh, brand-new, newborn, immature, young, beginning, hot off the press*, just out, newfangled.—*Ant.* OLD, stale, musty. **2** [Not preserved] unsalted, uncured, unsmoked, unpickled, uncanned. **3** [Unspoiled] uncontaminated, green, not stale, good, undecayed, well-preserved, odor-free, in good condition, unblemished, unspotted, preserved, new, virgin, unimpaired.—*Ant.* DECAYED, spoiled, contaminated. **4** [Not faded] colorful, vivid, sharp; see BRIGHT 1, DEFINITE 2. **5** [Not salt; *said of water*] potable, drinkable, cool, clear, pure, clean, sweet, fit to drink, safe.—*Ant.* DIRTY, brackish, briny. **6** [Refreshed] restored, rested, rehabilitated, like new, unused, new, relaxed, stimulated, relieved, freshened, revived.—*Ant.* TIRED, worn-out, exhausted. **7** [Inexperienced] green, untried, unskilled; see INEXPERIENCED.

freshman *n.* beginner, novice, underclassman; see AMATEUR.

fret[1] ***v.*** disturb, agitate, vex; see BOTHER 2.

friar *n.* brother, padre, father; see MONK.

friction *n.* **1** [The rubbing of two bodies] attrition, abrasion, erosion; see GRINDING. **2** [Trouble between individuals or groups] animosity, conflict, discord; see HATRED.

fried *a.* grilled, deep-fried, French-fried, sautéed, pan-fried, stir-fried, browned; see also DONE 2.

friend *n.* familiar, schoolmate, playmate, best friend, roommate, companion, intimate, confidant, comrade, mate, amigo, compadre, fellow, pal*, chum*, crony*, goombah*, buddy*, sidekick*.—*Ant.* ENEMY, foe, stranger. —**make** or **be friends with** befriend, stand by, become familiar with; see ASSOCIATE 1.

friendless *a.* deserted, alone, forlorn; see ABANDONED.

friendliness *n.* kindness, amiability, geniality; see FRIENDSHIP.

friendly *a.* kind, kindly, helpful, sympathetic, well-disposed, neighborly, well-intentioned, sociable, civil, peaceful, loving, affectionate, fond, warmhearted, attentive, brotherly, agreeable, genial, amiable, amicable, affable, benevolent, accommodating, unoffensive, pleasant, tender, companionable, with open arms, cordial, familiar, intimate, close, devoted, dear, attached, loyal, faithful, steadfast, true, responsive, understanding, congenial, approachable, cheerful, convivial, good-humored, good-natured, generous, gracious, cooperative, wholehearted, bighearted, chummy*, folksy*, thick*, arm in arm.—*Ant.* UNFRIENDLY, antagonistic, spiteful.

friendship *n.* harmony, friendliness, brotherly love; see FELLOWSHIP 1.

fright *n.* panic, dread, horror; see FEAR.

frighten *v.* scare, scare away, scare off, dismay, terrify, cow, shock, intimidate, threaten, badger, petrify, panic, demoralize, disrupt, give cause for alarm, terrorize, horrify, astound, awe, perturb, disturb, startle, frighten out of one's wits, take someone's breath away, chill to the bone, make someone's hair stand on end, make someone's blood run cold, make someone's flesh creep, scare one stiff*, curdle the blood.

frightened *a.* terrorized, scared, startled; see AFRAID.

frightful *a.* **1** [Causing fright] fearful, horrifying, dreadful; see TERRIBLE

[in a frightful hurry] —**fright′ful·ly** ***adv.*** —**fright′ful·ness** ***n.***
frig·id (frij′id) ***adj.*** ⟦< L *frigus*, coldness⟧ **1** extremely cold **2** not warm or friendly **3** sexually unresponsive: said of a woman —**fri·gid·i·ty** (fri jid′ə tē) ***n.*** —**frig′id·ly** ***adv.***
Frigid Zone either of two zones (**North Frigid Zone** or **South Frigid Zone**) between the polar circles and the poles
frill (fril) ***n.*** ⟦< ?⟧ **1** any unnecessary ornament **2** a ruffle —**frill′y, -i·er, -i·est,** ***adj.***
fringe (frinj) ***n.*** ⟦< LL *fimbria*⟧ **1** a border of threads, etc. hanging loose or tied in bunches **2** an outer edge; border **3** a marginal or minor part —***vt.*** **fringed, fring′ing** to be or make a fringe for —***adj.*** **1** at the outer edge **2** additional **3** minor
fringe benefit any form of employee compensation other than wages, as insurance or a pension
frip·per·y (frip′ər ē) ***n.***, *pl.* **-ies** ⟦< OFr *frepe*, a rag⟧ **1** cheap, gaudy clothes **2** showy display in dress, manners, etc.
Fris·bee (friz′bē) ⟦< "Mother *Frisbie's*" pie tins⟧ *trademark for* a saucer-shaped plastic disk sailed back and forth in a simple game —***n.*** [*also* **f-**] **1** such a disk **2** the game
fri·sé (frē zā′, fri-) ***n.*** ⟦Fr < *friser*, to curl⟧ an upholstery fabric with a thick pile in loops
Fri·sian (frizh′ən) ***n.*** the West Germanic language of an island chain, the Frisian Islands, along the coast of N Netherlands, Germany, & Denmark
frisk (frisk) ***vi.*** ⟦< OHG *frisc*, lively⟧ to move about in a lively way; frolic —***vt.*** [Slang] to search (a person) for weapons, etc. by passing the hands quickly over the person's clothing
frisk·y (fris′kē) ***adj.*** **-i·er, -i·est** lively; frolicsome —**frisk′i·ly** ***adv.*** —**frisk′i·ness** ***n.***
frit·ter[1] (frit′ər) ***vt.*** ⟦< L *frangere*, to break⟧ to waste (money, time, etc.) bit by bit: usually with *away*
frit·ter[2] (frit′ər) ***n.*** ⟦< L *frigere*, to fry⟧ a small cake of fried batter, usually containing corn, fruit, etc.
friv·o·lous (friv′ə ləs) ***adj.*** ⟦< L *frivolus*, silly⟧ **1** of little value; trivial **2** silly and light-minded; giddy —**fri·vol·i·ty** (fri väl′ə tē), *pl.* **-ties,** ***n.*** —**friv′o·lous·ly** ***adv.***
frizz or **friz** (friz) ***vt.***, ***vi.*** **frizzed, friz′zing** ⟦Fr *friser*⟧ to form into small, tight curls —***n.*** hair, etc. that is frizzed —**friz′zy, -zi·er, -zi·est,** ***adj.***
friz·zle[1] (friz′əl) ***vi.***, ***vt.*** **-zled, -zling** ⟦< FRY[1]⟧ to sizzle, as in frying
friz·zle[2] (friz′əl) ***n.***, ***vt.***, ***vi.*** **-zled, -zling** FRIZZ —**friz′zly** ***adj.***
fro (frō) ***adv.*** ⟦< ON *frā*⟧ backward; back: now only in TO AND FRO (at TO)
frock (fräk) ***n.*** ⟦< OFr *froc*⟧ **1** a robe worn by friars, monks, etc. **2** a dress
frog (frôg, fräg) ***n.*** ⟦OE *frogga*⟧ **1** a tailless, leaping amphibian with long hind legs and webbed feet **2** a fancy loop of braid used to fasten clothing —**frog in one's throat** temporary hoarseness
frog′man′ ***n.***, *pl.* **-men′** (-men′) a person trained and equipped for underwater demolition, exploration, etc.
frol·ic (fräl′ik) ***n.*** ⟦< MDu *vrō*, merry⟧ **1** a lively party or game **2** merriment; fun —***vi.*** **-icked, -ick·ing** **1** to make merry; have fun **2** to romp about; gambol —**frol′ick·er** ***n.***
frol′ic·some (-səm) ***adj.*** playful; merry
from (frum) ***prep.*** ⟦OE⟧ **1** beginning at; starting with *[from noon to midnight]* **2** out of *[from her purse]* **3** originating with *[a letter from me]* **4** out of the possibility of or use of *[kept from going]* **5** as not being like *[to know good from evil]* **6** because of *[to tremble from fear]*
frond (fränd) ***n.*** ⟦< L *frons*, leafy branch⟧ the leaf of a fern or palm
front (frunt) ***n.*** ⟦< L *frons*, forehead⟧ **1** *a)* outward behavior *[a bold front]* *b)* [Inf.] an appearance of social standing, wealth, etc. **2** the part facing forward **3** the first part; beginning **4** a forward or leading position **5** the land bordering a lake, street, etc. **6** the advanced battle area in warfare **7** an area of activity *[the home front]* **8** a person or group used to hide another's activity **9** *Meteorol.* the boundary between two differing air masses —***adj.*** at, to, in, on, or of the front —***vt.***, ***vi.*** **1** to face **2** to serve as a front (*for*) —**in front of** before —**fron′tal** ***adj.***
front·age (frunt′ij) ***n.*** **1** the front part of a building **2** the front boundary line of a lot or the length of this line **3** land bordering a street, lake, etc.
fron·tier (frun tir′) ***n.*** ⟦see FRONT⟧ **1** the border between two countries **2** the part of a country which borders an unexplored region **3** any new field of learning, etc. or any part of a field that is not fully investigated —***adj.*** of, on, or near a frontier —**fron·tiers′man** (-tirz′mən), *pl.* **-men** (-mən), ***n.***
fron·tis·piece (frunt′is pēs′) ***n.*** ⟦ult. < L *frons*, front + *specere*, to look⟧ an illustration facing the title page of a book
front office the management or administration, as of a company
front′-run′ner ***n.*** a leading contestant
front′-wheel′ drive an automotive design in which only the front wheels receive driving power
frost (frôst, fräst) ***n.*** ⟦OE < *freosan*, to freeze⟧ **1** a temperature low enough to cause freezing **2** frozen dew or vapor; rime —***vt.*** **1** to cover with frost **2** to cover with frosting **3** to give a frostlike, opaque surface to (glass) —**frost′y, -i·er, -i·est,** ***adj.***
Frost (frôst, fräst), **Robert** (**Lee**) (rä′bərt) 1874-1963; U.S. poet
frost′bite′ ***vt.*** **-bit′, -bit′ten, -bit′ing** to injure the tissues of (a body part) by exposing to intense cold —***n.*** injury caused by such exposure
frost′ing ***n.*** **1** a mixture of sugar, butter, flavoring, etc. for covering a cake; icing **2** a dull finish on glass, metal, etc.
frost line the limit of penetration of soil by frost
froth (frôth, fräth) ***n.*** ⟦< ON *frotha*⟧ **1** foam **2** foaming saliva **3** light, trifling talk, ideas, etc. —***vi.*** to foam —**froth′y, -i·er, -i·est,** ***adj.***
frou·frou (frōō′frōō′) ***n.*** ⟦Fr⟧ [Inf.] excessive ornateness
fro·ward (frō′wərd, -ərd) ***adj.*** ⟦see FRO & -WARD⟧ not easily controlled; willful; contrary —**fro′ward·ness** ***n.***
frown (froun) ***vi.*** ⟦< OFr *froigne*, sullen face⟧ **1** to contract the brows, as in displeasure **2** to show disapproval: with *on* or *upon* —***n.*** a frowning
frow·zy (frou′zē) ***adj.*** **-zi·er, -zi·est** ⟦< ?⟧ dirty and untidy; slovenly —**frow′zi·ly** ***adv.*** —**frow′zi·ness** ***n.***
froze (frōz) ***vi.***, ***vt.*** *pt. of* FREEZE
fro·zen (frō′zən) ***vi.***, ***vt.*** *pp. of* FREEZE —***adj.*** **1** turned into or covered with ice; solidified by cold **2** damaged or killed by freezing **3** preserved by freezing: said as of food **4** made motionless **5** kept at a fixed level **6** not readily convertible into cash *[frozen assets]*
frozen custard a food resembling ice cream, but softer and with less butterfat

THESAURUS

1, 2. **2** [Very unpleasant] calamitous, shocking, terrible; see OFFENSIVE 2.
frigid ***a.*** **1** [Thermally cold] freezing, frosty, refrigerated; see COLD 1. **2** [Unresponsive] unloving, distant, chilly; see COLD 2, INDIFFERENT.
fringe ***n.*** hem, trimming, border; see EDGE 1.
frisky ***a.*** spirited, dashing, playful; see ACTIVE.
frivolity ***n.*** silliness, levity, folly; see FUN.
frivolous ***a.*** superficial, petty, trifling; see TRIVIAL.
frog ***n.*** amphibian, tree frog, toad, bullfrog, horned frog, horned toad, polliwog.
from ***prep.*** in distinction to, out of, beginning with; see OF.
front ***a.*** fore, forward, frontal, foremost, head, headmost, leading, in the foreground.—*Ant.* BACK, rear, hindmost.
front ***n.*** **1** [The forward part or surface] exterior, forepart, anterior, bow, foreground, face, head, breast, frontal area.—*Ant.* REAR, posterior, back. **2** [The fighting line] front line, no man's land, advance position, line of battle, vanguard, outpost, field of fire, advance guard. **3** [The appearance one presents before others] mien, demeanor, aspect, countenance, face, presence, expression, figure, exterior. —**in front of** before, preceding, leading; see AHEAD.
frontier ***n.*** hinterland, remote districts, outskirts; see COUNTRY 1.
frost ***n.*** frozen dew, permafrost, rime; see ICE.
frosting ***n.*** icing, topping, finish, covering, coating.
frosty ***a.*** frigid, freezing, chilly; see COLD 1.
froth ***n.*** bubbles, scum, fizz, effervescence, foam, ferment, head, lather, suds, spray.
frothy ***a.*** fizzing, bubbling, foaming, soapy, sudsy, bubbly, fizzy, foamy, having a head.
frown ***n.*** scowl, grimace, wry face, gloomy countenance, forbidding aspect, dirty look.
frown ***v.*** scowl, grimace, pout, glare, sulk, glower, gloom, look stern.—*Ant.* SMILE, laugh, grin.
frozen ***a.*** chilled, frosted, iced; see COLD 1, 2.

fruc·ti·fy (fruk′tə fī′) ***vi.***, ***vt.*** **-fied′**, **-fy′ing** ⟦< L *fructificare*⟧ to bear or cause to bear fruit
fruc·tose (fruk′tōs′, frook′-) ***n.*** ⟦< L *fructus*, fruit + -OSE[1]⟧ a sugar found in sweet fruits and in honey
fru·gal (fro͞o′gəl) ***adj.*** ⟦< L *frugi*, fit for food⟧ **1** not wasteful; thrifty **2** inexpensive or meager —**fru·gal′i·ty** (-gal′ə tē), *pl.* **-ties**, ***n.*** —**fru′gal·ly** ***adv.***
fruit (fro͞ot) ***n.*** ⟦< L *fructus*⟧ **1** any plant product, as grain or vegetables: *usually used in pl.* **2** *a)* an edible plant structure, often sweet, containing the seeds inside a juicy pulp: many true fruits that are not sweet, as tomatoes, are popularly called *vegetables* *b) Bot.* the mature seed-bearing part of a flowering plant **3** the result or product of any action
fruit′cake′ ***n.*** a rich cake containing nuts, preserved fruit, citron, spices, etc.
fruit fly any of various small flies whose larvae feed on fruits and vegetables
fruit′ful (-fəl) ***adj.*** **1** bearing much fruit **2** productive; prolific **3** profitable
fru·i·tion (fro͞o ish′ən) ***n.*** **1** the bearing of fruit **2** a coming to fulfillment; realization
fruit′less (-lis) ***adj.*** **1** without results; unsuccessful **2** bearing no fruit; sterile; barren —**fruit′less·ly** ***adv.*** —**fruit′less·ness** ***n.***
frump (frump) ***n.*** ⟦prob. < Du *rompelen*, rumple⟧ a dowdy woman —**frump′ish** ***adj.*** —**frump′y**, **-i·er**, **-i·est**, ***adj.***
frus·trate (frus′trāt′) ***vt.*** **-trat′ed**, **-trat′ing** ⟦< L *frustra*, in vain⟧ **1** to cause to have no effect **2** to prevent from achieving a goal or gratifying a desire —**frus·tra′tion** ***n.***
fry[1] (frī) ***vt.***, ***vi.*** **fried**, **fry′ing** ⟦< L *frigere*, to fry⟧ to cook in a pan over direct heat, usually in hot fat —***n.***, *pl.* **fries** **1** [*pl.*] fried potatoes **2** a social gathering at which food is fried and eaten *[a fish fry]*
fry[2] (frī) ***pl.n.***, *sing.* **fry** ⟦< OFr *freier,* to rub, spawn⟧ young fish
fry′er ***n.*** **1** a utensil for deep-frying **2** a chicken for frying
FSLIC *abbrev.* Federal Savings and Loan Insurance Corporation
ft *abbrev.* foot; feet
Ft *abbrev.* Fort
FTC *abbrev.* Federal Trade Commission
fuch·sia (fyo͞o′shə) ***n.*** ⟦after L. *Fuchs* (1501-66), Ger botanist⟧ **1** a shrubby plant with pink, red, or purple flowers **2** purplish red
fud·dle (fud′'l) ***vt.*** **-dled**, **-dling** ⟦< ?⟧ to confuse or stupefy as with alcoholic liquor —***n.*** a fuddled state
fud·dy-dud·dy (fud′ē dud′ē) ***n.***, *pl.* **-dies** [Inf.] a fussy or old-fashioned person
fudge (fuj) ***n.*** ⟦< ?⟧ a soft candy made of butter, milk, sugar, chocolate or other flavoring, etc. —***vi.*** **fudged**, **fudg′ing** **1** to refuse to commit oneself; hedge **2** to be dishonest; cheat
fu·el (fyo͞o′əl, fyo͞ol) ***n.*** ⟦ult. < L *focus*, fireplace⟧ **1** coal, oil, gas, wood, etc., burned to supply heat or power **2** material from which nuclear energy can be obtained **3** anything that intensifies strong feeling —***vt.***, ***vi.*** **fu′eled** or **fu′elled**, **fu′el·ing** or **fu′el·ling** to supply with or get fuel
fuel injection a system for injecting a fine spray of fuel into the combustion chambers of an engine
fu·gi·tive (fyo͞o′ji tiv) ***adj.*** ⟦< L *fugere*, to flee⟧ **1** fleeing, as from danger or justice **2** fleeting —***n.*** one who is fleeing from justice, etc. —**fu′gi·tive·ly** ***adv.***
fugue (fyo͞og) ***n.*** ⟦< L *fugere*, to flee⟧ a musical work in which a theme is taken up successively and developed by the various parts or voices in counterpoint
-ful (fəl; *for 2, usually* fool) ⟦< FULL[1]⟧ *suffix* **1** *a)* full of, having *[joyful]* *b)* having the qualities of or tendency to *[helpful]* **2** the quantity that will fill *[handful]*
ful·crum (fool′krəm, ful′-) ***n.***, *pl.* **-crums** or **-cra** (-krə) ⟦L, a support⟧ the support on which a lever turns in raising something
ful·fill (fool fil′) ***vt.*** **-filled′**, **-fill′ing** ⟦OE *fullfyllan*⟧ **1** to carry out (a promise, etc.) **2** to do (a duty, etc.); obey **3** to satisfy (a condition) Brit. sp. **ful·fil′**, **-filled′**, **-fill′ing** —**ful·fill′ment** or **ful·fil′ment** ***n.***
full[1] (fool) ***adj.*** ⟦OE⟧ **1** having in it all there is space for; filled **2** having eaten all that one wants **3** having a great deal or number (*of*) **4** complete *[a full dozen]* **5** having reached the greatest size, extent, etc. *[a full moon]* **6** plump; round *[a full face]* **7** with wide folds; flowing *[a full skirt]* —***n.*** the greatest amount, extent, etc. —***adv.*** **1** to the greatest degree; completely **2** directly; exactly —**full′ness** or **ful′ness** ***n.***
full[2] (fool) ***vt.***, ***vi.*** ⟦< L *fullo*, cloth fuller⟧ to shrink and thicken (wool cloth) —**full′er** ***n.***
full′back′ ***n.*** *Football* one of the running backs, used typically for blocking an opponent
full′-blood′ed ***adj.*** **1** of unmixed breed or race **2** vigorous
full′-blown′ ***adj.*** **1** in full bloom **2** fully developed; matured
full′-bore′ ***adv.*** to the greatest degree or extent —***adj.*** all-out
full′-fledged′ ***adj.*** completely developed or trained; of full status
full moon the moon when it reflects light as a full disk
full′-scale′ ***adj.*** **1** according to the original or standard scale **2** to the utmost degree; all-out
full′-size′ ***adj.*** **1** of the usual or standard size **2** of a large size Also **full′-sized′**
full′-throat′ed ***adj.*** **1** having or producing deep, rich sound **2** complete and unmitigated
full′-time′ ***adj.*** of or engaged in work, study, etc. that takes all of one's regular working hours
full′y ***adv.*** **1** completely; thoroughly **2** at least
ful·mi·nate (ful′mə nāt′) ***vi.*** **-nat′ed**, **-nat′ing** ⟦< L *fulmen*, lightning⟧ to express strong disapproval —**ful′mi·na′tion** ***n.***
ful·some (fool′səm) ***adj.*** ⟦see FULL[1] & -SOME[1], but infl. by ME *ful*, foul⟧ disgusting, esp. because excessive
fum·ble (fum′bəl) ***vi.***, ***vt.*** **-bled**, **-bling** ⟦prob. < ON *famla*⟧ **1** to grope (*for*) or handle (a thing) clumsily **2** to lose one's grasp on (a football, etc.) —***n.*** a fumbling —**fum′bler** ***n.***

THESAURUS

frugal ***a.*** thrifty, prudent, parsimonious; see CAREFUL.
frugality ***n.*** carefulness, conservation, management; see ECONOMY.
fruit ***n.*** berry, grain, nut, root; see also VEGETABLE. *Common fruits include the following:* apple, pear, peach, plum, nectarine, tangerine, orange, grapefruit, citron, banana, pineapple, watermelon, cantaloupe, honeydew melon, papaya, mango, guava, kiwi, coconut, grape, lime, lemon, persimmon, kumquat, pomegranate, raspberry, blackberry, blueberry, cranberry, loganberry, huckleberry, date, fig, apricot, cherry, raisin, avocado, gooseberry, strawberry.
fruitful ***a.*** prolific, productive, fecund; see FERTILE.
fruitless ***a.*** vain, unprofitable, empty; see FUTILE.
frustrate ***v.*** defeat, foil, balk; see PREVENT.
frustration ***n.*** disappointment, impediment, failure; see DEFEAT.
fry[1,2] ***v.*** sauté, sear, singe, brown, grill, pan-fry, deep-fry, French-fry, sizzle; see also COOK. —**small fry** children, infants, toddlers; see BABY, CHILD.
fudge ***n.*** penuche, chocolate fudge, divinity; see CANDY.
fuel ***n.*** propellant, combustible, firing material. *Fuels include the following:* coal, gas, oil, coke, charcoal, anthracite, propane, bituminous coal, peat, slack, stoker coal, lignite, carbon, turf, cordwood, firewood, log, kindling, timber, diesel oil, crude oil, fuel oil, natural gas, gasoline, kerosene, wax.
fuel ***v.*** fill up, tank up*, gas up*; see FILL 1.
fugitive ***n.*** outlaw, refugee, truant, runaway, exile, vagabond, waif, stray, derelict, outcast, recluse, hermit.
fulfill ***v.*** accomplish, effect, complete; see ACHIEVE.
fulfilled ***a.*** accomplished, completed, achieved, realized, effected, finished, obtained, perfected, concluded, attained, reached, actualized, executed, brought about, performed, carried out, put into effect, made good, brought to a close.—*Ant.* DISAPPOINTED, unfulfilled, unrealized.
fulfillment ***n.*** attainment, accomplishment, realization; see ACHIEVEMENT.
full[1] ***a.*** **1** [Filled] running over, abundant, weighted, satisfied, saturated, crammed, packed, stuffed, jammed, glutted, gorged, loaded, chock-full, stocked, satiated, crowded, stuffed to the gills*, jampacked*, crawling with*, to the brim, packed like sardines*.—*Ant.* EMPTY, void, exhausted. **2** [Well-supplied] abundant, complete, copious, ample, plentiful, sufficient, adequate, competent, lavish, extravagant, profuse.—*Ant.* INADEQUATE, scanty, insufficient. **3** [Not limited] broad, unlimited, extensive; see ABSOLUTE 1, 2. —**in full** **1** for the entire amount, fully, thoroughly; see COMPLETELY. **2** complete, entire, inclusive; see WHOLE 1.
fully ***a.*** entirely, thoroughly, wholly; see COMPLETELY.
fumble ***n.*** mistake, blunder, dropped ball; see ERROR.
fumble ***v.*** mishandle, bungle, mismanage; see BOTCH.

fume (fyo͞om) ***n.*** ⟦< L *fumus*⟧ [*often pl.*] a gas, smoke, or vapor, esp. if offensive or suffocating —***vi.*** **fumed, fum′ing** **1** to give off fumes **2** to show anger

fu·mi·gate (fyo͞o′mə gāt′) ***vt.*** **-gat′ed, -gat′ing** ⟦< L *fumus*, smoke + *agere*, do⟧ to expose to fumes, esp. so as to disinfect or kill the vermin in —**fu′mi·ga′tion** ***n.*** —**fu′mi·ga′tor** ***n.***

fum·y (fyo͞om′ē) ***adj.*** **-i·er, -i·est** full of or producing fumes; vaporous

fun (fun) ***n.*** ⟦< ME *fonne*, foolish⟧ **1** *a)* lively, joyous play or playfulness *b)* pleasure **2** a source of amusement —***adj.*** [Inf.] intended for pleasure or amusement —**make fun of** to ridicule

func·tion (fuŋk′shən) ***n.*** ⟦< L *fungi*, to perform⟧ **1** the normal or characteristic action of anything **2** a special duty required in work **3** a formal ceremony or social occasion **4** a thing that depends on and varies with something else —***vi.*** to act in a required manner; work; be used —**func′tion·less** ***adj.***

func′tion·al ***adj.*** **1** of a function **2** performing a function **3** *Med.* affecting a function of some organ without apparent organic changes

functional illiterate a person who cannot read well enough to carry out everyday activities

func′tion·ar′y (-shə ner′ē) ***n.***, *pl.* **-ies** an official performing some function

function word a word, as an article or conjunction, serving mainly to show grammatical relationship

fund (fund) ***n.*** ⟦L *fundus*, bottom⟧ **1** a supply that can be drawn upon; stock **2** *a)* a sum of money set aside for a purpose *b)* [*pl.*] ready money —***vt.*** **1** to put or convert into a long-term debt that bears interest **2** to provide funds for (a project, retirement of a debt, etc.)

fun·da·men·tal (fun′də ment′'l) ***adj.*** ⟦see prec.⟧ of or forming a foundation or basis; basic; essential —***n.*** a principle, theory, law, etc. serving as a basis —**fun′da·men′tal·ly** ***adv.***

fun′da·men′tal·ism′ ***n.*** [*sometimes* **F-**] religious beliefs based on a literal interpretation of the Bible —**fun′da·men′tal·ist** ***n., adj.***

fund′rais′er (-rā′zər) ***n.*** **1** one soliciting money for a charity, political party, etc. **2** an event held to obtain such money —**fund′rais′ing** ***n.***

fu·ner·al (fyo͞o′nər əl) ***n.*** ⟦< L *funus*⟧ the ceremonies connected with burial or cremation of a dead person

funeral director one who manages a funeral home

funeral home (or **parlor**) an establishment where the bodies of the dead are prepared for burial or cremation and where funeral services can be held

fu·ne·re·al (fyo͞o nir′ē əl) ***adj.*** suitable for a funeral; sad and solemn; dismal —**fu·ne′re·al·ly** ***adv.***

fun·gi·cide (fun′jə sīd′) ***n.*** ⟦see -CIDE⟧ any substance that kills fungi

fun·gus (fuŋ′gəs) ***n.***, *pl.* **fun·gi** (fun′jī′) or **fun′gus·es** ⟦< L⟧ any of various plants or plantlike organisms, as molds, mildews, mushrooms, etc., that lack chlorophyll, stems, and leaves and reproduce by spores —**fun′gal** or **fun′gous** ***adj.***

fu·nic·u·lar (fyo͞o nik′yo͞o lər) ***n.*** ⟦< L *funiculus*, little rope⟧ a mountain railway with counterbalanced cable cars on parallel sets of rails: also **funicular railway**

funk (fuŋk) ***n.*** ⟦< ? Fl *fonck*, dismay⟧ **1** [Inf.] a state of great fear; panic **2** [Inf.] a depressed mood **3** popular music derived from rhythm and blues

funk·y (fuŋ′kē) ***adj.*** **-i·er, -i·est** ⟦orig., earthy⟧ **1** *Jazz* having an earthy style derived from early blues **2** [Slang] unconventional, eccentric, offbeat, etc.

fun·nel (fun′əl) ***n.*** ⟦ult. < L *fundere*, to pour⟧ **1** a tapering tube with a cone-shaped mouth, for pouring things into small-mouthed containers **2** the smokestack of a steamship —***vi., vt.*** **-neled** or **-nelled, -nel·ing** or **-nel·ling** to move or pour as through a funnel

fun·nies (fun′ēz) ***pl.n.*** [Inf.] comic strips

fun·ny (fun′ē) ***adj.*** **-ni·er, -ni·est** **1** causing laughter; humorous **2** [Inf.] *a)* strange *b)* tricky —**fun′ni·ly** ***adv.*** —**fun′ni·ness** ***n.***

funny bone a place on the elbow where a sharp impact on a nerve causes a tingling sensation

funny farm [Slang] an institution for the mentally ill

fur (fʉr) ***n.*** ⟦< OFr *fuerre*, sheath⟧ **1** the soft, thick hair covering certain animals **2** a processed skin bearing such hair —***adj.*** of fur —**furred** ***adj.***

fur·be·low (fʉr′bə lō′) ***n.*** ⟦ult. < Fr *falbala*⟧ **1** a flounce or ruffle **2** a showy, useless decorative addition

fur·bish (fʉr′bish) ***vt.*** ⟦< OFr *forbir*⟧ **1** to polish; burnish **2** to renovate

Fu·ries (fyoor′ēz) ***pl.n.*** *Gr. & Rom. Myth.* the three terrible female spirits who punish the perpetrators of unavenged crimes

fu·ri·ous (fyoor′ē əs) ***adj.*** **1** full of fury; very angry **2** very great, intense, wild, etc. —**fu′ri·ous·ly** ***adv.***

furl (fʉrl) ***vt.*** ⟦< L *firmus*, FIRM[1] + *ligare*, to tie⟧ to roll up (a sail, flag, etc.) tightly and make secure

fur·long (fʉr′lôŋ′) ***n.*** ⟦< OE *furh*, a furrow + *lang*, LONG[1]⟧ a measure of distance equal to $\frac{1}{8}$ of a mile

fur·lough (fʉr′lō) ***n.*** ⟦< Du *verlof*⟧ a leave of absence, esp. for military personnel —***vt.*** to grant a furlough to

fur·nace (fʉr′nəs) ***n.*** ⟦< L *fornax*, furnace⟧ an enclosed structure in which heat is produced, as by burning fuel

fur·nish (fʉr′nish) ***vt.*** ⟦< OFr *furnir*⟧ **1** to supply with furniture, etc.; equip **2** to supply; provide

fur′nish·ings ***pl.n.*** **1** the furniture, carpets, etc. as for a house **2** things to wear [*men's furnishings*]

fur·ni·ture (fʉr′ni chər) ***n.*** ⟦Fr *fourniture*⟧ **1** the things in a room, etc. which equip it for living, as chairs, beds, etc. **2** necessary equipment

THESAURUS

fun ***n.*** play, game, sport, jest, amusement, relaxation, pastime, diversion, frolic, mirth, entertainment, solace, merriment, pleasure, caper, foolery, joke, absurdity, playfulness, laughter, festivity, carnival, tomfoolery, ball*, escapade, antic, romp, prank, comedy, teasing, celebration, holiday, rejoicing, good humor, joking, enjoyment, gladness, good cheer, delight, glee, treat, lark, recreation, joy, time of one's life, blast*, big time*, picnic*, riot*.—*Ant.* UNHAPPINESS, tedium, sorrow. —**for** (or **in**) **fun** for amusement, not seriously, playfully; see HAPPILY. —**make fun of** mock, satirize, poke fun at; see RIDICULE.

function ***n.*** employment, capacity, faculty; see USE 1.

function ***v.*** perform, run, work; see OPERATE 2.

functional ***a.*** occupational, utilitarian, useful; see PRACTICAL.

fund ***n.*** endowment, trust fund, capital; see GIFT 1.

fundamental ***a.*** basic, underlying, primary, first, rudimentary, elemental, supporting, elementary, cardinal, organic, theoretical, structural, sustaining, central, original.—*Ant.* SUPERFICIAL, incidental, consequent.

fundamentally ***a.*** basically, radically, centrally; see ESSENTIALLY.

funds ***n.*** capital, wealth, cash, collateral, money, assets, currency, savings, revenue, wherewithal, proceeds, hard cash, stocks and bonds, money on hand, money in the bank, accounts receivable, property, means, affluence, belongings, resources, securities, stakes, earnings, winnings, possessions, profits, dividends, nest egg; see also MONEY.

funeral ***n.*** interment, last rites, burial, burial ceremony, entombment, requiem, cremation.

fungus ***n.*** mushroom, mold, rust; see DECAY, PARASITE 1.

funnel ***n.*** duct, shaft, conduit; see PIPE 1.

funny ***a.*** **1** [Stirring to laughter] laughable, comic, comical, whimsical, amusing, entertaining, diverting, humorous, witty, jesting, jocular, waggish, droll, facetious, clever, mirthful, ludicrous, jolly, risible, madcap, absurd, ridiculous, sly, sportive, playful, merry, joyful, joyous, good-humored, glad, gleeful, hilarious, jovial, farcical, joking, sidesplitting.—*Ant.* SAD, serious, melancholy. **2** [*Out of the ordinary] curious, odd, unusual; see SUSPICIOUS 2.

fur ***n.*** pelt, hide, hair, coat, brush. *Types of fur include the following:* sable, mink, chinchilla, karakul, seal, muskrat, ermine, monkey, beaver, skunk, otter, marten, stone marten, weasel, squirrel, leopard, raccoon, wolverine; white fox, blue fox, red fox, etc.; sheepskin, bearskin, calfskin, rabbit, coney. —**make the fur fly*** fight, bicker, stir up trouble; see EXCITE.

furious ***a.*** enraged, raging, fierce; see ANGRY.

furnace ***n.*** heater, heating system, boiler, hot-air furnace, steam furnace, hot-water furnace, oil burner, gas furnace, electric furnace, kiln, blast furnace, open-hearth furnace, stove, forge.

furnish ***v.*** fit out, equip, stock; see PROVIDE 1.

furnished ***a.*** supplied, provided, fitted out; see EQUIPPED.

furniture ***n.*** movables, household goods, home furnishings. *Furniture includes the following—home:* table, chair, rug, carpeting, drapes, sofa, davenport, love seat, settee, ottoman, couch, cabinet, picture, chest, bureau, buffet, cupboard, bed, dresser, mirror, commode, chiffonier, tapestry, footstool, secretary, highboy, sideboard, clock, bookcase; *office:* desk, filing cabinet, stool, chair, table, counter, workstation, printer stand.

fu·ror (fyoor′ôr′) ***n.*** ⟦< L⟧ **1** fury; frenzy **2** *a)* a widespread enthusiasm; craze *b)* a commotion or uproar Also [Chiefly Brit.] **fu′rore′**

fur·ri·er (fur′ē ər) ***n.*** one who processes furs or deals in fur garments

fur·ring (fur′iŋ) ***n.*** thin strips of wood fixed on a wall, floor, etc. before adding boards or plaster

fur·row (fur′ō) ***n.*** ⟦< OE *furh*⟧ **1** a groove made in the ground by a plow **2** anything like this, as a deep wrinkle —***vt.*** to make furrows in —***vi.*** to become wrinkled

fur·ry (fur′ē) ***adj.*** **-ri·er**, **-ri·est** **1** of or like fur **2** covered with fur —**fur′ri·ness** ***n.***

fur·ther (fur′thər) ***adj.*** ⟦OE *furthor*⟧ **1** *alt. compar. of* FAR **2** additional **3** more distant; farther —***adv.*** **1** *alt. compar. of* FAR **2** to a greater degree or extent **3** in addition **4** at or to a greater distance; farther —***vt.*** to give aid to; promote In sense 3 of the *adj.* and sense 4 of the *adv.*, FARTHER is more commonly used —**fur′ther·ance** ***n.***

fur′ther·more′ ***adv.*** in addition; besides; moreover

fur·thest (fur′thist) ***adj.*** **1** *alt. superl. of* FAR **2** most distant; farthest: also **fur′ther·most′** —***adv.*** **1** *alt. superl. of* FAR **2** at or to the greatest distance or degree

fur·tive (fur′tiv) ***adj.*** ⟦< L *fur*, a thief⟧ done or acting in a stealthy manner; sneaky —**fur′tive·ly** ***adv.*** —**fur′tive·ness** ***n.***

fu·ry (fyoor′ē) ***n.***, *pl.* **-ries** ⟦< L *furere*, to rage⟧ **1** violent anger; wild rage **2** violence; vehemence

furze (furz) ***n.*** ⟦OE *fyrs*⟧ a prickly evergreen shrub native to Europe

fuse[1] (fyo͞oz) ***vt.***, ***vi.*** **fused**, **fus′ing** ⟦< L *fundere*, to shed⟧ **1** to melt **2** to unite as if by melting together

fuse[2] (fyo͞oz) ***n.*** ⟦< L *fusus*, spindle⟧ **1** a tube or wick filled with combustible material, for setting off an explosive charge **2** *Elec.* a strip of easily melted metal placed in a circuit: it melts and breaks the circuit if the current becomes too strong

fu·see (fyo͞o zē′) ***n.*** ⟦Fr *fusée*, a rocket⟧ a colored flare used as a signal by railroad workers, truck drivers, etc.

fu·se·lage (fyo͞o′sə läzh′, -läj′) ***n.*** ⟦Fr⟧ the body of an airplane, exclusive of the wings, tail assembly, and engines

fu·si·ble (fyo͞o′zə bəl) ***adj.*** that can be fused or easily melted

fu·si·lier or **fu·sil·eer** (fyo͞o′zə lir′) ***n.*** ⟦Fr⟧ [Historical] a soldier armed with a flintlock musket

fu·sil·lade (fyo͞o′sə läd′, -lād′) ***n.*** ⟦Fr < *fusiller*, to shoot⟧ a simultaneous or rapid and continuous discharge of many firearms

fu·sion (fyo͞o′zhən) ***n.*** ⟦L *fusio*⟧ **1** a fusing or melting together **2** a blending; coalition **3** NUCLEAR FUSION **4** a style of popular music blending elements of jazz, rock, etc.

fuss (fus) ***n.*** ⟦prob. echoic⟧ **1** nervous, excited activity; bustle **2** a nervous state **3** a quarrel **4** a showy display of approval, etc. —***vi.*** **1** to bustle about or worry over trifles **2** to whine, as a baby

fuss′budg′et (-buj′it) ***n.*** ⟦prec. + BUDGET⟧ [Inf.] a fussy person: also [Inf., Chiefly Brit.] **fuss′pot′** (-pät′)

fuss′y ***adj.*** **-i·er**, **-i·est** **1** *a)* worrying over trifles *b)* hard to please *c)* whining, as a baby **2** full of unnecessary details —**fuss′i·ly** ***adv.*** —**fuss′i·ness** ***n.***

fus·tian (fus′chən) ***n.*** ⟦< L *fustis*, wooden stick⟧ pompous, pretentious talk or writing; bombast

fus·ty (fus′tē) ***adj.*** **-ti·er**, **-ti·est** ⟦< OFr *fust*, a cask⟧ **1** musty; moldy **2** old-fashioned —**fus′ti·ly** ***adv.*** —**fus′ti·ness** ***n.***

fut *abbrev.* future

fu·tile (fyo͞ot′'l) ***adj.*** ⟦< L *futilis*, lit., that easily pours out⟧ useless; vain —**fu′tile·ly** ***adv.*** —**fu·til·i·ty** (fyo͞o til′ə tē), *pl.* **-ties**, ***n.***

fu·ton (fo͞o′tän′) ***n.*** ⟦Sino-Jpn⟧ a thin mattress like a quilt, placed as on the floor or a platform frame for use as a bed

fu·ture (fyo͞o′chər) ***adj.*** ⟦< L *futurus*, about to be⟧ **1** that is to be or come **2** indicating time to come *[the future tense]* —***n.*** **1** the time that is to come **2** what is going to be **3** the chance to succeed, etc. **4** [*usually pl.*] a contract for a commodity bought or sold for delivery at a later date —**fu′tur·is′tic** ***adj.***

fu·tu·ri·ty (fyo͞o toor′ə tē, -tyoor′-) ***n.***, *pl.* **-ties** **1** the future **2** a future condition or event **3** a race for two-year-old horses in which the entries are selected before birth: in full **futurity race**

fu·tur·ol·o·gy (fyo͞o′chər äl′ə jē) ***n.*** ⟦FUTUR(E) + -OLOGY⟧ the study of probable or presumed future conditions as extrapolated from known facts —**fu′tur·ol′o·gist** ***n.***

futz (futs) ***vi.*** ⟦? < Yiddish⟧ [Slang] to trifle or fool (*around*)

fuzz (fuz) ***n.*** ⟦< ?⟧ **1** loose, light particles of down, wool, etc.; fine hairs or fibers —**the fuzz** [Slang] a policeman or the police —**fuzz′y**, **-i·er**, **-i·est**, ***adj.***

fuzzy logic ⟦< *fuzzy (set)*, coined (1965) by L. A. Zadeh, U.S. scientist⟧ a type of logic used in computers for processing imprecise or variable data

-fy (fī) ⟦< L *facere*, do⟧ *suffix* **1** to make *[liquefy]* **2** to cause to have *[glorify]* **3** to become *[putrefy]*

FYI *abbrev.* for your information

THESAURUS

furor ***n.*** tumult, excitement, stir; see DISTURBANCE 2.

further ***a.*** more, at a greater distance, in addition; see DISTANT.

furthermore ***a.*** moreover, too, in addition; see BESIDES.

furthest ***a.*** most remote, most distant, remotest, farthest, uttermost, outermost, ultimate, extreme, outmost.

fury ***n.*** wrath, fire, rage; see ANGER.

fuse[2] ***n.*** wick, tinder, kindling; see FUEL. —**blow a fuse*** become angry, lose one's temper, rant; see RAGE 1.

fuss ***n.*** trouble, complaint, bother; see DISTURBANCE 2.

fuss ***v.*** whine, whimper, object; see COMPLAIN.

fussy ***a.*** fastidious, particular, meticulous; see CAREFUL.

futile ***a.*** vain, useless, in vain, fruitless, hopeless, impractical, worthless, unprofitable, to no effect, not successful, to no purpose, unneeded, unsatisfactory, unsatisfying, ineffective, ineffectual, unproductive, idle, empty, hollow, unreal.—*Ant.* HOPEFUL, practical, effective.

futility ***n.*** uselessness, falseness, hollowness, frivolity, idleness, emptiness, fruitlessness, hopelessness, worthlessness, illusion, folly, unimportance, carrying water in a sieve, wild-goose chase, running around in circles, carrying coals to Newcastle.—*Ant.* IMPORTANCE, fruitfulness, significance.

future ***a.*** coming, impending, imminent, destined, fated, prospective, to come, in the course of time, expected, inevitable, approaching, eventual, ultimate, planned, scheduled, budgeted, booked, looked toward, likely, coming up, in the cards.—*Ant.* PAST, completed, recorded.

future ***n.*** infinity, eternity, world to come, subsequent time, coming time, events to come, prospect, tomorrow, the hereafter, by and by.—*Ant.* PAST, historic ages, recorded time. —**in the future** eventually, sometime, in due time; see FINALLY 2, SOMEDAY.

fuzz ***n.*** nap, fluff, fur; see HAIR 1.

fuzzy ***a.*** **1** [Like or covered with fuzz] hairy, woolly, furry; see HAIRY. **2** [Not clear] blurred, indistinct, out of focus, hazy, imprecise, foggy; see also OBSCURE 1, HAZY.

G

g or **G** (jē) ***n.***, *pl.* **g's, G's** the seventh letter of the English alphabet
G[1] (jē) ***n.*** *Music* the fifth tone in the scale of C major
G[2] *trademark for* a film rating indicating content suitable for persons of all ages
G[3] *abbrev.* **1** game(s) **2** German **3** goal(s) **4** gram(s) **5** guard **6** gulf Also, except for 2 & 6, **g**
Ga *Chem. symbol for* gallium
GA Georgia
gab (gab) ***n.***, ***vt.*** **gabbed, gab'bing** ⟦ON *gabba*, to mock⟧ [Inf.] chatter
gab·ar·dine (gab'ər dēn') ***n.*** ⟦< OFr *gaverdine*, kind of cloak⟧ a twilled cloth of wool, cotton, etc., with a fine, diagonal weave: Brit. sp. **gab'er·dine'**
gab·ble (gab'əl) ***vi.***, ***vt.*** **-bled, -bling** ⟦< GABB⟧ to talk or utter rapidly or incoherently —***n.*** such talk
gab·by (gab'ē) ***adj.*** **-bi·er, -bi·est** [Inf.] talkative —**gab'bi·ness** ***n.***
gab'fest' (-fest') ***n.*** [Inf.] an informal gathering of people to talk with one another
ga·ble (gā'bəl) ***n.*** ⟦< Gmc⟧ a triangular part of a wall enclosed by the sloping sides of a peaked roof —**ga'bled** ***adj.***
Ga·bon (ga bōn') country on the W coast of Africa: 103,347 sq. mi.; pop. 1,012,000
Ga·bri·el (gā'brē əl) ***n.*** *Bible* one of the archangels, the herald of good news
gad (gad) ***vi.*** **gad'ded, gad'ding** ⟦ME *gadden*, to hurry⟧ to wander about in an idle or restless way —**gad'der** ***n.***
gad'a·bout' ***n.*** one who gads about, looking for fun, etc.
gad'fly' ***n.***, *pl.* **-flies'** ⟦see GOAD & FLY[2]⟧ **1** a large fly that bites livestock **2** one who annoys others, esp. by rousing them from complacency
gadg·et (gaj'it) ***n.*** ⟦< ?⟧ any small mechanical contrivance or device
Gael·ic (gā'lik) ***adj.*** of the Celtic people of Ireland, Scotland, or the Isle of Man —***n.*** **1** the Celtic language of Scotland **2** the language group that includes GAELIC (*n.* 1), IRISH (*n.* 1), etc.
gaff (gaf) ***n.*** ⟦< OProv *gaf* or Sp *gafa*⟧ **1** a large hook on a pole for landing fish **2** a spar supporting a fore-and-aft sail
gaffe (gaf) ***n.*** ⟦Fr⟧ a blunder
gaf·fer (gaf'ər) ***n.*** a person in charge of lighting on the set of a film
gag (gag) ***vt.*** **gagged, gag'ging** ⟦echoic⟧ **1** to cause to retch **2** to keep from speaking, as by stopping up the mouth of —***vi.*** to retch —***n.*** **1** something put into or over the mouth to prevent talking, etc. **2** any restraint of free speech **3** a joke
gage[1] (gāj) ***n.*** ⟦< OFr, a pledge⟧ a glove, etc. thrown down as by a knight as a challenge to fight
gage[2] (gāj) ***n.***, ***vt.*** **gaged, gag'ing** *alt. sp. of* GAUGE
gag·gle (gag'əl) ***n.*** ⟦echoic⟧ **1** a flock of geese **2** any group or cluster
gai·e·ty (gā'ə tē) ***n.***, *pl.* **-ties** **1** the quality of being GAY (*adj.* 1); cheerfulness **2** merrymaking
gai·ly (gā'lē) ***adv.*** in a gay manner; specif., *a*) merrily *b*) brightly
gain (gān) ***n.*** ⟦< OFr *gaaigne*⟧ **1** an increase; specif., *a*) [*often pl.*] profit *b*) an increase in advantage **2** acquisition —***vt.*** **1** to earn **2** to win **3** to attract **4** to get as an addition, profit, or advantage **5** to make an increase in **6** to get to; reach —***vi.*** **1** to make progress **2** to increase in weight —**gain on** to draw nearer to (an opponent in a race, etc.)
gain'er ***n.*** **1** a person or thing that gains **2** a fancy dive forward, but with a backward somersault
gain'ful ***adj.*** producing gain; profitable —**gain'ful·ly** ***adv.***
gain·say (gān'sā') ***vt.*** **-said'** (-sed'), **-say'ing** ⟦< OE *gegn*, against + *secgan*, to say⟧ **1** to deny **2** to contradict —**gain'say'er** ***n.***
gait (gāt) ***n.*** ⟦< ON *gata*, path⟧ **1** manner of walking or running **2** any of the various foot movements of a horse, as a trot, pace, canter, etc.
gai·ter (gāt'ər) ***n.*** ⟦< Fr *guêtre*⟧ a cloth or leather covering for the instep, ankle, and lower leg
gal[1] (gal) ***n.*** [Slang] a girl or woman
gal[2] *abbrev.* gallon(s)
ga·la (gā'lə, gal'ə) ***n.*** ⟦ult. < It *gala*⟧ a celebration —***adj.*** festive
gal·a·bi·a or **gal·a·bi·ya** (gal'ə bē'ə, gə lä'bē ə) ***n.*** ⟦< Ar⟧ *var. of* DJELLABA
Gal·a·had (gal'ə had') ***n.*** *Arthurian Legend* the knight who, because of his purity, finds the Holy Grail
gal·ax·y (gal'ək sē) ***n.***, *pl.* **-ies** ⟦< Gr *gala*, milk⟧ **1** [*often* **G-**] MILKY WAY **2** a large, independent system of stars **3** a group of illustrious people —**ga·lac·tic** (gə lak'tik) ***adj.***
gale (gāl) ***n.*** ⟦< ?⟧ **1** a strong wind **2** an outburst *[a gale of laughter]*
ga·le·na (gə lē'nə) ***n.*** ⟦L, lead ore⟧ native lead sulfide, a soft, lead-gray mineral with a metallic luster
Gal·i·lee (gal'ə lē'), **Sea of** lake in NE Israel
Gal·i·le·o (gal'ə lē'ō, -lā'-) 1564-1642; It. astronomer & physicist
gall[1] (gôl) ***n.*** ⟦OE *galla*⟧ **1** BILE (sense 1) **2** something bitter or distasteful **3** bitter feeling **4** impudence
gall[2] (gôl) ***n.*** ⟦see fol.⟧ a sore on the skin caused by chafing —***vt.*** **1** to make sore by rubbing **2** to annoy; vex
gall[3] (gôl) ***n.*** ⟦< L *galla*⟧ a tumor on plant tissue caused by stimulation by fungi, insects, etc.
gal·lant (gal'ənt; *for adj.* 3 & *n.*, *usually* gə lant', -länt') ***adj.*** ⟦< OFr *galer*, to make merry⟧ **1** stately; imposing **2** brave and noble **3** polite and attentive to women —***n.*** **1** [Now Rare] a high-spirited, stylish man **2** a man attentive and polite to women
gal·lant·ry (gal'ən trē) ***n.***, *pl.* **-ries** **1** heroic courage **2** the behavior of a gallant **3** a courteous act or remark
gall·blad·der (gôl'blad'ər) ***n.*** a membranous sac closely attached to the liver, in which excess gall, or bile, is stored
gal·le·on (gal'ē ən) ***n.*** ⟦ult. < Gr *galeos*, shark⟧ a large sailing ship of the 15th and 16th c.
gal·le·ri·a (gal'ə rē'ə) ***n.*** a large arcade or court, sometimes with a glass roof
gal·ler·y (gal'ər ē) ***n.***, *pl.* **-ies** ⟦< ML *galeria*⟧ **1** a covered walk or porch open at one side or having the roof supported by pillars **2** a long, narrow, outside balcony **3** *a*) a balcony in a theater, etc.; esp., the highest balcony with the cheapest seats *b*) the people in these seats **4** the spectators at a sports event, etc. **5** a place for exhibiting or selling works of art; specif., a display room in a museum
gal·ley (gal'ē) ***n.***, *pl.* **-leys** ⟦< Gr *galeos*, shark⟧ **1** a long, low ship of ancient times, propelled by oars and sails **2** a ship's kitchen **3** *Printing* *a*) a shallow tray for holding

THESAURUS

gab* ***n.*** gossip, idle talk, prattle; see NONSENSE 1. —**gift of (the) gab*** loquacity, volubility, verbal ability; see ELOQUENCE.

gab* ***v.*** gossip, jabber, chatter; see BABBLE.

gadget ***n.*** mechanical contrivance, object, contraption; see DEVICE 1.

gag ***v.*** **1** [To stop the mouth] choke, muzzle, muffle, obstruct, stifle, throttle, tape up, deaden. **2** [To retch] be nauseated, sicken, choke; see VOMIT.

gaiety ***n.*** jollity, mirth, exhilaration; see HAPPINESS.

gaily ***a.*** showily, brightly, vivaciously, spiritedly, brilliantly, splendidly, gaudily, expensively, colorfully, extravagantly, garishly, in a sprightly manner.—*Ant.* PEACEFULLY, quietly, modestly.

gain ***n.*** increase, accrual, accumulation; see ADDITION 1.

gain ***v.*** **1** [To increase] augment, expand, enlarge; see GROW 1, INCREASE. **2** [To advance] progress, overtake, move forward; see ADVANCE 1. **3** [To achieve] attain, realize, reach; see SUCCEED 1.

gainful ***a.*** lucrative, productive, useful; see PROFITABLE.

gainfully ***a.*** productively, profitably, usefully; see PROFITABLY.

gait ***n.*** walk, run, motion, step, tread, stride, pace, tramp, march, carriage, movements.

galaxy ***n.*** cosmic system, star cluster, nebula; see STAR.

gale ***n.*** hurricane, windstorm, typhoon; see STORM, WIND.

gall[1] ***n.*** effrontery, insolence, impertinence; see RUDENESS.

gall[2] ***v.*** annoy, irk, irritate; see BOTHER 2.

gallant ***a.*** bold, intrepid, courageous; see BRAVE.

gallantry ***n.*** heroism, valor, bravery; see COURAGE.

gallery ***n.*** **1** [An elevated section of seats] mezzanine, upstairs, balcony; see UPSTAIRS. **2** [Onlookers, especially from the gallery] spectators, audience, public; see LISTENER. **3** [A room for showing works of art] salon, museum, exhibition room, studio, hall, exhibit, showroom.

composed type *b*) proof printed from such type (in full, **galley proof**)

Gal·lic (gal′ik) ***adj.*** **1** of ancient Gaul or its people **2** French

Gal·li·cism (gal′i siz′əm) ***n.*** ⟦< prec.⟧ [*also* **g-**] a French idiom, custom, etc.

gal·li·um (gal′ē əm) ***n.*** ⟦named after L *Gallia*, France⟧ a bluish-white, metallic chemical element with a low melting point, used in semiconductors, lasers, etc.

gal·li·vant (gal′ə vant′) ***vi.*** ⟦arbitrary elaboration of GALLANT⟧ to go about in search of amusement

gal·lon (gal′ən) ***n.*** ⟦< OFr *jalon*⟧ a liquid measure equal to 4 quarts

gal·lop (gal′əp) ***vi.***, ***vt.*** ⟦< OFr *galoper*⟧ to go, or cause to go, at a gallop —***n.*** the fastest gait of a horse, etc., a succession of leaping strides

gal·lows (gal′ōz) ***n.***, *pl.* **-lows** or **-lows·es** ⟦OE *galga*⟧ an upright frame with a crossbeam and a rope, for hanging condemned persons

gall·stone (gôl′stōn′) ***n.*** a small, solid mass sometimes formed in the gallbladder or bile duct

ga·lore (gə lôr′) ***adj.*** ⟦Ir *go leōr*, enough⟧ in abundance; plentifully *[to attract crowds galore]*

ga·losh or **ga·loshe** (gə läsh′) ***n.*** ⟦< OFr *galoche*⟧ a high, warmly lined overshoe of rubber and fabric

gal·van·ic (gal van′ik) ***adj.*** ⟦after L. *Galvani* (1737-98), It physicist⟧ **1** of or producing direct current from a chemical reaction, as in a battery **2** startling

gal·va·nize (gal′və nīz′) ***vt.*** **-nized′**, **-niz′ing** **1** to stimulate as if by electric shock; rouse; stir **2** to plate (metal) with zinc

gal′va·nom′e·ter (-näm′ət ər) ***n.*** an instrument for detecting and measuring a small electric current

Gam·bi·a (gam′bē ə) country on the W coast of Africa: 4,361 sq. mi.; pop. 1,026,000

gam·bit (gam′bit) ***n.*** ⟦< Sp *gambito*, a tripping⟧ **1** *Chess* an opening in which a pawn, etc. is sacrificed to get an advantage in position **2** an action intended to gain an advantage

gam·ble (gam′bəl) ***vi.*** **-bled**, **-bling** ⟦ME *gamen*, to play⟧ **1** to play games of chance for money, etc. **2** to take a risk for some advantage —***vt.*** to risk in gambling; bet —***n.*** an undertaking involving risk —**gam′bler** ***n.***

gam·bol (gam′bəl) ***n.*** ⟦< It *gamba*, leg⟧ a gamboling; frolic —***vi.*** **-boled** or **-bolled**, **-bol·ing** or **-bol·ling** to jump and skip about in play; frolic

gam·brel (roof) (gam′brəl) a roof with two slopes on each of its two sides

game[1] (gām) ***n.*** ⟦OE *gamen*⟧ **1** any form of play; amusement **2** *a*) any specific amusement or sport involving competition under rules *b*) a single contest in such a competition **3** the number of points required for winning **4** a scheme; plan **5** wild birds or animals hunted for sport or food **6** [Inf.] a business or job, esp. one involving risk —***vi.*** **gamed**, **gam′ing** to play cards, etc. for stakes; gamble —***adj.*** **1** designating or of wild birds or animals hunted for sport or food **2** *a*) plucky; courageous *b*) enthusiastic; ready (*for* something) —**the game is up** failure is certain —**game′ly** ***adv.*** —**game′ness** ***n.***

game[2] (gām) ***adj.*** ⟦< ?⟧ lame or injured *[a game leg]*

game′cock′ ***n.*** a specially bred rooster trained for cockfighting

game′keep′er ***n.*** a person who takes care of game birds and animals, as on an estate

game plan **1** the strategy planned before a game **2** any long-range strategy

game point **1** the situation when the next point scored could win a game **2** the winning point

games·man·ship (gāmz′mən ship′) ***n.*** skill in using ploys to gain an advantage

game·ster (gām′stər) ***n.*** a gambler

gam·ete (gam′ēt, gə mēt′) ***n.*** ⟦< Gr *gamos*, marriage⟧ a reproductive cell that unites with another to form the cell that develops into a new individual

gam·in (gam′in) ***n.*** ⟦Fr⟧ **1** a neglected child who roams the streets **2** a girl with saucy charm: also **ga·mine** (ga mēn′)

gam·ma (gam′ə) ***n.*** the third letter of the Greek alphabet (Γ, γ)

gamma glob·u·lin (gläb′yoo lin) that fraction of blood serum which contains most antibodies

gamma ray an electromagnetic radiation with a very short wavelength, produced as by the reactions of nuclei

gam·ut (gam′ət) ***n.*** ⟦< Gr letter *gamma*, for the lowest note of the medieval scale⟧ **1** any complete musical scale **2** the entire range or extent, as of emotions

gam·y (gām′ē) ***adj.*** **-i·er**, **-i·est** **1** having the strong flavor of cooked game **2** slightly tainted **3** risqué **4** coarse or crude —**gam′i·ness** ***n.***

gan·der (gan′dər) ***n.*** ⟦OE *gan(d)ra*⟧ **1** a male goose **2** [Slang] a look: chiefly in **take a gander**

Gan·dhi (gän′dē), **Mo·han·das** (mō hän′dəs) 1869-1948; Hindu nationalist leader: called *Mahatma Gandhi*

gang (gaŋ) ***n.*** ⟦< OE *gangan*, to go⟧ a group of people working or acting together; specif., a group of criminals or juvenile delinquents —**gang up on** [Inf.] to attack as a group

Gan·ges (gan′jēz) river in N India & Bangladesh

gan·gling (gaŋ′gliŋ) ***adj.*** ⟦< ?⟧ thin, tall, and awkward: also **gan′gly**

gan·gli·on (gaŋ′glē ən) ***n.***, *pl.* **-gli·a** (-ə) or **-gli·ons** ⟦ult. < Gr, tumor⟧ a mass of nerve cells from which nerve impulses are transmitted

gang′plank′ ***n.*** a movable ramp by which to board or leave a ship

gan·grene (gaŋ′grēn′, gaŋ grēn′) ***n.*** ⟦< Gr *gran*, gnaw⟧ decay of body tissue when the blood supply is obstructed —**gan′gre·nous** (-grə nəs) ***adj.***

gang·ster (gaŋ′stər) ***n.*** a member of a gang of criminals —**gang′ster·ism′** ***n.***

gang′way′ ***n.*** ⟦OE *gangweg*⟧ **1** a passageway **2** *a*) an opening in a ship's bulwarks for loading, etc. *b*) GANGPLANK —***interj.*** clear the way!

gant·let (gônt′lit, gänt′-, gant′-) ***n.*** ⟦< Swed *gata*, lane + *lopp*, a run⟧ **1** a former punishment in which the offender ran between two rows of men who struck him **2** a series of troubles Now sp. equally *gauntlet*

gan·try (gan′trē) ***n.***, *pl.* **-tries** ⟦< L *canterius*, beast of burden⟧ **1** a framework, often on wheels, for a traveling crane **2** a wheeled framework with a crane, platforms, etc., for readying a rocket to be launched

GAO *abbrev.* General Accounting Office

gaol (jāl) ***n.*** *Brit. sp. of* JAIL

gap (gap) ***n.*** ⟦< ON *gapa*, to gape⟧ **1** an opening made by breaking or parting **2** a mountain pass or ravine **3** a blank space; lacuna **4** a lag or disparity

gape (gāp) ***vi.*** **gaped**, **gap′ing** ⟦< ON *gapa*⟧ **1** to open the

THESAURUS

gallon ***n.*** 3.78 liters, half a peck, four quarts, eight pints.

gallop ***v.*** run, spring, leap, jump, go at a gallop, bound, hurdle, swing, stride, lope, canter, amble, trot.

galoshes ***n.*** overshoes, rubbers, boots; see SHOE.

gamble ***n.*** chance, lot, hazard; see CHANCE 1.

gamble ***v.*** game, wager, bet, play, plunge, play at dice, bet against, speculate, back, lay money on, lay odds on, try one's luck, go for broke*, shoot craps; see also RISK.

gambler ***n.*** backer, sharper, cardsharp*, speculator, confidence man, bettor, bookmaker, croupier, banker, player, sport*, highroller*, shark*, shill*, bookie*, con man*.

gambling ***n.*** betting, staking, venturing, gaming, laying money on, speculating.

game[1] ***a.*** spirited, hardy, resolute; see BRAVE.

game[1] ***n.*** **1** [Entertainment] *Card games include the following:* poker, rummy, gin rummy, pinochle, whist, euchre, bridge, contract bridge, duplicate bridge, five hundred, casino, war, seven-up, cribbage, solitaire, patience, canasta, old maid, hearts, twenty-one, blackjack, baccarat. *Children's games include:* hide-and-seek, tag, hopscotch, jacks, ball, fox and geese, marbles, crack the whip, statues, London Bridge, ring around the roses, drop the handkerchief, blindman's buff, follow the leader, Simon says, catch, post office, favors, musical chairs, mumbletypeg, cops and robbers, soldier, cowboys and Indians, mother-may-I, spin the bottle. *Board games include:* chess, checkers, Chinese checkers, backgammon, go, pachisi; Monopoly, Ouija (trademarks). **2** [Sport] play, recreation, merrymaking; see SPORT 1. **3** [Wild meat, fish, or fowl] quarry, prey, wildlife; see FISH, FOWL, MEAT. —**ahead of the game*** winning, doing well, thriving; see SUCCESSFUL. —**play the game*** behave properly, act according to custom, do what is expected; see BEHAVE.

gang ***n.*** horde, band, troop; see ORGANIZATION 2.

gangster ***n.*** gunman, underworld leader, racketeer; see CRIMINAL.

gang up on* ***v.*** combat, overwhelm, join forces against; see ATTACK.

gap ***n.*** **1** [A breach] cleft, break, rift; see HOLE 1. **2** [A break in continuity] hiatus, recess, lull; see PAUSE. **3** [A mountain pass] way, chasm, hollow, cleft, ravine, gorge, arroyo, canyon, passageway, notch, gully, gulch.

mouth wide, as in yawning **2** to stare with the mouth open **3** to open wide —*n.* **1** a gaping **2** a wide opening —**gap′ing·ly** *adv.*

gar (gär) *n., pl.* **gar** or **gars** ⟦< OE *gar*, a spear⟧ a freshwater fish with a long, beaklike snout: also **gar′fish′**

ga·rage (gə räzh′, -räj′) *n.* ⟦Fr < *garer*, to protect⟧ **1** a shelter for motor vehicles **2** a business place where motor vehicles are stored, repaired, etc.

garage sale a sale of used or unwanted household articles, etc.

garb (gärb) *n.* ⟦< It *garbo*, elegance⟧ clothing; style of dress *[clerical garb]* —*vt.* to clothe

gar·bage (gär′bij) *n.* ⟦ME, entrails of fowls⟧ **1** spoiled or waste food **2** any worthless, offensive, etc. matter

gar·ble (gär′bəl) *vt.* **-bled**, **-bling** ⟦< Ar *gharbāl*, a sieve⟧ to distort or confuse (a story, etc.)

gar·çon (gȧr sōn′) *n., pl.* ***-çons′*** (-sōn′) ⟦Fr⟧ a waiter

gar·den (gärd′'n) *n.* ⟦< Frankish⟧ **1** a piece of ground for growing vegetables, flowers, etc. **2** an area of fertile land: also **garden spot** **3** [*often pl.*] a public, parklike place, sometimes having displays of animals or plants —*vi.* to take care of a garden —*adj.* of, for, or grown in a garden —**gar′den·er** *n.*

gar·de·ni·a (gär dēn′yə) *n.* ⟦after A. *Garden* (1730-91), Am botanist⟧ a plant with fragrant, waxy flowers

gar′den-va·ri′e·ty *adj.* ordinary; commonplace

Gar·field (gär′fēld), **James A·bram** (jāmz ā′brəm) 1831-81; 20th president of the U.S. (1881): assassinated

Gar·gan·tu·a (gär gan′cho͞o ə) *n.* a giant king in a satire by Rabelais —**gar·gan′tu·an** *adj.*

gar·gle (gär′gəl) *vt., vi.* **-gled**, **-gling** ⟦< Fr *gargouille*, throat⟧ to rinse (the throat) with a liquid kept in motion by the expulsion of air from the lungs —*n.* a liquid for gargling

gar·goyle (gär′goil′) *n.* ⟦see prec.⟧ a waterspout formed like a fantastic creature, projecting from a building

Gar·i·bal·di (gar′ə bôl′dē), **Giu·sep·pe** (jo͞o zep′pe) 1807-82; It. patriot & general

gar·ish (gar′ish, ger′-) *adj.* ⟦prob. < ME *gauren*, to stare⟧ too bright or gaudy; showy —**gar′ish·ly** *adv.* —**gar′ish·ness** *n.*

gar·land (gär′lənd) *n.* ⟦< OFr *garlande*⟧ a wreath of flowers, leaves, etc. —*vt.* to decorate with garlands

Gar·land (gär′lənd) city in NE Texas: pop. 181,000

gar·lic (gär′lik) *n.* ⟦< OE *gar*, a spear + *leac*, leek⟧ **1** an herb of the lily family **2** its strong-smelling bulb, used as seasoning —**gar′lick·y** *adj.*

gar·ment (gär′mənt) *n.* ⟦see GARNISH⟧ any article of clothing

gar·ner (gär′nər) *vt.* ⟦< L *granum*, grain⟧ **1** to gather and store **2** to get or earn

gar·net (gär′nit) *n.* ⟦< ML *granatum*⟧ a hard, glasslike mineral: red varieties are often used as gems

gar·nish (gär′nish) *vt.* ⟦< OFr *garnir*, furnish⟧ **1** to decorate **2** to decorate (food) with something that adds color or flavor **3** *Law* to attach (a debtor's property, wages, etc.) so that it can be used to pay the debt —*n.* **1** a decoration **2** something used to garnish food, as parsley

gar·nish·ee (gär′ni shē′) *vt.* **-eed′**, **-ee′ing** ⟦< prec.⟧ GARNISH (*vt.* 3): now rare in legal usage

gar′nish·ment *n.* *Law* a proceeding by which a creditor seeks to attach a debtor's wages, etc.

gar·ret (gar′it) *n.* ⟦< OFr *garite*, watchtower⟧ an attic

gar·ri·son (gar′ə sən) *n.* ⟦< OFr *garir*, to watch⟧ **1** troops stationed in a fort or fortified place **2** a military post or station —*vt.* to station (troops) in (a fortified place) for its defense

gar·rote (gə rät′, -rōt′) *n.* ⟦Sp⟧ **1** a cord, thong, etc. used in strangling a person in a surprise attack **2** a strangling in this way —*vt.* **-rot′ed** or **-rot′ted**, **-rot′ing** or **-rot′ting** to execute or attack by such strangling Also **ga·rotte′** or **gar·rotte′** —**gar·rot′er** *n.*

gar·ru·lous (gar′ə ləs) *adj.* ⟦< L *garrire*, to chatter⟧ talking much, esp. about unimportant things —**gar·ru·li·ty** (gə ro͞o′lə tē) or **gar′ru·lous·ness** *n.* —**gar′ru·lous·ly** *adv.*

gar·ter (gärt′ər) *n.* ⟦< OFr *garet*, the back of the knee⟧ an elastic band or strap for holding a stocking in place

garter belt a belt of elastic fabric with hanging garters, worn by women

garter snake a small, harmless snake common in North America

Gar·y (ger′ē) city in NW Indiana: pop. 117,000

gas (gas) *n., pl.* **gas′es** or **gas′ses** ⟦coined < Gr *chaos*, space⟧ **1** the fluid form of a substance in which it can expand indefinitely; vapor **2** any mixture of flammable gases used for lighting or heating **3** any gas used as an anesthetic **4** any poisonous substance dispersed in the air, as in war **5** [Inf.] GASOLINE —*vt.* **gassed**, **gas′sing** to injure or kill by gas —**gas up** [Inf.] to supply (a vehicle) with gasoline —**gas′e·ous** (-ē əs) *adj.*

gas chamber a room in which people are put to be killed with poison gas

gash (gash) *vt.* ⟦< Gr *charassein*, to cut⟧ to make a long, deep cut in; slash —*n.* a long, deep cut

gas·ket (gas′kit) *n.* ⟦prob. < OFr *garcete*, small cord⟧ a piece or ring of rubber, metal, etc. used to make a joint leakproof

gas mask a filtering mask worn to prevent the breathing in of poisonous gases

gas·o·hol (gas′ə hôl′) *n.* a motor fuel mixture of gasoline and alcohol

gas·o·line (gas′ə lēn′, gas′ə lēn′) *n.* ⟦< *gas* + L *oleum*, oil⟧ a volatile, flammable liquid distilled from petroleum, used chiefly as a fuel in internal-combustion engines: also **gas′o·lene′**

gasp (gasp) *vi.* ⟦< ON *geispa*, to yawn⟧ to inhale suddenly, as in surprise, or breathe with effort —*vt.* to say with gasps —*n.* a gasping

gas station SERVICE STATION

gas′sy *adj.* **-si·er**, **-si·est** **1** full of gas; esp., flatulent **2** like gas

gas·tric (gas′trik) *adj.* ⟦GASTR(O)- + -IC⟧ of, in, or near the stomach

gastric juice the clear, acid digestive fluid produced by glands in the stomach lining

gas·tri·tis (gas trīt′is) *n.* ⟦fol. + -ITIS⟧ inflammation of the stomach

gastro- ⟦< Gr *gastēr*⟧ *combining form* stomach (and)

gas·tron·o·my (gas trän′ə mē) *n.* ⟦< Gr *gastēr*, stomach + *nomos*, a rule⟧ the art or science of good eating —**gas′tro·nom′ic** (-trə näm′ik) or **gas′tro·nom′i·cal** *adj.*

gas·tro·pod (gas′trō päd′) *n.* ⟦GASTRO- + -POD⟧ a mollusk of the class including snails, slugs, etc.

gate (gāt) *n.* ⟦OE⟧ **1** a movable structure controlling passage through an opening in a fence or wall **2** a gateway **3** a movable barrier **4** a structure controlling the flow of water, as in a canal **5** the total amount or number of paid admissions to a performance —**give** (or **get**) **the gate** [Slang] to subject (or be subjected) to dismissal

-gate (gāt) ⟦< *(Water)gate*, political scandal, after the *Watergate*, building in Washington, D.C., site of 1972 burglary⟧ *combining form* a scandal marked by charges of corruption on the part of public officials, etc.

gate′-crash′er *n.* [Inf.] one who attends a social affair without an invitation or attends a performance without paying

gate′fold′ *n.* an oversize page, as in a magazine, bound so it can be unfolded and opened out

THESAURUS

garage *n.* parking space, parking garage, parking, parking lot, carport.

garbage *n.* refuse, waste, rubbish; see TRASH 1.

garden *n.* vegetable patch, melon patch, cultivated area, truck garden, enclosure, field, plot, bed, herb garden, rock garden, rose garden, formal garden, kitchen garden, hotbed, greenhouse, patio, terrace, backyard, nursery, flower garden, garden spot, oasis.

gardener *n.* vegetable grower, caretaker, landscaper; see FARMER.

gargantuan *a.* enormous, huge, immense; see LARGE 1.

gargle *v.* swash, rinse the mouth, use a mouthwash; see CLEAN.

garish *a.* showy, gaudy, ostentatious; see ORNATE.

garment *n.* dress, attire, apparel; see CLOTHES.

garnish *v.* embellish, beautify, deck; see DECORATE.

gas *n.* **1** [A state of matter] vapor, volatile substance, fumes, aeriform fluid, gaseous mixture. **2** [Gasoline] propellant, petrol (British), motor fuel; see GASOLINE. **3** [Poisonous gas] systemic poison, mustard gas, tear gas; see POISON. **4** [An anesthetic] ether, general anesthetic, chloroform, nitrous oxide, laughing gas. **5** [A fuel] natural gas, propane, bottled gas, acetylene, coal gas; see also FUEL. —**step on the gas*** drive faster, hasten, move fast; see HURRY 1.

gaseous *a.* vaporous, effervescent, in the form of gas; see LIGHT 5.

gash *n.* slash, slice, wound; see CUT.

gasoline *n.* petrol, motor fuel, propellant, gas, juice*, low-octane gasoline, high-octane gasoline, ethyl gasoline, gasohol.

gasp *v.* labor for breath, gulp, have difficulty in breathing, pant, puff, wheeze, blow, snort.

gate *n.* entrance, ingress, passage, way, bar, turnstile, revolving door, barrier; see also DOOR.

gate'way' *n.* **1** an entrance as in a wall, fitted with a gate **2** a means of access

gath·er (ga*th*'ər) *vt.* ⟦OE *gad(e)rian*⟧ **1** to bring together in one place or group **2** to get gradually; accumulate **3** to collect by picking; harvest **4** to infer; conclude **5** to draw (cloth) into folds or puckers —*vi.* **1** to assemble **2** to increase —*n.* a pucker or fold —**gath'er·er** *n.*

gath'er·ing *n.* **1** a meeting; crowd **2** a gather in cloth

ga·tor or **'ga·tor** (gā'tər) *n. short for* ALLIGATOR

gauche (gōsh) *adj.* ⟦Fr < MFr *gauchir*, become warped⟧ lacking social grace; awkward; tactless

gau·che·rie (gō'shə rē) *n.* gauche behavior or a gauche act

gau·cho (gou'chō) *n., pl.* **-chos** ⟦AmSp⟧ a South American cowboy

gaud·y (gô'dē) *adj.* **-i·er, -i·est** ⟦< ME *gaude*, trinket⟧ bright and showy, but lacking in good taste —**gaud'i·ly** *adv.* —**gaud'i·ness** *n.*

gauge (gāj) *n.* ⟦NormFr⟧ **1** a standard measure or criterion **2** any device for measuring **3** the distance between the rails of a railroad **4** the size of the bore of a shotgun **5** the thickness of sheet metal, wire, etc. —*vt.* **gauged, gaug'ing** **1** to measure the size, amount, etc. of **2** to judge

Gaul[1] (gôl) *n.* a member of the people of ancient Gaul

Gaul[2] (gôl) ancient division of the Roman Empire, in W Europe

Gaul'ish *n.* the Celtic language of ancient Gaul

gaunt (gônt) *adj.* ⟦ME *gawnte*⟧ **1** thin and bony; haggard, as from great hunger **2** looking grim or forbidding —**gaunt'ness** *n.*

gaunt·let[1] (gônt'lit, gänt'-) *n.* ⟦< OFr *gant*, glove⟧ **1** a knight's armored glove **2** a long glove with a flaring cuff —**throw down the gauntlet** to challenge, as to combat

gaunt·let[2] (gônt'lit, gänt'-) *n. see* GANTLET

gauze (gôz) *n.* ⟦< Fr *gaze* < Ar *ḳazz*, silk⟧ any very thin, transparent, loosely woven material, as of cotton or silk —**gauz'y, -i·er, -i·est,** *adj.*

gave (gāv) *vt., vi. pt. of* GIVE

gav·el (gav'əl) *n.* ⟦? < Scot *gable*, fork⟧ a small mallet rapped on the table, as by a presiding officer, to call for attention, etc.

ga·votte (gə vät') *n.* ⟦Fr⟧ a 17th-c. dance like the minuet, but livelier

gawk (gôk) *vi.* ⟦prob. < *gowk*, stupid person⟧ to stare stupidly

gawk·y (gô'kē) *adj.* **-i·er, -i·est** ⟦see prec.⟧ clumsy; ungainly —**gawk'i·ly** *adv.* —**gawk'i·ness** *n.*

gay (gā) *adj.* ⟦OFr *gai*⟧ **1** joyous and lively; merry **2** bright; brilliant *[gay colors]* **3** homosexual —*n.* a homosexual; esp., a homosexual man

gay·e·ty (gā'ə tē) *n., pl.* **-ties** *alt. sp. of* GAIETY

gay·ly (gā'lē) *adv. alt. sp. of* GAILY

gaze (gāz) *vi.* **gazed, gaz'ing** ⟦< Scand⟧ to look steadily; stare —*n.* a steady look

ga·ze·bo (gə zē'bō, -zā'-) *n., pl.* **-bos** or **-boes** ⟦< prec.⟧ a summerhouse, windowed balcony, etc. from which one can gaze at the scenery around it

ga·zelle (gə zel') *n.* ⟦< Ar *ghazāl*⟧ a small, swift antelope of Africa and Asia, with large, lustrous eyes

ga·zette (gə zet') *n.* ⟦Fr < It dial. *gazeta*, a small coin, price of the newspaper⟧ **1** a newspaper: now mainly in newspaper titles **2** in England, an official publication —*vt.* **-zet'ted, -zet'ting** [Brit.] to publish or announce in a gazette

gaz·et·teer (gaz'ə tir') *n.* a dictionary or index of geographical names

ga·zil·lion (gə zil'yən) *n.* [Slang] a very large, indefinite number

gaz·pa·cho (gäs pä'chō, gäz-) *n.* ⟦Sp⟧ a cold Spanish soup of chopped raw tomatoes, cucumbers, onions, and peppers, mixed with oil, vinegar, etc.

GB *abbrev.* **1** gigabyte(s) **2** Great Britain

Ge *Chem. symbol for* germanium

gear (gir) *n.* ⟦prob. < ON *gervi*, preparation⟧ **1** clothing **2** equipment, esp. for some task **3** *a)* a toothed wheel designed to mesh with another *b)* [*often pl.*] a system of such gears meshed together to pass motion along *c)* a specific adjustment of such a system *d)* a part of a mechanism with a specific function *[the steering gear]* —*vt.* **1** to connect by or furnish with gears **2** to adapt (one thing) to conform with another *[to gear supply to demand]* —**in** (or **out of**) **gear** **1** (not) connected to the motor **2** (not) in proper working order

gear'shift' *n.* the lever for engaging or disengaging any of several sets of transmission gears to a motor, etc.

gear'wheel' *n.* a toothed wheel in a system of gears; cogwheel

geck·o (gek'ō) *n., pl.* **-os** or **-oes** ⟦prob. < Malay⟧ a tropical lizard with suction pads on its feet

GED[1] *trademark for* General Educational Development

GED[2] *abbrev.* general equivalency diploma

gee (jē) *interj.* ⟦< JE(SUS)⟧ [Slang] used to express surprise, wonder, etc.

geek (gēk) *n.* [Slang] a person considered to be different from others in a negative way, as in being socially awkward —**geek'y, -i·er, -i·est,** *adj.*

geese (gēs) *n. pl. of* GOOSE

gee whiz an exclamation used to express surprise, enthusiasm, protest, etc.

gee·zer (gē'zər) *n.* ⟦< GUISE⟧ [Slang] an old man

ge·fil·te fish (gə fil'tə) ⟦E Yiddish⟧ chopped, seasoned fish, boiled and served in balls or cakes

Gei·ger counter (gī'gər) ⟦after H. *Geiger* (1882-1945), Ger physicist⟧ an instrument for detecting and counting ionizing particles, as from radioactive ores

gei·sha (gā'shə) *n., pl.* **-sha** or **-shas** ⟦Sino-Jpn *gei*, art + *sha*, person⟧ a Japanese woman trained in singing, conversation, etc. to serve as a hired companion to men

gel (jel) *n.* ⟦< fol.⟧ **1** a jellylike substance formed from a colloidal solution **2** any of various jellylike preparations for setting hair, brushing teeth, etc. —*vi.* **gelled, gel'ling** to form a gel

gel·a·tin (jel'ə tin) *n.* ⟦< L *gelare*, freeze⟧ a tasteless, odorless substance extracted by boiling bones, horns, etc., or a similar vegetable substance: dissolved and cooled, it forms a jellylike substance used in foods, photographic film, etc.: also **gel'a·tine** (-tēn, -tin) —**ge·lat·i·nous** (jə lat''n əs) *adj.*

geld (geld) *vt.* **geld'ed** or **gelt, geld'ing** ⟦< ON *geldr*, barren⟧ to castrate (esp. a horse)

geld'ing *n.* a castrated horse

gel·id (jel'id) *adj.* ⟦< L *gelu*, frost⟧ extremely cold; frozen

gem (jem) *n.* ⟦< L *gemma*, a bud⟧ **1** a cut and polished gemstone or a pearl **2** someone or something very precious or valuable

THESAURUS

gather *v.* **1** [To come together] assemble, meet, gather around, congregate, flock in, pour in, rally, crowd, throng, come together, convene, collect, unite, reunite, associate, hold a meeting, hold a reunion, swarm, huddle, draw in, group, converge, accrete, concentrate.—*Ant.* SCATTER, disperse, part. **2** [To bring together] collect, aggregate, amass; see ACCUMULATE, ASSEMBLE 2. **3** [To conclude] infer, deduce, find; see ASSUME.

gathered *a.* assembled, met, congregated, joined, rallied, crowded together, thronged, collected, united, associated, swarmed, huddled, grouped, massed, amassed, accumulated, picked, garnered, harvested, stored, combined, brought together, convened, convoked, summoned, compiled, mobilized, lumped together, raked up, concentrated, heaped, stacked, piled, stowed away.—*Ant.* SCATTERED, dispersed, separated.

gathering *n.* assembly, meeting, conclave, caucus, parley, council, conference, band, congregation, company, rally, crowd, throng, bunch, collection, union, association, society, committee, legislature, house, senate, parliament, swarm, huddle, group, powwow*, body, mass, herd, turnout, flock, coven, combination, convention, discussion, panel, reunion, meet, congress, attendance, multitude, audience, horde, mob, crush, party, social gathering, crew, gang, school, bevy, troop, drove, concentration, convocation, get-together, bull session*.

gaudy *a.* showy, flashy, tawdry; see ORNATE.

gauge *n.* scale, criterion, standard; see MEASURE 2.

gauge *v.* check, weigh, calibrate, calculate; see also MEASURE 1.

gaunt *a.* emaciated, scraggy, skinny; see THIN 2.

gauze *n.* veil, bandage, cheesecloth; see DRESSING 3.

gawk *v.* stare, ogle, gaze; see LOOK 2.

gay *a.* **1** [Happy] cheerful, merry, vivacious; see HAPPY. **2** [Homosexual] homophile, homoerotic, lesbian; see HOMOSEXUAL.

gaze *v.* stare, watch, gape; see LOOK 2.

gear *n.* **1** [Equipment] material, tackle, things; see EQUIPMENT. **2** [A geared wheel] cog, cogwheel, pinion, toothed wheel, sprocket. —**in gear** usable, efficient, productive; see WORKING 1. —**out of gear** inefficient, not working, broken; see USELESS 1.

gem *n.* **1** [A jewel] precious stone, bauble, ornament; see JEWEL. *Types of gems include the following:* diamond, emerald, ruby, pearl, brilliant, aquamarine, amethyst, topaz, turquoise, jade, opal, sapphire, garnet, carnelian, jacinth, beryl, cat's-eye, chryso-

Gem·i·ni (jem′ə nī′, -nē′) ***n.*** ⟦L, twins⟧ the third sign of the zodiac

gem′stone′ ***n.*** any mineral that can be used in a piece of jewelry when cut and polished

ge·müt·lich (gə müt′liH) ***adj.*** ⟦Ger⟧ agreeable, cheerful, cozy, etc.

gen *abbrev.* general

Gen *abbrev.* **1** General **2** *Bible* Genesis

-gen (jən, jen) ⟦< Gr *-genēs*, born⟧ *suffix* **1** something that produces *[hydrogen]* **2** something produced (in a specified way)

gen·darme (zhän därm′) ***n.*** ⟦Fr < *gens d'armes*, men-at-arms⟧ a French police officer

gen·der (jen′dər) ***n.*** ⟦< L *genus*, origin⟧ **1** *Gram.* the classification by which words are grouped as masculine, feminine, or neuter **2** the fact of being a male or female human being, esp. as it affects a person's self-image, social relationships, etc.

gen′dered ***adj.*** affected by issues of GENDER (*n.* 2)

gene (jēn) ***n.*** ⟦see -GEN⟧ any of the units in the chromosomes by which hereditary characteristics are transmitted

ge·ne·al·o·gy (jē′nē äl′ə jē) ***n.***, *pl.* **-gies** ⟦< Gr *genea*, race + *-logia*, -LOGY⟧ **1** a recorded history of a person's ancestry **2** the study of family descent **3** lineage **—ge′ne·a·log′i·cal** (-ə läj′i kəl) ***adj.*** **—ge′ne·al′o·gist** ***n.***

gen·er·a (jen′ər ə) ***n.*** *pl. of* GENUS

gen·er·al (jen′ər əl) ***adj.*** ⟦< L *genus*, class⟧ **1** of, for, or from all; not local, special, or specialized **2** of or for a whole genus, kind, etc. **3** widespread *[general* unrest*]* **4** most common; usual **5** not specific or precise *[*in *general* terms*]* **6** highest in rank *[*attorney *general]* **—*n.*** a military officer ranking above a colonel, specif. one ranking above a lieutenant general **—in general 1** usually **2** without specific details **—gen′er·al·ship′ *n.***

general assembly [*often* **G- A-**] **1** the legislative assembly in some U.S. states **2** the deliberative assembly of the United Nations

general delivery delivery of mail at the post office to addressees who call for it

gen·er·al·is·si·mo (jen′ər ə lis′i mō′) ***n.***, *pl.* **-mos′** ⟦It⟧ in some countries, the commander in chief of the armed forces

gen·er·al·i·ty (jen′ər al′ə tē) ***n.***, *pl.* **-ties 1** the quality of being general **2** a general or vague statement, idea, etc. **3** the main body

gen·er·al·ize (jen′ər əl īz′) ***vt.*** **-ized′**, **-iz′ing 1** to state in terms of a general law **2** to infer or derive (a general law) from (particular instances) **—*vi.* 1** to formulate general principles **2** to talk in generalities

gen′er·al·ly ***adv.*** **1** widely; popularly **2** usually **3** not specifically

general practitioner a practicing physician who does not specialize in a particular field of medicine

gen·er·ate (jen′ər āt′) ***vt.*** **-at′ed**, **-at′ing** ⟦< L *genus*, race⟧ **1** to produce (offspring); beget **2** to bring into being **—gen′er·a′tive** (-āt′iv, -ə tiv) ***adj.***

gen′er·a′tion ***n.*** **1** the producing of offspring **2** production **3** a single stage in the succession of descent **4** the average period (*c.* 30 years) between human generations **5** all the people born and living at about the same time **—gen′er·a′tion·al *adj.***

generation gap the differences in attitudes, experiences, etc. between contemporary older and younger generations

Generation X (eks) the generation of persons born in the 1960s and 1970s

gen′er·a′tor ***n.*** a machine for changing mechanical energy into electrical energy; dynamo

ge·ner·ic (jə ner′ik) ***adj.*** ⟦< L *genus*, race, kind⟧ **1** of a whole kind, class, or group; inclusive **2** without a brand name **—*n.*** a product, as a drug, without a brand name: *often used in pl.* **—ge·ner′i·cal·ly *adv.***

gen·er·ous (jen′ər əs) ***adj.*** ⟦< L *generosus*, noble⟧ **1** noble-minded; magnanimous **2** willing to give or share; unselfish **3** large; ample **—gen·er·os·i·ty** (jen′ər äs′ə tē) ***n.*** **—gen′er·ous·ly *adv.***

gen·e·sis (jen′ə sis) ***n.*** ⟦Gr⟧ **1** the beginning; origin **2** [**G-**] the first book of the Bible

gene therapy the experimental treatment of diseases with new chemicals or organisms created by the recombining of units of DNA

genetic code the arrangement of chemical substances in DNA or RNA that determines the characteristics of an organism

ge·net·ics (jə net′iks) ***n.*** ⟦ult. < GENESIS⟧ the branch of biology dealing with heredity and variation in animal and plant species **—ge·net′ic *adj.*** **—ge·net′i·cal·ly *adv.*** **—ge·net′i·cist** (-ə sist) ***n.***

Ge·ne·va (jə nē′və) city in SW Switzerland: pop. 174,000

Gen·ghis Khan (geŋ′gis kän′, jeŋ′-) 1162?-1227; Mongol conqueror

gen·ial (jēn′yəl) ***adj.*** ⟦see GENIUS⟧ **1** good for life and growth *[a genial* climate*]* **2** cheerful and friendly; amiable **—ge·ni·al·i·ty** (jē′nē al′ə tē) ***n.*** **—gen′ial·ly *adv.***

ge·nie (jē′nē) ***n.*** ⟦< Fr < Ar *jinnī*⟧ JINNI

gen·i·tal (jen′i təl) ***adj.*** ⟦< L *genere*, beget⟧ of reproduction or the sexual organs

gen′i·tals ***pl.n.*** ⟦see prec.⟧ the reproductive organs; esp., the external sex organs: also **gen′i·ta′li·a** (-tā′lē ə, -tāl′ yə)

gen·i·tive (jen′i tiv) ***n.*** ⟦< Gr *genos*, genus⟧ *Gram.* a case expressing possession, source, etc., or referring to a part of a whole

gen·i·to·u·ri·nar·y (jen′i tō yoor′ə ner′ē) ***adj.*** of the genital and urinary organs

gen·i·us (jēn′yəs) ***n.*** ⟦L, guardian spirit⟧ **1** particular spirit or nature of a nation, place, age, etc. **2** natural

THESAURUS

prase, chalcedony, agate, bloodstone, moonstone, onyx, sard, lapis lazuli, chrysolite, carbuncle, coral. **2** [Anything excellent, especially if small and beautiful] jewel, pearl of great price, paragon, ace, nonpareil, perfection, ideal.

gender ***n.*** sexuality, sort, variety; see KIND 2, SEX 3.

genealogy ***n.*** derivation, lineage, extraction; see FAMILY.

general ***a.*** **1** [Having wide application] comprehensive, comprehending, widespread, universal, limitless, unlimited, extensive, ecumenical, all-embracing, ubiquitous, unconfined, broad, taken as a whole, not particular, not specific, blanket, inclusive, wide, catholic, infinite, worldwide, endless.—*Ant.* SPECIAL, particular, limited. **2** [Of common occurrence] usual, customary, prevailing; see COMMON 1. **3** [Not specific] indefinite, uncertain, imprecise; see VAGUE 2. —**in general** generally, usually, ordinarily; see REGULARLY.

generality ***n.*** abstraction, universality, sweeping statement; see LAW 4.

generalize ***v.*** theorize, speculate, postulate; see UNDERSTAND.

generally ***a.*** usually, commonly, ordinarily; see REGULARLY.

generate ***v.*** form, make, beget, create; see also PRODUCE 1.

generation ***n.*** **1** [The act of producing offspring] procreation, reproduction, breeding; see BIRTH. **2** [One cycle in the succession of parents and children] age, stage, crop, rank, age group; Silent Generation, baby boomers, boomers*, Generation X, Generation Y. **3** [The time required for a generation] span, 30 years, period; see AGE 3.

generic ***a.*** universal, general, nonproprietary; see UNIVERSAL 3, GENERAL 1.

generosity ***n.*** hospitality, benevolence, charity, liberality, philanthropy, altruism, unselfishness; see also KINDNESS 2.—*Ant.* GREED, miserliness, stinginess.

generous ***a.*** **1** [Openhanded] bountiful, liberal, charitable, altruistic, munificent, freehanded, beneficent, unselfish, hospitable, philanthropic, prodigal, lavish, profuse, unsparing, unstinting.—*Ant.* STINGY, close, tightfisted. **2** [Considerate] kindly, magnanimous, reasonable; see KIND.

generously ***a.*** **1** [With a free hand] bountifully, liberally, lavishly, unsparingly, unstintingly, in full measure, handsomely, freely, profusely, abundantly, munificently, charitably, copiously, with open hands.—*Ant.* SELFISHLY, grudgingly, sparingly. **2** [With an open heart] charitably, liberally, magnanimously, wholeheartedly, unreservedly, nobly, majestically, royally, honestly, candidly, enthusiastically, unselfishly, disinterestedly, chivalrously, benevolently, genially, warmly.—*Ant.* SELFISHLY, coldly, heartlessly.

genetic ***a.*** sporogenous, hereditary, genic, patrimonial; see also HISTORICAL.

genetics ***n.*** heredity, inheritance, eugenics; see HEREDITY.

genial ***a.*** cordial, kind, warm-hearted; see FRIENDLY.

genitals ***n.*** organs, sexual organs, genitalia, private parts, reproductive organs, privates.

genius ***n.*** **1** [The highest degree of intellectual capacity] ability, talent, intellect, brains, intelligence, inspiration, imagination, gift, aptitude, wisdom, astuteness, penetration, grasp, discernment, acumen, acuteness, perspicacity, power, capability, accomplishment, sagacity, understanding, reach, enthusiasm, creative gift,

ability; strong inclination *(for)* **3** great mental capacity and inventive ability **4** one having such capacity or ability

Gen·o·a (jen′ə wə) seaport in NW Italy: pop. 679,000

gen·o·cide (jen′ə sīd′) ***n.*** ⟦< Gr *genos,* race + -CIDE⟧ the systematic killing of a whole people or nation —**gen′o·ci′dal** ***adj.***

gen·re (zhän′rə) ***n.*** ⟦Fr < L *genus,* a kind⟧ **1** a kind, or type, as of works of literature, art, or popular fiction **2** painting in which everyday subjects are treated realistically

gent (jent) ***n.*** [Inf.] a gentleman

gen·teel (jen tēl′) ***adj.*** ⟦< Fr *gentil*⟧ polite or well-bred; now, esp., affectedly refined, polite, etc. —**gen·teel′ly** ***adv.***

gen·tian (jen′shən) ***n.*** ⟦< L *gentiana*⟧ a plant typically having fringed, blue flowers

gen·tile (jen′tīl′) [*also* **G-**] ***n.*** ⟦< L *gentilis,* of the same clan⟧ any person not a Jew —***adj.*** not Jewish

gen·til·i·ty (jen til′i tē) ***n.*** ⟦see fol.⟧ the quality of being genteel

gen·tle (jent′'l) ***adj.*** **-tler, -tlest** ⟦< L *gentilis,* of the same clan⟧ **1** of the upper classes **2** generous; kind **3** tame *[a gentle dog]* **4** kindly; patient **5** not harsh or rough *[a gentle tap]* **6** gradual *[a gentle slope]* —**gen′tle·ness** ***n.*** —**gen′tly** ***adv.***

gen′tle·folk′ ***pl.n.*** people of high social standing: also **gen′tle·folks′**

gen′tle·man (-mən) ***n.,*** *pl.* **-men** (-mən) **1** [Obs.] a man of good family and high social standing **2** a courteous, gracious, and honorable man **3** any man: a polite term, esp. as (in pl.) a form of address —**gen′tle·man·ly** ***adj.*** —**gen′tle·wom′an,** *pl.* **-wom′en,** ***fem.n.***

gen·tri·fy (jen′tri fī′) ***vt.*** **-fied′, -fy′ing** ⟦< fol. + -FY⟧ **1** to convert (an aging neighborhood) into a more affluent one, as by remodeling homes **2** to raise to a higher status —**gen′tri·fi·ca′tion** ***n.***

gen·try (jen′trē) ***n.*** ⟦see GENTLE⟧ people of high social standing

gen·u·flect (jen′yə flekt′) ***vi.*** ⟦< L *genu,* knee + *flectere,* to bend⟧ to bend the knee, as in worship —**gen′u·flec′tion** ***n.***

gen·u·ine (jen′yo͞o in) ***adj.*** ⟦L *genuinus,* inborn⟧ **1** not counterfeit or artificial; real; true **2** sincere —**gen′u·ine·ly** ***adv.*** —**gen′u·ine·ness** ***n.***

ge·nus (jē′nəs) ***n.,*** *pl.* **gen·er·a** (jen′ər ə) or **ge′nus·es** ⟦L, race, kind⟧ **1** a class; kind; sort **2** a category used in classifying plants or animals that are similar in structure

geo- ⟦< Gr *gē*⟧ *combining form* earth, of the earth

ge·o·cen·tric (jē′ō sen′trik) ***adj.*** **1** viewed as from the center of the earth **2** having the earth as a center —**ge′o·cen′tri·cal·ly** ***adv.***

ge·ode (jē′ōd′) ***n.*** ⟦< Gr *geoidēs,* earthlike⟧ a globular stone with a cavity lined with crystals or silica

ge·o·des·ic (jē′ə des′ik) ***adj.*** **1** GEODETIC (sense 1) **2** *a)* designating the shortest line between two points on a curved surface *b)* of the geometry of such lines **3** having a surface formed of straight bars in a grid of polygons *[geodesic dome]*

ge·o·det·ic (jē′ə det′ik) ***adj.*** **1** of or concerned with the measurement of the earth and its surface **2** GEODESIC (sense 2)

ge·og·ra·phy (jē äg′rə fē) ***n.*** ⟦< Gr *gē,* earth + *graphein,* write⟧ **1** the science dealing with the earth's surface, continents, climates, plants, animals, resources, etc. **2** the physical features of a region —**ge·og′ra·pher** ***n.*** —**ge′o·graph′i·cal** (-ə graf′i kəl) or **ge′o·graph′ic** ***adj.*** —**ge′o·graph′i·cal·ly** ***adv.***

ge·ol·o·gy (jē äl′ə jē) ***n.*** ⟦see GEO- & -LOGY⟧ the science dealing with the development of the earth's crust, its rocks and fossils, etc. —**ge′o·log′ic** (-ə läj′ik) or **ge′o·log′i·cal** ***adj.*** —**ge′o·log′i·cal·ly** ***adv.*** —**ge·ol′o·gist** ***n.***

ge·o·mag·net·ic (jē′ō mag net′ik) ***adj.*** of the magnetic properties of the earth —**ge′o·mag′ne·tism′** ***n.***

ge·om·e·try (jē äm′ə trē) ***n.*** ⟦< Gr *gē,* earth + *metrein,* to measure⟧ the branch of mathematics dealing with the properties, measurement, and relationships of points, lines, planes, and solids —**ge′o·met′ric** (-ə me′trik) or **ge′o·met′ri·cal** ***adj.*** —**ge′o·met′ri·cal·ly** ***adv.***

ge·o·phys·ics (jē′ō fiz′iks) ***n.*** the science dealing with the effects of weather, winds, tides, earthquakes, etc. on the earth —**ge′o·phys′i·cal** ***adj.*** —**ge′o·phys′i·cist** ***n.***

George III (jôrj) 1738-1820; king of Great Britain & Ireland (1760-1820)

George′town′ section of Washington, DC

Geor·gia (jôr′jə) **1** Southern state of the SE U.S.: 57,910 sq. mi.; pop. 6,478,000; cap. Atlanta: abbrev *GA* **2** country in W Asia: formerly part of the U.S.S.R.: 26,900 sq. mi.; pop. 5,456,000 —**Geor·gian** (jôr′jən) ***adj., n.***

ge·o·sta·tion·ar·y (jē′ō stā′shə ner′ē) ***adj.*** designating or of a satellite orbiting the earth at a speed which keeps it always above the same point on the earth's surface: also **ge′o·syn′chro·nous** (-siŋ′krə nəs)

ge′o·syn′cline′ (-sin′klīn′) ***n.*** a very large depression in the earth's surface

ge′o·ther′mal (-thur′məl) ***adj.*** ⟦GEO- + Gr *thermē,* heat⟧ of the heat inside the earth: sometimes **ge′o·ther′mic** (-thur′mik)

Ger *abbrev.* **1** German **2** Germany

ge·ra·ni·um (jə rā′nē əm) ***n.*** ⟦< Gr *geranos,* a crane⟧ **1** a common garden plant with showy red, white, etc. flowers **2** a related wildflower

ger·bil (jur′bəl) ***n.*** ⟦ult. < Ar⟧ a small rodent with long hind legs, often kept as a pet

ger·i·at·rics (jer′ē a′triks) ***n.*** ⟦< Gr *gēras,* old age + -IATRICS⟧ the branch of medicine dealing with the diseases of old age —**ger′i·at′ric** ***adj.***

germ (jurm) ***n.*** ⟦< L *germen*⟧ **1** the rudimentary form from which a new organism is developed; seed; bud **2** any microscopic disease-bearing organism; esp., one of the bacteria **3** an origin *[the germ of an idea]*

Ger·man (jur′mən) ***n.*** **1** a person born or living in Germany **2** the language of Germany, Austria, etc. —***adj.*** of Germany or its people, language, etc.

ger·mane (jər mān′) ***adj.*** ⟦see GERM⟧ truly relevant; pertinent

Ger·man·ic (jər man′ik) ***adj.*** designating or of GERMANIC (*n.* 2) —***n.*** **1** [Obs.] the original language of the German people **2** the group of languages descended from it, including English

ger·ma·ni·um (jər mā′nē əm) ***n.*** ⟦< L *Germania,* Germany⟧ a nonmetallic chemical element used in making transistors, etc.

German measles RUBELLA

German shepherd a large dog with a bushy tail and erect ears, originally used to herd sheep, now often used as a guard dog

Ger·ma·ny (jur′mə nē) country in NC Europe: formerly

THESAURUS

knack, bent, turn. **2** [One having genius] gifted person, prodigy, Einstein; see ARTIST, AUTHOR, PHILOSOPHER, POET, WRITER.

gentility ***n.*** decorum, propriety, refinement; see BEHAVIOR.

gentle ***a.*** **1** [Soft] tender, smooth, sensitive; see FAINT 3, SOFT 2, 3. **2** [Kind] tender, considerate, benign; see KIND. **3** [Tamed] domesticated, housebroken, disciplined, educated, trained, civilized, tractable, biddable, pliable, taught, cultivated, tame.—*Ant.* WILD, savage, untamed.

gentleman ***n.*** man of honor, man of his word, sir, cavalier, don, nobleman, gentleman and a scholar.

gentlemanly ***a.*** polite, polished, gallant; see REFINED 2.

gentleness ***n.*** tenderness, softness, delicacy, smoothness, fragility, sweetness.—*Ant.* ROUGHNESS, hardness, imperviousness.

gently ***a.*** considerately, tenderly, benevolently; see GENEROUSLY 2.

genuine ***a.*** **1** [Authentic; *said of things*] real, true, actual, original, veritable, unadulterated, official, whole, accurate, proved, tested, good, bona fide, natural, unimpeachable, pure, unquestionable, authenticated, existent, essential, substantial, factual, palpable, exact, precise, positive, valid, literal, sound, plain, certain, legitimate, legit*, for real*, honest-to-goodness*.—*Ant.* VULGAR, spurious, sham. **2** [Sincere] unaffected, unquestionable, certain, absolute, unimpeachable, definite, incontrovertible, well-established, known, reliable, bona fide, staunch, trustworthy, valid, positive, frank, honest, candid.

geographical ***a.*** terrestrial, geographic, geophysical; see PHYSICAL 1, WORLDLY.

geography ***n.*** earth science, geology, topography, economic geography, political geography, geopolitics, geopolitical study, physiography, geochemistry, geophysics, natural history, cartography; see also SCIENCE 1.

geometrical ***a.*** square, regular, even, proportional, many-sided, multilateral, bilateral, triangular, trilateral, quadrilateral.

germ ***n.*** microbe, antibody, bacterium, disease germ, microorganism, virus, pathogen, retrovirus, prion, infectious agent, toxin, bug*.

German ***a.*** Germanic, Teutonic, Prussian, Saxon, Bavarian.

partitioned (1949-90) into the **Federal Republic of Germany**, also called *West Germany*, and the **German Democratic Republic**, also called *East Germany:* 137,822 sq. mi.; pop. 80,975,000

germ cell an ovum or sperm cell

ger·mi·cide (jur′mə sīd′) ***n.*** ⟦< GERM + -CIDE⟧ any antiseptic, etc. used to destroy germs —**ger′mi·ci′dal** ***adj.***

ger·mi·nal (jur′mə nəl) ***adj.*** **1** of or like germ cells **2** in the first stage of growth

ger′mi·nate′ (-nāt′) ***vi., vt.*** **-nat′ed, -nat′ing** ⟦< L *germen*, a sprout⟧ **1** to sprout or cause to sprout, as from a seed **2** to start developing —**ger′mi·na′tion** ***n.***

germ′y ***adj.*** **-i·er, -i·est** full of germs

ger·on·tol·o·gy (jer′ən täl′ə jē) ***n.*** ⟦< Gr *gerōn*, old man + -LOGY⟧ the study of aging and the problems of the aged —**ger′on·to·log′i·cal** (-tə läj′i kəl) ***adj.*** —**ger′on·tol′o·gist** ***n.***

ger·ry·man·der (jer′ē man′dər) ***vt., vi.*** ⟦after Elbridge *Gerry*, governor of MA (1812) + (SALA)MANDER (from the shape of the county redistricted then)⟧ to divide (a voting area) unfairly, so as to give one political party an advantage

ger·und (jer′ənd) ***n.*** ⟦< L *gerere*, carry out⟧ *Gram.* an English verbal noun ending in *-ing*

Ge·sta·po (gə stä′pō) ***n.*** ⟦< Ger *Ge(heime) Sta(ats)po(lizei)*, secret state police⟧ the terrorist secret police force of Nazi Germany

ges·ta·tion (jes tā′shən) ***n.*** ⟦< L *gerere*, to bear⟧ the act or period of carrying young in the uterus; pregnancy —**ges′tate′, -tat′ed, -tat′ing,** ***vt.***

ges·tic·u·late (jes tik′yoo lāt′) ***vi.*** **-lat′ed, -lat′ing** ⟦see fol.⟧ to make gestures, esp. with the hands —**ges·tic′u·la′tion** ***n.***

ges·ture (jes′chər) ***n.*** ⟦< L *gerere*, to bear⟧ **1** a movement of part of the body to express or emphasize ideas, emotions, etc. **2** any act or remark conveying a state of mind, intention, etc., often made merely for effect —***vi.*** **-tured, -tur·ing** to make gestures

get (get) ***vt.*** **got, got′ten** or **got, get′ting** ⟦< ON *geta*⟧ **1** to come into the state of having; receive, obtain, acquire, etc. **2** to arrive at *[get* home early*]* **3** to go and bring *[get* your books*]* **4** to catch **5** to persuade *[get* him to leave*]* **6** to cause to be *[get* the jar open*]* **7** to prepare *[*to *get* lunch*]* **8** to manage or contrive *[*to *get* to do something*]* **9** [Inf.] *a)* to be obliged (with *have* or *has*) *[*he's *got* to pass*]* *b)* to possess (with *have* or *has*) *[*he's *got* red hair*]* *c)* to strike, kill, baffle, defeat, etc. *d)* to understand **10** [Slang] to cause an emotional response in *[*her singing *gets* me*]* —***vi.*** **1** to come, go, or arrive *[*when I *get* to work*]* **2** to come to be *[*to *get* caught*]* *Get* is used as an auxiliary for emphasis in passive constructions *[*to *get* praised*]* —***n.*** the young of an animal —**get anywhere** to have any success —**get around 1** to move from place to place; circulate: also **get about 2** to circumvent **3** to influence as by flattery —**get away 1** to go away **2** to escape —**get away with** [Inf.] to do without being discovered or punished —**get by** [Inf.] to survive; manage —**get it** [Inf.] **1** to understand **2** to be punished —**get off 1** to come off, down, or out of **2** to leave or start **3** to escape or help to escape —**get on 1** to go on or into **2** to put on **3** to proceed **4** to grow older **5** to succeed —**get out 1** to go out or away **2** to take out **3** to be disclosed **4** to publish —**get over 1** to recover from **2** to forget —**get through 1** to finish **2** to manage to survive —**get together 1** to assemble **2** [Inf.] to reach an agreement —**get up 1** to rise (from sleep, etc.) **2** to organize

get′a·way′ ***n.*** **1** the act of starting, as in a race **2** the act of escaping

get′-go′ ***n.*** [Inf.] beginning: used chiefly in **from the get-go**

get′-to·geth′er ***n.*** an informal social gathering or meeting

Get·tys·burg (get′iz burg′) town in S Pennsylvania: site of a crucial Civil War battle (July, 1863)

get′-up′ ***n.*** [Inf.] costume; dress

GeV *abbrev.* one billion electron-volts

gew·gaw (gyoo′gô′) ***n.*** ⟦ME⟧ a trinket

gey·ser (gī′zər) ***n.*** ⟦< ON *gjosa*, to gush⟧ a spring from which columns of boiling water and steam gush into the air at intervals

Gha·na (gä′nə) country on the W coast of Africa: 92,099 sq. mi.; pop. 12,296,000

ghast·ly (gast′lē) ***adj.*** **-li·er, -li·est** ⟦< OE *gast*, spirit⟧ **1** horrible; frightful **2** ghostlike; pale **3** [Inf.] very bad —**ghast′li·ness** ***n.***

gher·kin (gur′kin) ***n.*** ⟦< Pers *angārah*, watermelon⟧ a small pickled cucumber

ghet·to (get′ō) ***n., pl.*** **-tos** or **-toes** ⟦It⟧ **1** a section of some European cities to which Jews were once restricted **2** any section of a city in which many members of a minority group live, or to which they are restricted as by social discrimination

ghet′to·ize′ (-īz′) ***vt.*** **-ized′, -iz′ing 1** to restrict to a ghetto **2** to make into a ghetto

ghost (gōst) ***n.*** ⟦< OE *gast*⟧ **1** *Folklore* the disembodied spirit of a dead person, appearing as a pale, shadowy apparition **2** a slight trace; shadow *[*not a *ghost* of a chance*]* —**give up the ghost** to die —**ghost′ly** ***adj.***

ghost′writ′er ***n.*** one who writes books, articles, etc. for another who professes to be the author —**ghost′write′, -wrote′, -writ′ten, -writ′ing,** ***vt., vi.***

ghoul (gool) ***n.*** ⟦< Ar *ghāla*, to seize⟧ *Muslim Folklore* an evil spirit that robs graves and feeds on the dead —**ghoul′ish** ***adj.*** —**ghoul′ish·ness** ***n.*** —**ghoul′ish·ly** ***adv.***

GHQ *abbrev.* General Headquarters

GI (jē′ī′) ***adj.*** **1** government issue: designating clothing, etc. issued to military personnel **2** [Inf.] of or characteristic of the U.S. armed forces *[*a *GI* haircut*]* —***n., pl.*** **GI's** or **GIs** [Inf.] a U.S. enlisted soldier

gi·ant (jī′ənt) ***n.*** ⟦< Gr *gigas*⟧ **1** any imaginary being of superhuman size **2** a person or thing of great size, strength, intellect, etc. —***adj.*** like a giant —**gi′ant·ess** ***fem.n.***

gib·ber (jib′ər) ***vi., vt.*** ⟦echoic⟧ to speak rapidly and incoherently

THESAURUS

germinate ***v.*** generate, sprout, develop; see GROW 1.

gestation ***n.*** incubation, gravidity, fecundation; see PREGNANCY.

gesture ***n.*** gesticulation, indication, signal; see SIGN 1.

gesture ***v.*** make a sign, motion, signal, pantomime, act out, use sign language, use one's hands, indicate, signalize, point, nod; see also MOVE 1.

get ***v.*** **1** [To obtain] gain, procure, occupy, reach, capture, recover, take, grab, accomplish, attain, win, secure, achieve, collect, purchase, earn, receive, realize, possess, get possession of, take title to, acquire. **2** [To become] grow, develop into, go; see BECOME. **3** [To receive] be given, take, accept; see RECEIVE 1. **4** [To induce] persuade, talk into, compel; see URGE 2. **5** [*To overcome] beat, vanquish, overpower; see DEFEAT 2, 3. **6** [To prepare] make, arrange, dress; see PREPARE 1. **7** [To contract; *said of bodily disorders*] catch, succumb to, get sick; see CATCH 4. **8** [To learn] acquire, gain, receive; see LEARN. **9** [*To understand] comprehend, perceive, know; see UNDERSTAND 1. **10** [*To irritate] annoy, provoke, vex; see BOTHER 2. **11** [To arrive] come to, reach, land; see ARRIVE. —**get away** flee, run away, elude; see ESCAPE. —**get by*** manage, get along, do well enough; see SURVIVE 1. —**get it*** **1** [To understand] comprehend, perceive, know; see UNDERSTAND 1. **2** [To be punished] suffer, get what is coming to one, be reprimanded, suffer for, catch it*, get in trouble. —**get off 1** [To go away] depart, escape, go; see LEAVE 1. **2** [To dismount] alight, dismount, disembark; see DESCEND. —**get on 1** [To mount] go up, mount, scale; see CLIMB. **2** [To succeed] manage, do well enough, get along; see SUCCEED 1. **3** [To age] grow older, advance in years, approach retirement; see AGE. —**get out 1** [To leave] go, depart, take one's leave; see LEAVE 1. **2** [To escape] break out, run away, flee; see ESCAPE. —**get over** overcome, recuperate from, survive; see RECOVER 3. —**get through 1** [To complete] discharge, enact, finish; see ACHIEVE. **2** [To endure] live through, survive, subsist; see ENDURE 1, 2. —**get together 1** [To gather] collect, accumulate, congregate; see ASSEMBLE 2. **2** [To reach an agreement] come to terms, settle, make a bargain; see AGREE. —**get up 1** [To climb] ascend, mount, go up; see CLIMB. **2** [To arise] get out of bed, rise, turn out; see ARISE 1.

getting ***n.*** taking, obtaining, gaining, catching, earning, winning, seizing, securing, capturing, mastering, confiscating, appropriating.

ghastly ***a.*** **1** [Terrifying] hideous, horrible, frightening; see FRIGHTFUL. **2** [*Unpleasant] repulsive, disgusting, abhorrent; see OFFENSIVE 2.

ghost ***n.*** vision, specter, apparition, spirit, demon, shade, phantom, phantasm, poltergeist, appearance, spook; see also DEVIL.

giant ***a.*** monstrous, colossal, enormous; see LARGE 1.

giant ***n.*** ogre, Cyclops, Titan, colossus, Goliath, Hercules, Atlas, mammoth, behemoth, monster, whale, elephant, leviathan, mountain, hulk; see also MONSTER 1.

gib'ber·ish *n.* unintelligible chatter

gib·bet (jib'it) *n.* ⟦< OFr *gibet*⟧ **1** a gallows **2** a structure from which bodies of executed criminals were hung and exposed to public scorn —*vt.* to hang on a gibbet

gib·bon (gib'ən) *n.* ⟦Fr⟧ a small, slender, long-armed ape of India, S China, and the East Indies

Gib·bon (gib'ən), **Ed·ward** (ed'wərd) 1737-94; Eng. historian

gibe (jīb) *vi., vt.* **gibed, gib'ing** ⟦< ?⟧ to jeer or taunt —*n.* a jeer or taunt

gib·let (jib'lit) *n.* ⟦< OFr *gibelet*, stew made of game⟧ any of the edible internal parts of a fowl, as the gizzard or heart

Gi·bral·tar (ji brôl'tər) British colony occupying a peninsula consisting mostly of a rocky hill (**Rock of Gibraltar**) at the S tip of Spain

gid·dy (gid'ē) *adj.* **-di·er, -di·est** ⟦< OE *gydig*, insane⟧ **1** having or causing a whirling, unsteady sensation; dizzy **2** frivolous —**gid'di·ly** *adv.* —**gid'di·ness** *n.*

Gid·e·on (gid'ē ən) *n. Bible* a judge of Israel and a victorious leader in battle

gift (gift) *n.* ⟦< OE *giefan*, give⟧ **1** something given; present **2** the act of giving **3** a natural ability —*vt.* **1** to present a gift to **2** to present as a gift

gift'ed *adj.* **1** having a natural ability; talented **2** of superior intelligence

gig[1] (gig) *n.* ⟦ME *gigge*, whirligig⟧ **1** a light, two-wheeled open carriage **2** a long, light ship's boat

gig[2] (gig) *n.* ⟦< ?⟧ [Slang] a job, esp. one performing jazz or rock

gi·ga·byte (gig'ə bīt') *n.* 2^{30} bytes, or, loosely, one billion bytes

gi·gan·tic (jī gan'tik) *adj.* ⟦see GIANT⟧ huge; enormous; immense

gig·gle (gig'əl) *vi.* **-gled, -gling** ⟦< Du *giggelen*⟧ to laugh with high, quick sounds in a silly or nervous way —*n.* such a sound —**gig'gly, -gli·er, -gli·est,** *adj.*

gig·o·lo (jig'ə lō') *n., pl.* **-los'** ⟦Fr⟧ a man paid to be a woman's escort

Gi·la monster (hē'lə) ⟦after the *Gila* River, AZ⟧ a stout, poisonous lizard of SW U.S. deserts

gild (gild) *vt.* **gild'ed** or **gilt, gild'ing** ⟦< OE *gyldan*⟧ **1** to coat with gold leaf or a gold color **2** to make seem more attractive or valuable than it is —**gild'er** *n.* —**gild'ing** *n.*

gill[1] (gil) *n.* ⟦ME *gile*⟧ the breathing organ of most water animals, as fish

gill[2] (jil) *n.* ⟦< LL *gillo*, cooling vessel⟧ a unit of liquid measure equal to ¼ pint

gilt (gilt) *vt. alt. pt. & pp. of* GILD —*n.* gold leaf or color —*adj.* coated with gilt

gilt'-edged' *adj.* of the highest quality *[gilt-edged securities]*: also **gilt'-edge'**

gim·bal (gim'bəl, jim'-) *n.* ⟦< L *gemellus*, twin⟧ *[often pl.]* a device consisting of a pivoted ring or rings mounted on a fixed frame, used as to keep a ship's compass level

gim·crack (jim'krak') *adj.* ⟦< ME *gibbecrak*, an ornament⟧ showy but cheap and useless —*n.* a gimcrack thing —**gim'crack'er·y** *n.*

gim·let (gim'lit) *n.* ⟦< MDu *wimmel*⟧ a small tool for making holes

gim·mick (gim'ik) *n.* ⟦< ?⟧ [Inf.] **1** a tricky device **2** an attention-getting device or feature, as for promoting a product —**gim'mick·y** *adj.*

gimp·y (gim'pē) *adj.* ⟦prob. < Norw dial. *gimpa*, to rock⟧ [Inf.] lame; limping

gin[1] (jin) *n.* ⟦ult. < L *juniperus*, juniper⟧ a distilled alcoholic liquor typically flavored with juniper berries

gin[2] (jin) *n.* ⟦< OFr *engin*, engine⟧ **1** a snare, as for game **2** COTTON GIN —*vt.* **ginned, gin'ning** to remove seeds from (cotton) with a gin

gin[3] (jin) *n.* GIN RUMMY

gin·ger (jin'jər) *n.* ⟦< Gr *zingiberi*⟧ **1** a tropical herb with rhizomes used esp. as a spice **2** this spice **3** [Inf.] vigor; spirit —**gin'ger·y** *adj.*

ginger ale a carbonated soft drink flavored with ginger

gin'ger·bread' *n.* **1** a cake flavored with ginger and molasses **2** showy ornamentation

gin'ger·ly *adv.* very carefully —*adj.* very careful; cautious

gin'ger·snap' *n.* a crisp cookie flavored with ginger and molasses

ging·ham (giŋ'əm) *n.* ⟦< Malay *ginggang*⟧ a cotton cloth, usually woven in stripes, checks, or plaids

gin·gi·vi·tis (jin'jə vīt'is) *n.* ⟦< L *gingiva*, the gum + -ITIS⟧ inflammation of the gums

gink·go (giŋ'kō) *n., pl.* **-goes** ⟦Jpn *ginkyo*⟧ an Asian tree with fan-shaped leaves: also **ging'ko**

gin rummy (jin) a variety of the card game rummy

gip (jip) *n., vt., vi. alt. sp. of* GYP

Gip·sy (jip'sē) *n.* GYPSY

gi·raffe (jə raf') *n.* ⟦< Ar *zarāfa*⟧ a large African ruminant with a very long neck and long legs

gird (gurd) *vt.* **gird'ed** or **girt, gird'ing** ⟦OE *gyrdan*⟧ **1** to encircle or fasten with a belt **2** to surround **3** to prepare (oneself) for action

gird·er (gur'dər) *n.* a large wooden or steel beam for supporting joists, the framework of a building, etc.

gir·dle (gurd''l) *n.* ⟦OE *gyrdel*⟧ **1** [Archaic] a belt for the waist **2** anything that encircles **3** a woman's elasticized undergarment for supporting the waist and hips —*vt.* **-dled, -dling** to encircle or bind, as with a girdle

girl (gurl) *n.* ⟦ME *girle*, youngster⟧ **1** a female child **2** a young, unmarried woman **3** a female servant **4** [Inf.] a woman of any age **5** [Inf.] a sweetheart —**girl'hood'** *n.* —**girl'ish** *adj.*

girl'friend' *n.* [Inf.] **1** a sweetheart of a boy or man **2** a girl who is someone's friend **3** a woman friend of a woman

Girl Scout a member of the **Girl Scouts of the United States of America**, a girls' organization providing healthful, character-building activities

girt[1] (gurt) *vt. alt. pt. & pp. of* GIRD

girt[2] (gurt) *vt.* to fasten with a girth

girth (gurth) *n.* ⟦< ON *gyrtha*, encircle⟧ **1** a band put around the belly of a horse, etc. to hold a saddle or pack **2** the circumference, as of a tree trunk

gist (jist) *n.* ⟦< OFr *giste*, point at issue⟧ the essence or main point, as of an article or argument

give (giv) *vt.* **gave, giv'en, giv'ing** ⟦OE *giefan*⟧ **1** to make a gift of **2** to hand over *[to give the porter a bag]* **3** to hand over in or for payment **4** to pass (regards, etc.) along **5** to cause to have *[to give pleasure]* **6** to act as

THESAURUS

gibberish *n.* jargon, chatter, claptrap; see NONSENSE 1.

giddy *a.* high, towering, lofty; see STEEP.

gift *n.* **1** [A present] presentation, donation, grant, gratuity, alms, endowment, bequest, bounty, charity, favor, legacy, award, reward, offering, souvenir, token, remembrance, courtesy, bonus, subsidy, tribute, subvention, contribution, subscription, relief, ration, benefit, tip, allowance, handout. **2** [An aptitude] faculty, capacity, capability; see ABILITY. —**look a gift horse in the mouth** carp, criticize, be ungrateful; see JUDGE.

gifted *a.* smart, skilled, talented; see ABLE.

gigantic *a.* massive, immense, huge; see LARGE 1.

giggle *n.* titter, chuckle, snicker; see LAUGH.

gild *v.* varnish, whitewash, paint in rosy colors; see PAINT 2.

gimmick* *n.* catch*, deceptive device, method; see TRICK.

girder *n.* truss, rafter, mainstay; see BEAM 1.

girdle *n.* belt, cincher, sash; see UNDERWEAR.

girdle *v.* encircle, enclose, clasp; see SURROUND 1.

girl *n.* young woman, schoolgirl, miss, lass, coed, damsel, maid, mademoiselle (French), *señorita* (Spanish), maiden, tomboy, chick*, filly*, skirt*, dame*, babe*.

girlish *a.* juvenile, naive, unsophisticated, fresh, unaffected; see also YOUNG 1.—*Ant.* MATURE, matronly, sophisticated.

girth *n.* circumference, distance around, bigness; see SIZE 2.

gist *n.* substance, essence, significance; see BASIS, SUMMARY.

give *v.* **1** [To transfer] grant, bestow, confer, impart, present, endow, bequeath, award, dispense, subsidize, contribute, hand out, dole out, hand in, hand over, deliver, let have, tip, pass down, convey, deed, sell, will, make over to, put into the hands of, contribute to, consign, relinquish, cede, lease, invest, dispose of, part with, lay upon, turn over, come through with*, come across with*, shell out*, fork over*, kick in*, palm off*.—*Ant.* MAINTAIN, withhold, take. **2** [To yield under pressure] give way, retreat, collapse, fall, contract, shrink, recede, open, relax, sag, bend, flex, crumble, yield.—*Ant.* RESIST, remain rigid, stand firm. **3** [To allot] assign, dispense, deal; see DISTRIBUTE. **4** [To pass on] communicate, transmit, transfer; see SEND 1. **5** [To administer] minister, provide with, dispense; see PROVIDE 1. —**give away** **1** [*To reveal] betray, divulge, disclose; see REVEAL. **2** [To give] bestow, award, present; see GIVE 1. —**give back** return, refund, reimburse; see REPAY 1. —**give in** capitulate, submit, surrender; see ADMIT 2, YIELD 1. —**give out** **1** [To emit] emanate,

host or sponsor of **7** to produce; supply *[cows give milk]* **8** to devote or sacrifice **9** to concede; yield **10** to offer *[to give advice]* **11** to perform *[to give a concert]* **12** to utter *[to give a reply]* **13** to inflict (punishment, etc.) —***vi.*** **1** to bend, move, yield, etc. from force or pressure **2** to make gifts, donations, etc. —***n.*** a bending, moving, etc. under pressure —**give away 1** to make a gift of **2** to present (the bride) to the bridegroom **3** [Inf.] to reveal or betray —**give forth** (or **off**) to emit —**give in** to yield —**give it to** [Inf.] to beat or scold —**give or take** plus or minus —**give out 1** to emit **2** to make public **3** to distribute **4** to become worn out, etc. —**give up 1** to hand over **2** to cease **3** to stop trying **4** to despair of **5** to sacrifice —**giv′er** ***n.***

give′-and-take′ ***n.*** **1** mutual concession **2** repartee or banter

give′a·way′ ***n.*** **1** an unintentional revelation **2** something given free or sold cheap **3** an instance of giving something away free **4** a radio or television program giving prizes

give′back′ ***n.*** a previously negotiated workers' benefit relinquished to management, as for some concession

giv·en (giv′ən) ***vt.***, ***vi.*** *pp. of* GIVE —***adj.*** **1** accustomed (*to*) by habit, etc.; prone (*to*) **2** specified; stated **3** assumed; granted —***n.*** something assumed or accepted as fact

given name a person's first name

giz·mo (giz′mō) ***n.***, *pl.* **-mos** ⟦< ?⟧ [Slang] a gadget: also sp. **gis′mo**

giz·zard (giz′ərd) ***n.*** ⟦< L *gigeria*, cooked entrails of poultry⟧ the muscular second stomach of a bird

Gk *abbrev.* Greek

gla·cé (gla sā′) ***adj.*** ⟦< L *glacies*, ice⟧ **1** glossy, as silk **2** candied, as fruits —***vt.*** **-céed′**, **-cé′ing** to glaze (fruits, etc.)

gla·cial (glā′shəl) ***adj.*** of or like ice or glaciers —**gla′cial·ly** ***adv.***

gla·cier (glā′shər) ***n.*** ⟦< L *glacies*, ice⟧ a large mass of ice and snow moving slowly down a mountain or valley

glad (glad) ***adj.*** **glad′der**, **glad′dest** ⟦OE *glæd*⟧ **1** happy **2** causing joy **3** very willing **4** bright —**glad′ly** ***adv.*** —**glad′ness** ***n.***

glad·den (glad′′n) ***vt.*** to make glad

glade (glād) ***n.*** ⟦ME⟧ an open space in a forest

glad hand [Inf.] a cordial or effusive welcome —**glad′-hand′er** ***n.***

glad·i·a·tor (glad′ē āt′ər) ***n.*** ⟦L < *gladius*, sword⟧ **1** in ancient Rome, a man, often a slave, who fought in an arena as a public show **2** any person taking part in a fight —**glad′i·a·to′ri·al** (-ə tôr′ē əl) ***adj.***

glad·i·o·lus (glad′ē ō′ləs) ***n.***, *pl.* **-lus·es** or **-li′** (-lī′) ⟦L, small sword⟧ a plant of the iris family with swordlike leaves and tall spikes of funnel-shaped flowers: also **glad′i·o′la** (-lə), *pl.* **-las**

glad·some (glad′səm) ***adj.*** joyful or cheerful —**glad′some·ly** ***adv.***

glam·or·ize (glam′ər īz′) ***vt.*** **-ized′**, **-iz′ing** to make glamorous: also sp. **glam′our·ize′** —**glam′or·i·za′tion** ***n.***

glam·our (glam′ər) ***n.*** ⟦Scot var. of *grammar*, magic⟧ **1** seemingly mysterious allure; bewitching charm **2** elegance, luxury, etc. Also sp. **glam′or** —**glam′or·ous** or **glam′our·ous** ***adj.***

glance (glans) ***vi.*** **glanced**, **glanc′ing** ⟦ME *glansen*⟧ **1** to strike a surface obliquely and go off at an angle: with *off* **2** to flash **3** to take a quick look —***n.*** **1** a glancing off **2** a flash **3** a quick look

gland (gland) ***n.*** ⟦< L *glans*, acorn⟧ any organ or group of cells that produces secretions, as insulin, or excretions, as urine —**glan·du·lar** (glan′jə lər) ***adj.***

glans (glanz) ***n.*** ⟦L, lit., acorn⟧ **1** the head of the penis **2** the tip of the clitoris

glare (gler) ***vi.*** **glared**, **glar′ing** ⟦ME *glaren*⟧ **1** to shine with a steady, dazzling light **2** to stare fiercely —***n.*** **1** a steady, dazzling light **2** a fierce stare **3** a bright, glassy surface, as of ice

glar′ing ***adj.*** **1** dazzlingly bright **2** too showy **3** staring fiercely **4** flagrant *[a glaring error]* —**glar′ing·ly** ***adv.***

Glas·gow (glas′kō, glaz′gō) seaport in SC Scotland: district pop. 663,000

glas·nost (gläs′nôst) ***n.*** ⟦Russ, lit., openness⟧ Soviet official policy after 1985 of publicly acknowledging internal problems

glass (glas) ***n.*** ⟦OE *glæs*⟧ **1** a hard, brittle substance, usually transparent, made by fusing silicates with soda, lime, etc. **2** GLASSWARE **3** *a)* a glass article, as a drinking container *b)* [*pl.*] eyeglasses or binoculars **4** the amount held by a drinking glass —***vt.*** to equip with glass panes; glaze —***adj.*** of or made of glass —**glass′ful′** ***n.***

glass ceiling an unofficial policy that prevents women or minorities from advancing within a company, organization, etc.

glass′ware′ ***n.*** articles made of glass

glass′y ***adj.*** **-i·er**, **-i·est** **1** like glass, as in smoothness **2** expressionless *[a glassy stare]* —**glass′i·ly** ***adv.*** —**glass′i·ness** ***n.***

glau·co·ma (glô kō′mə) ***n.*** ⟦< Gr *glaukos*, gleaming⟧ any of various eye disorders marked by increased pressure within the eye causing impaired vision, etc.

glaze (glāz) ***vt.*** **glazed**, **glaz′ing** ⟦ME *glasen*⟧ **1** to fit (windows, etc.) with glass **2** to give a hard, glossy finish

THESAURUS

expend, exude; see EMIT, SMELL 1. **2** [To distribute] dole out, hand out, pass out; see DISTRIBUTE. **3** [To publish] proclaim, make known, announce; see ADVERTISE, DECLARE. **4** [To weaken] faint, fail, break down; see TIRE 1, WEAKEN 1. —**give up 1** [To surrender] stop fighting, cede, hand over; see YIELD 1. **2** [To stop] quit, halt, cease; see END 1.

given ***a.*** granted, supplied, donated, bestowed, presented, awarded, bequeathed, dispensed, handed out, contributed, offered.—*Ant.* KEPT, taken, withheld.

giver ***n.*** provider, supplier, donator; see DONOR.

giving ***n.*** donating, granting, supplying, awarding, presenting, dispensing, passing out, handing out, contributing, conferring, distributing, remitting, transferring, consigning, yielding, giving up, furnishing, allowing, expending, offering, tipping, parting with, pouring forth, discharging, emitting.—*Ant.* GETTING, taking, appropriating.

glacial ***a.*** icy, frozen, polar; see COLD 1.

glacier ***n.*** ice floe, floe, iceberg, berg, glacial mass, snow slide, icecap, ice field, ice stream, glacial table.

glad ***a.*** exhilarated, animated, jovial; see HAPPY.

gladly ***a.*** joyously, happily, gaily, blithely, cheerfully, ecstatically, blissfully, contendedly, readily, gratefully, enthusiastically, merrily, heartily, willingly, zealously, pleasantly, pleasurably, zestfully, complacently, delightfully, gleefully, cheerily, warmly, passionately, ardently, lovingly, cordially, genially, sweetly, joyfully, with relish, with satisfaction, with full agreement, with full approval, with delight.—*Ant.* SADLY, unwillingly, gloomily.

gladness ***n.*** cheer, mirth, delight; see HAPPINESS.

glamorous ***a.*** fascinating, alluring, captivating, bewitching, dazzling; see also CHARMING.

glamour ***n.*** allurement, charm, attraction; see BEAUTY 1.

glance ***n.*** glimpse, sight, fleeting impression; see LOOK 3.

glance ***v.*** **1** [To look] see, peep, glimpse; see LOOK 2. **2** [To ricochet] skip, slide, rebound; see BOUNCE.

gland ***n.*** endocrine organ, pancreas, kidney, liver, testicle, spleen. *Kinds of glands include the following:* simple, compound, tubular, sacular, ductless, adrenal, carotid, endocrine, lymphatic, parathyroid, parotid, pineal, pituitary, thyroid, thymus, sweat, lacrimal, salivary, mammary, seminal, prostate.

glare ***v.*** **1** [To shine fiercely] beam, glow, radiate; see SHINE 1, 2. **2** [To stare fiercely] pierce, glower, scowl; see FROWN, LOOK 2.

glaring ***a.*** **1** [Shining] blinding, dazzling, blazing; see BRIGHT 1. **2** [Obvious] evident, conspicuous, obtrusive; see OBVIOUS 2.

glass ***n.*** *Objects called glass include the following:* tumbler, goblet, beaker, chalice, cup, looking glass, mirror, barometer, thermometer, hourglass, windowpane, watch crystal, monocle, telescope, microscope, spyglass, burning glass, eye-glass, lens, optical glass.

glasses ***n.*** spcctacles, eyeglasses, bifocals, trifocals, aviator glasses, sunglasses, goggles, field glasses, opera glasses, contact lenses, specs*.

glassware ***n.*** crystal, glasswork, glass; see GLASS. *Types of common glassware include the following:* tumbler, jug, decanter, bottle, fruit jar, tableware, glass ovenware, vase, flower bowl, goblet, sherbet glass, wine glass, liqueur glass, champagne glass, cocktail glass, highball glass, old-fashioned glass, brandy snifter, shot glass, parfait glass, beer mug.

glassy ***a.*** vitreous, lustrous, polished; see SMOOTH 1.

glaze ***n.*** enamel, polish, varnish; see FINISH 2.

glaze ***v.*** coat, enamel, gloss over; see SHINE 3.

glazed ***a.*** glassy, translucent, transparent, enameled, varnished, filmed over, shiny, encrusted, burnished, lustrous, smooth.—*Ant.*

to (pottery, etc.) 3 to cover (foods) with a coating of sugar syrup, etc. —***vi.*** to become glassy or glossy —***n.*** 1 a glassy finish or coating 2 a thin coating of ice

gla·zier (glā′zhər) ***n.*** one whose work is fitting glass in windows, etc.

gleam (glēm) ***n.*** ⟦OE *glæm*⟧ 1 a flash or beam of light 2 a faint light 3 a reflected brightness, as from a polished surface 4 a faint manifestation, as of hope, understanding, etc. —***vi.*** 1 to shine with a gleam 2 to appear suddenly —**gleam′y *adj.***

glean (glēn) ***vt., vi.*** ⟦< Celt⟧ 1 to collect (grain left by reapers) 2 to collect (facts, etc.) gradually —**glean′ings *pl.n.***

glee (glē) ***n.*** ⟦OE *gleo*⟧ lively joy; merriment —**glee′ful *adj.***

glee club a group that sings part songs, etc.

glen (glen) ***n.*** ⟦medieval Scot⟧ a narrow, secluded valley

Glen·dale (glen′dāl) city in SW California: pop. 180,000

glen plaid [*also* **G- p-**] a plaid pattern with thin cross-barred stripes

glib (glib) ***adj.*** **glib′ber, glib′best** ⟦< or akin to Du *glibberig*, slippery⟧ speaking or spoken smoothly, often too smoothly to be convincing —**glib′ly *adv.*** —**glib′ness *n.***

glide (glīd) ***vi.*** **glid′ed, glid′ing** ⟦OE *glidan*⟧ 1 to move smoothly and easily 2 *Aeronautics* to descend with little or no engine power —***vt.*** to cause to glide —***n.*** 1 a gliding 2 a disk or ball, as of nylon, under a furniture leg to allow easy sliding

glid·er (glīd′ər) ***n.*** 1 an engineless aircraft carried along by air currents 2 a porch swing suspended in a frame

glim·mer (glim′ər) ***vi.*** ⟦< OE *glæm*, gleam⟧ 1 to give a faint, flickering light 2 to appear faintly —***n.*** 1 a faint, flickering light 2 a faint manifestation —**glim′mer·ing *n.***

glimpse (glimps) ***vt.*** **glimpsed, glimps′ing** ⟦< OE *glæm*, gleam⟧ to catch a brief, quick view of —***vi.*** to look quickly (*at*) —***n.*** a brief, quick view

glint (glint) ***vi.*** ⟦ME *glenten*⟧ to gleam or glitter —***n.*** a gleam, flash, etc.

glis·san·do (gli sän′dō) ***n.***, *pl.* **-di** (-dē) or **-dos** ⟦as if It < Fr *glisser*, to slide⟧ *Music* a sliding effect achieved by a rapid sounding of tones

glis·ten (glis′ən) ***vi.*** ⟦OE *glisnian*⟧ to shine with reflected light, as a wet surface

glitch (glich) ***n.*** ⟦< Ger *glitsche*, a slip⟧ [Slang] a mishap, error, etc.

glit·ter (glit′ər) ***vi.*** ⟦prob. < ON *glitra*⟧ 1 to shine brightly; sparkle 2 to be brilliant or showy —***n.*** 1 a bright, sparkling light 2 striking or showy brilliance 3 bits of glittering material —**glit′ter·y *adj.***

glitz (glits) ***n.*** ⟦< ?⟧ [Inf.] gaudy or glittery showiness —**glitz′y, -i·er, -i·est, *adj.***

gloam·ing (glōm′iŋ) ***n.*** ⟦< OE *glom*⟧ evening dusk; twilight

gloat (glōt) ***vi.*** ⟦prob. < ON *glotta*, grin scornfully⟧ to gaze or think with malicious pleasure: often with *over*

glob (gläb) ***n.*** ⟦prob. < GLOBULE⟧ a rounded mass or lump, as of jelly

glob·al (glō′bəl) ***adj.*** 1 worldwide 2 complete or comprehensive —**glob′al·ly *adv.***

glob′al·ism′ (-iz′əm) ***n.*** a policy, outlook, etc. that is worldwide in scope

global warming a slight, continuing rise in atmospheric temperature, usually attributed to an intensifying of the greenhouse effect

globe (glōb) ***n.*** ⟦< L *globus*, a ball⟧ 1 anything spherical or somewhat spherical 2 the earth, or a model of the earth

globe′-trot′ter *n.* one who travels widely about the world —**globe′-trot′ting *n., adj.***

glob·u·lar (gläb′yə lər) ***adj.*** 1 spherical 2 made up of globules

glob′ule′ (-yo͞ol′) ***n.*** ⟦< L *globulus*⟧ 1 a tiny ball or globe 2 a drop of liquid

glock·en·spiel (gläk′ən spēl′) ***n.*** ⟦Ger *glocke*, bell + *spiel*, to play⟧ a percussion instrument with tuned metal bars in a frame, played with small hammers

gloom (glo͞om) ***n.*** ⟦prob. < Scand⟧ 1 darkness; dimness 2 deep sadness; dejection —**gloom′y, -i·er, -i·est, *adj.***

glop (gläp) ***n.*** ⟦< ? GL(UE) + (SL)OP⟧ [Inf.] any soft, gluey substance —**glop′py *adj.***

glo·ri·fy (glôr′ə fī′) ***vt.*** **-fied′, -fy′ing** ⟦< L *gloria*, glory + *facere*, to make⟧ 1 to give glory to 2 to exalt (God), as in worship 3 to honor; extol 4 to make seem better, greater, etc. than is so —**glo′ri·fi·ca′tion *n.***

glo′ri·ous (-ē əs) ***adj.*** 1 having, giving, or deserving glory 2 splendid 3 [Inf.] very delightful or enjoyable —**glo′ri·ous·ly *adv.***

glo·ry (glôr′ē) ***n.***, *pl.* **-ries** ⟦< L *gloria*⟧ 1 great honor or fame, or its source 2 adoration 3 great splendor, prosperity, etc. 4 heavenly bliss —***vi.*** **-ried, -ry·ing** to exult (*in*)

gloss[1] (glôs, gläs) ***n.*** ⟦< ? Scand⟧ 1 the shine of a polished surface 2 a deceptive outward show —***vt.*** 1 to give a shiny surface to 2 to hide (an error, etc.) or make seem right or trivial: often with *over* —**gloss′y, -i·er, -i·est, *adj.***

gloss[2] (glôs, gläs) ***n.*** ⟦< Gr *glōssa*, tongue⟧ a note of comment or explanation, as in a footnote —***vt.*** to provide glosses for

glos·sa·ry (glôs′ə rē, gläs′-) ***n.***, *pl.* **-ries** ⟦see prec.⟧ a list of difficult terms with explanations, as for a book

glos·so·la·li·a (gläs′ō lā′lē ə, glôs′-) ***n.*** ⟦< Gr *glōssa*, tongue + *lalein*, to speak⟧ an uttering of unintelligible sounds, as in a religious ecstasy

glot·tis (glät′is) ***n.*** ⟦ModL < Gr *glōssa*, tongue⟧ the opening between the vocal cords in the larynx —**glot′tal *adj.***

glove (gluv) ***n.*** ⟦OE *glof*⟧ 1 a covering for the hand, with separate sheaths for the fingers and thumb 2 a baseball player's mitt 3 a padded mitten worn by boxers —***vt.*** **gloved, glov′ing** to cover with a glove

glow (glō) ***vi.*** ⟦OE *glowan*⟧ 1 to give off a bright light as a result of great heat 2 to give out a steady light 3 to give out heat 4 to be elated 5 to be bright with color 6 to be ruddy, flushed, etc., as from enthusiasm —***n.*** 1 a light given off, as a result of great heat 2 steady, even light 3 brightness, warmth, ardor, etc. —**glow′ing *adj.*** —**glow′ing·ly *adv.***

glow·er (glou′ər) ***vi.*** ⟦prob. < ON⟧ to stare with sullen anger; scowl —**glow′er·ing *adj.***

glow′worm′ (glō′-) ***n.*** a wingless, luminescent female or larva of the firefly

glu·cose (glo͞o′kōs′) ***n.*** ⟦Fr < Gr *gleûkos*, sweetness⟧ 1 a crystalline sugar occurring naturally in fruits, honey, etc. 2 a sweet syrup prepared by the hydrolysis of starch

THESAURUS

ROUGH, fresh, unglazed.

glee *n.* joviality, merriment, mirth; see HAPPINESS.

gleeful *a.* joyous, jolly, merry; see HAPPY.

glide *n.* floating, continuous motion, smooth movement, flow, slide, drift, swoop, skimming, flight, soaring, slither.

glide *v.* float, slide, drift, waft, skim, skip, trip, fly, coast, flit, wing, soar, coast along, slide along, skim along.—*Ant.* HIT, rattle, lurch.

glimmer *n.* gleam, flash, flicker; see LIGHT 1.

glimpse *n.* flash, impression, sight; see LOOK 3.

glisten *v.* sparkle, shimmer, flicker; see SHINE 1.

glitter *n.* sparkle, twinkle, gleam; see LIGHT 1.

glitter *v.* twinkle, shimmer, sparkle; see SHINE 1.

globe *n.* balloon, orb, spheroid; see BALL 1.

gloom *n.* woe, sadness, depression, dejection, melancholy, melancholia, dullness, despondency, misery, sorrow, morbidity, pessimism, foreboding, low spirits, cheerlessness, heaviness of mind, weariness, apprehension, misgiving, distress, affliction, despair, anguish, grief, horror, mourning, bitterness, chagrin, discouragement, the blues*, the dumps*.—*Ant.* HAPPINESS, optimism, gaiety.

gloomy *a.* dreary, depressing, discouraging; see DISMAL.

glorify *v.* laud, commend, acclaim; see PRAISE 1.

glorious *a.* famous, renowned, famed, well-known, distinguished, splendid, excellent, noble, exalted, grand, illustrious, notable, celebrated, esteemed, honored, eminent, remarkable, brilliant, great, heroic, memorable, apotheosized, immortal, time-honored, admirable, praiseworthy, remarkable; see also FAMOUS.—*Ant.* UNIMPORTANT, inglorious, ignominious.

glory *n.* 1 [Renown] honor, distinction, reputation; see FAME. 2 [Splendor] grandeur, radiance, majesty, brilliance, richness, beauty, fineness.—*Ant.* tawdriness, meanness, baseness.

glossy *a.* shining, reflecting, lustrous; see BRIGHT 1.

glove *n.* mitten, mitt, gauntlet; see CLOTHES.

glow *n.* warmth, shine, ray; see HEAT 1, LIGHT 1.

glow *v.* gleam, redden, radiate; see BURN, SHINE 1.

glowing *a.* gleaming, lustrous, phosphorescent; see BRIGHT 1.

glue (glōō) ***n.*** ⟦< LL *glus*⟧ **1** a sticky, viscous liquid made from animal gelatin, used as an adhesive **2** any similar substance —***vt.*** **glued**, **glu'ing** to make stick as with glue —**glu'ey**, **-i·er**, **-i·est**, ***adj.***

glum (glum) ***adj.*** **glum'mer**, **glum'mest** ⟦prob. < ME *glomen*, look morose⟧ gloomy; sullen —**glum'ly** ***adv.*** —**glum'ness** ***n.***

glut (glut) ***vi.*** **glut'ted**, **glut'ting** ⟦< L *gluttire*, to swallow⟧ to eat to excess —***vt.*** **1** to feed, fill, etc. to excess **2** to supply (the market) beyond demand —***n.*** **1** a glutting or being glutted **2** a supply greater than the demand

glu·ten (glōōt'''n) ***n.*** ⟦L, glue⟧ a gray, sticky, nutritious mixture of proteins found in wheat, etc. —**glu'ten·ous** ***adj.***

glu·ti·nous (glōōt''n əs) ***adj.*** ⟦see prec.⟧ gluey; sticky —**glu'ti·nous·ly** ***adv.***

glut·ton (glut''n) ***n.*** ⟦see GLUT⟧ **1** one who eats to excess **2** one with a great capacity for something —**glut'ton·ous** ***adj.*** —**glut'ton·ous·ly** ***adv.***

glut'ton·y ***n.***, *pl.* **-ies** the habit or act of eating too much

glyc·er·in (glis'ər in) ***n.*** ⟦< Gr *glykeros*, sweet⟧ *nontechnical term for* GLYCEROL: also **glyc'er·ine**

glyc·er·ol (glis'ər ôl', -ōl') ***n.*** ⟦< prec.⟧ a colorless, syrupy liquid made from fats and oils: used in skin lotions, in making explosives, etc.

gly·co·gen (glī'kə jən) ***n.*** ⟦< Gr *glykys*, sweet + -GEN⟧ a substance in animal tissues that is changed into glucose as the body needs it

GM *abbrev.* General Manager

Gmc *abbrev.* Germanic

gnarl (närl) ***n.*** ⟦< ME *knorre*⟧ a knot on a tree trunk or branch —***vt.*** to make knotted; twist

gnarled ***adj.*** **1** knotty and twisted **2** roughened, hardened, etc.: said as of hands Also **gnarl'y**, **-i·er**, **-i·est**

gnash (nash) ***vt.***, ***vi.*** ⟦prob. < ON⟧ to grind (the teeth) together, as in anger —***n.*** a gnashing

gnat (nat) ***n.*** ⟦OE *gnæt*⟧ any of various small, two-winged insects, which often bite

gnaw (nô) ***vt.*** ⟦OE *gnagen*⟧ **1** to bite away bit by bit; consume **2** to harass or vex —***vi.*** **1** to bite repeatedly: with *on, away,* etc. **2** to produce a corroding, tormenting, etc. effect: with *on, at,* etc. —**gnaw'ing** ***n.***

gneiss (nīs) ***n.*** ⟦< OHG *gneisto*, a spark⟧ a granitelike rock formed of layers of quartz, mica, etc.

gnome (nōm) ***n.*** ⟦< Gr *gnōmē*, thought⟧ *Folklore* a dwarf who dwells in the earth and guards its treasures —**gnom'ish** ***adj.***

GNP *abbrev.* gross national product

gnu (nōō) ***n.*** ⟦< the native name⟧ a large African antelope with an oxlike head and a horselike tail

go (gō) ***vi.*** **went**, **gone**, **go'ing** ⟦< OE *gan*⟧ **1** to move along; travel; proceed **2** to work properly; operate *[*the clock is *going]* **3** to act, sound, etc. as specified *[*the balloon *went* "pop"*]* **4** to turn out; result *[*the war *went* badly*]* **5** to pass: said of time **6** to pass from person to person **7** to become *[*to *go* mad*]* **8** to be expressed, sung, etc. *[*as the saying *goes]* **9** to harmonize; agree *[*blue *goes* with gold*]* **10** to be accepted, valid, etc. **11** to leave; depart **12** to come to an end; fail *[*his eyesight is *going]* **13** to be allotted (*to*) or sold (*for*) **14** to extend, reach, etc. **15** to be able to pass (*through*), fit (*into*), etc. **16** to belong *[*socks *go* in that drawer*]* —***vt.*** **1** to travel along *[*to *go* the wrong way*]* **2** [Inf.] to furnish (bail) for an arrested person **3** [Inf.] to say *[*he *goes* "Wow!"*]* —***n.***, *pl.* **goes** **1** a success *[*to make a *go* of marriage*]* **2** [Inf.] animation; energy **3** [Inf.] a try; attempt —**go back on** [Inf.] **1** to betray **2** to break (a promise, etc.) —**go for** **1** to try to get **2** [Inf.] to attack **3** [Inf.] to be attracted by —**go in for** [Inf.] to engage or indulge in —**go into** to be contained in *[*5 *goes into* 10 twice*]* —**go off** **1** to depart **2** to explode —**go on** **1** to proceed; continue **2** to happen **3** [Inf.] to chatter —**go out** **1** to be extinguished, become outdated, etc. **2** to attend social affairs, etc. —**go over** **1** to examine thoroughly **2** to do again **3** [Inf.] to be successful —**go through** **1** to endure; experience **2** to look through —**go through with** to pursue to the end —**go together** **1** to match; harmonize **2** [Inf.] to date only each other —**go under** to fail, as in business —**let go** **1** to let escape **2** to release one's hold **3** to dismiss from a job; fire —**let oneself go** to be unrestrained —**on the go** [Inf.] in constant motion or action —**to go** [Inf.] **1** to be taken out: said of food in a restaurant **2** still to be done, etc.

goad (gōd) ***n.*** ⟦OE *gad*⟧ **1** a sharp-pointed stick used in driving oxen **2** any driving impulse; spur —***vt.*** to drive as with a goad; urge on

THESAURUS

glue ***n.*** paste, mucilage, cement; see ADHESIVE.

glue ***v.*** paste, bond, cement; see REPAIR.

glum ***a.*** moody, morose, sullen; see SAD 1.

glut ***n.*** oversupply, overabundance, excess; see EXCESS 1.

glut ***v.*** **1** [To oversupply] overwhelm, overstock, fill; see FLOOD. **2** [To overeat] stuff, cram, gorge, eat one's fill, gobble up, eat out of house and home*, fill, feast, wolf, bolt, devour, eat like a horse*.—*Ant.* DIET, starve, fast.

glutton ***n.*** gourmand, overeater, pig; see BEAST 2.

gluttony ***n.*** voracity, piggishness, intemperance; see GREED.

gnarled ***a.*** knotted, twisted, contorted; see BENT.

gnaw ***v.*** crunch, chomp, masticate; see BITE, CHEW.

go ***v.*** **1** [To leave] quit, withdraw, take leave, depart, move, set out, go away, take off, start, leave, vanish, retire, vacate, flee, get out, fly, run along, say goodbye, escape, run away, abandon, abdicate, clear out*, pull out, push off*, scram*, split*, blow*, beat it*, take a powder*, get along*, fade away; see also LEAVE 1. **2** [To proceed] travel, progress, proceed; see ADVANCE 1, MOVE 1. **3** [To function] work, run, perform; see OPERATE 2. **4** [To fit or suit] conform, accord, harmonize; see AGREE, FIT 1. **5** [To extend] stretch, cover, spread; see REACH 1. **6** [To elapse] be spent, waste away, transpire; see PASS 2. **7** [To fail] diminish, stop working, die; see FAIL 1. **8** [To continue] maintain, carry on, persist; see CONTINUE 1. **9** [To die] pass away, depart, succumb; see DIE. **10** [To end] terminate, finish, conclude; see STOP 2. **11** [To endure] persevere, go on, persist; see ENDURE 1. —**as people** (or **things**) **go** in comparison with others, by all standards, according to certain criteria; see ACCORDING TO. —**from the word "go"** from the outset, at the start, beginning with; see FIRST. —**go after** **1** [To chase] seek, try to catch, hunt; see PURSUE 1. **2** [To follow in time] come after, supersede, supplant; see SUCCEED 2. —**go against** be opposed to, contradict, counteract; see OPPOSE 1, 2. —**go ahead** move on, proceed, progress; see ADVANCE 1. —**go back on** desert, be unfaithful, forsake; see ABANDON 2. —**go by** move onward, make one's way, proceed; see PASS 1. —**go down** **1** [To sink] descend, decline, submerge; see SINK 1. **2** [To lose] be defeated, submit, succumb; see FAIL 1, LOSE 3. **3** [To decrease] fall, decline, lessen; see DECREASE 1. —**go for** **1** [To reach for] try to get, aim at, clutch at; see REACH 2. **2** [*To attack] rush upon, run at, spring at; see ATTACK. **3** [*To like] be fond of, fancy, care for; see LIKE 2. —**go in for*** **1** [To advocate] endorse, favor, back; see PROMOTE 1. **2** [To like] care for, be fond of, fancy; see LIKE 1. —**go off** **1** [To leave] quit, depart, part; see LEAVE 1. **2** [To explode] blow up, detonate, discharge; see EXPLODE. —**go on** **1** [To act] execute, behave, conduct; see ACT 1, 2. **2** [To happen] occur, come about, take place; see HAPPEN 2. **3** [To persevere] persist, continue, bear; see ENDURE 1. **4** [*To talk] chatter, converse, speak; see TALK 1. —**go out** cease, die, darken, flicker out, flash out, become dark, become black, burn out, stop shining. —**go over** **1** [To rehearse] repeat, say something repeatedly, practice; see REHEARSE 3. **2** [To examine] look at, investigate, analyze; see EXAMINE, STUDY. —**go through** **1** [To inspect] search, audit, investigate; see EXAMINE. **2** [To undergo] withstand, survive, suffer; see ENDURE 2. **3** [To spend] consume, deplete, expend; see SPEND. —**go through with** fulfill, finish, follow through with; see ACHIEVE, COMPLETE. —**go together** **1** [To harmonize] be suitable, match, fit; see AGREE. **2** [To keep company] go steady*, escort, go with; see DATE 2, KEEP COMPANY (WITH). —**go under** **1** [Drown] sink, drown, suffocate; see DIE. **2** [To become bankrupt] default, go broke, go bankrupt; see LOSE 2. —**go with** **1** [*To keep company with] escort, attend, be with; see ACCOMPANY, DATE 2, KEEP COMPANY (WITH) at COMPANY. **2** [To be appropriate to] match, correspond, not clash, go well with, harmonize, complement, fit; see also AGREE. —**have a go at*** attempt, endeavor, try one's hand at; see TRY 1. —**let go** set free, give up, release; see ABANDON 1. —**let oneself go** be unrestrained, free oneself, have fun; see RELAX. —**no go*** impossible, worthless, without value; see USELESS 1. —**on the go*** in constant motion, moving, busy; see ACTIVE.

goad ***v.*** prod, urge, prick, prompt, spur, drive, whip, press, push, impel, force, stimulate, provoke, tease, excite, needle*, nag, noodge*, instigate, arouse, animate, encourage, bully, coerce; see also URGE 2.—*Ant.* RESTRAIN, curb, rein in.

go′-a·head′ *n.* permission or a signal to proceed: usually with *the*

goal (gōl) *n.* ⟦ME *gol*, boundary⟧ **1** the place at which a race, trip, etc. is ended **2** an end that one strives to attain **3** in some games, *a*) the line or net over or into which the ball or puck must go to score *b*) the score made

goal′keep′er *n.* in some games, a player stationed at a goal to prevent the ball or puck from entering it: also **goal′ie** or **goal′tend′er**

goat (gōt) *n.* ⟦OE *gat*⟧ **1** a cud-chewing mammal with hollow horns, closely related to sheep, antelopes, etc. **2** a lecherous man **3** [Inf.] a scapegoat —**get someone's goat** [Inf.] to annoy someone

goat·ee (gō tē′) *n.* a small, pointed beard on a man's chin

goat′herd′ *n.* one who herds goats

goat′skin′ *n.* the skin of a goat, or leather made from this skin

gob[1] (gäb) *n.* ⟦< OFr *gobe*, mouthful⟧ **1** a soft lump or mass **2** [*pl.*] [Inf.] a large quantity

gob[2] (gäb) *n.* ⟦< ?⟧ [Slang] a sailor in the U.S. Navy

gob·ble[1] (gäb′əl) *n.* ⟦echoic⟧ the throaty sound made by a male turkey —*vi.* **-bled, -bling** to make this sound

gob·ble[2] (gäb′əl) *vt., vi.* **-bled, -bling** ⟦< OFr *gobet*, mouthful⟧ **1** to eat quickly and greedily **2** to seize eagerly; snatch (*up*)

gob′ble·dy·gook′ (-dē gook′) *n.* ⟦? echoic of turkey cries⟧ [Slang] pompous, wordy talk or writing that is meaningless

gob·bler (gäb′lər) *n.* a male turkey

go′-be·tween′ *n.* one who makes arrangements between each of two sides; intermediary

Go·bi (gō′bē) large desert plateau in E Asia, chiefly in Mongolia

gob·let (gäb′lit) *n.* ⟦< OFr *gobel*⟧ a drinking glass with a base and stem

gob·lin (gäb′lin) *n.* ⟦< ML *gobelinus*⟧ *Folklore* an evil or mischievous spirit

go′-by′ *n.* [Inf.] an intentional disregard or slight

god (gäd, gôd) *n.* ⟦OE⟧ **1** any of various beings conceived of as supernatural and immortal; esp., a male deity **2** an idol **3** a person or thing deified **4** [**G-**] in monotheistic religions, the creator and ruler of the universe; Supreme Being —**god′like′** *adj.*

god′child′ *n., pl.* **-chil′dren** the person a godparent sponsors

god′daugh′ter *n.* a female godchild

god·dess (gäd′is) *n.* **1** a female god **2** a woman of great beauty, charm, etc.

god′fa′ther *n.* **1** a male godparent **2** [*often* **G-**] *a*) [Inf.] the head of a Mafia crime syndicate *b*) [Slang] a very influential or authoritative person

god′head′ *n.* **1** godhood **2** [**G-**] God: usually with *the*

god′hood′ *n.* the state of being a god; divinity

Go·di·va (gə dī′və) *n. Eng. Legend* an 11th-c. noblewoman who rode naked through the streets so that her husband would abolish a heavy tax

god′less *adj.* **1** irreligious; atheistic **2** wicked —**god′less·ness** *n.*

god′ly *adj.* **-li·er, -li·est** devoted to God; devout —**god′li·ness** *n.*

god′moth′er *n.* a female godparent

god′par′ent *n.* a person who sponsors a child, as at baptism, taking responsibility for its faith

god′send′ *n.* anything unexpected and needed or desired that comes at the opportune moment, as if sent by God

god′son′ *n.* a male godchild

God·win Aus·ten (gäd′win ôs′tən) mountain in the Himalayas: 2d highest mountain in the world: 28,250 ft.: commonly called *K2*

Goe·the (gö′tə; *E* gur′tə), **Jo·hann Wolf·gang von** (yō′hän vôlf′gäŋk fôn) 1749-1832; Ger. poet & dramatist

go·fer or **go-fer** (gō′fər) *n.* ⟦from being asked to *go for* something⟧ [Slang] an employee who performs menial tasks, as running errands

go-get·ter (gō′get′ər) *n.* [Inf.] an enterprising and aggressive person who usually achieves ambitions, goals, etc.

gog·gle (gäg′əl) *vi.* **-gled, -gling** ⟦ME *gogelen*⟧ to stare with bulging eyes —*n.* [*pl.*] large spectacles to protect the eyes against dust, wind, sparks, etc. —*adj.* bulging or rolling: said of the eyes

go′-go′ *adj.* ⟦short for *à gogo* < Fr, in plenty⟧ **1** of dancing to rock music, as in discothèques **2** of a dancer performing erotic movements to rock music, as in a bar

go·ing (gō′iŋ) *n.* **1** a departure **2** the condition of the ground or land as it affects traveling, walking, etc. **3** [Slang] current situation *[*tough *going* in the trial*]* —*adj.* **1** moving; working **2** conducting its business successfully *[*a *going* concern*]* **3** available **4** commonly accepted; current *[*the *going* rate*]* —**be going to** will or shall

go′ing-ov′er *n.* [Inf.] **1** a thorough inspection **2** a severe scolding or beating

go′ings-on′ *pl.n.* [Inf.] actions or events, esp. when disapproved of

goi·ter (goit′ər) *n.* ⟦< L *guttur*, throat⟧ an enlargement of the thyroid gland, often visible as a swelling in the front of the neck: also [Chiefly Brit.] **goi′tre**

gold (gōld) *n.* ⟦OE⟧ **1** a heavy, yellow, metallic, highly malleable chemical element: it is a precious metal **2** money; wealth **3** bright yellow

THESAURUS

goal *n.* object, aim, intent; see END 2, PURPOSE 1.

goat *n.* nanny goat, buck, kid; see ANIMAL. —**get one's goat*** annoy, irritate, anger; see BOTHER 2.

gobble[2] *v.* bolt, cram, stuff; see EAT 1.

go-between *n.* middleman, referee, mediator; see AGENT, MESSENGER.

god *n.* deity, divinity, divine being, spirit, numen, power, demigod, oversoul, prime mover, godhead, omnipotence, world soul, universal life force, infinite spirit. *Greek gods and their Roman counterparts include:* Zeus or Jupiter or Jove, Phoebus or Apollo, Ares or Mars, Hermes or Mercury, Poseidon or Neptune, Hephaestus or Vulcan, Dionysius or Bacchus, Hades or Pluto or Dis, Faunus or Pan, Kronos or Saturn, Eros or Cupid. *Norse gods include:* Balder, Bragi, Tyr, Frey, Loki, Odin or Woden or Wotan, Thor. *Egyptian gods include:* Ra, Amon, Amon-Re, Bes, Horus, Osiris, Ptah, Set, Thoth. *Hindu gods include:* Ganesha, Indra, Kama, Krishna, Rama, Vishnu, Siva, Shakti, Skanda, Varuna, Hanuman. *Babylonian and Semitic gods include:* Bel, Marduk, Shamash, Baal, Dagon, Molech. *Other gods include:* Mithras (Persian), Ashur (Assyrian), Tiki (Polynesian), Quetzalcoatl (Aztec). For specific female deities see also GODDESS.

God *n.* **1** [The Judeo-Christian deity] Lord, Jehovah, Yahweh, the Almighty, the King of Kings, the Godhead, the Creator, the Maker, the Supreme Being, the Ruler of Heaven, Our Father in Heaven, Almighty God, God Almighty, the Deity, the Divinity, Providence, the All-knowing, the Infinite Spirit, the First Cause, the Lord of Lords, the Supreme Soul, the All-wise, the All-merciful, the All-powerful; the Trinity, the Holy Trinity, Threefold Unity; Father, Son, and Holy Spirit; God the Son, Jesus Christ, Christ, Jesus, Jesus of Nazareth, the Nazarene, the Messiah, the Savior, the Redeemer, the Son of God, the Son of Man, the Son of Mary, the Lamb of God, Immanuel, Emmanuel, the King of the Jews, the Prince of Peace, the Good Shepherd, the Way, the Door, the Truth, the Life, the Light, the Christ Child, the Holy Spirit, the Spirit of God. **2** [The supreme deity of other religions] Allah (Islam); Brahma (Hinduism); Buddha (Buddhism); Mazda or Ormazd (Zoroastrianism).

goddess *n.* female deity, she-god, beauty; see GOD. *Greek goddesses and their Roman counterparts include the following:* Hera or Juno, Ceres or Demeter, Proserpina or Persephone, Tellus or Gaea, Vesta or Hestia, Artemis or Diana, Minerva or Athena, Aphrodite or Venus. *Hindu and Brahmanic goddesses include:* Devi, Maya, Kali, Parvati, Sarasvati. *Norse goddesses include:* Freya, Frigg, Idun, the Norns. *Other goddesses include:* the Goddess; Isis, Hather (Egyptian); Ashtoreth, Astarte (Semitic).

godly *a.* righteous, devout, pious; see HOLY 1.

going *a.* flourishing, thriving, profitable; see SUCCESSFUL. —**be going to** shall, be intending to, be prepared to; see WILL 3. —**get someone going*** annoy, excite, enrage; see BOTHER 2. —**have something going for one*** have an advantage, be talented, have opportunity; see SUCCEED 1. —**keep going** progress, promote, proceed; see ADVANCE 1, IMPROVE 2. —**going strong*** flourishing, surviving, thriving; see SUCCESSFUL.

gold *a.* yellow, golden, gold-colored, red-gold, greenish gold, flaxen, wheat-colored, deep tan, tawny.

gold *n.* **1** [A color] dark yellow, bright yellow, tawny; see COLOR, GOLD *a.* **2** [A precious metal] green gold, white gold, red gold, gold foil, gold leaf, gold plate, filled gold, commercial gold, gold alloy, cloth of gold, gold thread, gold wire; see also METAL. —**as good as gold*** very good, valuable, secure; see EXCELLENT.

gold'brick' ***n.*** [Mil. Slang] one who avoids work: also **gold'brick'er** —***vi.*** [Mil. Slang] to shirk a duty or avoid work

gol·den (gōl'dən) ***adj.*** **1** made of or containing gold **2** bright-yellow **3** very valuable; excellent **4** flourishing **5** marking the 50th year *[golden* anniversary*]* **6** favorable *[*a *golden* opportunity*]*

golden ag·er (ā'jər) [*also* **G- A-**] [Inf.] an elderly person, specif. one 65 or older and retired

Golden Fleece *Gr. Myth.* the fleece of gold captured by Jason

Golden Gate strait between San Francisco Bay & the Pacific

gold'en·rod' ***n.*** a North American plant with long, branching stalks bearing clusters of small, yellow flowers

golden rule the precept that one should act toward others as one would want them to act toward oneself

gold'-filled' ***adj.*** made of a base metal overlaid with gold

gold'finch' ***n.*** ⟦OE *goldfinc*⟧ any of various yellow-and-black finches

gold'fish' ***n.***, *pl.* **-fish'** a small, golden-yellow or orange fish, often kept in ponds or aquariums

gold leaf gold beaten into very thin sheets, used for gilding

gold'smith' ***n.*** an artisan who makes and repairs articles of gold

gold standard a monetary standard in which the basic currency unit equals a specified quantity of gold

golf (gôlf, gälf) ***n.*** ⟦? < Du *kolf*, a club⟧ an outdoor game played with a small, hard ball and a set of clubs, the object being to hit the ball into each of a series of 9 or 18 holes with the fewest possible strokes —***vi.*** to play golf —**golf'er** ***n.***

golf course (or **links**) a tract of land for playing golf

Go·li·ath (gə lī'əth) ***n.*** *Bible* the Philistine giant killed by David

gol·ly (gäl'ē) ***interj.*** used to express surprise, wonder, etc.: orig. a euphemism for *God*

Go·mor'rah ***n.*** *see* SODOM AND GOMORRAH

-gon (gän, gən) ⟦< Gr *gōnia*, an angle⟧ *combining form* a figure having (a specified number of) angles

go·nad (gō'nad') ***n.*** ⟦< Gr *gonē*, a seed⟧ an animal organ or gland that produces reproductive cells; esp., an ovary or testis

gon·do·la (gän'də lə, gän dō'lə) ***n.*** ⟦It⟧ **1** a narrow boat used on the canals of Venice **2** a railroad freight car with no top and, often, with low sides **3** a cabin suspended under an airship or balloon

gon'do·lier' (-lir') ***n.*** a man who propels a gondola

gone (gôn, gän) ***vi.***, ***vt.*** *pp. of* GO —***adj.*** ⟦ME *gon* < OE *gan*⟧ **1** departed **2** ruined **3** lost **4** dead **5** used up; consumed **6** ago; past

gon·er (gôn'ər) ***n.*** a person or thing certain to die, be ruined, etc.

gong (gôŋ, gäŋ) ***n.*** ⟦Malay *guṅ*⟧ a slightly convex metallic disk that gives a loud, resonant tone when struck

gon·or·rhe·a or **gon·or·rhoe·a** (gän'ə rē'ə) ***n.*** ⟦< Gr *gonos*, semen + *rheein*, to flow⟧ a venereal disease with inflammation of the genital organs

goo (gōō) ***n.*** [Inf.] **1** anything sticky, or sticky and sweet **2** excessive sentimentality —**goo'ey, -i·er, -i·est,** ***adj.***

goo·ber (gōō'bər) ***n.*** ⟦< Afr *nguba*⟧ [Chiefly South] a peanut

good (good) ***adj.*** **bet'ter, best** ⟦OE *gōd*⟧ **1** effective; efficient **2** beneficial **3** valid; real *[good* money*]* **4** healthy or sound *[good* eyesight, *good* investments*]* **5** honorable *[*one's *good* name*]* **6** enjoyable, pleasant, etc. **7** reliable **8** thorough **9** excellent **10** virtuous, devout, kind, dutiful, etc. **11** proper; correct **12** skilled **13** considerable *[*a *good* many*]* **14** at least *[*waiting a *good* six hours*]* —***n.*** something good; worth, benefit, etc. —***adv.*** [Inf. or Dial.] well; fully —**as good as** virtually; nearly —**for good (and all)** permanently —**good and** [Inf.] very or altogether —**good for 1** able to endure or be used for (a period of time) **2** worth **3** able to pay or give —**no good** useless; worthless

good'bye' or **good'-bye'** (-bī') ***interj.***, ***n.***, *pl.* **-byes'** ⟦contr. of *God be with ye*⟧ farewell: also sp. **good'by'**, **good'-by'**

good faith good intentions; sincerity

Good Friday the Friday before Easter, commemorating the Crucifixion

good'-heart'ed ***adj.*** kind and generous —**good'-heart'ed·ly** ***adv.*** —**good'-heart'ed·ness** ***n.***

Good Hope, Cape of cape at the SW tip of Africa

good humor a cheerful, agreeable mood —**good'-hu'mored** ***adj.*** —**good'-hu'mored·ly** ***adv.***

good'-look'ing ***adj.*** handsome or beautiful

good'ly ***adj.*** **-li·er, -li·est 1** of good appearance or quality **2** ample

good'-na'tured ***adj.*** agreeable; affable —**good'-na'tured·ly** ***adv.***

good'ness ***n.*** the state or quality of being good; virtue, kindness, etc. —***interj.*** used to express surprise or wonder: orig. a euphemism for *God*

goods (goodz) ***pl.n.*** **1** movable personal property **2** merchandise; wares **3** fabric; cloth —**get** (or **have**) **the goods on** [Slang] to discover (or know) something incriminating about

good Sa·mar·i·tan (sə mer'ə tən) one who helps another or others unselfishly: see Luke 10:30-37

good'-sized' ***adj.*** ample; fairly big

good'-tem'pered ***adj.*** amiable

good turn a friendly, helpful act; favor

good'will' ***n.*** **1** benevolence **2** willingness **3** the value of a business as a result of patronage, reputation, etc., beyond its tangible assets Also **good will**

good'y ***n.***, *pl.* **-ies** [Inf.] something good to eat, as a piece

THESAURUS

golf ***n.*** match play, medal play, open tournament, skins game, Scotch doubles, nine holes, eighteen holes, front nine, back nine, game; see also SPORT 1.

gone ***a.*** **1** [Having left] gone out, gone away, moved, removed, traveling, transferred, displaced, shifted, withdrawn, retired, left, taken leave, departed, deserted, abandoned, quit, disappeared, not here, no more, flown, run off, decamped.—*Ant.* HERE, returned, remained. **2** [Being no longer in existence] dead, vanished, dissipated, disappeared, dissolved, burned up, disintegrated, decayed, rotted away, extinct. —**far gone 1** advanced, deeply involved, absorbed; see INTERESTED 2. **2** crazy, mad, eccentric; see INSANE.

good ***a.*** **1** [Moral] upright, just, honest, worthy, respectable, noble, ethical, fair, guiltless, blameless, pure, truthful, decent, kind, conscientious, honorable, charitable. **2** [Kind] considerate, tolerant, generous; see KIND. **3** [Proper] suitable, becoming, desirable; see FIT 1. **4** [Reliable] trustworthy, dependable, loyal; see RELIABLE. **5** [Sound] safe, solid, stable; see RELIABLE. **6** [Pleasant] agreeable, satisfying, enjoyable; see PLEASANT 1, 2. **7** [Qualified] suited, competent, suitable; see ABLE. **8** [Of approved quality] choice, select, high-grade; see EXCELLENT. **9** [Healthy] sound, normal, vigorous; see HEALTHY. **10** [Obedient] dutiful, tractable, well-behaved; see OBEDIENT 1. **11** [Genuine] valid, real, sound; see GENUINE 1. **12** [Delicious] tasty, flavorful, tasteful; see DELICIOUS. **13** [Considerable] great, big, immeasurable; see LARGE 1, MUCH. **14** [Favorable] approving, commendatory, commending; see FAVORABLE 3. —**as good as** in effect, virtually, nearly; see ALMOST. —**for good** permanently, for all time, henceforth; see FOREVER. —**good for 1** [Helpful] useful, beneficial, salubrious; see HELPFUL 1. **2** [Financially sound] safe, creditworthy, sound; see VALID 2. —**make good 1** [To repay] compensate, adjust, reimburse; see PAY 1, REPAY 1. **2** [To justify] maintain, support, uphold; see SUPPORT 2. **3** [To succeed] arrive, pay off, prove oneself; see PAY 2, SUCCEED 1.

good ***n.*** **1** [A benefit] welfare, gain, asset; see ADVANTAGE. **2** [That which is morally approved] ethic, merit, ideal; see VIRTUE 1. —**come to no good** come to a bad end, get into trouble, have difficulty; see FAIL 1. —**no good** useless, valueless, unserviceable; see WORTHLESS. —**to the good** favorable, advantageous, beneficial; see PROFITABLE.

goodbye ***interj.*** farewell, fare you well, God bless you and keep you, God be with you, adieu, adios, ciao*, so long, bye, bye-bye*, see you later, take it easy*, have a nice day.

good humor ***n.*** cordiality, levity, geniality; see HAPPINESS.

good-looking ***a.*** clean-cut, attractive, impressive; see BEAUTIFUL, HANDSOME.

good-natured ***a.*** cordial, kindly, amiable; see FRIENDLY.

goodness ***n.*** decency, morality, honesty; see VIRTUE 1, 2.

goods ***n.*** **1** [Effects] equipment, personal property, possessions; see PROPERTY 1. **2** [Commodities] merchandise, materials, wares; see COMMODITY.

goodwill ***n.*** benevolence, charity, kindness, cordiality, sympathy, tolerance, helpfulness, altruism.—*Ant.* HATRED, malevolence, animosity.

of candy —*interj.* used to express approval or delight: mainly a child's term

good'y-good'y [Inf.] *adj.* affectedly moral or pious —*n.* a goody-goody person

goof (go͞of) [Inf.] *n.* **1** a stupid or silly person **2** a mistake; blunder —*vi.* **1** to err or blunder **2** to waste time, shirk duties, etc.: with *off* or *around* —**goof'y, -i·er, -i·est,** *adj.*

gook (go͝ok, go͞ok) *n.* ⟦GOO + (GUN)K⟧ [Slang] any sticky or slimy substance

goon (go͞on) *n.* [Slang] **1** a ruffian or thug **2** a grotesque or stupid person

goop (go͞op) *n.* ⟦GOO + (SOU)P⟧ [Slang] any sticky, semi-liquid substance

goose (go͞os) *n., pl.* **geese** ⟦< OE *gos*⟧ **1** a long-necked, web-footed waterfowl like a duck but larger **2** its flesh as food **3** a silly person —**cook someone's goose** [Inf.] to spoil someone's chances

goose'ber'ry *n., pl.* **-ries** **1** a small, sour berry **2** the shrub it grows on

goose bumps a momentary roughened condition of the skin, induced by cold, fear, etc.: also **goose flesh** (or **pimples**)

GOP (jē'ō'pē') *n.* ⟦G(rand) O(ld) P(arty)⟧ *name for* REPUBLICAN PARTY

go·pher (gō'fər) *n.* ⟦< ? Fr *gaufre*, honeycomb: from its burrowing⟧ **1** a burrowing rodent with wide cheek pouches **2** a striped ground squirrel of the prairies of North America

gore[1] (gôr) *n.* ⟦OE *gor*, filth⟧ blood from a wound, esp. when clotted

gore[2] (gôr) *vt.* **gored, gor'ing** ⟦< OE *gar*, a spear⟧ **1** to pierce with or as with a horn or tusk **2** to insert gores in —*n.* a tapering piece of cloth inserted in a skirt, sail, etc. to give it fullness

gorge (gôrj) *n.* ⟦< L *gurges*, whirlpool⟧ **1** the throat or gullet **2** the contents of the stomach **3** resentment, disgust, etc. **4** a deep, narrow pass between steep heights —*vi., vt.* **gorged, gorg'ing** to eat greedily or swallow gluttonously

gor·geous (gôr'jəs) *adj.* ⟦< OFr *gorgias*⟧ **1** brilliantly showy; magnificent **2** [Inf.] beautiful, delightful, etc. —**gor'geous·ly** *adv.*

go·ril·la (gə ril'ə) *n.* ⟦ult. < name in an ancient W Afr language⟧ the largest, and most powerful, of the great apes, native to Africa

Gor·ki or **Gor'ky** (gôr'kē) *name* (1932-90) *for* NIZHNY NOVGOROD

gor·mand·ize (gôr'mən dīz') *vi., vt.* **-ized', -iz'ing** ⟦< Fr *gourmandise*, gluttony⟧ to eat like a glutton

go'-round' *n.* one of a series of actions, encounters, etc., often involving conflict

gorp (gôrp) *n.* a mixture of raisins, nuts, etc. eaten as by hikers for quick energy

gorse (gôrs) *n.* ⟦OE *gorst*⟧ FURZE

gor·y (gôr'ē) *adj.* **-i·er, -i·est** **1** covered with gore; bloody **2** with much bloodshed —**gor'i·ness** *n.*

gosh (gäsh, gôsh) *interj.* used to express surprise, wonder, etc.: a euphemism for *God*

gos·ling (gäz'liŋ) *n.* a young goose

gos·pel (gäs'pəl) *n.* ⟦< OE *gōdspel*, good news⟧ **1** [*often* **G-**] the teachings of Jesus and the Apostles **2** [**G-**] any of the first four books of the New Testament **3** anything proclaimed or accepted as the absolute truth: also **gospel truth**

gos·sa·mer (gäs'ə mər) *n.* ⟦ME *gosesomer*, lit., goose summer⟧ **1** a filmy cobweb **2** a very thin, filmy cloth —*adj.* light, thin, and filmy

gos·sip (gäs'əp) *n.* ⟦< Late OE *godsibbe*, godparent⟧ **1** one who chatters idly about others **2** such talk —*vi.* to be a gossip —**gos'sip·y** *adj.*

got (gät) *vt., vi. pt. & alt. pp. of* GET

Goth (gäth, gôth) *n.* a member of a Germanic people that conquered most of the Roman Empire in the 3d, 4th, and 5th c. A.D.

Goth·ic (gäth'ik) *adj.* **1** of the Goths or their language **2** designating or of a style of architecture developed in W Europe between the 12th and 16th c., with pointed arches, steep roofs, etc. **3** [*sometimes* **g-**] uncivilized **4** [*sometimes* **g-**] of a type of fiction that uses remote, gloomy settings and a sinister atmosphere to suggest mystery —*n.* **1** the East Germanic language of the Goths **2** Gothic style, esp. in architecture

got·ten (gät''n) *vt., vi. alt. pp. of* GET

Gou·da (cheese) (go͞o'də, gou'-) ⟦after *Gouda*, Netherlands⟧ a mild cheese sometimes coated with red wax

gouge (gouj) *n.* ⟦< LL *gulbia*⟧ **1** a chisel for cutting grooves or holes in wood **2** such a groove or hole —*vt.* **gouged, goug'ing** **1** to make a groove, etc. in (something) as with a gouge **2** to scoop out **3** [Inf.] to cheat out of money —**goug'er** *n.*

gou·lash (go͞o'läsh') *n.* ⟦< Hung *gulyás*⟧ a beef or veal stew seasoned with paprika

gou·ra·mi (go͞o rä'mē, goor'ə mē) *n., pl.* **-mies** or **-mi** ⟦Malay *gurami*⟧ any of various freshwater tropical fishes; esp., a food fish of SE Asia

gourd (gôrd, goord) *n.* ⟦< L *cucurbita*⟧ **1** any trailing or climbing plant of a family that includes the squash, melon, etc. **2** the fruit of one inedible species or its dried, hollowed-out shell, used as a cup, dipper, etc.

gour·mand (goor mänd') *n.* ⟦OFr⟧ one who indulges in good food and drink excessively

gour·met (goor'mā, gôr-) *n.* ⟦Fr < OFr, *gormet*, wine taster⟧ one who likes and is an excellent judge of fine food and drink

gout (gout) *n.* ⟦< L *gutta*, a drop⟧ a form of arthritis characterized by painful swelling of the joints, esp. in the big toe —**gout'y, -i·er, -i·est,** *adj.*

gov or **Gov** *abbrev.* **1** government **2** governor

gov·ern (guv'ərn) *vt., vi.* ⟦< Gr *kybernan*, to steer⟧ **1** to exercise authority over; rule, control, etc. **2** to influence the action of; guide **3** to determine —**gov'ern·a·ble** *adj.*

gov'ern·ance (-ər nəns) *n.* the action, function, or power of government

gov'ern·ess (-ər nis) *n.* a woman employed in a private home to train and teach the children

gov·ern·ment (guv'ərn mənt, -ər mənt) *n.* **1** the exercise of authority over a state, organization, etc.; control; rule

THESAURUS

goof* *v.* err, make a mistake, flub*; see FAIL 1.

goose *n.* gray goose, snow goose, Canada goose; see BIRD.

gorge *n.* chasm, abyss, crevasse; see RAVINE.

gorge *v.* glut, devour, stuff oneself; see EAT 1, FILL 1.

gorgeous *a.* superb, sumptuous, impressive; see BEAUTIFUL, GRAND.

gory *a.* blood-soaked, bloodstained, bloody; see OFFENSIVE 2.

gospel *n.* **1** [A record of Christ] New Testament, Christian Scripture, Evangel; see BIBLE. **2** [Belief or statement supposedly infallible] creed, certainty, dogma; see DOCTRINE, FAITH 2, TRUTH.

gossip *n.* **1** [Idle talk] babble, chatter, meddling, small talk, malicious talk, hearsay, rumor, scandal, news, slander, defamation, injury, blackening, skinny*, the grapevine. **2** [One who indulges in gossip] snoop*, busybody, meddler, tattler, newsmonger, scandalmonger, muckraker, backbiter, chatterbox, talkative person, babbler.

gossip *v.* tattle, prattle, tell tales, talk idly, chat, chatter, rumor, report, tell secrets, blab, babble, repeat.

gouge *v.* scoop, chisel, channel; see DIG 1.

govern *v.* command, administer, reign, rule, legislate, oversee, assume command, hold office, administer the laws, exercise authority, be in power, supervise, direct, dictate, tyrannize.

governed *a.* commanded, administered, under authority, supervised, directed, dictated to, conducted, guided, piloted, mastered, led, driven, subjugated, subordinate, determined, guided, influenced, swayed, inclined, regulated, directed, ordered, dependent, obedient, under someone's jurisdiction.—*Ant.* UNRULY, self-determined, capricious.

governing *a.* commanding, administrative, executive, authoritative, supervisory, regulatory, controlling, directing, overseeing, dictatorial, conducting, guiding, mastering, dominating, dominant, determining, supreme, influential, presidential, absolute, ruling, checking, curbing, inhibiting, limiting.—*Ant.* SUBORDINATE, powerless, tributary.

government *n.* **1** [The process of governing] rule, control, command, regulation, direction, dominion, sway, authority, jurisdiction, sovereignty, direction, power, management, authorization, mastery, supervision, superintendence, supremacy, domination, influence, politics, state, political practice; see also ADMINISTRATION 2. **2** [The instrument of governing] administration, assembly, legislature, congress, cabinet, executive power, bureaucracy, authority, party, council, parliament, senate, department of justice, soviet, synod, convocation, convention, court, house. *Types of government include the following:* absolute monarchy, dictatorship, empire, tyranny, fascism, imperialism, colonialism, despotism, constitutional monarchy, oligarchy, aristocracy, theocracy, republic, democracy, popular government, rep-

2 a system of ruling, political administration, etc. 3 those who conduct the affairs of a state, etc.; administration —**gov'ern·men'tal** ***adj.***

gov·er·nor (guv'ə nər, -ər nər) ***n.*** **1** one who governs; esp., *a)* one appointed to govern a province, etc. *b)* the elected head of any state of the U.S. **2** a mechanical device for automatically controlling the speed of an engine —**gov'er·nor·ship'** ***n.***

governor general *pl.* **governors general** or **governor generals** a governor who has subordinate or deputy governors

govt or **Govt** *abbrev.* government

gown (goun) ***n.*** ⟦< LL *gunna*⟧ **1** a long, loose outer garment; specif., *a)* a nightgown *b)* a long, flowing robe worn by judges, clergymen, scholars, etc. **2** a woman's formal dress

GP or **gp** *abbrev.* general practitioner

gr *abbrev.* **1** grain(s) **2** gross

Gr *abbrev.* **1** Greece **2** Greek

grab (grab) ***vt.*** **grabbed**, **grab'bing** ⟦prob. < MDu *grabben*⟧ **1** to snatch suddenly **2** to get by unscrupulous methods **3** [Slang] to impress greatly —***n.*** a grabbing —**grab'ber** ***n.***

grab'by ***adj.*** **-bi·er**, **-bi·est** [Inf.] greedy; avaricious

grace (grās) ***n.*** ⟦< L *gratus*, pleasing⟧ **1** beauty or charm of form, movement, or expression **2** goodwill; favor **3** a delay granted for payment of an obligation **4** a short prayer of thanks for a meal **5** [**G-**] a title of an archbishop, duke, or duchess **6** the love and favor of God toward human beings —***vt.*** **graced**, **grac'ing** **1** to decorate **2** to dignify —**in the good** (or **bad**) **graces of** in favor (or disfavor) with

grace'ful ***adj.*** having beauty of form, movement, etc. —**grace'ful·ly** ***adv.*** —**grace'ful·ness** ***n.***

grace'less ***adj.*** **1** lacking any sense of what is proper **2** clumsy or inelegant —**grace'less·ly** ***adv.*** —**grace'less·ness** ***n.***

gra·cious (grā'shəs) ***adj.*** ⟦see GRACE⟧ **1** having or showing kindness, courtesy, charm, etc. **2** compassionate **3** polite to supposed inferiors **4** marked by luxury, ease, etc. *[gracious* living*]* —**gra'cious·ly** ***adv.*** —**gra'cious·ness** ***n.***

grack·le (grak'əl) ***n.*** ⟦L *graculus*, jackdaw⟧ any of several blackbirds somewhat smaller than a crow

grad[1] (grad) ***n.*** [Inf.] a graduate

grad[2] *abbrev.* **1** graduate **2** graduated

gra·da·tion (grā dā'shən) ***n.*** **1** an arranging in grades, or stages **2** a gradual change by stages **3** a step or degree in a graded series

grade (grād) ***n.*** ⟦< L *gradus*⟧ **1** a stage or step in a progression **2** *a)* a degree in a scale of quality, rank, etc. *b)* a group of people of the same rank, merit, etc. **3** *a)* the degree of rise or descent of a sloping surface *b)* such a surface **4** any of the divisions of a school curriculum, usually by years **5** a mark or rating on an examination, etc. —***vt.*** **grad'ed**, **grad'ing** **1** to classify by grades; sort **2** to give a GRADE (*n.* 5) to **3** to make (ground) level or evenly sloped, as for a road —**make the grade** to succeed

grade crossing the place where a railroad intersects another railroad or a roadway on the same level

grade school ELEMENTARY SCHOOL

grade separation a crossing with an overpass or underpass

gra·di·ent (grā'dē ənt) ***n.*** ⟦< L *gradi*, to step⟧ **1** a slope, as of a road **2** the degree of such slope

grad·u·al (gra'jo͞o əl) ***adj.*** ⟦< L *gradus*, a step⟧ taking place by degrees; developing little by little —**grad'u·al·ly** ***adv.*** —**grad'u·al·ness** ***n.***

grad'u·al·ism' ***n.*** the principle of promoting gradual rather than rapid change

grad·u·ate (gra'jo͞o it; *for v.*, -āt') ***n.*** ⟦< L *gradus*, a step⟧ one who has completed a course of study at a school or college —***vt.*** **-at'ed**, **-at'ing** **1** to give a degree or diploma to upon completion of a course of study **2** [Inf.] to become a graduate of *[*to *graduate* college*]* **3** to mark with degrees for measuring **4** to classify into grades according to amount, size, etc. —***vi.*** to become a graduate of a school, etc. —***adj.*** **1** having been graduated from a school, etc. **2** of or for degrees above the bachelor's —**grad'u·a'tor** ***n.***

grad'u·a'tion ***n.*** **1** a graduating from a school or college **2** the ceremony connected with this

graf·fi·ti (grə fēt'ē) ***pl.n.***, *sing.* **-to** (-ō) ⟦It < L: see fol.⟧ [*now usually with sing. v.*] inscriptions or drawings on a wall or other public surface

graft (graft) ***n.*** ⟦ult. < Gr *grapheion*, stylus⟧ **1** *a)* a shoot or bud of one plant or tree inserted into another, where it grows permanently *b)* the inserting of such a shoot **2** the transplanting of skin, bone, etc. **3** *a)* the dishonest use of one's position to gain money, etc., as in politics *b)* anything so gained —***vt.***, ***vi.*** to insert (a graft) —**graft'er** ***n.***

gra·ham (grā'əm, gram) ***adj.*** ⟦after S. *Graham*, 19th-c.

THESAURUS

resentative government, social democracy, communism, socialism, party government. *Divisions of government include:* state, province, kingdom, territory, colony, dominion, commonwealth, soviet, republic, shire, city, county, town, village, township, municipality, borough, commune, canton, ward, district, department, parish.

governmental ***a.*** political, administrative, executive, regulatory, bureaucratic, legal, supervisory, sovereign, presidential, official, gubernatorial, national.

governor ***n.*** director, leader, head, presiding officer, ruler; see also LEADER 2.

gown ***n.*** garb, garment, clothes; see DRESS 2.

grab ***v.*** clutch, grasp, take; see SEIZE 1, 2.

grace ***n.*** **1** [The quality of being graceful] suppleness, ease of movement, nimbleness, agility, pliancy, smoothness, form, poise, dexterity, symmetry, balance, style, harmony.—*Ant.* AWKWARDNESS, stiffness, maladroitness. **2** [Mercy] forgiveness, love, charity; see MERCY. —**in the bad graces of** in disfavor, rejected, disapproved; see HATED. —**in the good graces of** favored, accepted, admired; see APPROVED.

graceful ***a.*** **1** [*Said of movement*] supple, agile, lithe, pliant, nimble, elastic, springy, easy, dexterous, adroit, smooth, controlled, light-footed, athletic, willowy, poised, practiced, skilled, rhythmic, sprightly, elegant.—*Ant.* AWKWARD, fumbling, stiff. **2** [*Said of objects*] elegant, neat, well-proportioned, trim, balanced, symmetrical, dainty, pretty, harmonious, beautiful, comely, seemly, handsome, fair, delicate, tasteful, slender, decorative, artistic, exquisite, statuesque.—*Ant.* UGLY, shapeless, cumbersome. **3** [*Said of conduct*] cultured, seemly, becoming; see POLITE.

gracefully ***a.*** lithely, agilely, harmoniously, daintily, nimbly, elegantly, trimly, symmetrically, beautifully, delicately, tastefully, artistically, easily, dexterously, smoothly, skillfully, fairly, adroitly, handsomely, rhythmically, exquisitely, neatly, delightfully, charmingly, imaginatively, becomingly, suitably, pleasingly, appropriately, happily, decoratively, prettily.—*Ant.* AWKWARDLY, insipidly, grotesquely.

gracious ***a.*** **1** [Genial] amiable, courteous, condescending; see POLITE. **2** [Merciful] tender, loving, charitable; see KIND.

grade ***n.*** **1** [An incline] slope, inclined plane, gradient, slant, inclination, pitch, ascent, descent, ramp, upgrade, downgrade, climb, elevation, height; see also HILL. **2** [An embankment] fill, causeway, dike; see DAM. **3** [Rank or degree] class, category, classification; see DEGREE 2. **4** [A division of a school] standard, form, rank; see GATHERING. —**make the grade** win, prosper, achieve; see SUCCEED 1.

grade ***v.*** rate, assess, assort; see RANK 3.

gradual ***a.*** creeping, regular, continuous; see REGULATED.

gradually ***a.*** step by step, by degrees, steadily, increasingly, slowly, regularly, a little at a time, little by little, bit by bit, inch by inch, by installments, in small doses, continually, continuously, progressively, successively, sequentially, constantly, unceasingly, imperceptibly, deliberately.—*Ant.* QUICKLY, haphazardly, by leaps and bounds.

graduate ***n.*** recipient of a degree, recipient of a certificate, recipient of a diploma, alumnus, alumna, former student, holder of a degree, bearer of a degree, holder of a certificate, bearer of a certificate, baccalaureate, grad*, alum*.

graduate ***v.*** receive a degree, receive a certificate, receive a diploma, be awarded a degree, be awarded a certificate, be awarded a diploma, earn a degree, earn a certificate, earn a diploma, become an alumna, become an alumnus, get out, finish one's schooling; get a B.A., M.A., Ph.D., M.D., etc.; get a sheepskin*.

graduated ***a.*** **1** [Granted a degree] certified, ordained, passed; see OFFICIAL 1. **2** [Arranged or marked according to a scale] graded, sequential, progressive; see ORGANIZED.

graduation ***n.*** commencement, convocation, granting of diplomas, promotion, bestowal of honors, commissioning.

U.S. dietary reformer⟧ designating or made of whole-wheat flour *[graham crackers]*

Grail (grāl) ***n.*** ⟦< ML *gradalis*, cup⟧ *Medieval Legend* the cup used by Jesus at the Last Supper: also **Holy Grail**

grain (grān) ***n.*** ⟦< L *granum*⟧ **1** the small, hard seed of any cereal plant, as wheat or corn **2** cereal plants **3** a tiny, solid particle, as of salt or sand **4** a tiny bit **5** the smallest unit in the system of weights used in the U.S. **6** *a)* the arrangement or direction of fibers, layers, etc. of wood, leather, etc. *b)* the markings or texture due to this **7** disposition; nature

grain'y ***adj.*** **-i·er, -i·est 1** having a clearly defined grain: said as of wood **2** coarsely textured; granular **—grain'i·ness *n.***

gram[1] (gram) ***n.*** ⟦< Gr *gramma*, small weight⟧ the basic unit of mass in the metric system, equal to 0.03527 ounce

gram[2] *abbrev.* grammar

-gram (gram) ⟦< Gr *gramma*, writing⟧ *combining form* something written *[telegram]*

gram·mar (gram'ər) ***n.*** ⟦< Gr *gramma*, writing⟧ **1** language study dealing with the forms of words and with their arrangement in sentences **2** a system of rules for speaking and writing a given language **3** one's manner of speaking or writing as judged by such rules **—gram·mar·i·an** (grə mer'ē ən) ***n.*** **—gram·mat'i·cal** (-mat'i kəl) ***adj.*** **—gram·mat'i·cal·ly *adv.***

grammar school [Now Rare] ELEMENTARY SCHOOL

gran·a·ry (gran'ə rē, grān'-) ***n.***, *pl.* **-ries** ⟦< L *granum*, grain⟧ a building for storing threshed grain

grand (grand) ***adj.*** ⟦< L *grandis*, large⟧ **1** higher in rank than others *[a grand duke]* **2** most important; main *[the grand ballroom]* **3** imposing in size, beauty, and extent **4** distinguished; illustrious **5** complete; overall *[the grand total]* **6** [Inf.] excellent; delightful **—*n.***, *pl.* **grand** [Slang] a thousand dollars **—grand'ly *adv.***

grand- *combining form* of the generation older (or younger) than *[grandmother, grandson]*

grand'child' ***n.***, *pl.* **-chil'dren** a child of one's son or daughter

grand'daugh'ter ***n.*** a daughter of one's son or daughter

grande dame (grӓnd dӓm') ⟦Fr⟧ a woman, esp. an older one, of great dignity

gran·dee (gran dē') ***n.*** ⟦Sp & Port *grande*: see GRAND⟧ a man of high rank

gran·deur (gran'jər, -joor'; -dyoor') ***n.*** ⟦see GRAND⟧ **1** splendor; magnificence **2** moral or intellectual greatness

grand'fa'ther ***n.*** **1** the father of one's father or mother **2** a forefather **—*vt.*** [Inf.] to exempt (a practice, person, etc.) from a new law or regulation

grandfather (or **grandfather's**) **clock** a large clock with a pendulum, in a tall, narrow case

gran·dil·o·quent (gran dil'ə kwənt) ***adj.*** ⟦< L *grandis*, grand + *loqui*, speak⟧ using pompous, bombastic words **—gran·dil'o·quence *n.*** **—gran·dil'o·quent·ly *adv.***

gran·di·ose (gran'dē ōs') ***adj.*** ⟦< L *grandis*, great⟧ **1** having grandeur; imposing **2** pompous and showy **—gran'di·os'i·ty** (-äs'ə tē) ***n.***

grand jury a jury that investigates accusations and indicts persons for trial if there is sufficient evidence

grand'ma' ***n.*** [Inf.] GRANDMOTHER

grand'mas'ter ***n.*** a chess player of the highest rating

grand'moth'er ***n.*** **1** the mother of one's father or mother **2** a female ancestor

grand opera opera in which the whole text is set to music

grand'pa' ***n.*** [Inf.] GRANDFATHER

grand'par'ent ***n.*** a grandfather or grandmother

grand piano a large piano with strings set horizontally in a wing-shaped case

Grand Rapids city in SW Michigan: pop. 189,000

grand slam 1 *Baseball* a home run hit when there is a runner on each base **2** *Bridge* the winning of all the tricks in a deal

grand'son' ***n.*** a son of one's son or daughter

grand'stand' ***n.*** the main seating structure for spectators at a sporting event

grange (grānj) ***n.*** ⟦< L *granum*, grain⟧ a farm **—the Grange** a fraternal organization, originally of farmers, in the U.S.

gran·ite (gran'it) ***n.*** ⟦< L *granum*, grain⟧ a hard, grainy igneous rock consisting mainly of feldspar and quartz **—gra·nit·ic** (grə nit'ik) ***adj.***

gran·ny or **gran·nie** (gran'ē) ***n.***, *pl.* **-nies** [Inf.] **1** a grandmother **2** an old woman **—*adj.*** of a style like that formerly worn by elderly women *[granny glasses]*

gran·o·la (grə nō'lə) ***n.*** ⟦< ? L *granum*, grain⟧ a breakfast cereal of rolled oats, wheat germ, sesame seeds, brown sugar or honey, dried fruit or nuts, etc.

grant (grant) ***vt.*** ⟦ult. < L *credere*, believe⟧ **1** to give (what is requested, as permission) **2** to give or transfer by legal procedure **3** to admit as true; concede **—*n.*** **1** a granting **2** something granted, as property or a right **—take for granted** to consider as true, already settled, etc. **—grant'er *n.***

Grant (grant), **Ulysses S(impson)** 1822-85; 18th president of the U.S. (1869-77): Union commander in the Civil War

grant'-in-aid' ***n.***, *pl.* **grants'-in-aid'** a grant of funds, as by the federal government to a state or by a foundation to a scientist, artist, etc., to support a specific project

grants'man·ship' ***n.*** skill in acquiring grants-in-aid

gran·u·lar (gran'yə lər) ***adj.*** **1** containing or consisting of grains **2** like grains or granules **—gran'u·lar'i·ty** (-ler'ə tē) ***n.***

gran'u·late' (-lāt') ***vt.***, ***vi.*** **-lat'ed, -lat'ing** to form into grains or granules **—gran'u·la'tion *n.***

gran·ule (gran'yool) ***n.*** ⟦< L *granum*, grain⟧ a small grain or particle

grape (grāp) ***n.*** ⟦< OFr *graper*, to gather with a hook⟧ **1** a small, round, juicy berry, growing in clusters on a woody vine **2** a grapevine **3** a dark purplish red

grape'fruit' ***n.*** a large, round, sour citrus fruit with a yellow rind

grape hyacinth a small plant of the lily family, with spikes of small, bell-shaped flowers of blue or white

grape'shot' ***n.*** a cluster of small iron balls, formerly fired from a cannon

THESAURUS

grain ***n.*** **1** [Seeds of domesticated grasses] cereals, corn, small grain, seed. *Varieties of grain include the following:* rice, wheat, oats, barley, maize, corn, rye, millet, Indian corn, hybrid corn, popcorn. **2** [Character imparted by fiber] texture, warp and woof, warp and weft, tendency, fabric, tissue, current, direction, tooth, nap. **—against the grain** disturbing, irritating, bothersome; see OFFENSIVE 2.

grammar ***n.*** syntax, morphology, structure, syntactic structure, sentence structure, language pattern, sentence pattern, linguistic science, generative grammar, stratificational grammar, transformational grammar, universal grammar, tagmemics, synthetic grammar, inflectional grammar, analytic grammar, traditional grammar, structural linguistics; see also LANGUAGE. *Terms in grammar include the following:* tense, mood, voice, person, gender, number, word, phrase, clause, aspect, case, modification, incorporation, inflection, concord, agreement, sentence, nexus, coordination, subordination, structure, phrase structure, phoneme, phonemics, string, head word, morpheme, transform.

grammatical ***a.*** **1** [Having to do with grammar] linguistic, syntactic, morphological, logical, philological, analytic, analytical. **2** [Conforming to rules of grammar] grammatically correct, conventional, accepted; see CONVENTIONAL 1.

grand ***a.*** lofty, stately, dignified, elevated, high, regal, noble, illustrious, sublime, great, ambitious, august, majestic, solemn, grave, preeminent, extraordinary, monumental, stupendous, huge, chief, commanding, towering, overwhelming, impressive, imposing, awe-inspiring, mighty, terrific*.—*Ant.* POOR, low, mediocre.

grandeur ***n.*** splendor, magnificence, pomp, circumstance, impressiveness, eminence, distinction, fame, glory, brilliancy, richness, luxury, stateliness, beauty, ceremony, importance, celebrity, solemnity, fineness, majesty, sublimity, nobility, scope, dignity, elevation, preeminence, height, greatness, might, breadth, immensity, amplitude, vastness.

grandfather ***n.*** elder, forefather, ancestor, patriarch, grandpa*, granddaddy*, grandpappy*, gramps*.

grandmother ***n.*** matriarch, dowager, ancestor, nana*, grandma*, gram*, granny*.

grant ***n.*** gift, boon, reward, present, allowance, stipend, donation, matching grant, benefaction, gratuity, endowment, concession, bequest, privilege, subsidy.—*Ant.* DISCOUNT, deprivation, deduction.

grant ***v.*** **1** [To permit] yield, cede, impart; see ALLOW. **2** [To accept as true] concede, accede, acquiesce; see ACKNOWLEDGE 2.

granted ***a.*** **1** [Awarded] conferred, bestowed, awarded; see GIVEN. **2** [Allowed] accepted, admitted, acknowledged; see ASSUMED. **—take for granted** accept, presume, consider settled; see ASSUME.

grape ***n.*** wine grape, raisin, Concord grape; see FRUIT.

grape'vine' ***n.*** **1** a woody vine bearing grapes **2** a secret means of spreading information **3** a rumor

graph (graf) ***n.*** ⟦< *graph(ic formula)*⟧ a diagram representing quantitative information and relationships, such as successive changes in a variable quantity —***vt.*** to represent by a graph

-graph (graf) ⟦< Gr *graphein*, to write⟧ *combining form* **1** something that writes or records *[telegraph]* **2** something written, etc. *[monograph]*

graph·ic (graf'ik) ***adj.*** ⟦< Gr *graphein*, to write⟧ **1** described in realistic detail; vivid **2** of those arts (**graphic arts**) that include any form of visual artistic representation, esp. painting, drawing, etching, etc. Also **graph'i·cal** —**graph'i·cal·ly** ***adv.***

graph'ics ***n.*** **1** design as employed in the graphic arts **2** the graphic arts

graph·ite (graf'īt') ***n.*** ⟦< Gr *graphein*, to write⟧ a soft, black form of carbon used in pencils, electrodes, etc.

graph·ol·o·gy (graf äl'ə jē) ***n.*** ⟦< Fr: see GRAPHIC & -LOGY⟧ the study of handwriting, esp. as a clue to character —**graph·ol'o·gist** ***n.***

-gra·phy (grə fē) ⟦< Gr *graphein*, to write⟧ *combining form* **1** a process or method of writing or graphically representing *[calligraphy]* **2** a descriptive science *[geography]*

grap·nel (grap'nəl) ***n.*** ⟦< Prov *grapa*, a hook⟧ a small anchor with several curved, pointed arms

grap·ple (grap'əl) ***n.*** ⟦OFr *grapil*⟧ **1** GRAPNEL **2** a hand-to-hand fight —***vt.*** **-pled, -pling** to grip and hold —***vi.*** **1** to use a GRAPNEL **2** to wrestle **3** to try to cope (*with*)

grappling iron (or **hook**) GRAPNEL

grasp (grasp) ***vt.*** ⟦ME *graspen*⟧ **1** to grip, as with the hand **2** to take hold of eagerly; seize **3** to comprehend —***vi.*** **1** to try to seize: with *at* **2** to accept eagerly: with *at* —***n.*** **1** a grasping; grip **2** control; possession **3** the power to hold or seize **4** comprehension —**grasp'a·ble** ***adj.***

grasp'ing ***adj.*** avaricious; greedy

grass (gras, gräs) ***n.*** ⟦OE *græs*⟧ **1** a plant with long, narrow leaves, jointed stems, and seedlike fruit, as wheat or rye **2** any of various green plants with narrow leaves, growing densely in meadows, lawns, etc. **3** pasture or lawn **4** [Slang] marijuana —**grass'y, -i·er, -i·est,** ***adj.***

grass'hop'per ***n.*** any of various winged, plant-eating insects with powerful hind legs for jumping

grass roots [Inf.] **1** the common people **2** the basic source or support, as of a movement —**grass'-roots'** ***adj.***

grass widow a woman divorced or separated from her husband

grate[1] (grāt) ***vt.*** **grat'ed, grat'ing** ⟦< OFr *grater*⟧ **1** to grind into particles by scraping **2** to rub against (an object) or grind (the teeth) together with a harsh sound **3** to irritate; annoy; fret —***vi.*** **1** to rub with or make a rasping sound **2** to be irritating —**grat'er** ***n.***

grate[2] (grāt) ***n.*** ⟦< L *cratis*, a hurdle⟧ **1** GRATING[1] **2** a frame of metal bars for holding fuel in a fireplace, etc. **3** a fireplace

grate·ful (grāt'fəl) ***adj.*** ⟦obs. *grate*, pleasing (< L *gratus*)⟧ **1** thankful **2** welcome —**grate'ful·ly** ***adv.*** —**grate'ful·ness** ***n.***

grat·i·fy (grat'i fī') ***vt.*** **-fied', -fy'ing** ⟦< L *gratus*, pleasing + *-ficare*, -FY⟧ **1** to please or satisfy **2** to indulge; humor —**grat'i·fi·ca'tion** ***n.*** —**grat'i·fy'ing** ***adj.***

grat·ing[1] (grāt'iŋ) ***n.*** a framework of bars set in a window, door, etc.

grat'ing[2] ***adj.*** **1** rasping **2** irritating

gra·tis (grat'is, grät'-) ***adv., adj.*** ⟦L < *gratia*, a favor⟧ free of charge

grat·i·tude (grat'i to͞od') ***n.*** ⟦< L *gratus*, pleasing⟧ thankful appreciation for favors or benefits received

gra·tu·i·tous (grə to͞o'i təs, -tyo͞o'-) ***adj.*** ⟦< L *gratus*, pleasing⟧ **1** given free of charge **2** uncalled-for —**gra·tu'i·tous·ly** ***adv.***

gra·tu'i·ty (-tē) ***n.***, *pl.* **-ties** a gift of money for a service; tip

gra·va·men (grə vā'mən) ***n.***, *pl.* **-mens** or **gra·vam'i·na** (-vam'i nə) ⟦LL, a burden⟧ *Law* the essential part of a complaint or accusation

grave[1] (grāv) ***adj.*** **grav'er, grav'est** ⟦< L *gravis*, heavy⟧ **1** important **2** serious *[a grave illness]* **3** solemn or sedate **4** somber; dull —**grave'ly** ***adv.*** —**grave'ness** ***n.***

grave[2] (grāv) ***n.*** ⟦< OE *grafan*, to dig⟧ **1** *a)* a hole in the ground in which to bury a dead body *b)* any burial place; tomb **2** death —***vt.*** **graved, grav'en** or **graved, grav'ing** **1** [Archaic] to sculpture or engrave **2** to impress sharply

grave accent (gräv, grāv) a mark (ˋ) showing stress, the quality of a vowel, etc.

grav·el (grav'əl) ***n.*** ⟦< OFr *grave*, coarse sand⟧ a loose mixture of pebbles and rock fragments coarser than sand

grav'el·ly (-ē) ***adj.*** **1** full of or like gravel **2** harsh or rasping *[a gravelly voice]*

grav·en (grāv'ən) ***vt.*** *alt. pp. of* GRAVE[2]

grave'stone' ***n.*** a tombstone

grave'yard' ***n.*** a cemetery

graveyard shift [Inf.] work shift at night, esp. one starting at midnight

grav·id (grav'id) ***adj.*** ⟦< L *gravis*, heavy⟧ pregnant

gra·vim·e·ter (grə vim'ət ər) ***n.*** ⟦< L *gravis*, heavy + Fr *-mètre*, -METER⟧ **1** a device for determining specific gravity **2** an instrument for measuring the earth's gravitational pull

grav·i·tate (grav'i tāt') ***vi.*** **-tat'ed, -tat'ing** **1** to move or tend to move in accordance with the force of gravity **2** to be attracted (*toward*)

grav'i·ta'tion ***n.*** **1** a gravitating **2** *Physics* the force by which every mass attracts and is attracted by every other mass —**grav'i·ta'tion·al** ***adj.***

grav·i·ty (grav'i tē) ***n.***, *pl.* **-ties** ⟦< L *gravis*, heavy⟧ **1** graveness; seriousness **2** weight *[specific gravity]* **3** *Physics* gravitation; esp., the pull on all bodies in the earth's sphere toward the earth's center

gra·vy (grā'vē) ***n.***, *pl.* **-vies** ⟦< ?⟧ **1** the juice given off by meat in cooking **2** a sauce made from this juice **3** [Slang] any benefit beyond what is expected

gray (grā) ***n.*** ⟦< OE *græg*⟧ a color that is a blend of black and white —***adj.*** **1** of this color **2** having hair this color

THESAURUS

graph ***n.*** diagram, chart, linear representation; see DESIGN, PLAN 1.

graphic ***a.*** **1** [Pictorial] visible, illustrated, descriptive, photographic, visual, depicted, limned, seen, drawn, portrayed, traced, sketched, outlined, pictured, painted, engraved, etched, chiseled, penciled, printed.—*Ant.* UNREAL, imagined, chimerical. **2** [Vivid] forcible, telling, picturesque, intelligible, comprehensible, clear, explicit, striking, definite, distinct, precise, expressive, eloquent, moving, stirring, concrete, energetic, colorful, strong, figurative, poetic.—*Ant.* OBSCURE, ambiguous, abstract.

grasp ***v.*** **1** [To clutch] grip, enclose, clasp; see SEIZE 1, 2. **2** [To comprehend] perceive, apprehend, follow; see UNDERSTAND 1.

grasp ***n.*** hold, clutch, cinch; see GRIP 2.

grass ***n.*** **1** [Plant for food, grazing, etc.] *Wild grasses include the following:* Johnson grass, salt grass, bluegrass, foxtail, buffalo grass, sandbur, crab grass, deer grass, bunch grass, meadow grass, fescue, orchard grass, pampas grass, June grass, redtop, river grass, ribbon grass, sweet grass, cattail, wild rice. **2** [Grassed area] grassland, meadow, lawn, sward, turf, pasture, prairie, hayfield; see also FIELD 1, YARD 1. **3** [*A drug] marijuana, cannabis, pot*; see DRUG.

grassy ***a.*** grass-grown, verdant, green, reedy, lush, matted, tangled, carpeted, sowed, luxuriant, deep.

grate[1] ***v.*** rasp, grind, abrade; see RUB 1.

grateful ***a.*** appreciative, pleased, obliged; see THANKFUL.

gratefully ***a.*** appreciatively, thankfully, obligingly, delightedly, responsively, admiringly.—*Ant.* RUDELY, ungratefully, thanklessly.

gratitude ***n.*** thankfulness, appreciation, acknowledgment, response, sense of indebtedness, feeling of obligation, responsiveness, thanks, praise, recognition, honor, thanksgiving, grace.—*Ant.* INDIFFERENCE, ingratitude, thanklessness.

grave[1] ***a.*** **1** [Important] momentous, weighty, consequential; see IMPORTANT 1. **2** [Dangerous] critical, serious, ominous; see DANGEROUS. **3** [Solemn] serious, sober, earnest; see SOLEMN.

grave[2] ***n.*** vault, sepulcher, tomb, pit, crypt, mausoleum, catacomb, long home*, six feet of earth, final resting place, place of interment, mound, burial place, charnel house, last home*. —**make one turn (over) in one's grave** do something shocking, sin, err; see MISBEHAVE.

gravel ***n.*** sand, pebbles, shale, macadam, screenings, crushed rock, washings, alluvium, tailings.

graveyard ***n.*** burial ground, necropolis, churchyard; see CEMETERY.

gravity ***n.*** **1** [Weight] heaviness, pressure, force; see PRESSURE 1. **2** [Importance] seriousness, concern, significance; see IMPORTANCE.

gravy ***n.*** sauce, dressing, brown gravy, white gravy, milk gravy, pan gravy, chicken gravy, meat gravy.

gray ***a.*** neutral, dusky, silvery,

3 *a*) darkish; dull *b*) dreary; dismal 4 designating a vague, intermediate area —*vt.*, *vi.* to make or become gray —**gray'ish** *adj.* —**gray'ness** *n.*

gray'beard' *n.* an old man

gray matter 1 grayish nerve tissue of the brain and spinal cord 2 [Inf.] intellectual capacity; brains

graze[1] (grāz) *vt.* **grazed, graz'ing** ⟦< OE *græs*, grass⟧ 1 to put livestock to feed on (growing grass, etc.) 2 to tend (feeding livestock) —*vi.* to feed on growing grass, etc.

graze[2] (grāz) *vt.*, *vi.* **grazed, graz'ing** ⟦prob. < prec.⟧ to scrape or rub lightly in passing —*n.* a grazing

Gr Brit or **Gr Br** Great Britain

grease (grēs; *for v., also* grēz) *n.* ⟦< L *crassus*, fat⟧ 1 melted animal fat 2 any thick, oily substance or lubricant —*vt.* **greased, greas'ing** to smear or lubricate with grease

grease'paint' *n.* greasy coloring matter used in making up for the stage

greas·y (grē'sē, -zē) *adj.* **-i·er, -i·est** 1 soiled with grease 2 containing much grease 3 oily —**greas'i·ness** *n.*

great (grāt) *adj.* ⟦OE⟧ 1 of much more than ordinary size, extent, etc. *[the Great Lakes]* 2 much above the average; esp., *a*) intense *[great pain]* *b*) eminent *[a great writer]* 3 most important; main 4 [Inf.] skillful: often with *at* 5 [Inf.] excellent; fine —*n.* a distinguished person —**great'ly** *adv.* —**great'ness** *n.*

great- *combining form* older (or younger) by one generation *[great-aunt, great-great-grandson]*

great ape any of a family of primates consisting of the gorilla, chimpanzee, and orangutan

Great Britain principal island of the United Kingdom, including England, Scotland, & Wales

Great Dane a very large, muscular dog with a short, smooth coat

great'-grand'child' *n.*, *pl.* **-chil'dren** a child of any of one's grandchildren

great'-grand'par'ent *n.* a parent of any of one's grandparents

great'heart'ed *adj.* 1 brave; fearless 2 generous; unselfish

Great Lakes chain of five freshwater lakes in EC North America

Great Salt Lake shallow saltwater lake in NW Utah

grebe (grēb) *n.* ⟦Fr *grèbe*⟧ a diving and swimming bird with broadly lobed webbed feet

Gre·cian (grē'shən) *adj.*, *n.* GREEK

Greco- ⟦< L *Graecus*⟧ *combining form* Greek, Greek and *[Greco-Roman]*

Greece (grēs) country in the S Balkan Peninsula, on the Mediterranean: 50,949 sq. mi.; pop. 10,260,000

greed (grēd) *n.* ⟦< fol.⟧ excessive desire, esp. for wealth; avarice

greed·y (grēd'ē) *adj.* **-i·er, -i·est** ⟦OE *grædig*⟧ 1 desiring more than one needs or deserves 2 having too strong a desire for food and drink; gluttonous —**greed'i·ly** *adv.* —**greed'i·ness** *n.*

Greek (grēk) *n.* 1 a person born or living in Greece 2 the language, ancient or modern, of the Greeks —*adj.* of Greece or its people, language, etc.

green (grēn) *adj.* ⟦OE *grene*⟧ 1 of the color of growing grass 2 overspread with green plants or foliage 3 sickly or bilious 4 unripe 5 inexperienced or naive 6 not dried or seasoned 7 [Inf.] jealous —*n.* 1 the color of growing grass 2 [*pl.*] green leafy vegetables, as spinach 3 an area of smooth turf *[a putting green]* —**green'ish** *adj.* —**green'ly** *adv.* —**green'ness** *n.*

green'back' *n.* any piece of U.S. paper money printed in green ink on the back

Green Bay city & port in Wisconsin: pop 96,000

green bean the edible, immature green pod of the kidney bean

green'belt' *n.* a beltlike area around a city, reserved for park land or farms

green'er·y *n.* green vegetation; verdure

green'-eyed' *adj.* very jealous

green'gro'cer *n.* [Brit.] a retail dealer in fresh vegetables and fruit

green'horn' *n.* 1 an inexperienced person 2 a person easily deceived

green'house' *n.* a heated building, mainly of glass, for growing plants

greenhouse effect the warming of the earth and its lower atmosphere, caused by trapped solar radiation

Green·land (grēn'lənd) self-governing Danish island northeast of North America

green light [Inf.] permission to proceed with some undertaking —**green'light'**, **-light'ed** or **-lit'**, **-light'ing**, *vt.*

green manure a crop, as of clover, plowed under to fertilize the soil

green onion an immature onion with green leaves, often eaten raw; scallion

green pepper the green immature fruit of a red pepper, esp. the bell pepper

green power money as the source of economic power

Greens·bor·o (grēnz'bur'ō) city in NC North Carolina: pop. 184,000

green'sward' *n.* green, grassy turf

green thumb a talent for growing plants

Green·wich (gren'ich; *chiefly Brit,* grin'ij) borough of London, on the prime meridian: pop. 208,000

Green·wich Village (gren'ich) section of New York City: noted as a center for artists, writers, etc.

green'wood' *n.* a forest in leaf

greet (grēt) *vt.* ⟦OE *gretan*⟧ 1 to address with friendliness 2 to meet or receive (a person, event, etc.) in a specified way 3 to come or appear to; meet —**greet'er** *n.*

THESAURUS

dingy, somber, shaded, drab, leaden, grayish, ashen, grizzled. *Shades of gray include the following:* blue-gray, silver-gray, smoke-gray, slate, charcoal, mouse-colored, iron-gray, lead, ash-gray, pepper-and-salt, dusty, smoky.

gray *n.* shade, drabness, dusk; see COLOR.

graze[1,2] *v.* 1 [To touch or score lightly] brush, scrape, rub; see TOUCH 1. 2 [To pasture] browse, feed, crop, gnaw, nibble, bite, uproot, pull grass, forage, eat, munch, ruminate, chew cud.

grazing *a.* cropping, feeding, gnawing, nibbling, biting, uprooting, pasturing, pulling grass, foraging, eating, munching, ruminating, chewing cud.

grease *n.* oil, wax, lubricant, salve, petrolatum, petroleum jelly, animal fat, lard, shortening, suet, hydrogenated oil, axle grease, suint; see also OIL 1.

grease *v.* oil, lubricate, smear, salve, coat with oil, cream, pomade, grease the wheels, anoint, swab.

greasy *a.* creamy, oleaginous, fatty; see OILY 1.

great *a.* 1 [Eminent] noble, grand, majestic, dignified, exalted, commanding, famous, renowned, widely acclaimed, famed, celebrated, distinguished, noted, conspicuous, elevated, prominent, high, stately, honorable, magnificent, glorious, regal, royal, kingly, imposing, preeminent, unrivaled, fabulous, fabled, legendary, storied.—*Ant.* OBSCURE, retired, anonymous. 2 [Large] numerous, big, vast; see LARGE 1. 3 [*Excellent] exceptional, first-rate, top-notch*; see EXCELLENT.

greatly *a.* exceedingly, considerably, hugely; see VERY.

greatness *n.* 1 [Eminence] prominence, renown, importance; see FAME. 2 [Size] bulk, extent, largeness; see SIZE 2.

greed *n.* greediness, selfishness, eagerness, voracity, excess, gluttony, piggishness, indulgence, hoggishness, niggardliness, acquisitiveness, intemperance, covetousness, desire.—*Ant.* GENEROSITY, liberality, kindness.

greedy *a.* avid, grasping, rapacious, selfish, miserly, parsimonious, close, closefisted, tight, tightfisted, niggardly, exploitative, grudging, devouring, ravenous, omnivorous, intemperate, gobbling, indulging one's appetites, mercenary, stingy, covetous, grabby*, penny-pinching.—*Ant.* GENEROUS, munificent, bountiful.

Greek *a.* Grecian, Hellenic, Hellenistic, Minoan, Dorian, Attic, Athenian, Spartan, Peloponnesian, Ionian, Corinthian, Thessalian, Boeotian, Homeric, ancient, classic; see also CLASSICAL 2.

Greek *n.* 1 [A citizen of Greece] Hellene, Athenian, Spartan; see EUROPEAN. 2 [The Greek language] Hellenic, Ionic, koine; see LANGUAGE 1.

green *a.* 1 [Of the color green] *Tints and shades of green include the following:* emerald, blue-green, sage, aquamarine, chartreuse, lime, kelly, bronze-green, yellow-green, bottle-green, pea-green, sea-green, apple-green, grass-green, forest-green, moss-green, spinach-green, pine-green, olive-green, jade. 2 [Verdant] growing, leafy, grassy, flourishing, lush. 3 [Immature] young, growing, unripe, sprouting, maturing, developing, half-formed, fresh.—*Ant.* MATURE, ripe, gone to seed. 4 [Inexperienced] youthful, callow, raw; see INEXPERIENCED.

green *n.* greenness, verdure, virescence; see COLOR.

greet *v.* welcome, speak to, salute, address, hail, recognize, embrace, shake hands, nod, receive, call to, stop, acknowledge, bow to, approach, give one's love, hold out one's hand, herald, bid good day, bid hello, bid

greet'ing *n.* 1 the act or words of one who greets 2 [*often pl.*] a message of regards
greeting card CARD[1] (*n.* 1d)
gre·gar·i·ous (grə ger'ē əs) *adj.* ⟦< L *grex*, herd⟧ 1 living in herds 2 fond of the company of others; sociable —**gre·gar'i·ous·ly** *adv.* —**gre·gar'i·ous·ness** *n.*
Gre·go·ri·an calendar (grə gôr'ē ən) the calendar now widely used, introduced by Pope Gregory XIII in 1582
Gregorian chant ⟦after Pope Gregory I⟧ a kind of plainsong formerly widely used in the Roman Catholic Church
grem·lin (grem'lin) *n.* ⟦prob. < Dan *gram*, a devil⟧ a small imaginary creature humorously blamed for malfunctions or disruptions
Gre·na·da (grə nā'də) country on an island group in the West Indies: 133 sq. mi.; pop. 95,000
gre·nade (grə nād') *n.* ⟦Fr < OFr, pomegranate⟧ a small bomb detonated by a fuse and usually thrown by hand
gren·a·dier (gren'ə dir') *n.* 1 [Archaic] a soldier who threw grenades 2 a member of a special regiment or corps
gren·a·dine (gren'ə dēn') *n.* ⟦Fr⟧ a red syrup made from pomegranate juice
grew (grōō) *vi., vt. pt. of* GROW
grey (grā) *n., adj., vt., vi. chiefly Brit. sp. of* GRAY
grey'hound' *n.* a tall, slender, swift dog with a narrow head
grid (grid) *n.* ⟦short for GRIDIRON⟧ 1 a framework of parallel bars; grating 2 a metallic plate in a storage battery 3 an electrode, in spiral or gridlike shape, for controlling the flow of electrons in an electron tube
grid·dle (grid''l) *n.* ⟦< L *craticula*, gridiron⟧ a flat, heavy metal pan for cooking pancakes, etc.
grid'dle·cake' *n.* a pancake
grid·i·ron (grid'ī'ərn) *n.* ⟦see GRIDDLE⟧ 1 GRILL (*n.* 1) 2 a football field
grid'lock' *n.* a traffic jam in which no vehicle can move in any direction
grief (grēf) *n.* ⟦see GRIEVE⟧ 1 intense emotional suffering caused as by a loss 2 a cause of such suffering —**come to grief** to fail or be ruined
griev·ance (grēv'əns) *n.* 1 a circumstance thought to be unjust and ground for complaint 2 complaint against a real or imagined wrong
grieve (grēv) *vi., vt.* **grieved**, **griev'ing** ⟦< L *gravis*, heavy⟧ to feel or cause to feel grief
griev·ous (grēv'əs) *adj.* 1 causing grief 2 showing or full of grief 3 severe 4 deplorable; atrocious —**griev'ous·ly** *adv.*
grif·fin (grif'in) *n.* ⟦< Gr *gryps*⟧ a mythical monster, part lion and part eagle
grill (gril) *n.* ⟦see GRIDDLE⟧ 1 a unit for broiling meat, etc., consisting of a framework of metal bars or wires 2 a large griddle 3 grilled food 4 a restaurant that specializes in grilled foods —*vt.* 1 to broil 2 to question relentlessly
grille (gril) *n.* ⟦see GRIDDLE⟧ an open grating forming a screen
grim (grim) *adj.* **grim'mer**, **grim'mest** ⟦OE *grimm*⟧ 1 hard and unyielding; stern 2 appearing forbidding, harsh, etc. 3 repellent; ghastly —**grim'ly** *adv.* —**grim'ness** *n.*
gri·mace (gri mās', grim'is) *n.* ⟦Fr⟧ a distortion of the face, as in expressing pain, disgust, etc. —*vi.* **-maced'**, **-mac'ing** to make grimaces
grime (grīm) *n.* ⟦prob. < Fl *grijm*⟧ dirt rubbed into or covering a surface, as of the skin —**grim'y**, **-i·er**, **-i·est**, *adj.* —**grim'i·ness** *n.*
Grimm (grim) 1 **Ja·kob** (**Ludwig Karl**) (yä'kôp) 1785-1863; Ger. philologist 2 **Wil·helm** (**Karl**) (vil'helm) 1786-1859; Ger. philologist: brother of Jakob, with whom he collected fairy tales
grin (grin) *vi.* **grinned**, **grin'ning** ⟦< OE *grennian*, bare the teeth⟧ 1 to smile broadly as in amusement 2 to show the teeth in pain, scorn, etc. —*n.* the act or look of grinning
grind (grīnd) *vt.* **ground**, **grind'ing** ⟦OE *grindan*⟧ 1 to crush or chop into fine particles; pulverize 2 to oppress 3 to sharpen or smooth by friction 4 to rub (the teeth, etc.) together gratingly 5 to operate by turning the crank of —*n.* 1 a grinding 2 long, difficult work or study 3 [Inf.] a student who studies hard —**grind out** to produce by steady or laborious effort
grind·er (grīn'dər) *n.* 1 a person or thing that grinds 2 [*pl.*] [Inf.] the teeth 3 *chiefly New England var. of* HERO SANDWICH
grind'stone' *n.* a revolving stone disk for sharpening tools or polishing things —**keep one's nose to the grindstone** to work hard and steadily
grip (grip) *n.* ⟦< OE *grīpan*, seize⟧ 1 a secure grasp; firm hold 2 the manner of holding a club, bat, etc. 3 the power of grasping firmly 4 mental grasp 5 firm control 6 a handle 7 a small traveling bag —*vt.* **gripped** or **gript**, **grip'ping** 1 to take firmly and hold fast 2 to get and hold the attention of —*vi.* to get a grip —**come to grips** to struggle (*with*) —**grip'per** *n.*
gripe (grīp) *vt.* **griped**, **grip'ing** ⟦OE *grīpan*, seize⟧ 1 to cause sharp pain in the bowels of 2 [Slang] to annoy —*vi.* [Slang] to complain —*n.* 1 a sharp pain in the bowels: *usually used in pl.* 2 [Slang] a complaint —**grip'er** *n.*
grippe (grip) *n.* ⟦Fr⟧ *former term for* INFLUENZA
gris-gris (grē'grē') *n., pl.* **gris'-gris'** ⟦of Afr orig.⟧ an amulet, charm, or spell of African origin
gris·ly (griz'lē) *adj.* **-li·er**, **-li·est** ⟦OE *grislic*⟧ terrifying; ghastly —**gris'li·ness** *n.*
grist (grist) *n.* ⟦OE⟧ grain that is to be or has been ground
gris·tle (gris'əl) *n.* ⟦OE⟧ cartilage, esp. as found in meat —**gris'tly** (-lē) *adj.*
grist'mill' *n.* a mill for grinding grain
grit (grit) *n.* ⟦< OE *greot*⟧ 1 rough particles, as of sand 2 coarse sandstone 3 stubborn courage; pluck —*vt.* **grit'ted**, **grit'ting** to clench or grind (the teeth) as in determination —*vi.* to make a grating sound —**grit'ty**, **-ti·er**, **-ti·est**, *adj.*

THESAURUS

welcome, exchange greetings, usher in, attend, pay one's respects.—*Ant.* IGNORE, snub, slight.

greeting *n.* welcome, address, notice, speaking to, ushering in, acknowledgment, one's compliments, regards. *Common greetings include the following:* hello, how do you do, how are you, good morning, good day, good afternoon, good evening, hi*, hey*, yo*.

grey *a.* dun, drab, grayish; see GRAY.

grief *n.* sorrow, sadness, regret, melancholy, mourning, misery, trouble, anguish, despondency, pain, worry, harassment, anxiety, woe, heartache, malaise, disquiet, discomfort, affliction, gloom, unhappiness, desolation, despair, agony, torture, purgatory.—*Ant.* HAPPINESS, exhilaration, pleasure.

grievance *n.* complaint, injury, case; see OBJECTION.

grieve *v.* lament, bewail, sorrow for; see MOURN.

grill *v.* roast, sauté, barbecue; see COOK.

grim *a.* 1 [Sullen] sour, crusty, gloomy, sulky, morose, churlish, forbidding, glum, grumpy, scowling, grouchy, crabby, glowering, stubborn, cantankerous.—*Ant.* HAPPY, cheerful, gay. 2 [Stern] austere, strict, harsh; see SEVERE 1. 3 [Relentless] unrelenting, implacable, inexorable; see SEVERE 2.

grimace *n.* smirk, smile, sneer; see EXPRESSION 4.

grime *n.* soil, smudge, dirt; see FILTH.

grimy *a.* begrimed, dingy, soiled; see DIRTY 1.

grin *n.* smirk, simper, delighted look; see SMILE.

grin *v.* smirk, simper, beam; see SMILE.

grind *v.* crush, powder, mill, grate, granulate, disintegrate, rasp, scrape, file, abrade, pound, reduce to fine particles, crunch, roll out, pound out, chop up, crumble.—*Ant.* ORGANIZE, mold, solidify.

grinding *a.* abrasive, crushing, pulverizing, grating, rasping, rubbing, milling, powdering, cracking, bone-crushing, crunching, splintering, shivering, smashing, crumbling, scraping, chopping, wearing away, eroding.

grip *n.* 1 [The power and the application of the power to grip] grasp, hold, manual strength, clutch, clasp, catch, cinch, vise, clench, clinch, embrace, handhold, fist, handshake, anchor, squeeze, wrench, grab, fixing, fastening, crushing, clamp, vicelike grip, jaws. 2 [Something suited to grasping] knocker, knob, ear; see HANDLE 1. 3 [A traveling bag] valise, suitcase, satchel; see BAG. —**come to grips** engage, encounter, cope with; see FIGHT, TRY 1.

grip *v.* clutch, grasp, clasp; see SEIZE 1.

gripe* *n.* complaint, grievance, beef*; see OBJECTION.

gripe* *v.* grumble, mutter, fuss; see COMPLAIN.

grit *n.* sand, dust, crushed rock; see GRAVEL.

gritty *a.* rough, abrasive, sandy, rasping, lumpy, gravelly, muddy, dusty, powdery, granular, crumbly, loose, scratchy.

grits (grits) ***pl.n.*** ⟦OE *grytte*⟧ [*often with sing. v.*] coarsely ground grain; esp., hominy
griz·zled (griz′əld) ***adj.*** ⟦< OFr *gris*, gray⟧ **1** gray or streaked with gray **2** having gray hair
griz′zly (-lē) ***adj.*** **-zli·er, -zli·est** grayish; grizzled
grizzly (bear) a large, brown bear of W North America
groan (grōn) ***vi., vt.*** ⟦< OE *granian*⟧ to utter (with) a deep sound expressing pain, distress, etc. —***n.*** such a sound
gro·cer (grō′sər) ***n.*** ⟦< OFr *grossier*⟧ a dealer in food and household supplies
gro′cer·y ***n.***, *pl.* **-ies** **1** a grocer's store **2** [*pl.*] the food and supplies sold by a grocer
grog (gräg) ***n.*** ⟦after Old *Grog*, nickname of an 18th-c. Brit admiral⟧ **1** rum diluted with water **2** any alcoholic liquor
grog′gy ***adj.*** **-gi·er, -gi·est** ⟦< prec. + -Y[2]⟧ **1** [Archaic] intoxicated **2** dizzy **3** sluggish or dull —**grog′gi·ly** ***adv.*** —**grog′gi·ness** ***n.***
groin (groin) ***n.*** ⟦prob. < OE *grynde*, abyss⟧ **1** the fold where the abdomen joins either thigh **2** *Archit.* the sharp, curved edge at the junction of two vaults
grom·met (gräm′it) ***n.*** ⟦< obs. Fr *gromette*, a curb⟧ **1** a ring of rope **2** a metal eyelet in cloth, etc.
groom (groom) ***n.*** ⟦ME *grom*, boy⟧ **1** one whose work is tending horses **2** a bridegroom —***vt.*** **1** to clean and curry (a horse, etc.) **2** to make neat and tidy **3** to train for a particular purpose
groove (groov) ***n.*** ⟦< ON *grof*, a pit⟧ **1** a long, narrow furrow cut with a tool **2** any channel or rut **3** a settled routine —***vt.*** **grooved, groov′ing** to make a groove in
groov′y ***adj.*** **-i·er, -i·est** [Slang] very pleasing or attractive
grope (grōp) ***vi.*** **groped, grop′ing** ⟦< OE *grapian*, to touch⟧ to feel or search about blindly or uncertainly —***vt.*** **1** to seek or find (one's way) by groping **2** [Slang] to fondle sexually —**grop′er** ***n.*** —**grop′ing·ly** ***adv.***
gros·beak (grōs′bēk′) ***n.*** ⟦Fr: see GROSS & BEAK⟧ a songbird with a thick, strong, conical bill
gros·grain (grō′grān′) ***n.*** ⟦Fr, lit., coarse grain⟧ a ribbed silk or rayon fabric for ribbons, etc.
gross (grōs) ***adj.*** ⟦< LL *grossus*, thick⟧ **1** fat and coarse-looking **2** flagrant; very bad **3** lacking in refinement **4** vulgar; coarse **5** with no deductions; total **6** [Slang] disgusting —***n.*** **1** *pl.* **gross′es** overall total **2** *pl.* **gross** twelve dozen —***vt., vi.*** to earn (a specified total amount) before expenses are deducted —**gross out** [Slang] to disgust —**gross′ly** ***adv.***
gross national product the total value of a nation's annual output of goods and services
gro·tesque (grō tesk′) ***adj.*** ⟦< It *grotta*, grotto: from designs found in caves⟧ **1** distorted or fantastic in appearance, shape, etc. **2** ridiculous; absurd —**gro·tesque′ly** ***adv.***
grot·to (grät′ō) ***n.***, *pl.* **-toes** or **-tos** ⟦< It < L *crypta*, crypt⟧ **1** a cave **2** a cavelike summerhouse, shrine, etc.
grouch (grouch) ***vi.*** ⟦< ME *grucchen*⟧ to grumble or complain sulkily —***n.*** **1** one who grouches **2** a sulky mood —**grouch′y, -i·er, -i·est,** ***adj.*** —**grouch′i·ly** ***adv.*** —**grouch′i·ness** ***n.***
ground[1] (ground) ***n.*** ⟦OE *grund*, bottom⟧ **1** the solid surface of the earth **2** soil; earth **3** [*often pl.*] a tract of land [*grounds* of an estate] **4** area, as of discussion **5** [*often pl.*] basis; foundation **6** valid reason or motive: *often used in pl.* **7** the background, as in a design **8** [*pl.*] sediment [coffee *grounds*] **9** the connection of an electrical conductor with a ground —***adj.*** of, on, or near the ground —***vt.*** **1** to set on the ground **2** to cause to run aground **3** to base; found; establish **4** to instruct in the first principles of **5** *a*) to keep (an aircraft or pilot) from flying *b*) [Inf.] to punish (a teenager) by not permitting him or her to leave home for dates, etc. **6** *Elec.* to connect (a conductor) to a ground —***vi.*** **1** to run ashore **2** *Baseball* to be put out on a grounder: usually with *out* —**break ground** **1** to dig; excavate **2** to plow **3** to start building —**gain (or lose) ground** to gain (or lose) in achievement, popularity, etc. —**give ground** to retreat; yield —**hold** (or **stand**) **one's ground** to remain firm, not yielding
ground[2] (ground) ***vt., vi.*** *pt. & pp. of* GRIND
ground control personnel and equipment on the ground, for guiding airplanes and spacecraft in takeoff, landing, etc.
ground cover low, dense-growing plants used for covering bare ground
ground crew a group of workers who maintain and repair aircraft
ground′er ***n.*** *Baseball* a batted ball that travels along the ground: also **ground ball**
ground floor that floor of a building approximately level with the ground; first floor —**in on the ground floor** [Inf.] in at the start (of a business, etc.)
ground glass nontransparent glass with a surface that has been ground to diffuse light
ground′hog′ ***n.*** WOODCHUCK: also **ground hog**
ground′less ***adj.*** without reason or cause
ground rule **1** *Baseball* a rule adapted to playing conditions in a specific ballpark **2** any basic rule
ground′swell′ ***n.*** **1** a violent rolling of the ocean **2** a wave of popular feeling
ground′wa′ter ***n.*** water found underground
ground′work′ ***n.*** a foundation; basis
group (groop) ***n.*** ⟦< It *gruppo*⟧ a number of persons or things gathered or classified together —***vt., vi.*** to form into a group or groups
grou·per (groo′pər) ***n.*** ⟦Port *garupa*⟧ a large sea bass found in warm seas
group·ie (groo′pē) ***n.*** [Inf.] **1** a female fan of rock groups or other popular personalities, who follows them about **2** a fan; devotee
group therapy (or **psychotherapy**) a form of treatment for a group of patients with similar emotional problems, as by group discussions

THESAURUS

groan ***n.*** moan, sob, grunt; see CRY 1.
groan ***v.*** moan, murmur, keen; see CRY 1.
groceries ***n.*** food, edibles, produce, comestibles, foodstuffs, perishables, vegetables, staples, green groceries, fruits, dairy products, processed foods, frozen foods, freeze-dried foods, dried foods, packaged foods, canned foods.
grocery ***n.*** food store, vegetable market, supermarket; see MARKET 1.
groggy ***a.*** sleepy, dizzy, reeling; see TIRED.
groom ***n.*** bridegroom, married man, newlywed; see HUSBAND.
groom ***v.*** rub down, comb, brush; see PREPARE 1.
groove ***n.*** channel, trench, gouge, depression, scratch, canal, valley, notch, furrow, rut, incision, slit, gutter, ditch, crease. —**in the groove*** efficient, skillful, operative; see WORKING 1.
grope ***v.*** fumble, touch, feel blindly; see FEEL 1.
gross ***a.*** **1** [Fat] corpulent, obese, huge; see FAT. **2** [Obscene] foul, swinish, indecent; see LEWD 1, 2. **3** [Without deduction] in sum, total, entire; see WHOLE 1.
gross ***n.*** total, aggregate, total amount; see WHOLE.
gross ***v.*** earn, bring in, take in; see EARN 2.
grotesque ***a.*** malformed, ugly, distorted; see DEFORMED.
grouch ***n.*** complainer, grumbler, growler, bear*, sourpuss*, sorehead*, crab*, crank*, bellyacher*.
grouch ***v.*** mutter, grumble, gripe*; see COMPLAIN.
grouchy ***a.*** surly, ill-tempered, crusty; see IRRITABLE.
ground[1] ***n.*** **1** [Soil] sand, dirt, clay; see EARTH 2. **2** [An area] spot, terrain, territory; see AREA. —**break ground** begin construction, initiate, commence; see BEGIN 1. —**cover ground** move, go on, progress; see ADVANCE 1. —**from the ground up** thoroughly, wholly, entirely; see COMPLETELY. —**gain ground** move, go on, progress; see ADVANCE 1. —**get off the ground** start, commence, come into being; see BEGIN 2. —**hold** (or **stand**) **one's ground** maintain one's position, defend, sustain; see ENDURE 2. —**lose ground** lag, fall behind, drop back; see LAG. —**run into the ground*** exaggerate, do too much, press; see OVERDO 1.
ground[1] ***v.*** **1** [To bring to the ground] floor, bring down, prostrate; see TRIP 2. **2** [To restrict] punish, take away priveleges, force to stay home; see RESTRICT. **3** [To instruct in essentials] train, indoctrinate, educate; see TEACH.
grounds ***n.*** **1** [Real estate] lot, environs, territory; see PROPERTY 2. **2** [Basis] reasons, arguments, proof; see BASIS. **3** [Sediment] dregs, lees, leavings; see RESIDUE.
groundwork ***n.*** background, base, origin; see BASIS, FOUNDATION 2.
group ***n.*** **1** [A gathering of persons] assembly, assemblage, crowd; see GATHERING. **2** [Collected things] accumulation, assortment, combination; see COLLECTION. **3** [An organized body of people] association, club, society; see ORGANIZATION 2.
group ***v.*** file, assort, arrange; see CLASSIFY.

grouse[1] (grous) ***n.***, *pl.* **grouse** ⟦< ?⟧ a game bird with a plump body and mottled feathers

grouse[2] (grous) ***vi.* groused, grous′ing** ⟦< ?⟧ [Inf.] to complain

grout (grout) ***n.*** ⟦ME⟧ a thin mortar used as between tiles

grove (grōv) ***n.*** ⟦< OE *graf*⟧ a group of trees, without undergrowth

grov·el (gräv′əl, gruv′-) ***vi.* -eled** or **-elled, -el·ing** or **-el·ling** ⟦< ME *grufelinge*, down on one's face⟧ **1** to lie or crawl in a prostrate position, esp. abjectly **2** to behave abjectly —**grov′el·er** or **grov′el·ler *n.***

grow (grō) ***vi.* grew, grown, grow′ing** ⟦< OE *growan*⟧ **1** to come into being or be produced naturally **2** to develop or thrive, as a living thing **3** to increase in size, quantity, etc. **4** to become *[to grow weary]* —***vt.*** to cause to or let grow; raise; cultivate —**grow on** [Inf.] to come gradually to seem more likable, attractive, etc. to —**grow up** to mature —**grow′er *n.***

growl (groul) ***n.*** ⟦ME *groulen*⟧ a rumbling, menacing sound such as an angry dog makes —***vi., vt.*** to make, or express by, such a sound

grown (grōn) ***vi., vt.*** *pp. of* GROW —***adj.*** having completed its growth; mature

grown′-up′ *adj., n.* adult: also, for *n.*, **grown′up′**

growth (grōth) ***n.*** **1** a growing or developing **2** *a)* increase in size, etc. *b)* the full extent of this **3** something that grows or has grown **4** a tumor or other abnormal mass of tissue

grub (grub) ***vi.* grubbed, grub′bing** ⟦ME *grubben*⟧ **1** to dig in the ground **2** to work hard —***vt.*** **1** to clear (ground) of roots **2** to uproot —***n.*** **1** a wormlike larva, esp. of a beetle **2** [Slang] food

grub′by *adj.* -bi·er, -bi·est dirty; untidy —**grub′bi·ness *n.***

grub′stake′ *n.* ⟦GRUB, *n.* 2 + STAKE⟧ [Inf.] **1** money or supplies advanced, as to a prospector **2** money advanced for any enterprise

grudge (gruj) ***vt.* grudged, grudg′ing** ⟦< OFr *grouchier*⟧ **1** BEGRUDGE **2** to give with reluctance —***n.*** a feeling of resentment or ill will over some grievance —**grudg′ing·ly *adv.***

gru·el (gro͞o′əl) ***n.*** ⟦< ML *grutum*, meal⟧ thin porridge made by cooking meal in water or milk

gru′el·ing or **gru′el·ling *adj.*** ⟦prp. of obs. v. *gruel*, punish⟧ very trying; exhausting

grue·some (gro͞o′səm) ***adj.*** ⟦< dial. *grue*, to shudder + -SOME[1]⟧ causing horror or disgust; grisly

gruff (gruf) ***adj.*** ⟦< Du *grof*⟧ **1** rough or surly; brusquely rude **2** harsh and throaty; hoarse —**gruff′ly *adv.*** —**gruff′ness *n.***

grum·ble (grum′bəl) ***vi.* -bled, -bling** ⟦prob. < Du *grommelen*⟧ **1** to growl **2** to mutter in discontent **3** to rumble —***vt.*** to express by grumbling —***n.*** a grumbling —**grum′bler *n.***

grump·y (grum′pē) ***adj.* -i·er, -i·est** ⟦prob. echoic⟧ grouchy; peevish

grunge (grunj) ***n.*** [Slang] garbage or dirt

grun·gy (grun′jē) ***adj.* -gi·er, -gi·est** [Slang] dirty, messy, etc.

grun·ion (grun′yən) ***n.*** ⟦prob. < Sp *gruñón*, grumbler⟧ a fish of the California coast: it spawns on sandy beaches

grunt (grunt) ***vi., vt.*** ⟦< OE *grunian*⟧ to utter (with) the deep, hoarse sound of a hog —***n.*** **1** this sound **2** [Slang] one whose job involves routine tasks, strenuous labor, etc.; specif., a U.S. infantryman

Gru·yère (cheese) (gro͞o yer′, grē-) ⟦after *Gruyère*, Switzerland⟧ *[often* **g- c-***]* a light-yellow Swiss cheese, rich in butterfat

Gua·da·la·ja·ra (gwäd′'l ə här′ə) city in W Mexico: capital of Jalisco: pop. 1,626,000

Guam (gwäm) island in the W Pacific: an unincorporated territory of the U.S.: 209 sq. mi.; pop. 133,000

Guang·zhou (gwäŋ′jō) seaport in SE China: pop. 3,182,000

gua·nine (gwä′nēn′) ***n.*** ⟦< fol. + -INE[3]⟧ a crystalline base contained in the nucleic acids of all tissue

gua·no (gwä′nō) ***n.***, *pl.* **-nos** ⟦Sp < AmInd (Peru)⟧ manure of seabirds, used as fertilizer

guar *abbrev.* guaranteed

guar·an·tee (gar′ən tē′) ***n.*** **1** GUARANTY (sense 1) **2** *a)* a pledge to replace something if it is not as represented *b)* an assurance that something will be done as specified **3** a guarantor —***vt.* -teed′, -tee′ing** **1** to give a guarantee for **2** to promise

guar·an·tor (gar′ən tôr′) ***n.*** one who gives a guaranty or guarantee

guar′an·ty (-tē) ***n.***, *pl.* **-ties** ⟦< OFr *garant*, a warrant⟧ **1** a pledge or security for another's debt or obligation **2** an agreement that secures the existence or maintenance of something —***vt.* -tied, -ty·ing** GUARANTEE

guard (gärd) ***vt.*** ⟦< OFr *garder*⟧ **1** to watch over and protect; defend **2** to keep from escaping or from trouble **3** to control or restrain —***vi.*** **1** to keep watch (*against*) **2** to act as a guard —***n.*** **1** defense; protection **2** a posture of readiness for defense **3** any device to protect against injury or loss **4** a person or group that guards **5** *Basketball* either of two players who are the main ball handlers **6** *Football* either of two players next to the center —**on (one's) guard** vigilant

guard′ed *adj.* **1** kept safe **2** cautious *[a guarded reply]* —**guard′ed·ly *adv.***

THESAURUS

grovel *v.* crawl, beg, sneak, stoop, kneel, crouch before, kowtow to, sponge, cower, snivel, beseech, wheedle, flatter, cater to, humor, pamper, curry favor with, court, act up to, play up to, beg for mercy, prostrate oneself, be a toady, soft-soap*, butter up*, make up to, kiss someone's feet*, lick someone's boots*, knuckle under, polish the apple*, eat dirt*, brown-nose*.—*Ant.* HATE, spurn, scorn.

grow *v.* **1** [To become larger] increase, expand in size, swell, inflate, wax, thrive, gain, enlarge, advance, dilate, stretch, mount, build, burst forth, burgeon, spread, multiply, develop, mature, flourish, grow up, rise, sprout, shoot up, jump up, start up, spring up, spread like wildfire.—*Ant.* WITHER, lessen, shrink. **2** [To change slowly] become, develop, alter, tend, pass, evolve, flower, shift, flow, progress, advance; get bigger, larger, etc.; wax, turn into, improve, mellow, age, better, ripen into, blossom, open out, resolve itself into, mature. **3** [To cultivate] raise, nurture, tend, nurse, foster, produce, plant, breed.—*Ant.* HARM, impede, neglect.

growing *a.* increasing, ever-widening, expanding, budding, germinating, maturing, waxing, enlarging, amplifying, swelling, developing, mushrooming, spreading, thriving, flourishing, stretching, living, sprouting, viable, organic, animate, spreading like wildfire.—*Ant.* CONTRACTION, withering, shrinking.

growl *n.* snarl, gnarl, moan, bark, woof, bellow, rumble, roar, howl, grumble, grunt.

growl *v.* snarl, bark, gnarl; see CRY 2.

grown *a.* of age, adult, grown up; see MATURE.

grown-up *n.* adult, grown person, big person, grown man, grown woman.

growth *n.* **1** [The process of growing] extension, organic development, germination; see INCREASE. **2** [The result of growing] completion, adulthood, fullness; see MAJORITY 2. **3** [A swelling] tumor, cancer, mole, lump, cyst, sty, neoplasm, goose egg*, outgrowth, thickening.

grubby *a.* dirty, sloppy, grimy; see DIRTY 1.

grudge *n.* spite, rancor, animosity; see HATRED.

grudge *v.* begrudge, resent, give reluctantly; see ENVY.

grueling *a.* exhausting, tiring, fatiguing; see DIFFICULT 1, 2.

gruesome *a.* grim, grisly, horrible*; see FRIGHTFUL, OFFENSIVE 2.

gruff *a.* harsh, grating, rough; see HOARSE.

grumble *v.* whine, protest, fuss; see COMPLAIN.

grumpy *a.* sullen, grouchy, morose; see IRRITABLE.

grunt *v.* snort, squawk, squeak; see CRY 2.

guarantee *v.* attest, testify, vouch for, declare, assure, answer for, be responsible for, pledge, give bond, go bail, wager, stake, give a guarantee, stand behind, back, sign for, become surety for, endorse, secure, notarize, make certain, warrant, insure, witness, prove, reassure, support, affirm, confirm, cross one's heart.

guaranteed *a.* warranted, certified, bonded, secured, endorsed, insured, pledged, confirmed, assured, approved, attested, sealed, certificated, protected, affirmed, surefire*.—*Ant.* ANONYMOUS, unsupported, unendorsed.

guaranty *n.* warrant, warranty, bond, contract, certificate, charter, testament, security.

guard *n.* sentry, sentinel, protector; see WATCHMAN. —**off one's guard** unaware, unprotected, defenseless; see UNPREPARED. —**on one's guard** alert, mindful, vigilant; see READY 2.

guard *v.* watch, observe, protect, patrol, picket, police, look out, look after, see after, tend, keep in view, keep an eye on, attend, overlook, hold in custody, stand over, babysit, care for, see to, chaperone, oversee, ride herd on*, keep tabs on*.—*Ant.* NEGLECT, disregard, forsake.

guarded *a.* **1** [Protected] safeguarded, secured, defended; see SAFE 1. **2** [Cautious] circumspect, atten-

guard'house' *n. Mil.* **1** a building used by a guard when not walking a post **2** a jail for temporary confinement

guard'i·an (-ē ən) *n.* **1** one who guards or protects; custodian **2** a person legally in charge of the affairs of a minor or of a person of unsound mind —*adj.* protecting —**guard'i·an·ship'** *n.*

guard'rail' *n.* a protective railing

Gua·te·ma·la (gwät'ə mä'lə) country in Central America: 42,042 sq. mi.; pop. 6,054,000

gua·va (gwä'və) *n.* ⟦< native name⟧ a yellow, pear-shaped tropical American fruit

gua·ya·be·ra (gwä'yä ber'ä) *n.* ⟦AmSp⟧ a kind of loosefitting shirt worn with the shirttail outside the trousers

gu·ber·na·to·ri·al (go͞o'bər nə tôr'ē əl) *adj.* ⟦L *gubernator*, governor⟧ of a governor or the office of governor

Guern·sey (gurn'zē) *n., pl.* **-seys** ⟦after *Guernsey*, one of the Channel Islands⟧ a breed of dairy cattle, usually fawn-colored with white markings

guer·ril·la (gə ril'ə) *n.* ⟦Sp, dim. of *guerra*, war⟧ a member of a small defensive force of irregular soldiers, making surprise raids: also sp. **gue·ril'la**

guess (ges) *vt., vi.* ⟦ME *gessen*⟧ **1** to form a judgment or estimate of (something) without actual knowledge; surmise **2** to judge correctly by doing this **3** to think or suppose —*n.* **1** a guessing **2** something guessed; conjecture —**guess'er** *n.*

guess'work' *n.* **1** a guessing **2** a judgment, result, etc. arrived at by guessing

guest (gest) *n.* ⟦< ON *gestr*⟧ **1** a person entertained at the home, club, etc. of another **2** any paying customer of a hotel, restaurant, etc. —*adj.* **1** for guests **2** performing by special invitation *[a guest* artist*]*

guff (guf) *n.* ⟦echoic⟧ [Slang] **1** nonsense **2** brash or insolent talk

guf·faw (gə fô') *n.* ⟦echoic⟧ a loud, coarse burst of laughter —*vi.* to laugh in this way

guid·ance (gīd''ns) *n.* **1** a guiding; leadership **2** advice or assistance

guide (gīd) *vt.* **guid'ed, guid'ing** ⟦< OFr *guider*⟧ **1** to point out the way for; lead **2** to direct the course of; control —*n.* **1** one whose work is conducting tours, etc. **2** a controlling device **3** a book of basic instruction

guide'book' *n.* a book containing directions and information for tourists

guided missile a military missile whose course is controlled as by electronic signals

guide'line' *n.* a principle by which to determine a course of action

guild (gild) *n.* ⟦< OE *gieldan*, to pay⟧ an association for mutual aid and the promotion of common interests

guil·der (gil'dər) *n.* ⟦< MDu *gulden*, golden⟧ the monetary unit of the Netherlands

guile (gīl) *n.* ⟦< OFr⟧ slyness and cunning in dealing with others —**guile'ful** *adj.* —**guile'less** *adj.*

guil·lo·tine (gil'ə tēn', gē'ə-; *for v., usually* gil'ə tēn', gē'ə-) *n.* ⟦Fr: after J. *Guillotin* (1738-1814), Fr physician who advocated its use⟧ an instrument for beheading, having a heavy blade dropped between two grooved uprights —*vt.* **-tined', -tin'ing** to behead with a guillotine

guilt (gilt) *n.* ⟦OE *gylt*, a sin⟧ **1** the state of having done a wrong or committed an offense **2** a feeling of self-reproach from believing that one has done a wrong —**guilt'less** *adj.*

guilt'y *adj.* **-i·er, -i·est** **1** having guilt **2** legally judged an offender **3** of or showing guilt *[a guilty* look*]* —**guilt'i·ly** *adv.* —**guilt'i·ness** *n.*

guin·ea (gin'ē) *n.* ⟦first coined of gold from *Guinea*⟧ a former English gold coin equal to 21 shillings

Guin·ea (gin'ē) country on the W coast of Africa: 94,926 sq. mi.; pop. 7,300,000

Guin'ea-Bis·sau' (-bi sou') country on the W coast of Africa: 13,948 sq. mi.; pop. 777,000

guinea fowl (or **hen**) ⟦orig. imported from *Guinea*⟧ a domestic fowl with a rounded body and speckled feathers

guinea pig ⟦prob. orig. brought to England by ships plying between England, *Guinea*, and South America⟧ **1** a small, plump rodent, often used in biological experiments **2** any subject used in an experiment

guise (gīz) *n.* ⟦< OHG *wisa*, manner⟧ **1** manner of dress; garb **2** outward appearance **3** a false appearance; pretense

gui·tar (gi tär') *n.* ⟦ult. < Gr *kithara*, lyre⟧ a musical instrument with usually six strings plucked with the fingers or a plectrum —**gui·tar'ist** *n.*

gulch (gulch) *n.* ⟦prob. < dial., to swallow greedily⟧ a deep, narrow ravine

gulf (gulf) *n.* ⟦ult. < Gr *kolpos*, bosom⟧ **1** a large area of ocean reaching into land **2** a wide, deep chasm **3** a wide gap or separation

Gulf Stream warm ocean current flowing from the Gulf of Mexico northward and then eastward toward Europe

gull[1] (gul) *n.* ⟦< Celt⟧ a white and gray water bird with webbed feet

gull[2] (gul) *n.* ⟦ME, lit., unfledged bird⟧ a person easily tricked; dupe —*vt.* to cheat or trick

gul·let (gul'ət) *n.* ⟦< L *gula*, throat⟧ **1** the esophagus **2** the throat

gul·li·ble (gul'ə bəl) *adj.* easily gulled; credulous —**gul'li·bil'i·ty** *n.*

gul·ly (gul'ē) *n., pl.* **-lies** ⟦see GULLET⟧ a small, narrow ravine

gulp (gulp) *vt.* ⟦prob. < Du *gulpen*⟧ to swallow hastily or greedily —*vi.* to catch the breath as in swallowing —*n.* a gulping or swallowing

gum[1] (gum) *n.* ⟦< LL *gumma*⟧ **1** a sticky substance found in certain trees and plants **2** an adhesive **3** CHEWING GUM —*vt.* **gummed, gum'ming** to coat or unite with gum —**gum up** [Slang] to cause to go awry —**gum'my, -mi·er, -mi·est,** *adj.*

gum[2] (gum) *n.* ⟦OE *goma*⟧ [*often pl.*] the firm flesh surrounding the base of the teeth —*vt.* **gummed, gum'ming** to chew with toothless gums

gum arabic a gum from certain acacias, used in medicine, candy, etc.

gum·bo (gum'bō) *n.* ⟦< Bantu name for okra⟧ a soup thickened with okra

THESAURUS

tive, overcautious; see CAREFUL.

guardian *n.* **1** [One who regulates or protects] overseer, safeguard, curator, guard, protector, preserver, trustee, custodian, keeper, patrol, warden, defender, supervisor, babysitter, sponsor, superintendent, sentinel. **2** [A foster parent] adoptive parent, legal guardian, nanny; see FATHER 1, MOTHER 1.

guerrilla *a.* clandestine, underground, independent; see FIGHTING.

guerrilla *n.* irregular soldier, underground resistance fighter, revolutionary; see SOLDIER.

guess *n.* conjecture, surmise, supposition, theory, hypothesis, presumption, opinion, postulate, estimate, suspicion, guesswork, guesstimate*, view, belief, assumption, speculation, fancy, inference, conclusion, deduction, induction, shot in the dark*.

guess *v.* conjecture, presume, infer, suspect, speculate, imagine, surmise, theorize, hazard a guess, suggest, figure, venture, suppose, presume, imagine, think likely, reckon*, calculate. —**guess at** reckon*, calculate, survey; see ESTIMATE.

guessing *n.* guesswork, supposition, imagination, fancy, inference, deduction, presupposition, reckoning, surmise, theorizing, taking for granted, postulating, assuming, presuming, jumping to conclusions.

guest *n.* visitor, caller, house guest, dinner guest, luncheon guest, visitant, company.

guidance *n.* direction, leadership, supervision; see ADMINISTRATION 2.

guide *n.* pilot, captain, pathfinder, scout, escort, courier, director, explorer, guru, conductor, pioneer, leader, superintendent.

guide *v.* conduct, escort, show the way; see LEAD 1.

guilt *n.* culpability, blame, error, fault, crime, sin, offense, liability, criminality, sinfulness, misconduct, misbehavior, malpractice, delinquency, transgression, indiscretion, weakness.—*Ant.* INNOCENCE, blamelessness, honor.

guilty *a.* found guilty, guilty as charged, guilty as sin*, condemned, sentenced, criminal, censured, impeached, incriminated, indicted, liable, condemned, convictable, judged, damned, doomed, at fault, sinful, to blame, in the wrong, in error, wrong, blamable, reproachable, chargeable.—*Ant.* INNOCENT, blameless, right.

gulch *n.* gully, ditch, gorge; see RAVINE.

gulf *n.* **1** [Chasm] abyss, gap, depth; see RAVINE. **2** [An arm of the sea] inlet, sound, cove; see BAY.

gullible *a.* innocent, trustful, simple; see NAIVE.

gully *n.* ditch, chasm, crevasse; see RAVINE.

gulp *v.* swig, choke down, chug*; see SWALLOW.

gum[1] *n.* resin, glue, pitch, tar, pine tar, amber, wax. *Commercial gums include the following:* chewing gum, sealing wax, rosin, mucilage, chicle, latex, gum arabic.

gummy *a.* sticky, cohesive, viscid; see STICKY.

gum'drop' ***n.*** a small, firm candy made of sweetened gelatin, etc.

gump·tion (gump'shən) ***n.*** ⟦< Scot⟧ [Inf.] courage and initiative

gun (gun) ***n.*** ⟦< ME *gonnilde*, cannon < ON⟧ **1** any weapon with a metal tube from which a projectile is discharged by the force of an explosive **2** any similar device not discharged by an explosive *[an air gun]* **3** anything like a gun in shape or use —***vi.*** **gunned, gun'ning** to shoot or hunt with a gun —***vt.*** **1** [Inf.] to shoot (a person) **2** [Slang] to advance the throttle of (an engine) —**gun for** [Slang] to try to get —**jump the gun** [Inf.] to begin before the proper time —**stick to one's guns** [Inf.] to be resolute —**under the gun** [Inf.] in a tense situation, often one involving a deadline

gun'boat' ***n.*** a small armed ship

gun'fight' ***n.*** a fight between persons using pistols or revolvers —**gun'fight'er** ***n.***

gun'fire' ***n.*** the firing of guns

gung-ho (guŋ'hō') ***adj.*** ⟦Chin *kung-ho*, lit., work together⟧ [Inf.] enthusiastic

gunk (guŋk) ***n.*** ⟦< ?⟧ [Slang] any viscous or thick, messy substance

gun'man (-mən) ***n.***, *pl.* **-men** (-mən) an armed gangster or hired killer

gun'met'al ***n.*** **1** a bronze with a dark tarnish **2** its dark-gray color

gun'ner ***n.*** **1** a soldier, etc. who helps fire artillery **2** a naval warrant officer in charge of guns, missiles, etc.

gun'ner·y ***n.*** the science of making and using heavy guns and projectiles

gun·ny (gun'ē) ***n.***, *pl.* **-nies** ⟦< Sans *gōnī*, a sack⟧ a coarse fabric of jute or hemp

gun'ny·sack' ***n.*** a sack made of gunny

gun'play' ***n.*** an exchange of gunshots, as between gunmen and police

gun'point' ***n.*** used chiefly in **at gunpoint**, under threat of being shot with a gun at close range

gun'pow'der ***n.*** an explosive powder used in guns, for blasting, etc.

gun'ship' ***n.*** a heavily armed helicopter used to assault enemy ground forces

gun'shot' ***n.*** the shooting of a gun

gun'-shy' ***adj.*** **1** easily frightened at the firing of a gun *[a gun-shy dog]* **2** wary, mistrustful, etc., as because of a previous experience

gun'smith' ***n.*** one who makes or repairs small guns

gun·wale (gun'əl) ***n.*** ⟦< bulwarks supporting a ship's guns⟧ the upper edge of the side of a ship or boat

gup·py (gup'ē) ***n.***, *pl.* **-pies** ⟦after R. J. L. *Guppy*, of Trinidad⟧ a very small freshwater fish of the West Indies, etc.

gur·gle (gur'gəl) ***vi.*** **-gled, -gling** ⟦< L *gurgulio*, gullet⟧ to make a bubbling sound —***n.*** such a sound

gur·ney (gur'nē) ***n.***, *pl.* **-neys** ⟦< ?⟧ a hospital stretcher on wheels

gu·ru (gōō'rōō'; *also* gōō rōō') ***n.*** ⟦< Sans *guruḥ*, venerable⟧ in Hinduism, one's personal spiritual advisor or teacher

gush (gush) ***vi.*** ⟦ME *guschen*⟧ **1** to flow out plentifully **2** to have a sudden flow **3** to talk or write effusively —***vt.*** to cause to gush —***n.*** a gushing —**gush'y, -i·er, -i·est,** ***adj.***

gush'er ***n.*** **1** one who gushes **2** an oil well from which oil spouts forth

gus·set (gus'it) ***n.*** ⟦< OFr *gousset*⟧ a triangular piece inserted in a garment, etc. to make it stronger or roomier

gus·sy or **gus·sie** (gus'ē) ***vt., vi.*** **-sied, -sy·ing** ⟦nickname for *Augusta*, a feminine name⟧ [Slang] to dress (*up*) in a fine or showy way

gust (gust) ***n.*** ⟦< ON *gjosa*, to gush⟧ **1** a sudden, strong rush of air **2** a sudden outburst of rain, laughter, etc. —**gust'y, -i·er, -i·est,** ***adj.***

gus·ta·to·ry (gus'tə tôr'ē) ***adj.*** ⟦< L *gustus*, taste⟧ of the sense of taste

gus·to (gus'tō) ***n.*** ⟦see prec.⟧ **1** zest; relish **2** great vigor or liveliness

gut (gut) ***n.*** ⟦< OE *geotan*, to pour⟧ **1** [*pl.*] the entrails **2** the stomach or belly **3** the intestine **4** tough cord made from animal intestines **5** [*pl.*] [Inf.] daring; courage —***vt.*** **gut'ted, gut'ting** **1** to remove the intestines from **2** to destroy the interior of —***adj.*** [Slang] **1** basic **2** easy

gut'less ***adj.*** [Inf.] lacking courage

guts·y (gut'sē) ***adj.*** **-i·er, -i·est** [Inf.] courageous, forceful, etc.

gut·ter (gut'ər) ***n.*** ⟦< L *gutta*, a drop⟧ **1** a channel to carry off water, as along the eaves of a roof or the side of a street **2** a place or condition characterized by squalor —***vi.*** to flow in a stream

gut·tur·al (gut'ər əl) ***adj.*** ⟦L *guttur*, throat⟧ harsh; rasping: said of vocal sounds

guv (guv) ***n.*** *slang var. of* GOVERNOR

guy[1] (gī) ***n.*** ⟦< OFr *guier*, to guide⟧ a rope, chain, etc. used to steady or guide something —***vt.*** to guide or steady with a guy

guy[2] (gī) [Inf.] ***n.*** ⟦after *Guy* Fawkes, Eng conspirator⟧ **1** a man or boy **2** any person —***vt.*** to make fun of; ridicule

Guy·a·na (gī an'ə) country in NE South America: 83,000 sq. mi.; pop. 730,000

guz·zle (guz'əl) ***vi., vt.*** **-zled, -zling** ⟦< ? OFr *gosier*, throat⟧ to drink greedily or immoderately

gym (jim) ***n.*** [Inf.] **1** *short for* GYMNASIUM **2** PHYSICAL EDUCATION

gym·na·si·um (jim nā'zē əm) ***n.***, *pl.* **-si·ums** or **-si·a** (-ə) ⟦< Gr *gymnos*, naked⟧ a room or building equipped for physical training and sports

gym·nas·tics (jim nas'tiks) ***n.*** a sport combining tumbling and acrobatic feats —**gym'nast'** ***n.*** —**gym·nas'tic** ***adj.*** —**gym·nas'ti·cal·ly** ***adv.***

gym·no·sperm (jim'nō spurm', -nə-) ***n.*** ⟦< Gr *gymnos*, naked + *sperma*, seed⟧ any of a large division of seed plants, as seed ferns, conifers, etc., having the ovules not enclosed within an ovary

GYN *abbrev.* **1** gynecologic(al) **2** gynecologist **3** gynecology

gy·ne·col·o·gy (gī'nə käl'ə jē) ***n.*** ⟦< Gr *gynē*, woman + -LOGY⟧ the branch of medicine dealing with women's diseases, etc. —**gy'ne·co·log'ic** (-kə läj'ik) or **gy'ne·co·log'i·cal** ***adj.*** —**gy'ne·col'o·gist** ***n.***

gyp (jip) [Inf.] ***n.*** ⟦prob. < GYPSY⟧ **1** a swindle **2** a swindler: also **gyp'per** or **gyp'ster** —***vt., vi.*** **gypped, gyp'ping** to swindle; cheat

gyp·sum (jip'səm) ***n.*** ⟦< Gr *gypsos*⟧ a sulfate of calcium used to make plaster of Paris and cement

Gyp·sy (jip'sē) ***n.***, *pl.* **-sies** ⟦< *Egipcien*, Egyptian: orig. thought to be from Egypt⟧ **1** [*also* **g-**] a member of a wandering Caucasoid people, perhaps orig. from India,

THESAURUS

gun ***n.*** *Types include the following:* rifle, automatic rifle, repeating rifle, repeater, recoilless rifle, air rifle, BB gun, shotgun, sawed-off shotgun, musket, handgun, assault rifle, semiautomatic pistol, squirrel gun, carbine, long rifle, laser gun, revolver, pistol, rod*; see also MACHINE GUN. —**jump the gun*** start too soon, act inappropriately, give oneself away; see BEGIN 1, HURRY 1.

gunfire ***n.*** bombardment, artillery support, air support, air strike, mortar fire, heavy arms attack, explosion, shooting, shot, report, artillery, volley, discharge, detonation, blast, firing, burst, barrage, cannonade, fire superiority, salvo, firepower.

gunman ***n.*** killer, assassin, hit man*; see CRIMINAL.

gunner ***n.*** machine gunner, turret gunner, ball-turret gunner, tail gunner, rocketeer, missile launcher, bazooka launcher, sniper, sharpshooter, aerial gunner, artilleryman, cannoneer.

gurgle ***v.*** ripple, murmur, pour; see FLOW.

gush ***v.*** pour, well, spew; see FLOW.

gusto ***n.*** fervor, vigor, ardor; see ZEAL.

gut ***n.*** small intestine, large intestine, duodenum; see INTESTINES.

guts ***n.*** **1** [Bowels] viscera, insides, belly; see INTESTINES. **2** [*Fortitude] pluck, hardihood, effrontery; see COURAGE. —**hate someone's guts*** detest, loathe, despise; see HATE.

gutter ***n.*** canal, gully, sewer, watercourse, channel, dike, drain, moat, trough; see also TRENCH.

guttural ***a.*** throaty, gruff, deep; see HOARSE.

guy[2]* ***n.*** chap, lad, person; see FELLOW 1, MAN 2, PERSON 1.

guzzle ***v.*** swill, quaff, swig; see DRINK 1.

gymnasium ***n.*** health center, recreation center, playing floor, exercise room, sports center, field house, court, athletic club, arena, coliseum, theater, circus, stadium, ring, rink, pit, gym*.

gymnast ***n.*** acrobat, tumbler, jumper; see ATHLETE.

gymnastics ***n.*** trapeze performance, floor exercises, acrobatics, aerobatics, therapeutics, body-building exercises, tumbling, vaulting; work on the rings, parallel bars, balance beam, horse, etc.

gyp* ***n.*** cheat, fraud, trick; see FAKE, TRICK 1.

gypsy ***n.*** tramp, wanderer, itinerant; see TRAVELER.

with dark skin and black hair **2** the language of this people; Romany **3** [**g-**] one who looks or lives like a Gypsy

gypsy cab [Inf.] an unlicensed taxicab operated by an independent driver

gypsy moth a moth in the E U.S.: its larvae feed on leaves, damaging trees

gy·rate (jī′rāt′) ***vi.*** **-rat′ed, -rat′ing** ⟦< Gr *gyros*, a circle⟧ to move in a circular or spiral path; whirl —**gy·ra′tion** ***n.*** —**gy′ra′tor** ***n.***

gy·ro (yir′ō, jī′rō′) ***n.***, *pl.* **-ros** ⟦see prec.⟧ **1** layers of lamb and beef roasted and sliced **2** a pita sandwich of this Also **gy·ros** (yir′ôs)

gyro- ⟦see GYRATE⟧ *combining form* gyrating *[gyroscope]*

gy·ro·scope (jī′rō skōp′, -rə-) ***n.*** ⟦prec. + -SCOPE⟧ a wheel mounted in a set of rings so that its axis is free to turn in any direction: when the wheel is spun rapidly, it will keep its original plane of rotation

H

h or **H** (āch) ***n.***, *pl.* **h's, H's** the eighth letter of the English alphabet

H[1] or **h** *abbrev.* **1** height **2** high **3** *Baseball* hit(s) **4** hour(s) **5** hundred(s) **6** husband

H[2] *Chem. symbol for* hydrogen

ha (hä) ***interj.*** ⟦echoic⟧ used to express surprise, wonder, anger, triumph, etc.

ha·be·as cor·pus (hā′bē əs kôr′pəs) ⟦L, (that) you have the body⟧ *Law* a writ requiring that a detained person be brought before a court to decide the legality of the detention

hab·er·dash·er (hab′ər dash′ər) ***n.*** ⟦< ME⟧ a dealer in men's hats, shirts, neckties, etc. —**hab′er·dash′er·y *n.***

ha·bil·i·ment (hə bil′ə mənt) ***n.*** ⟦< MFr *habiller*, to clothe⟧ **1** [*usually pl.*] clothing; attire **2** [*pl.*] equipment; trappings

hab·it (hab′it) ***n.*** ⟦< L *habere*, to have⟧ **1** a distinctive costume, as of a nun **2** a thing done often and, hence, easily **3** a usual way of doing **4** an addiction, esp. to narcotics

hab′it·a·ble *adj.* fit to be lived in

hab·i·tat (hab′i tat′) ***n.*** ⟦L, it inhabits⟧ **1** the region where a plant or animal naturally lives **2** the place where a person is ordinarily found

hab·i·ta·tion (hab′i tā′shən) ***n.*** **1** an inhabiting **2** a dwelling; home

hab′it-form′ing *adj.* resulting in the formation of a habit or in addiction

ha·bit·u·al (hə bich′o͞o əl) ***adj.*** **1** done or acquired by habit **2** steady; inveterate *[a habitual smoker]* **3** much seen, done, or used; usual —**ha·bit′u·al·ly *adv.*** —**ha·bit′u·al·ness *n.***

ha·bit′u·ate′ (-āt′) ***vt.*** **-at′ed, -at′ing** to accustom (*to*) —**ha·bit′u·a′tion *n.***

ha·bit′u·é′ (-ā′) ***n.*** ⟦Fr⟧ one who frequents a certain place

ha·ci·en·da (hä′sē en′də) ***n.*** ⟦Sp < L *facere*, do⟧ in Spanish America, a large estate or ranch, or its main house

hack[1] (hak) ***vt.*** ⟦OE *haccian*⟧ to chop or cut crudely, roughly, etc. —***vi.*** **1** to make rough cuts **2** to give harsh, dry coughs —***n.*** **1** a gash **2** a harsh, dry cough

hack[2] (hak) ***n.*** ⟦< HACKNEY⟧ **1** a horse for hire **2** an old, worn-out horse **3** one hired to do routine or dull writing **4** a coach for hire **5** [Inf.] a taxicab —***adj.*** **1** employed as, or done by, a hack *[hack writer]* **2** trite; hackneyed

hack′er *n.* **1** an unskilled golfer, etc. **2** a talented amateur user of computers

hack·le (hak′əl) ***n.*** ⟦ME *hechele*⟧ **1** the neck feathers of a rooster, pigeon, etc. **2** [*pl.*] the hairs on a dog's neck and back that bristle

hack·ney (hak′nē) ***n.***, *pl.* **-neys** ⟦after *Hackney*, England⟧ **1** a horse for driving or riding **2** a carriage for hire

hack′neyed′ (-nēd′) ***adj.*** made trite by overuse

hack′saw′ *n.* a fine-toothed saw for cutting metal: also **hack saw**

had (had) ***vt.*** *pt. & pp. of* HAVE

had·dock (had′ək) ***n.***, *pl.* **-dock** or **-docks** ⟦ME *hadok*⟧ an Atlantic food fish, related to the cod

Ha·des (hā′dēz′) ***n.*** ⟦Gr *Haidēs*⟧ **1** *Gr. Myth.* the home of the dead **2** [*often* **h-**] hell

haft (haft, häft) ***n.*** ⟦OE *hæft*⟧ the handle or hilt of a knife, ax, etc.

hag (hag) ***n.*** ⟦< OE *hægtes*⟧ **1** a witch **2** an ugly, often vicious old woman —**hag′gish *adj.***

hag·gard (hag′ərd) ***adj.*** ⟦MFr *hagard*, untamed (hawk)⟧ having a wild, wasted, worn look; gaunt

hag·gle (hag′əl) ***vi.*** **-gled, -gling** ⟦< Scot *hag*, to hack⟧ to argue about terms, price, etc. —***n.*** a haggling —**hag′gler *n.***

Hague (hāg), **The** political capital of the Netherlands (cf. AMSTERDAM): pop. 445,000

hah (hä) ***interj.***, ***n.*** HA

hai·ku (hī′ko͞o′) ***n.*** ⟦Jpn⟧ **1** a Japanese verse form of three unrhymed lines of 5, 7, and 5 syllables, respectively **2** *pl.* **-ku′** a poem in this form

hail[1] (hāl) ***vt.*** ⟦< ON *heill*, whole, sound⟧ **1** to greet with cheers; acclaim **2** to call out to *[to hail a cab]* —***n.*** a greeting —***interj.*** used to signify tribute, greeting, etc. —**hail from** to be from

hail[2] (hāl) ***n.*** ⟦OE *hægel*⟧ **1** frozen raindrops falling during thunderstorms **2** a shower of or like hail —***vt., vi.*** to pour down like hail

hail′stone′ *n.* a pellet of hail

hail′storm′ *n.* a storm with hail

hair (her, har) ***n.*** ⟦OE *hær*⟧ **1** any of the threadlike outgrowths from the skin **2** a growth of these, as on the human head **3** a very small space, degree, etc. **4** a threadlike growth on a plant —**get in someone's hair** [Slang] to annoy someone —**split hairs** to quibble —**hair′less *adj.*** —**hair′like′ *adj.***

hair′ball′ *n.* a ball of hair that may form in the stomach of a cow, cat, or other animal that licks its coat

hair′breadth′ (-bredth′) ***n.*** an extremely small space or amount —***adj.*** very narrow; close Also **hairs′breadth′** or **hair's′-breadth′**

hair′cut′ *n.* the act of, or a style of, cutting the hair

hair′do′ (-do͞o′) ***n.***, *pl.* **-dos′** the style in which hair is arranged; coiffure

hair′dress′er *n.* one whose work is dressing, or arranging, hair

-haired (herd) having (a specified kind of) hair *[short-haired]*

hair′line′ *n.* **1** a very thin line **2** the outline of the hair on the head

hair′piece′ *n.* a toupee or wig

hair′pin′ *n.* a small, bent piece of wire, etc., for keeping the hair in place —***adj.*** U-shaped *[a hairpin turn in the road]*

hair′-rais′ing *adj.* terrifying or shocking

hair′split′ting *adj.*, ***n.*** making petty distinctions

hair′spring′ *n.* a slender, hairlike coil spring, as in a watch

hair′y *adj.* **-i·er, -i·est** covered with hair —**hair′i·ness *n.***

Hai·ti (hāt′ē) country occupying the W portion of the

THESAURUS

habit *n.* **1** [A customary action] mode, wont, routine, rule, characteristic, practice, disposition, way, fashion, manner, propensity, bent, turn, proclivity, predisposition, susceptibility, weakness, bias, persuasion, second nature; see also CUSTOM. **2** [An obsession] addiction, fixation, hang-up*; see OBSESSION.

habitat *n.* locality, territory, natural surroundings; see ENVIRONMENT, HOME 1, POSITION 1.

habitual *a.* ingrained, confirmed, frequent, periodic, continual, routine, mechanical, automatic, seasoned, permanent, perpetual, fixed, rooted, systematic, recurrent, repeated, periodical, methodical, disciplined, practiced, accustomed, established, set, repetitious, cyclic, reiterated, settled, trite, stereotyped, in a groove, in a rut.—*Ant.* DIFFERENT, exceptional, extraordinary.

hack[1] ***v.*** chop, whack, mangle; see CUT 1.

hack[1,2] ***n.*** **1** [A literary drudge] pulp-story writer, ghostwriter, propagandist, commercial writer, popular novelist; see also WRITER. **2** [*Commercial driver, especially of a taxicab] cab driver, chauffeur, cabby*; see DRIVER. **3** [A cut] notch, nick, cleavage; see CUT 1.

hag *n.* crone, witch, withered old woman, shrew, ogress, hellcat, fishwife, harridan, old bag*, battle-ax*; see also WITCH.

haggle *v.* deal, wrangle, argue; see BUY, SELL.

hail[1] ***v.*** cheer, welcome, honor; see GREET. —**hail from** come from, be born in, be a native of; see BEGIN 2.

hail[2] ***n.*** hailstorm, sleet, ice pellets, icy rain; see also RAIN 1.

hair *n.* **1** [Threadlike growth] locks, wig, moustache, whiskers, eyebrow, eyelash, sideburn, mane, fluff; see also BEARD, FUR. **2** [Anything suggesting the thickness of a hair] a hairbreadth, a narrow margin, hair trigger, hairspring, splinter, shaving, sliver; see also BIT 1. —**get in one's hair*** irritate, annoy, disturb; see BOTHER 2. —**let one's hair down*** be informal, have fun, let oneself go; see RELAX. —**make one's hair stand on end** terrify, scare, horrify; see FRIGHTEN.

haircut *n.* trim, trimming, bob, crew cut, flattop*, pageboy, pigtails, French roll, bun, ponytail, braid, feathercut, bangs, butch*, buzz cut*.

hairdo *n.* coiffure, hairdressing, hair style; see HAIRCUT.

hairless *n.* cleanshaven, beardless, smooth-faced; see BALD, SMOOTH 3.

hairpin *n.* bobby pin, hair clip, barrette; see FASTENER.

hairsplitting *a.* unimportant, scrupulous, subtle; see TRIVIAL, IRRELEVANT, UNIMPORTANT.

hairy *a.* bristly, shaggy, woolly, unshorn, downy, fleecy, whiskered, tufted, unshaven, bearded, bewhiskered, furry, fuzzy, hirsute, fluffy.—*Ant.* BALD, hairless, smooth.

island of Hispaniola, West Indies: 10,700 sq. mi.; pop. 5,054,000 —**Hai·tian** (hā′shən) ***adj., n.***

hake (hāk) ***n.*** ⟦prob. < ON⟧ a marine food fish related to the cod

hal·berd (hal′bərd) ***n.*** ⟦ult. < MHG *helmbarte*⟧ a combined spear and battle-ax of the 15th-16th c.

hal·cy·on (hal′sē ən) ***adj.*** ⟦< Gr *alkyōn*, kingfisher (fabled calmer of the sea)⟧ tranquil, happy, idyllic, etc. *[halcyon days]*

hale[1] (hāl) ***adj.*** **hal′er, hal′est** ⟦OE *hal*⟧ vigorous and healthy

hale[2] (hāl) ***vt.*** **haled, hal′ing** ⟦< OFr *haler*⟧ to force (a person) to go *[haled* him into court*]*

half (haf, häf) ***n., pl.*** **halves** ⟦OE *healf*⟧ **1** either of the two equal parts of something **2** either of the two equal parts of some games —***adj.*** **1** being a half **2** incomplete; partial —***adv.*** **1** to the extent of a half **2** partly *[half* done*]* **3** at all: used with *not [*not *half* bad*]*

half- *combining form* **1** one half *[half-*life*]* **2** partly *[half-*baked*]*

half′-and-half′ ***n.*** something that is half of one thing and half of another, as a mixture of milk and cream —***adj.*** combining two things equally —***adv.*** in two equal parts

half′back′ ***n.*** *Football* one of the running backs, typically smaller and faster than a fullback

half′-breed′ ***n.*** one whose parents are of different ethnic types: an offensive term

half brother a brother through one parent only

half dollar a coin of the U.S. or Canada, worth 50 cents

half′heart′ed ***adj.*** with little enthusiasm, determination, interest, etc. —**half′heart′ed·ly** ***adv.***

half′-life′ ***n.*** the constant time period required for the disintegration of half of the atoms in a sample of a radioactive substance: also **half life**

half′-mast′ ***n.*** the position of a flag halfway down its staff, esp. as a sign of mourning

half note *Music* a note having one half the duration of a whole note

half·pen·ny (hāp′nē, hā′pən ē) ***n., pl.*** **-pence** (hā′pəns) or **-pen·nies** a former British coin equal to half a penny

half sister a sister through one parent only

half sole a sole (of a shoe or boot) from the arch to the toe

half′track′ ***n.*** an army truck, armored vehicle, etc. with tractor treads instead of rear wheels

half′way′ ***adj.*** **1** midway between two points, etc. **2** partial *[halfway* measures*]* —***adv.*** **1** to the midway point **2** partially —**meet halfway** to be willing to compromise (with)

halfway house a place for helping people adjust to society after being imprisoned, hospitalized, etc.

half′-wit′ ***n.*** a stupid or silly person; fool —**half′-wit′ted** ***adj.***

hal·i·but (hal′ə bət) ***n., pl.*** **-but** or **-buts** ⟦ME *hali*, holy + *butt*, a flounder (so called because eaten on holidays)⟧ a large, edible flounder found in northern seas

Hal·i·fax (hal′ə faks′) capital of Nova Scotia, Canada: pop. 114,000

hal·ite (hal′īt′, hā′līt′) ***n.*** rock salt

hal·i·to·sis (hal′i tō′sis) ***n.*** ⟦< L *halitus*, breath⟧ bad-smelling breath

hall (hôl) ***n.*** ⟦OE *heall*⟧ **1** the main dwelling on an estate **2** a public building with offices, etc. **3** a large room for gatherings, exhibits, etc. **4** a college building **5** a vestibule at the entrance of a building **6** an area onto which rooms open

hal·le·lu·jah or **hal·le·lu·iah** (hal′ə lo͞o′yə) ***interj.*** ⟦< Heb < *hallelū*, praise (imper.) + *yāh*, Jehovah⟧ used to express praise, thanks, etc., esp. in a hymn or prayer —***n.*** a hymn of praise to God

hall·mark (hôl′märk′) ***n.*** ⟦< the mark stamped on gold and silver articles at Goldsmith's Hall⟧ a mark or symbol of genuineness or high quality

hal·loo (hə lo͞o′) ***n., interj.*** (a shout or call) used esp. to attract attention —***vi., vt.*** **-looed′, -loo′ing** to call out (to)

hal·low (hal′ō) ***vt.*** ⟦OE *halgian*⟧ to make or regard as holy

hal′lowed (-ōd) ***adj.*** holy or sacred

Hal·low·een or **Hal·low·e′en** (hal′ə wēn′, häl′-) ***n.*** ⟦contr. < *all hallow even*⟧ the evening of Oct. 31, followed by All Saints' Day: now celebrated with masquerading, etc.

hal·lu·ci·nate (hə lo͞o′si nāt′) ***vi., vt.*** **-nat′ed, -nat′ing** ⟦see fol.⟧ to have or cause to have hallucinations

hal·lu·ci·na·tion (hə lo͞o′si nā′shən) ***n.*** ⟦< L *hallucinari*, to wander mentally⟧ **1** the apparent perception of sights, sounds, etc. that are not actually present **2** the thing perceived —**hal·lu′ci·na·to′ry** (-nə tôr′ē) ***adj.***

hal·lu·ci·no·gen (hə lo͞o′si nə jən) ***n.*** a drug or other substance that produces hallucinations —**hal·lu′ci·no·gen′ic** ***adj.***

hall′way′ ***n.*** a passageway; corridor

ha·lo (hā′lō) ***n., pl.*** **-los** or **-loes** ⟦< Gr *halōs*, circular threshing floor⟧ **1** a ring of light, as around the sun **2** a symbolic ring of light around the head of a saint, etc., as in pictures

hal·o·gen (hal′ə jən) ***n.*** ⟦< Gr *hals*, salt⟧ any of the five nonmetallic chemical elements fluorine, chlorine, bromine, astatine, and iodine

halt[1] (hôlt) ***n., vi., vt.*** ⟦< Ger *halt machen*⟧ stop

halt[2] (hôlt) ***vi.*** ⟦< OE *healt*⟧ **1** [Archaic] to limp **2** to hesitate —***adj.*** lame —**the halt** those who are lame

hal·ter (hôl′tər) ***n.*** ⟦OE *hælftre*⟧ **1** a rope or strap for tying or leading an animal **2** a hangman's noose **3** a woman's upper garment, held up by a loop around the neck

halve (hav, häv) ***vt.*** **halved, halv′ing** **1** to divide into two equal parts **2** to reduce to half

halves (havz, hävz) ***n. pl. of*** HALF —**by halves** halfway; imperfectly —**go halves** to share expenses equally

hal·yard (hal′yərd) ***n.*** ⟦< ME *halier*: see HALE[2]⟧ a rope or tackle for raising or lowering a flag, sail, etc.

ham (ham) ***n.*** ⟦OE *hamm*⟧ **1** the back of the thigh **2** the upper part of a hog's hind leg, salted, smoked, etc. **3** [Inf.] an amateur radio operator **4** [Slang] an actor who overacts —**ham′my, -mi·er, -mi·est,** ***adj.***

Ham·burg (ham′bərg) seaport in N Germany: pop. 1,603,000

THESAURUS

half ***a.*** partial, divided by two, equally distributed in halves, mixed, divided, halved, bisected; see also HALFWAY.—*Ant.* FULL, all, whole.

half ***n.*** equal share, moiety, fifty percent; see SHARE. —**by half** considerably, many, very much; see MUCH. —**in half** into halves, split, divided; see HALF. —**not the half of it** not all of it, partial, incomplete; see UNFINISHED.

halfback ***n.*** running back, rusher, offensive back; see FOOTBALL PLAYER.

half dollar ***n.*** fifty cents, fifty-cent piece, four bits*; see MONEY 1.

halfhearted ***a.*** lukewarm, indecisive, wishy-washy*; see INDIFFERENT.

halfway ***a.*** midway, half the distance, in the middle, incomplete, unsatisfactory, partially, fairly, imperfectly, in part, partly, nearly, insufficiently, to a degree, to some extent, comparatively, moderately, at half the distance, in some measure, middling; see also HALF.—*Ant.* COMPLETELY, wholly, entirely.

hall ***n.*** **1** [A large public or semipublic building or room] legislative chamber, assembly room, meeting place, banquet hall, town hall, concert hall, dance hall, music hall, arena, ballroom, clubroom, church, salon, lounge, chamber, stateroom, gymnasium, dining hall, armory, amphitheater, council chamber, reception room, waiting room, lecture room, gallery, gym*, mess hall. **2** [An entranceway] foyer, corridor, hallway; see ENTRANCE 2, ROOM 2.

hallelujah ***interj.*** alleluia, praise God, praise the Lord; see YELL.

hallmark ***n.*** symbol, seal, certification; see EMBLEM.

hallowed ***a.*** sacred, sacrosanct, consecrated; see DIVINE.

hallway ***n.*** foyer, entranceway, corridor; see ENTRANCE 2.

halt[1] ***v.*** pull up, check, terminate, suspend, put an end to, interrupt, break into, block, cut short, adjourn, hold off, cause to halt, stem, deter, bring to a standstill, stall, bring to an end, curb, stop, restrict, arrest, hold in check, defeat, thwart, hamper, frustrate, suppress, clog, intercept, extinguish, blockade, obstruct, repress, inhibit, hinder, barricade, impede, overthrow, vanquish, override, dam, upset, stand in the way of, baffle, contravene, overturn, reduce, counteract, quell, prohibit, outdo, put down, finish, forbid, oppose, crush, nip in the bud, break it up, put on the brakes*, hold on*, throw a wet blanket on*, throw a monkey wrench in the works*, clip someone's wings*, tie someone's hands*, take the wind out of someone's sails, squelch*.—*Ant.* BEGIN, start, instigate.

halter ***n.*** leash, bridle, rein; see ROPE.

halve ***v.*** split, bisect, cut in two; see DIVIDE.

ham ***n.*** **1** [Smoked pork thigh] sugar-cured ham, Virginia ham, picnic ham; see MEAT. **2** [*An incompetent actor] one who overacts, hambone*, one who chews the scenery*; see AMATEUR.

ham·burg·er (ham′bur′gər) ***n.*** ⟦after *Hamburg*, Germany⟧ **1** ground beef **2** a cooked patty of such meat, often in a sandwich Also **ham′burg** (-bərg)

Ham·il·ton[1] (ham′əl tən), **Alexander** 1755?-1804; Am. statesman

Ham·il·ton[2] (ham′əl tən) city & port in SE Ontario, Canada: pop. 322,000

ham·let (ham′lit) ***n.*** ⟦< OFr *hamelete* < LowG *hamm*, enclosed area⟧ a very small village

Ham·let (ham′lit) ***n.*** the title hero of a tragedy by Shakespeare

ham·mer (ham′ər) ***n.*** ⟦OE *hamor*⟧ **1** a tool for pounding, having a metal head and a handle **2** a thing like this in shape or use, as the part of a gun that strikes the firing pin **3** one of the three small bones in the middle ear —***vt.***, ***vi.*** **1** to strike repeatedly, as with a hammer **2** to drive, force, or shape, as with hammer blows —**hammer (away) at** to keep emphasizing —**ham′mer·er** ***n.***

hammer and sickle the emblem of Communist parties in some countries

ham′mer·head′ ***n.*** **1** the head of a hammer **2** a shark with a mallet-shaped head having an eye at each end

ham′mer·toe′ ***n.*** a toe that is deformed, with its first joint bent downward

ham·mock (ham′ək) ***n.*** ⟦Sp *hamaca*, of WInd orig.⟧ a kind of bed of canvas, etc. swung from ropes at both ends

ham·per[1] (ham′pər) ***vt.*** ⟦ME *hampren*⟧ to hinder; impede; encumber

ham·per[2] (ham′pər) ***n.*** ⟦< OFr *hanap*, a cup⟧ a large basket, usually covered

ham·ster (ham′stər) ***n.*** ⟦< OHG *hamustro*⟧ a rodent of Europe and Asia, used in scientific experiments or kept as a pet

ham·string (ham′striŋ′) ***n.*** a tendon at the back of the knee —***vt.*** **-strung′**, **-string′ing** **1** to disable by cutting a hamstring **2** to lessen the power of

hand (hand) ***n.*** ⟦OE⟧ **1** the body part attached to the wrist, used for grasping **2** a side or direction *[*at my right *hand]* **3** [*pl.*] possession or care *[*the land is in my *hands]* **4** control *[*to strengthen one's *hand]* **5** an active part *[*take a *hand* in the work*]* **6** a promise to marry **7** skill **8** one having a special skill **9** manner of doing something **10** handwriting **11** applause **12** help *[*to lend a *hand]* **13** a hired worker *[*a farm *hand]* **14** a source *[*to get news at first *hand]* **15** anything like a hand, as a pointer on a clock **16** the breadth of a hand **17** *Card Games a)* the cards held by a player at one time *b)* a round of play —***adj.*** of, for, or controlled by the hand —***vt.*** **1** to give as with the hand **2** to help or conduct with the hand —**at hand** near —**hand in hand** together —**hand it to** [Slang] to give credit to —**hand over fist** [Inf.] easily and in large amounts —**hands down** easily —**on hand** **1** near **2** available **3** present —**on the one** (or **other**) **hand** from one (or the opposed) point of view

hand′bag′ ***n.*** a woman's purse

hand′ball′ ***n.*** a game in which players bat a small rubber ball against a wall with their hands

hand′bar′row ***n.*** a frame carried by two people holding handles at the ends

hand′bill′ ***n.*** a small printed notice to be passed out by hand

hand′book′ ***n.*** a compact reference book; manual

hand′breadth′ ***n.*** the breadth of the human palm, about 4 inches

hand′car′ ***n.*** a small, open car, originally hand-powered, used on railroads

hand′cart′ ***n.*** a small cart moved by hand

hand′clasp′ ***n.*** HANDSHAKE

hand′craft′ ***n.*** HANDICRAFT —***vt.*** to make skillfully by hand —**hand′craft′ed** ***adj.***

hand′cuff′ ***n.*** either of a pair of connected rings for shackling the wrists of a prisoner: *usually used in pl.* —***vt.*** to put handcuffs on; manacle

-hand·ed (han′did) *combining form* having or involving (a specified kind or number of) hands *[*right-*handed*, two-*handed]*

Han·del (han′dəl), **George Fri·der·ic** (frē′dər ik, -drik) 1685-1759; Eng. composer, born in Germany

hand′ful′ ***n.***, *pl.* **-fuls′** **1** as much or as many as the hand will hold **2** a few; not many **3** [Inf.] someone or something that is hard to manage

hand′gun′ ***n.*** any firearm that is held and fired with one hand, as a pistol

hand′-held′ ***adj.*** small enough to be held in the hand while being used

hand·i·cap (hand′dē kap′) ***n.*** ⟦< *hand in cap*, former kind of lottery⟧ **1** a competition in which difficulties are imposed on, or advantages given to, the various contestants to equalize their chances **2** such a difficulty or advantage **3** *a)* any hindrance *b)* a physical disability —***vt.*** **-capped′**, **-cap′ping** **1** to give a handicap to **2** to hinder —**the handicapped** those who are physically disabled or mentally retarded

hand′i·capped′ ***adj.*** physically disabled

hand′i·cap′per ***n.*** a person, as a sportswriter, who tries to predict the winners in horse races

hand·i·craft (han′dē kraft′) ***n.*** skill with the hands, or work calling for it

hand′i·work′ ***n.*** **1** HANDWORK **2** anything made or done by a particular person

hand·ker·chief (haŋ′kər chif′) ***n.*** ⟦HAND + KERCHIEF⟧ a small cloth used for wiping the nose, face, etc., or worn for ornament

THESAURUS

hamburger ***n.*** ground round, ground beef, burger; see MEAT.

hammer ***n.*** maul, mallet, mace, ball-peen hammer, sheet-metal hammer, tack hammer, claw hammer, meat tenderizer, gavel, triphammer, jackhammer, sledge; see also STICK, TOOL 1.

hammer ***v.*** strike, bang, pound away at; see BEAT 1, HIT.

hamper[1] ***v.*** impede, thwart, embarrass; see HINDER.

hand ***n.*** **1** [The termination of the arm] fingers, palm, grip, grasp, hold, knuckles, paw*; see also FIST. **2** [A workman] helper, worker, hired hand; see LABORER. **3** [Handwriting] chirography, script, penmanship; see HANDWRITING. **4** [Aid] help, guidance, instruction; see HELP 1. **5** [Applause] ovation, reception, handclapping; see PRAISE 2. **6** [Round of cards] deal, round, trick; see GAME 1. —**at hand** immediate, approximate, close by; see NEAR 1. —**by hand** handcrafted, handmade, manual; see HOMEMADE. —**change hands** transfer, pass on, shift; see GIVE 1. —**from hand to hand** shifted, given over, changed; see TRANSFERRED. —**from hand to mouth** from day to day, by necessity, in poverty; see POOR 1. —**hand in hand** closely associated, working together, related; see TOGETHER 2, UNITED. —**in hand** under control, in order, all right; see MANAGED 2. —**join hands** unite, associate, agree; see JOIN 1. —**keep one's hand in** carry on, continue, stay in practice; see PRACTICE 1. —**lay hands on** get, acquire, grasp; see SEIZE 1, 2. —**lend a hand** assist, aid, succor; see HELP. —**not lift a hand** do nothing, be lazy, not try; see NEGLECT 1, 2. —**off one's hands** out of one's responsibility, no longer one's concern, not accountable for; see IRRESPONSIBLE. —**on hand** ready, close by, usable; see AVAILABLE. —**on one's hands** in one's care or responsibility, chargeable to one, accountable to; see RESPONSIBLE 1. —**on the other hand** otherwise, conversely, from the opposite position; see OTHERWISE 1, 2. —**out of hand** out of control, wild, unmanageable; see UNRULY. —**take in hand** take responsibility for, take over, handle; see TRY 1. —**throw up one's hands** give up, resign, quit; see YIELD 1. —**wash one's hands of** be done with, reject, refuse to take responsibility for; see DENOUNCE.

hand ***v.*** deliver, give to, return; see GIVE 1. —**hand around** hand out, pass around, allot; see DISTRIBUTE, GIVE 1. —**hand in** deliver, submit, return; see GIVE 1, OFFER 1. —**hand out** give to, deliver, distribute; see GIVE 1, PROVIDE 1. —**hand over** deliver, surrender, give up; see GIVE 1, YIELD 1.

handbag ***n.*** lady's pocketbook, bag, clutch purse; see PURSE.

handbook ***n.*** textbook, vade mecum, guidebook; see BOOK.

handful ***n.*** a small quantity, some, a sprinkling; see FEW.

handicap ***n.*** **1** [A disadvantage] hindrance, obstacle, block; see BARRIER. **2** [A physical injury] impairment, affliction, disability; see IMPEDIMENT 2, INJURY.

handicapped ***a.*** thwarted, crippled, disabled, impeded, burdened, hampered, obstructed, encumbered, put at a disadvantage, checked, blocked, limited, restrained, wounded, curbed, put behind; see also DISABLED, RESTRICTED.—*Ant.* HELPED, aided, supported.

handily ***a.*** skillfully, deftly, smoothly; see CLEVERLY, EASILY.

handiwork ***n.*** handicraft, creation, handwork; see WORKMANSHIP.

handkerchief ***n.*** kerchief, hankie*, snotrag*; see TOWEL.

han·dle (han′dəl) ***n.*** ⟦OE < *hand*⟧ that part of a tool, etc. by which it is held, lifted, etc. —***vt.*** **-dled, -dling 1** to touch, lift, operate, etc. with the hand **2** to manage; control **3** to deal with; treat **4** to sell or deal in —***vi.*** to respond to control *[the car handles well]* —**han′dler *n.***

han′dle·bar′ *n.* [*often pl.*] a curved metal bar with handles on the ends, for steering a bicycle, etc.

hand′made′ *adj.* made by hand, not by machine

hand′maid′en *n.* [Archaic] a woman or girl servant: also **hand′maid′**

hand′-me-down′ *n.* [Inf.] a used garment, etc. passed on to another person

hand′out′ *n.* **1** a gift of food, clothing, etc., as to a beggar **2** a leaflet handed out **3** a news release

hand′pick′ *vt.* **1** to pick by hand **2** to choose with care or for a purpose

hand′rail′ *n.* a rail serving as a guard or support, as along a staircase

hand′set′ *n.* a telephone mouthpiece and receiver in a single unit

hand′shake′ *n.* a gripping of each other's hand in greeting, agreement, etc.

hands′-off′ *adj.* designating or of a policy, etc. of not interfering or intervening

hand·some (han′səm, hand′-) ***adj.*** ⟦orig., easily handled⟧ **1** large; considerable **2** generous; gracious **3** good-looking, esp. in a manly or impressive way —**hand′some·ness *n.***

hand′spring′ *n.* an acrobatic feat in which one turns over in midair with one or both hands touching the ground

hand′-to-hand′ *adj.* at close quarters: said of fighting

hand′-to-mouth′ *adj.* needing to consume all that is obtained

hand′work′ *n.* work done or made by hand

hand′-wring′ing or **hand′wring′ing *n.*** expression of distress or anxiety

hand′writ′ing *n.* **1** writing done by hand, with a pen, a pencil, etc. **2** a style of such writing —**hand′writ′ten *adj.***

hand′y *adj.* **-i·er, -i·est 1** close at hand; easily reached **2** easily used; convenient **3** clever with the hands; deft —**hand′i·ly *adv.*** —**hand′i·ness *n.***

hand′y·man′ (-man′) ***n.***, *pl.* **-men′** (-men′) a man who does odd jobs

hang (haŋ) ***vt.*** **hung, hang′ing**; for *vt.* 3 & *vi.* 5, **hanged** is preferred pt. & pp. ⟦OE *hangian*⟧ **1** to attach from above with no support from below; suspend **2** to attach (a door, etc.) so as to permit free motion at the point of attachment **3** to kill by suspending from a rope about the neck **4** to attach (wallpaper, etc.) to walls **5** to let (one's head) droop downward **6** to deadlock (a jury) —***vi.*** **1** to be attached above with no support from below **2** to hover in the air **3** to swing freely **4** to fall or drape: said as of cloth **5** to die by hanging **6** to droop; bend —***n.*** the way that a thing hangs —**get** (or **have**) **the hang of 1** to learn (or have) the knack of **2** to understand the meaning or idea of —**hang around** (or **about**) [Inf.] to loiter around —**hang back** (or **off**) to be reluctant, as from shyness —**hang in** (**there**) [Inf.] to persevere —**hang loose** [Slang] to be relaxed, easygoing, etc. —**hang on 1** to go on; persevere **2** to depend on **3** to listen attentively to —**hang out** [Slang] to spend much time —**hang up 1** to put on a hanger, hook, etc. **2** to end a telephone call by replacing the receiver **3** to delay

hang·ar (haŋ′ər) ***n.*** ⟦Fr⟧ a repair shed or shelter for aircraft

hang′dog′ *adj.* abject or ashamed

hang′er *n.* **1** one who hangs things **2** a thing on which something is hung

hang gliding the sport of gliding through the air while hanging suspended by a harness from a large type of kite (**hang glider**)

hang′ing *adj.* that hangs —***n.*** **1** a killing by hanging **2** something hung on a wall, etc.

hang′man (-mən) ***n.***, *pl.* **-men** (-mən) one who hangs convicted criminals

hang′nail′ *n.* ⟦OE *angnægl*, a corn (on the toe)⟧ a bit of torn skin hanging next to a fingernail

hang′o′ver *n.* headache, nausea, etc. as an aftereffect of drinking much alcoholic liquor

hang′-up′ *n.* [Slang] an emotional or psychological problem, difficulty, etc.

hank (haŋk) ***n.*** ⟦prob. < Scand⟧ a skein of yarn or thread

han·ker (haŋ′kər) ***vi.*** ⟦prob. < Du⟧ to long or yearn: used with *for* —**han′ker·ing *n.***

han·ky-pan·ky (haŋ′kē paŋ′kē) ***n.*** [Inf.] trickery or deception, as with illicit sex

Ha·noi (ha noi′) capital of Vietnam, in the N part: pop. 2,571,000

han·som (**cab**) (han′səm) ⟦after J. A. *Hansom* (1803-82), Eng inventor⟧ a two-wheeled covered carriage pulled by one horse, with the driver's seat above and behind

Ha·nuk·kah (khä′noo kä′, -kə; hä′-) ***n.*** ⟦< Heb *chanuka*, lit., dedication⟧ an 8-day Jewish festival commemorating the rededication of the Temple: also **Ha′nu·ka′**

hap (hap) ***n.*** ⟦< ON *happ*⟧ luck

hap·haz·ard (hap′haz′ərd) ***adj.*** not planned; random —***adv.*** by chance

hap·less (hap′lis) ***adj.*** unlucky

hap·loid (hap′loid′) ***adj.*** *Biol.* having the full number of chromosomes normally occurring in the mature germ cell, or half the number of the usual somatic cell —***n.*** a haploid cell or gamete

hap′ly *adv.* [Archaic] by chance; perhaps

hap·pen (hap′ən) ***vi.*** ⟦ME *happenen*⟧ **1** to take place; occur **2** to be, occur, or come by chance **3** to have the luck or occasion *[I happened to see it]* —**happen on** (or **upon**) to meet or find by chance

THESAURUS

handle *n.* **1** [A holder] handhold, hilt, grasp, crank, knob, stem, grip, arm; see also HOLDER. **2** [*A title] nickname, designation, moniker*; see NAME 1, TITLE 3. —**fly off the handle** become angry, lose one's temper, blow off steam*; see RAGE 1.

handle *v.* **1** [To deal in] retail, market, offer for sale; see SELL. **2** [To touch] finger, check, examine; see FEEL 1, TOUCH 1. **3** [To deal with] treat, manage, operate; see MANAGE 1.

handling *n.* treatment, approach, styling; see MANAGEMENT.

handmade *a.* made by hand, handicraft, handcrafted; see HOMEMADE.

hand-me-down *n.* secondhand article, discard; old clothes, etc.; see SECONDHAND.

handout *n.* contribution, donation, aid; see GIFT 1, GRANT.

handsome *a.* smart, impressive, stately, good-looking, attractive, athletic, personable, strong, muscular, robust, well-dressed, sharp*; see also BEAUTIFUL.—*Ant.* UGLY, homely, unsightly.

hand-to-hand *a.* face-to-face, facing, *mano a mano* (Spanish); see NEAR 1.

handwriting *n.* penmanship, hand, chirography, writing, cursive, script, longhand, scrawl, scribble, manuscript, calligraphy, scratching*, chicken scratch*.

handwritten *a.* in writing, in longhand, not typed; see REPRODUCED, WRITTEN 2.

handy *a.* **1** [Near] nearby, at hand, close by; see NEAR 1. **2** [Useful] beneficial, advantageous, gainful; see HELPFUL 1, PROFITABLE, USABLE.

hang *v.* **1** [To suspend] dangle, attach, drape, hook up, hang up, nail to the wall, put on a clothesline, fix, pin up, tack up, drape on the wall, fasten up; see also FASTEN.—*Ant.* DROP, throw down, let fall. **2** [To be suspended] overhang, wave, flap, be loose, droop, flop, be in midair, swing, dangle, be fastened, hover, stay up.—*Ant.* FALL, come down, drop. **3** [To kill by hanging] execute, lynch, string up*; see KILL 1. —**hang around*** associate with, get along with, have relations with; see KEEP COMPANY (WITH) at COMPANY. —**hang on** persist, remain, continue; see ENDURE 1, 2. —**hang out*** loiter, spend time, haunt; see VISIT.

hanged *a.* lynched, strung up*, brought to the gallows; see EXECUTED 2.

hanger *n.* coat hook, nail, peg, coat hanger, clothes hanger, holder, clothes rod, wire hanger, collapsible hanger; see also HOLDER.

hanging *a.* dangling, swaying, swinging, overhanging, projecting, suspended, fastened to, pendulous, drooping.

hang-up* *n.* problem, phobia, qualm; see DIFFICULTY 1, 2.

haphazard *a.* offhand, casual, random, careless, slipshod, incidental, unthinking, unconscious, uncoordinated, reckless, unconcerned, unpremeditated, loose, indiscriminate, unrestricted, irregular, blind, purposeless, unplanned, hit-or-miss, willy-nilly; see also AIMLESS.—*Ant.* CAREFUL, studied, planned.

happen *v.* **1** [To be by chance] come up, come about, turn up, crop up, chance, occur unexpectedly, come face to face with, befall, be just one's luck. **2** [To occur] take place, come to pass, arrive, ensue, befall, come after, arise, take effect, come into existence, recur, come into being, spring, proceed, follow, come about, fall, repeat, appear, go on, turn out, become known, be found, come to mind, transpire, come off, go down*; see also RESULT.

hap′pen·ing ***n.*** occurrence; event
hap′pen·stance′ (-stans′) ***n.*** [Inf.] a chance or accidental happening
hap·py (hap′ē) ***adj.*** **-pi·er, -pi·est** ⟦< HAP⟧ **1** lucky; fortunate **2** having, showing, or causing great pleasure or joy **3** suitable and clever; apt —**hap′pi·ly** ***adv.*** —**hap′pi·ness** ***n.***
hap′py-go-luck′y ***adj.*** easygoing
happy hour a time, as in the late afternoon, when a bar features drinks at reduced prices
har·a-kir·i (här′ə kir′ē) ***n.*** ⟦Jpn < *hara*, belly + *kiri*, a cutting⟧ ritual suicide by cutting the abdomen
ha·rangue (hə raŋ′) ***n.*** ⟦< OIt *aringo*, site for public assemblies⟧ a long, blustering speech; tirade —***vi.***, ***vt.*** **-rangued′, -rangu′ing** to speak or address in a harangue
har·ass (har′əs, hə ras′) ***vt.*** ⟦< OFr *harer*, to set a dog on⟧ **1** to worry or torment **2** to trouble by repeated raids or attacks —**har′ass·ment** ***n.***
Har·bin (här′bin) city in NE China: pop. 2,519,000
har·bin·ger (här′bin jər) ***n.*** ⟦< OFr *herberge*, a shelter⟧ a forerunner; herald
har·bor (här′bər) ***n.*** ⟦< OE *here*, army + *beorg*, shelter⟧ **1** a shelter **2** a protected inlet for anchoring ships; port —***vt.*** **1** to shelter or house **2** to hold in the mind *[to harbor envy]* —***vi.*** to take shelter Brit. sp. **har′bour**
hard (härd) ***adj.*** ⟦OE *heard*⟧ **1** firm and unyielding to the touch; solid and compact **2** powerful *[a hard blow]* **3** difficult to do, understand, or deal with **4** *a)* unfeeling *[a hard heart]* *b)* unfriendly *[hard feelings]* **5** harsh; severe **6** having mineral salts that interfere with lathering **7** energetic *[a hard worker]* **8** containing much alcohol *[hard liquor]* **9** addictive and harmful *[heroin is a hard drug]* **10** *a)* of currency, not credit (said of money) *b)* readily accepted as foreign exchange *[a hard currency]* —***adv.*** **1** energetically *[work hard]* **2** with strength *[hit hard]* **3** with difficulty *[hard-earned]* **4** close; near *[we live hard by]* **5** so as to be solid *[frozen hard]* **6** fully *[turn hard right]* —**hard and fast** invariable; strict —**hard of hearing** partially deaf —**hard up** [Inf.] in great need of money —**hard′ness** ***n.***
hard′back′ ***n.*** a hardcover book
hard′ball′ ***n.*** BASEBALL
hard′-bit′ten ***adj.*** tough; dogged
hard′-boiled′ ***adj.*** **1** boiled until solid: said of an egg **2** [Inf.] unfeeling; tough; callous
hard copy a computer printout, often supplied along with or instead of a video screen display
hard′-core′ ***adj.*** absolute; unqualified
hard′cov′er ***adj.***, ***n.*** (designating) any book bound in a stiff cover
hard disk a computer disk with a rigid metal base
hard drive a computer drive for hard disks
hard·en (härd′'n) ***vt.***, ***vi.*** to make or become hard —**hard′en·er** ***n.***
hard hat **1** a protective helmet worn by construction workers, miners, etc. **2** [Slang] such a worker
hard′head′ed ***adj.*** **1** shrewd and unsentimental; practical **2** stubborn; dogged
hard′heart′ed ***adj.*** unfeeling; cruel
har·di·hood (här′dē hood′) ***n.*** boldness
Har·ding (här′diŋ), **War·ren G(amaliel)** (wôr′ən, wär′-) 1865-1923; 29th president of the U.S. (1921-23)
hard′-line′ ***adj.*** aggressive; unyielding, as in politics, etc.
hard′-lin′er (-ər) ***n.*** one who takes a hard-line position
hard·ly (härd′lē) ***adv.*** **1** only just; scarcely **2** probably not; not likely
hard′-nosed′ ***adj.*** [Inf.] tough and stubborn or shrewd
hard′-pressed′ ***adj.*** confronted with a difficulty
hard·scrab·ble (härd′skrab′əl) ***adj.*** producing or earning only a very small amount; barren *[a hardscrabble farm, life, etc.]*
hard sell high-pressure salesmanship
hard′ship′ ***n.*** a thing hard to bear, as poverty
hard′stand′ ***n.*** a paved area for parking aircraft or other vehicles
hard′tack′ ***n.*** unleavened bread made in large, hard wafers
hard′top′ ***n.*** a motor vehicle having a rigid top
hard′ware′ ***n.*** **1** articles made of metal, as tools, nails, or fittings **2** the mechanical, magnetic, and electronic devices of a computer
hard′wood′ ***n.*** **1** any tough, heavy timber with a compact texture **2** the wood of any tree with broad, flat leaves, as the oak or maple
har·dy (här′dē) ***adj.*** **-di·er, -di·est** ⟦< OFr *hardir*, to make bold⟧ **1** bold and resolute **2** robust; vigorous —**har′di·ly** ***adv.*** —**har′di·ness** ***n.***

THESAURUS

happening ***n.*** incident, affair, event; see EVENT.

happily ***a.*** joyously, gladly, joyfully, cheerily, gaily, laughingly, smilingly, jovially, merrily, brightly, vivaciously, hilariously, with pleasure, peacefully, blissfully, cheerfully, gleefully, playfully, heartily, lightheartedly, lightly, to one's delight, optimistically, with all one's heart, with relish, with good will, in a happy manner, with zeal, with good grace, zestfully, with open arms, sincerely, willingly, freely, graciously, tactfully, lovingly, agreeably.—*Ant.* SADLY, morosely, dejectedly.

happiness ***n.*** mirth, merrymaking, cheer, merriment, joyousness, vivacity, laughter, delight, gladness, good spirits, hilarity, playfulness, exuberance, gaiety, cheerfulness, goodwill, rejoicing, exhilaration, glee, geniality, good cheer, lightheartedness, joy, pleasure, contentment; see also JOY.

happy ***a.*** joyous, joyful, merry, mirthful, glad, gleeful, delighted, cheerful, gay, laughing, contented, genial, satisfied, enraptured, congenial, cheery, jolly, hilarious, sparkling, enchanted, transported, rejoicing, blissful, jovial, delightful, delirious, exhilarated, pleased, gratified, peaceful, comfortable, intoxicated, debonair, light, bright, ecstatic, charmed, pleasant, hearty, overjoyed, lighthearted, radiant, vivacious, sunny, smiling, content, animated, lively, spirited, exuberant, good-humored, elated, jubilant, rollicking, playful, thrilled, fun-loving, carefree, at peace, in good spirits, in high spirits, happy as a lark, in ecstasy, beside oneself, bubbling over, tickled pink*, tickled to death*, tickled silly*, happy-go-lucky, in seventh heaven.—*Ant.* SAD, sorrowful, melancholy.

happy-go-lucky ***a.*** cheerful, easygoing, carefree; see IRRESPONSIBLE.

harass ***v.*** tease, vex, irritate; see BOTHER 2.

harbinger ***n.*** indication, sign, signal; see MESSENGER, SIGNAL.

harbor ***n.*** port, pier, inlet; see DOCK.

harbor ***v.*** **1** [To protect] shelter, provide refuge, secure; see DEFEND 2. **2** [To consider] entertain, cherish, regard; see CONSIDER.

hard ***a.*** **1** [Solid] unyielding, thick, heavy, strong, impermeable, tough, tempered, hardened, dense; see also FIRM 2. **2** [Difficult] arduous, tricky, impossible, trying, tedious, complex, abstract, puzzling, troublesome, laborious; see also DIFFICULT 1, 2. **3** [Cruel] perverse, unrelenting, vengeful; see CRUEL. **4** [Severe] harsh, exacting, grim; see SEVERE 1, 2. **5** [With difficulty] strenuously, laboriously, with great effort; see CAREFULLY 1, VIGOROUSLY. —**be hard on** treat severely, be harsh toward, be painful to; see ABUSE. —**hard of hearing** almost deaf, having a hearing problem, in need of a hearing aid; see DEAF. —**hard up*** in trouble, poverty-stricken, strapped*; see POOR 1.

hard-core ***a.*** dedicated, steadfast, unwavering; see FAITHFUL.

harden ***v.*** steel, temper, solidify, precipitate, crystallize, freeze, coagulate, clot, granulate, make firm, make compact, make tight, make hard, petrify, starch, cure, bake, dry, flatten, cement, compact, concentrate, sun, fire, fossilize, vulcanize, toughen, concrete, encrust; see also STIFFEN.—*Ant.* SOFTEN, unloose, melt.

hardened ***a.*** **1** [Made hard] compacted, stiffened, stiff; see FIRM 2. **2** [Inured to labor or hardship] accustomed, conditioned, tough; see HABITUAL.

hardening ***n.*** thickening, crystallization, setting; see SOLIDIFICATION.

hardheaded ***a.*** willful, stubborn, headstrong; see STUBBORN.

hardhearted ***a.*** cold, unfeeling, heartless; see CRUEL.

hardly ***a.*** scarcely, barely, just, merely, imperceptibly, not noticeably, gradually, not markedly, no more than, not likely, not a bit, almost not, only just, with difficulty, with trouble, by a narrow margin, not by a great deal, seldom, almost not at all, but just, in no manner, by no means, little, infrequently, somewhat, not quite, here and there, simply, not much, rarely, slightly, sparsely, not often, once in a blue moon*, by the skin of one's teeth*; see also ONLY.—*Ant.* EASILY, without difficulty, readily.

hard-nosed ***a.*** stubborn, unyielding, hardheaded; see OBSTINATE, RESOLUTE.

hardship ***n.*** trial, sorrow, worry; see DIFFICULTY 2, GRIEF.

hardware ***n.*** domestic appliances, fixtures, metal manufactures, casting, plumbing, metalware, implements, tools, housewares, fittings, aluminum ware, cutlery, house furnishings, kitchenware, household utensils, equipment.

hardy ***a.*** tough, toughened, in good shape, in good condition, hardened, resistant, solid, staunch, seasoned, capable of endurance, able-bodied, physically fit, well-equipped, acclima-

hare (her, har) ***n.*** ⟦OE *hara*⟧ a mammal related to and resembling the rabbit

hare′brained′ ***adj.*** having or showing little sense, flighty, etc.

Ha·re Krishna (hä′rē) ⟦< Hindi⟧ a member of a cult stressing devotion to Krishna

hare′lip′ ***n.*** CLEFT LIP

ha·rem (her′əm, har′-) ***n.*** ⟦Ar *ḥarīm*, lit., prohibited (place)⟧ **1** the part of a Muslim household in which the women live **2** the women in a harem

hark (härk) ***vi.*** ⟦ME *herkien*⟧ to listen carefully: usually in the imperative —**hark back** to go back in thought or speech

hark·en (här′kən) ***vi.*** HEARKEN

Har·le·quin (här′li kwin, -kin) ***n.*** **1** a comic character in pantomime, who wears a mask and diamond-patterned tights of many colors **2** [**h-**] a clown

har·lot (här′lət) ***n.*** ⟦< OFr, rogue⟧ PROSTITUTE —**har′lot·ry** (-lə trē) ***n.***

harm (härm) ***n.*** ⟦OE *hearm*⟧ hurt; injury; damage —***vt.*** to do harm to

harm′ful ***adj.*** causing harm; hurtful —**harm′ful·ly** ***adv.*** —**harm′ful·ness** ***n.***

harm′less ***adj.*** causing no harm —**harm′less·ly** ***adv.*** —**harm′less·ness** ***n.***

har·mon·ic (här män′ik) ***adj.*** of or in harmony —***n.*** *Music* a pure tone making up a composite tone —**har·mon′i·cal·ly** ***adv.***

har·mon′i·ca (-i kə) ***n.*** a small wind instrument with metal reeds that vibrate and produce tones when air is blown or sucked across them

har·mo·ni·ous (här mō′nē əs) ***adj.*** **1** having parts arranged in an orderly or pleasing way **2** having similar ideas, interests, etc. **3** having musical tones combined to give a pleasing effect —**har·mo′ni·ous·ly** ***adv.***

har·mo·nize (här′mə nīz′) ***vi.*** **-nized′**, **-niz′ing** **1** to be in harmony **2** to sing in harmony —***vt.*** to make harmonious —**har′mo·ni·za′tion** ***n.*** —**har′mo·niz′er** ***n.***

har·mo·ny (här′mə nē) ***n.***, *pl.* **-nies** ⟦< Gr *harmos*, a fitting⟧ **1** pleasing arrangement of parts in color, size, etc. **2** agreement in action, ideas, etc.; friendly relations **3** the sounding of two or more tones together in a chord, esp. when satisfying

har·ness (här′nis) ***n.*** ⟦< OFr *harneis*, armor⟧ **1** the combination of leather straps and metal pieces by which a horse, etc. is fastened to a vehicle, etc. **2** anything like this —***vt.*** **1** to put a harness on **2** to control so as to use the power of

harp (härp) ***n.*** ⟦OE *hearpe*⟧ a musical instrument having strings stretched vertically in an open, triangular frame and played by plucking —***vi.*** **1** to play a harp **2** to persist in talking or writing tediously (*on* or *upon* something) —**harp′ist** ***n.***

Har·pers Ferry (här′pərz) town in West Virginia: site of an antislavery raid (1859): pop. 300

har·poon (här po͞on′) ***n.*** ⟦< ON *harpa*, to squeeze⟧ a barbed spear with a line attached to it, used for spearing whales, etc. —***vt.*** to strike or catch with a harpoon

harp·si·chord (härp′si kôrd′) ***n.*** ⟦< It *arpa*, harp + *corda*, CORD⟧ a pianolike keyboard instrument whose strings are plucked rather than struck —**harp′si·chord′ist** ***n.***

Har·py (här′pē) ***n.***, *pl.* **-pies** ⟦< Gr *harpazein*, to snatch⟧ **1** *Gr. Myth.* any of several monsters, part woman and part bird **2** [**h-**] *a*) a greedy person *b*) a shrewish woman

har·ri·dan (har′i dən) ***n.*** ⟦prob. < Fr *haridelle*, worn-out horse⟧ a nasty, bad-tempered old woman

har·ri·er (har′ē ər) ***n.*** ⟦< HARE + -IER⟧ **1** a small hound used for hunting hares **2** a cross-country runner

Har·ris·burg (har′is burg′) capital of Pennsylvania, in the S part: pop. 52,000

Har·ri·son (har′ə sən) **1 Ben·ja·min** (ben′jə mən) 1833-1901; 23d president of the U.S. (1889-93): grandson of William Henry **2 William Henry** 1773-1841; 9th president of the U.S. (1841)

har·row (har′ō) ***n.*** ⟦prob. < ON⟧ a heavy frame with spikes or disks, used for breaking up and leveling plowed ground, etc. —***vt.*** **1** to draw a harrow over (land) **2** to cause mental distress to —**har′row·ing** ***adj.***

har·ry (har′ē) ***vt.*** **-ried**, **-ry·ing** ⟦< OE *here*, army⟧ **1** to raid and ravage or rob **2** to torment or worry

harsh (härsh) ***adj.*** ⟦ME *harsk*⟧ **1** unpleasantly rough or sharp to the eye, ear, taste, or touch **2** offensive to the mind or feelings **3** cruel or severe —**harsh′ly** ***adv.*** —**harsh′ness** ***n.***

hart (härt) ***n.*** ⟦OE *heorot*⟧ a full-grown, male European red deer

har·te·beest (här′tə bēst′, härt′bēst′) ***n.*** ⟦obs. Afrik < *harte*, hart + *beest*, beast⟧ a large African antelope with long horns curved backward

Hart·ford (härt′fərd) capital of Connecticut, in the central part: pop. 140,000

har·um-scar·um (her′əm sker′əm) ***adj.*** ⟦< ?⟧ reckless or irresponsible —***adv.*** in a harum-scarum way

har·vest (här′vist) ***n.*** ⟦OE *hærfest*⟧ **1** the time of the year when grain, fruit, etc. are gathered in **2** a season's crop **3** the gathering in of a crop **4** the outcome of any effort —***vt.***, ***vi.*** to gather in (a crop, etc.) —**har′vest·er** ***n.***

has (haz; *before "to"* has) ***vt.*** *3d pers. sing., pres. indic., of* HAVE

has′-been′ ***n.*** [Inf.] a person or thing whose popularity is past

hash (hash) ***vt.*** ⟦< Fr *hacher*, to chop⟧ to chop up (meat or vegetables) for cooking —***n.*** **1** a chopped mixture of cooked meat and vegetables, usually baked **2** a mixture

THESAURUS

tized, rugged, mighty, well, fit, robust, hearty, sound, fresh, hale, brawny, able, vigorous, powerful, firm, sturdy, solid, substantial; see also STRONG.—*Ant.* WEAK, unaccustomed, unhabituated.

harm ***n.*** **1** [Injury] hurt, damage, impairment; see INJURY. **2** [Evil] wickedness, outrage, foul play; see ABUSE, EVIL 1, WRONG.

harm ***v.*** injure, wreck, cripple; see HURT.

harmed ***a.*** damaged, injured, wounded; see HURT.

harmful ***a.*** injurious, detrimental, hurtful, noxious, evil, mischievous, ruinous, adverse, sinister, subversive, incendiary, virulent, cataclysmic, corroding, toxic, baleful, painful, wounding, crippling, bad, malicious, malignant, sinful, pernicious, unwholesome, corrupting, menacing, dire, prejudicial, damaging, corrupt, vicious, insidious, treacherous, catastrophic, disastrous, wild, murderous, destructive, unhealthy, killing, fatal, mortal, serious, dangerous, fraught with evil, doing harm, doing evil, sore, distressing, diabolic, brutal, unhealthful, satanic, grievous, lethal, venomous, cruel, unfortunate, disadvantageous, felonious, objectionable, fiendish, unlucky, malign, devilish, corrosive.

harmless ***a.*** pure, innocent, painless, powerless, controllable, manageable, safe, sure, reliable, trustworthy, sanitary, germproof, sound, sterile, disarmed.—*Ant.* HARMFUL, injurious, poisonous.

harmonica ***n.*** mouth organ, mouth harp, harp*; see MUSICAL INSTRUMENT.

harmonious ***a.*** **1** [In tune musically] melodious, tuneful, musical, rhythmical, melodic, symphonic, in tune. **2** [Congruous] agreeable to, corresponding, suitable, adapted, similar, like, peaceful, cooperative, in step, in accordance with, in concord with, in favor with, in harmony with, on a footing with, friendly, conforming, well-matched, evenly balanced, symmetrical, congruent; see also FIT.—*Ant.* OPPOSED, incongruous, incompatible.

harmonize ***v.*** blend, arrange, put to harmony, adapt, set, orchestrate, tune, sing a duet, sing in harmony.

harmony ***n.*** **1** [Musical concord] chord, consonance, accord, symphony, harmonics, counterpoint, concert, music, chorus, blending, unity, accordance, chime, overtone, musical pattern, musical blend. **2** [Social concord] compatibility, equanimity, unanimity; see AGREEMENT 1, PEACE 2.

harness ***n.*** tackle, gear, yoke, apparatus, bridle, rigging, fittings; see also EQUIPMENT.

harness ***v.*** fetter, saddle, yoke, outfit, bridle, hold in leash, hitch up, control, limit, cinch, strap, collar, put in harness, rig up, rig out, tie, secure, rein in, curb, check, constrain.

harp ***n.*** lyre, psaltery, zither; see MUSICAL INSTRUMENT.

harp on ***v.*** repeat, pester, nag; see COMPLAIN, TALK 1.

harsh ***a.*** discordant, jangling, cacophonous, grating, rusty, dissonant, strident, creaking, clashing, sharp, jarring, jangled, clamorous, cracked, hoarse, out of tune, unmelodious, rasping, screeching, earsplitting, disturbing, noisy, flat, sour, out of key, tuneless, unmusical, off-key; see also SHRILL.

harshly ***a.*** sternly, powerfully, grimly; see BRUTALLY, FIRMLY 2, LOUDLY, SERIOUSLY 1, 2.

harshness ***n.*** crudity, brutality, roughness; see ANGER, CRUELTY, TYRANNY.

harvest ***n.*** reaping, yield, produce; see CROP, FRUIT, GRAIN 1, VEGETABLE.

harvest ***v.*** gather, accumulate, pile up, collect, garner, crop, cut, pluck, pick, cull, take in, draw in, glean, gather in the harvest, hoard, mow.—*Ant.* SOW, plant, seed.

hash ***n.*** ground meat and vegetables, leftovers, casserole; see MEAT, STEW.

3 a muddle; mess **4** [Slang] hashish —**hash out** [Inf.] to settle by long discussion —**hash over** [Inf.] to discuss at length

hash·ish (hash′ēsh′, ha shēsh′) ***n.*** ⟦Ar *ḥashīsh*, dried hemp⟧ a narcotic and intoxicant made from hemp

hasp (hasp, häsp) ***n.*** ⟦OE *hæsp*⟧ a hinged fastening for a door, etc.; esp., a metal piece fitted over a staple and held in place by a pin or padlock

has·sle (has′əl) ***n.*** ⟦< ?⟧ [Inf.] **1** a heated argument; squabble **2** a troublesome situation —***vi.*** **-sled, -sling** [Inf.] to have a hassle —***vt.*** [Slang] to annoy, harass, etc.

has·sock (has′ək) ***n.*** ⟦OE *hassuc*, (clump of) coarse grass⟧ a firm cushion used as a footstool or seat

hast (hast) ***vt.*** *archaic 2d pers. sing., pres. indic., of* HAVE: used with *thou*

haste (hāst) ***n.*** ⟦OFr⟧ **1** quickness of motion; rapidity **2** careless or reckless hurrying —**make haste** to hurry

has·ten (hās′ən) ***vt.*** to cause to be or come faster; speed up —***vi.*** to move or act swiftly; hurry

hast·y (hās′tē) ***adj.*** **-i·er, -i·est** **1** done with haste; hurried **2** done, made, or acting rashly or too quickly —**hast′i·ly** ***adv.*** —**hast′i·ness** ***n.***

hat (hat) ***n.*** ⟦OE *hætt*⟧ a head covering, usually with a brim and a crown —**pass the hat** to take up a collection —**talk through one's hat** [Inf.] to talk nonsense —**throw one's hat into the ring** to enter a contest, esp. one for political office —**under one's hat** [Inf.] strictly confidential

hatch[1] (hach) ***vt.*** ⟦ME *hacchen*⟧ **1** to bring forth (young) from (an egg or eggs) **2** to contrive (a plan, plot, etc.) —***vi.*** **1** to bring forth young: said of eggs **2** to emerge from the egg

hatch[2] (hach) ***n.*** ⟦OE *hæcc*, grating⟧ **1** HATCHWAY **2** a lid for a hatchway

hatch′back′ ***n.*** ⟦prec. + BACK⟧ an automobile with a rear section that swings up, giving wide entry to a storage area

hat′check′ ***adj.*** of or working in a checkroom for hats, coats, etc.

hatch′er·y ***n.***, *pl.* **-ies** a place for hatching eggs, esp. of fish or poultry

hatch·et (hach′it) ***n.*** ⟦< OFr *hache*, an ax⟧ a small ax with a short handle —**bury the hatchet** to make peace

hatchet job [Inf.] a biased, malicious attack on another's character

hatch′way′ ***n.*** an opening in a ship's deck, or in a floor or roof

hate (hāt) ***vt.*** **hat′ed, hat′ing** ⟦OE *hatian*⟧ **1** to have strong dislike or ill will for **2** to wish to avoid *[to hate fights]* —***vi.*** to feel hatred —***n.*** **1** a strong feeling of dislike or ill will; hatred **2** a person or thing hated —**hat′er** ***n.***

hate′ful ***adj.*** **1** causing or deserving hate; loathsome **2** nasty, unpleasant, etc. —**hate′ful·ly** ***adv.*** —**hate′ful·ness** ***n.***

hath (hath) ***vt.*** *archaic 3d pers. sing., pres. indic., of* HAVE

ha·tred (hā′trid) ***n.*** strong dislike or ill will; hate

hat·ter (hat′ər) ***n.*** one who makes, sells, or cleans hats, esp. men's hats

hau·berk (hô′bərk) ***n.*** ⟦< Frankish *hals*, neck + *bergan*, to protect⟧ a medieval coat of armor, usually of chain mail

haugh·ty (hôt′ē) ***adj.*** **-ti·er, -ti·est** ⟦< OFr *haut*, high⟧ having or showing great pride in oneself and contempt for others; arrogant —**haugh′ti·ly** ***adv.*** —**haugh′ti·ness** ***n.***

haul (hôl) ***vt.*** ⟦< OFr *haler*⟧ **1** to move by pulling; drag **2** to transport by wagon, truck, etc. —***n.*** **1** the act of hauling; pull **2** [Inf.] the amount gained, earned, etc. at one time **3** the distance over which something is transported —**haul off** [Inf.] to draw the arm back before hitting —**in** (or **over**) **the long haul** over a long period of time

haunch (hônch, hänch) ***n.*** ⟦< OFr *hanche* < Gmc⟧ **1** the hip, buttock, and upper thigh together **2** an animal's loin and leg together

haunt (hônt) ***vt.*** ⟦< OFr *hanter*, to frequent⟧ **1** to visit often or continually **2** to recur repeatedly to *[haunted by memories]* —***n.*** a place often visited

haunt′ed ***adj.*** supposedly frequented by ghosts

haunt′ing ***adj.*** not easily forgotten

haute cou·ture (ōt′ko͞o to͝or′) ⟦Fr, high sewing⟧ high fashion for women

haute cui·sine (ōt′kwē zēn′) ⟦Fr, high kitchen⟧ **1** the preparation of fine food by skilled chefs **2** food prepared in this way

THESAURUS

hash over* ***v.*** debate, argue about, review; see DISCUSS.

hassle* ***n.*** quarrel, squabble, row; see DISPUTE.

hassle* ***v.*** pester, annoy, harass; see BOTHER 2.

haste ***n.*** hurry, scramble, bustle, scurry, precipitation, flurry, hurly-burly, impetuosity, rashness, dispatch, impetuousness, foolhardiness, want of caution, hustling, press, recklessness, rush, hastiness, carelessness, irrationality, rashness, giddiness, impatience, heedlessness, plunge, testiness, excitation, abruptness, anticipation.—*Ant.* PRUDENCE, caution, attention. —**in haste** hastening, in a hurry, moving fast; see FAST. —**make haste** hasten, act quickly, speed up; see HURRY 1.

hasten ***v.*** **1** [To make haste] rush, fly, sprint; see HURRY 1. **2** [To expedite] accelerate, speed up, advance, move up, quicken, stimulate, hurry up, push, make short work of, urge, goad, press, agitate, push ahead, put into action, get started, drive on, set in motion, take in hand, blast off, gear up; see also SPEED.—*Ant.* DELAY, defer, put off.

hastily ***a.*** **1** [Rapidly] hurriedly, speedily, fast; see QUICKLY. **2** [Carelessly] thoughtlessly, recklessly, rashly; see CARELESSLY.

hasty ***a.*** **1** [Hurried] quick, speedy, swift; see FAST 1. **2** [Careless] ill-advised, precipitate, foolhardy; see CARELESS, RASH.

hat ***n.*** headgear, millinery, headpiece, helmet, chapeau, bonnet. *Coverings for the head include the following—for men:* cap, yarmulke, derby, straw hat, felt hat, sombrero, cowboy hat, top hat, bowler, Panama hat, fedora, beret, turban; *for women:* hood, snood, cowl, kerchief, beret, bandanna, cloche, boater, bonnet, turban, pillbox, scarf, babushka. —**take one's hat off to** salute, cheer, congratulate; see PRAISE 1. —**talk through one's hat*** chatter, talk nonsense, make foolish statements; see BABBLE. —**throw one's hat into the ring** enter a contest, run for office, enter politics; see CAMPAIGN. —**under one's hat*** confidential, private, hidden; see SECRET 1.

hatch[1] ***v.*** bear, lay eggs, bring forth; see PRODUCE 1.

hate ***n.*** ill will, animosity, enmity; see HATRED.

hate ***v.*** **1** [To detest] abhor, abominate, loathe, scorn, despise, have an aversion toward, look at with loathing, spit upon, curse, dislike intensely, shudder at, not care for, have enough of, be repelled by, feel repulsion for, have no use for, object to, bear a grudge against, shun, denounce, resent, curse, be sick of, be tired of, reject, revolt against, deride, have no stomach for, disfavor, look down upon, hold in contempt, be disgusted with, view with horror, be down on*, have it in for*.—*Ant.* LOVE, adore, worship. **2** [To dislike; *often used with infinitive or participle*] object to, shudder at, not like; see DISLIKE.

hated ***a.*** despised, loathed, abhorred, detested, disliked, cursed, unpopular, avoided, shunned, out of favor, condemned; see also UNDESIRABLE.

hateful ***a.*** odious, detestable, repugnant; see OFFENSIVE 2, UNDESIRABLE.

hater ***n.*** despiser, racist, antagonist; see BIGOT, ENEMY.

hatred ***n.*** abhorrence, loathing, rancor, detestation, antipathy, repugnance, repulsion, disgust, contempt, intense dislike, scorn, abomination, distaste, disapproval, horror, hard feelings, displeasure, ill will, bitterness, antagonism, animosity, pique, grudge, malice, malevolence, revulsion, prejudice, spite, revenge, hate, venom, envy, spleen, coldness, hostility, alienation, bad blood, chip on one's shoulder*, grudge; see also ANGER.—*Ant.* DEVOTION, friendship, affection.

haughty ***a.*** arrogant, disdainful, proud; see EGOTISTIC.

haul ***n.*** **1** [A pull] tug, lift, wrench; see PULL 1. **2** [The distance something is hauled] trip, voyage, yards; see DISTANCE 3. **3** [*Something obtained, especially loot] find, spoils, take; see BOOTY.

haul ***v.*** pull, drag, bring; see DRAW 1.

haunt ***v.*** **1** [To frequent persistently] habituate, visit often, hang around; see LOITER. **2** [To prey upon] recur in someone's mind, obsess, torment, beset, possess, trouble, weigh on someone's mind, craze, madden, hound, terrify, plague, vex, harass, prey on, pester, worry, tease, terrorize, frighten, annoy, cause regret, cause sorrow, molest, appall, agitate, drive someone nuts*; see also BOTHER 2, DISTURB.

haunted ***a.*** frequented, visited by, preyed upon; see TROUBLED.

haunting ***a.*** eerie, unforgettable, seductive; see FRIGHTFUL, REMEMBERED.

hau·teur (hō tur′) ***n.*** ⟦Fr < *haut*, high⟧ disdainful pride; haughtiness
Ha·van·a[1] (hə van′ə) ***n.*** a cigar made of Cuban tobacco
Havana[2] capital of Cuba: pop. 2,078,000
have (hav; *before "to"* haf) ***vt.*** **had, hav′ing** ⟦OE *habban*⟧ **1** to hold; own; possess *[to have* money, a week *has* 7 days*]* **2** to experience *[have* a good time*]* **3** to hold mentally *[to have* an idea*]* **4** to state *[so rumor has* it*]* **5** to get, take, consume, etc. *[have* a drink*]* **6** to bear or beget (offspring) **7** to engage in *[to have* a fight*]* **8** to cause to or cause to be *[have* her sing*]* **9** to permit; tolerate *[I won't have* this noise!*]* **10** [Inf.] *a)* to hold at a disadvantage *b)* to deceive; cheat *Have* is used as an auxiliary to express completed action (Ex.: I *had* left) and with infinitives to express obligation or necessity (Ex.: we *have* to go). *Have got* often replaces *have*. *Have* is conjugated in the present indicative: (I) *have*, (he, she, it) *has*, (we, you, they) *have* —***n.*** a wealthy person or nation —**have it out** to settle an issue by fighting or discussion —**have on** to be wearing
ha·ven (hā′vən) ***n.*** ⟦OE *hæfen*⟧ **1** a port **2** any sheltered place; refuge
have-not (hav′nät′) ***n.*** a person or nation with little or no wealth
hav·er·sack (hav′ər sak′) ***n.*** ⟦< Ger *habersack*, lit., sack of oats⟧ a canvas bag for rations, etc., worn over one shoulder
hav·oc (hav′ək, -äk′) ***n.*** ⟦< OFr *havot*⟧ great destruction and devastation —**play havoc with** to devastate; ruin
haw[1] (hô) ***n.*** ⟦OE *haga*⟧ **1** the berry of the hawthorn **2** HAWTHORN
haw[2] (hô) ***vi.*** ⟦echoic⟧ *see* HEM AND HAW *under* HEM[2]
Ha·wai·i (hə wä′ē, -wī′ē) **1** state of the U.S., consisting of a group of islands (**Hawaiian Islands**) in the N Pacific: 6,423 sq. mi.; pop. 1,108,000; cap. Honolulu: abbrev. *HI* **2** the largest of these islands —**Ha·wai′ian** (-yən) ***adj., n.***
hawk[1] (hôk) ***n.*** ⟦OE *hafoc*⟧ **1** a bird of prey with short, rounded wings, a long tail, and a hooked beak and claws **2** an advocate of war
hawk[2] (hôk) ***vt.*** ⟦< HAWKER⟧ to advertise or peddle (goods) in the streets by shouting
hawk[3] (hôk) ***vi., vt.*** ⟦echoic⟧ to clear the throat (of) audibly
hawk′er ***n.*** ⟦< Old LowG *hoker*⟧ a peddler or huckster
hawk′-eyed′ (-īd′) ***adj.*** keen-sighted
haw·ser (hô′zər) ***n.*** ⟦< OFr *haucier* < L *altus*, high⟧ a large rope used as for mooring a ship
haw·thorn (hô′thôrn′) ***n.*** ⟦< OE *haga*, hedge + THORN⟧ a thorny shrub or small tree of the rose family, with flowers and small, red fruits
Haw·thorne (hô′thôrn′), **Na·than·iel** (nə than′yəl) 1804-64; U.S. writer
hay (hā) ***n.*** ⟦< OE *hieg*⟧ grass, clover, etc. cut and dried for fodder —***vi.*** to mow and dry grass, etc. for hay —**hit the hay** [Slang] to go to bed to sleep
hay′cock′ ***n.*** a small, conical heap of hay drying in a field
Hay·dn (hīd′'n), **(Franz) Jo·seph** (yō′zef) 1732-1809; Austrian composer
Hayes (hāz), **Ruth·er·ford B(irchard)** (ruth′ər fərd) 1822-93; 19th president of the U.S. (1877-81)
hay fever an allergy to pollen, causing inflammation of the eyes and respiratory tract
hay′loft′ ***n.*** a loft, or upper story, in a barn or stable, for storing hay
hay′mow′ (-mou′) ***n.*** **1** a pile of hay in a barn **2** HAYLOFT
hay′stack′ ***n.*** a large heap of hay piled up outdoors
hay′wire′ ***adj.*** [Inf.] **1** out of order; disorganized **2** crazy —**go haywire** [Inf.] **1** to behave erratically **2** to become crazy
haz·ard (haz′ərd) ***n.*** ⟦< OFr *hasard*, game of dice⟧ **1** risk; danger **2** an obstacle on a golf course —***vt.*** to risk
haz′ard·ous ***adj.*** risky; dangerous
haze[1] (hāz) ***n.*** ⟦prob. < HAZY⟧ **1** a thin cloud of fog, smoke, etc. in the air **2** a slight vagueness of mind —***vi., vt.*** **hazed, haz′ing** to make or become hazy: often with *over*
haze[2] (hāz) ***vt.*** **hazed, haz′ing** ⟦< ?⟧ to initiate or discipline by forcing to do ridiculous or painful things
ha·zel (hā′zəl) ***n.*** ⟦OE *hæsel*⟧ **1** a shrub or tree of the birch family, with edible nuts **2** a reddish brown —***adj.*** **1** light reddish-brown **2** greenish-gray or greenish-brown: said of eyes
ha′zel·nut′ ***n.*** FILBERT
ha·zy (hā′zē) ***adj.*** **-zi·er, -zi·est** ⟦prob. < OE *hasu*, dusky⟧ **1** somewhat foggy or smoky **2** somewhat vague —**ha′zi·ly** ***adv.*** —**ha′zi·ness** ***n.***
H-bomb (āch′bäm′) ***n.*** HYDROGEN BOMB
hdqrs *abbrev.* headquarters
HDTV *abbrev.* high-definition television
he (hē) ***pron.***, *pl. see* THEY ⟦OE⟧ **1** the man, boy, or male animal previously mentioned **2** anyone *[he* who laughs last laughs best*]* —***n.*** a male
He *Chem. symbol for* helium
head (hed) ***n.*** ⟦OE *heafod*⟧ **1** the part of the body containing the brain, jaws, eyes, ears, nose, mouth, etc. **2** the mind; intelligence **3** *pl.* **head** a unit of counting *[ten head* of cattle*]* **4** the main side of a coin: often **heads** **5** the uppermost part or thing; top **6** the topic or title of a section, chapter, etc. **7** the foremost or projecting part; front **8** the part designed for holding, striking, etc. *[the head* of a nail*]* **9** the part of a tape recorder that records or plays back the magnetic signals on the tape **10** the membrane across the end of a drum, etc. **11** the source of a river, etc. **12** froth, as on beer **13** a position of

THESAURUS

have ***v.*** **1** [To be in possession of] possess, keep, retain, guard, use, maintain, control, treasure, keep title to, hold; see also OWN 1. **2** [To bear] beget, give birth to, bring forth; see PRODUCE 1. **3** [*To have sexual intercourse with] seduce, sleep with*, deflower; see COPULATE. —**have on** be clothed in, be wearing, try on; see WEAR 1. —**have something on someone** be able to expose, have special knowledge of, be able to control; see CONVICT, KNOW 1. —**have to** be compelled to, be forced to, should, ought, be someone's duty to, be up to, have got to; see also MUST.

haven ***n.*** port, harbor, roadstead; see REFUGE 1, SHELTER.

having ***a.*** owning, possessing, enjoying, holding, controlling; see also COMMANDING.

havoc ***n.*** devastation, plunder, ruin; see DESTRUCTION 2.

hawk[1] ***n.*** **1** [A member of the Accipitridae] bird of prey, osprey, falcon; see BIRD. **2** [A warlike person] militarist, chauvinist, warmonger; see CONSERVATIVE, RADICAL.

hay ***n.*** fodder, roughage, forage, feed; see also GRASS 1. *Hay includes the following:* red clover, wild hay, timothy, alsike, sweet clover, swamp hay, alfalfa, oat hay, millet. —**hit the hay*** go to bed, rest, recline; see SLEEP.

hazard ***n.*** risk, peril, jeopardy; see DANGER.

hazard ***v.*** stake, try, guess; see CHANCE, GAMBLE, RISK.

hazardous ***a.*** perilous, uncertain, precarious; see DANGEROUS.

haze[1] ***n.*** mist, smog, cloudiness; see FOG.

hazy ***a.*** cloudy, foggy, murky, misty, unclear, overcast, steaming, filmy, gauzy, vaporous, smoky, dim, dull, indistinct, smoggy, fumy, crepuscular, bleary, nebulous, shadowy, dusky, obscure, thick, opaque, frosty, veiled, blurred, semitransparent, blurry, faint; see also DARK 1.—*Ant.* CLEAR, bright, cloudless.

he ***pron.*** this one, the male, the above-named, this man, this boy, that man, that boy, this male animal, that male animal, third person masculine singular.

head ***n.*** **1** [The skull] brainpan, scalp, crown, bean*, noggin*, noodle*. **2** [A leader or supervisor] commander, commanding officer, ruler; see LEADER 2. **3** [The top] summit, peak, crest; see TOP 1. **4** [*The beginning] front, start, source; see ORIGIN 2. **5** [An attachment] cap, bottle top, cork; see COVER 1. **6** [*Intelligence] brains, foresight, ingenuity; see JUDGMENT 1. **7** [*Drug addict] habitual user of drugs, acidhead*, pothead*; see ADDICT. —**come to a head** culminate, reach a crisis, come to a climax; see CLIMAX. —**get it through one's head** learn, comprehend, see; see UNDERSTAND 1. —**go to someone's head** stir mentally, stimulate, intoxicate; see EXCITE. —**hang** (or **hide**) **one's head** repent, be sorry, grieve; see REGRET 1. —**head off** block off, interfere with, intervene; see STOP 1. —**head over heels** entirely, precipitately, unreservedly; see COMPLETELY. —**keep one's head** remain calm, keep one's self-control, hold one's emotions in check; see RESTRAIN. —**lose one's head** become excited, become angry, rave; see RAGE 1. —**make head or tail of** comprehend, apprehend, see; see UNDERSTAND 1. —**one's head off** greatly, extremely, considerably; see MUCH. —**on** (or **upon**) **someone's head** burdensome, taxing, strenuous; see DIFFICULT 1. —**out of** (or **off**) **one's head*** crazy, delirious, raving; see INSANE. —**over someone's head** incomprehensible, not understandable, hard; see DIFFICULT 2.

head ***v.*** direct, oversee, supervise; see COMMAND 2, MANAGE 1.

leadership or honor **14** a leader, ruler, etc. **15** *Bot.* a dense cluster of small flowers **16** [Slang] a person dedicated to, addicted to, etc. some interest, activity, etc. —*adj.* **1** most important; principal **2** at the top or front **3** striking against the front *[head winds]* —*vt.* **1** to be the chief of; command **2** to lead; precede **3** to cause to go in a specified direction —*vi.* to set out; travel —**come to a head 1** to be about to suppurate, as a boil **2** to culminate, or reach a crisis —**go to someone's head 1** to confuse or intoxicate someone **2** to make someone vain —**head off** to get ahead of and intercept —**head over heels** deeply; completely —**heads up!** [Inf.] look out! —**keep** (or **lose**) **one's head** to keep (or lose) one's poise, self-control, etc. —**on** (or **upon**) **someone's head** as someone's responsibility or misfortune —**over someone's head 1** too difficult for someone to understand **2** to a higher authority —**turn one's head** to make one vain —**head'less** *adj.*

head'ache' *n.* **1** a continuous pain in the head **2** [Inf.] a cause of worry, annoyance, or trouble

head'board' *n.* a board that forms the head of a bed, etc.

head cold a common cold with congestion of the nasal passages

head'dress' *n.* a decorative head covering

-head·ed (hed'id) *combining form* having a (specified kind or number of) head or heads *[lightheaded, two-headed]*

head'er *n.* **1** a pipe, etc. that brings other pipes together, as in an exhaust system **2** in word processing, text repeated at the top of each page **3** [Inf.] a headlong fall or dive

head'first' *adv.* **1** with the head in front; headlong **2** recklessly; rashly —*adj.* with the head first

head'gear' *n.* a hat, cap, etc.

head'ing *n.* **1** something forming the head, top, or front **2** the title, topic, etc., as of a chapter **3** the direction in which a ship, plane, etc. is moving

head'land (-lənd) *n.* a cape or point of land reaching out into the water; promontory

head'light' *n.* a light with a reflector and lens, at the front of a vehicle

head'line' *n.* printed lines at the top of a newspaper article, giving the topic —*vt.* **-lined', -lin'ing 1** to give (a performer, etc.) featured billing or publicity **2** to be the featured performer, etc. in

head'long' (-lôŋ') *adv., adj.* ⟦ME *hedelinge(s)*⟧ **1** with the head first **2** with uncontrolled speed or force **3** reckless(ly); rash(ly)

head'mas'ter *n.* the male principal of a private school —**head'mis'tress** *fem.n.*

head'-on' *adj., adv.* **1** with the head or front foremost *[a head-on collision]* **2** directly *[to meet a problem head-on]*

head'phone' *n.* [*usually pl.*] a listening device for a radio, stereo, etc. worn over the head to position its speakers over the ears

head'quar'ters *pl.n.* [*with sing. or pl. v.*] **1** the main office, or center of operations, of one in command, as in an army **2** the main office in any organization

head'rest' *n.* a support for the head

head'room' *n.* space overhead, as in a doorway, tunnel, etc.

head start an early start or other competitive advantage

head'stone' *n.* a stone marker placed at the head of a grave

head'strong' *adj.* determined to do as one pleases

head'wa'ters *pl.n.* the small streams that are the sources of a river

head'way' *n.* **1** forward motion **2** progress or success

head'y *adj.* **-i·er, -i·est 1** intoxicating **2** having, using, etc. good judgment or intelligence

heal (hēl) *vt., vi.* ⟦OE *hælan*⟧ **1** to make or become well or healthy again **2** to cure (a disease) or mend, as a wound —**heal'er** *n.*

health (helth) *n.* ⟦OE *hælth*⟧ **1** physical and mental well-being; freedom from disease, etc. **2** condition of body or mind *[poor health]* **3** a wish for one's health and happiness, as in a toast **4** soundness, as of a society or culture

health'care' *n.* the prevention and treatment of illness or injury on an ongoing basis

health food food thought to be especially healthful; specif., food grown with natural fertilizers and free of chemical additives

health'ful *adj.* helping to produce or maintain health; wholesome

health'y *adj.* **-i·er, -i·est 1** having good health **2** showing or resulting from good health *[a healthy color]* **3** HEALTHFUL —**health'i·ness** *n.*

heap (hēp) *n.* ⟦< OE *heap*, a troop⟧ **1** a pile or mass of jumbled things **2** [*often pl.*] [Inf.] a large amount —*vt.* **1** to make a heap of **2** to give in large amounts **3** to fill (a plate, etc.) full or to overflowing —*vi.* to rise in a heap

hear (hir) *vt.* **heard** (hurd), **hear'ing** ⟦OE *hieran*⟧ **1** to be aware of (sounds) by the ear **2** to listen to **3** to conduct a hearing of (a law case, etc.) **4** to be informed of; learn —*vi.* **1** to be able to hear sounds **2** to be told (*of* or *about*) —**hear from** to get a letter, etc. from —**not hear of** to refuse to consider —**hear'er** *n.*

THESAURUS

headache *n.* **1** [A pain in the head] migraine, sick headache, neuralgia; see PAIN 2. **2** [*A source of vexation and difficulty] problem, jumble, mess; see DIFFICULTY 1, 2, TROUBLE 1.

headed *a.* in transit, in motion, en route, going, directed, started, aimed, slated for, on the way to, pointed toward, consigned to, on the road to.

heading *n.* headline, subtitle, address, caption, legend, head, banner head, subject, capital, superscription, headnote, display line, preface, prologue, streamer, preamble, topic, designation, specification.

headless *a.* **1** [Unthinking] witless, fatuous, brainless; see DULL 3, STUPID. **2** [Without a head] decapitated, lifeless, truncated; see DEAD 1.

headlight *n.* searchlight, beacon, spotlight; see LIGHT 3.

headline *n.* heading, caption, title; see HEADING.

headquarters *n.* main office, home office, chief office, central station, central place, distribution center, police station, meeting place, meeting house, manager's office, quarters, base, military station, military town, post, center of operations, base of operations, HQ.

headstone *n.* gravestone, marker, stone; see GRAVE.

headstrong *a.* determined, strong-minded, obstinate; see STUBBORN.

headway *n.* advance, increase, promotion; see PROGRESS 1.

heal *v.* restore, renew, treat, attend, make healthy, return to health, fix, repair, regenerate, bring around, cure, nurse, care for, take care of, renovate, set right, make better, ease, remedy, purify, rejuvenate, medicate, make clean, dress a wound, rebuild, revive, rehabilitate, work a cure, cause to heal, resuscitate, salve, help to get well, ameliorate, doctor*, put someone on his or her feet again, breathe new life into*.—*Ant.* EXPOSE, make ill, infect.

healing *a.* restorative, invigorating, medicinal; see HEALTHFUL.

health *n.* vigor, wholeness, good condition, healthfulness, good health, fitness, bloom, soundness of body, physical fitness, tone, hardiness, well-being, stamina, energy, full bloom, rosy cheeks*, good shape*, clean bill of health*; see also STRENGTH.

healthful *a.* nutritious, restorative, sanitary, hygienic, salutary, invigorating, tonic, stimulating, bracing, salubrious, wholesome, beneficial, health-giving, nutritive, nourishing, energy-giving, fresh, pure, clean, corrective, cathartic, sedative, regenerative, substantial, sustaining, benign, healthy, good for someone, desirable, harmless, innocuous, healing, preventive, disease-free, unpolluted, unadulterated, favorable.—*Ant.* UNHEALTHY, sickly, unwholesome.

healthy *a.* sound, trim, all right, normal, robust, hale, vigorous, well, hearty, athletic, rosy-cheeked, hardy, able-bodied, virile, muscular, blooming, sturdy, safe and sound, in good condition, in full possession of one's faculties, in good health, full of pep*, never feeling better, fresh, whole, firm, lively, undecayed, flourishing, good, physically fit, clear-eyed, in fine fettle, youthful, free from disease, fine, fine and dandy*, hunky-dory*, in the pink*, rugged, fit as a fiddle; see also SANE 1, STRONG 1.—*Ant.* UNHEALTHY, ill, diseased.

heap *n.* pile, mass, stack; see QUANTITY.

heap *v.* pile, add, lump; see LOAD 1, PACK 2.

hear *v.* **1** [To perceive by ear] listen to, give attention, attend to, make out, become aware of, catch, apprehend, take in, eavesdrop, detect, perceive by the ear, overhear, take cognizance of, keep one's ears open, have the sense of hearing, read loud and clear, strain one's ears, listen in, get an earful*. **2** [To receive information aurally] overhear, eavesdrop, find out; see LISTEN. **3** [To hold a hearing] preside over, put on trial, summon to court; see JUDGE. —**hear from** get word from, be informed, learn through; see RECEIVE 1. —**hear of** know about, be aware of, discover; see KNOW 1, 3. —**not hear of** not allow, refuse to consider, reject; see FORBID.

heard *a.* perceived, witnessed, caught, made out, understood, heeded, noted, made clear.

hearer *n.* listener, bystander, witness; see LISTENER.

hear'ing *n.* **1** the act or process of perceiving sounds **2** the ability to hear **3** an opportunity to be heard **4** an appearance before a judge, investigative committee, etc. **5** the distance a sound will carry *[within hearing]*

heark·en (härk'ən) *vi.* ⟦OE *heorknian*⟧ [Now Literary] to listen carefully; pay heed: with *to*

hear·say (hir'sā') *n.* rumor; gossip

hearse (hʉrs) *n.* ⟦< L *hirpex*, a harrow⟧ a vehicle used in a funeral for carrying the corpse

heart (härt) *n.* ⟦OE *heorte*⟧ **1** the hollow, muscular organ that circulates the blood by alternate dilation and contraction **2** the central, vital, or main part; core **3** the human heart considered as the center of emotions, personality attributes, etc.; specif., *a)* inmost thought and feeling *b)* love, sympathy, etc. *c)* spirit or courage **4** a conventionalized design of a heart (♥) **5** any of a suit of playing cards marked with such symbols in red —**after someone's own heart** that pleases someone perfectly —**at heart** in one's innermost nature —**by heart** by or from memorization —**set one's heart on** to have a fixed desire for —**take to heart 1** to consider seriously **2** to be troubled by

heart'ache' *n.* sorrow or grief

heart attack any sudden instance of heart failure; esp., a coronary

heart'beat' *n.* **1** one full contraction and dilation of the heart **2** a moment; instant

heart'break' *n.* overwhelming sorrow, grief, etc. —**heart'break'ing** *adj.* —**heart'bro'ken** *adj.*

heart'break'er *n.* one that causes heartbreak

heart'burn' *n.* a burning, acid sensation beneath the breastbone

-heart·ed (härt'id) ⟦ME⟧ *combining form* having a (specified kind of) heart *[stouthearted]*

heart·en (härt''n) *vt.* to encourage

heart failure the inability of the heart to pump enough blood to supply the body tissues adequately

heart'felt' *adj.* sincere; genuine

hearth (härth) *n.* ⟦OE *heorth*⟧ **1** the stone or brick floor of a fireplace **2** *a)* the fireside *b)* family life; home

heart'land' *n.* a geographically central area having crucial importance

heart'less *adj.* unkind; unfeeling —**heart'less·ly** *adv.* —**heart'less·ness** *n.*

heart'-rend'ing *adj.* causing much grief or mental anguish

heart'sick' *adj.* sick at heart; extremely unhappy or despondent

heart'strings' *pl.n.* deepest feelings or affections

heart'-to-heart' *adj.* intimate and candid

heart'warm'ing *adj.* causing genial feelings

heart'y *adj.* **-i·er, -i·est 1** warm and friendly; cordial **2** strongly felt; unrestrained *[hearty laughter]* **3** strong and healthy **4** nourishing and plentiful *[a hearty meal]* —**heart'i·ly** *adv.* —**heart'i·ness** *n.*

heat (hēt) *n.* ⟦OE *hætu*⟧ **1** the quality of being hot; hotness, or the perception of this **2** much hotness **3** hot weather or climate **4** the warming of a house, etc. **5** *a)* strong feeling; ardor, anger, etc. *b)* the period of this **6** a single bout, round, or trial **7** the period of sexual excitement in animals, esp. females **8** [Slang] coercion —*vt.*, *vi.* **1** to make or become warm or hot **2** to make or become excited

heat'ed *adj.* **1** hot **2** vehement or angry —**heat'ed·ly** *adv.*

heat'er *n.* an apparatus for giving heat; stove, furnace, radiator, etc.

heath (hēth) *n.* ⟦OE *hæth*⟧ **1** a tract of open wasteland, esp. in the British Isles **2** any of various shrubs that grow on heaths, as heather

hea·then (hē'thən) *n.*, *pl.* **-thens** or **-then** ⟦OE *hæthen*⟧ **1** anyone not a Jew, Christian, or Muslim **2** a person regarded as irreligious, uncivilized, etc. —*adj.* **1** pagan **2** irreligious, uncivilized, etc. —**hea'then·ish** *adj.*

heath·er (heth'ər) *n.* ⟦ME *haddyr*⟧ a plant of the heath family, esp. common in the British Isles, with small, bell-shaped, purplish-pink flowers

heating pad a pad consisting of an electric heating element covered with fabric, for applying heat to the body

heat lightning lightning without thunder, seen on hot evenings

heat'stroke' *n.* a condition of high fever, collapse, etc. resulting from exposure to intense heat

heat wave 1 unusually hot weather **2** a period of such weather

heave (hēv) *vt.* **heaved** or (esp. *Naut.*) **hove, heav'ing** ⟦OE *hebban*⟧ **1** to lift, esp. with effort **2** to lift in this

THESAURUS

hearing *n.* **1** [An opportunity to be heard] audition, interview, test, fair hearing, tryout, conference, audit, notice, performance, consultation, council, reception, presentation, audience, attention; see also TRIAL 2. **2** [The act of hearing] detecting, recording, distinguishing; see LISTENING. **3** [The faculty for hearing] ear, auditory faculty, perception, listening ear, sense of hearing, audition, act of perceiving sound, acoustic sensation. **4** [Range of hearing] earshot, hearing distance, reach, sound, carrying distance, range, auditory range; see also EXTENT.

hearsay *n.* noise, scandal, report; see GOSSIP 1, RUMOR.

heart *n.* **1** [The pump in the circulatory system] vital organ, vascular organ, blood pump, cardiac organ, ticker*; see also ORGAN 2. **2** [Feeling] response, sympathy, sensitivity; see EMOTION, FEELING 4, PITY. **3** [The center] core, middle, pith; see CENTER 1. **4** [The most important portion] gist, essence, root; see SOUL 1. **5** [Courage] fortitude, gallantry, spirit; see COURAGE, MIND 1, SOUL 2. —**after one's own heart** suitable, pleasing, lovable; see PLEASANT 2. —**break someone's heart** grieve, disappoint, pain; see HURT. —**by heart** from memory, memorized, learned; see REMEMBERED. —**change of heart** change of mind, reversal, alteration; see CHANGE 1. —**do someone's heart good** please, make content, delight; see SATISFY 1. —**eat one's heart out** worry, regret, nurse one's troubles; see BROOD 2. —**from (the bottom of) one's heart** deeply, honestly, frankly; see SINCERELY. —**have a heart** be kind, empathize, take pity; see SYMPATHIZE. —**lose one's heart to** love, cherish, adore; see FALL IN LOVE (WITH) at LOVE. —**set someone's heart at rest** calm, placate, soothe; see COMFORT 1. —**set one's heart on** long for, need, desire; see WANT 1. —**take to heart** think about, take into account, believe; see CONSIDER. —**wear one's heart on one's sleeve** disclose, divulge, confess; see REVEAL. —**with all one's heart** honestly, deeply, frankly; see SINCERELY.

heartache *n.* sorrow, despair, anguish; see GRIEF, REGRET.

heartbeat *n.* pulsation, throb of the heart, cardiovascular activity; see BEAT 1.

heartbreaking *a.* unbearable, deplorable, joyless; see PITIFUL, TRAGIC.

heartbroken *a.* melancholy, sorrowful, doleful; see SAD 1.

heartburn *n.* indigestion, nervous stomach, stomach upset; see ILLNESS 2.

hearth *n.* **1** [A fireplace] grate, fireside, hearthstone; see FIREPLACE. **2** [Home] dwelling, abode, residence; see HOME 1.

heartily *a.* enthusiastically, earnestly, cordially; see SERIOUSLY 2, SINCERELY.

heartless *a.* unkind, unthinking, insensitive; see CRUEL, RUTHLESS.

hearty *a.* warm, zealous, sincere, cheery, cheerful, jovial, wholehearted, neighborly, well-meant, animated, jolly, ardent, genial, glowing, enthusiastic, genuine, avid, passionate, deep, intense, exuberant, profuse, eager, devout, deep-felt, unfeigned, fervent, warm-hearted, authentic, impassioned, heartfelt, responsive; see also FRIENDLY.—*Ant.* FALSE, mock, sham.

heat *n.* **1** [Warmth] torridity, high temperature, hot wind, heat wave, fever, hot weather, temperature, hotness, warmness, sultriness, white heat, torridness, tropical heat, dog days; see also WARMTH.—*Ant.* COLD, frost, frigidity. **2** [Fervor] ardor, passion, excitement; see DESIRE 2. **3** [Sources of heat] flame, radiation, solar energy; see ENERGY 2, FIRE 1, 2.

heat *v.* **1** [To make hot] warm, fire, heat up, inflame, kindle, enkindle, subject to heat, put on the fire, make hot, make warm, scald, thaw, boil, char, roast, chafe, seethe, toast, oxidize, set fire to, melt, cauterize, reheat, steam, incinerate, sear, singe, scorch, fry, turn on the heat; see also BURN, COOK, IGNITE.—*Ant.* COOL, freeze, chill. **2** [To become hot] glow, warm up, rise in temperature, grow hot, blaze, flame, seethe, burst into flame, kindle, ignite, thaw, swelter, perspire.

heated *a.* **1** [Warmed] cooked, fried, burnt; see BAKED, BURNED. **2** [Fervent] fiery, ardent, avid; see EXCITED, PASSIONATE 2.

heater *n.* radiator, car heater, electric heater; see FURNACE.

heathen *n.* infidel, non-Christian, atheist; see BARBARIAN.

heave *n.* throw, hurl, fling, cast, wing, toss; see also PITCH 2.

heave *v.* rock, bob, pitch, go up and down, lurch, roll, reel, sway, swell, expand, be raised, swirl, throb, ebb and flow, wax and wane, slosh, wash;

way and throw **3** to utter (a sigh, etc.) with effort —*vi.* **1** to swell up **2** to rise and fall rhythmically **3** *a)* to vomit *b)* to pant; gasp —*n.* the act or effort of heaving —**heave to** *Naut.* to stop

heave′-ho′ (-hō′) *n.* [Inf.] dismissal, as from a job: chiefly in **give** (or **get**) **the** (**old**) **heave-ho**

heav·en (hev′ən) *n.* ⟦OE *heofon*⟧ **1** [*usually pl.*] the visible sky; firmament **2** [*often* **H-**] *Theol. a)* a state or place of complete happiness, etc. attained by the good after death *b)* the abode of God, his angels, and the blessed *c)* God **3** any place of great beauty or state of great happiness —**heav′en·ly** *adj.*

heav′en·ward *adv., adj.* toward heaven: also **heav′en·wards** *adv.*

heav·y (hev′ē) *adj.* **-i·er, -i·est** ⟦OE *hefig*⟧ **1** hard to lift because of great weight **2** of more than the usual, expected, or defined weight **3** larger, greater, or more intense than usual *[a heavy* blow, a *heavy* vote*]* **4** to an unusual extent *[a heavy* drinker*]* **5** hard to do *[heavy* work*]* **6** sorrowful *[a heavy* heart*]* **7** burdened with sleep *[heavy* eyelids*]* **8** hard to digest *[a heavy* meal*]* **9** clinging; penetrating *[a heavy* odor*]* **10** cloudy; gloomy *[a heavy* sky*]* **11** designating any large, basic industry that uses massive machinery **12** [Slang] serious and, often, depressing —*adv.* in a heavy manner —*n., pl.* **-ies** **1** *Theater* a villain **2** [Slang] an important person —**heav′i·ly** *adv.* —**heav′i·ness** *n.*

heav′y-du′ty *adj.* made to withstand great strain, bad weather, etc.

heav′y-hand′ed *adj.* **1** clumsy or tactless **2** oppressive or tyrannical

heav′y-heart′ed *adj.* sad; depressed

heav′y·set′ *adj.* having a stout or stocky build

heav′y·weight′ *n.* **1** one weighing more than average; esp., a boxer in the heaviest weight class **2** [Inf.] a very influential or important person

He·bra·ic (hē brā′ik, hi-) *adj.* of or characteristic of the Hebrews, their language, or culture; Hebrew

He·brew (hē′bro͞o′) *n.* **1** *a)* a member of an ancient Semitic people; Israelite *b)* a Jew **2** *a)* the ancient Semitic language of the Israelites *b)* its modern form, the language of Israel —*adj.* **1** of Hebrew or the Hebrews **2** JEWISH

Heb·ri·des (heb′rə dēz′) group of islands off the W coast of Scotland

heck (hek) *interj., n.* [Inf.] *euphemism for* HELL

heck·le (hek′əl) *vt.* **-led, -ling** ⟦ME *hechele*⟧ to harass (a speaker) by interrupting with questions or taunts —**heck′ler** *n.*

hec·tare (hek′ter′) *n.* ⟦Fr⟧ a metric unit of area, 10,000 square meters

hec·tic (hek′tik) *adj.* ⟦< Gr *hektikos*, habitual⟧ **1** feverish; flushed **2** confused, rushed, excited, etc. —**hec′ti·cal·ly** *adv.*

Hec·tor (hek′tər) *n.* in Homer's *Iliad*, a Trojan hero, killed by Achilles —*vt., vi.* [**h-**] to browbeat; bully

hedge (hej) *n.* ⟦OE *hecg*⟧ **1** a dense row of shrubs, etc. forming a boundary **2** any fence or barrier **3** a hedging —*vt.* **hedged, hedg′ing** **1** to put a hedge around **2** to hinder or guard as with a barrier: often with *in* **3** to try to avoid loss in (a bet, etc.) by making counterbalancing bets, etc. —*vi.* to avoid giving a direct answer

hedge fund a partnership of investors who pool large sums for speculating in securities

hedge′hog′ *n.* **1** a small, insect-eating mammal of the Old World, with sharp spines on the back **2** the American porcupine

he·don·ism (hēd′′n iz′əm) *n.* ⟦< Gr *hēdonē*, pleasure + -ISM⟧ the self-indulgent pursuit of pleasure as a way of life —**he′don·ist** *n.* —**he′do·nis′tic** *adj.*

-he·dron (hē′drən) ⟦< Gr⟧ *combining form* a geometric figure or crystal having (a specified number of) surfaces

heed (hēd) *vt., vi.* ⟦OE *hedan*⟧ to pay close attention (to) —*n.* close attention —**heed′ful** *adj.* —**heed′less** *adj.* —**heed′less·ly** *adv.* —**heed′less·ness** *n.*

hee·haw (hē′hô′) *n., vi.* ⟦echoic⟧ bray

heel[1] (hēl) *n.* ⟦OE *hela*⟧ **1** the back part of the foot, under the ankle **2** that part of a stocking, shoe, etc. at the heel **3** anything like a heel in location, shape, crushing power, etc. **4** [Inf.] a despicable person —*vt.* **1** to furnish with a heel **2** to follow closely **3** [Inf.] to provide (a person) with money, etc. —*vi.* to follow along at the heels of someone —**down at** (**the**) **heel** (or **heels**) shabby; seedy —**kick up one's heels** have fun —**on** (or **upon**) **the heels of** close behind

heel[2] (hēl) *vi.* ⟦OE *hieldan*⟧ to lean to one side: said esp. of a ship —*vt.* to cause (a ship) to heel

heft (heft) [Inf.] *n.* ⟦< base of HEAVE⟧ **1** weight; heaviness **2** importance; influence —*vt.* to try to judge the weight of by lifting

heft′y *adj.* **-i·er, -i·est** [Inf.] **1** heavy **2** large and powerful **3** big —**heft′i·ness** *n.*

he·gem·o·ny (hi jem′ə nē) *n., pl.* **-nies** ⟦< Gr *hēgeisthai*, to lead⟧ leadership or dominance, esp. that of one state or nation over others

he·gi·ra (hi jī′rə) *n.* ⟦< Ar *hijrah*, flight⟧ **1** [*often* **H-**] Mohammed's flight from Mecca in A.D. 622 **2** a journey, esp. one made to escape

Hei·del·berg (hīd′′l burg′) city in SW Germany: site of a famous university: pop. 140,000

heif·er (hef′ər) *n.* ⟦OE *heahfore*⟧ a young cow that has not borne a calf

height (hīt) *n.* ⟦< OE *heah*, high⟧ **1** the topmost point **2** the highest limit; extreme **3** the distance from the bottom to the top **4** elevation above a given level; altitude **5** a relatively great distance above a given level **6** [*often pl.*] an elevation; hill

height′en (-′n) *vt., vi.* **1** to bring or come to a higher position **2** to make or become larger, greater, etc.

Heim·lich maneuver (hīm′lik) ⟦after H. J. *Heimlich*, 20th-c. U.S. surgeon⟧ an emergency technique for dis-

THESAURUS

see also WAVE 3.—*Ant.* REST, lie still, quiet.

heaven *n.* **1** [The sky; *often plural*] firmament, stratosphere, heights, atmosphere, azure, beyond, heavenly spheres, upstairs*. **2** [The abode of the blessed] Paradise, the Great Beyond, Elysian fields, bliss, the Abode of the Dead, the Home of the Gods, Heavenly Home, God's Kingdom, Valhalla, the Holy City, Nirvana, the throne of God, the New Jerusalem, the afterworld, the heavenly city, the city of God, our eternal home, the Kingdom of Heaven, the next world, the world to come, our Father's house, the world beyond the grave, the happy hunting grounds*, the eternal rest*, Kingdom Come, the hereafter.—*Ant.* HELL, underworld, inferno. **3** [A state of great comfort] bliss, felicity, harmony; see HAPPINESS.

heavenly *a.* **1** [Concerning heaven] divine, celestial, supernal; see ANGELIC, HOLY 1. **2** [*Much approved of or liked] blissful, sweet, enjoyable; see EXCELLENT, PLEASANT 1, 2.

heavily *a.* laboriously, tediously, weightily, massively, ponderously, gloomily, with difficulty, wearily, profoundly, densely; see also GRADUALLY.—*Ant.* LIGHTLY, gently, easily.

heaviness *n.* burden, denseness, ballast; see DENSITY, MASS 1, WEIGHT 1.

heavy *a.* **1** [Weighty] bulky, massive, unwieldy, ponderous, huge, overweight, top-heavy, of great weight, burdensome, weighty, stout, big, hard to carry, dense, fat, substantial, ample, hefty*, chunky; see also LARGE 1.—*Ant.* LIGHT, buoyant, featherlight. **2** [Burdensome] troublesome, oppressive, vexatious; see DIFFICULT 1, DISTURBING. **3** [Dull] listless, slow, apathetic; see DULL 4, INDIFFERENT. **4** [Gloomy] dejected, cloudy, overcast; see DARK 1, DISMAL, SAD 1.

heavy-handed *a.* oppressive, harsh, coercive; see CRUEL, SEVERE 2.

heckle *v.* torment, disturb, pester; see BOTHER 2, RIDICULE.

hectic *a.* unsettled, boisterous, restless; see CONFUSED 2, DISORDERED.

hedge *n.* shrubbery, bushes, thicket; see PLANT.

heel[1] *n.* **1** [Hind part of the foot] hock, back of the foot, Achilles tendon; see FOOT 2. **2** [The portion of the shoe under the heel] low heel, high heel, stacked heel; see BOTTOM, FOUNDATION 2, SHOE. **3** [*A worthless individual] scamp, skunk*, trickster; see RASCAL. —**down at the heel(s)** shabby, seedy, rundown; see WORN 2. —**kick up one's heels** be lively, have fun, enjoy oneself; see PLAY 1, 2. —**on** (or **upon**) **the heels of** close behind, in back of, behind; see FOLLOWING. —**take to one's heels** run away, flee, take flight; see ESCAPE.

heel[1] *v.* follow, stay by someone's heel, attend; see OBEY.

hefty* *a.* sturdy, husky, stout, beefy, strapping, substantial, massive; see also STRONG 1.

heifer *n.* yearling, baby cow, calf; see ANIMAL, COW.

height *n.* elevation, extent upward, prominence, loftiness, highness, perpendicular distance, upright distance, tallness, stature; see also EXPANSE, EXTENT, LENGTH 1.—*Ant.* DEPTH, breadth, width.

heighten *v.* **1** [Increase] sharpen, redouble, emphasize; see INCREASE, STRENGTHEN. **2** [Raise] lift, elevate, uplift; see RAISE 1.

lodging an object stuck in the windpipe, using air forced up the windpipe by applying sharp pressure to the abdomen

hei·nous (hā′nəs) ***adj.*** ⟦< OFr *hair*, to hate⟧ outrageously evil —**hei′nous·ly *adv.*** —**hei′nous·ness *n.***

heir (er) ***n.*** ⟦< L *heres*⟧ one who inherits or is entitled to inherit another's property, title, etc.

heir apparent *pl.* **heirs apparent** the heir whose right to inherit cannot be denied if the heir outlives the ancestor and the ancestor dies intestate

heir′ess (-is) ***n.*** a female heir, esp. to great wealth

heir′loom′ ***n.*** ⟦see HEIR & LOOM[1]⟧ any treasured possession handed down from generation to generation

heist (hīst) [Slang] ***n.*** ⟦< HOIST⟧ a robbery —***vt.*** to rob or steal

held (held) ***vt.***, ***vi.*** *pt. & pp. of* HOLD[1]

Hel·e·na (hel′ə nə) capital of Montana: pop. 25,000

Helen of Troy *Gr. Legend* the beautiful wife of the king of Sparta: the Trojan War is started because of her abduction by Paris to Troy

hel·i·cal (hel′i kəl) ***adj.*** ⟦< Gr *helix*, spiral⟧ shaped like a helix; spiral

hel·i·cop·ter (hel′i käp′tər) ***n.*** ⟦< Gr *helix*, spiral + *pteron*, wing⟧ a vertical-lift aircraft, capable of hovering or moving in any direction, having a motor-driven, horizontal rotor —***vi.***, ***vt.*** to travel or convey by helicopter

he·li·o·cen·tric (hē′lē ō sen′trik) ***adj.*** ⟦< Gr *hēlios*, the sun + *kentron*, a point⟧ having or regarding the sun as the center

he·li·o·trope (hē′lē ə trōp′) ***n.*** ⟦< Gr *hēlios*, the sun + *trepein*, to turn⟧ **1** a plant with fragrant clusters of small, white or reddish-purple flowers **2** reddish purple —***adj.*** reddish-purple

hel·i·port (hel′i pôrt′) ***n.*** ⟦HELI(COPTER) + (AIR)PORT⟧ an airport for helicopters: also **hel′i·pad′** (-pad′)

he·li·um (hē′lē əm) ***n.*** ⟦< Gr *hēlios*, the sun⟧ a chemical element, a colorless, odorless, very light, nonreactive gas having the lowest known boiling and melting points

he·lix (hē′liks) ***n.***, *pl.* **-lix·es** or **hel·i·ces** (hel′i sēz′) ⟦L & Gr⟧ a spiral

hell (hel) ***n.*** ⟦< OE *helan*, to hide⟧ **1** [*often* **H-**] *Theol.* the state or place of total and final separation from God and so of eternal misery and suffering, arrived at by those who die unrepentant in grave sin **2** any place or condition of evil, pain, etc. —**catch** (or **get**) **hell** [Slang] to receive a severe scolding, punishment, etc.

hell′bent′ or **hell′-bent′** ***adj.*** [Slang] **1** recklessly determined **2** moving fast or recklessly

hell′cat′ ***n.*** an evil, spiteful woman

hel·le·bore (hel′ə bôr′) ***n.*** ⟦< Gr *helleboros*⟧ a plant with buttercuplike flowers, whose rhizomes were once used in medicine

Hel·len·ic (hə len′ik) ***adj.*** **1** Greek **2** of the history, language, or culture of the ancient Greeks —**Hel·len·ism** (hel′ən iz′əm) ***n.*** —**Hel′len·is′tic *adj.***

hell·gram·mite or **hell·gra·mite** (hel′grəm īt′) ***n.*** ⟦< ?⟧ a dark-brown, aquatic fly larva, often used as fish bait

hel·lion (hel′yən) ***n.*** ⟦< Scot dial. *hallion*, a low fellow⟧ [Inf.] a person fond of deviltry; troublemaker

hell′ish *adj.* **1** devilish; fiendish **2** [Inf.] very unpleasant —**hell′ish·ly *adv.*** —**hell′ish·ness *n.***

hel·lo (he lō′, hel′ō′) ***interj.*** used to express greeting

helm (helm) ***n.*** ⟦OE *helma*⟧ **1** the wheel or tiller by which a ship is steered **2** the control or leadership of an organization, government, etc.

hel·met (hel′mət) ***n.*** ⟦< OFr *helme*⟧ a protective, rigid head covering for use in combat, certain sports, etc.

helms·man (helmz′mən) ***n.***, *pl.* **-men** (-mən) one who steers a ship

hel·ot (hel′ət) ***n.*** ⟦after *Helos*, ancient Greek town⟧ a serf or slave

help (help) ***vt.*** ⟦OE *helpan*⟧ **1** to make things easier or better for; aid; assist **2** to relieve *[to help a cough]* **3** to keep from; avoid *[can't help crying]* **4** to serve or wait on (a customer, etc.) —***vi.*** to give aid; be useful —***n.*** **1** a helping; aid; assistance **2** relief **3** one that helps; esp., a hired person or persons; servant(s), farmhand(s), etc. —***interj.*** used to summon assistance, esp. urgently —**help oneself to** to take without asking —**help out** to help in getting or doing something —**help′er *n.***

help′ful *adj.* giving help; useful —**help′ful·ly *adv.*** —**help′ful·ness *n.***

help′ing *n.* a portion of food served to one person

help′less *adj.* **1** not able to help oneself; weak **2** lacking help or protection **3** incompetent or ineffective —**help′less·ly *adv.*** —**help′less·ness *n.***

help′mate′ *n.* ⟦< fol.⟧ a helpful companion; specif., a wife or husband

help′meet′ *n.* ⟦misreading of "an *help meet* for him" (Genesis 2:18)⟧ HELPMATE

Hel·sin·ki (hel′siŋ kē) capital of Finland: pop. 516,000

THESAURUS

heir *n.* future possessor, legal heir, heir apparent, successor, descendant, one who inherits, heiress, beneficiary, inheritor, crown prince.

heiress *n.* female inheritor, crown princess, wealthy girl; see HEIR.

heirloom *n.* inheritance, legacy, bequest; see GIFT 1.

held *a.* grasped, controlled, occupied, guarded, taken, gripped, clutched, defended, stuck, detained, sustained, believed.—*Ant.* LOST, released, freed.

hell *n.* **1** [Place of the dead, especially of the wicked dead; *often capitalized*] underworld, inferno, place of departed spirits, the lower world, the grave, infernal regions, abyss, Satan's Kingdom, purgatory, nether world, hellfire, Hades, bottomless pit, perdition, place of the lost, place of torment, limbo, the hereafter.—*Ant.* HEAVEN, earth, paradise. **2** [A condition of torment] trial, agony, ordeal; see CRISIS, DIFFICULTY 1, 2, EMERGENCY. —**catch** (or **get**) **hell*** get into trouble, be scolded, receive punishment; see GET IT 2. —**for the hell of it*** for no reason, for the fun of it, playfully; see LIGHTLY. —**hell of a*** helluva*, extremely, very bad or good; see POOR 2, EXCELLENT. —**hell on*** hard on, prejudiced against, strict with; see CRUEL, HARMFUL.

hellish *a.* diabolical, fiendish, destructive; see BAD 1.

hello *interj.* how do you do?, greetings, welcome, how are you?, good morning, good day, hi*, hey*, howdy*, hi there*, hi-ya*, *bonjour* (French), *buenos días* (Spanish), ciao*, shalom*, how goes it?.—*Ant.* GOODBYE, farewell, so long.

helmet *n.* football helmet, diver's helmet, hard hat; see HAT.

help *n.* **1** [Assistance] advice, comfort, aid, favor, support, gift, reward, charity, encouragement, advancement, subsidy, service, relief, care, endowment, cooperation, guidance. **2** [Employees] aides, representatives, hired help; see ASSISTANT, FACULTY 2, STAFF 2. **3** [Physical relief] maintenance, sustenance, nourishment; see RELIEF 4, REMEDY.

help *v.* assist, uphold, advise, encourage, stand by, cooperate, intercede for, befriend, accommodate, work for, back up, maintain, sustain, benefit, bolster, lend a hand, do a service, see through, do one's part, give a hand, be of use, come to the aid of, be of some help, help along, do a favor, promote, back, advocate, abet, stimulate, further, stick up for*, take under one's wing, go to bat for*, side with, give a lift, boost, pitch in*; see also SUPPORT 2.—*Ant.* OPPOSE, rival, combat. —**cannot help but** be obliged to, cannot fail to, have to; see MUST. —**cannot help oneself** be compelled to, have a need to, be the victim of habit; see MUST. —**help oneself** aid oneself, promote oneself, further oneself, live by one's own efforts, get on, get along. —**help oneself to** take, grab, pick up; see SEIZE 1, 2, STEAL. —**so help me (God)** as God is my witness, by God, I swear; see OATH 1.

helped *a.* aided, maintained, supported, advised, befriended, relieved, assisted, sustained, nursed, encouraged, accompanied, taken care of, subsidized, upheld.—*Ant.* HURT, impeded, harmed.

helpful *a.* **1** [Useful] valuable, important, significant, crucial, essential, cooperative, symbiotic, serviceable, profitable, advantageous, favorable, convenient, suitable, practical, operative, usable, applicable, conducive, improving, bettering, of service, all-purpose, desirable, instrumental, contributive, good for, to someone's advantage, at someone's command; see also CONVENIENT 1.—*Ant.* USELESS, ineffective, impractical. **2** [Curative] healthy, salutary, restorative; see HEALTHFUL. **3** [Obliging] accommodating, considerate, neighborly; see KIND.

helping *n.* serving, plateful, portion; see FOOD, MEAL 2, SHARE.

helping *a.* aiding, assisting, cooperating, collaborating, synergistic, working, being assistant to, being consultant to, in cooperation with, in combination with, contributing to, accessory to, going along with, in cahoots with*, thick as thieves*; see also HELPFUL 1.

helpless *a.* **1** [Dependent] feeble, unable, invalid; see DEPENDENT 2, DISABLED, WEAK 1, 5. **2** [Incompetent] incapable, unfit, inexpert; see INCOMPETENT.

helplessness *n.* **1** [Disability] poor health, frailty, convalescence; see ILLNESS 1, WEAKNESS 1. **2** [Incompetence] incapacity, disorder, failure; see WEAKNESS 1.

hel·ter-skel·ter (hel′tər skel′tər) ***adv.*** in haste and confusion —***adj.*** disorderly

helve (helv) ***n.*** ⟦OE *helfe*⟧ the handle of a tool, esp. of an ax

Hel·ve·tian (hel vē′shən) ***adj.***, ***n.*** Swiss

hem[1] (hem) ***n.*** ⟦OE⟧ the border on a garment, etc. made by folding the edge and sewing it down —***vt.*** **hemmed, hem′ming** to fold back the edge of and sew down —**hem in 1** to encircle **2** to confine

hem[2] (hem) ***interj.***, ***n.*** the sound made in clearing the throat —***vi.*** **hemmed, hem′ming 1** to make this sound, as in trying to get attention **2** to grope about in speech for the right words: usually used in the phrase **hem and haw**

he·ma- *combining form* HEMO-

he′-man′ ***n.*** [Inf.] a strong, virile man

hem·a·tite (hem′ə tīt′, hē′mə-) ***n.*** ⟦< Gr *haimatitēs*, bloodlike⟧ native ferric oxide, an important iron ore

he·ma·tol·o·gy (hē′mə täl′ə jē) ***n.*** ⟦< Gr *haima*, blood + -LOGY⟧ the study of blood and blood diseases —**he′ma·tol′o·gist** ***n.***

he′ma·to′ma (-tō′mə) ***n.***, *pl.* **-mas** or **-ma·ta** (-mə tə) ⟦< Gr *haima*, blood + *-ōma*, a mass⟧ a tumorlike collection of blood outside a blood vessel

heme (hēm) ***n.*** ⟦ult. < Gr *haima*, blood⟧ the iron-containing pigment in hemoglobin

hemi- ⟦Gr *hēmi-*⟧ *prefix* half *[hemisphere]*

Hem·ing·way (hem′iŋ wā′), **Er·nest** (ʉr′nist) 1899-1961; U.S. writer

hem·i·sphere (hem′i sfir′) ***n.*** ⟦< Gr *hēmisphairion*⟧ **1** half of a sphere, globe, celestial body, etc. **2** any of the halves (northern, southern, eastern, or western) of the earth —**hem′i·spher′i·cal** (-sfer′i kəl) or **hem′i·spher′ic** ***adj.***

hem′line′ ***n.*** the bottom edge of a dress, skirt, coat, etc.

hem·lock (hem′läk′) ***n.*** ⟦OE *hemlic*⟧ **1** *a)* a poisonous European plant related to parsley *b)* a poison made from this plant **2** *a)* an evergreen tree of the pine family *b)* the wood of this tree

hemo- ⟦< Gr *haima*⟧ *combining form* blood

he·mo·glo·bin (hē′mə glō′bin) ***n.*** ⟦< prec. + GLOBULE⟧ the red coloring matter of the red blood corpuscles

he·mo·phil·i·a (hē′mə fil′ē ə) ***n.*** ⟦< HEMO- + -PHILE⟧ a hereditary disorder in which the blood fails to clot normally, causing prolonged bleeding from even minor cuts —**he′mo·phil′i·ac′** (-ak′) ***n.***

hem·or·rhage (hem′ər ij′, hem′rij′) ***n.*** ⟦< Gr *haima*, blood + *rhēgnynai*, to break⟧ the escape of large quantities of blood from a blood vessel; heavy bleeding —***vi.*** **-rhaged′, -rhag′ing** (-ij′iŋ) to have a hemorrhage —**hem′or·rhag′ic** (-aj′ik) ***adj.***

hem·or·rhoid (hem′ər oid′, hem′roid′) ***n.*** ⟦< Gr *haima*, blood + *rheein*, to flow⟧ a painful swelling of a vein in the region of the anus, often with bleeding: *usually used in pl.* —**hem′or·rhoi′dal** ***adj.***

he·mo·stat (hē′mō stat′) ***n.*** ⟦see HEMO- & STATIC⟧ anything used to stop bleeding, as a surgical clamp

hemp (hemp) ***n.*** ⟦OE *hænep*⟧ **1** a tall Asiatic plant having tough fiber **2** the fiber, used to make rope, sailcloth, etc. **3** a substance, as marijuana, made from its leaves and flowers

hem′stitch′ ***n.*** an ornamental stitch, used esp. at a hem, made by pulling out several parallel threads and tying the cross threads into small bunches —***vt.*** to put hemstitches on

hen (hen) ***n.*** ⟦OE *henn*⟧ **1** the female of the domesticated chicken **2** the female of various other birds

hence (hens) ***adv.*** ⟦< OE *heonan*, from here⟧ **1** from this place; away *[go hence]* **2** from this time *[a year hence]* **3** as a result; therefore

hence·forth′ ***adv.*** from this time on; after this: also **hence′for′ward**

hench·man (hench′mən) ***n.***, *pl.* **-men** (-mən) ⟦< OE *hengest*, stallion + *-man*⟧ a trusted helper or follower

hen·na (hen′ə) ***n.*** ⟦Ar *ḥinnā′*⟧ **1** an Old World plant with tiny, white or red flowers **2** a dye extracted from its leaves, used to tint the hair auburn **3** reddish brown —***adj.*** reddish-brown —***vt.*** **-naed, -na·ing** to tint with henna

hen·peck (hen′pek′) ***vt.*** to nag and domineer over (one's husband) —**hen′pecked′** ***adj.***

Hen·ry VIII (hen′rē) 1491-1547; king of England (1509-47)

hep (hep) ***adj.*** [Slang] *var. of* HIP[2]

hep·a·rin (hep′ə rin) ***n.*** ⟦< Gr *hēpar*, liver⟧ a substance found in the liver, that slows the clotting of blood

he·pat·ic (hi pat′ik) ***adj.*** ⟦< Gr *hēpar*, liver⟧ of or like the liver

hep·a·ti·tis (hep′ə tīt′is) ***n.*** ⟦< Gr *hēpar*, liver + -ITIS⟧ inflammation of the liver

her (hʉr) ***pron.*** ⟦OE *hire*⟧ *objective form of* SHE —***poss. pronominal adj.*** of, belonging to, or done by her

He·ra (hir′ə, her′ə) ***n.*** *Gr. Myth.* the wife of Zeus and queen of the gods

her·ald (her′əld) ***n.*** ⟦< OFr *heralt*⟧ **1** [Historical] an official who made proclamations, carried state messages, etc. **2** one who announces significant news, etc. **3** a forerunner; harbinger —***vt.*** to announce, foretell, etc.

he·ral·dic (hə ral′dik) ***adj.*** of heraldry or heralds

her′ald·ry ***n.*** **1** the study of coats of arms, genealogies, etc. **2** ceremony or pomp

herb (ʉrb, hʉrb) ***n.*** ⟦< L *herba*⟧ **1** any seed plant whose stem withers away annually **2** any plant used as a medicine, seasoning, or flavoring —**her·ba·ceous** (hər bā′shəs, ər-) ***adj.*** —**herb′al** ***adj.***

herb·al·ist (hʉr′bəl ist, ʉr′-) ***n.*** one who grows or deals in herbs

her·bi·cide (hʉr′bə sīd′, ʉr′-) ***n.*** any chemical substance used to destroy plants, esp. weeds —**her′bi·ci′dal** ***adj.***

her·bi·vore (hʉr′bə vôr′) ***n.*** ⟦Fr⟧ a herbivorous animal

her·biv·o·rous (hər biv′ər əs) ***adj.*** ⟦< L *herba*, herb + *vorare*, devour⟧ feeding chiefly on grass or other plants

her·cu·le·an (hər kyoo̅′lē ən, hʉr′kyoo̅ lē′ən) ***adj.*** *[sometimes* **H-**] **1** having the great size or strength of Hercules **2** calling for great strength, size, or courage

Her·cu·les (hʉr′kyoo̅ lēz′) ***n.*** **1** *Gr. & Rom. Myth.* a hero famous for feats of strength **2** [**h-**] a very large, strong man

herd (hʉrd) ***n.*** ⟦OE *heord*⟧ **1** a number of cattle or other animals feeding or living together **2** *a)* a crowd *b)* the common people; masses (a contemptuous term) —***vt.***, ***vi.*** to gather or move as a herd

herds·man (hʉrdz′mən) ***n.***, *pl.* **-men** (-mən) one who keeps or tends a herd

here (hir) ***adv.*** ⟦OE *her*⟧ **1** at or in this place: often used as an intensive *[John here is an actor]* **2** to or into this place *[come here]* **3** at this point; now **4** in earthly life —***n.*** this place —**neither here nor there** irrelevant

here′a·bout′ ***adv.*** in this general vicinity: also **here′a·bouts′**

here·af′ter ***adv.*** **1** from now on; in the future **2** following this —***n.*** **1** the future **2** the state after death

THESAURUS

hem[1] ***n.*** border, skirting, edging; see EDGE 1, FRINGE, RIM.

hemisphere ***n.*** half of the globe, Western Hemisphere, Eastern Hemisphere, Northern Hemisphere, Southern Hemisphere, territory; see also EARTH 1.

hemorrhage ***n.*** discharge, bleeding, blood flow; see ILLNESS 1, INJURY.

hen ***n.*** female chicken, pullet, egger*; see BIRD, FOWL.

hence ***a.*** **1** [Therefore] consequently, for that reason, on that account; see SO 2, THEREFORE. **2** [From now] henceforth, henceforward, from here; see HEREAFTER.

henpeck ***v.*** bully, nag, intimidate; see BOTHER 2, THREATEN.

henpecked ***a.*** dominated by a wife, subjected to nagging, browbeaten, intimidated, passive, constrained, compliant, in bondage, yielding, without independence, acquiescent, in subjection, subject, resigned, submissive, docile, meek, cringing, unresisting, unassertive, led by the nose, under someone's thumb, at someone's beck and call, tied to someone's apron strings, nagged, in harness; see also OBEDIENT 1.

herb ***n.*** seasoning, flavoring, spice, medicine. *Herbs include the following:* ginger, peppermint, spearmint, thyme, savory, mustard, chives, cardamom, sweet basil, parsley, anise, cumin, fennel, caraway, rosemary, tarragon, oregano, wintergreen, coriander, cilantro, wormwood, marjoram, bay leaf, dill, sage, lavender, borage, camomile, chervil, digitalis, chicory; see also SPICE.

herd ***n.*** flock, drove, pack, brood, swarm, lot, bevy, covey, gaggle, nest, flight, school, clan; see also GATHERING.

herdsman ***n.*** shepherd, herder, sheepherder; see COWBOY, RANCHER.

here ***a.*** in this place, hereabout, in this direction, on this spot, over here, up here, down here, right here, on hand, on board, on deck*, within reach. **—here and there** often, in various places, sometimes; see EVERYWHERE, SCATTERED.

hereafter ***a.*** hence, henceforth, from now on, after this, in the future, hereupon, in the course of time.

hereafter ***n.*** underworld, abode of the dead, the Great Beyond; see HEAVEN 2, HELL 1.

here·by′ ***adv.*** by this means

he·red·i·tar·y (hə red′i ter′ē) ***adj.*** **1** *a*) of, or passed down by, inheritance from an ancestor *b*) having title, etc. by inheritance **2** of, or passed down by, heredity

he·red·i·ty (hə red′i tē) ***n.***, *pl.* **-ties** ⟦< L *heres*, heir⟧ the transmission of characteristics from parent to offspring by means of genes

here·in′ ***adv.*** **1** in here **2** in this writing

here·of′ ***adv.*** of or concerning this

here's (hirz) *contr.* here is

her·e·sy (her′ə sē) ***n.***, *pl.* **-sies** ⟦< Gr *hairesis*, selection, sect⟧ **1** a religious belief opposed to the orthodox doctrines of a church **2** any opinion opposed to official or established views

her′e·tic (-tik) ***n.*** one who professes a heresy; esp., a church member who holds beliefs opposed to church dogma —**he·ret·i·cal** (hə ret′i kəl) ***adj.*** —**he·ret′i·cal·ly** ***adv.***

here′to·fore′ ***adv.*** up until now

here′up·on′ ***adv.*** **1** immediately following this; at once **2** concerning this subject, etc.

here·with′ ***adv.*** **1** along with this **2** by this method or means

her·it·a·ble (her′it ə bəl) ***adj.*** that can be inherited

her·it·age (her′i tij) ***n.*** **1** property that is or can be inherited **2** tradition, etc. handed down from one's ancestors or the past

her·maph·ro·dite (hər maf′rə dīt′) ***n.*** ⟦after *Hermaphroditos*, son of Hermes and Aphrodite, who became united in a single body with a nymph⟧ a person, animal, or plant with the sexual organs of both the male and the female —**her·maph′ro·dit′ic** (-dit′ik) ***adj.***

Her·mes (hur′mēz′) ***n.*** *Gr. Myth.* the god who is the messenger of the other gods

her·met·ic (hər met′ik) ***adj.*** ⟦after prec. (reputed founder of alchemy)⟧ airtight: also **her·met′i·cal** —**her·met′i·cal·ly** ***adv.***

her·mit (hur′mit) ***n.*** ⟦< Gr *erēmos*, desolate⟧ one who lives alone in a secluded spot; recluse

her′mit·age (-mə tij) ***n.*** a secluded retreat, as the place where a hermit lives

hermit crab a soft-bodied crab that lives in an empty mollusk shell

her·ni·a (hur′nē ə) ***n.***, *pl.* **-as** or **-ae′** (-ē′, -ī′) ⟦L⟧ the protrusion of all or part of an organ, esp. the intestine, through a tear in the wall of the surrounding structure; rupture —**her′ni·al** ***adj.***

her′ni·ate′ (-āt′) ***vi.*** **-at′ed**, **-at′ing** to protrude so as to form a hernia —**her′ni·a′tion** ***n.***

he·ro (hir′ō, hē′rō′) ***n.***, *pl.* **-roes** ⟦< Gr *hērōs*⟧ **1** any person, esp. a man, admired for courage, nobility, etc. **2** the central male character in a novel, play, etc.

He·rod·o·tus (hə räd′ə təs) 484?-425? B.C.; Gr. historian

he·ro·ic (hi rō′ik) ***adj.*** **1** of or like a hero **2** of or about a hero and his deeds **3** daring and risky —***n.*** [*pl.*] heroic behavior, talk, or deeds —**he·ro′i·cal·ly** ***adv.***

her·o·in (her′ō in) ***n.*** ⟦Ger, orig. a trademark⟧ a habit-forming narcotic derived from morphine

her·o·ine (her′ō in) ***n.*** a female hero in life or literature

her′o·ism′ ***n.*** the qualities and actions of a hero or heroine

her·on (her′ən) ***n.*** ⟦< OFr *hairon*⟧ a wading bird with a long neck, long legs, and a long, tapered bill

hero sandwich a long roll sliced and filled with meats, cheeses, vegetables, etc.

her·pes (hur′pēz′) ***n.*** ⟦L < Gr *herpein*, to creep⟧ a viral disease causing small blisters on the skin and mucous membranes

herpes sim·plex (sim′pleks′) a recurrent, incurable form of herpes usually affecting the mouth, lips, face, or genitals

herpes zos·ter (zäs′tər) ⟦< HERPES + Gr *zōstēr*, a girdle⟧ a viral infection of certain sensory nerves, causing pain and an eruption of blisters; shingles

her·pe·tol·o·gy (hur′pə täl′ə jē) ***n.*** ⟦< Gr *herpeton*, reptile⟧ the branch of zoology having to do with the study of reptiles and amphibians —**her′pe·tol′o·gist** ***n.***

Herr (her) ***n.***, *pl.* ***Her′ren*** (-ən) ⟦Ger⟧ **1** Mr.; Sir: a German title of respect **2** a man; gentleman

her·ring (her′iŋ) ***n.*** ⟦OE *hæring*⟧ a small, silvery food fish of the North Atlantic

her′ring·bone′ ***n.*** **1** the spine of a herring, having numerous thin, parallel bony extensions on each side **2** a pattern with such a design, or anything having such a pattern, as a twill weave

hers (hurz) ***pron.*** that or those belonging to her: poss. form of SHE *[hers are better]*

her·self′ (hər-) ***pron.*** a form of SHE, used as an intensive *[she went herself]*, as a reflexive *[she hurt herself]*, or with the meaning "her true self" *[she is not herself today]*

hertz (hurts) ***n.***, *pl.* **hertz** ⟦after H. R. *Hertz*, 19th-c. Ger physicist⟧ the international unit of frequency, equal to one cycle per second

Hertz·i·an waves (hert′sē ən, hurt′-) ⟦see prec.⟧ [*sometimes* **h- w-**] radio waves or other electromagnetic radiation resulting from the oscillations of electricity in a conductor

he's (hēz) *contr.* **1** he is **2** he has

hes·i·tant (hez′i tənt) ***adj.*** hesitating or undecided; doubtful —**hes′i·tan·cy** ***n.*** —**hes′i·tant·ly** ***adv.***

hes′i·tate′ (-tāt′) ***vi.*** **-tat′ed**, **-tat′ing** ⟦< L *haerere*, to stick⟧ **1** to stop because of indecision **2** to pause **3** to be reluctant *[I hesitate to ask]* **4** to pause continually in speaking —**hes′i·tat′ing·ly** ***adv.*** —**hes′i·ta′tion** ***n.***

hetero- ⟦Gr *hetero-*⟧ *combining form* other, another, different: also **heter-**

het·er·o·dox (het′ər ə däks′) ***adj.*** ⟦< prec. + Gr *doxa*, opinion⟧ opposed to the usual beliefs, esp. in religion; unorthodox —**het′er·o·dox′y**, *pl.* **-ies**, ***n.***

het·er·o·ge·ne·ous (het′ər ə jē′nē əs) ***adj.*** ⟦< HETERO- + Gr *genos*, a kind⟧ **1** differing in structure, quality, etc.; dissimilar **2** composed of unlike parts

het′er·o·sex′u·al (-sek′sho͞o əl) ***adj.*** **1** of or characterized by sexual desire for those of the opposite sex **2** *Biol.* of different sexes —***n.*** a heterosexual individual —**het′er·o·sex·u·al′i·ty** ***n.***

heu·ris·tic (hyo͞o ris′tik) ***adj.*** ⟦< Gr *heuriskein*, invent⟧ helping to learn, as by a method of education based on following rules to find answers

hew (hyo͞o) ***vt.*** **hewed**, **hewed** or **hewn**, **hew′ing** ⟦OE *heawan*⟧ **1** to chop or cut with an ax, knife, etc.; hack **2**

THESAURUS

hereby ***a.*** with these means, with this, thus, herewith.

hereditary ***a.*** inherited, maternal, paternal; see GENETIC.

heredity ***n.*** inheritance, ancestry, hereditary transmission, genetics, eugenics.

heresy ***n.*** nonconformity, dissidence, protestantism, dissent, heterodoxy, sectarianism, agnosticism, schism, unorthodoxy, secularism.

heretic ***n.*** schismatic, apostate, sectarian; see CYNIC.

heritage ***n.*** **1** [Inheritance] legacy, birthright, heirship, ancestry, right, dowry; see also DIVISION 2, HEREDITY, SHARE. **2** [Tradition] convention, endowment, cultural inheritance; see CULTURE 1, CUSTOM, FASHION 2, METHOD, SYSTEM.

hermit ***n.*** holy man, ascetic, anchorite, solitary, recluse, eremite, anchoress, pillar saint.

hero ***n.*** **1** [One distinguished for action] brave man, model, conqueror, victorious general, god, martyr, champion, prize athlete, master, brave, warrior, saint, man of courage, star, popular figure, great man, knight-errant, a man among men, man of the hour; see also HEROINE 1. **2** [Principal male character in a literary composition] protagonist, male lead, leading man; see ACTOR.

heroic ***a.*** valiant, valorous, fearless; see BRAVE, NOBLE 1, 2.

heroine ***n.*** **1** [A female hero] brave woman, champion, goddess, ideal, intrepid woman, courageous woman, woman of heroic character, woman of the hour; see also HERO 1. **2** [Leading female character in a literary composition] protagonist, leading lady, female lead; see ACTOR.

heroism ***n.*** rare fortitude, valor, bravery; see COURAGE, STRENGTH.

hesitancy ***n.*** wavering, delaying, procrastination; see DELAY, PAUSE.

hesitant ***a.*** **1** [Doubtful] skeptical, unpredictable, irresolute; see DOUBTFUL, UNCERTAIN. **2** [Slow] delaying, wavering, dawdling; see LAZY 1, SLOW 2.

hesitantly ***a.*** dubiously, falteringly, shyly; see CAUTIOUSLY.

hesitate ***v.*** falter, fluctuate, vacillate, pause, stop, hold off, hold back, be dubious, be uncertain, flounder, alternate, ponder, think about, defer, delay, think it over, change one's mind, recoil, not know what to do, pull back, catch one's breath, weigh, consider, hang back, swerve, debate, shift, wait, deliberate, linger, balance, think twice, drag one's feet*, hem and haw, blow hot and cold, dillydally, straddle the fence, leave up in the air.—*Ant.* RESOLVE, decide, conclude.

hesitation ***n.*** **1** [Doubt] equivocation, skepticism, irresolution; see DOUBT, UNCERTAINTY 2. **2** [Delay] wavering, delaying, dawdling; see DELAY, PAUSE.

to make or shape in this way —*vi.* to conform (*to* a line, rule, principle, etc.)

hex (heks) ***n.*** ⟦Pennsylvania Ger *hexe*, witch⟧ a sign, spell, etc. believed to bring bad luck —***vt.*** to cause to have bad luck

hexa- ⟦< Gr *hex*, six⟧ *combining form* six: also **hex-**

hex·a·gon (heks′ə gän′) ***n.*** ⟦< Gr *hex*, six + *gōnia*, an angle⟧ a plane figure with six angles and six sides —**hex·ag·o·nal** (hek sag′ə nəl) ***adj.***

hex·am·e·ter (hek sam′ə tər) ***n.*** ⟦see HEXA- & METER[1]⟧ a line of verse containing six metrical feet

hey (hā) ***interj.*** used to attract attention, express surprise, etc.

hey·day (hā′dā′) ***n.*** the time of greatest health, vigor, etc.; prime

Hg ⟦L *hydrargyrum*⟧ *Chem. symbol for* mercury

hgt *abbrev.* height

HHS *abbrev.* (Department of) Health and Human Services

hi (hī) ***interj.*** [Inf.] hello

HI Hawaii

Hi·a·le·ah (hī′ə lē′ə) city in SE Florida.: pop. 188,000

hi·a·tus (hī āt′əs) ***n.***, *pl.* **-tus·es** or **-tus** ⟦L < *hiare*, to gape⟧ **1** a gap or break, as where a part is missing **2** any gap or interruption, as in time

hi·ba·chi (hi bä′chē) ***n.***, *pl.* **-chis** ⟦Jpn < *hi*, fire + *bachi*, bowl⟧ a small charcoal-burning grill

hi·ber·nate (hī′bər nāt′) ***vi.*** **-nat′ed**, **-nat′ing** ⟦< L *hibernus*, wintry⟧ to spend the winter in a dormant state —**hi′ber·na′tion** ***n.***

hi·bis·cus (hī bis′kəs, hi-) ***n.*** ⟦< L⟧ a plant of the mallow family, with large, colorful flowers

hic·cup (hik′up′, -əp) ***n.*** ⟦echoic⟧ a sudden contraction of the diaphragm that causes the glottis to close, producing an abrupt sound —***vi.*** **-cuped′** or **-cupped′**, **-cup′ing** or **-cup′ping** to make a hiccup Also sp. **hic′cough′**

hick (hik) ***n.*** ⟦altered < *Richard*⟧ [Inf.] an awkward, unsophisticated person regarded as typical of rural areas: a contemptuous term

hick·ey (hik′ē) ***n.***, *pl.* **-eys** or **-ies** [Inf.] any device or gadget

hick·o·ry (hik′ə rē, hik′rē) ***n.***, *pl.* **-ries** ⟦< AmInd *pawcohiccora*⟧ **1** a North American tree of the walnut family **2** its hard, tough wood **3** its hard, edible nut: usually **hickory nut**

hid·den (hid′'n) ***vt.***, ***vi.*** ⟦OE *gehydd*⟧ *alt. pp. of* HIDE[1] —***adj.*** concealed; secret

hide[1] (hīd) ***vt.*** **hid** (hid), **hid′den** or **hid**, **hid′ing** ⟦OE *hydan*⟧ **1** to put or keep out of sight; conceal **2** to keep secret **3** to keep from sight by obscuring, etc. —***vi.*** to conceal oneself

hide[2] (hīd) ***n.*** ⟦OE *hid*⟧ an animal skin or pelt, either raw or tanned

hide′a·way′ ***n.*** [Inf.] a place where one can hide, be secluded, etc.

hide′bound′ ***adj.*** obstinately conservative and narrow-minded

hid·e·ous (hid′ē əs) ***adj.*** ⟦< OFr *hide*, fright⟧ horrible; very ugly; dreadful —**hid′e·ous·ly** ***adv.*** —**hid′e·ous·ness** ***n.***

hide′-out′ ***n.*** [Inf.] a hiding place

hie (hī) ***vi.***, ***vt.*** **hied**, **hie′ing** or **hy′ing** ⟦OE *higian*⟧ to hasten: usually used reflexively

hi·er·ar·chy (hī′ər är′kē) ***n.***, *pl.* **-chies** ⟦< Gr *hieros*, sacred + *archos*, ruler⟧ **1** church government by clergy in graded ranks **2** the highest officials in such a system **3** a group of persons or things arranged in order of rank, grade, etc. —**hi′er·ar′chi·cal** (-ki kəl) ***adj.***

hi·er·o·glyph·ic (hī′ər ō glif′ik, hī′rō-) ***n.*** ⟦< Gr *hieros*, sacred + *glyphein*, to carve⟧ **1** a picture or symbol representing a word, syllable, or sound, used by the ancient Egyptians and others **2** [*usually pl.*] picture writing **3** a symbol, etc. that is hard to understand —***adj.*** of or like hieroglyphics

hi·er·o·phant (hī′ər ō fant′) ***n.*** ⟦< Gr *hieros*, sacred + *phainein*, to show⟧ in ancient Greece, a priest of a mystery cult

hi-fi (hī′fī′) ***n.*** a radio, phonograph, etc. having high fidelity —***adj.*** of or having high fidelity of sound reproduction

high (hī) ***adj.*** ⟦OE *heah*⟧ **1** lofty; tall **2** extending upward a (specified) distance **3** reaching to, situated at, or done from a height **4** above others in rank, position, etc.; superior **5** grave *[high* treason*]* **6** greater in size, amount, degree, etc. than usual *[high* prices*]* **7** luxurious *[high* living*]* **8** raised in pitch *[a high* note*]* **9** slightly tainted: said of meat, esp. game **10** excited *[high* spirits*]* **11** [Slang] *a)* drunk *b)* under the influence of a drug —***adv.*** in or to a high level, place, degree, etc. —***n.*** **1** a high level, place, etc. **2** an area of high barometric pressure **3** the gear of a motor vehicle, etc. producing the greatest speed **4** [Slang] a condition of euphoria induced as by drugs —**high and low** everywhere —**high on** [Inf.] enthusiastic about —**on high** in heaven

high′ball′ ***n.*** whiskey or brandy mixed with water, soda water, ginger ale, etc.

high′born′ ***adj.*** of noble birth

high′boy′ ***n.*** a high chest of drawers mounted on legs

high′brow′ ***n.*** one having or affecting highly cultivated tastes; intellectual —***adj.*** of or for a highbrow

high′chair′ ***n.*** a baby's chair with long legs and, usually, a tray for food

high′-def′i·ni′tion ***adj.*** designating TV transmission

THESAURUS

hey ***interj.*** you there, say, hey there, hi*, hi there*; see also HALT, HELLO.

heyday ***n.*** adolescence, bloom, prime of life; see YOUTH 1.

hibernate ***v.*** sleep through the winter, lie dormant, hole up*; see SLEEP.

hidden ***a.*** secluded, out of sight, covert, concealed, undercover, occult, in the dark, in a haze, in a fog, in darkness, masked, screened, veiled, cloaked, obscured, disguised, invisible, clouded, sealed, unobserved, blotted, impenetrable, unseen, eclipsed, camouflaged, shrouded, shadowy, unknown, buried, undetected, deep, unsuspected, inscrutable, illegible, puzzling, unobserved, out of view, dim, clandestine, subterranean, cloistered, suppressed, dark, inward, underground, unrevealed, withheld, surreptitious, underhand, kept in the dark, under wraps; see also PRIVATE.—*Ant.* OBVIOUS, open, apparent.

hide[1] ***v.*** **1** [To conceal] shroud, curtain, veil, camouflage, cover, mask, cloak, not give away, screen, blot out, bury, suppress, withhold, keep underground, stifle, keep secret, hush up, shield, eclipse, not tell, lock up, put out of sight, put out of the way, hold back, keep from, secrete, smuggle, shadow, conceal from sight, keep out of sight, stow away, protect, hoard, store, seclude, reserve, tuck away, cache, harbor, envelop, closet, conceal, hush, obscure, wrap, shelter, throw a veil over, keep in the dark, keep under one's hat*, seal one's lips*, put the lid on*, salt away*; see also DISGUISE.—*Ant.* EXPOSE, lay bare, uncover. **2** [To keep oneself concealed] disguise oneself, change one's identity, cover one's traces, keep out of sight, go underground, lie in ambush, sneak, travel incognito, take refuge, disappear, prowl, burrow, skulk, avoid notice, lie in wait, hibernate, lie concealed, lie low, conceal oneself, lurk, shut oneself up, seclude oneself, lie hidden, keep out of the way, stay in hiding, hide out*, cover up, duck*, keep in the background; see also DECEIVE.

hide[2] ***n.*** pelt, rawhide, pigskin, horsehide, cowhide, suede, kidskin, chamois, bearskin, goatskin, jacket, sheepskin, sealskin, snakeskin, alligator skin, calfskin; see also FUR, LEATHER, SKIN. —**neither hide nor hair** nothing whatsoever, no indication, not at all; see NOTHING.

hideous ***a.*** ghastly, grisly, frightful; see UGLY 1.

hiding ***a.*** concealing, in concealment, out of sight; see HIDDEN.

hierarchy ***n.*** regime, bureaucracy, chain of command; see GOVERNMENT 1, 2.

high ***a.*** **1** [Tall] towering, gigantic, big, colossal, tremendous, great, giant, huge, formidable, immense, tall, long, sky-scraping, steep, sky-high; see also LARGE 1.—*Ant.* SHORT, diminutive, undersized. **2** [Elevated] lofty, uplifted, soaring, aerial, high-reaching, flying, hovering, overtopping, jutting; see also RAISED 1.—*Ant.* LOW, depressed, underground. **3** [Exalted] eminent, leading, powerful; see DISTINGUISHED 2, NOBLE 1, 2. **4** [Expensive] high-priced, costly, precious; see EXPENSIVE. **5** [To an unusual degree] great, extraordinary, special; see UNUSUAL 1, 2. **6** [Shrill] piercing, sharp, penetrating; see LOUD 1, SHRILL. **7** [*Drunk] intoxicated, tipsy, inebriated; see DRUNK. **8** [*Under the influence of drugs] stoned*, freaked out*, wasted*, turned on*, on a trip*, tripping*, hyped-up*, spaced-out*, zonked out*. —**high and low** in every nook and corner, in all possible places, exhaustively; see COMPLETELY, EVERYWHERE.

higher ***a.*** taller, more advanced, superior to, over, larger than, ahead, surpassing, bigger, greater; see also ABOVE 1, BEYOND.—*Ant.* SHORTER, smaller, inferior.

highest ***a.*** topmost, superlative, supreme, maximal, most, top, maximum, head, preeminent, capital, chief, paramount, tiptop, top-notch*.

with greater clarity of image and sound than that of standard television
high'-end' *adj.* [Inf.] expensive and of very high quality
high'er-up' *n.* [Inf.] a person of higher rank or position
high'fa·lu'tin (-fə lo͞ot''n) *adj.* [Inf.] pretentious or pompous: also sp. **high'fa·lu'ting**
high fidelity in radio, sound recording, etc., nearly exact reproduction of sound
high'-five' *n.* [Inf.] a slapping of the upraised open hand of another person, as in celebration
high'-flown' *adj.* **1** extravagantly ambitious **2** bombastic
high frequency any radio frequency between 3 and 30 megahertz
High German the group of West Germanic dialects spoken in central and S Germany
high'hand'ed *adj.* overbearing —**high'hand'ed·ly** *adv.* —**high'hand'ed·ness** *n.*
high'-hat' (-hat'; *for v., usually,* -hat') *adj.* [Slang] snobbish —*vt.* **-hat'ted, -hat'ting** [Slang] to snub
high'land (-lənd) *n.* a region with many hills or mountains —**the Highlands** mountainous region occupying most of N Scotland —**High'land·er** *n.*
high'-lev'el *adj.* **1** of or by persons of high office or rank **2** in a high office
high'light' *n.* **1** a part on which light is brightest: also **high light** **2** the most important or interesting part, scene, etc. —*vt.* **1** to give highlights to **2** to give prominence to; emphasize
high'light'er *n.* a pen with a broad felt tip for marking passages as in a textbook
high'ly *adv.* **1** very much **2** favorably **3** at a high level, wage, etc.
high'-mind'ed *adj.* having high ideals, principles, etc. —**high'-mind'ed·ly** *adv.*
high'ness *n.* **1** height **2** [H-] a title used in speaking to or of a member of a royal family
high'-pres'sure *adj.* **1** having or withstanding high pressure **2** using forcefully persuasive or insistent methods —*vt.* **-sured, -sur·ing** [Inf.] to urge with such methods
high'-pro'file' *adj.* well-known, highly publicized, etc.
high'-rise' *adj.* tall and having many stories —*n.* a high-rise building
high road **1** [Chiefly Brit.] a highway **2** an easy or direct way Also **high'road'** *n.*
high roller **1** a person who gambles for high stakes **2** a person who spends money freely
high school a secondary school that includes grades 10, 11, 12, and sometimes 9
high seas open ocean waters outside the territorial limits of any nation
high sign a secret signal, given as in warning
high'-spir'it·ed (-spir'i tid) *adj.* **1** courageous **2** spirited; fiery **3** lively; merry
high'-strung' *adj.* highly sensitive or nervous and tense
high tech (tek) **1** of specialized, complex technology: in full **high technology** **2** furnishings, fashions, etc. whose design or look suggests industrial use —**high'-tech'** *adj.*
high'-ten'sion *adj.* having or carrying a high voltage
high tide the highest level to which the tide rises
high time time beyond the proper time but before it is too late
high'way' *n.* **1** a public road **2** a main road; thoroughfare
high'way·man (-mən) *n., pl.* **-men** (-mən) a man who formerly robbed travelers on a highway
high wire a cable stretched high above the ground, on which aerialists perform
hi·jack (hī'jak') *vt.* **1** to steal (goods in transit, etc.) by force **2** to seize control forcibly of (an aircraft, etc.), esp. in order to go to a nonscheduled destination —**hi'jack'er** *n.*
hike (hīk) *vi.* **hiked, hik'ing** ⟦< dial. *heik*⟧ to take a long walk —*vt.* [Inf.] **1** to pull up; hoist **2** to raise (prices, etc.) —*n.* **1** a long walk **2** [Inf.] a rise —**hik'er** *n.*
hi·lar·i·ous (hi ler'ē əs) *adj.* ⟦< Gr *hilaros*, cheerful⟧ **1** noisily merry **2** very funny —**hi·lar'i·ous·ly** *adv.* —**hi·lar'i·ty** (-i tē) *n.*
hill (hil) *n.* ⟦OE *hyll*⟧ **1** a natural raised part of the earth's surface, smaller than a mountain **2** a small pile, heap, or mound
hill'bil'ly *n., pl.* **-lies** ⟦prec. + *Billy*⟧ [Inf.] one who lives in or comes from the mountains or backwoods of the South, specif. Appalachia: sometimes a contemptuous term
hill'side' *n.* the side of a hill
hill'top' *n.* the top of a hill
hill'y *adj.* **-i·er, -i·est** full of hills —**hill'i·ness** *n.*
hilt (hilt) *n.* ⟦OE⟧ the handle of a sword, dagger, tool, etc.
him (him) *pron.* ⟦OE⟧ *objective form of* HE
Hi·ma·la·yas (him'ə lā'əz) mountain system of SC Asia, mostly in India & China —**Hi'ma·la'yan** *adj.*
him·self' *pron.* a form of HE, used as an intensive *[he went himself]*, as a reflexive *[he hurt himself]*, or with the meaning "his true self" *[he is not himself today]*
hind[1] (hīnd) *adj.* ⟦see HINDER[2]⟧ back; rear
hind[2] (hīnd) *n.* ⟦OE⟧ the female of the red deer
Hind *abbrev.* **1** Hindi **2** Hindu
hin·der[1] (hin'dər) *vt.* ⟦OE *hindrian*⟧ **1** to keep back; stop **2** to impede; thwart
hind·er[2] (hīn'dər) *adj.* ⟦OE⟧ [Now Rare] rear
Hin·di (hin'dē) *n.* the main (and official) language of India
hind'most' *adj.* farthest back; last
hind'quar'ter *n.* either of the two hind legs and the adjoining part of a carcass of veal, beef, etc.
hin·drance (hin'drəns) *n.* **1** the act of hindering **2** an obstacle
hind'sight' *n.* ability to see, after the event, what should have been done
Hin·du (hin'do͞o') *n.* a follower of Hinduism —*adj.* designating or of the Hindus or Hinduism
Hin'du·ism' *n.* the principal religion of India
Hin·du·stan (hin'do͞o stan') **1** region in N India **2** the entire Indian subcontinent **3** the republic of India

THESAURUS

highly *a.* extremely, profoundly, deeply; see VERY.
highness *n.* **1** [Quality of being high] length, tallness, loftiness; see HEIGHT. **2** [Term of respect, usually to royalty; *often capitalized*] majesty, lordship, ladyship; see ROYALTY.
high-pressure *a.* forceful, potent, compelling; see POWERFUL 1.
high school *n.* public school, secondary school, preparatory school, prep school, private academy, military school, upper grades, trade school, seminary, junior high school, senior high school, vocational school; see also SCHOOL 1.
high-spirited *a.* daring, dauntless, reckless; see BRAVE.
high-strung *a.* nervous, tense, impatient; see RESTLESS.
highway *n.* roadway, parkway, superhighway, freeway, turnpike, toll road, state highway, thruway, expressway, interstate; see also ROAD 1.
hijack *v.* highjack, skyjack, capture; see SEIZE 2.
hike *n.* trip, backpacking, tour; see JOURNEY, WALK 3.
hike *v.* **1** [To tramp] take a hike, tour, explore; see TRAVEL, WALK 1. **2** [*To raise] lift, advance, pull up; see INCREASE.
hiking *a.* hitchhiking, backpacking, exploring; see WALKING.
hilarious *a.* amusing, lively, witty; see ENTERTAINING, FUNNY 1.
hill *n.* mound, knoll, butte, bluff, promontory, precipice, cliff, range, rising ground, headland, upland, mesa, hillock, acropolis, downgrade, inclination, descent, slope, ascent, slant, grade, incline, height, highland, rise, foothill, dune, climb, elevation, ridge, heap, hillside, upgrade, hilltop, vantage point, gradient, summit; see also MOUNTAIN 1.
hillside *n.* grade, gradient, acclivity; see HILL.
hilltop *n.* peak, height, elevation; see HILL, TOP 1.
hilly *a.* steep, sloping, rugged; see MOUNTAINOUS, ROUGH 1.—*Ant.* LEVEL, even, regular.
hinder[1] *v.* impede, obstruct, interfere with, check, retard, fetter, block, thwart, bar, clog, encumber, burden, cripple, handicap, cramp, preclude, inhibit, shackle, interrupt, arrest, curb, resist, oppose, baffle, deter, hamper, frustrate, outwit, stop, counteract, offset, neutralize, tie up, hold up, embarrass, delay, postpone, keep back, set back, dam, close, box in, end, terminate, shut out, choke, intercept, bottleneck, defeat, trap, control, conflict with, deadlock, hold back, clash with, be an obstacle to, cross, exclude, limit, shorten, go against, prohibit, withhold, slow down, stall, bring to a standstill, smother, disappoint, spoil, gag, annul, silence, invalidate, detain, stalemate, taboo, suspend, set against, clip someone's wings*, tie someone's hands*, get in the way of, throw a monkey wrench into the works*, knock the props from under*.—*Ant.* HELP, assist, aid.
hindrance *n.* obstacle, intervention, trammel; see BARRIER, INTERFERENCE 1.

hinge (hinj) ***n.*** ⟦< ME *hengen*, to hang⟧ **1** a joint on which a door, lid, etc. swings **2** a natural joint, as of the shell of a clam —***vt.* hinged, hing′ing** to attach by a hinge —***vi.*** to hang as on a hinge; depend

hint (hint) ***n.*** ⟦prob. < OE *hentan*, to grasp⟧ a slight indication; indirect suggestion —***vt., vi.*** to give a hint (of)

hin·ter·land (hin′tər land′) ***n.*** ⟦Ger⟧ **1** the land behind that bordering a coast or river **2** a remote area

hip[1] (hip) ***n.*** ⟦OE *hype*⟧ the part of the body around the joint formed by each thighbone and the pelvis

hip[2] (hip) ***adj.* hip′per, hip′pest** ⟦< ? HEP⟧ [Slang] **1** sophisticated; aware; fashionable **2** of hippies

hip′-hop′ ***n.*** a style of music and dance that originated among inner-city African-American youths in the 1980s

hip·pie (hip′ē) ***n.*** [Slang] a young person of the 1960s and 1970s who, in a state of alienation from conventional society, turned variously to mysticism, psychedelic drugs, etc.

hip·po (hip′ō) ***n.***, *pl.* **-pos** [Inf.] HIPPOPOTAMUS

Hip·poc·ra·tes (hi päk′rə tēz′) 460?-377? B.C.; Gr. physician

Hip·po·crat·ic oath (hip′ə krat′ik) the oath, attributed to Hippocrates, generally taken by medical school graduates: it sets forth their ethical code

hip·po·drome (hip′ə drōm′) ***n.*** ⟦< Gr *hippos*, horse + *dromos*, course⟧ an arena for circuses, games, etc.

hip·po·pot·a·mus (hip′ə pät′ə məs) ***n.***, *pl.* **-a·mus·es, -a·mi′** (-mī′), or **-a·mus** ⟦< Gr *hippos*, a horse + *potamos*, river⟧ a large, plant-eating mammal with a heavy, thick-skinned body and short legs: it lives chiefly in or near African rivers

hip·py (hip′ē) ***n.***, *pl.* **-pies** *alt. sp. of* HIPPIE

hire (hīr) ***n.*** ⟦< OE *hyr*, wages⟧ **1** the amount paid in hiring **2** a hiring —***vt.* hired, hir′ing** to pay for the services of (a person) or the use of (a thing) —**hire out** to work for pay

hire′ling (-liŋ) ***n.*** one who will follow anyone's orders for pay; mercenary

Hi·ro·shi·ma (hir′ə shē′mə, hi rō′shi mə) seaport in SW Honshu, Japan: largely destroyed (Aug. 6, 1945) by a U.S. atomic bomb, the first ever used in warfare: pop. 1,077,000

hir·sute (hʉr′so͞ot′, hər so͞ot′) ***adj.*** ⟦L *hirsutus*⟧ hairy; shaggy

his (hiz) ***pron.*** ⟦OE⟧ that or those belonging to him: poss. form of HE *[his are better]* —***poss. pronominal adj.*** of, belonging to, or done by him

His·pan·ic (hi span′ik) ***adj.*** **1** Spanish or Spanish-and-Portuguese **2** of or relating to Hispanics —***n.*** a Spanish-speaking person of Latin American origin who lives in the U.S. For *adj.* 2 and the *n., Latino* and *Latina* are now often preferred

His·pan·io·la (his′pən yō′lə) island in the West Indies, between Cuba & Puerto Rico

hiss (his) ***vi.*** ⟦echoic⟧ **1** to make a sound like that of a prolonged *s* **2** to show disapproval by hissing —***vt.*** to say or indicate by hissing —***n.*** the act or sound of hissing

his·sy fit (his′ē) [Dial.] a fit of anger: usually in **have** (or **throw**) **a hissy fit**: also **his′sy *n.*,** *pl.* **-sies**

hist[1] (st) ***interj.*** [Inf.] used to attract attention

hist[2] *abbrev.* history

his·ta·mine (his′tə mēn′, -min′) ***n.*** ⟦< Gr *histos*, web + AMMONIA⟧ an ammonia derivative in all organic matter: it is released in allergic reactions, lowers the blood pressure, etc.

his·tol·o·gy (his täl′ə jē) ***n.*** ⟦< Gr *histos*, web + -LOGY⟧ *Biol.* the microscopic study of tissue structure —**his·tol′o·gist *n.***

his·to·ri·an (his tôr′ē ən) ***n.*** a writer of, or authority on, history

his·tor′ic (-ik) ***adj.*** having, or likely to have, lasting importance

his·tor′i·cal (-i kəl) ***adj.*** **1** of or concerned with history **2** based on people or events of the past **3** established by history; factual —**his·tor′i·cal·ly *adv.***

historical present the present tense used for the narration of past events

his·to·ric·i·ty (his′tə ris′ə tē) ***n.*** historical authenticity

his·to·ri·og·ra·phy (his tôr′ē äg′rə fē) ***n.*** the study of the techniques of historical research

his·to·ry (his′tə rē, -trē) ***n.***, *pl.* **-ries** ⟦< Gr *histōr*, knowing⟧ **1** an account of what has happened, esp. in the life of a people, country, etc. **2** all recorded past events **3** the branch of knowledge that deals systematically with the past **4** a known or recorded past *[the odd history of his coat]*

his·tri·on·ic (his′trē än′ik) ***adj.*** ⟦< L *histrio*, actor⟧ **1** of acting or actors **2** overacted or overacting; affected

his′tri·on′ics ***pl.n.*** [*sometimes with sing. v.*] **1** dramatics **2** an artificial manner, display of emotion, etc.

hit (hit) ***vt., vi.* hit, hit′ting** ⟦< ON *hitta*, meet with⟧ **1** to come against (something) with force; knock **2** to give a blow (to); strike **3** to strike with a missile **4** to affect strongly *[a town hard hit by floods]* **5** to come (upon) by accident or after search **6** to arrive at *[stocks hit a new high]* **7** *Baseball* to get (a hit) —***n.*** **1** a blow that strikes its mark **2** a collision **3** a successful and popular song, book, etc. **4** an instance of finding particular data in a computer search **5** [Slang] a murder **6** [Slang] a dose of a drug, a drink of liquor, etc. **7** *Baseball* BASE HIT —**hit it off** to get along well together —**hit′ter *n.***

THESAURUS

hinge *n.* hook, pivot, juncture, articulation, link, elbow, ball-and-socket joint, knee, butt hinge, strap hinge, articulated joint, flap; see also JOINT 1.

hinge *v.* connect, add, couple; see JOIN 1.

hint *n.* allusion, inkling, insinuation, implication, reference, advice, observation, reminder, communication, notice, information, announcement, inside information, tip, clue, token, idea, omen, scent, cue, trace, notion, whisper, taste, suspicion, evidence, innuendo, symptom, sign, bare suggestion, impression, supposition, premonition, broad hint, gentle hint, word to the wise, indication, tip-off, pointer*; see also SUGGESTION 1.

hint *v.* touch on, allude to, intimate, inform, hint at, imply, foreshadow, remind, impart, bring up, recall, cue, prompt, insinuate, indicate, wink, advise, cause to remember, make an allusion to, jog the memory, give a hint of, suggest, make mention of, remark in passing, drop a hint, whisper, give an inkling of, tip off*.—*Ant.* HIDE, conceal, cover. —**hinted at** signified, intimated, referred to; see IMPLIED, SUGGESTED.

hip[1] ***n.*** side, hipbone, pelvis; see BONE.

hip[2]* ***a.*** aware, informed, enlightened; see MODERN 1, OBSERVANT.

hippie *n.* bohemian, nonconformist, flower child*; see RADICAL.

hire *v.* engage, sign up, draft, obtain, secure, enlist, give a job to, take on, put to work, bring in, occupy, use, fill a position, appoint, delegate, authorize, empower, retain, commission, book, utilize, select, pick, contract, procure, fill an opening, find help, find a place for, exploit, make use of, use another's services, add to the payroll.—*Ant.* DISMISS, discharge, fire.

hired *a.* contracted, signed up, given work; see BUSY, EMPLOYED, ENGAGED 3.

hiring *n.* engaging, contracting, employing; see EMPLOYER.

hiss *n.* buzz, sibilance, escape of air; see NOISE 1.

hiss *v.* sibilate, fizz, seethe; see SOUND.

historical *a.* factual, traditional, chronicled; see OLD 3, PAST 1.

history *n.* annals, records, archives, recorded history, chronicle, historical knowledge, historical writings, historical evidence, oral history, genealogy, narrative; see also RECORD 1, SOCIAL SCIENCE. —**make history** accomplish, do something important, achieve; see SUCCEED 1.

hit *a.* shot, struck, slugged, cuffed, slapped, smacked, clouted*, punched, boxed, slammed, knocked, beaten, whipped, poked, pounded, thrashed, spanked, banged, smashed, tapped, rapped, whacked, thumped, kicked, swatted, mugged, knocked out; see also HURT.—*Ant.* UNTOUCHED, unhurt, unscathed.

hit *n.* **1** [A blow] slap, rap, punch; see BLOW. **2** [A popular success] favorite, sellout*, smash; see SUCCESS 2. **3** [In baseball, a batted ball that cannot be fielded] base hit or single, two-base hit or double, three base-hit or triple, home run, Texas leaguer*, two-bagger*, three-bagger*, homer*.

hit *v.* **1** [To strike] knock, sock*, slap, jostle, butt, knock against, scrape, bump, run against, thump, collide with, bump into, punch, punish, hammer, strike down, bang, whack, jab, tap, smack, kick at, pelt, flail, thrash, cuff, kick, rap, clout*, club, bat around, lash out at, hit at, hit out at, let have it, crack, pop*, bash*; see also BEAT 1. **2** [To fire in time; *said of an internal combustion motor*] catch, go, run; see OPERATE 2. **3** [In baseball, to hit safely] make a hit, get on, get on base. —**hit it off** get along well, become friends, become friendly; see AGREE, LIKE 1, 2. —**hit upon** realize, come upon, stumble on; see DISCOVER, FIND, RECOGNIZE 1. —**hit or miss** at random, uncertainly, sometimes; see SCATTERED.

hit-and-run (hit′'n run′) ***adj.*** hitting a person, car, etc. with a moving vehicle and fleeing the scene immediately: also **hit′-skip′**

hitch (hich) ***vi.*** ⟦ME *hicchen*⟧ **1** to move jerkily **2** to become fastened or caught **3** [Slang] to hitchhike —***vt.*** **1** to move, pull, etc. with jerks **2** to fasten with a hook, knot, etc. —***n.*** **1** a tug; jerk **2** a limp **3** a hindrance; obstacle **4** a fastening or catch **5** [Slang] a period of time served **6** a kind of knot

hitch′hike′ ***vi.*** **-hiked′**, **-hik′ing** to travel by asking for rides from passing drivers —**hitch′hik′er** ***n.***

hith·er (hi*th*′ər) ***adv.*** ⟦< OE *hider*⟧ to this place; here

hith′er·to′ ***adv.*** until this time

Hit·ler (hit′lər), **Ad·olf** (ad′ôlf′, ä′dôlf′) 1889-1945; Nazi dictator of Germany (1933-45), born in Austria —**Hit·ler′i·an** (-lir′ē ən) ***adj.***

hit man [Inf.] a hired murderer

hit′-or-miss′ ***adj.*** haphazard; random

HIV ***n.*** a retrovirus that infects human T cells and causes AIDS

hive (hīv) ***n.*** ⟦< OE *hyfe*⟧ **1** a shelter for a colony of bees; beehive **2** a colony of bees; swarm **3** a crowd of busy people **4** a place of great activity —***vt.*** **hived**, **hiv′ing** to gather (bees) into a hive —***vi.*** to enter a hive

hives (hīvz) ***pl.n.*** ⟦orig. Scot dial.⟧ [*with sing. or pl. v.*] an allergic skin condition characterized by itching, burning, and the formation of smooth patches

HMO ***n.***, *pl.* **HMO's** ⟦*h*(*ealth*) *m*(*aintenance*) *o*(*rganization*)⟧ a healthcare system in which an organization hires medical professionals to provide services for its subscribers

HMS *abbrev.* **1** Her (or His) Majesty's Service **2** Her (or His) Majesty's Ship

hoa·gie or **hoa·gy** (hō′gē) ***n.***, *pl.* **-gies** HERO SANDWICH

hoard (hôrd) ***n.*** ⟦OE *hord*⟧ a supply stored up and hidden —***vi.***, ***vt.*** to accumulate and store away (money, goods, etc.) —**hoard′er** ***n.*** —**hoard′ing** ***n.***

hoar·frost (hôr′frôst′) ***n.*** FROST (sense 2)

hoarse (hôrs) ***adj.*** **hoars′er**, **hoars′est** ⟦OE *has*⟧ **1** harsh and grating in sound **2** having a rough, husky voice —**hoarse′ly** ***adv.*** —**hoarse′ness** ***n.***

hoar·y (hôr′ē) ***adj.*** **-i·er**, **-i·est** ⟦< OE har⟧ **1** white or gray **2** having white or gray hair from old age **3** very old Also **hoar** —**hoar′i·ness** ***n.***

hoax (hōks) ***n.*** ⟦< ? HOCUS-POCUS⟧ a trick or fraud; esp., a practical joke —***vt.*** to deceive with a hoax

hob·ble (häb′əl) ***vi.*** **-bled**, **-bling** ⟦ME *hobelen*⟧ to go unsteadily; limp —***vt.*** **1** to cause to limp **2** to hamper (a horse, etc.) by tying two feet together **3** to hinder —***n.*** **1** a limp **2** a rope, etc. used to hobble a horse

hob·by (häb′ē) ***n.***, *pl.* **-bies** ⟦ME *hobi*⟧ **1** HOBBYHORSE **2** something that one likes to do in one's spare time —**hob′by·ist** ***n.***

hob′by·horse′ ***n.*** **1** a child's toy consisting of a stick with a horse's head **2** ROCKING HORSE **3** an idea with which one is preoccupied

hob·gob·lin (häb′gäb′lin) ***n.*** ⟦*hob*, elf or goblin + GOBLIN⟧ **1** an elf **2** a bugbear

hob′nail′ ***n.*** ⟦*hob*, a peg + NAIL⟧ a short nail with a broad head, put on the soles of heavy shoes to prevent wear or slipping —***vt.*** to put hobnails on

hob′nob′ (-näb′) ***vi.*** **-nobbed′**, **-nob′bing** ⟦< ME *habben*, have + *nabben*, not to have⟧ to be on close terms (*with*)

ho·bo (hō′bō) ***n.***, *pl.* **-bos** or **-boes** **1** a migratory worker **2** a tramp

Ho Chi Minh City (hō′chē′min′) seaport in S Vietnam: formerly (as *Saigon*) capital of South Vietnam (1954-76): pop. 3,420,000

hock[1] (häk) ***n.*** ⟦< OE *hoh*, heel⟧ the joint bending backward in the hind leg of a horse, ox, etc.

hock[2] (häk) ***vt.***, ***n.*** ⟦< Du *hok*, prison⟧ [Slang] PAWN[1] —**in** (or **out of**) **hock** [Slang] in (or out of) debt

hock·ey (häk′ē) ***n.*** ⟦prob. < OFr *hoquet*, bent stick⟧ **1** a team game played on ice skates, with curved sticks and a hard rubber disk (*puck*) **2** a similar game played on foot on a field, with a small ball; field hockey

hock′shop′ ***n.*** [Slang] PAWNSHOP

ho·cus-po·cus (hō′kəs pō′kəs) ***n.*** ⟦imitation L⟧ **1** meaningless words used as a formula by conjurers **2** a magician's trick or tricks **3** trickery

hod (häd) ***n.*** ⟦prob. < MDu *hodde*⟧ **1** a V-shaped device with a long handle, used for carrying bricks, mortar, etc. on the shoulder **2** a coal scuttle

hodge·podge (häj′päj′) ***n.*** ⟦< OFr *hochepot*, a stew⟧ a jumbled mixture

Hodg·kin's disease (häj′kinz) ⟦after T. *Hodgkin*, 19th-c. Eng physician⟧ a chronic disease of unknown cause characterized by progressive enlargement of the lymph nodes

hoe (hō) ***n.*** ⟦< OHG *houwan*, to cut⟧ a tool with a thin blade set across the end of a long handle, for weeding, loosening soil, etc. —***vt.***, ***vi.*** **hoed**, **hoe′ing** to weed, cultivate, etc. with a hoe

hoe′cake′ ***n.*** a thin bread made of cornmeal

hoe′down′ ***n.*** **1** a lively, rollicking dance **2** a party with such dances

hog (hôg, häg) ***n.*** ⟦OE *hogg*⟧ **1** any swine, esp. a domesticated adult ready for market **2** [Inf.] a selfish, greedy, gluttonous, or filthy person —***vt.*** **hogged**, **hog′ging** [Slang] to take all of or an unfair share of —**go** (**the**) **whole hog** [Slang] to go all the way —**high on** (or **off**) **the hog** [Inf.] in a luxurious or costly way —**hog′gish** ***adj.*** —**hog′gish·ly** ***adv.***

ho·gan (hō′gôn′, -gən) ***n.*** ⟦< AmInd⟧ a Navajo Indian dwelling, built of earth walls supported by timbers

hogs·head (hôgz′hed′) ***n.*** **1** a large barrel or cask holding from 63 to 140 gallons **2** a liquid measure, esp. one equal to 63 gallons

hog′tie′ ***vt.*** **-tied′**, **-ty′ing** or **-tie′ing** **1** to tie the four feet or the hands and feet of **2** [Inf.] to make incapable of effective action

hog′wash′ ***n.*** **1** refuse fed to hogs; swill **2** insincere talk, writing, etc.

ho-hum (hō′hum′) ***interj.*** used to show boredom: an utterance suggesting a yawn —***adj.*** [Inf.] boring or tiresome

hoi pol·loi (hoi′pə loi′) ⟦Gr, the many⟧ the common people; the masses

hoist (hoist) ***vt.*** ⟦< Du *hijschen*⟧ to raise aloft; lift, esp. with a pulley, crane, etc. —***n.*** **1** a hoisting **2** an apparatus for lifting; elevator; tackle

hoke (hōk) ***vt.*** **hoked**, **hok′ing** ⟦< fol.⟧ [Slang] to treat in a sentimental or crudely comic way: usually with *up* —**hok′ey** ***adj.***

ho·kum (hō′kəm) ***n.*** ⟦< HOCUS(-POCUS)⟧ [Slang] **1** trite sentiment, crude humor, etc. **2** nonsense or humbug

hold[1] (hōld) ***vt.*** **held**, **hold′ing** ⟦OE *haldan*⟧ **1** to keep in the hands, arms, etc.; grasp **2** to keep in a certain posi-

THESAURUS

hit-and-run *a.* leaving without offering assistance, fugitive, illegally departed; see ILLEGAL.

hitch *n.* **1** [A knot] loop, noose, yoke; see KNOT 1, TIE 1. **2** [A difficulty] block, obstacle, tangle; see DIFFICULTY.

hitch *v.* tie up, strap, hook; see FASTEN, JOIN 1.

hitchhike *v.* take a lift, hitch a ride, thumb a ride; see RIDE 1, TRAVEL.

hive *n.* apiary, swarm, beehive; see COLONY.

hoard *v.* store up, acquire, keep; see ACCUMULATE, SAVE 3.

hoarse *a.* grating, rough, uneven, harsh, raucous, discordant, gruff, husky, thick, growling, croaking, cracked, guttural, dry, piercing, scratchy, indistinct, squawking, jarring, rasping.—*Ant.* PURE, sweet, mellifluous.

hoax *n.* falsification, fabrication, deceit; see DECEPTION, LIE.

hobby *n.* avocation, pastime, diversion, side interest, leisure-time activity, specialty, whim, fancy, whimsy, labor of love, play, craze, sport, amusement, craft, fun, art, game, sideline; see also ENTERTAINMENT.

hobo *n.* vagrant, vagabond, tramp; see BEGGAR.

hock[2]* *v.* sell temporarily, pledge, deposit; see PAWN, SELL.

hockey *n.* ice hockey, field hockey, hockey game; see GAME 1, SPORT 3.

hodgepodge *n.* jumble, combination, mess; see MIXTURE 1.

hoe *n.* digger, scraper, garden hoe; see TOOL 1.

hog *n.* **1** [A pig] swine, sow, boar, shoat, razorback, wild boar, wart hog, peccary, porker, piggy, pork; see also ANIMAL. **2** [A person whose habits resemble a pig's] pig, glutton, filthy person; see SLOB. —**high on** (or **off**) **the hog*** luxuriously, extravagantly, richly; see EXPENSIVE.

hogtie *v.* fetter, shackle, tie up; see BIND.

hogwash *n.* foolishness, absurdity, ridiculousness; see NONSENSE 1.

hoist *n.* crane, lift, derrick; see ELEVATOR 1.

hold[1] *v.* **1** [To have in one's grasp] grasp, grip, clutch, carry, embrace, cling to, detain, enclose, restrain, confine, check, take hold of, contain, hold down, hold on to, not let go, hang on, squeeze, press, hug, handle, have in hand, keep in hand, retain, keep, clasp, hold fast, hold tight, keep a firm hold on, tie, take, catch; see also SEIZE 1.—*Ant.* DROP, let fall, release. **2** [To have in one's possession] keep, retain, possess; see HAVE 1. **3** [To remain

tion or condition **3** to restrain or control; keep back **4** to possess; occupy *[to hold an office]* **5** to guard; defend *[hold the fort]* **6** to carry on (a meeting, etc.) **7** to contain *[the jar holds a pint]* **8** to regard; consider *[I hold the story to be true]* **9** *Law* to decide; decree —***vi.*** **1** to go on being firm, loyal, etc. **2** to remain unbroken or unyielding *[the rope held]* **3** to be true or valid *[this rule holds for any case]* **4** to continue *[the wind held steady]* —***n.*** **1** a grasping or seizing; grip **2** a thing to hold on by **3** a dominating force *[she has a hold over him]* —**catch (get, lay,** or **take) hold of** to take, seize, acquire, etc. —**hold forth** to preach; lecture —**hold on** [Inf.] stop! wait! —**hold out** **1** to last; endure **2** to stand firm **3** to offer **4** [Inf.] to refuse to give (what is to be given) —**hold over** **1** to postpone **2** to keep for an additional period —**hold up** **1** to prop up **2** to show **3** to last; endure **4** to stop; delay **5** to stop forcibly and rob —**hold'er** ***n.***

hold[2] (hōld) ***n.*** ⟦< HOLE or < MDu *hol*⟧ **1** the interior of a ship below decks, where the cargo is carried **2** the compartment for cargo in an aircraft

hold'ing ***n.*** **1** land, esp. a farm, rented from another **2** [*pl.*] property owned, as stocks and bonds

hold'o'ver ***n.*** [Inf.] one staying on from a previous period

hold'up' ***n.*** **1** a delay **2** the act of stopping forcibly and robbing

hole (hōl) ***n.*** ⟦OE *hol*⟧ **1** a hollow place; cavity **2** an animal's burrow; den **3** a small, dingy, squalid place **4** an opening in anything; break; gap; tear **5** *Golf a)* a small cup sunk into a green, into which the ball is to be hit *b)* a section of a course including the tee, fairway, and green —**hole up** [Inf.] **1** to hibernate **2** to shut oneself in **3** to hide out —**in the hole** [Inf.] financially embarrassed or behind

-hol·ic (häl'ik) *combining form* -AHOLIC

hol·i·day (häl'ə dā') ***n.*** **1** a religious festival; holy day **2** a day of freedom from labor, often one set aside by law **3** [*often pl.*] [Chiefly Brit.] a vacation —***adj.*** of or for a holiday; joyous; gay

ho·li·er-than-thou (hō'lē ər *th*ən *th*ou') ***adj.*** annoyingly self-righteous

ho·li·ness (hō'lē nis) ***n.*** **1** a being holy **2** [**H-**] a title of the pope

ho·lis·tic (hō lis'tik) ***adj.*** of or dealing with wholes or integrated systems rather than with their parts —**ho·lis'ti·cal·ly** ***adv.***

Hol·land (häl'ənd) NETHERLANDS —**Hol'land·er** ***n.***

hol·lan·daise sauce (häl'ən dāz') ⟦Fr, of Holland⟧ a creamy sauce made of butter, egg yolks, lemon juice, etc.

hol·ler (häl'ər) ***vi., vt., n.*** [Inf.] shout or yell

hol·low (häl'ō) ***adj.*** ⟦OE *holh*⟧ **1** having a cavity inside; not solid **2** shaped like a bowl; concave **3** sunken *[hollow cheeks]* **4** empty or worthless *[hollow praise]* **5** hungry **6** deep-toned and muffled —***n.*** **1** a hollow place; cavity **2** a valley —***vt., vi.*** to make or become hollow —**hol'low·ness** ***n.***

hol·ly (häl'ē) ***n., pl.*** **-lies** ⟦OE *holegn*⟧ an evergreen shrub or tree with stiff, glossy, sharp-pointed leaves and bright-red berries

hol'ly·hock' (-häk') ***n.*** ⟦< OE *halig*, holy + *hoc*, mallow⟧ a tall plant of the mallow family, with large, showy flowers

Hol·ly·wood (häl'ē wood') section of Los Angeles, California, once the site of many U.S. film studios

Holmes (hōmz, hōlmz), **Ol·i·ver Wen·dell** (äl'ə vər wen'dəl) 1841-1935; associate justice, U.S. Supreme Court (1902-32)

hol·o·caust (häl'ə kôst', hō'lə-) ***n.*** ⟦< Gr *holos*, whole + *kaustos*, burnt⟧ a great destruction of life, esp. by fire —**the Holocaust** [*also* **the h-**] the systematic killing of millions of European Jews by the Nazis

Hol·o·cene (häl'ō sēn', hō'lə-) ***adj.*** ⟦< Gr *holos*, whole + *kainos*, recent⟧ designating the present epoch of geologic time

hol·o·gram (häl'ə gram', hō'lə-) ***n.*** a photographic image produced by holography

hol'o·graph' (-graf') ***n.*** ⟦< Gr *holos*, whole + *graphein*, to write⟧ a document, letter, etc. in the handwriting of the person under whose name it appears

hol'o·graph'ic (-graf'ik) ***adj.*** **1** of or in the form of a holograph **2** of holography

ho·log·ra·phy (hō läg'rə fē) ***n.*** ⟦< Gr *holos*, whole + -GRAPHY⟧ a method of making three-dimensional photographs using a laser beam

Hol·stein (hōl'stēn', -stīn') ***n.*** ⟦after the region of Schleswig-*Holstein*, Germany⟧ a breed of large, black-and-white dairy cattle

hol·ster (hōl'stər) ***n.*** ⟦Du⟧ a pistol case attached to a belt, saddle, etc.

ho·ly (hō'lē) ***adj.*** **-li·er** or **-li·est** ⟦OE *halig*⟧ [*often* **H-**] **1** dedicated to religious use; sacred **2** spiritually pure; sinless **3** deserving deep respect, awe, etc.

THESAURUS

firm] resist, persevere, keep staunch; see CONTINUE 1, ENDURE 2. **4** [To adhere] attach, cling, take hold; see FASTEN, STICK 1. **5** [To be valid] exist, continue, operate; see BE 1.—*Ant.* STOP, expire, be out of date. **6** [To contain] have the capacity for, carry, accommodate; see INCLUDE 1. **7** [To support; *often used with "up"*] sustain, brace, buttress, prop, lock, stay, shoulder, uphold, bear up; see also SUPPORT 1. —**hold back** **1** [To restrain] inhibit, control, curb; see CHECK 1, PREVENT, RESTRAIN. **2** [To refrain] desist, hesitate, forbear; see ABSTAIN, AVOID. —**hold fast** clasp, lock, clamp; see FASTEN, STICK 1. —**hold off** be above, keep aloof, stave off; see AVOID, PREVENT. —**hold out** **1** [To offer] proffer, tempt with, grant; see GIVE 1, OFFER 1. **2** [To endure] suffer, hold on, withstand; see CONTINUE 1, ENDURE 2. —**hold out for*** persist, go on supporting, stand firmly for; see CONTINUE 1. —**hold over** do again, show again, play over; see REPEAT 1. —**hold up** **1** [To show] exhibit, raise high, elevate; see DISPLAY. **2** [To delay] stop, delay, interfere with; see HINDER, INTERRUPT. **3** [To rob at gunpoint] waylay, burglarize, steal from; see ROB. **4** [To support] brace, prop, shoulder; see HOLD 7, SUPPORT 1.

holder ***n.*** **1** [Something used in holding] sheath, container, holster, bag, sack, clip, handle, rack, knob, stem; see also CONTAINER, FASTENER. **2** [An owner or occupant] leaseholder, renter, dweller; see OWNER, RESIDENT, TENANT.

holdings ***n.*** lands, possessions, security; see ESTATE, PROPERTY 1.

holdover ***n.*** remnant, relic, surplus; see REMAINDER.

holdup ***n.*** robbery, burglary, stickup*; see CRIME, THEFT.

hole ***n.*** **1** [A perforation or cavity] notch, puncture, slot, eyelet, keyhole, porthole, buttonhole, peephole, loophole, air hole, window, crack, rent, split, tear, cleft, opening, fissure, gap, gash, rift, rupture, fracture, break, leak, aperture, space, chasm, breach, slit, nick, cut, chink, incision, orifice, eye, crater, mouth, gorge, throat, gullet, cranny, dent, opening, depression, indentation, impression, corner, pockmark, pocket, dimple, dip, drop, gulf, depth, pit, abyss, hollow, chasm, crevasse, mine, shaft, chamber, valley, ravine, burrow, rift, cell, niche. **2** [A cave] burrow, den, lair; see sense 1. **3** [*Serious difficulty] impasse, tangle, mess; see CRISIS, DIFFICULTY 1, EMERGENCY. —**in a hole*** in trouble, suffering, caught; see ABANDONED. —**in the hole*** broke*, without money, in debt; see POOR 1.

holiday ***n.*** feast day, fiesta, legal holiday, holy day, festival, centennial, carnival, jubilee, red-letter day; see also ANNIVERSARY, CELEBRATION. *Common holidays include the following:* Sunday, Independence Day, Patriot's Day, Canada Day, Veterans Day, Memorial Day, Mardi Gras, New Year's Day, Saint Valentine's Day, Christmas, Easter, Boxing Day (British), Thanksgiving Day, May Day, Washington's Birthday, Lincoln's Birthday, Presidents' Day, Martin Luther King Day, Columbus Day, Labor Day, Halloween, Election Day, Cinco de Mayo (Mexican); *Jewish:* Passover, Purim, Shavuot, Yom Kippur, Rosh Hashana, Hanukkah.

holiness ***n.*** devoutness, humility, saintliness; see DEVOTION, WORSHIP 1.

hollow ***a.*** **1** [Concave] curving inward, bell-shaped, curved, carved out, sunken, depressed, arched, vaulted, cup-shaped, excavated, hollowed-out, indented, cupped; see also BENT, ROUND 2.—*Ant.* RAISED, convex, elevated. **2** [Sounding as though from a cave] cavernous, echoing deep, resonant, booming, roaring, rumbling, reverberating, muffled, dull, resounding, sepulchral, vibrating, low, ringing, deep-toned, thunderous; see also LOUD 1.—*Ant.* DEAD, mute, silent.

hollow ***n.*** dale, bowl, basin; see VALLEY.

hollow (out) ***v.*** excavate, indent, remove earth; see DIG 1, SHOVEL.

holy ***a.*** **1** [Sinless] devout, pious, blessed, righteous, moral, just, good, angelic, godly, reverent, venerable, immaculate, pure, spotless, clean, humble, saintly, innocent, godlike, saintlike, perfect, faultless, undefiled, untainted, chaste, upright, virtuous, revered, sainted, heaven-sent, believing, profoundly good, sanctified, devotional, spiritual, unstained, pure in heart, dedicated, unspotted; see also FAITHFUL, RELIGIOUS 2.—*Ant.* BAD, wicked, sinful. **2** [Concerned with worship] devotional, religious, ceremonial; see DIVINE.

Holy Communion a Christian rite in which bread and wine are consecrated and received as the body and blood of Jesus or as symbols of them

Holy Land PALESTINE

Holy Roman Empire empire of WC Europe, from A.D. 962 until 1806

Holy Spirit (or **Ghost**) the third person of the Trinity; spirit of God

hom·age (häm′ij, äm′-) ***n.*** ⟦< L *homo*, man⟧ anything given or done to show reverence, honor, etc.

hom·burg (häm′bərg) ***n.*** ⟦after *Homburg*, Prussia⟧ a man's felt hat with a crown dented front to back and a stiff, curved brim

home (hōm) ***n.*** ⟦OE *hām*⟧ **1** the place where one lives **2** the place where one was born or reared **3** a place thought of as home **4** a household and its affairs **5** an institution for orphans, the aged, etc. **6** the natural environment of an animal, plant, etc. **7** HOME PLATE —***adj.*** **1** of one's home or country; domestic **2** central *[home* office*]* —***adv.*** **1** at, to, or in the direction of home **2** to the point aimed at *[*to drive a nail *home]* —**at home 1** in one's home **2** at ease —**bring home to** to impress upon —**home′less *adj.*** —**home′like′ *adj.***

home′boy′ *masc.n.* [Slang] **1** a boy or man from one's neighborhood, town, etc. **2** a close male friend —**home′girl′ *fem.n.***

home′-care′ *adj.* of medical care, etc. provided in a person's home

home economics the science and art of homemaking, nutrition, etc.

home′land′ *n.* the country in which one was born or makes one's home

home′ly *adj.* -li·er, -li·est 1 suitable for home life; everyday **2** crude **3** plain or unattractive —**home′li·ness *n.***

home′made′ *adj.* made, or as if made, at home

home′mak′er *n.* one who manages a household

ho·me·op·a·thy (hō′mē äp′ə thē) ***n.*** the treatment of a disease using, in small doses, drugs that produce symptoms like those of the disease —**ho′me·o·path′ic** (-ə path′ ik) ***adj.***

home page a website or the initial page of a website

home plate *Baseball* the base that the batter stands beside: it is the last base touched in scoring a run

Ho·mer (hō′mər) semilegendary Gr. epic poet of *c.* 8th c. B.C. —**Ho·mer·ic** (hō mer′ik) ***adj.***

home run *Baseball* a hit that allows the batter to touch all bases and score a run: also [Inf.] **hom′er *n.***

home′sick′ *adj.* unhappy at being away from home —**home′sick′ness *n.***

home′spun′ *n.* coarse loosely-woven cloth —***adj.*** **1** spun at home **2** plain; homely

home′stead′ (-sted′) ***n.*** **1** a place where a family makes its home **2** a tract of land granted by the U.S. government to a settler —**home′stead′er *n.***

home′stretch′ *n.* **1** the part of a racetrack between the last turn and the finish line **2** the final part of any undertaking

home′ward *adv.*, *adj.* toward home *[homeward* bound*]*: also **home′wards *adv.***

home′work′ *n.* **1** work, esp. piecework, done at home **2** lessons to be done outside the classroom **3** preparation for some project: usually in **do one's homework**

home′y *adj.* hom′i·er, hom′i·est familiar, cozy, etc. —**home′y·ness *n.***

hom·i·cide (häm′ə sīd′) ***n.*** ⟦< L *homo*, a man + *caedere*, to kill⟧ **1** the killing of one person by another **2** a person who kills another —**hom′i·ci′dal *adj.***

hom·i·let·ics (häm′ə let′iks) ***pl.n.*** ⟦see fol.⟧ the art of preparing and delivering sermons

hom·i·ly (häm′ə lē) ***n.***, *pl.* **-lies** ⟦< Gr *homilos*, assembly⟧ **1** a sermon **2** a solemn, moralizing talk or writing

homing pigeon a pigeon trained to find its way home from distant places

hom·i·nid (häm′ə nid) ***n.*** ⟦< L *homo*, a man⟧ a human, extinct or living

hom·i·ny (häm′ə nē) ***n.*** ⟦< AmInd⟧ dry corn hulled and coarsely ground (**hominy grits**): it is boiled for food

homo- ⟦< Gr *homos*⟧ *combining form* same, equal, like

ho·mo·ge·ne·ous (hō′mō jē′nē əs, häm′ō-) ***adj.*** ⟦see prec. & GENUS⟧ **1** the same in structure, quality, etc.; similar **2** composed of similar parts —**ho′mo·ge·ne′i·ty** (-jə nē′ə tē, -nā′-) ***n.***

ho·mog·e·nize (hə mäj′ə nīz′) ***vt.* -nized′, -niz′ing** to make homogeneous, or more uniform throughout; specif., to process (milk) so that fat particles are so finely emulsified that the cream does not separate

hom·o·graph (häm′ə graf′, hō′mə-) ***n.*** ⟦HOMO- + -GRAPH⟧ a word with the same spelling as another but with a different meaning and origin

ho·mol·o·gous (hō mäl′ə gəs) ***adj.*** ⟦Gr *homologos*, agreeing⟧ matching in structure, position, etc.

hom·o·nym (häm′ə nim′) ***n.*** ⟦< Gr *homos*, same + *onyma*, name⟧ a word with the same pronunciation as another but with a different meaning, origin, and, usually, spelling

ho·mo·pho·bi·a (hō′mə fō′bē ə) ***n.*** ⟦HOMO(SEXUAL) + -PHOBIA⟧ irrational hatred or fear of homosexuals or homosexuality —**ho′mo·pho′bic** (-fō′bik) ***adj.***

Ho·mo sa·pi·ens (hō′mō sā′pē enz′) ⟦ModL *homo*, man + *sapiens*, prp. of *sapere*, to know⟧ mankind; human being

ho·mo·sex·u·al (hō′mō sek′sho͞o əl, -mə-) ***adj.*** of or having sexual desire for those of the same sex —***n.*** a homosexual person —**ho′mo·sex′u·al′i·ty** (-al′ə tē) ***n.***

Hon *abbrev.* honorable

Hon·du·ras (hän do͝or′əs) country in Central America: 43,277 sq. mi.; pop. 4,444,000

hone (hōn) ***n.*** ⟦OE *han*, a stone⟧ a hard stone used to sharpen cutting tools —***vt.* honed, hon′ing** to sharpen, as with a hone

hon·est (än′ist) ***adj.*** ⟦< L *honor*, honor⟧ **1** truthful; trustworthy **2** *a)* sincere or fair *[honest* effort*]* *b)* gained by fair means *[*an *honest* living*]* **3** being what it seems **4**

THESAURUS

Holy Spirit *n.* Holy Ghost, the Dove, third person of the Trinity; see GOD.

homage *n.* respect, adoration, deference; see DEVOTION, REVERENCE, WORSHIP 1.

home *a.* in one's home, at ease, at rest, homely, domestic, familiar, homey, in the bosom of one's family, down home, in one's element; see also COMFORTABLE 1.

home *n.* **1** [A dwelling place] house, dwelling, residence, habitation, tenement, abode, lodging, quarters, homestead, domicile, dormitory, apartment house, flat*, living quarters, chalet, shelter, asylum, hut, cabin, cottage, mansion, castle, summer home, rooming house, place, address, hovel, lodge, hotel, inn, farmhouse, tent, pad*, hangout*, digs*, nest; see also APARTMENT. **2** [An asylum] orphanage, sanatorium, mental hospital; see HOSPITAL. —**at home** relaxed, at ease, familiar; see COMFORTABLE 1, HOME. —**bring home to** make clear to, convince, impress upon; see EMPHASIZE. —**come home** come back, return home, go back; see RETURN 1. —**leave home** run off, play truant, depart; see LEAVE 1.

homeless *a.* desolate, outcast, destitute, vagrant, wandering, itinerant, friendless, banished, derelict, without a country, exiled, having no home, vagabond, forsaken, unsettled, unwelcome, dispossessed, disinherited, left to shift for oneself, without a roof over one's head; see also ABANDONED, POOR 1.—*Ant.* ESTABLISHED, at home, settled.

homely *a.* **1** [Unpretentious] snug, simple, cozy; see MODEST 2. **2** [Ill-favored] plain, unattractive, not good-looking; see UGLY 1.

homemade *a.* homespun, domestic, do-it-yourself, self-made, made at home, home, not foreign.

home run *n.* four-base hit, round-tripper*, homer*; see SCORE 1.

homesick *a.* nostalgic, pining, yearning for home, ill with longing, unhappy, alienated, rootless; see also LONELY.

homesickness *n.* nostalgia, isolation, unhappiness; see LONELINESS.

homespun *a.* handcrafted, domestic, handspun; see HOMEMADE.

homestead *n.* house, ranch, estate; see HOME 1, PROPERTY 2.

homeward *a.* toward home, back home, on the way home, homewards, home, homeward bound, to one's family, to one's native land.

homework *n.* outside assignment, study, preparation; see EDUCATION 1.

homey *a.* enjoyable, livable, familiar; see COMFORTABLE 2, PLEASANT 2.

homosexual *a.* gay, same-sex, bisexual, lesbian, Sapphic, homoerotic, epicene.

homosexual *n.* lesbian, gay, gay man, bisexual, Sapphist.

honest *a.* **1** [Truthful] true, trustworthy, correct, exact, verifiable, undisguised, candid, straightforward, aboveboard, just, frank, impartial, respectful, factual, sound, reasonable, unimpeachable, legitimate, unquestionable, realistic, true-to-life, naked, plain, square, honest as the day is long*, on the level*, kosher*, fair and square*, straight.—*Ant.* deceptive, false, misleading. **2** [Frank] candid, straightforward, aboveboard; see sense 1 and FRANK. **3** [Fair] just, equitable, impartial; see FAIR 1.

frank and open [an *honest* face] —**hon'est·ly** ***adv.*** —**hon'es·ty** ***n.***

hon·ey (hun'ē) ***n.***, *pl.* **-eys** ⟦OE *hunig*⟧ **1** a sweet, syrupy substance that bees make as food from the nectar of flowers **2** sweetness **3** darling

hon'ey·comb' ***n.*** the structure of six-sided wax cells made by bees to hold their honey or eggs —***vt.*** to cause to have holes like a honeycomb —***adj.*** of or like a honeycomb: also **hon'ey·combed'**

hon'ey·dew' melon a variety of melon with a smooth, whitish rind and sweet, greenish flesh

hon'ey·lo'cust ***n.*** a North American tree having featherlike foliage and large, twisted pods

hon'ey·moon' ***n.*** the vacation spent together by a newly married couple —***vi.*** to have or spend a honeymoon —**hon'ey·moon'er** ***n.***

hon'ey·suck'le (-suk'əl) ***n.*** a plant with small, fragrant flowers of red, yellow, or white

Hong Kong or **Hong·kong** (häŋ'käŋ', hôŋ'kôŋ') administrative region of China, on the South China Sea: formerly a British colony

honk (hôŋk, häŋk) ***n.*** ⟦echoic⟧ **1** the call of a wild goose **2** a similar sound, as of an automobile horn —***vi., vt.*** to make or cause to make such a sound

hon·ky-tonk (hôŋ'kē tôŋk') ***n.*** **1** [Old Slang] a cheap, noisy nightclub **2** [Slang] a bar, esp. one where country music if played —***adj.*** designating music played on a piano with a tinkling sound

Hon·o·lu·lu (hän'ə lo͞o'lo͞o) capital of Hawaii: seaport on Oahu: pop. 365,000

hon·or (än'ər) ***n.*** ⟦L⟧ **1** high regard or respect; esp., *a)* glory; fame *b)* good reputation **2** adherence to principles considered right; integrity **3** chastity **4** high rank; distinction **5** [**H-**] a title of certain officials, as judges **6** something done or given as a token of respect **7** a source of respect and fame —***vt.*** **1** to respect greatly **2** to show high regard for **3** to do or give something in honor of **4** to accept and pay [to *honor* a check] Brit. sp. **hon'our** —**do the honors** to act as host

hon'or·a·ble ***adj.*** **1** worthy of being honored **2** honest; upright **3** bringing honor —**hon'or·a·bly** ***adv.***

hon·o·ra·ri·um (än'ə rer'ē əm) ***n.***, *pl.* **-ri·ums** or **-ri·a** (-ə) ⟦L⟧ a payment as to a professional person for services on which no fee is set

hon·or·ar·y (än'ə rer'ē) ***adj.*** **1** given as an honor **2** designating or in an office held as an honor, without service or pay —**hon'or·ar'i·ly** ***adv.***

hon'or·if'ic (-ə rif'ik) ***adj.*** ⟦< L *honor* + *facere*, to make⟧ conferring honor; showing respect

Hon·shu (hän'sho͞o') largest of the islands forming Japan

hood (ho͝od) ***n.*** ⟦OE *hod*⟧ **1** a covering for the head and neck, often part of a coat, etc. **2** anything resembling a hood, as the metal cover over an automobile engine —***vt.*** to cover as with a hood —**hood'ed** ***adj.***

-hood (ho͝od) ⟦OE *had*⟧ *suffix* **1** state or quality [*childhood*] **2** the whole group of [*priesthood*]

hood·lum (ho͝od'ləm, ho͞od'-) ***n.*** ⟦prob. < Ger dial. *hudilump*, wretch⟧ a lawless person, as a member of a gang of criminals

hoo·doo (ho͞o'do͞o') ***n.***, *pl.* **-doos'** ⟦var. of VOODOO⟧ **1** VOODOO **2** [Inf.] bad luck or its cause

hood'wink' ***vt.*** ⟦HOOD + WINK⟧ to mislead by trickery; dupe

hoo·ey (ho͞o'ē) ***interj., n.*** ⟦echoic⟧ [Slang] nonsense

hoof (ho͞of, ho͝of) ***n.***, *pl.* **hoofs** or **hooves** (ho͞ovz, ho͝ovz) ⟦OE *hof*⟧ the horny covering on the feet of cattle, horses, etc., or the entire foot —***vt., vi.*** [Inf.] to walk: often with *it* —**hoofed** ***adj.***

hook (ho͝ok) ***n.*** ⟦OE *hoc*⟧ **1** a bent piece of metal, etc. used to catch, hold, or pull something **2** a fishhook **3** something shaped like a hook **4** something moving in a hooklike path, as a punch delivered with the elbow bent —***vt.*** to catch, fasten, throw, etc. with a hook —***vi.*** **1** to curve as a hook does **2** to be fastened or caught by a hook —**by hook or by crook** by any means, honest or dishonest —**hook up** to connect (a radio, etc.) —**off the hook** [Inf.] out of trouble

hook·ah or **hook·a** (ho͝ok'ə, ho͞o'kə) ***n.*** ⟦Ar *ḥuqqa*⟧ a tobacco pipe with a tube for drawing the smoke through a vessel of water to cool it

hooked (ho͝okt) ***adj.*** **1** like a hook **2** made with a hook [*hooked* rug] **3** [Slang] *a)* obsessed with or addicted to (often with *on*) *b)* married

hook'er ***n.*** [Slang] a prostitute

hook'up' ***n.*** the arrangement and connection of parts, circuits, etc., as in a radio

hook'worm' ***n.*** a small, parasitic, intestinal roundworm with hooks around the mouth

hook'y ***n.*** [Inf.] used only in **play hooky**, be a truant

hoo·li·gan (ho͞o'li gən) ***n.*** ⟦< ? *Hooligan*, a family name⟧ [Slang] a hoodlum

hoop (ho͞op) ***n.*** ⟦OE *hop*⟧ **1** a circular band for holding together the staves of a barrel, etc. **2** anything like this, as a metal basketball rim —***vt.*** to bind or fasten as with a hoop

hoop·la (ho͞op'lä') ***n.*** ⟦< ?⟧ [Inf.] **1** great excitement **2** showy publicity

hoop skirt a skirt worn over a framework of hoops

hoo·ray (hoo rā', hə-; ho͞o-) ***interj., n., vi., vt.*** *var. of* HURRAY

hoose·gow (ho͞os'gou') ***n.*** ⟦< Sp *juzgado*, court of justice⟧ [Slang] a jail

Hoo·sier (ho͞o'zhər) ***n.*** [Inf.] a person born or living in Indiana

hoot (ho͞ot) ***n.*** ⟦echoic⟧ **1** the sound that an owl makes **2** any sound like this, as a shout of scorn **3** [Inf.] an amusing person, thing, etc. —***vi.*** to utter a hoot —***vt.*** to express (scorn) of (someone) by hooting —**hoot'er** ***n.***

hoot·en·an·ny (ho͞ot''n an'ē) ***n.***, *pl.* **-nies** a meeting of folk singers, as for public entertainment

Hoo·ver (ho͞o'vər), **Her·bert** (**Clark**) (hur'bərt) 1874-1964; 31st president of the U.S. (1929-33)

hop[1] (häp) ***vi.*** **hopped**, **hop'ping** ⟦OE *hoppian*⟧ **1** to make a short leap or leaps on one foot **2** to leap with both, or all, feet at once, as a frog **3** [Inf.] *a)* to go briskly *b)* to take a short trip —***vt.*** **1** to jump over **2** to

THESAURUS

honestly ***a.*** **1** [In an honest manner] uprightly, fairly, genuinely; see JUSTLY 1, SINCERELY. **2** [Really] indeed, truly, naturally; see REALLY 1.

honesty ***n.*** honor, fidelity, scrupulousness, trustworthiness, self-respect, straightforwardness, confidence, soundness, right, principle, truthfulness, candor, frankness, openness, morality, goodness, responsibility, loyalty, faithfulness, good faith, probity, courage, moral strength, virtue, reliability, character, conscience, worth, conscientiousness, trustiness, faith, justice.—*Ant.* DISHONESTY, deception, deceit.

honey ***n.*** comb honey, extracted honey, wild honey; see FOOD.

honk ***n.*** croak, quack, blare; see NOISE 1.

honk ***v.*** blare, trumpet, bellow; see SOUND.

honor ***n.*** **1** [Respect] reverence, esteem, worship, adoration, veneration, high regard, trust, faith, confidence, recognition, praise, attention, deference, notice, consideration, renown, reputation, elevation, credit, tribute, popularity; see also ADMIRATION.—*Ant.* DISGRACE, opprobrium, disrepute. **2** [Integrity] courage, character, truthfulness; see HONESTY. —**do the honors** act as host or hostess, present, host; see SERVE. —**on** (or **upon**) **one's honor** by one's faith, on one's word, staking one's good name; see SINCERELY.

honor ***v.*** **1** [To treat with respect] worship, sanctify, venerate; see PRAISE 1. **2** [To recognize worth] esteem, value, look up to; see ADMIRE. **3** [To recognize as valid] clear, pass, accept; see ACKNOWLEDGE 2.

honorable ***a.*** upright, reputable, creditable; see DISTINGUISHED 2, FAMOUS, NOBLE 2, 3.

honorably ***a.*** nobly, fairly, virtuously; see JUSTLY 1.

honored ***a.*** respected, revered, decorated, privileged, celebrated, reputable, well-known, esteemed, eminent, distinguished, dignified, noble, recognized, highly regarded, venerated; see also FAMOUS.—*Ant.* CORRUPT, disgraced, shamed.

hood ***n.*** **1** [Covering worn over the head] cowl, shawl, bonnet, protector, veil, capuchin, kerchief, mantle; see also HAT. **2** [A covering for vehicles and the like] engine cover, bonnet (British), canopy; see COVER 1. **3** [*A criminal] gangster, hoodlum, crook*; see CRIMINAL.

hoodlum ***n.*** outlaw, gangster, crook*; see CRIMINAL.

hoof ***n.*** ungula, animal foot, paw; see FOOT 2.

hook ***n.*** latch, catch, clasp; see FASTENER.

hook ***v.*** **1** [To curve in the shape of a hook] angle, crook, curve; see ARCH. **2** [To catch on a hook] pin, catch, secure; see FASTEN. —**hooked up** connected, linked together, attached; see JOINED. —**hook up** combine, connect, attach; see JOIN 1, UNITE.

hookup ***n.*** attachment, connection, consolidation; see LINK, UNION 1.

hoop ***n.*** loop, band, circlet; see CIRCLE 1.

hoot ***n.*** howl, whoop, boo; see CRY 2.

hop[1] ***n.*** spring, bounce, leap; see JUMP 1.

hop[1] ***v.*** leap, skip, jump on one leg; see BOUNCE, JUMP 1.

get aboard —*n.* 1 a hopping 2 [Inf.] *a*) a dance *b*) a short flight in an airplane

hop[2] (häp) *n.* ⟦< MDu *hoppe*⟧ 1 a twining vine with flowers borne in small cones 2 [*pl.*] the dried ripe cones, used for flavoring beer, ale, etc. —**hop up** to stimulate, as by a drug

hope (hōp) *n.* ⟦OE *hopa*⟧ 1 a feeling that what is wanted will happen; desire accompanied by expectation 2 the object of this 3 a person or thing on which one may base some hope —*vt.* **hoped, hop'ing** to want and expect —*vi.* to have hope (*for*) —**hope'ful** *adj.* —**hope'ful·ly** *adv.* —**hope'less** *adj.* —**hope'less·ly** *adv.*

hop'head' *n.* [Slang] a drug addict

hop·per (häp'ər) *n.* 1 one that hops 2 any hopping insect 3 a box, tank, etc. from which the contents can be emptied slowly and evenly

hop·sack·ing (häp'sak'iŋ) *n.* a sturdy fabric resembling coarse material used for bags, that is made into coats, suits, etc. Also **hop'sack'**

hop·scotch (häp'skäch') *n.* a children's game in which a player hops from section to section of a figure drawn on the ground

Hor·ace (hôr'is, här'-) 65-8 B.C.; Rom. poet

horde (hôrd) *n.* ⟦ult. < Tatar *urdu*, a camp⟧ a crowd or throng; swarm —*vi.* **hord'ed, hord'ing** to form or gather in a horde

hore·hound (hôr'hound') *n.* ⟦OE *harhune*⟧ 1 a bitter plant of the mint family 2 medicine or candy made from its juice

ho·ri·zon (hə rī'zən) *n.* ⟦< Gr *horos*, boundary⟧ 1 the line where the sky seems to meet the earth 2 [*usually pl.*] the limit of one's experience, interest, etc.

hor·i·zon·tal (hôr'i zänt''l) *adj.* 1 parallel to the plane of the horizon; not vertical 2 flat and even; level —**hor'i·zon'tal·ly** *adv.*

hor·mone (hôr'mōn') *n.* ⟦< Gr *hormē*, impulse⟧ a substance formed in some organ of the body and carried to another part, where it takes effect —**hor·mo'nal** *adj.*

horn (hôrn) *n.* ⟦OE⟧ 1 a hard, bonelike projection growing on the head of a cow, goat, etc. 2 the substance horns are made of 3 anything like a horn in position, shape, etc. 4 any brass instrument; specif., FRENCH HORN 5 a device sounded to give a warning —*adj.* made of horn —**horn in** (**on**) to intrude or meddle (in) —**horned** *adj.* —**horn'less** *adj.* —**horn'like'** *adj.*

Horn, Cape southernmost point of South America, on an island of Chile

horn·blende (hôrn'blend') *n.* ⟦Ger⟧ a hard, heavy, dark-colored mineral

horned toad a small, scaly, insect-eating lizard with hornlike spines: also **horned lizard**

hor·net (hôr'nit) *n.* ⟦OE *hyrnet*⟧ a large, yellow and black wasp

horn of plenty CORNUCOPIA

horn'pipe' *n.* ⟦ME⟧ a lively dance formerly popular with sailors

horn·y (hôr'nē) *adj.* **-i·er, -i·est** 1 made of horn 2 toughened and calloused [*horny* hands] 3 [Slang] easily aroused sexually

ho·rol·o·gy (hō räl'ə jē) *n.* ⟦< Gr *hōra*, hour + -LOGY⟧ the science of measuring time or making timepieces

hor·o·scope (hôr'ə skōp') *n.* ⟦< Gr *hōra*, hour + *skopos*, watcher⟧ a chart of the zodiacal signs and positions of planets, etc., esp. at the time of a person's birth, used by an astrologer to make a forecast

hor·ren·dous (hô ren'dəs) *adj.* ⟦see HORRID⟧ horrible; frightful

hor·ri·ble (hôr'ə bəl) *adj.* ⟦see fol.⟧ 1 causing horror; terrible; dreadful 2 [Inf.] very bad, ugly, unpleasant, etc. —**hor'ri·bly** *adv.*

hor·rid (hôr'id) *adj.* ⟦< L *horrere*, to bristle, shake, be afraid⟧ 1 causing horror; terrible 2 very bad, ugly, unpleasant, etc. —**hor'rid·ly** *adv.*

hor·rif·ic (hô rif'ik, hə-) *adj.* horrifying

hor·ri·fy (hôr'ə fī') *vt.* **-fied', -fy'ing** 1 to cause to feel horror 2 [Inf.] to shock or disgust

hor·ror (hôr'ər) *n.* ⟦see HORRID⟧ 1 the strong feeling caused by something frightful or shocking 2 strong dislike 3 something that causes horror

hors de com·bat (ôr də kōn bá') ⟦Fr, out of combat⟧ disabled

hors d'oeuvre (ôr'durv') *pl.* **hors' d'oeuvres'** ⟦Fr, lit., outside of work⟧ an appetizer, as canapés, served before a meal

horse (hôrs) *n.* ⟦OE *hors*⟧ 1 a large, four-legged, solid-hoofed animal with flowing mane and tail, domesticated for drawing loads, carrying riders, etc. 2 a frame with legs to support something —*adj.* of or on horses —**hold**

THESAURUS

hope *n.* 1 [Reliance upon the future] faith, expectation, confidence; see ANTICIPATION, OPTIMISM 2. 2 [The object of hope] wish, goal, dream; see DESIRE 1, END 2, PURPOSE 1.

hope *v.* be hopeful, lean on, wish, desire, live in hope, rely, depend, count on, aspire to, doubt not, keep one's fingers crossed, hope for the best, be of good cheer, pray, cherish the hope, look forward to, await, dream, presume, watch for, bank on, foresee, promise oneself, suppose, deem likely, believe, suspect, surmise, hold, be assured, feel confident, anticipate, be prepared for, make plans for, have faith, rest assured, be sure of, be reassured, take heart, hope to hell*, knock on wood*; see also EXPECT 1, TRUST 1.

hopeful *a.* 1 [Optimistic] expectant, assured, sanguine, buoyant, enthusiastic, trustful, reassured, emboldened, full of hope, cheerful, anticipating, expecting, in hopes of, forward-looking, lighthearted, serene, calm, poised, comfortable, eager, elated, looking through rose-colored glasses; see also CONFIDENT, TRUSTING. 2 [Encouraging] promising, reassuring, favorable, bright, cheering, flattering, gracious, opportune, timely, fortunate, propitious, auspicious, well-timed, fit, suitable, convenient, beneficial, fair, uplifting, heartening, inspiring, exciting, pleasing, fine, lucky, stirring, making glad, helpful, rose-colored, rosy, animating, attractive, satisfactory, refreshing, probable, good, conducive, advantageous, pleasant, of promise, happy, cheerful.—*Ant.* UNFORTUNATE, discouraging, unfavorable.

hopefully *a.* 1 [Optimistically] confidently, expectantly, with confidence, with hope, trustingly, naively, with some reassurance, trustfully; see also BOLDLY 1, POSITIVELY 1, SURELY.—*Ant.* HOPELESSLY, doubtfully, gloomily. 2 [Probably] conceivably, expectedly, feasibly; see PROBABLY.

hopeless *a.* unfortunate, threatening, bad, sinister, unyielding, incurable, past hope, past cure, vain, irreversible, irreparable, without hope, with no hope, down in the mouth*, impracticable, ill-fated, disastrous, menacing, foreboding, unfavorable, dying, worsening, past saving, tragic, fatal, desperate, helpless, lost, to no avail, gone, empty, idle, useless, pointless, worthless; see also ABANDONED, IMPOSSIBLE.—*Ant.* FAVORABLE, heartening, cheering.

hopelessly *a.* cynically, pessimistically, despondently, dejectedly, desperately, emptily, darkly, gloomily, dismally, desolately; see also SADLY.—*Ant.* HOPEFULLY, confidently, expectantly.

horde *n.* pack, throng, swarm; see CROWD, GATHERING.

horizon *n.* range, border, limit; see BOUNDARY, EXTENT.

horizontal *a.* 1 [Level] plane, aligned, parallel to the horizon; see FLAT 1, LEVEL 3, STRAIGHT 1. 2 [Even] flush, uniform, regular; see FLAT 1, SMOOTH 1.

horn *n.* 1 [A wind instrument] *Horns include the following:* bugle, trombone, saxophone, cornet, clarinet, bassoon, pipe, fife, flute, picolo, oboe, English horn, French horn, tuba, sousaphone, baritone, alphorn, shofar, ram's horn, hunting horn; see also MUSICAL INSTRUMENT. 2 [Hard process protruding from the head of certain animals] antler, outgrowth, pronghorn, frontal bone, spine, spike, point; see also BONE. —**horn in** (**on**)* intrude, impose upon, get in on; see ENTER, MEDDLE 1. —**lock horns** disagree, conflict, defy; see OPPOSE 1.

horny *a.* 1 [Callous] hard, firm, bony; see TOUGH 2. 2 [*Sexually excited] sensual, aroused, lecherous; see EXCITED, LEWD 2.

horrendous *a.* horrible, frightful, terrifying; see POOR 2, TERRIBLE 1.

horrible *a.* 1 [Offensive] repulsive, dreadful, disgusting; see OFFENSIVE 2. 2 [Frightful] shameful, shocking, awful; see FRIGHTFUL, TERRIBLE 1.

horrid *a.* hideous, disturbing, shameful; see OFFENSIVE 2, PITIFUL.

horror *n.* awe, terror, fright; see FEAR.

horse *n.* nag, draft animal, plow horse, racer, saddle horse, steed, mount, charger, pony, mustang, bronco, quarter horse, piebald, pinto, palomino, Arabian, stallion, gelding, hack, mare, Thoroughbred, pacer, trotter, courser; see also ANIMAL. —**from the horse's mouth*** originally, from an authority, according to the original source of the information; see OFFICIALLY 1. —**hold one's horses*** curb one's impatience, slow down, relax; see RESTRAIN. —**horse around*** fool around, cavort, cause trouble; see MISBEHAVE, PLAY 2. —**on one's high horse*** arrogant, haughty, disdainful; see EGOTISTIC.

one's horses [Slang] to curb one's impatience —**horse around** [Slang] to engage in horseplay
horse′back′ ***n.*** the back of a horse —***adv.*** on horseback
horse chestnut **1** a flowering tree with large leaves and glossy brown seeds **2** its seed
horse′feath′ers ***n., interj.*** [Slang] nonsense
horse′fly′ ***n.***, *pl.* **-flies′** a large fly that sucks the blood of horses, etc.
horse′hair′ ***n.*** **1** hair from the mane or tail of a horse **2** a stiff fabric made from this hair
horse′hide′ ***n.*** **1** the hide of a horse **2** leather made from this
horse′laugh′ ***n.*** a loud, boisterous, usually derisive laugh; guffaw
horse′man (-mən) ***n.***, *pl.* **-men** (-mən) a man skilled in the riding, managing, or care of horses —**horse′man·ship′** ***n.*** —**horse′wom′an**, *pl.* **-wom′en**, ***fem.n.***
horse opera [Slang] WESTERN (*n.*)
horse′play′ ***n.*** rough, boisterous fun
horse′pow′er ***n.***, *pl.* **-pow′er** a unit for measuring the power of engines, etc., equal to 746 watts or 33,000 foot-pounds per minute
horse′rad′ish ***n.*** **1** a plant with a pungent, white, fleshy root **2** a relish made of the grated root
horse sense [Inf.] common sense
horse′shoe′ ***n.*** **1** a flat, U-shaped metal plate nailed to a horse's hoof to protect it **2** anything shaped like this **3** [*pl., with sing. v.*] a game in which players toss horseshoes at two stakes
horseshoe crab a sea arthropod shaped like the base of a horse's foot, with a long, spinelike tail
horse′tail′ ***n.*** a common rushlike plant found in moist areas
horse′whip′ ***n.*** a whip for driving horses —***vt.*** **-whipped′**, **-whip′ping** to lash with a horsewhip
hors·y (hôr′sē) ***adj.*** **-i·er**, **-i·est** **1** of, like, or suggesting a horse **2** of or like people who are fond of horses, fox-hunting, horse racing, etc. Also **hors′ey**
hor·ta·to·ry (hôr′tə tôr′ē) ***adj.*** ⟦< L *hortari*, incite⟧ exhorting; advising
hor·ti·cul·ture (hôr′tə kul′chər) ***n.*** ⟦< L *hortus*, garden + *cultura*, cultivation⟧ the art or science of growing flowers, fruits, and vegetables —**hor′ti·cul′tur·al** ***adj.***
ho·san·na (hō zan′ə, -zä′nə) ***n., interj.*** ⟦< Heb *hōshīʿāh nnā*, lit., save, we pray⟧ an exclamation of praise to God
hose (hōz) ***n.***, *pl.* **hose** or, for 2, usually **hos′es** ⟦OE *hosa*⟧ **1** [*pl.*] stockings or socks **2** a flexible tube used to convey fluids —***vt.*** **hosed**, **hos′ing** to water with a hose: often with *down*
ho·sier·y (hō′zhər ē) ***n.*** stockings
hos·pice (häs′pis) ***n.*** ⟦< L *hospes*, host, guest⟧ **1** a shelter for travelers **2** a homelike facility for the care of terminally ill patients
hos·pi·ta·ble (häs′pit ə bəl, häs pit′-) ***adj.*** ⟦see prec.⟧ friendly and solicitous toward guests, new arrivals, etc. —**hos′pi·ta·bly** ***adv.***
hos·pi·tal (häs′pit′l) ***n.*** ⟦< L *hospes*, host, guest⟧ an institution providing medical treatment for people who are ill, injured, pregnant, etc.
hos·pi·tal·i·ty (häs′pi tal′ə tē) ***n.***, *pl.* **-ties** the act, practice, or quality of being hospitable
hos·pi·tal·ize (häs′pit′l īz′) ***vt.*** **-ized′**, **-iz′ing** to put in, or admit to, a hospital —**hos′pi·tal·i·za′tion** ***n.***
host[1] (hōst) ***n.*** ⟦< ML *hostia*⟧ a wafer of the bread used in the Eucharist
host[2] (hōst) ***n.*** ⟦< L *hospes*, host, guest⟧ **1** one who entertains guests, esp. at home **2** a person who keeps an inn or hotel **3** any organism on or in which a parasitic organism lives —***vi., vt.*** to act as host (to)
host[3] (hōst) ***n.*** ⟦< ML *hostis*, army⟧ **1** an army **2** a great number
hos·tage (häs′tij) ***n.*** ⟦< OFr⟧ a person kept or given as a pledge until certain conditions are met
hos·tel (häs′təl) ***n.*** ⟦< L *hospes*, host, guest⟧ an inn: also **hos′tel·ry** (-rē), *pl.* **-ries**
hos′tel·er ***n.*** a traveler who stops at hostels
host·ess (hōs′tis) ***n.*** **1** a woman who entertains guests, esp. at home; sometimes, the host's wife **2** a woman employed in a restaurant to supervise serving, seating, etc.
hos·tile (häs′təl) ***adj.*** ⟦< L *hostis*, enemy⟧ **1** of or characteristic of an enemy **2** unfriendly; antagonistic —**hos′tile·ly** ***adv.***
hos·til·i·ty (häs til′ə tē) ***n.***, *pl.* **-ties** **1** a feeling of enmity, ill will, etc. **2** *a*) an expression of enmity, ill will, etc. *b*) [*pl.*] warfare
hos·tler (häs′lər, äs′-) ***n.*** ⟦contr. of HOSTELER⟧ one who takes care of horses at an inn, stable, etc.
hot (hät) ***adj.*** **hot′ter**, **hot′test** ⟦OE *hat*⟧ **1** *a*) having a temperature higher than that of the human body *b*) having a relatively high temperature **2** producing a burning sensation *[hot* pepper*]* **3** characterized by strong feeling or intense activity, etc.; specif., *a*) impetuous *[a hot* temper*]* *b*) violent *[a hot* battle*]* *c*) lustful *d*) very controversial **4** following closely *[in hot* pursuit*]* **5** electrically charged *[a hot* wire*]* **6** [Inf.] recent; fresh *[hot* news*]* **7** [Slang] *a*) recently stolen or smuggled *b*) excellent; good —**make it hot for** [Inf.] to make things uncomfortable for —**hot′ly** ***adv.*** —**hot′ness** ***n.***
hot air [Slang] empty talk
hot′bed′ ***n.*** **1** a bed of earth covered with glass and heated, as by manure, for forcing plants **2** a place of rapid growth or extensive activity
hot′blood′ed ***adj.*** easily excited; excitable
hot′box′ ***n.*** an overheated bearing on an axle or shaft
hot cake a pancake —**sell like hot cakes** [Inf.] to be sold rapidly and in large quantities
hot dog [Inf.] a wiener, esp. one served hot in a long, soft roll
ho·tel (hō tel′) ***n.*** ⟦< OFr *hostel*, hostel⟧ an establishment providing lodging and, usually, meals for travelers, etc.
ho·tel·ier (hō tel′yər) ***n.*** ⟦Fr *hôtelier*⟧ an owner or manager of a hotel
hot flash the sensation of a wave of heat passing over the body, often experienced by women during menopause
hot′foot′ ***vi.*** [Inf.] to hurry; hasten: with *it*
hot′head′ed ***adj.*** **1** quick-tempered **2** impetuous —**hot′head′** ***n.***
hot′house′ ***n.*** GREENHOUSE

THESAURUS

horseman ***n.*** equestrian, rider, jockey; see COWBOY.
horseplay ***n.*** clowning, play, fooling around; see FUN, JOKE.
horsepower ***n.*** strength, pull, power; see ENERGY 2.
hose ***n.*** **1** [Stocking] stockings, socks, pantyhose; see HOSIERY. **2** [A flexible conduit] garden hose, fire hose, line, tubing; see also PIPE 1, TUBE 1.
hosiery ***n.*** stockings, nylons, hose, seamless hose, full-fashioned hose, socks, anklets, tights, pantyhose, knee socks, bobby socks*, sport socks, sox, support hose.
hospitable ***a.*** cordial, courteous, open; see FRIENDLY.
hospital ***n.*** clinic, infirmary, sanatorium, sanitarium, dispensary, mental hospital, army hospital, city hospital, public hospital, veterans' hospital, teaching hospital, university hospital, treatment center, rehabilitation center, surgery center, maternity hospital, medical center, lying-in hospital, health service, outpatient ward, sick bay.
hospitality ***n.*** good cheer, companionship, good fellowship; see ENTERTAINMENT, WELCOME.
host[2] ***v.*** receive, treat, wine and dine; see ENTERTAIN 2.
host[2,3] ***n.*** **1** [A person who entertains] man of the house, woman of the house, entertainer, toastmaster, master of ceremonies, mistress of ceremonies, hostess, emcee. **2** [A large group] throng, multitude, army; see CROWD, GATHERING. **3** [Organism on which a parasite subsists] victim, host body, animal; see PARASITE 1.
hostage ***n.*** security, captive, victim of a kidnapping; see PRISONER.
hostess ***n.*** society lady, socialite, clubwoman, social leader, entertainer, lady of the house, toastmistress, mistress of ceremonies.
hostile ***a.*** antagonistic, hateful, opposed; see UNFRIENDLY.
hostility ***n.*** abhorrence, aversion, bitterness; see HATRED.
hot ***a.*** **1** [Having a high temperature] torrid, burning, fiery, flaming, blazing, very warm, baking, roasting, smoking, scorching, blistering, searing, sizzling, tropical, warm, broiling, red-hot, grilling, piping hot, white-hot, scalding, parching, sultry, on fire, at a high temperature, incandescent, smoldering, thermal, toasting, simmering, blazing hot*, boiling hot*, like an oven*, hotter than blazes*; see also BOILING, COOKING, MOLTEN.—*Ant.* COLD, frigid, chilly. **2** [Aroused] furious, ill-tempered, indignant; see ANGRY. **3** [*Erotic] spicy, salacious, carnal; see SENSUAL 2. —**get hot*** become excited, become enthusiastic, burn with fervor, get angry, rave; see also RAGE 1. —**hot under the collar*** furious, mad, resentful; see ANGRY. —**make it hot for*** create discomfort for, cause trouble for, vex; see DISTURB.
hotel ***n.*** stopping place, inn, lodging house, bed-and-breakfast, boarding-house, hostel, motel, motor hotel, resort, tavern, spa, rooming house, boatel, flophouse*.
hotheaded ***a.*** unmanageable, wild,

hot line an emergency telephone line between government leaders or to a social agency
hot plate a small portable stove for cooking food
hot potato [Inf.] a troubling problem that no one wants to handle
hot rod [Slang] an automobile, often an old one, rebuilt for great speed —**hot rod'der**
hot seat [Slang] **1** ELECTRIC CHAIR **2** a difficult situation
hot'shot' *n.* [Slang] one seen as an expert or as very aggressive: often used ironically
hot'-tem'pered *adj.* having a fiery temper
Hot·ten·tot (hät''n tät') *n.* **1** a member of a nomadic people of SW Africa **2** the language of this people
hot tub a large wooden tub in which several people can soak in hot water together
hound (hound) *n.* ⟦OE *hund*, dog⟧ **1** any of several breeds of hunting dog **2** any dog —*vt.* **1** to hunt or chase with or as with hounds **2** to urge on
hounds·tooth check (houndz'tooth') a pattern of irregular broken checks, used in woven material
hour (our) *n.* ⟦< Gr *hōra*⟧ **1** one of the twenty-four parts of a day; sixty minutes **2** the time for a particular activity [lunch *hour*] **3** [*pl.*] a period fixed for work, etc. [office *hours*] **4** the time of day [the *hour* is 2:30] **5** *Educ.* a credit, equal to one hour spent in class per week —**after hours** after the regular hours for business, school, etc. —**hour after hour** every hour
hour'glass' *n.* an instrument for measuring time by the trickling of sand, etc. from one glass bulb to another
hour hand the short hand of a clock or watch, which indicates the hours
hou·ri (hoo'rē, hou'-) *n.*, *pl.* **-ris** ⟦< Ar *ḥūrīyah*, black-eyed woman⟧ a beautiful nymph of the Muslim Paradise
hour'ly *adj.* **1** happening every hour **2** done during an hour **3** frequent —*adv.* **1** once an hour **2** often
house (hous; *for v.* houz) *n.*, *pl.* **hous·es** (hou'ziz) ⟦OE *hus*⟧ **1** a building to live in; specif., a building occupied by one family or person **2** the people who live in a house; household **3** [*often* **H-**] a family as including kin, ancestors, and descendants, esp. a royal family **4** shelter, living or storage space, etc. **5** *a*) a theater *b*) the audience in a theater **6** a business firm **7** [*often* **H-**] a legislative assembly —*adj.* of a salad dressing, wine, etc. at a particular restaurant —*vt.* **housed, hous'ing 1** to provide a house or lodgings for **2** to cover, shelter, etc. —**keep house** to take care of a home —**on the house** at the expense of the establishment
house'boat' *n.* a large, flat-bottomed boat used as a residence
house'bound' *adj.* confined to one's home, as by illness
house'break'ing *n.* the act of breaking into and entering another's house to commit theft or another felony
house'bro'ken *adj.* trained to live in a house (i.e., to urinate, etc. in a special place or outside): said of a dog, cat, etc.
house'fly' *n.*, *pl.* **-flies'** a two-winged fly found in and around houses
house'guest' *n.* a person who stays overnight in another's home
house'hold' *n.* **1** all those living in one house **2** the home and its affairs —**house'hold'er** *n.*
household word a common saying or thing, familiar to nearly everyone
house'hus'band *n.* a married man whose job is keeping house and taking care of domestic affairs
house'keep'er *n.* one who runs a home, esp. a woman hired to do this
house'maid' *n.* a maid who does housework
House of Commons the lower house of the legislature of Great Britain or Canada
House of Lords the upper house of the legislature of Great Britain
House of Representatives the lower house of the legislature of the U.S. and most of the states of the U.S.
house'plant' *n.* a plant grown indoors, mainly for decoration
house'wares' (-werz') *pl.n.* articles for household use, esp. in the kitchen
house'warm'ing *n.* a party to celebrate moving into a new home
house'wife' *n.*, *pl.* **-wives'** a married woman whose job is keeping house and taking care of domestic affairs
house'work' *n.* the work involved in keeping house; cleaning, cooking, etc.
hous·ing (hou'ziŋ) *n.* **1** the providing of shelter or lodging **2** shelter or lodging **3** houses collectively **4** *Mech.* a frame, box, etc. for containing some part, mechanism, etc.
Hous·ton (hyoos'tən) city & port in SE Texas: pop. 1,630,000
hove (hōv) *vt.*, *vi. alt. pt. & pp. of* HEAVE
hov·el (huv'əl, häv'-) *n.* ⟦ME⟧ any small, miserable dwelling; hut
hov·er (huv'ər, häv'-) *vi.* ⟦< ME *hoven*, to stay (suspended)⟧ **1** to flutter in the air near one place **2** to linger close by **3** to waver (*between*)
how (hou) *adv.* ⟦OE *hu*⟧ **1** in what manner or way **2** in what state or condition **3** for what reason **4** to what extent, degree, etc. *How* is also used as an intensive —**how about something** (or **someone**)? [Inf.] what is your opinion, etc. concerning something (or someone)?
how·be·it (hou bē'it) *adv.* [Archaic] however it may be; nevertheless
how·dah (hou'də) *n.* ⟦< Hindi *hauda*⟧ a seat for riding on the back of an elephant or camel
how·ev'er *adv.* **1** in whatever manner **2** to whatever degree **3** nevertheless
how·itz·er (hou'it sər) *n.* ⟦< Czech *houfnice*, orig., a sling⟧ a short cannon, firing shells in a high trajectory
howl (houl) *vi.* ⟦ME *hulen*⟧ **1** to utter the long, wailing cry of wolves, dogs, etc. **2** to utter a similar cry of pain, anger, etc. **3** to shout or laugh in scorn, mirth, etc. —*vt.* **1** to utter with a howl **2** to drive by howling —*n.* **1** the wailing cry of a wolf, dog, etc. **2** any similar sound **3** [Inf.] a joke
howl'er *n.* **1** one that howls **2** [Inf., Chiefly Brit.] a ludicrous blunder
how·so·ev·er (hou'sō ev'ər) *adv.* **1** to whatever degree or extent **2** by whatever means
hoy·den (hoid''n) *n.* ⟦< ? Du⟧ a bold, boisterous girl; tomboy
Hoyle (hoil) *n.* a book of rules for card games, orig. com-

THESAURUS

reckless; see RASH, UNRULY.
hound *n.* greyhound, bloodhound, beagle; see ANIMAL, DOG.
hound *v.* badger, provoke, annoy; see BOTHER 2.
hour *n.* time unit, sixty minutes, man-hour, horsepower hour, class hour, supper hour, study hour, rush hour; see also TIME 1. —**hour after hour** continually, steadily, on and on; see REGULARLY.
hourly *a.* each hour, every hour, every sixty minutes; see FREQUENTLY, REGULARLY.
house *n.* **1** [A habitation] dwelling, apartment house, residence; see APARTMENT, HOME 1. **2** [A family] line, family tradition, ancestry; see FAMILY. **3** [A legislative body] congress, council, parliament; see LEGISLATURE. —**bring down the house*** receive applause, create enthusiasm, please; see EXCITE. —**clean house** arrange, put in order, tidy up; see CLEAN. —**keep house** manage a home, run a house, be a housekeeper; see MANAGE 1. —**like a house on fire** (or **afire**) actively, vigorously, energetically; see QUICKLY. —**on the house** without expense, gratis, complimentary; see FREE 4.
household *n.* family unit, house, domestic establishment; see FAMILY, HOME 1.
housekeeper *n.* homemaker, caretaker, serving woman; see SERVANT.
housewife *n.* mistress, lady of the house, housekeeper, home economist, homemaker, family manager, wife and mother; see also WIFE.
housework *n.* housecleaning, spring cleaning, chores, window-washing, sweeping, cooking, baking, dusting, dishwashing, vacuuming, tidying up, putting things away, discarding trash, tending plants, minor repairs, recycling, mopping, washing, laundering, bed-making, sewing, ironing, mending; see also JOB 2.
housing *n.* habitation, home construction, housing development, low-cost housing, house-building program, sheltering, installation, abode, domicile, house, accommodations, quarters, roof, dwelling, lodging, pad*, residence, headquarters; see also HOME 1, SHELTER.
hover *v.* float, flutter, be in midair; see FLY 1, HANG 2.
how *a.*, *conj.* in what way, to what degree, by what method, in what manner, according to what specifications, from what source, by whose help, whence, wherewith, by virtue of what, whereby, through what agency, by what means.
however *a.* still, yet, nevertheless, in spite of this, despite that, nonetheless, notwithstanding, without regard to that.
howl *n.* wail, lament, shriek; see CRY 1, YELL.
howl *v.* bawl, wail, lament; see CRY 1, YELL.

piled by E. Hoyle (1672-1769) —**according to Hoyle** according to the rules

HP *abbrev.* horsepower: usually written **hp**

HQ or **hq** *abbrev.* headquarters

hr *abbrev.* hour

HR *abbrev.* **1** *Baseball* home run(s) **2** House of Representatives

HRH *abbrev.* Her (or His) Royal Highness

HS *abbrev.* high school

ht *abbrev.* height

HTML *abbrev.* Hypertext Markup Language

Huang He (hwäŋ′ hu′) river in N China, flowing into the Yellow Sea

hua·ra·ches (wə rä′chēz, hə-) ***pl.n.*** ⟦MexSp⟧ flat sandals with uppers made of straps or woven leather strips

hub (hub) ***n.*** ⟦< ?⟧ **1** the center part of a wheel **2** a center of activity

hub·bub (hub′bub′) ***n.*** ⟦prob. < Gael exclamation⟧ an uproar; tumult

hub′cap′ ***n.*** a tight cap over the hub of a wheel, esp. on an automobile

hu·bris (hyo͞o′bris) ***n.*** ⟦Gr *hybris*⟧ arrogance caused by excessive pride

huck·le·ber·ry (huk′əl ber′ē) ***n.***, *pl.* **-ries** ⟦prob. ult. < ME *hurtilberye*⟧ **1** a shrub with blue berries **2** this berry

huck·ster (huk′stər) ***n.*** ⟦< MDu *hoeken*, peddle⟧ **1** a peddler **2** [Inf.] one engaged in advertising —***vt.*** to peddle

HUD *abbrev.* (Department of) Housing and Urban Development

hud·dle (hud′'l) ***vi.***, ***vt.*** **-dled**, **-dling** ⟦< ?⟧ **1** to crowd close together **2** to draw (oneself) up —***n.*** **1** a confused crowd or heap **2** [Inf.] a private conference **3** *Football* a grouping of a team to get signals before a play

Hud·son (hud′sən) river in E New York

Hudson Bay inland sea in NE Canada; arm of the Atlantic

hue[1] (hyo͞o) ***n.*** ⟦< OE *heow*⟧ **1** color **2** a particular shade or tint of a color

hue[2] (hyo͞o) ***n.*** ⟦< OFr *hu*, outcry⟧ a shouting: now only in **hue and cry**

huff (huf) ***vi.*** to blow; puff —***n.*** a state of smoldering anger or resentment —**huff′y**, **-i·er**, **-i·est**, ***adj.***

hug (hug) ***vt.*** **hugged**, **hug′ging** ⟦prob. < ON *hugga*, to comfort⟧ **1** to clasp closely and fondly in the arms; embrace **2** to cling to (a belief, etc.) **3** to keep close to —***vi.*** to embrace each other —***n.*** a close embrace

huge (hyo͞oj) ***adj.*** **hug′er**, **hug′est** ⟦< OFr *ahuge*⟧ very large; gigantic; immense —**huge′ly** ***adv.***

Hu·go (hyo͞o′gō), **Vic·tor** (**Marie**) (vik′tər) 1802-85; Fr. poet, novelist, & playwright

Hu·gue·not (hyo͞o′gə nät′) ***n.*** a French Protestant of the 16th or 17th c.

huh (hu, hun) ***interj.*** [Inf.] used to express contempt, surprise, etc., or to ask a question

hu·la (ho͞o′lə) ***n.*** ⟦Haw⟧ a native Hawaiian dance: also **hu′la-hu′la**

hulk (hulk) ***n.*** ⟦< Gr *holkas*, towed ship⟧ **1** the hull of an old, dismantled ship **2** a big, clumsy person or thing

hulk′ing ***adj.*** bulky and clumsy

hull (hul) ***n.*** ⟦OE *hulu*⟧ **1** the outer covering of a seed or fruit, as the husk of grain or shell of a nut **2** the frame or main body of a ship, airship, etc. **3** any outer covering —***vt.*** to take the hulls off (nuts, etc.) —**hull′er** ***n.***

hul·la·ba·loo (hul′ə bə lo͞o′) ***n.*** ⟦echoic⟧ noise and confusion; hubbub

hum (hum) ***vi.*** **hummed**, **hum′ming** ⟦echoic⟧ **1** to make a low, continuous, murmuring sound **2** to sing with closed lips **3** [Inf.] to be full of activity —***vt.*** to sing (a tune) with closed lips —***n.*** a continuous murmur

hu·man (hyo͞o′mən) ***adj.*** ⟦< L *humanus*⟧ of, characteristic of, or having the qualities typical of people, or human beings —***n.*** a person: also **human being** —**hu′man·ness** ***n.***

hu·mane (hyo͞o mān′) ***adj.*** ⟦var. of prec.⟧ **1** kind, tender, merciful, etc. **2** civilizing; refining —**hu·mane′ly** ***adv.*** —**hu·mane′ness** ***n.***

hu·man·ism (hyo͞o′mə niz′əm) ***n.*** **1** any system of thought based on the interests and ideals of humanity **2** [**H-**] the intellectual movement that stemmed from the study of the Greek and Latin classics during the Middle Ages —**hu′man·ist** ***n.***, ***adj.*** —**hu′man·is′tic** ***adj.*** —**hu′man·is′ti·cal·ly** ***adv.***

hu·man·i·tar·i·an (hyo͞o man′ə ter′ē ən) ***n.*** a person devoted to promoting the welfare of humanity; philanthropist —***adj.*** helping humanity —**hu·man′i·tar′i·an·ism′** ***n.***

hu·man·i·ty (hyo͞o man′ə tē) ***n.***, *pl.* **-ties** **1** the fact or quality of being human or humane **2** people —**the humanities** literature, philosophy, history, etc., as distinguished from the sciences

hu·man·ize (hyo͞o′mə nīz′) ***vt.*** **-ized′**, **-iz′ing** to make or become human or humane —**hu′man·i·za′tion** ***n.*** —**hu′man·iz′er** ***n.***

hu′man·kind′ ***n.*** mankind; people

hu′man·ly ***adv.*** **1** in a human manner **2** within human ability or knowledge

hu′man·oid′ (-mə noid′) ***adj.*** nearly human —***n.*** a nearly human creature

hum·ble (hum′bəl) ***adj.*** **-bler**, **-blest** ⟦< L *humilis*, low⟧ **1** having or showing a consciousness of one's shortcomings; modest **2** lowly; unpretentious —***vt.*** **-bled**, **-bling** **1** to lower in condition or rank; abase **2** to lower in pride; make modest —**hum′ble·ness** ***n.*** —**hum′bly** ***adv.***

THESAURUS

hub ***n.*** core, heart, middle; see CENTER 1.

hubbub ***n.*** turmoil, fuss, disorder; see CONFUSION, NOISE 2, UPROAR.

huddle ***v.*** crouch, press close, crowd, bunch, draw, together, mass, cluster, throng, nestle, cuddle, hug, curl up, snuggle.

hue[1] ***n.*** color, shade, dye; see TINT.

huff ***n.*** annoyance, offense, perturbation; see ANGER, RAGE 1.

huffy ***a.*** offended, piqued, huffish; see ANGRY, INSULTED, IRRITABLE.

hug ***n.*** embrace, squeeze, tight grip, caress, clinch*, bearhug; see also TOUCH 2.

hug ***v.*** embrace, squeeze, clasp, press, love, hold, be near to, cling, fold in the arms, clutch, seize, envelop, enfold, nestle, welcome, cuddle, press to the bosom, snuggle.

huge ***a.*** tremendous, enormous, immense; see LARGE 1.

hulk ***n.*** bulk, hunk, lump; see MASS 1, PART 1.

hull ***n.*** **1** [The body of a vessel] framework, covering, main structure; see FRAME 1. **2** [A shell] peel, husk, shuck; see SHELL 1.

hullabaloo ***n.*** tumult, chaos, clamor; see CONFUSION, NOISE 2, UPROAR.

hum ***v.*** buzz, drone, murmur, sing low, hum a tune, croon, sing without words, moan, make a buzzing sound, whir, vibrate, purr.

human ***a.*** anthropoid, animal, biped, civilized, man-made, anthropomorphic, manlike, humanlike, of mankind, belonging to mankind, mortal, humanistic, individual, man's, personal, humane; see also ANIMAL.—*Ant.* DIVINE, bestial, nonhuman.

human being ***n.*** being, human, mortal; see MAN 1, PERSON 1, WOMAN 1.

humane ***a.*** benevolent, sympathetic, understanding, pitying, compassionate, kindhearted, human, tenderhearted, forgiving, gracious, charitable, gentle, tender, friendly, generous, lenient, tolerant, democratic, good-natured, liberal, openminded, broad-minded, altruistic, philanthropic, helpful, magnanimous, amiable, genial, cordial, unselfish, warmhearted, bighearted, softhearted, good; see also KIND.—*Ant.* CRUEL, barbaric, inhuman.

humanitarian ***n.*** altruist, philanthropist, benefactor; see PATRON.

humanity ***n.*** **1** [The human race] human beings, mankind, human race; see MAN 1. **2** [An ideal of human behavior] tolerance, sympathy, understanding; see KINDNESS 1, VIRTUE 1, 2.

humble ***a.*** **1** [Meek] lowly, submissive, gentle, quiet, unassuming, diffident, simple, retiring, bashful, shy, timid, reserved, deferential, self-conscious, soft-spoken, sheepish, mild, withdrawn, unpretentious, hesitant, fearful, tentative, poor in spirit, sedate, unpresuming, manageable, ordinary, unambitious, commonplace, free from pride, without arrogance, peaceable, obedient, passive, tame, restrained, unostentatious, unimportant, gentle as a lamb, resigned, subdued, tolerant, eating humble pie; see also MODEST 2.—*Ant.* PROUD, haughty, conceited. **2** [Lowly] unpretentious, unassuming, modest, seemly, becoming, homespun, natural, low, proletarian, servile, undistinguished, pitiful, sordid, shabby, underprivileged, meager, beggarly, commonplace, unimportant, insignificant, small, poor, rough, hard, base, meek, little, of low birth, obscure, inferior, plain, common, homely, simple, uncouth, miserable, scrubby, ordinary, humdrum, trivial, vulgar.—*Ant.* NOBLE, upper-class, privileged.

humble ***v.*** shame, mortify, chasten, demean, demote, lower, crush, bring low, put to shame, silence, reduce, humiliate, embarrass, degrade, overcome, strike dumb, put down, pull down, bring down, snub, discredit, deflate, upset, make ashamed, take down a peg, pull rank on*, squelch*, squash*.—*Ant.* PRAISE, exalt, glorify.

humbly ***a.*** meekly, submissively,

hum·bug (hum′bug′) ***n.*** ⟦< ?⟧ **1** fraud; sham; hoax **2** an impostor —***vt.*** **-bugged′**, **-bug′ging** to dupe; deceive —***interj.*** nonsense!

hum·drum (hum′drum′) ***adj.*** ⟦echoic⟧ dull

hu·mer·us (hyo͞o′mər əs) ***n.***, *pl.* **-mer·i′** (-ī′) ⟦L⟧ the bone of the upper arm or forelimb —**hu′mer·al** ***adj.***

hu·mid (hyo͞o′mid) ***adj.*** ⟦< L *umere*, be moist⟧ damp; moist

hu·mid·i·fy (hyo͞o mid′ə fī′) ***vt.*** **-fied′**, **-fy′ing** to make humid; dampen —**hu·mid′i·fi′er** ***n.***

hu·mid′i·ty (-ə tē) ***n.*** **1** moistness; dampness **2** the amount of moisture in the air

hu·mi·dor (hyo͞o′mə dôr′) ***n.*** a case or jar for keeping tobacco moist

hu·mil·i·ate (hyo͞o mil′ē āt′) ***vt.*** **-at′ed**, **-at′ing** ⟦< L *humilis*, humble⟧ to hurt the pride or dignity of; mortify —**hu·mil′i·a′tion** ***n.***

hu·mil′i·ty (-ə tē) ***n.*** the state or quality of being humble

hum·ming·bird (hum′iŋ burd′) ***n.*** a very small, brightly colored bird with narrow wings that vibrate rapidly, often with a humming sound

hum·mock (hum′ək) ***n.*** ⟦< ?⟧ a low, rounded hill; knoll —**hum′mock·y** ***adj.***

hum·mus (hum′əs) ***n.*** ⟦Turk *humus*⟧ a Middle Eastern puree of chickpeas, garlic, etc.

hu·mon·gous (hyo͞o mäŋ′gəs, -muŋ′-) ***adj.*** ⟦? a blend of HUGE + MONSTROUS⟧ [Slang] enormous

hu·mor (hyo͞o′mər) ***n.*** ⟦< L *humor*, fluid: after former belief in four body fluids (*humors*) held responsible for one's disposition⟧ **1** mood; state of mind **2** whim; caprice **3** a comical quality **4** *a)* the ability to appreciate or express what is funny, amusing, etc. *b)* the expression of this —***vt.*** to comply with the mood or whim of; indulge Brit. sp. **hu′mour** —**out of humor** not in a good mood —**hu′mor·ist** ***n.*** —**hu′mor·less** ***adj.***

hu′mor·ous ***adj.*** funny; amusing; comical —**hu′mor·ous·ly** ***adv.***

hump (hump) ***n.*** ⟦prob. < LowG⟧ a rounded, protruding lump, as on a camel's back —***vt.*** to hunch; arch —**over the hump** [Inf.] past the worst or most difficult part

hump′back′ ***n.*** **1** a humped, deformed back **2** HUNCHBACK (sense 2) **3** a large whale with long flippers and a raised back —**hump′backed′** ***adj.***

hu·mus (hyo͞o′məs) ***n.*** ⟦L, earth⟧ the dark part of the soil, from partially decayed leaves, etc.

Hun (hun) ***n.*** a member of a warlike Asiatic people that invaded Europe in the 4th and 5th c. A.D.

hunch (hunch) ***vt.*** ⟦< ?⟧ to arch into a hump —***vi.*** to move forward jerkily —***n.*** **1** a hump **2** a feeling not based on known facts; premonition

hunch·back (hunch′bak′) ***n.*** **1** HUMPBACK (sense 1) **2** a person having a back with a hump —**hunch′backed′** ***adj.***

hun·dred (hun′drəd) ***n.***, ***adj.*** ⟦OE⟧ ten times ten; 100; C —**hun′dredth** (-drədth) ***adj.***, ***n.***

hun′dred·fold′ ***adj.***, ***adv.*** (having) a hundred times as much or as many

hun′dred·weight′ ***n.*** a unit of weight equal to 100 pounds in the U.S. and 112 pounds in Great Britain

hung (huŋ) ***vt.***, ***vi.*** *pt. & pp. of* HANG —**hung over** [Slang] having a hangover —**hung up** (**on**) [Slang] disturbed, frustrated, or obsessed (by)

Hung *abbrev.* **1** Hungarian **2** Hungary

Hun·gar·i·an (huŋ ger′ē ən) ***n.*** **1** the language of Hungary **2** a person born or living in Hungary —***adj.*** of Hungary or its people, language, etc.

Hun·ga·ry (huŋ′gə rē) country in SC Europe: 35,911 sq. mi.; pop. 10,375,000

hun·ger (huŋ′gər) ***n.*** ⟦OE *hungor*⟧ **1** discomfort caused by a need for food **2** starvation **3** a desire for food **4** any strong desire —***vi.*** **1** to be hungry **2** to desire —**hun′gry**, **-gri·er**, **-gri·est**, ***adj.*** —**hun′gri·ly** ***adv.***

hunger strike the refusal of a prisoner, demonstrator, etc. to eat until certain demands are met

hung jury a jury unable to reach a verdict

hunk (huŋk) ***n.*** ⟦Fl *hunke*⟧ [Inf.] a large piece

hun·ker (huŋ′kər) ***vi.*** ⟦< dial.⟧ to squat or crouch: often with *down* —***n.*** [*pl.*] haunches or buttocks

hunt (hunt) ***vt.***, ***vi.*** ⟦OE *huntian*⟧ **1** to kill or catch (game) for food or sport **2** to try to find; search (for) **3** to chase —***n.*** **1** a hunting **2** a group of people who hunt together **3** a search —**hunt′er** or **hunts′man** (-mən), *pl.* **-men** (-mən), ***n.*** —**hunt′ress** ***fem.n.***

Hun·ting·ton Beach (hun′tiŋ tən) city in SW California: pop. 182,000

Hunts·ville (hunts′vil) city in N Alabama: pop. 160,000

hur·dle (hurd′'l) ***n.*** ⟦OE *hyrdel*⟧ **1** a framelike barrier over which horses or runners must leap in a race **2** an

THESAURUS

simply, obscurely, apologetically.

humbug ***n.*** lie, fraud, faker; see DECEPTION, NONSENSE 1.

humdrum ***a.*** monotonous, tedious, uninteresting; see DULL 4.

humid ***a.*** stuffy, sticky, muggy; see CLOSE 5, WET 1.

humidity ***n.*** moisture, wetness, dampness, mugginess, dankness, heaviness, sogginess, thickness, fogginess, wet, sultriness, steaminess, steam, evaporation, dewiness, stickiness, moistness; see also RAIN 1.

humiliate ***v.*** debase, chasten, mortify, make a fool of, put to shame, humble, degrade, crush, shame, confuse, snub, confound, lower, dishonor, depress, fill with shame, break, demean, bring low, conquer, make ashamed, vanquish, take down a peg; see also DISGRACE, EMBARRASS.

humiliation ***n.*** chagrin, mortification, degradation; see DISGRACE, EMBARRASSMENT, SHAME 2.

humility ***n.*** meekness, timidity, submissiveness, servility, reserve, subservience, subjection, humbleness, submission, obedience, passiveness, nonresistance, resignation, bashfulness, shyness, inferiority complex.—*Ant.* PRIDE, vainglory, conceit.

humor ***n.*** **1** [Comedy] amusement, jesting, raillery, joking, merriment, clowning, farce, facetiousness, whimsy, black humor; see also ENTERTAINMENT, FUN. **2** [An example of humor] witticism, pleasantry, banter; see JOKE. **3** [The ability to appreciate comedy] sense of humor, wittiness, high spirits, jolliness, gaiety, joyfulness, playfulness, happy frame of mind.

humor ***v.*** indulge, pamper, baby, play up to, gratify, please, pet, coddle, spoil, comply with, appease, placate, soften, be playful with; see also COMFORT 1.—*Ant.* ANGER, provoke, enrage.

humorous ***a.*** comical, comic, entertaining; see FUNNY 1.

humorously ***a.*** comically, ridiculously, playfully, absurdly, ludicrously, amusingly, jokingly, ironically, satirically, facetiously, merrily, genially, jovially, in a comical manner, in an amusing manner, just for fun.

hump ***n.*** protuberance, mound, bump, swelling, camel hump, humpback, hunchback, hummock, protrusion, knob, prominence, eminence, projection, swell, hunch, lump, dune.

hunch ***n.*** idea, notion, feeling, premonition, forecast, presentiment, instinct, expectation, anticipation, precognition, prescience, forewarning, clue, foreboding, hint, portent, apprehension, misgiving, qualm, suspicion, inkling, glimmer; see also THOUGHT 2.

hundred ***n.*** ten tens, five score, century; see NUMBER.

hung ***a.*** suspended, swaying, dangling; see HANGING. —**hung up*** **1** [Troubled] disturbed, distressed, confused; see TROUBLED. **2** [Intent] absorbed, engrossed, preoccupied; see THOUGHTFUL 1.

hunger ***n.*** craving, longing, yearning, mania, lust, desire for food, famine, starvation, ravenousness, appetite, hungriness, panting, drought, want, greediness, void, sweet tooth*.—*Ant.* SATISFACTION, satiety, glut.

hungry ***a.*** starved, famished, ravenous, desirous, hankering, unsatisfied, unfilled, starving, insatiate, voracious, half-starved, omnivorous, piggish, hoggish, on an empty stomach*, hungry as a wolf*, empty*.—*Ant.* FULL, satisfied, fed.

hunk ***n.*** lump, large piece, good-sized bit, portion, a fair quantity, a good bit, chunk, bunch, mass, clod, a pile, thick slice, morsel, a lot, slice, gob, nugget, block, loaf, wad; see also PIECE 1.

hunt ***n.*** chase, shooting, field sport; see HUNTING, SPORT 3.

hunt ***v.*** **1** [To pursue with intent to kill] follow, give chase, stalk, hound, trail, dog, seek, capture, kill, shoot, track, heel, shadow, chase, hunt out, snare, look for, fish, fish for, poach, gun for*, go gunning for*; see also TRACK 1. **2** [To try to find] investigate, probe, look for; see SEEK.

hunted ***a.*** pursued, followed, tracked, sought, trailed, chased, stalked, hounded, tailed, wanted, driven out, searched for.

hunter ***n.*** huntsman, stalker, chaser, sportsman, pursuer, big-game hunter, gunner, poacher, horsewoman, huntress, horseman, archer, trapper, deerstalker, angler, fisherman, bowman, shooter.

hunting ***n.*** the chase, the hunt, sporting, shooting, stalking, preying, trapping, big-game hunting, deer hunting, fox hunting, pheasant shooting, angling, fishing, steeplechase, riding to hounds; see also SPORT 3.

hurdle ***n.*** barricade, obstacle, blockade; see BARRIER.

hurdle ***v.*** jump over, scale, leap over; see JUMP 1.

obstacle —*vt.* **-dled, -dling 1** to jump over **2** to overcome (an obstacle) —**hur′dler** *n.*

hur·dy-gur·dy (hur′dē gur′dē) *n., pl.* **-dies** ⟦? echoic⟧ popularly, a barrel organ

hurl (hurl) *vt.* ⟦prob. < ON⟧ **1** to throw with force or violence **2** to cast down **3** to utter vehemently —*vi.* [Inf.] *Baseball* to pitch —**hurl′er** *n.*

hurl·y-burl·y (hur′lē bur′lē) *n., pl.* **-burl′ies** a turmoil; uproar

Hu·ron (hyoor′än), **Lake** second largest of the Great Lakes, between Michigan & Canada

hur·rah (hə rä′, -rô′) *n., interj., vi., vt.* HURRAY

hur·ray (hə rā′) *n., interj.* ⟦echoic⟧ (exclamation) used to express joy, approval, etc. —*vi., vt.* to shout "hurray" (for); cheer

hur·ri·cane (hur′i kān′) *n.* ⟦< WInd *huracan*⟧ a violent tropical cyclone

hurricane lamp 1 an oil lamp or candlestick with a glass chimney to protect the flame **2** an electric lamp like this

hur·ry (hur′ē) *vt.* **-ried, -ry·ing** ⟦prob. akin to HURL⟧ **1** to move or send with haste **2** to cause to occur or be done more rapidly or too rapidly **3** to urge to act soon or too soon —*vi.* to move or act with haste —*n.* **1** rush; urgency **2** eagerness to do, go, etc. quickly —**hur′ried·ly** *adv.*

hurt (hurt) *vt.* **hurt, hurt′ing** ⟦< OFr *hurter*, to hit⟧ **1** to cause pain or injury to **2** to harm **3** to offend —*vi.* **1** to cause injury, pain, etc. **2** to have pain; be sore —*n.* **1** a pain or injury **2** harm; damage —*adj.* injured; damaged

hurt′ful *adj.* causing hurt; harmful

hur·tle (hurt′'l) *vi., vt.* **-tled, -tling** ⟦ME *hurtlen*⟧ to move or throw with great speed or much force

hus·band (huz′bənd) *n.* ⟦< ON *hūs*, house + *bondi*, freeholder⟧ a married man —*vt.* to manage economically; conserve

hus′band·ry *n.* **1** thrift **2** farming

hush (hush) *vt.* ⟦< ME *huscht*, quiet (adj.)⟧ **1** to make quiet or silent **2** to soothe; lull —*vi.* to become quiet or silent —*n.* quiet; silence —*interj.* used to call for silence

hush′-hush′ *adj.* [Inf.] very secret

hush puppy a small ball of fried cornmeal dough

husk (husk) *n.* ⟦prob. < MDu *huus*, house⟧ **1** the dry outer covering of various fruits or seeds, as of an ear of corn **2** any dry, rough, or useless covering —*vt.* to remove the husk from

hus·ky[1] (hus′kē) *n., pl.* **-kies** ⟦< a var. of ESKIMO⟧ [*also* **H-**] a dog of any of several breeds for pulling sleds in the Arctic

husk·y[2] (hus′kē) *adj.* **-i·er, -i·est 1** hoarse; rough **2** ⟦< toughness of a *husk*⟧ big and strong

hus·sar (hoo zär′) *n.* ⟦< Serb *husar*⟧ a European light-armed cavalryman, usually with a brilliant dress uniform

hus·sy (huz′ē, hus′-) *n., pl.* **-sies** ⟦< ME *huswife*, housewife⟧ **1** a woman of low morals **2** a bold, saucy girl

hus·tings (hus′tiŋz) *pl.n.* ⟦< ON *hūsthing*, house council⟧ [*usually with sing. v.*] the process of, or a place for, political campaigning

hus·tle (hus′əl) *vt.* **-tled, -tling** ⟦Du *husselen*, shake up⟧ **1** to push about; jostle **2** to force in a rough, hurried manner —*vi.* **1** to move hurriedly **2** [Inf.] to work energetically **3** [Slang] to obtain money aggressively or dishonestly —*n.* **1** a hustling **2** [Inf.] energetic action; drive —**hus′tler** *n.*

hut (hut) *n.* ⟦< OHG *hutta*⟧ a very plain or crude little house or cabin

hutch (huch) *n.* ⟦< ML *hutica*, chest⟧ **1** a chest or cupboard **2** a pen or coop for small animals **3** a hut

hutz·pah (hoots′pə) *n.* CHUTZPAH

huz·zah or **huz·za** (hə zä′) *n., interj., vi., vt. archaic var. of* HURRAH (see HURRAY)

HVAC *abbrev.* heating, ventilating, and air conditioning

hwy *abbrev.* highway

hy·a·cinth (hī′ə sinth′) *n.* ⟦< Gr *hyakinthos*⟧ a plant of the lily family, with spikes of bell-shaped flowers

hy·brid (hī′brid) *n.* ⟦L *hybrida*⟧ **1** the offspring of two animals or plants of different varieties, species, etc. **2** anything of mixed origin —*adj.* of or like a hybrid —**hy′brid·ism′** *n.*

hy·brid·ize (hī′bri dīz′) *vi., vt.* **-ized′, -iz′ing** to produce or cause to produce hybrids; crossbreed

Hy·der·a·bad (hī′dər ə bad′, -bäd′) city in SC India: pop. 2,546,000

hy·dra (hī′drə) *n., pl.* **-dras** or **-drae′** (-drē′) ⟦< Gr, water serpent⟧ a small, freshwater polyp with a soft, tubelike body

hy·dran·ge·a (hī drān′jə, -dran′-; -jē ə) *n.* ⟦< HYDR(O)- + Gr *angeion*, vessel⟧ a shrub with large, showy clusters of white, blue, or pink flowers

hy·drant (hī′drənt) *n.* ⟦< Gr *hydōr*, water⟧ a large pipe with a valve for drawing water from a water main; fireplug

hy·drate (hī′drāt′) *n.* ⟦HYDR(O)- + -ATE[1]⟧ a chemical compound of water and some other substance

hy·drau·lic (hī drô′lik) *adj.* ⟦ult. < Gr *hydōr*, water + *aulos*, tube⟧ **1** of hydraulics **2** operated by the movement and force of liquid [*hydraulic* brakes] —**hy·drau′li·cal·ly** *adv.*

hy·drau′lics *n.* the science dealing with the mechanical properties of liquids, as water, in motion and their application in engineering

THESAURUS

hurl *v.* cast, fling, heave; see THROW 1.

hurrah *interj.* three cheers, hurray, yippee; see CHEER 2, CRY 1, ENCOURAGEMENT, YELL 1.

hurricane *n.* typhoon, tempest, monsoon; see STORM.

hurry *interj.* run, hasten, move, hustle, get a move on*, on the double*.

hurry *n.* dispatch, haste, rush; see SPEED.

hurry *v.* **1** [To act quickly] hasten, be quick, make haste, scurry, scuttle, fly, tear, dash, sprint, be in a hurry, lose no time, move quickly, move rapidly, bolt, bustle, rush, make short work of, scoot*, work at high speed, dash on, hurry about, hurry off, hurry up, run off, waste no time, plunge, skip, gallop, zoom, dart, spring, make good time, whip, go by forced marches, speed, work under pressure, run like mad*, go at full tilt, make strides, act on a moment's notice, step on the gas*, floor it*, get cracking*, step on it*, shake a leg*.—*Ant.* DELAY, lose time, procrastinate. **2** [To move rapidly] fly, bustle, dash off; see RACE 1, RUN 1, 2. **3** [To urge others] push, spur, goad; see DRIVE 1, URGE 2.

hurrying *a.* speeding, in a hurry, running; see FAST.

hurt *a.* injured, damaged, harmed, marred, wounded, in critical condition, impaired, shot, struck, bruised, stricken, battered, mauled, hit, stabbed, mutilated, disfigured, bleeding, burned, in pain, suffering, distressed, tortured, unhappy, grazed, scratched, nicked, winged; see also WOUNDED.

hurt *n.* **1** [A wound] blow, gash, ache; see INJURY, PAIN 1. **2** [Damage] ill-treatment, harm, persecution; see DAMAGE 1, DISASTER, MISFORTUNE.

hurt *v.* **1** [To cause pain] cramp, squeeze, cut, bruise, tear, torment, afflict, kick, puncture, do violence to, slap, abuse, flog, whip, torture, gnaw, stab, pierce, maul, cut up, harm, injure, wound, lacerate, sting, bite, inflict pain, burn, crucify, tweak, thrash, punch, pinch, spank, punish, trounce, scourge, lash, cane, switch, work over*, wallop*, slug*.—*Ant.* EASE, comfort, soothe. **2** [To harm] maltreat, injure, spoil; see DAMAGE, DESTROY. **3** [To give a feeling of pain] ache, throb, sting; see sense 1.

hurtful *a.* aching, injurious, bad; see DANGEROUS, DEADLY, HARMFUL.

husband *n.* spouse, married man, mate, bedmate, helpmate, consort, bridegroom, breadwinner, provider, man, common-law husband, hubby*, lord and master*, the man of the house, old man*, groom, cuckold; see also MAN 2.

hush *interj.* quiet, be quiet, pipe down*; see SHUT UP 1.

hush *n.* peace, stillness, quiet; see SILENCE 1.

hush *v.* silence, gag, stifle; see QUIET 2. —**hush (up)** cover, conceal, suppress; see HIDE 1.

husk *n.* shuck, covering, outside; see COVER 1, SHELL 1.

husky[2] *a.* **1** [Hoarse] throaty, growling, gruff; see HOARSE. **2** [Strong] muscular, sinewy, strapping; see STRONG 1.

hustle* *v.* act quickly, rush, push; see HURRY 1, RACE 1, RUN 1, SPEED.

hustler* *n.* **1** [A professional gambler] gamester, bookmaker, plunger*; see GAMBLER. **2** [A prostitute] whore, harlot, call girl; see PROSTITUTE. **3** [An energetic worker] dynamo, go-getter, workaholic; see EXECUTIVE, ZEALOT.

hut *n.* shanty, lean-to, shack, bungalow, bunkhouse, refuge, lodge, dugout, hovel, cottage, cabin, hogan, tepee, log cabin, wigwam, dump*; see also HOME 1, SHELTER.

hybrid *a.* crossed, alloyed, crossbred, interbred, mongrel, cross, half-blooded, heterogeneous, intermingled, half-and-half.

hybrid *n.* crossbreed, cross, mixture, composite, half-blood, combination, mestizo, outcross; see also MIXTURE 1.

hydrant *n.* fire hydrant, fireplug, spigot; see FAUCET.

hydraulics *n.* science of liquids in motion, hydrodynamics, hydrology;

hydro- ⟦< Gr *hydōr*, WATER⟧ *combining form* **1** water *[hydrometer]* **2** hydrogen
hy·dro·car·bon (hī′drə kär′bən) ***n.*** any compound containing only hydrogen and carbon
hy·dro·chlo·ric acid (hī′drə klôr′ik) a strong, highly corrosive acid that is a water solution of the gas hydrogen chloride
hy·dro·e·lec·tric (hī′drō ē lek′trik) ***adj.*** producing, or relating to the production of, electricity by water power —**hy′dro·e′lec′tric′i·ty** ***n.***
hy·dro·foil (hī′drə foil′) ***n.*** ⟦HYDRO- + (AIR)FOIL⟧ **1** a winglike structure that lifts and carries a watercraft just above the water at high speed **2** such a watercraft
hy·dro·gen (hī′drə jən) ***n.*** ⟦see HYDRO- & -GEN⟧ a flammable, colorless, odorless, gaseous chemical element: the lightest known substance
hy·drog·e·nate (hī dräj′ə nāt′) ***vt.*** **-nat′ed, -nat′ing** to combine with or treat with hydrogen *[vegetable oil is hydrogenated to make a solid fat]*
hydrogen bomb an extremely destructive nuclear bomb in which an atomic bomb explosion starts a nuclear fusion explosion of heavy hydrogen atoms
hydrogen peroxide a colorless liquid used as a bleach or disinfectant
hy·drol·o·gy (hī dräl′ə jē) ***n.*** ⟦see HYDRO- & -LOGY⟧ the study of the earth's waters, their distribution, and the cycle involving evaporation, precipitation, flow, etc.
hy·drol′y·sis (-ə sis) ***n.***, *pl.* **-ses′** (-sēz′) ⟦HYDRO- + -LYSIS⟧ a chemical reaction in which a substance reacts with water so as to be changed into one or more other substances
hy·drom·e·ter (hī dräm′ət ər) ***n.*** ⟦HYDRO- + -METER⟧ an instrument for measuring the specific gravity of liquids —**hy·drom′e·try** ***n.***
hy·dro·pho·bi·a (hī′drə fō′bē ə) ***n.*** ⟦see HYDRO- & -PHOBIA⟧ **1** an abnormal fear of water **2** ⟦from symptomatic inability to swallow liquids⟧ RABIES
hy·dro·phone (hī′drə fōn′) ***n.*** ⟦HYDRO- + -PHONE⟧ an instrument for registering the distance and direction of sound transmitted through water
hy′dro·plane′ (-plān′) ***n.*** **1** a small, high-speed motorboat with hydrofoils or a flat bottom **2** SEAPLANE
hy′dro·pon′ics (-pän′iks) ***n.*** ⟦< HYDRO- & Gr *ponos*, labor⟧ the science of growing plants in nutrient-rich solutions —**hy′dro·pon′ic** ***adj.***
hy′dro·sphere′ (-sfir′) ***n.*** ⟦HYDRO- + *-sphere*, a layer of the earth's atmosphere⟧ all the water on the surface of the earth, including oceans, etc.
hy′dro·ther′a·py ***n.*** the treatment of disease, etc. by the use of water
hy·drous (hī′drəs) ***adj.*** ⟦HYDR(O)- + -OUS⟧ containing water, esp. in chemical combination
hy·drox·ide (hī dräk′sīd′) ***n.*** ⟦HYDR(O)- + OXIDE⟧ a compound consisting of an element or radical combined with the radical OH
hy·e·na (hī ē′nə) ***n.*** ⟦< Gr *hyaina*⟧ a wolflike, flesh-eating animal of Africa and Asia, with a shrill cry
hy·giene (hī′jēn′) ***n.*** ⟦< Gr *hygiēs*, healthy⟧ **1** the science of maintaining health **2** cleanliness
hy·gi·en·ic (hī jen′ik) ***adj.*** **1** of hygiene or health **2** sanitary —**hy′gi·en′i·cal·ly** ***adv.***
hy·grom·e·ter (hī gräm′ət ər) ***n.*** ⟦< Gr *hygros*, wet + *metron*, a measure⟧ an instrument for measuring humidity
hy·men (hī′mən) ***n.*** ⟦Gr *hymēn*, membrane⟧ the thin mucous membrane that closes part or sometimes all of the opening of the vagina
hy·me·ne·al (hī′mə nē′əl) ***adj.*** ⟦< Gr *Hymēn*, god of marriage⟧ of marriage
hymn (him) ***n.*** ⟦< Gr *hymnos*⟧ a song of praise, esp. in honor of God
hym·nal (him′nəl) ***n.*** a collection of hymns: also **hymn′book′**
hype[1] (hīp) ***vt.*** **hyped, hyp′ing** [Slang] to stimulate, excite, etc. by or as by a drug injection: usually with *up*
hype[2] (hīp) [Inf.] ***n.*** ⟦? < HYPERBOLE⟧ **1** deception **2** excessive promotion —***vt.*** **hyped, hyp′ing** to promote in a sensational way
hy·per (hī′pər) ***adj.*** [Inf.] high-strung; keyed up
hyper- ⟦< Gr *hyper*⟧ *prefix* over, above, excessive
hy·per·ac·tive (hi′per ac′tiv) ***adj.*** abnormally active —**hy′per·ac·tiv′i·ty** ***n.***
hy·per·bo·la (hī pur′bə lə) ***n.***, *pl.* **-las** or **-lae′** (-lē′) ⟦< Gr *hyperbolē*, a throwing beyond, excess⟧ *Geom.* a curve formed by the intersection of a cone with a plane more steeply inclined than its side
hy·per·bo·le (hī pur′bə lē) ***n.*** ⟦see prec.⟧ exaggeration for effect, not meant to be taken literally —**hy·per·bol·ic** (hī′pər bäl′ik) ***adj.***
hy·per·crit·i·cal (hī′pər krit′i kəl) ***adj.*** too critical
hy′per·ex·tend′ (-ek stend′) ***vt.*** to injure (a knee, etc.) by bending it beyond its normal straightened position
hy′per·gly·ce′mi·a (-glī sē′mē ə) ***n.*** ⟦< HYPER- + Gr *glykys*, sweet + -EMIA⟧ an abnormally high amount of sugar in the blood
hy′per·sen′si·tive (-sen′sə tiv) ***adj.*** excessively sensitive —**hy′per·sen′si·tiv′i·ty** ***n.***
hy′per·ten′sion (-ten′shən) ***n.*** abnormally high blood pressure
hy′per·text′ (-tekst′) ***n.*** computer data organized so that related items can be accessed easily
hy′per·thy′roid·ism′ (-thī′roid iz′əm) ***n.*** excessive activity of the thyroid gland, causing nervousness, rapid pulse, etc. —**hy′per·thy′roid′** ***adj.***, ***n.***
hy′per·ven′ti·la′tion (-vent′'l ā′shən) ***n.*** extremely rapid or deep breathing that may cause dizziness, fainting, etc. —**hy′per·ven′ti·late′, -lat′ed, -lat′ing,** ***vi.***, ***vt.***
hy·phen (hī′fən) ***n.*** ⟦< Gr *hypo-*, under + *hen*, one⟧ a mark (-) used between the parts of a compound word or the syllables of a divided word
hy·phen·ate (hī′fə nāt′) ***vt.*** **-at′ed, -at′ing** to connect or write with a hyphen —**hy′phen·a′tion** ***n.***
hyp·no·sis (hip nō′sis) ***n.***, *pl.* **-ses′** (-sēz′) ⟦< Gr *hypnos*, sleep + -OSIS⟧ a trancelike condition usually induced by another person, in which the subject responds to suggestions made by that person
hyp·not′ic (-nät′ik) ***adj.*** **1** causing sleep; soporific **2** of, like, or inducing hypnosis —***n.*** any agent causing sleep —**hyp·not′i·cal·ly** ***adv.***
hyp′no·tism′ (-nə tiz′əm) ***n.*** the act or practice of inducing hypnosis —**hyp′no·tist** ***n.***
hyp′no·tize′ (-tīz′) ***vt.*** **-tized′, -tiz′ing** to induce hypnosis in
hy·po (hī′pō) ***n.***, *pl.* **-pos** *short for* HYPODERMIC
hypo- ⟦Gr < *hypo*, under⟧ *prefix* **1** under, beneath *[hypodermic]* **2** less than
hy·po·chon·dri·a (hī′pə kän′drē ə) ***n.*** ⟦LL, pl., abdomen (supposed seat of the condition)⟧ abnormal anxiety over one's health, often with imaginary illnesses —**hy′po·chon′dri·ac′** (-ak′) ***adj.***, ***n.***
hy·poc·ri·sy (hi päk′rə sē) ***n.***, *pl.* **-sies** ⟦< Gr *hypokrisis*, acting a part⟧ a pretending to be what one is not, or to feel what one does not feel; esp., a pretense of virtue, piety, etc.
hyp·o·crite (hip′ə krit′) ***n.*** ⟦see prec.⟧ one who pretends to be pious, virtuous, etc. without really being so —**hyp′o·crit′i·cal** ***adj.***

THESAURUS

see SCIENCE 1.

hygiene ***n.*** cleanliness, hygienics, preventive medicine, public health, sanitary measures; see also HEALTH, CLEANLINESS.

hygienic ***a.*** healthful, sanitary, clean; see PURE 2, STERILE 3.

hymn ***n.*** chant, psalm, spiritual; see SONG.

hyperbole ***n.*** overstatement, figure of speech, distortion; see EXAGGERATION.

hypnosis ***n.*** trance, anesthesia, lethargy; see SLEEP.

hypnotic ***a.*** sleep-inducing, narcotic, anesthetic, soporific, sleep-producing, soothing, calmative, trance-inducing.

hypnotism ***n.*** bewitchment, suggestion, hypnotherapy, deep sleep, self-hypnosis, autohypnosis, hypnotic suggestion, charm, fascination.

hypnotize ***v.*** mesmerize, lull to sleep, dull the will, hold under a spell, bring under one's control, stupefy, drug, soothe, fascinate, anesthetize, subject to suggestion, make drowsy.

hypnotized ***a.*** entranced, mesmerized, enchanted; see CHARMED.

hypochondria ***n.*** anxiety, imagined ill-health, neurosis; see PRETENSE 1.

hypochondriac ***n.*** worrier, neurotic, self-tormentor; see FAKE.

hypocrisy ***n.*** affectation, deception, bad faith, hollowness, display, lip service, bigotry, sham, fraud, pretense of virtue, quackery, empty ceremony, sanctimony, cant; see also DISHONESTY, LIE.—*Ant.* VIRTUE, devotion, piety.

hypocrite ***n.*** pretender, fraud, faker, deceiver, charlatan, bigot, quack, pharisee, sham, actor, cheat, informer, trickster, confidence man, malingerer, humbug, impostor, swindler, informer, rascal, traitor, wolf in sheep's clothing, masquerader, four-flusher*, two-timer*, two-face*; see also FAKE.

hypocritical ***a.*** deceptive, double-dealing, insincere; see DISHONEST.

hy·po·der·mic (hī′pə dur′mik) ***adj.*** ⟦< HYPO- + Gr *derma*, skin⟧ injected under the skin —***n.*** a hypodermic syringe or injection

hypodermic syringe a syringe attached to a hollow needle (**hypodermic needle**) and used for the injection of a medicine or drug under the skin

hy·po·gly·ce·mi·a (hī′pō glī sē′mē ə) ***n.*** ⟦< HYPO- + Gr *glykys*, sweet + -EMIA⟧ an abnormally low amount of sugar in the blood

hy·pot·e·nuse (hī pät′′n o͞os′) ***n.*** ⟦< Gr *hypo-*, under + *teinein*, to stretch⟧ the side of a right-angled triangle located opposite the right angle

hy·po·thal·a·mus (hī′pō thal′ə məs) ***n.***, *pl.* **-mi′** (-mī′) ⟦see HYPO- & THALAMUS⟧ the part of the brain that regulates many basic body functions, as temperature

hy′po·ther′mi·a (-thur′mē ə) ***n.*** ⟦< HYPO- + Gr *thermē*, heat⟧ a subnormal body temperature —**hy′po·ther′mal** ***adj.***

hy·poth·e·sis (hī päth′ə sis) ***n.***, *pl.* **-ses′** (-sēz′) ⟦< Gr *hypo-*, under + *tithenai*, to place⟧ an unproved theory, etc. tentatively accepted to explain certain facts —**hy·poth′e·size′** (-sīz′), **-sized′**, **-siz′ing**, ***vi.***, ***vt.***

hy·po·thet·i·cal (hī′pə thet′i kəl) ***adj.*** based on a hypothesis; assumed; supposed —**hy′po·thet′i·cal·ly** ***adv.***

hy·po·thy·roid·ism (hī′pō thī′roid iz′əm) ***n.*** deficient activity of the thyroid gland, causing sluggishness, puffiness, etc. —**hy′po·thy′roid′** ***adj.***, ***n.***

hys·sop (his′əp) ***n.*** ⟦< Heb *ēzōbh*⟧ a fragrant, blue-flowered herb of the mint family

hys·ter·ec·to·my (his′tər ek′tə mē) ***n.***, *pl.* **-mies** ⟦< Gr *hystera*, uterus + -ECTOMY⟧ surgical removal of all or part of the uterus

hys·te·ri·a (hi ster′ē ə, -stir′-) ***n.*** ⟦< Gr *hystera*, uterus: orig. thought to occur more often in women than in men⟧ **1** a psychiatric condition characterized by excitability, anxiety, the simulation of organic disorders, etc. **2** any outbreak of wild, uncontrolled feeling: also **hys·ter′ics** —**hys·ter′i·cal** or **hys·ter′ic** ***adj.*** —**hys·ter′i·cal·ly** ***adv.***

Hz *abbrev.* hertz

THESAURUS

hypothesis ***n.*** supposition, theory, assumption; see GUESS, OPINION 1.

hypothetical ***a.*** **1** [Supposed] imagined, uncertain, vague; see ASSUMED, LIKELY 1. **2** [Characterized by hypothesis] postulated, academic, philosophical; see LOGICAL.

hysteria ***n.*** delirium, agitation, feverishness; see CONFUSION, EXCITEMENT, NERVOUSNESS.

hysterical ***a.*** convulsed, uncontrolled, raving, delirious, unnerved, neurotic, emotional, rabid, emotionally disordered, distracted, fuming, distraught, unrestrained, possessed, fanatical, irrepressible, convulsive, carried away, seething, beside oneself, rampant, out of one's wits, mad, uncontrollable, agitated, raging, frenzied, spasmodic, confused, tempestuous, maddened, crazy, impetuous, crazed, furious, violent, impassioned, panic-stricken, nervous, vehement, overwrought, fiery, passionate, jittery*, wild-eyed, on a crying jag*; see also ANGRY, EXCITED, TROUBLED.

I

i or **I** (ī) ***n.***, *pl.* **i's, I's** the ninth letter of the English alphabet
I[1] (ī) ***n.*** a Roman numeral for 1
I[2] (ī) ***pron.*** ⟦OE *ic*⟧ the person speaking or writing
I[3] *abbrev.* **1** island(s) **2** isle(s)
I[4] *Chem. symbol for* iodine
IA *abbrev.* Iowa
-i·al (ē əl, yəl) ⟦L *-ialis*⟧ *suffix* -AL
i·amb (ī′amb′, -am′) ***n.*** ⟦< Gr *iambos*⟧ a metrical foot of one unaccented syllable followed by one accented one
i·am·bic (ī am′bik) ***adj.*** ⟦< Gr *iambikos*⟧ of or made up of iambs —***n.*** an iamb
-i·at·rics (ē a′triks′) ⟦< Gr *iatros*, physician⟧ *combining form* treatment of disease *[pediatrics]*
-i·a·try (ī′ə trē) ⟦< Gr *iatreia*, healing⟧ *combining form* medical treatment *[psychiatry]*
I·be·ri·a (ī bir′ē ə) peninsula in SW Europe, comprising Spain & Portugal: also **Iberian Peninsula** —**I·be′ri·an** ***adj.***, ***n.***
i·bex (ī′beks′) ***n.***, *pl.* **i′bex′es** or **i·bi·ces** (ī′bə sēz′) ⟦L⟧ a wild goat of the Old World, with large, backward-curved horns
ibid. *abbrev.* ⟦L *ibidem*⟧ in the same place, i.e., the book, page, etc. just cited: also **ib.**
-i·bil·i·ty (ə bil′ə tē) ⟦L *-ibilitas*⟧ *suffix* -ABILITY
i·bis (ī′bis) ***n.*** ⟦Egypt *hb*⟧ a large wading bird found chiefly in tropical regions
-i·ble (i bəl, ə bəl) ⟦L *-ibilis*⟧ *suffix* -ABLE
Ib·sen (ib′sən), **Hen·rik** (hen′rik) 1828-1906; Norw. playwright
i·bu·pro·fen (ī′byo͞o prō′fən) ***n.*** a drug used to reduce fever and relieve pain, esp. arthritic pain
-ic (ik) ⟦< Gr *-ikos*⟧ *suffix* **1** *a)* of, having to do with *[volcanic]* *b)* like *[angelic]* *c)* produced by *[anaerobic]* *d)* consisting of, containing *[dactylic]* *e)* having, showing *[lethargic]* **2** a person or thing: *a)* having *[paraplegic]* *b)* supporting *[heretic]* *c)* producing *[hypnotic]* Also **-i·cal** (i kəl, ə kəl)
ICBM ***n.*** an intercontinental ballistic missile
ICC *abbrev.* Interstate Commerce Commission
ice (īs) ***n.*** ⟦OE *īs*⟧ **1** water frozen solid by cold **2** a frozen dessert of fruit juice, sugar, etc. **3** [Slang] diamonds —***vt.* iced, ic′ing** **1** to change into ice; freeze **2** to cool with ice **3** to cover with icing —***vi.*** to freeze: often with *up* or *over* —**break the ice** to make a start, as in getting acquainted —**cut no ice** [Inf.] to have no influence —**on thin ice** [Inf.] in danger
Ice *abbrev.* **1** Iceland **2** Icelandic
ice′berg′ (-burg′) ***n.*** ⟦prob. < Du *ijsberg*, ice mountain⟧ a great mass of ice broken off from a glacier and floating in the sea
ice′bound′ ***adj.*** held fast or shut in by ice
ice′box′ ***n.*** a refrigerator, esp. one using ice
ice′break′er ***n.*** a sturdy boat for cutting channels through ice
ice′cap′ ***n.*** a mass of glacial ice that spreads slowly from a center
ice cream ⟦orig., *iced cream*⟧ a sweet, frozen food of flavored cream or milk —**ice′-cream′** ***adj.***
ice floe a piece of floating sea ice
ice hockey *see* HOCKEY (sense 1)
Ice·land (īs′lənd) country on an island in the North Atlantic, southeast of Greenland: 39,758 sq. mi.; pop. 229,000 —**Ice′land·er** ***n.***
Ice·lan·dic (īs lan′dik) ***n.*** the Germanic language of Iceland —***adj.*** of Iceland or its people, language, etc.
ice·man (īs′man′, -mən) ***n.***, *pl.* **-men′** (-men′, -mən) one who sells or delivers ice
ice milk a frozen dessert like ice cream, but with less butterfat
ice skate *see* SKATE[1] (*n.* 1) —**ice′-skate′, -skat′ed, -skat′ing,** ***vi.***
ich·thy·ol·o·gy (ik′thē äl′ə jē) ***n.*** ⟦< Gr *ichthys*, a fish + -LOGY⟧ the branch of zoology dealing with fish —**ich′thy·ol′o·gist** ***n.***
i·ci·cle (ī′sik′əl, -sə kəl) ***n.*** ⟦< OE īs, ice + *gicel*, piece of ice⟧ a hanging piece of ice, formed by the freezing of dripping water
ic·ing (īs′iŋ) ***n.*** a mixture variously of sugar, butter, flavoring, egg whites, etc. for covering a cake; frosting
ick·y (ik′ē) ***adj.* -i·er, -i·est** ⟦< STICKY⟧ [Slang] **1** unpleasantly sticky or sweet **2** disgusting
i·con (ī′kän′) ***n.*** ⟦< Gr *eikōn*, image⟧ **1** *a)* an image; figure *b)* a stylized figure on a computer screen, representing a function **2** *Eastern Orthodox Ch.* a sacred image or picture of Jesus, Mary, etc. **3** one that is revered or that represents an era, etc. —**i·con′ic** ***adj.***
i·con·o·clast (ī kän′ə klast′) ***n.*** ⟦< *c.* 6th-c. Gr *eikōn*, image + *klaein*, to break⟧ one who attacks widely accepted ideas, beliefs, etc. —**i·con′o·clasm′** ***n.*** —**i·con′o·clas′tic** ***adj.***
-ics (iks) ⟦-IC + -S (pl.)⟧ *suffix* [*usually with sing. v.*] art, science, study *[mathematics]*
ICU *abbrev.* intensive care unit
i·cy (ī′sē) ***adj.* i′ci·er, i′ci·est** **1** full of or covered with ice **2** of or like ice; specif., *a)* slippery *b)* very cold **3** cold in manner; unfriendly —**i′ci·ly** ***adv.*** —**i′ci·ness** ***n.***
id (id) ***n.*** ⟦L, it⟧ *Psychoanalysis* that part of the psyche which is the source of psychic energy
ID[1] (ī′dē′) ***n.***, *pl.* **ID's** or **IDs** [Inf.] a document, as a license to drive a car, serving as identification
ID[2] *abbrev.* identification
id. *abbrev.* ⟦L *idem*⟧ the same
I·da·ho (ī′də hō′) Mountain State of the NW U.S.: 82,751 sq. mi.; pop. 1,007,000; cap. Boise: abbrev. **ID** —**I′da·ho′an** ***adj.***, ***n.***
i·de·a (ī dē′ə) ***n.*** ⟦L < Gr, appearance of a thing⟧ **1** a thought; mental conception or image **2** an opinion or belief **3** a plan; scheme **4** meaning or significance
i·de·al (ī dē′əl, -dēl′) ***adj.*** ⟦see prec.⟧ **1** existing as an idea, model, etc. **2** thought of as perfect **3** imaginary —***n.*** **1** a conception of something in its most excellent form **2** a perfect model **3** a noble goal or principle
i·de′al·ism′ ***n.*** **1** behavior or thought based on a conception of things as one thinks they should be **2** a striving to achieve one's ideals —**i·de′al·ist** ***n.*** —**i′de·al·is′tic** ***adj.***
i·de·al·ize (ī dē′əl īz′) ***vt.* -ized′, -iz′ing** to regard or show as perfect or more nearly perfect than is true —**i·de′al·i·za′tion** ***n.*** —**i·de′al·iz′er** ***n.***
i·de′al·ly ***adv.*** **1** in an ideal manner; perfectly **2** in theory
i·den·ti·cal (ī den′ti kəl) ***adj.*** ⟦< L *idem*, the same⟧ **1** the very same **2** exactly alike —**i·den′ti·cal·ly** ***adv.***
i·den·ti·fi·ca·tion (ī den′tə fi kā′shən) ***n.*** **1** an identifying or being identified **2** anything by which one can be identified

THESAURUS

I[2] ***pron.*** myself, yours truly*, first person; see CHARACTER 2.

ICBM ***n.*** Intercontinental Ballistic Missile, guided missile, nuclear weapon; see ROCKET, WEAPON.

ice ***n.*** crystal, hail, floe, glacier, icicle, ice cube, cube ice, dry ice, black ice, white ice, crushed ice, iceberg, permafrost; see also FROST. —**break the ice** make a start, initiate, commence; see BEGIN 1. —**on ice*** in reserve, held, in abeyance; see SAVED 2. —**on thin ice*** in a dangerous situation, imperiled, insecure; see ENDANGERED.

ice ***v.*** frost, coat, mist; see FREEZE 1.

iceberg ***n.*** ice field, berg, floe; see ICE.

icebox ***n.*** cooler, freezer, fridge*; see REFRIGERATOR.

ice cream ***n.*** frozen dessert, ice, ice milk, frozen custard, soft serve, sherbet, sorbet, frozen yogurt, gelato, *glace* (French), spumoni, sundae, parfait; see also DESSERT.

icy ***a.*** frozen over, iced, freezing, glacial, frostbound, frosted, frosty, smooth as glass; see also SLIPPERY.

idea ***n.*** **1** [A concept] conception, plans, view, fancy, impression, image, understanding, observation, belief, feeling, opinion, guess, inference, theory, hypothesis, supposition, assumption, intuition, conjecture, design, approach, mental impression, notion. **2** [Fancy] whimsy, whim, fantasy; see FANCY 1, IMAGINATION. **3** [Meaning] sense, import, purport; see MEANING.

ideal ***a.*** **1** [Typical] prototypical, model, archetypical; see TYPICAL. **2** [Perfect] supreme, fitting, exemplary; see EXCELLENT, PERFECT.

ideal ***n.*** paragon, goal, prototype; see MODEL 1.

idealism ***n.*** principle, conscience, philosophy; see ETHICS.

idealistic ***a.*** lofty, utopian, exalted; see IMPRACTICAL, NOBLE 1.

idealize ***v.*** romanticize, glorify, put on a pedestal; see ADMIRE, DREAM 2.

identical ***a.*** like, twin, indistinguishable; see ALIKE.

identification ***n.*** **1** [The act of identifying] classifying, naming, cataloging; see CLASSIFICATION, DESCRIPTION. **2** [Means of identifying] credentials, letter of introduction, testi-

i·den·ti·fy (ī den′tə fī′) ***vt.*** **-fied′, -fy′ing** **1** to make identical; treat as the same **2** to fix the identity of *[to identify* a biological specimen*]* **3** to connect or associate closely

i·den·ti·ty (ī den′tə tē) ***n.,*** *pl.* **-ties** **1** the state or fact of being the same **2** *a)* the state or fact of being a specific person or thing; individuality *b)* the state of being as described

identity crisis the state of being uncertain about oneself regarding character, goals, etc., esp. in adolescence

id·e·o·gram (id′ē ō gram′, ī′dē-) ***n.*** ⟦see IDEA & -GRAM⟧ a symbol representing an object or idea without expressing the word for it: also **id′e·o·graph′** (-graf′)

i·de·ol·o·gy (ī′dē äl′ə jē, id′ē-) ***n.,*** *pl.* **-gies** ⟦see IDEA & -LOGY⟧ the doctrines, etc. on which a particular political or social system is based —**i′de·o·log′i·cal** ***adj.*** —**i′de·ol′o·gist** ***n.***

ides (īdz) ***pl.n.*** ⟦< L *idus*⟧ *[often with sing. v.]* in the ancient Roman calendar, the 15th day of March, May, July, or October, or the 13th of the other months

id·i·o·cy (id′ē ə sē) ***n.*** **1** great foolishness or stupidity **2** *pl.* **-cies** an idiotic act or remark

id·i·om (id′ē əm) ***n.*** ⟦< Gr *idios,* one's own⟧ **1** the language or dialect of a people, region, class, etc. **2** the usual way that the words of a language are joined to express thought **3** a phrase or expression with an unusual syntactic pattern or with a meaning differing from the literal meaning of its parts **4** a characteristic style, as in art or music —**id′i·o·mat′ic** (-ə mat′ik) ***adj.***

id·i·o·path·ic (id′ē ə′path′ik) ***adj.*** ⟦< Gr *idiopatheia,* feeling for oneself alone⟧ of a disease whose cause is unknown

id·i·o·syn·cra·sy (id′ē ō siŋ′krə sē) ***n.,*** *pl.* **-sies** ⟦< Gr *idio-,* one's own + *synkrasis,* a mixing⟧ any personal peculiarity, mannerism, etc. —**id′i·o·syn·crat′ic** (-sin krat′ik) ***adj.***

id·i·ot (id′ē ət) ***n.*** ⟦< Gr *idiōtēs,* ignorant person⟧ a very foolish or stupid person —**id′i·ot′ic** (-ät′ik) ***adj.*** —**id′i·ot′i·cal·ly** ***adv.***

i·dle (īd′'l) ***adj.*** **i′dler, i′dlest** ⟦OE *idel,* empty⟧ **1** useless; futile *[an idle wish]* **2** unfounded *[idle rumors]* **3** *a)* unemployed; not busy *b)* inactive; not in use **4** lazy —***vi.*** **i′dled, i′dling** **1** to move slowly or aimlessly **2** to be unemployed or inactive **3** to operate without transmitting power *[the motor idled]* —***vt.*** **1** to waste: usually with *away* **2** to cause (a motor, etc.) to idle —**i′dle·ness** ***n.*** —**i′dler** ***n.*** —**i′dly** ***adv.***

i·dol (īd′'l) ***n.*** ⟦< Gr *eidōlon,* image⟧ **1** an image of a god, used as an object of worship **2** any object of ardent or excessive devotion

i·dol·a·try (ī däl′ə trē) ***n.,*** *pl.* **-tries** **1** worship of idols **2** excessive reverence for or devotion to a person or thing —**i·dol′a·ter** ***n.*** —**i·dol′a·trous** ***adj.***

i·dol·ize (īd′'l īz′) ***vt.*** **-ized′, -iz′ing** **1** to make an idol of **2** to love or admire excessively

i·dyll or **i·dyl** (īd′'l; *Brit* id′'l) ***n.*** ⟦< Gr *eidos,* a form⟧ **1** a short poem, etc. describing a simple, peaceful scene of rural life **2** a scene or incident suitable for this —**i·dyl·lic** (ī dil′ik) ***adj.***

IE *abbrev.* Indo-European

-ie (ē) ⟦earlier form of -Y[1]⟧ *suffix* **1** small or little (one, as specified) *[lassie]* **2** *a)* one that is as specified *[softie]* *b)* one connected with *[groupie]*

i.e. *abbrev.* ⟦L *id est*⟧ that is (to say)

-i·er (ē′ər, yər, ir, ər) ⟦< L *-arius*⟧ *suffix* a person concerned with (a specified action or thing) *[bombardier]*

if (if) ***conj.*** ⟦OE *gif*⟧ **1** on condition that; in case that *[if I were you, I would quit]* **2** allowing that *[if she was there, I didn't see her]* **3** whether *[ask him if he knows her]*

if·fy (if′ē) ***adj.*** **-fi·er, -fi·est** [Inf.] not definite; containing doubtful elements

ig·loo (ig′lo͞o′) ***n.,*** *pl.* **-loos′** ⟦Esk *igdlu,* snow house⟧ an Eskimo hut, usually dome-shaped and built of blocks of packed snow

ig·ne·ous (ig′nē əs) ***adj.*** ⟦< L *ignis,* a fire⟧ **1** of fire **2** produced by volcanic action or intense heat *[igneous rock]*

ig·nite (ig nīt′) ***vt.*** **-nit′ed, -nit′ing** ⟦see prec.⟧ to set fire to —***vi.*** to catch on fire; start burning —**ig·nit′a·ble** or **ig·nit′i·ble** ***adj.***

ig·ni·tion (ig nish′ən) ***n.*** **1** an igniting or being ignited **2** the key-operated switch or system for igniting the explosive mixture in the cylinder of an internal-combustion engine

ig·no·ble (ig nō′bəl) ***adj.*** ⟦< L *in-,* not + *nobilis* (< earlier *gnobilis,* known)⟧ not noble; base; mean —**ig·no′bly** ***adv.***

ig·no·min·y (ig′nə min′ē) ***n.*** ⟦< L *in-,* no, not + *nomen,* name⟧ loss of reputation; shame; disgrace —**ig′no·min′i·ous** ***adj.*** —**ig′no·min′i·ous·ly** ***adv.***

ig·no·ra·mus (ig′nə rā′məs, -ram′əs) ***n.,*** *pl.* **-mus·es** an ignorant person

ig·no·rant (ig′nə rənt) ***adj.*** ⟦see fol.⟧ **1** lacking knowledge or experience **2** caused by or showing lack of knowledge **3** unaware (*of*) —**ig′no·rance** ***n.*** —**ig′no·rant·ly** ***adv.***

ig·nore (ig nôr′) ***vt.*** **-nored′, -nor′ing** ⟦< L *in-,* not + *gnarus,* knowing⟧ to disregard; pay no attention to

i·gua·na (i gwä′nə) ***n.*** ⟦Sp < WInd⟧ a large tropical American lizard

IL Illinois

il- *prefix* **1** IN-[1] **2** IN-[2] Used before *l*

-ile (il, əl, 'l, īl) *suffix* of or like

Il·i·ad (il′ē əd) ***n.*** ⟦< Gr *Ilios,* Troy⟧ a Greek epic poem, ascribed to Homer, about the Trojan War

ilk (ilk) ***n.*** ⟦< OE *ilca,* same⟧ kind; sort; class: only in **of that** (or **his, her,** etc.) **ilk**

ill (il) ***adj.*** **worse, worst** ⟦< ON *illr*⟧ **1** bad *[ill repute, ill will, ill omen]* **2** not well; sick —***n.*** an evil or a disease —***adv.*** **worse, worst** **1** badly **2** scarcely *[I can ill afford it]* —**ill at ease** uneasy; uncomfortable

THESAURUS

mony, letter of credit, badge, papers, ID; see also PASSPORT.

identify ***v.*** classify, catalog, analyze; see DESCRIBE, NAME 1, 2.

identity ***n.*** identification, character, individuality, uniqueness, antecedents, true circumstances, parentage, status, citizenship, nationality, connections; see also NAME 1.

ideology ***n.*** beliefs, ideas, philosophy; see CULTURE 2, ETHICS.

idiot ***n.*** simpleton, nincompoop, booby; see FOOL.

idiotic ***a.*** thickwitted, dull, moronic; see STUPID.

idle ***a.*** unoccupied, fallow, vacant, deserted, not in use, barren, void, empty, abandoned, still, quiet, motionless, inert, dead, rusty, dusty, out of action, out of a job, out of work, resting; see also UNEMPLOYED.—*Ant.* ACTIVE, busy, engaged.

idle ***v.*** slack, shirk, slow down; see LOAF.

idleness ***n.*** loitering, time-killing, dawdling, inertia, inactivity, indolence, sluggishness, unemployment, dormancy, lethargy, stupor, loafing.—*Ant.* ACTION, industry, occupation.

idol ***n.*** graven image, god, effigy, false god, figurine, fetish, totem, golden calf, pagan deity.

idolatry ***n.*** infatuation, fervor, transport; see ZEAL.

idolize ***v.*** glorify, adore, canonize; see WORSHIP.

if ***conj.*** provided that, with the condition that, supposing that, conceding that, on the assumption that, granted that, assuming that, whenever, wherever. —**as if** as though, assuming that, in a way; see AS IF at AS.

iffy ***a.*** unsettled, doubtful, not sure; see UNCERTAIN.

ignite ***v.*** kindle, light, strike a light, start up, burst into flames, touch off, touch a match to, set off; see also BURN.

ignition ***n.*** **1** [Igniting] combustion, bursting into flame, kindling; see FIRE 1. **2** [A system for igniting] distributor, firing system, wiring system; see ENGINE, MACHINE, MOTOR.

ignorance ***n.*** unconsciousness, incomprehension, bewilderment, incapacity, inexperience, disregard, illiteracy, denseness, stupidity, dumbness, empty-headedness, unintelligence, rawness, blindness, simplicity, insensitivity, shallowness, fog, vagueness, half-knowledge, lack of education, a little learning.—*Ant.* ABILITY, learning, erudition.

ignorant ***a.*** **1** [Unaware] unconscious of, uninformed, unknowing, uninitiated, inexperienced, unwitting, unmindful, disregardful, misinformed, unsuspecting, unaware of, unmindful of, mindless, witless, not conversant with, unintelligent, obtuse, thick, dense, unscientific, birdbrained*, lowbrow*, sappy*, green; see also sense 2 and DULL 3, SHALLOW 2, STUPID.—*Ant.* INTELLIGENT, alert, aware. **2** [Untrained] illiterate, uneducated, unlettered, untaught, uninstructed, uncultivated, unenlightened, untutored, unschooled, unread, benighted, shallow, superficial, gross, coarse, vulgar, crude, green, knowing nothing, misinformed, misguided, just beginning, apprenticed, unbriefed; see also INEXPERIENCED, NAIVE, UNAWARE.—*Ant.* LEARNED, cognizant, tutored.

ignore ***v.*** disregard, overlook, pass over; see DISCARD, NEGLECT 2.

ill ***a.*** **1** [Bad] harmful, evil, noxious; see BAD 1. **2** [Sick] unwell, ailing, unhealthy; see SICK. —**ill at ease** anxious, uneasy, uncomfortable; see DOUBTFUL, RESTLESS, SUSPICIOUS 1, 2.

ill ***n.*** depravity, misfortune, mischief; see EVIL 2, INSULT, WRONG.

ill·ad·vised (il′əd vīzd′) ***adj.*** showing or resulting from poor advice; unwise
ill′-bred′ ***adj.*** rude; impolite
il·le·gal (i lē′gəl) ***adj.*** prohibited by law; against the law —**il·le·gal·i·ty** (il′ē gal′i tē), *pl.* **-ties,** ***n.*** —**il·le′gal·ly** ***adv.***
il·leg·i·ble (i lej′ə bəl) ***adj.*** hard or impossible to read because badly written or printed —**il·leg′i·bly** ***adv.***
il·le·git·i·mate (il′ə jit′ə mət) ***adj.*** **1** born of parents not married to each other **2** not legal or logical —**il′le·git′i·ma·cy** (-mə sē), *pl.* **-cies,** ***n.***
ill-fat·ed (il′fāt′id) ***adj.*** **1** certain to have an evil fate or unlucky end **2** unlucky
ill′-fa′vored ***adj.*** ugly or unpleasant
ill′-got′ten ***adj.*** obtained unlawfully or dishonestly
il·lib·er·al (i lib′ər əl) ***adj.*** **1** narrow-minded **2** not generous
il·lic·it (i lis′it) ***adj.*** ⟦< L *illicitus,* not allowed⟧ unlawful; improper —**il·lic′it·ly** ***adv.*** —**il·lic′it·ness** ***n.***
il·lim·it·a·ble (i lim′i tə bəl) ***adj.*** without limit; immeasurable
Il·li·nois (il′ə noi′) Midwestern state of the U.S.: 55,646 sq. mi.; pop. 11,431,000; cap. Springfield: abbrev. IL —**Il′li·nois′an** ***adj., n.***
il·liq·uid (i lik′wid) ***adj.*** not readily convertible into cash
il·lit·er·a·cy (i lit′ər ə sē) ***n.*** **1** a being illiterate **2** *pl.* **-cies** a mistake in grammar suggesting this
il·lit·er·ate (i lit′ər it) ***adj.*** uneducated; esp., not knowing how to read or write —***n.*** an illiterate person
ill-man·nered (il′man′ərd) ***adj.*** having bad manners; rude; impolite
ill nature a disagreeable or mean disposition —**ill′-na′tured** ***adj.***
ill′ness ***n.*** the condition of being in poor health; sickness; disease
il·log·i·cal (i läj′i kəl) ***adj.*** not logical or reasonable —**il·log′i·cal·ly** ***adv.***
ill-starred (il′stärd′) ***adj.*** unlucky
ill′-suit′ed ***adj.*** not suited or appropriate
ill′-tem′pered ***adj.*** sullen; irritable
ill′-timed′ ***adj.*** inopportune
ill′-treat′ ***vt.*** to treat unkindly, unfairly, etc. —**ill′-treat′ment** ***n.***
il·lu·mi·nate (i lo͞o′mə nāt′) ***vt.*** **-nat′ed, -nat′ing** ⟦< L *in-,* in + *luminare,* to light⟧ **1** to give light to; light up **2** *a)* to make clear; explain *b)* to inform **3** to decorate with lights **4** to decorate (a page border, etc.) by hand —**il·lu′mi·na·ble** (-nə bəl) ***adj.***
il·lu′mi·na′tion ***n.*** **1** an illuminating **2** the intensity of light per unit of area
il·lu′mine (-mən) ***vt.*** **-mined, -min·ing** to light up
illus *abbrev.* **1** illustrated **2** illustration **3** illustrator
ill-us·age (il′yo͞o′sij) ***n.*** unkind or cruel treatment; abuse: also **ill usage**
ill′-use′ (-yo͞oz′; *for n.,* -yo͞os′) ***vt.*** **-used′, -us′ing** to treat unkindly; abuse —***n.*** ILL-USAGE
il·lu·sion (i lo͞o′zhən) ***n.*** ⟦< L *illudere,* to mock⟧ **1** a false idea or conception **2** an unreal or misleading appearance or image —**il·lu′so·ry** (-sə rē) or **il·lu′sive** (-siv) ***adj.***
il·lus·trate (il′ə strāt′) ***vt.*** **-trat′ed, -trat′ing** ⟦< L *in-,* in + *lustrare,* illuminate⟧ **1** to explain; make clear, as by examples **2** to furnish (books, etc.) with explanatory or decorative pictures, etc. —**il′lus·tra′tor** ***n.***
il′lus·tra′tion (-strā′shən) ***n.*** **1** an illustrating **2** an example, etc. used to help explain **3** a picture, diagram, etc. used to decorate or explain
il·lus·tra·tive (i lus′trə tiv, il′ə strāt′iv) ***adj.*** serving as an illustration or example
il·lus·tri·ous (i lus′trē əs) ***adj.*** ⟦< L *illustris,* clear⟧ distinguished; famous; outstanding —**il·lus′tri·ous·ly** ***adv.*** —**il·lus′tri·ous·ness** ***n.***
ill will hostility; hate; dislike
I'm (īm) *contr.* I am
im- *prefix* **1** IN-[1] **2** IN-[2] Used before *b, m,* or *p*
im·age (im′ij) ***n.*** ⟦< L *imago*⟧ **1** a representation of a person or thing; esp., a statue **2** the visual impression of something in a mirror, through a lens, etc. **3** a copy **4** *a)* a mental picture; idea *b)* the concept of a person, product, etc. held by the general public **5** a metaphor or simile —***vt.*** **-aged, -ag·ing** **1** to make a representation of **2** to reflect **3** to imagine
im·age·ry (im′ij rē) ***n.*** **1** mental images **2** figurative language
i·mag·i·na·ble (i maj′i nə bəl) ***adj.*** that can be imagined
i·mag′i·nar′y (-ner′ē) ***adj.*** existing only in the imagination; unreal
i·mag′i·na′tion (-nā′shən) ***n.*** **1** *a)* the act or power of forming mental images of what is not present *b)* the act or power of creating new ideas by combining previous experiences **2** the ability to understand the imaginative creations of others **3** resourcefulness
i·mag′i·na·tive (-nə tiv) ***adj.*** **1** having, using, or showing imagination **2** of or resulting from imagination —**i·mag′i·na·tive·ly** ***adv.***

THESAURUS

illegal ***a.*** illicit, unlawful, contraband, unwarranted, banned, unconstitutional, outside the law, extralegal, outlawed, not legal, unauthorized, unlicensed, lawless, actionable, illegitimate, prohibited, forbidden, criminal, against the law, not approved, uncertified, smuggled, bootlegged, hot*.—*Ant.* LEGAL, lawful, authorized.

illegible ***a.*** faint, unintelligible, difficult to read; see CONFUSED 2, OBSCURE 1.

illegibly ***a.*** faintly, unintelligibly, indistinctly; see CONFUSED 2.

illegitimate ***a.*** **1** [Unlawful] contraband, wrong, illicit; see BAD 1, ILLEGAL. **2** [Born of unmarried parents] born out of wedlock, unlawfully begotten, fatherless; see BASTARD.

illicit ***a.*** unlawful, prohibited, unauthorized; see BAD 1, ILLEGAL, WRONG 1.

illiteracy ***n.*** lack of education, inability to read and write, inadequacy; see IGNORANCE.

illiterate ***a.*** uneducated, unenlightened, unlettered; see IGNORANT 2.

ill-mannered ***a.*** impolite, uncouth, rough; see RUDE 2.

illness ***n.*** **1** [Poor health] sickness, failing health, seizure, ailing, disease, ailment, infirmity, disorder, relapse, attack, fit, convalescence, complaint, delicate health, collapse, breakdown, confinement, disturbance, ill health; see also WEAKNESS 1. **2** [A particular disease] sickness, ailment, malady, ache, infection, stroke, allergy; see also COLD 2, IMPEDIMENT 2, PAIN 2.

illogical ***a.*** irrational, unreasonable, absurd, fallacious, specious, incorrect, inconsistent, false, unscientific, contradictory, untenable, unsound, preposterous, invalid, self-contradictory, unproved, groundless, implausible, hollow, irrelevant, inconclusive, prejudiced, biased, unconnected, without foundation, not following, without rhyme or reason; see also WRONG 2.—*Ant.* LOGICAL, sound, reasonable.

ill-suited ***a.*** inappropriate, not harmonious, mismatched; see UNSUITABLE.

ill-tempered ***a.*** cross, touchy, querulous; see IRRITABLE, SULLEN.

illuminate ***v.*** **1** [To make light(er)] lighten, irradiate, illume; see BRIGHTEN 1, LIGHT 1. **2** [To explain] interpret, elucidate, clarify; see EXPLAIN.

illumination ***n.*** **1** [A light] gleam, flame, brilliance, lighting; see also FLASH, LIGHT 1, 3. **2** [Instruction] teaching, education, elucidation; see KNOWLEDGE 1.

illusion ***n.*** fancy, hallucination, mirage, apparition, ghost, delusion, figment of the imagination, image, trick of vision, myth, make-believe; see also DREAM.

illustrate ***v.*** picture, represent, portray, depict, imitate; see also DRAW 2, PAINT 1.

illustrated ***a.*** pictorial, decorated, portrayed; see DESCRIPTIVE.

illustration ***n.*** engraving, tailpiece, frontispiece, cartoon, vignette, etching, inset picture, news photo; see also PICTURE 3.

illustrative ***a.*** symbolic, representative, pictorial; see DESCRIPTIVE, EXPLANATORY, GRAPHIC 1, 2.

ill will ***n.*** malevolence, dislike, hostility; see BLAME, HATRED, OBJECTION.

image ***n.*** **1** [Mental impression] concept, conception, perception; see IDEA 1, THOUGHT 2. **2** [Representation] effigy, form, drawing, model, illustration, portrait, photograph, reproduction, copy, likeness, facsimile, counterpart, replica; see also PICTURE 2.

imagery ***n.*** illustration, metaphor, representation; see COMPARISON.

imaginable ***a.*** conceivable, comprehensible, credible, thinkable, possible, plausible, believable, reasonable; see also LIKELY 1.—*Ant.* UNBELIEVABLE, unimaginable, inconceivable.

imaginary ***a.*** fancied, illusory, visionary, shadowy, dreamy, dreamlike, hypothetical, theoretical, deceptive, imagined, hallucinatory, whimsical, fabulous, nonexistent, apocryphal, fantastic, mythological, fictitious, legendary, imaginative; see also UNREAL.—*Ant.* REAL, factual, existing.

imagination ***n.*** intelligence, thoughtfulness, inventiveness, conception, mental agility, wit, sensitivity, fancy, visualization, realization, cognition, awareness, dramatization, insight; see also MIND 1.

imaginative ***a.*** creative, inventive, resourceful; see ARTISTIC, ORIGINAL 2.

i·mag·ine (i maj′in) ***vt.***, ***vi.*** **-ined, -in·ing** ⟦< L *imago*, image⟧ **1** to make a mental image (of); conceive in the mind **2** to suppose; think

im′ag·ing ***n.*** the production of images, esp. by electronic means as in a CAT scan, ultrasound, etc.

i·mam (i mäm′) ***n.*** [*often* **I-**] a Muslim leader, as of prayer, or ruler: often used as a title

im·bal·ance (im bal′əns) ***n.*** lack of balance, as in proportion or force

im·be·cile (im′bə sil) ***n.*** ⟦< L *imbecilis*, feeble⟧ a foolish or stupid person —***adj.*** foolish or stupid: also **im′be·cil′ic** (-sil′ik) —**im′be·cil′i·ty** ***n.***

im·bed (im bed′) ***vt.*** *var. of* EMBED

im·bibe (im bīb′) ***vt.*** **-bibed′, -bib′ing** ⟦< L *in-*, in + *bibere*, to drink⟧ **1** to drink (esp. alcoholic liquor) **2** to take in with the senses or mind —***vi.*** to drink, esp. alcoholic liquor

im·bro·glio (im brōl′yō) ***n.***, *pl.* **-glios** ⟦It < *imbrogliare*, embroil⟧ **1** an involved and confusing situation **2** a confused misunderstanding

im·bue (im byo͞o′) ***vt.*** **-bued′, -bu′ing** ⟦< L *imbuere*, to wet⟧ **1** to dye **2** to permeate (*with* ideas, emotions, etc.)

im·i·tate (im′i tāt′) ***vt.*** **-tat′ed, -tat′ing** ⟦< L *imitari*⟧ **1** to seek to follow the example of **2** to mimic **3** to reproduce in form, color, etc. **4** to resemble —**im′i·ta′tor** ***n.***

im′i·ta′tion (-tā′shən) ***n.*** **1** an imitating **2** the result of imitating; copy —***adj.*** not real; sham *[imitation* leather*]* —**im′i·ta′tive** ***adj.***

im·mac·u·late (i mak′yə lit) ***adj.*** ⟦< L *in-*, not + *macula*, a spot⟧ **1** perfectly clean **2** without a flaw or error **3** pure; innocent; sinless —**im·mac′u·late·ly** ***adv.*** —**im·mac′u·late·ness** ***n.***

im·ma·nent (im′ə nənt) ***adj.*** ⟦< L *in-*, in + *manere*, remain⟧ **1** operating within; inherent **2** present throughout the universe: said of God —**im′ma·nence** ***n.*** —**im′ma·nent·ly** ***adv.***

im·ma·te·ri·al (im′ə tir′ē əl) ***adj.*** **1** not consisting of matter **2** not pertinent; unimportant

im·ma·ture (im′ə to͞or′, -cho͞or′) ***adj.*** **1** not mature; not completely developed **2** not finished or perfected —**im′ma·tu′ri·ty** ***n.***

im·meas·ur·a·ble (i mezh′ər ə bəl) ***adj.*** that cannot be measured; boundless; vast —**im·meas′ur·a·bly** ***adv.***

im·me·di·a·cy (i mē′dē ə sē) ***n.*** a being immediate; esp., direct relevance to the present time, purpose, etc.

im·me·di·ate (i mē′dē it) ***adj.*** ⟦see IN-[2] & MEDIATE⟧ **1** not separated in space; closest **2** without delay; instant **3** next in order or relation **4** direct; firsthand —**im·me′di·ate·ly** ***adv.***

im·me·mo·ri·al (im′e môr′ē əl) ***adj.*** extending back beyond memory or record; ancient

im·mense (i mens′) ***adj.*** ⟦< L *in-*, not + *metiri*, to measure⟧ very large; vast; huge —**im·mense′ly** ***adv.*** —**im·men′si·ty** ***n.***

im·merse (i murs′) ***vt.*** **-mersed′, -mers′ing** ⟦< L *immergere*⟧ **1** to plunge into or as if into a liquid **2** to baptize by submerging in water **3** to absorb deeply; engross *[immersed* in study*]* —**im·mer′sion** (-mur′zhən, -shən) ***n.***

immersion heater an electric coil or rod immersed in water to heat it

im·mi·grant (im′ə grənt) ***n.*** one who immigrates —***adj.*** immigrating

im′mi·grate′ (-grāt′) ***vi.*** **-grat′ed, -grat′ing** ⟦see IN-[1] & MIGRATE⟧ to come into a new country, etc., esp. to settle there —**im′mi·gra′tion** ***n.***

im·mi·nent (im′ə nənt) ***adj.*** ⟦< L *in-*, on + *minere*, to project⟧ likely to happen without delay; impending

im·mo·bile (i mō′bəl) ***adj.*** **1** firmly placed; stable **2** motionless —**im′mo·bil′i·ty** ***n.*** —**im·mo′bi·lize′** (-bə līz′), **-lized′, -liz′ing,** ***vt.***

im·mod·er·ate (i mäd′ər it) ***adj.*** without restraint; unreasonable; excessive

im·mod·est (i mäd′ist) ***adj.*** **1** indecent **2** not shy; forward —**im·mod′est·ly** ***adv.*** —**im·mod′es·ty** ***n.***

im·mo·late (im′ə lāt′) ***vt.*** **-lat′ed, -lat′ing** ⟦< L *immolare*, sprinkle with sacrificial meal⟧ to kill as a sacrifice —**im′mo·la′tion** ***n.***

im·mor·al (i môr′əl) ***adj.*** **1** not moral **2** lewd —**im·mor′al·ly** ***adv.***

im·mo·ral·i·ty (im′ôr al′i tē) ***n.*** **1** a being immoral **2** *pl.* **-ties** an immoral act or practice; vice

im·mor·tal (i môrt′'l) ***adj.*** **1** not mortal; living forever **2** enduring **3** having lasting fame —***n.*** an immortal being —**im·mor·tal·i·ty** (im′môr tal′i tē) ***n.***

im·mor′tal·ize′ (-īz′) ***vt.*** **-ized′, -iz′ing** to make immortal, as in fame

im·mov·a·ble (i mo͞ov′ə bəl) ***adj.*** **1** firmly fixed **2** unyielding; steadfast

im·mune (i myo͞on′) ***adj.*** ⟦< L *in-*, without + *munia*, duties⟧ **1** exempt from or protected against something disagreeable or harmful **2** not susceptible to some specified disease

THESAURUS

imagine ***v.*** conceive, picture, conjure up, envisage, envision, see in one's mind, invent, fabricate, formulate, devise, think of, make up, conceptualize, dream, dream up*, perceive, dramatize, create.

imagined ***a.*** not real, insubstantial, thought-up; see FALSE 1, 2, 3, IMAGINARY.

imbalance ***n.*** lack of balance, disproportion, inequality; see IRREGULARITY.

imbibe ***v.*** ingest, sip, guzzle; see DRINK 1, SWALLOW.

imitate ***v.*** **1** [To mimic] impersonate, mirror, copy, mime, ape, simulate, duplicate, act, repeat, echo, parody, emulate, do like*, reflect, pretend, play a part, take off*. **2** [To copy] duplicate, counterfeit, falsify; see COPY, REPRODUCE 2. **3** [To resemble] be like, simulate, parallel; see RESEMBLE.

imitated ***a.*** copied, duplicated, mimicked, mocked, aped, counterfeited, caricatured, parodied.

imitation ***a.*** copied, feigned, bogus; see FALSE 3.

imitation ***n.*** **1** [The act of imitating] simulation, counterfeiting, copying, duplication, patterning after, picturing, representing, mimicry, aping, impersonation, echoing, matching, mirroring, paralleling; see also COPY. **2** [An object made by imitating] counterfeit, mime, sham, fake, picture, replica, echo, reflection, match, parallel, resemblance, transcription, image, mockery, takeoff*, caricature, parody, satire, substitution, forgery; see also COPY.—*Ant.* ORIGINAL, novelty, pattern.

imitative ***a.*** forged, sham, deceptive; see FALSE 2, 3.

imitator ***n.*** follower, copier, impersonator, mime, mimic, pretender, counterfeiter, forger, copycat.

immaculate ***a.*** unsullied, spotless, stainless; see BRIGHT 1, CLEAN 1.

immature ***a.*** youthful, sophomoric, half-grown; see NAIVE.

immaturity ***n.*** imperfection, incompleteness, childlike behavior; see INSTABILITY.

immediate ***a.*** instantaneous, instant, quick, direct, fast, on the moment, at this moment, at the present time, next, prompt; see also FOLLOWING.—*Ant.* SOMEDAY, later, any time.

immediately ***a.*** at once, without delay, instantly, directly, right away, at the first opportunity, at short notice, now, this instant, speedily, quickly, promptly, on the spot, on the dot, rapidly, instantaneously, shortly, on the double*, in a jiffy*; see also URGENTLY.—*Ant.* LATER, in the future, in a while.

immense ***a.*** gigantic, tremendous, enormous; see LARGE 1.

immensity ***n.*** infinity, vastness, greatness; see EXTENT.

immerse ***v.*** submerge, dip, douse, plunge, sink, cover with water, drown, bathe, steep, drench, dunk, souse; see also SOAK 1.

immersed ***a.*** drowned, plunged, bathed; see DIPPED, SOAKED, WET 1.

immigrant ***n.*** newcomer, naturalized citizen, adoptive citizen; see ALIEN, EMIGRANT.

immigrate ***v.*** migrate, resettle, seek political asylum; see ENTER.

immigration ***n.*** colonization, settlement, migration; see ENTRANCE 1.

imminent ***a.*** approaching, in store, about to happen; see COMING 1, DESTINED.

immodest ***a.*** brazen, shameless, bold; see EGOTISTIC, RUDE 2.

immoral ***a.*** sinful, corrupt, shameless; see BAD 1.

immorality ***n.*** vice, depravity, dissoluteness; see EVIL 1.

immorally ***a.*** sinfully, wickedly, unrighteously; see WRONGLY.

immortal ***a.*** **1** [Deathless] undying, permanent, imperishable, endless, timeless, everlasting, death-defying, unfading, never-ending, perennial, constant, ceaseless, indestructible, enduring; see also ETERNAL.—*Ant.* MORTAL, perishable, corrupt. **2** [Illustrious] celebrated, eminent, glorious; see FAMOUS.

immortality ***n.*** deathlessness, everlasting life, permanence, endlessness, timelessness, divinity, indestructibility, continuity, perpetuation, endless life, unlimited existence, perpetuity; see also ETERNITY.—*Ant.* DEATH, mortality, decease.

immovable ***a.*** solid, stable, fixed; see FIRM 1.

immune ***a.*** free, unaffected by, hardened to, unsusceptible, privileged, not liable, excused; see also SAFE 1.

im·mu·ni·ty (i myōōn′ə tē) ***n.***, *pl.* **-ties 1** exemption from something burdensome, as a legal obligation **2** resistance to infection or a specified disease

im·mu·nize (im′yōō nīz′) ***vt.*** **-nized′**, **-niz′ing** to make immune, as by inoculation —**im′mu·ni·za′tion** ***n.***

im·mu·nol·o·gy (im′yōō näl′ə jē) ***n.*** the branch of science dealing with immunity, as to infection or a disease, and with the body mechanisms producing it —**im′mu·nol′o·gist** ***n.***

im·mure (i myoor′) ***vt.*** **-mured′**, **-mur′ing** ⟦< L *in-*, in + *murus*, wall⟧ to shut up within walls; confine

im·mu·ta·ble (i myōōt′ə bəl) ***adj.*** unchangeable —**im·mu′ta·bly** ***adv.***

imp (imp) ***n.*** ⟦< Gr *em-*, in + *phyton*, growth⟧ **1** a young demon **2** a mischievous child —**imp′ish** ***adj.***

im·pact (im pakt′; *for n.* im′pakt′) ***vt.*** ⟦< L *impingere*, press firmly together⟧ **1** to force tightly together **2** to affect — ***vi.*** **1** to hit with force **2** to have an effect (*on*) — ***n.*** **1** a violent contact **2** the power to move feelings, influence thinking, etc.

im·pact′ed ***adj.*** lodged in the jaw: said of a tooth

im·pair (im per′) ***vt.*** ⟦< L *in-*, intens. + *pejor*, worse⟧ to make worse, less, etc. —**im·pair′ment** ***n.***

im·pa·la (im pä′lə) ***n.***, *pl.* **-la** or **-las** a reddish antelope of central and S Africa

im·pale (im pāl′) ***vt.*** **-paled′**, **-pal′ing** ⟦< L *in-*, on + *palus*, a pole⟧ to pierce through with, or fix on, something pointed —**im·pale′ment** ***n.***

im·pal·pa·ble (im pal′pə bəl) ***adj.*** **1** not perceptible to the touch **2** too subtle to be easily understood

im·pan·el (im pan′əl) ***vt.*** **-eled** or **-elled**, **-el·ing** or **-el·ling** to choose (a jury) in a law case —**im·pan′el·ment** ***n.***

im·part (im pärt′) ***vt.*** ⟦see IN-[1] & PART⟧ **1** to give a part of **2** to make known; reveal

im·par·tial (im pär′shəl) ***adj.*** without bias; fair —**im·par′ti·al′i·ty** (-shē al′i tē) ***n.*** —**im·par′tial·ly** ***adv.***

im·pass·a·ble (im pas′ə bəl) ***adj.*** that cannot be passed or traveled over

im·passe (im′pas′, im pas′) ***n.*** ⟦Fr⟧ a situation offering no escape or resolution, as a deadlocked argument

im·pas·sioned (im pash′ənd) ***adj.*** passionate; fiery; ardent

im·pas·sive (im pas′iv) ***adj.*** not feeling or showing emotion; calm —**im·pas·siv·i·ty** (im′pa siv′i tē) ***n.***

im·pas·to (im päs′tō) ***n.*** ⟦It⟧ painting in which the paint is laid thickly on the canvas

im·pa·tient (im pā′shənt) ***adj.*** lacking patience; specif., *a*) annoyed because of delay, opposition, etc. *b*) restlessly eager to do something, etc. —**im·pa′tience** ***n.***

im·peach (im pēch′) ***vt.*** ⟦< L *in-*, in + *pedica*, a fetter⟧ **1** to discredit (a person's honor, etc.) **2** to charge (a public official) with wrongdoing —**im·peach′a·ble** ***adj.*** —**im·peach′ment** ***n.***

im·pec·ca·ble (im pek′ə bəl) ***adj.*** ⟦< L *in-*, not + *peccare*, to sin⟧ without defect or error; flawless —**im·pec′ca·bil′i·ty** ***n.*** —**im·pec′ca·bly** ***adv.***

im·pe·cu·ni·ous (im′pi kyōō′nē əs) ***adj.*** ⟦< L *in-*, not + *pecunia*, money⟧ having no money; poor

im·ped·ance (im pēd′′ns) ***n.*** ⟦< fol. + -ANCE⟧ the resistance in an electric circuit to a flow of alternating current

im·pede (im pēd′) ***vt.*** **-ped′ed**, **-ped′ing** ⟦< L *in-*, in + *pes*, foot⟧ to hinder the progress of; obstruct

im·ped·i·ment (im ped′ə mənt) ***n.*** anything that impedes; specif., a speech defect

im·ped′i·men′ta (-men′tə) ***pl.n.*** encumbrances, as baggage or supplies

im·pel (im pel′) ***vt.*** **-pelled′**, **-pel′ling** ⟦< L *in-*, in + *pellere*, to drive⟧ **1** to drive or move forward **2** to force, compel, or urge —**im·pel′ler** ***n.***

im·pend (im pend′) ***vi.*** ⟦< L *in-*, in + *pendere*, hang⟧ to be about to happen; be imminent *[impending* disaster*]* —**im·pend′ing** ***adj.***

im·pen·e·tra·ble (im pen′i trə bəl) ***adj.*** **1** that cannot be penetrated **2** that cannot be solved or understood

im·pen·i·tent (im pen′ə tənt) ***adj.*** without regret, shame, or remorse

im·per·a·tive (im per′ə tiv) ***adj.*** ⟦< L *imperare*, to command⟧ **1** indicating authority or command **2** necessary; urgent **3** designating or of the mood of a verb that expresses a command, etc. —***n.*** a command

im·per·cep·ti·ble (im′pər sep′tə bəl) ***adj.*** not easily perceived by the senses or the mind; very slight, subtle, etc. —**im′per·cep′ti·bly** ***adv.***

im′per·cep′tive (-tiv) ***adj.*** not perceiving —**im′per·cep′tive·ness** ***n.***

im·per·fect (im pur′fikt) ***adj.*** **1** not complete **2** not perfect **3** designating a verb tense that indicates a past action or state as uncompleted or continuous —**im·per′fect·ly** ***adv.***

im·per·fec·tion (im′pər fek′shən) ***n.*** **1** a being imperfect **2** a defect; fault

im·pe·ri·al (im pir′ē əl) ***adj.*** ⟦< L *imperium*, empire⟧ **1** of an empire, emperor, or empress **2** having supreme authority **3** majestic; august **4** of great size or superior quality —***n.*** a small, pointed chin beard

imperial gallon the standard British gallon, equal to 4.546 liters (about 1⅕ U.S. gallons)

im·pe′ri·al·ism′ ***n.*** **1** imperial state or authority **2** the policy of forming and maintaining an empire, as by establishing colonies **3** the policy of seeking to dominate the affairs of weaker countries —**im·pe′ri·al·ist** ***n.***, ***adj.*** —**im·pe′ri·al·is′tic** ***adj.***

im·per·il (im per′əl) ***vt.*** **-iled** or **-illed**, **-il·ing** or **-il·ling** to put in peril; endanger

im·pe·ri·ous (im pir′ē əs) ***adj.*** ⟦< L *imperium*, empire⟧ **1** overbearing, arrogant, etc. **2** urgent; imperative —**im·pe′ri·ous·ly** ***adv.***

im·per·ish·a·ble (im per′ish ə bəl) ***adj.*** not perishable; indestructible

im·per·ma·nent (im pur′mə nənt) ***adj.*** not permanent; temporary —**im·per′ma·nent·ly** ***adv.***

im·per·son·al (im pur′sə nəl) ***adj.*** **1** without reference to any particular person **2** not existing as a person *[*an *impersonal* force*]* **3** designating or of a verb occurring only in the third person singular, usually with *it* as subject —**im·per′son·al·ly** ***adv.***

im·per·son·ate (im pur′sə nāt′) ***vt.*** **-at′ed**, **-at′ing** to assume the role of or pretend to be, for purposes of entertainment or fraud —**im·per′son·a′tion** ***n.*** —**im·per′son·a′tor** ***n.***

im·per·ti·nent (im purt′′n ənt) ***adj.*** **1** not pertinent **2** insolent; impudent —**im·per′ti·nence** ***n.***

THESAURUS

immunity ***n.*** **1** [Exemption] favor, privilege, license; see FREEDOM 2. **2** [Freedom from disease] resistance, immunization, protection, active immunity, passive immunity; see also SAFETY 1.

impact ***n.*** shock, impression, contact; see COLLISION.

impair ***v.*** spoil, injure, hurt; see BREAK 2, DAMAGE, DESTROY.

impart ***v.*** **1** [To give] bestow, grant, present; see ALLOW, GIVE 1. **2** [To make known] tell, announce, divulge; see ADMIT 2, REVEAL.

impartial ***a.*** unbiased, unprejudiced, disinterested; see EQUAL, FAIR 1.

impartiality ***n.*** objectivity, candor, justice; see EQUALITY, FAIRNESS.

impasse ***n.*** deadlock, standstill, cessation; see PAUSE.

impatience ***n.*** agitation, restlessness, anxiety; see EXCITEMENT, NERVOUSNESS.

impatient ***a.*** anxious, eager, feverish; see RESTLESS.

impeach ***v.*** criticize, charge, arraign, denounce, indict, discredit, reprimand, accuse, incriminate, try, bring charges against, question; see also BLAME.—*Ant.* FREE, acquit, absolve.

impediment ***n.*** **1** [An obstruction] hindrance, obstacle, difficulty; see BARRIER. **2** [An obstruction in speech] speech impediment, speech difficulty, stutter, stammer, lisp, halting, cleft palate.

impending ***a.*** in the offing, threatening, menacing; see OMINOUS.

impenetrable ***a.*** **1** [Dense] impervious, hard, compact; see FIRM 2, THICK 3. **2** [Incomprehensible] unintelligible, inscrutable, unfathomable; see OBSCURE 1.

imperative ***a.*** **1** [Necessary] inescapable, compelling, crucial; see IMPORTANT 1, NECESSARY, URGENT 1. **2** [Authoritative] masterful, commanding, dominant; see AGGRESSIVE, POWERFUL 1.

imperfect ***a.*** flawed, incomplete, deficient; see FAULTY.

imperfection ***n.*** fault, flaw, stain; see BLEMISH.

imperialism ***n.*** empire, international domination, power politics; see POWER 2.

impersonal ***a.*** detached, disinterested, cold; see INDIFFERENT.

impersonate ***v.*** mimic, portray, act out, pose as, pass for, double for, put on an act, pretend to be, act the part of, take the part of, act a part, dress as, represent; see also IMITATE 1.

impersonation ***n.*** imitation, role, enactment; see PERFORMANCE.

impertinence ***n.*** impudence, insolence, disrespect; see RUDENESS.

impertinent ***a.*** saucy, insolent, impudent; see RUDE 2.

im·per·turb·a·ble (im′pər tur′bə bəl) ***adj.*** that cannot be disconcerted, disturbed, or excited

im·per·vi·ous (im pur′vē əs) ***adj.*** **1** incapable of being penetrated, as by moisture **2** not affected by: with *to*

im·pe·ti·go (im′pə tī′gō) ***n.*** ⟦see IMPETUS⟧ a contagious skin disease characterized by pustules

im·pet·u·ous (im pech′o͞o əs) ***adj.*** ⟦see fol.⟧ acting or done suddenly with little thought; rash **—im·pet′u·os′i·ty** (-äs′ i tē) ***n.*** **—im·pet′u·ous·ly** ***adv.***

im·pe·tus (im′pə təs) ***n.***, *pl.* **-tus·es** ⟦< L *in-*, in + *petere*, rush at⟧ **1** the force with which a body moves against resistance **2** driving force or motive; incentive

im·pi·e·ty (im pī′ə tē) ***n.*** **1** lack of reverence for God **2** *pl.* **-ties** an impious act or remark

im·pinge (im pinj′) ***vi.*** **-pinged′**, **-ping′ing** ⟦< L *in-*, in + *pangere*, to strike⟧ **1** to strike, hit, etc. (*on* or *upon*) **2** to encroach (*on* or *upon*) **—im·pinge′ment** ***n.***

im·pi·ous (im′pē əs) ***adj.*** not pious; specif., lacking reverence for God

im·plac·a·ble (im plak′ə bəl, -plā′kə-) ***adj.*** not to be placated or appeased; relentless **—im·plac′a·bly** ***adv.***

im·plant (im plant′; *for n.* im′plant′) ***vt.*** **1** to plant firmly **2** to fix firmly in the mind **3** to insert surgically **—*n.*** an implanted organ, etc.

im·plau·si·ble (im plô′zə bəl) ***adj.*** not plausible **—im·plau′si·bly** ***adv.***

im·ple·ment (im′plə mənt; *for v.*, -ment′) ***n.*** ⟦< L *in-*, in + *plere*, to fill⟧ something used in a given activity; tool, instrument, etc. **—*vt.*** to carry into effect; accomplish **—im′ple·men·ta′tion** (-mən tā′shən) ***n.***

im·pli·cate (im′pli kāt′) ***vt.*** **-cat′ed**, **-cat′ing** ⟦see IMPLY⟧ to show to be party to a crime, etc. **—im′pli·ca′tive** ***adj.***

im′pli·ca′tion (-kā′shən) ***n.*** **1** an implicating or being implicated **2** an implying or being implied **3** something implied

im·plic·it (im plis′it) ***adj.*** ⟦see IMPLY⟧ **1** suggested though not plainly expressed; implied **2** necessarily involved though not apparent; inherent **3** without reservation or doubt **—im·plic′it·ly** ***adv.***

im·plode (im plōd′) ***vt.***, ***vi.*** **-plod′ed**, **-plod′ing** ⟦< IN-[1] + (EX)PLODE⟧ to burst or cause to burst inward **—im·plo′sion** (-plō′zhən) ***n.*** **—im·plo′sive** (-plō′siv) ***adj.***

im·plore (im plôr′) ***vt.*** **-plored′**, **-plor′ing** ⟦< L *in-*, intens. + *plorare*, cry out⟧ **1** to ask earnestly for **2** to beg (a person) to do something **—im·plor′ing·ly** ***adv.***

im·ply (im plī′) ***vt.*** **-plied′**, **-ply′ing** ⟦< L *in-*, in + *plicare*, to fold⟧ **1** to have as a necessary part, condition, etc. **2** to indicate indirectly; hint; suggest

im·po·lite (im′pə līt′) ***adj.*** not polite; discourteous **—im′po·lite′ly** ***adv.***

im·pol·i·tic (im päl′ə tik′) ***adj.*** not politic; unwise

im·pon·der·a·ble (im pän′dər ə bəl) ***adj.*** that cannot be weighed, measured, explained, etc. **—*n.*** anything imponderable

im·port (im pôrt′, *also, and for n. always* im′pôrt′) ***vt.*** ⟦< L *in-*, in + *portare*, carry⟧ **1** to bring in (goods) from another country, especially for sale **2** to mean; signify **—*n.*** **1** something imported **2** meaning; signification **3** importance **—im′por·ta′tion** ***n.*** **—im·port′er** ***n.***

im·por·tant (im pôrt′′nt) ***adj.*** ⟦see IMPORT⟧ **1** meaning a great deal; having much significance or value **2** having, or acting as if having, power, authority, etc. **—im·por′tance** ***n.*** **—im·por′tant·ly** ***adv.***

im·por·tu·nate (im pôr′chə nət) ***adj.*** persistent in asking or demanding

im·por·tune (im′pôr to͞on′) ***vt.***, ***vi.*** **-tuned′**, **-tun′ing** ⟦< L *importunus*, troublesome⟧ to urge or entreat persistently or repeatedly **—im′por·tu′ni·ty**, *pl.* **-ties**, ***n.***

im·pose (im pōz′) ***vt.*** **-posed′**, **-pos′ing** ⟦< L *in-*, on + *ponere*, to place⟧ **1** to place (a burden, tax, etc. *on* or *upon*) **2** to force (oneself) on others **—impose on** (or **upon**) **1** to take advantage of **2** to cheat or defraud **—im′po·si′tion** (-pə zish′ən) ***n.***

im·pos′ing ***adj.*** impressive because of great size, strength, dignity, etc. **—im·pos′ing·ly** ***adv.***

im·pos·si·ble (im päs′ə bəl) ***adj.*** **1** not capable of being, being done, or happening **2** not capable of being endured, used, etc. because disagreeable or unsuitable **—im·pos′si·bil′i·ty**, *pl.* **-ties**, ***n.*** **—im·pos′si·bly** ***adv.***

im·post (im′pōst′) ***n.*** ⟦see IMPOSE⟧ a tax; esp., a duty on imported goods

im·pos·tor or **im·post′er** (im päs′tər) ***n.*** ⟦see IMPOSE⟧ one who deceives or cheats others by pretending to be what he or she is not

im·pos′ture (-chər) ***n.*** the act or practice of an impostor; fraud

im·po·tent (im′pə tənt) ***adj.*** **1** lacking physical strength **2** ineffective; powerless **3** unable to engage in sexual intercourse: said of males **—im′po·tence** or **im′po·ten·cy** ***n.*** **—im′po·tent·ly** ***adv.***

im·pound (im pound′) ***vt.*** **1** to shut up (an animal) in a pound **2** to take and hold in legal custody **3** to gather and enclose (water), as for irrigation

THESAURUS

impervious ***a.*** impenetrable, watertight, sealed; see TIGHT 2.

impetus ***n.*** force, cause, stimulus; see INCENTIVE, PURPOSE 1, REASON 3.

impious ***a.*** sinful, profane, blasphemous; see BAD 1.

implant ***v.*** stick in, insert, root; see PLANT.

implement ***n.*** utensil, instrument, device; see EQUIPMENT, MACHINE, TOOL 1.

implicate ***v.*** connect, cite, associate, tie up with, charge, link, catch up in, relate, compromise; see also BLAME.

implicated ***a.*** under suspicion, suspected, known to have been involved; see GUILTY, INVOLVED, SUSPICIOUS 1, 2.

implication ***n.*** **1** [Assumption] hint, indication, suggestion; see ASSUMPTION 1, GUESS. **2** [A link] connection, involvement, entanglement; see JOINT 1, LINK, UNION 1.

implicit ***a.*** unquestionable, certain, absolute; see DEFINITE 1, INEVITABLE.

implied ***a.*** implicit, indicated, foreshadowed, involved, tacit, signified, figured, intended, meant, alluded to, latent, hidden, insinuated, hinted at, understood, symbolized, potential, indirectly meant, undeclared; see also SUGGESTED.

imply ***v.*** **1** [To indicate] intimate, hint at, suggest; see HINT, MENTION, REFER 2. **2** [To mean] import, indicate, signify; see INTEND 2, MEAN 1.

impolite ***a.*** discourteous, moody, churlish; see IRRITABLE, RUDE 2, SULLEN.

import ***v.*** introduce, bring in, buy abroad; see CARRY 1, SEND 1.

importance ***n.*** import, force, consequence, bearing, denotation, gist, effect, distinction, influence, usefulness, moment, weightiness, momentousness, emphasis, standing, stress, accent, weight, concern, attention, interest, seriousness, point, substance, relevance, sum and substance; see also MEANING.—*Ant.* INSIGNIFICANCE, triviality, emptiness.

important ***a.*** **1** [Weighty; *said usually of things*] significant, considerable, momentous, essential, great, decisive, critical, major, chief, paramount, primary, foremost, principal, influential, marked, of great consequence, ponderous, of importance, never to be overlooked, of note, valuable, crucial, substantial, vital, serious, grave, relevant, pressing, far-reaching, extensive, conspicuous, heavy, big-league*, big; see also NECESSARY.—*Ant.* TRIVIAL, inconsequential, unimportant. **2** [Eminent; *said usually of persons*] illustrious, well-known, influential; see FAMOUS. **3** [Relevant] material, influential, significant; see FIT 1, RELATED 2, RELEVANT.

imported ***a.*** shipped in, produced abroad, exotic, alien; see also FOREIGN.—*Ant.* NATIVE, domestic, made in America.

impose ***v.*** force upon, inflict, foist; see FORCE. **—impose on** (or **upon**) intrude, interrupt, presume; see BOTHER 2, DISTURB.

imposing ***a.*** stirring, exciting, overwhelming; see IMPRESSIVE.

imposition ***n.*** demand, restraint, encumbrance; see COMMAND, PRESSURE 2.

impossibility ***n.*** hopelessness, impracticality, impracticability, difficulty, unworkability, unlikelihood, failure; see also FUTILITY.

impossible ***a.*** inconceivable, vain, unachievable, unattainable, out of the question, too much, insurmountable, useless, inaccessible, unworkable, preposterous, unimaginable, unobtainable, not to be thought of, hardly possible, like finding a needle in a haystack*, a hundred to one*; see also FUTILE, HOPELESS.—*Ant.* REASONABLE, possible, likely.

impostor ***n.*** pretender, charlatan, quack; see CHEAT.

impotence ***n.*** **1** [Sterility] unproductiveness, frigidity, infecundity; see EMPTINESS. **2** [Weakness] inability, feebleness, infirmity; see WEAKNESS 1.

impotent ***a.*** **1** [Weak] powerless, inept, infirm; see UNABLE, WEAK 1. **2** [Sterile] barren, frigid, unproductive; see STERILE 1.

impound ***v.*** appropriate, take, usurp; see SEIZE 2.

impounded ***a.*** kept, seized, confiscated; see HELD, RETAINED 1.

im·pov·er·ish (im päv′ər ish) ***vt.*** ⟦< L *in-*, in + *pauper*, poor⟧ **1** to make poor **2** to deprive of strength, resources, etc. —**im·pov′er·ish·ment *n.***

im·prac·ti·ca·ble (im prak′ti kə bəl) ***adj.*** not capable of being carried out in practice

im·prac·ti·cal (im prak′ti kəl) ***adj.*** not practical

im·pre·ca·tion (im′pri kā′shən) ***n.*** ⟦< L *in-*, on + *precari*, pray⟧ a curse

im·pre·cise (im′pri sīs′) ***adj.*** not precise; vague —**im′pre·cise′ly *adv.*** —**im′pre·ci′sion** (-sizh′ən) ***n.***

im·preg·na·ble (im preg′nə bəl) ***adj.*** **1** that cannot be captured or entered by force **2** unyielding —**im·preg′na·bil′i·ty *n.*** —**im·preg′na·bly *adv.***

im·preg·nate (im preg′nāt′) ***vt.*** **-nat′ed, -nat′ing** **1** to make pregnant; fertilize **2** to saturate **3** to imbue (*with* ideas, etc.) —**im′preg·na′tion *n.***

im·pre·sa·ri·o (im′prə sä′rē ō′) ***n.***, *pl.* **-os** ⟦It⟧ one who manages an opera, organizes concert series, etc.

im·press[1] (im pres′) ***vt.*** ⟦< IN-[1] + PRESS[2]⟧ **1** to force (a person) into military service **2** to seize for public use

im·press[2] (im pres′; *for n.* im′pres′) ***vt.*** ⟦see IMPRINT⟧ **1** to stamp; imprint **2** to affect strongly the mind or emotions of **3** to fix in the memory: with *on* or *upon* —***n.*** **1** an impressing **2** an imprint

im·press′i·ble (-ə bəl) ***adj.*** that can be impressed —**im·press′i·bil′i·ty *n.***

im·pres·sion (im presh′ən) ***n.*** **1** an impressing **2** *a)* a mark, imprint, etc. *b)* an effect produced on the mind **3** a vague notion **4** an amusing impersonation; mimicking

im·pres′sion·a·ble ***adj.*** easily impressed or influenced; sensitive

im·pres′sion·ism′ ***n.*** a theory of art, music, etc. whose aim is to capture a brief, immediate impression —**im·pres′sion·ist *n.*** —**im·pres′sion·is′tic *adj.***

im·pres·sive (im pres′iv) ***adj.*** tending to impress the mind or emotions; eliciting wonder or admiration —**im·pres′sive·ly *adv.***

im·pri·ma·tur (im′pri mät′ər) ***n.*** ⟦ModL, lit., let it be printed⟧ **1** permission to publish a book, etc., as granted by a Catholic bishop **2** any sanction or approval

im·print (im print′; *for n.* im′print′) ***vt.*** ⟦< L *in-*, on + *premere*, to press⟧ to mark or fix as by pressing or stamping —***n.*** **1** a mark made by imprinting **2** a lasting effect **3** a note in a book giving facts of its publication

im·pris·on (im priz′ən) ***vt.*** to put in or as in prison —**im·pris′on·ment *n.***

im·prob·a·ble (im präb′ə bəl) ***adj.*** not probable; unlikely —**im′prob·a·bil′i·ty**, *pl.* **-ties**, ***n.*** —**im·prob′a·bly *adv.***

im·promp·tu (im prämp′to͞o′) ***adj.***, ***adv.*** ⟦< L *in promptu*, in readiness⟧ without preparation; offhand

im·prop·er (im präp′ər) ***adj.*** **1** not suitable; unfit **2** incorrect **3** not in good taste —**im·prop′er·ly *adv.***

im·pro·pri·e·ty (im′prō prī′ə tē) ***n.***, *pl.* **-ties** **1** a being improper **2** an improper act, word usage, etc.

im·prove (im pro͞ov′) ***vt.*** **-proved′, -prov′ing** ⟦< Anglo-Fr *en-*, in + *prou*, gain⟧ **1** to make better **2** to make (real estate) more valuable by cultivation, construction, etc. —***vi.*** to become better —**improve on** (or **upon**) to do or make better than —**im·prov′a·ble *adj.***

im·prove′ment ***n.*** **1** an improving or being improved **2** an addition or change that improves something

im·prov·i·dent (im präv′ə dənt) ***adj.*** lacking foresight or thrift —**im·prov′i·dence *n.*** —**im·prov′i·dent·ly *adv.***

im·pro·vise (im′prə vīz′) ***vt.***, ***vi.*** **-vised′, -vis′ing** ⟦< L *in-*, not + *providere*, foresee⟧ **1** to compose and perform without preparation **2** to make or do with whatever is at hand —**im·prov′i·sa′tion** (-präv′i zā′shən) ***n.*** —**im·prov′i·sa′tion·al *adj.***

im·pru·dent (im pro͞od′′nt) ***adj.*** not prudent; rash —**im·pru′dence *n.***

im·pu·dent (im′pyo͞o dənt) ***adj.*** ⟦< L *in-*, not + *pudere*, feel shame⟧ shamelessly bold; insolent —**im′pu·dence *n.*** —**im′pu·dent·ly *adv.***

im·pugn (im pyo͞on′) ***vt.*** ⟦< L *in-*, against + *pugnare*, to fight⟧ to challenge as false or questionable

im·pulse (im′puls′) ***n.*** ⟦see IMPEL⟧ **1** *a)* an impelling force; impetus *b)* the motion or effect caused by such a force **2** *a)* incitement to action by a stimulus *b)* a sud-

THESAURUS

impoverish ***v.*** make poor, bankrupt, exhaust; see DESTROY.

impoverished ***a.*** poverty-stricken, bankrupt, broke*; see POOR 1, RUINED 3.

impractical ***a.*** unreal, unrealistic, unworkable, improbable, illogical, unreasonable, absurd, wild, abstract, impossible, idealistic, unfeasible, out of the question.—*Ant.* PRACTICAL, logical, reasonable.

impregnate ***v.*** **1** [To permeate] fill up, pervade, overflow; see FILL 2, SOAK 1. **2** [To beget] procreate, inseminate, reproduce; see FERTILIZE 2.

impregnated ***a.*** **1** [Full] saturated, shot through, full of; see FULL 1. **2** [Pregnant] expecting*, in a family way*, with child; see PREGNANT.

impress[2] ***v.*** **1** [To make an impression] indent, emboss, imprint; see DENT, MARK 1, PRINT 2. **2** [To attract attention] stand out, be conspicuous, cause a stir, create an impression, make an impression on, direct attention to, make an impact upon, engage the thoughts of, engage the attention of, be listened to, find favor with, make a hit*, make a dent in; see also FASCINATE.

impressed ***a.*** aroused, awakened, awed; see AFFECTED 1, EXCITED.

impression ***n.*** **1** [An imprint] print, footprint, fingerprint, dent, mold, indentation, depression, cast, form, track, pattern; see also MARK 1. **2** [An effect] response, consequence, reaction; see RESULT. **3** [A notion based on scanty evidence] theory, conjecture, supposition; see GUESS, OPINION 1.

impressionable ***a.*** susceptible, suggestible, receptive; see AFFECTED 1.

impressive ***a.*** stirring, moving, inspiring, effective, affecting, eloquent, impassioned, thrilling, exciting, intense, well-done, dramatic, absorbing, deep, profound, penetrating, remarkable, extraordinary, notable, important, momentous, vital; see also PROFOUND.—*Ant.* DULL, uninteresting, common.

imprint ***n.*** **1** [A printed identification] firm name, banner, trademark, heading; see also EMBLEM, SIGNATURE. **2** [An impression] dent, indentation, print; see MARK 1.

imprint ***v.*** print, stamp, designate; see MARK 1, 2.

imprison ***v.*** jail, lock up, confine, incarcerate, immure, impound, detain, keep in, hold, intern, shut in, lock in, box in, fence in, cage, send to prison, keep as captive, hold captive, hold hostage, enclose, keep in custody, put behind bars, put away*, send up*.—*Ant.* FREE, liberate, release.

imprisoned ***a.*** arrested, jailed, incarcerated; see CONFINED 3.

imprisonment ***n.*** captivity, isolation, incarceration, duress, bondage; see also CONFINEMENT.—*Ant.* FREEDOM, liberty, emancipation.

improbable ***a.*** not likely, doubtful, not to be expected; see UNLIKELY.

improper ***a.*** ill-advised, unsuited, incongruous, out of place, ludicrous, incorrect, preposterous, unwarranted, undue, imprudent, abnormal, irregular, inexpedient, unseasonable, inadvisable, untimely, inopportune, unfit, malapropos, unfitting, inappropriate, unbefitting, ill-timed, awkward, inharmonious, inapplicable, odd; see also UNSUITABLE.

improperly ***a.*** poorly, inappropriately, clumsily; see AWKWARDLY, BADLY 1, INADEQUATELY.

improve ***v.*** **1** [To make better] mend, update, refine; see CHANGE 1, REPAIR. **2** [To become better] regenerate, advance, progress, renew, augment, gain strength, develop, get better, grow better, grow, make progress, widen, increase, mellow, mature, come along, get on, look up, shape up*, pick up, perk up, come around, make headway, snap out of*; see also CHANGE 2, RECOVER 3.—*Ant.* WEAKEN, worsen, grow worse. —**improve on** (or **upon**) make better, develop, refine; see CORRECT, REPAIR.

improved ***a.*** corrected, bettered, amended, mended, reformed, elaborated, refined, modernized, brought up-to-date, enhanced, repaired, bolstered, rectified, remodeled, reorganized, made over, better for, doctored up*, polished up*; see also CHANGED 2.

improvement ***n.*** **1** [The process of becoming better] amelioration, betterment, rectification, change, alteration, reformation, progression, advance, advancement, development, growth, rise, civilization, gain, cultivation, increase, enrichment, promotion, elevation, regeneration, recovery, renovation, reorganization, amendment, reform, revision, elaboration, refinement, modernization, enhancement, remodeling.—*Ant.* DECAY, deterioration, retrogression. **2** [That which has been improved] addition, supplement, repair, extra, attachment, correction, reform, remodeling, refinement, luxury, advance, latest thing, last word*; see also CHANGE 1.

improving ***a.*** reconstructing, repairing, elaborating, bettering, correcting, developing, remodeling, fixing, on the mend.

impudence ***n.*** insolence, impertinence, effrontery; see RUDENESS.

impudent ***a.*** forward, insolent, shameless; see RUDE 2.

impugn ***v.*** question, attack, challenge, call into question, contradict, assail, knock*; see also DOUBT.

impulse ***n.*** **1** [A throb] surge, pulse, pulsation; see BEAT 1. **2** [A sudden urge] fancy, whim, caprice, motive, motivation, spontaneity, drive, appeal, notion, inclination, dis-

den inclination to act **3** a brief surge in an electric current

im·pul·sion (im pul′shən) ***n.*** **1** an impelling or being impelled **2** IMPULSE (sense 1*a*) **3** IMPULSE (sense 2)

im·pul·sive (im pul′siv) ***adj.*** **1** driving forward **2** likely to act on impulse —**im·pul′sive·ly** ***adv.***

im·pu·ni·ty (im pyo͞o′ni tē) ***n.*** ⟦< L *in-*, without + *poena*, punishment⟧ exemption from punishment, harm, etc.

im·pure (im pyo͝or′) ***adj.*** **1** unclean; dirty **2** immoral; obscene; **3** mixed with foreign matter; adulterated —**im·pure′ly** ***adv.*** —**im·pure′ness** ***n.***

im·pu′ri·ty (-pyo͝or′ə tē) ***n.*** **1** a being impure **2** *pl.* **-ties** an impure thing or part

im·pute (im pyo͞ot′) ***vt.*** **-put′ed, -put′ing** ⟦< L *in-*, in, to + *putare*, to think⟧ to attribute (esp. a fault or misconduct) to another —**im′pu·ta′tion** (-pyo͞o tā′shən) ***n.***

in[1] (in) ***prep.*** ⟦OE⟧ **1** contained by *[in* the room*]* **2** wearing *[*dressed *in* furs*]* **3** during *[*done *in* a day*]* **4** at the end of *[*due *in* an hour*]* **5** not beyond *[in* sight*]* **6** employed, enrolled, etc. at *[in* college*]* **7** out of a group of *[*one *in* ten*]* **8** amidst *[in* a storm*]* **9** affected by *[in* trouble*]* **10** with regard to *[*to vary *in* size*]* **11** using *[*speak *in* English*]* **12** because of; for *[*to cry *in* pain*]* **13** into *[*come *in* the house*]* **14** living or located at (*in* Rome) —***adv.*** **1** to the inside *[*he went *in]* **2** to or at a certain place **3** so as to be contained by a certain space, condition, etc. **4** inside one's home, etc. (to stay *in*) —***adj.*** **1** that is in power *[*the *in* group*]* **2** inner; inside **3** gathered, counted, etc. **4** [Inf.] currently smart, popular, etc. —***n.*** **1** one that is in power: *usually used in pl.* **2** [Inf.] special influence; pull —**have it in for** [Inf.] to hold a grudge against —**ins and outs** all the details and intricacies —**in that** because; since —**in with** associated with

in[2] *abbrev.* inch(es)

IN Indiana

in-[1] ⟦< the prep. IN[1] or L *in*, in⟧ *prefix* in, into, within, on, toward *[inbreed]*

in-[2] ⟦L⟧ *prefix* no, not, without, NON- The following list includes some common compounds formed with *in-*, with no special meanings; they will be understood if "not" or "lack of" is used with the meaning of the base word:

inability
inaccessible
inaccuracy
inaccurate
inaction
inactive
inadequacy
inadequate
inadmissible
inadvisable
inanimate
inapplicable
inappropriate
inapt
inaudible
inauspicious
incapable
incautious
incivility
incombustible
incommensurate
incommunicable
incomprehensible
inconceivable
inconclusive
inconsistency
inconsistent
incorrect
incurable
indecorous
indefinable
indiscernible
indisputable
indistinct
indistinguishable
indivisible
inedible
ineffective
ineffectual
inefficacious
inelastic
ineligible
inequality
inequitable
inequity
inexact
inexcusable
inexpensive
infertile
inharmonious
inhospitable
inhumane
injudicious
inopportune
inseparable
insignificance
insignificant
insolvable
insufficient
insurmountable
insusceptible
invariable

-in (in) *combining form* a mass action or gathering of a (specified) type *[*pray-*in*, be-*in]*

in ab·sen·ti·a (in ab sen′shə, -shē ə) ⟦L⟧ although not present *[*to receive an award *in absentia]*

in·ac·ti·vate (in ak′tə vāt′) ***vt.*** **-vat′ed, -vat′ing** to make inactive —**in·ac′ti·va′tion** ***n.***

in·ad·vert·ent (in′ad vurt′′nt, -əd-) ***adj.*** not on purpose; accidental —**in′ad·vert′ence** ***n.*** —**in′ad·vert′ent·ly** ***adv.***

in·al·ien·a·ble (in āl′yən ə bəl) ***adj.*** ⟦see ALIEN⟧ that may not be taken away or transferred —**in·al′ien·a·bly** ***adv.***

in·am·o·ra·ta (in am′ə rät′ə) ***n.*** ⟦It⟧ a sweetheart or lover: said of a woman

in·ane (in ān′) ***adj.*** ⟦L *inanis*, empty⟧ lacking sense; silly —**in·an′i·ty** (-an′i tē) ***n.***

in·ar·tic·u·late (in′är tik′yo͞o lit, -yə-) ***adj.*** **1** without the articulation of normal speech *[*an *inarticulate* cry*]* **2** not able to speak; mute **3** unable to speak clearly or coherently **4** unexpressed or unexpressible

in·as·much as (in′əz much′ az′) **1** since; because **2** to the extent that

in·at·ten·tion (in′ə ten′shən) ***n.*** failure to pay attention; negligence —**in′at·ten′tive** ***adj.***

in·au·gu·ral (in ô′gyə rəl) ***adj.*** ⟦Fr⟧ **1** of an inauguration **2** first in a series —***n.*** **1** a speech made at an inauguration **2** an inauguration

in·au′gu·rate′ (-rāt′) ***vt.*** **-rat′ed, -rat′ing** ⟦< L *inaugurare*, to practice augury⟧ **1** to induct into office with a formal ceremony **2** to make a formal beginning of **3** to dedicate formally —**in·au′gu·ra′tion** ***n.***

in·au·then·tic (in′ô then′tik) ***adj.*** not authentic

in·board (in′bôrd′) ***adv.***, ***adj.*** **1** inside the hull of a ship or boat **2** close to the fuselage of an aircraft —***n.*** a boat with an inboard motor

in·born (in′bôrn′) ***adj.*** present in the organism at birth; innate

THESAURUS

position, wish, whimsy, inspiration, hunch, flash, thought.

impulsive ***a.*** offhand, unpremeditated, extemporaneous; see AUTOMATIC, SPONTANEOUS.

impulsively ***a.*** imprudently, hastily, abruptly; see CARELESSLY, RASHLY.

impure ***a.*** **1** [Adulterated] not pure, loaded, weighted, salted, diluted, debased, contaminated, mixed, watered down, polluted, corrupted, tainted, cut, adulterated, doctored*, tampered with; see also UNCLEAN. **2** [Not chaste] unclean, unchaste, corrupt; see BAD 1, LEWD 2.

impurity ***n.*** **1** [Lewdness] indecency, profligacy, pornography; see LEWDNESS. **2** [Filth] dirt, defilement, excrement; see FILTH, POLLUTION.

in[1] ***prep.*** **1** [Within] surrounded by, in the midst of, within the boundaries of, in the area of, within the time of, concerning the subject of, as a part of, inside, inside of, enclosed in, not out of; see also WITHIN. **2** [Into] to the center of, to the midst of, in the direction of, within the extent of, under, near, against; see also INTO, TOWARD. **3** [While engaged in] in the act of, during the process of, while occupied with; see DURING, MEANWHILE, WHILE 1. —**have it in for*** wish to harm, be out to destroy, detest; see HATE 1.

inability ***n.*** **1** [Lack of competence] incapacity, incompetence, shortcoming; see FAILURE 1, WEAKNESS 1. **2** [A temporary lack] disability, failure, frailty; see LACK 2, NECESSITY 2.

inaccessible ***a.*** unobtainable, unworkable, out of reach; see AWAY, BEYOND, DIFFICULT 2, DISTANT, RARE 2, REMOTE 1, SEPARATED.

inaccuracy ***n.*** exaggeration, mistake, deception; see ERROR.

inaccurate ***a.*** fallacious, in error, incorrect; see MISTAKEN 1, WRONG 2.

inactive ***a.*** dormant, stable, still; see IDLE, MOTIONLESS 1.

inadequacy ***n.*** **1** [Inferiority] ineptitude, incompetence, insufficiency; see WEAKNESS 1. **2** [A defect] flaw, drawback, shortcoming; see BLEMISH, DEFECT, LACK 2.

inadequate ***a.*** lacking, scanty, short, insufficient, meager, failing, unequal, not enough, sparing, stinted, stunted, feeble, sparse, too little, small, thin, deficient, incomplete, inconsiderable, spare, bare, niggardly, miserly, scarce, barren, depleted, low, weak, impotent, unproductive, dry, sterile, imperfect, defective, lame, skimpy*; see also UNSATISFACTORY.—*Ant.* ENOUGH, adequate, sufficient.

inadequately ***a.*** insufficiently, not enough, partly, partially, incompletely, scantily, deficiently, perfunctorily, ineffectively, inefficiently, ineptly, not up to standards, not up to specifications, not up to requirements, meagerly, not in sufficient quantity, not of sufficient quality, to a limited degree, below par, not up to snuff*; see also BADLY 1.

inadvisable ***a.*** unsuitable, inappropriate, inconvenient; see IMPROPER, WRONG 2.

inane ***a.*** pointless, foolish, ridiculous; see ILLOGICAL, SILLY, STUPID.

inanimate ***a.*** dull, inert, inoperative; see IDLE, MOTIONLESS 1.

inappropriate ***a.*** improper, irrelevant, inapplicable; see UNSUITABLE.

inarticulate ***a.*** **1** [Mute] reticent, wordless, mute; see DUMB 1. **2** [Indistinct] unintelligible, inaudible, vague; see OBSCURE 1.

inasmuch as ***conj.*** in view of, the fact that, seeing that, while; see also BECAUSE, SINCE 1.

inattentive ***a.*** indifferent, preoccupied, negligent; see CARELESS, DIVERTED.

inaudible ***a.*** low, indistinct, silent; see OBSCURE 1, VAGUE.

inaugurate ***v.*** introduce, initiate, originate; see BEGIN 1.

inauguration ***n.*** initiation, commencement, introduction; see INSTALLATION 1.

inborn ***a.*** innate, intrinsic, inbred; see NATIVE 1.

in·bound (in′bound′) ***adj.*** traveling or going inward —***vt.***, ***vi.*** *Basketball* to put (the ball) in play from out of bounds
in·bred (in′bred′) ***adj.*** **1** innate; inborn **2** resulting from inbreeding
in·breed (in′brēd′) ***vt.*** **-bred′**, **in′breed′ing** to breed by continual mating of individuals of the same or closely related stocks —***vi.*** **1** to engage in such breeding **2** to become too refined, effete, etc. —**in′·breed′ing** ***n.***
inc *abbrev.* **1** incorporated: also **Inc. 2** increase
In·ca (iŋ′kə) ***n.*** a member of the highly civilized Indian people that dominated ancient Peru until the Spanish conquest —**In′can** ***adj.***
in·cal·cu·la·ble (in kal′kyo͞o lə bəl) ***adj.*** **1** that cannot be calculated; too great or too many to be counted **2** unpredictable —**in·cal′cu·la·bly** ***adv.***
in·can·des·cent (in′kən des′ənt) ***adj.*** ⟦< L *in-*, in + *candere*, to shine⟧ **1** glowing with intense heat **2** very bright —**in′can·des′cence** ***n.***
incandescent lamp a lamp with a filament in a vacuum heated to incandescence by an electric current
in·can·ta·tion (in′kan tā′shən) ***n.*** ⟦< L *in-*, intens. + *cantare*, to sing⟧ words chanted in magic spells or rites
in·ca·pac·i·tate (in′kə pas′ə tāt′) ***vt.*** **-tat′ed**, **-tat′ing** to make unable or unfit
in′ca·pac′i·ty ***n.*** lack of capacity, power, or fitness
in·car·cer·ate (in kär′sər āt′) ***vt.*** **-at′ed**, **-at′ing** ⟦< L *in*, in + *carcer*, prison⟧ to imprison —**in·car′cer·a′tion** ***n.***
in·car·na·dine (in kär′nə dīn′) ***vt.*** **-dined′**, **-din′ing** to make red
in·car·nate (in kär′nit; *also, and for v. always*, -nāt′) ***adj.*** ⟦< L *in-*, in + *caro*, flesh⟧ endowed with a human body; personified —***vt.*** **-nat′ed**, **-nat′ing** **1** to give bodily form to **2** to be the type or embodiment of —**in′car·na′tion** ***n.***
in·cen·di·ar·y (in sen′dē er′ē) ***adj.*** ⟦< L *incendium*, a fire⟧ **1** having to do with the willful destruction of property by fire **2** designed to cause fires, as certain bombs **3** willfully stirring up strife, riot, etc. —***n.***, *pl.* **-ar′ies** **1** one who willfully stirs up strife, riot, etc. **2** an incendiary bomb, etc.
in·cense[1] (in′sens′) ***n.*** ⟦< L *in-*, in + *candere*, to burn⟧ **1** any substance burned to produce a pleasant odor **2** the odor from this
in·cense[2] (in sens′) ***vt.*** **-censed′**, **-cens′ing** ⟦see prec.⟧ to make very angry
in·cen·tive (in sent′iv) ***n.*** ⟦< L *in-*, in, on + *canere*, sing⟧ a stimulus; motive
in·cep·tion (in sep′shən) ***n.*** ⟦see INCIPIENT⟧ the beginning of something; start
in·cer·ti·tude (in sʉrt′ə to͞od′) ***n.*** **1** doubt **2** insecurity
in·ces·sant (in ses′ənt) ***adj.*** ⟦< L *in-*, not + *cessare*, cease⟧ never ceasing; continuing without stopping; constant — **in·ces′sant·ly** ***adv.***
in·cest (in′sest′) ***n.*** ⟦< L *in-*, not + *castus*, chaste⟧ sexual intercourse between persons too closely related to marry legally —**in·ces·tu·ous** (in ses′tyo͞o əs, -cho͞o-) ***adj.*** —**in·ces′tu·ous·ly** ***adv.*** —**in·ces′tu·ous·ness** ***n.***
inch (inch) ***n.*** ⟦< L *uncia*, twelfth part⟧ a measure of length equal to $\frac{1}{12}$ foot: symbol, ″ —***vt.***, ***vi.*** to move very slowly, or by degrees —**every inch** in all respects —**inch by inch** gradually: also **by inches** —**within an inch of** very close to
in·cho·ate (in kō′it) ***adj.*** ⟦< L *inchoare*, begin⟧ **1** just begun; rudimentary **2** not yet clearly formed
in·ci·dence (in′sə dəns) ***n.*** **1** the degree or range of occurrence or effect **2** [Inf.] an instance
in′ci·dent (-dənt) ***adj.*** ⟦< L *in-*, on + *cadere*, to fall⟧ **1** likely to happen as a result **2** falling upon or affecting *[incident* rays*]* —***n.*** **1** an event, esp. a minor one **2** a minor conflict
in′ci·den′tal (-dent′'l) ***adj.*** **1** happening in connection with something more important; casual **2** secondary or minor —***n.*** **1** something incidental **2** [*pl.*] miscellaneous items
in′ci·den′tal·ly ***adv.*** **1** in an incidental manner **2** by the way
in·cin·er·ate (in sin′ər āt′) ***vt.***, ***vi.*** **-at′ed**, **-at′ing** ⟦< L *in*, in + *cinis*, ashes⟧ to burn to ashes; burn up —**in·cin′er·a′tion** ***n.***
in·cin′er·a′tor ***n.*** a furnace for burning trash
in·cip·i·ent (in sip′ē ənt) ***adj.*** ⟦< L *in-*, in + *capere*, to take⟧ just beginning to exist or appear —**in·cip′i·ence** ***n.***
in·cise (in sīz′) ***vt.*** **-cised′**, **-cis′ing** ⟦< L *in-*, into + *caedere*, to cut⟧ to cut into with a sharp tool; specif., to engrave or carve
in·ci·sion (in sizh′ən) ***n.*** **1** an incising **2** a cut; specif., one made surgically
in·ci·sive (in sī′siv) ***adj.*** **1** cutting into **2** sharp; penetrating —**in·ci′sive·ly** ***adv.*** —**in·ci′sive·ness** ***n.***
in·ci·sor (in sī′zər) ***n.*** any of the front cutting teeth between the canines
in·cite (in sīt′) ***vt.*** **-cit′ed**, **-cit′ing** ⟦< L *in-*, on + *citare*, to urge⟧ to urge to action; rouse —**in·cite′ment** ***n.***
incl *abbrev.* **1** including **2** inclusive
in·clem·ent (in klem′ənt) ***adj.*** ⟦< L *in-*, on + *clemens*, lenient⟧ **1** rough; stormy **2** lacking mercy; harsh —**in·clem′en·cy**, *pl.* **-cies**, ***n.***
in·cli·na·tion (in′klə nā′shən) ***n.*** **1** a bending, leaning, or sloping **2** an inclined surface; slope **3** *a)* a bias; tendency *b)* a preference
in·cline (in klīn′; *for n., usually* in′klīn′) ***vi.*** **-clined′**, **-clin′ing** ⟦< L *in-*, on + *clinare*, to lean⟧ **1** to lean; slope **2** to have a tendency **3** to have a preference or liking —***vt.*** **1** to cause to lean, slope, etc. **2** to make willing; influence —***n.*** a slope; grade
inclined plane a sloping plane surface, esp. one sloping slightly
in·close (in klōz′) ***vt.*** **-closed′**, **-clos′ing** ENCLOSE —**in·clo′sure** (-klō′zhər) ***n.***
in·clude (in klo͞od′) ***vt.*** **-clud′ed**, **-clud′ing** ⟦< L *in-*, in + *claudere*, to close⟧ **1** to have as part of a whole; contain

THESAURUS

inbred ***a.*** innate, inborn, ingrained; see NATIVE 1.
incalculable ***a.*** unpredictable, unforeseen, unfixed; see UNCERTAIN.
incandescent ***a.*** radiant, glowing, brilliant; see BRIGHT 1.
incapable ***a.*** unsuited, poor, inadequate; see INCOMPETENT, INEXPERIENCED, NAIVE.
incapacity ***n.*** inadequacy, insufficiency, inability; see WEAKNESS 1.
incense[1] ***n.*** scent, fragrance, essence; see PERFUME.
incentive ***n.*** spur, inducement, motive, stimulus, stimulation, impetus, provocation, enticement, temptation, bait, consideration, excuse, rationale, urge, influence, lure, persuasion, inspiration, encouragement, insistence, instigation, incitement, reason why; see also PURPOSE 1.
incessant ***a.*** ceaseless, continuous, monotonous; see CONSTANT.
incessantly ***a.*** steadily, monotonously, perpetually; see REGULARLY.
inch ***n.*** **1** [Twelfth of a foot] fingerbreadth, 2.54 centimeters, 1/36 yard; see MEASURE 1. **2** [Small degree] jot, little bit, iota; see BIT 2. —**by inches** slowly, by degrees, step by step; see GRADUALLY. —**every inch** in all respects, thoroughly, entirely; see COMPLETELY.
inch ***v.*** creep, barely move, make some progress; see CRAWL.
inchoate ***a.*** incipient, rudimentary, preliminary, beginning; see also UNFINISHED 1.
incident ***n.*** episode, happening, occurrence; see EVENT.
incidental ***a.*** subsidiary, relative to, contributing to; see RELATED 2, SUBORDINATE.
incidentally ***a.*** subordinately, by chance, by the way, as a side effect, as a byproduct, unexpectedly, not by design, remotely; see also ACCIDENTALLY.
incidentals ***n.*** minor needs, incidental expenses, per diem; see EXPENSES, NECESSITY 2.
incinerate ***v.*** cremate, parch, burn up; see BURN.
incise ***v.*** engrave, chisel, carve; see CUT 1.
incision ***n.*** gash, slash, surgery; see CUT 1, HOLE 1.
incite ***v.*** arouse, rouse, impel, stimulate, instigate, provoke, excite, spur, goad, persuade, influence, induce, taunt, activate, animate, inspirit, coax, stir up, motivate, prompt, urge on, inspire, force, work up*, talk into*, egg on, fan the flame*; see also URGE 2.—*Ant.* DISCOURAGE, dissuade, check.
incited ***a.*** driven, pushed, motivated; see URGED 2.
inclination ***n.*** **1** [A tendency] bias, bent, propensity, predilection, penchant, attachment, capability, capacity, aptness, leaning, fondness, disposition, liking, preference, movement, susceptibility, weakness, drift, trend, turn, slant, impulse, attraction, affection, desire, temperament, whim, idiosyncrasy, urge, persuasion. **2** [A slant] pitch, slope, incline, angle, ramp, bank, list; see also GRADE 1.
incline ***n.*** slope, inclined plane, approach; see GRADE 1, INCLINATION 2.
incline ***v.*** **1** [To lean] bow, nod, bend; see LEAN 1. **2** [To tend toward] prefer, be disposed, be predisposed; see FAVOR.
inclined ***a.*** prone, tending, willing; see LIKELY 4.
include ***v.*** **1** [To contain] hold, admit, cover, embrace, involve, consist of, take in, entail, incorporate, constitute, accommodate, comprise, be comprised of*, be composed of, embody, be

2 to make part of a whole 3 to take into account —**in·clu′sion** (-klo͞o′zhən) ***n.***

in·clu′sive (-klo͞o′siv) ***adj.*** 1 taking everything into account 2 including the terms or limits mentioned [the third to the fifth *inclusive*] —**inclusive of** including —**in·clu′sive·ly** ***adv.***

in·cog·ni·to (in′käg nē′tō′, in käg′ni tō′) ***adj., adv.*** ⟦It < L *in-*, not + *cognitus*, known⟧ with true identity unrevealed or disguised

in·co·her·ent (in′kō hir′ənt, -her′-) ***adj.*** 1 not logically connected; disjointed 2 characterized by speech, etc. like this —**in′co·her′ence** ***n.*** —**in′co·her′ent·ly** ***adv.***

in·come (in′kum′) ***n.*** money, etc. received in a given period, as wages, rent, interest, etc.

in·com·mu·ni·ca·do (in′kə myo͞o′ni kä′dō) ***adj., adv.*** ⟦Sp⟧ not allowed or willing to communicate with others

in·com·pa·ra·ble (in käm′pə rə bəl) ***adj.*** 1 having no basis of comparison 2 beyond comparison; matchless

in·com·pat·i·ble (in′kəm pat′ə bəl) ***adj.*** not compatible; specif., unable to live together harmoniously —**in′com·pat′i·bil′i·ty**, *pl.* **-ties**, ***n.***

in·com·pe·tent (in käm′pə tənt) ***adj.*** without adequate ability, knowledge, fitness, etc. —***n.*** an incompetent person —**in·com′pe·tence** ***n.*** —**in·com′pe·tent·ly** ***adv.***

in·com·plete (in′kəm plēt′) ***adj.*** 1 lacking a part or parts 2 unfinished —***n.*** *Educ.* a grade, etc. indicating assigned work is not complete

in·con·gru·ous (in käŋ′gro͞o əs) ***adj.*** 1 lacking harmony or agreement of parts, etc. 2 inappropriate —**in′con·gru′i·ty** (-kän gro͞o′i tē) ***n.***

in·con·se·quen·tial (in kän′si kwen′shəl) ***adj.*** unimportant; trivial

in·con·sid·er·a·ble (in′kən sid′ər ə bəl) ***adj.*** trivial; small

in′con·sid′er·ate (-it) ***adj.*** without thought or consideration for others; thoughtless —**in′con·sid′er·ate·ly** ***adv.*** —**in′con·sid′er·ate·ness** or **in′con·sid′er·a′tion** (-ər ā′shən) ***n.***

in·con·sol·a·ble (in′kən sōl′ə bəl) ***adj.*** that cannot be consoled

in·con·spic·u·ous (in′kən spik′yo͞o əs) ***adj.*** attracting little attention

in·con·stant (in kän′stənt) ***adj.*** not constant; changeable, irregular, etc. —**in·con′stan·cy** ***n.***

in·con·test·a·ble (in′kən tes′tə bəl) ***adj.*** unquestionable; indisputable —**in′con·test′a·bil′i·ty** ***n.*** —**in′con·test′a·bly** ***adv.***

in·con·ti·nent (in känt′′n ənt) ***adj.*** 1 without self-restraint, esp. in sexual activity 2 unable to restrain a natural discharge, as of urine —**in·con′ti·nence** ***n.***

in·con·ven·ience (in′kən vēn′yəns) ***n.*** 1 lack of comfort, ease, etc. 2 anything inconvenient —***vt.*** **-ienced**, **-ienc·ing** to cause inconvenience to

in′con·ven′ient (-yənt) ***adj.*** not favorable to one's comfort; causing bother, etc.

in·cor·po·rate (in kôr′pə rāt′) ***vt.*** **-rat′ed**, **-rat′ing** ⟦see IN-[1] & CORPORATE⟧ 1 to combine; include; embody 2 to bring together into a single whole; merge 3 to form into a corporation —***vi.*** 1 to combine into a single whole 2 to form a corporation —**in·cor′po·ra′tion** ***n.***

in·cor·ri·gi·ble (in kôr′ə jə bəl) ***adj.*** ⟦< LL *incorrigibilis*⟧ that cannot be corrected or reformed, esp. because set in bad habits —**in·cor′ri·gi·bil′i·ty** ***n.*** —**in·cor′ri·gi·bly** ***adv.***

in·cor·rupt·i·ble (in′kə rup′tə bəl) ***adj.*** that cannot be corrupted, esp. morally

in·crease (in krēs′, in′krēs′) ***vi.*** **-creased′**, **-creas′ing** ⟦< L *in-*, in + *crescere*, grow⟧ to become greater in size, amount, degree, etc. —***vt.*** to make greater in size, etc. —***n.*** 1 an increasing or becoming increased 2 the result or amount of an increasing —**on the increase** increasing

THESAURUS

made up of, number among, carry, bear; see also COMPOSE 1.—*Ant.* BAR, omit, stand outside of. 2 [To place into or among] enter, introduce, take in, incorporate, make room for, build in, work in, inject, interject, add on, insert, combine, make a part of, make allowance for, give consideration to, count in.—*Ant.* DISCARD, exclude, reject.

included *a.* counted, numbered, admitted, covered, involved, constituted, embodied, inserted, entered, incorporated, combined, placed, fused, merged; see also WITHIN.—*Ant.* REFUSED, excluded, left out.

including *a.* together with, along with, as well as, in conjunction with, not to mention, to say nothing of, among other things, with the addition of, in addition to, comprising, containing, counting, made up of, incorporating.—*Ant.* BESIDES, not counting, aside from.

incoherence *n.* unintelligibility, dissimilarity, incongruity; see INCONSISTENCY.

incoherent *a.* mumbling, stammering, confused, speechless, puzzling, indistinct, faltering, stuttering, unintelligible, muttered, mumbled, jumbled, gasping, breathless, tongue-tied, muffled, indistinguishable, incomprehensible, disconnected, muddled.—*Ant.* CLEAR, eloquent, distinct.

incoherently *a.* inarticulately, unclearly, illogically, drunkenly, confusedly, spasmodically, chaotically, randomly, ineptly, unsystematically, aimlessly, casually, sloppily, ambiguously, equivocally, illegibly, incomprehensibly, unrecognizably, uncertainly, inaudibly; see also WILDLY.

income *n.* earnings, salary, wages, returns, profit, dividends, assets, proceeds, benefits, receipts, gains, commission, rent, royalty, honorarium, net income, gross income, taxable income, cash, take; see also PAY 2.—*Ant.* EXPENSE, expenditures, outgo.

incomparable *a.* unequaled, exceptional, superior; see EXCELLENT, PERFECT.

incompatibility *n.* variance, conflict, animosity; see DISAGREEMENT 1.

incompatible *a.* inconsistent, contrary, clashing, inappropriate, contradictory, disagreeing, inconstant, unadapted, opposite, jarring, discordant, incoherent, inadmissible; see also OPPOSED, UNSUITABLE.

incompetence *n.* inadequacy, inexperience, ineptitude; see WEAKNESS 1.

incompetent *a.* incapable, inefficient, unskillful, not qualified, inadequate, unfit, unskilled, bungling, inexpert, ineffectual, unsuitable, untrained, clumsy, awkward, uninitiated, raw, inexperienced, unadapted, not equal to, amateurish; see also UNABLE.—*Ant.* ABLE, fit, qualified.

incomplete *a.* rough, half-done, under construction; see UNFINISHED 1.

inconceivable *a.* unimaginable, fantastic, incredible; see IMPOSSIBLE.

inconclusive *a.* indecisive, unresolved, unsettled; see INADEQUATE, UNSATISFACTORY.

incongruous *a.* uncoordinated, unconnected, contradictory; see ILLOGICAL, UNSUITABLE.

inconsequential *a.* unimportant, immaterial, insignificant; see IRRELEVANT, TRIVIAL, UNNECESSARY.

inconsiderate *a.* boorish, impolite, discourteous; see RUDE 2, THOUGHTLESS 2.

inconsistency *n.* discrepancy, disagreement, dissimilarity, disparity, variance, incongruity, inequality, divergence, deviation, disproportion, paradox; see also DIFFERENCE 1.—*Ant.* SIMILARITY, consistency, congruity.

inconsistent *a.* contradictory, illogical, incoherent; see ILLOGICAL.

inconspicuous *a.* concealed, indistinct, retiring; see HIDDEN, OBSCURE 1, 3, SECRETIVE.

inconspicuously *a.* secretly, surreptitiously, not openly; see SLYLY.

inconvenience *n.* bother, trouble, awkward detail; see DIFFICULTY 1.

inconvenient *a.* bothersome, awkward, badly arranged; see DISTURBING.

incorporate *v.* add, combine, fuse; see INCLUDE 2, JOIN 1.

incorporated *a.* entered, placed, fused; see INCLUDED, JOINED.

incorporation *n.* embodiment, adding, fusion; see ADDITION 1.

incorrect *a.* inaccurate, not trustworthy, false; see MISTAKEN 1, UNRELIABLE, WRONG 2.

incorrectly *a.* mistakenly, inaccurately, clumsily; see BADLY 1, WRONGLY.

increase *n.* development, spread, enlargement, expansion, escalation, elaboration, swelling, addition, incorporation, inflation, extension, heightening, dilation, multiplication, rise, broadening, advance, intensification, deepening, swell, amplification, progression, improvement, boost, hike*, jump, boom; see also PROGRESS 1.—*Ant.* REDUCTION, decline, decrease. —**on the increase** growing, developing, spreading; see INCREASING.

increase *v.* extend, enlarge, expand, dilate, broaden, widen, thicken, deepen, heighten, build, lengthen, magnify, add on to, augment, escalate, let out, branch out, further, mark up, sharpen, build up, raise, enhance, amplify, reinforce, supplement, annex, double, triple, stretch, multiply, intensify, exaggerate, prolong, redouble, boost, step up, rev up*.—*Ant.* DECREASE, reduce, abridge.

increased *a.* marked up, raised, heightened, elevated, added on to, doubled.

increasing *a.* developing, maturing, multiplying, broadening, widening, intensifying, heightening, growing, dominant, advancing, growing louder, sharpening, accentuating, aggravating, emphasizing, accelerating, deepening, flourishing, rising, expanding, enlarging, accumulating, piling up, shooting up, getting big, swelling, on the rise, on the increase, booming; see also GROWING.

in·creas′ing·ly *adv.* more and more
in·cred·i·ble (in kred′ə bəl) *adj.* **1** not credible **2** seeming too unusual to be possible —**in·cred′i·bly** *adv.*
in·cred·u·lous (in krej′oo ləs) *adj.* **1** unwilling to believe **2** showing doubt or disbelief —**in·cre·du·li·ty** (in′krə dōō′ lə tē) *n.*
in·cre·ment (in′krə mənt, iŋ′-) *n.* ⟦< L *incrementum*⟧ **1** an increase **2** amount of increase
in·crim·i·nate (in krim′i nāt′) *vt.* **-nat′ed, -nat′ing** ⟦< L *in-*, in + *crimen*, offense⟧ **1** to accuse of a crime **2** to involve in, or make appear guilty of, a crime or fault —**in·crim′i·na′tion** *n.*
in·crust (in krust′) *vt., vi.* ENCRUST —**in·crus·ta·tion** (in′ krus tā′shən) *n.*
in·cu·bate (in′kyōō bāt′, iŋ′-) *vt.* **-bat′ed, -bat′ing** ⟦< L *in-*, on + *cubare*, to lie⟧ **1** to sit on and hatch (eggs) **2** to heat, etc. so as to hatch or grow, as in an incubator **3** to develop, as by planning —*vi.* to undergo incubation —**in′cu·ba′tion** *n.*
in′cu·ba′tor *n.* **1** a heated container for hatching eggs **2** any similar device, as for protecting premature babies, growing cell cultures, etc.
in·cu·bus (in′kyə bəs, iŋ′-) *n.* ⟦LL⟧ **1** a nightmare **2** an oppressive burden
in·cul·cate (in kul′kāt′, in′kul-) *vt.* **-cat′ed, -cat′ing** ⟦< L *in-*, in + *calcare*, trample underfoot⟧ to impress upon the mind, as by persistent urging —**in′cul·ca′tion** *n.*
in·cul·pate (in kul′pāt′, in′kul-) *vt.* **-pat′ed, -pat′ing** ⟦< L *in*, on + *culpa*, blame⟧ INCRIMINATE
in·cum·ben·cy (in kum′bən sē) *n., pl.* **-cies** tenure of office
in·cum′bent (-bənt) *adj.* ⟦< L *in-*, on + *cubare*, lie down⟧ currently in office —*n.* one currently in office —**incumbent on** (or **upon**) resting upon as a duty or obligation
in·cum′ber (-bər) *vt.* ENCUMBER —**in·cum′brance** (-brəns) *n.*
in·cu·nab·u·la (in′kyōō nab′yōō lə) *pl.n., sing.* **-u·lum** (-ləm) ⟦< L *in-*, in + *cunabula*, pl., a cradle⟧ books printed before 1500
in·cur (in kur′) *vt.* **-curred′, -cur′ring** ⟦< L *in-*, in + *currere*, to run⟧ **1** to acquire (something undesirable) **2** to bring upon oneself
in·cu·ri·ous (in kyoor′ē əs) *adj.* not curious; uninterested
in·cur·sion (in kur′zhən) *n.* ⟦see INCUR⟧ an invasion or raid
ind *abbrev.* **1** independent **2** index
Ind *abbrev.* **1** India **2** Indian
in·debt·ed (in det′id) *adj.* **1** in debt **2** owing gratitude, as for a favor
in·debt′ed·ness *n.* **1** a being indebted **2** the amount owed
in·de·cent (in dē′sənt) *adj.* not decent; specif., *a)* improper *b)* morally offensive; obscene —**in·de′cen·cy** *n.* —**in·de′cent·ly** *adv.*
in·de·ci·pher·a·ble (in′dē sī′fər ə bəl) *adj.* that cannot be deciphered
in·de·ci·sion (in′dē sizh′ən) *n.* inability to decide; vacillation
in′de·ci′sive (-sī′siv) *adj.* **1** not conclusive or final **2** showing indecision —**in′de·ci′sive·ly** *adv.* —**in′de·ci′sive·ness** *n.*
in·deed (in dēd′) *adv.* certainly; truly —*interj.* used to express surprise, doubt, sarcasm, etc.
in·de·fat·i·ga·ble (in′di fat′i gə bəl) *adj.* ⟦< L *in-*, not + *defatigare*, tire out⟧ that cannot be tired out
in·de·fen·si·ble (in′dē fen′sə bəl) *adj.* **1** that cannot be defended **2** that cannot be justified
in·def·i·nite (in def′ə nit) *adj.* not definite; specif., *a)* having no exact limits *b)* not precise in meaning; vague *c)* blurred; indistinct *d)* uncertain *e)* *Gram.* not limiting or specifying *[*"a" and "an" are *indefinite* articles*]* —**in·def′i·nite·ly** *adv.*
in·del·i·ble (in del′ə bəl) *adj.* ⟦< L *in-*, not + *delere*, destroy⟧ **1** that cannot be erased, blotted out, etc. **2** leaving an indelible mark
in·del·i·cate (in del′i kit) *adj.* lacking propriety or modesty; coarse —**in·del′i·ca·cy**, *pl.* **-cies**, *n.*
in·dem·ni·fy (in dem′ni fī′) *vt.* **-fied′, -fy′ing** ⟦< L *indemnis*, unhurt + -FY⟧ **1** to insure against loss, damage, etc. **2** to repay for (loss or damage) —**in·dem′ni·fi·ca′tion** *n.*
in·dem′ni·ty (-tē) *n., pl.* **-ties** **1** insurance against loss, damage, etc. **2** repayment for loss, damage, etc.
in·dent[1] (in dent′) *vt.* ⟦< L *in*, in + *dens*, tooth⟧ **1** to notch **2** to space (a line, paragraph, etc.) in from the margin of a page
in·dent[2] (in dent′) *vt.* ⟦IN-[1] + DENT⟧ to make a dent in
in·den·ta·tion (in′den tā′shən) *n.* **1** a being indented **2** a notch, cut, inlet, etc. **3** a dent **4** a spacing in from a margin, or a blank space so made
in·den·ture (in den′chər) *n.* **1** a written contract **2** [*often pl.*] a contract binding a person to work for another —*vt.* **-tured, -tur·ing** to bind by indenture
in·de·pend·ence (in′dē pen′dəns) *n.* a being independent; freedom from the influence or control of others
In·de·pend·ence (in′dē pen′dəns) city in W Missouri: pop. 112,000
Independence Day the anniversary of the adoption of the Declaration of Independence on July 4, 1776
in′de·pend′ent (-dənt) *adj.* **1** free from the influence or control of others; specif., *a)* self-governing *b)* self-reliant *c)* not adhering to any political party *d)* not connected with others *[*an *independent* grocer*]* **2** not depending on another for financial support —*n.* one who is independent in thinking, action, etc. —**in′de·pend′ent·ly** *adv.*
independent clause a clause that can function as a complete sentence
in′-depth′ *adj.* detailed; thorough
in·de·scrib·a·ble (in′di skrīb′ə bəl) *adj.* beyond the power of description —**in′de·scrib′a·bly** *adv.*
in·de·struct·i·ble (in′di struk′tə bəl) *adj.* that cannot be destroyed —**in′de·struct′i·bil′i·ty** *n.*
in·de·ter·mi·nate (in′dē tur′mi nit, -di-) *adj.* **1** indefinite; vague **2** doubtful or inconclusive —**in′de·ter′mi·na·cy** (-nə sē) *n.*
in·dex (in′deks′) *n., pl.* **-dex′es** or **-di·ces′** (-di sēz′) ⟦L, indicator⟧ **1** forefinger: in full **index finger** **2** a pointer or indicator **3** an indication *[*an *index* of ability*]* **4** an alphabetical list of names, subjects, etc. indicating

THESAURUS

increasingly *a.* with continuing acceleration, more and more, with steady increase; see MORE 1, 2.
incredible *a.* unbelievable, improbable, ridiculous; see IMPOSSIBLE.
incriminate *v.* implicate, blame, charge; see IMPLICATE.
incriminating *a.* damning, damaging, accusatory; see SUSPICIOUS 2.
inculcate *v.* instill, implant, impress upon; see TEACH.
incurable *a.* fatal, serious, hopeless; see DEADLY.
indebted *a.* obligated, grateful, appreciative; see RESPONSIBLE 1, THANKFUL.
indebtedness *n.* deficit, responsibility, obligation; see DEBT.
indecency *n.* impurity, immodesty, vulgarity, impropriety, obscenity, raciness, four-letter word, lewdness, foulness; see also EVIL 1.—*Ant.* CHASTITY, purity, delicacy.
indecent *a.* immoral, shocking, shameless; see BAD 1, LEWD 2, SHAMEFUL 1, 2.
indecision *n.* hesitation, question, irresolution; see DOUBT, UNCERTAINTY 2.
indecisive *a.* irresolute, unstable, wishy-washy*; see DOUBTFUL.
indeed *a.* in fact, of course, certainly; see REALLY 1, SURELY.
indeed *interj.* really?, honestly?, is that so?; see OH.
indefensible *a.* bad, unforgivable, unpardonable; see WRONG 1.
indefinite *a.* unsure, unsettled, loose; see UNCERTAIN, VAGUE 2.
indefinitely *a.* **1** [Vaguely] loosely, unclearly, ambiguously, indistinctly, incoherently, obscurely, indecisively, incompletely, lightly, briefly, momentarily, generally; see also VAGUELY.—*Ant.* POSITIVELY, clearly, exactly. **2** [Without stated limit] endlessly, continually, considerably; see FREQUENTLY, REGULARLY.
indelible *a.* ingrained, enduring, strong; see PERMANENT.
indent[1] *v.* make a margin, paragraph, space inward; see ORDER 3.
indentation *n.* imprint, recession, depression; see DENT.
independence *n.* sovereignty, autonomy, license; see FREEDOM 1, 2.
independent *a.* self-ruling, autonomous, sovereign; see FREE 1.
independently *a.* alone, autonomously, unilaterally, without support, separately, exclusively, individually, by oneself, on one's own*; see also FREELY 2.
indestructible *a.* unchangeable, durable, immortal; see PERMANENT.
index *n.* **1** [An indicator] formula, rule, average; see MODEL 2. **2** [An alphabetical arrangement] tabular matter, book index, guide to publications, bibliography, contents, catalog, card file, book list, appendix, end list, directory, dictionary; see also FILE 1, LIST, RECORD 1.
index *v.* alphabetize, arrange, tabulate; see FILE 1, LIST 1, RECORD 1.

pages where found, as in a book **5** a number used to measure change in prices, wages, etc. —***vt.*** to make or be an index of or for

index fund a mutual fund tied to a particular stock-market index

In·di·a (in′dē ə) **1** region in S Asia, south of the Himalayas **2** republic in the central & S part of this region: 1,222,243 sq. mi.; pop. 846,303,000

India ink a black liquid ink

In′di·an ***n.*** **1** a person born or living in India or the East Indies **2** AMERICAN INDIAN —***adj.*** **1** of India, or the East Indies, their people, etc. **2** of the American Indians, their culture, etc.

In·di·an·a (in′dē an′ə) Midwestern state of the U.S.: 35,870 sq. mi.; pop. 5,544,000; cap. Indianapolis: abbrev. *IN* —**In′di·an′an** or **In′di·an′i·an** (-an′ē ən) ***adj., n.***

In·di·an·ap·o·lis (in′dē ə nap′ə lis) capital of Indiana, in the central part: pop. 742,000

Indian corn CORN[1] (sense 2)

Indian file SINGLE FILE

Indian Ocean ocean south of Asia, between Africa & Australia

Indian summer mild, warm weather following the first frosts of late autumn

India paper **1** a thin, absorbent paper for taking proofs from engraved plates **2** a thin, opaque printing paper, as for Bibles

in·di·cate (in′di kāt′) ***vt.*** **-cat′ed, -cat′ing** ⟦< L *in-*, in + *dicare*, declare⟧ **1** to direct attention to; point out **2** to be a sign of; signify **3** to show the need for **4** to express briefly or generally —**in′di·ca′tion** ***n.***

in·dic·a·tive (in dik′ə tiv) ***adj.*** **1** giving an indication **2** designating or of the mood of a verb used to express an act, state, etc. as actual, or to ask a question of fact —***n.*** the indicative mood

in·di·ca·tor (in′di kāt′ər) ***n.*** one that indicates; specif., a gauge, dial, etc. that measures

in·dict (in dīt′) ***vt.*** ⟦ult. < L *in*, against + *dicere*, speak⟧ to charge with a crime —**in·dict′ment** ***n.***

in·dif·fer·ent (in dif′ər ənt, -dif′rənt) ***adj.*** **1** neutral **2** unconcerned; apathetic **3** of no importance **4** average —**in·dif′fer·ence** ***n.*** —**in·dif′fer·ent·ly** ***adv.***

in·dig·e·nous (in dij′ə nəs) ***adj.*** ⟦< L *indegena*, a native⟧ existing or growing naturally in a region or country; native

in·di·gent (in′di jənt) ***adj.*** ⟦< L *indegere*, to be in need⟧ poor; needy —***n.*** an indigent person —**in′di·gence** ***n.*** —**in′di·gent·ly** ***adv.***

in·di·gest·i·ble (in′di jes′tə bəl) ***adj.*** not easily digested

in′di·ges′tion (-jes′chən) ***n.*** **1** difficulty in digesting food **2** discomfort caused by this

in·dig·nant (in dig′nənt) ***adj.*** ⟦< L *in-*, not + *dignus*, worthy⟧ feeling or expressing anger, esp. at unjust or mean action —**in·dig′nant·ly** ***adv.***

in·dig·na·tion (in′dig nā′shən) ***n.*** righteous anger

in·dig·ni·ty (in dig′nə tē) ***n.***, *pl.* **-ties** an insult or affront to one's dignity or self-respect

in·di·go (in′di gō′) ***n.***, *pl.* **-gos′** or **-goes′** ⟦Sp < Gr *Indikos*, Indian⟧ **1** a blue dye obtained from certain plants or made synthetically **2** a deep violet blue —***adj.*** of this color

in·di·rect (in′də rekt′) ***adj.*** **1** not straight **2** not straight to the point **3** dishonest *[indirect* dealing*]* **4** not immediate; secondary *[*an *indirect* result*]* —**in′di·rect′ly** ***adv.*** —**in′di·rect′ness** ***n.***

indirect object *Gram.* the word or words denoting the person or thing indirectly affected by the action of the verb (Ex.: *him* in "give *him* the ball")

in·dis·creet (in′di skrēt′) ***adj.*** not prudent, as in speech or action; unwise

in′dis·cre′tion (-skresh′ən) ***n.*** **1** lack of discretion; imprudence **2** an indiscreet act or remark

in·dis·crim·i·nate (in′di skrim′i nit) ***adj.*** **1** mixed or random **2** not making careful distinctions —**in′dis·crim′i·nate·ly** ***adv.***

in·dis·pen·sa·ble (in′di spen′sə bəl) ***adj.*** absolutely necessary

in·dis·posed (in′di spōzd′) ***adj.*** **1** slightly ill **2** unwilling; disinclined —**in·dis·po·si·tion** (in′dis pə zish′ən) ***n.***

in·dis·sol·u·ble (in′di säl′yoo bəl) ***adj.*** that cannot be dissolved or destroyed; lasting

in·dite (in dīt′) ***vt.*** **-dit′ed, -dit′ing** ⟦see INDICT⟧ to compose and write

in·di·vid·u·al (in′də vij′oo əl) ***adj.*** ⟦< L < *in-*, not + *dividere*, to divide⟧ **1** existing as a separate thing or being; single **2** of, for, by, or relating to a single person or thing —***n.*** **1** a single thing or being **2** a person

in′di·vid′u·al·ism′ ***n.*** **1** individuality **2** the doctrine that

THESAURUS

Indian ***a.*** Native American, pre-Columbian, Amerindian; see INDIAN, *n.* 1.

Indian ***n.*** **1** [An indigenous person of the Americas] Native American, American aborigine, American Indian, Amerindian, red man*. *Terms for Indian groups having had historical or social importance include the following—United States and Canada: Arctic Indians:* Eskimo, Inuit, Aleut; *Eastern Woodlands Indians:* Iroquois or Six Nations, Mohawk, Oneida, Onondaga, Tuscarora, Seneca, Cayuga, Huron, Algonquin, Mahican, Delaware, Ojibwa or Chippewa, Sauk, Fox, Potawatomi, Seminole, Cherokee, Choctaw, Chickasaw, Creek, Natchez, Winnebago; *Plains Indians:* Sioux or Dakota, Oglala, Mandan, Iowa, Omaha, Comanche, Crow, Osage, Kiowa, Arapaho, Cheyenne, Pawnee, Blackfoot; *Great Basin Indians:* Ute, Paiute, Shoshone, Bannock; *West Coast Indians:* Athabascan, Costanoan, Chinook, Nez Percé, Tlingit, Flathead, Kwakiutl, Bella Coola, Klamath, Luiseño, Pomo; *Southwest Indians:* Navajo, Apache, Hopi, Pueblo, Zuni; *Mexico and Central America:* Maya, Aztec, Toltec, Nahuatl; *South America:* Inca, Quechua, Carib, Tupí, Arawak. **2** [A native of India] South Asian, Asian Indian, Dravidian, Hindu, Muslim, Buddhist, Jain, Sikh.

indicate ***v.*** **1** [To signify] symbolize, betoken, intimate; see MEAN 1. **2** [To designate] show, point to, register; see NAME 2.

indication ***n.*** evidence, sign, implication; see HINT, SUGGESTION 1.

indicator ***n.*** notice, pointer, symbol; see SIGN 1.

indict ***v.*** charge, face with charges, arraign; see BLAME.

indictment ***n.*** detention, censure, incrimination; see BLAME.

indifference ***n.*** unconcern, nonchalance, aloofness, coldness, insensitivity, callousness, alienation, disregard, neutrality, isolationism, heedlessness, detachment, dullness, sluggishness, stupor, coldbloodedness, disdain, cool*.

indifferent ***a.*** listless, cold, cool, unemotional, unsympathetic, heartless, unresponsive, unfeeling, uncommunicative, nonchalant, impassive, detached, callous, uninterested, stony, reticent, remote, reserved, distant, unsocial, scornful, apathetic, heedless, unmoved, not inclined toward, neutral, uncaring, aloof, silent, disdainful, haughty, superior, condescending, snobbish, arrogant, not caring about; see also UNMOVED 2.—*Ant.* EXCITED, aroused, warm.

indifferently ***a.*** **1** [Rather badly] poorly, not very well done, in a mediocre manner; see BADLY 1, INADEQUATELY. **2** [In an indifferent manner] nonchalantly, coolly, detachedly; see CALMLY.

indigestible ***a.*** inedible, rough, hard, unripe, green, tasteless, unhealthy, unhealthful, putrid, heavy, unwholesome, undercooked, raw, poisonous, toxic, moldy, bad-smelling, rotten, uneatable, icky*.—*Ant.* DELICIOUS, appetizing, tasty.

indigestion ***n.*** heartburn, nausea, acid indigestion; see ILLNESS 1, PAIN 2.

indignant ***a.*** upset, displeased, piqued; see ANGRY.

indirect ***a.*** roundabout, out-of-the-way, tortuous, twisting, long, complicated, devious, erratic, sidelong, zigzag, crooked, backhanded, obscure, sinister, rambling, long-winded, secondary, implied, oblique.—*Ant.* DIRECT, straight, immediate.

indirectly ***a.*** by implication, by indirection, in a roundabout way, secondhand, from a secondary source, not immediately, discursively, obliquely.—*Ant.* IMMEDIATELY, primarily, directly.

indiscreet ***a.*** naive, inopportune, misguided; see RASH, TACTLESS.

indiscretion ***n.*** recklessness, tactlessness, rashness; see CARELESSNESS.

indiscriminate ***a.*** random, confused, chaotic; see AIMLESS.

indispensable ***a.*** required, needed, essential; see NECESSARY.

indisputable ***a.*** undoubted, undeniable, unquestionable; see CERTAIN 2.

indistinct ***a.*** vague, confused, indefinite; see OBSCURE 1.

indistinguishable ***a.*** **1** [Identical] like, same, equivalent; see ALIKE, EQUAL. **2** [Indistinct] vague, invisible, dull; see OBSCURE 1, UNCERTAIN.

individual ***a.*** specific, personal, special, proper, own, particular, definite, lone, alone, solitary, original, distinct, distinctive, personalized, individualized, exclusive, select, single, only, reserved, separate, sole; see also PRIVATE, SPECIAL.—*Ant.* PUBLIC, collective, social.

individual ***n.*** human being, self, somebody; see CHILD, MAN 2, PERSON 1, WOMAN 1.

the state exists for the individual **3** the leading of one's life in one's own way —**in'di·vid'u·al·ist** ***n.***, ***adj.*** —**in'di·vid'u·al·is'tic** ***adj.***

in'di·vid'u·al'i·ty (-al'ə tē) ***n.***, *pl.* **-ties** **1** the sum of the characteristics that set one person or thing apart **2** the condition of being different from others

in'di·vid'u·al·ize' (-īz') ***vt.*** **-ized', -iz'ing** **1** to make individual **2** to treat as an individual —**in'di·vid'u·al·i·za'tion** ***n.***

in'di·vid'u·al·ly ***adv.*** **1** as individuals; separately **2** distinctively

In·do·chi·na (in'dō chī'nə) **1** large peninsula south of China, including Myanmar, Thailand, etc. **2** E part of this peninsula, consisting of Laos, Cambodia, & Vietnam

in·doc·tri·nate (in däk'trə nāt') ***vt.*** **-nat'ed, -nat'ing** to instruct in, or imbue with, doctrines, theories, etc. —**in·doc'tri·na'tion** ***n.***

In·do-Eu·ro·pe·an (in'dō yoor'ə pē'ən) ***adj.*** designating a family of languages including most of those of Europe and many of those of Asia

in·do·lent (in'də lənt) ***adj.*** ⟦< L *in-*, not + *dolere*, feel pain⟧ idle; lazy —**in'do·lence** ***n.*** —**in'do·lent·ly** ***adv.***

in·dom·i·ta·ble (in däm'i tə bəl) ***adj.*** ⟦< L *in-*, not + *domitare*, to tame⟧ not easily discouraged or defeated

In·do·ne·sia (in'də nē'zhə) republic in the Malay Archipelago, consisting of Java, Sumatra, & most of Borneo: 741,098 sq. mi.; pop. 179,379,000

In'do·ne'sian ***n.*** **1** a person born or living in Indonesia **2** the official Malay language of Indonesia —***adj.*** of Indonesia, its people, language, etc.

in'door' ***adj.*** living, belonging, etc. in a building

in'doors' ***adv.*** in or into a building

in·dorse (in dôrs') ***vt.*** **-dorsed', -dors'ing** ENDORSE

in·du·bi·ta·ble (in dōō'bi tə bəl) ***adj.*** that cannot be doubted; certain —**in·du'bi·ta·bly** ***adv.***

in·duce (in dōōs') ***vt.*** **-duced', -duc'ing** ⟦< L *in-*, in + *ducere*, to lead⟧ **1** to persuade **2** to bring on or about; cause **3** to draw (a conclusion) from particular facts **4** to bring about (an electric or magnetic effect) in a body by placing it within a field of force —**in·duc'er** ***n.***

in·duce'ment ***n.*** **1** an inducing or being induced **2** a motive; incentive

in·duct (in dukt') ***vt.*** ⟦see INDUCE⟧ **1** to place formally in an office, a society, etc. **2** to enroll (esp. a draftee) in the armed forces

in·duct'ance ***n.*** the property of an electric circuit by which a varying current in it produces a magnetic field that induces voltages in the same or a nearby circuit

in·duct·ee (in'duk tē') ***n.*** a person inducted, esp. into the armed forces

in·duc·tion (in duk'shən) ***n.*** **1** an inducting or being inducted **2** reasoning from particular facts to a general conclusion **3** the inducing of an electric or magnetic effect by a field of force —**in·duc'tive** ***adj.***

in·dulge (in dulj') ***vt.*** **-dulged', -dulg'ing** ⟦L *indulgere*, be kind to⟧ **1** to satisfy (a desire) **2** to gratify the wishes of; humor —***vi.*** to give way to one's own desires —**in·dulg'er** ***n.***

in·dul·gence (in dul'jəns) ***n.*** **1** an indulging or being indulgent **2** a thing indulged in **3** a favor or privilege **4** *R.C.Ch.* remission of punishment still due for a sin committed but forgiven

in·dul'gent (-jənt) ***adj.*** indulging or inclined to indulge; kind or lenient, often to excess —**in·dul'gent·ly** ***adv.***

in·dus·tri·al (in dus'trē əl) ***adj.*** **1** having to do with industry, its workers, etc. **2** made as for industrial use —**in·dus'tri·al·ly** ***adv.***

industrial arts the mechanical and technical skills used in industry

in·dus'tri·al·ism' ***n.*** social and economic structure characterized by large industries, machine production, etc.

in·dus'tri·al·ist ***n.*** one who owns or controls an industrial enterprise

in·dus'tri·al·ize' (-īz') ***vt.***, ***vi.*** **-ized', -iz'ing** **1** to establish or develop industrialism (in) **2** to organize as an industry —**in·dus'tri·al·i·za'tion** ***n.***

industrial park a planned area for industrial use, usually on the outskirts of a city

Industrial Revolution [*often* **i- r-**] the societal change resulting from the introduction of machinery and large-scale production; esp., this change in England from *c.* 1760

in·dus·tri·ous (in dus'trē əs) ***adj.*** diligent; hardworking —**in·dus'tri·ous·ly** ***adv.*** —**in·dus'tri·ous·ness** ***n.***

in·dus·try (in'dəs trē) ***n.***, *pl.* **-tries** ⟦< L *industrius*, active⟧ **1** earnest, steady effort **2** *a)* any particular branch of productive, esp. manufacturing, enterprise *b)* manufacturing enterprises collectively **3** any large-scale business activity *[the tourist industry]* **4** the owners and managers of industry

-ine[1] (īn, in, ēn, ən) ⟦< L *-inus*⟧ *suffix* of, having the nature of, like *[aquiline, crystalline]*

-ine[2] (in, ən) ⟦< L *-ina*⟧ *suffix* forming abstract nouns *[discipline, doctrine]*

-ine[3] (ēn, in, īn, ən) ⟦< L *-inus*⟧ *suffix* forming chemical names, as of *a)* halogens *[iodine]* *b)* alkaloids or nitrogenous bases *[morphine]*

in·e·bri·ate (in ē'brē āt'; *for n.*, -it') ***vt.*** **-at'ed, -at'ing** ⟦< L *in-*, intens. + *ebrius*, drunk⟧ to make drunk —***n.*** a drunkard —**in·e'bri·a'tion** ***n.***

in·ed·u·ca·ble (in ej'ōō kə bəl, -ej'ə-) ***adj.*** thought to be incapable of being educated

in·ef·fa·ble (in ef'ə bəl) ***adj.*** ⟦< L *in-*, not + *effabilis*, utterable⟧ **1** inexpressible **2** too sacred to be spoken

in·ef·fi·cient (in'e fish'ənt) ***adj.*** not producing the desired effect with minimum energy, time, etc. —**in'ef·fi'cien·cy** ***n.*** —**in'ef·fi'cient·ly** ***adv.***

in·el·e·gant (in el'ə gənt) ***adj.*** not elegant; crude —**in·el'e·gant·ly** ***adv.***

THESAURUS

individuality ***n.*** personality, distinctiveness, particularity, separateness, dissimilarity, singularity, air, manner, habit, eccentricity, way of doing things; see also ORIGINALITY.

individually ***a.*** separately, severally, one by one, one at a time, personally, exclusively, singly, by oneself, alone, independently, without help, distinctively, apart; see also ONLY 1.—*Ant.* TOGETHER, collectively, cooperatively.

indoctrinate ***v.*** inculcate, imbue, implant; see CONVINCE, INFLUENCE, TEACH.

indoctrination ***n.*** propagandism, instruction, brainwashing; see EDUCATION 1, TRAINING.

indoors ***a.*** in the house, at home, under a roof; see INSIDE 2, WITHIN.

induce ***v.*** produce, effect, make; see BEGIN 1.

induced ***a.*** **1** [Brought about] effected, achieved, caused; see FINISHED 1. **2** [Inferred] thought, concluded, reasoned; see CONSIDERED, DETERMINED 1.

induct ***v.*** conscript, initiate, draft; see ENLIST 1, RECRUIT 1.

inducted ***a.*** conscripted, called up, drafted; see INITIATED 2.

induction ***n.*** **1** [Logical reasoning] inference, rationalization, conclusion, judgment, conjecture; see also REASON 2. **2** [The process of electrical attraction] electric induction, magnetic induction, electromagnetic action; see ELECTRICITY. **3** [The process of being initiated] initiation, introduction, ordination, consecration, entrance into service.

indulge ***v.*** **1** [To humor] pamper, spoil, coddle; see ENTERTAIN 1, HUMOR. **2** [To take part in] go in for, revel, give way to; see JOIN 2.

indulgence ***n.*** **1** [Humoring] coddling, pampering, petting, fondling, babying, spoiling, placating, pleasing, toadying, favoring, kowtowing, gratifying. **2** [Revelry] intemperance, overindulgence, self-indulgence; see GREED, WASTE 1.

indulgent ***a.*** fond, considerate, tolerant; see KIND.

industrial ***a.*** manufacturing, manufactured, mechanized, automated, industrialized, in industry, factory-made, machine-made, modern, streamlined, technical; see also MECHANICAL 1.—*Ant.* HOMEMADE, handmade, domestic.

industrious ***a.*** intent, involved, diligent; see ACTIVE, BUSY 1.

industriously ***a.*** diligently, energetically, busily; see CAREFULLY 1, VIGOROUSLY.

industry ***n.*** **1** [Attention to work] activity, persistence, application, patience, intentness, perseverance, enterprise, hard work, zeal, energy, dynamism, pains, inventiveness; see also ATTENTION.—*Ant.* LAZINESS, lethargy, idleness. **2** [Business as a division of society] big business, management, corporate officers, shareholders, high finance, entrepreneurs, capital, private enterprise, monied interests, stockholders.

inebriated ***a.*** intoxicated, tipsy, plastered*; see DRUNK.

ineffective ***a.*** not effective, worthless, neutralized; see INCOMPETENT, WEAK 1, 2.

inefficiency ***n.*** incompetence, incapability, wastefulness; see FAILURE 1, WEAKNESS 1.

inefficient ***a.*** extravagant, prodigal, improvident; see WASTEFUL.

ineligible ***a.*** unsuitable, inappropriate, unavailable; see INCOMPETENT, UNFIT.

in·e·luc·ta·ble (in′i luk′tə bəl) ***adj.*** ⟦< L *in-*, not + *eluctari*, to struggle⟧ not to be avoided or escaped; inevitable —**in′e·luc′ta·bly** ***adv.***

in·ept (in ept′) ***adj.*** ⟦< L *in-*, not + *aptus*, apt⟧ **1** unsuitable; unfit **2** foolish **3** awkward; clumsy —**in·ep′ti·tude′** (-ep′tə to͞od′) ***n.*** —**in·ept′ness** ***n.***

in·ert (in urt′) ***adj.*** ⟦< L *in-*, not + *ars*, skill⟧ **1** without power to move or to resist **2** inactive; dull; slow **3** exhibiting little or no chemical activity *[an inert gas]*

in·er·tia (in ur′shə) ***n.*** ⟦see prec.⟧ **1** *Physics* the tendency of matter to remain at rest or to continue in a fixed direction unless affected by some outside force **2** a disinclination to move or act —**in·er′tial** ***adj.***

in·es·cap·a·ble (in′e skāp′ə bəl) ***adj.*** that cannot be escaped or avoided

in·es·ti·ma·ble (in es′tə mə bəl) ***adj.*** too great to be properly measured

in·ev·i·ta·ble (in ev′i tə bəl) ***adj.*** ⟦< L *in-*, not + *evitabilis*, avoidable⟧ certain to happen; unavoidable —**in·ev′i·ta·bil′i·ty** ***n.*** —**in·ev′i·ta·bly** ***adv.***

in·ex·haust·i·ble (in′eg zôs′tə bəl) ***adj.*** **1** that cannot be used up or emptied **2** tireless

in·ex·o·ra·ble (in eks′ə rə bəl) ***adj.*** ⟦< L *in-*, not + *exorare*, move by entreaty⟧ **1** that cannot be influenced by persuasion or entreaty; unrelenting **2** that cannot be altered, checked, etc. —**in·ex′o·ra·bly** ***adv.***

in·ex·pe·ri·ence (in′ek spir′ē əns) ***n.*** lack of experience or of the knowledge or skill resulting from experience —**in′ex·pe′ri·enced** ***adj.***

in·ex·pert (in ek′spərt, in′ek spurt′) ***adj.*** not expert; unskillful

in·ex·pli·ca·ble (in eks′pli kə bəl) ***adj.*** that cannot be explained or understood

in·ex·press·i·ble (in′eks pres′ə bəl) ***adj.*** that cannot be expressed; indescribable

in·ex·tin·guish·a·ble (in′ek stiŋ′gwish ə bəl) ***adj.*** that cannot be put out or stopped

in ex·tre·mis (in′ eks trē′mis) ⟦L, in extremity⟧ at the point of death

in·ex·tri·ca·ble (in eks′tri kə bəl) ***adj.*** **1** that one cannot extricate oneself from **2** that cannot be untied **3** so complicated as to be unsolvable

in·fal·li·ble (in fal′ə bəl) ***adj.*** ⟦see IN-[2] & FALLIBLE⟧ **1** incapable of error **2** dependable; reliable —**in·fal′li·bil′i·ty** ***n.*** —**in·fal′li·bly** ***adv.***

in·fa·mous (in′fə məs) ***adj.*** **1** having a very bad reputation; notorious **2** causing a bad reputation; scandalous

in′fa·my (-mē) ***n.***, *pl.* **-mies** **1** very bad reputation; disgrace **2** great wickedness **3** an infamous act

in·fan·cy (in′fən sē) ***n.***, *pl.* **-cies** **1** the state or period of being an infant **2** the earliest stage of anything

in·fant (in′fənt) ***n.*** ⟦< L *in-*, not + *fari*, speak⟧ a very young child; baby —***adj.*** **1** of or for infants **2** in a very early stage

in·fan·ti·cide (in fan′tə sīd′) ***n.*** **1** the murder of a baby **2** a person guilty of this

in·fan·tile (in′fən tīl′) ***adj.*** **1** of infants **2** like an infant; babyish

in·fan·try (in′fən trē) ***n.***, *pl.* **-tries** ⟦< L *infans*, child⟧ **1** that branch of an army consisting of soldiers trained to fight on foot **2** such soldiers collectively —**in′fan·try·man** (-mən), *pl.* **-men**, ***n.***

in·farct (in färkt′) ***n.*** ⟦< L *in-*, in + *farcire*, to stuff⟧ an area of dying or dead tissue resulting from inadequate blood flow to that area: also **in·farc′tion** (-färk′shən)

in·fat·u·at·ed (in fach′o͞o āt′id) ***adj.*** ⟦< L *in-*, intens. + *fatuus*, foolish⟧ completely carried away by foolish love or affection

in·fat′u·a′tion ***n.*** a being infatuated

in·fect (in fekt′) ***vt.*** ⟦< L *inficere*, to stain⟧ **1** to contaminate or cause to become diseased by contact with a disease-producing organism or matter **2** to imbue with one's feelings, beliefs, etc.

in·fec·tion (in fek′shən) ***n.*** **1** an infecting or being infected **2** an infectious disease

in·fec′tious (-shəs) ***adj.*** **1** likely to cause infection **2** designating a disease that can be communicated by certain bacteria, viruses, etc. **3** tending to affect others, as a laugh —**in·fec′tious·ly** ***adv.*** —**in·fec′tious·ness** ***n.***

in·fe·lic·i·tous (in′fə lis′ə təs) ***adj.*** not felicitous; unfortunate or unsuitable —**in′fe·lic′i·ty**, *pl.* **-ties**, ***n.***

in·fer (in fur′) ***vt.*** **-ferred′**, **-fer′ring** ⟦< L *in-*, in + *ferre*, to carry⟧ **1** to conclude by reasoning from something known or assumed **2** to imply: still sometimes regarded as a loose usage —**in·fer·ence** (in′fər əns) ***n.***

in·fer·en·tial (in′fər en′shəl) ***adj.*** based on or having to do with inference

in·fe·ri·or (in fir′ē ər) ***adj.*** ⟦< L *inferus*, low⟧ **1** located below or lower down **2** lower in order, status, etc. **3** lower in quality than: with *to* **4** poor in quality —***n.*** an inferior person or thing —**in·fe′ri·or′i·ty** (-ôr′ə tē) ***n.***

in·fer·nal (in fur′nəl) ***adj.*** ⟦< L *inferus*, below⟧ **1** of hell or Hades **2** hellish; fiendish

in·fer·no (in fur′nō) ***n.***, *pl.* **-nos** ⟦see prec.⟧ **1** HELL **2** any place characterized by flames or great heat

in·fest (in fest′) ***vt.*** ⟦< L *infestus*, hostile⟧ **1** to overrun in large numbers, usually so as to be harmful **2** to be parasitic in or on —**in′fes·ta′tion** ***n.*** —**in·fest′er** ***n.***

in·fi·del (in′fə del′) ***n.*** ⟦< L *in-*, not + *fidelis*, faithful⟧ **1** one who does not believe in a particular religion **2** one who has no religion

in·fi·del·i·ty (in′fə del′ə tē) ***n.*** **1** unfaithfulness, esp. in marriage **2** *pl.* **-ties** an unfaithful act

in·field (in′fēld′) ***n.*** **1** the diamond-shaped area enclosed by the four base lines on a baseball field **2** the players (**in′field′ers**) whose field positions are there

in·fight·ing (in′fīt′iŋ) ***n.*** **1** fighting, esp. boxing, at close range **2** personal conflict within a group —**in′fight′er** ***n.***

THESAURUS

ineluctable ***a.*** certain, inescapable, unavoidable; see INEVITABLE.

inept ***a.*** clumsy, gauche, ungraceful; see AWKWARD.

inequality ***n.*** disparity, dissimilarity, irregularity; see CONTRAST, DIFFERENCE 1, VARIATION 2.

inert ***a.*** still, dormant, inactive; see IDLE.

inertia ***n.*** passivity, indolence, inactivity; see LAZINESS.

inevitable ***a.*** fated, sure, unavoidable, impending, inescapable, necessary, unpreventable, irresistible, destined, assured, unalterable, compulsory, obligatory, binding, irrevocable, inexorable, without fail, undeniable, fateful, doomed, determined, decreed, fixed, ordained, foreordained, decided, sure as shooting*, in the cards, come rain or shine*.—*Ant.* DOUBTFUL, contingent, indeterminate.

inevitably ***a.*** unavoidably, inescapably, surely; see NECESSARILY.

inexcusable ***a.*** unpardonable, reprehensible, indefensible; see WRONG 1.

inexpensive ***a.*** thrifty, low-priced, modest; see CHEAP 1, ECONOMICAL 2.

inexperience ***n.*** naiveté, inability, greenness; see IGNORANCE.

inexperienced ***a.*** unused to, unaccustomed, unadapted, unskilled, unlicensed, untried, youthful, undeveloped, naive, amateur, untrained, untutored, inefficient, fresh, ignorant, innocent, uninformed, unacquainted, undisciplined, new, immature, tender, wet behind the ears*, soft, raw, green.—*Ant.* EXPERIENCED, seasoned, hardened.

inexplicable ***a.*** unexplainable, incomprehensible, puzzling; see OBSCURE 1.

infallibility ***n.*** supremacy, impeccability, consummation; see PERFECTION.

infallible ***a.*** perfect, reliable, unquestionable; see ACCURATE 1, 2, CERTAIN 2.

infamous ***a.*** shocking, disgraceful, heinous; see OFFENSIVE 2, SHAMEFUL 2.

infancy ***n.*** cradle, babyhood, early childhood; see CHILDHOOD.

infant ***n.*** small child, tot, little one; see BABY, CHILD.

infantile ***a.*** babyish, childlike, juvenile; see CHILDISH.

infantry ***n.*** foot soldiers, infantrymen, combat troops; see ARMY 1, 2.

infect ***v.*** defile, taint, spoil; see POISON.

infection ***n.*** **1** [The spread of disease] contagion, communicability, epidemic, taint, corruption; see also POLLUTION. **2** [Disease] virus, impurity, germs; see GERM.

infectious ***a.*** transferable, diseased, communicable; see CATCHING, CONTAGIOUS, DANGEROUS.

infer ***v.*** reason, gather, reach the conclusion that; see ASSUME, UNDERSTAND 1.

inference ***n.*** deduction, conclusion, answer; see JUDGMENT 3, RESULT.

inferior ***a.*** mediocre, common, second-rate; see POOR 2.

inferiority ***n.*** deficiency, mediocrity, inadequacy; see FAILURE 1, WEAKNESS 1.

infest ***v.*** **1** [To contaminate] pollute, infect, defile; see CORRUPT, DIRTY. **2** [To swarm] overrun, swarm about, crowd, press, harass, teem, fill, flood, throng, flock, be thick as flies*; see also SWARM.

infested ***a.*** **1** [Overrun] swarming with, full of, overwhelmed; see FULL 1. **2** [Diseased] wormy, having parasites, ill; see SICK.

infielder ***n.*** first baseman, second baseman, third baseman; see BASEBALL PLAYER.

in·fil·trate (in fil′trāt′, in′fil trāt′) ***vi.***, ***vt.*** **-trat′ed, -trat′ing** **1** to filter or pass gradually through or into **2** to penetrate (enemy lines, a region, etc.) gradually or stealthily, so as to attack or to seize control from within —**in′fil·tra′tion** ***n.*** —**in′fil·tra′tor** ***n.***

in·fi·nite (in′fə nit) ***adj.*** ⟦see IN-[2] & FINITE⟧ **1** lacking limits or bounds; endless **2** very great; vast —***n.*** something infinite —**in′fi·nite·ly** ***adv.***

in·fin·i·tes·i·mal (in′fin i tes′i məl) ***adj.*** ⟦< L *infinitus*, infinite⟧ too small to be measured —**in′fin·i·tes′i·mal·ly** ***adv.***

in·fin·i·tive (in fin′i tiv) ***n.*** ⟦see INFINITE⟧ the form of a verb without reference to person, number, or tense: typically with *to*, as in "I want *to go*" —**in·fin′i·ti′val** (-tī′vəl) ***adj.***

in·fin′i·tude′ (-to͞od′, -tyo͞od′) ***n.*** ⟦< L *infinitus*, INFINITE, prob. infl. by MAGNITUDE⟧ **1** a being infinite **2** an infinite quantity

in·fin′i·ty (-tē) ***n.***, *pl.* **-ties** ⟦< L *infinitas*⟧ **1** the quality of being infinite **2** unlimited space, time, etc. **3** an indefinitely large quantity

in·firm (in furm′) ***adj.*** **1** weak; feeble, as from old age **2** not firm; unstable; frail; shaky —**in·firm′ly** ***adv.*** —**in·firm′ness** ***n.***

in·fir·ma·ry (in fur′mə rē) ***n.***, *pl.* **-ries** a school dispensary

in·fir′mi·ty (-mə tē) ***n.***, *pl.* **-ties** (a) physical weakness or defect

in·flame (in flame′) ***vt.***, ***vi.*** **-flamed′, -flam′ing** ⟦see IN-[1] & FLAME⟧ **1** to arouse, excite, etc. or become aroused, excited, etc. **2** to undergo or cause to undergo inflammation

in·flam·ma·ble (in flam′ə bəl) ***adj.*** **1** FLAMMABLE **2** easily excited —**in·flam′ma·bil′i·ty** ***n.***

in·flam·ma·tion (in′flə mā′shən) ***n.*** **1** an inflaming or being inflamed **2** redness, pain, heat, and swelling in the body, due to injury, disease, etc.

in·flam·ma·to·ry (in flam′ə tôr′ē) ***adj.*** **1** rousing excitement, anger, etc. **2** *Med.* of or caused by inflammation

in·flate (in flāt′) ***vt.*** **-flat′ed, -flat′ing** ⟦< L *in-*, in + *flare*, to blow⟧ **1** to blow full as with air or gas **2** to puff up with pride **3** to increase beyond what is normal; specif., to cause inflation of (money, credit, etc.) —***vi.*** to become inflated —**in·flat′a·ble** ***adj.***

in·fla′tion ***n.*** **1** an inflating or being inflated **2** *a*) an increase in the amount of money and credit in relation to the supply of goods and services *b*) an excessive or persistent increase in the general price level as a result of this, causing a decline in purchasing power —**in·fla′tion·ar′y** ***adj.***

in·flect (in flekt′) ***vt.*** ⟦< L *in-*, in + *flectere*, to bend⟧ **1** to vary the tone of (the voice) **2** *Gram.* to change the form of (a word) by inflection

in·flec·tion (in flek′shən) ***n.*** **1** a change in the tone of the voice **2** the change of form in a word to indicate number, case, tense, etc. Brit. sp. **in·flex′ion** —**in·flec′tion·al** ***adj.***

in·flex·i·ble (in flek′sə bəl) ***adj.*** not flexible; stiff, rigid, fixed, unyielding, etc. —**in·flex′i·bil′i·ty** ***n.***

in·flict (in flikt′) ***vt.*** ⟦< L *in-*, on + *fligere*, to strike⟧ **1** to cause (pain, wounds, etc.) as by striking **2** to impose (a punishment, etc.) *on* or *upon* —**in·flic′tion** ***n.*** —**in·flic′tive** ***adj.***

in-flight (in′flīt′) ***adj.*** done, shown, etc. while an aircraft is in flight *[in-flight* movies*]*

in·flo·res·cence (in′flō res′əns, -flô-) ***n.*** *Bot.* **1** the producing of blossoms **2** the arrangement of flowers on a stem **3** a flower cluster **4** flowers collectively

in·flu·ence (in′flo͞o əns) ***n.*** ⟦< L *in-*, in + *fluere*, to flow⟧ **1** power to affect others **2** power to produce effects because of wealth, high position, etc. **3** one that has influence —***vt.*** **-enced, -enc·ing** to have influence or an effect on

in′flu·en′tial (-en′shəl) ***adj.*** exerting influence, esp. great influence

in·flu·en·za (in′flo͞o en′zə) ***n.*** ⟦It, an influence⟧ an acute, contagious viral disease, characterized by inflammation of the respiratory tract, fever, and muscular pain

in·flux (in′fluks′) ***n.*** ⟦see INFLUENCE⟧ a flowing in or streaming in

in·fo (in′fō) ***n.*** [Slang] *short for* INFORMATION (sense 2)

in·fold (in fōld′) ***vt.*** *var. of* ENFOLD

in·fo·mer·cial (in′fō mur′shəl) ***n.*** ⟦INFO(RMATION) + (COM)MERCIAL⟧ a long TV commercial made to resemble a talk show, interview, etc.

in·form (in fôrm′) ***vt.*** ⟦see IN-[1] & FORM⟧ to give knowledge of something to —***vi.*** to give information, esp. in accusing another

in·for·mal (in fôr′məl) ***adj.*** not formal; specif., *a*) not according to fixed customs, rules, etc. *b*) casual, relaxed, etc. *c*) not requiring formal dress *d*) designating or of the words, phrases, etc. characteristic of speech or writing that is casual, ordinary, etc. —**in′for·mal′i·ty** (-mal′ə tē), *pl.* **-ties**, ***n.*** —**in·for′mal·ly** ***adv.***

in·form·ant (in fôr′mənt) ***n.*** a person who gives information; specif., an informer

THESAURUS

infiltrate ***v.*** permeate, pervade, penetrate; see JOIN 2.

infinite ***a.*** incalculable, unbounded, boundless, unconfined, countless, interminable, measureless, inexhaustible, bottomless, without end, limitless, tremendous, immense, having no limit, never-ending, immeasurable; see also ENDLESS, UNLIMITED.—*Ant.* RESTRICTED, limited, bounded.

infinite ***n.*** boundlessness, infinity, the unknown; see ETERNITY, SPACE 1.

infinitely ***a.*** extremely, very much, unbelievably; see VERY.

infinity ***n.*** boundlessness, endlessness, the beyond, limitlessness, expanse, extent, continuum, continuity, eternity, infinite space; see also SPACE 1.

infirmary ***n.*** clinic, sickroom, sick bay; see HOSPITAL.

infirmity ***n.*** frailty, deficiency, debility; see WEAKNESS 1.

inflame ***v.*** **1** [To arouse emotions] incense, irritate, disturb; see EXCITE. **2** [To cause physical soreness] redden, chafe, swell; see HURT 1. **3** [To burn] kindle, set on fire, scorch; see BURN, IGNITE.

inflamed ***a.*** **1** [Stirred to anger] aroused, incited, angered; see ANGRY. **2** [Congested] raw, blistered, swollen; see HURT, PAINFUL 1, SORE 1.

inflammable ***a.*** flammable, combustible, burnable, liable to burn, risky, unsafe, hazardous, dangerous.—*Ant.* SAFE, fireproof, nonflammable.

inflammation ***n.*** congestion, soreness, infection; see PAIN 2, SORE.

inflate ***v.*** **1** [To fill with air or gas] pump up, expand, swell; see FILL 1. **2** [To increase] exaggerate, bloat, cram, expand, balloon, distend, swell up, widen, augment, spread out, enlarge, magnify, exalt, build up, raise, maximize, overestimate; see also STRETCH 1, SWELL.

inflated ***a.*** distended, swollen, extended, dilated, puffed, filled, grown, stretched, spread, enlarged, amplified, augmented, pumped up, exaggerated, bloated, crammed, magnified, overestimated, pompous, verbose.—*Ant.* REDUCED, deflated, minimized.

inflation ***n.*** **1** [Increase] expansion, extension, buildup; see INCREASE. **2** [General rise in price levels] financial crisis, boom, rising prices; see RISE 3.

inflection ***n.*** pronunciation, enunciation, intonation; see ACCENT, SOUND 2.

inflexibility ***n.*** stability, toughness, rigidity, stiffness, ossification, fossilization, solidity, crystallization; see also FIRMNESS.

inflexible ***a.*** rigid, hardened, taut; see FIRM 2, STIFF 1.

inflict ***v.*** deliver, strike, dispense; see CAUSE.

influence ***n.*** control, weight, authority, supremacy, command, domination, esteem, political influence, monopoly, rule, fame, prominence, prestige, character, reputation, force, importance, money, power behind the throne*, pull*, clout*; see also LEADERSHIP, POWER 2.

influence ***v.*** sway, affect, impress, carry weight, be influential, determine, make oneself felt, have influence over, lead to believe, bring pressure to bear, bribe, seduce, talk someone into, alter, change, act upon, act on, lead, brainwash, direct, modify, regulate, rule, compel, urge, incite, bias, prejudice, train, channel, mold, form, shape, exert influence, get at*, be recognized, induce, convince, cajole, persuade, motivate, have an in*, pull strings, have a finger in the pie*, lead by the nose*, fix*.

influenced ***a.*** changed, swayed, persuaded; see AFFECTED 1.

influential ***a.*** prominent, substantial, powerful; see FAMOUS.

influx ***n.*** introduction, penetration, coming in; see ENTRANCE 1.

inform ***v.*** instruct, apprise, teach; see TELL 1.

informal ***a.*** intimate, relaxed, frank, open, straightforward, ordinary, everyday, inconspicuous, habitual, free, extemporaneous, spontaneous, congenial, easygoing, unrestrained, unconventional; see also FRIENDLY.—*Ant.* RESTRAINED, ceremonial, ritualistic.

informality ***n.*** casualness, familiarity, ease; see COMFORT.

in·for·ma·tion (in′fər mā′shən) ***n.*** **1** a being informed **2** something told or facts learned; news or knowledge **3** data stored in or retrieved from a computer
information science the science dealing with the collection, storage, and retrieval of information
in·form·a·tive (in fôr′mə tiv) ***adj.*** giving information; instructive
in·formed′ ***adj.*** having or based on knowledge or education
in·form′er ***n.*** one who secretly gives evidence against another
in·fo·tain·ment (in′fō tān′mənt) ***n.*** ⟦INFO(RMATION) + (ENTER)TAINMENT⟧ TV programming of information, as about celebrities, in a dramatic or sensational style
infra- ⟦< L⟧ *prefix* below, beneath
in·frac·tion (in frak′shən) ***n.*** ⟦see INFRINGE⟧ a violation of a law, pact, etc.
in·fra·red (in′frə red′) ***adj.*** designating or of those invisible rays just beyond the red of the visible spectrum: they have a penetrating heating effect
in′fra·son′ic (-sän′ik) ***adj.*** of a frequency of sound below the range audible to the human ear
in′fra·struc′ture (-struk′chər) ***n.*** basic installations and facilities, as roads, power plants, transportation and communication systems, etc.
in·fre·quent (in frē′kwənt) ***adj.*** not frequent; happening seldom; rare; uncommon —**in·fre′quen·cy** or **in·fre′quence** ***n.*** —**in·fre′quent·ly** ***adv.***
in·fringe (in frinj′) ***vt.*** **-fringed′**, **-fring′ing** ⟦< L *in-*, in + *frangere*, to break⟧ to break (a law or pact) —**infringe on** (or **upon**) to encroach on (the rights, etc. of others) —**in·fringe′ment** ***n.***
in·fu·ri·ate (in fyoor′ē āt′) ***vt.*** **-at′ed**, **-at′ing** ⟦< L *in-*, in + *furia*, rage⟧ to make very angry; enrage
in·fuse (in fyo͞oz′) ***vt.*** **-fused′**, **-fus′ing** ⟦< L *in-*, in + *fundere*, pour⟧ **1** to instill or impart (qualities, etc.) **2** to fill; inspire **3** to steep (tea leaves, etc.) to extract the essence —**in·fus′er** ***n.*** —**in·fu′sion** ***n.***
-ing (iŋ) ⟦< OE⟧ *suffix* used to form the present participle or verbal nouns *[talking, painting]*
in·gath·er·ing (in′gath′ər iŋ) ***n.*** a gathering together
in·gen·ious (in jēn′yəs) ***adj.*** ⟦< L *in-*, in + *gignere*, to produce⟧ **1** clever, resourceful, etc. **2** made or done in a clever or original way —**in·gen′ious·ly** ***adv.***
in·gé·nue (an′zhə no͞o′, än′-) ***n.*** ⟦Fr, ingenuous⟧ *Theater* the role of an inexperienced young woman, or an actress in this role
in·ge·nu·i·ty (in′jə no͞o′ə tē, -nyo͞o′-) ***n.*** the quality of being ingenious; cleverness
in·gen·u·ous (in jen′yo͞o əs) ***adj.*** ⟦< L *in-*, in + *gignere*, to produce⟧ **1** frank; open **2** simple; naive —**in·gen′u·ous·ly** ***adv.*** —**in·gen′u·ous·ness** ***n.***
in·gest (in jest′) ***vt.*** ⟦< L *in-*, into + *gerere*, carry⟧ to take (food, etc.) into the body, as by swallowing, inhaling, or absorbing —**in·ges′tion** ***n.***
in·glo·ri·ous (in glôr′ē əs) ***adj.*** shameful; disgraceful
in·got (iŋ′gət) ***n.*** ⟦prob. < OFr *lingo*, tongue⟧ a mass of metal cast into a bar or other convenient shape
in·grained (in′grānd′) ***adj.*** **1** firmly established, as habits **2** inveterate *[an ingrained liar]*
in·grate (in′grāt′) ***n.*** ⟦< L *in-*, not + *gratus*, grateful⟧ an ungrateful person
in·gra·ti·ate (in grā′shē āt′) ***vt.*** **-at′ed**, **-at′ing** ⟦< L *in-*, in + *gratia*, favor⟧ to bring (oneself) into another's favor —**in·gra′ti·a′tion** ***n.***
in·grat·i·tude (in grat′i to͞od′) ***n.*** lack of gratitude; ungratefulness
in·gre·di·ent (in grē′dē ənt) ***n.*** ⟦see fol.⟧ **1** any of the things that a mixture is made of **2** a component
in·gress (in′gres′) ***n.*** ⟦< L *in-*, into + *gradi*, to go⟧ entrance
in·grown (in′grōn′) ***adj.*** grown inward, esp. into the flesh, as a toenail
in·gui·nal (iŋ′gwi nəl) ***adj.*** ⟦< L *inguen*, groin⟧ of or near the groin
in·hab·it (in hab′it) ***vt.*** ⟦< L *in-*, in + *habitare*, dwell⟧ to live in —**in·hab′it·a·ble** ***adj.***
in·hab′it·ant (-i tənt) ***n.*** a person or animal inhabiting a specified place
in·hal·ant (in hāl′ənt) ***n.*** a medicine, etc. to be inhaled
in·ha·la·tor (in′hə lāt′ər) ***n.*** **1** INHALER (*n.* 3) **2** RESPIRATOR (sense 2)
in·hale (in hāl′) ***vt.***, ***vi.*** **-haled′**, **-hal′ing** ⟦< L *in-*, in + *halare*, breathe⟧ to breathe in (air, vapor, etc.) —**in·ha·la·tion** (in′hə lā′shən) ***n.***
in·hal·er (in hāl′ər) ***n.*** **1** one who inhales **2** RESPIRATOR (sense 1) **3** a device used in inhaling medicinal vapors
in·here (in hir′) ***vi.*** **-hered′**, **-her′ing** ⟦< L *in-*, in + *haerere*, to stick⟧ to be inherent
in·her·ent (in hir′ənt, -her′-) ***adj.*** existing in someone or something as a natural and inseparable quality —**in·her′ent·ly** ***adv.***
in·her·it (in her′it) ***vt.***, ***vi.*** ⟦< L *in*, in + *heres*, heir⟧ **1** to receive (property, etc.) as an heir **2** to have (certain characteristics) as by heredity —**in·her′i·tor** ***n.***
in·her·it·ance (in her′i təns) ***n.*** **1** the action of inheriting **2** something inherited
in·hib·it (in hib′it) ***vt.*** ⟦< L *in-*, in, on + *habere*, to hold⟧ to check or repress
in·hi·bi·tion (in′hi bish′ən, in′i-) ***n.*** **1** an inhibiting or being inhibited **2** a mental process that restrains an action, emotion, or thought
in′-house′ ***adj.***, ***adv.*** (done) within an organization, company, etc. rather than outside it
in·hu·man (in hyo͞o′mən) ***adj.*** not having worthy human characteristics; heartless, cruel, brutal, etc. —**in′hu·man′i·ty** (-man′ə tē) ***n.***
in·im·i·cal (i nim′i kəl) ***adj.*** ⟦< L *in-*, not + *amicus*, friend⟧ **1** hostile; unfriendly **2** in opposition; adverse
in·im·i·ta·ble (i nim′i tə bəl) ***adj.*** that cannot be imitated or matched
in·iq·ui·ty (i nik′wi tē) ***n.*** ⟦< L *in-*, not + *aequus*, equal⟧ **1** wickedness **2** *pl.* **-ties** a wicked or unjust act —**in·iq′ui·tous** ***adj.***
in·i·tial (i nish′əl) ***adj.*** ⟦< L *in-*, into, in + *ire*, go⟧ of or at the beginning; first —***n.*** the first letter of a name —***vt.***

THESAURUS

information ***n.*** **1** [Derived knowledge] acquired facts, evidence, knowledge, reports, details, results, notes, documents, testimony, facts, figures, statistics, measurements, conclusions, deductions, plans, field notes, lab notes, learning, erudition; see also KNOWLEDGE 1. **2** [News] report, notice, message; see NEWS 1, 2.
informative ***a.*** instructive, enlightening, accurate; see DETAILED.
infraction ***n.*** nonobservance, infringement, breach; see VIOLATION.
infrastructure ***n.*** foundation, basic structure, base; see FOUNDATION 2.
infrequent ***a.*** sparse, occasional, scarce; see RARE 2.
infrequently ***a.*** occasionally, rarely, hardly ever; see SELDOM.
infringe ***v.*** transgress, violate, trespass; see MEDDLE 1.
infuriate ***v.*** irritate, enrage, provoke; see ANGER.
infuriated ***a.*** furious, enraged, incensed; see ANGRY.
ingenious ***a.*** resourceful, skillful, gifted; see ABLE, INTELLIGENT.
ingenuity ***n.*** inventiveness, imagination, productiveness; see ORIGINALITY.
ingrained ***a.*** congenital, inborn, indelible; see NATIVE 1.
ingratitude ***n.*** disloyalty, ungratefulness, callousness, boorishness, lack of appreciation, inconsiderateness, thoughtlessness; see also RUDENESS.—*Ant.* GRATITUDE, appreciation, consideration.
ingredient ***n.*** constituent, component, element; see FUNDAMENTAL.
ingredients ***n.*** parts, elements, additives, constituents, pieces, components, makings, fixings*.
inhabit ***v.*** occupy, stay in, live in; see DWELL.
inhabitant ***n.*** occupant, dweller, settler, denizen, lodger, permanent resident, roomer, boarder, occupier, householder, addressee, inmate, tenant, settler, colonist, squatter, native; see also CITIZEN, RESIDENT.—*Ant.* ALIEN, transient, nonresident.
inhabited ***a.*** settled, owned, lived in, dwelt in, sustaining human life, peopled, occupied, colonized, developed, pioneered.
inhale ***v.*** breathe in, smell, sniff; see BREATHE.
inherent ***a.*** innate, inborn, inbred; see NATURAL 1, NATIVE 1.—*Ant.* SUPERFICIAL, incidental, extrinsic.
inherently ***a.*** naturally, intrinsically, by birth; see ESSENTIALLY.
inherit ***v.*** succeed to, acquire, receive, obtain, get one's inheritance, fall heir to, come into, come in for*, take over, receive an endowment; see also GET 1.—*Ant.* LOSE, be disowned, miss.
inheritance ***n.*** bequest, legacy, heritage; see GIFT 1.
inhibit ***v.*** repress, frustrate, hold back; see HINDER, RESTRAIN.
inhibition ***n.*** prevention, restraint, hindrance; see BARRIER, INTERFERENCE 1.
inhuman ***a.*** mean, heartless, cold-blooded; see CRUEL, FIERCE, RUTHLESS.
inhumanity ***n.*** savagery, barbarity, brutality; see CRUELTY, EVIL 1, TYRANNY.
initial ***a.*** basic, primary, elementary; see FIRST, FUNDAMENTAL.

-tialed or -tialled, -tial·ing or -tial·ling to mark with initials —in·i′tial·ly *adv.*

in·i·ti·ate (i nish′ē āt′) *vt.* -at′ed, -at′ing ⟦see prec.⟧ **1** to bring into practice or use **2** to teach the fundamentals of a subject to **3** to admit as a member into a fraternity, club, etc., esp. with a special or secret ceremony —in·i′ti·a′tion *n.* —in·i′ti·a·to′ry (-ə tôr′ē) *adj.*

in·i·ti·a·tive (i nish′ə tiv, -ē ə tiv) *n.* **1** the action of taking the first step or move **2** ability in originating new ideas or methods **3** the introduction of proposed legislation, as by voters' petitions

in·ject (in jekt′) *vt.* ⟦< L *in-*, in + *jacere*, to throw⟧ **1** to force (a fluid) into a cavity or chamber; esp., to introduce (a liquid) into a vein, tissue, etc. with a syringe **2** to introduce (a remark, quality, etc.) —in·jec′tion *n.* —in·jec′tor *n.*

in·junc·tion (in juŋk′shən) *n.* ⟦< L *in-*, in + *jungere*, join⟧ **1** a command; order **2** a court order prohibiting or ordering a given action

in·jure (in′jər) *vt.* -jured, -jur·ing ⟦see INJURY⟧ **1** to do harm or damage to; hurt **2** to wrong or offend

in·ju·ri·ous (in joor′ē əs) *adj.* injuring or likely to injure; harmful

in·ju·ry (in′jə rē) *n., pl.* -ries ⟦< L *in-*, not + *jus*, right⟧ **1** harm or damage **2** an injurious act

in·jus·tice (in jus′tis) *n.* **1** a being unjust **2** an unjust act; wrong

ink (iŋk) *n.* ⟦< Gr *en-*, in + *kaiein*, to burn⟧ **1** a colored liquid used for writing, printing, etc. **2** a dark, liquid secretion ejected by cuttlefish, squid, etc. —*vt.* to cover, mark, or color with ink

ink′blot′ *n.* any of the patterns made by blots of ink that are used in the RORSCHACH TEST

ink·ling (iŋk′liŋ′) *n.* ⟦ME *ingkiling*⟧ **1** a hint **2** a vague notion

ink′well′ *n.* a container for ink

ink′y *adj.* -i·er, -i·est **1** like ink in color; dark; black **2** covered with ink —ink′i·ness *n.*

in·laid (in′lād′, in lād′) *adj.* set into a surface or formed, decorated, etc. by inlaying

in·land (in′lənd; *for n. & adv.*, -land′, -lənd) *adj.* of or in the interior of a region —*n.* an inland region —*adv.* into or toward this region

in-law (in′lô′) *n.* ⟦< *mother-* (or *father-*, etc.) *in-law*⟧ [Inf.] a relative by marriage

in·lay (in′lā′, in lā′; *for n.* in′lā′) *vt.* -laid′, -lay′ing **1** to set (pieces of wood, etc.) into a surface, specif. for decoration **2** to decorate thus —*n., pl.* -lays′ **1** inlaid decoration or material **2** a shaped filling, as of gold, cemented into the cavity of a tooth

in·let (in′let′) *n.* a narrow strip of water extending into a body of land

in′-line′ skate a kind of roller skate with its wheels in a line from toe to heel

in·mate (in′māt′) *n.* a person confined with others in a prison or mental institution

in·most (in′mōst′) *adj.* INNERMOST

inn (in) *n.* ⟦OE⟧ **1** a hotel or motel **2** a restaurant or tavern: now usually only in the names of such places

in·nards (in′ərdz) *pl.n.* ⟦< INWARDS⟧ [Inf. or Dial.] the inner organs or parts

in·nate (i nāt′, in′āt′) *adj.* ⟦< L *in-*, in + *nasci*, be born⟧ inborn; natural

in·ner (in′ər) *adj.* **1** farther within **2** of the mind or spirit *[inner* peace*]* **3** more secret

inner circle the small, exclusive, most influential part of a group

inner city the central sections of a large city, esp. when crowded or run-down

inner ear the part of the ear consisting of the semicircular canals, vestibule, and cochlea

in′ner·most′ *adj.* **1** farthest within **2** most secret

in′ner·sole′ *n.* INSOLE

in′ner·spring′ mattress a mattress with built-in coil springs

in·ning (in′iŋ) *n.* ⟦< OE *innung*, getting in⟧ *[pl. for Cricket] Baseball, Cricket* **1** a team's turn at bat **2** a numbered round of play in which both teams have a turn at bat

inn′keep′er *n.* the owner of an inn

in·no·cent (in′ə sənt) *adj.* ⟦< L *in-*, not + *nocere*, to harm⟧ **1** free from sin, evil, etc.; specif., not guilty of a specific crime **2** harmless **3** knowing no evil **4** without guile —*n.* an innocent person, as a child —in′no·cence *n.* —in′no·cent·ly *adv.*

in·noc·u·ous (i näk′yoo əs) *adj.* ⟦see prec.⟧ **1** harmless **2** not controversial or offensive —in·noc′u·ous·ly *adv.* —in·noc′u·ous·ness *n.*

in·no·va·tion (in′ə vā′shən) *n.* ⟦< L *in-*, in + *novus*, new⟧ **1** the process of introducing new methods, devices, etc. **2** a new method, custom, device, etc. —in′no·vate′, -vat′ed, -vat′ing, *vi., vt.* —in′no·va′tive *adj.* —in′no·va′tor *n.*

in·nu·en·do (in′yoo en′dō) *n., pl.* -does or -dos ⟦< L *in-*, in + *-nuere*, to nod⟧ a hint or sly remark, usually derogatory; insinuation

in·nu·mer·a·ble (i noo′mer ə bəl) *adj.* too numerous to be counted

THESAURUS

initially *a.* at first, in the beginning, originally; see FIRST.

initiate *v.* open, start, inaugurate; see BEGIN 1.

initiated *a.* **1** [Introduced into] sponsored, originated, entered, brought into, admitted, put into, instituted; see also PROPOSED. **2** [Having undergone initiation] installed, inducted, confirmed, grounded, instructed, approved, admitted, passed, made part of, made a member of, received, introduced, acknowledged, accepted, drafted, called up.

initiation *n.* baptism, induction, indoctrination; see INTRODUCTION 3.

initiative *n.* action, enterprise, first step; see RESPONSIBILITY 1.

inject *v.* inoculate, introduce, mainline*; see VACCINATE.

injection *n.* dose, vaccination, inoculation; see TREATMENT 2.

injure *v.* harm, damage, wound; see HURT 1.

injured *a.* spoiled, damaged, harmed; see HURT, WOUNDED.

injurious *a.* detrimental, damaging, bad; see DANGEROUS, DEADLY, HARMFUL, POISONOUS.

injury *n.* harm, sprain, damage, mutilation, blemish, cut, gash, twinge, contusion, puncture, break, scrape, scratch, stab, impairment, bite, fracture, hemorrhage, sting, bruise, sore, cramp, trauma, abrasion, burn, lesion, swelling, wound, scar, laceration, affliction, deformation; see also PAIN 1.

injustice *n.* wrongdoing, malpractice, offense, crime, villainy, injury, unfairness, miscarriage of justice, infringement, violation, abuse, criminal negligence, transgression, grievance, inequality, tort, outrage, maltreatment, bum rap*, breach, damage, infraction, a crying shame*; see also EVIL 1, WRONG.—*Ant.* RIGHT, just decision, fairness.

ink *n.* dye, paint, watercolor; see COLOR.

inkling *n.* indication, clue, suspicion; see HINT, SUGGESTION 1.

inland *a.* toward the interior, backcountry, backland, hinterland, interior, midland, provincial, domestic, inward; see also CENTRAL.—*Ant.* FOREIGN, international, outlying.

inmate *n.* patient, convict, captive; see PRISONER.

inn *n.* tavern, hostel, bed-and-breakfast; see BAR 2, HOTEL, MOTEL, RESORT 2.

inner *a.* innate, inherent, essential, inward, internal, interior, inside, nuclear, central, spiritual, private, personal, inmost, intimate, subconscious, intrinsic, deep-seated, deep-rooted, intuitive.—*Ant.* OUTER, surface, external.

innocence *n.* **1** [Freedom from guilt] guiltlessness, blamelessness, integrity, clear conscience, faultlessness, clean hands*; see also HONESTY.—*Ant.* GUILT, culpability, dishonesty. **2** [Freedom from guile] frankness, candidness, sincerity, plainness, forthrightness, inoffensiveness; see also SIMPLICITY 1. **3** [Lack of experience] purity, virginity, naiveté; see CHASTITY, IGNORANCE, VIRTUE 1.

innocent *a.* **1** [Guiltless] blameless, not guilty, impeccable, faultless, safe, upright, free of guilt, uninvolved, above suspicion, clean*; see also HONEST 1.—*Ant.* GUILTY, culpable, blameworthy. **2** [Without guile] open, fresh, guileless; see FRANK, CHILDISH, NAIVE, NATURAL 3, SIMPLE 1. **3** [Morally pure] sinless, unblemished, pure, unsullied, undefiled, spotless, wholesome, upright, unimpeachable, clean, virtuous, virginal, immaculate, impeccable, righteous, uncorrupted, irreproachable, stainless, unstained, moral, angelic.—*Ant.* DISHONEST, sinful, corrupt. **4** [Harmless] innocuous, powerless, inoffensive; see HARMLESS, SAFE 1.

innocently *a.* without guilt, with good intentions, ignorantly, with the best of intentions; see also POLITELY.

innovation *n.* modernization, alteration, addition; see CHANGE 1.

innuendo *n.* aside, intimation, insinuation; see HINT, SUGGESTION 1.

in·oc·u·late (i näk′yə lāt′) ***vt.*** **-lat′ed, -lat′ing** ⟦< L *in-*, in + *oculus*, eye⟧ to inject a serum, vaccine, etc. into, esp. in order to create immunity —**in·oc′u·la′tion** ***n.***

in·of·fen·sive (in′ə fen′siv) ***adj.*** causing no harm or annoyance; not objectionable —**in′of·fen′sive·ly** ***adv.***

in·op·er·a·ble (in äp′ər ə bəl) ***adj.*** not operable; specif., incapable of being treated by surgery

in·op·er·a·tive (in äp′ər ə tiv, -ər āt′iv) ***adj.*** not working or functioning

in·or·di·nate (in ôrd′′n it) ***adj.*** ⟦ult. < L *in-*, not + *ordo*, order⟧ excessive; immoderate —**in·or′di·nate·ly** ***adv.***

in·or·gan·ic (in′ôr gan′ik) ***adj.*** not organic; specif., designating or of matter not animal or vegetable; not living

in·pa·tient (in′pā′shənt) ***n.*** a patient who stays in a hospital, etc. while receiving treatment

in·put (in′poot′) ***n.*** **1** what is put in; specif., *a)* power put into a machine, etc. *b)* data or programs entered into a computer **2** opinion; advice —***vt.*** **-put′, -put′ting** to enter (data) into a computer —**in′put′ter** ***n.***

in·quest (in′kwest′) ***n.*** ⟦see INQUIRE⟧ a judicial inquiry, esp. before a jury, as a coroner's investigation of a death

in·qui·e·tude (in kwī′ə tood′) ***n.*** restlessness; uneasiness

in·quire (in kwīr′) ***vi.*** **-quired′, -quir′ing** ⟦< L *in-*, into + *quaerere*, seek⟧ **1** to ask a question or questions **2** to investigate: usually with *into* —***vt.*** to seek information about —**in·quir′er** ***n.***

in·quir·y (in′kwər ē, in kwīr′ē) ***n.***, *pl.* **-ies** **1** an inquiring; investigation **2** a question

in·qui·si·tion (in′kwə zish′ən) ***n.*** **1** an investigation or inquest **2** [I-] *R.C.Ch.* the tribunal established in the 13th c. for suppressing heresy and heretics **3** any relentless questioning or harsh suppression —**in·quis·i·tor** (in kwiz′ə tər) ***n.***

in·quis·i·tive (in kwiz′ə tiv) ***adj.*** **1** inclined to ask many questions **2** unnecessarily curious; prying —**in·quis′i·tive·ness** ***n.***

in re (in rē′, -rā′) ⟦L⟧ in the matter (of)

-in-res′i·dence *combining form* appointed to work at, and usually residing at, an institution, as a college, for a certain period

in·road (in′rōd′) ***n.*** an encroachment: usually used in plural

ins *abbrev.* insurance

in·sane (in sān′) ***adj.*** **1** not sane; mentally ill or deranged **2** of or for insane people **3** very foolish, extravagant, etc. —**in·sane′ly** ***adv.*** —**in·san′i·ty** (-san′ə tē) ***n.***

in·sa·ti·a·ble (in sā′shə bəl, -shē ə bəl) ***adj.*** ⟦see IN-[2] & SATIATE⟧ that cannot be satisfied —**in·sa′ti·a·bil′i·ty** ***n.*** —**in·sa′ti·a·bly** ***adv.***

in·scribe (in skrīb′) ***vt.*** **-scribed′, -scrib′ing** ⟦< L *in-*, in + *scribere*, write⟧ **1** to mark or engrave (words, etc.) on (a surface) **2** *a)* to dedicate (a book, etc.) to someone *b)* to autograph **3** to fix in the mind —**in·scrip′tion** (-skrip′shən) ***n.***

in·scru·ta·ble (in skroot′ə bəl) ***adj.*** ⟦< L *in-*, not + *scrutari*, examine⟧ not easily understood; enigmatic —**in·scru′ta·bly** ***adv.***

in·seam (in′sēm′) ***n.*** an inner seam; specif., the seam from the crotch to the bottom of a trouser leg

in·sect (in′sekt′) ***n.*** ⟦< L *insectum*, lit., notched⟧ any of a large class of small, usually winged, invertebrates, as beetles, flies, or wasps, having three pairs of legs

in·sec·ti·cide (in sek′tə sīd′) ***n.*** any substance used to kill insects —**in·sec′ti·ci′dal** ***adj.***

in·sec·ti·vore (in sek′tə vôr′) ***n.*** ⟦see fol.⟧ any of various small mammals, as moles and shrews, that are active mainly at night and that feed principally on insects

in·sec·tiv·o·rous (in′sek tiv′ə rəs) ***adj.*** ⟦< INSECT + L *vorare*, devour⟧ feeding chiefly on insects

in·se·cure (in′si kyoor′) ***adj.*** **1** not safe from danger **2** feeling anxiety **3** not firm or dependable —**in′se·cure′ly** ***adv.*** —**in′se·cu′ri·ty**, *pl.* **-ties**, ***n.***

in·sem·i·nate (in sem′ə nāt′) ***vt.*** **-nat′ed, -nat′ing** ⟦< L *in-*, in + *semen*, seed⟧ **1** to sow seeds in; esp., to impregnate **2** to imbue (with ideas, etc.) —**in·sem′i·na′tion** ***n.***

in·sen·sate (in sen′sāt′, -sit) ***adj.*** **1** not feeling sensation **2** foolish **3** cold; insensitive

in·sen·si·ble (in sen′sə bəl) ***adj.*** **1** unable to perceive with the senses **2** unconscious **3** unaware; indifferent **4** so small as to be virtually imperceptible —**in·sen′si·bil′i·ty** ***n.***

in·sen′si·tive (-sə tiv) ***adj.*** **1** not sensitive; not responsive **2** tactless —**in·sen′si·tive·ly** ***adv.*** —**in·sen′si·tiv′i·ty** ***n.***

in·sen·tient (in sen′shənt, -shē ənt) ***adj.*** not sentient; not having life, consciousness, or feeling —**in·sen′tience** ***n.***

in·sert (in surt′; *for n.* in′surt′) ***vt.*** ⟦< L *in-*, in + *serere*, join⟧ to put or fit (something) into something else —***n.*** anything inserted or for insertion —**in·ser′tion** ***n.***

in·set (in set′; *for n.* in′set′) ***vt.*** **-set′, -set′ting** to set in; insert —***n.*** something inserted

in·shore (in′shôr′, in shôr′) ***adv.***, ***adj.*** in, near, or toward the shore

in·side (in′sīd′, in′sīd′, in sīd′) ***n.*** **1** the inner side, surface, or part **2** [*pl.*] [Inf.] the internal organs of the body —***adj.*** **1** internal **2** known only to insiders; secret —***adv.*** **1** on or to the inside; within **2** indoors —***prep.*** in or within —**inside of** within the space or time of —**inside out** **1** reversed **2** [Inf.] thoroughly

in·sid·er (in′sīd′ər, in sīd′ər) ***n.*** **1** one inside a given place or group **2** one having secret or confidential information

in·sid·i·ous (in sid′ē əs) ***adj.*** ⟦< L *insidiae*, an ambush⟧ **1** characterized by treachery or slyness **2** more dangerous than seems evident

THESAURUS

inoculate ***v.*** immunize, inject, vaccinate; see TREAT 3.

inoculation ***n.*** vaccination, injection, shot; see TREATMENT 2.

inoffensive ***a.*** innocuous, pleasant, peaceable; see CALM 1, FRIENDLY.

input ***n.*** information, knowledge, facts; see DATA.

inquire ***v.*** make an inquiry, probe, interrogate; see ASK, QUESTION.

inquiry ***n.*** probe, analysis, hearing; see EXAMINATION.

inquisitive ***a.*** curious, inquiring, speculative, questioning, meddling, searching, probing, intrusive, challenging, analytical, scrutinizing, prying, presumptuous, impertinent, snoopy*, nosy*; see also INTERESTED 1.—*Ant.* INDIFFERENT, unconcerned, aloof.

insane ***a.*** **1** [Deranged] crazy, crazed, wild, raging, frenzied, lunatic, balmy, schizophrenic, psychotic, psychopathic, delusional, paranoid, maniacal, raving, demented, rabid, unhinged, mentally unsound, mentally ill, suffering from hallucinations, daft, possessed, stark mad, out of one's mind, obsessed, touched, cracked*, screwy*, nutty*, nuts*, schizo*, loco*, wacko*, wacky*, haywire*, batty*, bonkers*, unglued*, off one's rocker*, not all there*; see also SICK.—*Ant.* SANE, rational, sensible. **2** [Utterly foolish] madcap, daft, idiotic; see STUPID.

insanely ***a.*** furiously, psychopathically, fiercely; see CRAZILY, VIOLENTLY, WILDLY.

insanity ***n.*** mental derangement, delusions, hysteria, obsession, compulsion, madness, dementia, lunacy, psychosis, neurosis, phobia, mania.—*Ant.* SANITY, reason, normality.

inscription ***n.*** engraving, epitaph, legend; see WRITING 2.

insect ***n.*** bug, beetle, mite, vermin, arthropod, cootie*; see also PEST 1. *Creatures commonly called insects include the following:* spider, ant, bee, flea, fly, mosquito, gnat, silverfish, hornet, leafhopper, squash bug, earwig, mayfly, walking stick, dragonfly, termite, cicada, aphid, mantis, beetle, butterfly, moth, wasp, locust, bedbug, caterpillar, grasshopper, cricket, bumblebee, honeybee, cockroach, potato bug, corn borer, ladybug, boll weevil, stinkbug, firefly, Japanese beetle, yellow jacket; see also FLY 1, SPIDER.

insecticide ***n.*** bug spray*, insect poison, pesticide; see POISON.

insecure ***a.*** anxious, vague, uncertain; see TROUBLED.

insecurity ***n.*** **1** [Anxiety] vacillation, indecision, instability; see DOUBT, UNCERTAINTY 2. **2** [Danger] risk, hazard, vulnerability; see CHANCE 1, DANGER.

inseparable ***a.*** indivisible, as one, tied up, intertwined, integrated, integral, interwoven, entwined, whole, connected, attached, conjoined, united; see also JOINED, UNIFIED.—*Ant.* DIVISIBLE, separable, apart.

insert ***n.*** supplement, advertisement, new material; see ADDITION 1.

insert ***v.*** introduce, inject, place inside; see INCLUDE 2.

inserted ***a.*** introduced, added, stuck in; see INCLUDED.

insertion ***n.*** insert, injection, inclusion; see ADDITION 1.

inside ***a.*** **1** [Within] inner, in, within the boundaries of, bounded, surrounded by; see also INNER, UNDER.—*Ant.* BEYOND, after, outside. **2** [Within doors] indoors, under a roof, in the privacy of one's own home, out of the open, behind closed doors, under a shelter; see also WITHIN.—*Ant.* OUTSIDE, out-of-doors, in the open.

inside ***n.*** inner wall, sheathing, plaster, facing, stuffing, wadding; see also LINING.

insides ***n.*** interior, inner portion, bowels, recesses, belly, gut, womb, heart, soul, breast; see also CENTER 1, STOMACH.

in·sight (in′sīt′) ***n.*** **1** the ability to see and understand clearly the inner nature of things, esp. by intuition **2** an instance of such understanding

in·sig·ni·a (in sig′nē ə) ***pl.n.***, *sing.* **in·sig′ne** (-nē) ⟦ult. < L *in-*, in + *signum*, a mark⟧ badges, emblems, or distinguishing marks, as of rank or membership —***sing.n.***, *pl.* **in·sig′ni·as** such a badge, etc.

in·sin·cere (in′sin sir′) ***adj.*** not sincere; deceptive or hypocritical —**in′sin·cere′ly** ***adv.*** —**in′sin·cer′i·ty** (-ser′ə tē), *pl.* **-ties**, ***n.***

in·sin·u·ate (in sin′yo͞o āt′) ***vt.*** **-at′ed, -at′ing** ⟦< L *in-*, in + *sinus*, a curve⟧ **1** to introduce or work into gradually, indirectly, etc. **2** to hint or suggest indirectly; imply —**in·sin′u·a′tion** ***n.*** —**in·sin′u·a′tive** ***adj.*** —**in·sin′u·a′tor** ***n.***

in·sip·id (in sip′id) ***adj.*** ⟦< L *in-*, not + *sapidus*, savory⟧ **1** without flavor; tasteless **2** not exciting or interesting; dull

in·sist (in sist′) ***vi.*** ⟦< L *in-*, in, on + *sistere*, to stand⟧ to take and maintain a stand: often with *on* or *upon* —***vt.*** **1** to demand strongly **2** to declare firmly —**in·sist′ing·ly** ***adv.***

in·sist′ent ***adj.*** insisting; persistent —**in·sist′ence** ***n.*** —**in·sist′ent·ly** ***adv.***

in si·tu (in sī′to͞o′) ⟦L⟧ in position; in its original place

in·so·far (in′sō fär′) ***adv.*** to such a degree or extent: usually with *as*

in·sole (in′sōl′) ***n.*** **1** the inside sole of a shoe **2** a removable inside sole put in for comfort

in·so·lent (in′sə lənt) ***adj.*** ⟦< L *in-*, not + *solere*, be accustomed⟧ boldly disrespectful; impudent —**in′so·lence** ***n.***

in·sol·u·ble (in säl′yə bəl) ***adj.*** **1** that cannot be solved **2** that cannot be dissolved —**in·sol′u·bil′i·ty** ***n.***

in·sol·vent (in säl′vənt) ***adj.*** not solvent; unable to pay debts; bankrupt —**in·sol′ven·cy** ***n.***

in·som·ni·a (in säm′nē ə) ***n.*** ⟦< L *in-*, without + *somnus*, sleep⟧ abnormal inability to sleep —**in·som′ni·ac′** (-ak′) ***n., adj.***

in·so·much (in′sō much′) ***adv.*** **1** to such a degree or extent; so: with *that* **2** inasmuch (*as*)

in·sou·ci·ant (in so͞o′sē ənt) ***adj.*** ⟦Fr < *in-*, not + *soucier*, to care⟧ calm and untroubled; carefree

in·spect (in spekt′) ***vt.*** ⟦< L *in-*, at + *specere*, look at⟧ **1** to look at carefully **2** to examine or review officially —**in·spec′tion** ***n.***

in·spec′tor ***n.*** **1** one who inspects **2** an officer on a police force, ranking next below a superintendent or police chief

in·spi·ra·tion (in′spə rā′shən) ***n.*** **1** an inspiring or being inspired mentally or emotionally **2** *a)* any stimulus to creative thought or action *b)* an inspired idea, action, etc. —**in′spi·ra′tion·al** ***adj.***

in·spire (in spīr′) ***vt.*** **-spired′, -spir′ing** ⟦< L *in-*, in, on + *spirare*, breathe⟧ **1** to inhale **2** to stimulate or impel, as to some creative effort **3** to motivate as by divine influence **4** to arouse (a thought or feeling) in (someone) **5** to occasion or cause —***vi.*** **1** to inhale **2** to give inspiration

in·spir·it (in spir′it) ***vt.*** to put spirit into; cheer; hearten

inst *abbrev.* **1** institute **2** institution

in·sta·bil·i·ty (in′stə bil′ə tē) ***n.*** lack of firmness, determination, etc.

in·stall or **in·stal** (in stôl′) ***vt.*** **-stalled′, -stall′ing** ⟦< ML *in-*, in + *stallum*, a place⟧ **1** to place in an office, rank, etc., with ceremony **2** to establish in a place **3** to fix in position for use *[to install new fixtures]* —**in·stal·la·tion** (in′stə lā′shən) ***n.*** —**in·stall′er** ***n.***

in·stall′ment or **in·stal′ment** ***n.*** **1** an installing or being installed **2** any of the parts of a sum of money to be paid at regular specified times **3** any of several parts, as of a serial

installment plan a credit system by which debts, as for purchased articles, are paid in installments

in·stance (in′stəns) ***n.*** ⟦see fol.⟧ **1** an example; case **2** a step in proceeding; occasion *[in the first instance]* —***vt.*** **-stanced, -stanc·ing** to give as an example; cite —**at the instance of** at the suggestion or instigation of

in·stant (in′stənt) ***adj.*** ⟦< L *in-*, in, upon + *stare*, to stand⟧ **1** immediate **2** soluble, concentrated, or precooked for quick preparation: said of a food or beverage —***n.*** **1** a moment **2** a particular moment —**the instant** as soon as

in·stan·ta·ne·ous (in′stən tā′nē əs) ***adj.*** done or happening in an instant —**in′stan·ta′ne·ous·ly** ***adv.***

in·stan·ter (in stan′tər) ***adv.*** ⟦L⟧ *Law* immediately

in′stant·ly ***adv.*** immediately

in·state (in stāt′) ***vt.*** **-stat′ed, -stat′ing** ⟦IN-[1] + STATE⟧ to put in a particular position, rank, etc.; install

in·stead (in sted′) ***adv.*** ⟦IN[1] + STEAD⟧ in place of the one mentioned —**instead of** in place of

in·step (in′step′) ***n.*** the top surface of the foot, between the ankle and the toes

in·sti·gate (in′stə gāt′) ***vt.*** **-gat′ed, -gat′ing** ⟦< L *in-*, on + *-stigare*, to prick⟧ **1** to urge on to some action **2** to foment (rebellion, etc.) —**in′sti·ga′tion** ***n.*** —**in′sti·ga′tor** ***n.***

in·still or **in·stil** (in stil′) ***vt.*** **-stilled′, -still′ing** ⟦< L *in-*, in + *stilla*, a drop⟧ **1** to put in drop by drop **2** to put (an idea, etc.) *in* or *into* gradually

THESAURUS

insight ***n.*** intuition, acuteness, perspicacity; see JUDGMENT 1.

insignia ***n.*** ensign, logo, symbol; see EMBLEM.

insignificance ***n.*** unimportance, worthlessness, indifference, triviality, nothingness, smallness, pettiness, matter of no consequence, nothing to speak of, nothing particular, trifling matter, drop in the bucket*, molehill.

insignificant ***a.*** inconsequential, petty, trifling; see TRIVIAL, UNIMPORTANT.

insincere ***a.*** deceitful, pretentious, shifty; see DISHONEST, FALSE 1, HYPOCRITICAL, SLY.

insincerity ***n.*** deceit, treachery, mendacity; see DECEPTION, DISHONESTY, HYPOCRISY.

insinuate ***v.*** imply, suggest, purport; see HINT, MENTION, PROPOSE 1, REFER 2.

insinuation ***n.*** implication, veiled remark, innuendo; see HINT, SUGGESTION 1.

insistence ***n.*** persistence, perseverance, obstinacy; see DETERMINATION.

insistent ***a.*** persistent, obstinate, continuous; see STUBBORN.

insist upon ***v.*** expect, demand, order; see ASK.

insolvent ***a.*** bankrupt, failed, broke*; see RUINED 3.—*Ant.* RUNNING, solvent, in good condition.

inspect ***v.*** scrutinize, probe, investigate; see EXAMINE.

inspected ***a.*** tested, checked, authorized; see APPROVED, INVESTIGATED.

inspection ***n.*** inventory, investigation, inquiry; see EXAMINATION 1.

inspector ***n.*** police inspector, chief detective, investigating officer, customs officer, immigration inspector, government inspector, checker, FBI agent, narc*, postal inspector; see also POLICE OFFICER.

inspiration ***n.*** **1** [An idea] notion, hunch, whim; see FANCY 1, IMPULSE 2, THOUGHT 2. **2** [A stimulant to creative activity] stimulus, motivation, influence; see INCENTIVE.

inspire ***v.*** fire, be the cause of, start off, urge, stimulate, cause, put one in the mood, give one the idea for, motivate, give an impetus.

inspired ***a.*** roused, animated, motivated, stimulated, energized, stirred, excited, exhilarated, influenced, set going, started, activated, moved; see also ENCOURAGED.

inspiring ***a.*** illuminating, encouraging, revealing; see EXCITING, STIMULATING.

instability ***n.*** inconstancy, changeability, immaturity, variability, inconsistency, irregularity, imbalance, unsteadiness, restlessness, anxiety, fluctuation, alternation, disquiet, fitfulness, impermanence, transience, vacillation, hesitation, oscillation, volatility, flightiness, capriciousness, wavering, fickleness; see also CHANGE 1, UNCERTAINTY 2.

install ***v.*** set up, establish, build in, put in, place, invest, introduce, inaugurate, furnish with, fix up.

installation ***n.*** **1** [The act of installing] placing, induction, ordination, inauguration, launching, coronation, establishment. **2** [That which has been installed] machinery, wiring, lighting, insulation, power, operating system, heating system, furnishings, foundation, base.

installed ***a.*** set up, started, put in; see ESTABLISHED 1, FINISHED 1.

installment ***n.*** periodic payment, down payment, tranche; see PART 1, PAYMENT 1.

instance ***n.*** case, situation, occurrence; see EXAMPLE. —**for instance** as an example, by way of illustration, case in point; see FOR EXAMPLE.

instant ***n.*** short while, second, flash, split second, wink of the eye, jiffy*; see also MOMENT 1. —**on the instant** instantly, without delay, right now; see IMMEDIATELY.

instantly ***a.*** directly, at once, without delay; see IMMEDIATELY.

instead ***a.*** in place of, as a substitute, as an alternative, on second thought, in lieu of, on behalf of, alternatively; see also RATHER 2. —**instead of** rather than, in place of, as a substitute for, in lieu of, as an alternative for.

instill ***v.*** inject, infiltrate, inoculate, impregnate, inseminate, implant, inspire, impress, brainwash*, introduce, inculcate, indoctrinate, impart, insert, cultivate, imbue, put into someone's head*; see also TEACH.—*Ant.* REMOVE, draw out, extract.

in·stinct (in′stiŋkt′) ***n.*** ⟦< L *instinguere*, to impel⟧ **1** (an) inborn tendency to behave in a way characteristic of a species **2** a natural or acquired tendency; knack —**in·stinc′tive** ***adj.*** —**in·stinc′tu·al** ***adj.***

in·sti·tute (in′stə to͞ot′) ***vt.*** **-tut′ed**, **-tut′ing** ⟦< L *in-*, in, on + *statuere*, to cause to set up⟧ **1** to set up; establish **2** to start; initiate —***n.*** something instituted; specif., *a)* an organization for the promotion of art, science, etc. *b)* a school or college specializing in some field —**in′sti·tut′er** or **in′sti·tu′tor** ***n.***

in·sti·tu·tion (in′stə to͞o′shən) ***n.*** **1** an instituting or being instituted **2** an established law, custom, etc. **3** *a)* an organization having a public character, as a school, church, bank, or hospital *b)* the building housing it **4** a person or thing long established in a place —**in′sti·tu′tion·al** ***adj.***

in′sti·tu′tion·al·ize′ (-īz′) ***vt.*** **-ized′**, **-iz′ing** **1** to make into an institution **2** to place in an institution, as for treatment —**in′sti·tu′tion·al·i·za′tion** ***n.***

in·struct (in strukt′) ***vt.*** ⟦< L *in-*, in + *struere*, pile up⟧ **1** to teach; educate **2** to inform **3** to order or direct

in·struc′tion (-struk′shən) ***n.*** **1** an instructing; education **2** something taught **3** any of the steps to be followed, as in operating something: *usually used in pl.* —**in·struc′tion·al** ***adj.***

in·struc′tive ***adj.*** giving knowledge

in·struc′tor ***n.*** **1** a teacher **2** a college teacher of the lowest rank

in·stru·ment (in′strə mənt) ***n.*** ⟦see INSTRUCT⟧ **1** a thing by means of which something is done **2** a tool or implement **3** any of various devices for indicating, measuring, controlling, etc. **4** any of various devices producing musical sound **5** *Law* a formal document

in′stru·men′tal (-mənt′'l) ***adj.*** **1** serving as a means; helpful **2** of, performed on, or written for a musical instrument or instruments

in′stru·men′tal·ist ***n.*** a person who performs on a musical instrument

in′stru·men·tal′i·ty (-men′tal′ə tē) ***n.***, *pl.* **-ties** a means; agency

in′stru·men·ta′tion (-tā′shən) ***n.*** **1** the writing or scoring of music for instruments **2** the use of or an equipping with instruments

instrument flying the flying of an aircraft by the use of instruments only

in·sub·or·di·nate (in′sə bôrd′'n it) ***adj.*** not submitting to authority; disobedient —**in′sub·or′di·na′tion** ***n.***

in·sub·stan·tial (in′səb stan′shəl) ***adj.*** not substantial; specif., *a)* not real; imaginary *b)* weak or flimsy

in·suf·fer·a·ble (in suf′ər ə bəl) ***adj.*** intolerable; unbearable

in·su·lar (in′sə lər) ***adj.*** ⟦< L *insula*, island⟧ **1** of or like an island or islanders **2** narrow-minded; illiberal

in′su·late′ (-lāt′) ***vt.*** **-lat′ed**, **-lat′ing** ⟦< L *insula*, island⟧ **1** to set apart; isolate **2** to cover with a nonconducting material in order to prevent the escape of electricity, heat, sound, etc.

in′su·la′tion ***n.*** **1** an insulating or being insulated **2** material for this

in·su·lin (in′sə lin) ***n.*** ⟦< L *insula*, island⟧ **1** a hormone vital to carbohydrate metabolism, secreted by the islets of Langerhans **2** an extract from the pancreas of sheep, oxen, etc., used in the treatment of diabetes

insulin shock the abnormal condition caused by an excess of insulin: it is characterized by tremors, cold sweat, convulsions, and coma

in·sult (in sult′; *for n.* in′sult′) ***vt.*** ⟦< L *in-*, on + *salire*, to leap⟧ to subject to an act, remark, etc. meant to hurt the feelings or pride —***n.*** an insulting act, remark, etc.

in·su·per·a·ble (in so͞o′pər ə bəl) ***adj.*** ⟦< L *insuperabilis*⟧ that cannot be overcome

in·sup·port·a·ble (in′sə pôrt′ə bəl) ***adj.*** **1** intolerable; unbearable **2** incapable of being upheld, proved, etc.

in·sur·ance (in shoor′əns) ***n.*** **1** an insuring or being insured against loss **2** a contract (**insurance policy**) purchased to guarantee compensation for a specified loss by fire, death, etc. **3** the amount for which something is insured **4** the business of insuring against loss

in·sure (in shoor′) ***vt.*** **-sured′**, **-sur′ing** ⟦ME *ensuren*: see ENSURE⟧ **1** to take out or issue insurance on **2** ENSURE —**in·sur′a·ble** ***adj.***

in·sured′ ***n.*** a person whose life, property, etc. is insured against loss

in·sur′er ***n.*** a person or company that insures others against loss

in·sur′gence (-jəns) ***n.*** a rising in revolt; uprising: also **in·sur′gen·cy**, *pl.* **-cies**

in·sur·gent (in sur′jənt) ***adj.*** ⟦< L *in-*, upon + *surgere*, rise⟧ rising up against established authority —***n.*** an insurgent person

in·sur·rec·tion (in′sə rek′shən) ***n.*** ⟦see INSURGENT⟧ a rising up against established authority; rebellion —**in′sur·rec′tion·ist** ***n.***

int *abbrev.* **1** interest **2** interjection **3** international

in·tact (in takt′) ***adj.*** ⟦< L *in-*, not + *tactus*, touched⟧ unimpaired or uninjured; kept or left whole

in·ta·glio (in tal′yō′) ***n.***, *pl.* **-glios′** ⟦It < *in-*, in + *tagliare*, to cut⟧ a design carved or engraved below the surface

in·take (in′tāk′) ***n.*** **1** a taking in **2** the amount taken in **3** the place in a pipe, etc. where a fluid is taken in

in·tan·gi·ble (in tan′jə bəl) ***adj.*** **1** that cannot be touched; incorporeal **2** of certain business assets, esp. goodwill, having monetary value but no material being **3** that cannot be easily defined; vague —***n.*** something intangible

THESAURUS

instinct ***n.*** drive, sense, intuition; see FEELING 4.

instinctive ***a.*** spontaneous, reflex, normal; see NATURAL 2.

instinctively ***a.*** inherently, intuitively, by instinct; see NATURALLY 2.

institute ***v.*** found, organize, launch; see ESTABLISH 2.

institution ***n.*** system, company, association; see BUSINESS 4, OFFICE 3, UNIVERSITY.

institutionalize ***v.*** standardize, incorporate into a system, make official; see ORDER 3, REGULATE 2, SYSTEMATIZE.

instruct ***v.*** educate, give lessons, guide; see TEACH.

instructed ***a.*** advised, informed, told; see EDUCATED, LEARNED 1.

instruction ***n.*** guidance, preparation, direction; see EDUCATION 1.

instructions ***n.*** orders, plans, directive; see ADVICE, DIRECTIONS.

instructor ***n.*** professor, tutor, lecturer; see TEACHER.

instrument ***n.*** means, apparatus, implement; see CONTROL 2, DEVICE 1, MACHINE, TOOL 1.

instrumental ***a.*** partly responsible for, contributory, conducive; see EFFECTIVE, HELPFUL 1, NECESSARY.

insubordinate ***a.*** disobedient, dissident, defiant; see REBELLIOUS.

insubordination ***n.*** disobedience, defiance, disregard; see DISOBEDIENCE.

insubstantial ***a.*** petty, slight, inadequate; see FLIMSY, POOR 2.

insufficient ***a.*** skimpy, meager, thin; see INADEQUATE, UNSATISFACTORY.

insufficiently ***a.*** barely, incompletely, partly; see BADLY 1, INADEQUATELY.

insulate ***v.*** protect, coat, treat, apply insulation, tape up, glass in, pad, caulk, weatherstrip, paint.

insulation ***n.*** nonconductor, protector, covering, packing, lining, resistant material, weatherproofing, padding, caulking.

insult ***n.*** indignity, offense, affront, abuse, outrage, impudence, insolence, blasphemy, mockery, derision, impertinence, discourtesy, invective, disrespect, slight, slander, libel, slap in the face; see also RUDENESS.—*Ant.* PRAISE, tribute, homage.

insult ***v.*** revile, libel, offend, outrage, vilify, humiliate, mock, vex, tease, irritate, annoy, aggravate, provoke, taunt, ridicule, abuse, deride, jeer, step on one's toes; see also CURSE, SLANDER.

insulted ***a.*** slandered, libeled, reviled, disgraced, defamed, vilified, cursed, dishonored, mocked, ridiculed, jeered at, humiliated, mistreated, offended, hurt, outraged, affronted, slighted, shamed; see also HURT.—*Ant.* PRAISED, admired, extolled.

insulting ***a.*** outrageous, offensive, degrading, humiliating, debasing, embarrassing, humbling, deriding, contemptuous.—*Ant.* RESPECTFUL, complimentary, honoring.

insurance ***n.*** indemnity, assurance, warrant, backing, allowance, safeguard, protection, coverage, support, something to fall back on*; see also SECURITY 2.

insure ***v.*** warrant, protect, cover; see GUARANTEE.

insured ***a.*** safeguarded, defended, warranteed; see GUARANTEED, PROTECTED.

insurmountable ***a.*** unconquerable, unbeatable, hopeless; see IMPOSSIBLE.

insurrection ***n.*** riot, revolt, rebellion; see DISORDER, REVOLUTION 2.

intact ***a.*** together, entire, uninjured; see WHOLE 2.

intake ***n.*** **1** [Contraction] alteration, shortening, constriction; see ABBREVIATION, REDUCTION 1. **2** [Profit] harvest, gain, accumulation; see PROFIT 2.

intangible ***a.*** indefinite, unsure, hypothetical; see UNCERTAIN, VAGUE 2.

in·te·ger (in′tə jər) ***n.*** ⟦L, whole⟧ a whole number (e.g., 5, -10) or zero

in·te·gral (in′tə grəl; *often* in teg′rəl) ***adj.*** ⟦see prec.⟧ **1** necessary for completeness; essential **2** made up of parts forming a whole

in′te·grate′ (-grāt′) ***vt.***, ***vi.*** **-grat′ed**, **-grat′ing** ⟦< L *integer*, whole⟧ **1** to make or become whole or complete **2** to bring (parts) together into a whole **3** *a)* to remove barriers imposing segregation upon (racial groups) *b)* to abolish segregation in —**in′te·gra′tion** ***n.*** —**in′te·gra′tive** ***adj.***

integrated circuit an electronic circuit with many interconnected circuit elements formed on a single body, or chip, of semiconductor material

in·teg·ri·ty (in teg′rə tē) ***n.*** ⟦see INTEGER⟧ **1** completeness **2** unimpaired condition; soundness **3** honesty, sincerity, etc.

in·teg·u·ment (in teg′yoo mənt) ***n.*** ⟦< L *in-*, upon + *tegere*, to cover⟧ an outer covering; skin, shell, rind, etc.

in·tel·lect (in′tə lekt′) ***n.*** ⟦< L *inter-*, between + *legere*, choose⟧ **1** the ability to reason or understand **2** high intelligence **3** a very intelligent person

in·tel·lec·tu·al (in′tə lek′choo əl) ***adj.*** **1** of, involving, or appealing to the intellect **2** requiring intelligence **3** having intellectual interests or tastes **4** showing high intelligence —***n.*** one with intellectual interests or tastes —**in′tel·lec′tu·al·ly** ***adv.*** —**in′tel·lec′tu·al′i·ty** ***n.***

in′tel·lec′tu·al·ize′ (-īz′) ***vt.*** **-ized′**, **-iz′ing** to examine or interpret rationally, often without regard for emotional considerations

intellectual property something produced by the mind, the rights to which may be protected by a copyright, patent, etc.

in·tel·li·gence (in tel′ə jəns) ***n.*** ⟦see INTELLECT⟧ **1** *a)* the ability to learn or understand *b)* the ability to cope with a new situation **2** news or information **3** those engaged in gathering secret, esp. military, information

intelligence quotient *see* IQ

in·tel′li·gent (-jənt) ***adj.*** having or showing intelligence; clever, wise, etc. —**in·tel′li·gent·ly** ***adv.***

in·tel′li·gent′si·a (-jent′sē ə) ***pl.n.*** ⟦< Russ⟧ [*also with sing. v.*] intellectuals collectively

in·tel·li·gi·ble (in tel′i jə bəl) ***adj.*** that can be understood; clear —**in·tel′li·gi·bil′i·ty** ***n.*** —**in·tel′li·gi·bly** ***adv.***

in·tem·per·ate (in tem′pər it, -prit) ***adj.*** **1** not temperate or moderate; excessive **2** drinking too much alcoholic liquor —**in·tem′per·ance** ***n.***

in·tend (in tend′) ***vt.*** ⟦< L *in-*, at + *tendere*, to stretch⟧ **1** to plan; have in mind as a purpose **2** to mean (something) to be or be used (*for*) **3** to mean; signify

in·tend′ed ***n.*** [Inf.] one's prospective spouse; fiancé(e)

in·tense (in tens′) ***adj.*** ⟦see INTEND⟧ **1** very strong *[an intense light]* **2** strenuous; earnest *[intense thought]* **3** characterized by much action, strong emotion, etc. —**in·tense′ly** ***adv.***

in·ten·si·fy (in ten′sə fī′) ***vt.***, ***vi.*** **-fied′**, **-fy′ing** to make or become intense or more intense —**in·ten′si·fi·ca′tion** ***n.***

in·ten′si·ty ***n.***, *pl.* **-ties** **1** a being intense **2** great energy or vehemence, as of emotion **3** the amount of force or energy of heat, light, sound, etc.

in·ten′sive ***adj.*** **1** of or characterized by intensity; thorough **2** designating very attentive care given to critically ill patients **3** *Gram.* giving force or emphasis *["very" is an intensive adverb]* —***n.*** *Gram.* an intensive word, prefix, etc. —**in·ten′sive·ly** ***adv.*** —**in·ten′sive·ness** ***n.***

-in·ten′sive *combining form* intensively using or requiring large amounts of (a specified thing) *[energy-intensive]*

in·tent (in tent′) ***adj.*** ⟦see INTEND⟧ **1** firmly directed; earnest **2** having one's attention or purpose firmly fixed *[intent on going]* —***n.*** **1** an intending **2** something intended; purpose or meaning —**to all intents and purposes** in almost every respect; practically; virtually —**in·tent′ly** ***adv.*** —**in·tent′ness** ***n.***

in·ten·tion (in ten′shən) ***n.*** **1** determination to act in a specified way **2** anything intended; purpose

in·ten′tion·al ***adj.*** done purposely —**in·ten′tion·al·ly** ***adv.***

in·ter (in tur′) ***vt.*** **-terred′**, **-ter′ring** ⟦< L *in*, in + *terra*, earth⟧ to put (a dead body) into a grave or tomb; bury

inter- ⟦L⟧ *prefix* **1** between or among: the second element of the compound is singular in form *[interstate]* **2** with or on each other (or one another) *[interact]*

in·ter·act (in′tər akt′) ***vi.*** to act on one another —**in′ter·ac′tion** ***n.***

in′ter·ac′tive (-ak′tiv) ***adj.*** **1** acting on one another **2** designating or of programming or electronic equipment, as for TV, which allows viewers to participate, as by making a response **3** of or involving the continual exchange of information between the computer and the user at a video screen

in·ter·breed (in′tər brēd′, in′tər brēd′) ***vt.***, ***vi.*** **-bred′**, **-breed′ing** HYBRIDIZE

in′ter·cede′ (-sēd′) ***vi.*** **-ced′ed**, **-ced′ing** ⟦< L *inter-*, between + *cedere*, go⟧ **1** to plead or make a request in behalf of another **2** to mediate; intervene

in′ter·cept′ (-sept′) ***vt.*** ⟦< L *inter-*, between + *capere*, take⟧ **1** to seize or stop in its course *[to intercept a message]* **2** *Math.* to cut off or mark off between two points, lines, etc. —**in′ter·cep′tion** ***n.***

in′ter·ces′sion (-sesh′ən) ***n.*** an interceding; mediation or

THESAURUS

integrate ***v.*** unify, combine, desegregate; see MIX 1, UNITE.

integrated ***a.*** nonsegregated, not segregated, for both black and white, interracial, nonracial, for all races, diverse, multicultural, combined; see also FREE 1, 2, OPEN 3.

integration ***n.*** unification, combination, cooperation; see ALLIANCE 1, MIXTURE 1, UNION 1.

integrity ***n.*** uprightness, honor, probity; see HONESTY.

intellect ***n.*** intelligence, brain, mentality; see MIND 1.

intellectual ***a.*** mental, cerebral, rarefied; see INTELLIGENT, LEARNED 1.

intellectual ***n.*** genius, philosopher, academician, highbrow, member of the intelligentsia, egghead*, brain*, Einstein*; see also ARTIST, PHILOSOPHER, SCIENTIST, WRITER.

intelligence ***n.*** **1** [Understanding] perspicacity, discernment, comprehension; see JUDGMENT 1. **2** [Secret information] report, statistics, facts, inside information, classified information, info*; see also KNOWLEDGE 1, NEWS 1, SECRET. **3** [The mind] intellect, brain, mentality; see MIND 1.

intelligent ***a.*** clever, bright, exceptional, gifted, astute, smart, brilliant, perceptive, well-informed, resourceful, profound, penetrating, original, keen, imaginative, inventive, reasonable, capable, able, ingenious, knowledgeable, creative, responsible, understanding, alert, quick-witted, clear-headed, quick, sharp, witty, ready, perspicacious, calculating, comprehending, discerning, discriminating, knowing, intellectual, studious, contemplative, having a head on his or her shoulders*, talented, apt, wise, shrewd, smart as a whip*, on the ball*, on the beam*, not born yesterday*.—*Ant.* DULL, slow-minded, shallow.

intelligently ***a.*** skillfully, admirably, reasonably, logically, judiciously, capably, diligently, sharply, astutely, discerningly, knowingly, knowledgeably, farsightedly, sensibly, prudently, alertly, keenly, resourcefully, aptly, discriminatingly; see also EFFECTIVELY.—*Ant.* BADLY, foolishly, stupidly.

intelligible ***a.*** plain, clear, obvious; see UNDERSTANDABLE.

intend ***v.*** **1** [To propose] plan, purpose, aim, expect, be resolved, be determined to, aspire to, have in mind, hope to, contemplate, think, aim at, take into one's head. **2** [To destine for] design, mean, devote to, reserve, appoint, set apart, aim at, aim for; see also ASSIGN, DEDICATE. **3** [To mean] indicate, signify, denote; see MEAN 1.

intended ***a.*** designed, advised, expected, predetermined, calculated, dedicated, prearranged, predestined, meant; see also PLANNED, PROPOSED.

intense ***a.*** intensified, deep, profound, extraordinary, exceptional, heightened, marked, vivid, ardent, powerful, passionate, impassioned, diligent, hard, full, great, exaggerated, violent, excessive, acute, keen, piercing, cutting, bitter, severe, concentrated, intensive, forceful, sharp, biting, stinging, shrill, high-pitched, strenuous, fervent, earnest, zealous, vehement, harsh, strong, brilliant.

intensely ***a.*** deeply, profoundly, strongly; see VERY.

intensify ***v.*** heighten, sharpen, emphasize, augment, enhance; see also STRENGTHEN, INCREASE.

intensity ***n.*** strain, force, concentration, power, vehemence, passion, fervor, ardor, severity, acuteness, depth, deepness, forcefulness, high pitch, sharpness, emphasis, magnitude.

intensive ***a.*** accelerated, sped up, hard; see FAST 1, SEVERE 1, 2.

intention ***n.*** aim, end, plan; see PURPOSE 1.

intentional ***a.*** intended, meditated, prearranged; see DELIBERATE.

intentionally ***a.*** specifically, purposely, willfully; see DELIBERATELY.

intently ***a.*** hard, with concentration, keenly; see CLOSELY.

intercept ***v.*** cut off, stop, ambush, block, catch, take away, appropriate, hijack, head off; see also PREVENT.

interception ***n.*** seizing, stopping,

prayer in behalf of another —**in'ter·ces'sor** (-ses'ər) ***n.*** —**in'ter·ces'so·ry** ***adj.***

in·ter·change (in'tər chānj'; *for n.* in'tər chānj') ***vt.*** **-changed'**, **-chang'ing** **1** to give and take mutually; exchange **2** to put (each of two things) in the other's place **3** to alternate —***n.*** **1** an interchanging **2** a junction which allows movement of traffic between highways on different levels, as a cloverleaf —**in'ter·change'a·ble** ***adj.***

in'ter·col·le'gi·ate (-kə lē'jit) ***adj.*** between or among colleges and universities

in·ter·com (in'tər käm') ***n.*** a radio or telephone intercommunication system, as between rooms

in'ter·com·mu'ni·cate' (-kə myōō'ni kāt') ***vt.***, ***vi.*** **-cat'ed**, **-cat'ing** to communicate with or to one another —**in'ter·com·mu'ni·ca'tion** ***n.***

in'ter·con·nect' (-kə nekt') ***vt.***, ***vi.*** to connect or be connected with one another —**in'ter·con·nec'tion** ***n.***

in'ter·con'ti·nen'tal (-känt''n ent''l) ***adj.*** **1** between or among continents **2** able to travel from one continent to another: said as of a missile

in'ter·cos'tal (-käs'təl, -kôs'-) ***adj.*** between the ribs —***n.*** an intercostal muscle, etc.

in·ter·course (in'tər kôrs') ***n.*** ⟦see INTER- & COURSE⟧ **1** communication or dealings between or among people, countries, etc. **2** SEXUAL INTERCOURSE

in'ter·de·nom'i·na'tion·al (-dē näm'ə nā'shən əl) ***adj.*** between or among religious denominations

in'ter·de'part·men'tal (-dē'pärt ment''l) ***adj.*** between or among departments

in'ter·de·pend'ence (-dē pen'dəns) ***n.*** mutual dependence —**in'ter·de·pend'ent** ***adj.***

in·ter·dict (in'tər dikt'; *for n.* in'tər dikt') ***vt.*** ⟦< L *inter-*, between + *dicere*, speak⟧ **1** to prohibit (an action) **2** to restrain from doing or using something —***n.*** an official prohibition —**in'ter·dic'tion** ***n.***

in'ter·dis'ci·pli·nar'y (-dis'ə pli ner'ē) ***adj.*** involving two or more disciplines, or branches of learning

in·ter·est (in'trist; *for v., also,* -tə rest') ***n.*** ⟦< L *inter-*, between + *esse*, be⟧ **1** a right to, or a share in, something **2** anything in which one has a share **3** [*often pl.*] advantage; benefit **4** [*usually pl.*] those having a common concern or power in some industry, cause, etc. *[the steel interests]* **5** *a)* a feeling of concern, curiosity, etc. about something *b)* the power of causing this feeling *c)* something causing this feeling **6** *a)* money paid for the use of money *b)* the rate of such payment —***vt.*** **1** to involve or excite the interest or attention of **2** to cause to have an interest or take part in —**in the interest(s) of** for the sake of

in'ter·est·ed ***adj.*** **1** having an interest or share **2** influenced by personal interest; biased **3** feeling or showing interest

in'ter·est·ing ***adj.*** exciting curiosity or attention; of interest

in·ter·face (in'tər fās') ***n.*** **1** a plane forming the common boundary between two parts of matter or space **2** a point or means of interaction between two systems, groups, etc. —***vt.***, ***vi.*** **-faced'**, **-fac'ing** to interact with (another system, group, etc.)

in'ter·faith' (-fāth') ***adj.*** between or involving persons adhering to different religions

in·ter·fere (in'tər fir') ***vi.*** **-fered'**, **-fer'ing** ⟦ult. < L *inter-*, between + *ferire*, to strike⟧ **1** to clash; collide **2** *a)* to come in or between; intervene *b)* to meddle **3** to hinder an opposing player in any of various illegal ways —**interfere with** to hinder —**in'ter·fer'ence** ***n.***

in·ter·fer·on (in'tər fir'än') ***n.*** ⟦INTERFER(E) + *-on*, arbitrary suffix⟧ a cellular protein produced in response to infection by a virus and acting to inhibit viral growth

in'ter·gen'er·a'tion·al (-jen'ə rā'shə nəl) ***adj.*** of or involving persons of different generations

in·ter·im (in'tər im) ***n.*** ⟦< L *inter*, between⟧ the period of time between; meantime —***adj.*** temporary

in·te·ri·or (in tir'ē ər) ***adj.*** ⟦< L *inter*, between⟧ **1** situated within; inner **2** inland **3** private —***n.*** **1** the interior part, as of a building or country **2** the internal, or domestic, affairs of a country

interior decoration the art or business of decorating and furnishing the interiors of houses, offices, etc. —**interior decorator**

in·te'ri·or·ize' (-īz') ***vt.*** **-ized'**, **-iz'ing** to make (a concept, value, etc.) part of one's inner nature

interj *abbrev.* interjection

in·ter·ject (in'tər jekt') ***vt.*** ⟦< L *inter-*, between + *jacere*, to throw⟧ to throw in between; interrupt with; insert

in'ter·jec'tion (-jek'shən) ***n.*** **1** an interjecting **2** something interjected **3** *Gram.* an exclamation or other word(s) inserted into an utterance without grammatical connection to it

in'ter·lace' (-lās') ***vt.***, ***vi.*** **-laced'**, **-lac'ing** to lace or weave together

in'ter·lard' (-lärd') ***vt.*** ⟦see INTER- & LARD⟧ to intersperse; diversify *[to interlard a talk with quotations]*

in·ter·leu·kin (in'tər lōō'kin) ***n.*** any of several proteins derived from many cell types and affecting the activity of other cells, as in stimulating the growth of T cells

in'ter·line' (-līn') ***vt.*** **-lined'**, **-lin'ing** to put an inner lining under the ordinary lining of (a garment)

in'ter·lock' (-läk') ***vt.***, ***vi.*** to lock together; join with one another

in·ter·loc·u·to·ry (in'tər läk'yōō tôr'ē, -yə-) ***adj.*** *Law* not final *[an interlocutory divorce decree]*

in·ter·lop·er (in'tər lō'pər) ***n.*** ⟦INTER- + *-loper* < Du *lopen*, to run⟧ one who meddles

in·ter·lude (in'tər lōōd') ***n.*** ⟦< L *inter*, between + *ludus*, a play⟧ **1** anything that fills time between two events, as music between acts of a play **2** intervening time

in'ter·mar'ry (-mar'ē) ***vi.*** **-ried**, **-ry·ing** **1** to become connected by marriage: said of different clans, races, etc. **2** to marry: said of closely related persons —**in'ter·mar'riage** ***n.***

in'ter·me'di·ar'y (-mē'dē er'ē) ***adj.*** **1** acting as a go-between or mediator **2** intermediate —***n.***, *pl.* **-ar'ies** a go-between; mediator

in'ter·me'di·ate (-mē'dē it) ***adj.*** ⟦< L *inter-*, between + *medius*, middle⟧ **1** in the middle; in between **2** of an automobile larger than a compact but smaller than the standard size —***n.*** an intermediate automobile

in·ter·ment (in tur'mənt) ***n.*** the act of interring; burial

in·ter·mez·zo (in'tər met'sō') ***n.***, *pl.* **-zos'** or **-zi'** (-sē') ⟦It <

THESAURUS

interposing; see INTERFERENCE 1.

interchange ***n.*** **1** [The act of giving and receiving reciprocally] barter, trade, reciprocation; see EXCHANGE 1. **2** [A highway intersection] cloverleaf, intersection, off-ramp; see HIGHWAY, ROAD 1.

intercourse ***n.*** **1** [Communication] association, dealings, interchange; see COMMUNICATION. **2** [Sex act] coitus, coition, sexual relations; see COPULATION, SEX 4.

interest ***n.*** **1** [Concern] attention, curiosity, excitement; see ATTENTION. **2** [Advantage] profit, benefit, gain; see ADVANTAGE. **3** [Money charged for a loan, etc.] cost of borrowing, cost of money*, finance charges; see EXPENSE. —**in the interest(s) of** for the sake of, on behalf of, in order to promote; see FOR.

interest ***v.*** intrigue, amuse, please; see ENTERTAIN 1, FASCINATE.

interested ***a.*** **1** [Having one's interest aroused] stimulated, attentive, curious, drawn, touched, moved, affected, inspired, sympathetic to, responsive, struck, impressed, roused, awakened, stirred, open to suggestion, all for, all wrapped up in.—*Ant.* BORED, tired, annoyed. **2** [Concerned with or engaged in] occupied, engrossed, partial, prejudiced, biased, taken, obsessed with, absorbed in; see also INVOLVED.—*Ant.* INDIFFERENT, impartial, disinterested.

interesting ***a.*** pleasing, pleasurable, fine, satisfying, fascinating, arresting, engaging, readable, absorbing, compelling, riveting, stirring, affecting, exotic, unusual, impressive, attractive, captivating, enchanting, beautiful, inviting, winning, magnetic, delightful, amusing, genial, refreshing; see also EXCITING.—*Ant.* DULL, shallow, boring.

interfere ***v.*** intervene, interpose, interlope; see MEDDLE 1.

interference ***n.*** **1** [Taking forcible part in the affairs of others] meddling, interruption, prying, trespassing, tampering, barging in, back-seat driving; see also INTERRUPTION. **2** [That which obstructs] obstruction, check, obstacle; see BARRIER, RESTRAINT 2.

interior ***a.*** inner, internal, inward; see CENTRAL, INSIDE 2.

interior ***n.*** **1** [Inside] inner part, lining, heart; see CENTER 1, INSIDE. **2** [The inside of a building] rooms, halls, stairway, vestibule, lobby, chapel, choir, gallery, basement, inner sanctum, sanctum sanctorum.

interjection ***n.*** **1** [Insertion] interpolation, insinuation, inclusion; see ADDITION 1. **2** [Exclamation] utterance, ejaculation, exclamation; see CRY 1.

intermediate ***a.*** mean, between, medium, halfway, compromising, neutral, standard, median, moderate, average; see also CENTRAL, COMMON 1, MIDDLE.

L: see INTERMEDIATE] a short piece of music, as between parts of a composition

in·ter·mi·na·ble (in tur′mi nə bəl) ***adj.*** lasting, or seeming to last, forever; endless —**in·ter′mi·na·bly** ***adv.***

in·ter·min·gle (in′tər miŋ′gəl) ***vt.***, ***vi.*** **-gled**, **-gling** to mix together; mingle

in·ter·mis·sion (in′tər mish′ən) ***n.*** [< L *inter-*, between + *mittere*, send] an interval of time between periods of activity, as between acts of a play

in′ter·mit′tent (-mit′′nt) ***adj.*** [see prec.] stopping and starting at intervals; periodic

in·tern (in′turn′; *for vt.* in turn′, in′turn′) ***n.*** [< L *internus*, inward] **1** a doctor serving as assistant resident in a hospital generally just after graduation from medical school **2** a student, etc. doing supervised temporary work in a field to gain experience —***vi.*** to serve as an intern —***vt.*** to detain or confine (foreign persons, etc.), as during a war —**in·tern′ment** ***n.*** —**in′tern′ship′** ***n.***

in·ter·nal (in tur′nəl) ***adj.*** [< L *internus*] **1** of or on the inside; inner **2** to be taken inside the body *[internal* remedies*]* **3** intrinsic *[internal* evidence*]* **4** domestic *[internal* revenue*]* —**in·ter′nal·ly** ***adv.***

in·ter′nal-com·bus′tion engine an engine, as in an automobile, powered by the explosion of a fuel-and-air mixture within the cylinders

in·ter′nal·ize′ (-īz′) ***vt.*** **-ized′**, **-iz′ing** to make (others' ideas, etc.) a part of one's thinking —**in·ter′nal·i·za′tion** ***n.***

internal medicine the branch of medicine that deals with the diagnosis and nonsurgical treatment of diseases

internal revenue governmental income from taxes on income, profits, etc.

in·ter·na·tion·al (in′tər nash′ə nəl) ***adj.*** **1** between or among nations **2** concerned with the relations between nations **3** for the use of all nations **4** of or for people in various nations —**in′ter·na′tion·al·ize′**, **-ized′**, **-iz′ing**, ***vt.*** —**in′ter·na′tion·al·ly** ***adv.***

International Phonetic Alphabet a set of phonetic symbols for international use: each symbol represents a single human speech sound

in·ter·ne·cine (in′tər nē′sin) ***adj.*** [< L *inter-*, between + *necare*, kill] deadly or harmful to both sides of a group in a conflict

In·ter·net (in′tər net′) ***n.*** an extensive computer network linking thousands of smaller networks: also with *the*

in·tern·ist (in′turn′ist, in turn′ist) ***n.*** a doctor who specializes in INTERNAL MEDICINE

in·ter·of·fice (in′tər ôf′is) ***adj.*** between or among the offices of an organization

in′ter·per′son·al (-pur′sə nəl) ***adj.*** between persons *[interpersonal* relationships*]*

in′ter·plan′e·tar′y (-plan′ə ter′ē) ***adj.*** between planets

in′ter·play′ (-plā′) ***n.*** action, effect, or influence on each other or one another

in·ter·po·late (in tur′pə lāt′) ***vt.*** **-lat′ed**, **-lat′ing** [< L *inter-*, between + *polire*, to polish] **1** to change (a text, etc.) by inserting new material **2** to insert between or among others —**in·ter′po·la′tion** ***n.***

in·ter·pose (in′tər pōz′) ***vt.***, ***vi.*** **-posed′**, **-pos′ing** **1** to place or come between **2** to intervene (with) **3** to interrupt (with) —**in′ter·po·si′tion** (-pə zish′ən) ***n.***

in·ter·pret (in tur′prət) ***vt.*** [< L *interpres*, agent, broker] **1** to explain or translate **2** to construe *[to interpret* a silence as contempt*]* **3** to give one's own conception of (a work of art), as in performance or criticism —***vi.*** to explain or translate —**in·ter′pre·ta′tion** ***n.*** —**in·ter′pret·er** ***n.***

in·ter′pre·tive (-prə tiv) ***adj.*** that interprets; explanatory: also **in·ter′pre·ta′tive** (-tāt′iv)

in·ter·ra·cial (in′tər rā′shəl) ***adj.*** between, among, or for members of different races: also **in′ter·race′**

in′ter·re·late′ (-rē lāt′) ***vt.***, ***vi.*** **-lat′ed**, **-lat′ing** to make or be mutually related —**in′ter·re·lat′ed** ***adj.***

in·ter·ro·gate (in ter′ə gāt′) ***vi.***, ***vt.*** **-gat′ed**, **-gat′ing** [< L *inter-*, between + *rogare*, ask] to ask questions (of), esp. formally —**in·ter′ro·ga′tion** ***n.*** —**in·ter′ro·ga′tor** ***n.***

in·ter·rog·a·tive (in′tə räg′ə tiv) ***adj.*** asking a question: also **in′ter·rog′a·to′ry** (-ə tôr′ē)

in·ter·rupt (in′tə rupt′) ***vt.*** [< L *inter-*, between + *rumpere*, to break] **1** to break into (a discussion, etc.) or to break in upon (a speaker, worker, etc.) **2** to make a break in the continuity of —***vi.*** to interrupt an action, talk, etc. —**in′ter·rup′tion** ***n.***

in·ter·scho·las·tic (in′tər skə las′tik) ***adj.*** between or among schools

in·ter·sect (in′tər sekt′) ***vt.*** [< L *inter-*, between + *secare*, to cut] to divide into two parts by passing through or across —***vi.*** to cross each other

in′ter·sec′tion (-sek′shən) ***n.*** **1** an intersecting **2** the place where two lines, roads, etc. meet

in′ter·serv′ice (-sur′vis) ***adj.*** between or among branches of the armed forces

in′ter·ses′sion (-sesh′ən) ***n.*** a short session between regular sessions of a college year, for concentrating on specialized projects

in·ter·sperse (in′tər spurs′) ***vt.*** **-spersed′**, **-spers′ing** [< L *inter-*, among + *spargere*, scatter] **1** to put here and there; scatter **2** to vary with things scattered here and there

in′ter·state′ (-stāt′) ***adj.*** between or among states, esp. of the U.S. —***n.*** one of a network of U.S. highways

in′ter·stel′lar (-stel′ər) ***adj.*** between or among the stars

in·ter·stice (in tur′stis) ***n.***, *pl.* **-sti·ces′** (-stə siz′, -sēz′) [< L *inter-*, between + *sistere*, to set] a crack; crevice

in′ter·twine′ (-twīn′) ***vt.***, ***vi.*** **-twined′**, **-twin′ing** to twine together

in′ter·ur′ban (-ur′bən) ***adj.*** between cities or towns —***n.*** an interurban railway, etc.

in·ter·val (in′tər vəl) ***n.*** [< L *inter-*, between + *vallum*, wall] **1** a space between things; gap **2** the time between events **3** the difference in pitch between two tones —**at intervals** **1** once in a while **2** here and there

in·ter·vene (in′tər vēn′) ***vi.*** **-vened′**, **-ven′ing** [< L *inter-*, between + *venire*, come] **1** to come or be between **2** to occur between two events, etc. **3** to come between to modify, settle, or hinder some action, etc.

in′ter·ven′tion (-ven′shən) ***n.*** **1** an intervening **2** interference, esp. of one country in the affairs of another

THESAURUS

intermission ***n.*** interim, break, interlude; see PAUSE, RECESS 1.

intermittent ***a.*** periodic, coming and going, recurrent; see CHANGING, IRREGULAR 1.

internal ***a.*** **1** [Within] inside, inward, interior, private, intrinsic, innate, inherent, under the surface, intimate, subjective, enclosed, circumscribed; see also INNER.—*Ant.* OUTER, external, outward. **2** [Within the body] intestinal, physiological, physical, neurological, abdominal, visceral.—*Ant.* FOREIGN, alien, external.

internally ***a.*** within, beneath the surface, inwardly, deep down, spiritually, mentally, invisibly, out of sight; see also INSIDE 1, WITHIN.

international ***a.*** worldwide, global, worldly, world, intercontinental, between nations, all over the world, universal, all-embracing, foreign, cosmopolitan; see also UNIVERSAL 3.—*Ant.* DOMESTIC, national, internal.

internationally ***a.*** cooperatively, globally, universally, around the world, not provincial; see also ABROAD, EVERYWHERE.

interpret ***v.*** give one's impression of, render, play, perform, depict, delineate, enact, portray, make sense of, read into, improvise on, reenact, mimic, gather from, view as, give one an idea about, make something of*; see also DEFINE, DESCRIBE.

interpretation ***n.*** account, rendition, exposition, statement, diagnosis, description, representation, definition, presentation, argument, answer, solution, take*; see also EXPLANATION.

interpreter ***n.*** commentator, writer, journalist, talking head, member of the chattering classes, artist, editor, reviewer, biographer, analyst, scholar, spokesman, delegate, speaker, exponent, demonstrator, philosopher, professor, translator, linguist, language expert.

interrogate ***v.*** cross-examine, grill, give the third degree*; see EXAMINE, QUESTION.

interrogation ***n.*** inquiry, query, investigation; see EXAMINATION 1.

interrupt ***v.*** intrude, intervene, cut in on, break into, interfere, infringe, cut off, break someone's train of thought, come between, butt in*, burst in.

interrupted ***a.*** stopped, checked, held up, obstructed, delayed, interfered with, disordered, hindered, suspended, cut short.

interruption ***n.*** check, break, gap, hiatus, suspension, intrusion, obstruction; see also DELAY, INTERFERENCE 1.

intersect ***v.*** cut across, come together, run through; see DIVIDE.

interstate ***a.*** between two states, among the states, national; see NATIONAL 2.

interval ***n.*** period, interlude, interim; see PAUSE.

intervene ***v.*** step in, intercede, mediate; see NEGOTIATE 1, RECONCILE 2.

intervention ***n.*** **1** [The act of intervening] intercession, interruption, breaking in; see INTERFERENCE 1, INTRUSION. **2** [Armed interference] invasion, military occupation, armed aggression; see ATTACK.

in'ter·view' (-vyo͞o') ***n.*** **1** a meeting of people face to face to confer **2** *a)* a meeting in which a person is asked about personal views, etc., as by a reporter *b)* a published, taped, or filmed account of this —***vt.*** to have an interview with —**in'ter·view·ee'** ***n.*** —**in'ter·view'er** ***n.***

in'ter·weave' (-wēv') ***vt., vi.*** **-wove', -wo'ven, -weav'ing** **1** to weave together **2** to connect closely

in·tes·ta·cy (in tes'tə sē) ***n.*** the fact or state of dying intestate

in·tes·tate (in tes'tāt', -tit) ***adj.*** ⟦< L *in-*, not + *testari*, make a will⟧ having made no will

in·tes·tine (in tes'tən) ***n.*** ⟦< L *intus*, within⟧ [*usually pl.*] the lower part of the alimentary canal, extending from the stomach to the anus and consisting of the SMALL INTESTINE and the LARGE INTESTINE; bowels —**in·tes'tin·al** ***adj.***

in·ti·mate (in'tə mət; *for vt.*, -māt') ***adj.*** ⟦< L *intus*, within⟧ **1** most private or personal **2** very close or familiar **3** deep and thorough —***n.*** an intimate friend —***vt.*** **-mat'ed, -mat'ing** to hint or imply —**in'ti·ma·cy** (-mə sē), *pl.* **-cies**, ***n.*** —**in'ti·mate·ly** ***adv.*** —**in'ti·ma'tion** ***n.***

in·tim·i·date (in tim'ə dāt') ***vt.*** **-dat'ed, -dat'ing** ⟦< L *in-*, in + *timidus*, afraid⟧ to make afraid, as with threats —**in·tim'i·da'tion** ***n.***

intl *abbrev.* international: also **intnl**

in·to (in'to͞o) ***prep.*** ⟦OE⟧ **1** from the outside to the inside of *[into* a room*]* **2** continuing to the midst of *[*to talk *into* the night*]* **3** to the form, substance, or condition of *[*divided *into* parts*]* **4** so as to strike *[*to run *into* a wall*]* **5** [Inf.] involved or interested in *[*she's *into* jazz now*]*

in·tol·er·a·ble (in täl'ər ə bəl) ***adj.*** unbearable; too severe, painful, etc. to be endured —**in·tol'er·a·bly** ***adv.***

in·tol'er·ant (-ənt) ***adj.*** unwilling to tolerate others' beliefs, etc. —**intolerant of** not able or willing to tolerate —**in·tol'er·ance** ***n.***

in·to·na·tion (in'tō nā'shən, -tə-) ***n.*** **1** an intoning **2** the quality of producing tones in or out of tune with regard to a given standard of pitch **3** variations in pitch within an utterance

in·tone (in tōn') ***vt., vi.*** **-toned', -ton'ing** to speak or recite in a singing tone; chant —**in·ton'er** ***n.***

in to·to (in tō'tō) ⟦L⟧ as a whole

in·tox·i·cate (in täk'si kāt') ***vt.*** **-cat'ed, -cat'ing** ⟦< L *in-*, in + *toxicum*, poison⟧ **1** to make drunk **2** to excite greatly —**in·tox'i·cant** ***n.*** —**in·tox'i·ca'tion** ***n.***

intra- ⟦L, within⟧ *prefix* within, inside

in·tra·cit·y (in'trə sit'ē) ***adj.*** of or within a large municipality, often, specif. the inner city

in·trac·ta·ble (in trak'tə bəl) ***adj.*** hard to manage; unruly or stubborn

in·tra·der·mal (in'trə dur'məl) ***adj.*** within the skin or between the layers of the skin

in'tra·mu'ral (-myoor'əl) ***adj.*** ⟦INTRA- + MURAL⟧ between or among members of the same school, college, etc. *[intramural* athletics*]*

in·tra·net (in'trə net') ***n.*** a private Internet computer network for one organization, company, etc.

in·tran·si·gent (in tran'sə jənt, -zə-) ***adj.*** ⟦< L *in-*, not + *transigere*, to settle⟧ refusing to compromise —**in·tran'si·gence** ***n.***

in·tran·si·tive (in tran'sə tiv, -zə-) ***adj.*** not transitive; designating a verb that does not require a direct object —**in·tran'si·tive·ly** ***adv.***

in·tra·u·ter·ine (contraceptive) device (in'trə yo͞ot'ər in) any of various devices, as a plastic loop, inserted in the uterus as a contraceptive

in'tra·ve'nous (-vē'nəs) ***adj.*** ⟦INTRA- + VENOUS⟧ directly into a vein —**in'tra·ve'nous·ly** ***adv.***

in·trench (in trench') ***vt.*** ENTRENCH

in·trep·id (in trep'id) ***adj.*** ⟦< L *in-*, not + *trepidus*, alarmed⟧ bold; fearless; brave —**in·trep'id·ly** ***adv.***

in·tri·cate (in'tri kit) ***adj.*** ⟦< L *in-*, in + *tricae*, vexations⟧ **1** hard to follow or understand because full of puzzling parts, details, etc. **2** full of elaborate detail —**in'tri·ca·cy** (-kə sē), *pl.* **-cies**, ***n.*** —**in'tri·cate·ly** ***adv.***

in·trigue (in trēg'; *for n., also* in'trēg') ***vi.*** **-trigued', -trigu'ing** ⟦see prec.⟧ to plot secretly or underhandedly —***vt.*** to excite the interest or curiosity of —***n.*** **1** a secret or underhanded plotting **2** a secret or underhanded plot or scheme **3** a secret love affair —**in·trigu'er** ***n.*** —**in·trigu'ing** ***adj.*** —**in·trigu'ing·ly** ***adv.***

in·trin·sic (in trin'sik, -zik) ***adj.*** ⟦< L *intra-*, within + *secus*, following⟧ belonging to the real nature of a thing; inherent —**in·trin'si·cal·ly** ***adv.***

intro- ⟦L⟧ *prefix* into, within, inward

in·tro·duce (in'trə do͞os') ***vt.*** **-duced', -duc'ing** ⟦< L *intro-*, in + *ducere*, to lead⟧ **1** to put in; insert **2** to bring in as a new feature **3** to bring into use or fashion **4** *a)* to make acquainted; present *[introduce* me to her*]* *b)* to give experience of *[*they *introduced* him to music*]* **5** to bring forward **6** to start; begin *[*to *introduce* a talk with a joke*]*

in'tro·duc'tion (-duk'shən) ***n.*** **1** an introducing or being introduced **2** the preliminary section of a book, speech, etc.; preface

in'tro·duc'to·ry (-duk'tə rē) ***adj.*** serving to introduce; preliminary

in·tro·it (in trō'it, in'troit') ***n.*** ⟦< L *intro-*, in + *ire*, to go⟧ **1** a psalm or hymn at the opening of a Christian worship service **2** [I-] *R.C.Ch.* the first variable part of the Mass

in·tro·spec·tion (in'trə spek'shən) ***n.*** ⟦< L *intro-*, within +

THESAURUS

interview ***n.*** meeting, audience, conference; see COMMUNICATION, CONVERSATION.

interview ***v.*** converse with, get someone's opinion, consult with, interrogate, hold an inquiry, give an oral examination to, get something for the record.

intestines ***n.*** entrails, bowels, viscera, vitals, digestive organs, guts; see also INSIDES.

intimacy ***n.*** closeness, familiarity, confidence; see AFFECTION, FRIENDSHIP.

intimate ***a.*** familiar, confidential, trusted; see PRIVATE, SECRET 1, SPECIAL.

intimate ***n.*** associate, constant companion, close friend; see FRIEND, LOVER 1.

intimate ***v.*** suggest, imply, hint; see HINT.

intimately ***a.*** closely, personally, informally, familiarly, confidentially, without reserve, privately; see also LOVINGLY, SECRETLY.—*Ant.* OPENLY, unreservedly, publicly.

into ***prep.*** inside, in the direction of, through, to, to the middle of; see also IN 1, 2, TOWARD, WITHIN.

intolerable ***a.*** insufferable, unendurable, unbearable; see IMPOSSIBLE, OFFENSIVE 2, PAINFUL 1, UNDESIRABLE.

intolerance ***n.*** racism, chauvinism, bigotry; see FANATICISM, PREJUDICE.

intolerant ***a.*** dogmatic, narrow, bigoted; see PREJUDICED, STUPID.

intoxicant ***n.*** **1** [Alcohol] alcoholic drink, liquor, booze*; see DRINK 2. **2** [Drug] narcotic, hallucinogen, dope*; see DRUG.

intoxicate ***v.*** befuddle, inebriate, muddle; see CONFUSE.

intoxicated ***a.*** inebriated, high*, stoned*; see DIZZY, DRUNK.

intoxication ***n.*** infatuation, inebriation, intemperance; see DRUNKENNESS.

intricacy ***n.*** complication, elaborateness, complexity; see CONFUSION, DIFFICULTY 1, 2.

intricate ***a.*** involved, tricky, abstruse; see COMPLEX 2, DIFFICULT 1, 2, OBSCURE 1.

intrigue ***n.*** scheme, conspiracy, ruse; see TRICK 1.

intrigue ***v.*** delight, please, attract; see CHARM, ENTERTAIN 1, FASCINATE.

intrigued ***a.*** attracted, delighted, pleased; see CHARMED, ENTERTAINED, FASCINATED.

intriguing ***a.*** engaging, attractive, delightful; see BEAUTIFUL, CHARMING, HANDSOME, PLEASANT 1.

introduce ***v.*** **1** [To bring in] import, carry in, transport; see CARRY, SEND 1. **2** [To present] set forth, submit, advance; see OFFER 1, PROPOSE 1. **3** [To make strangers acquainted] present, give an introduction, make known, put on speaking terms with, do the honors, break the ice, hook up*. **4** [To insert] put in, add, enter; see INCLUDE 2.

introduced ***a.*** **1** [Brought in] made known, put on the market, advanced, proposed, offered, imported, popularized; see also RECEIVED. **2** [Made acquainted] acquainted with, befriended, acknowledged, recognized, on speaking terms, not unknown to one another; see also FAMILIAR WITH.

introduction ***n.*** **1** [The act of bringing in] admittance, initiation, installation; see ENTRANCE 1. **2** [The act of making strangers acquainted] presentation, debut, meeting, formal acquaintance, preliminary encounter. **3** [Introductory knowledge] first acquaintance, elementary statement, first contact, start, awakening, first taste, baptism, preliminary training, basic principles; see also KNOWLEDGE 1. **4** [An introductory explanation] preface, preamble, foreword, prologue, prelude, overture; see also EXPLANATION. **5** [A work supplying introductory knowledge] primer, manual, handbook; see BOOK.

introductory ***a.*** initial, opening, early, prior, starting, beginning, preparatory, primary, original, provisional.—*Ant.* PRINCIPAL, substantial, secondary.

specere, to look⟧ a looking into one's own mind, feelings, etc. —**in'tro·spec'tive** *adj.*

in·tro·vert (in'trə vurt') *n.* ⟦< L *intro-*, within + *vertere*, to turn⟧ one who is introspective rather than being interested in others —**in'tro·ver'sion** (-vur'zhən) *n.* —**in'tro·vert'ed** *adj.*

in·trude (in trōōd') *vt.*, *vi.* **-trud'ed, -trud'ing** ⟦< L *in-*, in + *trudere*, to push⟧ to force (oneself) upon others unasked —**in·trud'er** *n.*

in·tru·sion (in trōō'zhən) *n.* an intruding —**in·tru'sive** (-siv) *adj.* —**in·tru'sive·ly** *adv.* —**in·tru'sive·ness** *n.*

in·trust (in trust') *vt.* ENTRUST

in·tu·bate (in'tōō bāt') *vt.* **-bat'ed, -bat'ing** to insert a tube into (an orifice or hollow organ) to admit air, etc.

in·tu·i·tion (in'tōō ish'ən) *n.* ⟦< L *in-*, in + *tueri* to view⟧ the direct knowing of something without the conscious use of reasoning —**in·tu·i·tive** (in tōō'i tiv) *adj.*

In·u·it (in'ōō it) *n.* ⟦Esk⟧ ESKIMO: now the preferred term, esp. in Canada

in·un·date (in'ən dāt') *vt.* **-dat'ed, -dat'ing** ⟦< L *in-*, in + *unda*, a wave⟧ to cover with or as with a flood; deluge —**in'un·da'tion** *n.*

in·ure (in yoor') *vt.* **-ured', -ur'ing** ⟦ME *in ure*, in practice⟧ to accustom to pain, trouble, etc.

in u·ter·o (in yōōt'ər ō) ⟦L⟧ in the uterus

in·vade (in vād') *vt.* **-vad'ed, -vad'ing** ⟦< L *in-*, in + *vadere*, to come, go⟧ **1** to enter forcibly or hostilely **2** to intrude upon; violate —**in·vad'er** *n.*

in·va·lid[1] (in'və lid) *adj.* ⟦< L *in-*, not + *validus*, strong⟧ **1** weak and sickly **2** of or for invalids —*n.* one who is ill or disabled

in·val·id[2] (in val'id) *adj.* not valid

in·val'i·date' (-ə dāt') *vt.* **-dat'ed, -dat'ing** to make invalid; deprive of legal force —**in·val'i·da'tion** *n.*

in·val·u·a·ble (in val'yōō ə bəl) *adj.* too valuable to be measured; priceless —**in·val'u·a·bly** *adv.*

in·va·sion (in vā'zhən) *n.* an invading or being invaded, as by an army

in·va'sive (-siv) *adj.* **1** having to do with (an) invasion **2** penetrating into the body

in·vec·tive (in vek'tiv) *n.* ⟦see fol.⟧ a violent verbal attack; vituperation

in·veigh (in vā') *vi.* ⟦< L *in-*, in + *vehere*, carry⟧ to make a violent verbal attack; rail (*against*)

in·vei·gle (in vā'gəl) *vt.* **-gled, -gling** ⟦< MFr *aveugler*, to blind⟧ to entice or trick into doing or giving something —**in·vei'gler** *n.*

in·vent (in vent') *vt.* ⟦< L *in-*, in + *venire*, come⟧ **1** to think up [*to invent* excuses] **2** to think out or produce (a new device, process, etc.); originate —**in·ven'tor** *n.*

in·ven'tion (-ven'shən) *n.* **1** an inventing **2** the power of inventing **3** something invented

in·ven'tive (-tiv) *adj.* **1** of invention **2** skilled in inventing —**in·ven'tive·ly** *adv.* —**in·ven'tive·ness** *n.*

in·ven·to·ry (in'vən tôr'ē) *n.*, *pl.* **-ries** ⟦see INVENT⟧ **1** an itemized list of goods, property, etc., as of a business **2** the store of goods, etc. for such listing; stock —*vt.* **-ried, -ry·ing** to make an inventory of

in·verse (in vurs', in'vurs') *adj.* inverted; directly opposite —*n.* any inverse thing —**in·verse'ly** *adv.*

in·ver·sion (in vur'zhən) *n.* **1** an inverting or being inverted **2** something inverted; reversal **3** *Meteorol.* a temperature reversal in which a layer of warm air traps cooler air near the surface of the earth

in·vert (in vurt') *vt.* ⟦< L *in-*, to + *vertere*, to turn⟧ **1** to turn upside down **2** to reverse the order, position, direction, etc. of

in·ver·te·brate (in vur'tə brit, -brāt') *adj.* not vertebrate; having no backbone —*n.* any invertebrate animal

in·vest (in vest') *vt.* ⟦< L *in-*, in + *vestis*, clothing⟧ **1** to clothe **2** to install in office with ceremony **3** to furnish with power, authority, etc. **4** to put (money) into business, stocks, etc. in order to get a profit —*vi.* to invest money —**in·ves'tor** *n.*

in·ves·ti·gate (in ves'tə gāt') *vi.*, *vt.* **-gat'ed, -gat'ing** ⟦< L *in-*, in + *vestigare*, to track⟧ to search (into); inquire —**in·ves'ti·ga'tor** *n.*

in·ves'ti·ga'tion (-gā'shən) *n.* an investigating; careful search; systematic inquiry

in·ves'ti·ture (-chər) *n.* a formal investing, as with an office

in·vest·ment (in vest'mənt) *n.* **1** an investing or being invested **2** *a*) money invested *b*) anything in which money is or may be invested

in·vet·er·ate (in vet'ər it) *adj.* ⟦< pp. of L *inveterare*, to age⟧ **1** firmly established **2** habitual —**in·vet'er·a·cy** *n.*

in·vid·i·ous (in vid'ē əs) *adj.* ⟦< L *invidia*, envy⟧ such as to excite ill will; giving offense, as by discriminating unfairly —**in·vid'i·ous·ly** *adv.* —**in·vid'i·ous·ness** *n.*

in·vig·or·ate (in vig'ər āt') *vt.* **-at'ed, -at'ing** to give vigor to; fill with energy —**in·vig'or·a'tion** *n.*

in·vin·ci·ble (in vin'sə bəl) *adj.* ⟦< L *invincibilis*, not easily overcome⟧ that cannot be overcome; unconquerable —**in·vin'ci·bil'i·ty** *n.*

in·vi·o·la·ble (in vī'ə lə bəl) *adj.* **1** not to be violated; not to be profaned or injured; sacred **2** indestructible —**in·vi'o·la·bil'i·ty** *n.*

in·vi'o·late (-lit) *adj.* not violated; kept sacred or unbroken

THESAURUS

intrude *v.* interfere, interrupt, interpose; see MEDDLE 1.

intruder *n.* prowler, thief, burglar, unwelcome guest, meddler, invader, snooper, interloper, unwanted person, interferer, interrupter, trespasser; see also ROBBER, TROUBLE 1.

intrusion *n.* interruption, forced entrance, trespass, intervention, meddling, encroachment, invasion, infraction, overstepping, transgression, nose-in*, horn-in*, muscle-in*; see also INTERFERENCE 1.

intuition *n.* presentiment, foreknowledge, inspiration; see FEELING 4.

intuitive *a.* prescient, emotional, instinctive; see AUTOMATIC, NATURAL 1, SPONTANEOUS.

invade *v.* **1** [To enter with armed force] lay siege to, penetrate, fall on; see ATTACK. **2** [To encroach upon] infringe on, trespass, interfere with; see MEDDLE 1.

invader *n.* trespasser, alien, attacking force; see ATTACKER, ENEMY.

invalid[1] *n.* disabled person, incurable, paralytic, chronically ill person, valetudinarian, crippled person; see also PATIENT.

invalid[2] *a.* irrational, unreasonable, fallacious; see ILLOGICAL, WRONG 2.

invalidate *v.* annul, refute, nullify; see CANCEL.

invaluable *a.* priceless, expensive, dear; see VALUABLE.

invariable *a.* unchanging, uniform, static; see CONSTANT, REGULAR 3.

invariably *a.* perpetually, constantly, habitually; see CUSTOMARILY, REGULARLY.

invasion *n.* forced entrance, intrusion, aggression; see ATTACK.

invent *v.* **1** [To create or discover] originate, devise, fashion, form, project, design, find, improvise, contrive, execute, come upon, conceive, author, plan, think up, make up, bear, turn out, forge, make, hatch, dream up*, cook up*. **2** [To fabricate] misrepresent, fake, make believe; see LIE 1.

invention *n.* contrivance, contraption, design; see DISCOVERY.

inventive *a.* productive, imaginative, fertile; see ARTISTIC, ORIGINAL 2.

inventor *n.* author, originator, creator; see ARCHITECT, ARTIST.

inventory *n.* **1** [A list] stock book, itemization, register; see INDEX 2, LIST, RECORD 1. **2** [The act of taking stock] inspection, examination, investigation; see SUMMARY.

inventory *v.* take stock of, count, audit; see FILE 1, LIST 1, RECORD 1.

invert *v.* **1** [To upset] overturn, turn upside-down, tip; see UPSET 1. **2** [To reverse] change, rearrange, transpose; see EXCHANGE.

invest *v.* lay out, spend, put one's money into, provide capital for, give money over, buy stocks, make an investment, buy into, sink money in*, put up the dough*; see also BUY.

investigate *v.* look into, interrogate, review; see EXAMINE, STUDY.

investigated *a.* examined, tried, tested, inspected, searched, questioned, probed, considered, measured, checked, studied, researched, made the subject of an investigation, worked on, thought out, thought through, scrutinized, put to the test, gone over, gone into, cross-examined.

investigation *n.* inquiry, search, research; see EXAMINATION 1.

investigator *n.* reviewer, examiner, auditor; see DETECTIVE, INSPECTOR.

investment *n.* grant, loan, expenditure, expense, backing, speculation, financing, finance, purchase, advance, bail, interest. *Types of investment include the following:* stocks, bonds, shares, securities, property, real estate, mortgage, capital, mutual funds, hedge funds, debentures, futures, precious metals, gems.

invigorate *v.* stimulate, freshen, exhilarate; see ANIMATE, EXCITE.

invigorating *a.* refreshing, exhilarating, bracing; see STIMULATING.

invincible *a.* unconquerable, insuperable, impregnable; see POWERFUL 1, STRONG 1, 2.

invisibility *n.* obscurity, concealment, camouflage, indefiniteness, seclusion, cloudiness, haziness, foggi-

in·vis·i·ble (in viz′ə bəl) ***adj.*** **1** not visible; that cannot be seen **2** out of sight **3** imperceptible —**in·vis′i·bil′i·ty** ***n.*** —**in·vis′i·bly** ***adv.***

in·vi·ta·tion (in′və tā′shən) ***n.*** **1** an inviting **2** a message used in inviting

in′vi·ta′tion·al ***adj.*** only for those invited to take part: said as of an art show

in·vite (in vīt′; *for n.* in′vīt′) ***vt.*** **-vit′ed**, **-vit′ing** ⟦< L *invitare*⟧ **1** to ask to come somewhere or do something **2** to ask for **3** to give occasion for *[*action that *invites* scandal*]* **4** to tempt; entice —***n.*** [Inf.] an invitation —**in′vit·ee′** ***n.***

in·vit′ing ***adj.*** tempting; enticing

in vi·tro (in vē′trō′) ⟦L, in glass⟧ isolated from the living organism and artificially maintained, as in a test tube

in·vo·ca·tion (in′və kā′shən) ***n.*** an invoking of God, the Muses, etc.

in·voice (in′vois′) ***n.*** ⟦prob. < ME *envoie*, message⟧ a list of goods shipped or services rendered, stating prices, etc.; bill —***vt.*** **-voiced′**, **-voic′ing** to present an invoice for or to

in·voke (in vōk′) ***vt.*** **-voked′**, **-vok′ing** ⟦< L *in-*, in, on + *vocare*, to call⟧ **1** to call on (God, the Muses, etc.) for blessing, help, etc. **2** to resort to (a law, ruling, etc.) as pertinent **3** to conjure **4** to beg for; implore

in·vol·un·tar·y (in väl′ən ter′ē) ***adj.*** **1** not done by choice **2** not consciously controlled —**in·vol′un·tar′i·ly** ***adv.*** —**in·vol′un·tar′i·ness** ***n.***

in·vo·lu·tion (in′və lo͞o′shən) ***n.*** **1** an involving or being involved **2** a complication; intricacy

in·volve (in välv′, -vôlv′) ***vt.*** **-volved′**, **-volv′ing** ⟦< L *in-*, in + *volvere*, to roll⟧ **1** to make intricate or complicated **2** to entangle in difficulty, danger, etc.; implicate **3** to affect or include *[*the riot *involved* thousands*]* **4** to require *[*saving *involves* thrift*]* **5** to make busy; occupy *[involved* the class in research*]* —**in·volved′** ***adj.*** —**in·volve′ment** ***n.***

in·vul·ner·a·ble (in vul′nər ə bəl) ***adj.*** **1** that cannot be wounded or injured **2** proof against attack —**in·vul′ner·a·bil′i·ty** ***n.***

in·ward (in′wərd) ***adj.*** **1** situated within; internal **2** mental or spiritual **3** directed toward the inside **4** sensitive, subtle, reticent, etc. —***adv.*** **1** toward the inside **2** into the mind or soul Also **in′wards** ***adv.***

in′ward·ly ***adv.*** **1** in or on the inside **2** in the mind or spirit **3** toward the inside

in′-your′-face′ ***adj.*** [Slang] done in a direct, often aggressive way; assertive; daring

I/O *abbrev.* input/output

i·o·dine (ī′ə dīn′, -din) ***n.*** ⟦< Gr *iōdēs*, violetlike⟧ **1** a nonmetallic chemical element, used in medicine, etc. **2** a tincture of iodine, used as an antiseptic

i′o·dize′ (-dīz′) ***vt.*** **-dize′**, **-diz′ing** to treat with iodine

i·on (ī′ən, -än′) ***n.*** ⟦ult. < Gr *ienai*, to go⟧ an electrically charged atom or group of atoms

-ion (ən) ⟦< L *-io*⟧ *suffix* **1** the act or condition of **2** the result of

I·on·ic (ī än′ik) ***adj.*** designating or of a Greek or Roman style of architecture, distinguished by ornamental scrolls on the capitals

i·on·ize (ī′ən īz′) ***vt.***, ***vi.*** **-ized′**, **-iz′ing** to dissociate into ions, as a salt dissolved in water, or become electrically charged, as a gas under radiation —**i′on·i·za′tion** ***n.*** —**i′on·iz′er** ***n.***

i·on·o·sphere (ī än′ə sfir′) ***n.*** the outer layers of the earth's atmosphere, with some electron and ion content

i·o·ta (ī ōt′ə) ***n.*** **1** the ninth letter of the Greek alphabet (Ι, ι) **2** a very small quantity; jot

IOU (ī′ō′yo͞o′) ***n.***, *pl.* **IOU's** ⟦for *I owe you*⟧ a signed paper bearing the letters *IOU*, acknowledging a specified debt

-i·ous (ē əs, yəs, əs) ⟦see -OUS⟧ *suffix* characterized by *[furious]*

I·o·wa (ī′ə wə) Midwestern state of the U.S.: 55,875 sq. mi.; pop. 2,777,000; cap. Des Moines: abbrev. *IA* —**I′o·wan** ***adj.***, ***n.***

ip·e·cac (ip′i kak′) ***n.*** ⟦< AmInd (Brazil) name⟧ an emetic made as from the dried roots of a South American plant

IPO *abbrev.* initial public offering

ip·so fac·to (ip′sō fak′tō) ⟦L⟧ by that very fact

IQ ***n.***, *pl.* **IQ's** ⟦I(NTELLIGENCE) Q(UOTIENT)⟧ a number intended to indicate a person's intelligence, based on a test

I·qa·lu·it (ē kä′lo͞o ēt′) capital of Nunavut, Canada: pop. 4,200

Ir[1] *abbrev.* **1** Ireland **2** Irish

Ir[2] *Chem. symbol for* iridium

ir- *prefix* **1** IN-[1] **2** IN-[2] Used before *r*

IRA (ī′är′ā′; ī′rə) ***n.***, *pl.* **IRA's** ⟦*I(ndividual) R(etirement) A(ccount)*⟧ a personal retirement plan with taxes on the earnings deferred until funds are withdrawn

I·ran (i ran′, -rän′) country in SW Asia: 634,293 sq. mi.; pop. 49,445,000: former name PERSIA —**I·ra·ni·an** (i rā′nē ən, ī-; -rä′-) ***adj.***, ***n.***

I·raq (i räk′, -rak′) country in SW Asia, at the head of the Persian Gulf: 169,235 sq. mi.; pop. 16,335,000 —**I·ra·qi** (i rä′kē, -rak′ē), *pl.* **-qis**, ***n.***, ***adj.***

i·ras·ci·ble (i ras′ə bəl) ***adj.*** ⟦see fol.⟧ easily angered; hot-tempered

i·rate (ī rāt′, ī′rāt′) ***adj.*** ⟦< L *ira*, anger⟧ angry; wrathful; incensed —**i·rate′ly** ***adv.*** —**i·rate′ness** ***n.***

ire (īr) ***n.*** ⟦< L *ira*⟧ anger; wrath

Ire·land (īr′lənd) **1** one of the British Isles, west of Great Britain **2** republic comprising most of this island: 27,137 sq. mi.; pop. 3,560,000

i·ren·ic (ī ren′ik) ***adj.*** ⟦< Gr *eirēnē*, peace⟧ promoting peace

ir·i·des·cent (ir′i des′ənt) ***adj.*** ⟦< Gr *iris*, rainbow⟧ having or showing an interplay of rainbowlike colors —**ir′i·des′cence** ***n.***

i·rid·i·um (ī rid′ē əm) ***n.*** ⟦see fol.⟧ a white metallic chemical element

i·ris (ī′ris) ***n.***, *pl.* **i′ris·es** ⟦Gr, rainbow⟧ **1** the round, pigmented membrane surrounding the pupil of the eye **2** a plant with sword-shaped leaves and a showy flower

I·rish (ī′rish) ***adj.*** of Ireland or its people, language, etc. —***n.*** **1** the Celtic language of Ireland **2** the English dialect of Ireland —**the Irish** the people of Ireland —**I′rish·man** (-mən), *pl.* **-men** (-mən), ***n.*** —**I′rish·wom′an**, *pl.* **-wom′en**, ***fem.n.***

Irish coffee brewed coffee with Irish whiskey, topped with whipped cream

Irish Sea arm of the Atlantic between Ireland & Great Britain

irk (urk) ***vt.*** ⟦ME *irken*, be weary of⟧ to annoy, irritate, tire out, etc.

THESAURUS

ness, mistiness, duskiness, darkness, gloom, intangibility, disappearance, vagueness, indefiniteness.

invisible ***a.*** imperceptible, out of sight, microscopic, beyond the visual range, unseen, undisclosed, vaporous, gaseous.—*Ant.* REAL, substantial, material.

invisibly ***a.*** imperceptibly, out of sight, undetectably; see VAGUELY.

invitation ***n.*** note, card, message, encouragement, proposition, proposal, call, petition, overture, offer, solicitation, temptation, attraction, lure, prompting, urge, pressure, reason, motive, ground.

invite ***v.*** bid, request, beg, suggest, encourage, entice, solicit, pray, petition, persuade, insist, press, ply, propose, appeal to, implore, call upon, ask, have over, have in, formally invite, send an invitation to; see also ASK.

invited ***a.*** asked, requested, solicited, persuaded, bade, summoned; see also WELCOME.

inviting ***a.*** appealing, alluring, tempting, attractive, captivating, agreeable, open, encouraging, delightful, pleasing, persuasive, magnetic, fascinating, provocative, bewitching.—*Ant.* PAINFUL, unbearable, insufferable.

involuntary ***a.*** unintentional, uncontrolled, instinctive; see AUTOMATIC, HABITUAL.

involve ***v.*** draw into, compromise, implicate, entangle, embroil, link, connect, incriminate, associate, relate, suggest, prove, comprise, point to, commit, bring in.

involved ***a.*** brought into difficulties, entangled in a crime, incriminated, embarrassed, embroiled, caught up in; see also INCLUDED.

involvement ***n.*** **1** [Difficulty] quandary, predicament, embarrassment; see DIFFICULTY 1, 2. **2** [Engrossment] intentness, study, preoccupation; see REFLECTION 1.

invulnerable ***a.*** strong, invincible, secure; see SAFE 1.

inward ***a.*** **1** [Moving into] penetrating, ingoing, through, incoming, entering, inbound, infiltrating, inflowing. **2** [Placed within] inside, internal, interior; see IN 1, WITHIN. **3** [Private] spiritual, meditative, intimate; see PRIVATE, RELIGIOUS 2.

inwardly ***a.*** from within, fundamentally, basically; see NATURALLY, WITHIN.

iota ***n.*** grain, particle, speck; see BIT 1.

irate ***a.*** enraged, furious, incensed; see ANGRY.

Irish ***a.*** Celtic, Gaelic, Hibernian*; see EUROPEAN.

irk ***v.*** annoy, harass, disturb; see BOTHER 1, 2.

irk′some (-səm) ***adj.*** that tends to irk; tiresome or annoying

i·ron (ī′ərn) ***n.*** ⟦OE *iren*⟧ **1** a metallic chemical element, the most common of all metals **2** any device of iron; esp., such a device with a flat undersurface, heated for pressing cloth **3** [*pl.*] iron shackles **4** firm strength; power **5** any of certain golf clubs with angled metal heads —***adj.*** **1** of iron **2** like iron; strong; firm —***vt.***, ***vi.*** to press with a hot iron —**iron out** to smooth out; eliminate

i′ron·clad′ ***adj.*** **1** covered or protected with iron **2** difficult to change or break *[an ironclad lease]*

iron curtain **1** [*often* **I- C-**] a barrier of secrecy and censorship seen as isolating the U.S.S.R., etc.: often with *the* **2** any similar barrier

i′ron-fist′ed (-fis′tid) ***adj.*** despotic and brutal

i·ron·ic (ī rän′ik) ***adj.*** **1** meaning the contrary of what is expressed **2** using irony **3** opposite to what is or might be expected Also **i·ron′i·cal** —**i·ron′i·cal·ly** ***adv.***

i·ron·man (ī′ərn man′) ***n.***, *pl.* **-men′** (-men′) [*often* **I-**] a man of great physical strength

i′ron·ware′ ***n.*** things made of iron

i·ro·ny (ī′rə nē, ī′ər nē) ***n.***, *pl.* **-nies** ⟦< Gr *eirōn*, dissembler in speech⟧ **1** expression in which the intended meaning of the words is the direct opposite of their usual sense **2** an event or result that is the opposite of what is expected

Ir·o·quois (ir′ə kwoi′) ***n.***, *pl.* **-quois′** (-kwoi′, -kwoiz′) a member of a confederation of North American Indian peoples that lived in upstate New York —***adj.*** of the Iroquois —**Ir′o·quoi′an** ***n.***, ***adj.***

ir·ra·di·ate (i rā′dē āt′) ***vt.*** **-at′ed**, **-at′ing** **1** to shine upon; light up **2** to enlighten **3** to radiate **4** to expose to X-rays or other radiant energy —***vi.*** to emit rays; shine —**ir·ra′di·a′tion** ***n.***

ir·ra·tion·al (i rash′ə nəl) ***adj.*** **1** lacking the power to reason **2** senseless; unreasonable; absurd —**ir·ra′tion·al′i·ty** (-ə nal′ə tē), *pl.* **-ties**, ***n.*** —**ir·ra′tion·al·ly** ***adv.***

ir·re·claim·a·ble (ir′i klām′ə bəl) ***adj.*** that cannot be reclaimed

ir·rec·on·cil·a·ble (i rek′ən sīl′ə bəl) ***adj.*** that cannot be brought into agreement; incompatible

ir·re·cov·er·a·ble (ir′i kuv′ər ə bəl) ***adj.*** that cannot be recovered, rectified, or remedied

ir·re·deem·a·ble (ir′i dēm′ə bəl) ***adj.*** **1** that cannot be bought back **2** that cannot be converted into coin: said as of certain paper money **3** that cannot be changed or reformed

ir·ref·u·ta·ble (i ref′yo͞o tə bəl, ir′i fyo͞ot′ə bəl) ***adj.*** indisputable —**ir·ref′u·ta·bly** ***adv.***

ir·re·gard·less (ir′i gärd′lis) ***adj.***, ***adv.*** REGARDLESS: a nonstandard or humorous usage

ir·reg·u·lar (i reg′yə lər) ***adj.*** **1** not conforming to an established rule, standard, etc. **2** not straight, even, or uniform **3** *Gram.* not inflected in the usual way —**ir·reg′u·lar′i·ty**, *pl.* **-ties**, ***n.***

ir·rel·e·vant (i rel′ə vənt) ***adj.*** not pertinent; not to the point —**ir·rel′e·vance** ***n.*** —**ir·rel′e·vant·ly** ***adv.***

ir·re·li·gious (ir′i lij′əs) ***adj.*** **1** not religious **2** indifferent or hostile to religion **3** profane; impious —**ir′re·li′gious·ly** ***adv.***

ir·re·me·di·a·ble (ir′i mē′dē ə bəl) ***adj.*** that cannot be remedied or corrected —**ir′re·me′di·a·bly** ***adv.***

ir·rep·a·ra·ble (i rep′ə rə bəl) ***adj.*** that cannot be repaired, mended, etc.

ir·re·place·a·ble (ir′i plās′ə bəl) ***adj.*** that cannot be replaced

ir′re·press′i·ble (-pres′ə bəl) ***adj.*** that cannot be repressed

ir′re·proach′a·ble (-prō′chə bəl) ***adj.*** blameless; faultless

ir′re·sist′i·ble (-zis′tə bəl) ***adj.*** that cannot be resisted; too strong, fascinating, etc. to be withstood —**ir′re·sist′i·bly** ***adv.***

ir·res·o·lute (i rez′ə lo͞ot′) ***adj.*** not resolute; wavering; indecisive —**ir·res′o·lu′tion** (-lo͞o′shən) ***n.***

ir·re·spec·tive (ir′i spek′tiv) ***adj.*** regardless (*of*)

ir′re·spon′si·ble (-spän′sə bəl) ***adj.*** **1** not responsible for actions **2** lacking a sense of responsibility —**ir′re·spon′si·bil′i·ty** ***n.***

ir′re·triev′a·ble (-trēv′ə bəl) ***adj.*** that cannot be retrieved —**ir′re·triev′a·bly** ***adv.***

ir·rev·er·ence (i rev′ər əns) ***n.*** lack of reverence; disrespect —**ir·rev′er·ent** ***adj.***

ir·re·vers·i·ble (ir′i vʉr′sə bəl) ***adj.*** that cannot be reversed; esp., that cannot be annulled or turned back

ir·rev·o·ca·ble (i rev′ə kə bəl) ***adj.*** that cannot be revoked or undone —**ir·rev′o·ca·bly** ***adv.***

ir·ri·ga·ble (ir′i gə bəl) ***adj.*** that can be irrigated

ir·ri·gate (ir′ə gāt′) ***vt.*** **-gat′ed**, **-gat′ing** ⟦< L *in-*, in + *rigare*, to water⟧ **1** to supply (land) with water, as by means of artificial ditches **2** *Med.* to wash out (a cavity, wound, etc.) —**ir′ri·ga′tion** ***n.***

ir·ri·ta·ble (ir′i tə bəl) ***adj.*** **1** easily annoyed or provoked **2** *Med.* excessively sensitive to a stimulus —**ir′ri·ta·bil′i·ty** ***n.*** —**ir′ri·ta·bly** ***adv.***

ir′ri·tant (-tənt) ***adj.*** causing irritation —***n.*** a thing that irritates

THESAURUS

iron ***a.*** ferrous, ironclad, hard, robust, strong, unyielding, dense, inflexible, heavy; see also FIRM 2, THICK 3.

iron ***n.*** pig iron, cast iron, wrought iron, sheet iron, coke; see also METAL.

iron ***v.*** use a steam iron on, press, mangle, roll, finish, smooth out; see also SMOOTH. —**iron out** compromise, settle differences, smooth over; see AGREE, NEGOTIATE 1.

ironic ***a.*** contradictory, twisted, ridiculous, mocking, satiric, sardonic, paradoxical, critical, derisive, exaggerated, caustic, biting, incisive, scathing, satirical, bitter; see also SARCASTIC.

irony ***n.*** satire, wit, ridicule, mockery, quip, banter, derision, criticism, paradox, twist, humor, reproach, repartee, back-handed compliment; see also SARCASM.

irrational ***a.*** **1** [Illogical] unreasonable, specious, fallacious; see ILLOGICAL, WRONG 2. **2** [Stupid] senseless, silly, ridiculous; see STUPID.

irrationally ***a.*** illogically, unreasonably, stupidly; see FOOLISHLY.

irregular ***a.*** **1** [Not even] uneven, spasmodic, fitful, uncertain, random, unsettled, inconstant, unsteady, fragmentary, unsystematic, occasional, infrequent, fluctuating, wavering, intermittent, sporadic, changeable, capricious, variable, erratic, shifting, unmethodical, jerky, up and down.—*Ant.* REGULAR, even, punctual. **2** [Not customary] unique, extraordinary, abnormal; see UNUSUAL 2. **3** [Questionable] strange, overt, debatable; see QUESTIONABLE 2, SUSPICIOUS 2. **4** [Not regular in form or in outline] not uniform, unsymmetrical, uneven, asymmetrical, unequal, craggy, hilly, saw-toothed, broken, jagged, notched, eccentric, bumpy, meandering, variable, wobbly, lumpy, off balance, off center, lopsided, pockmarked, scarred, bumpy, sprawling, out of proportion; see also BENT.

irregularity ***n.*** peculiarity, singularity, abnormality, strangeness, uniqueness, exception, excess, malformation, deviation, allowance, exemption, privilege, nonconformity, innovation, oddity, eccentricity, anomaly, rarity; see also CHARACTERISTIC.—*Ant.* CUSTOM, regularity, rule.

irregularly ***a.*** periodically, at irregular intervals, intermittently, fitfully, off and on; see also UNEXPECTEDLY.

irrelevant ***a.*** inapplicable, impertinent, off the topic, inappropriate, inapt, unrelated, extraneous, unconnected, inapropos, off the point, foreign, beside the question, out of order, out of place, pointless, beside the point, not pertaining to, without reference to, out of the way, remote, neither here nor there; see also TRIVIAL, UNNECESSARY.

irreparable ***a.*** incurable, hopeless, irreversible; see BROKEN 1, RUINED 1, DESTROYED.

irresistible ***a.*** compelling, overpowering, invincible; see OVERWHELMING, POWERFUL 1.

irresponsible ***a.*** untrustworthy, capricious, flighty, fickle, thoughtless, rash, undependable, unstable, loose, lax, immoral, shiftless, unpredictable, wild, devil-may-care; see also UNRELIABLE.—*Ant.* RESPONSIBLE, trustworthy, dependable.

irrevocable ***a.*** permanent, indelible, set in stone; see CERTAIN 2, INEVITABLE.

irrigate ***v.*** water, pass water through, inundate; see FLOOD.

irrigation ***n.*** watering, flooding, inundation; see FLOOD.

irritability ***n.*** anger, peevishness, impatience; see ANGER, ANNOYANCE.

irritable ***a.*** sensitive, touchy, testy, peevish, ill-tempered, huffy, petulant, tense, resentful, fretting, carping, crabbed, hypercritical, quick-tempered, easily offended, glum, complaining, brooding, dissatisfied, snarling, grumbling, surly, gloomy, ill-natured, morose, moody, snappish, waspish, in bad humor, cantankerous, fretful, hypersensitive, annoyed, piqued, cross, churlish, grouchy, sulky, sullen, high-strung, thin-skinned, grumpy; see also ANGRY.—*Ant.* PLEASANT, agreeable, good-natured.

irritant ***n.*** bother, burden, nuisance; see ANNOYANCE.

ir′ri·tate′ (-tāt′) *vt.* **-tat′ed, -tat′ing** ⟦< L *irritare*, excite⟧ **1** to provoke to anger; annoy **2** to make inflamed or sore —**ir′ri·ta′tion** *n.*

ir·rupt (i rupt′) *vi.* ⟦< L *in-*, in + *rumpere*, to break⟧ to burst suddenly or violently (*into*) —**ir·rup′tion** *n.* —**ir·rup′tive** *adj.*

IRS *abbrev.* Internal Revenue Service

Ir·ving (ʉr′viŋ) city in NW Texas: pop. 155,000

is[1] (iz) *vi.* ⟦OE⟧ *3d pers. sing., pres. indic., of* BE

is[2] *abbrev.* **1** island(s) **2** islet(s)

I·saac (ī′zək) *n. Bible* one of the patriarchs, son of Abraham, and father of Jacob and Esau

I·sa·iah (ī zā′ə) *n. Bible* **1** a Hebrew prophet of the 8th c. B.C. **2** the book containing his teachings

-ise (īz) *suffix chiefly Brit. sp. of* -IZE

-ish (ish) ⟦< OE *-isc*⟧ *suffix* **1** of (a specified people) *[Irish]* **2** somewhat *[tallish]* **3** [Inf.] approximately *[thirtyish]* **4** like or characteristic of

Ish·tar (ish′tär′) *n.* the Babylonian and Assyrian goddess of fertility

i·sin·glass (ī′zin glas′, -ziŋ-) *n.* ⟦prob. < MDu *huizen*, sturgeon + *blas*, bladder⟧ mica, esp. in thin sheets

I·sis (ī′sis) *n.* the Egyptian goddess of fertility

isl *abbrev.* **1** island **2** isle

Is·lam (is′läm′, iz′-) *n.* ⟦Ar *islām*, lit., submission (to God's will)⟧ **1** the Muslim religion, a monotheistic religion founded by Mohammed **2** Muslims collectively or the lands in which they predominate —**Is·lam′ic** (-läm′ik) *adj.*

Is·lam·a·bad (is läm′ə bäd′) capital of Pakistan, in the NE part: pop. 201,000

is·land (ī′lənd) *n.* ⟦< OE *igland*, lit., island land: sp. after *isle*⟧ **1** a land mass smaller than a continent and surrounded by water **2** anything like this in position or isolation

is′land·er *n.* a person born or living on an island

isle (īl) *n.* ⟦< L *insula*⟧ an island, esp. a small island

is·let (ī′lit) *n.* a very small island

islets (or **islands**) **of Lang·er·hans** (läŋ′ər häns′) ⟦after P. *Langerhans* (1847-88), Ger histologist⟧ endocrine cells in the pancreas that produce the hormone insulin

ism (iz′əm) *n.* a doctrine, theory, system, etc. whose name ends in *-ism*

-ism (iz′əm) ⟦< Gr *-ismos*⟧ *suffix* **1** act or result of *[terrorism]* **2** condition, conduct, or qualities of *[patriotism]* **3** theory of *[socialism]* **4** devotion to *[nationalism]* **5** an instance of *[witticism]*

is·n't (iz′ənt) *contr.* is not

ISO *abbrev.* International Standards Organization

iso- ⟦< Gr *isos*⟧ *combining form* equal, similar, identical *[isomorph]*

i·so·bar (ī′sō bär′) *n.* ⟦< prec. + Gr *baros*, weight⟧ a line on a map connecting points of equal barometric pressure

i·so·late (ī′sə lāt′; *for n., usually*, -lit) *vt.* **-lat′ed, -lat′ing** ⟦< It *isola* (< L *insula*), island⟧ to set apart from others; place alone —*n.* a person or thing that is isolated —**i′so·lat′ed** *adj.* —**i′so·la′tion** *n.* —**i′so·la′tor** *n.*

i′so·la′tion·ist *n.* one who opposes the involvement of a country in international alliances, etc. —*adj.* of isolationists —**i′so·la′tion·ism′** *n.*

i·so·mer (ī′sə mər) *n.* ⟦< Gr *isos*, equal + *meros*, a part⟧ any of two or more chemical compounds whose molecules contain the same atoms but in different arrangements —**i′so·mer′ic** (-mer′ik) *adj.*

i′so·met′ric (-met′rik) *adj.* ⟦< Gr *isos*, equal + *metron*, measure⟧ **1** equal in measure **2** of isometrics —*n.* [*pl.*] exercise in which muscles are briefly tensed in opposition to other muscles or to an immovable object —**i′so·met′ri·cal·ly** *adv.*

i·sos·ce·les (ī säs′ə lēz′) *adj.* ⟦< Gr *isos*, equal + *skelos*, leg⟧ designating a triangle with two equal sides

i·so·tope (ī′sə tōp′) *n.* ⟦< ISO- + Gr *topos*, place⟧ any of two or more forms of an element having the same atomic number but different atomic weights

ISP *n., pl.* **ISPs** ⟦*I(nternet) s(ervice) p(rovider)*⟧ a company that provides access to the Internet

Is·ra·el[1] (iz′rē əl) *n. Bible* Jacob

Is·ra·el[2] (iz′rē əl) **1** ancient land of the Hebrews at the SE end of the Mediterranean **2** kingdom in the N part of this land **3** country between the Mediterranean Sea & Jordan: 8,463 sq. mi.; pop. 4,038,000

Is·rae·li (iz rā′lē) *n.* a person born or living in modern Israel —*adj.* of modern Israel or its people

Is·ra·el·ite (iz′rē ə līt′) *n.* any of the people of ancient Israel; Hebrew

is·su·ance (ish′o͞o əns) *n.* an issuing; issue

is·sue (ish′o͞o) *n.* ⟦< L *ex-*, out + *ire*, go⟧ **1** an outgoing; outflow **2** a result; consequence **3** offspring **4** a point under dispute **5** a sending or giving out **6** all that is put forth at one time *[an issue of bonds, a periodical, etc.]* —*vi.* **-sued, -su·ing** **1** to go or flow out; emerge **2** to result (*from*) or end (*in*) —*vt.* **1** to give or deal out *[to issue supplies]* **2** to publish —**at issue** in dispute —**take issue** to disagree —**is′su·er** *n.*

-ist (ist, əst) ⟦< Gr *-istēs*⟧ *suffix* **1** one who does, makes, or practices *[satirist]* **2** one skilled in or occupied with *[druggist, violinist]* **3** an adherent of *[anarchist]*

Is·tan·bul (is′tan bo͝ol′, -tän-) seaport in NW Turkey: pop. 5,476,000

isth·mus (is′məs) *n., pl.* **-mus·es** or **-mi′** (-mī′) ⟦< Gr *isthmos*, a neck⟧ a narrow strip of land having water at each side and connecting two larger bodies of land

it (it) *pron., pl. see* THEY ⟦< OE *hit*⟧ **1** the animal or thing previously mentioned **2** *it* is also used as: *a)* the subject of an impersonal verb *[it is snowing]* *b)* a subject or object of indefinite sense in various idiomatic constructions *[it's all right, he lords it over us]* —*n.* the player, as in tag, who must try to catch another —**with it** [Slang] alert, informed, or hip

It or **Ital** *abbrev.* **1** Italian **2** Italy

IT *abbrev.* information technology

I·tal·ian (i tal′yən) *adj.* of Italy or its people, language, etc. —*n.* **1** a person born or living in Italy **2** the Romance language of Italy

i·tal·ic (i tal′ik, ī-) *adj.* ⟦< its early use in *Italy*⟧ designating a type in which the characters slant upward to the right (Ex.: *this is italic type*) —*n.* [*usually pl., sometimes with sing. v.*] italic type or print: abbrev. **ital**

i·tal·i·cize (i tal′ə sīz′, ī-) *vt.* **-cized′, -ciz′ing** to print in italics

It·a·ly (it′'l ē) country in S Europe: 116,333 sq. mi.; pop. 56,778,000

itch (ich) *vi.* ⟦OE *giccan*⟧ **1** to feel a tingling of the skin, with the desire to scratch **2** to have a restless desire —*vt.* [Inf.] SCRATCH —*n.* **1** an itching **2** a restless desire —**itch′y, -i·er, -i·est,** *adj.*

THESAURUS

irritate *v.* **1** [To bother] provoke, exasperate, pester; see BOTHER 1, CONFUSE, DISTURB. **2** [To inflame] redden, chafe, swell, erupt, pain, sting; see also BURN, HURT 1, ITCH.

irritated *a.* disturbed, upset, bothered; see TROUBLED.

irritating *a.* annoying, bothersome, trying; see DISTURBING.

irritation *n.* **1** [The result of being irritated] soreness, tenderness, rawness; see FEELING 4. **2** [A disturbed mental state] excitement, upset, provocation; see ANGER, ANNOYANCE.

is[1] *v.* lives, breathes, subsists, transpires, happens, amounts to, equals, comprises, signifies, means.

island *n.* **1** [Land surrounded by water] isle, sandbar, archipelago; see LAND 1. **2** [An isolated spot] haven, retreat, sanctuary; see REFUGE 1, SHELTER.

isolate *v.* confine, detach, seclude; see DIVIDE.

isolated *a.* secluded, apart, backwoods, insular, provincial, segregated, confined, withdrawn, rustic, separate, lonely, forsaken, hidden, remote, out-of-the-way, lonesome, Godforsaken, rare, infrequent; see also ALONE, PRIVATE, SOLITARY.

isolation *n.* detachment, solitude, loneliness, seclusion, segregation, confinement, separation, self-sufficiency, obscurity, retreat, privacy; see also WITHDRAWAL.

issue *n.* **1** [Question] point, matter, problem, concern, point in question, argument; see also MATTER. **2** [Result] upshot, culmination, effect; see RESULT. **3** [Edition] number, copy, impression; see COPY. —**at issue** in dispute, unsettled, controversial; see CONTROVERSIAL. —**take issue** differ, disagree, take a stand against; see OPPOSE 1.

issue *v.* **1** [To emerge] flow out, proceed, come forth; see APPEAR 1. **2** [To be a result of] rise from, spring, originate; see BEGIN 2, RESULT. **3** [To release] circulate, announce, send out; see ADVERTISE, DECLARE, PUBLISH 1.

issued *a.* circulated, broadcast, televised, made public, announced, published, sent out, disseminated, spread; see also DISTRIBUTED.

it *pron.* such a thing, that which, that object, this thing, the subject; see also THAT, THIS.

Italian *a.* Latin, Etruscan, Roman, Florentine, Milanese, Venetian, Neapolitan, Sicilian.

italicize *v.* stress, underline, print in italic type, draw attention to; see also DISTINGUISH 1, EMPHASIZE.

itch *n.* tingling, prickling, crawling, creeping sensation, rawness, psoriasis, scabbiness.

-ite (īt) ⟦< Gr *-itēs*⟧ *suffix* **1** an inhabitant of *[Akronite]* **2** an adherent of *[laborite]* **3** a manufactured product *[dynamite]*
i·tem (īt′əm) ***n.*** ⟦< L *ita*, so, thus⟧ **1** an article; unit; separate thing **2** a bit of news or information
i′tem·ize′ (-īz′) ***vt.*** **-ized′**, **-iz′ing** to specify the items of; set down by items —**i′tem·i·za′tion** ***n.***
it·er·ate (it′ər āt′) ***vt.*** **-at′ed**, **-at′ing** ⟦< L *iterum*, again⟧ to utter or do again —**it′er·a′tion** ***n.***
i·tin·er·ant (ī tin′ər ənt) ***adj.*** ⟦< L *iter*, a walk⟧ traveling from place to place —***n.*** a traveler
i·tin′er·ar′y (-er′ē) ***n.***, *pl.* **-ar′ies** **1** a route **2** a record of a journey **3** a detailed plan for a journey
-i·tis (īt′is) ⟦< Gr *-itis*⟧ *suffix* inflammation of (a specified part or organ) *[neuritis]*
its (its) ***pron.*** that or those belonging to it —***poss. pronominal adj.*** of, belonging to, or done by it
it's (its) *contr.* **1** it is **2** it has
it·self (it self′) ***pron.*** a form of IT, used as an intensive *[the work itself is easy]*, as a reflexive *[the dog bit itself]*, or with the meaning "its true self" *[the bird is not itself today]*
it·ty-bit·ty (it′ē bit′ē) ***adj.*** ⟦baby talk < *little bit*⟧ [Inf.] very small; tiny: also **it·sy-bit·sy** (it′sē bit′sē)
-i·ty (ə tē, i-) ⟦< L *-itas*⟧ *suffix* state, quality, or instance *[chastity]*
IUD *abbrev.* intrauterine (contraceptive) device
IV[1] ***n.***, *pl.* **IVs** ⟦< I(NTRA)V(ENOUS)⟧ *Med.* **1** a procedure in which a hypodermic needle is inserted into a vein to supply blood, nutrients, etc. **2** the apparatus used for this, including the bag of fluid, tubing, and needle
IV[2] *abbrev.* intravenous(ly)
-ive (iv) ⟦< L *-ivus*⟧ *suffix* **1** of or having the nature of *[sportive]* **2** tending to *[retrospective]*
i·vied (ī′vēd) ***adj.*** covered or overgrown with ivy
i·vo·ry (ī′vər ē, īv′rē) ***n.***, *pl.* **-ries** ⟦ult. < Egypt *ȝbw*⟧ **1** the hard, white substance forming the tusks of elephants, walruses, etc. **2** any substance like ivory **3** creamy white —***adj.*** **1** of or like ivory **2** creamy-white
Ivory Coast country on the W coast of Africa: 123,855 sq. mi.; pop. 10,813,000
ivory tower a retreat away from reality or practical affairs
i·vy (ī′vē) ***n.***, *pl.* **i′vies** ⟦OE *ifig*⟧ **1** a climbing vine with a woody stem and evergreen leaves **2** any of various similar climbing plants
-ize (īz) ⟦< Gr *-izein*⟧ *suffix* **1** to cause to be *[sterilize]* **2** to become (like) *[crystallize]* **3** to combine with *[oxidize]* **4** to engage in *[soliloquize]*

THESAURUS

itch ***v.*** creep, prickle, be irritated, crawl, tickle; see also TINGLE.
item ***n.*** piece, article, matter; see DETAIL, PART 1.
itemize ***v.*** inventory, enumerate, number; see DETAIL, LIST 1.
itemized ***a.*** counted, particularized, enumerated; see DETAILED.
itinerant ***a.*** roving, nomadic, peripatetic; see VAGRANT, WANDERING 1.
itinerant ***n.*** nomad, wanderer, vagrant; see TRAMP 1.
itinerary ***n.*** course, travel plans, route; see PATH, PLAN 2, PROGRAM 2, WAY 2.

J

j or **J** (jā) ***n.***, *pl.* **j's, J's** the tenth letter of the English alphabet

jab (jab) ***vt.***, ***vi.*** **jabbed, jab'bing** ⟦< ME *jobben*, to peck⟧ **1** to poke, as with a sharp instrument **2** to punch with short, straight blows —***n.*** a quick thrust or blow

jab·ber (jab'ər) ***vi.***, ***vt.*** ⟦prob. echoic⟧ to speak or say quickly, incoherently, or foolishly; chatter —***n.*** chatter —**jab'ber·er *n.***

ja·bot (zha bō') ***n.*** ⟦Fr, bird's crop⟧ a ruffle or frill down the front of a blouse, etc.

jack (jak) ***n.*** ⟦< the name *Jack*⟧ **1** [*often* **J-**] a man or boy **2** any of various machines used to lift something heavy a short distance *[an automobile jack]* **3** a playing card with a picture of a royal male servant or soldier **4** a small flag flown on a ship's bow to show nationality **5** any of the small, 6-pronged metal pieces tossed and picked up in a game (**jacks**) **6** *Elec.* a plug-in receptacle used to make electrical contact —***vt.*** to raise by means of a jack: usually with *up* —**jack up** [Inf.] to raise (prices, wages, etc.)

jack- [see prec.] *combining form* **1** male *[jackass]* **2** large or strong *[jackknife]* **3** boy; fellow *[jack-in-the-box]*

jack·al (jak'əl) ***n.*** ⟦< Sans⟧ a wild dog of Asia and N Africa

jack·ass (jak'as') ***n.*** ⟦JACK- + ASS⟧ **1** a male donkey **2** a fool

jack'boot' (-bo͞ot') ***n.*** ⟦JACK- + BOOT¹⟧ a long, heavy military boot that covers the knee

jack'daw' (-dô') ***n.*** ⟦JACK- + ME *dawe*, jackdaw⟧ a small European crow

jack·et (jak'it) ***n.*** ⟦< Ar *shakk*⟧ **1** a short coat **2** an outer covering, as the removable paper cover on a book, the metal casing of a bullet, etc.

Jack Frost frost or cold weather personified

jack'ham'mer ***n.*** a portable type of pneumatic hammer, used for breaking up concrete, rock, etc.

jack'-in-the-box' ***n.***, *pl.* **-box'es** a toy consisting of a box from which a figure on a spring jumps up when the lid is lifted: also **jack'-in-a-box'**

jack'-in-the-pul'pit (-po͝ol'pit) ***n.***, *pl.* **-pits** a plant with a flower spike partly arched over by a hoodlike covering

jack'knife' ***n.***, *pl.* **-knives'** **1** a large pocketknife **2** a dive in which the diver keeps knees unbent, touches the feet, and then straightens out —***vi.***, ***vt.*** **-knifed', -knif'ing** to bend or fold at the middle or at a connection

jack'-of-all-trades' ***n.***, *pl.* **jacks'-** [*often* **J-**] one who can do many kinds of work acceptably

jack-o'-lan·tern (jak'ə lant'ərn) ***n.***, *pl.* **-terns** a hollow pumpkin cut to look like a face and used esp. as a decoration at Halloween

jack'pot' ***n.*** ⟦*jack*, playing card + *pot*⟧ **1** cumulative stakes, as in poker **2** any large prize, etc.

jack rabbit a large hare of W North America, with long ears and strong hind legs

Jack·son¹ (jak'sən), **An·drew** (an'dro͞o') 1767-1845; 7th president of the U.S. (1829-37)

Jack·son² (jak'sən) capital of Mississippi, in the SW part: pop. 197,000

Jack·son·ville (jak'sən vil') port in NE Florida: pop. 673,000

Ja·cob (jā'kəb) ***n.*** *Bible* a son of Isaac

jac·quard (jak'ärd, jə kärd') ***n.*** ⟦after J. M. *Jacquard* (1752-1834), Fr inventor⟧ [*sometimes* **J-**] a fabric with a figured weave

Ja·cuz·zi (jə ko͞o'zē) ⟦< *Jacuzzi*, U.S. developers⟧ *trademark for* a kind of whirlpool bath

jade (jād) ***n.*** ⟦< Sp (*piedra de*) *ijada*, (stone of) the side: supposed to cure pains in the side⟧ **1** a hard, greenish, ornamental gemstone **2** a medium green color

jad·ed (jād'id) ***adj.*** **1** tired; worn-out **2** dulled or satiated —**jad'ed·ly *adv.*** —**jad'ed·ness *n.***

jade plant a thick-leaved plant native to S Africa and Asia

jag¹ (jag) ***n.*** ⟦ME *jagge*⟧ a sharp, toothlike projection

jag² (jag) ***n.*** ⟦< ?⟧ [Slang] a drunken spree

jag·ged (jag'id) ***adj.*** having sharp projecting points; notched or ragged —**jag'ged·ly *adv.*** —**jag'ged·ness *n.***

jag·uar (jag'wär') ***n.*** ⟦Port < AmInd (Brazil)⟧ a large, leopardlike cat found from SW U.S. to Argentina

jai a·lai (hī'lī', hī'ə lī') ⟦< Basque *jai*, celebration + *alai*, merry⟧ a game like handball, played with a basketlike racket

jail (jāl) ***n.*** ⟦ult. < L *cavea*, cage⟧ a prison, esp. for minor offenders or persons awaiting trial —***vt.*** to put or keep in jail

jail'break' ***n.*** a breaking out of jail

jail'er or **jail'or** ***n.*** a person in charge of a jail or of prisoners

Ja·kar·ta (jə kär'tə) capital of Indonesia, on Java island: pop. *c.* 6,503,000

ja·la·pe·ño (hä'lə pān'yō) ***n.*** ⟦Mex⟧ a kind of hot pepper, orig. from Mexico

Ja·lis·co (hä lēs'kô) state of W Mexico, on the Pacific: 30,941 sq. mi.; pop. 5,303,000

ja·lop·y (jə läp'ē) ***n.***, *pl.* **-lop'ies** ⟦< ?⟧ [Slang] an old, ramshackle car

jal·ou·sie (jal'ə sē') ***n.*** ⟦Fr < It *gelosia*, jealousy⟧ a window, shade, or door formed of adjustable horizontal slats of wood, metal, or glass

jam¹ (jam) ***vt.*** **jammed, jam'ming** ⟦< ?⟧ **1** to squeeze into a confined space **2** to crush **3** to crowd **4** to crowd into or block (a passageway, etc.) **5** to make stick so that it cannot move or work **6** to make (radio broadcasts, etc.) unintelligible, as by sending out other signals on the same wavelength —***vi.*** **1** *a)* to become stuck fast *b)* to become unworkable because of jammed parts **2** to become squeezed into a confined space **3** [Inf.] *Jazz* to improvise, as in a gathering of musicians (**jam session**) —***n.*** **1** a jamming or being jammed *[a traffic jam]* **2** [Inf.] a difficult situation

jam² (jam) ***n.*** ⟦< ? prec.⟧ fruit boiled with sugar to a thick mixture

Ja·mai·ca (jə mā'kə) country on an island in the West Indies, south of Cuba: 4,411 sq. mi.; pop. 2,374,000 —**Ja·mai'can *adj.*, *n.***

jamb (jam) ***n.*** ⟦< LL *gamba*, hoof⟧ a side post of a doorway, window, etc.

jam·bo·ree (jam'bə rē') ***n.*** ⟦< ?⟧ **1** a noisy party, gathering, etc. **2** a large assembly of Boy Scouts from many places

James (jāmz), **Henry** 1843-1916; U.S. novelist, in England

James·town (jāmz'toun') former village in Virginia: the 1st permanent English colonial settlement in America (1607)

jam·packed (jam'pakt') ***adj.*** [Inf.] tightly packed

jan·gle (jaŋ'gəl) ***vi.*** **-gled, -gling** ⟦< OFr *jangler*⟧ to make a harsh, usually metallic sound —***vt.*** **1** to cause to jangle **2** to irritate *[to jangle someone's nerves]* —***n.*** a jangling —**jan'gler *n.***

THESAURUS

jab *n.* poke, punch, hit; see BLOW.

jabber *v.* gibber, babble, mutter; see MURMUR 1, SOUND.

jack *n.* automobile jack, pneumatic jack, hydraulic jack; see DEVICE 1, TOOL 1. —**jack up*** lift, add to, hike*; see INCREASE, RAISE 1.

jacket *n.* tunic, jerkin, parka; see CAPE 2, CLOTHES, COAT 1.

jackknife *n.* clasp knife, case knife, pocket knife; see KNIFE.

jack-of-all-trades *n.* handyman, factotum, versatile person; see LABORER, WORKMAN.

jackpot *n.* bonanza, find, winnings; see LUCK 1, PROFIT 2, SUCCESS 2.

jagged *a.* serrated, ragged, rugged; see IRREGULAR 4, ROUGH 1.

jail *n.* penitentiary, cage, cell, dungeon, bastille, pound, reformatory, stockade, detention camp, gaol (British), concentration camp, penal institution, house of detention, lockup, the big house*, pen*, stir*, clink*, jug*, can*; see also PRISON.

jail *v.* confine, lock up, incarcerate, sentence, impound, detain, arrest, put behind bars, put in the clink*, throw away the keys*; see also IMPRISON.—*Ant.* FREE, liberate, discharge.

jailed *a.* arrested, incarcerated, in jail; see CONFINED 3, HELD, UNDER ARREST.

jam¹ *v.* **1** [To force one's way] jostle, squeeze, crowd, throng, press, thrust, pack; see also PUSH 1. **2** [To compress] bind, squeeze, push; see COMPRESS, PACK 2, PRESS 1.

jam¹,² *n.* **1** [Preserves] conserve, fruit butter, spread, marmalade; blackberry jam, plum jam, strawberry jam, etc.; see also JELLY. **2** [*A troublesome situation] fix*, dilemma, problem; see DIFFICULTY 1.

jammed *a.* **1** [Stuck fast] wedged, caught, frozen; see TIGHT 2. **2** [Thronged] crowded, busy, congested; see FULL 1.

jan·i·tor (jan′i tər) ***n.*** ⟦L, doorkeeper⟧ one who takes care of a building, doing routine repairs, etc. —**jan′i·to′ri·al** (-i tôr′ē əl) ***adj.***

Jan·u·ar·y (jan′yo͞o er′ē) ***n.***, *pl.* **-ar′ies** ⟦< L < *Janus*, Roman god who was a patron of beginnings and endings⟧ the first month of the year, having 31 days: abbrev. *abbrev.* **Jan.**

ja·pan (jə pan′) ***n.*** ⟦orig. made in Japan⟧ a lacquer giving a hard, glossy finish

Ja·pan (jə pan′) **1** island country in the Pacific, off the E coast of Asia: 145,841 sq. mi.; pop. 123,612,000 **2 Sea of** arm of the Pacific, between Japan & E Asia

Jap·a·nese (jap′ə nēz′) ***adj.*** of Japan or its people, language, etc. —***n.*** **1** *pl.* **-nese′** a person born or living in Japan **2** the language of Japan

Japanese beetle a shiny, green-and-brown beetle, orig. from Japan, damaging to crops

jape (jāp) ***vi.*** **japed, jap′ing** ⟦< OFr *japer,* to howl⟧ **1** to joke **2** to play tricks —***n.*** **1** a joke **2** a trick

jar[1] (jär) ***vi.*** **jarred, jar′ring** ⟦ult. echoic⟧ **1** to make a harsh sound; grate **2** to have an irritating effect (*on* one) **3** to vibrate from an impact **4** to clash; conflict —***vt.*** to jolt —***n.*** **1** a grating sound **2** a vibration due to impact **3** a jolt

jar[2] (jär) ***n.*** ⟦< Ar *jarrah,* earthen container⟧ **1** a container made of glass, earthenware, etc., with a large opening **2** as much as a jar will hold: also **jar′ful′**

jar·di·niere (jär′də nir′) ***n.*** ⟦< Fr < *jardin*, a garden⟧ an ornamental pot or stand for flowers or plants

jar·gon (jär′gən) ***n.*** ⟦< MFr, a chattering⟧ **1** unintelligible talk **2** the specialized vocabulary of those in the same work, way of life, etc.

jas·mine (jaz′min, jas′-) ***n.*** ⟦< Pers *yāsamīn*⟧ any of certain plants of warm regions, with fragrant flowers of yellow, red, or white

Ja·son (jā′sən) ***n.*** *Gr. Myth.* the leader of the Argonauts: cf. ARGONAUT

jas·per (jas′pər) ***n.*** ⟦< Gr *iaspis*⟧ an opaque variety of colored quartz, usually reddish

jaun·dice (jôn′dis) ***n.*** ⟦< L *galbus*, yellow⟧ a diseased condition in which the eyeballs, skin, and urine become abnormally yellowish as a result of increased bile in the blood —***vt.*** **-diced, -dic·ing** **1** to cause to have jaundice **2** to make bitter through envy, etc.

jaunt (jônt) ***vi.*** ⟦< ?⟧ to take a short pleasure trip —***n.*** such a trip

jaun·ty (jôn′tē) ***adj.*** **-ti·er, -ti·est** ⟦< Fr *gentil*, genteel⟧ showing an easy confidence; sprightly or perky —**jaun′ti·ly** ***adv.*** —**jaun′ti·ness** ***n.***

Ja·va[1] (jä′və, jav′ə) ***n.*** **1** a coffee grown on Java **2** [*often* **j-**] [Slang] any coffee

Java[2] (jä′və, jav′ə) large island of Indonesia —**Jav·a·nese** (jä′və nēz′), *pl.* **-nese′, *adj.*, *n.***

jav·e·lin (jav′lin, jav′ə lin) ***n.*** ⟦MFr *javeline*⟧ a light spear, esp. one thrown for distance in an athletic contest

jaw (jô) ***n.*** ⟦< OFr *joue*, cheek⟧ **1** either of the two bony parts that hold the teeth and frame the mouth **2** either of two movable parts that grasp or crush something, as in a vise —***vi.*** [Slang] to talk

jaw′bone′ ***n.*** a bone of a jaw, esp. of the lower jaw —***vt.***, ***vi.*** **-boned′, -bon′ing** to try to persuade by using the influence of one's office or position

jaw′break′er ***n.*** **1** a hard, usually round candy **2** [Slang] a word hard to pronounce

jaw′less fish a jawless fish with an eel-like body and a circular sucking mouth, as the lamprey

jay (jā) ***n.*** ⟦< LL *gaius*, jay⟧ any of several birds, usually strikingly colored, as the blue jay

jay′walk′ ***vi.*** to walk across a street without obeying traffic rules and signals —**jay′walk′er** ***n.***

jazz (jaz) ***n.*** ⟦< ?⟧ **1** a kind of syncopated, highly rhythmic music originated by Southern blacks in the late 19th c. **2** [Slang] talk, acts, etc. regarded disparagingly —***vt.*** [Slang] to enliven or embellish: usually with *up*

jazz′y ***adj.*** **-i·er, -i·est** **1** of or like jazz **2** [Slang] lively, flashy, etc.

JD *abbrev.* **1** ⟦L *Jurum Doctor*⟧ Doctor of Laws: also **J.D.** **2** juvenile delinquent: also **jd**

jeal·ous (jel′əs) ***adj.*** ⟦see ZEAL⟧ **1** watchful in guarding *[jealous* of one's rights*]* **2** *a)* resentfully suspicious of rivalry *[*a *jealous* lover*]* *b)* resentfully envious *c)* resulting from such feelings *[*a *jealous* rage*]* —**jeal′ous·ly** ***adv.***

jeal′ous·y ***n.*** **1** the quality or condition of being jealous **2** *pl.* **-ous·ies** a jealous feeling

jean (jēn) ***n.*** ⟦< L *Genua*, Genoa, city in Italy⟧ **1** a durable, twilled cotton cloth **2** [*pl.*] trousers of this or of denim

jeep (jēp) ***n.*** ⟦< creature in comic strip by E. C. Segar (1894-1938)⟧ a small, rugged military vehicle of WWII —**[J-]** *trademark for* a similar vehicle for civilian use

jeer (jir) ***vt.***, ***vi.*** ⟦< ? CHEER⟧ to make fun of (a person or thing) in a rude, sarcastic manner; scoff (at) —***n.*** a jeering remark

Jef·fer·son (jef′ər sən), **Thom·as** (täm′əs) 1743-1826; 3d president of the U.S. (1801-09)

Jefferson City capital of Missouri: pop. 35,000

Je·ho·vah (ji hō′və) ***n.*** ⟦< Heb⟧ God

je·june (ji jo͞on′) ***adj.*** ⟦L *jejunus*, empty⟧ **1** not interesting or satisfying **2** not mature; childish

je·ju·num (jē jo͞o′nəm) ***n.***, *pl.* **-na** (-nə) ⟦< L *jejunus,* empty⟧ the middle part of the small intestine

jell (jel) ***vi.***, ***vt.*** ⟦< L *gelare*, freeze⟧ **1** to become, or make into, jelly **2** [Inf.] to crystallize *[*plans haven't *jelled* yet*]*

jell·o (jel′ō) ***n.*** ⟦< *Jell-O*, a trademark⟧ a flavored gelatin used as a dessert, etc.

jel·ly (jel′ē) ***n.***, *pl.* **-lies** ⟦< L *gelare,* freeze⟧ **1** a soft, gelatinous food made from cooked fruit syrup or meat juice **2** any substance like this —***vi.***, ***vt.*** **-lied, -ly·ing** JELL (sense 1)

jelly bean a small, bean-shaped, gelatinous candy: also **jel′ly·bean′** ***n.***

jel′ly·fish′ ***n.***, *pl.* **-fish′** or (for different species) **-fish′es** **1** a sea animal with an umbrella-shaped, jellylike body and long tentacles **2** [Inf.] a weak-willed person

jel′ly·roll′ ***n.*** a thin sheet of sponge cake spread with jelly and rolled up

jeop·ard·ize (jep′ər dīz′) ***vt.*** **-ized′, -iz′ing** to put in jeopardy

jeop′ard·y (-dē) ***n.*** ⟦< OFr *jeu parti,* lit., a game with even chances⟧ great danger or risk

jer·e·mi·ad (jer′ə mī′ad′, -əd) ***n.*** a long lamentation or complaint: in allusion to the *Lamentations of Jeremiah*

Jer′e·mi′ah (-ə) ***n.*** *Bible* a Hebrew prophet of the 7th and 6th c. B.C.

Jer·i·cho (jer′i kō′) city in W Jordan: site of an ancient city in Canaan

jerk (jurk) ***n.*** ⟦< ?⟧ **1** a sharp, abrupt pull, twist, etc. **2** a sudden muscular contraction **3** [Slang] a person

THESAURUS

janitor ***n.*** building custodian, watchman, doorman; see ATTENDANT, CUSTODIAN.

jar[1] ***v.*** jolt, bounce, bump; see CRASH 4, HIT 1.

jar[1,2] ***n.*** **1** [A glass or earthen container] crock, pot, fruit jar, can, vessel, basin, beaker, jug, cruet, vat, decanter, pitcher, bottle, flagon, flask, vial, vase, chalice, urn; see also CONTAINER. **2** [A jolt] jounce, thud, thump; see BUMP 1.

jargon ***n.*** **1** [Trite speech] banality, patter, hackneyed terms, overused words, commonplace phrases, shopworn language, trite vocabulary, hocus-pocus; see also LANGUAGE 1. **2** [Specialized vocabulary or pronunciation, etc.] argot, patois, lingo, broken English, idiom, pidgin English, vernacular, colloquialism, coined words, localism, rhyming slang, doubletalk, officialese, newspeak, journalese; see also DIALECT, SLANG.

jarring ***a.*** **1** [Discordant] unharmonious, grating, rasping; see HARSH, LOUD 1, 2, SHRILL. **2** [Jolting] bumpy, rough, uneven; see UNSTABLE 1.

jaunt ***n.*** excursion, trip, tour; see JOURNEY, WALK 3.

jaw ***n.*** jawbone, muzzle, jowl, mandible, maxilla, chops; see also BONE.

jaywalk ***v.*** cross against a light, cut across, cross illegally.

jazz ***n.*** Dixieland, ragtime, modern jazz, traditional jazz, improvisation, hot music, bop, bebop, hard bop, mainstream, fusion, free jazz, swing, big-band, cool jazz, boogie-woogie; see also MUSIC 1.

jealous ***a.*** possessive, demanding, monopolizing, envious, watchful, resentful, mistrustful, doubting, apprehensive; see also SUSPICIOUS 1.—*Ant.* TRUSTING, confiding, believing.

jealousy ***n.*** resentment, possessiveness, suspicion; see DOUBT, ENVY.

jell ***v.*** set, crystallize, condense; see FREEZE 1, HARDEN, STIFFEN, THICKEN.

jelly ***n.*** jell, extract, preserve, gelatin; apple jelly, currant jelly, raspberry jelly, etc.; see also JAM 1.

jellyfish ***n.*** medusa, coelenterate, hydrozoan; see FISH.

jeopardize ***v.*** imperil, expose, venture; see ENDANGER, RISK.

jeopardy ***n.*** risk, peril, exposure; see CHANCE 1, DANGER.

jerk ***n.*** **1** [A twitch] tic, shrug, wiggle, shake, quiver, flick, jiggle; see also BUMP 1. **2** [*A contemptible person] scoundrel, rat*, creep*; see FOOL,

regarded as disagreeable, contemptible, etc. —*vi., vt.* **1** to move with a jerk; pull sharply **2** to twitch

jer·kin (jur′kin) *n.* ⟦< ?⟧ a short, closefitting jacket, often sleeveless

jerk′wa′ter *adj.* [Inf.] small, unimportant, etc. *[a jerkwater town]*

jerk·y[1] (jur′kē) *adj.* **jerk′i·er, jerk′i·est** **1** moving by jerks; spasmodic **2** [Slang] foolish, mean, etc. —**jerk′i·ly** *adv.*

jer·ky[2] (jur′kē) *n.* ⟦< Sp *charqui*⟧ meat preserved by being sliced into strips and dried in the sun

jer·ry-built (jer′ē bilt′) *adj.* built poorly, of cheap materials

jer·sey (jur′zē) *n., pl.* **-seys** ⟦after *Jersey,* one of the Channel Islands⟧ **1** [**J-**] any of a breed of reddish-brown dairy cattle, orig. from Jersey **2** a soft, knitted cloth **3** a close-fitting, knitted upper garment

Jer·sey City (jur′zē) city in NE New Jersey, across the Hudson from New York City: pop. 229,000

Je·ru·sa·lem (jə ro͞oz′ə ləm) capital of Israel (the country): pop. 591,000

jest (jest) *n.* ⟦< L *gerere,* perform⟧ **1** a mocking remark; taunt **2** a joke **3** fun; joking **4** something to be laughed at —*vi.* **1** to jeer **2** to joke

jest′er *n.* one who jests; esp., a man employed to amuse a medieval ruler

Jes·u·it (jezh′o͞o it, jez′-) *n.* a member of the Society of Jesus, a Roman Catholic religious order for men, founded in 1534

Je·sus (jē′zəz, -zəs) *c.* 8-4 B.C.-A.D. 29?; founder of the Christian religion: also **Jesus Christ**

jet[1] (jet) *vt., vi.* **jet′ted, jet′ting** ⟦< L *jacere,* to throw⟧ **1** to gush out in a stream **2** to travel or convey by jet airplane —*n.* **1** a stream of liquid or gas suddenly emitted **2** a spout or nozzle for emitting a jet **3** a jet-propelled airplane: in full **jet (air)plane** —*adj.* driven by jet propulsion

jet[2] (jet) *n.* ⟦after *Gagas,* town in Asia Minor⟧ **1** a hard, black mineral like coal, polished and used in jewelry **2** a lustrous black —*adj.* black like jet

jet lag a disruption of the daily body rhythms, associated with high-speed travel by jet airplane to distant time zones —**jet′-lagged′** *adj.*

jet′port′ *n.* a large airport with long runways, for use by jetliners

jet propulsion propulsion of airplanes, boats, etc. by the forcing of compressed outside air and hot exhaust gases through a jet nozzle —**jet′-pro·pelled′** (-prə peld′) *adj.*

jet·sam (jet′səm) *n.* ⟦var. of JETTISON⟧ cargo thrown overboard to lighten a ship in danger

jet set fashionable people who frequently travel, often by jet, as for pleasure —**jet′-set′ter** *n.*

Jet Ski *trademark for* a motorcyclelike watercraft propelled by a jet of water —[**j- s-**] any such watercraft

jet stream high-velocity winds moving from west to east, high above the earth

jet·ti·son (jet′ə sən) *vt.* ⟦< L *jactare,* to throw⟧ **1** to throw (goods) overboard so as to lighten a ship in danger **2** to discard

jet·ty (jet′ē) *n., pl.* **-ties** ⟦see JET[1]⟧ **1** a wall built out into the water to restrain currents, protect a harbor, etc. **2** a landing pier

Jew (jo͞o) *n.* ⟦< Heb *yehūdī,* citizen of Judah⟧ **1** a person descended, or regarded as descended, from the ancient Hebrews **2** a person whose religion is Judaism

jew·el (jo͞o′əl) *n.* ⟦ult. < L *jocus,* a joke⟧ **1** a valuable ring, necklace, etc., esp. one set with gems **2** a precious stone; gem **3** any person or thing that is very precious or valuable **4** a small gem used as a bearing in a watch —*vt.* **-eled** or **-elled, -el·ing** or **-el·ling** to decorate or set with jewels

jewel box a thin plastic case used to hold a compact disk

jew′el·er or **jew′el·ler** (-ər) *n.* ⟦ME *jueler* < OFr *joieleor* < *joel:* see JEWEL⟧ one who makes, repairs, or deals in jewelry, watches, etc.

jew′el·ry *n.* ornaments such as rings, bracelets, etc., collectively

Jew·ish (jo͞o′ish) *adj.* of or having to do with Jews or Judaism —*n.* loosely, Yiddish —**Jew′ish·ness** *n.*

Jew·ry (jo͞o′rē) *n.* the Jewish people

jew's-harp or **jews'-harp** (jo͞oz′härp′) *n.* ⟦< Du *jeugdtromp,* child's trumpet⟧ a small, metal musical instrument held between the teeth and plucked to produce twanging tones

Jez·e·bel (jez′ə bel′) *n. Bible* a wicked queen of Israel

Ji·ang Ze·min (jē äŋ′ zə min′) 1926- ; president of China (1993-)

jib (jib) *n.* ⟦Dan *gib*⟧ a triangular sail secured forward of the mast or foremast

jibe[1] (jīb) *vi.* **jibed, jib′ing** ⟦< Du *gijpen*⟧ **1** to shift from one side of a ship to the other, as a fore-and-aft sail **2** to change the course of a ship so that the sails jibe **3** [Inf.] to be in agreement or accord: often with *with*

jibe[2] (jīb) *vi., vt.,* **jibed, jib′ing,** *n.* GIBE

jif·fy (jif′ē) *n., pl.* **-fies** ⟦< ?⟧ [Inf.] a very short time: also **jiff**

jig (jig) *n.* ⟦prob. < MFr *giguer,* to dance⟧ **1** a fast, springy dance in triple time, or music for this **2** a device used to guide a tool —*vi., vt.* **jigged, jig′ging** to dance (a jig) —**in jig time** [Inf.] very quickly —**the jig is up** [Slang] no chance is left

jig·ger (jig′ər) *n.* **1** a small glass, usually of $1\frac{1}{2}$ ounces, used to measure liquor **2** the contents of a jigger

jig·gle (jig′əl) *vt., vi.* **-gled, -gling** ⟦< JIG⟧ to move in quick, slight jerks —*n.* a jiggling

jig·saw (jig′sô′) *n.* a saw with a narrow blade set in a frame, for cutting curves, etc.

jigsaw puzzle a puzzle consisting of a picture cut up into irregularly shaped pieces, which must be put together again

jilt (jilt) *vt.* ⟦< *Jill,* sweetheart⟧ to reject or cast off (a previously accepted lover, etc.)

Jim Crow ⟦name of an early black minstrel song⟧ [*also* **j- c-**] [Inf.] discrimination against or segregation of blacks —**Jim′-Crow′** *vt., adj.*

jim·my (jim′ē) *n., pl.* **-mies** ⟦< *James*⟧ a short crowbar, used as by burglars to pry open windows, etc. —*vt.* **-mied, -my·ing** to pry open with or as with a jimmy

jim·son weed (jim′sən) ⟦< *Jamestown weed*⟧ a poisonous weed with white or purplish, trumpet-shaped flowers

jin·gle (jiŋ′gəl) *vi.* **-gled, -gling** ⟦echoic⟧ to make light, ringing sounds, as small bells —*vt.* to cause to jingle —*n.* **1** a jingling sound **2** a catchy verse or song with easy rhythm, simple rhymes, etc.

jin·go·ism (jiŋ′gō iz′əm) *n.* ⟦< phrase *by jingo* in patriotic Brit song⟧ chauvinistic advocacy of an aggressive, warlike foreign policy —**jin′go·ist** *n.* —**jin′go·is′tic** *adj.*

jin·ni (ji nē′, jin′ē) *n., pl.* **jinn** ⟦Ar⟧ *Muslim Folklore* a supernatural being that can influence human affairs

jin·rik·i·sha (jin rik′shô′) *n.* ⟦Jpn < *jin,* a man + *riki,* power + *sha,* carriage⟧ a small, two-wheeled carriage, pulled by a man, esp. formerly in East Asia: also sp. **jin·rick′sha′** or **jin·rik′sha′**

jinx (jiŋks) [Inf.] *n.* ⟦< Gr *iynx,* the wryneck (bird used in black magic)⟧ a person or thing supposed to bring bad luck —*vt.* to be a jinx to

jit·ney (jit′nē) *n., pl.* **-neys** ⟦< ? Fr *jeton,* a token⟧ a small bus or a car carrying passengers for a low fare

jit·ter·bug (jit′ər bug′) *n.* a fast, acrobatic dance for couples, esp. in the 1940s —*vi.* **-bugged′, -bug′ging** to do this dance

THESAURUS

RASCAL.

jerk *v.* **1** [To undergo a spasm] have a convulsion, quiver, shiver; see SHAKE 1, TWITCH 2. **2** [To move an object with a quick tug] snatch, grab, flick; see SEIZE 1, 2.

jester *n.* comedian, buffoon, joker; see ACTOR, CLOWN, FOOL.

jet[1] *n.* **1** [A stream of liquid or gas] spray, stream, spurt; see FOUNTAIN 1. **2** [A jet-propelled airplane] turbojet, turboprop, SST; see PLANE 3. *Types of jets include the following:* 737, 747, 757, 767, 777, DC-10, MD-80, Concorde.

jet[1] *v.* **1** [To gush out in a stream] spout, squirt, spurt; see FLOW. **2** [To travel by jet airplane] take a jet, go by jet, fly; see TRAVEL.

Jew *n.* Hebrew, Israelite, Semite.

jewel *n.* bauble, gem, trinket; see DIAMOND. *Jewels include the following:* emerald, amethyst, sapphire, opal, pearl, jade, aquamarine, moonstone, agate, ruby, turquoise, topaz, garnet, jasper, coral, peridot, lapis lazuli, bloodstone, onyx, zircon.

jeweler *n.* goldsmith, diamond setter, lapidary; see ARTIST, CRAFTSMAN, SPECIALIST.

jewelry *n.* gems, jewels, baubles, trinkets, adornments, frippery, ornaments, costume jewelry, bangles; see also JEWEL.

Jewish *a.* Hebrew, Semitic, Yiddish.

jibe[1]* *v.* agree, match, correspond; see RESEMBLE, AGREE.

jiggle *v.* shake, twitch, wiggle; see JERK 2.

jingle *n.* tinkle, jangle, clank; see NOISE 1.

jingle *v.* tinkle, clink, rattle; see SOUND.

jinx* *n.* evil eye, hex, curse, spell; see also CHANCE 1.

jit·ters (jit′ərz) ***pl.n.*** [Inf.] an uneasy, nervous feeling; fidgets: with *the* —**jit′ter·y** ***adj.***

jive (jīv) [Slang] ***n.*** ⟦< JIBE[2]⟧ foolish, exaggerated, or insincere talk —***adj.*** insincere, fraudulent, etc.

Joan of Arc (jōn əv ärk), Saint (1412-31); Fr. military heroine: burned at the stake for witchcraft

job (jäb) ***n.*** ⟦< ?⟧ **1** a piece of work done for pay **2** a task; duty **3** the thing or material being worked on **4** employment; work —***adj.*** hired or done by the job —***vt., vi.*** **jobbed, job′bing** **1** to deal in (goods) as a jobber **2** to let or sublet (work, contracts, etc.) —**job′hold′er** ***n.*** —**job′less** ***adj.***

Job (jōb) ***n.*** *Bible* a man who suffered much but kept his faith in God

job action a refusal by a group of employees (esp. a group forbidden by law to strike) to perform their duties in an effort to win certain demands

job·ber (jäb′ər) ***n.*** **1** one who buys goods in quantity and sells them to dealers; wholesaler **2** one who works by the job or does piecework

job lot an assortment of goods for sale as one quantity

jock (jäk) ***n.*** **1** *short for: a)* JOCKEY *b)* JOCKSTRAP **2** [Slang] a male athlete

jock·ey (jäk′ē) ***n.***, *pl.* **-eys** ⟦< Scot dim. of JACK⟧ one whose work is riding horses in races —***vt., vi.*** **-eyed, -ey·ing** **1** to cheat; swindle **2** to maneuver for position or advantage

jock·strap (jäk′strap′) ***n.*** ⟦slang *jock,* penis + STRAP⟧ an elastic belt with a pouch for supporting the genitals, worn by male athletes

jo·cose (jō kōs′) ***adj.*** ⟦< L *jocus,* a joke⟧ joking or playful —**jo·cose′ly** ***adv.*** —**jo·cos′i·ty** (-käs′ə tē), *pl.* **-ties**, or **jo·cose′ness** ***n.***

joc·u·lar (jäk′yə lər) ***adj.*** ⟦< L *jocus,* a joke⟧ joking; full of fun —**joc′u·lar′i·ty** (-lar′ə tē), *pl.* **-ties**, ***n.***

joc·und (jäk′ənd) ***adj.*** ⟦< L *jucundus,* pleasant⟧ cheerful; genial —**joc′und·ly** ***adv.***

jodh·purs (jäd′pərz) ***pl.n.*** ⟦after *Jodhpur,* former state in India⟧ riding breeches made loose and full above the knees and closefitting below

jog[1] (jäg) ***vt.*** **jogged, jog′ging** ⟦ME *joggen,* to spur (a horse)⟧ **1** to give a little shake to; nudge **2** to rouse (the memory) —***vi.*** to move along at a slow, steady, jolting pace or trot; specif., to engage in jogging as a form of exercise —***n.*** **1** a little shake or nudge **2** a slow, steady, jolting motion or trot **3** a jogging —**jog′ger** ***n.***

jog[2] (jäg) ***n.*** ⟦var. of JAG[1]⟧ **1** a projecting or notched part in a surface or line **2** a sharp change of direction

jog′ging ***n.*** trotting slowly and steadily as a form of exercise

jog·gle (jäg′əl) ***vt., vi.*** **-gled, -gling** ⟦< JOG[1]⟧ to shake or jolt slightly —***n.*** a slight jolt

Jo·han·nes·burg (jō han′is burg′) city in NE South Africa: pop. 713,000

john (jän) ***n.*** [Slang] **1** a toilet **2** [*also* **J-**] a prostitute's customer

John (jän) ***n.*** *Bible* **1** a Christian apostle, the reputed author of the fourth Gospel **2** this book

John Bull *personification of* England or an Englishman

John Doe (dō) a fictitious name used in legal papers for an unknown person

John·son (jän′sən) **1 An·drew** (an′drōō′) 1808-75; 17th president of the U.S. (1865-69) **2 Lyn·don Baines** (lin′dən bānz′) 1908-73; 36th president of the U.S. (1963-69) **3 Samuel** 1709-84; Eng. lexicographer & writer

John the Baptist *Bible* the forerunner and baptizer of Jesus

join (join) ***vt., vi.*** ⟦< L *jungere*⟧ **1** to bring or come together (with); connect; unite **2** to become a part or member of (a club, etc.) **3** to participate (*in* a conversation, etc.)

join′er ***n.*** a carpenter who finishes interior woodwork

joint (joint) ***n.*** ⟦< L *jungere*⟧ **1** a place where, or way in which, two things are joined **2** any of the parts of a jointed whole **3** a large cut of meat with the bone still in it **4** [Slang] a cheap bar, restaurant, etc., or any house, building, etc. **5** [Slang] a marijuana cigarette —***adj.*** **1** common to two or more *[joint* property*]* **2** sharing with another *[*a *joint* owner*]* —***vt.*** **1** to connect by or provide with a joint or joints **2** to cut (meat) into joints —**out of joint** **1** dislocated **2** disordered

joint′ly ***adv.*** in common

joist (joist) ***n.*** ⟦< OFr *giste,* a bed⟧ any of the parallel beams that hold up the planks of a floor or the laths of a ceiling

joke (jōk) ***n.*** ⟦L *jocus*⟧ **1** anything said or done to arouse laughter, as a funny anecdote **2** a thing done or said merely in fun **3** a person or thing to be laughed at —***vi.*** **joked, jok′ing** to make jokes —**jok′ing·ly** ***adv.***

jok′er ***n.*** **1** one who jokes: also **joke′ster** **2** a cunningly worded provision, as in a legal document, intended to deceive **3** a playing card with the image of a jester on it **4** [Slang] a contemptibly foolish or inept person

jok′ey ***adj.*** comical or lighthearted: also **jok′y** —**jok′i·ness** ***n.***

jol·li·ty (jäl′ə tē) ***n.*** a being jolly

jol·ly (jäl′ē) ***adj.*** **-li·er, -li·est** ⟦OFr *joli*⟧ **1** full of high spirits and good humor; merry **2** [Inf.] enjoyable —***vt., vi.*** **-lied, -ly·ing** [Inf.] to try to make (a person) feel good, as by coaxing: often with *along* —**jol′li·ly** ***adv.*** —**jol′li·ness** ***n.***

jolt (jōlt) ***vt.*** ⟦< earlier *jot*⟧ **1** to shake up, as with a bumpy ride **2** to shock or surprise —***vi.*** to move along in a bumpy manner —***n.*** **1** a sudden jerk, bump, etc. **2** a shock or surprise

Jo·nah (jō′nə) ***n.*** **1** *Bible* a Hebrew prophet: cast over-

THESAURUS

job *n.* **1** [Gainful employment] situation, place, position, appointment, operation, task, line, calling, vocation, career, craft, pursuit, office, function, livelihood; see also BUSINESS 1, PROFESSION 1, TRADE 2, WORK 2. **2** [Something to be done] task, business, action, act, mission, assignment, affair, concern, obligation, enterprise, undertaking, project, chore, errand, care, matter in hand, commission, function, responsibility, office, tour of duty, operation; see also DUTY 1. **3** [The amount of work done] assignment, day's work, output; see DUTY 1. —**odd jobs** miscellaneous duties, chores, occasional labor; see WORK 2. —**on the job** busy, engaged, occupied; see BUSY 1.

jog[1] ***n.*** **1** [A slow run] trot, amble, pace; see RUN 1. **2** [A bump] nudge, poke, shake; see BLOW, BUMP 1. —**jog someone's memory** bring up, recall, suggest; see REMIND.

jog[1] ***v.*** run, do roadwork, trot; see RUN 1.

join *v.* **1** [To unite] put together, blend, combine, bring in contact with, touch, connect, couple, mix, assemble, bind together, fasten, attach, annex, pair with, link, yoke, marry, wed, copulate, cement, weld, clasp, fuse, lock, grapple, clamp, entwine; see also UNITE.—*Ant.* SEPARATE, sunder, sever. **2** [To enter the company of] go to, seek, associate with, join forces, go to the aid of, place by the side of, follow, register, team up with, take up with, be in, sign on, sign up, go in with, fall in with, consort, enlist, fraternize, throw in with*, pair with, affiliate, side with, make one of, take part in, seek a place among, advance toward, seek reception, hook up*, go to meet.—*Ant.* DESERT, leave, abandon. **3** [*To adjoin] lie next to, neighbor, border, fringe, verge upon, be adjacent to, open into, be close to, bound, lie beside, be at hand, touch, skirt, parallel, rim, hem.

joined *a.* linked, yoked, coupled, allied, akin, intertwined, blended, connected, united, federated, banded, wedded, married, mixed, tied together, combined, touching, cemented, welded, fused, locked, clipped together, accompanying, associated, confederated, mingled, spliced, affixed, attached, joint, incorporated, involved, inseparable, affiliated, related, pieced together, coupled with, bound up with; see also UNIFIED.—*Ant.* SEPARATED, disparate, apart.

joint *n.* **1** [A juncture] union, coupling, hinge, tie, swivel, link, connection, point of union, bond, splice, bend, hyphen, junction, bridge; see also BOND 1. **2** [A section] piece, unit, portion; see LINK, PART 3. **3** [*A cheap bar, restaurant, etc.] hangout*, dive*, hole in the wall*; see BAR 2, RESTAURANT. **4** [*A marijuana cigarette] roach*, doobie*, reefer*, stick*; see also DRUG. —**out of joint** dislocated, disjointed, wrong; see DISORDERED.

jointly *a.* conjointly, mutually, combined; see TOGETHER.

joke *n.* prank, put-on*, game, sport, frolic, practical joke, jest, pun, witticism, play on words, quip, pleasantry, banter, drollery, retort, repartee, crack*, wisecrack*, clowning, caper, mischief, escapade, tomfoolery, play, antic, spree, farce, monkeyshine*, shenanigan*, horseplay, stunt, gag*; see also TRICK 1.

joke *v.* jest, quip, banter, laugh, raise laughter, poke fun, play, frolic, play tricks, pun, twit, trick, fool, make merry, play the fool, wisecrack*, pull someone's leg*.

joking *a.* humorous, facetious, not serious; see FUNNY 1.

jokingly *a.* facetiously, amusingly, not seriously; see HUMOROUSLY.

jolly *a.* gay, merry, joyful; see HAPPY.

jolt *n.* **1** [A bump] jar, punch, bounce; see BLOW, BUMP 1. **2** [A surprise] jar, start, shock; see SURPRISE 2, WONDER 1.

board and swallowed by a big fish, he was later cast up unharmed **2** one who brings bad luck

Jones (jōnz), **John Paul** 1747-92; Am. naval officer in the Revolutionary War, born in Scotland

jon·quil (jäŋ′kwil, jän′-) ***n.*** ⟦< L *juncus*, a rush⟧ a species of narcissus with small, yellow flowers

Jon·son (jän′sən), **Ben** (ben) 1572?-1637; Eng. dramatist & poet

Jor·dan (jôrd′'n) **1** river in the Near East, flowing into the Dead Sea **2** country east of Israel: 37,738 sq. mi.; pop. 2,133,000 —**Jor·da·ni·an** (jôr dā′nē ən) ***adj.***, ***n.***

Jo·seph (jō′zəf, -səf) ***n.*** *Bible* **1** one of Jacob's sons, who became a high official in Egypt **2** the husband of Mary, mother of Jesus

josh (jäsh) ***vt.***, ***vi.*** ⟦< ?⟧ [Inf.] to tease; banter

Josh·u·a (jäsh′yōō ə, -ōō-) ***n.*** *Bible* Moses' successor, who led the Israelites into the Promised Land

jos·tle (jäs′əl) ***vt.***, ***vi.*** **-tled**, **-tling** ⟦see JOUST⟧ to push, as in a crowd; shove roughly —***n.*** a jostling

jot (jät) ***n.*** ⟦< Gr *iōta*, the smallest letter⟧ a very small amount —***vt.*** **jot′ted**, **jot′ting** to make a brief note of: usually with *down* —**jot′ter** ***n.***

joule (jōōl) ***n.*** ⟦after J. P. *Joule*, 19th-c. Eng physicist⟧ *Physics* a unit of work or energy

jounce (jouns) ***vt.***, ***vi.*** **jounced**, **jounc′ing** ⟦< ?⟧ to jolt or bounce —***n.*** a jolt —**jounc′y** ***adj.***

jour·nal (jʉr′nəl) ***n.*** ⟦< L *diurnalis*, daily⟧ **1** a daily record of happenings, as a diary **2** a newspaper or periodical **3** *Bookkeeping* a book for recording transactions in the order in which they occur **4** ⟦orig. Scot⟧ the part of an axle or shaft that turns in a bearing

jour′nal·ese′ (-ēz′) ***n.*** a facile style of writing found in many newspapers, magazines, etc.

jour′nal·ism′ ***n.*** the work of gathering news for, or producing, a newspaper, etc. —**jour′nal·ist** ***n.*** —**jour′nal·is′tic** ***adj.***

jour·ney (jʉr′nē) ***n.***, *pl.* **-neys** ⟦< OFr *journee*; ult. < L *dies*, day⟧ a traveling from one place to another; trip —***vi.*** **-neyed**, **-ney·ing** to travel —**jour′ney·er** ***n.***

jour′ney·man (-mən) ***n.***, *pl.* **-men** (-mən) ⟦ME < *journee*, day's work + *man*⟧ **1** a worker qualified to work at a specified trade **2** any sound, experienced, but not brilliant performer

joust (joust) ***n.*** ⟦ult. < L *juxta*, close to⟧ a combat with lances between two knights on horseback —***vi.*** to engage in a joust

jo·vi·al (jō′vē əl) ***adj.*** ⟦< LL *Jovialis*, of Jupiter: from astrological notion of planet's influence⟧ full of playful good humor —**jo′vi·al′i·ty** (-al′ə tē) ***n.*** —**jo′vi·al·ly** ***adv.***

jowl[1] (joul) ***n.*** ⟦OE *ceafl*, jaw⟧ **1** the lower jaw **2** the cheek, esp. of a hog

jowl[2] (joul) ***n.*** ⟦OE *ceole*, throat⟧ [*usually pl.*] the fleshy hanging part under the jaw —**jowl′y** ***adj.***

joy (joi) ***n.*** ⟦ult. < L *gaudium*, joy⟧ **1** a very glad feeling; happiness; delight **2** anything causing this

Joyce (jois), **James** 1882-1941; Ir. novelist

joy′ful ***adj.*** feeling, expressing, or causing joy; glad —**joy′ful·ly** ***adv.***

joy′ous ***adj.*** joyful; happy —**joy′ous·ly** ***adv.***

joy ride [Inf.] an automobile ride, often at a reckless speed, taken for pleasure, sometimes, specif., in a stolen car —**joy rider** —**joy riding**

joy′stick′ ***n.*** **1** [Slang] the control stick of an airplane **2** a device with a lever for controlling a cursor, etc. as in a video game

JP *abbrev.* Justice of the Peace

Jpn *abbrev.* **1** Japan **2** Japanese

Jr *abbrev.* junior: also **jr**

ju·bi·lant (jōō′bə lənt) ***adj.*** ⟦< L *jubilum*, wild shout⟧ joyful and triumphant; elated; rejoicing

ju·bi·la·tion (jōō′bə lā′shən) ***n.*** **1** a rejoicing **2** a happy celebration

ju·bi·lee (jōō′bə lē′) ***n.*** ⟦< Heb *yōbēl*, a ram's horn (trumpet)⟧ **1** a 50th or 25th anniversary **2** a time of rejoicing **3** jubilation

Ju·dah[1] (jōō′də) ***n.*** *Bible* one of Jacob's sons

Ju·dah[2] (jōō′də) ancient kingdom in the S part of Palestine

Ju·da·ism (jōō′dā iz′əm, -dē-, -də-) ***n.*** the Jewish religion —**Ju·da′ic** (-dā′ik) ***adj.***

Judas (jōō′dəs) ***n.*** **1** *Bible* the disciple who betrayed Jesus for money: in full **Judas Is·car·i·ot** (is ker′ē ət) **2** a traitor or betrayer

Ju·de·a (jōō dē′ə) ancient region of S Palestine

Judeo- *combining form* Jewish

judge (juj) ***n.*** ⟦< L *jus*, law + *dicere*, say⟧ **1** a public official with authority to hear and decide cases in a court of law **2** a person designated to determine the winner, settle a controversy, etc. **3** a person qualified to decide on the relative worth of anything **4** a governing leader of the Israelites before the time of the kings —***vt.***, ***vi.*** **judged**, **judg′ing** **1** to hear and pass judgment on in a court of law **2** to determine the winner of (a contest) or settle (a controversy) **3** to form an opinion about **4** to criticize or censure **5** to think or suppose —**judge′ship′** ***n.***

judg·ment (juj′mənt) ***n.*** **1** a judging; deciding **2** a legal decision; order given by a judge, etc. **3** an opinion **4** the ability to come to an opinion **5** [J-] *short for* LAST JUDGMENT Also **judge′ment**

judg·men′tal (-ment′'l) ***adj.*** making judgments as to value, etc., often, specif., judgments considered to be lacking in tolerance, objectivity, etc.

Judgment Day *Theol.* the time of God's final judgment of all people

THESAURUS

jostle ***v.*** nudge, elbow, shoulder; see PRESS 1, PUSH 1.

jot ***v.*** scribble, indicate, list; see RECORD 1, WRITE 1.

journal ***n.*** **1** [A daily record] diary, almanac, chronicle; see RECORD 1. **2** [A periodical] publication, annual, daily; see MAGAZINE, NEWSPAPER.

journalism ***n.*** reportage, news coverage, the fourth estate; see WRITING 3.

journalist ***n.*** investigative reporter, correspondent, columnist, stringer; see also ANNOUNCER, REPORTER, WRITER.

journey ***n.*** trip, visit, run, passage, tour, excursion, jaunt, pilgrimage, voyage, crossing, expedition, patrol, beat, venture, adventure, drive, flight, cruise, course, route, sojourn, travels, trek, migration, caravan, roaming, quest, safari, exploration, hike, airing, outing, march, picnic, survey, mission, ride.

journey ***v.*** tour, jaunt, take a trip; see TRAVEL.

jovial ***a.*** affable, amiable, merry; see HAPPY.

jowl[1] ***n.*** dewlap, chin, cheek; see JAW.

joy ***n.*** mirth, cheerfulness, delight, pleasure, gratification, treat, diversion, sport, refreshment, revelry, frolic, playfulness, gaiety, geniality, good humor, merriment, merrymaking, levity, rejoicing, liveliness, high spirits, good spirits, jubilation, celebration, ecstasy; see also LAUGHTER.—*Ant.* COMPLAINING, weeping, wailing.

joyful ***a.*** joyous, cheery, glad; see HAPPY.

joyous ***a.*** blithe, glad, gay; see HAPPY.

Judaism ***n.*** Jewish religion, Hebraism, Zionism; see RELIGION 2.

Judas ***n.*** betrayer, fraud, informer; see HYPOCRITE, TRAITOR.

judge ***n.*** **1** [A legal official] justice, executive judge, magistrate, justice of the peace, chief justice, associate justice, judiciary, circuit judge, county judge, judge of the district court, appellate judge. **2** [A connoisseur] expert, arbiter of taste, master of discernment; see CRITIC 2, SPECIALIST.

judge ***v.*** adjudge, adjudicate, rule on, pass on, sit in judgment, sentence, give a hearing to, hold the scales; see also CONDEMN, CONVICT.

judged ***a.*** found guilty or innocent, convicted, settled; see DETERMINED 1, GUILTY.

judgment ***n.*** **1** [Discernment] discrimination, taste, shrewdness, sapience, understanding, knowledge, wit, keenness, sharpness, critical faculty, rational faculty, reason, rationality, intuition, mentality, acuteness, intelligence, awareness, experience, profundity, depth, brilliance, sanity, intellectual power, capacity, comprehension, mother wit, quickness, readiness, grasp, apprehension, perspicacity, soundness, genius, good sense, common sense, astuteness, prudence, wisdom, gray matter*, brains, savvy*, horse sense*.—*Ant.* STUPIDITY, simplicity, naiveté. **2** [The act of judging] decision, appraisal, consideration, examination, weighing, sifting the evidence, determination, inspection, assessment, estimate, estimation, probing, appreciation, evaluation, review, contemplation, analysis, inquiry, inquisition, inquest, search, quest, pursuit, scrutiny, exploration, close study, observation, exhaustive inquiry; see also EXAMINATION 1. **3** [A pronouncement] conclusion, appraisal, estimate, opinion, report, view, summary, belief, idea, conviction, inference, resolution, deduction, induction, determination, decree, fiat, *fatwa* (Arabic), supposition, commentary, finding, recommendation; see also VERDICT.

Judgment Day ***n.*** doomsday, Day of Judgment, retribution, visitation, chastisement, correction, castigation, mortification, end of the world, last day, day of reckoning; see also JUDG-

ju·di·ca·to·ry (jo͞o′di kə tôr′ē) ***adj.*** ⟦see JUDGE⟧ having to do with administering justice —***n.***, *pl.* **-ries** a law court, or law courts collectively

ju′di·ca·ture (-chər) ***n.*** **1** the administering of justice **2** jurisdiction **3** judges or courts collectively

ju·di·cial (jo͞o dish′əl) ***adj.*** **1** of judges, courts, or their functions **2** allowed, enforced, etc. by a court **3** befitting a judge **4** fair; impartial

ju·di·ci·ar·y (jo͞o dish′ē er′ē) ***adj.*** of judges or courts —***n.***, *pl.* **-ar′ies** **1** the part of government that administers justice **2** judges collectively

ju·di′cious (-dish′əs) ***adj.*** having or showing sound judgment —**ju·di′cious·ly** ***adv.***

ju·do (jo͞o′dō) ***n.*** ⟦Jpn < *jū*, soft + *dō*, way⟧ a form of jujitsu

jug (jug) ***n.*** ⟦a pet form of *Judith* or *Joan*⟧ **1** a large container for liquids, with a small opening and a handle **2** [Slang] a jail

jug·ger·naut (jug′ər nôt′) ***n.*** ⟦< Sans *Jagannātha*, lord of the world⟧ a relentless, irresistible force

jug·gle (jug′əl) ***vt.*** **-gled**, **-gling** ⟦< L *jocus*, a joke⟧ **1** to perform skillful tricks of sleight of hand with (balls, etc.) **2** to catch or hold awkwardly **3** to manipulate so as to deceive —***vi.*** to toss up balls, etc. and keep them in the air —**jug′gler** ***n.***

jug·u·lar (jug′yo͞o lər) ***adj.*** ⟦< L *jugum*, a yoke⟧ of the neck or throat —***n.*** JUGULAR VEIN

jugular vein either of two large veins in the neck carrying blood from the head

juice (jo͞os) ***n.*** ⟦< L *jus*, broth, juice⟧ **1** the liquid part of a plant, fruit, etc. **2** a liquid in or from animal tissue **3** [Inf.] vitality **4** [Slang] *a)* electricity *b)* alcoholic liquor *c)* power or influence —***vt.*** **juiced**, **juic′ing** to extract juice from —***vi.*** [Slang] to drink alcoholic beverages to excess

juiced (jo͞ost) ***adj.*** [Slang] drunk; intoxicated

juic·er (jo͞o′sər) ***n.*** **1** a device for extracting juice from fruit **2** [Slang] a drunkard

juic·y (jo͞o′sē) ***adj.*** **-i·er**, **-i·est** **1** full of juice **2** [Inf.] *a)* full of interest *[juicy gossip]* *b)* highly profitable —**juic′i·ness** ***n.***

ju·jit·su (jo͞o jit′so͞o′) ***n.*** ⟦< Jpn *jū*, soft, pliant + *jutsu*, art⟧ a Japanese system of wrestling in which an opponent's strength and weight are used against him or her

ju·ju·be (jo͞o′jo͞o bē′) ***n.*** ⟦< Gr *zizyphon*, name of a fruit⟧ a fruit-flavored, jellylike lozenge

ju·jut·su (jo͞o jit′so͞o′, -jut′-) ***n.*** JUJITSU

juke·box (jo͞ok′bäks′) ***n.*** ⟦< Am black *juke*, wicked⟧ a coin-operated player for records, CD's, etc. as in a bar

ju·lep (jo͞o′ləp) ***n.*** ⟦< Pers *gul*, rose + *āb*, water⟧ MINT JULEP

ju·li·enne (jo͞o′lē en′) ***adj.*** ⟦Fr⟧ cut into strips: said of vegetables, etc.: also **ju′li·enned′** (-end′)

Ju·li·et (jo͞o′lē et′, jo͞o′lē et′) ***n.*** the heroine of Shakespeare's tragedy *Romeo and Juliet*

Ju·ly (joo lī′) ***n.*** ⟦< L < *Julius* Caesar⟧ the seventh month of the year, having 31 days: abbrev. *abbrev.* **Jul**

jum·ble (jum′bəl) ***vt.***, ***vi.*** **-bled**, **-bling** ⟦? blend of JUMP + TUMBLE⟧ to mix or be mixed in a confused heap —***n.*** a confused mixture or heap

jum·bo (jum′bō) ***n.***, *pl.* **-bos** ⟦< Am black *jamba*, elephant⟧ a large person, animal, or thing —***adj.*** very large

jump (jump) ***vi.*** ⟦< ?⟧ **1** to spring or leap from the ground, a height, etc. **2** to jerk; bob **3** to move or act eagerly: often with *at* **4** to pass suddenly, as to a new topic **5** to rise suddenly, as prices **6** [Slang] to be lively —***vt.*** **1** *a)* to leap over *b)* to pass over **2** to cause to leap **3** to leap upon **4** to cause (prices, etc.) to rise **5** [Inf.] *a)* to attack suddenly *b)* to react to prematurely **6** [Slang] to leave suddenly *[to jump town]* —***n.*** **1** a jumping **2** a distance jumped **3** a sudden transition **4** a sudden rise, as in prices **5** a sudden, nervous start —**get** (or **have**) **the jump on** [Slang] to get (or have) an advantage over —**jump bail** to forfeit bail by running away

jump·er[1] (jum′pər) ***n.*** **1** one that jumps **2** a short wire to make a temporary electrical connection

jump·er[2] (jum′pər) ***n.*** ⟦< dial. *jump*, short coat⟧ **1** a loose jacket **2** a sleeveless dress for wearing over a blouse, etc.

jumper cables a pair of thick, insulated electrical wires with clamplike terminals, used to jump-start a motor vehicle with a dead battery

jump′-start′ ***vt.*** **1** to start (a motor-vehicle engine) with jumper cables **2** [Inf.] to energize, revive, etc. —***n.*** a starting in such a way

jump′suit′ ***n.*** **1** a coverall worn by paratroops, etc. **2** a lounging outfit like this

jump·y (jum′pē) ***adj.*** **-i·er**, **-i·est** **1** moving in jumps or jerks **2** easily startled **3** nervous —**jump′i·ly** ***adv.*** —**jump′i·ness** ***n.***

jun·co (juŋ′kō′) ***n.***, *pl.* **-cos′** ⟦< Sp⟧ a small bird with a gray or black head

junc·tion (juŋk′shən) ***n.*** ⟦< L *jungere*, join⟧ **1** a joining or being joined **2** a place of joining, as of roads —**junc′tion·al** ***adj.***

junc·ture (juŋk′chər) ***n.*** **1** a junction **2** a point of time **3** a crisis

June (jo͞on) ***n.*** ⟦< L *Junius*, of *Juno*⟧ the sixth month of the year, having 30 days: abbrev. *abbrev.* **Jun**

Ju·neau (jo͞o′nō′) capital of Alaska: seaport on the SE coast: pop. 27,000

jun·gle (juŋ′gəl) ***n.*** ⟦< Sans *jaṅgala*, wasteland⟧ **1** land densely covered with trees, vines, etc., as in the tropics **2** [Slang] a situation in which people struggle fiercely for survival

jun·ior (jo͞on′yər) ***adj.*** ⟦L < *juvenis*, young⟧ **1** the younger: written *Jr.* after a son's name if it is the same as his father's **2** of more recent position or lower status *[a junior partner]* **3** of juniors —***n.*** **1** one who is younger, of lower rank, etc. **2** a student in the next-to-last year, as of college

junior college a school offering courses two years beyond high school

junior high school a school usually including grades 7, 8, and 9

ju·ni·per (jo͞o′ni pər) ***n.*** ⟦L *juniperus*⟧ an evergreen shrub or tree with berrylike cones

junk[1] (juŋk) ***n.*** ⟦< ?⟧ **1** old metal, paper, rags, etc. that might be reusable in some way **2** [Inf.] worthless stuff; trash **3** [Slang] heroin —***vt.*** [Inf.] to scrap; discard —**junk′y**, **-i·er**, **-i·est**, ***adj.***

junk[2] (juŋk) ***n.*** ⟦< Malay *adjong*⟧ a Chinese or Japanese flat-bottomed ship

THESAURUS

MENT 1, 2.

judicial ***a.*** juridical, court-ordered, equitable; see LAWFUL.

judiciary ***n.*** justices, bench, bar; see COURT 2.

judicious ***a.*** well-advised, prudent, sensible; see DISCREET, RATIONAL 1.—*Ant.* RASH, ill-advised, hasty.

jug ***n.*** crock, flask, pitcher; see CONTAINER.

juggle ***v.*** **1** [To keep in the air by tossing] toss, keep in motion, bobble; see BALANCE 2. **2** [To alter, usually so as to deceive] shuffle, trick, delude; see DECEIVE.

juice ***n.*** sap, extract, fluid; see LIQUID.

juicy ***a.*** **1** [Succulent] moist, wet, watery, humid, dewy, sappy, dank, dripping, sodden, soaked, liquid, oily, syrupy; see also WET.—*Ant.* DRY, dehydrated, bone-dry. **2** [*Full of interest] spicy, piquant, intriguing, racy, risqué, fascinating, colorful. **3** [*Profitable] lucrative, remunerative, fruitful; see PROFITABLE.

jumble ***n.*** clutter, mess, hodgepodge; see CONFUSION, MIXTURE 1.

jumbo ***a.*** immense, mammoth, gigantic; see LARGE 1.

jump ***n.*** **1** [A leap up or across] skip, hop, rise, pounce, lunge, jumping, broad jump, high jump, vault, bounce, hurdle, spring, bound, caper. **2** [A leap down] plunge, plummet, fall; see DIVE, DROP 2. **3** [Distance jumped] leap, stretch, vault; see HEIGHT, LENGTH 1. **4** [*An advantage] upper hand, edge, head start; see ADVANTAGE. **5** [A sudden rise] ascent, spurt, spike; see INCREASE, RISE 3.

jump ***v.*** **1** [To leap across or up] vault, leap over, spring, lurch, lunge, pop up, bound, hop, skip, high-jump, broad-jump, hurdle, top. **2** [To leap down] drop, plummet, plunge; see DIVE, FALL 1. **3** [To pass over] skip, traverse, remove, nullify; see also CANCEL, CROSS 1. **4** [*To accost belligerently] attack suddenly, assault, mug*; see ATTACK.

jumping ***a.*** vaulting, hopping, skipping; see ACTIVE.

jumpy ***a.*** sensitive, restless, nervous; see EXCITED.

junction ***n.*** **1** [A meeting] joining, coupling, reunion; see JOINT 1, UNION 1. **2** [A place of meeting, especially of roads] crossroads, crossing, intersection; see ROAD 1.

jungle ***n.*** wilderness, rain forest, tropical forest; see FOREST.

junior ***a.*** subordinate, lesser, lower; see SUBORDINATE.

junk[1] ***n.*** waste, garbage, filth; see TRASH 1.

junk[1]* ***v.*** dump, scrap, wreck; see DISCARD.

junk bond [Inf.] a speculative BOND (*n.* 6), often issued to finance the takeover of a corporation

junk·er (juŋ′kər) ***n.*** [Slang] an old, dilapidated car or truck

Jun·ker (yooŋ′kər) ***n.*** ⟦Ger⟧ [Historical] a Prussian of the militaristic landowning class

jun·ket (juŋ′kit) ***n.*** ⟦ME *joncate,* cream cheese⟧ **1** milk sweetened, flavored, and thickened into curd **2** a picnic **3** an excursion, esp. one by an official at public expense —***vi.*** to go on a junket —**jun′ket·eer′** (-ki tir′) or **jun′ket·er** ***n.***

junk food snack food with chemical additives and little food value

junk·ie or **junk·y** (juŋ′kē) ***n.***, *pl.* **-ies** ⟦< JUNK[1], *n.* 3⟧ [Slang] **1** a narcotics addict **2** one who is addicted to a specified activity, food, etc.

junk mail advertisements, solicitations, etc. mailed in large quantities

Ju·no (jo͞o′nō) ***n.*** *Gr. Myth.* the wife of Jupiter and queen of the gods

jun·ta (ho͝on′tə, jun′-) ***n.*** ⟦Sp < L *jungere,* join⟧ a group of political intriguers, esp. military men, in power after a coup d'état

Ju·pi·ter (jo͞o′pit ər) ***n.*** **1** the chief Roman god **2** the largest planet of the solar system: see PLANET

Ju·ras·sic (jo͞o ras′ik) ***adj.*** ⟦< Fr, after *Jura* Mountains, between France and Switzerland⟧ of the geologic period characterized by the dominance of dinosaurs

ju·rid·i·cal (jo͞o rid′i kəl, jo͝o-) ***adj.*** ⟦< L *jus,* law + *dicere,* declare⟧ of judicial proceedings or law

ju·ried (jo͝or′ēd) ***adj.*** of a competition in which the winners are selected by a jury

ju·ris·dic·tion (jo͝or′is dik′shən) ***n.*** ⟦see JURIDICAL⟧ **1** legal authority **2** the range of authority

ju·ris·pru·dence (jo͝or′is pro͞od′′ns) ***n.*** ⟦< L *jus,* law + *prudentia,* a foreseeing⟧ **1** the science or philosophy of law **2** a division of law *[medical jurisprudence]*

ju·rist (jo͝or′ist) ***n.*** ⟦< L *jus,* law⟧ **1** an expert in law or writer on law **2** JUDGE (*n.* 1)

ju·ror (jo͝or′ər, -ôr′) ***n.*** a member of a jury

ju·ry (jo͝or′ē) ***n.***, *pl.* **-ries** ⟦L *jurare,* to swear⟧ **1** a group of people sworn to hear evidence in a law case and to give a decision **2** a committee that decides winners in a contest

just (just) ***adj.*** ⟦< L *jus,* law⟧ **1** right or fair *[a just decision]* **2** righteous *[a just man]* **3** deserved *[just praise]* **4** lawful **5** proper **6** correct or true **7** accurate; exact —***adv.*** **1** exactly *[just one o'clock]* **2** nearly **3** only *[just a taste]* **4** barely *[just missed him]* **5** a very short time ago *[she's just left]* **6** immediately *[just east of here]* **7** [Inf.] really *[just beautiful]* —**just the same** [Inf.] nevertheless —**just′ly** ***adv.*** —**just′ness** ***n.***

jus·tice (jus′tis) ***n.*** **1** a being righteous **2** fairness **3** rightfulness **4** reward or penalty as deserved **5** the use of authority to uphold what is just **6** the administration of law **7** *a)* JUDGE (*n.* 1) *b)* JUSTICE OF THE PEACE —**do justice to** to treat fairly

justice of the peace a local magistrate who decides minor cases, performs marriages, etc.

jus·ti·fy (jus′tə fī′) ***vt.*** **-fied′**, **-fy′ing** ⟦< L *justus,* just + *facere,* to do⟧ **1** to show to be just, right, etc. **2** *Theol.* to free from blame or guilt **3** to supply grounds for —**jus′ti·fi′a·ble** ***adj.*** —**jus′ti·fi·ca′tion** (-fi kā′shən) ***n.***

Jus·tin·i·an I (jus tin′ē ən) A.D. 483-565; ruler of Byzantine Empire (527-565): codified Roman law

jut (jut) ***vi., vt.*** **jut′ted**, **jut′ting** ⟦prob. var. of JET[1]⟧ to stick out; project —***n.*** a part that juts

jute (jo͞ot) ***n.*** ⟦< Sans *jūṭa,* matted hair⟧ **1** a strong fiber used for making burlap, rope, etc. **2** a S Asian plant yielding this fiber

ju·ve·nile (jo͞o′və nīl′, -nəl) ***adj.*** ⟦< L *juvenis,* young⟧ **1** young; immature **2** of or for young persons —***n.*** **1** a young person **2** an actor who plays youthful roles **3** a book for children —**ju′ve·nil′i·ty** (-nil′i tē), *pl.* **-ties**, ***n.***

juvenile delinquency antisocial or illegal behavior by minors, usually 18 years of age or younger —**juvenile delinquent**

jux·ta·pose (juks′tə pōz′) ***vt.*** **-posed′**, **-pos′ing** ⟦< Fr < L *juxta,* beside + POSE⟧ to put side by side —**jux′ta·po·si′tion** ***n.***

JV *abbrev.* junior varsity

THESAURUS

junkie* ***n.*** drug addict, dope addict*, doper*; see ADDICT.

jurisdiction ***n.*** authority, range, supervision, control, discretion, province, commission, scope, arbitration, reign, domain, bailiwick, extent, empire, sovereignty.

jurist ***n.*** legal scholar, justice, judge; see LAWYER.

jury ***n.*** tribunal, panel, board; see COURT 2.

just ***a.*** **1** [Precisely] exactly, correctly, perfectly; see ACCURATE. **2** [Hardly] barely, scarcely, by very little; see HARDLY. **3** [Only] merely, simply, no more than; see ONLY 2. **4** [Recently] just a while ago, lately, a moment ago; see RECENTLY. **5** [Fair] impartial, equitable, righteous; see FAIR 1. —**just the same** nevertheless, however, in spite of that; see BUT 1.

justice ***n.*** **1** [Fairness] right, truth, equity; see FAIRNESS. **2** [Lawfulness] legality, equity, prescriptive right, statutory right, established right, legitimacy, sanction, legalization, constitutionality, authority, code, charter, decree, rule, legal process, authorization; see also CUSTOM, LAW 1, POWER 2.—*Ant.* WRONG, illegality, illegitimacy. **3** [The administration of law] adjudication, settlement, arbitration, hearing, legal process, due process, judicial procedure, jury trial, trial by jury, regulation, decision, pronouncement, review, appeal, sentence, consideration, taking evidence, litigation, prosecution; see also JUDGMENT 2, LAW 1, TRIAL 2.—*Ant.* DISORDER, lawlessness, despotism. **4** [A judge] magistrate, umpire, chancellor; see JUDGE 1. —**do justice to** esteem, pay tribute to, honor; see ADMIRE, CONSIDER, RESPECT 2. —**do oneself justice** be fair to oneself, give oneself credit, behave in a worthy way; see APPROVE.

justifiable ***a.*** proper, suitable, probable; see FIT 1, LOGICAL.

justification ***n.*** excuse, defense, rationale; see APPEAL 1, EXPLANATION.

justify ***v.*** **1** [To vindicate] absolve, acquit, clear; see EXCUSE. **2** [To give reasons for] support, apologize for, excuse; see DEFEND, EXPLAIN.

justly ***a.*** **1** [Honorably] impartially, honestly, frankly, candidly, straightforwardly, reasonably, fairly, moderately, temperately, evenhandedly, rightly, equitably, tolerantly, charitably, respectably, lawfully, legally, legitimately, rightfully, properly, duly, in justice, as it ought to be. **2** [Exactly] properly, precisely, rationally; see ACCURATELY.

jut ***v.*** extend, bulge, stick out; see PROJECT 1.

juvenile ***a.*** youthful, adolescent, teenage; see YOUNG 1.

k or **K** (kā) ***n.***, *pl.* **k's, K's** the eleventh letter of the English alphabet

K[1] ***n.*** **1** *Comput.* KILOBYTE **2** [Inf.] a thousand dollars

K[2] *abbrev.* **1** karat (carat) **2** kilometer **3** kindergarten **4** *Baseball* strikeout **5** *Comput.* the number 1,024, or 2^{10} Also, for 1 & 2, **k**

K[3] ⟦ModL *kalium*⟧ *Chem. symbol for* potassium

Ka·bu·ki (kä bo͞o′kē) ***n.*** [*also* **k-**] a form of Japanese drama, chiefly in formalized pantomime

kad·dish (käd′ish) ***n.*** ⟦Aram *kadish,* lit., holy⟧ *Judaism* a hymn in praise of God, recited at the daily service or as a mourner's prayer

kaf·fee·klatsch (kä′fā kläch′, kô′fē klach′) ***n.*** ⟦Ger < *kaffee,* coffee + *klatsch,* gossip⟧ [*also* **K-**] an informal gathering to drink coffee and chat

Kai·ser (kī′zər) ***n.*** ⟦ME *caiser*, emperor < L *Caesar*⟧ the title of the former rulers of Austria and Germany

kaiser roll ⟦Ger *kaisersemmel*, kaiser bun⟧ a large, round roll with a hard crust

kale (kāl) ***n.*** ⟦var. of COLE⟧ a hardy cabbage with spreading leaves

ka·lei·do·scope (kə lī′də skōp′) ***n.*** ⟦< Gr *kalos,* beautiful + *eidos,* form + -SCOPE⟧ **1** a small tube containing bits of colored glass reflected by mirrors so that symmetrical patterns appear when the tube is rotated **2** anything that constantly changes —**ka·lei′do·scop′ic** (-skäp′ik) ***adj.***

ka·mi·ka·ze (kä′mə kä′zē) ***adj.*** ⟦Jpn, divine wind⟧ of a suicidal attack by a WWII Japanese airplane pilot

kan·ga·roo (kaŋ′gə ro͞o′) ***n.*** ⟦< ?⟧ a leaping marsupial of Australia and nearby islands, with short forelegs and strong, large hind legs

kangaroo court [Inf.] an irregular court, usually disregarding normal legal procedure

Kan·sas (kan′zəs) Midwestern state of the U.S.: 81,823 sq. mi.; pop. 2,478,000; cap. Topeka: abbrev. *KS* —**Kan′san** ***adj.***, ***n.***

Kansas City **1** city in W Missouri, on the Missouri River: pop. 435,000 **2** city opposite this, in NE Kansas: pop. 150,000

Kant (känt), **Im·man·u·el** (i man′yo͞o el′) 1724-1804; Ger. philosopher

ka·o·lin (kā′ə lin) ***n.*** ⟦Fr < Chin name of hill where found⟧ a white clay used in porcelain, etc.

ka·pok (kā′päk′) ***n.*** ⟦Malay⟧ the silky fibers around the seeds of certain tropical trees, used for stuffing mattresses, etc.

kap·pa (kap′ə) ***n.*** the tenth letter of the Greek alphabet (Κ, κ)

ka·put (kə poot′, -po͞ot′) ***adj.*** ⟦Ger *kaputt*⟧ [Slang] ruined, destroyed, etc.

Ka·ra·chi (kə rä′chē) seaport in S Pakistan: former capital: pop. 5,076,000

kar·a·kul (kar′ə kul′, -kəl) ***n.*** ⟦ult. < Turkic *qara köl*, dark lake⟧ **1** a sheep native to central Asia **2** the curly black fur from the fleece of its lambs: usually sp. *caracul*

ka·ra·o·ke (kar′ē ō′kē) ***n.*** a form of entertainment in which bar patrons, etc. take turns singing while a special device plays prerecorded music

kar·at (kar′ət) ***n.*** ⟦var. of CARAT⟧ one 24th part (of pure gold)

ka·ra·te (kə rät′ē) ***n.*** ⟦Jpn⟧ a Japanese system of self-defense by sharp, quick blows with the hands and feet

kar·ma (kär′mə) ***n.*** ⟦Sans, act⟧ **1** *Buddhism, Hinduism* the totality of one's acts in each state of one's existence **2** loosely, fate

kart (kärt) ***n.*** ⟦< CART⟧ a small, flat, motorized vehicle, used in racing (**kart′ing**)

ka·ty·did (kāt′ē did′) ***n.*** ⟦echoic of the male's shrill sound⟧ a large, green tree insect

kay·ak (kī′ak′) ***n.*** ⟦Esk⟧ a canoe, originally used by Eskimos, with only a small opening in its shell for the paddler —***vi.*** to go in a kayak —**kay′ak′er** ***n.***

kay·o (kā′ō′) [Slang] ***vt.*** **-oed′**, **-o′ing** ⟦< KO⟧ *Boxing* to knock out —***n.*** *Boxing* a knockout

Ka·zakh·stan (kä′zäk stän′) country in W Asia: formerly a republic of the U.S.S.R.: 1,049,155 sq. mi.; pop. 16,464,000

ka·zoo (kə zo͞o′) ***n.*** ⟦echoic⟧ a toy musical instrument that makes buzzing tones when hummed into

KB *abbrev.* kilobyte(s)

kc *abbrev.* kilocycle(s)

Keats (kēts), **John** 1795-1821; Eng. poet

ke·bab or **ke·bob** (kə bäb′) ***n.*** ⟦Ar *kabāb*⟧ any of the small pieces of marinated meat used in making shish kebab

keel (kēl) ***n.*** ⟦< ON *kjǫlr*⟧ the chief timber or piece extending along the length of the bottom of a boat or ship —**keel over** **1** to capsize **2** to fall over suddenly —**on an even keel** upright or steady

keen[1] (kēn) ***adj.*** ⟦OE *cene,* wise⟧ **1** having a sharp edge or point *[a keen knife]* **2** cutting *[a keen wind]* **3** very perceptive *[keen eyes]* **4** shrewd **5** eager **6** intense —**keen′ly** ***adv.*** —**keen′ness** ***n.***

keen[2] (kēn) ***vt., vi.*** ⟦< Ir *caoinim,* I wail⟧ to make a mournful, wailing sound

keep (kēp) ***vt.*** **kept**, **keep′ing** ⟦OE *cæpan,* behold⟧ **1** to celebrate; observe *[to keep the Sabbath]* **2** to fulfill (a promise, etc.) **3** to protect; guard; take care of; tend **4** to preserve **5** to provide for; support **6** to make regular entries in *[to keep a diary]* **7** to maintain in a specified state, position, etc. *[to keep prices down]* **8** to hold for the future; retain **9** to hold and not let go; detain, withhold, restrain, etc. **10** to stay in or on (a course, place, etc.) —***vi.*** **1** to stay in a specified state, position, etc. **2** to continue; go on **3** to refrain *[to keep from eating]* **4** to stay fresh; not spoil —***n.*** **1** food and shelter; support **2** the inner stronghold of a castle —**for keeps** [Inf.] **1** with the winner keeping what he wins **2** permanently —**keep to oneself** **1** to avoid others **2** to refrain from telling —**keep up** **1** to maintain in good condition **2** to continue **3** to maintain the pace **4** to remain informed about: with *on* or *with*

keep′er ***n.*** **1** one that keeps; specif., *a)* a guard *b)* a guardian *c)* a custodian **2** [Inf.] something worth keeping

keep′ing ***n.*** **1** observance (of a rule, holiday, etc.) **2** care; charge —**in keeping with** in conformity or accord with

keep′sake′ ***n.*** something kept, or to be kept, in memory of the giver

THESAURUS

keen[1] ***a.*** **1** [Sharp] pointed, edged, acute; see SHARP 1. **2** [Astute] bright, clever, shrewd; see INTELLIGENT. **3** [Eager] ardent, interested, intent; see ZEALOUS.

keenly ***a.*** acutely, sharply, penetratingly; see CLEARLY 1, 2, VERY, VIGOROUSLY.

keep ***v.*** **1** [To hold] retain, grip, own, possess, have, take, seize, save, grasp; see also HOLD 1. **2** [To maintain] preserve, conserve, care for; see MAINTAIN 3. **3** [To continue] persist in, carry on, sustain; see CONTINUE 1, ENDURE 1. **4** [To operate] administer, run, direct; see MANAGE 1. **5** [To tend] care for, minister to, attend; see TEND 1. **6** [To remain] stay, continue, abide; see SETTLE 5, 6. **7** [To store] deposit, hoard, retain, preserve, reserve, put away, conserve, warehouse, stash away*, put away, cache; see also SAVE 3, STORE. **8** [To prevent; *used with "from"*] stop, block, avert; see HINDER, PREVENT. **9** [To stay in good condition] not spoil, last, hold up; see PRESERVE 3. —**for keeps*** permanently, always, perpetually; see FOREVER. —**keep after** **1** [To pursue] track, trail, follow; see PURSUE 1. **2** [To nag] push, remind, pester; see BOTHER 2, DISTURB. —**keep at** persist, persevere, endure; see CONTINUE 1. —**keep away** **1** [To remain] stay away, hold back, keep one's distance; see WAIT 1. **2** [To restrain] keep off, hold back, defend oneself from; see HINDER, PREVENT, RESTRICT. —**keep back** **1** [To delay] check, hold, postpone; see DELAY, HINDER, SUSPEND. **2** [To restrict] enclose, inhibit, oppose; see FORBID, RESTRICT. —**keep down** reduce, deaden, muffle; see SOFTEN, DECREASE 2. —**keep from** **1** [To abstain] desist, refrain, avoid; see ABSTAIN. **2** [To prevent] prohibit, forestall, impede; see HINDER, PREVENT. —**keep on** finish, repeat, pursue; see CONTINUE 1, ENDURE 1. —**keep to oneself** be a recluse, be a hermit, cultivate solitude, avoid human companionship, stay away, keep one's own counsel; see also HIDE. —**keep up** support, care for, safeguard; see SUSTAIN 2. —**keep up with** keep step with, keep pace with, run with; see COMPETE.

keeper ***n.*** guard, official, attendant; see WARDEN, WATCHMAN.

keeping ***n.*** care, custody, guard; see PROTECTION 2. —**in keeping with** similar to, much the same as, in conformity with; see ALIKE.

keepsake ***n.*** memento, token, souvenir; see REMINDER.

keg (keg) ***n.*** ⟦< ON *kaggi,* keg⟧ **1** a small barrel **2** a unit of weight for nails, equal to 100 lb.

kelp (kelp) ***n.*** ⟦ME *culp*⟧ a large, coarse, brown seaweed, rich in iodine

Kel·vin (kel′vin) ***adj.*** ⟦after 1st Baron *Kelvin,* 19th-c. Brit physicist⟧ designating or of a scale of temperature measured from absolute zero (-273.16°C)

ken (ken) ***vt.*** **kenned, ken′ning** ⟦OE *cennan,* cause to know⟧ [Scot.] to know —***n.*** range of knowledge

Ken·ne·dy (ken′ə dē), **John Fitz·ger·ald** (fits jer′əld) 1917-63; 35th president of the U.S. (1961-63): assassinated

ken·nel (ken′əl) ***n.*** ⟦< L *canis,* dog⟧ **1** a doghouse **2** [*often pl.*] a place where dogs are bred or kept —***vt.*** **-neled** or **-nelled, -nel·ing** or **-nel·ling** to keep in a kennel

Ken·tuck·y (kən tuk′ē) EC state of the U.S.: 39,732 sq. mi.; pop. 3,685,000; cap. Frankfort: abbrev. *KY* —**Ken·tuck′i·an** ***adj., n.***

Ken·ya (ken′yə, kēn′-) country on the E coast of Africa: 224,961 sq. mi.; pop. 29,295,000

kept (kept) ***vt., vi.*** *pt. & pp. of* KEEP —***adj.*** maintained so as to be a sexual partner *[a kept woman]*

ker·a·tin (ker′ə tin) ***n.*** ⟦< Gr *keras,* horn⟧ a tough, fibrous protein, the basic substance of hair, nails, etc.

kerb (kurb) ***n.*** *Brit. sp. of* CURB (*n.* 3)

ker·chief (kur′chif) ***n.*** ⟦< OFr *covrir,* to cover + *chef,* head⟧ **1** a piece of cloth worn over the head or around the neck **2** a handkerchief

ker·nel (kur′nəl) ***n.*** ⟦< OE *cyrnel*⟧ **1** a grain or seed, as of corn **2** the inner, softer part of a nut, etc. **3** the central, most important part; essence

ker·o·sene (ker′ə sēn′) ***n.*** ⟦Gr *kēros,* wax⟧ a thin oil distilled from petroleum, used as a fuel, solvent, etc.: also **ker′o·sine′**

kes·trel (kes′trəl) ***n.*** ⟦echoic of its cry⟧ a small European falcon

ketch (kech) ***n.*** ⟦ME *cache*⟧ a small sailing vessel rigged fore-and-aft

ketch·up (kech′əp) ***n.*** ⟦? Malay *kēchap,* sauce⟧ a sauce for meat, fish, etc.; esp., a thick sauce (**tomato ketchup**) of tomatoes, onions, spices, etc.

ket·tle (ket′'l) ***n.*** ⟦< L *catinus,* container for food⟧ **1** a metal container for boiling or cooking things **2** a teakettle

ket′tle·drum′ ***n.*** a hemispheric percussion instrument of copper with a parchment top that can be tightened or loosened to change the pitch

Kev·lar (kev′lär′) *trademark for* a tough, light, synthetic fiber used in bulletproof vests, boat hulls, etc.

key[1] (kē) ***n.,*** *pl.* **keys** ⟦OE *cæge*⟧ **1** a device for moving the bolt of a lock and thus locking or unlocking something **2** any of the buttons, levers, etc. pressed in operating a piano, typewriter, etc. **3** a thing that explains or solves something else, as a code, the legend of a map, etc. **4** an essential person or thing **5** tone or style of expression **6** *Music* a system of related tones based on a keynote and forming a given scale —***adj.*** essential; important —***vt.*** **keyed, key′ing 1** to furnish with a key **2** to regulate the tone or pitch of **3** to bring into harmony —**key in** to input (data) by means of a keyboard —**key up** to make tense or excited

key[2] (kē) ***n.,*** *pl.* **keys** ⟦Sp *cayo*⟧ a reef or low island

key′board′ ***n.*** **1** the row or rows of keys of a piano, typewriter, computer terminal, etc. **2** a musical instrument with a keyboard —***vt., vi.*** to write (text) or input (data) by means of a keyboard —**key′board′er** ***n.***

key′hole′ ***n.*** an opening (in a lock) into which a key is inserted

key′note′ ***n.*** **1** the lowest, basic note or tone of a musical scale **2** the basic idea or ruling principle —***vt.*** **-not′ed, -not′ing 1** to give the keynote of **2** to give the keynote speech at —**key′not′er** ***n.***

keynote speech (or **address**) a speech, as at a convention, setting forth the main line of policy

key′pad′ ***n.*** the keys or push buttons on a computer keyboard, telephone, etc.

key′stone′ ***n.*** **1** the central, topmost stone of an arch **2** the main part or principle

key′stroke′ ***n.*** any of the strokes made in operating a keyboard

Key West island off S Florida, in the Gulf of Mexico

kg *abbrev.* kilogram(s)

kha·ki (kak′ē, kä′kē) ***adj.*** ⟦< Pers *khāk,* dust⟧ **1** dull yellowish-brown **2** made of khaki (cloth) —***n.,*** *pl.* **-kis 1** a dull yellowish brown **2** strong, twilled cloth of this color **3** [*often pl.*] a khaki uniform or pants

khan (kän, kan) ***n.*** ⟦< Mongolian *qan,* lord⟧ **1** a title of Tatar or Mongol rulers in the Middle Ages **2** a title of various dignitaries in Iran, Afghanistan, etc.

Khar·kov (kär′kôf′) city in NE Ukraine: pop. 1,611,000

Khar·toum (kär to͞om′) capital of Sudan, on the Nile: pop. 476,000

kHz *abbrev.* kilohertz

kib·butz (ki bo͞ots′, -bo͝ots′) ***n.,*** *pl.* **kib·but·zim** (kē′bo͞o tsēm′) ⟦ModHeb⟧ an Israeli collective settlement, esp. a collective farm

kib·itz·er (kib′it sər) ***n.*** ⟦Yiddish < Ger *kiebitz*⟧ [Inf.] **1** an onlooker at a card game, etc., esp. one who volunteers advice **2** a giver of unwanted advice or meddler in others' affairs —**kib′itz** ***vi.***

ki·bosh (kī′bäsh′, ki bäsh′) ***n.*** ⟦< ?⟧ used chiefly in **put the kibosh on,** to check, squelch, etc.

kick (kik) ***vi.*** ⟦ME *kiken*⟧ **1** to strike out with the foot **2** to recoil, as a gun **3** [Inf.] to complain **4** *Football* to kick the ball —***vt.*** **1** to strike with the foot **2** to drive, force, etc., as by kicking **3** to score (a goal, etc.) by kicking **4** [Slang] to get rid of (a habit) —***n.*** **1** an act or method of kicking **2** a sudden recoil **3** a complaint **4** [Inf.] an intoxicating effect **5** [*often pl.*] [Inf.] pleasure —**kick in** [Slang] to pay (one's share) —**kick over** to start up, as an automobile engine —**kick′er** ***n.***

kick′back′ ***n.*** [Slang] **1** a giving back of part of money received as payment, often because of coercion or a previous agreement **2** the money so returned

kick′off′ ***n.*** **1** *Football* a kick that puts the ball into play **2** a beginning, as of a campaign

kick′stand′ ***n.*** a pivoted metal bar that can be kicked down to support a bicycle, etc. in an upright position

kick′-start′ ***vt.*** **1** to start (a motorcycle, etc.) with a lever attached to a pedal that one kicks downward **2** [Inf.] to start, energize, revive, etc.

kick′y ***adj.*** **-i·er, -i·est** [Slang] **1** fashionable **2** exciting

kid (kid) ***n.*** ⟦ME *kide*⟧ **1** a young goat **2** leather from the skin of young goats **3** [Inf.] a child —***adj.*** [Inf.] younger *[my kid sister]* —***vt., vi.*** **kid′ded, kid′ding** [Inf.] to tease or fool playfully

kid′die or **kid′dy** (-ē) ***n.,*** *pl.* **-dies** ⟦dim. of prec., *n.* 3⟧ [Inf.] a child

kid·nap (kid′nap′) ***vt.*** **-napped′** or **-naped′, -nap′ping** or **-nap′ing** ⟦KID, *n.* 3 + dial. *nap,* to snatch⟧ to seize and

THESAURUS

keg ***n.*** cask, drum, vat; see BARREL, CONTAINER.

kennel ***n.*** doghouse, den, pound; see ENCLOSURE 1, PEN 1.

kept ***a.*** **1** [Preserved] put up, pickled, stored; see PRESERVED 2. **2** [Retained] maintained, withheld, held, reserved, guarded, watched over, on file, at hand; see also SAVED 2. **3** [Observed] obeyed, honored, continued, discharged, maintained, carried on; see also FULFILLED.—*Ant.* ABANDONED, dishonored, forgotten.

kernel ***n.*** nut, core, heart; see GRAIN 1, SEED.

ketchup ***n.*** tomato sauce, catsup, condiment; see RELISH.

kettle ***n.*** caldron, saucepan, stewpot; see POT 1.

key[1] ***n.*** **1** [Instrument to open a lock] latchkey, opener, master key, passkey, skeleton key. **2** [A means of solution] clue, code, indicator; see ANSWER 2.

keyboard ***n.*** keypad, console, row of keys; see CONTROL 2.

keyed up ***a.*** stimulated, spurred on, nervous; see EXCITED.

keynote ***a.*** main, leading, official; see IMPORTANT 1, PRINCIPAL.

kick ***n.*** **1** [A blow with the foot] boot, swift kick, jolt, jar, hit; see also BLOW. **2** [In sports, a kicked ball] punt, drop kick, placekick; see sense 1. **3** [*Pleasant reaction] joy, pleasant sensation, refreshment; see ENJOYMENT.

kick ***v.*** **1** [To give a blow with the foot] boot, jolt, punt, drop-kick, placekick, kick off; see also BEAT 1, HIT 1. **2** [*To object] make a complaint, criticize, carp; see COMPLAIN, OPPOSE 1. —**kick around** (or **about**) mistreat, treat badly, misuse; see ABUSE. —**kick off** start, open, get under way; see BEGIN 1. —**kick out*** reject, throw out, eject; see DISMISS, REMOVE 1.

kickoff ***n.*** opening, beginning, launching; see ORIGIN 2.

kid ***n.*** **1** [The young of certain animals] young goat, young antelope, yearling; see ANIMAL. **2** [*A child] son, daughter, tot; see BOY, CHILD, GIRL.

kid* ***v.*** tease, pretend, fool; see BOTHER 2, JOKE.

kidnap ***v.*** abduct, ravish, capture, steal, rape, carry away, hold for ransom, shanghai, carry off, make off with, make away with, grab, spirit away, pirate, snatch*, bundle off.—*Ant.* RESCUE, ransom, release.

kidnapped ***a.*** made off with,

hold (a person) by force or fraud, as in order to get a ransom —**kid'nap'per** or **kid'nap'er** ***n.***

kid·ney (kid'nē) ***n.***, *pl.* **-neys** ⟦< ?⟧ **1** either of a pair of glandular organs that separate water and waste products from the blood and excrete them as urine **2** an animal's kidney, used as food **3** *a)* disposition *b)* class; kind

kidney bean the kidney-shaped seed of the common garden bean

kidney stone a hard mineral deposit sometimes formed in the kidney

kid'skin' ***n.*** leather from the skin of young goats

kiel·ba·sa (kēl bä'sə, kil-) ***n.***, *pl.* **-si** (-sē) or **-sas** ⟦Pol⟧ a Polish smoked sausage

Ki·ev (kē'ef', -ev') capital of Ukraine, on the Dnepr: pop. 2,587,000

kill (kil) ***vt.*** ⟦< ? OE *cwellan*⟧ **1** to cause the death of; slay **2** to destroy; put an end to **3** to defeat or veto (legislation) **4** to spend (time) on trivial matters **5** to turn off (an engine, etc.) **6** to stop publication of —***n.*** **1** the act of killing **2** an animal or animals killed —**kill'er** ***n.***

killer bee AFRICANIZED BEE

killer whale a large dolphin that hunts in packs and preys on large fish, seals, etc.

kill'ing ***adj.*** **1** causing death; deadly **2** exhausting; fatiguing —***n.*** **1** slaughter; murder **2** [Inf.] a sudden great profit

kill'joy' ***n.*** one who destroys or lessens other people's enjoyment: also **kill'-joy'**

kiln (kil, kiln) ***n.*** ⟦< L *culina,* cookstove⟧ a furnace or oven for drying, burning, or baking bricks, pottery, etc.

ki·lo (kē'lō, kil'ō) ***n.***, *pl.* **-los** ⟦Fr⟧ **1** KILOGRAM **2** KILOMETER

kilo- ⟦< Gr *chilioi*⟧ *combining form* one thousand

kil·o·byte (kil'ə bīt') ***n.*** 1,024 bytes, or, loosely, 1,000 bytes

kil'o·cy'cle (-sī'kəl) ***n.*** *former term for* KILOHERTZ

kil'o·gram' (-gram') ***n.*** 1,000 grams

kil'o·hertz' (-herts', -hurts') ***n.***, *pl.* **-hertz'** 1,000 hertz

kil'o·li'ter (-lēt'ər) ***n.*** 1,000 liters, or one cubic meter

kil·o·me·ter (kə läm'ət ər, kil'ə mēt'ər) ***n.*** 1,000 meters

kil·o·ton (kil'ə tun') ***n.*** the explosive force of 1,000 tons of TNT

kil'o·watt' (-wät') ***n.*** 1,000 watts

kilt (kilt) ***n.*** ⟦prob. < ON⟧ a knee-length, pleated tartan skirt worn sometimes by men of the Scottish Highlands

kil·ter (kil'tər) ***n.*** ⟦< ?⟧ [Inf.] good condition; proper order: now chiefly in **out of kilter**

ki·mo·no (kə mō'nə) ***n.***, *pl.* **-nos** ⟦Jpn⟧ **1** a robe with wide sleeves and a sash, part of the traditional Japanese costume **2** a woman's dressing gown

kin (kin) ***n.*** ⟦OE *cynn*⟧ relatives; family

-kin (kin) ⟦< MDu *-ken*⟧ *suffix* little *[lambkin]*

kind (kīnd) ***n.*** ⟦OE *cynd*⟧ **1** a natural group or division **2** essential character **3** sort; variety; class —***adj.*** sympathetic, gentle, benevolent, etc. —**in kind** in the same way —**kind of** [Inf.] somewhat; rather —**of a kind** alike

kin·der·gar·ten (kin'dər gärt''n) ***n.*** ⟦Ger < *kinder,* child + *garten,* garden⟧ a school or class for young children, usually four to six years old, that develops basic skills and social behavior by games, music, handicrafts, etc. —**kin'der·gart'ner** or **kin'der·gar'ten·er** (-gärt'nər) ***n.***

kind'heart'ed ***adj.*** kind

kin·dle (kin'dəl) ***vt.*** **-dled, -dling** ⟦< ON *kynda*⟧ **1** to set on fire; ignite **2** to excite (interest, feelings, etc.) —***vi.*** **1** to catch fire **2** to become excited

kin·dling (kind'liŋ) ***n.*** material, as bits of dry wood, for starting a fire

kind·ly (kīnd'lē) ***adj.*** **-li·er, -li·est** **1** kind; gracious **2** agreeable; pleasant —***adv.*** **1** in a kind, gracious manner **2** agreeably; favorably **3** please *[kindly* shut the door*]* —**kind'li·ness** ***n.***

kind'ness ***n.*** **1** the state, quality, or habit of being kind **2** a kind act

kin·dred (kin'drid) ***n.*** ⟦< OE *cynn,* kin + *ræden,* condition⟧ relatives or family —***adj.*** of like nature; similar *[kindred* spirits*]*

kine (kīn) ***pl.n.*** ⟦< OE *cy,* cows⟧ [Archaic] cows; cattle

ki·net·ic (ki net'ik) ***adj.*** ⟦< Gr *kinein,* to move⟧ of or resulting from motion

kin·folk (kin'fōk') ***pl.n.*** family; relatives; kin: also **kin'folks'**

king (kiŋ) ***n.*** ⟦< OE *cyning*⟧ **1** a male ruler of a nation **2** a man who is supreme in some field **3** something supreme in its class **4** a playing card with a picture of a king on it **5** *Chess* the chief piece —***adj.*** chief (in size, importance, etc.) —**king'ly** ***adj.***

King (kiŋ), **Mar·tin Luther, Jr.** (märt''n) 1929-68; U.S. clergyman & leader in the civil rights movement: assassinated

king'dom (-dəm) ***n.*** **1** a country headed by a king or queen; monarchy **2** a realm; domain *[*the *kingdom* of poetry*]* **3** any of three divisions into which all natural objects have been classified *[*the animal, vegetable, and mineral *kingdoms]*

king'fish'er ***n.*** a short-tailed diving bird that feeds chiefly on fish

King James Version AUTHORIZED VERSION

THESAURUS

abducted, ravished, stolen, carried away, held for ransom, shanghaied, waylaid, manhandled, seized, held under illegal restraint; see also CAPTURED.—*Ant.* FREE, rescued, freed.

kidney ***n.*** excretory organ, urinary organ, abdominal organ; see ORGAN 2.

kill ***v.*** **1** [To deprive of life] slay, slaughter, murder, assassinate, massacre, butcher, hang, lynch, electrocute, dispatch, execute, knife, sacrifice, shoot, strangle, poison, choke, smother, suffocate, asphyxiate, drown, behead, guillotine, crucify, dismember, decapitate, disembowel, quarter, tear limb from limb, destroy, give the death blow, give the coup de grâce, put to death, deprive of life, put an end to, exterminate, stab, cut the throat of, shoot down, mangle, cut down, bring down, mow down, machine-gun, liquidate, put someone out of his or her misery, starve, do away with, commit murder, bump off*, rub out*, wipe out*, do in*, knock off*, finish off*, blow someone's brains out*, put to sleep*, brain*, whack*, zap*.—*Ant.* RESCUE, resuscitate, animate. **2** [To cancel] annul, nullify, counteract; see CANCEL. **3** [To turn off] turn out, shut off, stop; see HALT, TURN OFF. **4** [To veto] cancel, prohibit, refuse; see FORBID.

killer ***n.*** murderer, manslayer, gunman, gangster, shooter, butcher, executioner, hit man*, homicide, poisoner, exterminator, hangman, assassin, slayer, sniper, cutthroat, thug, Cain; see also CRIMINAL.

killing ***a.*** mortal, lethal, fatal; see DEADLY.

killing ***n.*** slaying, assassination, slaughter; see CRIME.

kin ***n.*** blood relation, member of the family, sibling; see FAMILY, RELATIVE.

kind ***a.*** tender, well-meaning, considerate, charitable, loving, pleasant, amiable, soft, softhearted, compassionate, sympathetic, understanding, solicitous, sweet, generous, helpful, obliging, neighborly, accommodating, indulgent, delicate, tactful, gentle, tenderhearted, kindhearted, good-natured, inoffensive, benevolent, altruistic, lenient, easygoing, patient, tolerant, mellow, genial, sensitive, courteous, agreeable, thoughtful, well-disposed.—*Ant.* ROUGH, brutal, harsh.

kind ***n.*** **1** [Class] classification, species, genus; see CLASS 1. **2** [Type] sort, variety, description, stamp, character, tendency, gender, habit, breed, set, tribe, denomination, persuasion, manner, connection, designation. —**kind of*** somewhat, rather, sort of*; see MODERATELY.

kindergarten ***n.*** class for small children, pre-elementary grade, preschool; see SCHOOL 1.

kindhearted ***a.*** amiable, generous, good; see HUMANE, KIND.

kindle ***v.*** light, catch fire, set fire; see BURN, IGNITE.

kindling ***n.*** firewood, tinder, twigs; see FUEL, WOOD 2.

kindly ***a.*** generous, helpful, good; see HUMANE, KIND.

kindness ***n.*** **1** [The quality of being kind] tenderness, good intentions, consideration, sympathy, sweetness, helpfulness, tact, benignity, mildness, courtesy, thoughtfulness, humanity, courteousness, understanding, compassion, unselfishness, altruism, warmheartedness, softheartedness, politeness, kindliness, clemency, benevolence, goodness, philanthropy, charity, friendliness, affection, loving-kindness, cordiality, mercy, amiability, forbearance, graciousness, kindheartedness, virtue.—*Ant.* CRUELTY, brutality, selfishness. **2** [A kindly act] relief, charity, benevolence, philanthropy, favor, good deed, good turn, self-sacrifice, mercy, lift, boost; see also HELP 1.—*Ant.* INJURY, transgression, wrong.

kindred ***n.*** kin, relations, relatives; see FAMILY.

king ***n.*** **1** [A male sovereign] monarch, tyrant, prince, autocrat, czar, tsar, potentate, caesar, lord, emperor, overlord, crowned head, imperator, majesty, highness, mogul, *rex* (Latin), sultan, caliph, shah, rajah, maharajah; see also RULER 1.—*Ant.* SERVANT, slave, subordinate. **2** [A very superior being] lord, chief, head; see LEADER 2.

kingdom ***n.*** realm, domain, country, empire, lands, possessions, principality, state, dominions, monarchy, nation, subject territory.

King Lear (lir) the title character of a tragedy by Shakespeare
king'pin' ***n.*** **1** the pin at the front of a triangle of bowling pins **2** [Inf.] the essential person or thing
king'-size' ***adj.*** larger than the regular kind: also **king'-sized'**
kink (kiŋk) ***n.*** ⟦< Scand⟧ **1** a short twist, curl, or bend in a rope, wire, hair, etc. **2** a painful cramp in the neck, back, etc. **3** a mental twist; eccentricity —***vi.***, ***vt.*** to form or cause to form a kink or kinks
kink'y ***adj.*** **-i·er**, **-i·est** **1** tightly curled **2** [Slang] weird, eccentric, etc.; specif., sexually abnormal
kin·ship (kin'ship') ***n.*** **1** family relationship **2** close connection
kins·man (kinz'mən) ***n.***, *pl.* **-men** (-mən) a relative; esp., a male relative —**kins'wom'an**, *pl.* **-wom'en**, ***n.***
ki·osk (kē'äsk') ***n.*** ⟦< Pers *kūshk,* palace⟧ a small, open structure used as a newsstand, etc.
kip·per (kip'ər) ***vt.*** ⟦< ?⟧ to cure (herring, salmon, etc.) by salting and drying or smoking —***n.*** a kippered herring, etc.
Kir·i·bati (kir'ə bas') country on a group of islands in the WC Pacific, on the equator: 277 sq. mi.; pop. 72,000
kirk (kurk) ***n.*** [Scot. or North Eng.] a church
kis·met (kiz'met) ***n.*** ⟦< Ar *qasama,* to divide⟧ fate; destiny
kiss (kis) ***vt.***, ***vi.*** ⟦OE *cyssan*⟧ **1** to touch or caress with the lips as an act of affection, greeting, etc. **2** to touch lightly or gently —***n.*** **1** an act of kissing **2** a light, gentle touch **3** any of various candies —**kiss'a·ble** ***adj.***
kit (kit) ***n.*** ⟦ME *kyt,* tub⟧ **1** *a)* personal equipment, esp. as packed for travel *b)* a set of tools *c)* equipment for some particular activity, etc. *d)* a set of parts to be assembled **2** a box, bag, etc. for carrying such parts, equipment, or tools —**the whole kit and caboodle** [Inf.] the whole lot
kitch·en (kich'ən) ***n.*** ⟦ult. < L *coquere,* to cook⟧ a room or place for the preparation and cooking of food
Kitch·e·ner (kich'ə nər) city in SE Ontario, Canada: pop. 178,000
kitch'en·ette' or **kitch'en·et'** (-et') ***n.*** a small, compact kitchen
kitch'en·ware' (-wer') ***n.*** kitchen utensils
kite (kīt) ***n.*** ⟦< OE *cyta*⟧ **1** any of several long-winged birds of prey **2** a light wooden frame covered with paper or cloth, to be flown in the wind at the end of a string
kith (kith) ***n.*** ⟦< OE *cyth*⟧ friends: now only in **kith and kin** *a)* friends and relatives *b)* relatives
kitsch (kich) ***n.*** ⟦Ger, gaudy trash⟧ pretentious but shallow art or writing —**kitsch'y** ***adj.***
kit·ten (kit''n) ***n.*** ⟦< OFr dim. of *chat,* cat⟧ a young cat —**kit'ten·ish** ***adj.***
kit·ty[1] (kit'ē) ***n.***, *pl.* **-ties** **1** a kitten **2** *a pet name for* a cat
kit·ty[2] (kit'ē) ***n.***, *pl.* **-ties** ⟦prob. < KIT⟧ **1** the stakes in a poker game **2** money pooled for some purpose
kit·ty-cor·nered (kit'ē kôr'nərd) ***adj.***, ***adv.*** CATER-CORNERED: also **kit'ty-cor'ner**
ki·wi (kē'wē) ***n.***, *pl.* **-wis** ⟦echoic of its cry⟧ **1** a flightless bird of New Zealand **2** [*also* **K-**] a hairy, egg-sized fruit with sweet, green pulp
KKK *abbrev.* Ku Klux Klan
Klee·nex (klē'neks') *trademark for* soft tissue paper used as a handkerchief, etc. —***n.*** [*occas.* **k-**] a piece of such paper
klep·to·ma·ni·a (klep'tō mā'nē ə) ***n.*** ⟦< Gr *kleptēs,* thief + -MANIA⟧ a persistent, abnormal impulse to steal —**klep'to·ma'ni·ac'** ***n.***, ***adj.***
klieg light (klēg) ⟦after A. & J. *Kliegl,* who developed it in 1911⟧ a very bright arc light used on motion picture sets
Klon·dike (klän'dīk') gold-mining region in W Yukon Territory, Canada
klutz (kluts) ***n.*** ⟦< Yiddish *klots,* lit., wooden block⟧ [Slang] a clumsy or stupid person
km *abbrev.* kilometer(s)
knack (nak) ***n.*** ⟦ME *knak,* sharp blow⟧ **1** a clever expedient **2** ability to do something easily
knack·wurst (näk'wurst') ***n.*** ⟦Ger < *knacken,* to burst + *wurst,* sausage⟧ a thick, highly seasoned sausage
knap·sack (nap'sak') ***n.*** ⟦< Du *knappen,* eat + *zak,* a sack⟧ a bag of leather, canvas, or nylon for carrying equipment or supplies on the back
knave (nāv) ***n.*** ⟦< OE *cnafa,* boy⟧ **1** a dishonest, deceitful person; rogue **2** JACK (*n.* 3) —**knav'ish** ***adj.***
knav·er·y (nāv'ər ē) ***n.***, *pl.* **-ies** rascality; dishonesty
knead (nēd) ***vt.*** ⟦< OE *cnedan*⟧ **1** to work (dough, clay, etc.) into a pliable mass by folding, pressing, and squeezing **2** to massage —**knead'er** ***n.***
knee (nē) ***n.*** ⟦< OE *cneow*⟧ **1** the joint between the thigh and the lower leg **2** anything shaped like a bent knee —***vt.*** **kneed**, **knee'ing** to hit or touch with the knee
knee'cap' ***n.*** PATELLA
knee'-deep' ***adj.*** **1** up to the knees *[knee-deep* mud*]* **2** very much involved
knee'-jerk' ***adj.*** ⟦< the reflex when the knee is tapped⟧ [Inf.] characterized by or reacting with an automatic, predictable response
kneel (nēl) ***vi.*** **knelt** or **kneeled**, **kneel'ing** ⟦< OE *cneow,* knee⟧ to bend or rest on a knee or the knees
kneel'er ***n.*** a cushion, stool, etc. to kneel on in a church pew
knell (nel) ***vi.*** ⟦< OE *cnyllan*⟧ **1** to ring slowly; toll **2** to sound ominously —***vt.*** to call or announce by or as by a knell —***n.*** **1** the sound of a bell rung slowly, as at a funeral **2** an omen of death, failure, etc.
knelt (nelt) ***vi.*** *alt. pt. and pp. of* KNEEL
knew (no͞o) ***vt.***, ***vi.*** *pt. of* KNOW
knick·ers (nik'ərz) ***pl.n.*** ⟦after D. *Knickerbocker,* fictitious Du author of W. Irving's *History of New York*⟧ loose breeches gathered just below the knees: also **knick'er·bock'ers** (-ər bäk'ərz)
knick·knack (nik'nak') ***n.*** ⟦< KNACK⟧ a small ornamental article
knife (nīf) ***n.***, *pl.* **knives** ⟦< OE *cnif*⟧ **1** a cutting instrument with a sharp-edged blade set in a handle **2** a cutting blade, as in a machine —***vt.*** **knifed**, **knif'ing** **1** to cut or stab with a knife **2** [Inf.] to injure or defeat by treachery —**under the knife** [Inf.] undergoing surgery
knight (nīt) ***n.*** ⟦< OE *cniht,* boy⟧ **1** in medieval times, a man formally raised to special military rank and pledged to chivalrous conduct **2** in Great Britain, a man who for some achievement is given honorary rank entitling him to use *Sir* before his given name **3** a chess

THESAURUS

kingship ***n.*** supremacy, sovereignty, majesty; see POWER 2, ROYALTY.
king-size ***a.*** big, large-size, giant; see BROAD 1, LARGE 1.
kink ***n.*** **1** [A twist] tangle, crimp, crinkle; see CURL, CURVE. **2** [A difficulty] hitch, defect, complication; see DIFFICULTY 1.
kinky ***a.*** **1** [Full of kinks] fuzzy, curled, crimped; see CURLY. **2** [*Bizarre] weird, odd, sick*; see UNUSUAL 2.
kinship ***n.*** affiliation, affinity, cohesion, unity, familiarity, intimacy, connection, alliance; see also FAMILY, RELATIONSHIP.
kiss ***n.*** embrace, endearment, touch of the lips, caress, French kiss, smooch*, smack*, peck*; see also TOUCH 2.
kiss ***v.*** salute, osculate, make love, play post office*, smack*, smooch*, pet*, neck*, make out*, blow a kiss*; see also LOVE 2.
kit ***n.*** **1** [Equipment] material, tools, outfit; see EQUIPMENT. **2** [A pack] backpack, knapsack, satchel; see BAG, CONTAINER.
kitchen ***n.*** scullery, galley, canteen, cook's room, kitchenette, mess.
kite ***n.*** box kite, Chinese kite, tailless kite; see TOY 1.
kitten ***n.*** pussycat, kitty, baby cat; see ANIMAL, CAT.
knack ***n.*** trick, skill, faculty; see ABILITY.
knapsack ***n.*** backpack, kit, rucksack; see BAG, CONTAINER.
knead ***v.*** work, mix, squeeze; see PRESS 1.
knee ***n.*** knee joint, crook, bend, hinge, kneecap, articulation of the femur and the tibia; see also BONE.
kneel ***v.*** bend the knee, rest on the knees, genuflect, bend, stoop, bow down, curtsy.
knickknack ***n.*** gadget, bric-a-brac, curio, ornament, trifle, bauble, trinket, plaything, showpiece, gewgaw*; see also TOY 1.
knife ***n.*** blade, cutter, sword, bayonet, cutting edge, dagger, stiletto, lance, machete, poniard, scalpel, edge, dirk, sickle, scythe, saber, scimitar, broadsword, point, pigsticker*, shiv*; see also RAZOR. *Knives include the following:* carving, chopping, table, dinner, dessert, grapefruit, fish, pocket, hunting, Bowie, butcher, skinning, surgical, paper, pruning, oyster, putty, palette, bread, cake, serving, Boy Scout, Swiss Army.
knife ***v.*** **1** [To stab] slash, lance, thrust through; see HURT 1, KILL 1, STAB. **2** [*To injure in an underhanded way] trick, give a coward's blow, strike below the belt; see DECEIVE.
knight ***n.*** cavalier, champion, knight-errant; see ARISTOCRAT.

piece shaped like a horse's head —*vt.* to make (a man) a knight

knight'-er'rant (-er'ənt) *n., pl.* **knights'-er'rant** **1** a medieval knight wandering in search of adventure **2** a chivalrous or quixotic person

knight'hood' *n.* **1** the rank, status, or vocation of a knight **2** knights collectively

knight'ly *adj.* of, like, or befitting a knight; chivalrous, brave, etc.

knit (nit) *vt., vi.* **knit'ted** or **knit, knit'ting** ⟦< OE *cnotta*, a knot⟧ **1** to make (a fabric) by looping yarn or thread together with special needles **2** to join or grow together closely and firmly: said as of a broken bone **3** to draw or become drawn together in wrinkles: said of the brows —**knit'ter** *n.*

knit'wear' *n.* knitted clothing

knob (näb) *n.* ⟦ME *knobbe*⟧ **1** a rounded lump or protuberance **2** *a)* a handle, usually round, of a door, drawer, etc. *b)* a similar device used to control a radio, TV, etc.

knob'by *adj.* **-bi·er, -bi·est** **1** covered with knobs **2** like a knob

knock (näk) *vi.* ⟦< OE *cnocian*⟧ **1** to strike a blow **2** to rap on a door **3** to bump; collide **4** to make a thumping noise: said of an engine, etc. —*vt.* **1** to hit; strike **2** to make by hitting *[to knock a hole in a wall]* **3** [Inf.] to find fault with —*n.* **1** a knocking **2** a hit; rap **3** a thumping noise in an engine, etc., as because of faulty combustion **4** [Inf.] an adverse criticism —**knock about** (or **around**) [Inf.] to wander about —**knock down** **1** to hit so as to cause to fall **2** to take apart **3** to indicate the sale of (an article) at an auction —**knock off** **1** [Inf.] to stop working **2** [Inf.] to deduct **3** [Slang] to kill, overcome, etc. —**knock out** to make unconscious or exhausted —**knock together** to make or compose hastily or crudely

knock'er *n.* one that knocks; esp., a small ring, knob, etc. on a door for use in knocking

knock'-kneed' (-nēd') *adj.* having legs that bend inward at the knees

knock'out' *n.* **1** a knocking out or being knocked out **2** [Slang] a very attractive person or thing **3** *Boxing* a victory won when the opponent is unable to continue to fight, as because of having been knocked unconscious

knock·wurst (näk'wʉrst') *n. alt. sp. of* KNACKWURST

knoll (nōl) *n.* ⟦OE *cnoll*⟧ a small hill; mound

knot (nät) *n.* ⟦< OE *cnotta*⟧ **1** a lump in a thread, etc., formed by a tightened loop or a tangle **2** a fastening made by tying together pieces of string, rope, etc. **3** an ornamental bow of ribbon, etc. **4** a small group or cluster **5** something that ties closely; esp., the bond of marriage **6** a problem; difficulty **7** a hard lump on a tree where a branch grows out, or a cross section of such a lump in a board **8** *Naut.* a unit of speed of one nautical mile (6,076.12 feet) an hour —*vt., vi.* **knot'ted, knot'ting** **1** to make or form a knot (in) **2** to entangle or become entangled —**tie the knot** [Inf.] to get married

knot'hole' *n.* a hole in a board, etc. where a knot has fallen out

knot'ty *adj.* **-ti·er, -ti·est** ⟦ME⟧ **1** full of knots *[knotty pine]* **2** hard to solve; puzzling *[a knotty problem]*

know (nō) *vt.* **knew, known, know'ing** ⟦< OE *cnawan*⟧ **1** to be well informed about **2** to be aware of *[to know that one is loved]* **3** to be acquainted with **4** to recognize or distinguish *[to know right from wrong]* —*vi.* **1** to have knowledge **2** to be sure or aware —**in the know** [Inf.] having confidential information

know'-how' *n.* [Inf.] technical skill

know'ing *adj.* **1** having knowledge **2** shrewd; clever **3** implying shrewd or secret understanding *[a knowing look]* —**know'ing·ly** *adv.*

know'-it-all' *n.* [Inf.] one claiming to know much about almost everything

knowl·edge (näl'ij) *n.* **1** the fact or state of knowing **2** range of information or understanding **3** what is known; learning **4** the body of facts, etc. accumulated by humanity —**to** (**the best of**) **one's knowledge** as far as one knows

knowl'edge·a·ble *adj.* having knowledge or intelligence —**knowl'edge·a·bly** *adv.*

known (nōn) *vt., vi. pp. of* KNOW —*adj.* **1** familiar **2** recognized, proven, etc. *[a known expert]*

Knox·ville (näks'vil') city in E Tennessee: pop. 165,000

knuck·le (nuk'əl) *n.* ⟦< or akin to MDu & LowG *knokel*, dim. of *knoke*, bone⟧ **1** a joint of the finger; esp., the joint connecting a finger to the rest of the hand **2** the knee or hock joint of an animal, used as food —**knuckle down** to work hard or seriously —**knuckle under** to yield; give in

knuck'le·head' *n.* [Inf.] a stupid person

knurl (nʉrl) *n.* ⟦prob. < *knur*, a knot + GNARL⟧ **1** a knot, knob, etc. **2** any of a series of small beads or ridges, as along the edge of a coin —*vt.* to make knurls on

KO (kā'ō') [Slang] *vt.* **KO'd, KO'ing** *Boxing* to knock out —*n., pl.* **KO's** *Boxing* a knockout Also **K.O.** or **k.o.**

ko·a·la (kō ä'lə) *n.* ⟦< native name⟧ a tree-dwelling Australian marsupial with thick, gray fur

Ko·di·ak (kō'dē ak') island off the SW coast of Alaska

kohl·ra·bi (kōl rä'bē) *n., pl.* **-bies** ⟦< It *cavolo rapa*⟧ a vegetable related to the cabbage, with an edible, turniplike stem

ko·la (kō'lə) *n.* COLA (sense 1)

THESAURUS

knit *v.* **1** [To form by knitting] crochet, purl, spin, web, loop; see also SEW, WEAVE 1. **2** [To combine or join closely] intermingle, connect, affiliate; see JOIN 1.

knitted *a.* knit, purled, crocheted; see WOVEN.

knob *n.* **1** [A projection] hump, bulge, knot, node, bump, protuberance; see also LUMP. **2** [A door handle] doorknob, latch, door latch; see HANDLE 1.

knobby *a.* knobbed, lumpy, bumpy; see BENT, CROOKED 1.

knock *n.* rap, thump, whack; see BEAT 1, BLOW, INJURY.

knock *v.* tap, rap, thump; see BEAT 2, HIT 1, HURT 1. —**knock down** thrash, drub, kayo*; see BEAT 1, HIT 1, KNOCK OUT 2. —**knock off*** **1** [To kill] murder, stab, shoot; see KILL 1. **2** [To accomplish] complete, finish, eliminate; see ACHIEVE, SUCCEED 1. **3** [To stop] quit, leave, halt; see STOP 2. —**knock oneself out*** slave, labor, do one's utmost; see WORK 1. —**knock out** **1** [To anesthetize] etherize, put to sleep, drug; see DEADEN. **2** [To strike down] strike senseless, render unconscious, knock someone out of his or her senses, knock cold*, kayo*, knock for a loop*, put out like a light*. —**knock up*** impregnate, make pregnant, inseminate; see FERTILIZE 2.

knockout *n.* **1** [A blow that knocks unconscious] knockout punch, final blow, kayo*; see BLOW. **2** [*A success] excellent thing, sensation, perfection; see SUCCESS 1.

knot *n.* **1** [An arrangement of strands] tie, clinch, hitch, splice, ligature, bond. **2** [A hard or twisted portion] snarl, gnarl, snag, bunch, coil, entanglement, tangle, twist.

knot *v.* bind, tie, hitch; see FASTEN.

knotted *a.* tied, twisted, tangled, snarled, entangled, bunched, clustered, looped, hitched, spliced, fastened, bent, warped, clinched, banded, lassoed, braided, linked, involved.—*Ant.* FREE, loose, separate.

know *v.* **1** [To possess information] be cognizant, be acquainted, be informed, be in possession of the facts, have knowledge of, be schooled in, be versed in, understand, appreciate, be conversant with, recognize, know full well, have at one's fingertips, be master of, know by heart, know inside out*, be instructed, awaken to, keep up on, have information about, know what's what*, know all the answers, have someone's number*, have the jump on*, have down cold*, know one's stuff*, know the score*, know the ropes*.—*Ant.* NEGLECT, be oblivious to, overlook. **2** [To understand] comprehend, apprehend, see into; see UNDERSTAND 1. **3** [To recognize] perceive, discern, be familiar with, have the friendship of, acknowledge, be accustomed to, associate with, get acquainted. —**know how** be able, have the necessary background, be trained; see UNDERSTAND 1.

know-how* *n.* skill, background, wisdom; see ABILITY, EXPERIENCE, KNOWLEDGE 1.

knowing *a.* sharp, clever, acute; see INTELLIGENT, REASONABLE 1.

knowingly *a.* intentionally, purposely, consciously; see DELIBERATELY.

knowledge *n.* **1** [Information] lore, learning, scholarship, facts, wisdom, instruction, book learning, erudition, culture, data, enlightenment, expertise, intelligence, light, theory, science, principles, philosophy, awareness, insight, education, substance, store of learning, know-how*; see also INFORMATION 1.—*Ant.* IGNORANCE, emptiness, pretension. **2** [Culture] tradition, cultivation, learning; see EXPERIENCE, REFINEMENT 2.

known *a.* **1** [Open] discovered, disclosed, revealed; see OBVIOUS 1, PUBLIC 1. **2** [Established] well-known, published, recognized, notorious, received, accepted, noted, proverbial, certified, down pat*; see also FAMILIAR.

knuckle under *v.* give in, give up, acquiesce; see YIELD 1.

kook (ko͝ok) ***n.*** ⟦prob. < CUCKOO⟧ [Slang] a person regarded as silly, eccentric, etc. —**kook'y** or **kook'ie, -i·er, -i·est,** ***adj.***

kook·a·bur·ra (ko͝ok'ə bur'ə) ***n.*** ⟦< native name⟧ an Australian kingfisher with a harsh cry like loud laughter

ko·peck or **ko·pek** (kō'pek') ***n.*** ⟦Russ < *kopye,* a lance⟧ a 100th part of a ruble

Ko·ran (kə ran', kôr'an') ***n.*** ⟦< Ar *qur'ān,* book⟧ the sacred book of Islam

Ko·re·a (kə rē'ə) peninsula & country northeast of China: divided (1948) into *a)* **Korean People's Democratic Republic** (**North Korea**): 47,399 sq. mi.; pop. 23,030,000 *b)* **Republic of Korea** (**South Korea**): 38,326 sq. mi.; pop. 43,412,000 —**Ko·re'an** ***adj.***, ***n.***

ko·sher (kō'shər) ***adj.*** ⟦< Heb *kāshēr,* proper⟧ *Judaism* clean or fit to eat according to the dietary laws

kow·tow (kou'tou') ***vi.*** ⟦Chin *k'o-t'ou,* lit., bump head⟧ to show great deference, respect, etc. (*to*)

KP *abbrev.* kitchen police: a detail to assist the cooks in an army kitchen

kraal (kräl) ***n.*** ⟦Afrik⟧ **1** a village of South African native people **2** in South Africa, an enclosure for cattle or sheep

Krem·lin (krem'lin) ***n.*** ⟦< Russ *kryeml'*⟧ **1** the citadel of Moscow, housing many Russian, or, formerly, Soviet, government offices **2** the Russian, or, formerly, Soviet, government

Krish·na (krish'nə) ***n.*** a Hindu god, an incarnation of Vishnu

kro·na (krō'nə) ***n.***, *pl.* **-nor'** (-nôr') ⟦ult. < L *corona*, crown⟧ the monetary unit of Sweden

kró·na (krō'nə) ***n.***, *pl.* **-nur** (-nər) ⟦see prec.⟧ the monetary unit of Iceland

kro·ne (krō'nə) ***n.***, *pl.* **-ner** (-nər) ⟦see KRONA⟧ the monetary unit of Denmark and Norway

KS Kansas

K2 GODWIN AUSTEN

ku·chen (ko͞o'kən) ***n.*** ⟦Ger, cake⟧ a coffeecake made of yeast dough, often with raisins, nuts, etc.

ku·dos (kyo͞o'däs', ko͞o'-) ***n.*** ⟦Gr *kydos*⟧ credit for an achievement; glory; fame: often wrongly taken to be the plural (*pron.* -dōz) of an assumed word *"kudo"*

kud·zu (ko͝od'zo͞o') ***n.*** ⟦Jpn⟧ a fast-growing perennial vine with large, three-part leaves

Ku Klux Klan (ko͞o' kluks' klan') ⟦< Gr *kyklos,* circle⟧ a U.S. secret society that is anti-black, anti-Semitic, anti-Catholic, etc., and uses terrorist methods

kum·quat (kum'kwät') ***n.*** ⟦< Mandarin *chin-chü*, lit., golden orange⟧ a small, orange-colored, oval fruit with a sour pulp and a sweet rind

kung fu (ko͝oŋ' fo͞o', go͞oŋ'-) ⟦< Chin⟧ a Chinese system of self-defense, like karate but with circular movements

Ku·wait (ko͞o wāt') independent Arab state in E Arabia: 6,880 sq. mi.; pop. 1,697,000 —**Ku·wai'ti** (-wāt'ē) ***adj.***, ***n.***

kvetch (kə vech') ***vi.*** ⟦< Yiddish⟧ [Slang] to complain in a nagging way

kW or **kw** *abbrev.* kilowatt(s)

Kwang·chow (kwäŋ'chō') *a former transliteration of* GUANGZHOU

Kwan·zaa (kwän'zä) ***n.*** ⟦ult. < Swahili⟧ an African-American cultural festival, Dec. 26 through Jan. 1

KY Kentucky

Kyo·to (kē ōt'ō) city in S Honshu, Japan: pop. 1,473,000

Kyr·gyz·stan (kir'gi stan') country in south-central Asia: formerly a republic of the U.S.S.R.: 77,180 sq. mi.; pop. 4,463,000

THESAURUS

kook* ***n.*** eccentric, crackpot*, loony*, cuckoo*, ding-a-ling*, nut*, screwball*, crazy*, weirdo*, wacko*, flake*, dingbat*.

kudos ***n.*** credit, glory, fame; see PRAISE 2, HONOR 1.

L

l[1] or **L** (el) ***n.***, *pl.* **l's, L's** the 12th letter of the English alphabet
l[2] *abbrev.* **1** latitude **2** left **3** length **4** line **5** liter(s) **6** long **7** loss(es)
L[1] (el) ***n.***, *pl.* **L's** **1** an extension forming an L with the main structure **2** a Roman numeral for 50
L[2] *abbrev.* **1** Lake **2** large **3** Latin **4** left **5** length **6** liter(s) **7** longitude **8** ⟦L *libra*, pl. *librae*⟧ pound(s): now usually £
la (lä) ***n.*** ⟦< L⟧ *Music* the sixth tone of the diatonic scale
LA **1** Los Angeles **2** Louisiana
lab (lab) ***n.*** [Inf.] a laboratory
la·bel (lā′bəl) ***n.*** ⟦OFr, a rag⟧ **1** a card, paper, etc. marked and attached to an object to indicate its contents, owner, destination, etc. **2** a term of generalized classification —***vt.*** **-beled** or **-belled**, **-bel·ing** or **-bel·ling** **1** to attach a label to **2** to classify as
la·bi·al (lā′bē əl) ***adj.*** ⟦< L *labium*, lip⟧ **1** of the lips **2** *Phonetics* articulated with one or both lips: said as of (f), (b), and (ü)
la′bi·um (-əm) ***n.***, *pl.* **-bi·a** (-ə) ⟦L, lip⟧ a lip or liplike organ
la·bor (lā′bər) ***n.*** ⟦< L⟧ **1** physical or mental exertion; work **2** a specific task **3** all wage-earning workers **4** labor unions collectively **5** the process of childbirth —***vi.*** **1** to work **2** to work hard **3** to move slowly and with difficulty **4** to be burdened with a liability or limitation (with *under*) **5** to be in childbirth —***vt.*** to develop in too great detail; belabor
lab·o·ra·to·ry (lab′rə tôr′ē) ***n.***, *pl.* **-ries** ⟦see prec.⟧ a room, building, etc. for scientific experimentation or research
Labor Day the first Monday in September, a legal holiday honoring working people
la·bored (lā′bərd) ***adj.*** made or done with great effort; strained
la′bor·er ***n.*** one who labors; esp., a wage-earning worker whose work is largely hard physical labor
la·bo·ri·ous (lə bôr′ē əs) ***adj.*** **1** involving much hard work; difficult **2** LABORED —**la·bo′ri·ous·ly** ***adv.***
labor union an association of workers to promote and protect the welfare, rights, etc. of its members
la·bour (lā′bər) ***n.***, ***vi.***, ***vt.*** *Brit. sp. of* LABOR
Lab·ra·dor (lab′rə dôr′) **1** region along the Atlantic in NE Canada: the mainland part of Newfoundland **2** large peninsula between the Atlantic & Hudson Bay, containing this region & Quebec
Labrador retriever a retriever with a short, dense, black, yellow, or brown coat
la·bur·num (lə bur′nəm) ***n.*** ⟦< L⟧ a small tree or shrub of the pea family, with drooping yellow flowers
lab·y·rinth (lab′ə rinth′) ***n.*** ⟦< Gr *labyrinthos*⟧ a structure containing winding passages hard to follow without losing one's way; maze
lac (lak) ***n.*** ⟦< Sans *lākṣā*⟧ a resinous substance secreted on certain trees in India, etc. by a certain kind of insect: source of shellac
lace (lās) ***n.*** ⟦< L *laqueus*, noose⟧ **1** a string, etc. used to draw together and fasten the parts of a shoe, corset, etc. **2** a fine netting of cotton, silk, etc., woven in ornamental designs —***vt.*** **laced, lac′ing** **1** to fasten with a lace **2** to weave together; intertwine **3** to hit hard **4** to add a dash of alcoholic liquor to (a drink)
lac·er·ate (las′ər āt′) ***vt.*** **-at′ed, -at′ing** ⟦< L *lacer*, lacerated⟧ to tear jaggedly; mangle (flesh, etc.) —**lac′er·a′tion** ***n.***
lace′work′ ***n.*** lace, or any openwork decoration like lace
lach·ry·mal (lak′ri məl) ***adj.*** ⟦< L *lacrima*, TEAR[2]⟧ **1** of or producing tears **2** LACRIMAL (sense 1)
lach′ry·mose′ (-mōs′) ***adj.*** ⟦see prec.⟧ shedding, or causing to shed, tears; tearful or sad
lack (lak) ***n.*** ⟦< or akin to medieval LowG *lak*⟧ **1** the fact or state of not having enough or not having any **2** the thing that is needed —***vt.***, ***vi.*** to be deficient in or entirely without (something)
lack·a·dai·si·cal (lak′ə dā′zi kəl) ***adj.*** ⟦< archaic *lackaday*, an exclamation of regret, etc.⟧ showing lack of interest or spirit; listless
lack·ey (lak′ē) ***n.***, *pl.* **-eys** ⟦< Sp *lacayo*⟧ **1** a male servant of low rank, usually in some sort of livery or uniform **2** a servile follower; toady
lack·lus·ter (lak′lus′tər) ***adj.*** **1** lacking brightness; dull **2** lacking vitality; boring Also [Chiefly Brit.] **lack′lus′tre**
la·con·ic (lə kän′ik) ***adj.*** ⟦< Gr *Lakōn*, a Spartan⟧ terse in expression; concise —**la·con′i·cal·ly** ***adv.***
lac·quer (lak′ər) ***n.*** ⟦< Fr < Port *laca*, lac⟧ **1** a coating substance made of shellac, gum resins, etc. dissolved in ethyl alcohol or other solvent that evaporates rapidly **2** a resinous varnish obtained from certain E Asian trees —***vt.*** to coat with lacquer
lac·ri·mal (lak′ri məl) ***adj.*** **1** of or near the glands that secrete tears **2** LACHRYMAL (sense 1)
la·crosse (lə krôs′) ***n.*** ⟦CdnFr, lit., the crutch⟧ a ballgame played by two teams using long-handled, pouched rackets
lac·tate (lak′tāt′) ***vi.*** **-tat′ed, -tat′ing** to secrete milk
lac·ta·tion (lak tā′shən) ***n.*** ⟦< L *lac*, milk⟧ **1** the secretion of milk by a mammary gland **2** the period during which milk is secreted
lac·te·al (lak′tē əl) ***adj.*** ⟦< L *lac*, milk⟧ of or like milk; milky
lac·tic (lak′tik) ***adj.*** ⟦< L *lac*, milk⟧ of or obtained from milk
lactic acid a clear, syrupy acid formed when milk sours
lac·tose (lak′tōs′) ***n.*** ⟦< L *lac*, milk⟧ a sugar found in milk: used in foods
la·cu·na (lə kyo͞o′nə) ***n.***, *pl.* **-nas** or **-nae** (-nē) ⟦L, a ditch⟧ a blank space; esp., a missing portion in a text, etc.
lac·y (lās′ē) ***adj.*** **-i·er, -i·est** of or like lace —**lac′i·ness** ***n.***
lad (lad) ***n.*** ⟦ME *ladde*⟧ a boy; youth
lad·der (lad′ər) ***n.*** ⟦OE *hlæder*⟧ **1** a framework consisting of two sidepieces connected by a series of rungs, for use in climbing up or down **2** any means of climbing

THESAURUS

label ***n.*** tag, marker, mark, stamp, hallmark, insignia, design, number, identification, description, sticker, emblem, ticket; see also NAME 1.

label ***v.*** specify, mark, identify; see NAME 1, 2.

labeled ***a.*** identified, tagged, stamped; see MARKED 1, 2.

labor ***n.*** **1** [The act of doing work] activity, toil, operation; see WORK 2. **2** [Work to be done] task, employment, undertaking; see JOB 2. **3** [Exertion required in work] exertion, energy, industry, diligence, strain, stress, drudgery; see also EFFORT, EXERCISE 1. **4** [The body of workers] laborers, workers, workingmen, workingwomen, wage earners, proletariat, work force, labor force, working people, employees.—*Ant.* EMPLOYER, capitalist, businessman. **5** [Childbirth] parturition, giving birth, labor pains; see BIRTH.

labor ***v.*** toil, strive, get cracking*; see WORK 1.

laboratory ***n.*** workroom, lab*, research facility, testing room; see also OFFICE 3.

laborer ***n.*** day laborer, unskilled worker, hand, manual laborer, ranch hand, farmhand, worker, blue-collar worker, serf, apprentice, hired man, transient worker, toiler, seasonal laborer, ditch digger, pick-and-shovel man, roustabout, stevedore, miner, street cleaner, wage slave, robot, peon, flunky, lackey, hireling, hack, beast of burden*.

labor union ***n.*** organized labor, American Federation of Labor and Congress of Industrial Organizations (AFL-CIO), craft union, industrial union, trade union, local, labor party; see also ORGANIZATION 2.

lace ***n.*** **1** [Ornamental threadwork] tatting, crocheted lace, edging; see DECORATION 2. **2** [Material for binding through openings] thong, cord, band; see ROPE.

lace ***v.*** strap, bind, close; see FASTEN, TIE 2.

lacing ***n.*** bond, hitch, tie; see FASTENER, KNOT 1.

lack ***n.*** **1** [The state of being lacking] destitution, absence, need, shortage, paucity, deprivation, deficiency, scarcity, insufficiency, inadequacy, privation, poverty, distress, scantiness.—*Ant.* PLENTY, sufficiency, abundance. **2** [That which is lacking] need, decrease, want, loss, depletion, shrinkage, shortage, defect, inferiority, paucity, stint, curtailment, reduction; see also NECESSITY 2.—*Ant.* WEALTH, overflow, satisfaction.

lack ***v.*** want, require, have need of; see NEED.

lacking ***a.*** needed, deprived of, missing; see WANTING.

lacy ***a.*** sheer, thin, gauzy; see TRANSPARENT 1.

lad ***n.*** fellow, youth, stripling; see BOY, CHILD.

ladder ***n.*** *Ladders include the following:* stepladder, rope ladder, ship's ladder, aerial ladder, extension ladder, step stool, gangway, fire escape; see also STAIRS.

lad·die (lad'ē) ***n.*** [Chiefly Scot.] a young lad
lad·en (lād''n) ***adj.*** ⟦< OE⟧ **1** loaded **2** burdened
la-di-da (lä'dē dä') ***adj.*** ⟦imitative⟧ [Inf.] affectedly refined
lad·ing (lād'iŋ) ***n.*** a load; cargo; freight
la·dle (lād''l) ***n.*** ⟦OE *hlædel*⟧ a long-handled, cuplike spoon —***vt.*** **-dled, -dling** to dip out with a ladle
la·dy (lād'ē) ***n.***, *pl.* **-dies** ⟦< OE *hlaf*, loaf + *dæge*, kneader⟧ **1** *a)* a woman of high social position *b)* a woman who is polite, refined, etc. **2** any woman: used (in pl.) to address a group **3** [**L-**] a British title given to women of certain ranks —***adj.*** [Inf.] female
la'dy·bug' ***n.*** a small, roundish beetle with a spotted back: also **la'dy·bird'**
la'dy·fin'ger ***n.*** a small spongecake shaped somewhat like a finger
la'dy-in-wait'ing ***n.***, *pl.* **la'dies-in-wait'ing** a woman waiting upon a queen or princess
la'dy·like' ***adj.*** like or suitable for a lady; refined; well-bred
la'dy·love' ***n.*** a female sweetheart
la'dy·ship' ***n.*** **1** the rank or position of a lady **2** [*usually* **L-**] a title used in speaking to or of a woman holding the rank of lady
la'dy-slip'per ***n.*** an orchid with flowers that somewhat resemble slippers: also **la'dy's-slip'per**
la·e·trile (lā'ə tril') ***n.*** any of several compounds obtained chiefly from apricot kernels, claimed by some to be effective in treating cancer
La·fa·yette (lä'fē et', -fā-), Marquis **de** 1757-1834; Fr. general: served (1777-81) in the American Revolutionary army
lag (lag) ***vi.*** **lagged, lag'ging** ⟦< ?⟧ **1** to fall behind or move slowly; loiter **2** to become less intense —***n.*** **1** a falling behind **2** the amount of this
la·ger (beer) (lä'gər) ⟦Ger *lagerbier*, storehouse beer⟧ a beer aged at a low temperature
lag·gard (lag'ərd) ***n.*** ⟦< LAG + -ARD⟧ a slow person, esp. one who falls behind —***adj.*** slow; falling behind
la·gniappe or **la·gnappe** (lan yap', lan'yap') ***n.*** ⟦Creole < Fr & Sp⟧ a gratuity
la·goon (lə go͞on') ***n.*** ⟦< L *lacuna*, pool⟧ **1** a shallow lake or pond, esp. one connected with a larger body of water **2** the water enclosed by a circular coral reef **3** an area of shallow salt water separated from the sea by sand dunes
La·hore (lə hôr') city in NE Pakistan: pop. 2,953,000
laid (lād) ***vt.***, ***vi.*** *pt. & pp. of* LAY[1]
laid'-back' ***adj.*** [Slang] relaxed, easygoing, etc.; not frenetic or hurried
lain (lān) ***vi.*** *pp. of* LIE[1]
lair (ler) ***n.*** ⟦OE *leger*⟧ a resting place of a wild animal; den
lais·sez faire (les'ā fer') ⟦Fr, allow to do⟧ noninterference; specif., absence of government control over industry and business
la·i·ty (lā'i tē) ***n.***, *pl.* **-ties** ⟦< LAY[3]⟧ laymen collectively
lake (lāk) ***n.*** ⟦< L *lacus*⟧ **1** a large inland body of usually fresh water **2** a pool of oil or other liquid
lake'front' ***n.*** the land along the shore of a lake —***adj.*** near, at, or of the lakefront
lal·ly·gag (lä'lē gag') ***vi.*** **-gagged', -gag'ging** [Inf.] LOLLYGAG
lam (lam) [Slang] ***n.*** ⟦< ?⟧ headlong flight —***vi.*** **lammed, lam'ming** to flee; escape —**on the lam** in flight, as from the police
la·ma (lä'mə) ***n.*** ⟦Tibetan *blama*⟧ a priest or monk in Lamaism
La·ma·ism (lä'mə iz'əm) ***n.*** a form of Buddhism in Tibet and Mongolia
la·ma·ser·y (lä'mə ser'ē) ***n.***, *pl.* **-ies** a monastery of lamas
La·maze (lə mäz') ***n.*** ⟦after F. *Lamaze*, 20th-c. Fr physician⟧ a training program in natural childbirth, involving the help of the father
lamb (lam) ***n.*** ⟦OE⟧ **1** a young sheep **2** its flesh, used as food **3** a gentle, innocent, or gullible person
lam·baste (lam bāst', -bast') ***vt.*** **-bast'ed, -bast'ing** ⟦< *lam*, to beat + *baste*, to flog⟧ [Inf.] **1** to beat soundly **2** to scold or denounce severely
lamb·da (lam'də) ***n.*** the 11th letter of the Greek alphabet (Λ, λ)
lam·bent (lam'bənt) ***adj.*** ⟦< L *lambere*, to lick⟧ **1** playing lightly over a surface: said of a flame, etc. **2** glowing softly **3** light and graceful *[lambent* wit*]* —**lam'ben·cy** ***n.***
lamb'kin ***n.*** a little lamb: sometimes applied to a child, etc. as a term of affection
lame (lām) ***adj.*** ⟦OE *lama*⟧ **1** crippled; esp., having an injury that makes one limp **2** stiff and painful **3** poor; ineffectual *[a lame* excuse*]* —***vt.*** **lamed, lam'ing** to make lame —**lame'ly** ***adv.*** —**lame'ness** ***n.***
la·mé (la mā', lä-) ***n.*** ⟦< Fr *lame*, metal plate⟧ a cloth interwoven with metal threads, as of gold
lame duck an elected official whose term ends after someone else has been elected to the office
la·mel·la (lə mel'ə) ***n.***, *pl.* **-lae** (-ē) or **-las** ⟦L⟧ a thin plate, scale, or layer
la·ment (lə ment') ***vi.***, ***vt.*** ⟦< L *lamentum*, a wailing⟧ to feel or express deep sorrow (for); mourn —***n.*** **1** a lamenting **2** an elegy, dirge, etc. mourning some loss or death —**lam·en·ta·ble** (lam'ən tə bəl, lə men'-) ***adj.*** —**lam·en·ta·tion** (lam'ən tā'shən) ***n.***
lam·i·na (lam'i nə) ***n.***, *pl.* **-nae'** (-nē') or **-nas** ⟦L⟧ a thin scale or layer, as of metal, tissue, etc.
lam·i·nate (lam'i nāt'; *for adj. usually*, -nit) ***vt.*** **-nat'ed, -nat'ing** ⟦see prec.⟧ **1** to cover with one or more thin layers **2** to make by building up in layers —***adj.*** LAMINATED —**lam'i·na'tion** ***n.***
lam'i·nat'ed ***adj.*** **1** built in thin sheets or layers **2** covered with a thin protective layer, as of clear plastic
lamp (lamp) ***n.*** ⟦< Gr *lampein*, to shine⟧ **1** a container with a wick for burning oil, etc. to produce light or heat **2** any device for producing light or heat, as an electric light bulb **3** a holder or base for such a device
lamp'black' ***n.*** fine soot used as a black pigment
lam·poon (lam po͞on') ***n.*** ⟦< Fr *lampons*, let us drink: used as a refrain⟧ a satirical writing attacking someone —***vt.*** to attack in a lampoon
lamp·post (lamp'pōst') ***n.*** a post supporting a street lamp
lam·prey (lam'prē) ***n.***, *pl.* **-preys** ⟦< ML *lampreda*⟧ an eel-like fish with a jawless, sucking mouth
la·na·i (lə nä'ē, -nī') ***n.*** ⟦Haw⟧ a veranda or open-sided living room
lance (lans) ***n.*** ⟦< L *lancea*⟧ **1** a long, wooden spear with a sharp metal head **2** *a)* LANCER *b)* LANCET **3** any instrument like a lance —***vt.*** **lanced, lanc'ing** **1** to pierce with a lance **2** to cut open (a boil, etc.) with a lancet
Lan·ce·lot (län'sə lət, -lät') ***n.*** the most celebrated of the Knights of the Round Table
lanc·er (lans'ər) ***n.*** a cavalry soldier armed with a lance
lan·cet (lan'sit) ***n.*** ⟦< OFr dim. of *lance*, lance⟧ a small, pointed surgical knife, usually two-edged

THESAURUS

ladle ***n.*** skimmer, scoop, dipper; see SILVERWARE.
lady ***n.*** **1** [A woman] female, adult, matron; see WOMAN 1. **2** [A woman of gentle breeding] gentlewoman, well-bred woman, woman of quality, cultured woman, highborn lady, mistress of an estate, noblewoman, titled lady; see also WOMAN 1.
ladylike ***a.*** womanly, cultured, well-bred; see POLITE, REFINED 2.
lag ***n.*** slackness, slowness, tardiness, falling behind, sluggishness, backwardness.—*Ant.* PROGRESS, progression, advance.
lag ***v.*** dawdle, linger, fall back, loiter, tarry, straggle, get behind, slacken, slow up, fall behind, procrastinate, plod, trudge, lounge, shuffle, falter, stagger, limp, get no place fast*; see also DELAY.—*Ant.* HURRY, hasten, keep pace with.
lagoon ***n.*** inlet, sound, pool; see BAY, LAKE.
lair ***n.*** cave, home, den; see PEN 1.
lake ***n.*** pond, creek, loch, pool, lagoon, inland sea; see also SEA. *Famous lakes include the following:* Geneva, Lucerne, Great Salt, Superior, Huron, Michigan, Erie, Ontario, Champlain, Finger Lakes, Tahoe, Tanganyika, Nyasa, Loch Lomond, Victoria, Baikal, Great Slave, Titicaca, Great Bear, Loch Ness, Caspian Sea, Aral Sea.
lamb ***n.*** young sheep, young one, yeanling; see ANIMAL.
lame ***a.*** **1** [Forced to limp] crippled, unable to walk, halt, weak, paralyzed, impaired, handicapped, limping; see also DEFORMED, DISABLED. **2** [Weak; *usually used figuratively*] inefficient, ineffective, faltering; see UNSATISFACTORY, WANTING.
lamp ***n.*** light, light bulb, lighting device; see LIGHT 3. *Types and forms of lamps include the following:* wick, oil, gas, electric, table, hanging, safety, gooseneck, three-way, floor, miner's, arc, incandescent, halogen, fluorescent; sunlamp, streetlamp, night light, flashlight, chandelier, lantern.
lampoon ***n.*** satire, pasquinade, travesty, parody, burlesque.

land (land) ***n.*** ⟦OE⟧ **1** the solid part of the earth's surface **2** a country or nation **3** ground or soil **4** real estate — ***vt.*** **1** to put on shore from a ship **2** to bring to a particular place or condition *[it landed him in jail]* **3** to set (an aircraft) down on land or water **4** to catch *[to land a fish]* **5** [Inf.] to get or secure *[to land a job]* **6** [Inf.] to deliver (a blow) — ***vi.*** **1** to leave a ship and go on shore **2** to come to a port, etc.: said of a ship **3** to arrive at a specified place **4** to come to rest

land contract a real estate contract in which a buyer makes payments over a specified period until the full price is paid, after which the seller transfers his interest to the buyer

land'ed ***adj.*** owning land *[landed gentry]*

land'fall' ***n.*** **1** a sighting of land from a ship at sea **2** the land sighted

land'fill' ***n.*** **1** a place used to dispose of garbage, rubbish, etc. by burying it in the ground **2** garbage, etc. so disposed of

land grant a grant of land by the government for a railroad, state college, etc.

land'hold'er ***n.*** an owner of land —**land'hold'ing** ***adj., n.***

land'ing ***n.*** **1** the act of coming to shore **2** a place where a ship or boat is loaded or unloaded **3** a platform at the end of a flight of stairs **4** the act of alighting, as after a flight or jump

landing gear the system of parts on an aircraft or spacecraft used for support or mobility on land or water

land'locked' ***adj.*** **1** surrounded by land, as a country **2** cut off from the sea and confined to fresh water *[landlocked salmon]*

land'lord' ***n.*** **1** a person who leases land, houses, etc. to others **2** a man who keeps a rooming house, inn, etc. — **land'la'dy**, *pl.* **-dies**, ***fem.n.***

land'lub'ber (-lub'ər) ***n.*** one who has had little experience at sea

land'mark' ***n.*** **1** an object that marks the boundary of a piece of land **2** any prominent feature of the landscape, distinguishing a locality **3** an important event or turning point

land'mass' ***n.*** a very large area of land; esp., a continent

land office a government office that handles the sales of public lands

land'-of'fice business [Inf.] a booming business

land'scape' (-skāp') ***n.*** ⟦< Du *land*, land + *-schap*, -ship⟧ **1** a picture of natural, inland scenery **2** an expanse of natural scenery —***vt.* -scaped', -scap'ing** to make (a plot of ground) more attractive, as by adding a lawn, trees, bushes, etc. —**land'scap'er** ***n.***

land'slide' ***n.*** **1** the sliding of a mass of earth or rocks down a slope **2** the mass sliding down **3** an overwhelming victory, esp. in an election

land'ward (-wərd) ***adv., adj.*** toward the land: also **land'wards** ***adv.***

lane (lān) ***n.*** ⟦OE *lanu*⟧ **1** a narrow way, path, road, etc. **2** a path or route designated, for reasons of safety, for ships, aircraft, automobiles, etc. **3** *Bowling* a long, narrow strip of polished wood, along which the balls are rolled

lan·guage (laŋ'gwij) ***n.*** ⟦< L *lingua*, tongue⟧ **1** human speech or the written symbols for speech **2** *a)* any means of communicating *b)* a special set of symbols used in a computer **3** the speech of a particular nation, etc. *[the French language]* **4** the particular style of verbal expression characteristic of a person, group, profession, etc.

lan·guid (laŋ'gwid) ***adj.*** ⟦< L *languere*, be weary⟧ **1** without vigor or vitality; weak **2** listless; indifferent **3** slow; dull —**lan'guid·ly** ***adv.***

lan'guish (-gwish) ***vi.*** ⟦see prec.⟧ **1** to become weak; droop **2** to live under distressing conditions *[to languish in poverty]* **3** to long; pine **4** to put on an air of sentimental tenderness

lan·guor (laŋ'gər) ***n.*** ⟦see LANGUID⟧ lack of vigor or vitality; weakness; listlessness —**lan'guor·ous** ***adj.***

lank (laŋk) ***adj.*** ⟦OE *hlanc*⟧ **1** long and slender **2** straight and limp: said of hair

lank·y (laŋ'kē) ***adj.*** **-i·er, -i·est** awkwardly tall and lean

lan·o·lin (lan'ə lin') ***n.*** ⟦< L *lana*, wool + *oleum*, oil⟧ a fatty substance obtained from wool and used in ointments, cosmetics, etc.

Lan·sing (lan'siŋ) capital of Michigan, in the SC part: pop. 127,000

THESAURUS

land ***n.*** **1** [The solid surface of the earth] ground, soil, dirt, clay, loam, gravel, subsoil, clod, sand, rock, mineral, pebble, stone, dry land, valley, desert, hill, bank, seaside, shore, beach, crag, cliff, boulder, ledge, peninsula, delta, promontory; see also EARTH 2, MOUNTAIN 1, PLAIN.—*Ant.* SEA, stream, ocean. **2** [Land as property] estate, tract, ranch, farm, home, lot, real estate; see also AREA, PROPERTY 2. **3** [A country] state, province, region; see NATION 1.

land ***v.*** **1** [To come into port; *said of a ship*] dock, berth, moor, make port, tie up, come to land, drop anchor, put in; see also ARRIVE.—*Ant.* LEAVE, weigh anchor, cast off. **2** [To go ashore] disembark, come ashore, arrive, alight, leave the boat or ship, go down the gangplank, hit the beach*. **3** [To bring an airplane to earth] touch down, ground, take down, alight, come in, settle, level off, come down, descend, make a forced landing, crash-land, nose over, overshoot, splash down, check in, undershoot, pancake, settle her down hot*, fishtail down; see also ARRIVE.

landing ***n.*** **1** [The act of reaching shore] arriving, docking, making port, anchoring, mooring, dropping anchor; see also ARRIVAL 1. **2** [The place where landing on the shore is possible] marina, pier, wharf; see DOCK. **3** [The act of reaching the earth] setting down, grounding, getting in, arriving, reaching an airport, splashing down, completing a mission, settling, splashdown.

landlady ***n.*** homeowner, apartment manager, innkeeper; see OWNER, LANDLORD.

landlord ***n.*** homeowner, apartment manager, realtor, landowner, lessor, property owner, innkeeper; see also OWNER.

landmark ***n.*** **1** [A notable relic] remnant, vestige, historic structure; see MONUMENT 1, RELIC. **2** [A point from which a course may be taken] vantage point, mark, blaze, guide, marker, stone, tree, hill, mountain, bend, promontory.

landscape ***n.*** scene, scenery, panorama; see VIEW.

landscape ***v.*** lay out a garden or yard, finish up, put in the lawn and shrubbery; see DECORATE.

landslide ***n.*** slide, avalanche, rock slide; see DESCENT 2.

lane ***n.*** way, alley, passage; see PATH, ROAD 1.

language ***n.*** **1** [A means of communication] voice, utterance, expression, vocalization, sound, phonation, tongue, mother tongue, articulation, metalanguage, physical language; language of diplomacy, language of chemistry, language of flowers, etc.; accent, word, sign, signal, pantomime, gesture, vocabulary, diction, dialect, idiom, local speech, broken English, pidgin English, patois, vernacular, lingua franca, gibberish, pig Latin; see also DIALECT, JARGON 2, WRITING 1, 2. **2** [The study of language] semantics, psycholinguistics, morphology, phonology, phonemics, morphemics, phonics, phonetics, letters, linguistic studies, history of language, etymology, dialectology, linguistic geography; see also GRAMMAR, LINGUISTICS, LITERATURE 1. *Indo-European languages include the following—Germanic:* Old English or Anglo-Saxon, English, German, Yiddish, Dutch, Afrikaans, Old Norse, Danish, Swedish, Norwegian; *Celtic:* Welsh or Cymric, Irish or Erse, Gaelic or Scots Gaelic; *Italic:* Latin; *Romance:* Portuguese, Spanish, Provençal, French, Italian, Romanian; *Greek:* Attic, Ionic, Doric, Koine; *Slavic:* Russian, Belorussian, Ukrainian, Polish, Czech, Slovak, Slovenian, Macedonian, Serbo-Croatian, Bulgarian; *Baltic:* Lithuanian, Latvian; *Iranian:* Old Persian, Avestan, Pehlevi, Kurdish, Persian, Pashto or Afghan; *Indic:* Sanskrit, Pali, Prakrits, Hindi, Bengali, Gujarati, Hindustani, Urdu; *other branches:* Albanian, Armenian. *Other Eurasian languages include the following—Uralic:* Finnish, Estonian, Hungarian; *Altaic:* Turkish, Mongolian. *African and Asian languages include the following—Afro-Asiatic or Haimo-Semitic:* Aramaic, Phoenician, Hebrew, Arabic, Egyptian, Coptic; *Niger-Congo:* Bantu, Yoruba, Swahili, Zulu, Xhosa, Swazi; *other languages:* Masai, Bushman-Hottentot. *Asian and Malayo-Polynesian languages include the following*—Japanese, Korean; *Sino-Tibetan:* Burmese, Tibetan, Mandarin, Cantonese; *Kadai:* Thai, Siamese, Laotian, Lao; *Malayao-Polynesian:* Malay, Indonesian, Javanese, Tagalog, Filipino, Papuan. *North American languages include the following*—Nahuatl, Dakota, Zapotec, Navajo, Caddo, Cherokee, Choctaw, Arapaho. —**speak the same language** understand one another, communicate, get along; see AGREE.

languor ***n.*** lethargy, listlessness, lassitude; see INDIFFERENCE, LAZINESS.

lanky ***a.*** lean, bony, rangy; see THIN 2.

lan·tern (lan′tərn) ***n.*** ⟦ult. < Gr *lampein*, to shine⟧ a transparent case for holding and shielding a light

lan′tern-jawed′ ***adj.*** having long, thin jaws and sunken cheeks

lan·yard (lan′yərd) ***n.*** ⟦< OFr *lasne*, noose⟧ a short rope used on board ship for holding or fastening something

La·os (lä′ōs′) country in the NW part of Indochina: 91,400 sq. mi.; pop. 3,722,000 —**La·o·tian** (lā ō′shən) ***adj.***, ***n.***

lap[1] (lap) ***n.*** ⟦OE *læppa*⟧ **1** the front part, from the waist to the knees, of a sitting person **2** the part of the clothing covering this **3** that in which a person or thing is cared for **4** *a)* an overlapping *b)* a part that overlaps **5** one complete circuit of a racetrack —***vt.*** **lapped, lap′ping** **1** to fold (*over* or *on*) **2** to wrap; enfold **3** to overlap **4** to get a lap ahead of (an opponent) in a race —***vi.*** **1** to overlap **2** to extend beyond something in space or time: with *over*

lap[2] (lap) ***vi.***, ***vt.*** **lapped, lap′ping** ⟦OE *lapian*⟧ **1** to drink (a liquid) by dipping it up with the tongue as a dog does **2** to strike gently with a light splash: said of waves —***n.*** **1** a lapping **2** the sound of lapping

La Paz (lə päz′) city & seat of government of Bolivia: pop. 711,000

lap′board′ ***n.*** a board placed on the lap for use as a table or desk

lap dog any pet dog small enough to be held in the lap: also written **lap′dog′** ***n.***

la·pel (lə pel′) ***n.*** ⟦dim. of LAP[1]⟧ the front part of a coat folded back and forming a continuation of the collar

lap·i·dar·y (lap′ə der′ē) ***n.***, *pl.* **-dar′ies** ⟦< L *lapis*, a stone⟧ one who cuts and polishes precious stones —***adj.*** **1** of the art of a lapidary **2** precise and elegant *[lapidary prose]*

lap·in (lap′in) ***n.*** ⟦Fr, rabbit⟧ rabbit fur, often dyed to resemble other skins

lap·is laz·u·li (lap′is laz′yo͞o lī′, -lazh′-; -lē′) ⟦< L *lapis*, a stone + ML *lazulus*, azure⟧ an azure, opaque, semiprecious stone

Lap·land (lap′land′) region of N Europe, including the N parts of Norway, Sweden, & Finland

Lapp (lap) ***n.*** ⟦Swed⟧ a member of a people living in Lapland: also **Lap′land′er**

lap·pet (lap′it) ***n.*** ⟦dim. of LAP[1]⟧ a loose flap or fold of a garment or head covering

lapse (laps) ***n.*** ⟦< L *labi*, to slip⟧ **1** a small error **2** *a)* a moral slip *b)* a falling into a lower condition **3** a passing, as of time **4** the termination as of a privilege through failure to meet requirements —***vi.*** **lapsed, laps′ing** **1** to fall into a specified state *[he lapsed into silence]* **2** to backslide **3** to elapse **4** to come to an end; stop **5** to become void because of failure to meet requirements

lap′top′ ***n.*** a small, light, portable microcomputer having, in a single unit, a CPU, keyboard, screen, etc., and, usually, a rechargeable battery

lar·board (lär′bərd) ***adj.***, ***n.*** ⟦< OE *hladan*, lade + *bord*, side⟧ (of) the port side of a ship

lar·ce·ny (lär′sə nē) ***n.***, *pl.* **-nies** ⟦ult. < L *latro*, robber⟧ the unlawful taking of another's property; theft —**lar′ce·nist** ***n.*** —**lar′ce·nous** ***adj.***

larch (lärch) ***n.*** ⟦< L *larix*⟧ **1** a tree of the pine family that sheds its needles annually **2** its tough wood

lard (lärd) ***n.*** ⟦< L *lardum*⟧ a white, soft solid made by melting the fat of hogs —***vt.*** **1** to put strips of fat pork, bacon, etc. on (meat, etc.) before cooking **2** to embellish *[a talk larded with jokes]*

lard′er ***n.*** **1** a place where food supplies are kept; pantry **2** food supplies; provisions

large (lärj) ***adj.*** **larg′er, larg′est** ⟦< L *largus*⟧ **1** of great extent or amount; big, bulky, spacious, etc. **2** bigger than others of its kind **3** operating on a big scale *[a large producer]* —***adv.*** in a large way *[write large]* —**at large** **1** free; not confined **2** taken altogether **3** representing no particular district *[a congressman at large]* —**large′ness** ***n.*** —**larg′ish** ***adj.***

large′heart′ed ***adj.*** generous; kindly

large intestine the relatively large section of the intestines of vertebrates, including the cecum, colon, and rectum

large′ly ***adv.*** for the most part; mainly

large′-scale′ ***adj.*** **1** drawn to a large scale **2** of wide scope; extensive

lar·gess or **lar·gesse** (lär jes′, lär′jis) ***n.*** ⟦see LARGE⟧ **1** generous giving **2** a gift or gifts generously given

lar·go (lär′gō) ***adj.***, ***adv.*** ⟦It, slow⟧ *Music* slow and stately: also written ***largo***

lar·i·at (lar′ē ət) ***n.*** ⟦Sp *la reata*, the rope⟧ **1** a rope used for tethering grazing horses, etc. **2** LASSO

lark[1] (lärk) ***n.*** ⟦< OE *læwerce*⟧ any of a large family of chiefly Old World birds, esp. the skylark

lark[2] (lärk) ***vi.*** ⟦? < ON *leika*⟧ to play or frolic —***n.*** a frolic or spree

lark·spur (lärk′spur′) ***n.*** DELPHINIUM

lar·va (lär′və) ***n.***, *pl.* **-vae′** (-vē′) or **-vas** ⟦L, ghost⟧ the early form of any animal that changes structurally when it becomes an adult *[the tadpole is the larva of the frog]* —**lar′val** ***adj.***

lar·yn·gi·tis (lar′in jīt′is) ***n.*** an inflammation of the larynx, often with a temporary loss of voice

lar·ynx (lar′iŋks) ***n.***, *pl.* **lar′ynx·es** or **la·ryn·ges** (lə rin′jēz′) ⟦< Gr⟧ the structure at the upper end of the trachea, containing the vocal cords

la·sa·gna (lə zän′yə) ***n.*** ⟦It⟧ a dish of wide noodles baked in layers with tomato sauce, ground meat, and cheese

las·civ·i·ous (lə siv′ē əs) ***adj.*** ⟦< L *lascivus*, wanton⟧ **1** characterized by or expressing lust **2** exciting lust

la·ser (lā′zər) ***n.*** ⟦*l(ight) a(mplification by) s(timulated) e(mission of) r(adiation)*⟧ a device containing a substance whose atoms or molecules can be raised to a higher energy state, so that it emits light in an intense, narrow beam

la′ser·disc′ ***n.*** a videodisc for recording audio and video data to be read by a laser beam: also **la′ser·disk′**, **laser disc**, or **laser disk**

lash[1] (lash) ***n.*** ⟦< ?⟧ **1** the flexible striking part of a whip **2** a stroke as with a whip **3** an eyelash —***vt.*** **1** to strike or drive as with a lash **2** to jerk or swing sharply *[the cat lashed her tail]* **3** to censure or rebuke —***vi.*** to make strokes as with a whip —**lash out** **1** to strike out violently **2** to speak angrily

lash[2] (lash) ***vt.*** ⟦see LACE⟧ to fasten or tie with a rope, etc.

lass (las) ***n.*** ⟦prob. < ON *lǫskr*, weak⟧ a young woman

las·sie (las′ē) ***n.*** [Scot.] a young woman

las·si·tude (las′i to͞od′) ***n.*** ⟦< L *lassus*, faint⟧ weariness; languor

las·so (las′ō) ***n.***, *pl.* **-sos** or **-soes** ⟦< Sp < L *laqueus*, noose⟧ a rope with a sliding noose used to catch cattle, etc. —***vt.*** **-soed, -so·ing** to catch with a lasso

last[1] (last) ***adj.*** **1** *alt. superl. of* LATE **2** being or coming after all others in place or time; final **3** only remaining

THESAURUS

lap[1] ***n.*** **1** [That portion of the body that is formed when one sits down] knees, legs, thighs, front. **2** [The portion that overlaps] extension, overlap, fold; see FLAP. **3** [Part of a race] circuit, round, loop; see DISTANCE 3, RACE 3. —**drop into someone's lap** transfer responsibility, shift blame, pass the buck*; see GIVE 1. —**in the lap of luxury** very wealthy, living elegantly, prospering; see RICH 1.

lapse ***n.*** slip, mistake, failure; see ERROR.

lapse ***v.*** slip, deteriorate, decline; see WEAKEN 1.

larceny ***n.*** burglary, thievery, robbery; see CRIME, THEFT.

large ***a.*** **1** [Of great size] huge, wide, grand, great, considerable, substantial, vast, massive, immense, spacious, bulky, colossal, gigantic, mountainous, immeasurable, plentiful, copious, populous, ample, abundant, liberal, comprehensive, lavish, swollen, bloated, puffy, obese, monstrous, towering, mighty, magnificent, enormous, giant, tremendous, monumental, stupendous, voluminous, cumbersome, ponderous, gross, immoderate, extravagant, super*, booming, bumper, whopping*; see also BIG 1, BROAD 1, DEEP 2, EXTENSIVE, HIGH 1.—*Ant.* LITTLE, small, tiny. **2** [Involving great plans] extensive, extended, considerable; see GENERAL 1.

largely ***a.*** **1** [In large measure] mostly, mainly, chiefly; see PRINCIPALLY. **2** [In a large way] extensively, abundantly, comprehensively; see WIDELY.

largeness ***n.*** magnitude, proportion, breadth; see MEASURE 1, MEASUREMENT 2, QUANTITY, SIZE.

lariat ***n.*** lasso, tether, line; see ROPE.

lark[1] ***n.*** songbird, warbler, skylark; see BIRD.

larva ***n.*** maggot, grub, caterpillar; see WORM.

lash[1] ***v.*** cane, scourge, strap; see BEAT 1, HIT 1.

lass ***n.*** young woman, damsel, maiden; see GIRL, WOMAN.

lasso ***n.*** tether, lariat, noose; see ROPE.

last[1] ***a.*** **1** [Final] ultimate, utmost, lowest, meanest, least, end, extreme, remotest, furthest, outermost, farthest, uttermost, concluding, hindmost, far, far-off, ulterior, once and for all, definitive, after all others, ending, at the end, terminal, eventual,

4 most recent *[last* month*]* **5** least likely *[*the *last* person to suspect*]* **6** conclusive *[*the *last* word*]* —***adv.*** **1** after all others **2** most recently **3** finally; in conclusion —***n.*** the one coming last —**at (long) last** after a long time; finally

last[2] (last) ***vi.*** ⟦OE *læstan*⟧ to remain in existence, use, etc.; endure —***vt.*** **1** to continue during **2** to be enough for

last[3] (last) ***n.*** ⟦< OE *last*, footstep⟧ a form shaped like the foot, used in making or repairing shoes

last hurrah a final attempt or appearance

last′ing ***adj.*** that lasts a long time —**last′ing·ly** ***adv.***

Last Judgment *Theol.* the final judgment at the end of the world

last′ly ***adv.*** in conclusion; finally

last straw ⟦< the straw that broke the camel's back⟧ a final trouble that results in a defeat, loss of patience, etc.: with *the*

Las Ve·gas (läs vā′gəs) city in SE Nevada: pop. 258,000

lat *abbrev.* latitude

Lat *abbrev.* Latin

latch (lach) ***n.*** ⟦< OE *læccan*⟧ a fastening for a door, gate, or window; esp., a bar that fits into a notch —***vt., vi.*** to fasten with a latch —**latch onto** [Inf.] to get or obtain

late (lāt) ***adj.*** **lat′er** or **lat′ter, lat′est** or **last** ⟦OE *læt*⟧ **1** happening, coming, etc. after the usual or expected time, or at a time far advanced in a period *[late* to class, *late* Victorian*]* **2** recent **3** having recently died —***adv.*** **lat′er, lat′est** or **last** **1** after the expected time **2** at or until an advanced time of the day, year, etc. **3** toward the end of a period **4** recently —**of late** recently —**late′ness** ***n.***

late′ly ***adv.*** recently; not long ago

la·tent (lāt′'nt) ***adj.*** ⟦< L *latere*, lurk⟧ lying hidden and undeveloped in a person or thing —**la′ten·cy** ***n.***

lat·er·al (lat′ər əl) ***adj.*** ⟦< L *latus*, a side⟧ of, at, from, or toward the side; sideways —**lat′er·al·ly** ***adv.***

la·tex (lā′teks′) ***n.*** ⟦L, a fluid⟧ **1** a milky liquid in certain plants and trees: used esp. as the basis of rubber **2** a suspension in water of particles of rubber or plastic: used in adhesives, paints, etc.

lath (lath) ***n., pl.*** **laths** (la*th*z, laths) ⟦< ME⟧ **1** any of the thin, narrow strips of wood used as a foundation for plaster, etc. **2** any foundation for plaster

lathe (lā*th*) ***n.*** ⟦prob. < MDu *lade*⟧ a machine for shaping wood, metal, etc. by holding and turning it rapidly against the edge of a cutting tool —***vt.*** **lathed, lath′ing** to shape on a lathe

lath·er (la*th*′ər) ***n.*** ⟦OE *leathor*, soap⟧ **1** the foam formed by soap and water **2** foamy sweat, as on a racehorse **3** [Slang] an excited state —***vt., vi.*** to cover with or form lather —**lath′er·y** ***adj.***

Lat·in (lat′'n) ***adj.*** ⟦< *Latium*, ancient country in central Italy⟧ **1** of ancient Rome or its people, language, etc. **2** designating or of the languages derived from Latin, the peoples that speak them, their countries, etc. —***n.*** **1** a person born or living in ancient Rome **2** the language of ancient Rome **3** a person whose language is derived from Latin, as a Spaniard, Italian, or Latin American

Latin America that part of the Western Hemisphere south of the U.S. where Spanish, Portuguese, & French are the official languages —**Latin American**

La·ti·no (la tē′nō) ***n., pl.*** **-nos** ⟦< L *Latinus*, LATIN⟧ a Latin American, esp. one who lives in the U.S. —***adj.*** of or relating to Latinos Now often preferred to *Hispanic* —**La·ti′na** (-nə) ***fem.n.***

lat·ish (lāt′ish) ***adj., adv.*** somewhat late

lat·i·tude (lat′ə to͞od′) ***n.*** ⟦< L *latus*, wide⟧ **1** freedom from narrow restrictions **2** *a)* distance, measured in degrees, north or south from the equator *b)* a region with reference to this distance

la·trine (lə trēn′) ***n.*** ⟦< L *lavare*, to wash⟧ a toilet for the use of a large number of people, as in an army camp

lat·te (lä′tā) ***n.*** ⟦It⟧ espresso coffee mixed with steamed milk

lat·ter (lat′ər) ***adj.*** ⟦orig. compar. of LATE⟧ **1** *alt. compar. of* LATE **2** *a)* later; more recent *b)* nearer the end or close **3** being the last mentioned of two

lat·tice (lat′is) ***n.*** ⟦< OHG *latta*, lath⟧ an openwork structure of crossed strips of wood, metal, etc. used as a screen, support, etc.

lat′tice·work′ ***n.*** **1** a lattice **2** lattices collectively

Lat·vi·a (lat′vē ə) country in N Europe: formerly a republic of the U.S.S.R.: 24,595 sq. mi.; pop. 2,606,000 —**Lat′vi·an** ***adj., n.***

laud (lôd) ***vt.*** ⟦< L *laus*, glory⟧ to praise; extol

laud′a·ble ***adj.*** praiseworthy; commendable

lau·da·num (lôd′'n əm) ***n.*** ⟦< L *ladanum*, a dark resin⟧ **1** [Archaic] any of various opium preparations **2** a solution of opium in alcohol

laud·a·to·ry (lôd′ə tôr′ē) ***adj.*** expressing praise; commendatory

laugh (laf) ***vi.*** ⟦< OE *hleahhan*⟧ to make the sounds and facial movements that express mirth, ridicule, etc. —***n.*** **1** the act or sound of laughing **2** a cause of laughter **3** [*pl.*] [Inf.] mere diversion or pleasure —**laugh at** **1** to be amused by **2** to make fun of

laugh′a·ble ***adj.*** amusing or ridiculous —**laugh′a·bly** ***adv.***

laugh′ing·stock′ ***n.*** an object of ridicule

laugh′ter ***n.*** the action or sound of laughing

launch[1] (lônch) ***vt.*** ⟦< L *lancea*, a lance⟧ **1** to hurl or send forth with some force *[*to *launch* a rocket*]* **2** to slide (a

THESAURUS

settling, resolving, decisive, crowning, climactic, closing, finishing, irrefutable.—*Ant.* FIRST, foremost, beginning. **2** [Most recent] latest, newest, current, freshest, immediate, in the fashion, modish, the last word*, trendy*; see also FASHIONABLE, MODERN 1.—*Ant.* OLD, stale, outmoded.

last[1] ***n.*** tail end, last one, ending; see END 4. —**at (long) last** after a long time, in the end, ultimately; see FINALLY 2. —**see the last of** see for the last time, dispose of, get rid of; see END 1.

last[2] ***v.*** **1** [To endure] remain, carry on, survive, hold out, suffer, stay, overcome, persist, stick it out*, stick with it*, go on; see also CONTINUE 1, ENDURE 1, 2. **2** [To be sufficient] hold out, be adequate, be enough, serve, do, accomplish the purpose, answer; see also SATISFY 3.

lasting ***a.*** enduring, abiding, constant; see PERMANENT.

latch ***n.*** catch, hook, bar; see FASTENER, LOCK 1.

latch ***v.*** lock, cinch, close up; see CLOSE 4, FASTEN.

late ***a.*** **1** [Tardy] too late, held up, overdue, stayed, postponed, put off, not on time, belated, behind time, lagging, delayed, backward, not in time; see also SLOW 2, 3.—*Ant.* EARLY, punctual, on time. **2** [Recently dead] defunct, deceased, departed; see DEAD 1. **3** [Recent] new, just out, recently published; see FRESH 1. **4** [Far into the night] nocturnal, night-loving, advanced, tardy, toward morning, after midnight. —**of late** lately, in recent times, a short time ago; see RECENTLY.

lately ***a.*** a short time ago, in recent times, of late; see RECENTLY.

lateness ***n.*** belatedness, procrastination, hesitation, tardiness, protraction, prolongation, slowness, backwardness, advanced hour, late date.—*Ant.* ANTICIPATION, earliness, promptness.

latent ***a.*** underdeveloped, potential, dormant, inactive.

later ***a.*** succeeding, next, more recent; see FOLLOWING.

lateral ***a.*** oblique, sidelong, side by side; see SIDE.

latest ***a.*** most recent, immediately prior, just finished; see LAST 1, 2.

lather ***n.*** suds, foam, bubbles; see FROTH.

Latin ***a.*** **1** [Pertaining to ancient Rome or to its language] of Rome, classical, Italic; see ROMAN. **2** [Pertaining to southwestern Europe] Roman, Mediterranean, speaking Romance languages; see EUROPEAN.

Latin ***n.*** language of Rome, classical Latin, church Latin; see LANGUAGE 2.

latitude ***n.*** meridional distance, degree, measure, degrees of latitude; see also MEASURE 1.

latter ***a.*** late, last, recent; see FOLLOWING, LAST 1.

laugh ***n.*** mirth, merriment, amusement, rejoicing, shout, chuckle, chortle, cackle, peal of laughter, horselaugh, guffaw, titter, snicker, giggle, roar, snort; see also LAUGHTER.—*Ant.* CRY, sob, whimper. —**have the last laugh** defeat finally, beat in the end, overcome all obstacles; see WIN 1.

laugh ***v.*** chuckle, chortle, guffaw, laugh off, snicker, titter, giggle, burst out laughing, shriek, roar, beam, grin, smile, smirk, shout, die laughing*, break up*, crack up*, howl, roll in the aisles*, be in stitches; see also SMILE.—*Ant.* CRY, sob, weep. —**laugh at** deride, taunt, make fun of; see RIDICULE. —**no laughing matter** serious, grave, significant; see IMPORTANT 1.

laughable ***a.*** ludicrous, comic, comical; see FUNNY 1.

laughing ***a.*** chortling, giggling, chuckling; see HAPPY.

laughter ***n.*** chortling, chuckling, guffawing, tittering, giggling, shouting, roaring, howling, snorting; see also LAUGH.—*Ant.* CRY, weeping, wailing.

launch[1] ***v.*** **1** [To initiate] originate, start, set going; see BEGIN 1. **2** [To send off] set in motion, propel, thrust, fire off, send forth, eject; see also

new vessel) into the water **3** to set in operation or on some course; start *[to launch an attack]* —***vi.*** **1** to start something new: often with *out* or *forth* **2** to plunge (*into*) —***n.*** a launching —***adj.*** designating or of vehicles, sites, etc. used in launching spacecraft or missiles

launch[2] (lônch) ***n.*** ⟦Sp or Port *lancha*⟧ an open, or partly enclosed, motorboat

launch'pad' or **launch pad** ***n.*** the platform from which a rocket, guided missile, etc. is launched: also **launching pad**

laun·der (lôn'dər) ***vt.*** ⟦< L *lavare*, to wash⟧ **1** to wash, or wash and iron (clothes, etc.) **2** to exchange or invest (illegally gotten money) so as to conceal its source —**laun'der·er** ***n.*** —**laun'dress** (-dris) ***fem.n.***

laun·dro·mat (lôn'drə mat') ***n.*** ⟦< *Laundromat*, a former service mark⟧ a self-service laundry: also **laun·der·mat** (lôn'dər mat')

laun·dry (lôn'drē) ***n.***, *pl.* **-dries** **1** a place for laundering **2** clothes, etc. laundered or to be laundered

laun'dry·man' (-man', -mən) ***n.***, *pl.* **-men'** (-man', -mən) a man who works in or for a laundry, esp. one who collects and delivers laundry

lau·re·ate (lôr'ē it) ***adj.*** ⟦< L *laurus*, laurel⟧ honored, as with a crown of laurel —***n.*** POET LAUREATE

lau·rel (lôr'əl) ***n.*** ⟦< L *laurus*⟧ **1** an evergreen tree or shrub of S Europe, with large, glossy leaves **2** its foliage, esp. as woven into wreaths once used to crown the victors in contests **3** [*pl.*] fame; honor **4** any of various trees and shrubs resembling the true laurel

la·va (lä'və, lav'ə) ***n.*** ⟦It < L *labi*, to slide⟧ **1** melted rock issuing from a volcano **2** such rock when solidified by cooling

La·val (lə val') city in SW Quebec, Canada, near Montreal: pop. 330,000

lav·a·liere or **lav·a·lier** (lav'ə lir', lä'və-) ***n.*** ⟦< Fr⟧ an ornament on a chain, worn around the neck

lav·a·to·ry (lav'ə tôr'ē) ***n.***, *pl.* **-ries** ⟦< L *lavare*, to wash⟧ a room with a washbowl and a toilet

lave (lāv) ***vt.***, ***vi.*** **laved**, **lav'ing** ⟦< L *lavare*⟧ [Old Poet.] to wash or bathe

lav·en·der (lav'ən dər) ***n.*** ⟦< ML *lavandria*⟧ **1** a fragrant European plant of the mint family with spikes of pale-purplish flowers **2** its dried flowers and leaves, used to perfume clothes, etc. **3** a pale purple —***adj.*** pale-purple

lav·ish (lav'ish) ***adj.*** ⟦< OFr *lavasse*, downpour⟧ **1** very generous; prodigal **2** very abundant —***vt.*** to give or spend generously —**lav'ish·ly** ***adv.***

law (lô) ***n.*** ⟦OE *lagu*⟧ **1** *a)* all the rules of conduct established by the authority or custom of a nation, etc. *b)* any one of such rules **2** obedience to such rules **3** the study of such rules; jurisprudence **4** the seeking of justice in courts under such rules **5** the profession of lawyers, judges, etc. **6** *a)* a sequence of natural events occurring with unvarying uniformity under the same conditions *b)* the stating of such a sequence **7** any rule expected to be observed *[the laws of health]* —**the Law** **1** the Mosaic law, or the part of the Jewish Scriptures containing it **2** [**the l-**] [Inf.] a policeman or the police

law'-a·bid'ing ***adj.*** obeying the law

law'break'er ***n.*** a person who violates the law —**law'break'ing** ***adj.***, ***n.***

law'ful ***adj.*** **1** in conformity with the law **2** recognized by law *[lawful debts]* —**law'ful·ly** ***adv.***

law'giv'er ***n.*** a lawmaker; legislator

law'less ***adj.*** **1** not regulated by the authority of law **2** not in conformity with law; illegal **3** not obeying the law; unruly —**law'less·ness** ***n.***

law'mak'er ***n.*** one who makes or helps to make laws; esp., a legislator

lawn[1] (lôn) ***n.*** ⟦< OFr *launde*, heath⟧ land covered with grass kept closely mowed, esp. around a house

lawn[2] (lôn) ***n.*** ⟦after *Laon*, city in France⟧ a fine, sheer cloth of linen or cotton

lawn bowling a bowling game played on a smooth lawn with wooden balls

lawn mower a machine for cutting the grass of a lawn

Law·rence (lôr'əns), **D**(avid) **H**(erbert) 1885-1930; Eng. novelist & poet

law'suit' ***n.*** a suit between private parties in a law court

law·yer (lô'yər) ***n.*** one whose profession is advising others in matters of law or representing them in lawsuits

lax (laks) ***adj.*** ⟦< L *laxus*⟧ **1** loose; slack; not tight **2** not strict or exact —**lax'ly** ***adv.***

lax·a·tive (lak'sə tiv) ***adj.*** ⟦see prec.⟧ making the bowels loose and relieving constipation —***n.*** any laxative medicine

lax·i·ty (lak'si tē) ***n.*** lax quality or condition

lay[1] (lā) ***vt.*** **laid**, **lay'ing** ⟦< OE *lecgan*⟧ **1** to cause to fall with force; knock down **2** to place or put in a resting position: often with *on* or *in* **3** to put down (bricks, carpeting, etc.) in the correct position or way **4** to place;

THESAURUS

DRIVE 1, 2, PROPEL.

launched ***a.*** started, sent, set in motion; see BEGIN, DRIVEN.

launder ***v.*** cleanse, do the wash, wash and iron; see CLEAN, WASH 2.

laundry ***n.*** ironing, washing, clothes; see WASH 1.

lavatory ***n.*** restroom, bathroom, washroom; see BATH 2, TOILET.

lavender ***a.***, ***n.*** lilac, pale purple, bluish-red; see COLOR, PURPLE.

lavish ***a.*** generous, unstinted, unsparing; see PLENTIFUL 1, 2.

lavish ***v.*** scatter freely, give generously, squander; see SPEND, WASTE 2.

lavishly ***a.*** profusely, richly, expensively; see CARELESSLY, FOOLISHLY, WASTEFULLY.

law ***n.*** **1** [The judicial system] judicial procedure, legal process, the legal authorities, the police, due process, precept, summons, notice, warrant, search warrant, warrant of arrest, subpoena. **2** [Bodies of law] code, constitution, criminal law, statute law, civil law, martial law, military law, commercial law, probate law, statutory law, statutes, civil code, ordinances, equity, cases, common law, canon law, decisions, unwritten law, natural law. **3** [An enactment] statute, edict, decree, ordinance, judicial decision, ruling, injunction, summons, act, enactment, requirement, demand, canon, regulation, bylaw, commandment, mandate, dictate, instruction, legislation; see also COMMAND, ORDER 1. **4** [A principle] foundation, fundamental, origin, source, ultimate cause, truth, axiom, maxim, ground, base, rule, theorem, guide, precept, usage, postulate, proposition, generalization, assumption, hard and fast rule; see also REASON 3. **5** [Officers appointed to enforce the law] sheriff, state police, city police; see JUDGE 1, LAWYER, POLICE. —**lay down the law** establish rules, command, prohibit; see ORDER 1.

lawbreaker ***n.*** felon, offender, violator; see CRIMINAL.

lawful ***a.*** legalized, legitimate, statutory, passed, decreed, judged, rightful, just, valid, authorized, licit, commanded, ruled, ordered, constitutional, legislated, enacted, official, enforced, protected, vested, within the law, legitimized, established; see also LEGAL, PERMITTED.—*Ant.* ILLEGAL, unlawful, illegitimate.

lawfully ***a.*** licitly, in accordance with the law, by law; see LEGALLY.

lawless ***a.*** **1** [Without law] wild, untamed, uncivilized, savage, barbarous, fierce, violent, tempestuous, disordered, agitated, disturbed, warlike; see also UNCONTROLLED.—*Ant.* CULTURED, cultivated, controlled. **2** [Not restrained by law] riotous, insubordinate, disobedient; see UNRULY.

lawlessness ***n.*** irresponsibility, terrorism, chaos; see DISORDER, DISTURBANCE 2.

lawmaker ***n.*** lawgiver, member of Congress, councilman; see LEGISLATOR.

lawn[1] ***n.*** green, grassplot, grassland; see GRASS 2, YARD 1.

lawsuit ***n.*** action, prosecution, suit; see CLAIM, TRIAL 2.

lawyer ***n.*** legal advisor, defense attorney, jurist, member of the bar, public defender, defender, prosecuting attorney, prosecutor, attorney, solicitor, counsel, counselor, counselor-at-law, barrister, advocate, professor of law, attorney at law, attorney general, district attorney, DA, Philadelphia lawyer*, legal eagle*, shyster*, mouthpiece*.

lax ***a.*** slack, remiss, soft; see CARELESS, INDIFFERENT.

laxative ***n.*** physic, purgative, diuretic, cathartic, purge, remedy, cure, dose; see also MEDICINE 2. *Common laxatives include the following:* castor oil, mineral oil, agar, cascara sagrada, flaxseed, milk of magnesia, croton oil, epsom salts, cascarin compound.

lay[1] ***v.*** **1** [To knock down] trounce, defeat, club; see BEAT 1, HIT 1. **2** [To place] put, locate, settle, deposit, plant, lodge, store, stow, situate, deposit; see also SET 1. **3** [To put in order] arrange, organize, systematize; see ORDER 3. —**lay aside** **1** [To place] deposit, put, place; see SET 1. **2** [To save] lay away, collect, keep; see SAVE 3, STORE. —**lay away** lay aside, keep, collect; see STORE. —**lay down** **1** [To declare] assert, state, affirm; see DECLARE, REPORT 1, SAY. **2** [To bet] game, put up, wager; see BET, GAMBLE. —**lay off** **1** [To discharge employees, usually temporarily] fire, discharge, let go; see DISMISS, OUST. **2** [*To stop] cease, halt, desist; see END 1, STOP 2. —**lay out** lend, put out at interest, put up; see INVEST, SPEND. —**lay over** delay, stay over, break a journey; see STOP 1. —**lay up** **1** [To save] conserve, preserve, hoard;

put; set [to *lay* emphasis on accuracy] **5** to produce (an egg) **6** to allay, suppress, etc. **7** to bet (a specified sum, etc.) **8** to devise [to *lay* plans] **9** to present or assert [to *lay* claim to property] —***n.*** the way or position in which something is situated [the *lay* of the land] —**lay aside** to put away for future use; save: also **lay away** or **lay by** —**lay in** to get and store away —**lay into** [Slang] to attack with blows or words —**lay off 1** to discharge (an employee), esp. temporarily **2** [Slang] to cease —**lay open 1** to cut open **2** to expose —**lay out 1** to spend **2** to arrange according to a plan **3** to spread out (clothes, etc.) ready for wear, etc. —**lay over** to stop a while in a place before going on —**lay up 1** to store for future use **2** to confine to a sickbed

lay[2] (lā) ***vi.*** *pt. of* LIE[1]

lay[3] (lā) ***adj.*** ⟦< Gr *laos*, the people⟧ **1** of a layman **2** not belonging to a given profession

lay[4] (lā) ***n.*** ⟦ME & OFr *lai*⟧ **1** a short poem, esp. a narrative poem, orig. for singing **2** [Obs.] a song

lay'a·way' ***n.*** a method of buying by making a deposit on something which is delivered only after full payment

lay'er ***n.*** **1** a person or thing that lays **2** a single thickness, fold, etc.

lay·ette (lā et') ***n.*** ⟦< MDu *lade*, chest⟧ a complete outfit of clothes, bedding, etc. for a newborn baby

lay·man (lā'mən) ***n.***, *pl.* **-men** (-mən) a person not a clergyman or one not belonging to a given profession: also **lay'per'son** —**lay'wom'an**, *pl.* **-wom'en**, ***fem.n.***

lay'off' ***n.*** temporary unemployment, or the period of this

lay'out' ***n.*** **1** the manner in which anything is laid out; specif., the makeup of a newspaper, advertisement, etc. **2** the thing laid out

lay'o'ver ***n.*** a stop during a journey

Laz·a·rus (laz'ə rəs) ***n.*** *Bible* a man raised from the dead by Jesus

laze (lāz) ***vi.***, ***vt.*** **lazed**, **laz'ing** to idle or loaf

la·zy (lā'zē) ***adj.*** **-zi·er**, **-zi·est** ⟦prob. < medieval LowG or MDu⟧ **1** not eager or willing to work or exert oneself **2** sluggish —***vi.***, ***vt.*** **-zied**, **-zy·ing** LAZE —**la'zi·ly** ***adv.*** —**la'zi·ness** ***n.***

la'zy·bones' ***n.*** [Inf.] a lazy person

Lazy Su·san (so͞o'zən) a rotating tray for food

lb *symbol* ⟦abbrev. for LIBRA⟧ pound; pounds: also, for the plural, **lbs**

l.c. *abbrev.* ⟦L *loco citato*⟧ in the place cited

LCD ***n.*** ⟦*l(iquid-)c(rystal) d(isplay)*⟧ a device for alphanumeric displays, as on digital watches, using a crystalline liquid

LD *abbrev.* **1** learning disability **2** learning-disabled

lea (lē) ***n.*** ⟦OE *leah*⟧ [Old Poet.] a meadow

leach (lēch) ***vt.*** ⟦prob. < OE *leccan*, to water⟧ **1** to wash (some material) with a filtering liquid **2** to extract (a soluble substance) from some material —***vi.*** to dissolve and be washed away

lead[1] (lēd) ***vt.*** **led**, **lead'ing** ⟦OE *lædan*⟧ **1** to direct, as by going before or along with, by physical contact, pulling a rope, etc.; guide **2** to guide by influence **3** to be the head of (an expedition, orchestra, etc.) **4** to be at the head of [to *lead* one's class] **5** to be ahead of in a contest **6** to live; spend [to *lead* a hard life] —***vi.*** **1** to show the way, as by going before **2** to tend in a certain direction: with *to, from*, etc. **3** to bring as a result: with *to* [hate *led* to war] **4** to be or go first —***n.*** **1** the role or example of a leader **2** first or front place **3** the amount or distance ahead [to hold a safe *lead*] **4** anything that leads, as a clue **5** the leading role in a play, etc. **6** the right of playing first in cards or the card played **7** the most important news story, as in a newspaper or telecast —**lead off** to begin —**lead on** to lure —**lead up to** to prepare the way for

lead[2] (led) ***n.*** ⟦OE⟧ **1** a heavy, soft, bluish-gray metallic chemical element **2** a weight for measuring depth at sea **3** bullets **4** a stick of graphite, used in pencils —***adj.*** of or containing lead —***vt.*** to cover, line, or weight with lead

lead·ed (led'əd) ***adj.*** containing a lead compound: said of gasoline

lead·en (led''n) ***adj.*** **1** of lead **2** heavy **3** sluggish **4** gloomy **5** gray

lead·er (lēd'ər) ***n.*** one that leads; guiding head —**lead'er·ship'** ***n.***

lead·ing (lēd'iŋ) ***adj.*** **1** that leads; guiding **2** principal; chief

leading question a question put in such a way as to suggest the answer sought

lead time (lēd) the period of time between the decision to make a product and the start of production

leaf (lēf) ***n.***, *pl.* **leaves** ⟦OE⟧ **1** any of the flat, thin parts, usually green, growing from the stem of a plant **2** a sheet of paper **3** a very thin sheet of metal **4** a hinged or removable section of a table top —***vi.*** **1** to bear leaves **2** to turn the pages of a book: with *through* —**leaf'less** ***adj.***

leaf'let (-lit) ***n.*** **1** a small or young leaf **2** a separate sheet of printed matter, often folded

leaf'stalk' ***n.*** the part of a leaf supporting the blade and attached to the stem

leaf'y ***adj.*** **-i·er**, **-i·est** having many or broad leaves [a *leafy* vegetable]

league[1] (lēg) ***n.*** ⟦< L *ligare*, bind⟧ **1** an association of nations, groups, etc. for promoting common interests **2** *Sports* a group of teams organized to play one another —***vt.***, ***vi.*** **leagued**, **leagu'ing** to form into a league

THESAURUS

see SAVE 3, STORE. **2** [To disable] injure, harm, beat up*; see HURT.

layer ***n.*** thickness, fold, band, overlay, lap, overlap, seam, floor, story, tier, zone, stripe, coating, flap, panel.

layman ***n.*** nonprofessional, novice, layperson; see AMATEUR, RECRUIT.

laymen ***n.*** laity, converts, congregation, neophytes, parish, parishioners, the faithful, communicants, members, believers; see also FOLLOWING.

layout ***n.*** arrangement, design, draft; see ORGANIZATION 2, PLAN 1, PURPOSE 1.

layover ***n.*** break, stop, rest; see DELAY, PAUSE.

lazily ***a.*** indolently, nonchalantly, slackly; see GRADUALLY, SLOWLY.

laziness ***n.*** indolence, sloth, lethargy, inactivity, slackness, sluggishness, dullness, heaviness, inertia, drowsiness, passivity, listlessness, laxness, negligence, sleepiness, dreaminess, weariness, apathy, indifference, tardiness, shiftlessness, procrastination; see also IDLENESS.—*Ant.* ACTION, promptitude, agility.

lazy ***a.*** **1** [Indolent] idle, remiss, sluggish, lagging, apathetic, loafing, dallying, passive, asleep on the job, procrastinating, neglectful, indifferent, dilatory, tardy, slack, inattentive, careless, flagging, weary, tired.—*Ant.* ACTIVE, businesslike, indefatigable. **2** [Slow] slothful, inactive, lethargic; see SLOW 1, 2.

lead[1] ***a.*** leading, head, foremost; see BEST, FIRST, PRINCIPAL.

lead[1] ***n.*** **1** [The position at the front] head, advance, first place, point, edge, front rank, first line, scout, outpost, scouting party, patrol, advance position, forerunner; see also FRONT.—*Ant.* END, rear, last place. **2** [Leadership] direction, guidance, headship; see LEADERSHIP. **3** [A clue] evidence, trace, hint; see PROOF 1, SIGN 1. **4** [A leading role] principal part, important role, chief character; see ROLE. —**in the lead** ahead, winning, leading; see TRIUMPHANT. —**take the lead** direct, guide, head; see LEAD 1.

lead[1] ***v.*** **1** [To conduct] guide, steer, pilot, show the way, point the way, show in, point out, escort, accompany, protect, guard, safeguard, watch over, drive, discover the way, find a way through, be responsible for.—*Ant.* FOLLOW, be conveyed, be piloted. **2** [To exercise leadership] direct, command, supervise; see MANAGE 1. **3** [To extend] traverse, pass along, span; see REACH 1. —**lead on** lure, entice, intrigue; see DECEIVE. —**lead up to** prepare for, introduce, make preparations for; see BEGIN 2, PROPOSE 1.

lead[2] ***n.*** metallic lead, galena, blue lead; see ELEMENT 2, METAL.

leaden ***a.*** **1** [Made of lead] plumbous, pewter, galena; see METALLIC 1. **2** [Heavy] burdensome, oppressive, weighty; see HEAVY 1. **3** [Lead-colored] dull, pewter, blue-gray; see GRAY.

leader ***n.*** **1** [A guide] conductor, lead, pilot; see GUIDE. **2** [One who provides leadership] general, commander, director, manager, head, officer, captain, master, mistress, chieftain, governor, ruler, admiral, chief, administrator, chairman, chairperson, chair, president, boss, supervisor, executive director, brains*; see also EXECUTIVE.

leadership ***n.*** authority, control, administration, effectiveness, superiority, supremacy, skill, initiative, foresight, energy, capacity; see also INFLUENCE, POWER 2.

leading ***a.*** foremost, chief, dominant; see BEST, PRINCIPAL.

leaf ***n.*** leaflet, needle, blade, stalk, scale, floral leaf, seed leaf, sepal, petal. —**turn over a new leaf** make a new start, redo, begin again; see CHANGE 2.

leaflet ***n.*** handbill, circular, broadside; see PAMPHLET.

leafy ***a.*** leafed out, in leaf, shaded; see SHADY.

league[1] ***n.*** band, group, unit; see ORGANIZATION 2.

league² (lēg) ***n.*** ⟦ult. < OE *leowe*, mile⟧ a measure of distance, about three miles

leak (lēk) ***vi.*** ⟦< ON *leka*, to drip⟧ **1** to let a fluid out or in accidentally **2** to pass in or out of a container thus **3** to become known gradually, by accident, etc. —***vt.*** to allow to leak —***n.*** **1** an accidental crack, etc. that lets something out or in **2** any accidental means of escape **3** leakage **4** a disclosure of confidential information —**leak'y, -i·er, -i·est,** ***adj.***

leak'age ***n.*** **1** a leaking **2** that which leaks or the amount that leaks

lean¹ (lēn) ***vi.*** **leaned** or [Chiefly Brit.] **leant** (lent), **lean'ing** ⟦OE *hlinian*⟧ **1** to bend or slant from an upright position **2** to bend the body so as to rest part of one's weight on something **3** to rely (*on* or *upon*) **4** to tend (*toward* or *to*) —***vt.*** to cause to lean —**lean'er** ***n.***

lean² (lēn) ***adj.*** ⟦OE *hlæne*⟧ **1** with little flesh or fat; thin; spare **2** meager —**lean'ness** ***n.***

lean'ing ***n.*** a tendency; inclination

lean'-to' ***n.***, *pl.* **-tos'** a structure whose sloping roof abuts another building, a wall, etc.

leap (lēp) ***vi.*** **leapt** (lept, lēpt) or **lept** or **leaped, leap'ing** ⟦OE *hleapan*⟧ **1** to jump; spring; bound **2** to accept eagerly something offered: with *at* —***vt.*** **1** to pass over by a jump **2** to cause to leap —***n.*** **1** a jump; spring **2** the distance covered in a jump **3** a sudden transition —**leap'er** ***n.***

leap'frog' ***n.*** a game in which each player in turn leaps over the bent backs of the other players —***vt., vi.*** **-frogged', -frog'ging** to leap or jump in or as in this way; skip (*over*)

leap year every fourth year, containing an extra day in February

learn (lurn) ***vt., vi.*** **learned** (lurnd) or [Chiefly Brit.] **learnt** (lurnt), **learn'ing** ⟦OE *leornian*⟧ **1** to get knowledge of (a subject) or skill in (an art, trade, etc.) by study, experience, etc. **2** to come to know; hear (*of* or *about*) **3** to memorize —**learn'er** ***n.***

learn·ed (lurn'id; *for 2* lurnd) ***adj.*** **1** having or showing much learning **2** acquired by study, experience, etc.

learn'ing ***n.*** **1** the acquiring of knowledge or skill **2** acquired knowledge or skill

learning disability any of several conditions, believed to involve the nervous system, that interfere with mastering a skill such as reading or writing —**learn'ing-dis·a'bled** ***adj.***

lease (lēs) ***n.*** ⟦< L *laxus*, loose⟧ a contract by which a landlord rents lands, buildings, etc. to a tenant for a specified time —***vt.*** **leased, leas'ing** to give or get by a lease —**leas'er** ***n.***

lease'hold' ***n.*** **1** the act of holding by lease **2** land, buildings, etc. held by lease

leash (lēsh) ***n.*** ⟦< L *laxus*, loose⟧ a cord, strap, etc. by which a dog or the like is held in check —***vt.*** to check or control as by a leash

least (lēst) ***adj.*** ⟦OE *læst*⟧ **1** *alt. superl. of* LITTLE **2** smallest or slightest in size, degree, etc. —***adv.*** **1** *superl. of* LITTLE **2** in the smallest degree —***n.*** the smallest in amount, importance, etc. —**at (the) least** **1** at the lowest **2** at any rate —**not in the least** not at all

least'wise' ***adv.*** [Inf.] at least; anyway: also [Chiefly Dial.] **least'ways'**

leath·er (leth'ər) ***n.*** ⟦< OE *lether-*⟧ animal skin prepared for use by removing the hair and tanning —***adj.*** of leather

leath'er·neck' ***n.*** ⟦< former leather-lined uniform collar⟧ [Slang] a U.S. Marine

leath'er·y ***adj.*** like leather; tough and flexible —**leath'er·i·ness** ***n.***

leave¹ (lēv) ***vt.*** **left, leav'ing** ⟦OE *læfan*, let remain⟧ **1** to allow to remain *[leave it open]* **2** to have remaining behind or after one **3** to bequeath **4** to go away from **5** to abandon **6** [Chiefly Dial.] to let *[leave us go]* —***vi.*** to go away or set out —**leave off** to stop —**leave out** to omit —**leav'er** ***n.***

leave² (lēv) ***n.*** ⟦OE *leaf*⟧ **1** permission **2** *a)* permission to be absent from duty *b)* the period for which this is granted —**take leave of** to say goodbye to —**take one's leave** to depart

leave³ (lēv) ***vi.*** **leaved, leav'ing** to bear leaves; leaf

leav·en (lev'ən) ***n.*** ⟦< L *levare*, raise⟧ **1** LEAVENING (sense 1) **2** LEAVENING (sense 2) —***vt.*** **1** to make (dough) rise **2** to spread through, causing gradual change

leav'en·ing ***n.*** **1** a substance, as baking powder or yeast, used to make dough rise **2** a tempering or modifying quality or thing **3** a causing to be leavened

Leav·en·worth (lev'ən wurth') city in NE Kansas: pop 38,000: site of a federal prison

leave of absence permission to be absent from work or duty, esp. for a long time; also, the period for which this is granted

leaves (lēvz) ***n.*** *pl. of* LEAF

leave'-tak'ing ***n.*** a parting; farewell

THESAURUS

leak ***n.*** **1** [Loss through leakage] leakage, loss, flow, seepage, escape, falling off, expenditure, decrease; see also WASTE 1. **2** [An aperture through which a leak may take place] puncture, chink, crevice; see HOLE 1. **3** [Surreptitious news] news leak, exposé, slip; see NEWS 1, 2.

leak ***v.*** **1** [To escape by leaking] drip, ooze, seep; see FLOW. **2** [To permit leakage] be cracked, be split, have a fissure, be out of order, have a slow leak.

leaky ***a.*** punctured, cracked, split; see BROKEN 1, OPEN 4.

lean¹ ***v.*** **1** [To incline] slope, slant, sag, sink, decline, list, tip, bow, roll, veer, droop, drift, pitch, be slanted, be off; see also BEND, TILT. **2** [To tend] favor, be disposed, incline; see TEND 2. —**lean on** **1** [To be supported by] rest on, be held up by, bear on, put one's weight on, hang on, fasten on; see also LEAN 1. **2** [To rely upon] believe in, count on, put faith in; see TRUST 1.

lean² ***a.*** **1** [Thin] lank, slender, slim; see THIN 2. **2** [Containing little fat] fibrous, muscular, sinewy, meaty, free from fat, all-meat, protein-rich.

leaning ***a.*** inclining, tilting, out of perpendicular; see OBLIQUE.

lean-to ***n.*** shelter, shanty, cabin; see HUT.

leap ***v.*** spring, vault, bound; see BOUNCE, JUMP 1.

learn ***v.*** acquire, receive, get, take in, drink in, pick up, read, master, ground oneself in, pore over, gain information, ascertain, determine, unearth, hear, find out, learn by heart, memorize, be taught a lesson, improve one's mind, build one's background, get up on*, get the signal*; see also STUDY.

learned ***a.*** **1** [Having great learning; *said of people*] scholarly, erudite, academic, accomplished, conversant with, lettered, instructed, collegiate, well-informed, bookish, pedantic, professorial; see also CULTURED, EDUCATED.—*Ant.* IGNORANT, incapable, illiterate. **2** [Showing evidence of learning; *said of writings*] deep, sound, solemn; see PROFOUND.

learning ***n.*** lore, scholarship, training; see EDUCATION 1, KNOWLEDGE 1.

lease ***n.*** rental agreement, permission to rent, charter; see CONTRACT, RECORD 1.

lease ***v.*** let, charter, rent out; see RENT 1.

leash ***n.*** cord, chain, strap; see ROPE.

least ***a.*** **1** [Smallest] tiniest, infinitesimal, microscopic; see MINUTE 1. **2** [Least important] slightest, piddling, next to nothing; see TRIVIAL, UNIMPORTANT. **3** [In the lowest degree] minimal, most inferior, bottom; see LOWEST, MINIMUM. —**at (the) least** in any event, with no less than, at any rate; see ANYHOW. —**not in the least** not at all, in no way, not in the slightest degree; see NEVER.

leather ***n.*** tanned hide, parchment, calfskin, horsehide, buckskin, deerskin, vellum, suede, kid, patent leather, buffalo hide, goatskin, sheepskin, rawhide, cowhide, snakeskin, sharkskin, lizard, shoe leather, glove leather, chamois, alligator hide; see also HIDE, SKIN.

leave¹ ***v.*** **1** [To go away] go, depart, take leave, withdraw, move, set out, come away, go forth, take off, start, step down, quit a place, part company, defect, vanish, walk out, walk away, get out, get away, slip out, slip away, break away, break out, ride off, ride away, go off, go out, go away, move out, move away, vacate, abscond, flee, flit, migrate, fly, run along, embark, say goodbye, emigrate, clear out*, cut out*, pull out, push off*, cast off, scram*, split*, sign out, check out, beat it*, take a powder*, pull up stakes*.—*Ant.* ARRIVE, get to, reach. **2** [To abandon] back out, forsake, desert; see ABANDON 2. **3** [To allow to remain] let stay, leave behind, let continue, let go, drop, lay down, omit, forget; see also NEGLECT 1, 2.—*Ant.* SEIZE, take away, keep. **4** [To allow to fall to another] bequeath, hand down, transmit; see GIVE 1. —**leave out** cast aside, reject, dispose of; see DISCARD, ELIMINATE. —**leave to** bequeath, hand down, pass on; see GIVE 1.

leave² ***n.*** **1** [Permission] consent, dispensation, allowance; see PERMISSION. **2** [Authorized absence] leave of absence, holiday, furlough; see VACATION. —**on leave** away, gone, on a vacation; see ABSENT. —**take one's leave** go away, depart, remove oneself; see LEAVE 1.

leav·ings (lēv′iŋz) ***pl.n.*** leftovers, remnants, refuse, etc.
Leb·a·non (leb′ə nän′) country in SW Asia, on the Mediterranean: 4,036 sq. mi.; pop. 2,760,000 —**Leb′a·nese′** (-nēz′), *pl.* **-nese′**, ***adj.***, ***n.***
lech·er (lech′ər) ***n.*** ⟦OFr *lechier*, live debauchedly⟧ a lewd, grossly sensual man —**lech′er·ous** ***adj.*** —**lech′er·y** ***n.***
lec·i·thin (les′i thin) ***n.*** ⟦< Gr *lekithos*, egg yolk⟧ a nitrogenous, fatty compound found in animal and plant cells: used in medicine, foods, etc.
lec·tern (lek′tərn) ***n.*** ⟦< L *legere*, to read⟧ a reading stand
lec·ture (lek′chər) ***n.*** ⟦< L *legere*, read⟧ **1** an informative talk to a class, etc. **2** a lengthy scolding —***vt.***, ***vi.*** **-tured**, **-tur·ing** **1** to give a lecture (to) **2** to scold —**lec′tur·er** ***n.***
led (led) ***vt.***, ***vi.*** *pt. & pp. of* LEAD[1]
LED (el′ē′dē′) ***n.*** ⟦*l(ight-)e(mitting) d(iode)*⟧ a semiconductor diode that emits light when voltage is applied: used as in lamps and digital watches
ledge (lej) ***n.*** ⟦ME *legge*⟧ **1** a shelf or shelflike projection **2** a projecting ridge of rocks
ledg·er (lej′ər) ***n.*** ⟦ME *legger*⟧ a book of final entry, in which a record of debits and credits is kept
lee (lē) ***n.*** ⟦OE *hleo*, shelter⟧ **1** shelter **2** *Naut.* the side or direction away from the wind —***adj.*** of or on the side away from the wind
Lee (lē), **Rob·ert E(dward)** (räb′ərt) 1807-70; commander in chief of the Confederate army
leech (lēch) ***n.*** ⟦OE *læce*⟧ **1** a bloodsucking worm living in water and used, esp. formerly, to bleed patients **2** one who clings to another for personal advantage —***vi.*** to cling (*onto*) thus
leek (lēk) ***n.*** ⟦OE *leac*⟧ a vegetable that resembles a thick green onion
leer (lir) ***n.*** ⟦OE *hleor*⟧ a sly, sidelong look showing lust, malicious triumph, etc. —***vi.*** to look with a leer —**leer′ing·ly** ***adv.***
leer′y ***adj.*** **-i·er**, **-i·est** wary; suspicious
lees (lēz) ***pl.n.*** ⟦< ML *lia*⟧ dregs or sediment, as of wine
lee·ward (lē′wərd′; *naut.* lo͞o′ərd) ***adj.*** away from the wind —***n.*** the side or direction away from the wind —***adv.*** toward the lee
Lee·ward Islands (lē′wərd) N group of islands in the Lesser Antilles of the West Indies
lee·way (lē′wā′) ***n.*** **1** the leeward drift of a ship or aircraft from its course **2** [Inf.] *a*) margin of time, money, etc. *b*) room for freedom of action
left[1] (left) ***adj.*** ⟦< OE *lyft*, weak⟧ **1** of or on the side that is toward the west when one faces north **2** closer to the left side of one who is facing the thing mentioned —***n.*** **1** the left side **2** [*often* **L-**] *Politics* a liberal or radical position, party, etc.: often with *the* —***adv.*** on or toward the left hand or side
left[2] (left) ***vt.***, ***vi.*** *pt. & pp. of* LEAVE[1]
left′-hand′ ***adj.*** **1** on or toward the left **2** of, for, or with the left hand
left′-hand′ed ***adj.*** **1** using the left hand more skillfully than the right **2** done with or made for use with the left hand **3** ambiguous or backhanded [*a left-handed compliment*] —***adv.*** **1** with the left hand [*to write left-handed*] **2** in such a way that the bat, club, etc. swings rightward
left′ist ***n.***, ***adj.*** liberal or radical
left′o′ver ***n.*** **1** something remaining unused, etc. **2** [*usually pl.*] food left from a previous meal —***adj.*** remaining unused, uneaten, etc.
left wing the more liberal or radical section of a political party, group, etc. —**left′-wing′** ***adj.*** —**left′-wing′er** ***n.***
left′y ***n.***, *pl.* **-ies** [Slang] a left-handed person
leg (leg) ***n.*** ⟦ON *leggr*⟧ **1** one of the parts of the body by means of which humans and animals stand and walk **2** the part of a garment covering the leg **3** anything like a leg in shape or use **4** a stage, as of a trip —***vi.*** **legged**, **leg′ging** [Inf.] to walk or run: chiefly in the phrase **leg it**
leg·a·cy (leg′ə sē) ***n.***, *pl.* **-cies** ⟦ult. < L *lex*, law⟧ **1** money or property left to someone by a will **2** anything handed down as from an ancestor
le·gal (lē′gəl) ***adj.*** ⟦< L *lex*, law⟧ **1** of or based upon law **2** permitted by law **3** of or for lawyers —**le′gal·ly** ***adv.***
le′gal·ese′ (-ēz′) ***n.*** the special language of legal forms, etc., often considered incomprehensible
legal holiday a holiday set by law
le′gal·ism′ ***n.*** strict or too strict adherence to the law —**le′gal·is′tic** ***adj.***
le·gal·i·ty (li gal′i tē) ***n.***, *pl.* **-ties** quality, condition, or instance of being legal or lawful
le·gal·ize (lē′gəl īz′) ***vt.*** **-ized′**, **-iz′ing** to make legal or lawful —**le′gal·i·za′tion** ***n.***
legal pad a pad of lined writing paper, 8 ½ by 13 or 14 inches
legal tender money acceptable by law in payment of an obligation
leg·ate (leg′it) ***n.*** ⟦< L *lex*, law⟧ an envoy or ambassador
leg·a·tee (leg′ə tē′) ***n.*** one to whom a legacy is bequeathed
le·ga·tion (li gā′shən) ***n.*** **1** a diplomatic minister and staff collectively **2** the headquarters of such a group
le·ga·to (li gät′ō) ***adj.***, ***adv.*** ⟦< L *ligare*, to tie⟧ *Music* in a smooth, even style, with no breaks between notes: also written ***legato***
leg·end (lej′ənd) ***n.*** ⟦< L *legere*, read⟧ **1** a story or body of stories handed down for generations and popularly believed to have a historical basis **2** a notable person or the stories told about his or her exploits **3** an inscription on a coin, etc. **4** a title, key, etc. accompanying an illustration or map
leg·end·ar·y (lej′ən der′ē) ***adj.*** **1** of, based on, or presented in legends **2** famous or remarkable
leg·er·de·main (lej′ər di mān′) ***n.*** ⟦< Fr *leger de main*, light of hand⟧ **1** sleight of hand **2** trickery

THESAURUS

leavings ***n.*** remains, residue, garbage; see TRASH 1.
lecture ***n.*** **1** [A speech] discourse, instruction, lesson; see SPEECH 3. **2** [A reprimand] rebuke, talking-to, dressing-down.
lecture ***v.*** **1** [To give a speech] talk, instruct, expound; see ADDRESS 2, TEACH. **2** [To rebuke] reprimand, admonish, give a going-over*, give a piece of one's mind*; see also SCOLD.
led ***a.*** taken, escorted, guided; see ACCOMPANIED.
ledge ***n.*** shelf, mantel, strip, bar, step, ridge, reef, rim, bench, edge, walk.
leech ***n.*** **1** [A parasite] tapeworm, hookworm, bloodsucker; see PARASITE 1. **2** [Dependent] parasite, hanger-on, sponger*; see WEAKLING.
leeward ***a.*** protected, screened, safe; see CALM 2.
leeway ***n.*** space, margin, latitude; see EXTENT.
left[1] ***n.*** left hand, left side, left part, port, not the right, not the center; see also POSITION 1.
left[1,2] ***a.*** **1** [Opposite to right] leftward, left-hand, near, sinister, larboard, port, portside.—*Ant.* RIGHT, right-hand, starboard. **2** [Remaining] staying, continuing, over; see EXTRA. **3** [Radical] left-wing, liberal, progressive; see RADICAL 2, REVOLUTIONARY 1. **4** [Departed] gone out, absent, lacking; see GONE 1. —**left out** omitted, neglected, removed; see LOST 1.
leftist ***n.*** socialist, anarchist, communist; see LIBERAL, RADICAL.
leftover ***a.*** remaining, unwanted, unused, residual, uneaten, unconsumed, untouched, perfectly good; see also EXTRA.
leftovers ***n.*** leavings, scraps, debris; see FOOD, TRASH 1.
left-wing ***a.*** leftist, not conservative, reform; see LIBERAL, RADICAL 2.
leg ***n.*** part, member, lower appendage, hind leg, foreleg, back leg, front leg, left leg, right leg, shank; see also LIMB 2. —**not have a leg to stand on*** be unreasonable, make rash statements, have no defense; see MISTAKE. —**on one's (or its) last legs*** decaying, not far from breakdown, old; see DYING 2, WORN 2. —**pull someone's leg*** make fun of, fool, play a trick on; see DECEIVE.
legal ***a.*** constitutional, permissible, allowable, allowed, proper, legalized, sanctioned, legitimate, right, just, justifiable, justified, fair, authorized, accustomed, due, rightful, warranted, admitted, sound, granted, acknowledged, equitable, within the law, protected, enforced, judged, decreed, statutory, contractual, customary, chartered, clean*, legit*, straight*, on the up and up*; see also LAWFUL, PERMITTED.—*Ant.* ILLEGAL, unlawful, prohibited.
legality ***n.*** legitimacy, lawfulness, authority; see LAW 1.
legalize ***v.*** authorize, formulate, sanction; see APPROVE.
legally ***a.*** lawfully, legitimately, permissibly, licitly, enforcibly, allowably, admittedly, constitutionally, with due process of law, by statute, by law, in the eyes of the law, in accordance with law, in accordance with the constitution; see also RIGHTFULLY.—*Ant.* illegally, illicitly, unconstitutionally.
legend ***n.*** folk tale, saga, fable; see MYTH, STORY.
legendary ***a.*** fabulous, mythical, mythological, fanciful, imaginative, created, invented, allegorical, apocryphal, improbable, dubious, not historical, doubtful, romantic, storied, unverifiable; see also IMAGINARY.
legerdemain ***n.*** deceit, trickery, sleight of hand; see DECEPTION, TRICK 1.

-leg·ged (leg′id, legd) *combining form* having (a specified number or kind of) legs *[short-legged]*

leg·ging (leg′iŋ, -in) ***n.*** **1** a covering for the lower leg **2** [*pl.*] a child's outer garment with legs **3** [*pl.*] a garment like tights but without feet

leg·gy (leg′ē) ***adj.*** **-gi·er, -gi·est** **1** having long legs **2** [Inf.] having long, spindly stems

leg·horn (leg′hôrn′, -ərn) ***n.*** ⟦after *Leghorn*, It seaport⟧ [*sometimes* **L-**] any of a breed of small chicken

leg·i·ble (lej′ə bəl) ***adj.*** ⟦< L *legere*, read⟧ that can be read —**leg′i·bil′i·ty** ***n.*** —**leg′i·bly** ***adv.***

le·gion (lē′jən) ***n.*** ⟦< L *legere*, choose⟧ **1** a large group of soldiers; army **2** a large number; multitude —**le′gion·naire′** (-jə ner′) ***n.***

leg·is·late (lej′is lāt′) ***vi.*** **-lat′ed, -lat′ing** ⟦see fol.⟧ to make or pass a law or laws —***vt.*** to cause to be, go, etc. by making laws —**leg′is·la′tor** ***n.***

leg′is·la′tion ***n.*** ⟦< L *lex*, law + *latio*, a bringing⟧ **1** the making of laws **2** the law or laws made

leg′is·la′tive ***adj.*** **1** of legislation or a legislature **2** having the power to make laws

leg′is·la′ture (-chər) ***n.*** a body of persons given the power to make laws

le·git·i·mate (lə jit′ə mət; *for v.*, -māt′) ***adj.*** ⟦< L *lex*, law⟧ **1** born of parents married to each other **2** lawful **3** *a*) reasonable *b*) justifiable **4** conforming to accepted rules, standards, etc. **5** of stage plays, as distinguished from films, vaudeville, etc. —***vt.*** **-mat′ed, -mat′ing** LEGITIMIZE —**le·git′i·ma·cy** (-mə sē) ***n.*** —**le·git′i·mate·ly** ***adv.***

le·git′i·ma·tize′ (-mə tīz′) ***vt.*** **-tized′, -tiz′ing** LEGITIMIZE

le·git′i·mize′ (-mīz′) ***vt.*** **-mized′, -miz′ing** to make or declare legitimate —**le·git′i·mi·za′tion** ***n.***

leg·man (leg′man′) ***n.***, *pl.* **-men′** (-mən′) **1** a news reporter who transmits information from the scene **2** an assistant who does routine tasks outside the office

leg′room′ ***n.*** adequate space for the legs while seated, as in a car

leg·ume (leg′yo͞om′, li gyo͞om′) ***n.*** ⟦< L *legere*, gather⟧ **1** any of an order of plants having seeds growing in pods, including peas, beans, etc. **2** the pod or seed of such a plant —**le·gu·mi·nous** (lə gyo͞o′mə nəs) ***adj.***

leg′work′ ***n.*** [Inf.] necessary, routine work, typically involving walking, as part of a job

lei (lā, lā′ē) ***n.***, *pl.* **leis** ⟦Haw⟧ in Hawaii, a garland of flowers, generally worn about the neck

Leip·zig (līp′sig) city in E Germany: pop. 494,000

lei·sure (lē′zhər, lezh′ər) ***n.*** ⟦< L *licere*, be permitted⟧ free time during which one may indulge in rest, recreation, etc. —***adj.*** **1** free and unoccupied **2** done or used during one's leisure

lei′sure·ly ***adj.*** without haste; slow —***adv.*** in an unhurried manner

leit·mo·tif or **leit·mo·tiv** (līt′mō tēf′) ***n.*** ⟦Ger *leitmotiv* < *leiten*, to guide + *motiv*, motive⟧ a dominant theme, as in a musical composition

lem·ming (lem′iŋ) ***n.*** ⟦< ON *læmingi*⟧ a small arctic rodent with a short tail

lem·on (lem′ən) ***n.*** ⟦< Pers *līmūn*⟧ **1** a small, sour, yellow citrus fruit **2** the spiny, semitropical tree that it grows on **3** [Slang] something that is defective —***adj.*** yellow

lem′on·ade′ (-ād′) ***n.*** a drink made of lemon juice, sugar, and water

le·mur (lē′mər) ***n.*** ⟦< L *lemures*, ghosts⟧ a small, tree-dwelling primate with large eyes

lend (lend) ***vt.*** **lent, lend′ing** ⟦< OE *læn*, a loan⟧ **1** to let another use or have (a thing) temporarily **2** to let out (money) at interest **3** to give; impart —***vi.*** to make loans —**lend itself** (or **oneself**) **to** to be useful for or adapted to —**lend′er** ***n.***

length (leŋkth) ***n.*** ⟦< OE *lang*, long⟧ **1** the distance from end to end of a thing **2** extent in space or time **3** a long stretch or extent **4** a piece of a certain length —**at length** **1** finally **2** for a long time or in great detail

length′en ***vt.***, ***vi.*** to make or become longer

length′wise′ ***adv.***, ***adj.*** in the direction of the length: also **length′ways′**

length′y ***adj.*** **-i·er, -i·est** long; esp., too long —**length′i·ly** ***adv.***

le·ni·ent (lēn′yənt, lē′nē ənt) ***adj.*** ⟦< L *lenis*, soft⟧ not harsh or severe; merciful —**le′ni·en·cy** or **le′ni·ence** ***n.*** —**le′ni·ent·ly** ***adv.***

Len·in (len′in), **V**(**ladimir**) **I**(**lyich**) 1870-1924; Russ. leader of the Communist revolution of 1917

Len′in·grad′ (-grad′) *name* (1924-91) *for* ST. PETERSBURG (Russia)

len·i·tive (len′ə tiv) ***adj.*** ⟦< L *lenire*, to soften⟧ lessening pain or distress

lens (lenz) ***n.*** ⟦L, lentil: < its shape⟧ **1** a curved piece of glass, plastic, etc. for bringing together or spreading rays of light passing through it: used in optical instruments to form an image **2** a similar transparent part of the eye: it focuses light rays upon the retina **3** any device used to focus microwaves, sound waves, etc.

lent (lent) ***vt.***, ***vi.*** *pt. & pp. of* LEND

Lent (lent) ***n.*** ⟦OE *lengten*, the spring⟧ *Christianity* the forty weekdays of fasting and penitence from Ash Wednesday to Easter —**Lent′en** or **lent′en** ***adj.***

len·til (lent′'l) ***n.*** ⟦< L *lens*⟧ **1** a kind of legume, with small, edible seeds **2** this seed

Le·o (lē′ō) ***n.*** ⟦L, lion⟧ the fifth sign of the zodiac

le·o·nine (lē′ə nīn′) ***adj.*** ⟦< L *leo*, lion⟧ of or like a lion

leop·ard (lep′ərd) ***n.*** ⟦< Gr *leōn*, lion + *pardos*, panther⟧ any of various large, ferocious cats, including the jaguar; esp., one with a black-spotted, tawny coat, found in Africa and Asia

le·o·tard (lē′ə tärd′) ***n.*** ⟦after J. *Léotard*, 19th-c. Fr aerial performer⟧ a tightfitting garment for acrobats, dancers, etc.

lep·er (lep′ər) ***n.*** ⟦< Gr *lepros*, scaly⟧ a person having leprosy

lep·re·chaun (lep′rə kôn′, -kän′) ***n.*** ⟦< Old Ir *lu*, little + *corp*, body⟧ *Ir. Folklore* a fairy who can reveal hidden treasure

THESAURUS

legible ***a.*** distinct, readable, plain; see CLEAR 2.

legion ***n.*** multitude, body, group; see CROWD, GATHERING.

legislate ***v.*** make laws, pass, constitute; see ENACT.

legislation ***n.*** bill, enactment, act; see LAW 3.

legislative ***a.*** lawmaking, enacting, decreeing, ordaining, lawgiving, congressional, parliamentary, senatorial, by the legislature.

legislator ***n.*** lawmaker, lawgiver, assemblyman, representative, member of congress, congressman, congresswoman, senator, member of parliament, floor leader, councilman, councilwoman, alderman; see also EXECUTIVE.

legislature ***n.*** lawmakers, congress, parliament, chamber, assembly, senate, house, elected representatives, soviet, plenum, lawmaking body, voice of the people.

legitimate ***a.*** **1** [In accordance with legal provisions] licit, statutory, authorized; see LAWFUL, LEGAL. **2** [Logical] reasonable, probable, consistent; see LOGICAL, UNDERSTANDABLE. **3** [Authentic] verifiable, valid, reliable; see GENUINE 1, 2.

leisure ***n.*** freedom, free time, spare time, spare moments, relaxation, recreation, ease, recess, holiday, leave of absence, convenience, idle hours, opportunity; see also REST 1, VACATION.—*Ant.* WORK, toil, travail. —**at leisure** idle, at rest, not busy; see RESTING 1. —**at one's leisure** when one has time, at one's convenience, at an early opportunity; see WHENEVER.

leisurely ***a.*** slow, unhurried, deliberate, calm, taking one's time, gradual, lethargic, sluggish, indolent.—*Ant.* FAST, rapid, hasty.

lemon ***n.*** citrus fruit, juicy fruit, food; see FRUIT.

lend ***v.*** advance, provide with, let out, furnish, permit to borrow, trust with, lend on security, extend credit, entrust, accommodate.—*Ant.* BORROW, repay, pay back.

lender ***n.*** moneylender, bank, loan company; see BANKER, DONOR.

length ***n.*** **1** [Linear distance] space, measure, span, reach, range, longitude, remoteness, magnitude, compass, portion, dimension, unit, radius, diameter, longness, mileage, stretch, extensiveness, spaciousness, distance, height, expansion; see also EXPANSE, EXTENT.—*Ant.* NEARNESS, shortness, closeness. **2** [Duration] period, interval, season, year, month, week, day, minute, limit; see also TIME 1. —**at length** **1** [Finally] after a while, at last, in the end; see FINALLY 2. **2** [Fully] in full, extensively, without omission; see COMPLETELY.

lengthen ***v.*** **1** [To make longer] extend, stretch, protract; see INCREASE. **2** [To grow longer] extend itself, increase, expand; see GROW 1.

lengthwise ***a.*** longitudinally, the long way, along, endlong*, from end to end, from stem to stern, overall, from head to foot, from top to bottom; see also ALONGSIDE.

lengthy ***a.*** tedious, not brief, long; see DULL 4.

lenient ***a.*** soft, mild, tolerant; see KIND.

lens ***n.*** microscope, camera, spectacles; see GLASS.

leopard ***n.*** panther, hunting leopard, jaguar; see ANIMAL, CAT 2.

lep·ro·sy (lep′rə sē) ***n.*** ⟦see LEPER⟧ a progressive infectious disease of the skin, flesh, nerves, etc., characterized by ulcers, white scaly scabs, deformities, etc. —**lep′rous** ***adj.***

lept (lept) ***vi.***, ***vt.*** *alt. pt. of* LEAP

lep·ton (lep′tän′) ***n.*** ⟦< Gr *leptos*, thin⟧ any of certain atomic particles, as the electron or neutrino

les·bi·an (lez′bē ən) ***n.*** ⟦after *Lesbos*, Gr. island home of the poetess Sappho⟧ a homosexual woman —**les′bi·an·ism′** ***n.***

lèse-ma·jest·é (lez′ma′zhes tā′, -maj′is tē) ***n.*** ⟦Fr < L *laesa majestas*, injured majesty⟧ **1** a crime or offense against the sovereign **2** any lack of proper respect as toward one in authority

le·sion (lē′zhən) ***n.*** ⟦< L *laedere*, to harm⟧ an injury of an organ or tissue resulting in impairment of function

Le·sot·ho (le so͞o′to͞o) country in SE Africa, surrounded by South Africa: 11,720 sq. mi.; pop. 1,578,000

less (les) ***adj.*** ⟦OE *læs(sa)*⟧ **1** *alt. compar. of* LITTLE **2** not so much **3** fewer —***adv.*** **1** *compar. of* LITTLE **2** to a smaller extent —***n.*** a smaller amount —***prep.*** minus —**less and less** decreasingly

-less (lis, ləs) ⟦OE *leas*, free⟧ *suffix* **1** without **2** not able to **3** not able to be ___ed

les·see (les ē′) ***n.*** ⟦see LEASE⟧ one to whom a lease is given; tenant

less′en ***vt.***, ***vi.*** to make or become less; decrease

less′er ***adj.*** **1** *alt. compar. of* LITTLE **2** smaller, less, or less important

les·son (les′ən) ***n.*** ⟦< L *legere*, to read⟧ **1** an exercise for a student to learn **2** something learned for one's safety, etc. **3** [*pl.*] course of instruction **4** a selection from the Bible read as part of a religious service

les·sor (les′ôr′) ***n.*** ⟦see LEASE⟧ one who gives a lease; landlord

lest (lest) ***conj.*** ⟦< OE *thy læs the*, lit., by the less that⟧ for fear that

let[1] (let) ***vt.*** **let, let′ting** ⟦OE *lætan*, leave behind⟧ **1** to leave: now only in **let alone, let be** **2** *a)* to rent *b)* to assign (a contract) **3** to cause to escape *[to let blood]* **4** to allow; permit Also used as an auxiliary in commands or suggestions *[let us go]* —***vi.*** to be rented *[a house to let]* —**let down** **1** to lower **2** to slow up **3** to disappoint —**let off** **1** to give forth **2** to deal leniently with —**let on** [Inf.] **1** to indicate one's awareness **2** to pretend —**let out** **1** to release **2** to rent out **3** to make a garment larger —**let up** **1** to relax **2** to cease

let[2] (let) ***n.*** ⟦< OE *lettan*, make late⟧ *Law* an obstacle: in **without let or hindrance**

-let (lit, lət) ⟦Fr *-el* + *-et*, dim. suffixes⟧ *suffix* small *[piglet]*

let′down′ ***n.*** **1** a slowing up **2** a disappointment

le·thal (lē′thəl) ***adj.*** ⟦< L *letum*, death⟧ causing death; fatal

leth·ar·gy (leth′ər jē) ***n.***, *pl.* **-gies** ⟦< Gr *lēthē*, oblivion + *argos*, idle⟧ **1** an abnormal drowsiness **2** sluggishness, apathy, etc. —**le·thar·gic** (li thär′jik) ***adj.*** —**le·thar′gi·cal·ly** ***adv.***

let's (lets) *contr.* let us

let·ter (let′ər) ***n.*** ⟦< L *littera*⟧ **1** any character in an alphabet **2** a written or printed message, usually sent by mail **3** [*pl.*] *a)* literature *b)* learning; knowledge **4** the literal meaning —***vt.*** to mark with letters —**let′ter·er** ***n.***

letter carrier a postal employee who delivers mail

let′ter·head′ ***n.*** the name, address, etc. as a heading on stationery

let′ter·ing ***n.*** the act of making or inscribing letters, or such letters

let′ter-per′fect ***adj.*** entirely correct

let·tuce (let′əs) ***n.*** ⟦< L *lac*, milk⟧ **1** a plant with crisp, green leaves **2** the leaves, much used for salads

let·up (let′up′) ***n.*** [Inf.] **1** a slackening **2** a stop or pause

leu·ke·mi·a (lo͞o kē′mē ə) ***n.*** ⟦see fol. & -EMIA⟧ a disease characterized by an abnormal increase in the number of leukocytes: also sp. **leu·kae′mi·a**

leu·ko·cyte (lo͞o′kō sīt′, -kə-) ***n.*** ⟦< Gr *leukos*, white + *kytos*, hollow⟧ a colorless cell in the blood, etc. that destroys disease-causing organisms; white blood cell

lev·ee (lev′ē) ***n.*** ⟦ult. < L *levare*, to raise⟧ an embankment to prevent a river from flooding bordering land

lev·el (lev′əl) ***n.*** ⟦< L *libra*, a balance⟧ **1** an instrument for determining an even horizontal plane **2** a horizontal plane or line *[sea level]* **3** a horizontal area **4** normal position with reference to height *[water seeks its level]* **5** position in a scale of values *[income level]* —***adj.*** **1** perfectly flat and even **2** not sloping **3** even in height (*with*) **4** equal in importance, advancement, quality, etc. **5** calm or steady —***vt.***, ***vi.*** **-eled** or **-elled**, **-el·ing** or **-el·ling** **1** to make or become level **2** to demolish **3** to aim (a gun, etc.) —**level with** [Slang] to be honest with —**lev′el·er** or **lev′el·ler** ***n.***

lev′el·head′ed ***adj.*** having an even temper and sound judgment

lev·er (lev′ər, lē′vər) ***n.*** ⟦< L *levare*, to raise⟧ **1** a bar used as a pry **2** a means to an end **3** a device consisting of a bar turning about a fixed point, using force at a second point to lift a weight at a third

lev′er·age (-ij) ***n.*** **1** the action or mechanical power of a lever **2** means of accomplishing something —***vt.*** **-aged, -ag·ing** *Finance* to speculate in (a business venture) with borrowed funds

le·vi·a·than (lə vī′ə thən) ***n.*** ⟦< Heb *liwyāthān*⟧ **1** *Bible* a sea monster **2** anything huge

Le·vi's (lē′vīz′) ⟦after *Levi* Strauss, U.S. manufacturer⟧

THESAURUS

lesbian ***n.*** gay, Sapphist, homosexual woman; see HOMOSEXUAL.

less ***a.*** smaller, lower, lesser, minor, fewer, reduced, in decline, depressed, inferior, secondary, subordinate, beneath, minus, deficient, diminished, shortened, limited, not so much as, not as much; see also SHORTER.—*Ant.* MORE, more than, longer.

lessen ***v.*** **1** [To grow less] diminish, dwindle, decline; see DECREASE 1. **2** [To make less] reduce, diminish, lower; see DECREASE 2.

lessening ***a.*** decreasing, declining, waning, dropping, diminishing, abating, slowing down, dwindling, sinking, sagging, subsiding, moderating, slackening, ebbing, lowering, shrinking, drying up, shriveling up, softening, weakening, decaying, narrowing down, drooping, wasting, running low, running down, dying away, dying down, wearing off, wearing out, wearing away, wearing down, falling off, slacking off, growing less and less, losing momentum, slumping, plunging, plummeting, going down, in reverse, getting worse, getting slower.

lesser ***a.*** inferior, minor, secondary; see SUBORDINATE.

lesson ***n.*** drill, assignment, reading; see JOB 2.

let[1] ***v.*** **1** [To permit] suffer, give permission, condone, approve, authorize, consent, permit, tolerate; see also ALLOW. **2** [To rent] lease, hire, sublet; see RENT 1. —**let down** disappoint, disillusion, not support; see ABANDON 2, FAIL 1. —**let in** admit, allow to enter, give admission to; see RECEIVE 4. —**let off** leave, excuse, let go, remove; see also ABANDON 1. —**let on*** imply, indicate, suggest; see HINT. —**let out** liberate, let go, eject; see FREE. —**let up** cease, release, slow down; see SLOW 1, STOP 2.

letdown ***n.*** frustration, setback, disillusionment; see DISAPPOINTMENT 1.

lethal ***a.*** fatal, mortal, malignant; see DEADLY, HARMFUL, POISONOUS.

letter ***n.*** **1** [A unit of the alphabet] capital, upper-case letter, lower-case letter, small letter, digraph, rune; see also CONSONANT, VOWEL. **2** [A written communication] note, epistle, missive, message, memorandum, report, line. *Types of letters include the following:* business, form, circular, chain, cover, fan, love, thank-you, registered, airmail, open, personal; billet-doux, postcard, e-mail, fax, letter of resignation, invitation, direct mail advertising, junk mail*. —**to the letter** just as directed, accurately, precisely; see PERFECTLY.

letup ***n.*** interval, recess, respite; see PAUSE.

level ***a.*** **1** [Smooth] polished, rolled, planed; see FLAT 1, SMOOTH 1. **2** [Of an even height] regular, equal, uniform, flush, of the same height, same, constant, straight, balanced, steady, stable, trim, precise, exact, matched, unbroken, on a line, lined up, aligned, uninterrupted, continuous; see also SMOOTH 1.—*Ant.* IRREGULAR, uneven, crooked. **3** [Horizontal] plane, leveled, lying prone, in the same plane, on one plane; see also FLAT 1. —**one's level best*** one's best, the best one can do, all one's effort; see BEST. —**on the level*** fair, sincere, truthful; see HONEST 1.

level ***v.*** **1** [To straighten] surface, bulldoze, equalize; see SMOOTH, STRAIGHTEN. **2** [To demolish] ruin, waste, wreck; see DESTROY. **3** [*To be honest with] be frank with, come to terms, be open and aboveboard; see DECLARE. —**level off** level out, find a level, reach an equilibrium; see DECREASE 1, STRAIGHTEN.

levelheaded ***a.*** wise, practical, prudent; see RATIONAL 1, REASONABLE 1.

lever ***n.*** lifter, pry, leverage, pry bar, pinch bar, crowbar, handspike, arm, advantage; see also TOOL 1.

leverage ***n.*** purchase, lift, hold; see SUPPORT 2.

levied ***a.*** exacted, taken, collected; see TAXED 1.

trademark for trousers of heavy denim —**pl.n.** such trousers: also written **Le'vis** or **le'vis**

lev·i·ta·tion (lev'ə tā'shən) **n.** ⟦< L *levis*, light⟧ the illusion of raising a body in the air with no support —**lev'i·tate', -tat'ed, -tat'ing, vt., vi.**

Le·vit·i·cus (lə vit'i kəs) **n.** the third book of the Pentateuch

Lev·it·town (lev'it toun') city in SE New York: post-WWII planned community of mass-produced houses: pop. 53,000

lev·i·ty (lev'i tē) **n.**, *pl.* **-ties** ⟦< L *levis*, light⟧ gaiety, esp. improper gaiety; frivolity

lev·y (lev'ē) **n.**, *pl.* **lev'ies** ⟦< L *levare*, to raise⟧ **1** an imposing and collecting of a tax, fine, etc. **2** the amount imposed **3** compulsory enlistment for military service **4** a group so enlisted —**vt. -ied, -y·ing 1** to impose (a tax, fine, etc.) **2** to enlist (troops) **3** to wage (war)

lewd (lo͞od) **adj.** ⟦OE *læwede*, unlearned⟧ indecent; lustful; obscene —**lewd'ly adv.** —**lewd'ness n.**

lex·i·cog·ra·phy (lek'sə käg'rə fē) **n.** ⟦see fol. & -GRAPHY⟧ the act, art, or work of writing a dictionary —**lex'i·cog'ra·pher n.**

lex·i·con (lek'si kän') **n.** ⟦< Gr *lexis*, word⟧ **1** a dictionary **2** a special vocabulary —**lex'i·cal adj.**

Lex·ing·ton (lek'siŋ tən) city in NC Kentucky: with the county in which it is located, pop. 225,000

lg *abbrev.* large

Li *Chem. symbol for* lithium

li·a·bil·i·ty (lī'ə bil'ə tē) **n.**, *pl.* **-ties 1** the state of being liable **2** anything for which a person is liable **3** a debt of a person or business **4** something that works to one's disadvantage

li·a·ble (lī'ə bəl) **adj.** ⟦< L *ligare*, bind⟧ **1** legally bound or responsible **2** subject to *[liable* to heart attacks*]* **3** likely to *[liable* to get hurt*]*

li·ai·son (lē ā'zän', -zən) **n.** ⟦< L *ligare*, bind⟧ **1** a linking up, as of units of a military force **2** an illicit love affair

li·ar (lī'ər) **n.** one who tells lies

lib (lib) **n.** [Inf.] *short for* LIBERATION

li·ba·tion (lī bā'shən) **n.** ⟦< L *libare*, pour out⟧ **1** the ritual of pouring out wine or oil in honor of a god **2** this liquid **3** an alcoholic drink

li·bel (lī'bəl) **n.** ⟦< L *liber*, book⟧ **1** any written or printed matter tending to injure a person's reputation unjustly **2** the act or crime of publishing such a thing —**vt. -beled** or **-belled, -bel·ing** or **-bel·ling** to make a libel against —**li'bel·er** or **li'bel·ler n.** —**li'bel·ous** or **li'bel·lous adj.**

lib·er·al (lib'ər əl) **adj.** ⟦< L *liber*, free⟧ **1** generous **2** ample; abundant **3** not literal or strict **4** tolerant; broad-minded **5** favoring reform or progress —**n.** one who favors reform or progress —**lib'er·al·ism' n.** —**lib'er·al·ly adv.** —**lib'er·al·ness n.**

liberal arts literature, languages, history, etc. as courses or a course of study

lib'er·al'i·ty (-al'i tē) **n.**, *pl.* **-ties 1** generosity **2** broad-mindedness

lib'er·al·ize' (-əl īz') **vt., vi. -ized', -iz'ing** to make or become liberal —**lib'er·al·i·za'tion n.**

lib·er·ate (lib'ər āt') **vt. -at'ed, -at'ing** ⟦< L *liber*, free⟧ to release from slavery, oppression, enemy occupation, etc. —**lib'er·a'tion n.** —**lib'er·a'tor n.**

Li·ber·i·a (lī bir'ē ə) country on the W coast of Africa: founded (1821) as settlement for freed U.S. slaves: 38,250 sq. mi.; pop. 2,102,000 —**Li·ber'i·an adj., n.**

lib·er·tar·i·an (lib'ər ter'ē ən) **n.** an advocate of full individual freedom of thought and action

lib·er·tine (lib'ər tēn') **n.** ⟦< L *liber*, free⟧ one who is sexually promiscuous —**adj.** licentious

lib·er·ty (lib'ər tē) **n.**, *pl.* **-ties** ⟦< L *liber*, free⟧ **1** freedom from slavery, captivity, etc. **2** a particular right, freedom, etc. **3** a too free or impertinent action or attitude **4** permission given to a sailor to go ashore See also CIVIL LIBERTIES —**at liberty 1** not confined **2** permitted (to do or say something) **3** not busy or in use —**take liberties 1** to be too familiar or impertinent **2** to deal inaccurately (*with* facts, data, etc.)

li·bid·i·nous (li bid''n əs) **adj.** ⟦see fol.⟧ lustful; lascivious

li·bi·do (li bē'dō) **n.** ⟦< L, pleasure⟧ **1** the sexual urge **2** *Psychoanalysis* psychic energy; specif., that comprising the positive, loving instincts

Li·bra (lē'brə) **n.** ⟦L, balance, scales⟧ the seventh sign of the zodiac

li·brar·i·an (lī brer'ē ən) **n.** one in charge of a library or trained in library science

li·brar·y (lī'brer'ē) **n.**, *pl.* **-ies** ⟦< L *liber*, book⟧ **1** a collection of books, etc. **2** a room or building for, or an institution in charge of, such a collection

li·bret·to (li bret'ō) **n.**, *pl.* **-tos** or **-ti** (-ē) ⟦It < L *liber*, book⟧ the words, or text, of an opera, oratorio, etc. —**li·bret'tist n.**

Lib·y·a (lib'ē ə) country in N Africa, on the Mediterranean: 679,358 sq. mi.; pop. 3,637,000 —**Lib'y·an adj., n.**

lice (līs) **n.** *pl. of* LOUSE

li·cense (lī'səns) **n.** ⟦< L *licere*, be permitted⟧ **1** formal or legal permission to do something specified **2** a document, etc. indicating such permission **3** freedom to deviate from rule, practice, etc. *[poetic license]* **4** excessive freedom, constituting an abuse of liberty Brit. sp. **li'cence** —**vt. -censed, -cens·ing** to permit formally

li·cen·see (lī'səns ē') **n.** a person to whom a license is granted

li·cen·ti·ate (lī sen'shē it, -āt') **n.** a person having a professional license

THESAURUS

levy *n.* toll, duty, customs; see TAX 1.

lewd *a.* **1** [Suggestive of lewdness] ribald, smutty, indecent; see sense 2 and SENSUAL 2. **2** [Inclined to lewdness] lustful, wanton, lascivious, libidinous, licentious, lecherous, profligate, dissolute, carnal, sensual, debauched, depraved, unchaste, corrupt, unbridled, ruttish, nymphomaniacal, prurient, concupiscent, incontinent, incestuous, goatish, raunchy*, horny*, in heat*; see also VULGAR.—*Ant.* PURE, chaste, modest.

lewdly *a.* wantonly, shockingly, indecently, lasciviously, lecherously, libidinously, unchastely, carnally, dissolutely, immodestly, voluptuously, sensually, incontinently, indelicately, in a lewd manner, with lewd gestures, in a suggestive manner.

lewdness *n.* indecency, unchastity, incontinence, vulgarity, lechery, wantonness, lasciviousness, sensuality, licentiousness, voluptuousness, lecherousness, profligacy, dissoluteness, lustfulness, prurience, ribaldry, concupiscence, obscenity, scurrility, coarseness, carnal passion, grossness, sensuous desire, salaciousness, pornography, lust, depravity, carnality, nymphomania, corruption, raunchiness*, dirtiness, incest, indelicacy, eroticism, erotism, smut, impurity, debauchery.—*Ant.* MODESTY, continence, decency.

liability *n.* obligation, indebtedness, answerability; see RESPONSIBILITY 2.

liable *a.* **1** [Responsible] answerable, subject, accountable; see RESPONSIBLE 1. **2** [Likely] tending, apt, inclined; see LIKELY 4.

liar *n.* prevaricator, false witness, deceiver, perjurer, trickster, misleader, falsifier, storyteller*, equivocator, fibber, fabricator; see also CHEAT.

libel *n.* calumny, slander, lying; see LIE.

liberal *a.* tolerant, receptive, nonconformist, progressive, advanced, left, radical, leftist, reformist, broad-minded, understanding, permissive, indulgent, impartial, unprejudiced, reasonable, rational, unbiased, detached, dispassionate, unconventional, avant-garde, left-wing, objective, magnanimous; see also FAIR 1.—*Ant.* PREJUDICED, intolerant, biased.

liberal *n.* individualist, insurgent, rebel, revolutionary, nonconformist, progressive, leftist, independent, believer in civil rights, reformer, socialist, eccentric, freethinker, left-winger; see also RADICAL.

liberate *v.* set free, loose, release; see FREE.

liberation *n.* release, freedom, deliverance; see RESCUE 1.

liberty *n.* **1** [Freedom from bondage] deliverance, emancipation, enfranchisement; see RESCUE 1. **2** [Freedom from activity or obligation] rest, leave, relaxation; see FREEDOM 2, LEISURE, RECREATION. **3** [Freedom to choose] permission, alternative, decision; see CHOICE, SELECTION 1. **4** [The rights supposedly natural to human beings] freedom, independence, power of choice; see DEMOCRACY. —**at liberty** unrestricted, unlimited, not confined; see FREE 1, 2. —**take liberties** be impertinent, act too freely, use carelessly; see ABUSE.

librarian *n.* keeper, caretaker, curator; see EXECUTIVE.

library *n.* books, book collection, manuscripts, manuscript collection, archives, institution, public library, private library, book room, lending library, reference collection, museum, treasury, memorabilia, rare books, reading room.

license *n.* **1** [Unbridled use of freedom] looseness, excess, immoderation; see FREEDOM 2. **2** [A formal permission] permit, form, identification, tag, card, consent, grant; see also PERMISSION.

license *v.* permit, authorize, accredit; see ALLOW.

li·cen·tious (lī sen′shəs) ***adj.*** ⟦see LICENSE⟧ sexually unrestrained; lascivious —**li·cen′tious·ness *n.***

li·chen (lī′kən) ***n.*** ⟦< Gr *leichein*, to lick⟧ a plant resembling moss but actually a combination of fungus and algae, growing in patches on rock, wood, soil, etc.

lic·it (lis′it) ***adj.*** ⟦< L *licitus*, permitted⟧ lawful —**lic′it·ly *adv.***

lick (lik) ***vt.*** ⟦OE *liccian*⟧ **1** to pass the tongue over **2** to pass lightly over like a tongue **3** [Inf.] *a*) to thrash *b*) to vanquish —***vi.*** to move lightly, as a flame —***n.*** **1** a licking with the tongue **2** a small quantity **3** *short for* SALT LICK **4** [Inf.] a sharp blow —**lick up** to consume as by licking

lic·o·rice (lik′ə rish) ***n.*** ⟦< Gr *glykys*, sweet + *rhiza*, root⟧ **1** a black flavoring extract made from the root of a European plant **2** candy flavored with this extract or in imitation of it

lid (lid) ***n.*** ⟦OE *hlid*⟧ **1** a movable cover, as for a box, pot, etc. **2** *short for* EYELID **3** [Inf.] a restraint

lid·ded (lid′id) ***adj.*** **1** having a lid **2** having (a specified kind of) eyelids *[heavy-lidded]*

lie[1] (lī) ***vi.*** **lay, lain, ly′ing** ⟦OE *licgan*⟧ **1** to be or put oneself in a reclining or horizontal position **2** to rest on a support in a horizontal position **3** to be in a specified condition **4** to be situated *[Canada lies to the north]* **5** to extend **6** to be or be found —***n.*** the way in which something is situated; lay

lie[2] (lī) ***vi.*** **lied, ly′ing** ⟦OE *leogan*⟧ to make a statement that one knows is false —***vt.*** to bring, put, accomplish, etc. by lying *[to lie his way into office]* —***n.*** a false statement made with intent to deceive

Lieb·frau·milch (lēb′frou milk′) ***n.*** ⟦Ger⟧ a white wine

Liech·ten·stein (lik′tən stīn′) country between Switzerland & Austria: 62 sq. mi.; pop. 29,000

lie detector a polygraph used on persons suspected of lying

lief (lēf) ***adv.*** ⟦< OE *leof*, dear⟧ willingly; gladly: only in **would** (or **had**) **as lief**

liege (lēj) ***adj.*** ⟦OFr⟧ loyal; faithful —***n.*** *Feudal Law* **1** a lord or sovereign **2** a subject or vassal

li·en (lēn, lē′ən) ***n.*** ⟦Fr < L *ligare*, to bind⟧ a legal claim on another's property as security for the payment of a debt

lieu (lo͞o) ***n.*** ⟦< L *locus*⟧ place: chiefly in **in lieu of**, instead of

Lieut *abbrev.* Lieutenant

lieu·ten·ant (lo͞o ten′ənt) ***n.*** ⟦< Fr *lieu*, place + *tenant*, holding⟧ **1** one who acts for a superior **2** *U.S. Mil.* an officer ranking below a captain: see FIRST LIEUTENANT, SECOND LIEUTENANT **3** *U.S. Navy* an officer ranking just above a lieutenant junior grade —**lieu·ten′an·cy *n.***

lieutenant colonel *U.S. Mil.* an officer ranking just above a major

lieutenant commander *U.S. Navy* an officer ranking just above a lieutenant

lieutenant general *U.S. Mil.* an officer ranking just above a major general

lieutenant governor an elected official of a U.S. state who ranks below and substitutes for the governor

lieutenant junior grade *U.S. Navy* an officer ranking just above an ensign

life (līf) ***n.***, *pl.* **lives** ⟦OE *lif*⟧ **1** that property of plants and animals (ending at death) which makes it possible for them to take in food, get energy from it, grow, etc. **2** the state of having this property **3** a human being *[100 lives were lost]* **4** living things collectively *[plant life]* **5** the time a person or thing is alive or exists **6** one's manner of living *[a life of ease]* **7** the people and activities of a given time, place, etc. *[military life]* **8** *a*) one's animate existence *b*) a biography **9** the source of liveliness *[the life of the party]* **10** vigor; liveliness

life belt a life preserver in belt form

life′blood′ ***n.*** **1** the blood necessary to life **2** a vital element

life′boat′ ***n.*** one of the small boats carried by a ship for use in an emergency

life′-form′ ***n.*** a particular type of organism, often one that is unusual or newly found

life′guard′ ***n.*** a swimmer employed as at a beach to prevent drownings

life insurance insurance in which a stipulated sum is paid at the death of the insured

life jacket (or **vest**) a life preserver like a sleeveless jacket or vest

life′less ***adj.*** **1** without life; specif., *a*) inanimate *b*) dead **2** dull

life′like′ ***adj.*** resembling real life or a real person or thing

life′line′ ***n.*** **1** a rope or line for saving life, as one thrown to a person in the water **2** a very important commercial route

life′long′ ***adj.*** lasting or not changing during one's whole life

life net a strong net used as by firefighters to catch people jumping from a burning building

life preserver a buoyant device for saving a person from drowning by keeping the body afloat

lif′er ***n.*** [Slang] a person sentenced to prison for life

life raft a small, inflatable raft for emergency use at sea

life′sav′er ***n.*** **1** a lifeguard **2** [Inf.] a help in time of need

life′-size′ ***adj.*** as big as the person or thing represented *[a life-size portrait]*: also **life′-sized′**

life′style′ ***n.*** an individual's way of living

life′-sup·port′ ***adj.*** *Med.* for providing support needed to maintain life *[a life-support system]*

THESAURUS

lick *v.* **1** [To pass the tongue over] stroke, rub, touch, pass over, pass across, caress, wash, graze, brush, glance, tongue, fondle. **2** [To play over; *said of flames*] rise and fall, fluctuate, leap; see BURN, DART, WAVE 3. **3** [*To beat] whip, trim*, thrash; see BEAT 1. **4** [*To defeat] overcome, vanquish, frustrate; see DEFEAT 3.

lid *n.* cap, top, roof; see COVER 1, HOOD 1.

lie[1,2] ***v.*** **1** [To utter an untruth] falsify, prevaricate, tell a lie, deceive, mislead, misinform, exaggerate, distort, concoct, equivocate, be untruthful, be a liar, break one's word, bear false witness, go back on, say one thing and mean another, misrepresent, dissemble, perjure oneself, delude, invent.—*Ant.* DECLARE, tell the truth, be honest. **2** [To be situated] extend, be on, be beside, be located, be fixed, be established, be placed, be seated, be set, be level, be smooth, be even, exist in space, stretch along, reach along, spread along. **3** [To be prostrate] be flat, be prone, sprawl, loll, be stretched out; see also REST 1.—*Ant.* STAND, be upright, sit. **4** [To assume a prostrate position] lie down, recline, stretch out, go to bed, turn in, retire, take a nap, take a siesta, hit the sack*, hit the hay*; see also REST 1, SLEEP.—*Ant.* RISE, get up, arise. —**take lying down** submit, surrender, be passive; see YIELD 1.

lie[2] ***n.*** falsehood, untruth, fiction, inaccuracy, misstatement, myth, fable, deceptiveness, misrepresentation, lying, prevarication, falsification, falseness, defamation, tall story*, fabrication, deception, slander, aspersion, tale, perjury, libel, forgery, distortion, fib, white lie, fish story*, whopper*.—*Ant.* TRUTH, veracity, truthfulness.

life *n.* **1** [The fact or act of living] being, entity, growth, animation, endurance, survival, presence, living, consciousness, breath, continuance, flesh and blood, viability, metabolism, vitality, vital spark; see also EXPERIENCE.—*Ant.* DEATH, discontinuance, nonexistence. **2** [The sum of one's experiences] life experience, conduct, behavior, way of life, reaction, response, participation, enjoyment, joy, suffering, happiness, tide of events, circumstances, realization, knowledge, enlightenment, attainment, development, growth, personality. **3** [A biography] life story, memoir, memorial; see BIOGRAPHY, STORY. **4** [Duration] lifetime, one's natural life, period of existence, duration of life, endurance, continuance, span, history, career, course, era, epoch, century, decade, days, generation, time, period, life span, season, cycle, record; see also TIME 1. **5** [One who promotes gaiety] animator, entertainer, life of the party; see HOST 1, HOSTESS. **6** [Vital spirit] vital force, vital principle, *élan vital* (French); see EXCITEMENT, ZEAL. —**as large** (or **big**) **as life** actually, really, in actual fact; see TRULY. —**for dear life** intensely, desperately, for all one is worth; see STRONGLY. —**for life** for the duration of one's life, for a long time, as long as one lives; see FOREVER. —**for the life of me*** by any means, as if one's life were at stake, whatever happens; see ANYHOW. —**life or death** decisive, necessary, critical; see IMPORTANT 1. —**matter of life and death** crisis, grave concern, something vitally important; see IMPORTANCE. —**not on your life*** by no means, certainly not, never; see NO. —**take one's own life** kill oneself, die by one's own hand, commit suicide. —**true to life** true to reality, realistic, real; see GENUINE 1.

lifeless *a.* **1** [Without life] inert, inanimate, departed; see DEAD 1. **2** [Lacking spirit] lackluster, listless, heavy; see DULL 3, 4, SLOW 2.

lifelike *a.* simulated, exact, imitative; see GRAPHIC 1, 2.

life'time' *n.* **1** the period of time that someone lives or that a thing lasts **2** a very long time

life'work' *n.* the work to which a person's life is devoted

lift (lift) *vt.* ⟦< ON *lopt*, air⟧ **1** to bring up to a higher position; raise **2** to raise in rank, condition, etc.; exalt **3** to pay off (a mortgage, debt, etc.) **4** to end (a blockade, etc.) **5** [Slang] to steal —*vi.* **1** to exert strength in raising something **2** to rise; go up —*n.* **1** a lifting or rising **2** the distance something is lifted **3** lifting power or influence **4** elevation of mood **5** a ride in the direction one is going **6** help of any kind **7** *a)* [Brit.] ELEVATOR *b)* SKI LIFT

lift'off' *n.* **1** the initial vertical takeoff of a rocket, helicopter, etc. **2** the time this occurs

lig·a·ment (lig'ə mənt) *n.* ⟦< L *ligare*, bind⟧ a band of tissue connecting bones or holding organs in place

lig·a·ture (lig'ə chər) *n.* ⟦< L *ligare*, bind⟧ **1** a tying or binding together **2** a tie, bond, etc. **3** two or more letters united, as *æ, th* **4** *Surgery* a thread used to tie up an artery, etc.

light[1] (līt) *n.* ⟦OE *leoht*⟧ **1** *a)* the form of radiant energy acting on the retina of the eye to make sight possible *b)* ultraviolet or infrared radiation **2** brightness; illumination **3** h source of light, as the sun, a lamp, etc. **4** daylight **5** a thing used to ignite something **6** a window or windowpane **7** knowledge; enlightenment **8** public view *[to bring new facts to light]* **9** aspect *[viewed in another light]* —*adj.* **1** having light; bright **2** pale in color; fair —*adv.* palely *[a light blue color]* —*vt.* **light'ed** or **lit**, **light'ing** **1** to ignite *[to light a bonfire]* **2** to cause to give off light **3** to furnish with light **4** to brighten; animate —*vi.* **1** to catch fire **2** to be lighted: usually with *up* —**in the light of** considering —**see the light (of day)** **1** to come into existence **2** to come to public view **3** to understand

light[2] (līt) *adj.* ⟦OE *leoht*⟧ **1** having little weight; not heavy, esp. for its size **2** less than usual in weight, amount, force, etc. *[a light blow]* **3** not serious or profound **4** easy to bear *[a light tax]* **5** easy to do *[light work]* **6** merry; happy **7** dizzy; giddy **8** containing fewer calories **9** moderate *[a light meal]* **10** moving with ease *[light on one's feet]* **11** producing small products *[light industry]* —*adv.* LIGHTLY —*vi.* **light'ed** or **lit**, **light'ing** **1** to come to rest after traveling through the air **2** to come or happen (*on* or *upon*) —**light into** [Inf.] to attack —**light out** [Inf.] to depart suddenly —**make light of** to treat as unimportant

light'en[1] *vt., vi.* **1** to make or become light or brighter **2** to shine; flash

light'en[2] *vt., vi.* **1** to make or become lighter in weight **2** to make or become more cheerful

light'er[1] *n.* a person or thing that starts something burning

light'er[2] *n.* ⟦< MDu *licht*, LIGHT[2]⟧ a large barge used to load or unload ships anchored in a harbor

light'-fin'gered *adj.* **1** skillful at stealing **2** likely to steal

light'-foot'ed *adj.* stepping lightly and gracefully

light'head'ed *adj.* **1** giddy; dizzy **2** flighty; frivolous

light'heart'ed *adj.* free from care; cheerful —**light'heart'ed·ly** *adv.* —**light'heart'ed·ness** *n.*

light heavyweight a boxer with a maximum weight of 175 lb.

light'house' *n.* a tower with a very bright light to guide ships at night

light'ing *n.* the act or manner of giving light, or illuminating

light'ly *adv.* **1** with little weight or pressure; gently **2** to a small degree or amount **3** nimbly; deftly **4** cheerfully **5** with indifference

light meter an instrument to measure intensity of light, used in photography

light'-mind'ed *adj.* silly; frivolous

light'ness[1] *n.* **1** the amount of light; brightness **2** paleness in color

light'ness[2] *n.* **1** a being light, not heavy **2** mildness, nimbleness, cheerfulness, etc.

light'ning (-niŋ) *n.* a flash of light in the sky caused by the discharge of atmospheric electricity

lightning bug FIREFLY

lightning rod a metal rod placed high on a building and grounded to divert lightning from the structure

light opera OPERETTA

light'weight' *n.* a boxer with a maximum weight of 135 lb. —*adj.* light in weight

light'-year' *n.* a unit of distance equal to the distance light travels in one year, *c.* 6 trillion miles

lig·nite (lig'nīt') *n.* ⟦< L *lignum*, wood⟧ a soft coal, brownish-black in color and retaining the texture of the original wood

lik·a·ble (līk'ə bəl) *adj.* pleasant, genial, etc.: also **like'a·ble** —**lik'a·ble·ness** or **lik'a·bil'i·ty** *n.*

THESAURUS

lifetime *a.* lifelong, continuing, enduring; see PERMANENT.

lifetime *n.* existence, endurance, continuance; see LIFE 4, RECORD 2.

lift *n.* **1** [The work of lifting] pull, lifting, ascension, raising, weight, foot-pounds, elevation, escalation, ascent, mounting. **2** [A ride] transportation, drive, passage; see JOURNEY. **3** [Aid] encouragement, assistance, support; see HELP 1.

lift *v.* hoist, elevate, heave; see RAISE 1.

light[1] *n.* **1** [The condition opposed to darkness] radiance, brilliance, splendor, glare, brightness, clearness, lightness, incandescence, shine, luster, sheen, sparkle, glitter, glimmer, flood of light, blare, radiation, gleam.—*Ant.* DARKNESS, blackness, blankness. **2** [Emanations from a source of light] radiation, stream, blaze; see FLASH, RAY. **3** [A source of light] lamp, lantern, match, candle, sun, planet, star, moon, lightning, torch, flashlight, chandelier, spotlight, light bulb, halo, corona. **4** [Day] daylight, sun, sunrise; see DAY 1. **5** [Aspect] point of view, condition, standing; see CIRCUMSTANCES 2. —**in (the) light of** with knowledge of, because of, in view of; see CONSIDERING. —**see the light (of day)** **1** come into being, exist, begin; see BE. **2** comprehend, realize, be aware; see UNDERSTAND 1.

light[1,2] *a.* **1** [Having illumination] illuminated, radiant, luminous; see BRIGHT 1. **2** [Having color] vivid, rich, bright; see CLEAR 2. **3** [Having little content] superficial, slight, frivolous; see TRIVIAL, UNIMPORTANT. **4** [Having gaiety and spirit] lively, merry, animated; see ACTIVE. **5** [Having little weight] airy, fluffy, feathery, slender, downy, floating, lighter than air, light as air, floatable, light as a feather, frothy, buoyant, dainty, thin, sheer, insubstantial, ethereal, graceful, weightless.—*Ant.* HEAVY, ponderous, weighty. **6** [Digestible] slight, edible, moderate; see EATABLE. **7** [Small in quantity or number] wee, small, tiny, minute, thin, inadequate, insufficient, hardly enough, not much, hardly any, not many, slender, scanty, slight, sparse, fragmentary, fractional; see also FEW.—*Ant.* LARGE, great, immense. —**make light of** make fun of, mock, belittle; see NEGLECT 1, RIDICULE.

light[1,2] *v.* **1** [To provide light] illuminate, illumine, lighten, give light to, shine upon, furnish with light, light up, turn on the electricity, make visible, provide adequate illumination, switch on a light, floodlight, make bright, flood with light, fill with light; see also BRIGHTEN 1.—*Ant.* SHADE, put out, darken. **2** [To cause to ignite] set fire to, spark, kindle; see BURN, IGNITE. **3** [To become ignited] take fire, become inflamed, flame; see BURN, IGNITE. **4** [To come to rest from flight or travel] descend, come down, stop; see ARRIVE. —**light into*** rebuke, blame, assault; see SCOLD.

lighted *a.* **1** [Illuminated] brilliant, alight, glowing; see BRIGHT 1. **2** [Burning] blazing, flaming, aflame; see BURNING.

lighten[2] *v.* unburden, make lighter, reduce the load of, lessen the weight of, uplift, buoy up, alleviate, take off a load, remove, take from, pour out, throw overboard, reduce, cut down, put off, make buoyant, take off weight, eradicate, shift, change; see also UNLOAD.—*Ant.* LOAD, burden, overload.

lighter[1] *n.* cigarette lighter, igniter, flame; see LIGHT 3, MATCH 1.

lightheaded *a.* **1** [Giddy] inane, fickle, frivolous; see SILLY. **2** [Faint] tired, delirious, dizzy; see WEAK 1.

lighthearted *a.* gay, joyous, cheerful; see HAPPY.

lighting *n.* brilliance, flame, brightness; see FLASH, LIGHT 1, 3.

lightly *a.* delicately, airily, buoyantly, daintily, readily, gently, subtly, mildly, softly, tenderly, carefully, leniently, effortlessly, smoothly, blandly, sweetly, comfortably, restfully, peacefully, quietly; see also EASILY.—*Ant.* HEAVILY, ponderously, roughly.

lightness[1,2] *n.* **1** [Illumination] sparkle, blaze, shine; see FLASH, LIGHT 1, 3. **2** [The state of being light] airiness, etherealness, downiness, thinness, sheerness, fluffiness. **3** [Agility] balance, deftness, nimbleness; see AGILITY, GRACE 1.

lightning *n.* electrical discharge, bolt, streak of lightning, fireball, thunderbolt; see also ELECTRICITY.

likable *a.* agreeable, amiable, attractive; see FRIENDLY.

like[1] (līk) ***adj.*** ⟦OE *gelic*⟧ having the same characteristics; similar; equal —***adv.*** [Inf.] likely *[like* as not, he'll go*]* —***prep.*** **1** similar to **2** similarly to *[*to sing *like* a bird*]* **3** characteristic of *[*not *like* her to cry*]* **4** in the mood for *[*to feel *like* sleeping*]* **5** indicative of *[*it looks *like* rain*]* **6** as for example *[*fruit, *like* pears and plums*]* —***conj.*** [Inf.] **1** as *[*it's just *like* he said*]* **2** as if *[*it looks *like* he's late*]* —***n.*** an equal or counterpart *[*I've never met her *like]* —**nothing like** not at all like —**something like** almost like —**the like** others of the same kind —**the like** (or **likes**) **of** [Inf.] any person or thing like

like[2] (līk) ***vi.*** **liked, lik'ing** ⟦OE *lician*⟧ to be inclined *[*do as you *like]* —***vt.*** **1** to be pleased with; enjoy **2** to wish *[*I'd *like* to go*]* —***n.*** [*pl.*] preferences or tastes —**lik'er** ***n.***

-like (līk) *suffix* like, characteristic of *[homelike*, bull-*like]*

like·li·hood (līk'lē ho͝od') ***n.*** a being likely to happen; probability

like·ly (līk'lē) ***adj.*** **-li·er, -li·est** ⟦OE *geliclic*⟧ **1** credible *[*a *likely* cause*]* **2** reasonably to be expected *[likely* to rain*]* **3** suitable *[*a *likely* place to swim*]* —***adv.*** probably *[*she'll *likely* go*]*

like'-mind'ed ***adj.*** having the same ideas, plans, tastes, etc. —**like'-mind'ed·ness** ***n.***

lik·en (līk'ən) ***vt.*** to compare

like'ness ***n.*** **1** a being like **2** (the same) form **3** a copy, portrait, etc.

like'wise' ***adv.*** ⟦< *in like wise*⟧ **1** in the same manner **2** also; too

lik·ing (līk'iŋ) ***n.*** **1** fondness; affection **2** preference; taste; pleasure

li·lac (lī'lək, -läk', -lak') ***n.*** ⟦ult. < Pers *līlak*, bluish⟧ **1** a shrub with large clusters of tiny, fragrant flowers **2** pale purple —***adj.*** pale-purple

Lil·li·pu·tian (lil'ə pyo͞o'shən) ***adj.*** ⟦after *Lilliput*, place in J. Swift's *Gulliver's Travels*⟧ **1** tiny **2** petty

lilt (lilt) ***n.*** ⟦ME *lilten*, to sound⟧ a light, swingy rhythm or tune —**lilt'ing** ***adj.***

lil·y (lil'ē) ***n.***, *pl.* **lil'ies** ⟦< L *lilium*⟧ **1** a plant grown from a bulb and having typically trumpet-shaped flowers **2** its flower **3** any similar plant, as the waterlily —***adj.*** like a lily, as in whiteness, purity, etc.

lil'y-liv'ered ***adj.*** cowardly; timid

lily of the valley *pl.* **lilies of the valley** a low plant with a spike of white, bell-shaped flowers

Li·ma (lē'mə) capital of Peru: pop. 5,706,000

li·ma bean (lī'mə) ⟦after *Lima*, Peru⟧ **1** a bean with broad pods **2** its broad, flat, edible seed

limb (lim) ***n.*** ⟦OE lim⟧ **1** an arm, leg, or wing **2** a large branch of a tree —**out on a limb** [Inf.] in a precarious position —**limb'less** ***adj.***

lim·ber (lim'bər) ***adj.*** ⟦< ? prec.⟧ **1** easily bent; flexible **2** able to bend the body easily; supple —***vt.***, ***vi.*** to make or become limber

lim·bo (lim'bō) ***n.***, *pl. for 2 & 3* **-bos** ⟦< L (*in*) *limbo*, (on) the border⟧ **1** [*usually* **L-**] in some Christian theologies, the abode after death of unbaptized infants, etc. **2** an indefinite state **3** a condition of neglect, oblivion, etc.

Lim·burg·er (cheese) (lim'burg'ər) a semisoft cheese with a strong odor, originally from Limburg, Belgium

lime[1] (līm) ***n.*** ⟦OE *lim*⟧ a white substance, calcium oxide, obtained from limestone, etc. and used in mortar and cement and to neutralize acid soil —***vt.*** **limed, lim'ing** to treat with lime

lime[2] (līm) ***n.*** ⟦< Ar *līmah*⟧ a small, lemon-shaped, greenish-yellow citrus fruit with a juicy, sour pulp

lime'ade' (-ād') ***n.*** a drink made of lime juice, sugar, and water

lime'light' ***n.*** **1** a brilliant light created by the incandescence of lime, formerly used in theaters **2** a prominent position before the public

lim·er·ick (lim'ər ik) ***n.*** ⟦prob. after *Limerick*, Ir county⟧ a rhymed nonsense poem of five lines

lime'stone' ***n.*** rock consisting mainly of calcium carbonate

lim·i·nal (lim'i nəl) ***adj.*** at a boundary or transitional point between two conditions, stages, etc.

lim·it (lim'it) ***n.*** ⟦< L *limes*⟧ **1** the point, line, etc. where something ends; boundary **2** [*pl.*] bounds **3** the greatest amount allowed —***vt.*** to set a limit to; restrict —**lim'i·ta'tion** ***n.*** —**lim'it·er** ***n.*** —**lim'it·less** ***adj.***

lim'it·ed ***adj.*** **1** *a)* restricted *b)* narrow in scope *c)* brief **2** making a restricted number of stops: said of a train, bus, etc.

limn (lim) ***vt.*** **limned, limn·ing** (lim'iŋ, -niŋ) ⟦< L *illuminare*, to illuminate⟧ **1** to paint or draw **2** to describe

lim·nol·o·gy (lim näl'ə jē) ***n.*** ⟦< Gr *limnē*, marsh + -LOGY⟧ the science that deals with the physical, etc. properties and features of fresh waters, esp. lakes, etc.

lim·o (lim'ō) ***n.***, *pl.* **-os** [Inf.] LIMOUSINE

lim·ou·sine (lim'ə zēn') ***n.*** ⟦Fr, lit., cloak⟧ a large, luxurious sedan, esp. one driven by a chauffeur

limp (limp) ***vi.*** ⟦< OE *limpan*⟧ to walk with or as with a lame leg —***n.*** a lameness in walking —***adj.*** lacking firmness; wilted, flexible, etc. —**limp'ly** ***adv.*** —**limp'ness** ***n.***

THESAURUS

like[1] ***a.*** similar, same, alike, near, close, matching, equaling, not unlike, akin, related, analogous, twin, corresponding, allied, much the same, in the same form, of the same form, comparable, identical, parallel, homologous, consistent, approximating.—*Ant.* UNLIKE, different, unrelated.

like[1] ***prep.*** similar to, same as, near to, resembling, allied to, in the manner of; see also LIKE, *a.*

like[1] ***n.*** counterpart, resemblance, equal; see SIMILARITY. —**and the like** and so forth, and so on, similar kinds; see OTHERS. —**more like it*** acceptable, good, improved; see BETTER 1. —**nothing like** dissimilar, contrasting, opposed; see UNLIKE. —**something like** similar, resembling, akin; see LIKE *a.*

like[2] ***v.*** **1** [To enjoy] take delight in, relish, derive pleasure from, be keen on, be pleased by, revel in, indulge in, rejoice in, find agreeable, find appealing, be gratified by, take satisfaction in, savor, fancy, dote on, take an interest in, develop interest for, delight in, regard with favor, have a liking for, love, have a taste for, care to, get a kick out of*, be tickled by, eat up*, go in for*.—*Ant.* ENDURE, detest, dislike. **2** [To be fond of] have a fondness for, admire, take a fancy to, feel affectionately toward, adore, prize, esteem, hold dear, care about, care for, approve of, be pleased with, take to, have a soft spot in one's heart for, hanker for, dote on, have a yen for*, become attached to, be sweet on*, have eyes for*; see also LOVE 1.—*Ant.* HATE, disapprove, dislike. **3** [To be inclined] choose, feel disposed, wish, desire, have a preference for, prefer, fancy, feel like, incline toward, want.

liked ***a.*** popular, loved, admired; see BELOVED, HONORED.

likely ***a.*** **1** [Probable] apparent, probable, seeming, credible, possible, feasible, presumable, conceivable, reasonable, workable, attainable, achievable, believable, rational, thinkable, imaginable, ostensible, plausible, anticipated, expected, imminent.—*Ant.* IMPOSSIBLE, doubtful, questionable. **2** [Promising] suitable, apt, assuring; see FIT 1, HOPEFUL 2. **3** [Believable] plausible, true, acceptable; see CONVINCING. **4** [Apt] inclined, tending, disposed, predisposed, prone, liable, subject to, on the verge of, in the habit of, given to, in favor of, having a weakness for.

likeness ***n.*** **1** [Similarity] resemblance, correspondence, affinity; see SIMILARITY. **2** [A representation] portrait, image, effigy; see COPY, PICTURE 3.

likewise ***a.*** in like manner, furthermore, moreover; see BESIDES.

liking ***n.*** desire, fondness, devotion; see AFFECTION, LOVE 1.

limb ***n.*** **1** [A tree branch] arm, bough, offshoot; see BRANCH 2. **2** [A bodily appendage] part, wing, fin, flipper, member; see also ARM 1, LEG.

limber ***a.*** nimble, spry, deft; see AGILE, GRACEFUL 1.

limit ***n.*** **1** [The boundary] end, frontier, border; see BOUNDARY. **2** [The ultimate] utmost, farthest point, farthest reach, destination, goal, conclusion, extremity, eventuality, termination, absolute, the bitter end, deadline, cutoff point; see also END 4.—*Ant.* ORIGIN, start.

limit ***v.*** bound, confine, curb; see DEFINE 1, RESTRICT.

limitation ***n.*** **1** [The act of limiting] restriction, restraint, control; see ARREST, INTERFERENCE 1, INTERRUPTION, PREVENTION. **2** [That which limits] condition, definition, qualification, reservation, control, curb, check, injunction, bar, obstruction, stricture, taboo, inhibition, modification; see also ARREST, BARRIER, BOUNDARY, REFUSAL, RESTRAINT 2.—*Ant.* FREEDOM, latitude, liberty. **3** [A shortcoming] inadequacy, insufficiency, deficiency, shortcoming, weakness, want, blemish, defect, lack, imperfection, failing, frailty, flaw; see also FAULT 1.—*Ant.* STRENGTH, perfection, ability.

limited ***a.*** **1** [Restricted] confined, checked, curbed; see BOUND 1, 2, RESTRICTED. **2** [Having only moderate capacity] cramped, insufficient, short; see FAULTY, INADEQUATE, POOR 2, UNSATISFACTORY.

limitless ***a.*** unending, boundless, immeasurable; see ENDLESS, INFINITE, UNLIMITED.

limp ***a.*** pliant, soft, flaccid, flabby, supple, pliable, limber, relaxed, flexible, droopy, unsubstantial, bending

limp·et (lim′pit) ***n.*** ⟦< ML *lempreda*⟧ a mollusk that clings to rocks, etc.

lim·pid (lim′pid) ***adj.*** ⟦< L *limpidus*⟧ perfectly clear; transparent —**lim·pid′i·ty** ***n.***

lim·y (līm′ē) ***adj.*** **-i·er, -i·est** of, like, or containing lime

lin·age (līn′ij) ***n.*** the number of written or printed lines, as on a page

linch·pin (linch′pin′) ***n.*** ⟦OE *lynis*, linchpin⟧ **1** a pin in an axle to keep the wheel from coming off **2** anything holding together the parts of a whole

Lin·coln[1] (liŋ′kən), **Abraham** 1809-65; 16th president of the U.S. (1861-65): assassinated

Lin·coln[2] (liŋ′kən) capital of Nebraska, in the SE part: pop. 192,000

lin·den (lin′dən) ***n.*** ⟦OE⟧ a tree with heart-shaped leaves

line[1] (līn) ***n.*** ⟦< L *linea*, lit., linen thread⟧ **1** a cord, rope, wire, etc. **2** any wire, pipe, etc., or system of these, conducting fluid, electricity, etc. **3** a thin, threadlike mark **4** a border or boundary **5** a limit **6** outline; contour **7** a row of persons or things, as of printed letters across a page **8** a succession of persons or things **9** lineage **10** a transportation system of buses, ships, etc. **11** the course a moving thing takes **12** a course of conduct, action, explanation, etc. **13** a person's trade or occupation **14** a stock of goods **15** a short letter, note, etc. **16** [*pl.*] all the speeches of a character in a play **17** the forward combat position in warfare **18** *Football* the players in the forward row **19** *Math.* the path of a moving point —***vt.*** **lined, lin′ing 1** to mark with lines **2** to form a line along —**bring** (or **come**) **into line** to bring (or come) into alignment or conformity —**draw the** (or **a**) **line** to set a limit —**hold the line** to stand firm —**in line for** being considered for —**line up** to form, or bring into, a line

line[2] (līn) ***vt.*** **lined, lin′ing** ⟦< L *linum*, flax⟧ to put, or serve as, a lining in

lin·e·age (lin′ē ij) ***n.*** ⟦see LINE[1]⟧ **1** direct descent from an ancestor **2** ancestry; family

lin·e·al (lin′ē əl) ***adj.*** **1** in the direct line of descent from an ancestor **2** hereditary **3** of lines; linear

lin·e·a·ment (lin′ē ə mənt) ***n.*** ⟦< L *linea*, line⟧ a distinctive feature, esp. of the face: *usually used in pl.*

lin·e·ar (lin′ē ər) ***adj.*** **1** of, made of, or using a line or lines **2** logical and not complex **3** in relation to length only

line·back·er (līn′bak′ər) ***n.*** *Football* a defensive player directly behind the line

line drive a baseball hit in a straight line parallel to the ground

line′man (-mən) ***n.***, *pl.* **-men** (-mən) **1** one who sets up and repairs telephone lines, electric power lines, etc. **2** *Football* a player in the line

lin·en (lin′ən) ***n.*** ⟦< OE *lin*, flax: see LINE[2]⟧ **1** thread or cloth made of flax **2** [*often pl.*] sheets, cloths, etc. of linen, or of cotton, etc.

lin·er (līn′ər) ***n.*** **1** a steamship, airplane, etc. in regular service for a specific line **2** LINE DRIVE **3** a cosmetic applied in a fine line, as along the eyelid

lines·man (līnz′mən) ***n.***, *pl.* **-men** (-mən) **1** *Football* an official who marks the yardage gained or lost **2** *Tennis* an official who decides whether the ball is inside or outside the lines

line′up′ ***n.*** an arrangement of persons or things in or as in a line

-ling (liŋ) ⟦OE⟧ *suffix* **1** small *[duckling]* **2** unimportant or contemptible *[hireling]*

lin·ger (liŋ′gər) ***vi.*** ⟦OE *lengan*, to delay⟧ **1** to continue to stay, esp. through reluctance to leave **2** to loiter —**lin′ger·er** ***n.*** —**lin′ger·ing** ***adj.***

lin·ge·rie (län′zhə rā′) ***n.*** ⟦Fr⟧ women's underwear and nightclothes of silk, nylon, etc.

lin·go (liŋ′gō) ***n.***, *pl.* **-goes** ⟦< L *lingua*, tongue⟧ [Inf.] a dialect, jargon, etc. that one is not familiar with

lin·gua fran·ca (liŋ′gwə fraŋ′kə) a hybrid language used for communication by speakers of different languages

lin·gual (liŋ′gwəl) ***adj.*** ⟦see LANGUAGE⟧ of, or pronounced with, the tongue

lin·gui·ne (liŋ gwē′nē) ***n.*** ⟦< It *lingua*, tongue⟧ pasta in thin, flat, narrow strips: also sp. **lin·gui′ni**

lin·guist (liŋ′gwist) ***n.*** ⟦< L *lingua*, tongue⟧ a specialist in linguistics

lin·guis′tics (-gwis′tiks) ***n.*** **1** the science of language **2** the study of the structure, development, etc. of a particular language —**lin·guis′tic** ***adj.***

lin·i·ment (lin′ə mənt) ***n.*** ⟦< L *linere*, to smear⟧ a soothing medicated liquid for the skin

lin·ing (līn′iŋ) ***n.*** the material covering an inner surface

link (liŋk) ***n.*** ⟦< Scand⟧ **1** any of the loops making up a chain **2** *a)* a section of something like a chain *[a link of sausage]* *b)* an element in a series *[a weak link in the evidence]* **3** anything that connects *[a link with the past]* —***vt., vi.*** to join; connect

THESAURUS

readily, plastic, yielding, lax, slack, loose, flimsy.—*Ant.* STIFF, rigid, wooden.

limp ***v.*** walk lamely, proceed slowly, shuffle, lag, stagger, totter, dodder, hobble, falter.

line[1] ***n.*** **1** [A row] array, list, rank, file, catalog, order, group, arrangement, ridge, range, seam, series, sequence, succession, procession, chain, train, string, column, formation, division, queue, channel, furrow, scar, trench, groove, mark, thread, fissure, crack, straight line. **2** [A mark] outline, tracing, stroke; see MARK 1. **3** [A rope] string, cable, towline; see ROPE, WIRE 1. **4** [Lineal descent] ancestry, pedigree, lineage; see FAMILY, HEREDITY. **5** [A borderline] border, mark, limit; see BOUNDARY, EDGE 1. **6** [Matter printed in a row of type] row, words, letters; see COPY. **7** [A military front] disposition, formation, position; see FRONT 2. **8** [A transportation system] trunk line, bus line, steamship line, railroad line, airline. **9** [Goods handled by a given company] wares, merchandise, produce; see MATERIAL 2. **10** [*Talk intended to influence another] rhetoric, lecture, propaganda, advertising; see also CONVERSATION, SPEECH 3. —**all along the line** at every turn, completely, constantly; see EVERYWHERE. —**bring** (or **come** or **get**) **into line** align, make uniform, regulate; see ORDER 3. —**draw the** (or **a**) **line** set a limit, prohibit, restrain; see RESTRICT. —**get a line on*** find out about, investigate, expose; see DISCOVER. —**in line** agreeing, conforming, uniform; see REGULAR 3. —**in line for** being considered for, ready, thought about; see CONSIDERED. —**in line with** similar to, in accord with, consonant; see HARMONIOUS 2, FIT 1. —**lay** (or **put**) **it on the line** speak frankly, define, clarify; see EXPLAIN. —**on a line** straight, even, level; see DIRECT 1, STRAIGHT 1. —**out of line** misdirected, not uniform, not even; see IRREGULAR 1, 4. —**read between the lines** read meaning into, discover a hidden meaning, figure out; see UNDERSTAND 1.

line[1,2] ***v.*** **1** [To provide a lining] interline, stuff, wad, panel, pad, quilt, fill. **2** [To provide lines] trace, delineate, outline; see DRAW 2, MARK 1. **3** [To be in a line] border, edge, outline, rim, bound, fall in, fall into line, fringe, follow. **4** [To arrange in a line] align, queue, marshal, arrange, range, array, group, set out, bring into a line with others, fix, place, draw up; see also LINE UP.—*Ant.* SCATTER, disarrange, disperse. —**line up** fall in, form in line, take one's proper place in line, queue up, form ranks, get in line, get set, get into formation.

linear ***a.*** long, elongated, successive; see DIRECT 1, STRAIGHT 1.

lined ***a.*** interlined, stuffed, coated; see FULL 1.

linen ***n.*** material, sheeting, linen cloth; see GOODS. *Articles called linens include the following:* handkerchiefs, towels, bedding, sheets, pillowcases, underwear, comforters, dishtowels, tablecloths, napkins, doilies.

lineup ***n.*** starters, entrants, first string; see LIST.

linger ***v.*** tarry, saunter, lag, hesitate, trail, vacillate, delay, plod, trudge, falter, dawdle, procrastinate, stay, shuffle, crawl, loll, take one's time, wait, putter, be tardy, dillydally, sit around, hang around*; see also LOITER.—*Ant.* HURRY, hasten, speed.

lingerie ***n.*** women's underwear, undergarments, unmentionables*; see CLOTHES, UNDERWEAR.

linguist ***n.*** student of language, language expert, philologist, lexicographer, polyglot, translator, grammarian, etymologist; see also SCIENTIST.

linguistics ***n.*** grammar, semantics, phonology, etymology, prosody, morphology, syntax, philology; see also GRAMMAR, LANGUAGE 2.

liniment ***n.*** ointment, cream, lotion; see MEDICINE 2, SALVE.

lining ***n.*** interlining, inner coating, inner surface, filling, quilting, stuffing, wadding, padding, sheathing, covering, wall, reinforcement, partition, paneling.

link ***n.*** ring, loop, coupling, coupler, section, seam, weld, bond, hitch, intersection, copula, connective, connection, fastening, splice, knot, interconnection, junction, joining, ligature, articulation; see also JOINT 1.

link ***v.*** connect, associate, combine; see JOIN 1.

linked ***a.*** connected, combined, associated; see JOINED.

linking ***a.*** combining, joining, associating; see CONNECTING.

link′age *n.* **1** a linking **2** a series or system of links
linking verb a verb that functions chiefly as a connection between a subject and a predicate (Ex.: *be, seem, become*)
links (liŋks) *pl.n.* ⟦OE *hlinc*, a slope⟧ GOLF COURSE
link′up′ *n.* a linking together
Lin·nae·us (li nē′əs), **Car·o·lus** (kar′ə ləs) 1707-78; Swed. botanist
lin·net (lin′it) *n.* ⟦< L *linum*, flax: it feeds on flaxseed⟧ a small finch of either an Old World or New World species
li·no·le·um (li nō′lē əm) *n.* ⟦< L *linum*, flax + *oleum*, oil⟧ **1** a smooth, washable floor covering, formerly much used, esp. in kitchens **2** any floor covering like linoleum
lin·seed (lin′sēd′) *n.* ⟦OE *linsæd*⟧ the seed of flax; flaxseed
linseed oil a yellowish oil extracted from flaxseed, used in oil paints, etc.
lint (lint) *n.* ⟦< L *linum*, flax⟧ bits of thread, fluff, etc. from cloth or yarn —**lint′y**, **-i·er**, **-i·est**, *adj.*
lin·tel (lin′təl) *n.* ⟦ult. < L *limen*, threshold⟧ the horizontal crosspiece over a door, window, etc.
li·on (lī′ən) *n.* ⟦< Gr *leōn*⟧ **1** a large, powerful cat, found in Africa and SW Asia **2** a person of great courage or strength **3** a celebrity —**li′on·ess** *fem.n.*
li′on·heart′ed *adj.* very brave
li·on·ize (lī′ə nīz′) *vt.* **-ized′**, **-iz′ing** to treat as a celebrity
lip (lip) *n.* ⟦OE *lippa*⟧ **1** either of the two fleshy folds forming the edges of the mouth **2** anything like a lip, as the rim of a pitcher **3** [Slang] insolent talk —*adj.* spoken, but insincere *[lip* worship*]* —**keep a stiff upper lip** [Inf.] to bear pain or distress bravely
lip·id (lip′id) *n.* ⟦< Gr *lipos*, fat⟧ any of a group of organic compounds consisting of the fats and other similar substances: also **lip·ide** (lip′īd′, -id)
lip·o·suc·tion (lip′ō suk′shən) *n.* ⟦< LIPID + SUCTION⟧ surgical removal of fatty tissue under the skin by means of suction
lip·py (lip′ē) *adj.* **-pi·er**, **-pi·est** [Slang] impudent; insolent —**lip′pi·ness** *n.*
lip reading the act or skill of recognizing words by watching a speaker's lips: it is taught esp. to the deaf —**lip′-read′** *vt., vi.* —**lip reader**
lip service insincere words of support, etc.
lip′stick′ *n.* a small stick of cosmetic paste for coloring the lips
lip′-sync′ or **lip′-synch′** (-siŋk′) *vt., vi.* ⟦< *lip sync(hronization)*⟧ to move the lips silently so as to seem to be speaking or singing (something recorded)
liq·ue·fy (lik′wi fī′) *vt., vi.* **-fied′**, **-fy′ing** ⟦< L *liquere*, be liquid + *facere*, make⟧ to change into a liquid —**liq′ue·fac′tion** (-fak′shən) *n.*
li·queur (li kʉr′, -koor′) *n.* ⟦Fr⟧ a sweet, syrupy, flavored alcoholic liquor
liq·uid (lik′wid) *adj.* ⟦< L *liquidus*⟧ **1** readily flowing; fluid **2** clear; limpid **3** flowing smoothly and musically, as verse **4** readily convertible into cash —*n.* a substance that, unlike a solid, flows readily but, unlike a gas, does not expand indefinitely —**liq·uid′i·ty** *n.*
liq·ui·date (lik′wi dāt′) *vt.* **-dat′ed**, **-dat′ing** ⟦see prec.⟧ **1** to settle the accounts of (a business) by apportioning assets and debts **2** to pay (a debt) **3** to convert into cash **4** to get rid of, as by killing —**liq′ui·da′tion** *n.* —**liq′ui·da′tor** *n.*
liq′uid·ize′ (-wid īz′) *vt.* **-ized′**, **-iz′ing** to cause to become liquid
liq·ui·fy (lik′wi fī′) *vt., vi.* **-fied′**, **-fy′ing** *alt. sp. of* LIQUEFY
liq·uor (lik′ər) *n.* ⟦L⟧ **1** any liquid **2** an alcoholic drink, esp. a distilled drink, as whiskey or rum
li·ra (lir′ə) *n., pl.* **li′re** (-ā) or **li′ras** ⟦< L *libra*, a pound⟧ the monetary unit of Italy
Lis·bon (liz′bən) capital of Portugal: pop. 817,000
lisle (līl) *n.* ⟦after *Lisle* (now *Lille*), city in France⟧ **1** a fine, hard, extra-strong cotton thread **2** a fabric woven of lisle
lisp (lisp) *vi.* ⟦< OE *wlisp*, a lisping⟧ **1** to substitute the sounds (th) and (*th*) for the sounds of *s* and *z*, respectively **2** to speak imperfectly —*vt.* to utter with a lisp —*n.* the act or sound of lisping
lis·some or **lis·som** (lis′əm) *adj.* ⟦< *lithesome*⟧ lithe, supple, limber, agile, etc.
list[1] (list) *n.* ⟦< OE *liste*, border⟧ a series of names, numbers, etc. set forth in order —*vt.* to enter in a list, directory, etc.
list[2] (list) *vi.* ⟦prob. ult. < OE *lust*, desire⟧ to tilt to one side: said of a ship, etc. —*n.* such a tilting
lis·ten (lis′ən) *vi.* ⟦< OE *hlysnan*⟧ **1** to make a conscious effort to hear **2** to give heed; take advice —**lis′ten·er** *n.*
list′ing *n.* **1** the making of a list **2** an entry in a list
list′less (-lis) *adj.* ⟦< OE *lust*, desire + -LESS⟧ indifferent because of illness, dejection, etc.; languid —**list′less·ly** *adv.* —**list′less·ness** *n.*
list price retail price as given in a list or catalog
lists (lists) *pl.n.* ⟦< ME *liste*, border⟧ a fenced area in which knights jousted
Liszt (list), **Franz** (fränts) 1811-86; Hung. composer & pianist
lit[1] (lit) *vt., vi. alt. pt. & pp. of* LIGHT[1]
lit[2] *abbrev.* **1** liter(s) **2** literally **3** literary **4** literature
lit·a·ny (lit′'n ē) *n., pl.* **-nies** ⟦< Gr *litē*, a request⟧ a series of fixed invocations and responses, used as a prayer
li·tchi (lē′chē′) *n.* ⟦< Chin⟧ the raisinlike fruit of a Chinese evergreen tree, enclosed in a papery shell
lite (līt) *adj. informal sp. of* LIGHT[2] (*adj.* 8)
li·ter (lēt′ər) *n.* ⟦< Gr *litra*, a pound⟧ the basic metric unit of volume, equal to 1 cubic decimeter or 61.0237 cubic inches: Brit. sp. **li′tre**
lit·er·a·cy (lit′ər ə sē) *n.* the ability to read and write
lit·er·al (lit′ər əl) *adj.* ⟦< L *littera*, a letter⟧ **1** following exactly the wording of the original *[a literal* translation*]* **2** in a basic or strict sense *[the literal* meaning*]* **3** prosaic; matter-of-fact *[a literal* mind*]* **4** restricted to the facts *[the literal* truth*]* —**lit′er·al·ly** *adv.*
lit·er·ar·y (lit′ər er′ē) *adj.* **1** of or having to do with literature or books **2** familiar with or versed in literature

THESAURUS

lint *n.* thread, fluff, fiber; see DUST.
lion *n.* king of beasts, king of the jungle, lioness; see ANIMAL, CAT 2.
lip *n.* edge of the mouth, liplike part, labium; see MOUTH 1. —**keep a stiff upper lip*** take heart, be encouraged, remain strong; see ENDURE 2.
liquid *a.* **1** [In a state neither solid nor gaseous] watery, molten, damp, moist, aqueous, liquefied, dissolved, melted, thawed; see also FLUID, WET 1. **2** [Having qualities suggestive of fluids] flowing, running, splashing, thin, moving, viscous, sappy, diluting; see also FLUID, JUICY.
liquid *n.* liquor, fluid, juice, sap, extract, secretion, flow; see also WATER 1.
liquidate *v.* **1** [To change into money] sell, convert, change; see EXCHANGE. **2** [To abolish] annul, cancel, destroy; see ABOLISH, ELIMINATE.
liquor *n.* whiskey, booze*, alcohol; see COCKTAIL, DRINK 2.
lisp *v.* mispronounce, sputter, stutter; see UTTER.
lissome *a.* lithe, supple, flexible; see AGILE, FLEXIBLE.
list[1] *n.* roll, record, schedule, agenda, arrangement, enrollment, slate, draft, panel, brief, invoice, register, memorandum, inventory, account, outline, tally, bulletin, directory, roster, subscribers, subscription list, muster, poll, ballot, table of contents, menu, dictionary, thesaurus, glossary, lexicon, vocabulary, docket.
list[1,2] *v.* **1** [To enter in a list] set down, arrange, bill, catalogue, schedule, enter, note, add, place, file, record, insert, enroll, register, tally, inventory, index, draft, enumerate, tabulate, book, take a census, poll, slate, keep count of, run down, call the roll.—*Ant.* REMOVE, wipe out, obliterate. **2** [To lean] pitch, slant, incline; see LEAN 1.
listed *a.* filed, cataloged, indexed; see RECORDED.
listen *v.* attend, keep one's ears open, be attentive, listen in, pick up, overhear, monitor, tap, give attention to, give ear, listen to, pay attention, hear, tune in*, lend an ear*, strain one's ears*.—*Ant.* IGNORE, be deaf to, turn a deaf ear to.
listener *n.* spy, student, monitor, spectator, audience, eavesdropper, witness.
listening *a.* hearing, paying attention, interested, involved, attentive, heeding, overhearing, straining to hear, receiving, lending an ear*.—*Ant.* INDIFFERENT, giving no attention, inattentive.
listless *a.* passive, sluggish, lifeless; see INDIFFERENT, SLOW 2.
lit[1] *a.* illuminated, resplendent, lighted; see BRIGHT 1, BURNING.
literacy *n.* scholarship, ability to read and write, verbal competence; see EDUCATION 1, KNOWLEDGE 1.
literal *a.* true, verbatim, exact; see ACCURATE 2.
literally *a.* really, actually, precisely, exactly, completely, indisputably, correctly, strictly, to the letter, faithfully, rigorously, straight, unmistakably, truly, not metaphorically, not figuratively, word for word, verbatim, letter by letter.—*Ant.* FREELY, figuratively, fancifully.
literary *a.* scholarly, bookish, literate; see LEARNED 1.

lit·er·ate (lit′ər it) ***adj.*** ⟦< L *littera*, a letter⟧ **1** able to read and write **2** well-educated —***n.*** a literate person

lit·e·ra·ti (lit′ə rät′ē) ***pl.n.*** ⟦It < L *litterati*: see prec.⟧ writers, scholars, etc.

lit·er·a·ture (lit′ər ə chər′) ***n.*** ⟦< L *littera*, a letter⟧ **1** *a)* all writings in prose or verse of an imaginative character *b)* all such writings having permanent value, excellence of form, etc. *c)* all the writings of a particular time, country, etc. *d)* all the writings on a particular subject **2** any printed matter

lithe (līth) ***adj.*** **lith′er, lith′est** ⟦OE *lithe*, soft⟧ bending easily; flexible; supple: also **lithe′some** (-səm)

lith·i·um (lith′ē əm) ***n.*** ⟦< Gr *lithos*, stone⟧ a soft, silver-white, chemical element

lithium carbonate a white, powdery salt, used in making glass, dyes, etc. and in treating manic-depressive disorders

lith·o·graph (lith′ə graf′) ***n.*** a print made by lithography —***vi., vt.*** to make (prints or copies) by this process —**li·thog·ra·pher** (li thäg′rə fər) ***n.***

li·thog·ra·phy (li thäg′rə fē) ***n.*** ⟦< Gr *lithos*, stone + -GRAPHY⟧ printing from a flat stone or metal plate, parts of which have been treated to repel ink —**lith·o·graph·ic** (lith′ə graf′ik) ***adj.***

lith·o·sphere (lith′ō sfir′) ***n.*** ⟦< Gr *lithos*, stone + *sphaira*, sphere⟧ the solid, rocky part of the earth; earth's crust

Lith·u·a·ni·a (lith′o͞o ā′nē ə) country in N Europe: formerly a republic of the U.S.S.R.: 25,170 sq. mi.; pop. 3,675,000 —**Lith′u·a′ni·an** ***adj., n.***

lit·i·gant (lit′i gənt) ***n.*** ⟦see fol.⟧ a party to a lawsuit

lit′i·gate′ (-gāt′) ***vt., vi.*** **-gat′ed, -gat′ing** ⟦< L *lis*, dispute + *agere*, do⟧ to contest in a lawsuit —**lit′i·ga′tion** ***n.*** —**lit′i·ga′tor** ***n.***

li·ti·gious (li tij′əs) ***adj.*** ⟦see prec.⟧ **1** *a)* given to carrying on lawsuits *b)* quarrelsome **2** of lawsuits —**li·ti′gious·ness** ***n.***

lit·mus (lit′məs) ***n.*** ⟦< ON *litr*, color + *mosi*, moss⟧ a purple coloring matter obtained from various lichens: paper treated with it (**litmus paper**) turns blue in bases and red in acids

litmus test a test in which a single factor determines the finding

LittD or **Litt.D.** *abbrev.* Doctor of Letters

lit·ter (lit′ər) ***n.*** ⟦< L *lectus*, a couch⟧ **1** a framework enclosing a couch on which a person can be carried **2** a stretcher for carrying the sick or wounded **3** straw, hay, etc. used as bedding for animals **4** granular clay used in an indoor receptacle (**litter box**) to absorb cat waste **5** the young borne at one time by a dog, cat, etc. **6** things lying about in disorder, esp. bits of rubbish —***vt.*** **1** to make untidy **2** to scatter about carelessly

lit′ter·bug′ (-bug′) ***n.*** [Inf.] one who litters public places with rubbish, etc.

lit·tle (lit′'l) ***adj.*** **lit′tler** or **less** or **less′er, lit′tlest** or **least** ⟦OE *lytel*⟧ **1** small in size, amount, degree, etc. **2** short in duration; brief **3** small in importance or power *[the rights of the little man]* **4** narrow-minded *[a little mind]* —***adv.*** **less, least** **1** slightly; not much **2** not in the least —***n.*** a small amount, degree, etc. —**little by little** gradually — **make** (or **think**) **little of** to consider as not very important —**lit′tle·ness** ***n.***

Little Dipper, the a dipper-shaped group of stars containing the North Star

Little Rock capital of Arkansas: pop. 176,000

lit·to·ral (lit′ə rəl) ***adj.*** ⟦< L *litus*, seashore⟧ of or along the shore

lit·ur·gy (lit′ər jē) ***n.***, *pl.* **-gies** ⟦ult. < Gr *leōs, laos*, people + *ergon*, work⟧ prescribed ritual for public worship —**li·tur·gi·cal** (lə tur′ji kəl) ***adj.***

liv·a·ble (liv′ə bəl) ***adj.*** **1** fit or pleasant to live in *[a livable house]* **2** endurable: said as of a way of life Also **live′a·ble**

live[1] (liv) ***vi.*** **lived, liv′ing** ⟦OE *libban*⟧ **1** to have life **2** *a)* to remain alive *b)* to endure **3** to pass one's life in a specified manner **4** to enjoy life *[to know how to live]* **5** to feed *[to live on fruit]* **6** to reside —***vt.*** **1** to carry out in one's life *[to live one's faith]* **2** to spend; pass *[to live a useful life]* —**live down** to live so as to wipe out the shame of (a misdeed, etc.) —**live up to** to live or act in accordance with (one's ideals, etc.)

live[2] (līv) ***adj.*** ⟦< ALIVE⟧ **1** having life **2** of present interest *[a live issue]* **3** still burning *[a live spark]* **4** unexploded *[a live shell]* **5** carrying electrical current *[a live wire]* **6** *a)* in person *b)* broadcast, recorded, etc. during the actual performance **7** *Sports* in play *[a live ball]*

live·bear·er (līv′ber′ər) ***n.*** any of various small, tropical, American, freshwater fishes, as the guppy and molly

-lived (līvd, livd) *combining form* having (a specified kind of) life *[long-lived]*

live′-in′ ***adj.*** living in someone's residence as a domestic, lover, etc.

live·li·hood (līv′lē ho͝od′) ***n.*** ⟦< OE *lif*, life + *-lad*, course⟧ means of living or of supporting life

live·long (liv′lôŋ′) ***adj.*** ⟦ME *lefe longe*, lit., lief long: *lief* is merely intens.⟧ long in passing; whole *[the livelong day]*

live·ly (līv′lē) ***adj.*** **-li·er, -li·est** ⟦OE *liflic*⟧ **1** full of life; vigorous **2** full of spirit; exciting **3** animated, cheerful, vivacious, etc. **4** vivid; keen **5** bounding back with great resilience *[a lively ball]* —**live′li·ness** ***n.***

liv·en (līv′ən) ***vt., vi.*** to make or become lively; cheer: often with *up*

liv·er (liv′ər) ***n.*** ⟦OE *lifer*⟧ **1** the largest glandular organ in vertebrate animals: it secretes bile and is important in metabolism **2** the liver of cattle, fowl, etc., used as food

Liv·er·pool (liv′ər po͞ol′) seaport in NW England: county district pop. 452,000

liv·er·wurst (liv′ər wurst′) ***n.*** ⟦< Ger *leber*, liver + *wurst*, sausage⟧ a sausage containing ground liver

liv·er·y (liv′ər ē) ***n.***, *pl.* **-er·ies** ⟦ME, gift of clothes to a servant⟧ **1** an identifying uniform as of a servant **2** *a)* the care and feeding of horses for a fee *b)* the keeping

THESAURUS

literate ***a.*** informed, scholarly, able to read and write; see EDUCATED, INTELLIGENT, LEARNED 1.

literature ***n.*** **1** [Artistic production in language] letters, lore, belles-lettres, literary works, literary productions, the humanities, classics, books, writings. **2** [Written matter treating a given subject] article, discourse, composition, treatise, dissertation, thesis, paper, treatment, essay, discussion, research, observation, comment, critique, findings, abstract, report, summary, précis.

litter ***n.*** **1** [Trash] rubbish, debris, waste; see TRASH 1. **2** [The young of certain animals] piglets, puppies, kittens; see OFFSPRING.

litter ***v.*** scatter, discard, spread; see DIRTY.

litterbug ***n.*** slob*, pig, polluter; see SLOB.

little ***a.*** **1** [Small in size] minute, diminutive, small, tiny, wee, undersized, stubby, truncated, stunted, limited, cramped, imperceptible, light, slight, microscopic, short, runty, shriveled, toy, miniature, puny, pygmy, dwarfed, bantam, half pint*, pocket-sized, pint-sized.—*Ant.* LARGE, big, huge. **2** [Inadequate] wanting, deficient, insufficient; see INADEQUATE. **3** [Few in number] scarce, not many, hardly any; see FEW. **4** [Brief] concise, succinct, abrupt; see SHORT 2. **5** [Small in importance] trifling, shallow, petty, superficial, frivolous, irrelevant, meaningless, slight, paltry, insignificant, inconsiderable; see also TRIVIAL, UNIMPORTANT. **6** [Small in character] base, weak, shallow, small-minded, prejudiced, bigoted, low, sneaky, mean, petty; see also VULGAR. **7** [Weak] stunted, runty, undersized; see WEAK 1. —**make little of** make fun of, mock, abuse; see RIDICULE.

little ***n.*** some, a few, trifle; see BIT 1.

livable ***a.*** habitable, endurable, inhabitable; see BEARABLE, COMFORTABLE 2.

live[1] ***v.*** **1** [To have life] exist, continue, subsist, prevail, survive, breathe, be alive; see also BE 1. **2** [To enjoy life] relish, savor, experience, love, delight in, make every moment count, experience life to the fullest, live it up*, make the most of life, have a meaningful existence, take pleasure in, get a great deal from life.—*Ant.* SUFFER, endure pain, be discouraged. **3** [To dwell] live in, inhabit, settle; see DWELL. **4** [To gain subsistence] earn a living, support oneself, earn money, get ahead, provide for one's needs, make ends meet, subsist, maintain oneself; see also SURVIVE 1. **5** [To persist in human memory] remain, be remembered, last; see ENDURE 1. —**live and let live** be tolerant, accept, ignore; see ALLOW. —**live at** inhabit, reside, occupy; see DWELL. —**live down** overcome, survive, outgrow; see ENDURE 2. —**live on** be supported, earn, subsist on; see LIVE 4. —**live up to** meet expectations, do well, give satisfaction; see SATISFY 3. —**where one lives*** personally, in a vulnerable area, at one's heart; see PERSONALLY 2.

live[2] ***a.*** **1** [Active] energetic, lively, dynamic; see ACTIVE. **2** [Not dead] aware, conscious, existing; see ALIVE. **3** [Not taped or filmed] broadcast direct, unrehearsed, on stage; see REAL 2.

livelihood ***n.*** career, occupation, job; see PROFESSION 1.

lively ***a.*** vigorous, brisk, industrious; see ACTIVE.

of horses or vehicles for hire *c)* a stable for this (usually **livery stable**) **3** a place where boats can be rented

lives (līvz) ***n.*** *pl. of* LIFE

live·stock (līv′stäk′) ***n.*** domestic animals raised for use and sale

liv·id (liv′id) ***adj.*** ⟦< L *lividus*⟧ **1** discolored by a bruise; black-and-blue **2** grayish-blue: sometimes taken to mean pale or red *[livid* with rage*]* **3** enraged

liv·ing (liv′iŋ) ***adj.*** **1** alive; having life **2** in active operation or use *[*a *living* institution*]* **3** of persons alive *[*within *living* memory*]* **4** true; lifelike **5** of life *[living* conditions*]* —***n.*** **1** a being alive **2** livelihood **3** manner of existence —**the living** those that are still alive

living room a room in a home, with sofas, chairs, etc., used for social activities, entertaining guests, etc.

living wage a wage sufficient to maintain a reasonable level of comfort

living will a document directing that the signer's life not be artificially supported during a terminal illness

liz·ard (liz′ərd) ***n.*** ⟦< L *lacerta*⟧ any of various slender, scaly reptiles with four legs and a tail, as the chameleon and iguana

ll *abbrev.* lines

LL *abbrev.* Late Latin

-'ll (əl) *suffix* will or shall: used in contractions *[she'll* sing*]*

lla·ma (lä′mə) ***n.*** ⟦Sp < AmInd (Peru)⟧ a South American beast of burden related to the camel but smaller

lla·no (lä′nō) ***n.***, *pl.* **-nos** ⟦Sp < L *planus*, plain⟧ any of the level, grassy plains of Spanish America

LLB or **LL.B.** *abbrev.* Bachelor of Laws

LLD or **LL.D.** *abbrev.* Doctor of Laws

lo (lō) ***interj.*** ⟦OE *la*⟧ look! see!

load (lōd) ***n.*** ⟦< OE *lad*, a course, journey⟧ **1** an amount carried at one time **2** something borne with difficulty; burden **3** [*often pl.*] [Inf.] a great amount or number **4** *Finance* an amount added to the price of mutual fund shares to cover costs, etc. —***vt.*** **1** to put (a load) into or upon (a carrier) **2** to burden; oppress **3** to supply in large quantities **4** to put a charge of ammunition into (a firearm) **5** *Comput.* to transfer (a program or data) into main memory from a disk, etc. —**load′er** ***n.*** —**load′ing** ***n.***

load·star (lōd′stär′) ***n.*** LODESTAR

load·stone (lōd′stōn′) ***n.*** LODESTONE

loaf[1] (lōf) ***n.***, *pl.* **loaves** (lōvz) ⟦OE *hlaf*⟧ **1** a portion of bread baked in one piece **2** any food baked in this shape

loaf[2] (lōf) ***vi.*** ⟦prob. < fol.⟧ to spend time idly; idle, dawdle, etc.

loaf′er ***n.*** ⟦prob. < Ger *landläufer*, a vagabond⟧ one who loafs; idler

Loaf′er *trademark for* a casual shoe like a moccasin —***n.*** [l-] a shoe similar to this

loam (lōm) ***n.*** ⟦OE *lam*⟧ a rich soil, esp. one composed of clay, sand, and some organic matter —**loam′y, -i·er, -i·est,** ***adj.***

loan (lōn) ***n.*** ⟦< ON *lān*⟧ **1** the act of lending **2** something lent, esp. money at interest —***vt.***, ***vi.*** to lend

loan′er ***n.*** **1** one who loans something **2** an automobile, TV, etc. lent in place of one left for repair

loan shark [Inf.] one who lends money at illegal rates of interest

loan′word′ ***n.*** a word of one language taken into and used in another

loath (lōth) ***adj.*** ⟦< OE *lath*, hostile⟧ reluctant *[*to be *loath* to depart*]*

loathe (lō*th*) ***vt.*** **loathed, loath′ing** ⟦< OE *lathian*, be hateful⟧ to feel intense dislike or disgust for; abhor

loath′ing ***n.*** intense dislike, disgust, or hatred; abhorrence

loath′some ***adj.*** causing loathing; disgusting

loaves (lōvz) ***n.*** *pl. of* LOAF[1]

lob (läb) ***vt.***, ***vi.*** **lobbed, lob′bing** ⟦< ME *lobbe*, heavy⟧ to toss or hit (a ball) in a high curve —**lob′ber** ***n.***

lob·by (läb′ē) ***n.***, *pl.* **-bies** ⟦LL *lobia*⟧ **1** an entrance hall, as of a hotel or theater **2** a group of lobbyists representing the same interest —***vi.*** **-bied, -by·ing** to act as a lobbyist

lob′by·ist ***n.*** a person, acting on behalf of a group, who tries to get legislators to support certain measures

lobe (lōb) ***n.*** ⟦< Gr *lobos*⟧ a rounded projecting part, as the lower part of the ear or any of the divisions of the lung

lo·bot·o·my (lō bät′ə mē) ***n.***, *pl.* **-mies** ⟦< prec. + -TOMY⟧ a surgical incision into a lobe of the brain: now rarely used as a treatment

lob·ster (läb′stər) ***n.*** ⟦< OE *loppe*, spider + *-estre*, -ster⟧ an edible sea crustacean usually with four pairs of legs and a pair of large pincers

lobster tail the tail of any of various crustaceans, prepared as food

lo·cal (lō′kəl) ***adj.*** ⟦< L *locus*, a place⟧ **1** of, characteristic of, or confined to a particular place **2** of or for a particular part of the body *[local* anesthesia*]* **3** making all stops along its run *[*a *local* bus*]* —***n.*** **1** a local train, bus, etc. **2** a branch, as of a labor union —**lo′cal·ly** ***adv.***

lo·cale (lō kal′) ***n.*** ⟦OFr *local*⟧ a place or locality, esp. with reference to events, etc. associated with it

lo·cal·i·ty (lō kal′ə tē) ***n.***, *pl.* **-ties** a place; district; neighborhood

lo·cal·ize (lō′kəl īz′) ***vt.*** **-ized′, -iz′ing** to limit, confine, or trace to a particular place —**lo′cal·i·za′tion** ***n.***

lo·cate (lō′kāt′, lō kāt′) ***vt.*** **-cat′ed, -cat′ing** ⟦< L *locus*, a place⟧ **1** to establish in a certain place *[*offices *located*

THESAURUS

livestock ***n.*** cows, sheep, domestic animals; see CATTLE, HERD.

living ***a.*** **1** [Alive] existing, breathing, having being; see ALIVE. **2** [Vigorous] awake, brisk, alert; see ACTIVE.

living ***n.*** **1** [A means of survival] existence, sustenance, maintenance; see SUBSISTENCE 2. **2** [Those not dead; *usually used with "the"*] the world, everyone, people; see ANIMAL, PERSON, PLANT.

living room ***n.*** lounge, front room, den; see ROOM 2.

load ***n.*** **1** [A physical burden] weight, encumbrance, truckload, carload, wagonload, shipload, cargo, haul, bale, charge, pack, mass, payload, shipment, contents, capacity, bundle.—*Ant.* LIGHTNESS, buoyancy, weightlessness. **2** [Responsibility] charge, obligation, trust; see DUTY 1. **3** [A charge; *said especially of firearms*] shot, clip, round; see AMMUNITION. **4** [A measure] quantity, portion, amount; see MEASUREMENT 2, QUANTITY.

load ***v.*** **1** [To place a load] arrange, stow away, store, burden, stuff, put goods in, put goods on, containerize, pile, heap, fill, cram, put aboard, stack, pour in, take on cargo; see also PACK 1.—*Ant.* UNLOAD, unpack, take off cargo. **2** [To overload] encumber, saddle, weigh down; see BURDEN. **3** [To charge; *said especially of firearms*] insert a clip, ready, make ready to fire; see SHOOT 1.

loaded ***a.*** **1** [Supplied with a load] laden, burdened, weighted; see FULL 1. **2** [Ready to discharge; *said of firearms*] charged, primed, ready to shoot. **3** [*Intoxicated] inebriated, drunken, under the influence; see DRUNK.

loaf[1] ***n.*** roll, bun, pastry; see BREAD, CAKE 2.

loaf[2] ***v.*** idle, trifle, lounge, kill time, be inactive, be slothful, be lazy, take it easy, not lift a finger, putter, rest, dally, let down, slack off, vegetate, loll, malinger, drift, relax, slack, shirk, waste time, slow down, evade, dillydally, stand around, dream, goof off, goof around, goldbrick*, bum*, stall, piddle.

loafer ***n.*** idler, lounger, lazy person, ne'er-do-well, good-for-nothing, lazybones, malingerer, waster, slacker, shirker, wanderer, bum*, goldbrick*, deadbeat*.

loafing ***a.*** careless, apathetic, shirking; see LAZY 1.

loan ***n.*** lending, advance, giving credit, mortgage, time payment, installment loan, student loan, car loan, home equity loan, personal loan.

loan ***v.*** provide with, share, furnish; see LEND.

loaned ***a.*** lent, advanced, invested, granted, furnished, put out at interest, let, risked, leased; see also GIVEN.—*Ant.* BORROWED, rented, taken.

lobby ***n.*** vestibule, entryway, foyer; see HALL 1, ROOM 2.

lobby ***v.*** induce, put pressure on, promote; see INFLUENCE.

local ***a.*** **1** [Associated with a locality] sectional, divisional, territorial, district, provincial, neighborhood, town, civic, small-town, grass-roots, parochial, geographical; see also REGIONAL. **2** [Restricted to a locality] limited, confined, bounded; see RESTRICTED.

locale ***n.*** vicinity, territory, district; see AREA, REGION 1.

locality ***n.*** **1** [Area] district, section, sector; see AREA, REGION 1. **2** [Position] spot, location, site; see POSITION 1. **3** [Neighborhood] block, vicinity, district; see NEIGHBORHOOD.

locally ***a.*** regionally, sectionally, provincially, in the neighborhood, in the town, close by, nearby.

locate ***v.*** **1** [To determine a location] discover, search out, find, come across, position, ferret out, stumble on, discover the location of, get at, hit upon, come upon, lay one's hands on, track down, unearth, establish, determine, station, place; see also FIND. **2** [To take up residence] settle down, establish oneself, inhabit; see DWELL,

downtown*]* **2** to discover the position of **3** to show the position of *[*to *locate* Guam on a map*]* —*vi.* [Inf.] to settle *[*she *located* in Ohio*]*

lo·ca'tion *n.* **1** a locating or being located **2** position; place —**on location** *Film* in an outdoor setting, away from the studio

loc. cit. *abbrev.* ⟦L *loco citato*⟧ in the place cited

loch (läk, läkh) *n.* ⟦< Gael & Old Ir⟧ [Scot.] **1** a lake **2** an arm of the sea

lock[1] (läk) *n.* ⟦< OE *loc*, a bolt⟧ **1** a mechanical device for fastening a door, strongbox, etc. as with a key or combination **2** an enclosed part of a canal, etc. equipped with gates for changing the water level to raise or lower boats **3** the mechanism of a firearm that explodes the charge —*vt.* **1** to fasten with a lock **2** to shut (*up, in,* or *out*) by means of a lock **3** to link *[*to *lock* arms*]* **4** to jam together so as to make immovable —*vi.* **1** to become locked **2** to interlock

lock[2] (läk) *n.* ⟦OE *loc*⟧ a curl of hair

lock'er *n.* **1** a chest, closet, etc. which can be locked **2** a large compartment for freezing and storing foods

lock·et (läk'it) *n.* ⟦< OFr *loc*, a latch, lock⟧ a small, hinged case of gold, etc. for holding a picture, lock of hair, etc.: usually worn on a necklace

lock'jaw' *n.* a form of tetanus, in which the jaws become firmly closed

lock'out' *n.* the shutdown of a plant to bring the workers to an agreement

lock'smith' *n.* one whose work is making or repairing locks and making keys

lock'up' *n.* a jail

lo·co (lō'kō) *adj.* ⟦Sp, mad⟧ [Slang] crazy; demented

loco disease a nervous disease of horses, cattle, etc. caused by locoweed poison

lo·co·mo·tion (lō'kə mō'shən) *n.* ⟦< L *locus*, a place + MOTION⟧ motion, or the power of moving, from one place to another

lo'co·mo'tive (-mōt'iv) *adj.* of locomotion —*n.* an electric, steam, or diesel engine on wheels, designed to push or pull a railroad train

lo·co·weed (lō'kō wēd') *n.* a plant of W North America that causes the loco disease of cattle, horses, etc.

lo·cus (lō'kəs) *n., pl.* **lo'ci'** (-sī') ⟦L⟧ **1** a place **2** *Math.* a line, plane, etc. every point of which satisfies a given condition

lo·cust (lō'kəst) *n.* ⟦< L *locusta*⟧ **1** a large grasshopper often traveling in swarms and destroying vegetation **2** SEVENTEEN-YEAR LOCUST **3** a tree of the E or Central U.S., with clusters of fragrant, white flowers

lo·cu·tion (lō kyōō'shən) *n.* ⟦< L *loqui*, speak⟧ a word, phrase, or expression

lode (lōd) *n.* ⟦< OE *lad*, course⟧ a vein, stratum, etc. of metallic ore

lode'star' *n.* a star by which one directs one's course; esp., the North Star

lode'stone' *n.* a strongly magnetic variety of iron ore

lodge (läj) *n.* ⟦< OFr *loge*, arbor⟧ **1** *a)* a small house for some special use *[*a hunting *lodge]* *b)* a resort hotel or motel **2** the local chapter or hall of a fraternal society —*vt.* **lodged**, **lodg'ing** **1** to house temporarily **2** to shoot, thrust, etc. firmly (*in*) **3** to bring (a complaint, etc.) before legal authorities **4** to confer (powers) upon: with *in* —*vi.* **1** to live (*with* or *in*) as a paying guest **2** to come to rest and stick firmly (*in*)

lodg'er *n.* one who lives in a rented room in another's home

lodg'ing *n.* **1** a place to live in, esp. temporarily **2** [*pl.*] a room or rooms rented in a private home

loft (lôft, läft) *n.* ⟦< ON *lopt*, upper room, air⟧ **1** the space just below the roof of a house, barn, etc. **2** an upper story of a warehouse or factory; specif., a dwelling space, artist's studio, etc. in such an upper story **3** a gallery *[*a choir *loft]* **4** height given to a ball hit or thrown —*vt.* to send (a ball) into a high curve

loft bed a bed on a platform or balcony allowing the use of the floor area below as part of a living room, etc.

loft'y *adj.* **-i·er, -i·est** **1** very high **2** elevated; noble **3** haughty; arrogant —**loft'i·ness** *n.*

log[1] (lôg, läg) *n.* ⟦ME *logge*⟧ **1** a section of the trunk or of a large branch of a felled tree **2** a device for measuring the speed of a ship **3** a record of progress, speed, etc., specif. one kept on a ship's voyage or aircraft's flight —*vt.* **logged**, **log'ging** **1** to saw (trees) into logs **2** to record in a log **3** to sail or fly (a specified distance) —*vi.* to cut down trees and remove the logs —**log on** (or **off**) to enter the necessary information to begin (or end) a session on a computer terminal

log[2] (lôg, läg) *n. short for* LOGARITHM

-log (lôg, läg) *combining form* -LOGUE

lo·gan·ber·ry (lō'gən ber'ē) *n., pl.* **-ries** ⟦after J. H. *Logan*, who developed it (1881)⟧ **1** a hybrid bramble developed from the blackberry and the red raspberry **2** its purplish-red fruit

log·a·rithm (lôg'ə rith əm, läg'-) *n.* ⟦< Gr *logos*, ratio + *arithmos*, number⟧ *Math.* the exponent expressing the power to which a fixed number must be raised to produce a given number —**log'a·rith'mic** *adj.*

loge (lōzh) *n.* ⟦OFr: see LODGE⟧ **1** a theater box or mezzanine section **2** a luxury suite in a stadium or arena

log'ger *n.* a person whose work is felling trees for use as lumber, etc.

log'ger·head' *n.* ⟦dial. *logger*, block of wood + HEAD⟧ used chiefly in **at loggerheads**, in sharp disagreement

log·ic (läj'ik) *n.* ⟦ult. < Gr *logos*, word⟧ **1** correct reasoning, or the science of this **2** way of reasoning *[*bad *logic]* **3** what is expected by the working of cause and effect **4** *Comput.* the system of switching functions, circuits, or devices —**lo·gi·cian** (lō jish'ən) *n.*

log'i·cal (-i kəl) *adj.* ⟦ML *logicalis*⟧ **1** based on or using logic **2** expected because of what has gone before —**log'i·cal·ly** *adv.*

lo·gis·tics (lō jis'tiks) *n.* ⟦< Fr *loger*, to quarter, lodge⟧ the military science of procuring, maintaining, and transporting materiel and personnel —**lo·gis'tic** or **lo·gis'ti·cal** *adj.* —**lo·gis'ti·cal·ly** *adv.*

log'jam' *n.* **1** an obstacle formed by logs jamming together in a stream **2** piled-up work, etc. that obstructs progress **3** a deadlock

log·o (lō'gō) *n.* ⟦< Gr *logos*, a word⟧ a distinctive company signature, trademark, etc.: also **log·o·type** (lôg'ə tīp', läg'-)

log'roll'ing *n.* **1** mutual exchange of favors, esp. among legislators **2** the sport of balancing oneself on a floating log while rotating it with one's feet

-logue (lôg, läg) ⟦see LOGIC⟧ *combining form* a (specified kind of) speaking or writing *[Decalogue]*

lo·gy (lō'gē) *adj.* **-gi·er, -gi·est** ⟦< ? Du *log*, dull⟧ [Inf.] dull or sluggish

-lo·gy (lə jē) ⟦see LOGIC⟧ *combining form* **1** a (specified

THESAURUS

SETTLE 5.

located *a.* **1** [Discovered] traced, found, detected; see DISCOVERED. **2** [Situated] positioned, seated, fixed; see PLACED.

location *n.* **1** [A position] place, spot, section; see POSITION 1. **2** [A site] zone, place, scene; see AREA, NEIGHBORHOOD.

lock[1] *v.* bolt, bar, secure; see FASTEN. —**lock up** confine, put behind bars, shut up; see IMPRISON.

lock[1,2] *n.* **1** [A device for locking] hook, catch, latch, bolt, deadbolt, bar, hasp, fastening, padlock, safety catch, clamp, clasp, tumblers, barrier, device, fixture, grip; see also FASTENER. **2** [A tuft of hair] tress, ringlet, curl; see HAIR 1. —**under lock and key** locked up, imprisoned, in jail; see CONFINED 3.

locked *a.* secured, padlocked, closed; see TIGHT 2.

locker *n.* cabinet, footlocker, cupboard; see CLOSET, FURNITURE.

locket *n.* memento case, pendant, keepsake; see JEWELRY, NECKLACE.

lockup *n.* prison, jail, penitentiary; see JAIL.

lodge *n.* inn, hostel, ski lodge; see HOTEL, MOTEL, RESORT 2.

lodge *v.* **1** [To become fixed] catch, stay, remain; see STICK 1. **2** [To take (temporary) residence] room, stay over, stop over; see DWELL.

lodger *n.* guest, roomer, resident; see TENANT.

lodging *n.* **1** [Place of protection] sanctuary, retreat, asylum; see REFUGE 1, SHELTER. **2** [A (temporary) living place; *usually plural*] room, apartment, suite; see HOTEL, MOTEL, RESORT 2.

lofty *a.* tall, elevated, towering; see HIGH 2, RAISED 1.

log[1] *n.* **1** [The main stem of a fallen or cut tree] timber, trunk, lumber; see WOOD 2. **2** [The record of a voyage] journal, account, diary; see RECORD 1.

logic *n.* reasoning, deduction, induction; see THOUGHT 1, PHILOSOPHY 1.

logical *a.* coherent, consistent, probable, sound, valid, pertinent, germane, legitimate, cogent, relevant, congruent with, as it ought to be; see also REASONABLE 1.

logically *a.* rationally, by reason, inevitably; see REASONABLY 1, 2.

logy* *a.* dull, sluggish, drowsy; see LAZY 1.

kind of) speaking *[eulogy]* **2** the science, doctrine, or theory of *[biology]*

loin (loin) ***n.*** ⟦< L *lumbus*⟧ **1** [*usually pl.*] the lower part of the back between the hipbones and the ribs **2** the front part of the hindquarters of beef, lamb, etc. **3** [*pl.*] the hips and the lower abdomen regarded as the region of strength, etc.

loin'cloth' ***n.*** a cloth worn about the loins, as by some peoples in warm climates

loi·ter (loit'ər) ***vi.*** ⟦< MDu *loteren*⟧ **1** to spend time idly; linger **2** to move slowly and idly —**loi'ter·er** ***n.***

loll (läl) ***vi.*** ⟦< MDu *lollen*, mumble, doze⟧ **1** to lean or lounge about lazily **2** to hang loosely; droop *[*the camel's tongue *lolled* out*]* —***vt.*** to let hang loosely

lol·li·pop or **lol·ly·pop** (läl'ē päp') ***n.*** ⟦prob. < dial. *lolly*, the tongue + *pop*⟧ a piece of hard candy on the end of a stick

lol·ly·gag (läl'ē gag') ***vi.*** **-gagged'**, **-gag'ging** ⟦var. of *lallygag* < ?⟧ [Inf.] to waste time in trifling or aimless activity

Lon·don (lun'dən) **1** capital of England, the United Kingdom, & the Commonwealth: pop. 7,567,000 **2** city in SE Ontario, Canada: pop. 326,000

lone (lōn) ***adj.*** ⟦< *alone*⟧ **1** by oneself; solitary **2** isolated

lone'ly ***adj.*** **-li·er, -li·est** **1** solitary or isolated **2** unhappy at being alone —**lone'li·ness** ***n.***

lon·er (lōn'ər) ***n.*** [Inf.] one who prefers to be independent of others, as by living or working alone

lone'some ***adj.*** **1** having or causing a lonely feeling **2** unfrequented

long[1] (lôŋ) ***adj.*** ⟦< OE⟧ **1** measuring much in space or time **2** in length *[*six feet *long]* **3** of greater than usual length, quantity, etc. *[*a *long* list*]* **4** tedious; slow **5** far-reaching *[*a *long* view of the matter*]* **6** well-supplied *[long* on excuses*]* —***adv.*** **1** for a long time **2** from start to finish *[*all day *long]* **3** at a remote time *[long* ago*]* —**as** (or **so**) **long as** **1** during the time that **2** seeing that; since **3** provided that —**before long** soon

long[2] (lôŋ) ***vi.*** ⟦< OE *langian*⟧ to feel a strong yearning; wish earnestly

long[3] *abbrev.* longitude

Long Beach seaport in SW California, on the Pacific: pop. 429,000

long distance a telephone service for calls to and from distant places —**long'-dis'tance** ***adj., adv.***

lon·gev·i·ty (län jev'ə tē, lôn-) ***n.*** ⟦< L *longus*, long + *aevum*, age⟧ long life

long'-faced' ***adj.*** glum

long'hair' ***adj.*** [Inf.] of intellectuals or intellectual tastes

long'hand' ***n.*** ordinary handwriting, as distinguished from shorthand or typed characters

long'ing ***n.*** strong desire; yearning —***adj.*** feeling or showing a yearning

Long Island island in SE New York, in the Atlantic south of Connecticut

lon·gi·tude (län'jə to͞od') ***n.*** ⟦< L *longus*, long⟧ distance east or west of the prime meridian, expressed in degrees or by the difference in time

lon'gi·tu'di·nal (-to͞od''n əl) ***adj.*** **1** of or in length **2** running or placed lengthwise **3** of longitude

long jump *Sports* a jump for distance made with a running start

long'-lived' (-līvd', -livd') ***adj.*** having or tending to have a long life span

long'-range' ***adj.*** **1** having a range of a great distance **2** taking the future into consideration

long·shore·man (lôŋ'shôr'mən) ***n.***, *pl.* **-men** (-mən) ⟦< *alongshore* + MAN⟧ a person who works on a waterfront loading and unloading ships; stevedore

long shot [Inf.] **1** in betting, a choice that is little favored and, hence, carries great odds **2** a venture with only a slight chance of success, but offering great rewards

long'-stand'ing ***adj.*** having continued for a long time

long'-suf'fer·ing ***adj.*** bearing trouble, etc. patiently for a long time

long'-term' ***adj.*** for or extending over a long time

long ton TON (sense 2)

Lon·gueuil (lôŋ gāl') city in S Quebec: suburb of Montreal: pop. 128,000

long'-wind'ed (-win'did) ***adj.*** **1** speaking or writing at great length **2** tiresomely long

look (look) ***vi.*** ⟦< OE *locian*⟧ **1** to direct one's eyes in order to see **2** to search **3** to appear; seem **4** to be facing in a specified direction —***vt.*** **1** to direct one's eyes on **2** to have an appearance befitting *[*to *look* the part*]* —***n.*** **1** a looking; glance **2** appearance; aspect **3** [Inf.] *a)* [*usually pl.*] appearance *b)* [*pl.*] personal appearance —***interj.*** **1** see! **2** pay attention! —**look after** to take care of —**look down on** (or **upon**) to regard with contempt —**look for** to expect —**look forward to** to anticipate —**look in (on)** to pay a brief visit (to) —**look into** to investigate —**look out** to be careful —**look over** to examine —**look to** **1** to take care of **2** to rely on —**look up** **1** to search for as in a reference book **2** [Inf.] to call on —**look up to** to admire —**look'er** ***n.***

look'er-on' ***n.***, *pl.* **look'ers-on'** an observer or spectator; onlooker

looking glass a (glass) mirror

look'out' ***n.*** **1** a careful watching **2** a place for keeping watch **3** a person detailed to watch **4** [Inf.] concern

look'-see' ***n.*** [Inf.] a quick look

loom[1] (lo͞om) ***n.*** ⟦< OE *(ge)loma*, tool⟧ a machine for weaving thread or yarn into cloth

THESAURUS

loiter ***v.*** saunter, stroll, dawdle, delay, lag, shuffle, waste time, procrastinate, tarry, fritter away time, loll, loaf, dabble, wait, pause, dilly-dally, hang back, trail, drag, ramble, idle; see also LINGER.—*Ant.* HURRY, hasten, stride along.

lone ***a.*** solitary, lonesome, deserted; see ALONE.

loneliness ***n.*** detachment, separation, solitude, desolation, isolation, aloneness, lonesomeness, forlornness.

lonely ***a.*** abandoned, homesick, forlorn, forsaken, friendless, deserted, desolate, homeless, left, lone, lonesome, solitary, empty, companionless, without company, unwanted, withdrawn, renounced, secluded, unattended, by oneself, apart, reclusive, single, rejected, unaccompanied; see also ALONE.—*Ant.* ACCOMPANIED, escorted, associated.

lonesome ***a.*** solitary, forlorn, alone; see HOMESICK, LONELY.

long[1] ***a.*** **1** [Extended in space] lengthy, extended, outstretched, elongated, interminable, boundless, endless, unending, limitless, stretching, great, high, deep, drawn out, enlarged, expanded, spread, tall, lofty, towering, lengthened, stringy, rangy, lanky, gangling, far-reaching, distant, running, faraway, far-off, remote; see also LARGE 1.—*Ant.* SHORT, small, stubby. **2** [Extended in time] protracted, prolonged, enduring, unending, meandering, long-winded, spun out, lengthy, for ages, delayed, tardy, dilatory, without end, perpetual, forever and a day, lasting, continued, long-lived, sustained, lingering; day after day, hour after hour, etc.—*Ant.* SHORT, brief, fleeting. **3** [Tedious] hard, boring, prolonged; see DULL 4. **4** [Having (a certain commodity) in excess] rich, profuse, abundant; see PLENTIFUL 1. —**as** (or **so**) **long as** seeing that, provided, since; see BECAUSE. —**before long** in the near future, immediately, shortly; see SOON. —**long and short of it** gist, totality, outcome; see RESULT, WHOLE.

long[2] ***v.*** desire, yearn for, wish; see WANT 1.

longing ***n.*** yearning, pining, hunger; see DESIRE 1, WISH.

long-lived ***a.*** long-lasting, perpetual, enduring; see PERMANENT.

look ***n.*** **1** [Appearance] features, demeanor, shape; see EXPRESSION 4, LOOKS. **2** [An effort to see] gaze, stare, gander, scrutiny, inspection, examination, contemplation, speculation, attending, noticing, regarding, marking, observation, reconnaissance, keeping watch, once-over*, look-see*; see also ATTENTION. **3** [A quick use of the eyes] glance, survey, squint, glimpse, peek, peep, leer, flash.

look ***v.*** **1** [To appear] seem to be, look like, resemble; see SEEM. **2** [To endeavor to see] view, gaze, glance at, scan, stare, behold, contemplate, watch, survey, scrutinize, regard, inspect, discern, spy, observe, attend, examine, mark, gape, give attention, peer, ogle, have an eye on, study, peep, look at, take a gander at*, get a load of*; see also SEE 1. —**it looks like** probably, it seems that there will be, it seems as if; see SEEM. —**look after** look out for, support, watch; see GUARD. —**look into** investigate, study, probe; see EXAMINE. —**look up** come upon, research, find; see DISCOVER, SEARCH, SEEK. —**look up to** respect, idolize, honor; see ADMIRE.

lookout ***n.*** **1** [A place of vantage] watchtower, tower, observatory, patrol station, post, crow's-nest, observation tower. **2** [One stationed at a lookout] observer, sentinel, scout; see WATCHMAN.

looks* ***n.*** appearance, countenance, aspect, manner, demeanor, face, expression, features, form, shape, posture, bearing, presence.

loom² (lo͞om) ***vi.*** ⟦< ?⟧ to come into sight indistinctly, esp. threateningly
loon¹ (lo͞on) ***n.*** ⟦< ON *lomr*⟧ a fish-eating, diving bird, similar to a duck
loon² (lo͞on) ***n.*** ⟦< ?⟧ a stupid or crazy person
loon′ie ***n.*** ⟦< LOON¹, depicted on the reverse⟧ [Cdn.] the Canadian one-dollar coin
loon′y ***adj.*** **-i·er, -i·est** ⟦< LUNATIC⟧ [Slang] crazy; demented
loop (lo͞op) ***n.*** ⟦ME *loup*⟧ **1** the figure made by a line, thread, etc. that curves back to cross itself **2** anything forming this figure **3** an intrauterine contraceptive device **4** a segment of movie film or magnetic tape joined end to end —***vt.*** **1** to make a loop in or of **2** to fasten with a loop —***vi.*** to form a loop or loops
loop′hole′ ***n.*** ⟦prob. < MDu *lupen*, to peer + HOLE⟧ **1** a hole in a wall for looking or shooting through **2** a means of evading an obligation, etc.
loop′y ***adj.*** **-i·er, -i·est** [Slang] **1** slightly crazy **2** confused
loose (lo͞os) ***adj.*** **loos′er, loos′est** ⟦< ON *lauss*⟧ **1** not confined or restrained; free **2** not firmly fastened **3** not tight or compact **4** not precise; inexact **5** sexually immoral **6** [Inf.] relaxed —***adv.*** loosely —***vt.*** **loosed, loos′ing** **1** to set free; unbind **2** to make less tight, compact, etc. **3** to relax **4** to release (an arrow, etc.) —**on the loose** not confined; free —**loose′ly** ***adv.*** —**loose′ness** ***n.***
loose ends unsettled details —**at loose ends** unsettled, idle, etc.
loose′-leaf′ ***adj.*** having leaves, or sheets, that can be removed or replaced easily
loos·en (lo͞os′ən) ***vt., vi.*** to make or become loose or looser
loos·ey-goos·ey (lo͞o′sē go͞o′sē) [Slang] ***adj.*** relaxed; easy —***adv.*** in a loose, relaxed way
loot (lo͞ot) ***n.*** ⟦Hindi *lūṭ*⟧ **1** goods stolen or taken by force; plunder **2** [Slang] money, gifts, etc. —***vt., vi.*** to plunder
lop¹ (läp) ***vt.*** **lopped, lop′ping** ⟦< OE *loppian*⟧ **1** to trim (a tree, etc.) by cutting off branches, etc. **2** to remove by or as by cutting off: usually with *off*
lop² (läp) ***vi.*** **lopped, lop′ping** ⟦prob. akin to LOB⟧ to hang down loosely
lope (lōp) ***vi.*** **loped, lop′ing** ⟦< ON *hlaupa*, to leap⟧ to move with a long, swinging stride —***n.*** such a stride
lop·sid·ed (läp′sīd′id) ***adj.*** noticeably heavier, bigger, or lower on one side
lo·qua·cious (lō kwā′shəs) ***adj.*** ⟦< L *loqui*, speak⟧ very talkative —**lo·qua′cious·ness** ***n.*** —**lo·quac′i·ty** (-kwas′ə tē) ***n.***
lord (lôrd) ***n.*** ⟦< OE *hlaf*, loaf + *weard*, keeper⟧ **1** a ruler; master **2** the head of a feudal estate **3** [**L-**] *a)* God *b)* Jesus Christ **4** in Great Britain, a titled nobleman —**lord it over** to be overbearing toward
lord′ly ***adj.*** **-li·er, -li·est** **1** noble; grand **2** haughty —***adv.*** in the manner of a lord —**lord′li·ness** ***n.***
Lord′s Day [*sometimes* **L- d-**] Sunday: with *the*
lord′ship′ ***n.*** **1** the rank or authority of a lord **2** rule; dominion **3** the territory of a lord **4** [*often* **L-**] a title used in speaking to or of a lord
Lord′s Prayer the prayer beginning *Our Father*: Matt. 6:9-13
lore (lôr) ***n.*** ⟦< OE *lar*⟧ knowledge; learning, esp. of a traditional nature
lor·gnette (lôr nyet′) ***n.*** ⟦Fr < OFr *lorgne*, squinting⟧ eyeglasses, or opera glasses, attached to a handle
lo·ris (lō′ris, lôr′is) ***n.*** ⟦ult. < Du *loer*, a clown⟧ a small, slow-moving, large-eyed Asiatic lemur that lives in trees and is active at night
lor·ry (lôr′ē) ***n.***, *pl.* **-ries** ⟦prob. < dial. *lurry*, to pull⟧ [Brit.] a motor truck
Los Al·a·mos (lôs al′ə mōs′) town in NC New Mexico: site of nuclear energy facility where the atomic bomb was developed: pop. 11,000
Los An·ge·les (lôs an′jə ləs) city & seaport on the SW coast of California: pop. 3,486,000 (met. area, incl. Long Beach, 8,863,000)
lose (lo͞oz) ***vt.*** **lost, los′ing** ⟦OE *losian*⟧ **1** to become unable to find *[to lose one's keys]* **2** to have taken from one by accident, death, removal, etc. **3** to fail to keep *[to lose one's temper]* **4** to fail to see, hear, or understand **5** to fail to have, get, etc. *[to lose one's chance]* **6** to fail to win **7** to cause the loss of **8** to wander from (one's way, etc.) **9** to squander —***vi.*** to suffer (a) loss —**lose oneself** to become absorbed —**los′er** ***n.***
loss (lôs, läs) ***n.*** ⟦ME *los*⟧ **1** a losing or being lost **2** the damage, trouble, etc. caused by losing **3** the person, thing, or amount lost —**at a loss to** uncertain how to
lost (lôst, läst) ***vt., vi.*** *pt. & pp. of* LOSE —***adj.*** **1** ruined; destroyed **2** not to be found; missing **3** no longer held, seen, heard, etc. **4** not gained or won **5** having wandered astray **6** wasted

THESAURUS

loom² ***v.*** **1** [To appear] come into view, come on the scene, arrive; see APPEAR 1. **2** [To appear large or imposing] menace, overshadow, hulk, emerge, shadow, top, tower, impress, hang over, emanate, seem huge, be near, hover, approach, come forth; see also THREATEN.

loop ***n.*** ring, orbit, circuit; see CIRCLE 1. —**knock** (or **throw**) **for a loop*** confuse, disturb, startle; see SHOCK 2.

loop ***v.*** curve, connect, tie together; see BEND.

loophole ***n.*** avoidance, means of escape, escape clause; see LIE, TRICK 1.

loose ***a.*** **1** [Unbound] unfastened, undone, untied, insecure, relaxed, unattached, unconnected, disconnected, untethered, unbuttoned, unclasped, unhooked, unsewed, unstuck, slack, loosened, baggy, unconfined, unlatched, unlocked, unbolted, unscrewed, unhinged, worked free; see also FREE 3.—*Ant.* TIGHT, confined, bound. **2** [Movable] unattached, free, wobbly; see MOVABLE. **3** [Vague] disconnected, random, detached; see OBSCURE 1, VAGUE 2. **4** [Wanton] dissolute, licentious, disreputable; see LEWD 2. —**on the loose*** unconfined, unrestrained, wild; see FREE. —**set** (or **turn**) **loose** set free, release, untie; see FREE.

loosen ***v.*** **1** [To make loose] extricate, untie, unbind, undo, disentangle, let go, unlock, release, unfix; see also FREE. **2** [To become loose] relax, slacken, work free, break up, let go, become unstuck.—*Ant.* TIGHTEN, tighten up, become rigid.

loot ***n.*** spoils, plunder, take*; see BOOTY.

loot ***v.*** plunder, thieve, pilfer; see ROB, STEAL.

lop¹ ***v.*** trim, prune, chop; see CUT 1.

lopsided ***a.*** uneven, unbalanced, crooked; see IRREGULAR 4.

lord ***n.*** **1** [A master] ruler, governor, prince; see LEADER 2. **2** [A member of the nobility] nobleman, count, peer; see ARISTOCRAT, ROYALTY.

Lord ***n.*** Divinity, the Supreme Being, Jehovah; see GOD 1.

lordly ***a.*** grand, dignified, honorable; see NOBLE 1, 2, 3.

lore ***n.*** enlightenment, wisdom, learning; see KNOWLEDGE 1.

lose ***v.*** **1** [To bring about a loss] mislay, misfile, misplace, disturb, disorder, confuse, mix, scatter, mess, muss, disorganize, forget, be careless with. **2** [To incur loss] suffer, miss, be deprived of, fail to keep, suffer loss, be impoverished from, become poorer by, let slip through the fingers*; see also WASTE 1.—*Ant.* PROFIT, improve, gain. **3** [To fail to win] suffer defeat, be defeated, go down in defeat, succumb, fall, be the loser, miss, have the worst of it, be humbled, take defeat at the hands of, be outdistanced; see also FAIL 1.—*Ant.* WIN, triumph, be victorious. **4** [To suffer financially] squander, expend, deplete; see SPEND, WASTE 2.

loser ***n.*** sufferer, victim, prey, failure, defeated, vanquished, dispossessed, underdog, disadvantaged, underprivileged, fallen.—*Ant.* WINNER, victor, conqueror.

losing ***a.*** **1** [*Said of one who loses*] failing, having the worst of it, on the way out; see RUINED 1. **2** [*Said of an activity in which one must lose*] futile, desperate, lost; see HOPELESS.

loss ***n.*** **1** [The act or fact of losing] ruin, destruction, mishap, misfortune, giving up, ill fortune, accident, calamity, trouble, disaster, sacrifice, catastrophe, trial, failure. **2** [Damage caused by losing something] hurt, injury, wound; see DAMAGE 1, 2. **3** [The result of unprofitable activity] privation, want, bereavement, deprivation, need, destitution, being without, lack, waste, deterioration, impairment, degeneration, decline, disadvantage, wreck, wreckage, undoing, annihilation, bane, end, undoing, disorganization, breaking up, suppression, relapse.—*Ant.* ADVANTAGE, advancement, supply. —**at a loss** confused, puzzled, unsure; see UNCERTAIN.

losses ***n.*** casualties, damage, deaths; see DESTRUCTION 2.

lost ***a.*** **1** [Not to be found] misplaced, mislaid, missing, hidden, obscured, gone astray, nowhere to be found, strayed, lacking, wandered off, absent, forfeited, vanished, wandering, without, gone out of one's possession.—*Ant.* FOUND, come back, returned. **2** [Ignorant of the way] perplexed, bewildered, ignorant; see DOUBTFUL 1. **3** [Destroyed] demolished, devastated, wasted; see DESTROYED, RUINED 1. **4** [No longer to be gained] gone, passed, costly; see UNPROFITABLE. **5** [Helpless] feeble, sickly, disabled; see WEAK 1, 3. —**get lost*** go away, leave, begone.

lot (lät) ***n.*** ⟦< OE *hlot*⟧ **1** the deciding of a matter by chance, as by drawing counters **2** the decision thus arrived at **3** one's share by lot **4** fortune *[her unhappy lot]* **5** a plot of ground **6** a group of persons or things **7** [*often pl.*] [Inf.] a great number or amount *[a lot of cars, lots of fun]* **8** [Inf.] sort *[he's a bad lot]* —**a (whole) lot** a great deal; very much: somewhat informal — **draw** (or **cast**) **lots** to decide by lot

Lo·thar·i·o (lō ther′ē ō′) ***n.***, *pl.* **-i·os′** ⟦after the rake in the play *The Fair Penitent* (1703)⟧ [*often* **l-**] a seducer of women; rake

lo·tion (lō′shən) ***n.*** ⟦< L *lavare*, to wash⟧ a liquid preparation used, as on the skin, for cleansing, healing, etc.

lots ***adv.*** a great deal; very much: somewhat informal

lot·ter·y (lät′ər ē) ***n.***, *pl.* **-ies** ⟦< MDu *lot*, lot⟧ **1** a game of chance in which people buy numbered tickets on prizes, winners being chosen by lot **2** a drawing, event, etc. based on chance

lot·to (lät′ō) ***n.*** ⟦It < MDu: see LOT⟧ a game resembling bingo

lo·tus (lōt′əs) ***n.*** ⟦< Gr *lōtos*⟧ **1** *Gr. Legend* a plant whose fruit induced forgetfulness **2** any of several tropical waterlilies

lotus position in yoga, an erect sitting position with the legs crossed close to the body

loud (loud) ***adj.*** ⟦< OE *hlud*⟧ **1** strongly audible: said of sound **2** making a loud sound **3** noisy **4** emphatic *[loud denials]* **5** [Inf.] flashy —***adv.*** in a loud manner — **loud′ly** ***adv.*** —**loud′ness** ***n.***

loud′mouthed′ (-mouthd′, -moutht′) ***adj.*** talking in a loud, irritating voice

loud′speak′er ***n.*** SPEAKER (*n.* 2)

Lou·is (lo͞o′ē; *Fr* lwē) **1 Louis XIV** 1638-1715; king of France (1643-1715) **2 Louis XV** 1710-74; king of France (1715-74) **3 Louis XVI** 1754-93; king of France (1774-92): guillotined

Lou·i·si·an·a (loo ē′zē an′ə) Southern state of the U.S.: 43,566 sq. mi.; pop. 4,220,000; cap. Baton Rouge: abbrev. *LA* —**Lou·i′si·an′i·an** or **Lou·i′si·an′an** ***adj.***, ***n.***

Lou·is·ville (lo͞o′ə vəl) city in N Kentucky: pop. 270,000

lounge (lounj) ***vi.*** **lounged**, **loung′ing** ⟦Scot dial. < ? *lungis*, a laggard⟧ **1** to move, sit, lie, etc. in a relaxed way **2** to spend time in idleness —***n.*** **1** a room with comfortable furniture for lounging **2** a couch or sofa

lounge′wear′ ***n.*** loose-fitting clothing for casual wear, esp. at home

louse (lous) ***n.***, *pl.* **lice** ⟦< OE *lus*⟧ **1** a small, wingless insect parasitic on humans and other animals **2** any similar insect parasitic on plants **3** *pl.* **lous′es** [Slang] a mean, contemptible person —**louse up** [Slang] to spoil; ruin

lous·y (lou′zē) ***adj.*** **-i·er**, **-i·est** **1** infested with lice **2** [Slang] *a)* disgusting *b)* poor; inferior **3** well supplied (*with*) —**lous′i·ness** ***n.***

lout (lout) ***n.*** ⟦prob. < or akin to ME *lutien*, to lurk⟧ a clumsy, stupid fellow —**lout′ish** ***adj.***

lou·ver (lo͞o′vər) ***n.*** ⟦< MDu *love*, gallery⟧ **1** an opening, window, etc. fitted with a series of sloping slats arranged so as to admit light and air but shed rain **2** any of these slats

love (luv) ***n.*** ⟦< OE *lufu*⟧ **1** strong affection or liking for someone or something **2** a passionate affection of one person for another **3** the object of such affection; a sweetheart or lover **4** *Tennis* a score of zero —***vt.***, ***vi.*** to feel love (for) —**fall in love (with)** to begin to feel love (for) —**in love** feeling love —**make love** **1** to woo, embrace, etc. **2** to have sexual intercourse —**lov′a·ble** or **love′a·ble** ***adj.*** —**love′less** ***adj.***

love′bird′ ***n.*** any of various small Old World parrots often kept as cage birds

love′lorn′ (-lôrn′) ***adj.*** ⟦LOVE + obs. *lorn*, lost⟧ sad because not loved in return

love′ly ***adj.*** **-li·er**, **-li·est** **1** beautiful **2** [Inf.] highly enjoyable —**love′li·ness** ***n.***

lov·er (luv′ər) ***n.*** **1** a person who greatly enjoys something **2** one who loves; specif., either partner in a sexual relationship, often an illicit one **3** [*pl.*] a couple in love with, or in a sexual relationship with, each other

love seat a small sofa for two people

lov′ing ***adj.*** feeling or expressing love —**lov′ing·ly** ***adv.***

THESAURUS

lot ***n.*** **1** [A small parcel of land] parcel, part, division, patch, clearing, piece of ground, plat, plot, field, tract, block, portion, parking lot, piece, property, acreage. **2** [A number of individual items, usually alike] batch, group, set; see LOAD 1. **3** [Destiny] doom, fortune, fate; see CHANCE 1. **4** [*A great quantity] large amount, abundance, plenty, considerable amount, great numbers, bundle, bunch, cluster, group, pack, large numbers, very much, very many, quite a lot, quite a bit, a good deal, a whole bunch*, loads*, oodles*; see also PLENTY.

lotion ***n.*** liniment, hand lotion, cream, moisturizer, after-shave; see also COSMETIC, MEDICINE 2, SALVE.

loud ***a.*** **1** [Having volume of sound] deafening, ringing, ear-piercing, ear-splitting, booming, intense, resounding, piercing, blaring, sonorous, resonant, crashing, deep, full, powerful, emphatic, thundering, heavy, big, deep-toned, thunderous, roaring, enough to wake the dead*; see also SHRILL.—*Ant.* SOFT, faint, feeble. **2** [Producing loud sounds] clamorous, noisy, uproarious, blatant, vociferous, turbulent, tumultuous, blustering, lusty, loud-voiced, boisterous, bombastic, raucous; see also HARSH.—*Ant.* QUIET, soft-voiced, calm. **3** [*Lacking manners and refinement] loudmouthed, brash, offensive; see RUDE 2, VULGAR. **4** [*Lacking good taste, especially in colors] garish, flashy, gaudy; see ORNATE.

loudly ***a.*** audibly, fully, powerfully, crashingly, shrilly, deafeningly, piercingly, resonantly, emphatically, vehemently, thunderingly, thunderously, in full cry, clamorously, noisily, uproariously, blatantly, at the top of one's lungs.

loudspeaker ***n.*** speaker, amplifier, public address system, PA, high-fidelity speaker, high-frequency speaker, low-frequency speaker, tweeter, woofer, bullhorn.

lounge ***v.*** idle, repose, kill time; see LOAF, REST 1.

lousy ***a.*** **1** [Having lice] infested with lice, crawling with lice, pediculous, pedicular; see also CREEPING. **2** [*Bad] horrible, miserable, faulty; see OFFENSIVE 2.

lovable ***a.*** adorable, sweet, lovely; see FRIENDLY.

love ***n.*** **1** [Passionate and tender devotion] attachment, devotedness, passion, infatuation, yearning, flame, rapture, enchantment, ardor, emotion, sentiment, fondness, tenderness, adoration, puppy love, crush*; see also AFFECTION.—*Ant.* HATE, aversion, antipathy. **2** [Affection based on esteem] respect, regard, appreciation; see ADMIRATION. **3** [A lively and enduring interest] involvement, concern, enjoyment; see DEVOTION. **4** [A beloved] dear one, loved one, cherished one; see LOVER 1. —**fall in love (with)** become enamored, lose one's heart, take a fancy to, have eyes for, take a liking to, become attached to, become fond of, fancy. —**for the love of** for the sake of, with fond concern for, because of; see FOR. —**in love** enamored, infatuated, charmed; see LOVING. —**make love** fondle, embrace, sleep with; see COPULATE, LOVE 2. —**not for love or money** under no conditions, by no means, no; see NEVER.

love ***v.*** **1** [To be passionately devoted] adore, be in love with, care for, hold dear, choose, fancy, be enchanted by, be passionately attached to, have affection for, dote on, glorify, idolize, prize, be fascinated by, hold high, think the world of, treasure, prefer, yearn for, be fond of, admire, long for, flip over*, fall for*, be nuts about*, be crazy about*, go for*.—*Ant.* HATE, detest, loathe. **2** [To express love by caresses] cherish, fondle, kiss, make love to, embrace, cling to, clasp, hug, take into one's arms, hold, pet, stroke, draw close, bring to one's side; see also KISS.—*Ant.* REFUSE, reject, spurn. **3** [To possess a deep and abiding interest] enjoy, delight in, relish; see ADMIRE, LIKE 1.

loved ***a.*** desired, cherished, adored; see BELOVED.

loveliness ***n.*** appeal, charm, fairness; see BEAUTY 1.

lovely ***a.*** **1** [Beautiful] attractive, pretty, gorgeous; see sense 2 and BEAUTIFUL, HANDSOME. **2** [Charming] engaging, enchanting, captivating; see CHARMING. **3** [*Very pleasing] nice, splendid, delightful; see PLEASANT 1, 2.

lover ***n.*** **1** [A suitor] sweetheart, admirer, escort, paramour, fiancé, fiancée, gentleman friend, significant other, flame, boyfriend*, girlfriend*, steady*. **2** [A willing student or practitioner] enthusiast, fan, hobbyist; see ZEALOT. **3** [An epithet for a beloved] beloved, sweetheart, dear; see DARLING.

loving ***a.*** admiring, respecting, valuing, liking, fond, tender, kind, enamored, attached, devoted, appreciative, attentive, thoughtful, passionate, ardent, amiable, warm, amorous, affectionate, anxious, concerned, sentimental, earnest, benevolent, cordial, caring, considerate, loyal, generous.

lovingly ***a.*** tenderly, devotedly, adoringly, warmly, ardently, fervently, zealously, earnestly, loyally, generously, kindly, thoughtfully, dotingly, fondly, affectionately, passionately, longingly, rapturously, admiringly, respectfully, reverently, with

loving cup a large drinking cup with two handles, often given as a trophy

low[1] (lō) ***adj.*** ⟦< ON *lagr*⟧ **1** not high or tall **2** below the normal level *[low ground]* **3** shallow **4** less in size, degree, etc. than usual *[low speed]* **5** deep in pitch **6** depressed in spirits **7** not of high rank; humble **8** vulgar; coarse **9** poor; inferior **10** not loud —***adv.*** in or to a low level, degree, etc. —***n.*** **1** a low level, degree, etc. **2** an arrangement of gears giving the lowest speed and greatest power **3** *Meteorol.* an area of low barometric pressure —**lay low** to overcome or kill —**lie low** to keep oneself hidden —**low'ness** ***n.***

low[2] (lō) ***n., vi.*** ⟦< OE *hlowan*⟧ MOO

low'born' ***adj.*** of humble birth

low'boy' ***n.*** a chest of drawers mounted on short legs

low'brow' ***n.*** one considered to lack cultivated tastes —***adj.*** of or for a lowbrow

Low Countries the Netherlands, Belgium, & Luxembourg

low·down (lō'doun'; *for adj.*, -doun') ***n.*** [Slang] the true, pertinent facts: with *the* —***adj.*** [Inf.] mean; contemptible

low'-end' ***adj.*** [Inf.] **1** inexpensive and low in quality **2** having only the basic features

low·er[1] (lō'ər) ***adj.*** ⟦compar. of LOW[1]⟧ **1** below in place, rank, etc. **2** less in amount, degree, etc. **3** farther south —***vt.*** **1** to let or put down *[lower the window]* **2** to reduce in height, amount, etc. **3** to bring down in respect, etc. —***vi.*** to become lower

low·er[2] (lou'ər) ***vi.*** ⟦ME *louren*⟧ **1** to scowl or frown **2** to appear dark and threatening: said as of the sky —**low'er·ing** ***adj.*** —**low'er·ing·ly** ***adv.***

low·er·case (lō'ər kās') ***n.*** small-letter type used in printing, as distinguished from capital letters —***adj.*** of or in lowercase

low'er·class'man (-klas'mən) ***n.**, pl.* **-men** (-mən) a student in the freshman or sophomore class of a high school or college

low frequency any radio frequency between 30 and 300 kilohertz

Low German **1** the group of dialects of N Germany **2** the branch of Germanic languages including English, Dutch, Flemish, etc.

low'-grade' ***adj.*** of low quality, degree, etc.

low'-key' ***adj.*** of low intensity, tone, etc.; subdued: also **low'-keyed'**

low'land (-lənd, -land') ***n.*** land below the level of the surrounding land —***adj.*** of, in, or from such a region —**the Lowlands** lowland region of SC Scotland

low'life' ***n.**, pl.* **-lifes'** a vulgar or undignified person

low'ly ***adj.*** **-li·er, -li·est** **1** of low position or rank **2** humble; meek —**low'li·ness** ***n.***

low'-mind'ed ***adj.*** having or showing a coarse, vulgar mind

low'-spir'it·ed ***adj.*** sad; depressed

low tide the lowest level reached by the ebbing tide

lox[1] (läks) ***n.*** ⟦< Yiddish < Ger *lachs*, salmon⟧ a kind of smoked salmon

lox[2] (läks) ***n.*** ⟦*l(iquid) ox(ygen)*⟧ liquid oxygen, esp. when used in rockets: also **LOX**

loy·al (loi'əl) ***adj.*** ⟦see LEGAL⟧ **1** faithful to one's country, friends, ideals, etc. **2** showing such faithfulness —**loy'al·ly** ***adv.*** —**loy'al·ty**, *pl.* **-ties**, ***n.***

loy'al·ist ***n.*** one who supports the government during a revolt

loz·enge (läz'ənj) ***n.*** ⟦< OFr *losenge*⟧ a cough drop, candy, etc., orig. diamond-shaped

LP ***n.*** ⟦*L(ong) P(laying)*⟧ a phonograph record having microgrooves, for playing at 33⅓ revolutions per minute

LPN ***n.**, pl.* **LPNs** licensed practical nurse

Lr *Chem. symbol for* lawrencium

LSD ***n.*** ⟦*l(y)s(ergic acid) d(iethylamide)*⟧ a chemical compound used in the study of mental disorders and as a psychedelic drug

Lt *abbrev.* Lieutenant

Ltd or **ltd** *abbrev.* limited

lu·au (lo͞o'ou') ***n.*** a Hawaiian feast

Lub·bock (lub'ək) city in NW Texas: pop. 186,000

lube (lo͞ob) ***n.*** **1** a lubricating oil for machinery: also **lube oil** **2** [Inf.] a lubrication

lu·bri·cant (lo͞o'bri kənt) ***adj.*** reducing friction by providing a smooth film over parts coming into contact —***n.*** a lubricant oil, etc.

lu'bri·cate' (-kāt') ***vt.*** **-cat'ed, -cat'ing** ⟦< L *lubricus*, smooth⟧ **1** to make slippery or smooth **2** to apply a lubricant to (machinery, etc.) —***vi.*** to serve as a lubricant —**lu'bri·ca'tion** ***n.*** —**lu'bri·ca'tor** ***n.***

lu·cid (lo͞o'sid) ***adj.*** ⟦< L *lucere*, to shine⟧ **1** [Old Poet.] shining **2** transparent **3** sane **4** clear; readily understood —**lu·cid'i·ty** ***n.*** —**lu'cid·ly** ***adv.***

Lu·ci·fer (lo͞o'sə fər) ***n.*** Satan

Lu·cite (lo͞o'sīt') ⟦< L *lux*, light⟧ *trademark for* an acrylic resin that is molded into transparent or translucent sheets, rods, etc.

luck (luk) ***n.*** ⟦prob. < MDu *gelucke*⟧ **1** the seemingly chance happening of events that affect someone; fortune; lot **2** good fortune —**luck out** [Inf.] to be lucky —**luck'less** ***adj.***

luck'y ***adj.*** **-i·er, -i·est** **1** having good luck **2** resulting fortunately **3** believed to bring good luck —**luck'i·ly** ***adv.*** —**luck'i·ness** ***n.***

lu·cra·tive (lo͞o'krə tiv) ***adj.*** ⟦< L *lucrum*, riches⟧ producing wealth or profit; profitable

lu·cre (lo͞o'kər) ***n.*** ⟦< L *lucrum*, riches⟧ riches; money: chiefly humorously derogatory

lu·cu·brate (lo͞o'kə brāt', -kyo͞o-) ***vi.*** **-brat'ed, -brat'ing** ⟦< L *lucubrare*, to work by candlelight⟧ to work, study, or write laboriously, esp. late at night —**lu'cu·bra'tion** ***n.***

lu·di·crous (lo͞o'di krəs) ***adj.*** ⟦< L *ludus*, a game⟧ causing laughter because absurd or ridiculous —**lu'di·crous·ly** ***adv.*** —**lu'di·crous·ness** ***n.***

luff (luf) ***vi.*** ⟦< ME *lof*⟧ to turn the bow of a ship toward the wind

lug (lug) ***vt.*** **lugged, lug'ging** ⟦prob. < Scand⟧ to carry or drag (something heavy) —***n.*** **1** an earlike projection by which a thing is held or supported **2** a heavy bolt, used, with a nut (**lug nut**), to secure a wheel to an axle

THESAURUS

love, attentively.

low[1] ***a.*** **1** [Close to the earth] squat, flat, level, low-lying, prostrate, crouched, below, not far above the horizon, low-hanging, knee-high, beneath, under, depressed, sunken, inferior, lying under.—*Ant.* HIGH, lofty, elevated. **2** [Quiet] muffled, hushed, soft; see FAINT 3. **3** [Low in spirits] dejected, moody, blue; see SAD 1. **4** [Vulgar] base, mean, coarse; see VULGAR. **5** [Ill] faint, dizzy, feeble; see SICK, WEAK 1. **6** [Inexpensive] economical, affordable, low-priced; see CHEAP 1. —**lay low** bring to ruin, overcome, kill; see DESTROY. —**lie low** wait, conceal oneself, take cover; see HIDE 2.

lower[1] ***a.*** beneath, inferior, under; see LOW 1.

lower[1] ***v.*** bring low, cast down, depress; see DECREASE 1, 2, DROP 2.

lowest ***a.*** shortest, littlest, smallest, slightest, least, rock-bottom, ground, base; see also MINIMUM.

low-key ***a.*** subdued, relaxed, laid-back*; see CALM.

lowly ***a.*** unpretentious, unassuming, meek; see HUMBLE 2.

loyal ***a.*** true, dependable, firm; see FAITHFUL.

loyally ***a.*** faithfully, conscientiously, truly, devotedly, constantly, sincerely, obediently, resolutely, earnestly, staunchly, steadfastly, in good faith.

loyalty ***n.*** allegiance, faithfulness, fidelity, trustworthiness, constancy, integrity, attachment, sincerity, adherence, bond, tie, honor, reliability, good faith, conscientiousness, dependability, commitment, support, zeal, ardor, earnestness, resolution, obedience, duty, honesty, truthfulness; see also DEVOTION.—*Ant.* INDIFFERENCE, disloyalty, faithlessness.

lubricant ***n.*** cream, ointment, oil; see GREASE.

lubricate ***v.*** oil, put grease on or in, lube*; see GREASE.

luck ***n.*** **1** [Good fortune] good luck, prosperity, wealth, streak of luck, windfall, success, advantage, profit, triumph, victory, win, happiness, blessings, godsend, opportunity, lucky break, break, the breaks*.—*Ant.* FAILURE, ill-fortune, bad luck. **2** [Chance] unforeseen occurrence, happenstance*, fate; see ACCIDENT, CHANCE 1. —**good luck** prosperity, fortune, affluence; see SUCCESS 2. —**in luck** lucky, successful, prosperous; see FORTUNATE. —**out of luck** unlucky, in misfortune, in trouble; see UNFORTUNATE. —**press** (or **push**) **one's luck** gamble, take risks, chance; see RISK. —**try one's luck** attempt, risk, endeavor; see TRY 1.

luckily ***a.*** opportunely, happily, favorably; see FORTUNATELY.

lucky ***a.*** **1** [Enjoying good luck] blessed, wealthy, victorious, happy, favored, winning, in luck, successful, prosperous; see also FORTUNATE. **2** [Supposed to bring good luck] providential, propitious, auspicious; see MAGIC.

lucrative ***a.*** fruitful, productive, gainful; see PROFITABLE.

ludicrous ***a.*** comical, odd, absurd; see FUNNY 1.

lug ***v.*** carry, tug, lift; see DRAW 1.

lug·gage (lug′ij) ***n.*** ⟦< prec.⟧ suitcases, trunks, etc.; baggage

lu·gu·bri·ous (lə go͞o′brē əs) ***adj.*** ⟦< L *lugere*, mourn⟧ very sad or mournful, esp. in an exaggerated way —**lu·gu′bri·ous·ly** ***adv.*** —**lu·gu′bri·ous·ness** ***n.***

Luke (lo͝ok) ***n.*** *Bible* **1** an early Christian, the reputed author of the third Gospel **2** this Gospel

luke·warm (lo͞ok′wôrm′) ***adj.*** ⟦< ME *luke*, tepid + *warm*, warm⟧ **1** slightly warm **2** lacking enthusiasm —**luke′warm′ly** ***adv.*** —**luke′warm′ness** ***n.***

lull (lul) ***vt.*** ⟦ME *lullen*⟧ **1** to calm by gentle sound or motion **2** to bring into a specified condition by soothing and reassuring —***vi.*** to become calm —***n.*** a short period of calm

lull′a·by′ (-ə bī′) ***n.***, *pl.* **-bies′** ⟦< ME, echoic⟧ a song for lulling a baby to sleep

lum·ba·go (lum bā′gō) ***n.*** ⟦L < *lumbus*, loin⟧ pain in the lower back

lum·bar (lum′bär) ***adj.*** ⟦< L *lumbus*, loin⟧ of or near the loins

lum·ber[1] (lum′bər) ***n.*** ⟦< ? pawnbrokers of *Lombardy*, Italy; hence, stored articles⟧ timber sawed into boards, etc. —***vi.*** to cut down timber and saw it into lumber —**lum′ber·er** ***n.*** —**lum′ber·ing** ***n.***

lum·ber[2] (lum′bər) ***vi.*** ⟦< ? Scand⟧ to move heavily and noisily —**lum′ber·ing** ***adj.***

lum′ber·jack′ (-jak′) ***n.*** LOGGER

lum′ber·man (-mən) ***n.***, *pl.* **-men** (-mən) one who deals in lumber

lu·mi·nar·y (lo͞o′mə ner′ē) ***n.***, *pl.* **-nar′ies** ⟦< L *lumen*, a light⟧ **1** a body that gives off light, such as the sun **2** a famous or notable person

lu·mi·nes·cence (lo͞o′mə nes′əns) ***n.*** ⟦< L *lumen*, a light + -ESCENCE⟧ the giving off of light without heat, as in fluorescence or phosphorescence —**lu′mi·nes′cent** ***adj.***

lu·mi·nous (lo͞o′mə nəs) ***adj.*** ⟦< L *lumen*, a light⟧ **1** giving off light; bright **2** clear; readily understood —**lu′mi·nos′i·ty** (-näs′ə tē) ***n.***

lum·mox (lum′əks) ***n.*** ⟦< ?⟧ [Inf.] a clumsy, stupid person

lump[1] (lump) ***n.*** ⟦ME *lompe*⟧ **1** an indefinitely shaped mass of something **2** a swelling **3** [*pl.*] [Inf.] hard blows, criticism, etc. —***adj.*** in a lump or lumps —***vt.*** **1** to put together in a lump or lumps **2** to treat or deal with in a mass —***vi.*** to become lumpy —**lump′i·ness** ***n.*** —**lump′y**, **-i·er**, **-i·est**, ***adj.***

lump[2] (lump) ***vt.*** ⟦< ?⟧ [Inf.] to have to put up with (something disagreeable) *[like it or lump it]*

lump sum a gross, or total, sum paid at one time

lu·na·cy (lo͞o′nə sē) ***n.*** ⟦< LUNATIC⟧ **1** insanity **2** great folly or a foolish act

lu·nar (lo͞o′nər) ***adj.*** ⟦< L *luna*, the moon⟧ of or like the moon

lu·na·tic (lo͞o′nə tik) ***adj.*** ⟦< L *luna*, the moon⟧ **1** insane or for insane persons **2** utterly foolish —***n.*** an insane person

lunch (lunch) ***n.*** ⟦< ? Sp *lonja*, slice of ham⟧ a light meal; esp., the midday meal between breakfast and dinner —***vi.*** to eat lunch

lunch·eon (lun′chən) ***n.*** a lunch; esp., a formal lunch

lunch·eon·ette (lun′chən et′) ***n.*** a place where light lunches are served

luncheon meat meat processed in the form of loaves, sausages, etc. and ready to eat: also [Inf.] **lunch′meat′** ***n.***

lung (luŋ) ***n.*** ⟦OE *lungen*⟧ either of the two spongelike breathing organs in the thorax of vertebrates

lunge (lunj) ***n.*** ⟦< Fr *allonger*, lengthen⟧ **1** a sudden thrust as with a sword **2** a sudden plunge forward —***vi.***, ***vt.*** **lunged**, **lung′ing** to move, or cause to move, with a lunge

lung·fish (luŋ′fish′) ***n.***, *pl.* **-fish′** or (for different species) **-fish′es** any of various fishes having lungs as well as gills

lunk·head (luŋk′hed′) ***n.*** ⟦prob. echoic alteration of LUMP[1] + HEAD⟧ [Inf.] a stupid person: also **lunk**

lu·pine (lo͞o′pīn′; *for n.*, -pin) ***adj.*** ⟦< L *lupus*, wolf⟧ of or like a wolf —***n.*** a plant with long spikes of white, rose, yellow, or blue flowers

lu·pus (lo͞o′pəs) ***n.*** ⟦< L, a wolf⟧ any of various diseases with skin lesions

lurch[1] (lurch) ***vi.*** ⟦< ?⟧ **1** to pitch or sway suddenly to one side **2** to stagger —***n.*** a lurching movement

lurch[2] (lurch) ***n.*** ⟦prob. < OFr *lourche*, duped⟧ a difficult situation: only in **leave someone in the lurch**

lure (lo͝or) ***n.*** ⟦< OFr *loirre*⟧ **1** anything that tempts or entices **2** a bait used in fishing —***vt.*** **lured**, **lur′ing** to attract; tempt; entice

lu·rid (lo͝or′id) ***adj.*** ⟦L *luridus*, ghastly⟧ **1** glowing through a haze: said as of flames enveloped by smoke **2** shocking; sensational —**lu′rid·ly** ***adv.*** —**lu′rid·ness** ***n.***

lurk (lurk) ***vi.*** ⟦ME *lurken*⟧ to stay hidden, ready to attack, spring out, etc.

lus·cious (lush′əs) ***adj.*** ⟦ME *lucius*⟧ **1** highly gratifying to taste or smell; delicious **2** delighting any of the senses —**lus′cious·ness** ***n.***

lush[1] (lush) ***adj.*** ⟦< ? OFr *lasche*, lax⟧ **1** of or showing luxuriant growth **2** rich, abundant, extravagant, etc. —**lush′ness** ***n.***

lush[2] (lush) ***n.*** [Slang] an alcoholic

lust (lust) ***n.*** ⟦OE, pleasure⟧ **1** bodily appetite; esp., excessive sexual desire **2** overwhelming desire *[a lust for power]* —***vi.*** to feel an intense desire —**lust′ful** ***adj.*** —**lust′ful·ly** ***adv.*** —**lust′ful·ness** ***n.***

lus·ter (lus′tər) ***n.*** ⟦< L *lustrare*, illumine⟧ **1** gloss; sheen **2** brightness; radiance **3** brilliant beauty or fame; glory Also [Chiefly Brit.] **lus′tre**

lus′trous (-trəs) ***adj.*** having luster; shining

lust·y (lus′tē) ***adj.*** **-i·er**, **-i·est** full of vigor; robust —**lust′i·ly** ***adv.*** —**lust′i·ness** ***n.***

lute (lo͞ot′) ***n.*** ⟦ult. < Ar *al‘ūd*, the wood⟧ an old stringed instrument like the guitar, with a rounded body

lu·te·nist (lo͞ot′′n ist) ***n.*** a lute player: also **lu′ta·nist**

Lu·ther (lo͞o′thər), **Mar·tin** (märt′′n) 1483-1546; Ger. Reformation leader

Lu′ther·an ***adj.*** of the Protestant denomination founded by Luther —***n.*** a member of a Lutheran Church —**Lu′ther·an·ism′** ***n.***

lut·ist (lo͞ot′ist) ***n.*** LUTENIST

Lux·em·bourg (luk′səm burg′) grand duchy in W Europe, north of France: 999 sq. mi.; pop. 401,000

lux·u·ri·ant (lug zho͝or′ē ənt) ***adj.*** ⟦see LUXURY⟧ **1** growing with vigor and in abundance **2** having rich ornamentation, etc. —**lux·u′ri·ance** ***n.***

lux·u′ri·ate′ (-āt′) ***vi.*** **-at′ed**, **-at′ing** **1** to live in great luxury **2** to revel (*in*) —**lux·u′ri·a′tion** ***n.***

THESAURUS

luggage ***n.*** trunks, bags, suitcases; see BAGGAGE.

lukewarm ***a.*** cool, tepid, room-temperature; see WARM 1.

lull ***n.*** quiet, stillness, calm; see SILENCE 1, PAUSE.

lull ***v.*** calm, quiet down, bring repose; see QUIET 1, 2.

lullaby ***n.*** good-night song, bedtime song, cradlesong; see SONG.

lumber[1] ***n.*** cut timber, logs, sawed timber, forest products, boards, hardwood, softwood, lumbering products; see also WOOD 2.

luminescence ***n.*** fluorescence, incandescence, radiance; see LIGHT 1.

luminous ***a.*** lighted, glowing, radiant; see BRIGHT 1.

lump[1] ***n.*** handful, protuberance, bunch, bump, hump, block, bulk, chunk, piece, portion, section; see also HUNK.

lumpy ***a.*** knotty, clotty, uneven; see IRREGULAR 4, THICK 1, 3.

lunacy ***n.*** madness, dementia, mania; see INSANITY.

lunatic ***a.*** **1** [Insane] demented, deranged, psychotic; see INSANE. **2** [Foolish] irrational, idiotic, senseless; see STUPID.

lunatic ***n.*** crazy person, psychotic, insane person; see MADMAN.

lunch ***n.*** meal, luncheon, brunch, refreshment, sandwich, snack, high tea.

lunch ***v.*** dine, have lunch, take a lunch break; see EAT 1.

lunge ***v.*** surge, lurch, bound; see JUMP 1.

lurch[1] ***v.*** stagger, weave, lunge; see TOTTER.

lure ***n.*** bait, decoy, fake; see CAMOUFLAGE, TRICK 1.

lure ***v.*** enchant, bewitch, allure; see CHARM, FASCINATE.

lurid ***a.*** **1** [Shocking] startling, ghastly, sensational; see UNUSUAL, OFFENSIVE 2. **2** [Vivid] distinct, extreme, deep; see INTENSE.

lurk ***v.*** wait, crouch, conceal oneself; see HIDE 2.

lurking ***a.*** hiding out, sneaking, hidden; see HIDDEN.

luscious ***a.*** sweet, tasty, palatable; see DELICIOUS.

lush[1] ***a.*** **1** [Green] verdant, dense, grassy; see GREEN 2. **2** [Delicious] rich, juicy, succulent; see DELICIOUS. **3** [Elaborate] extensive, luxurious, ornamental; see ELABORATE 1, ORNATE.

lust ***n.*** appetite, passion, sensuality; see DESIRE 2.

lust (after) ***v.*** long for, desire, hunger for; see WANT 1.

luster ***n.*** glow, brilliance, radiance; see LIGHT 1.

lustrous ***a.*** shiny, radiant, glowing; see BRIGHT 1.

lusty ***a.*** hearty, robust, vigorous; see HEALTHY.

luxuriant ***a.*** lush, dense, abundant;

lux·u'ri·ous (-əs) ***adj.*** **1** fond of or indulging in luxury **2** constituting luxury; rich, comfortable, etc. —**lux·u'ri·ous·ly** ***adv.***

lux·u·ry (luk'shə rē, lug'zhə rē) ***n.***, *pl.* **-ries** ⟦< L *luxus*⟧ **1** the use and enjoyment of the best and most costly things **2** anything contributing to such enjoyment, usually something not necessary —***adj.*** characterized by luxury

Lu·zon (lo͞o zän') main island of the Philippines

-ly[1] (lē) ⟦< OE *-lic*⟧ *suffix* **1** like or characteristic of *[manly]* **2** happening (once) every (specified period of time) *[monthly, hourly]*

-ly[2] (lē) ⟦< OE *-lice*⟧ *suffix* **1** in a (specified) manner or direction, to a (specified) extent, in or at a (specified) time or place *[harshly, inwardly, hourly]* **2** in the (specified) order *[thirdly]*

ly·ce·um (lī sē'əm) ***n.*** ⟦< Gr *Lykeion*, grove at Athens where Aristotle taught⟧ **1** a lecture hall **2** an organization presenting lectures, etc.

Ly·cra (lī'krə) *trademark for* a spandex fabric used in underwear, athletic apparel, etc.

lye (lī) ***n.*** ⟦OE *leag*⟧ any strongly alkaline substance, used in cleaning, making soap, etc.

ly·ing[1] (lī'iŋ) ***vi.*** *prp. of* LIE[1]

ly·ing[2] (lī'iŋ) ***vt., vi.*** *prp. of* LIE[2] —***adj.*** false; not truthful —***n.*** the telling of a lie or lies

ly'ing-in' ***n.*** confinement in childbirth —***adj.*** of or for childbirth

lymph (limf) ***n.*** ⟦L *lympha*, spring water⟧ a clear, yellowish body fluid resembling blood plasma, found in the spaces between cells and in the lymphatic vessels

lym·phat·ic (lim fat'ik) ***adj.*** containing lymph

lymph node any of the small, compact structures lying in groups along the course of the lymphatic vessels

lym·pho·cyte (lim'fō sīt') ***n.*** a leukocyte formed in lymphatic tissue, important in the synthesis of antibodies

lymph·oid (lim'foid') ***adj.*** of or like lymph or the tissue of the lymph nodes

lym·pho·ma (lim fō'mə) ***n.*** any of a group of diseases resulting from the proliferation of malignant lymphoid cells

lynch (linch) ***vt.*** ⟦after W. *Lynch*, vigilante in VA in 1780⟧ to murder (an accused person) by mob action and without lawful trial, as by hanging —**lynch'ing** ***n.***

lynx (liŋks) ***n.*** ⟦< Gr *lynx*⟧ a wildcat found throughout the Northern Hemisphere, having a short tail and tufted ears

lynx'-eyed' (-īd') ***adj.*** keen-sighted

Lyon (lyōn) city in EC France: pop. 415,000

ly·on·naise (lī'ə nāz') ***adj.*** ⟦Fr⟧ prepared with sliced onions

lyre (līr) ***n.*** ⟦< Gr *lyra*⟧ a small stringed instrument of the harp family, used by the ancient Greeks

lyr·ic (lir'ik) ***adj.*** ⟦< Gr *lyrikos*⟧ **1** suitable for singing; specif., designating or of poetry expressing the poet's personal emotion **2** of or having a high voice with a light, flexible quality *[a lyric tenor]* —***n.*** **1** a lyric poem **2** [*usually pl.*] the words of a song

lyr'i·cal (-i kəl) ***adj.*** **1** LYRIC **2** expressing rapture or great enthusiasm

lyr'i·cism' (-ə siz'əm) ***n.*** lyric quality or style

lyr'i·cist (-ə sist) ***n.*** a writer of lyrics, esp. lyrics for popular songs

ly·ser·gic acid (lī sur'jik) *see* LSD

-ly·sis (lə sis, li-) ⟦< Gr *lysis*, a loosening⟧ *combining form* a loosening, dissolution, dissolving, destruction *[catalysis, electrolysis]*

-lyte (līt) ⟦< Gr *lyein*, dissolve⟧ *combining form* a substance undergoing decomposition *[electrolyte]*

THESAURUS

see GREEN 2.

luxurious ***a.*** comfortable, easy, affluent; see EXPENSIVE, RICH 2.

luxury ***n.*** **1** [Indulgence of the senses, regardless of the cost] gratification, costliness, expensiveness, richness, idleness, leisure, high living, lavishness; see also INDULGENCE 1.—*Ant.* POVERTY, deprivation, lack. **2** [An indulgence beyond one's means] extravagance, exorbitance, wastefulness; see EXCESS 1, WASTE 1.

lying[1,2] ***a.*** **1** [In the act of lying] falsifying, prevaricating, swearing falsely, committing perjury, fibbing, equivocating, inventing, misrepresenting.—*Ant.* FRANK, truthful, honest. **2** [Given to lying] deceitful, unreliable, double-dealing; see DISHONEST. **3** [Not reliable] unsound, tricky, treacherous; see FALSE 2. **4** [Prostrate] supine, reclining, resting, horizontal, reposing, recumbent, flat, fallen, prone, powerless.

lynch ***v.*** hang, string up*, murder; see KILL 1.

lyric ***n.*** **1** [Verses set to music] the words, the lyrics, the verse; see POEM. **2** [A short, songlike poem] lyrical poem, ode, sonnet, hymn, nursery rhyme; see also POETRY, SONG, VERSE 1.

M

m¹ or **M** (em) ***n.***, *pl.* **m's, M's** the 13th letter of the English alphabet
m² *abbrev.* **1** married **2** masculine **3** medium **4** meter(s) **5** mile(s) **6** minute(s)
M¹ (em) ***n.*** a Roman numeral for 1,000
M² *abbrev.* **1** male **2** married **3** medium **4** Monday **5** Monsieur
ma (mä) ***n.*** [Inf.] MOTHER (*n.* 1)
MA *abbrev.* **1** Massachusetts **2** ⟦L *Magister Artium*⟧ Master of Arts: also **M.A.**
ma'am (mam, mäm) *contr.* ***n.*** [Inf.] madam: used in direct address
ma·ca·bre (mə käb'rə, mə käb') ***adj.*** ⟦< OFr (*danse*) *Macabré*, (dance) of death⟧ grim and horrible; gruesome
mac·ad·am (mə kad'əm) ***n.*** ⟦after J. L. *McAdam* (1756-1836), Scot engineer⟧ small broken stones used in making roads, esp. such stones mixed with tar or asphalt
Ma·cao (mə kou') administrative zone of China, near Hong Kong: formerly under Portuguese administration
mac·a·ro·ni (mak'ə rō'nē) ***n.*** ⟦It *maccaroni*, ult. < Gr *makar*, blessed⟧ pasta in the form of tubes, etc.
mac·a·roon (mak'ə ro͞on') ***n.*** ⟦see prec.⟧ a small, chewy cookie made with crushed almonds or coconut
ma·caw (mə kô') ***n.*** ⟦prob. < AmInd (Brazil)⟧ a large, bright-colored parrot of Central and South America
Mac·beth (mək beth') ***n.*** the title character of a tragedy by Shakespeare
Mac·ca·bees (mak'ə bēz') ***n.*** a family of Jewish patriots who headed a successful revolt against the Syrians (175-164 B.C.)
mace¹ (mās) ***n.*** ⟦OFr *masse*⟧ **1** a heavy, spiked war club, used in the Middle Ages **2** a staff used as a symbol of authority by certain officials
mace² (mās) ***n.*** ⟦< ML *macis*⟧ a spice made from the husk of the nutmeg
Mace (mās) ⟦< MACE¹⟧ *trademark for* a gas, sold in aerosol containers, that temporarily stuns its victims —***n.*** [*often* **m-**] such a substance, or a container of it —***vt.*** **Maced, Mac'ing** [*often* **m-**] to spray with Mace
Mac·e·do·ni·a (mas'ə dō'nē ə) **1** ancient kingdom in SE Europe **2** country in the Balkan Peninsula: 9,928 sq. mi.; pop. 1,937,000 —**Mac'e·do'ni·an *adj.*, *n.***
mac·er·ate (mas'ər āt') ***vt.*** **-at'ed, -at'ing** ⟦< L *macerare*, soften⟧ **1** to soften and separate into parts by soaking in liquid **2** to steep (fruit or vegetables), as in wine **3** loosely, to tear, chop, etc. into bits —**mac'er·a'tion *n.***
ma·che·te (mə shet'ē, -chet'ē) ***n.*** ⟦Sp < L *marcus*, hammer⟧ a large knife used for cutting sugar cane, underbrush, etc., esp. in Central and South America
Mach·i·a·vel·li·an (mak'ē ə vel'ē ən, mäk'-) ***adj.*** ⟦after N. *Machiavelli* (1469-1527), It statesman⟧ crafty; deceitful
mach·i·na·tion (mak'ə nā'shən) ***n.*** ⟦< L *machinari*, to plot⟧ a plot or scheme, esp. one with evil intent: *usually used in pl.*
ma·chine (mə shēn') ***n.*** ⟦< Gr *mēchos*, contrivance⟧ **1** a structure consisting of a framework with various moving parts, for doing some kind of work **2** an organization functioning like a machine **3** the controlling group in a political party **4** *Mech.* a device, as the lever, that transmits, or changes the application of, energy —***adj.*** **1** of machines **2** done by machinery —***vt.*** **-chined', -chin'ing** to make, shape, etc. by machinery
machine gun an automatic gun, firing a rapid stream of bullets
machine language a language entirely in binary digits, used directly by a computer
ma·chin·er·y (mə shēn'ər ē, -shēn'rē) ***n.***, *pl.* **-ies** **1** machines collectively **2** the working parts of a machine **3** the means for keeping something going
ma·chin'ist ***n.*** one who makes, repairs, or operates machinery
ma·chis·mo (mä chēz'mō) ***n.*** ⟦Sp < *macho*, masculine + *-ismo*, -ISM⟧ overly assertive or exaggerated masculinity
Mach number (mäk) ⟦after E. *Mach* (1838-1916), Austrian physicist⟧ [*also* **m- n-**] a number indicating the ratio of an object's speed to the speed of sound in the surrounding medium
ma·cho (mä'chō) ***adj.*** ⟦Sp, masculine⟧ exhibiting or characterized by machismo
mack·er·el (mak'ər əl) ***n.***, *pl.* **-el** or **-els** ⟦< OFr *maquerel*⟧ an edible fish of the North Atlantic
Mack·i·naw (coat) (mak'ə nô') ⟦after *Mackinac* Island in N Lake Huron⟧ [*also* **m-**] a short, heavy, double-breasted woolen coat, usually plaid
mack·in·tosh (mak'in täsh') ***n.*** ⟦after C. *Macintosh*, 19th-c. Scot inventor⟧ a raincoat, orig., one made of rubberized cloth
Ma·con (mā'kən) city in central Georgia: pop. 107,000
mac·ra·mé (mak'rə mā') ***n.*** ⟦Fr, ult. < Ar *miqramah*, a veil⟧ a coarse fringe or lace made as of cord knotted in designs
macro- ⟦< Gr *makros*, long⟧ *combining form* long, large, enlarged
mac·ro·bi·ot·ics (mak'rō bī ät'iks) ***pl.n.*** ⟦< prec. + Gr *bios*, life⟧ [*with sing. v.*] the study of prolonging life, as by special diets —**mac'ro·bi·ot'ic *adj.***
mac'ro·cosm' (-käz'əm) ***n.*** ⟦see MACRO- & COSMOS⟧ **1** the universe **2** any large, complex entity
ma·cron (mā'krən) ***n.*** ⟦< Gr *makros*, long⟧ a mark (¯) placed over a vowel to indicate its pronunciation
mad (mad) ***adj.*** **mad'der, mad'dest** ⟦< OE (*ge*)*mædan*, make mad⟧ **1** insane **2** frantic *[mad* with fear*]* **3** foolish and rash **4** infatuated *[*he's *mad* about her*]* **5** wildly amusing **6** having rabies *[*a *mad* dog*]* **7** angry: often with *at* —**mad'ly *adv.*** —**mad'ness *n.***
Mad·a·gas·car (mad'ə gas'kər) island country off the SE coast of Africa: 226,658 sq. mi.; pop. 13,469,000
mad·am (mad'əm) ***n.***, *pl.* **mad'ams**; for 1, usually **mes·dames** (mā däm', -dam') ⟦Fr *madame*, orig. *ma dame*, my lady⟧ **1** a woman; lady: a polite term of address **2** a woman in charge of a brothel
ma·dame (mə däm', -dam'; mad'əm; *Fr* mȧ dȧm') ***n.***, *pl.* **mes·dames** (mā däm', -dam'; *Fr* mā dȧm') ⟦Fr: see prec.⟧ **1** a married woman: French title equivalent to *Mrs.* **2** a distinguished woman: used in English as a title of respect
mad·cap (mad'kap') ***n.*** ⟦MAD + CAP¹, figurative for head⟧ a reckless, impulsive person —***adj.*** reckless and impulsive
mad·den (mad''n) ***vt.***, ***vi.*** to make or become insane, angry, or wildly excited —**mad'den·ing *adj.*** —**mad'den·ing·ly *adv.***
mad·der (mad'ər) ***n.*** ⟦OE *mædere*⟧ **1** any of various related plants, esp. a vine with yellow flowers and a red root **2** a red dye made from this root
made (mād) ***vt.***, ***vi.*** *pt. & pp. of* MAKE
ma·de·moi·selle (mad'ə mə zel'; *Fr* mȧd mwȧ zel') ***n.***, *pl.* **-selles'**; Fr. ***mes·de·moi·selles*** (mād mwȧ zel') ⟦Fr < *ma*, my + *demoiselle*, young lady⟧ an unmarried woman or girl: French title equivalent to *Miss*
made'-to-or'der ***adj.*** made to conform to the customer's specifications
made'-up' ***adj.*** **1** put together **2** invented; false *[*a *made-up* story*]* **3** with cosmetics applied
mad'house' ***n.*** **1** an insame asylum **2** any place of turmoil, noise, etc.

THESAURUS

ma* ***n.*** mama*, mommy*, mom*; see MOTHER 1.
machine ***n.*** instrument, appliance, vehicle, computer, mechanism, implement, gadget; see also DEVICE 1, ENGINE, MOTOR, TOOL 1.
machine gun ***n.*** submachine gun, automatic rifle, semiautomatic rifle, tommy gun, burp gun*, Gatling gun, assault rifle, Uzi, M16, AK-47; see also GUN, WEAPON.
machinery ***n.*** appliances, implements, tools; see APPLIANCE, DEVICE 1, ENGINE, MACHINE, MOTOR.
mad ***a.*** **1** [Insane] demented, deranged, psychotic; see INSANE. **2** [Angry] provoked, enraged, exasperated; see ANGRY. **3** [Afflicted with rabies] rabid, hydrophobic, foaming at the mouth; see SICK. —**get mad** lose one's temper, become angry, rant and rave; see GET ANGRY.
madden ***v.*** annoy, infuriate, enrage; see ANGER.
maddening ***a.*** annoying, infuriating, offensive; see DISTURBING.
made ***a.*** fashioned, shaped, finished; see BUILT, FORMED, MANUFACTURED. —**have** (or **have got**) **it made*** succeed, be assured, be prosperous; see SUCCEED 1.
made-up ***a.*** **1** [False] invented, concocted, devised, fabricated, exaggerated, prepared, fictitious; see also FALSE 2, 3, UNREAL. **2** [Marked by the use of makeup] rouged, powdered, painted, colored, freshened, reddened.
madhouse ***n.*** mental hospital, asylum, bedlam; see HOSPITAL.

Mad·i·son[1] (mad′ə sən), **James** 1751-1836; 4th president of the U.S. (1809-17)

Mad·i·son[2] (mad′ə sən) capital of Wisconsin: pop. 191,000

mad′man′ (-man′, -mən) ***n.**, pl.* **-men′** (-men′, -mən) an insane person —**mad′wom′an**, *pl.* **-wom′en**, ***fem.n.***

Ma·don·na (mə dän′ə) ***n.*** ⟦It < *ma*, my + *donna*, lady⟧ **1** Mary, mother of Jesus **2** a picture or statue of Mary

ma·dras (ma′drəs, mə dras′) ***n.*** ⟦after fol.⟧ a fine, firm cotton cloth, usually striped or plaid

Ma·dras (mə dras′, -dräs′) seaport on the SE coast of India: pop. 4,289,000: now officially *Chennai*

Ma·drid (mə drid′) capital of Spain, in the central part: pop. 3,159,000

mad·ri·gal (ma′dri gəl) ***n.*** ⟦< It⟧ a part song, without accompaniment, popular in the 15th to 17th c.

mael·strom (māl′strəm) ***n.*** ⟦< Du *malen*, to grind + *stroom*, a stream⟧ **1** a large or violent whirlpool **2** an agitated state of mind, affairs, etc.

ma·es·tro (mīs′trō) ***n.**, pl.* **-tros** or **-tri** (-trē) ⟦It < L *magister,* master⟧ a master in any art; esp., a great composer or conductor of music

Ma·fi·a (mä′fē ə) ***n.*** ⟦It *maffia*⟧ a secret society engaged in illegal activities

Ma·fi·o·so (mä′fē ō′sō) ***n.**, pl.* **-si** (-sē) [*also* **m-**] a member of the Mafia

mag·a·zine (mag′ə zēn′) ***n.*** ⟦< Ar *makhzan,* storehouse⟧ **1** a military supply depot **2** a space in which explosives are stored, as in a fort **3** a supply chamber, as in a rifle or camera **4** a periodical publication containing stories, articles, etc.

Ma·gel·lan (mə jel′ən), **Fer·di·nand** (furd″n and′) 1480?-1521; Port. navigator in the service of Spain

ma·gen·ta (mə jen′tə) ***n.*** ⟦after *Magenta,* town in Italy⟧ **1** a purplish-red dye **2** purplish red —***adj.*** purplish-red

mag·got (mag′ət) ***n.*** ⟦ME *magotte*⟧ a wormlike insect larva, as of the housefly —**mag′got·y** ***adj.***

Ma·gi (mā′jī′) ***pl.n.**, sing.* **-gus** (-gəs) ⟦< Old Pers *magus,* magician⟧ the wise men who came bearing gifts to the infant Jesus

mag·ic (maj′ik) ***n.*** ⟦< Gr *magikos,* of the Magi, ancient Persian priests⟧ **1** the use of charms, spells, etc. in seeking or pretending to control events **2** any mysterious power *[*the *magic* of love*]* **3** the art of producing illusions by sleight of hand, etc. —***adj.*** **1** of, produced by, or using magic **2** producing extraordinary results, as if by magic —**mag′i·cal** ***adj.*** —**mag′i·cal·ly** ***adv.***

magic bullet an invention, discovery, etc. that solves a particular problem; esp., a medicine that can cure a disease

ma·gi·cian (mə jish′ən) ***n.*** ⟦< OFr *magicien*⟧ an expert in magic

mag·is·te·ri·al (maj′is tir′ē əl) ***adj.*** **1** of or suitable for a magistrate or master **2** authoritative —**mag′is·te′ri·al·ly** ***adv.***

mag·is·trate (maj′is trāt′) ***n.*** ⟦< L *magister,* master⟧ **1** a civil officer empowered to administer the law **2** a minor official, as a justice of the peace

mag·ma (mag′mə) ***n.*** ⟦< Gr *massein,* knead⟧ liquid or molten rock in the earth, which solidifies to produce igneous rock

Mag·na Car·ta or **Mag·na Char·ta** (mag′nə kär′tə) ⟦ML, great charter⟧ the charter, granted in 1215, that guarantees certain civil and political liberties to the English people

mag·nan·i·mous (mag nan′ə məs) ***adj.*** ⟦< L *magnus,* great + *animus,* soul⟧ generous in overlooking injury or insult; rising above pettiness; noble —**mag′na·nim′i·ty** (-nə nim′ə tē) ***n.*** —**mag·nan′i·mous·ly** ***adv.***

mag·nate (mag′nāt) ***n.*** ⟦< L *magnus,* great⟧ a very influential person, esp. in business

mag·ne·sia (mag nē′zhə, -shə) ***n.*** ⟦ModL, ult. < Gr *Magnēsia,* ancient Gr city⟧ magnesium oxide, a white powder, used as a mild laxative and antacid

mag·ne′si·um (-zē əm) ***n.*** ⟦ModL: see prec.⟧ a lightweight, metallic chemical element

mag·net (mag′nit) ***n.*** ⟦see MAGNESIA⟧ **1** any piece of iron or certain other materials that has the property of attracting similar material **2** one that attracts

mag·net·ic (mag net′ik) ***adj.*** **1** having the properties of a magnet **2** of, producing, or caused by magnetism **3** of the earth's magnetism **4** that can be magnetized **5** powerfully attractive —**mag·net′i·cal·ly** ***adv.***

magnetic field a physical field arising from an electric charge in motion, producing a force on a moving electric charge

magnetic tape a thin plastic ribbon with a magnetized coating for recording sounds, digital computer data, etc.

mag·net·ism (mag′nə tiz′əm) ***n.*** **1** the property, quality, or condition of being magnetic **2** the force to which this is due **3** personal charm

mag′net·ite′ (-tīt′) ***n.*** ⟦< Ger⟧ black iron oxide, an important iron ore

mag′net·ize′ (-tīz′) ***vt.*** **-ized′**, **-iz′ing** **1** to give magnetic properties to (steel, iron, etc.) **2** to charm (a person) —**mag′net·i·za′tion** ***n.***

mag·ne·to (mag nēt′ō) ***n.**, pl.* **-tos** an electric generator, often a small one, in which one or more permanent magnets produce the magnetic field

mag·ne·tom·e·ter (mag′nə täm′ət ər) ***n.*** **1** an instrument for measuring magnetic forces **2** such an instrument used as to detect concealed metal weapons at airports, etc.

magnet school a public school offering new and special courses to attract students from a broad urban area so as to bring about desegregation

mag·nif·i·cent (mag nif′ə sənt) ***adj.*** ⟦< L *magnus*, great + *facere*, do⟧ **1** splendid, stately, or sumptuous, as in form **2** exalted: said of ideas, etc. **3** [Inf.] excellent —**mag·nif′i·cence** ***n.*** —**mag·nif′i·cent·ly** ***adv.***

mag·ni·fy (mag′nə fī′) ***vt.*** **-fied′**, **-fy′ing** ⟦see prec.⟧ **1** to exaggerate **2** to increase the apparent size of, esp. with a lens **3** [Archaic] to praise —***vi.*** to have the power of increasing the apparent size of an object —**mag′ni·fi·ca′tion** ***n.*** —**mag′ni·fi′er** ***n.***

mag′ni·tude′ (-to͞od′) ***n.*** ⟦< L *magnus,* great⟧ **1** greatness of size, extent, etc. **2** *a)* size *b)* loudness (of sound) *c)* importance **3** the degree of brightness of a star, etc.

mag·no·li·a (mag nō′lē ə, -nōl′yə) ***n.*** ⟦after P. *Magnol*

THESAURUS

madly ***a.*** rashly, crazily, hastily; see VIOLENTLY, WILDLY.

madman ***n.*** lunatic, psychopath, maniac, insane person, deranged person, psychiatric patient, nut*, screwball*, oddball*, psycho*, loony*, wacko*, schizo*, cuckoo*.

madness ***n.*** derangement, aberration, delusion; see INSANITY.

magazine ***n.*** publication, pamphlet, booklet, manual, circular, journal, periodical, weekly, monthly, quarterly, annual, bulletin, transactions, review, supplement, gazette, report, brochure, pulp, zine, glossy*, slick*.

maggot ***n.*** grub, slug, larva; see PARASITE 1, WORM.

magic ***a.*** magical, mystic, diabolic, Satanic, necromantic, fiendish, demoniac, malevolent, shamanist, voodooistic, conjuring, spellbinding, enchanting, fascinating, cryptic, transcendental, supernatural, alchemistic, spooky, ghostly, haunted, weird, uncanny, eerie, disembodied, immaterial, astral, spiritualistic, psychic, supersensory, otherworldly, fairylike, mythical, mythic, charmed, spellbound, enchanted, under a spell, bewitched, entranced, cursed, prophetic, telepathic, clairvoyant, telekinetic, parapsychological; see also MYSTERIOUS 2.

magic ***n.*** **1** [The controlling of supernatural powers] occultism, legerdemain, necromancy, incantation, spell, wizardry, alchemy, superstition, enchantment, sorcery, prophecy, divination, astrology, taboo, witchcraft, black magic, voodooism, fire worship; see also WITCHCRAFT. **2** [An example of magic] incantation, prediction, soothsaying, fortunetelling, foreboding, exorcism, ghost dance.

magical ***a.*** occult, enchanting, mystic; see MAGIC, MYSTERIOUS 2.

magician ***n.*** enchanter, necromancer, conjurer, seer, soothsayer, diviner, sorcerer, wizard, warlock, medicine man, shaman, exorcist; see also PROPHET, WITCH.

magnet ***n.*** lodestone, magnetite, magnetic iron ore, natural magnet, artificial magnet, bar magnet, electromagnet, horseshoe magnet.

magnetic ***a.*** irresistible, captivating, fascinating; see CHARMING.

magnetism ***n.*** lure, influence, charm; see ATTRACTION.

magnificence ***n.*** grandeur, majesty, stateliness, nobleness, glory, radiance, grace, beauty, style, flourish, luxuriousness, glitter, nobility, greatness, lavishness, brilliance, splendor, richness, pomp; see also GRANDEUR.—*Ant.* DULLNESS, simplicity, unostentatiousness.

magnificent ***a.*** exalted, great, majestic; see GRAND.

magnify ***v.*** amplify, blow up, expand; see INCREASE.

magnitude ***n.*** **1** [Size] extent, breadth, dimension; see MEASURE 1, MEASUREMENT 2, QUANTITY, SIZE. **2** [Importance] greatness, consequence, significance; see DEGREE 2, IMPORTANCE.

(1638-1715), Fr botanist⟧ a tree with large, fragrant flowers of white, pink, or purple
mag·num (mag′nəm) ***n.*** ⟦< L *magnus,* great⟧ **1** a wine bottle holding 1.5 liters **2** [*usually* **M-**] a firearm, esp. a revolver, that fires magnum cartridges —***adj.*** of or pertaining to a cartridge having great explosive force for its size
mag·num o·pus (mag′nəm ō′pəs) ⟦L⟧ a great work; masterpiece
mag·pie (mag′pī′) ***n.*** ⟦< *Mag,* dim. of *Margaret* + *pie,* magpie⟧ **1** a noisy, black-and-white bird related to the jay **2** a person who chatters
Mag·yar (mag′yär′) ***n.*** **1** a member of the main ethnic group of Hungary **2** the language of this people
ma·ha·ra·jah or **ma·ha·ra·ja** (mä′hə rä′jə) ***n.*** ⟦< Sans *mahā,* great + *rājā,* king⟧ [Historical] in India, a prince, specif. the ruler of a native state —**ma′ha·ra′ni** or **ma′ha·ra′nee** (-nē) ***fem.n.***
ma·ha·ri·shi (mä′hə rish′ē) ***n.*** ⟦Hindi < *mahā,* great + *ṛshi,* sage⟧ a Hindu teacher of mysticism
ma·hat·ma (mə hat′mə, -hät′-) ***n.*** ⟦< Sans *mahā,* great + *ātman,* soul⟧ in India, any of a class of wise and holy persons held in special regard
mah-jongg or **mah·jong** (mä′jôŋ′, -zhôŋ′) ***n.*** ⟦< Chin *ma-ch'iao,* sparrow, a figure on one of the tiles⟧ a game of Chinese origin played with small pieces called *tiles*
Mah·ler (mä′lər), **Gus·tav** (goos′täf′) 1860-1911; Austrian composer & conductor
ma·hog·a·ny (mə häg′ə nē, -hôg′-) ***n.,*** *pl.* **-nies** ⟦< ?⟧ **1** *a)* a tropical American tree *b)* the reddish-brown wood of this tree **2** reddish brown
Ma·hom·et (mə häm′it) *var. of* MOHAMMED
ma·hout (mə hout′) ***n.*** ⟦< Hindi⟧ in India, an elephant driver or keeper
maid (mād) ***n.*** **1** [Now Chiefly Literary] a girl or young unmarried woman **2** a female servant
maid·en (mād′'n) ***n.*** ⟦OE *mægden*⟧ [Now Rare] a girl or young unmarried woman —***adj.*** **1** of or for a maiden **2** unmarried or virgin **3** untried **4** first *[a maiden* voyage*]* —**maid′en·hood′** ***n.*** —**maid′en·ly** ***adj.***
maid′en·hair′ (fern) a delicate fern
maid′en·head′ (-hed′) ***n.*** the hymen
maiden name the surname that a married woman had when not yet married
maid of honor an unmarried woman acting as chief attendant to a bride
maid′ser′vant ***n.*** a female servant
mail[1] (māl) ***n.*** ⟦< OHG *malaha,* wallet⟧ **1** letters, packages, etc. transported and delivered by the post office **2** a postal system —***adj.*** of mail —***vt.*** to send by mail —**mail′er** ***n.***
mail[2] (māl) ***n.*** ⟦< L *macula,* mesh of a net⟧ flexible body armor made of small metal rings, scales, etc.
mail′box′ ***n.*** **1** a box into which mail is put when delivered **2** a box into which mail is put for collection Also **mail box**
mail carrier a person who carries and delivers mail
mail′man′ (-man′, -mən) ***n.,*** *pl.* **-men′** (-men′, -mən) a man who is a mail carrier
mail order an order for goods to be sent by mail —**mail′-or′der** ***adj.***
maim (mām) ***vt.*** ⟦OFr *mahaigner*⟧ to disable; mutilate
main (mān) ***n.*** ⟦OE *mægen,* strength⟧ **1** a principal pipe in a distribution system for water, gas, etc. **2** [Old Poet.] the ocean —***adj.*** chief in size, importance, etc.; principal —**by main force** (or **strength**) by sheer force (or strength) —**in the main** mostly; chiefly —**with might and main** with all one's strength
main clause *Gram.* INDEPENDENT CLAUSE
main drag [Slang] the principal street of a city or town
Maine (mān) New England state of the U.S.: 30,865 sq. mi.; pop. 1,228,000; cap. Augusta: abbrev. *ME* —**Main·er** (mā′nər) ***n.***
main·frame (mān′frām′) ***n.*** **1** the central processing unit of a large computer **2** a very large computer, to which several terminals may be connected
main′land′ (-land′, -lənd) ***n.*** the principal land mass of a continent, as distinguished from nearby islands —**main′land′er** ***n.***
main′line′ ***n.*** the principal road, course, etc. —***vt.*** **-lined′, -lin′ing** [Slang] to inject (a narcotic drug) directly into a large vein
main′ly ***adv.*** chiefly; principally
main′mast′ (-mast′; *naut.,* -məst) ***n.*** the principal mast of a vessel
main′sail′ (-sāl′; *naut.,* -səl) ***n.*** the principal sail of a vessel, set from the mainmast
main′spring′ ***n.*** **1** the principal spring in a clock, watch, etc. **2** the chief motive or cause
main′stay′ ***n.*** **1** the supporting line extending forward from the mainmast **2** a chief support
main′stream′ ***n.*** a major trend or line of thought, action, etc. —***vt.*** to cause to undergo mainstreaming
main′stream′ing ***n.*** the placement of disabled people into regular school classes, workplaces, etc.
main·tain (mān tān′) ***vt.*** ⟦< L *manu tenere,* hold in the hand⟧ **1** to keep or keep up; carry on **2** to keep in continuance or in a certain state, as of repair **3** to affirm or assert **4** to support by providing what is needed —**main·tain′a·ble** ***adj.***
main·te·nance (mānt′'n əns) ***n.*** a maintaining or being maintained
mai tai (mī′ tī′) ⟦Tahitian, lit., good⟧ [*often* **M- T-**] a cocktail of rum, fruit juices, etc.
mai·tre d′ (māt′ər dē′) ⟦< fol.⟧ [Inf.] MAÎTRE D'HÔTEL
maî·tre d'hô·tel (me tr′ dô tel′) ⟦Fr, master of the house⟧ a supervisor of waiters and waitresses
maize (māz) ***n.*** ⟦< WInd *mahiz*⟧ **1** *chiefly Brit. name for* CORN[1] (*n.* 2) **2** yellow
Maj *abbrev.* Major
ma·jes·tic (mə jes′tik) ***adj.*** grand; stately —**ma·jes′ti·cal·ly** ***adv.***
maj·es·ty (maj′is tē) ***n.,*** *pl.* **-ties** ⟦< L *magnus,* great⟧ **1** [**M-**] a title used in speaking to or of a sovereign **2** grandeur
ma·jol·i·ca (mə jäl′i kə) ***n.*** ⟦It⟧ Italian glazed pottery
ma·jor (mā′jər) ***adj.*** ⟦L, compar. of *magnus,* great⟧ **1** greater in size, amount, importance, etc. **2** *Music* designating an interval greater than the corresponding minor by a half tone —***vi.*** *Educ.* to specialize (*in* a field of study) —***n.*** **1** *U.S. Mil.* an officer ranking just above a captain **2** a field of study in which a student specializes
ma′jor-do′mo (-dō′mō) ***n.,*** *pl.* **-mos** ⟦< L *major,* greater + *domus,* house⟧ a man in charge of a great household

THESAURUS

maid ***n.*** **1** [A female servant] maidservant, nursemaid, housemaid, chambermaid, domestic, cleaning lady; see also SERVANT. **2** [A girl] child, maiden, schoolgirl; see GIRL, WOMAN 1.
maiden ***a.*** earliest, beginning, initial; see FIRST.
maiden name ***n.*** family name, inherited name, surname; see NAME 1.
mail[1] ***n.*** letter, missive, snail mail, communication, correspondence, airmail letters, postal card, junk mail, postcard, printed matter, e-mail; see also LETTER 2.
mail[1] ***v.*** post, send by mail, drop into a mailbox; see SEND 1.
mailed ***a.*** posted, sent by post, delivered, in the mail, shipped, consigned, dispatched, sent by mail, dropped in a mailbox, e-mailed; see also SENT.
maim ***v.*** mutilate, disable, disfigure; see DAMAGE, HURT.
main ***a.*** **1** [Principal] chief, dominant, first, authoritative, significant, most important, superior, foremost, central, leading; see also MAJOR 1. **2** [Only] utter, pure, simple; see ABSOLUTE.
mainland ***n.*** shore, beach, dry land; see LAND 1, REGION 1.
mainly ***a.*** chiefly, largely, essentially; see PRINCIPALLY.
maintain ***v.*** **1** [To uphold] hold up, advance, keep; see SUPPORT 2, SUSTAIN 1. **2** [To assert] state, affirm, attest; see DECLARE, REPORT 1, SAY. **3** [To keep ready for use] preserve, keep, conserve, repair, withhold, renew, reserve, defer, hold back, have in store, care for, save, put away, set aside, store up, keep for, lay aside, lay away, set by, keep on hand, keep in reserve, set apart, keep up, keep aside, control, hold over, manage, direct, have, own, sustain, secure, stick to, stand by; see also KEEP 1.—*Ant.* WASTE, neglect, consume. **4** [To continue] carry on, persevere, keep on; see CONTINUE 1. **5** [To support] provide for, take care of, keep; see SUPPORT 3, SUSTAIN 2.
maintenance ***n.*** sustenance, livelihood, resources; see PAY 1, 2, SUBSISTENCE 2.
majestic ***a.*** dignified, sumptuous, exalted; see GRAND, NOBLE 1, 3.
majesty ***n.*** **1** [Grandeur] splendor, magnificence, greatness; see GRANDEUR. **2** [A form of address; *usually capital*] Lord, King, Emperor, Prince, Royal Highness, Highness, Sire, Eminence, Queen.
major ***a.*** **1** [Greater] higher, larger, dominant, primary, upper, exceeding, extreme, ultra, over, above; see also SUPERIOR. **2** [Important] significant, main, influential; see IMPORTANT 1, PRINCIPAL.

ma'jor·ette' (-et') ***n.*** a girl or woman with a baton, who leads or accompanies a marching band; drum majorette

major general *pl.* **major generals** *U.S. Mil.* an officer ranking just above a brigadier general

ma·jor·i·ty (mə jôr'ə tē) ***n.***, *pl.* **-ties** ⟦see MAJOR⟧ **1** [*also with pl. v.*] the greater number; more than half of a total **2** the number by which the votes cast for the candidate who receives more than half the votes, exceed the remaining votes **3** full legal age **4** the military rank of a major

major scale a musical scale with semitones between the third and fourth and the seventh and eighth tones, and whole tones in all other positions

make (māk) ***vt.* made, mak'ing** ⟦OE *macian*⟧ **1** to bring into being; build, create, produce, etc. **2** to cause to be or become *[made* king, *made* sad*]* **3** to prepare for use *[make* the beds*]* **4** to amount to *[*two pints *make* a quart*]* **5** to have the qualities of *[*to *make* a fine leader*]* **6** to acquire; earn **7** to cause the success of *[*that venture *made* her*]* **8** to regard as the meaning (*of*) *[*what do you *make* of that?*]* **9** to execute, do, etc. *[*to *make* a speech*]* **10** to cause or force: with an infinitive without *to [make* him behave*]* **11** to arrive at; reach *[*the ship *made* port*]* **12** [Inf.] to get on or in *[*to *make* the team*]* —***vi.*** **1** to behave as specified *[make* bold*]* **2** to cause something to be as specified *[make* ready*]* —***n.*** **1** the way in which something is made; style **2** a type or brand —**make away with** to steal —**make believe** to pretend —**make someone's day** [Slang] to give pleasure that will be the high point of someone's day —**make do** to manage with what is available —**make for** **1** to go toward **2** to help effect —**make good** **1** to repay or replace **2** to fulfill **3** to succeed —**make it** [Inf.] to achieve a certain thing —**make off with** to steal —**make out** **1** to see with difficulty **2** to understand **3** to fill out (a blank form, etc.) **4** to (try to) show or prove to be **5** to succeed; get along **6** [Slang] *a*) to kiss and caress as lovers *b*) to have sexual intercourse —**make over** **1** to change; renovate **2** to transfer the ownership of —**make something of** **1** to treat as of great importance **2** [Inf.] to make an issue of —**make up** **1** to put together **2** to form; constitute **3** to invent **4** to complete by providing what is lacking **5** to compensate (*for*) **6** to become friendly again after a quarrel **7** to put on cosmetics, etc. —**make up one's mind** to come to a decision —**make up to** to try to win over, as by flattering —**mak'er** ***n.***

make'-be·lieve' ***n.*** pretense; feigning —***adj.*** pretended; feigned

make'o'ver ***n.*** **1** a renovation **2** a change in someone's appearance made by altering makeup, hairstyle, etc.

make'shift' ***n.*** a temporary substitute or expedient —***adj.*** that will do as a temporary substitute

make'up' or **make'-up'** ***n.*** **1** the way something is put together; composition **2** nature; disposition **3** the cosmetics, etc. used by an actor **4** cosmetics generally

make'-work' ***adj.*** that serves no other purpose than to give an idle or unemployed person something to do *[*a *make-work* project*]*

mal- ⟦< L *malus,* bad⟧ *prefix* bad or badly, wrong, ill

mal·ad·just·ed (mal'ə jus'tid) ***adj.*** poorly adjusted; specif., unable to adjust to the stresses of daily life —**mal'ad·just'ment** ***n.***

mal·a·droit (mal'ə droit') ***adj.*** ⟦Fr: see MAL- & ADROIT⟧ awkward; clumsy; bungling —**mal'a·droit'ly** ***adv.***

mal·a·dy (mal'ə dē) ***n.***, *pl.* **-dies** ⟦< VL *male habitus,* badly kept⟧ a disease; illness

ma·laise (ma lāz') ***n.*** ⟦Fr < *mal,* bad + *aise,* ease⟧ a vague feeling of illness

mal·a·mute (mal'ə myo͞ot') ***n.*** ⟦< *Malemute,* an Eskimo tribe⟧ a strong dog developed as a sled dog by Alaskan Eskimos

mal·a·prop·ism (mal'ə präp'iz'əm) ***n.*** ⟦after Mrs. *Malaprop* in Sheridan's *The Rivals* (1775)⟧ a ludicrous misuse of words that sound alike

ma·lar·i·a (mə ler'ē ə) ***n.*** ⟦It < *mala aria,* bad air⟧ an infectious disease transmitted by the anopheles mosquito, characterized by severe chills and fever —**ma·lar'i·al** ***adj.***

ma·lar·key or **ma·lar·ky** (mə lär'kē) ***n.*** ⟦< ?⟧ [Slang] nonsensical talk

mal·a·thi·on (mal'ə thī'än') ***n.*** ⟦< chemical names⟧ an organic insecticide

Ma·la·wi (mä'lä wē') country in SE Africa: 45,747 sq. mi.; pop. 7,983,000

Ma·lay (mā'lā', mə lā') ***n.*** **1** the language of a large group of indigenous peoples of the Malay Peninsula and the Malay Archipelago, now the official language of Malaysia and Indonesia **2** a member of any of these peoples —***adj.*** of these peoples or their language or culture

Mal·a·ya·lam (mal'ə yä'ləm) ***n.*** a language of the SW coast of India

Malay Archipelago large group of islands between SE Asia & Australia

Malay Peninsula peninsula in SE Asia

Ma·lay·sia (mə lā'zhə) **1** MALAY ARCHIPELAGO **2** country in SE Asia, mostly on the Malay Peninsula: 127,317 sq. mi.; pop. 17,567,000 —**Ma·lay'sian** ***adj., n.***

mal·con·tent (mal'kən tent') ***adj.*** ⟦OFr: see MAL- & CONTENT[1]⟧ dissatisfied or rebellious —***n.*** a malcontent person

Mal·dives (mal'dīvz) country on a group of islands (**Mal'dive Islands**) in the Indian Ocean: 115 sq. mi.; pop. 213,000

male (māl) ***adj.*** ⟦< L *mas,* a male⟧ **1** designating or of the sex that fertilizes the ovum **2** of, like, or suitable for men or boys; masculine **3** having a part shaped to fit into a corresponding hollow part (called *female*): said of electric plugs, etc. —***n.*** a male person, animal, or plant

mal·e·dic·tion (mal'ə dik'shən) ***n.*** ⟦see MAL- & DICTION⟧ a curse

mal'e·fac'tor (-fak'tər) ***n.*** ⟦< L *male,* evil + *facere,* do⟧ an evildoer or criminal —**mal'e·fac'tion** ***n.***

ma·lef·i·cent (mə lef'ə sənt) ***adj.*** ⟦< L: see prec.⟧ harmful; evil —**ma·lef'i·cence** ***n.***

ma·lev·o·lent (mə lev'ə lənt) ***adj.*** ⟦< L *male,* evil + *velle,* to wish⟧ wishing evil or harm to others; malicious —**ma·lev'o·lence** ***n.***

THESAURUS

majority ***n.*** **1** [The larger part] bulk, more than half, preponderance, most, best, gross, lion's share, greater number. **2** [Legal maturity] legal age, adulthood, voting age; see MANHOOD 1.

make ***v.*** **1** [To manufacture] construct, fabricate, assemble, fashion, form, shape, mold, compose, compile, create, effect, produce; see also BUILD, MANUFACTURE. **2** [To total] add up to, come to, equal; see AMOUNT TO. **3** [To create] originate, actualize, effect, generate, compose, plan, devise, construct, cause, conceive; see also COMPOSE 2, CREATE , INVENT 1, PRODUCE 2. **4** [To acquire] gain, get, secure; see GET 1. **5** [To force] constrain, compel, coerce; see FORCE. **6** [To cause] start, effect, initiate; see BEGIN 1, CAUSE. **7** [To wage] carry on, conduct, engage in; see ACT 2. **8** [To prepare] get ready, arrange, fix; see COOK, PREPARE 1. —**make believe** feign, simulate, counterfeit; see DREAM 2, PRETEND 1, 2. —**make do** get by, manage, accept; see ENDURE 2, SURVIVE 1, USE 1. —**make it*** achieve, triumph, accomplish; see SUCCEED 1. —**make off with** abduct, rob, kidnap; see STEAL. —**make out** **1** [To understand] perceive, recognize, see; see UNDERSTAND 1. **2** [To succeed] accomplish, achieve, prosper; see SUCCEED 1. **3** [To see] discern, perceive, detect; see DISCOVER, SEE 1. —**make over** **1** [To improve] amend, correct, restore; see IMPROVE 1, REDECORATE, REMODEL. **2** [To rebuild] renovate, reconstruct, refurbish; see REPAIR, RESTORE 3. —**make up** **1** [To compose] compound, combine, mingle; see JOIN 1, MIX 1. **2** [To constitute] comprise, belong to, go into the making of, be contained in, be an element of, be a portion of, include, consist of; see also COMPOSE 1. **3** [To invent] fabricate, devise, fashion; see COMPOSE 2, CREATE, INVENT 1. **4** [To reconcile] conciliate, pacify, accommodate; see RECONCILE 2. **5** [To apply cosmetics] apply face powder, apply lipstick, apply eye shadow, etc.; powder, beautify, do up*, put one's face on. —**make up one's mind** choose, pick, elect; see DECIDE, RESOLVE.

make-believe ***a.*** fraudulent, pretended, acted; see FALSE 3, FANTASTIC, UNREAL.

make-believe ***n.*** sham, unreality, fairy tale; see FANTASY, PRETENSE 2.

makeshift ***a.*** substitute, alternative, stopgap; see TEMPORARY.

makeup ***n.*** **1** [Cosmetics] greasepaint, mascara, eyeliner, powder, foundation, eye shadow, lipstick, lip gloss, rouge, blush, war paint*; see also COSMETIC. **2** [Composition] construction, structure, arrangement; see COMPOSITION, DESIGN, FORMATION.

making ***n.*** performing, conception, formulation, devising, producing, constituting, causation, fashioning, building, origination, shaping, forging, designing, planning, fabrication, composition; see also PRODUCTION 1.

male ***a.*** manlike, virile, macho; see MASCULINE.

male ***n.*** fellow, man, guy; see BOY, FATHER 1.

mal·fea·sance (mal fē′zəns) ***n.*** ⟦< Fr *mal,* evil + *faire,* do⟧ wrongdoing, esp. by a public official

mal·for·ma·tion (mal′fôr mā′shən) ***n.*** faulty or abnormal formation of a body or part —**mal·formed′** ***adj.***

mal·func·tion (mal fuŋk′shən) ***vi.*** to fail to function as it should —***n.*** an instance of malfunctioning

Ma·li (mä′lē) country in W Africa: 478,841 sq. mi.; pop. 9,820,000

mal·ice (mal′is) ***n.*** ⟦< L *malus,* bad⟧ **1** active ill will; desire to harm another **2** *Law* evil intent

ma·li·cious (mə lish′əs) ***adj.*** having, showing, or caused by malice; spiteful —**ma·li′cious·ly** ***adv.***

ma·lign (mə līn′) ***vt.*** ⟦< L *male,* ill + *genus,* born⟧ to speak evil of; slander —***adj.*** **1** malicious **2** evil; baleful **3** very harmful

ma·lig′nan·cy (-nən sē) ***n.*** **1** malignant quality **2** *pl.* **-cies** a malignant tumor

ma·lig·nant (mə lig′nənt) ***adj.*** ⟦see MALIGN⟧ **1** having an evil influence **2** wishing evil **3** very harmful **4** causing or likely to cause death; specif., cancerous —**ma·lig′ni·ty** (-nə tē), *pl.* **-ties**, ***n.***

ma·lin·ger (mə liŋ′gər) ***vi.*** ⟦< Fr *malingre,* sickly⟧ to feign illness so as to escape duty —**ma·lin′ger·er** ***n.***

mall (môl) ***n.*** ⟦< *maul,* mallet: from use in a game on outdoor lanes⟧ **1** a shaded walk or public promenade **2** *a*) a shop-lined street for pedestrians only *b*) an enclosed shopping center

mal·lard (mal′ərd) ***n.*** ⟦< OFr *malart*⟧ the common wild duck

mal·le·a·ble (mal′ē ə bəl) ***adj.*** ⟦< L *malleus,* a hammer⟧ **1** that can be hammered, pounded, or pressed into various shapes without breaking **2** adaptable —**mal′le·a·bil′i·ty** ***n.***

mal·let (mal′ət) ***n.*** ⟦< L *malleus,* a hammer⟧ **1** a short-handled hammer with a wooden head, for driving a chisel, etc. **2** any similar, long-handled hammer, as for use in croquet or polo **3** a small hammer for playing a xylophone, etc.

mal·low (mal′ō) ***n.*** ⟦< L *malva*⟧ any of a family of plants, including the hollyhock, cotton, and okra, with large, showy flowers

mal·nour·ished (mal nur′isht) ***adj.*** improperly nourished

mal·nu·tri·tion (mal′no͞o trish′ən) ***n.*** faulty or inadequate nutrition or nourishment

mal′oc·clu′sion (-ə klo͞o′zhən) ***n.*** improper meeting of the upper and lower teeth

mal·o′dor·ous (-ō′dər əs) ***adj.*** having a bad odor; stinking

mal·prac′tice (-prak′tis) ***n.*** professional misconduct or improper practice, esp. by a physician

malt (môlt) ***n.*** ⟦OE *mealt*⟧ barley or other grain soaked until it sprouts, then dried in a kiln: used in brewing and distilling —***adj.*** made with malt

Mal·ta (môl′tə) country on a group of islands in the Mediterranean, south of Sicily: 122 sq. mi.; pop. 376,000

malt′ed (milk) a drink made by mixing a preparation of powdered malt and dried milk, with milk, ice cream, etc.

Mal·tese (môl tēz′) ***n.*** **1** the language of Malta, closely related to Arabic **2** *pl.* **Mal·tese′** a person born or living in Malta —***adj.*** of Malta or its people, language, etc.

malt liquor beer, ale, or the like made from malt by fermentation

mal·treat (mal trēt′) ***vt.*** ⟦see MAL- & TREAT⟧ to treat roughly, unkindly, or brutally; abuse —**mal·treat′ment** ***n.***

ma·ma or **mam′ma** (mä′mə, mə mä′) ***n.*** *child's term for* MOTHER

mam·mal (mam′əl) ***n.*** ⟦< L *mamma,* breast⟧ any of a large group of warmblooded vertebrates the females of which have milk-secreting glands (**mam′ma·ry glands**) for feeding their offspring —**mam·ma·li·an** (mə mā′lē ən) ***adj.***, ***n.***

mam·mo·gram (mam′ə gram′) ***n.*** an X-ray obtained by mammography

mam·mog·ra·phy (mə mäg′rə fē) ***n.*** ⟦< L *mamma,* breast + -GRAPHY⟧ an X-ray technique for detecting breast tumors before they can be seen or felt

mam·mon (mam′ən) ***n.*** ⟦< Aram⟧ [*often* **M-**] riches regarded as an object of worship and greedy pursuit

mam·moth (mam′əth) ***n.*** ⟦< Russ *mamont*⟧ an extinct elephant with long tusks and hairy skin —***adj.*** huge; enormous

man (man) ***n.***, *pl.* **men** (men) ⟦OE *mann*⟧ **1** a human being; person **2** the human race; mankind **3** an adult male person **4** an adult male servant, employee, etc. **5** a husband or male lover **6** any of the pieces used in chess, checkers, etc. —***vt.*** **manned**, **man′ning** **1** to furnish with a labor force for work, defense, etc. **2** to take one's station in or at **3** to strengthen; brace *[to man oneself for an ordeal]* —**as a** (or **one**) **man** in unison; unanimously —**to a man** with no exception

Man (man), **Isle of** one of the British Isles, between Northern Ireland & England

-man (mən, man) *combining form* man or person of a (specified) kind, in a (specified) activity, etc.: now often replaced by -PERSON or -WOMAN

man·a·cle (man′ə kəl) ***n.*** ⟦< L *manus,* hand⟧ a handcuff: *usually used in pl.* —***vt.*** **-cled**, **-cling** **1** to put handcuffs on **2** to restrain

man·age (man′ij) ***vt.*** **-aged**, **-ag·ing** ⟦< L *manus,* hand⟧ **1** to control the movement or behavior of **2** to have charge of; direct *[to manage a hotel]* **3** to succeed in accomplishing —***vi.*** **1** to carry on business **2** to contrive to get along —**man′age·a·ble** ***adj.***

managed care a plan or system for providing medical services at reduced costs to patients who agree to use specified doctors and hospitals

man′age·ment ***n.*** **1** a managing or being managed **2** the persons managing a business, institution, etc.

man′ag·er ***n.*** one who manages; esp., one who manages a business, etc.

THESAURUS

malformed ***a.*** distorted, grotesque, abnormal; see DEFORMED, TWISTED 1.

malfunction ***n.*** slip, bad performance, glitch*; see FAILURE 1.

malice ***n.*** spite, animosity, resentment; see EVIL 1, HATRED.

malicious ***a.*** wicked, spiteful, hateful; see BAD 1.

malignant ***a.*** **1** [Diseased] cancerous, lethal, poisonous; see DEADLY. **2** [Harmful] deleterious, corrupt, subversive; see DANGEROUS, HARMFUL.

malpractice ***n.*** negligence, misbehavior, neglect; see CARELESSNESS, VIOLATION.

mama* ***n.*** mom*, ma*, mommy*; see MOTHER 1.

mammal ***n.*** quadraped, suckler, beast; see ANIMAL.

man ***n.*** **1** [The human race] mankind, human beings, humanity, human species, human nature, persons, mortals, individuals, earthlings, men and women, civilized society, creatures, fellow creatures, people, folk, society, *Homo sapiens* (Latin). **2** [An adult male] he, gentleman, Sir, Mr., fellow, mister, master, chap*, guy*; see also BOY. **3** [Anyone] human being, an individual, fellow creature; see PERSON 1. **4** [An employee] hand, worker, representative; see EMPLOYEE. **5** [Husband] married man, spouse, partner; see HUSBAND. —**as a** (or **one**) **man** in unison, united, all together; see UNANIMOUSLY. —**be one's own man** be independent, stand alone, be free; see ENDURE 1. —**to a man** all, everyone, with no exception; see EVERYBODY.

man ***v.*** garrison, protect, fortify; see DEFEND 1, GUARD.

manage ***v.*** **1** [To direct] lead, oversee, instruct, mastermind, engineer, show, dominate, execute, handle, watch, guide, supervise, conduct, pilot, steer, run, minister, regulate, administer, delegate, manipulate, officiate, superintend, preside, control, operate, maneuver, maintain, care for, take over, take care of, carry on, watch over, have in one's charge, look after, see to, run the show*, call the shots*, run a tight ship*.—*Ant.* OBEY, follow, take orders. **2** [To contrive] accomplish, bring about, effect; see ACHIEVE, SUCCEED 1. **3** [To get along] bear up, survive, get by; see ENDURE 2.

manageable ***a.*** controllable, docile, compliant, governable, teachable, tractable, willing, obedient, submissive, yielding, adaptable, flexible, dutiful, humble, meek, easy; see also GENTLE 3, OBEDIENT 1, WILLING.—*Ant.* REBELLIOUS, unwilling, defiant.

managed ***a.*** **1** [Trained] handled, guided, persuaded, influenced, driven, counseled, urged, taught, instructed, coached, groomed, primed; see also EDUCATED, TRAINED.—*Ant.* WILD, undisciplined, unrestrained. **2** [Governed] ruled, controlled, dominated, commanded, directed, swayed, mastered, run, regulated, ordered, compelled, supervised, piloted, cared for, taken care of; see also GOVERNED.—*Ant.* FREE, ungoverned, unsupervised.

management ***n.*** **1** [Direction] command, supervision, superintendence, government, guidance, conduct, organization, handling, policy, order, power, control; see also COMMAND. **2** [Those who undertake management; *usually preceded by "the"*] directors, administrators, executives; see ADMINISTRATION 2.

manager ***n.*** director, handler, superintendent, supervisor; see also EXECUTIVE.

man·a·ge·ri·al (man′ə jir′ē əl) ***adj.*** of a manager or management

ma·ña·na (mä nyä′nä) ***n., adv.*** ⟦Sp⟧ tomorrow or (at) an indefinite future time

Ma·nas·sas (mə nas′əs) city in NE Virginia: site of two Civil War battles: pop. 28,000

man·a·tee (man′ə tē′) ***n.*** ⟦< WInd native name⟧ a large aquatic mammal of tropical waters

Man·ches·ter (man′ches′tər) city & port in NW England: county district pop. 405,000

Man·chu (man cho͞o′, man′cho͞o) ***n.*** **1** *pl.* **-chus′** or **-chu′** a member of a Mongolian people of Manchuria that ruled China from 1644 to 1912 **2** the language of this people —***adj.*** of the Manchus, their language, etc.

Man·chu·ri·a (man cho͝or′ē ə) region in NE China —**Man·chu′ri·an** ***adj., n.***

man·da·rin (man′də rin) ***n.*** ⟦< Sans *mantrin,* counselor⟧ **1** a high official in the Chinese empire **2** [**M-**] the main dialect of Chinese

man·date (man′dāt′) ***n.*** ⟦< L *mandare,* to command⟧ **1** an order or command **2** [Historical] *a)* a League of Nations commission to a country to administer some region *b)* this region **3** the will of voters as expressed in an election —***vt.*** **-dat′ed, -dat′ing** to require as by law

man·da·to·ry (man′də tôr′ē) ***adj.*** authoritatively commanded; obligatory

man·di·ble (man′də bəl) ***n.*** ⟦< L *mandere,* chew⟧ the jaw; specif., *a)* the lower jaw of a vertebrate *b)* either jaw of a beaked animal

man·do·lin (man′də lin′) ***n.*** ⟦< Gr *pandoura,* kind of lute⟧ a lute-like musical instrument with four to six pairs of strings

man·drake (man′drāk′) ***n.*** ⟦< Gr *mandragoras*⟧ a poisonous plant of the nightshade family

man·drill (man′dril) ***n.*** ⟦MAN + *drill,* kind of monkey⟧ a baboon of W Africa: the male has blue and scarlet patches on the face and rump

mane (mān) ***n.*** ⟦OE *manu*⟧ the long hair growing on the neck of the horse, lion, etc. —**maned** ***adj.***

man′-eat′er ***n.*** an animal that eats human flesh —**man′-eat′ing** ***adj.***

ma·neu·ver (mə no͞o′vər) ***n.*** ⟦< L *manu operare,* to work by hand⟧ **1** a planned and controlled movement of troops, warships, etc. **2** a skillful change of direction **3** a skillful or shrewd move; stratagem —***vi., vt.*** **1** to perform or cause to perform a maneuver or maneuvers **2** to manage or plan skillfully **3** to move, get, make, etc. by some scheme —**ma·neu′ver·a·ble** ***adj.***

man·ful (man′fəl) ***adj.*** manly; brave, resolute, etc. —**man′ful·ly** ***adv.***

man·ga·nese (maŋ′gə nēs′, -nēz′) ***n.*** ⟦ult. < ML *magnesia*: see MAGNESIA⟧ a grayish-white, metallic chemical element, used in alloys

mange (mānj) ***n.*** ⟦< OFr *mangeue,* an itch⟧ a skin disease of mammals, causing itching, hair loss, etc.

man·ger (mān′jər) ***n.*** ⟦< L *mandere,* chew⟧ a box or trough to hold fodder for horses or cattle to eat

man·gle[1] (maŋ′gəl) ***vt.*** **-gled, -gling** ⟦prob. < OFr *mehaigner,* maim⟧ **1** to mutilate by roughly cutting, tearing, crushing, etc. **2** to spoil; botch; mar

man·gle[2] (maŋ′gəl) ***n.*** ⟦< Gr *manganon,* war machine⟧ a machine for pressing and smoothing sheets, etc. between rollers

man·go (maŋ′gō) ***n.***, *pl.* **-goes** or **-gos** ⟦< Tamil *mān-kāy*⟧ **1** the yellow-red, somewhat acid fruit of a tropical tree **2** this tree

man·grove (maŋ′grōv) ***n.*** ⟦< WInd name⟧ a tropical tree of swampy areas, usually with roots that rise out of the water

man·gy (mān′jē) ***adj.*** **-gi·er, -gi·est** **1** having mange **2** filthy, low, etc. —**man′gi·ness** ***n.***

man·han·dle (man′han′dəl) ***vt.*** **-dled, -dling** to handle roughly

Man·hat·tan[1] (man hat′′n) ***n.*** ⟦after fol.⟧ [*often* **m-**] a cocktail made of whiskey and sweet vermouth

Man·hat·tan[2] (man hat′′n) island in SE New York: borough of New York City: pop. 1,488,000

man′hole′ ***n.*** a hole through which one can enter a sewer, conduit, etc.

man′hood′ ***n.*** **1** the state or time of being a man **2** manly qualities; manliness **3** men collectively

man′-hour′ ***n.*** a time unit equal to one hour of work done by one person

man′hunt′ ***n.*** a hunt for a fugitive

ma·ni·a (mā′nē ə) ***n.*** ⟦Gr, madness⟧ **1** wild or violent mental disorder **2** an excessive enthusiasm

-ma·ni·a (mā′nē ə) ⟦see prec.⟧ *combining form* **1** a (specified) type of mental disorder **2** an intense enthusiasm for

ma·ni·ac (mā′nē ak′) ***adj.*** wildly insane —***n.*** a violently insane person —**ma·ni·a·cal** (mə nī′ə kəl) ***adj.***

man·ic (man′ik) ***adj.*** **1** having, characterized by, or like mania **2** [Inf.] very excited, elated, etc. —**man′ic·al·ly** ***adv.***

man′ic-de·pres′sive (-dē pres′iv) ***adj.*** BIPOLAR (sense 2)

man·i·cure (man′i kyo͝or′) ***n.*** ⟦< L *manus,* a hand + *cura,* care⟧ a trimming, polishing, etc. of the fingernails —***vt.*** **-cured′, -cur′ing** **1** to trim, polish, etc. (fingernails) **2** [Inf.] to trim, clip, etc. meticulously —**man′i·cur′ist** ***n.***

man·i·fest (man′ə fest′) ***adj.*** ⟦< L *manifestus,* lit., struck by the hand⟧ apparent to the senses or the mind; obvious —***vt.*** to show plainly; reveal —***n.*** an itemized list of a craft's cargo or passengers —**man′i·fest′ly** ***adv.***

man′i·fes·ta′tion (-fes tā′shən) ***n.*** **1** a manifesting or being manifested **2** something that manifests or is manifested

man′i·fes′to (-fes′tō) ***n.***, *pl.* **-toes** or **-tos** ⟦It < *manifestare,* to manifest⟧ a public declaration of intention by an important person or group

man·i·fold (man′ə fōld′) ***adj.*** ⟦see MANY & -FOLD⟧ **1** having many forms, parts, etc. **2** of many sorts —***n.*** a pipe with several outlets, as for conducting cylinder exhaust from an engine

man·i·kin (man′i kin) ***n.*** ⟦Du *manneken* < *man,* man + *-ken,* -KIN⟧ **1** a little man; dwarf **2** an anatomical model of the human body, used as in art classes **3** MANNEQUIN

Ma·nil·a (mə nil′ə) capital & seaport of the Philippines, in SW Luzon: pop. 1,630,000 (met. area, 7,929,000)

Manila hemp ⟦after prec.⟧ [*often* **m- h-**] a strong fiber from the leafstalks of a Philippine plant, used for making rope, paper, etc.

Manila paper [*often* **m- p-**] a strong, buff-colored paper, orig. made of Manila hemp

man in the street the average person

ma·nip·u·late (mə nip′yo͞o lāt′, -yə-) ***vt.*** **-lat′ed, -lat′ing** ⟦ult. < L *manus,* a hand + *plere,* to fill⟧ **1** to handle skillfully **2** to manage artfully or shrewdly, often in an unfair way **3** to falsify (figures, etc.) for one's own purposes —**ma·nip′u·la′tion** ***n.***

Man·i·to·ba (man′ə tō′bə) province of SC Canada: 250,946 sq. mi.; pop. 1,114,000; cap. Winnipeg: abbrev. *MB* —**Man′i·to′ban** ***adj., n.***

man·kind (man′kind′) ***n.*** **1** the human race **2** all human males

THESAURUS

managing ***n.*** directing, supervising, governing, superintending, advising, overseeing, controlling, taking charge of, caring for, administering, executing, organizing, regulating, leading, piloting, steering, handling, charging, manipulating; see also OPERATING.

mandate ***n.*** command, decree, order; see COMMAND.

mandatory ***a.*** compulsory, forced, obligatory; see NECESSARY.

man-eating ***a.*** cannibal, carnivorous, omnivorous; see DANGEROUS, DEADLY.

maneuver ***n.*** **1** [A movement, usually military] stratagem, movement, procedure; see PLAN 2, TACTICS. **2** [A trick] subterfuge, finesse, ruse; see TRICK 1. **3** [Extensive practice in arms; *plural*] imitation war, exercise, war games; see DRILL 3, EXERCISE 1, PARADE 1.

maneuver ***v.*** plot, scheme, move, manage, contrive, design, devise, trick, cheat, conspire, finesse, angle for; see also PLAN 1.

mangle[1] ***v.*** tear, lacerate, wound, injure, cripple, maim, rend, disfigure, cut, slit, butcher, hack, slash, slice, carve, bruise, mutilate; see also HURT 1.

manhandle ***v.*** damage, maul, mistreat; see ABUSE, BEAT 1.

manhood ***n.*** **1** [Male maturity] legal age, coming of age, prime of life, middle age, voting age, majority, adulthood. **2** [Manly qualities] virility, resoluteness, honor, gallantry, nobility, forcefulness, daring, boldness, tenacity, self-reliance, potency.

mania ***n.*** craze, lunacy, madness; see DESIRE 1, INSANITY, OBSESSION.

maniac ***n.*** lunatic, insane person, crazy person; see MADMAN.

manipulate ***v.*** handle, shape, mold; see FORM 1, MANAGE 1, PLAN 1.

manipulation ***n.*** guidance, use, direction; see MANAGEMENT 1.

mankind ***n.*** humanity, human race, society; see MAN 1.

man·ly (man′lē) ***adj.*** **-li·er, -li·est** having the qualities regarded as suitable for a man; virile, brave, etc. —**man′li·ness** ***n.***

man′-made′ ***adj.*** artificial or synthetic

Mann (tō′mäs), **Thom·as** 1875-1955; Ger. novelist, in the U.S. 1938-52

man·na (man′ə) ***n.*** ⟦< Heb *mān*⟧ **1** *Bible* food miraculously provided for the Israelites in the wilderness **2** anything badly needed that comes unexpectedly

man·ne·quin (man′ə kin) ***n.*** ⟦see MANIKIN⟧ **1** a model of the human body, used as by tailors **2** a woman who models clothes in stores, etc.

man·ner (man′ər) ***n.*** ⟦< L *manus,* a hand⟧ **1** a way in which something is done or happens **2** a way, esp. a usual way, of acting **3** [*pl.*] *a*) ways of social behavior *[*bad *manners]* *b*) polite ways of social behavior *[*to learn *manners]* **4** kind; sort

man′nered (-ərd) ***adj.*** **1** having manners of a specified sort *[*ill-*mannered]* **2** artificial, stylized, etc.

man′ner·ism′ ***n.*** **1** excessive use of some distinctive manner or style in art, literature, etc. **2** a peculiarity of manner in behavior, speech, etc.

man′ner·ly ***adj.*** polite

man·ni·kin (man′ə kin) ***n.*** *alt. sp. of* MANIKIN

man·nish (man′ish) ***adj.*** like a man or man's: used in referring to a woman having characteristics generally attributed to men

ma·noeu·vre (mə nōō′vər) ***n.***, ***vi.***, ***vt.*** **-vred, -vring** *chiefly Brit. sp. of* MANEUVER

man of letters a writer, scholar, editor, etc., esp. in the field of literature

man′-of-war′ ***n.***, *pl.* **men′-of-war′** an armed naval vessel; warship

ma·nom·e·ter (mə näm′ət ər) ***n.*** ⟦Fr < Gr *manos,* rare (as in "thin, sparse") + Fr *-mètre,* -METER⟧ an instrument for measuring the pressure of gases or liquids

man on the street *var. of* MAN IN THE STREET

man·or (man′ər) ***n.*** ⟦< L *manere,* remain, dwell⟧ **1** in England, an estate **2** the main house on an estate —**ma·no·ri·al** (mə nôr′ē əl) ***adj.***

man′pow′er ***n.*** **1** power furnished by human strength **2** the collective strength or availability for work of the people of an area, nation, etc.

man·qué (män kā′) ***adj.*** ⟦Fr < *manquer,* be lacking⟧ unfulfilled; would-be *[*a poet *manqué]*

man·sard (roof) (man′särd) ⟦after F. *Mansard,* 17th-c. Fr architect⟧ a roof with two slopes on each of four sides, the lower steeper than the upper

manse (mans) ***n.*** ⟦see MANOR⟧ the residence of a minister; parsonage

man′ser′vant ***n.***, *pl.* **men′ser′vants** a male servant: also **man servant**

-man·ship (mən ship) *combining form* talent or skill (esp. in gaining advantage) in connection with *[grantsmanship]*

man·sion (man′shən) ***n.*** ⟦< L *manere,* remain, dwell⟧ a large, imposing house

man′-sized′ ***adj.*** [Inf.] of a size fit for a man; big: also **man′-size′**

man′slaugh′ter (-slôt′ər) ***n.*** the killing of a human being by another, esp. when unlawful but without malice

man·ta (man′tə) ***n.*** ⟦Sp < LL *mantum,* a cloak⟧ a giant ray, with winglike pectoral fins: also **manta ray**

man·tel (man′təl) ***n.*** ⟦var. of MANTLE⟧ **1** the facing of stone, etc. about a fireplace, including a projecting shelf **2** this shelf Also **man′tel·piece′**

man·til·la (man til′ə, -tē′ə) ***n.*** ⟦Sp: see MANTA⟧ a woman's scarf, as of lace, worn over the hair and shoulders

man·tis (man′tis) ***n.***, *pl.* **-tis·es** or **-tes′** (-tēz′) ⟦< Gr, prophet⟧ an insect with forelegs often held up together as if praying

man·tis·sa (man tis′ə) ***n.*** ⟦L, (useless) addition⟧ the decimal part of a logarithm

man·tle (man′təl) ***n.*** ⟦< L *mantellum*⟧ **1** a loose, sleeveless cloak: sometimes used figuratively to connote authority **2** anything that envelops or conceals **3** a small hood which when placed over a flame gives off incandescent light —***vt.*** **-tled, -tling** to cover as with a mantle —***vi.*** to blush

man′-to-man′ ***adj.*** frank; candid

man·tra (man′trə, män′-) ***n.*** ⟦Sans⟧ a chant of a Vedic hymn, text, etc.

man·u·al (man′yōō əl) ***adj.*** ⟦< L *manus,* a hand⟧ **1** of the hands **2** made, done, or worked by hand **3** involving skill or hard work with the hands —***n.*** **1** a handy book of facts, etc. for use as a guide, reference, etc. **2** prescribed drill in the handling of a weapon —**man′u·al·ly** ***adv.***

man·u·fac·ture (man′yōō fak′chər, -yə-) ***n.*** ⟦< L *manus,* a hand + *facere,* make⟧ **1** the making of goods, esp. by machinery and on a large scale **2** the making of something in any way, esp. when regarded as merely mechanical —***vt.*** **-tured, -tur·ing** **1** to make, esp. by machinery **2** to make up (excuses, etc.); fabricate —**man′u·fac′tur·er** ***n.***

man·u·mit (man′yōō mit′) ***vt.*** **-mit′ted, -mit′ting** ⟦< L *manus,* a hand + *mittere,* send⟧ to free from slavery —**man′u·mis′sion** ***n.***

ma·nure (mə nōōr′) ***vt.*** **-nured′, -nur′ing** ⟦< OFr *manouvrer,* work with the hands⟧ to put manure on or into —***n.*** animal excrement, etc. used to fertilize soil

man·u·script (man′yōō skript′, -yə-) ***adj.*** ⟦< L *manus,* hand + *scriptus,* written⟧ written by hand or typewritten —***n.*** **1** a written or typewritten document, book, etc., esp. one submitted to a publisher **2** writing as opposed to print

Manx (maŋks) ***n.*** the Celtic language of the Isle of Man, now nearly extinct —***adj.*** of the Isle of Man or its people, etc.

THESAURUS

manly ***a.*** masculine, courageous, fearless, firm, noble, valiant, intrepid, gallant, resolute, bold, confident, dauntless, self-reliant; see also MASCULINE.—*Ant.* COWARDLY, timid, effeminate.

man-made ***a.*** manufactured, artificial, synthetic, unnatural, counterfeit, not organic, ersatz, false, not genuine.

manner ***n.*** **1** [Personal conduct] mien, deportment, demeanor; see BEHAVIOR. **2** [Customary action] use, way, practice; see CUSTOM, HABIT 1. **3** [Method] mode, fashion, style; see METHOD. **—in a manner of speaking** in a way, so to speak, so to say; see RATHER.

mannerism ***n.*** idiosyncrasy, pretension, peculiarity; see CHARACTERISTIC, QUIRK.

mannerly ***a.*** polished, considerate, charming; see POLITE.

manners ***n.*** **1** [Personal behavior] conduct, deportment, bearing; see BEHAVIOR. **2** [Culture] etiquette, decorum, refinement; see COURTESY 1, CULTURE 2, ELEGANCE.

manpower ***n.*** workers, laborers, work force; see LABOR 4.

mansion ***n.*** villa, stately home, hall; see ESTATE, HOME 1.

manslaughter ***n.*** killing, homicide, slaying; see CRIME, MURDER.

mantel ***n.*** fireplace, mantelpiece, chimney piece; see SHELF 2.

manual ***a.*** hand-operated, not automatic, by hand; see OLD-FASHIONED.

manual ***n.*** guidebook, reference book, textbook; see BOOK.

manufacture ***n.*** fashioning, forming, assembling; see PRODUCTION 1.

manufacture ***v.*** make, construct, fabricate, produce, form, fashion, carve, mold, cast, frame, put together, turn out, stamp out, print out, cut out, have in production, have on the assembly line, mass-produce, print, shape, execute, accomplish, complete, tool, machine, mill, make up; see also BUILD.—*Ant.* DESTROY, demolish, tear down.

manufactured ***a.*** made, produced, constructed, fabricated, erected, fashioned, shaped, forged, turned out, mass-produced, tooled, executed, done, assembled, ready for the market, in shape, complete, completed; see also BUILT, FORMED.

manufacturer ***n.*** maker, producer, fabricator, constructor, builder, operator, craftsman, corporation, entrepreneur, company, business.

manufacturing ***n.*** fabrication, building, construction, assembling, preparing for market, putting in production, continuing production, keeping in production, forging, formation, mass production, composition, accomplishment, completion, finishing, doing, turning out; see also PRODUCTION 1.—*Ant.* DESTRUCTION, wreck, demolition.

manure ***n.*** guano, plant-food, compost; see DUNG, FERTILIZER.

manuscript ***n.*** composition, parchment, tablet, paper, document, original, copy, typescript, translation, facsimile, book, script; see also WRITING 2.

man·y (men′ē) ***adj.*** **more, most** ⟦OE *manig*⟧ numerous —***pl.n.*** a large number (of persons or things) —***pron.*** many persons or things

Ma·o·ri (mä′ō rē, mou′rē) ***n.*** **1** *pl.* **-ris** or **-ri** a member of a Polynesian people native to New Zealand **2** the language of this people —***adj.*** of the Maoris or their language, etc.

Mao Tse-tung (mou′ dzu′doon′) 1893-1976; Chinese Communist leader: Pinyin *Mao Zedong* —**Mao′ism′** ***n.*** —**Mao′ist** ***adj., n.***

map (map) ***n.*** ⟦< L *mappa,* napkin, cloth⟧ **1** a representation of all or part of the earth's surface, showing countries, bodies of water, cities, etc. **2** a representation of the sky, showing the stars, etc. —***vt.*** **mapped, map′ping 1** to make a map of **2** to plan

ma·ple (mā′pəl) ***n.*** ⟦OE *mapel*⟧ **1** any of a large group of trees with two-winged fruits, grown for wood, sap, or shade **2** the hard, light-colored wood **3** the flavor of the syrup or sugar made from the sap

mar (mär) ***vt.*** **marred, mar′ring** ⟦OE *mierran,* hinder⟧ to injure or damage so as to make imperfect, etc.; spoil

mar·a·bou (mar′ə boo′) ***n.*** ⟦Fr < Ar *murābit,* hermit⟧ a large-billed African stork

ma·ra·ca (mə rä′kə) ***n.*** ⟦Port *maracá* < native name in Brazil⟧ a percussion instrument that is a dried gourd or a gourd-shaped rattle with pebbles, etc. in it

mar·a·schi·no (mar′ə shē′nō, -skē′-) ***n.*** ⟦It < *marasca,* kind of cherry⟧ a liqueur made from a sour cherry

maraschino cherries cherries in a syrup flavored with maraschino or imitation maraschino

mar·a·thon (mar′ə thän′) ***n.*** ⟦after *Marathon,* plain in ancient Greece⟧ **1** a race on foot, 26 miles and 385 yards in length **2** any contest or endeavor testing endurance —**mar′a·thon′er** ***n.***

ma·raud (mə rôd′) ***vi., vt.*** ⟦< Fr *maraud,* vagabond⟧ to raid and plunder —**ma·raud′er** ***n.***

mar·ble (mär′bəl) ***n.*** ⟦< Gr *marmaros,* white stone⟧ **1** a hard limestone, white, colored, or mottled, which takes a high polish **2** a piece of this stone, used in sculpture, etc. **3** anything like marble in hardness, coldness, coloration, etc. **4** *a)* a little ball of stone, glass, etc. *b)* [*pl., with sing. v.*] a children's game played with such balls **5** [*pl.*] [Slang] mental soundness; wits —***adj.*** of or like marble —***vt.*** **-bled, -bling** to make (book edges) look mottled like marble

mar′bled ***adj.*** **1** mottled or streaked **2** streaked with fat: said of meat

mar′ble·ize′ (-īz′) ***vt.*** **-ized′, -iz′ing** to make look like marble

mar′bling ***n.*** a streaked or mottled appearance like that of marble

march[1] (märch) ***vi.*** ⟦Fr *marcher*⟧ **1** to walk with regular steps, as in military formation **2** to advance steadily —***vt.*** to cause to march —***n.*** **1** a marching **2** a steady advance; progress **3** a regular, steady step **4** the distance covered in marching **5** a piece of music with a beat suitable for marching —**on the march** marching or advancing —**steal a march on** to get an advantage over secretly —**march′er** ***n.***

march[2] (märch) ***n.*** ⟦< OFr⟧ a border or frontier

March (märch) ***n.*** ⟦< L *Mars,* the god Mars⟧ the third month of the year, having 31 days: abbrev. **Mar.**

March hare a hare in breeding time, proverbially an example of madness

marching orders 1 orders to march, go, or leave **2** notice of dismissal

mar·chion·ess (mär′shən is) ***n.*** **1** the wife or widow of a marquess **2** a lady of the rank of a marquess

Mar·co·ni (mär kō′nē), **Gu·gliel·mo** (goo lyel′mō) 1874-1937; It. physicist: developed wireless telegraphy

Mar·di Gras (mär′dē grä′) ⟦Fr, fat Tuesday⟧ [*sometimes* **M- g-**] the last day before Lent: a day of carnival in New Orleans, etc.

mare[1] (mer) ***n.*** ⟦< OE *mere*⟧ a mature female horse, mule, donkey, etc.

ma·re[2] (mä′rā′) ***n., pl.*** **ma·ri·a** (mä′rē ə) ⟦L, sea⟧ a large, dark area on the moon

mare's-nest (merz′nest′) ***n.*** **1** a hoax **2** a jumble; mess

mar·ga·rine (mär′jə rin) ***n.*** ⟦Fr⟧ a spread or cooking fat of vegetable oils processed, often with milk or whey, to the consistency of butter

mar·gin (mär′jən) ***n.*** ⟦< L *margo*⟧ **1** a border; edge **2** the blank border of a printed or written page **3** an amount beyond what is needed **4** provision for increase, error, etc. **5** the amount or degree by which things differ **6** the difference between the cost and the selling price of goods **7** collateral deposited with a broker, either to meet legal requirements or to insure against loss on contracts, as for buying stocks

mar′gin·al ***adj.*** **1** of, in, or near the margin **2** limited or minimal

mar·gi·na·li·a (mär′jə nā′lē ə) ***pl.n.*** notes written or printed in the margin

mar′gin·al·ize′ ***vt.*** **-ized′, -iz′ing** to exclude or ignore

ma·ri·a·chi (mär′ē ä′chē) ***n., pl.*** **-chis** ⟦MexSp < Fr *mariage,* marriage: from playing at wedding celebrations⟧ **1** a member of a strolling band of musicians in Mexico **2** such a band **3** its music

Mar·i·an (mer′ē ən, mar′-) ***adj.*** of the Virgin Mary

Ma·rie An·toi·nette (mə rē′ an′twə net′) 1755-93; wife of Louis XVI: queen of France (1774-92): guillotined

mar·i·gold (mar′ə gōld′) ***n.*** ⟦< *Marie* (prob. the Virgin Mary) + GOLD⟧ a plant of the composite family, with red, yellow, or orange flowers

mar·i·jua·na or **mar·i·hua·na** (mar′ə wä′nə) ***n.*** ⟦AmSp⟧ **1** HEMP (*n.* 1) **2** its dried leaves and flowers, smoked for euphoric effects

ma·rim·ba (mə rim′bə) ***n.*** ⟦< native name in Africa⟧ a kind of xylophone with a resonant tube beneath each bar

ma·ri·na (mə rē′nə) ***n.*** ⟦< L *mare,* sea⟧ a small harbor with docks, services, etc. for pleasure craft

mar·i·nade (mar′ə nād′) ***n.*** ⟦Fr < Sp *marinar,* to pickle⟧ a spiced pickling solution for steeping meat, fish, etc., often before cooking —***vt.*** **-nad′ed, -nad′ing** MARINATE

mar·i·nate (mar′ə nāt′) ***vt.*** **-nat′ed, -nat′ing** ⟦< It *marinare,* to pickle⟧ to steep in a marinade

ma·rine (mə rēn′) ***adj.*** ⟦< L *mare,* sea⟧ **1** of or found in the sea **2** *a)* maritime; nautical *b)* naval —***n.*** **1** a member of a military force trained for service at sea **2** [*often* **M-**] a member of the MARINE CORPS

THESAURUS

many ***a.*** numerous, multiplied, manifold, multitudinous, multifarious, diverse, sundry, profuse, innumerable, multiple, numberless, a world of, countless, uncounted, alive with, teeming, in heaps, several, of every description, prevalent, no end of, no end to, everywhere, crowded, common, usual, plentiful, abundant, galore; see also VARIOUS.—*Ant.* FEW, meager, scanty.

many ***n.*** a great number, abundance, thousands*; see PLENTY. —**a good** (or **great**) **many** a great number, abundance, thousands*; see PLENTY. —**as many** as much as, an equal number, a similar amount; see SAME.

many-sided ***a.*** **1** [Multilateral] polyhedral, geometric, trilateral, quadrilateral, tetrahedral; see also GEOMETRICAL. **2** [Gifted] endowed, talented, adaptable; see ABLE, VERSATILE.

map ***n.*** chart, graph, plat, sketch, delineation, drawing, picture, portrayal, draft, tracing, outline, projection. —**put on the map** make famous, bring fame to, glorify; see ESTABLISH 2. —**wipe off the map** eliminate, put out of existence, ruin; see DESTROY.

map ***v.*** outline, draft, chart; see PLAN 2.

mar ***v.*** **1** [To damage slightly] harm, bruise, scratch; see BREAK 2, DAMAGE. **2** [To impair] deform, deface, warp; see DESTROY.

marble ***a.*** petrified, granitelike, unyielding; see ROCK *n.* 1, STONE.

marble ***n.*** **1** [Metamorphic limestone] *Marbles include the following:* Parian, Pentelic, Carrian, Serpentine, Algerian, Tecali (onyx marbles), Tuscan, Gibraltar, Vermont, Georgia, fire, black, ophicalcite; see also STONE. **2** [A piece of carved marble] carving, figurine, figure; see ART, SCULPTURE, STATUE. **3** [A ball used in marbles] cat's-eye, shooter*, aggie; see TOY 1.

march[1] ***n.*** **1** [The act of marching] progression, movement, advancing, advancement, countermarch, parade, hike, trudge; see also STEP 1, WALK 3. **2** [The distance or route marched] walk, trek, hike; see JOURNEY. **3** [Music for marching] martial music, wedding march, processional; see MUSIC. —**on the march** proceeding, advancing, tramping; see MOVING 1.

march[1] ***v.*** move, advance, step out, go on, proceed, step, tread, tramp, patrol, prowl, parade, trudge, file, range, strut, progress, go ahead, forge ahead.—*Ant.* PAUSE, halt, retreat.

mare[1] ***n.*** female horse, filly, jenny; see ANIMAL, HORSE.

margin ***n.*** border, lip, shore; see BOUNDARY, EDGE 1.

marginal ***a.*** rimming, borderline, peripheral; see BORDERING.

marijuana ***n.*** weed*, grass*, pot*; see DRUG.

marine ***a.*** maritime, of the sea, oceanic; see MARITIME, NAUTICAL.

Marine Corps a branch of the United States armed forces trained for land, sea, and aerial combat
mar·i·ner (mar′ə nər) ***n.*** a sailor
mar·i·o·nette (mar′ē ə net′, mer′-) ***n.*** ⟦Fr < *Marie*, Mary⟧ a jointed puppet moved by strings or wires
mar·i·tal (mar′ət'l) ***adj.*** ⟦< L *maritus*, a husband⟧ of marriage; matrimonial —**mar′i·tal·ly *adv.***
mar·i·time (mar′ə tīm′) ***adj.*** ⟦< L *mare*, sea⟧ **1** on, near, or living near the sea **2** of sea navigation, shipping, etc.
mar·jo·ram (mär′jə rəm) ***n.*** ⟦prob. ult. < Gr *amarakos*⟧ a fragrant herb of the mint family, used in cooking
mark[1] (märk) ***n.*** ⟦OE *mearc*, boundary⟧ **1** a line, dot, spot, scratch, etc. on a surface **2** a printed or written symbol *[punctuation marks]* **3** a brand or label on an article showing the maker, etc. **4** an indication of some quality **5** a grade *[a mark of B in Latin]* **6** a standard of quality **7** impression; influence **8** an object of known position, serving as a guide **9** a line, dot, etc. indicating position, as on a graduated scale **10** an object aimed at; target **11** a goal; end; aim —***vt.*** **1** to put or make a mark or marks on **2** to identify as by a mark **3** to indicate by a mark **4** to show plainly *[her smile marked her joy]* **5** to set off; characterize **6** to listen to *[mark my words]* **7** to grade; rate —**make one's mark** to achieve fame —**mark down** (or **up**) to mark for sale at a reduced (or an increased) price —**mark time** **1** to keep time while at a halt by lifting the feet as if marching **2** to suspend progress for a time —**mark′er *n.***
mark[2] (märk) ***n.*** ⟦< ON *mǫrk*⟧ DEUTSCHE MARK
Mark (märk) ***n.*** *Bible* **1** one of the four Evangelists, the reputed author of the second Gospel **2** this Gospel
mark′down′ *n.* **1** a selling at a reduced price **2** the amount of reduction in price
marked (märkt) ***adj.*** **1** having a mark or marks **2** noticeable; obvious —**mark·ed·ly** (märk′id lē) ***adv.***
mar·ket (mär′kit) ***n.*** ⟦ult. < L *merx*, merchandise⟧ **1** a gathering of people for buying and selling things **2** an open space or a building where goods are shown for sale: also **mar′ket·place′** **3** a shop for the sale of provisions *[a meat market]* **4** a region in which goods can be bought and sold *[the European market]* **5** trade; buying and selling **6** demand (for goods, etc.) *[a good market for tea]* —***vt.*** **1** to offer for sale **2** to sell —***vi.*** to buy provisions —**mar′ket·a·ble *adj.*** —**mar′ket·eer′** (-kə tir′) ***n.*** —**mar′ket·er *n.***
mar·ket·ing *n.* **1** a buying or selling in a market **2** the total of activities involved in the moving of goods from the producer to the consumer, including selling, advertising, etc.
market share a company's percentage of the total sales of some commodity
Mark·ham (mär′kəm) city in SE Ontario, Canada: pop. 173,000
mark′ing *n.* **1** a mark or marks **2** the characteristic arrangement of marks, as of an animal
marks·man (märks′mən) ***n.***, *pl.* **-men** (-mən) a person who shoots, esp. one who shoots well —**marks′man·ship′ *n.***
mark′up′ *n.* **1** a selling at an increased price **2** the amount of increase in price
mar·lin (mär′lin) ***n.***, *pl.* **-lin** or **-lins** ⟦< fol.: from the shape⟧ a large, slender deep-sea fish
mar·line·spike (mär′lin spīk′) ***n.*** ⟦< Du *marlijn*, small cord + SPIKE[1]⟧ a pointed metal tool for separating the strands of a rope in splicing
mar·ma·lade (mär′mə lād′) ***n.*** ⟦ult. < Gr *meli*, honey + *mēlon*, apple⟧ a jamlike preserve of oranges, etc.
mar·mo·set (mär′mə zet′, -set′) ***n.*** ⟦< OFr *marmouset*, grotesque figure⟧ a small monkey of South and Central America
mar·mot (mär′mət) ***n.*** ⟦prob. < L *mus montanus*, mountain mouse⟧ any of a group of thick-bodied rodents, as the woodchuck
ma·roon[1] (mə ro͞on′) ***n.***, ***adj.*** ⟦Fr *marron*, chestnut⟧ dark brownish red
ma·roon[2] (mə ro͞on′) ***vt.*** ⟦< AmSp *cimarrón*, wild⟧ **1** to put (a person) ashore in a lonely place and abandon that person **2** to leave abandoned, helpless, etc.
marque (märk) ***n.*** ⟦Fr, a sign⟧ a distinctive emblem on an automobile
mar·quee (mär kē′) ***n.*** ⟦< Fr *marquise*, awning⟧ a rooflike projection over an entrance, as to a theater
mar·quess (mär′kwis) ***n.*** ⟦var. of MARQUIS⟧ **1** a British nobleman ranking above an earl **2** MARQUIS
mar·que·try (mär′kə trē) ***n.*** ⟦Fr, ult. < *marque*, a mark⟧ decorative inlaid work, as in furniture
mar·quis (mär′kwis) ***n.*** ⟦< ML *marchisus*, prefect⟧ in some European countries, a nobleman ranking above an earl or count
mar·quise (mär kēz′) ***n.*** **1** the wife or widow of a marquis **2** a lady of the rank of a marquis
mar·qui·sette (mär′ki zet′, -kwi-) ***n.*** ⟦see MARQUEE⟧ a thin, meshlike fabric used for curtains, etc.
mar·riage (mar′ij) ***n.*** **1** the state of being married **2** the act of marrying; wedding **3** a close union —**mar′riage·a·ble *adj.***
mar·ried (mar′ēd) ***adj.*** **1** being husband and wife **2** having a husband or wife **3** of marriage —***n.*** a married person
mar·row (mar′ō) ***n.*** ⟦OE *mearg*⟧ the soft, fatty tissue that fills the cavities of most bones
mar·ry (mar′ē) ***vt.*** **-ried**, **-ry·ing** ⟦< L *maritus*, husband⟧ **1** to join as husband and wife **2** to take as husband or wife **3** to unite —***vi.*** to get married —**marry off** to give in marriage
Mars (märz) ***n.*** **1** the Roman god of war **2** a planet of the solar system: see PLANET
Mar·seille (mär sā′) seaport in SE France: pop. 801,000 Eng. sp. **Mar·seilles′**

THESAURUS

marital ***a.*** conjugal, connubial, nuptial; see MARRIED.

maritime ***a.*** naval, marine, oceanic, seagoing, hydrographic, seafaring, aquatic, pelagic, Neptunian; see also NAUTICAL.

mark[1] ***n.*** **1** [The physical result of marking] brand, stamp, blaze, imprint, impression, line, trace, check, stroke, streak, dot, point, nick. **2** [A target] butt, prey, bull's-eye. **3** [Effect] manifestation, consequence, value; see RESULT. —**hit the mark** achieve, accomplish, do well; see SUCCEED 1. —**make one's mark** accomplish, prosper, become famous; see SUCCEED 1. —**miss the mark** be unsuccessful, err, mistake; see FAIL 1.

mark[1] ***v.*** **1** [To make a mark] brand, stamp, imprint, blaze, print, check, chalk, label, sign, identify, check off, trace, stroke, streak, dot, point, nick, x, underline. **2** [To designate] earmark, point out, stake out, indicate, check off, mark off, signify, denote; see also MEAN 1. **3** [To distinguish] characterize, demarcate, qualify; see DISTINGUISH 1. **4** [To put prices upon] ticket, label, tag; see PRICE. —**mark down** reduce, put on sale, cut the price of; see PRICE. —**mark time** put off, postpone, kill time; see DELAY, WAIT 1. —**mark up** raise the price, adjust, add to; see INCREASE.

marked ***a.*** **1** [Carrying a mark] branded, signed, sealed, stamped, imprinted, inscribed, characterized by, distinguished by, recognized by, identified by. **2** [Priced] labeled, price-marked, marked down, marked up, ticketed, priced, tagged; see also COSTING.

marker ***n.*** **1** [A label] ticket, price mark, seal, brand, stamp, boundary mark, tombstone; see also LABEL. **2** [A writing instrument] pencil, pen, felt tip pen; see PEN 2.

market ***n.*** **1** [A place devoted to sale] trading post, mart, shopping mall, emporium, exchange, city market, public market, supermarket, meat market, fish market, stock market, stock exchange, fair, dime store, drugstore, discount store, department store, variety store, bazaar, warehouse, warehouse club, flea market, business, delicatessen; see also SHOP, STORE. **2** [The state of trade] supply and demand, market, sales; see BUSINESS 1, 4, DEMAND 2. —**be in the market (for)** want to buy, be willing to purchase, need; see WANT 1. —**on the market** salable, ready for purchase, available; see FOR (or ON or UP FOR) SALE.

market ***v.*** trade, exchange, barter; see SELL.

markup ***n.*** raise, margin, gross profit; see INCREASE, PROFIT 2.

marriage ***n.*** wedding, ceremony, nuptials, pledging, mating, matrimony, conjugality, union, match, arrangement, wedlock, wedded state, wedded bliss, holy matrimony, sacrament.

married ***a.*** wedded, espoused, mated, united, given in marriage, pledged in marriage, living in the married state, in the state of matrimony, hitched*.—*Ant.* SINGLE, unwedded, unmarried.

marry ***v.*** **1** [To take a spouse] wed, enter the matrimonial state, take wedding vows, pledge in marriage, mate, lead to the altar, take the vows, become one, tie the knot*, get hitched*.—*Ant.* DIVORCE, separate, reject. **2** [To join in wedlock] unite, give, join in matrimony, pronounce man and wife, pair up with, couple; see also JOIN 1.—*Ant.* DIVORCE, annul, separate.

marsh (märsh) ***n.*** ⟦OE *merisc*⟧ a tract of low, wet, soft land; swamp; bog —**marsh'y, -i·er, -i·est,** ***adj.***

mar·shal (mär'shəl) ***n.*** ⟦< OHG *marah*, horse + *scalh*, servant⟧ **1** in various foreign armies, a general officer of the highest rank **2** an official in charge of ceremonies, parades, etc. **3** in the U.S., *a)* a federal officer appointed to a judicial district with duties like those of a sheriff *b)* the head of some police or fire departments —***vt.*** **-shaled** or **-shalled, -shal·ing** or **-shal·ling** **1** to arrange (troops, ideas, etc.) in order **2** to guide

Mar·shall (mär'shəl), **John** 1755-1835; U.S. chief justice (1801-35)

Marshall Islands country on a group of islands in the W Pacific: formerly part of a U.S. territory: 70 sq. mi.; pop. 43,000

marsh·mal·low (märsh'mel'ō) ***n.*** ⟦orig. made of the root of a mallow found in marshes⟧ a soft, spongy confection of sugar, gelatin, etc.

mar·su·pi·al (mär so͞o'pē əl) ***adj.*** ⟦< Gr *marsypos*, pouch⟧ of a group of mammals that carry their incompletely developed young in an external abdominal pouch on the mother —***n.*** such an animal, as a kangaroo or opossum

mart (märt) ***n.*** ⟦MDu *markt*⟧ a market

mar·ten (märt''n) ***n.*** ⟦< OFr *martre*⟧ **1** a small mammal like a weasel, with soft, thick fur **2** the fur

mar·tial (mär'shəl) ***adj.*** ⟦< L *martialis*, of Mars⟧ **1** of or suitable for war **2** warlike; bold **3** military —**mar'tial·ly** ***adv.***

martial arts systems of self-defense originating in E Asia, such as karate or kung fu, also engaged in for sport

martial law temporary rule by military authorities over civilians, as during a war

Mar·tian (mär'shən) ***adj.*** of Mars —***n.*** a being from or living on Mars, as in science fiction

mar·tin (märt''n) ***n.*** ⟦Fr⟧ any of several birds of the swallow family

mar·ti·net (märt''n et') ***n.*** ⟦after *Martinet*, 17th-c. Fr general⟧ a very strict disciplinarian

mar·ti·ni (mär tē'nē) ***n., pl.*** **-nis** ⟦< ?⟧ a cocktail made of gin (or vodka) and dry vermouth

mar·tyr (märt'ər) ***n.*** ⟦< Gr *martyr,* a witness⟧ **1** one who chooses to suffer or die for one's faith or principles **2** one who suffers great pain or misery for a long time —***vt.*** to kill or persecute for a belief —**mar'tyr·dom** ***n.***

mar·vel (mär'vəl) ***n.*** ⟦< L *mirari*, wonder at⟧ a wonderful thing —***vi.*** **-veled** or **-velled, -vel·ing** or **-vel·ling** to be filled with wonder —***vt.*** to wonder at or about: followed by a clause

mar'vel·ous (-və ləs) ***adj.*** **1** causing wonder; extraordinary, etc. **2** fine; splendid Also [Chiefly Brit.] **mar'vel·lous** —**mar'vel·ous·ly** ***adv.***

Marx (märks), **Karl** (kärl) 1818-83; Ger. founder of modern socialism

Marx'ism' ***n.*** the system of thought developed by Karl Marx and Friedrich Engels (1820-95, Ger. socialist leader & writer), serving as a basis for socialism and communism —**Marx'ist** or **Marx'i·an** ***adj., n.***

Mar·y (mer'ē) ***n.*** *Bible* mother of Jesus

Mar·y·land (mer'ə lənd) state of the E U.S.: 9,775 sq. mi.; pop. 4,781,000; cap. Annapolis: abbrev. *MD* —**Mar'y·land·er** (-lən dər, -lan'-) ***n.***

Mary Mag·da·lene (mag'də lən) *Bible* a repentant woman whom Jesus forgave

mar·zi·pan (mär'zi pan') ***n.*** ⟦Ger < It *marzapane*⟧ a confection that is a paste of ground almonds, sugar, and egg white, variously shaped

masc or **mas** *abbrev.* masculine

mas·car·a (mas kar'ə) ***n.*** ⟦< It *maschera*, mask⟧ a cosmetic for darkening the eyelashes —***vt.*** **-car'aed, -car'a·ing** to put mascara on

mas·cot (mas'kät') ***n.*** ⟦< Prov *masco*, sorcerer⟧ **1** any person, animal, or thing supposed to bring good luck **2** any person, animal, or thing adopted, as by a sports team, as a symbol

mas·cu·line (mas'kyə lin) ***adj.*** ⟦< L *mas*, male⟧ **1** male; of men or boys **2** suitable to or having qualities regarded as typical of men; strong, vigorous, manly, etc. **3** mannish: said of women **4** *Gram.* designating or of the gender of words referring to males as well as to other words to which no sex is attributed —**mas'cu·lin'i·ty** ***n.***

mash (mash) ***n.*** ⟦< OE *mascwyrt*⟧ **1** crushed malt or meal soaked in hot water for making wort **2** a mixture of watered bran, meal, etc. for feeding horses, etc. **3** any soft mass —***vt.*** **1** to change into a soft mass by beating, crushing, etc. **2** to crush and injure

mask (mask) ***n.*** ⟦< Fr < It *maschera*⟧ **1** a covering to conceal or protect the face **2** anything that conceals or disguises **3** *a)* a molded likeness of the face *b)* a grotesque representation of a face, worn to amuse or frighten —***vt.*** to conceal or cover with or as with a mask —**masked** ***adj.***

mas·o·chism (mas'ə kiz'əm) ***n.*** ⟦after L. von Sacher-*Masoch* (1835-95), Austrian writer⟧ the getting of pleasure, often sexual pleasure, from being hurt or humiliated —**mas'o·chist** ***n.*** —**mas'o·chis'tic** ***adj.*** —**mas'o·chis'ti·cal·ly** ***adv.***

ma·son (mā'sən) ***n.*** ⟦< ML *macio*⟧ **1** one whose work is building with stone, brick, etc. **2** [**M-**] FREEMASON

Ma·son-Dix·on line (mā'sən dik'sən) ⟦after C. *Mason* & J. *Dixon*, who surveyed it, 1763-67⟧ boundary line between Pennsylvania & Maryland, regarded as separating the North from the South

Ma·son·ic (mə sän'ik) ***adj.*** [*also* **m-**] of Freemasons or Freemasonry

ma·son·ry (mā'sən rē) ***n.*** **1** a mason's trade **2** *pl.* **-ries** something built, as by a mason, of stone, brick, etc. **3** [*usually* **M-**] FREEMASONRY

masque (mask) ***n.*** ⟦see MASK⟧ **1** MASQUERADE (*n.* 1) **2** a former kind of dramatic entertainment, with lavish costumes, music, etc. —**masqu'er** ***n.***

mas·quer·ade (mas'kə rād') ***n.*** ⟦see MASK⟧ **1** a ball or party at which masks and fancy costumes are worn **2** *a)* a disguise *b)* an acting under false pretenses —***vi.*** **-ad'ed, -ad'ing** **1** to take part in a masquerade **2** to act under false pretenses

mass (mas) ***n.*** ⟦< Gr *maza*, barley cake⟧ **1** a quantity of matter of indefinite shape and size; lump **2** a large quantity or number *[a* mass *of bruises]* **3** bulk; size **4** the main part **5** *Physics* the quantity of matter in a body as measured by its inertia —***adj.*** of or for the masses or for a large number —***vt., vi.*** to gather or form into a mass —**the masses** the common people

Mass (mas) ***n.*** ⟦< L *missa* in the words said by the priest: *ite, missa est (contio)*, go, (the meeting) is dismissed⟧ [*also* **m-**] *R.C.Ch.* the service that includes the Eucharist

Mas·sa·chu·setts (mas'ə cho͞o'sits) New England state of

THESAURUS

marsh ***n.*** morass, bog, quagmire; see SWAMP.

marshy ***a.*** swampy, wet, sloppy; see MUDDY 1, 2.

martial ***a.*** warlike, soldierly, combative; see AGGRESSIVE.

martyr ***n.*** sufferer, offering, scapegoat; see SAINT, VICTIM.

martyrdom ***n.*** agony, suffering, ordeal; see TORTURE.

marvel ***n.*** miracle, phenomenon, curiosity; see WONDER 2.

marvel ***v.*** stare, stand in awe, stare with open mouth; see WONDER 1.

marvelous ***a.*** fabulous, astonishing, spectacular; see UNUSUAL 1.

masculine ***a.*** brawny, macho, male, virile, potent, vigorous, forceful, aggressive, muscular, powerful; see also MANLY.

masculinity ***n.*** virility, power, manliness; see MANHOOD 2, STRENGTH.

mash ***n.*** mix, pulp, paste; see FEED, MIXTURE 1.

mash ***v.*** crush, bruise, squash, chew, masticate, smash, pound, reduce, squeeze, brew, pulverize; see also GRIND, PRESS 1.

mashed ***a.*** crushed, pressed, mixed, pulpy, battered, pounded, smashed, macerated, squashed, softened, reduced, spongy, pasty, pulverized, masticated, chewed, bruised; made into a powder, made into a paste, etc.—*Ant.* WHOLE, hard, uncrushed.

mask ***n.*** **1** [A disguise] cover, false face, veil, hood, costume, domino; see also CAMOUFLAGE, DISGUISE. **2** [A protection] gas mask, catcher's mask, face mask, fencing mask, fireman's mask, respirator; see also PROTECTION 2. **3** [A masquerade] revel, party, carnival; see PARTY 1.

mask ***v.*** cloak, conceal, veil; see DISGUISE, HIDE 1.

masquerade ***n.*** masque, masked ball, Mardi Gras; see DANCE 1, ENTERTAINMENT, PARTY 1.

mass ***n.*** **1** [A body of matter] lump, bulk, piece, portion, section, batch, block, body, core, clot, coagulation, wad, gob; see also HUNK. **2** [A considerable quantity] heap, volume, crowd; see QUANTITY, SIZE 2. **3** [Size] magnitude, volume, span; see EXTENT, SIZE 2. —**the masses** the proletariat, the rank and file, the multitude; see PEOPLE 3.

Mass ***n.*** eucharistic rite, Catholic service, Eucharist, Lord's Supper, Holy Communion, ceremony, observance; High Mass, Low Mass, Solemn High Mass, Requiem Mass, Votive Mass; see also CELEBRATION, WORSHIP 1.

the U.S.: 7,838 sq. mi.; pop. 6,016,000; cap. Boston: abbrev. *MA*

mas·sa·cre (mas′ə kər) ***n.*** ⟦< OFr *maçacre*, butchery⟧ the indiscriminate, merciless killing of many people or animals —***vt.*** **-cred, -cring** (-kər iŋ, -kriŋ) to kill in large numbers

mas·sage (mə säzh′) ***n.*** ⟦Fr < Ar *massa*, to touch⟧ a rubbing, kneading, etc. of part of the body, as to stimulate circulation or relieve tension —***vt.*** **-saged′, -sag′ing** to give a massage to

mas·seur (mə sur′, -soor′) ***n.*** ⟦Fr⟧ a man whose work is giving massages —**mas·seuse** (mə sooz′, -soos′) ***fem.n.***

mas·sive (mas′iv) ***adj.*** **1** forming or consisting of a large mass; big and solid **2** large and imposing —**mas′sive·ly** ***adv.*** —**mas′sive·ness** ***n.***

mass media those means of communication that reach and influence large numbers of people, as newspapers, radio, and TV

mass noun a noun denoting an abstraction or something that cannot be counted (Ex.: *love, water, news*)

mass number the number of neutrons and protons in the nucleus of an atom

mass production quantity production of goods, esp. by machinery and division of labor —**mass′-pro·duce′, -duced′, -duc′ing,** ***vt.***

mast (mast) ***n.*** ⟦OE *mæst*⟧ **1** a tall vertical spar used to support the sails, yards, radar, etc. on a ship **2** a vertical pole

mas·tec·to·my (mas tek′tə mē) ***n.***, *pl.* **-mies** the surgical removal of all or part of a breast

mas·ter (mas′tər) ***n.*** ⟦< L *magister*⟧ **1** a man who rules others or has control over something; specif., *a*) one who is head of a household *b*) an employer *c*) one who owns a slave or an animal *d*) the captain of a merchant ship **2** *a*) a person very skilled and able in some work, profession, science, etc.; expert *b*) an artist regarded as great **3** [**M-**] a title applied to a boy too young to be addressed as *Mr.* —***adj.*** **1** being a master **2** of a master **3** chief; main; controlling —***vt.*** **1** to become master of **2** to become an expert in (an art, science, etc.)

mas′ter·ful ***adj.*** **1** acting the part of a master; domineering **2** expert; skillful —**mas′ter·ful·ly** ***adv.***

master key a key that will open every one of a set of locks

mas′ter·ly ***adj.*** expert; skillful

mas′ter·mind′ ***n.*** a very clever person, esp. one who plans or runs a project —***vt.*** to be the mastermind of

Master of Arts (or **Science,** etc.) a degree given by a college or university to one who has completed a prescribed course at the first level of graduate study: also **master's (degree)**

master of ceremonies one who supervises or presides over a ceremony, program, etc.

mas′ter·piece′ ***n.*** ⟦< Ger *meisterstück*⟧ **1** a thing made or done with masterly skill **2** the greatest work of a person or group

master sergeant *U.S. Mil.* a noncommissioned officer of high rank

mas′ter·stroke′ ***n.*** a masterly action, move, or achievement

mas′ter·work′ ***n.*** MASTERPIECE

mas′ter·y ***n.***, *pl.* **-ies** **1** rule; control **2** ascendancy or victory **3** expert skill or knowledge

mast′head′ ***n.*** **1** the top part of a ship's mast **2** a box or section in a newspaper or magazine, giving the owner, editors, etc.

mas·ti·cate (mas′ti kāt′) ***vt.*** **-cat′ed, -cat′ing** ⟦ult. < Gr *mastax*, mouth⟧ to chew —**mas′ti·ca′tion** ***n.***

mas·tiff (mas′tif) ***n.*** ⟦< L *mansuetus*, tame⟧ a large, powerful dog with a short, thick coat

mas·to·don (mas′tə dän′) ***n.*** ⟦< Gr *mastos*, breast + *odous*, tooth: from the nipplelike processes on its molar⟧ a large, extinct mammal resembling the elephant but larger

mas·toid (mas′toid′) ***adj.*** ⟦< Gr *mastos*, breast + *-eidēs*, -OID⟧ designating, of, or near a projection of the temporal bone behind the ear —***n.*** the mastoid projection

mas·tur·bate (mas′tər bāt′) ***vi.*** **-bat′ed, -bat′ing** ⟦< L *masturbari*⟧ to manipulate the genitals for sexual gratification —**mas′tur·ba′tion** ***n.***

mat[1] (mat) ***n.*** ⟦< LL *matta*⟧ **1** a flat piece of cloth, rubber, woven straw, etc. used for protection, as on a floor or under a vase **2** a thickly padded floor covering, esp. one used for wrestling, etc. **3** anything densely interwoven or growing in a thick tangle —***vt., vi.*** **mat′ted, mat′ting** **1** to cover as with a mat **2** to form into a thick tangle —**go to the mat** [Inf.] to engage in a struggle or dispute

mat[2] (mat) ***n.*** ⟦< OFr⟧ **1** MATTE **2** a border, as of cardboard, put around a picture —***vt.*** **mat′ted, mat′ting** to frame with a mat

mat[3] (mat) ***n.*** [Inf.] *Printing* a matrix

mat·a·dor (mat′ə dôr′) ***n.*** ⟦< Sp *matar*, to kill⟧ a bullfighter whose specialty is killing the bull

match[1] (mach) ***n.*** ⟦< OFr *mesche*⟧ a slender piece of wood, cardboard, etc. tipped with a substance that catches fire by friction

match[2] (mach) ***n.*** ⟦OE (*ge*)*mæcca*, mate⟧ **1** any person or thing equal or similar to another **2** two persons or things that go well together **3** a contest or game **4** a marriage or mating —***vt.*** **1** to put in opposition (*with*); pit (*against*) **2** to be equal or similar to **3** to make or get a counterpart or equivalent to **4** to fit (one thing) to another —***vi.*** to be equal, similar, suitable, etc.

match′book′ ***n.*** a folder of book matches

match′less ***adj.*** having no equal

match′mak′ing ***n.*** the arranging of marriages, or of boxing matches, etc. —**match′mak′er** ***n.***

match′stick′ ***n.*** a thin strip of wood, cardboard, etc., as or like that of a match

mate (māt) ***n.*** ⟦< MDu⟧ **1** a companion or fellow worker **2** one of a matched pair **3** *a*) a husband or wife *b*) the male or female of paired animals **4** an officer of a merchant ship, ranking below the captain —***vt., vi.*** **mat′ed, mat′ing** **1** to join as a pair **2** to couple in marriage or sexual union

THESAURUS

massacre ***n.*** butchering, killing, slaughter; see MURDER.

massacre ***v.*** exterminate, decimate, annihilate; see KILL 1.

massage ***v.*** stimulate, caress, rub down; see RUB 1.

massive ***a.*** huge, heavy, cumbersome; see LARGE 1.

mass production ***n.*** automation, mass-producing, assembly-line methods; see MANUFACTURING, PRODUCTION 1.

mast ***n.*** spar, pole, flagstaff, post, timber, trunk; see also POST.

master ***a.*** leading, supreme, main; see EXCELLENT, MAJOR 1, PRINCIPAL.

master ***n.*** **1** [One who directs others] chief, director, boss; see EXECUTIVE, LEADER 2. **2** [A teacher] instructor, preceptor, mentor; see TEACHER. **3** [One who possesses great skill] genius, maestro, sage, past master, champion, prima donna, connoisseur, fellow, doctor; see also ARTIST.—*Ant.* DISCIPLE, beginner, undergraduate.

master ***v.*** **1** [To conquer] subdue, rule, humble; see SUCCEED 1. **2** [To become proficient in] gain mastery in, understand, comprehend; see LEARN, STUDY.

masterful ***a.*** commanding, expert, skillful; see EXCELLENT.

masterpiece ***n.*** model, standard, classic, gem, showpiece, cream of the crop, masterwork, magnum opus, *chef-d'ouevre* (French).

mastery ***n.*** **1** [Control] dominance, sovereignty, government; see COMMAND, POWER 2. **2** [Ability to use to the full] skill, capacity, proficiency; see ABILITY, EDUCATION 1.

mat[1] ***n.*** covering, floor covering, doormat, place mat, runner, doily, table mat, place setting, web, mesh, cloth, straw mat; see also COVER 1, RUG.

mat[1] ***v.*** braid, tangle, snarl; see TWIST, WEAVE 1.

match[1,2] ***n.*** **1** [An instrument to produce fire] safety match, sulphur match, matchstick, fusee*; see also LIGHT 3. **2** [An article that is like another] peer, equivalent, mate, analogue, counterpart, approximation; see also EQUAL. **3** [A formal contest] race, event, rivalry; see COMPETITION, SPORT 3.

match[2] ***v.*** **1** [To find or make equals] equalize, liken, equate, make equal, pair, coordinate, level, even, match up, balance, mate, marry, unite; see also EQUAL. **2** [To be alike] harmonize, suit, be twins, be counterparts, be doubles, check with, go together, go with, rhyme with, take after; see also AGREE, RESEMBLE.—*Ant.* DIFFER, be unlike, bear no resemblance. **3** [To meet in contest] equal, keep pace with, compete with; see COMPETE.

matched ***a.*** doubled, similar, equated, evened, coordinated, harmonized, paired, mated; see also ALIKE, BALANCED 1.—*Ant.* UNLIKE, unequal, different.

matching ***a.*** comparable, analogous, parallel; see EQUAL.

mate ***n.*** **1** [One of a pair] complement, analogue, counterpart; see MATCH 2. **2** [A companion] playmate, classmate, buddy; see FRIEND. **3** [A marriage partner] spouse, bride, groom, bedmate, the old man*, the old lady*; see also HUSBAND, WIFE.

ma·te·ri·al (mə tir′ē əl) ***adj.*** ⟦< L *materia,* matter⟧ **1** of matter; physical *[a material object]* **2** of the body or bodily needs, comfort, etc.; not spiritual **3** important, pertinent, etc. —***n.*** **1** what a thing is, or may be, made of; elements or parts **2** cloth; fabric **3** [*pl.*] tools, articles, etc. needed to make or do something

ma·te′ri·al·ism′ ***n.*** **1** the doctrine that everything in the world, including thought, can be explained in terms of matter alone **2** the tendency to be more concerned with material than with spiritual or intellectual values —**ma·te′ri·al·ist** ***n., adj.*** —**ma·te′ri·al·is′tic** ***adj.***

ma·te′ri·al·ize′ (-īz′) ***vt.*** **-ized′**, **-iz′ing** to give material form to —***vi.*** **1** to become fact; be realized **2** to take on bodily form: said of spirits, etc. —**ma·te′ri·al·i·za′tion** ***n.***

ma·te′ri·al·ly ***adv.*** **1** physically **2** to a great extent; substantially

ma·te·ri·el or **ma·té·ri·el** (mə tir′ē el′) ***n.*** ⟦Fr⟧ the necessary materials and tools; specif., military weapons, equipment, etc.

ma·ter·nal (mə tur′nəl) ***adj.*** ⟦< L *mater,* mother⟧ **1** of, like, or from a mother **2** related through the mother's side of the family —**ma·ter′nal·ly** ***adv.***

ma·ter′ni·ty (-nə tē) ***n.*** the state of being a mother; motherhood —***adj.*** **1** for pregnant women **2** for the care of mothers and their newborn babies

math[1] (math) ***n.*** [Inf.] mathematics

math[2] *abbrev.* mathematics

math·e·mat·i·cal (math′ə mat′i kəl) ***adj.*** ⟦< Gr *manthanein,* learn⟧ **1** of, like, or concerned with mathematics **2** very precise, accurate, etc. —**math′e·mat′i·cal·ly** ***adv.***

math·e·mat·ics (math′ə mat′iks) ***n.*** ⟦see prec. & -ICS⟧ the science dealing with quantities, forms, etc. and their relationships, by the use of numbers and symbols —**math′e·ma·ti′cian** (-mə tish′ən) ***n.***

mat·i·nee or **mat·i·née** (mat′'n ā′) ***n.*** ⟦< Fr *matin,* morning⟧ an afternoon performance of a play, etc.

mat·ins (mat′'nz) ***pl.n.*** ⟦< L *matutinus,* of the morning⟧ [*often* **M-**] [*usually with sing. v.*] a church service of morning prayer

Ma·tisse (mȧ tēs′), **Hen·ri** (än rē′) 1869-1954; Fr. painter

matri- ⟦< L *mater*⟧ *combining form* mother: also **matr-**

ma·tri·arch (mā′trē ärk′) ***n.*** ⟦prec. + -ARCH⟧ **1** a woman who rules a family, tribe, etc. **2** a highly respected elderly woman —**ma′tri·ar′chal** (-är′kəl) ***adj.*** —**ma′tri·arch′y**, *pl.* **-ies**, ***n.***

mat·ri·cide (ma′trə sīd′) ***n.*** **1** the murdering of one's mother **2** a person who does this —**mat′ri·ci′dal** ***adj.***

ma·tric·u·late (mə trik′yōō lāt′, -yə-) ***vt., vi.*** **-lat′ed**, **-lat′ing** ⟦< LL: see MATRIX⟧ to enroll, esp. as a student in a college —**ma·tric′u·la′tion** ***n.***

mat·ri·mo·ny (ma′trə mō′nē) ***n.***, *pl.* **-nies** ⟦< L *mater,* mother⟧ **1** the act or rite of marriage **2** married life —**mat′ri·mo′ni·al** ***adj.***

ma·trix (mā′triks′) ***n.***, *pl.* **ma·tri·ces** (mā′trə sēz′, ma′trə-) or **ma′trix′es** ⟦< L *mater,* mother⟧ that within which something originates or develops

ma·tron (mā′trən) ***n.*** ⟦< L *mater,* mother⟧ **1** a wife or widow, esp. one with a mature appearance and manner **2** a woman manager of the domestic arrangements of a hospital, prison, etc. —**ma′tron·ly** ***adj.***

matron of honor a married woman acting as chief attendant to a bride

matte (mat) ***n.*** ⟦var. of MAT[2]⟧ a dull surface or finish —***adj.*** not shiny Also **matt**

mat·ted (mat′id) ***adj.*** closely tangled in a dense mass *[matted hair]*

mat·ter (mat′ər) ***n.*** ⟦< L *materia*⟧ **1** what a thing is made of; material **2** whatever occupies space and is perceptible to the senses **3** any specified substance *[coloring matter]* **4** material of thought or expression **5** an amount or quantity *[a matter of a few days]* **6** *a)* a thing or affair *b)* cause or occasion *[no laughing matter]* **7** importance *[it's of no matter]* **8** trouble; difficulty: with *the [what's the matter?]* **9** mail —***vi.*** to be of importance —**as a matter of fact** *see this phrase at* FACT —**no matter 1** it is not important **2** regardless of

mat′ter-of-fact′ ***adj.*** sticking to facts; literal, unimaginative, etc.

Mat·thew (math′yōō′) ***n.*** *Bible* **1** a Christian apostle, reputed author of the first Gospel **2** this Gospel: abbrev. **Matt.**

mat·ting (mat′iŋ) ***n.*** **1** a woven fabric of fiber, as straw, for mats, etc. **2** mats collectively

mat·tock (mat′ək) ***n.*** ⟦OE *mattuc*⟧ a tool like a pickax, for loosening the soil, digging roots, etc.

mat·tress (ma′trəs) ***n.*** ⟦< Ar *maṭraḥ,* cushion⟧ a casing of strong cloth filled with cotton, foam rubber, coiled springs, etc., used on a bed

ma·ture (mə toor′, -choor′) ***adj.*** ⟦< L *maturus,* ripe⟧ **1** full-grown; ripe **2** fully developed, perfected, etc. **3** due: said of a note, bond, etc. —***vt., vi.*** **-tured′**, **-tur′ing** to make or become mature —**mat·u·ra·tion** (mach′ə rā′shən) ***n.*** —**ma·ture′ly** ***adv.*** —**ma·tu′ri·ty** ***n.***

mat·zo (mät′sə, -sō) ***n.***, *pl.* **mat′zot**, **mat′zoth** (-sōt), or **mat′zos** ⟦Heb *matstsāh,* unleavened⟧ **1** thin, crisp unleavened bread eaten during the Passover **2** a piece of this

maud·lin (môd′lin) ***adj.*** ⟦< ME *Maudeleyne,* (Mary) Magdalene (often represented as weeping)⟧ foolishly, often tearfully, sentimental

maul (môl) ***n.*** ⟦< L *malleus,* a hammer⟧ a heavy hammer for driving stakes, etc. —***vt.*** **1** to bruise or lacerate **2** to handle roughly; manhandle

maun·der (môn′dər) ***vi.*** ⟦< earlier *mander,* to grumble⟧ to talk or move in a confused way

THESAURUS

material ***a.*** palpable, sensible, corporeal; see PHYSICAL 1, REAL 2, TANGIBLE.

material ***n.*** **1** [Matter] body, corporeality, substance; see ELEMENT 2, MATTER 1. **2** [Unfinished matter; *often plural*] raw material, stuff, stock, staple, ore, stockpile, crop, supply, accumulation; see also ALLOY, ELEMENT 2, GOODS, METAL, MINERAL, PLASTIC, ROCK 1, WOOL.

materialistic ***a.*** possessive, acquisitive, opportunistic; see GREEDY, WORLDLY.

materialize ***v.*** be realized, take on form, become real, actualize, become concrete, metamorphose, reintegrate; see also BECOME.—*Ant.* DISSOLVE, disintegrate, disperse.

maternal ***a.*** parental, sympathetic, protective; see MOTHERLY.

maternity ***n.*** parenthood, motherhood, motherliness; see PARENT.

mathematical ***a.*** arithmetical, numerical, digital; see NUMERICAL.

mathematics ***n.*** science of real numbers, science of numbers, computation, reckoning, calculation, new math, math. *Types of mathematics include the following:* arithmetic, algebra, plane geometry, solid geometry, spherical geometry, trigonometry, trig*, analytical geometry, calculus, differential calculus, integral calculus, applied mathematics, statistics, topology, geodesy, Fourier analysis, game theory, set theory, number theory, systems analysis, quadratics.

matriarch ***n.*** female ruler, dowager, matron; see QUEEN.

matrimony ***n.*** conjugality, wedlock, union; see MARRIAGE.

matron ***n.*** lady, wife, mother; see WOMAN 1.

matronly ***a.*** middle-aged, dignified, sedate; see MATURE, MOTHERLY.

matted ***a.*** snarled, rumpled, disordered; see TANGLED, TWISTED 1.

matter ***n.*** **1** [Substance] body, material, substantiality, corporeality, constituents, stuff, object, thing, physical world; see also ELEMENT 2.—*Ant.* NOTHING, nothingness, immateriality. **2** [Subject] interest, focus, resolution; see SUBJECT, THEME 1. **3** [An affair] undertaking, circumstance, concern; see AFFAIR 1. —**as a matter of fact** in fact, in actuality, truly; see REALLY 1. —**for that matter** in regard to that, as far as that is concerned, concerning that; see AND. —**no matter** it does not matter, it is of no concern, regardless of; see REGARDLESS 2.

matter ***v.*** signify, be substantive, carry weight, weigh, be important, have influence, import, imply, express, be of consequence, involve, be worthy of notice; see also MEAN 1.

matter-of-fact ***a.*** objective, prosaic, feasible; see PRACTICAL.

mattress ***n.*** innerspring, springs, box spring, bedding, cushion, crib mattress; see also BED.

mature ***a.*** full-grown, middle-aged, grown, grown-up, of age, in full bloom, womanly, manly, matronly, developed, prepared, settled, cultivated, cultured, sophisticated; see also EXPERIENCED.—*Ant.* YOUNG, adolescent, immature.

mature ***v.*** grow up, become a man, become a woman, come of age, become experienced, settle down, ripen, reach perfection, attain majority, culminate, become wise, become perfected, grow skilled, fill out; see also AGE, DEVELOP 1.

matured ***a.*** grown, full-grown, aged; see FINISHED.

maturity ***n.*** **1** [Mental competence] development, sophistication, cultivation, culture, civilization, advancement, mental power, capability. **2** [Physical development] prime of life, post-pubescence, adulthood; see MAJORITY 2. **3** [Ripeness] readiness, mellowness, sweetness; see DEVELOPMENT.

maul ***v.*** mangle, manhandle, batter;

Mau·ri·ta·ni·a (môr′ə tā′nē ə) country in NW Africa, on the Atlantic: 398,000 sq. mi.; pop. 1,864,000

Mau·ri·ti·us (mô rish′ē əs, -rish′əs) island country in the Indian Ocean: 788 sq. mi.; pop. 1,059,000

mau·so·le·um (mô′sə lē′əm, mä′-; -zə-) ***n.***, *pl.* **-le′ums** or **-le′a** (-ə) ⟦after the tomb of King *Mausolus*, in ancient Asia Minor⟧ **1** a large, imposing tomb **2** a building with spaces for entombing a number of bodies

mauve (mōv, môv) ***n.*** ⟦Fr, mallow⟧ any of several shades of pale purple —***adj.*** of such a color

mav·er·ick (mav′ər ik) ***n.*** ⟦after S. *Maverick*, 19th-c. Texan whose cattle had no brand⟧ **1** an unbranded animal, esp. a lost calf **2** [Inf.] one who takes an independent stand, as in politics

maw (mô) ***n.*** ⟦OE *maga*⟧ **1** [Archaic] the stomach **2** the throat, jaws, or mouth of a voracious animal

mawk·ish (môk′ish) ***adj.*** ⟦< ON *mathkr*, maggot⟧ sentimental in a weak, insipid way —**mawk′ish·ly** ***adv.***

max[1] (maks) [Slang] ***n., adj.*** maximum —**to the max** to the greatest possible degree

max[2] *abbrev.* maximum

maxi- ⟦< MAXI(MUM)⟧ *combining form* maximum, very large, very long

max·il·la (mak sil′ə) ***n.***, *pl.* **-lae** (-ē) ⟦L⟧ the upper jawbone —**max′il·lar′y** (-sə ler′ē) ***adj.***

max·im (mak′sim) ***n.*** ⟦< LL *maxima* (*propositio*), the greatest (premise)⟧ a concise rule of conduct

max·i·mize (mak′sə mīz′) ***vt.*** **-mized′**, **-miz′ing** to increase to the maximum

max·i·mum (mak′sə məm) ***n.***, *pl.* **-mums** or **-ma** (-mə) ⟦< L superl. of *magnus*, great⟧ **1** the greatest quantity, number, etc. possible or permissible **2** the highest degree or point reached —***adj.*** greatest possible, permissible, or reached —**max′i·mal** (-məl) ***adj.***

may (mā) ***v.aux.*** *pt.* **might** ⟦OE *mæg*⟧ used to express *a)* possibility *[it may rain]* *b)* permission *[you may go]* (see also CAN[1]) *c)* contingency *[they died that we may be free]* *d)* a wish or hope *[may he live]*

May (mā) ***n.*** ⟦< L *Maius*⟧ the fifth month of the year, having 31 days

Ma·ya (mä′yə, mī′ə) ***n.*** ⟦Sp < native name⟧ **1** *pl.* **-ya** or **-yas** a member of an American Indian people of Central America that had a highly developed civilization **2** the language of this people —**Ma′yan** ***adj., n.***

may·be (mā′bē) ***adv.*** ⟦ME (for *it may be*)⟧ perhaps

May Day May 1: a traditional spring festival, now also a labor holiday in many countries

may′flow′er ***n.*** **1** an early spring flower, as the trailing arbutus **2** [**M-**] the ship on which the Pilgrims came to America (1620)

may′fly′ ***n.***, *pl.* **-flies′** ⟦thought to be prevalent in May⟧ a delicate insect with gauzy wings

may·hem (mā′hem, -əm) ***n.*** ⟦see MAIM⟧ **1** *Law* the offense of maiming a person **2** any deliberate destruction

may·o (mā′ō) ***n.*** [Inf.] *short for* MAYONNAISE

may·on·naise (mā′ə nāz′) ***n.*** ⟦after *Mahón*, port on a Sp island⟧ a creamy sauce of egg yolks, oil, vinegar, etc. beaten together

may·or (mā′ər) ***n.*** ⟦< L *major*, greater⟧ the chief administrative official of a city, town, etc. —**may·or·al** (mā′ər əl, mā ôr′əl) ***adj.***

may′or·al·ty ***n.***, *pl.* **-ties** the office or term of office of a mayor

may·pole (mā′pōl′) ***n.*** [*often* **M-**] a high pole with flowers, streamers, etc., for dancing around on May Day

Ma·za·tlán (mä′sät län′) seaport & resort on the Pacific coast of Mexico: pop. 314,000

maze (māz) ***n.*** ⟦< OE *amasian*, to amaze⟧ **1** a confusing, intricate network of pathways **2** a confused state

maz·el tov (mä′zəl tōv′, -tôf′) ⟦Heb, good luck⟧ used to express congratulations: also **maz′el·tov′** ***interj.***

ma·zur·ka or **ma·zour·ka** (mə zur′kə) ***n.*** ⟦Pol⟧ a lively Polish folk dance in 3/4 or 3/8 time

MB *abbrev.* **1** Manitoba **2** megabyte(s): also **mb**

MBA or **M.B.A.** *abbrev.* Master of Business Administration

MC *abbrev.* **1** Master of Ceremonies **2** Member of Congress

Mc·Kin·ley[1] (mə kin′lē), **William** 1843-1901; 25th president of the U.S. (1897-1901): assassinated

Mc·Kin·ley[2] (mə kin′lē), **Mount** mountain in Alaska: highest peak in North America: 20,320 ft.: popularly called *Denali*

MD *abbrev.* **1** ⟦L *Medicinae Doctor*⟧ Doctor of Medicine: also **M.D.** **2** Maryland

mdse *abbrev.* merchandise

me (mē) ***pron.*** ⟦OE⟧ *objective form of* I[2]

ME Maine

mead[1] (mēd) ***n.*** ⟦OE *meodu*⟧ an alcoholic liquor made of fermented honey and water

mead[2] (mēd) ***n.*** [Old Poet.] *var. of* MEADOW

mead·ow (med′ō) ***n.*** ⟦< OE *mæd*⟧ **1** a grassland where the grass is grown for hay **2** low, level grassland

mea·ger (mē′gər) ***adj.*** ⟦< L *macer*, lean⟧ **1** thin; lean **2** poor; not full or rich; inadequate Brit. sp. **mea′gre** —**mea′ger·ly** ***adv.*** —**mea′ger·ness** ***n.***

meal[1] (mēl) ***n.*** ⟦OE *mæl*⟧ **1** any of the times for eating, as lunch or dinner **2** the food served at such a time

meal[2] (mēl) ***n.*** ⟦OE *melu*⟧ **1** any edible grain, coarsely ground *[cornmeal]* **2** any substance similarly ground —**meal′y**, **-i·er**, **-i·est**, ***adj.***

meal·y-mouthed (mēl′ē mouthd′) ***adj.*** not outspoken or blunt; euphemistic

mean[1] (mēn) ***vt.*** **meant** (ment), **mean′ing** ⟦OE *mænan*⟧ **1** to have in mind; intend *[he means to go]* **2** to intend to express *[say what you mean]* **3** to signify; denote *[the German word "ja" means "yes"]* —***vi.*** to have a (specified) degree of importance, effect, etc. *[honors mean little to him]* —**mean well** to have good intentions

mean[2] (mēn) ***adj.*** ⟦OE (*ge*)*mæne*⟧ **1** low in quality or value; paltry **2** poor in appearance; shabby **3** petty **4** stingy **5** pettily bad-tempered, disagreeable, etc. **6** [Slang] *a)* hard to cope with *b)* skillful —**mean′ly** ***adv.*** —**mean′ness** ***n.***

THESAURUS

see BEAT 1, HIT 1.

maxim ***n.*** aphorism, adage, epithet; see PROVERB, SAYING51.

maximum ***a.*** supreme, highest, greatest; see BEST.

maximum ***n.*** supremacy, height, pinnacle, preeminence, culmination, matchlessness, preponderance, apex, acme, peak, greatest number, highest degree, summit; see also CLIMAX.—*Ant.* MINIMUM, foot, bottom.

may ***v.*** **1** [Grant permission] be permitted to, be allowed to, can, be privileged to, be authorized to, be at liberty to. **2** [Concede possibility] will, shall, be going to, should, be conceivable, be possible, be practicable, be within reach, be obtainable; see also WILL 3.

maybe ***a.*** perhaps, possibly, it might be, it could be, maybe so, as it may be, conceivably, God willing.—*Ant.* HARDLY, scarcely, probably not.

mayor ***n.*** magistrate, Lord Mayor, burgomaster, His Honor, Her Honor, president of a city council, civil administrator, civil judge, city father; see also EXECUTIVE.

maze ***n.*** tangle, entanglement, twist, winding, convolution, intricacy, confusion, meandering, labyrinth, puzzle.—*Ant.* ORDER, disentanglement, simplicity.

meadow ***n.*** grass, pasture, lea, mead*, mountain meadow, upland pasture, meadowland, bottom land, bottoms, pasturage; hay meadow, clover meadow, bluegrass meadow, etc.; salt marsh, steppe, heath, pampa, savanna; see also FIELD 1.

meager ***a.*** lank, lanky, gaunt, starved, emaciated, lean, bony, slender, slim, spare, little, bare, scant, stinted, lacking, wanting, scrawny, withered, lithe, narrow, tenuous, skinny; see also THIN 2.—*Ant.* FAT, plump, stout.

meal[1,2] ***n.*** **1** [Ground feed] bran, farina, grits, fodder, provender, forage; see also FEED, FLOUR, GRAIN 1. *Types of meal include the following:* corn meal, corn grits, hominy, corn starch, barley meal, oatmeal, soybean meal, soybean flour. **2** [The quantity of food taken at one time] repast, feast, refreshment, mess, eats*, grub*, chow*, spread*, square meal*, snack. *Meals include the following:* breakfast, dinner, lunch, banquet, brunch, snack, tea, high tea (British), picnic, luncheon, dessert, midnight supper; see also BREAKFAST, DINNER, LUNCH.

mean[1] ***v.*** **1** [To have as meaning] indicate, spell, denote, signify, add up, determine, symbolize, imply, involve, speak of, touch on, stand for, drive at, point to, connote, suggest, express, designate, intimate, betoken, purport. **2** [To have in mind] anticipate, propose, expect; see INTEND 1. **3** [To design for] destine for, aim at, set apart; see INTEND 2.

mean[2] ***a.*** **1** [Small-minded] base, low, debased; see VULGAR. **2** [Of low estate] servile, pitiful, shabby; see HUMBLE 2. **3** [Vicious] spiteful, malicious, cruel, unkind, shameless, dishonorable, degraded, contemptible, evil, infamous, treacherous, crooked, faithless, unfaithful, ill-tempered, bad-tempered, dangerous, despicable, degenerate, knavish, unscrupulous, hard as nails.

mean[3] (mēn) ***adj.*** ⟦< L *medius*, middle⟧ **1** halfway between extremes **2** average —***n.*** **1** what is between extremes **2** *Math.* a number between the smallest and largest values of a set of quantities; esp., an average

me·an·der (mē an′dər) ***vi.*** ⟦< Gr *Maiandros*, a winding river in Asia Minor⟧ **1** to take a winding course: said of a stream **2** to wander idly —***n.*** an aimless wandering

mean·ie or **mean·y** (mē′nē) ***n.***, *pl.* **-ies** [Inf.] one who is mean, selfish, etc.

mean′ing ***n.*** what is meant; what is intended to be signified, understood, indicated, etc.; import; sense *[*the *meaning* of a word*]* —**mean′ing·ful** ***adj.*** —**mean′ing·less** ***adj.***

means (mēnz) ***pl.n.*** ⟦< MEAN[3], *n.*⟧ **1** [*with sing. or pl. v.*] that by which something is done or obtained; agency *[*a *means* of travel*]* **2** resources; wealth —**by all means** **1** without fail **2** certainly —**by means of** by using —**by no means** not at all

means test an investigation of a person's financial resources, to determine that person's eligibility for welfare payments, etc.

meant (ment) ***vt.***, ***vi.*** *pt. & pp. of* MEAN[1]

mean′time′ ***adv.*** **1** in or during the intervening time **2** at the same time —***n.*** the intervening time Also **mean′while′**

mea·sles (mē′zəlz) ***n.*** ⟦ME *maseles*⟧ **1** an acute, infectious, communicable viral disease, usually of children, characterized by small, red spots on the skin, high fever, etc. **2** a similar but milder disease; esp., rubella (*German measles*)

mea·sly (mēz′lē) ***adj.*** **-sli·er**, **-sli·est** [Inf.] contemptibly slight or worthless

meas·ure (mezh′ər) ***n.*** ⟦< L *metiri*, to measure⟧ **1** the extent, dimensions, capacity, etc. of anything **2** a determining of this; measurement **3** *a)* a unit of measurement *b)* any standard of valuation **4** a system of measurement **5** an instrument for measuring **6** a definite quantity measured out **7** a course of action *[*reform *measures]* **8** a statute; law **9** a rhythmical pattern or unit; specif., the notes and rests between two bars on a musical staff —***vt.*** **-ured**, **-ur·ing** **1** to find out or estimate the extent, dimensions, etc. of, esp. by a standard **2** to mark off by measuring: often with *off* or *out* **3** to be a measure of —***vi.*** **1** to take measurements **2** to be of a specified dimension, etc. —**beyond measure** exceedingly —**for good measure** as a bonus or something extra —**measure up to** to reach (a standard, etc.) —**meas′ur·a·ble** ***adj.*** —**meas′ur·a·bly** ***adv.*** —**meas′ure·less** ***adj.***

meas′ured ***adj.*** **1** determined or marked off by a standard **2** regular or steady *[measured* steps*]* **3** careful and guarded: said of speech, etc.

meas′ure·ment ***n.*** **1** a measuring or being measured **2** extent or quantity determined by measuring **3** a system of measuring or of measures

meat (mēt) ***n.*** ⟦OE *mete*⟧ **1** food: now archaic except in **meat and drink** **2** the flesh of animals, esp. of mammals, used as food **3** the edible, inner part *[*the *meat* of a nut*]* **4** the substance or essence —**meat′y**, **-i·er**, **-i·est**, ***adj.***

meat′-and-po·ta′toes ***adj.*** [Inf.] **1** basic; fundamental **2** ordinary; everyday

meat′pack′ing ***n.*** the process or industry of preparing the meat of animals for market

Mec·ca[1] (mek′ə) ***n.*** ⟦after fol.⟧ [*often* **m-**] any place many people feel drawn to *[*a tourist *mecca]*

Mecca[2] (mek′ə) city in W Saudi Arabia: birthplace of Mohammed & hence a holy city of Islam: pop. 618,000

me·chan·ic (mə kan′ik) ***n.*** ⟦< Gr *mēchanē*, machine⟧ a worker skilled in using tools, repairing machines, etc.

me·chan′i·cal ***adj.*** **1** having to do with machinery or tools **2** produced or operated by machinery or a mechanism **3** of the science of mechanics **4** machinelike; lacking warmth, spontaneity, etc. —**me·chan′i·cal·ly** ***adv.***

me·chan′ics ***n.*** **1** the science of motion and of the action

THESAURUS

mean[3] ***n.*** middle, median, midpoint; see AVERAGE, CENTER 1.

meander ***v.*** twist and turn, zigzag, snake; see RAMBLE 2, WIND 3, WALK 1.

meaning ***n.*** sense, import, purport, purpose, definition, object, implication, application, intent, suggestion, denotation, connotation, aim, drift, context, significance, essence, worth, intrinsic value, interest.—*Ant.* NONSENSE, aimlessness, absurdity.

meaningful ***a.*** significant, exact, essential; see IMPORTANT 1.

meaningless ***a.*** vague, absurd, insignificant; see TRIVIAL, UNIMPORTANT.

meanness ***n.*** **1** [The quality of being mean] small-mindedness, debasement, degradation, degeneracy, unscrupulousness, stinginess, disrepute, malice, unworthiness, ill-temper, unkindness, covetousness, avarice, miserliness; see also GREED.—*Ant.* GENEROSITY, nobility, worthiness. **2** [A mean action] belittling, defaming, groveling, cheating, sneaking, quarreling, scolding, taking advantage of, deceiving, coveting, grudging, dishonoring, defrauding, shaming, degrading, stealing.

means ***n.*** **1** [An instrumentality or instrumentalities] machinery, mechanism, agency, organ, channel, medium, factor, agent, power, organization; see also METHOD, SYSTEM. **2** [Wealth] resources, substance, property; see WEALTH. —**by all means** of course, certainly, indeed; see SURELY, YES. —**by any means** in any way, at all, somehow; see ANYHOW. —**by means of** with the aid of, somehow, through; see BY 2. —**by no (manner of) means** in no way, not possible, definitely not; see NEVER, NO.

meanwhile ***a.*** meantime, during the interval, in the interim, ad interim (Latin), for the time being, until, till, up to, in the meantime, when; see also DURING.

measurable ***a.*** weighable, definite, limited, determinable, knowable, recognizable, detectable, calculable, real, present, fathomable, assessible.

measure ***n.*** **1** [A unit of measurement] dimension, capacity, weight, volume, distance, degree, quantity, area, mass, frequency, density, intensity, rapidity, speed, caliber, bulk, sum, duration, magnitude, amplitude, size, pitch, ratio, depth, scope, height, strength, breadth, amplification. *Common units of measure include the following—linear:* inch, foot, yard, rod, mile, millimeter, centimeter, meter, kilometer; *surface:* square inch, square foot, square yard, acre, square rod, square mile, hectare; *volume:* fluid ounce, fluid dram, pint, quart, gallon, milliliter, liter; *weight:* ounce, pound, ton, milligram, gram, kilogram; *relationship:* horsepower, baud, revolutions per minute (rpm), miles per hour (mph), feet per second (fps), per second per second, erg, foot-pound, kilowatt-hour, acre-foot, decibel, man-hour, ohm, watt, volt, octane number. **2** [Anything used as a standard] rule, test, trial, example, standard, yardstick, norm, pattern, type, model; see also CRITERION. **3** [A beat] rhythm, tempo, time, step, throb, stroke, accent, meter, cadence, tune, melody, stress, vibration, division; see also BEAT 2. —**for good measure** added, as a bonus, additionally; see EXTRA. —**in full measure** completely, sufficiently, amply; see ADEQUATELY. —**take measures** take action, do things to accomplish a purpose, take steps; see ACT 1.

measure ***v.*** **1** [To apply a standard of measurement] rule, weigh, mark, lay out, grade, graduate, gauge, sound, pitch, beat, stroke, time, mark off, scale, rank, even, level, gradate, line, align, line out, regulate, portion, set a standard, average, equate, square, calibrate, block in, survey, map. **2** [To contain by measurement] hold, cover, contain; see INCLUDE 1.

measured ***a.*** **1** [Steady] orderly, systematic, deliberate; see REGULAR 3. **2** [Determined] checked, evaluated, calculated; see DETERMINED 1.

measurement ***n.*** **1** [The act of measuring] estimation, analysis, computation; see JUDGMENT 2. **2** [The result of measuring] distance, dimension, weight, degree, pitch, time, height, depth, density, volume, area, length, measure, thickness, quantity, magnitude, extent, range, scope, reach, amount, capacity, frequency, intensity, pressure, speed, caliber, grade, span, step, strength, mass. **3** [A set of measures] inch, foot, yard; see MEASURE 1.

meat ***n.*** beef, pork, flesh, veal, mutton, lamb, chicken, turkey, goose, duck, rabbit, venison, horsemeat; see also FOOD. *Cuts and forms of meat include the following:* roast, cutlet, steak, filet, leg, shoulder, loin, sirloin, tenderloin, rib, round, chuck, brisket, shank, rump, flank, chop, liver, brains, kidneys, heart, bacon, tripe, shank, sausage, frankfurter, ground meat, chipped meat, dried meat, salted meat, pickled meat.

mechanic ***n.*** machinist, technician, skilled worker; see WORKMAN.

mechanical ***a.*** **1** [Concerning machinery] engineering, production, manufacturing, tooling, tuning, implementing, fabricating, forging, machining, building, construction, constructing. **2** [Like a machine] made to a pattern, machinelike, stereotyped, standardized, without variation, robotic, unchanging, monotonous.—*Ant.* ORIGINAL, varied, changing. **3** [Operated by the use of machinery] power-driven, involuntary, programmed; see AUTOMATED, AUTOMATIC.

mechanically ***a.*** automatically, unreasoningly, unchangeably; see REGULARLY.

of forces on bodies **2** knowledge of machinery —***pl.n.*** [*sometimes with sing. v.*] the technical part *[*the *mechanics* of writing*]*

mech·a·nism (mek′ə niz′əm) ***n.*** ⟦< Gr *mēchanē*, machine⟧ **1** the working parts of a machine **2** any system of interrelated parts **3** any physical or mental process by which a result is produced —**mech′a·nis′tic** ***adj.***

mech′a·nize′ (-nīz′) ***vt.*** **-nized′**, **-niz′ing** **1** to make mechanical **2** to equip (an industry) with machinery or (an army, etc.) with motor vehicles, tanks, etc. —**mech′a·ni·za′tion** ***n.***

med *abbrev.* **1** medical **2** medicine **3** medium

med·al (med′'l) ***n.*** ⟦< LL *medialis*, medial⟧ **1** a small, flat piece of inscribed metal commemorating some event or awarded for some distinguished action, merit, etc. **2** a similar piece of metal bearing a religious figure or symbol

med′al·ist ***n.*** one awarded a medal

me·dal·lion (mə dal′yən) ***n.*** ⟦Fr *médaillon*⟧ **1** a large medal **2** a design, portrait, etc. resembling a medal

med·dle (med′'l) ***vi.*** **-dled**, **-dling** ⟦< L *miscere*, to mix⟧ to interfere in another's affairs —**med′dler** ***n.*** —**med′dle·some** (-səm) ***adj.***

me·di·a (mē′dē ə) ***n.*** *alt. pl. of* MEDIUM: see MEDIUM (*n.* 3) —**the media** [*usually with sing. v.*] all the means of communication such as newspapers, radio, and TV

me·di·al (mē′dē əl) ***adj.*** ⟦< L *medius*⟧ **1** of or in the middle **2** average

me·di·an (mē′dē ən) ***adj.*** **1** middle; intermediate **2** designating the middle number in a series —***n.*** **1** a median number, point, line, etc. **2** the strip of land separating the lanes of opposing traffic of a divided highway: in full **median strip**

me·di·ate (mē′dē āt′) ***vi.*** **-at′ed**, **-at′ing** ⟦< L *medius*, middle⟧ to be an intermediary —***vt.*** to settle (differences) between persons, nations, etc. by friendly or diplomatic intervention —**me′di·a′tion** ***n.*** —**me′di·a′tor** ***n.***

med·ic (med′ik) ***n.*** [Inf.] **1** a physician or surgeon **2** a medical officer who gives first aid in combat

Med′ic·aid′ (-i kād′) ***n.*** ⟦MEDIC(AL) + AID⟧ [*also* **m-**] a state and federal health program for paying certain medical expenses of persons of low income

med′i·cal (-i kəl) ***adj.*** of or connected with the practice or study of medicine —**med′i·cal·ly** ***adv.***

medical jurisprudence the application of medical knowledge to questions of law

Med·i·care (med′i ker′) ***n.*** ⟦MEDI(CAL) + CARE⟧ [*also* **m-**] a federal health program for paying certain medical expenses of the aged and the needy

med′i·cate′ (-kāt′) ***vt.*** **-cat′ed**, **-cat′ing** ⟦< L *medicari*, heal⟧ to treat with medicine —**med′i·ca′tion** ***n.***

me·dic·i·nal (mə dis′ən əl) ***adj.*** of, or having the properties of, medicine

med·i·cine (med′i sən) ***n.*** ⟦< L *medicus*, physician⟧ **1** the science and art of treating and preventing disease **2** any substance, as a drug, used in treating disease, relieving pain, etc.

medicine man among North American Indians, etc., a man supposed to have supernatural powers for healing the sick, etc.

me·di·e·val (mē′dē ē′vəl, mi dē′vəl) ***adj.*** ⟦< L *medius*, middle + *aevum*, age⟧ of or characteristic of the Middle Ages

me·di·o·cre (mē′dē ō′kər) ***adj.*** ⟦< L *medius*, middle + *ocris*, peak⟧ **1** ordinary; average **2** inferior —**me′di·oc′ri·ty** (-äk′rə tē), *pl.* **-ties**, ***n.***

med·i·tate (med′ə tāt′) ***vt.*** **-tat′ed**, **-tat′ing** ⟦< L *meditari*⟧ to plan —***vi.*** to think deeply —**med′i·ta′tion** ***n.*** —**med′i·ta′tive** ***adj.***

Med·i·ter·ra·ne·an (med′ə tə rā′nē ən) ***adj.*** **1** *a)* of the large sea (**Mediterranean Sea**) surrounded by Europe, Africa, & Asia *b)* of the regions near this sea **2** designating furniture made to simulate heavy, ornately carved Renaissance furniture —***n.*** a Mediterranean person

me·di·um (mē′dē əm) ***n.***, *pl.* **-di·ums** or **-di·a** (-ə) ⟦L < *medius*, the middle⟧ **1** an intermediate thing or state **2** an intervening thing through which a force acts **3** *pl. usually* **me′dia** any means, agency, etc.; specif., a means of communication that reaches the general public: a singular form **media** (*pl.* **medias**) is now often used **4** any surrounding substance or environment **5** *pl.* **me′di·ums** one through whom messages are supposedly sent from the dead —***adj.*** intermediate in size, quality, etc.

med·ley (med′lē) ***n.***, *pl.* **-leys** ⟦< L *miscere*, to mix⟧ **1** a mixture of dissimilar things **2** a musical piece made up of various tunes or passages

me·dul·la (mi dul′ə) ***n.***, *pl.* **-las** or **-lae** (-ē) ⟦L, marrow⟧ *Anat.* **1** a widening of the spinal cord forming the lowest part of the brain: in full **medulla ob·lon·ga·ta** (äb′läŋ

THESAURUS

mechanism ***n.*** working parts, mechanical action, the works; see DEVICE 1, TOOL 1.

mechanize ***v.*** equip, computerize, industrialize, motorize, automate, put on the assembly line, make mechanical, robotize, introduce machinery into.

medal ***n.*** award, commemoration, badge; see DECORATION 3.

medallion ***n.*** ornament, emblem, necklace; see JEWELRY.

meddle ***v.*** **1** [To interfere in others' affairs] interfere, obtrude, interlope, intervene, pry, snoop, nose, impose oneself, infringe, break in upon, make it one's business, abuse one's rights, push in, chime in, force an entrance, encroach, intrude, be officious, obstruct, impede, hinder, encumber, busy oneself with, come uninvited, tamper with, inquire, be curious, kibitz*, stick one's nose in*, monkey with*, bust in*, muscle in*, barge in, have a finger on*, butt in*, horn in*; see also INTERRUPT.—*Ant.* NEGLECT, ignore, let along. **2** [To handle others' things] tamper, molest, pry, fool with, trespass, use improperly.

meddlesome ***a.*** obtrusive, interfering, officious, meddling, intrusive, impertinent, interposing, interrupting, obstructive, impeding, hindering, encumbering, curious, tampering, prying, snooping, troublesome, snoopy*, nosy*, kibitzing*, chiseling*.

meddling ***n.*** interfering, interrupting, snooping; see INTERFERENCE 1, RUDENESS.

media ***n.*** radio, television, newspapers, magazines, journalism, news, reporters, reportage, *paparazzi* (Italian), the networks, cable, programming, audiovisual devices.

medic* ***n.*** physician, practitioner, surgeon; see DOCTOR, MEDICINE 1.

medical ***a.*** healing, medicinal, curative, therapeutic, restorative, prophylactic, preventive, alleviating, medicating, pharmaceutical, sedative, narcotic, tonic, disinfectant, corrective, pathological, cathartic, health-bringing, demulcent, balsamic, emollient.—*Ant.* HARMFUL, destructive, disease-giving.

medication ***n.*** remedy, pill, vaccination; see MEDICINE 2.

medicinal ***a.*** curative, healing, therapeutic; see HEALTHFUL.

medicine ***n.*** **1** [The healing profession] healers, practitioners, doctors, physicians, nurses, EMT's, medics*, surgeons, osteopaths, homeopaths, chiropractors. **2** [A medical preparation] drug, dose, dosage, potion, prescription, pill, tablet, caplet, capsule, draft, patent medicine, remedy, cure, antipoison, antibiotic, medication, vaccination, inoculation, injection, draught, herb, specific, nostrum, elixir, tonic, balm, salve, lotion, ointment, emetic, shot. **3** [The study and practice of medicine] medical science, physic, healing art, medical profession. *Branches of medicine include the following:* surgery, therapy, therapeutics, anesthesiology, internal medicine, family practice, general practice, psychiatry, psychotherapy, ophthalmology, obstetrics, gynecology, pediatrics, sports medicine, audiology, orthopedics, neurology, cardiology, dermatology, pathology, endocrinology, immunology, hematology, urology, inhalation therapy, diagnostics, radiotherapy, geriatrics, veterinary medicine.

medieval ***a.*** pertaining to the Middle Ages, feudal, antiquated; see OLD 3.

mediocre ***a.*** **1** [Ordinary] average, typical, unexceptional; see COMMON 1. **2** [Low in quality] not good enough, inferior, second-rate; see POOR 2.

mediocrity ***n.*** **1** [Ordinariness] commonplaceness, commonness, averageness; see REGULARITY. **2** [Substandard quality] inferiority, triviality, second-rateness.

meditate ***v.*** **1** [To muse] ponder, study, contemplate, muse over, revolve, say to oneself, reflect, view, brood over, dream; see also THINK 1. **2** [To think over] weigh, consider, speculate; see THINK 1.

meditation ***n.*** musing, contemplation, reflection; see REFLECTION 1, THOUGHT 1.

medium ***a.*** commonplace, average, ordinary; see COMMON 1.

medium ***n.*** **1** [A means] mechanism, means, agent; see MEANS 1, PART 3. **2** [A means of expression] symbol, sign, token, interpretation, manifestation, revelation, evidence, mark, statement; see also COMMUNICATION, SPEECH 2. **3** [A supposed channel of supernatural knowledge] oracle, seer, spiritualist; see PROPHET.

medley ***n.*** mingling, assortment, conglomeration; see MIXTURE 1, VARIETY 1.

gät′ə) **2** the inner substance of an organ, as of the kidney

meek (mēk) ***adj.*** ⟦< ON *miukr*, gentle⟧ **1** patient and mild **2** too submissive; spiritless —**meek′ly** ***adv.*** —**meek′ness** ***n.***

meer·schaum (mir′shəm, -shôm′) ***n.*** ⟦Ger, sea foam⟧ **1** a white, claylike, heat-resistant mineral used for tobacco pipes, etc. **2** a pipe made of this

meet[1] (mēt) ***vt.*** **met, meet′ing** ⟦OE *metan*⟧ **1** to come upon; encounter **2** to be present at the arrival of *[to meet a bus]* **3** to come into contact with **4** to be introduced to **5** to contend with; deal with **6** to experience *[to meet disaster]* **7** to be perceived by (the eye, etc.) **8** *a)* to satisfy (a demand, etc.) *b)* to pay (a bill, etc.) —***vi.*** **1** to come together **2** to come into contact, etc. **3** to be introduced **4** to assemble —***n.*** a meeting as for a sporting competition —**meet with 1** to experience **2** to receive

meet[2] (mēt) ***adj.*** ⟦OE *(ge)mæte*, fitting⟧ [Now Rare] suitable; proper

meet′ing ***n.*** **1** a coming together **2** a gathering of people **3** a junction

mega- ⟦Gr < *megas*, great⟧ *combining form* **1** large, great, powerful **2** one million Also **meg-**

meg·a·byte (meg′ə bīt′) ***n.*** ⟦prec. + BYTE⟧ a unit of storage capacity in a computer system, equal to 2^{20} bytes, or, loosely, one million bytes

meg′a·hertz′ (-hurts′) ***n.***, *pl.* **-hertz′** ⟦MEGA- + HERTZ⟧ one million hertz

meg·a·lo·ma·ni·a (meg′ə lō mā′nē ə) ***n.*** ⟦< Gr *megas*, large + -MANIA⟧ a mental disorder characterized by delusions of grandeur, power, etc. —**meg′a·lo·ma′ni·ac** ***adj., n.***

meg·a·lop·o·lis (meg′ə läp′ə lis) ***n.*** ⟦Gr, great city⟧ a vast, continuously urban area, including any number of cities

meg·a·phone (meg′ə fōn′) ***n.*** ⟦MEGA- + -PHONE⟧ a cone-shaped device for increasing the volume of the voice

meg′a·ton′ (-tun′) ***n.*** ⟦MEGA- + TON⟧ the explosive force of a million tons of TNT

Me·kong (mā′käŋ′, -kôŋ′) river in SE Asia, flowing into the South China Sea

mel·a·mine (mel′ə mēn′) ***n.*** ⟦Ger *melamin*⟧ a white, crystalline compound used in making synthetic resins

mel·an·cho·li·a (mel′ən kō′lē ə) ***n.*** a mental disorder, often psychotic, characterized by extreme depression

mel′an·chol′y (-käl′ē) ***n.***, *pl.* **-ies** ⟦< Gr *melas*, black + *cholē*, bile⟧ sadness and depression of spirits —***adj.*** **1** sad and depressed **2** causing sadness —**mel′an·chol′ic** ***adj.***

Mel·a·ne·sia (mel′ə nē′zhə) group of islands in the S Pacific —**Mel′a·ne′sian** ***adj., n.***

mé·lange (mā lônzh′, -lônj′) ***n.*** ⟦Fr < *mêler*, to mix⟧ a mixture; medley

mel·a·nin (mel′ə nin) ***n.*** ⟦< Gr *melas*, black⟧ a blackish pigment found in skin, hair, etc.

mel′a·no′ma (-nō′mə) ***n.***, *pl.* **-mas** or **-ma·ta** (-mə tə) ⟦< Gr *melas*, black + *-ōma*, mass⟧ a skin tumor derived from cells capable of melanin formation

Mel·ba toast (mel′bə) ⟦after N. *Melba* (1861-1931), Australian soprano⟧ [*also* **m- t-**] very crisp, thinly sliced toast

Mel·bourne (mel′bərn) seaport in SE Australia: pop. 2,833,000

meld (meld) ***vt., vi.*** ⟦< MELT + WELD⟧ to blend; merge

me·lee or **mê·lée** (mā′lā′, mā lā′) ***n.*** ⟦Fr⟧ a confused fight or hand-to-hand struggle

mel·io·rate (mēl′yə rāt′) ***vt., vi.*** **-rat′ed, -rat′ing** ⟦< L *melior*, better⟧ to make or become better

mel·lif·lu·ous (mə lif′lo͞o əs) ***adj.*** ⟦< L *mel*, honey + *fluere*, to flow⟧ sounding sweet and smooth: also **mel·lif′lu·ent** —**mel·lif′lu·ence** ***n.***

mel·low (mel′ō) ***adj.*** ⟦ME *melwe*, ripe⟧ **1** full-flavored: said of wine, etc. **2** full, rich, soft, etc.; not harsh: said of sound, light, etc. **3** made gentle, understanding, etc. by age **4** [Inf.] genial, as from drinking liquor —***vt., vi.*** to make or become mellow

me·lo·di·ous (mə lō′dē əs) ***adj.*** **1** producing melody **2** pleasing to hear; tuneful —**me·lo′di·ous·ly** ***adv.***

mel·o·dra·ma (mel′ə drä′mə, -dram′ə) ***n.*** ⟦< Fr < Gr *melos*, song + LL *drama*, drama⟧ a drama with exaggerated conflicts and emotions, stereotyped characters, etc. —**mel′o·dra·mat′ic** (-drə mat′ik) ***adj.***

mel′o·dra·mat′ics (-drə mat′iks) ***pl.n.*** melodramatic behavior

mel·o·dy (mel′ə dē) ***n.***, *pl.* **-dies** ⟦< Gr *melos*, song + *aeidein*, sing⟧ **1** pleasing sounds in sequence **2** *Music a)* a tune, song, etc. *b)* the leading part in a harmonic composition —**me·lod·ic** (mə läd′ik) ***adj.*** —**me·lod′i·cal·ly** ***adv.***

mel·on (mel′ən) ***n.*** ⟦< Gr *mēlon*, apple⟧ the large, juicy, thick-skinned, many-seeded fruit of certain trailing plants, as the watermelon or cantaloupe

melt (melt) ***vt., vi.*** ⟦OE *m(i)eltan*⟧ **1** to change from a solid to a liquid state, generally by heat **2** to dissolve **3** to disappear or cause to disappear gradually **4** to soften; become gentle, tender, etc.

melt′down′ ***n.*** a dangerous situation in which a nuclear reactor begins to melt its fuel rods

melting pot a country, etc. in which people of various nationalities and races are assimilated

Mel·ville (mel′vil), **Her·man** (hur′mən) 1819-91; U.S. novelist

mem·ber (mem′bər) ***n.*** ⟦< L *membrum*⟧ **1** a limb or other part of a person, animal, or plant **2** a distinct part of a whole **3** a person belonging to some group, society, etc.

THESAURUS

meek ***a.*** **1** [Humble] unassuming, plain, mild; see HUMBLE 1, MODEST 2. **2** [Long-suffering] passive, resigned, uncomplaining; see PATIENT 1. **3** [Lacking spirit] submissive, compliant, subdued; see DOCILE, RESIGNED.

meekness ***n.*** submissiveness, mildness, timidity; see HUMILITY.

meet[1] ***n.*** match, athletic event, tournament; see EVENT, COMPETITION.

meet[1] ***v.*** **1** [To come together] converge, assemble, crowd, rally, convene, collect, associate, unite, swarm, get together, enter in; see also GATHER 1. **2** [To go to a place of meeting] resort, be present at, gather together, convene, congregate, muster, appear; see also ASSEMBLE 1, ATTEND.—*Ant.* LEAVE, disperse, scatter. **3** [To touch] reach, coincide, adhere; see JOIN 1. **4** [To become acquainted] make the acquaintance of, be presented to, be introduced, present oneself to, make oneself known to, get next to*, get to know; see also FAMILIARIZE (ONESELF WITH). **5** [To fulfill] answer, fit, suffice; see SATISFY 3. **6** [To encounter] fall in with, come upon, meet by accident, come across, meet face to face, face up to, bump into, touch shoulders with, meet at every turn, engage, join, battle, match, push, brush against, shove; see also FACE 1, FIGHT.—*Ant.* ABANDON, turn one's back on, leave. —**meet with** observe, experience, suffer; see FIND.

meeting ***n.*** **1** [The act of coming together] encounter, juxtaposition, joining, juncture, unifying, unification, adherence, convergence, confrontation, contacting, connection, conflict, accord, agreement.—*Ant.* SEPARATION, departure, dispersal. **2** [A gathering, usually of people] conference, assemblage, rally; see GATHERING.

melancholy ***a.*** depressed, unhappy, dispirited; see SAD 1.

melancholy ***n.*** unhappiness, wistfulness, despair; see DEPRESSION 2, GRIEF, SADNESS.

meld ***v.*** blend, merge, unite; see MIX 1, UNITE.

mellow ***a.*** **1** [Ripe] sweet, soft, perfected; see RIPE 1. **2** [Culturally mature] cultured, fully developed, broad-minded; see MATURE.

mellowed ***a.*** mature, ripened, softened; see RIPE 1, SOFT 3.

melodious ***a.*** agreeable, pleasing, resonant; see HARMONIOUS 1, MUSICAL 1.

melodrama ***n.*** play, theater, sitcom*; see DRAMA.

melodramatic ***a.*** artificial, spectacular, sensational; see EXAGGERATED.

melody ***n.*** **1** [The quality of being melodious] concord, euphony, resonance; see HARMONY 1. **2** [A melodious arrangement] air, lyric, strain; see SONG.

melon ***n.*** watermelon, cantaloupe, muskmelon; see FOOD, FRUIT.

melt ***v.*** **1** [To liquefy] thaw, fuse, blend, merge, soften, flow, run, disintegrate, waste away; see also DISSOLVE.—*Ant.* FREEZE, harden, coagulate. **2** [To relent] forgive, show mercy, become lenient; see YIELD 1. **3** [To decrease] vanish, pass away, go; see DECREASE 1.

melted ***a.*** softened, thawed, liquefied, dwindled, blended, merged, wasted away, disintegrated, vanished, decreased, diminished, tempered, relaxed.

melting ***a.*** softening, liquefying, reducing; see SOFT 2.

member ***n.*** **1** [A person or group] constituent, charter member, active member, member in good standing, honorary member, affiliate, brother, sister, comrade, chapter, post, branch, lodge, district, company, battalion, regiment, division. **2** [A part] portion, segment, fragment; see DIVISION 1, PART 1. **3** [A part of the body] organ, arm, leg; see LIMB 2.

mem'ber·ship' *n.* **1** the state of being a member: with *in* **2** members collectively, as of a group **3** the number of members

mem·brane (mem'brān') *n.* ⟦< L *membrum,* member⟧ a thin, soft layer, esp. of animal or plant tissue, that covers or lines an organ, part, etc. —**mem'bra·nous** (-brə nəs) *adj.*

me·men·to (mə men'tō) *n., pl.* **-tos** or **-toes** ⟦< L *meminisse,* remember⟧ a souvenir

mem·o (mem'ō) *n., pl.* **-os** *short for* MEMORANDUM

mem·oirs (mem'wärz') *pl.n.* ⟦< L *memoria,* memory⟧ **1** an autobiography **2** a record of events based on the writer's personal knowledge

mem·o·ra·bil·i·a (mem'ə rə bil'ē ə, -bil'yə; -bēl'-) *pl.n.* ⟦L⟧ things serving as a record or reminder

mem·o·ra·ble (mem'ə rə bəl) *adj.* worth remembering; notable; remarkable —**mem'o·ra·bly** *adv.*

mem·o·ran·dum (mem'ə ran'dəm) *n., pl.* **-dums** or **-da** (-də) ⟦L⟧ **1** a short note written to remind one of something **2** an informal written communication, as in an office **3** *Law* a short written statement of the terms of an agreement, etc.

me·mo·ri·al (mə môr'ē əl) *adj.* ⟦< L *memoria,* memory⟧ serving to help people remember —*n.* anything meant to help people remember a person or event, as a monument or holiday —**me·mo'ri·al·ize'** (-īz'), **-ized'**, **-iz'ing**, *vt.*

Memorial Day a legal holiday in the U.S. (the last Monday in May in most States) in memory of members of the armed forces killed in war

mem·o·rize (mem'ə rīz') *vt.* **-rized'**, **-riz'ing** to commit to memory —**mem'o·ri·za'tion** *n.*

mem·o·ry (mem'ə rē, mem'rē) *n., pl.* **-ries** ⟦< L *memor,* mindful⟧ **1** the power or act of remembering **2** all that one remembers **3** something remembered **4** the period of remembering *[within my memory]* **5** commemoration **6** storage capacity, as of a computer or disk

Mem·phis (mem'fis) city in SW Tennessee: pop. 610,000

men (men) *n. pl. of* MAN

men·ace (men'əs) *n.* ⟦< L *minari,* threaten⟧ **1** a threat **2** [Inf.] one who is a nuisance —*vt., vi.* **-aced**, **-ac·ing** to threaten —**men'ac·ing·ly** *adv.*

mé·nage or **me·nage** (mā näzh', mə-) *n.* ⟦Fr < L *mansio,* house⟧ a household

me·nag·er·ie (mə naj'ər ē, -nazh'-) *n.* ⟦see prec.⟧ a collection of wild animals kept in cages, etc. for exhibition

mend (mend) *vt.* ⟦< ME *amenden,* amend⟧ **1** to repair **2** to make better; reform —*vi.* **1** to improve, esp. in health **2** to heal, as a fracture —*n.* **1** a mending **2** a mended place —**on the mend** improving, esp. in health —**mend'er** *n.*

men·da·cious (men dā'shəs) *adj.* ⟦< L *mendax*⟧ not truthful; lying —**men·dac'i·ty** (-das'ə tē), *pl.* **-ties**, *n.*

Men·del (men'dəl), **Gre·gor** (grā'gôr) 1822-84; Austrian monk & geneticist

Men·dels·sohn (men'dəl sən, -sōn'), **Fe·lix** (fā'liks) 1809-47; Ger. composer

men·di·cant (men'di kənt) *adj.* ⟦< L *mendicus,* needy⟧ begging —*n.* **1** a beggar **2** a mendicant friar

men'folk' (-fōk') *pl.n.* [Inf. or Dial.] men: also **men'folks'**

men·ha·den (men hād''n) *n., pl.* **-den** or **-dens** ⟦< AmInd⟧ a common fish of the W Atlantic, used for bait or for making oil and fertilizer

me·ni·al (mē'nē əl) *adj.* ⟦< L *mansio,* house⟧ **1** of or fit for servants **2** servile; low —*n.* **1** a domestic servant **2** a servile, low person —**me'ni·al·ly** *adv.*

me·nin·ges (mə nin'jēz') *pl.n., sing.* **me·ninx** (mē'niŋks') ⟦< Gr *mēninx,* membrane⟧ the three membranes that envelop the brain and the spinal cord —**me·nin'ge·al** (-jē əl) *adj.*

men·in·gi·tis (men'in jīt'is) *n.* ⟦ModL: see prec. & -ITIS⟧ inflammation of the meninges

me·nis·cus (mə nis'kəs) *n., pl.* **-cus·es** or **-ci'** (-ī') ⟦< Gr dim. of *mēnē,* the moon⟧ **1** a crescent or crescent-shaped thing **2** the convex or concave upper surface of a column of liquid

Men·non·ite (men'ən īt') *n.* ⟦after *Menno* Simons, 16th-c. Du reformer⟧ a member of an evangelical Christian sect that opposes military service and favors plain living and dress

men·o·pause (men'ə pôz') *n.* ⟦< Gr *mēn,* month + *pauein,* to end⟧ the permanent cessation of menstruation

me·no·rah (mə nō'rə, -nôr'ə) *n.* ⟦Heb *menora,* lamp stand⟧ a candelabrum with seven (or nine) branches: a symbol of Judaism

men·ses (men'sēz') *pl.n.* ⟦L, pl. of *mensis,* month⟧ the periodic flow, usually monthly, of blood from the uterus

men·stru·ate (men'strōō āt') *vi.* **-at'ed**, **-at'ing** ⟦< L *mensis,* month⟧ to have a discharge of the menses —**men'strual** (-strəl) *adj.* —**men'stru·a'tion** *n.*

men·su·ra·tion (men'shə rā'shən) *n.* ⟦< L *mensura,* measure⟧ a measuring

-ment (mənt, mint) ⟦< L *-mentum*⟧ *suffix* **1** a result **2** a means of **3** an act **4** a state *[enchantment]*

men·tal (ment''l) *adj.* ⟦< L *mens,* the mind⟧ **1** of, for, by, or in the mind **2** of, having, or related to mental illness **3** for the mentally ill *[a mental hospital]* —**men'tal·ly** *adv.*

men'tal·ist *n.* MIND READER

men·tal·i·ty (men tal'i tē) *n., pl.* **-ties** **1** mental capacity or power **2** mental attitude or outlook

mental reservation a qualification (of a statement) that one makes to oneself but does not express

mental retardation a condition, usually congenital, characterized by subnormal intelligence

men·ta·tion (men tā'shən) *n.* ⟦< L *mens,* mind + -ATION⟧ the act or process of using the mind

men·thol (men'thôl') *n.* ⟦Ger < L *mentha,* MINT[2]⟧ a white, crystalline alcohol obtained from oil of peppermint and used in medicine, cosmetics, etc. —**men'tho·lat'ed** (-thə lāt'id) *adj.*

men·tion (men'shən) *n.* ⟦< L *mens,* the mind⟧ **1** a brief reference **2** a citing for honor —*vt.* to refer to briefly or

THESAURUS

membership *n.* club, society, association; see MEMBER 1.

memorable *a.* **1** [Historic] momentous, critical, unforgettable, crucial, famous, illustrious, distinguished, great, notable, significant, decisive, enduring, lasting, monumental, eventful, interesting; see also FAMOUS. **2** [Unusual] remarkable, exceptional, singular; see sense 1 and UNUSUAL 1.

memorandum *n.* notice, record, memo; see NOTE 2, REMINDER.

memorial *a.* dedicatory, remembering, commemorative; see REMEMBERED.

memorial *n.* remembrance, testimonial, tablet, slab, pillar, tombstone, headstone, column, monolith, mausoleum, record, memento, inscription, statue; see also CELEBRATION, CEREMONY 2, MONUMENT.

memorize *v.* fix in the memory, record, commemorate, memorialize, retain, commit to memory, imprint in one's mind, bear in mind, give word for word, get down pat*, have in one's head*, have at one's fingertips, learn by heart; see also LEARN, REMEMBER 2.—*Ant.* NEGLECT, forget, fail to remember.

memory *n.* **1** [The power to call up the past] recollection, retrospection, reminiscence, thought, consciousness, subconsciousness, unconscious memory, retentive memory, photographic memory, visual memory, auditory memory; see also MIND 1. **2** [That which can be recalled] mental image, picture, vision; see THOUGHT 2. —**in memory** in commemoration, in honor, in memoriam; see REMEMBERED.

menace *n.* **1** [A threat] caution, intimidation, foretelling; see WARNING. **2** [An imminent danger] hazard, peril, threat; see DANGER.

menace *v.* intimidate, portend, loom; see THREATEN.

menacing *a.* imminent, impending, threatening; see DANGEROUS, OMINOUS, SINISTER.

mend *v.* **1** [To repair] heal, patch, fix; see REPAIR. **2** [To improve] aid, remedy, cure; see CORRECT.

mended *a.* restored, put in shape, patched, patched up, renovated, refreshed, renewed, corrected, helped, bettered, lessened, remedied, cured, relieved, rectified, rejuvenated, remodeled, altered, changed, fixed, regulated, rebuilt, regenerated, reorganized, revived, touched up, doctored*; see also REPAIRED.

menial *a.* common, servile, abject; see HUMBLE 1, 2.

mental *a.* **1** [Concerning the mind] reasoning, cerebral, thinking; see RATIONAL 1, THOUGHTFUL 1. **2** [Existing only in the mind] subjective, subliminal, subconscious, telepathic, psychic, clairvoyant, imaginative; see also IMAGINARY.—*Ant.* OBJECTIVE, BODILY, SENSUAL.

mentality *n.* intellect, comprehension, reasoning; see MIND 1.

mentally *a.* rationally, psychically, intellectually; see REASONABLY 1.

mention *n.* notice, naming, specifying; see REMARK. —**not to mention** in addition, too, without even mentioning; see ALSO.

mention *v.* notice, specify, cite, introduce, state, declare, quote, refer to, discuss, touch on, instance, intimate, notify, communicate, suggest, make known, point out, bring up, speak of, throw out, toss off; see also TELL 1.—*Ant.* OVERLOOK, take no notice of, disregard.

incidentally —**make mention of** to mention —**not to mention** without even mentioning

men·tor (men′tər, -tôr′) ***n.*** ⟦after *Mentor*, friend and advisor of Odysseus⟧ **1** a wise advisor **2** a teacher or coach

men·u (men′yo͞o) ***n.***, *pl.* **-us** ⟦Fr, small, detailed⟧ **1** a detailed list of the foods served at a meal or those available at a restaurant **2** a list, as on a computer screen, of the various choices available to the user

me·ow or **me·ou** (mē ou′) ***n.*** ⟦echoic⟧ the characteristic vocal sound made by a cat —***vi.*** to make such a sound

mer·can·tile (mʉr′kən tīl′, -til) ***adj.*** ⟦Fr⟧ of or characteristic of merchants or trade

mer·ce·nar·y (mʉr′sə ner′ē) ***adj.*** ⟦< L *merces,* wages⟧ working or done for payment only —***n.***, *pl.* **-ies** a soldier hired to serve in a foreign army

mer′cer·ize′ (-īz′) ***vt.*** **-ized′**, **-iz′ing** ⟦after J. *Mercer* (1791-1866), Eng calico dealer⟧ to treat (cotton thread or fabric) with a sodium hydroxide solution to strengthen it, give it a silky luster, etc.

mer·chan·dise (mʉr′chən dīz′; *for n., also,* -dīs′) ***n.*** ⟦see fol.⟧ things bought and sold; goods; commodities —***vt.***, ***vi.*** **-dised′**, **-dis′ing** **1** to buy and sell **2** to promote the sale of (a product) Also, for v., **mer′chan·dize′** (-dīz′), **-dized′**, **-diz′ing** —**mer′chan·dis′er** or **mer′chan·diz′er** ***n.***

mer·chant (mʉr′chənt) ***n.*** ⟦ult. < L *merx,* wares⟧ **1** one whose business is buying and selling goods **2** a retail dealer; storekeeper —***adj.*** mercantile; commercial

mer′chant·man (-mən) ***n.***, *pl.* **-men** (-mən) a ship used in commerce

merchant marine **1** all of a nation's commercial ships **2** their personnel

mer·ci (mer sē′) ***interj.*** ⟦Fr⟧ thank you

mer·ci·ful (mʉr′si fəl) ***adj.*** having or showing mercy; compassionate; lenient —**mer′ci·ful·ly** ***adv.***

mer′ci·less ***adj.*** without mercy; pitiless —**mer′ci·less·ly** ***adv.***

mer·cu·ri·al (mər kyoor′ē əl) ***adj.*** **1** of or containing mercury **2** quick, changeable, fickle, etc.

Mer·cu·ry (mʉr′kyoor ē) ***n.*** **1** *Rom. Myth.* the messenger of the gods **2** a small planet in the solar system: see PLANET **3** [**m-**] a heavy, silver-white metallic chemical element, liquid at ordinary temperatures, used in thermometers, etc. —**mer·cu·ric** (mər kyoor′ik) ***adj.*** —**mer·cu′rous** ***adj.***

mer·cy (mʉr′sē) ***n.***, *pl.* **-cies** ⟦< L *merces,* payment⟧ **1** a refraining from harming offenders, enemies, etc. **2** imprisonment rather than death for a capital crime **3** a disposition to forgive or be kind **4** the power to forgive **5** kind or compassionate treatment **6** a lucky thing; blessing —**at the mercy of** completely in the power of

mercy killing EUTHANASIA

mere (mir) ***adj.*** *superl.* **mer′est** ⟦< L *merus,* pure⟧ nothing more or other than *[a mere boy]*

mere′ly ***adv.*** only; no more than

mer·e·tri·cious (mer′ə trish′əs) ***adj.*** ⟦< L *meretrix,* a prostitute⟧ **1** attractive in a flashy way **2** superficially plausible; specious

mer·gan·ser (mər gan′sər) ***n.*** ⟦< L *mergus,* diver (bird) + *anser,* goose⟧ a fish-eating, diving duck with a long bill

merge (mʉrj) ***vi.***, ***vt.*** **merged**, **merg′ing** ⟦L *mergere,* to dip⟧ **1** to lose or cause to lose identity by being absorbed or combined **2** to unite; combine

merg·er (mʉr′jər) ***n.*** a merging; specif., a combining of two or more companies into one

me·rid·i·an (mə rid′ē ən) ***n.*** ⟦< L *meridies,* noon⟧ **1** the highest point of power, etc. **2** *a)* a circle on the earth's surface passing through the geographical poles and any given point *b)* any of the lines of longitude

me·ringue (mə raŋ′) ***n.*** ⟦Fr⟧ egg whites beaten with sugar until stiff: used as a pie covering, etc.

me·ri·no (mə rē′nō) ***n.***, *pl.* **-nos** ⟦Sp⟧ **1** any of a breed of hardy, white-faced sheep with long, fine wool **2** the wool **3** yarn or cloth made of it

mer·it (mer′it) ***n.*** ⟦< L *merere,* deserve⟧ **1** worth; value; excellence **2** something deserving reward, praise, etc. **3** [*pl.*] intrinsic rightness or wrongness —***vt.*** to deserve

mer·i·to·ri·ous (mer′i tôr′ē əs) ***adj.*** having merit; deserving reward, praise, etc. —**mer′i·to′ri·ous·ly** ***adv.***

Mer·lin (mʉr′lin) ***n.*** *Arthurian Legend* a magician and seer, helper of King Arthur

mer·maid (mʉr′mād′) ***n.*** ⟦< OE *mere,* sea + MAID⟧ an imaginary sea creature with the head and upper body of a woman and the tail of a fish —**mer′man′** (-man′), *pl.* **-men′** (-mən′), ***masc.n.***

mer·ri·ment (mer′i mənt) ***n.*** a merrymaking; gaiety and fun; mirth

mer·ry (mer′ē) ***adj.*** **-ri·er**, **-ri·est** ⟦< OE *myrge,* pleasing⟧ **1** full of fun; lively **2** festive —**make merry** to be festive and have fun —**mer′ri·ly** ***adv.*** —**mer′ri·ness** ***n.***

mer′ry-go-round′ ***n.*** **1** a circular, revolving platform with forms of animals as seats on it, used at carnivals, etc. **2** a busy series of activities

mer′ry·mak′ing ***n.*** a having fun; festivity —**mer′ry·mak′er** ***n.***

me·sa (mā′sə) ***n.*** ⟦Sp < L *mensa*, a table⟧ a small, high plateau with steep sides

Me·sa (mā′sə) city in SC Arizona: pop. 288,000

mes·cal (mes kal′) ***n.*** ⟦< Sp < AmInd(Mex)⟧ a small cactus of N Mexico and the SW U.S.

mes·ca·line (mes′kə lin) ***n.*** ⟦< AmInd(Mex) *mexcalli*, a spineless cactus⟧ a psychedelic drug obtained from the mescal

mes·clun (mes′klən) ***n.*** ⟦Fr⟧ a mixture of salad greens and herbs

mes·dames (mā däm′; *Fr,* -dȧm′) ***n.*** *pl. of* MADAME, MADAM (sense 1), or MRS.

mes·de·moi·selles (mād mwȧ zel′) ***n.*** *pl. of* MADEMOISELLE

mesh (mesh) ***n.*** ⟦prob. < MDu *mæsche*⟧ **1** any of the open spaces of a net, screen, etc. **2** a net or network **3** a netlike material, as for stockings **4** the engagement of the teeth of gears —***vt.***, ***vi.*** **1** to entangle or become entangled **2** to engage or become engaged: said of gears **3** to interlock

mes·mer·ize (mez′mər īz′, mes′-) ***vt.*** **-ized′**, **-iz′ing** ⟦after F. A. *Mesmer* (1734-1815), Ger physician⟧ **1** to hypnotize **2** to spellbind —**mes′mer·ism′** ***n.*** —**mes′mer·ist** ***n.***

Mes·o·a·mer·i·ca (mes′ō ə mer′i kə, mez′-) region including parts of modern Mexico and Central America, formerly inhabited by the Maya, the Aztecs, etc.

mes·on (mes′än′, mez′-) ***n.*** ⟦< Gr *mesos*, middle + (ELECTR)ON⟧ any of a group of unstable subatomic particles having a mass between those of an electron and a proton

Mes·o·po·ta·mi·a (mes′ə pə tā′mē ə) ancient country in SW Asia, between the upper Tigris & Euphrates rivers

Mes·o·zo·ic (mes′ə zō′ik, mez′-) ***adj.*** ⟦< Gr *mesos*, middle + ZO(O)- + -IC⟧ designating the geologic era (*c.* 240 to 66

THESAURUS

mentioned ***a.*** noticed, cited, specified, named, quoted, introduced, referred to, discussed, declared, revealed, brought up, considered, communicated, made known, spoken of; see also TOLD.

menu ***n.*** bill of fare, cuisine, food; see LIST.

merchandise ***n.*** wares, commodities, stock; see COMMODITY.

merchandise ***v.*** market, distribute, promote; see SELL.

merchant ***n.*** trader, storekeeper, retailer, shopkeeper, wholesaler, exporter, shipper, dealer, jobber, tradesman; see also BUSINESSMAN.

merciful ***a.*** lenient, feeling, compassionate, softhearted, mild, tolerant, kindly, indulgent; see also KIND.—*Ant.* CRUEL, pitiless, unsparing.

merciless ***a.*** pitiless, unsparing, relentless; see CRUEL, FIERCE, RUTHLESS.

mercy ***n.*** leniency, lenience, softheartedness, mildness, clemency, amnesty, pardon, tenderness, gentleness, compassion, ruth*; see also GENEROSITY, TOLERANCE 1.—*Ant.* INDIFFERENCE, intolerance, selfishness. —**at the mercy of** in the power of, vulnerable to, controlled by; see SUBJECT.

mere ***a.*** small, minor, insignificant; see LITTLE 1, POOR 2.

merely ***a.*** slightly, solely, simply; see HARDLY, ONLY 3.

merge ***v.*** fuse, join, blend; see MIX 1, UNITE.

merger ***n.*** amalgamation, consolidation, alliance; see ORGANIZATION 2.

merit ***n.*** **1** [Worth] credit, benefit, advantage; see QUALITY 3, VALUE 3. **2** [A creditable quality] worthiness, excellence, honor; see CHARACTER 2, VIRTUE 1.

merit ***v.*** be worth, warrant, justify; see DESERVE.

merited ***a.*** earned, proper, fitting; see DESERVED, FIT 1.

merrily ***a.*** joyfully, gleefully, genially; see CHEERFULLY, HAPPILY.

merriment ***n.*** joy, cheerfulness, gaiety; see HAPPINESS, HUMOR 3.

merry ***a.*** festive, joyous, mirthful; see HAPPY. —**make merry** frolic, revel, enjoy; see PLAY 1.

mesa ***n.*** plateau, table, tableland, butte, table mountain; see also HILL, MOUNTAIN 1.

mesh ***v.*** coincide, suit, coordinate; see AGREE, FIT 1.

million years ago) characterized by dinosaurs and by the appearance of flowering plants, mammals, birds, etc.

mes·quite or **mes·quit** (me skēt′) ***n.*** ⟦< AmInd(Mex) *mizquitl*⟧ a thorny tree or shrub of Mexico and the SW U.S.

mess (mes) ***n.*** ⟦< L *missus,* course (at a meal)⟧ **1** a portion of food for a meal **2** a group of people who regularly eat together, as in the army **3** the meal they eat **4** a jumble **5** a state of trouble, disorder, or confusion **6** [Inf.] a person in such a state **7** [Inf.] an untidy place —***vt.*** **1** to make dirty or untidy **2** to muddle; botch Often with *up* —***vi.*** **1** to eat as one of a mess **2** to make a mess **3** to putter or meddle (*in* or *with*) —**mess′y, -i·er, -i·est,** ***adj.*** —**mess′i·ly** ***adv.*** —**mess′i·ness** ***n.***

mes·sage (mes′ij) ***n.*** ⟦< L *mittere,* send⟧ **1** a communication sent by speech, in writing, etc. **2** the chief idea that an artist, writer, etc. seeks to communicate in a work —**get the message** [Inf.] to understand a hint, etc.

mes·sen·ger (mes′ən jər) ***n.*** one who carries a message or goes on an errand

messenger RNA a single-stranded form of RNA, derived from DNA, that carries the genetic information needed to form proteins

mess hall a room or building where soldiers, etc. regularly have meals

Mes·si·ah (mə sī′ə) ***n.*** ⟦< Heb *māshīaḥ,* anointed⟧ **1** *Judaism* the expected deliverer of the Jews **2** *Christianity* Jesus **3** [**m-**] any expected savior or liberator —**Mes′si·an′ic** or **me·si·an·ic** (mes′ē an′ik) ***adj.***

mes·sieurs (mes′ərz; *Fr* mā syö′) ***n. pl.*** *of* MONSIEUR

Messrs (mes′ərz) *abbrev.* messieurs: now used chiefly as the pl. of MR.

mes·ti·zo (me stē′zō) ***n.***, *pl.* **-zos** or **-zoes** ⟦Sp < L *miscere,* to mix⟧ a person of mixed parentage, esp. Spanish and American Indian

met[1] (met) ***vt., vi.*** *pt. & pp. of* MEET[1]

met[2] *abbrev.* metropolitan

meta- ⟦< Gr *meta,* after⟧ *prefix* **1** changed *[metathesis]* **2** after, beyond, higher *[metaphysics]*

me·tab·o·lism (mə tab′ə liz′əm) ***n.*** ⟦< Gr *meta,* beyond + *ballein,* throw⟧ the chemical and physical processes continuously going on in living organisms and cells, including the changing of food into living tissue and the changing of living tissue into waste products and energy —**met·a·bol·ic** (met′ə bäl′ik) ***adj.*** —**me·tab′o·lize′** (-līz′), **-lized′, -liz′ing,** ***vt., vi.***

met·a·car·pus (met′ə kär′pəs) ***n.***, *pl.* **-pi′** (-pī′) ⟦< Gr *meta,* over + *karpos,* wrist⟧ the part of the hand between the wrist and the fingers —**met′a·car′pal** ***adj., n.***

met·al (met′'l) ***n.*** ⟦< Gr *metallon,* a mine⟧ **1** *a*) any of a class of chemical elements, as iron or gold, that have luster, can conduct heat and electricity, etc. *b*) an alloy of such elements, as brass **2** anything consisting of metal —**me·tal·lic** (mə tal′ik) ***adj.***

met·al·lur·gy (met′ə lʉr′jē) ***n.*** ⟦< Gr *metallon,* metal + *ergon,* work⟧ the science of separating metals from their ores and preparing them for use, by smelting, refining, etc. —**met′al·lur′gi·cal** ***adj.*** —**met′al·lur′gist** ***n.***

met·a·mor·phose (met′ə môr′fōz′, -fōs′) ***vt., vi.*** **-phosed′, -phos′ing** to change in form; transform

met′a·mor′pho·sis (-môr′fə sis) ***n.***, *pl.* **-ses′** (-sēz′) ⟦< Gr *meta,* over + *morphē,* form⟧ **1** a change of form, structure, substance, or function; specif., the physical change undergone by some animals during development, as of the tadpole to the frog **2** a marked change of character, appearance, condition, etc. —**met′a·mor′phic** ***adj.***

met·a·phor (met′ə fôr′) ***n.*** ⟦< Gr *meta,* over + *pherein,* to bear⟧ a figure of speech in which one thing is spoken of as if it were another (Ex.: "all the world's a stage") —**met′a·phor′ic** or **met′a·phor′i·cal** ***adj.***

met·a·phys·i·cal (met′ə fiz′i kəl) ***adj.*** **1** of, or having the nature of, metaphysics **2** very abstract or subtle **3** supernatural

met′a·phys′ics (-iks) ***n.*** ⟦< Gr *meta (ta) physika,* after (the) *Physics* (of Aristotle)⟧ **1** the branch of philosophy that seeks to explain the nature of being and reality **2** speculative philosophy in general

me·tas·ta·sis (mə tas′tə sis) ***n.***, *pl.* **-ses′** (-sēz′) ⟦< Gr *meta,* after + *histanai,* to place⟧ the spread of disease from one part of the body to another, esp. the spread of cancer cells by way of the bloodstream —**me·tas′ta·size′** (-sīz′), **-sized′, -siz′ing,** ***vi.***

met·a·tar·sus (met′ə tär′səs) ***n.***, *pl.* **-si′** (-sī′) ⟦< Gr *meta,* over + *tarsos,* flat of the foot⟧ the part of the human foot between the ankle and the toes —**met′a·tar′sal** ***adj., n.***

me·tath·e·sis (mə tath′ə sis) ***n.***, *pl.* **-ses′** (-sēz′) ⟦< Gr *meta,* over + *tithenai,* to place⟧ transposition, specif. of sounds in a word

mete (mēt) ***vt.*** **met′ed, met′ing** ⟦OE *metan,* to measure⟧ to allot; distribute: usually with *out*

me·tem·psy·cho·sis (mi tem′sī kō′sis) ***n.***, *pl.* **-ses′** (-sēz′) ⟦< Gr *meta,* over + *en,* in + *psychē,* soul⟧ transmigration of souls

me·te·or (mēt′ē ər, -ôr′) ***n.*** ⟦< Gr *meta,* beyond + *eōra,* a hovering⟧ **1** the streak of light, etc. observed when a meteoroid enters the earth's atmosphere; shooting star **2** loosely, a meteoroid or meteorite

me′te·or′ic (-ôr′ik) ***adj.*** **1** of a meteor **2** like a meteor; momentarily brilliant, swift, etc.

me′te·or·ite′ (-ər īt′) ***n.*** that part of a meteoroid that survives passage through the atmosphere of a planet and falls to its surface

me′te·or·oid′ (-ər oid′) ***n.*** a small, solid body traveling through outer space, seen as a meteor when in the earth's atmosphere

me′te·or·ol′o·gy (-ə räl′ə jē) ***n.*** ⟦see METEOR & -LOGY⟧ the science of the atmosphere and its phenomena; study of weather —**me′te·or·o·log′i·cal** (-ə läj′i kəl) ***adj.*** —**me′te·or·ol′o·gist** ***n.***

me·ter[1] (mēt′ər) ***n.*** ⟦< Gr *metron,* a measure⟧ **1** rhythm in verse; measured arrangement of syllables according to stress **2** the basic pattern of beats in a piece of music **3** ⟦Fr *mètre*⟧ the basic metric unit of length, equal to 39.3701 inches

me·ter[2] (mēt′ər) ***n.*** ⟦METE + -ER⟧ **1** an apparatus for measuring and recording the quantity of gas, water, etc. passing through it **2** PARKING METER

-me·ter (mēt′ər, mi tər) ⟦< Gr *metron,* a measure⟧ *combining form* a device for measuring *[barometer]*

meth·a·done (meth′ə dōn′) ***n.*** ⟦< its chemical name⟧ a synthetic narcotic drug used in medicine to treat heroin and morphine addicts

meth·ane (meth′ān′) ***n.*** ⟦< METHYL⟧ a colorless, odorless, flammable gas formed by the decomposition of vegetable matter, as in marshes

meth·a·nol (meth′ə nôl′) ***n.*** ⟦< METHAN(E) + (ALCOH)OL⟧ a colorless, flammable, poisonous liquid used as a fuel, solvent, antifreeze, etc.

me·thinks (mē thiŋks′) ***v.impersonal*** *pt.* **-thought′** (-thôt′) ⟦OE *me,* to me + *thyncth,* it seems⟧ [Archaic] it seems to me

THESAURUS

mess ***n.*** **1** [A mixture] combination, compound, blend; see MIXTURE 1. **2** [A confusion] jumble, muss, chaos, clutter, clog, congestion, snag, scramble, complexity, mayhem, shambles, hodgepodge; see also CONFUSION, DISORDER.

message ***n.*** news, information, intelligence; see ADVICE, BROADCAST, COMMUNICATION, DIRECTIONS. —**get the message*** get the hint, comprehend, perceive; see UNDERSTAND 1.

messenger ***n.*** bearer, minister, herald, carrier, courier, runner, crier, gopher*, errand boy, intermediary, envoy, emissary, angel, prophet, nuncio, go-between; see also AGENT.

Messiah ***n.*** Saviour, Redeemer, Son of Man, Jesus Christ; see also CHRIST, GOD 1.

mess up ***v.*** spoil, ruin, foul up*, damage; see also BOTCH, DESTROY.

messy ***a.*** rumpled, untidy, slovenly; see DIRTY, DISORDERED.

metal ***n.*** element, native rock, ore deposit, free metal, refined ore, smelted ore. *Types of metal include the following:* gold, silver, copper, iron, aluminum, manganese, nickel, lead, cobalt, platinum, zinc, tin, barium, cadmium, chromium, tungsten, mercury, molybdenum, sodium, potassium, radium, magnesium, calcium, titanium, uranium, gallium, rubidium, vanadium.

metallic ***a.*** **1** [Made of metal] hard, rocklike, iron, leaden, silvery, golden, metallurgic, mineral, geologic. **2** [Suggestive of metal; *said especially of sound*] ringing, resounding, resonant, bell-like, tinny, clanging.

metaphor ***n.*** trope, simile, figure of speech; see COMPARISON.

metaphorical ***a.*** figurative, symbolical, allegorical; see DESCRIPTIVE, GRAPHIC 1, 2.

metaphysical ***a.*** mystical, abstract, spiritual; see DIFFICULT 2.

meteor ***n.*** falling star, shooting star, meteorite, fireball, meteroid.

meteorology ***n.*** weather science, climatology, aerology; see CLIMATE, SCIENCE 1, WEATHER.

meter[1] ***n.*** measure, rhythm, tempo, metrical feet, common meter, long meter, ballad meter, tetrameter, pentameter, sprung rhythm, dipodic rhythm.

meth·od (meth′əd) ***n.*** ⟦< Fr < Gr *meta,* after + *hodos,* a way⟧ **1** a way of doing anything; procedure; process **2** orderliness in doing things or handling ideas
me·thod·i·cal (mə thäd′i kəl) ***adj.*** characterized by method; orderly; systematic —**me·thod′i·cal·ly** ***adv.***
Meth·od·ist (meth′ə dist) ***n.*** a member of a Protestant Christian denomination that developed from the teachings of John Wesley —**Meth′od·ism′** ***n.***
meth·od·ol·o·gy (meth′ə däl′ə jē) ***n.***, *pl.* **-gies** a system of methods, as in a science
Me·thu·se·lah (mə tho͞o′zə lə) ***n.*** *Bible* a patriarch who lived 969 years
meth·yl (meth′əl) ***n.*** ⟦< Gr *methy,* wine + *hylē,* wood⟧ a hydrocarbon radical found in methanol
methyl alcohol METHANOL
me·tic·u·lous (mə tik′yo͞o ləs, -yə-) ***adj.*** ⟦< L *metus,* fear⟧ extremely or excessively careful about details; scrupulous or finicky —**me·tic′u·lous·ly** ***adv.***
mé·tier (mā tyā′) ***n.*** ⟦Fr, a trade⟧ work that one is particularly suited for
me·tre (mēt′ər) ***n.*** *Brit. sp. of* METER[1]
met·ric (me′trik) ***adj.*** **1** METRICAL **2** *a)* of the METER[1] (sense 3) *b)* of the metric system
met·ri·cal (me′tri kəl) ***adj.*** **1** of or composed in meter or verse **2** of or used in measurement —**met′ri·cal·ly** ***adv.***
met·ri·cate (me′tri kāt′) ***vt.*** **-cat′ed, -cat′ing** to change over to the metric system —**met′ri·ca′tion** ***n.***
metric system a decimal system of weights and measures in which the kilogram (2.2046 pounds), the meter (39.3701 inches), and the liter (1,000 cubic centimeters or 1.0567 quarts) are the basic units
met·ro[1] (me′trō) ***adj.*** *short for* METROPOLITAN
met·ro[2] (me′trō) ***n.***, *pl.* **-ros** ⟦ult. < *metro(politan)*⟧ [*often* **M-**] a subway
met·ro·nome (me′trə nōm′) ***n.*** ⟦< Gr *metron,* measure + *nomos,* law⟧ a device that beats time at a desired rate, as for piano practice
me·trop·o·lis (mə träp′ə lis) ***n.*** ⟦< Gr *mētēr,* mother + *polis,* city⟧ **1** the main city of a country, state, etc. **2** any large or important city —**met·ro·pol·i·tan** (me′trə päl′i tən) ***adj.***
met·tle (met′'l) ***n.*** ⟦var. of METAL⟧ spirit; courage; ardor —**on one's mettle** prepared to do one's best
met′tle·some (-səm) ***adj.*** full of mettle; spirited; ardent, brave, etc.
mew (myo͞o) ***n.*** ⟦echoic⟧ the characteristic vocal sound made by a cat —***vi.*** to make this sound
mewl (myo͞ol) ***vi.*** ⟦< prec.⟧ to cry weakly, like a baby; whimper
mews (myo͞oz) ***pl.n.*** ⟦< L *mutare,* to change⟧ [*usually with sing. v.*] [Chiefly Brit.] stables or carriage houses in a court or alley
Mex *abbrev.* **1** Mexican **2** Mexico
Mex·i·ca·li (mek′si kä′lē) city in NW Mexico, on the U.S. border: pop. 602,000
Mex·i·co (mek′si kō′) **1** country in North America, south of the U.S.: 759,529 sq. mi.; pop. 81,250,000 **2 Gulf of** arm of the Atlantic, east of Mexico —**Mex′i·can** ***adj.***, ***n.***
Mexico City capital of Mexico: pop. 8,831,000 (met. area, 15,048,000)
mez·za·nine (mez′ə nēn′, mez′ə nēn′) ***n.*** ⟦< It *mezzano,* middle⟧ **1** a low-ceilinged story between two main stories, usually in the form of a balcony over the main floor **2** the first few rows of the balcony in some theaters
mez·zo-so·pra·no (met′sō sə pran′ō) ***n.***, *pl.* **-nos** or **-ni** (-ē) ⟦It < *mezzo,* medium + SOPRANO⟧ **1** the range of a female voice between soprano and contralto **2** a voice or singer with such a range
MFA or **M.F.A.** *abbrev.* Master of Fine Arts
mfg *abbrev.* manufacturing
mfr *abbrev.* **1** manufacture **2** manufacturer
Mg *Chem. symbol for* magnesium
mg *abbrev.* milligram(s)
Mgr or **mgr** *abbrev.* manager
MHz *abbrev.* megahertz
mi (mē) ***n.*** ⟦ML⟧ *Music* the third tone of the diatonic scale
mi *abbrev.* **1** mile(s) **2** mill(s)
MI *abbrev.* **1** Michigan **2** middle initial
Mi·am·i (mī am′ē) city on the SE coast of Florida: pop. 359,000 —**Mi·am′i·an** ***n.***
mi·as·ma (mī az′mə, mē-) ***n.*** ⟦< Gr *miainein,* pollute⟧ **1** a vapor as from marshes, formerly supposed to poison the air **2** an unwholesome atmosphere or influence
mi·ca (mī′kə) ***n.*** ⟦L, a crumb⟧ a mineral that crystallizes in thin, flexible layers, resistant to heat and electricity
mice (mīs) ***n.*** *pl. of* MOUSE
Mi·chel·an·ge·lo (mī′kəl an′jə lō′, mik′əl-) 1475-1564; It. sculptor, painter, & architect
Mich·i·gan (mish′i gən) **1** Midwestern state of the U.S.: 58,110 sq. mi.; pop. 9,295,000; cap. Lansing: abbrev. *MI* **2 Lake** one of the Great Lakes, between Michigan & Wisconsin —**Mich′i·gan′der** (-gan′dər) ***n.*** —**Mich′i·ga′ni·an** (-gā′nē ən) or **Mich′i·gan·ite′** ***adj.***, ***n.***
Mick·ey Finn (mik′ē fin′) ⟦< ?⟧ [*also* **m- f-**] [Slang] a drink of liquor to which a narcotic, etc. has been added, given to an unsuspecting person: often shortened to **Mick′ey** or **mick′ey** ***n.***, *pl.* **-eys**
micro- ⟦< Gr *mikros,* small⟧ *combining form* **1** little, small *[microcosm]* **2** enlarging *[microscope]* **3** involving microscopes *[microsurgery]* **4** one millionth *[microsecond]* Also **micr-**
mi·crobe (mī′krōb′) ***n.*** ⟦< Gr *mikros,* small + *bios,* life⟧ a microorganism, esp. one causing disease
mi·cro·bi·ol·o·gy (mī′krō bī äl′ə jē) ***n.*** the branch of biology dealing with microorganisms —**mi′cro·bi·ol′o·gist** ***n.***
mi′cro·brew′er·y ***n.***, *pl.* **-er·ies** a small brewery producing high-quality beer for local consumption
mi′cro·chip′ ***n.*** CHIP (*n.* 5)
mi′cro·com·put′er ***n.*** a small, inexpensive computer having a microprocessor and used in the home, etc.
mi′cro·cosm′ (-käz′əm) ***n.*** ⟦see MICRO- & COSMOS⟧ something regarded as a world in miniature
mi′cro·dot′ ***n.*** a copy, as of written or printed matter, photographically reduced to pinhead size, used in espionage, etc.
mi′cro·ec′o·nom′ics ***n.*** a branch of economics dealing with certain specific factors affecting an economy, as the behavior of individual consumers
mi′cro·fiche′ (-fēsh′) ***n.***, *pl.* **-fich′es** or **-fiche′** ⟦Fr < *micro-,* MICRO- + *fiche,* small card⟧ a small sheet of microfilm containing a group of microfilmed pages
mi′cro·film′ ***n.*** film on which documents, etc. are photographed in a reduced size for storage, etc. —***vt.***, ***vi.*** to photograph on microfilm
mi′cro·man′age ***vt.*** **-aged, -ag·ing** to manage or control closely, often so closely as to be counterproductive
mi·crom·e·ter (mī kräm′ət ər) ***n.*** ⟦< Fr: see MICRO- & -METER⟧ a tool for measuring very small distances, angles, etc.
mi·cron (mī′krän′) ***n.*** ⟦< Gr *mikros,* small⟧ one millionth of a meter
Mi·cro·ne·sia (mī′krə nē′zhə) country on a group of islands in the Pacific east of the Philippines: 271 sq. mi.; pop. 108,000 —**Mi′cro·ne′sian** ***adj.***, ***n.***
mi·cro·or·gan·ism (mī′krō ôr′gə niz′əm) ***n.*** a microscopic animal, plant, bacterium, virus, etc.
mi·cro·phone (mī′krə fōn′) ***n.*** ⟦MICRO- + -PHONE⟧ an instrument for converting sound waves into an electric signal
mi·cro·proc·es·sor (mī′krō prä′ses′ər) ***n.*** a chip that functions to control the operation of a microcomputer
mi·cro·scope (mī′krə skōp′) ***n.*** ⟦see MICRO- & -SCOPE⟧ an instrument consisting of a combination of lenses, for making very small objects, as microorganisms, look larger
mi′cro·scop′ic (-skäp′ik) ***adj.*** **1** so small as to be invisible or obscure except through a microscope; minute **2** of, with, or like a microscope —**mi′cro·scop′i·cal·ly** ***adv.***
mi·cro·sur·ger·y (mī′krō sur′jər ē) ***n.*** surgery performed using a microscope and minute instruments or laser beams
mi′cro·wave′ ***adj.*** **1** designating equipment, etc. using

THESAURUS

method ***n.*** mode, style, standard operating procedure, fashion, way, means, process, proceeding, adjustment, disposition, practice, routine, technique, attack, mode of operation, manner of working, ways and means, habit, custom, manner, formula, course, MO*, rule; see also SYSTEM.
methodical ***a.*** well-regulated, systematic, exact; see ORDERLY 2, REGULAR 3.
métier ***n.*** forte, area of expertise, occupation; see JOB 1, PROFESSION 1.
metropolis ***n.*** capital, megalopolis, municipality; see CENTER 2, CITY.
metropolitan ***a.*** city, municipal, cosmopolitan; see MODERN 2, URBAN.
microbe ***n.*** microorganism, bacterium, bacillus; see GERM.
microphone ***n.*** sound transmitter, receiver, pickup instrument, mike*, bug*, wire*, walkie-talkie.
microscope ***n.*** lens, magnifying glass, optical instrument, scope. *Microscopes include the following:* high-powered, compound, photographic, electron, electronic.
microscopic ***a.*** diminutive, tiny, infinitesimal; see LITTLE 1, MINUTE 1.

microwaves for radar, communications, etc. **2** designating an oven that cooks quickly using microwaves —***vt.*** **-waved′**, **-wav′ing** to cook in a microwave oven —***n.*** **1** an electromagnetic wave with a frequency of about 300,000 megahertz to 300 megahertz **2** a microwave oven

mid[1] (mid) ***adj.*** ⟦OE *midd-*⟧ middle

mid[2] (mid) ***prep.*** [Old Poet.] amid: also **'mid**

mid- *combining form* middle, middle part of *[mid-*May*]*

mid′air′ ***n.*** any point in space not in contact with the ground or any other surface

Mi·das (mī′dəs) *Gr. Myth.* a king granted the power to turn everything he touches into gold

mid′course′ ***adj.*** happening in the middle of a flight, journey, or course of action

mid′day′ ***n.***, ***adj.*** ⟦OE *middæg*⟧ noon

mid·dle (mid′'l) ***adj.*** ⟦OE *middel*⟧ **1** halfway between two given points, times, etc. **2** intermediate **3** [**M-**] designating a stage in language development intermediate between *Old* and *Modern [Middle* English*]* —***n.*** **1** a middle point, part, time, etc. **2** something intermediate **3** the middle part of the body; waist

middle age the time between youth and old age —**mid′dle-aged′** ***adj.***

Middle Ages the period of European history between ancient and modern times, A.D. 476-*c.* 1450

Middle America the American middle class, seen as being conventional or conservative

mid′dle·brow′ (-brou′) ***n.*** [Inf.] one regarded as having conventional, middle-class tastes or opinions —***adj.*** of or for a middlebrow

middle class the social class between the aristocracy or very wealthy and the lower working class —**mid′dle-class′** ***adj.***

middle ear the part of the ear including the eardrum and the adjacent cavity containing three small bones

Middle East area from Afghanistan to Libya, including Arabia, Cyprus, & Asiatic Turkey —**Middle Eastern**

Middle English the English language between *c.* 1100 and *c.* 1500

mid′dle·man′ (-man′) ***n.***, *pl.* **-men′** (-men′) **1** a trader who buys from a producer and sells at wholesale or retail **2** a go-between

mid′dle·most′ ***adj.*** MIDMOST

mid′dle-of-the-road′ ***adj.*** avoiding extremes, esp. political extremes

middle school a school with three or four grades, variously including grades 5 through grade 8

mid′dle·weight′ ***n.*** a boxer with a maximum weight of 160 pounds

Middle West MIDWEST —**Middle Western**

mid·dling (mid′liŋ) ***adj.*** of middle size, quality, etc.; medium —***adv.*** [Inf.] fairly; moderately

mid·dy (mid′ē) ***n.***, *pl.* **-dies** ⟦< MIDSHIPMAN⟧ a loose blouse with a sailor collar, worn by women and children

Mid·east′ MIDDLE EAST —**Mid·east′ern** ***adj.***

midge (mij) ***n.*** ⟦OE *mycg*⟧ a small, gnatlike insect

midg·et (mij′it) ***n.*** **1** a very small person **2** anything very small of its kind —***adj.*** very small of its kind

mid·land (mid′lənd) ***n.*** the middle region of a country; interior —***adj.*** in or of the midland

mid′most′ ***adj.*** exactly in the middle, or nearest the middle

mid′night′ ***n.*** twelve o'clock at night —***adj.*** **1** of or at midnight **2** like midnight; very dark

mid′point′ ***n.*** a point at or close to the middle or center

mid·riff (mid′rif) ***n.*** ⟦< OE *midd-*, MID[1] + *hrif,* belly⟧ **1** DIAPHRAGM (sense 1) **2** the middle part of the torso, between the abdomen and the chest

mid·ship·man (mid′ship′mən) ***n.***, *pl.* **-men** (-mən) a student in training to be a naval officer

mid-size or **mid·size** (mid′sīz′) ***adj.*** of a size intermediate between large and small *[a mid-size* car*]*

midst (midst) ***n.*** the middle; central part —***prep.*** [Old Poet.] in the midst of; amid —**in our** (or **your** or **their**) **midst** among us (or you or them) —**in the midst of** **1** in the middle of **2** during

mid·stream (mid′strēm′) ***n.*** the middle of a stream

mid′sum′mer ***n.*** **1** the middle of summer **2** the time of the summer solstice, about June 21

mid′term′ ***adj.*** in the middle of the term —***n.*** [Inf.] a midterm examination, as at a college

mid′town′ ***adj.*** of or in the central part of a city, esp. a large city —***n.*** a midtown area

mid′way′ ***n.*** that part of a fair where sideshows, etc. are located —***adj.***, ***adv.*** in the middle of the way or distance; halfway

Mid·west′ region of the NC U.S. between the Rocky Mountains & the E border of Ohio & the S borders of Kansas & Missouri —**Mid·west′ern** ***adj.***

mid′wife′ (-wīf′) ***n.***, *pl.* **-wives′** ⟦< ME *mid,* with + *wif,* woman⟧ a person who helps women in childbirth —**mid′wife′ry** (-wif′rē) ***n.***

mid′win′ter ***n.*** **1** the middle of winter **2** the time of the winter solstice, about Dec. 22

mid′year′ ***adj.*** in the middle of the year —***n.*** [Inf.] a midyear examination, as at a college

mien (mēn) ***n.*** ⟦short for DEMEAN[2]⟧ one's appearance, bearing, or manner

miff (mif) ***vt.*** ⟦prob. orig. cry of disgust⟧ [Inf.] to offend

MIG (mig) ***n.*** ⟦after *Mi(koyan)* & *G(urevich)*, its Soviet designers⟧ a high-speed, high-altitude jet fighter plane: also **MiG**

might[1] (mīt) ***v.aux.*** ⟦OE *mihte*⟧ **1** *pt.* of MAY **2** used as an auxiliary generally equivalent to MAY *[it might* rain*]*

might[2] (mīt) ***n.*** ⟦OE *miht*⟧ strength, power, or vigor

might′y ***adj.*** **-i·er**, **-i·est** **1** powerful; strong **2** remarkably large, etc.; great —***adv.*** [Inf.] very —**might′i·ly** ***adv.*** —**might′i·ness** ***n.***

mi·gnon·ette (min′yə net′) ***n.*** ⟦< Fr *mignon,* small⟧ a plant with spikes of small greenish, whitish, or reddish flowers

mi·graine (mī′grān′) ***n.*** ⟦< Gr *hēmi-,* half + *kranion,* skull⟧ an intense, periodic headache, usually limited to one side of the head

mi·grant (mī′grənt) ***adj.*** migrating —***n.*** **1** one that migrates **2** a farm laborer who moves from place to place to harvest seasonal crops

mi·grate (mī′grāt′) ***vi.*** **-grat′ed**, **-grat′ing** ⟦< L *migrare*⟧ **1** to settle in another country or region **2** to move to another region with the change in seasons, as many birds do —**mi·gra·to·ry** (mī′grə tôr′ē) ***adj.***

mi·gra·tion (mī grā′shən) ***n.*** **1** a migrating **2** a group of people, birds, etc., migrating together

mi·ka·do (mi kä′dō) ***n.***, *pl.* **-dos** ⟦< Jpn *mi,* an honorific title + *kado,* gate⟧ [*often* **M-**] the emperor of Japan: title no longer used

mike (mīk) [Inf.] ***n.*** a microphone —***vt.*** **miked**, **mik′ing** to record, amplify, etc. with a microphone

mil[1] (mil) ***n.*** ⟦L *mille,* thousand⟧ a unit of linear measure, equal to $\frac{1}{1000}$ inch

mil[2] (mil) ***n.*** [Slang] *short for* million

Mi·lan (mi lan′, -län′) city in NW Italy: pop. 1,602,000

milch (milch) ***adj.*** ⟦ME *milche*⟧ kept for milking *[milch* cows*]*

THESAURUS

middle ***a.*** mean, midway, medial, average, equidistant; see also CENTRAL, HALFWAY, INTERMEDIATE.

middle ***n.*** mean, core, nucleus, heart, navel, midst, marrow, pivot, axis, medium, halfway point, midpoint; see also CENTER 1.

middle age ***n.*** adulthood, prime, maturity; see MAJORITY 2.

middle-aged ***a.*** in midlife, in one's prime, matronly; see MATURE.

middle-class ***a.*** white-collar, bourgeois, substantial; see COMMON 1, POPULAR 3, 4.

midget ***n.*** pygmy, dwarf, little person, Lilliputian.

midnight ***n.*** dead of night, stroke of midnight, twelve o'clock, twelve midnight, noon of night, witching hour; see also NIGHT 1. —**burn the midnight oil** stay up late, work late, keep late hours; see STUDY, WORK 1.

midst ***n.*** midpoint, nucleus, middle; see CENTER 1. —**in the midst of** in the course of, engaged in, in the middle of; see AMONG, CENTRAL.

midway ***a.*** in an intermediate position, halfway, in the middle of the way; see CENTRAL, INTERMEDIATE, MIDDLE.

might[2] ***n.*** power, force, vigor; see STRENGTH.

mightily ***a.*** energetically, strongly, forcibly; see POWERFULLY, VIGOROUSLY.

mighty ***a.*** **1** [Strong] powerful, stalwart, muscular; see STRONG 1. **2** [Powerful through influence] great, all-powerful, omnipotent; see POWERFUL 1. **3** [Imposing] great, extensive, impressive, gigantic, magnificent, towering, dynamic, notable, extraordinary, grand, considerable, monumental, tremendous; see also LARGE 1.—*Ant.* PLAIN, unimpressive, ordinary. **4** [*To a high degree] exceedingly, greatly, extremely; see VERY.

migrate ***v.*** move, emigrate, immigrate; see LEAVE 1.

migration ***n.*** emigration, immigration, trek; see DEPARTURE, JOURNEY, MOVEMENT 2.

migratory ***a.*** wandering, migrant, vagrant; see TEMPORARY.

mild (mīld) ***adj.*** ⟦OE *milde*⟧ **1** gentle or kind; not severe **2** having a soft, pleasant flavor *[a mild cheese]* —**mild′ly** ***adv.*** —**mild′ness** ***n.***

mil·dew (mil′do͞o′) ***n.*** ⟦OE *meledeaw,* honeydew⟧ a fungus that attacks some plants or appears on damp cloth, etc. as a whitish coating —***vt., vi.*** to affect or be affected with mildew

mile (mīl) ***n.*** ⟦< L *milia* (*passuum*), thousand (paces)⟧ a unit of linear measure equal to 5,280 feet

mile′age ***n.*** **1** an allowance per mile for traveling expenses **2** total miles traveled **3** the average number of miles that can be traveled, as per gallon of fuel

mile′post′ ***n.*** a signpost showing the distance in miles to or from a place

mil′er ***n.*** one who competes in mile races

mile′stone′ ***n.*** **1** a stone set up to show the distance in miles to or from a place **2** a significant event in history, in a career, etc.

mi·lieu (mēl yʉ′, -yo͞o′, -yo͞o′; mil-) ***n.***, *pl.* **-lieus′** ⟦Fr < L *medius*, middle + *locus*, a place⟧ environment; esp., social setting

mil·i·tant (mil′i tənt) ***adj.*** ⟦< L *miles*, soldier⟧ **1** fighting **2** ready to fight, esp. for some cause —***n.*** a militant person —**mil′i·tan·cy** ***n.*** —**mil′i·tant·ly** ***adv.***

mil·i·ta·rism (mil′ə tə riz′əm) ***n.*** **1** military spirit **2** a policy of aggressive military preparedness —**mil′i·ta·rist** ***n.*** —**mil′i·ta·ris′tic** ***adj.***

mil′i·ta·rize′ (-rīz′) ***vt.*** **-rized′**, **-riz′ing** to equip and prepare for war

mil·i·tar·y (mil′ə ter′ē) ***adj.*** ⟦< L *miles*, soldier⟧ **1** of, for, or done by soldiers **2** of, for, or fit for war **3** of the army —**the military** the armed forces

military police soldiers assigned to police duties in the army

mil·i·tate (mil′ə tāt′) ***vi.*** **-tat′ed**, **-tat′ing** ⟦< L *militare*, be a soldier⟧ to operate or work (*against*)

mi·li·tia (mə lish′ə) ***n.*** ⟦< L *miles*, soldier⟧ **1** an army composed of citizens rather than professional soldiers, called up in time of emergency **2** a group of disaffected citizens organized like an army and opposing federal authority —**mi·li′tia·man** (-mən), *pl.* **-men** (-mən), ***n.***

milk (milk) ***n.*** ⟦OE *meolc*⟧ **1** a white fluid secreted by the mammary glands of female mammals for suckling their young **2** cow's milk, etc., drunk by humans as a food or used to make butter, cheese, etc. **3** any liquid like this, as the liquid in coconuts —***vt.*** **1** to squeeze milk from (a cow, goat, etc.) **2** to extract money, ideas, etc. from as if by milking —**milk′er** ***n.***

milk glass a nearly opaque whitish glass

milk′maid′ ***n.*** a girl or woman who milks cows or works in a dairy

milk′man′ (-man′) ***n.***, *pl.* **-men′** (-mən′) a man who sells or delivers milk for a dairy

milk of magnesia a milky-white suspension of magnesium hydroxide in water, used as a laxative and antacid

milk′shake′ ***n.*** a drink made of milk, flavoring, and ice cream, mixed or shaken until frothy

milk′sop′ (-säp′) ***n.*** a man thought of as timid, ineffectual, effeminate, etc.

milk tooth any of the temporary, first teeth of a child or young animal

milk′weed′ ***n.*** any of a group of plants with a milky juice

milk′y ***adj.*** **-i·er**, **-i·est** **1** like milk; esp., white as milk **2** of or containing milk —**milk′i·ness** ***n.***

Milky Way the galaxy containing our sun: seen as a broad, faintly luminous band of very distant stars and interstellar gas arching across the night sky

mill[1] (mil) ***n.*** ⟦< L *mola,* millstone⟧ **1** a building with machinery for grinding grain into flour or meal **2** any of various machines for grinding, crushing, cutting, etc. **3** a factory *[a textile mill]* —***vt.*** **1** to grind, form, etc. by or in a mill **2** to raise and ridge the edge of (a coin) —***vi.*** to move (*around* or *about*) confusedly —**in the mill** in preparation —**through the mill** [Inf.] through a hard, painful, instructive experience, test, etc.

mill[2] (mil) ***n.*** ⟦< L *mille,* thousand⟧ $\frac{1}{10}$ of a cent: unit used in calculating

mill′age ***n.*** taxation in mills per dollar of valuation

mil·len·ni·um (mi len′ē əm) ***n.***, *pl.* **-ni·ums** or **-ni·a** (-ə) ⟦< L *mille,* thousand + *annus,* year⟧ **1** a thousand years **2** *Christian Theol.* the period of a thousand years during which Christ will reign on earth: with *the* **3** any period of great happiness, peace, etc.

mill′er ***n.*** one who owns or operates a mill, esp. a flour mill

mil·let (mil′it) ***n.*** ⟦< L *milium*⟧ **1** a cereal grass whose grain is used for food in Europe and Asia **2** any of several similar grasses

milli- ⟦< L *mille,* thousand⟧ *combining form* one thousandth part of *[millimeter]*

mil·li·gram (mil′i gram′) ***n.*** one thousandth of a gram

mil′li·li′ter (-lēt′ər) ***n.*** one thousandth of a liter: Brit. sp. **mil′li·li′tre**

mil′li·me′ter (-mēt′ər) ***n.*** one thousandth of a meter: Brit. sp. **mil′li·me′tre**

mil·li·ner (mil′i nər) ***n.*** ⟦< *Milaner*, vendor of dress wares from Milan⟧ one who makes or sells women's hats

mil·li·ner·y (mil′i ner′ē) ***n.*** **1** women's hats, headdresses, etc. **2** the work or business of a milliner

mil·lion (mil′yən) ***n.*** ⟦< L *mille,* thousand⟧ a thousand thousands; 1,000,000

mil′lion·aire′ (-yə ner′) ***n.*** a person whose wealth comes to at least a million dollars, pounds, francs, etc.

mil·li·pede (mil′i pēd′) ***n.*** ⟦< L *mille,* thousand + *pes*, foot⟧ a many-legged arthropod with an elongated body

mill′race′ ***n.*** the channel in which water runs to turn the wheel driving the machinery in a mill

mill′stone′ ***n.*** **1** either of a pair of round, flat stones used for grinding grain, etc. **2** a heavy burden

mill′stream′ ***n.*** the water flowing in a millrace

mill′wright′ ***n.*** a worker who builds, installs, or repairs the machinery in a mill

milt (milt) ***n.*** ⟦prob. < Scand⟧ the sex glands or sperm of male fishes

Mil·ton (milt′'n), **John** 1608-74; Eng. poet

Mil·wau·kee (mil wô′kē) city & port in SE Wisconsin, on Lake Michigan: pop. 628,000

mime (mīm) ***n.*** ⟦< Gr *mimos*, imitator⟧ **1** the representation of an action, mood, etc. by gestures, not words **2** a mimic or pantomimist —***vt.*** **mimed**, **mim′ing** to mimic or pantomime

mim·e·o·graph (mim′ē ə graf′) ***n.*** ⟦< Gr *mimeomai,* I imitate⟧ a machine for making copies of graphic matter by means of an inked stencil —***vt.*** to make (such copies) of

mi·met·ic (mi met′ik, mī-) ***adj.*** ⟦< Gr *mimeisthai,* to imitate⟧ **1** imitative **2** characterized by mimicry

mim·ic (mim′ik) ***adj.*** ⟦< Gr *mimos,* actor⟧ imitative —***n.*** an imitator; esp., an actor skilled in mimicry —***vt.***

THESAURUS

mild ***a.*** **1** [Gentle; *said especially of persons*] meek, easygoing, patient; see KIND. **2** [Temperate; *said especially of weather*] bland, untroubled, tropical, peaceful, summery, tepid, cool, balmy, breezy, gentle, soft, lukewarm, clear, moderate, mellow, fine, uncloudy, sunny, warm.—*Ant.* ROUGH, COLD, STORMY. **3** [Easy; *said especially of burdens or punishment*] soft, light, tempered; see MODERATE 4. **4** [Not irritating] bland, soothing, soft, smooth, gentle, moderate, emollient, easy, mellow, delicate, temperate.

mildly ***a.*** gently, meekly, calmly, genially, tranquilly, softly, lightly, moderately, tenderly, compassionately, tolerantly, patiently, temperately, indifferently, quietly.—*Ant.* VIOLENTLY, harshly, roughly.

mildness ***n.*** tolerance, tenderness, gentleness; see KINDNESS 1.

mile ***n.*** 5,280 feet, 1.6 kilometers, statute mile, geographical mile, nautical mile, Admiralty mile; see also DISTANCE 3, MEASURE 1.

militant ***a.*** combative, belligerent, offensive; see AGGRESSIVE.

militant ***n.*** rioter, violent objector, demonstrator; see RADICAL.

military ***a.*** armed, martial, soldierly; see AGGRESSIVE.

militia ***n.*** military force, civilian army, National Guard; see ARMY 1.

milk ***n.*** fluid, juice, sap; see LIQUID. *Types of milk include the following:* whole, skim, low-fat, raw, pasteurized, homogenized, certified; loose, condensed, dried, evaporated, powdered; two-percent, four-percent, etc.; goat's, mare's, mother's; cream, half-and-half, buttermilk, baby formula, kefir. —**cry over spilt milk** mourn, lament, sulk; see REGRET.

milky ***a.*** opaque, pearly, cloudy; see WHITE 1.

mill[1] ***n.*** **1** [A factory] manufactory, plant, millhouse; see FACTORY. **2** [A machine for grinding, crushing, pressing, etc.] *Types of mills include the following:* flour, coffee, cotton, weaving, spinning, powder, rolling, cider, cane, lapidary, sawmill, gristmill, coin press.

millionaire ***n.*** person of means, capitalist, tycoon, billionaire, magnate, plutocrat, Croesus, nabob, Midas, robber baron, fat cat*.—*Ant.* BEGGAR, poor person, pauper.

mimic ***n.*** mime, impersonator, comedian; see ACTOR, IMITATOR.

mimic ***v.*** **1** [To imitate] copy, simu-

-icked, -ick·ing **1** to imitate, often so as to ridicule **2** to copy or resemble closely

mim·ic·ry (mim′ik rē) ***n.***, *pl.* **-ries** the practice or art of, or a way of, mimicking

mi·mo·sa (mi mō′sə) ***n.*** ⟦see MIME⟧ a tree, shrub, or herb growing in warm regions and usually having spikes of white, yellow, or pink flowers

min *abbrev.* **1** minimum **2** minute(s)

min·a·ret (min′ə ret′) ***n.*** ⟦< Ar *manāra(t)*, lighthouse⟧ a high, slender tower attached to a mosque

min·a·to·ry (min′ə tôr′ē) ***adj.*** ⟦< L *minari,* threaten⟧ menacing

mince (mins) ***vt.*** **minced, minc′ing** ⟦< L *minutus,* small⟧ **1** to cut up (meat, etc.) into small pieces **2** to lessen the force of *[to mince no words]* —***vi.*** to speak, act, or walk with an affected daintiness —**minc′ing** ***adj.***

mince′meat′ ***n.*** a mixture of chopped apples, spices, suet, raisins, etc., and sometimes meat, used as a pie filling

mind (mīnd) ***n.*** ⟦< OE *(ge)mynd*⟧ **1** memory *[to bring to mind a story]* **2** opinion *[speak your mind]* **3** the seat of consciousness, in which thinking, feeling, etc. takes place **4** intellect **5** PSYCHE (*n.* 2) **6** reason; sanity —***vt.*** **1** to pay attention to; heed **2** to obey **3** to take care of *[mind the baby]* **4** to be careful about *[mind the stairs]* **5** to care about; object to *[they don't mind the noise]* —***vi.*** **1** to pay attention **2** to be obedient **3** to be careful **4** to care; object —**bear** (or **keep**) **in mind** to remember —**change one's mind** to change one's opinion, purpose, etc. —**have in mind** to intend —**never mind** don't be concerned —**on someone's mind** **1** filling someone's thoughts **2** worrying someone —**out of one's mind** **1** insane **2** frantic (*with* worry, etc.)

mind′-blow′ing ***adj.*** [Slang] **1** causing shock, etc.; overwhelming **2** hard to comprehend

mind′-bog′gling ***adj.*** [Slang] **1** hard to comprehend **2** surprising, overwhelming, etc.

mind′ed ***adj.*** having a (specified kind of) mind: used in compounds *[high-minded]*

mind′ful (-fəl) ***adj.*** having in mind; aware or careful (*of*) —**mind′ful·ly** ***adv.*** —**mind′ful·ness** ***n.***

mind′less (-lis) ***adj.*** stupid or foolish

mind reader one who seems or professes to be able to perceive another's thoughts

mind's eye the imagination

mine[1] (mīn) ***pron.*** ⟦OE min⟧ that or those belonging to me: poss. form of I[2] *[this is mine; mine are better]*

mine[2] (mīn) ***n.*** ⟦< Fr⟧ **1** a large excavation made in the earth, from which to extract ores, coal, etc. **2** a deposit of ore, coal, etc. **3** any great source of supply **4** *Mil. a)* a tunnel dug under an enemy's fort, etc., in which an explosive is placed *b)* an explosive charge hidden underground or in the sea, for destroying enemy vehicles, ships, etc. —***vt.***, ***vi.*** **mined, min′ing** **1** to dig (ores, etc.) from (the earth) **2** to dig or lay military mines in or under **3** to undermine

min′er ***n.*** one whose work is digging coal, ore, etc. in a mine

min·er·al (min′ər əl) ***n.*** ⟦< ML *minera,* ore⟧ **1** an inorganic substance found naturally in the earth, as metallic ore **2** any substance that is neither vegetable nor animal —***adj.*** of or containing a mineral

mineral jelly PETROLATUM

min·er·al·o·gy (min′ər äl′ə jē) ***n.*** the scientific study of minerals —**min′er·al′o·gist** ***n.***

mineral oil a colorless, tasteless oil derived from petroleum, used as a laxative

mineral water water impregnated with mineral salts or gases

Mi·ner·va (mi nur′və) ***n.*** *Rom. Myth.* the goddess of wisdom

mi·ne·stro·ne (min′ə strō′nē) ***n.*** ⟦It.: ult. < L *ministrare,* serve⟧ a thick vegetable soup in a meat broth

min·gle (miŋ′gəl) ***vt.*** **-gled, -gling** ⟦< OE *mengan,* to mix⟧ to mix together; blend —***vi.*** **1** to become mixed or blended **2** to join or unite with others

mini- ⟦< MINI(ATURE)⟧ *combining form* miniature, very small, very short *[miniskirt]*

min·i·a·ture (min′ē ə chər, min′i chər) ***n.*** ⟦< L *miniare,* to paint red⟧ **1** a small painting, esp. a portrait **2** a copy or model on a very small scale —***adj.*** done on a very small scale

min′i·a·tur·ize′ (-īz′) ***vt.*** **-ized′, -iz′ing** to make in a small and compact form —**min′i·a·tur′i·za′tion** ***n.***

min·i·bike (min′ē bīk′) ***n.*** a compact motorcycle, usually used as an off-road vehicle

min′i·cam′ (-kam′) ***n.*** a portable TV camera for telecasting or videotaping news events, etc.

min′i·com·put′er (-kəm pyo͞ot′ər) ***n.*** a computer intermediate in size, power, etc. between a mainframe and a microcomputer

min·i·mal (min′i məl) ***adj.*** **1** smallest or least possible **2** of minimalism —**min′i·mal·ly** ***adv.***

min′i·mal·ism′ ***n.*** a movement in art, music, etc. in which

THESAURUS

late, impersonate; see IMITATE. **2** [To mock] make fun of, burlesque, caricature; see RIDICULE.

mimicry ***n.*** mime, pretense, mockery; see IMITATION 2.

mind ***n.*** **1** [Intellectual potentiality] soul, spirit, intellect, brain, consciousness, thought, mentality, intuition, perception, conception, intelligence, intellectuality, capacity, judgment, understanding, wisdom, genius, talent, reasoning, instinct, wit, mental faculties, intellectual faculties, creativity, ingenuity, intellectual powers, gray matter*, brainpower. **2** [Purpose] intention, inclination, determination; see PURPOSE 1. —**bear** (or **keep**) **in mind** heed, recollect, recall; see REMEMBER 1. —**be in one's right mind** be mentally well, be rational, be sane; see SANE. —**be of one mind** have the same opinion, concur, be in accord; see AGREE. —**call to mind** recall, recollect, bring to mind; see REMEMBER 1. —**change one's mind** alter one's opinion, change one's views, decide against, modify one's ideas. —**give someone a piece of one's mind** rebuke, chide, criticize; see SCOLD. —**have a good mind to** be inclined to, propose, intend to; see INTEND 1. —**have half a mind to** be inclined to, propose, intend to; see INTEND 1. —**have in mind** **1** [To remember] recall, recollect, think of; see REMEMBER 1, THINK 1. **2** [To intend] expect, plan on, propose; see ANTICIPATE, INTEND 1. —**know one's own mind** know oneself, be deliberate, have a plan; see KNOW 1. —**make up one's mind** form a definite opinion, choose, finalize; see DECIDE. —**meeting of the minds** concurrence, unity, harmony; see AGREEMENT 1. —**on one's mind** occupying one's thoughts, causing concern, worrying one; see IMPORTANT 1. —**out of one's mind** mentally ill, raving, mad; see INSANE. —**take one's mind off** turn one's attention from, divert, change; see DISTRACT.

mind ***v.*** **1** [To obey] be under the authority of, heed, do as one is told; see BEHAVE, OBEY. **2** [To give one's attention] heed, regard, be attentive to; see ATTEND. **3** [To be careful] tend, watch out for, take care, be wary, be concerned for, mind one's *p's* and *q's**; see also CONSIDER.—*Ant.* NEGLECT, ignore, be careless. **4** [*To remember] recollect, recall, bring to mind; see REMEMBER 1. **5** [To dislike] object to, take exception, be opposed to; see DISLIKE. —**never mind** forget it, it doesn't matter, ignore it, don't bother, let it go, drop it*; see also STOP.

minded ***a.*** disposed, inclined, leaning toward; see WILLING.

mindful ***a.*** attentive, heedful, watchful; see CAREFUL.

mindless ***a.*** **1** [Careless] inattentive, oblivious, neglectful; see CARELESS, INDIFFERENT, RASH. **2** [Stupid] foolish, senseless, unintelligent; see STUPID.

mine[1] ***pron.*** my own, belonging to me, possessed by me, mine by right, owned by me, left to me, from me, by me; see also OUR.

mine[2] ***n.*** **1** [A source of natural wealth] pit, well, shaft, diggings, excavation, workings, quarry, deposit, vein, lode, ore bed, placer, pay dirt, bonanza, strip mine, open-pit mine, surface mine, hard-rock mine. **2** [An explosive charge] land mine, ambush, trap; see BOMB, EXPLOSIVE, WEAPON.

mine[2] ***v.*** excavate, work, quarry; see DIG 1.

miner ***n.*** excavator, digger, driller, dredger, mine worker, prospector, mucker, driller, placer miner, hard-rock miner, mine superintendent, mining engineer, sourdough*, forty-niner*; see also LABORER, WORKMAN.

mineral ***a.*** geologic, rock, metallurgic; see METALLIC 1.

mineral ***n.*** geologic rock, rock deposit, ore deposit, igneous rock, metamorphic rock, magma, petroleum, crystal; see also METAL, ROCK 1. *Common minerals include the following:* quartz, feldspar, mica, basalt, coal, hornblende, pyroxene, olivine, calcite, dolomite, pyrite, chalcopyrite, barite, garnet, diopside, gypsum, staurolite, tourmaline, obsidian, malachite, azurite, limonite, galena, aragonite, magnetite, ilmenite, serpentine, epidote, fluorite, cinnabar, talc, bauxite, corundum, cryolite, spinel, sheelite, wolframite, graphite, diatomite, pitchblende.

mingle ***v.*** combine, blend, merge; see MIX 1.

miniature ***a.*** diminutive, small, tiny; see LITTLE 1, MINUTE 1.

only the simplest design, forms, etc. are used, often repetitiously —**min′i·mal·ist** ***adj., n.***
min′i·mal·ize′ (-īz′) ***vt.*** **-ized′, -iz′ing** to reduce to basic components
min·i·mize (min′i mīz′) ***vt.*** **-mized′, -miz′ing** to reduce to or estimate at a minimum
min′i·mum (-məm) ***n.***, *pl.* **-mums** or **-ma** (-mə) ⟦L, least⟧ **1** the smallest quantity, number, etc. possible or permissible **2** the lowest degree or point reached —***adj.*** smallest possible, permissible, or reached
min·ion (min′yən) ***n.*** ⟦Fr *mignon,* darling⟧ **1** a favorite, esp. one who is a servile follower: term of contempt **2** a subordinate official
min·is·cule (min′i skyo͞ol′) ***adj.*** *disputed var. of* MINUSCULE
min·i·se·ries (min′ē sir′ēz) ***n.***, *pl.* **-ries** a TV drama broadcast serially in a limited number of episodes
min·i·skirt (min′ē skurt′) ***n.*** a very short skirt ending well above the knee
min·is·ter (min′is tər) ***n.*** ⟦L, a servant⟧ **1** a person appointed to head a governmental department **2** a diplomat representing his or her government in a foreign nation **3** one authorized to conduct religious services in a church —***vi.*** **1** to serve as a minister in a church **2** to give help (*to*) —**min′is·te′ri·al** (-tir′ē əl) ***adj.*** —**min′is·trant** (-trənt) ***adj., n.***
min′is·tra′tion (-trā′shən) ***n.*** the act of giving help or care; service
min′is·try (-is trē) ***n.***, *pl.* **-tries** **1** the act of ministering, or serving **2** *a)* the office or function of a religious minister *b)* ministers of religion collectively; clergy **3** *a)* the department under a minister of government *b)* the minister's term of office *c)* the ministers of a government as a group
min·i·van (min′ē van′) ***n.*** a passenger vehicle like a van but smaller, usually with windows all around and removable rear seats: also **min′i-van**
mink (miŋk) ***n.*** ⟦< Scand⟧ **1** a slim, erminelike carnivore living in water part of the time **2** its valuable, white to brown fur
Min·ne·ap·o·lis (min′ē ap′ə lis) city in E Minnesota: pop. 368,000 (met. area, incl. St. Paul, 2,464,000)
Min·ne·so·ta (min′ə sōt′ə) Midwestern state of the U.S.: 79,617 sq. mi.; pop. 4,375,000; cap. St. Paul: abbrev. *MN* —**Min′ne·so′tan** ***adj., n.***
min·now (min′ō) ***n.*** ⟦< OE *myne*⟧ any of various, usually small, freshwater fishes used commonly as bait
Mi·no·an (mi nō′ən) ***adj.*** ⟦after *Minos,* mythical king of Crete⟧ of an advanced prehistoric culture in Crete from *c.* 3000 to *c.* 1100 B.C.
mi·nor (mī′nər) ***adj.*** ⟦< L⟧ **1** lesser in size, amount, importance, etc. **2** *Music* lower than the corresponding major by a half tone —***vi.*** *Educ.* to have a secondary field of study (*in*) —***n.*** **1** a person under full legal age **2** *Educ.* a secondary field of study
mi·nor·i·ty (mī nôr′ə tē, mi-) ***n.***, *pl.* **-ties** **1** the lesser part or smaller number **2** a racial, religious, or political group that differs from the larger, controlling group **3** the period or state of being under full legal age
minor scale an eight-tone musical scale with a semitone between the second and third tones
Min·o·taur (min′ə tôr′) ***n.*** *Gr. Myth.* a monster with the body of a man and the head of a bull
min·ox·i·dil (min äk′sə dil) ***n.*** a drug that dilates blood vessels, used in treating high blood pressure and baldness
min·strel (min′strəl) ***n.*** ⟦see MINISTER⟧ **1** a medieval traveling singer **2** a member of a comic variety show (**minstrel show**) in which the performers blacken their faces —**min′strel·sy** (-sē), *pl.* **-sies**, ***n.***
mint[1] (mint) ***n.*** ⟦< L < *Moneta*, epithet for Juno, whose temple was the Roman mint⟧ **1** a place where a government coins money **2** a large amount —***adj.*** new, as if freshly minted —***vt.*** to coin (money) —**mint′age** (-ij) ***n.***
mint[2] (mint) ***n.*** ⟦< Gr *mintha*⟧ **1** an aromatic plant whose leaves are used for flavoring **2** a candy flavored with mint
mint julep an iced drink of bourbon, sugar, and mint leaves
min·u·end (min′yo͞o end′) ***n.*** ⟦< L *minuere*, lessen⟧ the number from which another is to be subtracted
min·u·et (min′yo͞o et′) ***n.*** ⟦< Fr < OFr *menu*, small: from the small steps taken⟧ **1** a slow, stately dance **2** the music for this
mi·nus (mī′nəs) ***prep.*** ⟦< L *minor*, less⟧ **1** reduced by subtraction of; less *[four minus two]* **2** [Inf.] without *[minus a toe]* —***adj.*** **1** involving subtraction *[a minus sign]* **2** negative **3** less than *[a grade of A minus]* —***n.*** a sign (−), indicating subtraction or negative quantity: in full **minus sign**
mi·nus·cule (mi nus′kyo͞ol′, min′i skyo͞ol′) ***adj.*** ⟦L *minusculus*⟧ very small
min·ute[1] (min′it) ***n.*** ⟦see fol.⟧ **1** the sixtieth part of an hour, or of a degree of an arc **2** a moment **3** a specific point in time **4** [*pl.*] an official record of a meeting, etc. —**the minute (that)** just as soon as
mi·nute[2] (mī no͞ot′, -nyo͞ot′) ***adj.*** ⟦< L *minor*, less⟧ **1** very small **2** of little importance **3** of or attentive to tiny details; precise —**mi·nute′ly** ***adv.***
min′ute hand the longer hand of a clock, indicating the minutes
min′ute·man′ (-man′) ***n.***, *pl.* **-men′** (-men′) [*also* **M-**] a member of the American citizen army at the time of the American Revolution
min′ute steak a small, thin steak that can be cooked quickly
mi·nu·ti·ae (mi no͞o′shə, -nyo͞o′-) ***pl.n.***, *sing.* **-tia** (-shə) ⟦see MINUTE[2]⟧ small or unimportant details
minx (miŋks) ***n.*** ⟦< ?⟧ a pert, saucy girl
mir·a·cle (mir′ə kəl) ***n.*** ⟦< L *mirus,* wonderful⟧ **1** an event or action that apparently contradicts known scientific laws **2** a remarkable thing
mi·rac·u·lous (mi rak′yo͞o ləs, -yə-) ***adj.*** **1** having the nature of, or like, a miracle **2** able to work miracles —**mi·rac′u·lous·ly** ***adv.*** —**mi·rac′u·lous·ness** ***n.***

THESAURUS

minimize *v.* lessen, depreciate, reduce; see DECREASE 2.
minimum *a.* smallest, tiniest, merest, lowest, least.
minimum *n.* smallest, least, lowest, narrowest, atom, molecule, particle, dot, jot, iota, spark, shadow, gleam, grain, scruple.
mining *n.* excavating, hollowing, opening, digging, boring, drilling, delving, burrowing, tunneling, honeycombing, placer mining, hard-rock mining, prospecting.
minister *n.* **1** [One authorized to conduct Christian worship] pastor, parson, preacher, clergyman, rector, monk, abbot, prelate, canon, curate, vicar, deacon, chaplain, servant of God, shepherd, churchman, cleric, padre, ecclesiastic, bishop, archbishop, confessor, reverend, diocesan, divine, missionary; see also PRIEST.—*Ant.* LAYMAN, church member, parishioner. **2** [A high servant of the state] ambassador, consul, liaison officer; see DIPLOMAT, REPRESENTATIVE 2, STATESMAN.
minister to *v.* administer to, tend to, wait on; see HELP.
ministry *n.* **1** [The functions of the clergy] preaching, prayer, spiritual leadership; see RELIGION 2. **2** [The clergy] the cloth, clergymen, ecclesiastics, clerics, the clerical order, priesthood, clericals, prelacy, vicarage. **3** [A department of state] bureau, agency, executive branch; see DEPARTMENT.
minor *a.* secondary, lesser, insignificant; see TRIVIAL, UNIMPORTANT.
minor *n.* person under eighteen or twenty-one, underage person, boy, girl, child, infant, little one, lad, schoolboy, schoolgirl; see also YOUTH 3.
minority *n.* **1** [An outnumbered group] opposition, less than half, the outvoted, the few, the outnumbered, ethnic minority, religious minority, the losing side, splinter group. **2** [The time before one is of legal age] childhood, immaturity, adolescence; see YOUTH 1.
mint[1] *v.* strike, coin, issue; see PRINT 2.
minus *a.* diminished, negative, deficient; see LESS.
minute[1] *n.* sixty seconds, unit of time, moment, short time, second, flash, twinkling, breath, jiffy*, bat of an eye*; see also TIME 1.—*Ant.* FOREVER, eternity, long time. —**in a minute** before long, shortly, presently; see SOON. —**the minute that** as soon as, the second that, at the time that; see WHEN 2. —**up to the minute** modern, contemporary, up-to-date; see FASHIONABLE, NEW 1, 2.
minute[2] *a.* **1** [Extremely small] microscopic, diminutive, wee, tiny, atomic, subatomic, miniature, puny, microbic, molecular, exact, precise, fine, inconsiderable, teeny*, weeny*, teeny-weeny*, teensy*, itty-bitty*, invisible; see also LITTLE 1.—*Ant.* LARGE, huge, immense. **2** [Trivial] immaterial, nonessential, paltry; see TRIVIAL, UNIMPORTANT. **3** [Exact] particular, circumstantial, specialized; see DETAILED, ELABORATE 2.
miracle *n.* marvel, revelation, supernatural occurrence; see WONDER 2.
miraculous *a.* **1** [Caused by divine intervention] supernatural, marvelous, superhuman, beyond understanding, phenomenal, awesome,

mi·rage (mi räzh′) ***n.*** ⟦< VL *mirare,* look at⟧ an optical illusion, caused by the refraction of light, in which a distant object appears to be nearby, inverted, etc.

mire (mīr) ***n.*** ⟦< ON *myrr*⟧ **1** an area of wet, soggy ground **2** deep mud —***vt.*** **mired, mir′ing** **1** to cause to get stuck as in mire **2** to soil with mud, etc. —***vi.*** to sink in mud —**mir′y, -i·er, -i·est,** ***adj.***

mir·ror (mir′ər) ***n.*** ⟦< L *mirare,* look at⟧ **1** a smooth, reflecting surface; esp., a glass coated as with silver on the back **2** anything giving a true representation —***vt.*** to reflect, as in a mirror

mirth (murth) ***n.*** ⟦< OE *myrig,* pleasant⟧ joyfulness or gaiety, esp. when shown by laughter —**mirth′ful** ***adj.*** —**mirth′less** ***adj.***

MIRV (murv) ***n.***, *pl.* **MIRV's** ⟦*m(ultiple) i(ndependently targeted) r(eentry) v(ehicle)*⟧ an intercontinental ballistic missile whose several warheads can be launched individually

mis- ⟦< OE *mis-* or OFr *mes-*⟧ *prefix* **1** wrong(ly), bad(ly) **2** no, not

mis·ad·ven·ture (mis′əd ven′chər) ***n.*** a mishap; an instance of bad luck

mis·an·thrope (mis′ən thrōp′) ***n.*** ⟦Gr *misein,* to hate + *anthrōpos,* man⟧ a person who hates or distrusts all people: also **mis·an·thro·pist** (mi san′thrə pist) —**mis′an·throp′ic** (-thräp′ik) ***adj.*** —**mis·an′thro·py** ***n.***

mis′ap·ply′ ***vt.*** **-plied′, -ply′ing** to use badly, improperly, or wastefully

mis′ap·pre·hend′ (-ap rē hend′) ***vt.*** to misunderstand —**mis′ap·pre·hen′sion** ***n.***

mis′ap·pro′pri·ate′ ***vt.*** **-at′ed, -at′ing** to appropriate to a wrong or dishonest use —**mis′ap·pro′pri·a′tion** ***n.***

mis′be·got′ten ***adj.*** **1** wrongly or unlawfully begotten; illegitimate **2** badly conceived

mis′be·have′ ***vt., vi.*** **-haved′, -hav′ing** to behave (oneself) wrongly —**mis′be·hav′ior** ***n.***

misc *abbrev.* **1** miscellaneous **2** miscellany

mis·cal′cu·late′ ***vt., vi.*** **-lat′ed, -lat′ing** to calculate incorrectly; miscount or misjudge —**mis′cal·cu·la′tion** ***n.***

mis·call′ ***vt.*** to call by a wrong name

mis·car·ry (mis kar′ē, mis′kar′ē) ***vi.*** **-ried, -ry·ing** **1** to go wrong; fail: said of a plan, etc. **2** to fail to arrive: said of mail, freight, etc. **3** to give birth to a fetus before it has developed enough to live —**mis·car′riage** ***n.***

mis·cast′ ***vt.*** **-cast′, -cast′ing** to cast (an actor or a play) unsuitably

mis·ce·ge·na·tion (mi sej′ə nā′shən) ***n.*** ⟦< L *miscere,* to mix + *genus,* race⟧ marriage or sexual relations between a man and woman of different races

mis·cel·la·ne·ous (mis′ə lā′nē əs) ***adj.*** ⟦< L *miscere,* to mix⟧ consisting of various kinds or qualities

mis·cel·la·ny (mis′ə lā′nē) ***n.***, *pl.* **-nies** a miscellaneous collection, esp. of literary works

mis·chance′ ***n.*** bad luck

mis·chief (mis′chif) ***n.*** ⟦< OFr *mes-,* MIS- + *chief,* end⟧ **1** harm or damage **2** a cause of harm or annoyance **3** *a)* a prank *b)* playful teasing

mis·chie·vous (mis′chə vəs) ***adj.*** **1** causing mischief; specif., *a)* harmful *b)* prankish **2** inclined to annoy with playful tricks —**mis′chie·vous·ly** ***adv.*** —**mis′chie·vous·ness** ***n.***

mis·ci·ble (mis′ə bəl) ***adj.*** ⟦< L *miscere,* to mix⟧ that can be mixed

mis·con·ceive (mis′kən sēv′) ***vt., vi.*** **-ceived′, -ceiv′ing** to misunderstand —**mis′con·cep′tion** (-sep′shən) ***n.***

mis·con′duct ***n.*** **1** bad or dishonest management **2** willfully improper behavior

mis·con·strue (mis′kən strōō′) ***vt.*** **-strued′, -stru′ing** to misinterpret —**mis′con·struc′tion** (-struk′shən) ***n.***

mis·count (mis kount′; *for n.* mis′kount′) ***vt., vi.*** to count incorrectly —***n.*** an incorrect count

mis·cre·ant (mis′krē ənt) ***adj.*** ⟦< OFr *mes-,* MIS- + *croire,* believe⟧ villainous —***n.*** a criminal; villain

mis·deal (mis dēl′; *for n.* mis′dēl′) ***vt., vi.*** **-dealt′, -deal′ing** to deal (playing cards) incorrectly —***n.*** an incorrect deal

mis·deed′ ***n.*** a wrong or wicked act; crime, sin, etc.

mis·de·mean·or (mis′də mēn′ər) ***n.*** *Law* any minor offense bringing a lesser punishment than a felony

mis′di·rect′ ***vt.*** to direct wrongly or badly —**mis′di·rec′tion** ***n.***

mis·do′ing ***n.*** wrongdoing

mi·ser (mī′zər) ***n.*** ⟦< L, wretched⟧ a greedy, stingy person who hoards money for its own sake —**mi′ser·ly** ***adj.*** —**mi′ser·li·ness** ***n.***

mis·er·a·ble (miz′ər ə bəl, miz′rə bəl) ***adj.*** **1** in misery **2** causing misery, discomfort, etc. **3** bad; inadequate **4** pitiable —**mis′er·a·bly** ***adv.***

mis·er·y (miz′ər ē) ***n.***, *pl.* **-ies** ⟦see MISER⟧ **1** a condition of great suffering; distress **2** a cause of such suffering; pain, poverty, etc.

mis·file′ ***vt.*** **-filed′, -fil′ing** to file (papers, etc.) in the wrong place

mis′fire′ ***vi.*** **-fired′, -fir′ing** **1** to fail to go off or ignite properly: said as of a firearm or engine **2** to fail to achieve a desired effect —***n.*** a misfiring

mis·fit (mis fit′; *for n.* mis′fit′) ***vt., vi.*** **-fit′ted, -fit′ting** to fit badly —***n.*** **1** an improper fit **2** a maladjusted person

mis·for′tune ***n.*** **1** ill fortune; trouble **2** a mishap, calamity, etc.

mis·giv′ing ***n.*** a disturbed feeling of fear, doubt, etc.: *usually used in pl.*

mis·gov′ern ***vt.*** to govern badly —**mis′gov′ern·ment** ***n.***

mis·guide′ (-gīd′) ***vt.*** **-guid′ed, -guid′ing** to lead into error or misconduct; mislead —**mis·guid′ance** ***n.*** —**mis′guid′ed·ly** ***adv.***

mis·han′dle ***vt.*** **-dled, -dling** to handle badly or roughly; abuse or mismanage

mis·hap (mis′hap′) ***n.*** an unlucky or unfortunate accident

mis·hear′ ***vt., vi.*** **-heard′, -hear′ing** to hear wrongly

mish·mash (mish′mash′) ***n.*** a jumble

THESAURUS

unimaginable, stupendous, wondrous; see also MYSTERIOUS 2.—*Ant.* NATURAL, familiar, imaginable. **2** [So unusual as to suggest a miracle] extraordinary, freakish, monstrous; see UNUSUAL 1, 2.

mirage ***n.*** phantasm, delusion, hallucination; see FANTASY, ILLUSION.

mirror ***n.*** looking glass, speculum, reflector, polished metal, hand glass, pier glass, mirroring surface, hand mirror, full-length mirror; see also GLASS.

mirth ***n.*** frolic, jollity, entertainment; see FUN.

misbehave ***v.*** do wrong, sin, fail, trip, blunder, offend, trespass, behave badly, misdo, misstep, err, lapse, be delinquent, be at fault, be culpable, be guilty, be bad, forget oneself, be dissolute, be indecorous, carry on*, be naughty, go astray, sow one's wild oats, cut up*.—*Ant.* BEHAVE, be good, do well.

miscalculate ***v.*** blunder, miscount, err; see MISTAKE.

miscarriage ***n.*** malfunction, defeat, mistake; see FAILURE 1.

miscellaneous ***a.*** **1** [Lacking unity] diverse, disparate, unmatched; see UNLIKE. **2** [Lacking order] mixed, muddled, scattered; see CONFUSED 2, DISORDERED.

mischief ***n.*** troublesomeness, harmfulness, prankishness, playfulness, impishness, misbehavior, misconduct, fault, transgression, wrongdoing, misdoing, naughtiness, mischief-making, friskiness.—*Ant.* DIGNITY, demureness, sedateness.

mischievous ***a.*** playful, roguish, prankish; see NAUGHTY, RUDE 2.

misconception ***n.*** delusion, blunder, fault; see ERROR, MISTAKE 2, MISUNDERSTANDING 1.

misconduct ***n.*** misbehavior, offense, wrongdoing; see EVIL 2, MISCHIEF.

misdemeanor ***n.*** misconduct, misbehavior, misdeed; see CRIME.

miser ***n.*** extortioner, usurer, misanthropist, stingy person, skinflint, Scrooge, money-grubber.—*Ant.* BEGGAR, spendthrift, waster.

miserable ***a.*** distressed, afflicted, sickly, ill, wretched, sick, ailing, unfortunate, uncomfortable, suffering, hurt, wounded, tormented, tortured, in pain, strained, injured, convulsed; see also TROUBLED.—*Ant.* HELPED, aided, comfortable.

miserably ***a.*** poorly, unsatisfactorily, imperfectly; see BADLY 1, INADEQUATELY.

miserly ***a.*** covetous, parsimonious, closefisted; see STINGY.

misery ***n.*** **1** [Pain] distress, suffering, agony; see PAIN 2. **2** [Dejection] worry, despair, desolation; see DEPRESSION 2, GRIEF, SADNESS.

misfit ***n.*** maladjusted person, maverick, loner, dropout, nonconformist, oddball*, sociopath.

misfortune ***n.*** misadventure, ill luck, ill fortune, disadvantage, mischance, disappointment, adversity, discomfort, burden, annoyance, nuisance, unpleasantness, inconvenience, worry, anxiety; see also DIFFICULTY 1.—*Ant.* ADVANTAGE, good fortune, stroke of fortune.

misgiving ***n.*** apprehension, qualm, reservation; see DOUBT, UNCERTAINTY 2.

misguided ***a.*** misled, deceived, benighted; see MISTAKEN 1.

mishap ***n.*** accident, mischance, misadventure; see CATASTROPHE, DISASTER, MISFORTUNE.

mis′in·form′ *vt.* to supply with false or misleading information —**mis′in′for·ma′tion** *n.*

mis′in·ter′pret *vt.* to interpret wrongly; understand or explain incorrectly —**mis′in·ter′pre·ta′tion** *n.*

mis·judge′ *vt., vi.* **-judged′**, **-judg′ing** to judge wrongly or unfairly —**mis·judg′ment** *n.*

mis·la′bel *vt.* **-beled** or **-belled**, **-bel·ing** or **-bel·ling** to label incorrectly or improperly

mis·lay′ (-lā′) *vt.* **-laid′**, **-lay′ing** to put in a place that is then forgotten

mis·lead′ *vt.* **-led′**, **-lead′ing** **1** to lead in a wrong direction **2** to deceive **3** to lead into wrongdoing

mis·man′age *vt., vi.* **-aged**, **-ag·ing** to manage badly or dishonestly —**mis·man′age·ment** *n.*

mis·match (mis mach′; *for n.* mis′mach′) *vt.* to match badly or unsuitably —*n.* a bad match

mis·name′ *vt.* **-named′**, **-nam′ing** to give an inappropriate name to

mis·no·mer (mis nō′mər) *n.* ⟦< OFr < *mes-*, MIS- + *nommer*, to name⟧ a wrong name

mi·sog·y·ny (mi säj′ə nē) *n.* ⟦< Gr *misein*, to hate + *gynē*, woman⟧ hatred of women —**mi·sog′y·nist** *n.*

mis·place (mis plās′) *vt.* **-placed′**, **-plac′ing** **1** to put in a wrong place **2** to bestow (one's trust, etc.) unwisely **3** MISLAY

mis·play (mis plā′; *for n.* mis′plā′) *vt., vi.* to play wrongly or badly, as in games or sports —*n.* a wrong or bad play

mis·print (mis print′; *for n.* mis′print′) *vt.* to print incorrectly —*n.* a printing error

mis·pri′sion (-prizh′ən) *n.* ⟦< OFr *mesprendre,* take wrongly⟧ misconduct or neglect of duty by a public official

mis′pro·nounce′ *vt., vi.* **-nounced′**, **-nounc′ing** to pronounce differently from the accepted pronunciations —**mis′pro·nun′ci·a′tion** *n.*

mis·quote′ *vt., vi.* **-quot′ed**, **-quot′ing** to quote incorrectly —**mis′quo·ta′tion** *n.*

mis·read′ (-rēd′) *vt., vi.* **-read′** (-red′), **-read′ing** (-rēd′iŋ) to read wrongly, esp. so as to misunderstand

mis′rep·re·sent′ *vt.* to represent falsely; give an untrue idea of —**mis′rep·re·sen·ta′tion** *n.*

mis·rule (mis ro͞ol′) *vt.* **-ruled′**, **-rul′ing** to rule badly; misgovern —*n.* misgovernment

miss[1] (mis) *vt.* ⟦OE *missan*⟧ **1** to fail to hit, meet, do, attend, see, hear, etc. **2** to let (a chance, etc.) go by **3** to avoid *[*he just *missed* being hit*]* **4** to notice or feel the absence or loss of **5** to lack *[*this book is *missing* a page*]* —*vi.* **1** to fail to hit something **2** to fail to be successful **3** to misfire: said as of an engine —*n.* a failure to hit, obtain, etc.

miss[2] (mis) *n., pl.* **miss′es** ⟦< MISTRESS⟧ **1** [**M-**] a title used before the name of an unmarried woman or a girl **2** a young unmarried woman or a girl

mis·sal (mis′əl) *n.* ⟦< LL *missa,* Mass⟧ [*often* **M-**] a book of prayers, readings, etc. authorized by the Roman Catholic Church for the celebration of Mass

mis·shape′ *vt.* **-shaped′**, **-shap′ing** to shape badly; deform —**mis·shap′en** *adj.*

mis·sile (mis′əl) *n.* ⟦< L *mittere*, send⟧ an object, as a spear, bullet, or rocket, designed to be thrown, fired, or launched toward a target

mis′sile·ry or **mis′sil·ry** (-rē) *n.* **1** the science of building and launching guided missiles **2** such missiles

miss·ing (mis′iŋ) *adj.* absent; lost

mis·sion (mish′ən) *n.* ⟦< L *mittere,* send⟧ **1** a sending out or being sent out to perform a special service **2** *a)* a group of persons sent by a religious body to spread its religion, esp. in a foreign land *b)* its headquarters **3** a diplomatic delegation **4** a group of technicians, specialists, etc. sent to a foreign country **5** the special duty for which one is sent **6** a special task to which one devotes one's life; calling

mis′sion·ar′y (-er′ē) *adj.* of religious missions or missionaries —*n., pl.* **-ies** a person sent on a religious mission

Mis·sis·sip·pi (mis′ə sip′ē) **1** river in the central U.S., flowing from NC Minnesota to the Gulf of Mexico **2** Southern state of the U.S.: 47,689 sq. mi.; pop. 2,573,000; cap. Jackson: abbrev. *MS* —**Mis′sis·sip′pi·an** *adj., n.*

mis·sive (mis′iv) *n.* ⟦< L *mittere,* send⟧ a letter or written message

Mis·sou·ri (mi zoor′ē, -ə) **1** river in the central U.S., flowing from SW Montana into the Mississippi **2** Midwestern state of the U.S.: 68,898 sq. mi.; pop. 5,117,000; cap. Jefferson City: abbrev. *MO* —**Mis·sou′ri·an** *adj., n.*

mis·spell′ *vt., vi.* **-spelled′** or **-spelt′**, **-spell′ing** to spell incorrectly

mis·spend′ *vt.* **-spent′**, **-spend′ing** to spend improperly or wastefully

mis·state′ *vt.* **-stat′ed**, **-stat′ing** to state incorrectly or falsely —**mis·state′ment** *n.*

mis′step′ *n.* **1** a wrong or awkward step **2** a mistake in conduct

mist (mist) *n.* ⟦OE⟧ **1** a large mass of water vapor, less dense than a fog **2** anything that dims or obscures —*vt., vi.* to make or become misty

mis·take (mi stāk′) *vt.* **-took′**, **-tak′en**, **-tak′ing** ⟦< ON *mistaka,* take wrongly⟧ to understand or perceive

THESAURUS

misinform *v.* mislead, report inaccurately to, misstate; see DECEIVE, LIE.

misinterpret *v.* falsify, distort, miscalculate; see MISTAKE, MISUNDERSTAND.

misinterpretation *n.* distortion, misreckoning, delusion; see MISTAKE 2, MISUNDERSTANDING 1.

misjudge *v.* **1** [To make a wrong judgment, usually of a person] be overcritical, be unfair, come to a hasty conclusion; see MISUNDERSTAND. **2** [To make an inaccurate estimate] miss, miscalculate, misconceive, misthink, misconstrue, overestimate, underestimate, bark up the wrong tree*; see also MISTAKE.—*Ant.* UNDERSTAND, estimate, calculate.

misjudgment *n.* miscalculation, misinterpretation, misconception; see MISTAKE 2.

mislay *v.* lose, disarrange, displace; see MISPLACE.

mislead *v.* delude, cheat, defraud, bilk, take in, outwit, trick, entangle, advise badly, victimize, lure, beguile, hoax, dupe, bait, misrepresent, bluff, give a bum steer*, throw off the scent*, bamboozle, hoodwink, put on*; see also DECEIVE.

misled *a.* misguided, deluded, wronged; see DECEIVED, MISTAKEN 1.

mismanage *v.* bungle, blunder, mess up, foul up*; see also FAIL 1.

mismatched *a.* incompatible, discordant, inconsistent; see UNFIT.

misplace *v.* mislay, displace, shuffle, disarrange, remove, disturb, take out of its place, confuse, mix, scatter, unsettle, disorganize; see also LOSE 2.—*Ant.* FIND, LOCATE, place.

misplaced *a.* displaced, mislaid, out of place; see LOST 1.

mispronounce *v.* falter, misspeak, mumble; see HESITATE, STAMMER.

misrepresent *v.* distort, falsify, misstate; see DECEIVE, LIE 1, MISLEAD.

misrepresentation *n.* untruth, deceit, disguise; see DECEPTION, LIE.

miss[1] *v.* **1** [To feel a want] desire, crave, yearn; see NEED, WANT 1. **2** [To fail to catch] snatch at, drop, fumble, have butterfingers*, muff*, boot*.—*Ant.* CATCH, grab, hold. **3** [To fail to hit] miss one's aim, miss the mark, be wide of the mark, overshoot, undershoot, fan the air*.—*Ant.* HIT, shoot, get.

miss[1,2] *n.* **1** [A failure] slip, blunder, mishap; see MISTAKE 2. **2** [A young woman] lass, young lady, female; see GIRL.

missed *a.* **1** [Not found or noticed] gone, misplaced, mislaid, forgotten, unrecalled, unnoticed, not in sight, put away, in hiding, hidden, strayed, moved, removed, unseen; see also LOST 1.—*Ant.* REMEMBERED, found, located. **2** [Longed for] needed, desired, wished for, pined for, wanted, yearned for, clung to, craved for, hungered for.—*Ant.* HATED, disliked, unwanted.

misshapen *a.* distorted, disfigured, twisted; see DEFORMED.

missile *n.* cartridge, projectile, ammunition; see BULLET, SHOT 1, WEAPON. *Terms for types of missiles include the following:* Polaris, Poseidon, RPV or remotely piloted vehicle, Minuteman, guided missile, cruise missile, ICBM or intercontinental ballistic missile, ABM or antiballistic missile, MIRV or multiple independently targeted reentry vehicle.

missing *a.* disappeared, lacking, removed; see ABSENT, LOST 1.

mission *n.* aim, resolution, goal; see PURPOSE 1.

missionary *n.* apostle, evangelist, preacher; see MESSENGER, MINISTER 1.

misspent *a.* wasted, squandered, thrown away; see WASTED.

mist *n.* cloud, rain, haze; see FOG.

mistake *n.* **1** [A blunder] false step, blunder, slip, error, omission, failure, confusion, wrongdoing, sin, crime, goof*; see also ERROR. **2** [A misunderstanding] misapprehension, confusion, muddle, misconception, delusion, illusion, overestimation, underestimation, impression, confounding, misinterpretation, perversion, perplexity, bewilderment, misjudgment; see also EXAGGERATION, MISUNDERSTANDING 1.—*Ant.* KNOWLEDGE, certainty, interpretation.

mistake *v.* err, blunder, slip, lapse, miss, overlook, omit, underestimate, overestimate, substitute, misjudge,

wrongly —*n.* an idea, answer, act, etc. that is wrong; error or blunder —**mis·tak'a·ble** *adj.*

mis·tak'en *adj.* 1 wrong; having an incorrect understanding 2 incorrect: said of ideas, etc. —**mis·tak'en·ly** *adv.*

mis·ter[1] (mis'tər) *n.* ⟦< MASTER⟧ [**M-**] a title used before the name of a man or his office and usually written *Mr.*

mist'er[2] *n.* a bottle for directing a fine spray of water onto a houseplant, etc.

mis·time (mis tīm') *vt.* **-timed', -tim'ing** to do or say at the wrong time

mis·tle·toe (mis'əl tō') *n.* ⟦< OE *mistel,* mistletoe + *tan,* a twig⟧ a parasitic evergreen plant with yellowish flowers and poisonous, white berries

mis·took (mis to͝ok') *vt., vi. pt. of* MISTAKE

mis·treat' *vt.* to treat wrongly or badly —**mis·treat'ment** *n.*

mis·tress (mis'tris) *n.* ⟦< OFr, fem. of *maistre,* master⟧ 1 a woman who is head of a household or institution 2 a woman, nation, etc. that has control, power, etc. 3 a woman in a sexual relationship with, and typically supported by, a man without being married to him 4 [**M-**] [Obs.] a title used before the name of a woman: now replaced by *Mrs., Miss,* or *Ms.*

mis'tri'al *n. Law* a trial made void, as by an error in the proceedings or by the inability of the jury to reach a verdict

mis·trust' *n.* lack of trust or confidence —*vt., vi.* to have no trust in; doubt —**mis·trust'ful** *adj.*

mist'y *adj.* **-i·er, -i·est** 1 of, like, or covered with mist 2 blurred, as by mist; vague —**mist'i·ly** *adv.* —**mist'i·ness** *n.*

mis'un·der·stand' *vt.* **-stood', -stand'ing** to fail to understand correctly; misinterpret

mis'un·der·stand'ing *n.* 1 a failure to understand 2 a quarrel or disagreement

mis·use (mis yo͞oz'; *for n.,* -yo͞os') *vt.* **-used', -us'ing** 1 to use improperly 2 to treat badly or harshly —*n.* incorrect or improper use

mite (mīt) *n.* ⟦OE⟧ 1 a tiny arachnid, often parasitic upon animals or plants 2 a very small sum of money 3 a very small creature or object

mi·ter (mīt'ər) *n.* ⟦< Gr *mitra,* headband⟧ 1 a tall, ornamented cap worn by bishops and abbots 2 *Carpentry* a joint formed by fitting together two pieces beveled to form a corner: now usually **miter joint**

mit·i·gate (mit'ə gāt') *vt., vi.* **-gat'ed, -gat'ing** ⟦< L *mitis,* soft⟧ 1 to make or become less severe, less painful, etc. 2 ⟦< confusion with MILITATE⟧ to operate or work (*against*): a loose usage —**mit'i·ga'tion** *n.*

mi·to·sis (mī tō'sis) *n.* ⟦< Gr *mitos,* thread⟧ the process by which a cell divides into two with the nucleus of each new cell having the full number of chromosomes —**mi·tot'ic** (-tät'ik) *adj.*

mitt (mit) *n.* ⟦< fol.⟧ 1 a woman's glove covering the hand and forearm, but only part of the fingers 2 [Slang] a hand 3 *a) Baseball* a padded glove, worn for protection *b)* a boxing glove

mit·ten (mit''n) *n.* ⟦< OFr *mitaine*⟧ a glove with a thumb but no separately divided fingers

mix (miks) *vt.* ⟦< L *miscere*⟧ 1 to blend together in a single mass 2 to make by blending ingredients *[to mix a drink]* 3 to combine *[to mix work and play]* 4 to blend electronically (recorded sounds, etc.) on (a tape, etc.) —*vi.* 1 to be mixed or blended 2 to get along together —*n.* 1 a mixture 2 a commercial mixture of ingredients *[a cake mix]* 3 MIXER (*n.* 4) 4 the blend of sounds in a recording, etc. —**mix up** 1 to mix thoroughly 2 to confuse 3 to involve or implicate (*in*): usually used in the passive —**mix'a·ble** *adj.*

mixed (mikst) *adj.* 1 blended 2 made up of different parts, classes, races, etc., or of both sexes 3 confused; muddled

mixed number a number consisting of a whole number and a fraction, as $3\frac{2}{3}$

mixed'-up' *adj.* confused, troubled, etc.

mix'er *n.* 1 a person with reference to the ability to get along with others 2 a machine for mixing ingredients together 3 a social dance for helping people meet one another 4 a beverage for mixing with alcoholic beverages

mix·ture (miks'chər) *n.* 1 a mixing or being mixed 2 something made by mixing

mix'-up' *n.* a confusion; tangle

miz·zen·mast (miz'ən mast'; *naut.,* -məst) *n.* ⟦< L *medius,* middle⟧ the mast third from the bow in a ship

mkt *abbrev.* market

ml *abbrev.* milliliter(s)

Mlle *abbrev.* Mademoiselle

mm *abbrev.* millimeter(s)

MM *abbrev.* Messieurs

Mme *abbrev.* Madame

Mmes *abbrev.* mesdames

Mn *Chem. symbol for* manganese

MN Minnesota

mne·mon·ic (nē män'ik) *adj.* ⟦< Gr *mnēmōn,* mindful⟧ of or helping the memory

mo *abbrev.* month

Mo *Chem. symbol for* molybdenum

MO *abbrev.* 1 Missouri 2 ⟦L *modus operandi*⟧ mode of operation

moan (mōn) *n.* ⟦prob. < OE *mænan,* complain⟧ a low, mournful sound, as of sorrow or pain —*vi., vt.* 1 to utter or say with a moan 2 to complain (about)

THESAURUS

misapprehend, misconceive, misunderstand, confound, misinterpret, confuse, botch, bungle, have the wrong impression, tangle, snarl, slip up, make a mess of*, miss the boat*, put one's foot in one's mouth*.—*Ant.* SUCCEED, be accurate, explain.

mistaken *a.* 1 [In error] misinformed, deceived, confounded, confused, having the wrong impression, deluded, misinformed, misguided, at fault, off the track; see also WRONG 2. 2 [Ill-advised] unadvised, duped, fooled, misled, tricked, unwarranted; see also DECEIVED. 3 [Taken for another] wrongly identified, unrecognized, confused with, taken for, in a case of mistaken identity, misnamed, misconstrued.

mister[1] *n.* Mr., man, sir, *monsieur* (French), *Herr* (German), *signor* (Italian), *señor* (Spanish).

mistreat *v.* harm, injure, wrong; see ABUSE.

mistress *n.* 1 [A woman in authority] housekeeper, chaperone, manager; see LADY 2. 2 [An illicit lover] courtesan, paramour, kept woman; see PROSTITUTE.

mistrust *v.* suspect, distrust, be skeptical of; see DOUBT.

misty *a.* dim, foggy, hazy, murky, shrouded, obscure; see also DARK 1.

misunderstand *v.* err, misconceive, misinterpret, miscomprehend, misjudge, miscalculate, misconstrue, be perplexed, be bewildered, be confused, be confounded, have the wrong impression, fail to understand, misapprehend, overestimate, underestimate, be misled, be unfamiliar with, have the wrong slant on*, have something not register; see also MISTAKE.—*Ant.* UNDERSTAND, grasp, apprehend.

misunderstanding *n.* 1 [Misapprehension] delusion, miscalculation, confusion, misinterpretation, confounding; see also MISTAKE 2.—*Ant.* UNDERSTANDING, conception, apprehension. 2 [Disagreement] debate, dissension, quarrel; see DISAGREEMENT 1, DISPUTE.

misunderstood *a.* misinterpreted, badly interpreted, misconceived; see MISTAKEN 1, WRONG 2.

mitigate *v.* alleviate, lessen, moderate; see DECREASE, RELIEVE 2.

mitten *n.* mitt, gauntlet, glove; see CLOTHES.

mix *v.* 1 [To blend] fuse, merge, coalesce, brew, unite, combine, cross, interbreed, amalgamate, incorporate, alloy, mingle, marry, compound, intermingle, weave, interweave, throw together, adulterate, infiltrate, twine, knead, stir, suffuse, instill, transfuse, synthesize, stir around, infuse, saturate, season. 2 [To confuse] mix up, jumble, tangle; see CONFUSE. 3 [To associate] fraternize, get along, consort; see JOIN 2.

mixed *a.* 1 [Commingled] blended, fused, mingled, compounded, combined, amalgamated, united, brewed, merged, transfused, crossed, assimilated, married, woven, kneaded, incorporated.—*Ant.* SEPARATED, severed, raveled. 2 [Various] miscellaneous, unselected, diverse; see VARIOUS. 3 [Confused] mixed up, jumbled, disordered; see CONFUSED 2.

mixer *n.* blender, food processor, juicer, eggbeater, cake mixer, food mixer, cocktail shaker, converter, carburetor, cement mixer, paint mixer; see also MACHINE.

mixture *n.* 1 [A combination] blend, compound, composite, amalgam, miscellany, mishmash, mingling, medley, marriage, pastiche, mix, potpourri, alloy, fusion, jumble, brew, merger, hybrid, crossing, infiltration, transfusion, infusion, mélange, saturation, assimilation, incorporation, hodgepodge. 2 [A mess] mix-up, muddle, disorder; see CONFUSION.

mix-up *n.* turmoil, chaos, commotion; see CONFUSION, DISORDER.

moan *n.* plaint, groan, wail; see CRY 1.

moan *v.* groan, wail, whine; see CRY 1.

moat (mōt) ***n.*** ⟦< OFr *mote*, a mound⟧ a deep, broad ditch, often filled with water, around a fortress or castle

mob (mäb) ***n.*** ⟦< L *mobile* (*vulgus*), movable (crowd)⟧ **1** a disorderly, lawless crowd **2** any crowd **3** the masses: contemptuous term **4** [Inf.] a gang of criminals —***vt.*** **mobbed, mob′bing 1** to crowd around and attack, annoy, etc. **2** to throng; crowd into

mo·bile (mō′bəl, -bīl′; *for n.*, -bēl′) ***adj.*** ⟦< L *movere,* to move⟧ **1** moving or movable **2** movable by means of a motor vehicle *[a mobile* X-ray unit*]* **3** that can change rapidly or easily; adaptable **4** characterized by ease in change of social status —***n.*** a piece of abstract sculpture that aims to depict movement, as by an arrangement of thin forms, rings, etc. suspended and set in motion by air currents —**mo·bil′i·ty** (-bil′ə tē) ***n.***

Mo·bile (mō bēl′) seaport in SW Alabama: pop. 196,000

-mo·bile (mō bēl′) ⟦< (AUTO)MOBILE⟧ *combining form* motorized vehicle *[bookmobile]*

mo·bile home (mō′bəl) a movable dwelling set more or less permanently at a location: cf. MOTOR HOME

mo′bi·lize′ (-bə līz′) ***vt., vi.*** **-lized′, -liz′ing** to make or become organized and ready, as for war —**mo′bi·li·za′tion** ***n.***

mob·ster (mäb′stər) ***n.*** [Slang] a gangster

moc·ca·sin (mäk′ə sən) ***n.*** ⟦< AmInd⟧ **1** a heelless slipper of soft, flexible leather **2** any similar heeled slipper

mo·cha (mō′kə) ***n.*** a choice grade of coffee grown orig. in Arabia —***adj.*** flavored with coffee or coffee and chocolate

mock (mäk) ***vt.*** ⟦< OFr *mocquer*⟧ **1** to ridicule **2** to mimic, as in fun or derision —***vi.*** to express scorn, ridicule, etc. —***adj.*** sham; imitation; pretended —***adv.*** falsely or insincerely

mock′er·y (-ər ē) ***n.***, *pl.* **-ies 1** a mocking **2** a person or thing receiving or deserving ridicule **3** a false or derisive imitation

mock′ing·bird′ ***n.*** a bird of the U.S. that imitates the calls of other birds

mock′-up′ ***n.*** ⟦< Fr *maquette*⟧ a model built to scale, often full-sized, for teaching, testing, etc.

mod (mäd) ***adj.*** ⟦< MOD(ERN)⟧ up-to-date, fashionable, stylish, etc.

mode (mōd) ***n.*** ⟦< L *modus*⟧ **1** a manner or way of acting, doing, or being **2** customary usage or current fashion **3** *Gram.* MOOD[2]

mod·el (mäd′'l) ***n.*** ⟦< L *modus,* a measure⟧ **1** a small representation of a planned or existing object **2** a hypothetical description, often based on an analogy, used in analyzing something **3** a person or thing regarded as a standard of excellence to be imitated **4** a style or design **5** *a)* one who poses for an artist or photographer *b)* one employed to display clothes by wearing them —***adj.*** **1** serving as a model **2** representative of others of the same style, etc. *[a model* home*]* —***vt.*** **-eled** or **-elled, -el·ing** or **-el·ling 1** *a)* to make a model of *b)* to plan or form after a model **2** to display (clothes) by wearing —***vi.*** to serve as a MODEL (*n.* 5)

mo·dem (mō′dəm) ***n.*** ⟦MO(DULATOR) + DEM(ODULATION)⟧ a device that converts data for transmission, as by telephone, to data-processing equipment

mod·er·ate (mäd′ər it; *for v.*, -āt′) ***adj.*** ⟦< L *moderare,* restrain⟧ **1** within reasonable limits; avoiding extremes **2** mild; calm **3** of medium quality, amount, etc. —***n.*** one holding moderate opinions —***vt., vi.*** **-at′ed, -at′ing 1** to make or become moderate **2** to preside over (a meeting, etc.) —**mod′er·ate·ly** ***adv.***

mod′er·a′tion ***n.*** **1** a moderating **2** avoidance of extremes **3** calmness

mod′er·a′tor ***n.*** one who presides at an assembly, debate, etc.

mod·ern (mäd′ərn) ***adj.*** ⟦< L *modo,* just now⟧ **1** of the present or recent times; specif., up-to-date **2** [*often* **M-**] designating the most recent form of a language —***n.*** a person living in modern times, having modern ideas, etc. —**mo·der·ni·ty** (mä dʉr′nə tē) ***n.***

Modern English the English language since about the mid-15th c.

mod′ern·ism′ ***n.*** (a) modern usage, practice, thought, etc. —**mod′ern·ist** ***n., adj.*** —**mod′ern·is′tic** ***adj.***

mod′ern·ize′ ***vt., vi.*** **-ized′, -iz′ing** to make or become modern —**mod′ern·i·za′tion** ***n.***

THESAURUS

mob ***n.*** **1** [A disorderly crowd of people] swarm, rabble, throng, press, multitude, populace, horde, riot, rout, host, lawless element; see also CROWD, GATHERING. **2** [The lower classes] bourgeoisie, plebeians, proletariat; see PEOPLE 3.

mob ***v.*** throng, crowd, swarm; see ATTACK, REBEL.

mobile ***a.*** unstationary, loose, free; see MOVABLE.

mobility ***n.*** changeability, versatility, flow; see MOVEMENT 1.

mobilize ***v.*** assemble, muster, gather; see ENLIST 1.

moccasin ***n.*** heelless shoe, slipper, sandal; see SHOE.

mock ***a.*** counterfeit, sham, pretended; see FALSE 3, UNREAL.

mock ***v.*** **1** [To ridicule] deride, scorn, taunt; see RIDICULE. **2** [To mimic] mime, burlesque, caricature; see IMITATE.

mockery ***n.*** disparagement, imitation, sham; see RIDICULE.

model ***n.*** **1** [A person worthy of imitation] archetype, prototype, exemplar, role model, paradigm, ideal, good man, good woman, good example, hero, demigod, saint. **2** [Anything that serves as a copy] original, text, guide, copy, tracing, facsimile, duplicate, pattern, template, design, gauge, ideal, shape, form, specimen, mold, principle, basis, standard, sketch, painting, precedent, archetype, prototype; see also CRITERION. **3** [A duplicate on a small scale] miniature, image, illustration, representation, reduction, statue, figure, figurine, effigy, mock-up, skeleton, portrait, photograph, relief, print, engraving; see also COPY, DUPLICATE. **4** [One who poses professionally] poser, sitter, mannequin; see NUDE.

model ***v.*** **1** [To form] shape, mold, fashion; see CREATE, FORM 1. **2** [To imitate a model] trace, duplicate, sketch, reduce, represent, print, counterfeit, caricature, parody; see also ILLUSTRATE, PAINT 1. **3** [To serve as a model] sit, be a role model, set an example; see POSE 2. **4** [To demonstrate] show off, wear, parade in; see DISPLAY.

moderate ***a.*** **1** [Not expensive] inexpensive, low-priced, reasonable; see CHEAP 1, ECONOMICAL 2. **2** [Not violent] modest, cool, tranquil; see CALM 1, RESERVED 3. **3** [Not radical] tolerant, judicious, nonpartisan, liberal, middle-of-the-road, unopinionated, undogmatic, not given to extremes, measured, low-key, evenly balanced, neutral, impartial, centrist, conventional, in the mean, average, restrained, sound, cautious, respectable, middle-class, compromising; see also CONSERVATIVE.—*Ant.* RADICAL, unbalanced, partial. **4** [Not intemperate] pleasant, gentle, soft, balmy, inexcessive, tepid, easy, not rigorous, not severe, temperate, favorable, tolerable, bearable, tame, untroubled, unruffled, monotonous, even; see also FAIR 3, MILD 2.—*Ant.* SEVERE, rigorous, bitter. **5** [Not indulgent] sparing, frugal, abstemious, regulated, self-denying, abstinent, non-indulgent, self-controlled, disciplined, careful, on the wagon*, sworn off*, teetotalling; see also SOBER.—*Ant.* WASTEFUL, excessive, self-indulgent.

moderate ***v.*** abate, modify, decline; see DECREASE 1.

moderately ***a.*** tolerantly, tolerably, temperately, somewhat, to a degree, enough, to some extent, to a certain extent, a little, to some degree, fairly, not exactly, in moderation, within reason, within bounds, within reasonable limits, as far as could be expected, within the bounds of reason, in reason; see also REASONABLY 2, SLIGHTLY.—*Ant.* MUCH, extremely, remarkably.

moderation ***n.*** **1** [Restraint] toleration, steadiness, sobriety, coolness, the golden mean, quiet, temperance, patience, fairness, justice, constraint, forbearance, poise, balance; see also RESTRAINT 1. **2** [The act of moderating] mediation, regulation, limitation; see RESTRAINT 2.

modern ***a.*** **1** [Up-to-date] stylish, modish, chic, smart, up-to-the-minute, current, recent, of the present, prevailing, prevalent, faddish, avant-garde, present-day, latest, most recent, advanced, modernistic, streamlined, breaking with tradition, new, newest, untraditional, contemporary, in vogue, in use, common, newfangled, just out, cool*, sharp*, smooth*, state-of-the-art, mod, trendy*; see also FASHIONABLE.—*Ant.* OLD-FASHIONED, out-of-date, out-of-style. **2** [Having the comforts of modern life] high-tech, modernized, renovated, functional, with modern conveniences, done over, having modern improvements; see also CONVENIENT 1, IMPROVED. **3** [Concerning recent times] contemporary, contemporaneous, recent, concurrent, present-day, coincident, twentieth-century, twenty-first-century, latter-day, mechanical, of the Machine Age, of the Space Age, of the Computer Age, automated, of modern times; see also NEW 1, 2, NOW 1.—*Ant.* OLD, medieval, primordial.

mod·est (mäd′ist) ***adj.*** ⟦< L *modus,* a measure⟧ **1** not vain or boastful **2** shy or reserved **3** decorous; decent **4** unpretentious —**mod′est·ly** ***adv.*** —**mod′es·ty** ***n.***

mod·i·cum (mäd′i kəm) ***n.*** ⟦< L, moderate⟧ a small amount; bit

mod·i·fy (mäd′ə fī′) ***vt.*** **-fied′**, **-fy′ing** ⟦< L *modificare,* to limit⟧ **1** to change partially in character, form, etc. **2** to limit slightly **3** *Gram.* to limit in meaning —**mod′i·fi·ca′tion** ***n.*** —**mod′i·fi′er** ***n.***

mod·ish (mōd′ish) ***adj.*** fashionable; stylish —**mo′dish·ly** ***adv.*** —**mod′ish·ness** ***n.***

mod·u·lar (mäj′ə lər) ***adj.*** of modules

mod′u·late′ (-lāt′) ***vt.*** **-lat′ed**, **-lat′ing** ⟦< L *modus,* a measure⟧ **1** to regulate or adjust **2** to vary the pitch, intensity, etc. of (the voice) **3** *Radio* to vary the frequency of (radio waves, etc.) —**mod′u·la′tion** ***n.*** —**mod′u·la′tor** ***n.***

mod·ule (mäj′o͞ol′) ***n.*** ⟦Fr < L *modus,* a measure⟧ **1** a standard or unit of measurement, as of building materials **2** any of a set of units to be variously fitted together **3** a detachable unit with a specific function, as in a spacecraft

mo·gul (mō′gul′) ***n.*** ⟦Pers *Mughul,* Mongol⟧ a powerful or important person

mo·hair (mō′her′) ***n.*** ⟦< Ar *mukhayyar,* fine cloth⟧ **1** the hair of the Angora goat **2** yarn or fabric made of this

Mo·ham·med (mō ham′id) A.D. 570?-632; Arab prophet: founder of Islam

Mo·ham′med·an ***adj.*** of Mohammed or Islam —***n.*** MUSLIM Term used, esp. formerly, by non-Muslims —**Mo·ham′med·an·ism′** ***n.***

moi·e·ty (moi′ə tē) ***n.***, *pl.* **-ties** ⟦< L *medius,* middle⟧ **1** a half **2** an indefinite part

moire (mwär, môr) ***n.*** ⟦Fr⟧ a fabric, esp. silk, etc., having a wavy pattern: also **moi·ré** (mwä rā′, mô-)

moist (moist) ***adj.*** ⟦< L *mucus,* mucus⟧ slightly wet; damp —**moist′ly** ***adv.*** —**moist′ness** ***n.***

mois·ten (mois′ən) ***vt.***, ***vi.*** to make or become moist

mois′ture (-chər) ***n.*** water or other liquid causing a slight wetness

mois′tur·ize′ (-īz′) ***vt.***, ***vi.*** **-ized′**, **-iz′ing** to make (the skin, air, etc.) moist —**mois′tur·iz′er** ***n.***

Mo·ja·ve Desert (mō hä′vē) desert in SE California: also sp. **Mo·ha′ve Desert**

mo·lar (mō′lər) ***adj.*** ⟦< L *mola,* millstone⟧ designating a tooth or teeth adapted for grinding —***n.*** a molar tooth

mo·las·ses (mə las′iz) ***n.*** ⟦< L *mel,* honey⟧ a thick, dark syrup produced during the refining of sugar

mold[1] (mōld) ***n.*** ⟦< L *modus,* a measure⟧ **1** a hollow form for giving a certain shape to something plastic or molten **2** a frame on which something is modeled **3** a pattern; model **4** something that is formed in or on a mold **5** distinctive character —***vt.*** **1** to make in or on a mold **2** to form; shape

mold[2] (mōld) ***n.*** ⟦ME *moul*⟧ **1** a fungus producing a furry growth on the surface of organic matter **2** this growth —***vi.*** to become moldy

mold[3] (mōld) ***n.*** ⟦OE *molde*⟧ loose, soft soil rich in decayed organic matter

mold·er (mōl′dər) ***vi.*** ⟦< OE *molde,* dust⟧ to crumble into dust

mold·ing (mōl′diŋ) ***n.*** **1** the act of one that molds **2** something molded **3** a shaped strip of wood, etc., as around the upper walls of a room

Mol·do·va (môl dō′və) country in E Europe: formerly a republic of the U.S.S.R.: 13,000 sq. mi.; pop. 4,339,000

mold′y ***adj.*** **-i·er**, **-i·est** **1** covered or overgrown with mold **2** musty or stale —**mold′i·ness** ***n.***

mole[1] (mōl) ***n.*** ⟦OE *mal*⟧ a small, congenital spot on the human skin, usually dark-colored and raised

mole[2] (mōl) ***n.*** ⟦ME *molle*⟧ **1** a small, burrowing mammal with soft fur **2** a spy in an enemy intelligence agency, etc. who infiltrates long before engaging in spying

mole[3] (mōl) ***n.*** ⟦< L *moles,* a dam⟧ a breakwater

mol·e·cule (mäl′i kyo͞ol′) ***n.*** ⟦< ModL dim. of L *moles,* a mass⟧ **1** the smallest particle of an element or compound that can exist in the free state and still retain the characteristics of the substance **2** a small particle —**mo·lec·u·lar** (mō lek′yo͞o lər) ***adj.***

mole′hill′ ***n.*** a small ridge of earth, formed by a burrowing mole

mole′skin′ ***n.*** a napped cotton fabric

mo·lest (mə lest′) ***vt.*** ⟦< L *moles,* a burden⟧ **1** to annoy or to meddle with so as to trouble or harm **2** to make improper sexual advances to **3** to assault or attack (esp. a child) sexually —**mo·les·ta·tion** (mō′les tā′shən) ***n.*** —**mo·lest′er** ***n.***

Mo·lière (mōl yer′) 1622-73; Fr. dramatist

mol·li·fy (mäl′ə fī′) ***vt.*** **-fied′**, **-fy′ing** ⟦< L *mollis,* soft + *facere,* make⟧ **1** to soothe; appease **2** to make less severe or violent

mol·lusk (mäl′əsk) ***n.*** ⟦< L *mollis,* soft⟧ any of a group of invertebrates, as an oyster or snail, having a soft body, often in a shell

mol·ly (mäl′ē) ***n.***, *pl.* **-lies** ⟦after F. N. *Mollien* (1758-1850), Fr statesman⟧ any of various brightly colored fishes often kept in aquariums: also **mol′lie**

mol·ly·cod·dle (mäl′ē käd′'l) ***n.*** ⟦< *Molly,* dim. of *Mary* + CODDLE⟧ a man or boy used to being coddled, protected, etc. —***vt.*** **-dled**, **-dling** to pamper; coddle

molt (mōlt) ***vi.*** ⟦< L *mutare,* to change⟧ to shed hair, skin, horns, etc. prior to replacement by a new growth: said of reptiles, birds, etc.

mol·ten (mōlt′'n) ***vt.***, ***vi.*** ⟦ME⟧ *archaic pp. of* MELT —***adj.*** melted by heat

mo·lyb·de·num (mə lib′də nəm) ***n.*** ⟦ult. < Gr *molybdos,* lead⟧ a silvery metallic chemical element, used in alloys

mom (mäm) ***n.*** [Inf.] MOTHER

mo·ment (mō′mənt) ***n.*** ⟦< L *momentum,* movement⟧ **1** an indefinitely brief period of time; instant **2** a definite point in time **3** a brief time of importance **4** importance

mo·men·tar·i·ly (mō′mən ter′ə lē) ***adv.*** **1** for a short time **2** in an instant **3** at any moment

THESAURUS

modest ***a.*** **1** [Humble] unassuming, meek, diffident; see HUMBLE 1, RESIGNED. **2** [Not showy] unpretentious, plain, unostentatious, unobtrusive, demure, quiet, seemly, proper, decorous, simple, natural, unassuming, humble, tasteful, unadorned, unaffected, homely. **3** [Moderate] reasonable, inexpensive, average; see CHEAP 1, ECONOMICAL 2. **4** [Proper] pure, chaste, seemly; see DECENT 2, HONEST 1. **5** [Lowly] plain, simple, unaffected; see HUMBLE 2.

modestly ***a.*** unobtrusively, retiringly, quietly, unpretentiously, diffidently, bashfully, unassumingly, chastely, virtuously, purely, shyly, demurely.—*Ant.* BOLDLY, boastfully, pretentiously.

modesty ***n.*** **1** [Unassuming or humble attitude] humility, delicacy, reticence, unobtrusiveness, meekness; see also COURTESY 1, DIGNITY, RESTRAINT 1.—*Ant.* VANITY, conceit, egotism. **2** [Shyness] inhibition, timidity, diffidence; see SHYNESS. **3** [Chastity] decency, innocence, celibacy; see CHASTITY, VIRTUE 1.

modicum ***n.*** trifle, fraction, particle; see BIT.

modification ***n.*** qualification, alteration, correction; see ADJUSTMENT, CHANGE 2.

modified ***a.*** varied, mutated, adjusted; see CHANGED 2.

modify ***v.*** **1** [To change] alter, modify, vary; see BECOME, CHANGE 2. **2** [To moderate] mitigate, restrain, curb; see DECREASE 2, RESTRICT.

moist ***a.*** humid, dank, moistened; see WET 1.

moisten ***v.*** sprinkle, dampen, saturate, drench, waterlog, steep, sog, sop, dip, rinse, wash over, wet down, water down, squirt, shower, rain on, splash, splatter, bathe, steam, spray, sponge.

moisture ***n.*** precipitation, mist, drizzle; see FOG, WATER 1.

mold[1,2] ***n.*** **1** [A form] matrix, cavity, shape, frame, pattern, design, template, die, cast, cup, image, kind, molding, casting, reproduction, form, pottery, shell, core. **2** [A parasitic growth] mildew, rust, parasite, fungus, lichen; see also DECAY.

mold[1,2] ***v.*** **1** [To give physical shape to] make, round into, fashion; see FORM 1. **2** [To decay through the action of mold] rot, mildew, rust; see SPOIL.

moldy ***a.*** musty, mildewed, dank; see ROTTEN 1.

mole[1] ***n.*** flaw, birthmark, blotch; see BLEMISH.

molecular ***a.*** miniature, microscopic, atomic; see LITTLE 1, MINUTE 1.

molecule ***n.*** particle, fragment, unit; see ATOM, BIT 1.

molest ***v.*** bother, interrupt, break in upon, intrude, encroach upon, annoy, worry, irritate, plague, badger, bait, pester, hinder, tease, irk, vex, trouble, harass, assault, assault sexually, confuse, perturb, frighten, terrify, scare; see also BOTHER 2.

mollycoddle ***v.*** pamper, coddle, spoil, overindulge; see also BABY.

molten ***a.*** heated, melted, fused, liquefied, running, fluid, seething; see also HOT 1.—*Ant.* COLD, cool, solid.

moment ***n.*** **1** [A brief time] minute, instant, millisecond, trice, second, bit, while, flash, jiffy*; see also MINUTE . **2** [Importance] significance, note, consequence; see IMPORTANCE.

momentarily ***a.*** immediately, right now, instantly; see NOW 1.

mo·men·tar·y (mō′mən ter′ē) ***adj.*** lasting for only a moment; passing

mo·men·tous (mō men′təs) ***adj.*** of great moment; very important —**mo·men′tous·ness** ***n.***

mo·men·tum (mō men′təm) ***n.***, *pl.* **-tums** or **-ta** (-tə) ⟦L: see MOMENT⟧ the impetus of a moving object, equal to the product of its mass and its velocity

mom·my (mäm′ē) ***n.***, *pl.* **-mies** *child's term for* MOTHER

Mon *abbrev.* Monday

Mon·a·co (män′ə kō) country on the Mediterranean: an independent principality & an enclave in SE France: .75 sq. mi.; pop. 30,000

mon·arch (män′ərk, -ärk′) ***n.*** ⟦< Gr *monos,* alone + *archein,* to rule⟧ **1** a hereditary ruler; king, queen, etc. **2** a large butterfly of North America, having black-edged orange wings —**mo·nar·chi·cal** (mə när′ki kəl) ***adj.***

mon′ar·chist (-ər kist) ***n.*** one who favors monarchical government

mon′ar·chy (-kē) ***n.***, *pl.* **-chies** a government or state headed by a monarch

mon·as·ter·y (män′ə ster′ē) ***n.***, *pl.* **-ies** ⟦< Gr *monos,* alone⟧ the residence of a group of monks, etc. who have withdrawn from the world for religious reasons

mo·nas·tic (mə nas′tik) ***adj.*** of or like that of a monastery, monk, nun, etc.: also **mo·nas′ti·cal** —**mo·nas′ti·cism′** (-tə siz′əm) ***n.***

mon·au·ral (män ôr′əl) ***adj.*** of sound reproduction in which only one source of sound is used

Mon·day (mun′dā) ***n.*** ⟦OE *monandæg,* moon's day⟧ the second day of the week: abbrev. *Mon*

mon·e·tar·y (män′ə ter′ē) ***adj.*** ⟦< L *moneta,* a MINT[1]⟧ **1** of the coinage or currency of a country **2** of money —**mon′e·tar′i·ly** ***adv.***

mon·ey (mun′ē) ***n.***, *pl.* **-eys** or **-ies** ⟦< L *moneta,* a MINT[1]⟧ **1** stamped pieces of metal, or any paper notes, authorized by a government as a medium of exchange **2** property; wealth —**in the money** [Slang] **1** among the winners in a race, etc. **2** wealthy —**make money** to gain profits; become wealthy —**put money into** to invest money in

mon′ey·bag′ ***n.*** **1** a bag for money **2** [*pl., with sing. v.*] [Inf.] a rich person

mon·eyed (mun′ēd) ***adj.*** rich; wealthy

mon′ey·mak′er ***n.*** **1** one successful at acquiring money **2** something profitable —**mon′ey·mak′ing** ***adj., n.***

money market the short-term system for lending and borrowing funds, especially by governments and large corporations

money market fund a mutual fund that puts funds into short-term investments, as government treasury bills

money order an order for payment of a specified sum of money, issued for a fee at one post office, bank, etc. and payable at another

mon·ger (muŋ′gər) ***n.*** ⟦< OE *mangere*⟧ [Chiefly Brit.] a dealer or trader: usually in compounds

Mon·gol (mäŋ′gəl) ***n.*** a person born or living in Mongolia —***adj.*** MONGOLIAN

Mon·go·li·a (mäŋ gō′lē ə) **1** region in EC Asia, consisting of the country of Mongolia and a region of China (*Inner Mongolia*) **2** country in EC Asia: 604,250 sq. mi.; pop. 2,096,000

Mon·go·li·an (mäŋ gō′lē ən) ***n.*** **1** MONGOL **2** a family of languages spoken in Mongolia —***adj.*** **1** of Mongolia or its peoples, languages, etc. **2** [Obs.] affected with Down syndrome

Mon·gol·ic (mäŋ gäl′ik) ***adj.*** *var. of* MONGOLIAN

Mon·gol·oid (mäŋ′gəl oid′) ***adj.*** **1** *var. of* MONGOLIAN **2** designating or of one of the major geographical varieties of human beings, including most of the peoples of Asia **3** [*often* **m-**] [Old-fashioned] affected with Down syndrome —***n.*** **1** a member of the Mongoloid population of human beings **2** [*often* **m-**] [Old-fashioned] one affected with Down syndrome

mon·goose (mäŋ′go͞os′) ***n.***, *pl.* **-goos′es** ⟦< native name in India⟧ a civetlike Old World carnivore that kills snakes, rodents, etc.

mon·grel (mäŋ′grəl) ***n.*** ⟦< OE *mengan,* to mix⟧ an animal or plant, esp. a dog, of mixed breed —***adj.*** of mixed breed, origin, character, etc.

mon·ied (mun′ēd) ***adj.*** MONEYED

mon·i·ker (män′i kər) ***n.*** ⟦< ?⟧ [Slang] a person's name: also **mon′ick·er**

mo·ni·tion (mō nish′ən) ***n.*** ⟦< L *monere,* warn⟧ admonition; warning

mon·i·tor (män′i tər) ***n.*** ⟦< L *monere,* warn⟧ **1** a student chosen to help the teacher **2** any device for regulating the performance of a machine, an aircraft, etc. **3** *Comput.* a video screen for displaying data, images, etc. **4** *Radio, TV* a receiver for checking the quality of transmission —***vt., vi.*** to watch or check on (a person or thing)

monk (muŋk) ***n.*** ⟦< Gr *monos,* alone⟧ a man who is a member of an ascetic religious order

mon·key (muŋ′kē) ***n.***, *pl.* **-keys** ⟦< ? Fr or Sp *mona,* ape + LowG *-ke,* -KIN⟧ **1** a primate having a flat, hairless face and a long tail **2** loosely, another, similar primate, as a chimpanzee —***vi.*** [Inf.] to play, trifle, or meddle (*around* or *with*)

monkey business [Inf.] foolishness, mischief, or deceit

mon′key·shines′ (-shīnz′) ***pl.n.*** [Inf.] playful tricks or pranks

monkey wrench a wrench with an adjustable jaw —**throw a monkey wrench into** [Inf.] to disrupt the orderly functioning of

monk's cloth a heavy cloth with a basket weave, used for drapes, etc.

mon·o (män′ō) ***adj.*** *short for* MONOPHONIC —***n.*** *short for* MONONUCLEOSIS

mono- ⟦< Gr *monos,* single⟧ *prefix* one, alone, single

mon·o·chrome (män′ə krōm′) ***adj.*** ⟦< MONO- + -CHROME⟧ in one color or shades of one color

mon·o·cle (män′ə kəl) ***n.*** ⟦ult. < Gr *monos,* single + L *oculus,* eye⟧ an eyeglass for one eye only

mon·o·clon·al (män′ō klōn′əl) ***adj.*** of cells derived or cloned from one cell

mon·o·cot·y·le·don (män′ō kät′ə lēd′′n) ***n.*** *Bot.* a plant having an embryo with only one cotyledon, or seed leaf: also **mon′o·cot′**

mo·nog·a·my (mə näg′ə mē) ***n.*** ⟦ult. < Gr *monos,* single + *gamos,* marriage⟧ the practice or state of being married to only one person at a time —**mo·nog′a·mous** ***adj.***

mon·o·gram (män′ə gram′) ***n.*** ⟦< Gr *monos,* single + *gramma,* letter⟧ the initials of a name, combined in a single design —***vt.*** **-grammed′**, **-gram′ming** to put a monogram on

mon′o·graph′ (-graf′) ***n.*** ⟦MONO- + -GRAPH⟧ a book or long article, esp. a scholarly one, on a single subject

mon·o·lin·gual (män′ō liŋ′gwəl) ***adj.*** using or knowing only one language

mon·o·lith (män′ə lith′) ***n.*** ⟦< Gr *monos,* single + *lithos,*

THESAURUS

momentary ***a.*** fleeting, quick, passing, flitting, flashing, transient, impermanent, shifting, ephemeral, vanishing, cursory, temporary, dreamlike, in the blink of an eye, in the wink of an eye.—*Ant.* ETERNAL, continual, ceaseless.

momentum ***n.*** impulse, force, drive; see ENERGY 2.

mommy* ***n.*** mom*, female parent, mama*; see MOTHER 1, PARENT.

monarch ***n.*** hereditary ruler, sovereign, autocrat; see KING 1.

monarchy ***n.*** kingship, sovereignty, command; see POWER 2.

monastery ***n.*** abbey, priory, religious community; see CHURCH 1.

monetary ***a.*** pecuniary, financial, fiscal; see COMMERCIAL.

money ***n.*** **1** [A medium of monetary exchange] gold, silver, cash, currency, check, bills, notes, specie, legal tender, Almighty Dollar*, gravy*, wampum*, shekels*, dough*, long green*, coins*, lucre, folding money*, wad*, bucks*, hard cash*, bread*. *Money includes the following:* dollar, pound, franc, lira, peso, ruble, krone, yuan, yen, euro, schilling, real, deutsche mark, drachma, rupee, shekel, won, sol, złoty, escudo, rand, peseta. **2** [Wealth] funds, capital, property; see WEALTH. **3** [Merged interest] financiers, corporate interests, capitalists; see BUSINESS 4. **4** [Pay] payment, salary, wages; see PAY 2. —**for one's money*** for one's choice, in one's opinion, to one's mind; see PERSONALLY 2. —**in the money*** wealthy, flush*, loaded*; see RICH 1. —**make money** gain profits, become wealthy, earn; see PROFIT 2. —**one's money's worth** full value, gain, benefit; see VALUE 1, 3. —**put money into** invest in, support, underwrite; see INVEST.

mongrel ***n.*** mutt*, cur, crossbreed, mixed breed.

monk ***n.*** hermit, religious, ascetic, solitary, recluse, abbot, prior; see also PRIEST.

monkey ***n.*** *Monkeys include the following:* marmoset, tamarin, capuchin; squirrel, proboscis, howler, spider, woolly, etc. monkey; macaque, baboon, mandrill, colobus.

monkey* ***v.*** pry, fool around, tamper with; see MEDDLE 2.

monkey business* ***n.*** deceit, conniving, misconduct; see DECEPTION, LIE.

stone⟧ **1** a single large block of stone, as one made into an obelisk **2** any massive, unyielding structure —**mon'o·lith'ic** ***adj.***

mon·o·logue or **mon·o·log** (män'ə lôg') ***n.*** ⟦< Gr *monos,* single + *legein,* speak⟧ **1** a long speech **2** a soliloquy **3** a skit, etc. for one actor only

mon·o·ma·ni·a (män'ō mā'nē ə) ***n.*** an excessive interest in or enthusiasm for some one thing; craze —**mon'o·ma'ni·ac'** (-mā'nē ak') ***n.*** —**mon'o·ma·ni'a·cal** (-mə nī'ə kəl) ***adj.***

mon·o·nu·cle·o·sis (män'ō no͞o'klē ō'sis) ***n.*** ⟦MONO- + NUCLE(US) + -OSIS⟧ an acute disease, with fever, swollen lymph nodes, etc.

mon'o·phon'ic (-fän'ik) ***adj.*** of sound reproduction using a single channel to carry sounds

mo·nop·o·list (mə näp'ə list) ***n.*** one who has a monopoly or favors monopoly —**mo·nop'o·lis'tic** ***adj.***

mo·nop'o·lize' (-līz') ***vt.*** **-lized', -liz'ing** **1** to get, have, or exploit a monopoly of **2** to get full control of *[he monopolized* the conversation*]*

mo·nop'o·ly (-lē) ***n., pl.*** **-lies** ⟦< Gr *monos,* single + *pōlein,* sell⟧ **1** exclusive control of a commodity or service in a given market **2** such control granted by a government **3** something held as a monopoly **4** a company that has a monopoly

mon·o·rail (män'ə rāl') ***n.*** **1** a single rail that is a track for cars suspended from it or balanced on it **2** a railway with such a track

mon·o·so·di·um glu·ta·mate (män'ō sō'dē əm glo͞o'tə māt') a white powder made from vegetable protein, used to intensify flavor in foods

mon·o·syl·la·ble (män'ō sil'ə bəl) ***n.*** a word of one syllable —**mon'o·syl·lab'ic** (-si lab'ik) ***adj.***

mon'o·the·ism' (-thē iz'əm) ***n.*** ⟦MONO- + THEISM⟧ the belief that there is only one God —**mon'o·the·ist'** ***n.*** —**mon'o·the·is'tic** ***adj.***

mon·o·tone (män'ə tōn') ***n.*** ⟦see MONO- & TONE⟧ **1** utterance of successive words without change of pitch or key **2** tiresome sameness of style, color, etc. **3** a single, unchanging tone

mo·not·o·nous (mə nät''n əs) ***adj.*** **1** going on in the same tone **2** having no variety **3** tiresome because unvarying —**mo·not'o·ny** ***n.***

Mon·roe (mən rō'), **James** (jāmz) 1758-1831; 5th president of the U.S. (1817-25)

mon·sieur (mə syʉr'; *Fr* mə syö') ***n., pl.*** **mes·sieurs** (mes'ərz; *Fr* mā syö') ⟦Fr, lit., my lord⟧ **1** a man; gentleman **2** [M-] French title, equivalent to *Mr.* or *Sir*

Mon·si·gnor (män sēn'yər) ***n., pl.*** **-gnors** ⟦It, lit., my lord⟧ *R.C.Ch.* a title of certain Roman Catholic prelates

mon·soon (män so͞on') ***n.*** ⟦< Ar *mausim,* a season⟧ **1** a seasonal wind of the Indian Ocean and S Asia **2** the rainy season during which this wind blows from the southwest

mon·ster (män'stər) ***n.*** ⟦< L *monere,* warn⟧ **1** any grotesque imaginary creature **2** a very wicked person **3** any huge animal or thing —***adj.*** huge

mon·strance (män'strəns) ***n.*** ⟦ult. < L *monstrare,* to show⟧ *R.C.Ch.* a receptacle for displaying the consecrated Host

mon·strous (män'strəs) ***adj.*** **1** huge; enormous **2** greatly malformed **3** horrible; hideous **4** evil —**mon·stros'i·ty** (-sträs'ə tē), *pl.* **-ties**, ***n.***

mon·tage (män täzh') ***n.*** ⟦Fr < *monter,* to mount⟧ **1** a composite picture **2** a rapid sequence of film scenes, often superimposed

Mon·taigne (män tān'), **Mi·chel de** (mē shel' də) 1533-92; Fr. essayist

Mon·tan·a (män tan'ə) Mountain State of the NW U.S.: 145,556 sq. mi.; pop. 799,000; cap. Helena: abbrev. *MT* —**Mon·tan'an** ***adj., n.***

Mon·te Car·lo (mänt'ə kär'lō) town in Monaco: gambling resort: pop. 13,000

Mon·tes·so·ri method (mänt'ə sôr'ē) ⟦after M. *Montessori* (1870-1952), It educator⟧ a method of teaching young children, emphasizing training of the senses

Mon·te·vi·de·o (mänt'ə və dā'ō) capital & seaport of Uruguay: pop. 1,247,000

Mont·gom·er·y (munt gum'ər ē, -gum'rē) capital of Alabama: pop. 188,000

month (munth) ***n.*** ⟦OE *monath*⟧ **1** any of the twelve divisions of the calendar year **2** a period of four weeks or 30 days **3** one twelfth of the solar year

month'ly ***adj.*** done, happening, payable, etc. every month —***n., pl.*** **-lies** a periodical published once a month —***adv.*** once a month; every month

Mon·ti·cel·lo (män'tə sel'ō, -chel'ō) home & burial place of Thomas Jefferson, in central Virginia

Mont·pel·ier (mänt pēl'yər) capital of Vermont: pop. 8,200

Mon·tre·al (män'trē ôl') city & seaport in SW Quebec, Canada, on an island in the St. Lawrence River: pop. 1,016,000

mon·u·ment (män'yo͞o mənt) ***n.*** ⟦< L *monere,* remind⟧ **1** something set up to keep alive the memory of a person or event, as a tablet or statue **2** a work of enduring significance

mon'u·men'tal (-ment''l) ***adj.*** **1** of or serving as a monument **2** like a monument; massive, enduring, etc. **3** very great; colossal

moo (mo͞o) ***n., pl.*** **moos** ⟦echoic⟧ a cow's vocal sound —***vi.*** **mooed, moo'ing** to make this sound

mooch (mo͞och) ***vi., vt.*** ⟦ult. < OFr *muchier,* to hide⟧ [Slang] to get (food, money, etc.) by begging, imposition, etc. —**mooch'er** ***n.***

mood[1] (mo͞od) ***n.*** ⟦< OE *mod,* mind⟧ **1** a particular state of mind or feeling **2** a predominant or pervading feeling or spirit

mood[2] (mo͞od) ***n.*** ⟦< MODE⟧ a characteristic of verbs that indicates whether the action expressed is regarded as a fact, supposition, or command

mood'y ***adj.*** **-i·er, -i·est** **1** changing in mood **2** gloomy —**mood'i·ly** ***adv.*** —**mood'i·ness** ***n.***

moon (mo͞on) ***n.*** ⟦OE *mona*⟧ [*often* **M-**] **1** the celestial body that revolves around the earth once about every 29½ days **2** anything shaped like the moon (i.e., an orb or

THESAURUS

monolithic ***a.*** solid, unified, inflexible, unyielding; see also FIRM 1, UNITED.

monologue ***n.*** talk, speech, discourse; see ADDRESS 1.

monopolize ***v.*** engross, acquire, exclude, own exclusively, absorb, consume, manage, have, hold, corner, restrain, patent, copyright, corner the market.—*Ant.* INCLUDE, give, invite.

monopoly ***n.*** trust, syndicate, cartel; see BUSINESS 1.

monotonous ***a.*** **1** [Tiresome] tedious, wearisome, wearying; see DULL 4. **2** [Having but one tone] monotonic, unvarying, lacking variety, in one key, unchanged, reiterated, recurrent, single, uniform.—*Ant.* VARIOUS, varying, multiple.

monotony ***n.*** invariability, likeness, tediousness, tedium, similarity, continuity, continuance, oneness, evenness, levelness, flatness, the same old thing; see also BOREDOM.—*Ant.* VARIETY, difference, variability.

monsoon ***n.*** typhoon, hurricane, tempest; see STORM.

monster ***n.*** **1** [A great or imaginary beast] beastlike creature, centaur, monstrosity, sphinx, chimera, unicorn, dragon, griffin, cyclops, phoenix, mermaid, sea serpent, rhinoceros, elephant, werewolf. **2** [An unnatural creation] abnormality, monstrosity, malformation; see FREAK. **3** [An inhuman person] brute, beast, cruel person; see CRIMINAL, RASCAL.

monstrous ***a.*** **1** [Huge] stupendous, prodigious, enormous; see LARGE 1. **2** [Unnatural] abnormal, preposterous, uncanny; see UNNATURAL 1, UNUSUAL 2.

month ***n.*** measure of time, thirty days, one-twelfth of a year, four weeks. *Months of the year are the following:* January, February, March, April, May, June, July, August, September, October, November, December.

monthly ***a.*** once a month, every month, from month to month, menstrual, recurrent, cyclic, cyclical, repeated, rhythmic; punctually, steadily, methodically, periodically; see also REGULARLY.

monument ***n.*** **1** [Anything erected to preserve a memory] tomb, shaft, column, pillar, headstone, tombstone, gravestone, mausoleum, obelisk, shrine, statue, building, tower, monolith, tablet, slab, stone; see also MEMORIAL. **2** [A landmark in the history of creative work] work of art, magnum opus, permanent contribution; see ACHIEVEMENT, MASTERPIECE.

monumental ***a.*** lofty, impressive, majestic; see GRAND, GREAT 1.

mood[1,2] ***n.*** **1** [A state of mind] state, condition, frame of mind, temper, humor, disposition, inclination, caprice, whim, fancy, pleasure, freak, wish, desire, bent, propensity, tendency; see also ATTITUDE. **2** [Grammatical mode] aspect, inflection, mode. *Moods in English grammar include the following:* indicative, subjunctive, imperative.

moody ***a.*** pensive, unhappy, low-spirited; see SAD 1.

moon ***n.*** celestial body, heavenly body, planet, planetoid, satellite, crescent, new moon, half-moon, full moon, old moon, Luna*, Diana*, moon goddess, harvest moon, blue moon.

crescent) **3** any natural satellite of a planet —***vi.*** to behave in an idle or abstracted way

moon′beam′ ***n.*** a ray of moonlight

moon′light′ ***n.*** the light of the moon —***vi.*** to engage in moonlighting

moon′light′ing ***n.*** the holding of a second job along with one's main job

moon′lit′ ***adj.*** lighted by the moon

moon′scape′ (-skāp′) ***n.*** ⟦MOON + (LAND)SCAPE⟧ the surface of the moon or a representation of it

moon′shine′ ***n.*** **1** MOONLIGHT **2** [Inf.] whiskey unlawfully distilled —**moon′shin′er** ***n.***

moon′shot′ ***n.*** the launching of a spacecraft to the moon

moon′stone′ ***n.*** a feldspar with a pearly luster, used as a gem

moon′struck′ ***adj.*** **1** crazed; lunatic **2** romantically dreamy

moon′walk′ ***n.*** a walking about by an astronaut on the surface of the moon

moor[1] (moor) ***n.*** ⟦OE *mor*⟧ [Brit.] open wasteland covered with heather and often marshy

moor[2] (moor) ***vt.*** ⟦< ? MDu *maren,* to tie⟧ **1** to hold (a ship, etc.) in place by cables attached as to a pier **2** to secure —***vi.*** to moor a ship, etc.

Moor (moor) ***n.*** a member of a Muslim people of NW Africa —**Moor′ish** ***adj.***

moor′ing ***n.*** **1** [*often pl.*] the cables, etc. by which a ship is moored **2** [*pl.*] a place where a ship is moored

moose (mo͞os) ***n., pl.*** **moose** ⟦< AmInd⟧ a large deer of N regions, the male of which has broad, flat antlers

moot (mo͞ot) ***adj.*** ⟦< OE *mot*, a meeting⟧ **1** debatable **2** resolved and thus not worthy of discussion

mop (mäp) ***n.*** ⟦earlier *mappe*⟧ **1** a bundle of rags or yarns, a sponge, etc. fastened to the end of a stick, as for washing floors **2** anything suggesting this, as a thick head of hair —***vt.*** **mopped, mop′ping** to wash or wipe with a mop —**mop up** [Inf.] **1** to finish **2** to clear remnants of beaten enemy forces from

mope (mōp) ***vi.*** **moped, mop′ing** ⟦akin to MDu *mopen*⟧ to be gloomy and apathetic —**mop′ey, mop′y,** or **mop′ish** ***adj.***

mop·pet (mäp′it) ***n.*** ⟦< ME *moppe,* rag doll⟧ [Inf.] a little child

mo·raine (mə rān′) ***n.*** ⟦Fr⟧ a mass of rocks, sand, etc. left by a glacier

mor·al (môr′əl, mär′-) ***adj.*** ⟦< L *mos*, pl. *mores*, morals⟧ **1** dealing with, or capable of distinguishing between, right and wrong **2** of, teaching, or in accordance with the principles of right and wrong **3** good in conduct or character; specif., sexually virtuous **4** involving sympathy without action [*moral* support] **5** virtually such because of effects on thoughts or attitudes [a *moral* victory] **6** based on probability [a *moral* certainty] —***n.*** **1** a moral lesson taught by a fable, event, etc. **2** [*pl.*] principles or standards with respect to right or wrong in conduct —**mor′al·ly** ***adv.***

mo·rale (mə ral′) ***n.*** mental condition related to courage, confidence, enthusiasm, etc.

mor·al·ist (môr′əl ist) ***n.*** **1** a teacher of or writer on morals **2** one who seeks to impose personal morals on others —**mor′al·is′tic** ***adj.***

mo·ral·i·ty (mō ral′i tē, mə-) ***n., pl.*** **-ties** **1** rightness or wrongness, as of an action **2** right or moral conduct **3** moral principles

mor·al·ize (môr′əl īz′) ***vi.*** **-ized′, -iz′ing** to think, write, etc. about moral questions, often in a self-righteous or tedious way

mo·rass (mə ras′) ***n.*** ⟦< OFr *maresc*⟧ a bog; marsh; swamp: often used figuratively of a difficult or troublesome situation

mor·a·to·ri·um (môr′ə tôr′ē əm) ***n., pl.*** **-ri·ums** or **-ri·a** (-ə) ⟦< L *mora,* a delay⟧ **1** a legal authorization to delay payment of money due **2** any authorized delay of a specified activity

mo·ray (eel) (môr′ā) ⟦< Gr *myraina*⟧ a voracious, brilliantly colored eel

mor·bid (môr′bid) ***adj.*** ⟦< L *morbus,* disease⟧ **1** of or caused by disease; diseased **2** resulting as from a diseased state of mind **3** gruesome [*morbid* details] —**mor·bid′i·ty** ***n.*** —**mor′bid·ly** ***adv.***

mor·dant (môr′dənt) ***adj.*** ⟦< L *mordere,* to bite⟧ caustic; sarcastic —***n.*** a substance that fixes colors in dyeing —**mor′dan·cy** ***n.*** —**mor′dant·ly** ***adv.***

more (môr) ***adj.*** ⟦OE *mara*⟧ **1** greater in amount, degree, or number: comparative of MUCH or MANY **2** additional [take *more* tea] —***n.*** **1** a greater amount or degree **2** [*with pl. v.*] a greater number (*of*) **3** something additional —***adv.*** **1** in or to a greater degree or extent **2** in addition

more·o′ver ***adv.*** in addition to what has been said; besides

mo·res (môr′ēz′, -āz′) ***pl.n.*** ⟦L, customs⟧ ways of thinking, behaving, etc. that develop the force of law because most people follow them

morgue (môrg) ***n.*** ⟦Fr⟧ **1** a place where the bodies of unknown dead persons or those dead of unknown causes are temporarily kept **2** the file of back numbers, photographs, etc. kept as in a newspaper's office

mor·i·bund (môr′i bund′) ***adj.*** ⟦< L *mori,* to die⟧ dying

Mor·mon (môr′mən) ***n.*** a member of the Church of Jesus Christ of Latter-day Saints, founded (1830) in the U.S. —**Mor′mon·ism′** ***n.***

morn (môrn) ***n.*** [Old Poet.] morning

morn·ing (môr′niŋ) ***n.*** ⟦OE *morgen*⟧ the first or early part of the day, from midnight, or esp. dawn, to noon

morning glory a twining vine with trumpet-shaped flowers

morning sickness nausea, vomiting, etc. affecting many women early in pregnancy, occurring usually in the morning

mo·roc·co (mə rä′kō) ***n.*** ⟦< fol.⟧ a fine, soft leather

Mo·roc·co (mə rä′kō) kingdom on the NW coast of Africa: 274,461 sq. mi.; pop. 25,897,000 —**Mo·roc′can** ***adj., n.***

THESAURUS

moonlight ***n.*** effulgence, radiance, luminescence; see LIGHT 3.

moonshine ***n.*** **1** [Moonlight] effulgence, radiance, luminosity; see LIGHT 3. **2** [Whiskey distilled illicitly] mountain dew*, hooch*, white lightning*; see WHISKEY.

moot ***a.*** unsettled, debatable, disputable; see UNCERTAIN.

mop ***n.*** swab, duster, sweeper; see BROOM.

mop ***v.*** swab, wipe, rub, dab, pat, polish, wash, dust, wipe up; see also CLEAN. —**mop up*** finish off, dispatch, clean up; see DEFEAT 2, ELIMINATE.

mope ***v.*** fret, pine away, grieve, sorrow, sink, lose heart, brood, pine, yearn, despair, grumble, chafe, lament, regret, look glum, sulk, pull a long face*.—*Ant.* CELEBRATE, revive, cheer up.

moral ***a.*** **1** [Characterized by conventional virtues] trustworthy, kindly, courteous, respectable, proper, scrupulous, conscientious, good, truthful, decent, just, honorable, honest, high-minded, saintly, pure, worthy, correct, seemly, aboveboard, dutiful, principled, conscientious, chaste, ethical; see also NOBLE 1, 2, RELIABLE.—*Ant.* LYING, DISHONEST, unscrupulous. **2** [Having to do with approved relationships between the sexes] virtuous, immaculate, decent; see CHASTE, INNOCENT 2.

morale ***n.*** assurance, resolve, spirit; see CONFIDENCE.

morality ***n.*** righteousness, uprightness, ethics; see VIRTUE 1.

morally ***a.*** **1** [In accordance with accepted standards of conduct] conscientiously, truthfully, honestly, honorably, appropriately, respectably, courteously, scrupulously, ethically, correctly, in a principled manner, uprightly, righteously, trustworthily, decently, properly, in a manner approved by society; see also JUSTLY 1, SINCERELY.—*Ant.* WRONGLY, worthlessly, dishonorably. **2** [In a chaste manner] chastely, virtuously, purely; see MODESTLY.

morals ***n.*** ideals, customs, standards, mores, policies, beliefs, dogmas, social standards, principles; see also ETHICS.

morbid ***a.*** **1** [Diseased] sickly, unhealthy, ailing; see SICK. **2** [Pathological] gloomy, depressed, melancholic; see SAD 1.

more ***a.*** **1** [Additional] some more, over and above, more than that, in addition, further, besides, added; see also EXTRA.—*Ant.* LESS, less than, subtracted from. **2** [Greater in quantity, amount, degree, or quality] more numerous, exceeding, many more, much more, extra, expanded, augmented, increased, major, extended, enhanced, added to, larger, higher, wider, deeper, heavier, stronger, above the mark.—*Ant.* weaker, lessened, decreased.

moreover ***a.*** further, by the same token, furthermore; see BESIDES.

morning ***n.*** **1** [Dawn] morn, daybreak, break of day, first blush of morning, daylight, cockcrow, sunup, the wee small hours*, crack of dawn*. **2** [The time before noon] forenoon, morningtide*, after midnight, before noon, breakfast time, before lunch. —**good morning** good day, good morrow*, greetings; see HELLO.

mornings ***a.*** in the morning, every morning, before noon; see DAILY, REGULARLY.

mo·ron (môr′än′) ***n.*** ⟦< Gr *mōros,* foolish⟧ a very foolish or stupid person —**mo·ron′ic** ***adj.***

mo·rose (mə rōs′) ***adj.*** ⟦< L *mos,* manner⟧ ill-tempered; gloomy, sullen, etc. —**mo·rose′ly** ***adv.***

morph (môrf) ***vt., vi.*** to transform or be transformed as by morphing

mor·pheme (môr′fēm′) ***n.*** ⟦< Gr *morphē,* a form⟧ the smallest meaningful unit in a language, as an affix or base

mor·phine (môr′fēn′) ***n.*** ⟦after *Morpheus,* Gr god of dreams⟧ an alkaloid derived from opium and used in medicine to relieve pain

morph′ing ***n.*** ⟦< (META)MORPH(OSIS) + *-ing*⟧ a film or video process in which persons or objects seem to change form through a continuous series of images created by a computer

mor·phol·o·gy (môr fäl′ə jē) ***n.*** ⟦Ger < Gr *morphē,* form + Ger *-logie,* -LOGY⟧ the study of form and structure, as in biology or linguistics

mor·row (mär′ō, môr′-) ***n.*** ⟦< OE *morgen,* morning⟧ [Archaic] **1** morning **2** the next day

Morse (môrs) ***adj.*** ⟦after S. *Morse,* 19th-c. U.S. inventor⟧ [*often* **m-**] designating or of a code of dots and dashes used in telegraphy

mor·sel (môr′səl) ***n.*** ⟦< L *morsum,* a bite⟧ a small piece or amount, as of food

mor·tal (môrt′'l) ***adj.*** ⟦< L *mors,* death⟧ **1** that must eventually die **2** of a human being seen as a being who must eventually die **3** of death **4** causing physical or spiritual death; deadly; fatal **5** very intense *[mortal* terror*]* —***n.*** a human being —**mor′tal·ly** ***adv.***

mor·tal·i·ty (môr tal′ə tē) ***n.*** **1** the mortal nature of human beings **2** death on a large scale, as from war **3** the ratio of deaths to population

mor·tar (môrt′ər) ***n.*** ⟦< L *mortarium*⟧ **1** a bowl in which substances are pulverized with a pestle **2** a short-barreled cannon which hurls shells in a high trajectory **3** a mixture of cement or lime with sand and water, used to bind bricks or stones

mor′tar·board′ ***n.*** **1** a square board for holding mortar **2** an academic cap with a square, flat top

mort·gage (môr′gij) ***n.*** ⟦< OFr *mort,* dead + *gage,* pledge⟧ **1** the pledging of property to a creditor as security for the payment of a debt **2** the deed by which this is done —***vt.*** **-gaged, -gag·ing** **1** to pledge (property) by a mortgage **2** to put an advance claim on *[*to *mortgage* one's future*]* —**mort′ga·gor** or **mort′gag·er** (-gi jər) ***n.***

mort′ga·gee′ (-gə jē′) ***n.*** a person to whom property is mortgaged

mor·ti·cian (môr tish′ən) ***n.*** ⟦< L *mors,* death⟧ FUNERAL DIRECTOR

mor·ti·fy (môrt′ə fī′) ***vt.*** **-fied′, -fy′ing** ⟦< L *mors,* death + *facere,* make⟧ **1** to subdue (physical desires) by self-denial, fasting, etc. **2** to humiliate —**mor′ti·fi·ca′tion** ***n.***

mor·tise (môrt′is) ***n.*** ⟦< Ar *murtazza,* joined⟧ a hole or recess cut, as in a piece of wood, to receive a projecting part *(tenon)* shaped to fit into it

mor·tu·ar·y (môr′cho͞o er′ē) ***n.,*** *pl.* **-ies** a place where dead bodies are kept before burial or cremation; morgue or funeral home

mo·sa·ic (mō zā′ik) ***n.*** ⟦< L *musivus,* artistic⟧ **1** the making of pictures or designs by inlaying small bits of colored stone, etc. in mortar **2** a picture or design so made

Mo·sa·ic (mō zā′ik) ***adj.*** of Moses or the laws, etc. attributed to him

Mos·cow (mäs′kō, -kou′) capital of Russia, in the W part: pop. 8,769,000

Mo·ses (mō′zəz, -zəs) ***n.*** *Bible* the leader and lawgiver who brought the Israelites out of slavery in Egypt

mo·sey (mō′zē) ***vi.*** ⟦prob. < VAMOOSE⟧ [Slang] to stroll or amble along

Mos·lem (mäz′ləm) ***n., adj.*** MUSLIM

mosque (mäsk) ***n.*** ⟦< Ar *masjid,* temple⟧ a Muslim place of worship

mos·qui·to (mə skēt′ō) ***n.,*** *pl.* **-toes** or **-tos** ⟦Sp & Port < L *musca,* a fly⟧ a two-winged insect, the female of which sucks blood from animals, including humans

moss (môs, mäs) ***n.*** ⟦OE *mos,* a swamp⟧ a very small, green plant that grows in velvety clusters on rocks, trees, etc. —**moss′y, -i·er, -i·est,** ***adj.***

moss′back′ ***n.*** [Inf.] an old-fashioned or very conservative person

most (mōst) ***adj.*** ⟦OE *mast*⟧ **1** greatest in amount, degree, or number: superlative of MUCH or MANY **2** in the greatest number of instances *[most* fame is fleeting*]* —***n.*** **1** the greatest amount, quantity, or degree **2** [*with pl. v.*] the greatest number *(of)* —***adv.*** in or to the greatest degree or extent

most′ly ***adv.*** **1** for the most part **2** chiefly; principally **3** usually

mote (mōt) ***n.*** ⟦OE *mot*⟧ a speck, as of dust

mo·tel (mō tel′) ***n.*** ⟦< MO(TOR) + (HO)TEL⟧ a hotel for motorists

moth (môth) ***n.,*** *pl.* **moths** (môthz, môths) ⟦OE *moththe*⟧ a four-winged, chiefly night-flying insect, similar to the butterfly: the larvae of one kind feed on wool, etc.

moth′ball′ ***n.*** a small ball, as of naphthalene, the fumes of which repel moths from woolens, etc. —**in mothballs** put into storage or reserve

moth·er (mu*th*′ər) ***n.*** ⟦OE *modor*⟧ **1** a female parent **2** the origin or source of something **3** [*often* **M-**] a woman who is the head (**mother superior**) of a religious establishment —***adj.*** **1** of or like a mother **2** native *[mother* tongue*]* —***vt.*** **1** to be the mother of **2** to care for as a mother does —**moth′er·hood′** ***n.*** —**moth′er·less** ***adj.***

Mother Goose the imaginary creator of a collection of nursery rhymes

moth′er-in-law′ ***n.,*** *pl.* **moth′ers-in-law′** the mother of one's husband or wife

moth′er·land′ ***n.*** one's native land

moth′er·ly ***adj.*** of or like a mother; protective, nurturing, etc. —**moth′er·li·ness** ***n.***

moth′er-of-pearl′ ***n.*** the hard internal layer of the shell of the pearl oyster, etc., used to make buttons, etc.

mother tongue one's native language

mo·tif (mō tēf′) ***n.*** ⟦Fr: see MOTIVE⟧ **1** *Art, Literature, Music* a main theme for development **2** a repeated figure in a design

mo·tile (mōt′'l) ***adj.*** ⟦< L *movere,* to move⟧ *Biol.* capable of or exhibiting spontaneous motion —**mo·til′i·ty** ***n.***

mo·tion (mō′shən) ***n.*** ⟦< L *movere,* to move⟧ **1** a moving from one place to another; movement **2** a moving of a part of the body; specif., a gesture **3** a proposal formally made in an assembly —***vi.*** to make a meaningful move-

THESAURUS

moron ***n.*** imbecile, idiot, goose, simpleton, dullard, dolt, blockhead, cretin, dunce, dunderhead*, numskull, loony*, dummy*; see also FOOL.—*Ant.* PHILOSOPHER, sage, scientist.

moronic ***a.*** foolish, slow, dumb*; see STUPID.

morsel ***n.*** bite, chunk, piece; see BIT 1, PART 1.

mortal ***a.*** **1** [Causing death] malignant, fatal, lethal; see DEADLY, POISONOUS. **2** [Subject to death] human, transient, temporal, passing, frail, impermanent, perishable, fading, passing away, momentary; see also TEMPORARY.—*Ant.* ETERNAL, perpetual, everlasting.

mortal ***n.*** creature, being, human; see ANIMAL, MAN 1.

mortality ***n.*** dying, extinction, ending; see DEATH, DESTRUCTION 1.

mortgage ***n.*** lease, title, debt; see CONTRACT.

mortuary ***n.*** morgue, funeral parlor, funeral home; see FUNERAL.

moss ***n.*** lichen, Iceland moss, peat moss; see PLANT.

mossy ***a.*** tufted, velvety, plushy, downy, smooth, fresh, damp, moist, resilient, soft, covered, overgrown.—*Ant.* DRY, bare, prickly.

most ***a.*** nearly all, all but, not quite all, maximum, greatest, utmost, in the majority. —**at the most** in toto, not more than, at the outside; see MOST. —**make the most of** exploit, utilize, take advantage of; see USE 1.

mostly ***a.*** **1** [Frequently] often, many times, in many instances; see FREQUENTLY, REGULARLY. **2** [Largely] chiefly, essentially, for the most part; see PRINCIPALLY.

motel ***n.*** motor inn, inn, cabins, stopping place, roadhouse, court, motor court; see also HOTEL, RESORT 2.

moth ***n.*** silkworm moth, gypsy moth, clothes moth; see INSECT.

mother ***n.*** **1** [A female parent] parent, matriarch, dam*, mama, mammy*, mum*, ma*, mom*, mommy*, maw*, mater*; see also PARENT, RELATIVE. **2** [The source] fountainhead, source, beginning; see ORIGIN 2.

mother-in-law ***n.*** spouse's mother, mother by marriage, in-law*; see RELATIVE.

motherly ***a.*** maternal, devoted, careful, watchful, kind, warm, gentle, tender, sympathetic, supporting, protective, nurturing, caretaking; see also LOVING.

motion ***n.*** **1** [A movement] change, act, action; see MOVEMENT 2. **2** [The state of moving] passage, translating, changing; see MOVEMENT 1. **3** [An act formally proposed] suggestion, consideration, proposition; see PLAN 2. —**in motion** traveling, going, under way; see MOVING 1.

ment of the hand, etc.; gesture —*vt.* to direct by a meaningful gesture —**go through the motions** to do something as from habit, without enthusiasm, enjoyment, etc. —**in motion** moving —**mo'tion·less** *adj.*

motion picture FILM (*n.* 4)

motion sickness nausea, vomiting, etc. caused by the motion of a car, boat, etc.

mo·ti·vate (mōt'ə vāt') *vt.* **-vat'ed, -vat'ing** to provide with, or affect as, a motive; incite —**mo'ti·va'tion** *n.* —**mo'ti·va'tion·al** *adj.*

mo·tive (mōt'iv) *n.* ⟦< L *movere,* to move⟧ **1** an inner drive, impulse, etc. that causes one to act; incentive **2** MOTIF (sense 1)

-mo·tive (mōt'iv) *combining form* moving, of motion *[automotive]*

mot·ley (mät'lē) *adj.* ⟦< ?⟧ **1** of many colors **2** of many different or clashing elements

mo·to·cross (mō'tō krôs') *n.* ⟦Fr⟧ a cross-country race for lightweight motorcycles

mo·tor (mōt'ər) *n.* ⟦L < *movere,* to move⟧ **1** anything that produces motion **2** an engine; esp., an internal-combustion engine **3** a machine for converting electric energy into mechanical energy —*adj.* **1** producing motion **2** of or powered by a motor **3** of, by, or for motor vehicles **4** of or involving muscular movements *[motor* skills*]* —*vi.* to travel by automobile

mo'tor·bike' *n.* [Inf.] **1** a motor-driven bicycle **2** a light motorcycle

mo'tor·boat' *n.* a small motor-driven boat

mo'tor·cade' (-kād') *n.* ⟦MOTOR + -CADE⟧ an automobile procession

mo'tor·car' *n.* [Now Chiefly Brit.] an automobile

mo'tor·cy'cle (-sī'kəl) *n.* a two-wheeled vehicle propelled by an internal-combustion engine

motor home a motor vehicle with a truck chassis, outfitted as a traveling home

mo·tor·ist (mōt'ər ist) *n.* one who drives an automobile or travels by automobile

mo'tor·ize' (-īz') *vt.* **-ized', -iz'ing** to equip with a motor or with motor-driven vehicles

motor vehicle an automotive vehicle, esp. an automobile, truck, or bus

mot·tle (mät'’l) *vt.* **-tled, -tling** ⟦< MOTLEY⟧ to mark with blotches, etc. of different colors

mot·to (mät'ō) *n., pl.* **-toes** or **-tos** ⟦It, a word⟧ a word or saying that expresses the goals, ideals, etc. of a nation, group, etc.

mould (mōld) *n., vt., vi. chiefly Brit. sp. of* MOLD[1], MOLD[2], MOLD[3]

mould'ing *n. chiefly Brit. sp. of* MOLDING

mould'y *adj. chiefly Brit. sp. of* MOLDY

moult (mōlt) *vi. chiefly Brit. sp. of* MOLT

mound (mound) *n.* ⟦< ? MDu *mond,* protection⟧ a heap or bank of earth, sand, etc. —*vt.* to heap up

mount[1] (mount) *n.* ⟦< L *mons*⟧ a mountain

mount[2] (mount) *vi.* ⟦< L *mons,* mountain⟧ **1** to climb; ascend **2** to climb up on something, as onto a horse **3** to increase in amount —*vt.* **1** to go up; ascend *[to mount* stairs*]* **2** to get up on (a horse, platform, etc.) **3** to provide with horses *[mounted* police*]* **4** to place or fix (a jewel, picture, etc.) on or in the proper support, backing, etc. **5** to arrange (a dead animal, etc.) for exhibition **6** to place (a gun) into proper position for use **7** to prepare for and undertake (an expedition, etc.) —*n.* **1** the act of mounting **2** a horse, etc. for riding **3** the support, setting, etc. on or in which a thing is mounted

moun·tain (mount'’n) *n.* ⟦ult. < L *mons*⟧ **1** a natural raised part of the earth, larger than a hill **2** a large pile, amount, etc. —*adj.* of or in the mountains

mountain bike a heavy-duty bicycle with wide tires for use on and off regular road surfaces

moun'tain·eer' (-ir') *n.* **1** one who lives in a mountainous region **2** a mountain climber

mountain goat a long-haired, goatlike antelope of the Rocky Mountains

mountain lion COUGAR

moun'tain·ous *adj.* **1** full of mountains **2** huge

mountain sickness weakness, nausea, etc. caused by thin air at high altitudes

Mountain State any of the eight states of the W U.S. through which the Rocky Mountains pass; Montana, Idaho, Wyoming, Nevada, Utah, Colorado, Arizona, or New Mexico

moun·te·bank (mount'ə baŋk') *n.* ⟦It *montambanco,* lit., mounted on a bench: orig. a person on a bench, or platform, selling quack medicines⟧ a charlatan or quack

mount'ed *adj.* **1** on horseback, a bicycle, etc. **2** on or in a mounting

mount'ing *n.* something serving as a backing, support, setting, etc.

THESAURUS

motionless *a.* **1** [Not moving] still, unmoving, dead, deathly still, inert, stock-still, stagnant, quiet.—*Ant.* MOVING, CHANGING, shifting. **2** [Firm] unmovable, fixed, stationary; see FIRM 1.

motion picture *n.* moving picture, cinema, film; see MOVIE.

motivate *v.* impel, inspire hope, stimulate, incite, propel, spur, goad, move, induce, prompt, arouse, whet, instigate, fire up*, provoke, cause, touch off, egg on, trigger; see also DRIVE 1, EXCITE, URGE 2.

motive *n.* cause, purpose, idea; see REASON 3.

motor *n.* machine, device, instrument; see ENGINE. *Types of motors include the following:* internal-combustion engine, diesel engine, steam engine, external-combustion engine; radial, airplane, automobile, truck, AC electric, DC electric.

motorboat *n.* speedboat, putt-putt*, powerboat, racer; see also BOAT. *Types of motorboats include the following:* open, outboard, electric-powered, gasoline-powered; cruiser, runabout.

motorcycle *n.* motorized two-wheeled vehicle, cycle, hog*, bike*, chopper*; see also VEHICLE.

motorist *n.* automobile operator, traveler, car pool member; see DRIVER.

motorized *a.* motor-driven, motor-powered, electric-driven, gasoline-driven, oil-driven, motor-equipped, motor-operated.

motto *n.* maxim, adage, saw, epigram, aphorism, sentiment, slogan, catchword, axiom; see also PROVERB, SAYING. *Familiar mottoes include the following:* in God we trust, *e pluribus unum* (Latin), time flies, seize the day, make hay while the sun shines, rest in peace, peace be with you, one for all and all for one, home sweet home, God bless our home, don't tread on me, give me liberty or give me death, all or nothing, you can't take it with you, all men are created equal, for God and country, what's worth doing is worth doing well, don't give up the ship, don't fire until you see the whites of their eyes; remember the Alamo, remember the Maine, remember Pearl Harbor, etc.; my country, right or wrong; praise the Lord and pass the ammunition, put your trust in God and keep your powder dry; abandon hope, all ye who enter here; to err is human, to forgive, divine; liberty, equality, fraternity; I came, I saw, I conquered; Pikes Peak or bust*.

mound *n.* pile, heap, knoll; see HILL.

mount[2] *v.* **1** [To rise] ascend, arise, uprise; see RISE 1. **2** [To climb] ascend, scale, clamber; see CLIMB.

mountain *n.* **1** [A lofty land mass] mount, elevation, peak, sierra, butte, hill, alp, range, ridge, pike, bluff, headland, volcano, crater, tableland, mesa, plateau, height, crag, precipice, cliff, earth mass.—*Ant.* VALLEY, ravine, flatland. *Famous chains of mountains include the following:* Alps, Himalayas, Caucasus, Urals, Pyrenees, Andes, Rockies, Canadian Rockies, Appalachians, Cascades, Adirondacks, White Mountains, Sierra Nevada, Sierra Madre, Ozarks, Smokies, Cordilleras, Apennines. *Famous peaks include the following:* Mont Blanc, Mt. Etna, Vesuvius, the Matterhorn, Pikes Peak, Mt. Whitney, Mt. Shasta, Mt. Washington, Mt. McKinley, Krakatau, Pelée, Popocatépetl, Mt. Everest, Annapurna, Mount of Olives, Mt. Sinai, Fuji, Mt. Kilimanjaro, Mt. St. Helens, Mt. Rainier, K2. **2** [A pile] mass, mound, glob; see HEAP.

mountaineer *n.* mountain man, mountain dweller, hillman, highlander, uplander, native of mountains, mountain climber, rock climber, mountain guide, mountain scaler, hillbilly*.

mountainous *a.* mountainlike, with mountains, difficult, barbarous, wild, untamed, strange, remote, uncivilized, rude, unpopulated, solitary, unfamiliar, isolated, steep, lofty, hilly, alpine, upland, elevated, volcanic, towering, craggy, rugged.—*Ant.* LOW, small, flat.

mounted *a.* **1** [On horseback] seated, riding, in the saddle, cavalry, horsed*, up.—*Ant.* AFOOT, unhorsed, dismounted. **2** [Firmly fixed] supported, set, attached; see FIRM 1. **3** [Backed] pasted on, set off, strengthened; see REINFORCED.

mourn (môrn) ***vi., vt.*** ⟦OE *murnan*⟧ **1** to feel or express sorrow for (something regrettable) **2** to grieve for (someone who has died) **—mourn'er *n.***

mourn'ful *adj.* **1** feeling or expressing grief or sorrow **2** causing sorrow

mourn'ing *n.* **1** the expression of grief, esp. at someone's death **2** black clothes, etc., worn as such an expression **3** the period during which one mourns

mouse (mous; *for v., also* mouz) ***n., pl.*** **mice** ⟦OE *mus*⟧ **1** any of many small rodents, esp. a species that commonly infests buildings **2** a timid person **3** [Slang] a black eye **4** a hand-held device for controlling the video display of a computer **—*vi.* moused, mous'ing** to hunt mice

mousse (mo͞os) ***n.*** ⟦Fr, foam⟧ **1** a light, chilled dessert made with egg white, whipped cream, etc. **2** an aerosol foam used to keep hair in place, etc. **—*vt.* moussed, mouss'ing** to style (hair) using mousse

mous·tache (mus'tash', məs tash') ***n. alt. sp. of*** MUSTACHE

mous·y (mous'ē, mouz'-) ***adj.* -i·er, -i·est** of or like a mouse; specif., quiet, timid, drab, etc.: also **mous'ey —mous'i·ness *n.***

mouth (mouth; *for v.* mouth) ***n., pl.*** **mouths** (mouthz) ⟦OE *muth*⟧ **1** the opening in the head through which food is taken in and sounds are made **2** any opening regarded as like this [the *mouth* of a jar, river, etc.] **—*vt.* 1** to say, esp. insincerely **2** to form (a word) with the mouth silently **—down in** (or **at**) **the mouth** [Inf.] unhappy **—mouth off** [Slang] to talk loudly, impudently, etc.

mouth'ful' *n., pl.* -fuls' 1 as much as the mouth can hold **2** as much as is usually taken into the mouth **3** [Slang] a pertinent remark: chiefly in **say a mouthful**

mouth organ HARMONICA

mouth'piece' *n.* **1** a part, as of a musical instrument, held in or to the mouth **2** a person, periodical, etc. which expresses the views as of a group

mouth'wash' *n.* a flavored, often antiseptic liquid for rinsing the mouth

mouth'wa'ter·ing *adj.* appetizing; tasty

mouth'y *adj.* -i·er, -i·est talkative, esp. in a bombastic or rude way **—mouth'i·ness *n.***

mou·ton (mo͞o'tän') ***n.*** ⟦Fr, sheep⟧ lambskin or sheepskin made to resemble beaver, seal, etc.

mov·a·ble (mo͞o'və bəl) ***adj.*** that can be moved from one place to another **—*n.* 1** something movable **2** *Law* personal property, esp. furniture: *usually used in pl.* Also **move'a·ble**

move (mo͞ov) ***vt.* moved, mov'ing** ⟦< L *movere*⟧ **1** to change the place or position of **2** to set or keep in motion **3** to cause (*to do, say,* etc.) **4** to arouse the emotions, etc. of **5** to propose formally, as in a meeting **—*vi.* 1** to change place or position **2** to change one's residence **3** to be active **4** to make progress **5** to take action **6** to be, or be set, in motion **7** to make a formal application (*for*) **8** to evacuate: said of the bowels **9** to be sold: said of goods **—*n.* 1** act of moving **2** an action toward some goal **3** a change of residence **4** *Chess, Checkers, etc.* the act of moving a piece, or one's turn to move **—move up** to promote or be promoted **—on the move** [Inf.] moving about from place to place

move'ment *n.* **1** a moving or manner of moving **2** an evacuation (of the bowels) **3** a change in the location of troops, etc. **4** organized action by people working toward a goal **5** the moving parts of a mechanism, as of a clock **6** *Music a*) a principal division of a symphony, etc. *b*) rhythm

mov·er (mo͞o'vər) ***n.*** one that moves; specif., one whose work is moving furniture, etc. for those changing residence

mov'ie (-vē) ***n.*** ⟦< *moving picture*⟧ FILM (*n.* 4) **—the movies 1** the film industry **2** a showing of a film

moving van a large van for transporting belongings, as of a person moving to a new residence

THESAURUS

mourn *v.* deplore, grieve, fret, sorrow, rue, regret, bemoan, sigh, long for, miss, droop, languish, yearn, pine, anguish, complain, agonize, weep, suffer, wring one's hands, be brokenhearted, be in distress, be sad.—*Ant.* CELEBRATE, rejoice, be happy.

mourner *n.* lamenter, griever, keener, weeper, wailer, sorrower, pallbearer, friend of the deceased, member of the family.

mournful *a.* sorrowful, mourning, unhappy; see SAD 1.

mourning *n.* **1** [The act of expressing grief] sorrowing, grieving, yearning, sorrow, lamentation, pining, sighing, regretting, deploring, weeping over, wailing, crying, moaning, murmuring, complaining, sobbing; see also DEPRESSION 2, GRIEF, SADNESS.—*Ant.* CELEBRATION, rejoicing, being glad. **2** [Symbols of mourning] black, sackcloth and ashes, arm band, mourning veil, widow's weeds, black suit, black tie.

mouse *n.* rodent, vermin, rat; see ANIMAL.

mouth *n.* **1** [The principal facial opening] *Parts of the mouth include the following:* lips, roof, floor, tongue, jaws, gums, teeth, soft palate, alveolar ridge, hard palate, uvula. **2** [Any opening resembling a mouth] orifice, entrance, aperture; see ENTRANCE 2. **3** [The end of a river] estuary, firth, delta, portal, harbor, roads, sound, tidewater. **—down in** (or **at**) **the mouth*** depressed, discouraged, unhappy; see SAD 1. **—have a big mouth*** talk loudly, exaggerate, brag; see TALK 1.

mouthful *n.* portion, piece, morsel; see BITE 1.

movable *a.* not fastened, portable, adjustable, adaptable, not fixed, transportable, ambulatory, mobile, detachable, turnable, removable, separable, transferable, loose, unfastened, free, unattached, in parts, in sections, knocked down, on wheels.—*Ant.* FIXED, fastened, stationary.

move *n.* action, transit, progress; see MOVEMENT 1, 2. **—get a move on*** go faster, start moving, get cracking*; see HURRY 1. **—on the move*** moving, busy, acting; see ACTIVE.

move *v.* **1** [To be in motion] go, walk, run, glide, travel, drift, budge, stir, shift, pass, cross, roll, flow, march, travel, progress, proceed, traverse, drive, ride, fly, hurry, head for, bustle, climb, crawl, leap, hop to it*, get a move on*, scooch*, get going, get cracking*; see also ADVANCE 1.—*Ant.* STOP, remain stationary, stay quiet. **2** [To set in motion] impel, actuate, propel; see PUSH 2. **3** [To arouse the emotions of] influence, stir, instigate, stimulate, touch, play on, sway, induce, rouse, prevail upon, work upon, strike a sympathetic chord; see also DRIVE 1, ENCOURAGE, EXCITE.—*Ant.* QUIET, lull, pacify. **4** [To take up another residence] pack up, move out, move in; see LEAVE 1. **5** [To propose an action formally] suggest, introduce, submit; see PROPOSE 1. **—move up** go forward, do well, get ahead; see ADVANCE 1, RISE 1.

moved *a.* **1** [Transported] conveyed, carried, taken, shifted, transferred, reassigned, changed, flown, driven, drawn, pushed, lifted, elevated, lowered, let down, displaced, withdrawn, replaced, sent abroad, trucked, hauled, dragged; see also SENT. **2** [Gone to a different residence] emigrated, migrated, vacated, removed, departed, gone away, changed residences, left, gone for good; see also GONE 1.—*Ant.* RESIDENT, remaining, still here. **3** [Proposed] recommended, submitted, introduced; see PROPOSED, SUGGESTED. **4** [Excited] disturbed, stimulated, upset; see EXCITED.

movement *n.* **1** [The act of moving] move, transit, passage, progress, journey, advance, mobility, change, shift, alteration, ascension, descent, propulsion, flow, flux, action, flight, wandering, journeying, voyaging, migration, emigration, immigration, transplanting, evolving, shifting, changing, locomotion, drive, evolution, undertaking, regression.—*Ant.* QUIET, rest, fixity. **2** [An example of movement] journey, trip, immigration, migration, march, crusade, patrol, sweep, emigration, evolution, unrest, transition, change, transfer, displacement, withdrawal, ascension, descent, progression, regression, transportation, removal, departure, shift, flight, slip, slide, step, footfall, stride, gesture, act, action, pilgrimage, expedition, locomotion. **3** [A trend] drift, tendency, bent; see INCLINATION 1.

movie *n.* moving picture, motion picture, photoplay, cinema, film, show, screenplay, cartoon, animated cartoon, serial, comedy, foreign film, travelogue, short, documentary, feature film, videotape, flick*; see also DRAMA.

movies *n.* **1** [A showing of a moving picture] motion picture, film, photoplay; see MOVIE. **2** [The motion picture industry] moving pictures, the cinematic industry, Hollywood, the screen world, the silver screen*, the industry*, pictures*, the flicks*, celluloids*.

moving *a.* **1** [In motion] going, changing, progressing, advancing, shifting, evolving, withdrawing, rising, going down, descending, ascending, getting up, traveling, journeying, on the march, moving up, starting, proceeding, flying, climbing, uptempo, on the jump*, going great guns*. **2** [Going to another residence] migrating, emigrating, vacating, removing, departing, leaving, going away, changing residences. **3** [Exciting] affecting, emotional, touching; see EXCITING.

mow[1] (mō) ***vt.***, ***vi.*** **mowed**, **mowed** or **mown** (mōn), **mow'ing** ⟦OE *mawan*⟧ to cut down (grass, etc.) from (a lawn, etc.) —**mow down** **1** to cause to fall like cut grass **2** to overwhelm (an opponent) —**mow'er** ***n.***

mow[2] (mou) ***n.*** ⟦OE *muga*⟧ a heap of hay, etc., esp. in a barn

Mo·zam·bique (mō'zəm bēk') country in SE Africa: 308,642 sq. mi.; pop. 11,674,000

Mo·zart (mō'tsärt'), **Wolf·gang A·ma·de·us** (vôlf'gäŋk' ä'mä dā'o͝os) 1756-91; Austrian composer

MP *abbrev.* **1** Member of Parliament **2** Military Police

mpg *abbrev.* miles per gallon

mph *abbrev.* miles per hour

Mr. or **Mr** (mis'tər) *abbrev.* mister: used before a man's name or title: pl. *Messrs*

MRI ***n.*** ⟦*m(agnetic) r(esonance) i(maging)*⟧ imaging by means of atomic nuclei in a strong magnetic field, used in medical diagnosis

Mrs. or **Mrs** (mis'iz) *abbrev.* mistress: now used before a married woman's name: pl. *Mmes*

MS *abbrev.* **1** manuscript: also **ms** **2** Master of Science: also **M.S.**, **MSc**, or **M.Sc.** **3** Mississippi **4** multiple sclerosis

Ms. or **Ms** (miz) *abbrev.* a title, free of reference to marital status, used in place of *Miss* or *Mrs.*

MSG *abbrev.* monosodium glutamate

Msgr *abbrev.* Monsignor

MST *abbrev.* Mountain Standard Time

MSW or **M.S.W.** *abbrev.* Master of Social Work

Mt *abbrev.* **1** Mount **2** Mountain

MT *abbrev.* **1** Montana **2** megaton **3** Mountain Time

mtg *abbrev.* **1** meeting **2** mortgage: also **mtge**

MTV *trademark for* Music Television

mu (mo͞o, myo͞o) ***n.*** the 12th letter of the Greek alphabet (Μ, μ)

much (much) ***adj.*** **more**, **most** ⟦< OE *mycel*⟧ great in quantity, degree, etc. —***adv.*** **more**, **most** **1** to a great degree or extent *[much* happier*]* **2** nearly *[much* the same*]* —***n.*** **1** a great amount **2** something great or outstanding *[*not *much* to look at*]*

mu·ci·lage (myo͞o'si lij') ***n.*** ⟦< L *mucere*, be moldy⟧ **1** a thick, sticky substance in certain plants **2** any watery solution of gum, glue, etc. used as an adhesive

muck (muk) ***n.*** ⟦ME *muk*⟧ **1** moist manure **2** black earth with decaying matter, used as fertilizer **3** mud; dirt; filth —**muck'y**, **-i·er**, **-i·est**, ***adj.***

muck'rake' ***vi.*** **-raked'**, **-rak'ing** ⟦see prec. & RAKE[1]⟧ to search for and publicize real or alleged corruption in politics, etc. —**muck'rak'er** ***n.***

mu·cous (myo͞o'kəs) ***adj.*** **1** of, containing, or secreting mucus **2** slimy

mucous membrane a mucus-secreting lining of certain body cavities

mu·cus (myo͞o'kəs) ***n.*** ⟦L⟧ the thick, slimy substance secreted by the mucous membranes for moistening and protection

mud (mud) ***n.*** ⟦ME⟧ **1** wet, soft, sticky earth **2** defamatory remarks

mud·dle (mud''l) ***vt.*** **-dled**, **-dling** ⟦< prec.⟧ **1** to mix up; bungle **2** to confuse mentally; befuddle —***vi.*** to act or think confusedly —***n.*** **1** a mess, jumble, etc. **2** mental confusion

mud'dle-head'ed ***adj.*** confused

mud'dy ***adj.*** **-di·er**, **-di·est** **1** full of or spattered with mud **2** not clear; cloudy *[muddy* coffee*]* **3** confused, obscure, etc. *[muddy* thinking*]* —***vt.***, ***vi.*** **-died**, **-dy·ing** to make or become muddy —**mud'di·ness** ***n.***

mud flat low, muddy land that floods at high tide

mud'sling'ing ***n.*** the making of unscrupulous, malicious attacks, as against a political opponent —**mud'sling'er** ***n.***

mu·ez·zin (myo͞o ez'in) ***n.*** ⟦< Ar *adhana*, proclaim⟧ a Muslim crier who calls the people to prayer

muff (muf) ***n.*** ⟦< Fr *moufle*, mitten⟧ **1** a cylindrical covering, as of fur, to warm the hands **2** any bungled action —***vt.*** to bungle; specif., to miss (a catch, etc.)

muf·fin (muf'ən) ***n.*** ⟦< ?⟧ a quick bread baked in a cup-shaped mold

muf·fle (muf'əl) ***vt.*** **-fled**, **-fling** ⟦prob. < OFr *moufle*, mitten⟧ **1** to wrap or cover so as to keep warm, deaden sound, etc. **2** to deaden (a sound)

muf'fler (-lər) ***n.*** **1** a scarf worn around the throat, as for warmth **2** a device for deadening noise, esp. of a car's exhaust

muf·ti (muf'tē) ***n.***, *pl.* **-tis** ⟦< Ar⟧ ordinary clothes, esp. when worn by one usually wearing a uniform

mug (mug) ***n.*** ⟦prob. < Scand⟧ **1** a cup made of earthenware or metal, with a handle **2** as much as a mug will hold **3** [Slang] the face —***vt.*** **mugged**, **mug'ging** to assault, usually with intent to rob —***vi.*** [Slang] to grimace, esp. in overacting —**mug'ger** ***n.***

mug·gy (mug'ē) ***adj.*** **-gi·er**, **-gi·est** ⟦< dial. *mug*, mist⟧ hot, damp, and close —**mug'gi·ness** ***n.***

mug shot a police photograph of the face of a criminal or suspect

Mu·ham·mad (mo͞o ham'əd) *var. of* MOHAMMED

muk·luk (muk'luk') ***n.*** ⟦Esk *muklok*, a seal⟧ an Eskimo boot of sealskin or reindeer skin

mu·lat·to (mə lät'ō, -lat'ō) ***n.***, *pl.* **-toes** or **-tos** ⟦Sp & Port *mulato*⟧ a person who has one black parent and one white parent

mul·ber·ry (mul'ber'ē, -bər ē) ***n.***, *pl.* **-ries** ⟦< OE *morberie*⟧ **1** a tree with purplish-red, edible, berrylike fruit **2** the fruit

mulch (mulch) ***n.*** ⟦ME *molsh*, soft⟧ leaves, straw, etc., spread around plants to prevent freezing of roots, etc. —***vt.*** to apply mulch to

mulct (mulkt) ***vt.*** ⟦< L *mul(c)ta*, a fine⟧ **1** to fine **2** to take (money, etc.) from (someone) by fraud —***n.*** a fine

mule[1] (myo͞ol) ***n.*** ⟦< L *mulus*⟧ **1** the offspring of a jackass and a female horse **2** [Inf.] a stubborn person **3** [Slang] a drug smuggler

mule[2] (myo͞ol) ***n.*** ⟦< L *mulleus*, red shoe⟧ a lounging slipper that does not cover the heel

mu·le·teer (myo͞o'lə tir') ***n.*** ⟦OFr *muletier*⟧ a driver of mules: also [Inf.] **mule skin·ner** (skin'ər)

mul'ish ***adj.*** stubborn; obstinate

mull[1] (mul) ***vt.***, ***vi.*** ⟦ME *mullen*, to grind⟧ to ponder (*over*)

THESAURUS

mow[1] ***v.*** scythe, reap, cut; see HARVEST.

much ***a.*** **1** [To a great degree or extent] considerably, greatly, vastly, enormously, significantly, notably, remarkably; see also ESPECIALLY 1. **2** [Great in amount or degree] abundant, satisfying, enough, sufficient, adequate, considerable, substantial, ample, everywhere, copious, voluminous, plentiful, profuse, complete, lavish, generous, immeasurable, endless, countless, extravagant, hell of a lot*.—*Ant.* INADEQUATE, insufficient, limited. —**as much as** practically, virtually, in effect; see ALMOST, EQUAL. —**too much** excess, waste, extravagance, overabundance, superfluity, preposterousness, overcharge, ever so much, more than can be used, vastness, prodigiousness, immensity; see also EXCESS 1.—*Ant.* LACK, want, shortage.

much ***n.*** a great quantity, abundance, quantities, a great deal, riches, wealth, volume, very much, breadth, plentifulness, fullness, completeness, lavishness, a lot*, lots*, quite a bit*, gobs*, thousands*, tons*, oodles*; see also PLENTY.—*Ant.* LITTLE, penury, scarcity. —**make much of** treat as of great importance, expand, exaggerate; see OVERDO 1. —**not much of a** inferior, mediocre, unsatisfactory; see POOR 2.

muck ***n.*** refuse, dung, waste; see TRASH 1.

mucus ***n.*** phlegm, slime, expectoration, spit, snot*.

mud ***n.*** dirt, muck, clay, mire, slush, silt, muddiness, stickiness, ooze, bog, marsh, swamp.

muddle ***n.*** trouble, disarrangement, disarray; see CONFUSION, DISORDER.

muddle ***v.*** stir up, disarrange, entangle, foul, mix, jumble, derange, shake up, mess, botch, clutter, snarl, complicate, disorder; see also CONFUSE.

muddled ***a.*** uncertain, addled, perplexed; see CONFUSED 2.

muddy ***a.*** **1** [Containing sediment] stirred, dull, dark, cloudy, murky, indistinct, roiled, roily, confused, obscure, opaque; see also DIRTY 1.—*Ant.* CLEAR, translucent, pellucid. **2** [Deep with mud] sloppy, swampy, soggy, sodden, slushy, watery, boggy, soaked.—*Ant.* DRY, barren, parched.

muffle ***v.*** deaden, mute, stifle; see DECREASE 2, SOFTEN.

muffled ***a.*** suppressed, stifled, indistinct; see OBSCURE 1.

muffler ***n.*** chest protector, scarf, neckpiece, babushka, neckerchief, kerchief, neckband, neckcloth, Ascot, choker, mantle, stole; see also CLOTHES.

mug ***n.*** vessel, stein, flagon; see CUP.

muggy ***a.*** damp, humid, moist; see WET 1.

mule[1] ***n.*** hinny, donkey, burro; see ANIMAL.

mull[1] ***v.*** reflect, meditate, ponder; see THINK 1.

mull² (mul) *vt.* ⟦< ?⟧ to heat, sweeten, and spice (wine, cider, etc.)

mul·let (mul′it) *n.* ⟦< L *mullus*⟧ an edible, spiny-finned fish of fresh and salt waters

mul·li·gan stew (mul′i gən) a stew made of bits of meat and vegetables, esp. as by hobos

mul·li·ga·taw·ny (mul′i gə tô′nē) *n.* ⟦Tamil *milagutaṇṇir*, lit., pepper water⟧ an East Indian soup of meat, etc., flavored with curry

mul·lion (mul′yən) *n.* ⟦prob. < OFr *moien*, median⟧ a vertical dividing bar, as between windowpanes

multi- ⟦L < *multus*, many⟧ *combining form* **1** having many **2** more than two **3** many times more than

mul·ti·cul·tur·al·ism (mul′tē kul′chər əl iz′əm) *n.* the practice of giving equal emphasis to the needs and contributions of all cultural groups, esp. traditionally underrepresented minority groups, in a society —**mul′ti·cul′tur·al** *adj.*

mul′ti·fac′et·ed (-fas′ət id) *adj.* having a variety of features, parts, etc. *[a multifaceted* career*]*

mul·ti·far·i·ous (mul′tə far′ē əs) *adj.* ⟦< L⟧ having many kinds of parts or elements; diverse

mul·ti·lat·er·al (mul′ti lat′ər əl) *adj.* involving more than two parties, nations, etc.

mul′ti·lin′gual *adj.* of, in, or capable of using several languages

mul′ti·me′di·a (-mē′dē ə) *adj.* combining or using several media, as film and live performance or TV, radio, and printed matter

mul′ti·mil′lion·aire′ *n.* one whose wealth amounts to many millions of dollars, pounds, etc.

mul′ti·na′tion·al *adj.* **1** of many nations **2** having offices, etc. in many nations —*n.* a multinational corporation

mul·ti·ple (mul′tə pəl) *adj.* ⟦< L *multiplex*⟧ **1** having many parts, elements, etc. **2** shared by or involving many —*n.* a number which is a product of some specified number and another number

mul′ti·ple-choice′ *adj.* listing several answers from which the correct one is to be chosen

multiple sclerosis a disease of the central nervous system, with loss of muscular coordination, etc.

mul·ti·plex (mul′tə pleks′) *adj.* ⟦L, multiple⟧ designating a system for sending two or more signals simultaneously over a common circuit, etc. —*n.* a film-theater complex with three or more screens —**mul′ti·plex′er** or **mul′ti·plex′or** *n.*

mul′ti·pli·cand′ (-pli kand′) *n.* a number to be multiplied by another

mul′ti·pli·ca′tion (-pli kā′shən) *n.* a multiplying or being multiplied; specif., the process of finding the quantity obtained by repeated additions of a specified quantity a specified number of times

mul′ti·plic′i·ty (-plis′ə tē) *n.* a great number or variety (*of*)

mul′ti·pli′er (-plī′ər) *n.* the number by which another is to be multiplied

mul′ti·ply′ (-plī′) *vt., vi.* **-plied′**, **-ply′ing** ⟦see MULTIPLE⟧ **1** to increase in number, degree, etc. **2** to find the product (of) by multiplication

mul·ti·proc·es·sor (mul′ti prä′ses′ər) *n.* a computer system capable of processing many programs at once

mul′ti·stage′ *adj.* having more than one stage, as a missile, process, etc.

mul·ti·tude (mul′tə to͞od′) *n.* ⟦< L *multus*, many⟧ a large number; host

mul′ti·tu′di·nous (-to͞od′n əs) *adj.* very numerous; many

mum¹ (mum) *n.* [Inf.] a chrysanthemum

mum² (mum) *adj.* ⟦ME *momme*⟧ silent; not speaking

mum·ble (mum′bəl) *vt., vi.* **-bled**, **-bling** ⟦ME *momelen*⟧ to speak or say indistinctly; mutter —*n.* a mumbled utterance —**mum′bler** *n.*

mum·bo jum·bo (mum′bō jum′bō) ⟦of Afr orig.⟧ meaningless ritual, talk, etc.

mum·mer (mum′ər) *n.* ⟦< OFr *momo*, grimace⟧ an actor, esp. one who wears a mask or costume

mum·mi·fy (mum′ə fī′) *vt., vi.* **-fied′**, **-fy′ing** to make into or become (like) a mummy

mum·my (mum′ē) *n., pl.* **-mies** ⟦ult. < Pers *mum*, wax⟧ a dead body preserved by embalming, as by the ancient Egyptians

mumps (mumps) *n.* ⟦< obs. *mump*, a grimace⟧ an acute communicable disease characterized by swelling of the salivary glands

mun *abbrev.* municipal

munch (munch) *vt., vi.* ⟦ME *monchen*⟧ to chew steadily, often with a crunching sound

mun·dane (mun′dān′, mun dān′) *adj.* ⟦< L *mundus*, world⟧ **1** of the world; worldly **2** commonplace, ordinary, etc. —**mun′dane′ly** *adv.*

Mu·nich (myo͞o′nik) city in SE Germany: pop. 1,256,000

mu·nic·i·pal (myo͞o nis′ə pəl) *adj.* ⟦< L *municeps*, inhabitant of a free town⟧ of or having to do with a city, town, etc. or its local government

mu·nic′i·pal′i·ty (-pal′ə tē) *n., pl.* **-ties** a city, town, etc. having its own incorporated government

mu·nif·i·cent (myo͞o nif′ə sənt) *adj.* ⟦< L *munus*, a gift + *facere*, make⟧ very generous; lavish —**mu·nif′i·cence** *n.*

mu·ni·tions (myo͞o nish′ənz) *pl.n.* ⟦< L *munire*, fortify⟧ weapons and ammunition for war

mu·ral (myoor′əl) *adj.* ⟦< L *murus*, wall⟧ of, on, or for a wall —*n.* a picture, esp. a large one, painted directly on a wall —**mu′ral·ist** *n.*

mur·der (mur′dər) *n.* ⟦OE *morthor*⟧ **1** the unlawful and malicious or premeditated killing of a person **2** [Inf.] something very hard, unsafe, etc. to do or deal with —*vt.* **1** to kill (a person) unlawfully and with malice **2** to spoil, mar, etc., as in performance *[to murder* a song*]* —**mur′der·er** *n.* —**mur′der·ess** *fem.n.*

mur′der·ous *adj.* **1** of or characteristic of murder; brutal **2** capable or guilty of, or intending, murder —**mur′der·ous·ly** *adv.*

murk (murk) *n.* ⟦< ON *myrkr*, dark⟧ darkness; gloom

murk′y *adj.* **-i·er**, **-i·est** dark or gloomy —**murk′i·ness** *n.*

mur·mur (mur′mər) *n.* ⟦< L⟧ **1** a low, steady sound **2** a mumbled complaint **3** *Med.* an abnormal sound in the

THESAURUS

multiple *a.* **1** [Various] complicated, more than one, many, manifold, compound, having many uses, multifold, multitudinous, aggregated, many-sided, versatile, increased, varied, compound, added; see also VARIOUS.—*Ant.* SIMPLE, UNITED, centralized. **2** [Repeated] recurring, repetitious, duplicated; see MULTIPLIED.

multiplication *n.* duplication, reproduction, addition, increase, repetition, compounding, recurrence, amplification, making more, reproducing, repeating, augmenting; see also MATHEMATICS.—*Ant.* REDUCTION, subtraction, decrease.

multiplied *a.* compounded, added, reproduced, amplified, repeated, augmented, duplicated, reduplicated, made many.—*Ant.* REDUCED, divided, decreased.

multiply *v.* **1** [To increase] add, augment, double; see INCREASE. **2** [To bring forth young] generate, produce, populate; see REPRODUCE 3. **3** [To employ multiplication as an arithmetical process] square, cube, raise to a higher power; see INCREASE.

multitude *n.* throng, drove, mob; see CROWD, GATHERING, PEOPLE 3.

mumble *v.* mutter, utter, whine, whimper, grumble, murmur, maunder, ramble on, whisper, speak indistinctly, say to oneself; see also HESITATE, STAMMER.—*Ant.* SAY, articulate, enunciate.

mumbo jumbo *n.* gibberish, double talk, drivel; see NONSENSE 1.

munch *v.* crunch, bite, crush; see CHEW, EAT.

mundane *a.* normal, ordinary, everyday; see WORLDLY.

municipal *a.* self-governing, metropolitan, city, town, community, local, civil, incorporated, corporate; see also PUBLIC.—*Ant.* PRIVATE, national, state.

municipality *n.* district, village, borough; see CITY, TOWN 1.

munitions *n.* materiel, weapons, ordnance; see AMMUNITION, BOMB, BULLET, CANNON, EXPLOSIVE, GUN, MACHINE GUN, ROCKET, SHOT 1.

murder *n.* killing, homicide, death, destruction, annihilation, carnage, terrorism, mayhem, dispatching, putting an end to, slaying, shooting, knifing, assassination, lynching, crime, felony, killing with malice aforethought, murder in the first degree, first-degree murder, contract killing, murder in the second degree, murder in the third degree, massacre, genocide, butchery, patricide, parricide, matricide, infanticide, fratricide, genocide, suicide, foul play. —**get away with murder*** escape punishment, take flight, avoid punishment; see EVADE.

murder *v.* **1** [To kill unlawfully] slay, assassinate, butcher; see KILL 1. **2** [*To ruin, especially by incompetence] spoil, mar, misuse; see BOTCH, DESTROY, FAIL 1.

murdered *a.* killed, assassinated, massacred; see DEAD 1.

murderer *n.* slayer, assassin, butcher; see CRIMINAL, KILLER.

murderous *a.* killing, cruel, criminal; see DEADLY.

murky *a.* dim, dusky, dingy; see DARK 1, DIRTY 1.

murmur *v.* **1** [To make a low, continuous sound] ripple, moan, trickle, burble, babble, tinkle, gurgle,

body, esp. in the heart —*vi.* to make a murmur —*vt.* to say in a murmur

mus·cat (mus′kət) ***n.*** ⟦< LL *muscus,* musk⟧ a sweet European grape

mus′ca·tel′ (-kə tel′) ***n.*** a sweet wine made from the muscat

mus·cle (mus′əl) ***n.*** ⟦< L *musculus,* lit., little mouse⟧ **1** any body organ consisting of fibrous tissue that can be contracted and expanded to produce bodily movements **2** this tissue **3** muscular strength —***vi.*** **-cled, -cling** [Inf.] to force one's way (*in*)

mus′cle-bound′ ***adj.*** having some of the muscles enlarged and less elastic, as from too much exercise

mus·cu·lar (mus′kyoo lər, -kyə-) ***adj.*** **1** of, consisting of, or done by muscles **2** having well-developed muscles; strong —**mus′cu·lar′i·ty** (-lar′ə tē) ***n.***

muscular dys·tro·phy (dis′trə fē) a chronic disease characterized by a progressive wasting of the muscles

mus·cu·la·ture (mus′kyoo lə chər, -kyə-) ***n.*** ⟦Fr⟧ the muscular system of a body, limb, etc.

muse (myooz) ***vi.*** **mused, mus′ing** ⟦< OFr *muser,* ponder⟧ to think deeply; meditate

Muse (myooz) ***n.*** ⟦< Gr *mousa*⟧ **1** *Gr. Myth.* any of the nine goddesses of literature and of the arts and sciences **2** [**m-**] the spirit thought to inspire a poet or other artist

mu·sette (bag) (myoo zet′) ⟦< OFr, bagpipe⟧ a bag with a shoulder strap, carried as by soldiers

mu·se·um (myoo zē′əm) ***n.*** ⟦< Gr *mousa,* Muse⟧ a place for preserving and exhibiting artistic or historical objects

mush[1] (mush) ***n.*** ⟦prob. var. of MASH⟧ **1** a thick porridge of boiled meal **2** any thick, soft mass **3** [Inf.] maudlin sentimentality —**mush′y, -i·er, -i·est,** ***adj.***

mush[2] (mush) ***interj.*** ⟦prob. < Fr *marchons,* let's go⟧ a shout to urge on sled dogs —***vi.*** to travel on foot over snow with a dog sled

mush′room′ ***n.*** ⟦< LL *mussirio*⟧ any of various fleshy fungi, typically with a stalk capped by an umbrellalike top; esp., any edible variety —***adj.*** of or like a mushroom —***vi.*** to grow or spread rapidly

mu·sic (myoo′zik) ***n.*** ⟦< Gr *mousikē* (*technē*), art of the Muses⟧ **1** the art of combining tones to form expressive compositions **2** such compositions **3** any rhythmic sequence of pleasing sounds —**face the music** [Inf.] to accept the consequences

mu′si·cal (-zi kəl) ***adj.*** **1** of or for music **2** melodious or harmonious **3** fond of or skilled in music **4** set to music —***n.*** a play or film with a musical score featuring songs and dances —**mu′si·cal·ly** ***adv.***

mu·si·cale (myoo′zi kal′) ***n.*** ⟦Fr⟧ a social affair featuring a musical program

mu·si·cian (myoo zish′ən) ***n.*** one skilled in music; esp., a performer

mu′si·col′o·gy (-zi käl′ə jē) ***n.*** the study of the history, forms, etc. of music —**mu′si·col′o·gist** ***n.***

musk (musk) ***n.*** ⟦< Sans *muṣka,* testicle⟧ a strong-smelling animal secretion, used in perfumes —**musk′y, -i·er, -i·est,** ***adj.***

mus·kel·lunge (mus′kə lunj′) ***n.*** ⟦< AmInd⟧ a very large, edible pike of North America: also **mus′kie** (-kē)

mus·ket (mus′kət) ***n.*** ⟦< L *musca,* a fly⟧ a former kind of firearm with a long barrel and smooth bore

mus·ket·eer (mus′kə tir′) ***n.*** a soldier armed with a musket

musk′mel′on ***n.*** any of various sweet, juicy melons, as the cantaloupe

musk ox a hardy ox of arctic North America with a long, coarse coat and a musklike odor

musk′rat′ ***n.*** **1** an American water rodent with webbed hind feet and a musklike odor **2** its fur

Mus·lim (muz′ləm, mooz′-, moos′-) ***n.*** ⟦Ar, true believer < *aslama,* to resign oneself (to God)⟧ an adherent of Islam —***adj.*** of Islam or the Muslims

mus·lin (muz′lin) ***n.*** ⟦after *Mosul,* city in Iraq⟧ a strong, plain-woven cotton cloth

muss (mus) ***n.*** ⟦prob. var. of MESS⟧ [Inf.] a mess; disorder —***vt.*** to make messy or disordered: often with *up* —**muss′y, -i·er, -i·est,** ***adj.***

mus·sel (mus′əl) ***n.*** ⟦< OE *muscle*⟧ any of various bivalve mollusks; specif., an edible variety

must (must) ***v.aux.*** *pt.* **must** ⟦< OE *moste*⟧ used to express: **1** necessity *[I must go]* **2** probability *[it must be Joe]* **3** certainty *[all men must die]* —***n.*** [Inf.] something that must be done, had, etc.

mus·tache (mus′tash′, məs tash′) ***n.*** ⟦ult. < Gr *mystax*⟧ hair growing on the upper lip; esp., the hair that a man has let grow

THESAURUS

meander, flow gently; see also HUM, WHISPER.—*Ant.* SOUND, peal, clang. **2** [To mutter] mumble, rumble, growl; see MUTTER 2.

muscle ***n.*** fiber, flesh, tissue, brawn, beef*.

muscular ***a.*** brawny, powerful, husky; see STRONG 1.

muse ***v.*** ponder, meditate, reflect; see THINK 1.

museum ***n.*** institution, building, hall, place of exhibition, foundation, art gallery, library, picture gallery, archives, treasury, storehouse, repository, vault, aquarium, menagerie, zoological garden, zoo, botanical garden, herbarium, arboretum.

mush[1] ***n.*** **1** [Boiled meal] Indian meal, hasty pudding, hominy, cereal, grain; see also FOOD. **2** [*Sentimentality] sentimentalism, excessive sentiment, mawkishness, affectation, superficiality, romanticism, puppy love, hearts and flowers*, sob story*.

mushroom ***n.*** toadstool, fungus, *champignon* (French); see FOOD, PLANT.

mushroom ***v.*** augment, spread, sprout; see GROW 1, INCREASE.

mushy ***a.*** **1** [Soft] pulpy, gooey*, muddy; see SOFT 2. **2** [*Sentimental] romantic, maudlin, effusive; see EMOTIONAL, SENTIMENTAL.

music ***n.*** **1** [A combination of tone and rhythm] melody, tune, air, strain, harmonics, song, measure, refrain, phrasing; see also BEAT 2, HARMONY 1. *Terms used in music include the following:* scale, clef, note, tone, pitch, sharp, flat, major, minor, key, mode, bridge, theme, movement, orchestration, instrumentation, variation, improvisation, rhythm, accent, beat, down-beat, up-beat, off-beat, chord, counterpoint, timbre, volume, resonance; see also SONG. *Musical forms for instruments include the following:* symphony, concerto, suite; trio, quartet, quintet, etc.; overture, prelude, sonata, mass, scherzo, nocturne, fugue, étude, tone poem, variations, rhapsody, serenade, ballade, march; see also OVERTURE 2. *Musical dance forms include the following:* waltz, tango, foxtrot, rhumba, polka, minuet, ballet; see also DANCE 1. *General styles of music include the following:* classical, longhair*, serious, medieval, modern, folk, primitive, popular, national, sacred, baroque, romantic, jazz, blues, rhythm-and-blues, gospel, fusion, boogie-woogie, folk-rock, heavy metal, acid rock, rock-and-roll, pop, bebop, bop, soul, ragtime, swing, funk, rap, hip-hop, punk, New Age, minimalist, serial, country; see also JAZZ. **2** [Responsiveness to music] music appreciation, sensitivity, aesthetic sense; see APPRECIATION 2, FEELING 4. **—face the music*** accept the consequences of one's actions, suffer, undergo; see ENDURE 2.

musical ***a.*** **1** [Having the qualities of music] tuneful, sweet, pleasing, agreeable, symphonic, lyric, mellow, vocal, choral, consonant, rhythmical; see also HARMONIOUS 1.—*Ant.* HARSH, tuneless, discordant. **2** [Having aptitude for music] having perfect pitch, talented, musically inclined; see ARTISTIC.

musical ***n.*** musicale, musical comedy, burlesque; see PERFORMANCE, SHOW 1.

musical instrument ***n.*** *Types of musical instruments include the following:* recorder, grand piano, spinet, lyre, bells, flute, piccolo, violin, fiddle*, oboe, clarinet, bassoon, fife, English horn, maracas, sousaphone, alpenhorn, shofar, bagpipe, trombone, French horn, tuba, cornet, trumpet, saxophone, dulcimer, harpsichord, harmonica, organ, harp, tambourine, ukelele, guitar, electric guitar, banjo, mandolin, lute, viola, cello, double bass, xylophone, marimba, cymbal, drum, balalaika, accordion, concertina, tom-tom, sitar, calliope.

musician ***n.*** player, performer, composer; see ARTIST. *Musicians include the following:* singer, instrumentalist, soloist, soprano, alto, contralto, coloratura, mezzo-soprano, countertenor, tenor, baritone, bass, conductor, director, leader, basso profundo, folk singer, drummer, pianist, violinist, cellist, guitarist, bassist, keyboardist, organist, saxophonist, woodwind player, percussionist, brass player, jazzman.

muss* ***n.*** chaos, disarrangement, mess; see CONFUSION, DISORDER.

muss ***v.*** rumple, tousle, dishevel, ruffle, crumple, jumble, disarrange, disturb, mess up; see also TANGLE.

mussy* ***a.*** messy, chaotic, rumpled; see TANGLED.

must* ***n.*** requirement, need, obligation; see NECESSITY 2.

must ***v.*** ought to, should, have to, have got to, be compelled to, be obliged to, be required to, be destined to, be ordered to, be made to, have no choice but to, have as one's fate; see also NEED.

mustache ***n.*** mustachio, handle-

mus·tang (mus′taŋ′) ***n.*** ⟦< L *mixtus,* a mingling⟧ a small wild horse of the SW plains
mus·tard (mus′tərd) ***n.*** ⟦< OFr⟧ **1** an herb with yellow flowers and round seeds in slender pods **2** a pungent seasoning made from the ground seeds
mustard gas ⟦< its mustardlike odor⟧ an oily liquid used in warfare for its blistering and disabling effects
mus·ter (mus′tər) ***vt.*** ⟦< L *monstrare,* to show⟧ **1** to assemble (troops, etc.) **2** to collect; summon: often with *up* —***vi.*** to assemble, as troops —***n.*** **1** a gathering or assembling, as of troops for inspection **2** the persons or things assembled —**muster in** (or **out**) to enlist in (or discharge from) military service —**pass muster** to meet the required standards
mus·ty (mus′tē) ***adj.*** **-ti·er, -ti·est** ⟦< ? MOIST⟧ **1** having a stale, moldy smell or taste **2** stale or trite; antiquated —**mus′ti·ly** ***adv.*** —**mus′ti·ness** ***n.***
mu·ta·ble (myōōt′ə bəl) ***adj.*** ⟦< L *mutare,* to change⟧ **1** that can be changed **2** inconstant; fickle —**mu′ta·bil′i·ty** ***n.*** —**mu′ta·bly** ***adv.***
mu·tant (myōōt′'nt) ***adj.*** of mutation —***n.*** an animal or plant with inheritable characteristics that differ from those of the parents; sport
mu·ta·tion (myōō tā′shən) ***n.*** **1** a change, as in form, nature, etc. **2** a sudden variation in some inheritable characteristic of an animal or plant —**mu′tate′, -tat′ed, -tat′ing,** ***vi., vt.***
mute (myōōt) ***adj.*** ⟦< L *mutus*⟧ **1** not speaking; silent **2** unable to speak —***n.*** **1** a deaf-mute **2** a device that softens the sound of a musical instrument —***vt.*** **mut′ed, mut′ing** to soften the sound of
mu·ti·late (myōōt′'l āt′) ***vt.*** **-lat′ed, -lat′ing** ⟦< L *mutilus,* maimed⟧ to cut off, damage, or mar an important part of —**mu′ti·la′tion** ***n.*** —**mu′ti·la′tor** ***n.***
mu·ti·ny (myōōt′'n ē) ***n., pl.*** **-nies** ⟦< L *movere,* to move⟧ revolt against constituted authority; esp., rebellion of soldiers or sailors against their officers —***vi.*** **-nied, -ny·ing** to take part in a mutiny —**mu′ti·neer′** ***n.*** —**mu′ti·nous** ***adj.***
mutt (mut) ***n.*** [Slang] a mongrel dog
mut·ter (mut′ər) ***vi., vt.*** ⟦ME *moteren*⟧ **1** to speak or say in low, indistinct tones **2** to grumble —***n.*** **1** a muttering **2** something muttered
mut·ton (mut′'n) ***n.*** ⟦< OFr, a ram⟧ the flesh of a sheep, esp. a grown sheep, used as food
mu·tu·al (myōō′chōō əl) ***adj.*** ⟦< L *mutare,* to exchange⟧ **1** *a*) done, felt, etc. by each of two or more for or toward the other or others *b*) of each other **2** in common *[*our *mutual* friend*]* —**mu′tu·al·ly** ***adv.***
mutual fund **1** a fund of securities owned jointly by investors who have purchased shares of it **2** a corporation which manages such a fund or funds
mu·tu·el (myōō′chōō əl) ***n.*** PARIMUTUEL
muu·muu (mōō′mōō′) ***n.*** ⟦< Haw⟧ a long, loose dress of Hawaiian style
Mu·zak (myōō′zak′) *trademark for* a system of transmitting recorded background music to stores, etc. —***n.*** this music, variously regarded as unobtrusive, bland, monotonous, etc.
muz·zle (muz′əl) ***n.*** ⟦< ML *musum*⟧ **1** the mouth, nose, and jaws of a dog, horse, etc. **2** a device put over the mouth of an animal to prevent its biting or eating **3** the front end of the barrel of a firearm —***vt.*** **-zled, -zling** **1** to put a muzzle on (an animal) **2** to prevent from talking
MX missile (em′eks′) ⟦< *m(issile), (e)x(perimental)*⟧ a U.S. ICBM armed with several nuclear warheads
my (mī) ***poss. pronominal adj.*** ⟦< OE *min*⟧ of, belonging to, or done by me
Myan·mar (myän′mär′) country in SE Asia: 261,228 sq. mi.; pop. 35,314,000
my·col·o·gy (mī käl′ə jē) ***n.*** the study of fungi —**my·col′o·gist** ***n.***
my·e·li·tis (mī′ə līt′is) ***n.*** ⟦< Gr *myelos,* marrow + -ITIS⟧ inflammation of the spinal cord or the bone marrow
My·lar (mī′lär′) *trademark for* a strong, thin polyester used for recording tapes, fabrics, etc. —***n.*** [*occas.* **m-**] this substance
my·na or **my·nah** (mī′nə) ***n.*** ⟦Hindi *mainā*⟧ any of various tropical birds of Southeast Asia: some can mimic speech
my·o·pi·a (mī ō′pē ə) ***n.*** ⟦< Gr *myein,* to close + *ōps,* eye⟧ nearsightedness —**my·op′ic** (-äp′ik) ***adj.***
myr·i·ad (mir′ē əd) ***n.*** ⟦< Gr *myrios,* countless⟧ a great number —***adj.*** countless; innumerable
myr·mi·don (mur′mə dän′, -dən) ***n.*** ⟦after name of a Gr tribe led by Achilles⟧ an unquestioning follower
myrrh (mur) ***n.*** ⟦< Ar *murr*⟧ a fragrant gum resin of Arabia and E Africa, used in incense, etc.
myr·tle (murt′'l) ***n.*** ⟦< Gr *myrtos*⟧ **1** an evergreen shrub with white or pink flowers and dark berries **2** any of various other plants, as the periwinkle
my·self (mī self′) ***pron.*** a form of I, used as an intensive *[*I went *myself],* as a reflexive *[*I hurt *myself],* or with the meaning "my true self" *[*I am not *myself* today*]*
mys·te·ri·ous (mis tir′ē əs) ***adj.*** of, containing, implying, or characterized by mystery —**mys·te′ri·ous·ly** ***adv.*** —**mys·te′ri·ous·ness** ***n.***
mys·ter·y (mis′tə rē) ***n., pl.*** **-ies** ⟦< Gr *mystērion,* secret rite⟧ **1** something unexplained or secret **2** a story involving unknown persons, facts, etc. *[*a murder *mystery]* **3** secrecy
mys·tic (mis′tik) ***adj.*** **1** of esoteric rites or doctrines **2** MYSTICAL **3** mysterious —***n.*** one who professes to undergo mystical experiences
mys′ti·cal (-ti kəl) ***adj.*** **1** spiritually significant or symbolic **2** of mystics or mysticism **3** occult —**mys′ti·cal·ly** ***adv.***
mys·ti·cism (mis′tə siz′əm) ***n.*** **1** belief in the possibility of attaining direct communion with God or knowledge of spiritual truths, as by meditation **2** obscure thinking or belief
mys′ti·fy′ (-fī′) ***vt.*** **-fied′, -fy′ing** to puzzle or perplex —**mys′ti·fi·ca′tion** ***n.***

THESAURUS

bar*, soup strainer*; see BEARD, WHISKERS.
muster ***v.*** gather, marshal, summon; see ASSEMBLE 1.
musty ***a.*** moldy, fusty, rank; see ROTTEN 1.
mutation ***n.*** deviation, modification, variation; see CHANGE 1, VARIETY 1, 2.
mute ***a.*** **1** [Without power of speech] tongueless, deaf-mute, aphasic, inarticulate, voiceless, tongue-tied; see also DUMB 1, QUIET.—*Ant.* VOCAL, noisy, unimpaired. **2** [Suddenly deprived of speech] speechless, wordless, silent; see BEWILDERED, SURPRISED.
mutilate ***v.*** **1** [To maim] cut, batter, scratch; see WEAKEN 2. **2** [To damage] injure, deface, ravage; see DAMAGE, HURT 1.
mutilated ***a.*** disfigured, distorted, maimed; see DEFORMED.
mutiny ***n.*** insurrection, revolt, resistance; see REVOLUTION 2.
mutter ***v.*** **1** [To make a low, mumbling sound] rumble, growl, snarl; see SOUND. **2** [To speak as if to oneself] murmur, grunt, grumble, sputter, whisper, speak inarticulately, speak indistinctly, speak in an undertone, swallow one's words*; see also MUMBLE, MURMUR 1. **3** [To complain] grumble, moan, groan; see COMPLAIN.
mutual ***a.*** **1** [Reciprocal] interchangeable, two-sided, give-and-take; see COMPLEMENTARY. **2** [Common] joint, shared, belonging equally to each; see COMMON 5.
mutually ***a.*** commonly, cooperatively, jointly, reciprocally, in combination, by common consent, in conjunction; see also TOGETHER 2.
muzzle ***v.*** **1** [To fasten a muzzle upon] wrap, muffle, enclose; see BIND 1, GAG 1. **2** [To silence] gag, restrain, restrict, repress, suppress, check, stop, stop someone's mouth, hush, still, shush*; see also QUIET 2.
myriad ***a.*** variable, infinite, innumerable; see ENDLESS, MULTIPLE 1.
myself ***pron.*** me, me personally; the speaker, the writer, etc.; on my own authority, on my own responsibility, yours truly*, me myself.
mysterious ***a.*** **1** [Puzzling] enigmatic, uncanny, strange; see DIFFICULT 2, OBSCURE 1, UNNATURAL 1. **2** [Concerning powers beyond those supposedly natural] mystic, occult, dark, mystifying, transcendental, abstruse, arcane, inscrutable, metaphysical, mystical, magical, dark, veiled, strange, astrological, unknowable, unfathomable, esoteric, cryptic, oracular, incredible; see also MAGIC. **3** [Not generally known] obscure, hidden, ambiguous; see SECRET 1.
mystery ***n.*** **1** [The quality of being mysterious] inscrutability, occultism, abstruseness; see MAGIC 1, 2, STRANGENESS. **2** [Something difficult to know] riddle, conundrum, enigma; see DIFFICULTY 2, PUZZLE 1. **3** [A trick] sleight-of-hand, magic trick, magic; see TRICK 1. **4** [A mystery story] detective story, mystery play, mystery movie; see STORY.
mystic ***a.*** occult, transcendental, spiritual; see MYSTERIOUS 2, SECRET 1.
mysticism ***n.*** occultism, cabala, quietism, orphism.
mystify ***v.*** perplex, trick, hoodwink; see DECEIVE, LIE 1.

mys·tique (mis tēk′) ***n.*** ⟦Fr, mystic⟧ a complex of quasi-mystical attitudes and feelings surrounding some person, institution, etc.

myth (mith) ***n.*** ⟦< Gr *mythos*⟧ **1** a traditional story serving to explain some phenomenon, custom, etc. **2** mythology **3** any fictitious story, person, or thing —**myth′i·cal** ***adj.***

my·thol·o·gy (mi thäl′ə jē) ***n.***, *pl.* **-gies** **1** the study of myths **2** myths collectively, as of a specific people —**myth·o·log·i·cal** (mith′ə läj′i kəl) ***adj.***

THESAURUS

mystique ***n.*** attitude, complex, nature; see CHARACTER 1, TEMPERAMENT.

myth ***n.*** fable, folk tale, legend, lore, saga, folk ballad, allegory, parable, tale; see also STORY.

mythical ***a.*** mythological, fabricated, fictitious; see FALSE 3, UNREAL.

mythological ***a.*** whimsical, fictitious, chimerical; see FANTASTIC, IMAGINARY.

mythology ***n.*** belief, tradition, stories of gods and heroes; see RELIGION 1.

N

n[1] or **N** (en) ***n.***, *pl.* **n's, N's** the 14th letter of the English alphabet

n[2] *abbrev.* **1** name **2** neuter **3** new **4** nominative **5** noun **6** number

N[1] *abbrev.* **1** Navy **2** north **3** northern **4** November

N[2] *Chem. symbol for* nitrogen

Na ⟦L *natrium*⟧ *Chem. symbol for* sodium

NA *abbrev.* North America

NAACP *abbrev.* National Association for the Advancement of Colored People

nab (nab) ***vt.*** **nabbed, nab'bing** ⟦prob. < dial. *nap*, to snatch⟧ [Inf.] **1** to snatch or seize **2** to arrest or catch (a felon or wrongdoer)

na·bob (nā'bäb') ***n.*** ⟦< Ar *nā'ib*, deputy⟧ a very rich or important man

na·cre (nā'kər) ***n.*** ⟦Fr < Ar *naqqārah*, small kettledrum⟧ MOTHER-OF-PEARL

na·dir (nā'dər, -dir') ***n.*** ⟦< Ar *naẓīr*, opposite⟧ **1** the point opposite the zenith and directly below the observer **2** the lowest point

nae (nā) [Scot.] ***adv.*** no; not —***adj.*** no

nag[1] (nag) ***vt.***, ***vi.*** **nagged, nag'ging** ⟦< ON *gnaga*⟧ **1** to annoy by continual scolding, urging, etc. **2** to keep troubling *[nagged* by doubts*]* —***n.*** one who nags: also **nag'ger**

nag[2] (nag) ***n.*** ⟦ME *nagge*⟧ an old or inferior horse

Na·ga·sa·ki (nä'gə sä'kē) seaport in SW Japan: U.S. atomic-bomb target (1945): pop. 438,000

Na·go·ya (nä'gô yä') seaport in S Honshu, Japan: pop. 2,088,000

nai·ad (nā'ad', nī'-) ***n.*** ⟦< Gr *naein*, to flow⟧ [*also* **N-**] *Gr. & Rom. Myth.* a nymph living in a spring, river, etc.

nail (nāl) ***n.*** ⟦< OE *nægl*⟧ **1** the thin, horny growth at the ends of fingers and toes **2** a tapered, pointed piece of metal driven with a hammer, as to join pieces of wood —***vt.*** **1** to fasten, secure, etc. with or as with nails **2** [Inf.] to catch, capture, etc. **3** [Inf.] to hit hard

nail'-bit'er (-bīt'ər) ***n.*** [Inf.] a suspenseful drama, sports event, etc.

Nai·ro·bi (nī rō'bē) capital of Kenya: pop. 1,346,000

na·ive or **na·ïve** (nä ēv') ***adj.*** ⟦Fr < L *nativus*, natural⟧ **1** unaffectedly simple **2** credulous —**na·ive'ly** or **na·ïve'ly** ***adv.*** —**na·ive·té'** or **na·ïve·té'** (-tā') ***n.***

na·ked (nā'kid) ***adj.*** ⟦OE *nacod*⟧ **1** completely unclothed; nude **2** without covering **3** without additions, disguises, etc.; plain *[*the *naked* truth*]* —**na'ked·ly** ***adv.*** —**na'ked·ness** ***n.***

nam·by-pam·by (nam'bē pam'bē) ***adj.*** ⟦18th-c. play on name *Ambrose*⟧ weak, insipid, indecisive, etc. —***n.***, *pl.* **-bies** a namby-pamby person

name (nām) ***n.*** ⟦OE *nama*⟧ **1** a word or phrase by which a person, thing, or class is known; title **2** a word or words considered descriptive; epithet, often an abusive one **3** reputation **4** appearance only, not reality *[*chief in *name* only*]* —***adj.*** well-known —***vt.*** **named, nam'ing** **1** to give a name to **2** to mention by name **3** to identify by the right name *[name* the oceans*]* **4** to appoint to an office, etc. **5** to specify (a date, price, etc.) —**in the name of** by the authority of

name'less ***adj.*** **1** not having a name **2** left unnamed **3** indescribable

name'ly ***adv.*** that is to say; to wit

name'sake' ***n.*** a person with the same name as another, esp. if named after the other

Na·mib·i·a (nə mib'ē ə) country in S Africa: 318,251 sq. mi.; pop. 1,402,000 —**Na·mib'i·an** ***adj.***, ***n.***

Nan·jing (nän'jiŋ') city in E China, on the Chang: pop. 2,091,000

Nan·king (nan'kiŋ', nän'-) *a former transliteration of* NANJING

nan·ny goat (nan'ē) ⟦< fem. name *Nan*⟧ a female goat

na·no·sec·ond (nan'ə sek'ənd) ***n.*** one billionth of a second

nap[1] (nap) ***vi.*** **napped, nap'ping** ⟦OE *hnappian*⟧ to sleep lightly for a short time —***n.*** a brief, light sleep

nap[2] (nap) ***n.*** ⟦ME *noppe*⟧ the downy or hairy surface of cloth or suede formed by short hairs or fibers —**nap'less** ***adj.***

na·palm (nā'päm') ***n.*** ⟦*na*(*phthene*) + *palm*(*itate*)⟧ a jellylike substance used in flame throwers and fire bombs —***vt.*** to attack or burn with napalm

nape (nāp) ***n.*** ⟦ME⟧ the back of the neck

naph·tha (naf'thə, nap'-) ***n.*** ⟦< Pers *neft*, pitch⟧ a flammable liquid distilled from petroleum, used as a fuel, solvent, etc.

naph'tha·lene' (-lēn') ***n.*** ⟦< prec.⟧ a white crystalline hydrocarbon distilled from coal tar, used in moth repellents, dyes, etc.

nap·kin (nap'kin) ***n.*** ⟦< L *mappa*⟧ **1** a small piece of cloth or paper used while eating to protect the clothes and wipe the lips **2** any small cloth, towel, etc.

THESAURUS

nab* ***v.*** grab, take, snatch; see SEIZE 2.

nag[1] ***v.*** vex, annoy, pester; see BOTHER 2.

nail ***n.*** brad, pin, peg, stud, spike; see also TACK 1.

nail ***v.*** **1** [To hammer] drive, pound, spike; see HIT 1. **2** [To fasten with nails] secure, hold, clinch; see FASTEN. **3** [*To arrest] capture, detain, apprehend; see ARREST, SEIZE 2. —**hard as nails** callous, unfeeling, remorseless; see CRUEL. —**hit the nail on the head*** say what is exactly right, be accurate, come to the point; see DEFINE 2.

naive ***a.*** unaffected, childish, childlike, plain, artless, innocent, untrained, countrified, callow, natural, unschooled, ignorant, untaught, unworldly, provincial, unsophisticated, guileless, spontaneous, instinctive, impulsive, simple-minded, innocuous, unsuspecting, unsuspicious, harmless, gullible, credulous, trusting, original, fresh, unpolished, rude, primitive, ingenuous, sincere, open, candid, forthright, aboveboard, romantic, fanciful, unpretentious, transparent, straightforward, uncomplicated, easily imposed upon; see also INEXPERIENCED.—*Ant.* EXPERIENCED, sophisticated, complicated.

naively ***a.*** childishly, innocently, stupidly; see FOOLISHLY, OPENLY 1.

naiveté ***n.*** simplicity, childishness, inexperience; see INNOCENCE 2.

naked ***a.*** **1** [Nude] unclothed, undressed, stripped, unclad, unrobed, disrobed, leafless, hairless, bare, undraped, exposed, having nothing on, unappareled, denuded, unveiled, uncovered, uncloaked, stark naked, topless, bald, in one's birthday suit*, in the buff, peeled*, without a stitch, in the raw. **2** [Unadorned] plain, simple, artless; see MODEST 2, NATURAL 3.

nakedness ***n.*** nudity, bareness, undress, exposure, the raw, nudism.

name ***n.*** **1** [A title] proper name, Christian name, given name, cognomen, appellation, designation, first name, family name, title, denomination, surname, last name, middle name, confirmation name, moniker*, sign, handle*. **2** [Reputation] renown, honor, repute; see FAME. **3** [An epithet] nickname, pen name, pseudonym, sobriquet, stage name, nom de plume, nom de guerre, pet name, fictitious name, alias. **4** [A famous person] star, hero, a person of renown; see CELEBRITY. —**call names** swear at, insult, slander; see SCOLD. —**in the name of** by authority of, in reference to, as representative of; see FOR. —**know only by name** be familiar with, not know personally, have heard of; see KNOW 3. —**to one's name** belonging to one, in one's possession, possessed by one; see OWNED.

name ***v.*** **1** [To give a name] call, christen, baptize, style, term, label, identify, designate, classify, denominate, title, entitle, nickname, characterize, label, dub; see also DESCRIBE, DEFINE. **2** [To indicate by name] refer to, specify, signify, denote, single out, mark, suggest, connote, point to, note, remark, index, list, cite; see also MENTION. **3** [To appoint] elect, nominate, select; see DELEGATE 1.

named ***a.*** **1** [Having as a name] called, designated, entitled, titled, termed, specified, styled, denominated, christened, baptized, nicknamed, labeled, tagged*, dubbed. **2** [Chosen] appointed, commissioned, delegated, authorized, nominated, elected, invested, vested, assigned, ordained, entrusted, picked, selected, decided upon, settled on, picked out, preferred, favored, supported, approved, certified, called, anointed, consecrated, sanctioned, drafted, opted, declared, announced, singled out.

nameless ***a.*** inconspicuous, undistinguished, obscure; see UNKNOWN 2.

namely ***a.*** specifically, to wit, that is to say, particularly, by way of explanation, strictly speaking, in other words, in plain English.

nap[1,2] ***n.*** **1** [A short sleep] siesta, cat nap, doze; see SLEEP. **2** [The finish of certain goods, especially fabric] pile, shag, surface; see GRAIN 2, OUTSIDE 1, TEXTURE 1.

napkin ***n.*** paper napkin, serviette*, table linen; see TOWEL.

Na·ples (nā′pəlz) seaport in S Italy: pop. 1,072,000
Na·po·le·on (nə pō′lē ən) *see* BONAPARTE, Napoleon
narc (närk) ***n.*** ⟦< NARC(OTIC)⟧ [Slang] a police agent who enforces laws dealing with narcotics
nar·cis·sism (när′sə siz′əm) ***n.*** ⟦< fol.⟧ self-love; specif., excessive interest in one's own appearance, comfort, etc. —**nar′cis·sist** ***n., adj.*** —**nar′cis·sis′tic** ***adj.***
Nar·cis·sus (när sis′əs) ***n.*** **1** *Gr. Myth.* a youth who falls in love with his reflection in a pool and changes into the narcissus **2** *pl.* **-cis′sus, -cis′sus·es,** or **-cis′si** (-ī) [n-] any of various bulb plants whose flowers have six parts and a cuplike or tubelike center
nar·co·sis (när kō′sis) ***n., pl.*** **-ses′** (-sēz′) unconsciousness caused by a narcotic
nar·cot·ic (när kät′ik) ***n.*** ⟦< Gr *narkē*, numbness⟧ a drug, as morphine, used to relieve pain and induce sleep: narcotics are often addictive —***adj.*** of or having to do with narcotics
nar·co·tize (när′kə tīz′) ***vt.*** **-tized′, -tiz′ing** to subject to a narcotic —**nar′co·ti·za′tion** ***n.***
nark (närk) ***n.*** [Slang] *alt. sp. of* NARC
nar·rate (nar′āt′, na rāt′) ***vt., vi.*** **-rat′ed, -rat′ing** ⟦< L *narrare*, tell⟧ to tell (a story), relate (events), etc.
nar·ra·tion (na rā′shən) ***n.*** **1** a narrating **2** a narrative
nar·ra·tive (nar′ə tiv) ***adj.*** in story form —***n.*** **1** a story; account **2** the art or practice of narrating
nar·row (nar′ō) ***adj.*** ⟦OE *nearu*⟧ **1** small in width; not wide **2** limited in meaning, size, amount, etc. **3** limited in outlook; not liberal **4** with limited margin *[a narrow* escape*]* —***vi., vt.*** to decrease or limit in width, extent, etc. —***n.*** [*usually pl.*] a narrow passage; strait
nar′row·cast′ (-kast′) ***vt., vi.*** **-cast′, -cast′ing** to transmit by cable TV to a selected audience —***n.*** a narrowcasting
nar′row-mind′ed ***adj.*** limited in outlook; bigoted; prejudiced —**nar′row-mind′ed·ness** ***n.***
nar·whal (när′wəl) ***n.*** ⟦< ON *nahvalr*, lit., corpse whale⟧ a small arctic whale: the male has a long, spiral tusk
nar·y (ner′ē) ***adj.*** ⟦< *ne'er a*, never a⟧ [Dial.] not any; no: with *a* or *an [nary* a doubt*]*
NASA (nas′ə) *abbrev.* National Aeronautics and Space Administration
na·sal (nā′zəl) ***adj.*** ⟦< L *nasus*, nose⟧ **1** of the nose **2** uttered so that the breath passes through the nose
na′sal·ize′ (-īz′) ***vt., vi.*** **-ized′, -iz′ing** to pronounce or speak with a nasal sound —**na′sal·i·za′tion** ***n.***
NASCAR (nas′kär′) *trademark for* National Association for Stock Car Auto Racing
nas·cent (nas′ənt, nā′sənt) ***adj.*** ⟦< L *nasci*, be born⟧ **1** coming into being **2** beginning to form or develop: said of ideas, etc.
Nash·ville (nash′vil) capital of Tennessee: pop. 511,000
nas·tur·tium (nə stur′shəm) ***n.*** ⟦< L *nasus*, nose + *torquere*, to twist: from its pungent odor⟧ **1** a plant with trumpet-shaped, red, yellow, or orange flowers **2** its flower
nas·ty (nas′tē) ***adj.*** **-ti·er, -ti·est** ⟦< ?⟧ **1** filthy **2** morally offensive **3** very unpleasant **4** mean; malicious —**nas′ti·ly** ***adv.*** —**nas′ti·ness** ***n.***
na·tal (nāt′'l) ***adj.*** ⟦< L *nasci*, be born⟧ of or relating to one's birth
na·tion (nā′shən) ***n.*** ⟦< L *natus*, born⟧ **1** a stable community of people with a territory, culture, and language in common **2** the people united under a single government; country
na·tion·al (nash′ə nəl) ***adj.*** of or affecting a nation as a whole —***n.*** a citizen —**na′tion·al·ly** ***adv.***
National Guard the organized militia forces of the individual U.S. states, part of the U.S. Army when called into active federal service
na′tion·al·ism′ ***n.*** **1** devotion to one's nation; patriotism **2** the advocacy of national independence —**na′tion·al·ist** ***n., adj.*** —**na′tion·al·is′tic** ***adj.***
na′tion·al′i·ty (-nal′ə tē) ***n., pl.*** **-ties** **1** the status of belonging to a nation by birth or naturalization **2** a national group, esp. of immigrants
na′tion·al·ize′ (-nə līz′) ***vt.*** **-ized′, -iz′ing** **1** to make national **2** to transfer ownership or control of (land, industries, etc.) to the government —**na′tion·al·i·za′tion** ***n.***
na′tion·wide′ ***adj.*** by or throughout the whole nation; national
na·tive (nāt′iv) ***adj.*** ⟦< L *natus*, born⟧ **1** inborn **2** belonging to a locality or country by birth, production, or growth **3** being, or connected with, the place of one's birth *[*one's *native* land or language*]* **4** as found in nature; natural **5** of or characteristic of the original inhabitants of a place —***n.*** **1** a person born in the place indicated **2** an original inhabitant **3** an indigenous plant or animal
Native American AMERICAN INDIAN
na′tive-born′ ***adj.*** of a specified place by birth
na·tiv·i·ty (nə tiv′ə tē) ***n., pl.*** **-ties** ⟦see NATIVE⟧ birth — **the Nativity** the birth of Jesus
natl *abbrev.* national
NATO (nā′tō) ***n.*** North Atlantic Treaty Organization
nat·ty (nat′ē) ***adj.*** **-ti·er, -ti·est** ⟦< ? NEAT⟧ trim and stylish —**nat′ti·ly** ***adv.***
nat·u·ral (nach′ər əl) ***adj.*** ⟦< L *naturalis*, by birth⟧ **1** of or dealing with nature **2** produced or existing in nature; not artificial **3** innate; not acquired **4** true to nature;

THESAURUS

narcotic ***n.*** depressant, sedative, opiate; see DRUG.
narrate ***v.*** detail, describe, depict; see REPORT 1, TELL 1.
narrative ***a.*** storylike, historical, sequential; see CHRONOLOGICAL.
narrow ***a.*** **1** [Lacking breadth] close, cramped, tight, confined, shrunken, compressed, slender, fine, linear, threadlike, tapering, tapered, slim, scant, scanty, lanky, small, meager; see also THIN 1.—*Ant.* BROAD, wide, extensive. **2** [Lacking tolerance] dogmatic, narrow-minded, parochial; see CONSERVATIVE, CONVENTIONAL 3, PREJUDICED. **3** [Lacking a comfortable margin] close, near, precarious; see DANGEROUS, ENDANGERED, UNSAFE.
narrowly ***a.*** nearly, closely, by a narrow margin; see ALMOST.
narrow-minded ***a.*** bigoted, biased, provincial; see CONSERVATIVE, CONVENTIONAL 3, PREJUDICED.
narrowness ***n.*** **1** [A physical restriction] confinement, thinness, restriction; see BARRIER, INTERFERENCE 1. **2** [A mental restriction] intolerance, bigotry, bias; see PREJUDICE, STUBBORNNESS.
nasty ***a.*** **1** [Offensive to the senses] foul, gross, revolting; see OFFENSIVE 2, VULGAR. **2** [Indecent] immoral, immodest, smutty; see LEWD 1, SHAMEFUL 1. **3** [Unkind] sarcastic, critical, mean; see CRUEL, FIERCE, RUTHLESS.
nation ***n.*** **1** [An organized state] realm, country, commonwealth, republic, democracy, state, monarchy, dominion, body politic, land, domain, empire, kingdom, principality, sovereignty, colony; see also GOVERNMENT 1. **2** [A people having some unity] populace, community, public; see POPULATION, RACE 2, SOCIETY 2.
national ***a.*** **1** [Concerning a nation] ethnic, political, sovereign, state, social, civic, civil, societal, communal, royal, imperial, federal; see also GOVERNMENTAL, PUBLIC 2. **2** [Operative throughout a nation] nationwide, countrywide, interstate, internal, social, widespread, sweeping; see also GENERAL 1.
nationalism ***n.*** provincialism, chauvinism, allegiance; see LOYALTY, PATRIOTISM.
nationality ***n.*** native land, country, citizenship; see ORIGIN 2.
nationally ***a.*** politically, governmentally, as a state, as a country, publicly, of the people, throughout the country, transcending state boundaries, for the general welfare.
native ***a.*** **1** [Natural] innate, inherent, inborn, implanted, inbred, ingrained, congenital, fundamental, hereditary, inherited, essential, constitutional; see also NATURAL 1.—*Ant.* UNNATURAL, foreign, alien. **2** [Characteristic of a region] aboriginal, indigenous, original, primitive, primary, primeval, vernacular, domestic, local, found locally; see also REGIONAL.—*Ant.* IMPORTED, brought in, transplanted.
native ***n.*** **1** [Aborigine] original inhabitant, indigenous inhabitant, tribesman; see MAN 1. **2** [Citizen] national, inhabitant, occupant; see CITIZEN, RESIDENT.
natural ***a.*** **1** [Rooted in nature] intrinsic, original, essential, true, fundamental, inborn, ingrained, inherent, instinctive, implanted, innate, inbred, incarnate, subjective, inherited, congenital, genetic; see also NATIVE 1.—*Ant.* FOREIGN, alien, acquired. **2** [To be expected] normal, typical, characteristic, usual, customary, habitual, accustomed, involuntary, spontaneous, uncontrolled, uncontrollable, familiar, common, universal, prevailing, prevalent, general, probable, uniform, constant, consistent, ordinary, logical, reasonable, anticipated, looked for, hoped for, counted on, relied on; see also REGULAR 3.—*Ant.* UNKNOWN, unexpected, unheard-of. **3** [Not affected] ingenuous, simple, artless, innocent, unstudied, spontaneous, impulsive, childlike, unfeigned, open, frank, candid, unsophisticated, unpolished, homey, unpretentious, forthright, sincere, straightforward, being oneself, unsuspecting, credulous, trusting, plain, direct, rustic; see also

lifelike **5** normal *[a natural result]* **6** free from affectation; at ease **7** *Music* neither sharped nor flatted —***n.*** [Inf.] a person or thing sure to be successful

natural childbirth childbirth without anesthesia but with prior training

natural gas a mixture of gaseous hydrocarbons, chiefly methane, occurring naturally in the earth and used as fuel

natural history the study of the animal, vegetable, and mineral world

nat'u·ral·ism' ***n.*** **1** action or thought based on natural desires **2** *Literature, Art, etc.* the realistic portrayal of persons or things

nat'u·ral·ist ***n.*** one who studies animals and plants

nat'u·ral·ize' (-īz') ***vt.*** **-ized', -iz'ing** to confer citizenship upon (an alien) —**nat'u·ral·i·za'tion** ***n.***

nat'u·ral·ly ***adv.*** **1** in a natural manner **2** by nature; innately **3** of course

natural number any positive integer, as 1, 2, or 3

natural resource a form of wealth supplied by nature, as coal, oil, or water power

natural science the systematized knowledge of nature, including biology, chemistry, physics, etc.

natural selection the evolutionary process by which the most adaptable species survive

na·ture (nā'chər) ***n.*** ⟦< L *natus*, born⟧ **1** the essential quality of a thing; essence **2** inherent tendencies of a person **3** kind; type **4** *a)* the physical universe *b)* [*sometimes* **N-**] the power, force etc. that seems to regulate this **5** the primitive state of humans **6** natural scenery —**by nature** naturally; inherently

Naug·a·hyde (nôg'ə hīd') ⟦arbitrary coinage⟧ *trademark for* an imitation leather, used for upholstery, luggage, etc. —***n.*** [**n-**] this material

naught (nôt) ***n.*** ⟦OE *nawiht*⟧ **1** nothing **2** *alt. sp. of* NOUGHT

naugh·ty (nôt'ē) ***adj.*** **-ti·er, -ti·est** ⟦ME *naugti*⟧ **1** mischievous or disobedient **2** indelicate; improper —**naugh'ti·ly** ***adv.*** —**naugh'ti·ness** ***n.***

Na·u·ru (nä o͞o'ro͞o) country on an island in the W Pacific, south of the equator: 8 sq. mi.; pop. 8,000

nau·sea (nô'shə, -zhə; -sē ə, -zē ə) ***n.*** ⟦< Gr *nausia*, seasickness⟧ **1** a sick feeling in the stomach, with an impulse to vomit **2** disgust; loathing

nau'se·ate' (-shē āt', -zhē-, -sē-, -zē-) ***vt.*** **-at'ed, -at'ing** to cause to feel nausea

nau·seous (nô'shəs, -zē əs, -sē-) ***adj.*** **1** causing nausea **2** feeling nausea; nauseated: usage objected to by some

nau·ti·cal (nôt'i kəl) ***adj.*** ⟦< Gr *naus*, ship⟧ of sailors, ships, or navigation —**nau'ti·cal·ly** ***adv.***

nautical mile a unit of linear measure used in navigation, equal to 1.1508 miles or 1,852 meters

nau·ti·lus (nôt''l əs) ***n.***, *pl.* **-lus·es** or **-li'** (-ī') ⟦< Gr *naus*, a ship⟧ a tropical mollusk with a spiral shell divided into many chambers —[**N-**] *trademark for* a type of mechanical weight-lifting equipment

Nav·a·jo (nav'ə hō') ***n.*** *pl.* **-jos', -jo'**, or **-joes'** a member of a North American Indian people of the SW U.S.: also sp. **Nav'a·ho'**

na·val (nā'vəl) ***adj.*** ⟦< L *navis*, a ship⟧ of, having, characteristic of, or for a navy, its ships, etc.

nave (nāv) ***n.*** ⟦< L *navis*, a ship⟧ the main part of a church, from the chancel to the principal entrance

na·vel (nā'vəl) ***n.*** ⟦OE *nafela*⟧ the small scar in the abdomen marking the place where the umbilical cord was attached to the fetus

navel orange a seedless orange with a navel-like hollow at its apex

nav·i·ga·ble (nav'i gə bəl) ***adj.*** **1** wide or deep enough for the passage of ships **2** that can be steered —**nav'i·ga·bil'i·ty** ***n.***

nav·i·gate (nav'ə gāt') ***vt.***, ***vi.*** **-gat'ed, -gat'ing** ⟦< L *navis*, a ship + *agere*, to lead⟧ **1** to steer or direct (a ship or aircraft) **2** to travel through or over (water, air, etc.) in a ship or aircraft **3** [Inf.] to walk or make one's way (on or through)

nav'i·ga'tion (-gā'shən) ***n.*** **1** the science of locating the position and plotting the course of ships and aircraft **2** traffic by ship

nav'i·ga'tor ***n.*** one skilled or employed in the navigation of a ship or aircraft

na·vy (nā'vē) ***n.***, *pl.* **-vies** ⟦< L *navis*, a ship⟧ **1** all the warships of a nation **2** [*often* **N-**] a nation's entire military sea force, including ships, personnel, stores, etc. **3** NAVY BLUE

navy bean ⟦from use in U.S. *Navy*⟧ a small white variety of kidney bean

navy blue very dark, purplish blue

nay (nā) ***adv.*** ⟦< ON *ne*, not + *ei*, ever⟧ **1** no: now used only in voice votes **2** not that only, but also *[I permit, nay encourage it]* —***n.*** **1** a denial **2** a negative vote or a person voting negatively

nay·say·er (nā'sā'ər) ***n.*** one who opposes, refuses, or denies, esp. habitually

Na·zi (nät'sē) ***adj.*** ⟦Ger contr. of the party name⟧ designating or of the German fascist political party which ruled Germany under Hitler (1933-45) —***n.*** a member of this party

NB New Brunswick

n.b. *abbrev.* ⟦L *nota bene*⟧ note well: also **NB**

NC North Carolina

NCO *abbrev.* noncommissioned officer

NC-17 *trademark for* a film rating indicating that no one under 17 may be admitted

ND North Dakota

Ne *Chem. symbol for* neon

NE *abbrev.* **1** Nebraska **2** northeast **3** northeastern

Ne·an·der·thal (nē an'dər thôl') ***adj.*** ⟦after a Ger valley⟧ **1** designating or of a widespread form of early human being of the Pleistocene Epoch **2** primitive or regressive

THESAURUS

NAIVE.—*Ant.* ORNATE, pretentious, sophisticated. **4** [Concerning the physical universe] actual, tangible, according to nature; see PHYSICAL 1, REAL.

naturalist ***n.*** botanist, zoologist, biologist; see SCIENTIST.

naturally ***interj.*** certainly, absolutely, of course; see SURELY, YES.

naturally ***a.*** **1** [In an unaffected manner] artlessly, spontaneously, innocently, candidly, openly, honestly, disingenuously, impulsively, freely, readily, easily, without restraint, directly; see also SIMPLY, SINCERELY.—*Ant.* AWKWARDLY, restrainedly, clumsily. **2** [As a matter of course] casually, according to expectation, as anticipated, characteristically, typically, normally, commonly, usually, ordinarily, habitually, by nature, instinctively, intuitively, by birth, uniformly, generally, consistently; see also REGULARLY.—*Ant.* STRANGELY, astonishingly, amazingly.

nature ***n.*** **1** [The external universe] cosmos, creation, macrocosm; see UNIVERSE. **2** [The complex of essential qualities] characteristics, quality, constitution; see CHARACTER 1, ESSENCE 1. **3** [Natural surroundings] outside world, out-of-doors, scenery, natural setting, view, seascape, landscape, the outdoors, natural scenery, the great outdoors; see also ENVIRONMENT, REALITY. **4** [Natural forces] natural law, natural order, underlying cause, cosmic process, physical energy, kinetic energy, potential energy, water power, fission, fusion, atomic power, the sun, radiation, rays; see also ENERGY 2. **5** [Vital forces in an organism] creation, generation, regeneration; see LIFE 1, 2, STRENGTH. **6** [Kind] species, sort, type; see KIND 2, VARIETY 1, 2. —**by nature** inherently, by birth, as a matter of course; see NATURALLY 2. —**of** (or **in**) **the nature of** similar to, having the essential character of, as compared to; see LIKE.

naughty ***a.*** wayward, disobedient, mischievous, impish, fiendish, badly behaved, roguish, bad, unmanageable, ungovernable, insubordinate, froward, wanton, recalcitrant; see also RUDE 2, UNRULY.

nausea ***n.*** motion sickness, queasiness, vomiting; see ILLNESS 2.

nauseate ***v.*** sicken, offend, repulse; see BOTHER 2, DISGUST, DISTURB.

nauseous* ***a.*** queasy, ill, squeamish; see SICK.

nautical ***a.*** oceangoing, marine, naval, oceanic, deep-sea, aquatic, sailing, seafaring, seaworthy, seagoing, boating, yachting, cruising, whaling, oceanographic, rowing, navigating; see also MARITIME.

naval ***a.*** seagoing, marine, aquatic; see MARITIME, NAUTICAL.

navel ***n.*** bellybutton*, depression, umbilicus; see CENTER 1.

navigable ***a.*** passable, deep enough, open; see SAFE 1.

navigate ***v.*** pilot, steer, cruise, sail, head out for, ride out, lay a course, operate; see also DRIVE 2.

navigation ***n.*** navigating, seamanship, yachting, piloting, aeronautics, flying, sailing, seafaring, ocean travel, exploration, voyaging, shipping, cruising, plotting a course, boating, pilotage, dead reckoning.

navigator ***n.*** seaman, explorer, mariner; see PILOT 1, SAILOR.

navy ***n.*** fleet, carrier group, squadron, flotilla, armada, task force, submarine force, ships, amphibious force, coast guard.

—*n.* **1** a Neanderthal human being **2** one who is crude, primitive, etc.

neap (nēp) ***adj.*** ⟦OE *nep-* in *nepflod,* neap tide⟧ designating either of the two lowest high tides in the month —***n.*** neap tide

Ne·a·pol·i·tan (nē′ə päl′ə tən) ***adj.*** of Naples —***n.*** a person born or living in Naples

Neapolitan ice cream brick ice cream in layers of different flavors and colors

near (nir) ***adv.*** ⟦OE compar. of *neah,* nigh⟧ **1** at a short distance in space or time **2** closely; intimately —***adj.*** **1** close in distance or time **2** close in relationship; akin **3** close in friendship **4** close in degree *[*a *near* escape*]* **5** short or direct *[*the *near* way*]* —***prep.*** close to —***vt., vi.*** to draw near (to); approach —**near′ness *n.***

near′by′ *adj., adv.* near; close at hand

Near East countries near the E end of the Mediterranean, including those of SW Asia, the Arabian Peninsula, & NE Africa

near′ly *adv.* almost; not quite

near miss 1 a result that is nearly but not quite successful **2** a near escape

near′sight′ed *adj.* having better vision for near objects than for objects that are distant; myopic —**near′sight′ed·ness *n.***

neat (nēt) ***adj.*** ⟦< L *nitere,* to shine⟧ **1** unmixed; undiluted *[*whiskey *neat]* **2** clean and tidy **3** skillful and precise **4** well-proportioned **5** cleverly said or done **6** [Slang] nice, pleasing, etc. —**neat′ly *adv.*** —**neat′ness *n.***

neat′en *vt.* to make clean, tidy, orderly, etc.: often with *up*

'neath or **neath** (nēth) ***prep.*** [Old Poet.] *short for* BENEATH

neb·bish (neb′ish) ***n.*** ⟦< Yiddish *nebekh,* pity⟧ one who is pitifully inept, shy, dull, etc.

Ne·bras·ka (nə bras′kə) Midwestern state of the U.S.: 76,878 sq. mi.; pop. 1,578,000; cap. Lincoln: abbrev. *NE* —**Ne·bras′kan *adj., n.***

neb·u·la (neb′yə lə) ***n., pl.*** **-lae′** (-lē′) or **-las** ⟦L, mist⟧ a cloud of interstellar gas or dust, or, formerly, any hazy, distant celestial object, as a star cluster —**neb′u·lar *adj.***

neb′u·lous (-ləs) ***adj.*** unclear; vague

nec·es·sar·i·ly (nes′ə ser′ə lē) ***adv.*** **1** because of necessity **2** as a necessary result

nec′es·sar′y (-ser′ē) ***adj.*** ⟦< L *ne-,* not + *cedere,* give way⟧ **1** essential; indispensable **2** inevitable **3** required —***n.,*** *pl.* **-sar′ies** something necessary

ne·ces·si·tate (nə ses′ə tāt′) ***vt.*** **-tat′ed, -tat′ing** to make necessary or unavoidable

ne·ces′si·ty (-tē) ***n., pl.*** **-ties** ⟦see NECESSARY⟧ **1** natural causation; fate **2** great need **3** something that cannot be done without —**of necessity** necessarily

neck (nek) ***n.*** ⟦OE *hnecca*⟧ **1** that part of a human or animal joining the head to the body **2** the part of a garment near the neck **3** a necklike part; specif., *a)* a narrow strip of land *b)* the narrowest part of a bottle, etc. *c)* a strait —***vt., vi.*** [Slang] to hug, kiss, and caress passionately —**neck and neck** very close, as in a race

neck·er·chief (nek′ər chif, -chēf′) ***n.*** ⟦see prec. & KERCHIEF⟧ a handkerchief or scarf worn around the neck

neck′lace (-lis) ***n.*** ⟦NECK + LACE⟧ an ornamental string of beads, chain of gold, etc., worn around the neck

neck′tie′ *n.* a band worn around the neck under a collar and tied in front

neck′wear′ *n.* articles worn about the neck, as neckties or scarves

ne·crol·o·gy (ne kräl′ə jē) ***n., pl.*** **-gies** ⟦ult. < Gr *nekros,* corpse + -LOGY⟧ a list of people who have died

nec·ro·man·cy (nek′rə man′sē) ***n.*** ⟦< Gr *nekros,* corpse + *manteia,* divination⟧ **1** divination by alleged communication with the dead **2** black magic; sorcery —**nec′ro·man′cer *n.***

ne·cro·sis (ne krō′sis) ***n., pl.*** **-ses′** (-sēz′) ⟦< Gr *nekros,* corpse⟧ the death or decay of tissue in a part of the body

nec·tar (nek′tər) ***n.*** ⟦< Gr *nektar*⟧ **1** *Gr. & Rom. Myth.* the drink of the gods **2** any very delicious beverage **3** the sweetish liquid in many flowers, used by bees to make honey

nec·tar·ine (nek′tə rēn′, nek′tə rēn′) ***n.*** ⟦< prec.⟧ a kind of smooth-skinned peach

nee or **née** (nā; *now often* nē) ***adj.*** ⟦Fr⟧ born *[*Mrs. Helen Jones, *nee* Smith*]*

need (nēd) ***n.*** ⟦OE *nied*⟧ **1** necessity **2** a lack of something useful, required, or desired *[*to have *need* of a rest*]* **3** something required or desired that is lacking *[*your daily *needs]* **4** *a)* a condition in which help is required *[*a friend in *need] b)* poverty —***vt.*** **1** to have need of; require **2** to be obliged; must *[*she needs to be careful*]* —

THESAURUS

near *a.* **1** [Not distant in space] close, nigh*, proximate, adjacent, adjoining, neighboring, not remote, close at hand, contiguous, handy, nearby, next door to, at close quarters, beside, side by side, in close proximity; see also BORDERING.—*Ant.* DISTANT, removed, far off. **2** [Not distant in relationship] touching, close, akin; see FRIENDLY, RELATED 3. **3** [Not distant in time] at hand, approaching, next; see COMING 1, EXPECTED.

nearly *a.* practically, just about*, approximately; see ALMOST.

nearness *n.* **1** [Nearness in time or space] closeness, proximity, vicinity, approximation, approach, intimacy, close quarters, resemblance, likeness, handiness, imminence, immediacy, threat, menace.—*Ant.* DISTANCE, remoteness, difference. **2** [Nearness in feeling] familiarity, affection, intimacy; see ADMIRATION, FRIENDSHIP.

neat *a.* **1** [Clean and orderly] tidy, trim, prim, spruce, dapper, smart, correct, shipshape, methodical, regular, orderly, systematic, spotless, nice, meticulous, elegant, spick-and-span, immaculate, chic, well-groomed, exact, precise, proper, neat as a pin, in good order, spruced up; see also CLEAN 1.—*Ant.* DISORDERED, messy, slovenly. **2** [Clever] dexterous, deft, skillful, expert, proficient, apt, ready, artful, nimble, quick, agile, adept, speedy, finished, practiced, easy, effortless; see also ABLE.—*Ant.* AWKWARD, clumsy, fumbling.

neatly *a.* **1** [So as to present a neat appearance] tidily, systematically, methodically, correctly, exactly, uniformly, levelly, flatly, smoothly, regularly, precisely, immaculately; see also EVENLY 1, ORGANIZED. **2** [In an adroit manner] skillfully, deftly, agilely; see CLEVERLY, EASILY.

neatness *n.* cleanness, tidiness, orderliness; see CLEANLINESS.

necessarily *a.* vitally, fundamentally, importantly, indispensably, unavoidably, undeniably, certainly, as a matter of course, inescapably, irresistibly, inevitably, assuredly, significantly, undoubtedly, indubitably, positively, unquestionably, no doubt, without fail, of necessity, of course, beyond someone's control, come what may, by its own nature, from within, by definition; see also SURELY.

necessary *a.* important, needed, requisite, expedient, needful, indispensable, required, urgent, wanted, imperative, prerequisite, pressing, vital, fundamental, quintessential, cardinal, significant, momentous, compulsory, mandatory, basic, paramount, obligatory, essential, compelling, binding, incumbent upon someone, all-important, specified, unavoidable, decisive, crucial, elementary, chief, principal, prime, intrinsic, fixed, constant, permanent, inherent, ingrained, innate, without choice.

necessitate *v.* compel, constrain, oblige; see FORCE.

necessity *n.* **1** [The state of being required] need, essentiality, indispensability; see REQUIREMENT 2. **2** [That which is needed] need, want, requisite, vital part, essential, demand, imperative, fundamental, claim; see also LACK 2. **3** [The state of being forced by circumstances] exigency, pinch, stress, urgency, destitution, extremity, privation, obligation, matter of life and death; see also EMERGENCY, POVERTY 1. **—of necessity** inevitably, importantly, surely; see NECESSARILY.

neck *n.* **1** [The juncture of the head and the trunk] cervical vertebrae, nape, scruff; see THROAT. **2** [The part of a dress at the neck] neckband, neckline, collar; see DRESS 1, 2. **—risk one's neck** endanger oneself, gamble, take a chance; see RISK. **—stick one's neck out** endanger oneself, take a chance, gamble; see RISK.

necklace *n.* ornament, accessory, string of beads, jewels, chain, neckband, pearls, diamonds, choker; see also JEWELRY.

necktie *n.* neckwear, cravat, ascot; see TIE 2.

need *n.* **1** [Poverty] want, destitution, pennilessness; see POVERTY 1. **2** [Lack] insufficiency, shortage, inadequacy; see LACK 1, 2. **3** [A requirement] obligation, necessity, urgency; see REQUIREMENT 2. **—if need be** if it is required, if the occasion demands, if necessary; see IF.

need *v.* lack, require, feel the necessity for, be in need of, suffer privation, be in want, be destitute, be short, be inadequate, have occasion for, have use for, miss, be without, do without, be needy, be poor, be deficient in, go hungry, live from hand to mouth, feel the pinch*, be down and out*, be hard up*, be up against it*; see also WANT 2.—*Ant.* OWN, have, hold. **—have need to** have to, be obligated to, have reason to; see MUST.

needed *a.* wanted, required, desired; see NECESSARY.

vi. to be in need —**have need to** to be required to —**if need be** if it is required
need'ful *adj.* necessary; required
nee·dle (nēd''l) *n.* ⟦OE *nædl*⟧ **1** a small, slender, pointed piece of steel with a hole for thread, used for sewing **2** a slender rod of steel, bone, etc. used for crocheting or knitting **3** STYLUS (sense 2*b*) **4** the pointer of a compass, gauge, etc. **5** the thin, short, pointed leaf of the pine, spruce, etc. **6** the sharp, slender metal tube at the end of a hypodermic syringe —*vt.* **-dled, -dling** [Inf.] **1** to goad; prod **2** to tease —**nee'dler** *n.*
nee'dle·point' *n.* **1** embroidery of woolen threads upon canvas **2** lace made on a paper pattern, with a needle: in full **needlepoint lace**
need'less *adj.* not needed; unnecessary *[needless* cruelty*]* —**need'less·ly** *adv.*
nee'dle·work' *n.* work done with a needle; embroidery, crocheting, sewing, etc.
need·n't (nēd''nt) *contr.* need not
needs (nēdz) *adv.* ⟦OE *nedes*⟧ of necessity: with *must [*he must *needs* obey*]*
need'y *adj.* **-i·er, -i·est** very poor —**need'i·ness** *n.*
ne'er (ner) *adv.* [Old Poet.] never
ne'er'-do-well' *n.* a shiftless, irresponsible person
ne·far·i·ous (nə fer'ē əs) *adj.* ⟦< L *ne-*, not + *fas*, lawful⟧ very wicked; villainous —**ne·far'i·ous·ly** *adv.* —**ne·far'i·ous·ness** *n.*
ne·gate (ni gāt') *vt.* **-gat'ed, -gat'ing** ⟦< L *negare*, deny⟧ **1** to deny **2** to make ineffective
ne·ga·tion (ni gā'shən) *n.* **1** the act or an instance of denying **2** the lack or opposite of something positive
neg·a·tive (neg'ə tiv) *adj.* **1** expressing denial or refusal; saying "no" **2** opposite to or lacking in that which is positive *[*a *negative* force*]* **3** *Math.* designating a quantity less than zero, or one to be subtracted **4** *Med.* not showing the presence of a condition, infection, etc. **5** *Photog.* reversing the relation of light and shade of the subject **6** *Elec. a)* of, generating, or charged with negative electricity *b)* having an excess of electrons —*n.* **1** a negative word, reply, etc. **2** the point of view that opposes the positive **3** the plate in a battery having an excess of electrons flowing out toward the positive **4** an exposed and developed photographic film or plate on which light and shadow are reversed —**in the negative** with a negative answer —**neg'a·tive·ly** *adv.* —**neg'a·tiv'i·ty** *n.*
ne·glect (ni glekt') *vt.* ⟦< L *neg-*, not + *legere*, gather⟧ **1** to ignore or disregard **2** to fail to attend to properly **3** to leave undone —*n.* **1** a neglecting **2** lack of proper care **3** the state of being neglected —**ne·glect'ful** *adj.*
neg·li·gee (neg'lə zhā') *n.* ⟦< Fr *négliger*, to neglect⟧ a woman's loosely fitting dressing gown
neg·li·gent (neg'lə jənt) *adj.* **1** habitually failing to do the required thing; neglectful **2** careless, inattentive, etc. —**neg'li·gence** *n.*
neg'li·gi·ble (-jə bəl) *adj.* that can be neglected or disregarded; trifling
ne·go·ti·ate (ni gō'shē āt') *vi.* **-at'ed, -at'ing** ⟦< L *negotium*, business⟧ to discuss a matter with a view to reaching agreement —*vt.* **1** to settle (a business transaction, treaty, etc.) **2** to transfer or sell (bonds, stocks, etc.) **3** to succeed in crossing, passing, etc. —**ne·go'ti·a·ble** (-shē ə bəl, -shə bəl) *adj.* —**ne·go'ti·a'tion** *n.* —**ne·go'ti·a'tor** *n.*
neg·ri·tude (neg'rə to͞od', nē'grə-) *n.* ⟦Fr *négritude*⟧ *[also* **N-**] an awareness and affirmation by black people of their distinctive cultural heritage
Ne·gro (nē'grō) *n.*, *pl.* **-groes** ⟦Sp & Port *negro*, black⟧ **1** a member of any of the indigenous dark-skinned peoples of Africa **2** a person having some African ancestors; a black person —*adj.* of or for Negroes
Ne'groid' (-groid') *adj.* designating or of one of the major groups of human beings, including most of the peoples of Africa
Neh·ru (nā'ro͞o), **Ja·wa·har·lal** (jə wä'hər läl') 1889-1964; prime minister of India (1947-64)
neigh (nā) *vi.* ⟦OE *hnægan*⟧ to utter the characteristic cry of a horse —*n.* this cry; a whinny
neigh·bor (nā'bər) *n.* ⟦OE *neah*, nigh + *gebur*, freeholder⟧ **1** one who lives or is situated near another **2** a fellow human being —*vt.*, *vi.* to live or be situated near (someone or something) Brit. sp. **neigh'bour** —**neigh'bor·ing** *adj.*
neigh'bor·hood' *n.* **1** a particular community, district, or area **2** the people living near one another —**in the neighborhood of** [Inf.] **1** near **2** about; approximately
neigh'bor·ly *adj.* like or appropriate to neighbors; friendly, helpful, etc. —**neigh'bor·li·ness** *n.*
nei·ther (nē'*th*ər, nī'-) *adj.*, *pron.* ⟦OE *na-hwæther*, lit., not whether⟧ not one or the other (of two); not either *[neither* boy went; *neither* of them was invited*]* —*conj.* not either *[*I could *neither* laugh nor cry*]*
nem·a·tode (nem'ə tōd') *n.* ⟦ult. < Gr *nēma*, thread⟧ a long, cylindrical, unsegmented worm; roundworm
nem·e·sis (nem'ə sis) *n.*, *pl.* **-ses'** (-sēz') ⟦< Gr *nemein*,

THESAURUS

needle *n.* awl, spike, hypodermic needle, syringe, phonograph needle, stylus, electric needle, probe, skewer, pin, darning needle, sewing needle, knitting needle.

needle* *v.* provoke, goad, tease; see BOTHER 2.

needless *a.* unwanted, excessive, groundless; see UNNECESSARY, USELESS 1.

needy *a.* destitute, indigent, penniless; see POOR 1.

negate *v.* repeal, retract, nullify; see CANCEL.

negation *n.* opposition, contradiction, repudiation; see DENIAL, REFUSAL.

negative *a.* **1** [Involving a refusal] denying, contradictory, contrary, disavowing, contravening, rejecting, disallowing.—*Ant.* FAVORABLE, encouraging, accepting. **2** [Lacking positive qualities] absent, removed, neutralizing, counteractive, annulling, invalidating.—*Ant.* EMPHATIC, validating, affirmative.

negative *n.* **1** [A refusal] contradiction, disavowal, refutation; see DENIAL, REFUSAL. **2** [A negative image] film, plate, developed film; see IMAGE 2, PICTURE 2.

neglect *n.* **1** [The act of showing indifference to a person] slight, disregard, thoughtlessness, disrespect, carelessness, scorn, oversight, heedlessness, inattention, unconcern, inconsideration, disdain, coolness; see also INDIFFERENCE. **2** [The act of neglecting responsibilities] negligence, slovenliness, neglectfulness; see CARELESSNESS.

neglect *v.* **1** [To treat with indifference] slight, scorn, overlook, disregard, disdain, detest, rebuff, affront, despise, ignore, depreciate, spurn, underestimate, undervalue, shake off, make light of, laugh off, keep one's distance, pass over, pass up, have nothing to do with, let alone, let go, not care for, pay no attention to, pay no heed, leave alone, not give a darn*, leave well enough alone, let it ride*, keep at arm's length.—*Ant.* CONSIDER, appreciate, value. **2** [To fail to attend to responsibilities] pass over, defer, procrastinate, suspend, dismiss, discard, let slip, miss, skip, omit, skimp, gloss over, be remiss, be derelict, ignore, trifle, postpone, lose sight of, look the other way, let it go, not trouble oneself with, evade, be careless, be irresponsible.—*Ant.* WATCH, care for, attend to.

neglected *a.* slighted, disregarded, scorned, disdained, despised, affronted, overlooked, ignored, spurned, omitted, undervalued, deferred, dismissed, passed over, postponed, evaded, deteriorated, underestimated, declined, lapsed, uncared-for, unwatched, unheeded, depreciated, unconsidered, shaken off, unused, unwanted, tossed aside, abandoned, forgotten, out in the cold, dropped, put on the shelf.—*Ant.* CONSIDERED, cared for, heeded.

negligence *n.* disregard, inconsideration, disrespect; see CARELESSNESS, INDIFFERENCE, NEGLECT 1.

negligent *a.* indifferent, inattentive, neglectful; see CARELESS.

negotiate *v.* **1** [To make arrangements for] arrange, bargain, confer, consult, parley, transact, mediate, make peace, contract, settle, adjust, conciliate, accommodate, arbitrate, referee, umpire, compromise, bring to terms, make terms, make the best of, treat with, moderate, work out, dicker*, haggle, bury the hatchet*. **2** [To transfer] barter, allocate, transmit; see ASSIGN, SELL.

negotiation *n.* compromise, intervention, mediation; see AGREEMENT.

Negro *n.* black, African, African-American, Afro-American, Afro-Asian, black person, person of color.

neighbor *n.* acquaintance, companion, associate, next-door neighbor, nearby resident; see also FRIEND.

neighborhood *n.* environs, block, vicinity, locality, proximity, district, area, parish, ward, precinct, community, region, zone, section, suburb, tract. —**in the neighborhood of*** about, approximately, close to; see NEAR 1.

neighboring *a.* adjacent, adjoining, contiguous; see BORDERING, NEAR 1.

neighborly *a.* sociable, hospitable, helpful; see FRIENDLY.

neither *a.*, *conj.* nor yet, also not, not either, not, not at all.

neither *pron.* not one or the other, not either one, no one, nobody, neither one, not this one, nor this nor that, no one of two, not the one, not any one; see also NONE 1, NOTHING.

deal out⟧ **1** *a*) just punishment *b*) one who imposes this **2** anyone or anything that seems inevitably to defeat or frustrate someone

neo- ⟦< Gr *neos*⟧ *combining form* [*often* **N-**] **1** new, recent **2** in a new or different way

ne·o·clas·sic (nē′ō klas′ik) ***adj.*** designating or of a revival of classic style and form in art, literature, etc.: also **ne′o·clas′si·cal** —**ne′o·clas′si·cism′** ***n.***

ne′o·co·lo′ni·al·ism′ ***n.*** exploitation by a foreign power of a region that has ostensibly achieved independence

ne·ol·o·gism (nē äl′ə jiz′əm) ***n.*** ⟦see NEO-, -LOGY, & -ISM⟧ a new word or a new meaning for an established word

ne·on (nē′än′) ***n.*** ⟦ult. < Gr *neos*, new⟧ a nonreactive, gaseous chemical element found in small amounts in the earth's atmosphere

ne·o·nate (nē′ō nāt′) ***n.*** ⟦ModL < *neo-*, NEO- + L *natus*, born⟧ a newborn infant —**ne′o·na′tal** ***adj.***

neon lamp a tube containing neon, which glows red when an electric current is sent through it

ne·o·phyte (nē′ō fīt′) ***n.*** ⟦< Gr *neos*, new + *phyein*, to produce⟧ **1** a new convert **2** a beginner; novice

ne·o·plasm (nē′ō plaz′əm) ***n.*** ⟦< NEO- + Gr *plassein*, to form⟧ an abnormal growth of tissue, as a tumor

ne′o·prene′ (-prēn′) ***n.*** a synthetic rubber resistant to oil, heat, etc.

Ne·pal (nə pôl′, -päl′) country in the Himalayas: 56,827 sq. mi.; pop. 18,462,000 —**Nep·a·lese** (nep′ə lēz′) ***adj.***, ***n.***

neph·ew (nef′yo͞o) ***n.*** ⟦< L *nepos*⟧ the son of one's brother or sister, or of one's brother-in-law or sister-in-law

ne·phri·tis (nə frīt′əs) ***n.*** ⟦< Gr *nephros*, kidney + -ITIS⟧ a disease of the kidneys, characterized by inflammation

ne·phro·sis (nə frō′sis) ***n.*** ⟦< Gr *nephros*, kidney + -OSIS⟧ a degenerative disease of the kidneys, characterized by edema

ne plus ul·tra (nā plus ul′trə) ⟦L, no more beyond⟧ the ultimate

nep·o·tism (nep′ə tiz′əm) ***n.*** ⟦< L *nepos*, nephew⟧ favoritism shown to relatives, esp. in providing jobs —**nep′o·tis′tic** ***adj.***

Nep·tune (nep′to͞on′) ***n.*** **1** the Roman god of the sea **2** the planet eighth in distance from the sun: see PLANET

nep·tu·ni·um (nep to͞o′nē əm) ***n.*** ⟦after prec.⟧ a radioactive chemical element produced by irradiating uranium atoms

nerd (nʉrd) ***n.*** [Slang] a person regarded as dull, ineffective, etc. —**nerd′y** ***adj.***

Ne·ro (nir′ō) A.D. 37-68; emperor of Rome (54-68)

nerve (nʉrv) ***n.*** ⟦< L *nervus*⟧ **1** any of the cordlike fibers carrying impulses between body organs and the central nervous system **2** coolness in danger; courage **3** [*pl.*] nervousness **4** [Inf.] impudent boldness —***vt.*** **nerved, nerv′ing** to give strength or courage to —**get on someone's nerves** [Inf.] to make someone irritable or exasperated

nerve center a control center; headquarters

nerve gas a poisonous gas causing paralysis of the respiratory and nervous systems

nerve′less ***adj.*** **1** without strength, vigor, etc.; weak **2** not nervous; cool; controlled —**nerve′less·ly** ***adv.***

nerve′-rack′ing or **nerve′-wrack′ing** (-rak′iŋ) ***adj.*** very trying to one's patience or equanimity

nerv·ous (nʉr′vəs) ***adj.*** **1** animated **2** of or made up of nerves **3** emotionally tense, restless, etc. **4** fearful —**nerv′ous·ly** ***adv.*** —**nerv′ous·ness** ***n.***

nervous system all the nerve cells and nervous tissues in an organism, including, in the vertebrates, the brain, spinal cord, nerves, etc.

nerv′y ***adj.*** **-i·er, -i·est** **1** bold **2** [Inf.] brazen; impudent

-ness (nis, nəs) ⟦OE *-nes(s)*⟧ *suffix* state, quality, or instance of being [*togetherness, sadness*]

nest (nest) ***n.*** ⟦OE⟧ **1** the structure or place where a bird lays its eggs and shelters its young **2** the place used by insects, fish, etc. for spawning or breeding **3** a cozy place; retreat **4** *a*) a haunt or den *b*) the people who frequent such a place [*a nest of thieves*] **5** a set of things, each fitting within the one next larger —***vi.***, ***vt.*** **1** to build or settle in (a nest) **2** to fit (an object) closely within another

nest egg money, etc. put aside as a reserve or to establish a fund

nes·tle (nes′əl) ***vi.*** **-tled, -tling** ⟦OE *nestlian*⟧ **1** to settle down comfortably **2** to press close for comfort or in affection **3** to lie sheltered —***vt.*** to cause to rest snugly

nest·ling (nest′liŋ) ***n.*** a young bird not yet ready to leave the nest

net[1] (net) ***n.*** ⟦OE *nett*⟧ **1** a loose fabric of woven or knotted string, etc., used to snare birds, fish, etc. **2** a trap; snare **3** a loose fabric of woven or knotted threads, etc., esp. one used to hold, protect, etc. [*a hairnet*] **4** [*usually* **N-**] [Inf.] *Comput. short for* INTERNET: with *the* —***vt.*** **net′ted, net′ting** to snare or enclose, as with a net

net[2] (net) ***adj.*** ⟦Fr, clear⟧ remaining after deductions or allowances have been made —***n.*** a net amount, profit, weight, price, etc. —***vt.*** **net′ted, net′ting** to clear as profit, etc.

neth·er (ne*th*′ər) ***adj.*** ⟦OE *neothera*⟧ lower or under [*the nether world*]

Neth·er·lands (ne*th*′ər ləndz) country in W Europe: 16,033 sq. mi.; pop. 15,340,000: usually used with *the* —**Neth′er·land′er** (-land′ər, -lən dər) ***n.***

neth′er·most′ ***adj.*** lowest

net′ting ***n.*** NET[1] (*n.* 1 & 3)

net·tle (net′'l) ***n.*** ⟦OE *netele*⟧ a weed with stinging hairs —***vt.*** **-tled, -tling** to irritate; annoy; vex

net′tle·some (-səm) ***adj.*** that nettles, or irritates

net′work′ ***n.*** **1** an arrangement of parallel wires, etc. crossed at intervals by others so as to leave open spaces **2** anything like this, as a system of interconnected roads, individuals, or computer terminals **3** *Radio, TV* a chain of transmitting stations —***adj.*** broadcast over the stations of a network

net′work′ing ***n.*** **1** the developing of contacts or exchanging of information, as to further a career **2** the interconnection of computer systems

neu·ral (no͝or′əl) ***adj.*** ⟦NEUR(O)- + -AL⟧ of a nerve, nerves, or the nervous system

neu·ral·gi·a (no͞o ral′jə) ***n.*** ⟦see NEURO- & -ALGIA⟧ severe pain along a nerve —**neu·ral′gic** (-jik) ***adj.***

neu·ras·the·ni·a (no͝or′əs thē′nē ə) ***n.*** ⟦< NEURO- + Gr *asthenia*, weakness⟧ a former category of mental disorder, characterized by fatigue, anxiety, etc. —**neu′ras·then′ic** (-then′ik) ***adj.***, ***n.***

neu·ri·tis (no͞o rīt′əs) ***n.*** ⟦fol. + -ITIS⟧ inflammation of a nerve or nerves —**neu·rit′ic** (-rit′ik) ***adj.***

neuro- ⟦< Gr *neuron*, nerve⟧ *combining form* of a nerve or the nervous system: also **neur-**

neu·rol·o·gy (no͞o räl′ə jē) ***n.*** ⟦prec. + -LOGY⟧ the branch of medicine dealing with the nervous system and its

THESAURUS

nephew ***n.*** brother's son, sister's son, grandnephew*, great-nephew, brother-in-law's son, sister-in-law's son, nephew by marriage; see also NIECE, RELATIVE.

nerve ***n.*** **1** [The path of nervous impulses] nerve fiber, nerve tissue, nerve cells, neurons, nerve endings. *Types of nerves include the following:* motor, sensory, efferent, afferent; effector, receptor. **2** [Courage] resolution, spirit, mettle; see COURAGE. **3** [*Impudence] temerity, audacity, effrontery; see RUDENESS.

nerve-racking ***a.*** exhausting, horrible, wearisome; see DIFFICULT 1, PAINFUL 1.

nerves ***n.*** strain, tension, hysteria, stress, butterflies*; see also NERVOUSNESS. —**get on someone's nerves*** exasperate, irritate, annoy; see BOTHER 2.

nervous ***a.*** **1** [Excitable] sensitive, irritable, impatient, moody, peevish, restless, uneasy, impulsive, rash, hasty, reckless, touchy, readily upset, high-strung, neurotic; see also UNSTABLE 2. **2** [Excited] agitated, bothered, annoyed; see EXCITED.

nervousness ***n.*** stimulation, agitation, animation, intoxication, sensitivity, delirium, excitability, irascibility, impulsiveness, impetuosity, moodiness, anger, elation, discomfiture, hastiness, vehemence, impatience, feverishness, stage fright, butterflies in the stomach*, the jitters*, the shakes*; see also EMBARRASSMENT, EXCITEMENT.—*Ant.* REST, calm, relaxation.

nest ***n.*** den, cradle, incubator; see RETREAT 2.

nest egg* ***n.*** personal savings, personal property, money, something for a rainy day*; see also MONEY 1, SAVINGS.

nestle ***v.*** cuddle, snuggle, settle down, take shelter, lie close, make oneself snug, huddle, move close to, lie against, curl up to.

net[1] ***n.*** screen, mesh, fabric; see WEB. *Varieties of nets include the following:* fishing, seine, gill, mosquito, tennis, ping-pong, volleyball, basketball, hockey, bird, butterfly, drift, hand, scoop; hairnet, dragnet.

net[2] ***a.*** clear, final, remaining, exclusive, irreducible, undeductible.

net[2] ***v.*** make, clear, gain above expenses; see PROFIT 2.

network ***n.*** **1** [System of channels] tracks, circuitry, channels, system, labyrinth, arrangement; see also CHAIN, WIRING. **2** [Netting] fiber, weave, mesh; see GOODS, WEB.

diseases —**neu·ro·log·i·cal** (noor'ə läj'i kəl) ***adj.*** —**neu·rol'o·gist** ***n.***
neu·ro·mus·cu·lar (noor'ō mus'kyoo lər) ***adj.*** of or involving both nerves and muscles
neu·ron (noor'än') ***n.*** the nerve cell body and all its processes
neu·ro·sis (noo rō'sis) ***n.***, *pl.* **-ses'** (-sēz') ⟦NEUR(O)- + -OSIS⟧ any of various mental disorders characterized by anxiety, compulsions, phobias, etc.
neu·ro·sur·ger·y (noor'ō sur'jər ē) ***n.*** the branch of surgery involving the brain or spinal cord —**neu'ro·sur'geon** ***n.***
neu·rot·ic (noo rät'ik) ***adj.*** of, characteristic of, or having a neurosis —***n.*** a neurotic person —**neu·rot'i·cal·ly** ***adv.***
neu·ro·trans·mit·ter (noor'ō trans'mit'ər) ***n.*** a biochemical substance that transmits or inhibits nerve impulses at a synapse
neu·ter (noot'ər) ***adj.*** ⟦< L *ne-*, not + *uter*, either⟧ **1** *Biol.* *a)* having no sexual organ *b)* having undeveloped sexual organs in the adult **2** *Gram.* designating or of the gender of words that are neither masculine nor feminine —***vt.*** to castrate or spay (an animal)
neu·tral (noo'trəl) ***adj.*** ⟦see prec.⟧ **1** supporting neither side in a quarrel or war **2** of neither extreme in type, kind, etc.; indefinite **3** having little or no decided color; not vivid —***n.*** **1** a neutral person or nation **2** a neutral color **3** *Mech.* a disengaged position of gears —**neu'tral·ly** ***adv.***
neu'tral·ism' (-iz'əm) ***n.*** a policy of remaining neutral, esp. in international conflicts —**neu'tral·ist** ***adj.***, ***n.***
neu·tral'i·ty (-tral'ə tē) ***n.*** **1** a being neutral **2** the status or policy of a neutral nation
neu·tral·ize (noo'trə līz') ***vt.*** **-ized'**, **-iz'ing** to destroy or counteract the effectiveness, force, etc. of —**neu'tral·i·za'tion** ***n.*** —**neu'tral·iz'er** ***n.***
neutral spirits ethyl alcohol of 190 proof or over, used in blended whiskeys, liqueurs, etc.
neu·tri·no (noo trē'nō) ***n.***, *pl.* **-nos** ⟦It, little neutron⟧ any of three leptons having almost no mass
neu·tron (noo'trän') ***n.*** ⟦< NEUTRAL⟧ an elementary particle in the nucleus of an atom, carrying no electrical charge
neutron bomb a small thermonuclear bomb that would release large numbers of neutrons intended to kill enemy soldiers without destroying buildings, etc.
neutron star a collapsed star of extremely high density composed almost entirely of neutrons
Ne·vad·a (nə vad'ə, -väd'ə) Mountain State of the W U.S.: 109,806 sq. mi.; pop. 1,202,000; cap. Carson City: abbrev. *NV* —**Ne·vad'an** ***adj.***, ***n.***
nev·er (nev'ər) ***adv.*** ⟦< OE *ne*, not + *æfre*, ever⟧ **1** not ever; at no time **2** not at all; in no case
nev'er·more' ***adv.*** never again
nev'er-nev'er land an unreal or unrealistic place or situation
nev'er·the·less' (-*th*ə les') ***adv.*** in spite of that; however
Ne·vis (nē'vis, nev'is) island of the West Indies: see ST. KITTS AND NEVIS
ne·vus (nē'vəs) ***n.***, *pl.* **ne'vi'** (-vī') ⟦< L *naevus*⟧ a birthmark or mole
new (noo) ***adj.*** ⟦OE *niwe*⟧ **1** appearing, thought of, developed, made, etc. for the first time **2** different from (the) one in the past *[a new hairdo]* **3** strange; unfamiliar **4** *a)* recently grown; fresh *b)* harvested early *[new potatoes]* **5** unused **6** modern; recent **7** more; additional **8** starting as a repetition of a cycle, series, etc. *[the new moon]* **9** having just reached a position, rank, etc. *[a new arrival]* —***adv.*** **1** again **2** recently —**new'ness** ***n.***
New Age [*often* **n- a-**] of or pertaining to a cultural movement variously combining belief in reincarnation, astrology, meditation, etc.
New·ark (noo'ərk) city in NE New Jersey: pop. 275,000
new blood new people as a potential source of new ideas, vigor, etc.
new'born' ***adj.*** **1** recently born **2** reborn —***n.*** a newborn infant
New Bruns·wick (brunz'wik) province of SE Canada: 28,354 sq. mi.; pop. 738,000; cap. Fredericton: abbrev. *NB*
new'com'er (-kum'ər) ***n.*** a recent arrival
New Deal the principles and policies adopted by President F. D. Roosevelt in the 1930s to advance economic recovery and social welfare
New Delhi capital of India, adjacent to the old city of Delhi: pop. 301,000
new·el (noo'əl) ***n.*** ⟦ult. < L *nux*, nut⟧ **1** the pillar around which the steps of a winding staircase turn **2** the post that supports the handrail of a flight of stairs: also **newel post**
New England the six NE states of the U.S.: Maine, Vermont, New Hampshire, Massachusetts, Rhode Island, and Connecticut —**New Eng'land·er**
new'fan'gled (-faŋ'gəld) ***adj.*** ⟦ME *newe*, new + *-fangel* < OE *fon*, to take⟧ new; novel: a humorously derogatory term
new'found' (-found') ***adj.*** newly gained or acquired
New·found·land (noo'fənd lənd, -land') province of Canada, including an island off the E coast & Labrador: 143,501 sq. mi.; pop. 552,000; cap. St. John's: abbrev. *NF*
New Guinea large island in the East Indies, north of Australia
New Hamp·shire (hamp'shir) New England state of the U.S.: 8,993 sq. mi.; pop. 1,109,000; cap. Concord: abbrev. *NH* —**New Hamp'shir·ite'**
New Ha·ven (hā'vən) city in S Connecticut: pop. 130,000
New Jer·sey (jur'zē) state of the E U.S.: 7,417 sq. mi.; pop. 7,730,000; cap. Trenton: abbrev. *NJ* —**New Jer'sey·ite'**
new'ly ***adv.*** recently; lately
new'ly·wed' ***n.*** a recently married person
New Mexico Mountain State of the SW U.S.: 121,335 sq. mi.; pop. 1,515,000; cap. Santa Fe: abbrev. *NM* —**New Mexican**
new moon the moon when it is between the earth and the sun, with its dark side toward the earth: it is followed by a thin crescent phase
New Or·le·ans (ôr'lē ənz, -lənz; ôr lēnz') city & port in SE Louisiana: pop. 497,000
New·port News (noo'pôrt') seaport in SE Virginia: pop. 171,000
news (nooz) ***n.*** **1** new information; information previously unknown **2** *a)* recent happenings *b)* reports of these **3** *short for* NEWSCAST —**make news** to do something apt to be reported as news
news'boy' ***n.*** a boy who sells or delivers newspapers

THESAURUS

neurosis ***n.*** compulsion, instability, mental disorder; see NERVOUSNESS, OBSESSION.
neurotic ***a.*** disturbed, unstable, high-strung; see TROUBLED.
neurotic ***n.*** paranoid, compulsive person, victim of depression; see ILLNESS 1.
neutral ***a.*** **1** [Not fighting] noncombatant, nonpartisan, on the sidelines, nonparticipating, inactive, disengaged, uninvolved, standing by, inert, on the fence.—*Ant.* ENGAGED, involved, active. **2** [Without opinion] unbiased, open-minded, impartial; see INDIFFERENT. **3** [Without distinctive color] drab, indeterminate, vague; see DULL 2.
never ***a.*** not ever, at no time, not at any time, not in the least, not in any way, in no way, not at all, not under any condition, nevermore, never again, no way*.
nevertheless ***a.*** however, nonetheless, notwithstanding; see ALTHOUGH, BUT 1.
new ***a.*** **1** [Recent] current, brand-new, newborn, young, newfangled*, latest, just out; see also FRESH 1. **2** [Modern] modish, popular, faddish, up to the minute, contemporary, latest; see also FASHIONABLE, MODERN 1. **3** [Novel] unique, original, bizarre; see UNUSUAL 1, 2. **4** [Different] unlike, dissimilar, distinct; see UNLIKE. **5** [Additional] further, increased, supplementary; see EXTRA. **6** [Inexperienced] green, unseasoned, untrained; see INCOMPETENT, INEXPERIENCED. **7** [Recently] newly, freshly, lately; see RECENTLY.
newcomer ***n.*** immigrant, outsider, foreigner, tenderfoot, maverick*, Johnny-come-lately*; see also ALIEN, STRANGER.
newfangled* ***a.*** novel, unique, new; see FASHIONABLE, MODERN 1.
newly ***a.*** lately, anew, afresh; see RECENTLY.
newlywed ***n.*** bride, bridegroom, honeymooner; see HUSBAND, WIFE.
newness ***n.*** uniqueness, modernity, recentness; see ORIGINALITY.
news ***n.*** **1** [Information] intelligence, tidings, advice, discovery, recognition, the scoop*, the goods*, headlines, front-page news; see also DATA, KNOWLEDGE 1. **2** [A specific report] telling, narration, recital, account, description, message, copy, communication, release, communiqué, telegram, cable, radiogram, broadcast, telecast, bulletin, dispatch, news story, scoop*, big news*, eye opener*; see also ANNOUNCEMENT. —**make news** become famous, accomplish, create events; see EXPOSE, REVEAL.

news'cast' ***n.*** a radio or television news broadcast —**news'cast'er** ***n.***
news'deal'er ***n.*** a retailer of newspapers, magazines, etc.
news'let'ter ***n.*** a bulletin issued regularly to subscribers, employees, club members, etc., containing news of upcoming events, etc.
news'man' (-man', -mən) ***n.***, *pl.* **-men'** (-men', -mən) a newscaster or reporter, esp. a male
news'pa'per ***n.*** a regular publication, usually daily or weekly, containing news, opinions, advertising, etc.
news'pa'per·man' (-man') ***n.***, *pl.* **-men'** (-men') **1** a person, esp. a man, who works for a newspaper as a reporter, editor, etc. **2** a newspaper owner or publisher —**news'pa'per·wom'an**, *pl.* **-wom'en**, ***fem.n.***
news'print' ***n.*** a cheap, low-grade paper used chiefly for newspapers
news'stand' ***n.*** a stand at which newspapers, magazines, etc. are sold
news'wom'an ***n.***, *pl.* **-wom'en** a female newscaster or reporter
news'wor'thy (-wur'*th*ē) ***adj.*** timely and important or interesting
news'y ***adj.*** **-i·er**, **-i·est** [Inf.] containing much news
newt (no͞ot) ***n.*** ⟦by merging of ME (*a*)*n eute*, a newt⟧ any of various small, amphibious salamanders
New Testament the part of the Bible that contains the life and teachings of Jesus and his followers
new·ton (no͞ot''n) ***n.*** ⟦after fol.⟧ a unit of force
New·ton (no͞ot''n), Sir **Isaac** 1642-1727; Eng. mathematician & natural philosopher
New World the Western Hemisphere
New Year's (Day) Jan. 1
New Year's Eve the evening before New Year's Day
New York (yôrk) **1** state of the NE U.S.: 47,224 sq. mi.; pop. 17,990,000; cap. Albany: abbrev. *NY* **2** city & port in SE New York: pop. 7,323,000 (met. area, 8,547,000): often **New York City** —**New York'er**
New Zea·land (zē'lənd) country made up of two large islands in the S Pacific, southeast of Australia: 104,454 sq. mi.; pop. 3,435,000 —**New Zea'land·er**
next (nekst) ***adj.*** ⟦OE *neahst*, superl. of *neah*, nigh⟧ nearest; immediately preceding or following —***adv.*** **1** in the nearest time, place, rank, etc. **2** on the first subsequent occasion
next'-door' ***adj.*** in or at the next house, building, etc.
nex·us (nek'səs) ***n.***, *pl.* **nex'us·es** or **nex'us** ⟦L⟧ a connection, tie, or link
NF Newfoundland
NH New Hampshire
Ni *Chem. symbol for* nickel
ni·a·cin (nī'ə sin) ***n.*** ⟦NI(COTINIC) AC(ID) + *-in*⟧ NICOTINIC ACID
Ni·ag·ara Falls (nī ag'rə) large waterfall on a river (**Niagara**) flowing from Lake Erie into Lake Ontario
nib (nib) ***n.*** ⟦< ME *nebb*, a bird's beak⟧ a point, esp. a pen point
nib·ble (nib'əl) ***vt.***, ***vi.*** **-bled**, **-bling** ⟦ME *nebyllen*⟧ **1** to eat (food) with quick, small bites **2** to bite (*at*) lightly and intermittently —***n.*** a small bite —**nib'bler** ***n.***
nibs (nibz) ***n.*** ⟦< ?⟧ [Inf.] a self-important person: preceded by *his* or *her*
Nic·a·ra·gua (nik'ə rä'gwə) country in Central America: 50,452 sq. mi.; pop. 4,395,000 —**Nic'a·ra'guan** ***adj.***, ***n.***
nice (nīs) ***adj.*** **nic'er**, **nic'est** ⟦< L *nescius*, ignorant⟧ **1** fastidious; refined **2** delicate; precise; subtle *[a nice distinction]* **3** calling for care, tact, etc. **4** pleasant, attractive, kind, good, etc.: a generalized term of approval —**nice'ly** ***adv.*** —**nice'ness** ***n.***
ni·ce·ty (nī'sə tē) ***n.***, *pl.* **-ties** **1** precision; accuracy **2** fastidiousness; refinement **3** a subtle or minute detail, distinction, etc.
niche (nich) ***n.*** ⟦Fr < L *nidus*, a nest⟧ **1** a recess in a wall, for a statue, vase, etc. **2** an especially suitable place or position **3** a specialized business market
nicht wahr? (niHt vär') ⟦Ger, not true?⟧ isn't that so?
nick (nik) ***n.*** ⟦ME *nyke*⟧ a small cut, chip, etc. made on a surface —***vt.*** **1** to make a nick or nicks in **2** to wound superficially —**in the nick of time** exactly when needed
nick·el (nik'əl) ***n.*** ⟦< Ger *kupfernickel*, copper devil: the copperlike ore contains no copper⟧ **1** a hard, silver-white, metallic chemical element, much used in alloys **2** a U.S. or Canadian coin of nickel and copper, equal to five cents
nick·el·o·de·on (nik'əl ō'dē ən) ***n.*** ⟦prec. + (*mel*)*odeon*, a small keyboard organ⟧ a coin-operated player piano or early type of jukebox
nick·er (nik'ər) ***vi.***, ***n.*** NEIGH
nick·name (nik'nām') ***n.*** ⟦by merging of ME (*a*)*n ekename*, a surname⟧ **1** a substitute, often descriptive, name given in fun, etc., as "Shorty" **2** a familiar form of a proper name, as "Dick" for "Richard" —***vt.*** **-named'**, **-nam'ing** to give a nickname to
nic·o·tine (nik'ə tēn') ***n.*** ⟦Fr, after J. *Nicot*, 16th-c. Fr diplomat who introduced tobacco into France⟧ a toxic alkaloid found in tobacco leaves
nic'o·tin'ic acid (-tin'ik) a white, crystalline substance, a member of the vitamin B complex
niece (nēs) ***n.*** ⟦< L *neptis*⟧ the daughter of one's brother or sister or of one's brother-in-law or sister-in-law
Nie·tzsche (nē'chə), **Fried·rich** (frē'driH) 1844-1900; Ger. philosopher
nif·ty (nif'tē) ***adj.*** **-ti·er**, **-ti·est** ⟦prob. < *magnificent*⟧ [Slang] attractive, smart, stylish, etc.
Ni·ger (nī'jər) country in WC Africa, north of Nigeria: 489,191 sq. mi.; pop. 7,250,000
Ni·ger·i·a (nī jir'ē ə) country on the W coast of Africa: 356,669 sq. mi.; pop. 88,515,000 —**Ni·ger'i·an** ***adj.***, ***n.***
nig·gard (nig'ərd) ***n.*** ⟦prob. < Scand⟧ a stingy person; miser —**nig'gard·ly** ***adj.***, ***adv.*** —**nig'gard·li·ness** ***n.***
nig·gle (nig'əl) ***vi.*** **-gled**, **-gling** ⟦prob. akin to Norw *nigla*⟧ to be finicky —**nig'gler** ***n.*** —**nig'gling** ***adj.***, ***n.***
nigh (nī) ***adv.***, ***adj.***, ***prep.*** ⟦OE *neah*⟧ [Now Chiefly Dial.] NEAR

THESAURUS

newscast ***n.*** news broadcasting, telecast, newscasting; see ANNOUNCEMENT, NEWS 2.
newscaster ***n.*** news analyst, commentator, broadcaster, anchor; see also REPORTER, WRITER.
newspaper ***n.*** publication, daily paper, journal, press, fourth estate, public press, sheet, tabloid, gazette; see also RECORD 1. *Varieties of newspapers include the following:* daily, weekly, biweekly, metropolitan, rural, national, tabloid, alternative, trade, provincial, community. *Parts of newspapers include the following:* front page, editorial page, local news, national news, state news, international news, magazine, comics pages, TV listings, ads, classified advertising, columnists, sports pages, business section, society page, entertainment, obituaries, arts, living, food, women's section, boilerplate.
newspaperman ***n.*** newsperson, journalist, member of the editorial department; see AUTHOR, EDITOR, REPORTER, WRITER.
next ***a.*** **1** [Following in order] succeeding, resulting, subsequent, ensuing; see also FOLLOWING. **2** [Adjacent] beside, close, alongside, on one side, on the side, adjoining, neighboring, meeting, touching, bordering on, cheek by jowl, side by side, attached, abutting, back to back, to the left, to the right; see also NEAR 1.
nibble ***n.*** morsel, peck, cautious bite; see BIT 1, BITE 1.
nibble ***v.*** nip, gnaw, snack; see BITE 1, EAT 1.
nice ***a.*** **1** [Approved] likable, superior, admirable; see EXCELLENT. **2** [Behaving in a becoming manner] pleasing, agreeable, winning, refined, cultured, amiable, delightful, charming, inviting, pleasant, cordial, courteous, considerate, kind, kindly, helpful, gracious, obliging, genial, gentle, unassuming, modest, demure; see also FRIENDLY.—*Ant.* RUDE, indecorous, crude.
nicely ***a.*** **1** [In a welcome manner] pleasantly, perfectly, pleasingly, amiably, winningly, creditably, acceptably, excellently, distinctively, happily, admirably, desirably, pleasurably, attractively, likably, enjoyably, beautifully, graciously, finely; see also AGREEABLY.—*Ant.* BADLY, unfortunately, unsuccessfully. **2** [In a becoming manner] charmingly, winsomely, invitingly; see MODESTLY, POLITELY.
niceness ***n.*** discernment, taste, refinement; see CARE 1, DISCRETION, KINDNESS 1.
niche ***n.*** cranny, corner, cubbyhole; see HOLE 1.
nick ***n.*** indentation, notch, slit; see CUT 1, DENT.
nick ***v.*** indent, notch, slit; see CUT 1, DENT.
nickel ***n.*** **1** silvery metal, chemical element, plating material; see ELEMENT 2, METAL, MINERAL. **2** [A coin made of nickel] five-cent piece, coin, five cents; see MONEY 1.
niece ***n.*** sister's daughter, brother's daughter, niece by marriage, grandniece, great-niece, sister-in-law's daughter, brother-in-law's daughter; see also NEPHEW, RELATIVE.
niggling ***a.*** trifling, petty, piddling; see TRIVIAL, UNIMPORTANT.

night (nīt) ***n.*** ⟦OE *niht*⟧ **1** the period of darkness from sunset to sunrise **2** any period or condition of darkness or gloom
night blindness imperfect vision in the dark or in dim light
night'cap' ***n.*** **1** a cap worn to bed, esp. formerly **2** [Inf.] an alcoholic drink taken just before going to bed
night'clothes' ***n.*** clothes to be worn in bed, as pajamas
night'club' ***n.*** a place of entertainment for eating, drinking, dancing, etc. at night
night crawl'er a large earthworm that comes to the surface at night
night'fall' ***n.*** the time in the evening when daylight is last visible; dusk
night'gown' ***n.*** a loose gown worn in bed by women or girls
night'hawk' ***n.*** **1** any of various usually nocturnal birds that feed on insects **2** NIGHT OWL
night'ie (-ē) ***n.*** [Inf.] NIGHTGOWN
night·in·gale (nīt''n gāl') ***n.*** ⟦< OE *niht*, night + *galan*, sing⟧ a small European thrush: the male sings melodiously, esp. at night
Night·in·gale (nīt''n gāl'), **Florence** 1820-1910; Eng. nurse: regarded as the founder of modern nursing
night life pleasure-seeking activity at night, as in nightclubs
night'ly ***adj.*** done or occurring every night —***adv.*** night after night; every night
night'mare' (-mer') ***n.*** ⟦ME < *niht*, night + *mare*, demon⟧ **1** a frightening dream **2** any frightening experience —**night'mar'ish** ***adj.***
night owl a person who works at night or otherwise stays up late
night'shade' ***n.*** **1** a chiefly tropical plant with five-lobed leaves and flowers of various colors **2** BELLADONNA
night'shirt' ***n.*** a loose garment like a long shirt, worn in bed
night'spot' ***n.*** *inf. var. of* NIGHTCLUB
night stand a small bedside table
night'stick' ***n.*** a policeman's club; billy
night'time' ***n.*** the time between dusk and dawn
night'wear' ***n.*** NIGHTCLOTHES
NIH *abbrev.* National Institutes of Health
ni·hil·ism (nī'ə liz'əm, nē'-) ***n.*** ⟦< L *nihil*, nothing⟧ the general rejection of customary beliefs in morality, religion, etc. —**ni'hil·ist** ***n.*** —**ni'hil·is'tic** ***adj.***
Ni·hon (nē'hôn) *Jpn. name for* JAPAN
nil (nil) ***n.*** ⟦L, contr. of *nihil*⟧ nothing
Nile (nīl) river in NE Africa, flowing through Egypt into the Mediterranean
nim·ble (nim'bəl) ***adj.*** **-bler, -blest** ⟦< OE *niman*, to take⟧ **1** quick-witted; alert **2** moving quickly and lightly —**nim'bly** ***adv.***
nim·bus (nim'bəs) ***n.***, *pl.* **-bi'** (-bī') or **-bus·es** ⟦L⟧ **1** any rain-producing cloud **2** a halo around the head of a saint, etc., as in a painting
Nim·rod (nim'räd') ***n.*** *Bible* a mighty hunter
nin·com·poop (nin'kəm po͞op') ***n.*** ⟦< ?⟧ a stupid, silly person; fool
nine (nīn) ***adj.***, ***n.*** ⟦OE *nigon*⟧ one more than eight; 9; IX —**ninth** (nīnth) ***adj.***, ***n.***
nine'pins' ***n.*** a British version of the game of tenpins, played with nine pins
nine'teen' ***adj.***, ***n.*** nine more than ten; 19; XIX —**nine'teenth'** (-tēnth') ***adj.***, ***n.***
nine·ty (nīn'tē) ***adj.***, ***n.***, *pl.* **-ties** nine times ten; 90; XC (or LXXXX) —**the nineties** the numbers or years, as of a century, from 90 through 99 —**nine'ti·eth** (-ith) ***adj.***, ***n.***
nin·ny (nin'ē) ***n.***, *pl.* **-nies** ⟦< *(a)n inn(ocent)*⟧ a fool; dolt
nip[1] (nip) ***vt.*** **nipped, nip'ping** ⟦prob. < earlier LowG *nippen*⟧ **1** to pinch or bite **2** to sever (shoots, etc.) by clipping **3** to check the growth of **4** to have a painful or injurious effect on because of cold —***n.*** **1** a nipping; pinch; bite **2** a stinging, as in cold air **3** stinging cold; frost —**nip and tuck** so close as to leave the outcome in doubt
nip[2] (nip) ***n.*** ⟦prob. < Du *nippen*, to sip⟧ a small drink of liquor —***vt.***, ***vi.*** **nipped, nip'ping** to drink in nips
nip·per (nip'ər) ***n.*** **1** anything that nips **2** [*pl.*] pliers, pincers, etc. **3** the claw of a crab or lobster
nip·ple (nip'əl) ***n.*** ⟦prob. < earlier *neb*, a beak⟧ **1** the small protuberance on a breast or udder through which, in the female, the milk passes; teat **2** the teatlike part in the cap of a baby's bottle
Nip·pon (nip'än', ni pän') *var. of* NIHON
Nip·pon·ese (nip'ə nēz') ***adj.***, ***n.***, *pl.* **-ese'** JAPANESE
nip·py (nip'ē) ***adj.*** **-pi·er, -pi·est** bitingly cold
nir·va·na (nir vä'nə) ***n.*** ⟦< Sans⟧ [*also* **N-**] **1** *Buddhism* the state of perfect blessedness **2** a place or condition of great bliss
ni·sei (nē'sā') ***n.***, *pl.* **-sei'** or **-seis'** ⟦Jpn, second generation⟧ [*also* **N-**] a native U.S. or Canadian citizen born of immigrant Japanese parents
nit (nit) ***n.*** ⟦OE *hnitu*⟧ **1** the egg of a louse or similar insect **2** a young louse, etc.
nite (nīt) ***n.*** *inf. sp. of* NIGHT
ni·ter (nīt'ər) ***n.*** ⟦< Gr *nitron*⟧ potassium nitrate or sodium nitrate, used in making explosives, fertilizers, etc.; saltpeter: also [Chiefly Brit.] **ni'tre**
nit-pick·ing (nit'pik'iŋ) ***adj.***, ***n.*** stressing petty details; niggling —**nit'-pick'er** ***n.***
ni·trate (nī'trāt') ***n.*** a salt of nitric acid, as sodium nitrate —***vt.*** **-trat'ed, -trat'ing** to combine with nitric acid or, esp., to make into a nitrate
ni·tric acid (nī'trik) a colorless, corrosive acid containing nitrogen
ni·tro·cel·lu·lose (nī'trō sel'yo͞o lōs') ***n.*** a substance obtained by treating cellulose with nitric acid, used in making explosives, lacquers, etc.
ni·tro·gen (nī'trə jən) ***n.*** ⟦< Fr: see NITER & -GEN⟧ a colorless, odorless, gaseous chemical element forming nearly four fifths of the atmosphere —**ni·trog'e·nous** (-träj'ə nəs) ***adj.***
ni·tro·glyc·er·in or **ni·tro·glyc·er·ine** (nī'trō glis'ər in) ***n.*** a thick, explosive oil prepared by treating glycerin with nitric and sulfuric acids: used in making dynamite
ni·trous oxide (nī'trəs) a colorless gas containing nitrogen, used as an anesthetic and in aerosols
nit·ty-grit·ty (nit'ē grit'ē) ***n.*** [Slang] the actual, basic facts, issues, etc.
nit'wit' ***n.*** ⟦? NIT + WIT[1]⟧ a stupid or silly person
nix (niks) [Slang] ***adv.*** ⟦Ger *nichts*⟧ **1** no **2** not at all —***interj.*** **1** stop! **2** I forbid, disagree, etc. —***vt.*** to disapprove of or put a stop to
Nix·on (nik'sən), **Richard M(ilhous)** 1913-94; 37th president of the U.S. (1969-74): resigned
Nizh·ny Nov·go·rod (nēzh'nē nôv'gə rət) city in central European Russia: pop. 1,438,000
NJ New Jersey
NM New Mexico
no[1] (nō) ***adv.*** ⟦< OE *ne a*, not ever⟧ **1** not at all *[no* worse*]* **2** nay; not so: used to deny, refuse, or disagree —***adj.*** not any; not one *[no* errors*]* —***n.***, *pl.* **noes** or **nos** **1** a refusal or denial **2** a negative vote or voter
no[2] *abbrev.* ⟦L *numero*⟧ number
No·ah (nō'ə) ***n.*** *Bible* the patriarch commanded by God to build the ARK (sense 3)
No·bel prizes (nō bel') ⟦after A. B. *Nobel*, 19th-c. Swed inventor who established them⟧ annual international prizes given for distinction in physics, chemistry, economics, medicine, and literature, and for promoting peace
no·bil·i·ty (nō bil'ə tē) ***n.***, *pl.* **-ties** **1** a being noble **2** high rank in society **3** the class of people of noble rank

THESAURUS

night ***n.*** **1** [The diurnal dark period] after dark, evening, from dusk to dawn, nightfall, after nightfall, twilight, nighttime, bedtime, midnight, before dawn, the dark hours, dead of night. **2** [The dark] blackness, duskiness, gloom; see DARKNESS 1. —**good night** sleep well, have a good evening, nighty-night*; see GOODBYE.

nightclub ***n.*** casino, discotheque, cabaret; see BAR 2, RESTAURANT.

nightly ***a.*** nocturnal, in the hours of night, every twenty-four hours, during the hours of darkness, at night, each night, every night, by night; see also REGULAR, REGULARLY.—*Ant.* DAILY, by day, diurnal.

nightmare ***n.*** bad dream, horror, incubus; see DREAM.

nighttime ***n.*** darkness, bedtime, dark of night; see NIGHT 1.

nimble ***a.*** **1** [Agile] quick, spry, active; see AGILE, GRACEFUL 1. **2** [Alert] quick-witted, bright, clever; see INTELLIGENT.

nip[1] ***v.*** nibble, snap, munch; see BITE 1, PINCH.

nipple ***n.*** mamilla, mammary gland, teat; see BREAST 2.

nitwit ***n.*** blockhead, dummy*, dimwit*; see FOOL.

no[1] ***a.***, ***interj.*** absolutely not, not at all, by no means, the answer is in the negative, not by any means, none, nay, not, not a, not one, not any, *non*(French), *nein* (German), *nyet* (Russian), nix*; see also NEGATIVE 2, NEITHER, NEVER.

nobility ***n.*** [*Usually used with "the"*] ruling class, gentry, peerage; see ARISTOCRACY, ROYALTY.

no·ble (nō′bəl) ***adj.*** **-bler, -blest** ⟦< L *nobilis,* well-known⟧ **1** having high moral qualities **2** excellent **3** grand; stately **4** of high hereditary rank —***n.*** one having hereditary rank or title —**no′ble·ness** ***n.*** —**no·bly** (nō′ blē) ***adv.***

no′ble·man (-mən) ***n.***, *pl.* **-men** (-mən) a member of the nobility; peer

no·blesse o·blige (nō bles′ ō blēzh′) ⟦Fr, nobility obliges⟧ the inferred obligation of people of high rank to behave nobly toward others

no·bod·y (nō′bäd′ē, -bud′ē, -bə dē) ***pron.*** not anybody; no one —***n.***, *pl.* **-ies** a person of no importance

no-brain·er (nō′brān′ər) ***n.*** something so obvious, simple, etc. as to require little thought

noc·tur·nal (näk tʉr′nəl) ***adj.*** ⟦< L *nox,* night⟧ **1** of the night **2** functioning, done, or active during the night —**noc·tur′nal·ly** ***adv.***

noc·turne (näk′tʉrn′) ***n.*** ⟦Fr⟧ a romantic or dreamy musical composition thought appropriate to night

nod (näd) ***vi.*** **nod′ded, nod′ding** ⟦ME *nodden*⟧ **1** to bend the head forward quickly, as in agreement, greeting, etc. **2** to let the head fall forward because of drowsiness —***vt.*** **1** to bend (the head) forward quickly **2** to signify (assent, etc.) by doing this —***n.*** a nodding

node (nōd) ***n.*** ⟦L *nodus*⟧ **1** a knot; knob; swelling **2** that part of a stem from which a leaf starts to grow —**nod·al** (nōd′'l) ***adj.***

nod·ule (näj′o͞ol′) ***n.*** ⟦L *nodulus*⟧ a small knot or rounded lump

No·el or **No·ël** (nō el′) ***n.*** ⟦Fr < L *natalis,* natal⟧ CHRISTMAS

no′-fault′ ***adj.*** **1** designating a form of automobile insurance in which those injured collect damages without blame being fixed **2** designating a form of divorce granted without blame being charged

nog·gin (näg′in) ***n.*** ⟦prob. < Brit dial. *nog,* strong ale⟧ **1** a small cup or mug **2** [Inf.] the head

no′-good′ ***adj.*** [Slang] contemptible

noir (nwär) ***n.*** ⟦Fr, black⟧ a film, novel, etc. pessimistic or cynical in mood and often dealing with urban crime —**noir′ish** ***adj.***

noise (noiz) ***n.*** ⟦< OFr⟧ **1** din of voices; clamor **2** any sound; specif., a loud, disagreeable sound —***vt.*** **noised, nois′ing** to spread (a report, rumor, etc.) *about, around,* etc.

noise′less ***adj.*** with little or no noise; very quiet —**noise′less·ly** ***adv.***

noi·some (noi′səm) ***adj.*** ⟦see ANNOY & -SOME[1]⟧ **1** injurious to health; harmful **2** foul-smelling

nois·y (noiz′ē) ***adj.*** **-i·er, -i·est** **1** making noise **2** full of noise —**nois′i·ly** ***adv.*** —**nois′i·ness** ***n.***

no-load (nō′lōd′) ***adj.*** designating mutual funds charging no commissions on sales

no·mad (nō′mad′) ***n.*** ⟦< Gr *nemein,* to pasture⟧ **1** any of a people having no permanent home, but moving about constantly, as in search of pasture **2** a wanderer —**no·mad′ic** ***adj.***

no man's land the unoccupied region separating opposing armies

nom de plume (näm′ də plo͞om′) ⟦Fr⟧ a pen name

Nome (nōm) city in W Alaska: pop. 3,500

no·men·cla·ture (nō′mən klā′chər) ***n.*** ⟦< L *nomen,* a name + *calare,* to call⟧ the system of names used in a science, etc. or for the parts of a device

-nom·ics (näm′iks) *combining form* economics: also **-om′ics**

nom·i·nal (näm′ə nəl) ***adj.*** ⟦< L *nomen,* a name⟧ **1** in name only, not in fact *[a nominal leader]* **2** relatively very small —**nom′i·nal·ly** ***adv.***

nom′i·nate′ (-nāt′) ***vt.*** **-nat′ed, -nat′ing** ⟦< L *nomen,* a name⟧ **1** to appoint to an office or position **2** to name as a candidate for election —**nom′i·na′tion** ***n.***

nom′i·na·tive (-nə tiv) ***n.*** *Gram.* the case of the subject of a verb

nom′i·nee′ (-ə nē′) ***n.*** a person who is nominated

non- ⟦< L *non,* not⟧ *prefix* not: less emphatic than IN-[2] and UN-, which often give a word a strong opposite or reverse meaning: the terms in the following list will be understood if "not" is used before the meaning of the base word:

nonabrasive
nonabsorbent
nonactive
nonaddictive
nonadministrative
nonaggression
nonaggressive
nonalcoholic
nonallergenic
nonallergic
nonassignable
nonathletic
nonattendance
nonautomotive
nonavailability
nonbasic
nonbeliever
nonbelligerent
nonbreakable
nonburnable
non-Catholic
nonchargeable
nonclerical
nonclinical
noncollectable
noncombustible
noncommercial
noncommunicable
non-Communist
noncompeting
noncompetitive
noncompliance
noncomplying
nonconducting
nonconforming
nonconsecutive
nonconstructive
noncontagious
noncontributory
noncontroversial
nonconvertible
noncorroding
noncorrosive
noncriminal
noncritical
noncrystalline
noncumulative
nondeductible

THESAURUS

noble ***a.*** **1** [Possessing an exalted mind and character] generous, princely, magnanimous, magnificent, courtly, lofty, elevated, splendid, excellent, supreme, eminent, lordly, dignified, great, good, superior, great-hearted, high-minded, honorable, distinguished, liberal, tolerant, gracious, humane, benevolent, charitable, sympathetic, bounteous, brilliant, extraordinary, remarkable, devoted, heroic, resolute, valorous; see also WORTHY.—*Ant.* CORRUPT, low, ignoble. **2** [Possessing excellent qualities or properties] meritorious, virtuous, worthy, valuable, useful, first-rate, refined, cultivated, chivalrous, trustworthy, candid, liberal, gracious, princely, magnanimous, generous, sincere, truthful, constant, faithful, upright, honest, warmhearted, true, incorruptible, distinctive, reputable, respectable, admirable, good, aboveboard, fair, just, estimable; see also EXCELLENT, PERFECT 2.—*Ant.* POOR, inferior, second-rate. **3** [Belonging to the nobility] titled, aristocratic, patrician, highborn, well-born, blue-blooded, of gentle birth, imperial, lordly, highbred, princely, of good breed, kingly; see also ROYAL.—*Ant.* COMMON, plebeian, lowborn. **4** [Grand] stately, impressive, imposing; see GRAND.

nobly ***a.*** **1** [Majestically] aristocratically, illustriously, royally; see GENEROUSLY 2, POLITELY. **2** [Honorably] fairly, respectably, honestly; see JUSTLY 1.

nobody ***n.*** **1** [No one at all] no person, no one, not anybody; see NONE 1. **2** [A person of little importance] upstart, cipher, nonentity, whippersnapper, no great shakes*, nix*, zero*.

nocturnal ***a.*** at night, night-loving, nighttime; see LATE 4, NIGHTLY.

nod ***n.*** slight bow, aknowledgement, gesture of agreement; see GREETING.

nod ***v.*** **1** [To make a nodding movement] assent, signal, greet, bend, curtsy, incline the head, bow, nod yes, acquiesce, consent, respond, concur, acknowledge, recognize; see also AGREE, APPROVE.—*Ant.* DENY, dissent, disagree. **2** [To become sleepy or inattentive] drowse, nap, drift off; see SLEEP.

noise ***n.*** **1** [A sound] sound, something heard, impact of sound waves. *Kinds of noises include the following—brief, loud noises:* bang, boom, crash, thud, blast, roar, bellow, blat, shout, peal, cry, yelp, squawk, blare, clang, ring, shot, sonic boom, jangle, eruption, explosion, detonation; *brief, faint noises:* peep, squeak, squawk, cackle, cluck, tweet, clink, tinkle, pop, whisper, stage whisper, sigh, splash, swish, sob, whine, whimper, plunk, plop, ping, rustle, murmur, stirring; *continuing noises:* reverberation, ringing, tone, tune, clanging, tinkling, resonance, cacophony, rattle, whir, whistle, dissonance, discord, shouting, roaring, bellowing, rumble, rumbling, grunting, murmuring, drone, droning, purr, thundering, whine, screeching, screaming, banging, clanging, hum, humming, laughing, chuckle, swishing, rustling, ripple, strumming, beating, pattering, clattering, trilling, whinneying, neighing, cawing, cackling. **2** [Clamor] racket, fracas, din; see UPROAR.

noiseless ***a.*** **1** [Containing no noise] silent, still, soundless; see QUIET. **2** [Making no noise] voiceless, speechless, wordless; see DUMB 1, MUTE 1.

noiselessly ***a.*** inaudibly, quietly, without a sound; see SILENTLY.

noisy ***a.*** clamorous, vociferous, boisterous; see LOUD 1, 2.

nomad ***n.*** wanderer, migrant, vagabond; see TRAVELER.

nominal ***a.*** professed, pretended, in name only; see GIVEN, NAMED 1.

nominate ***v.*** propose as a candidate, designate for election, put up; see CHOOSE, DECIDE.

nominated ***a.*** designated, called, suggested; see APPROVED, NAMED 2.

nomination ***n.*** naming, designation, proposal; see APPOINTMENT 1.

nondelivery
nondepartmental
nondepreciating
nondestructive
nondetachable
nondisciplinary
nondiscrimination
nondramatic
nondrinker
nondrying
noneducational
noneffective
nonenforceable
non-English
nonessential
nonexchangeable
nonexclusive
nonexempt
nonexistence
nonexistent
nonexplosive
nonfactual
nonfading
nonfat
nonfatal
nonfiction
nonfictional
nonflammable
nonflowering
nonfluctuating
nonflying
nonfreezing
nonfunctional
nongovernmental
nongranular
nonhazardous
nonhereditary
nonhuman
nonidentical
noninclusive
nonindependent
nonindustrial
noninfected
noninflammatory
noninflationary
nonintellectual
noninterference
nonintoxicating
nonirritating
nonjudicial
nonlegal
nonliterary
nonmagnetic
nonmalignant
nonmember
nonmigratory
nonmilitant
nonmilitary
nonnarcotic
nonnegotiable
nonnumerical
nonobjective
nonobligatory
nonobservance
nonobservant
nonoccupational
nonoccurrence
nonofficial
nonoperational
nonoperative
nonpaying
nonpayment
nonperishable
nonphysical
nonpoisonous
nonpolitical
nonporous
nonprejudicial
nonprescriptive
nonproductive
nonprofessional
nonprofitable
nonpunishable
nonracial
nonreactive
nonreciprocal
nonreciprocating
nonrecoverable
nonrecurring
nonredeemable
nonrefillable
nonreligious
nonrenewable
nonrepresentational
nonresidential
nonresidual
nonresistant
nonreturnable
nonrhythmic
nonrigid
nonsalaried
nonscientific
nonscoring
nonseasonal
nonsecular
nonsensitive
nonsmoker
nonsocial
nonspeaking
nonspecializing
nonspiritual
nonstaining
nonstandard
nonsticking
nonstrategic
nonstriking
nonstructural
nonsuccessive
nonsupporting
nonsustaining
nonsympathizer
nontaxable
nontechnical
nontheatrical
nonthinking
nontoxic
nontransferable
nontransparent
nontropical
nonuniform
nonuser
nonvenomous
nonverbal
nonvirulent
nonvocal
nonvocational
nonvoter
nonvoting
nonwhite
nonyielding

non·age (nän′ij, nō′nij) ***n.*** ⟦see prec. & AGE⟧ the state of being under full legal age

non·a·ge·nar·i·an (nän′ə jə ner′ē ən) ***n.*** ⟦< L *nonaginta*, ninety⟧ a person between the ages of 90 and 100

non′a·ligned′ (-ə līnd′) ***adj.*** not aligned with either side in a conflict —**non′a·lign′ment** ***n.***

no′-name′ ***adj.*** not famous or distinguished

non′bind′ing (-bīn′diŋ) ***adj.*** not holding one to an obligation, promise, etc.

non′-book′ ***n.*** a book produced cheaply and quickly, often in response to a current fad, etc.

nonce (näns) ***n.*** ⟦by merging of ME (*for then*) *ones*, lit., (for the) once⟧ the present use, occasion, or time: chiefly in **for the nonce**

nonce word a word coined and used for a single occasion

non·cha·lant (nän′shə länt′) ***adj.*** ⟦Fr, ult. < L *non*, not + *calere*, be warm⟧ casually indifferent —**non′cha·lance′** (-läns′) ***n.***

non·com (nän′käm′) ***n.*** [Inf.] *short for* NONCOMMISSIONED OFFICER

non·com·bat·ant (nän′kəm bat′′nt) ***n.*** **1** a member of the armed forces not engaged in actual combat **2** any civilian in wartime

non′com·mis′sioned officer (-kə mish′ənd) an enlisted person of any of various grades in the armed forces: in the U.S. Army, from corporal to sergeant major inclusive

non′com·mit′tal (-kə mit′l) ***adj.*** not committing one to a definite point of view or course of action

non com·pos men·tis (nän′ käm′pəs men′tis) ⟦L⟧ *Law* not of sound mind

non′con·duc′tor (-kən duk′tər) ***n.*** a substance that does not readily transmit sound, heat, or, esp., electricity

non′con·form′ist (-kən fôr′mist) ***n.*** **1** one who does not conform to prevailing beliefs and practices **2** [**N-**] a British Protestant who is not Anglican —**non′con·form′i·ty** ***n.***

non′cus·to′di·al (-kəs tō′dē əl) ***adj.*** without custody, as of one's children after divorce

non·dair·y (nän′der′ē) ***adj.*** containing no milk or milk products

non·de·script (nän′di skript′) ***adj.*** ⟦< L *non*, not + *describere*, describe⟧ **1** belonging to no definite class or type; hard to classify or describe **2** not interesting; colorless

none (nun) ***pron.*** ⟦< OE *ne*, not + *an*, one⟧ **1** no one; not anyone **2** [*with pl. v.*] not any *[*there are *none* on the table*]* —***n.*** not any (of); no part *[*I want *none* of it*]* —***adv.*** not at all *[none* the worse for wear*]*

non·en·ti·ty (nän′en′tə tē) ***n.***, *pl.* **-ties** a person or thing of little or no importance

none·the·less (nun′*th*ə les′) ***adv.*** nevertheless: also **none the less**

non·e·vent (nän′ē vent′) ***n.*** [Inf.] an event that is boring or deliberately staged, as for publicity

non′fer′rous (-fer′əs) ***adj.*** **1** not containing iron **2** designating or of metals other than iron

non′in·ter·ven′tion (-in′tər ven′shən) ***n.*** refusal to interfere; esp., a refusal by one nation to interfere in another's affairs

non′in·va′sive (-in vā′siv) ***adj.*** *Med.* not entering the skin or a body cavity

non′judg·men′tal (-juj ment′′l) ***adj.*** objective; tolerant

non′met′al (-met′′l) ***n.*** any chemical element, as oxygen, carbon, nitrogen, fluorine, etc., lacking the characteristics of a metal —**non′me·tal′lic** ***adj.***

no′-no′ ***n.***, *pl.* **-nos′** [Slang] something forbidden or considered unwise to do, say, etc.

no′-non′sense ***adj.*** practical and serious

non·pa·reil (nän′pə rel′) ***adj.*** ⟦Fr < *non*, not + *pareil*, equal⟧ unequaled; unrivaled; peerless

non′par′ti·san (-pärt′ə zən) ***adj.*** not partisan; esp., not connected with any single political party

non′per′son (-pʉr′sən) ***n.*** a person officially ignored by the government

non·plus (nän plus′) ***vt.*** **-plused′** or **-plussed′**, **-plus′ing** or **-plus′sing** ⟦L *non*, not + *plus*, more⟧ to greatly perplex or bewilder

non′prof′it (-präf′it) ***adj.*** not established or done to earn a profit: said as of a charity

THESAURUS

nonchalance ***n.*** apathy, disregard, insouciance; see INDIFFERENCE.

nonchalant ***a.*** **1** [Cool and casual] uncaring, unconcerned, untroubled, apathetic, unfeeling, impassive, imperturbable, easygoing, listless, lackadaisical, unruffled, lukewarm, composed, collected, aloof, detached, calm, serene, placid, disinterested, easy, effortless, light, smooth, neutral, laid-back*.—*Ant.* WARM, ardent, enthusiastic. **2** [Careless] neglectful, negligent, trifling; see CARELESS.

nonchalantly ***a.*** coolly, indifferently, casually; see CALMLY.

nonconformist ***n.*** rebel, eccentric, maverick, iconoclast, loner, malcontent, dissenter, demonstrator, hippie, protester, dissident, a different breed; see also RADICAL.

nonconformity ***n.*** dissent, opposition, difference; see INDIVIDUALITY.

none ***pron.*** **1** [No person or persons] no one, not one, not anyone, no one at all, not a person, not a soul, neither one nor the other; see also NEITHER.—*Ant.* MANY, some, a few. **2** [No thing or things] not a thing, not anything, not any; see NOTHING.

nonetheless ***a.*** nevertheless, in spite of that, anyway; see ALTHOUGH, BUT 1.

nonexistent ***a.*** missing, unsubstantial, fictitious; see IMAGINARY, UNREAL.

no-nonsense ***a.*** matter-of-fact, serious, purposeful, dedicated, resolute; see also PRACTICAL.

nonpartisan ***a.*** unprejudiced, unbiased, independent; see NEUTRAL 1.

nonpayment ***n.*** failure, delinquency, bankruptcy; see DEFAULT.

nonproductive ***a.*** unproductive, futile, ineffectual; see IDLE, USELESS 1.

nonprofit ***a.*** charitable, public-service, not-for-profit; see GENEROUS.

non'res'i·dent (-rez'ə dənt) ***adj.*** not residing in the locality where one works, attends school, etc. —***n.*** a nonresident person

non're·stric'tive (-ri strik'tiv) ***adj.*** *Gram.* designating a clause, phrase, or word felt as not essential to the sense, usually set off by commas (Ex.: John, *who is tall,* is Bill's brother)

non'sched'uled (-skej'o͞old) ***adj.*** licensed for commercial air flights as demand warrants rather than on a schedule

non'sec·tar'i·an (-sek ter'ē ən) ***adj.*** not confined to any specific religion

non·sense (nän'sens') ***n.*** words, actions, etc. that are absurd or meaningless —***interj.*** how absurd!: an exclamation —**non·sen'si·cal** (-sen'si kəl) ***adj.***

non se·qui·tur (nän' sek'wi tər) ⟦L, it does not follow⟧ **1** *Logic* a conclusion which does not follow from the premises **2** a remark having no bearing on what has just been said

non'skid' (-skid') ***adj.*** having a surface made so as to reduce slipping or skidding

non'-start'er (-stärt'ər) ***n.*** [Slang] **1** an expected occurrence, project, etc. that fails to materialize **2** a worthless idea

non'stop' (-stäp') ***adj., adv.*** without a stop

non'sup·port' (-sə pôrt') ***n.*** failure to provide for a legal dependent

non'un'ion (-yo͞on'yən) ***adj.*** **1** not belonging to a labor union **2** not made or serviced by union workers

non'vi'o·lence (-vī'ə ləns) ***n.*** an abstaining from violence or the use of force, as in efforts to obtain civil rights —**non'vi'o·lent** ***adj.***

noo·dle[1] (no͞od''l) ***n.*** ⟦< ?⟧ [Slang] the head

noo·dle[2] (no͞od''l) ***n.*** ⟦Ger *nudel*⟧ a flat, narrow strip of dry dough, usually made with egg and served in soup, etc.

nook (no͝ok) ***n.*** ⟦ME *nok*⟧ **1** a corner or separate part of a room **2** a small, secluded spot

noon (no͞on) ***n.*** ⟦< L *nona* (*hora*), ninth (hour)⟧ twelve o'clock in the daytime; midday —***adj.*** of or at noon Also **noon'time'** or **noon'day'**

no one not anyone; nobody

noose (no͞os) ***n.*** ⟦< L *nodus*, knot⟧ a loop in a rope, etc. formed by a slipknot so that the loop tightens as the rope is pulled

nor (nôr) ***conj.*** ⟦ME < *ne-*, not, + *or*, other⟧ and not; and not either *[*I can neither go *nor* stay*]*

Nor·dic (nôr'dik) ***adj.*** ⟦OE *north*, north⟧ of a Caucasoid physical type exemplified by the tall, blond Scandinavians

Nor·folk (nôr'fək) seaport in SE Virginia: pop. 261,000

norm (nôrm) ***n.*** ⟦L *norma*, rule⟧ a standard or model for a group

nor·mal (nôr'məl) ***adj.*** **1** conforming with an accepted standard or norm; natural; usual **2** average in intelligence, etc. —***n.*** **1** anything normal **2** the usual state, amount, etc. —**nor'mal·cy** (-sē) or **nor·mal'i·ty** (-mal'ə tē) ***n.*** —**nor'mal·ize'**, **-ized'**, **-iz'ing**, ***vt., vi.*** —**nor'mal·i·za'tion** ***n.***

nor'mal·ly ***adv.*** **1** in a normal manner **2** under normal circumstances

Nor·man (nôr'mən) ***n.*** ⟦< OFr⟧ **1** a member of the people of Normandy that conquered England in 1066 **2** a person born or living in Normandy —***adj.*** of Normandy or its people, etc.

Nor·man·dy (nôr'mən dē) historical region in NW France, on the English Channel

norm·a·tive (nôr'mə tiv) ***adj.*** of or establishing a norm

Norse (nôrs) ***adj., n.*** ⟦prob. < Du *noord*, north⟧ **1** SCANDINAVIAN **2** (of) the Scandinavian group of languages

Norse'man (-mən) ***n.***, *pl.* **-men** (-mən) a member of any of the medieval Scandinavian peoples

north (nôrth) ***n.*** ⟦OE⟧ **1** the direction to the right of one facing the sunset (0° or 360° on the compass) **2** a region in or toward this direction —***adj.*** **1** in, of, toward, or facing the north **2** from the north *[*a *north* wind*]* —***adv.*** in or toward the north —**the North** that part of the U.S. north of Maryland, the Ohio River, and Missouri

North America N continent in the Western Hemisphere: *c.* 9,400,000 sq. mi.; pop. *c.* 449,000,000 —**North American**

North Car·o·li·na (kar'ə lī'nə) state of the SE U.S.: 48,718 sq. mi.; pop. 6,629,000; cap. Raleigh: abbrev. *NC* —**North Car'o·lin'i·an** (-lin'ē ən)

North Da·ko·ta (də kōt'ə) Midwestern state of the U.S.: 68,994 sq. mi.; pop. 639,000; cap. Bismarck: abbrev. *ND* —**North Da·ko'tan**

north'east' ***n.*** **1** the direction halfway between north and east **2** a region in or toward this direction —***adj.*** **1** in, of, or toward the northeast **2** from the northeast *[*a *northeast* wind*]* —***adv.*** in or toward the northeast —**north'east'er·ly** ***adj., adv.*** —**north'east'ern** ***adj.*** —**north'east'ward** ***adj., adv.*** —**north'east'wards** ***adv.***

north·er·ly (nôr*th*'ər lē) ***adj., adv.*** **1** toward the north **2** from the north

north·ern (nôr'*th*ərn) ***adj.*** **1** in, of, or toward the north **2** from the north **3** [**N-**] of the North

north'ern·er ***n.*** a person born or living in the north

Northern Hemisphere the half of the earth north of the equator

Northern Ireland division of the United Kingdom, in the NE part of the island of Ireland: 5,467 sq. mi.; pop. 1,578,000

northern lights [*also* **N- L-**] the aurora borealis

Northern Ma·ri·an·a Islands (mer'ē an'ə) group of islands in the W Pacific: a commonwealth associated with the U.S.: land area *c.* 179 sq. mi.; pop. 43,000: also **Northern Marianas**

North Pole the northern end of the earth's axis

North Sea arm of the Atlantic, between Great Britain & the N European mainland

North Star POLARIS

north'ward ***adv., adj.*** toward the north: also **north'wards** ***adv.***

north'west' ***n.*** **1** the direction halfway between north and west **2** a region in or toward this direction —***adj.*** **1** in, of, or toward the northwest **2** from the northwest *[*a *northwest* wind*]* —***adv.*** in or toward the northwest —

THESAURUS

nonresident ***a.*** absentee, out-of-state, living abroad; see FOREIGN.

nonsense ***n.*** **1** [Matter that has no meaning] balderdash, rubbish, trash, scrawl, inanity, senselessness, buncombe, bunkum*, idle chatter, prattle, rant, bombast, claptrap, bull*, baloney*, hooey*, bunk*, poppycock*, guff*, hot air*. **2** [Frivolous behavior] unsteadiness, flightiness, stupidity, thoughtlessness, fickleness, foolishness, giddiness, rashness, infatuation, extravagance, imprudence, madness, irrationality, senselessness, inconsistency, shallowness.—*Ant.* CONSIDERATION, steadiness, thoughtfulness. **3** [Pure fun] absurdity, antics, monkey business*; see FUN.

nonstop ***a.*** uninterrupted, unbroken, continuous; see CONSTANT.

nonviolent ***a.*** pacifist, engaging in passive resistance, without violence; see CALM 1, QUIET.

nook ***n.*** niche, cubbyhole, cranny; see HOLE 1.

noon ***n.*** noontime, noontide, noonday, midday, twelve noon, meridian, noon hour; see also TIME 1, 2.

no one ***pron.*** no person, not anybody, nobody; see NEITHER, NONE 1.

noose ***n.*** loop, running knot, lasso; see KNOT 1, ROPE.

nor ***conj.*** and not, not any, not either, not one, nor yet; see also NEITHER.

normal ***a.*** **1** [Usual] ordinary, run-of-the-mill, typical; see COMMON 1, CONVENTIONAL 1, 3. **2** [Regular] routine, orderly, methodical; see REGULAR 3. **3** [Sane] lucid, wholesome, right-minded; see RATIONAL, REASONABLE, SANE 1. **4** [Showing no abnormal bodily condition] in good health, whole, sound; see HEALTHY.

normally ***a.*** usually, commonly, ordinarily; see FREQUENTLY, REGULARLY.

north ***a.*** **1** [Situated to the north] northward, northern, in the north, on the north side of, northerly, northmost, northernmost, toward the North Pole. **2** [Moving toward the north] northerly, northbound, northward, to the north, headed north, in a northerly direction; see also SOUTH 2. **3** [Coming from the north] northerly, southbound, headed south, out of the north, moving toward the equator, moving toward the South Pole; see also SOUTH 3. **4** [Associated with the north] polar, frozen, boreal; see COLD 1.

north ***n.*** tundra, northern section, northland, Northern Hemisphere, the north country, the north woods, arctic regions, polar regions, the frozen north, land of ice and snow; see also DIRECTION 1.

northeast ***a.*** NE, northeastern, northeasterly, northeastward, north-northeast, northeast by east, northeast by north; see also DIRECTION 1.

northerly ***a.*** boreal, northern, polar; see NORTH 2.

northern ***a.*** northerly, arctic, polar; see NORTH 1.

northwest ***a.*** NW, northwestern, northwesterly, northwestward, north-northwest, northwest by west, northwest by north; see also DIRECTION 1.

north′west′er·ly *adj., adv.* —**north′west′ern** *adj.* —**north′west′ward** *adj., adv.* —**north′west′wards** *adv.*

Northwest Territories division of N Canada: 552,909 sq. mi.; pop. 39,000; cap. Yellowknife: abbrev. *NT*

North York (yôrk) city in SE Ontario, Canada: part of metropolitan Toronto: pop. 590,000

Norw *abbrev.* **1** Norway **2** Norwegian

Nor·way (nôr′wā′) country in N Europe: 125,001 sq. mi.; pop. 4,248,000

Nor·we·gian (nôr wē′jən) *n.* **1** the language of Norway **2** a person born or living in Norway —*adj.* of Norway or its people, language, etc.

nose (nōz) *n.* ⟦OE *nosu*⟧ **1** the part of the face above the mouth, having two openings for breathing and smelling; in animals, the snout, muzzle, etc. **2** the sense of smell **3** anything like a nose in shape or position —*vt.* **nosed, nos′ing 1** to nuzzle **2** to push (a way, etc.) with the front forward —*vi.* **1** to pry inquisitively **2** to move forward —**nose out 1** to defeat by a very small margin **2** to discover, as by smelling —**on the nose** [Slang] precisely

nose′bleed′ *n.* a bleeding from the nose

nose cone the cone-shaped foremost part of a rocket or missile

nose dive 1 a swift, steep downward plunge of an airplane, nose first **2** any sudden, sharp drop, as in profits —**nose′-dive′, -dived′, -div′ing,** *vi.*

nose drops medication administered through the nose with a dropper

nose·gay (nōz′gā′) *n.* ⟦NOSE + GAY (obs. sense "bright object")⟧ a small bouquet

nose guard *Football* the defensive lineman directly opposite the offensive center: also **nose tackle**

nosh (näsh) *vt., vi.* ⟦< Yiddish < Ger *nashchen*, to nibble⟧ [Slang] to eat (a snack) —*n.* [Slang] a snack —**nosh′er** *n.*

no′-show′ *n.* one who fails to claim or cancel a reservation

nos·tal·gi·a (nä stal′jə) *n.* ⟦< Gr *nostos*, a return + -ALGIA⟧ a longing for something far away or long ago —**nos·tal′gic** (-jik) *adj.*

nos·tril (näs′trəl) *n.* ⟦< OE *nosu*, nose + *thyrel*, hole⟧ either of the external openings of the nose

nos·trum (näs′trəm) *n.* ⟦L, ours⟧ **1** a quack medicine **2** a panacea

nos·y or **nos·ey** (nō′zē) *adj.* **-i·er, -i·est** [Inf.] prying; inquisitive

not (nät) *adv.* ⟦< ME *nought*⟧ in no manner, to no degree, etc.

no·ta·ble (nōt′ə bəl) *adj.* ⟦< L *notare*, to note⟧ worthy of notice; remarkable; outstanding —*n.* a person of distinction —**no′ta·bly** *adv.*

no·ta·rize (nōt′ə rīz′) *vt.* **-rized′, -riz′ing** to certify or attest (a document) as a notary public

no′ta·ry (-rē) *n., pl.* **-ries** ⟦< L *notare*, to note⟧ an official authorized to certify or attest documents, take affidavits, etc.: in full **notary public**

no·ta·tion (nō tā′shən) *n.* **1** the use of signs or symbols to represent words, quantities, etc. **2** any such system of signs or symbols, as in mathematics or music **3** a brief note or noting

notch (näch) *n.* ⟦prob. < ME (*a*)*n oche*, a notch⟧ **1** a V-shaped cut in an edge or surface **2** a narrow pass with steep sides **3** [Inf.] a step; degree —*vt.* to cut a notch or notches in

note (nōt) *n.* ⟦< L *nota*, a mark⟧ **1** a distinguishing feature *[a note* of sadness*]* **2** importance, distinction, etc. *[a* person of *note]* **3** a brief writing to aid the memory; memorandum **4** a comment or explanation; annotation **5** notice; heed *[*worthy of *note]* **6** a short, informal letter **7** a written acknowledgment of a debt **8** *Music a)* a tone of definite pitch *b)* a symbol for a tone, indicating its duration and pitch —*vt.* **not′ed, not′ing 1** to heed; observe **2** to set down in writing **3** to mention particularly —**compare notes** to exchange views

note′book′ *n.* **1** a book in which notes, or memorandums, are kept **2** a small laptop computer

not·ed (nōt′id) *adj.* renowned; famous

note′wor′thy *adj.* worthy of note; outstanding; remarkable —**note′wor′thi·ness** *n.*

noth·ing (nuth′iŋ) *pron.* ⟦OE *na thing*⟧ **1** no thing; not anything **2** a person or thing considered of little or no importance —*n.* **1** nothingness **2** a thing that does not exist **3** a person or thing considered of little or no importance **4** a zero; cipher —*adv.* not at all; in no way —**for nothing 1** free **2** in vain **3** without reason

noth′ing·ness *n.* **1** the condition of not existing **2** insignificance **3** unconsciousness or death

no·tice (nōt′is) *n.* ⟦see NOTE⟧ **1** announcement or warning **2** a brief article about a book, play, etc. **3** a sign giving some public information, warning, etc. **4** attention; heed **5** a formal warning of intention to end an agreement or contract at a certain time —*vt.* **-ticed, -tic·ing** to observe; pay attention to —**take notice** to pay attention

no′tice·a·ble *adj.* readily noticed; conspicuous —**no′tice·a·bly** *adv.*

no·ti·fy (nōt′ə fī′) *vt.* **-fied′, -fy′ing** ⟦< L *notus*, known + *facere*, make⟧ to give notice to; inform —**no′ti·fi·ca′tion** (-fi kā′shən) *n.*

THESAURUS

nose *n.* **1** [The organ of smell] nasal organ, nasal cavity, nares, nasal passages, nostrils, olfactory nerves, snoot*, schnoz*, beak*, bill; see also ORGAN 2. **2** [A projection] snout, nozzle, muzzle; see BEAK. —**by a nose** by a very small margin, too close for comfort, barely; see ALMOST. —**look down one's nose at*** disdain, snub, be disgusted by; see ABUSE. —**on the nose*** precisely, to the point, correctly; see ACCURATE. —**turn up one's nose at** sneer at, refuse, scorn; see ABUSE. —**under one's (very) nose** in plain sight, visible, at one's fingertips; see OBVIOUS 1.

nostalgia *n.* remorse, wistfulness, sentimentality; see LONELINESS.

nostalgic *a.* lonesome, regretful, sentimental; see HOMESICK, LONELY.

nosy* *a.* meddlesome, snooping*, unduly curious; see INQUISITIVE, INTERESTED 2.

not *a.* no, in no manner, to no degree, non-, un-, in-; see also NEGATIVE 2.

notable *a.* distinguished, important, striking; see FAMOUS, UNUSUAL 1.

notch *n.* indentation, nick, indent; see CUT 1, DENT, GROOVE.

notch *v.* indent, nick, chisel; see CUT 1, DENT.

notched *a.* nicked, jagged, sawtoothed; see IRREGULAR 4, ROUGH 1.

note *n.* **1** [A representation] sign, figure, mark; see REPRESENTATION. **2** [A brief record] notation, jotting, scribble, reminder, scrawl, annotation, agenda, entry, memorandum, journal, inscription, calendar, diary; see also NOTES, SUMMARY. **3** [A brief communication] dispatch, word, announcement; see LETTER 2. **4** [A musical tone, or its symbol] tone, key, pitch, whole note, half note, quarter note, eighth note, sixteenth note, grace note, triplet, interval, degree, step, sharp, flat, natural; see also MUSIC 1.

note *v.* **1** [To notice] remark, heed, perceive; see REGARD 1, SEE 1. **2** [To record] write down, enter, transcribe; see RECORD 1, WRITE.

notebook *n.* memorandum book, record book, diary; see JOURNAL 1, RECORD 1.

noted *a.* well-known, celebrated, notorious; see FAMOUS.

notes *n.* commentary, interpretation, explanation, findings, recordings, field notes, observations; see also DATA, RECORDS. —**compare notes** exchange views, confer, go over; see DISCUSS.

nothing *n.* nonexistence, emptiness, nothingness, inexistence, nonbeing, nullity, zero, extinction, oblivion, obliteration, annihilation, nonentity, trifle.

nothing *pron.* no thing, not anything, naught, trifle, no part, no trace. —**for nothing 1** gratis, without cost, unencumbered; see FREE 4. **2** in vain, for naught, emptily; see UNNECESSARY. —**have nothing on** have no evidence, be without proof, be only guessing; see GUESS. —**in nothing flat*** in almost no time at all, speedily, rapidly; see QUICKLY. —**think nothing of** minimize, underplay, disregard; see NEGLECT 1.

nothingness *n.* **1** [Void] vacuum, blank, hollowness; see EMPTINESS, NOTHING. **2** [Worthlessness] pettiness, unimportance, smallness; see INSIGNIFICANCE.

notice *n.* **1** [A warning] note, notification, intimation; see SIGN 1, WARNING. **2** [An announcement] remark, comments, information; see DECLARATION, ANNOUNCEMENT, REPORT 1. —**serve notice** give warning, notify, announce; see DECLARE. —**take notice** observe, become aware, pay attention; see SEE 1.

notice *v.* mark, remark, look at; see SEE 1.

noticeable *a.* observable, appreciable, conspicuous; see OBVIOUS 1.

noticed *a.* observed, remarked, seen; see RECORDED.

notify *v.* declare, announce, inform; see ADVERTISE, COMMUNICATE, TELL 1.

no·tion (nō′shən) ***n.*** ⟦see NOTE⟧ **1** a general idea **2** a belief; opinion **3** an inclination; whim **4** [*pl.*] small, useful articles, as needles and thread, sold in a store —**no′tion·al** ***adj.***
no·to·ri·e·ty (nōt′ə rī′ə tē) ***n.*** a being notorious
no·to·ri·ous (nō tôr′ē əs) ***adj.*** ⟦see NOTE⟧ widely known, esp. unfavorably —**no·to′ri·ous·ly** ***adv.***
not·with·stand·ing (nät′with stan′diŋ, -with-) ***prep.*** in spite of —***adv.*** nevertheless —***conj.*** although
nou·gat (no͞o′gət) ***n.*** ⟦< Prov *noga*, nut⟧ a confection of sugar paste with nuts
nought (nôt) ***n.*** ⟦< OE *ne*, not + *awiht*, aught⟧ *Arith.* the figure zero (0)
noun (noun) ***n.*** ⟦< L *nomen*, a name⟧ *Gram.* a word that names or denotes a person, thing, place, action, quality, etc.
nour·ish (nur′ish) ***vt.*** ⟦< L *nutrire*⟧ **1** to provide with substances necessary to life and growth **2** to foster; promote —**nour′ish·ing** ***adj.***
nour′ish·ment (-mənt) ***n.*** **1** a nourishing or being nourished **2** food
nou·veau riche (no͞o′vō rēsh′) *pl.* **nou·veaux riches** (no͞o′ vō rēsh′) ⟦Fr⟧ a newly rich person, esp. one lacking culture, taste, or social grace
no·va (nō′və) ***n.***, *pl.* **-vas** or **-vae** (-vē) ⟦< L, new⟧ a star that brightens intensely and then gradually dims
No·va Sco·tia (nō′və skō′shə) province of SE Canada: 21,425 sq. mi.; pop. 909,000; cap. Halifax: abbrev. *NS* —**No′va Sco′tian**
nov·el (näv′əl) ***adj.*** ⟦< L dim. of *novus*, new⟧ new and unusual —***n.*** a relatively long fictional prose narrative
nov′el·ette′ (-et′) ***n.*** a short novel
nov′el·ist ***n.*** one who writes novels
nov′el·ize′ (-īz′) ***vt.*** **-ized′**, **-iz′ing** to make into or like a novel; specif., to use (a film script) as the basis of a novel
nov′el·ty ***n.***, *pl.* **-ties** **1** the quality of being novel; newness **2** something new, fresh, or unusual **3** a small, often cheap, cleverly made article: *usually used in pl.*
No·vem·ber (nō vem′bər) ***n.*** ⟦< L *novem*, nine: ninth month in Roman year⟧ the 11th month of the year, having 30 days: abbrev. **Nov.**
no·ve·na (nō vē′nə) ***n.*** ⟦< L *novem*, nine⟧ *R.C.Ch.* the offering of special prayers and devotions for nine days
nov·ice (näv′is) ***n.*** ⟦< L *novus*, new⟧ **1** a person on probation in a religious order before taking final vows **2** a person new to something; beginner
no·vi·tiate (nō vish′it) ***n.*** the period or state of being a novice
No·vo·cain (nō′və kān′) ⟦L *nov(us)*, new + (C)OCAIN(E)⟧ *trademark for* PROCAINE
now (nou) ***adv.*** ⟦OE *nu*⟧ **1** *a)* at the present time *b)* at once **2** at that time; then **3** with things as they are *[now we'll never know]* —***conj.*** since; seeing that —***n.*** the present time *[that's all for now]* —***adj.*** of the present time —**just now** recently —**now and then** (or **again**) occasionally
now′a·days′ (-ə dāz′) ***adv.*** at the present time
no·way (nō′wā′) ***adv.*** by no means; not at all: now often **no way**, used with the force of an interjection
no′where′ ***adv.*** not in, at, or to any place —**nowhere near** not by a wide margin
no-win (nō′win′) ***adj.*** designating or of a situation, policy, etc. that cannot lead to success no matter what measures are taken
no′wise′ (-wīz′) ***adv.*** in no manner; noway
nox·ious (näk′shəs) ***adj.*** ⟦< L *nocere*, to hurt⟧ harmful to health or morals; injurious or unwholesome —**nox′ious·ness** ***n.***
noz·zle (näz′əl) ***n.*** ⟦dim. of *nose*⟧ the spout at the end of a hose, pipe, etc.
Np *Chem. symbol for* neptunium
NR *abbrev.* not rated: said of films
NS Nova Scotia
NT *abbrev.* **1** New Testament **2** Northwest Territories
-n't *suffix* not: used with certain verbs in contractions *[aren't]*
nth (enth) ***adj.*** of the indefinitely large or small quantity represented by *n*
nt wt *abbrev.* net weight
nu (no͞o, nyo͞o) ***n.*** the 13th letter of the Greek alphabet (N, ν)
NU Nunavut
nu·ance (no͞o′äns′) ***n.*** ⟦Fr < *nuer*, to shade⟧ a slight variation in tone, color, meaning, etc. —**nu′anced′** ***adj.***
nub (nub) ***n.*** ⟦var. of *knub*, knob⟧ **1** a lump or small piece **2** [Inf.] the main point; gist
nub·bin (nub′in) ***n.*** ⟦dim. of prec.⟧ a small thing
nub·by (nub′ē) ***adj.*** **-bi·er**, **-bi·est** having a rough, knotted surface *[a nubby fabric]*
nu·bile (no͞o′bəl, -bīl′) ***adj.*** ⟦< L *nubere*, marry⟧ **1** marriageable **2** sexually attractive Said of a young woman
nu·cle·ar (no͞o′klē ər) ***adj.*** **1** of, like, or forming a nucleus **2** of or relating to atomic nuclei *[nuclear energy]* **3** of or operated by the use of nuclear energy *[nuclear weapons]* **4** of or involving nuclear weapons *[nuclear warfare]*
nuclear energy the energy released from an atom in nuclear reactions, esp. in nuclear fission or nuclear fusion
nuclear family a basic social unit consisting of parents and their children living in one household
nuclear fission the splitting of the nuclei of atoms, accompanied by conversion of part of their mass into energy, as in the atomic bomb
nuclear fusion the fusion of lightweight atomic nuclei into a nucleus of heavier mass with a resultant loss in the combined mass, which is converted into energy, as in the hydrogen bomb
nuclear physics the branch of physics dealing with the structure of atomic nuclei, nuclear forces, etc.
nuclear reactor a device for creating a controlled nuclear chain reaction using atomic fuel, as for the production of energy
nuclear winter a hypothetical condition following nuclear war in which sunlight is cut off by clouds of smoke and dust, resulting in very low temperatures, destruction of life forms, etc.
nu·cle·ate (no͞o′klē it; *for v.*, -āt′) ***adj.*** having a nucleus —***vt.***, ***vi.*** **-at′ed**, **-at′ing** to form into a nucleus —**nu′cle·a′tion** ***n.***
nu·cle·ic acid (no͞o klē′ik, -klā′-) any of a group of essential complex organic acids found in all living cells: the two types are DNA and RNA

THESAURUS

notion ***n.*** **1** [Opinion] idea, sentiment, assumption; see OPINION 1, THOUGHT 2. **2** [Conception] concept, insight, impression; see AWARENESS, KNOWLEDGE 1.
notoriety ***n.*** repute, renown, name; see FAME.
notorious ***a.*** ill-famed, infamous, disreputable; see BAD 1.
notwithstanding ***a.***, ***prep.*** despite, in spite of, in any case; see ALTHOUGH, BUT 1.
noun ***n.*** substantive, common noun, proper noun; see LABEL, NAME 1.
nourish ***v.*** feed, supply, sustain; see PROVIDE 1, SUPPORT 3.
nourishing ***a.*** healthy, nutritious, full of vitamins; see HEALTHFUL.
nourishment ***n.*** nurture, nutriment, provender; see FOOD.
novel ***a.*** new, odd, strange; see UNIQUE, UNUSUAL 1, 2.
novel ***n.*** narrative, bestseller, fiction; see BOOK, STORY. *Types of novels include the following:* romance, detective story, love story, novella, adventure story, ghost story, mystery, western, science fiction, fantasy; historical, regional, naturalistic, Gothic, biographical, psychological, pornographic, satirical, epistolary, experimental, adventure, etc., novel; thriller, porn*.
novelist ***n.*** fiction writer, storyteller, narrative writer, writer of novels, writer of prose fiction, hack, genre writer, pulp writer; see also AUTHOR, WRITER.
novelty ***n.*** **1** [The quality of being novel] recentness, modernity, freshness; see ORIGINALITY. **2** [Something popular because it is new] innovation, origination, creation; see FAD.
novice ***n.*** beginner, learner, neophyte; see AMATEUR.
now ***a.*** **1** [At the present] at this time, right now, at the moment, just now, momentarily, this day, these days, here and now. **2** [In the immediate future] promptly, in a moment, in a minute; see SOON. **3** [Immediately] at once, momentarily, instantly; see IMMEDIATELY. —**now and then** (or **again**) sometimes, infrequently, occasionally; see SELDOM.
nowadays ***a.*** in these days, in this age, at the present time; see NOW 1.
noway ***a.*** not at all, on no account, by no means, not a bit of it, nowhere near, in no respect.
nowhere ***a.*** not anywhere, not in any place, not at any place, nowhere at all, in no place, to no place.
nozzle ***n.*** spout, outlet, vent; see END 4.
nuance ***n.*** subtlety, refinement, distinction; see DIFFERENCE 1.
nub* ***n.*** gist, crux, core, nitty-gritty*; see also ESSENCE 1.
nuclear bomb ***n.*** nuclear warhead, hydrogen bomb, H-bomb, atomic bomb, A-bomb, neutron bomb, atomic weapon, nuclear weapon; see also ARMS.

nucleo- *combining form* **1** nucleus **2** nuclear **3** nucleic acid Also **nucle-**

nu·cle·o·lus (no͞o klē′ə ləs) ***n.***, *pl.* **-li′** (-lī′) ⟦< LL, dim. of L *nucleus*⟧ a conspicuous, usually spherical, dense body in the nucleus of most cells, consisting of protein and RNA

nu·cle·us (no͞o′klē əs) ***n.***, *pl.* **-cle·i′** (-ī′) or **-cle·us·es** ⟦< L, kernel⟧ **1** a central thing or part around which others are grouped; core **2** any center of growth or development **3** the central part of an atom **4** the central mass of protoplasm in a cell

nude (no͞od) ***adj.*** ⟦L *nudus*⟧ naked; bare —***n.*** **1** a nude human figure, esp. in a work of art **2** the state of being nude *[in the nude]* —**nu′di·ty** ***n.***

nudge (nuj) ***vt.*** **nudged, nudg′ing** ⟦< ?⟧ to push gently, esp. with the elbow, in order to get the attention of, hint slyly, etc. —***n.*** a gentle push

nud·ism (no͞o′diz′əm) ***n.*** the practice or cult of going nude for hygienic reasons —**nud′ist** ***n., adj.***

nu·ga·to·ry (no͞o′gə tôr′ē) ***adj.*** ⟦< L *nugari*, to trifle⟧ **1** trifling; worthless **2** not operative; invalid

nug·get (nug′ət) ***n.*** ⟦prob. < dial. *nug*, a lump⟧ a lump; esp., a lump of native gold

nui·sance (no͞o′səns) ***n.*** ⟦< L *nocere*, annoy⟧ an act, thing, or person causing trouble, annoyance, etc.

nuke (no͞ok) [Slang] ***n.*** ⟦< NUCLEAR⟧ a nuclear weapon —***vt.*** **nuked, nuk′ing** to attack with nuclear weapons

null (nul) ***adj.*** ⟦< L *nullus*, none⟧ **1** without legal force; invalid: usually in the phrase **null and void** **2** amounting to naught **3** of no value, effect, etc.

nul·li·fy (nul′ə fī′) ***vt.*** **-fied′, -fy′ing** ⟦< L *nullus*, none + *facere*, to make⟧ **1** to make legally null or valueless **2** to cancel out —**nul′li·fi·ca′tion** ***n.***

numb (num) ***adj.*** ⟦< ME *nimen*, to take⟧ deadened; insensible —***vt.*** to make numb —**numb′ly** ***adv.*** —**numb′ness** ***n.***

num·ber (num′bər) ***n.*** ⟦< L *numerus*⟧ **1** a symbol or word showing how many or which one in a series (Ex.: 2, 35, four, ninth) **2** [*pl.*] ARITHMETIC **3** the sum of persons or things; total **4** *a)* [*often pl.*] many *b)* [*pl.*] numerical superiority **5** quantity **6** *a)* a single issue of a periodical *b)* a single song, dance, etc. in a program of entertainment **7** [Inf.] a person or thing singled out **8** *Gram.* the form of a word as indicating either singular or plural —***vt.*** **1** to count; enumerate **2** to give a number to **3** to include as one of a group **4** to limit the number of **5** to have or comprise; total —***vi.*** to be included —**a number of** several or many; some —**beyond** (or **without**) **number** too numerous to be counted —**the numbers** an illegal lottery based on certain numbers published in newspapers: also **numbers game** (or **racket**)

num′ber·less ***adj.*** countless

Num·bers (num′bərz) ***n.*** the fourth book of the Pentateuch in the Bible: abbrev. **Num.**

nu·mer·al (no͞o′mər əl) ***adj.*** ⟦< L *numerus*, number⟧ of or denoting a number or numbers —***n.*** a figure, a letter, or a group of figures or letters, expressing a number

nu′mer·ate (-it) ***adj.*** [Chiefly Brit.] able to understand basic mathematical concepts, etc.

nu′mer·a′tor (-āt′ər) ***n.*** the part of a fraction above the line

nu·mer·i·cal (no͞o mer′i kəl) ***adj.*** **1** of, or having the nature of, number **2** in or by numbers **3** expressed by numbers, not letters —**nu·mer′i·cal·ly** ***adv.***

nu·mer·ol·o·gy (no͞o′mər äl′ə jē) ***n.*** divination by numbers, as with birth dates

nu·mer·ous (no͞o′mər əs) ***adj.*** **1** consisting of many persons or things **2** very many

nu·mi·nous (no͞o′mə nəs) ***adj.*** ⟦< L *numen*, deity⟧ having a deeply spiritual or mystical effect

nu·mis·mat·ics (no͞o′miz mat′iks, -mis-) ***n.*** ⟦< L *numisma*, a coin⟧ the study or collection of coins, medals, paper money, etc. —**nu·mis′ma·tist** (-mə tist) ***n.***

num·skull (num′skul′) ***n.*** ⟦NUM(B) + SKULL⟧ a dunce

nun (nun) ***n.*** ⟦< LL *nonna*⟧ a woman devoted to a religious life, esp. one living in a convent under vows

Nu·na·vut (no͞o′nə vo͞ot′) territory of N Canada: 770,000 sq. mi.; pop. 25,000; cap. Iqaluit: abbrev. *NU*

nun·ci·o (nun′shō′, -sē ō′) ***n.***, *pl.* **-ci·os′** ⟦< It < L *nuntius*, messenger⟧ a papal ambassador to a foreign state

nun·ner·y (nun′ər ē) ***n.***, *pl.* **-ies** *former term for* CONVENT

nup·tial (nup′shəl, -chəl) ***adj.*** ⟦< L *nubere*, marry⟧ of marriage or a wedding —***n.*** [*pl.*] a wedding

nurse (nʉrs) ***n.*** ⟦< L *nutrire*, nourish⟧ **1** a woman hired to care for another's children **2** a person trained to care for the sick, assist surgeons, etc. —***vt.*** **nursed, nurs′ing** **1** to suckle (an infant) **2** to take care of (a child, invalid, etc.) **3** to nourish, foster, etc. **4** to try to cure *[to nurse a cold]* **5** to use or handle so as to protect or conserve —***vi.*** **1** to feed at the breast; suckle **2** to serve as a nurse

nurse′maid′ ***n.*** a woman hired to care for a child or children

nurs·er·y (nʉrs′ə rē) ***n.***, *pl.* **-ies** **1** a room set aside for children **2** a place where parents may temporarily leave children to be cared for **3** a place where young trees or other plants are raised for transplanting, etc.

nurs′er·y·man (-mən) ***n.***, *pl.* **-men** (-mən) one who owns or works in a tree nursery

nursery rhyme a poem for children

nursery school PRESCHOOL

nursing home a residence providing care for the infirm, chronically ill, disabled, etc.

nur·ture (nʉr′chər) ***n.*** ⟦< L *nutrire*, nourish⟧ training; rearing —***vt.*** **-tured, -tur·ing** **1** to nourish **2** to train, educate, rear, etc. —**nur′tur·er** ***n.***

nut (nut) ***n.*** ⟦OE *hnutu*⟧ **1** a dry, one-seeded fruit, consisting of a kernel, often edible, in a woody shell, as the walnut **2** the kernel itself **3** loosely, any hard-shell, relatively nonperishable fruit, as the peanut **4** a small

THESAURUS

nucleus ***n.*** **1** [Essence] core, gist, kernel; see ESSENCE 1, MATTER 1. **2** [Center] hub, focus, pivot; see CENTER 1.

nude ***a.*** stripped, unclothed, bare; see NAKED 1.

nude ***n.*** naked body, naked man, naked woman, nudist, pinup, artist's model, sculpture, sketch, painting, stripper*, peeler*.

nudge ***n.*** tap, poke, shove; see BUMP 1, PUSH, TOUCH 2.

nudge ***v.*** poke, bump, tap; see PUSH 1, TOUCH 1.

nudity ***n.*** bareness, nudeness, undress; see NAKEDNESS.

nugget ***n.*** lump, bullion, chunk; see GOLD, ROCK 1.

nuisance ***n.*** **1** [A bother] annoyance, vexation, bore; see TROUBLE 2. **2** [An offense against the public] breach, infraction, affront; see CRIME. **3** [An unpleasant or unwelcome person] problem child, frump, bother, holy terror*, bad egg*, insect*, louse*, pain in the neck*, poor excuse*, bum*; see also TROUBLE 1.

null ***a.*** invalid, vain, unsanctioned; see VOID.

numb ***a.*** **1** [Insensible] deadened, dead, unfeeling, numbed, asleep, senseless, anesthetized, comatose; see also PARALYZED. **2** [Insensitive] apathetic, lethargic, callous; see INDIFFERENT.

numb ***v.*** paralyze, stun, dull; see DEADEN.

number ***n.*** amount, sum total, totality, aggregate, whole, whole number, product, measurable quantity, estimate, the lot, plenty, abundance; see also QUANTITY. **—get** (or **have**) **someone's number*** find out about, discover someone's true character, come to know someone; see UNDERSTAND 1. **—someone's number is up*** someone's time to die has arrived, someone's time has come, someone's destiny is fulfilled; see DOOMED. **—without number** too numerous to be counted, innumerable, countless; see MANY.

number ***v.*** count, calculate, enumerate; see ADD 1, TOTAL.

numbered ***a.*** designated, enumerated, checked, specified, indicated; see also MARKED 1.

numbness ***n.*** deadness, anesthesia, dullness, insensitivity, insensibility, paralysis, loss of sensation.

numeral ***n.*** character, cipher, digit; see NUMBER.

numerical ***a.*** arithmetical, statistical, fractional, exponential, logarithmic, differential, integral, digital, mathematical, binary.

numerous ***a.*** copious, various, diverse; see INFINITE, MANY.

nun ***n.*** sister, religious, ascetic, anchorite, prioress, mother superior, abbess; see also MINISTRY.

nuptials ***n.*** wedding, matrimony, marriage ceremony; see MARRIAGE.

nurse ***n.*** **1** [One who cares for the sick] attendant, male nurse, licensed practical nurse, LPN, private nurse, registered nurse, RN, floor nurse, night nurse, day nurse, doctor's assistant, student nurse, nurse's aide, therapist, Red Cross nurse, Florence Nightingale*. **2** [One who cares for the young] nursemaid, babysitter, nanny; see ATTENDANT.

nurse ***v.*** attend to, aid, medicate; see HEAL, SUSTAIN 2, TEND 1, TREAT 2.

nursery ***n.*** **1** [A place for children] child's room, playroom, nursery school; see SCHOOL 1. **2** [A place for plants] hothouse, potting shed, greenhouse; see BUILDING.

nurture ***v.*** nourish, care for, provide for; see FEED, SUSTAIN 2.

nut ***n.*** **1** [The dry fruit] seed, kernel, stone; see FRUIT. *Common nuts include the following:* acorn, beechnut, peanut, hazelnut, black walnut, English walnut, almond, pecan, filbert, pistachio, cashew, hickory nut,

metal block with a threaded hole for screwing onto a bolt, etc. **5** [Slang] *a*) a crazy or eccentric person *b*) a devotee; fan

nut case [Slang] one who is eccentric or crazy: also **nut'case'** ***n.***

nut'crack'er ***n.*** **1** an instrument for cracking nutshells **2** a crowlike bird that feeds on nuts

nut'hatch' ***n.*** a small nut-eating bird with a sharp beak

nut'meat' ***n.*** the kernel of a nut

nut'meg' (-meg') ***n.*** ⟦< L *nux*, nut + LL *muscus*, musk⟧ the aromatic seed of an East Indian tree, grated and used as a spice

nu·tri·a (no͞o'trē ə) ***n.*** ⟦Sp < L *lutra*, otter⟧ the soft, brown fur of a South American rodent

nu·tri·ent (no͞o'trē ənt) ***adj.*** ⟦< L *nutrire*, nourish⟧ nourishing —***n.*** anything nutritious

nu'tri·ment (-trə mənt) ***n.*** anything that nourishes; food

nu·tri·tion (no͞o trish'ən) ***n.*** ⟦see NUTRIENT⟧ **1** the process by which an organism takes in and assimilates food **2** anything that nourishes; food **3** the study of diet and health —**nu·tri'tion·al** ***adj.*** —**nu·tri'tion·al·ly** ***adv.*** —**nu'tri·tive** (-trə tiv) ***adj.***

nu·tri'tious (-trish'əs) ***adj.*** nourishing

nuts (nuts) [Slang] ***adj.*** crazy; foolish —***interj.*** used to express disgust, scorn, refusal, etc.: often in the phrase **nuts to someone** (or **something**) —**be nuts about** **1** to be greatly in love with **2** to be very enthusiastic about

nuts and bolts [Inf.] the basic elements or practical aspects of something —**nuts'-and-bolts'** ***adj.***

nut'shell' ***n.*** the shell enclosing the kernel of a nut —**in a nutshell** in concise form; in a few words

nut'ty ***adj.*** **-ti·er, -ti·est** **1** containing nuts **2** having a nutlike flavor **3** [Slang] *a*) very enthusiastic *b*) foolish, crazy, etc. —**nut'ti·ness** ***n.***

nuz·zle (nuz'əl) ***vt.***, ***vi.*** **-zled, -zling** ⟦< ME *nose*, NOSE⟧ **1** to push (against) or rub with the nose, snout, etc. **2** to nestle; snuggle —**nuz'zler** ***n.***

NV Nevada

NW *abbrev.* **1** northwest **2** northwestern

NY New York

NYC or **N.Y.C.** New York City

ny·lon (nī'län') ***n.*** ⟦arbitrary coinage⟧ **1** an elastic, very strong synthetic material that is made into fiber, yarn, bristles, etc. **2** [*pl.*] stockings made of this

nymph (nimf) ***n.*** ⟦< Gr *nymphē*⟧ **1** *Gr. & Rom. Myth.* any of a group of minor nature goddesses, living in rivers, trees, etc. **2** a lovely young woman **3** the young of an insect with incomplete metamorphosis

nym·pho·ma·ni·a (nim'fō mā'nē ə) ***n.*** uncontrollable desire by a woman for sexual intercourse —**nym'pho·ma'ni·ac'** ***adj.***, ***n.***

THESAURUS

chestnut, butternut, pine nut, pignolia, kola nut, Brazil nut, betel nut. **2** [A threaded metal block] bolt nut, screw nut, lock nut, cap, ratchet nut; see also BOLT. **3** [*An eccentric or insane person] eccentric, fanatic, maniac; see ZEALOT.

nutriment ***n.*** nourishment, provisions, sustenance; see FOOD.

nutrition ***n.*** diet, nourishment, victuals; see FOOD, SUBSISTENCE 1.

nutritive ***a.*** edible, wholesome, nutritious; see HEALTHFUL.

nuts* ***a.*** crazy, deranged, ridiculous; see INSANE, UNUSUAL 2.

nuzzle ***v.*** caress, cuddle, nudge; see NESTLE.

nylon ***n.*** synthetic, polyamide product, synthetic fiber; see PLASTIC.

nymph ***n.*** nature goddess, sprite, mermaid; see FAIRY.

o or **O** (ō) ***n.***, *pl.* **o's, O's** the 15th letter of the English alphabet

O[1] (ō) ***n.***, *pl.* **O's** **1** the numeral zero **2** a blood type

O[2] (ō) ***interj.*** **1** used in direct address *[O Lord!]* **2** OH

O[3] *abbrev.* **1** Ocean **2** *Physics* ohm **3** Old **4** *Baseball* out(s)

O[4] *Chem. symbol for* oxygen

-o (ō) *suffix* forming slangy words, as slang nouns from adjectives *[weirdo, sicko]*

oaf (ōf) ***n.*** ⟦< ON *alfr,* elf⟧ a stupid, clumsy fellow; lout —**oaf'ish** ***adj.***

O·a·hu (ō ä'hōō) chief island of Hawaii

oak (ōk) ***n.*** ⟦OE *ac*⟧ **1** a large hardwood tree with nuts called *acorns* **2** its wood —***adj.*** of oak —**oak'en** ***adj.***

Oak·land (ōk'lənd) seaport in W California: pop. 372,000

Oak Ridge city in E Tennessee: center for atomic research: pop. 27,000

oa·kum (ō'kəm) ***n.*** ⟦< OE *a-*, out + *camb*, a comb⟧ stringy hemp fiber gotten by taking apart old ropes, used as a caulking material

oar (ôr) ***n.*** ⟦OE *ar*⟧ a long pole with a broad blade at one end, used in rowing —**oars·man** (ôrz'mən), *pl.* **-men,** ***n.***

oar'lock' ***n.*** a device, often U-shaped, for holding an oar in place in rowing

OAS *abbrev.* Organization of American States

o·a·sis (ō ā'sis) ***n.***, *pl.* **-ses'** (-sēz') ⟦< Gr, fertile spot⟧ a fertile place in a desert, resulting from the presence of water

oat (ōt) ***n.*** ⟦OE *ate*⟧ [*usually pl.*] **1** a hardy cereal grass **2** its edible grain —**oat'en** ***adj.***

oat'cake' ***n.*** a thin, flat cake made of oatmeal

oath (ōth) ***n.***, *pl.* **oaths** (ōt*h*z, ōths) ⟦OE *ath*⟧ **1** a declaration based on an appeal to God that one will speak the truth, keep a promise, etc. **2** a swearword; curse

oat'meal' ***n.*** **1** oats ground or rolled into meal or flakes **2** a porridge of this

OB *abbrev.* **1** obstetrician **2** obstetrics

ob. *abbrev.* ⟦L *obiit*⟧ he (or she) died

ob- ⟦< L *ob*⟧ *prefix* **1** to, toward, before *[obtrude]* **2** against *[obstinate]* **3** upon, over *[obscure]* **4** completely *[obdurate]*

ob·bli·ga·to (äb'li gät'ō) ***n.***, *pl.* **-tos** or **-ti** (-ē) ⟦see OBLIGE⟧ a musical accompaniment, usually by a solo instrument

ob·du·rate (äb'door it) ***adj.*** ⟦< L *obduratus* < *ob-*, intens. + *durus*, hard⟧ **1** hardhearted **2** stubborn; obstinate —**ob'du·ra·cy** (-ə sē) ***n.***

o·be·di·ent (ō bē'dē ənt) ***adj.*** obeying or willing to obey —**o·be'di·ence** ***n.*** —**o·be'di·ent·ly** ***adv.***

o·bei·sance (ō bā'səns, -bē'-) ***n.*** ⟦< OFr *obeir*, obey⟧ **1** a gesture of respect, as a bow **2** homage; deference —**o·bei'sant** ***adj.***

ob·e·lisk (äb'ə lisk, ō'bə-) ***n.*** ⟦< Gr *obelos*, needle⟧ a tall, four-sided stone pillar tapering to its pyramidal top

o·bese (ō bēs') ***adj.*** ⟦< L *obesus* < *ob-* (see OB-) + *edere*, to eat⟧ very fat; stout —**o·be'si·ty** (-ə tē) ***n.***

o·bey (ō bā') ***vt.*** ⟦< L *obedire* < *ob-* (see OB-) + *audire*, hear⟧ **1** to carry out the orders of **2** to carry out (an order, etc.) **3** to be guided by *[to obey one's conscience]* —***vi.*** to be obedient

ob·fus·cate (äb'fəs kāt', äb fus'kāt') ***vt.*** **-cat'ed, -cat'ing** ⟦< L *obfuscatus* < *ob-* (see OB-) + *fuscus*, dark⟧ to obscure; confuse —**ob'fus·ca'tion** ***n.***

ob·i·ter dic·tum (äb'i tər dik'təm, ō bi-) *pl.* **ob'i·ter dic'ta** (-tə) an incidental remark

o·bit·u·ar·y (ō bich'ōō er'ē) ***n.***, *pl.* **-ar'ies** ⟦< L *obire*, to die⟧ a notice of someone's death, usually with a brief biography: also **o·bit** (ō'bit)

obj *abbrev.* **1** object **2** objective

ob·ject (äb'jikt; *for v.* äb jekt') ***n.*** ⟦< ML *objectum*, thing thrown in the way < L *objectus* < *ob-* (see OB-) + *jacere*, to throw⟧ **1** a thing that can be seen or touched **2** a person or thing to which action, feeling, etc. is directed **3** purpose; goal **4** *Gram.* a noun or other substantive receiving the action of a verb or governed by a preposition —***vt.*** to state by way of objection —***vi.*** to feel or express disapproval or opposition —**ob·jec'tor** ***n.***

ob·jec·tion (əb jek'shən) ***n.*** **1** a feeling or expression of opposition or disapproval **2** a reason for objecting

ob·jec'tion·a·ble ***adj.*** **1** open to objection **2** disagreeable; offensive

ob·jec·tive (əb jek'tiv) ***adj.*** **1** existing as an object or fact, independent of the mind; real **2** determined by the realities of the thing dealt with rather than the thoughts of the writer or speaker **3** without bias or prejudice **4** *Gram.* designating or of the case of an object of a preposition or verb —***n.*** something aimed at —**ob·jec'tive·ly** ***adv.*** —**ob·jec·tiv·i·ty** (äb'jek tiv'ə tē) or **ob·jec'tive·ness** ***n.***

object lesson an actual or practical demonstration or exemplification of some principle

ob·jet d'art (äb'zhā där') *pl.* **ob'jets d'art'** (-zhā-) ⟦Fr⟧ a small object of artistic value, as a figurine

ob·jur·gate (äb'jər gāt') ***vt.*** **-gat'ed, -gat'ing** ⟦< L *objurgatus* < *ob-* (see OB-) + *jurgare*, chide⟧ to upbraid sharply; rebuke

ob·late (äb'lāt') ***adj.*** ⟦ModL *oblatus*, thrust forward⟧ *Geom.* flattened at the poles

THESAURUS

oak ***n.*** **1** [An oak tree] white oak, pin oak, cork oak; see TREE. **2** [Oak wood] hardwood, oaken wood, oak paneling; see WOOD 2.

oar ***n.*** pole, paddle, scull; see TOOL 1.

oasis ***n.*** green area, fertile area, irrigated land, watered tract, garden spot, desert garden, water hole, watering place, desert resting place; see also REFUGE 1, RETREAT 2.

oath ***n.*** **1** [An attestation of the truth] affirmation, declaration, affidavit, vow, sworn statement, testimony, word, contract, pledge; see also PROMISE 1.—*Ant.* DENIAL, disavowal, lie. **2** [The name of the Lord taken in vain] malediction, swearword, blasphemy; see CURSE.

obedience ***n.*** docility, submission, compliance; see WILLINGNESS.

obedient ***a.*** **1** [Dutiful] loyal, law-abiding, governable, resigned, devoted, respectful, controllable, attentive, obliging, willing, tractable, deferential, under control, at one's command, at one's beck and call, on a string*, wrapped around one's little finger*; see also FAITHFUL.—*Ant.* UNRULY, disobedient, undutiful. **2** [Docile] pliant, acquiescent, compliant; see DOCILE.

obediently ***a.*** dutifully, submissively, loyally; see WILLINGLY.

obese ***a.*** corpulent, plump, stout; see FAT.

obey ***v.*** submit, answer to, respond, act upon, act on, bow to, surrender, yield, perform, do, carry out, attend to orders, do what one is told, accept, consent, do what is expected of one, do one's duty, do as one says, serve, concur, assent, conform, acquiesce, mind, take orders, do one's bidding, comply, fulfill; see also AGREE.—*Ant.* REBEL, disobey, mutiny.

obfuscate ***v.*** obscure, make unclear, bewilder; see MUDDLE, CONFUSE.

object ***n.*** **1** [A corporeal body] article, something, gadget; see THING 1. **2** [A purpose] objective, aim, wish; see PURPOSE 1. **3** [One who receives] recipient, target, victim; see RECEIVER.

object ***v.*** protest, take exception to, dispute; see COMPLAIN.

objection ***n.*** disapproval, scruple, hesitation, question, criticism, complaint, charge, accusation, reprimand, exception, admonition, reproach, dispute, opposition, adverse comment, rejection, ban, countercharge, grievance, contradiction, censure, abuse, scolding, denunciation, lecture, disagreement, difference, disdain, insistence, condemnation, grumbling, faultfinding, reproof, dissent, insinuation, complaining, frown, blame, sarcasm, wail, groan, murmur, lament, regret, aspersion, beef*, gripe*, demurring, reluctance, unwillingness, rejection, dislike, dissatisfaction, discontent, displeasure, low opinion, abhorrence, dubiousness; see also DOUBT.—*Ant.* PERMISSION, acceptance, desire.

objectionable ***a.*** **1** [Revolting] gross, repugnant, abhorrent; see OFFENSIVE 2. **2** [Undesirable] unacceptable, unsatisfactory, inexpedient; see UNDESIRABLE.

objective ***a.*** **1** [Existing independently of the mind] actual, external, material, scientific, sure, extrinsic, measurable, extraneous, reified, tactile, corporeal, bodily, palpable, physical, sensible, outward, outside, determinable, unchangeable, invariable; see also REAL 2.—*Ant.* MENTAL, subjective, introspective. **2** [Free from personal bias] detached, impersonal, unbiased; see ACCURATE 2, FAIR 1.

objective ***n.*** goal, aim, aspiration; see PURPOSE 1.

objectively ***a.*** impartially, indifferently, neutrally, open-mindedly, dispassionately, justly, equitably, detachedly, soberly, accurately, candidly, considerately, not subjectively, with objectivity, with impartiality, with consideration, with good judgment, without prejudice, without bias, without partiality, without passion.

ob·la·tion (äb lā′shən) ***n.*** ⟦< L *oblatus*, offered⟧ an offering or sacrifice to God or a god
ob·li·gate (äb′li gāt′) ***vt.*** **-gat′ed, -gat′ing** ⟦see OBLIGE⟧ to bind by a promise, sense of duty, etc.
ob′li·ga′tion (-gā′shən) ***n.*** **1** an obligating or being obligated **2** a binding contract, promise, responsibility, etc. **3** the binding power of a contract, etc. **4** a being indebted for a favor, etc.
ob·lig·a·to·ry (ə blig′ə tôr′ē, äb′lə gə-) ***adj.*** legally or morally binding
o·blige (ə blīj′) ***vt.*** **o·bliged′, o·blig′ing** ⟦< L *obligare* < *ob-* (see OB-) + *ligare*, to bind⟧ **1** to compel by moral, legal, or physical force **2** to make indebted for a favor; do a favor for
o·blig′ing ***adj.*** helpful; accommodating —**o·blig′ing·ly** ***adv.***
ob·lique (ō blēk′) ***adj.*** ⟦< L *obliquus* < *ob-* (see OB-) + *liquis*, awry⟧ **1** slanting **2** indirect or evasive —**ob·lique′ly** ***adv.*** —**ob·liq·ui·ty** (ə blik′wə tē) or **ob·lique′ness** ***n.***
ob·lit·er·ate (ə blit′ər āt′) ***vt.*** **-at′ed, -at′ing** ⟦< L *obliteratus* < *ob-* (see OB-) + *littera*, a letter⟧ **1** to blot out; efface **2** to destroy —**ob·lit′er·a′tion** ***n.***
ob·liv·i·on (ə bliv′ē ən) ***n.*** ⟦< L *oblivisci*, to forget⟧ **1** forgetfulness **2** the condition of being forgotten
ob·liv′i·ous (-əs) ***adj.*** forgetful or indifferent: usually with *to* or *of*
ob·long (äb′lôŋ′) ***adj.*** ⟦< L *oblongus*, rather long < *ob-* (see OB-) + *longus*, long⟧ longer than broad; specif., rectangular and longer in one direction —***n.*** an oblong figure
ob·lo·quy (äb′lə kwē) ***n.***, *pl.* **-quies** ⟦< L *obloqui* < *ob-* (see OB-) + *loqui*, speak⟧ **1** widespread censure or abuse **2** disgrace resulting from this
ob·nox·ious (əb näk′shəs, äb-) ***adj.*** ⟦< L *obnoxiosus* < *ob-* (see OB-) + *noxa*, harm⟧ very unpleasant; offensive; repugnant —**ob·nox′ious·ly** ***adv.*** —**ob·nox′ious·ness** ***n.***
o·boe (ō′bō) ***n.*** ⟦< Fr *haut*, high (pitch) + *bois*, wood⟧ a double-reed woodwind instrument having a high, penetrating tone —**o′bo·ist** ***n.***
obs *abbrev.* obsolete
ob·scene (äb sēn′) ***adj.*** ⟦< L *obscenus*, filthy⟧ **1** offensive to modesty or decency; lewd **2** repulsive —**ob·scen′i·ty** (-sen′ə tē), *pl.* **-ties**, ***n.***
ob·scur·ant·ism (äb′skyoor′ən tiz′əm) ***n.*** **1** opposition to human progress **2** a being deliberately obscure or vague
ob·scure (əb skyoor′) ***adj.*** ⟦< L *obscurus*, covered over⟧ **1** dim; dark **2** not easily seen; faint **3** vague; ambiguous *[an obscure answer]* **4** inconspicuous or hidden **5** not well-known *[an obscure actor]* —***vt.*** **-scured′, -scur′ing** to make obscure —**ob·scure′ly** ***adv.*** —**ob·scu′ri·ty** ***n.***
ob·se·quies (äb′si kwēz′) ***pl.n.*** ⟦< L *obsequium*, compliance, substituted for L *exsequiae*, funeral⟧ funeral rites
ob·se·qui·ous (əb sē′kwē əs) ***adj.*** ⟦< L *obsequi*, to comply with⟧ servile or fawning
ob·serv·ance (əb zurv′əns) ***n.*** **1** the observing of a law, custom, etc. **2** a customary act, rite, etc.
ob·serv′ant (-ənt) ***adj.*** **1** strict in observing a law, custom, etc. **2** paying careful attention **3** perceptive or alert
ob·ser·va·tion (äb′zər vā′shən) ***n.*** **1** *a)* the act or power of noticing *b)* something noticed **2** a being seen **3** a noting and recording of facts, as for research **4** a comment or remark
ob·serv·a·to·ry (əb zurv′ə tôr′ē) ***n.***, *pl.* **-ries** a building equipped for astronomical research, esp. one with a large telescope
ob·serve (əb zurv′) ***vt.*** **-served′, -serv′ing** ⟦< L *observare* < *ob-* (see OB-) + *servare*, to keep⟧ **1** to adhere to (a law, custom, etc.) **2** to celebrate (a holiday, etc.) **3** *a)* to notice (something) *b)* to pay special attention to **4** to say; remark **5** to examine scientifically —**ob·serv′a·ble** ***adj.*** —**ob·serv′er** ***n.***
ob·sess (əb ses′) ***vt.*** ⟦< L *obsessus* < *ob-* (see OB-) + *sedere*, sit⟧ to haunt or trouble in mind; preoccupy —***vi.*** to be obsessed or preoccupied: usually with *about, over*, or *on* —**ob·ses′sive** ***adj.*** —**ob·ses′sive·ly** ***adv.***
ob·ses′sion (-sesh′ən) ***n.*** **1** a being obsessed **2** an idea, desire, etc. that obsesses one
ob·sid·i·an (əb sid′ē ən) ***n.*** ⟦ModL *obsidianus*, ult. after *Obsius*, finder of a similar stone in ancient times⟧ a hard, dark, volcanic glass
ob·so·les·cent (äb′sə les′ənt) ***adj.*** becoming obsolete —**ob′so·les′cence** ***n.***
ob·so·lete (äb′sə lēt′) ***adj.*** ⟦< L *obsoletus* < *ob-* (see OB-) + *exolescere*, to grow out of use⟧ **1** no longer in use **2** out-of-date

THESAURUS

obligate ***v.*** bind, restrict, constrain; see FORCE.
obligation ***n.*** responsibility, burden, debt; see DUTY 1.
obligatory ***a.*** required, essential, binding; see NECESSARY.
oblige ***v.*** **1** [To accommodate] assist, aid, contribute; see ACCOMMODATE 1, HELP. **2** [To require] compel, coerce, bind; see FORCE, REQUIRE 2.
obliged ***a.*** compelled, obligated, required; see BOUND 2.
obliging ***a.*** amiable, accommodating, helpful; see KIND.
obligingly ***a.*** helpfully, thoughtfully, graciously; see AGREEABLY.
oblique ***a.*** inclined, inclining, diverging, leaning, sloping, angled, askew, asymmetrical, turned, twisted, awry, askance, distorted, off level, sideways, slanted, tipping, tipped, at an angle, on the bias; see also BENT, CROOKED 1.—*Ant.* STRAIGHT, vertical, perpendicular.
oblivion ***n.*** nonexistence, obscurity, void; see EMPTINESS, NOTHING.
oblivious ***a.*** abstracted, preoccupied, absorbed; see ABSENT-MINDED, DREAMY.
oblong ***a.*** elongated, rectangular, oval, elliptical, egg-shaped.—*Ant.* SQUARE, round, circular.
obnoxious ***a.*** annoying, disagreeable, displeasing; see OFFENSIVE 2.
obscene ***a.*** indecent, smutty, pornographic; see LEWD 2.
obscenity ***n.*** vulgarity, impropriety, smut; see INDECENCY, LEWDNESS.
obscure ***a.*** **1** [Vague] indistinct, ambiguous, indefinite, indecisive, unintelligible, impenetrable, inscrutable, unfathomable, unclear, vague, undefined, intricate, illegible, incomprehensible, hazy, dark, dim, inexplicable, inconceivable, unbelievable, incredible, complicated, illogical, unreasoned, mixedup, doubtful, questionable, dubious, inexact, unreasoned, loose, ill-defined, unidentified, invisible, undisclosed, perplexing, cryptic, escaping notice, mystical, secret, enigmatic, concealed, mysterious, esoteric, puzzling, lacking clarity, unreadable, contradictory, out of focus, unrelated, clear as mud*, over one's head, deep, far out*; see also COMPLEX 2, CONFUSED 2, CONFUSING, DIFFICULT 2.—*Ant.* CLEAR, definite, distinct. **2** [Dark] cloudy, dense, hazy; see DARK 1. **3** [Little known] unknown, rare, hidden, covered, remote, reticent, secretive, seldom seen, unseen, inconspicuous, humble, invisible, mysterious, deep, cryptic, enigmatic, esoteric, arcane, undisclosed, dark; see also DISTANT, IRRELEVANT, PROFOUND.
obscure ***v.*** **1** [To dim] shadow, cloud, screen; see SHADE 2. **2** [To conceal] cover, veil, wrap up; see DISGUISE, HIDE 1.
obscurely ***a.*** dimly, darkly, indistinctly; see VAGUELY.
obscurity ***n.*** vagueness, dimness, fuzziness; see UNCERTAINTY 1, 2.
observable ***a.*** perceptible, noticeable, discernible; see OBVIOUS 1.
observance ***n.*** **1** [A custom] ritual, practice, rite; see CUSTOM. **2** [Attention] awareness, observation, notice; see ATTENTION.
observant ***a.*** keen, alert, penetrating, wide-awake, discerning, perceptive, sharp, eager, interested, discovering, detecting, discriminating, judicious, searching, understanding, questioning, deducing, sensitive, surveying, considering, clearsighted, comprehending, bright, on the ball*, on one's toes*; see also INTELLIGENT.—*Ant.* THOUGHTLESS, unobservant, insensitive.
observation ***n.*** **1** [The power of observing] seeing, recognizing, perception; see SIGHT 1. **2** [A remark] comment, note, commentary; see REMARK, SPEECH 3.
observe ***v.*** **1** [To watch] scrutinize, inspect, examine; see SEE, WATCH. **2** [To comment] note, remark, mention; see COMMENT. **3** [To commemorate] dedicate, solemnize, keep; see CELEBRATE 1. **4** [To abide by] conform to, comply, adopt; see FOLLOW 2, OBEY.
observed ***a.*** **1** [Noticed] seen, noted, marked; see RECOGNIZED. **2** [Commemorated] kept, celebrated, recalled; see REMEMBERED.
observer ***n.*** watcher, watchman, sentinel, lookout, sentry, guard, detective, policeman, policewoman, spy, spectator, eyewitness, beholder, onlooker, bystander, passerby, meddler, peeper, voyeur, prying person, peeping Tom*; see also WITNESS.
obsess ***v.*** dominate, possess, hound; see HAUNT 2.
obsessed ***a.*** haunted, beset, controlled; see TROUBLED.
obsession ***n.*** fixation, fascination, passion, fancy, craze, delusion, mania, infatuation, fixed idea, compulsion, bee in one's bonnet*, hang-up*; see also FANTASY.
obsolete ***a.*** antiquated, archaic, out-of-date; see OLD 1, 2, OLD-FASHIONED.

ob·sta·cle (äb′stə kəl) ***n.*** ⟦< L *obstaculum* < *ob-* (see OB-) + *stare,* to stand⟧ anything that stands in the way; obstruction

ob·stet·rics (əb stet′riks) ***n.*** ⟦< L *obstetrix,* midwife⟧ the branch of medicine concerned with the care and treatment of women during pregnancy and childbirth —**ob·stet′ric** or **ob·stet′ri·cal** ***adj.*** —**ob·ste·tri·cian** (äb′stə trish′ən) ***n.***

ob·sti·nate (äb′stə nət) ***adj.*** ⟦< L *obstinare,* to resolve on⟧ **1** determined to have one's own way; stubborn **2** hard to treat or cure *[an obstinate* fever*]* —**ob′sti·na·cy** (-nə sē) ***n.*** —**ob′sti·nate·ly** ***adv.***

ob·strep·er·ous (əb strep′ər əs) ***adj.*** ⟦< L *obstreperus* < *ob-* (see OB-) + *strepere,* to roar⟧ noisy or unruly, esp. in resisting —**ob·strep′er·ous·ly** ***adv.*** —**ob·strep′er·ous·ness** ***n.***

ob·struct (əb strukt′) ***vt.*** ⟦< L *obstructus* < *ob-* (see OB-) + *struere,* to pile up⟧ **1** to block or stop up (a passage) **2** to hinder (progress, etc.) **3** to cut off from view —**ob·struc′tive** ***adj.*** —**ob·struc′tive·ly** ***adv.*** —**ob·struc′tive·ness** ***n.***

ob·struc′tion (-struk′shən) ***n.*** **1** an obstructing **2** anything that obstructs; hindrance

ob·struc′tion·ist ***n.*** one who obstructs progress —***adj.*** that obstructs progress

ob·tain (əb tān′) ***vt.*** ⟦< L *obtinere* < *ob-* (see OB-) + *tenere,* to hold⟧ to get possession of by trying; procure —***vi.*** to prevail or be in effect —**ob·tain′a·ble** ***adj.*** —**ob·tain′ment** ***n.***

ob·trude (əb tro͞od′, äb-) ***vt.*** **-trud′ed, -trud′ing** ⟦< L *obtrudere* < *ob-* (see OB-) + *trudere,* to thrust⟧ to force (oneself, one's opinions, etc.) upon others unasked or unwanted —***vi.*** to obtrude oneself (*on* or *upon*) —**ob·tru′sion** ***n.*** —**ob·tru′sive** ***adj.*** —**ob·tru′sive·ly** ***adv.*** —**ob·tru′sive·ness** ***n.***

ob·tuse (äb to͞os′, əb-) ***adj.*** ⟦< L *obtundere,* to strike upon, blunt⟧ **1** blunt **2** greater than 90° and less than 180° *[an obtuse* angle*]* **3** slow to understand —**ob·tuse′ly** ***adv.*** —**ob·tuse′ness** ***n.***

ob·verse (äb vʉrs′; *also, and for n. always,* äb′vʉrs′) ***adj.*** ⟦< L *obversus* < *ob-* (see OB-) + *vertere,* to turn⟧ **1** turned toward the observer **2** forming a counterpart —***n.*** **1** the side, as of a coin or medal, bearing the main design **2** a counterpart

ob·vi·ate (äb′vē āt′) ***vt.*** **-at′ed, -at′ing** ⟦see fol.⟧ to do away with or prevent by effective measures; make unnecessary —**ob′vi·a′tion** ***n.***

ob·vi·ous (äb′vē əs) ***adj.*** ⟦L *obvius,* in the way⟧ easy to see or understand; evident —**ob′vi·ous·ly** ***adv.*** —**ob′vi·ous·ness** ***n.***

oc- *prefix* OB-: used before *c [occur]*

oc·a·ri·na (äk′ə rē′nə) ***n.*** ⟦It < LL *auca,* goose: from its shape⟧ a small wind instrument with finger holes and a mouthpiece

occas *abbrev.* occasional(ly)

oc·ca·sion (ə kā′zhən, ō-) ***n.*** ⟦< L *occasio* < *ob-* (see OB-) + *cadere,* to fall⟧ **1** a favorable time; opportunity **2** an event, etc. that makes something else possible **3** *a)* a happening *b)* a particular time **4** a special time or event **5** need arising from circumstances —***vt.*** to cause —**on occasion** sometimes

oc·ca′sion·al ***adj.*** **1** of or for special occasions **2** happening now and then; infrequent —**oc·ca′sion·al·ly** ***adv.***

oc·ci·dent (äk′sə dənt, -dent′) ***n.*** ⟦< L *occidere,* to fall: with reference to the setting sun⟧ [Old Poet.] the west —**the Occident** Europe and the Americas —**oc′ci·den′tal** or **Oc′ci·den′tal** ***adj.***, ***n.***

oc·clude (ə klo͞od′) ***vt.*** **-clud′ed, -clud′ing** ⟦< L *occludere* < *ob-* (see OB-) + *claudere,* to shut⟧ **1** to close or block (a passage) **2** to shut in or out —***vi.*** *Dentistry* to meet with the cusps fitting closely —**oc·clu′sion** (-klo͞o′zhən) ***n.*** —**oc·clu·sive** (ə klo͞o′siv) ***adj.***

oc·cult (ə kult′) ***adj.*** ⟦< L *occulere,* to conceal⟧ **1** hidden **2** secret **3** mysterious **4** of mystic arts, such as magic, astrology, etc.

oc·cu·pan·cy (äk′yo͞o pən sē) ***n.***, *pl.* **-cies** an occupying; a taking or keeping in possession

oc′cu·pant (-pənt) ***n.*** one who occupies

oc·cu·pa·tion (äk′yo͞o pā′shən) ***n.*** **1** an occupying or being occupied **2** that which occupies one's time; work; profession —**oc′cu·pa′tion·al** ***adj.***

oc·cu·py (äk′yo͞o pī′) ***vt.*** **-pied′, -py′ing** ⟦< L *occupare* < *ob-* (see OB-) + *capere,* seize⟧ **1** to take possession of by settlement or seizure **2** to hold possession of; specif., *a)* to dwell in *b)* to hold (a position or office) **3** to take up (space, time, etc.) **4** to employ (oneself, one's mind, etc.)

oc·cur (ə kʉr′) ***vi.*** **-curred′, -cur′ring** ⟦< L *occurrere* < *ob-* (see OB-) + *currere,* to run⟧ **1** to be found; exist **2** to come to mind *[an idea occurred* to me*]* **3** to take place; happen

oc·cur′rence (-əns) ***n.*** **1** the act or fact of occurring **2** an event; incident

o·cean (ō′shən) ***n.*** ⟦< Gr *Ōkeanos*⟧ **1** the body of salt water that covers about 71% of the earth's surface **2**

THESAURUS

obstacle ***n.*** restriction, obstruction, hindrance; see BARRIER.

obstinate ***a.*** firm, headstrong, opinionated; see STUBBORN.

obstinately ***a.*** doggedly, bullheadedly, persistently; see STUBBORNLY.

obstruct ***v.*** stop, interfere, bar; see HINDER, PREVENT.

obstruction ***n.*** difficulty, trouble, roadblock; see BARRIER, IMPEDIMENT 1.

obtain ***v.*** **1** [To gain possession of] take, acquire, seize; see GET 1. **2** [To pertain] be pertinent to, appertain to, bear upon; see CONCERN 1.

obtainable ***a.*** ready, attainable, achievable; see AVAILABLE.

obvious ***a.*** **1** [Clearly apparent to the eye] clear, visible, apparent, public, transparent, observable, perceptible, exposed, noticeable, plain, conspicuous, overt, glaring, prominent, standing out, light, bright, open, unmistakable, evident, recognizable, discernible, in evidence, in view, in sight, perceivable, discoverable, distinguishable, palpable, distinct, clear as a bell*, clear as day*, hitting one in the face*; see also DEFINITE 2.—*Ant.* OBSCURE, hidden, indistinct. **2** [Clearly apparent to the mind] lucid, apparent, conclusive, explicit, understood, intelligible, comprehensible, self-evident, indisputable, unquestionable, undeniable, proverbial, aphoristic, reasonable, broad, unambiguous, on the surface, as plain as the nose on someone's face*, going without saying*, staring someone in the face*, open-and-shut; see also UNDERSTANDABLE.—*Ant.* PROFOUND, ambiguous, equivocal.

obviously ***interj.*** of course, yes, evidently; see SURELY.

obviously ***a.*** without doubt, unmistakably, certainly; see CLEARLY 1, 2.

occasion ***n.*** **1** [An event] occurrence, incident, happening; see EVENT. **2** [An opportunity] chance, excuse, opening; see OPPORTUNITY 1, POSSIBILITY 2. —**on occasion** once in a while, sometimes, occasionally; see HARDLY, SELDOM.

occasional ***a.*** **1** [Occurring at odd times] sporadic, random, infrequent; see IRREGULAR 1. **2** [Intended for special use] uncommon, particular, specific; see EXCLUSIVE, SPECIAL.

occasionally ***a.*** infrequently, at random, irregularly; see HARDLY, SELDOM.

occult ***a.*** secret, magical, supernatural; see MYSTERIOUS 2.

occupancy ***n.*** possession, occupation, title; see DEED 2, OWNERSHIP.

occupant ***n.*** lessee, inhabitant, renter; see RESIDENT, TENANT.

occupation ***n.*** **1** [The act of occupying] seizure, entering, invasion; see ATTACK, CAPTURE. **2** [A vocation] calling, craft, chosen work; see JOB 1, PROFESSION 1, TRADE 2.

occupational ***a.*** professional, career, vocational, technical, workaday, official, industrial.

occupied ***a.*** **1** [Busy] engaged, working, engrossed; see BUSY 1. **2** [Full] in use, leased, taken; see RENTED.

occupy ***v.*** **1** [To take possession of] conquer, take over, invade; see GET 1, SEIZE 2. **2** [To fill space] remain, tenant, reside, live in, hold, take up, pervade, keep, own, command, be in command, extend, control, maintain, permeate; see also FILL 2.—*Ant.* EMPTY, remove, move. **3** [To absorb attention] engage, engross, monopolize, interest, arrest, absorb, take up, utilize, involve, keep busy, busy; see also FASCINATE.

occupying ***a.*** **1** [Filling a place] holding, remaining, situated, posted, assigned to, tenanting, residing, living in, taking up, possessing, pervading, covering, settled on, controlling, maintaining, commanding, sitting, staying, established in, established at, owning, set up*; see also PLACED.—*Ant.* GONE, leaving, removing. **2** [Engaging attention] absorbing, engrossing, monopolizing, engaging, arresting, working at, attracting, focusing, drawing, exacting, requiring; see also EXCITING, INTERESTING.

occur ***v.*** take place, transpire, befall; see HAPPEN 1, 2. —**occur to** come to mind, present itself, offer itself, suggest itself, spring, issue, rise, appear, catch one's attention, strike one, pass through one's mind, impress one, enter one's mind, cross one's mind, crop up.

occurrence ***n.*** happening, incident, episode; see EVENT.

ocean ***n.*** great sea, high seas, salt water, seashore, seaside, shores, the

any of its four principal divisions: the Atlantic, Pacific, Indian, or Arctic Ocean **3** a great quantity **—o·ce·an·ic** (ō'shē an'ik) ***adj.***

o'cean·go'ing (-gō'iŋ) ***adj.*** of, or made for, travel on the ocean

O·ce·an·i·a (ō'shē an'ē ə) islands in the Pacific, including Melanesia, Micronesia, & Polynesia **—O'ce·an'i·an** ***adj., n.***

o·cean·og·ra·phy (ō'shə näg'rə fē) ***n.*** the study of the environment in the ocean, its plants and animals, etc. —**o'cean·o'graph'ic** (-nō'graf'ik) ***adj.*** **—o'cean·og'ra·pher** ***n.***

o'cean·ol'o·gy (-näl'ə jē) ***n.*** the study of the sea in all its aspects, including oceanography, undersea exploration, etc.

o·ce·lot (äs'ə lət, -lät') ***n.*** ⟦Fr < AmInd⟧ a spotted wildcat of North and South America

o·cher or **o·chre** (ō'kər) ***n.*** ⟦< Gr *ōchros,* pale-yellow⟧ **1** a yellow or reddish-brown clay containing iron, used as a pigment **2** its color

o'clock (ə kläk', ō-) ***adv.*** of or according to the clock *[nine o'clock* at night*]*

octa- ⟦< Gr *oktō,* eight⟧ *combining form* eight *[octagon]*

oc·ta·gon (äk'tə gän') ***n.*** ⟦< Gr: see prec. & -GON⟧ a plane figure with eight angles and eight sides **—oc·tag'o·nal** (-tag'ə nəl) ***adj.***

octane number (or **rating**) (äk'tān') a number representing the antiknock properties of a gasoline, etc.

oc·tave (äk'tiv, -tāv') ***n.*** ⟦< L *octavus,* eighth⟧ **1** any group of eight **2** *Music a)* the eighth tone of a diatonic scale, or a tone seven degrees above or below a given tone *b)* the interval of seven degrees between a tone and either of its octaves *c)* the series of tones within this interval, or the keys of an instrument producing such a series

oc·ta·vo (äk tā'vō, -tä'-) ***n., pl.*** **-vos** ⟦< L *(in) octavo,* (in) eight⟧ **1** the page size (usually 6 by 9 in.) of a book made up of printer's sheets folded into eight leaves **2** a book of such pages

oc·tet or **oc·tette** (äk tet') ***n.*** ⟦OCT(A)- + (DU)ET⟧ **1** a composition for eight voices or instruments **2** the eight performers of this

Oc·to·ber (äk tō'bər) ***n.*** ⟦< L *octo,* eight: eighth month in Roman calendar⟧ the tenth month of the year, having 31 days: abbrev. **Oct.**

oc·to·ge·nar·i·an (äk'tə ji ner'ē ən) ***n.*** ⟦< L *octoginta,* eighty⟧ a person between the ages of 80 and 90

oc·to·pus (äk'tə pəs) ***n., pl.*** **-pus·es** or **-pi'** (-pī') ⟦< Gr *oktō,* eight + *pous,* foot⟧ a mollusk with a soft body and eight arms covered with suckers

oc·u·lar (äk'yoo lər) ***adj.*** ⟦< L *oculus,* eye⟧ **1** of, for, or like the eye **2** by eyesight

oc'u·list (-list) ***n.*** *former term for* OPHTHALMOLOGIST

OD[1] (ō'dē') [Slang] ***n., pl.*** **ODs** or **OD's** an overdose, esp. of a narcotic —***vi.*** **OD'd** or **ODed, OD'ing** or **ODing** to take an overdose, esp. a fatal overdose of a narcotic

OD[2] or **O.D.** *abbrev.* ⟦L⟧ Doctor of Optometry

o·da·lisque or **o·da·lisk** (ō'də lisk') ***n.*** ⟦Fr < Turk *ōdalik,* chambermaid⟧ a female slave or concubine in a harem

odd (äd) ***adj.*** ⟦< ON *oddi*⟧ **1** remaining or separated from a pair, set, etc. **2** having a remainder of one when divided by two **3** with a few more: usually in hyphenated compounds *[*sixty-*odd* years ago*]* **4** occasional *[odd* jobs*]* **5** peculiar or eccentric **—odd'ly** ***adv.*** **—odd'ness** ***n.***

odd'ball' ***adj., n.*** [Slang] strange or eccentric (person)

odd'i·ty (-ə tē) ***n.*** **1** strangeness **2** *pl.* **-ties** an odd person or thing

odds (ädz) ***pl.n.*** **1** difference in favor of one side over the other; advantage **2** an equalizing advantage in betting, based on a bettor's assumed chance of winning and expressed as a ratio *[odds* of 3 to 1*]* **—at odds** quarreling

odds and ends scraps; remnants

odds'mak'er ***n.*** an expert who estimates the odds in betting, etc.

odds'-on' ***adj.*** having a good chance of winning *[*an *odds-on* favorite*]*

ode (ōd) ***n.*** ⟦< Gr *ōidē,* song⟧ a lyric poem characterized by lofty feeling, elaborate form, and dignified style

-ode (ōd) ⟦< Gr *hodos*⟧ *suffix* way, path *[electrode]*

O·des·sa (ō des'ə) seaport in S Ukraine, on the Black Sea: pop. 1,101,000

O·din (ō'din) ***n.*** *Norse Myth.* the chief deity, god of art, war, and the dead

o·di·ous (ō'dē əs) ***adj.*** ⟦< L *odium,* hatred⟧ disgusting; offensive **—o'di·ous·ly** ***adv.*** **—o'di·ous·ness** ***n.***

o·di·um (ō'dē əm) ***n.*** ⟦< L *odi,* I hate⟧ **1** hatred **2** the disgrace brought on by hateful action

o·dom·e·ter (ō däm'ət ər) ***n.*** ⟦< Gr *hodometros* < *hodos,* way + *metron,* a measure⟧ an instrument for measuring the distance traveled by a vehicle

o·dor (ō'dər) ***n.*** ⟦L⟧ a smell; scent; aroma Brit. sp. **o'dour —o'dor·less** ***adj.*** **—o'dor·ous** ***adj.***

o·dor·if·er·ous (ō'dər if'ər əs) ***adj.*** ⟦< L *odor,* odor + *ferre,* to bear⟧ giving off an odor, now often, specif., a strong or offensive one

O·dys·se·us (ō dis'ē əs, ō dis'yoos') ***n.*** ⟦Gr⟧ the hero of the *Odyssey,* one of the Greek leaders in the Trojan War

Od·ys·sey (äd'i sē) ***n.*** **1** an ancient Greek epic poem, ascribed to Homer, about the wanderings of Odysseus after the fall of Troy **2** *pl.* **-seys** [**o-**] any extended journey

OE *abbrev.* Old English

Oed·i·pal (ed'i pəl, ē'di-) ***adj.*** [*also* **o-**] of or relating to the Oedipus complex

Oed·i·pus (ed'i pəs, ē'di-) ***n.*** *Gr. Myth.* a king who unwittingly kills his father and marries his mother

Oedipus complex *Psychoanalysis* the unconscious tendency of a child to be attached to the parent of the opposite sex

oe·nol·o·gy (ē näl'ə jē) ***n.*** ⟦< Gr *oinos,* wine + -LOGY⟧ the science or study of wines and winemaking **—oe·nol'o·gist** ***n.***

oe·no·phile (ē'nə fīl') ***n.*** a connoisseur of wine

o'er (ō'ər, ôr) ***prep., adv.*** [Old Poet.] OVER

oeu·vre (ë'vr') ***n., pl.*** **-vres** (-vr') ⟦Fr⟧ all the works of a writer, artist, or composer

of (uv) ***prep.*** ⟦OE⟧ **1** from; specif., *a)* coming from *[*men *of* Ohio*]* *b)* resulting from *[*to die *of* fever*]* *c)* at a distance from *[*east *of* the city*]* *d)* by *[*the poems *of* Poe*]* *e)* separated from *[*robbed *of* his money*]* *f)* from the whole constituting *[*one *of* her hats*]* *g)* made from *[*a sheet *of* paper*]* **2** belonging to *[*the pages *of* a book*]* **3** *a)* possessing *[*a man *of* wealth*]* *b)* containing *[*a bag *of* nuts*]* **4** specified as *[*a height *of* six feet*]* **5** characterized by *[*a man *of* honor*]* **6** concerning; about *[*think *of* me*]* **7** during *[of* recent years*]*

of- *prefix* OB-: used before *f [offer]*

off (ôf) ***adv.*** ⟦ME var. of *of*⟧ **1** so as to be away, at a distance, etc. **2** so as to be no longer on, attached, etc.

THESAURUS

mighty deep, the main, the great waters, the seven seas; see also SEA.—*Ant.* EARTH, lake, river. *Oceans include the following:* Atlantic, Pacific, Arctic, Antarctic, Indian.

oceanic ***a.*** marine, aquatic, pelagic; see MARITIME, NAUTICAL.

odd ***a.*** **1** [Unusual] peculiar, unique, strange; see UNUSUAL 2. **2** [Miscellaneous] fragmentary, different, varied; see VARIOUS. **3** [Single] unpaired, sole, unmatched; see ALONE. **4** [Not even] remaining, over and above, leftover; see IRREGULAR 1, 4.

oddly ***a.*** curiously, ridiculously, inexplicably; see STRANGELY, FOOLISHLY.

odds ***n.*** **1** [An advantage] allowance, edge, benefit, difference, superiority, place money*, show money*; see also ADVANTAGE. **2** [A probability] favor, superiority, chances; see CHANCE 1. **—at odds** disagreeing, at variance, discordant; see QUARRELSOME.

odds and ends ***n.*** miscellany, scraps, particles; see REMNANTS.

odor ***n.*** perfume, fragrance, aroma; see SMELL 1, 2.

odorless ***a.*** flat, scentless, unaromatic, unperfumed, unscented, without odor, odor-free, unfragrant, lacking fragrance.

odorous ***a.*** **1** [Having an offensive odor] smelly, stinking, putrid; see OFFENSIVE 2, ROTTEN 1. **2** [Having a pleasant odor] spicy, sweet-smelling, fragrant; see SWEET 3.

of ***prep.*** from, out of, out from, away from, proceeding from, coming from, going from, about, concerning, as concerns, appropriate to, pertaining to, peculiar to, attributed to, characterized by, regarding, as regards, in regard to, referring to, in reference to, belonging to, related to, having relation to, native to, consequent to, based on, akin to, connected with; see also ABOUT 2.

off ***a., prep.*** **1** [Situated at a distance] ahead, behind, up front, to one side, divergent, beside, aside, below, beneath, above, far, absent, not here, removed, apart, in the distance, at a distance, gone, away; see also DISTANT.—*Ant.* HERE, at hand, present. **2** [Moving away] into the distance, away from, farther away, disappearing, vanishing, removing, turning aside; see also AWAY.—*Ant.* APPROACHING, returning, coming. **3** [Started] initiated, commenced, origi-

[take off your hat] **3** (a specified distance) away in space or time *[20 yards off]* **4** so as to be no longer in operation, etc. *[turn the motor off]* **5** so as to be less, etc. *[5% off for cash]* **6** away from one's work *[take a week off]* —***prep.*** **1** (so as to be) no longer (or not) on, attached, etc. *[off the road]* **2** from the substance of *[live off the land]* **3** away from *[a mile off shore]* **4** branching out from *[an alley off Main Street]* **5** relieved from *[off duty]* **6** not up to the usual standard, etc. of *[off one's game]* —***adj.*** **1** not on or attached **2** not in operation **3** on the way *[off to bed]* **4** away from work *[we are off today]* **5** not up to the usual standard, etc. **6** more remote *[on the off chance]* **7** in (specified) circumstances *[to be well off]* **8** wrong *[his figures are off]* —***vt.*** [Slang] to kill; murder —***interj.*** go away! —**off and on** now and then

-off (ôf, äf) *combining form* a contest of skill in a (specified) activity or field *[a chili cook-off]*

of·fal (ôf'əl) ***n.*** ⟦ME *ofall,* lit., off-fall⟧ **1** [*with sing. or pl. v.*] the entrails, etc. of a butchered animal **2** refuse; garbage

off'beat' ***n.*** *Music* a beat having a weak accent —***adj.*** [Inf.] unconventional, unusual, strange, etc.

off'-col'or ***adj.*** **1** varying from the standard color **2** improper; risqué

of·fend (ə fend') ***vi.*** ⟦< L *offendere,* to strike against < *ob-* (see OB-) + *fendere,* to hit⟧ **1** to commit a sin or crime **2** to create resentment, anger, etc. —***vt.*** **1** to hurt the feelings of; insult **2** to be displeasing to (the taste, sense, etc.) —**of·fend'er** ***n.***

of·fense (ə fens', ô'fens') ***n.*** **1** a sin or crime **2** a creating of resentment, displeasure, etc. **3** a feeling hurt, angry, etc. **4** something that causes anger, etc. **5** the act of attacking **6** the side that is attacking or seeking to score in any contest Brit. sp. **of·fence'** —**take offense** to become offended

of·fen'sive ***adj.*** **1** attacking or for attack **2** unpleasant; disgusting **3** insulting —***n.*** **1** attitude or position of attack: often with *the* **2** an attack —**of·fen'sive·ly** ***adv.*** —**of·fen'sive·ness** ***n.***

of·fer (ôf'ər, äf'-) ***vt.*** ⟦< L *offerre* < *ob-* (see OB-) + *ferre,* to bear⟧ **1** to present in worship *[to offer prayers]* **2** to present for acceptance *[to offer help]* **3** to suggest; propose **4** to show or give signs of *[to offer resistance]* **5** to bid (a price, etc.) —***n.*** the act of offering or thing offered

of'fer·ing ***n.*** **1** the act of making an offer **2** something offered; specif., *a)* a gift *b)* presentation in worship

of'fer·to'ry (-tôr'ē) ***n.***, *pl.* **-ries** [*often* **O-**] **1** *a)* the part of a Eucharistic service in which the bread and wine are offered to God *b)* the prayers said, or music used, then **2** *a)* the part of a church service during which money offerings are collected *b)* the collection itself

off'hand' ***adv.*** without preparation; extemporaneously —***adj.*** **1** said or done offhand **2** casual, curt, etc. Also **off'hand'ed**

off'-hour' ***adj.*** not for or during rush hour or other busy periods

of·fice (ôf'is, äf'-) ***n.*** ⟦< L *officium*⟧ **1** a service done for another **2** a duty, esp. as a part of one's work **3** a position of authority or trust, as in government **4** *a)* the place where the affairs of a business, etc. are carried on *b)* the people working there **5** [*often* **O-**] a religious service or set of prayers

of'fice·hold'er ***n.*** a government official

of·fi·cer (ôf'i sər, äf'-) ***n.*** **1** anyone holding an office, or position of authority, in a government, business, club, etc. **2** a police officer **3** one holding a position of authority, esp. by commission, in the armed forces

of·fi·cial (ə fish'əl) ***adj.*** **1** of or holding an office, or position of authority **2** authorized or authoritative **3** formal —***n.*** a person holding office —**of·fi'cial·dom** (-dəm) ***n.*** —**of·fi'cial·ly** ***adv.***

of·fi·ci·ate (ə fish'ē āt') ***vi.*** **-at'ed, -at'ing** **1** to perform the duties of an office **2** to perform the functions of a priest, minister, rabbi, etc. at a religious ceremony

of·fi·cious (ə fish'əs) ***adj.*** ⟦see OFFICE⟧ offering unwanted

THESAURUS

nated; see BEGUN. **4** [Mistaken] erring, in error, confused; see MISTAKEN 1, WRONG 2. **5** [*Crazy] odd, peculiar, strange; see INSANE. **6** [*Not employed] not on duty, on vacation, gone; see UNEMPLOYED.

off and on ***a.*** now and then, sometimes, occasionally; see SELDOM.

off-color ***a.*** racy, spicy, indelicate; see RISQUÉ.

offend ***v.*** annoy, affront, outrage; see BOTHER 2.

offended ***a.*** vexed, provoked, exasperated; see ANGRY, INSULTED.

offense ***n.*** **1** [A misdeed] misdemeanor, malfeasance, transgression; see CRIME, SIN. **2** [An attack] assault, aggression, battery; see ATTACK. *Styles of offense in football include the following:* running attack, ground attack, passing attack, aerial attack, shotgun, T formation, wishbone, razzle-dazzle, T, I formation, I, wing T, run and shoot, pro, red zone, goal line, tight end, H-back, West Coast. **3** [Resentment] umbrage, pique, indignation; see ANGER.

offensive ***a.*** **1** [Concerned with an attack] assaulting, attacking, invading; see AGGRESSIVE. **2** [Revolting] disgusting, horrid, repulsive, shocking, gross*, dreadful, detestable, repugnant, obnoxious, hideous, horrible, displeasing, disagreeable, repellent, nauseating, invidious, nauseous*, distasteful, unspeakable, accursed, unutterable, terrible, grisly, ghastly, bloody, gory, hateful, low, foul, corrupt, bad, indecent, nasty, dirty, unclean, filthy, sickening, malignant, rancid, putrid, vile, impure, beastly, monstrous, coarse, loathsome, abominable, stinking, reeking, obscene, smutty, damnable, distressing, irritating, unpleasant, contaminated, frightful, unattractive, forbidding, repelling, incompatible, unsavory, intolerable, unpalatable, dissatisfactory, unpleasing, unsuited, objectionable, beneath contempt, icky*, lousy*; see also REVOLTING.—*Ant.* PLEASANT, agreeable, likable. **3** [Insolent] impertinent, impudent, insulting; see RUDE 2.

offensive ***n.*** position of attack, invasion, assault; see ATTACK.

offer ***n.*** proposal, presentation, proposition; see SUGGESTION 1.

offer ***v.*** **1** [To present] proffer, tender, administer, donate, put forth, advance, extend, submit, hold out, grant, allow, award, volunteer, accord, place at someone's disposal, lay at someone's feet, put up; see also CONTRIBUTE, GIVE 1.—*Ant.* REFUSE, withhold, keep. **2** [To propose] suggest, submit, advise; see PROPOSE 1.

offering ***n.*** contribution, donation, present; see GIFT 1.

offhand ***a.*** at the moment, unprepared, impromptu, improvised, by ear, informal, extemporaneous, extemporary, spontaneous, unpremeditated, unstudied, unrehearsed.

office ***n.*** **1** [A position involving responsibility] position, post, occupation; see JOB 1, PROFESSION 1, TRADE 2. **2** [A function] performance, province, service; see DUTY 1. **3** [A place in which office work is done] room, office building, factory, bureau, agency, warehouse, facility, school building; see also BUILDING, DEPARTMENT. *Types of offices include the following:* government, principal's, counseling, secretarial, insurance, data processing, real estate, brokerage, law, bank, foreign, consular, doctor's, dentist's; advertising agency, booking office, box office. —**hold office** be in office, direct, rule; see GOVERN, MANAGE 1.

officer ***n.*** **1** [An executive] manager, director, president; see EXECUTIVE, LEADER 2. **2** [One who enforces the law] magistrate, military police, deputy; see POLICE OFFICER. **3** [One holding a responsible post in the armed forces] *American officers include the following — Army commissioned and special officers:* Commander in Chief, Five-star General, Four-star General, Three-star General, Two-star General, General of the Army, Lieutenant General, Major General, Brigadier General, Colonel, Lieutenant Colonel, Major, Captain, First Lieutenant, Second Lieutenant, Chief of Staff; *Navy commissioned officers:* Admiral of the Fleet, Fleet Admiral, Admiral, Rear Admiral, Vice Admiral, Captain, Commander, Lieutenant Commander, Lieutenant; Lieutenant, junior grade; Ensign; *Army noncommissioned officers:* Chief Warrant Officer; Warrant Officer, junior grade; Master Sergeant, First Sergeant, Technical Sergeant, Staff Sergeant, Sergeant, Corporal.

official ***a.*** **1** [Having to do with one's office] formal, fitting, suitable, precise, established, according to precedent, according to protocol, proper, correct, accepted, recognized, customary; see also CONVENTIONAL 1, 3, FIT 1.—*Ant.* INFORMAL, ill-fitting, unceremonious. **2** [Authorized] ordered, endorsed, sanctioned; see APPROVED. **3** [Reliable] authoritative, authentic, trustworthy; see CERTAIN 3, GENUINE 1, RELIABLE.

official ***n.*** **1** [Administrator] controller, director, manager; see EXECUTIVE, LEADER 2. **2** [A sports official] referee, judge, linesman; see UMPIRE.

officially ***a.*** **1** [In an official manner] regularly, formally, in an orderly manner, suitably, according to form, ceremoniously, in set form, precisely, according to precedent, conventionally, in an established manner, as prescribed, according to protocol, all in order, correctly, properly, customarily. **2** [With official approval] authoritatively, with authorization, sanctioned; see APPROVED.

advice or services; meddlesome, esp. overbearingly so —**of·fi′cious·ly** ***adv.*** —**of·fi′cious·ness** ***n.***

off·ing (ôf′iŋ) ***n.*** ⟦< OFF⟧ used chiefly in **in the offing**, at some indefinite future time

off′-key′ ***adj.*** **1** *Music* flat or sharp **2** not harmonious

off′-lim′its ***adj.*** ruled to be a place that cannot be entered, etc. by a specified group

off′-line′ ***adj.*** designating or of equipment not directly connected to and controlled by the central processing unit of a computer

off′load′ ***vt.***, ***vi.*** UNLOAD (1*a*, 2*b*, 4)

off′-put′ting ***adj.*** [Chiefly Brit.] distracting, annoying, etc.

off′-road′ ***adj.*** designating or of a vehicle for use off regular highways, streets, etc.

off′-sea′son ***n.*** a time of the year when the usual activity is reduced or not carried on

off·set (ôf set′; *for n.* ôf′set′) ***vt.*** **-set′**, **-set′ting** to balance, compensate for, etc. —***n.*** **1** a thing that offsets another **2** OFFSET PRINTING

offset printing a printing process in which the inked impression is first made on a rubber-covered roller, then transferred to paper

off′shoot′ ***n.*** anything that derives from a main source; specif., a shoot growing from the main stem of a plant

off′shore′ ***adj.*** **1** moving away from the shore **2** at some distance from the shore **3** engaged in outside the U.S. as by U.S. banks or manufacturers *[offshore* investments*]* —***adv.*** **1** away from the shore **2** outside the U.S. *[*to borrow *offshore]*

off′side′ ***adj.*** *Sports* not in the proper position for play: also **off′sides′**

off′spring′ ***n.***, *pl.* **-spring′** or **-springs′** a child or children; progeny; young

off′stage′ ***n.*** the part of the stage not seen by the audience —***adj.*** in or from this —***adv.*** to the offstage

off′-the-wall′ ***adj.*** [Slang] very unusual, unconventional, eccentric, etc.

off′-track′ ***adj.*** designating or of legalized betting on horse races, carried on away from the racetrack

off′-white′ ***adj.*** grayish-white or yellowish-white

off year **1** a year in which a major election does not take place **2** a year of little production

oft (ôft) ***adv.*** ⟦OE⟧ *literary var. of* OFTEN

of·ten (ôf′ən, -tən) ***adv.*** ⟦ME var. of prec.⟧ many times; frequently: also **of′ten·times′**

o·gle (ō′gəl) ***vi.***, ***vt.*** **o′gled**, **o′gling** ⟦prob. < LowG *oog*, an eye⟧ to keep looking (at) flirtatiously —***n.*** an ogling look —**o′gler** ***n.***

o·gre (ō′gər) ***n.*** ⟦Fr⟧ **1** in fairy tales and folklore, a man-eating giant **2** a hideous, cruel man

oh (ō) ***interj.***, ***n.***, *pl.* **oh's** or **ohs** an exclamation of surprise, fear, pain, etc.

O·hi·o (ō hī′ō) **1** river flowing from W Pennsylvania into the Mississippi **2** Midwestern state of the U.S.: 40,952 sq. mi.; pop. 10,847,000; cap. Columbus: abbrev. **OH** —**O·hi′o·an** ***adj.***, ***n.***

ohm (ōm) ***n.*** ⟦after G. S. *Ohm* (1789-1854), Ger physicist⟧ unit of electrical resistance

ohm′me′ter ***n.*** an instrument for measuring electrical resistance in ohms

o·ho (ō hō′) ***interj.*** used to express surprise or triumph

-o·hol·ic (ə häl′ik) *combining form* -AHOLIC

-oid (oid) ⟦< Gr *eidos*, a form⟧ *suffix* like or resembling *[crystalloid]*

oil (oil) ***n.*** ⟦< L *oleum*⟧ **1** any of various greasy, combustible, liquid substances obtained from animal, vegetable, and mineral matter **2** PETROLEUM **3** *a)* OIL COLOR *b)* OIL PAINTING —***vt.*** to lubricate or supply with oil —***adj.*** of, from, or like oil

oil′cloth′ ***n.*** cloth made waterproof by being treated with oil or paint

oil color paint made by grinding a pigment in oil: also **oil paint**

oil′man (-mən) ***n.***, *pl.* **-men** (-mən) an entrepreneur or executive in the petroleum industry

oil painting **1** a picture painted in oil colors **2** the art of painting in oil colors

oil shale shale from which oil can be extracted by distillation

oil′skin′ ***n.*** **1** cloth made waterproof by treatment with oil **2** [*often pl.*] a garment or outfit made of this

oil well a well that supplies petroleum

oil·y (oi′lē) ***adj.*** **-i·er**, **-i·est** **1** of, like, or containing oil **2** greasy **3** too suave or smooth; unctuous —**oil′i·ness** ***n.***

oink (oiŋk) ***n.*** ⟦echoic⟧ the grunt of a pig —***vi.*** to make this sound

oint·ment (oint′mənt) ***n.*** ⟦< L *unguentum*, a salve⟧ a fatty substance used on the skin for healing or cosmetic purposes; salve

OK or **O.K.** (ō kā′) [Inf.] ***adj.***, ***adv.***, ***interj.*** ⟦< "oll korrect," facetious misspelling of *all correct*⟧ all right; correct —***n.***, *pl.* **OK's** or **O.K.'s** approval —***vt.*** **OK'd** or **O.K.'d**, **OK'ing** or **O.K.'ing** to approve or endorse Also **o'kay′**

O·kla·ho·ma (ō′klə hō′mə) state of the SC U.S.: 68,679 sq. mi.; pop. 3,146,000; cap. Oklahoma City: abbrev. **OK** —**O′kla·ho′man** ***adj.***, ***n.***

Oklahoma City capital of Oklahoma: pop. 445,000

o·kra (ō′krə) ***n.*** ⟦< WAfr name⟧ **1** a plant with sticky green pods **2** the pods, used in soups, stews, etc.

Ok·to·ber·fest (äk tō′bər fest′) ***n.*** ⟦Ger⟧ a beer-drinking festival held in Germany and elsewhere in the fall

old (ōld) ***adj.*** **old′er** or **eld′er**, **old′est** or **eld′est** ⟦OE *ald*⟧ **1** having lived or existed for a long time **2** of aged people **3** of a specified age *[*two years *old]* **4** not new **5** worn out by age or use **6** former **7** experienced *[*an *old* hand*]* **8** ancient **9** [*often* **O-**] designating the earliest form of a language *[Old* English*]* **10** designating the earlier or earliest of two or more *[*the *Old* World*]* —***n.*** **1** time long

THESAURUS

offset ***v.*** counterbalance, compensate, allow for; see BALANCE 2.

offspring ***n.*** progeny, issue, descendants, children, kids, siblings, lineage, generation, brood, seed, family, heirs, offshoots, succession, successors, next generation; see also BABY, CHILD.

often ***a.*** usually, many times, oftentimes; see FREQUENTLY.

oh ***interj.*** indeed, oh-oh, oops; oh, no; oh, yes; see also NO, YES.

oil ***n.*** **1** [Liquid, greasy substance] melted fat, unction, lubricant; see GREASE. *Common oils include the following:* vegetable, animal, mineral, saturated, polyunsaturated, volatile, essential, machine, crude, lubricating, cottonseed, olive, castor, palm, corn, safflower, coconut, whale, canola, peanut, tung, wintergreen, linseed, drying, nondrying, soybean, sesame, cod-liver, fish; lard, tallow, oleo, lanolin, turpentine. **2** [Liquid substance used for power or illumination] petroleum, kerosene, coal oil, crude oil, liquid coal, fossil oil; see also FUEL.

oil ***v.*** lubricate, smear, coat with oil; see GREASE.

oily ***a.*** **1** [Rich with oil] fatty, greasy, buttery, oil-soaked, rich, lardy, oleaginous, soapy, soothing, creamy, oil-bearing.—*Ant.* DRY, dried, gritty. **2** [Having a surface suggestive of oil] oiled, waxy, sleek, slippery, polished, lustrous, bright, brilliant, gleaming, glistening, shining; see also SMOOTH 1, 2.—*Ant.* ROUGH, dull, unpolished. **3** [Unctuous] fulsome, suave, flattering; see AFFECTED 2, TREACHEROUS.

ointment ***n.*** unguent, lotion, cream; see MEDICINE 2.

OK* ***interj.*** all right, correct, surely; see YES.

OK* ***n.*** approval, endorsement, affirmation; see PERMISSION.

OK* ***v.*** confirm, condone, notarize; see APPROVE, ENDORSE 2.

old ***a.*** **1** [No longer vigorous] aged, elderly, patriarchal, matriarchal, mature, gray, venerable, not young, of long life, past one's prime, far advanced in years, matured, having lived long, full of years, seasoned, infirm, inactive, enfeebled, decrepit, superannuated, exhausted, tired, impaired, broken-down, wasted, doddering, senile, ancient, having one foot in the grave, gone to seed.—*Ant.* YOUNG, fresh, youthful. **2** [Worn] time-worn, worn-out, thin, patched, ragged, faded, used, in holes, rubbed off, mended, broken-down, fallen to pieces, fallen in, given way, out of use, rusted, crumbled, dilapidated, battered, shattered, shabby, castoff, decayed, decaying, stale, useless, tattered, in rags, torn, moth-eaten.—*Ant.* FRESH, new, unused. **3** [Ancient] archaic, time-honored, prehistoric, bygone, early, antique, forgotten, immemorial, antediluvian, olden, remote, past, distant, former, of old, gone by, classic, medieval, in the Middle Ages, out of the dim past, primordial, primeval, before history, dateless, unrecorded, handed down, of earliest time, of the old order, ancestral, traditional, time out of mind, in the dawn of history, old as the hills; see also senses 1, 2.—*Ant.* MODERN, recent, late.

older ***a.*** elder, senior, former, preceding, prior, more aged, less young, not so new, earlier, first, firstborn, having come before, more ancient, lower, of an earlier time, of an earlier vintage, of a former period; see also OLD 3.—*Ant.* YOUNG, newer, of a later vintage.

oldest ***a.*** most aged, initial, primeval; see FIRST, ORIGINAL 1.

past *[days of old]* **2** something old: with *the* —**old'ness** ***n.***

Old Church Sla·von·ic (slə vän'ik) the South Slavic language now used only as a liturgical language by Orthodox Slavs: also called **Old Church Slavic** or **Old Bulgarian**

old country the country, esp. in Europe, from which an immigrant came

old·en (ōl'dən) ***adj.*** [Old Poet.] (of) old

Old English the Germanic language of the Anglo-Saxons, spoken in England from *c.* A.D. 400 to *c.* 1100

old'-fash'ioned ***adj.*** suited to or favoring the styles, ideas, etc. of past times —***n.*** [*also* **Old-Fashioned**] a cocktail made with whiskey, bitters, and bits of fruit

old fogy or **old fogey** *see* FOGY

Old French the French language from *c.* A.D. 800 to *c.* 1550

Old Glory *name for* the flag of the United States

old'-growth' ***adj.*** designating or of a forest having very large, very old trees

old guard ⟦transl. < Fr⟧ [*sometimes* **O- G-**] the conservative element of a group, party, etc.

old hat [Slang] old-fashioned or stale

Old High German the High German language before the 12th c.

old·ie or **old·y** (ōl'dē) ***n.***, *pl.* **-ies** [Inf.] an old joke, saying, song, movie, etc.

old lady [Slang] **1** one's mother **2** one's wife

old'-line' ***adj.*** long-established, traditional, conservative, etc.

Old Low German the Low German language before the 12th c.

old maid **1** a woman, esp. an older woman, who has never married: mildly disparaging **2** a prim, prudish, fussy person

old man [Slang] **1** one's father **2** one's husband **3** [*usually* **O- M-**] any man in authority: with *the*

old master **1** any of the great European painters before the 18th c. **2** a painting by any of these

Old Norse the Germanic language of the Scandinavians before the 14th c.

Old Saxon the Low German dialect of the Saxons before the 10th c.

old school a group of people who cling to traditional or conservative ideas, methods, etc.

old'ster (-stər) ***n.*** [Inf.] an old or elderly person

Old Testament *Christian designation for* the Holy Scriptures of Judaism, the first of the two general divisions of the Christian Bible

old'-time' ***adj.*** **1** of past times **2** of long standing

old'-tim'er ***n.*** [Inf.] a long-time resident, employee, member, etc.

old'-tim'ey (-tīm'ē) ***adj.*** [Inf.] reminiscent of the past, usually in a positive way

old'-world' ***adj.*** of or from the Eastern Hemisphere, esp. Europe

o·lé (ô lā') ***interj.***, ***n.*** ⟦Sp⟧ used to express approval, triumph, joy, etc.

o·le·ag·i·nous (ō'lē aj'i nəs) ***adj.*** ⟦< L *olea,* olive tree⟧ oily; unctuous

o·le·an·der (ō'lē an'dər) ***n.*** ⟦ML⟧ a poisonous evergreen shrub with fragrant white, pink, or red flowers and narrow, leathery leaves

o·le·o·mar·ga·rine or **o·le·o·mar·ga·rin** (ō'lē ō mär'jə rin) ***n.*** ⟦< L *oleum,* oil + MARGARINE⟧ *former term for* MARGARINE: also **o'le·o'**

ol·fac·to·ry (äl fak'tə rē, ōl-) ***adj.*** ⟦< L *olere,* have a smell + *facere,* make⟧ of the sense of smell

ol·i·gar·chy (äl'i gär'kē) ***n.***, *pl.* **-chies** ⟦< Gr *oligos,* few + -ARCHY⟧ **1** government in which ruling power belongs to a few persons **2** a state governed in this way **3** the persons ruling such a state —**ol'i·gar'chic** ***adj.***

ol·ive (äl'iv) ***n.*** ⟦< L *oliva*⟧ **1** *a)* an evergreen tree of S Europe and the Near East *b)* its small, oval fruit, eaten green or ripe as a relish or pressed, when ripe, to extract its oil (**olive oil**) **2** the yellowish-green color of the unripe fruit

olive branch the branch of the olive tree, a symbol of peace

O·lym·pi·a (ō lim'pē ə) capital of Washington: pop. 34,000

O·lymp·ic games (ō lim'pik) ⟦< *Olympia,* plain in Greece, site of ancient games⟧ an international athletic competition now held every two years, alternating between summer games and winter games: also **O·lym'pics**

O·lym·pus (ō lim'pəs), **Mount** mountain in N Greece: in Greek mythology, the home of the gods —**O·lym'pi·an** (-pē ən) ***adj.***, ***n.***

om (ōm) ***n.*** ⟦Sans⟧ *Hinduism* a word intoned as during meditation

O·ma·ha (ō'mə hô) city in E Nebraska: pop. 336,000

O·man (ō män') country on the SE coast of Arabia: 119,499 sq. mi.; pop. 2,070,000 —**O·man'i** (-ē) ***adj.***, ***n.***

om·buds·man (äm'bədz mən) ***n.***, *pl.* **-men** (-mən) ⟦Swed < *ombud,* a deputy⟧ a public official appointed to investigate citizens' complaints

o·me·ga (ō mā'gə) ***n.*** ⟦Gr ō + *mega,* great, i.e., long *o*: see OMICRON⟧ the 24th & final letter of the Greek alphabet (Ω, ω)

om·e·let or **om·e·lette** (äm'lət) ***n.*** ⟦< L *lamella,* small plate⟧ eggs beaten and cooked flat in a pan

o·men (ō'mən) ***n.*** ⟦L⟧ a thing or happening supposed to foretell a future event, either good or evil

om·i·cron (äm'i krän', ō'mi-) ***n.*** ⟦Gr *o mikron,* small *o*: see OMEGA⟧ the 15th letter of the Greek alphabet (O, o)

om·i·nous (äm'ə nəs) ***adj.*** of or serving as an evil omen; threatening —**om'i·nous·ly** ***adv.***

o·mis·sion (ō mish'ən) ***n.*** **1** an omitting **2** something omitted

o·mit (ō mit') ***vt.*** **o·mit'ted**, **o·mit'ting** ⟦< L *omittere* < *ob-* (see OB-) + *mittere,* send⟧ **1** to fail to include; leave out **2** to fail to do; neglect

omni- ⟦L < *omnis,* all⟧ *combining form* all, everywhere

om·ni·bus (äm'ni bəs) ***n.***, *pl.* **-bus·es** ⟦< L, for all⟧ **1** BUS **2** a collection of stories, articles, etc., as on one theme —***adj.*** including many things

om·nip·o·tent (äm nip'ə tənt) ***adj.*** ⟦< L *omnis,* all + *potens,* able⟧ having unlimited power or authority; all-powerful —**the Omnipotent** God —**om·nip'o·tence** ***n.***

om·ni·pres·ent (äm'ni prez'ənt) ***adj.*** present in all places at the same time —**om'ni·pres'ence** ***n.***

om·nis·cient (äm nish'ənt) ***adj.*** ⟦< L *omnis,* all + *sciens,* knowing⟧ knowing all things —**the Omniscient** God —**om·nis'cience** ***n.***

om·niv·o·rous (äm niv'ə rəs) ***adj.*** ⟦< L *omnis,* all + *vorare,* devour⟧ **1** eating any sort of food, esp. both animal and vegetable food **2** taking in everything indiscriminately —**om·niv'o·rous·ly** ***adv.*** —**om·niv'o·rous·ness** ***n.***

on (än, ôn) ***prep.*** ⟦OE⟧ **1** in contact with, supported by, or covering **2** in the surface of *[scars on it]* **3** *a)* near to *[on my left]* *b)* having as its location *[a house on Main Street]* **4** at the time of *[on Monday]* **5** connected with

THESAURUS

old-fashioned ***a.*** antiquated, out-of-date, obsolete, obsolescent, outmoded, *démodé* (French), unfashionable, traditional, unstylish, passé, Victorian, not modern, old-time, time-honored, not current, antique, ancient, no longer prevailing, bygone, archaic, grown old, primitive, quaint, amusing, odd, neglected, outworn, of long standing, unused, past, behind the times, gone by, of the old school, extinct, out, gone out, out of it*; see also OLD 3.—*Ant.* MODERN, fashionable, stylish.

old lady* ***n.*** female spouse, woman, female relative; see MOTHER 1, PARENT, WIFE.

old man* ***n.*** head of the house, male spouse, man; see FATHER 1, HUSBAND, PARENT.

Old Testament ***n.*** Torah, Hebrew Scripture, Jewish Law; see BIBLE.

old-time ***a.*** outmoded, ancient, obsolete; see OLD-FASHIONED.

Old World ***n.*** Europe, Asia, Eastern Hemisphere; see EAST 2.

Olympics ***n.*** Olympic Games, world championships, international amateur athletic competion; see COMPETITION, SPORT 3.

omen ***n.*** portent, augury, indication; see SIGN 1.

ominous ***a.*** threatening, forbidding, foreboding, menacing, dark, suggestive, fateful, premonitory, dire, grim, gloomy, haunting, perilous, ill-starred, ill-fated, impending, fearful, prophetic; see also DANGEROUS, DISMAL, DOOMED.—*Ant.* FAVORABLE, encouraging, auspicious.

omission ***n.*** **1** [The act of omitting] overlooking, missing, leaving out; see CARELESSNESS, EXCLUSION, NEGLECT 1.—*Ant.* ADDITION, mention, insertion. **2** [Something omitted] need, want, imperfection; see LACK 2.

omit ***v.*** **1** [To fail to include] leave out, reject, exclude; see BAR 2, DISMISS, ELIMINATE. **2** [To neglect] ignore, slight, overlook; see DISREGARD, NEGLECT 2.

omitted ***a.*** unmentioned, left out, overlooked; see MISSED 1, NEGLECTED.

on ***a.***, ***prep.*** **1** [Upon] above, in contact with, touching, supported by, situated upon, resting upon, on top of, about, held by, moving across, moving over, covering; see also UPON 1.—*Ant.* UNDER, underneath, below. **2** [Against] in contact with, close to,

[on the team] **6** engaged in *[on a trip]* **7** in a state of *[on parole]* **8** as a result of *[a profit on the sale]* **9** in the direction of *[light shone on us]* **10** through the use of *[live on bread]* **11** concerning *[an essay on war]* **12** onto **13** at the expense of *[a drink on the house]* **14** [Inf.] using; addicted to *[on drugs]* —***adv.*** **1** in a situation of contacting, being supported by, or covering **2** in a direction toward *[he looked on]* **3** forward *[move on]* **4** without stopping *[she sang on]* **5** into action or operation *[turn on the light]* —***adj.*** **1** in action or operation *[the TV is on]* **2** [Slang] performing very well *[she is really on today]* —**and so on** and more like the preceding —**on and off** intermittently —**on and on** for a long time; continuously —**on to** [Slang] aware of the real nature or meaning of

ON Ontario

once (wuns) ***adv.*** ⟦ME *ones*⟧ **1** one time only **2** at any time; ever **3** formerly *[a once famous woman]* **4** by one degree *[a cousin once removed]* —***conj.*** as soon as *[once he is tired, he will quit]* —***n.*** one time *[go this once]* —**at once 1** immediately **2** at the same time —**once (and) for all** conclusively —**once in a while** now and then

once'-o'ver ***n.*** [Inf.] a quick look

on·co·gene (äŋ'kə jēn') ***n.*** ⟦< Gr *onkos*, a mass + GENE⟧ a gene that, when activated as by a virus, may cause a normal cell to become cancerous

on·col·o·gy (än käl'ə jē, äŋ-) ***n.*** ⟦< Gr *onkos*, a mass + -LOGY⟧ the branch of medicine dealing with tumors —**on·col'o·gist** ***n.***

on·com·ing (än'kum'iŋ) ***adj.*** coming nearer in position or time

on·co·vi·rus (äŋ'kə vī'rəs) ***n.*** a virus that causes cancer

one (wun) ***adj.*** ⟦OE *an*⟧ **1** being a single thing or unit **2** united *[with one accord]* **3** a certain but unnamed *[take one path or the other, one day last week]* **4** the same **5** unique; only *[the one solution]* —***n.*** **1** the first and lowest cardinal number; 1; I **2** a single person or thing —***pron.*** **1** a certain person or thing **2** any person or thing —**at one** in accord —**one another** each one the other or others; each other —**one by one** individually in succession

one'-di·men'sion·al ***adj.*** having one dominant aspect, quality, etc. and hence narrow, limited, etc.

O'Neill (ō nēl'), **Eu·gene** (yōō jēn') 1888-1953; U.S. playwright

one'ness ***n.*** **1** singleness; unity **2** unity of mind, feeling, etc.

one'-on-one' ***adj.***, ***adv.*** in direct personal confrontation

on·er·ous (än'ər əs) ***adj.*** ⟦< L *onus*, a load⟧ burdensome; oppressive

one·self' ***pron.*** a person's own self: also **one's self** —**be oneself 1** to function normally **2** to be natural —**by oneself** alone

one'-sid'ed ***adj.*** **1** on, having, or involving only one side **2** unfair **3** unequal *[a one-sided race]*

one'-stop' ***adj.*** designating or of a store, bank, etc. that offers a complete range of goods or services

one'time' ***adj.*** former: also **one'-time'**

one'-track' ***adj.*** [Inf.] limited in scope

one'-up' ***adj.*** [Inf.] having an advantage (over another)

one-up'man·ship' (-up'mən ship') ***n.*** [Inf.] skill in seizing an advantage over others

one'-way' ***adj.*** moving, or allowing movement, in one direction only

on'go'ing ***adj.*** going on; progressing

on·ion (un'yən) ***n.*** ⟦< L *unus*, one⟧ **1** a plant of the lily family with an edible bulb **2** this bulb, having a strong, sharp smell and taste

on'ion·skin' ***n.*** a tough, thin, translucent paper

on'line' ***adj.*** designating or of equipment directly connected to and controlled by the central processing unit of a computer: also **on'-line'**

on'look'er ***n.*** a spectator

on·ly (ōn'lē) ***adj.*** ⟦< OE *an*, one + *-lic*, -ly⟧ **1** alone of its or their kind; sole **2** alone in superiority; best —***adv.*** **1** and no other; and no more; solely **2** (but) in the end *[to meet one crisis, only to face another]* **3** as recently as —***conj.*** [Inf.] except that; but —**only too** very; exceedingly

on·o·mat·o·poe·ia (än'ō mat'ō pē'ə, -mät'-) ***n.*** ⟦< Gr *onoma*, a name + *poiein*, make⟧ the formation of words by imitating sounds (Ex.: *buzz*)

on'rush' ***n.*** a headlong dash forward

on'set' ***n.*** **1** an attack **2** a start

on·slaught (än'slôt') ***n.*** ⟦< Du *slagen*, to strike⟧ a violent attack

on'stream' or **on'-stream'** ***adv.*** into operation or production *[a new refinery coming onstream]*

On·tar·i·o (än ter'ē ō) **1** province of SC Canada: 412,580 sq. mi.; pop. 10,754,000; cap. Toronto: abbrev. *ON* **2 Lake** smallest of the Great Lakes, between New York & Ontario, Canada —**On·tar'i·an** ***adj.***, ***n.***

on·to (än'tōō) ***prep.*** **1** to a position on **2** [Slang] aware of the real meaning or nature of

on·tog·e·ny (än täj'ə nē) ***n.*** ⟦ult. < Gr *einai*, to be + *-genēs*, born⟧ the life cycle of a single organism

o·nus (ō'nəs) ***n.*** ⟦L⟧ **1** a burden, unpleasant duty, etc. **2** blame

on'ward ***adv.*** toward or at a position ahead; forward: also **on'wards** —***adj.*** advancing

on·yx (än'iks) ***n.*** ⟦< Gr, fingernail⟧ a type of agate with alternate colored layers

oo·dles (ōōd''lz) ***pl.n.*** ⟦< ?⟧ [Inf.] a great amount; very many

ooze[1] (ōōz) ***n.*** ⟦OE *wos*, sap⟧ **1** an oozing **2** something that oozes —***vi.*** **oozed, ooz'ing** to flow or leak out slowly —***vt.*** to give forth (a fluid)

ooze[2] (ōōz) ***n.*** ⟦OE *wase*⟧ soft mud or slime, as at the bottom of a lake

op- *prefix* OB-: used before *p [oppress]*

o·pal (ō'pəl) ***n.*** ⟦< Sans *úpalaḥ*, (precious) stone⟧ an iridescent mineral of various colors: some varieties are semiprecious —**o·pal·es·cent** (ō'pəl es'ənt) ***adj.***

o·paque (ō pāk') ***adj.*** ⟦< L *opacus*, shady⟧ **1** not transparent **2** dull or dark **3** hard to understand —**o·pac·i·ty** (ō pas'ə tē) or **o·paque'ness** ***n.*** —**o·paque'ly** ***adv.***

THESAURUS

leaning on; see NEXT 2. **3** [Toward] in the direction of, to, at; see APPROACHING, TOWARD. **4** [Forward] onward, ahead, advancing; see FORWARD 1. **5** [Near] beside, close to, adjacent to; see BORDERING, NEAR 1. —**and so on** and so forth, also, in addition; see AND.

on and off ***a.*** now and then, sometimes, infrequently; see SELDOM.

once ***a.*** **1** [One time] this time, but once, once only, before, one time before, just this once, not more than once, never again, a single time, one time previously, on one occasion, only one time.—*Ant.* FREQUENTLY, twice, many times. **2** [Formerly] long ago, previously, earlier; see FORMERLY. —**all at once** simultaneously, all at the same time, unanimously; see TOGETHER 2. —**at once** now, quickly, this moment; see IMMEDIATELY. —**for once** for at least one time, once only, uniquely; see ONCE 1. —**once and for all** with finality, permanently, unalterably; see FINALLY 1. —**once in a while** sometimes, occasionally, on occasion; see SELDOM.

once-over* ***n.*** look, inspection, checkup; see EXAMINATION 1.

oncoming ***a.*** impending, expected, imminent; see APPROACHING.

one ***a.*** individual, peculiar, lone, specific, separate, single, singular, odd, one and only, precise, definite, sole, uncommon; see also SPECIAL, UNIQUE, UNUSUAL 2.—*Ant.* COMMON, several, imprecise.

one ***n.*** unit, 1, whole, person, thing, identity, ace, integer, item, example, digit, singleness, individual, individuality, individuation.—*Ant.* MANY, plural, several. —**all one** making no difference, insignificant, of no importance; see UNIMPORTANT. —**at one** in accord, agreeing, of the same opinion; see UNITED. —**tie one on*** go on a drinking spree, get drunk, imbibe; see DRINK 2.

oneness ***n.*** integrity, harmony, indivisibility; see UNITY 1.

one-sided ***a.*** **1** [Unilateral] single, uneven, partial; see IRREGULAR 4. **2** [Prejudiced] biased, partial, narrow-minded; see PREJUDICED, UNFAIR.

one-way ***a.*** directional, with no return, restricted; see NARROW 1.

ongoing ***a.*** open-ended, continuous, in process; see REGULAR 3.

only ***a.*** **1** [Solely] exclusively, uniquely, wholly, entirely, particularly, and no other, and no more, and nothing else, nothing but, totally, utterly, first and last, one and only; see also SINGLY. **2** [Merely] just, simply, plainly, barely, solely; see also HARDLY. **3** [Sole] single, companionless, without another, by oneself, isolated, apart, unaccompained, exclusive, unique; see also ALONE.

onset ***n.*** incipience, opening, start; see ORIGIN 2.

onto ***a.***, ***prep.*** **1** [To] toward, in contact with, adjacent; see AGAINST 1. **2** [Upon] over, out upon, above; see UPON 1.

onward ***a.*** on ahead, beyond, in front of; see FORWARD 1, MOVING 1.

ooze[1] ***v.*** seep, exude, leak; see FLOW.

ooze[2] ***n.*** slime, fluid, mire; see MUD.

opaque ***a.*** not transparent, dim, dusky, darkened, murky, gloomy, smoky, thick, misty, cloudy, clouded, shady, muddy, dull, blurred, frosty, filmy, foggy, sooty, dirty, dusty, coated over, covered.—*Ant.* CLEAR,

op art (äp) a style of abstract painting creating optical effects, as the illusion of movement

op. cit. *abbrev.* ⟦L *opere citato*⟧ in the work cited

OPEC (ō′pek′) ***n.*** Organization of Petroleum Exporting Countries

Op-Ed (äp′ed′) ***adj.*** ⟦*Op(posite) Ed(itorial page)*⟧ designating or on a page in a newspaper featuring a wide variety of columns, letters, etc.

o·pen (ō′pən) ***adj.*** ⟦OE⟧ **1** not closed, covered, clogged, or shut **2** not enclosed *[open* fields*]* **3** spread out; unfolded *[*an *open* book*]* **4** having gaps, holes, etc. **5** free to be entered, used, etc. *[*an *open* meeting*]* **6** not decided *[*an *open* question*]* **7** not closed to new ideas, etc. *[*an *open* mind*]* **8** generous **9** free from legal or discriminatory restrictions *[open* season, *open* housing*]* **10** not conventional *[open* marriage*]* **11** not already taken *[*the job is *open]* **12** not secret; public **13** frank; candid *[*an *open* manner*]* —***vt., vi.*** **1** to cause to be, or to become, open **2** to spread out; expand; unfold **3** to begin; start **4** to start operating —**open to** **1** willing to receive, discuss, etc. **2** liable to **3** available to —**the open** **1** the outdoors **2** public knowledge —**o′pen·er** ***n.*** —**o′pen·ly** ***adv.*** —**o′pen·ness** ***n.***

open air the outdoors —**o′pen-air′** ***adj.***

o′pen-and-shut′ ***adj.*** easily decided

o′pen-end′ed (-en′did) ***adj.*** unlimited

o′pen-eyed′ (-īd′) ***adj.*** with the eyes wide open, as in surprise or watchfulness

o′pen-faced′ ***adj.*** **1** having a frank, honest face **2** designating a sandwich without a top slice of bread Also **o′pen-face′**

o′pen-hand′ed ***adj.*** generous

o′pen-heart′ed ***adj.*** **1** not reserved; frank **2** kindly; generous

o′pen-hearth′ ***adj.*** designating or using a furnace with a wide hearth and low roof, for making steel

o′pen-heart′ surgery surgery on the heart during which the blood is diverted, circulated, and oxygenated by mechanical means

open house **1** an informal reception at one's home **2** a time when an institution is open to visitors

o′pen·ing ***n.*** **1** an open place; hole; gap **2** a clearing **3** a beginning **4** start of operations **5** a favorable chance **6** an unfilled job

o′pen-mind′ed ***adj.*** having a mind open to new ideas; unprejudiced

o′pen·work′ ***n.*** ornamental work, as in cloth, with openings in it

op·er·a[1] (äp′ə rə, äp′rə) ***n.*** ⟦< L, a work⟧ a play having its text set to music and sung to orchestral accompaniment —**op′er·at′ic** (-ə rat′ik) ***adj.***

o·pe·ra[2] (ō′pə rə, äp′ə rə) ***n.*** *pl. of* OPUS

op·er·a·ble (äp′ər ə bəl) ***adj.*** ⟦see OPERATE & -ABLE⟧ **1** able to function **2** that can be treated by surgery

opera glasses a small binocular telescope used in theaters, etc.

op·er·ate (äp′ə rāt′) ***vi.*** **-at′ed, -at′ing** ⟦< L *operari,* to work⟧ **1** to be in action; act; work **2** to have an effect **3** to perform a surgical operation —***vt.*** **1** to put or keep in action **2** to direct; manage

op′er·a′tion (-rā′shən) ***n.*** ⟦< L *operatio*⟧ **1** the act or method of operating **2** a being in action or at work **3** a process or action that is part of a series in some work **4** any surgical procedure to remedy a physical ailment

THESAURUS

transparent, translucent.

open ***a.*** **1** [Not closed] unclosed, accessible, clear, open to view, uncovered, disclosed, divulged, introduced, initiated, begun, full-blown, unfurled, susceptible, ajar, gaping, wide, rent, torn, spacious, unshut, expansive, extensive, spread out, revealed; see also senses 2, 4.—*Ant.* CLOSED, tight, shut. **2** [Not obstructed] unlocked, unbarred, unbolted, unblocked, unfastened, cleared away, made passable, unsealed, unobstructed, unoccupied, vacated, unburdened, emptied; see also sense 1.—*Ant.* TAKEN, barred, blocked. **3** [Not forbidden] free of entrance, unrestricted, allowable, free of access, public, welcoming; see also PERMITTED.—*Ant.* REFUSED, forbidden, restricted. **4** [Not protected] insecure, unsafe, unguarded, unsecluded, liable, exposed, uncovered, apart, unshut, unroofed, conspicuous, unhidden, unconcealed, subject to, sensitive; see also sense 1 and UNSAFE.—*Ant.* SAFE, secluded, secure. **5** [Not decided] in question, up for discussion, debatable; see QUESTIONABLE 1, UNCERTAIN. **6** [Frank] plain, candid, straightforward; see FRANK.

open ***v.*** **1** [To begin] start, inaugurate, initiate; see BEGIN 1, 2. **2** [To move aside a prepared obstruction] unbar, unlock, unclose, clear, admit, reopen, open the lock, lift the latch, free, loosen, disengage, unfasten, undo, unbolt, turn the key, turn the knob.—*Ant.* CLOSE, shut, lock. **3** [To make an opening] force an entrance, breach, cut in, tear down, push in, shatter, destroy, burst in, break open, cave in, burst out from, penetrate, pierce, force one's way into, smash, punch a hole into, slit, puncture, crack, muscle in*, jimmy*; see also FORCE, REMOVE 1.—*Ant.* REPAIR, seal, mend. **4** [To make available] make accessible, put on sale, put on view, open to the public, make public, put forward, free, make usable, prepare, present, make ready.—*Ant.* REMOVE, put away, lock up. **5** [To expose to fuller view] unroll, unfold, uncover; see EXPOSE 1, REVEAL.

opened ***a.*** unlocked, made open, not closed; see FREE 3, OPEN 2.

open-ended ***a.*** going on, without specified limits, optional; see CONSTANT, UNCERTAIN.

opening ***a.*** initial, beginning, primary; see FIRST.

opening ***n.*** **1** [A hole] break, crack, tear; see HOLE 1. **2** [An opportunity] chance, availability, occasion; see OPPORTUNITY 1, POSSIBILITY 2.

openly ***a.*** **1** [Frankly] naturally, simply, artlessly, naively, unsophisticatedly, out in the open, candidly, aboveboard, straightforwardly, honestly, unreservedly, fully, readily, willingly, without restraint, plainly, without reserve, to one's face, in public, face to face; see also SINCERELY.—*Ant.* SECRETLY, furtively, surreptitiously. **2** [Shamelessly] immodestly, brazenly, not caring, regardlessly, insensibly, unconcernedly, crassly, insolently, flagrantly, wantonly, unblushingly, notoriously, without pretense, in defiance of the law; see also CARELESSLY, LEWDLY.—*Ant.* CAREFULLY, prudently, discreetly.

open-minded ***a.*** tolerant, fair-minded, just; see FAIR 1, LIBERAL.

opera[1] ***n.*** musical drama, libretto, score, operetta, grand opera, light opera, comic opera, rock opera, opera performance; see also PERFORMANCE.

operate ***v.*** **1** [To keep in operation] manipulate, conduct, administer; see MANAGE 1. **2** [To be in operation] function, work, serve, carry on, run, revolve, act, behave, fulfill, turn, roll, spin, pump, lift, perform, burn, move, progress, advance, proceed, go, contact, engage, transport, convey, click*, tick*.—*Ant.* STOP, stall, break down. **3** [To produce an effect] react, act on, influence, bring about, determine, turn, bend, contrive, work, accomplish, fulfill, finish, complete, benefit, compel, promote, concern, enforce, take effect, have effect, work on, succeed, get results, get across; see also ACHIEVE, PRODUCE 1. **4** [To perform a surgical operation] remove diseased tissue, amputate, transplant; see TREAT 2.

operated ***a.*** conducted, handled, run, carried on, regulated, ordered, maintained, supervised, superintended, governed, administered, transacted, performed, conveyed, transported, moved, determined, achieved, contrived, accomplished, fulfilled, promoted, enforced, worked, served, guided, executed, sustained, used, practiced, put into effect, finished, driven, brought about, bent, manipulated, negotiated; see also DIRECTED, MANAGED 2.

operating ***a.*** managing, conducting, directing, executing, manipulating, administering, ordering, regulating, supervising, running, wielding, transacting, guiding, putting into effect, sustaining, maintaining, performing, practicing, revolving, promoting, determining, moving, turning, spinning, driving, contriving, fulfilling, accomplishing, finishing, effecting, bringing about, serving, enforcing, in operation, at work; see also USING.

operation ***n.*** **1** [The act of causing to function] execution, guidance, superintendence, carrying out, ordering, order, control, maintenance, handling, administration, manipulating, manipulation, supervision, agency, enforcement, advancement, regulating, running, supervising, directing, transacting, conducting; see also MANAGEMENT 1, REGULATION 1. **2** [An action] performance, act, employment, labor, service, carrying on, transaction, deed, doing, proceeding, handiwork, workmanship, enterprise, movement, progress, development, engagement, undertaking; see also ACTION 1, WORK 2. **3** [A method] process, formula, procedure; see METHOD, PLAN 2. **4** [Surgical treatment] surgery, transplant, amputation, dismemberment, vivisection, dissection, biopsy, emergency operation, acupuncture, exploratory operation, section, resection, incision, excision, removal, tonsillectomy, appendectomy, hysterectomy, plastic surgery, cesarean section, coronary bypass, rhinoplasty, keratotomy, laparotomy, mastectomy, trache-

op'er·a'tion·al *adj.* **1** of or having to do with the operation of a device, system, process, etc. **2** *a)* that can be used or operated *b)* in use; operating

op'er·a·tive' (-rə tiv', -rāt'iv) *adj.* **1** in operation **2** effective **3** connected with physical work or mechanical action

op'er·a'tor (-rāt'ər) *n.* **1** one who operates a machine *[a telephone operator]* **2** one engaged in commercial or industrial operations **3** [Slang] a clever, persuasive person

op·er·et·ta (äp'ə ret'ə) *n.* ⟦It, dim. of *opera,* OPERA[1]⟧ an amusing opera with spoken dialogue

oph·thal·mic (äf thal'mik) *adj.* ⟦< Gr *ophthalmos,* the eye⟧ of or involving the eye

oph·thal·mol·o·gy (äf'thal mäl'ə jē, äp'thə-) *n.* ⟦< Gr *ophthalmos,* the eye + -LOGY⟧ the branch of medicine dealing with the eye and its diseases —**oph'thal·mol'o·gist** *n.*

o·pi·ate (ō'pē it) *n.* ⟦ML *opiatum*⟧ **1** a drug containing, or derived from, opium **2** anything that quiets, soothes, or deadens

o·pine (ō pīn') *vt., vi.* **o·pined', o·pin'ing** ⟦< L *opinari,* think⟧ to express (an opinion)

o·pin·ion (ə pin'yən) *n.* ⟦< L *opinari,* think⟧ **1** a belief based not on certainty but on what seems true or probable **2** an evaluation, estimation, etc. **3** formal expert judgment

o·pin'ion·at'ed (-āt'id) *adj.* holding obstinately to one's opinions

o·pi·um (ō'pē əm) *n.* ⟦< Gr *opos,* vegetable juice⟧ a narcotic drug prepared from the seed of a certain poppy

o·pos·sum (ə päs'əm) *n.* ⟦< AmInd, white beast⟧ a small, nocturnal, tree-dwelling American marsupial that becomes motionless when frightened

op·po·nent (ə pō'nənt) *n.* ⟦< L *ob-* (see OB-) + *ponere,* to place⟧ one who opposes, as in a game; adversary

op·por·tune (äp'ər to͞on') *adj.* ⟦< L *ob-* (see OB-) + *portus,* PORT[1]⟧ **1** suitable: said of time **2** well-timed

op'por·tun'ism' *n.* the adapting of one's actions, thoughts, etc. to circumstances, as in politics, without regard for principles —**op'por·tun'ist** *n., adj.* —**op'por·tun·is'tic** (-to͞o nis'tik) *adj.*

op·por·tu·ni·ty (äp'ər to͞o'nə tē) *n., pl.* **-ties 1** a combination of circumstances favorable for the purpose **2** a good chance, as to advance oneself

op·pose (ə pōz') *vt.* **-posed', -pos'ing** ⟦< L *ob-* (see OB-) + *ponere,* to place⟧ **1** to place opposite **2** to contend with; resist —**op·pos'a·ble** *adj.*

op·po·site (äp'ə zit) *adj.* ⟦< L *ob-* (see OB-) + *ponere,* to place⟧ **1** set against; in a contrary direction: often with *to* **2** entirely different; exactly contrary —*n.* anything opposed —*prep.* across from —**op'po·site·ly** *adv.*

opposite number one whose position, rank, etc. parallels another's in a different place or organization

op'po·si'tion (-zish'ən) *n.* **1** an opposing **2** resistance, contrast, hostility, etc. **3** *a)* one that opposes *b)* [*often* **O-**] a political party opposing the party in power

op·press (ə pres') *vt.* ⟦< L *ob-* (see OB-) + *premere,* to press⟧ **1** to weigh heavily on the mind of; worry **2** to keep down by the cruel or unjust use of authority —**op·pres'sor** *n.*

op·pres·sion (ə presh'ən) *n.* **1** an oppressing or being oppressed **2** a thing that oppresses **3** physical or mental distress

op·pres·sive (ə pres'iv) *adj.* **1** causing discomfort **2** tyrannical **3** distressing —**op·pres'sive·ly** *adv.*

op·pro·bri·ous (ə prō'brē əs) *adj.* expressing opprobrium; abusive

op·pro'bri·um (-əm) *n.* ⟦< L *ob-* (see OB-) + *probrum,* a disgrace⟧ **1** the disgrace attached to shameful conduct **2** contempt for something regarded as inferior

opt (äpt) *vi.* ⟦< L *optare,* to wish⟧ to make a choice: often with *for* —**opt out (of)** to choose not to be or continue in (some activity, organization, etc.)

op·tic (äp'tik) *adj.* ⟦< Gr *ōps,* an eye⟧ of the eye or sense of sight

THESAURUS

otomy, open-heart surgery, abortion, autopsy, the knife*; see also MEDICINE 3.

operator *n.* **1** [One who operates a machine] engineer, worker, skilled employee; see LABORER, WORKMAN. *Kinds of operators include the following:* telephone, computer, switchboard, PBX, information, long-distance, emergency. **2** [One who operates workable property] executive, supervisor, director; see EXECUTIVE. **3** [*Manipulator] speculator, scoundrel, fraud; see RASCAL.

opinion *n.* **1** [A belief] notion, view, point of view, sentiment, conception, idea, surmise, impression, inference, conjecture, inclination, fancy, imagining, supposition, suspicion, assumption, guess, theory, thesis, theorem, postulate, hypothesis, persuasion, presumption, presupposition, mind; see also BELIEF. **2** [A considered judgment] estimation, estimate, view, summary, belief, idea, resolution, determination, recommendation, finding, conviction, conclusion; see also JUDGMENT 3, VERDICT.

opinionated *a.* bigoted, stubborn, unyielding; see OBSTINATE, PREJUDICED.

opium *n.* opiate, soporific, dope*; see DRUG.

opponent *n.* **1** [A rival] competitor, contender, challenger, candidate, equal, entrant, the opposition, aspirant, bidder.—*Ant.* SUPPORTER, defender, abettor. **2** [An opposing contestant] antagonist, contestant, litigant; see PLAYER 1. **3** [An enemy] foe, adversary, assailant; see ENEMY.

opportunity *n.* **1** [Favorable circumstances] chance, occasion, happening, event, excuse, suitable circumstance, probability, good fortune, luck, break; see also POSSIBILITY 2. **2** [A suitable time] occasion, moment, right time; see TIME 2.

oppose *v.* **1** [To hold a contrary opinion] object, disapprove, debate, dispute, disagree, contradict, argue, deny, run counter to, protest, defy, cross, speak against, confront, thwart, neutralize, reverse, turn the tables, be opposed to, oppose change, not have any part of, face down, interfere with, disapprove of, cry out against, disagree with, not conform, run against, run counter to, come in conflict with, go contrary to, frown at, not accept, call into question, conflict with, grapple with, doubt, be against, be unwilling, reject, dislike, take exception, repudiate, question, probe, resist, confound, confute, refute, buck*, turn thumbs down*; see also sense 2 and DARE 2, FACE 1.—*Ant.* AGREE, approve, accept. **2** [To fight] resist, battle, encounter, assault, attack, assail, storm, protest, clash, meet, skirmish, engage, contest, face, restrain, go against, turn against, uphold, defend, rebel, revolt, mutiny, strike back, combat, run counter to, defy, snub, grapple with, fight off, withstand, repel, guard, counterattack, struggle, outflank, antagonize, retaliate, impede, overpower, take on all comers*, lock horns with; see also FIGHT.

opposed *a.* antagonistic to, averse, adverse, opposite, contrary, hostile to, at odds, counter to, at cross purposes, up against, against the grain; see also OPPOSITE 2.

opposing *a.* **1** [In the act of opposition] conflicting, unfriendly, clashing; see OPPOSED. **2** [Situated opposite] face to face with, facing, fronting; see OPPOSITE 3.

opposite *a.* **1** [Contrary] antithetical, diametric, reversed; see UNLIKE. **2** [In conflict] adverse, inimical, antagonistic, rival, unfavorable, averse, argumentative, contradictory, hostile; see also AGAINST 1. **3** [So situated as to seem to oppose] facing, fronting, in front of, on different sides of, on opposite sides, in opposition to, contrasting, on the other side of, contrary, over against, front to front, back to back, nose to nose, face to face, on the farther side, opposing, diametrical, eyeball to eyeball*.—*Ant.* MATCHED, on the same side, side by side.

opposite *n.* contradiction, contrary, converse, direct opposite, opposition, vice versa, antithesis, antonym, counter term, counterpart, inverse, reverse, adverse, the opposite pole, the other extreme, the other side, the opposite idea.—*Ant.* EQUAL, like, similar thing.

opposition *n.* **1** [The act of opposing] hostilities, conflict, combat; see BATTLE, FIGHT 1. **2** [The attitude suggestive of opposition] dislike, disagreement, hostility, antagonism, defiance, antipathy, abhorrence, aversion, constraint, restriction, restraint, hindrance, discord, distaste, disfavor, dissatisfaction, discontent, displeasure, irritation, offense, chagrin, humiliation, anger, loathing, disapproval, complaint, repugnance; see also HATRED, RESENTMENT.—*Ant.* SUPPORT, enthusiasm, accord. **3** [The individual or group that opposes] antagonist, disputant, adversary; see ENEMY, OPPONENT 1.

oppress *v.* suppress, harass, maltreat; see ABUSE, BOTHER 2.

oppressed *a.* misused, downtrodden, enslaved; see HURT.

oppression *n.* tyranny, hardness, domination, coercion, dictatorship, fascism, persecution, severity, harshness, abuse, conquering, subjugation, subduing, torture, compulsion, force, torment, martial law; see also CRUELTY.—*Ant.* FREEDOM, liberalism, voluntary control.

opt (for) *v.* select, vote, pick; see CHOOSE, DECIDE.

op·ti·cal (äp′ti kəl) ***adj.*** **1** of the sense of sight; visual **2** of optics **3** for aiding vision —**op′ti·cal·ly** ***adv.***
optical disc (or **disk**) any disk on which data, as computer files or music, is stored in the form of microscopic pits to be read by a laser
op·ti·cian (äp tish′ən) ***n.*** one who makes or sells eyeglasses, etc.
op·tics (äp′tiks) ***n.*** the branch of physics dealing with light and vision
op·ti·mism (äp′tə miz′əm) ***n.*** ⟦< L *optimus,* best⟧ **1** the belief that good ultimately prevails over evil **2** the tendency to take the most hopeful view of matters —**op′ti·mist** ***n.*** —**op′ti·mis′tic** ***adj.*** —**op′ti·mis′ti·cal·ly** ***adv.***
op′ti·mum (-məm) ***n.***, *pl.* **-mums** or **-ma** (-mə) ⟦see prec.⟧ the best or most favorable degree, condition, etc. —***adj.*** most favorable; best: also **op′ti·mal** (-məl)
op·tion (äp′shən) ***n.*** ⟦< L *optare,* to wish⟧ **1** a choosing; choice **2** the right of choosing **3** something that is or can be chosen **4** the right to buy, sell, or lease at a fixed price within a specified time —**op′tion·al** ***adj.***
op·tom·e·try (äp täm′ə trē) ***n.*** ⟦< Gr *optikos,* optic + *metron,* a measure⟧ the profession of testing and examining the eyes and prescribing glasses to correct vision problems —**op·tom′e·trist** ***n.***
op·u·lent (äp′yoo lənt, -yə-) ***adj.*** ⟦< L *ops,* riches⟧ **1** very wealthy **2** abundant —**op′u·lence** ***n.***
o·pus (ō′pəs) ***n.***, *pl.* **o·pe·ra** (ō′pə rə, äp′ə rə) or **o′pus·es** ⟦L, a work⟧ a work; composition; esp., any of the numbered musical works of a composer
or (ôr) ***conj.*** ⟦OE *oththe*⟧ a coordinating conjunction introducing: *a*) an alternative *[* red *or* blue*]* or the last in a series of choices *b*) a synonymous word or phrase *[*oral, *or* spoken*]*
-or (ər, ôr) ⟦< L⟧ *suffix* a person or thing that (does a specified thing) *[inventor]*
OR Oregon
or·a·cle (ôr′ə kəl) ***n.*** ⟦< L *orare,* pray⟧ **1** among the ancient Greeks and Romans, *a*) the place where, or medium by which, deities were consulted *b*) the revelation of a medium or priest **2** *a*) a person of great knowledge *b*) statements of such a person —**o·rac·u·lar** (ō rak′yoo lər) ***adj.***
o·ral (ôr′əl) ***adj.*** ⟦< L *os,* the mouth⟧ **1** uttered; spoken **2** of or near the mouth —**o′ral·ly** ***adv.***
oral history **1** the gathering of personal recollections in tape recorded interviews **2** a historical account based on this
or·ange (ôr′inj, är′-) ***n.*** ⟦< Sans *naranga*⟧ **1** a round, edible, reddish-yellow citrus fruit, with a sweet, juicy pulp **2** the evergreen tree it grows on **3** reddish yellow
or′ange·ade′ ***n.*** a drink made of orange juice, water, and sugar
o·rang·u·tan (ô raŋ′oo tan′) ***n.*** ⟦< Malay *orañ,* man + *utan,* forest⟧ an ape of Borneo and Sumatra with shaggy, reddish-brown hair and very long arms
o·rate (ō rāt′, ôr′āt′) ***vi.*** **-rat′ed, -rat′ing** to make an oration; speak in a pompous or bombastic way
o·ra·tion (ō rā′shən, ô-) ***n.*** ⟦< L *orare,* speak⟧ a formal speech, esp. one given at a ceremony
or·a·tor (ôr′ət ər, är′-) ***n.*** an eloquent public speaker
or·a·to·ri·o (ôr′ə tôr′ē ō′) ***n.***, *pl.* **-os′** ⟦It, small chapel⟧ a long, dramatic musical work, usually on a religious theme, sung but not acted out
or·a·to·ry (ôr′ə tôr′ē, är′-) ***n.***, *pl.* **-ries** ⟦< L *oratoria*⟧ skill in public speaking —**or′a·tor′i·cal** ***adj.***
orb (ôrb) ***n.*** ⟦L *orbis,* a circle⟧ a sphere, esp. a celestial body, as the sun or moon
or·bit (ôr′bit) ***n.*** ⟦< L *orbis,* a circle⟧ **1** the path of a celestial body during its revolution around another **2** the path of an artificial satellite or spacecraft around a celestial body —***vi.***, ***vt.*** to move in, or put into, an orbit —**or′bit·al** ***adj.***
or·chard (ôr′chərd) ***n.*** ⟦OE *ortgeard*⟧ **1** land for growing fruit trees **2** the trees
or·ches·tra (ôr′kis trə, -kes′-) ***n.*** ⟦< Gr *orcheisthai,* to dance⟧ **1** the space in front of a theater stage, where the musicians sit: in full **orchestra pit** **2** the seats on the main floor of a theater **3** *a*) a group of musicians playing together *b*) their instruments —**or·ches′tral** (-kes′trəl) ***adj.***
or′ches·trate′ (-trāt′) ***vt.***, ***vi.*** **-trat′ed, -trat′ing** **1** to arrange (music) for an orchestra **2** to coordinate or arrange (something) —**or′ches·tra′tion** ***n.***
or·chid (ôr′kid) ***n.*** ⟦< Gr *orchis,* testicle: from the shape of the roots⟧ **1** a perennial plant having flowers with three petals, one of which is lip-shaped **2** this flower **3** pale purple
or·dain (ôr dān′) ***vt.*** ⟦< L *ordo,* an order⟧ **1** to decree; establish; enact **2** to invest with the office of minister, priest, or rabbi —**or·dain′ment** ***n.***
or·deal (ôr dēl′) ***n.*** ⟦OE *ordal*⟧ any difficult or painful experience
or·der (ôr′dər) ***n.*** ⟦< L *ordo,* straight row⟧ **1** social position **2** a state of peace; orderly conduct **3** arrangement of things or events; series **4** a definite plan; system **5** a military, monastic, or social brotherhood **6** a condition

THESAURUS

optical ***a.*** ocular, seeing, visible; see VISUAL.
optimism ***n.*** **1** [Belief in the essential goodness of the universe] confidence, philosophy of goodness, belief in progress; see FAITH 1. **2** [An inclination to expect or to hope for the best] cheerfulness, hope, hopefulness, confidence, assurance, encouragement, happiness, brightness, enthusiasm, good cheer, trust, calmness, elation, expectancy, expectation, anticipation, certainty.—*Ant.* GLOOM, despair, melancholy.
optimist ***n.*** Pollyanna, dreamer, positivist.
optimistic ***a.*** cheerful, sanguine, assured; see CONFIDENT, HOPEFUL 1, TRUSTING.
option ***n.*** **1** [A choice] selection, alternative, dilemma; see CHOICE. **2** [A privilege to purchase] right, prerogative, grant, claim, license, lease, franchise, advantage, security, immunity, benefit, title, prior claim, dibs*.
optional ***a.*** discretionary, elective, noncompulsory, free, unrestricted, arbitrary, not required, with no strings attached*, take it or leave it*; see also VOLUNTARY.—*Ant.* NECESSARY, compulsory, enforced.
or ***conj.*** **1** [A suggestion of choice] and as an alternative, and as a substitute, and on the other hand; see EITHER.—*Ant.* NOR, neither, without choice. **2** [A suggestion of correction] or not, or not exactly, but on the contrary, or rather; see also INSTEAD.
oral ***a.*** vocal, verbal, uttered, voiced, unwritten, phonetic, sounded, articulated, pronounced, not written, by word of mouth; see also SPOKEN.—*Ant.* WRITTEN, PRINTED, unspoken.
orange ***a.*** reddish, ocherous, glowing; see ORANGE, *n.* 2.
orange ***n.*** **1** [Color] red-yellow, apricot, tangerine, burnt orange, peach, coral, salmon; see also COLOR. **2** [Fruit] citrus fruit, tropical fruit, juice orange; see FOOD, FRUIT.
orbit ***n.*** **1** [Path described by one body revolving around another] ellipse, circle, ring, circuit, apogee, course, perigee, lap, round, cycle, curve, flight path; see also REVOLUTION 1. **2** [Range of activity or influence] range, field, boundary; see AREA.
orbit ***v.*** **1** [To revolve around another body] encircle, encompass, ring, move in a circuit, go around, revolve; see also CIRCLE. **2** [To put into orbit] fire, blast off, project; see LAUNCH 2.
orbited ***a.*** sent into orbit, put up, rocketed; see DRIVEN, SENT.
orchard ***n.*** fruit trees, fruit farm, apple orchard; see FARM.
orchestra ***n.*** musical ensemble, symphony, instrumental ensemble, chamber orchestra; see also BAND.
ordain ***v.*** **1** [To establish] install, institute, appoint; see ENACT. **2** [To destine] determine, foreordain, predestine; see INTEND 2. **3** [To invest with priestly functions] install, confer holy orders upon, consecrate, anoint, delegate, invest; see also BLESS.
ordained ***a.*** **1** [Ordered] commanded, determined, established by law; see ESTABLISHED 2, ORDERED 2. **2** [Invested into the ministry] consecrated, anointed, received into the ministry; see NAMED 2.
ordeal ***n.*** tribulation, distress, suffering; see DIFFICULTY 1, 2.
order ***n.*** **1** [A command] direction, demand, decree, rule, edict, charge, requirement, ordinance, act, warrant, mandate, injunction; see also COMMAND, LAW 3. **2** [Sequence] progression, succession, procession; see LINE 1, SEQUENCE 1, SERIES. **3** [Orderly arrangement] regulation, plan, disposition, management, establishment, method, distribution, placement, scale, rule, computation, adjustment, adaptation, ordering, ranging, standardizing, lining up, trimming, grouping, composition, assortment, disposal, scheme, form, routine, array, procedure, index, regularity, uniformity, symmetry, harmony, layout, lineup, setup; see also CLASSIFICATION, SYSTEM.—*Ant.* CONFUSION, disarray, displacement. **4** [Organization] society, sect, company; see ORGANIZATION 2. **5** [A formal agreement to purchase] reserve, application, requisition, request, stipulation, booking, layaway, arrangement; see also BUYING, RESERVATION 1. **6** [Kind] rank, hierarchy, degree; see CLASS 1, CLASSIFICATION. **7** [Custom-

in which everything is in its place and working properly **7** condition in general *[in working order]* **8** an authoritative command, instruction, etc. **9** a class; kind **10** an established method, as of conduct in meetings, etc. **11** *a)* a request to supply something *[an order for books]* *b)* the goods supplied **12** *[usually pl.]* the position of ordained minister, priest, etc. *[to take holy orders]* —***vt.**, **vi.*** **1** to put or keep (things) in order; arrange **2** to command **3** to request (something to be supplied) —**in** (or **out of**) **order 1** in (or not in) proper position **2** in (or not in) good condition **3** in (or not in) accordance with the rules —**in order that** so that —**in order to** for the purpose of —**in short order** quickly —**on the order of** similar to —**to order** in accordance with the buyer's specifications

or′der·ly ***adj.*** **1** neat or tidy **2** well-behaved —***n.**, pl.* **-lies 1** an enlisted person assigned to perform personal services for an officer **2** a male hospital attendant —**or′der·li·ness** ***n.***

or·di·nal (ôrd′'n əl) ***adj.*** ⟦< L *ordo,* order⟧ expressing order in a series —***n.*** any number showing order in a series (e.g., first, tenth): in full **ordinal number**

or·di·nance (ôrd′'n əns) ***n.*** ⟦< L *ordo,* an order⟧ a statute or regulation, esp. a municipal one

or·di·nar·i·ly (ôrd′'n er′ə lē) ***adv.*** usually; as a rule

or·di·nar·y (ôrd′'n er′ē) ***adj.*** ⟦< L *ordo,* an order⟧ **1** customary; usual **2** familiar; unexceptional; common —**out of the ordinary** unusual

or·di·nate (ôrd′'n it, -āt′) ***n.*** ⟦< L *(linea) ordinate (applicata),* line applied in ordered manner⟧ *Math.* the vertical distance of a point from a horizontal axis

or·di·na·tion (ôrd′'n ā′shən) ***n.*** an ordaining or being ordained to the clergy

ord·nance (ôrd′nəns) ***n.*** ⟦< ORDINANCE⟧ **1** artillery **2** all military weapons, ammunition, etc.

or·dure (ôr′jər) ***n.*** ⟦< L *horridus,* horrid⟧ dung; filth

ore (ôr) ***n.*** ⟦OE *ar,* brass⟧ a natural combination of minerals, esp. one from which a metal or metals can be profitably extracted

o·reg·a·no (ô reg′ə nō, ə-) ***n.*** ⟦< Sp < Gr *origanon*⟧ an herb of the mint family, with fragrant leaves used for seasoning

Or·e·gon (ôr′i gən, -gän′) NW coastal state of the U.S.: 97,060 sq. mi.; pop. 2,842,000; cap. Salem: abbrev. *OR* —**Or′e·go′ni·an** (-gō′nē ən) ***adj.**, **n.***

or·gan (ôr′gən) ***n.*** ⟦< Gr *organon,* an implement⟧ **1** a keyboard musical instrument with sets of graduated pipes through which compressed air is passed, causing sound by vibration **2** in animals and plants, a part adapted to perform a specific function **3** a means for performing some action **4** a means of communicating ideas, as a periodical

or·gan·dy or **or·gan·die** (ôr′gən dē) ***n.**, pl.* **-dies** ⟦Fr *organdi*⟧ a very sheer, crisp cotton fabric

or·gan·elle (ôr′gə nel′) ***n.*** ⟦< L *organum,* tool + dim. of *-ellus*⟧ a discrete structure within a cell, as a chloroplast, having specialized functions, a distinctive chemical composition, etc.

or·gan·ic (ôr gan′ik) ***adj.*** **1** of or having to do with a bodily organ **2** inherent; inborn **3** systematically arranged **4** designating or of any chemical compound containing carbon **5** of, like, or derived from living organisms **6** grown with only natural fertilizers —**or·gan′i·cal·ly** ***adv.***

or·gan·ism (ôr′gə niz′əm) ***n.*** any living thing

or′gan·ist ***n.*** an organ player

or·gan·i·za·tion (ôr′gə ni zā′shən) ***n.*** **1** an organizing or being organized **2** any organized group, as a club —**or′gan·i·za′tion·al** ***adj.***

or·gan·ize (ôr′gə nīz′) ***vt.*** **-ized′, -iz′ing 1** to provide with an orderly structure or arrangement **2** to arrange for **3** to institute; establish **4** to persuade to join a cause, group, etc. —***vi.*** to become organized —**or′gan·iz′er** ***n.***

or·gan·za (ôr gan′zə) ***n.*** a thin, stiff fabric of rayon, silk, etc.

THESAURUS

ary method] ritual, rite, plan; see CUSTOM. —**in order** working, efficient, operative; see EFFECTIVE. —**in order to** so as to, as a means to, so that; see FOR. —**in short order** rapidly, without delay, soon; see QUICKLY. —**on order** requested, on the way, sent for; see ORDERED 1. —**out of order** broken-down, defective, faulty; see BROKEN 2.

order ***v.*** **1** [To give a command] direct, command, instruct, bid, tell, demand, impose, give directions, dictate, decree; see also REQUIRE 2. **2** [To authorize a purchase] secure, reserve, request; see BUY, OBTAIN 1. **3** [To put in order] arrange, plan, furnish, regulate, establish, manage, systematize, space, file, put away, classify, distribute, alphabetize, regularize, pattern, formalize, settle, fix, locate, dress up, sort out, index, put to rights, set guidelines for, adjust, adapt, set in order, assign, place, align, standardize, group; see also ORGANIZE 1.—*Ant.* CONFUSE, disarrange, disarray.

ordered ***a.*** **1** [On order] requested, requisitioned, sent for, spoken for, engaged, booked, arranged for, retained, written for, telephoned for; see also RESERVED 1. **2** [Commanded] directed, ordained, charged, dictated, regulated, decreed, ruled, enjoined, stipulated, bidden, imposed, authorized, exacted, forbidden, required, as ordered, under someone's jurisdiction, by order; see also APPROVED, REQUESTED.—*Ant.* NEGLECTED, omitted, revoked. **3** [Put in order] arranged, regulated, placed; see CLASSIFIED, ORGANIZED.

orderly ***a.*** **1** [Ordered; *said of objects and places*] well-kept, tidy, arranged; see CLEAN 1, NEAT 1. **2** [Methodical; *said of persons*] systematic, correct, formal, businesslike, exact, tidy, neat, thorough, precise; see also CAREFUL.—*Ant.* IRREGULAR, inaccurate, unmethodical.

ordinance ***n.*** direction, mandate, authorization; see LAW 3.

ordinarily ***a.*** usually, generally, habitually; see FREQUENTLY, REGULARLY.

ordinary ***a.*** **1** [In accordance with a regular order or sequence] customary, normal, regular, constant, usual, habitual, routine, mundane, everyday; see also COMMON 1, POPULAR 1, 3, TRADITIONAL. **2** [Lacking distinction] average, mediocre, familiar, natural, everyday, accepted, typical, commonplace, characteristic, prosaic, simple, banal, bland, trite, monotonous, stale, tedious, plain, normal; see also COMMON 1, CONVENTIONAL 3, DULL 4. —**out of the ordinary** extraordinary, uncommon, special; see UNUSUAL 2.

ore ***n.*** unrefined rock, ore bed, native mineral; see MINERAL.

organ ***n.*** **1** [An instrument] medium, means, way; see TOOL 1. **2** [A part of an organism having a specialized use] vital part, vital structure, process; see GLAND. *Human organs include the following:* brain, heart, eye, ear, nose, tongue, lung, kidney, stomach, intestine, pancreas, gallbladder, liver, spleen, bladder, colon, reproductive organ, genitals. **3** [A musical instrument] wind instrument, keyboard instrument, calliope, hurdy-gurdy, pipe organ, harmonium, electronic organ, accordion, harmonica, mouth organ, synthesizer; see also MUSICAL INSTRUMENT.

organic ***a.*** basic, vital, essential; see FUNDAMENTAL, NATURAL 1.

organically ***a.*** by nature, inevitably, wholly; see ESSENTIALLY, NATURALLY 2.

organism ***n.*** person, organic structure, physiological individual; see ANIMAL, BODY 1, PLANT.

organization ***n.*** **1** [The process or manner of organizing] establishment, plan, planning, ordering, creation, grouping, design, provision, working out, assembling, construction, regulation, systematization, system, method, coordination, adjustment, harmony, unity, correlation, standard, standardization, settlement, arrangement, disposition, alignment, institution, foundation, preparation, direction, structure, situation, formation, association, uniformity; see also CLASSIFICATION, ORDER 3.—*Ant.* CONFUSION, bedlam, chance. **2** [An organized body] aggregation, association, federation, combine, corporation, union, institute, trust, cartel, confederation, monopoly, combination, machine, business, industry, company, society, league, club, fraternity, sorority, house, order, alliance, party, cooperative, guild, profession, trade, coalition, syndicate, fellowship, lodge, brotherhood, sisterhood, confederacy, affiliation, body, band, team, squad, crew, clique, circle, set, troupe, group; see also SYSTEM.

organize ***v.*** **1** [To put in order] arrange, fix, straighten, standardize, compose, combine, systematize, methodize, coordinate, adjust, put in order, line up, regulate; see also CLASSIFY, ORDER 3. **2** [To form an organization] establish, build, found; see PLAN 2.

organized ***a.*** established, methodized, coordinated, systematized, systematic, constituted, directed, adjusted, assigned, distributed, grouped, fixed up, standardized, in order, in succession, in good form, placed, put away, orderly, in sequence, arranged, prepared, made ready, constructed, settled, composed, framed, planned, ranked, put in order, ordered, regulated, ranged, disposed, formulated, formed, fashioned, shaped, made, projected, designed, harmonized, related, correlated, founded, associated; see also CLASSIFIED.

or·gasm (ôr′gaz′əm) ***n.*** ⟦< Gr *organ,* to swell⟧ the climax of a sexual act

or·gy (ôr′jē) ***n.***, *pl.* **-gies** ⟦< Gr *orgia,* secret rites⟧ **1** a wild party, esp. with sexual activity **2** unrestrained indulgence in any activity

o·ri·el (ôr′ē əl, ôr′-) ***n.*** ⟦< ML *oriolum,* porch⟧ a bay window resting on a bracket or a corbel

o·ri·ent (ôr′ē ənt; *for v.*, -ent′, -ənt) ***n.*** ⟦< L *oriri,* arise: used of the rising sun⟧ [Old Poet.] the east —***vt.*** to adjust (oneself) to a particular situation, with regard to direction or position, etc. —**the Orient** the East, or Asia; esp. the Far East —**o′ri·en·ta′tion *n.***

O′ri·en′tal (-ent′'l) ***adj.*** of the Far East or its people, etc. —***n.*** a person born in the Far East or a member of a people of that region Now often regarded as a term of disparagement

or·i·fice (ôr′ə fis, är′-) ***n.*** ⟦< L *os,* a mouth + *facere,* make⟧ a mouth of a tube, cavity, etc.; opening

orig *abbrev.* **1** origin **2** original **3** originally

o·ri·ga·mi (ôr′ə gä′mē) ***n.*** ⟦Jpn⟧ the Japanese art of folding paper to form flowers, animals, etc.

or·i·gin (ôr′ə jin, är′-) ***n.*** ⟦< L *oriri,* to rise⟧ **1** a coming into existence or use; beginning **2** parentage; birth **3** source; root; cause

o·rig·i·nal (ə rij′i nəl) ***adj.*** **1** first; earliest **2** never having been before; new; novel **3** capable of creating something new **4** being that from which copies are made —***n.*** **1** a primary type that has given rise to varieties **2** an original work, as of art or literature —**o·rig′i·nal′i·ty** (-nal′ə tē) ***n.*** —**o·rig′i·nal·ly *adv.***

o·rig′i·nate′ (-nāt′) ***vt.*** **-nat′ed**, **-nat′ing** to bring into being; esp., to invent —***vi.*** to begin; start —**o·rig′i·na′tion *n.*** —**o·rig′i·na′tor *n.***

O-ring (ō′riŋ′) ***n.*** a ring-shaped seal of rubber, plastic, etc., used to prevent leaks

o·ri·ole (ôr′ē ōl′) ***n.*** ⟦< L *aurum,* gold⟧ a bright-orange and black American bird that builds a hanging nest

O·ri·on (ō rī′ən) ***n.*** a very bright equatorial constellation

Or·lon (ôr′län′) *trademark for* a synthetic acrylic fiber similar to nylon, or a fabric made from this fiber

or·mo·lu (ôr′mə lo͞o′) ***n.*** ⟦Fr *or moulu,* ground gold⟧ a copper and tin alloy used to imitate gold

or·na·ment (ôr′nə mənt; *for v.*, -ment′) ***n.*** ⟦< L *ornare,* adorn⟧ **1** anything that adorns; decoration **2** one whose character or talent adds luster to the surroundings, etc. —***vt.*** to decorate —**or′na·men′tal *adj.*** —**or′na·men·ta′tion *n.***

or·nate (ôr nāt′) ***adj.*** ⟦< L *ornare,* adorn⟧ heavily ornamented; showy —**or·nate′ly *adv.*** —**or·nate′ness *n.***

or·ner·y (ôr′nər ē) ***adj.*** ⟦< ORDINARY⟧ [Inf.] **1** mean; nasty **2** obstinate —**or′ner·i·ness *n.***

or·ni·thol·o·gy (ôr′nə thäl′ə jē) ***n.*** ⟦< Gr *ornis,* bird + -LOGY⟧ the branch of zoology dealing with birds —**or′ni·thol′o·gist *n.***

o·ro·tund (ôr′ə tund′) ***adj.*** ⟦< L *os,* mouth + *rotundas,* round⟧ **1** resonant: said of the voice **2** bombastic or pompous

or·phan (ôr′fən) ***n.*** ⟦< Gr *orphanos*⟧ a child whose parents are dead —***adj.*** **1** being an orphan **2** of or for orphans —***vt.*** to cause to become an orphan

or′phan·age (-ij) ***n.*** an institution that is a home for orphans

Or·phe·us (ôr′fē əs) ***n.*** *Gr. Myth.* a poet-musician with magic musical powers

or·ris (ôr′is, är′-) ***n.*** ⟦< Gr *iris,* iris⟧ a European iris, esp. one with a root (**or′ris·root′**) pulverized for perfumery, etc.

ortho- ⟦< Gr *orthos,* straight⟧ *combining form* **1** straight *[orthodontics]* **2** proper; correct *[orthography]* Also **orth-**

or·tho·don·tics (ôr′thə dän′tiks) ***n.*** ⟦< ORTH(O)- + Gr *odōn,* tooth + -ICS⟧ the branch of dentistry concerned with correcting tooth irregularities: also **or′tho·don′tia** (-dän′shə, -shē ə) —**or′tho·don′tist *n.***

or·tho·dox (ôr′thə däks′) ***adj.*** ⟦< Gr *orthos,* straight + *doxa,* opinion⟧ conforming to the usual beliefs or established doctrines; approved or conventional —**or′tho·dox′y**, *pl.* **-ies**, ***n.***

or·thog·ra·phy (ôr thäg′rə fē) ***n.***, *pl.* **-phies** ⟦< Gr: see ORTHO- & -GRAPHY⟧ **1** correct spelling **2** spelling as a subject for study —**or·tho·graph·ic** (ôr′thə graf′ik) ***adj.***

or·tho·pe·dics or **or·tho·pae·dics** (ôr′thə pē′diks) ***n.*** ⟦< Gr *orthos,* straight + *paideia,* training of children⟧ the branch of medicine dealing with deformities, diseases, and injuries of the bones, joints, muscles, etc. —**or′tho·pe′dic** or **or′tho·pae′dic *adj.*** —**or′tho·pe′dist** or **or′tho·pae′dist *n.***

-o·ry (ôr′ē, ər ē) ⟦< L *-orius*⟧ *suffix* **1** of, having the nature of *[sensory]* **2** a place or thing for *[crematory]*

OS *abbrev.* Old Saxon

O·sa·ka (ō′sä kə) seaport in S Honshu, Japan: pop. 2,648,000

os·cil·late (äs′ə lāt′) ***vi.*** **-lat′ed**, **-lat′ing** ⟦< L *oscillum,* a swing⟧ **1** to swing to and fro **2** to vacillate **3** *Physics* to vary regularly between high and low values: said as of an electric current —**os′cil·la′tion *n.*** —**os′cil·la′tor *n.***

os·cil·lo·scope (ə sil′ə skōp′) ***n.*** ⟦< L *oscillare,* to swing + -SCOPE⟧ an instrument that visually displays an electrical wave on a fluorescent screen

os·cu·late (äs′kyo͞o lāt′, -kyə-) ***vt.***, ***vi.*** **-lat′ed**, **-lat′ing** ⟦< L

THESAURUS

Orient ***n.*** **1** [Eastern Asia] Far East, Asia, China, India, Japan, Vietnam, Thailand, Laos, Hong Kong, Cambodia, Korea, Myanmar, the mysterious East, land of the rising sun.—*Ant.* Occident, Europe, West. **2** [Southwestern Asia] Near East, Middle East, Levant, Egypt, Fertile Crescent, Turkey, Syria, Lebanon, Israel, Jordan, Iraq, Iran, Persia, Muslim world, Arabia, the Golden Crescent; see also EAST 2.

orientation ***n.*** familiarization, bearings, introduction; see ADJUSTMENT, INTRODUCTION 3, 4.

origin ***n.*** **1** [The act of beginning] rise, start, foundation; see BIRTH. **2** [The place or time of beginning] source, spring, issue, fountain, inlet, derivation, root, stem, shoot, twig, sapling, portal, door, gate, gateway, fountainhead, wellspring, font, fount, birthplace, cradle, nest, womb, reservoir, infancy, babyhood, childhood, youth.—*Ant.* RESULT, outcome, issue. **3** [Cause] seed, germ, stock, parentage, ancestry, parent, ancestor, egg, sperm, embryo, principle, element, nucleus, first cause, author, creator, prime mover, producer, causation, source, influence, generator, occasion, root, spring, antecedent, motive, inspiration; see also CAUSE.—*Ant.* RESULT, consequence, conclusion.

original ***a.*** **1** [Pertaining to the source] primary, primeval, primordial, rudimentary, elementary, inceptive, in embryo, fundamental, primitive, initial, beginning, commencing, starting, opening, dawning, incipient; see also FIRST.—*Ant.* LATE, recent, developed. **2** [Creative] originative, productive, causal, causative, generative, imaginative, inventive, thoughtful, ingenious, innovative, unconventional, clever, fresh, nonconformist, formative, resourceful, ready, quick, seminal, envisioning, sensitive, archetypal, inspiring, devising, conceiving, fertile, fashioning, molding.—*Ant.* STUPID, imitative, unproductive. **3** [Not copied] primary, principal, first, genuine, new, firsthand, uncopied, fresh, novel, independent, one, sole, lone, single, solitary, authentic, unique, pure, rare, unusual, not translated, not copied, not imitated, real, absolute.—*Ant.* IMITATED, copied, repeated.

originality ***n.*** creativeness, inventiveness, creative spirit, creativity, nonconformity, modernity, intellectual, independence, innovation, invention, ingenuity, conception, authenticity, novelty, freshness, newness, individuality, brilliance; see also IMAGINATION.

originally ***a.*** **1** [In an original manner] imaginatively, creatively, ingeniously, inventively, startlingly, freshly, in a new fashion, independently, artistically. **2** [In the beginning] first, incipiently, basically; see FORMERLY.

originate ***v.*** start, introduce, found; see BEGIN 1.

originated ***a.*** introduced, started, commenced; see BEGUN.

ornament ***n.*** embellishment, adornment, beautification; see DECORATION 2.

ornamental ***a.*** **1** [Intended for ornament] fancy, luxurious, showy; see ELABORATE 1, ORNATE. **2** [Beautiful] delicate, exquisite, lovely; see BEAUTIFUL.

ornate ***a.*** showy, gaudy, sumptuous, lavish, bright, colored, tinseled, jeweled, embroidered, glossy, burnished, polished, gorgeous, pompous, stylish, magnificent, adorned, trimmed, gilded, embellished, inlaid, garnished, flowered, glowing, vivid, radiant, fine, alluring, dazzling, sparkling, shining, flashing, glistening, glamorous, artificial, pretentious, baroque, rococo, tawdry, flashy; see also ELABORATE 1.

orphan ***n.*** foundling, ragamuffin, parentless child, orphaned child, waif, stray; see also CHILD.

orphanage ***n.*** orphans' home, institution, foundling home; see SCHOOL 1.

orthodox ***a.*** customary, standard, doctrinal; see CONSERVATIVE, CONVENTIONAL 1, 3.

osculum, little mouth⟧ to kiss: a facetious usage —**os′cu·la′tion** ***n.***

-ose[1] (ōs) ⟦Fr < (*gluc*)*ose*⟧ *suffix* **1** a carbohydrate *[sucrose]* **2** the product of a protein hydrolysis

-ose[2] (ōs) ⟦L *-osus*⟧ *suffix* full of, like

Osh·kosh (äsh′käsh′) city in E Wisconsin: pop. 55,000

o·sier (ō′zhər) ***n.*** ⟦< ML *auseria*, willow⟧ a willow with branches used for baskets and furniture

-o·sis (ō′sis) ⟦< Gr⟧ *suffix* **1** condition, action *[hypnosis]* **2** an abnormal or diseased condition *[psychosis]*

Os·lo (äz′lō, äs′-) seaport & capital of Norway: pop. 459,000

os·mo·sis (äs mō′sis, äz-) ***n.*** ⟦< Gr *ōsmos*, impulse⟧ **1** the tendency of fluids to pass through a membrane so as to equalize concentrations on both sides **2** the movement of fluids through a membrane **3** an apparently effortless absorption of ideas, feelings, etc. —**os·mot′ic** (-mät′ik) ***adj.***

os·prey (äs′prē, -prā) ***n.***, *pl.* **-preys** ⟦< L *os*, a bone + *frangere*, to break⟧ a large diving bird that feeds mainly on fish

os·si·fy (äs′ə fī′) ***vt.***, ***vi.*** **-fied′**, **-fy′ing** ⟦< L *os*, a bone + -FY⟧ **1** to change into bone **2** to fix rigidly in a custom, practice, etc. —**os′si·fi·ca′tion** ***n.***

os·ten·si·ble (ä sten′sə bəl) ***adj.*** ⟦< L *ostendere*, to show⟧ apparent; seeming —**os·ten′si·bly** ***adv.***

os·ten·ta·tion (äs′tən tā′shən) ***n.*** ⟦< L *ostendere*, to show⟧ showy display; pretentiousness —**os′ten·ta′tious** ***adj.***

osteo- ⟦< Gr *osteon*, a bone⟧ *combining form* bone or bones

os·te·o·ar·thri·tis (äs′tē ō′är thrīt′is) ***n.*** ⟦prec. + ARTHRITIS⟧ a common form of arthritis marked by cartilage degeneration and bone enlargement

os·te·op·a·thy (äs′tē äp′ə thē) ***n.*** ⟦ModL: see OSTEO- & -PATHY⟧ a school of medicine and surgery that emphasizes the interrelationship of muscles and bones to other body systems —**os·te·o·path** (äs′tē ə path′) ***n.*** —**os′te·o·path′ic** ***adj.***

os·te·o·po·ro·sis (äs′tē ō′pə rō′sis) ***n.*** ⟦OSTEO- + L *porus*, a pore + -OSIS⟧ a bone disorder marked by porous, brittle bones

os·to·my (äs′tə mē) ***n.***, *pl.* **-mies** any surgery connecting a hollow organ to the outside of the body or to another hollow organ

os·tra·cize (äs′trə sīz′) ***vt.*** **-cized′**, **-ciz′ing** ⟦< Gr *ostrakon*, a shell or potsherd (cast as a ballot)⟧ to banish from a group, society, etc. —**os′tra·cism′** (-siz′əm) ***n.***

os·trich (äs′trich, ôs′-) ***n.*** ⟦< L *avis*, bird + *struthio*, ostrich⟧ a large, swift-running bird of Africa and SW Asia

OT *abbrev.* **1** Old Testament **2** overtime

O·thel·lo (ō thel′ō) ***n.*** the title character of a tragedy by Shakespeare

oth·er (u*th*′ər) ***adj.*** ⟦OE⟧ **1** being the remaining one or ones *[*Bill and the *other* boys*]* **2** different or distinct from that or those referred to or implied *[*use your *other* foot*]* **3** additional *[*he has no *other* coat*]* —***pron.*** **1** the other one **2** some other one *[*do as *others* do*]* —***adv.*** otherwise *[*he can't do *other* than go*]* —**the other day** (or **night**, etc.) on a recent day (or night, etc.)

oth′er·wise′ ***adv.*** **1** in another manner; differently *[*she believes *otherwise]* **2** in all other respects *[*he is *otherwise* intelligent*]* **3** in other circumstances **4** if not *[*do it now; *otherwise*, you'll forget it*]* —***adj.*** different

oth′er·world′ly ***adj.*** being apart from earthly interests; spiritual

o·ti·ose (ō′shē ōs′) ***adj.*** ⟦< L *otium*, leisure⟧ **1** futile **2** useless

Ot·ta·wa (ät′ə wə, -wä′) capital of Canada, in SE Ontario: pop. 323,000

ot·ter (ät′ər) ***n.*** ⟦OE *oter*⟧ **1** a furry, carnivorous mammal with webbed feet **2** its fur

ot·to·man (ät′ə mən) ***n.*** ⟦Fr *ottomane*⟧ a low, cushioned seat or footstool

ouch (ouch) ***interj.*** used to express sudden pain

ought (ôt) ***v.aux.*** used with infinitives and meaning: **1** to be compelled by obligation, duty, or desirability *[*you *ought* to eat more*]* **2** to be expected *[*it *ought* to be over soon*]*

oui (wē) ***adv.***, ***interj.*** ⟦Fr⟧ yes

Oui·ja (wē′jə, -jē) ⟦< prec. + Ger *ja*, yes⟧ *trademark for* a board with the alphabet and various symbols on it and a sliding pointer: believed by some to convey messages from spirits

ounce (ouns) ***n.*** ⟦< L *uncia*, a twelfth⟧ **1** a unit of weight, $\frac{1}{16}$ pound avoirdupois or $\frac{1}{12}$ pound troy **2** fluid ounce, $\frac{1}{16}$ pint

our (our) ***poss. pronominal adj.*** ⟦OE *ure*⟧ of, belonging to, or done by us

ours (ourz) ***pron.*** that or those belonging to us: poss. form of WE *[*that book is *ours*; *ours* are better*]*

our·selves (our selvz′) ***pron.*** a form of WE, used as an intensive *[*we went *ourselves]*, as a reflexive *[*we saw *ourselves* in the mirror*]*, or with the meaning "our true selves" *[*we are not *ourselves* when we are sick*]*

-ous (əs) ⟦< L *-osus*⟧ *suffix* having, full of, characterized by *[beauteous]*

oust (oust) ***vt.*** ⟦< L *ostare*, obstruct⟧ to force out; expel; dispossess

oust′er ***n.*** an ousting or being ousted

out (out) ***adv.*** ⟦OE *ut*⟧ **1** away or removed from a place, position, etc. **2** into the open air **3** into existence or activity *[*disease broke *out]* **4** *a*) to a conclusion *[*argue it *out]* *b*) completely *[*tired *out]* **5** into sight or notice *[*the moon came *out]* **6** from existence or activity *[*fade *out]* **7** aloud *[*sing *out]* **8** beyond a regular surface, condition, etc. *[*stand *out]* **9** into disuse *[*long skirts went *out]* **10** from a group or stock *[*pick *out]* **11** [Slang] into uncon-

THESAURUS

ostentatious ***a.*** showy, pretentious, pompous; see EGOTISTIC.

ostracize ***v.*** exile, expel, outlaw; see BANISH.

other ***a.*** being one of two, remaining, another, the other, some other, former, recent, future, besides, additional, different, separate, distinct, opposite, across from; see also EXTRA.

other ***pron.*** one of two, another one, some other, the one remaining, the part remaining, the alternate, the alternative; see also ANOTHER.—*Ant.* THIS, that, the first choice.

others ***pron.*** unnamed persons, the remainder, some, a few, any others, a number, a handful, a small number, not many, hardly any, two or three, more than one, many, a great number, a great many, they, folks, the rest; see also EVERYBODY.—*Ant.* NONE, no one, not any.

otherwise ***a.*** **1** [In another way] in a different way, contrarily, in an opposed way, under other conditions, in different circumstances, on the other hand, in other respects, in other ways.—*Ant.* LIKE, so, in like manner. **2** [Introducing an alternative threat] unless you do, with this exception, except on these conditions, barring this, in any other circumstances, except that, without this, unless ... then, other than; see also UNLESS.—*Ant.* THEREFORE, hence, as a result.

ought (to) ***v.*** should, have to, need to, had better, might, will, shall; it is necessary, is fitting, is becoming, is expedient, behooves, is reasonable, is logical, is natural, requires, is in need of; see also MUST.

ounce ***n.*** measure, troy ounce, avoirdupois ounce, fluid ounce, one sixteenth of a pound (avoirdupois), one sixteenth of a pint, one twelfth of a pound (troy); see also MEASURE 1.

our ***poss. pronominal adj.*** of our own, belonging to us, owned by us, used by us, due to us, a part of us, of interest to us, done by us, accomplished by us, in our employ, with us, near us, of us.

ourselves ***pron.*** us, the speakers, individually, personally, privately, without help, our own selves*; see also WE.

oust ***v.*** eject, discharge, dispossess, evict, dislodge, remove, deprive, expel, drive out, force out, show the door, chase out, cast out, depose, dethrone, disinherit, banish, boot out*, bundle off, send packing*, give the gate*, pack off*.

ousted ***a.*** deposed, fired, defeated; see BEATEN 1, DISCHARGED.

out ***a.***, ***prep.*** **1** [In motion from within] out of, away from, from, from within, out from, out toward, outward, on the way.—*Ant.* IN, in from, into. **2** [Not situated within] not inside, not within, on the outer side, on the surface, external, extrinsic, outer, outdoors, out-of-doors, unconcealed, open, exposed, in the open; see also OUTSIDE, WITHOUT.—*Ant.* WITHIN, inside, on the inner side. **3** [Beyond] distant, removed, removed from; see AWAY, BEYOND. **4** [Continued to the limit or near it] ended, accomplished, fulfilled; see DONE 1, FINISHED 1. **5** [Not at home or at one's office] not in, away, busy, on vacation, at lunch, gone, left; see also ABSENT.—*Ant.* IN, receiving, not busy. **6** [*Unconscious] insensible, out cold, blotto*; see UNCONSCIOUS. **7** [Wanting] lacking, missing, without; see WANTING 1. —**all out*** wholeheartedly, with great effort, entirely; see COMPLETELY. —**out of** **1** [Having none in stock] not having any of, without, needing to reorder; see SOLD OUT. **2** [From] out from, away from, from within; see FROM. **3** [Beyond] outside, on the outskirts, on the border of; see BEYOND.

out* ***n.*** means of escape, way out, excuse; see ESCAPE, EXPLANATION.

sciousness **12** *Baseball* in a manner that results in an out *[to fly out]* —*adj.* **1** external: usually in combination *[outpost]* **2** beyond regular limits **3** away from work, etc. **4** in error *[out in one's estimates]* **5** not in use, operation, etc. **6** [Inf.] having suffered a financial loss *[out twenty dollars]* **7** [Inf.] outmoded **8** *Baseball* having failed to get on base —*prep.* **1** out of **2** along, and away from a central location —*n.* **1** something that is out **2** [Slang] a way out; excuse **3** *Baseball* the failure of a player to reach base safely —*vi.* to become known *[the truth will out]* —*vt.* [Inf.] to identify (a person) publicly as a homosexual —**on the outs** [Inf.] on unfriendly terms —**out for** trying to get or do —**out of 1** from inside of **2** beyond **3** from (material, etc.) *[made out of stone]* **4** because of *[out of spite]* **5** having no *[out of gas]* **6** so as to deprive —**out to** trying to

out- *combining form* **1** at or from a point away, outside, etc. *[outpatient]* **2** going away or forth, outward *[outbound]* **3** better or more than *[outdo]*

out'age *n.* an interruption of operation, as of electric power

out'-and-out' *adj.* thorough

out'back' *n.* any remote, sparsely settled region viewed as uncivilized

out'bid' *vt.* **-bid', -bid'ding** to bid or offer more than (someone else)

out'board' *adj.* outside the hull of a ship or boat *[an outboard motor]*

out'bound' *adj.* outward bound

out'break' *n.* a breaking out; sudden occurrence, as of disease or rioting

out'build'ing *n.* a structure, as a shed, separate from the main building

out'burst' *n.* a sudden release, as of feeling or energy

out'cast' *adj.* driven out; rejected —*n.* a person rejected, as by society

out'class' *vt.* to surpass

out'come' *n.* result; consequence

out'crop' *n.* **1** the emergence of a mineral at the earth's surface **2** the mineral that so emerges

out'cry' *n., pl.* **-cries'** **1** a crying out **2** a strong objection

out'dat'ed *adj.* no longer current

out'dis'tance *vt.* **-tanced, -tanc·ing** to get ahead of, as in a race

out'do' *vt.* **-did', -done', -do'ing** to exceed or surpass —**outdo oneself** to do better than one expected to do

out'door' *adj.* **1** being or taking place outdoors **2** of or fond of the outdoors

out'doors' *adv.* in or into the open; outside —*n.* any area outside a building

out'er *adj.* farther out or away

out'er·most' *adj.* farthest out

outer space space beyond the earth's atmosphere or beyond the solar system

out'er·wear' *n.* garments, as overcoats, worn over the usual clothing

out'field' *n.* *Baseball* **1** the playing area beyond the infield **2** the players (**out'field'ers**) positioned there

out'fit' *n.* **1** the equipment used in an activity **2** clothing worn together; ensemble **3** a group associated in an activity —*vt.* **-fit'ted, -fit'ting** to furnish as with an outfit —**out'fit'ter** *n.*

out'flank' *vt.* to go around and beyond the flank of (enemy troops)

out'fox' *vt.* to outsmart

out'go' *n., pl.* **-goes'** that which is paid out; expenditure

out'go'ing *adj.* **1** *a)* leaving *b)* retiring from office **2** sociable, friendly, etc.

out'grow' *vt.* **-grew', -grown', -grow'ing** **1** to grow faster or larger than **2** to lose in becoming mature **3** to grow too large for

out'growth' *n.* **1** a growing out or that which grows out **2** a result or development

out'guess' *vt.* to outwit in anticipating

out'house' *n.* a small outdoor structure used as a toilet, having a seat with a hole over a deep pit

out'ing *n.* **1** a pleasure trip **2** an outdoor walk, ride, etc.

out'land'ish (-lan'dish) *adj.* very odd or strange; fantastic; bizarre

out'last' *vt.* to endure longer than

out'law' *n.* a habitual or notorious criminal —*vt.* to declare illegal

out'lay' *n.* **1** a spending (*of* money, etc.) **2** money, etc. spent

out'let' *n.* **1** a passage for letting something out **2** a means of expression *[an outlet for anger]* **3** a retail store selling defective or surplus goods at a discount: in full **outlet store** **4** a point in an electric circuit where a plug can be inserted to connect with a power supply

out'line' *n.* **1** a line bounding the limits of an object **2** a sketch showing only contours **3** [*also pl.*] a general plan

THESAURUS

outage *n.* interruption of service, blackout, dimout, brownout, failure of electrical service; see also INTERRUPTION.

out-and-out *a.* complete, entire, total; see COMPLETELY.

outbid *v.* offer higher than, raise the price, bid something up; see PAY 1.

outbreak *n.* **1** [A sudden violent appearance] eruption, explosion, outburst, disruption, burst, bursting forth, detonation, thunder, commotion, rending, break, breaking out, breaking forth, gush, gushing forth, outpouring, pouring forth, tumult, discharge, blast, blowup, crash, roar, earthquake, squall, paroxysm, spasm, convulsion, fit, effervescence, boiling, flash, flare, crack.—*Ant.* PEACE, tranquillity, quiet. **2** [Sudden violence] fury, mutiny, brawl; see DISORDER, REVOLUTION 2.

outburst *n.* discharge, upheaval, eruption; see DISTURBANCE 2, OUTBREAK 1.

outcast *a.* vagabond, driven out, hounded, untouchable, rejected, thrown aside, pushed out, disgraced, hunted, not accepted by society, cast out, degraded, expelled, outlawed, cast away, exiled, expatriated, serving a life sentence, having a price on one's head.

outcast *n.* fugitive, pariah, untouchable; see REFUGEE.

outcome *n.* issue, upshot, consequence; see END 2, RESULT.

outcrop *n.* bared soil, exposed surface, projecting land mass; see EARTH 2, LAND 1.

outcry *n.* complaint, clamor, scream; see OBJECTION.

outdated *a.* outmoded, out of fashion, antiquated; see OLD 3.

outdo *v.* surpass, best, beat; see EXCEED.

outdone *a.* defeated, bettered, improved upon; see BEATEN 1.

outdoor *a.* outside, airy, out-of-doors, open-air, out of the house, out in the open, free, unrestricted, rustic, free and easy, healthful; see also OUTDOORS.—*Ant.* interior, indoor, in the house.

outdoors *a.* out-of-doors, outdoor, without, out of the house, outside, on the outside, in the yard, in the open, in the garden, into the street.

outdoors *n.* the out-of-doors, natural scenery, fresh air, garden, patio, woods, hills, mountains, stream, Mother Nature, the great outdoors, countryside, the country, environment, nature.—*Ant.* INSIDE, domestic matters, household concerns.

outer *a.* outward, without, external, exterior, foreign, alien to, beyond, exposed; see also OUTSIDE.—*Ant.* INNER, inward, inside.

outer space *n.* infinity, the heavens, the universe; see SPACE 1.

outfield *n.* left field, deep left, center field, deep center, right field, deep right; see also BASEBALL, FIELD 2.

outfielder *n.* right fielder, center fielder, left fielder; see BASEBALL PLAYER.

outfit *n.* trappings, paraphernalia, gear; see EQUIPMENT.

outfit *v.* equip, fit out, supply; see PROVIDE 1.

outflank *v.* bypass, surround, outmaneuver; see DEFEAT 2, PASS 1.

outgo *n.* costs, losses, outflow; see EXPENSES.

outgoing *a.* sociable, civil, kind; see FRIENDLY.

outgrowth *n.* end result, outcome, effect; see END 2, RESULT.

outhouse *n.* latrine, privy, shed; see TOILET.

outing *n.* excursion, airing, drive; see VACATION.

outlandish *a.* odd, strange, foreign; see UNUSUAL.

outlast *v.* outlive, outwear, remain; see ENDURE 1, SURVIVE 1.

outlaw *n.* fugitive, bandit, desperado; see CRIMINAL.

outlaw *v.* make illegal, stop, ban; see BANISH, CONDEMN.

outlawed *a.* stopped, banned, prevented; see ILLEGAL.

outlet *n.* **1** [An opening] break, crack, exit; see HOLE 1. **2** [An electric terminal] socket, double socket, triple socket, wall plug, floor plug, electric service connection.

outline *n.* **1** [A skeletonized plan] frame, sketch, framework; see PLAN 1. **2** [The line surrounding an object; *often plural*] contour, side, boundary; see EDGE 1, FRAME 2. **3** [A shape seen in outline] silhouette, profile, configuration, shape, figure, formation, aspect, appearance; see also FORM 1.

outline *v.* **1** [To draw] sketch, paint, describe; see DRAW 2. **2** [To plan] block out, draft, sketch; see PLAN 2.

4 a systematic summary —*vt.* **-lined′**, **-lin′ing** **1** to draw in outline **2** to give or write the main points of
out′live′ *vt.* **-lived′**, **-liv′ing** to live or endure longer than; outlast
out′look′ *n.* **1** the view from a place **2** viewpoint **3** expectation or prospect
out′ly′ing *adj.* relatively far out from a certain point; remote
out′ma·neu′ver or **out′ma·noeu′vre** *vt.* **-vered** or **-vred**, **-ver·ing** or **-vring** to outwit by maneuvering
out′match′ *vt.* to be superior to; outdo
out′mod′ed *adj.* no longer in fashion or accepted; obsolete
out′num′ber *vt.* to exceed in number
out′-of-date′ *adj.* no longer in style or use; old-fashioned
out′-of-doors′ *adj.* OUTDOOR —*adv.*, *n.* OUTDOORS
out′-of-the-way′ *adj.* **1** secluded **2** not common; unusual
out′-of-town′er *n.* a visitor from another town or city
out′pa′tient *n.* a patient treated at a hospital, etc. without becoming an inpatient
out′place′ment *n.* assistance in finding a new job, provided to an employee by the employer
out′play′ *vt.* to play better than
out′post′ *n.* **1** *Mil. a)* a small group stationed at a distance from the main force *b)* the station occupied by such a group *c)* a foreign base **2** a frontier settlement
out′put′ *n.* **1** the work done or amount produced, esp. over a given period **2** information delivered by a computer **3** *Elec.* the useful voltage, current, or power delivered
out′rage′ *n.* ⟦ult. < L *ultra*, beyond⟧ **1** an extremely vicious or violent act **2** a deep insult or offense **3** great anger, etc. aroused by this —*vt.* **-raged′**, **-rag′ing** **1** to commit an outrage upon or against **2** to cause outrage in
out′ra′geous (-rā′jəs) *adj.* **1** involving or doing great injury or wrong **2** very offensive or shocking — **out′ra′geous·ly** *adv.* —**out′ra′geous·ness** *n.*
out′rank′ *vt.* to exceed in rank
ou·tré (o͞o trā′) *adj.* ⟦Fr⟧ **1** exaggerated **2** eccentric; bizarre
out·reach (out′rēch′; *for v., also* out′rēch′) *vt.*, *vi.* to reach farther (than) —*n.* a reaching out —*adj.* designating or of a program extending assistance, services, etc. to people in the community
out′rid′er *n.* **1** a rider on horseback who accompanies a stagecoach, etc. **2** a cowboy riding a range, as to keep cattle from straying **3** a forerunner
out′rig′ger (-rig′ər) *n.* **1** a timber rigged out from the side of certain canoes to prevent tipping **2** a canoe of this type
out·right (out′rīt′, out′rīt′) *adj.* **1** without reservation **2** complete —*adv.* **1** entirely **2** openly **3** at once

out′run′ *vt.* **-ran′**, **-run′**, **-run′ning** **1** to run faster than **2** to exceed
out′sell′ *vt.* **-sold′**, **-sell′ing** to sell in greater amounts than
out′set′ *n.* a setting out; beginning
out′shine′ *vt.* **-shone′** or **-shined′**, **-shin′ing** **1** to shine brighter or longer than (another) **2** to surpass; excel
out·side (out′sīd′, out′sīd′) *n.* **1** the outer side or part; exterior **2** outward appearance **3** any area not inside —*adj.* **1** of or on the outside; outer **2** extreme [an *outside* estimate] **3** slight [an *outside* chance] —*adv.* **1** on or to the outside **2** outdoors —*prep.* **1** on or to the outer side of **2** beyond the limits of —**outside of** **1** outside **2** [Inf.] other than
out·sid·er (out′sīd′ər, out′sīd′ər) *n.* one who is not included in a given group
out′size′ *n.* an unusually large size —*adj.* unusually large
out′skirts′ *pl.n.* districts remote from the center, as of a city
out′smart′ *vt.* to overcome by cunning or cleverness; outwit —**outsmart oneself** to have one's efforts at cunning or cleverness result in one's own disadvantage
out′source′ *vt.* **-sourced′**, **-sourc′ing** to transfer (manufacturing tasks, etc.) to outside contractors, esp. in order to reduce operating costs
out′spo′ken *adj.* **1** unrestrained in speech **2** spoken boldly or candidly
out′spread′ *adj.* spread out; extended
out′stand′ing *adj.* **1** prominent; distinguished **2** unpaid; uncollected **3** issued and sold: said of stocks and bonds
out′sta′tion *n.* a post or station in a remote or unsettled area
out′stretch′ *vt.* to stretch out; extend
out′strip′ *vt.* **-stripped′**, **-strip′ping** **1** to go at a faster pace than **2** to excel; surpass
out′take′ *n.* a filmed scene, defective recording, etc. not used as or in the final version
out′vote′ *vt.* **-vot′ed**, **-vot′ing** to defeat in a vote
out′ward *adj.* **1** having to do with the outside; outer **2** clearly apparent **3** away from the interior —*adv.* toward the outside: also **out′wards** —**out′ward·ly** *adv.*
out′wear′ *vt.* **-wore′**, **-worn′**, **-wear′ing** to outlast
out′weigh′ *vt.* **1** to weigh more than **2** to be more important than
out′wit′ *vt.* **-wit′ted**, **-wit′ting** to get the better of by cleverness
o·va (ō′və) *n. pl. of* OVUM
o·val (ō′vəl) *adj.* ⟦< L *ovum*, egg⟧ egg-shaped; elliptical —*n.* anything oval
o·va·ry (ō′və rē) *n.*, *pl.* **-ries** ⟦< L *ovum*, egg⟧ **1** a female

THESAURUS

outlined *a.* **1** [Marked in outline] bounded, edged, bordered, circumscribed, marked, delineated, surrounded, banded, configurated. **2** [Given in summary] charted, summarized, surveyed; see PLANNED.
outlive *v.* live longer than, outlast, survive; see ENDURE 1.
outlook *n.* **1** [Point of view] scope, vision, standpoint; see VIEWPOINT. **2** [Apparent future] probability, prospects, likelihood, possibility, chances, opportunity, appearances, probable future, openings, normal course of events, probabilities, risk, law of averages.
outlying *a.* afar, far-off, external; see DISTANT.
outnumbered *a.* exceeded, bested, overcome; see BEATEN 1.
out-of-date *a.* obsolete, passé, antiquated; see OLD-FASHIONED.
out-of-the-way *a.* far-off, secluded, isolated; see DISTANT.
outplay *v.* overcome, surpass, beat; see DEFEAT 3.
outpost *n.* forward position, listening post, point of attack; see BOUNDARY, POSITION 1.
output *n.* yield, amount, crop; see PRODUCE.
outrage *n.* indignity, abuse, affront; see INSULT.
outrage *v.* offend, wrong, affront; see ABUSE, INSULT.
outrageous *a.* wanton, notorious, shameless, disgraceful, brazen, barefaced, gross, scandalous, disorderly, insulting, affronting, abusive, oppressive, dishonorable, injurious, glaring, offensive, heinous, intolerable, execrable, unspeakable, shameful, horrifying, immoderate, extreme, flagrant, contemptible, ignoble, malevolent, odious, monstrous, atrocious, nefarious, vicious, iniquitous, wicked, shocking, violent, unbearable, villainous, infamous, corrupt, degenerate, criminal, sinful, vile, abominable.—*Ant.* EXCELLENT, laudable, honorable.
outright *a.* out-and-out, unmitigated, unconditional; see COMPLETELY, OBVIOUS 1.
outset *n.* start, beginning, source; see ORIGIN 2.
outside *a.* extreme, outermost, farthest, apart from, external, away from, farther; see also OUTER.—*Ant.* INNER, inside, interior.
outside *n.* **1** [An outer surface] exterior, outer side, surface, skin, cover, covering, topside, upper side, front side, face, appearance, outer aspect, seeming.—*Ant.* INSIDE, interior, inner side. **2** [The limit] outline, border, bounds; see BOUNDARY, EDGE 1, END 4. —**at the outside** at the most, at the absolute limit, not more than; see MOST.
outsider *n.* foreigner, stranger, refugee; see ALIEN.
outskirts *n.* border, suburbs, limits; see BOUNDARY, EDGE 1.
outspoken *a.* blunt, candid, artless; see FRANK.
outspread *a.* spread out, expanded, extended; see WIDESPREAD.
outstanding *a.* conspicuous, leading, notable; see DISTINGUISHED 2.
outward *a.* **1** [In an outward direction] out, toward the edge, from within; see OUTER, OUTSIDE. **2** [To outward appearance] on the surface, visible, to the eye; see OBVIOUS 1, OPEN 1.
outwear *v.* remain after, last longer than, outlast; see CONTINUE 1, ENDURE 1, SURVIVE 1.
outweigh *v.* **1** [To exceed in weight] overbalance, overweigh, weigh more than, go beyond; see also BURDEN. **2** [To exceed in importance] excel, surpass, outrun; see EXCEED.
outwit *v.* baffle, trick, bewilder; see CONFUSE, DECEIVE.
outwitted *a.* tricked, outsmarted, taken*; see DECEIVED.
oval *a.* egg-shaped, elliptical, ellipsoid; see OBLONG.

reproductive gland producing eggs **2** *Bot.* the enlarged, hollow part of the pistil, containing ovules —**o·var·i·an** (ō ver′ē ən) ***adj.***

o·vate (ō′vāt′) ***adj.*** egg-shaped; oval

o·va·tion (ō vā′shən) ***n.*** ⟦< L *ovare,* celebrate a triumph⟧ enthusiastic applause or an enthusiastic public welcome

ov·en (uv′ən) ***n.*** ⟦OE *ofen*⟧ a compartment or receptacle for baking, roasting, heating, etc.

ov′en·proof′ ***adj.*** able to withstand the high temperatures of an oven without being damaged

o·ver (ō′vər) ***prep.*** ⟦OE *ofer*⟧ **1** *a)* in, at, or to a position above *b)* across and down from *[to fall over a cliff]* **2** so as to cover *[shutters over the windows]* **3** upon *[to cast a spell over someone]* **4** above in authority, power, etc. **5** on or to the other side of *[fly over the lake]* **6** throughout *[over the whole city]* **7** during *[over the years]* **8** more than *[over ten cents]* **9** in preference to **10** concerning —***adv.*** **1** *a)* above or across *b)* across the brim or edge **2** more *[three hours or over]* **3** from start to finish *[think it over]* **4** *a)* from an upright position *[to fall over]* *b)* upside down *[turn the cup over]* **5** again *[do it over]* **6** at, on, to, or in a specified place *[over in Spain]* **7** from one belief, etc. to another *[win him over]* —***adj.*** **1** upper, outer, superior, excessive, or extra *[overseer]* **2** finished; past **3** having reached the other side **4** [Inf.] as a surplus; extra

over- *combining form* **1** above in position, rank, etc. *[overlord]* **2** passing across or beyond *[overrun]* **3** excessively *[oversell]* The list below includes some common compounds formed with *over-* that can be understood if "too much" or "excessively" is added to the meaning of the base word:

overabundance	**overgenerous**
overactive	**overheat**
overambitious	**overindulge**
overanxious	**overindulgence**
overbid	**overload**
overburden	**overpay**
overcautious	**overpopulate**
overconfident	**overproduce**
overcook	**overproduction**
overcritical	**overrefined**
overcrowd	**overripe**
overdevelop	**oversell**
overeager	**oversensitive**
overeat	**overspecialize**
overemphasize	**overspend**
overenthusiastic	**overstimulate**
overexercise	**overstock**
overexert	**overstrict**
overexpose	**oversupply**
overextend	**overtire**

o′ver·a·chieve′ ***vi.*** **-chieved′, -chiev′ing** **1** to do better, as in school, than expected **2** to drive oneself to reach unreasonable goals —**o′ver·a·chieve′ment** ***n.*** —**o′ver·a·chiev′er** ***n.***

o′ver·act′ ***vt., vi.*** to act (a dramatic role) with exaggeration

o·ver·age[1] (ō′vər āj′) ***adj.*** over the age fixed as a standard

o·ver·age[2] (ō′vər ij) ***n.*** ⟦OVER + -AGE⟧ a surplus or excess

o·ver·all (ō′vər ôl′, ō′vər ôl′) ***adj.*** **1** from end to end **2** including everything; total —***adv.*** **1** from end to end **2** in general

o′ver·alls′ (-ôlz′) ***pl.n.*** loose trousers extending up over the chest, worn, usually over other clothing, to protect against dirt

o′ver·arch′ing ***adj.*** including or linking all that is within its scope *[an overarching theory]*

o′ver·awe′ ***vt.*** **-awed′, -aw′ing** to overcome or subdue by inspiring awe

o′ver·bal′ance ***vt.*** **-anced, -anc·ing** OUTWEIGH

o′ver·bear′ing ***adj.*** arrogant; domineering

o′ver·bite′ ***n.*** a dental condition in which the upper incisors and canines project over the lower ones to an abnormal extent

o′ver·blown′ (-blōn′) ***adj.*** **1** overdone; excessive **2** pompous or bombastic

o′ver·board′ ***adv.*** from a ship into the water —**go overboard** [Inf.] to go to extremes

o′ver·book′ ***vt., vi.*** to issue more reservations for (a flight, hotel, etc.) than there are accommodations

o′ver·cast′ ***adj.*** cloudy; dark: said of the sky

o·ver·charge (ō′vər chärj′; *also, and for n. always,* ō′vər chärj′) ***vt., vi.*** **-charged′, -charg′ing** **1** to charge too high a price (to) **2** to overload —***n.*** **1** an excessive charge **2** too full a load

o′ver·cloud′ ***vt., vi.*** to make or become cloudy, gloomy, etc.

o′ver·coat′ ***n.*** a heavy coat worn over the usual clothing for warmth

o′ver·come′ ***vt.*** **-came′, -come′, -com′ing** **1** to get the better of in competition, etc. **2** to master, prevail over, or surmount —***vi.*** to win

o′ver·de·ter′mine ***vt.*** **-mined, -min·ing** to bring about through many causes or factors

o′ver·do′ ***vt.*** **-did′, -done′, -do′ing** **1** to do too much **2** to exaggerate **3** to overcook —***vi.*** to exhaust oneself by doing too much

o′ver·dose′ ***n.*** too large a dose —***vi.*** to take too large an amount of a narcotic, etc.

o′ver·draw′ ***vt.*** **-drew′, -drawn′, -draw′ing** to draw on in excess of the amount credited to the drawer —**o′ver·draft′** ***n.***

o′ver·dress′ ***vt., vi.*** to dress too warmly, too showily, or too formally

o′ver·dub′ ***n.*** a recording of sounds, music, etc. superimposed on another recording —***vt., vi.*** **-dubbed′, -dub′bing** to add (sounds, music, etc.) to (a recording)

o′ver·due′ ***adj.*** past the time for payment, arrival, etc.

o′ver·es′ti·mate′ ***vt.*** **-mat′ed, -mat′ing** to set too high an estimate on or for

o′ver·flight′ ***n.*** the flight of an aircraft over a foreign territory, as in reconnaissance

o·ver·flow (ō′vər flō′; *also, and for n. always,* ō′vər flō′) ***vt.*** **1** to flow across; flood **2** to flow over the brim of —***vi.***

THESAURUS

oven ***n.*** baking compartment, toaster oven, broiler; see FURNACE, STOVE.

over ***a., prep.*** **1** [Situated above] aloft, overhead, up beyond, covering, roofing, protecting, upper, higher than, farther up, upstairs, in the sky, straight up, high up, up there, in the clouds, among the stars, in heaven, just over, up from, outer, on top of; see also ABOVE.—*Ant.* under, below, beneath. **2** [Passing above] overhead, aloft, up high; see ACROSS. **3** [Again] once more, afresh, another time; see AGAIN. **4** [Beyond] past, farther on, out of sight; see BEYOND. **5** [Done] accomplished, ended, completed; see DONE 1, FINISHED 1. **6** [*In addition] over and above, extra, additionally; see BESIDES. **7** [Having authority] superior to, in authority, above; see HIGHER, SUPERIOR.

overabundance ***n.*** surplus, profusion, superfluity; see EXCESS 1.

overall ***a.*** complete, thorough, comprehensive; see GENERAL 1.

overalls ***n.*** protective garment, jumpsuit, coveralls; see CLOTHES, PANTS 1.

overbearing ***a.*** despotic, tyrannical, dictatorial; see ABSOLUTE 3.

overblown ***a.*** excessive, magnified, overdone; see EXAGGERATED.

overboard ***a.*** over the side, out of the boat, into the water; see WET 1. —**go overboard*** go to extremes, get carried away, go off the deep end*; see OVERDO 1.

overcast ***a.*** cloudy, gloomy, not clear or fair; see DARK 1.

overcoat ***n.*** topcoat, greatcoat, raincoat; see CLOTHES, COAT 1.

overcome ***a.*** conquered, overwhelmed, overthrown; see BEATEN 1.

overcome ***v.*** overwhelm, best, vanquish, conquer, outdo, surpass, overpower, overwhelm, beat, trounce, subdue, master; see also DEFEAT 2, 3, WIN 1.

overconfident ***a.*** reckless, imprudent, heedless; see CARELESS, RASH.

overcritical ***a.*** domineering, harsh, hypercritical; see SEVERE 1, 2.

overcrowd ***v.*** crowd, stuff, fill; see PACK 2, PRESS 1.

overcrowded ***a.*** congested, overbuilt, overpopulated; see FULL 1.

overdo ***v.*** **1** [To do too much] magnify, amplify, overestimate, overreach, stretch, go too far, overrate, exaggerate, go to extremes, overstate, enlarge, enhance, exalt, bite off more than one can chew*, run into the ground*, do to death, go overboard*, burn the candle at both ends, lay it on*, have too many irons in the fire; see also EXCEED.—*Ant.* NEGLECT, underdo, slacken. **2** [To overtax oneself physically] tire, fatigue, exhaust; see WEARY 2.

overdone ***a.*** excessive, too much, pushed too far; see EXAGGERATED.

overdose ***n.*** excessive dose, too much, overtreatment; see EXCESS 1.

overdrawn ***a.*** exhausted, depleted, all paid out; see GONE 2.

overdue ***a.*** delayed, belated, tardy; see LATE 1.

overeat ***v.*** overindulge, stuff, gorge; see EAT 1.

overemphasize ***v.*** exaggerate, make a big thing of*, make something out of nothing*; see EMPHASIZE, EXCEED.

overestimate ***v.*** overvalue, overprice, overrate; see EXAGGERATE, EXCEED.

overflow ***n.*** **1** [The act of overflowing] redundancy, inundation, overproduction; see FLOOD. **2** [That which

1 to run over 2 to be superabundant —*n.* 1 an overflowing 2 the amount that overflows 3 an outlet for overflowing liquids

o′ver·grow′ *vt.* **-grew′**, **-grown′**, **-grow′ing** to overspread with foliage so as to cover —*vi.* to grow too fast or beyond normal size —**o′ver·grown′** *adj.* —**o′ver·growth′** *n.*

o′ver·hand′ *adj.*, *adv.* with the hand raised above the elbow or the arm above the shoulder

o·ver·hang (ō′vər haŋ′; *also, and for n. always,* ō′vər haŋ′) *vt.*, *vi.* **-hung′**, **-hang′ing** to hang over or project beyond (something) —*n.* the projection of one thing over or beyond another

o·ver·haul (ō′vər hôl′; *also, and for n. always,* ō′vər hôl′) *vt.* 1 *a)* to check thoroughly for needed repairs *b)* to restore (a motor, etc.) to good working order 2 to catch up with —*n.* an overhauling

o·ver·head (ō′vər hed′; *for adv.* ō′vər hed′) *adj.* 1 above the head 2 in the sky 3 on a higher level, with reference to related objects —*n.* the general, continuing costs of a business, as of rent, maintenance, etc. —*adv.* above the head; aloft

o′ver·hear′ *vt.* **-heard′**, **-hear′ing** to hear (something spoken or a speaker) without the speaker's knowledge or intention

o′ver·joy′ *vt.* to give great joy to; delight —**o′ver·joyed′** *adj.*

o′ver·kill′ *n.* much more of something than is necessary, appropriate, etc.

o′ver·land′ (-land′, -lənd) *adv.*, *adj.* by, on, or across land

o·ver·lap (ō′vər lap′; *also, and for n. always,* ō′vər lap′) *vt.*, *vi.* **-lapped′**, **-lap′ping** to extend over a part of (something) so as to coincide with this part —*n.* an overlapping part or amount

o′ver·lay′ *vt.* **-laid′**, **-lay′ing** 1 to lay or spread over 2 to cover, as with a decorative layer

o′ver·lie′ *vt.* **-lay′**, **-lain′**, **-ly′ing** to lie on or over

o′ver·look′ *vt.* 1 to look at from above 2 to give a view of from above 3 *a)* to fail to notice *b)* to ignore; neglect 4 to excuse

o′ver·lord′ *n.* person having great authority over others

o′ver·ly *adv.* too or too much

o′ver·mas′ter *vt.* to overcome; subdue

o′ver·much′ *adj.*, *adv.*, *n.* too much

o·ver·night (ō′vər nīt′, ō′vər nīt′) *adv.* 1 during the night 2 suddenly —*adj.* 1 done or going on during the night 2 staying through the night [an *overnight* guest] 3 of or for a brief trip [an *overnight* bag]

o′ver·pass′ *n.* a bridge, etc. over a road, railway, etc.

o′ver·play′ *vt.* to overact, overdo, or overemphasize

o′ver·pow′er *vt.* to get the better of; subdue or overwhelm —**o′ver·pow′er·ing** *adj.*

o′ver·price′ *vt.* **-priced′**, **-pric′ing** to offer for sale at too high a price

o′ver·pro·tect′ *vt.* to protect more than necessary; specif., to exercise excessive, damaging control over (one's child, etc.) in trying to shield from hurt, disappointment, etc.

o′ver·qual′i·fied′ *adj.* having more knowledge, education, etc. than needed for a particular job

o′ver·rate′ *vt.* **-rat′ed**, **-rat′ing** to rate or estimate too highly

o′ver·reach′ *vt.* to reach beyond or above —**overreach oneself** to fail because of trying to do too much

o′ver·re·act′ *vi.* to react in an overly emotional way

o′ver·ride′ *vt.* **-rode′**, **-rid′den**, **-rid′ing** 1 to prevail over 2 to disregard or nullify

o′ver·rule′ *vt.* **-ruled′**, **-rul′ing** 1 to set aside or decide against by virtue of higher authority; annul; reverse 2 to prevail over

o′ver·run′ *vt.* **-ran′**, **-run′**, **-run′ning** 1 to spread out over so as to cover 2 to swarm over, as vermin do 3 to extend beyond (certain limits)

o′ver·seas′ *adv.* over or beyond the sea —*adj.* 1 foreign 2 over or across the sea

o′ver·see′ *vt.* **-saw′**, **-seen′**, **-see′ing** to supervise; superintend —**o′ver·se′er** (-sē′ər) *n.*

o′ver·sexed′ (-sekst′) *adj.* having exceptional sexual drive or interest in sex

o′ver·shad′ow *vt.* 1 *a)* to cast a shadow over *b)* to darken 2 to be more important than by comparison

o′ver·shoe′ *n.* a boot of rubber, etc. worn over the regular shoe to protect against cold or dampness

o′ver·shoot′ *vt.* **-shot′**, **-shoot′ing** 1 to shoot or pass beyond (a target, mark, etc.) 2 to exceed

o′ver·sight′ *n.* a careless mistake or omission

o′ver·sim′pli·fy′ *vt.*, *vi.* **-fied′**, **-fy′ing** to simplify to the point of distortion —**o′ver·sim′pli·fi·ca′tion** *n.*

o′ver·size′ *adj.* 1 too large 2 larger than the usual Also **o′ver·sized′**

o′ver·sleep′ *vi.* **-slept′**, **-sleep′ing** to sleep longer than intended

o′ver·spread′ *vt.* **-spread′**, **-spread′ing** to spread or cover over

o′ver·state′ *vt.* **-stat′ed**, **-stat′ing** to exaggerate —**o′ver·state′ment** *n.*

o′ver·stay′ *vt.* to stay beyond the time or limit of

THESAURUS

overflows] superfluity, surplus, extra quantity; see EXCESS 1.

overflow *v.* 1 [To flow over the top, or out at a vent] spill over, run over, pour out, cascade, spout forth, jet, spurt, drain, leak, squirt, spray, shower, gush, shoot, issue, rush, wave, surge, brim over, bubble over; see also LEAK 1. 2 [To flow out upon] inundate, water, wet; see FLOOD.

overflowing *a.* abundant, in plenty, bountiful; see PLENTIFUL 2.

overgrown *a.* disproportionate, excessive, huge; see LARGE 1.

overgrowth *n.* growth, abundance, luxuriance; see EXCESS 1.

overhang *v.* jut, be suspended, dangle over; see PROJECT 1.

overhaul *v.* modernize, fix, renew; see REPAIR.

overhead *a.* above, aloft, hanging; see OVER 1.

overhear *v.* hear intentionally, hear unintentionally, catch; see EAVESDROP, HEAR 1.

overheard *a.* listened to, recorded, discovered; see HEARD.

overheat *v.* heat too much, bake, blister; see HEAT 2.

overindulgence *n.* overeating, drinking to excess, eating or drinking too much; see DRUNKENNESS, EATING, GREED.

overjoyed *a.* enraptured, transported, thrilled; see EXCITED, HAPPY.

overlap *n.* extension, overlay, addition; see FLAP.

overlap *v.* overlie, overhang, lap over, fold over, extend alongside, project over, overlay; see also PROJECT 1.

overload *v.* oppress, weigh down, encumber; see BURDEN, LOAD 1.

overlook *v.* 1 [To occupy a commanding height] look over, top, survey, inspect, watch over, look out, view, give upon, give on, front on, command. 2 [To ignore deliberately] slight, make light of, disdain; see NEGLECT 1. 3 [To fail to see] miss, leave out, neglect; see NEGLECT 2.

overlooked *a.* missed, left out, forgotten; see NEGLECTED.

overlooking *a.* 1 [Providing a view] looking over, looking out on, commanding; see SEEING. 2 [Disregarding] missing, neglecting, forgetting.

overnight *a.* one night, lasting one night, during the night; see LATE 4.

overpass *n.* span, footbridge, skywalk; see BRIDGE 1.

overpower *v.* overwhelm, master, subjugate; see DEFEAT 2, 3.

overpowering *a.* irresistible, uncontrollable, overwhelming; see INTENSE.

overproduction *n.* excess, excessive production, overstock; see PRODUCTION 1.

overrate *v.* build up, magnify, overestimate; see EXAGGERATE, EXCEED.

overrated *a.* not very good, overblown, not satisfactory; see POOR 2, UNSATISFACTORY.

overreact *v.* make too much of, blow out of proportion, go overboard*; see EXAGGERATE.

override *v.* 1 [To dismiss] pass over, not heed, take no account of; see DISREGARD, NEGLECT 1. 2 [To thwart] make void, reverse, annul; see CANCEL, REVOKE.

overrule *v.* invalidate, rule against, override; see CANCEL, REVOKE.

overrun *v.* 1 [To defeat] overwhelm, invade, occupy; see DEFEAT 2. 2 [To infest] ravage, invade, overwhelm; see INFEST 2.

overseas *a.* away, across the ocean, in foreign countries; see ABROAD.

oversee *v.* superintend, supervise, look after; see MANAGE 1.

overseer *n.* supervisor, manager, superintendent; see FOREMAN.

overshadow *v.* domineer, tower above, predominate; see DOMINATE.

overshoes *n.* galoshes, rubbers, arctics; see SHOE.

overshoot *v.* overreach, overdo, overact; see EXCEED.

oversight *n.* failure, omission, mistake; see ERROR.

oversleep *v.* sleep late, miss the alarm, stay in bed; see SLEEP.

overspecialize *v.* limit oneself, specialize too much, be a specialist; see RESTRAIN, RESTRICT.

overstay *v.* stay too long, tarry, stop, outstay one's welcome; see also REMAIN 1.

o′ver·step′ ***vt.*** **-stepped′, -step′ping** to go beyond the limits of
o′ver·strung′ ***adj.*** high-strung; tense
o′ver·stuff′ ***vt.*** **1** to stuff with too much of something **2** to upholster with deep stuffing
o·vert (ō vʉrt′, ō′vʉrt′) ***adj.*** ⟦< L *aperire,* to open⟧ not hidden; apparent; open **—o·vert′ly** ***adv.***
o′ver·take′ ***vt.*** **-took′, -tak′en, -tak′ing** **1** to catch up with **2** to come upon suddenly
o′ver·tax′ ***vt.*** **1** to tax too heavily **2** to make excessive demands on
o′ver-the-count′er ***adj.*** **1** designating or of securities sold directly to buyers **2** sold legally without prescription: said of some drugs
o′ver-the-top′ ***adj.*** outrageously or ridiculously excessive
o·ver·throw (ō′vər thrō′; *also & for n.* ō′vər thrō′) ***vt.*** **-threw′, -thrown′, -throw′ing** **1** to overcome; conquer **2** to throw beyond **—*n.*** **1** an overthrowing or being overthrown **2** destruction; end
o′ver·time′ ***n.*** **1** time beyond the established limit, as of working hours **2** pay for work done in such time **—*adj.*, *adv.*** of, for, or during overtime
o′ver·tone′ ***n.*** **1** a faint, higher tone accompanying a fundamental tone produced by a musical instrument **2** an implication; nuance: *usually used in pl.*
o·ver·ture (ō′vər chər) ***n.*** ⟦< L *apertura,* opening⟧ **1** an introductory proposal or offer **2** a musical introduction to an opera, etc.
o′ver·turn′ ***vt.*** **1** to turn over **2** to conquer **—*vi.*** to tip over; capsize
o′ver·ween′ing (-wēn′iŋ) ***adj.*** ⟦< OE *ofer,* over + *wenan,* to think⟧ **1** arrogant **2** excessive
o·ver·weight (ō′vər wāt′, ō′vər wāt′) ***adj.*** above the normal or allowed weight
o′ver·whelm′ ***vt.*** **1** to pour down upon and bury beneath **2** to crush; overpower **—o′ver·whelm′ing** ***adj.***
o·ver·work (ō′vər wʉrk′, ō′vər wʉrk′) ***vt.*** to work or use to excess **—*vi.*** to work too hard or too long **—*n.*** severe or burdensome work
o·ver·wrought (ō′vər rôt′) ***adj.*** **1** very nervous or excited **2** too elaborate
Ov·id (äv′id) 43 B.C.-A.D. 17?; Rom. poet
o·vi·duct (ō′vi dukt′, äv′i-) ***n.*** ⟦< L *ovum,* egg + DUCT⟧ a tube through which the ova pass from an ovary to the uterus
o·vip·a·rous (ō vip′ə rəs) ***adj.*** ⟦< L *ovum,* egg + *parere,* to bear⟧ producing eggs which hatch after leaving the female's body
o·void (ō′void′) ***adj.*** ⟦< L *ovum,* egg + -OID⟧ egg-shaped **—*n.*** anything ovoid
ov·u·late (äv′yə lāt′) ***vi.*** **-lat′ed, -lat′ing** ⟦< L *ovum,* egg⟧ to produce and discharge ova from the ovary **—ov′u·la′tion** ***n.***
ov·ule (äv′yo͞ol′, ō′vyo͞ol′) ***n.*** ⟦< L *ovum,* egg⟧ a small egg or seed, esp. one in an early stage of development **—ov′u·lar** ***adj.***
o·vum (ō′vəm) ***n.***, *pl.* **o·va** (ō′və) ⟦L, egg⟧ a mature female germ cell
ow (ou) ***interj.*** a cry of pain
owe (ō) ***vt.*** **owed, ow′ing** ⟦OE *agan,* to own⟧ **1** to be indebted to the amount of **2** to have the need to do, give, etc., as because of gratitude **3** to be indebted *to* someone for the existence of
ow·ing (ō′iŋ) ***adj.*** ⟦ME *owynge*⟧ due; unpaid **—owing to** because of
owl (oul) ***n.*** ⟦OE *ule*⟧ **1** a predatory night bird having a large, flat face, large eyes, and a short, hooked beak **2** a person of nocturnal habits, solemn appearance, etc. **—owl′ish** ***adj.***
owl′et (-it) ***n.*** a young or small owl
own (ōn) ***adj.*** ⟦OE *agan,* possess⟧ belonging or relating to oneself or itself *[his own book]* **—*n.*** that which belongs to oneself *[that is her own]* **—*vt.*** **1** to possess; have **2** to admit; acknowledge **—*vi.*** to confess (*to*) **—on one's own** [Inf.] by one's own efforts **—own′er** ***n.*** **—own′er·ship′** ***n.***
ox (äks) ***n.***, *pl.* **ox′en** ⟦OE *oxa*⟧ any of certain cud-chewing, cattlelike mammals, esp. a castrated, domesticated bull used as a draft animal
ox′blood′ ***n.*** a deep-red color
ox′bow′ (-bō′) ***n.*** the U-shaped part of an ox yoke which passes under and around the animal's neck
ox·ford (äks′fərd) ***n.*** ⟦after *Oxford,* England⟧ [*sometimes* **O-**] **1** a low shoe laced over the instep: also **oxford shoe** **2** a cotton or rayon fabric with a basketlike weave: also **oxford cloth**
Ox·ford (äks′fərd) city in SC England; site of Oxford University: county district pop. 110,000
ox·i·dant (äk′si dənt) ***n.*** an oxidizing agent
ox·i·da·tion (äk′si dā′shən) ***n.*** an oxidizing or being oxidized
ox·ide (äk′sīd′) ***n.*** ⟦Fr⟧ a compound of oxygen with another element or a radical
ox·i·dize (äk′si dīz′) ***vt.*** **-dized′, -diz′ing** to unite with oxygen, as in burning or rusting **—*vi.*** to become oxidized **—ox′i·diz′er** ***n.***
ox·y·a·cet·y·lene (äk′sē ə set′′l ēn′) ***adj.*** of or using a mixture of oxygen and acetylene, as for producing a hot flame used in welding
ox·y·gen (äk′si jən) ***n.*** ⟦Fr *oxygène*⟧ a colorless, odorless, gaseous chemical element: it is essential to life processes and to combustion
ox′y·gen·ate′ (-jə nāt′) ***vt.*** **-at′ed, -at′ing** to treat or combine with oxygen **—ox′y·gen·a′tion** ***n.***
oxygen tent a transparent enclosure filled with oxygen, fitted around a bed patient to aid breathing
ox·y·mo·ron (äk′si môr′än′) ***n.***, *pl.* **-mo′ra** (-rə) ⟦< Gr

THESAURUS

overstep ***v.*** violate, encroach, trespass; see EXCEED, MEDDLE 1.
overt ***a.*** apparent, out in the open, patent; see OBVIOUS.
overtake ***v.*** overhaul, catch up with, get to; see REACH 1.
overtaken ***a.*** caught up with, reached, apprehended; see BEATEN 1, CAPTURED.
overthrow ***v.*** overcome, overrun, overpower; see DEFEAT 2.
overthrown ***a.*** overcome, overwhelmed, vanquished; see BEATEN 1.
overtime ***n.*** extra pay, additional wages, late hours; see PAY 2.
overtone ***n.*** tone, implication, hint; see MEANING, SUGGESTION 1.
overture ***n.*** **1** [Preliminary negotiations; *sometimes plural*] approach, offer, tender; see SUGGESTION 1. **2** [A musical introduction] prelude, prologue, *Vorspiel* (German), voluntary, proem, preface; see also INTRODUCTION 3.
overturn ***v.*** reverse, upturn, overthrow; see UPSET 1.
overweight ***a.*** ample, fat, obese; see HEAVY 1.
overwhelm ***v.*** **1** [To defeat] overcome, overthrow, conquer; see DEFEAT 2, 3, WIN 1. **2** [To astonish] puzzle, bewilder, confound; see CONFUSE, SURPRISE.
overwhelmed ***a.*** beaten, worsted, submerged; see BEATEN 2.
overwhelming ***a.*** overpowering, ruinous, overthrowing, crushing, smashing, extinguishing, invading, ravaging, overriding, upsetting, inundating, drowning, deluging, surging, obliterating, dissolving, wrecking, erasing, effacing, expunging, burying, immersing, engulfing, engrossing, covering; see also HARMFUL, TRIUMPHANT.
overwork ***n.*** extra work, overtime, exhaustion; see ABUSE.
overwork ***v.*** overdo, exhaust, wear out; see BURDEN, WEARY 1.
overworked ***a.*** overburdened, too busy, worked too hard; see TIRED.
overwrought ***a.*** nervous, agitated, high-strung; see EXCITED.
owe ***v.*** be under obligation, be indebted to, be obligated to, have an obligation, be bound, get on credit, feel bound, be bound to pay, be contracted to, be in debt for, have signed a note for, have borrowed, have lost.
owed ***a.*** owing, becoming due, outstanding; see DUE, UNPAID 1.
owl ***n.*** bird of prey, night bird, nocturnal bird; see BIRD.
own ***a.*** personal, individual, owned, very own*; see also PRIVATE.
own ***v.*** **1** [To possess] hold, have, enjoy, fall heir to, have title to, have rights to, be master of, occupy, control, dominate, have a claim upon, reserve, retain, keep, have in hand, have a deed for.—*Ant.* LACK, want, need. **2** [To acknowledge] assent to, grant, recognize; see ADMIT 2, DECLARE.
own ***n.*** one's own possession, something personal, what belongs to one. **—come into one's own** receive what one deserves, gain proper recognition, thrive; see PROFIT 2. **—of one's own** personal, private, belonging to one; see OWNED. **—on one's own** by oneself, acting independently, singly; see INDEPENDENTLY.
owned ***a.*** possessed, had, bought, held, purchased, kept, inherited, enjoyed, in hand, bound over, in the possession of, among the possessions of.
owner ***n.*** one who has, keeper, buyer, purchaser, heir, heiress, proprietor, landlord, landlady, sharer, partner, title holder, master, heir apparent.
ownership ***n.*** possession, having, holding, claim, deed, title, control, buying, purchasing, proprietorship, occupancy, use, residence, tenancy, dominion.

oxys, sharp + *mōros*, foolish⟧ a figure of speech in which contradictory ideas or terms are combined (Ex.: thunderous silence)

oys·ter (ois′tər) ***n.*** ⟦< Gr *ostreon*⟧ an edible bivalve mollusk with an irregular shell

oz *symbol* ounce(s)

o·zone (ō′zōn′) ***n.*** ⟦Fr < Gr *ozein*, to smell⟧ **1** an unstable, pale-blue form of oxygen with a strong odor, formed by an electrical discharge in air and used as a bleaching agent, water purifier, etc. **2** [Slang] pure, fresh air

ozone layer the layer of ozone within the stratosphere that absorbs much ultraviolet radiation

THESAURUS

oyster ***n.*** bivalve, mollusk, seafood; see FISH, SHELLFISH.

P

p[1] or **P** (pē) ***n.***, *pl.* **p's, P's** the 16th letter of the English alphabet

p[2] *abbrev.* **1** page **2** participle **3** past **4** per **5** pint

P[1] *abbrev.* petite

P[2] *Chem. symbol for* phosphorus

pa (pä) ***n.*** [Inf.] FATHER

PA *abbrev.* **1** Pennsylvania **2** public address (system)

pab·lum (pab'ləm) ***n.*** ⟦< *Pablum,* trademark for a soft, bland baby food⟧ simplistic or bland writing, ideas, etc.

PAC ***n.***, *pl.* **PAC's** political action committee

pace (pās) ***n.*** ⟦< L *passus,* a step⟧ **1** a step in walking, etc. **2** the length of a step or stride **3** the rate of speed in walking, etc. **4** rate of progress, etc. **5** a gait **6** the gait of a horse in which both legs on the same side are raised together —***vt.*** **paced, pac'ing 1** to walk back and forth across **2** to measure by paces **3** to set the pace for (a runner, etc.) —***vi.*** **1** to walk with regular steps **2** to move at a pace: said of a horse —**put through one's paces** to test one's ability, skills, etc. —**pac'er** ***n.***

pace'mak'er ***n.*** **1** one that leads the way: also **pace'set'ter** (-set'ər) **2** an electronic device placed in the body to regulate the heartbeat

pach·y·derm (pak'ə durm') ***n.*** ⟦< Gr *pachys,* thick + *derma,* skin⟧ a large, thick-skinned, hoofed animal, as the elephant or rhinoceros

pach·y·san·dra (pak'ə san'drə) ***n.*** ⟦< ModL name of genus⟧ a low, hardy evergreen plant often used for a ground cover in the shade

pa·cif·ic (pə sif'ik) ***adj.*** ⟦see PACIFY⟧ **1** making peace **2** of a peaceful nature; tranquil; calm

Pa·cif·ic (pə sif'ik) largest of the earth's oceans, between Asia and the American continents

pac·i·fi·er (pas'ə fī'ər) ***n.*** **1** one that pacifies **2** a nipple or teething ring for babies

pac'i·fism' (-fiz'əm) ***n.*** opposition to the use of force under any circumstances; specif., refusal to participate in war —**pac'i·fist** ***n.***, ***adj.***

pac·i·fy (pas'ə fī') ***vt.*** **-fied', -fy'ing** ⟦< L *pax,* peace + *facere,* make⟧ to make peaceful, calm, nonhostile, etc. —**pac'i·fi·ca'tion** ***n.***

pack[1] (pak) ***n.*** ⟦< MDu *pak*⟧ **1** a bundle of things tied up for carrying **2** a number of similar persons or things; specif., *a)* a group *[*a *pack* of lies*]* *b)* a package of a standard number *[*a *pack* of cigarettes*]* *c)* a number of wild animals living together —***vt.*** **1** to make a pack of **2** *a)* to put together in a box, trunk, etc. *b)* to fill (a box, etc.) **3** to crowd; cram *[*the hall was *packed]* **4** to fill in tightly, as for prevention of leaks **5** to carry in a pack **6** to send (*off*) *[*to *pack* him off to school*]* **7** [Slang] to carry (a gun, etc.) **8** [Slang] to be able to deliver (a punch, etc.) with force —***vi.*** **1** to make up packs **2** to put one's clothes, etc. into luggage for a trip **3** to crowd together **4** to settle into a compact mass —***adj.*** used for carrying packs, loads, etc. *[*a *pack* animal*]* —**send packing** to dismiss abruptly

pack[2] (pak) ***vt.*** to choose (a jury, etc.) so as to get desired results

pack·age (pak'ij) ***n.*** **1** a wrapped or boxed thing or group of things; parcel **2** a number of items, plans, etc. offered as a unit —***vt.*** **-aged, -ag·ing 1** to make a package of **2** to offer or present in an enticing way —**pack'ag·er** ***n.***

package store a store where alcoholic beverages are sold by the bottle

pack'et (-it) ***n.*** **1** a small package **2** a boat that travels a regular route carrying passengers, freight, and mail: in full **packet boat**

pack'ing ***n.*** **1** the act or process of a person or thing that packs **2** any material used to pack

pack'ing·house' ***n.*** a plant where meats, etc. are processed and packed for sale

pack rat 1 a North American rat that often hides small articles in its nest **2** [Inf.] one who hoards miscellaneous items

pack'sad'dle ***n.*** a saddle with fastenings to secure the load carried by a pack animal

pact (pakt) ***n.*** ⟦< L *pax,* peace⟧ an agreement; compact

pad[1] (pad) ***n.*** ⟦echoic⟧ the dull sound of a footstep —***vi.*** **pad'ded, pad'ding** to walk, esp. with a soft step

pad[2] (pad) ***n.*** ⟦? var. of POD⟧ **1** anything soft to protect against friction, pressure, etc.; cushion **2** the cushionlike sole of an animal's paw **3** the floating leaf of a water plant, as the waterlily **4** a number of sheets of paper glued along one edge; tablet **5** [Slang] the place where one lives —***vt.*** **pad'ded, pad'ding 1** to stuff or cover with soft material **2** to lengthen (a speech, etc.) with unnecessary material **3** to fill (an expense account, etc.) with invented or inflated entries

pad'ding ***n.*** anything used to pad

pad·dle[1] (pad''l) ***n.*** ⟦ME *padell,* small spade⟧ **1** a short pole with a wide blade at one or both ends, used to propel a canoe, kayak, etc. **2** an implement shaped like this, used to hit a ball, beat something, etc. —***vt.***, ***vi.*** **-dled, -dling 1** to propel (a canoe, etc.) with a paddle **2** to beat as with a paddle; spank —**pad'dler** ***n.***

pad·dle[2] (pad''l) ***vi.*** **-dled, -dling** ⟦prob. < PAD[1]⟧ to move the hands or feet about in the water, as in playing —**pad'dler** ***n.***

paddle ball a game like handball played with a short-handled paddle

paddle wheel a wheel with boards around it for propelling a steamboat

pad·dock (pad'ək) ***n.*** ⟦OE *pearruc,* enclosure⟧ **1** a small enclosure near a stable, in which horses are exercised **2** an enclosure at a racetrack, where horses are saddled

pad·dy (pad'ē) ***n.***, *pl.* **-dies** ⟦Malay *padi,* rice in the husk⟧ a rice field

pad·lock (pad'läk') ***n.*** a removable lock with a hinged link to be passed through a staple, chain, or eye —***vt.*** to fasten or close up as with a padlock

pa·dre (pä'drā') ***n.*** ⟦< L *pater*⟧ **1** father: the title of a priest in Italy, Spain, etc. **2** [Inf.] a priest or chaplain

pae·an (pē'ən) ***n.*** ⟦< Gr *paian,* hymn⟧ a song of joy, triumph, etc.

THESAURUS

pa* ***n.*** male parent, papa*, dad*; see FATHER 1, PARENT.

pace ***n.*** step, velocity, movement; see SPEED. —**change of pace** variation, alteration, diversity; see CHANGE 1. —**keep pace (with)** go at the same speed, maintain the same rate of progress, keep up with; see EQUAL. —**set the pace** begin, initiate, establish criteria; see LEAD 1.

pace ***v.*** determine, pace off, step off; see MEASURE 1.

pacifist ***n.*** dove, peace lover, conscientious objector; see RADICAL, RESISTER.

pacify ***v.*** conciliate, appease, placate; see QUIET 1.

pack[1] ***n.*** **1** [A package] bundle, parcel, load; see PACKAGE. **2** [Kit] outfit, baggage, luggage; see EQUIPMENT. **3** [A group] number, gang, mob; see CROWD. **4** [A medical dressing] application, hot pack, ice pack; see DRESSING 3. **5** [A set of cards] bridge deck, pinochle deck, set; see DECK 2.

pack[1] ***v.*** **1** [To prepare for transportation] prepare, gather, collect, ready, get ready, put in order, stow away, tie, bind, brace, fasten.—*Ant.* UNDO, untie, take out. **2** [To stow compactly] stuff, squeeze, bind, compress, condense, arrange, ram, cram, jam, insert, press, contract, put away.—*Ant.* SCATTER, loosen, fluff up.

package ***n.*** parcel, packet, burden, load, kit, bunch, sheaf, pack, batch, bag, case, roll, wrapped object, box, carton, crate, bundle, bale, can, tin, sack, bottle; see also CONTAINER.

packed ***a.*** **1** [Ready for storage or shipment] prepared, bundled, wrapped; see READY 2. **2** [Pressed together] compact, compressed, pressed down; see FULL 1.

packet ***n.*** pack, receptacle, parcel; see CONTAINER, PACKAGE.

packing ***n.*** preparation, arrangement, compression, consignment, disposal, disposition, sorting, grading, laying away.

pact ***n.*** settlement, compact, bargain; see TREATY.

pad[2] ***n.*** **1** [Material for writing] scratchpad, scratch paper, notepad, stationery, notepaper, legal pad; see also PAPER 4, TABLET 2. **2** [An article that cushions] cushion, support, pallet; see PILLOW, MAT. **3** [*A residence] room, apartment, living quarters; see HOME.

pad[2] ***v.*** **1** [To stuff] pack, fill out, pad out; see FILL 1. **2** [To increase] inflate, build up, falsify; see DECEIVE, INCREASE.

padded ***a.*** stuffed, filled, quilted; see FULL 1.

padding ***n.*** stuffing, wadding, waste; see FILLING.

paddle[1] ***n.*** oar, pole, scull; see TOOL 1.

paddle[1] ***v.*** **1** [To propel by paddling] scull, boat, cruise, drift, navigate, shoot rapids, run rapids; see also DRIVE 2. **2** [To beat, usually rather lightly] spank, thrash, rap; see BEAT 1, PUNISH.

padlock ***n.*** latch, fastener, catch; see LOCK 1.

pa·gan (pā′gən) ***n.*** ⟦< L *paganus,* peasant⟧ **1** a heathen **2** one who has no religion —***adj.*** of pagans —**pa′gan·ism′** ***n.***

page[1] (pāj) ***n.*** ⟦< L *pangere,* fasten⟧ **1** *a)* one side of a leaf of a book, etc. *b)* an entire leaf in a book, etc. **2** [*often pl.*] a record of events **3** WEB PAGE —***vi.*** **paged, pag′ing** to look (*through*) by turning the pages

page[2] (pāj) ***n.*** ⟦OFr⟧ a boy attendant —***vt.*** **paged, pag′ing** **1** to try to find by calling out the name of **2** to contact with a pager

pag·eant (paj′ənt) ***n.*** ⟦ME *pagent,* stage scene⟧ **1** a spectacular exhibition, parade, etc. **2** an elaborate outdoor drama celebrating a historical event

pag′eant·ry (-ən trē) ***n.***, *pl.* **-ries** **1** grand spectacle; gorgeous display **2** empty show or display

pag·er (pā′jər) ***n.*** a portable electronic device used to contact people for messages

pag·i·na·tion (paj′ə nā′shən) ***n.*** **1** the numbering of pages **2** the arrangement and number of pages

pa·go·da (pə gō′də) ***n.*** ⟦prob. < Pers *but,* idol + *kadah,* house⟧ in India and the Far East, a temple in the form of a pyramidal tower of several stories

paid (pād) ***vt., vi.*** *pt. & pp. of* PAY —***adj.*** **1** settled by payment **2** with pay *[a paid vacation]*

pail (pāl) ***n.*** ⟦< OE *pægel,* wine vessel⟧ **1** a container, usually with a handle, for holding liquids, etc.; bucket **2** the amount held by a pail: also **pail′ful′**, *pl.* **-fuls′**

pain (pān) ***n.*** ⟦< Gr *poinē,* penalty⟧ **1** physical or mental suffering caused by injury, disease, grief, anxiety, etc. **2** [*pl.*] great care *[take pains with one's work]* —***vt.*** to cause pain to; hurt —**on** (or **under**) **pain of** at the risk of a penalty —**pain′ful** ***adj.*** —**pain′ful·ly** ***adv.*** —**pain′less** ***adj.***

Paine (pān), **Thom·as** (täm′əs) 1737-1809; Am. Revolutionary patriot & writer

pain′kill′er ***n.*** [Inf.] a medicine that relieves pain

pains·tak·ing (pānz′tā′kiŋ) ***adj.*** requiring or showing great care; very careful

paint (pānt) ***vt.*** ⟦< L *pingere*⟧ **1** *a)* to make (a picture, etc.) in colors applied to a surface *b)* to depict with paints **2** to describe vividly **3** to cover or decorate with paint —***vi.*** to paint pictures —***n.*** **1** a mixture of a pigment with oil, water, etc., used as a covering or coloring **2** a dried coat of paint

paint′er ***n.*** **1** an artist who paints pictures **2** one whose work is covering walls, etc. with paint

paint′ing ***n.*** a painted picture

pair (per) ***n.***, *pl.* **pairs** or **pair** ⟦< L *par,* equal⟧ **1** two corresponding things associated or used together *[a pair of shoes]* **2** a single unit of two corresponding parts *[a pair of pants]* **3** any two persons or animals regarded as a unit —***vi., vt.*** **1** to form a pair (of) **2** to mate

pais·ley (pāz′lē) ***adj.*** ⟦after *Paisley,* Scotland⟧ [*also* **P-**] having an intricate, multicolored pattern of swirls, etc.

pa·ja·mas (pə jä′məz, -jam′əz) ***pl.n.*** ⟦< Pers *pāi,* a leg + *jāma,* garment⟧ a loosely fitting sleeping or lounging suit consisting of jacket (or blouse) and trousers

Pa·ki·stan (pak′i stan′, pä′ki stän′) country in S Asia, west of India: 307,293 sq. mi.; pop. 131,500,000 —**Pak′i·stan′i** (-ē) ***adj., n.***

pal (pal) ***n.*** ⟦Romany, brother, ult. < Sans⟧ [Inf.] a close friend

pal·ace (pal′əs) ***n.*** ⟦< L *Palatium,* one of the Seven Hills of Rome⟧ **1** the official residence of a king, etc. **2** any large, magnificent building

pal·at·a·ble (pal′it ə bəl) ***adj.*** pleasant or acceptable to the taste or mind

pal·ate (pal′it) ***n.*** ⟦< L *palatum*⟧ **1** the roof of the mouth **2** sense of taste —**pal′a·tal** (-it′l) ***adj.***

pa·la·tial (pə lā′shəl) ***adj.*** ⟦see PALACE⟧ **1** of, suitable for, or like a palace **2** magnificent; stately

pal·a·tine (pal′ə tīn′, -tin) ***adj.*** ⟦see PALACE⟧ designating or of a count or earl who ruled in his own territory

Pa·lau (pä lou′) country on a group of islands in the W Pacific: 630 sq. mi.; pop. 15,000

pa·lav·er (pə lav′ər) ***n.*** ⟦Port *palavra,* a word⟧ talk, esp. idle talk —***vi.*** to talk idly

pale[1] (pāl) ***adj.*** **pal′er, pal′est** ⟦< L *pallidus*⟧ **1** of a whitish or colorless complexion **2** faint; dim **3** feeble; weak

THESAURUS

pagan ***a.*** unchristian, non-Christian, polytheistic, pantheistic, idolatrous, heathenish.

pagan ***n.*** pantheist, heathen, doubter, scoffer, unbeliever, atheist, polytheist, nonbeliever, non-Christian, non-Jew, non-Muslim.

paganism ***n.*** heathenism, agnosticism, idolatry; see ATHEISM.

page[1] ***n.*** leaf, sheet, folio, side, surface, recto, verso.

page[1,2] ***v.*** **1** [To call] hunt for, seek for, call the name of; see SUMMON. **2** [To mark the pages] number, check, paginate; see CHECK 2.

pageant ***n.*** exhibition, celebration, pomp; see PARADE 1.

paid ***a.*** rewarded, paid off, reimbursed, indemnified, remunerated, solvent, unindebted, unowed, recompensed, salaried, hired, out of debt, refunded; see also REPAID.

pail ***n.*** pot, receptacle, bucket; see CONTAINER.

pain ***n.*** **1** [Suffering, physical or mental] hurt, anguish, distress, discomfort, agony, misery, martyrdom, wretchedness, shock, torture, torment, passion; see also INJURY.—*Ant.* HEALTH, well-being, ease. **2** [Suffering, usually physical] ache, twinge, catch, throe, spasm, cramp, torture, malady, sickness, laceration, soreness, fever, burning, torment, distress, agony, affliction, discomfort, hurt, wound, strain, sting, burn, crick; see also ILLNESS 1, INJURY. **3** [Suffering, usually mental] despondency, worry, anxiety; see DEPRESSION 2, GRIEF, SADNESS. —**feeling no pain*** intoxicated, inebriated, stoned*; see DRUNK. —**take pains** make an effort, care, endeavor; see TRY 1.

pain ***v.*** distress, grieve, trouble; see HURT 1.

painful ***a.*** **1** [Referring to physical anguish] raw, aching, throbbing, burning, torturing, hurtful, biting, piercing, sharp, severe, caustic, tormenting, smarting, extreme, grievous, stinging, bruised, sensitive, tender, irritated, distressing, inflamed, burned, unpleasant, ulcerated, abscessed, uncomfortable; see also SORE 1.—*Ant.* HEALTHY, comfortable, well. **2** [Referring to mental anguish] worrying, depressing, saddening; see DISTURBING.

paint ***n.*** **1** [Pigment] coloring material, chroma, chlorophyll; see COLOR. *Paints and colorings include the following—artist's materials:* oil, acrylic, pastel, crayon, charcoal, watercolor, tempera; *architectural finishes:* house paint, enamel, varnish, redwood stain, oil, wax, whitewash, latex, polyurethane, luminous paint, plastic paint, cold-water paint, flat paint, high-gloss paint, metallic paint, barn paint, interior paint, exterior paint, white lead. **2** [Covering] overlay, varnish, lacquer; see FINISH 2.

paint ***v.*** **1** [To represent by painting] portray, paint in oils, sketch, outline, picture, depict, limn, catch a likeness, design, shade, tint, wash; see also DRAW 2. **2** [To protect or decorate by painting] coat, decorate, apply, brush, tint, touch up, ornament, gloss over, swab, daub, slap on; see also COVER 1, SPREAD 3.

painted ***a.*** **1** [Portrayed] outlined, pictured, drawn, sketched, designed, depicted. **2** [Finished] coated, enameled, covered, decorated, ornamented, brushed over, tinted, washed, daubed, touched up, smeared; see also FINISHED 1.

painter ***n.*** **1** [House painter] interior decorator, dauber, paintslinger*; see WORKMAN. **2** [An artist] craftsman, artisan, illustrator, draftsman, sketcher, limner, cartoonist, watercolorist, painter in oils, fresco painter, portrait painter, landscape painter; see also ARTIST. *Major painters include the following:* Giotto, Sandro Botticelli, Jan van Eyck, Albrecht Dürer, Hieronymus Bosch, Pieter Brueghel (the elder), Leonardo da Vinci, Raphael, Michelangelo, Titian, Tintoretto, El Greco, Peter Paul Rubens, Anthony Van Dyck, Rembrandt van Rijn, Jan Vermeer, Sir Joshua Reynolds, Thomas Gainsborough, J.M.W. Turner, Diego Velázquez, Francisco Goya, Eugène Delacroix, Auguste Renoir, Edgar Degas, James Whistler, Winslow Homer, John Singer Sargent, Edouard Manet, Claude Monet, Paul Cézanne, Vincent van Gogh, Paul Gauguin, Henri de Toulouse-Lautrec, Pablo Picasso, Henri Matisse, Paul Klee, Salvador Dali, Jackson Pollock.

painting ***n.*** **1** [A work of art] oil painting, watercolor, abstract design, landscape, sketch, picture, likeness, artwork, canvas, mural, fresco, depiction, delineation; see also ART. **2** [The act of applying paint] enameling, covering, coating; see ART.

pair ***n.*** couple, mates, two, two of a kind, twosome, twins, fellows, duality, brace.

pair ***v.*** combine, match, balance; see JOIN 1, 2.

pajamas ***n.*** nightwear, lounging pajamas, lounging robe, pj's*, jammies*, nightie*; see also CLOTHES.

pal* ***n.*** chum*, bosom friend, buddy*; see FRIEND.

palace ***n.*** royal residence, manor, mansion; see CASTLE.

pale[1] ***a.*** **1** [Wan] pallid, sickly, anemic, bloodless, ghastly, cadaverous, haggard, deathlike, ghostly; see also DULL 2. **2** [Lacking color] white, colorless, bleached; see DULL 2.

pale[1] ***v.*** grow pale, lose color,

—*vi.* **paled**, **pal′ing** to become pale —**pale′ly** *adv.* — **pale′ness** *n.*

pale² (pāl) *n.* ⟦< L *palus*, a stake⟧ **1** a pointed stake used in fences **2** a boundary; restriction: now chiefly figurative

pale′face′ *n.* a white person: a term allegedly first used by North American Indians

pa·le·on·tol·o·gy (pā′lē ən täl′ə jē) *n.* ⟦< Fr⟧ the branch of geology studying prehistoric life by means of fossils —**pa′le·on·tol′o·gist** *n.*

Pa′le·o·zo′ic (-ə zō′ik) *adj.* ⟦< Gr *palaios*, ancient + ZO(O)- + -IC⟧ designating the geologic era (*c.* 570-240 million years ago) characterized by the first fishes, reptiles, and land plants

Pal·es·tine (pal′əs tīn′) historical region in SW Asia at the E end of the Mediterranean, including modern Israel & Jordan

Pal′es·tin′i·an (-tin′ē ən) *n.* a person, esp. an Arab, born or living in Palestine —*adj.* of Palestine or the Palestinians

pal·ette (pal′it) *n.* ⟦Fr < L *pala*, a shovel⟧ **1** a thin board on which an artist arranges and mixes paints **2** the colors used as for a painting

pal·frey (pôl′frē) *n.*, *pl.* **-freys** ⟦ult. < Gr *para*, beside + L *veredus*, post horse⟧ [Archaic] a saddle horse, esp. a gentle one for a woman

pal·i·mo·ny (pal′ə mō′nē) *n.* ⟦PAL + (AL)IMONY⟧ an allowance or a property settlement claimed by or granted to one member of an unmarried couple who separate after having lived together

pal·imp·sest (pal′imp sest′) *n.* ⟦< Gr *palimpsēstos*, lit., rubbed again⟧ a parchment previously written upon that bears traces of the erased texts

pal·in·drome (pal′in drōm′) *n.* ⟦< Gr *palindromos*, running back⟧ a word, phrase, or sentence that reads the same backward or forward (Ex.: madam)

pal·ing (pāl′iŋ) *n.* a fence made of pales

pal·i·sade (pal′ə sād′) *n.* ⟦< Fr < L *palus*, a stake⟧ **1** any of a row of large, pointed stakes forming a fence as for fortification **2** such a fence **3** [*pl.*] a line of steep cliffs

pall¹ (pôl) *vi.* **palled**, **pall′ing** ⟦ME *pallen*, appall⟧ **1** to become cloying, insipid, boring, etc. **2** to become satiated

pall² (pôl) *n.* ⟦< L *pallium*, a cover⟧ **1** a cloth covering for a coffin **2** a dark or gloomy covering

pall·bear·er (pôl′ber′ər) *n.* ⟦prec. + BEARER⟧ one of the persons who attend or carry the coffin at a funeral

pal·let¹ (pal′it) *n.* ⟦see PALETTE⟧ a low, portable platform used for stacking materials, as in a warehouse

pal·let² (pal′it) *n.* ⟦< L *palea*, chaff⟧ a small bed or a pad filled as with straw and used on the floor

pal·li·ate (pal′ē āt′) *vt.* **-at′ed**, **-at′ing** ⟦< L *pallium*, a cloak⟧ **1** to lessen the severity of without curing; alleviate **2** to make (an offense) appear less serious; excuse — **pal′li·a′tion** *n.* —**pal′li·a′tive** (-āt′iv, -ə tiv) *adj.*, *n.*

pal·lid (pal′id) *adj.* ⟦L *pallidus*, pale⟧ faint in color; pale —**pal′lid·ly** *adv.*

pal·lor (pal′ər) *n.* ⟦< L *pallere*, be pale⟧ unnatural paleness

palm¹ (päm) *n.* ⟦< L *palma*: from its handlike leaf⟧ **1** any of a large group of tropical or subtropical trees or shrubs with a branchless trunk and a bunch of large leaves at the top **2** a leaf of such a tree carried as a symbol of victory, etc.

palm² (päm) *n.* ⟦< L *palma*⟧ the inner surface of the hand between the fingers and wrist —*vt.* to hide (something) in the palm, as in a sleight-of-hand trick —**palm off** [Inf.] to pass off by fraud

pal·met·to (pal met′ō) *n.*, *pl.* **-tos** or **-toes** any of certain palms with fan-shaped leaves

palm·is·try (päm′is trē) *n.* ⟦prob. < ME *paume*, PALM² + *maistrie*, mastery⟧ fortunetelling by interpreting the lines, etc. on the palm of a person's hand —**palm′ist** *n.*

Palm Springs resort city in SW California: pop. 40,000

Palm Sunday the Sunday before Easter, commemorating Jesus' entry into Jerusalem, when palm branches were strewn before him

palm′top′ *n.* a small, portable computer for storing personal information, sending e-mail, etc.

palm·y (päm′ē) *adj.* **-i·er**, **-i·est** **1** of, like, or full of palm trees **2** prosperous *[palmy* days*]*

pal·o·mi·no (pal′ə mē′nō) *n.*, *pl.* **-nos** ⟦AmSp < Sp, dove-colored⟧ a golden or cream-colored horse with a white tail

pal·pa·ble (pal′pə bəl) *adj.* ⟦< L *palpare*, to touch⟧ **1** that can be touched, felt, etc. **2** easily perceived by the senses; perceptible **3** obvious; plain —**pal′pa·bly** *adv.*

pal·pi·tate (pal′pə tāt′) *vi.* **-tat′ed**, **-tat′ing** ⟦< L *palpare*, to feel⟧ **1** to beat rapidly, as the heart **2** to throb — **pal′pi·ta′tion** *n.*

pal·sy (pôl′zē) *n.*, *pl.* **-sies** ⟦ult. < L *paralysis*, paralysis⟧ paralysis of a muscle, sometimes with involuntary tremors —*vt.* **-sied**, **-sy·ing** to affect with or as with palsy

pal·try (pôl′trē) *adj.* **-tri·er**, **-tri·est** ⟦prob. < LowG *palte*, rag⟧ almost worthless; trifling —**pal′tri·ness** *n.*

pam·pa (pam′pə, päm′-) *n.* ⟦AmSp < AmInd *pampa*, plain, field⟧ an extensive, treeless plain of Argentina

pam·per (pam′pər) *vt.* ⟦ME *pampren*, to feed too much < LowG⟧ to be overindulgent with; coddle

pam·phlet (pam′flit) *n.* ⟦< OFr *Pamphilet*, shortened name of a ML poem⟧ a thin, unbound booklet, often on some topic of current interest —**pam′phlet·eer′** (-flə tir′) *n.*

pan¹ (pan) *n.* ⟦OE *panne*⟧ **1** any broad, shallow container used in cooking, etc. **2** a pan-shaped part or object —*vt.* **panned**, **pan′ning** **1** [Inf.] to criticize unfavorably **2** *Mining* to wash (gravel) in a pan, as to separate (gold) — *vi. Mining* to wash gravel in a pan, searching for gold — **pan out** [Inf.] to turn out; esp., to succeed

pan² (pan) *Film, TV, etc.* *vt.*, *vi.* **panned**, **pan′ning** ⟦< PAN(ORAMA)⟧ to move (a camera) so as to get a panoramic effect —*n.* the act of panning

Pan (pan) *n. Gr. Myth.* a god of fields, forests, flocks, and shepherds, represented as having the legs of a goat

pan- ⟦< Gr *pan*, all, every⟧ *combining form* **1** all *[pantheism]* **2** **[P-]** of, comprising, or uniting every *[Pan-*American*]*

pan·a·ce·a (pan′ə sē′ə) *n.* ⟦< Gr *pan*, all + *akos*, healing, medicine⟧ a supposed remedy for all ills

pa·nache (pə nash′, -näsh′) *n.* ⟦Fr, ult. < L *pinna*, feather⟧ dashing elegance of manner or style

Pan·a·ma (pan′ə mä′, -mô′) country in Central America, a strip of land connecting Central & South America: 29,761 sq. mi.; pop. 2,329,000 —**Pan′a·ma′ni·an** (-mā′nē ən) *adj.*, *n.*

Panama Canal ship canal across Panama, connecting the Atlantic & Pacific

Panama (hat) [*also* **p-**] a hand-woven hat made with strawlike strips of the leaves of a tropical plant

Pan′-A·mer′i·can *adj.* of North, South, and Central America, collectively

pan·cake (pan′kāk′) *n.* a flat cake of batter fried on a griddle or in a pan

pan·chro·mat·ic (pan′krō mat′ik) *adj.* sensitive to light of all colors *[panchromatic* film*]*

pan·cre·as (pan′krē əs, paŋ′-) *n.* ⟦< Gr *pan*, all + *kreas*, flesh⟧ a large gland that secretes a digestive juice into the small intestine and produces insulin —**pan′cre·at′ic** (-at′ik) *adj.*

pan·da (pan′də) *n.* ⟦< native name in Nepal⟧ **1** a black-and-white, bearlike mammal of China: in full **giant panda** **2** a reddish, raccoonlike mammal of the Himalayas: in full **lesser panda**

pan·dem·ic (pan dem′ik) *adj.* ⟦< Gr *pan*, all + *dēmos*, the people⟧ epidemic over a large region

pan·de·mo·ni·um (pan′də mō′nē əm) *n.* ⟦< name of demons' abode in Milton's *Paradise Lost* < Gr *pan*, all + *daimōn*, evil spirit⟧ wild disorder or noise

pan·der (pan′dər) *n.* ⟦< L *Pandarus*, lovers' go-between in Chaucer, etc.⟧ **1** a procurer; pimp **2** one who helps others to satisfy their vices, etc. Also **pan′der·er** —*vi.* to act as a pander (*to*)

THESAURUS

blanch; see WHITEN 1.

paleness *n.* whiteness, anemia, colorlessness; see ILLNESS 1.

paltry *a.* small, insignificant, trifling; see UNIMPORTANT.

pamper *v.* spoil, indulge, pet, cater to, humor, gratify, yield to, coddle, overindulge, please, spare the rod and spoil the child*.

pamphlet *n.* booklet, brochure, pocketbook, chapbook, leaflet, bulletin, circular, broadside, handbill; see also ANNOUNCEMENT.

pan¹ *n.* vessel, container, pail, bucket, baking pan, gold pan; see also CONTAINER. *Kitchen pans include the following:* kettle, stewpan, saucepan, double boiler, roaster, casserole, cake pan, bread pan, pie pan, cookie sheet, frying pan, skillet, dishpan.

pan¹* *v.* criticize, review unfavorably, jeer at; see BLAME. —**pan out*** turn out, work, be a success; see SUCCEED 1.

panacea *n.* relief, cure, elixir; see REMEDY 2.

pancake *n.* flapjack, hot cake, griddlecake; see FOOD.

pandemonium *n.* uproar, anarchy, riot; see CONFUSION.

P & H *abbrev.* postage and handling

Pan·do·ra (pan dôr′ə) ***n.*** ⟦< Gr *pan,* all + *dōron,* gift⟧ *Gr. Myth.* the first mortal woman: she opens a box, letting all human ills into the world

pane (pān) ***n.*** ⟦< L *pannus,* piece of cloth⟧ a sheet of glass in a frame of a window, etc.

pan·e·gyr·ic (pan′ə jir′ik) ***n.*** ⟦< Gr *panēgyris,* public meeting⟧ **1** a formal speech or piece of writing praising a person or event **2** high praise

pan·el (pan′əl) ***n.*** ⟦see PANE⟧ **1** *a)* a section or division, usually rectangular, forming a part of a wall, door, etc. *b)* a board for instruments or controls **2** a lengthwise strip in a skirt, etc. **3** a list of persons summoned for jury duty **4** a group of persons selected for judging, discussing, etc. —***vt.*** **-eled** or **-elled**, **-el·ing** or **-el·ling** to provide with panels

pan′el·ing or **pan′el·ling** ***n.*** **1** panels collectively **2** sheets of plastic, wood, etc. from which to cut panels

pan′el·ist ***n.*** a member of a PANEL (*n.* 4)

panel truck an enclosed pickup truck

pang (paŋ) ***n.*** ⟦< ?⟧ a sudden, sharp pain, physical or emotional

pan·han·dle[1] (pan′han′dəl) ***n.*** a strip of land projecting like the handle of a pan

pan·han·dle[2] (pan′han′dəl) ***vi.*** **-dled**, **-dling** [Inf.] to beg on the streets —**pan′han′dler** ***n.***

pan·ic (pan′ik) ***n.*** ⟦< Gr *panikos,* of Pan, as inspirer of sudden fear⟧ a sudden, unreasoning fear, often spreading quickly —***vt.*** **-icked**, **-ick·ing** to affect with panic —***vi.*** to show panic —**pan′ick·y** ***adj.***

pan′ic-strick′en ***adj.*** badly frightened: also **pan′ic-struck′**

pan·nier or **pan·ier** (pan′yər, -ē ər) ***n.*** ⟦< L *panis,* bread⟧ a large basket for carrying loads on the back

pa·no·cha (pə nō′chə) ***n.*** ⟦AmSp, ult. < L *panis,* bread⟧ **1** a coarse Mexican sugar **2** *var. of* PENUCHE

pan·o·ply (pan′ə plē) ***n.***, *pl.* **-plies** ⟦< Gr *pan,* all + *hopla,* arms⟧ **1** a complete suit of armor **2** any complete or magnificent covering or array

pan·o·ram·a (pan′ə ram′ə) ***n.*** ⟦< PAN- + Gr *horama,* a view⟧ **1** a wide view in all directions **2** a constantly changing scene —**pan′o·ram′ic** ***adj.***

pan·sy (pan′zē) ***n.***, *pl.* **-sies** ⟦< Fr *penser,* think⟧ a small plant of the violet family, with velvety petals

pant (pant) ***vi.*** ⟦ult. < L *phantasia,* nightmare⟧ **1** to breathe rapidly and heavily, as from running fast **2** to yearn eagerly: with *for* or *after* —***vt.*** to gasp out —***n.*** any of a series of rapid, heavy breaths; gasp

pan·ta·loons (pan′tə lo͞onz′) ***pl.n.*** ⟦< It: ult. after St. *Pantalone*⟧ [Historical] trousers

pan·the·ism (pan′thē iz′əm) ***n.*** ⟦< Gr *pan,* all + *theos,* a god + -ISM⟧ **1** the doctrine that all forces, manifestations, etc. of the universe are God **2** the worship of all gods —**pan′the·ist** ***n.***

pan·the·on (pan′thē än′) ***n.*** ⟦< Gr *pan,* all + *theos,* a god⟧ **1** all the gods of a people **2** [*often* **P-**] a building in which famous dead persons of a nation are entombed or commemorated

pan·ther (pan′thər) ***n.*** ⟦< Gr *panthēr*⟧ **1** a leopard, specif. one that is black **2** COUGAR

pant·ies (pan′tēz) ***pl.n.*** women's or children's short underpants: also **pant′ie** or **pant′y** ***n.***

pan·to·mime (pan′tə mīm′) ***n.*** ⟦ult. < Gr *pan,* all + *mimos,* a mimic⟧ **1** a drama played without words, using only action and gestures **2** action or gestures without words —***vt.***, ***vi.*** **-mimed′**, **-mim′ing** to express or act in pantomime —**pan′to·mim′ist** (-mīm′ist) ***n.***

pan·to·then·ic acid (pan′tō then′ik) ⟦< Gr *pantothen,* from every side⟧ a viscous oil, part of the vitamin B complex, occurring widely in animal and plant tissues and thought essential for cell growth

pan·try (pan′trē) ***n.***, *pl.* **-tries** ⟦< L *panis,* bread⟧ a small room off the kitchen, where cooking ingredients and utensils, china, etc. are kept

pants (pants) ***pl.n.*** ⟦< PANTALOONS⟧ **1** trousers **2** drawers or panties

pant′suit′ ***n.*** matched pants and jacket for women: also **pants suit**

pant·y·hose (pan′tē hōz′) ***n.*** women's hose that extend to the waist, forming a one-piece garment

pant′y·waist′ (-wāst′) ***n.*** [Slang] a sissy

pap (pap) ***n.*** ⟦ME⟧ **1** any soft food for babies or invalids **2** any oversimplified or tasteless writing, ideas, etc.

pa·pa (pä′pə, pə pä′) ***n.*** ⟦< baby talk⟧ *child's term for* FATHER

pa·pa·cy (pā′pə sē) ***n.***, *pl.* **-cies** ⟦LL *papa,* pope⟧ **1** the rank of pope **2** the term of office of a pope **3** the governing of the Roman Catholic Church by the pope, its head

pa·pal (pā′pəl) ***adj.*** of or relating to a pope or the papacy

pa·pa·raz·zi (pä′pä rät′tsē) ***pl.n.*** photographers who take candid shots of celebrities

pa·paw (pə pô′, pô′pô′) ***n.*** ⟦< fol.⟧ **1** PAPAYA **2** *a)* a tree of central and S U.S. with an oblong, yellowish, edible fruit *b)* its fruit

pa·pa·ya (pə pī′ə) ***n.*** ⟦Sp < WInd name⟧ **1** a tropical American tree with a large, oblong, yellowish-orange fruit **2** its fruit

pa·per (pā′pər) ***n.*** ⟦ult. < Gr *papyros,* papyrus⟧ **1** a thin, flexible material in sheets, made from rags, wood, etc. and used for writing or printing on, for packaging, etc. **2** a single sheet of this **3** an official document **4** an essay, dissertation, etc. **5** a newspaper **6** wallpaper **7** [*pl.*] credentials —***adj.*** **1** of, or made of, paper **2** like paper; thin —***vt.*** to cover with wallpaper —**pa′per·y** ***adj.***

pa′per·back′ ***n.*** a book bound in paper covers

pa′per·boy′ ***n.*** a boy who sells or delivers newspapers —**pa′per·girl′** ***fem.n.***

paper clip a flexible clasp for holding loose sheets of paper together

pa′per·hang′er ***n.*** a person whose work is covering walls with wallpaper

paper tiger a person, nation, etc. that seems to pose a threat but is really powerless

THESAURUS

pane ***n.*** window glass, stained glass, mirror; see GLASS.

panel ***n.*** ornament, tablet, inset; see DECORATION 2.

pang ***n.*** throb, sting, bite; see PAIN 2.

panhandle[2*] ***v.*** solicit, ask alms, bum*; see BEG.

panhandler* ***n.*** vagrant, bum*, mendicant; see BEGGAR.

panic ***n.*** dread, alarm, fright; see FEAR.

panic-stricken ***a.*** terrified, hysterical, fearful; see AFRAID.

panorama ***n.*** spectacle, scenery, prospect; see VIEW.

pant ***v.*** wheeze, throb, breathe heavily; see BREATHE, GASP.

panties ***n.*** pants, underpants, briefs; see UNDERWEAR.

pantomime ***n.*** sign, sign language, dumb show*, mimicry, play without words, acting without speech, charade, mime.

pantry ***n.*** storeroom, larder, cupboard; see CLOSET, ROOM 2.

pants ***n.*** **1** [Trousers] breeches, britches*, slacks, jeans, overalls, cords, shorts, corduroys, pantaloons, bell-bottoms, riding breeches, chaps, short pants, knee pants, knickers, bloomers, sweat pants, jodhpurs, dungarees, harem pants, stretch pants, leggings; see also CLOTHES. **2** [Underclothing] shorts, briefs, panties; see CLOTHES, UNDERWEAR.

papa* ***n.*** dad*, daddy*, male parent; see FATHER 1, PARENT.

paper ***n.*** **1** [A piece of legal or official writing] document, official document, legal paper; see RECORD 1. *Papers include the following:* abstract, affidavit, bill, certificate, citation, contract, credentials, data, deed, diploma, indictment, grant, orders, passport, visa, plea, records, safe-conduct, subpoena, summons, testimony, voucher, warrant, will, warranty, decree, writ, receipt. **2** [A newspaper] journal, daily, weekly; see NEWSPAPER. **3** [A piece of writing] essay, article, thesis; see WRITING 2. **4** [A manufactured product] *Paper products include the following—writing material:* typing paper, typewriter paper, stationery, bond paper, letterhead, personal stationery, ruled paper, second sheet, handmade paper, parchment, vellum, onionskin, carbon paper, notepad, notecard, tablet, file card, computer paper, notebook; *printing paper:* coated stock, poster, linen finish, vellum, parchment, India; 50-pound, 60-pound, etc.; newsprint; *miscellaneous:* rice, crepe, butcher's, wrapping, tissue, brown, tar, roofing, tracing, graph, filter, toilet, wax, waxed, blotting, scrap, photographic, etc. paper; cardboard, paper bag, wallpaper, cellophane, paper towel, cleansing tissue. —**on paper** **1** recorded, signed, official; see WRITTEN 2. **2** in theory, assumed to be feasible, not yet in practice; see THEORETICAL.

paper ***v.*** hang, paste up, plaster; see COVER 1.

paperback ***n.*** softcover, pocket book, reprint; see BOOK.

papers ***n.*** **1** [Evidence of identity or authorization] naturalization papers, identification card, ID; see IDENTIFICATION 2, PASSPORT. **2** [Documentary materials] writings, documents, effects; see RECORD 1.

paper trail written records that serve as evidence of a person's actions
pa′per·weight′ ***n.*** any small, heavy object set on papers to keep them from being scattered
pa′per·work′ ***n.*** the keeping of records, etc. incidental to some task
pa·pier-mâ·ché (pā′pər mə shā′) ***n.*** ⟦Fr < *papier*, paper + *mâcher*, to chew⟧ a material made of paper pulp mixed with size, glue, etc., and molded into various objects when moist
pa·pil·la (pə pil′ə) ***n.***, *pl.* **-lae** (-ē) ⟦L < *papula*, pimple⟧ any small nipplelike projection of tissue, as on the surface of the tongue —**pap·il·lar·y** (pap′ə ler′ē) ***adj.***
pa·poose (pa po͞os′, pa-) ***n.*** ⟦< AmInd⟧ a North American Indian baby
pa·pri·ka (pə prē′kə) ***n.*** ⟦Hung, ult. < Gr *peperi*, pepper⟧ a mild or hot, red, powdered condiment ground from the fruit of certain pepper plants
Pap test (pap) ⟦after G. *Papanicolaou*, 20th-c. U.S. anatomist⟧ a test for uterine cancer
Pap·u·a New Guinea (pap′yo͞o ə) country occupying the E half of the island of New Guinea & nearby islands: 178,703 sq. mi.; pop. 3,689,000
pa·py·rus (pə pī′rəs) ***n.***, *pl.* **-ri′** (-rī′) or **-rus·es** ⟦< Gr *papyros*⟧ **1** a tall water plant of Egypt **2** a writing material made from the pith of this plant by the ancients
par (pär) ***n.*** ⟦L, an equal⟧ **1** the established value of a currency in terms of the money of another country **2** an equal status, level, etc.: usually in **on a par (with)** **3** the average state, condition, etc. *[work that is above par]* **4** the face value of stocks, etc. **5** *Golf* the number of strokes established as a skillful score for a hole or course —***adj.*** **1** of or at par **2** average
par *abbrev.* **1** paragraph **2** parish
para- *prefix* **1** beside, beyond *[parapsychology]* **2** helping, accessory *[paramedical]*
par·a·ble (par′ə bəl) ***n.*** ⟦< Gr *parabolē*, analogy < *para-*, beside + *ballein*, to throw⟧ a short, simple story teaching a moral lesson
pa·rab·o·la (pə rab′ə lə) ***n.*** ⟦see prec.⟧ *Geom.* a curve formed by the intersection of a cone with a plane parallel to its side —**par·a·bol·ic** (par′ə bäl′ik) ***adj.***
par·a·chute (par′ə sho͞ot′) ***n.*** ⟦Fr < *para-*, protecting + *chute*, a fall⟧ a cloth contrivance usually shaped like an umbrella when expanded, and used to retard the speed of one dropping from an airplane, etc. —***vt.***, ***vi.*** **-chut′ed**, **-chut′ing** to drop by parachute —**par′a·chut′ist** ***n.***
pa·rade (pə rād′) ***n.*** ⟦< L *parare*, prepare⟧ **1** ostentatious display **2** a review of marching troops **3** any organized procession or march, as for display —***vt.*** **-rad′ed**, **-rad′ing** **1** to march or walk through, as for display **2** to show off *[to parade one's knowledge]* —***vi.*** **1** to march in a parade **2** to walk about ostentatiously
par·a·digm (par′ə dīm′) ***n.*** ⟦< Gr *para-*, beside + *deigma*, example⟧ **1** an example or model **2** a generally accepted concept that explains a complex idea, set of data, etc. **3** *Gram.* an example of a declension or conjugation, giving all the inflections of a word
Par·a·dise (par′a dīs′) ***n.*** ⟦< Gr *paradeisos*, garden⟧ **1** the garden of Eden **2** heaven **3** [**p-**] any place or state of great happiness
par·a·dox (par′ə däks′) ***n.*** ⟦< Gr *para-*, beyond + *doxa*, opinion⟧ **1** a statement that seems contradictory, etc. but may be true in fact **2** a statement that is self-contradictory and, hence, false —**par′a·dox′i·cal** ***adj.*** —**par′a·dox′i·cal·ly** ***adv.***
par·af·fin (par′ə fin) ***n.*** ⟦Ger < L *parum*, too little + *affinis*, akin: from its inertness⟧ a white, waxy substance obtained from petroleum and used for making candles, sealing jars, etc.
par·a·gon (par′ə gän′) ***n.*** ⟦< It *paragone*, touchstone⟧ a model of perfection or excellence
par·a·graph (par′ə graf′) ***n.*** ⟦< Gr *para-*, beside + *graphein*, write⟧ **1** a distinct section of a piece of writing, begun on a new line and often indented **2** a brief item in a newspaper, etc. —***vt.*** to arrange in paragraphs
Par·a·guay (par′ə gwā′, -gwī′) inland country in SC South America: 157,042 sq. mi.; pop. 4,120,000 —**Par′a·guay′an** ***adj.***, ***n.***
par·a·keet (par′ə kēt′) ***n.*** ⟦prob. < MFr *perrot*, parrot⟧ a small, slender parrot with a long tail
par·a·le·gal (par′ə lē′gəl) ***adj.*** designating or of persons trained to aid lawyers but not licensed to practice law —***n.*** such a person
par·al·lax (par′ə laks′) ***n.*** ⟦< Gr *para-*, beyond + *allassein*, to change⟧ the apparent change in the position of an object resulting from a change in the viewer's position
par·al·lel (par′ə lel′) ***adj.*** ⟦< Gr *para-*, side by side + *allēlos*, one another⟧ **1** extending in the same direction and at the same distance apart, as so never to meet **2** similar or corresponding —***n.*** **1** a parallel line, surface, etc. **2** any person or thing similar to another; counterpart **3** any comparison showing likeness **4** any of the imaginary lines parallel to the equator and representing degrees of latitude: in full **parallel of latitude** —***vt.*** **-leled′** or **-lelled′**, **-lel′ing** or **-lel′ling** **1** to be parallel with **2** to match; equal —**par′al·lel′ism′** ***n.***
par′al·lel′o·gram′ (-ə gram′) ***n.*** a four-sided plane figure having the opposite sides parallel and equal
parallel parking the parking of vehicles close to and parallel to the curb
pa·ral·y·sis (pə ral′ə sis) ***n.***, *pl.* **-ses′** (-sēz′) ⟦< Gr *paralyein*, to loosen or weaken at the side⟧ **1** partial or complete loss of voluntary motion or of sensation in part or all of the body **2** any condition of helpless inactivity —**par·a·lyt·ic** (par′ə lit′ik) ***adj.***, ***n.***
par·a·lyze (par′ə līz′) ***vt.*** **-lyzed′**, **-lyz′ing** **1** to cause paralysis in **2** to make ineffective or powerless
par·a·me·ci·um (par′ə mē′sē əm, -shē əm) ***n.***, *pl.* **-ci·a** (-ə) ⟦< Gr *paramēkēs*, oval⟧ an elongated protozoan that moves by means of cilia
par·a·med·ic (par′ə med′ik) ***n.*** a person in paramedical work
par′a·med′i·cal (-med′i kəl) ***adj.*** ⟦PARA- + MEDICAL⟧ of auxiliary medical personnel, as midwives and nurses' aides
pa·ram·e·ter (pə ram′ət ər) ***n.*** ⟦< Gr *para-*, beside + *metron*, a measure⟧ **1** any of a set of interdependent variables **2** *a*) a boundary or limit *b*) a characteristic (*usually used in pl.*)
par·a·mil·i·tar·y (par′ə mil′ə ter′ē) ***adj.*** ⟦PARA- + MILITARY⟧ of forces working along with, or in place of, a regular military organization
par·a·mount (par′ə mount′) ***adj.*** ⟦< OFr *par*, by + *amont*, uphill⟧ ranking higher than any other; chief
par·a·mour (par′ə moor′) ***n.*** ⟦< OFr *par amour*, with love⟧ a lover or mistress; esp., the illicit sexual partner of a married man or woman
par·a·noi·a (par′ə noi′ə) ***n.*** ⟦< Gr *para-*, beside + *nous*, the

THESAURUS

paperwork ***n.*** office work, desk work, keeping one's desk clear, keeping records, filing, preparing reports, writing, editing, research, letter writting, billing, filling out forms, taking dictation, typing, keeping books.
papery ***a.*** flimsy, insubstantial, slight; see POOR 2.
par ***n.*** standard, level, norm; see MODEL 2.
parable ***n.*** fable, moral story, allegory; see STORY.
parachute ***n.*** chute, seat pack parachute, lap pack parachute, harness and pack, umbrella*, silk*.
parachute ***v.*** fall, bail out, hit the silk*; see DIVE.
parade ***n.*** **1** [A procession] march, motorcade, spectacle, ceremony, demonstration, review, line of floats, line of march, pageant, ritual. **2** [An ostentatious show] show, ostentation, ceremony; see DISPLAY.
parade ***v.*** demonstrate, display, exhibit; see MARCH.
paradise ***n.*** **1** [Heaven] kingdom come, celestial home, the other world; see HEAVEN. **2** [The home of Adam and Eve] Garden of Eden, Eden, the Garden.
paradox ***n.*** seeming contradiction, enigma, ambiguity; see PUZZLE 1.
paragon ***n.*** ideal, perfection, best; see MODEL 1.
paragraph ***n.*** passage, section, division of thought, topic, statement, verse, article, item, notice.
parallel ***a.*** **1** [Equidistant at all points] side by side, never meeting, running parallel, coextending, lateral, laterally, in the same direction, extending equally. **2** [Similar in kind, position, or the like] identical, equal, conforming; see ALIKE.
parallel ***n.*** resemblance, likeness, correspondence; see SIMILARITY.
parallel ***v.*** match, correspond, correlate; see EQUAL.
paralysis ***n.*** insensibility, loss of motion, loss of sensation; see ILLNESS 2.
paralytic ***a.*** inactive, paralyzed, immobile; see DISABLED, SICK.
paralytic ***n.*** paralysis victim, disabled person, paralyzed person; see PATIENT.
paralyze ***v.*** strike with paralysis, make inert, take away sensation; see DEADEN.
paralyzed ***a.*** insensible, benumbed, stupefied, inert, inactive, unmoving, helpless, torpid; see also DISABLED.

mind] a mental disorder characterized by delusions, as of grandeur or, esp., persecution —**par'a·noid'** *adj.*, *n.*

par·a·pet (par'ə pet', -pət) *n.* [< It *parare,* to guard + *petto,* breast] **1** a wall or bank for screening troops from enemy fire **2** a low wall or railing

par·a·pher·na·li·a (par'ə fər nāl'yə, -nā'lē ə) *pl.n.* [< Gr *para-,* beyond + *phernē,* dowry] [*often with sing. v.*] **1** personal belongings **2** equipment

par·a·phrase (par'ə frāz') *n.* [< Gr *para-,* beside + *phrazein,* say] a rewording of the meaning of something spoken or written —*vt.*, *vi.* **-phrased'**, **-phras'ing** to express (something) in a paraphrase

par·a·ple·gi·a (par'ə plē'jē ə, -jə) *n.* [< Gr *para-,* beside + *plēgē,* a stroke] paralysis of the lower half of the body —**par'a·ple'gic** (-plē'jik) *adj.*, *n.*

par'a·pro·fes'sion·al *n.* [see PARA-] a trained assistant to licensed professionals, as in medicine

par'a·psy·chol'o·gy *n.* [see PARA-] psychology that investigates psychic phenomena, such as telepathy

par'a·sail' *n.* [< PARACHUTE] a kind of parachute worn by a person who is pulled by a boat, car, etc. fast enough to glide in the air —**par'a·sail'ing** *n.*

par·a·site (par'ə sīt') *n.* [< Gr *para-,* beside + *sitos,* food] **1** one who lives at others' expense without making any useful return **2** a plant or animal that lives on or in another organism, usually with harmful effects —**par'a·sit'ic** (-sit'ik) *adj.*

par·a·sol (par'ə sôl') *n.* [< It *parare,* ward off + *sole,* sun] a lightweight umbrella used for protection from the sun's rays

par·a·sym·pa·thet·ic (par'ə sim'pə thet'ik) *adj.* [PARA- + SYMPATHETIC] *Physiology* designating the part of the autonomic nervous system whose functions include constricting the pupils of the eyes, slowing the heartbeat, and stimulating some digestive glands

par·a·thi·on (par'ə thī'än') *n.* [PARA- + Gr *theion,* sulfur] a highly poisonous insecticide

par·a·thy'roid' (-thī'roid') *adj.* [PARA- + THYROID] designating or of the small glands near the thyroid that regulate calcium and phosphorus metabolism

par·a·troops (par'ə tro͞ops') *pl.n.* [< PARA(CHUTE) + TROOP] troops trained and equipped to parachute into a combat area —**par'a·troop'er** *n.*

par·boil (pär'boil') *vt.* [< L *per,* through + *bullire,* to boil: infl. by *part*] to boil until partly cooked

par·cel (pär'səl) *n.* [ult. < L *pars,* part] **1** a small, wrapped bundle; package **2** a piece (of land) —*vt.* **-celed** or **-celled**, **-cel·ing** or **-cel·ling** to separate into parts and distribute: with *out*

parcel post a mail service for parcels not over a specified weight and size

parch (pärch) *vt.* [< ?] **1** to make hot and dry **2** to make very thirsty —*vi.* to become very dry, hot, thirsty, etc.

parch·ment (pärch'mənt) *n.* [< L (*charta*) *Pergamena,* (paper) of Pergamum, city in Asia Minor] **1** the skin of a sheep, goat, etc. prepared as a surface for writing **2** paper like parchment **3** a manuscript on parchment

par·don (pärd''n) *vt.* [< L *per-,* through + *donare,* give] **1** to release from further punishment **2** to forgive (an offense) **3** to excuse (a person) for a fault, etc. —*n.* **1** forgiveness **2** an official document granting a pardon —**par'don·a·ble** *adj.*

pare (per) *vt.* **pared**, **par'ing** [< L *parare,* prepare] **1** to cut or trim away (the rind, skin, etc.) of; peel **2** to reduce gradually: often with *down*

par·e·gor·ic (par'ə gôr'ik) *n.* [< Gr *parēgoros,* soothing] a tincture of opium, used to relieve diarrhea

par·ent (per'ənt) *n.* [< L *parere,* beget] **1** a person in relation to his or her offspring; a mother or father **2** any organism in relation to its offspring **3** a source; origin —*adj.* of a corporation in relation to a subsidiary that it owns —**pa·ren·tal** (pə rent''l) *adj.* —**par'ent·hood'** *n.*

par'ent·age *n.* descent from parents or ancestors; lineage

pa·ren·the·sis (pə ren'thə sis) *n.*, *pl.* **-ses'** (-sēz') [< Gr *para-,* beside + *entithenai,* to insert] **1** a word, clause, etc. added as an explanation or comment within a sentence **2** either or both of the curved lines, ( ), used to set this off —**par·en·thet·i·cal** (par'ən thet'i kəl) or **par'en·thet'ic** *adj.*

par'ent·ing *n.* the work or skill of a parent in raising a child or children

pa·re·sis (pə rē'sis) *n.*, *pl.* **-ses'** (-sēz') [Gr < *parienai,* relax] **1** partial paralysis **2** a brain disease caused by syphilis of the central nervous system

par ex·cel·lence (ek'sə läns) [< Fr] in the greatest degree of excellence

par·fait (pär fā') *n.* [Fr, lit., perfect] a frozen dessert of cream, eggs, etc., or of layers of ice cream, crushed fruit, etc. in a tall glass

pa·ri·ah (pə rī'ə) *n.* [< Tamil *paraiyan,* drummer] **1** a member of one of the lowest social castes in India **2** any outcast

par·i·mu·tu·el (par'ə myo͞o'cho͞o əl) *n.* [Fr, lit., a mutual bet] a system of betting on races in which the winning bettors share the net of each pool in proportion to their wagers

par·ing (per'iŋ) *n.* a piece pared off

Par·is[1] (par'is) *n.* *Gr. Legend* a prince of Troy: see HELEN OF TROY

Par·is[2] (par'is; *Fr* pä rē') capital of France: pop. 2,166,000 —**Pa·ri·sian** (pə rizh'ən, -rē'zhən) *adj.*, *n.*

par·ish (par'ish) *n.* [< Gr *paroikia,* diocese] **1** a part of a diocese, under the charge of a priest or minister **2** the congregation of a church **3** a civil division in Louisiana, like a county

pa·rish·ion·er (pə rish'ə nər) *n.* a member of a parish

par·i·ty (par'ə tē) *n.* [< L *par,* equal] **1** equality in power, value, etc. **2** equality of value at a given ratio between different kinds of money, etc.

park (pärk) *n.* [< ML *parricus*] **1** wooded land held as part of an estate or preserve **2** an area of public land, with walks, playgrounds, etc., for recreation **3** the system in an automatic transmission that locks the drive wheels of a motor vehicle —*vt.*, *vi.* **1** to leave (a vehicle) in a place temporarily **2** to maneuver (a vehicle) into a space where it can be left temporarily

par·ka (pär'kə) *n.* [< Russ, fur coat] a heavy jacket with a hood

parking meter a timing device installed near a parking space: drivers pay to park there for a certain length of time by inserting coins in it

Par·kin·son's disease (pär'kin sənz) [after J. *Parkinson* (1755-1824), Eng physician] a degenerative disease of later life, causing a rhythmic tremor and muscular rigidity

THESAURUS

paranoid *a.* affected by paranoia, unreasonably distrustful, overly suspicious, having a persecution complex.

paraphernalia *n.* gear, material, apparatus; see EQUIPMENT.

parasite *n.* **1** [A plant or animal living on another] bacteria, bacterium, parasitoid, saprophyte, epiphyte. **2** [A hanger-on] dependent, freeloader*, sponger*; see SLAVE.

parcel *n.* bundle, packet, carton; see PACKAGE.

parch *v.* dessicate, dehydrate, dry up; see DRY 1.

parched *a.* burned, withered, dried; see DRY 1.

parchment *n.* vellum, goatskin, sheepskin; see PAPER 4.

pardon *n.* **1** [The reduction or removal of punishment] absolution, grace, remission, amnesty, exoneration, discharge; see also MERCY.—*Ant.* PUNISHMENT, condemnation, conviction. **2** [Forgiveness] excusing, forbearance, conciliation; see FORGIVENESS, KINDNESS 1.

pardon *v.* **1** [To reduce punishment] exonerate, clear, absolve, reprieve, acquit, set free, liberate, discharge, rescue, justify, suspend charges, put on probation, grant amnesty to; see also FREE, RELEASE.—*Ant.* PUNISH, chastise, sentence. **2** [To forgive] condone, overlook, exculpate; see EXCUSE, FORGIVE.

pardoned *a.* forgiven, freed, excused, released, granted amnesty, given a pardon, reprieved, granted a reprieve, acquitted, let off, sprung*; see also DISCHARGED, FREE 1.—*Ant.* ACCUSED, convicted, condemned.

pare *v.* peel, trim, scrape; see CUT 1, SHAVE, SKIN.

parent *n.* immediate forebear, procreator, progenitor, stepparent, foster parent; see also FATHER 1, MOTHER 1.

parental *a.* paternal, maternal, familial; see GENETIC.

parentheses *n.* brackets, braces, punctuation marks; see PUNCTUATION.

parish *n.* archdiocese, congregation, diocese; see AREA, CHURCH 3.

park *n.* **1** [A place designated for outdoor recreation] square, plaza, lawn, green, village green, promenade, tract, recreational area, national park, national monument, enclosure, woodland, meadow. **2** [A place designed for outdoor storage] car park*, parking space, lot; see GARAGE, PARKING LOT.

parked *a.* standing, left, put, lined up, in rows, by the curb, in the parking lot, stored, halted, unmoving.

parking lot *n.* lot, space, parking space, parking garage, parking area, parking facility, parking slot, off-street parking.

park'way' ***n.*** a broad roadway landscaped with trees, bushes, etc.
par·lance (pär'ləns) ***n.*** ⟦< OFr *parler*, speak⟧ language or idiom
par·lay (pär'lā) ***vt., vi.*** ⟦< It *paro*, a pair⟧ to bet (an original wager plus its winnings) on another race, etc. —***n.*** a parlayed bet
par·ley (pär'lē) ***vi.*** ⟦< Fr *parler*, speak⟧ to confer, esp. with an enemy —***n.***, *pl.* **-leys** a conference, as to settle a dispute or discuss terms
par·lia·ment (pär'lə mənt) ***n.*** ⟦< OFr *parler*, speak⟧ **1** an official government council **2** [**P-**] the national legislative body of certain countries, esp. Great Britain
par'lia·men·tar'i·an (-men ter'ē ən) ***n.*** one skilled in parliamentary rules or debate
par'lia·men'ta·ry (-ment'ə rē, -men'trē) ***adj.*** **1** of or by a parliament **2** conforming to the rules of a parliament
par·lor (pär'lər) ***n.*** ⟦< OFr *parler*, speak⟧ **1** [Old-fashioned] any living room **2** any of certain kinds of business establishment *[*a beauty *parlor]*
Parmesan (cheese) (pär'mə zän', -zhän') ⟦after *Parma*, It city⟧ a very hard, dry cheese orig. of Italy
par·mi·gia·na (pär'mə zhä'nə, pär'mə zhän') ***adj.*** prepared with Parmesan cheese
pa·ro·chi·al (pə rō'kē əl) ***adj.*** ⟦see PARISH⟧ **1** of or in a parish or parishes **2** narrow in scope; provincial
parochial school a school supported and run by a church
par·o·dy (par'ə dē) ***n.***, *pl.* **-dies** ⟦< Gr *para-*, beside + *ōidē*, song⟧ a humorous imitation of a literary or musical work or style —***vt.*** **-died, -dy·ing** to make a parody of
pa·role (pə rōl') ***n.*** ⟦< LL *parabola*, a speech⟧ the release of a prisoner whose sentence has not expired, on condition of future good behavior —***vt.*** **-roled', -rol'ing** to release on parole
par·ox·ysm (par'ək siz'əm) ***n.*** ⟦< Gr *para-*, beyond + *oxynein*, sharpen⟧ **1** a sudden attack of a disease **2** a sudden outburst as of laughter
par·quet (pär kā') ***n.*** ⟦Fr, < MFr *parchet*, dim. of *parc*, park⟧ **1** the main floor of a theater: usually called *orchestra* **2** a flooring of parquetry —***vt.*** **-queted'** (-kād'), **-quet'ing** (-kā'iŋ) to make of parquetry
parquet circle the part of a theater beneath the balcony on the main floor
par·quet·ry (pär'kə trē) ***n.*** inlaid wooden flooring in geometric forms
par·ri·cide (par'ə sīd') ***n.*** ⟦< L *paricida*: see -CIDE⟧ **1** the act of murdering one's parent, close relative, etc. **2** one who does this
par·rot (par'ət) ***n.*** ⟦Fr dial. *perrot*⟧ **1** a tropical bird with a hooked bill and brightly colored feathers: some parrots can learn to imitate human speech **2** one who parrots what others say —***vt.*** to repeat without understanding
par·ry (par'ē) ***vt.*** **-ried, -ry·ing** ⟦prob. ult. < L *parare*, prepare⟧ **1** to ward off (a blow, etc.) **2** to evade (a question, etc.) —***n.***, *pl.* **-ries** a parrying
parse (pärs) ***vt., vi.*** **parsed, pars'ing** ⟦< L *pars* (*orationis*), part (of speech)⟧ to separate (a sentence) into its parts, giving the form and function of each part
par·si·mo·ny (pär'sə mō'nē) ***n.*** ⟦< L *parcere*, to spare⟧ stinginess; extreme frugality —**par'si·mo'ni·ous** ***adj.***
pars·ley (pärs'lē) ***n.*** ⟦< Gr *petros*, stone + *selinon*, celery⟧ a plant with aromatic, often curled leaves used to flavor or garnish some foods
pars·nip (pärs'nip') ***n.*** ⟦< L *pastinare*, dig up⟧ **1** a plant with a long white root used as a vegetable **2** its root
par·son (pär'sən) ***n.*** ⟦see PERSON⟧ **1** an Anglican minister having a parish **2** [Inf.] any minister
par'son·age ***n.*** the dwelling provided by a church for its minister
part (pärt) ***n.*** ⟦< L *pars*⟧ **1** a portion, division, etc. of a whole *[*a *part* of a book*]* **2** an essential, separable element *[*automobile *parts]* **3** a portion or share; specif., *a*) a share of work *[*to do one's *part]* *b*) [*usually pl.*] talent; ability *[*a man of *parts]* *c*) a role in a play *d*) any of the voices or instruments in a musical ensemble, or the score for this **4** [*usually pl.*] a portion of a country **5** a dividing line formed in combing the hair —***vt.*** **1** to break or divide into parts **2** to comb (the hair) so as to leave a part **3** to break or hold apart —***vi.*** **1** to break or divide into parts **2** to separate and go different ways **3** to cease associating **4** to go away; leave: with *from* —***adj.*** partial —**for one's part** as far as one is concerned —**for the most part** mostly —**in part** partly —**part with** to relinquish —**take part** to participate —**take someone's part** to side with someone
par·take (pär tāk') ***vi.*** **-took', -tak'en, -tak'ing** ⟦< *part taker*⟧ **1** to participate (*in* an activity) **2** to eat or drink something, esp. with others: usually with *of* —**par·tak'er** ***n.***
part·ed (pärt'id) ***adj.*** separated; divided
par·terre (pär ter') ***n.*** ⟦Fr < *par*, on + *terre*, earth⟧ **1** a garden with the flower beds and path in a pattern **2** PARQUET CIRCLE
par·the·no·gen·e·sis (pär'thə nō'jen'ə sis) ***n.*** ⟦see fol. & GENESIS⟧ reproduction from an unfertilized ovum, seed, or spore
Par'the·non' (-nän') ***n.*** ⟦< Gr *parthenos*, a virgin (i.e., Athena)⟧ the Doric temple of Athena on the Acropolis
par·tial (pär'shəl) ***adj.*** ⟦< L *pars*, a part⟧ **1** favoring one person, faction, etc. more than another; biased **2** not complete —**partial to** fond of —**par'ti·al'i·ty** (-shē al'ə tē) ***n.*** —**par'tial·ly** ***adv.***
par·tic·i·pate (pär tis'ə pāt') ***vi.*** **-pat'ed, -pat'ing** ⟦< L *pars*, a part + *capere*, to take⟧ to have or take a share with others (*in* some activity) —**par·tic'i·pant** ***adj., n.*** —**par·tic'i·pa'tion** ***n.*** —**par·tic'i·pa'tor** ***n.*** —**par·tic'i·pa·to'ry** (-pə tôr'ē) ***adj.***
par·ti·ci·ple (pärt'i sip'əl) ***n.*** ⟦see prec.⟧ a verbal form having characteristics of both verb and adjective —**par'ti·cip'i·al** (-sip'ē əl) ***adj.***
par·ti·cle (pärt'i kəl) ***n.*** ⟦< L *pars*, a part⟧ **1** a tiny fragment or trace **2** a short, usually invariable part of

THESAURUS

Parliament ***n.*** national legislative body of Great Britain, House of Commons, House of Lords; see GOVERNMENT 1, LEGISLATURE.
parliamentary ***a.*** congressional, administrative, lawmaking; see GOVERNMENTAL, LEGISLATIVE.
parochial ***a.*** provincial, insular, sectional; see LOCAL 1, REGIONAL.
parody ***n.*** travesty, burlesque, mimicry; see JOKE.
parody ***v.*** mimic, copy, caricature; see IMITATE 1, JOKE.
parole ***v.*** discharge, let out, liberate; see FREE, RELEASE.
parrot ***n.*** **1** [A bird] parakeet, lovebird, cockatoo; see BIRD. **2** [One who copies others] plagiarist, mimic, ape, impersonator, impostor, mocker, copycat; see also IMITATOR.
parson* ***n.*** clergyman, cleric, preacher; see MINISTER 1.
part ***n.*** **1** [A portion] piece, fragment, fraction, section, sector, member, segment, division, allotment, apportionment, ingredient, element, slab, subdivision, particle, installment, component, constituent, bit, slice, scrap, chip, chunk, lump, sliver, splinter, shaving, molecule, atom, electron, proton, neutron; see also SHARE.—*Ant.* WHOLE, total, aggregate. **2** [A part of speech] grammatical form, word class, function word; see NOUN, VERB. **3** [A machine part] molding, casting, fitting, lever, shaft, cam, spring, band, belt, chain, pulley, clutch, spare part, replacement; see also BOLT, GEAR, MACHINE, WHEEL 1. **4** [A character in a drama] hero, heroine, character; see ROLE. —**for the most part** mainly, mostly, to the greatest extent; see MOST. —**in part** partially, somewhat, to some extent; see PARTLY, UNFINISHED 1. —**on one's part** privately, as far as one is concerned, coming from one; see PERSONALLY 2. —**play a part** share, join, take part; see PARTICIPATE 1. —**take part** associate, cooperate, follow; see JOIN 2, PARTICIPATE 1, SHARE 2.
part ***v.*** **1** [To put apart] separate, break, sever; see DIVIDE. **2** [To depart] withdraw, take leave, part company; see LEAVE 1. —**part from** separate, part, break up with; see LEAVE 1. —**part with** let go of, suffer loss, give up; see LOSE 2.
partake ***v.*** participate, divide, take; see SHARE 2.
parted ***a.*** divided, severed, sundered; see SEPARATED.
partial ***a.*** **1** [Not complete] not total, incomplete, half done; see UNFINISHED 1. **2** [Showing favoritism] unfair, influenced, biased; see PREJUDICED.
partiality ***n.*** fondness, inclination, preference; see AFFECTION.
partially ***a.*** to some degree, somewhat, in part; see PARTLY.
participant ***n.*** member, partner, sharer; see ASSOCIATE.
participate ***v.*** **1** [To take part in] share, partake, aid, cooperate, join in, come in, associate with, be a party to, have a hand in, concur, take an interest in, take part in, enter into, have to do with, get into the act*, go into, chip in*; see also JOIN 2.—*Ant.* RETIRE, withdraw, refuse. **2** [To engage in a contest] play, strive, engage; see COMPETE.
participation ***n.*** joining in, sharing, support, aid, assistance, encouragement, seconding, help, standing by, taking part; see also PARTNERSHIP.
particle ***n.*** jot, scrap, atom, molecule, fragment, piece, shred; see also BIT 1.

speech, as an article or preposition **3** *Physics* a subatomic particle that cannot be divided

par·ti-col·ored (pär'tē kul'ərd) ***adj.*** ⟦< Fr *parti,* divided + COLORED⟧ having different colors in different parts

par·tic·u·lar (pär tik'yə lər) ***adj.*** ⟦< L *particula,* particle⟧ **1** of or belonging to a single person, group, or thing **2** regarded separately; specific **3** unusual **4** exacting; fastidious —***n.*** a distinct fact, item, detail, etc. —**in particular** especially —**par·tic'u·lar'i·ty** (-lar'ə tē), *pl.* **-ties,** ***n.***

par·tic'u·lar·ize' (-lər īz') ***vt., vi.*** **-ized', -iz'ing** to give particulars or details (of) —**par·tic'u·lar·i·za'tion** ***n.***

par·tic'u·lar·ly ***adv.*** **1** in detail **2** especially **3** specifically

par·tic'u·late (-lit, -lāt') ***adj.*** of or formed of separate tiny particles

part'ing ***adj.*** **1** dividing; separating **2** departing **3** given, spoken, etc. at parting —***n.*** **1** a breaking or separating **2** a departure

par·ti·san (pärt'ə zən) ***n.*** ⟦< L *pars,* a part⟧ **1** a strong supporter of a faction, party, etc. **2** a guerrilla fighter —***adj.*** of or like a partisan Also sp. **par'ti·zan** —**par'ti·san·ship'** ***n.***

par·ti·tion (pär tish'ən) ***n.*** ⟦< L *partitio*⟧ **1** division into parts **2** something that divides, as a wall separating rooms —***vt.*** **1** to divide into parts; apportion **2** to divide by a partition

part'ly ***adv.*** not fully or completely

part·ner (pärt'nər) ***n.*** ⟦< ME⟧ **1** one who joins in an activity with another or others; specif., one of two or more persons jointly owning a business **2** a spouse **3** either of two persons not married to each other but in an intimate, spouse-like relationship **4** either of two persons dancing together **5** either of two players on the same side or team —**part'ner·ship'** ***n.***

part of speech any of the classes to which a word can be assigned as by form, function, or meaning; noun, verb, adverb, etc.

par·took (pär to͝ok') ***vi.*** *pt. of* PARTAKE

par·tridge (pär'trij) ***n.*** ⟦< Gr *perdix*⟧ any of several short-tailed game birds, esp. one with an orange-brown head and grayish neck

part song a song for several voices, usually without accompaniment

part'-time' ***adj.*** designating, of, or engaged in work, study, etc. taking less time than a regular or full schedule

part'-tim'er ***n.*** a part-time employee, student, etc.

par·tu·ri·tion (pär'to͞o rish'ən) ***n.*** ⟦< L *parere,* bring forth⟧ childbirth

part'way' ***adv.*** to some degree, but not fully

par·ty (pär'tē) ***n.,*** *pl.* **-ties** ⟦< L *pars,* a part⟧ **1** a group of people working to promote a political platform or group of candidates, a cause, etc. **2** a group acting together to accomplish a task **3** a gathering for social entertainment **4** one concerned in an action, plan, lawsuit, etc. *[a party to the action]* **5** [Inf.] a person —***vi.*** **-tied, -ty·ing** to attend or hold social parties

par'ty·go'er (-gō'ər) ***n.*** a person who attends a party or many parties

party line **1** a single circuit connecting two or more telephone users with the exchange **2** the policies of a political party

par·ve·nu (pär'və no͞o') ***n.*** ⟦< L *pervenire,* arrive⟧ a newly rich person who is considered an upstart

Pas·a·de·na (pas'ə dē'nə) city in SW California: pop. 132,000

pas·chal (pas'kəl) ***adj.*** ⟦< LL < Gr < Heb *pesach,* Passover⟧ **1** of Passover **2** of Easter

pa·sha (pə shä', pä'shə) ***n.*** ⟦Turk⟧ [Historical] in Turkey, a title of rank or honor placed after the name

pass (pas) ***vi.*** ⟦< L *passus,* a step⟧ **1** to go or move forward, through, etc. **2** to go or be conveyed from one place, form, condition, etc. to another **3** *a)* to cease *b)* to depart **4** to die: usually with *away* or *on* **5** to go by **6** to elapse *[an hour passed]* **7** to make a way: with *through* or *by* **8** to be accepted without question **9** to be approved, as by a legislature **10** to go through a test, course, etc. successfully **11** to give a judgment, sentence, etc.: with *on* or *upon* **12** *Card Games* to decline a chance to bid —***vt.*** **1** to go by, beyond, over, or through; specif., *a)* to leave behind *b)* to go through (a test, course, etc.) successfully **2** to cause or allow to go, move, or proceed; specif., *a)* to ratify; enact *b)* to spend (time) *c)* to excrete **3** to cause to move from place to place; circulate **4** to give (an opinion or judgment) —***n.*** **1** an act of passing; passage **2** a condition; situation *[a strange pass]* **3** *a)* a ticket, etc. giving permission to come or go freely or without charge *b) Mil.* a brief leave of absence **4** a motion of the hand, as in card tricks or hypnotism, or as if to strike **5** a tentative attempt **6** a narrow passage, etc., esp. between mountains **7** [Inf.] an overly familiar attempt to embrace or kiss **8** *Sports* a

THESAURUS

particular ***a.*** **1** [Specific] distinct, singular, appropriate; see SPECIAL. **2** [Accurate] precise, minute, exact; see ACCURATE 2.

particular ***n.*** fact, specification, item; see DETAIL. —**in particular** expressly, particularly, individually; see ESPECIALLY 1.

particularly ***a.*** unusually, individually, expressly; see ESPECIALLY 1.

parting ***n.*** leavetaking, goodbye, farewell; see DEPARTURE.

partisan ***n.*** adherent, supporter, disciple; see FOLLOWER.

partition ***n.*** **1** [Division] apportionment, separation, severance; see DISTRIBUTION. **2** [That which divides or separates] bar, obstruction, divider; see BARRIER, WALL 1.

partly ***a.*** in part, partially, to a degree, measurably, somewhat, noticeably, notably, in some part, incompletely, insufficiently, inadequately, up to a certain point, so far as possible, not entirely, as much as could be expected, to some extent, within limits, slightly, to a slight degree, in some ways, only in details, in a general way, not strictly speaking, in bits and pieces, by fits and starts, at best, at worst, at most, at least, at the outside.—*Ant.* COMPLETELY, wholly, entirely.

partner ***n.*** co-worker, ally, comrade; see ASSOCIATE.

partnership ***n.*** alliance, cooperation, company, combination, corporation, connection, brotherhood, society, lodge, club, fellowship, fraternity, confederation, band, body, crew, clique, gang, ring, faction, party, community, conjunction, joining, companionship, friendship, sisterhood, sorority; see also ALLIANCE 1, UNION 1.

part of speech ***n.*** grammatical form, word class, function word; see ADJECTIVE, GRAMMAR, PRONOUN, VERB, WORD 1.

partway ***a.*** started, toward the middle, somewhat; see BEGUN, SOME.

party ***n.*** **1** [A social affair] at-home, tea, luncheon, dinner party, dinner, cocktail hour, surprise party, house party, social, reception, banquet, feast, affair, gathering, function, fete, ball, recreation, amusement, entertainment, festive occasion, carouse, diversion, performance, high tea, binge*, spree*, blowout*, bash*. **2** [A group of people] multitude, mob, company; see CROWD, GATHERING. **3** [A political organization] organized group, body, electorate, combine, combination, bloc, ring, junta, partisans, cabal; see also FACTION. **4** [*A specified but unnamed individual] party of the first part, someone, individual; see PERSON 1, SOMEBODY.

pass ***n.*** **1** [An opening through mountains] gorge, ravine, crossing, track, way, path, passageway; see also GAP 3. **2** [A document assuring permission to pass] ticket, permit, passport, visa, order, admission, furlough, permission, right, license. **3** [In sports, the passing of the ball from one player to another] toss, throw, fling; see PITCH 2. **4** [*An advance] approach, sexual overture, proposition; see SUGGESTION 1.

pass ***v.*** **1** [To move past] go by, run by, run past, flit by, come by, shoot ahead of, catch, come to the front, go beyond, roll on, fly past, reach, roll by, cross, flow past, go in opposite directions; see also MOVE 1. **2** [To elapse] transpire, slip away, slip by, pass away, pass by, fly, fly by, run out, drag. **3** [To complete a course successfully] satisfy the requirements, be graduated, pass with honors; see SUCCEED 1. **4** [To hand to others] transfer, relinquish, hand over; see GIVE 1. **5** [To enact] legislate, establish, vote in; see ENACT. **6** [To become enacted] carry, become law, become valid, be ratified, be established, be ordained, be sanctioned. **7** [To exceed] excel, transcend, go beyond; see EXCEED. **8** [To spend time] fill, occupy oneself, while away; see SPEND. **9** [To proceed] progress, get ahead, move on, go on; see also ADVANCE 1. **10** [To emit] give off, send forth, exude; see EMIT. —**bring to pass** bring about, initiate, start; see CAUSE. —**come to pass** occur, develop, come about; see HAPPEN 2. —**pass away** depart, expire, pass on; see DIE. —**pass by** travel, move past, depart from; see LEAVE 1, PASS 1. —**pass off** pass for, make a pretense of, palm off*; see PRETEND 1. —**pass on** expire, depart, succumb; see DIE. —**pass out** **1** [To faint] swoon, lose consciousness, black out; see FAINT. **2** [To distribute] hand out, circulate, deal out; see DISTRIBUTE, GIVE 1. —**pass over** dismiss, overlook, neglect; see DISREGARD. —**pass up*** dismiss, let go by, reject; see DENY, REFUSE.

transfer of a ball, etc. to another player during play —**come** (or **bring**) **to pass** to (cause to) happen —**pass for** to be accepted as —**pass off** to cause to be accepted through deceit —**pass out** **1** to distribute **2** to faint —**pass over** to disregard; ignore —**pass up** [Inf.] to refuse or let go by —**pass'er** ***n.***

pass'a·ble ***adj.*** **1** that can be passed, traveled over, etc. **2** adequate; fair —**pass'a·bly** ***adv.***

pas·sage (pas'ij) ***n.*** **1** a passing; specif., *a)* migration *b)* transition *c)* the enactment of a law **2** permission or right to pass **3** a voyage **4** a means of passing; road, passageway, etc. **5** an exchange, as of blows or words **6** a portion of a book, musical composition, etc.

pas'sage·way' ***n.*** a narrow way for passage, as a hall or alley

pass'book' ***n.*** BANKBOOK

pas·sé (pa sā', pä-) ***adj.*** ⟦Fr, past⟧ out-of-date; old-fashioned

pas·sel (pas'əl) ***n.*** ⟦< PARCEL⟧ [Inf. or Dial.] a group, esp. a fairly large one

pas·sen·ger (pas'ən jər) ***n.*** ⟦< OFr *passage,* passage⟧ a person traveling in a train, boat, car, etc.

pass'er·by' ***n.***, *pl.* **pass'ers·by'** one who passes by: also **pass'er-by'**, *pl.* **pass'ers-by'**

pass'-fail' ***adj.*** *Educ.* designating a grading system recording "pass" or "fail" instead of a letter or number grade

pass'ing ***adj.*** **1** going by, beyond, etc. **2** fleeting **3** casual *[*a *passing* remark*]* **4** satisfying given requirements *[*a *passing* grade*]* —***n.*** the act of one that passes; specif., death —**in passing** incidentally

pas·sion (pash'ən) ***n.*** ⟦< L *pati,* endure⟧ **1** any emotion, as hate, love, or fear **2** intense emotional excitement, as rage, enthusiasm, or lust **3** the object of any strong desire **4** [**P-**] the sufferings of Jesus, beginning after the Last Supper and continuing to his death on the Cross

pas'sion·ate (-ə nit) ***adj.*** **1** having or showing strong feelings **2** hot-tempered **3** ardent; intense **4** sensual —**pas'sion·ate·ly** ***adv.***

pas·sive (pas'iv) ***adj.*** ⟦see PASSION⟧ **1** inactive, but acted upon **2** offering no resistance; submissive **3** *Gram.* denoting the voice of a verb whose subject is the recipient (object) of the action —**pas'sive·ly** ***adv.*** —**pas·siv·i·ty** (pa siv'ə tē) ***n.***

pas'sive-ag·gres'sive ***adj.*** *Psychol.* showing disguised resistance to others' expectations, as by procrastination or inefficiency

passive resistance opposition to a government, etc. by refusal to comply or by nonviolent acts such as fasting

pass'key' ***n.*** **1** *a)* MASTER KEY *b)* SKELETON KEY **2** any private key

Pass·o·ver (pas'ō'vər) ***n.*** a Jewish holiday commemorating deliverance of the ancient Hebrews from slavery in Egypt

pass'port' ***n.*** a government document carried by a citizen traveling abroad, certifying identity and citizenship

pass'word' ***n.*** **1** a secret term used for identification, as in passing a guard **2** any means of gaining entrance

past (past) ***vi.***, ***vt.*** *rare pp. of* PASS —***adj.*** **1** gone by; ended **2** of a former time **3** immediately preceding **4** *Gram.* indicating an action completed, or a condition in existence, at a former time *[*the *past* tense*]* —***n.*** **1** time gone by **2** the history of a person, group, etc. **3** a personal background that is hidden or questionable —***prep.*** beyond in time, space, etc. —***adv.*** to and beyond some point

pas·ta (päs'tə) ***n.*** ⟦It⟧ **1** a flour paste or dough of which spaghetti, etc. is made **2** any food made of this

paste (pāst) ***n.*** ⟦< Gr *pastē,* porridge⟧ **1** dough for making pastry, etc. **2** any soft, moist, smooth preparation *[toothpaste]* **3** a mixture of flour, water, etc. used as an adhesive **4** the hard, brilliant glass of artificial gems —***vt.*** **past'ed**, **past'ing** **1** to make adhere with paste **2** [Slang] to hit

paste'board' ***n.*** a stiff material made as of layers of paper pasted together

pas·tel (pas tel') ***n.*** ⟦< LL *pasta,* paste⟧ **1** a crayon of ground coloring matter **2** a picture drawn with such crayons **3** a soft, pale shade of a color —***adj.*** soft and pale: said of colors

pas·tern (pas'tərn) ***n.*** ⟦< L *pastor,* shepherd⟧ the part of the foot of a horse, dog, etc. just above the hoof or toes

Pas·teur (pas tʉr'), **Louis** 1822-95; Fr. chemist & bacteriologist

pas·teur·ize (pas'chər īz', -tər-) ***vt.*** **-ized'**, **-iz'ing** ⟦after prec.⟧ to destroy bacteria in (milk, etc.) by heating to a prescribed temperature for a specified time —**pas'teur·i·za'tion** ***n.***

pas·tiche (pas tēsh') ***n.*** ⟦Fr⟧ an artistic composition made up of bits from various sources

pas·time (pas'tīm') ***n.*** a way of spending spare time; diversion

past master ⟦for *passed master*⟧ a person of long experience in an occupation, art, etc.; expert

pas·tor (pas'tər) ***n.*** ⟦L, a shepherd⟧ a priest or minister in charge of a congregation —**pas'tor·ate** (-it) ***n.***

pas'to·ral (-tə rəl) ***adj.*** **1** of or relating to a pastor **2** of shepherds **3** of rustic life **4** peaceful; simple

past participle *Gram.* a participle used *a)* to express completed action (Ex.: *gone* in "he has gone") *b)* to form the passive voice (Ex.: *done* in "the deed was done") *c)* as an adjective (Ex.: *fried* in "fried fish")

pas·tra·mi (pə strä'mē) ***n.*** ⟦E Yiddish, ult. < Turk *basdyrma,* dried meat⟧ highly spiced smoked beef

pas·try (pās'trē) ***n.***, *pl.* **-tries** ⟦see PASTE & -ERY⟧ **1** pies, tarts, etc. with crusts baked from flour dough made with shortening **2** broadly, all fancy baked goods

pas·tur·age (pas'chər ij) ***n.*** PASTURE

pas·ture (pas'chər) ***n.*** ⟦< L *pascere,* to feed⟧ **1** grass, etc. used as food by grazing animals **2** ground suitable for grazing —***vt.*** **-tured**, **-tur·ing** to put (cattle, etc.) out to graze in a pasture

past·y (pās'tē) ***adj.*** **-i·er**, **-i·est** of or like paste in color or texture

THESAURUS

passable ***a.*** open, fair, penetrable, navigable, accessible, traveled, easy, broad, graded; see also AVAILABLE.

passage ***n.*** **1** [A journey] voyage, crossing, trek; see JOURNEY. **2** [A passageway] way, exit, entry; see ENTRANCE 2. **3** [A reading] section, portion, paragraph; see QUOTATION 1.

passé ***a.*** obsolete, out-of-date, outmoded; see OLD-FASHIONED.

passenger ***n.*** commuter, tourist, traveler; see RIDER 1.

passerby ***n.*** witness, viewer, bystander; see OBSERVER.

passing ***a.*** **1** [In the act of going past] crossing, going by, gliding by, flashing by, speeding by, going in opposite directions, passing in the night; see also MOVING 1. **2** [Of brief duration] fleeting, transitory, transient; see TEMPORARY.

passion ***n.*** lust, craving, sexual excitement; see DESIRE 2, EMOTION.

passionate ***a.*** **1** [Excitable] vehement, hotheaded, tempestuous; see sense 2. **2** [Ardent] intense, impassioned, loving, fervent, moving, inspiring, dramatic, melodramatic, romantic, poignant, enthusiastic, tragic, stimulating, wistful, stirring, thrilling, warm, burning, glowing, vehement, deep, affecting, eloquent, spirited, fiery, expressive, forceful, heated, hot. **3** [Intense] strong, vehement, violent; see INTENSE.

passive ***a.*** **1** [Being acted upon] receptive, stirred, influenced; see AFFECTED 1. **2** [Not active] inactive, inert, lifeless; see IDLE.

passport ***n.*** pass, license, permit, safe-conduct, visa, travel permit, authorization, warrant, credentials; see also IDENTIFICATION 2.

password ***n.*** countersign, signal, phrase, secret word, watchword, identification, open sesame.

past ***a.*** **1** [Having occurred previously] former, preceding, gone by, foregoing, elapsed, anterior, antecedent, prior. **2** [No longer serving] ex-, retired, earlier; see PRECEDING.

past ***n.*** **1** [Past time] antiquity, long ago, the past, past times, old times, years ago, good old days, ancient times, former times, days gone by, auld lang syne, days of old, yesterday.—*Ant.* FUTURE, tomorrow, the present. **2** [Past events] memories, happenings, events; see HISTORY.

past ***prep.*** through, farther than, behind; see BEYOND.

paste ***n.*** adhesive, glue, mucilage; see CEMENT.

paste ***v.*** glue, fix, affix, repair, patch; see also STICK 1.

pastime ***n.*** recreation, amusement, sport; see ENTERTAINMENT, HOBBY.

pastor ***n.*** priest, rector, member of the clergy; see MINISTER 1.

pastry ***n.*** baked goods, dainty, delicacy, goodies*, cake; see also BREAD. *Pastries include the following:* French, Danish; tart, pie, turnover, torte, cream puff, éclair, strudel, puff pastry, phyllo, brioche, napoleon, croissant, quiche Lorraine, petit four, roll, bun, baklava, patty shell, patisserie, Linzer torte, Cornish pasty, empanada, calzone, sweet roll.

pasture ***n.*** grazing land, pasturage, hayfield; see FIELD 1, MEADOW.

pasty ***a.*** wan, pallid, sickly, ashen, anemic; see also PALE 1, DULL 2.

pat[1] (pat) ***n.*** ⟦prob. echoic⟧ **1** a gentle tap or stroke with the hand or a flat object **2** the sound made by this **3** a small lump, as of butter —***vt.*** **pat'ted, pat'ting 1** to tap or stroke gently, esp. with the hand **2** to shape or apply by patting —***adj.*** **1** exactly suitable **2** so glibly plausible as to seem contrived —**pat on the back 1** a compliment **2** to praise —**stand pat** to refuse to change an opinion, etc.

pat[2] *abbrev.* **1** patent **2** patented

patch (pach) ***n.*** ⟦ME *pacche*⟧ **1** a piece of material applied to mend a hole or strengthen a weak spot **2** a bandage **3** an area or spot *[patches* of blue sky*]* **4** a small plot of land **5** a scrap; bit **6** an adhesive pad containing a drug or hormone that is absorbed through the skin —***vt.*** **1** to put a patch on **2** to produce crudely or hurriedly —**patch up** to settle (differences, a quarrel, etc.)

patch test *Med.* a test for allergy, made by attaching a sample of a substance to the skin and observing the reaction

patch'work' ***n.*** needlework, as a quilt, made of patches of cloth sewn together at their edges

patch'y ***adj.*** **-i·er, -i·est 1** made up of patches **2** not consistent or uniform; irregular —**patch'i·ness** ***n.***

pate (pāt) ***n.*** ⟦< ?⟧ the head, esp. the top of the head: a humorous term

pâ·té (pä tā') ***n.*** ⟦Fr⟧ a meat paste or pie

pa·tel·la (pə tel'ə) ***n.***, *pl.* **-las** or **-lae** (-ē) ⟦< L *patina,* a pan⟧ a movable bone at the front of the human knee

pat·ent (pat''nt; *also for adj. 1 & 2,* pāt'-) ***adj.*** ⟦< L *patere,* be open⟧ **1** obvious; plain **2** of or having to do with patents —***n.*** **1** a document granting the exclusive right to produce or sell an invention, etc. for a specified time **2** *a)* the right so granted *b)* the thing protected by such a right —***vt.*** to secure a patent for

patent leather (pat''nt) leather with a hard, glossy finish: formerly patented

patent medicine (pat''nt) a trademarked medical preparation

pa·ter·nal (pə tur'nəl) ***adj.*** ⟦< L *pater,* father⟧ **1** of, like, or from a father **2** related through the father's side of the family —**pa·ter'nal·ly** ***adv.***

pa·ter'nal·ism' ***n.*** the governing or controlling of a country, employees, etc. in a manner suggesting a father's relationship with his children —**pa·ter'nal·is'tic** ***adj.***

pa·ter'ni·ty (-nə tē) ***n.*** **1** the state of being a father **2** male parentage

pa·ter·nos·ter (pät'ər näs'tər) ***n.*** ⟦L, our father⟧ the Lord's Prayer, esp. in Latin: often **Pater Noster**

path (path) ***n.*** ⟦OE *pæth*⟧ **1** a way worn by footsteps **2** a walk for the use of people on foot **3** a line of movement **4** a course of conduct, thought, etc. —**path'less** ***adj.***

pa·thet·ic (pə thet'ik) ***adj.*** ⟦see PATHOS⟧ **1** arousing pity, sorrow, etc.; pitiful **2** pitifully unsuccessful, etc. —**pa·thet'i·cal·ly** ***adv.***

pathetic fallacy in literature, the attribution of human feelings and characteristics to inanimate things (Ex.: the angry sea)

patho- ⟦< Gr: see PATHOS⟧ *combining form* suffering, disease, feeling: also **path-**

path·o·gen (path'ə jən) ***n.*** ⟦prec. + -GEN⟧ a microorganism, etc. capable of causing disease —**path'o·gen'ic** (-jen'ik) ***adj.***

pa·thol·o·gy (pə thäl'ə jē) ***n.***, *pl.* **-gies** ⟦< Gr *pathologia:* see fol. & -LOGY⟧ **1** the branch of medicine that deals with the nature of disease, esp. with structural and functional effects **2** any abnormal variation from a sound condition —**path·o·log·i·cal** (path'ə läj'i kəl) ***adj.*** —**pa·thol'o·gist** ***n.***

pa·thos (pā'thäs') ***n.*** ⟦Gr, suffering, disease, feeling⟧ the quality in something which arouses pity, sorrow, sympathy, etc.

path'way' ***n.*** PATH

-pa·thy (pə thē) ⟦< Gr: see PATHOS⟧ *combining form* **1** feeling *[telepathy]* **2** (treatment of) disease *[osteopathy]*

pa·tience (pā'shəns) ***n.*** a being patient; calm endurance

pa'tient (-shənt) ***adj.*** ⟦< L *pati,* endure⟧ **1** enduring pain, trouble, etc. without complaining **2** calmly tolerating delay, confusion, etc. **3** diligent; persevering —***n.*** one receiving medical care —**pa'tient·ly** ***adv.***

pat·i·na (pat''n ə, pə tē'nə) ***n.*** ⟦Fr < It⟧ a fine greenish crust on bronze or copper, formed by oxidation

pa·ti·o (pat'ē ō', pät'-) ***n.***, *pl.* **-os'** ⟦Sp⟧ **1** a courtyard open to the sky **2** a paved area adjoining a house, for outdoor lounging, dining, etc.

pa·tois (pa'twä') ***n.***, *pl.* **-tois'** (-twäz') ⟦Fr⟧ a provincial or local dialect

pat pend *abbrev.* patent pending

patri- ⟦< Gr *patēr*⟧ *combining form* father: also **patr-**

pa·tri·arch (pā'trē ärk') ***n.*** ⟦< Gr *patēr,* father + *archein,* to rule⟧ **1** the father and head of a family or tribe, as Abraham, Isaac, or Jacob in the Bible **2** a man of great age and dignity **3** [*often* **P-**] a high-ranking bishop, as in the Eastern Orthodox Church —**pa'tri·ar'chal** ***adj.***

pa'tri·arch'y (-är'kē) ***n.***, *pl.* **-ies 1** a form of social organization in which the father is head of the family, descent being traced through the male line **2** rule or domination by men

pa·tri·cian (pə trish'ən) ***n.*** ⟦< L *pater,* father⟧ an aristocrat

pat·ri·cide (pa'trə sīd') ***n.*** **1** the murdering of one's father **2** a person who does this —**pat'ri·ci'dal** ***adj.***

pat'ri·mo'ny (-mō'nē) ***n.***, *pl.* **-nies** ⟦< L *pater,* father⟧ property inherited from one's father or ancestors —**pat'ri·mo'ni·al** ***adj.***

pa·tri·ot (pā'trē ət) ***n.*** ⟦< Gr *patris,* fatherland⟧ one who loves and zealously supports one's own country —**pa'tri·ot'ic** (-ät'ik) ***adj.*** —**pa'tri·ot'i·cal·ly** ***adv.*** —**pa'tri·ot·ism'** ***n.***

pa·trol (pə trōl') ***vt.***, ***vi.*** **-trolled', -trol'ling** ⟦Fr *patrouiller*⟧ to make a regular, repeated circuit (of) in guarding —***n.*** **1** a patrolling **2** a person or group patrolling

patrol car a police car used to patrol an area

THESAURUS

pat[1] ***v.*** **1** [To strike lightly] tap, beat, slap; see HIT 1. **2** [To strike lightly and affectionately] stroke, pet, rub; see TOUCH 2.

patch ***n.*** piece, bit, scrap, spot, application.

patch ***v.*** darn, mend, cover; see REPAIR. —**patch up** appease, adjust, compensate; see SETTLE 7.

patchwork ***n.*** jumble, hodgepodge, muddle; see CONFUSION, DISORDER.

patent ***n.*** patent right, protection, concession, control, limitation, license, copyright, privilege; see also RIGHT 1.

patent ***v.*** license, secure, control, limit, monopolize, safeguard, exclude, copyright.

patented ***a.*** copyrighted, patent applied for, trademarked, under patent, under copyright, patent pending; see also RESTRICTED.

paternal ***a.*** patrimonial, fatherly, protective, benevolent.

paternity ***n.*** progenitorship, parenthood, fatherhood; see FATHER 1.

path ***n.*** trail, way, track, shortcut, footpath, crosscut, footway, roadway, cinder track, byway, pathway, bridle path; see also ROUTE 1.

pathetic ***a.*** touching, affecting, moving; see PITIFUL.

patience ***n.*** **1** [Willingness to endure] forbearance, fortitude, composure, submission, endurance, nonresistance, self-control, passiveness, bearing, serenity, humility, yielding, poise, sufferance, long-suffering, moderation, leniency; see also RESIGNATION 1.—*Ant.* NERVOUSNESS, fretfulness, restlessness. **2** [Ability to continue] submission, perseverance, persistence; see ENDURANCE.

patient ***a.*** **1** [Enduring without complaint] submissive, meek, forbearing, mild-tempered, composed, tranquil, serene, long-suffering, unruffled, imperturbable, passive, easygoing, tolerant, gentle, unresentful; see also RESIGNED.—*Ant.* IRRITABLE, violent, resentful. **2** [Quietly persistent in an activity] steady, dependable, calm, stable, composed, unwavering, quiet, serene, unimpassioned, enduring; see also RELIABLE.—*Ant.* RESTLESS, irrepressible, feverish.

patient ***n.*** case, inmate, victim, sufferer, sick person, medical case, surgical case, outpatient, bed patient, emergency ward patient, convalescent, hospital case, hospitalized person, subject.

patiently ***a.*** **1** [Suffering without complaint] enduringly, bravely, impassively, resignedly, numbly, forbearingly, tolerantly, submissively, meekly; see also CALMLY. **2** [Continuing without impatience] steadily, firmly, unabatingly; see REGULARLY.

patio ***n.*** porch, courtyard, square; see YARD 1.

patriarch ***n.*** male ruler, head of family, ancestor; see CHIEF.

patriot ***n.*** lover of one's country, good citizen, statesman, nationalist, volunteer, loyalist, jingoist, chauvinist.

patriotic ***a.*** devoted, zealous, public-spirited, consecrated, dedicated, jingoistic, chauvinistic.

patriotism ***n.*** love of country, public spirit, good citizenship, nationality, nationalism; see also LOYALTY.

patrol ***n.*** guard, watch, protection; see ARMY 2.

patrol ***v.*** watch, walk, inspect; see GUARD.

pa·trol'man (-mən) ***n.**, pl.* **-men** (-mən) a police officer who patrols a certain area
patrol wagon an enclosed truck used by police to carry prisoners
pa·tron (pā'trən) ***n.*** ⟦< L *pater*, father⟧ **1** a protector; benefactor **2** a person, usually wealthy, who sponsors and supports some person, activity, etc. **3** a regular customer **—pa'tron·ess** ***fem.n.***
pa·tron·age (pā'trə nij, pa'-) ***n.*** **1** support, encouragement, etc. given by a patron **2** *a)* clientele *b)* business; trade **3** *a)* the power to grant political favors *b)* such favors
pa·tron·ize (pā'trə nīz', pa'-) ***vt.*** **-ized', -iz'ing** **1** to sponsor; support **2** to be kind or helpful to, but in a haughty or snobbish way **3** to be a regular customer of
patron saint a saint looked upon as a special guardian
pat·ro·nym·ic (pa'trə nim'ik) ***n.*** ⟦< Gr *patēr*, father + *onyma*, name⟧ a name showing descent from a given person (Ex.: *Johnson*, son of John)
pat·sy (pat'sē) ***n.**, pl.* **-sies** [Slang] a person easily imposed upon or victimized
pat·ter[1] (pat'ər) ***vi.*** ⟦< PAT[1]⟧ to make, or move so as to make, a patter **—*n.*** a series of quick, light taps *[the patter of rain]*
pat·ter[2] (pat'ər) ***vi.*** ⟦< PATERNOSTER⟧ to speak rapidly or glibly **—*n.*** **1** glib, rapid speech, as of salespeople or comedians **2** idle chatter
pat·tern (pat'ərn) ***n.*** ⟦< OFr *patrun*, patron⟧ **1** a person or thing worthy of imitation **2** a model or plan used in making things **3** a design **4** a regular way of acting or doing **5** a predictable route, movement, etc. **—*vt.*** to make or do in imitation of a pattern
pat·ty (pat'ē) ***n.**, pl.* **-ties** ⟦Fr *pâté*, pie⟧ **1** a small pie **2** a small, flat cake of ground meat, fish, etc.
patty shell a small pastry case for a single portion of creamed fish, etc.
pau·ci·ty (pô'sə tē) ***n.*** ⟦< L *paucus*, few⟧ **1** smallness of number or amount **2** scarcity
Paul (pôl) (original name *Saul*) (died A.D. 67?); the Apostle of Christianity to the Gentiles: author of several Letters in the New Testament: also **Saint Paul**
Paul Bun·yan (bun'yən) *American Folklore* a giant lumberjack who performs superhuman feats
paunch (pônch) ***n.*** ⟦< L *pantex*, belly⟧ a potbelly **— paunch'y *adj.***
pau·per (pô'pər) ***n.*** ⟦L⟧ an extremely poor person, esp. one who lives on charity **—pau'per·ize', -ized', -iz'ing, *vt.***
pause (pôz) ***n.*** ⟦< Gr *pauein*, to bring to an end⟧ a temporary stop or rest **—*vi.*** **paused, paus'ing** to make a pause; stop
pave (pāv) ***vt.*** **paved, pav'ing** ⟦< L *pavire*, to beat⟧ to cover the surface of (a road, etc.), as with concrete **— pave the way (for)** to prepare the way (for)
pave'ment ***n.*** a paved surface, as of concrete; specif., a paved road, etc.
pa·vil·ion (pə vil'yən) ***n.*** ⟦< L *papilio*, tent⟧ **1** a large tent **2** a building, often partly open, for exhibits, etc., as at a fair or park **3** any of a group of related buildings, as of a hospital
Pav·lov (pav'lôv'), **I·van** (i vän') 1849-1936; Russ. physiologist
paw (pô) ***n.*** ⟦< OFr *poue*⟧ **1** the foot of a four-footed animal having claws **2** [Inf.] a hand **—*vt.*, *vi.*** **1** to touch, dig, hit, etc. with paws or feet **2** to handle clumsily or roughly
pawl (pôl) ***n.*** ⟦< ?⟧ a device, as a hinged tongue which engages cogs in a wheel, allowing rotation in only one direction
pawn[1] (pôn) ***n.*** ⟦< L *pannus*, cloth⟧ **1** anything given as security, as for a debt **2** the state of being pledged *[a ring in pawn]* **—*vt.*** **1** to give as security **2** to wager or risk
pawn[2] (pôn) ***n.*** ⟦< ML *pedo*, foot soldier⟧ **1** a chess piece of the lowest value **2** a person used to advance another's purposes
pawn'bro'ker ***n.*** a person licensed to lend money at interest on personal property left as security
pawn'shop' ***n.*** a pawnbroker's shop
paw·paw (pô'pô') ***n.*** *var. of* PAPAW
pay (pā) ***vt.*** **paid** or [Obs.] (except in PAY OUT) **payed, pay'ing** ⟦< L *pacare*, pacify⟧ **1** to give to (a person) what is due, as for goods or services **2** to give (what is due) in return, as for goods or services **3** to settle (a debt, etc.) **4** *a)* to give (a compliment, etc.) *b)* to make (a visit, etc.) **5** to be profitable to **—*vi.*** **1** to give due compensation **2** to be profitable **—*n.*** money paid; esp., wages or salary **— *adj.*** **1** operated by the insertion of coins *[a pay phone]* **2** designating a service, etc. paid for by fees *[pay TV]* **—in the pay of** employed and paid by **—pay back** **1** to repay **2** to retaliate upon **—pay down** to pay (part of the price) at purchase as an installment **—pay for** to suffer or atone for (a wrong) **—pay off** **1** to pay all that is owed on or to **2** to yield full recompense **3** [Inf.] to succeed **— pay out** to let out (a rope, cable, etc.) **—pay up** to pay in full or on time **—pay'er *n.***
pay'a·ble ***adj.*** **1** that can be paid **2** due to be paid (*on* a specified date)
pay'check' ***n.*** a check in payment of wages or salary
pay'day' ***n.*** the day on which salary or wages are paid
pay dirt soil, ore, etc. rich in minerals **—hit** (or **strike**) **pay dirt** [Inf.] to discover a source of wealth, success, etc.
pay·ee (pā ē') ***n.*** one to whom a payment is made or owed
pay'load' ***n.*** **1** a cargo **2** a load, as a warhead or satel-

THESAURUS

patrolman ***n.*** police, police officer, constable; see POLICE OFFICER.
patron ***n.*** philanthropist, benefactor, helper, protector, encourager, champion, backer, advocate, defender, guide, leader, friend, ally, sympathizer, well-wisher, partisan, buyer, angel*, sugar daddy*, booster.—*Ant.* ENEMY, obstructionist, adversary.
patronage ***n.*** **1** [Trade] commerce, trading, shopping; see BUSINESS 1. **2** [Condescension] patronization, deference, toleration; see PRIDE 2.
patronize ***v.*** **1** [To trade with] frequent, buy from, shop with; see BUY, SELL. **2** [To assume a condescending attitude] talk down to, be overbearing, stoop, be gracious to, favor, pat on the back, play the snob, snub, lord it over; see also CONDESCEND.
patronizing ***a.*** condescending, snobbish, stooping; see EGOTISTIC, POLITE.
pattern ***n.*** original, guide, copy; see MODEL 2.
pauper ***n.*** poor person, indigent, destitute person; see BEGGAR.
pause ***n.*** lull, rest, stop, halt, truce, stay, respite, standstill, stand, deadlock, stillness, intermission, suspension, discontinuance, breathing space, hitch, hesitancy, interlude, hiatus, interim, lapse, cessation, stopover, interval, rest period, gap, stoppage.
pause ***v.*** delay, halt, rest, catch one's breath, cease, hold back, reflect, deliberate, suspend, think twice, discontinue, interrupt; see also HESITATE.
pave ***v.*** lay concrete, lay asphalt, macadamize; see COVER 1.
paved ***a.*** hard-surfaced, flagged, cobblestone, asphalt, concrete, brick, bricked, surfaced with wood blocks; see also COVERED 1.
pavement ***n.*** hard surface, paving, paving stone, paving tile, flagging. *Road surfaces include the following:* concrete, asphalt, blacktop, stone, brick, tile, macadam, gravel, cobblestone, wood blocks, flagstone.
paving ***n.*** hard surface, concrete, paved highway; see PAVEMENT.
paw ***n.*** forefoot, talon, hand; see CLAW.
paw ***v.*** **1** [To strike wildly] clutch, grasp, smite; see HIT 1. **2** [To scrape with the front foot] scratch, rake, claw; see DIG 1.
pawn[1] ***v.*** deposit, pledge, hock*; see SELL.
pawned ***a.*** deposited, pledged, hocked*; see SOLD OUT.
pay ***n.*** **1** [Monetary return] profit, proceeds, interest, return, recompense, indemnity, reparation, rake-off*, reward, consideration, defrayment.—*Ant.* EXPENSE, disbursement, outlay. **2** [Wages] compensation, salary, payment, hire, remuneration, commission, fee, stipend, earnings, settlement, consideration, reimbursement, reward, time, time and a half, double time, overtime.
pay ***v.*** **1** [To give payment] pay up, compensate, recompense, make payment, reward, remunerate, discharge, pay a bill, foot the bill*, refund, settle, get even with, reckon with, put down, make restitution, make reparation, hand over, repay, liquidate, handle, take care of, give, confer, bequeath, defray, meet, disburse, clear, adjust, satisfy, reimburse, kick in*, plunk down*, put up*, pay as you go, fork out*, fork over*, ante up*, even the score*, chip in*.—*Ant.* DECEIVE, swindle, victimize. **2** [To produce a profit] return, pay off, pay out, show profit, yield profit, show gain, pay dividends.—*Ant.* FAIL, lose, become bankrupt. **3** [To retaliate] repay, punish, requite; see REVENGE. **—pay for** atone for, make amends for, do penance for, compensate for, make up for, make satisfaction for, expiate, make reparation for, give satisfaction for, pay the penalty for, make compensation for.

lite, carried by an aircraft, rocket, etc. but not essential to its flight operations

pay′mas′ter *n.* the official in charge of paying employees

pay′ment *n.* **1** a paying or being paid **2** something that is paid

pay′off′ *n.* **1** a settlement, reckoning, or payment **2** [Inf.] a bribe **3** [Inf.] a climax or culmination

pay·o·la (pā ō′lə) *n.* [Slang] a bribe, as to a disc jockey for unfairly promoting a certain record

pay′out′ *n.* **1** a paying out; disbursement **2** an amount paid out; dividend

pay′-per-view′ *adj. TV* of a system for paying for single showings of films or programs, as by cable or satellite —*n.* such a system

pay phone (or **station**) a public telephone, usually coin-operated

pay′roll′ *n.* **1** a list of employees to be paid, with the amount due to each **2** the total amount needed for this

Pb ⟦L *plumbum*⟧ *Chem. symbol for* lead

PBX *n.* ⟦*p*(*rivate*) *b*(*ranch*) (*e*)*x*(*change*)⟧ a telephone system within an organization, having outside lines

PC[1] *n., pl.* **PCs** or **PC's** PERSONAL COMPUTER

PC[2] *abbrev.* politically correct or political correctness

pct *abbrev.* percent

PCV valve ⟦*p*(*ositive*) *c*(*rankcase*) *v*(*entilation*)⟧ a valve regulating the pollution control system of a motor vehicle

pd *abbrev.* paid

Pd *Chem. symbol for* palladium

PE *abbrev.* **1** physical education **2** Prince Edward Island

pea (pē) *n., pl.* **peas** ⟦< ME *pese,* a pea, taken as pl.; ult. < Gr *pison*⟧ **1** a climbing plant with green pods **2** its small round seed, used as a vegetable

peace (pēs) *n.* ⟦< L *pax*⟧ **1** freedom from war **2** an agreement to end war **3** law and order **4** harmony; concord **5** serenity or quiet —**hold** (or **keep**) **one's peace** to be silent —**peace′a·ble** *adj.*

peace′ful *adj.* **1** not quarrelsome **2** free from disturbance; calm **3** of or in a time of peace —**peace′ful·ly** *adv.*

peace′mak′er *n.* a person who makes peace, as by settling quarrels —**peace′mak′ing** *n., adj.*

peace officer an officer entrusted with maintaining law and order, as a sheriff

peace pipe a ceremonial pipe smoked by American Indians as part of a peace conference

peace′time′ *n.* a time of freedom from war —*adj.* of such a time

peach (pēch) *n.* ⟦< L *Persicum* (*malum*), Persian (apple)⟧ **1** a tree with round, juicy, orange-yellow fruit having a fuzzy skin and a rough pit **2** its fruit **3** the color of this fruit **4** [Slang] a well-liked person or thing

pea·cock (pē′käk′) *n.* ⟦< L *pavo,* peacock⟧ the male of a pheasantlike bird (**pea′fowl′**), with a long, showy tail that can be spread out like a fan —**pea′hen′** *fem.n.*

pea jacket (pē) ⟦< Du *pijjekker*⟧ a hip-length, double-breasted coat of heavy woolen cloth, worn orig. by seamen

peak (pēk) *n.* ⟦var. of Brit dial. *pike,* prob. < ON *pic*⟧ **1** a pointed end or top, as of a cap or roof **2** *a*) the summit of a hill or mountain ending in a point *b*) a mountain with such a summit **3** the highest or utmost point of anything —*adj.* maximum —*vi.* to come to a peak

peak·ed (pē′kid) *adj.* ⟦< ?⟧ thin and drawn, or weak and pale, as from illness

peal (pēl) *n.* ⟦ME *apele,* appeal⟧ **1** the loud ringing of a bell or bells **2** a set of tuned bells **3** a loud, prolonged sound, as of thunder or laughter —*vi., vt.* to sound in a peal; ring

pea′nut′ *n.* **1** a vine related to the pea, with underground pods containing edible seeds **2** the pod or any of its seeds **3** [*pl.*] [Slang] a trifling sum of money

peanut butter a food paste or spread made by grinding roasted peanuts

pear (per) *n.* ⟦< L *pirum*⟧ **1** a tree with greenish-yellow, brown, or reddish fruit **2** the juicy fruit, round at the base and narrowing toward the stem

pearl (purl) *n.* ⟦< L *perna,* sea mussel⟧ **1** a smooth, hard, usually white or bluish-gray object, a roundish growth formed within the shell of some oysters and other mollusks: used as a gem **2** MOTHER-OF-PEARL **3** any person or thing like a pearl in beauty, value, etc. **4** bluish-gray —**pearl′y, -i·er, -iest,** *adj.*

Pearl Harbor inlet on the S coast of Oahu, Hawaii: site of a U.S. naval base bombed by Japan on Dec. 7, 1941

peas·ant (pez′ənt) *n.* ⟦< LL *pagus,* district⟧ **1** a small farmer or farm laborer, as in Europe or Asia **2** a person regarded as boorish, ignorant, etc. —**peas′ant·ry** *n.*

peat (pēt) *n.* ⟦< ML *peta,* piece of turf⟧ partly decayed plant matter from ancient swamps, used for fuel

peat moss peat composed of residues of mosses, used as mulch

peb·ble (peb′əl) *n.* ⟦< OE *papol-*(*stan*), pebble (stone), prob. echoic⟧ a small stone worn smooth and round, as by running water —**peb′bly, -bli·er, -bli·est,** *adj.*

pe·can (pē kän′, -kan′; pi-; pē′kän′, -kan′) *n.* ⟦< AmInd⟧ **1** an edible nut with a thin, smooth shell **2** the tree it grows on

pec·ca·dil·lo (pek′ə dil′ō) *n., pl.* **-loes** or **-los** ⟦< Sp < L *peccare,* to sin⟧ a small fault or offense

pec·ca·ry (pek′ə rē) *n., pl.* **-ries** ⟦< native name⟧ a piglike animal of North and South America, with sharp tusks

peck[1] (pek) *vt.* ⟦ME *picken,* to pick⟧ **1** to strike, as with a beak **2** to make by doing this [*to peck a hole*] **3** to pick up with the beak —*vi.* to make strokes as with a pointed object —*n.* **1** a stroke so made **2** [Inf.] a quick, casual kiss —**peck at** [Inf.] **1** to eat very little of **2** to criticize constantly

peck[2] (pek) *n.* ⟦< OFr *pek*⟧ a unit of dry measure, ¼ bushel or eight quarts

pecking order a hierarchy of members of a group, based on status, relative power, etc.

pec·tin (pek′tin) *n.* ⟦< Gr *pēktos,* congealed⟧ a carbohydrate, obtained from certain fruits, which yields a gel that is the basis of jellies and jams

pec·to·ral (pek′tə rəl) *adj.* ⟦< L *pectus,* breast⟧ of or located in or on the chest or breast

pec·u·la·tion (pek′yoo lā′shən) *n.* ⟦ult. < L *peculium,* private property⟧ embezzlement

pe·cu·liar (pi kyool′yər) *adj.* ⟦< L *peculium*: see prec.⟧ **1** of only one person, thing, etc.; exclusive **2** special **3** odd; strange —**pe·cu′liar·ly** *adv.*

THESAURUS

payment *n.* **1** [The act of paying] recompense, reimbursement, restitution, subsidy, return, redress, refund, remittance, reparation, disbursement, money down, amends, cash, salary, wage, sum, payoff, repayment, defrayment, retaliation; see also PAY 1. **2** [An installment] portion, part, amount; see DEBT.

payoff *n.* settlement, conclusion, reward; see PAY 1, PAYMENT 1.

payroll *n.* employees, workers, pay list; see FACULTY 2, STAFF 2.

peace *n.* **1** [The state of being without war] armistice, pacification, conciliation, order, concord, amity, union, unity, reconciliation, brotherhood, love, unanimity; see also AGREEMENT 1, FRIENDSHIP.—*Ant.* WAR, warfare, battle. **2** [State of being without disturbance] calm, repose, quiet, tranquillity, harmony, lull, hush, congeniality, equanimity, silence, stillness; see also REST 1.—*Ant.* FIGHT, noisiness, quarrel. **3** [Mental or emotional calm] calmness, repose, harmony, concord, contentment, sympathy; see also COMPOSURE, RESERVE 2, TRANQUILLITY.—*Ant.* DISTRESS, disturbance, agitation. —**at peace** peaceful, quiet, tranquil; see CALM 1, 2. —**hold** (or **keep**) **one's peace** be silent, keep quiet, not speak; see SHUT UP 1. —**make peace** end hostilities, settle, reconcile; see QUIET 1.

peaceable *a.* conciliatory, pacific, peaceful; see FRIENDLY.

peaceful *a.* **1** [At peace] quiet, tranquil, serene; see CALM 1, 2. **2** [Inclined toward peace] well-disposed, sociable, amiable; see FRIENDLY.

peacefully *a.* **1** [Calmly] tranquilly, quietly, composedly; see CALMLY. **2** [Without making trouble] harmoniously, placatingly, inoffensively, temperately, civilly; see also MODESTLY.

peak *n.* **1** [A mountain] summit, top, crown; see MOUNTAIN 1. **2** [The maximum] zenith, highest point, greatest quantity; see HEIGHT, TIP 1, TOP 1.

peaked *a.* pointed, topped, triangle-topped; see SHARP 1.

pearl *n.* nacre, gem, cultured pearl; see JEWEL.

peasant *n.* small farmer, farm laborer, farm worker; see FARMER, LABORER, WORKMAN.

pebble *n.* small stone, gravel, cobblestone; see ROCK 1, STONE.

peck[1] *v.* nip, pick, tap; see BITE 1, PINCH.

peck[1,2] *n.* **1** [A slight, sharp blow] pinch, tap, rap; see BLOW. **2** [One fourth of a bushel] eight quarts, quarter-bushel, large amount; see MEASURE 1, QUANTITY.

peculiar *a.* **1** [Unusual] wonderful, singular, outlandish; see STRANGE, UNUSUAL 2. **2** [Characteristic of only one] strange, uncommon, eccentric; see CHARACTERISTIC, UNIQUE.

pe·cu·li·ar·i·ty (pi kyo͞o′lē er′ə tē) ***n.*** **1** a being peculiar **2** *pl.* **-ties** something that is peculiar, as a trait

pe·cu·ni·ar·y (pi kyo͞o′nē er′ē) ***adj.*** ⟦< L *pecunia,* money⟧ of or involving money

ped·a·gogue or **ped·a·gog** (ped′ə gäg′) ***n.*** ⟦< Gr *paidagōgos* < *pais,* child + *agein,* to lead⟧ a teacher, esp. a pedantic one

ped′a·gog′y (-gäj′ē, -gō′jē) ***n.*** the art or science of teaching; esp., instruction in teaching methods —**ped′a·gog′ic** or **ped′a·gog′i·cal** ***adj.***

ped·al (ped′'l) ***adj.*** ⟦< L *pes,* FOOT⟧ of the foot or feet —***n.*** a lever operated by the foot, as on a bicycle or organ —***vt.***, ***vi.*** **-aled** or **-alled**, **-al·ing** or **-al·ling** to operate by pedals; use the pedals of

ped·ant (ped′'nt) ***n.*** ⟦ult. < Gr *paidagōgos*: see PEDAGOGUE⟧ **1** one who emphasizes trivial points of learning **2** a narrow-minded teacher who insists on exact adherence to rules —**pe·dan′tic** ***adj.*** —**ped′ant·ry** ***n.***

ped·dle (ped′'l) ***vt.***, ***vi.*** **-dled**, **-dling** ⟦< ? ME *ped,* basket⟧ to go from place to place selling (small articles) —**ped′dler** ***n.***

-pede (pēd) ⟦< L *pes*⟧ *combining form* foot or feet *[centipede]*

ped·er·as·ty (ped′ər as′tē) ***n.*** ⟦< Gr *paiderastēs,* lover of boys⟧ sodomy between males, esp. between a man and a boy —**ped′er·ast′** ***n.***

ped·es·tal (ped′əs təl) ***n.*** ⟦< It *piè,* foot + *di,* of + *stal,* a rest⟧ a bottom support of a pillar, statue, etc.

pe·des·tri·an (pi des′trē ən) ***adj.*** ⟦< L *pes,* foot⟧ **1** going or done on foot **2** of or for pedestrians **3** ordinary and dull; prosaic —***n.*** one who goes on foot; walker

pe·di·at·rics (pē′dē a′triks) ***n.*** ⟦< Gr *pais,* child + *iatros,* physician⟧ the branch of medicine dealing with the care of infants and children —**pe′di·a·tri′cian** (-ə trish′ən) ***n.*** —**pe′di·at′ric** ***adj.***

ped·i·cab (ped′i kab′) ***n.*** ⟦< L *pes,* foot + CAB⟧ a three-wheeled carriage, esp. formerly in SE Asia, pedaled like a bicycle by the driver

ped·i·cure (ped′i kyoor′) ***n.*** ⟦< L *pes,* FOOT + *cura,* care⟧ a trimming, polishing, etc. of the toenails

ped·i·gree (ped′i grē′) ***n.*** ⟦< MFr *pié de grue,* lit., crane's foot: from lines in genealogical tree⟧ **1** a list of ancestors **2** descent; lineage **3** a known line of descent, esp. of a purebred animal —**ped′i·greed′** ***adj.***

ped·i·ment (ped′i mənt) ***n.*** ⟦< earlier *periment,* prob. < PYRAMID⟧ an ornamental gable or triangular piece on the front of a building, over a doorway, etc.: see PORTICO, illus.

pe·dom·e·ter (pē däm′ət ər, pi-) ***n.*** ⟦< L *pes,* foot + Gr *metron,* a measure⟧ an instrument carried to measure the distance walked

ped·o·phil·i·a (ped′ə fil′ē ə) ***n.*** ⟦< Gr *pais,* child + *philos,* loving⟧ an abnormal condition in which an adult has a sexual desire for children —**pe′do·phile′** ***n.***

pe·dun·cle (pē duŋ′kəl, pē′duŋ′-) ***n.*** ⟦< L *pes,* foot⟧ a stalklike part in some plants, animals, etc.

peek (pēk) ***vi.*** ⟦ME *piken*⟧ to look quickly and furtively —***n.*** such a look

peel (pēl) ***vt.*** ⟦< L *pilare,* make bald⟧ to cut away (the rind, skin, etc.) of —***vi.*** **1** to shed skin, etc. **2** to come off in layers or flakes —***n.*** the rind or skin of fruit —**peel′er** ***n.***

peel′ing ***n.*** a peeled-off strip

peen (pēn) ***n.*** ⟦prob. < Scand⟧ the end of a hammerhead opposite the flat striking surface, usually ball-shaped or wedge-shaped

peep[1] (pēp) ***vi.*** ⟦echoic⟧ to make the short, high-pitched cry of a young bird —***n.*** a peeping sound

peep[2] (pēp) ***vi.*** ⟦ME *pepen*⟧ **1** to look through a small opening or from a place of hiding **2** to appear gradually or partially —***n.*** a brief look; furtive glimpse —**peep′er** ***n.***

peep′hole′ ***n.*** a hole to peep through

peeping Tom ⟦after legendary tailor who peeped at Lady GODIVA⟧ one who gets sexual pleasure from furtively watching others

peer[1] (pir) ***n.*** ⟦< L *par,* an equal⟧ **1** a person or thing of the same rank, ability, etc.; an equal **2** a British noble —**peer′age** (-ij) ***n.*** —**peer′ess** ***fem.n.***

peer[2] (pir) ***vi.*** ⟦< ? APPEAR⟧ **1** to look closely, as in trying to see more clearly **2** to appear partially

peer′less ***adj.*** without equal

peeve (pēv) [Inf.] ***vt.*** **peeved**, **peev′ing** to make peevish; annoy —***n.*** an annoyance

pee·vish (pē′vish) ***adj.*** ⟦ME *pevische*⟧ irritable; fretful; cross —**pee′vish·ly** ***adv.*** —**pee′vish·ness** ***n.***

pee·wee (pē′wē′) ***n.*** ⟦< ?⟧ [Inf.] an unusually small person or thing

peg (peg) ***n.*** ⟦ME *pegge*⟧ **1** a short piece of wood, metal, etc. used to hold parts together, hang things on, etc. **2** a step or degree **3** [Inf.] a throw —***vt.*** **pegged**, **peg′ging** **1** to fasten, fix, secure, mark, etc. with pegs **2** [Inf.] to throw —**peg away (at)** to work steadily (at)

Peg·a·sus (peg′ə səs) ***n.*** *Gr. Myth.* a winged horse

peg′board′ ***n.*** a piece of boardlike material with rows of holes for hooks or pegs to hold displays, tools, etc.

peign·oir (pān wär′, pen-) ***n.*** ⟦Fr⟧ a woman's full, loose dressing gown

Pei·ping (bā′piŋ′) *a former transliteration of* BEIJING

pe·jo·ra·tive (pi jôr′ə tiv) ***adj.*** ⟦< L *pejor,* worse⟧ disparaging or derogatory —**pe·jo′ra·tive·ly** ***adv.***

Pe·king (pē′kiŋ′) *a former transliteration of* BEIJING

Pe·king·ese (pē′kə nēz′) ***n.***, *pl.* **-ese′** a small dog with a long, straight coat, short legs, and a short, wrinkled muzzle: also **Pe′kin·ese′** (-kə nēz′)

pe·koe (pē′kō) ***n.*** ⟦< Chin dial. *pek-ho,* white down (on the leaves used)⟧ a black tea of Sri Lanka and India

pe·lag·ic (pi laj′ik) ***adj.*** ⟦< Gr *pelagos,* sea⟧ of the open sea or ocean

pelf (pelf) ***n.*** ⟦< ? MFr *pelfre,* booty⟧ money or wealth regarded with contempt

pel·i·can (pel′i kən) ***n.*** ⟦< Gr *pelekan*⟧ a large, web-footed water bird with an expandable pouch in the lower bill for scooping up fish

pel·la·gra (pə lā′grə, -lag′rə) ***n.*** ⟦It ult. < L *pellis,* skin + Gr *agra,* seizure⟧ a chronic disease caused by a lack of nicotinic acid in the diet, characterized by skin eruptions and mental disorders

pel·let (pel′it) ***n.*** ⟦< L *pila,* a ball⟧ **1** a little ball, as of clay or medicine **2** a bullet, piece of lead shot, etc.

pell-mell (pel′mel′) ***adv.***, ***adj.*** ⟦< OFr *mesler,* to mix⟧ **1** in a jumble **2** in wild, disorderly haste; headlong Also **pell′mell′**

pel·lu·cid (pə lo͞o′sid) ***adj.*** ⟦< L *per,* through + *lucere,* to shine⟧ **1** transparent; clear **2** easy to understand

pelt[1] (pelt) ***vt.*** ⟦ME *pelten*⟧ **1** to throw things at **2** to beat repeatedly —***vi.*** to strike heavily or steadily: said as of hard rain

pelt[2] (pelt) ***n.*** ⟦prob. < OFr *pel,* a skin⟧ the skin of a fur-bearing animal, esp. when stripped from the carcass

pel·vis (pel′vis) ***n.***, *pl.* **-vis·es** or **-ves′** (-vēz′) ⟦L, basin⟧ **1** the basinlike cavity in the posterior part of the trunk in many vertebrates: in humans, it supports the spinal column and rests on the legs **2** the bones forming this cavity —**pel′vic** ***adj.***

pem·mi·can (pem′i kən) ***n.*** ⟦< AmInd⟧ a concentrated food made of dried beef, suet, dried fruit, etc.

THESAURUS

peculiarity ***n.*** distinctiveness, singularity, unusualness; see CHARACTERISTIC.

pedal ***n.*** treadle, foot lever, accelerator; see LEVER.

peddle ***v.*** hawk, vend, trade; see SELL.

peddler ***n.*** hawker, vendor, seller; see BUSINESSMAN.

pedestal ***n.*** stand, foundation, footstall, plinth; see also COLUMN 1, SUPPORT 2.

pedestrian ***n.*** traveler on foot, walker, hiker; see WALKING *a.*

peek ***n.*** peep, glimpse, glance; see LOOK 3.

peek ***v.*** glance, peep, glimpse; see SEE 1.

peel ***n.*** husk, bark, shell; see SKIN.

peel ***v.*** pare, strip, tear off, pull off, flay, uncover; see also SKIN.

peeling ***n.*** paring, strip, sliver; see SKIN.

peep[1,2] ***n.*** **1** [A peek] glimpse, glance, sight; see LOOK 3. **2** [A peeping sound] cheep, chirp, squeak; see CRY 2.

peep[1,2] ***v.*** **1** [To look cautiously] peek, glimpse, glance; see SEE 1. **2** [To make a peeping sound] cheep, chirp, squeak; see CRY 2.

peer[1] ***n.*** match, rival, companion; see EQUAL.

peer[2] ***v.*** gaze, inspect, scrutinize; see SEE 1.

peer group ***n.*** equals, social group, one's peers; see ASSOCIATE, EQUAL.

peeve* ***v.*** irritate, annoy, anger; see BOTHER 2.

peeved ***a.*** sullen, irritated, upset; see ANGRY.

peevish ***a.*** cross, fretful, fretting; see ANGRY.

peg ***n.*** pin, tack, fastener; see NAIL. —**take down a peg** humiliate, criticize, diminish; see HUMBLE.

pellet ***n.*** pill, bead, grain; see STONE.

pell-mell ***a.*** impetuously, hurriedly, indiscreetly; see FOOLISHLY.

pelt[2] ***n.*** skin, hair, wool; see HIDE.

pen[1] (pen) ***n.*** ⟦OE *penn*⟧ **1** a small enclosure for domestic animals **2** any small enclosure —***vt.*** **penned** or **pent**, **pen'ning** to enclose as in a pen

pen[2] (pen) ***n.*** ⟦< L *penna,* a feather⟧ a device used in writing, etc. with ink; specif., *a)* a device with a metal point split into two nibs *b)* BALLPOINT (PEN) *c)* FOUNTAIN PEN —***vt.*** **penned**, **pen'ning** to write with or as with a pen

pen[3] (pen) ***n.*** [Slang] a penitentiary

Pen or **pen** *abbrev.* peninsula

pe·nal (pē'nəl) ***adj.*** ⟦< Gr *poinē,* penalty⟧ of, for, constituting, or making a person liable to punishment

pe·nal·ize (pē'nə līz', pen'ə-) ***vt.*** **-ized', -iz'ing** to impose a penalty on; punish —**pe'nal·i·za'tion** ***n.***

pen·al·ty (pen'əl tē) ***n.***, *pl.* **-ties** **1** a punishment **2** the handicap, etc. imposed on an offender, as a fine

pen·ance (pen'əns) ***n.*** ⟦see PENITENT⟧ voluntary self-punishment to show repentance for wrongdoing, sins, etc.

pence (pens) ***n.*** [Brit.] *pl. of* PENNY

pen·chant (pen'chənt) ***n.*** ⟦Fr < *pencher,* to incline⟧ a strong liking

pen·cil (pen'səl) ***n.*** ⟦< L *penis,* a tail⟧ a rod-shaped instrument with a core of graphite, crayon, etc. that is sharpened to a point for writing, drawing, etc. —***vt.*** **-ciled** or **-cilled**, **-cil·ing** or **-cil·ling** to write, etc. with a pencil

pend (pend) ***vi.*** ⟦< L *pendere,* hang⟧ to await judgment or decision

pend·ant (pen'dənt) ***n.*** ⟦see prec.⟧ a hanging ornamental object, as one on a necklace or earring

pend·ent (pen'dənt) ***adj.*** ⟦see PEND⟧ **1** suspended **2** overhanging **3** undecided; pending

pend'ing ***adj.*** ⟦prp. of PEND, infl. by Fr *pendant,* L *pendens*⟧ **1** not decided **2** impending —***prep.*** until

pen·du·lous (pen'dyoo ləs, -joo-) ***adj.*** ⟦see PEND⟧ hanging freely; drooping

pen·du·lum (pen'dyoo ləm, -joo-) ***n.*** ⟦see PEND⟧ a weight hung so as to swing freely to and fro: used to regulate clock movements

pen·e·trate (pen'i trāt') ***vt.***, ***vi.*** **-trat'ed, -trat'ing** ⟦< L *penitus,* inward⟧ **1** to enter by or as by piercing **2** to have an effect throughout **3** to affect deeply **4** to understand —**pen'e·tra·ble** (-trə bəl) ***adj.*** —**pen'e·tra'tion** ***n.***

pen·e·trat·ing (pen'i trāt'iŋ) ***adj.*** **1** that penetrates **2** sharp; piercing **3** acute; discerning Also **pen'e·tra'tive** (-trāt'iv)

pen·guin (peŋ'gwin, pen'-) ***n.*** ⟦prob. < Welsh⟧ a flightless bird of the Southern Hemisphere with webbed feet and flippers for swimming

pen·i·cil·lin (pen'i sil'in) ***n.*** ⟦< L *penicillus,* brush⟧ an antibiotic obtained from certain molds or produced synthetically

pen·in·su·la (pə nin'sə lə) ***n.*** ⟦< L *paene,* almost + *insula,* isle⟧ a land area almost surrounded by water —**pen·in'su·lar** ***adj.***

pe·nis (pē'nis) ***n.***, *pl.* **-nis·es** or **-nes'** (-nēz') ⟦L⟧ the male organ of sexual intercourse —**pe'nile'** (-nīl') ***adj.***

pen·i·tent (pen'i tənt) ***adj.*** ⟦< L *paenitere,* repent⟧ sorry for having done wrong and willing to atone —***n.*** a penitent person —**pen'i·tence** ***n.*** —**pen'i·ten'tial** (-ten'shəl) ***adj.*** —**pen'i·tent·ly** ***adv.***

pen·i·ten·tia·ry (pen'i ten'shə rē) ***n.***, *pl.* **-ries** a state or federal prison for persons convicted of serious crimes

pen'knife' ***n.***, *pl.* **-knives'** (-nīvz') a small pocketknife

pen'light' or **pen'lite'** ***n.*** a flashlight about the size of a fountain pen

pen'man (-mən) ***n.***, *pl.* **-men** (-mən) one skilled in penmanship

pen'man·ship' ***n.*** handwriting as an art or skill

Penn (pen), **William** 1644-1718; Eng. Quaker: founder of Pennsylvania

pen name a pseudonym

pen·nant (pen'ənt) ***n.*** ⟦< PENNON⟧ **1** any long, narrow flag **2** such a flag symbolizing a championship, esp. in baseball

pen·ne (pen'ā') ***n.*** pasta in the form of tubes, cut diagonally on the ends

pen·ni·less (pen'ə lis) ***adj.*** without even a penny; extremely poor

pen·non (pen'ən) ***n.*** ⟦< L *penna,* a feather⟧ a flag or pennant

Penn·syl·va·ni·a (pen'səl vān'yə) state of the NE U.S.: 44,820 sq. mi.; pop. 11,882,000; cap. Harrisburg: abbrev. *PA* —**Penn'syl·va'ni·an** ***adj.***, ***n.***

pen·ny (pen'ē) ***n.***, *pl.* **-nies** or **pence** (pens) ⟦< OE *penig*⟧ **1** in the United Kingdom, $\frac{1}{100}$ of a pound **2** a U.S. or Canadian cent

penny arcade a building, as at an amusement park, with coin-operated games, etc.

penny pincher a miserly person —**pen'ny-pinch'ing** ***n.***, ***adj.***

pen'ny·weight' ***n.*** a unit of weight, equal to $\frac{1}{20}$ ounce troy weight

pen'ny-wise' ***adj.*** thrifty in small matters —**penny-wise and pound-foolish** thrifty in small matters but wasteful in major ones

pe·nol·o·gy (pē näl'ə jē) ***n.*** ⟦< Gr *poinē,* punishment + -LOGY⟧ the study of prison management and prison reform

pen pal a person, esp. a stranger in another country, with whom one exchanges letters

pen·sion (pen'shən) ***n.*** ⟦< L *pensio,* a paying⟧ a regular payment, not wages, as to one who is retired or disabled —***vt.*** to grant a pension to

pen'sion·er ***n.*** one who receives a pension

pen·sive (pen'siv) ***adj.*** ⟦< L *pensare,* consider⟧ thoughtful or reflective, often in a melancholy way —**pen'sive·ly** ***adv.*** —**pen'sive·ness** ***n.***

pent (pent) ***vt.*** *alt. pt. & pp. of* PEN[1] —***adj.*** held or kept in; penned: often with *up*

penta- ⟦< Gr *pente,* FIVE⟧ *combining form* five

pen·ta·gon (pen'tə gän') ***n.*** ⟦< Gr *penta-,* five + *gōnia,* an angle⟧ a plane figure with five angles and five sides —**the Pentagon** the pentagonal office building of the Defense Department, near Washington, DC —**pen·tag'o·nal** (-tag'ə nəl) ***adj.***

pen·tam·e·ter (pen tam'ət ər) ***n.*** ⟦see PENTA- & METER[1]⟧ a line of verse containing five metrical feet; esp., English iambic pentameter (Ex.: "Hĕ jésts| ăt scárs| whŏ név| ĕr félt| ă wóund")

Pen·ta·teuch (pen'tə took') ***n.*** ⟦< Gr *penta-,* five + *teuchos,* book⟧ the first five books of the Bible

pen·tath·lon (pen tath'län') ***n.*** ⟦< Gr *penta-,* five + *athlon,* a contest⟧ an athletic contest in which each contestant takes part in five events —**pen·tath'lete'** (-lēt') ***n.***

Pen·te·cost (pen'tə kôst') ***n.*** ⟦< Gr *pentēkostē* (*hēmera*),

THESAURUS

pen[1,2] ***v.*** **1** [To enclose] close in, confine, coop up*; see ENCLOSE. **2** [To write] compose, indite, commit to writing; see WRITE 1, 2.

pen[1,2,3] ***n.*** **1** [An enclosed place] coop, cage, corral, sty, close; see also ENCLOSURE 1. **2** [A writing instrument] *Pens include the following:* fountain, desk, drawing, ruling, artist's, reed, quill, steel, ballpoint, felt-tip. **3** [*A place of confinement] penitentiary, prison, concentration camp; see JAIL.

penalize ***v.*** scold, chasten, castigate; see PUNISH.

penalty ***n.*** fine, sentence, discipline; see PUNISHMENT.

penance ***n.*** mortification, purgation, repentance, retribution, compensation, atonement, fasting, suffering, sackcloth and ashes, hair shirt, reparation; see also PUNISHMENT.

pencil ***n.*** *Types of pencils include the following:* lead, mechanical, colored, drawing, indelible, charcoal, grease, eyebrow, cosmetic, drafting; chalk, crayon, stylus.

pendant ***n.*** earring, locket, lavaliere; see DECORATION 2, JEWELRY.

pending ***a.*** continuing, indeterminate, unfinished; see OMINOUS.

pendulum ***n.*** swing, pendant, suspended body; see DEVICE, MACHINE.

penetrable ***a.*** permeable, receptive, open, passable, accessible; see also POROUS.

penetrate ***v.*** bore, perforate, enter, insert, go through, make an entrance, stick into, jab, thrust, stab, force, make a hole, run through, punch, puncture, drive into, stick, drill, eat through, spear, impale, wound, gore, sting, sink into, knife, go through, pass through.—*Ant.* LEAVE, withdraw, turn aside.

penetrating ***a.*** **1** [Entering] piercing, going through, puncturing; see SHARP 1. **2** [Mentally keen] astute, shrewd, sharp; see INTELLIGENT.

penetration ***n.*** **1** [Act of entering] insertion, invasion, perforation; see ENTRANCE 1. **2** [Mental acuteness] discernment, perception, keen-sightedness; see INTELLIGENCE 1.

peninsula ***n.*** point, promontory, cape; see LAND 1.

penitentiary ***n.*** reformatory, penal institution, pen*; see JAIL, PRISON.

penniless ***a.*** poverty-stricken, lacking means, indigent; see POOR 1.

penny ***n.*** cent, copper, red cent*; see MONEY 1.

pension ***n.*** annuity, premium, payment, grant, social security, gift, subsidy, fixed income, reward; see also ALLOWANCE.

the fiftieth (day)⟧ a Christian festival on the seventh Sunday after Easter
Pen·te·cos·tal (pen′tə kôs′təl) ***adj.*** **1** of Pentecost **2** designating or of any of various Protestant fundamentalist sects often stressing direct inspiration by the Holy Spirit —**Pen′te·cos′tal·ism′** ***n.***
pent·house (pent′hous′) ***n.*** ⟦ult. < L *appendere*, append⟧ an apartment on the roof or on the top floor of a building
pent-up (pent′up′) ***adj.*** held in check; curbed *[pent-up* emotion*]*
pe·nu·che or **pe·nu·chi** (pə no͞o′chē) ***n.*** ⟦var. of PANOCHA⟧ a candy similar to fudge
pe·nul·ti·mate (pē nul′tə mət) ***adj.*** ⟦< L *paene*, almost + ULTIMATE⟧ next to the last
pe·nu·ri·ous (pe nyoor′ē əs, -noor′-) ***adj.*** ⟦see fol.⟧ miserly; stingy —**pe·nu′ri·ous·ly** ***adv.*** —**pe·nu′ri·ous·ness** ***n.***
pen·u·ry (pen′yo͞o rē, -yə-) ***n.*** ⟦< L *penuria,* want⟧ extreme poverty
pe·on (pē′än′) ***n.*** ⟦< ML *pedo,* foot soldier⟧ **1** in Spanish America, a member of the laboring class **2** in the SW U.S., a person forced into servitude to work off a debt —**pe′on·age** (-ə nij) ***n.***
pe·o·ny (pē′ə nē) ***n.***, *pl.* **-nies** ⟦< Gr *Paiōn,* Apollo as god of medicine: from its former medicinal use⟧ **1** a plant with large, showy, pink, white, red, or yellow flowers **2** the flower
peo·ple (pē′pəl) ***n.***, *pl.* **-ples** ⟦< L *populus,* nation, crowd⟧ all the persons of a racial or ethnic group; nation, race, etc. —***pl.n.*** **1** *pl. of* PERSON (sense 1) **2** the persons of a certain place, group, or class **3** one's family; relatives **4** the populace **5** persons considered indefinitely *[*what will *people* say?*]* **6** human beings —***vt.*** **-pled**, **-pling** to populate
Pe·or·i·a (pē ôr′ē ə) city in central Illinois: pop. 114,000
pep (pep) [Inf.] ***n.*** ⟦< fol.⟧ energy; vigor —***vt.*** **pepped**, **pep′ping** to fill with pep; invigorate: with *up* —**pep′py**, **-pi·er**, **-pi·est**, ***adj.***
pep·per (pep′ər) ***n.*** ⟦< Gr *peperi*⟧ **1** *a)* a pungent condiment ground from the dried fruits of an East Indian vine *b)* this vine **2** a plant with red or green, sweet or hot pods —***vt.*** **1** to season with ground pepper **2** to pelt with small objects
pep′per·corn′ ***n.*** the dried berry of the pepper
pepper mill a hand mill used to grind peppercorns
pep′per·mint′ ***n.*** **1** a plant of the mint family that yields a pungent oil used for flavoring **2** the oil **3** a candy flavored with this oil
pep·per·o·ni (pep′ər ō′nē) ***n.***, *pl.* **-nis** or **-ni** ⟦< It *peperoni*⟧ a hard, highly spiced Italian sausage
pepper shaker a container for ground pepper, with a perforated top
pep′per·y ***adj.*** **1** of, like, or highly seasoned with pepper **2** sharp or fiery, as words **3** hot-tempered
pep·sin (pep′sin) ***n.*** ⟦< Gr *peptein,* to digest⟧ a stomach enzyme, aiding in the digestion of proteins
pep talk a talk, as to an athletic team by its coach, to instill enthusiasm, determination, etc.
pep·tic (pep′tik) ***adj.*** ⟦see PEPSIN⟧ **1** of or aiding digestion **2** caused by digestive secretions *[*a *peptic* ulcer*]*
per (pur) ***prep.*** ⟦L⟧ **1** through; by; by means of **2** for each *[*fifty cents *per* yard*]* **3** [Inf.] according to
per- ⟦< prec.⟧ *prefix* **1** through, throughout **2** thoroughly
per·ad·ven·ture (pur′əd ven′chər) ***adv.*** ⟦< OFr *par*, by + *aventure,* chance⟧ [Archaic] possibly
per·am·bu·late (pər am′byo͞o lāt′) ***vt.***, ***vi.*** **-lat′ed**, **-lat′ing** ⟦< L *per,* through + *ambulare,* to walk⟧ to walk (through, over, etc.)
per·am′bu·la′tor (-lāt′ər) ***n.*** [Chiefly Brit.] a baby carriage
per an·num (pər an′əm) ⟦L⟧ yearly
per·cale (pər kāl′) ***n.*** ⟦Fr < Pers *pargāla,* scrap⟧ fine, closely woven cotton cloth, used for sheets, etc.
per cap·i·ta (pər kap′i tə) ⟦ML, lit., by heads⟧ for each person
per·ceive (pər sēv′) ***vt.***, ***vi.*** **-ceived′**, **-ceiv′ing** ⟦< L *per,* through + *capere,* take⟧ **1** to understand **2** to become aware (of) through the senses
per·cent (pər sent′) ***adv.***, ***adj.*** ⟦< L *per centum*⟧ in, to, or for every hundred: symbol, %: also **per cent** —***n.*** [Inf.] percentage
per·cent′age ***n.*** **1** a given part in every hundred **2** part; portion **3** [Inf.] advantage; profit
per·cen·tile (pər sen′tīl′, -sent′'l) ***n.*** *Statistics* any of 100 divisions of a series, each of equal frequency
per·cep·ti·ble (pər sep′tə bəl) ***adj.*** that can be perceived —**per·cep′ti·bly** ***adv.***
per·cep′tion (-shən) ***n.*** ⟦< L *percipere*, perceive⟧ **1** the mental grasp of objects, etc. through the senses **2** insight or intuition **3** the knowledge, etc. gotten by perceiving —**per·cep′tion·al** ***adj.***
per·cep′tive (-tiv) ***adj.*** **1** of perception **2** able to perceive quickly —**per·cep′tive·ly** ***adv.*** —**per·cep′tive·ness** ***n.***
per·cep′tu·al (-cho͞o əl) ***adj.*** of or involving perception
perch[1] (purch) ***n.***, *pl.* **-es** ⟦< Gr *perkē*⟧ **1** a small, spiny-finned, freshwater food fish **2** any of various other spiny-finned fishes
perch[2] (purch) ***n.*** ⟦< L *pertica,* pole⟧ **1** a horizontal pole, etc. serving as a roost for birds **2** any high resting place —***vi.***, ***vt.*** to rest or place on or as on a perch
per·chance (pər chans′) ***adv.*** ⟦< OFr *par*, by + *chance,* chance⟧ [Archaic] **1** by chance **2** perhaps
per·co·late (pur′kə lāt′) ***vt.*** **-lat′ed**, **-lat′ing** ⟦< L *per,* through + *colare,* to strain⟧ to filter (a liquid) through a porous substance —***vi.*** to ooze through a porous substance
per′co·la′tor (-lāt′ər) ***n.*** a coffeepot in which the boiling water bubbles up through a tube and filters back down through the ground coffee
per·cus·sion (pər kush′ən) ***n.*** ⟦< L *per-*, thoroughly + *quatere*, shake⟧ **1** the hitting of one body against another, as the hammer of a firearm against a powder cap (**percussion cap**) **2** the shock, vibration, etc. from this —***adj.*** of a musical instrument producing a tone when struck, as a drum, cymbal, etc.
per·cus′sion·ist ***n.*** a musician who plays percussion instruments
per di·em (pər dē′əm) ⟦L⟧ daily
per·di·tion (pər dish′ən) ***n.*** ⟦< L *perdere,* to lose⟧ *Theol.* **1** the loss of the soul **2** HELL
per·dure (pər door′) ***vi.*** **-dured′**, **-dur′ing** ⟦< L *perdurare,* to endure⟧ to remain in existence; last
per·e·gri·nate (per′ə gri nāt′) ***vt.***, ***vi.*** **-nat′ed**, **-nat′ing** ⟦see PILGRIM⟧ to travel (along, over, or through) —**per′e·gri·na′tion** ***n.***
per·e·grine (falcon) (per′ə grin) a swift falcon much used in falconry
per·emp·to·ry (pər emp′tə rē) ***adj.*** ⟦< L *perimere,* destroy⟧ **1** *Law* barring further action; final **2** that cannot be denied, delayed, etc., as a command **3** dogmatic; imperious
per·en·ni·al (pə ren′ē əl) ***adj.*** ⟦< L *per-*, through + *annus,* year⟧ **1** continuing for a long time **2** becoming active again and again **3** living more than two years: said of plants —***n.*** a perennial plant

THESAURUS

pent-up *a.* held in check, repressed, unexpressed; see HELD, RESTRICTED.
people *n.* **1** [Humankind] humanity, mankind, the human race; see MAN 1. **2** [A body of persons having racial or social ties] nationality, tribe, community; see RACE 2. **3** [The middle and lower classes of society] folk, proletariat, rabble, masses, the multitude, the majority, crowd, common people, common herd, rank and file, the underprivileged, the public, the man in the street, bourgeoisie, riffraff, the herd*, the many, the great unwashed*, hoi polloi, John Q. Public, Jane Q. Public. **4** [Family] close relatives, kin, siblings; see FAMILY. **5** [Society in general] they, anybody, the public; see EVERYBODY.
peopled *a.* lived in, dwelt in, sustaining human life; see INHABITED.
pep* *n.* energy, vigor, liveliness; see ACTION 1.
per *prep.* to each, for each, contained in each, according to*, through, by, by means of.
perceive *v.* **1** [See] observe, note, notice; see LOOK 2, SEE 1. **2** [Understand] comprehend, sense, grasp; see UNDERSTAND 1.
perceived *a.* seen, felt, touched; see UNDERSTOOD 1.
percent *a.* by the hundred, per hundred, in a hundred, percentile.
percentage *n.* percent, rate, rate per cent, portion, section, allotment, proportion, duty, discount, commission, winnings, cut*, rake-off*, payoff, slice*; see also DIVISION 2.
perceptible *a.* perceivable, discernible, cognizable; see OBVIOUS 1.
perception *n.* **1** [The act of perceiving] realizing, understanding, apprehending; see ATTENTION, JUDGMENT 2. **2** [The result of perceiving] insight, knowledge, observation; see ATTITUDE, OPINION 1, VIEWPOINT.
perceptive *a.* alert, incisive, keen; see CONSCIOUS, OBSERVANT.
perch[2] *n.* seat, pole, landing place, resting place.
perch[2] *v.* roost, settle down, land; see REST 1, SIT.

per·fect (pur′fikt; *for v.* pər fekt′) ***adj.*** ⟦< L *per-,* through + *facere,* do⟧ **1** complete in all respects; flawless **2** excellent, as in skill or quality **3** completely accurate **4** utter; absolute *[a perfect fool]* **5** *Gram.* expressing a state or action completed at the time of speaking —***vt.*** **1** to complete **2** to make perfect or nearly perfect —**per′fect·ly** ***adv.***

per·fec·ta (pər fek′tə) ***n.*** ⟦Sp, perfect⟧ a bet in which one wins if one correctly picks the first and second place finishers in a race

per·fect·i·ble (pər fek′tə bəl) ***adj.*** that can become, or be made, perfect

per·fec·tion (pər fek′shən) ***n.*** **1** the act of perfecting **2** a being perfect **3** a person or thing that is the perfect embodiment of some quality

per·fec′tion·ism′ ***n.*** obsessive striving for perfection —**per·fec′tion·ist** ***n., adj.***

per·fi·dy (pur′fə dē) ***n.,*** *pl.* **-dies** ⟦< L *per,* through + *fides,* faith⟧ betrayal of trust; treachery —**per·fid·i·ous** (pər fid′ē əs) ***adj.***

per·fo·rate (pur′fə rāt′) ***vt., vi.*** **-rat′ed, -rat′ing** ⟦< L *per,* through + *forare,* to bore⟧ **1** to make a hole or holes through (something), as by boring **2** to pierce with holes in a row —**per′fo·ra′tion** ***n.***

per·force (pər fôrs′) ***adv.*** ⟦< OFr: see PER & FORCE⟧ necessarily

per·form (pər fôrm′) ***vt.*** ⟦< OFr *parfournir*⟧ **1** to do (a task, etc.) **2** to fulfill (a promise, etc.) **3** to render or enact (a piece of music, dramatic role, etc.) —***vi.*** to execute an action or process, esp. in a PERFORMANCE (sense 4) —**per·form′er** ***n.***

per·form′ance ***n.*** **1** the act of performing **2** functional effectiveness **3** deed or feat **4** *a)* a formal exhibition or presentation, as a play *b)* one's part in this

performance art an art form combining elements of several art forms, as dance, film, etc., in a presentation of juxtaposed images on various themes

performing arts arts, such as drama, for performance before an audience

per·fume (pər fyoom′; *for n. usually* pur′fyoom′) ***vt.*** **-fumed′, -fum′ing** ⟦< L *per-,* intens. + *fumare,* to smoke⟧ **1** to scent **2** to put perfume on —***n.*** a pleasing odor, or a substance producing this, as a volatile oil extracted from flowers

per·fum′er·y (-fyoo′mə rē) ***n.,*** *pl.* **-ies** perfumes collectively

per·func·to·ry (pər fuŋk′tə rē) ***adj.*** ⟦< L *per-,* intens. + *fungi,* perform⟧ **1** done without care or interest; superficial **2** indifferent; unconcerned —**per·func′to·ri·ly** ***adv.***

per·go·la (pur′gə lə) ***n.*** ⟦< L *pergula*⟧ an arbor with a latticework roof

per·haps (pər haps′) ***adv.*** ⟦PER + pl. of *hap,* chance⟧ possibly; maybe

peri- ⟦Gr⟧ *prefix* **1** around; about **2** near

per·i·car·di·um (per′ə kär′dē əm) ***n.,*** *pl.* **-di·a** (-ə) ⟦< Gr *peri-,* around + *kardia,* heart⟧ in vertebrates, the thin, closed sac surrounding the heart —**per′i·car′di·al** ***adj.***

Per·i·cles (per′ə klēz′) 495?-429 B.C.; Athenian statesman & general

per·i·gee (per′ə jē′) ***n.*** ⟦< Gr *peri-,* near + *gē,* earth⟧ the point nearest to the earth in the orbit of the moon or of a man-made satellite

per·i·he·li·on (per′ə hē′lē ən) ***n.,*** *pl.* **-li·ons** or **-li·a** (-ə) ⟦< Gr *peri-,* around + *hēlios,* sun⟧ the point nearest the sun in the orbit of a planet, comet, or man-made satellite

per·il (per′əl) ***n.*** ⟦< L *periculum,* danger⟧ **1** exposure to harm or injury **2** something that may cause harm

per′il·ous (-ə ləs) ***adj.*** involving peril or risk; dangerous —**per′il·ous·ly** ***adv.***

pe·rim·e·ter (pə rim′ə tər) ***n.*** ⟦< Gr *peri-,* around + *metron,* measure⟧ **1** the outer boundary of a figure or area **2** the total length of this

per·i·ne·um (per′ə nē′əm) ***n.,*** *pl.* **-ne′a** (-ə) ⟦< Gr *perineon*⟧ the small area between the anus and the genitals

pe·ri·od (pir′ē əd) ***n.*** ⟦< Gr *periodos,* a cycle⟧ **1** the interval between successive occurrences of an event **2** a portion of time characterized by certain processes, etc. *[a period of change]* **3** any of the portions of time into which a game, school day, etc. is divided **4** the menses **5** an end, conclusion **6** *a)* the pause in speaking or a mark of punctuation (.) used at the end of a sentence *b)* the dot (.) following many abbreviations —***interj.*** an exclamation used for emphasis

pe·ri·od·ic (pir′ē äd′ik) ***adj.*** **1** appearing or recurring at regular intervals **2** intermittent

pe′ri·od′i·cal ***adj.*** **1** PERIODIC **2** published at regular intervals, as weekly, etc. **3** of a periodical —***n.*** a periodical publication —**pe′ri·od′i·cal·ly** ***adv.***

periodic table an arrangement of the chemical elements according to their atomic numbers

pe·ri·od·i·za·tion (pir′ē ə də zā′shən) ***n.*** the dividing, as of history, into chronological periods

per·i·o·don·tal (per′ē ə dänt′'l) ***adj.*** ⟦< PERI- + Gr *odōn,* tooth⟧ occurring around a tooth or affecting the gums

per·i·pa·tet·ic (per′i pə tet′ik) ***adj.*** ⟦< Gr *peri-,* around + *patein,* walk⟧ walking or moving about; itinerant

pe·riph·er·al (pə rif′ər əl) ***adj.*** **1** of or forming a periphery **2** outer; external —***n.*** a piece of equipment used with a computer to increase its range or efficiency, as a disk, etc.

pe·riph·er·y (pə rif′ər ē) ***n.,*** *pl.* **-ies** ⟦< Gr *peri-,* around + *pherein,* to bear⟧ **1** an outer boundary, esp. of a rounded object **2** surrounding space

pe·riph·ra·sis (pə rif′rə sis) ***n.,*** *pl.* **-ses′** (-sēz′) ⟦< Gr *peri-,* around + *phrazein,* to speak⟧ the use of many words where a few would do —**per·i·phras·tic** (per′ə fras′tik) ***adj.***

per·i·scope (per′ə skōp′) ***n.*** ⟦PERI- + -SCOPE⟧ an optical

THESAURUS

perfect ***a.*** **1** [Having all necessary qualities] complete, sound, entire; see ABSOLUTE 1, WHOLE 1, 2. **2** [Without defect] excelling, faultless, flawless, impeccable, immaculate, unblemished, foolproof, untainted, unspotted, absolute, classic, stainless, spotless, crowning, culminating, sublime, supreme, ideal, beyond all praise, beyond compare; see also EXCELLENT, PURE 2, WHOLE 2.—*Ant.* RUINED, damaged, faulty. **3** [Exact] precise, sharp, distinct; see ACCURATE 2.

perfect ***v.*** fulfill, realize, develop; see ACHIEVE, COMPLETE.

perfected ***a.*** completed, developed, mature, conclusive, full, elaborate, thorough; see also FINISHED 1, FULFILLED.

perfection ***n.*** completion, fulfillment, finishing, consummation, supremacy, ideal, ending, realization; see also ACHIEVEMENT.—*Ant.* RUIN, destruction, neglect.

perfectly ***a.*** excellently, supremely, ideally, fitly, correctly, flawlessly, faultlessly.—*Ant.* BADLY, poorly, incorrectly.

perforate ***v.*** drill, slit, stab; see PENETRATE.

perforation ***n.*** break, aperture, slit; see HOLE 1.

perform ***v.*** **1** [To accomplish an action] do, make, achieve, accomplish, fulfill, execute, transact, carry out, carry through, discharge, effect, enforce, administer, complete, consummate, operate, finish, realize, go about, go through with, put through, work out, devote oneself to, come through, be engrossed in, be engaged in, see to it, bring about, engage in, concern oneself with, have an effect, fall to, do justice to, do one's part, make a move, follow through, apply oneself to, deal with, do something, look to, take measures, act on, lose oneself in, make it one's business, dispose of, bring to pass, do what is expected of one, put into effect, occupy oneself with, take action, address oneself to, put in action, lift a finger*, keep one's hand in*, pull off*. **2** [To present a performance] give, present, enact, play, offer, impersonate, show, exhibit, display, act out, dramatize, execute, put on the stage, produce, act the part of, act one's part.

performance ***n.*** appearance, rehearsal, exhibition, offering, representation, spectacle, review, revue, opera, play, concert, display, show; see also DRAMA.

perfume ***n.*** scent, fragrance, aroma, odor, sweetness, bouquet, incense; see also SMELL 1. *Perfumes include the following:* attar of roses, sandalwood, bay, rosemary, bay rum, frankincense, myrrh, eau de Cologne, musk, toilet water, potpourri, patchouli, spice, sachet, lavender, rose geranium.

perhaps ***a.*** conceivably, possibly, reasonably; see MAYBE.

perilous ***a.*** precarious, unsafe, uncertain; see DANGEROUS.

perimeter ***n.*** margin, outline, border; see BOUNDARY, EDGE 1.

period ***n.*** **1** [A measure of time] epoch, time, era; see AGE 3. **2** [An end] limit, conclusion, close; see END 2. **3** [A mark of punctuation] point, full stop, full pause, dot; see also PUNCTUATION.

periodic ***a.*** rhythmic, intermittent, recurrent; see REGULAR 3.

periodical ***n.*** review, number, publication; see MAGAZINE, NEWSPAPER.

periodically ***a.*** rhythmically, systematically, annually; see REGULARLY.

peripheral ***a.*** external, outer, surface; see OUTSIDE.

periphery ***n.*** covering, perimeter, border; see OUTSIDE 1.

instrument which allows one to see around or over an obstacle: used on submarines, etc.

per·ish (per′ish) ***vi.*** ⟦< L *per-*, through + *ire,* go⟧ **1** to be destroyed or ruined **2** to die, esp. violently

per·ish·a·ble (per′ish ə bəl) ***adj.*** that may perish; esp., liable to spoil, as some foods —***n.*** something, esp. a food, liable to spoil

per·i·stal·sis (per′ə stal′sis, -stôl′-) ***n.***, *pl.* **-ses′** (-sēz′) ⟦< Gr *peri-*, around + *stellein,* to place⟧ the contractions and dilations of the alimentary canal, moving the contents onward —**per′i·stal′tic** ***adj.***

per·i·to·ne·um (per′ə tə nē′əm) ***n.***, *pl.* **-ne′a** (-ə) or **-ne′ums** ⟦< Gr *peri-*, around + *teinein,* to stretch⟧ the serous membrane lining the abdominal cavity

per′i·to·ni′tis (-nīt′is) ***n.*** inflammation of the peritoneum

per·i·wig (per′ə wig′) ***n.*** ⟦altered < Fr *perruque*⟧ a wig of a type formerly worn by men

per·i·win·kle[1] (per′ə wiŋ′kəl) ***n.*** ⟦< L *pervincire,* entwine⟧ a creeping plant with blue, white, or pink flowers

per·i·win·kle[2] (per′ə wiŋ′kəl) ***n.*** ⟦OE *pinewincle*⟧ a small saltwater snail with a spherical shell

per·jure (pʉr′jər) ***vt.*** **-jured, -jur·ing** ⟦< L *per,* through + *jurare,* swear⟧ to make (oneself) guilty of perjury —**per′jur·er** ***n.***

per·ju·ry (pʉr′jə rē) ***n.***, *pl.* **-ries** ⟦< L *perjurus,* false⟧ the willful telling of a lie while under oath

perk[1] (pʉrk) ***vt.*** ⟦ME *perken*⟧ **1** to raise (the head, ears, etc.) briskly **2** to give a smart, fresh, or vivacious look to Often with *up* —***vi.*** to become lively: with *up* —**perk′y, -i·er, -i·est,** ***adj.***

perk[2] (pʉrk) ***vt., vi.*** [Inf.] *short for* PERCOLATE

perk[3] (pʉrk) ***n.*** [Inf.] *short for* PERQUISITE

perm (pʉrm) [Inf.] ***n.*** *short for* PERMANENT —***vt.*** to give a permanent to

per·ma·frost (pʉr′mə frôst′) ***n.*** permanently frozen subsoil

per·ma·nent (pʉr′mə nənt) ***adj.*** ⟦< L *per,* through + *manere,* remain⟧ lasting or intended to last indefinitely or for a long time —***n.*** a long-lasting hair wave produced by use of chemicals or heat

per·me·a·ble (pʉr′mē ə bəl) ***adj.*** that can be permeated, as by fluids —**per′me·a·bil′i·ty** ***n.***

per′me·ate′ (-āt′) ***vt., vi.*** **-at′ed, -at′ing** ⟦< L *per,* through + *meare,* to glide⟧ to spread or diffuse; penetrate (*through* or *among*)

per·mis·si·ble (pər mis′ə bəl) ***adj.*** that can be permitted; allowable

per·mis·sion (pər mish′ən) ***n.*** the act of permitting; esp., formal consent

per·mis′sive (-mis′iv) ***adj.*** **1** that permits **2** allowing freedom; lenient —**per·mis′sive·ly** ***adv.*** —**per·mis′sive·ness** ***n.***

per·mit (pər mit′; *for n.* pʉr′mit′, pər mit′) ***vt.*** **-mit′ted, -mit′ting** ⟦< L *per,* through + *mittere,* send⟧ **1** to allow; consent to **2** to authorize —***vi.*** to give opportunity *[if time permits]* —***n.*** a license

per·mu·ta·tion (pʉr′myoo tā′shən) ***n.*** ⟦< L *per-*, intens. + *mutare,* change⟧ **1** any radical alteration **2** any of the total number of groupings possible within a group

per·ni·cious (pər nish′əs) ***adj.*** ⟦< L < *per,* thoroughly + *necare,* kill⟧ very harmful or destructive —**per·ni′cious·ly** ***adv.***

per·o·ra·tion (per′ə rā′shən) ***n.*** ⟦< L *per,* through + *orare,* speak⟧ the concluding part of a speech

per·ox·ide (pər äk′sīd′) ***n.*** ⟦< L *per,* through + OXIDE⟧ any oxide containing the oxygen group linked by a single bond; specif., hydrogen peroxide —***vt.*** **-id′ed, -id′ing** to bleach (hair, etc.) with hydrogen peroxide

per·pen·dic·u·lar (pʉr′pən dik′yoo lər, -yə-) ***adj.*** ⟦< L *perpendiculum,* plumb line⟧ **1** at right angles to a given plane or line **2** exactly upright; vertical —***n.*** a line or plane at right angles to another line or plane

per·pe·trate (pʉr′pə trāt′) ***vt.*** **-trat′ed, -trat′ing** ⟦< L *per,* thoroughly + *patrare,* to effect⟧ **1** to do (something evil, criminal, etc.) **2** to commit (a blunder, etc.) —**per′pe·tra′tion** ***n.*** —**per′pe·tra′tor** ***n.***

per·pet·u·al (pər pech′oo əl) ***adj.*** ⟦< L *perpetuus,* constant⟧ **1** lasting forever or for a long time **2** continuing without interruption; constant —**per·pet′u·al·ly** ***adv.***

per·pet′u·ate′ (-āt′) ***vt.*** **-at′ed, -at′ing** to make perpetual; cause to continue or be remembered —**per·pet′u·a′tion** ***n.***

per·pe·tu·i·ty (pʉr′pə too′ə tē) ***n.***, *pl.* **-ties** unlimited time; eternity —**in perpetuity** forever

per·plex (pər pleks′) ***vt.*** ⟦< L *per,* through + *plectere,* twist⟧ to make (a person) uncertain, doubtful, etc.; confuse —**per·plex′ing** ***adj.*** —**per·plex′i·ty,** *pl.* **-ties,** ***n.***

per·qui·site (pʉr′kwi zit) ***n.*** ⟦< L *per-*, intens. + *quaerere,* seek⟧ something in addition to regular pay for one's work, as a tip

per se (pʉr′ sā′, -sē′) ⟦L⟧ by (or in) itself; intrinsically

per·se·cute (pʉr′si kyoot′) ***vt.*** **-cut′ed, -cut′ing** ⟦< L *per,* through + *sequi,* follow⟧ to afflict constantly so as to injure or distress, as for reasons of religion, race, etc. —**per′se·cu′tion** ***n.*** —**per′se·cu′tor** ***n.***

per·se·vere (pʉr′sə vir′) ***vi.*** **-vered′, -ver′ing** ⟦< L *per-*, intens. + *severus,* severe⟧ to continue a course of action, etc. in spite of difficulty, opposition, etc. —**per′se·ver′ance** ***n.***

Per·sia (pʉr′zhə) *former name for* IRAN

Per·sian (pʉr′zhən, -shən) ***adj.*** of Persia or its people, language, etc. —***n.*** **1** person born or living in Persia **2** the language of Iran **3** a variety of domestic cat with a long, thick, glossy coat

Persian Gulf arm of the Indian Ocean, between Iran & Arabia

Persian lamb the pelt of karakul lambs

per·si·flage (pʉr′sə fläzh′) ***n.*** ⟦Fr < L *per,* through + *sifilare,* to hiss⟧ frivolous talk or writing

per·sim·mon (pər sim′ən) ***n.*** ⟦< AmInd⟧ **1** a hardwood tree with plumlike fruit **2** the fruit

THESAURUS

perish ***v.*** pass away, be lost, depart; see DIE.

perjure ***v.*** prevaricate, swear falsely, lie on the stand; see LIE 1.

perjury ***n.*** false statement, violation of an oath, willful falsehood; see LIE.

perk up ***v.*** **1** [Be refreshed] revive, recuperate, liven up; see RECOVER 3. **2** [Cheer or refresh] invigorate, animate, enliven; see RENEW 1, REVIVE 1.

permanence ***n.*** continuity, dependability, durability; see STABILITY 1.

permanent ***a.*** durable, enduring, abiding, uninterrupted, stable, continuing, lasting, firm, hard, tough, strong, hardy, robust, sound, sturdy, steadfast, imperishable, surviving, living, long-lived, long-standing, invariable, persevering, unyielding, persisting, resistant, impenetrable, recurring, constant, changeless, persistent, perennial.

permanently ***a.*** for all time, enduringly, lastingly; see FOREVER.

permeate ***v.*** pervade, saturate, fill; see FILTER 1.

permissible ***a.*** allowable, sanctioned, authorized; see PERMITTED.

permission ***n.*** leave, liberty, consent, assent, acceptance, letting, approbation, agreement, license, permit, authority, tolerance, toleration, authorization, approval, acknowledgment, admission, verification, recognition, concurrence, promise, avowal, support, corroboration, guarantee, guaranty, visa, encouragement, ratification, grace, authority, sanction, confirmation, endorsement, affirmation, assurance, empowering, legalization, grant, indulgence, trust, concession, adjustment, settlement, accord, nod*, OK*, rubber stamp*, the go-ahead*, high sign, green light*.—*Ant.* DENIAL, injunction, interdiction.

permissive ***a.*** allowing, lenient, agreeable; see KIND.

permit ***n.*** license, grant, consent; see PERMISSION.

permit ***v.*** sanction, tolerate, let; see ALLOW.

permitted ***a.*** granted, allowed, licensed, authorized, legalized, tolerated, empowered, sanctioned, conceded, consented, favored, suffered, chartered, accorded, let, indulged, privileged; see also APPROVED.—*Ant.* REFUSED, denied, prohibited.

perpendicular ***a.*** vertical, plumb, upright; see STRAIGHT 1.

perpetrate ***v.*** commit, act, do; see PERFORM 1.

perpetual ***a.*** **1** [Never stopping] continuous, unceasing, constant; see ENDLESS. **2** [Continually repeating] repetitious, repeating, recurrent; see CONSTANT.

perpetually ***a.*** enduringly, permanently, unceasingly; see FOREVER.

perplex ***v.*** puzzle, confound, bewilder; see CONFUSE.

perplexed ***a.*** troubled, uncertain, bewildered; see DOUBTFUL.

perplexing ***a.*** bewildering, confusing, mystifying; see DIFFICULT 2.

per se ***a.*** as such, intrinsically, alone, singularly, fundamentally, in essence, in itself, by itself, virtually; see also ESSENTIALLY.

persecute ***v.*** afflict, harass, victimize; see ABUSE.

persecution ***n.*** torture, torment, teasing, provoking; see also ABUSE.

perseverance ***n.*** grit, resolution, pluck; see DETERMINATION.

persevere ***v.*** persist, remain, pursue; see ENDURE 1.

per·sist (pər sist′, -zist′) ***vi.*** ⟦< L *per,* through + *sistere,* cause to stand⟧ **1** to refuse to give up, esp. when faced with opposition **2** to continue insistently **3** to endure; remain

per·sist′ent ***adj.*** **1** continuing, esp. in the face of opposition, etc. **2** continuing to exist or endure **3** constantly repeated —**per·sist′ence** ***n.***

per·snick·e·ty (pər snik′ə tē) ***adj.*** ⟦< Scot dial.⟧ [Inf.] too particular or precise; fussy

per·son (pur′sən) ***n.*** ⟦< L *persona*⟧ **1** a human being: now usually pluralized as *people* **2** the human body **3** personality; self **4** *Gram.* any of the three sets of pronouns and corresponding verb forms: see FIRST PERSON, SECOND PERSON, THIRD PERSON **5** *Law* any individual or incorporated group having certain legal rights and responsibilities —**in person** actually present

-per·son (pur′sən) *combining form* person in a (specified) activity: used to avoid the masculine implication of *-man [chairperson]*

per′son·a·ble ***adj.*** ⟦ME *personabilis*⟧ having a pleasing appearance and personality

per′son·age ***n.*** a person; esp., an important person; notable

per′son·al (-nəl) ***adj.*** **1** private; individual **2** done in person **3** involving human beings *[personal* relationships*]* **4** of the body or physical appearance **5** *a)* having to do with the character, conduct, etc. of a person *[*a *personal* remark*]* *b)* tending to make personal, esp. derogatory, remarks **6** *Gram.* indicating PERSON (sense 4) **7** *Law* of property (**personal property**) that is movable

personal computer MICROCOMPUTER

personal effects personal belongings, esp. those worn or carried

per·son·al·i·ty (pur′sə nal′ə tē) ***n.***, *pl.* **-ties** **1** distinctive individual qualities of a person, considered collectively **2** such qualities seen as being attractive to others **3** a notable person **4** [*pl.*] offensive remarks aimed at a person

per·son·al·ize (pur′sə nə līz′) ***vt.*** **-ized′**, **-iz′ing** **1** to apply to a particular person, esp. to oneself **2** to have marked with one's name, etc.

per′son·al·ly ***adv.*** **1** in person **2** as a person *[*I dislike him *personally]* **3** in one's own opinion **4** as though directed at oneself

per·so·na non gra·ta (pər sō′nə nōn grät′ə) ⟦L⟧ an unwelcome person

per·son·i·fy (pər sän′ə fī′) ***vt.*** **-fied′**, **-fy′ing** **1** to think of or represent (a thing) as a person **2** to typify; embody —**per·son′i·fi·ca′tion** ***n.***

per·son·nel (pur′sə nel′) ***n.*** ⟦Fr⟧ **1** persons employed in any work, enterprise, service, etc. **2** a personnel department or office —***adj.*** of or relating to the division within a business, etc. responsible for hiring and training employees, etc.

per·spec·tive (pər spek′tiv) ***n.*** ⟦< L *per,* through + *specere,* look⟧ **1** the art of picturing objects so as to show relative distance or depth **2** the appearance of objects as determined by their relative distance and positions **3** sense of proportion **4** *a)* a specific point of view in understanding things or events *b)* the ability to see things in a true relationship

per·spi·ca·cious (pur′spi kā′shəs) ***adj.*** ⟦see prec.⟧ having keen judgment; discerning —**per′spi·ca′cious·ly** ***adv.*** —**per′spi·cac′i·ty** (-kas′ə tē) ***n.***

per·spic·u·ous (pər spik′yoo̅ əs) ***adj.*** ⟦see PERSPECTIVE⟧ easily understood; lucid —**per·spi·cu·i·ty** (pur′spi kyoo̅′ə tē) ***n.***

per·spi·ra·tion (pur′spə rā′shən) ***n.*** **1** the action of perspiring **2** sweat

per·spire (pər spīr′) ***vt.***, ***vi.*** **-spired′**, **-spir′ing** ⟦< L *per-,* through + *spirare,* breathe⟧ to sweat

per·suade (pər swād′) ***vt.*** **-suad′ed**, **-suad′ing** ⟦< L *per-,* intens. + *suadere,* to urge⟧ to cause to do or believe something by reasoning, urging, etc.; induce or convince —**per·suad′er** ***n.***

per·sua·sion (pər swā′zhən) ***n.*** **1** a persuading or being persuaded **2** power of persuading **3** a strong belief **4** a particular religious belief

per·sua′sive ***adj.*** having the power, or tending, to persuade —**per·sua′sive·ly** ***adv.***

pert (purt) ***adj.*** ⟦< L *apertus,* open⟧ **1** impudent; saucy **2** chic and jaunty —**pert′ly** ***adv.***

per·tain (pər tān′) ***vi.*** ⟦< L *per-,* intens. + *tenere,* hold⟧ **1** to belong; be connected or associated **2** to be appropriate **3** to have reference

per·ti·na·cious (purt′′n ā′shəs) ***adj.*** ⟦< L *per-,* intens. + *tenax,* holding fast⟧ **1** holding firmly to some purpose, belief, etc. **2** hard to get rid of —**per′ti·nac′i·ty** (-as′ə tē) ***n.***

per·ti·nent (purt′′n ənt) ***adj.*** ⟦see PERTAIN⟧ having some connection with the matter at hand —**per′ti·nence** ***n.***

per·turb (pər turb′) ***vt.*** ⟦< L *per-,* intens. + *turbare,* disturb⟧ to cause to be alarmed, agitated, or upset —**per·tur·ba·tion** (pur′tər bā′shən) ***n.***

Pe·ru (pə roo̅′) country in W South America, on the Pacific: 480,041 sq. mi.; pop. 22,048,000 —**Pe·ru′vi·an** (-vē ən) ***adj.***, ***n.***

pe·ruke (pə roo̅k′) ***n.*** ⟦Fr *perruque*⟧ PERIWIG

pe·ruse (pə roo̅z′) ***vt.*** **-rused′**, **-rus′ing** ⟦prob. < L *per-,* intens. + ME *usen,* to use⟧ **1** to read carefully; study **2** to read in a leisurely way —**pe·rus′al** ***n.***

per·vade (pər vād′) ***vt.*** **-vad′ed**, **-vad′ing** ⟦< L *per,* through + *vadere,* go⟧ to spread or be prevalent throughout —**per·va′sive** (-vā′siv) ***adj.***

per·verse (pər vurs′) ***adj.*** ⟦see PERVERT⟧ **1** deviating from what is considered right or good **2** stubbornly con-

THESAURUS

persist *v.* persevere, keep on, insist; see CONTINUE 1, ENDURE 1.

persistence *n.* constancy, resolution, stamina; see ENDURANCE.

persistent *a.* tenacious, steadfast, determined; see RESOLUTE.

person *n.* **1** [An individual] human being, child, adult, someone, somebody, self, oneself, I, me, soul, spirit, character, individuality, personage, personality, identity; see also MAN 2, WOMAN 1. **2** [An individual enjoying distinction] distinguished person, personality, success; see CHARACTER 4. **3** [Bodily form] physique, frame, form; see BODY 1. —**in person** personally, in the flesh, present; see NEAR 1.

personable *a.* agreeable, pleasant, attractive; see CHARMING.

personage *n.* human being, someone, individual; see MAN 2, PERSON 1.

personal *a.* **1** [Private] secluded, secret, intimate; see PRIVATE. **2** [Individual] own, peculiar, particular; see INDIVIDUAL, SPECIAL. **3** [Pertaining to one's person] fleshly, corporeal, corporal; see BODILY.

personality *n.* **1** [The total of one's nature] self, oneself, being; see CHARACTER 2. **2** [Individual characteristics] disposition, nature, temper; see CHARACTER 1. **3** [A notable person] celebrity, star, personage; see CHARACTER 4.

personally *a.* **1** [Viewed in a personal manner] individually, privately, by oneself. **2** [From the point of view of the speaker] for me, myself, for myself, for my part, as I see it, according to my opinion; see also INDIVIDUALLY.—*Ant.* CERTAINLY, objectively, scientifically.

personify *v.* **1** [To impersonate] represent, live as, act out; see IMPERSONATE. **2** [To represent] copy, symbolize, exemplify; see REPRESENT 3.

personnel *n.* workers, employees, group; see STAFF 2.

perspective *n.* aspect, attitude, outlook; see VIEWPOINT.

perspiration *n.* water, exudation, beads of moisture; see SWEAT.

perspire *v.* secrete, exude, lather; see SWEAT.

persuade *v.* convince, move, induce, assure, cajole, incline, talk someone into something, win over, bring around, lead to believe, lead to do something, gain the confidence of, prevail upon, overcome another's resistance, wear down, bring a person to his or her senses, win an argument, make one's point, gain the confidence of, make someone see the light; see also INFLUENCE.—*Ant.* NEGLECT, dissuade, dampen.

persuaded *a.* convinced, won over, moved to, influenced, motivated, lured, impelled, wheedled, having succumbed to pressure, brought to see the light.

persuasion *n.* **1** [The act of persuading] inducing, influencing, enticing; see INFLUENCE. **2** [A belief] creed, tenet, religion; see FAITH.

persuasive *a.* convincing, alluring, luring, seductive, influential, winning, enticing, impelling, moving, actuating, efficient, effective, effectual, compelling, touching, forceful, potent, powerful, pointed, strong, energetic, forcible, plausible, inveigling; see also CONVINCING.

pertain *v.* relate to, belong to, refer to; see CONCERN 1.

pertaining to *a.* belonging to, appropriate to, connected with, having to do with.

pertinence *n.* consistency, congruity, relevance; see IMPORTANCE.

pertinent *a.* appropriate, suitable, related; see RELEVANT.

perturb *v.* pester, worry, irritate; see BOTHER 2.

perturbed *a.* uneasy, anxious, restless; see TROUBLED.

pervade *v.* suffuse, permeate, spread through; see PENETRATE.

perverse *a.* wayward, delinquent, capricious; see BAD 1.

trary 3 obstinately disobedient —**per·verse'ly** *adv.* —**per·verse'ness** or **per·ver'si·ty** *n.*
per·ver·sion (pər vur'zhən) *n.* 1 a perverting or being perverted 2 something perverted 3 any sexual act or practice considered abnormal
per·vert (pər vurt'; *for n.* pur'vurt') *vt.* ⟦< L *per-,* intens. + *vertere,* turn⟧ 1 to lead astray; corrupt 2 to misuse 3 to distort —*n.* one practicing sexual perversion
pe·se·ta (pə sāt'ə) *n.* ⟦Sp, dim. of *peso,* peso⟧ the monetary unit of Spain
pes·ky (pes'kē) *adj.* **-ki·er, -ki·est** ⟦prob. var. of *pesty*⟧ [Inf.] annoying; troublesome —**pes'ki·ness** *n.*
pe·so (pā'sō) *n., pl.* **-sos** ⟦Sp < L *pensum,* something weighed⟧ the monetary unit of various countries, including Mexico, Colombia, Chile, etc.
pes·si·mism (pes'ə miz'əm) *n.* ⟦< L *pejor,* worse⟧ 1 the belief that the evil in life outweighs the good 2 the tendency to expect the worst —**pes'si·mist** *n.* —**pes'si·mis'tic** *adj.* —**pes'si·mis'ti·cal·ly** *adv.*
pest (pest) *n.* ⟦< L *pestis,* plague⟧ a person or thing that is troublesome, destructive, etc.; specif., a rat, fly, weed, etc.
pes·ter (pes'tər) *vt.* ⟦< OFr *empestrer,* entangle⟧ to annoy; vex
pest'hole' *n.* a place infested with an epidemic disease
pes·ti·cide (pes'tə sīd') *n.* any chemical for killing insects, weeds, etc.
pes·tif·er·ous (pes tif'ər əs) *adj.* ⟦< L *pestis,* plague + *ferre,* to bear⟧ 1 noxious 2 [Inf.] annoying
pes·ti·lence (pes'tə ləns) *n.* 1 a deadly epidemic disease; plague 2 anything regarded as harmful
pes·ti·lent (pes'tə lənt) *adj.* ⟦< L *pestis,* plague⟧ 1 likely to cause death 2 dangerous to society *[*the *pestilent* threat of war*]* 3 annoying
pes·tle (pes'əl) *n.* ⟦< L *pinsere,* to pound⟧ a tool used to pound or grind substances, esp. in a mortar
pes·to (pes'tō) *n.* ⟦see prec.⟧ a sauce for pasta, of ground basil and garlic mixed with olive oil
pet[1] (pet) *n.* ⟦orig. Scot dial.⟧ 1 an animal that is domesticated and kept as a companion 2 a person treated with particular indulgence —*adj.* 1 kept or treated as a pet 2 especially liked 3 particular *[*a *pet* peeve*]* 4 showing fondness *[*a *pet* name*]* —*vt.* **pet'ted, pet'ting** to stroke or pat gently; caress —*vi.* [Inf.] to kiss, embrace, etc. as lovers do
pet[2] (pet) *n.* ⟦< ?⟧ a sulky mood
pet·al (pet''l) *n.* ⟦< Gr *petalos,* outspread⟧ any of the leaflike parts of a blossom
pe·tard (pi tärd') *n.* ⟦< Fr⟧ used chiefly in **hoist with** (or **by**) **one's own petard,** destroyed by the very thing with which one meant to destroy others
pet·cock (pet'käk') *n.* ⟦< L *pedere,* break wind + *cock,* valve⟧ a small valve for draining pipes, etc.
pe·ter (pēt'ər) *vi.* ⟦< ?⟧ [Inf.] to become gradually smaller, weaker, etc. and then disappear: with *out*
Pe·ter (pēt'ər) *n. Bible* (original name *Simon*) (died A.D. 64?); one of the twelve Apostles, a fisherman: reputed author of two Letters: also **Saint Peter**
Peter I 1672-1725; czar of Russia (1682-1725): called *Peter the Great*
pet·i·ole (pet'ē ōl') *n.* ⟦< L *pes,* FOOT⟧ LEAFSTALK
pe·tite (pə tēt') *adj.* ⟦Fr⟧ small and trim in figure: said of a woman
pe·tit four (pet'ē fôr') *pl.* **pe·tits fours** or **pe·tit fours** (pet'ē fôrz') ⟦Fr, lit., small oven⟧ a tiny, frosted cake
pe·ti·tion (pə tish'ən) *n.* ⟦< L *petere,* seek⟧ 1 a solemn, earnest request; entreaty 2 a formal document embodying such a request, often signed by many people 3 *Law* a written formal request asking for a specific court action —*vt.* to address a petition to —*vi.* to make a petition —**pe·ti'tion·er** *n.*
pe·tit jury (pet'ē) a group of citizens picked to decide the issues of a trial in court
pet·rel (pe'trəl) *n.* ⟦< ?⟧ a small sea bird with long wings
pet·ri·fy (pe'tri fī') *vt.* **-fied', -fy'ing** ⟦< L *petra,* rock + *facere,* make⟧ 1 to turn into stone 2 to harden or deaden 3 to paralyze, as with fear
petro- ⟦< Gr *petra,* rock⟧ *combining form* 1 rock or stone 2 petroleum 3 of or relating to the petroleum business
pet·ro·chem·i·cal (pe'trō kem'i kəl) *n.* a chemical with a petroleum base
pet'ro·dol'lars *pl.n.* revenue from the sale of petroleum
pet·rol (pe'trəl) *n.* ⟦see PETROLEUM⟧ *Brit. term for* GASOLINE
pet·ro·la·tum (pe'trə lāt'əm) *n.* ⟦< fol.⟧ a greasy, jellylike substance derived from petroleum and used in ointments, etc.: also **petroleum jelly**
pe·tro·le·um (pə trō'lē əm) *n.* ⟦< L *petra,* rock + *oleum,* oil⟧ an oily, liquid solution of hydrocarbons, occurring naturally in certain rock strata: it yields kerosene, gasoline, etc.
PET (scan) (pet) ⟦*p(ositron) e(mission) t(omography),* an X-ray technique⟧ a type of X-raying that shows metabolic activity, used to detect abnormalities, esp. of the brain: also **PETT scan**
pet·ti·coat (pet'ē kōt', pet'i-) *n.* ⟦< PETTY + COAT⟧ a woman's underskirt
pet·ti·fog·ger (pet'i fäg'ər, -fôg'-; pet'ē-) *n.* ⟦< PETTY + *fogger* < ?⟧ 1 a lawyer who handles petty cases, esp. unethically 2 one who quibbles —**pet'ti·fog', -fogged', -fog'ging,** *vi.*
pet·tish (pet'ish) *adj.* ⟦< PET[2]⟧ peevish; petulant —**pet'tish·ly** *adv.*
pet·ty (pet'ē) *adj.* **-ti·er, -ti·est** ⟦< OFr *petit*⟧ 1 relatively unimportant 2 small-minded; mean 3 relatively low in rank —**pet'ti·ness** *n.*
petty cash a cash fund for incidentals
petty officer *U.S. Navy* a naval enlisted person who is a noncommissioned officer
pet·u·lant (pech'ə lənt) *adj.* ⟦< L *petere,* to rush at⟧ impatient or irritable, esp. over a petty annoyance —**pet'u·lance** *n.* —**pet'u·lant·ly** *adv.*
pe·tu·ni·a (pə to͞on'yə) *n.* ⟦ult. < AmInd (Brazil)⟧ a plant with showy, funnel-shaped flowers
pew (pyo͞o) *n.* ⟦ult. < Gr *pous,* foot⟧ any of the benches with a back that are fixed in rows in a church
pe·wee (pē'wē') *n.* ⟦echoic of its call⟧ a small flycatcher
pew·ter (pyo͞ot'ər) *n.* ⟦OFr *peautre*⟧ 1 an alloy of tin with antimony, copper, lead, etc. 2 articles made of this
pe·yo·te (pā ōt'ē) *n.* ⟦AmSp < AmInd (Mexico) *peyotl,* caterpillar⟧ MESCAL: see also MESCALINE
pf or **pfd** *abbrev.* preferred
PFC or **Pfc** *abbrev.* Private First Class
pg *abbrev.* page
PG *trademark for* a film rating indicating parents may find some content unsuitable for children under 17
PG-13 *trademark for* a film rating indicating parents may

THESAURUS

perversion *n.* 1 [A distortion] involution, regression, abuse; see CONTORTION. 2 [Sexual deviation] corruption, debasement, depravity, wickedness, depredation, degeneration, degradation, bestiality, vice; see also LEWDNESS.
pervert *v.* ruin, vitiate, divert; see CORRUPT.
pervert *n.* sex maniac, sex criminal, rapist, molester, sodomizer, deviant, pederast, lecher.
perverted *a.* distorted, deviating, corrupt; see BAD 1.
pessimism *n.* doubt, cynicism, lack of hope; see DEPRESSION 2, GRIEF, SADNESS.
pessimistic *a.* 1 [Discouraging] worrisome, bleak, troubling; see DISMAL. 2 [Inclined to a discouraging view] hopeless, gloomy, cynical; see SAD 1.
pest *n.* 1 [Anything destructive] virus, germ, insect, bug, harmful bird, bird of prey, destructive animal. *Common pests include the following:* housefly, mosquito, flea, louse, mite, gnat, bedbug, tick, aphid, Japanese beetle, corn borer, boll weevil, squash bug, gypsy moth, cutworm, ant, wasp, meal moth, slug, snail, skunk, mouse, rat, gopher, prairie dog, woodchuck, groundhog, rabbit, mole, weasel, coyote, hawk. 2 [A nuisance] bore, tease, annoyance; see TROUBLE 1.
pester *v.* annoy, harass, provoke; see BOTHER 2.
pestilence *n.* epidemic, plague, sickness; see ILLNESS 1.
pet[1] *n.* 1 [A term of endearment] lover, dear, love; see DARLING. 2 [Favorite] darling, idol, adored one; see FAVORITE. 3 [A creature kept as an object of affection] *Common pets include the following:* pony, dog, cat, horse, goldfish, rabbit, hamster, guinea pig, mouse, canary, parrot, parakeet, tropical fish, turtle, gerbil.
pet[1] *v.* 1 [To caress] fondle, cuddle, pat; see TOUCH 1. 2 [*To make love] embrace, hug, neck*; see CARESS, KISS, LOVE 2.
petal *n.* flower part, bract, colored leaflike structure; see FLOWER.
petition *n.* prayer, request, supplication; see APPEAL 1.
petrified *a.* stone, hardened, mineralized; see FIRM 2.
petrify *v.* mineralize, clarify, solidify; see HARDEN.
petroleum *n.* crude oil, fuel, oil; see OIL.
petty *a.* small, insignificant, frivolous; see TRIVIAL, UNIMPORTANT.

find some content especially unsuitable for children under 13

pH (pē′āch′) ***n.*** ⟦< Fr *p(ouvoir) h(ydrogène)*, lit., hydrogen power⟧ the degree of acidity or alkalinity of a solution

pha·e·ton or **pha·ë·ton** (fā′ə tən) ***n.*** ⟦after *Phaetōn*, son of Helios, Gr sun god⟧ **1** a light, four-wheeled carriage **2** an early type of open automobile

phag·o·cyte (fag′ə sīt′) ***n.*** ⟦< Gr *phagein*, to eat + *kytos*, hollow⟧ any cell, esp. a leukocyte, that destroys foreign matter in the blood and tissues

pha·lan·ger (fə lan′jər) ***n.*** ⟦< Gr *phalanx*, bone between fingers or toes⟧ a small, tree-dwelling Australian marsupial

pha·lanx (fā′laŋks′) ***n.***, *pl.* **-lanx′es**; also, and for 3 always, **pha·lan·ges** (fə lan′jēz′) ⟦Gr, line of battle⟧ **1** an ancient close-ranked infantry formation **2** any massed group **3** any of the bones forming the fingers or toes

phal·lo·cen·tric (fal′ō sen′trik) ***adj.*** dominated by attitudes regarded as typically masculine

phal·lus (fal′əs) ***n.***, *pl.* **-li′** (-ī′) or **-lus·es** ⟦Gr *phallos*⟧ an image of the penis —**phal′lic** ***adj.***

phan·tasm (fan′taz′əm) ***n.*** ⟦< Gr *phantazein*, to show⟧ **1** a figment of the mind **2** a deceptive likeness

phan·tas·ma·go·ri·a (fan taz′mə gôr′ē ə) ***n.*** ⟦< Gr *phantasma*, phantasm + *ageirein*, assemble⟧ a rapid sequence of images, as in a dream

phan·tom (fan′təm) ***n.*** ⟦see PHANTASM⟧ **1** an apparition; specter **2** an illusion —***adj.*** of or like a phantom; illusory

Phar·aoh (far′ō, fā′rō′) ***n.*** [*sometimes* **p-**] the title of the kings of ancient Egypt

Phar·i·see (far′ə sē′) ***n.*** **1** a member of an ancient Jewish group that observed both the written and the oral law **2** ⟦< characterization in NT⟧ [**p-**] a self-righteous, hypocritical person —**phar′i·sa′ic** (-sā′ik) ***adj.***

phar·ma·ceu·ti·cal (fär′mə so͞ot′i kəl) ***adj.*** ⟦< Gr *pharmakon*, a drug⟧ of pharmacy or drugs: also **phar′ma·ceu′tic** —***n.*** a drug or medicine

phar′ma·ceu′tics (-iks) ***n.*** PHARMACY (sense 1)

phar·ma·cist (fär′mə sist) ***n.*** one licensed to practice pharmacy; druggist

phar′ma·col′o·gy (-käl′ə jē) ***n.*** ⟦< Gr *pharmakon*, a drug⟧ the science dealing with the effect of drugs on living organisms

phar′ma·co·pe′ia or **phar′ma·co·poe′ia** (-kō pē′ə) ***n.*** ⟦< Gr *pharmakon*, a drug + *poiein*, to make⟧ an official book listing drugs and medicines

phar·ma·cy (fär′mə sē) ***n.***, *pl.* **-cies** ⟦< Gr *pharmakon*, a drug⟧ **1** the art or profession of preparing drugs and medicines **2** a drugstore

phar·yn·gi·tis (far′in jīt′is) ***n.*** inflammation of the pharynx; sore throat

phar·ynx (far′iŋks) ***n.***, *pl.* **pha·ryn·ges** (fə rin′jēz′) or **phar′ynx·es** ⟦Gr *pharynx*, throat⟧ the cavity leading from the mouth and nasal passages to the larynx and esophagus —**pha·ryn·ge·al** (fə rin′jē əl) ***adj.***

phase (fāz) ***n.*** ⟦< Gr *phainesthai*, appear⟧ **1** any stage in a series or cycle of changes, as in the moon's illumination **2** an aspect or side, as of a problem —***vt.*** **phased**, **phas′ing** to introduce or carry out in stages: often with *in* or *into* —**in** (or **out of**) **phase** in (or not in) synchronization —**phase out** to bring or come to an end by stages

phase′out′ ***n.*** a phasing out; gradual termination or withdrawal

PhD or **Ph.D.** *abbrev.* ⟦L *Philosophiae Doctor*⟧ Doctor of Philosophy

pheas·ant (fez′ənt) ***n.*** ⟦< Gr *phasianos*, (bird) of *Phasis*, river in Asia⟧ a large game bird with a long, sweeping tail and brilliant feathers

phe·nac·e·tin (fē nas′ə tin) ***n.*** a white, crystalline powder used to reduce fever, relieve headaches, etc.

phe·no·bar·bi·tal (fē′nə bär′bi tôl′) ***n.*** an odorless, white, crystalline powder used as a sedative

phe·nol (fē′nōl′, -nôl′, -näl′) ***n.*** a white, crystalline compound, corrosive and poisonous, used to make synthetic resins, etc. and, in dilute solution (*carbolic acid*) as an antiseptic

phe·nol·phthal·ein (fē′nōl thal′ēn′, -ē in) ***n.*** a white to pale-yellow, crystalline powder used as a laxative, as an acid-base indicator in chemical analysis, etc.

phe·nom (fē′näm) ***n.*** ⟦< PHENOMENON⟧ [Slang] one who is very talented or skilled; specif., a young, very gifted athlete

phe·nom·e·non (fə näm′ə nən, -nän′) ***n.***, *pl.* **-na** (-nə); also, esp. for 2 and usually for 3, **-nons′** ⟦< Gr *phainesthai*, appear⟧ **1** any observable fact or event that can be scientifically described **2** anything very unusual **3** [Inf.] an extraordinary person; prodigy —**phe·nom′e·nal** ***adj.***

pher·o·mone (fer′ə mōn′) ***n.*** ⟦< Gr *pherein*, carry + (HOR)MONE⟧ a chemical substance secreted by certain animals, as ants, that conveys information to others of the same species

phi (fī, fē) ***n.*** the 21st letter of the Greek alphabet (Φ, φ)

phi·al (fī′əl) ***n.*** ⟦< Gr *phialē*, shallow bowl⟧ a small glass bottle; vial

Phil·a·del·phi·a (fil′ə del′fē ə) city & port in SE Pennsylvania: pop. 1,586,000

Philadelphia lawyer [Inf.] a shrewd or tricky lawyer

phi·lan·der (fi lan′dər, fə-) ***vi.*** ⟦ult. < Gr *philos*, loving + *anēr*, a man⟧ to engage lightly in love affairs: said of a man —**phi·lan′der·er** ***n.***

phi·lan·thro·py (fə lan′thrə pē) ***n.*** ⟦< Gr *philein*, to love + *anthrōpos*, human being⟧ **1** a desire to help mankind, esp. as shown by gifts to institutions, etc. **2** *pl.* **-pies** a philanthropic gift, institution, etc. —**phil·an·throp·ic** (fil′ən thräp′ik) ***adj.*** —**phi·lan′thro·pist** ***n.***

phi·lat·e·ly (fə lat′'l ē) ***n.*** ⟦< Fr < Gr *philos*, loving + *ateleia*, exemption from (further) tax (meaning "postage prepaid")⟧ the collection and study of postage stamps, postmarks, etc. —**phi·lat′e·list** ***n.***

-phile (fīl, fil) ⟦< Gr *philos*, loving⟧ *combining form* one that loves or is attracted to

Phil·har·mon·ic (fil′här män′ik) ***adj.*** ⟦ult. < Gr *philos*, loving + *harmonia*, harmony⟧ designating a group formed to sponsor a symphony orchestra —***n.*** an orchestra so sponsored

phi·lip·pic (fi lip′ik) ***n.*** ⟦< Gr *Philippos*, Philip, Macedonian king denounced by Demosthenes⟧ a bitter verbal attack

Phil·ip·pines (fil′ə pēnz′) country consisting of *c.* 7,100 islands (**Philippine Islands**) in the SW Pacific off the SE coast of Asia: 115,830 sq. mi.; pop. 60,559,000 —**Phil′ip·pine′** (-pēn′) ***adj.***

Phil·is·tine (fil′ə stēn′) ***n.*** **1** a member of a non-Semitic people of SW Palestine in biblical times **2** ⟦< a Ger slang word⟧ [*often* **p-**] a person regarded as smugly conventional, lacking culture, etc.

Phil·lips (fil′ips) ⟦after H. F. *Phillips* (?-1958), its U.S. developer⟧ *trademark for* a screwdriver (**Phillips screwdriver**) with a cross-shaped, pointed tip

philo- ⟦< Gr *philos*, loving⟧ *combining form* loving, liking

phil·o·den·dron (fil′ə den′drən) ***n.*** ⟦< Gr *philos*, loving + *dendron*, tree⟧ a tropical American vine used as a houseplant

phi·lol·o·gy (fi läl′ə jē) ***n.*** ⟦< Gr *philein*, to love + *logos*, word⟧ *former term for* LINGUISTICS —**phil·o·log·i·cal** (fil′ə läj′i kəl) ***adj.*** —**phi·lol′o·gist** ***n.***

phi·los·o·pher (fə läs′ə fər) ***n.*** ⟦< Gr *philos*, loving + *sophos*, wise⟧ **1** one who is an expert in philosophy **2** one who expounds a system of philosophy **3** one who meets difficulties calmly

phil·o·soph·ic (fil′ə säf′ik) ***adj.*** **1** of philosophy or philosophers **2** sensibly composed or calm Also **phil′o·soph′i·cal**

THESAURUS

phantom ***n.*** apparition, specter, shade; see GHOST.

phase ***n.*** condition, stage, appearance, point, aspect; see also STATE 2.

phase out ***v.*** slowly get rid of, gradually dispose of, weed out*; see ELIMINATE.

phenomenal ***a.*** extraordinary, unique, remarkable; see UNUSUAL 1.

phenomenon ***n.*** fact, experience, happening; see EVENT.

philanthropic ***a.*** kindhearted, benevolent, humanitarian; see HUMANE, KIND.

philosopher ***n.*** logician, wise person, wise man, thinker, scholar, sage, savant, Sophist, Solon. *Major philosophers include the following:* Socrates, Epicurus, Plato, Aristotle, Marcus Aurelius, Plotinus, St. Augustine, St. Thomas Aquinas, Thomas Hobbes, René Descartes, Baruch Spinoza, Gottfried Wilhelm von Leibniz, John Locke, George Berkeley, David Hume, Jean Jacques Rousseau, Immanuel Kant, G.W.F. Hegel, Arthur Schopenhauer, John Stuart Mill, Søren Kierkegaard, Karl Marx, Friedrich Nietzsche, William James, Martin Heidegger, Ludwig Wittgenstein, Jean-Paul Sartre.

philosophical ***a.*** **1** [Given to thought] reflective, cogitative, rational; see THOUGHTFUL 1. **2** [Embodying deep thought] erudite, thoughtful, deep; see LEARNED 1, PROFOUND.

phi·los·o·phize (fə läs′ə fīz′) ***vi.*** **-phized′**, **-phiz′ing** **1** to think or reason like a philosopher **2** to moralize, express truisms, etc.

phi·los·o·phy (fə läs′ə fē) ***n.*** ⟦see PHILOSOPHER⟧ **1** the study of the principles underlying conduct, thought, and the nature of the universe **2** the general principles of a field of knowledge **3** *pl.* **-phies** a particular system of principles for the conduct of life

phil·ter (fil′tər) ***n.*** ⟦< Gr *philein,* to love⟧ a magic potion, esp. one thought to arouse sexual love: also [Chiefly Brit.] **phil′tre** (-tər)

phle·bi·tis (flə bīt′is) ***n.*** ⟦< Gr *phleps*, vein + -ITIS⟧ inflammation of a vein

phle·bot·o·my (fli bät′ə mē) ***n.*** ⟦< Gr *pheps*, vein + *temnein*, to cut⟧ the practice of taking blood from the body for therapeutic purposes

phlegm (flem) ***n.*** ⟦< Gr *phlegma*, inflammation⟧ **1** thick mucus discharged from the throat, as during a cold **2** sluggishness or apathy

phleg·mat·ic (fleg mat′ik) ***adj.*** ⟦see prec.⟧ sluggish or unexcited —**phleg·mat′i·cal·ly** ***adv.***

phlo·em (flō′em′) ***n.*** ⟦< Gr *phloos*, bark⟧ the vascular tissue through which food is distributed in a plant

phlox (fläks) ***n.*** ⟦Gr, lit., a flame⟧ a North American plant with clusters of white, pink, or bluish flowers

-phobe (fōb) ⟦< Gr *phobos,* fear⟧ *combining form* one who fears or hates

pho·bi·a (fō′bē ə) ***n.*** ⟦see prec.⟧ an irrational, excessive, and persistent fear of some thing or situation —**pho′bic** ***adj.***

-pho·bi·a (fō′bē ə) ⟦Gr *-phobia* < *phobos,* fear⟧ *combining form* fear, dread, hatred

phoe·be (fē′bē) ***n.*** ⟦echoic, with sp. after *Phoebe*, Gr goddess of the moon⟧ an American bird with a grayish or brown back, that catches insects in flight

Phoe·ni·cia (fə nish′ə, -nē′shə) ancient region at the E end of the Mediterranean —**Phoe·ni′cian** ***adj.***, ***n.***

phoe·nix (fē′niks) ⟦< Gr *phoinix*⟧ *Egypt. Myth.* a bird that lives for 500 years and then sets itself on fire, rising renewed from the ashes

Phoe·nix (fē′niks) capital of Arizona: pop. 983,000

phone (fōn) ***n.***, ***vt.***, ***vi.*** **phoned**, **phon′ing** *short for* TELEPHONE

-phone (fōn) ⟦< Gr *phōnē,* a sound⟧ *combining form* **1** a device producing or transmitting sound **2** a telephone

phone card CALLING CARD (sense 2)

pho·neme (fō′nēm′) ***n.*** ⟦< Fr < Gr *phōnē,* voice⟧ *Linguistics* a set of related speech sounds with slight variations, that are heard as the same sound by native speakers —**pho·ne·mic** (fō nē′mik, fə-) ***adj.***

pho·net·ics (fō net′iks, fə-) ***n.*** ⟦< Gr *phōnē*, a sound⟧ the study of the production of speech sounds and their representation in written symbols —**pho·net′ic** ***adj.*** —**pho·ne·ti·cian** (fō′nə tish′ən) ***n.***

phon·ics (fän′iks) ***n.*** ⟦< Gr *phōnē*, a sound⟧ a phonetic method of teaching reading —**phon′ic** ***adj.***

phono- ⟦< Gr *phōnē,* a sound⟧ *combining form* sound, tone, speech *[phonology]*

pho·no·graph (fō′nə graf′) ***n.*** ⟦prec. + -GRAPH⟧ a device for reproducing sound recorded in a spiral groove on a revolving disk —**pho′no·graph′ic** ***adj.***

pho·nol·o·gy (fō näl′ə jē, fə-) ***n.*** ⟦PHONO- + -LOGY⟧ **1** the study of speech sounds **2** a description of the sounds of a given language —**pho′no·log′i·cal** (-nō läj′i kəl, -nə-) ***adj.*** —**pho·nol′o·gist** ***n.***

pho·ny (fō′nē) [Inf.] ***adj.*** **-ni·er**, **-ni·est** ⟦< Brit thieves' argot *fawney,* gilt ring⟧ not genuine; false —***n.***, *pl.* **-nies** something or someone not genuine; fraud; fake Also sp. **pho′ney** —**pho′ni·ness** ***n.***

phoo·ey (fo͞o′ē) ***interj.*** ⟦echoic⟧ used to express scorn, disgust, etc.

phos·phate (fäs′fāt′) ***n.*** ⟦Fr⟧ **1** a salt or ester of phosphoric acid **2** a fertilizer containing phosphates

phos·phor (fäs′fər, -fôr′) ***n.*** ⟦see PHOSPHORUS⟧ a phosphorescent or fluorescent substance

phos·pho·res·cence (fäs′fə res′əns) ***n.*** **1** the property of giving off a lingering emission of light after exposure to radiant energy such as light **2** a continuing luminescence without noticeable heat —**phos′pho·res′cent** ***adj.***

phos·phor·ic acid (fäs fôr′ik) any of several oxygen acids of phosphorus

phos·pho·rus (fäs′fə rəs) ***n.*** ⟦< Gr *phōs,* a light + *pherein,* to bear⟧ a nonmetallic chemical element, a waxy solid that ignites spontaneously at room temperature

pho·to (fōt′ō) ***n.***, *pl.* **-tos** *short for* PHOTOGRAPH

photo- *combining form* **1** ⟦< Gr *phōs*, a light⟧ of or produced by light **2** ⟦< PHOTOGRAPH⟧ photograph, photography

pho·to·cop·y (fōt′ō käp′ē) ***n.***, *pl.* **-ies** a photographic reproduction, as of a book page, made by a special device (**pho′to·cop′i·er**)

pho′to·e·lec′tric cell any device in which light controls an electric circuit that operates a mechanical device, as for opening doors

pho′to·en·grav′ing ***n.*** **1** a process by which photographs are reproduced on relief printing plates **2** such a plate, or a print made from it —**pho′to·en·grave′**, **-graved′**, **-grav′ing**, ***vt.*** —**pho′to·en·grav′er** ***n.***

photo finish a race finish so close that the winner can be determined only from a photograph of the finish

pho′to·fin′ish·ing ***n.*** the process of developing photographic film, making prints, etc.

pho′to·flash′ ***adj.*** designating a flashbulb, etc. electrically synchronized with the camera shutter

pho·to·gen·ic (fōt′ə jen′ik) ***adj.*** ⟦PHOTO- + *-genic*, suitable for⟧ likely to look attractive in photographs

pho·to·graph (fōt′ə graf′) ***n.*** a picture made by photography —***vt.*** to take a photograph of —***vi.*** to appear (as specified) in photographs —**pho·tog·ra·pher** (fə täg′rə fər) ***n.***

pho·tog·ra·phy (fə täg′rə fē) ***n.*** ⟦PHOTO- + -GRAPHY⟧ the art or process of producing pictorial images on a surface sensitive to light or other radiant energy, as on film in a camera —**pho·to·graph·ic** (fōt′ə graf′ik) ***adj.***

pho·ton (fō′tän′) ***n.*** ⟦PHOT(O)- + (ELECTR)ON⟧ a subatomic particle that is a quantum of electromagnetic energy, including light

pho′to·off′set′ ***n.*** offset printing in which the text or pictures are photographically transferred to a metal plate from which inked impressions are made on the roller

pho·to·stat (fōt′ə stat′) ***n.*** ⟦< former trademark⟧ **1** a device for making photocopies on special paper **2** a copy so made —***vt.*** **-stat′ed** or **-stat′ted**, **-stat′ing** or **-stat′ting** to make a photostat of

pho·to·syn·the·sis (fōt′ō sin′thə sis) ***n.*** the production of organic substances, esp. sugars, from carbon dioxide and water by the action of light on the chlorophyll in green plant cells

pho′to·syn′the·size′ (-sīz′) ***vi.***, ***vt.*** **-sized′**, **-siz′ing** to carry on, or produce by, photosynthesis

THESAURUS

philosophize ***v.*** ponder, weigh, deliberate; see THINK 1.

philosophy ***n.*** **1** [The study of knowledge] theory, reasoned doctrine, explanation of phenomena, logical concept, systematic view, theory of knowledge, early science, natural philosophy; see also KNOWLEDGE 1. *Fields of philosophy include the following:* aesthetics, logic, ethics, metaphysics, cosmology, epistemology, axiology, ontology. *Philosophic attitudes include the following:* idealism, realism, empiricism, existentialism, nihilism, transcendentalism, mechanism, naturalism, determinism, intuitionism, utilitarianism, nominalism, conceptualism, pragmatism, Kantianism, Hegelianism, absolutism, logical positivism. **2** [A fundamental principle] truth, axiom, conception; see BASIS, LAW 4, THEORY 1. **3** [A personal attitude or belief] outlook, view, position; see BELIEF, OPINION 1, VIEWPOINT.

phlegm ***n.*** spittle, sputum, mucus; see SALIVA.

phobia ***n.*** fear, neurosis, aversion; see HATRED, RESENTMENT.

phone ***n.*** pay phone, home phone, wall phone, desk phone, car phone, cellular phone, cellphone, cordless phone, speakerphone, fax; see also TELEPHONE.

phony* ***a.*** counterfeit, imitation, artificial; see FALSE 3.

photograph ***n.*** photo, print, portrait, image, likeness, snapshot, microcopy, microfilm, radiograph, X-ray, photomontage, photomural, electronic image, shot, pic*, close-up, candid; see also PICTURE 2, 3.

photograph ***v.*** take a picture, get a likeness, film, copy, reproduce, illustrate, make an exposure, make a picture, record, make a movie, microfilm, snap, shoot, get a close-up.

photographer ***n.*** picture-taker, cameraman, cinematographer; see ARTIST.

photographic ***a.*** **1** [Of photography] camera, video, film, cinematographic. **2** [Precise] exact, accurate, detailed; see GRAPHIC 1.

photography ***n.*** picture-taking, portrait photography, landscape photography, aerial photography, tactical photography, candid photography, microphotography, photomicrography, digital photography, videotaping.

phrase (frāz) ***n.*** ⟦< Gr *phrazein,* speak⟧ **1** a short, colorful expression **2** a group of words, not a full sentence or clause, conveying a single thought **3** a short, distinct musical passage —***vt.***, ***vi.*** **phrased**, **phras′ing** to express in words —**phras·al** (frā′zəl) ***adj.***

phra·se·ol·o·gy (frā′zē äl′ə jē) ***n.***, *pl.* **-gies** choice and pattern of words

phre·net·ic (fri net′ik) ***adj.*** ⟦< Gr *phrenētikos,* mad⟧ *archaic sp. of* FRENETIC

phre·nol·o·gy (fri näl′ə jē, frə-) ***n.*** ⟦< Gr *phrēn,* mind + -LOGY⟧ a system, popular esp. in the 19th c., based on the assumption that character can be analyzed based on the shape of the skull

phy·lac·ter·y (fi lak′tər ē) ***n.***, *pl.* **-ies** ⟦< Gr *phylaktērion,* safeguard⟧ TEFILLIN

phyl·lo (fē′lō, fī′-) ***n.*** ⟦< Gr *phyllon,* leaf⟧ dough in very thin sheets that becomes very flaky when baked

phy·log·e·ny (fī läj′ə nē) ***n.***, *pl.* **-nies** ⟦< Gr *phylon,* tribe + *-geneia,* origin⟧ the origin and evolution of a group or race of animals or plants

phy·lum (fī′ləm) ***n.***, *pl.* **-la** (-lə) ⟦< Gr *phylon,* tribe⟧ a major category in the classification of organisms, esp. animals

phys *abbrev.* **1** physical **2** physician **3** physics

phys·ic (fiz′ik) ***n.*** ⟦< Gr *physis,* nature⟧ a medicine, esp. a laxative

phys·i·cal (fiz′i kəl) ***adj.*** **1** of nature and all matter; material **2** of or according to the laws of nature **3** of, or produced by the forces of, physics **4** of the body as opposed to the mind —***n.*** a general medical examination —**phys′i·cal·ly** ***adv.***

physical anthropology a major division of anthropology that deals with the physical characteristics and evolution of humans

physical education instruction in physical exercise and in the care of the body, including sports, calisthenics, and hygiene

physical science any science dealing with nonliving matter or energy, as physics, chemistry, geology, or astronomy

physical therapy the treatment of disease, injury, etc. by physical means, as by exercise or massage

phy·si·cian (fi zish′ən) ***n.*** ⟦see PHYSIC⟧ a doctor of medicine

phys·ics (fiz′iks) ***n.*** ⟦see PHYSIC⟧ the science dealing with the properties, changes, interactions, etc. of matter and energy —**phys′i·cist** (-ə sist) ***n.***

phys·i·og·no·my (fiz′ē äg′nə mē) ***n.*** ⟦< Gr *physis,* nature + *gnōmōn,* one who knows⟧ facial features and expression

phys′i·ol′o·gy (-äl′ə jē) ***n.*** ⟦< Gr *physis,* nature + -LOGY⟧ the science dealing with the functions and vital processes of living organisms —**phys′i·o·log′i·cal** (-ə läj′i kəl) ***adj.*** —**phys′i·ol′o·gist** ***n.***

phys·i·o·ther·a·py (fiz′ē ō′ther′ə pē) ***n.*** PHYSICAL THERAPY —**phys′i·o·ther′a·pist** ***n.***

phy·sique (fi zēk′) ***n.*** ⟦Fr⟧ the structure or form of the body; build

pi (pī) ***n.*** **1** the 16th letter of the Greek alphabet (Π, π) **2** the symbol (π) designating the ratio of the circumference of a circle to its diameter, about 3.1416

pi·a·nis·si·mo (pē′ə nis′i mō′) ***adj.***, ***adv.*** ⟦It⟧ *Music* very soft(ly)

pi·an·ist (pē′ə nist, pē an′ist) ***n.*** one who plays the piano

pi·a·no[1] (pē ä′nō) ***adj.***, ***adv.*** ⟦It⟧ *Music* soft(ly)

pi·an·o[2] (pē an′ō) ***n.***, *pl.* **-os** ⟦< fol.⟧ a large, stringed keyboard instrument: each key operates a felt-covered hammer that strikes a corresponding wire or wires

pi·an·o·for·te (pē an′ō fôrt′, pē an′ō fôr′tā) ***n.*** ⟦It < *piano,* soft + *forte,* loud⟧ PIANO[2]

pi·as·ter (pē as′tər) ***n.*** ⟦ult. < L *emplastrum,* plaster⟧ a 100th part of a pound in Egypt, Lebanon, and Syria

pi·az·za (pē ät′sə; *for 2* pē az′ə) ***n.*** **1** in Italy, a public square **2** [Dial.] a large, covered porch

pi·broch (pē′bräk′) ***n.*** ⟦< Gael *piob,* bagpipe⟧ music for the bagpipe, usually of a martial kind

pi·ca (pī′kə) ***n.*** ⟦< ? ML, a directory⟧ a size of printing type, 12 point

pi·can·te (pē kän′tā) ***adj.*** ⟦Sp⟧ designating, prepared with, or served with a hot, spicy sauce

pic·a·resque (pik′ə resk′) ***adj.*** ⟦< Sp *pícaro,* rascal⟧ dealing with sharp-witted vagabonds or rogues and their adventures *[a picaresque novel]*

Pi·cas·so (pi kä′sō), **Pa·blo** (pä′blō) 1881-1973; Sp. painter & sculptor in France

pic·a·yune (pik′ə yo͞on′, pik′ə yo͞on′) ***adj.*** ⟦< Fr *picaillon,* small coin⟧ trivial or petty

pic·ca·lil·li (pik′ə lil′ē) ***n.*** ⟦prob. < PICKLE⟧ a relish of chopped vegetables, mustard, vinegar, and hot spices

pic·co·lo (pik′ə lō′) ***n.***, *pl.* **-los′** ⟦< It, small⟧ a small flute, pitched an octave above the ordinary flute

pick[1] (pik) ***n.*** ⟦OE *pic,* PIKE[2]⟧ **1** any of several pointed tools or instruments for picking, esp. a heavy one used in breaking up soil, rock, etc. **2** PLECTRUM

pick[2] (pik) ***vt.*** ⟦ME *picken*⟧ **1** to probe, scratch at, etc. so as to remove or clear something from **2** to gather (flowers, berries, etc.) **3** to prepare (a fowl) by removing the feathers **4** to choose; select **5** to provoke (a quarrel or fight) **6** to pluck (the strings) of (a guitar, etc.) **7** to open (a lock) with a wire, etc. instead of a key **8** to steal from (another's pocket, etc.) —***vi.*** **1** to use a pick **2** to select, esp. in a fussy way —***n.*** **1** the act of choosing or the choice made **2** the best —**pick at** to eat small amounts of, esp. fussily —**pick off** **1** to remove by picking **2** to hit with a carefully aimed shot —**pick on** [Inf.] to single out for criticism or abuse; annoy; tease —**pick out** to choose —**pick up** **1** to grasp and lift **2** to get, find, or learn, esp. by chance **3** to stop for and take along **4** to gain (speed) **5** to improve **6** [Inf.] to become acquainted with casually, esp. for sexual activity —**pick′er** ***n.***

pick·ax or **pick·axe** (pik′aks′) ***n.*** ⟦< OFr *picquois*⟧ a pick with a point at one end of the head and a chisel-like edge at the other

pick·er·el (pik′ər əl) ***n.***, *pl.* **-el** or **-els** ⟦ME < *pik,* PIKE[3]⟧ any of various small North American freshwater fishes

THESAURUS

phrase ***n.*** group of words, expression, slogan, catchword, maxim, word group. *Grammatical phrases include the following:* prepositional, participial, infinitive, noun, adjective, adverb, verb, restrictive, nonrestrictive.

phraseology ***n.*** style, manner, idiom; see DICTION.

physical ***a.*** **1** [Concerning matter] material, corporeal, visible, tangible, environmental, palpable, substantial, natural, concrete; see also REAL 2. **2** [Concerning the body] corporal, corporeal, fleshly; see BODILY. **3** [Concerning physics] mechanical, motive, electrical, sonic, vibratory, vibrational, thermal, radioactive, atomic, relating to matter, dynamic.

physical ***n.*** examination, physical examination, exam, checkup.

physically ***a.*** corporally, really, actually; see BODILY.

physician ***n.*** practitioner, doctor of medicine, osteopath; see DOCTOR.

physicist ***n.*** biophysicist, geophysicist, nuclear physicist; see SCIENTIST.

physics ***n.*** natural philosophy, science of the material world, science of matter and motion; see SCIENCE 1. *Divisions of physics include the following:* electronics, thermodynamics, acoustics, mechanics, dynamics, kinetics, optics, geophysics, spectroscopy, pneumatics, hydraulics, aerophysics, astrophysics, nuclear physics, theoretical physics, chaos theory.

physiology ***n.*** study of bodily processes, study of organic functions, biology; see SCIENCE 1.

physique ***n.*** build, structure, frame; see BODY 1.

pianist ***n.*** keyboardist, piano player, virtuoso; see MUSICIAN.

piano[2] ***n.*** grand, baby grand, upright, pianoforte, concert grand, spinet, clavichord, harpsichord, keyboard, electric piano, synthesizer, player piano; see also MUSICAL INSTRUMENT.

picayune ***a.*** trivial, petty, small; see TRIVIAL, UNIMPORTANT.

pick[1,2] ***n.*** **1** [An implement for picking] pickax, mattock, ice pick; see TOOL 1. **2** [A blow with a pointed instrument] peck, nip, dent; see BLOW. **3** [A selection] choice, election, preference; see CHOICE.

pick[1,2] ***v.*** **1** [To choose] select, pick out, separate; see CHOOSE. **2** [To gather] pluck, pull, harvest; see ACCUMULATE. **3** [To use a pointed instrument] dent, indent, strike; see HIT 1. —**pick a fight** provoke, start, foment; see FIGHT. —**pick off** knock out, get, shoot; see KILL 1. —**pick out** select, make a choice of, notice; see CHOOSE. —**pick up** **1** [To acquire incidentally] happen upon, find, secure; see GET 1. **2** [To take up in the hand or arms] lift, elevate, hold up; see RAISE 1. **3** [To receive] get, take, acquire; see RECEIVE 1. **4** [To increase] improve, do better, grow; see INCREASE. **5** [To improve physically] get better, get well, recover health; see RECOVER 3. **6** [*To call for] stop for, bring along, go to get, accompany, get; see also INVITE.

picked ***a.*** elite, special, exclusive; see EXCELLENT.

pick·et (pik′it) ***n.*** ⟦< Fr *pic,* PIKE²⟧ **1** a pointed stake used in a fence, as a hitching post, etc. **2** a soldier or soldiers stationed to guard against surprise attack **3** a person, as a member of a striking labor union, stationed outside a factory, store, etc. to demonstrate opposition, keep workers out, etc. —***vt.*** **1** to hitch (an animal) to a picket **2** to post as a military picket **3** to place pickets, or serve as a picket, at (a factory, etc.)

picket line a line or cordon of people serving as pickets

pick′ings ***pl.n.*** [*occas. sing.*] something picked; specif., *a*) scraps; remains *b*) something gotten by effort, often dishonestly

pick·le (pik′əl) ***n.*** ⟦< MDu *pekel*⟧ **1** any brine, vinegar, etc. used to preserve or marinate food **2** a vegetable, specif. a cucumber, preserved in this **3** [Inf.] an awkward situation —***vt.*** **-led, -ling** to treat or preserve in a pickle solution

pick′pock′et ***n.*** a thief who steals from pockets, as in a crowd

pick′up′ ***n.*** **1** a picking up **2** the process or power of increasing in speed **3** a small, open delivery truck **4** [Inf.] a casual acquaintance, esp. one formed for sexual purposes **5** [Inf.] improvement **6** *a*) a device for producing electric currents from the vibrations of a phonograph needle *b*) the pivoted arm holding this device —***adj.*** [Inf.] assembled informally for a single occasion

pick′y ***adj.*** **-i·er, -i·est** [Inf.] overly fastidious; fussy

pic·nic (pik′nik) ***n.*** ⟦< Fr⟧ a pleasure outing at which a meal is eaten outdoors —***vi.*** **-nicked, -nick·ing** to have a picnic —**pic′nick·er** ***n.***

pi·cot (pē′kō) ***n.***, *pl.* **-cots** ⟦< Fr *pic,* a point⟧ any of the small loops forming a fancy edge, as on lace

pic·to·graph (pik′tə graf′) ***n.*** **1** a picture or picturelike symbol used in a system of writing **2** a graph using pictures to convey data

pic·to·ri·al (pik tôr′ē əl) ***adj.*** **1** of, containing, or expressed in pictures **2** suggesting a mental image; vivid —**pic·to′ri·al·ly** ***adv.***

pic·ture (pik′chər) ***n.*** ⟦< L *pingere,* to paint⟧ **1** a likeness of a person, scene, etc. produced by drawing, painting, photography, etc. **2** a perfect likeness or image *[the picture of health]* **3** anything suggestive of a beautiful painting, drawing, etc. **4** a vivid description **5** FILM (*n.* 4) **6** the image on a TV screen —***vt.*** **-tured, -tur·ing** **1** to make a picture of **2** to show visibly **3** to describe **4** to imagine —**in** (or **out of**) **the picture** considered (or not considered) as being involved in a situation

pic′ture-per′fect ***adj.*** perfect or flawless

pic′tur·esque′ (-chər esk′) ***adj.*** like or suggesting a picture; beautiful, vivid, quaint, etc.

picture tube a cathode-ray tube in a TV receiver, monitor, etc., that produces visual images on its screen

picture window a large window that seems to frame the outside view

pid·dle (pid′'l) ***vi., vt.*** **-dled, -dling** ⟦< ?⟧ to dawdle; trifle

pid·dling (pid′liŋ) ***adj.*** insignificant; trifling

pid·dly (pid′lē) ***adj.*** PIDDLING

pidg·in (pij′in) ***n.*** ⟦supposed Chin pronunciation of *business*⟧ a mixed language for trade purposes, using words from one language and simplified grammar from another: **pidgin English** uses English words and Chinese or Melanesian syntax

pie (pī) ***n.*** ⟦ME⟧ a baked dish as of fruit or of meat, with an under crust or upper crust, or both —(**as**) **easy as pie** [Inf.] extremely easy

pie·bald (pī′bôld′) ***adj.*** ⟦< *pie,* magpie + BALD⟧ covered with patches of two colors —***n.*** a piebald horse, etc.

piece (pēs) ***n.*** ⟦OFr *pece*⟧ **1** a part broken or separated from the whole **2** a section of a whole regarded as complete in itself **3** any single thing, specimen, example, etc. *[a piece of music]* **4** a quantity, as of cloth, manufactured as a unit —***vt.*** **pieced, piec′ing** **1** to add pieces to, as in repairing **2** to join (*together*) the pieces of —**go to pieces** **1** to fall apart **2** to lose self-control

pièce de ré·sis·tance (pyes də rā zēs täns′) ⟦Fr, piece of resistance⟧ **1** the principal dish of a meal **2** the main item in a series

piece goods YARD GOODS

piece′meal′ ***adv.*** ⟦< ME *pece,* a piece + *-mele,* part⟧ piece by piece —***adj.*** made or done piecemeal

piece′work′ ***n.*** work paid for at a fixed rate (**piece rate**) per piece of work done

pie chart a graph in the form of a circle divided into sectors in which relative quantities are indicated by the sizes of the sectors

pied (pīd) ***adj.*** ⟦< *pie,* magpie⟧ spotted with various colors

pied-à-terre (pyā tȧ ter′) ***n.***, *pl.* ***pied-à-terre*** ⟦Fr, foot on the ground⟧ a residence, esp. one used only part of the time or temporarily

pie′-eyed′ ***adj.*** [Slang] intoxicated

pier (pir) ***n.*** ⟦< ML *pera*⟧ **1** a structure supporting the spans of a bridge **2** a structure built out over the water and supported by pillars: used as a landing place, pavilion, etc. **3** *Archit.* a heavy column used to support weight

THESAURUS

picket ***n.*** **1** [A stake] stake, pole, pillar; see POST. **2** [A watchman] patrolman, guard, union member, scout, lookout, sentry.

picket ***v.*** **1** [To strike] walk out, blockade, boycott; see STRIKE 2. **2** [To enclose] imprison, fence, corral; see ENCLOSE.

pickings ***n.*** profits, earnings, proceeds; see BOOTY.

pickle ***n.*** **1** [A relish] *Varieties of pickles include the following:* cucumber, beet, green tomato, dill, bread-and-butter, sweet, gherkin, kosher, mustard, garlic, sour, pickled peppers, pickled beans, pickled apricots, pickled watermelon rind, piccalilli, chutney, spiced currants, beet relish, chili sauce, catsup, ketchup, pickle relish, kimchi. **2** [*A troublesome situation] disorder, dilemma, evil plight; see DIFFICULTY 2.

pickpocket ***n.*** petty criminal, thief, purse snatcher; see CRIMINAL, ROBBER.

picnic ***n.*** barbecue, cookout, fish fry; see MEAL 2.

pictorial ***a.*** **1** [Having the quality of a picture] picturesque, scenic, striking; see GRAPHIC 1. **2** [Making use of pictures] detailed, embellished, illustrated; see DESCRIPTIVE.

picture ***n.*** **1** [A scene before the eye or the imagination] spectacle, panorama, pageant; see VIEW. **2** [A human likeness] portrait, representation, photo, photograph, snapshot, cartoon, image, sketch, caricature, effigy, statue, statuette, figure, icon, figurine, close-up. **3** [A pictorial representation] illustration, engraving, etching, woodcut, outline, cartoon, draft, hologram, fax, graph, halftone, still, ad*, crayon sketch, pastel, watercolor, poster, oil, chart, map, mosaic, blueprint, advertisement, facsimile, animation, tracing, photograph, lithograph, print; see also DESIGN, DRAWING, PAINTING 1. *Types of pictures, as works of art, include the following:* landscape, seascape, genre painting, cityscape, historical work, religious work, battle scene, triumphal entry, detail, icon, illumination, miniature, portrait, illustration, self-portrait, nude, fresco, mural, collage, cameo, figure, still life, photomural, poster, photomontage. **4** [A motion picture] cinema, film, show; see MOVIE. **5** [A description] depiction, delineation, portrayal; see DESCRIPTION. **6** [Adequate comprehension; *usually with "the"*] idea, understanding, survey; see KNOWLEDGE 1.

picture ***v.*** **1** [To depict] sketch, delineate, portray; see DRAW 2. **2** [To imagine] envision, think of, conceive; see IMAGINE.

picturesque ***a.*** pictorial, scenic, graphic, striking, arresting.

pie ***n.*** *Varieties of pies include the following—meat pies:* fish, chicken pot, lamb, pork, beef, steak-and-kidney, shepherd's; pasty; *Other savory pies:* spinach pie, calzone, pizza, quiche; *dessert pies:* apple, banana cream, chiffon, apricot, peach, pumpkin, raisin, custard, coconut cream, pecan, chess, rhubarb, chocolate cream, lemon meringue, key lime, mince, mincemeat, cherry, blueberry, strawberry, strawberry cream, butterscotch, plum; see also DESSERT. —**as easy as pie*** not difficult, simple, uncomplicated; see EASY 2.

piece ***n.*** **1** [Part] portion, share, section; see PART 1. **2** [Work of art] study, composition, creation; see ART. **3** [Musical, literary, or theatrical composition] suite, orchestration, production, opus, aria, song, study, arrangement, treatise, exposition, sketch, play, novel, discourse, discussion, treatment, essay, article, paper, memoir, homily, poem, theme, monograph, commentary, review, paragraph, critique, play, drama, melodrama, pageant, monologue, opera, overture, prelude, étude, ballet. —**go to pieces** **1** come apart, break up, fail; see BREAK DOWN 2. **2** quit, collapse, lose control; see CRY 1, WORRY 2. —**in pieces** shattered, damaged, busted*; see BROKEN 1, DESTROYED, RUINED 1, 2. —**piece together** combine, make, create; see ASSEMBLE 2. —**speak one's piece** air one's opinions, talk, reveal; see TELL 1.

pier ***n.*** wharf, landing, quay; see DOCK.

pierce (pirs) ***vt.*** **pierced, pierc′ing** ⟦< OFr *percer*⟧ **1** to pass into or through as a pointed instrument does; stab **2** to make a hole in **3** to force a way into; break through **4** to sound sharply through **5** to penetrate with the sight or mind —***vi.*** to penetrate

Pierce (pirs), **Franklin** 1804-69; 14th president of the U.S. (1853-57)

Pierre (pir) capital of South Dakota: pop. 13,000

pi·e·ty (pī′ə tē) ***n.***, *pl.* **-ties** ⟦< L *pius*, pious⟧ **1** devotion to religious duties, etc. **2** devotion to parents, family, etc. **3** a pious act

pif·fle (pif′əl) ***n.*** [Inf.] anything regarded as insignificant or nonsensical —**pif·fling** (pif′liŋ) ***adj.***

pig (pig) ***n.*** ⟦ME *pigge*⟧ **1** any swine, esp. the unweaned young of the thick-bodied domesticated species; hog **2** a greedy or filthy person

pi·geon (pij′ən) ***n.*** ⟦< L *pipire*, to chirp⟧ any of various related birds with a small head, a plump body, and short legs

pi′geon·hole′ ***n.*** a small, open compartment, as in a desk, for filing papers —***vt.*** **-holed′**, **-hol′ing** **1** to put in the pigeonhole of a desk, etc. **2** to put aside indefinitely **3** to classify

pi′geon-toed′ (-tōd′) ***adj.*** having the toes or feet turned in

pig·gish (pig′ish) ***adj.*** like a pig; gluttonous or filthy —**pig′gish·ness** ***n.***

pig·gy (pig′ē) ***n.***, *pl.* **-gies** a little pig: also sp. **pig′gie** —***adj.*** **-gi·er**, **-gi·est** PIGGISH

pig′gy·back′ ***adv.***, ***adj.*** **1** on the shoulders or back **2** by or of a transportation system in which truck trailers are carried on flatcars **3** carried by or connected with something else as an adjunct —***vt.*** **1** to carry piggyback **2** to place on something in piggyback fashion

pig′head′ed ***adj.*** stubborn

pig iron crude iron, as it comes from the blast furnace

pig·ment (pig′mənt) ***n.*** ⟦< L *pingere*, to paint⟧ **1** coloring matter used to make paints **2** any coloring matter in the tissues of plants or animals

pig·men·ta·tion (pig′mən tā′shən) ***n.*** coloration in plants or animals due to pigment in the tissue

Pig·my (pig′mē) ***n.***, *pl.* **-mies**, ***adj.*** PYGMY

pig′pen′ ***n.*** a pen where pigs are kept: also **pig′sty′** (-stī′), *pl.* **-sties′**

pig′skin′ ***n.*** **1** leather made from the skin of a pig **2** [Inf.] a football

pig′tail′ (-tāl′) ***n.*** a long braid of hair hanging at the back of the head

pike[1] (pīk) ***n.*** a highway: now chiefly in [Inf.] **come down the pike**, to happen or appear

pike[2] (pīk) ***n.*** ⟦Fr *pique*⟧ a weapon, formerly for foot soldiers, consisting of a metal spearhead on a long wooden shaft (**pike′staff′**)

pike[3] (pīk) ***n.***, *pl.* **pike** or **pikes** ⟦ME *pik*⟧ a slender, freshwater bony fish with a narrow, pointed head

pik·er (pīk′ər) ***n.*** ⟦< ? *Pike* County, Missouri⟧ [Slang] a person who does things in a petty or stingy way

pi·laf or **pi·laff** (pē′läf′) ***n.*** ⟦Pers *pilāv*⟧ a dish made of rice boiled in a seasoned liquid

pi·las·ter (pi las′tər) ***n.*** ⟦< L *pila*, a pile⟧ a supporting column projecting partially from a wall

Pi·late (pī′lət), **Pon·tius** (pun′chəs) 1st c. A.D.; Rom. procurator of Judea (26?-36?) who condemned Jesus to be crucified

pil·chard (pil′chərd) ***n.*** ⟦< ?⟧ **1** a small, oily marine fish, the commercial sardine of W Europe **2** any of several related fishes

pile[1] (pīl) ***n.*** ⟦< L *pila*, pillar⟧ **1** a mass of things heaped together **2** a heap of wood, etc. on which a corpse or sacrifice is burned **3** a large building **4** [Inf.] a large amount —***vt.*** **piled, pil′ing** **1** to heap up **2** to load **3** to accumulate Often with *up* —***vi.*** **1** to form a pile **2** to move in a mass: with *in, into, out, on, off*, etc.

pile[2] (pīl) ***n.*** ⟦< L *pilus*, hair⟧ a soft, velvety, raised surface of yarn loops, often sheared, as on a rug

pile[3] (pīl) ***n.*** ⟦OE *pil*⟧ a long, heavy beam driven into the ground to support a bridge, dock, etc.

pile driver (or **engine**) a machine for driving piles by raising and dropping a heavy weight on them

piles (pīlz) ***pl.n.*** ⟦< L *pila*, a ball⟧ hemorrhoids

pile′up′ ***n.*** **1** an accumulation of tasks, etc. **2** [Inf.] a collision involving several vehicles

pil·fer (pil′fər) ***vt.***, ***vi.*** ⟦< MFr *pelfre*, booty⟧ to steal (esp. small sums, etc.) —**pil′fer·age** (-ij) ***n.*** —**pil′fer·er** ***n.***

pil·grim (pil′grəm) ***n.*** ⟦< L *peregrinus*, foreigner⟧ **1** a wanderer **2** one who travels to a shrine or holy place as a religious act **3** [**P-**] any of the band of English Puritans who founded Plymouth Colony in 1620

pil′grim·age ***n.*** **1** a journey made by a pilgrim, esp. to a shrine or holy place **2** any long journey

pill (pil) ***n.*** ⟦< L *pila*, a ball⟧ a small ball, tablet, etc. of medicine to be swallowed whole —**the pill** (or **Pill**) [Inf.] any contraceptive drug for women, in the form of a pill

pil·lage (pil′ij) ***n.*** ⟦< MFr *piller*, to rob⟧ **1** a plundering **2** goods stolen or taken by force —***vt.***, ***vi.*** **-laged**, **-lag·ing** to plunder

pil·lar (pil′ər) ***n.*** ⟦< L *pila*, column⟧ **1** a slender, vertical structure used as a support or monument; column **2** a main support of something

pill′box′ ***n.*** **1** a small box for holding pills **2** an enclosed gun emplacement of concrete and steel

pil·lion (pil′yən) ***n.*** ⟦< L *pellis*, a skin⟧ an extra seat behind the saddle on a horse or motorcycle

pil·lo·ry (pil′ə rē) ***n.***, *pl.* **-ries** ⟦< OFr *pilori*⟧ a device consisting of a board with holes for the head and hands, in which petty offenders were formerly locked and exposed to public scorn —***vt.*** **-ried**, **-ry·ing** **1** to punish by placing in a pillory **2** to subject to public scorn or ridicule

pil·low (pil′ō) ***n.*** ⟦OE *pyle*⟧ a cloth case filled with down, foam rubber, etc., used as a support, as for the head in sleeping —***vt.*** to rest as on a pillow

pil′low·case′ ***n.*** a removable covering for a pillow: also **pil′low·slip′**

pi·lot (pī′lət) ***n.*** ⟦< Gr *pēdon*, oar⟧ **1** *a*) [Archaic] HELMSMAN *b*) a person licensed to direct ships into or out of a harbor or through difficult waters **2** a qualified operator of aircraft or spacecraft **3** a guide; leader **4** *a*) pilot light *b*) pilot film (or tape) —***vt.*** **1** to act as a pilot of, on, etc. **2** to guide —***adj.*** serving as a trial unit in testing

pilot film (or **tape**) a film (or videotape) of a single segment of a projected series of TV shows

pi′lot·house′ ***n.*** an enclosure for the helmsman on the upper deck of a ship

pilot light a small gas burner that is kept burning for use in lighting a main burner

Pil·sen·er or **Pil·sner** (pilz′nər) ***n.*** [*often* **p-**] a light lager beer

pi·men·to (pi men′tō) ***n.***, *pl.* **-tos** ⟦< Sp < L *pigmentum*, pigment⟧ a variety of sweet red pepper: also **pi·mien′to** (-myen′-, -men′-)

THESAURUS

pierce ***v.*** break into, stab, intrude; see PENETRATE.

piercing ***a.*** **1** [Shrill] deafening, earsplitting, sharp; see LOUD 1, SHRILL. **2** [Penetrating] entering, boring, puncturing; see SHARP 1.

piety ***n.*** reverence, duty, zeal; see DEVOTION.

pig ***n.*** piglet, sow, shoat; see ANIMAL, HOG 1.

pigeon ***n.*** dove, homing pigeon, turtledove; see BIRD.

piggish ***a.*** selfish, dirty, ravenous; see GREEDY.

pigheaded ***a.*** recalcitrant, insistent, obstinate; see STUBBORN.

pigment ***n.*** paint, coloring matter, dye; see COLOR.

pigskin* ***n.*** regulation football, the ball, the sphere*; see FOOTBALL.

pigtail ***n.*** plait, hairdo, braid; see HAIR 1.

piker* ***n.*** tightwad*, skinflint, cheapskate*; see MISER.

pile[1] ***n.*** heap, mass, quantity; see COLLECTION.

pile[1] ***v.*** heap, stack, gather; see ACCUMULATE, STORE.

pilgrim ***n.*** wayfarer, wanderer, sojourner; see TRAVELER.

pilgrimage ***n.*** travel, wayfaring, trip; see JOURNEY.

pill ***n.*** **1** [A tablet] capsule, gelcap, caplet; see MEDICINE 2. **2** [*A contraceptive tablet; *usually with "the"*] birth control pill, oral contraceptive, preventive; see DRUG.

pillage ***v.*** plunder, loot, rob; see DESTROY, STEAL.

pillar ***n.*** **1** [A column] pedestal, mast, shaft; see COLUMN 1, POST. **2** [A support] mainstay, reinforcement, buttress; see SUPPORT 2.

pillow ***n.*** feather pillow, down pillow, foam rubber cushion, pad, padding, rest, cushion, support, headrest.

pillowcase ***n.*** pillowslip, pillow casing, pillow cover; see COVER 1.

pilot ***n.*** **1** [Flier] airman, fighter pilot, commercial pilot, bomber pilot, automatic pilot, navigator. **2** [Guide] scout, leader, director; see GUIDE.

pilot ***v.*** guide, conduct, manage; see LEAD 1.

pimp (pimp) ***n.*** ⟦< ?⟧ a prostitute's agent —***vi.*** to act as a pimp

pim·ple (pim′pəl) ***n.*** ⟦< OE *piplian,* to break out in pimples⟧ a small, usually inflamed swelling of the skin —**pim′ply, -pli·er, -pli·est,** ***adj.***

pin (pin) ***n.*** ⟦OE *pinn*⟧ **1** a peg, as of wood, or a pointed piece of stiff wire, for fastening things together, etc. **2** anything like a pin **3** an ornament or badge with a pin or clasp for fastening to clothing **4** *Bowling* one of the bottle-shaped wooden objects at which the ball is rolled —***vt.*** **pinned, pin′ning 1** to fasten as with a pin **2** to hold firmly in one position —**pin down 1** to get (someone) to make a commitment, etc. **2** to determine (a fact, etc.) —**pin something on someone** [Inf.] to lay the blame for something on someone

PIN (pin) ***n.*** ⟦*p*(*ersonal*) *i*(*dentification*) *n*(*umber*)⟧ an identification number, as for use at an ATM

pin·a·fore (pin′ə fôr′) ***n.*** ⟦PIN + archaic *afore,* before⟧ a sleeveless garment worn over a dress

pi·ña·ta (pē nyä′tä) ***n.*** ⟦Sp, ult. < L *pinus,* pine tree⟧ in Mexico, a papier-mâché container hung from the ceiling in a game in which blindfolded children take turns trying to break it open and release the toys, candy, etc. inside

pin′ball′ machine a game machine consisting of an inclined board and a rolling ball that hits objects, etc. on it to score points

pince-nez (pans′nā′) ***n.*** ⟦Fr, nose-pincher⟧ *pl.* **pince′-nez′** (-nāz′; -nā′) eyeglasses kept in place by a spring gripping the bridge of the nose

pin·cers (pin′sərz) ***pl.n.*** ⟦< OFr *pincier,* to pinch⟧ **1** a tool formed of two pivoted parts, used in gripping things **2** a grasping claw, as of a crab

pinch (pinch) ***vt.*** ⟦ME *pinchen* < OFr *pincier*⟧ **1** to squeeze between a finger and the thumb or between two edges, surfaces, etc. **2** to press painfully upon (some part of the body) **3** to make cramped, thin, etc., as by hunger or cold **4** [Slang] *a*) to steal *b*) to arrest —***vi.*** **1** to squeeze painfully **2** to be stingy or frugal —***n.*** **1** a squeeze or nip **2** *a*) an amount grasped between finger and thumb *b*) a small amount **3** distress or difficulty **4** an emergency: usually in **in a pinch** —***adj.*** *Baseball* substitute

pinch′-hit′ ***vi.*** **-hit′, -hit′ting 1** *Baseball* to bat in place of the batter whose turn it is **2** to substitute in an emergency (*for*) —**pinch hitter**

pin curl a strand of hair kept curled with a bobby pin while it sets

pin′cush′ion ***n.*** a small cushion to stick pins in to keep them handy

pine[1] (pīn) ***n.*** ⟦< L *pinus*⟧ **1** an evergreen tree with cones and needle-shaped leaves **2** its wood

pine[2] (pīn) ***vi.*** **pined, pin′ing** ⟦< L *poena,* a pain⟧ **1** to waste (*away*) through grief, etc. **2** to yearn

pin·e·al body (pin′ē əl) ⟦< L *pinea,* pine cone⟧ a small, cone-shaped body in the brain that produces a hormone

pine·ap·ple (pīn′ap′əl) ***n.*** ⟦ME *pinappel,* pine cone⟧ **1** a juicy, edible tropical fruit somewhat resembling a pine cone **2** the plant it grows on

pine tar a thick, dark liquid obtained from pine wood, used in disinfectants, paints, etc.

pin′feath′er ***n.*** an undeveloped, emerging feather

ping (piŋ) ***n.*** ⟦echoic⟧ the sound made as by a bullet striking something sharply —***vi., vt.*** to make or cause to make this sound

Ping-Pong (piŋ′pôŋ′) ⟦echoic⟧ *trademark for* table-tennis equipment —***n.*** [*often* **ping-pong**] TABLE TENNIS

pin′head′ ***n.*** **1** the head of a pin **2** a person regarded as stupid or silly

pin′hole′ ***n.*** **1** a tiny hole as from a pin **2** a hole to stick a pin into

pin·ion (pin′yən) ***n.*** ⟦< L *pinna,* feather⟧ **1** a small cogwheel that meshes with a larger gear or with a RACK[1] (*n.* 2) **2** a wing; specif., the outer part of a bird's wing —***vt.*** **1** to bind the wings or arms of **2** to shackle

pink[1] (piŋk) ***n.*** ⟦< ?⟧ **1** any of certain plants with white, pink, or red flowers **2** the flower **3** pale red **4** the highest degree, finest example, etc. —***adj.*** **1** pale-red **2** [Inf.] somewhat leftist: a derogatory term —**in the pink** [Inf.] healthy; fit

pink[2] (piŋk) ***vt.*** ⟦ME *pynken*⟧ **1** to cut a saw-toothed edge on (cloth, etc.) **2** to prick or stab

pink′eye′ ***n.*** a contagious eye infection in which the eyeball and the lining of the eyelid are red and inflamed

pink·ie or **pink·y** (piŋ′kē) ***n.,*** *pl.* **-ies** the smallest finger

pink·ing shears (piŋ′kiŋ) shears with notched blades, for pinking edges of cloth

pink slip [Inf.] notice to an employee that he or she is fired

pin money a small sum of money, as for incidental minor expenses

pin·na·cle (pin′ə kəl) ***n.*** ⟦< L *pinna,* feather⟧ **1** a small turret or spire **2** a slender, pointed formation, as a mountain peak **3** the highest point

pin·nate (pin′āt′, -it) ***adj.*** ⟦< L *pinna,* feather⟧ *Bot.* with leaflets on each side of a common stem

pi·noch·le or **pi·noc·le** (pē′nuk′əl) ***n.*** ⟦< Fr *binocle,* pince-nez⟧ a card game played with a 48-card deck (two of every card above the eight)

pi·not noir (pē′nō nwär′, pē nō′-) [*also* **P- N-**] **1** the main red-wine grape of the Burgundy region **2** a dry red wine made from this grape

pin′point′ ***vt.*** to locate precisely —***adj.*** precise

pin′prick′ ***n.*** **1** a tiny puncture as by a pin **2** a minor annoyance

pins and needles a tingling feeling as in a numb limb —**on pins and needles** in anxious suspense

pin′set′ter ***n.*** a person or automatic device that sets up bowling pins on the alley: also **pin′spot′ter**

pin′stripe′ ***n.*** a pattern of very narrow stripes in suit fabrics, etc.

pint (pīnt) ***n.*** ⟦< ML⟧ a unit of measure equal to $\frac{1}{2}$ quart

pin·to (pin′tō) ***adj.*** ⟦< obs. Sp, spotted⟧ having patches of white and some other color —***n.,*** *pl.* **-tos** a pinto horse

pinto bean a kind of mottled kidney bean grown in the SW U.S.

pin′up′ ***adj.*** **1** that is or can be fastened to a wall **2** [Inf.] designating a sexually attractive person whose picture is often pinned up on walls

pin′wheel′ ***n.*** **1** a small wheel with vanes of paper, etc., pinned to a stick so as to revolve in the wind **2** a revolving fireworks device

Pin·yin (pin yin′) ***n.*** ⟦Chin *pinyin,* lit., phonetic sound⟧ [*also* **p-**] system for transliterating Chinese ideograms into the Latin alphabet

pi·o·neer (pī′ə nir′) ***n.*** ⟦< OFr *peonier,* foot soldier⟧ one who goes before, preparing the way for others, as an early settler —***vi.*** to be a pioneer —***vt.*** to be a pioneer in or of

pi·ous (pī′əs) ***adj.*** ⟦< L *pius*⟧ **1** having or showing religious devotion **2** only seemingly virtuous **3** sacred —**pi′ous·ly** ***adv.***

THESAURUS

pimp ***n.*** procurer, whoremonger, pander; see CRIMINAL.

pimple ***n.*** pustule, swelling, acne, whitehead, blackhead, inflammation, bump, lump, boil, carbuncle, blister, zit*; see also BLEMISH.

pin ***n.*** **1** [A device for fastening things by piercing or clasping] clip, catch, needle, bodkin, peg, clasp, nail, tack; see also FASTENER. *Pins include the following:* common, safety, straight, bobby, cotter pin; hatpin, hairpin, clothespin, pushpin. **2** [A piece of jewelry] tiepin, stickpin, brooch, badge, stud, sorority pin, fraternity pin, school pin; see also JEWELRY.

pin ***v.*** close, clasp, bind; see FASTEN.

pinch ***n.*** squeeze, compression, nip, nipping, grasp, grasping, pressure, cramp, contraction, confinement, limitation, hurt, torment. —**in a pinch** if necessary, in an emergency, under stress; see UNFORTUNATELY.

pinch ***v.*** **1** [To squeeze] nip, grasp, compress, press, cramp, grab, contract, confine, limit, torment; see also HURT 1. **2** [*To steal] take, rob, pilfer; see STEAL. **3** [*To arrest] apprehend, detain, hold; see ARREST.

pinch-hit ***v.*** replace, act for, succeed; see SUBSTITUTE.

pine[1] ***n.*** *Pines include the following:* white, jack, bristlecone, nut, loblolly, ponderosa, red, yellow, pitch, sugar, longleaf, lodgepole, Scotch pine; balsam fir, piñon; see also TREE, WOOD 2.

pink[1] ***a.*** rosy, reddish, pinkish, pale-red, salmon-colored, flesh-colored, flushed, ruddy.

pink[1] ***n.*** rose, red, blush-rose, salmon, shocking pink, blushing pink; see also COLOR.

pinnacle ***n.*** zenith, crest, summit; see CLIMAX.

pioneer ***a.*** pioneering, initial, untried; see BRAVE, EARLY 1, EXPERIMENTAL.

pioneer ***n.*** **1** [One who prepares the way] pathfinder, scout, explorer; see GUIDE. **2** [One in the vanguard of civilization] early settler, colonist, pilgrim, immigrant, colonizer, homesteader, squatter.

pioneer ***v.*** discover, explore, found; see COLONIZE, ESTABLISH 2, SETTLE 1.

pious ***a.*** divine, holy, devout; see RELIGIOUS 2.

pip[1] (pip) ***n.*** ⟦< PIPPIN⟧ a small seed, as of an apple

pip[2] (pip) ***n.*** ⟦< ?⟧ any of the figures or spots on playing cards, dice, or dominoes

pip[3] (pip) ***n.*** ⟦< L *pituita,* phlegm⟧ a contagious disease of fowl

pipe (pīp) ***n.*** ⟦< L *pipare,* chirp⟧ **1** a tube of wood, metal, etc. for making musical sounds **2** [*pl.*] the bagpipe **3** a long tube for conveying water, gas, etc. **4** a tube with a small bowl at one end in which tobacco is smoked **5** any tubular part, organ of the body, etc. —***vi.* piped, pip'ing 1** to play on a pipe **2** to utter shrill sounds —***vt.* 1** to play (a tune) on a pipe **2** to utter in a shrill voice **3** to bring, call, etc. by piping **4** to convey (water, gas, etc.) by pipes —**pipe down** [Slang] to stop shouting, talking, etc. —**pip'er *n.***

pipe dream [Inf.] a fantastic idea, vain hope or plan, etc.

pipe fitter a mechanic who installs and maintains plumbing pipes, etc.

pipe'line' ***n.*** **1** a line of pipes for conveying water, gas, oil, etc. **2** any means whereby something is passed on

pipe organ ORGAN (sense 1)

pi·pette or **pi·pet** (pi pet', pī-) ***n.*** a slender tube for taking up and measuring small amounts of a liquid

pip·ing (pīp'iŋ) ***n.*** **1** music made by pipes **2** a shrill sound **3** a pipelike fold of material for trimming seams, etc. —**piping hot** very hot

pip·it (pip'it) ***n.*** ⟦echoic⟧ a small bird with a slender bill, streaked breast, and the habit of walking rather than hopping

pip·pin (pip'in) ***n.*** ⟦< OFr *pepin,* seed⟧ any of several varieties of apple

pip·squeak (pip'skwēk') ***n.*** [Inf.] anyone or anything regarded as small or insignificant

pi·quant (pē'kənt) ***adj.*** ⟦Fr < *piquer,* to prick⟧ **1** agreeably pungent to the taste **2** exciting interest; stimulating —**pi'quan·cy** (-kən sē) ***n.***

pique (pēk) ***n.*** ⟦see prec.⟧ resentment at being slighted —***vt.* piqued, piqu'ing 1** to arouse such resentment in **2** to stir up; excite

pi·qué or **pi·que** (pē kā') ***n.*** ⟦see PIQUANT⟧ a cotton fabric with ribbed or corded wales

pi·ra·cy (pī'rə sē) ***n.***, *pl.* **-cies 1** robbery of ships on the high seas **2** the unauthorized use of copyrighted or patented work

pi·ra·nha (pi rä'nə) ***n.*** ⟦< Brazilian Port < AmInd (Brazil) *pirá,* fish + *sainha,* tooth⟧ any of various small, freshwater South American fishes: they hunt in schools, attacking any animals

pi·rate (pī'rət) ***n.*** ⟦< Gr *peirān,* to attack⟧ one who practices piracy —***vt.*, *vi.* -rat·ed, -rat·ing 1** to take (something) by piracy **2** to publish, reproduce, etc. (a book, recording, etc.) in violation of a copyright —**pi·rat'i·cal** (-rat' i kəl) ***adj.***

pi·ro·gi (pi rō'gē) ***n.***, *pl.* **-gi** or **-gies** ⟦Russ⟧ a small pastry turnover filled with meat, cheese, etc.

pir·ou·ette (pir'o͞o et') ***n.*** ⟦Fr, spinning top⟧ a whirling on one foot or the point of the toe —***vi.* -et'ted, -et'ting** to do a pirouette

pis·ca·to·ri·al (pis'kə tôr'ē əl) ***adj.*** ⟦< L *piscator,* fisherman⟧ of fishes or fishing

Pis·ces (pī'sēz') ***n.*** ⟦ L, pl. of *piscis,* fish⟧ the 12th sign of the zodiac

pis·mire (pis'mīr', piz'-) ***n.*** ⟦< ME *pisse,* urine + *mire,* ant⟧ [Archaic] an ant

piss·ant (pis'ant') ***adj.***, ***n.*** [Slang] insignificant and contemptible (person)

pis·tach·i·o (pi stash'ē ō) ***n.***, *pl.* **-os'** ⟦< OPers *pistah*⟧ **1** a small tree of the cashew family **2** its edible, greenish seed (**pistachio nut**)

pis·til (pis'təl) ***n.*** ⟦< L *pistillum,* pestle⟧ the seed-bearing organ of a flower —**pis'til·late'** ***adj.***

pis·tol (pis'təl) ***n.*** ⟦< Czech *pišt'al*⟧ a small firearm operated with one hand

pis'tol-whip' ***vt.*** **-whipped', -whip'ping** to beat with a pistol, esp. about the head

pis·ton (pis'tən) ***n.*** ⟦ult. < L *pinsere,* to pound⟧ the snug-fitting engine part that is forced back and forth within a cylinder by the pressure of combustion, steam, etc. and a reciprocating connecting rod (**piston rod**)

piston ring a split ring fitted into a groove around a piston to seal the cylinder, transfer heat, etc.

pit[1] (pit) ***n.*** ⟦< MDu *pitte*⟧ the hard stone, as of the plum, peach, or cherry, containing the seed —***vt.* pit'ted, pit'ting** to remove the pit from

pit[2] (pit) ***n.*** ⟦< L *puteus,* a well⟧ **1** a hole in the ground **2** an abyss **3** hell: used with *the* **4** a pitfall **5** an enclosed area in which animals are kept or made to fight **6** a small hollow in a surface, as a scar left by smallpox **7** the section for the orchestra in front of the stage **8** a work area for mechanics beside an auto-racing track —***vt.* pit'ted, pit'ting 1** to make pits or scars in **2** to set in competition (*against*)

pi·ta (pēt'ə) ***n.*** ⟦< Heb < Modern Greek⟧ a round, flat bread of the Middle East: also **pita bread**

pit·a·pat (pit'ə pat') ***adv.*** with rapid beating —***n.*** a rapid series of beats or taps

pit bull a short, heavy dog with powerful jaws

pitch[1] (pich) ***n.*** ⟦< L *pix*⟧ a black, sticky substance formed from coal tar, etc. and used for roofing, etc.

pitch[2] (pich) ***vt.*** ⟦ME *picchen*⟧ **1** to set up *[pitch* a tent*]* **2** *a)* to throw or toss *b)* to throw away **3** to fix at a certain point, degree, key, etc. **4** *Baseball a)* to throw (the ball) to the batter *b)* to act as pitcher for (a game, etc.) —***vi.* 1** to pitch a ball, etc. **2** to plunge forward or dip downward **3** to rise and fall, as a ship in rough water —***n.* 1** a throw or toss **2** anything pitched **3** a point or degree **4** the degree of slope **5** [Inf.] a line of talk for persuading **6** *Music, etc.* the highness or lowness of a sound due to vibrations of sound waves —**pitch in** [Inf.] **1** to begin working hard **2** to make a contribution —**pitch into** [Inf.] to attack

pitch'-black' ***adj.*** very black

pitch'blende' (-blend') ***n.*** ⟦< Ger *pech,* PITCH[1] + *blenden,* to blind⟧ a dark mineral, a major source of uranium

pitch'-dark' ***adj.*** very dark

pitched battle 1 a battle in which troop placement is relatively fixed beforehand **2** a hard-fought battle

pitch'er[1] ***n.*** ⟦< OFr *pichier*⟧ a container, usually with a handle and lip, for holding and pouring liquids

pitch'er[2] ***n.*** ⟦PITCH[2] + -ER⟧ the baseball player who pitches the ball to the batters

pitcher plant a plant with pitcherlike leaves that trap and digest insects

pitch'fork' ***n.*** a large, long-handled fork for lifting and tossing hay, etc.

pitch'man (-mən) ***n.***, *pl.* **-men** (-mən) **1** a hawker of novelties, as at a carnival **2** [Inf.] any high-pressure salesman

pitch pipe a small pipe that produces a fixed tone used as a standard in tuning instruments, etc.

pit·e·ous (pit'ē əs) ***adj.*** arousing or deserving pity —**pit'e·ous·ly** ***adv.***

THESAURUS

pipe ***n.*** **1** [A tube] pipeline, drainpipe, sewer, conduit, culvert, water pipe, aqueduct, trough, passage, duct, canal, vessel. **2** [A device for smoking] *Varieties of smoking pipes include the following:* meerschaum, corncob, Missouri meerschaum, bulldog pipe, briar pipe, clay pipe, hookah, water pipe, churchwarden, calabash, calumet, hash pipe*. **3** [A musical instrument] fife, flute, piccolo; see MUSICAL INSTRUMENT.

pipe down* ***v.*** become quiet, hush, speak lower; see STOP 2.

piracy ***n.*** pillage, holdup, robbery; see CRIME, THEFT.

pirate ***n.*** thief, freebooter, plunderer, pillager, marauder, privateer, soldier of fortune, buccaneer, sea rover; see also CRIMINAL, ROBBER.

pistol ***n.*** revolver, automatic, six-shooter*, rod*, six-gun*, Saturday night special*, iron*, forty-five, thirty-eight; see also GUN, WEAPON.

pit[2] ***n.*** abyss, cavity, depression; see HOLE 1.

pitch[1,2] ***n.*** **1** [Slope] slant, incline, angle; see GRADE 1, INCLINATION 2. **2** [A throw] toss, fling, hurl, heave, cast, pitched ball, ball, strike, delivery, offering. **3** [Musical frequency] frequency of vibration, rate of vibration, tone; see SOUND 2. **4** [A viscous liquid] resin, gum resin, coal tar; see GUM, TAR.

pitch[2] ***v.*** **1** [To throw] hurl, fling, toss; see THROW 1. **2** [To fall forward] plunge, flop, vault; see DIVE, FALL 1. **3** [To slope abruptly] rise, fall, tilt; see BEND, LEAN 1. —**pitch in*** volunteer, work, aid; see HELP. —**pitch into*** assault, blame, scold; see ATTACK, FIGHT.

pitcher[1,2] ***n.*** **1** [A utensil for pouring liquid] cream pitcher, milk pitcher, water pitcher, ewer, jar, carafe, jug, vessel, amphora; see also CONTAINER. **2** [In baseball, one who pitches to the batter] right-hand pitcher, right-hander, left-hand pitcher, left-hander, southpaw*, lefty*, righty*, reliever*, fireballer*, hurler*, ace*.

pitchfork ***n.*** fork, hayfork, three-tined fork; see TOOL 1.

pit'fall' *n.* ⟦< PIT² + OE *fealle*, a trap⟧ **1** a lightly covered pit for trapping animals **2** an unsuspected danger, etc.
pith (pith) *n.* ⟦OE *pitha*⟧ **1** the soft, spongy tissue in the center of certain plant stems **2** the essential part; gist
pith'y *adj.* **-i·er, -i·est 1** of, like, or full of pith **2** terse and full of meaning —**pith'i·ly** *adv.*
pit·i·ful (pit'i fəl) *adj.* **1** arousing or deserving pity **2** contemptible Also **pit·i·a·ble** (pit'ē ə bəl) —**pit'i·ful·ly** *adv.*
pit'i·less (-lis) *adj.* without pity
pi·ton (pē'tän') *n.* ⟦Fr < MFr, a spike⟧ a metal spike with an eye for a rope, driven into rock or ice for support in mountain climbing
pit stop 1 a temporary stop in the PIT² (*n.* 8) by a racing car **2** [Slang] *a*) a pause for food, etc. during a journey *b*) a visit to a restroom
pit·tance (pit''ns) *n.* ⟦< OFr *pitance*, food allowed a monk⟧ **1** a meager allowance of money **2** any small amount or share
pit·ter-pat·ter (pit'ər pat'ər) *n.* ⟦echoic⟧ a rapid succession of light tapping sounds
Pitts·burgh (pits'burg') city in SW Pennsylvania: pop. 370,000
pi·tu·i·tar·y (pi to͞o'ə ter'ē) *adj.* ⟦< L *pituita*, phlegm⟧ of a small, oval endocrine gland (**pituitary gland**) attached to the brain: it secretes hormones affecting growth, etc.
pit viper any of several poisonous vipers with a heat-sensitive pit on each side of the head
pit·y (pit'ē) *n.*, *pl.* **-ies** ⟦< L *pietas*, piety⟧ **1** sorrow for another's suffering or misfortune **2** a cause for sorrow or regret —*vt.*, *vi.* **-ied, -y·ing** to feel pity (for)
piv·ot (piv'ət) *n.* ⟦Fr⟧ **1** a point, shaft, etc. on which something turns **2** a person or thing on which something depends, etc. **3** a pivoting movement —*vt.* to provide with a pivot —*vi.* to turn as on a pivot —**piv'ot·al** *adj.*
pix·el (pik'səl) *n.* ⟦< *pic(ture)s* + *el(ement)*⟧ any of the dots that make up an image on a video screen
pix·ie or **pix·y** (pik'sē) *n.*, *pl.* **-ies** ⟦< Brit dial.⟧ a fairy, elf, etc.
pi·zazz or **piz·zazz** (pi zaz') *n.* [Inf.] **1** vigor **2** style, flair, etc.
piz·za (pēt'sə) *n.* ⟦It⟧ an Italian dish made by baking thin dough covered with tomatoes, cheese, etc.
piz·ze·ri·a (pēt'sə rē'ə) *n.* ⟦It⟧ a place where pizzas are made and sold
piz·zi·ca·to (pit'si kät'ō) *adj.* ⟦It⟧ *Music* plucked: a note to pluck the strings with the finger instead of bowing: also written ***piz'zi·ca'to***
pj's (pē'jāz') *pl.n. inf. var. of* PAJAMAS
pk *abbrev.* **1** pack **2** park **3** peck
pkg *abbrev.* package(s)
Pkwy or **Pky** *abbrev.* Parkway
pl *abbrev.* **1** place: also **Pl 2** plural
plac·ard (plak'ärd; -ərd) *n.* ⟦< MDu *placke*, a piece⟧ a notice for display in a public place —*vt.* to place placards on or in
pla·cate (plā'kāt') *vt.* **-cat'ed, -cat'ing** ⟦< L *placare*⟧ to appease; pacify —**pla·ca'tion** *n.*
place (plās) *n.* ⟦< Gr *plateia*, a street⟧ **1** a court or short street in a city **2** space; room **3** a region **4** *a*) the part of space occupied by a person or thing *b*) situation **5** a city, town, etc. **6** a residence **7** a building or space devoted to a special purpose *[a place* of amusement*]* **8** a particular point, part, position, etc. *[a sore place* on the leg, a *place* in history*]* **9** a step or point in a sequence **10** the proper position, time, etc. **11** a space, seat, etc. reserved or occupied by a person **12** a job or position **13** the duties of any position **14** the second position at the finish of a race —*vt.* **placed, plac'ing 1** *a*) to put in a particular place, condition, or relation *b*) to recognize or identify **2** to find employment for **3** to repose (trust) *in* a person or thing **4** to finish in (a specified position) in a race —*vi.* to finish second or among the first three in a race —**take place** to occur
pla·ce·bo (plə sē'bō) *n.*, *pl.* **-bos** or **-boes** ⟦< L, I shall please⟧ a harmless, unmedicated preparation given as a medicine, as to humor a patient
place mat a small mat serving as an individual table cover for a person at a meal
place'ment *n.* **1** a placing or being placed **2** location or arrangement
pla·cen·ta (plə sen'tə) *n.*, *pl.* **-tas** or **-tae** (-tē) ⟦ult. < Gr *plax*, a flat object⟧ the structure in the uterus through which the fetus is nourished: cf. AFTERBIRTH —**pla·cen'tal** *adj.*
plac·er (plas'ər) *n.* ⟦< Sp *placel*⟧ a deposit of gravel or sand containing particles of gold, etc. that can be washed out
place setting the dish, utensils, etc. used for setting one place at a table for a meal
plac·id (plas'id) *adj.* ⟦L *placidus*⟧ calm; quiet —**pla·cid·i·ty** (plə sid'ə tē) *n.* —**plac'id·ly** *adv.*
plack·et (plak'it) *n.* ⟦< ?⟧ a slit at the waist of a skirt or collar of a shirt, to make it easy to put on and take off
pla·gi·a·rize (plā'jə rīz') *vt.*, *vi.* **-rized', -riz'ing** ⟦< L *plagiarius*, kidnapper⟧ to take (ideas, writings, etc.) from (another) and pass them off as one's own —**pla'gi·a·rism'** (-riz'əm) *n.* —**pla'gi·a·rist** *n.*
plague (plāg) *n.* ⟦< Gr *plēgē*, a misfortune⟧ **1** any affliction or calamity **2** any deadly epidemic disease —*vt.* **plagued, plagu'ing 1** to afflict with a plague **2** to vex; torment
plaice (plās) *n.*, *pl.* **plaice** or **plaices** any of various American and European flounders
plaid (plad) *n.* ⟦Gael *plaide*, a blanket⟧ **1** cloth with a crossbarred pattern **2** any pattern of this kind —*adj.* having such a pattern
plain (plān) *adj.* ⟦< L *planus*, flat⟧ **1** open; clear *[in plain* view*]* **2** clearly understood; obvious **3** outspoken;

THESAURUS

pitfall *n.* snare, pit, blind; see TRAP 1.

pitiful *a.* miserable, mournful, sorrowful, woeful, distressed, distressing, deplorable, cheerless, joyless, pitiable, piteous, forlorn, wretched, comfortless, dismal, touching, pathetic, affecting, stirring, lamentable, poignant, heartbreaking, human, dramatic, impressive, tearful, gratifying, heartrending, depressing, afflicted, suffering, moving, vile; see also SAD 1.—*Ant.* HAPPY, cheerful, joyful.

pitiless *a.* unfeeling, heartless, cold; see INDIFFERENT.

pitter-patter *n.* thump, patter, tap; see NOISE 1.

pity *n.* sympathy, compassion, charity, softheartedness, tenderness, goodness, understanding, forbearance, mercy, kindness, warmheartedness, kindliness, brotherly love, unselfishness, benevolence, favor, condolence, commiseration, clemency, humanity.—*Ant.* HATRED, severity, ferocity. —**have** (or **take**) **pity on** show pity to, spare, pardon; see FORGIVE, PITY 2.

pity *v.* **1** [To feel pity] feel for, sympathize with, commiserate, be sorry for, bleed for, be sympathetic to, show sympathy, express sympathy for, grieve with, weep for; see also COMFORT, SYMPATHIZE. **2** [To be merciful to] spare, take pity on, show pity to, show forgiveness to, be merciful to, give quarter, pardon, reprieve, grant amnesty to; see also FORGIVE.—*Ant.* DESTROY, condemn, accuse.

pivot *v.* whirl, swivel, rotate; see TURN 1.

place *n.* **1** [Position] station, point, spot; see POSITION 1. **2** [Space] room, compass, stead, void, distance, area, seat, volume, berth, reservation, accommodation; see also EXTENT. **3** [Locality] spot, locus, site, community, district, suburb, country, section, habitat, home, residence, abode, house, quarters; see also AREA, NEIGHBORHOOD, REGION 1. **4** [Rank] status, position, station; see RANK 3. —**go places*** attain success, achieve, advance; see SUCCEED 1. —**in place** in order, timely, appropriate; see FIT 1. —**in place of** as a substitute for, instead of, taking the place of; see INSTEAD. —**out of place** inappropriate, unsuitable, not fitting; see IMPROPER. —**put someone in his** (or **her**) **place** humiliate, reprimand, shame; see HUMBLE. —**take place** occur, come into being, be; see HAPPEN 2. —**take the place of** replace, act in one's stead, serve as proxy for; see SUBSTITUTE.

place *v.* **1** [To put in a place] locate, assign, deposit; see PUT 1. **2** [To put in order] fix, arrange, group; see ORDER 3.

placed *a.* established, settled, fixed, located, rated, deposited, lodged, quartered, planted, set, arranged, stowed, stored, installed, situated, implanted, set up, ordered.

placement *n.* situation, position, arrangement; see ORGANIZATION 1.

plagiarism *n.* literary theft, forgery, fraud; see THEFT.

plague *n.* epidemic, pestilence, disease; see ILLNESS 2.

plague *v.* disturb, trouble, irk; see BOTHER 2.

plain *a.* **1** [Obvious] open, manifest, clear; see OBVIOUS 1, 2, UNDERSTANDABLE. **2** [Simple] unadorned, unostentatious, unpretentious; see MODEST 2. **3** [Ordinary] everyday, average, commonplace; see COMMON 1. **4** [Homely] plain-featured, coarse-featured, unattractive; see UGLY 1. **5** [In blunt language] outspoken, candid, impolite; see RUDE 2.

plain *n.* prairie, steppe, pampas,

straightforward **4** not luxurious or ornate **5** not complicated; simple **6** homely **7** pure; unmixed **8** common; ordinary *[a plain man]* —*n.* an extent of level country —*adv.* clearly —**plain'ly** *adv.* —**plain'ness** *n.*

plain'clothes' man a detective or police officer who wears civilian clothes while on duty: also **plain'clothes'man**, *pl.* **-men**

plain'song' *n.* a very old, plain kind of church music chanted in unison

plaint (plānt) *n.* ⟦< L *plangere,* to lament⟧ a complaint or lament

plain·tiff (plān'tif) *n.* ⟦see prec.⟧ one who brings a suit into a court of law

plain'tive (-tiv) *adj.* ⟦see PLAINT⟧ expressing sorrow or melancholy; mournful; sad

plait (plāt) *n.* ⟦< L *plicare,* to fold⟧ a braid of hair, etc. —*vt.* to braid

plan (plan) *n.* ⟦Fr, plan, foundation⟧ **1** a diagram showing the arrangement of a structure, piece of ground, etc. **2** a scheme for making, doing, or arranging something **3** any outline or sketch —*vt.* **planned, plan'ning 1** to make a plan of (a structure, etc.) **2** to devise a scheme for doing, etc. **3** to have in mind as a project or purpose —*vi.* to make plans —**plan'ner** *n.*

plane[1] (plān) *adj.* ⟦L *planus*⟧ **1** flat; level **2** of or having to do with flat surfaces or points, lines, etc. on them *[plane geometry]* —*n.* **1** a flat, level surface **2** a level of achievement, etc. **3** *short for* AIRPLANE

plane[2] (plān) *n.* ⟦< L *planus,* level⟧ a carpenter's tool for shaving a wood surface to make it smooth or level —*vt.* **planed, plan'ing** to smooth or level with a plane

plan·et (plan'it) *n.* ⟦< Gr *planan,* wander⟧ any celestial body that revolves about a star; esp., one of the sun's nine major planets: Mercury, Venus, Earth, Mars, Jupiter, Saturn, Uranus, Neptune, and Pluto —**plan'e·tar'y** (-ə ter'ē) *adj.*

plan·e·tar·i·um (plan'ə ter'ē əm) *n., pl.* **-i·ums** or **-i·a** (-ə) **1** a revolving projector used to simulate the past, present, or future motions or positions of the sun, planets, etc. on the inside of a large dome **2** the room or building containing this

plane tree any of various trees with ball-shaped fruits and bark that sheds in large patches; sycamore

plan·gent (plan'jənt) *adj.* ⟦< L *plangere,* to beat⟧ loud or resonant, and, often, mournful-sounding

plank (plaŋk) *n.* ⟦< LL *planca*⟧ **1** a long, broad, thick board **2** an item in the platform of a political party —*vt.* **1** to cover with planks **2** to broil and serve (steak, fish, etc.) on a board **3** [Inf.] to set (*down*) with force

plank'ing *n.* **1** planks in quantity **2** the planks of a structure

plank·ton (plaŋk'tən) *n.* ⟦< Gr *plazesthai,* wander⟧ the microscopic animal and plant life found floating in bodies of water

plant (plant) *n.* ⟦< L *planta,* a sprout⟧ **1** any of a group of living organisms, excluding animals, bacteria, and certain other simple organisms, typically having leaves, stems, and roots and the ability to carry on photosynthesis **2** an herb, as distinguished from a tree or shrub **3** the machinery, buildings, etc. of a factory, etc. —*vt.* **1** to put into the ground to grow **2** to set firmly in position **3** to settle; establish **4** [Slang] to place (a person or thing) in such a way as to trick, trap, etc.

plan·tain[1] (plan'tin) *n.* ⟦< L *plantago*⟧ a plant with basal leaves and spikes of tiny, greenish flowers

plan·tain[2] (plan'tin) *n.* ⟦< Sp *plátano,* banana tree⟧ a hybrid banana plant yielding a fruit that is usually cooked while green

plan·tar (plant'ər) *adj.* ⟦< L *planta,* sole⟧ of or on the sole of the foot

plan·ta·tion (plan tā'shən) *n.* ⟦< L *plantare,* to plant⟧ **1** an estate, as in a warm climate, cultivated by workers living on it **2** a large, cultivated planting of trees

plant·er (plant'ər) *n.* **1** the owner of a plantation **2** one that plants **3** a decorative container for plants

plant'ing *n.* **1** the act of putting seeds, etc. into soil **2** something planted

plant louse APHID

plaque (plak) *n.* ⟦Fr < MDu *placke,* disk⟧ **1** a flat, inscribed piece of wood or metal, used to commemorate an event, etc. **2** a thin film of matter on uncleaned teeth

plash (plash) *vt., vi., n.* ⟦echoic⟧ SPLASH

plas·ma (plaz'mə) *n.* ⟦Ger < Gr, something molded⟧ **1** the fluid part of blood, lymph, or milk **2** a high-temperature, ionized gas that is electrically neutral

plasma membrane a very thin living membrane surrounding a plant or animal cell

plas·ter (plas'tər) *n.* ⟦< Gr *emplassein,* to daub over⟧ **1** a pasty mixture, as of lime, sand, and water, that hardens when it dries, for coating walls, etc. **2** PLASTER OF PARIS **3** a pasty, medicinal preparation spread on cloth and applied to the body —*vt.* **1** to cover as with plaster **2** to apply like a plaster *[to plaster posters on walls]* **3** to make lie smooth and flat —**plas'ter·er** *n.*

plas'ter·board' *n.* thin board consisting of plaster of Paris covered with heavy paper, used in wide sheets for walls, etc.

plaster of Paris ⟦from use of gypsum from *Paris,* France⟧ a thick paste of gypsum and water that sets quickly: used for casts, statuary, etc.

plas·tic (plas'tik) *adj.* ⟦< Gr *plassein,* to form⟧ **1** molding or shaping matter; formative **2** that can be molded or shaped **3** made of plastic —*n.* **1** any of various nonme-

THESAURUS

expanse, open country, lowland, flat, level land, mesa, savanna, moorland, moor, heath, tundra, veldt, downs; see also FIELD 1, MEADOW.

plainly *a.* obviously, evidently, visibly; see CLEARLY 1, 2.

plan *n.* **1** [A preliminary sketch] draft, diagram, map, chart, timeline, design, outline, representation, form, drawing, view, projection, blueprint, rough draft, road map. **2** [A proposed sequence of action] plans, scheme, project, flowchart, outline, idea, handling, projection, undertaking, method, design, tactics, procedure, treatment, intention, policy, course of action, plot, conspiracy, expedient, strategy, stratagem, arrangement, way of doing things, angle*, the picture; see also PROGRAM 2, PURPOSE 1. **3** [Arrangement] layout, method, disposition; see ORDER 3. —**lay plans (for)** draft, design, think out; see FORM 1, INTEND 1, PLAN 2.

plan *v.* **1** [To plot an action in advance] prepare, scheme, devise, invent, outline, project, contrive, shape, design, map, plot a course, form a plan, think out, concoct, engineer, figure on, intrigue, conspire, frame, steer one's course, establish guidelines, set parameters, work up, work out, line up, plan an attack, come through, calculate on, make arrangements, take measures, bargain for, cook up*, put on ice*. **2** [To arrange in a preliminary way] outline, draft, sketch, lay out, map out, preprint, organize, prepare a sketch, chart, map, draw, trace, design, illustrate, depict, delineate, represent, shape, chalk out, rough in, block out, block in. **3** [To have in mind] propose, think, contemplate; see INTEND 1.

plane[1,2] *n.* **1** [A plane surface] level, extension, horizontal, flat, face, stratum. **2** [A tool for smoothing wood] electric planer, jointer, block plane; see TOOL 1. **3** [An airplane] aircraft, airliner, aeroplane, airship, heavier-than-air craft, shuttle, jet, jet plane. *Kinds of planes include the following:* propeller, jet, rocket, scout, observation, reconnaissance, transport, commercial, passenger; biplane, triplane, monoplane, racer, glider, bomber, seaplane, hydroplane, fighter, fighter-bomber, interceptor, turbojet, stratojet, helicopter, gunship, amphibian, sailplane.

plane[2] *v.* finish, smooth, level; see FLATTEN.

planet *n.* celestial body, heavenly body, luminous body, wandering star, planetoid, asteroid, star*. *The known planets are as follows:* Mercury, Venus, Earth, Mars, Jupiter, Saturn, Uranus, Neptune, Pluto, the asteroids.

plank *n.* board, planking, sheet; see LUMBER.

planned *a.* projected, budgeted, in the budget, provided for, on the drawing board, programmed, in the making, under consideration, on the docket, prospective, cut and dried, under advisement, prepared.

plant *n.* shrub, weed, bush, slip, shoot, cutting, sprout, seedling, plantlet, bulb, flower, tree, herb, grass, mushroom, fungus, moss, alga, seaweed.

plant *v.* put in the ground, sow, farm, set out, pot, start, transplant, seed, stock, colonize, settle, establish, locate.

plantation *n.* hacienda, estate, ranch; see FARM.

planted *a.* cultivated, sown, seeded, stocked, implanted, strewn, drilled.

plaster *n.* mortar, binding, plaster of Paris; see CEMENT.

plaster *v.* coat, bind, cement; see COVER 1.

plastic *a.* substitute, synthetic, cellulose; see SYNTHETIC.

plastic *n.* synthetic, artificial product, substitute, plastic material, processed material, polymerized substance, thermoplastic, cellophane, polyester, polystyrene, acrylic, polyethylene, acetate, celluloid, melamine, vinyl, nylon, PVC. *Trademarked plastics:* Neoprene, Orlon, Plexiglas, Lucite, Formica, Teflon, Styrofoam.

tallic compounds, synthetically produced, which can be molded and hardened for commercial use **2** [Inf.] a credit card or credit cards, or credit based on their use —**plas·tic'i·ty** (-tis'ə tē) ***n.***

plas'ti·cize' (-tə sīz') ***vt., vi.*** **-cized', -ciz'ing** to make or become plastic

plastic surgery surgery dealing with the repair of deformed or destroyed parts of the body, as by transferring skin, bone, etc. from other parts —**plastic surgeon**

plat (plat) ***n.*** ⟦var. of PLOT⟧ **1** a small piece of ground **2** a map or plan, as of a subdivision —***vt.*** **plat'ted, plat'ting** to make a map or plan of

plate (plāt) ***n.*** ⟦< Gr *platys*, broad⟧ **1** a smooth, flat, thin piece of metal, etc., specif. one on which an engraving is cut **2** an impression taken from an engraved surface **3** dishes, utensils, etc. of, or plated with, silver or gold **4** a shallow dish **5** the food in a dish; a course **6** a denture, specif. that part of it which fits to the mouth **7** *Baseball short for* HOME PLATE **8** *Photog.* a sheet of glass, metal, etc. coated with a film sensitive to light **9** *Printing* a cast to be printed from —***vt.*** **plat'ed, plat'ing 1** to coat with gold, silver, etc. **2** to cover with metal plates

pla·teau (pla tō') ***n.*** ⟦Fr: see prec.⟧ **1** an elevated tract of level land **2** a period of relative stability or little change

plate glass polished, clear glass in thick sheets, for windows, mirrors, etc.

plate·let (plāt'lit) ***n.*** a small blood cell involved in clotting

plat·en (plat''n) ***n.*** ⟦< OFr *plat*, flat⟧ **1** in a printing press, a flat metal plate which presses the paper against the type **2** a typewriter roller on which the keys strike

plate tec·ton·ics (tek tän'iks) *Geol.* the theory that the earth's surface consists of plates whose constant motion explains continental drift, etc.

plat·form (plat'fôrm') ***n.*** ⟦Fr *plate-forme*, lit., flat form⟧ **1** a raised horizontal surface, as a stage for speakers, etc. **2** a statement of policy, esp. of a political party

plat·i·num (plat''n əm) ***n.*** ⟦< Sp *plata*, silver⟧ a silvery, metallic chemical element, resistant to corrosion: used for jewelry, etc.

plat·i·tude (plat'ə to͞od') ***n.*** ⟦Fr < *plat*, flat, after *latitude*, etc.⟧ a commonplace or trite remark

Pla·to (plāt'ō) 427?-347? B.C.; Gr. philosopher

Pla·ton·ic (plə tän'ik) ***adj.*** **1** of Plato or his philosophy **2** [*usually* **p-**] not sexual but purely spiritual: said of a relationship, etc.

pla·toon (plə to͞on') ***n.*** ⟦Fr *peloton*, a ball, group⟧ **1** a military unit composed of two or more squads **2** *Sports* any of the specialized squads making up a team —***vt.*** *Sports* to alternate (players) at a position

plat·ter (plat'ər) ***n.*** ⟦< OFr *plat*, flat⟧ a large, shallow dish, usually oval, for serving food

plat·y (plat'ē) ***n.***, *pl.* **plat'y, plat'ys,** or **plat'ies** ⟦clipped < ModL *Platypoecilus*, genus name⟧ a brightly colored, freshwater fish of Central America: used in aquariums

plat·y·pus (plat'ə pəs) ***n.***, *pl.* **-pus·es** or **-pi'** (-pī') ⟦< Gr *platys*, flat + *pous*, foot⟧ a small, egg-laying water mammal of Australia, with webbed feet and a ducklike bill; duckbill

plau·dit (plô'dit) ***n.*** ⟦< L *plaudere*, applaud⟧ [*usually pl.*] applause

plau·si·ble (plô'zə bəl) ***adj.*** ⟦< L *plaudere*, applaud⟧ seemingly true, trustworthy, honest, etc. —**plau'si·bil'i·ty** ***n.***

play (plā) ***vi.*** ⟦OE *plegan*⟧ **1** to move lightly, rapidly, etc. *[sunlight played on the water]* **2** to engage in recreation **3** to take part in a game or sport **4** to trifle (*with* a thing or person) **5** to perform on a musical instrument **6** to give out sounds **7** to act in a specified way *[to play dumb]* **8** to act in a drama **9** to impose unscrupulously (*on* another's feelings) —***vt.*** **1** to take part in (a game or sport) **2** to oppose (a person, team, etc.) in a game **3** to do, as in fun *[to play tricks]* **4** to bet on **5** to cause to move, etc.; wield **6** to cause *[to play havoc]* **7** to perform (music, a drama, etc.) **8** to perform on (an instrument) **9** to act the part of *[to play Hamlet]* —***n.*** **1** motion or activity, esp. when free or rapid **2** freedom for motion or action **3** recreation; sport **4** fun; joking **5** the playing of a game **6** a move or act in a game **7** a dramatic composition or performance; drama —**in** (or **out of**) **play** *Sports* in (or not in) the condition for continuing play: said of a ball, etc. —**play down** to attach little importance to —**played out** exhausted —**play up** [Inf.] to give prominence to —**play up to** [Inf.] to try to please by flattery

play'act' ***vi.*** **1** to pretend **2** to behave in an affected or dramatic manner —**play'act'ing** ***n.***

play'back' ***n.*** **1** reproduction of sounds, images, etc. from a recorded disc, tape, etc. **2** the control or device for such reproduction

play'bill' ***n.*** **1** a poster advertising a play **2** a program of a play, listing the cast, etc.

play'boy' ***n.*** a man of means who is given to pleasure-seeking

play'er ***n.*** **1** one who plays a specified game, instrument, etc. **2** an actor

play'ful ***adj.*** **1** fond of play or fun **2** jocular —**play'ful·ly** ***adv.*** —**play'ful·ness** ***n.***

play'go'er (-gō'ər) ***n.*** one who goes to the theater frequently or regularly

play'ground' ***n.*** a place, often near a school, for outdoor recreation

play'house' ***n.*** **1** a theater for live dramatic productions **2** a small house for children to play in

playing cards cards used in playing various games, arranged in four suits

play'mate' ***n.*** a companion in games and recreation

play'off' ***n.*** a contest to break a tie or to decide a championship

play on words a pun or punning

play'pen' ***n.*** a portable enclosure for an infant to play or crawl in safely

play'thing' ***n.*** a toy

play'wright' (-rīt') ***n.*** one who writes plays

pla·za (plä'zə, plaz'ə) ***n.*** ⟦Sp < L *platea*, street⟧ **1** a public square in a city or town **2** a shopping center **3** a service area along a superhighway

THESAURUS

plate ***n.*** **1** [A flat surface] lamina, slice, stratum; see PLANE 1. **2** [A full-page illustration] photograph, lithograph, etching; see ILLUSTRATION, PICTURE 3. **3** [A flattish dish] dinner plate, soup plate, salad plate, casserole, dessert plate, platter, trencher, china, serving dish; see also DISH 1. **4** [Food served on a plate] helping, serving, course; see MEAL 2. **5** [In baseball, the base immediately in front of the catcher] home base, home plate, home; see BASE 4.

plate ***v.*** laminate, stratify, layer, scale, flake, overlay, gild, nickel, bronze, chrome, silver, enamel, encrust, cover.

plateau ***n.*** tableland, mesa, elevation; see HILL, PLAIN.

platform ***n.*** **1** [A stage] dais, pulpit, speaker's platform, rostrum, stand, floor, staging, terrace. **2** [A program] principles, policies, the party planks*; see PROGRAM 2.

platoon ***n.*** detachment, military unit, company; see ARMY 2.

platter ***n.*** tray, serving dish, meat platter; see DISH 1, PLATE 3.

plausible ***a.*** probable, credible, believable; see LIKELY 1.

play ***n.*** **1** [Amusement] enjoyment, diversion, pleasure; see ENTERTAINMENT. **2** [Recreation] relaxation, game, sport; see ENTERTAINMENT. **3** [Fun] frolic, happiness, sportiveness; see FUN. **4** [A drama] performance, musical, show; see DRAMA. **5** [Sport] exhibition, match, competition; see SPORT 1, 3. **6** [Action] activity, movement, working; see ACTION 1. —**make a play for*** make advances to, court, try to attract; see TRY 1.

play ***v.*** **1** [To amuse oneself] entertain oneself, revel, make merry, carouse, play games, rejoice, have a good time, idle away, horse around*.—*Ant.* MOURN, grieve, sulk. **2** [To frolic] frisk, sport, cavort, joke, dance, play games, make jokes, be a practical joker, show off, jump about, skip, gambol, caper.—*Ant.* DRAG, mope, droop. **3** [To produce music] perform, execute, work, cause to sound, finger, pedal, bow, plunk, tinkle, pipe, toot, blow, pump, fiddle, sound, strike, scrape, twang, pound, thump, shake, beat, pluck, clash. **4** [To engage in sport] participate, engage, practice; see COMPETE. **5** [To pretend] imagine, suppose, think; see PRETEND 1. —**play down** belittle, hold back, minimize; see RESTRAIN.

player ***n.*** **1** [One who takes part in a game] team member, athlete, sportsman, sportswoman, amateur, professional, gymnast, acrobat, swimmer, diver, trackman, champ*, pro*, semipro*, jock*; see also CONTESTANT. **2** [An actor] performer, entertainer, thespian; see ACTOR, ACTRESS.

playful ***a.*** joking, whimsical, comical; see FUNNY 1.

playground ***n.*** playing field, park, school ground, municipal playground, yard, schoolyard, diamond, gridiron.

playmate ***n.*** schoolmate, neighbor, companion; see FRIEND.

plaything ***n.*** gadget, amusement, trinket; see DOLL, GAME 1, TOY 1.

playwright ***n.*** scriptwriter, dramatist, tragedian; see AUTHOR, WRITER.

plea (plē) ***n.*** ⟦< L *placere*, to please⟧ **1** a statement in defense; excuse **2** a request; appeal **3** *Law* the response of a defendant to criminal charges

plea′-bar′gain ***vi.*** to engage in plea bargaining

plea bargaining pretrial negotiations in which the defendant agrees to plead guilty to a lesser charge if more serious charges are dropped

plead (plēd) ***vi.*** **plead′ed** or **pled** or **plead** (pled), **plead′ing** ⟦see PLEA⟧ **1** to present a plea in a law court **2** to make an appeal; beg —***vt.*** **1** to argue (a law case) **2** to answer (guilty or not guilty) to a charge **3** to offer as an excuse —**plead′er** ***n.***

pleas·ant (plez′ənt) ***adj.*** ⟦< Fr *plaisir*, to please⟧ **1** agreeable to the mind or senses; pleasing **2** having an agreeable manner, look, etc.; amiable —**pleas′ant·ly** ***adv.*** —**pleas′ant·ness** ***n.***

pleas′ant·ry (-ən trē) ***n.***, *pl.* **-ries** **1** a humorous remark **2** a polite social remark *[to exchange pleasantries]*

please (plēz) ***vt.*** **pleased**, **pleas′ing** ⟦< L *placere*⟧ **1** to be agreeable to; satisfy **2** to be the wish of *[it pleased him to go]* —***vi.*** **1** to be agreeable; satisfy **2** to have the wish; like *[to do as one pleases]* *Please* is also used in polite requests *[please sit down]*

pleas′ing ***adj.*** giving pleasure —**pleas′ing·ly** ***adv.***

pleas·ur·a·ble (plezh′ər ə bəl) ***adj.*** pleasant; enjoyable

pleas·ure (plezh′ər) ***n.*** **1** a pleased feeling; delight **2** one's wish, will, or choice **3** a thing that gives delight or satisfaction —**pleas′ure·ful** ***adj.***

pleat (plēt) ***n.*** ⟦ME *pleten*⟧ a flat double fold in cloth, etc. pressed or stitched in place —***vt.*** to lay and press (cloth) in a pleat or pleats

ple·be·ian (pli bē′ən) ***n.*** ⟦< L *plebs*, the common people⟧ **1** one of the common people **2** a vulgar, coarse person —***adj.*** vulgar or common

pleb·i·scite (pleb′ə sīt′) ***n.*** ⟦< L *plebs*, the common people + *scitum*, a decree⟧ a direct vote of the people on a political issue, such as independent nationhood or annexation

plec·trum (plek′trəm) ***n.***, *pl.* **-trums** or **-tra** (-trə) ⟦L < Gr *plēssein*, to strike⟧ a thin piece of metal, plastic, etc., for plucking the strings of a guitar, etc.; pick

pled (pled) ***vi.***, ***vt.*** *pt. & pp. of* PLEAD

pledge (plej) ***n.*** ⟦prob < OS *plegan*, to warrant⟧ **1** the condition of being given or held as security for a contract, payment, etc. **2** a person or thing given or held thus as security **3** a promise or agreement **4** something promised —***vt.*** **pledged**, **pledg′ing** **1** to give as security **2** to bind by a promise **3** to promise to give

Pleis·to·cene (plīs′tə sēn′) ***adj.*** ⟦< Gr *pleistos*, most + *kainos*, recent⟧ designating an epoch in the Cenozoic Era, characterized by the appearance of modern humans

ple·na·ry (plē′nə rē, plen′ə-) ***adj.*** ⟦< L *plenus*, full⟧ **1** full; complete **2** for attendance by all members *[a plenary session]*

plen·i·po·ten·ti·ar·y (plen′i pō ten′shē er′ē) ***adj.*** ⟦< L *plenus*, full + *potens*, powerful⟧ having or conferring full authority —***n.***, *pl.* **-ar′ies** a diplomat given full authority

plen·i·tude (plen′i to͞od′) ***n.*** ⟦< L *plenus*, full⟧ **1** fullness; completeness **2** abundance; plenty

plen·te·ous (plen′tē əs) ***adj.*** plentiful

plen·ti·ful (plen′ti fəl) ***adj.*** **1** having or yielding plenty **2** abundant —**plen′ti·ful·ly** ***adv.***

plen·ty (plen′tē) ***n.***, *pl.* **-ties** ⟦< L *plenus*, full⟧ **1** prosperity; opulence **2** a sufficient supply **3** a large number —***adv.*** [Inf.] fully; quite

pleth·o·ra (pleth′ə rə) ***n.*** ⟦< Gr *plēthein*, to be full⟧ an overabundance

pleu·ra (plo͝or′ə) ***n.***, *pl.* **-rae** (-ē) ⟦< Gr, rib, side⟧ the thin membrane that covers a lung and lines the chest cavity in mammals

pleu·ri·sy (plo͝or′ə sē) ***n.*** ⟦< Gr *pleura*, rib, side⟧ inflammation of the pleura, characterized by painful breathing

Plex·i·glas (plek′si glas′) *trademark for* a lightweight, transparent thermoplastic substance —***n.*** this material

plex·i·glass (plek′si glas′) ***n.*** a material like Plexiglas

plex·us (plek′səs) ***n.***, *pl.* **-us·es** or **-us** ⟦< L *plectere*, to twine⟧ a network of blood vessels, nerves, etc.

pli·a·ble (plī′ə bəl) ***adj.*** ⟦< L *plicare*, to fold⟧ **1** easily bent; flexible **2** easily influenced or persuaded **3** adaptable —**pli′a·bil′i·ty** ***n.***

pli·ant (plī′ənt) ***adj.*** **1** easily bent; pliable **2** compliant —**pli′an·cy** ***n.***

pli·ers (plī′ərz) ***pl.n.*** ⟦< PLY[1]⟧ small pincers for gripping small objects, bending wire, etc.: often **pair of pliers**

plight[1] (plīt) ***n.*** ⟦< OFr *pleit*, a fold⟧ a distressing situation

plight[2] (plīt) ***vt.*** ⟦< OE *pliht*, a pledge, danger⟧ to pledge, or bind by a pledge

plinth (plinth) ***n.*** ⟦< Gr *plinthos*, a brick⟧ the block at the base of a column, pedestal, etc.

PLO *abbrev.* Palestine Liberation Organization

plod (pläd) ***vi.*** **plod′ded**, **plod′ding** ⟦of echoic orig.⟧ **1** to move heavily and laboriously; trudge **2** to work steadily; drudge —**plod′der** ***n.***

plop (pläp) ***vt.***, ***vi.*** **plopped**, **plop′ping** ⟦echoic⟧ to drop with a sound like that of something flat falling into water —***n.*** such a sound

plot (plät) ***n.*** ⟦OE⟧ **1** a small area of ground **2** a secret, usually evil, scheme **3** the plan of action of a play, novel, etc.: also **plot′line′** —***vt.*** **plot′ted**, **plot′ting** **1** to

THESAURUS

plea ***n.*** **1** [An appeal] overture, request, supplication; see APPEAL 1. **2** [A form of legal defense] pleading, argument, case; see DEFENSE 2.

plead ***v.*** **1** [To beg] implore, beseech, solicit; see ASK, BEG. **2** [To enter a plea] present, allege, cite; see DECLARE. —**plead guilty** confess, repent, concede; see ADMIT 2.

pleading ***a.*** imploring, supplicating, desirous.

pleasant ***a.*** **1** [Affable] agreeable, attractive, obliging, charming, mild, amusing, kindly, mild-mannered, gracious, genial, amiable, polite, urbane, cheerful, sympathetic, civil, cordial, engaging, social, bland, diplomatic, civilized, good-humored, good-natured, soft, fun, delightful, jovial, jolly.—*Ant.* SULLEN, unsympathetic, unkind. **2** [Giving pleasure; *said of occasions, experiences, and the like*] gratifying, pleasurable, agreeable, cheering, amusing, welcome, refreshing, satisfying, all right, satisfactory, adequate, acceptable, comfortable, diverting, fascinating, adorable, enjoyable, delightful, sociable, lively, exciting, glad, festive, cheerful, entertaining, relaxing, joyous, joyful, merry, happy, pleasing, favorable, bright, sunny, brisk, sparkling, enlivening, colorful, light, humorous, comforting.—*Ant.* SAD, disagreeable, unhappy.

pleasantly ***a.*** pleasingly, charmingly, welcomely; see AGREEABLY.

please ***interj.*** if you please, if it pleases you, may it please you, by your leave.

please ***v.*** **1** [To give pleasure] gratify, satisfy, make up to; see ENTERTAIN. **2** [To desire] wish, demand, command; see WANT 1. —**if you please** if you will, if I may, by your leave; see PLEASE *interj.*

pleased ***a.*** gratified, satisfied, charmed; see HAPPY.

pleasing ***a.*** charming, agreeable, delightful; see PLEASANT 1.

pleasure ***n.*** **1** [Enjoyment] bliss, delight, ease; see HAPPINESS. **2** [Will] want, preference, wish; see DESIRE 1.

pleat ***n.*** pleating, tuck, crease; see FOLD.

pleat ***v.*** ruffle, crease, gather; see FOLD.

pledge ***n.*** guarantee, token, agreement; see PROMISE 1.

pledge ***v.*** swear, vow, declare; see PROMISE.

plentiful ***a.*** **1** [Bountiful] prolific, fruitful, profuse, lavish, liberal, unsparing, inexhaustible, replete, generous, abundant, extravagant, improvident, excessive, copious, superabundant, overliberal, superfluous, overflowing, flowing.—*Ant.* STINGY, niggardly, skimpy. **2** [Existing in plenty] sufficient, abundant, copious, ample, overflowing, large, chock-full, teeming, unlimited, well-provided, flowing, full, flush, lush with, pouring, fruitful, swarming, swimming, abounding.—*Ant.* POOR, scant, scanty.

plenty ***n.*** abundance, fruitfulness, fullness, lavishness, deluge, torrent, bounty, profusion, adequacy, flood, avalanche, limit, capacity, adequate stock, enough and to spare, everything, all kinds of, all one wants, all one can eat and drink, more than one knows what to do with, too much of a good thing, a good bit, all one needs, all one can use, a great deal, a lot*, lots*, oodles*.

pliable ***a.*** limber, supple, plastic; see FLEXIBLE.

pliant ***a.*** limber, supple, plastic; see FLEXIBLE.

pliers ***n.*** pinchers, wrench, pincers, tongs, forceps, tweezers.

plod ***v.*** trudge, hike, plug; see WALK 1.

plop ***v.*** thump, thud, bump; see SOUND.

plot ***n.*** **1** [An intrigue] conspiracy, scheme, artifice; see TRICK 1. **2** [The action of a story] plan, scheme, outline, design, development, progress, unfolding, movement, climax, events, incidents, suspense, structure, buildup, scenario. **3** [A piece of ground] parcel, land, division; see AREA, LOT 1.

plot ***v.*** **1** [To devise an intrigue] frame, contrive, scheme; see PLAN 1. **2**

mark or trace on a chart or map **2** to make secret plans for —***vi.*** to scheme —**plot·ter** ***n.***

plov·er (pluv′ər, plō′vər) ***n.*** ⟦< L *pluvia*, rain⟧ a bird living near the shore, having a short tail and long, pointed wings

plow (plou) ***n.*** ⟦OE *ploh*⟧ **1** a farm implement used to cut and turn up the soil **2** any implement like this, as a snowplow —***vt.*** **1** to cut and turn up (soil) with a plow **2** to make (one's way) through by or as if by plowing —***vi.*** **1** to use a plow **2** to move (*through, into*, etc.) with force **3** to plod **4** to begin work vigorously: with *into* Also, chiefly Brit., **plough** —**plow′man** (-mən), *pl.* **-men**, ***n.***

plow′share′ ***n.*** the cutting blade of a plow

ploy (ploi) ***n.*** ⟦? < (EM)PLOY⟧ an action intended to outwit someone

pluck (pluk) ***vt.*** ⟦OE *pluccian*⟧ **1** to pull off or out; pick **2** to snatch **3** to pull feathers or hair from **4** to pull at (a guitar string, etc.) and release quickly —***vi.*** to pull: often with *at* —***n.*** **1** a pulling; tug **2** courage

pluck′y ***adj.*** **-i·er**, **-i·est** brave; spirited —**pluck′i·ness** ***n.***

plug (plug) ***n.*** ⟦MDu *plugge*⟧ **1** an object used to stop up a hole, etc. **2** a cake of pressed tobacco **3** an electrical device, as with prongs, for making contact or closing a circuit **4** a kind of fishing lure **5** [Inf.] a free boost, advertisement, etc. **6** [Slang] an old, worn-out horse —***vt.*** **plugged**, **plug′ging** **1** to fill (a hole, etc.) with a plug **2** to insert a plug of **3** [Inf.] to advertise with a plug **4** [Slang] to shoot a bullet into —***vi.*** [Inf.] to work doggedly —**plug in** to connect (an electrical device) by inserting a plug into a jack, socket, etc.

plum (plum) ***n.*** ⟦OE *plume*⟧ **1** *a)* a tree bearing a smooth-skinned fruit with a flattened stone *b)* the fruit **2** a raisin *[plum* pudding*]* **3** the bluish-red color of some plums **4** something desirable

plum·age (plo͞o′mij) ***n.*** ⟦Fr < *plume*, a feather⟧ a bird's feathers

plumb (plum) ***n.*** ⟦< L *plumbum*, LEAD[2]⟧ a lead weight (**plumb bob**) hung at the end of a line (**plumb line**), used to determine how deep water is or whether a wall, etc. is vertical —***adj.*** perfectly vertical —***adv.*** **1** straight down **2** [Inf.] entirely —***vt.*** **1** to test or sound with a plumb **2** to probe or fathom —**out of** (or **off**) **plumb** not vertical

plumb·er (plum′ər) ***n.*** ⟦see prec.⟧ a skilled worker who installs and repairs pipes, fixtures, etc., as of water systems

plumber's helper [Inf.] PLUNGER (sense 2): also **plumber's friend**

plumb·ing (plum′iŋ) ***n.*** **1** the work of a plumber **2** the pipes and fixtures with which a plumber works

plume (plo͞om) ***n.*** ⟦< L *pluma*⟧ **1** a feather, esp. a large, showy one **2** a group of these —***vt.*** **plumed**, **plum′ing** **1** to adorn with plumes **2** to preen —**plum′y**, **-i·er**, **-i·est**, ***adj.***

plum·met (plum′it) ***n.*** ⟦see PLUMB⟧ **1** a plumb **2** a thing that weighs heavily —***vi.*** to fall straight downward

plump[1] (plump) ***adj.*** ⟦< MDu *plomp*, bulky⟧ full and rounded in form; chubby —**plump′ness** ***n.***

plump[2] (plump) ***vi.***, ***vt.*** ⟦echoic⟧ to drop or bump suddenly or heavily —***n.*** **1** a falling, bumping, etc. **2** the sound of this —***adv.*** **1** suddenly; heavily **2** straight down

plun·der (plun′dər) ***vt.***, ***vi.*** ⟦< Ger *plunder*, baggage⟧ **1** to rob or pillage **2** to take (property) by force or fraud —***n.*** **1** a plundering **2** things taken by force or fraud

plunge (plunj) ***vt.*** **plunged**, **plung′ing** ⟦see PLUMB⟧ to thrust or throw suddenly (*into* a liquid, condition, etc.) —***vi.*** **1** to dive or rush **2** to move violently and rapidly downward or forward **3** [Inf.] to gamble heavily —***n.*** **1** a dive or fall **2** [Inf.] a gamble

plung′er ***n.*** **1** one who plunges **2** a large rubber suction cup used to free clogged drains **3** any cylindrical device that operates with a plunging motion, as a piston

plunk (pluŋk) ***vt.*** ⟦echoic⟧ **1** to strum (a banjo, etc.) **2** to throw or put down heavily —***vi.*** **1** to give out a twanging sound **2** to fall heavily —***n.*** the sound made by plunking —**plunk down** [Inf.] to give in payment

plu·ral (ploor′əl) ***adj.*** ⟦< L *plus*, more⟧ more than one —***n.*** *Gram.* the form of a word designating more than one (Ex.: *hands, men*)

plu′ral·ism′ ***n.*** various ethnic, religious, etc. groups existing together in a nation or society —**plu′ral·ist** ***n.***, ***adj.*** —**plu′ral·is′tic** ***adj.***

plu·ral·i·ty (plo͞o ral′ə tē) ***n.***, *pl.* **-ties** **1** a being plural or numerous **2** *a)* the excess of votes in an election that the leading candidate has over the nearest rival *b)* a majority

plu·ral·ize (ploor′ə līz′) ***vt.***, ***vi.*** **-ized′**, **-iz′ing** to make plural

plus (plus) ***prep.*** ⟦L, more⟧ **1** added to *[*2 *plus* 2*]* **2** in addition to —***adj.*** **1** indicating addition **2** positive *[*a *plus* quantity*]* **3** somewhat higher than *[*a grade of B *plus]* **4** involving extra gain *[*a *plus* factor*]* **5** [Inf.] and more *[*personality *plus]* —***n.***, *pl.* **plus′es** or **plus′ses** **1** a sign (**plus sign**, +) indicating addition or positive quantity **2** something added **3** an advantage; benefit

plush (plush) ***n.*** ⟦< L *pilus*, hair⟧ a fabric with a soft, thick pile —***adj.*** [Inf.] luxurious: also **plush′y**, **-i·er**, **-i·est**

Plu·tarch (plo͞o′tärk′) A.D. 46?-120?; Gr. biographer & historian

Plu·to (plo͞ot′ō) **1** *Gr. & Rom. Myth.* the god of the lower world **2** the outermost planet: see PLANET

plu·toc·ra·cy (plo͞o täk′rə sē) ***n.***, *pl.* **-cies** ⟦< Gr *ploutos*, wealth + *kratein*, to rule⟧ **1** government by the wealthy **2** a group of wealthy people who control a government

plu·to·crat (plo͞ot′ə krat′) ***n.*** **1** a member of a plutocracy **2** one whose wealth is the source of control or influence —**plu′to·crat′ic** ***adj.***

plu·to·ni·um (plo͞o tō′nē əm) ***n.*** ⟦after PLUTO (planet)⟧ a radioactive metallic chemical element

plu·vi·al (plo͞o′vē əl) ***adj.*** ⟦< L *pluvia*, rain⟧ of, or having much, rain

ply[1] (plī) ***vt.*** **plied**, **ply′ing** ⟦< L *plicare*, to fold⟧ [Now Rare] to twist, fold, etc. —***n.***, *pl.* **plies** **1** a thickness or layer, as of cloth or plywood **2** one of the twisted strands in rope, yarn, etc.

ply[2] (plī) ***vt.*** **plied**, **ply′ing** ⟦contr. < APPLY⟧ **1** to use (a tool, faculty, etc.), esp. with energy **2** to work at (a trade) **3** to keep supplying, assailing, etc. (*with*) **4** to sail back and forth across —***vi.*** **1** to keep busy (*at*) **2** to travel regularly (*between* places)

Ply·mouth (plim′əth) town in SE Massachusetts: settled by the Pilgrims (1620): pop. 46,000

ply′wood′ ***n.*** ⟦PLY[1] + WOOD⟧ a construction material made of thin layers of wood glued together

PM *abbrev.* **1** ⟦L *post meridiem*⟧ after noon: used for the time from noon to midnight: also **P.M.** or **p.m.** or **pm** **2** Postmaster **3** Prime Minister

PMS *abbrev.* ⟦*p(re)m(enstrual) s(yndrome)*⟧ the physical and emotional symptoms that may precede menstruation

pneu·mat·ic (no͞o mat′ik) ***adj.*** ⟦< Gr *pneuma*, breath⟧ **1**

THESAURUS

[To plan] sketch, outline, draft; see PLAN 2.

plow ***n.*** *Plows include the following:* moldboard, gang, steam, tractor, double, straddle, sulky, wheel, shovel, hand; lister, hoe plow or horse-hoe, garden plow or wheel hoe, (corn) cultivator; see also TOOL 1.

plow ***v.*** **1** [To use a plow] break, furrow, cultivate, turn, plow up, turn over, till, ridge, break ground, do the plowing; see also FARM. **2** [To act like a plow] smash into, rush through, shove apart; see DIG 1, PUSH 1.

plug ***n.*** **1** [An implement to stop an opening] cork, stopper, stopple, filling, bung, lid, wedge. **2** [An electrical fitting] attachment plug, fitting, connection, wall plug, floor plug, plug fuse. **3** [A large pipe with a discharge valve] water plug, fire hydrant, fire plug; see PIPE 1.

plug ***v.*** stop, fill, obstruct, secure, ram, make tight, drive in; see also STOP 2.

plum ***n.*** *Plums and plumlike fruits include the following:* freestone, damson, greengage, Reine Claude, Sugar plum, French prune, Stanley prune; see also FRUIT.

plumber ***n.*** steamfitter, metalworker, handyman; see WORKMAN.

plumbing ***n.*** pipes, water pipes, sewage pipes, heating pipes, bathroom fixtures, sanitary provisions; see also PIPE 1.

plummet ***v.*** plunge, fall, nose-dive; see DIVE, FALL 1.

plump[1] ***a.*** obese, stout, fleshy; see FAT.

plunder ***v.*** burn, steal, lay waste; see RAID, RAVAGE.

plunge ***v.*** fall, throw oneself, rush; see DIVE, JUMP 1.

plural ***a.*** more than one, a number of, abundant; see MANY.

plurality ***n.*** majority, advantage in votes cast, greater amount; see LEAD 1, MAJORITY 1.

plus ***a.***, ***prep.*** added to, additional, additionally, increased by, with the addition of, surplus, positive; see also EXTRA.—*Ant.* LESS, minus, subtracted from.

plush* ***a.*** elegant, luxurious, sumptuous; see RICH 2.

PM or **P.M.** *abbrev.* post meridiem, postmeridian, after noon, afternoon, evening, before midnight, shank of the evening, sunset.

of or containing wind, air, or gases 2 filled with or worked by compressed air

pneu·mo·ni·a (nōō mōn′yə) ***n.*** ⟦< Gr *pneumōn*, lung < *pnein*, breathe⟧ inflammation of the lungs caused as by bacteria or viruses

Po (pō) river in N Italy, flowing from the Alps into the Adriatic

PO *abbrev.* **1** Post Office **2** post office box

poach[1] (pōch) ***vt.*** ⟦< MFr *poche*, pocket: the yolk is "pocketed" in the white⟧ to cook (fish, an egg without its shell, etc.) in or over boiling water

poach[2] (pōch) ***vt., vi.*** ⟦< MHG *puchen*, to plunder⟧ **1** to trespass on (private property), esp. to hunt or fish **2** to hunt or catch (game or fish) illegally **—poach′er *n.***

pock (päk) ***n.*** ⟦OE *pocc*⟧ **1** a pustule caused by smallpox, etc. **2** POCKMARK **—pocked *adj.***

pock·et (päk′it) ***n.*** ⟦< Fr *poque*, a pouch⟧ **1** a little bag or pouch, esp. one sewn into clothing, for carrying small articles **2** a pouchlike cavity or hollow **3** a small area or group *[a pocket of poverty]* **—*adj.*** **1** that can be carried in a pocket **2** small **—*vt.*** **1** to put into a pocket **2** to envelop; enclose **3** to take (money, etc.) dishonestly **4** to suppress *[to pocket one's pride]* **—pock′et·ful′**, *pl.* **-fuls′**, ***n.***

pock′et·book′ ***n.*** **1** a woman's purse or handbag **2** monetary resources

pock′et·knife′ ***n.***, *pl.* **-knives′** a knife with a blade or blades that fold into the handle

pock′mark′ ***n.*** a scar left by a pustule, as of smallpox

pod (päd) ***n.*** ⟦< ?⟧ a dry fruit or seed vessel, as of peas or beans

-pod (päd) ⟦< Gr *pous*, foot⟧ *combining form* **1** foot **2** (one) having (a specified number or kind of) feet Also **-pode** (pōd)

po·di·a·try (pō dī′ə trē) ***n.*** ⟦< Gr *pous*, foot + -IATRY⟧ the profession dealing with the care and treatment of the feet **—po·di′a·trist *n.***

po·di·um (pō′dē əm) ***n.*** ⟦L < Gr *pous*, foot⟧ **1** a small platform, as for an orchestra conductor **2** LECTERN

Poe (pō), **Ed·gar Al·lan** (ed′gər al′ən) 1809-49; U.S. poet & short-story writer

po·em (pō′əm) ***n.*** ⟦< Gr *poiein*, to make⟧ an arrangement of words, esp. a rhythmical composition, sometimes rhymed, in a style more imaginative than ordinary speech or prose

po·e·sy (pō′ə sē′) ***n.*** *old-fashioned var. of* POETRY

po·et (pō′ət) ***n.*** **1** one who writes poems or verses **2** one who displays imaginative power and beauty of thought, language, etc. **—po′et·ess *fem.n.***

po·et·as·ter (pō′ə tas′tər) ***n.*** ⟦< prec. + L *-aster*, dim. suffix⟧ a writer of mediocre verse

po·et·ic (pō et′ik) ***adj.*** **1** of or for poets or poetry **2** displaying the beauty, imaginative qualities, etc. found in good poetry Also **po·et′i·cal *adj.*** **—po·et′i·cal·ly *adv.***

poetic justice justice, as in stories, applied in an especially fitting way

poetic license deviation from strict fact or rules, for artistic effect

poet laureate the official poet of a nation, appointed to write poems celebrating national events, etc.

po·et·ry (pō′ə trē) ***n.*** **1** the art, theory, or structure of poems **2** poems **3** poetic qualities

po·grom (pō′grəm, -gräm′) ***n.*** ⟦< Russ, earlier, riot, storm⟧ an organized massacre, as of Jews in czarist Russia

poi (poi) ***n.*** ⟦Haw⟧ a Hawaiian food that is a paste of taro root

poign·ant (poin′yənt) ***adj.*** ⟦< L *pungere*, to prick⟧ **1** pungent **2** *a)* sharply painful to the feelings *b)* emotionally moving **3** sharp, biting, pointed, etc. **—poign′an·cy *n.***

poin·ci·an·a (poin′sē an′ə) ***n.*** ⟦after M. de *Poinci*, early governor of the Fr West Indies⟧ a small tropical tree or shrub with showy red, orange, or yellow flowers

poin·set·ti·a (poin set′ə, -set′ē ə) ***n.*** ⟦after J. R. *Poinsett*, 19th-c. U.S. ambassador to Mexico⟧ a tropical shrub with yellow flowers and petal-like red leaves

point (point) ***n.*** ⟦< L *pungere*, to prick⟧ **1** a dot in writing, etc. *[a decimal point]* **2** a position or location **3** the exact moment **4** a condition reached *[boiling point]* **5** a detail; item *[point by point]* **6** a distinguishing feature **7** a unit, as of value or game scores **8** a sharp end **9** a projecting piece of land; cape **10** the essential fact or idea *[the point of a joke]* **11** a purpose; object **12** a convincing idea or fact **13** a helpful hint **14** a mark showing direction on a compass **15** *Finance a)* a $1 change in the price of a stock *b)* a unit or amount equal to one percent **16** *Printing* a measuring unit for type, about $\frac{1}{72}$ of an inch **—*vt.*** **1** to sharpen to a point **2** to give (a story, etc.) emphasis: usually with *up* **3** to show: usually with *out [point out the way]* **4** to aim **—*vi.*** **1** to direct

THESAURUS

pneumonia ***n.*** pneumonitis, lung inflammation, lung infection; see ILLNESS 2.

poach[2] ***v.*** filch, pilfer, smuggle; see STEAL.

pock ***n.*** flaw, hole, mark; see BLEMISH, SCAR.

pocket ***a.*** small, tiny, miniature; see LITTLE 1, MINUTE 1.

pocket ***n.*** **1** [A cavity] hollow, opening, air pocket; see HOLE 1. **2** [A pouch sewn into a garment] pouch, bag, sac, pod. *Kinds of pockets include the following:* patch, slash, inset, watch, coin, invisible, pants, jacket, coat, vest, inner, outer, shirt. **3** [Small area] isolated group, enclave, survival; see AREA. **—in someone's pocket*** controlled, under control, regulated; see MANAGED.

pocket ***v.*** conceal, hide, enclose; see STEAL.

pocketbook ***n.*** wallet, pouch, coin purse; see BAG, PURSE.

pod ***n.*** seed vessel, bean pod, pea pod; see SEED.

poem ***n.*** poetry, lyric, sonnet, ballad, verse, quatrain, blank verse, free verse, song, composition, creation; see also WRITING 2.

poet ***n.*** writer, bard, versifier, minstrel, troubadour, maker of verses, lyrist, author of the lyric, dramatic poet, dramatist, lyric poet, writer of lyrics, lyricist, poetaster; see also ARTIST, WRITER. *Major poets include the following—British:* Geoffrey Chaucer, Edmund Spenser, William Shakespeare, John Donne, George Herbert, John Milton, Andrew Marvell, John Dryden, Alexander Pope, Robert Burns, William Blake, William Wordsworth, Samuel Taylor Coleridge, Lord Byron, John Keats, Percy Bysshe Shelley, John Clare, Alfred, Lord Tennyson, Robert Browning, Gerard Manley Hopkins, A.E. Housman, William Butler Yeats, T.S. Eliot, W.H. Auden, Dylan Thomas, Philip Larkin; *American:* Edgar Allan Poe, Walt Whitman, Emily Dickinson, Edwin Arlington Robinson, Robert Frost, Carl Sandburg, Ezra Pound, Wallace Stevens, E.E. Cummings, Robert Lowell, Marianne Moore; *Classical Greek:* Homer, Pindar, Aeschylus, Sophocles, Euripides; *Latin:* Virgil, Lucretius, Ovid, Horace, Catullus, Juvenal, Martial; *European:* Dante Alighieri, Petrarch, Ludovico Ariosto, François Villon, Jean de La Fontaine, Charles Baudelaire, Stéphane Mallarmé, Paul Verlaine, Arthur Rimbaud, Victor Hugo, Pedro Calderón, Federico García Lorca, Pablo Neruda, Luis Vaz de Camões, Wolfgang von Goethe, Friedrich Schiller, Heinrich Heine, Rainer Maria Rilke, Bertolt Brecht, Alexander Pushkin, Aleksandr Blok, Anna Akhmatova, Osip Mandelstam, Vladimir Mayakovski.

poetic ***a.*** poetical, lyric, lyrical, metrical, tuneful, elegiac, romantic, dramatic, iambic, dactylic, spondaic, trochaic, anapestic, imaginative, epic, rhapsodic.

poetry ***n.*** poem, song, versification, metrical composition, rime, rhyme, poesy, stanza, rhythmical composition, poetical writings. *Forms of verse include the following:* sonnet, Shakespearean sonnet, Petrarchan sonnet, Italian sonnet, Miltonic sonnet, Wordsworthian sonnet, Chaucerian stanza, Spenserian stanza, heroic couplet, Alexandrine, iambic pentameter, rhyme royal, ottava rima, couplet, distich, ode, epode, triolet, rondeau, rondel, rondelet, tanka, haiku, ballade, sestine, villanelle, limerick, blank verse, free verse, strophic verse, stanzaic verse, accentual verse, alliterative verse.

pogrom ***n.*** slaughter, mass murder, massacre, genocide; see also MURDER.

point ***n.*** **1** [A position or spot having no measurable extent] location, spot, locality; see POSITION 1. **2** [A sharp, tapered end] end, pointed end, needle point, pinpoint, barb, spur, spike, snag, spine, claw, tooth, calk, sticker; see also TIP 1. **3** [Anything having a point] sword, dagger, stiletto; see KNIFE, NEEDLE. **4** [Purpose] aim, object, intent; see PURPOSE 1. **5** [Meaning] force, drift, import; see MEANING. **6** [A detail] case, feature, point at issue; see CIRCUMSTANCE 1, DETAIL. **—at** (or **on**) **the point of** on the verge of, close to, almost; see NEAR 1. **—beside the point** immaterial, not pertinent, not germane; see IRRELEVANT. **—make a point of** stress, emphasize, make an issue of; see DECLARE. **—to the point** pertinent, apt, exact; see RELEVANT.

point ***v.*** **1** [To indicate] show, designate, denote; see NAME 2. **2** [To direct] guide, steer, influence; see LEAD 1. **—point out** indicate, show, denote; see NAME 2.

one's finger (*at* or *to*) **2** to call attention (*to*) **3** to be directed (*to* or *toward*) —**at the point of** very close to —**beside the point** irrelevant —**to the point** pertinent; apt

point'-blank' ***adj., adv.*** ⟦prec. + *blank* (white center of a target)⟧ **1** (aimed) straight at a mark **2** direct(ly); blunt(ly)

point'ed ***adj.*** **1** having a sharp end **2** sharp; incisive **3** aimed at someone: said as of a remark **4** very evident —**point'ed·ly** ***adv.***

poin·telle (pɑin tel') ***n.*** a lacy, loosely formed fabric, often of acrylic, used for blouses, sweaters, etc.

point'er ***n.*** **1** a long, tapered rod for pointing to things **2** an indicator on a meter, etc. **3** a large, muscular hunting dog with a smooth coat **4** [Inf.] a helpful hint or suggestion

poin·til·lism (pwan'tə liz'əm) ***n.*** ⟦Fr⟧ a style of painting using dots of color that blend together when seen from a distance —**poin'til·list** ***n., adj.***

point'less ***adj.*** **1** without a point **2** without meaning or force; senseless

point man **1** the soldier in the front position in a patrol **2** anyone in the forefront a movement of attacking or supporting a political program, etc.

point of view **1** the way in which something is viewed **2** a mental attitude or opinion

point'y ***adj.*** **-i·er, -i·est** **1** coming to a sharp point **2** many-pointed

poise (pɑiz) ***n.*** ⟦< L *pendere*, weigh⟧ **1** balance; stability **2** ease and dignity of manner **3** carriage, as of the body —***vt., vi.*** **poised, pois'ing** to balance or be balanced

poised ***adj.*** **1** calm; self-assured **2** readied

poi·son (pɑi'zən) ***n.*** ⟦< L *potio*, potion⟧ a substance that can cause illness or death when ingested even in small quantities —***vt.*** **1** to harm or kill with poison **2** to put poison into **3** to influence wrongfully —***adj.*** poisonous

poison ivy a plant having leaves of three leaflets and ivory-colored berries: it can cause a severe rash if touched

poi'son·ous ***adj.*** that can injure or kill by or as by poison —**poi'son·ous·ly** ***adv.***

poison pill any defensive measure which makes the takeover of a corporation prohibitively expensive

poke[1] (pōk) ***vt.*** **poked, pok'ing** ⟦< MDu *poken*⟧ **1** *a)* to prod, as with a stick *b)* [Slang] to hit **2** to make (a hole, etc.) by poking —***vi.*** **1** to jab (*at*) **2** to pry or search (*about* or *around*) **3** to move slowly (*along*) —***n.*** **1** a jab; thrust **2** [Slang] a blow with the fist —**poke fun at** to ridicule

poke[2] (pōk) ***n.*** ⟦OFr⟧ [Dial.] a sack

pok·er[1] (pōk'ər) ***n.*** ⟦< ? Ger *pochspiel*, lit., game of defiance⟧ a card game in which the players bet on the value of their hands

pok·er[2] (pō'kər) ***n.*** a rod, usually of iron, for stirring a fire

poker face an expressionless face, as of a poker player trying to conceal the nature of his or her hand

pok·y (pō'kē) ***adj.*** **-i·er, -i·est** ⟦POKE[1] + -Y[2]⟧ **1** slow, dull, etc. **2** small and uncomfortable [a *poky* room] Also **pok'ey**

pol (päl) ***n.*** [Slang] a politician

Pol *abbrev.* **1** Poland **2** Polish

Po·land (pō'lənd) country in EC Europe, on the Baltic Sea: 120,628 sq. mi.; pop. 38,309,000

po·lar (pō'lər) ***adj.*** **1** of or near the North or South pole **2** of a pole or poles

polar bear a large white bear of coastal arctic regions

Po·la·ris (pō lar'is) ***n.*** the bright star almost directly above the North Pole

po·lar·i·ty (pō lar'ə tē) ***n.***, *pl.* **-ties** **1** the tendency of bodies having opposite magnetic poles to have their ends point to the earth's magnetic poles **2** the tendency to turn, grow, think, etc. in contrary directions, as if because of magnetic repulsion

po·lar·i·za·tion (pō'lə ri zā'shən) ***n.*** **1** a polarizing or being polarized **2** *Optics* the condition of electromagnetic waves in which the motion of the wave is confined to one plane or one direction

po·lar·ize (pō'lə rīz') ***vt.*** **-ized', -iz'ing** to give polarity to —***vi.*** to acquire polarity; specif., to separate into opposed or antagonistic groups, viewpoints, etc.

Po·lar·oid (pō'lə rɑid') *trademark for:* **1** a transparent material capable of polarizing light **2** ⟦< *Polaroid* (*Land Camera*)⟧ *a)* a camera that produces a print within seconds *b)* such a print

pole[1] (pōl) ***n.*** ⟦< L *palus*, a stake⟧ a long, slender piece of wood, metal, etc. —***vt.*** **poled, pol'ing** to push along with a pole

pole[2] (pōl) ***n.*** ⟦< Gr *polos*⟧ **1** either end of any axis, as of the earth's axis **2** either of two opposed forces, parts, etc., as the ends of a magnet or the terminals of a battery

Pole (pōl) ***n.*** a person born or living in Poland

pole·cat (pōl'kat') ***n.*** ⟦prob. < OFr *poule*, hen + CAT⟧ **1** a small Old World weasel **2** SKUNK

po·lem·ic (pō lem'ik) ***adj.*** ⟦< Gr *polemos*, war⟧ of or involving dispute: also **po·lem'i·cal** —***n.*** a controversy

po·lem'ics ***n.*** [*sometimes with pl. v.*] the art or practice of disputation —**po·lem'i·cist** (-i sist) ***n.***

pole'star' Polaris, the North Star: usually **Pole Star** —***n.*** a guiding principle

pole vault a leap for height by jumping over a bar with the aid of a long pole —**pole'-vault'** ***vi.*** —**pole'-vault'er** ***n.***

po·lice (pə lēs') ***n.*** ⟦Fr: ult. < Gr *polis*, city⟧ **1** the governmental department (of a city, state, etc.) for keeping order, detecting crime, etc. **2** [*with pl. v.*] the members of such a department —***vt.*** **-liced', -lic'ing** **1** to control, protect, etc. with police or a similar force **2** to keep (a military camp, etc.) clean and orderly

po·lice'man (-mən) ***n.***, *pl.* **-men** (-mən) a member of a police force —**po·lice'wom'an**, *pl.* **-wom'en**, ***fem.n.***

police officer a member of a police force

THESAURUS

pointed ***a.*** **1** [Sharp] fine, keen, spiked; see SHARP 1. **2** [Biting or insinuating] caustic, tart, trenchant; see SARCASTIC.

pointer ***n.*** **1** [A pointing instrument] hand, rod, wand, baton, indicator, dial, gauge, index, mark, signal needle, register. **2** [A variety of dog] hunting dog, gun dog, game dog; see DOG. **3** [*A hint] clue, tip, warning; see HINT.

pointless ***a.*** **1** [Dull] uninteresting, prosaic, not pertinent; see IRRELEVANT, TRIVIAL, UNNECESSARY. **2** [Blunt] worn, obtuse, rounded; see DULL 1. **3** [Ineffective] useless, powerless, impotent; see INCOMPETENT, WEAK 1, 2.

point of view ***n.*** outlook, position, approach; see ATTITUDE.

poise ***n.*** balance, gravity, equilibrium; see COMPOSURE, DIGNITY.

poison ***n.*** virus, bane, toxin, infection, germ, bacteria, venom, oil, vapor, gas. *Poisons include the following:* rattlesnake, copperhead, black-widow-spider, tarantula venom; smallpox, yellow-fever, common-cold, flu virus; poison oak, poison ivy; carbon monoxide gas, cooking gas; arsenic, lead, strychnine; oxalic, sulfuric, hydrochloric, nitric, carbolic, prussic, hydrocyanic acid; cantharides, caustic soda, lye, belladonna, aconite, lead arsenate, blue vitriol or copper sulfate, nicotine.

poison ***v.*** infect, injure, kill, murder, destroy, corrupt, pervert, undermine, defile, harm, taint, make ill, cause violent illness in.—*Ant.* HELP, benefit, purify.

poisoned ***a.*** **1** [Suffering from poisoning] ill, indisposed, diseased; see SICK. **2** [Dying of poison] expiring, beyond recovery, succumbing; see DYING 1. **3** [Polluted with poison] contaminated, tainted, defiled, corrupted, venomous, virulent, impure, malignant, noxious, deadly, toxic; see also POISONOUS.—*Ant.* PURE, fresh, untainted.

poisonous ***a.*** bad, noxious, hurtful, dangerous, malignant, infective, venomous, virulent, vicious, corrupt, morbid, fatal, pestilential, toxic, deadly, destructive; see also HARMFUL.—*Ant.* HEALTHY, wholesome, nourishing.

poke[1] ***n.*** jab, thrust, punch; see BLOW.

poke[1] ***v.*** jab, punch, crowd; see PUSH 1.

polar ***a.*** glacial, frozen, frigid; see COLD 1.

pole[1] ***n.*** shaft, flagpole, flagstaff; see POST.

police ***n.*** law enforcement body, FBI, police officers, policemen, policewomen, police force, detective force, military police, Royal Canadian Mounted Police, New York's Finest*.

police ***v.*** watch, control, patrol; see GUARD.

police officer ***n.*** patrolman, patrolwoman, policeman, policewoman, officer, magistrate, process server, constable, cop*, copper*, flatfoot*, the fuzz*, the Man*, speed cop*, bobby*, pig*. *Police officers include the following:* beat patrolman, mounted police, motorcycle police, traffic police, squad-car police, municipal police, state police, highway patrol, detective, federal agent, federal investigator, fed*, narc*, FBI agent, prefect, inspector, member of the homicide squad, member of the vice squad.

police state a government that seeks to suppress political opposition by means of police
pol·i·cy[1] (päl′ə sē) ***n.***, *pl.* **-cies** ⟦see POLICE⟧ **1** wise management **2** a principle, plan, etc., as of a government
pol·i·cy[2] (päl′ə sē) ***n.***, *pl.* **-cies** ⟦< Gr *apodeixis*, proof⟧ a written insurance contract: in full **insurance policy**
pol′i·cy·hold′er ***n.*** a person to whom an insurance policy is issued
po·li·o·my·e·li·tis (pō′lē ō mī′ə līt′is) ***n.*** ⟦< Gr *polios*, gray + MYELITIS⟧ an acute infectious disease caused by viral inflammation of the gray matter of the spinal cord, often resulting in muscular paralysis: also **po′li·o′**
pol·ish (päl′ish) ***vt.*** ⟦< L *polire*⟧ **1** to smooth and brighten, as by rubbing **2** to refine (manners, style, etc.) —***vi.*** to take a polish —***n.*** **1** a surface gloss **2** elegance, refinement, etc. **3** a substance used to polish —**polish off** [Inf.] to finish (a meal, job, etc.) completely
Pol·ish (pōl′ish) ***adj.*** of Poland or its people, language, etc. —***n.*** the Slavic language of Poland
po·lite (pə līt′) ***adj.*** ⟦< L *polire*, to polish⟧ **1** cultured; refined **2** courteous; mannerly —**po·lite′ly** ***adv.*** —**po·lite′ness** ***n.***
pol·i·tesse (päl′i tes′) ***n.*** ⟦Fr⟧ politeness
pol·i·tic (päl′ə tik′) ***adj.*** ⟦see POLICE⟧ **1** having practical wisdom; prudent **2** expedient: said as of a plan —***vi.*** **-ticked′**, **-tick′ing** to campaign in politics
po·lit·i·cal (pə lit′i kəl) ***adj.*** **1** of, concerned with, or engaged in government, politics, etc. **2** of or characteristic of political parties or politicians —**po·lit′i·cal·ly** ***adv.***
politically correct holding orthodox liberal political views: usually used disparagingly to connote dogmatism, etc. —**political correctness**
political science the science of the principles, organization, and methods of government —**political scientist**
pol·i·ti·cian (päl′ə tish′ən) ***n.*** one actively engaged in politics: often used with implications of seeking personal or partisan gain, scheming, etc.
po·lit·i·cize (pə lit′ə sīz′) ***vt.*** **-cized′**, **-ciz′ing** to make political in tone, character, etc.
po·lit·i·co (pə lit′ə kō′) ***n.***, *pl.* **-cos′** ⟦< Sp or It⟧ POLITICIAN
pol·i·tics (päl′ə tiks) ***pl.n.*** [*with sing. or pl. v.*] **1** the science and art of government **2** political affairs **3** political methods, tactics, etc. **4** political opinions, etc. **5** factional scheming for power
pol′i·ty (-ə tē) ***n.***, *pl.* **-ties** ⟦see POLICE⟧ **1** governmental organization **2** a society with a government; state
Polk (pōk), **James K.** 1795-1849; 11th president of the U.S. (1845-49)
pol·ka (pōl′kə) ***n.*** ⟦Czech, Polish dance⟧ **1** a fast dance for couples **2** music for this
pol·ka dot (pō′kə, pōl′kə) any of a regular pattern of small, round dots on cloth
poll (pōl) ***n.*** ⟦ME *pol*⟧ **1** the head **2** a counting, listing, etc. of persons, esp. of voters **3** the number of votes recorded **4** [*pl.*] a place where votes are cast **5** a canvassing of people's opinions on some question —***vt.*** **1** to register the votes of **2** to require each member of (a jury, etc.) to declare individual votes **3** to receive (a specified number of votes) **4** to cast (a vote) **5** to canvass in a POLL (sense 5)
pol·len (päl′ən) ***n.*** ⟦L, dust⟧ the fine, dustlike mass of grains in the anthers of seed plants
pollen count the number of grains of pollen, esp. of ragweed, in a given volume of air at a specified time and place
pol·li·nate (päl′ə nāt′) ***vt.*** **-nat′ed**, **-nat′ing** to transfer pollen to the pistil of (a flower) —**pol′li·na′tion** ***n.*** —**pol′li·na′tor** ***n.***
pol·li·wog (päl′ē wäg′, -wôg′) ***n.*** ⟦< ME: see POLL + WIGGLE⟧ TADPOLE: also **pol′ly·wog′**
poll·ster (pōl′stər) ***n.*** one whose work is taking public-opinion polls
pol·lute (pə lo͞ot′) ***vt.*** **-lut′ed**, **-lut′ing** ⟦< L *polluere*⟧ to make unclean or impure —**pol·lu′tant** ***n.*** —**pol·lu′tion** ***n.***
Pol·ly·an·na (päl′ē an′ə) ***n.*** ⟦after the young heroine of a novel (1913) by E. H. Porter⟧ an excessively optimistic person
po·lo (pō′lō) ***n.*** ⟦ult. < Tibetan *pulu*, ball⟧ a game played on horseback by two teams, using a wooden ball and long-handled mallets
Po·lo (pō′lō), **Mar·co** (mär′kō) 1254-1324; Venetian traveler in E Asia
pol·o·naise (päl′ə nāz′) ***n.*** ⟦Fr (fem.), Polish⟧ a stately Polish dance
pol·ter·geist (pōl′tər gīst′) ***n.*** ⟦Ger < *poltern*, to rumble + *geist*, ghost⟧ a ghost supposed to be responsible for mysterious noisy disturbances
pol·troon (päl tro͞on′) ***n.*** ⟦< It *poltrone*⟧ a thorough coward
poly- ⟦< Gr⟧ *combining form* much, many
pol·y·clin·ic (päl′i klin′ik) ***n.*** ⟦POLY- + CLINIC⟧ a clinic or hospital for the treatment of various kinds of diseases
pol·y·es·ter (päl′ē es′tər) ***n.*** ⟦POLY(MER) + ESTER⟧ a polymeric resin used in making plastics, fibers, etc.
pol·y·eth·yl·ene (päl′ē eth′ə lēn′) ***n.*** ⟦POLY(MER) + ETHYLENE⟧ a thermoplastic resin used in making plastics, films, etc.
po·lyg·a·my (pə lig′ə mē) ***n.*** ⟦< Gr *poly-*, many + *gamos*, marriage⟧ the practice of having two or more spouses at the same time —**po·lyg′a·mist** ***n.*** —**po·lyg′a·mous** ***adj.***
pol·y·glot (päl′i glät′) ***adj.*** ⟦< Gr *poly-*, many + *glōtta*, tongue⟧ **1** knowing several languages **2** written in several languages —***n.*** a polyglot person
pol′y·gon′ (-gän′) ***n.*** ⟦< Gr: see POLY- & -GON⟧ a closed plane figure consisting of straight lines —**po·lyg·o·nal** (pə lig′ə nəl) ***adj.***
pol′y·graph′ (-graf′) ***n.*** ⟦see POLY- & -GRAPH⟧ a device measuring changes in respiration, pulse rate, etc.: see LIE DETECTOR
pol′y·he′dron (-hē′drən) ***n.*** ⟦< Gr: see POLY- & -HEDRON⟧ a solid figure with usually more than six plane surfaces
pol′y·math′ (-ə math′) ***n.*** ⟦< Gr *poly-*, much + *manthanein*, learn⟧ a person of great and varied learning
pol′y·mer (-mər) ***n.*** ⟦Ger < Gr *poly-*, many + *meros*, part⟧ a substance consisting of giant molecules formed from polymerization —**pol′y·mer′ic** (-mer′ik) ***adj.***

THESAURUS

police state ***n.*** dictatorship, autocracy, authoritarian government; see TYRANNY.
policy[1] ***n.*** course, procedure, method, system, strategy, tactics, administration, management, theory, doctrine, behavior, scheme, design, arrangement, organization, plan, order.
polish ***n.*** shine, burnish, glaze; see FINISH 2.
polish ***v.*** buff, burnish, finish; see SHINE 3.
polished ***a.*** **1** [Bright] glossy, shining, gleaming; see BRIGHT 1. **2** [Refined] polite, well-bred, cultured; see REFINED 2.
polite ***a.*** obliging, thoughtful, mannerly, attentive, pleasant, gentle, mild, nice, concerned, considerate, solicitous, bland, condescending, honey-tongued, amiable, gracious, cordial, considerate, good-natured, sympathetic, interested, smooth, diplomatic, kindly, kind, kindly disposed, affable, agreeable, civil, ladylike, respectful, amenable, gallant, genteel, gentlemanly, mannered, sociable, ingratiating, neighborly, friendly, respectful.—*Ant.* EGOTISTIC, insolent, pompous.
politely ***a.*** thoughtfully, considerately, attentively, solicitously, cordially, graciously, kindheartedly, amiably, compassionately, gently, urbanely, affably, agreeably, civilly, gallantly, sociably, elegantly, gracefully, charmingly, ingratiatingly, winningly, tactfully, in good humor, with good grace; see also RESPECTFULLY.
politeness ***n.*** refinement, culture, civility; see COURTESY 1.
political ***a.*** legislative, executive, administrative; see GOVERNMENTAL.
politician ***n.*** officeholder, office seeker, party member, partisan, legislator, congressman, member of parliament, politico.
politics ***n.*** practical government, functional government, statesmanship, diplomacy, domestic affairs, internal affairs, foreign affairs, matters of state, campaigning, getting votes, seeking nomination, electioneering, being up for election, running for office.
poll ***n.*** **1** [A census] vote, consensus, ballot; see CENSUS. **2** [A voting place; *usually plural*] ballot box, voting machines, polling place, polling area.
poll ***v.*** question, register, survey; see EXAMINE, LIST 1.
pollute ***v.*** contaminate, soil, stain; see DIRTY, POISON.
polluted ***a.*** corrupted, defiled, poisoned; see DIRTY 1.
pollution ***n.*** corruption, defilement, adulteration, blight, soiling, fouling, foulness, taint, tainting, polluting, decomposition, desecration, profanation, abuse, deterioration, rottenness, impairment, misuse, infection, besmearing, besmirching, smirching. *Some common pollutants of the air and water include the following:* sewage, soapsuds, garbage, factory waste, detergent, carbon monoxide, automobile or bus or truck exhaust, pesticides, factory smoke.
poltergeist ***n.*** spirit, spook, supernatural visitant; see GHOST.
polygamy ***n.*** polyandry, plural marriage, polygyny; see MARRIAGE.

po·lym·er·i·za·tion (pō lim′ər ə zā′shən) ***n.*** a chaining together of many simple molecules to form a more complex molecule with different properties —**po·lym′er·ize′** (-īz′), **-ized′**, **-iz′ing**, ***vt.***, ***vi.***

Pol·y·ne·sia (päl′i nē′zhə) group of Pacific islands, east of Micronesia, including Hawaii, etc. —**Pol′y·ne′sian** ***adj.***, ***n.***

pol·y·no·mi·al (päl′i nō′mē əl) ***n.*** ⟦POLY- + (BI)NOMIAL⟧ a mathematical expression containing three or more terms (Ex: $x^3 + 3x + 2$)

pol·yp (päl′ip) ***n.*** ⟦< Gr *poly-*, many + *pous*, foot⟧ **1** a cnidarian with many small tentacles at the top of a tubelike body **2** a growth of mucous membrane in the bladder, rectum, etc.

po·lyph·o·ny (pə lif′ə nē) ***n.*** ⟦< Gr *poly-*, many + *phōnē*, a sound⟧ *Music* a combining of independent, harmonizing melodies, as in a fugue; counterpoint —**pol·y·phon·ic** (päl′i fän′ik) ***adj.*** —**pol′y·phon′i·cal·ly** ***adv.***

pol·y·rhythm (päl′i rith′əm) ***n.*** *Music* **1** the simultaneous use of strongly contrasting rhythms **2** such a rhythm: *usually used in pl.* —**pol′y·rhyth′mic** ***adj.***

pol′y·sty′rene′ (-stī′rēn′) ***n.*** ⟦POLY(MER) + *styrene*, an organic compound⟧ a clear polymer used to make containers, etc.

pol·y·syl·lab·ic (päl′i si lab′ik) ***adj.*** **1** having four or more syllables **2** characterized by polysyllabic words —**pol′y·syl′la·ble** (-sil′ə bəl) ***n.***

pol′y·tech′nic (-tek′nik) ***n.***, ***adj.*** ⟦< Gr *poly-*, many + *technē*, art⟧ (school) providing instruction in many scientific and technical subjects

pol′y·the·ism′ (-thē iz′əm) ***n.*** ⟦< Gr *poly*, many + *theos*, god⟧ belief in more than one god —**pol′y·the·ist** ***adj.***, ***n.*** —**pol′y·the·is′tic** ***adj.***

pol·y·un·sat·u·rat·ed (päl′ē un sach′ə rāt′id) ***adj.*** designating any of certain vegetable and animal fats and oils with a low cholesterol content

pol′y·u·re·thane′ (-yoor′ə thān′) ***n.*** ⟦POLY- + URETHANE⟧ any of various synthetic polymers, used in cushions, coatings, etc.

pol·y·vi·nyl (päl′i vī′nəl) ***adj.*** designating or of any of a group of polymerized vinyl compounds

po·made (päm ād′, pō-) ***n.*** ⟦< It *pomo*, apple (orig. an ingredient)⟧ a perfumed ointment, as for the hair

pome·gran·ate (päm′gran′it, päm′ə-) ***n.*** ⟦ult. < L *pomum*, fruit + *granum*, seed⟧ **1** a round, red fruit with a hard rind and many seeds **2** the bush or tree it grows on

pom·mel (päm′əl; *for v.* pum′əl) ***n.*** ⟦< L *pomum*, fruit⟧ **1** the knob on the end of the hilt of some swords and daggers **2** the rounded, upward-projecting part at the front of a saddle —***vt.*** **-meled** or **-melled**, **-mel·ing** or **-mel·ling** PUMMEL

pomp (pämp) ***n.*** ⟦< Gr *pompē*, solemn procession⟧ **1** stately display **2** ostentatious show or display

pom·pa·dour (päm′pə dôr′) ***n.*** ⟦after Mme. *Pompadour*, mistress of Louis XV⟧ a hairdo in which the hair is brushed up high from the forehead

pom·pa·no (päm′pə nō′) ***n.***, *pl.* **-no′** or **-nos′** ⟦< Sp⟧ a food fish of North America and the West Indies

pom·pom (päm′päm′) ***n.*** ⟦see POMP⟧ an ornamental tuft of silk, etc., used on clothing, etc. or waved as by a cheerleader: also **pom′pon′** (-pän′)

pom·pous (päm′pəs) ***adj.*** pretentious; self-important —**pom·pos′i·ty** (-päs′ə tē) ***n.***

pon·cho (pän′chō) ***n.***, *pl.* **-chos** ⟦AmSp < AmInd, woolen cloth⟧ a cloak like a blanket with a hole in the middle for the head, esp. a waterproof one worn as a raincoat

pond (pänd) ***n.*** ⟦< ME *pounde*, enclosure⟧ a body of water smaller than a lake

pon·der (pän′dər) ***vt.***, ***vi.*** ⟦< L *ponderare*, weigh⟧ to think deeply (about); consider carefully

pon·der·o·sa (pine) (pän′dər ō′sə) ⟦< L *ponderosus*, very heavy⟧ a yellow pine of W North America

pon′der·ous ***adj.*** **1** very heavy **2** unwieldy **3** labored and dull

pone (pōn) ***n.*** ⟦< AmInd⟧ [Chiefly South] corn bread in the form of small ovals

pon·gee (pän jē′, pun-) ***n.*** ⟦< Mandarin Chin dial. *pen-chi*, one's own loom⟧ a soft, thin silk cloth, usually left in its natural light-brown color

pon·iard (pän′yərd) ***n.*** ⟦ult. < L *pugnus*, fist⟧ a dagger

pon·tiff (pänt′if) ***n.*** ⟦< L *pontifex*, high priest⟧ **1** a bishop **2** [P-] the pope

pon·tif·i·cal (pän tif′i kəl) ***adj.*** ⟦see prec.⟧ **1** having to do with a bishop, the pope, etc. **2** pompous, dogmatic, etc.

pon·tif′i·cate (-i kit; *for v.*, -kāt′) ***n.*** the office or term of a pontiff —***vi.*** **-cat′ed**, **-cat′ing** **1** to officiate as a pontiff **2** to be pompous or dogmatic

pon·toon (pän to͞on′) ***n.*** ⟦< L *pons*, a bridge⟧ **1** a flat-bottomed boat **2** any of a row of boats or floating objects used to support a temporary bridge **3** a float on an aircraft's landing gear

po·ny (pō′nē) ***n.***, *pl.* **-nies** ⟦prob. < L *pullus*, foal⟧ **1** a horse of any small breed **2** a small liqueur glass **3** [Inf.] a literal translation of a foreign work, used in doing schoolwork

po′ny·tail′ ***n.*** a hair style in which the hair is tied tightly at the back and hangs down

pooch (po͞och) ***n.*** ⟦< ?⟧ [Slang] a dog

poo·dle (po͞od′'l) ***n.*** ⟦Ger *pudel*⟧ a dog with a thick, wiry coat of tight curls in a solid color

pooh (po͞o) ***interj.*** used to express disdain, disbelief, or impatience

pooh-pooh (po͞o′po͞o′) ***vt.*** to treat disdainfully; make light of

pool[1] (po͞ol) ***n.*** ⟦OE *pol*⟧ **1** a small pond **2** a small collection of liquid, as a puddle **3** a tank for swimming

pool[2] (po͞ol) ***n.*** ⟦< LL *pulla*, hen⟧ **1** a game related to billiards, played on a table with six pockets **2** a combination of resources, funds, supplies, etc. for some common purpose **3** the parties forming such a combination —***vt.***, ***vi.*** to contribute to a common fund

poop[1] (po͞op) ***n.*** ⟦< L *puppis*, stern of a ship⟧ a raised deck at the stern of a sailing ship: also **poop deck**

poop[2] (po͞op) ***vt*** [Slang] to tire

poop[3] (po͞op) ***n.*** [Slang] current inside information

poor (poor) ***adj.*** ⟦< L *pauper*, poor⟧ **1** having little or no means to support oneself; needy **2** lacking in some quality; specif., *a)* inadequate *b)* inferior or worthless *c)* contemptible **3** worthy of pity; unfortunate —**the poor** poor, or needy, people —**poor′ly** ***adv.***

THESAURUS

pomp ***n.*** grandeur, affectation, splendor; see MAGNIFICENCE.

pompous ***a.*** arrogant, haughty, proud; see EGOTISTIC.

pond ***n.*** fishpond, millpond, lily pond; see LAKE, POOL 1.

ponder ***v.*** meditate, deliberate, consider; see THINK 1.

ponderous ***a.*** dull, weighty, lifeless; see HEAVY.

pony ***n.*** Shetland pony, bronco, mustang; see HORSE.

poodle ***n.*** French poodle, show dog, fancy dog; see DOG.

pool[1,2] ***n.*** **1** [Small body of liquid, usually water] puddle, mud puddle, pond, fishpond, millpond, swimming pool; see also LAKE. **2** [Supply] resources, supplies, amount available; see FUNDS. **3** [Game] snooker, eight ball, billiards; see GAME 1.

pool[2] ***v.*** combine, merge, blend; see JOIN 1.

poor ***a.*** **1** [Lacking worldly goods] indigent, penniless, moneyless, homeless, impecunious, destitute, needy, poverty-stricken, underprivileged, fortuneless, starved, pinched, reduced, beggared, empty-handed, meager, scanty, insolvent, ill-provided, ill-furnished, in want, suffering privation, in need, poor as a church mouse*, broke*, hard up*, down and out.— *Ant.* WEALTHY, well-to-do, affluent. **2** [Lacking excellence] pitiful, paltry, contemptible, miserable, pitiable, dwarfed, insignificant, diminutive, ordinary, common, mediocre, trashy, shoddy, worthless, sorry, base, mean, coarse, vulgar, inferior, imperfect, smaller, lesser, below par, subnormal, below average; second-rate, third-rate, fourth-rate, etc.; reduced, defective, deficient, lower, subordinate, minor, secondary, humble, secondhand, pedestrian, beggarly, tawdry, petty, unimportant, bad, cheap, flimsy, threadbare, badly made, less than good, unwholesome, lacking in quality, dowdy, second-class, shabby, gaudy, mass-produced, squalid, trivial, sleazy, trifling, unsuccessful, second-best, tasteless, insipid, rustic, crude, odd, rock-bottom, garish, flashy, showy, loud, unsightly, affected, ramshackle, tumbledown, glaring, artificial, newfangled, out-of-date, crummy*, junky*, two-bit*, raunchy*, corny*, cheesy*; see also INADEQUATE, UNSATISFACTORY. **3** [Lacking strength] puny, feeble, infirm; see WEAK 1. **4** [Lacking vigor or health] indisposed, impaired, imperfect; see SICK. **5** [Lacking fertility] infertile, unproductive, barren; see STERILE 1, 2, WORTHLESS.

poor ***n.*** the needy, forgotten man, the unemployed, the homeless, underdogs, the underprivileged, beggars, paupers, the impoverished masses, second-class citizen, have-nots; see also PEOPLE 3.

poorly ***a.*** defectively, crudely, unsuccessfully; see BADLY 1, INADEQUATELY.

poor'house' *n.* [Historical] a publicly supported institution for paupers

poor'-mouth' *vi.* [Inf.] to complain about one's lack of money

pop[1] (päp) *n.* ⟦echoic⟧ **1** a sudden, light explosive sound **2** any carbonated, nonalcoholic beverage —*vi.* **popped, pop'ping 1** to make, or burst with, a pop **2** to move, go, etc. suddenly **3** to open wide or bulge: said of the eyes **4** *Baseball* to hit the ball high into the infield —*vt.* **1** to cause to pop, as corn by heating it **2** to put suddenly [to *pop* one's head in] **3** [Slang] to swallow (a pill, etc.) — **pop'per** *n.*

pop[2] (päp) *n.* ⟦< PAPA⟧ [Inf.] FATHER

pop[3] (päp) *adj.* **1** of music popular with the general public **2** intended for the popular taste, esp. as exploited commercially [*pop* culture] **3** of a realistic art style using techniques and subjects adapted from commercial art, comic strips, posters, etc. —*n.* pop music, etc.

pop *abbrev.* **1** popular **2** popularly **3** population

pop'corn' *n.* **1** a variety of corn with hard grains that pop open into a white, puffy mass when heated **2** the popped grains

pope (pōp) *n.* ⟦< Gr *pappas*, father⟧ [*often* **P-**] *R.C.Ch.* the bishop of Rome and head of the Church

Pope (pōp), **Alexander** 1688-1744; Eng. poet

pop'gun' *n.* a toy gun that shoots a piece of cork, etc. by air compression, with a pop

pop·in·jay (päp'in jā') *n.* ⟦< Ar *babghā'*, a parrot⟧ a conceited person

pop·lar (päp'lər) *n.* ⟦< L *populus*⟧ **1** a tall tree of the willow family having soft wood **2** its wood

pop·lin (päp'lin) *n.* ⟦prob. after *Poperinge*, city in Flanders⟧ a sturdy ribbed fabric of cotton, silk, etc.

pop'o'ver *n.* a very light, puffy, hollow muffin

pop·py (päp'ē) *n., pl.* **-pies** ⟦< L *papaver*⟧ **1** a plant with a milky juice and variously colored flowers **2** its flower

pop'py·cock' (-käk') *n.* [Inf.] foolish talk; nonsense

poppy seed the small, dark seed of the poppy, used in baking, etc.

pops (päps) *adj.* of a symphony orchestra that plays light classical music or arrangements of popular music —*n.* a pops orchestra, concert, etc.

Pop·si·cle (päp'si kəl) ⟦blend of POP[1] + I(CICLE)⟧ *trademark for* a flavored ice frozen around a stick —*n.* [*also* **p-**] such a confection

pop-top (päp'täp') *n.* a container with a tab or ring pulled or pushed to make an opening in the top

pop·u·lace (päp'yə lis) *n.* ⟦< L *populus*⟧ **1** the common people; the masses **2** POPULATION (sense 1*a*)

pop·u·lar (päp'yə lər) *adj.* ⟦< L *populus*, the people⟧ **1** of, carried on by, or intended for people generally **2** not expensive [*popular* prices] **3** commonly accepted; prevalent **4** liked by many people —**pop'u·lar'i·ty** (-lar'ə tē) *n.* —**pop'u·lar·ly** *adv.*

pop·u·lar·ize (päp'yə lə rīz') *vt.* **-ized', -iz'ing** to make popular —**pop'u·lar·i·za'tion** *n.*

pop·u·late (päp'yə lāt') *vt.* **-lat'ed, -lat'ing** ⟦< L *populus*, the people⟧ **1** to inhabit **2** to supply with inhabitants

pop'u·la'tion *n.* **1** *a*) all the people in a country, region, etc. *b*) the number of these **2** a populating or being populated

population explosion the great and rapid increase in human population in modern times

pop·u·list (päp'yə list) *n.* a politician, etc. who claims to represent the common people: often used to suggest demagogy —*adj.* of a populist —**pop'u·lism'** *n.*

pop'u·lous (-ləs) *adj.* full of people; thickly populated

por·ce·lain (pôr'sə lin) *n.* ⟦< It *porcellana*⟧ a hard, white, translucent variety of ceramic ware

porch (pôrch) *n.* ⟦< L *porta*, gate⟧ **1** a covered entrance to a building **2** an open or enclosed gallery or room on the outside of a building

por·cine (pôr'sīn', -sin) *adj.* ⟦< L *porcus*, hog⟧ of or like pigs or hogs

por·cu·pine (pôr'kyə pīn') *n.* ⟦< L *porcus*, pig + *spina*, spine⟧ a rodent having coarse hair mixed with long, stiff, sharp spines

pore[1] (pôr) *vi.* **pored, por'ing** ⟦ME *poren*⟧ **1** to study carefully: with *over* **2** to ponder: with *over*

pore[2] (pôr) *n.* ⟦< Gr *poros*, passage⟧ a tiny opening, as in skin or plant leaves, for absorbing or discharging fluids

pork (pôrk) *n.* ⟦< L *porcus*, pig⟧ the flesh of a pig, used as food

pork barrel [Inf.] government appropriations for political patronage

pork'y *adj.* **-i·er, -i·est 1** of or like pork **2** fat **3** [Slang] saucy, cocky, etc.

porn (pôrn) *n., adj.* [Slang] *short for* PORNOGRAPHY, PORNOGRAPHIC: also **por·no** (pôr'nō)

por·nog·ra·phy (pôr näg'rə fē) *n.* ⟦< Gr *pornē*, a prostitute + *graphein*, write⟧ writings, pictures, etc. intended to arouse sexual desire —**por·nog'ra·pher** *n.* —**por'no·graph'ic** (-nə graf'ik) *adj.*

po·rous (pôr'əs) *adj.* full of pores, through which fluids, air, or light may pass —**po·ros·i·ty** (pō räs'ə tē) *n.*

por·phy·ry (pôr'fə rē) *n., pl.* **-ries** ⟦< Gr *porphyros*, purple⟧ any igneous rock with large, distinct crystals

por·poise (pôr'pəs) *n.* ⟦< L *porcus*, pig + *piscis*, a fish⟧ **1** a small whale with a blunt snout **2** a dolphin

por·ridge (pôr'ij) *n.* ⟦< POTTAGE by confusion with VL *porrata*, leek broth⟧ [Chiefly Brit.] a soft food of cereal or meal boiled in water or milk

por'rin·ger (-in jər) *n.* ⟦< Fr *potager*, soup dish: infl. by prec.⟧ a small, shallow bowl

port[1] (pôrt) *n.* ⟦< L *portus*, haven⟧ **1** a harbor **2** a city with a harbor where ships load and unload cargo

port[2] (pôrt) *n.* ⟦after *Oporto*, city in Portugal⟧ a sweet, dark-red wine

port[3] (pôrt) *vt.* ⟦< L *portare*, carry⟧ to hold (a rifle, etc.) diagonally in front of one, as for inspection

port[4] (pôrt) *n.* ⟦< PORT[1]⟧ the left side of a ship, etc. as one faces forward —*adj.* of or on this side

port[5] (pôrt) *n.* ⟦< L *porta*, door⟧ **1** PORTHOLE **2** an opening, as in a valve face, for the passage of steam, etc. **3** *Comput.* the circuit, outlet, etc. which connects a computer and its peripheral

Port *abbrev.* **1** Portugal **2** Portuguese

port·a·ble (pôr'tə bəl) *adj.* ⟦< L *portare*, carry⟧ **1** that can be carried **2** easily carried —*n.* something portable — **port'a·bil'i·ty** *n.*

por·tage (pôr'tij, pôr täzh') *n.* ⟦< L *portare*, carry⟧ **1** a carrying of boats and supplies overland between navigable lakes, rivers, etc. **2** any route over which this is done —*vt., vi.* **-taged, -tag·ing** to carry (boats, etc.) over a portage

por·tal (pôrt''l) *n.* ⟦< L *porta*, door⟧ a doorway, gate, or entrance

THESAURUS

pop[1] *n.* **1** [A slight explosive sound] report, burst, shot; see NOISE 1. **2** [A carbonated drink] soda pop, ginger ale, cola, tonic, root beer, soda, soda water, beverage, soft drink; see also DRINK 2.

pop[1] *v.* dart, leap, protrude; see JUMP 1.

Pope *n.* Pontiff, bishop of Rome, the Holy Father; see PRIEST.

poppy *n.* bloom, blossom, herb; see DRUG, FLOWER.

populace *n.* masses, citizenry, multitude; see MAN 1, PEOPLE 3.

popular *a.* **1** [Generally liked] favorite, well-liked, approved, pleasing, suitable, well-received, fashionable, stylish, beloved, likable, lovable, attractive, praised, promoted, recommended, in the public eye, celebrated, noted, admired, famous, run after*.—*Ant.* UNKNOWN, in disrepute, out of favor. **2** [Cheap] low-priced, inexpensive, marked down; see CHEAP 1, ECONOMICAL 2. **3** [Commonly accepted] general, familiar, in demand, prevalent, prevailing, current, in use, widespread, ordinary, adopted, embraced, having caught on, in the majority; see also FASHIONABLE, MODERN 1. **4** [Pertaining to the common people] proletarian, accessible, neighborly; see DEMOCRATIC, REPUBLICAN.

popularity *n.* approval, general esteem, widespread acceptance, following, prevalence, universality, repute, fame, demand, fashionableness, the rage*.

popularly *a.* commonly, usually, ordinarily; see REGULARLY.

populated *a.* crowded, teeming, populous, peopled, urban, occupied, filled; see also INHABITED.

population *n.* inhabitants, dwellers, citizenry, natives, group, residents, culture, community, state, populace; see also SOCIETY 2.

porch *n.* entrance, doorstep, stoop; see ENTRANCE 2.

pore[2] *n.* opening, foramen, orifice, vesicle; see also HOLE 1.

pork *n.* ham, bacon, chops; see MEAT.

pornographic *a.* immoral, dirty, obscene; see LEWD 2.

pornography *n.* vulgarity, obscenity, smut; see LEWDNESS.

porous *a.* pervious, permeable, acceptable; see OPEN 1.

port[1] *n.* haven, anchorage, gate; see DOCK.

portable *a.* transportable, transferable, compact; see MOVABLE.

portal *n.* gateway, opening, ingress; see DOOR, ENTRANCE 2, GATE.

port·cul·lis (pôrt kul′is) ***n.*** ⟦< MFr *porte*, gate + *coleïce*, sliding⟧ a heavy iron grating lowered to bar the gateway of a castle or fortified town

por·tend (pôr tend′) ***vt.*** ⟦< L *por-*, forth + *tendere*, to stretch⟧ **1** to be an omen of; presage **2** to signify

por·tent (pôr′tent′) ***n.*** **1** something that portends an event **2** significance

por·ten·tous (pôr ten′təs) ***adj.*** **1** portending evil; ominous **2** amazing **3** pompous; self-important —**por·ten′tous·ly** ***adv.***

por·ter[1] (pôr′tər) ***n.*** ⟦< L *porta*, gate⟧ a doorman or gatekeeper

por·ter[2] (pôr′tər) ***n.*** ⟦< L *portare*, carry⟧ **1** one who carries luggage, etc. for hire **2** an employee who sweeps, cleans, etc. in a bank, store, etc. **3** a railroad attendant for passengers as on a sleeper **4** a dark-brown beer

por′ter·house′ ***n.*** ⟦orig. a tavern: see PORTER[2], sense 4⟧ a choice cut of beef next to the sirloin: in full **porterhouse steak**

port·fo·li·o (pôrt fō′lē ō′) ***n.***, *pl.* **-li·os′** ⟦< L *portare*, carry + *folium*, leaf⟧ **1** a flat, portable case, for loose papers; briefcase **2** the office of a minister of state **3** a list of an investor's securities **4** a selection from an artist's, etc. work

port·hole (pôrt′hōl′) ***n.*** an opening in a ship's side to admit light and air

por·ti·co (pôr′ti kō′) ***n.***, *pl.* **-coes′** or **-cos′** ⟦< L *porticus*, porch⟧ a porch or covered walk, consisting of a roof supported by columns

por·tiere or **por·tière** (pôr tyer′) ***n.*** ⟦Fr < *porte*, door⟧ a curtain hung in a doorway

por′tion (-shən) ***n.*** ⟦< L *portio*⟧ **1** a part, esp. that allotted to a person; share **2** one's fate **3** a helping of food —***vt.*** to give out in portions

Port·land (pôrt′lənd) city & port in NW Oregon: pop. 439,000

port·ly (pôrt′lē) ***adj.*** **-li·er, -li·est** **1** large and stately **2** stout; corpulent —**port′li·ness** ***n.***

port·man·teau (pôrt man′tō) ***n.***, *pl.* **-teaus** or **-teaux** (-tōz) ⟦< Fr *porter*, carry + *manteau*, cloak⟧ a stiff suitcase that opens into two compartments

portmanteau word a word that is a combination of two other words (Ex.: *smog*, from *smoke* and *fog*)

por·to·bel·lo mushroom (pôr′tə bel′ō) a dark, flavorful mushroom with a broad cap: also **portobello** ***n.***, *pl.* **-los**

port of entry a place where customs officials check people and goods entering a country

Por·to Ri·co (pôr′tə rē′kō) *former var. of* PUERTO RICO —**Por′to Ri′can**

por·trait (pôr′trit, -trāt′) ***n.*** ⟦see PORTRAY⟧ **1** a painting, photograph, etc. of a person, esp. of the face **2** a description, portrayal, etc.

por′trai·ture (-tri chər) ***n.*** the practice or art of portraying

por·tray (pôr trā′) ***vt.*** ⟦< L *pro-*, forth + *trahere*, draw⟧ **1** to make a portrait of **2** to describe graphically **3** to play the part of as in a play or movie —**por·tray′al** ***n.***

Por·tu·gal (pôr′chə gəl) country in SW Europe, on the Atlantic: 35,456 sq. mi.; pop. 9,863,000

Por·tu·guese (pôr′chə gēz′, -gēs′) ***adj.*** of Portugal or its people, language, etc. —***n.*** **1** *pl.* **-guese′** a person born or living in Portugal **2** a Romance language of Portugal and Brazil

por·tu·lac·a (pôr′chə lak′ə) ***n.*** ⟦< L *portula*, small door: from the opening in its seed capsule⟧ a fleshy plant with yellow, pink, or purple flowers

pose (pōz) ***vt.*** **posed, pos′ing** ⟦< L *pausare*, to stop⟧ **1** to propose (a question, etc.) **2** to put (a model, etc.) in a certain attitude —***vi.*** **1** to assume a certain attitude, as in modeling for an artist **2** to strike attitudes for effect **3** set oneself up (*as*) *[to pose as an officer]* —***n.*** **1** a bodily attitude, esp. one held for an artist, etc. **2** a way of behaving assumed for effect

Po·sei·don (pō sī′dən) ***n.*** the Greek god of the sea

pos·er (pō′zər) ***n.*** one who poses; esp., a poseur

po·seur (pō zʉr′) ***n.*** ⟦Fr⟧ one who assumes attitudes or manners merely for effect

posh (päsh) ***adj.*** ⟦< ?⟧ [Inf.] luxurious and fashionable

pos·it (päz′it) ***vt.*** ⟦see fol.⟧ to suppose to be a fact; postulate

po·si·tion (pə zish′ən) ***n.*** ⟦< L *ponere*, to place⟧ **1** the way in which a person or thing is placed or arranged **2** one's attitude or opinion **3** the place where one is; location **4** the usual or proper place **5** rank, esp. high rank **6** a post of employment; job —***vt.*** to put into a certain position

pos·i·tive (päz′ə tiv) ***adj.*** ⟦see prec.⟧ **1** definitely set; explicit *[positive* instructions*]* **2** *a)* having the mind set; confident *b)* overconfident or dogmatic **3** showing agreement; affirmative **4** constructive *[positive* criticism*]* **5** regarded as having real existence *[a positive* good*]* **6** based on facts *[positive* proof*]* **7** *Elec. a)* of the kind of electricity predominating in a glass body after it has been rubbed with silk *b)* charged with positive electricity *c)* having a deficiency of electrons **8** *Gram.* of an adjective or adverb in its uncompared degree **9** *Math.* greater than zero **10** *Med.* showing the presence of a condition, infection, etc. **11** *Photog.* with the light and shade corresponding to those of the subject —***n.*** **1** something positive, as a degree, quality, quantity, photographic print, etc. **2** the plate in a battery having an excess of electrons flowing out toward the negative —**pos′i·tive·ly** ***adv.***

pos′i·tron′ (-trän′) ***n.*** ⟦POSI(TIVE) + (ELEC)TRON⟧ the positive antiparticle of an electron, having the same mass and magnitude of charge

poss *abbrev.* **1** possessive **2** possibly

pos·se (päs′ē) ***n.*** ⟦< L, be able⟧ [Historical] a band of men, usually armed, summoned to assist the sheriff in keeping the peace, etc.

pos·sess (pə zes′) ***vt.*** ⟦< L *possidere*⟧ **1** to have as belonging to one; own **2** to have as an attribute, quality, etc. **3** to gain control over *[possessed* by an idea*]* —**pos·ses′sor** ***n.***

pos·sessed′ ***adj.*** **1** owned **2** controlled, as if by a demon; crazed

pos·ses′sion (-zesh′ən) ***n.*** **1** a possessing or being possessed **2** anything possessed **3** [*pl.*] property **4** territory ruled by an outside country

pos·ses′sive (-zes′iv) ***adj.*** **1** of possession **2** showing or desiring possession, domination, control, influence, etc. **3** *Gram.* designating or of a case, form, or construction expressing possession (Ex: *my, Bill's*) —***n.*** *Gram.* **1** the

THESAURUS

portfolio ***n.*** **1** [A flat container] briefcase, attaché case, folder; see BAG, CONTAINER. **2** [Assets, especially stocks and bonds] holdings, securities, documents; see WEALTH.

portion ***n.*** section, piece, part; see DIVISION 2, SHARE.

portrait ***n.*** likeness, portraiture, representation; see PAINTING 1, PICTURE 4.

portray ***v.*** depict, characterize, reproduce; see DESCRIBE, REPRESENT 2.

portrayal ***n.*** depiction, replica, likeness; see DESCRIPTION, IMITATION 2.

pose ***n.*** artificial position, affectation, mannerism; see FAKE, PRETENSE 1.

pose ***v.*** **1** [To pretend] play a part, claim falsely, make believe; see ACT 1, PRETEND 1. **2** [To assume a pose for a picture] model, adopt a position, adopt a stance; see SIT.

posh* ***a.*** elegant, stylish, opulent; see RICH 2, FASHIONABLE.

position ***n.*** **1** [A physical position] location, locality, spot, seat, ground, environment, post, whereabouts, bearings, station, point, stand, space, surroundings, situation, site, geography, region, tract, district, scene, setting; see also AREA, PLACE 3. **2** [An intellectual position] view, belief, attitude; see JUDGMENT 3, OPINION 1. **3** [An occupational position] office, employment, occupation; see JOB 1, PROFESSION 1. **4** [A social position] station, state, status; see RANK 3. **5** [Posture] pose, carriage, bearing; see POSTURE 1.

positive ***a.*** **1** [Definite] decisive, actual, concrete; see DEFINITE 1, REAL 2. **2** [Emphatic] peremptory, assertive, obstinate; see EMPHATIC, RESOLUTE. **3** [Certain] sure, convinced, confident; see CERTAIN 1.

positively ***a.*** **1** [In a positive manner] assertively, uncompromisingly, dogmatically, arbitrarily, stubbornly, obstinately, emphatically, dictatorially, imperatively, absolutely, insistently, authoritatively, assuredly, confidently, unhesitatingly, with conviction. **2** [Without doubt] undoubtedly, unmistakably, undeniably; see SURELY.

posse ***n.*** detachment, armed band, police force; see POLICE.

possess ***v.*** hold, occupy, control; see MAINTAIN 3, OWN 1.

possessed ***a.*** **1** [Insane] mad, crazed, violent; see INSANE. **2** [Owned] kept, enjoyed, in one's possession; see HELD, OWNED.

possession ***n.*** **1** [Ownership] proprietary rights, hold, mastery; see OWNERSHIP. **2** [Property] personal property, real estate, something possessed; see PROPERTY 1, 2.

possessions ***n.*** belongings, goods, effects; see ESTATE, PROPERTY 1.

possessive case **2** a word or phrase in this case —**pos·ses'sive·ness** *n.*

pos·si·ble (päs'ə bəl) *adj.* ⟦< L *posse*, be able⟧ **1** that can be or exist **2** that may or may not happen **3** that can be done, selected, etc. **4** permissible —**pos'si·bil'i·ty** (-bil'ə tē), *pl.* **-ties**, *n.*

pos'si·bly (-blē) *adv.* **1** by any possible means **2** perhaps; maybe

pos·sum (päs'əm) *n.* [Inf.] OPOSSUM —**play possum** to pretend to be asleep, dead, ill, etc.

post[1] (pōst) *n.* ⟦< L *postis*⟧ **1** a piece of wood, metal, etc. set upright to support a building, sign, etc. **2** the starting point of a horse race —*vt.* **1** to put up (a poster, etc.) on (a wall, etc.) **2** to announce by posting notices *[to post a reward]* **3** to warn against trespassing on by posted notices **4** to put (a name) on a posted or published list

post[2] (pōst) *n.* ⟦< Fr < It *posto*⟧ **1** the place where a soldier, guard, etc. is stationed **2** a place where troops are garrisoned **3** the place assigned to one **4** a job or duty —*vt.* **1** to assign to a post **2** to put up (a bond, etc.)

post[3] (pōst) *n.* ⟦< Fr < It *posta*⟧ [Chiefly Brit.] (the) mail —*vi.* to travel fast; hasten —*vt.* **1** [Chiefly Brit.] to mail **2** to inform *[keep me posted]*

post- ⟦L < *post*, after⟧ *prefix* **1** after in time, later (than) *[postnatal]* **2** after in space, behind

post·age (pōs'tij) *n.* the amount charged for mailing a letter, etc., esp. as represented by stamps

post·al (pōs'təl) *adj.* ⟦Fr⟧ of mail or post offices

post-bel·lum (pōst bel'əm) *adj.* ⟦L⟧ after the war; specif., after the American Civil War

post'card' *n.* a card, usually with a picture on one side, for sending short messages by mail

post'date' *vt.* **-dat'ed**, **-dat'ing** **1** to assign a later date to than the actual date **2** to be subsequent to

post·er (pōs'tər) *n.* a large advertisement or notice posted publicly

pos·te·ri·or (päs tir'ē ər) *adj.* ⟦L < *post*, after⟧ **1** later; following **2** at the rear; behind —*n.* the buttocks

pos·ter·i·ty (päs ter'ə tē) *n.* ⟦see prec.⟧ **1** all of a person's descendants **2** all succeeding generations

post'grad'u·ate *adj.* of or taking a course of study after graduation, esp. after receipt of the bachelor's degree

post'haste' *adv.* with great haste

post'hole' *n.* a hole dug to hold the end of an upright post

post·hu·mous (päs'choo məs, -tyoo-) *adj.* ⟦< L *postumus*, last⟧ **1** published after the author's death **2** arising or continuing after one's death —**post'hu·mous·ly** *adv.*

post'hyp·not'ic *adj.* in the time after a hypnotic trance *[posthypnotic suggestion]*

pos·til·ion or **pos·til·lion** (pōs til'yən, päs-) *n.* ⟦Fr < It *posta*, a post⟧ one who rides the leading left-hand horse of a team drawing a carriage

post'in·dus'tri·al *adj.* of a society in which the economy has shifted from heavy industry to service industries, technology, etc.

Post'-it' *trademark for* small sheets of adhesive-backed paper for attaching notes —*n.* a sheet of this

post·lude (pōst'lood') *n.* ⟦POST- + (PRE)LUDE⟧ a concluding musical piece

post'man (-mən) *n. pl.* **-men** (-mən) MAIL CARRIER

post'mark' *n.* a post-office mark stamped on mail, canceling the postage stamp and recording the date and place —*vt.* to stamp with a postmark

post'mas'ter *n.* the manager of a post office

postmaster general *pl.* **postmasters general** the head of a government's postal system

post'me·rid'i·an (-mə rid'ē ən) *adj.* ⟦L⟧ after noon

post me·ri·di·em (mə rid'ē əm) ⟦L⟧ after noon: abbrev. *P.M.*, *p.m.*, *PM*, or *pm*

post'mod'ern·ism' *n.* an eclectic cultural and artistic trend in art, etc. of the late 20th c. —**post'mod'ern** *adj.* —**post'mod'ern·ist** *adj.*, *n.*

post-mor·tem (pōst'môr'təm) *adj.* ⟦L⟧ **1** after death **2** of a post-mortem —*n.* **1** AUTOPSY **2** an evaluation of some event just ended

post·na·sal drip (pōst'nā'zəl) a discharge of mucus from behind the nose onto the pharynx, due to a cold, allergy, etc.

post'na'tal (-nāt''l) *adj.* after birth

post office **1** the governmental department in charge of the mail **2** a place where mail is sorted, postage stamps are sold, etc.

post'op'er·a·tive (-äp'ər ə tiv) *adj.* occurring after a surgical operation

post'paid' *adj.* with postage prepaid

post'par'tum (-pär'təm) *adj.* ⟦L < *post-*, after + *parere*, to bear⟧ of the time after childbirth

post·pone (pōst pōn') *vt.* **-poned'**, **-pon'ing** ⟦< L *post-*, after + *ponere*, put⟧ to put off until later; delay —**post·pone'ment** *n.*

post'script' *n.* ⟦< L *post-*, after + *scribere*, write⟧ a note added below the signature in a letter

post time the scheduled starting time of a horse race

pos·tu·late (päs'chə lāt'; *for n.*, -lit) *vt.* **-lat'ed**, **-lat'ing** ⟦< L *postulare*, to demand⟧ to assume to be true, real, etc., esp. as a basis for argument —*n.* something postulated

pos·ture (päs'chər) *n.* ⟦MFr < L *ponere*, to place⟧ **1** the position or carriage of the body **2** a position assumed as in posing **3** an official stand or position *[our national posture]* —*vi.* to pose or assume an attitude merely for effect

post'war' *adj.* after the (or a) war

po·sy (pō'zē) *n.*, *pl.* **-sies** ⟦< POESY⟧ [Old-fashioned] a flower or bouquet

pot[1] (pät) *n.* ⟦OE *pott*⟧ **1** a round vessel for holding liquids, for cooking, etc. **2** a pot with its contents **3** [Inf.] all the money bet at a single time —*vt.* **pot'ted**, **pot'ting** to put into a pot —**go to pot** to go to ruin —**pot'ful'**, *pl.* **-fuls'**, *n.*

pot[2] (pät) *n.* ⟦< AmSp *potiguaya*⟧ [Slang] MARIJUANA

po·ta·ble (pōt'ə bəl) *adj.* ⟦< L *potare*, to drink⟧ drinkable —**po'ta·bil'i·ty** *n.*

pot'ash' *n.* ⟦< Du *pot*, POT[1] + *asch*, ASH[1]⟧ any of various potassium compounds used in fertilizers, soaps, etc.

po·tas·si·um (pə tas'ē əm) *n.* ⟦see prec.⟧ a soft, silver-white, metallic chemical element

po·ta·to (pə tāt'ō) *n.*, *pl.* **-toes** ⟦< WInd⟧ **1** the starchy tuber of a widely cultivated plant, eaten as a cooked vegetable **2** this plant

potato chip a very thin slice of potato fried crisp and then salted

pot'bel'lied *adj.* **1** having a potbelly **2** having bulging sides *[a potbellied stove]*

pot'bel'ly *n.*, *pl.* **-lies** a protruding belly

pot'boil'er *n.* a piece of writing, etc., done quickly and for money only

THESAURUS

possessor *n.* holder, proprietor, occupant; see OWNER.

possibility *n.* **1** [The condition of being possible] plausibility, feasibility, workableness; see CHANCE 2. **2** [A possible happening] hazard, chance, occasion, circumstance, hope, occurrence, hap, happening, outside chance, incident, instance; see also EVENT, OPPORTUNITY 1.

possible *a.* **1** [Within the realm of possibility] conceivable, imaginable, thinkable; see LIKELY 1. **2** [Acceptable] expedient, desirable, welcome; see PLEASANT 2. **3** [Contingent upon the future] indeterminate, fortuitous, adventitious; see LIKELY 1, UNCERTAIN.

possibly *a.* perhaps, by chance, potentially; see LIKELY 1, MAYBE, PROBABLY.

post[1] *n.* prop, support, pillar, pedestal, stake, stud, upright, doorpost; see also COLUMN 1, MAST.

postcard *n.* postal card, note, picture postcard; see LETTER 2.

poster *n.* placard, bill, sign, banner, sheet, billboard, handbill, broadside; see also ADVERTISEMENT.

posterior *a.* **1** [Subsequent] coming after, succeeding, next; see FOLLOWING. **2** [Behind] in back, last, after; see BACK.

posterity *n.* descendants, offspring, children; see FAMILY, OFFSPRING.

postman *n.* mailman, letter carrier, postal employee; see WORKMAN.

post office *n.* postal substation, postal service, PO; see MAIL.

postpone *v.* defer, put off, hold over; see DELAY, SUSPEND 2.

postponed *a.* deferred, delayed, put off, set for a later time, to be done later, withheld, shelved, tabled, adjourned, suspended; see also LATE 1.

postponement *n.* respite, suspension, adjournment; see DELAY, PAUSE.

posture *n.* **1** [Stance] pose, carriage, demeanor, aspect, presence, condition. **2** [Attitude] way of thinking, point of view, sentiment; see ATTITUDE.

postwar *a.* peacetime, post-bellum, after the war, peaceful.

pot[1,2] *n.* **1** [Container] vessel, kettle, saucepan, pan, jug, jar, mug, tankard, cup, can, crock, canister, receptacle, bucket, urn, pitcher, bowl, caldron, crucible, melting pot; see also CONTAINER. **2** [*Marijuana] *cannabis sativa* (Latin), grass*, weed*; see DRUG. —**go to pot** deteriorate, go to ruin, fall apart; see SPOIL.

potato *n.* tuber, white potato, sweet potato, yam, new potato, redskin potato, spud*, tater*.

pot'-bound' *adj.* having outgrown its container: said of a potted plant

po·tent (pōt''nt) *adj.* ⟦< L *posse*, be able⟧ **1** having authority or power **2** convincing; cogent **3** effective, as a drug **4** able to have sexual intercourse: said of a male —**po'ten·cy** *n.*

po·ten·tate (pōt''n tāt') *n.* a person having great power; ruler; monarch

po·ten·tial (pō ten'shəl) *adj.* ⟦see POTENT⟧ that can come into being; possible; latent —*n.* **1** something potential **2** the difference in voltage between two points in an electric circuit or field —**po·ten'ti·al'i·ty** (-shē al'ə tē), *pl.* **-ties**, *n.* —**po·ten'tial·ly** *adv.*

pot'herb' *n.* any herb whose leaves and stems are boiled and eaten or used as a flavoring

pot'hold'er *n.* a small pad, or piece of thick cloth, for handling hot pots, etc.

pot'hole' *n.* **1** a deep hole or pit **2** CHUCKHOLE

pot'hook' *n.* an S-shaped hook for hanging a pot over a fire

po·tion (pō'shən) *n.* ⟦< L *potare*, to drink⟧ a drink as of medicine, poison, or a supposedly magic substance

pot'luck' *n.* **1** whatever the family meal happens to be *[to take potluck]* **2** a dinner to which everyone brings a dish to share: in full **potluck dinner**

Po·to·mac (pə tō'mək) river in the E U.S., flowing into Chesapeake Bay

pot'pie' *n.* a meat pie made in a deep dish

pot·pour·ri (pō'poo rē', pät'poo rē') *n.* ⟦Fr < *pot*, a pot + *pourrir*, to rot⟧ **1** a mixture of dried flowers, spices, etc., kept for its fragrance **2** a medley or miscellany; mixture

pot roast a large cut of beef cooked in one piece by braising

pot·sherd (pät'shurd') *n.* ⟦see POT[1] & SHARD⟧ a piece of broken pottery

pot'shot' *n.* **1** an easy or random shot **2** a haphazard try **3** a random attack

pot·tage (pät'ij) *n.* ⟦< earlier Fr *pot*, a pot⟧ a kind of thick soup or stew

pot'ter *n.* one who makes earthenware pots, dishes, etc.

potter's field a burial ground for paupers or unknown persons

potter's wheel a rotating disk upon which clay is molded into bowls, etc.

pot'ter·y *n., pl.* **-ies** **1** a potter's workshop **2** the art of a potter; ceramics **3** pots, dishes, etc. made of clay hardened by heat

pot·ty (pät'ē) *n., pl.* **-ties** **1** a small pot used as a toilet for a child **2** a child's chair for toilet training with such a pot: in full **potty chair** **3** a toilet: a child's word

pouch (pouch) *n.* ⟦< earlier Fr *poche*⟧ **1** a small bag or sack *[a tobacco pouch]* **2** a mailbag **3** a saclike structure, as that on the abdomen of the kangaroo, etc. for carrying young —*vi.* to form a pouch

poul·tice (pōl'tis) *n.* ⟦< ML *pultes*, pap⟧ a hot, soft, moist mass applied to a sore part of the body —*vt.* **-ticed**, **-tic·ing** to apply a poultice to

poul·try (pōl'trē) *n.* ⟦< L *pullus*, chicken⟧ domestic fowls; chickens, ducks, etc.

pounce (pouns) *n.* ⟦ME *pownce*, talon⟧ a pouncing —*vi.* **pounced**, **pounc'ing** to swoop down or leap (*on*, *upon*, or *at*) in, or as in, seizing

pound[1] (pound) *n., pl.* **pounds**; sometimes, after a number, **pound** ⟦< L *pondus*, weight⟧ **1** a unit of weight equal to 16 oz. avoirdupois or 12 oz. troy: abbrev. *lb.* **2** the monetary unit of the United Kingdom: symbol, £ **3** the monetary unit of various other countries, as Egypt and Syria

pound[2] (pound) *vt.* ⟦OE *punian*⟧ **1** to beat to a pulp, powder, etc. **2** to hit hard —*vi.* **1** to deliver repeated, heavy blows (*at* or *on*) **2** to move with heavy steps **3** to throb

pound[3] (pound) *n.* ⟦< OE *pund-*⟧ a municipal enclosure for stray animals *[a dog pound]*

pound'cake' *n.* a rich cake made (orig. with a pound each) of flour, butter, sugar, etc.

pound sign a symbol (#) on a button on a telephone keypad

pour (pôr) *vt.* ⟦ME *pouren*⟧ **1** to cause to flow in a continuous stream **2** to emit, utter, etc. profusely or steadily —*vi.* **1** to flow freely, continuously, etc. **2** to rain heavily

pout (pout) *vi.* ⟦ME *pouten*⟧ **1** to thrust out the lips, as in sullenness **2** to sulk —*n.* the act of pouting —**pout'er** *n.*

pov·er·ty (päv'ər tē) *n.* ⟦< L *pauper*, poor⟧ **1** the condition or quality of being poor; need **2** deficiency; inadequacy **3** scarcity

pov'er·ty-strick'en *adj.* very poor

POW *n., pl.* **POW's** prisoner of war

pow·der (pou'dər) *n.* ⟦< L *pulvis*, dust⟧ **1** any dry substance in the form of fine, dustlike particles, produced by crushing, grinding, etc. **2** a specific kind of powder *[bath powder]* —*vt.* **1** to sprinkle, etc. with powder **2** to make into powder —**pow'der·y** *adj.*

powder keg **1** a keg for gunpowder **2** a potential source of violence, war, etc.

powder room a lavatory for women

pow·er (pou'ər) *n.* ⟦ult. < L *posse*, be able⟧ **1** ability to do or act **2** vigor; force; strength **3** *a)* authority; influence *b)* legal authority **4** physical force or energy *[electric power]* **5** a person or thing having great influence, force, or authority **6** a nation with influence over other nations **7** the product of the multiplication of a quantity by itself **8** the degree of magnification of a lens —*vt.* to supply with a source of power —*adj.* **1** operated by electricity, a fuel engine, etc. *[power tools]* **2** served by an auxiliary system that reduces effort *[power steering]* **3** carrying electricity

THESAURUS

potency *n.* **1** [Strength] power, energy, vigor; see MANHOOD 2, STRENGTH. **2** [Authority] influence, control, dominion; see COMMAND, POWER 2.

potent *a.* **1** [Strong] vigorous, robust, sturdy; see STRONG 1, 2. **2** [Powerful] mighty, great, influential; see POWERFUL 1.

potential *a.* implied, inherent, dormant; see LIKELY 1.

potentially *a.* conceivably, imaginably, possibly; see LIKELY 1, MAYBE, PROBABLY.

potion *n.* dose, draft, liquor; see DRINK 1, LIQUID, MEDICINE 2.

pottery *n.* ceramics, porcelain, crockery, earthenware, clayware; see also UTENSILS.

pouch *n.* sack, receptacle, poke*; see BAG, CONTAINER.

poultry *n.* domesticated birds, pullets, barnyard fowls; see FOWL.

pounce *v.* bound, surge, dart; see DIVE, JUMP 1.

pound[1,3] *n.* **1** [Measure of weight] sixteen ounces, Troy pound, avoirdupois pound, commercial pound, pint; see also MEASURE 1, WEIGHT 1. **2** [Kennel] coop, doghouse, cage; see PEN 1. **3** [British monetary unit] pound sterling, 100 pence, 20 shillings (formerly), quid*; see also MONEY 1.

pound[2] *v.* strike, crush, pulverize; see BEAT 1, HIT 1.

pour *v.* **1** [To flow] discharge, emit, issue; see DRAIN 3, FLOW. **2** [To allow to flow] replenish with, spill, splash; see EMPTY 2. **3** [To rain heavily] stream, flood, drench; see RAIN.

pouring *a.* streaming, gushing, spouting, rushing, raining, flooding, showering, discharging, emitting, issuing, escaping, emanating, welling out, spurting, spilling, shedding, draining, running down, running out; see also FLOWING.

pout *v.* mope, brood, sulk; see FROWN.

poverty *n.* **1** [Want of earthly goods] destitution, pennilessness, penury, indigence, pauperism, want, need, insufficiency, starvation, famine, privation, insolvency, broken fortune, straits, scantiness, deficiency, meagerness, aridity, sparingness, stint, depletion, emptiness, vacancy, deficit, debt, wolf at the door*, pinch*, bite*, tough going*; see also LACK 1.—*Ant.* WEALTH, prosperity, comfort. **2** [Want of any desirable thing] shortage, inadequacy, scarcity; see LACK 1.

poverty-stricken *a.* penniless, broke, bankrupt; see POOR 1, WANTING 1.

powder *n.* particles, film, powderiness, explosive powder, medicinal powder, cosmetic powder; see also COSMETIC, EXPLOSIVE, MEDICINE 2.

powdery *a.* sandy, gravelly, dusty; see GRITTY.

power *n.* **1** [Strength] vigor, energy, stamina; see STRENGTH. **2** [Controlling sway] authority, command, jurisdiction, dominion, ascendency, superiority, domination, dominance, mastery, control, sway, sovereignty, hegemony, prerogative, prestige, omnipotence, supreme authority, the last word, rule, law, warrant, supremacy, legal sanction, government, say-so*; see also INFLUENCE, LEADERSHIP. **3** [Ability; *often plural*] skill, endowment, capability; see ABILITY. **4** [Force] compulsion, coercion, duress; see PRESSURE 2, RESTRAINT 2. **5** [Energy] horsepower, potential, dynamism; see ENERGY 2. **—in power** ruling, authoritative, commanding; see POWERFUL 1. **—(the) powers that be** management, higher authorities, higher-ups*; see ADMINISTRATION 2.

pow'er·ful *adj.* strong, mighty, influential, etc. —**pow'er·ful·ly** *adv.*
pow'er·house' *n.* **1** a building where electric power is generated **2** [Inf.] a powerful person, team, etc.
pow·er·less (pou'ər lis) *adj.* without power; weak, unable, etc. —**pow'er·less·ly** *adv.*
power of attorney written legal authority for one person to act for another
pow'er·train' *n.* DRIVETRAIN
pow·wow (pou'wou') *n.* ⟦< AmInd⟧ **1** a conference of or with North American Indians **2** [Inf.] any conference
pox (päks) *n.* ⟦for *pocks*: see POCK⟧ **1** a disease characterized by skin eruptions, as smallpox **2** syphilis: with *the*
pp *abbrev.* **1** pages **2** parcel post **3** past participle **4** postpaid **5** prepaid Also, for 4 & 5, **ppd**
PP *abbrev.* parcel post
PPO *n., pl.* **PPO's** ⟦*p(referred) p(rovider) o(rganization)*⟧ a healthcare system having certain hospitals, doctors, etc. under contract at a reduced cost
ppr *abbrev.* present participle
P.P.S., p.p.s., PPS, or **pps** *abbrev.* ⟦L *post postscriptum*⟧ an additional postscript
pr *abbrev.* **1** pair(s) **2** price
Pr *abbrev.* Provençal
PR or **P.R.** *abbrev.* **1** public relations **2** Puerto Rico
prac·ti·ca·ble (prak'ti kə bəl) *adj.* **1** that can be put into practice; feasible **2** that can be used; useful —**prac'ti·ca·bil'i·ty** *n.* —**prac'ti·ca·bly** *adv.*
prac·ti·cal (prak'ti kəl) *adj.* **1** of or obtained through practice or action **2** useful **3** concerned with the application of knowledge to useful ends *[practical* science*]* **4** dealing realistically and sensibly with everyday matters **5** that is so in practice, if not in theory, law, etc. —**prac'ti·cal'i·ty** (-kal'ə tē), *pl.* **-ties,** *n.*
practical joke a trick played on someone in fun —**practical joker**
prac·ti·cal·ly (prak'tik lē, -tik ə lē) *adv.* **1** in a practical manner **2** from a practical viewpoint **3** in effect; virtually **4** [Inf.] nearly
practical nurse a nurse with less training than a registered nurse, often one licensed by a U.S. state (**licensed practical nurse**) for specified duties
prac·tice (prak'tis) *vt.* **-ticed, -tic·ing** ⟦< Gr *prassein*, do⟧ **1** to do or engage in frequently; make a habit of **2** to do repeatedly so as to become proficient **3** to work at, esp. as a profession —*vi.* to do something repeatedly so as to become proficient; drill Chiefly Brit. sp. **prac'tise** —*n.* **1** a practicing; habit, custom, etc. **2** *a)* repeated action to acquire proficiency *b)* proficiency so acquired **3** the actual doing of something **4** *a)* the exercise of a profession *b)* a business based on this
prac'ticed *adj.* experienced; skilled
prac·ti·cum (prak'ti kəm) *n.* ⟦see PRACTICE⟧ a course involving activities emphasizing the practical application of theory, as on-the-job experience in a field of study
prac·ti·tion·er (prak tish'ə nər) *n.* one who practices a profession
Prae·to·ri·an (prē tôr'ē ən) *adj.* ⟦< L *praetor*, magistrate⟧ of or belonging to the bodyguard (**Praetorian Guard**) of a Roman emperor
prag·mat·ic (prag mat'ik) *adj.* ⟦< Gr *pragma*, thing done⟧ **1** practical **2** testing the validity of all concepts by their practical results —**prag·mat'i·cal·ly** *adv.* —**prag'ma·tism'** (-mə tiz'əm) *n.* —**prag'ma·tist** *n.*
Prague (präg) capital of the Czech Republic: pop. 1,217,000
prai·rie (prer'ē) *n.* ⟦Fr < L *pratum*, meadow⟧ a large area of level or rolling, grassy land
prairie dog a small, burrowing rodent of North America
prairie schooner a box-shaped covered wagon
praise (prāz) *vt.* **praised, prais'ing** ⟦< L *pretium*, worth, price⟧ **1** to express approval or admiration of **2** to glorify (God, etc.), as in song —*n.* a praising or being praised; commendation
praise'wor'thy *adj.* worthy of praise —**praise'wor'thi·ly** *adv.* —**praise'wor'thi·ness** *n.*
pra·line (prā'lēn', prä'-) *n.* ⟦Fr⟧ any of various soft or crisp candies made of nuts, sugar, etc.
prance (prans) *vi.* **pranced, pranc'ing** ⟦< ?⟧ **1** to rise up, or move along, on the hind legs, as a horse does **2** to caper or strut —*n.* a prancing —**pranc'er** *n.* —**pranc'ing·ly** *adv.*
prank (praŋk) *n.* ⟦< ?⟧ a mischievous trick —**prank'ster** *n.*
prate (prāt) *vi., vt.* **prat'ed, prat'ing** ⟦< MDu *praten*⟧ to talk much and foolishly; chatter
prat·tle (prat''l) *vi., vt.* **-tled, -tling** ⟦LowG *pratelen*⟧ to prate or babble —*n.* chatter or babble
prawn (prôn) *n.* ⟦< ?⟧ a large shrimp or other similar crustacean
pray (prā) *vt.* ⟦< L *prex*, prayer⟧ **1** to implore *[*(I) *pray* (you) tell me*]* **2** to ask for by prayer —*vi.* to say prayers, as to God
prayer[1] (prer) *n.* **1** the act of praying **2** an entreaty; supplication **3** *a)* a humble request, as to God *b)* any set formula for this **4** [*often pl.*] a devotional service chiefly of prayers **5** something prayed for —**prayer'ful** *adj.* —**prayer'ful·ly** *adv.*

THESAURUS

powerful *a.* **1** [Wielding power] mighty, all-powerful, almighty, superhuman, omnipotent, overpowering, great, invincible, dominant, influential, authoritative, overruling, potent, forceful, forcible, compelling, ruling, prevailing, preeminent, commanding, supreme, highest, important, authoritarian, ruthless, having the upper hand, in control.—*Ant.* WEAK, incompetent, impotent. **2** [Strong] robust, stalwart, sturdy; see STRONG 1, 2. **3** [Effective] efficacious, effectual, convincing; see PERSUASIVE.
powerfully *a.* forcibly, forcefully, effectively, severely, intensely, with authority; see also VIGOROUSLY.
powerless *a.* impotent, feeble, infirm; see WEAK 1, 2.
practical *a.* matter-of-fact, pragmatic, unimaginative, practicable, feasible, workable, functional, useful, sound, unromantic, sound-thinking, down-to-earth, realistic, sensible, sane, reasonable, rational, to one's advantage, operative, utilitarian, possible, usable, serviceable, efficient, effective, working, in action, in operation, with both feet on the ground.—*Ant.* UNREAL, imaginative, impractical.
practically *a.* **1** [In a practical manner] unimaginatively, pragmatically, efficiently, functionally, sensibly, rationally, reasonably, realistically, with regard to use, feasibly; see also EFFECTIVELY. **2** [Virtually] for ordinary purposes, nearly, just about; see ALMOST.
practice *n.* **1** [A customary action] usage, use, wont; see CUSTOM. **2** [A method] mode, manner, fashion; see METHOD, SYSTEM. **3** [Educational repetition] exercise, drill, repetition, iteration, rehearsal, recitation, recounting, relating, tuneup*, prepping*. **4** [A practitioner's customers] clientele, patients, clients; see BUSINESS 4.
practice *v.* **1** [To seek improvement through repetition] drill, train, exercise, study, rehearse, repeat, recite, iterate, put in practice, make it one's business, work at, accustom oneself, polish up*, sharpen up*, build up. **2** [To employ one's professional skill] function, work at, employ oneself in; see WORK 2.
practiced *a.* trained, expert, exercised; see ABLE.
pragmatic *a.* realistic, utilitarian, logical; see PRACTICAL.
prairie *n.* steppe, savanna, grassland; see FIELD 1, MEADOW, PLAIN.
praise *n.* **1** [The act of praising] applause, approval, appreciation; see ADMIRATION. **2** [An expression of praise] laudation, eulogy, regard, applause, recommendation, handclapping, hurrahs, bravos, ovation, cheers, cries, whistling, tribute, compliment, acclaim, flattery, blessing, benediction, boost, rave.—*Ant.* BLAME, censure, condemnation.
praise *v.* **1** [To commend] recommend, applaud, cheer, acclaim, endorse, sanction, admire, eulogize, adulate, elevate, smile on, cajole, give an ovation to, clap, pay tribute to, do credit to, have a good word for, make much of, extend credit, advocate, compliment, appreciate, admire, celebrate, honor, congratulate, flatter, rave over, boost, give a big hand; see also APPROVE. **2** [To speak or sing in worship] glorify, adore, reverence; see WORSHIP.
praised *a.* admired, helped, flattered, worshiped, glorified, exalted, blessed, celebrated, paid tribute to, magnified.
prance *v.* cavort, frisk, gambol; see DANCE.
prank *n.* game, escapade, caper; see JOKE.
pray *v.* **1** [To ask or beg] importune, petition, plead; see ASK, BEG. **2** [To call upon God] hold communion with God, supplicate, implore, petition, entreat, bless.
prayer[1] *n.* **1** [An earnest request] entreaty, request, petition; see APPEAL 1. **2** [An address to a deity] invocation, act of devotion, supplication, devotions, benediction, litany. *Prayers include the following:* Lord's Prayer, Our Father, Hail Mary, Pater Noster, Ave Maria, grace, kaddish, matins, vespers, Angelus, general confession, Miserere, collects, hours, stations of the cross, evensong.

pray·er² (prā′ər) ***n.*** one who prays
praying mantis MANTIS
pre- ⟦< L *prae*, before⟧ *prefix* before in time, place, rank, etc.
preach (prēch) ***vi.*** ⟦< L *prae-*, before + *dicare*, proclaim⟧ **1** to give a religious sermon **2** to give moral advice, esp. in a tiresome manner —***vt.*** **1** to urge as by preaching **2** to deliver (a sermon) —**preach′ment** ***n.***
preach′er ***n.*** one who preaches; esp., a member of the Protestant clergy
preach′y ***adj.*** **-i·er, -i·est** [Inf.] given to or marked by preaching, or moralizing
pre·am·ble (prē′am′bəl) ***n.*** ⟦< L *prae-*, before + *ambulare*, go⟧ an introduction, esp. one to a constitution, statute, etc., stating its purpose
pre′ap·prove′ (-ə pro͞ov′) ***vt.*** **-proved′, -prov′ing** to authorize before an application is submitted
pre′ar·range′ (-ə rānj′) ***vt.*** **-ranged′, -rang′ing** to arrange beforehand
pre·can·cer·ous (prē kan′sər əs) ***adj.*** likely to become cancerous
pre·car·i·ous (prē ker′ē əs) ***adj.*** ⟦see PRAY⟧ dependent upon circumstances or chance; uncertain; risky —**pre·car′i·ous·ly** ***adv.***
pre·cau·tion (pri kô′shən) ***n.*** ⟦< L *prae-*, before + *cavere*, take care⟧ care taken beforehand, as against danger or failure —**pre·cau′tion·ar′y** ***adj.***
pre·cede (prē sēd′) ***vt., vi.*** **-ced′ed, -ced′ing** ⟦< L *prae-*, before + *cedere*, to go⟧ to be, come, or go before in time, place, rank, etc.
prec·e·dence (pres′ə dəns; prē sēd′′ns) ***n.*** the act, right, or fact of preceding in time, order, rank, etc.
prec·e·dent (pres′ə dənt) ***n.*** an act, statement, etc. that may serve as an example or justification for a later one
pre·ced′ing ***adj.*** that precedes
pre·cept (prē′sept′) ***n.*** ⟦< L *prae-*, before + *capere*, take⟧ a rule of moral conduct; maxim
pre·cep·tor (prē sep′tər) ***n.*** a teacher
pre·cinct (prē′siŋkt′) ***n.*** ⟦< L *prae-*, before + *cingere*, surround⟧ **1** [*usually pl.*] an enclosure between buildings, walls, etc. **2** [*pl.*] environs **3** *a*) police district *b*) a subdivision of a voting ward **4** a limited area
pre·ci·os·i·ty (presh′ē äs′ə tē, pres′-) ***n., pl.*** **-ties** ⟦see fol.⟧ affectation, esp. in language
pre·cious (presh′əs) ***adj.*** ⟦< L *pretium*, a price⟧ **1** of great price or value; costly **2** beloved; dear **3** very fastidious, affected, etc. —**pre′cious·ly** ***adv.***
precious stone a rare and costly gem: applied to the diamond, emerald, ruby, and sapphire
prec·i·pice (pres′i pis) ***n.*** ⟦< L *prae-*, before + *caput*, a head⟧ a vertical or overhanging rock face
pre·cip·i·tant (prē sip′i tənt) ***adj.*** ⟦see prec.⟧ PRECIPITATE
pre·cip·i·tate (prē sip′ə tāt′; *for adj. & n.*, -tit, -tāt′) ***vt.*** **-tat′ed, -tat′ing** ⟦see PRECIPICE⟧ **1** to hurl downward **2** to cause to happen before expected, needed, etc. **3** *Chem.* to separate (a soluble substance) out of a solution —***vi.*** **1** *Chem.* to be precipitated **2** *Meteorol.* to condense and fall as rain, snow, etc. —***adj.*** **1** acting or done hastily or rashly **2** very sudden or abrupt —***n.*** a substance precipitated out of a solution
pre·cip′i·ta′tion (-tā′shən) ***n.*** **1** a headlong fall or rush **2** rash haste; impetuosity **3** a bringing on suddenly **4** *Chem.* a precipitating or being precipitated from a solution **5** *Meteorol. a*) rain, snow, etc. *b*) the amount of this
pre·cip′i·tous (-təs) ***adj.*** **1** steep like a precipice **2** rash; impetuous
pré·cis (prā sē′) ***n., pl.*** **-cis′** (-sēz′) ⟦Fr: see fol.⟧ a concise abridgment; summary
pre·cise (prē sīs′) ***adj.*** ⟦< L *prae-*, before + *caedere*, to cut⟧ **1** accurately stated; definite **2** minutely exact **3** strict; scrupulous; fastidious —**pre·cise′ly** ***adv.*** —**pre·cise′ness** ***n.***
pre·ci·sion (prē sizh′ən) ***n.*** the quality of being precise; exactness —***adj.*** requiring exactness *[precision* work*]*
pre·clude (prē klo͞od′) ***vt.*** **-clud′ed, -clud′ing** ⟦< L *prae-*, before + *claudere*, to close⟧ to make impossible, esp. in advance; prevent —**pre·clu′sion** (-klo͞o′zhən) ***n.***
pre·co·cious (prē kō′shəs) ***adj.*** ⟦< L *prae-*, before + *coquere*, to cook⟧ matured earlier than usual *[a precocious* child*]* —**pre·coc′i·ty** (-käs′ə tē) ***n.***
pre·cog·ni·tion (prē′käg nish′ən) ***n.*** ⟦see PRE- & COGNITION⟧ *Parapsychology* the perception of an event, etc. before it occurs, esp. by extrasensory means —**pre·cog′ni·tive** (-nə tiv) ***adj.***
pre-Co·lum·bi·an (prē′kə lum′bē ən) ***adj.*** of any period in the Americas before Columbus's voyages
pre·con·ceive (prē′kən sēv′) ***vt.*** **-ceived′, -ceiv′ing** to form (an opinion) in advance —**pre′con·cep′tion** (-sep′shən) ***n.***
pre′con·di′tion (-dish′ən) ***vt.*** to prepare (someone) to behave, react, etc. in a certain way under certain conditions —***n.*** a condition required beforehand if something else is to occur
pre·cur·sor (prē kʉr′sər, prē′kʉr′-) ***n.*** ⟦< L *praecurrere*, run ahead⟧ **1** a forerunner **2** a predecessor —**pre·cur′so·ry** ***adj.***
pred·a·to·ry (pred′ə tôr′ē) ***adj.*** ⟦< L *praeda*, a prey⟧ **1** of or living by plundering or robbing **2** preying on other animals —**pred′a·tor** (-tər) ***n.***
pre·de·cease (prē′dē sēs′) ***vt.*** **-ceased′, -ceas′ing** to die before (someone else)
pred·e·ces·sor (pred′ə ses′ər) ***n.*** ⟦< L *prae-*, before + *decedere*, go away⟧ a person preceding another, as in office
pre·des·ti·na·tion (prē des′tə nā′shən) ***n.*** **1** *Theol.* the doctrine that *a*) God foreordained everything that would happen *b*) God predestines souls to salvation or to damnation **2** one's destiny
pre·des′tine (-des′tin) ***vt.*** **-tined, -tin·ing** to destine beforehand; foreordain
pre′de·ter′mine (-dē tʉr′min) ***vt.*** **-mined, -min·ing** to determine beforehand
pre·dic·a·ment (prē dik′ə mənt) ***n.*** ⟦see PREACH⟧ an unpleasant or embarrassing situation
pred·i·cate (pred′i kāt′; *for n. & adj.*, -kit) ***vt.*** **-cat′ed, -cat′ing** ⟦see PREACH⟧ **1** to affirm as a quality or attrib-

THESAURUS

prayer book ***n.*** liturgy, mass book, missal, missalette, hymnal, breviary, holy text, guide; see also BIBLE.
preach ***v.*** exhort, proselytize, evangelize, witness, moralize, teach, lecture, talk, harangue, inform, address.
preacher ***n.*** missionary, parson, clergyman; see MINISTER 1.
preamble ***n.*** prelude, preface, foreword; see INTRODUCTION 4.
precarious ***a.*** doubtful, uncertain, risky; see DANGEROUS.
precaution ***n.*** anticipation, forethought, regard; see CARE 1. —**take precautions** foresee, mind, be careful; see PREPARE 1, WATCH OUT.
precede ***v.*** go before, come first, be ahead of, move ahead of, take precedence over, preface, introduce, usher in, ring in, herald, forerun, head, lead, go ahead, scout, light the way, go in advance, come before, come to the front, forge ahead, head up.—*Ant.* SUCCEED, come after, come last.
precedence ***n.*** preference, precession, the lead; see ADVANTAGE.
precedent ***n.*** authoritative example, exemplar, pattern; see EXAMPLE 1, MODEL 1.
preceding ***a.*** antecedent, precedent, previous, other, prior, aforesaid, ahead of, earlier, former, forerunning, past, foregoing, above-mentioned, above-named, above-cited, aforementioned, before-mentioned, above, before, prefatory, front, forward, anterior, preliminary, preparatory, introductory, aforeknown, already indicated, previously mentioned.
precious ***a.*** **1** [Valuable] high-priced, costly, dear; see EXPENSIVE, VALUABLE. **2** [Beloved] cherished, inestimable, prized; see BELOVED, FAVORITE. **3** [Refined and delicate] overrefined, overnice, fragile; see DAINTY.
precipice ***n.*** crag, cliff, bluff; see HILL, MOUNTAIN.
precipitate ***v.*** accelerate, press, hurry; see HASTEN 2, SPEED.
precipitation ***n.*** **1** [Carelessness] rashness, presumption, impetuosity; see CARELESSNESS, RUDENESS. **2** [Condensation] hail, rain, snow; see STORM.
precise ***a.*** **1** [Exact] decisive, well-defined, strict; see ACCURATE 2, DEFINITE 1, 2. **2** [Fussily or prudishly careful] rigid, inflexible, uncompromising; see CAREFUL, SEVERE 1.
precisely ***a.*** correctly, exactly, definitely; see ACCURATE 2.
precision ***n.*** exactness, correctness, sureness; see ACCURACY.
preconception ***n.*** prejudice, bias, assumption; see INCLINATION 1.
predatory ***a.*** voracious, carnivorous, bloodthirsty; see GREEDY, HUNGRY.
predecessor ***n.*** antecedent, forerunner, ancestor; see PARENT.
predicament ***n.*** strait, quandary, plight, puzzle, perplexity, dilemma, scrape, corner, hole, impasse, tight situation, state, condition, position, lot, circumstance, mess, muddle, deadlock, pinch, crisis, bind*, fix*, pickle*, hot water*, jam*, spot*; see also DIFFICULTY 1, 2.
predicate ***n.*** verbal phrase, part of speech, verb; see VERB.
predicate ***v.*** assert, declare, state; see MEAN 1.

ute **2** to base (something) *on* or *upon* facts, conditions, etc. —***n.*** *Gram.* the word or words that make a statement about the subject —***adj.*** *Gram.* of a predicate —**pred'i·ca'tion** ***n.***

pre·dict (prē dikt') ***vt., vi.*** ⟦< L *prae-*, before + *dicere*, tell⟧ to say in advance (what one believes will happen); foretell —**pre·dict'a·ble** ***adj.*** —**pre·dic'tion** ***n.*** —**pre·dic'tor** ***n.***

pre·di·gest (prē'di jest', -dī-) ***vt.*** to treat (food) as with enzymes for easier digestion when eaten

pred·i·lec·tion (pred'ə lek'shən, prē'də-) ***n.*** ⟦< L *prae-*, before + *diligere*, prefer⟧ a partiality or preference (*for*)

pre·dis·pose (prē'di spōz') ***vt.*** **-posed', -pos'ing** to make receptive or susceptible (*to*); incline —**pre'dis·po·si'tion** (-dis pə zish'ən) ***n.***

pre·dom·i·nant (prē däm'ə nənt) ***adj.*** **1** having authority or influence over others; superior **2** most frequent; prevailing —**pre·dom'i·nance** ***n.*** —**pre·dom'i·nant·ly** ***adv.***

pre·dom·i·nate (prē däm'ə nāt') ***vi.*** **-nat'ed, -nat'ing 1** to have authority or influence (*over* others) **2** to be dominant in amount, number, etc.; prevail

pre·em·i·nent (prē em'ə nənt) ***adj.*** eminent above others; surpassing —**pre·em'i·nence** ***n.*** —**pre·em'i·nent·ly** ***adv.***

pre·empt or **pre-empt'** (prē empt') ***vt.*** ⟦ult. < L *prae-*, before + *emere*, buy⟧ **1** to gain the right to buy (public land) by settling on it **2** to seize before anyone else can **3** *Radio, TV* to replace (a scheduled program)

pre·emp'tion (-emp'shən) ***n.*** **1** a preempting **2** action taken to check other action beforehand —**pre·emp'tive** ***adj.***

preen (prēn) ***vt.*** ⟦< ME *proinen*, to dress up⟧ **1** to clean and trim (the feathers) with the beak **2** to dress up or adorn (oneself)

pre·ex·ist (prē'eg zist') ***vt., vi.*** to exist previously or before (another person or thing) —**pre'ex·ist'ence** ***n.***

pref *abbrev.* **1** preface **2** preferred **3** prefix

pre·fab (prē'fab') ***n.*** [Inf.] a prefabricated building

pre·fab·ri·cate (prē fab'ri kāt') ***vt.*** **-cat'ed, -cat'ing** to build (a house, etc.) in standardized sections for shipment and quick assembly

pref·ace (pref'is) ***n.*** ⟦< L *prae-*, before + *fari*, speak⟧ an introduction to a book, speech, etc. —***vt.*** **-aced, -ac·ing 1** to furnish with a preface **2** to introduce —**pref'a·to'ry** (-ə tôr'ē) ***adj.***

pre·fect (prē'fekt') ***n.*** ⟦< L *praeficere*, to set over⟧ any of various administrators —**pre'fec'ture** (-fek'chər) ***n.***

pre·fer (prē fur', pri-) ***vt.*** **-ferred', -fer'ring** ⟦< L *prae-*, before + *ferre*, to bear⟧ **1** to put before a court, etc. for consideration **2** to like better

pref·er·a·ble (pref'ər ə bəl) ***adj.*** more desirable —**pref'er·a·bly** ***adv.***

pref'er·ence (-əns) ***n.*** **1** a preferring or being preferred **2** something preferred **3** advantage given to one person, country, etc. over others —**pref'er·en'tial** (-ər en'shəl) ***adj.***

pre·fer·ment (prē fur'mənt) ***n.*** an advancement in rank, etc.; promotion

pre·fig·ure (prē fig'yər) ***vt.*** **-ured, -ur·ing** to suggest beforehand; foreshadow

pre·fix (prē'fiks'; *for v., also* prē fiks') ***vt.*** ⟦< L *prae-*, before + *figere*, fix⟧ to fix to the beginning of a word, etc.; esp., to add as a prefix —***n.*** a syllable, group of syllables, or word joined to the beginning of another word or a base to alter its meaning

preg·nant (preg'nənt) ***adj.*** ⟦< L *pregnans*⟧ **1** having (an) offspring developing in the uterus; with child **2** mentally fertile; inventive **3** full of meaning, etc. *[a pregnant silence]* **4** filled (*with*); abounding —**preg'nan·cy,** *pl.* **-cies,** ***n.***

pre·hen·sile (prē hen'səl) ***adj.*** ⟦< L *prehendere*, take⟧ adapted for seizing or grasping, esp. by wrapping around something: said as of a monkey's tail

pre·his·tor·ic (prē'his tôr'ik) ***adj.*** of the period before recorded history

pre·ig·ni·tion (prē'ig nish'ən) ***n.*** in an internal-combustion engine, ignition occurring before the intake valve is closed or before the spark plug fires

pre·judge (prē juj') ***vt.*** **-judged', -judg'ing** to judge beforehand or without all the evidence —**pre·judg'ment** ***n.***

prej·u·dice (prej'ə dis) ***n.*** ⟦< L *prae-*, before + *judicium*, judgment⟧ **1** a preconceived, usually unfavorable idea **2** an opinion held in disregard of facts that contradict it; bias **3** intolerance or hatred of other races, etc. **4** injury or harm as from some judgment —***vt.*** **-diced, -dic·ing 1** to injure or harm, as by some judgment **2** to cause to have prejudice; bias —**prej'u·di'cial** (-dish'əl) ***adj.***

prel·ate (prel'it) ***n.*** ⟦< L *praelatus*, placed before⟧ a high-ranking member of the clergy, as a bishop —**prel'a·cy,** *pl.* **-cies,** ***n.***

pre·lim·i·nar·y (prē lim'ə ner'ē, pri-) ***adj.*** ⟦< L *prae-*, before + *limen*, threshold⟧ leading up to the main action, discussion, etc.; introductory —***n.,*** *pl.* **-ies** [*often pl.*] a preliminary step, procedure, etc.

pre·lit·er·ate (prē lit'ər it) ***adj.*** of a society not having a written language

prel·ude (prel'yōōd', prā'lōōd') ***n.*** ⟦< Fr < L *prae-*, before + *ludere*, to play⟧ **1** a preliminary part **2** *Music a)* an introductory instrumental composition, as the overture to an opera *b)* a short, romantic composition

pre·mar·i·tal (prē mar'ət'l) ***adj.*** occurring before marriage

pre·ma·ture (prē'mə toor', -choor') ***adj.*** ⟦< L *prae-*, before + *maturus*, ripe⟧ happening, done, arriving, etc. before the proper or usual time; too early —**pre'ma·ture'ly** ***adv.***

pre·med'i·tate' (-med'ə tāt') ***vt., vi.*** **-tat'ed, -tat'ing** to think (out) or plan beforehand —**pre·med'i·ta'tion** ***n.***

pre·men·stru·al (prē men'strəl) ***adj.*** occurring before a menstrual period

pre·mier (pri mir', -myir') ***adj.*** ⟦Fr < L *primus*, first⟧ first

THESAURUS

predict ***v.*** prophesy, prognosticate, divine; see FORETELL.

predictable ***a.*** anticipated, foreseen, prepared for; see EXPECTED, LIKELY 1.

prediction ***n.*** prophecy, foresight, prognostication; see GUESS.

predominance ***n.*** supremacy, superiority, control; see COMMAND, POWER 2.

predominant ***a.*** **1** [Supreme in power] mighty, almighty, supreme; see POWERFUL 1. **2** [Of first importance] transcendent, surpassing, superlative; see PRINCIPAL.

predominate ***v.*** dominate, prevail, rule; see GOVERN, MANAGE 1.

prefab* ***n.*** prefabricated building, modular structure, standardized housing; see BUILDING.

prefabricate ***v.*** fabricate, preform, set up, coordinate, pre-assemble; see also ASSEMBLE 2.

preface ***n.*** prelude, prolegomenon, preliminary; see EXPLANATION, INTRODUCTION 4.

preface ***v.*** introduce, commence, precede; see BEGIN 1.

prefer ***v.*** single out, fix upon, fancy; see FAVOR.

preferable ***a.*** more eligible, more desirable, better; see EXCELLENT.

preferably ***a.*** by preference, by choice, by selection, in preference, first, sooner, before, optionally, at pleasure, willingly, at will; see also RATHER 2.

preference ***n.*** favorite, election, option, decision, selection, pick; see also CHOICE.

preferred ***a.*** chosen, selected, fancied, adopted, picked out, taken, elected, liked, favored, set apart, handpicked, singled out, endorsed, settled upon, sanctioned, decided upon.—*Ant.* NEGLECTED, unpreferred, overlooked.

pregnant ***a.*** gestating, gravid, fruitful, with child, big with child, hopeful, anticipating, in a family way*, expecting*, knocked up*.

prehistoric ***a.*** ancient, primeval, earliest; see OLD 3.

prejudge ***v.*** presuppose, forejudge, presume; see DECIDE.

prejudice ***n.*** partiality, unfairness, spleen, bias, detriment, enmity, prejudgment, dislike, disgust, aversion, antipathy, racism, bigotry, apartheid, misjudgment, pique, coolness, animosity, contemptuousness, bad opinion, displeasure, repugnance, revulsion, preconception, quirk, warp, twist.—*Ant.* ADMIRATION, appreciation, good opinion.

prejudiced ***a.*** preconceived, prepossessed, biased, directed against, influenced, inclined, leaning, conditioned, presupposing, predisposed, dogmatic, opinionated, partisan, extreme, hidebound, narrow, intolerant, canting, racist, sexist, chauvinistic, bigoted, blind, partial, narrow-minded, parochial, provincial, one-sided, not seeing an inch beyond one's nose, squinteyed, intolerant of, disliking, having a predilection, closed against, judging on slight knowledge, smug.—*Ant.* GENEROUS, open-minded, receptive.

preliminary ***a.*** preparatory, preceding, prefatory; see INTRODUCTORY.

prelude ***n.*** preface, prologue, overture; see INTRODUCTION 3.

premarital ***a.*** prenuptial, before marriage, during courtship; see BEFORE.

premature ***a.*** unanticipated, precipitate, rash; see EARLY 2, UNTIMELY.

prematurely ***a.*** too early, rash, precipitately; see EARLY 2, UNTIMELY.

in importance; foremost —*n.* a chief official; specif., a prime minister —**pre·mier′ship** *n.*

pre·mière or **pre·miere** (pri mir′, -myer′) *n.* ⟦Fr: see prec.⟧ a first performance of a play, movie, etc.

prem·ise (prem′is) *n.* ⟦< L *prae-*, before + *mittere*, send⟧ **1** a previous statement serving as a basis for an argument **2** [*pl.*] a piece of real estate —*vt.* **-ised**, **-is·ing** to state as a premise

pre·mi·um (prē′mē əm) *n., pl.* **-ums** ⟦< L *prae-*, before + *emere*, get, buy⟧ **1** a reward or prize, esp. as an inducement to buy **2** an additional amount paid or charged **3** a payment, as for an insurance policy **4** very high value [*to put a premium on wit*] —**at a premium** very valuable because of scarcity

prem·o·ni·tion (prēm′ə nish′ən, prē′mə-) *n.* ⟦< L *prae-*, before + *monere*, warn⟧ **1** a forewarning **2** a foreboding —**pre·mon·i·to·ry** (prē män′i tôr′ē) *adj.*

pre·na·tal (prē nāt′'l) *adj.* before birth

pre·nup·tial (prē nup′shəl) *adj.* before a marriage or wedding

pre·oc′cu·pied′ *adj.* completely absorbed in one's own thoughts; engrossed

pre·oc·cu·py (prē äk′yōō pī′) *vt.* **-pied′**, **-py′ing** ⟦< L *prae-*, before + *occupare*, seize⟧ to wholly occupy the thoughts of; engross —**pre·oc′cu·pa′tion** (-pā′shən) *n.*

pre·or·dain (prē′ôr dān′) *vt.* to ordain or decree beforehand

pre-owned′ *adj.* previously owned; used

prep[1] (prep) *adj. short for* PREPARATORY [*a prep school*] —*vt.* **prepped**, **prep′ping** to prepare (a patient) for surgery, etc.

prep[2] *abbrev.* **1** preparatory **2** preposition

pre·pack·age (prē pak′ij) *vt.* **-aged**, **-ag·ing** to package (foods, etc.) in standard units before selling

pre·paid (prē pād′) *vt. pt. & pp. of* PREPAY

prep·a·ra·tion (prep′ə rā′shən) *n.* **1** a preparing or being prepared **2** a preparatory measure **3** something prepared, as a medicine or cosmetic

pre·par·a·to·ry (prē par′ə tôr′ē, prep′ə rə-) *adj.* serving to prepare; introductory

preparatory school a private secondary school that prepares students for college

pre·pare (prē par′, pri-) *vt.* **-pared′**, **-par′ing** ⟦< L *prae-*, before + *parare*, get ready⟧ **1** to make ready **2** to equip or furnish **3** to put together [*to prepare dinner*] —*vi.* **1** to make things ready **2** to make oneself ready

pre·par′ed·ness (-par′id nəs) *n.* the state of being prepared, esp. for waging war

pre·pay′ *vt.* **-paid′**, **-pay′ing** to pay or pay for in advance —**pre·pay′ment** *n.*

pre·pon·der·ate (prē pän′dər āt′, pri-) *vi.* **-at′ed**, **-at′ing** ⟦< L *prae-*, before + *ponderare*, weigh⟧ to be superior in amount, power, etc. —**pre·pon′der·ance** *n.* —**pre·pon′der·ant** *adj.*

prep·o·si·tion (prep′ə zish′ən) *n.* ⟦< L *prae-*, before + *ponere*, to place⟧ a word, as *in*, *by*, or *to*, that connects a noun or pronoun to another element of a sentence —**prep′o·si′tion·al** *adj.*

pre·pos·sess (prē′pə zes′) *vt.* to bias, esp. favorably

pre′pos·sess′ing *adj.* that impresses favorably

pre·pos·ter·ous (prē päs′tər əs, pri-) *adj.* ⟦< L *prae-*, before + *posterus*, following⟧ absurd; ridiculous; laughable

prep·py or **prep·pie** (prep′ē) *n., pl.* **-pies** a student at or graduate of a preparatory school —*adj.* **-pi·er**, **-pi·est** of or like the clothes worn by such students

pre·puce (prē′pyōōs′) *n.* ⟦< L *praeputium*⟧ FORESKIN

pre·re·cord (prē′ri kôrd′) *vt. Film, Radio, TV* to record (music, a program, etc.) for later use

pre′re·cord′ed *adj.* designating or of a magnetic tape, as in a cassette, on which sound, etc. has been recorded before its sale

pre·req·ui·site (prē rek′wə zit, pri-) *adj.* required beforehand as a necessary condition —*n.* something prerequisite

pre·rog·a·tive (prē räg′ə tiv, pri-) *n.* ⟦< L *prae-*, before + *rogare*, ask⟧ an exclusive right or privilege

pres *abbrev.* present

Pres *abbrev.* President

pres·age (pres′ij; *for v., usually* prē sāj′, pri-) *n.* ⟦< L *prae-*, before + *sagire*, perceive⟧ **1** an omen; portent **2** a foreboding —*vt.* **-aged′**, **-ag′ing** to give warning of

pres·by·ter (prez′bi tər) *n.* ⟦see PRIEST⟧ **1** in the Presbyterian Church, an elder **2** in the Episcopal Church, a priest

Pres′by·te′ri·an (-tir′ē ən) *adj.* designating or of a church of a traditionally Calvinistic Protestant denomination governed by presbyters —*n.* a member of a Presbyterian church

pre′school′ *adj.* of or for a child between infancy and school age —*n.* a school for very young children, usually those three to five years of age —**pre′school′er** *n.*

pres·cience (prē′shəns, -shē əns) *n.* ⟦< L *prae-*, before + *scire*, know⟧ foreknowledge; foresight —**pres′cient** *adj.*

pre·scribe (prē skrīb′, pri-) *vt.* **-scribed′**, **-scrib′ing** ⟦< L *prae-*, before + *scribere*, write⟧ **1** to order; direct **2** to order as a medicine or treatment: said as of physicians

pre·script (prē′skript′) *n.* a prescribed rule —**pre·scrip′tive** *adj.*

pre·scrip·tion (prē skrip′shən, pri-) *n.* **1** something prescribed **2** *a)* a written direction for the preparation and use of medicine *b)* such a medicine

pres·ence (prez′əns) *n.* **1** the fact or state of being present **2** immediate surroundings [*in his presence*] **3** *a)* a person's bearing or appearance *b)* impressive bearing, personality, etc.

presence of mind ability to think and act quickly in an emergency

pres·ent (prez′ənt; *for v.* prē zent′, pri-) *adj.* ⟦< L *prae-*, before + *esse*, be⟧ **1** being at the specified place **2**

THESAURUS

premiere *n.* first night, beginning, opening; see PERFORMANCE.

premise *n.* proposition, principle, assumption; see BASIS, PROOF 1.

premises *n.* bounds, real estate, land; see PROPERTY 2.

premium *a.* prime, superior, select; see EXCELLENT.

premium *n.* remuneration, bonus, installment; see PRIZE.

premonition *n.* omen, portent, forewarning; see SIGN 1, WARNING.

preoccupation *n.* absorption, daydreaming, obsession; see FANTASY, THOUGHT 1.

preoccupied *a.* engrossed, distracted, absorbed; see ABSENT-MINDED, RAPT.

preparation *n.* **1** [The act of preparing] preparing, fitting, making ready, manufacture, readying, putting in order, establishment, compounding, adapting, rehearsal, incubation, gestation, formation, maturing, development, evolution, construction, building, furnishing, anticipation, buildup*. **2** [The state of being prepared] preparedness, readiness, fitness, adaptation, suitability, capacity, qualification, background, ripeness, mellowness, maturity, training, education, equipment. **3** [Something that is prepared] arrangement, product, compound; see MIXTURE 1.

prepare *v.* **1** [To make oneself ready] get ready, foresee, arrange, make preparations, make arrangements, fit, adapt, qualify, put in order, adjust, set one's house in order, prime, fix, settle, fabricate, appoint, furnish, elaborate, perfect, develop, prepare the ground, lay the foundations, block out, smooth the way, man, arm, cut out, warm up, lay the groundwork, contrive, devise, make provision, put in readiness, build up, provide for, provide against, make snug, be ready; see also ANTICIPATE, PLAN 1. **2** [To make other persons or things ready] outfit, equip, fit out; see PROVIDE 1. **3** [To cook and serve] concoct, dress, brew; see COOK, SERVE.

prepared *a.* **1** [Fitted] adapted, qualified, adjusted; see ABLE, FIT 1. **2** [Subjected to a special process or treatment] frozen, precooked, processed; see PRESERVED 2. **3** [Ready] available, on hand, in order; see READY 2.

prepossessing *a.* pleasing, captivating, attractive; see CHARMING, PLEASANT 1.

prerequisite *n.* essential, necessity, need; see REQUIREMENT 2.

prerogative *n.* privilege, advantage, exemption; see RIGHT 1.

prescribe *v.* guide, order, give directions; see ORDER 1.

prescription *n.* direction, medicinal recipe, formula; see MEDICINE 2.

presence *n.* **1** [The fact of being present] occupancy, occupation, residence, inhabitance, habitancy; see also ATTENDANCE 1. **2** [The vicinity of a person] propinquity, nearness, closeness; see NEIGHBORHOOD. **3** [One's appearance and behavior] carriage, port, demeanor; see APPEARANCE 1, BEHAVIOR.

presence of mind *n.* sensibility, alertness, acumen; see ATTENTION.

present *a.* **1** [Near in time] existing, being, in process, in duration, begun, started, commenced, going on, under consideration, at this time, contemporary, immediate, instant, prompt, at this moment, at present, today, nowadays, these days, already, even now, but now, just now, ongoing, for the time being, for the occasion; see also NOW 1.—*Ant.* PAST, over, completed. **2** [Near in space] in view, at hand, within reach; see NEAR 1.

present *n.* **1** [The present time] instant, this time, present moment;

existing or happening now **3** *Gram.* indicating action or state occurring now or action that is always the same *[present* tense*]* —***n.*** **1** the present time **2** the present tense **3** a gift —***vt.*** **pre·sent′** **1** to introduce (a person) **2** to exhibit; show **3** to offer for consideration **4** to give (a gift, etc.) to a person, etc. —**present arms** to hold a rifle vertically in front of the body

pre·sent·a·ble (prē zent′ə bəl, pri-) ***adj.*** **1** suitable for presentation **2** suitably groomed for meeting people

pres·en·ta·tion (prez′ən tā′shən, prē′zən-) ***n.*** **1** a presenting or being presented **2** something presented

pres′ent-day′ ***adj.*** of the present time

pre·sen·ti·ment (prē zent′ə mənt, pri-) ***n.*** ⟦see PRE- & SENTIMENT⟧ a feeling that something, esp. of an unfortunate nature, is about to take place

pres′ent·ly ***adv.*** **1** soon; shortly **2** at present; now: a usage objected to by some

pre·sent·ment (prē zent′mənt, pri-) ***n.*** presentation

present participle a participle used *a)* to express present or continuing action or existence (Ex.: he is *growing*) *b)* as an adjective (Ex.: a *growing* boy)

pres·er·va·tion·ist (prez′ər vā′shən ist) ***n.*** one who advocates positive measures to preserve historic buildings, wilderness lands, etc.

pre·serv·a·tive (prē zurv′ə tiv, pri-) ***adj.*** preserving —***n.*** anything that preserves *[*a *preservative* added to foods*]*

pre·serve (prē zurv′, pri-) ***vt.*** **-served′**, **-serv′ing** ⟦< L *prae-*, before + *servare*, to keep⟧ **1** to protect from harm, damage, etc. **2** to keep from spoiling **3** to prepare (food), as by canning, for future use **4** to carry on; maintain —***n.*** **1** [*usually pl.*] fruit preserved by cooking with sugar **2** a place where game, fish, etc. are maintained —**pres·er·va·tion** (prez′ər vā′shən) ***n.*** —**pre·serv′er** ***n.***

pre·set (prē set′) ***vt.*** **-set′**, **-set′ting** to set (automatic controls) beforehand

pre·shrink (prē shriŋk′) ***vt.*** **-shrank′** or **-shrunk′**, **-shrunk′** or **-shrunk′en**, **-shrink′ing** to shrink by a special process in manufacture, to minimize further shrinkage in laundering —**pre′shrunk′** ***adj.***

pre·side (prē zīd′, pri-) ***vi.*** **-sid′ed**, **-sid′ing** ⟦< L *prae-*, before + *sedere*, sit⟧ **1** to serve as chairman **2** to have control or authority (*over*)

pres·i·dent (prez′ə dənt) ***n.*** ⟦see PRESIDE⟧ **1** the highest executive officer of a company, club, etc. **2** [*often* **P-**] the chief executive (as in the U.S.), or the nominal head (as in Italy), of a republic —**pres′i·den·cy**, *pl.* **-cies**, ***n.*** —**pres′i·den′tial** (-den′shəl) ***adj.***

press[1] (pres) ***vt.*** ⟦< L *premere*⟧ **1** *a)* to act on with steady force or weight; push against, squeeze, compress, etc. *b)* to push against (a button, key, etc.) as in using an elevator, keyboard, etc. **2** to squeeze (juice, etc.) from **3** to iron (clothes, etc.) **4** to embrace closely **5** to urge persistently; entreat **6** to try to force **7** to emphasize **8** to distress or trouble *[*I'm *pressed* for time*]* **9** to urge on —***vi.*** **1** to exert pressure; apply weight **2** to go forward with determination **3** to crowd —***n.*** **1** pressure, urgency, etc. **2** a crowd **3** a machine for crushing, stamping, etc. **4** *a) short for* PRINTING PRESS *b)* a printing establishment *c)* newspapers, magazines, etc., or the persons who write for them *d)* publicity, etc. in newspapers, etc. **5** a closet for storing clothes, etc. —**press′er** ***n.***

press[2] (pres) ***vt.*** ⟦< L *praes*, surety + *stare*, to stand⟧ to force into service, esp. military or naval service

press agent one whose work is to get publicity for a client

press box a place for reporters at sports events, etc.

press conference a group interview granted to media personnel as by a celebrity

press′ing ***adj.*** calling for immediate attention; urgent

press′man (-mən) ***n.***, *pl.* **-men** (-mən) an operator of a printing press

press secretary one whose job is to deal with the news media on behalf of a prominent person

pres·sure (presh′ər) ***n.*** **1** a pressing or being pressed **2** a state of distress **3** a compelling influence *[*social *pressure]* **4** urgent demands; urgency **5** *Physics* force per unit of area exerted upon a surface, etc. —***vt.*** **-sured**, **-sur·ing** to exert pressure on

pressure cooker a container for quick cooking by steam under pressure

pressure group a group trying to influence government through lobbying, propaganda, etc.

pres′sur·ize′ (-īz′) ***vt.*** **-ized′**, **-iz′ing** to keep nearly normal atmosphere pressure inside (an airplane, etc.), as at high altitudes —**pres′sur·i·za′tion** ***n.***

pres·ti·dig·i·ta·tion (pres′tə dij′i tā′shən) ***n.*** ⟦Fr < *preste*, quick + L *digitus*, finger⟧ sleight of hand

pres·tige (pres tēzh′, -tēj′) ***n.*** ⟦< L *praestrigiae*, deceptions⟧ **1** the power to impress or influence **2** reputation based on high achievement, character, etc.

pres·ti′gious (-tij′əs, -tē′jəs) ***adj.*** having or imparting prestige or distinction

pres·to (pres′tō) ***adv.***, ***adj.*** ⟦It, quick⟧ **1** fast or at once **2** *Music* in fast tempo Also written **pres′to**

pre·stressed concrete (prē′strest′) concrete containing tensed steel cables for strength

pre·sume (prē zōōm′, pri-) ***v.*** **-sumed′**, **-sum′ing** ⟦< L *prae-*, before + *sumere*, take⟧ **1** to dare (to say or do something); venture **2** to take for granted; suppose —***vi.***

THESAURUS

see TODAY. **2** [A gift] grant, donation, offering; see GIFT 1.

present ***v.*** **1** [To introduce] make known, acquaint with, give an introduction; see INTRODUCE 3. **2** [To submit] donate, proffer, put forth; see OFFER 1. **3** [To give] grant, bestow, confer; see GIVE 1. **4** [To give a play, etc.] put on, do, offer; see ACT 3, PERFORM 2.

presentable ***a.*** attractive, prepared, satisfactory; see FIT 1.

presentation ***n.*** **1** [The act of presenting] bestowal, donation, delivering; see GIVING. **2** [Something presented] present, offering, remembrance; see GIFT 1.

presented ***a.*** bestowed, granted, conferred; see GIVEN.

presently ***a.*** directly, without delay, shortly; see IMMEDIATELY, SOON.

preservation ***n.*** security, safety, protection, conservation, maintenance, saving, keeping, storage, curing, tanning, freezing, freeze-drying, sugaring, pickling, evaporation, canning, refrigeration.

preserve ***v.*** **1** [To guard] protect, shield, save; see DEFEND 2. **2** [To maintain] keep up, care for, conserve; see MAINTAIN 3. **3** [To keep] can, conserve, process, save, put up, put down, store, cure, bottle, do up, season, salt, pickle, put in brine, put in vinegar, pot, tin, dry, smoke, corn, dry-cure, smoke-cure, freeze, freeze-dry, quick freeze, keep up, cold-pack, refrigerate, dehydrate, seal up, kipper, marinate, evaporate, embalm, mummify, mothball, fill.—*Ant.* WASTE, allow to spoil, let spoil.

preserved ***a.*** **1** [Saved] rescued, guarded, secured; see SAVED 1. **2** [Prepared for preservation] canned, corned, dried, freeze-dried, dehydrated, evaporated, smoked, seasoned, pickled, salted, brined, put up, conserved, cured, marinated, tinned, potted, bottled, embalmed, mummified.

preserves ***n.*** spread, marmalade, conserve; see JAM 1, JELLY.

preside ***v.*** direct, lead, emcee; see ADVISE, MANAGE 1.

presidency ***n.*** office of the president, chairmanship, position; see ADMINISTRATION 2.

president ***n.*** presiding officer, chief executive, prez*; see EXECUTIVE.

presidential ***a.*** official, regulatory, of the chief executive; see MANAGING.

press[1] ***n.*** **1** [The pressure of circumstances] rush, confusion, strain; see HASTE. **2** [Publishing as a social institution] the fourth estate, publishers, publicists, newsmen, newspapermen, journalists, journalistic writers, editors, correspondents, political writers, columnists, periodicals, papers, newspapers, the media.

press[1] ***v.*** **1** [To subject to pressure] thrust, crowd, bear upon, bear down on, squeeze, hold down, pin down, force down, crush, drive, weight, urge; see also PUSH 1.—*Ant.* RAISE, release, relieve. **2** [To smooth, usually by heat and pressure] finish, mangle, roll; see IRON, SMOOTH.

press conference ***n.*** interview, question-and-answer session, briefing; see ANNOUNCEMENT, HEARING 1.

pressing ***a.*** importunate, constraining, distressing; see IMPORTANT 1, URGENT 1.

pressure ***n.*** **1** [Physical pressure] force, burden, mass, load, encumbrance, stress, thrust, tension, squeeze; see also WEIGHT 1.—*Ant.* RELEASE, relief, deliverance. **2** [Some form of social pressure] compulsion, constraint, urgency, persuasion, stress, affliction, coercion, trouble, hardship, humiliation, misfortune, necessity, repression, confinement, unnaturalness, obligation, discipline.—*Ant.* AID, assistance, encouragement.

pressure ***v.*** press, compel, constrain; see URGE 2, 3.

prestige ***n.*** renown, effect, influence; see FAME.

presumably ***a.*** in all probability, credibly, likely; see PROBABLY.

presume ***v.*** consider, suppose, take for granted; see ASSUME.

to act presumptuously; take liberties —**pre·sum'a·ble** ***adj.*** —**pre·sum'a·bly** ***adv.***
pre·sump·tion (prē zump'shən, pri-) ***n.*** **1** a presuming; specif., *a)* an overstepping of proper bounds *b)* a taking of something for granted **2** the thing presumed **3** a reason for presuming —**pre·sump'tive** ***adj.***
pre·sump'tu·ous (-cho͞o əs) ***adj.*** too bold or forward
pre·sup·pose (prē'sə pōz') ***vt.*** **-posed', -pos'ing** **1** to suppose or assume beforehand **2** to require or imply as a preceding condition —**pre'sup·po·si'tion** (-sup ə zish'ən) ***n.***
pre·teen (prē'tēn') ***n.*** a child nearly a teenager
pre·tend (prē tend', pri-) ***vt.*** ⟦< L *prae-*, before + *tendere*, to stretch⟧ **1** to profess *[to pretend ignorance]* **2** to feign; simulate *[to pretend anger]* **3** to make believe *[to pretend to be astronauts]* —***vi.*** to lay claim (*to*) —**pre·tend'er** ***n.***
pre·tense (prē tens', pri-; prē'tens') ***n.*** **1** a claim; pretension **2** a false claim **3** a false show of something **4** a pretending, as at play Brit. sp. **pre·tence'**
pre·ten·sion (prē ten'shən, pri-) ***n.*** **1** a pretext **2** a claim **3** assertion of a claim **4** pretentiousness
pre·ten'tious (-shəs) ***adj.*** **1** making claims to some distinction, importance, etc. **2** affectedly grand; ostentatious —**pre·ten'tious·ly** ***adv.*** —**pre·ten'tious·ness** ***n.***
pret·er·it or **pret·er·ite** (pret'ər it) ***adj.*** ⟦< L *praeter-*, beyond + *ire*, go⟧ *Gram.* expressing past action or state —***n.*** the past tense
pre·term (prē'turm') ***adj.*** of premature birth
pre·ter·nat·u·ral (prēt'ər nach'ər əl) ***adj.*** ⟦ML *praeternaturalis*⟧ **1** differing from or beyond what is natural; abnormal **2** SUPERNATURAL
pre·test (prē test') ***vt., vi.*** to test in advance
pre·text (prē'tekst') ***n.*** ⟦< L *prae-*, before + *texere*, weave⟧ a false reason put forth to hide the real one
Pre·to·ri·a (prē tôr'ē ə) administrative capital of South Africa: pop. 526,000
pret·ti·fy (prit'i fī') ***vt.*** **-fied', -fy'ing** to make pretty
pret·ty (prit'ē) ***adj.*** **-ti·er, -ti·est** ⟦OE *prættig*, crafty⟧ attractive in a dainty, graceful way —***adv.*** fairly; somewhat —***vt.*** **-tied, -ty·ing** to make pretty: usually with *up* —**pret'ti·ly** ***adv.*** —**pret'ti·ness** ***n.***
pret·zel (pret'səl) ***n.*** ⟦< L *brachium*, an arm⟧ a hard, brittle, salted biscuit, often formed in a loose knot
pre·vail (prē vāl', pri-) ***vi.*** ⟦< L *prae-*, before + *valere*, be strong⟧ **1** to be victorious; triumph: often with *over* or *against* **2** to succeed **3** to be or become more widespread **4** to be prevalent —**prevail on** (or **upon** or **with**) to persuade
pre·vail'ing ***adj.*** **1** superior in strength or influence **2** prevalent
prev·a·lent (prev'ə lənt) ***adj.*** ⟦see PREVAIL⟧ widely existing; generally accepted, used, etc. —**prev'a·lence** ***n.***
pre·var·i·cate (pri var'i kāt') ***vi.*** **-cat'ed, -cat'ing** ⟦< L *prae-*, before + *varicare*, straddle⟧ **1** to evade the truth **2** to lie —**pre·var'i·ca'tion** ***n.*** —**pre·var'i·ca'tor** ***n.***
pre·vent (prē vent', pri-) ***vt.*** ⟦< L *prae-*, before + *venire*, come⟧ to stop or keep from doing or happening; hinder —**pre·vent'a·ble** or **pre·vent'i·ble** ***adj.*** —**pre·ven'tion** ***n.***
pre·ven'tive (-vent'iv) ***adj.*** preventing or serving to prevent —***n.*** anything that prevents Also **pre·vent'a·tive** (-vent'ə tiv)
pre·view (prē'vyo͞o') ***n.*** **1** an advance, restricted showing, as of a movie **2** a showing of scenes from a movie, etc. to advertise it Also sp. **pre'vue'**
pre·vi·ous (prē'vē əs) ***adj.*** ⟦< L *prae-*, before + *via*, a way⟧ occurring before; prior —**previous to** before —**pre'vi·ous·ly** ***adv.***
pre·war (prē'wôr') ***adj.*** before a (or the) war
prex·y (prek'sē) ***n., pl.*** **-ies** [Slang] the president, esp. of a college, etc.
prey (prā) ***n.*** ⟦< L *prehendere*, seize⟧ **1** an animal hunted for food by another animal **2** a victim **3** the mode of living by preying on other animals *[a bird of prey]* —***vi.*** **1** to plunder **2** to hunt other animals for food **3** to weigh as an obsession Generally used with *on* or *upon*
pri·ap·ic (prī ap'ik) ***adj.*** ⟦after *Priapos*, Gr god of procreation⟧ overly concerned with masculinity
price (prīs) ***n.*** ⟦< L *pretium*⟧ **1** the amount of money, etc. asked or paid for something; cost **2** value or worth **3** the cost, as in life, labor, etc., of obtaining some benefit —***vt.*** **priced, pric'ing** **1** to fix the price of **2** [Inf.] to find out the price of
price'less ***adj.*** of inestimable value; invaluable
price'y ***adj.*** [Inf.] expensive: also sp. **pri'cy**
prick (prik) ***n.*** ⟦OE *prica*, a point⟧ **1** a tiny puncture made by a sharp point **2** a sharp pain caused as by being pricked —***vt.*** **1** to make (a hole) in (something) with a sharp point **2** to pain sharply —**prick up one's ears** **1** to raise the ears erect **2** to listen closely
prick·le (prik'əl) ***n.*** ⟦OE *prica*, a point⟧ **1** a small, sharply pointed growth, as a thorn: also **prick'er** **2** a tingling

THESAURUS

presumption ***n.*** **1** [An assumption] conjecture, guess, hypothesis; see ASSUMPTION 1. **2** [Impudence] arrogance, audacity, effrontery; see RUDENESS.

pretend ***v.*** **1** [To feign] affect, simulate, claim falsely, imitate, counterfeit, sham, make as if, make as though, mislead, beguile, delude, pass off for, cheat, dupe, hoodwink, be deceitful, bluff, falsify, be hypocritical, fake, put on*, let on*, go through the motions, keep up appearances; see also DECEIVE. **2** [To make believe] mimic, fill a role, take a part, represent, portray, put on a front, play, make believe, act the part of, put on an act*, act a part, put on airs*, playact.

pretended ***a.*** feigned, counterfeit, assumed, affected, shammed, bluffing, simulated, lying, falsified, put on, concealed, covered, masked, cheating; see also FALSE 3.

pretense ***n.*** **1** [The act of pretending] affectation, misrepresentation, falsification, act, deceit, fabrication, trickery, double-dealing, misstatement, falsifying, simulation, excuse, insincerity, profession, ostentation, assumption, dissimulation, evasion, equivocation, prevarication, egotism, brazenness, arrogance, dandyism, foppery, servility, complacency, smugness, prudishness, coyness, formality, stiffness, blind, smoke screen; see also DISHONESTY, IMITATION.—*Ant.* HONESTY, candor, sincerity. **2** [Something pretended] falsehood, lie, falseness, affectation, mask, cloak, show, excuse, subterfuge, pretext, fraud, appearance, seeming, semblance, wile, ruse, sham, airs, claim, mannerism; see also DECEPTION, IMITATION 2.

prettily ***a.*** pleasingly, gently, daintily; see POLITELY.

pretty ***a.*** **1** [Attractive] comely, lovely, good-looking; see BEAUTIFUL. **2** [Pleasant] delightful, cheerful, pleasing; see PLEASANT 2. **3** [*Considerable] ample, sizable, notable; see LARGE 1, MUCH 1, 2. **4** [Somewhat] rather, tolerably, a little; see MODERATELY.

prevalence ***n.*** dissemination, occurrence, currency; see REGULARITY.

prevalent ***a.*** widespread, accepted, commonplace; see COMMON 1.

prevent ***v.*** preclude, obviate, forestall, anticipate, block, arrest, stop, thwart, repress, interrupt, halt, impede, check, avert, frustrate, balk, foil, retard, obstruct, counter, countercheck, counteract, inhibit, restrict, block off, limit, hold back, hold off, stop from, deter, intercept, override, circumvent, bar, ward off, keep from happening, nip in the bud, put a stop to, stave off, keep off, turn aside; see also HINDER, RESTRAIN.—*Ant.* HELP, aid, encourage.

prevented ***a.*** obviated, stopped, interfered with; see INTERRUPTED.

prevention ***n.*** anticipation, forestalling, arresting, obviating, bar, debarring, halt, impeding, retardation, repression, restraint, restriction, inhibition, interception, overriding, circumvention, hindering, counteraction, obstruction, opposition, stopping, thwarting, blocking, warding off, staving off, keeping off; see also REFUSAL.—*Ant.* AID, encouragement, help.

preventive ***a.*** deterrent, precautionary, prophylactic, averting, defensive.

previous ***a.*** antecedent, prior, former; see PRECEDING.

previously ***a.*** long ago, earlier, beforehand; see BEFORE.

prey ***n.*** quarry, hunted, game; see VICTIM.

prey on ***v.*** **1** [To destroy] seize, plunder, victimize; see DESTROY. **2** [To eat] feed on, devour, consume; see EAT 1.

price ***n.*** expenditure, outlay, expense, cost, value, worth, figure, dues, tariff, valuation, quotation, fare, hire, wages, return, disbursement, rate, appraisal, reckoning, equivalent, payment, demand, barter, consideration, amount, sticker price, asking price, estimate, output, ransom, reward, pay, par value, money's worth, price ceiling, ceiling; see also VALUE 1. —**at any price** whatever the cost, expense no object, anyhow; see REGARDLESS 2.

price ***v.*** fix the price of, appraise, assess; see RATE, VALUE 2.

priced ***a.*** valued, estimated, worth; see COSTING.

priceless ***a.*** invaluable, inestimable, without price; see VALUABLE.

prick ***n.*** puncture, stab, stick; see CUT.

prick ***v.*** pierce, puncture, stick; see CUT, HURT 1.

sensation —*vt.*, *vi.* **-led**, **-ling** to tingle —**prick′ly**, **-li·er**, **-li·est**, *adj.*

prickly heat a skin eruption caused by inflammation of the sweat glands

pride (prīd) *n.* ⟦< OE *prut*, proud⟧ **1** *a)* an unduly high opinion of oneself *b)* haughtiness; arrogance **2** dignity and self-respect **3** satisfaction in something done, owned, etc. **4** a person or thing in which pride is taken —**pride oneself on** to be proud of —**pride′ful** *adj.* —**pride′ful·ly** *adv.*

pri·er (prī′ər) *n.* one who pries

priest (prēst) *n.* ⟦< Gr *presbys*, old⟧ **1** a person of special rank who performs religious rites in a temple of God or a god **2** *R.C.Ch.* a clergyman ranking next below a bishop —**priest′hood′** *n.* —**priest′ly**, **-li·er**, **-li·est**, *adj.*

priest·ess (prēs′tis) *n.* a pagan female priest

prig (prig) *n.* ⟦< 16th-c. cant⟧ one who smugly affects great propriety or morality —**prig′gish** *adj.*

prim (prim) *adj.* **prim′mer**, **prim′mest** ⟦< ?⟧ stiffly formal, precise, or moral —**prim′ly** *adv.*

pri·ma·cy (prī′mə sē) *n.*, *pl.* **-cies** ⟦< L *primus*, first⟧ **1** a being first in time, rank, etc.; supremacy **2** the rank or office of a primate

pri·ma don·na (prē′mə dän′ə, prim′ə) *pl.* **pri′ma don′nas** ⟦It, lit., first lady⟧ the principal woman singer in an opera

pri·ma fa·ci·e (prī′mə fā′shə) ⟦L, lit., at first sight⟧ **1** self-evident **2** *Law* designating evidence that establishes a fact unless refuted

pri·mal (prī′məl) *adj.* ⟦< L *primus*, first⟧ **1** first in time; original **2** first in importance; chief **3** fundamental; basic *[primal* instincts*]*

pri·mar·i·ly (prī mer′ə lē) *adv.* **1** at first; originally **2** mainly; principally

pri·mar·y (prī′mer′ē) *adj.* ⟦< L *primus*, first⟧ **1** first in time or order; original **2** from which others are derived; fundamental *[primary* colors*]* **3** first in importance; chief —*n.*, *pl.* **-ries** **1** something first in order, importance, etc. **2** a preliminary election at which candidates are chosen for the final election

primary school **1** ELEMENTARY SCHOOL **2** a school including the first three elementary grades and, sometimes, kindergarten

primary stress (or **accent**) the heaviest stress (′) in pronouncing a word

pri·mate (prī′mit; *for 2*, -māt′) *n.* ⟦< L *primus*, first⟧ **1** an archbishop, or the highest-ranking bishop in a province, etc. **2** any of the order of mammals that includes humans, the apes, etc.

prime (prīm) *adj.* ⟦< L *primus*, first⟧ **1** first in time; original **2** first in rank or importance; chief; principal **3** first in quality **4** fundamental **5** *Math.* that can be evenly divided by no other whole number than itself and 1 —*n.* **1** the first or earliest part **2** the best or most vigorous period **3** the best part —*vt.* **primed**, **prim′ing** **1** to make ready; prepare **2** to get (a pump) into operation by pouring water into it **3** to undercoat, size, etc. before painting **4** to provide with facts, answers, etc. beforehand

prime meridian the meridian at Greenwich, England, from which longitude is measured east and west

prime minister in some countries, the chief executive of the government

prim·er[1] (prim′ər) *n.* ⟦< L *primus*, first⟧ **1** a simple book for teaching reading **2** any elementary textbook

prim·er[2] (prī′mər) *n.* a thing that primes; specif., *a)* an explosive cap, etc. used to set off a main charge *b)* a preliminary coat of paint, etc.

prime rate the most favorable interest rate charged on bank loans to large corporations: also **prime interest rate** or **prime lending rate**

prime time *Radio, TV* the hours when the largest audience is available

pri·me·val (prī mē′vəl) *adj.* ⟦< L *primus*, first + *aevum*, an age⟧ of the earliest times or ages; primordial

prim·i·tive (prim′i tiv) *adj.* ⟦< L *primus*, first⟧ **1** of the earliest times; original **2** crude; simple **3** primary; basic —*n.* a primitive person or thing

pri·mo·gen·i·ture (prī′mə jen′i chər) *n.* ⟦< L *primus*, first + *genitura*, a begetting⟧ the exclusive right of inheritance of the eldest son

pri·mor·di·al (prī môr′dē əl) *adj.* ⟦< L *primus*, first + *ordiri*, begin⟧ primitive; fundamental

primp (primp) *vt.*, *vi.* ⟦prob. < PRIM⟧ to groom or dress up in a fussy way

prim·rose (prim′rōz′) *n.* ⟦altered (after *rose*) < ML *primula*⟧ a plant with tubelike, often yellow flowers

primrose path **1** the path of pleasure, self-indulgence, etc. **2** a course of action that seems easy but that can lead to disaster

prince (prins) *n.* ⟦< L *princeps*, chief⟧ **1** a ruler ranking below a king; head of a principality **2** a son of a sovereign **3** any preeminent person

prince consort the husband of a reigning queen

Prince Edward Island island province of SE Canada: 2,185 sq. mi.; pop. 135,000; cap. Charlottetown: abbrev. *PE*

prince′ly *adj.* **-li·er**, **-li·est** **1** of a prince **2** magnificent; generous —**prince′li·ness** *n.*

prin·cess (prin′sis, -ses′) *n.* **1** a daughter of a sovereign **2** the wife of a prince

prin·ci·pal (prin′sə pəl) *adj.* ⟦see PRINCE⟧ first in rank, importance, etc. —*n.* **1** a principal person or thing **2** the head of a school **3** the amount of a loan, on which interest is computed —**prin′ci·pal·ly** *adv.*

prin′ci·pal′i·ty (-pal′ə tē) *n.*, *pl.* **-ties** the territory ruled by a prince

THESAURUS

prickly *a.* thorny, pointed, spiny; see SHARP 1.

pride *n.* **1** [The quality of being vain] conceit, vainglory, vanity, hubris, egoism, egotism, self-esteem, self-love, self-exaltation, self-glorification, self-admiration, pretension.—*Ant.* HUMILITY, self-effacement, unpretentiousness. **2** [Conduct growing from pride or conceit] haughtiness, vanity, disdain, condescension, patronizing, patronage, snobbery, superiority; see also sense 1. **3** [Sense of personal satisfaction] self-respect, self-satisfaction, self-sufficiency; see HAPPINESS. **4** [A source of satisfaction] treasure, jewel, pride and joy; see SATISFACTION 2.

pride oneself on *v.* take pride in, flatter oneself that, be proud of; see BOAST.

priest *n. Names for priests in various sects include the following:* father confessor, spiritual father, priest-vicar, high priest, minor canon, pontiff, vicar, bishop, monsignor, clergyman, rector, preacher, presbyter, elder, rabbi, lama, imam, monk, friar; see also MINISTER 1.

priesthood *n.* clergy, Holy Orders, monasticism; see MINISTRY 2.

priestly *a.* ecclesiastic, episcopal, ministerial; see CLERICAL 2.

prim *a.* stiff, formal, precise, demure, decorous, nice, orderly, tidy, cleanly, dapper, trim, spruce, pat; see also POLITE.

primarily *a.* mainly, fundamentally, in the first place; see PRINCIPALLY.

primary *a.* **1** [Earliest] primitive, initial, first; see ORIGINAL 1. **2** [Fundamental] elemental, basic, central; see FUNDAMENTAL. **3** [Principal] chief, prime, main; see PRINCIPAL.

primate *n.* gorilla, chimpanzee, orangutan, gibbon, great ape, lemur; see also MAN 1, MONKEY.

prime *a.* **1** [Principal] main, first, chief; see PRINCIPAL. **2** [Excellent] top, choice, superior; see EXCELLENT.

primitive *a.* **1** [Simple] rudimentary, elementary, first; see FUNDAMENTAL. **2** [Ancient] primeval, archaic, primordial; see OLD 3. **3** [Uncivilized] crude, rough, simple, rude, atavistic, uncivilized, savage, uncultured, natural, barbaric, barbarous, barbarian, fierce, untamed, uncouth, ignorant, undomesticated, wild, brutish, raw, untaught, green, unlearned, untutored, underdeveloped.

prince *n.* sovereign, ruler, monarch, potentate; see also ROYALTY.

princely *a.* **1** [Royal] sovereign, regal, august; see ROYAL. **2** [Suited to a prince] lavish, sumptuous, luxurious; see EXPENSIVE, HANDSOME, RICH 1, 2.

princess *n.* sovereign, monarch, infanta; see ROYALTY.

principal *a.* leading, chief, first, head, prime, main, foremost, cardinal, essential, capital, important, preeminent, highest, supreme, prominent, dominant, predominant, controlling, superior, prevailing, paramount, greatest, incomparable, unapproachable, peerless, matchless, unequaled, unrivaled, maximum, crowning, unparalleled, sovereign, second to none.—*Ant.* UNIMPORTANT, secondary, accessory.

principal *n.* chief, head, headmaster, master; see also EXECUTIVE.

principally *a.* chiefly, mainly, essentially, substantially, materially, eminently, preeminently, superlatively, supremely, vitally, especially, particularly, peculiarly, notably, importantly, fundamentally, dominantly, predominantly, basically, largely, first and foremost, in large measure, first of all, to a great degree, prevalently, generally, universally, mostly, above all, in the first place, for the most part, for the greatest part, before anything else, in the main.—*Ant.* SLIGHTLY, somewhat, tolerably.

principal parts the principal inflected forms of a verb: in English, the infinitive, past tense, and past participle (Ex: *drink, drank, drunk*)
prin·ci·ple (prin'sə pəl) ***n.*** ⟦see PRINCE⟧ **1** a fundamental truth, law, etc. upon which others are based **2** *a)* a rule of conduct *b)* adherence to such rules; integrity **3** a basic part **4** *a)* the scientific law explaining a natural action *b)* the method of a thing's operation
prin'ci·pled ***adj.*** having principles, as of conduct
print (print) ***n.*** ⟦< L *premere*, to press⟧ **1** a mark made on a surface by pressing or stamping **2** cloth printed with a design **3** the impression of letters, designs, etc. made by inked type or from a plate, block, etc. **4** a photograph, esp. one made from a negative —***vt.***, ***vi.*** **1** to stamp (a mark, letter, etc.) on a surface **2** to produce on (paper, etc.) the impression of inked type, etc. **3** to produce (a book, etc.) **4** to write in letters resembling printed ones **5** to make (a photographic print) —**in** (or **out of**) **print** still (or no longer) being sold by the publisher: said of books, etc. —**print'er** ***n.***
printed circuit an electrical circuit of conductive material, as in fine lines, applied to an insulating sheet
print'ing ***n.*** **1** the act of one that prints **2** something printed **3** all the copies printed at one time
printing press a machine for printing from inked type, plates, or rolls
print'out' ***n.*** the printed or typewritten output of a computer
pri·or (prī'ər) ***adj.*** ⟦L⟧ **1** earlier; previous **2** preceding in order or importance —***n.*** the head of a priory —**prior to** before in time
pri'or·ess (-is) ***n.*** a woman who heads a priory of nuns
pri·or·i·tize (prī ôr'ə tīz') ***vt.*** **-tized'**, **-tiz'ing** to arrange (items) in order of importance
pri·or·i·ty (prī ôr'ə tē) ***n.***, *pl.* **-ties** **1** a being prior; precedence **2** a prior right to get, buy, or do something **3** something to be given prior attention
pri·o·ry (prī'ə rē) ***n.***, *pl.* **-ries** a monastery governed by a prior, or a convent governed by a prioress
prism (priz'əm) ***n.*** ⟦< Gr *prizein*, to saw⟧ **1** *Geom.* a solid figure whose ends are parallel and equal in size and shape, and whose sides are parallelograms **2** a transparent, triangular prism used to disperse light into the spectrum —**pris·mat·ic** (priz mat'ik) ***adj.***
pris·on (priz'ən) ***n.*** ⟦< L *prehendere*, take⟧ a place of confinement for convicted criminals or persons who are awaiting trial
prison camp **1** a camp with minimum security for holding reliable prisoners **2** a camp for confining prisoners of war
pris'on·er ***n.*** one held captive or confined, esp. in prison
pris·sy (pris'ē) ***adj.*** **-si·er**, **-si·est** ⟦prob. PR(IM) + (S)ISSY⟧ [Inf.] very prim or prudish —**pris'si·ness** ***n.***
pris·tine (pris'tēn', pris tēn') ***adj.*** ⟦L *pristinus*, former⟧ **1** characteristic of the earliest period **2** unspoiled
prith·ee (prith'ē) ***interj.*** ⟦< *pray thee*⟧ [Archaic] I pray thee; please
pri·va·cy (prī'və sē) ***n.***, *pl.* **-cies** **1** a being private; seclusion **2** secrecy **3** one's private life
pri·vate (prī'vət) ***adj.*** ⟦< L *privus*, separate⟧ **1** of or concerning a particular person or group **2** not open to or controlled by the public *[a private* school*]* **3** for an individual person *[a private* room*]* **4** not holding public office *[a private* citizen*]* **5** secret *[a private* matter*]* —***n.*** **1** [*pl.*] the genitals: also **private parts** **2** the lowest-ranking enlisted man of either the U.S. Army or Marine Corps —**go private** to restore private corporate ownership by buying back publicly held stock —**in private** not publicly —**pri'vate·ly** ***adv.***
pri·va·teer (prī'və tir') ***n.*** **1** a privately owned ship commissioned in war to capture enemy ships **2** a commander or crew member of a privateer
private eye [Slang] a private detective
pri·va·tion (prī vā'shən) ***n.*** the lack of ordinary necessities or comforts
pri·va·tize (prī'və tīz') ***vt.*** **-tized'**, **-tiz'ing** to turn over (a public property, etc.) to private interests —**pri'va·ti'za'tion** ***n.***
priv·et (priv'it) ***n.*** ⟦< ?⟧ an evergreen shrub used for hedges
priv·i·lege (priv'ə lij, priv'lij) ***n.*** ⟦< L *privus*, separate + *lex*, law⟧ a special right, favor, etc. granted to some person or group —***vt.*** **-leged**, **-leg·ing** to grant a privilege to
priv·y (priv'ē) ***adj.*** private: now only in such phrases as **privy council**, a body of confidential advisers named by a ruler —***n.***, *pl.* **priv'ies** an outhouse —**privy to** privately informed about
prize[1] (prīz) ***vt.*** **prized**, **priz'ing** ⟦see PRICE⟧ to value highly; esteem —***n.*** **1** something given to the winner of a contest, etc. **2** anything worth striving for —***adj.*** **1** that has won or is worthy of a prize **2** given as a prize
prize[2] (prīz) ***n.*** ⟦< L *prehendere*, to take⟧ something taken by force, esp. a captured ship —***vt.*** **prized**, **priz'ing** to pry, as with a lever
prize'fight' ***n.*** a professional boxing match —**prize'fight'er** ***n.***
pro[1] (prō) ***adv.*** ⟦L, for⟧ favorably —***adj.*** favorable —***n.***, *pl.* **pros** **1** a person or vote on the affirmative side **2** an argument in favor of something
pro[2] (prō) ***adj.***, ***n.***, *pl.* **pros** *short for* PROFESSIONAL
pro-[1] ⟦Gr < *pro*, before⟧ *prefix* before in place or time
pro-[2] ⟦L < *pro*, forward⟧ *prefix* **1** moving forward or ahead of *[*proclivity*]* **2** forth *[*produce*]* **3** substituting for *[*pronoun*]* **4** defending, supporting *[*prolabor*]*
pro-am (prō'am') ***n.*** a sports competition for both amateurs and professionals
prob *abbrev.* **1** probably **2** problem
prob·a·bil·i·ty (präb'ə bil'ə tē) ***n.***, *pl.* **-ties** **1** a being probable; likelihood **2** something probable

THESAURUS

principle ***n.*** **1** [A fundamental law] underlying truth, basic doctrine, postulate; see LAW 4. **2** [A belief or set of beliefs; *often plural*] system, canon, teaching; see BELIEF, FAITH 2, POLICY.
print ***n.*** **1** [Printed matter] impression, reprint, issue; see COPY. **2** [A printed picture] engraving, lithograph, photograph; see PICTURE 3, SKETCH. —**in print** printed, available, obtainable; see PUBLISHED. —**out of print** OP, unavailable, remaindered; see SOLD OUT.
print ***v.*** **1** [To make an impression] impress, imprint, indent; see MARK 1. **2** [To reproduce by printing] run off, print up, issue, reissue, reprint, bring out, go to press, set type, compose, start the presses; see also PUBLISH 1.—*Ant.* TALK, write, inscribe. **3** [To simulate printing] letter, hand-letter, calligraph; see WRITE 2.
printed ***a.*** impressed, imprinted, engraved, stamped, embossed, lithographed, multilithed, xeroxed, printed by photo-offset, silkscreened; see also REPRODUCED.
printer ***n.*** typesetter, compositor, linotype operator; see WORKMAN.
printing ***n.*** **1** [A process of reproduction] typography, composition, typesetting, presswork. **2** [Printed matter] line, page, sheet; see PAGE. **3** [Publication] issuing, issue, distribution; see PUBLICATION 1.
prior ***a.*** antecedent, above-mentioned, foregoing; see PRECEDING.
priority ***n.*** superiority, preference, precedence; see ADVANTAGE.
prison ***n.*** penitentiary, reformatory, prison house, guardhouse, stockade; see also JAIL.
prisoner ***n.*** captive, convict, culprit, jailbird*, detainee, escapee, hostage, con*; see also DEFENDANT.
prisoner of war ***n.*** captive person, captured person, interned person, person in captivity, POW; see also PRISONER.
privacy ***n.*** seclusion, solitude, retreat, isolation, separateness, aloofness, separation, concealment; see also SECRECY.
private ***a.*** special, separate, retired, secluded, withdrawn, removed, not open, behind the scenes, off the record, privy, clandestine, single; see also INDIVIDUAL, OWN.—*Ant.* PUBLIC, open, exposed. —**in private** privately, personally, not publicly; see SECRETIVE, SECRETLY.
private ***n.*** enlisted man, infantryman; private first class, private second class, etc.; see also SAILOR, SOLDIER.
privately ***a.*** confidentially, clandestinely, alone; see PERSONALLY 1, SECRETLY.
private parts ***n.*** genitals, organs of reproduction, privates; see GENITALS.
privilege ***n.*** **1** [A customary concession] due, perquisite, prerogative; see RIGHT 1. **2** [An opportunity] chance, fortunate happening, event; see OPPORTUNITY 1.
privileged ***a.*** **1** [Wealthy] well-to-do, favored, affluent; see RICH 1. **2** [Confidential] classified, not public, top-secret; see SECRET 1.
prize[1] ***n.*** reward, advantage, privilege, possession, honor, inducement, premium, bounty, bonus, spoil, booty, plunder, pillage, loot, award, accolade, recompense, requital, acquisitions, laurel, decoration, medal, trophy, palm, crown, citation, scholarship, fellowship, feather in one's cap, title, championship, first place, blue ribbon, *prix* (French), payoff*, cake*, plum.
prize[1] ***v.*** regard highly, value, esteem; see VALUE 2.
probability ***n.*** likelihood, possibil-

prob·a·ble (präb′ə bəl) ***adj.*** ⟦< L *probare,* prove⟧ **1** likely to occur or be **2** reasonably so, but not proved —**prob′a·bly *adv.***

pro·bate (prō′bāt′) ***n.*** ⟦see PROBE⟧ the act or process of probating —***adj.*** having to do with probating *[probate* court*]* —***vt.*** **-bat′ed, -bat′ing** to establish officially that (a document, esp. a will) is genuine

pro·ba·tion (prō bā′shən) ***n.*** ⟦see PROBE⟧ **1** a testing, as of one's character, ability, etc. **2** the conditional suspension of a convicted person's sentence —**pro·ba′tion·ar′y *adj.***

pro·ba′tion·er ***n.*** a person on probation

probation officer an officer who watches over persons on probation

probe (prōb) ***n.*** ⟦< L *probare,* to test⟧ **1** a surgical instrument for exploring a wound, etc. **2** a searching examination **3** a device, as a spacecraft with instruments, used to get information about an environment —***vt.*** **probed, prob′ing 1** to explore (a wound, etc.) with a probe **2** to investigate thoroughly —***vi.*** to search

pro·bi·ty (prō′bə tē, präb′ə-) ***n.*** ⟦< L *probus,* good⟧ honesty; integrity

prob·lem (präb′ləm) ***n.*** ⟦< Gr *problēma*⟧ **1** a question proposed for solution **2** a perplexing or difficult matter, person, etc.

prob·lem·at·ic (präb′lə mat′ik) ***adj.*** **1** hard to solve **2** uncertain Also **prob′lem·at′i·cal**

pro·bos·cis (prō bäs′is) ***n., pl.*** **-cis·es** ⟦< Gr *pro-,* before + *boskein,* to feed⟧ an elephant's trunk, or any similar long, flexible snout

pro·caine (prō′kān′) ***n.*** ⟦PRO-[2] + (CO)CAINE⟧ a synthetic compound used as a local anesthetic

pro·ce·dure (prō sē′jər, prə-) ***n.*** the act or method of proceeding in an action —**pro·ce′dur·al *adj.***

pro·ceed (prō sēd′, prə-) ***vi.*** ⟦< L *pro-,* forward + *cedere,* go⟧ **1** to go on, esp. after stopping **2** to carry on some action **3** to take legal action (*against*) **4** to come forth or issue (*from*)

pro·ceed′ing ***n.*** **1** a going on with what one has been doing **2** a course of action **3** [*pl.*] a record of the business carried on, as by a learned society **4** [*pl.*] legal action

pro·ceeds (prō′sēdz′) ***pl.n.*** the sum derived from a sale, business venture, etc.

proc·ess (prä′ses′) ***n.*** ⟦see PROCEED⟧ **1** the course of being done: chiefly in **in process** **2** course (*of* time, etc.) **3** a continuing development involving many changes *[*the *process* of digestion*]* **4** a method of doing something, with all the steps involved **5** *Biol.* a projecting part **6** *Law* a court summons —***vt.*** to prepare by or subject to a special process —**pro′cess·or *n.***

pro·ces·sion (prō sesh′ən, prə-) ***n.*** ⟦see PROCEED⟧ a number of persons or things moving forward, as in a parade

pro·ces′sion·al ***n.*** a hymn sung at the beginning of a church service during the entrance of the clergy

pro′-choice′ ***adj.*** advocating the legal right to obtain an abortion —**pro′-choic′er *n.***

pro·claim (prō klām′) ***vt.*** ⟦< L *pro-,* before + *clamare,* cry out⟧ to announce officially; announce to be

proc·la·ma·tion (präk′lə mā′shən) ***n.*** **1** a proclaiming **2** something that is proclaimed

pro·cliv·i·ty (prō kliv′ə tē) ***n., pl.*** **-ties** ⟦< L *pro-,* before + *clivus,* a slope⟧ a tendency or inclination

pro·cras·ti·nate (prō kras′tə nāt′) ***vi., vt.*** **-nat′ed, -nat′ing** ⟦< L *pro-,* forward + *cras,* tomorrow⟧ to put off doing (something) until later; delay —**pro·cras′ti·na′tion *n.*** —**pro·cras′ti·na′tor *n.***

pro·cre·ate (prō′krē āt′) ***vt., vi.*** **-at′ed, -at′ing** ⟦< L *pro-,* before + *creare,* create⟧ to produce (young); beget (offspring) —**pro′cre·a′tion *n.***

proc·tor (präk′tər) ***n.*** ⟦see PROCURE⟧ one who supervises students, as at an examination —***vt.*** to supervise (an academic examination)

proc·u·ra·tor (präk′yoo rāt′ər) ***n.*** ⟦see fol.⟧ in the Roman Empire, the governor of a lesser province

pro·cure (prō kyoor′) ***vt.*** **-cured′, -cur′ing** ⟦< L *pro-,* before + *curare,* attend to⟧ to obtain; get —**pro·cur′a·ble *adj.*** —**pro·cure′ment *n.***

pro·cur′er ***n.*** a pimp

prod (präd) ***vt.*** **prod′ded, prod′ding** ⟦< ?⟧ **1** to jab as with a pointed stick **2** to goad into action —***n.*** **1** a jab or thrust **2** something that prods

prod·i·gal (präd′i gəl) ***adj.*** ⟦< L *pro-,* forth + *agere,* to drive⟧ **1** exceedingly or recklessly wasteful **2** extremely abundant —***n.*** a spendthrift —**prod′i·gal′i·ty** (-gal′ə tē), *pl.* **-ties, *n.***

pro·di·gious (prō dij′əs, prə-) ***adj.*** ⟦see fol.⟧ **1** wonderful; amazing **2** enormous; huge —**pro·di′gious·ly *adv.***

prod·i·gy (präd′ə jē) ***n., pl.*** **-gies** ⟦< L *prodigium,* omen⟧ an extraordinary person, thing, or act; specif., a child of genius

pro·duce (prə do͞os′; *for n.* prō′do͞os′) ***vt.*** **-duced′, -duc′ing** ⟦< L *pro-,* forward + *ducere,* to lead⟧ **1** to bring to view; show *[*to *produce* identification*]* **2** to bring forth; bear **3** to make or manufacture **4** to cause **5** to get (a play, etc.) ready for presentation —***vi.*** to yield something —***n.*** something produced; esp., fruit and vegetables —**pro·duc′er *n.***

prod·uct (präd′əkt) ***n.*** **1** something produced by nature, industry, or art **2** result; outgrowth **3** *Math.* the quantity obtained by multiplying two or more quantities together

pro·duc·tion (prə duk′shən) ***n.*** a producing or something produced

THESAURUS

ity, chance; see CHANCE, POSSIBILITY 2.

probable ***a.*** seeming, presumable, feasible; see LIKELY 1.

probably ***a.*** presumably, seemingly, apparently, believably, reasonably, imaginably, feasibly, practicably, expediently, plausibly, most likely, everything being equal, as like as not, in all likelihood, as the case may be, one can assume, like enough, no doubt, to all appearances, in all probability.—*Ant.* UNLIKELY, doubtfully, questionably.

problem ***n.*** **1** [A difficulty] dilemma, quandary, obstacle; see DIFFICULTY 1, 2. **2** [A question to be solved] query, intricacy, enigma; see PUZZLE 1.

procedure ***n.*** fashion, style, mode; see METHOD, SYSTEM.

proceed ***v.*** move, progress, continue; see ADVANCE 1.

proceeding ***n.*** [*Often plural*] process, transaction, deed, experiment, performance, measure, step, course, undertaking, venture, adventure, occurrence, incident, circumstance, happening, movement, operation, procedure, exercise, maneuver; see also ACTION 1.

proceeds ***n.*** gain, profit, yield; see RETURN 3.

process ***n.*** means, rule, manner; see METHOD. **—in (the) process of** while, when, in the course of; see DURING.

process ***v.*** treat, make ready, put through; see PREPARE 1.

processed ***a.*** treated, handled, fixed; see PRESERVED 2.

prod ***v.*** provoke, goad, shove; see PUSH 1.

prodigy ***n.*** marvel, portent, miracle, monster, enormity, spectacle, freak, curiosity, phenom*; see also WONDER 2. **—child prodigy** genius, gifted child, boy or girl wonder; see ARTIST, MUSICIAN, SCIENTIST, WRITER.

produce ***n.*** product, harvest, result, crop, return, effect, consequence, amount, profit, outcome, outgrowth, aftermath, gain, realization; see also BUTTER, CHEESE, CREAM 1, FOOD, FRUIT, GRAIN 1, MILK, VEGETABLE.

produce ***v.*** **1** [To bear] yield, bring forth, give birth to, propagate, bring out, come through, blossom, flower, deliver, generate, engender, breed, contribute, give, afford, furnish, return, render, fetch, bring in, present, offer, provide, contribute, sell for, bear fruit, accrue, allow, admit, proliferate, be delivered of, bring to birth, reproduce, foal, lamb, drop, calve, fawn, whelp, litter, hatch, usher into the world, spawn. **2** [To create by mental effort] originate, author, procreate, bring forth, conceive, concoct, engender, write, design, fabricate, imagine, turn out, churn out, devise; see also COMPOSE 2, CREATE, INVENT 1. **3** [To cause] effect, occasion, bring about; see BEGIN 1. **4** [To show] exhibit, present, unfold; see DISPLAY. **5** [To make] assemble, build, construct; see MANUFACTURE. **6** [To present a performance] present, play, put on; see ACT 3, PERFORM 2.

produced ***a.*** **1** [Created] originated, composed, made; see FORMED. **2** [Presented] performed, acted, put on; see SHOWN 1. **3** [Caused] occasioned, propagated, begot, bred, engendered, generated, hatched, induced.

product ***n.*** **1** [A result] output, outcome, outgrowth; see RESULT. **2** [Goods produced; *often plural*] stock, commodity, merchandise; see GOODS 1.

production ***n.*** **1** [The act of producing] origination, creation, authoring, reproduction, giving, bearing, rendering, giving forth, putting out, issuing, increasing, return, procreation, generation, engendering, blooming, blossoming; see also MAKING. **2** [The amount produced] crop, result, stock; see QUANTITY.

pro·duc'tive *adj.* 1 fertile 2 marked by abundant production 3 bringing as a result (with *of*) *[war is productive of misery]* —**pro·duc'tive·ly** *adv.* —**pro·duc·tiv·i·ty** (prō'dək tiv'ə tē) or **pro·duc'tive·ness** *n.*

prof (präf) *n.* [Inf.] *short for* PROFESSOR

Prof *abbrev.* Professor

pro·fane (prō fān') *adj.* ⟦< L *pro-*, before + *fanum*, temple⟧ 1 not connected with religion; secular 2 showing disrespect or contempt for sacred things —*vt.* **-faned'**, **-fan'ing** 1 to treat (sacred things) with irreverence or contempt 2 to debase; defile —**prof·a·na·tion** (präf'ə nā' shən) *n.* —**pro·fane'ly** *adv.* —**pro·fane'ness** *n.*

pro·fan'i·ty (-fan'ə tē) *n.* 1 a being profane 2 *pl.* **-ties** profane language; swearing

pro·fess (prō fes', prə-) *vt.* ⟦< L *pro-*, before + *fateri*, avow⟧ 1 to declare openly; affirm 2 to claim to have (some feeling, etc.): often insincerely 3 to declare one's belief in —**pro·fessed'** *adj.*

pro·fes·sion (prō fesh'ən, prə-) *n.* 1 a professing, or declaring; avowal 2 an occupation requiring advanced academic training, as medicine, law, etc. 3 all the persons in such an occupation

pro·fes'sion·al *adj.* 1 of or engaged in a profession 2 engaged in some sport or in a specified occupation for pay —*n.* a person who is professional —**pro·fes'sion·al·ly** *adv.*

pro·fes·sor (prō fes'ər, prə-) *n.* a college or university teacher, esp. one of the highest rank —**pro·fes·so·ri·al** (prō'fə sôr'ē əl, prä'-) *adj.* —**pro·fes'sor·ship'** *n.*

prof·fer (präf'ər) *vt.* ⟦< OFr: see PRO-[2] & OFFER⟧ to offer (usually something intangible) *[to proffer friendship]* —*n.* an offer

pro·fi·cient (prō fish'ənt, prə-) *adj.* ⟦< L *pro-*, forward + *facere*, make⟧ highly competent; skilled —**pro·fi'cien·cy** *n.* —**pro·fi'cient·ly** *adv.*

pro·file (prō'fīl') *n.* ⟦< It *profilare*, to outline⟧ 1 a side view of the face 2 a drawing of this 3 an outline 4 a short, vivid biography 5 a degree of public exposure *[keeping a low profile]* —*vt.* 1 to draw or write a profile 2 to identify by profiling

pro'fil'ing *n.* the use of a set of characteristics to identify those likely to belong to a certain group, as in detaining suspected criminals

prof·it (präf'it) *n.* ⟦see PROFICIENT⟧ 1 advantage; gain 2 [*often pl.*] financial gain; esp. the sum remaining after deducting costs —*vt.*, *vi.* 1 to be of advantage (to) 2 to benefit —**prof'it·a·bil'i·ty** *n.* —**prof'it·a·ble** *adj.* —**prof'it·a·bly** *adv.* —**prof'it·less** *adj.*

prof·it·eer (präf'i tir') *n.* one who makes excessive profits by charging exorbitant prices —*vi.* to be a profiteer

pro·fi·te·role (prə fit'ə rōl') *n.* a small cream puff

prof·li·gate (präf'li git) *adj.* ⟦< L *pro-*, forward + *fligere*, to drive⟧ 1 dissolute 2 recklessly wasteful —**prof'li·ga·cy** (-gə sē) *n.*

pro for·ma (prō fôr'mə) ⟦L⟧ for (the sake of) form; as a matter of form

pro·found (prō found', prə-) *adj.* ⟦< L *pro-*, forward + *fundus*, bottom⟧ 1 marked by intellectual depth 2 deeply felt *[profound grief]* 3 thoroughgoing *[profound changes]* —**pro·found'ly** *adv.* —**pro·fun'di·ty** (-fun'də tē), *pl.* **-ties**, *n.*

pro·fuse (prō fyo͞os', prə-) *adj.* ⟦< L *pro-*, forth + *fundere*, pour⟧ giving or given freely and abundantly —**pro·fuse'ly** *adv.* —**pro·fu'sion** (-fyo͞o'zhən) *n.*

pro·gen·i·tor (prō jen'ə tər) *n.* ⟦< L *pro-*, forth + *gignere*, beget⟧ 1 an ancestor in direct line 2 a precursor

prog·e·ny (präj'ə nē) *n.*, *pl.* **-nies** ⟦see prec.⟧ children; offspring

pro·ges·ter·one (prō jes'tər ōn') *n.* a female hormone secreted by the ovary or made synthetically

prog·na·thous (präg'nə thəs) *adj.* ⟦PRO-[1] + Gr *gnathos*, jaw⟧ having the jaws projecting beyond the upper face

prog·no·sis (präg nō'sis) *n.*, *pl.* **-no'ses'** (-sēz') ⟦< Gr *pro-*, before + *gignōskein*, know⟧ a prediction, esp. of the course of a disease

prog'nos'tic (-näs'tik) *adj.* ⟦see prec.⟧ 1 foretelling 2 of a medical prognosis

prog·nos'ti·cate' (-näs'ti kāt') *vt.* **-cat'ed**, **-cat'ing** ⟦see PROGNOSIS⟧ to foretell —**prog·nos'ti·ca'tion** *n.* —**prog·nos'ti·ca'tor** *n.*

pro·gram (prō'gram', -grəm) *n.* ⟦< Gr *pro-*, before + *graphein*, write⟧ 1 a list of the acts, speeches, musical pieces, etc. as of an entertainment 2 a plan or procedure 3 a scheduled radio or TV broadcast 4 a logical sequence of coded instructions specifying the operations to be performed by a computer 5 a series of operations used to control an electronic device —*vt.* **-grammed'** or **-gramed'**, **-gram'ming** or **-gram'ing** 1 to schedule in a program 2 to prepare (a textbook, etc.) for use in programmed instruction 3 to plan a computer program for 4 to furnish (a computer) with a program Also [Chiefly Brit.] **pro'gramme'** —**pro·gram·ma·ble** (prō'gram'ə bəl, prō gram'-) *adj.*, *n.* —**pro'gram'mer** or **pro'gram'er** *n.*

pro·gram·mat·ic (prō'grə mat'ik) *adj.* of or like a program; often, specif., predictable, mechanical, uninspired, etc.

programmed instruction instruction in which individual students answer questions about a unit of study at

THESAURUS

productive *a.* rich, fruitful, prolific; see FERTILE.

productivity *n.* richness, potency, fecundity; see FERTILITY.

profanity *n.* abuse, cursing, swearing; see CURSE 0.

profession *n.* 1 [A skilled or learned occupation] calling, business, avocation, vocation, career, employment, occupation, engagement, office, situation, position, lifework, chosen work, role, service, pursuit, undertaking, concern, post, berth, craft, sphere, field, walk of life; see also JOB 1, TRADE 2. 2 [A declaration] pretense, avowal, vow; see DECLARATION, OATH 1.

professional *a.* 1 [Skillful] expert, learned, adept; see ABLE. 2 [Well-qualified] acknowledged, known, licensed; see ABLE.

professional *n.* expert, trained personnel, specially trained person; see SPECIALIST.

professor *n.* educator, faculty member, sage; see TEACHER. *Teachers popularly called professors include the following:* full professor, associate professor, assistant professor, instructor, lecturer, graduate assistant, teaching assistant, tutor, school principal, fellow, teaching fellow, master docent.

proficiency *n.* learning, skill, knowledge; see ABILITY.

proficient *a.* skilled, expert, skillful; see ABLE.

profile *n.* silhouette, shape, figure; see FORM 1, OUTLINE 3.

profit *n.* 1 [Advantage] avail, good, value; see ADVANTAGE. 2 [Excess of receipts over expenditures] gain, returns, proceeds, receipts, take*, gate, acquisition, rake-off*, windfall, accumulation, saving, interest, remuneration, earnings.—*Ant.* LOSS, debits, costs.

profit *v.* 1 [To be of benefit] benefit, assist, avail; see HELP. 2 [To derive gain] benefit, capitalize on, cash in on, realize, clear, gain, reap profits, make a profit, be in the black, recover, thrive, prosper, harvest, make money.—*Ant.* LOSE, lose out on, miss out on.

profitable *a.* lucrative, useful, sustaining, aiding, remunerative, beneficial, gainful, advantageous, paying, successful, favorable, assisting, productive, serviceable, valuable, instrumental, practical, pragmatic, effective, to advantage, effectual, sufficient, paying its way, bringing in returns, making money, paying well, paying out, in the black; see also HELPFUL 1.—*Ant.* UNPROFITABLE, UNSUCCESSFUL, unproductive.

profitably *a.* lucratively, remuneratively, gainfully, usefully, advantageously, successfully, favorably, for money, productively, practically, effectively, effectually, sufficiently, sustainingly.

profiteer *n.* exploiter, chiseler, gouger*; see CHEAT.

profound *a.* 1 [Physically deep] fathomless, bottomless, subterranean; see DEEP 1. 2 [Intellectually deep] heavy, erudite, scholarly, mysterious, sage, serious, sagacious, penetrating, discerning, knowing, wise, knowledgeable, intellectual, enlightened, thorough, informed; see also LEARNED 1, SOLEMN.—*Ant.* SUPERFICIAL, shallow, flighty. 3 [Emotionally deep] heartfelt, deep-felt, great; see INTENSE.

profoundly *a.* deeply, extremely, thoroughly; see VERY.

program *n.* 1 [A list of subjects] schedule, menu, printed program; see LIST. 2 [A sequence of events] happenings, schedule, agenda, order of business, calendar, plans, business, affairs, details, arrangements, catalogue, curriculum, order of the day, series of events, itinerary, appointments, things to do, chores, preparations, meetings, getting and spending, all the thousand and one things; see also PLAN 2. 3 [An entertainment] performance, show, presentation; see PERFORMANCE.

program *v.* 1 [To schedule] slate, book, bill; see sense 2. 2 [To work out a sequence to be performed] feed in, activate a computer, compute, reckon, figure, calculate, estimate, enter, compile, feed, edit, process, extend, delete, add.

programmed *a.* scheduled, slated, lined up; see PLANNED.

their own rate, checking their own answers and advancing only after answering correctly

prog·ress (präg′res; *for v.* prō gres′, prə-) ***n.*** ⟦< L *pro-*, before + *gradi*, to step⟧ **1** a moving forward or onward **2** development **3** improvement —***vi.*** **1** to move forward or onward **2** to move forward toward completion **3** to improve

pro·gres·sion (prō gresh′ən, prə-) ***n.*** **1** a moving forward **2** a succession, as of events **3** *Math.* a series of numbers, each of which is obtained from its predecessor by the same rule

pro·gres′sive (-gres′iv, prə-) ***adj.*** **1** moving forward **2** continuing by successive steps **3** of or favoring progress, reform, etc. **4** *Gram.* indicating continuing action or state, as certain verb forms —***n.*** one who is progressive —**pro·gres′sive·ly** ***adv.***

pro·hib·it (prō hib′it, prə-) ***vt.*** ⟦< L *pro-*, before + *habere*, have⟧ **1** to forbid by law or an order **2** to prevent; hinder —**pro·hib′i·tive** ***adj.***

pro·hi·bi·tion (prō′i bish′ən) ***n.*** **1** a prohibiting **2** the forbidding by law of the manufacture or sale of alcoholic beverages —**pro′hi·bi′tion·ist** ***n.***

proj·ect (prä′jekt′; *for v.* prō jekt′, prə-) ***n.*** ⟦< L *pro-*, before + *jacere*, to throw⟧ **1** a proposal; scheme **2** an organized undertaking —***vt.*** **pro·ject′** **1** to propose (a plan) **2** to throw forward **3** to cause to jut out **4** to cause (a shadow, image, etc.) to fall upon a surface —***vi.*** to jut out —**pro·jec′tion** ***n.***

pro·jec·tile (prō jek′təl, prə-) ***n.*** **1** an object designed to be shot forward, as a bullet **2** anything thrown or hurled forward

projection booth a small chamber, as in a theater, from which images on film, slides, etc. are projected

pro·jec′tion·ist ***n.*** the operator of a film or slide projector

pro·jec′tor ***n.*** a machine for projecting images onto a screen

pro·lapse (prō laps′, prō′laps′) ***n.*** ⟦L *pro-*, forward + *labi*, to fall⟧ *Med.* the slipping out of place of an internal organ: said as of the uterus

pro·le·tar·i·at (prō′lə ter′ē ət) ***n.*** ⟦< L *proletarius*, a citizen of the lowest class⟧ the working class; esp., the industrial working class —**pro′le·tar′i·an** ***adj.***, ***n.***

pro′-life′ ***adj.*** opposing the legal right to abortion —**pro′-lif′er** ***n.***

pro·lif·er·ate (prō lif′ər āt′, prə-) ***vi.*** **-at′ed, -at′ing** ⟦ult. < L *proles*, offspring + *ferre*, to bear⟧ to increase rapidly —**pro·lif′er·a′tion** ***n.***

pro·lif·ic (prō lif′ik, prə-) ***adj.*** ⟦< L *proles*, offspring + *facere*, make⟧ **1** producing many young or much fruit **2** turning out many products of the mind —**pro·lif′i·cal·ly** ***adv.***

pro·lix (prō liks′, prō′liks′) ***adj.*** ⟦< L *prolixus*, extended⟧ wordy or long-winded —**pro·lix′i·ty** ***n.***

pro·logue (prō′lôg′) ***n.*** ⟦< Gr *pro-*, before + *logos*, discourse⟧ **1** an introduction to a poem, play, etc. **2** any preliminary act, event, etc.

pro·long (prō lôŋ′, prə-) ***vt.*** ⟦< L *pro-*, forth + *longus*, long⟧ to lengthen in time or space: also **pro·lon′gate′** (-gāt′), **-gat′ed, -gat′ing** —**pro·lon·ga·tion** (prō′lôŋ gā′shən) ***n.***

prom (präm) ***n.*** ⟦< fol.⟧ a dance, as of a particular class in a school

prom·e·nade (präm′ə nād′, -näd′) ***n.*** ⟦Fr < L *pro-*, forth + *minare*, to herd⟧ **1** a leisurely walk taken for pleasure, display, etc. **2** a public place for walking —***vi.***, ***vt.*** **-nad′ed, -nad′ing** to take a promenade (along or through)

Pro·me·the·us (prō mē′thē əs) ***n.*** *Gr. Myth.* a Titan who steals fire from heaven for the benefit of human beings

prom·i·nent (präm′ə nənt) ***adj.*** ⟦< L *prominere*, to project⟧ **1** sticking out; projecting **2** noticeable; conspicuous **3** widely and favorably known —**prom′i·nence** ***n.*** —**prom′i·nent·ly** ***adv.***

pro·mis·cu·ous (prō mis′kyoo͞ əs, prə-) ***adj.*** ⟦< L *pro-*, forth + *miscere*, to mix⟧ **1** consisting of different elements indiscriminately mingled **2** characterized by a lack of discrimination, esp. in sexual liaisons —**prom·is·cu·i·ty** (präm′is kyoo͞′ə tē), *pl.* **-ties**, ***n.*** —**pro·mis′cu·ous·ly** ***adv.***

prom·ise (präm′is) ***n.*** ⟦< L *pro-*, forth + *mittere*, send⟧ **1** an agreement to do or not to do something **2** indication, as of a successful future **3** something promised —***vi.***, ***vt.*** **-ised, -is·ing** **1** to make a promise of (something) **2** to give a basis for expecting (something)

Promised Land *Bible* Canaan, promised by God to Abraham and his descendants: Genesis 17:8

prom·is·so·ry (präm′i sôr′ē) ***adj.*** containing a promise

pro·mo (prō′mō) [Inf.] ***adj.*** of or engaged in the promotion or advertising of a product, etc. —***n.***, *pl.* **-mos** a recorded announcement, radio or TV commercial, etc. used in advertising, etc.

prom·on·to·ry (präm′ən tôr′ē) ***n.***, *pl.* **-ries** ⟦prob. < L *prominere*, to project⟧ a peak of high land that juts out into a body of water; headland

pro·mote (prə ōt′) ***vt.*** **-mot′ed, -mot′ing** ⟦< L *pro-*, forward + *movere*, to move⟧ **1** to raise to a higher position

THESAURUS

progress ***n.*** **1** [Movement forward] progression, advance, headway, impetus, forward course, development, velocity, pace, tempo, momentum, motion, rate, step, stride, current, flow, tour, circuit, transit, journey, voyage, march, expedition, locomotion, passage, course, procession, process, march of events, course of life, movement of the stars, motion through space.—*Ant.* STOP, stay, stand. **2** [Improvement] advancement, development, growth; see IMPROVEMENT 1. —**in progress** advancing, going on, continuing; see MOVING 1.

progress ***v.*** proceed, move onward, move on; see ADVANCE 1.

progressive ***a.*** **1** [In mounting sequence] advancing, mounting, rising; see MOVING 1. **2** [Receptive to new ideas] tolerant, lenient, open-minded; see LIBERAL.

prohibit ***v.*** interdict, ban, obstruct; see FORBID, PREVENT.

prohibited ***a.*** forbidden, restricted, proscribed; see ILLEGAL, REFUSED.

project ***n.*** outline, design, scheme; see PLAN 2.

project ***v.*** **1** [To thrust out] protrude, hang over, extend, jut, bulge, stick out, hang out, jut out, be prominent, be conspicuous.—*Ant.* WITHDRAW, regress, revert. **2** [To throw] pitch, heave, propel; see THROW 1.

projection ***n.*** **1** [Bulge] prominence, jut, protuberance, step, ridge, rim; see also BULGE. **2** [Forecast] prognostication, prediction, guess; see GUESS.

prolong ***v.*** continue, hold, draw out; see INCREASE.

prolonged ***a.*** extended, lengthened, continued; see DULL 4.

prominence ***n.*** **1** [A projection] jut, protrusion, bump; see BULGE, PROJECTION 1. **2** [Notability] renown, influence, distinction; see FAME.

prominent ***a.*** **1** [Physically prominent] protuberant, extended, jutting, conspicuous, protruding, projecting, noticeable, rugged, rough, obtrusive, standing out, sticking out, hilly, raised, relieved, rounded.—*Ant.* HOLLOW, depressed, sunken. **2** [Socially prominent] notable, preeminent, leading; see FAMOUS. **3** [Conspicuous] remarkable, striking, noticeable; see CONSPICUOUS.

promiscuity ***n.*** lechery, looseness, sexual immorality; see LEWDNESS.

promiscuous ***a.*** indiscriminate, sexually immoral, loose; see LEWD 2.

promise ***n.*** **1** [A pledge] assurance, agreement, pact, oath, engagement, covenant, consent, warrant, affirmation, swearing, plight, word, troth, vow, profession, guarantee, insurance, obligation, commitment, betrothal, espousal, plighted faith, marriage contract, giving one's word, gentleman's agreement, word of honor. **2** [Hope] outlook, good omen, potential; see ENCOURAGEMENT.

promise ***v.*** engage, declare, agree, vow, swear, consent, affirm, profess, undertake, pledge, covenant, contract, bargain, espouse, betroth, assure, guarantee, warrant, give assurance, give warranty, insure, cross one's heart, plight one's troth, bind oneself, commit oneself, obligate oneself, make oneself answerable, give security, underwrite, subscribe, lead someone to expect, answer for, pledge one's honor.—*Ant.* DECEIVE, deny, break faith.

promised ***a.*** pledged, sworn, vowed, agreed, covenanted, as agreed upon, undertaken, professed, consented, affirmed, insured, warranted, vouched for, underwritten, subscribed, stipulated, assured, ensured; see also GUARANTEED.

promising ***a.*** likely, assuring, encouraging; see HOPEFUL 2.

promote ***v.*** **1** [To further] forward, urge, encourage, profit, patronize, help, aid, assist, develop, support, boom, back, uphold, champion, advertise, market, merchandise, sell, advocate, cultivate, improve, push, bolster, develop, speed, foster, nourish, nurture, subsidize, befriend, mentor, benefit, subscribe to, favor, expand, improve, better, cooperate, get behind, boost.—*Ant.* DISCOURAGE, weaken, enfeeble. **2** [To advance in rank] raise, advance, elevate, graduate, move up, exalt, aggrandize, magnify, prefer, favor, increase, better, dignify.—*Ant.* HUMBLE, demote, reduce.

or rank 2 to further the growth, establishment, sales, etc. of —**pro·mo'tion** *n.* —**pro·mo'tion·al** *adj.*

pro·mot'er *n.* one who begins, organizes, and furthers an undertaking

prompt (prämpt) *adj.* ⟦< L *pro-*, forth + *emere*, take⟧ **1** ready, punctual, etc. **2** done, spoken, etc. without delay —*vt.* **1** to urge into action **2** to remind (a person) of something he or she has forgotten; specif., to help (an actor, etc.) with a cue **3** to inspire —**prompt'er** *n.* —**prompt'ly** *adv.* —**prompt'ness** or **promp'ti·tude'** *n.*

prom·ul·gate (präm'əl gāt', prō mul'gāt') *vt.* **-gat'ed, -gat'ing** ⟦< L *promulgare*, publish⟧ **1** to make known officially **2** to make widespread —**prom'ul·ga'tion** *n.*

pron *abbrev.* **1** pronoun **2** pronunciation

prone (prōn) *adj.* ⟦< L *pronus*⟧ **1** lying face downward or prostrate **2** disposed or inclined (*to*) *[prone* to error*]*

prong (prôŋ) *n.* ⟦ME *pronge*⟧ **1** any of the pointed ends of a fork; tine **2** any projecting part —**pronged** *adj.*

prong'horn' *n.* an animal of the W U.S. having curved horns and resembling both the deer and the antelope

pro·noun (prō'noun') *n.* ⟦< L *pro*, for + *nomen*, noun⟧ *Gram.* a word used in place of a noun (Ex.: *I, he, them, ours, which, yourself, anyone*) —**pro·nom'i·nal** (-näm'i nəl) *adj.*

pro·nounce (prə nouns', prō-) *vt.* **-nounced', -nounc'ing** ⟦< L *pro-*, before + *nuntiare*, announce⟧ **1** to declare officially, solemnly, etc. **2** to utter or articulate (a sound or word) —**pro·nounce'a·ble** *adj.*

pro·nounced' *adj.* clearly marked; decided *[a pronounced* change*]*

pro·nounce'ment *n.* a formal statement, as of an opinion

pron·to (prän'tō) *adv.* ⟦Sp: see PROMPT⟧ [Slang] at once; quickly

pro·nun·ci·a·tion (prə nun'sē ā'shən, prō-) *n.* **1** the act or manner of pronouncing words **2** an accepted way of pronouncing a word; also, a rendering of this in symbols

proof (pro͞of) *n.* ⟦see PROBE⟧ **1** a proving or testing of something **2** evidence that establishes the truth of something **3** the relative strength of an alcoholic liquor **4** *Photog.* a trial print of a negative **5** a sheet printed from set type, for checking errors, etc. —*adj.* of tested strength in resisting: with *against*

-proof (pro͞of) ⟦< prec.⟧ *combining form* **1** impervious to *[waterproof]* **2** protected from *[rustproof]* **3** resistant to *[fireproof]*

proof'read' (-rēd') *vt., vi.* to read and mark corrections on (printers' proofs, etc.) —**proof'read'er** *n.*

prop[1] (präp) *n.* ⟦< MDu *proppe*⟧ a support, as a pole, placed under or against something: often used figuratively —*vt.* **propped, prop'ping** **1** to support with or as with a prop: often with *up* **2** to lean (something) *against* a support

prop[2] (präp) *n.* PROPERTY (sense 4)

prop[3] (präp) *n. short for* PROPELLER

prop[4] *abbrev.* **1** proper(ly) **2** property **3** proposition **4** proprietor

prop·a·gan·da (präp'ə gan'də) *n.* ⟦ModL: see fol.⟧ **1** any widespread promotion of particular ideas, doctrines, etc. **2** ideas, etc. so spread —**prop'a·gan'dist** *n., adj.* —**prop'a·gan'dize'** (-dīz'), **-dized', -diz'ing,** *vt., vi.*

prop·a·gate (präp'ə gāt') *vt.* **-gat'ed, -gat'ing** ⟦< L *propago*, slip (of a plant)⟧ **1** to cause (a plant or animal) to reproduce itself **2** to reproduce (itself): said of a plant or animal **3** to spread (ideas, customs, etc.) —*vi.* to reproduce: said of plants or animals —**prop'a·ga'tion** *n.*

pro·pane (prō'pān') *n.* a gaseous hydrocarbon obtained from petroleum, used as a fuel

pro·pel (prə pel', prō-) *vt.* **-pelled', -pel'ling** ⟦< L *pro-*, forward + *pellere*, to drive⟧ to drive onward or forward

pro·pel'lant or **pro·pel'lent** *n.* one that propels; specif., the fuel for a rocket

pro·pel'ler *n.* a device having two or more blades in a revolving hub, for propelling a ship or aircraft

pro·pen·si·ty (prə pen'sə tē) *n., pl.* **-ties** ⟦< L *propendere*, hang forward⟧ a natural inclination or tendency

prop·er (präp'ər) *adj.* ⟦< L *proprius*, one's own⟧ **1** specially suitable; appropriate; fitting **2** naturally belonging (*to*) **3** conforming to a standard; correct **4** decent; decorous **5** in the most restricted sense *[*Chicago *proper* (i.e., apart from its suburbs)*]* **6** designating a noun that names a specific individual, place, etc. (Ex.: *Bill, Paris*) —**prop'er·ly** *adv.*

prop·er·ty (präp'ər tē) *n., pl.* **-ties** ⟦see prec.⟧ **1** ownership **2** something owned, esp. real estate **3** a characteristic or attribute **4** any of the movable articles used in a stage setting —**prop'er·tied** (-tēd) *adj.*

proph·e·cy (präf'ə sē) *n., pl.* **-cies** ⟦see PROPHET⟧ **1** prediction of the future, as by divine guidance **2** something predicted

proph'e·sy' (-sī') *vt., vi.* **-sied', -sy'ing** **1** to predict as by divine guidance **2** to predict in any way

proph·et (präf'it) *n.* ⟦< Gr *pro-*, before + *phanai*, speak⟧ **1** a religious leader regarded as, or claiming to be, divinely inspired **2** one who predicts the future —**proph'et·ess** *fem.n.*

pro·phet·ic (prə fet'ik, prō-) *adj.* **1** of or like a prophet **2** like or containing a prophecy —**pro·phet'i·cal·ly** *adv.*

pro·phy·lac·tic (prō'fə lak'tik) *adj.* ⟦< Gr *pro-*, before + *phylassein*, to guard⟧ preventive or protective; esp., preventing disease —*n.* **1** a prophylactic medicine, device, etc. **2** a condom

pro'phy·lax'is (-lak'sis) *n., pl.* **-lax'es'** (-sēz') **1** prophylactic treatment **2** *Dentistry* a cleaning of the teeth to remove plaque and tartar

THESAURUS

promotion *n.* **1** [Advancement in rank] preferment, elevation, raise, improvement, advance, lift, betterment, ennobling, favoring.—*Ant.* REMOVAL, demotion, lowering. **2** [Improvement] advancement, progression, development; see IMPROVEMENT 1, INCREASE.

prompt *a.* early, timely, precise; see PUNCTUAL.

prompt *v.* **1** [To instigate] arouse, provoke, inspire; see INCITE, URGE 2. **2** [To suggest] bring up, indicate, imply; see PROPOSE 1.

promptly *a.* on time, punctually, hastily; see IMMEDIATELY, QUICKLY.

prone *a.* inclined, predisposed, disposed; see LIKELY 4.

prong *n.* spine, spur, spike; see FASTENER.

pronoun *n. Pronouns include the following:* personal, possessive, demonstrative, relative, definite, indefinite, interrogative, intensive, reflexive, reciprocal, compound, emphatic, negative, universal.

pronounce *v.* **1** [To speak formally] proclaim, say, assert; see DECLARE. **2** [To articulate] enunciate, say phonetically, vocalize; see UTTER.

pronounced *a.* notable, noticeable, clear; see DEFINITE 2, OBVIOUS 1, 2, UNUSUAL 1.

pronouncement *n.* report, declaration, statement; see ANNOUNCEMENT.

pronunciation *n.* articulation, utterance, voicing; see DICTION.

proof *n.* **1** [Evidence] demonstration, verification, case, reasons, exhibits, credentials, data, warrant, confirmation, substantiation, attestation, corroboration, affidavit, facts, witness, testimony, deposition, trace, record, criterion. **2** [Process of proving] test, attempt, assay; see TRIAL 2.

prop[1] *n.* aid, assistance, strengthener; see POST.

propaganda *n.* promotion, publicity, advertisement, plug*, evangelism, proselytism, ballyhoo, disinformation, spin, PR.

propel *v.* impel forward, move, thrust; see DRIVE 2.

propellant *n.* charge, gunpowder, combustible; see EXPLOSIVE, FUEL.

propeller *n. Propellers include the following:* screw, Archimedean, fishtail, variable-pitch, feathering, marine, airplane, two-bladed, three-bladed, four-bladed, weedless, pusher, pulling.

propensity *n.* talent, capacity, competence; see ABILITY.

proper *a.* **1** [Suitable] just, decent, fitting; see FIT 1. **2** [Conventional] customary, usual, decorous; see CONVENTIONAL 1, 3. **3** [Prudish] prim, precise, strait-laced; see PRUDISH.

properly *a.* correctly, fitly, suitably; see WELL 3.

property *n.* **1** [Possessions] belongings, lands, assets, holdings, inheritance, capital, equity, investments, goods and chattels, earthly possessions, real property, personal property, taxable property, resources, private property, public property, wealth; see also BUSINESS 4, ESTATE, FARM, HOME 1. **2** [A piece of land] section, quarter section, subdivision, site, estate, tract, part, farm, park, ranch, homestead, yard, grounds, frontage, acres, acreage, premises, campus, grant, field, claim, holding, real estate, plot; see also LOT 1.

prophecy *n.* prediction, prognostication, augury; see IDEA 1.

prophesy *v.* predict, prognosticate, divine; see FORETELL.

prophet *n.* seer, oracle, soothsayer, prophetess, seeress, clairvoyant, wizard, augur, sibyl, sorcerer, predictor, forecaster, prognosticator, diviner, medium, witch, palmist, fortuneteller, magus, astrologer, horoscopist, channeler, spiritualist, table-rapper*.

prophetic *a.* predictive, occult, clairvoyant, oracular, sibylline.

pro·pin·qui·ty (prō piŋ′kwə tē) ***n.*** ⟦< L *propinquus*, near⟧ nearness

pro·pi·ti·ate (prō pish′ē āt′, prə-) ***vt.*** **-at′ed, -at′ing** ⟦see fol.⟧ to win the good will of; appease —**pro·pi′ti·a′tion** ***n.*** —**pro·pi′ti·a·to′ry** (-ē ə tôr′ē) ***adj.***

pro·pi·tious (prō pish′əs, prə-) ***adj.*** ⟦< L *pro-*, before + *petere*, seek⟧ **1** favorably inclined **2** favorable; auspicious

prop′jet′ ***n.*** TURBOPROP

pro·po·nent (prə pō′nənt, prō-) ***n.*** ⟦see PROPOSE⟧ one who espouses or supports a cause, etc.

pro·por·tion (prə pôr′shən, prō-) ***n.*** ⟦< L *pro*, for + *portio*, a part⟧ **1** the comparative relation in size, amount, etc. between things; ratio **2** a part, share, etc. in its relation to the whole **3** balance or symmetry **4** [*pl.*] dimensions —***vt.*** **1** to put in proper relation with something else **2** to arrange the parts of (a whole) so as to be harmonious —**pro·por′tion·al** or **pro·por′tion·ate** (-shə nit) ***adj.***

pro·pos·al (prə pōz′əl) ***n.*** **1** a proposing **2** a proposed plan, etc. **3** an offer of marriage

pro·pose (prə pōz′) ***vt.*** **-posed′, -pos′ing** ⟦< L *pro-*, forth + *ponere*, to place⟧ **1** to put forth for consideration, approval, etc. **2** to plan or intend —***vi.*** to offer marriage

prop·o·si·tion (präp′ə zish′ən) ***n.*** **1** something proposed; plan **2** [Inf.] a proposed deal, as in business **3** [Inf.] an undertaking, etc. to be dealt with **4** a subject to be discussed **5** *Math.* a problem to be solved

pro·pound (prə pound′, prō-) ***vt.*** ⟦see PROPOSE⟧ to put forward for consideration

pro·pri·e·tar·y (prə prī′ə tər ē, prō-) ***adj.*** ⟦see PROPERTY⟧ belonging to a proprietor, as under a patent, trademark, or copyright

pro·pri′e·tor ***n.*** an owner —**pro·pri′e·tor·ship′** ***n.*** —**pro·pri′e·tress** (-tris) ***fem.n.***

pro·pri′e·ty (-tē) ***n.***, *pl.* **-ties** ⟦see PROPER⟧ **1** the quality of being proper, fitting, etc. **2** conformity with accepted standards of behavior

pro·pul·sion (prə pul′shən) ***n.*** ⟦see PROPEL⟧ **1** a propelling or being propelled **2** something that propels —**pro·pul′sive** ***adj.***

pro·rate (prō rāt′, prō′rāt′) ***vt.***, ***vi.*** **-rat′ed, -rat′ing** ⟦< L *pro rata*, in proportion⟧ to divide or assess proportionally

pro·sa·ic (prō zā′ik) ***adj.*** ⟦< L *prosa*, prose⟧ commonplace; dull

pro·sce·ni·um (prō sē′nē əm) ***n.***, *pl.* **-ni·ums** or **-ni·a** (-ə) ⟦< Gr *pro-*, before + *skēnē*, tent⟧ in a theater, the plane separating the stage proper from the audience and including the arch (**proscenium arch**) and the curtain within it

pro·scribe (prō skrīb′) ***vt.*** **-scribed′, -scrib′ing** ⟦< L < *pro-*, before + *scribere*, write⟧ **1** to outlaw **2** to banish; exile **3** to denounce or forbid the use, etc. of —**pro·scrip′tion** (-skrip′shən) ***n.***

prose (prōz) ***n.*** ⟦< L *prorsus*, straight on⟧ ordinary language; writing that is not poetry

pros·e·cute (präs′ə kyo͞ot′) ***vt.*** **-cut′ed, -cut′ing** ⟦< L *pro-*, before + *sequi*, follow⟧ **1** to carry on **2** to conduct legal action against —**pros′e·cu′tion** ***n.*** —**pros′e·cu′tor** ***n.*** —**pros′e·cu·to′ri·al** ***adj.***

pros·e·lyte (präs′ə līt′) ***n.*** ⟦< Gr *prosēlytos*, a stranger⟧ one who has been converted from one religion, sect, etc. to another

pros·e·lyt·ize (präs′ə li tīz′) ***vi.***, ***vt.*** **-ized′, -iz′ing** **1** to try to convert (a person), esp. to one's religion **2** to persuade to do or join something —**pros′e·lyt·ism′** (-li tiz′əm) ***n.*** —**pros′e·lyt·iz′er** ***n.***

pro·sim·i·an (prō sim′ē ən) ***n.*** any of various small, arboreal primates

pros·o·dy (präs′ə dē) ***n.*** ⟦< Gr *prosōidia*, accent⟧ versification; study of meter, rhyme, etc.

pros·pect (präs′pekt′) ***n.*** ⟦< L *pro-*, forward + *specere*, to look⟧ **1** a broad view; scene **2** a viewpoint; outlook **3** anticipation **4** *a*) something expected *b*) [*usually pl.*] apparent chance for success **5** a likely customer, candidate, etc. —***vi.*** to explore or search (*for*) —**pros′pec′tor** ***n.***

pro·spec·tive (prə spek′tiv, prä-, prō-) ***adj.*** expected; likely

pro·spec′tus (-spek′təs) ***n.*** ⟦L: see PROSPECT⟧ a statement of the features of a new work, enterprise, etc.

pros·per (präs′pər) ***vi.*** ⟦< L *prospere*, fortunately⟧ to succeed; thrive

pros·per·i·ty (präs per′ə tē) ***n.***, *pl.* **-ties** prosperous condition; wealth

pros·per·ous (präs′pər əs) ***adj.*** **1** prospering; successful **2** wealthy —**pros′per·ous·ly** ***adv.***

pros·tate (präs′tāt′) ***adj.*** ⟦< Gr *prostatēs*, one standing before⟧ of or designating a gland surrounding the male urethra at the base of the bladder —***n.*** this gland: in full **prostate gland**

pros·the·sis (präs thē′sis) ***n.***, *pl.* **-ses′** (-sēz′) *Med.* **1** the replacement of a missing part of the body, as a limb, by an artificial substitute **2** such a substitute —**pros·thet′ic** (-thet′ik) ***adj.***

pros·ti·tute (präs′tə to͞ot′) ***n.*** ⟦< L *pro-*, before + *statuere*, cause to stand⟧ one who engages in promiscuous sexual activity for pay —***vt.*** **-tut′ed, -tut′ing** **1** to offer (oneself) as a prostitute **2** to sell (oneself, one's talents, etc.) for base purposes —**pros′ti·tu′tion** ***n.***

pros·trate (präs′trāt′) ***adj.*** ⟦< L *pro-*, before + *sternere*, stretch out⟧ **1** lying face downward **2** lying prone or supine **3** laid low; overcome —***vt.*** **-trat′ed, -trat′ing** **1** to lay flat on the ground **2** to lay low; subjugate —**pros·tra′tion** ***n.***

pros·y (prō′zē) ***adj.*** **-i·er, -i·est** prosaic; commonplace, dull, etc.

pro·tag·o·nist (prō tag′ə nist) ***n.*** ⟦< Gr *prōtos*, first + *agōnistēs*, actor⟧ the main character in a drama, novel, etc.

THESAURUS

propitious ***a.*** **1** [Favorable] auspicious, encouraging, promising; see HOPEFUL 2. **2** [Kindly] benignant, helpful, generous; see KIND.

proponent ***n.*** defender, advocate, champion; see PROTECTOR.

proportion ***n.*** relationship, dimension, share; see BALANCE 2, PART 1.

proportional ***a.*** proportionate, equivalent, comparable; see EQUAL.

proposal ***n.*** **1** [Offer] overture, recommendation, proposition; see SUGGESTION 1. **2** [Plan] scheme, program, prospectus; see PLAN 2.

propose ***v.*** **1** [To make a suggestion] suggest, offer, put forward, move, set forth, come up with, state, proffer, advance, propound, introduce, put to, contend, assert, tender, recommend, advise, counsel, lay before, submit, affirm, volunteer, press, urge upon, hold out, make a motion, lay on the line.—*Ant.* OPPOSE, dissent, protest. **2** [To mean] purpose, intend, aim; see MEAN 1. **3** [To propose marriage] offer marriage, ask in marriage, make a proposal, ask for the hand of, pop the question*.

proposed ***a.*** projected, prospective, scheduled, expected, arranged, advanced, suggested, advised, moved, put forward, submitted, recommended, urged, volunteered, pressed, intended, determined, anticipated, designed, schemed, purposed, considered, referred to, contingent; see also PLANNED.

proposition ***n.*** proposal, scheme, project; see PLAN 1.

proprietor ***n.*** owner, superintendent, operator; see MANAGER.

propriety ***n.*** aptness, suitability, advisability, accordance, agreeableness, compatibility, correspondence, consonance, appropriateness, congruity, modesty, seemliness, good breeding, decorum, rightness, dignity, concord, harmony, expedience; see also FITNESS.—*Ant.* INCONSISTENCY, incongruity, inappropriateness.

prose ***n.*** fiction, nonfiction, composition; see LITERATURE 1, 2, STORY, WRITING 2.

prosecute ***v.*** contest, indict, try; see SUE.

prosecution ***n.*** state, government, prosecuting attorney, state's attorney; see also LAWYER.

prospect ***n.*** **1** [A view] sight, landscape, vista; see VIEW. **2** [A probable future] expectancy, promise, hope; see OUTLOOK 2. **3** [A possible candidate] possibility, likely person, interested party; see CANDIDATE.

prospective ***a.*** considered, hoped for, promised; see PLANNED, PROPOSED.

prosper ***v.*** become rich, become wealthy, be enriched, thrive, turn out well, fare well, do well, be fortunate, have good fortune, flourish, get on, rise in the world, fatten, increase, bear fruit, bloom, blossom, flower, make money, make a fortune, benefit, advance, gain, make good, do well by oneself*, make one's mark, roll in the lap of luxury*, come along, do wonders; see also SUCCEED 1.

prosperity ***n.*** accomplishment, victory, successfulness; see SUCCESS 2.

prosperous ***a.*** flourishing, well-off, well-to-do; see RICH 1.

prostitute ***n.*** harlot, strumpet, lewd woman, whore, bawd, streetwalker, loose woman, fallen woman, courtesan, lady of the evening, sex worker, concubine, hustler, call girl, B-girl, tramp*, slut*, tart*, hooker*; see also CRIMINAL.

prostitution ***n.*** hustling, harlotry, hooking*, the life*; see also LEWDNESS.

protagonist ***n.*** leading character, lead, combatant; see HERO 1, IDOL.

pro·te·an (prōt′ē ən, prō tē′ən) ***adj.*** ⟦after *Proteus*, Gr god who changes his form⟧ readily taking on different forms

pro·tect (prə tekt′, prō-) ***vt.*** ⟦< L *pro-*, before + *tegere*, to cover⟧ to shield from injury, danger, etc.; defend —**pro·tec′tor** ***n.***

pro·tec′tion ***n.*** **1** a protecting or being protected **2** a person or thing that protects

pro·tec′tive ***adj.*** **1** protecting **2** *Economics* intended to protect domestic industry from foreign competition *[a protective tariff]* —**pro·tec′tive·ly** ***adv.*** —**pro·tec′tive·ness** ***n.***

pro·tec′tor·ate (-tər it) ***n.*** a weak state under the protection and control of a strong state

pro·té·gé (prōt′ə zhā′) ***n.*** ⟦Fr: see PROTECT⟧ a person guided and helped in his or her career by another person

pro·tein (prō′tēn′, prō′tē in) ***n.*** ⟦< Gr *prōtos*, first⟧ any of numerous nitrogenous substances occurring in all living matter and essential to diet

pro tem·po·re (prō tem′pə rē′) ⟦L⟧ for the time (being); temporarily: shortened to **pro tem**

pro·test (prō test′; *also, and for n. always* prō′test′) ***vt.*** ⟦< L *pro-*, forth + *testari*, affirm⟧ **1** to state positively **2** to speak strongly against —***vi.*** to express disapproval; object —***n.*** **1** an objection **2** a formal statement of objection —**prot·es·ta·tion** (prät′es tā′shən) ***n.*** —**pro′test′er** ***n.***

Prot·es·tant (prät′əs tənt) ***n.*** ⟦see prec.⟧ any Christian not belonging to the Roman Catholic Church or the Eastern Orthodox Church —**Prot′es·tant·ism′** ***n.***

proto- ⟦< Gr *prōtos*, first⟧ *combining form* **1** first in time, original **2** first in importance, chief

pro·to·col (prōt′ə kôl′) ***n.*** ⟦< Gr *prōtokollon*, contents page⟧ **1** an original draft of a document, etc. **2** the code of ceremonial forms accepted as correct in official dealings, as between heads of state or diplomatic officials

pro·ton (prō′tän′) ***n.*** ⟦< Gr *prōtos*, first⟧ an elementary particle in the nucleus of all atoms, carrying a unit positive charge of electricity

pro·to·plasm (prōt′ə plaz′əm) ***n.*** ⟦see PROTO- & PLASMA⟧ a semifluid, viscous colloid, the essential living matter of all animal and plant cells —**pro′to·plas′mic** (-plaz′mik) ***adj.***

pro·to·type (prōt′ə tīp′) ***n.*** the first thing or being of its kind; model

pro·to·zo·an (prōt′ə zō′ən) ***n.***, *pl.* **-zo′a** (-ə) ⟦< Gr *prōtos*, first + *zōion*, an animal⟧ any of various microscopic, single-celled animals: also **pro′to·zo′on′** (-än′), *pl.* **-zo′a** (-ə)

pro·tract (prō trakt′, prə-) ***vt.*** ⟦< L *pro-*, forward + *trahere*, draw⟧ to draw out; prolong —**pro·trac′tion** ***n.***

pro·trac·tor (prō′trak′tər) ***n.*** a graduated semicircular instrument for plotting and measuring angles

pro·trude (prō trood′, prə-) ***vt.***, ***vi.*** **-trud′ed**, **-trud′ing** ⟦< L *pro-*, forth + *trudere*, to thrust⟧ to jut out; project —**pro·tru′sion** (-troo′zhən) ***n.***

pro·tu·ber·ance (prō too′bər əns, prə-) ***n.*** a part or thing that protrudes; bulge —**pro·tu′ber·ant** ***adj.***

proud (proud) ***adj.*** ⟦< LL *prode*, beneficial⟧ **1** having a proper pride in oneself **2** arrogant; haughty **3** feeling or causing great pride or joy **4** caused by pride **5** stately; splendid *[a proud fleet]* —**proud of** highly pleased with —**proud′ly** ***adv.***

proud flesh ⟦from the notion of swelling up⟧ an abnormal growth of flesh around a healing wound

Proust (proost), **Mar·cel** (mär sel′) 1871-1922; Fr. novelist

prove (proov) ***vt.*** **proved**, **proved** or **prov′en**, **prov′ing** ⟦< L *probare*, to test⟧ **1** to test by experiment, a standard, etc. **2** to establish as true —***vi.*** to be found by experience or trial —**prov′a·bil′i·ty** ***n.*** —**prov′a·ble** ***adj.***

prov·e·nance (präv′ə nəns) ***n.*** ⟦< L *provenire*, come forth⟧ origin; source

Pro·ven·çal (prō′vən säl′) ***n.*** **1** the vernacular of S France, a Romance language **2** the medieval literary language of S France

prov·en·der (präv′ən dər) ***n.*** ⟦< L *praebere*, give⟧ **1** dry food for livestock **2** [Inf.] food

prov·erb (präv′ərb) ***n.*** ⟦< L *pro-*, PRO-[2] + *verbum*, word⟧ a short, traditional saying expressing an obvious truth —**pro·ver·bi·al** (prō vʉr′bē əl) ***adj.***

Prov′erbs ***n.*** a book of the Bible containing maxims

pro·vide (prə vīd′, prō-) ***vt.*** **-vid′ed**, **-vid′ing** ⟦< L *pro-*, PRO-[2] + *videre*, see⟧ **1** to make available; supply **2** to furnish (someone) *with* something **3** to stipulate —***vi.*** **1** to prepare (*for* or *against* a possible situation, etc.) **2** to furnish support (*for*) —**pro·vid′er** ***n.***

pro·vid′ed or **pro·vid′ing** ***conj.*** on the condition or understanding (*that*)

prov·i·dence (präv′ə dəns) ***n.*** **1** provident management **2** the benevolent guidance of God or nature **3** [**P-**] God

Prov·i·dence (präv′ə dəns) capital of Rhode Island: pop. 161,000

prov′i·dent (-dənt) ***adj.*** ⟦see PROVIDE⟧ **1** providing for the future **2** prudent or economical —**prov′i·dent·ly** ***adv.***

prov′i·den′tial (-den′shəl) ***adj.*** of, by, or as if decreed by divine providence

THESAURUS

protect ***v.*** shield, guard, preserve; see DEFEND 1, 2.

protected ***a.*** shielded, safeguarded, cared for, watched over, preserved, defended, guarded, secured, kept safe, sheltered, harbored, screened, fostered, cherished, curtained, shaded, disguised, camouflaged; see also COVERED 1, SAFE 1.—*Ant.* WEAK, insecure, unsheltered.

protection ***n.*** **1** [A covering] shield, screen, camouflage; see SHELTER. **2** [A surety] certainty, safeguard, safekeeping, assurance, invulnerability, reassurance, security, stability, strength; see also GUARANTY.—*Ant.* WEAKNESS, insecurity, frailty.

protector ***n.*** champion, defender, patron, sponsor, safeguard, benefactor, supporter, advocate, padrone, guardian angel, guard, shield, savior, standby, promoter, mediator, mentor, counsel, second, backer, upholder, sympathizer, big brother, big sister, angel*, cover*, front*, goombah*; see also GUARDIAN.

protest ***n.*** mass meeting, rally, demonstration, riot, clamor, tumult, turmoil, moratorium, sit-in, agitation, strike, sit-down strike, wildcat strike, work slowdown, work stoppage, job action, sickout, blue flu*.

protest ***v.*** demur, disagree, object; see OPPOSE 1.

Protestant ***n.*** *Protestant denominations include the following:* Evangelicals, Adventists, Baptists, Congregationalists, Anglicans, Episcopalians, Lutherans, Methodists, Presbyterians, Amish, Mennonites, Brethren, Christian Scientists, Jehovah's Witnesses, Quakers, Pentecostalists, United Church of Christ, Moravians, Reformed churches.

protester ***n.*** demonstrator, dissident, rebel; see RADICAL.

protrude ***v.*** come through, stick out, jut out; see PROJECT 1.

proud ***a.*** **1** [Having a creditable self-respect] self-respecting, self-sufficient, self-satisfied, ambitious, spirited, vigorous, high-spirited, great-hearted, fiery, dignified, honorable, stately, lordly, lofty-minded, high-minded, impressive, imposing, fine, splendid, looking one in the eye, on one's high horse*, high and mighty*, holding up one's head.—*Ant.* HUMBLE, unpretentious, unassuming. **2** [Egotistic] egotistical, vain, vainglorious; see EGOTISTIC. —**do oneself proud*** achieve, prosper, advance; see SUCCEED 1.

proudly ***a.*** boastfully, haughtily, conceitedly; see ARROGANTLY.

prove ***v.*** justify, substantiate, authenticate, corroborate, testify, explain, attest, show, warrant, uphold, determine, settle, fix, certify, back, sustain, validate, bear out, affirm, confirm, make evident, convince, evidence, be evidence of, witness, declare, have a case, manifest, demonstrate, document, establish, settle once and for all.

proved ***a.*** confirmed, established, demonstrated; see ESTABLISH 3.

proverb ***n.*** maxim, adage, aphorism, precept, saw, saying, motto, dictum, text, witticism, repartee, axiom, truism, byword, epigram, moral, folk wisdom, platitude.

proverbial ***a.*** current, general, unquestioned; see COMMON 1, DULL 4.

provide ***v.*** **1** [To supply] furnish, equip, grant, replenish, provide with, accommodate, care for, indulge with, favor with, contribute, give, outfit, stock, store, minister, administer, render, procure, afford, present, bestow, cater, rig up, fit out, fit up, provision, ration, implement.—*Ant.* REFUSE, take away, deny. **2** [To yield] render, afford, give; see PRODUCE 1. —**provide for** (or **against**) prepare for, arrange, plan ahead; see PREPARE 1.

provided (that) ***conj.*** on the assumption that, in the event, in the case that; see IF, SUPPOSING.

providence ***n.*** divine guidance, God's gifts, Nature's bounty; see GOD.

providing ***conj.*** provided, in the event that, on the assumption that; see IF, SUPPOSING.

providing ***n.*** provision, supplying, furnishing, equipping, replenishing, replenishment, contributing, outfitting, stocking, filling, procurement, affording, presenting, preparing, preparation, arrangement, planning, putting by, laying in, putting in readiness, granting, bestowing, giving, offering, tendering, accumulating,

prov·ince (präv′ins) ***n.*** ⟦< L *provincia*⟧ **1** an administrative division of a country; specif., of Canada **2** *a)* a district; territory *b)* [*pl.*] the parts of a country removed from the major cities **3** range of duties or work; sphere

pro·vin·cial (prə vin′shəl, prō-) ***adj.*** **1** of a province **2** having the ways, speech, etc. of a certain province **3** countrylike; rustic **4** narrow; limited —**pro·vin′cial·ism′** ***n.***

proving ground a place for testing new equipment, new theories, etc.

pro·vi·sion (prə vizh′ən, prō-) ***n.*** **1** a providing or preparing **2** something provided for the future **3** [*pl.*] a stock of food **4** a stipulation; proviso —***vt.*** to supply with provisions

pro·vi′sion·al ***adj.*** temporary —**pro·vi′sion·al·ly** ***adv.***

pro·vi·so (prə vī′zō′, prō-) ***n.***, *pl.* **-sos′** or **-soes′** ⟦see PROVIDE⟧ a condition or stipulation, or a clause making one

prov·o·ca·tion (präv′ə kā′shən) ***n.*** **1** a provoking **2** something that provokes; incitement

pro·voc·a·tive (prə väk′ə tiv, prō-) ***adj.*** provoking or tending to provoke, as to action, thought, or feeling —**pro·voc′a·tive·ly** ***adv.***

pro·voke (prə vōk′, prō-) ***vt.*** **-voked′**, **-vok′ing** ⟦< L *pro-*, forth + *vocare*, to call⟧ **1** to excite to some action or feeling **2** to anger or irritate **3** to stir up (action or feeling) **4** to evoke —**pro·vok′er** ***n.*** —**pro·vok′ing** ***adj.***

pro·vost (prō′vōst′) ***n.*** ⟦< L *praepositus*, chief⟧ a high executive official, as in some colleges

pro·vost guard (prō′vō′) a detail of military police under the command of an officer (**provost marshal**)

prow (prou) ***n.*** ⟦< Gr *prōira*⟧ the forward part of a ship, etc.

prow·ess (prou′is) ***n.*** ⟦< OFr *prouesse*⟧ **1** bravery; valor **2** superior ability, skill, etc.

prowl (proul) ***vi.***, ***vt.*** ⟦< ?⟧ to roam about furtively (in), as in search of prey or loot —***n.*** a prowling —**prowl′er** ***n.***

prowl car PATROL CAR

prox·im·i·ty (präk sim′ə tē) ***n.*** ⟦< L *prope*, near⟧ nearness

prox·y (präk′sē) ***n.***, *pl.* **-ies** ⟦< ME *procuracie*, function of a procurator⟧ **1** the authority to act for another, as in voting **2** one given such authority

Pro·zac (prō′zak′) *trademark for* a drug used in treating depression, eating disorders, etc.

prude (pro͞od) ***n.*** ⟦Fr < *prudefemme*, excellent woman⟧ one who is overly modest or proper in behavior, dress, etc. —**prud′er·y** ***n.*** —**prud′ish** ***adj.*** —**prud′ish·ness** ***n.***

pru·dent (pro͞o′dənt) ***adj.*** ⟦< L *providens*, provident⟧ **1** exercising sound judgment in practical matters **2** cautious in conduct; not rash **3** managing carefully —**pru′dence** ***n.*** —**pru·den·tial** (pro͞o den′shəl) ***adj.***

prune[1] (pro͞on) ***n.*** ⟦< Gr *proumnon*, plum⟧ a dried plum

prune[2] (pro͞on) ***vt.*** **pruned**, **prun′ing** ⟦< OFr *prooignier*⟧ **1** to trim dead or living parts from (a plant) **2** to cut out (unnecessary parts, etc.)

pru·ri·ent (proor′ē ənt) ***adj.*** ⟦< L *prurire*, to itch⟧ tending to excite lust; lewd —**pru′ri·ence** ***n.***

Prus·sia (prush′ə) former kingdom in N Europe & later the dominant state of the German Empire (1871-1919) —**Prus′sian** ***adj.***, ***n.***

pry[1] (prī) ***n.***, *pl.* **pries** ⟦< PRIZE[2]⟧ a lever or crowbar —***vt.*** **pried**, **pry′ing** **1** to raise or move with a pry **2** to obtain with difficulty

pry[2] (prī) ***vi.*** **pried**, **pry′ing** ⟦< ?⟧ to look closely and inquisitively; snoop

pry′er ***n.*** PRIER

PS *abbrev.* Public School

P.S., **p.s.**, or **PS** *abbrev.* postscript

psalm (säm) ***n.*** ⟦< Gr *psallein*, to pluck (a harp)⟧ **1** a sacred song or poem **2** [*usually* **P-**] any of the songs in praise of God constituting the Book of Psalms —**psalm′ist** ***n.***

Psalms (sämz) ***n.*** a book of the Bible consisting of 150 psalms

Psal·ter (sôl′tər) ***n.*** ⟦< Gr *psaltērion*, a harp⟧ **1** PSALMS **2** [*also* **p-**] a version of the Book of Psalms for use in religious services

pseu·do (so͞o′dō) ***adj.*** ⟦ME: see fol.⟧ sham; false; spurious

pseudo- ⟦< Gr *pseudein*, deceive⟧ *combining form* sham, counterfeit

pseu·do·nym (so͞o′də nim′) ***n.*** ⟦< Gr *pseudēs*, false + *onyma*, a name⟧ a fictitious name, esp. one assumed by an author; pen name

pshaw (shô) ***n.***, ***interj.*** (an exclamation) used to express impatience, disgust, etc.

psi[1] (sī, psē) ***n.*** the 23d letter of the Greek alphabet (Ψ, ψ)

psi[2] *abbrev.* pounds per square inch

psit·ta·co·sis (sit′ə kō′sis) ***n.*** ⟦< Gr *psittakos*, parrot + -OSIS⟧ a disease of birds, esp. parrots, often transmitted to humans

pso·ri·a·sis (sə rī′ə sis) ***n.*** ⟦ult. < Gr *psōra*, an itch⟧ a chronic skin disease characterized by scaly, reddish patches

psst (pst) ***interj.*** [Inf.] used to attract someone's attention quietly

PST *abbrev.* Pacific Standard Time

psych[1] (sīk) ***vt.*** **psyched**, **psych′ing** ⟦< PSYCHOANALYZE⟧ [Slang] **1** to outwit, overcome, etc. by psychological means: often with *out* **2** to prepare (oneself) psychologically: often with *up*

psych[2] *abbrev.* psychology

psych- *combining form* PSYCHO-

psy·che (sī′kē) ***n.*** ⟦Gr *psychē*⟧ **1** the soul **2** the mind regarded as an entity based ultimately upon physical processes but with its own complex processes **3** [**P-**] *Rom. Folklore* the wife of Cupid

psy·che·del·ic (sī′kə del′ik) ***adj.*** ⟦< prec. + Gr *dēloun*, make manifest⟧ **1** of or causing extreme changes in the conscious mind, as hallucinations **2** of or associated with psychedelic drugs

psy·chi·a·try (sī kī′ə trē) ***n.*** ⟦see PSYCHO- & -IATRY⟧ the branch of medicine dealing with disorders of the mind, including psychoses and neuroses —**psy·chi·at·ric** (sī′kē a′trik) ***adj.*** —**psy′chi′a·trist** ***n.***

psy·chic (sī′kik) ***adj.*** ⟦see PSYCHE⟧ **1** of the psyche, or mind **2** beyond known physical processes **3** apparently

THESAURUS

storing, saving.

province *n.* area, region, hinterland; see TERRITORY 2.

provincial *a.* rude, unpolished, narrow-minded; see RURAL.

provision *n.* **1** [Arrangement] preparation, outline, procurement; see PLAN 2. **2** [Supplies; *usually plural*] stock, store, emergency; see EQUIPMENT. **3** [A proviso] stipulation, prerequisite, terms; see REQUIREMENT 1.

provisional *a.* transient, passing, ephemeral; see TEMPORARY.

provisionally *a.* conditionally, on certain conditions, for the time being; see TEMPORARILY.

provocation *n.* incitement, stimulus, inducement; see INCENTIVE.

provocative *a.* alluring, arousing, controversial; see INTERESTING.

provoke *v.* **1** [To vex] irritate, put out, aggravate; see BOTHER 2. **2** [To incite] stir, rouse, arouse; see INCITE. **3** [To cause] make, produce, bring about; see BEGIN 1.

provoked *a.* exasperated, incensed, enraged; see ANGRY.

prowl *v.* slink, lurk, rove; see SNEAK.

proxy *n.* substitute, broker, representative; see AGENT, DELEGATE.

prude *n.* prig, puritan, old maid, prudish person, priss*, bluenose*, stick-in-the-mud*, spoilsport, wet blanket*, goody-goody*.

prudence *n.* caution, circumspection, judgment, providence, considerateness, judiciousness, deliberation, wisdom, foresight, forethought, care, carefulness, frugality, watchfulness, precaution, heedfulness, heed, economy, husbandry, concern, conservatism, conservation, discrimination, cunning, vigilance, coolness, calculation, presence of mind.—*Ant.* CARELESSNESS, imprudence, rashness.

prudent *a.* **1** [Cautious and careful] cautious, circumspect, wary; see CAREFUL, DISCREET. **2** [Sensible and wise] discerning, sound, reasonable; see CAREFUL.

prudish *a.* narrow-minded, illiberal, bigoted, prissy*, priggish, overrefined, fastidious, stiff, smug, stuffy, conventional, straitlaced, demure, narrow, puritanical, affected, artificial, scrupulous, pedantic, pretentious, strict, rigid, rigorous, simpering, finicking, finicky, squeamish, repressed, inhibited, uptight*, like a maiden aunt, like an old maid; see also PRIM.—*Ant.* SOCIABLE, broad-minded, genial.

pry[1,2] *v.* **1** [To move, with a lever] push, lift, raise, pull, move, tilt, hoist, heave, uplift, upraise, elevate, turn out, jimmy; see also FORCE, OPEN 2. **2** [To endeavor to discover; *often used with "into"*] search, ferret out, seek, reconnoiter, peep, peer, peek, snoop, gaze, look closely, spy, stare, gape, nose, be curious, inquire; see also MEDDLE 1.

pseudo *a.* imitation, faux, sham; see FALSE 3.

psyche *n.* subconscious, mind, ego; see CHARACTER 2.

psychiatrist *n.* analyst, therapist, shrink*; see DOCTOR.

psychiatry *n.* psychiatric medicine, psychotherapy, psychoanalysis; see MEDICINE 1, SCIENCE 1.

psychic *a.* **1** [Mental] analytic, intellectual, psychological; see MENTAL 2. **2** [Spiritual] telepathic, mys-

sensitive to forces beyond the physical world Also **psy'chi·cal** —*n.* **1** a person apparently sensitive to nonphysical forces **2** a MEDIUM (*n.* 5) —**psy'chi·cal·ly** *adv.*
psy·cho (sī'kō) *adj., n.* [Inf.] *short for* PSYCHOTIC, PSYCHOPATHIC, and PSYCHOPATH
psycho- ⟦see PSYCHE⟧ *combining form* the mind or mental processes
psy·cho·a·nal·y·sis (sī'kō ə nal'ə sis) *n.* a method of treating some mental disorders by analyzing repressed feelings, emotional conflicts, etc. through the use of free association, dream analysis, etc. —**psy'cho·an'a·lyst** (-an'ə list) *n.* —**psy'cho·an'a·lyze'** (-līz'), **-lyzed'**, **-lyz'ing**, *vt.*
psy'cho·bab'ble (-bab'əl) *n.* [Inf.] talk or writing that uses psychological terms and concepts in a trite or superficial way
psy'cho·gen'ic (-jen'ik) *adj.* ⟦see PSYCHO- & GENESIS⟧ originating in the mind or caused by mental conflicts
psy·chol·o·gy (sī käl'ə jē) *n., pl.* **-gies** ⟦see PSYCHO- & -LOGY⟧ **1** the science dealing with the mind and with mental and emotional processes **2** the science of human and animal behavior —**psy'cho·log'i·cal** (-kə läj'i kəl) *adj.* —**psy·chol'o·gist** *n.*
psy·cho·neu·ro·sis (sī'kō nōō rō'sis) *n., pl.* **-ses'** (-sēz') NEUROSIS
psy'cho·path' (-path') *n.* ⟦see PSYCHO- & -PATHY⟧ one who has a severe mental disorder and whose behavior is asocial —**psy'cho·path'ic** *adj.*
psy·cho·sis (sī kō'sis) *n., pl.* **-ses'** (-sēz') ⟦see PSYCHO- & -OSIS⟧ a mental disorder in which the personality is seriously disorganized and contact with reality is usually impaired —**psy·chot'ic** (-kät'ik) *adj.*
psy'cho·so·mat'ic (-sō mat'ik) *adj.* ⟦PSYCHO- + SOMATIC⟧ designating or of a physical disorder brought on, or made worse, by one's emotional state
psy'cho·ther'a·py (-ther'ə pē) *n.* ⟦PSYCHO- + THERAPY⟧ treatment of mental disorders by counseling, psychoanalysis, etc. —**psy'cho·ther'a·pist** *n.*
pt *abbrev.* **1** part **2** pint(s) **3** point
Pt[1] *abbrev.* **1** Point **2** Port
Pt[2] *Chem. symbol for* platinum
PT *abbrev.* Pacific Time
PTA *abbrev.* Parent-Teacher Association
ptar·mi·gan (tär'mi gən) *n.* ⟦< Scot *tarmachan*⟧ a grouse of northern regions
ptero- ⟦< Gr *pteron*, wing⟧ *combining form* feather, wing
pter·o·dac·tyl (ter'ə dak'təl) *n.* ⟦see prec. & DACTYL⟧ an extinct flying reptile with wings of skin stretched from the hind limbs to the long digits of each forelimb
Ptol·e·my (täl'ə mē) 2d c. A.D.; Greco-Egyptian astronomer & mathematician
pto·maine (tō'mān') *n.* ⟦< Gr *ptōma*, corpse⟧ an alkaloid substance, often poisonous, formed in decaying matter
Pu *Chem. symbol for* plutonium
pub (pub) *n.* ⟦< *pub(lic house)*⟧ [Inf.] a bar or tavern
pu·ber·ty (pyōō'bər tē) *n.* ⟦< L *puber*, adult⟧ the stage of physical development when sexual reproduction first becomes possible —**pu'ber·tal** *adj.*
pu·bes·cent (pyōō bes'ənt) *adj.* ⟦see prec.⟧ reaching or having reached puberty —**pu·bes'cence** *n.*
pu'bic (-bik) *adj.* of or in the region of the genitals
pub·lic (pub'lik) *adj.* ⟦ult. < L *populus*, the people⟧ **1** of the people as a whole **2** for the use or benefit of all *[a public park]* **3** acting officially for the people *[a public prosecutor]* **4** known by, open to, or available to most or all people *[to make public, a public company]* —*n.* **1** the people as a whole **2** a specific part of the people *[the reading public]* —**in public** openly —**pub'lic·ly** *adv.*
pub·li·can (pub'li kən) *n.* **1** in ancient Rome, a tax collector **2** [Brit.] a saloon proprietor
pub·li·ca·tion (pub'li kā'shən) *n.* ⟦see PUBLISH⟧ **1** public notification **2** the printing and distribution of books, magazines, etc. **3** something published, as a periodical or book
public defender an attorney employed at public expense to defend indigent people who are accused of crimes
public domain the condition of being free from copyright or patent
pub·li·cist (pub'lə sist) *n.* a person whose business is publicity
pub·lic·i·ty (pub lis'ə tē) *n.* **1** *a)* any information or action that brings a person, cause, etc. to public notice *b)* work concerned with such promotional matters **2** notice by the public
pub·li·cize (pub'lə sīz') *vt.* **-cized'**, **-ciz'ing** to give publicity to
public relations relations of an organization, etc. with the general public as through publicity
public school **1** in the U.S., an elementary or secondary school maintained by public taxes, free to students, and supervised locally **2** in England, a private boarding school
public servant a government official or a civil-service employee
pub'lic-spir'it·ed *adj.* having or showing zeal for the public welfare
public utility an organization supplying water, electricity, transportation, etc. to the public
pub·lish (pub'lish) *vt.* ⟦< L *publicare*⟧ **1** to make publicly known; announce **2** to issue (a printed work) for sale —*vi.* **1** to issue books, newspapers, printed music, etc. **2** to write books, etc. that are published —**pub'lish·er** *n.*
Puc·ci·ni (pōō chē'nē), **Gia·co·mo** (jä'kō mō') 1858-1924; It. operatic composer
puck (puk) *n.* ⟦< dial. *puck*, to strike⟧ the hard rubber disk used in ice hockey
puck·er (puk'ər) *vt., vi.* ⟦< POKE[2]⟧ to gather into wrinkles or small folds —*n.* a wrinkle or small fold made by puckering

THESAURUS

tic, immaterial; see SUPERNATURAL.
psycho* *a.* mad, crazy, psychopathic; see INSANE.
psychological *a.* emotional, mental, cognitive; see MENTAL 2.
psychologist *n.* psychiatrist, analyst, therapist; see DOCTOR, SCIENTIST.
psychology *n.* science of mind, study of personality, medicine, psychotherapy; see also SCIENCE 1, SOCIAL SCIENCE. *Divisions and varieties of psychology include the following:* rational, existential, functionalism, structural, self, dynamic, cognitive, developmental, physiological, abnormal, differential, Gestalt, Freudian, Adlerian, Jungian, analytic, comparative, child, animal, industrial or occupational, individual, social, family therapy, behaviorism, parapsychology.
psychopath *n.* lunatic, antisocial personality, sociopath; see MADMAN.
psychotic *a.* insane, mad, psychopathic; see INSANE 1.
puberty *n.* sexual development, pubescence, adolescence; see YOUTH 1.
public *a.* **1** [Available to the public] free to all, without charge, open, unrestricted, not private, known; see also FREE 4. **2** [Owned by the public] governmental, government, civil, civic, common, communal, publicly owned, municipal, metropolitan, state, federal, county, city.—*Ant.* PRIVATE, personal, restricted.
public *n.* society, the community, the masses; see PEOPLE 3. —**in public** candidly, plainly, aboveboard; see OPENLY 1.
publication *n.* **1** [The act of making public] writing, printing, broadcasting, announcement, notification, promulgation, issuing, statement, advertisement, communication, revelation, disclosure, discovery, making current, making available. **2** [Something published] news, tidings, information; see BOOK, MAGAZINE, NEWSPAPER.
publicity *n.* **1** [Public awareness] notoriety, currency, public relations; see DISTRIBUTION. **2** [Free advertising] PR copy, press release, proclamation; see PROPAGANDA. **3** [Activity intended to advertise] promotion, publicizing, advertising, PR; see also ADVERTISEMENT.
publicize *v.* announce, broadcast, promulgate; see ADVERTISE.
publicly *a.* candidly, plainly, aboveboard; see OPENLY 1.
public relations *n.* promotion, public image, favorable climate of opinion; see ADVERTISEMENT, PROPAGANDA, PUBLICITY 3.
public-spirited *a.* humanitarian, altruistic, openhanded; see GENEROUS 1.
publish *v.* **1** [To print and distribute] reprint, issue, reissue, get into print, hit the newsstands, e-publish, self-publish, distribute, bring out, write, do publishing, become a publisher, get out, put to press, put forth, be in the newspaper business, be in the book business, own a publishing house, send forth, give out; see also PRINT 2. **2** [To make known] announce, promulgate, disseminate; see ADVERTISE.
published *a.* written, printed, made public, circulated, proclaimed, promulgated, propagated, divulged, made current, made known, broadcast, circulated, spread abroad, disseminated, gotten out, appeared, released, presented, offered, voiced, noised abroad, brought before the public; see also ADVERTISED, ISSUED.—*Ant.* UNKNOWN, unpublished, unwritten.

puck·ish (puk′ish) ***adj.*** ⟦after *Puck*, elf in a Shakespeare play⟧ mischievous

pud·ding (po͝od′iŋ) ***n.*** ⟦ME *puddyng*, a sausage⟧ a soft, sweet food made of eggs, milk, fruit, etc.

pud·dle (pud′'l) ***n.*** ⟦dim. < OE *pudd*, a ditch⟧ a small pool of water, esp. stagnant, spilled, or muddy water

pud′dling (-liŋ) ***n.*** the making of wrought iron from pig iron melted and stirred in an oxidizing atmosphere

pudg·y (puj′ē) ***adj.*** **-i·er, -i·est** ⟦< Scot *pud*, belly⟧ short and fat

pueb·lo (pweb′lō) ***n., pl.*** **-los** (-lōz) ⟦Sp < L *populus*, people⟧ an Amerindian communal village, as in the SW U.S., of terraced adobe dwellings

pu·er·ile (pyo͞o′ər əl, pyoor′īl′) ***adj.*** ⟦< L *puer*, boy⟧ childish; silly —**pu′er·il′i·ty** ***n.***

Puer·to Ri·co (pwer′tə rē′kō, pôr′-) island in the West Indies: a commonwealth associated with the U.S.: 3,427 sq. mi.; pop. 3,522,000; cap. San Juan —**Puer′to Ri′can** (-kən)

puff (puf) ***n.*** ⟦OE *pyff*⟧ **1** a short, sudden gust or expulsion of air, breath, smoke, etc. **2** a draw at a cigarette, etc. **3** a light pastry filled with whipped cream, etc. **4** a soft pad *[a powder puff]* **5** a book review, etc. giving undue praise —***vi.*** **1** to blow in puffs **2** to breathe rapidly **3** to fill or swell (*out* or *up*) **4** to take puffs at a cigarette, etc. —***vt.*** **1** to blow, smoke, etc. in or with puffs **2** to swell; inflate **3** to praise unduly —**puff′y, -i·er, -i·est,** ***adj.*** —**puff′i·ness** ***n.***

puff′ball′ ***n.*** a fungus that bursts at the touch and discharges a brown powder

puff′er ***n.*** a small saltwater fish that can expand its body by swallowing water or air

puf·fin (puf′in) ***n.*** ⟦ME *poffin*⟧ a northern sea bird with a brightly colored, triangular beak

puff pastry rich, flaky pastry made of many thin layers of dough

pug (pug) ***n.*** ⟦< ? *Puck*: see PUCK⟧ any of a breed of small, short-haired, snub-nosed dog

pu·gil·ism (pyo͞o′jə iz′əm) ***n.*** ⟦L *pugil*, boxer⟧ the sport of boxing —**pu′gil·ist** ***n.*** —**pu′gil·is′tic** ***adj.***

pug·na·cious (pug nā′shəs) ***adj.*** ⟦< L *pugnare*, to fight⟧ eager and ready to fight; quarrelsome —**pug·na′cious·ly** ***adv.*** —**pug·nac′i·ty** (-nas′ə tē) ***n.***

pug nose a short, thick, turned-up nose —**pug′-nosed′** ***adj.***

puke (pyo͞ok) ***n., vt., vi.*** **puked, puk′ing** ⟦< ?⟧ [Inf.] VOMIT

puk·ka (puk′ə) ***adj.*** ⟦Hindi *pakka*, ripe⟧ **1** [Anglo-Ind.] first-rate **2** genuine; real

pul·chri·tude (pul′krə to͞od′) ***n.*** ⟦< L *pulcher*, beautiful⟧ physical beauty

pule (pyo͞ol) ***vi.*** **puled, pul′ing** ⟦echoic⟧ to whimper or whine, as a sick or fretful child does

pull (pool) ***vt.*** ⟦< OE *pullian*, to pluck⟧ **1** to exert force on so as to move toward the source of the force **2** to pluck out *[to pull a tooth]* **3** to rip; tear **4** to strain (a muscle) **5** [Inf.] to carry out; perform *[to pull a raid]* **6** [Inf.] to restrain *[to pull one's punches]* **7** [Inf.] to draw out (a gun, etc.) —***vi.*** **1** to exert force in dragging, tugging, or attracting something **2** to be capable of being pulled **3** to move (*away, ahead*, etc.) —***n.*** **1** the act, force, or result of pulling; a tugging, attracting, etc. **2** a difficult, continuous effort **3** something to be pulled, as a handle **4** [Inf.] *a*) influence *b*) drawing power —**pull for** [Inf.] to cheer on —**pull off** [Inf.] to accomplish —**pull oneself together** to regain one's poise, etc. —**pull out** to depart or withdraw —**pull through** [Inf.] to get over (an illness, etc.) —**pull up** **1** to bring or come to a stop **2** to move ahead —**pull′er** ***n.***

pull′back′ ***n.*** a pulling back; esp., a planned military withdrawal

pul·let (pool′it) ***n.*** ⟦ult. < L *pullus*, chicken⟧ a young hen

pul·ley (pool′ē) ***n., pl.*** **-leys** ⟦< medieval Gr *polos*, pivot⟧ a small wheel with a grooved rim in which a rope, belt, etc. runs, as to raise weights or transmit power

Pull·man (pool′mən) ***n.*** ⟦after G. M. *Pullman* (1831-97), U.S. inventor⟧ a railroad car with convertible berths for sleeping: also **Pullman car**

pull′out′ ***n.*** **1** a pulling out; esp. removal, withdrawal, etc. **2** something to be pulled out, as a magazine insert

pull′o′ver ***adj.*** that is put on by being pulled over the head —***n.*** a pullover sweater, shirt, etc.

pull′-up′ or **pull′up′** ***n.*** the act of chinning oneself

pul·mo·nar·y (pul′mə ner′ē) ***adj.*** ⟦< L *pulmo*, lung⟧ of the lungs

pul·mo·tor (pool′mō′tər) ***n.*** ⟦< L *pulmo*, lung + MOTOR⟧ an apparatus for applying artificial respiration

pulp (pulp) ***n.*** ⟦< L *pulpa*, flesh⟧ **1** a soft, moist, sticky mass **2** the soft, juicy part of a fruit or the pith inside a plant stem **3** the soft, sensitive tissue in the center of a tooth **4** ground-up, moistened fibers of wood, rags, etc., used to make paper —**pulp′y, -i·er, -i·est,** ***adj.***

pul·pit (pool′pit) ***n.*** ⟦< L *pulpitum*, a stage⟧ **1** a raised platform from which a member of the clergy preaches in a church **2** preachers collectively

pul·sar (pul′sär′) ***n.*** ⟦< PULSE⟧ any of several celestial objects that emit radio waves at short, regular intervals

pul·sate (pul′sāt′) ***vi.*** **-sat′ed, -sat′ing** ⟦< L *pulsare*, to beat⟧ **1** to beat or throb rhythmically **2** to vibrate; quiver —**pul·sa′tion** ***n.***

pulse (puls) ***n.*** ⟦< L *pulsus*, a beating⟧ **1** the regular beating in the arteries, caused by the contractions of the heart **2** any regular beat **3** a brief, abnormal burst or surge, as of electric current —***vi.*** **pulsed, puls′ing** to pulsate; throb

pul·ver·ize (pul′vər īz′) ***vt., vi.*** **-ized′, -iz′ing** ⟦< L *pulvis*, powder⟧ to grind or be ground into powder

pu·ma (pyo͞o′mə) ***n.*** ⟦AmSp⟧ COUGAR

pum·ice (pum′is) ***n.*** ⟦< L *pumex*⟧ a light, porous volcanic rock used for scouring, polishing, etc.

pum·mel (pum′əl) ***vt.*** **-meled** or **-melled, -mel·ing** or **-mel·ling** ⟦< POMMEL⟧ to hit with repeated blows, esp. with the fist

pump[1] (pump) ***n.*** ⟦< Sp *bomba*⟧ a machine that forces a liquid or gas into, or draws it out of, something —***vt.*** **1** to move (fluids) with a pump **2** to remove water, etc. from **3** to drive air into with a pump **4** to draw out, move up and down, pour forth, etc. as a pump does **5** [Inf.] to question persistently, or to elicit (information) by this —**pump′er** ***n.***

pump[2] (pump) ***n.*** ⟦prob. < Fr *pompe*, boot⟧ a low-cut shoe without straps or ties

pumped ***adj.*** [Slang] full of confidence, enthusiasm, etc.

pum·per·nick·el (pum′pər nik′əl) ***n.*** ⟦Ger⟧ a coarse, dark rye bread

pump·kin (pump′kin) ***n.*** ⟦< Gr *pepōn*, ripe⟧ a large, round, orange-yellow, edible gourdlike fruit that grows on a vine

THESAURUS

pudding ***n.*** mousse, custard, tapioca; see DESSERT.

puddle ***n.*** plash, mud puddle, rut; see POOL 1.

pudgy ***a.*** chubby, chunky, stout; see FAT.

puff ***n.*** whiff, sudden gust, quick blast; see WIND.

puff ***v.*** distend, enlarge, swell; see FILL 1, 2.

puffy ***a.*** **1** [Windy] airy, gusty, breezy; see WINDY. **2** [Swollen] distended, expanded, blown; see FULL 1.

puke* ***v.*** throw up, retch, upchuck*; see VOMIT.

pull ***n.*** **1** [The act of pulling] tow, drag, haul, jerk, twitch, wrench, extraction, drawing, rending, tearing, uprooting, weeding, row, paddle. **2** [Exerted force] work, strain, tug; see STRENGTH. **3** [*Influence] having friends in high places, knowing the right people, juice*; see INFLUENCE.

pull ***v.*** **1** [To exert force] tug, pull at, draw in; see WORK 1. **2** [To move by pulling] draw, ease, drag, lift, stretch, move, jerk, haul, tear, rend, gather; see also DRAW 1. **3** [To incline] slope, tend, move toward; see LEAN 1. —**pull away** depart, pull off, go; see LEAVE 1. —**pull off** **1** [To remove] detach, separate, yank off*; see REMOVE 1. **2** [*To achieve] accomplish, manage, succeed; see ACHIEVE. —**pull oneself together** recover, revive, get on one's feet; see IMPROVE 2. —**pull out** go, depart, stop participating; see LEAVE 1, STOP 2. —**pull through*** revive, get over something, triumph; see SURVIVE 1. —**pull up** **1** [To remove] dislodge, elevate, dig out; see REMOVE 1. **2** [To stop] arrive, come to a stop, get there; see STOP 1.

pulley ***n.*** sheave, block, lift, lifter, crowbar, lever, crow, pry; see also TOOL 1.

Pullman ***n.*** railroad sleeping car, chair car, sleeper, first-class accommodation, *wagon-lit* (French).

pulp ***n.*** pap, mash, sponge, paste, dough, batter, curd, jam, poultice.

pulpit ***n.*** **1** [The ministry] priesthood, clergy, ecclesiastics; see MINISTRY 2. **2** [A platform in a church] desk, rostrum, stage; see PLATFORM 1.

pulpy ***a.*** smooth, thick, pasty; see SOFT 1.

pulse ***n.*** pulsation, vibration, throb; see BEAT 1.

pump[1] ***n.*** air pump, vacuum pump, jet pump; see MACHINE, TOOL 1.

pump[1] ***v.*** elevate, draw out, tap; see DRAW 1.

pun (pun) ***n.*** ⟦< ? It *puntiglio*, fine point⟧ the humorous use of a word, or of different words sounded alike, so as to play on the various meanings —***vi.*** **punned, pun'ning** to make puns

punch[1] (punch) ***n.*** ⟦ult. < L *pungere*, to prick⟧ a tool driven against a surface that is to be stamped, pierced, etc. —***vt.*** **1** to pierce, stamp, etc. with a punch **2** to make (a hole) with or as with a punch

punch[2] (punch) ***vt.*** ⟦ME *punchen*⟧ **1** to prod with a stick **2** to herd (cattle) as by prodding **3** to strike with the fist —***n.*** **1** a thrusting blow with the fist **2** [Inf.] effective force —**punch in** (or **out**) to record with a time clock one's arrival (or departure)

punch[3] (punch) ***n.*** ⟦Hindi *pañca*, five⟧ a sweet drink made with fruit juices, sherbet, etc., often mixed with wine or liquor

punch'-drunk' ***adj.*** confused, unsteady, etc., as from many blows to the head in boxing

punch line the surprise line carrying the point of a joke

punch'y ***adj.*** **-i·er, -i·est** [Inf.] **1** forceful; vigorous **2** PUNCH-DRUNK

punc·til·i·ous (puŋk til'ē əs) ***adj.*** ⟦see fol.⟧ **1** very careful about fine points of behavior **2** very exact; scrupulous

punc·tu·al (puŋk'cho͞o əl) ***adj.*** ⟦< L *punctus*, a point⟧ on time; prompt —**punc'tu·al'i·ty** (-al'ə tē) ***n.*** —**punc'tu·al·ly** ***adv.***

punc'tu·ate' (-āt') ***vt.*** **-at'ed, -at'ing** ⟦see prec.⟧ **1** to use standardized marks (**punctuation marks**), as the period and comma, in (written matter) to clarify meaning **2** to interrupt *[a speech punctuated with applause]* **3** to emphasize —**punc'tu·a'tion** ***n.***

punc·ture (puŋk'chər) ***n.*** ⟦< L *pungere*, pierce⟧ **1** a piercing **2** a hole made by a sharp point —***vt., vi.*** **-tured, -tur·ing** to pierce or be pierced with or as with a sharp point

pun·dit (pun'dit) ***n.*** ⟦< Sans *paṇḍita*⟧ a person of great learning

pun·gent (pun'jənt) ***adj.*** ⟦< L *pungere*, pierce⟧ **1** producing a sharp sensation of taste and smell **2** sharp, biting, or stimulating *[pungent wit]* —**pun'gen·cy** ***n.*** —**pun'gent·ly** ***adv.***

pun·ish (pun'ish) ***vt.*** ⟦< L *punire*⟧ **1** to cause to undergo pain, loss, etc., as for a crime **2** to impose a penalty for (an offense) —**pun'ish·a·ble** ***adj.***

pun'ish·ment ***n.*** **1** a punishing or being punished **2** the penalty imposed **3** harsh treatment

pu·ni·tive (pyo͞o'ni tiv) ***adj.*** inflicting, or concerned with, punishment —**pu'ni·tive·ly** ***adv.***

punk[1] (puŋk) ***n.*** ⟦prob. < SPUNK⟧ **1** decayed wood used as tinder **2** a fungous substance that smolders when ignited, used to light fireworks, etc.

punk[2] (puŋk) ***n.*** ⟦< ?⟧ **1** [Slang] *a)* a young hoodlum *b)* a young person regarded as inexperienced, insignificant, etc. **2** PUNK ROCK —***adj.*** **1** [Slang] poor; inferior **2** of punk rock

punk rock a loud, fast, and deliberately offensive style of rock music

pun·ster (pun'stər) ***n.*** one who is fond of making puns

punt[1] (punt) ***n.*** ⟦< ? dial. *bunt*, to kick⟧ *Football* a kick in which the ball is dropped and kicked before it hits the ground —***vt., vi.*** to kick (a football) in this way

punt[2] (punt) ***n.*** ⟦< L *ponto*⟧ a flat-bottomed boat with square ends —***vt., vi.*** to propel (a punt) with a long pole

pu·ny (pyo͞o'nē) ***adj.*** **-ni·er, -ni·est** ⟦< OFr *puis*, after + *né*, born⟧ of inferior size, strength, or importance —**pu'ni·ness** ***n.***

pup (pup) ***n.*** **1** a young dog; puppy **2** a young fox, seal, etc.

pu·pa (pyo͞o'pə) ***n.***, *pl.* **-pae** (-pē) or **-pas** ⟦< L, a doll⟧ an insect in the stage between the last larval form and the adult form

pu·pil[1] (pyo͞o'pəl) ***n.*** ⟦< L *pupillus*, a ward⟧ a person taught under the supervision of a teacher or tutor

pu·pil[2] (pyo͞o'pəl) ***n.*** ⟦< L *pupilla*, figure reflected in the eye⟧ the contractile circular opening, apparently black, in the center of the iris of the eye

pup·pet (pup'ət) ***n.*** ⟦< L *pupa*, a doll⟧ **1** a small figure, as of a person, moved by strings or the hands, as in a performance (**puppet show**) **2** one whose actions, ideas, etc. are controlled by another —**pup'pet·ry** ***n.***

pup'pet·eer' (-ə tir') ***n.*** one who operates, designs, etc. puppets

pup·py (pup'ē) ***n.***, *pl.* **-pies** ⟦< medieval Fr *popee*, a doll⟧ a young dog

pup tent a small, portable tent

pur·blind (pur'blīnd') ***adj.*** ⟦ME *pur blind*, quite blind⟧ **1** partly blind **2** slow in understanding

pur·chase (pur'chəs) ***vt.*** **-chased, -chas·ing** ⟦< OFr *pour*, for + *chacier*, to chase⟧ to buy —***n.*** **1** anything bought **2** the act of buying **3** a firm hold applied to move something heavy or to keep from slipping —**pur'chas·a·ble** ***adj.*** —**pur'chas·er** ***n.***

pure (pyoor) ***adj.*** **pur'er, pur'est** ⟦< L *purus*⟧ **1** free from anything that adulterates, taints, etc.; unmixed **2** simple; mere **3** utter; absolute **4** faultless **5** blameless **6** virgin or chaste **7** abstract or theoretical *[pure physics]* —**pure'ly** ***adv.*** —**pure'ness** ***n.***

pure'bred' ***adj.*** belonging to a recognized breed with genetic attributes maintained through generations of unmixed descent —***n.*** a purebred animal or plant

pu·rée or **pu·ree** (pyoo rā') ***n.*** ⟦Fr: see PURE⟧ **1** cooked

THESAURUS

pun ***n.*** witticism, quip, play on words; see JOKE.

punch[1,2] ***v.*** **1** [To hit] strike, knock, thrust against; see HIT. **2** [To perforate] pierce, puncture, bore; see PENETRATE.

punch[2] ***n.*** thrust, knock, stroke; see BLOW.

punched ***a.*** perforated, dented, pierced, punctured, needled, stamped, imprinted, bored, wounded, bitten, tapped, impaled, spiked, gored, speared, stabbed, stuck.

punctual ***a.*** prompt, precise, particular, on time, on schedule, exact, timely, seasonable, regular, cyclic, dependable, recurrent, constant, steady, scrupulous, punctilious, meticulous, on the nose*.—*Ant.* CARELESS, unreliable, desultory.

punctuation ***n.*** *Marks of punctuation include the following:* period, colon, semicolon, comma, question mark, exclamation mark, parentheses, dash, brackets, apostrophe, hyphen, quotation marks, braces, ellipsis.

puncture ***n.*** punctured tire, flat tire, flat; see HOLE, TROUBLE 1.

puncture ***v.*** prick, perforate, pierce; see PENETRATE.

punish ***v.*** correct, discipline, chasten, chastise, sentence, reprove, lecture, penalize, fine, incarcerate, expel, execute, ostracize, exile, behead, hang, electrocute, dismiss, debar, whip, spank, paddle, trounce, switch, cuff, inflict a penalty, come down on, make an example of, rap on the knuckles, attend to, crack down on, make it hot for*, pitch into*, lay into*, give a dressing-down*, lower the boom on*, ground*, throw the book at*, blacklist, blackball; see also BEAT 1, IMPRISON, KILL 1, SCOLD.

punished ***a.*** corrected, disciplined, chastened, penalized, sentenced, reproved, chastised, castigated, lectured, scolded, imprisoned, incarcerated, expelled, exiled, dismissed, disbarred, defrocked, whipped, switched, cuffed, cracked down on, pitched into*, grounded*, given one's just deserts; see also BEATEN 1, CONFINED 3, EXECUTED 2.—*Ant.* RELEASED, cleared, exonerated.

punishment ***n.*** correction, discipline, reproof, penalty, infliction, suffering, deprivation, unhappiness, trial, penance, retribution, mortification, disciplinary action, fine, reparation, forfeiture, forfeit, confiscation, rap on the knuckles.—*Ant.* FREEDOM, exoneration, release.

puny ***a.*** feeble, inferior, diminutive; see WEAK 1.

pup ***n.*** puppy, whelp, young dog; see ANIMAL, DOG.

pupil[1] ***n.*** schoolboy, schoolgirl, learner; see STUDENT.

puppet ***n.*** manikin, figurine, moppet; see DOLL.

puppy ***n.*** pup, whelp, young dog; see ANIMAL, DOG.

purchase ***n.*** **1** [The act of buying] procurement, getting, obtaining, shopping, installment buying, bargaining, marketing, investing; see also BUYING. **2** [Something bought] buy, order, goods, shipment, acquisition, invoice, packages, delivery, articles, property, possession, gain, booty, acquirement, investment; see also BARGAIN, GOODS.

purchase ***v.*** obtain, acquire, buy up; see BUY.

purchaser ***n.*** shopper, consumer, procurer; see BUYER.

pure ***a.*** **1** [Not mixed] unmixed, unadulterated, unalloyed, unmingled, simple, clear, genuine, undiluted, classic, real, true, fair, bright, unclouded, transparent, lucid, straight, neat; see also CLEAR 2, GENUINE 1, SIMPLE 1.—*Ant.* MIXED, mingled, blended. **2** [Clean] immaculate, spotless, stainless, unspotted, germfree, unstained, unadulterated, unblemished, untarnished, unsoiled, disinfected, sterilized, uncontaminated, sanitary, unpolluted, purified, refined.—*Ant.* DIRTY, sullied, contaminated. **3** [Chaste] virgin, continent, celibate; see CHASTE. **4** [Absolute] sheer, utter, complete; see ABSOLUTE 1.

purely ***a.*** entirely, totally, essentially; see COMPLETELY.

food pressed through a sieve or whipped in a blender to a soft, smooth consistency **2** a thick soup made with this —*vt.* **-réed'** or **-reed'**, **-rée'ing** or **-ree'ing** to make a purée of

pur·ga·tive (pur'gə tiv) ***adj.*** purging —***n.*** a purging substance; cathartic

pur·ga·to·ry (pur'gə tôr'ē) ***n.***, *pl.* **-ries** ⟦see fol.⟧ [*often* **P-**] *Theol.* a state or place after death, in some Christian doctrine, for expiating sins by suffering —**pur'ga·to'ri·al** ***adj.***

purge (purj) ***vt.*** **purged**, **purg'ing** ⟦< L *purus*, clean + *agere*, do⟧ **1** to cleanse of impurities, etc. **2** to cleanse of sin **3** to rid (a nation, party, etc.) of (individuals held to be disloyal) **4** to empty (the bowels) —***n.*** **1** a purging **2** that which purges; esp., a cathartic —**purg'er** ***n.***

pu·ri·fy (pyoor'ə fī') ***vt.*** **-fied'**, **-fy'ing** ⟦see PURE & -FY⟧ **1** to rid of impurities, etc. **2** to free from guilt, sin, etc. —***vi.*** to become purified —**pu'ri·fi·ca'tion** ***n.***

Pu·rim (poor'im) ***n.*** ⟦Heb⟧ a Jewish holiday commemorating Esther's deliverance of the Jews from a massacre

pu·rine (pyoor'ēn, -in) ***n.*** ⟦Ger *purin*⟧ **1** a colorless, crystalline organic compound, from which is derived a group of compounds including uric acid and caffeine **2** a purine derivative, as adenine

pur·ism (pyoor'iz'əm) ***n.*** strict or excessive observance of precise usage or formal rules in language, style, etc. —**pur'ist** ***n.***

Pu·ri·tan (pyoor'i tən) ***n.*** ⟦see fol.⟧ **1** a member of a group in 16th-17th-c. England and America that wanted to make the Church of England simpler in its forms and stricter about morality **2** [**p-**] a person regarded as excessively strict in morals and religion —**pu'ri·tan'i·cal** (-tan'i kəl) ***adj.*** —**Pu'ri·tan·ism'** or **pu'ri·tan·ism'** ***n.***

pu'ri·ty (-tē) ***n.*** ⟦< LL *puritas*⟧ a being pure; specif., *a)* freedom from adulterating matter *b)* cleanness *c)* freedom from sin; chastity

purl[1] (purl) ***vi.*** ⟦< ? Scand⟧ to move in ripples or with a murmur —***n.*** the sound of purling water

purl[2] (purl) ***vt.***, ***vi.*** ⟦earlier *pirl*, prob. ult. < It⟧ to invert (stitches) in knitting

pur·lieu (purl'yoo') ***n.*** ⟦< OFr *pur-*, through + *aler*, go⟧ **1** [*pl.*] environs **2** an outlying part

pur·loin (pər loin', pur'loin') ***vt.***, ***vi.*** ⟦< OFr *pur-*, for + *loin*, far⟧ to steal

pur·ple (pur'pəl) ***n.*** ⟦ult. < Gr *porphyra*, shellfish yielding a dye⟧ **1** a dark bluish red **2** crimson cloth or clothing, esp. as a former emblem of royalty —***adj.*** **1** bluish-red **2** imperial **3** ornate *[purple prose]* **4** profane or obscene

pur·port (pur pôrt'; *for n.* pur'pôrt') ***vt.*** ⟦< OFr *por-*, forth + *porter*, to bear⟧ **1** to profess or claim as its meaning **2** to give the appearance, often falsely, of being, intending, etc. —***n.*** **1** meaning; sense **2** intention —**pur·port'ed** ***adj.*** —**pur·port'ed·ly** ***adv.***

pur·pose (pur'pəs) ***vt.***, ***vi.*** **-posed**, **-pos·ing** ⟦see PROPOSE⟧ to intend or plan —***n.*** **1** something one intends to get or do; aim **2** determination **3** the object for which something exists or is done —**on purpose** by design; intentionally —**pur'pose·ful** ***adj.*** —**pur'pose·less** ***adj.***

pur'pose·ly ***adv.*** with a definite purpose; intentionally; deliberately

pur'pos·ive ***adj.*** serving or having a purpose

purr (pur) ***n.*** ⟦echoic⟧ a low, vibratory sound made by a cat at ease —***vi.***, ***vt.*** to make, or express by, such a sound

purse (purs) ***n.*** ⟦< Gr *byrsa*, a hide⟧ **1** a small bag for carrying money **2** finances; money **3** a sum of money for a present or prize **4** a woman's handbag —***vt.*** **pursed**, **purs'ing** to draw (the lips) tightly, as in disapproval

purs·er (pur'sər) ***n.*** ⟦ME, purse-bearer⟧ a ship's officer in charge of accounts, tickets, etc.

pur·su·ance (pər soo'əns) ***n.*** a pursuing of a project, plan, etc.

pur·su'ant ***adj.*** [Now Rare] pursuing —**pursuant to** in accordance with

pur·sue (pər soo') ***vt.*** **-sued'**, **-su'ing** ⟦< L *pro-*, forth + *sequi*, follow⟧ **1** to follow in order to overtake or capture; chase **2** to follow (a specified course, action, etc.) **3** to strive for **4** to continue to annoy —**pur·su'er** ***n.***

pur·suit' (-soot') ***n.*** **1** a pursuing **2** an occupation, interest, etc.

pu·ru·lent (pyoor'ə lənt) ***adj.*** ⟦< L *pus*, pus⟧ of, like, or discharging pus —**pu'ru·lence** ***n.***

pur·vey (pər vā') ***vt.*** ⟦see PROVIDE⟧ to supply (esp. food) —**pur·vey'or** ***n.***

pur·view (pur'vyoo') ***n.*** ⟦< OFr *pourveü*, provided⟧ scope or extent, as of control or activity

pus (pus) ***n.*** ⟦L⟧ the yellowish-white liquid matter produced by an infection

push (poosh) ***vt.*** ⟦< L *pulsare*, to beat⟧ **1** to press against so as to move **2** to press or urge on **3** to urge the use, sale, etc. of —***n.*** **1** a pushing **2** a vigorous effort **3** an advance against opposition **4** [Inf.] aggressiveness; drive

push button a small knob pushed to operate something, as with electricity

push'er ***n.*** **1** one that pushes **2** [Slang] one who sells drugs, esp. narcotics, illegally

push'o'ver ***n.*** [Slang] **1** anything very easy to do **2** one easily persuaded, defeated, etc.

push'-up' or **push'up'** ***n.*** an exercise in which a prone person, with hands under shoulders, raises the body by pushing down on the palms

push'y ***adj.*** **-i·er**, **-i·est** [Inf.] annoyingly aggressive and persistent —**push'i·ness** ***n.***

pu·sil·lan·i·mous (pyoo'si lan'ə məs) ***adj.*** ⟦< L *pusillus*, tiny + *animus*, the mind⟧ timid; cowardly —**pu'sil·la·nim'i·ty** (-si lə nim'ə tē) ***n.***

puss (poos) ***n.*** ⟦< ?⟧ a cat: also **puss'y·cat'** or **puss'y**, *pl.* **-ies**

puss'y·foot' ***vi.*** [Inf.] **1** to move with stealth or caution, like a cat **2** to avoid committing oneself

pussy willow a willow bearing silvery, velvetlike catkins

THESAURUS

purification ***n.*** purifying, cleansing, purgation; see CLEANING.—*Ant.* POLLUTION, defilement, contamination.

purify ***v.*** cleanse, clear, refine, wash, disinfect, fumigate, deodorize, clarify, sublimate, purge, filter; see also CLEAN.

purity ***n.*** **1** [The state of being pure] pureness, cleanness, cleanliness, immaculateness, stainlessness, whiteness, clearness. **2** [Innocence] artlessness, guilelessness, blamelessness; see INNOCENCE 2. **3** [Chastity] abstemiousness, continence, self-command; see CHASTITY, VIRTUE 1.

purple ***a.*** purpled, reddish-blue, bluish-red; see COLOR. *Tints and shades of purple include the following:* lilac, violet, mauve, heliotrope, magenta, orchid, grape, puce, plum, lavender, pomegranate, royal purple, wine.

purpose ***n.*** **1** [Aim] intention, end, goal, mission, objective, object, idea, design, hope, resolve, meaning, view, scope, desire, dream, expectation, ambition, intent, destination, direction, scheme, prospective, proposal, target, aspiration; see also PLAN 2. **2** [Resolution] tenacity, constancy, persistence; see CONFIDENCE, DETERMINATION, FAITH 1. —**on purpose** purposefully, intentionally, designedly; see DELIBERATELY. —**to the purpose** to the point, pertinent, apt; see RELEVANT.

purpose ***v.*** aim, plan, propose; see INTEND 1.

purposeful ***a.*** obstinate, stubborn, persistent; see RESOLUTE.

purr ***v.*** hum, drone, sigh; see SOUND.

purse ***n.*** pouch, pocketbook, receptacle, moneybag, wallet, pocket, coin purse, billfold, money belt, sack, vanity case.

pursue ***v.*** **1** [To chase] seek, hound, track down, dog, shadow, search for, search out, stalk, run after, go after, hunt down, trail, follow close upon, move behind, scout out, nose around, poke around, keep on foot, follow up. **2** [To seek] strive for, aspire to, attempt; see TRY 1. **3** [To continue] persevere, proceed, carry on; see CONTINUE 1.

pursuit ***n.*** chase, race, pursuance; see HUNT.

pus ***n.*** infection, discharge, mucus; see MATTER 1.

push ***n.*** shove, force, bearing, propulsion, drive, inertia, exertion, weight, straining, shoving, thrusting, forcing, driving, inducement, mass, potential, reserve, impact, blow; see also PRESSURE.

push ***v.*** **1** [To press against] thrust, shove, butt, crowd, gore, ram, crush against, jostle, push out of one's way, shoulder, elbow, struggle, strain, exert, set one's shoulder to, rest one's weight on, put forth one's strength; see also FORCE. **2** [To move by pushing] impel, accelerate, drive onward, launch, start, set in motion, push forward, shift, start rolling, budge, stir, shove along; see also DRIVE 2. **3** [To promote] advance, expedite, urge; see PROMOTE 1.

pushover ***n.*** sucker*, easy pickings, fool; see VICTIM.

pussyfoot* ***v.*** evade, avoid, dodge, sidestep, tiptoe, dance around, hedge; see also AVOID, EVADE.

pus·tule (pus′chool′) ***n.*** ⟦L *pustula*⟧ a pus-filled blister or pimple

put (poot) ***vt.* put, put′ting** ⟦< or akin to OE *potian*, to push⟧ **1** *a)* to thrust; drive *b)* to propel with an overhand thrust [*to put the shot*] **2** to cause to be in a certain place, condition, relation, etc.; place; set **3** to impose (a tax, etc.) **4** to attribute; ascribe **5** to express [*put it plainly*] **6** to present for decision [*put the question*] **7** to bet (money) *on* —***n.*** *Finance* an option to sell a stock, etc. —***adj.*** [Inf.] fixed [*stay put*] —**put across** [Inf.] to cause to be understood or accepted —**put aside** (or **by**) **1** to reserve for later use **2** to discard —**put down 1** to crush; repress **2** to write down **3** [Slang] to belittle or humiliate —**put in for** to apply for —**put it** (or **something**) **over on** [Inf.] to deceive; trick —**put off 1** to postpone; delay **2** to evade; divert —**put on 1** to clothe oneself with **2** to pretend **3** to stage (a play) **4** [Slang] to fool; hoax —**put out 1** to expel; dismiss **2** to extinguish (a fire or light) **3** to inconvenience **4** *Baseball* to retire (a batter or runner) —**put through 1** to carry out **2** to cause to do or undergo —**put up 1** to offer **2** to preserve or can (fruits, etc.) **3** to build or erect **4** to provide lodgings for **5** to provide (money) **6** to arrange (the hair) with curlers, etc. **7** [Inf.] to incite *to* some action —**put up with** to tolerate

pu·ta·tive (pyoot′ə tiv) ***adj.*** ⟦< L *putare*, suppose⟧ generally considered or deemed such; reputed

put′-down′ ***n.*** [Slang] a belittling remark or crushing retort

Pu·tin (poo′tən), **Vlad·i·mir** (vlad′ə mir) 1952- ; president of Russia (2000-)

put′-on′ ***n.*** [Slang] a hoax

pu·tre·fy (pyoo′trə fī′) ***vt.***, ***vi.* -fied′, -fy′ing** ⟦see PUTRID & -FY⟧ to make or become putrid; rot —**pu′tre·fac′tion** (-fak′shən) ***n.***

pu·tres·cent (pyoo tres′ənt) ***adj.*** putrefying; rotting —**pu·tres′cence** ***n.***

pu·trid (pyoo′trid) ***adj.*** ⟦< L *putrere*, to rot⟧ rotten and foul-smelling

putt (put) ***n.*** ⟦< PUT, v.⟧ *Golf* a shot which attempts to roll the ball into the hole —***vt.***, ***vi.*** to hit (the ball) in making a putt

putt·er[1] (put′ər) ***n.*** *Golf* a short, straight-faced club used in putting

put·ter[2] (put′ər) ***vi.*** ⟦< OE *potian*, to push⟧ to busy oneself in an ineffective or aimless way (with *along, around*, etc.) —***vt.*** to fritter (*away*)

put·ty (put′ē) ***n.*** ⟦Fr *potée*, lit., potful⟧ a soft, plastic mixture of powdered chalk and linseed oil, used to fill small cracks, etc. —***vt.* -tied, -ty·ing** to cement or fill with putty

put′-up′ ***adj.*** [Inf.] planned secretly beforehand [*a put-up job*]

puz·zle (puz′əl) ***vt.* -zled, -zling** ⟦< ?⟧ to perplex; bewilder —***vi.* 1** to be perplexed **2** to exercise one's mind, as over a problem —***n.* 1** something that puzzles **2** a toy or problem for testing skill or ingenuity —**puzzle out** to solve by deep study —**puz′zle·ment** ***n.*** —**puz′zler** ***n.***

PVC ***n.*** ⟦*p*(*oly*)*v*(*inyl*) *c*(*hloride*)⟧ a type of polymer used in packaging materials, plumbing, etc.

Pvt *abbrev. Mil.* Private

PX *service mark for* a general store at an army base

Pyg·my (pig′mē) ***n.***, *pl.* **-mies** ⟦< Gr *pygmaios*, of a forearm's length⟧ **1** a member of any of several groups of African or Asian peoples of small stature **2** [**p-**] a dwarf —***adj.* 1** of the Pygmies **2** [**p-**] very small

py·ja·mas (pə jä′məz, -jam′əz) ***pl.n.*** *Brit. sp. of* PAJAMAS

py·lon (pī′län′) ***n.*** ⟦Gr *pylōn*, gateway⟧ **1** a gateway, as of an Egyptian temple **2** a towerlike structure supporting electric lines, marking a flight course, etc.

py·lo·rus (pī lôr′əs) ***n.***, *pl.* **-ri** (-rī) ⟦< Gr *pylōros*, gatekeeper⟧ the opening from the stomach into the duodenum —**py·lor′ic** ***adj.***

py·or·rhe·a (pī′ə rē′ə) ***n.*** ⟦< Gr *pyon*, pus + *rheein*, to flow⟧ a periodontal infection with formation of pus and loosening of teeth —**py′or·rhe′al** ***adj.***

pyr·a·mid (pir′ə mid) ***n.*** ⟦< Gr *pyramis*⟧ **1** a huge structure with a square base and four triangular sides meeting at the top, as a royal tomb of ancient Egypt **2** *Geom.* a solid figure with a polygonal base, the sides of which form the bases of triangular surfaces meeting at a common vertex —**py·ram·i·dal** (pi ram′i dəl) ***adj.***

pyre (pīr) ***n.*** ⟦< Gr *pyr*, fire⟧ a pile of wood on which a dead body is burned in funeral rites

Pyr·e·nees (pir′ə nēz′) mountain range between France & Spain

py·ret·ic (pī ret′ik) ***adj.*** ⟦< Gr *pyretos*, fever⟧ of, causing, or characterized by fever

Py·rex (pī′reks′) ⟦arbitrary coinage < *pie*⟧ *trademark for* a heat-resistant glassware used for cooking, lab work, etc.

py·rite (pī′rīt′) ***n.***, *pl.* **py·ri·tes** (pi rīt′ēz′, pī′rīts′) ⟦< Gr *pyritēs*, flint⟧ iron sulfide, a lustrous yellow mineral used as a source of sulfur

pyro- ⟦< Gr *pyr*, fire⟧ *combining form* fire, heat

py·ro·ma·ni·a (pī′rə mā′nē ə) ***n.*** ⟦ModL: see prec. & -MANIA⟧ a compulsion to start destructive fires —**py′ro·ma′ni·ac′** ***n.***, ***adj.***

py·ro·tech·nics (pī′rə tek′niks) ***pl.n.*** ⟦< Gr *pyr*, fire + *technē*, art⟧ **1** a display of fireworks **2** a dazzling display, as of wit

Pyr·rhic victory (pir′ik) ⟦after *Pyrrhus*, Gr king who won such victories over the Romans, 280 and 279 B.C.⟧ a too costly victory

Py·thag·o·ras (pi thag′ə rəs) 6th c. B.C.; Gr. philosopher & mathematician —**Py·thag′o·re′an** (-ə rē′ən) ***adj.***, ***n.***

py·thon (pī′thän′, -thən) ***n.*** ⟦< Gr *Pythōn*, a serpent slain by Apollo⟧ a large, nonpoisonous snake of Asia, Africa, and Australia, that squeezes its prey to death

THESAURUS

put ***v.*** **1** [To place] set, locate, deposit, plant, lodge, store, situate, fix, put in a place, lay, pin down, seat, settle. **2** [To establish] install, quarter, fix; see ESTABLISH 2. **3** [To deposit] invest in, insert, embed; see PLANT. —**put aside** deposit, save, hoard; see STORE. —**put down** silence, repress, crush; see DEFEAT 2, 3. —**put off** postpone, defer, retard; see DELAY. —**put on 1** [To pretend] feign, sham, make believe; see PRETEND 1. **2** [*To deceive] trick, confuse, confound; see DECEIVE. —**put through** do, manage, finish; see ACHIEVE. —**put up 1** [To preserve] can, smoke, pickle; see see PRESERVE 2. **2** [To build] erect, fabricate, construct; see BUILD. —**put up with** undergo, tolerate, stand; see ENDURE 2.

put-down* ***n.*** insult, slight, demeaning remark; see INSULT.

put-on* ***n.*** deception, device, con-job*; see TRICK 1.

putrid ***a.*** spoiled, decayed, putrified; see ROTTEN 1.

putter[2] ***v.*** dawdle, fritter, poke; see LOITER.

puzzle ***n.*** **1** [A problem] tangle, bafflement, question, frustration, intricacy, maze, issue, enigma, baffler, brainteaser, puzzler, query, mystery, dilemma, muddle, secret, riddle, ambiguity, difficulty, perplexity, confusion, entanglement, stickler*, paradox.—*Ant.* ANSWER, solution, key. **2** [A problem to be worked for amusement] *Varieties include the following:* riddle, cryptogram, crossword puzzle, jigsaw puzzle, anagram, acrostic, rebus, Chinese puzzle, palindrome.

puzzle ***v.*** **1** [To perplex] obscure, bewilder, complicate; see CONFUSE. **2** [To wonder] marvel, be surprised, be astonished; see WONDER 1. —**puzzle out** figure out, work out, decipher; see SOLVE.

puzzled ***a.*** perplexed, bewildered, mystified; see DOUBTFUL.

puzzling ***a.*** **1** [Obscure] uncertain, ambiguous, mystifying; see OBSCURE 1. **2** [Difficult] perplexing, abstruse, hard; see DIFFICULT 2.

pyramid ***n.*** tomb, shrine, mausoleum; see MONUMENT 1.

Q

q[1] or **Q** (kyoo) ***n.**, pl.* **q's, Q's** the 17th letter of the English alphabet

q[2] *abbrev.* **1** quart **2** question

Qa·tar (kä tär′) country on a peninsula of E Arabia, on the Persian Gulf: 4,416,000 sq. mi.; pop. 369,000

QC Quebec

Q.E.D. or **q.e.d.** *abbrev.* ⟦L *quod erat demonstrandum*⟧ which was to be demonstrated or proved

qt *abbrev.* quart(s)

q.t. ***n.*** ⟦< *q(uie)t*⟧ [Inf.] quiet: chiefly in **on the q.t.**, secretly: also **Q.T.**

qua (kwā, kwä) ***prep.*** ⟦L < *qui*, who⟧ in the function or character of; as *[*the President *qua* Commander in Chief*]*

quack[1] (kwak) ***vi.*** ⟦echoic⟧ to utter the sound or cry of a duck —***n.*** this sound

quack[2] (kwak) ***n.*** ⟦ult. < MDu *quacken*, to brag⟧ **1** a person who practices medicine fraudulently **2** one who falsely pretends to have knowledge or a skill —***adj.*** fraudulent —**quack′er·y *n.***

quad[1] (kwäd) ***n.** short for:* **1** QUADRANGLE **2** QUADRUPLET

quad[2] *abbrev.* **1** quadrangle **2** quadrant **3** quadruplicate

quad·ran·gle (kwä′draŋ′gəl) ***n.*** ⟦see QUADRI- & ANGLE[1]⟧ **1** *Geom.* a plane figure with four angles and four sides **2** an area surrounded on its four sides by buildings —**quad·ran′gu·lar *adj.***

quad·rant (kwä′drənt) ***n.*** ⟦< L *quadrans*, fourth part⟧ **1** an arc of 90° **2** a quarter section of a circle **3** an instrument formerly used in measuring angular elevation and altitude in navigation, etc.

quad·rat·ic (kwä drat′ik) ***adj.*** *Algebra* involving a quantity or quantities that are squared but none that are raised to a higher power

quad·ren·ni·al (kwä dren′ē əl) ***adj.*** ⟦< L *quadri-* (see fol.) + *annus*, year⟧ **1** happening every four years **2** lasting four years

quadri- ⟦L < *quattuor*, four⟧ *combining form* four, four times

quad·ri·ceps (kwä′dri seps′) ***n.*** ⟦< prec. + L *caput*, the head⟧ a muscle with four points of origin; esp., the large muscle at the front of the thigh

quad·ri·lat·er·al (kwä′dri lat′ər əl) ***adj.*** ⟦see QUADRI- & LATERAL⟧ four-sided —***n.*** *Geom.* a plane figure having four sides and four angles

qua·drille (kwə dril′, kwä-) ***n.*** ⟦Fr: ult. < L *quadra*, a square⟧ a square dance performed by four couples

quad·ri·ple·gi·a (kwä′dri plē′jē ə, -jə) ***n.*** ⟦ModL < QUADRI- + Gr *plēgē*, a stroke⟧ total paralysis of the body from the neck down —**quad′ri·ple′gic** (-plē′jik) ***adj.**, **n.***

quad·ru·ped (kwä′droo ped′) ***n.*** ⟦< L *quadru-*, four + *pes*, foot⟧ an animal, esp. a mammal, with four feet

quad·ru·ple (kwä droo′pəl) ***adj.*** ⟦< L *quadru-*, four + *-plus*, -fold⟧ **1** consisting of four **2** four times as much or as many —***n.*** an amount four times as much or as many —***vt.**, **vi.*** **-pled, -pling** to make or become four times as much or as many

quad·ru·plet (kwä droo′plit, -drup′lit) ***n.*** **1** any of four offspring from the same pregnancy **2** a collection or group of four, usually of one kind

quad·ru·pli·cate (kwä droo′pli kāt′; *for adj. & n.*, -kit, -kāt′) ***vt.*** **-cat′ed, -cat′ing** to make four identical copies of —***adj.*** **1** fourfold **2** being the last of four identical copies —***n.*** any one of such copies —**in quadruplicate** in four such copies —**quad·ru′pli·ca′tion *n.***

quaff (kwäf, kwaf) ***vt.**, **vi.*** ⟦prob. < LowG *quassen*, overindulge⟧ to drink deeply and heartily —***n.*** a quaffing

quag·mire (kwag′mīr′) ***n.*** ⟦*quag*, a bog + MIRE⟧ wet, boggy ground

qua·hog or **qua·haug** (kō′häg′) ***n.*** ⟦AmInd⟧ an edible clam of the E coast of North America

quail[1] (kwāl) ***vi.*** ⟦prob. < L *coagulare*, coagulate⟧ to recoil in fear

quail[2] (kwāl) ***n.*** ⟦< OFr *quaille*⟧ a small, short-tailed bird resembling a partridge

quaint (kwānt) ***adj.*** ⟦< OFr *cointe* < L *cognitus*, known⟧ **1** pleasingly odd or old-fashioned **2** unusual; curious **3** fanciful; whimsical —**quaint′ly *adv.*** —**quaint′ness *n.***

quake (kwāk) ***vi.*** **quaked, quak′ing** ⟦< OE *cwacian*⟧ **1** to tremble or shake **2** to shiver, as from fear or cold —***n.*** **1** a shaking or tremor **2** an earthquake —**quak′y, -i·er, -i·est, *adj.***

Quak·er (kwā′kər) ***n.*** ⟦< founder's admonition to "quake" at the word of the Lord⟧ *name for* a member of the SOCIETY OF FRIENDS

qual·i·fi·ca·tion (kwôl′ə fi kā′shən) ***n.*** **1** a qualifying or being qualified **2** a restriction; limiting condition **3** any skill, etc. that fits one for a job, office, etc.

qual·i·fied (kwôl′ə fīd′) ***adj.*** **1** fit; competent **2** limited; modified

qual′i·fi′er (-fī′ər) ***n.*** **1** one that qualifies **2** an adjective or adverb

qual′i·fy′ (-fī′) ***vt.*** **-fied′, -fy′ing** ⟦< L *qualis*, of what kind + *facere*, make⟧ **1** to make fit for a job, etc. **2** to make legally capable **3** to modify; restrict **4** to moderate; soften —***vi.*** to be or become qualified

qual′i·ta′tive (-tāt′iv) ***adj.*** having to do with quality or qualities —**qual′i·ta′tive·ly *adv.***

qual′i·ty (-tē) ***n.**, pl.* **-ties** ⟦< L *qualis*, of what kind⟧ **1** a characteristic element or attribute **2** basic nature; kind **3** the degree of excellence of a thing **4** excellence —***adj.*** of high quality

qualm (kwäm) ***n.*** ⟦OE *cwealm*, disaster⟧ **1** a sudden, brief feeling of sickness, faintness, etc. **2** a doubt; misgiving **3** a twinge of conscience

quan·da·ry (kwän′də rē, -drē) ***n.**, pl.* **-ries** ⟦prob. < L⟧ a state of uncertainty; dilemma

quan·ti·fy (kwänt′ə fī′) ***vt.*** **-fied′, -fy′ing** ⟦< L *quantus*, how much + *facere*, make⟧ **1** to determine or express the quantity of **2** to express as a quantity or number —**quan′ti·fi′er *n.***

quan′ti·ta′tive (-tāt′iv) ***adj.*** having to do with quantity

quan′ti·ty (-tē) ***n.**, pl.* **-ties** ⟦< L *quantus*, how great⟧ **1** an amount; portion **2** any indeterminate bulk or number **3** [*also pl.*] a great amount **4** that property by which a thing can be measured **5** a number or symbol expressing this property

quan·tum (kwän′təm) ***n.**, pl.* **-ta** (-tə) ⟦L, how much⟧ *Physics* a fixed, elemental unit of energy: the **quantum**

THESAURUS

quack[2] ***a.*** fraudulent, unprincipled, dissembling; see DISHONEST.

quack[2] ***n.*** rogue, charlatan, humbug; see CHEAT, IMPOSTOR.

quadrangle ***n.*** geometrical four-sided figure, parallelogram, square; see RECTANGLE.

quadrangular ***a.*** quadrilateral, four-sided, rectangular; see ANGULAR, SQUARE.

quadruped ***n.*** four-legged animal, quadrupedal animal, mammal; see ANIMAL.

quadruple ***a.*** fourfold, four-way, four times as great, consisting of four parts, quadruplex, four-cycle, four-ply, quadruplicate.

quaff ***v.*** gulp, swallow, guzzle; see DRINK 1, SWALLOW.

quaint ***a.*** fanciful, cute, pleasing, captivating, curious, antique, whimsical, picturesque, enchanting, baroque, Victorian, French Provincial, Early American, Colonial; see also CHARMING.—*Ant.* MODERN, up-to-date, fashionable.

quake ***n.*** temblor, tremor, shock; see EARTHQUAKE.

quake ***v.*** tremble, shrink, cower; see SHAKE 1.

qualification ***n.*** need, requisite, essential; see REQUIREMENT 1.

qualifications ***n.*** endowments, acquirements, attainments; see EXPERIENCE.

qualified ***a.*** **1** [Limited] conditional, modified, confined; see RESTRICTED. **2** [Competent] fitted, adequate, equipped; see ABLE.

qualify ***v.*** **1** [To limit] reduce, restrain, temper; see ALTER 1. **2** [To fulfill requirements] fit, suit, pass, pass muster, have the requisites, meet the demands, be endowed by nature for, measure up, meet the specifications.—*Ant.* FAIL, become unfit, be unsuited.

quality ***n.*** **1** [A characteristic] attribute, trait, endowment; see CHARACTERISTIC. **2** [Essential character] nature, essence, genius; see CHARACTER 2. **3** [Grade] class, kind, caliber, state, condition, merit, worth, excellence, stage, step, variety, standing, rank, group, place, position, repute.

qualm ***n.*** indecision, scruple, suspicion; see DOUBT, UNCERTAINTY 2.

quantity ***n.*** amount, number, bulk, mass, measure, extent, abundance, volume, capacity, lot, deal, pile, multitude, portion, carload, sum, profusion, mountain, load, barrel, shipment, consignment, bushel, supply, ton, ocean, flood, sea, flock, the amount of, score, swarm, quite a few, army, host, pack, crowd, bunch, heap*, mess*, slew*, gob*, batch, all kinds of*, all sorts of*; see also SIZE 2.

theory states that energy is radiated discontinuously in quanta

quantum jump (or **leap**) a sudden, extensive change

quar·an·tine (kwôr′ən tēn) ***n.*** ⟦< L *quadraginta,* forty⟧ **1** the period, orig. 40 days, during which a vessel suspected of carrying contagious disease is detained in port **2** any isolation imposed to keep contagious diseases, etc. from spreading —***vt.*** **-tined′**, **-tin′ing** to place under quarantine

quark (kwôrk) ***n.*** ⟦arbitrary coinage⟧ any of a set of elementary particles that bind together to form protons, neutrons, mesons, etc.

quar·rel (kwôr′əl) ***n.*** ⟦< L *queri,* complain⟧ **1** a cause for dispute **2** a dispute, esp. an angry one —***vi.*** **-reled** or **-relled**, **-rel·ing** or **-rel·ling** **1** to find fault **2** to dispute heatedly **3** to have a breach in friendship —**quar′rel·er** or **quar′rel·ler** ***n.*** —**quar′rel·some** ***adj.***

quar·ry[1] (kwôr′ē) ***n.,*** *pl.* **-ries** ⟦< OFr *cuiree,* parts of prey fed to dogs⟧ an animal, etc. being hunted

quar·ry[2] (kwôr′ē) ***n.,*** *pl.* **-ries** ⟦< L *quadrare,* to square⟧ a place where stone, slate, etc. is excavated —***vt.*** **-ried**, **-ry·ing** to excavate from a quarry

quart (kwôrt) ***n.*** ⟦< L *quartus,* fourth⟧ **1** ¼ gallon in liquid measure **2** ⅛ peck in dry measure

quar′ter (-ər) ***n.*** ⟦< L *quartus,* fourth⟧ **1** a fourth of something **2** *a*) one fourth of a year *b*) any of the three terms of about eleven weeks each in an academic year **3** one fourth of an hour **4** one fourth of a dollar; 25 cents, or a coin of this value **5** any leg of a four-legged animal, with the adjoining parts **6** a particular district or section **7** [*pl.*] lodgings **8** mercy granted to a surrendering foe **9** a particular source *[*news from high *quarters]* —***vt.*** **1** to divide into four equal parts **2** to provide lodgings for —***adj.*** constituting a quarter —**at close quarters** close together

quar′ter·back′ ***n.*** *Football* the offensive back who calls the play, passes the ball, etc.

quar′ter·deck′ ***n.*** the after part of the upper deck of a ship, usually for officers

quar′ter·fi′nal ***adj.*** coming just before the semifinals —***n.*** a quarterfinal match, etc.

quarter horse ⟦< its speed in a *quarter*-mile sprint⟧ any of a breed of muscular, solid-colored horse

quar′ter·ly ***adj.*** occurring regularly four times a year —***adv.*** once every quarter of the year —***n.,*** *pl.* **-lies** a publication issued every three months

quar′ter·mas′ter ***n.*** **1** *Mil.* an officer who provides troops with quarters, clothing, equipment, etc. **2** *Naut.* a petty officer or mate involved in steering and navigating a ship

quarter note *Music* a note having one fourth the duration of a whole note

quar·tet (kwôr tet′) ***n.*** ⟦ult. < L *quartus,* fourth⟧ **1** a group of four **2** *Music a*) a composition for four voices or instruments *b*) the four performers of this

quar·to (kwôrt′ō) ***n.,*** *pl.* **-tos** ⟦< L (*in*) *quarto,* (in) a fourth⟧ **1** the page size (about 9 by 12 in.) of a book made up of sheets each of which is folded twice to form four leaves, or eight pages **2** a book with pages of this size

quartz (kwôrts) ***n.*** ⟦Ger *quarz*⟧ a crystalline mineral, a form of silica, usually colorless and transparent

quartz crystal *Electronics* a piece of quartz cut and ground so as to vibrate at a particular frequency

qua·sar (kwā′zär′) ***n.*** ⟦< *quas*(*i-stell*)*ar* (*radio source*)⟧ a distant celestial object that emits immense quantities of light and radio waves

quash[1] (kwäsh) ***vt.*** ⟦< L *cassus,* empty⟧ *Law* to set aside (an indictment)

quash[2] (kwäsh) ***vt.*** ⟦< L *quatere,* to break⟧ to quell (an uprising)

qua·si (kwā′zī′, kwä′zē′) ***adv.*** ⟦L⟧ as if; seemingly; in part —***adj.*** seeming Often hyphenated as a prefix *[quasi-*legal*]*

quat·rain (kwä′trān′) ***n.*** ⟦< L *quattuor,* four⟧ a stanza of four lines

qua·ver (kwā′vər) ***vi.*** ⟦ME *cwafien*⟧ **1** to shake or tremble **2** to be tremulous: said of the voice —***n.*** a tremulous quality in a voice or tone

quay (kē) ***n.*** ⟦ult. < Celt⟧ a wharf, usually of concrete or stone

quea·sy (kwē′zē) ***adj.*** **-si·er**, **-si·est** ⟦ME *qwesye* < Gmc⟧ **1** affected with nausea **2** squeamish; easily nauseated

Que·bec (kwi bek′) **1** province of E Canada: 594,860 sq. mi.; pop. 7,139,000: abbrev. *QC* **2** its capital, on the St. Lawrence River: pop. 167,000

queen (kwēn) ***n.*** ⟦< OE *cwen*⟧ **1** the wife of a king **2** a female monarch in her own right **3** a woman noted for her beauty or accomplishments **4** the fully developed, reproductive female in a colony of bees, ants, etc. **5** a playing card with a picture of a queen on it **6** *Chess* the most powerful piece —**queen′ly**, **-li·er**, **-li·est**, ***adj.***

Queens (kwēnz) borough of New York City, on W Long Island: pop. 1,952,000

queen′-size′ ***adj.*** larger than usual, but smaller than king-size *[*a *queen-size* bed is 60 by 80 in.*]*

queer (kwir) ***adj.*** ⟦< ? Ger *quer,* crosswise⟧ **1** different from the usual; strange **2** [Inf.] eccentric —***vt.*** [Slang] to spoil the success of

quell (kwel) ***vt.*** ⟦OE *cwellan,* kill⟧ **1** to subdue **2** to quiet; allay

quench (kwench) ***vt.*** ⟦OE *cwencan*⟧ **1** to extinguish *[*to *quench* a fire with water*]* **2** to satisfy *[*to *quench* one's thirst*]* **3** to cool (hot steel, etc.) suddenly by plunging into water, etc. —**quench′less** ***adj.***

quer·u·lous (kwer′yo͞o ləs, -ə-) ***adj.*** ⟦< L *queri,* complain⟧ **1** inclined to find fault **2** full of complaint; peevish —**quer′u·lous·ly** ***adv.***

que·ry (kwir′ē) ***n.,*** *pl.* **-ries** ⟦< L *quaerere,* ask⟧ a question; inquiry —***vt.,*** ***vi.*** **-ried**, **-ry·ing** to question

quest (kwest) ***n.*** ⟦see prec.⟧ **1** a seeking **2** a journey in pursuit of a lofty goal —***vi.*** to go in pursuit

ques·tion (kwes′chən) ***n.*** ⟦see QUERY⟧ **1** an asking; inquiry **2** something asked **3** doubt; uncertainty **4** a

THESAURUS

quarantined ***a.*** shut up, under quarantine, hospitalized, restrained, separated; see also ISOLATED.

quarrel ***n.*** **1** [An angry dispute] wrangle, squabble, dissension; see DISAGREEMENT 1, DISPUTE. **2** [Objection] complaint, disapproval, disagreement; see OBJECTION.

quarrel ***v.*** wrangle, dispute, contend, fight, squabble, row, clash, altercate, dissent, bicker, struggle, strive, contest, object, complain, disagree, argue, charge, feud, engage in blows, mix it up with*, step on someone's toes, get tough with*, lock horns, have words with, have a brush with, have it out*, fall out with, break with*, hassle*; see also OPPOSE 1.—*Ant.* AGREE, concur, harmonize.

quarrelsome ***a.*** factious, irritable, combative, pugnacious, turbulent, unruly, passionate, violent, contentious, disputatious, fiery, cross, irascible, snappish, waspish, peevish, petulant, argumentative, litigious, churlish, cantankerous, thin-skinned, touchy, huffy, pettish, peppery, impassioned, hotheaded, excitable, hasty, tempestuous, with a chip on one's shoulder*.—*Ant.* AGREEABLE, CALM, peaceful.

quart ***n.*** two pints, thirty-two ounces, one-fourth gallon; see MEASURE 1.

quarter ***n.*** **1** [One of four equal parts] fourth, one-fourth part, portion, quadrant, division, three months, 90 days, school term, quarter of an hour, quarter section; see also PART 1. **2** [One quarter of a dollar; *United States*] twenty-five cents, one-fourth of a dollar, coin, two bits*; see also MONEY 1. **3** [A section of a community] neighborhood, district, section; see AREA. —**at close quarters** at close range, cramped, restricted; see NEAR 1.

quarter ***v.*** **1** [To divide into quarters] cleave, dismember, cut up; see CUT 1, DIVIDE. **2** [To provide living quarters] lodge, shelter, house; see SHELTER.

quarterly ***a.*** by quarters, once every three months, periodically; see REGULARLY.

quarters ***n.*** lodgings, housing, living quarters, accommodations, house, apartment, room, barracks, tent, lodge, cabins, cottage, car trailer.

quartet ***n.*** four persons, four voices, four musicians, string quartet.

quartz ***n.*** *Types of quartz include the following:* amethyst, chalcedony, rock crystal, rose quartz, smoky quartz, bloodstone, agate, onyx, sardonyx, carnelian, chrysoprase, prase, flint, jasper; see also ROCK 1.

quasi ***a.*** supposedly, to a certain extent, apparently; see ALMOST.

queasy ***a.*** squeamish, sick, uneasy; see UNCOMFORTABLE 1.

queen ***n.*** ruler, female ruler, female sovereign, empress, woman monarch, queen mother, regent, wife of a king, consort, queen consort, queen dowager, queen regent, fairy queen, May Queen, matriarch.

queer ***a.*** **1** [Odd] strange, peculiar, uncommon; see UNUSUAL 2. **2** [*Suspicious] doubtful, questionable, curious; see SUSPICIOUS 2.

quench ***v.*** **1** [To satisfy] slake, glut, gorge; see DRINK 1. **2** [To smother] stifle, dampen, douse; see MOISTEN.

quest ***n.*** journey, search, crusade; see EXAMINATION 1.

question ***n.*** **1** [A query] inquiry, interrogatory, interrogation, inquisi-

matter open to discussion 5 a difficult matter *[it's not a question of money]* 6 a point being debated before an assembly —***vt.*** 1 to ask questions of 2 to express doubt about 3 to dispute; challenge —***vi.*** to ask questions —**out of the question** impossible

ques'tion·a·ble ***adj.*** 1 that can be questioned or doubted 2 suspected of being immoral, dishonest, etc. 3 uncertain

question mark a mark of punctuation (?) put after a sentence, word, etc. to indicate a direct question or to express doubt, etc.

ques'tion·naire' (-chə ner') ***n.*** a written or printed set of questions used in gathering information from people

queue (kyoo͞) ***n.*** ⟦< L *cauda,* tail⟧ 1 a pigtail 2 [Chiefly Brit.] a line, as of persons waiting to be served 3 stored computer data or programs waiting to be processed —***vi.*** **queued, queu'ing** [Chiefly Brit.] to line up in a queue: often with *up*

quib·ble (kwib'əl) ***n.*** ⟦< L *qui,* who⟧ a petty evasion or criticism —***vi.*** **-bled, -bling** to evade the truth of a point under discussion by caviling

quiche (kēsh) ***n.*** a dish consisting of custard baked in a pastry shell with various ingredients, as bacon, cheese, or spinach

quick (kwik) ***adj.*** ⟦< OE *cwicu,* living⟧ 1 *a*) rapid; swift *[a quick walk]* *b*) prompt *[a quick reply]* 2 prompt to understand or learn *[a quick mind]* 3 easily stirred *[a quick temper]* —***adv.*** quickly; rapidly —***n.*** 1 the living: esp. in **the quick and the dead** 2 the sensitive flesh under the nails 3 the deepest feelings *[hurt to the quick]* —**quick'ly** ***adv.*** —**quick'ness** ***n.***

quick bread any bread leavened with baking powder, soda, etc. and baked as soon as the batter is mixed

quick'en ***vt.*** 1 to animate; enliven; revive 2 to cause to move more rapidly —***vi.*** 1 to become enlivened; revive 2 to begin to show signs of life, as a fetus 3 to become more rapid

quick'-freeze' ***vt.*** **-froze', -fro'zen, -freez'ing** to subject (food) to sudden freezing for long storage

quick'ie ***n.*** [Inf.] anything done or made quickly and, often, cheaply

quick'lime' ***n.*** unslaked lime

quick'sand' ***n.*** ⟦< ME: see QUICK & SAND⟧ a loose, deep sand deposit, engulfing heavy objects easily

quick'sil'ver ***n.*** mercury

quick'-tem'pered ***adj.*** easily angered

quick'-wit'ted ***adj.*** mentally nimble

quid (kwid) ***n.*** ⟦var. of CUD⟧ a piece, as of tobacco, to be chewed

quid pro quo (kwid' prō kwō') ⟦L⟧ one thing in return for another

qui·es·cent (kwī es'ənt) ***adj.*** ⟦< L *quiescere,* become quiet⟧ still; inactive —**qui·es'cence** ***n.***

qui·et (kwī'ət) ***adj.*** ⟦< L *quies,* rest⟧ 1 still; motionless 2 *a*) not noisy; hushed *b*) not speaking; silent 3 not easily excited 4 not showy 5 not forward; unobtrusive 6 peaceful and relaxing —***n.*** 1 calmness, stillness, etc. 2 a quiet or peaceful quality —***vt.*** to make quiet —***vi.*** to become quiet: usually with *down* —**qui'et·ly** ***adv.***

qui·e·tude (kwī'ə too͞d') ***n.*** a state of being quiet; calmness

qui·e·tus (kwī ēt'əs) ***n.*** ⟦< ML *quietus* (*est*), (he is) quit⟧ 1 discharge from debt, etc. 2 death

quill (kwil) ***n.*** ⟦prob. < LowG or MDu⟧ 1 a large, stiff feather 2 *a*) the hollow stem of a feather *b*) anything made from this, as a pen 3 a spine of a porcupine or hedgehog

quilt (kwilt) ***n.*** ⟦< L *culcita,* bed⟧ a bedcover filled with down, cotton, etc. and stitched together in lines or patterns —***vt.*** to stitch like a quilt —***vi.*** to make a quilt —**quilt'er** ***n.***

quince (kwins) ***n.*** ⟦< Gr *kydōnion*⟧ 1 a yellowish, apple-shaped fruit, used in preserves 2 the tree it grows on

qui·nel·la (kwi nel'ə, kē-) ***n.*** ⟦< AmSp < L *quinque,* five⟧ a form of betting in horse-racing, in which the bettor, to win, must pick the first two finishers, in whichever order they finish: also **qui·nie·la** (kē nye'lə)

qui·nine (kwī'nīn') ***n.*** ⟦< *quina,* cinchona bark⟧ a bitter, crystalline alkaloid extracted from cinchona bark, used for treating malaria

quin·tes·sence (kwin tes'əns) ***n.*** ⟦< ML *quinta essentia*⟧ the pure essence or perfect type

quin·tet or **quin·tette** (kwin tet') ***n.*** ⟦ult. < L *quintus,* a fifth⟧ 1 a group of five 2 *Music a*) a composition for five voices or instruments *b*) the five performers of this

quin·tu·ple (kwin too͞'pəl) ***adj.*** ⟦< L *quintus,* a fifth + *-plex,* -fold⟧ 1 consisting of five 2 five times as much or

THESAURUS

tion, feeler, inquest, rhetorical question, burning question, crucial question, leading question, academic question.—*Ant.* ANSWER, solution, reply. 2 [A puzzle] enigma, mystery, problem; see PUZZLE 1. 3 [A subject] issue, topic, discussion; see SUBJECT. —**beside the question** not germane, beside the point, unnecessary; see IRRELEVANT. —**beyond question** beyond dispute, without any doubt, sure; see CERTAIN 2. —**in question** open for discussion, in debate, at issue; see CONTROVERSIAL, QUESTIONABLE 1, UNCERTAIN. —**out of the question** not to be considered, by no means, no; see IMPOSSIBLE.

question ***v.*** 1 [To ask] inquire, interrogate, query, quest, seek, search, sound out, petition, solicit, ask about, catechize, show curiosity, pry into, debrief, ask a leading question, challenge, raise a question, make inquiry, quiz, cross-examine, probe, investigate, grill, put to the question, bring into question; see also ASK. 2 [To doubt] distrust, suspect, dispute; see DOUBT.

questionable ***a.*** 1 [Justifying doubt] doubtful, undefined, equivocal, disputable, obscure, occult, indecisive, controversial, vague, unsettled, open to doubt, indeterminate, debatable, unconfirmed, problematical, cryptic, apocryphal, hypothetical, mysterious, enigmatic, ambiguous, indefinite, contingent, provisional, paradoxical, under advisement, under examination, open to question, up for discussion, in question, to be decided, hard to believe, incredible, iffy*, fishy*; see also UNCERTAIN.—*Ant.* DEFINITE, undoubted, credible. 2 [Having a poor appearance or reputation] dubious, disreputable, notorious, of ill repute, unsatisfactory, of little account, thought ill of, under a cloud, ill-favored, unpopular, disagreeable, evil-looking, illegitimate, discreditable, unreliable, dishonest, untrustworthy, fly-by-night, shady*, fishy*; see also SUSPICIOUS 2.—*Ant.* HONORED, esteemed, liked.

questionnaire ***n.*** set of questions, inquiry, survey; see CENSUS.

quick ***a.*** 1 [Rapid] swift, expeditious, fleet; see FAST 1. 2 [Almost immediate] posthaste, prompt, instantaneous; see IMMEDIATE. 3 [Hasty] impetuous, mercurial, quick-tempered; see RASH. 4 [Alert] ready, sharp, vigorous; see ACTIVE.

quicken ***v.*** 1 [To hasten] speed, hurry, make haste; see HASTEN 2. 2 [To cause to hasten] expedite, urge, promote; see HASTEN 2.

quickly ***a.*** speedily, swiftly, fleetly, flying, wingedly, with dispatch, scurrying, hurrying, rushing, shooting, bolting, darting, flashing, dashing, suddenly, in haste, in a hurry, just now, this minute, in a moment, in an instant, right away, at a greater rate, without delay, against the clock, racing, galloping, loping, sweeping, lightfootedly, briskly, at once, like a bat out of hell*, on the double*, in a flash*, in a jiffy*, to beat the band*, at full blast, hellbent for leather*, hand over fist*, like mad*, by leaps and bounds, like a house on fire, full steam ahead*.—*Ant.* SLOWLY, sluggishly, creepingly.

quick-tempered ***a.*** temperamental, quarrelsome, irascible; see IRRITABLE.

quiet ***a.*** calm, peaceful, hushed, muffled, noiseless, still, stilled, mute, muted, mum, soundless, dumb, quieted, speechless, unspeaking, quiescent, taciturn, reserved, reticent, not excited, not anxious, not disturbed, silent, unexpressed, closemouthed, close, tight-lipped, uncommunicative, secretive.

quiet ***n.*** 1 [Rest] calm, tranquillity, relaxation; see PEACE 2. 2 [Silence] hush, stillness, speechlessness; see SILENCE 1.

quiet ***v.*** 1 [To make calm] calm, comfort, ease, cool, relax, compose, tranquilize, satisfy, please, pacify, mollify, console, subdue, reconcile, gratify, calm down, soften, moderate, smooth, ameliorate, lull, appease, restrain, sober, slacken, soothe.—*Ant.* EXCITE, stimulate, agitate. 2 [To make silent] still, deaden, silence, lower the sound level, muffle, mute, stop, check, restrain, suppress, break in, gag, muzzle, eliminate, repress, refute, confound, answer, quell, put the lid on*, button up*, choke off*, put the stopper on*.—*Ant.* SOUND, ring, cause to sound. —**quiet down** grow silent, be hushed, hush, be subdued, be suppressed, become speechless, fall quiet, break off, clam up*.

quietly ***a.*** 1 [Calmly] peacefully, serenely, confidently; see CALMLY. 2 [Almost silently] noiselessly, speechlessly, as quietly as possible; see SILENTLY. 3 [Without attracting attention] humbly, unostentatiously, simply; see MODESTLY.

quilt ***n.*** bed covering, coverlet, comforter, duvet, feather bed, puff, down puff, patchwork quilt, pieced quilt, bedspread, pad; see also COVER 1.

as many —*vt., vi.* **-pled, -pling** to make or become five times as much or as many

quin·tu·plet (kwin tup′lit, -to͞o′plit) *n.* **1** any of five offspring from the same pregnancy **2** a group of five, usually of one kind

quip (kwip) *n.* ⟦< L *quippe,* indeed⟧ a witty or sarcastic remark or reply —*vi.* **quipped, quip′ping** to utter quips —**quip′ster** *n.*

quire (kwīr) *n.* ⟦< L *quaterni,* four each⟧ a set of 24 or 25 sheets of paper of the same size and stock

quirk (kwurk) *n.* ⟦< ?⟧ **1** a sudden twist or turn **2** a peculiarity —**quirk′i·ness** *n.* —**quirk′y, -i·er, -i·est,** *adj.*

quirt (kwurt) *n.* ⟦AmSp *cuarta*⟧ a riding whip with a braided leather lash and a short handle

quis·ling (kwiz′liŋ) *n.* ⟦after V. *Quisling,* Norw collaborator with the Nazis⟧ a traitor

quit (kwit) *vt.* **quit, quit′ting** ⟦< ML *quittus,* free⟧ **1** to free (oneself) *of* **2** to stop having, using, or doing **3** to depart from **4** to resign from —*vi.* **1** to stop doing something **2** to give up one's job

quit′claim′ *n.* a deed relinquishing a claim, as to property

quite (kwīt) *adv.* ⟦see QUIT⟧ **1** completely **2** really; positively **3** very or fairly *[quite* warm*]* —**quite a few** (or **bit,** etc.) [Inf.] more than a few (or bit, etc.)

Qui·to (kē′tō) capital of Ecuador: pop. 1,101,000

quits (kwits) *adj.* ⟦< ML *quittus,* free⟧ on even terms, as by discharge of a debt, retaliation, etc. —**call it quits** [Inf.] **1** to stop working, etc. **2** to end an association

quit·tance (kwit′'ns) *n.* ⟦see QUIT⟧ **1** discharge from a debt **2** recompense

quit′ter *n.* [Inf.] one who quits or gives up easily, without trying hard

quiv·er[1] (kwiv′ər) *vi.* ⟦< OE *curifer-,* eager⟧ to shake tremulously; tremble —*n.* a quivering; tremor

quiv·er[2] (kwiv′ər) *n.* ⟦< OFr *coivre*⟧ a case for holding arrows

quix·ot·ic (kwik sät′ik) *adj.* ⟦after DON QUIXOTE⟧ extravagantly chivalrous or foolishly idealistic

quiz (kwiz) *n., pl.* **quiz′zes** ⟦prob. < L *quis,* what⟧ a questioning; esp., a short examination to test knowledge —*vt.* **quizzed, quiz′zing** to ask questions, or test the knowledge, of —**quiz′zer** *n.*

quiz′zi·cal (-i kəl) *adj.* **1** teasing **2** perplexed —**quiz′zi·cal·ly** *adv.*

quoin (koin, kwoin) *n.* ⟦var. of COIN⟧ **1** the external corner of a building; esp., any of the large stones at such a corner **2** a wedge-shaped block

quoit (kwoit) *n.* ⟦prob. < OFr *coite,* a cushion⟧ **1** a ring thrown in quoits **2** [*pl., with sing. v.*] a game somewhat like horseshoes, in which rings are thrown at a peg

quon·dam (kwän′dəm) *adj.* ⟦L⟧ former

Quon·set hut (kwän′sit) ⟦< *Quonset,* a trademark⟧ a prefabricated, metal shelter like a half cylinder on its flat side

quo·rum (kwôr′əm) *n.* ⟦< L *qui,* who⟧ the minimum number of members required to be present before an assembly can transact business

quot *abbrev.* quotation

quo·ta (kwōt′ə) *n.* ⟦< L *quota pars,* how large a part⟧ a share or proportion assigned to each of a number

quotation mark either of a pair of punctuation marks (" ... ") used to enclose a direct quotation

quote (kwōt) *vt.* **quot′ed, quot′ing** ⟦< L *quotus,* of what number⟧ **1** to repeat a passage from or statement of **2** to repeat (a passage, statement, etc.) **3** to state the price of (something) —*n.* [Inf.] **1** something quoted **2** QUOTATION MARK —**quot′a·ble** *adj.* —**quo·ta·tion** (kwō tā′shən) *n.*

quoth (kwōth) *vt.* ⟦< OE *cwethan,* speak⟧ [Archaic] said

quo·tid·i·an (kwō tid′ē ən) *adj.* ⟦< L *quotidie*⟧ **1** daily **2** ordinary

quo·tient (kwō′shənt) *n.* ⟦< L *quot,* how many⟧ *Math.* the result obtained when one number is divided by another

Qu·ran or **Qu·r′an** (ko͞o rän′) *n. var. of* KORAN

q.v. *abbrev.* ⟦L *quod vide*⟧ which see

THESAURUS

quip *n.* jest, witticism, one-liner; see JOKE.

quirk *n.* vagary, whim, caprice, fancy, whimsy, oddity, humor, turn, twist, knack, peculiarity, idiosyncrasy, foible, eccentricity, kink, crotchet, bee in one's bonnet*; see also CHARACTERISTIC, IRREGULARITY.

quit *v.* **1** [Abandon] surrender, renounce, relinquish; see ABANDON 1. **2** [To cease] discontinue, cease, halt, pause, stop, end, desist; see also STOP 2. **3** [To leave] go away from, depart, vacate; see LEAVE 1. **4** [To resign] leave, stop work, walk out, change jobs, cease work, give notice; see also RESIGN 2.

quite *a.* **1** [Completely] entirely, wholly, totally; see COMPLETELY. **2** [Really] truly, positively, actually; see REALLY 1. **3** [To a considerable degree] pretty, more or less, considerably; see VERY.

quitter *n.* shirker, dropout, deserter, goldbrick*, piker*, slacker.

quiver[1] *n.* shudder, shiver, tremble; see VIBRATION.

quiver[1] *v.* vibrate, shudder, shiver; see WAVE 3.

quiz *n.* test, questioning, exam; see EXAMINATION 2.

quiz *v.* question, test, cross-examine; see EXAMINE.

quorum *n.* enough to transact business, majority of the membership, legal minimum; see MEMBER.

quota *n.* portion, allowance, ration; see SHARE.

quotation *n.* **1** [Quoted matter] excerpt, passage, citation, cite*, citing, extract, recitation, repetition, sentence, quote, plagiarism. **2** [A quoted price] market price, current price, published price; see PRICE.

quote *v.* **1** [To repeat verbatim] recite, excerpt, extract; see SAY. **2** [To state a price] name a price, request, demand; see PRICE, VALUE 2.

quoted *a.* **1** [Repeated from some-one else] recited, excerpted, extracted, cited, instanced, copied. **2** [Offered or mentioned at a stated price] asked, stated, announced, published, named, marked, given, priced, ticketed, tagged.

R

r[1] or **R** (är) ***n.***, *pl.* **r's, R's** the 18th letter of the English alphabet
r[2] *abbrev.* radius
R[1] *trademark for* a film rating indicating that no one under 17 may be admitted unless accompanied by a parent or guardian
R[2] *abbrev.* **1** ⟦L *Rex*⟧ king **2** ⟦L *Regina*⟧ queen **3** Republican **4** right **5** River **6** Road **7** route **8** *Baseball* run(s): also **r**
Ra[1] (rä) ***n.*** *Egypt. Myth.* the sun god and chief deity
Ra[2] *Chem. symbol for* radium
rab·bet (rab′it) ***n.*** ⟦< OFr *rabattre,* beat down⟧ a cut made in a board so that another may be fitted into it —***vt.***, ***vi.*** to cut, or be joined by, a rabbet
rab·bi (rab′ī) ***n.***, *pl.* **-bis** ⟦< Heb *rabi,* my master⟧ an ordained teacher of the Jewish law
rab·bin·ate (rab′i nit, -nāt′) ***n.*** **1** the position of a rabbi **2** rabbis collectively —**rab·bi·ni·cal** (rə bin′i kəl) ***adj.***
rab·bit (rab′it) ***n.*** ⟦ME *rabette*⟧ a swift, burrowing mammal with soft fur and long ears
rabbit punch *Boxing* a short, sharp blow to the back of the neck
rab·ble (rab′əl) ***n.*** ⟦< ?⟧ a mob
rab′ble-rous′er (-rou′zər) ***n.*** one who tries to arouse people to violent action by appeals to emotions, prejudices, etc.
Ra·be·lais (rab′ə lā′), **Fran·çois** (frän swá′) 1494?-1553; Fr. satirist & humorist
Ra·be·lai·si·an (rab′ə lā′zhən, -zē ən) ***adj.*** ⟦after prec.⟧ broadly and coarsely humorous or satirical
rab·id (rab′id) ***adj.*** ⟦< L *rabere,* to rage⟧ **1** violent; raging **2** fanatic **3** of or having rabies
ra·bies (rā′bēz) ***n.*** ⟦L, madness⟧ an infectious disease characterized by convulsions, etc., transmitted to people by the bite of an infected animal
rac·coon (ra ko͞on′) ***n.*** ⟦< AmInd *aroughcun*⟧ **1** a small, tree-climbing, American mammal, with yellowish-gray fur and a black-ringed tail **2** its fur
race[1] (rās) ***n.*** ⟦< ON *rās,* a running⟧ **1** a competition of speed in running, etc. **2** any similar contest *[the race for mayor]* **3** a swift current of water, or its channel —***vi.*** **raced, rac′ing** **1** to take part in a race **2** to go or move swiftly —***vt.*** **1** to compete with in a race **2** to enter or run (a horse, etc.) in a race **3** to cause to go swiftly —**rac′er** ***n.***
race[2] (rās) ***n.*** ⟦Fr < It *razza*⟧ **1** any of the different varieties of human beings distinguished by physical traits, blood types, etc. **2** loosely, any geographical population sharing the same habits, ideas, etc. **3** any distinct group of people
race′horse′ ***n.*** a horse bred and trained for racing
ra·ceme (rā sēm′, rə-) ***n.*** ⟦L *racemus,* cluster of grapes⟧ a flower cluster having a central stem along which individual flowers grow on small stalks
race′track′ ***n.*** a course prepared for racing, esp. an oval track for horse races
race′way′ ***n.*** **1** a narrow channel for water **2** a racetrack for harness racing, drag racing, etc.
ra·cial (rā′shəl) ***adj.*** **1** of or characteristic of a RACE[2] **2** between races —**ra′cial·ly** ***adv.***
rac·i·ness (rā′sē nis) ***n.*** racy quality
racing form a chart, etc. of information about the horse races at a track or tracks
rac·ism (rā′siz′əm) ***n.*** the practice of racial discrimination, segregation, etc. —**rac′ist** ***n.***, ***adj.***
rack[1] (rak) ***n.*** ⟦< LowG *rack*⟧ **1** a framework, etc. for holding or displaying various things *[dish rack]* **2** a toothed bar into which a pinion, etc. meshes **3** an instrument of torture which stretches the victim's limbs —***vt.*** **1** to arrange in or on a rack **2** to torture on a rack **3** to torment —**rack one's brains** to try hard to think of something —**rack up** [Slang] to score or achieve
rack[2] (rak) ***n.*** ⟦var. of WRACK⟧ used only in **go to rack and ruin**, to become ruined
rack[3] (rak) ***n.*** ⟦< ? RACK[1]⟧ the rib section of mutton: in full **rack of lamb**
rack·et[1] (rak′it) ***n.*** ⟦prob. echoic⟧ **1** a noisy confusion **2** *a)* a method or scheme for obtaining money illegally *b)* [Inf.] any dishonest practice
rack·et[2] (rak′it) ***n.*** ⟦< Ar *rāḥa(t),* palm of the hand⟧ a light bat for tennis, etc., with a network, as of catgut or nylon, in an oval frame attached to a handle: also **rac′quet**
rack·et·eer (rak′ə tir′) ***n.*** one who obtains money illegally, as by fraud, extortion, etc. —**rack′et·eer′ing** ***n.***
rac·on·teur (rak′än tʉr′) ***n.*** ⟦Fr < *raconter,* to recount⟧ one skilled at telling stories or anecdotes
rac·quet·ball (rack′it bôl′) ***n.*** a game like handball, but played with a short racket
rac·y (rā′sē) ***adj.*** **-i·er, -i·est** ⟦RACE[2] + -Y[2]⟧ **1** having the taste or quality of the genuine type *[racy fruit]* **2** lively; spirited **3** pungent **4** risqué
rad (rad) ***n.*** ⟦< RAD(IATION)⟧ a dosage of absorbed radiation
ra·dar (rā′där′) ***n.*** ⟦*ra(dio) d(etecting) a(nd) r(anging)*⟧ an apparatus that transmits radio waves to a reflecting object, as an aircraft, to determine its location, speed, etc. by the reflected waves
ra′dar·scope′ ***n.*** an oscilloscope that displays reflected radar wave signals

THESAURUS

rabbi ***n.*** Jewish teacher, teacher, Hebrew theologian; see PRIEST.

rabbit ***n.*** hare, pika, bunny, Easter bunny; see also ANIMAL, RODENT. *Kinds of rabbits include the following:* jack rabbit, cottontail, snowshoe rabbit, coney.

rabble ***n.*** mob, masses, riffraff; see CROWD, PEOPLE 3.

rabid ***a.*** **1** [Fanatical] obsessed, zealous, extremist; see RADICAL 2. **2** [Insane] mad, raging, deranged; see INSANE. **3** [Affected with rabies] attacked by a mad dog, hydrophobic, foaming at the mouth; see SICK.

rabies ***n.*** canine madness, hydrophobia, lyssa; see ILLNESS 2.

race[1] ***v.*** **1** [To move at great speed] speed, hurry, run, pursue, chase, tear, bustle, spurt, post, zoom, press on, run swiftly, hasten, trip, fly, hustle, dash, rush, sprint, swoop, scuttle, dart, scamper, haste, plunge ahead, whiz, bolt, scramble, whisk, shoot, run like mad, burn up the road*, gun the motor*, skedaddle*. **2** [To compete] run a race, compete in a race, contend in running, follow a course, engage in a contest of speed, contend, sprint, enter a competition.

race[1,2] ***n.*** **1** [A major division of mankind] species, culture, variety, type, kind, strain, breed, family, cultural group, color; see also MAN 1. **2** [Roughly, people united by blood or custom] nationality, caste, sect, culture, variety, type, the people, mankind, tribe, group, ethnic stock, human race, class, kind, nation, folk, gene pool, pedigree, lineage, community, inhabitants, population, populace, public, clan, breeding population; see also HEREDITY, SOCIETY 2. **3** [A contest, usually in speed] competition, run, sprint, clash, meet, event, engagement, relay, footrace, horse race, competitive action, pursuit, rush, steeplechase, handicap, chase, match, derby, regatta, sweepstakes, marathon, heat, time trial; see also SPORT 3.

racial ***a.*** lineal, hereditary, ancestral, genetic, ethnic, genealogical, ethnological, phylogenic, national.

racism ***n.*** racial prejudice, racial bias, bigotry, racial discrimination, apartheid, segregation; see also PREJUDICE.

racist ***a.*** supremacist, discriminatory, bigoted; see CONSERVATIVE, PREJUDICED.

racist ***n.*** supremacist, believer in racism, racialist; see BIGOT, CONSERVATIVE.

rack[1] ***n.*** holder, receptacle, framework, stand, shelf, ledge, perch, frame, bracket, whatnot, arbor, box, counter, trestle, hat rack, clothes rack, bottle rack, gun rack, feed rack; see also FRAME 1.

racket[1] ***n.*** **1** [Disturbing noise] uproar, clatter, din; see DISTURBANCE 2, NOISE 2. **2** [Confusion accompanied by noise] disturbance, squabble, scuffle, fracas, clash, row, wrangle, agitation, babel, pandemonium, turbulence, clamor, outcry, hullabaloo, tumult, hubbub, commotion, blare, turmoil, stir, noisy fuss, uproar, clatter, babble, roar, shouting, rumpus, riot, squall, brawl, fight, pitched battle, free-for-all, to-do*, fuss. **3** [*A means of extortion] illegitimate business, confidence game, con game*; see CORRUPTION 2, CRIME, THEFT.

racketeer ***n.*** gang leader, mobster, gangster; see CRIMINAL.

racy ***a.*** **1** [Full of zest] spicy, sharp, spirited; see EXCITING. **2** [Not quite respectable] indecent, erotic, suggestive; see LEWD 2, SENSUAL 2.

radar ***n.*** radio detecting and ranging, radiolocation, Loran; see ELECTRONICS.

ra·di·al (rā′dē əl) ***adj.*** ⟦< L *radius*, ray⟧ **1** of or like a ray or rays; branching out from a center **2** of a radius

radial (ply) tire an automobile tire with plies of rubberized cords at right angles to the center line of the tread

ra·di·ant (rā′dē ənt) ***adj.*** ⟦< L *radius*, ray⟧ **1** shining brightly **2** showing pleasure, etc.; beaming **3** issuing (from a source) in or as in rays —**ra′di·ance** ***n.*** —**ra′di·ant·ly** ***adv.***

ra·di·ate (rā′dē āt′) ***vi.*** **-at′ed, -at′ing** ⟦< L *radius,* ray⟧ **1** to send out rays of heat, light, etc. **2** to branch out in lines from a center —***vt.*** **1** to send out (heat, light, etc.) in rays **2** to give forth or spread (happiness, love, etc.)

ra′di·a′tion ***n.*** **1** a radiating **2** the rays sent out **3** energy emitted as nuclear particles, etc.

radiation sickness sickness produced by overexposure to X-rays, radioactive matter, etc.

ra′di·a′tor ***n.*** **1** an apparatus for radiating heat, as into a room **2** a device for circulating coolant, etc., as for a car engine

rad·i·cal (rad′i kəl) ***adj.*** ⟦< L *radix*, root⟧ **1** fundamental; basic **2** favoring basic change, as in the social or economic structure —***n.*** **1** a person holding radical views **2** *Chem.* a group of two or more atoms acting as a single atom **3** *Math.* the sign (√) used with a quantity to show that its root is to be extracted —**rad′i·cal·ism′** ***n.*** —**rad′i·cal·ly** ***adv.***

ra·dic·chio (rə dē′kyō) ***n.***, *pl.* **-chios** ⟦It⟧ a variety of chicory used in salads

ra·di·i (rā′dē ī′) ***n.*** *alt. pl. of* RADIUS

ra·di·o (rā′dē ō′) ***n.*** ⟦< *radio(telegraphy)*⟧ **1** the transmission of sounds or signals by electromagnetic waves directly through space to a receiving set **2** *pl.* **-os′** such a set **3** broadcasting by radio as an industry, entertainment, etc. —***adj.*** **1** of, using, used in, or sent by radio **2** of electromagnetic wave frequencies between *c.* 10 kilohertz and *c.* 300,000 megahertz —***vt.***, ***vi.*** **-oed′, -o′ing** to transmit, or communicate with, by radio

radio- ⟦< L *radius,* ray⟧ *combining form* **1** ray, raylike **2** by radio **3** using radiant energy **4** radioactive *[radiotherapy]*

ra′di·o·ac′tive ***adj.*** giving off radiant energy in the form of particles or rays by the disintegration of atomic nuclei —**ra′di·o·ac·tiv′i·ty** ***n.***

radio astronomy astronomy dealing with radio waves in space in order to obtain information about the universe

ra′di·o·gram′ ***n.*** a message sent by radio

ra′di·o·i′so·tope′ ***n.*** a radioactive isotope of a chemical element

ra·di·ol·o·gy (rā′dē äl′ə jē) ***n.*** the use of radiant energy, as X-rays, in medical diagnosis and therapy —**ra′di·ol′o·gist** ***n.***

ra′di·o·paque′ (-ō pāk′) ***adj.*** ⟦RADIO- + (O)PAQUE⟧ not allowing the passage of X-rays, etc.

radio telescope a radio antenna for receiving and measuring radio waves from stars, spacecraft, etc.

ra′di·o·ther′a·py ***n.*** the treatment of disease by the use of X-rays or rays from a radioactive substance

rad·ish (rad′ish) ***n.*** ⟦< L *radix*, root⟧ **1** an annual plant with an edible root **2** the pungent root, eaten raw

ra·di·um (rā′dē əm) ***n.*** ⟦< L *radius,* ray⟧ a radioactive, metallic chemical element found in some uranium, which undergoes spontaneous atomic disintegration

ra·di·us (rā′dē əs) ***n.***, *pl.* **-di·i′** (-ī′) or **-us·es** ⟦L, ray⟧ **1** any straight line from the center to the periphery of a circle or sphere **2** the circular area limited by the sweep of such a line *[within a radius of two miles]* **3** the shorter, thicker bone of the forearm

ra·don (rā′dän′) ***n.*** ⟦< RADIUM⟧ a radioactive chemical element, a nonreactive gas, formed in the atomic disintegration of radium

RAF *abbrev.* Royal Air Force

raf·fi·a (raf′ē ə) ***n.*** ⟦< native name⟧ **1** a palm tree of Madagascar, with large leaves **2** fiber from its leaves, used as string or for weaving

raff·ish (raf′ish) ***adj.*** ⟦(RIFF)RAFF + -ISH⟧ **1** carelessly unconventional **2** vulgar; low

raf·fle (raf′əl) ***n.*** ⟦ME *rafle*⟧ a lottery in which each participant buys a chance to win a prize —***vt.*** **-fled, -fling** to offer as a prize in a raffle: often with *off*

raft[1] (raft) ***n.*** ⟦< ON *raptr,* a log⟧ **1** a flat, buoyant structure of logs, etc. fastened together **2** a flat-bottomed, inflatable boat —***vi.*** to travel on a raft

raft[2] (raft) ***n.*** ⟦< Brit dial. *raff*, rubbish⟧ [Inf.] a large quantity

raf·ter (raf′tər) ***n.*** ⟦OE *ræfter*⟧ any of the beams that slope from the ridge of a roof to the eaves

rag[1] (rag) ***n.*** ⟦< ON *rögg*, tuft of hair⟧ **1** a waste piece of cloth, esp. one old or torn **2** a small piece of cloth for dusting, etc. **3** [*pl.*] old, worn clothes

rag[2] (rag) ***vt.*** **ragged, rag′ging** ⟦< ?⟧ [Slang] to tease or scold: often with *on*

rag[3] (rag) ***n.*** a tune in ragtime

ra·ga (rä′gə) ***n.*** ⟦Sans *rāga*, color⟧ any of various melody patterns improvised on by Hindu musicians

rag·a·muf·fin (rag′ə muf′in) ***n.*** ⟦ME *Ragamoffyn,* name of a demon⟧ a poor, ragged child

rag′bag′ ***n.*** **1** a bag for rags **2** a collection of odds and ends

rage (rāj) ***n.*** ⟦< LL *rabia*, madness⟧ **1** a furious, uncontrolled anger **2** a great force, violence, etc. —***vi.*** **raged,**

THESAURUS

radial ***a.*** branched, outspread, radiated; see SPIRAL, SPREADING.

radiance ***n.*** brightness, brilliance, effulgence; see LIGHT 1.

radiant ***a.*** shining, luminous, beaming; see BRIGHT 1.

radiate ***v.*** **1** [To send forth from a center] scatter, shed, diffuse, spread, disperse, shoot in all directions, irradiate, emit in straight lines, transmit, disseminate, broadcast, dispel, strew, sprinkle, circulate, send out in rays from a point, throw out. **2** [To shed light or heat] shine, beam, light up, illumine, heat, warm, circulate, expand, widen, brighten, illuminate, irradiate, glitter, glisten, glow, glare, gleam, glimmer, flare, blaze, flicker, sparkle, flash, shimmer, reflect.

radiation ***n.*** **1** [Dissemination] propagation, dissipation, polarization, scattering, spread, diffraction, transmission, broadcast, emission, diffusion, dispersion, circulation, divergence, dispersal; see also DISTRIBUTION, EXTENT. **2** [Fallout] nuclear particles, radioactivity, radiant energy; see ENERGY 2.

radical ***a.*** **1** [Fundamental] original, basic, native; see FUNDAMENTAL, ORGANIC. **2** [Advocating violent change] extremist, fanatical, insurgent, revolutionary, iconoclastic, advanced, forward, progressive, abolitionist, militant, recalcitrant, mutinous, seditious, riotous, lawless, racist, insubordinate, anarchistic, unruly, nihilistic, communistic, liberal, leftist, left-wing, immoderate, freethinking, ultra, avant-garde, pink*, red; see also REBELLIOUS.—*Ant.* CONSERVATIVE, reformist, gradualist. **3** [Believing in violent political and social change] leftist, communistic, militant; see REVOLUTIONARY 1.

radical ***n.*** militant, rebel, agitator, insurgent, objector, revolutionist, revolutionary, insurrectionist, leftist, Bolshevik, anarchist, socialist, communist, nihilist, traitor, mutineer, firebrand, renegade, extremist, crusader, individualist, fascist, Nazi, misfit, iconoclast, eccentric, freethinker, rightist, hippie*, fanatic, demonstrator, rioter, fifth columnist, nonconformist, left-winger, right-winger, pinko*, red*.

radically ***a.*** **1** [Completely] wholly, thoroughly, entirely; see COMPLETELY. **2** [Originally] basically, primitively, firstly; see ESSENTIALLY, FORMERLY.

radio ***n.*** **1** [The study and practice of wireless communication] radio transmission, radio reception, signaling; see BROADCASTING, COMMUNICATION. **2** [A receiving device] wireless, ship's radio, radio set, tuner, receiver, car radio, dish, transistor radio, transistor, portable radio, pocket radio, walkie-talkie, cellular phone, cell-phone; see also ELECTRONICS.

radioactive ***a.*** active, energetic, dangerous, hot*; see also POISONOUS.

radioactivity ***n.*** radiant energy, radioactive particles, Roentgen rays; see ENERGY 2.

radius ***n.*** space, sweep, range; see BOUNDARY, EXPANSE.

raffle ***n.*** sweepstakes, pool, lottery; see GAMBLING.

raft[1] ***n.*** flatboat, barge, float, catamaran, life raft, swimming raft, rubber raft; see also BOAT.

rag[1] ***n.*** remnant, cloth, dishrag, discarded material, hand rag, tatter, shred; see also GOODS 1. **—chew the rag*** chat, converse, have a talk; see TALK 1.

rage ***n.*** **1** [A fit of anger] frenzy, tantrum, uproar, hysterics, explosion, storm, outburst, spasm, convulsion, eruption, furor, excitement, extreme agitation, madness, vehemence, fury, rampage, huff, wrath, raving, violent anger, ire, resentment, bitterness, gall, irritation, animosity, exasperation, passion, indignation, heat, temper, blowup*, fireworks, hissy*, conniption fit*. **2** [The object of enthusiasm and imitation] style, mode, fashion, vogue, craze, mania, the last word, the latest; see also FAD.

rage ***v.*** **1** [To give vent to anger] rant, fume, rave, foam, splutter, yell, scream, roar, rail at, boil over, shake, quiver, seethe, shout, scold, go into a tantrum, have a fit, run amok, run riot, fly apart, flare up, carry on, show violent anger, bluster, storm, be furious, fret, lose one's temper, go berserk, go into a tailspin, blow one's

rag′ing **1** to show violent anger in action or speech **2** to be forceful, violent, etc. **3** to spread unchecked, as a disease —**(all) the rage** a fad

ragg (rag) ***adj.*** designating or made of sturdy yarn having a speckled pattern

rag·ged (rag′id) ***adj.*** **1** shabby or torn from wear **2** wearing shabby or torn clothes **3** uneven; imperfect **4** shaggy *[ragged* hair*]* —**run ragged** to tire out; exhaust —**rag′ged·ness** ***n.***

rag′ged·y ***adj.*** tattered

rag·lan (rag′lən) ***n.*** ⟦after Lord *Raglan,* 19th-c. Brit general⟧ a loose coat with sleeves that continue in one piece to the collar —***adj.*** designating or having such a sleeve

ra·gout (ra go͞o′) ***n.*** ⟦< Fr *ragoûter,* revive the appetite of⟧ a highly seasoned stew of meat and vegetables

rag′time′ ***n.*** ⟦prob. < *ragged time*⟧ **1** a type of American music (*c.* 1890-1920), with strong syncopation in even time **2** its rhythm

rag′weed′ ***n.*** ⟦< its ragged-looking leaves⟧ a weed whose pollen is a common cause of hay fever

rah (rä) ***interj.*** hurrah: used as by cheerleaders

raid (rād) ***n.*** ⟦dial. var. of ROAD⟧ **1** a sudden, hostile attack, esp. by troops or bandits **2** a sudden invasion of a place by police, for discovering violations of the law —***vt.***, ***vi.*** to make a raid (on) —**raid′er** ***n.***

rail[1] (rāl) ***n.*** ⟦< L *regula,* a rule⟧ **1** a bar of wood, metal, etc. placed between posts as a barrier or support **2** any of the parallel metal bars forming a track for a railroad, etc. **3** railroad or railway —***vt.*** to supply with rails or a railing —***adj.*** of a railway or railroad

rail[2] (rāl) ***vi.*** ⟦< LL *ragere,* to bellow⟧ to speak bitterly; complain violently

rail[3] (rāl) ***n.*** ⟦< Fr *raaler,* to screech⟧ a marsh bird with a harsh cry

rail′ing ***n.*** **1** materials for rails **2** a fence, etc. made of rails and posts

rail·ler·y (rā′lər ē) ***n.***, *pl.* **-ies** ⟦see RAIL[2]⟧ light, good-natured ridicule

rail′road′ ***n.*** **1** a track of parallel steel rails for a train **2** a complete system of such tracks, trains, etc. —***vt.*** **1** to transport by railroad **2** [Inf.] to rush through quickly, so as to prevent careful consideration —***vi.*** to work on a railroad —**rail′road′er** ***n.*** —**rail′road′ing** ***n.***

rail′way′ ***n.*** **1** any track with rails for guiding wheels **2** RAILROAD

rai·ment (rā′mənt) ***n.*** ⟦see ARRAY & -MENT⟧ [Archaic] clothing; attire

rain (rān) ***n.*** ⟦OE *regn*⟧ **1** water falling in drops condensed from the atmosphere **2** the falling of such drops **3** a rapid falling of many small objects —***vi.*** **1** to fall: said of rain **2** to fall like rain —***vt.*** **1** to pour down **2** to give in large quantities —**rain out** to cause (an event) to be postponed because of rain —**rain′y**, **-i·er**, **-i·est**, ***adj.***

rain′bow′ (-bō′) ***n.*** ⟦OE *regnboga*⟧ an arc containing the colors of the spectrum, formed in the sky by the refraction, reflection, and dispersion of light in rain or fog

rain check a ticket stub to a ballgame, etc. allowing future admission if the event is rained out

rain′coat′ ***n.*** a water-repellent coat

rain′drop′ ***n.*** a single drop of rain

rain′fall′ ***n.*** **1** a falling of rain **2** the amount of rain over a given area during a given time

rain forest a dense, evergreen forest in a rainy tropical region

rain′storm′ ***n.*** a storm with heavy rain

rain′wa′ter ***n.*** water that is falling or has fallen as rain

raise (rāz) ***vt.*** **raised**, **rais′ing** ⟦< ON *reisa*⟧ **1** to cause to rise; lift **2** to construct; build **3** to increase in size, intensity, amount, degree, etc. *[*to *raise* prices, *raise* one's voice*]* **4** to provoke; inspire **5** to present for consideration *[raise* a question*]* **6** to collect (an army, money, etc.) **7** to end *[raise* a siege*]* **8** *a)* to cause to grow *b)* to rear (children) —***n.*** **1** a raising **2** an increase in salary or in a bet —**raise Cain** (or **hell**, etc.) [Slang] to create a disturbance

rai·sin (rā′zən) ***n.*** ⟦< L *racemus,* cluster of grapes⟧ a dried sweet grape

rai·son d'être (rā′zōn det′, det′rə) ⟦Fr⟧ reason for being; justification for existence

raj (räj) ***n.*** ⟦Hindi: see fol.⟧ in India, rule; government —**the Raj** the British government in, or its dominion over, India

ra·jah or **ra·ja** (rä′jə) ***n.*** ⟦< Sans *rāj,* to rule⟧ a prince in India

rake[1] (rāk) ***n.*** ⟦OE *raca*⟧ a long-handled tool with teeth at one end, for gathering loose hay, leaves, etc. —***vt.*** **raked**, **rak′ing** **1** to gather or smooth with a rake **2** to search through minutely **3** to direct gunfire along (a line of troops, etc.) —**rake in** to gather a great amount of rapidly —**rake up** to uncover facts or gossip about (the past, etc.)

rake[2] (rāk) ***n.*** ⟦contr. of *rakehell*⟧ a dissolute, debauched man

rake[3] (rāk) ***vi.***, ***vt.*** **raked**, **rak′ing** ⟦< ?⟧ to slant —***n.*** a slanting

rake′-off′ ***n.*** [Slang] a commission or rebate, esp. when illegitimate

rak·ish (rāk′ish) ***adj.*** ⟦< RAKE[3] + -ISH⟧ **1** having a trim appearance suggesting speed: said of a ship **2** dashing; jaunty —**rak′ish·ly** ***adv.***

THESAURUS

top*, gnash one's teeth, raise Cain*, raise the devil*, raise hell*, take on*, throw a fit*, fly off the handle*, explode, vent one's spleen, snap at, blow up*, blow a fuse*, cut loose*, have a hemorrhage*, make a fuss over, kick up a row*, have a nervous breakdown, let off steam*, get oneself into a lather*, lose one's head.—*Ant.* CRY, be calm, pout. **2** [To be out of control] explode, flare, roar; see BURN, RUN 1.

ragged ***a.*** tattered, in shreds, patched, badly worn, rough, worn out, broken, worn to rags, frayed, frazzled, threadbare, shoddy, out at the seams, shredded, battered, the worse for wear, worn to a thread, down at the heel, moth-eaten, full of holes, torn, badly dressed; see also SHABBY, WORN 2.—*Ant.* WHOLE, new, unworn.

raging ***a.*** furious, irate, enraged; see ANGRY.

raid ***n.*** **1** [A predatory attack] invasion, assault, forced entrance; see ATTACK. **2** [An armed investigation] seizure, surprise entrance, police raid, roundup, bust*; see also ARREST, CAPTURE.

raid ***v.*** assail, storm, assault; see ATTACK.

raider ***n.*** bandit, thief, looter; see CRIMINAL, PIRATE, ROBBER.

rail[1] ***n.*** **1** [A polelike structure] post, railing, barrier, picket, rail fence, siding, banister, paling, rest, hand rail, guardrail, brass rail; see also BAR 1, FENCE. **2** [A track; *often plural*] railway, monorail, railroad track; see RAILROAD.

railroad ***n.*** track, line, railway, trains, rails, elevated, underground, subway, commuter line, sidetrack, siding, passing track, loading track, feeder line, main line, double track, single track, trunk line, transcontinental railroad, el*; see also TRAIN.

railway ***n.*** track, line, route; see RAILROAD.

rain ***n.*** **1** [Water falling in drops] drizzle, mist, sprinkle, sprinkling, damp day, spring rain, rainfall, shower, precipitation, wet weather. **2** [A rainstorm] thunderstorm, thundershower, cloudburst; see STORM.

rain ***v.*** pour, drizzle, drop, fall, shower, sprinkle, mist, teem, spit, precipitate, patter, rain cats and dogs*, come down in bucketfuls; see also STORM.

raincoat ***n.*** trench coat, slicker, mackintosh; see COAT 1, CLOTHES.

rainy ***a.*** moist, coastal, drizzly; see STORMY, WET 2.

raise ***n.*** increase, salary increment, advance; see PROMOTION 1.

raise ***v.*** **1** [To lift] uplift, upraise, upheave, pull up, lift up, hold up, stand up, heave, set upright, put on its end, shove, boost, rear, mount, pry.—*Ant.* LOWER, bring down, take down. **2** [To nurture] bring up, rear, nurse, suckle, nourish, wean, breed, cultivate, train, foster; see also PROVIDE 1, SUPPORT 3. **3** [To collect or make available] gather, borrow, have ready; see ACCUMULATE, APPROPRIATE 2. **4** [To erect] construct, establish, put up; see BUILD. **5** [To ask] bring up, suggest, put; see ASK, PROPOSE 1. **6** [To advance in rank] exalt, dignify, honor; see PROMOTE 2. —**raise hell*** carry on*, celebrate, carouse; see DRINK 2.

raised ***a.*** **1** [Elevated] lifted, hoisted, built high, heightened, set high, in relief, erected, constructed, set up; see also BUILT.—*Ant.* REDUCED, lowered, taken down. **2** [Nurtured] reared, brought up, trained, prepared, educated, fostered, bred, nourished, nursed. **3** [Produced] harvested, cultivated, grown; see MADE.

rake[1] ***v.*** **1** [To use a rake] clear up, collect, scratch, gather, scrape, clean up, weed, clear, grade, level. **2** [To sweep with gunfire] strafe, machine-gun, blister; see SHOOT 1.

rake[1,2] ***n.*** **1** [A debauched person] lecher, philanderer, profligate; see DRUNKARD, RASCAL. **2** [A pronged implement] *Rakes include the following:* clam, lawn, garden, moss, hay, stubble, weeding, oyster, horse, revolving; leaf sweeper; see also TOOL 1.

Ra·legh or **Ra·leigh** (rô′lē, rä′lē), Sir **Wal·ter** (wôl′tər) 1552?-1618; Eng. explorer & poet

Ra·leigh (rô′lē, rä′lē) capital of North Carolina: pop. 212,000

ral·ly[1] (ral′ē) ***vt.***, ***vi.*** **-lied**, **-ly·ing** ⟦< OFr *re-*, again + *alier*, join⟧ **1** to bring back together in, or come back to, a state of order: said as of troops **2** to bring or come together for a common purpose **3** to recover; revive —***n.***, *pl.* **-lies** **1** a rallying or being rallied; esp., a gathering of people for some purpose **2** an organized automobile run designed to test driving skills

ral·ly[2] (ral′ē) ***vt.***, ***vi.*** **-lied**, **-ly·ing** ⟦see RAIL[2]⟧ to tease or ridicule

ram (ram) ***n.*** ⟦OE *ramm*⟧ **1** a male sheep **2** BATTERING RAM —***vt.*** **rammed**, **ram′ming** **1** to strike against with great force **2** to force into place; press down

RAM (ram) ***n.*** random-access memory

ram·ble (ram′bəl) ***vi.*** **-bled**, **-bling** ⟦< ME *romen*⟧ **1** to roam about; esp., to stroll about idly **2** to talk or write aimlessly **3** to spread in all directions, as a vine does —***n.*** a stroll

ram′bler (-blər) ***n.*** a person or thing that rambles; esp., a climbing rose

ram·bunc·tious (ram buŋk′shəs) ***adj.*** ⟦altered, (after RAM) < earlier *rambustious*⟧ disorderly, boisterous, unruly, etc. —**ram·bunc′tious·ness** ***n.***

ram·e·kin or **ram·e·quin** (ram′ə kin) ***n.*** ⟦< Fr < MDu⟧ a small individual baking dish

ra·men (rä′mən) ***pl.n.*** [*sometimes with sing. v.*] Japanese wheat noodles

ram·i·fy (ram′ə fī′) ***vt.***, ***vi.*** **-fied′**, **-fy′ing** ⟦< L *ramus,* a branch + *facere,* make⟧ to divide or spread out into branches or branchlike divisions —**ram′i·fi·ca′tion** ***n.***

ramp (ramp) ***n.*** ⟦< OFr *ramper*, to climb⟧ **1** a sloping surface, walk, etc. joining different levels **2** a means for boarding a plane, as a movable staircase **3** a sloping runway, as for launching boats

ram·page (ram′pāj′) ***vi.*** **-paged′**, **-pag′ing** to rush about wildly; rage —***n.*** an outbreak of violent, raging behavior: chiefly in **on the** (or **a**) **rampage**

ramp·ant (ram′pənt) ***adj.*** ⟦< OFr *ramper*, to climb⟧ growing unchecked; widespread

ram·part (ram′pärt′, -pərt) ***n.*** ⟦< Fr *re-*, again + *emparer*, fortify⟧ an embankment of earth surmounted by a parapet for defending a fort, etc.

ram′rod′ ***n.*** a rod for ramming down the charge in a muzzle-loading gun

ram·shack·le (ram′shak′əl) ***adj.*** ⟦< RANSACK⟧ loose and rickety; likely to fall to pieces

ran (ran) ***vi.***, ***vt.*** *pt. of* RUN

ranch (ranch) ***n.*** ⟦< Sp *rancho*, small farm⟧ **1** a large farm, esp. in the W U.S., for raising cattle, horses, or sheep **2** a style of house with all the rooms on one floor: in full **ranch house** —***vi.*** to work on or manage a ranch —**ranch′er** ***n.***

ranch dressing creamy buttermilk salad dressing

ran·cid (ran′sid) ***adj.*** ⟦< L *rancere,* to be rank⟧ smelling or tasting of stale fats or oils; spoiled

ran·cor (raŋ′kər) ***n.*** ⟦< L *rancere,* to be rank⟧ a continuing and bitter hate or ill will: Brit. sp. **ran′cour** —**ran′cor·ous** ***adj.*** —**ran′cor·ous·ly** ***adv.***

rand (rand) ***n.***, *pl.* **rand** the monetary unit of South Africa

R & B or **r & b** *abbrev.* rhythm and blues

R & D *abbrev.* research and development

ran·dom (ran′dəm) ***adj.*** ⟦< OFr *randir*, run violently⟧ purposeless; haphazard —**at random** haphazardly —**ran′dom·ly** ***adv.***

ran′dom-ac′cess ***adj.*** *Comput.* of a kind of memory that allows data to be directly accessible

ran′dom·ize′ (-īz′) ***vt.*** **-ized′**, **-iz′ing** to select or choose (items of a group) in a random order

ran·dy (ran′dē) ***adj.*** **-di·er**, **-di·est** [Chiefly Scot.] amorous; lustful

rang (raŋ) ***vi.***, ***vt.*** *pt. of* RING[1]

range (rānj) ***vt.*** **ranged**, **rang′ing** ⟦< OFr *renc*, a ring⟧ **1** to arrange in order; set in a row or rows **2** to place (esp. oneself) with others in a cause, etc. **3** to roam through —***vi.*** **1** to extend in a given direction **2** to roam **3** to vary between stated limits —***n.*** **1** a row, line, or series **2** a series of connected mountains **3** the distance that a weapon can fire its projectile **4** *a)* a place for shooting practice *b)* a place for testing rockets in flight **5** extent; scope **6** a large, open area for grazing livestock **7** the limits of possible variations of amount, degree, pitch, etc. *[a wide range of prices]* **8** a cooking stove

rang·er (rān′jər) ***n.*** **1** *a)* a mounted trooper who patrols a region *b)* [*often* **R-**] a soldier trained for raiding and close combat **2** a warden who patrols parks and forests

Ran·goon (ran go͞on′) *former name for* YANGON

rang·y (rān′jē) ***adj.*** **-i·er**, **-i·est** long-limbed and slender —**rang′i·ness** ***n.***

rank[1] (raŋk) ***n.*** ⟦< OFr *ranc*⟧ **1** a row, line, or series **2** a social class **3** a high position in society **4** an official

THESAURUS

rally[1] ***n.*** assembly, mass meeting, demonstration; see GATHERING.

rally[1] ***v.*** unite against, renew, redouble; see RETURN 1, REVENGE.

ram ***n.*** **1** [An object used to deliver a thrust] plunger, pump, beam, prow, hammerhead, weight, pole, shaft, lever, spike, battering ram, pile driver, tamping iron, punch, sledge hammer, rammer, tamper, monkey, bat, maul, hydraulic ram, spar, piston, drop weight, bow; see also BAR 1, HAMMER. **2** [A male sheep] buck, tup, bighorn; see ANIMAL.

ram ***v.*** **1** [To strike head-on] bump, collide, slam; see BUTT, HIT 1. **2** [To pack forcibly] cram, jam, stuff; see PACK 2.

ramble ***v.*** **1** [To saunter] stroll, promenade, roam; see WALK 1. **2** [To speak or write aimlessly] drift, stray, diverge, meander, gossip, talk nonsense, chatter, babble, digress, maunder, get off the subject, go on and on, expatiate, protract, enlarge, be diffuse, dwell on, amplify, go astray, drivel, rant and rave, talk off the top of one's head, go off on a tangent, beat around the bush.

rambling ***a.*** **1** [Strolling] hiking, roaming, roving; see WALKING, WANDERING 1. **2** [Incoherent] discursive, disconnected, confused; see INCOHERENT. **3** [Covering considerable territory without much plan] spread out, strewn, straggling, trailing, random, here and there, at length, unplanned, sprawling, gangling; see also SCATTERED.—*Ant.* PLANNED, closely formed, compact.

ramp ***n.*** incline, slope, grade; see HILL, INCLINATION 2.

rampant ***a.*** raging, uncontrolled, growing without check, violent, vehement, impetuous, rank, turbulent, wild, luxuriant, tumultuous, profuse, epidemic, pandemic, fanatical, plentiful, unruly, wanton, rife, prevalent, dominant, predominant, excessive, impulsive, impassioned, intolerant, unrestrained, extravagant, overabundant, sweeping the country, like wildfire.—*Ant.* MODEST, mild, meek.

ranch ***n.*** plantation, grange, farmstead, ranchland, ranch house, ranch buildings, hacienda, dude ranch, rancho, spread; see also FARM, PROPERTY 2.

rancher ***n.*** ranch owner, ranchman, stockman, breeder, cattle farmer, cowherder, shepherd, drover, stock breeder, horse trainer, herdsman, herder, ranchero, broncobuster*, granger, cattleman, cowboy, cowpoke*, ranch hand, cattle baron; see also FARMER.

rancid ***a.*** tainted, stale, bad; see ROTTEN 1.

random ***a.*** haphazard, chance, purposeless, thoughtless, careless, blind, casual, fickle, erratic, aleatory, hit-or-miss, eccentric, unpredictable, accidental; see also AIMLESS, IRREGULAR 1. —**at random** haphazardly, by chance, aimlessly; see ACCIDENTALLY.

range ***n.*** **1** [Distance] reach, span, horizontal projection; see EXPANSE. **2** [Extent] length, area, expanse; see EXTENT. **3** [A series of mountains] highlands, alps, sierras; see MOUNTAIN 1. **4** [Land open to grazing] pasture, grazing land, field; see COUNTRY 1. **5** [A kitchen stove] gas range, electric range, oven; see APPLIANCE, STOVE.

range ***v.*** **1** [To vary] differ, fluctuate, diverge from; see VARY. **2** [To traverse wide areas] encompass, reach, pass over, cover, stray, stroll, wander, ramble, explore, scour, search, traverse, roam, rove; see also CROSS 1, TRAVEL. **3** [To place in order] line up, classify, arrange; see ORDER 3.

rank[1] ***n.*** **1** [A row] column, file, string; see LINE 1. **2** [Degree] seniority, standing, station; see DEGREE 2. **3** [Social eminence] station, position, distinction, note, nobility, caste, privilege, standing, reputation, quality, situation, esteem, condition, state, place in society, status, circumstance, footing, grade, blood, family, pedigree, ancestry, stock, parentage, birth. —**pull (one's) rank on*** take advantage of, exploit, abuse subordinates; see GOVERN, HUMILIATE.

rank[1] ***v.*** **1** [To arrange in a row or rows] put in line, line up, place in formation; see ORDER 3. **2** [To evaluate comparatively] place, put, regard, judge, assign, give precedence to, fix, establish, settle, estimate, value, valuate, include, list, rate; see also CLASSIFY. **3** [To possess relative evaluation] be worth, stand, be at the head, have a place, go ahead of, come

grade *[the rank of major]* **5** a relative position in a scale *[a poet of the first rank]* **6** *a)* a row of soldiers, etc. placed side by side *b)* [*pl.*] the army; esp., enlisted soldiers —***vt.*** **1** to place in a rank **2** to assign a position to **3** to outrank —***vi.*** to hold a certain position —**rank and file** **1** enlisted soldiers **2** the common people, as distinguished from leaders

rank[2] (raŋk) ***adj.*** ⟦OE *ranc,* strong⟧ **1** growing vigorously and coarsely *[rank grass]* **2** strong and offensive in smell or taste **3** in bad taste **4** complete; utter *[rank deceit]*

rank'ing ***adj.*** **1** of the highest rank **2** prominent or outstanding

ran·kle (raŋ'kəl) ***vi., vt.*** **-kled, -kling** ⟦ult. < L dim. of *draco,* dragon⟧ **1** [Obs.] to fester **2** to cause, or cause to have, long-lasting anger, rancor, etc.

ran·sack (ran'sak') ***vt.*** ⟦< ON *rann,* house + *sœkja,* seek⟧ **1** to search thoroughly **2** to plunder

ran·som (ran'səm) ***n.*** ⟦see REDEEM⟧ **1** the redeeming of a captive by paying money or complying with demands **2** the price thus paid or demanded —***vt.*** to obtain the release of (a captive, etc.) by paying the demanded price

rant (rant) ***vi., vt.*** ⟦< obs. Du *ranten*⟧ to talk or say in a loud, wild, extravagant way —***n.*** loud, wild speech

rap (rap) ***vt.*** **rapped, rap'ping** ⟦prob. echoic⟧ **1** to strike quickly and sharply; tap **2** [Slang] to criticize sharply —***vi.*** **1** to knock sharply **2** [Slang] to talk —***n.*** **1** a quick, sharp knock **2** [Slang] blame or punishment **3** [Slang] a chat or serious discussion **4** a kind of popular music in which rhymed verses are chanted over repetitive rhythms

ra·pa·cious (rə pā'shəs) ***adj.*** ⟦< L *rapere,* seize⟧ **1** greedy; voracious **2** predatory —**ra·pa'cious·ly** ***adv.*** —**ra·pac'i·ty** (-pas'ə tē) ***n.***

rape[1] (rāp) ***n.*** ⟦prob. < L *rapere,* seize⟧ **1** the crime of having sexual intercourse with a person forcibly and without consent **2** the plundering (*of* a city, etc.), as in warfare —***vt.*** **raped, rap'ing** **1** to commit rape on; violate **2** to plunder or destroy —***vi.*** to commit rape —**rap'ist** ***n.***

rape[2] (rāp) ***n.*** ⟦< L *rapa,* turnip⟧ an annual plant whose leaves are used for fodder

Raph·a·el (rä'fā el', -fī-) 1483-1520; It. painter & architect

rap·id (rap'id) ***adj.*** ⟦< L *rapere,* to rush⟧ moving or occurring with speed; swift; quick —***n.*** [*usually pl.*] a part of a river where the current is swift —**ra·pid·i·ty** (rə pid'ə tē) ***n.*** —**rap'id·ly** ***adv.***

rapid transit a system of public transportation in an urban area, using electric trains along an unimpeded right of way

ra·pi·er (rā'pē ər) ***n.*** ⟦Fr *rapière*⟧ a light, sharp-pointed sword used only for thrusting

rap·ine (rap'in) ***n.*** ⟦< L *rapere,* seize⟧ plunder; pillage

rap·pel (ra pel') ***n.*** ⟦Fr, lit., a recall⟧ a descent by a mountain climber, using a double rope around the body to control the slide downward —***vi.*** **-pelled', -pel'ling** to make such a descent

rap'per ***n.*** a performer of rap music

rap·port (ra pôr') ***n.*** ⟦Fr⟧ close relationship; harmony

rap·proche·ment (ra'prōsh män') ***n.*** ⟦Fr⟧ an establishing of friendly relations

rap·scal·lion (rap skal'yən) ***n.*** ⟦< RASCAL⟧ ROGUE

rap sheet [Slang] one's police record of arrests and convictions

rapt (rapt) ***adj.*** ⟦< L *rapere,* seize⟧ **1** carried away with joy, love, etc. **2** completely engrossed (*in* meditation, study, etc.)

rap·tor (rap'tər, -tôr') ***n.*** ⟦< L *rapere,* to snatch⟧ a bird, as a hawk, that preys on other animals

rap·ture (rap'chər) ***n.*** the state of being carried away with joy, love, etc.; ecstasy —**rap'tur·ous** ***adj.*** —**rap'tur·ous·ly** ***adv.***

ra·ra a·vis (rer'ə ā'vis) *pl.* **ra·rae a·ves** (rer'ē ā'vēz) ⟦L, lit., strange bird⟧ an extraordinary person or thing

rare[1] (rer) ***adj.*** **rar'er, rar'est** ⟦< L *rarus*⟧ **1** not frequently encountered; scarce; unusual **2** unusually good; excellent **3** not dense *[rare atmosphere]* —**rare'ness** ***n.***

rare[2] (rer) ***adj.*** **rar'er, rar'est** ⟦OE *hrere*⟧ not completely cooked; partly raw: said esp. of meat —**rare'ness** ***n.***

rare[3] (rer) ***vi.*** **rared, rar'ing** [Inf.] to be eager: used in prp. *[raring to go]*

rare·bit (rer'bit) ***n.*** WELSH RABBIT

rar·e·fy (rer'ə fī') ***vt., vi.*** **-fied', -fy'ing** ⟦< L *rarus,* RARE[1] + *facere,* make⟧ to make or become less dense —**rar'e·fac'tion** (-fak'shən) ***n.***

rare·ly (rer'lē) ***adv.*** **1** infrequently; seldom **2** uncommonly

rar·i·ty (rer'ə tē) ***n.*** **1** a being rare; specif., *a)* scarcity *b)* lack of density **2** *pl.* **-ties** something remarkable or valuable because rare

ras·cal (ras'kəl) ***n.*** ⟦< OFr *rascaille,* rabble⟧ **1** a rogue **2** a mischievous child —**ras·cal'i·ty** (-kal'ə tē) ***n.*** —**ras'cal·ly** ***adj., adv.***

THESAURUS

first, forerun, antecede, have supremacy over, have the advantage of, precede, outrank, take the lead, take precedence over, belong, count among, be classed, stand in relationship.

rank[2] ***a.*** **1** [Having luxurious growth] wild, dense, lush; see GREEN 2, THICK 1. **2** [Having a foul odor] smelly, fetid, putrid, stinking, rancid, disagreeable, smelling, offensive, sour, foul, noxious, stale, tainted, gamy, musty, strong, rotten, moldy, turned, high, ill-smelling, nauseating, obnoxious, disgusting, reeking, malodorous, nasty, strong-smelling.—*Ant.* SWEET, fragrant, fresh.

ranked ***a.*** ordered, piled, neatly stacked; see ORGANIZED.

ransack ***v.*** **1** [To search thoroughly] rummage, explore, turn upside down, look all over, look high and low, leave no stone unturned, scour, seek everywhere, sound, spy, peer, look around, pry, scan, probe, look into, investigate, scrutinize; see also SEARCH. **2** [To loot] pillage, plunder, ravish, raid, rape, strip, rifle, forage, maraud, make off with, take away, seize, appropriate, spoil, poach, gut, rustle, lift*, thieve, ravage, pilfer, rob, steal, filch, pinch*.

ransom ***n.*** redemption money, compensation, payoff*; see BRIBE.

ransom ***v.*** release, rescue, deliver; see FREE.

rant ***v.*** rave, fume, rail; see RAGE 1, YELL.

rap ***n.*** knock, thump, slap; see BLOW. —**beat the rap*** avoid punishment, evade, be acquitted; see ESCAPE. —**bum rap*** unfair sentence, blame, frame-up*; see PUNISHMENT. —**take the rap*** be punished, suffer, take the blame; see PAY FOR.

rap ***v.*** **1** [To tap sharply] knock, strike, whack; see BEAT 1, HIT 1. **2** [*To talk, often compulsively] chatter, jabber, discuss; see BABBLE, TALK 1.

rape[1] ***n.*** seduction, violation, deflowering, criminal attack, assault, abduction, statutory offense, defilement, abuse, molestation, maltreatment, forcible violation of a woman, date rape; see also CRIME.

rape[1] ***v.*** violate, seize, compromise, force a woman, molest, ravish, attack, assault, defile, wrong, debauch, ruin, corrupt, seduce, maltreat, abuse.

rapid ***a.*** speedy, accelerated, hurried; see FAST 1.

rapidly ***a.*** fast, swiftly, posthaste; see IMMEDIATELY, QUICKLY.

rapist ***n.*** raper, ravager, ravisher; see RASCAL.

rapt ***a.*** enraptured, entranced, enchanted; see HAPPY.

rapture ***n.*** pleasure, enchantment, euphoria; see HAPPINESS.

rare[1,2] ***a.*** **1** [Uncommon] exceptional, singular, extraordinary; see UNUSUAL 1, 2. **2** [Scarce] sparse, few, scanty, meager, limited, short, expensive, precious, out of circulation, off the market, in great demand, occasional, uncommon, isolated, scattered, infrequent, deficient, almost unobtainable, few and far between; see also UNIQUE.—*Ant.* CHEAP, profuse, abounding. **3** [Choice] select, matchless, superlative; see EXCELLENT. **4** [Lightly cooked] not cooked, undercooked, not done, seared, braised, not overdone, nearly raw, underdone, red, moderately done, not thoroughly cooked; see also RAW 1.

rarely ***a.*** unusually, occasionally, once in a great while; see SELDOM.

rascal ***n.*** scoundrel, rogue, rake, knave, villain, robber, fraud, scamp, hypocrite, sneak, shyster*, cad, trickster, charlatan, swindler, grafter, cheat, black sheep, ruffian, tough, rowdy, bully, scalawag, mountebank, liar, blackguard, wretch, quack, tramp, beggar, bum*, idler, wastrel, prodigal, hooligan*, ne'er-do-well, reprobate, misdoer, felon, sinner, delinquent, recreant, malefactor, profligate, loafer, renegade, impostor, opportunist, vagrant, pretender, gambler, mischief-maker, sharper, faker, skunk*, bastard*, fink*, rat*, rotten egg*, con man*, con artist*, flimflammer*, dirty dog*, good-for-nothing, worm, two-timer*, stool pigeon*, double-dealer*, phony*, four-flusher*, slicker*; see also CRIMINAL.—*Ant.* HERO, GENTLEMAN, philanthropist.

rash[1] (rash) ***adj.*** ⟦ME *rasch*⟧ too hasty in acting or speaking; reckless —**rash'ly *adv.*** —**rash'ness *n.***

rash[2] (rash) ***n.*** ⟦< OFr *rascaille*, rabble⟧ **1** an eruption of spots on the skin **2** a sudden appearance of a large number of instances

rash'er *n.* ⟦< L *radere*, to scrape⟧ a thin slice of bacon, etc., or a serving of several such slices

rasp (rasp) ***vt.*** ⟦< OHG *raspon*, to scrape together⟧ **1** to scrape as with a file **2** to grate upon; irritate —***vi.*** **1** to grate **2** to make a rough, grating sound —***n.*** **1** a type of rough file **2** a rough, grating sound —**rasp'y, -i·er, -i·est, *adj.***

rasp·ber·ry (raz'ber'ē, -bər-) ***n.***, *pl.* **-ries** ⟦< earlier *raspis*⟧ **1** a small, juicy, edible reddish fruit of a plant related to the rose **2** this plant **3** [Slang] a sound of derision

rat (rat) ***n.*** ⟦OE *ræt*⟧ **1** a long-tailed rodent, resembling, but larger than, the mouse **2** [Slang] a sneaky, contemptible person; esp., an informer —***vi.*** **rat'ted, rat'ting** [Slang] to inform (*on*) —**smell a rat** to suspect a trick, plot, etc.

ratch·et (rach'it) ***n.*** ⟦< It *rocca*, distaff⟧ **1** a toothed wheel (in full **ratchet wheel**) or bar whose sloping teeth catch a pawl, preventing backward motion **2** such a pawl

rate[1] (rāt) ***n.*** ⟦< L *reri*, reckon⟧ **1** the amount, degree, etc. of anything in relation to units of something else *[rate* of pay*]* **2** price, esp. per unit —***vt.*** **rat'ed, rat'ing** **1** to appraise **2** to consider **3** [Inf.] to deserve —***vi.*** to have value, status, etc. —**at any rate** **1** in any event **2** anyway

rate[2] (rāt) ***vt., vi.*** **rat'ed, rat'ing** ⟦< L *reputare*, to count⟧ to scold; chide

rath·er (rath'ər) ***adv.*** ⟦OE *hræthe*, quickly⟧ **1** more willingly; preferably **2** with more justice, reason, etc. *[*I, *rather* than you, should pay*]* **3** more accurately *[*my son, or *rather*, stepson*]* **4** on the contrary **5** somewhat *[rather* hungry*]* —**rather than** instead of

rat'hole' *n.* a great waste of money, etc.

raths·kel·ler (rath'skel'ər) ***n.*** ⟦Ger < *rat*, council, town hall + *keller*, cellar⟧ a restaurant, usually below the street level, where beer is served

rat·i·fy (rat'ə fī') ***vt.*** **-fied', -fy'ing** ⟦< L *ratus*, reckoned + *facere*, make⟧ to approve; esp., to give official sanction to —**rat'i·fi·ca'tion *n.***

rat·ing (rāt'iŋ) ***n.*** **1** a rank or grade, as of military personnel **2** a placement in a certain rank or class **3** an evaluation; appraisal **4** *Film* a classification, based on content, restricting the age of those who may attend **5** *Radio, TV* the relative popularity of a program according to sample polls

ra·tio (rā'shō, -shē ō') ***n.***, *pl.* **-tios** ⟦L, a reckoning⟧ a fixed relation in degree, number, etc. between two similar things; proportion

ra·ti·oc·i·nate (rash'ē äs'ə nāt') ***vi.*** **-nat'ed, -nat'ing** ⟦see prec.⟧ to think or argue logically; reason —**ra'ti·oc'i·na'tion *n.***

ra·tion (rash'ən, rā'shən) ***n.*** ⟦see RATIO⟧ **1** a fixed portion; share **2** a fixed allowance of food, as a daily allowance for a soldier **3** [*pl.*] food supply —***vt.*** **1** to supply with rations **2** to distribute (food, clothing, etc.) in rations, as in times of scarcity

ra·tion·al (rash'ən əl) ***adj.*** ⟦see RATIO⟧ **1** of or based on reasoning **2** able to reason; reasoning **3** sensible or sane —**ra'tion·al'i·ty** (-ə nal'ə tē) ***n.*** —**ra'tion·al·ly *adv.***

ra·tion·ale (rash'ə nal') ***n.*** ⟦< L *rationalis*, rational⟧ **1** the reasons or rational basis for something **2** an explanation of principles

ra'tion·al·ism' *n.* the practice of accepting reason as the only authority in determining one's opinions or course of action —**ra'tion·al·ist *n., adj.*** —**ra'tion·al·is'tic *adj.***

ra'tion·al·ize' *vt., vi.* **-ized', -iz'ing** **1** to make or be rational or reasonable **2** to devise plausible explanations for (one's acts, beliefs, etc.), usually in self-deception —**ra'tion·al·i·za'tion *n.***

rat·line (rat'lin) ***n.*** ⟦< ?⟧ any of the horizontal ropes which join the shrouds of a ship and serve as a ladder: also sp. **rat'lin**

rat race [Slang] a mad scramble or intense struggle, as in the business world

rat·tan (ra tan') ***n.*** ⟦Malay *rotan*⟧ **1** a tall palm tree with long, slender, tough stems **2** its stem, used in making furniture, etc.

rat·tle (rat''l) ***vi.*** **-tled, -tling** ⟦prob. echoic⟧ **1** to make a series of sharp, short sounds **2** to chatter: often with *on* —***vt.*** **1** to cause to rattle **2** to confuse or upset —***n.*** **1** a series of sharp, short sounds **2** a series of horny rings at the end of a rattlesnake's tail **3** a baby's toy, a percussion instrument, etc. made to rattle when shaken

rat'tle·brain' *n.* a frivolous, talkative person —**rat'tle·brained' *adj.***

rat'tler *n.* a rattlesnake

rat'tle·snake' *n.* a poisonous American snake with horny rings at the end of the tail that rattle when shaken

rat'tle·trap' *n.* a rickety old car

rat'tling (-liŋ) ***adj.*** **1** that rattles **2** [Inf.] very fast, good, etc. —***adv.*** [Inf.] very *[*a *rattling* good time*]*

THESAURUS

rash[1] ***a.*** impetuous, impulsive, foolish, hotheaded, thoughtless, reckless, headstrong, bold, careless, determined, audacious, heedless, madcap, unthinking, headlong, incautious, wild, precipitant, overhasty, unwary, injudicious, venturous, foolhardy, imprudent, venturesome, adventurous, daring, jumping to conclusions, insuppressible, breakneck, irrational, fiery, furious, frenzied, passionate, immature, hurried, aimless, excited, feverish, tenacious, frantic, indiscreet, quixotic, ill-advised, unconsidered, without thinking, imprudent, unadvised, irresponsible, brash, precipitous, premature, sudden, harebrained, harum-scarum, devil-may-care, daredevil; see also RUDE 1.—*Ant.* CALM, cool, levelheaded.

rashly *a.* brashly, impulsively, unwisely, abruptly, foolishly, impetuously, incautiously, carelessly, precipitately, imprudently, recklessly, boldly, indiscreetly, inadvisedly, ill-advisedly, thoughtlessly, unthinkingly, furiously, hurriedly, heedlessly, boldly, unpreparedly, excitedly, overhastily, wildly, frantically, irrepressibly, without due consideration, without thinking, without forethought, in a hasty manner, passionately, fiercely, feverishly, headily; see also RUDELY.

rashness *n.* frenzy, recklessness, foolhardiness; see CARELESSNESS.

rasping *a.* hoarse, grating, grinding; see HARSH.

rat *n.* **1** [A rodent] mouse, muskrat, vermin; see PEST 1, RODENT. **2** [*A betrayer] informer, turncoat, fink*; see DESERTER, TRAITOR.

rate[1] ***n.*** **1** [Ratio] proportion, degree, standard, incidence, frequency, scale, fixed amount, quota, relation, relationship, comparison, relative weight, percentage, numerical progression; see also MEASURE 1, 2. **2** [Price] valuation, charge, cost; see PRICE. **3** [Speed] velocity, pace, tempo; see SPEED.

rate[1] ***v.*** **1** [To rank] judge, estimate, evaluate, grade, relate to a standard, fix, tag, calculate, assess, class, determine, appraise, guess at; see also MEASURE 1, PRICE, RANK 2. **2** [*To be well-thought-of] be a favorite, merit, rank; see SUCCEED 1.

rated *a.* ranked, classified, graded, classed, appraised, estimated, thought of, given a rating, weighted, measured; see also PLACED.

rather *a.* **1** [To some degree] fairly, somewhat, a little; see MODERATELY, REASONABLY 2. **2** [By preference] first, by choice, in preference, sooner, more readily, willingly, much sooner, just as soon, as a matter of choice; see also PREFERABLY.

rather *interj.* I should say, certainly, of course, by all means, most assuredly, no doubt about it, and how*, you're telling me*.

ratification *n.* acceptance, confirmation, sanction; see PERMISSION.

ratify *v.* sanction, establish, substantiate; see APPROVE, ENDORSE 2.

rating *n.* grade, relative standing, evaluation; see CLASS 1, DEGREE 2, RANK 2.

ratio *n.* proportion, quota, quotient; see DEGREE 1, RATE 1.

ration *n.* allotment, portion, quota; see DIVISION 2, SHARE.

ration *v.* proportion, allot, apportion; see DISTRIBUTE.

rational *a.* **1** [Acting in accordance with reason] stable, calm, cool, deliberate, discerning, discriminating, levelheaded, collected, logical, thoughtful, knowing, sensible, of sound judgment, having good sense, impartial, exercising reason, intelligent, wise, reasoning, prudent, circumspect, intellectual, reflective, philosophic, objective, farsighted, enlightened, well-advised, judicious, analytical, deductive, synthetic, conscious, balanced, sober, systematic; see also REASONABLE 1.—*Ant.* RASH, reckless, wild. **2** [Of a nature that appeals to reason] intelligent, sensible, wise; see REASONABLE 1. **3** [Sane] normal, lucid, responsible; see SANE 1.

rationalize *v.* explain away, vindicate, reconcile; see EXPLAIN.

rationally *a.* sensibly, normally, intelligently; see REASONABLY 1.

rattle *n.* clatter, noise, racket; see NOISE 1.

rattle *v.* **1** [To make a rattling sound] drum, clack, knock; see SOUND. **2** [To talk with little meaning] chatter, gush, prattle; see BABBLE. **3** [To disconcert] bother, put out, unnerve; see CONFUSE, DISTURB, EMBARRASS.

rat'trap' ***n.*** **1** a trap for rats **2** [Inf.] a dirty, run-down building
rat·ty (rat'ē) ***adj.*** **-ti·er, -ti·est** [Slang] shabby or run-down
rau·cous (rô'kəs) ***adj.*** ⟦L *raucus*⟧ **1** hoarse **2** loud and rowdy —**rau'cous·ly** ***adv.*** —**rau'cous·ness** ***n.***
raun·chy (rôn'chē) ***adj.*** **-chi·er, -chi·est** ⟦< ?⟧ [Slang] **1** dirty, sloppy, etc. **2** risqué, lustful, etc.
rav·age (rav'ij) ***n.*** ⟦see RAVISH⟧ destruction; ruin —***vt.*** **-aged, -ag·ing** to destroy violently; ruin
rave (rāv) ***vi.*** **raved, rav'ing** ⟦< OFr *raver,* roam⟧ **1** to talk incoherently or wildly **2** to talk with great enthusiasm (*about*) —***n.*** [Inf.] a very enthusiastic commendation
rav·el (rav'əl) ***vt., vi.*** **-eled** or **-elled, -el·ing** or **-el·ling** ⟦< MDu *ravelen*⟧ to separate into its parts, esp. threads; fray —***n.*** a raveled part in a fabric
ra·ven (rā'vən) ***n.*** ⟦OE *hræfn*⟧ the largest crow, with a straight, sharp beak —***adj.*** black and lustrous
rav·en·ing (rav'ə niŋ) ***adj.*** ⟦ult. < L *rapere,* seize⟧ greedily searching for prey *[ravening* wolves*]*
rav·e·nous (rav'ə nəs) ***adj.*** ⟦< L *rapere,* seize⟧ **1** greedily hungry **2** rapacious —**rav'e·nous·ly** ***adv.***
ra·vine (rə vēn') ***n.*** ⟦Fr, flood⟧ a long, deep hollow in the earth, esp. one worn by a stream; gorge
rav'ing ***adj.*** **1** that raves; frenzied **2** [Inf.] exciting enthusiastic admiration *[a raving* beauty*]* —***adv.*** so as to cause raving *[raving* mad*]*
ra·vi·o·li (rav'ē ō'lē) ***n., pl.*** **-li** or **-lis** ⟦It⟧ small casings of dough filled with meat, cheese, etc.
rav·ish (rav'ish) ***vt.*** ⟦< L *rapere,* seize⟧ **1** to seize and carry away forcibly **2** to rape (a woman) **3** to transport with joy or delight —**rav'ish·ment** ***n.***
rav'ish·ing ***adj.*** causing great joy
raw (rô) ***adj.*** ⟦OE *hreaw*⟧ **1** not cooked **2** in its natural condition; not processed *[raw* silk*]* **3** inexperienced *[a raw* recruit*]* **4** abraded and sore **5** uncomfortably cold and damp *[a raw* wind*]* **6** brutal, coarse, indecent, etc. **7** [Inf.] harsh or unfair *[a raw* deal*]* —**in the raw** **1** in the natural state **2** naked —**raw'ness** ***n.***
raw bar a place serving uncooked shellfish
raw'boned' (-bōnd') ***adj.*** lean; gaunt
raw'hide' ***n.*** **1** an untanned cattle hide **2** a whip made of this
ray[1] (rā) ***n.*** ⟦< L *radius*⟧ **1** any of the thin lines, or beams, of light that appear to come from a bright source **2** any of several lines radiating from a center **3** a tiny amount *[a ray* of hope*]* **4** a beam of radiant energy, radioactive particles, etc.
ray[2] (rā) ***n.*** ⟦< L *raia*⟧ a cartilaginous fish with a broad, flat body, widely expanded fins on both sides, and a whiplike tail
ray·on (rā'än) ***n.*** ⟦< RAY[1]⟧ **1** a textile fiber made from a cellulose solution **2** a fabric of such fibers
raze (rāz) ***vt.*** **razed, raz'ing** ⟦< L *radere,* to scrape⟧ to tear down completely; demolish
ra·zor (rā'zər) ***n.*** ⟦see prec.⟧ **1** a sharp-edged cutting instrument for shaving, cutting hair, etc. **2** SHAVER (sense 2)
razor wire sharp-edged wire, as for fences
razz (raz) ***vt.*** ⟦< RASPBERRY⟧ [Slang] to tease, ridicule, etc.
raz·zle-daz·zle (raz'əl daz'əl) ***n.*** [Slang] a flashy, deceptive display
razz·ma·tazz (raz'mə taz') ***n.*** ⟦prob. < prec.⟧ [Slang] **1** lively spirit **2** flashy display

RBI or **rbi** ***n., pl.*** **RBIs** *or* **RBI, rbi's** or **rbi** *Baseball* run batted in
RC *abbrev.* Roman Catholic
rd *abbrev.* **1** rod **2** round
Rd *abbrev.* Road
RD *abbrev.* Rural Delivery
RDA *abbrev.* Recommended Daily (*or* Dietary) Allowance: the amount of protein, vitamins, etc. suggested for various age groups
re[1] (rā) ***n.*** ⟦It⟧ *Music* the second tone of the diatonic scale
re[2] (rē, rā) ***prep.*** ⟦L < *res,* thing⟧ in the matter of; as regards
re- ⟦< Fr or L⟧ *prefix* **1** back **2** again; anew It is sometimes hyphenated, as before a word beginning with *e* or to distinguish between such forms as *re-cover* (to cover again) and RECOVER The words in the following list can be understood if "again" or "anew" is added to the meaning of the base word:

reacquaint
reacquire
readjust
readmit
reaffirm
realign
reappear
reapply
reappoint
reappraise
rearm
reassemble
reassert
reassess
reassign
reawaken
reborn
rebroadcast
rebuild
recharge
recheck
reclassify
recommence
reconquer
reconsign
reconvene
reconvert
recopy
re-cover
redecorate
rededicate
redesign
redetermine
redirect
rediscover
redistribution
redivide
redraw
reedit
reeducate
reelect
reembark
reemerge
reemphasize
reenact
reengage
reenlist
reenter
reestablish
reevaluate
reexamine
reexplain
refashion
refasten
refinance
reformulate
refuel
refurnish
rehear
reheat
rehire
reimpose
reinfect
reinsert
reinspect
reinvest
reissue
rekindle
relearn
reload
remake
remarry
rematch
remix
rename
renegotiate
renominate
renumber
reoccupy
reoccur
reopen
reorder
repack
repackage
repaint
repave
rephrase
replant
replay
re-press
reprint
republish
reread
rerelease
reroute
reschedule
resell
reset
resettle
reshuffle
respell
restate
restring
restudy
restyle
resubscribe

THESAURUS

raucous ***a.*** hoarse, loud, gruff; see HARSH.
raunchy* ***a.*** lustful, sexy*, suggestive; see LEWD 2.
ravage ***v.*** pillage, overrun, devastate, destroy, crush, desolate, despoil, overspread, wreck, waste, disrupt, disorganize, demolish, annihilate, overthrow, overwhelm, break up, pull down, smash, shatter, scatter, batter down, exterminate, extinguish, trample down, dismantle, stamp out, lay waste, lay in ruins, sweep away, raze, ruin, plunder, strip, impair, sack, consume, spoil, harry, ransack, maraud, prey, rape, rob, raid, pirate, seize, capture, gut, loot; see also DAMAGE.—*Ant.* BUILD, improve, rehabilitate.
rave ***v.*** **1** [To babble] gabble, jabber, rattle on; see BABBLE. **2** [To rage] storm, splutter, rail; see RAGE 1.
ravel ***v.*** untwist, come apart, wind out, untangle, disentangle, unsnarl, unbraid, untwine, unweave, unravel, fray, make plain; see also FREE, LOOSEN 2.
ravenous ***a.*** voracious, omnivorous, starved; see HUNGRY.
ravine ***n.*** gully, gorge, canyon, gulch, arroyo, valley, gap, chasm, abyss, break, crevice, crevasse, coulee.
raving ***a.*** violent, shouting, fuming; see INSANE.
raw ***a.*** **1** [Uncooked] fresh, rare, hard, unprepared, undercooked, fibrous, coarsegrained, unpasteurized, unbaked, unfried; see also RARE 4.—*Ant.* BAKED, cooked, fried. **2** [Unfinished] natural, untreated, crude, rough, newly cut, unprocessed, unrefined, untanned, coarse, newly mined, uncut, virgin; see also UNFINISHED 2.—*Ant.* REFINED, manufactured, processed. **3** [Untrained] immature, new, fresh; see INEXPERIENCED. **4** [Cold] biting, windy, bleak; see COLD 1. **5** [Without skin] peeled, skinned, dressed, galled, scraped, blistered, cut, wounded, pared, uncovered, chafed, bruised.—*Ant.* COVERED, coated, healed. **6** [Nasty] low, dirty, unscrupulous; see MEAN 3, VULGAR. —**in the raw** nude, bare, unclothed; see NAKED 1.
ray[1] ***n.*** beam, flash, light, stream, gleam, blaze, sunbeam, wave, moonbeam, radiation, flicker, spark, emanation, radiance, streak, shaft, pencil, patch, blink, glimmer, glitter, glint, sparkle.
razor ***n.*** shaving instrument, cutting edge, blade; see KNIFE. *Razors include the following:* double-edged, single-edged, disposable, straight-back, safety, hollow-ground, electric; electric shaver.

resupply	**reunite**
retell	**reupholster**
retest	**reuse**
rethink	**revitalize**
retrain	**reweigh**
retrial	**rework**

reach (rēch) ***vt.*** ⟦OE *ræcan*⟧ **1** to thrust out (the hand, etc.) **2** to extend to by thrusting out, etc. **3** to obtain and hand over *[reach* me the salt*]* **4** to go as far as; attain **5** to influence; affect **6** to get in touch with, as by telephone —***vi.*** **1** to thrust out the hand, etc. **2** to extend in influence, space, amount, etc. **3** to carry: said of sight, sound, etc. **4** to try to get something —***n.*** **1** a stretching or thrusting out **2** the power of, or the extent covered in, stretching, obtaining, etc. **3** a continuous extent, esp. of water

re·act (rē akt′) ***vi.*** **1** to act in return or reciprocally **2** to act in opposition **3** to act in a reverse way; go back to a former condition, stage, etc. **4** to respond to a stimulus **5** *Chem.* to act with another substance in a chemical change

re·act·ant (rē ak′tənt) ***n.*** any substance involved in a chemical reaction

re·ac·tion (rē ak′shən) ***n.*** **1** a return or opposing action, etc. **2** a response, as to a stimulus or influence **3** a movement back to a former or less advanced condition; extreme conservatism **4** a chemical change

re·ac′tion·ar′y (-shə ner′ē) ***adj.*** of, characterized by, or advocating reaction, esp. in politics —***n.***, *pl.* **-ies** an advocate of reaction, esp. in politics

re·ac·ti·vate (rē ak′tə vāt′) ***vt.***, ***vi.*** **-vat′ed**, **-vat′ing** to make or be made active again; specif., to return (a military unit, ship, etc.) to active status —**re·ac′ti·va′tion** ***n.***

re·ac′tive (-tiv) ***adj.*** **1** tending to react **2** of, from, or showing reaction —**re′ac·tiv′i·ty** ***n.***

re·ac′tor (-tər) ***n.*** NUCLEAR REACTOR

read[1] (rēd) ***vt.*** **read** (red), **read·ing** (rēd′iŋ) ⟦< OE *rædan*, to counsel⟧ **1** to get the meaning of (writing) by interpreting the characters **2** to utter aloud (written matter) **3** to understand or interpret **4** to foretell (the future) **5** [Brit.] to study *[*to *read* law*]* **6** to register: said as of a gauge **7** [Slang] to hear and understand *[*I *read* you*]* **8** *Comput.* to access (data) from (a disk, tape, etc.) —***vi.*** **1** to read something written **2** to learn by reading: with *about* or *of* **3** to contain certain words —**read into** to attribute (a particular meaning) to —**read out of** to expel from (a group) —**read′a·bil′i·ty** ***n.*** —**read′a·ble** ***adj.*** —**read′er** ***n.***

read[2] (red) ***vt.***, ***vi.*** *pt. & pp. of* READ[1] —***adj.*** informed by reading *[*well-*read]*

read·er·ship (rēd′ər ship′) ***n.*** the people who read a certain publication, author, etc.

read·i·ly (red′ə lē) ***adv.*** **1** willingly **2** easily

read·ing (rēd′iŋ) ***n.*** **1** the act of one who reads **2** material to be read **3** the amount measured by a barometer, thermometer, etc. **4** a particular interpretation or performance

read·out (rēd′out′) ***n.*** **1** the retrieving of information from a computer **2** information from a computer, thermostat, etc. displayed visually or recorded, as on tape

read·y (red′ē) ***adj.*** **-i·er**, **-i·est** ⟦OE *ræde*⟧ **1** prepared to act or be used immediately **2** willing **3** likely or liable; apt *[ready* to cry*]* **4** dexterous **5** prompt *[*a *ready* reply*]* **6** available at once *[ready* cash*]* —***vt.*** **-ied**, **-y·ing** to prepare —**at the ready** prepared for immediate use —**read′i·ness** ***n.***

read′y-made′ ***adj.*** made so as to be ready for use or sale at once: also, as applied to clothing, **read′y-to-wear′**

Rea·gan (rā′gən), **Ron·ald** (**Wilson**) (rän′əld) 1911- ; 40th president of the U.S. (1981-89)

re·a·gent (rē ā′jənt) ***n.*** *Chem.* a substance used to detect, measure, or react with another substance

re·al (rē′əl, rēl) ***adj.*** ⟦< L *res*, thing⟧ **1** existing as or in fact; actual; true **2** authentic; genuine **3** *Law* of or relating to permanent, immovable things *[real* property*]* —***adv.*** [Inf.] very —**for real** [Slang] real or really

real estate **1** land, including the buildings, etc. on it **2** the buying and selling of this

re·al·ism (rē′ə liz′əm) ***n.*** **1** a tendency to face facts and be practical **2** the picturing in art and literature of people

THESAURUS

reach ***n.*** compass, range, scope, grasp, stretch, extension, orbit, horizon, gamut; see also ABILITY.

reach ***v.*** **1** [To extend to] touch, span, encompass, pass along, continue to, roll on, stretch, go as far as, attain, equal, approach, lead, stand, terminate, end, overtake, join, come up to, sweep; see also SPREAD 2. **2** [To extend a part of the body to] lunge, strain, move, reach out, feel for, come at, make contact with, shake hands, throw out a limb, make for, put out, touch, strike, seize, grasp; see also STRETCH 1. **3** [To arrive] get to, come to, enter; see ARRIVE.

reaching ***a.*** **1** [Extending to a point] going up to, ending at, stretching, encompassing, taking in, spanning, spreading to, embracing, joining, sweeping on to. **2** [Arriving] coming to, landing, touching down; see LANDING 1. **3** [Extending a part of the body] stretching, straining, lunging; see EXTENDING.

react ***v.*** **1** [To act in response] reciprocate, respond, act; see ANSWER 1. **2** [To feel in response] be affected, be impressed, be involved; see FEEL 2.

reaction ***n.*** reply, rejoinder, reception, receptivity, response, return, feeling, opinion, reflection, backlash, attitude, retort, reciprocation, repercussion, result, reflex; see also ANSWER 1, OPINION 1. *Reactions to stimuli include the following:* contraction, expansion, jerk, knee jerk, cognition, shock, relapse, exhaustion, stupor, anger, disgust, revulsion, fear, illness, joy, laughter, wonder.

reactionary ***a.*** rigid, retrogressive, ultraconservative; see CONSERVATIVE.

reactionary ***n.*** die-hard, right-winger, untraconservative; see CONSERVATIVE.

read[1] ***a.*** examined, gone over, scanned; see UNDERSTOOD 1.

read[1] ***v.*** **1** [To understand by reading] comprehend, go through, peruse, scan, glance over, go over, gather, see, know, skim, perceive, apprehend, grasp, learn, flip through the pages, dip into, scratch the surface, bury oneself in; see also UNDERSTAND 1. **2** [To interpret] view, render, translate, decipher, make out, unravel, express, explain, expound, construe, paraphrase, restate, put; see also INTERPRET.

readable ***a.*** **1** [Capable of being read] clear, legible, coherent, distinct, intelligible, lucid, comprehensible, decipherable, unmistakable, plain, regular, orderly, fluent, tidy, flowing, precise, graphic, explicit, understandable, unequivocal, straightforward, simple. **2** [Likely to be read with pleasure] interesting, absorbing, fascinating, pleasurable, engrossing, satisfying, amusing, entertaining, enjoyable, rewarding, gratifying, pleasing, worth reading, pleasant, inviting, engaging, eloquent, well-written, smooth, exciting, attractive, clever, brilliant, ingenious, relaxing, stimulating, riveting, appealing.—*Ant.* DULL, dreary, depressing.

reader ***n.*** **1** [One who reads habitually] bookworm, bibliophile, scholar; see WRITER. **2** [A book intended for the study of reading] primer, graded text, selected readings; see BOOK.

readily ***a.*** quickly, immediately, promptly; see EAGERLY, EASILY, WILLINGLY.

readiness ***n.*** aptness, predisposition, eagerness; see WILLINGNESS, ZEAL.

reading ***n.*** **1** [Interpretation] version, treatment, commentary; see INTERPRETATION, TRANSLATION. **2** [A selection from written matter] excerpt, passage, section; see QUOTATION. **3** [A version] account, paraphrase, rendering; see LITERATURE 2, INTERPRETATION.

ready ***a.*** **1** [Prompt] quick, spontaneous, alert, wide-awake, swift, fleet, fast, sharp, immediate, instant, animated; see also ACTIVE, OBSERVANT, PUNCTUAL.—*Ant.* SLOW, dull, lazy. **2** [Prepared] fit, apt, skillful, ripe, handy, in readiness, waiting, on call, in line for, in position, on the brink of, equipped to do the job, open to, fixed for, on the mark, equal to, expectant, available, at hand, anticipating, in order, all systems go*, all squared away*, in a go condition*.—*Ant.* UNPREPARED, unready, unavailable. **3** [Enthusiastic] eager, willing, ardent; see ZEALOUS. —**make ready** put in order, prepare for something, equip; see PREPARE 1.

ready-made ***a.*** instant, prefabricated, built; see PRESERVED 2.

real ***a.*** **1** [Genuine] true, authentic, original; see GENUINE 1. **2** [Having physical existence] actual, solid, firm, substantive, material, live, substantial, existent, tangible, existing, present, palpable, factual, sound, concrete, corporal, corporeal, bodily, incarnate, embodied, physical, sensible, stable, in existence, perceptible, evident, undeniable, irrefutable, practical, true, true to life.—*Ant.* UNREAL, unsubstantial, hypothetical. **3** [*Very much] exceedingly, exceptionally, uncommonly; see VERY. —**for real*** actually, in fact, certainly; see REALLY 1.

real estate ***n.*** land, property, realty; see BUILDING, ESTATE, FARM, HOME 1.

realism ***n.*** authenticity, naturalness, actuality; see REALITY.

and things as they really appear to be —**re'al·ist** *n.* —**re'al·is'tic** *adj.* —**re'al·is'ti·cal·ly** *adv.*

re·al·i·ty (rē al'ə tē) *n., pl.* **-ties** **1** the quality or fact of being real **2** a person or thing that is real; fact —**in reality** in fact; actually

re·al·ize (rē'ə līz') *vt.* **-ized', -iz'ing** **1** to make real; achieve **2** to understand fully **3** to convert (assets, rights, etc.) into money **4** to gain; obtain *[to realize a profit]* **5** to be sold for (a specified sum) —**re'al·i·za'tion** *n.*

re'al-life' *adj.* actual; not imaginary

re'al·ly *adv.* **1** in reality **2** truly —*interj.* indeed: used to express surprise, doubt, etc.

realm (relm) *n.* ⟦see REGAL⟧ **1** a kingdom **2** a region; sphere

Re·al·tor (rē'əl tər, -tôr') *trademark for* a real estate broker or appraiser who is a member of the National Association of Realtors —*n.* [**r-**] a real estate agent

re·al·ty (rē'əl tē) *n.* REAL ESTATE

ream[1] (rēm) *n.* ⟦< Ar *rizma,* a bale⟧ **1** a quantity of paper varying from 480 to 516 sheets **2** [*pl.*] [Inf.] a great amount

ream[2] (rēm) *vt.* ⟦OE *reman*⟧ to enlarge (a hole) as with a reamer

ream'er *n.* **1** a sharp-edged tool for enlarging or tapering holes **2** a juicer

re·an·i·mate (rē an'ə māt') *vt.* **-mat'ed, -mat'ing** to give new life, power, or vigor to —**re·an'i·ma'tion** *n.*

reap (rēp) *vt., vi.* ⟦OE *ripan*⟧ **1** to cut (grain) with a scythe, reaper, etc. **2** to gather (a harvest) **3** to obtain as the reward of action, etc.

reap'er *n.* **1** one who reaps **2** a machine for reaping grain

re·ap·por·tion (rē'ə pôr'shən) *vt.* to apportion again; specif., to change the distribution of (a legislature) so that members represent constituents equally —**re'ap·por'tion·ment** *n.*

rear[1] (rir) *n.* ⟦see ARREARS⟧ **1** the back part **2** the position behind or at the back **3** the part of an army, etc. farthest from the enemy **4** [Slang] the buttocks —*adj.* of, at, or in the rear —**bring up the rear** to come at the end

rear[2] (rir) *vt.* ⟦OE *ræran*⟧ **1** to put upright; elevate **2** to build; erect **3** to grow or breed **4** to educate, train, etc. *[to rear a child]* —*vi.* **1** to rise on the hind legs, as a horse does **2** to rise (*up*), in anger, etc. **3** to rise high

rear admiral a naval officer ranking above a captain

rear-end' *vt.* to crash into, or cause one's vehicle to crash into, the back end of (another vehicle)

rear'most' *adj.* farthest in the rear

re·ar·range (rē'ə rānj') *vt.* **-ranged', -rang'ing** to arrange again or in a different way

rear'ward *adj.* at, in, or toward the rear —*adv.* toward the rear: also **rear'wards**

rea·son (rē'zən) *n.* ⟦< L *ratio,* a reckoning⟧ **1** an explanation of an act, idea, etc. **2** a cause or motive **3** the ability to think, draw conclusions, etc. **4** good sense **5** sanity —*vi., vt.* **1** to think logically (about); analyze **2** to argue or infer —**stand to reason** to be logical —**rea'son·ing** *n.*

rea'son·a·ble *adj.* **1** able to reason **2** fair; just **3** sensible **4** not excessive —**rea'son·a·bly** *adv.*

re·as·sure (rē'ə shoor') *vt.* **-sured', -sur'ing** to restore to confidence —**re'as·sur'ance** *n.*

re·bate (rē'bāt') *vt.* **-bat'ed, -bat'ing** ⟦< OFr *re-,* RE- + *abattre,* beat down⟧ to give back (part of a payment) —*n.* a return of part of a payment

Re·bek·ah (ri bek'ə) *n. Bible* the wife of Isaac: also sp. **Re·bec'ca**

reb·el (reb'əl; *for v.* ri bel') *n.* ⟦< L *re-,* again + *bellare,* wage war⟧ one who resists authority —*adj.* **1** rebellious

THESAURUS

realist *n.* pragmatist, naturalist, scientist; see PHILOSOPHER.

realistic *a.* **1** [Practical] pragmatic, sensible, rational; see PRACTICAL. **2** [Lifelike] true-to-life, faithful, representative; see GENUINE 1.

reality *n.* authenticity, factual basis, truth, actuality, realness, substantiality, existence, substance, materiality, being, presence, actual existence, sensibility, corporeality, solidity, perceptibility, true being, absoluteness, tangibility, palpability. —**in reality** in truth, truly, honestly; see REALLY 1.

realization *n.* understanding, comprehension, consciousness; see AWARENESS.

realize *v.* **1** [To bring to fulfillment] perfect, make good, actualize; see COMPLETE. **2** [To understand] recognize, apprehend, discern; see UNDERSTAND 1. **3** [To receive] acquire, make a profit from, obtain; see EARN 2, PROFIT 2, RECEIVE 1.

realized *a.* **1** [Fulfilled] completed, accomplished, done; see FINISHED 1. **2** [Earned] gained, gotten, acquired, received, accrued, made, reaped, harvested, gathered, inherited, profited, taken, cleared, obtained, gleaned, netted.

really *a.* **1** [In fact] actually, indeed, genuinely, certainly, surely, absolutely, positively, veritably, in reality, authentically, upon my honor, legitimately, precisely, literally, indubitably, unmistakably, in effect, undoubtedly, categorically, in point of fact, I assure you, be assured, believe me, as a matter of fact, of course, honestly, truly, admittedly, nothing else but, beyond any doubt, in actuality, unquestionably, as sure as you're alive*, no buts about it*, without a doubt. **2** [To a remarkable degree] surprisingly, remarkably, extraordinarily; see VERY.

really *interj.* indeed, honestly, for a fact, yes, is that so, are you sure, no fooling, cross your heart and hope to die, on your honor, you don't say*, ain't it the truth*, you said it*, do tell*, no kidding*.

realm *n.* domain, area, sphere; see DEPARTMENT, EXPANSE, REGION 1.

reappear *v.* come again, reenter, crop up again; see APPEAR 1, REPEAT 2.

rear[1] *n.* hind part, back seat, rear end, tail, tail end, posterior, rump, butt*; see also BACK 1.

rear[2] *v.* lift, elevate, bring up; see RAISE 1, SUPPORT 1.

rearrange *v.* do over, reorganize, shift; see ORDER 3, PREPARE 1.

reason *n.* **1** [The power of reasoning] intelligence, mind, sanity; see JUDGMENT 1. **2** [A process of reasoning] logic, dialectics, speculation, generalization, rationalism, argumentation, inference, induction, deduction, analysis, rationalization. **3** [A basis for rational action] end, object, rationale, intention, motive, ulterior motive, basis, wherefore, aim, intent, cause, design, ground, impetus, idea, motivation, root, incentive, goal, purpose, the why and wherefore; see also PURPOSE 1. **4** [The mind] brain, mentality, intellect; see MIND 1. —**by reason of** because of, for, by way of; see BECAUSE. —**in** (or **within**) **reason** in accord with what is reasonable, rationally, understandably; see REASONABLY 1. —**stand to reason** be feasible, seem all right, be logical; see CONVINCE. —**with reason** understandably, soundly, plausibly; see REASONABLY 1.

reason *v.* **1** [To think logically] reflect, deliberate, contemplate; see THINK 1. **2** [To seek a reasonable explanation] suppose, gather, conclude; see ASSUME. **3** [To discuss persuasively] argue, contend, debate; see DISCUSS.

reasonable *a.* **1** [Rational] sane, logical, levelheaded, intelligent, clear-cut, tolerant, endowed with reason, conscious, cerebral, thoughtful, reflective, capable of reason, reasoning, cognitive, percipient, discerning, discriminating, common-sense, consistent, broad-minded, liberal, generous, sensible, unprejudiced, unbiased, flexible, agreeable; see also RATIONAL 1.—*Ant.* PREJUDICED, intolerant, biased. **2** [Characterized by justice] fair, right, just; see HONEST 1. **3** [Likely to appeal to the reason] feasible, sound, plausible; see UNDERSTANDABLE. **4** [Moderate in price] inexpensive, reduced, fair; see CHEAP 1.

reasonably *a.* **1** [In a reasonable manner] rationally, sanely, logically, understandably, plausibly, sensibly, soundly, persuasively, fairly, justly, honestly, wisely, judiciously, plainly, intelligently, soberly, agreeably, in reason, within reason, within the limits of reason, as far as possible, as far as could be expected, as much as good sense dictates, within reasonable limitations, with due restraint. **2** [To a moderate degree] mildly, prudently, fairly, moderately, inexpensively, temperately, evenly, calmly, gently, leniently, sparingly, frugally, indulgently, tolerantly, within bounds.

reasoning *n.* thinking, rationalizing, drawing conclusions; see THOUGHT 1.

reassure *v.* convince, console, give confidence; see COMFORT 1, ENCOURAGE, GUARANTEE.

rebel *n.* insurrectionist, revolutionist, revolutionary, agitator, insurgent, traitor, seditionist, mutineer, subversive, subverter, anarchist, overthrower, nihilist, guerrilla, member of the uprising, rioter, terrorist, demagogue, revolter, separatist, malcontent, schismatic, dissenter, deserter, apostate, turncoat, counterrevolutionary, renegade, secessionist, underground worker; see also RADICAL.

rebel *v.* rise up, resist, revolt, turn against, defy, resist lawful authority, fight in the streets, strike, boycott, break with, overturn, mutiny, riot, take up arms against, start a confrontation, secede, renounce, combat, oppose, be insubordinate, be treason-

2 of rebels —*vi.* **re·bel′**, **-belled′**, **-bel′ling** **1** to resist authority **2** to feel or show strong aversion
re·bel·lion (ri bel′yən) *n.* **1** armed resistance to one's government **2** a defiance of any authority
re·bel′lious (-yəs) *adj.* **1** resisting authority **2** opposing control; defiant
re·birth (rē burth′) *n.* **1** a new or second birth **2** a reawakening; revival
re·boot (rē bo͞ot′) *vi.*, *vt. Comput.* to boot again, as to restore normal operation
re·bound (ri bound′; *for n.* rē′bound′) *vi.* to spring back, as upon impact —*n.* a rebounding, or a ball, etc. that rebounds —**on the rebound** **1** after it bounces back **2** just after being jilted
re·buff (ri buf′) *n.* ⟦< It *rabbuffare,* disarrange⟧ **1** an abrupt refusal of offered advice, help, etc. **2** any repulse —*vt.* **1** to snub **2** to check or repulse
re·buke (ri byo͞ok′) *vt.* **-buked′**, **-buk′ing** ⟦< OFr *re-,* back + *buchier,* to beat⟧ to scold in a sharp way; reprimand —*n.* a reprimand
re·bus (rē′bəs) *n.* ⟦L, lit., by things⟧ a puzzle consisting of pictures, etc. combined to suggest words or phrases
re·but (ri but′) *vt.* **-but′ted**, **-but′ting** ⟦< OFr *re-,* back + *buter,* to thrust⟧ to contradict or oppose, esp. in a formal manner by argument, proof, etc. —**re·but′tal** (-′l) *n.*
rec (rek) *n. short for* RECREATION: used in compounds, as **rec room**
re·cal·ci·trant (ri kal′si trənt) *adj.* ⟦< L *re-,* back + *calcitrare,* to kick⟧ **1** refusing to obey authority, etc. **2** hard to handle —**re·cal′ci·trance** *n.*
re·call (ri kôl′; *for n.* rē′kôl′) *vt.* **1** to call back **2** to remember **3** to take back; revoke —*n.* **1** a recalling **2** memory **3** the removal of, or right to remove, an official from office by popular vote
re·cant (ri kant′) *vt.*, *vi.* ⟦< L *re-,* back + *canere,* sing⟧ to renounce formally (one's beliefs, remarks, etc.) —**re·can·ta·tion** (rē′kan tā′shən) *n.*
re·cap[1] (rē kap′; *also, and for n. always,* rē′kap′) *vt.* **-capped′**, **-cap′ping** to put a new tread on (a worn tire) —*n.* such a tire
re·cap[2] (rē′kap′) *n.* a recapitulation, or summary —*vt.*, *vi.* **-capped′**, **-cap′ping** to recapitulate
re·ca·pit·u·late (rē′kə pich′ə lāt′) *vi.*, *vt.* **-lat′ed**, **-lat′ing** ⟦see RE- & CAPITULATE⟧ to repeat briefly; summarize —**re′ca·pit′u·la′tion** *n.*
re·cap·ture (rē kap′chər) *vt.* **-tured**, **-tur·ing** **1** to capture again; retake **2** to remember —*n.* a recapturing
recd or **rec'd** *abbrev.* received
re·cede (ri sēd′) *vi.* **-ced′ed**, **-ced′ing** ⟦see RE- & CEDE⟧ **1** to go, move, or slope backward **2** to diminish
re·ceipt (ri sēt′) *n.* ⟦see RECEIVE⟧ **1** *old-fashioned var. of* RECIPE **2** a receiving or being received **3** a written acknowledgment that something has been received **4** [*pl.*] the amount, as of money, received —*vt.* to write a receipt for (goods, etc.)
re·ceiv·a·ble (ri sē′və bəl) *adj.* **1** that can be received **2** due —*n.* [*pl.*] outstanding bills, loans, etc.
re·ceive (ri sēv′) *vt.* **-ceived′**, **-ceiv′ing** ⟦< L *re-,* back + *capere,* take⟧ **1** to take or get (something given, thrown, sent, etc.) **2** to experience; undergo [to *receive* acclaim] **3** to bear or hold **4** to react to in a specified way **5** to learn [to *receive* news] **6** to let enter **7** to greet (visitors, etc.)
re·ceived′ *adj.* accepted; considered as standard
re·ceiv′er *n.* one that receives; specif., *a*) a device that converts electrical waves or signals into audible or visual signals *b*) a football player designated to receive a forward pass *c*) one appointed by a court to administer or hold in trust property in bankruptcy or in a lawsuit —**re·ceiv′er·ship′** *n.*
re·cen·sion (ri sen′shən) *n.* ⟦< L *recensere,* revise⟧ a revision of a text based on a critical study of sources
re·cent (rē′sənt) *adj.* ⟦< L *recens*⟧ **1** done, made, etc. just before the present; new **2** of a time just before the present —**re′cent·ly** *adv.*
re·cep·ta·cle (ri sep′tə kəl) *n.* ⟦see RECEIVE⟧ a container
re·cep·tion (ri sep′shən) *n.* **1** *a*) a receiving or being received *b*) the manner of this **2** a social function for the receiving of guests **3** *Radio, TV* the receiving of signals, with reference to the quality of reproduction
re·cep′tion·ist *n.* an office employee who receives callers, etc.
re·cep′tive *adj.* able or ready to accept new ideas, suggestions, etc.
re·cep′tor *n.* a nerve ending or group of nerve endings specialized for receiving stimuli

THESAURUS

able, upset, overthrow, dethrone, disobey, raise hell*, run amok*.—*Ant.* OBEY, be contented, submit.

rebellion *n.* insurrection, revolt, defiance; see DISOBEDIENCE, REVOLUTION 2.

rebellious *a.* revolutionary, insurgent, counterrevolutionary, terrorist, warring, stubborn, contemptuous, insolent, scornful, intractable, unyielding, recalcitrant, insurrectionary, attacking, rioting, mutinous, dissident, factious, fractious, seditious, treasonable, traitorous, disobedient, refractory, defiant, resistant, riotous, insubordinate, sabotaging, treacherous, bellicose, seditious, disloyal, disaffected, alienated, ungovernable, restless, threatening, anarchistic, iconoclastic, individualistic, radical, independent-minded, quarrelsome.—*Ant.* CALM, DOCILE, peaceful.

rebirth *n.* resurrection, rejuvenation, rehabilitation; see REVIVAL 1.

rebound *v.* bounce back, ricochet, spring back; see BOUNCE.

rebuild *v.* **1** [To repair] touch up, patch, fix; see REPAIR. **2** [To restore] overhaul, replace, remake; see RECONSTRUCT.

rebuke *n.* condemnation, reproof, reprimand; see INSULT.

rebuke *v.* reprove, reprimand, censure; see OPPOSE 1.

recall *v.* **1** [To call to mind] recollect, think of, revive; see REMEMBER 1. **2** [To remove from office] discharge, disqualify, suspend; see DISMISS. **3** [To summon again] call back, reconvene, reassemble; see SUMMON.

recalled *a.* **1** [Remembered] recollected, brought to mind, summoned up; see REMEMBERED. **2** [Relieved of responsibility] stripped of office, dismissed, cast out, displaced, fired, replaced, ousted, suspended, laid off, cashiered, pensioned, let out, let go, removed, retired, impeached, kicked upstairs*, canned*, busted*, washed out*; see also DISCHARGED.

recapture *v.* regain, reobtain, reacquire; see RECOVER 1.

recede *v.* **1** [To go backward] fall back, shrink from, withdraw; see RETREAT. **2** [To sink] ebb, drift away, lower, turn down, abate, decline, go away, drop, fall off, lessen; see also DECREASE 1, FALL 2.—*Ant.* RISE, ascend, increase.

receipt *n.* **1** [The act of receiving] receiving, acquisition, acquiring, accession, acceptance, taking, arrival, getting, admitting, reception; see also ADMISSION 1.—*Ant.* DELIVERY, shipment, giving. **2** [An acknowledgement of receipt] letter, voucher, release, cancellation, slip, sales slip, signed notice, stub, discharge, declaration, paid bill; see also CERTIFICATE.

receive *v.* **1** [To take into one's charge] accept, be given, admit, get, gain, inherit, acquire, gather up, collect, obtain, reap, procure, derive, appropriate, seize, take possession, redeem, pocket, pick up, hold, come by, earn, take in, assume, draw, win, secure, come into, come in for, catch, get from; see also GET 1.—*Ant.* DISCARD, abandon, refuse. **2** [To endure] undergo, experience, suffer; see ENDURE 2. **3** [To support] bear, sustain, prop; see SUPPORT 1. **4** [To make welcome] accommodate, initiate, induct, install, make welcome, shake hands with, admit, permit, welcome home, accept, entertain, invite in, show in, usher in, let through, make comfortable, bring as a guest into, introduce, give a party, give access to, allow entrance to, roll out the red carpet for*, give the red-carpet treatment to*, get out the welcome mat for*; see also GREET.—*Ant.* VISIT, be a guest, call.

received *a.* taken, gotten, acquired, obtained, honored, brought in, signed for, admitted, collected, gathered; see also ACCEPTED, ACKNOWLEDGED.—*Ant.* GIVEN, disbursed, delivered.

receiver *n.* **1** [One who receives] customer, recipient, beneficiary; see HEIR. **2** [A device for receiving] telephone, cellphone, television, radio, satellite dish, radio telescope, walkie-talkie, headphone, car phone, beeper, pager, mission control, control center, listening device, transceiver, bug*.

recent *a.* **1** [Lately brought into being] fresh, novel, newly born; see MODERN 1, UNUSUAL 1, 2. **2** [Associated with modern times] contemporary, up-to-date, current; see MODERN 1, 3.

recently *a.* lately, in recent times, just now, just a while ago, not long ago, a short while ago, of late, newly, freshly, new, the other day, within the recent past.—*Ant.* ONCE, long ago, formerly.

receptacle *n.* box, wastebasket, holder; see CONTAINER.

reception *n.* **1** [The act of receiving] acquisition, acceptance, accession; see RECEIPT 2. **2** [The manner of receiving] greeting, encounter, meeting, reaction, response, introduction, welcome, salutation, induction, admission, disposition; see also GREETING. **3** [A social function] gathering, party, soiree; see GATHERING.

receptive *a.* responsive, sensitive,

re·cess (rē′ses; *also, & for v. usually,* ri ses′) ***n.*** ⟦< L *recedere,* recede⟧ **1** a hollow place, as in a wall **2** a hidden or inner place **3** a temporary halting as of work, a session, etc. —***vt.*** **1** to place in a recess **2** to halt temporarily —***vi.*** to take a recess

re·ces·sion (ri sesh′ən) ***n.*** **1** a going back; withdrawal **2** a temporary falling off of business activity

re·ces′sion·al ***n.*** a piece of music at the end of a church service played when the clergy, etc. march out

re·ces·sive (ri ses′iv) ***adj.*** **1** tending to recede **2** *Genetics* designating or of that one of any pair of hereditary factors which remains latent —***n.*** *Genetics* a recessive character or characters

re·cher·ché (rə sher′shā, -sher′shā′) ***adj.*** ⟦Fr⟧ **1** rare; choice **2** refined; esp., too refined

re·cid·i·vism (ri sid′ə viz′əm) ***n.*** ⟦< L *re-,* back + *cadere,* to fall⟧ habitual or chronic relapse, esp. into crime

rec·i·pe (res′ə pē′) ***n.*** ⟦L < *recipere,* receive⟧ **1** a list of materials and directions for preparing a dish or drink **2** a way to achieve something

re·cip·i·ent (ri sip′ē ənt) ***n.*** ⟦see RECEIVE⟧ one that receives

re·cip·ro·cal (ri sip′rə kəl) ***adj.*** ⟦< L *reciprocus,* returning⟧ **1** done, given, etc. in return **2** mutual *[reciprocal love]* **3** corresponding but reversed **4** corresponding or complementary —***n.*** **1** a complement, counterpart, etc. **2** *Math.* the quantity resulting from the division of 1 by the given quantity *[the reciprocal of 7 is $\frac{1}{7}$]*

re·cip′ro·cate′ (-kāt′) ***vt., vi.*** **-cat′ed, -cat′ing** **1** to give and get reciprocally **2** to do, feel, etc. in return **3** to move alternately back and forth —**re·cip′ro·ca′tion *n.***

rec·i·proc·i·ty (res′ə präs′ə tē) ***n.,*** *pl.* **-ties** **1** reciprocal state **2** mutual exchange; esp., exchange of special privileges between two countries

re·cit·al (ri sīt′'l) ***n.*** **1** a reciting **2** the account, story, etc. told **3** a musical or dance program

rec·i·ta·tion (res′ə tā′shən) ***n.*** **1** a reciting, as of facts, events, etc. **2** *a)* a saying aloud in public of something memorized *b)* a piece so presented **3** a reciting by pupils of answers to questions on a prepared lesson

rec′i·ta·tive′ (-tə tēv′) ***n.*** ⟦< It: see fol.⟧ a type of declamation, as for operatic dialogue, with the rhythms of speech, but in musical tones

re·cite (ri sīt′) ***vt., vi.*** **-cit′ed, -cit′ing** ⟦see RE- & CITE⟧ **1** to say aloud from memory, as a poem, lesson, etc. **2** to tell in detail; relate

reck·less (rek′lis) ***adj.*** ⟦OE *recceleas*⟧ careless; heedless —**reck′less·ly *adv.*** —**reck′less·ness *n.***

reck·on (rek′ən) ***vt.*** ⟦OE *-recenian*⟧ **1** to count; compute **2** to estimate **3** [Inf. or Dial.] to suppose —***vi.*** **1** to count up **2** [Inf.] to rely (*on*) —**reckon with** to take into consideration

reck′on·ing ***n.*** **1** count or computation **2** the settlement of an account

re·claim (ri klām′) ***vt.*** ⟦see RE- & CLAIM⟧ **1** to bring back (a person) from error, vice, etc. **2** to make (wasteland, etc.) usable **3** to recover (useful materials) from waste products —**rec·la·ma·tion** (rek′lə mā′shən) ***n.***

re·cline (ri klīn′) ***vt., vi.*** **-clined′, -clin′ing** ⟦< L *re-,* back + *clinare,* lean⟧ to lie or cause to lie down

re·clin′er ***n.*** an upholstered armchair with an adjustable back and seat for reclining: also **reclining chair**

rec·luse (rek′lo͞os, ri klo͞os′) ***n.*** ⟦< L *re-,* back + *claudere,* shut⟧ one who lives a secluded, solitary life

rec·og·ni·tion (rek′əg nish′ən) ***n.*** **1** a recognizing or being recognized **2** identification of a person or thing as having been known before

re·cog·ni·zance (ri käg′ni zəns, -kän′i-) ***n.*** ⟦< L *re-,* again + *cognoscere,* know⟧ *Law* a bond binding one to some act, as to appear in court

rec·og·nize (rek′əg nīz′) ***vt.*** **-nized′, -niz′ing** ⟦see prec.⟧ **1** to be aware of as someone or something known before **2** to know by some detail, as of appearance **3** to perceive **4** to accept as a fact *[to recognize defeat]* **5** to acknowledge as worthy of approval **6** to acknowledge the status of (a government, etc.) **7** to grant the right to speak in a meeting —**rec′og·niz′a·ble *adj.***

re·coil (ri koil′; *also for n.* rē′koil′) ***vi.*** ⟦< L *re-,* back + *culus,* buttocks⟧ **1** to draw back, as in fear, etc. **2** to spring or kick back, as a gun when fired —***n.*** a recoiling

rec·ol·lect (rek′ə lekt′) ***vt., vi.*** ⟦see RE- & COLLECT⟧ to remember, esp. with some effort —**rec′ol·lec′tion *n.***

re·com·bi·nant DNA (rē käm′bə nənt) DNA formed in the laboratory by splicing together pieces of DNA from different species, as to create new life forms

rec·om·mend (rek′ə mend′) ***vt.*** ⟦see RE- & COMMEND⟧ **1** to entrust **2** to suggest favorably as suited for some position, etc. **3** to make acceptable **4** to advise; counsel —**rec′om·men·da′tion *n.***

re·com·mit (rē′kə mit′) ***vt.*** **-mit′ted, -mit′ting** **1** to commit again **2** to refer (a question, bill, etc.) back to a committee

rec·om·pense (rek′əm pens′) ***vt.*** **-pensed′, -pens′ing** ⟦see RE- & COMPENSATE⟧ **1** to repay or reward **2** to compen-

THESAURUS

perceptive; see OBSERVANT, SYMPATHETIC.

recess *n.* **1** [An intermission] respite, rest, pause, interlude, break, cessation, stop, suspension, interval, coffee break, intervening period, halt, breather*. **2** [An indentation] break, dent, corner; see HOLE 1. **3** [A recessed space] cell, cubicle, nook; see ROOM 2.

recession *n.* unemployment, inflation, decline; see DEPRESSION 3.

recipe *n.* formula, receipt, instructions, prescription, cooking instructions, directions, method, procedure, compound.

recipient *n.* receiver, beneficiary, legatee; see HEIR.

recital *n.* presentation, concert, musical; see PERFORMANCE.

recitation *n.* **1** [The act of reciting] delivery, speaking, playing, narrating, reading, recounting, declaiming, discoursing, soliloquizing, discussion, holding forth, performance, recital, rehearsal, monologue, discourse. **2** [A compositon used for recitation] reading selection, performance piece, monologue; see SPEECH 3, WRITING 2.

recite *v.* **1** [To repeat formally] declaim, address, read, render, discourse, hold forth, enact, dramatize, deliver from memory, interpret, soliloquize. **2** [To report on a lesson] answer, give a report, explain; see DISCUSS, REPORT 1. **3** [To relate in detail] enumerate, enlarge, report, account for, give an account for, impart, convey, quote, communicate, utter, describe, relate, state, tell, mention, narrate, recount, retell, picture, delineate, portray; see also EXPLAIN, TELL 1.

reckless *a.* thoughtless, foolish, wild; see RASH.

recklessly *a.* dangerously, heedlessly, with abandon; see BRAVELY, CARELESSLY.

reckon *v.* consider, evaluate, judge; see ESTIMATE.

reclaim *v.* **1** [To bring into usable condition] restore, regenerate, redeem; see RECOVER 1. **2** [To reform] rehabilitate, mend, improve; see REFORM 3.

reclamation *n.* redemption, repair, repossession; see RECOVERY 3.

recognition *n.* **1** [The act of recognizing] recalling, remembering, identifying, perceiving, verifying, apprehending, acknowledging, noticing, recollection, memory, identification, recall, reidentification, cognizance, remembrance, realization. **2** [Tangible evidence of recognition] greeting, acknowledgment, identification, perception, admission, verification, comprehension, appreciation, renown, esteem, notice, attention, acceptance, regard, honor, credit.

recognize *v.* **1** [To know again] be familiar with, make out, distinguish, verify, recollect, sight, diagnose, place, espy, descry, recall, remember, see, perceive, admit knowledge of, notice; see also KNOW 1. **2** [To acknowledge] admit, appreciate, realize; see ALLOW. **3** [To acknowledge the legality of a government] exchange diplomatic representatives with, have diplomatic relations with, sanction, approve, extend formal recognition to; see also ACKNOWLEDGE 2.

recognized *a.* sighted, caught, realized, acknowledged, perceived, known, appreciated, admitted, recalled, remembered.

recoil *v.* turn away, shrink from, draw back; see RETREAT.

recollect *v.* recall, bring to mind, look back on; see REMEMBER 1.

recollection *n.* remembrance, reminiscence, consciousness; see MEMORY 1.

recommend *v.* **1** [To lend support or approval] agree to, sanction, hold up, commend, extol, compliment, applaud, advocate, celebrate, praise, speak highly of, acclaim, eulogize, confirm, laud, second, favor, back, stand by, magnify, glorify, exalt, think highly of, think well of, be satisfied with, esteem, value, prize, uphold, justify, endorse, go on record for, be all for, vouch for, front for, go to bat for*.—*Ant.* DENOUNCE, censure, renounce. **2** [To make a suggestion or prescription] prescribe, suggest, counsel; see ADVISE, URGE 2.

recommendation *n.* **1** [The act of recommending] guidance, counsel, direction; see ADVICE, SUGGESTION 1. **2** [A document that vouches for character or ability] certificate, testimonial, reference, letter of introduction, character reference, credentials, letter of recommendation, letter in support; see also LETTER 2.

recommended *a.* advocated, endorsed, suggested; see APPROVED.

sate (a loss, etc.) —**n.** **1** requital; reward **2** compensation

rec·on·cile (rek′ən sīl′) **vt.** **-ciled′**, **-cil′ing** ⟦see RE- & CONCILIATE⟧ **1** to make friendly again **2** to settle (a quarrel, etc.) **3** to make (ideas, accounts, etc.) consistent **4** to make acquiescent (*to*) —**rec′on·cil′a·ble** ***adj.*** —**rec′on·cil′i·a′tion** (-sil′ē ā′shən) **n.**

rec·on·dite (rek′ən dīt′) ***adj.*** ⟦< L *re-*, back + *condere*, to hide⟧ beyond ordinary understanding; abstruse

re·con·di·tion (rē′kən dish′ən) **vt.** to put back in good condition, as by repairing

re·con·nais·sance (ri kän′ə səns) **n.** ⟦Fr: see RECOGNIZANCE⟧ a survey of a region, as in seeking out information about enemy positions

rec·on·noi·ter (rek′ə noit′ər, rē′kə-) **vt.**, **vi.** to make a reconnaissance (of): also [Chiefly Brit.] **rec′on·noi′tre**, **-tred**, **-tring**

re·con·sid·er (rē′kən sid′ər) **vt.**, **vi.** to think over again, esp. with a view to changing a decision

re·con·sti·tute (rē kän′stə to͞ot′) **vt.** **-tut′ed**, **-tut′ing** to constitute again; specif., to restore (a dried or condensed substance) to its full liquid form by adding water

re·con·struct (rē′kən strukt′) **vt.** **1** to construct again; rebuild **2** to build up, as from remains, an image of the original

re′con·struc′tion **n.** **1** a reconstructing **2** [**R-**] the process or period, after the Civil War, of reestablishing the Southern States in the Union

re·cord (ri kôrd′; *for n. & adj.* rek′ərd) **vt.** ⟦< L *recordari*, remember⟧ **1** to write down for future use **2** to register, as on a graph **3** to register (sound or visual images) on a disc, tape, etc. for later reproduction —**n.** **rec′ord** **1** the condition of being recorded **2** anything written down and preserved; account of events **3** *a)* the known facts about anyone or anything *b)* the recorded offenses or crimes of a person **4** a grooved disc for playing on a phonograph **5** the best official performance achieved —***adj.*** **rec′ord** being the best, largest, etc. —**on** (or **off the**) **record** publicly (or confidentially) declared

re·cord′er **n.** **1** an official who keeps records **2** a machine or device that records; esp., a TAPE RECORDER **3** an early wind instrument

re·cord′ing **n.** **1** what is recorded, as on a disc or tape **2** a record, disc, etc.

re·count[1] (ri kount′) **vt.** ⟦see RE- & COUNT[1]⟧ to tell in detail; narrate

re·count[2] (rē′kount′; *for n.* rē′kount′) **vt.** to count again —**n.** a recounting, as of votes

re·coup (ri ko͞op′) **vt.** ⟦< Fr *re-*, again + *couper*, to cut⟧ to make up for or regain *[to recoup a loss]*

re·course (rē′kôrs′, ri kôrs′) **n.** ⟦see RE- & COURSE⟧ **1** a turning for aid, safety, etc. **2** that to which one turns seeking aid, safety, etc.

re·cov·er (ri kuv′ər) **vt.** ⟦< L *recuperare*⟧ **1** to get back (something lost, etc.) **2** to regain (health, etc.) **3** to make up for *[to recover losses]* **4** to save (oneself) from a fall, etc. **5** to reclaim (land from the sea, etc.) **6** *Sports* to get control of (a fumbled ball, etc.) —**vi.** **1** to regain health, balance, or control **2** *Sports* to regain control of a fumbled ball, etc.

re·cov′er·y **n.**, *pl.* **-ies** a recovering; specif., *a)* a regaining of something lost *b)* a return to health *c)* a retrieval of a capsule, etc. after a spaceflight

recovery room a hospital room where postoperative patients are kept for close observation and care

rec·re·ant (rek′rē ənt) [Archaic] ***adj.*** ⟦< OFr *recreire*, surrender allegiance⟧ **1** cowardly **2** disloyal —**n.** **1** a coward **2** a traitor

THESAURUS

reconcile *v.* **1** [To adjust] adapt, arrange, regulate; see ADJUST 1, 2. **2** [To bring into harmony] conciliate, assuage, pacify, propitiate, mitigate, make up, mediate, arbitrate, intercede, bring together, accustom oneself to, harmonize, accord, dictate peace, accommodate, appease, reunite, make peace between, bring to terms, bring into one's camp, win over, bury the hatchet, patch up, kiss and make up; see also SETTLE 7.—*Ant.* BOTHER, irritate, alienate.

reconciled *a.* settled, regulated, arranged; see DETERMINED 1.

reconciliation *n.* conciliation, settlement, rapprochement; see ADJUSTMENT, AGREEMENT 1.

reconsider *v.* reevaluate, think over, rearrange, consider again, recheck, reexamine, correct, amend, revise, retrace, rework, replan, review, withdraw for consideration, reweigh, amend one's judgment; see also CONSIDER.

reconstruct *v.* rebuild, remodel, construct again, make over, re-create, revamp, recondition, reconstitute, reestablish, restore, reproduce, refashion, reorganize, replace, overhaul, renovate, modernize, rework, construct from the original, copy, remake; see also BUILD, REPAIR.

reconstruction *n.* rebuilding, rehabilitation, restoration; see REPAIR.

record *n.* **1** [Documentary evidence] manuscript, inscription, transcription, account, history, legend, story, writing, written material, document. *Types of records include the following:* register, catalog, list, inventory, memo, memorandum, registry, schedule, chronicle, docket, scroll, archive, note, contract, statement, will, testament, petition, calendar, log, letter, memoir, reminiscence, dictation, confession, deposition, inscription, official record, sworn document, evidence, license, bulletin, gazette, newspaper, magazine, annual report, journal, *Congressional Record*, transactions, debates, bill, annals, presidential order, state paper, white paper, blue book, budget, report, entry, book, publication, autograph, signature, vital statistics, deed, paper, diary, stenographic notes, ledger, daybook, almanac, proceedings, minutes, description, affidavit, certificate, transcript, dossier, roll, tape, disk, microfilm, microfiche, floppy disk, CD. **2** [One's past] career, experience, work; see LIFE 2. **3** [A device for the reproduction of sound] recording, disk, phonograph record, LP, transcription, compact disc, CD, laserdisc, canned music*, cut, take, platter*. **—go on record** assert, attest, state; see DECLARE. **—off the record** confidential, unofficial, secret; see PRIVATE. **—on the record** recorded, stated, official; see PUBLIC 1.

record *v.* **1** [To write down] register, write in, jot down, set down, take down, put on record, transcribe, list, note, file, mark, inscribe, log, catalog, tabulate, put in writing, put in black and white, chronicle, keep accounts, keep an account of, make a written account of, matriculate, enroll, journalize, put on paper, preserve, make an entry in, chalk up, write up, enter, report, book, post, copy, document, insert, enumerate; see also WRITE 1. **2** [To indicate] point out, register, show; see NAME 2. **3** [To record electronically] tape, cut, photograph, make a record of, make a tape, tape-record, film, videotape, cut a record.

recorded *a.* listed, filed, on file, in black and white, in writing, inscribed, put down, registered, documented, entered, written, published, noted down, described, reported, cataloged, mentioned, certified, kept, chronicled, booked.

recorder *n.* dictaphone, recording instrument, cassette; see TAPE RECORDER.

recording *n.* documentation, recounting, reporting; see RECORD 1.

records *n.* documents, chronicles, archives, public papers, registers, annals, memorabilia, memoranda, lists, returns, statistics, diaries, accounts.

recover *v.* **1** [To obtain again] redeem, salvage, retrieve, rescue, reclaim, recoup, find again, recapture, repossess, bring back, win back, reacquire, obtain, regain, rediscover, resume, catch up; see also GET 1.—*Ant.* LOSE, let slip, fall behind. **2** [To improve one's condition] gain, increase, better; see IMPROVE 2, PROFIT 2.—*Ant.* FAIL, go bankrupt, give up. **3** [To regain health] rally, come around, come to, come out of it, get out of danger, improve, convalesce, heal, get the better of, overcome, start anew, be restored, mend, revive, be oneself again, perk up, gain strength, recuperate, get well, get over, get better, get through, return to form, make a comeback, get back in shape, snap out of it, pull through*.—*Ant.* DIE, fail, become worse.

recovered *a.* renewed, found, replaced, reborn, rediscovered, reawakened, retrieved, redeemed, reclaimed, regained, revived, returned, resumed; see also DISCOVERED.—*Ant.* LOST, missed, dropped.

recovery *n.* **1** [The act of returning to normal] reestablishment, resumption, restoration, reinstatement, return, rehabilitation, reconstruction, reformation, re-creation, replacement, readjustment, improving, getting back to normal; see also sense 2, IMPROVEMENT 1. **2** [The process of regaining health] convalescence, recuperation, revival, rebirth, renaissance, resurgence, resurrection, regeneration, cure, improvement, reawakening, renewal, resuscitation, rejuvenation, rehabilitation, return of health, comeback, physical improvement, healing, betterment. **3** [The act of regaining possession] repossession, retrieval, reclamation, redemption, indemnification, reparation, compensation, recapture, recouping, return, restoration, remuneration, reimbursement, retaking, recall.

rec·re·a·tion (rek'rē ā'shən) ***n.*** ⟦< L *recreare,* refresh⟧ any form of play, amusement, etc. used to relax or refresh the body or mind —**rec're·ate', -at'ed, -at'ing,** ***vt., vi.*** —**rec're·a'tion·al** ***adj.***

re·crim·i·nate (ri krim'ə nāt') ***vi.*** **-nat'ed, -nat'ing** ⟦< L *re-,* back + *crimen,* offense⟧ to answer an accuser by accusing that person in return —**re·crim'i·na'tion** ***n.***

re·cru·desce (rē'kro͞o des') ***vi.*** **-desced', -desc'ing** ⟦< L *re-,* again + *crudus,* raw⟧ to break out again after being inactive —**re'cru·des'cence** ***n.*** —**re'cru·des'cent** ***adj.***

re·cruit (ri kro͞ot') ***vt., vi.*** ⟦< L *re-,* again + *crescere,* grow⟧ **1** to enlist (personnel) into an army or navy **2** to enlist (new members) for an organization —***n.*** **1** a newly enlisted or drafted soldier, etc. **2** a new member of any group —**re·cruit'er** ***n.***

rec·tal (rek'təl) ***adj.*** of, for, or near the rectum

rec·tan·gle (rek'taŋ'gəl) ***n.*** ⟦< L *rectus,* straight + *angulus,* a corner⟧ a four-sided plane figure with four right angles —**rec·tan'gu·lar** (-gyə lər) ***adj.***

rec·ti·fy (rek'tə fī') ***vt.*** **-fied', -fy'ing** ⟦< L *rectus,* straight + *facere,* make⟧ **1** to put right; correct **2** *Elec.* to convert (alternating current) to direct current —**rec'ti·fi·ca'tion** ***n.*** —**rec'ti·fi'er** ***n.***

rec·ti·lin·e·ar (rek'tə lin'ē ər) ***adj.*** bounded or formed by straight lines

rec·ti·tude (rek'tə to͞od') ***n.*** ⟦< L *rectus,* right⟧ strict honesty; uprightness of character

rec·tor (rek'tər) ***n.*** ⟦< L *regere,* to rule⟧ **1** in some churches, a clergyman in charge of a parish **2** the head of certain schools, colleges, etc.

rec·to·ry (rek'tər ē) ***n., pl.*** **-ries** the house of a minister or priest

rec·tum (rek'təm) ***n., pl.*** **-tums** or **-ta** (-tə) ⟦< L *rectum (intestinum),* straight (intestine)⟧ the lowest, or last, segment of the large intestine

re·cum·bent (ri kum'bənt) ***adj.*** ⟦< L *re-,* back + *-cumbere,* lie down⟧ lying down; reclining

re·cu·per·ate (ri ko͞o'pə rāt') ***vt., vi.*** **-at'ed, -at'ing** ⟦< L *recuperare,* recover⟧ **1** to get well again **2** to recover (losses, etc.) —**re·cu'per·a'tion** ***n.*** —**re·cu'per·a'tive** (-pə rāt'iv, -pə rə tiv) ***adj.***

re·cur (ri kʉr') ***vi.*** **-curred', -cur'ring** ⟦< L *re-,* back + *currere,* run⟧ **1** to return in thought, talk, etc. **2** to occur again or at intervals —**re·cur'rence** ***n.*** —**re·cur'rent** ***adj.***

re·cy·cle (rē sī'kəl) ***vt.*** **-cled, -cling** **1** to pass through a cycle again **2** to use again and again, as the same water **3** *a)* to process in order to use again *[to recycle* paper*]* *b)* to gather up and turn in (newspapers, etc.) for such processing

red (red) ***n.*** ⟦OE *read*⟧ **1** the color of blood **2** any red pigment **3** [*often* **R-**] [Inf.] a communist —***adj.*** **red'der, red'dest** **1** of the color red **2** [*often* **R-**] communist —**in the red** losing money —**see red** [Inf.] to become angry —**red'dish** ***adj.*** —**red'ness** ***n.***

re·dact (ri dakt') ***vt.*** ⟦< L *redigere,* get in order⟧ to prepare for publication; edit —**re·dac'tion** ***n.*** —**re·dac'tor** ***n.***

red blood cell (or **corpuscle**) ERYTHROCYTE

red'-blood'ed ***adj.*** high-spirited and strong-willed; vigorous

red'cap' ***n.*** a baggage porter, as in a railroad station

red carpet a very grand or impressive welcome and entertainment: with *the* —**red'-car'pet** ***adj.***

red'coat' ***n.*** a British soldier in a uniform with a red coat, as during the American Revolution

Red Cross an international society for the relief of suffering in time of war or disaster

redd (red) ***vt., vi.*** **redd** or **redd'ed, redd'ing** ⟦< OE *hreddan,* take away⟧ [Inf. or Dial.] to put in order; tidy: usually with *up*

red deer a deer of Europe and Asia

red·den (red''n) ***vt.*** to make red —***vi.*** to become red; esp., to blush

re·deem (ri dēm') ***vt.*** ⟦< L *re(d)-,* back + *emere,* get⟧ **1** to buy or get back; recover **2** to pay off (a mortgage, etc.) **3** to turn in (a coupon, etc.) for a discount, premium, etc. **4** to ransom **5** to deliver from sin **6** to fulfill (a promise) **7** *a)* to make amends or atone for *b)* to restore (oneself) to favor —**re·deem'a·ble** ***adj.*** —**re·deem'er** ***n.*** —**re·demp·tion** (ri demp'shən) ***n.***

re·de·ploy (rē'di ploi') ***vt., vi.*** to move (troops, etc.) from one front or area to another —**re'de·ploy'ment** ***n.***

re·de·vel·op (rē'di vel'əp) ***vt.*** **1** to develop again **2** to rebuild or restore —**re'de·vel'op·ment** ***n.***

red'-flag' ***vt.*** **-flagged', -flag'ging** to mark or otherwise indicate as being risky, etc.

red'-hand'ed ***adv.*** in the very commission of crime or wrongdoing

red'head' ***n.*** a person with red hair

red herring ⟦< herring drawn across the trace in hunting to divert the hounds⟧ something used to divert attention from the basic issue

red'-hot' ***adj.*** **1** hot enough to glow **2** very excited, angry, etc. **3** very new

re·dis'trict ***vt.*** to divide anew into districts

red'-let'ter ***adj.*** designating a memorable or joyous day or event

red'lin'ing (-līn'iŋ) ***n.*** ⟦from outlining such areas in red on a map⟧ the refusal by some banks or companies to issue loans or insurance on property in certain neighborhoods

re·do (rē do͞o') ***vt.*** **-did', -done', -do'ing** **1** to do again **2** to redecorate

red·o·lent (red''l ənt) ***adj.*** ⟦< L *re(d)-,* intens. + *olere,* to smell⟧ **1** sweet-smelling **2** smelling *(of)* **3** suggestive *(of)* —**red'o·lence** ***n.***

re·dou·ble (rē dub'əl) ***vt., vi.*** **-bled, -bling** to make or become twice as much or twice as great

re·doubt (ri dout') ***n.*** ⟦see REDUCE⟧ **1** a breastwork **2** any stronghold

re·doubt'a·ble ***adj.*** ⟦< L *re-,* intens. + *dubitare,* to doubt⟧ formidable —**re·doubt'a·bly** ***adv.***

re·dound (ri dound') ***vi.*** ⟦< L *re(d)-,* intens. + *undare,* to surge⟧ **1** to have a result *(to* the credit or discredit of) **2** to come back; react *(upon)*

THESAURUS

recreation ***n.*** amusement, relaxation, diversion, play, fun, entertainment, enjoyment, festivity, hobby, holiday, vacation, pastime, pleasure, game, avocation, refreshment; see also SPORT 1.

recruit ***n.*** new person, novice, beginner, selectee, draftee, trainee, volunteer, enlisted person, serviceman, servicewoman, soldier, sailor, marine, rookie*; see also SOLDIER.

recruit ***v.*** **1** [To raise troops] draft, call up, select, supply, muster, deliver, sign up, induct, take in, find manpower, call to arms, bring into service; see also ENLIST 1. **2** [To gather needed resources] restore, store up, replenish; see GET 1.

rectangle ***n.*** geometrical figure, square, box, oblong, four-sided figure, right-angled parallelogram; see also FORM 1.

rectangular ***a.*** square, four-sided, right-angled; see ANGULAR.

rectitude ***n.*** integrity, trustworthiness, responsibility; see HONESTY.

recuperate ***v.*** heal, pull through, get back on one's feet; see RECOVER 3.

recur ***v.*** return, reappear, crop up again; see HAPPEN 2, REPEAT 1.

recurrent ***a.*** reoccurring, repetitive, habitual; see REPEATED 1.

recycle ***v.*** start over, start again, restart; see BEGIN 1, RESUME.

red ***n.*** *Tints and shades of red include the following:* scarlet, carmine, vermilion, crimson, cerise, cherry red, ruby, garnet, maroon, brick red, claret, rust, red gold, magenta, pink, fuchsia, coral red, blood red, russet, terra cotta, Chinese red, Congo red, Turkey red, aniline red, chrome red, rose, rose blush, old rose, fire engine red; see also COLOR. —**in the red** in debt, losing money, going broke*; see RUINED 3. —**see red*** become angry, lose one's temper, get mad; see RAGE 1.

red-blooded ***a.*** robust, vigorous, hearty; see HEALTHY.

redden ***v.*** flush, rouge, color, blush.

reddish ***a.*** flushed, somewhat red, rose; see RED, *n.*

redecorate ***v.*** refurbish, refresh, renew, paint, repaint, repaper, restore, recondition, remodel, renovate, revamp, reaarrange, touch up, patch up, plaster, refurnish, wallpaper, clean up, carpet, do over*, fix up*; see also DECORATE.

redeem ***v.*** **1** [To recover through a payment] buy back, repay, purchase; see GET 1. **2** [To save] liberate, set free, deliver; see RESCUE 1. —**redeem oneself** atone, give satisfaction, make amends; see PAY FOR.

redeemer ***n.*** rescuer, deliverer, liberator; see PROTECTOR.

redemption ***n.*** regeneration, salvation, rebirth; see RESCUE 1.

redheaded ***a.*** auburn-haired, red-haired, sandy-haired, titian-haired, strawberry-blonde, carrot-topped.

red-hot ***a.*** **1** [Burning] heated, sizzling, scorching; see BURNING, HOT 1. **2** [Raging] vehement, violent, furious; see EXTREME. **3** [Newest] latest, most recent, hippest*; see MODERN 1.

redo ***v.*** start over, redesign, rethink, go back to the drawing board, revamp, do over again, redecorate, remodel; see also REPEAT.

redone ***a.*** done over, refinished, fixed up; see IMPROVED.

re·dress (ri dres′; *for n., usually* rē′dres′) ***vt.*** ⟦see RE- & DRESS⟧ to compensate for (a wrong, etc.) —***n.*** **1** compensation **2** a redressing

Red Sea sea between NE Africa & W Arabia

red snapper a reddish, edible, deep-water fish

red tape ⟦< tape for tying official papers⟧ rules and details that waste time and effort

red tide sea water discolored by red algae poisonous to marine life

re·duce (ri do͞os′) ***vt.*** **-duced′**, **-duc′ing** ⟦< L *re-*, back + *ducere,* to lead⟧ **1** to lessen, as in size, price, etc. **2** to put into a different form **3** to lower, as in rank or condition —***vi.*** to lose weight, as by dieting

re·duc·tion (ri duk′shən) ***n.*** **1** a reducing or being reduced **2** anything made by reducing **3** the amount by which anything is reduced

re·dun·dant (ri dun′dənt) ***adj.*** ⟦see REDOUND⟧ **1** excess; superfluous **2** wordy **3** unnecessary to the meaning: said of words and affixes —**re·dun′dan·cy** ***n.***

red′wood′ ***n.*** **1** a giant evergreen of the Pacific coast **2** its reddish wood

re·ech·o or **re-ech·o** (rē ek′ō) ***vt.***, ***vi.*** **-oed**, **-o·ing** to echo back or again —***n.***, *pl.* **-oes** the echo of an echo

reed (rēd) ***n.*** ⟦OE *hreod*⟧ **1** a tall, slender grass **2** a rustic musical instrument made from a hollow stem **3** *Music* a thin strip of wood, plastic, etc. placed against the mouthpiece, as of a clarinet, and vibrated by the breath to produce a tone —**reed′y**, **-i·er**, **-i·est**, ***adj.***

reef[1] (rēf) ***n.*** ⟦prob. < ON *rif*, a rib⟧ a ridge of rock, coral, or sand at or near the surface of the water

reef[2] (rēf) ***n.*** ⟦ME *riff*⟧ a part of a sail which can be folded or rolled up and made fast to reduce the area exposed to the wind —***vt.***, ***vi.*** to reduce the size of (a sail) by taking in part of it

reef′er ***n.*** [Slang] a marijuana cigarette

reek (rēk) ***n.*** ⟦OE *rec*⟧ a strong, unpleasant smell —***vi.*** to have a strong, offensive smell

reel[1] (rēl) ***n.*** ⟦OE *hreol*⟧ **1** a spool on which wire, film, fishing line, etc. is wound **2** the quantity of wire, film, etc. usually wound on one reel —***vt.*** to wind on a reel —***vi.*** **1** to sway, stagger, etc. as from drunkenness or dizziness **2** to spin; whirl —**reel in** **1** to wind on a reel **2** to pull in (a fish) by using a reel —**reel off** to tell, write, etc. easily and quickly —**reel out** to unwind from a reel

reel[2] (rēl) ***n.*** ⟦prob. < prec.⟧ a lively dance

re·en·try or **re-en·try** (rē en′trē) ***n.***, *pl.* **-tries** a coming back, as of a space vehicle, into the earth's atmosphere

ref[1] (ref) ***n.***, ***vt.***, ***vi.*** [Inf.] *short for* REFEREE

ref[2] *abbrev.* **1** referee **2** reference **3** reformed **4** refund

re·face (rē fās′) ***vt.*** **-faced′**, **-fac′ing** to put a new facing or covering on

re·fec·tion (ri fek′shən) ***n.*** ⟦< L *re-*, again + *facere*, make⟧ a light meal; lunch

re·fec·to·ry (ri fek′tə rē) ***n.***, *pl.* **-ries** a dining hall, as in a monastery

re·fer (ri fʉr′) ***vt.*** **-ferred′**, **-fer′ring** ⟦< L *re-*, back + *ferre*, to bear⟧ **1** to submit (a quarrel, etc.) for settlement **2** to direct *to* someone or something for aid, information, etc. —***vi.*** **1** to relate or apply (*to*) **2** to direct attention (*to*) **3** to turn (*to*) for information, aid, etc. —**re·fer′rer** ***n.***

ref·er·ee (ref′ə rē′) ***n.*** **1** one to whom something is referred for decision **2** an official who enforces the rules in certain sports contests —***vt.***, ***vi.*** **-eed′**, **-ee′ing** to act as referee (in)

ref·er·ence (ref′ər əns, ref′rəns) ***n.*** **1** a referring or being referred **2** relation *[in reference to his letter]* **3** *a)* the directing of attention to a person or thing *b)* a mention **4** *a)* an indication, as in a book, of some other source of information *b)* such a source **5** *a)* one who can offer information or recommendation *b)* a statement of character, ability, etc. by such a person

ref·er·en·dum (ref′ə ren′dəm) ***n.***, *pl.* **-dums** or **-da** (-də) ⟦L: see REFER⟧ **1** the submission of a law to a direct vote of the people **2** the vote itself

ref·er·ent (ref′ər ənt) ***n.*** the thing referred to, esp. by a word or expression

re·fer·ral (ri fʉr′əl) ***n.*** **1** a referring or being referred **2** a person who is referred to another

re·fill (rē fil′; *for n.* rē′fil′) ***vt.***, ***vi.*** to fill again —***n.*** **1** a unit to refill a special container **2** a refilling of a medical prescription —**re·fill′a·ble** ***adj.***

re·fine (ri fīn′) ***vt.*** **-fined′**, **-fin′ing** ⟦RE- + *fine*, make fine⟧ **1** to free from impurities, etc. **2** to make more polished or elegant

re·fined′ ***adj.*** **1** made free from impurities; purified **2** cultivated, elegant, etc. **3** subtle, precise, etc.

re·fine′ment ***n.*** **1** *a)* a refining or being refined *b)* the result of this **2** delicacy or elegance of manners, etc. **3** an improvement **4** a fine distinction; subtlety

re·fin′er·y ***n.***, *pl.* **-er·ies** a plant for purifying materials, as oil, sugar, etc.

re·fin·ish (rē fin′ish) ***vt.*** to change or restore the finish of (furniture, etc.) —**re·fin′ish·er** ***n.***

THESAURUS

redress ***n.*** compensation, reparation, amends; see PAYMENT 1.

red tape ***n.*** **1** [Delay] wait, roadblock, holdup; see DELAY. **2** [Bureaucracy] paperwork, inflexible routine, officialdom; see GOVERNMENT 1, 2.

reduce ***v.*** **1** [To make less] lessen, diminish, cut down; see DECREASE 2. **2** [To defeat] conquer, overcome, subdue; see DEFEAT 2, 3. **3** [To humble] degrade, demote, abase; see HUMBLE, HUMILIATE.

reduced ***a.*** **1** [Made smaller] lessened, decreased, diminished, shortened, abridged, abbreviated, condensed, miniaturized, transistorized, compressed, economized, cut down, shrunk, subtracted, contracted, melted, boiled down.—*Ant.* SPREAD, enlarged, stretched. **2** [Made lower] lowered, abated, sunk, deflated, leveled, marked down, discounted, cheapened, weakened, debilitated, humbled, demoted, degraded, downgraded.—*Ant.* RAISED, heightened, elevated.

reduction ***n.*** **1** [The process of making smaller] contraction, abatement, reducing, refinement, diminution, lowering, lessening, shortening, condensation, decrease, loss, compression, depression, subtraction, discount, shrinkage, atrophy, constriction, modification, curtailment, abbreviation, miniaturization, abridgment, mitigation, remission, decline.—*Ant.* INCREASE, increasing, enlargement. **2** [An amount that constitutes reduction] decrease, rebate, cut; see DISCOUNT.

redundant ***a.*** wordy, bombastic, verbose; see DULL 3, 4.

reeducate ***v.*** reinstruct, readjust, rehabilitate; see TEACH.

reef[1] ***n.*** ridge, shoal, sand bar; see ROCK 2.

reek ***n.*** stench, stink, smell; see SMELL 2.

reek ***v.*** give off an odor, emit a stench, stink; see SMELL 1.

reel[1] ***n.*** spool, bobbin, spindle; see ROLL 2.

reexamine ***v.*** go back over, review, check thoroughly; see EXAMINE.

refer ***v.*** **1** [To concern] regard, relate, have relation, have to do with, apply, be about, answer to, involve, connect, be a matter of, have a bearing on, correspond with, bear upon, comprise, include, belong, pertain, have reference, take in, cover, point, hold, encompass, incorporate, touch, deal with; see also CONCERN 1. **2** [To mention] allude to, bring up, direct a remark, make reference, ascribe, direct attention, attribute, cite, quote, hint at, point to, notice, indicate, speak about, suggest, touch on, give as an example, associate, exemplify, instance, excerpt, extract; see also MENTION. **3** [To direct] send to, put in touch with, relegate, commit, submit to, assign, give a recommendation to, introduce, designate; see also LEAD 1. **—referred to** **1** [Mentioned] brought up, alluded to, spoken about; see MENTIONED, SUGGESTED. **2** [Directed] recommended, sent on, introduced to; see PROPOSED.

referee ***n.*** arbitrator, conciliator, judge; see UMPIRE.

reference ***n.*** **1** [An allusion] mention, citation, implication; see HINT. **2** [A book of reference] original text, source, informant; see BOOK, DICTIONARY. **3** [A person vouching for another] associate, employer, patron; see FRIEND.

refine ***v.*** **1** [To purify] clarify, strain, filter; see CLEAN, PURIFY. **2** [To improve] perfect, polish, hone; see EXPLAIN.

refined ***a.*** **1** [Purified] cleaned, cleansed, aerated, strained, washed, clean, rarefied, boiled down, distilled, clarified, processed, tried, drained; see also PURE.—*Ant.* RAW, crude, unrefined. **2** [Genteel] cultivated, civilized, polished, elegant, well-bred, gracious, enlightened, gentlemanly, ladylike, restrained, gentle, mannerly, high-minded, suave, urbane, courteous; see also POLITE.

refinement ***n.*** **1** [The act of refining] cleansing, clearing, purification; see CLEANING. **2** [Culture] civilization, cultivation, sophistication, breeding, enlightenment, wide knowledge, lore, erudition, science, scholarship, learning; see also CULTURE 1. **3** [Genteel feelings and behavior] elegance, politeness, polish, good manners, suavity, savoir-faire, courtesy, grace, gentleness, tact, cultivation, graciousness, civility, affability, taste, discrimination, fineness, delicacy, dignity, urbanity; see also CULTURE 2.

refinished ***a.*** redone, remodeled, fixed up; see CHANGED 2, REPAIRED.

re·fit (rē fit′) ***vt.***, ***vi.*** **-fit′ted**, **-fit′ting** to make or be made fit for use again by repairing, reequipping, etc.
re·flect (ri flekt′) ***vt.*** ⟦< L *re-,* back + *flectere,* to bend⟧ **1** to throw back (light, heat, or sound) **2** to give back an image of **3** to bring as a result *[to reflect* honor on the city*]* —***vi.*** **1** to throw back light, heat, etc. **2** to give back an image **3** to think seriously (*on* or *upon*) **4** to cast blame or discredit (*on* or *upon*) —**re·flec′tive** ***adj.***
re·flec′tion ***n.*** **1** a reflecting or being reflected **2** anything reflected **3** contemplation **4** a thoughtful idea or remark **5** blame; discredit
re·flec′tor ***n.*** a surface, object, etc. that reflects light, sound, heat, etc.
re·flex (rē′fleks′) ***adj.*** ⟦see REFLECT⟧ designating or of an involuntary action, as a sneeze, resulting from the direct transmission of a stimulus to a muscle or gland —***n.*** a reflex action
re·flex·ive (ri flek′siv) ***adj.*** **1** designating a grammatical relation in which a verb's subject and object refer to the same person or thing (Ex.: I wash myself) **2** designating a verb, pronoun, etc. in such a relation —**re·flex′ive·ly** ***adv.***
re·for·est (rē fôr′ist) ***vt.***, ***vi.*** to plant new trees on (land once forested) —**re′for·est·a′tion** ***n.***
re·form (ri fôrm′) ***vt.*** ⟦see RE- & FORM⟧ **1** to make better as by stopping abuses **2** to cause (a person) to behave better —***vi.*** to become better in behavior —***n.*** a reforming
re-form (rē fôrm′) ***vt.***, ***vi.*** to form again
ref·or·ma·tion (ref′ər mā′shən) ***n.*** a reforming or being reformed —**the Reformation** the 16th-c. religious movement that resulted in establishing the Protestant churches
re·form·a·to·ry (ri fôr′mə tôr′ē) ***n.***, *pl.* **-ries** an institution to which young offenders are sent to be reformed
re·form′er ***n.*** one who seeks to bring about political or social reform
re·fract (ri frakt′) ***vt.*** ⟦< L *refractus,* turned aside < *re-,* back + *frangere,* to break⟧ to cause (a ray of light, etc.) to undergo refraction
re·frac′tion ***n.*** the bending of a ray or wave of light, heat, or sound as it passes from one medium into another
re·frac·to·ry (ri frak′tər ē) ***adj.*** ⟦see REFRACT⟧ hard to manage; stubborn
re·frain[1] (ri frān′) ***vi.*** ⟦< L *re-,* back + *frenare,* to curb⟧ to hold back; keep oneself (*from* doing something)
re·frain[2] (ri frān′) ***n.*** ⟦see REFRACT⟧ a phrase or verse repeated at intervals in a song or poem
re·fresh (ri fresh′) ***vt.*** **1** to make fresh by cooling, wetting, etc. **2** to make (a person) feel cooler, stronger, etc., as by food, sleep, etc. **3** to replenish **4** to stimulate (the memory, etc.)
re·fresh′ing ***adj.*** **1** that refreshes **2** pleasingly new or different
re·fresh′ment ***n.*** **1** a refreshing or being refreshed **2** something that refreshes **3** [*pl.*] food or drink or both
re·frig·er·ant (ri frij′ər ənt) ***n.*** a substance used in refrigeration
re·frig·er·ate (ri frij′ə rāt′) ***vt.*** **-at′ed**, **-at′ing** ⟦< L *re-,* intens. + *frigus,* cold⟧ to make or keep cool or cold, as for preserving —**re·frig′er·a′tion** ***n.***
re·frig′er·a′tor ***n.*** a box or room in which food, drink, etc. are kept cool
ref·uge (ref′yo͞oj) ***n.*** ⟦< L *re-,* back + *fugere,* flee⟧ (a) shelter or protection from danger, difficulty, etc.
ref·u·gee (ref′yoo jē′, ref′yoo jē′) ***n.*** one who flees from home or country to seek refuge elsewhere
re·ful·gent (ri ful′jənt) ***adj.*** ⟦< L *re-,* back + *fulgere,* shine⟧ shining; radiant; glowing —**re·ful′gence** ***n.***
re·fund (ri fund′; *for n.* rē′fund′) ***vt.***, ***vi.*** ⟦< L *re-,* back + *fundere,* pour⟧ to give back (money, etc.); repay —***n.*** a refunding or the amount refunded
re·fur·bish (ri fur′bish) ***vt.*** ⟦RE- + FURBISH⟧ to renovate —**re·fur′bish·ment** ***n.***
re·fuse[1] (ri fyo͞oz′) ***vt.***, ***vi.*** **-fused′**, **-fus′ing** ⟦< L *re-,* back + *fundere,* pour⟧ **1** to decline to accept **2** to decline (to do

THESAURUS

reflect ***v.*** **1** [To contemplate] speculate, concentrate, weigh; see CONSIDER, THINK 1. **2** [To throw back] echo, reecho, repeat, match, take after, return, resonate, reverberate, copy, resound, reproduce, reply, be resonant, emulate, imitate, follow, catch, rebound, bounce. **3** [To throw back an image] mirror, shine, reproduce, show up on, flash, cast back, return, give forth.
reflection ***n.*** **1** [Thought] consideration, absorption, imagination, observation, thinking, contemplation, rumination, speculation, musing, deliberation, study, pondering, meditation, concentration, cogitation; see also THOUGHT 1. **2** [An image] impression, rays, light, shine, glitter, appearance, idea, reflected image, likeness, shadow, duplicate, picture, echo, representation, reproduction; see also COPY, IMAGE 2.
reflector ***n.*** shiny metal, glass, looking glass; see MIRROR.
reflex ***a.*** mechanical, unthinking, habitual; see AUTOMATIC, SPONTANEOUS.
reform ***n.*** reformation, betterment, new law; see IMPROVEMENT 2.
reform ***v.*** **1** [To change into a new form] reorganize, remodel, revise, repair, reconstruct, rearrange, transform, ameliorate, redeem, rectify, better, rehabilitate, improve, correct, cure, remedy, convert, mend, amend, restore, rebuild, reclaim, revolutionize, regenerate, refashion, renovate, renew, rework, reconstitute, make over, remake; see also CORRECT, REPAIR.—*Ant.* CORRUPT, degrade, botch. **2** [To correct evils] amend, clean out, give a new basis, abolish, repeal, uplift, ameliorate, rectify, regenerate, give new life to, remedy, stamp out, make better, standardize, bring up to code; see also IMPROVE 1. **3** [To change one's conduct for the better] resolve, mend, regenerate, uplift, make amends, make a new start, make resolutions, turn over a new leaf, go straight*, clean up one's act*, swear off; see also sense 2.
Reformation ***n.*** Renaissance, Lutheranism, Protestantism, Puritanism, Calvinism, Anglicanism, Unitarianism, Counter Reformation, Protestant Movement; see also REVOLUTION 2.
reformed ***a.*** **1** [Changed] altered, transformed, shifted, reconstituted, reorganized, shuffled, reestablished, revolutionized, rectified, amended, reset, reworked, renewed, regenerated, redone, rejiggered; see also CHANGED 2, IMPROVED.—*Ant.* preserved, degenerated, deteriorated. **2** [Changed for the better in behavior] converted, improved, redeemed, born-again, gone straight*, turned over a new leaf; see also POLITE, RIGHTEOUS 1.
refrain[1] ***v.*** cease, avoid, forbear; see ABSTAIN.
refrain[2] ***n.*** undersong*, theme, strain; see MUSIC 1, SONG.
refresh ***v.*** invigorate, animate, exhilarate; see RENEW 1.
refreshing ***a.*** invigorating, rousing, exhilarating; see STIMULATING.
refreshment ***n.*** snack, light meal, treat; see DRINK 1, FOOD.
refrigerate ***v.*** chill, make cold, freeze; see COOL.
refrigeration ***n.*** cooling, chilling, freezing; see PRESERVATION.
refrigerator ***n.*** fridge*, icebox, cooler, refrigerator car, cooling apparatus, refrigeration equipment, deep freezer, freezer, deepfreeze.
refuge ***n.*** **1** [A place of protection] shelter, asylum, sanctuary, covert, home, retreat, anchorage, nunnery, convent, monastery, poorhouse, safe place, hiding place, game preserve, safe haven, safe house, harbor, haven, fortress, stronghold, hideaway*, hideout*. **2** [A means of resort] alternative, resource, last resort; see ESCAPE.
refugee ***n.*** exile, expatriate, fugitive, emigrant, renegade, foreigner, castaway, derelict, defector, homeless person, leper, pariah, outlaw, prodigal, displaced person, alien, outcast.
refund ***n.*** return, reimbursement, repayment, remuneration, compensation, allowance, payment for expenses, rebate, discount, settlement, retribution, satisfaction, consolation, money back; see also PAYMENT 1.
refund ***v.*** pay back, reimburse, remit, return, repay, relinquish, make good, balance, recoup, adjust, reward, restore, redeem, make repayment to, compensate, recompense, make amends, redress, remunerate, give back, settle, honor a claim, kick back*, make good*, make up for; see also PAY 1.
refunded ***a.*** repaid, reimbursed, discharged; see PAID, RETURNED.
refusal ***n.*** repudiation, renunciation, rebuff, snub, rejection, nonacceptance, denial, disavowal, noncompliance, opposition, forbidding, veto, interdiction, proscription, ban, writ, exclusion, negation, repulse, withholding, disclaimer, nonconsent, unwillingness, regrets, declination, repulsion, reversal, dissent, prohibition, disfavor, disapproval, curb, restraint.
refuse[1] ***v.*** dissent, desist, repel, rebuff, scorn, pass up, reject, disallow, have no plans to, not anticipate, demur, protest, withdraw, hold back, withhold, shun, turn thumbs down on, evade, dodge, ignore, spurn, regret, turn down, turn from, beg to be excused, send regrets, not budge, cut out of the budget, not budget, not care to, refuse to receive, dispense with, not be at home to, say no, make excuses, disapprove, set aside, turn

something), to grant the request of (someone), etc. —**re·fus'al** ***n.***

ref·use[2] (ref'yo͞os, -yo͞oz) ***n.*** ⟦see prec.⟧ waste; trash; rubbish

re·fute (ri fyo͞ot') ***vt.*** **-fut'ed, -fut'ing** ⟦L *refutare,* repel⟧ to prove to be false or wrong —**re·fut'a·ble** ***adj.*** —**ref·u·ta·tion** (ref'yə tā'shən) ***n.***

reg *abbrev.* **1** registered **2** regular **3** regulation

re·gain (ri gān') ***vt.*** **1** to get back; recover **2** to get back to

re·gal (rē'gəl) ***adj.*** ⟦< L *rex,* king⟧ of, like, or fit for a monarch

re·gale (ri gāl') ***vt.*** **-galed', -gal'ing** ⟦< Fr *ré-* (see RE-) + OFr *gale,* joy⟧ to amuse or delight as with a story

re·ga·li·a (ri gāl'yə) ***pl.n.*** ⟦see REGAL⟧ **1** royal insignia **2** the insignia as of a rank or society **3** finery

re·gard (ri gärd') ***n.*** ⟦see RE- & GUARD⟧ **1** a steady look; gaze **2** consideration; concern **3** respect and affection **4** reference; relation *[in regard to your plan]* **5** [*pl.*] good wishes —***vi.*** **1** to look at attentively **2** to consider **3** to hold in affection and respect **4** to concern or involve —**as regards** concerning

re·gard'ing ***prep.*** concerning; about

re·gard'less ***adv.*** [Inf.] without regard for objections, etc.; anyway —**regardless of** in spite of

re·gat·ta (ri gät'ə) ***n.*** ⟦< It⟧ **1** a boat race **2** a series of boat races

re·gen·er·ate (ri jen'ə rit; *for v.,* -rāt') ***adj.*** ⟦see RE- & GENERATE⟧ **1** spiritually reborn **2** renewed or restored —***vt.*** **-at'ed, -at'ing** **1** to cause to be spiritually reborn **2** to cause to be completely reformed **3** to bring into existence again —***vi.*** to form again, or be made anew —**re·gen'er·a'tion** ***n.*** —**re·gen'er·a'tive** ***adj.***

re·gent (rē'jənt) ***n.*** ⟦< L *regere,* to rule⟧ **1** a person appointed to rule when a monarch is absent, too young, etc. **2** a member of a governing board, as of a university —**re'gen·cy** ***n.***

reg·gae (reg'ā) ***n.*** ⟦< ?⟧ a form of strongly syncopated popular Jamaican music

reg·i·cide (rej'ə sīd') ***n.*** ⟦< L *regis,* of a king + *-cida* (see -CIDE)⟧ **1** one who kills a monarch **2** the killing of a monarch

re·gime or **ré·gime** (rə zhēm', rā-) ***n.*** ⟦see fol.⟧ **1** a political system **2** an administration

reg·i·men (rej'ə mən) ***n.*** ⟦< L *regere,* to rule⟧ a system of diet, exercise, etc. to improve health

reg·i·ment (rej'ə mənt; *for v.,* -ment') ***n.*** ⟦< L *regere,* to rule⟧ a military unit, smaller than a division —***vt.*** **1** to organize systematically **2** to subject to strict discipline and control —**reg'i·men'tal** ***adj.*** —**reg'i·men·ta'tion** ***n.***

Re·gi·na (ri jī'nə) capital of Saskatchewan, Canada: pop. 180,000

re·gion (rē'jən) ***n.*** ⟦< L *regere,* to rule⟧ **1** a large, indefinite part of the earth's surface **2** a division or part, as of an organism —**re'gion·al** ***adj.***

re'gion·al·ism' ***n.*** **1** regional quality or character in life or literature **2** a word, etc. peculiar to some region

reg·is·ter (rej'is tər) ***n.*** ⟦< L *regerere,* to record⟧ **1** *a)* a list of names, items, etc. *b)* a book in which this is kept **2** a device for recording *[a cash register]* **3** an opening into a room by which the amount of warm or cold air passing through can be controlled **4** *Music* a part of the range of a voice or instrument —***vt.*** **1** to enter in a list **2** to indicate on or as on a scale **3** to show, as by facial expression *[to register surprise]* **4** to protect (mail) by paying a fee to have it handled by a special postal service —***vi.*** **1** to enter one's name in a list, as of voters **2** to enroll in a school **3** to make an impression —**reg'is·trant** (-trənt) ***n.***

registered nurse a trained nurse who has passed a state examination

reg·is·trar (rej'i strär') ***n.*** one who keeps records, as in a college

reg·is·tra·tion (rej'i strā'shən) ***n.*** **1** a registering or being registered **2** an entry in a register **3** the number of persons registered

reg'is·try (-is trē) ***n.***, *pl.* **-tries** **1** a registering **2** an office where registers are kept **3** an official record or list

reg·nant (reg'nənt) ***adj.*** **1** ruling **2** predominant **3** prevalent

re·gress (rē'gres; *for v.* ri gres') ***n.*** ⟦< L *re-,* back + *gradi,* go⟧ backward movement —***vi.*** to go back —**re·gres'sion** ***n.*** —**re·gres'sive** ***adj.***

re·gret (ri gret') ***vt.*** **-gret'ted, -gret'ting** ⟦< OFr *regreter,* mourn⟧ to feel sorry about (an event, one's acts, etc.) —***n.*** remorse, esp. over one's acts or omissions —**(one's)**

THESAURUS

away, beg off, brush off*, not buy*, hold off, turn one's back on, turn a deaf ear to; see also DENY.—*Ant.* ALLOW, admit, consent.

refuse[2] ***n.*** leavings, remains, residue; see TRASH 1.

refused ***a.*** declined, rejected, rebuffed, vetoed, repudiated, forbidden, denied, disowned, disavowed, forsaken, blocked, repelled, closed to, dismissed, turned down, not budgeted, not in the budget.—*Ant.* PERMITTED, allowed, consented to.

refute ***v.*** disprove, answer, prove false; see DENY.

regain ***v.*** recapture, retrieve, reacquire; see RECOVER 1.

regard ***n.*** **1** [A look] gaze, glance, once-over*; see LOOK 3. **2** [A favorable opinion] esteem, respect, honor, favor, liking, interest, fondness, attachment, deference, opinion, sympathy, estimation, appreciation, reverence, consideration, love, affection, value, devotion; see also ADMIRATION.

regard ***v.*** **1** [To look at] observe, notice, mark; see SEE 1. **2** [To have an attitude] surmise, look upon, view; see CONSIDER, THINK 1. **3** [To hold in esteem] respect, esteem, value; see ADMIRE.

regarding ***a., prep.*** concerning, with reference to, in relation to, as regards; see also ABOUT 2. —**as regards** concerning, regarding, respecting; see ABOUT 2. —**in regard to** as to, concerning, with regard to; see ABOUT 2, REGARDING.

regardless ***a.*** **1** [Indifferent] negligent, careless, unobservant, unheeding, inattentive, inconsiderate, reckless, inadvertent, unfeeling, deaf, blind, heedless, neglectful, mindless, insensitive, lax, listless, uninterested, unconcerned.—*Ant.* OBSERVANT, alert, vigilant. **2** [In spite of; *usually used with "of"*] despite, aside from, distinct from, without regard to, without considering, notwithstanding, at any cost, leaving aside; see also ALTHOUGH, BUT 1.

regards ***n.*** best wishes, compliments, greetings, salutations, remembrances, respects, love, deference, one's best, commendation, love and kisses*; see also GREETING.

regenerate ***v.*** restore, re-create, renew; see PRODUCE 2, REVIVE 1.

regeneration ***n.*** rebuilding, rehabilitation, renovation; see REPAIR.

regime ***n.*** administration, management, political system; see GOVERNMENT 2.

regiment ***n.*** corps, soldiers, military organization; see ARMY 2.

regimentation ***n.*** discipline, strictness, collectivization, organization, planned economy, standardization, regulation, uniformity, arrangement, mechanization, institutionalization, classification, division, lining up, adjustment, harmonization, grouping, ordering; see also RESTRAINT 2.

region ***n.*** **1** [An indefinite area] country, district, territory, section, sector, province, zone, realm, vicinity, quarter, locale, locality, environs, precinct, county, neighborhood, terrain, domain, range. **2** [A limited area] precinct, ward, block; see AREA. **3** [Scope] sphere, province, realm; see FIELD 3.

regional ***a.*** provincial, territorial, local, environmental, positional, geographical, parochial, sectional, topical, locational, insular, topographic.

register ***n.*** **1** [A list] file, registry, roll; see LIST, RECORD 1. **2** [A heating regulator] grate, hot-air vent, radiator; see APPLIANCE.

register ***v.*** **1** [To record] check in, enroll, file; see LIST 1, RECORD 1. **2** [To indicate] point to, designate, record; see NAME 2. **3** [To show] express, disclose, manifest; see DISPLAY. **4** [To enlist or enroll] go through registration, check into, make an entry, sign up for, check in, sign in, join.

registration ***n.*** **1** [The act of registering] enrolling, signing up, certification, matriculation, recording, listing, filing, cataloging, booking, noting down, stamping, authorizing, notarization; see also ENROLLMENT 1. **2** [Those who have registered] enrollment, turnout, registrants, voters, hotel guests, students, student body, delegation.

regress ***v.*** backslide, relapse, revert; see RETREAT, SINK 1.

regressive ***a.*** conservative, reverse, reactionary; see BACKWARD 1.

regret ***n.*** **1** [Remorse] concern, compunction, worry, repentance, self-reproach, self-condemnation, self-disgust, misgiving, regretfulness, nostalgia, self-accusation, contrition, qualm, scruple, penitence, bitterness, disappointment, dissatisfaction, uneasiness, discomfort, annoyance, spiritual disturbance; see also CARE 2.—*Ant.* COMFORT, satisfaction, ease. **2** [Grief] sorrow, pain, anxiety; see GRIEF.

regret ***v.*** **1** [To be sorry for] mourn, bewail, lament, cry over, rue, grieve, repent, have compunctions about, look back upon, feel conscience-stricken, moan, have a bad conscience, have qualms about, weep over, be disturbed over, feel uneasy about, laugh out of the other side of one's mouth*, kick oneself*, bite one's tongue*, cry over

regrets a polite declining of an invitation —**re·gret′ful** *adj.* —**re·gret′ta·ble** *adj.*

re·group′ *vt., vi.* **1** to reassemble or reorganize **2** to collect oneself, as after a setback

reg·u·lar (reg′yə lər) *adj.* ⟦< L *regula,* a rule⟧ **1** conforming to a rule, type, etc.; orderly; symmetrical **2** conforming to a fixed principle or procedure **3** customary or established **4** consistent *[a regular customer]* **5** functioning in a normal way *[a regular pulse]* **6** properly qualified *[a regular doctor]* **7** designating or of the standing army of a country **8** [Inf.] *a)* thorough; complete *[a regular nuisance]* *b)* pleasant, friendly, etc. —*n.* **1** a regular soldier or a player who is not a substitute **2** [Inf.] one who is regular in attendance **3** *Politics* a loyal party member —**reg′u·lar′i·ty** (-lar′ə tē), *pl.* **-ties,** *n.* —**reg′u·lar·ize′, -ized′, -iz′ing,** *vt.* —**reg′u·lar·ly** *adv.*

reg·u·late (reg′yə lāt′) *vt.* **-lat′ed, -lat′ing** ⟦< L *regula,* a rule⟧ **1** to control or direct according to a rule, principle, etc. **2** to adjust to a standard, rate, etc. **3** to adjust for accurate operation —**reg′u·la′tor** *n.* —**reg′u·la·to′ry** (-lə tôr′ē) *adj.*

reg′u·la′tion *n.* **1** a regulating or being regulated **2** a rule or law regulating conduct —*adj.* usual; regular

re·gur·gi·tate (ri gur′jə tāt′) *vi., vt.* **-tat′ed, -tat′ing** ⟦< ML *re-,* back + LL *gurgitare,* to flood⟧ to bring (partly digested food) back up to the mouth —**re·gur′gi·ta′tion** *n.*

re·hab (rē′hab′) *n. short for* REHABILITATION —*vt.* **-habbed′, -hab′bing** *short for* REHABILITATE

re·ha·bil·i·tate (rē′hə bil′ə tāt′) *vt.* **-tat′ed, -tat′ing** ⟦< L *re-,* back + *habere,* have⟧ **1** to restore to rank, reputation, etc. which one has lost **2** to put back in good condition **3** to bring or restore to a state of health, constructive activity, etc. —**re′ha·bil′i·ta′tion** *n.* —**re′ha·bil′i·ta′tive** *adj.*

re·hash (rē′hash′; *for v., also* rē hash′) *vt.* ⟦RE- + HASH⟧ to work up again or go over again —*n.* a rehashing

re·hearse (ri hurs′) *vt., vi.* **-hearsed′, -hears′ing** ⟦< OFr *re-,* again + *hercer,* to harrow⟧ to practice (a play, etc.) for public performance —**re·hears′al** *n.*

reign (rān) *n.* ⟦< L *regere,* to rule⟧ **1** royal power **2** dominance or sway **3** the period of rule, dominance, etc. —*vi.* **1** to rule as a sovereign **2** to prevail *[peace reigns]*

re·im·burse (rē′im burs′) *vt.* **-bursed′, -burs′ing** ⟦RE- + archaic *imburse,* to pay⟧ to pay back —**re′im·burse′ment** *n.*

rein (rān) *n.* ⟦see RETAIN⟧ **1** a narrow strap of leather attached in pairs to a horse's bit and manipulated to control the animal: *usually used in pl.* **2** [*pl.*] a means of controlling, etc. —**give (free) rein to** to allow to act without restraint

re·in·car·na·tion (rē′in kär nā′shən) *n.* ⟦see RE- & INCARNATE⟧ rebirth of the soul in another body —**re′in·car′nate′, -nat′ed, -nat′ing,** *vt.*

rein·deer (rān′dir′) *n., pl.* **-deer′** ⟦< ON *hreinn,* reindeer + *dȳr,* animal⟧ a large deer found in northern regions and domesticated there as a beast of burden

re·in·force (rē′in fôrs′) *vt.* **-forced′, -forc′ing** ⟦RE- + var. of ENFORCE⟧ **1** to strengthen (a military force) with more troops, ships, etc. **2** to strengthen, as by patching, propping, or adding new material —**re′in·force′ment** *n.*

re·in·state (rē′in stāt′) *vt.* **-stat′ed, -stat′ing** to restore to a former state, position, etc. —**re′in·state′ment** *n.*

re·it·er·ate (rē it′ə rāt′) *vt.* **-at′ed, -at′ing** ⟦< L *re-,* back + *iterare,* repeat⟧ to say or do again or repeatedly —**re·it′er·a′tion** *n.* —**re·it′er·a′tive** (-ə rāt′iv, -ər ə tiv) *adj.*

re·ject (ri jekt′; *for n.* rē′jekt) *vt.* ⟦< L *re-,* back + *jacere,* to throw⟧ **1** to refuse to take, agree to, use, believe, etc. **2** to discard —*n.* a rejected thing or person —**re·jec′tion** *n.*

re·jig·ger (rē jig′ər) *vt.* to adjust or alter the structure, terms, etc. of

re·joice (ri jois′) *vi., vt.* **-joiced′, -joic′ing** ⟦< OFr *re-,* again + *joïr,* be glad⟧ to be glad or happy

re·join (rē join′) *vt., vi.* **1** to join again; reunite **2** to answer

re·join·der (ri join′dər) *n.* ⟦see RE- & JOIN⟧ an answer, esp. to a reply

re·ju·ve·nate (ri jo͞o′və nāt′) *vt.* **-nat′ed, -nat′ing** ⟦< RE- + L *juvenis,* young⟧ to make feel or seem young again —**re·ju′ve·na′tion** *n.*

THESAURUS

spilt milk*.—*Ant.* CELEBRATE, be satisfied with, be happy. **2** [To disapprove of] deplore, be opposed to, deprecate; see DENOUNCE, DISLIKE.

regular *a.* **1** [In accordance with custom] customary, usual, routine; see CONVENTIONAL 1, 3. **2** [In accordance with law] normal, legitimate, lawful; see LEGAL. **3** [In accordance with an observable pattern] orderly, methodical, routine, symmetrical, precise, exact, systematic, arranged, organized, patterned, constant, congruous, consonant, consistent, invariable, formal, regulated, rational, rhythmic, periodic, measured, classified, in order, unconfused, harmonious, normal, natural, cyclic, successive, alternating, probable, recurrent, general, usual, expected, serial, automatic, mechanical, hourly, daily, monthly, weekly, annual, seasonal, yearly, diurnal, quotidian, anticipated, hoped for, counted on, generally occurring, in the natural course of events, punctual, steady, uniform.—*Ant.* IRREGULAR, sporadic, erratic.

regularity *n.* evenness, steadiness, uniformity, routine, constancy, consistency, invariability, recurrence, system, congruity, punctuality, homogeneity, rhythm, periodicity, rotation, conformity, proportion, symmetry, balance, cadence, harmony.

regularly *a.* customarily, habitually, punctually, systematically, unchangingly, as a rule, usually, commonly, as a matter of course, tirelessly, conventionally, ordinarily, repeatedly, frequently, faithfully, religiously, mechanically, automatically, normally, periodically, evenly, methodically, exactly, monotonously, rhythmically, steadily, typically, continually, like clockwork, cyclically, constantly, always, ceaselessly, time and time again, invariably, redundantly, hourly, incessantly, daily, 24/7*, perpetually, over and over again, weekly, monthly, annually, exactly; day in, day out.—*Ant.* IRREGULARLY, unevenly, brokenly.

regulate *v.* **1** [To control] rule, legislate, direct; see GOVERN, MANAGE 1. **2** [To adjust] arrange, methodize, classify, systematize, put in order, fix, settle, adapt, standardize, coordinate, allocate, readjust, reconcile, rectify, correct, improve, temper, set; see also ADJUST 1.

regulated *a.* fixed, adjusted, arranged, directed, controlled, supervised, methodized, systematized, settled, adapted, coordinated, reconciled, improved, standardized, tempered, ruled; see also CLASSIFIED, MANAGED 2, ORGANIZED.—*Ant.* CONFUSED, disarranged, upset.

regulation *n.* **1** [The act of regulating] handling, direction, control; see MANAGEMENT 1. **2** [A rule] principle, statute, ordinance; see COMMAND, LAW 3.

regulator *n.* control, thermostat, valve; see MACHINE.

rehabilitate *v.* restore, improve, reestablish; see RENEW 1.

rehabilitation *n.* rebuilding, reestablishment, remaking; see IMPROVEMENT 1, REPAIR.

rehearsal *n.* recitation, recital, trial performance, practice performance, experiment, test flight, reading, dress rehearsal, call; see also PERFORMANCE, PRACTICE 3.

rehearse *v.* **1** [To tell] describe, recount, relate; see TELL 1. **2** [To repeat] tell again, retell, do over, recapitulate, reenact; see also REPEAT 3. **3** [To practice for a performance] drill, experiment, hold rehearsals, speak from a script, run through, hold a reading, learn one's part; see also PRACTICE 1.

reign *v.* hold power, sit on the throne, wear the crown; see GOVERN, MANAGE 1.

reimburse *v.* repay, compensate, make reparations; see PAY 1, REFUND.

reimbursement *n.* compensation, restitution, recompense; see PAYMENT 1.

rein *n.* bridle strap, line, control; see ROPE. —**give (free) rein to** authorize, permit, condone; see ALLOW. —**keep a rein on** control, check, have authority over; see MANAGE 1.

reincarnation *n.* incarnation, transmigration of souls, rebirth; see BIRTH, RETURN 2.

reinforce *v.* buttress, bolster, augment; see STRENGTHEN.

reinforced *a.* supported, assisted, strengthened, augmented, buttressed, fortified, backed, built-up, stiffened, thickened, cushioned, lined; see also STRONG 2.

reinforcement *n.* **1** [Support] coating, concrete block, pillar; see SUPPORT 2. **2** [Military aid; *usually plural*] fresh troops, additional materiel, new ordnance; see HELP 1.

reject *v.* **1** [To refuse] repudiate, decline, renounce; see DENY, REFUSE. **2** [To discard] cast out, throw out, expel; see DISCARD.

rejected *a.* returned, given back, denied; see REFUSED.

rejection *n.* repudiation, denial, dismissal; see REFUSAL.

rejoice *v.* exult, enjoy, revel; see CELEBRATE 2.

rejuvenate *v.* reinvigorate, renew, refresh; see STRENGTHEN.

rejuvenation *n.* reinvigoration, stimulation, revivification; see

rel *abbrev.* **1** relative(ly) **2** religion

re·lapse (ri laps′; *for n., usually* rē′laps) ***vi.*** **-lapsed′, -laps′ing** ⟦see RE- & LAPSE⟧ to slip back into a former state, esp. into illness after apparent recovery —***n.*** a relapsing

re·late (ri lāt′) ***vt.*** **-lat′ed, -lat′ing** ⟦< L *relatus,* brought back⟧ **1** to tell the story of; narrate **2** to connect, as in thought or meaning —***vi.*** to have some connection or relation (*to*)

re·lat′ed ***adj.*** connected by kinship, origin, marriage, etc.

re·la′tion ***n.*** **1** a narrating **2** a narrative; account **3** connection, as in thought or meaning **4** connection by blood or marriage **5** a relative **6** [*pl.*] the connections between or among persons, nations, etc. —**in** (or **with**) **relation to** concerning; regarding —**re·la′tion·ship′** ***n.***

rel·a·tive (rel′ə tiv) ***adj.*** **1** related each to the other **2** pertinent; relevant **3** comparative *[living in relative comfort]* **4** meaningful only in relationship *["cold" is a relative term]* **5** *Gram.* that refers to an antecedent *[a relative pronoun]* —***n.*** one related by blood or marriage —**rel′a·tive·ly** ***adv.***

relative humidity the ratio of the amount of moisture in the air to the maximum amount possible at the given temperature

rel·a·tiv·i·ty (rel′ə tiv′ə tē) ***n.*** **1** a being relative **2** *Physics* the theory of the relative, rather than absolute, character of motion, velocity, mass, etc., and the interdependence of matter, time, and space

re·lax (ri laks′) ***vt., vi.*** ⟦< L *re-,* back + *laxare,* loosen⟧ **1** to make or become less firm, tense, severe, etc. **2** to rest, as from work —**re·lax′er** ***n.***

re·lax′ant ***adj.*** causing relaxation, esp. of muscles —***n.*** a relaxant drug

re·lax·a·tion (rē′lak sā′shən) ***n.*** **1** a relaxing or being relaxed **2** *a)* rest from work or effort *b)* recreation

re·lay (rē′lā′; *for v., also* ri lā′) ***n.*** ⟦< Fr *re-,* back + *laier,* to leave⟧ **1** a fresh supply of horses, etc., as for a stage of a journey **2** a relief crew of workers **3** a race (in full **relay race**) between teams, each member of which goes a part of the distance —***vt.*** **-layed′, -lay′ing** to get and pass on

re·lease (ri lēs′) ***vt.*** **-leased′, -leas′ing** ⟦see RELAX⟧ **1** to set free from confinement, work, pain, etc. **2** to let go *[to release an arrow]* **3** to permit to be issued, published, etc. —***n.*** **1** a releasing, as from prison **2** a film, news story, etc. released to the public **3** a written surrender of a claim, etc.

rel·e·gate (rel′ə gāt′) ***vt.*** **-gat′ed, -gat′ing** ⟦< L *re-,* away + *legare,* send⟧ **1** to exile or banish (*to*) **2** to consign or assign, esp. to an inferior position **3** to refer or hand over for decision —**rel′e·ga′tion** ***n.***

re·lent (ri lent′) ***vi.*** ⟦< L *re-,* again + *lentus,* pliant⟧ to become less severe, stern, or stubborn; soften

re·lent′less ***adj.*** **1** harsh; pitiless **2** not letting up; persistent —**re·lent′less·ly** ***adv.*** —**re·lent′less·ness** ***n.***

rel·e·vant (rel′ə vənt) ***adj.*** ⟦see RELIEVE⟧ relating to the matter under consideration; pertinent —**rel′e·vance** or **rel′e·van·cy** ***n.***

re·li·a·ble (ri lī′ə bəl) ***adj.*** that can be relied on; dependable —**re·li′a·bil′i·ty** ***n.*** —**re·li′a·bly** ***adv.***

re·li′ance (-əns) ***n.*** **1** a relying **2** trust, dependence, or confidence **3** a thing relied on —**re·li′ant** ***adj.***

rel·ic (rel′ik) ***n.*** ⟦see RELINQUISH⟧ **1** an object, custom, etc. surviving from the past **2** a souvenir **3** [*pl.*] ruins **4** the venerated remains, etc. of a saint

re·lief (ri lēf′) ***n.*** **1** a relieving of pain, anxiety, a burden, etc. **2** anything that lessens tension, or offers a pleasing

THESAURUS

REVIVAL 1.

relapse ***n.*** reversion, recidivism, return; see LOSS 3.

relapse ***v.*** lapse, retrogress, fall, backslide, revert, regress, suffer a relapse, deteriorate, degenerate, fall from grace, fall off, weaken, sink back, fall into again, slip back, slide back, be overcome, give in to again.

relate ***v.*** **1** [Tell] recount, recite, retell; see DESCRIBE, REPORT 1. **2** [Connect] bring into relation, associate, correlate; see COMPARE 1. —**relate to** be associated with, be connected with, affect; see CONCERN 1, REFER 1.

related ***a.*** **1** [Told] described, narrated, recounted; see TOLD. **2** [Connected] associated, in touch, with, linked, tied up, knit together, allied, affiliated, complementary, analogous, correspondent, akin, alike, like, parallel, correlated, intertwined, interrelated, similar, mutual, dependent, interdependent, interwoven, of that ilk, in the same category, reciprocal, interchangeable. **3** [Akin] kindred, of the same family, germane, fraternal, cognate, consanguine, of one blood; see also sense 2.

relation ***n.*** **1** [Relationship] connection, association, similarity; see RELATIONSHIP. **2** [A relative] family connection, sibling, kin; see RELATIVE. —**in relation to** concerning, with reference to, about; see REGARDING.

relationship ***n.*** relation, connection, tie, association, affinity, likeness, link, kinship, bond, dependence, relativity, proportion, rapport, analogy, homogeneity, interrelation, correlation, nearness, alliance, relevance, accord, hookup*, contact; see also SIMILARITY.—*Ant.* DIFFERENCE, dissimilarity, oppositeness.

relative ***a.*** dependent, contingent, applicable; see RELATED 2, RELEVANT. —**relative to** with respect to, concerning, relating to; see ABOUT 2.

relative ***n.*** kin, family connection, relation, member of the family, blood relation, next of kin, sibling, kinsman, kinswoman. *Relatives include the following:* mother, father, parent, grandmother, grandfather, grandparent, grandchild, grandson, granddaughter, great-grandmother, great-grandfather, ancestor, aunt, uncle, great-aunt, great-uncle, cousin, first cousin, second cousin, distant cousin, wife, husband, spouse, daughter, son, child, stepchild, stepparent, half brother, half sister, stepfather, stepmother, biological parent, adoptive parent, descendant, nephew, niece, brother, sister, kinsman, kinswoman, in-law*, mother-in-law, father-in-law, brother-in-law, sister-in-law.

relatively ***a.*** comparatively, approximately, nearly; see ALMOST.

relax ***v.*** repose, recline, settle back, make oneself at home, breathe easy*, take one's time, take a break, sit around*, stop work, lie down, unbend, be at ease, take a breather*; see also REST 1.

relaxation ***n.*** repose, reclining, loosening; see REST 1.

relaxed ***a.*** untroubled, carefree, at ease; see COMFORTABLE 1.

relay ***v.*** communicate, transfer, send forth, transmit, hand over, hand down, turn over, deliver, pass on; see also CARRY 1, SEND 1.

release ***n.*** **1** [Freedom] liberation, discharge, freeing; see FREEDOM 2. **2** [That which has been released; *usually, printed matter*] news story, publicity, news flash; see PROPAGANDA, STORY.

release ***v.*** liberate, let go, acquit; see FREE.

released ***a.*** **1** [Freed] discharged, dismissed, liberated; see FREE 1, 2. **2** [Announced] broadcast, stated, made public; see PUBLISHED.

relent ***v.*** soften, comply, relax; see YIELD 1.

relentless ***a.*** unmerciful, vindictive, hard; see RUTHLESS.

relevance ***n.*** connection, significance, pertinence; see IMPORTANCE.

relevant ***a.*** suitable, appropriate, fit, proper, pertinent to, becoming, pertaining to, apt, applicable, important, fitting, congruous, cognate, related, conforming, concerning, compatible, accordant, referring, harmonious, correspondent, consonant, congruent, consistent, correlated, associated, allied, relative, connected, to the point, bearing on the question, having direct bearing, having to do with, related to, on the nose.—*Ant.* IRRELEVANT, WRONG, not pertinent.

reliability ***n.*** dependability, trustworthiness, constancy, loyalty, faithfulness, sincerity, devotion, honesty, authenticity, steadfastness, fidelity, safety, security.

reliable ***a.*** firm, unimpeachable, sterling, strong, positive, stable, dependable, sure, solid, staunch, decisive, unequivocal, steadfast, definite, conscientious, constant, steady, trustworthy, faithful, loyal, good, true, devoted, tried, trusty, honest, honorable, candid, truehearted, responsible, high-principled, sincere, altruistic, determined, reputable, careful, proved, respectable, righteous, decent, incorrupt, truthful, upright, regular, all right, kosher*, OK*, on the up and up*, true-blue, safe, sound, guaranteed, certain, substantial, secure, unquestionable, conclusive, irrefutable, incontestable, unfailing, infallible, authentic, competent, assured, workable, foolproof, surefire.—*Ant.* DANGEROUS, insecure, undependable.

reliably ***a.*** assuredly, presumably, certainly; see PROBABLY, SURELY.

reliance ***n.*** confidence, trust, hope; see FAITH 1.

relic ***n.*** **1** [Something left from an earlier time] vestige, trace, survival, heirloom, antique, souvenir, keepsake, curio, memento, curiosity, token, testimonial, evidence, monument, trophy, remains, artifact, remembrance, bric-a-brac. **2** [A ruin] remnant, residue, remains, broken stone; see also DESTRUCTION 2, RUIN 2.

relief ***n.*** **1** [The act of bringing succor] alleviation, softening, comforting; see COMFORT. **2** [Aid] assistance, support, maintenance; see HELP 1. **3** [A relieved state of mind] satisfaction, relaxation, ease, release, happiness, contentment, cheer, restfulness, a

change **3** aid, esp. by a public agency to the needy **4** release from work or duty, or those bringing it **5** the projection of sculptured forms from a flat surface **6** the differences in height, collectively, of land forms shown as by lines on a map (**relief map**) —*adj. Baseball* designating a pitcher who replaces another during a game — **in relief** carved so as to project from a surface

re·lieve (ri lēv′) *vt.* **-lieved′**, **-liev′ing** ⟦< L *re-*, again + *levare,* to raise⟧ **1** to ease (pain, anxiety, etc.) **2** to free from pain, anxiety, a burden, etc. **3** to give or bring aid to **4** to set free from duty or work by replacing **5** to make less tedious, etc. by providing a pleasing change — **relieve oneself** to urinate or defecate

re·li·gion (ri lij′ən) *n.* ⟦< L *religio,* holiness⟧ **1** belief in and worship of God or gods **2** a specific system of belief, worship, etc., often involving a code of ethics

re·li′gi·os′i·ty (-ē äs′ə tē) *n.* a being religious, esp. excessively or sentimentally religious

re·li′gious (-əs) *adj.* **1** devout; pious **2** of or concerned with religion **3** conscientiously exact; scrupulous —*n., pl.* **-gious** a monk or nun —**re·li′gious·ly** *adv.*

re·lin·quish (ri liŋ′kwish) *vt.* ⟦< L *re-*, from + *linquere,* to leave⟧ **1** to give up (a plan, etc.) or let go (one's grasp, etc.) **2** to renounce or surrender (property, a right, etc.) —**re·lin′quish·ment** *n.*

rel·ish (rel′ish) *n.* ⟦< OFr *relais,* something remaining⟧ **1** an appetizing flavor **2** enjoyment; zest *[to listen with relish]* **3** a food, as pickles or raw vegetables, served with a meal to add flavor **4** a condiment of chopped pickles, spices, etc. for use as on hot dogs —*vt.* to enjoy; like

re·live (rē liv′) *vt.* **-lived′**, **-liv′ing** to experience again (a past event) as in the imagination

re·lo·cate (rē lō′kāt′) *vt., vi.* **-cat′ed**, **-cat′ing** to move to a new location —**re′lo·ca′tion** *n.*

re·luc·tant (ri luk′tənt) *adj.* ⟦< L *re-*, against + *luctari,* to struggle⟧ **1** unwilling; disinclined **2** marked by unwillingness *[a reluctant answer]* —**re·luc′tance** *n.* —**re·luc′tant·ly** *adv.*

re·ly (ri lī′) *vi.* **-lied′**, **-ly′ing** ⟦< L *re-*, back + *ligare,* bind⟧ to trust or depend: used with *on* or *upon*

rem (rem) *n., pl.* **rem** ⟦*r(oentgen) e(quivalent), m(an)*⟧ a dose of ionizing radiation with a biological effect equal to one roentgen of X-ray

REM (rem) *n., pl.* **REMs** ⟦*r(apid) e(ye) m(ovement)*⟧ the rapid, jerky movement of the eyeballs during stages of sleep associated with dreaming

re·main (ri mān′) *vi.* ⟦< L *re-*, back + *manere,* to stay⟧ **1** to be left over when the rest has been taken away, etc. **2** to stay **3** to continue *[to remain a cynic]* **4** to be left to be done, said, etc.

re·main′der *n.* **1** those remaining **2** what is left when a part is taken away **3** what is left when a smaller number is subtracted from a larger **4** what is left undivided when a number is divided by another that is not one of its factors

re·mains′ *pl.n.* **1** what is left after use, destruction, etc. **2** a dead body

re·mand (ri mand′) *vt.* ⟦< L *re-*, back + *mandare,* to order⟧ to send back (a prisoner, etc.) into custody

re·mark (ri märk′) *vt.* ⟦< Fr *re-*, again + *marquer,* to mark⟧ **1** to notice or observe **2** to say or write as a comment —*vi.* to make a comment: with *on* or *upon* —*n.* a brief comment

re·mark′a·ble *adj.* worthy of notice; extraordinary —**re·mark′a·bly** *adv.*

Rem·brandt (rem′brant′) 1606-69; Du. painter & etcher

re·me·di·al (ri mē′dē əl) *adj.* **1** providing a remedy **2** for correcting deficiencies: said as of some courses of study

re·me′di·ate′ (-āt′) *vt.* **-at′ed**, **-at′ing** to provide a remedy for

rem·e·dy (rem′ə dē) *n., pl.* **-dies** ⟦< L *re-*, again + *mederi,* heal⟧ **1** any medicine or treatment for a disease **2** something to correct a wrong —*vt.* **-died**, **-dy·ing** to cure, correct, etc.

re·mem·ber (ri mem′bər) *vt.* ⟦< L *re-*, again + *memorare,* bring to mind⟧ **1** to think of again **2** to bring back to

THESAURUS

load off one's mind; see also COMFORT. **4** [The person or thing that brings relief] diversion, relaxation, consolation, solace, reinforcement, supplies, food, shelter, clothing, release, respite, remedy, nursing, medicine, medical care, redress, reparations, indemnities, variety, change, cure; see also HELP 1. **5** [The raised portions of a sculptural decoration or map] projection, contour, configuration; see DECORATION 2.

relieve *v.* **1** [To replace] discharge, throw out, force to resign; see DISMISS. **2** [To lessen; *said especially of pain*] assuage, alleviate, soothe, comfort, allay, divert, free, ease, lighten, soften, diminish, mitigate, console, cure, aid, assist; see also DECREASE 2, HELP.

relieved *a.* **1** [Eased in mind] comforted, solaced, consoled, reassured, satisfied, soothed, relaxed, put at ease, restored, reconciled, appeased, placated, alleviated, mollified, disarmed, pacified, adjusted, propitiated, breathing easy*; see also COMFORTABLE 1.—*Ant.* SAD, worried, distraught. **2** [Deprived of something, or freed from it] replaced, dismissed, separated from, disengaged, released, made free of, rescued, delivered, supplanted, superseded, succeeded, substituted for, exchanged, interchanged. **3** [Lessened; *said especially of pain*] mitigated, palliated, softened, assuaged, eased, abated, diminished, salved, soothed, lightened, alleviated, drugged, anesthetized.

religion *n.* **1** [All that centers about human beings' belief in or relationship with a superior being or beings] belief, devotion, piety, spirituality, persuasion, godliness, sense of righteousness, morality, theology, faithfulness, devoutness, creed, myth, superstition, doctrine, cult, denomination, mythology, communion, sect, fidelity, conscientiousness, religious bent, ethical standard; see also FAITH 2. **2** [Organized worship or service of a deity] veneration, adoration, consecration, sanctification, prayer, rites, holy sacrifice, incantation, holiday, observance, orthodoxy; see also CEREMONY 2. *Religions include the following:* Christianity, Buddhism, Zen Buddhism, Hinduism, Islam, Judaism, Zoroastrianism, Shintoism, Confucianism, Taoism, Jainism, Bahaism, nature worship, Wicca, paganism, Sikhism, monotheism, ancestor worship, voodoo, Santeria, deism, theism, polytheism, dualism; see also CHURCH 3. —**get religion*** become converted, believe, change; see REFORM 2, 3.

religious *a.* **1** [Pertaining to religion] ethical, spiritual, moral, ecclesiastical, clerical, theological, canonical, divine, supernatural, holy, sacred, churchly, theistic, deistic, priestly, pontifical, pastoral, ministerial.—*Ant.* WORLDLY, secular, earthly. **2** [Devout] pious, puritanical, sanctimonious, pietistic, godly, god-fearing, orthodox, reverend, reverential, believing, faithful, fanatic, evangelistic, revivalistic, churchgoing; see also HOLY 1. **3** [Scrupulous] methodical, minute, thorough; see CAREFUL.

relish *n.* **1** [A condiment] flavoring, accent, pickle. *Relishes include the following:* catsup or ketchup, piccalilli, cucumber relish, pickle relish, mincemeat, pickled pears, pickled peaches, chutney, chili sauce, hot sauce, cranberry sauce. **2** [Obvious delight] gusto, joy, great satisfaction; see ZEAL.

relish *v.* enjoy, fancy, be fond of; see LIKE 1, 2.

reluctance *n.* disinclination, qualm, hesitation; see DOUBT.

reluctant *a.* disinclined, loath, unwilling, averse, opposed, tardy, backward, adverse, laggard, remiss, slack, squeamish, demurring, grudging, involuntary, uncertain, hanging back, hesitant, hesitating, diffident, with bad grace, indisposed, disheartened, discouraged, queasy.—*Ant.* WILLING, eager, disposed.

rely on (or **upon**) *v.* hope, have faith in, count on; see TRUST 1.

remain *v.* **1** [To stay] linger, abide, reside; see SETTLE 5. **2** [To endure] keep on, go on, prevail; see CONTINUE 1, ENDURE 1. **3** [To be left] remain standing, endure, outlast; see SURVIVE 1.

remainder *n.* remaining portion, leftovers, residue, remains, relic, remnant, dregs, surplus, leavings, balance, residuum, excess, overplus, scrap, fragment, small piece, carryover, rest, residual portion, average, salvage.

remains *n.* corpse, cadaver, relics; see BODY 2.

remake *v.* change, revise, alter; see CORRECT.

remark *n.* statement, saying, utterance, annotation, note, mention, reflection, illustration, point, conclusion, consideration, talk, observation, expression, comment, assertion, witticism.

remark *v.* say, mention, observe; see SAY, TALK 1.

remarkable *a.* exceptional, extraordinary, uncommon; see UNUSUAL 1.

remarkably *a.* exceptionally, singularly, notably; see ESPECIALLY, VERY.

remedy *n.* **1** [A medicine] antidote, pill, drug; see MEDICINE 2, TREATMENT 2. **2** [Effective help] relief, cure, redress, support, improvement, solution, plan, panacea, cure-all, assistance, counteraction; see also RELIEF 4.

remedy *v.* cure, help, aid; see HEAL.

remember *v.* **1** [To recall] recol-

mind by an effort; recall **3** to be careful not to forget **4** to mention (a person) to another as sending greetings —*vi.* to bear something in mind or call something back to mind

re·mem′brance (-brəns) ***n.*** **1** a remembering or being remembered **2** the power to remember **3** a souvenir

re·mind (ri mīnd′) ***vt., vi.*** to put (a person) in mind (*of* something); make remember —**re·mind′er** ***n.***

rem·i·nisce (rem′ə nis′) ***vi.*** **-nisced′, -nisc′ing** ⟦< fol.⟧ to think, talk, or write about remembered events

rem′i·nis′cence (-əns) ***n.*** ⟦Fr < L *re-*, again + *memini*, remember⟧ **1** a remembering **2** a memory **3** [*pl.*] an account of remembered experiences —**rem′i·nis′cent** ***adj.***

re·miss (ri mis′) ***adj.*** ⟦see REMIT⟧ careless; negligent —**re·miss′ness** ***n.***

re·mis·sion (ri mish′ən) ***n.*** ⟦see fol.⟧ **1** forgiveness; pardon **2** release from a debt, tax, etc. **3** an abating of pain, a disease, etc.

re·mit (ri mit′) ***vt.*** **-mit′ted, -mit′ting** ⟦< L *re-*, back + *mittere*, send⟧ **1** to forgive or pardon **2** to refrain from exacting (a payment), inflicting (punishment), etc. **3** to slacken; decrease **4** to send (money) in payment —**re·mit′tance** ***n.***

rem·nant (rem′nənt) ***n.*** ⟦see REMAIN⟧ what is left over, as a piece of cloth at the end of a bolt

re·mod·el (rē mäd′'l) ***vt.*** **-eled** or **-elled, -el·ing** or **-el·ling** to make over; rebuild

re·mon·strate (ri män′strāt′) ***vt.*** **-strat′ed, -strat′ing** ⟦< L *re-*, again + *monstrare*, to show⟧ to say in protest, objection, etc. —***vi.*** to protest; object —**re·mon′strance** (-strəns) ***n.***

re·morse (ri môrs′) ***n.*** ⟦< L *re-*, again + *mordere*, to bite⟧ a torturing sense of guilt for one's actions —**re·morse′ful** ***adj.*** —**re·morse′less** ***adj.***

re·mote (ri mōt′) ***adj.*** **-mot′er, -mot′est** ⟦< L *remotus*, removed⟧ **1** distant in space or time **2** distant in connection, relation, etc. **3** distantly related **4** aloof **5** slight [*a remote* chance] —**re·mote′ly** ***adv.***

remote control **1** control of aircraft, etc. from a distance, as by radio waves **2** a device to control a TV set, recorder, etc. from a distance

re·move (ri mo͞ov′) ***vt.*** **-moved′, -mov′ing** ⟦see RE- & MOVE⟧ **1** to move (something) from where it is; take away or off **2** to dismiss, as from office **3** to get rid of —***vi.*** to move away, as to another residence —***n.*** a step or degree away —**re·mov′a·ble** ***adj.*** —**re·mov′al** ***n.*** —**re·mov′er** ***n.***

re·mu·ner·ate (ri myo͞o′nə rāt′) ***vt.*** **-at′ed, -at′ing** ⟦< L *re-*, again + *munus*, gift⟧ to pay (a person) for (work, a loss, etc.) —**re·mu′ner·a′tion** ***n.*** —**re·mu′ner·a′tive** ***adj.***

ren·ais·sance (ren′ə säns′) ***n.*** ⟦Fr⟧ a rebirth; renascence —**the Renaissance** the great revival of art and learning in Europe in the 14th, 15th, and 16th centuries

Renaissance man (or **woman**) one skilled and knowledgeable in many fields

re·nal (rē′nəl) ***adj.*** ⟦< L *renes*, kidneys⟧ of or near the kidneys

re·nas·cence (ri nas′əns, -nās′-) ***n.*** ⟦< L *renasci*, be born again⟧ [*also* **R-**] RENAISSANCE

rend (rend) ***vt.*** **rent, rend′ing** ⟦OE *rendan*⟧ to tear or split with violence —***vi.*** to tear; split apart

ren·der (ren′dər) ***vt.*** ⟦ult. < L *re(d)-*, back + *dare*, give⟧ **1** to submit, as for approval or payment **2** to give in return or pay as due [*render* thanks] **3** to cause to be **4** to give (aid) or do (a service) **5** to depict, as by drawing **6** to play (music), act (a role), etc. **7** to translate **8** to melt down (fat) **9** to pronounce (a verdict)

ren·dez·vous (rän′dā vo͞o′) ***n.***, *pl.* **-vous′** (-vo͞oz′) ⟦< Fr *rendez-vous*, present yourself⟧ **1** a meeting place **2** an agreement to meet **3** the meeting itself —***vi., vt.*** **-voused′** (-vo͞od′), **-vous′ing** (-vo͞o′iŋ) to meet or assemble at a certain time or place

ren·di·tion (ren dish′ən) ***n.*** a rendering; performance, translation, etc.

ren·e·gade (ren′ə gād′) ***n.*** ⟦< L *re-*, again + *negare*, deny⟧ one who abandons a party, movement, etc. to join the opposition; turncoat

re·nege (ri nig′) ***vi.*** **-neged′, -neg′ing** ⟦see prec.⟧ to go back on a promise

re·new (ri no͞o′) ***vt.*** **1** to make new or fresh again **2** to reestablish; revive **3** to resume **4** to put in a fresh sup-

THESAURUS

lect, recognize, summon up, relive, dig into the past, refresh one's memory, be reminded of, think of, revive, bring to mind, call to mind, think over, think back, look back, brood over, conjure up, call up, carry one's thoughts back, look back upon, have memories of, commemorate, memorialize, reminisce.—*Ant.* LOSE, forget, neglect. **2** [To bear in mind] keep in mind, memorize, know by heart, learn, master, get, have impressed upon one's mind, fix in the mind, retain, treasure, hold dear, dwell upon, brood over, keep forever.—*Ant.* NEGLECT, ignore, disregard.

remembered ***a.*** thought of, recalled, recollected, rewarded, summoned up, brought to mind, memorialized, haunting one's thoughts, commemorated, dug up.—*Ant.* LOST, forgotten, overlooked.

remembrance ***n.*** **1** [Memory] recall, recollection, recognition; see MEMORY 1. **2** [A gift] memento, token, keepsake; see GIFT 1.

remind ***v.*** **1** [To bring into the memory] bring back, make one think of, intimate; see HINT. **2** [To call the attention of another] caution, point out, jog the memory of, mention to, call attention to, bring up, prompt, prod, stress, emphasize, note, stir up, put a bug in one's ear*, give a cue; see also WARN.

reminded ***a.*** warned, cautioned, prompted, put in mind of, made aware, advised, forewarned, notified, awakened, prodded.

reminder ***n.*** warning, notice, admonition, note, memorandum, memo, hint, suggestion, memento, token, keepsake, trinket, remembrance, souvenir.

remit ***v.*** make payment, forward, dispatch; see PAY 1.

remittance ***n.*** transmittal, money sent, enclosure; see PAYMENT 1.

remnant ***n.*** residue, leavings, what is left; see EXCESS 1, REMAINDER.

remnants ***n.*** scraps, odds and ends, leftovers, particles, surplus, vestiges, remains, leavings; see also EXCESS 1, REMAINDER.

remodel ***v.*** renovate, refurnish, refurbish, readjust, reconstruct, readapt, rearrange, redecorate, refashion, improve, reshape, recast, rebuild, modernize, repaint; see also REPAIR.

remodeled ***a.*** refurnished, redecorated, rebuilt; see CHANGED 2.

remorse ***n.*** compunction, contrition, self-reproach; see GRIEF, REGRET 1. —**without remorse** cruel, pitiless, relentless; see RUTHLESS.

remorseful ***a.*** contrite, penitent, repentant; see SORRY 1.

remorseless ***a.*** unyielding, unforgiving, vindictive; see SEVERE 1, 2.

remote ***a.*** **1** [Distant] far-off, faraway, out-of-the-way, removed, beyond, secluded, inaccessible, isolated, unknown, alien, foreign, undiscovered, off the beaten track, over the hills and far away, Godforsaken; see also DISTANT.—*Ant.* NEAR, close, accessible. **2** [Ancient] forgotten, past, aged; see OLD 3. **3** [Separated] unrelated, irrelevant, unconnected; see SEPARATED.

removal ***n.*** dismissal, discharge, expulsion, exile, deportation, banishment, elimination, extraction, dislodgment, evacuation, ejection, transference, eradication, extermination, replacement, the bounce*, the gate*.—*Ant.* ENTRANCE, induction, introduction.

remove ***v.*** **1** [To move physically] cart away, clear away, carry away, take away, tear away, brush away, transfer, transport, dislodge, uproot, excavate, displace, unload, discharge, lift up, doff, raise, evacuate, shift, switch, lift, push, draw away, draw in, withdraw, separate, extract, cut out, dig out, tear out, pull out, take out, smoke out, rip out, take down, tear off, draw off, take off, carry off, cart off, clear off, strike off, cut off, rub off, scrape off. **2** [To eliminate] get rid of, do away with, exclude; see ELIMINATE. **3** [To dismiss] discharge, displace, discard; see DISMISS.

removed ***a.*** **1** [Taken out] dislodged, extracted, eliminated, withdrawn, evacuated, ejected, pulled out, amputated, excised, expunged, extirpated.—*Ant.* LEFT, established, ignored. **2** [Distant] faraway, out-of-the-way, far-off; see DISTANT. **3** [Dismissed] banished, relieved of office, retired; see DISCHARGED, RECALLED 2.

rend ***v.*** rip, sever, tear; see BREAK 1.

render ***v.*** **1** [To give] present, hand over, distribute; see GIVE 1. **2** [To perform, especially a service] do, carry out, execute; see PERFORM 1. **3** [To interpret; *said especially of music*] play, perform, portray; see INTERPRET.

rendition ***n.*** interpretation, version, reading; see TRANSLATION.

renew ***v.*** **1** [To refresh] reawaken, regenerate, reestablish, rehabilitate, reinvigorate, replace, rebuild, reconstitute, remake, refinish, refurbish, redo, repeat, invigorate, exhilarate, restore, resuscitate, recondition, overhaul, replenish, go over, freshen, stimulate, recreate, remodel, revamp, redesign, modernize, rejuvenate, give new life to, recover, renovate, reintegrate, make a new beginning, bring up to date, do over, make like new; see also REVIVE 1. **2** [To repeat] resume, reiterate, recommence; see REPEAT 1.

ply of **5** to give or get an extension of *[renew a lease]* —**re·new'a·ble** ***adj.*** —**re·new'al** ***n.***

ren·net (ren'it) ***n.*** ⟦< ME *rennen,* coagulate⟧ an extract from the stomach of calves, etc. used to curdle milk

Re·no (rē'nō) city in W Nevada: pop. 134,000

Re·noir (rən wär', ren'wär'), **Pierre Au·guste** (pyer ô güst') 1841-1919; Fr. painter

re·nounce (ri nouns') ***vt.*** **-nounced', -nounc'ing** ⟦< L *re-,* back + *nuntiare,* tell⟧ **1** to give up formally (a claim, etc.) **2** to give up (a habit, etc.) **3** to disown —**re·nounce'ment** ***n.***

ren·o·vate (ren'ə vāt') ***vt.*** **-vat'ed, -vat'ing** ⟦< L *re-,* again + *novus,* new⟧ to make as good as new; restore —**ren'o·va'tion** ***n.*** —**ren'o·va'tor** ***n.***

re·nown (ri noun') ***n.*** ⟦< OFr *re-,* again + *nom(m)er,* to name < L *nominare*⟧ great fame or reputation —**re·nowned'** ***adj.***

rent[1] (rent) ***n.*** ⟦< L *reddita,* paid⟧ a stated payment at fixed intervals for the use of a house, land, etc. —***vt.*** to get or give use of in return for rent —***vi.*** to be let for rent —**for rent** available to be rented —**rent'er** ***n.***

rent[2] (rent) ***vt., vi.*** *pt. & pp. of* REND —***n.*** a hole or gap made by tearing

rent·al (rent''l) ***n.*** **1** an amount paid or received as rent **2** a house, car, etc. offered for rent **3** a renting —***adj.*** of or for rent

re·nun·ci·a·tion (ri nun'sē ā'shən) ***n.*** a renouncing, as of a right

re·or·gan·ize (rē ôr'gə nīz') ***vt., vi.*** **-ized', -iz'ing** to organize (a business, etc.) anew —**re·or'gan·i·za'tion** ***n.***

rep[1] (rep) ***n.*** ⟦Fr *reps* < Eng *ribs*⟧ a ribbed fabric

rep[2] (rep) ***n.*** a representative

rep[3] *abbrev.* **1** repeat **2** report(ed) **3** reporter

Rep *abbrev.* **1** Representative **2** Republican

re·paid (ri pād') ***vt., vi.*** *pt. & pp. of* REPAY

re·pair[1] (ri per') ***vt.*** ⟦< L *re-,* again + *parare,* prepare⟧ **1** to put back in good condition; fix; renew **2** to make amends for —***n.*** **1** a repairing **2** [*usually pl.*] work done in repairing **3** the state of being repaired *[kept in repair]* —**re·pair'a·ble** ***adj.***

re·pair[2] (ri per') ***vi.*** ⟦< L *re-,* back + *patria,* native land⟧ to go (*to* a place)

re·pair'man (-mən, -man') ***n., pl.*** **-men** (-mən, -men') one whose work is repairing things

rep·a·ra·tion (rep'ə rā'shən) ***n.*** ⟦see REPAIR[1]⟧ **1** a making of amends **2** [*usually pl.*] compensation, as for war damage

rep·ar·tee (rep'är tē', -tā') ***n.*** ⟦< Fr *repartir,* to return a blow quickly⟧ a series of quick, witty retorts; banter

re·past (ri past') ***n.*** ⟦< OFr *re-,* RE- + *past,* food⟧ food and drink; a meal

re·pa·tri·ate (rē pā'trē āt') ***vt., vi.*** **-at'ed, -at'ing** ⟦see REPAIR[2]⟧ to return to the country of birth, citizenship, etc. —**re·pa'tri·a'tion** ***n.***

re·pay (ri pā') ***vt.*** **-paid', -pay'ing** **1** to pay back **2** to make return to for (a favor, etc.) —**re·pay'ment** ***n.***

re·peal (ri pēl') ***vt.*** ⟦see RE- & APPEAL⟧ to revoke; cancel; annul —***n.*** revocation; abrogation

re·peat (ri pēt') ***vt.*** ⟦< L *re-,* again + *petere,* to demand⟧ **1** to say again **2** to recite (a poem, etc.) **3** to say (something) as said by someone else **4** to tell to someone else *[to repeat a secret]* **5** to do or make again —***vi.*** to say or do again —***n.*** **1** a repeating **2** anything said or done again, as a rebroadcast of a television program **3** *Music a)* a passage to be repeated *b)* a symbol for this —**re·peat'er** ***n.***

re·peat'ed ***adj.*** said, made, or done again, or often —**re·peat'ed·ly** ***adv.***

re·pel (ri pel') ***vt.*** **-pelled', -pel'ling** ⟦< L *re-,* back + *pellere,* to drive⟧ **1** to drive or force back **2** to reject **3** to cause dislike in; disgust **4** to be resistant to (water, dirt, etc.) —**re·pel'lent** ***adj., n.***

re·pent (ri pent') ***vi., vt.*** ⟦< L *re-,* again + *poenitere,* repent⟧ **1** to feel sorry for (an error, sin, etc.) **2** to feel such regret over (an action, intention, etc.) as to change one's mind (about) —**re·pent'ance** ***n.*** —**re·pent'ant** ***adj.***

re·per·cus·sion (rē'pər kush'ən) ***n.*** ⟦see RE- & PERCUSSION⟧ **1** reverberation **2** a far-reaching, often indirect reaction to some event

rep·er·toire (rep'ər twär') ***n.*** ⟦< Fr < L *reperire,* discover⟧ the stock of plays, songs, etc. that a company, singer, etc. is prepared to perform

rep'er·to'ry (-tôr'ē) ***n., pl.*** **-ries** **1** REPERTOIRE **2** the system of alternating several plays throughout a season with a permanent group of actors

rep·e·ti·tion (rep'ə tish'ən) ***n.*** ⟦< L *repetitio*⟧ **1** a repeating **2** something repeated —**rep'e·ti'tious** ***adj.*** —**re·pet·i·tive** (ri pet'ə tiv) ***adj.***

THESAURUS

3 [To replace] replenish, supplant, take over; see SUBSTITUTE.

renewal ***n.*** resurrection, new start, renovation; see REVIVAL 1.

renewed ***a.*** revived, readapted, refitted; see REPAIRED.

renounce ***v.*** disown, disavow, give up; see DENY, DISCARD.

renovate ***v.*** make over, remake, rehabilitate; see RENEW 1.

renovated ***a.*** renewed, remodeled, redone; see CLEAN 1, REPAIRED.

renovation ***n.*** remodeling, repair, restoration; see IMPROVEMENT 1.

rent[1] ***v.*** **1** [To sell the use of property] lease, lend, let, make available, allow the use of, take in roomers, sublet, put on loan. **2** [To obtain use by payment] hire, pay rent for, charter, contract, sign a contract for, engage, borrow, pay for services; see also PAY 1. —**for rent** on the market, renting, for hire, available, offered, advertised, to let.

rented ***a.*** leased, lent, hired, contracted, engaged, let, chartered, taken, on lease, out of the market.

reopen ***v.*** revive, reestablish, begin again; see OPEN 2, RENEW 1.

reorganization ***n.*** reestablishment, reconstitution, reorientation; see CHANGE 2, IMPROVEMENT 1.

reorganize ***v.*** rebuild, restructure, rearrange; see RECONSTRUCT.

repaid ***a.*** paid back, reimbursed, refunded; see PAID.

repair[1] ***n.*** reconstruction, substitution, reformation, rehabilitation, new part, patch, restoration, restored portion, replacement; see also IMPROVEMENT 1, 2.—*Ant.* BREAK, tear, fracture.

repair[1] ***v.*** fix, adjust, improve, correct, put into shape, reform, patch, rejuvenate, refurbish, retread, touch up, put in order, revive, refresh, renew, mend, darn, sew, revamp, rectify, ameliorate, renovate, reshape, rebuild, work over, fix up*.—*Ant.* WRECK, damage, smash.

repaired ***a.*** fixed, rearranged, adjusted, adapted, settled, remodeled, rectified, mended, corrected, righted, restored, renewed, remedied, improved, renovated, retouched, in working order, patched up, put together, put back into shape, sewn, reset, stitched up.—*Ant.* DAMAGED, worn, torn.

reparation ***n.*** indemnity, retribution, amends; see PAYMENT 1.

repay ***v.*** **1** [To pay back] reimburse, recompense, refund, return, indemnify, give back, make amends, requite, compensate, square oneself*, settle up; see also PAY 1. **2** [To retaliate] get even with, square accounts, reciprocate; see REVENGE.

repayment ***n.*** compensation, indemnity, restitution; see PAYMENT 1.

repeal ***n.*** annulment, cancellation, abolition; see WITHDRAWAL.

repeal ***v.*** annul, abolish, abrogate; see CANCEL.

repeat ***v.*** **1** [To do again] redo, remake, do over, rehash, reciprocate, return, rework, re-form, refashion, recast, reduplicate, renew, reconstruct, re-erect, go over again and again. **2** [To happen again] reoccur, recur, reappear, occur again, come again, return; see also HAPPEN 2. **3** [To say again] reiterate, restate, reissue, republish, reutter, echo, recite, reecho, rehearse, retell, go over, play back, recapitulate, drum into, rehash, come again; see also SAY.

repeated ***a.*** **1** [Done again] redone, remade, copied, imitated, reworked, refashioned, recast, done over, reciprocated, returned, reduplicated. **2** [Said again] reiterated, restated, reannounced, reuttered, recited, reproduced, seconded, paraphrased, reworded, retold.

repeatedly ***a.*** again and again, many times, time and again; see FREQUENTLY, REGULARLY.

repel ***v.*** **1** [To throw back] rebuff, resist, stand up against, oppose, check, repulse, put to flight, keep at bay, knock down, drive away, drive back, beat back, hold back, force back, push back, ward off, chase off, stave off, fight off.—*Ant.* FALL, fail, retreat. **2** [To cause aversion] nauseate, offend, revolt; see DISGUST. **3** [To reject] disown, dismiss, cast aside; see REFUSE.

repent ***v.*** be sorry, have qualms, be penitent; see APOLOGIZE, REGRET 1.

repentance ***n.*** sorrow, remorse, self-reproach; see REGRET 1.

repentant ***a.*** penitent, regretful, contrite; see SORRY 1.

repercussion ***n.*** consequence, reaction, effect; see RESULT.

repetition ***n.*** recurrence, reoccurrence, reappearance, reproduction, copy, rote, duplication, renewal, recapitulation, reiteration, return; see also WORDINESS.

repetitious ***a.*** boring, wordy, repeating; see DULL 4.

re·pine (ri pīn′) *vi.* **-pined′, -pin′ing** ⟦RE- + PINE[2]⟧ to feel or express unhappiness or discontent

re·place (ri plās′) *vt.* **-placed′, -plac′ing** 1 to put back in a former or the proper place 2 to take the place of 3 to provide an equivalent for —**re·place′a·ble** *adj.* —**re·place′ment** *n.*

re·plen·ish (ri plen′ish) *vt.* ⟦< L *re-*, again + *plenus*, full⟧ 1 to make full or complete again 2 to supply again —**re·plen′ish·ment** *n.*

re·plete (ri plēt′) *adj.* ⟦< L *re-*, again + *plere*, to fill⟧ 1 plentifully supplied 2 stuffed; gorged —**re·ple′tion** *n.*

rep·li·ca (rep′li kə) *n.* ⟦see REPLY⟧ a reproduction or close copy, as of a work of art

rep·li·cate (rep′li kāt′) *vt.* **-cat′ed, -cat′ing** ⟦see REPLY⟧ to repeat or duplicate

rep′li·ca′tion *n.* 1 a replicating 2 a reply; answer 3 a copy; reproduction

re·ply (ri plī′) *vi.* **-plied′, -ply′ing** ⟦< L *re-*, back + *plicare*, to fold⟧ to answer or respond —*n.*, *pl.* **-plies′** an answer or response

re·port (ri pôrt′) *vt.* ⟦< L *re-*, back + *portare*, carry⟧ 1 to give an account of, as for publication 2 to carry and repeat (a message, etc.) 3 to announce formally 4 to make a charge about (something) or against (someone) to one in authority —*vi.* 1 to make a report 2 to present oneself, as for work —*n.* 1 rumor 2 a statement or account 3 a formal presentation of facts 4 the noise of an explosion —**re·port′ed·ly** *adv.*

re·port·age (ri pôrt′ij, rep′ər täzh′) *n.* 1 the reporting of the news 2 journalistic writings

report card a periodic written report on a student's progress: often used figuratively

re·port′er *n.* one who reports; specif., one who gathers and reports news for a newspaper, etc. —**rep·or·to·ri·al** (rep′ər tôr′ē əl) *adj.*

re·pose[1] (ri pōz′) *vt.* **-posed′, -pos′ing** ⟦< L *re-*, again + *pausare*, to rest⟧ to lay or place for rest —*vi.* 1 to lie at rest 2 to rest from work, etc. 3 to lie dead —*n.* 1 *a*) rest *b*) sleep 2 composure 3 calm; peace —**re·pose′ful** *adj.*

re·pose[2] (ri pōz′) *vt.* **-posed′, -pos′ing** ⟦see fol.⟧ 1 to place (trust, etc.) *in* someone 2 to place (power, etc.) *in* the control of some person or group

re·pos·i·to·ry (ri päz′ə tôr′ē) *n.*, *pl.* **-ries** ⟦< L *re-*, back + *ponere*, to place⟧ a box, room, etc. in which things may be placed for safekeeping

re·pos·sess (rē′pə zes′) *vt.* to take back, as from a buyer who missed payments —**re′pos·ses′sion** *n.*

rep·re·hend (rep′ri hend′) *vt.* ⟦< L *re-*, back + *prehendere*, take⟧ to rebuke, blame, or censure

rep′re·hen′si·ble (-hen′sə bəl) *adj.* deserving to be reprehended —**rep′re·hen′si·bly** *adv.*

rep·re·sent (rep′ri zent′) *vt.* ⟦< L *re-*, again + *praesentare*, to present⟧ 1 to present to the mind 2 to present a likeness of 3 to describe 4 to stand for; symbolize 5 to be the equivalent of 6 to act (a role) 7 to act in place of, esp. by conferred authority 8 to serve as an example of

rep′re·sen·ta′tion *n.* 1 a representing or being represented, as in a legislative assembly 2 legislative representatives, collectively 3 a likeness, image, picture, etc. 4 [*often pl.*] a statement of facts, arguments, etc. meant to influence action, make protest, etc. —**rep′re·sen·ta′tion·al** *adj.*

rep′re·sent′a·tive *adj.* 1 representing 2 of or based on representation of the people by elected delegates 3 typical —*n.* 1 an example or type 2 one authorized to act for others; delegate, agent, salesman, etc. 3 [**R-**] a member of the lower house of Congress or of a state legislature

re·press (ri pres′) *vt.* ⟦see RE- & PRESS[1]⟧ 1 to hold back; restrain 2 to put down; subdue 3 *Psychiatry* to force (painful ideas, etc.) into the unconscious —**re·pres′sion** *n.* —**re·pres′sive** *adj.*

re·prieve (ri prēv′) *vt.* **-prieved′, -priev′ing** ⟦< Fr *reprendre*, take back⟧ 1 to postpone the punishment of, esp. the execution of 2 to give temporary relief to —*n.* a reprieving or being reprieved

rep·ri·mand (rep′rə mand′) *n.* ⟦< L *reprimere*, repress⟧ a severe or formal rebuke —*vt.* to rebuke severely or formally

re·pris·al (ri prī′zəl) *n.* ⟦see REPREHEND⟧ injury done in return for injury received

re·proach (ri prōch′) *vt.* ⟦< L *re-*, back + *prope*, near⟧ to accuse of a fault; rebuke —*n.* 1 shame, disgrace, etc. or a cause of this 2 rebuke or censure —**re·proach′ful** *adj.*

rep·ro·bate (rep′rə bāt′) *adj.* ⟦LL *reprobare*, reprove⟧ unprincipled or depraved —*n.* a reprobate person

re·proc·ess (rē präs′es) *vt.* to process again so as to reuse; esp., to recover plutonium, etc. from

re·pro·duce (rē′prə do͞os′) *vt.* **-duced′, -duc′ing** to produce again; specif., *a*) to produce by propagation *b*) to make a copy of —*vi.* to produce offspring —**re′pro·duc′i·ble** *adj.*

THESAURUS

replace *v.* 1 [To supply an equivalent for] replenish, repay, compensate for; see RECONSTRUCT, RENEW 1, REPAIR. 2 [To take the place of] take over, supplant, displace; see SUBSTITUTE. 3 [To put back in the same place] restore, reinstate, put back; see RETURN 2.

replaced *a.* 1 [Returned to the same place] restored, reinstated, reintegrated, recovered, recouped, reacquired, regained, repossessed, resumed, rewon, retrieved. 2 [Having another in one's place; *said of persons*] dismissed, cashiered, dislodged; see RECALLED 2. 3 [Having another in its place; *said of things*] renewed, interchanged, replenished; see CHANGED 1.

replica *n.* copy, likeness, model; see DUPLICATE, IMITATION 2.

reply *n.* response, return, retort; see ANSWER 1.

reply *v.* retort, rejoin, return; see ANSWER 1.

report *n.* 1 [A transmitted account] tale, narrative, description; see NEWS 1, 2, STORY. 2 [An official summary] statement, bulletin, release; see RECORD 1, SUMMARY. 3 [A loud, explosive sound] detonation, bang, blast; see NOISE 1.

report *v.* 1 [To deliver information] describe, recount, narrate, provide the details of, give an account of, set forth, inform, advise, communicate, retail, wire, cable, telephone, broadcast, notify, relate, state; see also TELL 1. 2 [To make a summary statement] summarize, publish, proclaim; see sense 1. 3 [To present oneself] be at hand, check in, come; see ARRIVE. 4 [To record] take minutes, take notes, note down; see RECORD 1.

reported *a.* stated, recited, recounted, narrated, described, set forth, announced, broadcast, made known, rumored, noted, expressed, proclaimed, according to rumor, revealed, communicated, disclosed, imparted, divulged, recorded, in the air, all over town*.—*Ant.* UNKNOWN, verified, certain.

reporter *n.* newspaperman, newspaperwoman, news writer, columnist, journalist, newsman, newswoman, anchorman, anchorwoman, anchor, newscaster, stringer, correspondent, interviewer, cub reporter, star reporter, news gatherer; see also WRITER.

represent *v.* 1 [To act as a delegate] be an agent for, serve, hold office, be deputy for, be attorney for, steward, act as broker, sell for, buy for, do business for, be spokesperson for, serve in a legislature for, be ambassador for, exercise power of attorney for. 2 [To present as a true interpretation] render, depict, portray; see ENACT. 3 [To serve as an equivalent of] copy, imitate, reproduce, symbolize, exemplify, typify, signify, substitute for, stand for, impersonate, personify.

representation *n.* description, narration, delineation; see COPY.

representative *n.* 1 [An emissary] deputy, salesman, messenger; see AGENT, DELEGATE. 2 [One who is elected to the lower legislative body] congressman, congresswoman, congressperson, assemblyman, assemblywoman, councilman, councilwoman, member of parliament, deputy, legislator, councilor; see also DIPLOMAT.

represented *a.* 1 [Depicted] portrayed, interpreted, pictured; see MADE. 2 [Presented] rendered, exhibited, displayed; see SHOWN 1.

repress *v.* control, curb, check; see HINDER, RESTRAIN.

reprimand *v.* reproach, denounce, criticize; see SCOLD.

reproach *n.* discredit, censure, rebuke; see BLAME.

reproach *v.* condemn, censure, scold; see BLAME.

reproduce *v.* 1 [To make an exact copy] photograph, print, xerox; see COPY. 2 [To make a second time] repeat, duplicate, recreate, recount, revive, reenact, redo, reawaken, relive, remake, reflect, follow, mirror, echo, reecho, represent. 3 [To multiply] procreate, engender, breed, generate, propagate, fecundate, hatch, father, beget, impregnate, bear, sire, repopulate, multiply, give birth.

reproduced *a.* copied, printed, traced, duplicated, transcribed, dittoed, recorded, multiplied, repeated, made identical, typed, set up, set in type, in facsimile, faxed, transferred, photographed, blueprinted, photostated, mimeographed, engraved, photoengraved, photocopied; see also MANUFACTURED.

re'pro·duc'tion (-duk'shən) ***n.*** **1** a reproducing **2** a copy, imitation, etc. **3** the process by which animals and plants produce new individuals —**re'pro·duc'tive** ***adj.***

re·proof (ri pro͞of') ***n.*** a reproving; rebuke: also **re·prov'al** (-pro͞o'vəl)

re·prove (ri pro͞ov') ***vt.*** **-proved', -prov'ing** ⟦see RE- & PROVE⟧ **1** to rebuke **2** to express disapproval of (something done or said)

rep·tile (rep'tīl') ***n.*** ⟦< L *repere,* to creep⟧ a coldblooded vertebrate covered as with scales, as a snake, lizard, turtle, or dinosaur —**rep·til·i·an** (rep til'ē ən) ***adj.***

re·pub·lic (ri pub'lik) ***n.*** ⟦< L *res,* thing + *publica,* public (adj.)⟧ a state or government, specif. one headed by a president, in which the power is exercised by officials elected by the voters

re·pub'li·can (-li kən) ***adj.*** **1** of or like a republic **2** [**R-**] of or belonging to the Republican Party —***n.*** **1** one who favors a republican form of government **2** [**R-**] a member of the Republican Party

Republican Party one of the two major political parties in the U.S.

re·pu·di·ate (ri pyo͞o'dē āt') ***vt.*** **-at'ed, -at'ing** ⟦< L *repudium,* separation⟧ **1** to refuse to have anything to do with **2** to refuse to accept or support (a belief, treaty, etc.) —**re·pu'di·a'tion** ***n.***

re·pug·nant (ri pug'nənt) ***adj.*** ⟦< L *re-,* back + *pugnare,* fight⟧ **1** contradictory **2** distasteful; offensive —**re·pug'nance** ***n.***

re·pulse (ri puls') ***vt.*** **-pulsed', -puls'ing** ⟦see REPEL⟧ **1** to drive back (an attack, etc.) **2** to refuse or reject with discourtesy, etc.; rebuff —***n.*** a repelling or being repelled

re·pul·sion (ri pul'shən) ***n.*** **1** a repelling or being repelled **2** strong dislike **3** *Physics* the mutual action by which bodies tend to repel each other

re·pul'sive (-siv) ***adj.*** causing strong dislike or aversion; disgusting —**re·pul'sive·ly** ***adv.*** —**re·pul'sive·ness** ***n.***

rep·u·ta·ble (rep'yə tə bəl) ***adj.*** having a good reputation —**rep'u·ta·bil'i·ty** ***n.*** —**rep'u·ta·bly** ***adv.***

rep·u·ta·tion (rep'yo͞o tā'shən) ***n.*** ⟦see fol.⟧ **1** estimation in which a person or thing is commonly held **2** favorable estimation **3** fame

re·pute (ri pyo͞ot') ***vt.*** **-put'ed, -put'ing** ⟦< L *re-,* again + *putare,* think⟧ to consider or regard *[reputed* to be rich*]* —***n.*** REPUTATION (senses 1 & 3)

re·put'ed ***adj.*** generally supposed to be such *[*the *reputed* owner*]* —**re·put'ed·ly** ***adv.***

re·quest (ri kwest') ***n.*** ⟦see REQUIRE⟧ **1** an asking for something **2** something asked for **3** the state of being asked for; demand —***vt.*** **1** to ask for **2** to ask (a person) to do something

Re·qui·em (rek'wē əm, rā'kwē-) ***n.*** ⟦< L, rest⟧ [*also* **r-**] **1** *R.C.Ch.* a Mass for a dead person or persons **2** a musical setting for this

re·quire (ri kwīr') ***vt.*** **-quired', -quir'ing** ⟦< L *re-,* again + *quaerere,* ask⟧ **1** to insist upon; demand **2** to order **3** to need —**re·quire'ment** ***n.***

req·ui·site (rek'wə zit) ***adj.*** ⟦see prec.⟧ required; necessary; indispensable —***n.*** something requisite

req·ui·si·tion (rek'wə zish'ən) ***n.*** **1** a requiring; formal demand **2** a formal written order, as for equipment —***vt.*** **1** to demand or take, as by authority **2** to submit a written request for

re·quite (ri kwīt') ***vt.*** **-quit'ed, -quit'ing** ⟦RE- + *quite,* obs. var. of QUIT⟧ to repay (someone) for (a benefit, service, etc. or an injury, wrong, etc.) —**re·quit'al** ***n.***

re·run (rē'run') ***n.*** the showing of a film or TV program after the first run or showing

re'sale' ***n.*** a selling of something bought to a third party

re·scind (ri sind') ***vt.*** ⟦< L *re-,* back + *scindere,* to cut⟧ to revoke or cancel (a law, etc.) —**re·scis'sion** (-sizh'ən) ***n.***

res·cue (res'kyo͞o) ***vt.*** **-cued, -cu·ing** ⟦ult. < L *re-,* again + *ex-,* off + *quatere,* to shake⟧ to free or save from danger, imprisonment, evil, etc. —***n.*** a rescuing; deliverance —**res'cu·er** ***n.***

re·search (rē'surch', ri surch') ***n.*** ⟦see RE- & SEARCH⟧ careful, systematic study and investigation in some field of knowledge —***vi., vt.*** to do research (on or in) —**re'search'er** ***n.***

re·sec·tion (ri sek'shən) ***n.*** ⟦< L *re-,* back + *secare,* to cut⟧ *Surgery* the removal of part of an organ, bone, etc.

re·sem·blance (ri zem'bləns) ***n.*** a similarity of appearance; likeness

re·sem'ble (-bəl) ***vt.*** **-bled, -bling** ⟦ult. < L *re-,* again + *simulare,* feign⟧ to be like or similar to

THESAURUS

reproduction ***n.*** **1** [A copy] imitation, print, offprint; see COPY. **2** [A photographic reproduction] photostat, photoengraving, rotogravure, telephoto, wirephoto, X-ray, candid photo, closeup, pic, pix, blowup, facsimile, fax.

reproductive ***a.*** generative, creative, conceptive; see GENETIC.

reptile ***n.*** serpent, lizard, turtle; see SNAKE.

republic ***n.*** democracy, democratic state, constitutional government, commonwealth, self-government, representative government; see also GOVERNMENT 2.

republican ***a.*** democratic, constitutional, popular; see CONSERVATIVE, DEMOCRATIC.

Republican ***n.*** registered Republican, GOP, Old Guard, Young Republican, Old Line Republican; see also CONSERVATIVE.

repudiate ***v.*** retract, repeal, revoke; see ABANDON 1.

repulse ***v.*** **1** [To throw back] set back, overthrow, resist; see REPEL 1. **2** [To rebuff] spurn, repel, snub; see REFUSE.

repulsion ***n.*** **1** [Rejection] rebuff, denial, snub; see REFUSAL. **2** [Aversion] hate, disgust, resentment; see HATRED.

repulsive ***a.*** **1** [Capable of repelling] offensive, resistant, unyielding, stubborn, opposing, retaliating, insurgent, counteracting, attacking, counterattacking, defensive, combative, aggressive, pugnacious; see also STUBBORN.—*Ant.* YIELDING, surrendering, capitulating. **2** [Disgusting] odious, forbidding, horrid; see OFFENSIVE 2.

reputable ***a.*** **1** [Enjoying a good reputation] distinguished, celebrated, honored; see IMPORTANT 2. **2** [Honorable] trustworthy, honest, worthy; see BRAVE, NOBLE 1, 2.

reputation ***n.*** **1** [Supposed character] reliability, trustworthiness, respectability, dependability, credit, esteem, estimation; see also CHARACTER 2. **2** [Good name] standing, prestige, regard, favor, account, respect, privilege, acceptability, social approval; see also HONOR 1. **3** [Fame] prominence, eminence, notoriety; see FAME.

request ***n.*** call, inquiry, petition, question, invitation, offer, solicitation, supplication, prayer, requisition, suit, entreaty, demand; see also APPEAL 1. **—by request** asked for, sought for, wanted; see REQUESTED.

request ***v.*** **1** [To ask] demand, inquire, call for; see ASK. **2** [To solicit] beseech, entreat, sue; see BEG.

requested ***a.*** asked, demanded, popular, wished, desired, sought, hunted, needed, solicited, requisitioned, in demand; see also WANTED.

require ***v.*** **1** [To need] want, lack, have need for; see NEED. **2** [To demand] exact, insist upon, expect; see ASK.

required ***a.*** requisite, imperative, essential; see NECESSARY.

requirement ***n.*** **1** [A prerequisite] preliminary condition, essential, imperative, element, requisite, provision, terms, necessity, stipulation, fundamental, first principle, precondition, reservation, specification, proviso, qualification, vital part, *sine qua non* (Latin); see also BASIS. **2** [A need] necessity, necessary, lack, want, demand, claim, obsession, preoccupation, prepossession, extremity, exigency, pinch, obligation, pressing concern, urgency, compulsion, exaction.

rescue ***n.*** **1** [The act of rescuing] deliverance, saving, release, extrication, liberation, ransom, redemption, freeing, salvation, reclamation, reclaiming, emancipation, disentanglement, recovering, heroism. **2** [An instance of rescue] action, deed, feat, performance, exploit, accomplishment, heroics; see also ACHIEVEMENT.

rescue ***v.*** **1** [To save] preserve, recover, redeem, recapture, salvage, retain, hold over, keep back, safeguard, ransom, protect, retrieve, withdraw, take to safety; see also SAVE 1.—*Ant.* LOSE, let slip from one's hands, relinquish. **2** [To free] deliver, liberate, release; see FREE.

research ***n.*** investigation, analysis, experimentation; see EXAMINATION 1, STUDY.

research ***v.*** read up on, do research, look up; see EXAMINE, STUDY.

resemblance ***n.*** likeness, correspondence, coincidence; see SIMILARITY.

resemble ***v.*** be like, look like, seem like, sound like, follow, take after, parallel, match, coincide, relate, mirror, approximate, give indication of, remind someone of, bring to mind, have all the signs of, be the very image of, be similar to, come close to, appear like, bear a resemblance to, come near, pass for, have all the earmarks of, echo, compare with, be comparable to, smack of*, be the spit and image of*, be a dead ringer for*; see also AGREE.—*Ant.* DIFFER, contradict, oppose.

re·sent (ri zent′) ***vt.*** ⟦ult. < L *re-*, again + *sentire*, to feel⟧ to feel or show displeasure and hurt or indignation over or toward —**re·sent′ful** ***adj.*** —**re·sent′ful·ly** ***adv.*** —**re·sent′ment** ***n.***

re·ser·pine (ri sur′pin, -pēn) ***n.*** ⟦Ger⟧ a crystalline alkaloid used in treating hypertension, mental illness, etc.

res·er·va·tion (rez′ər vā′shən) ***n.*** **1** a reserving or that which is reserved; specif., *a*) a withholding *b*) public land set aside for a special use, as for American Indians *c*) holding of a hotel room, etc. until called for **2** a limiting condition

re·serve (ri zurv′) ***vt.*** **-served′**, **-serv′ing** ⟦< L *re-*, back + *servare*, to keep⟧ **1** to keep back or set apart for later or special use **2** to keep back for oneself —***n.*** **1** something kept back or stored up, as for later use **2** the keeping one's thoughts, feelings, etc. to oneself **3** reticence; silence **4** [*pl.*] troops, players, etc. kept out of action for use as replacements **5** land set apart for a special purpose **6** cash, etc. held back to meet future demands —**in reserve** reserved for later use —**without reserve** subject to no limitation

re·served′ ***adj.*** **1** kept in reserve; set apart **2** self-restrained; reticent

re·serv′ist ***n.*** a member of a country's military reserves

res·er·voir (rez′ər vwär′, -vwôr′) ***n.*** ⟦< Fr: see RESERVE⟧ **1** a place where water is collected and stored for use **2** a receptacle for holding a fluid **3** a large supply

re·side (ri zīd′) ***vi.*** **-sid′ed**, **-sid′ing** ⟦< L *re-*, back + *sedere*, sit⟧ **1** to dwell for a long time; live (*in* or *at*) **2** to be present or inherent (*in*): said of qualities, etc.

res·i·dence (rez′i dəns) ***n.*** **1** a residing **2** the place where one resides —**res′i·den′tial** (-den′shəl) ***adj.***

res′i·den·cy (-dən sē) ***n.***, *pl.* **-cies** **1** RESIDENCE (sense 1) **2** a period of advanced, specialized medical or surgical training at a hospital

res′i·dent (-dənt) ***adj.*** residing; esp., living in a place while working, etc. —***n.*** **1** one who lives in a place, not just a visitor **2** a doctor who is serving a residency

re·sid·u·al (ri zij′o͞o əl) ***adj.*** of or being a residue; remaining —***n.*** **1** something remaining **2** [*often pl.*] the fee paid for reruns on television, etc.

res·i·due (rez′ə do͞o′) ***n.*** ⟦< L *residuus*, remaining⟧ that which is left after part is taken away; remainder

re·sid·u·um (ri zij′o͞o əm) ***n.***, *pl.* **-u·a** (-ə) RESIDUE

re·sign (ri zīn′) ***vt.***, ***vi.*** ⟦< L *re-*, back + *signare*, to sign⟧ to give up (a claim, position, etc.) —**resign oneself** (**to**) to become reconciled (to)

res·ig·na·tion (rez′ig nā′shən) ***n.*** **1** *a*) the act of resigning *b*) formal notice of this **2** patient submission

re·signed (ri zīnd′) ***adj.*** feeling or showing resignation; submissive —**re·sign′ed·ly** (-zīn′id lē) ***adv.***

re·sil·ient (ri zil′yənt) ***adj.*** ⟦< L *re-*, back + *salire*, to jump⟧ **1** springing back into shape, etc. **2** recovering strength, spirits, etc. quickly —**re·sil′ience** or **re·sil′ien·cy** ***n.***

res·in (rez′ən) ***n.*** ⟦< L *resina*⟧ **1** a substance exuded from various plants and trees and used in varnishes, plastics, etc. **2** ROSIN —**res′in·ous** ***adj.***

re·sist (ri zist′) ***vt.*** ⟦< L *re-*, back + *sistere*, to set⟧ **1** to withstand; fend off **2** to oppose actively; fight against —***vi.*** to oppose or withstand something —**re·sist′er** ***n.*** —**re·sist′i·ble** ***adj.***

re·sist′ance ***n.*** **1** a resisting **2** power to resist, as to ward off disease **3** opposition of some force, thing, etc. to another, as to the flow of an electric current —**re·sist′ant** ***adj.***

re·sist′less ***adj.*** **1** irresistible **2** unable to resist

re·sis′tor ***n.*** a device used in an electrical circuit to provide resistance

re·sole (rē sōl′) ***vt.*** **-soled′**, **-sol′ing** to put a new sole on (a shoe, etc.)

res·o·lute (rez′ə lo͞ot′) ***adj.*** ⟦see RE- & SOLVE⟧ fixed and firm in purpose; determined —**res′o·lute′ly** ***adv.***

res′o·lu′tion ***n.*** **1** the act or result of resolving something **2** a thing determined upon; decision as to future action **3** a resolute quality of mind **4** a formal statement of opinion or determination by an assembly, etc.

THESAURUS

resent ***v.*** frown on, be vexed by, be insulted by; see DISLIKE.

resentment ***n.*** exasperation, annoyance, irritation; see ANGER.

reservation ***n.*** **1** [The act of reserving] restriction, limitation, withholding; see RESTRAINT 2. **2** [An instrument for reserving] card, pass, license; see TICKET 1. **3** [The space reserved] seat, car, room, bus, train, plane, box, stall, place, parking spot, table, berth, compartment.

reserve ***n.*** **1** [A portion kept against emergencies] savings, insurance, resources, reserved funds, store, provisions, assets, supply, hoard, backlog, nest egg, something in the sock*, something for a rainy day; see also SECURITY 2. **2** [Calmness] backwardness, restraint, reticence, modesty, unresponsiveness, uncommunicativeness, caution, inhibition, coyness, demureness, aloofness. —**in reserve** withheld, out of circulation, stored away; see KEPT 2, RETAINED 1, SAVED 2.

reserve ***v.*** **1** [To save] store up, set aside, put away; see MAINTAIN 3, SAVE 3. **2** [To retain] keep, possess, have; see HOLD 1, OWN 1.

reserved ***a.*** **1** [Held on reservation] preempted, claimed, booked; see SAVED 2. **2** [Held in reserve] saved, withheld, kept aside, preserved, conserved, stored away, put in a safe, on ice*.—*Ant.* USED, spent, exhausted. **3** [Restrained] shy, modest, backward, reticent, secretive, quiet, composed, retiring, private, controlling oneself, mild, gentle, peaceful, soft-spoken, sedate, collected, serene, placid.—*Ant.* LOUD, ostentatious, boisterous.

reserves ***n.*** enlisted personnel, reinforcements, volunteers; see ARMY 2.

reservoir ***n.*** storage place, tank, reserve, store, pool, cistern, water supply.

reside ***v.*** dwell, stay, lodge; see OCCUPY 2.

residence ***n.*** house, habitation, living quarters; see APARTMENT, HOME 1.

resident ***n.*** house dweller, citizen, suburbanite, tenant, inhabitant, native, denizen, occupant, inmate, homeowner, renter, householder, dweller.

residual ***a.*** left over, remaining, surplus, continuing, extra, enduring, lingering.

residue ***n.*** residual, remainder, leavings, scraps, parings, shavings, debris, sewage, dregs, silt, slag, soot, scum; see also TRASH 1.

resign ***v.*** **1** [To relinquish] surrender, capitulate, give up; see ABANDON 1, YIELD 1. **2** [To leave one's employment] quit, separate oneself from, retire, step down, drop out, stand down, sign off, end one's services, leave, hand in one's resignation, cease work, give notice, walk.

resignation ***n.*** **1** [Mental preparation for something unwelcome] submission, humility, passivity, patience, deference, docility, submissiveness, abandonment, renunciation, acquiescence, endurance, compliance.—*Ant.* RESISTANCE, immovability, unwillingness. **2** [The act of resigning] retirement, departure, leaving, quitting, giving up, abdication, surrender, withdrawal, relinquishment, vacating, tendering one's resignation, giving up office.

resigned ***a.*** quiet, peaceable, docile, tractable, submissive, yielding, relinquishing, gentle, obedient, manageable, willing, agreeable, ready, amenable, pliant, compliant, easily managed, genial, cordial, satisfied, well-disposed, patient, unresisting, tolerant, calm, reconciled, adjusted, adapted, accommodated, tame, nonresisting, passive, philosophical, renouncing, unassertive, subservient, deferential.—*Ant.* REBELLIOUS, recalcitrant, resistant.

resilience ***n.*** elasticity, snap, recoil; see FLEXIBILITY.

resilient ***a.*** rebounding, elastic, springy; see FLEXIBLE.

resin ***n.*** pine tar, pitch, gum; see GUM.

resist ***v.*** withstand, remain, endure, bear, continue, persist, stay, be strong, be immune, brook, suffer, abide, tolerate, persevere, last, oppose, bear up against, stand up to, put up a struggle, hold off, repel, remain firm, die hard.—*Ant.* STOP, desist, cease.

resistance ***n.*** **1** [A defense] stand, holding, withstanding, warding off, rebuff, obstruction, defiance, striking back, coping, check, halting, protecting, protection, safeguard, shield, screen, cover, watch, fight, impeding, blocking, opposition; see also DEFENSE 1.—*Ant.* WITHDRAWAL, withdrawing, retirement. **2** [The power of remaining impervious to an influence] unsusceptibility, immunity, immovability, hardness, imperviousness, endurance, fixedness, fastness, stability, stableness, permanence. **3** [The power of holding back another substance] friction, attrition, impedance; see RESERVE 1. **4** [An opposition] underground movement; anti-Fascist, anti-Communist, anti-American, etc., movement; boycott, strike, walkout, slowdown, front, stand, guerrilla movement; see also REVOLUTION 2.

resister ***n.*** adversary, antagonist, opponent; see OPPOSITION 2.

resolute ***a.*** steadfast, firm, courageous; see DETERMINED 1.

resolutely ***a.*** with all one's heart, bravely, with a will; see FIRMLY 1, 2.

resolution ***n.*** **1** [Fixedness of mind] fortitude, perseverance, resolve; see DETERMINATION. **2** [A for-

re·solve (ri zälv′, -zôlv′) ***vt.* -solved′, -solv′ing** ⟦see RE- & SOLVE⟧ **1** to break up into separate parts **2** to change: used reflexively **3** to reach as a decision; determine *[to resolve to go]* **4** to solve (a problem) **5** to decide by vote —***n.*** **1** firm determination **2** a formal resolution —**re·solv′a·ble *adj.***

re·solved′ *adj.* determined; resolute

res·o·nant (rez′ə nənt) ***adj.*** ⟦< L *resonare,* resound⟧ **1** resounding **2** intensifying sound *[resonant walls]* **3** sonorous; vibrant *[a resonant voice]* —**res′o·nance *n.*** —**res′o·nate′** (-nāt′), **-nat′ed, -nat′ing, *vi., vt.***

res′o·na′tor *n.* a device that produces, or increases sound by, resonance

re·sort (ri zôrt′) ***vi.*** ⟦< OFr *re-,* again + *sortir,* go out⟧ to have recourse; turn (*to*) for help, etc. *[to resort to lies]* —***n.*** **1** a place to which people go often or generally, as on vacation **2** a source of help, support, etc.; recourse —**as a last resort** as the last available means

re·sound (ri zound′) ***vi.*** ⟦< L *resonare*⟧ **1** to reverberate **2** to make a loud, echoing sound —**re·sound′ing *adj.*** —**re·sound′ing·ly *adv.***

re·source (rē′sôrs′, ri sôrs′) ***n.*** ⟦< OFr *re-,* again + *sourdre,* spring up⟧ **1** something that lies ready for use or can be drawn upon for aid **2** [*pl.*] wealth; assets **3** resourcefulness

re·source′ful *adj.* able to deal effectively with problems, etc. —**re·source′ful·ness *n.***

re·spect (ri spekt′) ***vt.*** ⟦< L *re-,* back + *specere,* look at⟧ **1** to feel or show honor or esteem for **2** to show consideration for —***n.*** **1** honor or esteem **2** consideration or regard **3** [*pl.*] expressions of regard **4** a particular detail **5** reference; relation *[with respect to the problem]* —**re·spect′ful *adj.*** —**re·spect′ful·ly *adv.***

re·spect′a·ble *adj.* **1** worthy of respect or esteem **2** proper; correct **3** fairly good in quality or size **4** presentable —**re·spect′a·bil′i·ty *n.***

re·spect′ing *prep.* concerning; about

re·spec′tive *adj.* as relates individually to each one

re·spec′tive·ly *adv.* in regard to each, in the order named

res·pi·ra·tion (res′pə rā′shən) ***n.*** ⟦< L *re-,* back + *spirare,* breathe⟧ act or process of breathing —**res·pi·ra·to·ry** (res′pər ə tôr′ē, ri spī′rə-) ***adj.***

res′pi·ra′tor *n.* **1** a mask, as of gauze, to prevent the inhaling of harmful substances **2** an apparatus to maintain breathing by artificial means

res·pite (res′pit) ***n.*** ⟦see RESPECT⟧ **1** a delay or postponement **2** temporary relief, as from pain or work; lull

re·splend·ent (ri splen′dənt) ***adj.*** ⟦< L *re-,* again + *splendere,* to shine⟧ shining brightly; dazzling —**re·splend′ence *n.*** —**re·splend′ent·ly *adv.***

re·spond (ri spänd′) ***vi.*** ⟦< L *re-,* back + *spondere,* to pledge⟧ **1** to answer; reply **2** to react **3** to have a favorable reaction

re·spond′ent *adj.* responding —***n.*** *Law* a defendant

re·sponse (ri späns′) ***n.*** ⟦see RESPOND⟧ **1** something said or done in answer; reply **2** words sung or spoken by the congregation or choir replying to the clergyman **3** any reaction to a stimulus

re·spon·si·bil·i·ty (ri spän′sə bil′ə tē) ***n., pl.* -ties** **1** a being responsible; obligation **2** a thing or person that one is responsible for

re·spon′si·ble (-bəl) ***adj.*** **1** expected or obliged to account (*for*); answerable (*to*) **2** involving obligation or duties **3** that is the cause of something **4** able to distinguish between right and wrong **5** dependable; reliable —**re·spon′si·bly *adv.***

re·spon′sive *adj.* reacting readily, as to suggestion or appeal —**re·spon′sive·ness *n.***

rest[1] (rest) ***n.*** ⟦OE⟧ **1** sleep or repose **2** ease or inactivity after exertion **3** relief from anything distressing, tiring, etc. **4** absence of motion **5** a resting place **6** a support-

THESAURUS

mal statement of opinion] verdict, decision, recommendation, analysis, elucidation, interpretation, exposition, presentation, declaration, recitation, assertion, judgment.

resolve *v.* determine, settle on, conclude, purpose, propose, choose, fix upon, make up one's mind, take a firm stand, take one's stand, take a decisive step, make a point of, pass upon, decree, elect, remain firm, take the bull by the horns; see also DECIDE.

resort *n.* **1** [A relief in the face of difficulty] expedient, shift, makeshift, stopgap, substitute, surrogate, resource, device, refuge, recourse, hope, relief, possibility, opportunity. **2** [A place for rest or amusement] *Resorts include the following:* seaside, mountain, rest, camping, skiing, sports, winter, lake, summer, gambling; amusement park, nightclub, spa, health spa, restaurant, dance hall, club; see also HOTEL, MOTEL. —**as a last resort** in desperation, lastly, in the end; see FINALLY 1, 2.

resort to *v.* turn to, refer to, apply, go to, use, try, employ, utilize, have recourse to, benefit by, put to use, fall back on, make use of, take up.

resource *n.* reserve, supply, support, source, stock, store, means, expedient, stratagem, relief, resort, recourse, artifice, device, refuge.

resourceful *a.* original, ingenious, capable; see ACTIVE, INTELLIGENT.

resources *n.* means, money, stocks, bonds, products, revenue, riches, assets, belongings, effects, capital, collateral, credit, land, holdings, real estate, investments, income, savings; see also PROPERTY 1, RESERVE 1, WEALTH.

respect *n.* esteem, honor, regard; see ADMIRATION. —**pay one's respects** wait upon, show regard, be polite; see VISIT.

respect *v.* **1** [To esteem] regard, value, look up to; see ADMIRE. **2** [To treat with consideration] heed, notice, consider, note, recognize, defer to, do honor to, be kind to, show courtesy to, spare, take into account, attend, regard, uphold; see also APPRECIATE 1.—*Ant.* RIDICULE, mock, scorn.

respectability *n.* integrity, propriety, decency; see HONESTY, VIRTUE 1.

respectable *a.* upright, presentable, fair, moderate, mediocre, tolerable, passable, ordinary, virtuous, modest, honorable, worthy, estimable, decorous, seemly, admirable, correct, reputable, proper; see also DECENT 2, HONEST 1.

respected *a.* regarded, appreciated, valued; see HONORED.

respectful *a.* deferential, considerate, appreciative, courteous, admiring, reverent, attending, upholding, regarding, valuing, venerating, recognizing, deferring to, showing respect; see also POLITE.—*Ant.* RUDE, impudent, contemptuous.

respectfully *a.* deferentially, reverentially, decorously, ceremoniously, attentively, courteously, considerately, with all respect, with due respect, with the highest respect, in deference to; see also POLITELY.—*Ant.* RUDELY, disrespectfully, impudently.

respecting *a.* regarding, concerning, in relation to; see ABOUT 2.

respiration *n.* inhalation, exhalation, breathing; see BREATH.

respite *n.* reprieve, postponement, pause; see DELAY.

respond *v.* reply, retort, acknowledge; see ANSWER 1.

response *n.* statement, reply, acknowledgment; see ANSWER 1.

responsibility *n.* **1** [State of being reliable] trustworthiness, reliability, trustiness, dependability, loyalty, faithfulness, capableness, capacity, efficiency, competency, uprightness, firmness, steadfastness, stability, ability; see also HONESTY. **2** [State of being accountable] answerability, accountability, liability, subjection, engagement, pledge, contract, constraint, restraint; see also DUTY 1.—*Ant.* FREEDOM, exemption, immunity. **3** [Anything for which one is accountable] obligation, trust, contract; see DUTY 1.

responsible *a.* **1** [Charged with responsibility] accountable, answerable, liable, subject, bound, under obligation, constrained, tied, fettered, bonded, censurable, chargeable, obligated, obliged, compelled, contracted, hampered, held, pledged, sworn to, bound to, beholden to, under contract, engaged; see also BOUND 2.—*Ant.* FREE, unconstrained, unbound. **2** [Capable of assuming responsibility] trustworthy, trusty, reliable, capable, efficient, loyal, faithful, dutiful, dependable, tried, self-reliant, able, competent, qualified, effective, upright, firm, steadfast, steady, stable; see also ABLE.—*Ant.* IRRESPONSIBLE, capricious, unstable.

rest[1] ***v.*** **1** [To take one's rest] sleep, slumber, doze, repose, lie down, lounge, let down, ease off, recuperate, rest up, take a rest, take a break, break the monotony, lean, recline, relax, unbend, settle down, dream, drowse, take one's ease, be comfortable, stretch out, nap, nod, snooze*. **2** [To depend upon] be supported, be seated on, be based on; see DEPEND ON 2.

rest[1,2] ***n.*** **1** [Repose] quiet, quietness, quietude, ease, tranquillity, slumber, calm, calmness, peace, peacefulness, relaxation, sleep, recreation, coffee break, rest period, siesta, doze, nap, somnolence, dreaminess, comfort, breathing spell, lounging period, loafing period, vacation, lull, leisure, respite, composure; see also sense 2. **2** [State of inactivity] intermission, cessation, stillness, stop, stay, standstill, lull, discontinuance, interval, hush, silence, dead calm, stagnation, fixity, immobility, inactivity, motionlessness, pause, full stop, deadlock, recess, noon hour; see also sense 1, PEACE 2.—*Ant.* ACTIVITY, continuance, endurance. **3** [Anything

ing device **7** *Music* a measured interval of silence between tones, or a symbol for this —***vi.*** **1** to get ease and refreshment by sleeping or by ceasing from work **2** to be at ease **3** to be or become still **4** to lie, sit, or lean **5** to be placed or based (*in, on,* etc.) **6** to be found *[*the fault *rests* with him*]* **7** to rely; depend —***vt.*** **1** to give rest to **2** to put for ease, support, etc. *[rest* your head here*]* **3** *Law* to stop introducing evidence in (a case) —**lay to rest** to bury

rest[2] (rest) ***n.*** ⟦< L *restare,* remain⟧ **1** what is left **2** [*with pl. v.*] the others —***vi.*** to go on being *[rest* assured*]*

res·tau·rant (res′tə ränt′, res′tränt′) ***n.*** ⟦Fr: see RESTORE⟧ a place where meals can be bought and eaten

res·tau·ra·teur (res′tə rə tʉr′, -toor′) ***n.*** ⟦Fr⟧ one who owns or operates a restaurant: also **res·tau·ran·teur** (res′ tə rän′tʉr′, -toor′)

rest·ful (rest′fəl) ***adj.*** **1** full of or giving rest **2** quiet; peaceful

rest home a residence that provides care for aged persons or convalescents

res·ti·tu·tion (res′tə to͞o′shən) ***n.*** ⟦< L *re-,* again + *statuere,* set up⟧ **1** a giving back of something that has been lost or taken away **2** reimbursement, as for loss

res·tive (res′tiv) ***adj.*** ⟦< OFr *rester,* remain⟧ **1** unruly or balky **2** nervous under restraint; restless —**res′tive·ly *adv.*** —**res′tive·ness *n.***

rest′less *adj.* **1** unable to relax; uneasy **2** giving no rest; disturbed *[restless* sleep*]* **3** rarely quiet or still; active **4** discontented —**rest′less·ly *adv.*** —**rest′less·ness *n.***

res·to·ra·tion (res′tə rā′shən) ***n.*** **1** a restoring or being restored **2** something restored, as by rebuilding

re·stor·a·tive (ri stôr′ə tiv) ***adj.*** able to restore health, consciousness, etc. —***n.*** something that is restorative

re·store (ri stôr′) ***vt.* -stored′, -stor′ing** ⟦< L *re-,* again + *-staurare,* to erect⟧ **1** to give back (something taken, lost, etc.) **2** to return to a former or normal state, or to a position, rank, use, etc. **3** to bring back to health, strength, etc.

re·strain (ri strān′) ***vt.*** ⟦< L *re-,* back + *stringere,* draw tight⟧ **1** to hold back from action; check; suppress **2** to limit; restrict

re·straint (ri strānt′) ***n.*** **1** a restraining or being restrained **2** a means or instrument of restraining **3** confinement **4** control of emotions, impulses, etc.; reserve

re·strict (ri strikt′) ***vt.*** ⟦see RESTRAIN⟧ to keep within limits; confine —**re·strict′ed *adj.*** —**re·stric′tion *n.***

re·stric′tive *adj.* **1** restricting **2** *Gram.* designating a modifier, as a subordinate clause or phrase, that limits the reference of the word it modifies and is not set off by punctuation

rest′room′ *n.* a room in a public building, equipped with toilets, washbowls, etc.: also **rest room**

re·struc·ture (rē struk′chər) ***vt.* -tured, -tur·ing** **1** to plan or provide a new structure or organization for **2** to change the terms of (a loan, etc.)

re·sult (ri zult′) ***vi.*** ⟦< L *resultare,* to rebound⟧ **1** to happen as an effect **2** to end as a consequence (*in* something) —***n.*** **1** *a*) anything that comes about as an effect

THESAURUS

upon which an object rests] support, prop, pillar; see FOUNDATION 2. **4** [*The remainder] residue, surplus, remnant; see REMAINDER. **5** [Death] release, demise, mortality; see DEATH. —**at rest** in a state of rest, immobile, inactive; see RESTING 1. —**lay to rest** inter, assign to the grave, entomb; see BURY 1.

restaurant *n.* café, eatery, cafeteria, diner, hamburger stand. *Types of restaurants include the following;* café, hotel, dining room, inn, coffee shop, coffeehouse, chophouse, tearoom, luncheonette, lunch wagon, lunchroom, fast-food place, diner, takeout place, pizzeria, lunch bar, soda fountain, juice bar, sushi bar, raw bar, bar, tavern, steakhouse, hotdog stand, snack bar, automat, rotisserie, cabaret, nightclub, cafeteria, grill, oyster house, barbecue, spaghetti house, canteen, food court, dining car, wine bar, private club, wine cellar, bistro, ethnic restaurant, icecream parlor.

rested *a.* restored, refreshed, relaxed, strengthened, renewed, unwearied, unfatigued, untired, awake, revived, recovered, brought back, reanimated, revitalized, reintegrated, unworn.—*Ant.* TIRED, wearied, fatigued.

restful *a.* untroubling, untroubled, tranquil, tranquilizing, calm, peaceful, quiet, reposeful, serene, comfortable, easy, placid, mild, still, soothing, relaxing, restoring, refreshing, renewing, revitalizing, reviving.—*Ant.* LOUD, irritating, agitating.

resting *a.* **1** [Taking rest] relaxing, unwinding, reposing, composing oneself, reclining, lying down, sleeping, stretched out, at ease, quiet, dormant, comfortable, lounging, loafing, taking a breather*, enjoying a lull, sleeping, dozing, drowsing, napping, taking a siesta, recessing, taking a vacation, having a holiday. **2** [Situated] located, settled on, seated; see OCCUPYING 1, PLACED.

restitution *n.* compensation, return, restoration; see PAYMENT 1, REPARATION.

restless *a.* fidgety, skittish, feverish, sleepless, jumpy, nervous, unquiet, disturbed, uneasy, anxious, up in arms, discontented, vexed, agitated, angry, disaffected, estranged, alienated, resentful, recalcitrant, fractious, insubordinate, flurried, roving, transient, wandering, discontented, unsettled, roaming, nomadic, moving, straying, ranging, footloose, itinerant, gallivanting, meandering, traipsing, restive, peeved, annoyed, impatient, flustered, twitching, trembling, tremulous, rattled*, jittery*; see also ACTIVE, EXCITED, REBELLIOUS.—*Ant.* QUIET, sedate, calm.

restlessness *n.* uneasiness, discomfort, excitability; see EXCITEMENT, NERVOUSNESS.

restoration *n.* **1** [The act of restoring] revival, return, renewal; see RECOVERY 1. **2** [The act of reconstructing] rehabilitation, reconstruction, refurbishing; see REPAIR.

restore *v.* **1** [To give back] make restitution, replace, put back; see RETURN 2. **2** [To re-create] reestablish, revive, recover; see RENEW 1. **3** [To rebuild in a form supposed to be original] rebuild, alter, rehabilitate; see RECONSTRUCT, REPAIR. **4** [To bring back to health] refresh, cure, make healthy; see HEAL.

restrain *v.* check, control, curb, bridle, rein in, hem in, keep in, handle, regulate, keep in line, guide, direct, keep down, repress, harness, muzzle, hold in leash, govern, inhibit, hold, bind, deter, hold back, hamper, constrain, restrict, stay, gag, limit, impound, bottle up, tie down, pin down, pull back, contain, sit on*, come down on.

restrained *a.* under control, in check, on a leash; see HELD.

restraint *n.* **1** [Control over oneself] control, self-control, reserve, reticence, constraint, withholding, caution, coolness, forbearance, silence, secretiveness, stress, repression, self-restraint, stiffness, abstinence, self-denial, unnaturalness, self-repression, constrained manner, abstention, self-discipline, self-censorship; see also ATTENTION.—*Ant.* LAZINESS, slackness, laxity. **2** [An influence that checks or hinders] repression, deprivation, limitation, hindrance, reduction, abridgment, decrease, prohibition, confinement, check, barrier, obstacle, obstruction, restriction, bar, curb, blockade, order, command, instruction, coercion, impediment, compulsion, duress, force, violence, deterrence, determent, discipline, definition, moderation, tempering, qualifying.—*Ant.* FREEDOM, liberty, license.

restrict *v.* delimit, limit, circumscribe, assign, contract, shorten, narrow, decrease, enclose, keep in, keep within bounds, define, encircle, surround, shut in, tether, chain, diminish, reduce, moderate, modify, temper, qualify, come down on, pin down.—*Ant.* INCREASE, extend, expand.

restricted *a.* limited, confined, restrained, circumscribed, curbed, bound, prescribed, checked, bounded, inhibited, hampered, marked, defined, delimited, encircled, surrounded, shut in, hitched, tethered, chained, fastened, secured, bridled, held back, held down, reined in, controlled, governed, deterred, impeded, stayed, stopped, suppressed, repressed, prevented, fettered, deprived, obstructed, manacled, barred, blocked, dammed, clogged, frustrated, foiled, shrunken, narrowed, shortened, decreased, diminished, reduced, moderated, tempered, modified, qualified, out of bounds; see also BOUND 1, 2.

restriction *n.* constraint, limitation, stipulation; see RESTRAINT 2.

result *n.* consequence, issue, event, effect, outcome, finish, termination, consummation, completion, aftereffect, aftermath, upshot, sequel, sequence, fruit, fruition, eventuality, proceeds, emanation, outgrowth, returns, backwash, backlash, repercussion, settlement, determination, decision, arrangement, payoff*; see also END 2, 4.—*Ant.* ORIGIN, source, root.

result *v.* issue, grow from, spring from, rise from, proceed from, emanate from, germinate from, flow from, accrue from, arise from, derive from, come from, originate in, become of, spring, emerge, rise, ensue, emanate, effect, produce, follow, happen, occur, come about, come forth, come out, pan out, work out, end, finish, terminate, conclude.

b) [*pl.*] the desired effect **2** the number, etc. obtained by mathematical calculation —**re·sult'ant** *adj., n.*

re·sume (ri zo͞om') *vt.* **-sumed', -sum'ing** ⟦< L *re-*, again + *sumere,* take⟧ **1** to take or occupy again **2** to continue after interruption —*vi.* to proceed after interruption —**re·sump'tion** (-zump'shən) *n.*

ré·su·mé (rez'ə mā') *n.* ⟦Fr: see prec.⟧ a summary, esp. of employment experience: also written **resume** or **resumé**

re·sur·face (rē sʉr'fis) *vt.* **-faced, -fac·ing** to put a new surface on —*vi.* to come to the surface again

re·sur·gent (ri sʉr'jənt) *adj.* ⟦see fol.⟧ rising or tending to rise again —**re·sur'gence** *n.*

res·ur·rec·tion (rez'ə rek'shən) *n.* ⟦< L *resurgere,* rise again⟧ **1** a rising from the dead **2** a coming back into notice, use, etc.; revival —**the Resurrection** *Theol.* the rising of Jesus from the dead —**res'ur·rect'** *vt.*

re·sus·ci·tate (ri sus'ə tāt') *vt., vi.* **-tat'ed, -tat'ing** ⟦< L *re-*, again + *suscitare,* revive⟧ to revive when apparently dead or in a faint, etc. —**re·sus'ci·ta'tion** *n.* —**re·sus'ci·ta'tor** *n.*

ret *abbrev.* **1** retired **2** return(ed)

re·tail (rē'tāl') *n.* ⟦< OFr *re-*, again + *tailler,* to cut⟧ the sale of goods in small quantities directly to the consumer —*adj.* of or engaged in such sale —*adv.* at a retail price —*vt., vi.* to sell or be sold directly to the consumer —**re'tail'er** *n.*

re·tain (ri tān') *vt.* ⟦< L *re-*, back + *tenere,* to hold⟧ **1** to keep in possession, use, etc. **2** to hold in **3** to keep in mind **4** to hire by paying a retainer

re·tain'er *n.* **1** something that retains **2** a servant, attendant, etc. **3** a fee paid in advance to engage the services of a lawyer, etc.

retaining wall a wall for keeping earth from sliding or water from flooding

re·take (rē tāk'; *for n.* rē'tāk') *vt.* **-took', -tak'en, -tak'ing** **1** to take again; recapture **2** to photograph again —*n.* a scene, etc. rephotographed

re·tal·i·ate (ri tal'ē āt') *vi.* **-at'ed, -at'ing** ⟦< L *re-*, back + *talio,* punishment in kind⟧ to return like for like, esp. injury for injury —**re·tal'i·a'tion** *n.* —**re·tal'i·a·to'ry** *adj.*

re·tard (ri tärd') *vt.* ⟦< L *re-*, back + *tardare,* make slow⟧ to hinder, delay, or slow the progress of —**re·tar·da·tion** (rē'tär dā'shən) *n.*

re·tard'ant *n.* something that retards; esp., a substance that delays a chemical reaction —*adj.* that retards

re·tard'ed *adj.* slowed or delayed in development, esp. mentally

retch (rech) *vi.* ⟦OE *hræcan,* clear the throat⟧ to strain to vomit, esp. without bringing anything up

re·ten·tion (ri ten'shən) *n.* **1** a retaining or being retained **2** capacity for retaining **3** a remembering; memory —**re·ten'tive** *adj.*

ret·i·cent (ret'ə sənt) *adj.* ⟦< L *re-*, again + *tacere,* be silent⟧ disinclined to speak; taciturn —**ret'i·cence** *n.*

ret·i·na (ret''n ə) *n., pl.* **-nas** or **-nae'** (-ē') ⟦prob. < L *rete,* a net⟧ the innermost coat lining the eyeball, containing light-sensitive cells that are directly connected to the brain

ret·i·nue (ret''n o͞o') *n.* ⟦< OFr, ult. < L: see RETAIN⟧ a group of persons attending a person of rank or importance

re·tire (ri tīr') *vi.* **-tired', -tir'ing** ⟦< Fr *re-*, back + *tirer,* draw⟧ **1** to withdraw to a secluded place **2** to go to bed **3** to retreat, as in battle **4** to give up one's work, business, etc., esp. because of age —*vt.* **1** to pay off (bonds, etc.) **2** to cause to retire from a position, office, etc. **3** to withdraw from use **4** *Baseball* to put out (a batter, side, etc.) —**re·tir'ee'** *n.* —**re·tire'ment** *n.*

re·tired' *adj.* **1** secluded **2** *a*) no longer working, etc. as because of age *b*) of or for such retired persons

re·tir'ing *adj.* reserved; modest; shy

re·tool (rē to͞ol') *vt., vi.* **1** to adapt (factory machinery) for a different product **2** to reorganize to meet new or different needs or conditions

re·tort[1] (ri tôrt') *vt.* ⟦< L *re-*, back + *torquere,* to twist⟧ to say in reply —*vi.* to make a sharp, witty reply —*n.* a sharp, witty reply

re·tort[2] (ri tôrt') *n.* ⟦< ML *retorta*: see prec.⟧ a glass container with a long tube, in which substances are distilled

re·touch (rē tuch') *vt.* to touch up details in (a painting, essay, etc.) so as to improve or change it

re·trace (rē trās') *vt.* **-traced', -trac'ing** ⟦see RE- & TRACE[1]⟧ to go back over again [*to retrace* one's steps]

re·tract (ri trakt') *vt., vi.* ⟦< L *re-*, back + *trahere,* draw⟧ **1** to draw back or in **2** to withdraw (a statement, charge, etc.) —**re·tract'a·ble** or **re·trac'tile** (-trak'təl, -tīl') *adj.* —**re·trac'tion** *n.*

re·tread (rē tred'; *for n.* rē'tred') *vt., n.* RECAP[1]

re·treat (ri trēt') *n.* ⟦< L *retrahere:* see RETRACT⟧ **1** a withdrawal, as from danger **2** a safe, quiet place **3** a period of seclusion, esp. for spiritual renewal **4** *a*) the forced withdrawal of troops under attack *b*) a signal for this *c*) a signal, as by bugle, or a ceremony at sunset for lowering the national flag —*vi.* to withdraw; go back

re·trench (rē trench') *vi.* ⟦< Fr: see RE- & TRENCH⟧ to cut down expenses; economize —**re·trench'ment** *n.*

ret·ri·bu·tion (re'trə byo͞o'shən) *n.* ⟦< L *re-*, back + *tribuere,* to pay⟧ punishment for evil done —**re·trib·u·tive** (ri trib'yoo tiv) *adj.*

re·trieve (ri trēv') *vt.* **-trieved', -triev'ing** ⟦< OFr *re-*, again + *trouver,* find⟧ **1** to get back; recover **2** to restore

THESAURUS

resume *v.* take up again, reassume, begin again, recommence, reoccupy, go on with, renew, recapitulate, return, keep on, carry on, keep up; see also CONTINUE 2.—*Ant.* STOP, cease, discontinue.

résumé *n.* curriculum vitae, vita, CV, synopsis, abstract, précis, work history, biography; see also SUMMARY.

resurrection *n.* return to life, reanimation, reawakening, salvation, rebirth; see also RENEWAL.

retain *v.* **1** [To hold] cling to, grasp, clutch; see HOLD 1. **2** [To reserve services] employ, maintain, engage; see HIRE. **3** [To remember] recall, recollect, recognize; see REMEMBER 1.

retained *a.* **1** [Kept] had, held, possessed, owned, enjoyed, secured, saved, preserved, maintained, restrained, confined, curbed, detained, contained, received, admitted, included, withheld, put away, treasured, sustained, celebrated, remembered, commemorated; see also KEPT 2.—*Ant.* LOST, wasted, refused. **2** [Employed] hired, engaged, contracted for; see EMPLOYED.

retaliate *v.* fight back, return, repay; see REVENGE.

retaliation *n.* vengeance, reprisal, punishment; see REVENGE 1.

retard *v.* postpone, delay, impede; see HINDER.

retarded *a.* **1** [*Said of persons*] backward, slow, developmentally disabled; see DULL 3. **2** [*Said of activities*] delayed, slowed down, held back; see SLOW 1, 2, 3.

retire *v.* **1** [To draw away] withdraw, part, retreat; see LEAVE 1. **2** [To go to bed] lie down, turn in, rest; see SLEEP. **3** [To cease active life] resign, give up work, sever one's connections, leave active service, stop working, make vacant, lay down, hand over, lead a quiet life, sequester oneself, reach retirement age.

retired *a.* resigned, in retirement, emeritus, emerita, on a pension, on Social Security, having reached retirement age, laid down, handed over, withdrawn, retreated, removed, leading a quiet life, secluding oneself, separating oneself, aloof.—*Ant.* ACTIVE, working, busy.

retirement *n.* **1** [The act of retiring] removal, vacating, separation; see RESIGNATION 2. **2** [The state of being retired] seclusion, aloofness, apartness, separateness, privacy, concealment, solitude, solitariness, isolation, remoteness, loneliness, quiet, retreat, tranquillity, refuge, serenity, inactivity; see also SILENCE 1.—*Ant.* EXPOSURE, activity, association.

retort[1] *n.* counter, repartee, response; see ANSWER 1.

retort[1] *v.* reply, respond, snap back; see ANSWER 1.

retract *v.* withdraw, take back, take in; see REMOVE 1.

retraction *n.* denial, revocation, disowning; see DENIAL, CANCELLATION.

retreat *n.* **1** [The act of retreating] retirement, removal, evacuation, departure, escape, withdrawal, drawing back, reversal, retrogression, backing out, flight, recession, going, running away, eluding, evasion, avoidance, recoil.—*Ant.* ADVANCE, progress, progression. **2** [A place to which one retreats] seclusion, solitude, privacy, shelter, refuge, asylum, safe place, defense, sanctuary, security, cover, ark, harbor, port, haven, place of concealment, hiding place, hideaway*, resort, haunt, habitat, hermitage, cell, convent, cloister, abbey, monastery, home, cabin, lodge.—*Ant.* FRONT, exposed position, van.

retreat *v.* recede, retrograde, back out, retract, go, depart, recoil, shrink, quail, run, draw back, reel, start back, reverse, seclude oneself, keep aloof, hide, separate from, regress, resign, relinquish, lay down, hand over, withdraw, backtrack, leave, back off*, back down, chicken out*.—*Ant.* STAY, remain, continue.

retribution *n.* vengeance, reprisal, retaliation; see REVENGE 1.

retrieve *v.* regain, bring back, reclaim; see RECOVER 1.

3 to make good (a loss, error, etc.) 4 to access (data) stored in a computer 5 to find and bring back (killed or wounded game): said of dogs —*vi.* to retrieve game —**re·triev'al** *n.*

re·triev'er *n.* a dog trained to retrieve game

retro- ⟦< L⟧ *combining form* backward, back, behind

ret·ro·ac·tive (re'trō ak'tiv) *adj.* having an effect on things that are already past —**ret'ro·ac'tive·ly** *adv.*

ret·ro·fire (re'trə fīr') *vt.* **-fired', -fir'ing** to ignite (a retrorocket)

ret'ro·fit' (-fit') *n.* a change in design or equipment, as of an aircraft already in operation, so as to incorporate later improvements —*vt., vi.* **-fit'ted, -fit'ting** to modify with a retrofit

ret'ro·grade' (-grād') *adj.* ⟦< L: see RETRO- & GRADE⟧ 1 moving backward 2 going back to a worse condition

ret'ro·gress' (-gres') *vi.* ⟦< L: see prec.⟧ to move backward, esp. into a worse condition; degenerate —**ret'ro·gres'sion** *n.* —**ret'ro·gres'sive** *adj.*

ret·ro·rock·et or **ret·ro-rock·et** (re'trō räk'it) *n.* a small rocket, as on a spacecraft, producing thrust opposite to the direction of flight to reduce speed, as for maneuvering

ret·ro·spect (re'trə spekt') *n.* ⟦< L *retro-*, back + *specere*, to look⟧ contemplation of the past —**ret'ro·spec'tion** *n.*

ret'ro·spec'tive *adj.* looking back on the past —*n.* a representative show of an artist's lifetime work

ret·si·na (ret sē'nə) *n.* ⟦ModGr, prob. < It *resina*, resin⟧ a Greek wine flavored with pine resin

re·turn (ri turn') *vi.* ⟦< OFr: see RE- & TURN⟧ 1 to go or come back 2 to answer; reply —*vt.* 1 to bring, send, or put back 2 to do in reciprocation *[to return a visit]* 3 to yield (a profit, etc.) 4 to report officially 5 to elect or reelect —*n.* 1 a coming or going back 2 a bringing, sending, or putting back 3 something returned 4 a recurrence 5 repayment; requital 6 [*often pl.*] yield or profit, as from investments 7 an answer; reply 8 *a)* an official report *[election returns]* *b)* a form for computing income tax —*adj.* 1 of or for a return *[return postage]* 2 given, done, etc. in return —**in return** as a return; as an equivalent, response, etc. —**re·turn'a·ble** *adj.*

re·turn'ee' *n.* one who returns, as home from military service

Reu·ben (sandwich) (ro͞o'bən) a sandwich of rye bread, corned beef, sauerkraut, Swiss cheese, etc. served hot

re·u·ni·fy (rē yo͞o'nə fī') *vt., vi.* **-fied', -fy'ing** to unify again after being divided —**re·u'ni·fi·ca'tion** *n.*

re·un·ion (rē yo͞on'yən) *n.* a coming together again, as after separation

re-up (rē up') *vi.* **-upped', -up'ping** ⟦RE- + (*sign*) *up*⟧ [Mil. Slang] to reenlist

rev[1] (rev) *vt.* **revved, rev'ving** ⟦< REV(OLUTION)⟧ [Inf.] 1 to increase the speed of (an engine) 2 to accelerate, intensify, etc. Usually with *up*

rev[2] *abbrev.* 1 revenue 2 revise(d) 3 revolution

Rev *abbrev.* 1 *Bible* Revelation 2 Reverend

re·vamp (rē vamp') *vt.* to renovate; redo

re·veal (ri vēl') *vt.* ⟦< L *re-*, back + *velum*, veil⟧ 1 to make known (something hidden or secret) 2 to show; exhibit; display

rev·eil·le (rev'ə lē) *n.* ⟦< Fr < L *re-*, again + *vigilare*, to watch⟧ a signal on a bugle, drum, etc. in the morning to waken soldiers, etc.

rev·el (rev'əl) *vi.* **-eled** or **-elled, -el·ing** or **-el·ling** ⟦< MFr < L *rebellare*, to rebel: see REBEL⟧ 1 to be festive; make merry 2 to take much pleasure (*in*) —*n.* merrymaking —**rev'el·er** or **rev'el·ler** *n.* —**rev'el·ry**, *pl.* **-ries**, *n.*

rev·e·la·tion (rev'ə lā'shən) *n.* 1 a revealing 2 a striking disclosure 3 *Theol.* God's disclosure to humanity of divine truth, etc. —**[R-]** the last book of the New Testament

re·venge (ri venj') *vt.* **-venged', -veng'ing** ⟦< OFr: see RE- & VENGEANCE⟧ to inflict harm in return for (an injury, etc.) —*n.* 1 the act or result of revenging 2 desire to take vengeance —**re·venge'ful** *adj.*

rev·e·nue (rev'ə no͞o') *n.* ⟦< MFr, returned⟧ 1 return, as from investment; income 2 the income from taxes, licenses, etc., as of a city or nation

re·ver·ber·ate (ri vur'bə rāt') *vi., vt.* **-at'ed, -at'ing** ⟦< L *re-*, again + *verberare*, to beat⟧ to reecho or cause to reecho —**re·ver'ber·a'tion** *n.*

THESAURUS

return *a.* coming back, repeat, repeating, repetitive, recurring, reappearing, sent back, answering, replying, retorting, rotating, turning, rebounding, recurrent, intermittent, round-trip; see also REPEATED 1.

return *n.* 1 [The act of coming again] homecoming, arrival, reappearance; see sense 2. 2 [The fact or process of being returned] restoration, restitution, rejoinder, recompense, acknowledgment, answer, reaction, reversion, repetition, reverberation, reappearance, rotation, recurrence, resurgence, renewal, recovery, replacement, reoccurrence, rebound, recoil, reconsideration. 3 [Proceeds] profit, income, results, gain, avail, revenue, advantage, yield, accrual, accruement, interest.—*Ant.* FAILURE, loss, disadvantage. —**in return** in exchange, as payment, as an equivalent, as a reward, back, in response.

return *v.* 1 [To go back] come again, come back, recur, reappear, reoccur, repeat, revert, reconsider, reenter, reexamine, reinspect, bounce back, retrace one's steps, turn, rotate, revolve, renew, revive, recover, regain, rebound, circle back, double back, move back, turn back, reverberate, recoil, retrace, revisit, retire, retreat.—*Ant.* MOVE, advance, go forward. 2 [To put or send something back] bring back, toss back, roll back, hand back, give back, restore, replace, render, reseat, reestablish, reinstate, react, recompense, refund, repay, make restitution.—*Ant.* HOLD, keep, hold back. 3 [To answer] reply, respond, retort; see ANSWER 1. 4 [To repay] reimburse, recompense, refund; see REPAY 1. 5 [To yield a profit] pay off, show profit, pay dividends; see PAY 2. 6 [To reflect] echo, sound, mirror; see REFLECT 2, 3.

returned *a.* restored, given back, gone back, sent back, brought back, turned back, come back, repeated, reentered, rotated, revolved, rebounded, reverberated, refunded, acknowledged, answered, repaid, yielded; see also REFUSED.—*Ant.* KEPT, held, retained.

reunion *n.* reuniting, meeting again, rejoining, reconciliation, reconcilement, homecoming, restoration, harmonizing, bringing together, healing the breach, get-together.

reunite *v.* meet again, reassemble, reconvene, join, rejoin, become reconciled, have a reconciliation, be restored to one another, remarry, heal the breach, get together, patch it up, make up.—*Ant.* SEPARATE, go separate ways, be disrupted.

reveal *v.* disclose, betray a confidence, divulge, make known, confess, impart, publish, lay bare, betray, avow, admit, bring to light, acknowledge, give utterance to, bring out, let out, give out, make public, unfold, communicate, announce, declare, inform, notify, utter, make plain, break the news, broadcast, concede, come out with, explain, bring into the open, affirm, report, let the cat out of the bag, blab*, talk, rat*, stool*, make a clean breast of, put one's cards on the table, bring to light, show one's colors, get something out of one's system, give the low-down*, let on*, squeal*, blow the whistle*; see also TELL 1.

revelation *n.* 1 [A disclosure] divulgence, announcement, betrayal; see RECORD 1. 2 [Revealed divine truth] divine word, God's word, revealed truth; see DOCTRINE, FAITH 2.

revenge *n.* 1 [The act of returning an injury] vengeance, requital, reprisal, measure for measure, repayment, sortie, retaliation, retribution, avenging, counterinsurgency, getting even; see also ATTACK, FIGHT 1.—*Ant.* PARDON, forgiveness, excusing. 2 [The desire to obtain revenge] vindictiveness, rancor, malevolence; see HATRED.

revenge *v.* retaliate, vindicate, requite, take revenge, breathe vengeance, have accounts to settle, have one's revenge, pay back, make reprisal, get even with, punish for, repay, return like for like, retort, match, reciprocate, square accounts, settle up, take an eye for an eye, turn the tables on, get back at*, fight back, hit back at, be out for blood, give and take, give someone his or her just deserts, even the score, get*, fix*, get square with, return the compliment.—*Ant.* FORGIVE, condone, pardon.

revenue *n.* 1 [Income] return, earnings, result, yield, wealth, receipts, proceeds, resources, funds, credits, dividends, interest, salary, profits, means, fruits, rents; see also INCOME, PAY 1, 2.—*Ant.* EXPENSES, outgo, obligations. 2 [Governmental income] wealth, taxes, taxation; see INCOME, TAX 1. *Types of revenue include the following:* direct tax, indirect tax, bonds, loans, customs, duties, tariff, tax surcharge, excise, property tax, income tax, inheritance and death tax, land tax, poll tax, gasoline tax, school tax, franchise, license, grants, rates, bridge and road tolls, harbor dues, special taxation, patent stamps, stamp duties, registration duties, internal revenue, tax on spirits, tobacco tax, sin tax, lease of land, sale of land, subsidy.

re·vere (ri vir′) *vt.* **-vered′, -ver′ing** ⟦< L *re-,* again + *vereri,* to fear⟧ to regard with deep respect, love, etc.

Re·vere (ri vir′), **Paul** 1735-1818; Am. silversmith & patriot

rev·er·ence (rev′ə rəns) *n.* a feeling of deep respect, love, and awe —*vt.* **-enced, -enc·ing** to treat or regard with reverence; venerate —**rev′er·ent** or **rev′er·en′tial** (-ə ren′ shəl) *adj.* —**rev′er·ent·ly** *adv.*

rev·er·end (rev′ə rənd) *adj.* worthy of reverence: used with *the* as a title of respect for a member of the clergy *[*the *Reverend* A. B. Smith*]*

rev·er·ie (rev′ə rē) *n.* ⟦< Fr⟧ daydreaming or a daydream

re·vers (ri vir′, -ver′) *n., pl.* **-vers′** (-virz′, -verz′) ⟦Fr: see REVERT⟧ a part (of a garment) turned back to show the reverse side, as a lapel: also **re·vere′** (-vir′)

re·verse (ri vurs′) *adj.* ⟦see REVERT⟧ **1** turned backward; opposite or contrary **2** causing movement in the opposite direction —*n.* **1** the opposite or contrary **2** the back of a coin, medal, etc. **3** a change from good fortune to bad **4** a mechanism for reversing, as a gear on a machine —*vt.* **-versed′, -vers′ing 1** to turn backward, in an opposite position or direction, upside down, or inside out **2** to change to the opposite **3** *Law* to revoke or annul (a decision, etc.) —*vi.* to go or turn in the opposite direction —**re·ver′sal** (-vur′səl) *n.* —**re·vers′i·ble** *adj.* —**re·vers′i·bly** *adv.*

re·vert (ri vurt′) *vi.* ⟦< L *re-,* back + *vertere,* to turn⟧ **1** to go back, as to a former practice, state, subject, etc. **2** *Biol.* to return to a former or primitive type **3** *Law* to go back to a former owner or his or her heirs —**re·ver′sion** (-vur′zhən) *n.* —**re·vert′i·ble** *adj.*

re·vet·ment (ri vet′mənt) *n.* ⟦< Fr⟧ **1** a facing of stone, cement, etc., as to protect an embankment **2** RETAINING WALL

re·view (ri vyoo′) *n.* ⟦< L *re-,* again + *videre,* see⟧ **1** a looking at or looking over again **2** a general survey or report **3** a looking back on (past events, etc.) **4** reexamination, as of the decision of a lower court **5** a critical evaluation of a book, play, etc. **6** a formal inspection, as of troops on parade —*vt.* **1** to look back on **2** to survey in thought, speech, etc. **3** to inspect (troops, etc.) formally **4** to give a critical evaluation of (a book, etc.) **5** to study again —**re·view′er** *n.*

re·vile (ri vīl′) *vt.* **-viled′, -vil′ing** ⟦< OFr: see RE- & VILE⟧ to use abusive language to or about —**re·vile′ment** *n.* —**re·vil′er** *n.*

re·vise (ri vīz′) *vt.* **-vised′, -vis′ing** ⟦< L *re-,* back + *visere,* to survey⟧ **1** to read over carefully and correct, improve, or update **2** to change or amend —**re·vi′sion** (-vizh′ən) *n.*

Revised Standard Version a 20th-c. version of the Bible

re·vi′sion·ist *n.* a person who revises, or favors the revision of, some accepted theory, doctrine, etc. —*adj.* of revisionists or their policy or practice —**re·vi′sion·ism′** *n.*

re·vis·it (rē viz′it) *vt.* **1** to visit again **2** to reconsider or reevaluate

re·viv·al (ri vī′vəl) *n.* **1** a reviving or being revived **2** a bringing or coming back into use, being, etc. **3** a new presentation of an earlier play, etc. **4** restoration to vigor or activity **5** a meeting led by an evangelist to stir up religious feeling —**re·viv′al·ist** *n.*

re·vive (ri vīv′) *vi., vt.* **-vived′, -viv′ing** ⟦< L *re-,* again + *vivere,* to live⟧ **1** to return to life or consciousness **2** to return to health or vigor **3** to come or bring back into use, attention, popularity, etc.

re·viv·i·fy (ri viv′ə fī′) *vt.* **-fied′, -fy′ing** to put new life or vigor into —*vi.* to revive —**re·viv′i·fi·ca′tion** *n.*

re·voke (ri vōk′) *vt.* **-voked′, -vok′ing** ⟦< L *re-,* back + *vocare,* to call⟧ to withdraw, repeal, or cancel (a law, etc.) —**rev·o·ca·ble** (rev′ə kə bəl, ri vō′kə-) *adj.* —**rev′o·ca′tion** (-kā′shən) *n.*

re·volt (ri vōlt′) *n.* ⟦< Fr: see REVOLVE⟧ a rebelling against the government or any authority —*vi.* to rebel against authority —*vt.* to disgust —**re·volt′ing** *adj.* —**re·volt′ing·ly** *adv.*

rev·o·lu·tion (rev′ə loo′shən) *n.* ⟦see REVOLVE⟧ **1** the movement of a body in an orbit **2** a turning around an axis; rotation **3** a complete cycle of events **4** a complete change **5** overthrow of a government, social system, etc. —**rev′o·lu′tion·ar′y,** *pl.* **-ies,** *n., adj.* —**rev′o·lu′tion·ist** *n.*

Revolutionary War *see* AMERICAN REVOLUTION

rev′o·lu′tion·ize′ (-shə nīz′) *vt.* **-ized′, -iz′ing** to make a fundamental change in

re·volve (ri välv′, -vôlv′) *vt.* **-volved′, -volv′ing** ⟦< L *re-,* back + *volvere,* to roll⟧ to turn over in the mind —*vi.* **1** to move in a circle or orbit **2** to rotate —**re·volv′a·ble** *adj.*

THESAURUS

revere *v.* venerate, regard with deep respect, respect; see ADMIRE.

reverence *n.* respect, admiration, love, regard, approval, approbation, esteem, deference, awe, fear, veneration, honor, devotion, adoration; see also PRAISE 2.—*Ant.* HATRED, contempt, disdain.

reverent *a.* venerating, esteeming, honoring; see RESPECTFUL.

reversal *n.* renunciation, repudiation, repeal; see CANCELLATION, REFUSAL, WITHDRAWAL.

reverse *n.* **1** [The opposite] converse, other side, contrary; see OPPOSITE. **2** [A defeat] downfall, catastrophe, setback; see DEFEAT.

reverse *v.* **1** [To turn] go back, shift, invert; see TURN 2. **2** [To alter] turn around, modify, convert; see CHANGE 2. **3** [To annul] nullify, invalidate, repeal; see CANCEL. **4** [To exchange] transpose, rearrange, shift; see EXCHANGE 1.

reversed *a.* turned around, turned back, backward, end for end, inverted, contrariwise, out of order, regressive, retrogressive, undone, unmade.—*Ant.* ORDERED, established, in proper order.

revert *v.* go back, reverse, relapse; see RETURN 1.

review *n.* **1** [A reexamination] reconsideration, second thought, revision, retrospection, second view, reflection, study, survey, retrospect. **2** [A critical study] survey, critique, criticism; see EXAMINATION 1. **3** [A summary] synopsis, abstract, outline; see SUMMARY. **4** [A formal inspection] parade, inspection, dress parade, drill, march, procession, cavalcade, column, file, military display; see also DISPLAY.

review *v.* **1** [To correct] criticize, revise, reedit; see CORRECT. **2** [To inspect] analyze, reexamine, check thoroughly; see EXAMINE.

revise *v.* reconsider, rewrite, correct; see EDIT.

revised *a.* corrected, edited, amended, overhauled, improved, altered, changed, rectified, polished, redone, rewritten, reorganized, restyled, emended.

revision *n.* reexamination, correction, editing; see CORRECTION.

revival *n.* **1** [The act of reviving] renewal, renascence, renaissance, refreshment, arousal, awakening, rebirth, reversion, resurrection, enkindling, restoration, invigoration, vivification, resuscitation, reawakening, improvement, freshening, recovery, cheering, consolation. **2** [An evangelical service] tent meeting, prayer meeting, camp meeting; see CEREMONY.

revive *v.* **1** [To give new life] enliven, enkindle, refresh, renew, vivify, animate, reanimate, resuscitate, recondition, rejuvenate, bring to, bring around, wake up, resurrect, make whole, exhilarate, energize, invigorate, breathe new life into, regenerate, restore, touch up, repair.—*Ant.* DECREASE, wither, lessen. **2** [To take on new life] come around, come to, freshen, improve, recover, flourish, awake, reawaken, rouse, strengthen, overcome, come to life, grow well, be cured.—*Ant.* DIE, faint, weaken.

revoke *v.* recall, retract, disclaim; see CANCEL.

revolt *n.* uprising, mutiny, sedition; see REVOLUTION 2.

revolt *v.* **1** [To rebel] mutiny, rise up, resist; see REBEL. **2** [To repel] sicken, offend, nauseate; see DISGUST.

revolting *a.* awful, loathsome, repulsive; see OFFENSIVE 2, SHAMEFUL 1, 2.

revolution *n.* **1** [A complete turn or motion around something] turning, rotation, spin, turn, revolving, circuit, round, whirl, gyration, circumvolution, cycle, roll, reel, twirl, swirl, pirouette. **2** [An armed uprising] revolt, rebellion, mutiny, insurrection, riot, anarchy, outbreak, coup, coup d'état, destruction, overturn, upset, overthrow, reversal, rising, crime, violence, bloodshed, turbulence, insubordination, disturbance, reformation, plot, underground activity, guerrilla activity, public unrest, upheaval, tumult, disorder, turmoil, uproar, uprising, row, strife, strike, putsch, subversion, breakup, secession.—*Ant.* LAW, order, control.

revolutionary *a.* **1** [Concerned with a revolution] rebellious, mutinous, insurrectionary, destructive, anarchistic, subverting, insurgent, overturning, upsetting, destroying, reformist, subversive, seceding, riotous, agitating, disturbing, working underground, treasonable.—*Ant.* PATRIOTIC, loyal, constructive. **2** [New and unusual] novel, advanced, radical; see UNUSUAL 2.

revolutionary *n.* reformer, traitor, insurrectionist; see REBEL.

revolutionize *v.* recast, remodel, refashion; see REFORM 1.

revolve *v.* spin, rotate, twirl; see TURN 1.

re·volv'er ***n.*** a handgun with a revolving cylinder containing cartridges

re·vue (ri vyōō') ***n.*** ⟦Fr, review⟧ a musical show with skits, dances, etc., often parodying recent events

re·vul·sion (ri vul'shən) ***n.*** ⟦< L *re-*, back + *vellere,* to pull⟧ extreme disgust; loathing

re·ward (ri wôrd') ***n.*** ⟦< OFr *regarde*: see REGARD⟧ **1** something given in return for something done **2** money offered, as for capturing a criminal —***vt.*** to give a reward to (someone) for (service, etc.)

re·ward'ing ***adj.*** giving a sense of reward or worthwhile return

re·wind (rē wīnd') ***vt.*** **-wound', -wind'ing** to wind again; specif., to wind (film or tape) back on the original reel

re·word' ***vt.*** to change the wording of

re·write' ***vt., vi.*** **-wrote', -writ'ten, -writ'ing** **1** to write again **2** to revise (something written) **3** to write (news turned in) in a form suitable for publication

Rey·kja·vík (rā'kyə vēk', -vik') seaport & capital of Iceland: pop. 103,000

RFD *abbrev.* Rural Free Delivery

rhap·so·dize (rap'sə dīz') ***vi., vt.*** **-dized', -diz'ing** to speak or write in a rhapsodic manner

rhap'so·dy (-sə dē) ***n., pl.*** **-dies** ⟦< Gr *rhaptein,* stitch together + *ōidē,* song⟧ **1** any ecstatic or enthusiastic speech or writing **2** a musical composition of free, irregular form, suggesting improvisation —**rhap·sod'ic** (-säd'ik) or **rhap·sod'i·cal** ***adj.***

rhe·a (rē'ə) ***n.*** ⟦< Gr⟧ a large, flightless South American bird, like an ostrich but smaller

rhe·o·stat (rē'ə stat') ***n.*** ⟦< Gr *rheos,* current + -STAT⟧ a device for varying the resistance of an electric circuit, used as for dimming or brightening electric lights

rhesus (monkey) (rē'səs) ⟦< Gr proper name⟧ a brownish-yellow monkey of India: used in medical research

rhet·o·ric (ret'ə rik) ***n.*** ⟦< Gr *rhētōr,* orator⟧ **1** the art of using words effectively; esp., the art of prose composition **2** showy, elaborate language that is empty or insincere —**rhe·tor·i·cal** (ri tôr'i kəl) ***adj.*** —**rhet'o·ri'cian** (-ə rish'ən) ***n.***

rhetorical question a question asked only for rhetorical effect, no answer being expected

rheum (rōōm) ***n.*** ⟦< Gr *rheuma,* a flow⟧ watery discharge from the eyes, nose, etc., as in a cold

rheumatic fever an acute or chronic disease, usually of children, with fever, swelling of the joints, inflammation of the heart, etc.

rheu·ma·tism (rōō'mə tiz'əm) ***n.*** ⟦see RHEUM⟧ *nontechnical term for* a painful condition of the joints and muscles —**rheu·mat'ic** (-mat'ik) ***adj., n.*** —**rheu'ma·toid'** (-mə toid') ***adj.***

rheumatoid arthritis a chronic disease with painful swelling of joints, often leading to deformity

Rh factor (är'āch') ⟦first discovered in RH(ESUS) monkeys⟧ a group of antigens, usually present in human blood: people who have this factor are **Rh positive**; those who do not are **Rh negative**

Rhine (rīn) river in W Europe, flowing from E Switzerland through Germany & the Netherlands into the North Sea

rhine·stone (rīn'stōn') ***n.*** a bright, colorless artificial gem of hard glass, often cut like a diamond

Rhine wine a light white wine, esp. one produced in the valley of the Rhine

rhi·ni·tis (rī nīt'is) ***n.*** ⟦< Gr *rhis,* nose + -ITIS⟧ inflammation of the nasal mucous membrane

rhi·no (rī'nō) ***n., pl.*** **-nos** or **-no** *short for* RHINOCEROS

rhi·noc·er·os (rī näs'ər əs) ***n.*** ⟦< Gr *rhis,* nose + *keras,* horn⟧ a large, thick-skinned, plant-eating mammal of Africa and Asia, with one or two upright horns on the snout

rhi·zome (rī'zōm') ***n.*** ⟦< Gr *rhiza,* a root⟧ a horizontal stem on or under soil, bearing leaves near its tips and roots from its undersurface

rho (rō) ***n.*** the 17th letter of the Greek alphabet (Ρ, ρ)

Rhode Island (rōd) New England state of the U.S.: 1,045 sq. mi.; pop. 1,003,000; cap. Providence: abbrev. *RI* —**Rhode Islander**

Rhodes (rōdz) large Greek island in the Aegean

rho·do·den·dron (rō'də den'drən) ***n.*** ⟦< Gr *rhodon,* rose + *dendron,* tree⟧ any of various trees or shrubs, mainly evergreen, with showy flowers

rhom·boid (räm'boid') ***n.*** ⟦< Fr: see fol. & -OID⟧ a parallelogram with oblique angles and only the opposite sides equal

rhom·bus (räm'bəs) ***n., pl.*** **-bus·es** or **-bi'** (-bī') ⟦L < Gr *rhombos,* turnable object⟧ an equilateral parallelogram, esp. one with oblique angles

Rhone or **Rhône** (rōn) river flowing through SW Switzerland & France into the Mediterranean

rhu·barb (rōō'bärb') ***n.*** ⟦< Gr *rhēon,* rhubarb + *barbaron,* foreign⟧ **1** a plant with long, thick stalks that are cooked into a sauce, etc. **2** [Slang] a heated argument

rhyme (rīm) ***n.*** ⟦< OFr⟧ **1** a poem or verse with like recurring sounds, esp. at ends of lines **2** such verse, poetry, or likeness of sounds **3** a word like another in end sound —***vi.*** **rhymed, rhym'ing** **1** to make (rhyming) verse **2** to form a rhyme *["more" rhymes with "door"]* —***vt.*** **1** to put into rhyme **2** to use as a rhyme

rhym'er ***n.*** a maker of rhymes, esp. a rhymester

rhyme'ster ***n.*** a maker of trivial rhyme

rhythm (rith'əm) ***n.*** ⟦< Gr *rhythmos,* measure⟧ **1** movement, flow, etc. characterized by regular recurrence of beat, accent, etc. **2** the pattern of this in music, verse, etc. —**rhyth'mic** (-mik) or **rhyth'mi·cal** ***adj.*** —**rhyth'mi·cal·ly** ***adv.***

rhythm and blues the form of American popular music from which rock-and-roll derives

rhythm method a method of seeking birth control by abstaining from intercourse during the woman's probable ovulation period

RI Rhode Island

rib (rib) ***n.*** ⟦OE⟧ **1** any of the arched bones attached to the spine and enclosing the chest cavity **2** anything like a rib in appearance or function —***vt.*** **ribbed, rib'bing** **1** to strengthen or form with ribs **2** [Slang] to make fun of; kid

rib·ald (rib'əld) ***adj.*** ⟦< OHG *riban,* to rub⟧ coarse or vulgar in joking, speaking, etc. —**rib'ald·ry** ***n.***

rib·bon (rib'ən) ***n.*** ⟦< MFr *ruban*⟧ **1** a narrow strip of silk, rayon, etc. used for decoration, tying, etc. **2** [*pl.*] torn shreds **3** an inked strip for printing, as in a typewriter, etc.

rib'bon-cut'ting ***n.*** a ceremony to officially open a new building, construction site, etc.

rib'-eye' (steak) boneless beefsteak from the rib section

ri·bo·fla·vin (rī'bə flā'vin) ***n.*** ⟦< *ribose,* a sugar + L *flavus,* yellow⟧ a B vitamin found in milk, eggs, fruits, etc.: see VITAMIN B (COMPLEX)

rice (rīs) ***n.*** ⟦< Gr *oryza*⟧ **1** an aquatic cereal grass grown widely in warm climates, esp. in East Asia **2** the starchy grains of this grass, used as food —***vt.*** **riced, ric'ing** to make ricelike granules from (cooked potatoes, etc.) using a utensil with small holes (**ric'er**)

rich (rich) ***adj.*** ⟦< OFr⟧ **1** owning much money or property; wealthy **2** well-supplied (*with*); abounding (*in*) **3** valuable or costly **4** full of choice ingredients, as butter, sugar, etc. *[rich pastries]* **5** *a)* full and mellow (said of

THESAURUS

revolver ***n.*** automatic, gun, rod*; see PISTOL.

reward ***n.*** **1** [Payment] compensation, remuneration, recompense; see PAY 1, 2. **2** [A prize] premium, bonus, award; see PRIZE.

reward ***v.*** compensate, repay, remunerate; see PAY 1.

rewrite ***v.*** rework, revise, cut; see EDIT.

rhyme ***n.*** verse, rhyming verse, similarity of vowel sounds; see POETRY.

rhythm ***n.*** swing, accent, rise and fall; see BEAT 2.

rhythmic ***a.*** patterned, measured, balanced; see MUSICAL 1, REGULAR 3.

rib ***n.*** **1** [One part of the bony frame of the thorax] true rib, false rib, floating rib; see BONE. **2** [A rod] girder, bar, strip; see ROD 1, SUPPORT 2. **3** [A ridge] fin, nervure, vaulting; see sense 2.

ribbon ***n.*** strip, trimming, decoration; see BAND 1.

rich ***a.*** **1** [Possessed of wealth] wealthy, moneyed, affluent, well-to-do, well provided for, worth a million, well-off, well-fixed*, in clover, swimming in gravy*, in the money*.—*Ant.* POOR, poverty-stricken, destitute. **2** [Sumptuous] luxurious, magnificent, resplendent, lavish, embellished, ornate, costly, expensive, splendid, superb, elegant, gorgeous, valuable, precious, extravagant, grand; see also BEAUTIFUL.—*Ant.* CHEAP, plain, simple. **3** [Fertile] exuberant, lush, copious, plentiful, generous, fruitful, profuse, luxuriant, teeming, abundant, prolific, productive, fruit-bearing, propagating, yielding, breeding, superabounding, prodigal; see also FERTILE.—*Ant.* STERILE, unfruitful, barren. **4** [Having much butter, cream, sugar, seasoning, etc.] heavy, luscious, sweet, fatty, oily, creamy, buttery, juicy, succulent, fattening, filling, cloying, spicy, satisfying; see also DELICIOUS.—*Ant.* light, plain, low-fat.

sounds) *b)* deep; vivid (said of colors) *c)* very fragrant **6** abundant **7** yielding in abundance, as soil **8** [Inf.] very amusing —**the rich** wealthy people collectively —**rich'ly** *adv.* —**rich'ness** *n.*

Rich·ard I (rich'ərd) 1157-99; king of England (1189-99): called **Richard Coeur de Li·on** (kur' də lē'ən) or **Richard the Li'on-Heart'ed**

rich·es (rich'iz) *pl.n.* ⟦< OFr *richesse*⟧ wealth

Rich·mond (rich'mənd) capital of Virginia: pop. 203,000

Rich·ter scale (rik'tər) ⟦devised by C. *Richter* (1900-85), U.S. geologist⟧ a scale for measuring the magnitude of earthquakes

rick (rik) *n.* ⟦OE *hreac*⟧ a stack of hay, straw, etc.

rick·ets (rik'its) *n.* ⟦< ? Gr *rhachis,* spine⟧ a disease, chiefly of children, characterized by a softening and, often, bending of the bones

rick·et·y (rik'it ē) *adj.* feeble; weak; shaky

rick·shaw or **rick·sha** (rik'shô') *n.* JINRIKISHA

ric·o·chet (rik'ə shā') *n.* ⟦Fr⟧ the oblique rebound of a bullet, etc. after striking a surface at an angle —*vi.* **-cheted'** (-shād'), **-chet'ing** (-shā'iŋ) to make a ricochet

ri·cot·ta (ri kät'ə) *n.* ⟦It < L *recocta,* recooked⟧ a soft cheese made from whey, whole milk, or both

rid (rid) *vt.* **rid** or **rid'ded, rid'ding** ⟦< ON *rythja,* to clear (land)⟧ to free or relieve, as of something undesirable —**get rid of** to give or throw away or to destroy

rid·dance (rid''ns) *n.* a ridding or being rid —**good riddance** an expression of satisfaction at being rid of something

rid·den (rid''n) *vi., vt. pp. of* RIDE —*adj.* dominated: used in compounds *[fear-ridden]*

rid·dle[1] (rid''l) *n.* ⟦OE *rædels*⟧ **1** a puzzling question, etc. requiring some ingenuity to answer **2** any puzzling person or thing

rid·dle[2] (rid''l) *vt.* **-dled, -dling** ⟦< OE *hriddel,* a sieve⟧ **1** to make many holes in **2** to affect every part of *[riddled with errors]*

ride (rīd) *vi.* **rode, rid'den, rid'ing** ⟦OE *ridan*⟧ **1** to be carried along by a horse, in a vehicle, etc. **2** to be supported in motion (*on* or *upon*) *[tanks ride on treads]* **3** to admit of being ridden *[the car rides smoothly]* **4** to move or float on water **5** [Inf.] to continue undisturbed *[let the matter ride]* —*vt.* **1** to sit on or in and control so as to move along **2** to move over, along, or through (a road, area, etc.) by horse, car, etc. **3** to control, dominate, etc. *[ridden by doubts]* **4** [Inf.] to tease with ridicule, etc. —*n.* **1** a riding **2** a thing to ride at an amusement park

rid'er *n.* **1** one who rides **2** an addition or amendment to a document

rid'er·ship' *n.* the passengers of a particular transportation system

ridge (rij) *n.* ⟦< OE *hrycg,* animal's spine⟧ **1** the long, narrow crest of something **2** a long, narrow elevation of land **3** any raised narrow strip **4** the horizontal line formed by the meeting of two sloping surfaces —*vt., vi.* **ridged, ridg'ing** to mark or be marked with, or form into, ridges

ridge'pole' *n.* the horizontal beam at the ridge of a roof, to which the rafters are attached

rid·i·cule (rid'i kyōōl') *n.* ⟦< L *ridere,* to laugh⟧ **1** the act of making someone the object of scornful laughter **2** words or actions intended to produce such laughter —*vt.* **-culed', -cul'ing** to make fun of; deride; mock

ri·dic·u·lous (ri dik'yə ləs) *adj.* deserving ridicule —**ri·dic'u·lous·ly** *adv.* —**ri·dic'u·lous·ness** *n.*

rife (rīf) *adj.* ⟦OE *ryfe*⟧ **1** widespread **2** abounding *[rife with error]*

riff (rif) *n.* ⟦prob. altered < REFRAIN[2]⟧ *Jazz* a constantly repeated musical phrase —*vi. Jazz* to perform a riff

rif·fle (rif'əl) *n.* ⟦< ?⟧ **1** a ripple in a stream, produced by a reef, etc. **2** a certain way of shuffling cards —*vt., vi.* **-fled, -fling** to shuffle (playing cards) by letting a divided deck fall together as the corners are slipped through one's thumbs

riff·raff (rif'raf') *n.* ⟦< OFr⟧ those people regarded as worthless, disreputable, etc.

ri·fle[1] (rī'fəl) *vt.* **-fled, -fling** ⟦Fr *rifler,* to scrape⟧ to cut spiral grooves within (a gun barrel, etc.) —*n.* a gun, fired from the shoulder, with a rifled barrel to spin the bullet for greater accuracy

ri·fle[2] (rī'fəl) *vt.* **-fled, -fling** ⟦< OFr *rifler*⟧ to ransack and rob —**ri'fler** *n.*

ri'fle·man (-mən) *n., pl.* **-men** (-mən) a soldier armed with a rifle

ri·fling (rī'fliŋ) *n.* spiral grooves cut within a gun barrel to make the projectile spin

rift (rift) *n.* ⟦< Dan, fissure⟧ an opening caused by splitting; cleft —*vt., vi.* to burst open; split

rig (rig) *vt.* **rigged, rig'ging** ⟦< Scand⟧ **1** to fit (a ship, mast, etc.) with (sails, shrouds, etc.) **2** to assemble **3** to equip **4** to arrange dishonestly **5** [Inf.] to dress: with *out* —*n.* **1** the way sails, etc. are rigged **2** equipment; gear **3** oil-drilling equipment **4** a tractor-trailer

rig·a·ma·role (rig'ə mə rōl') *n. var. of* RIGMAROLE

rig'ging *n.* the ropes, chains, etc. for a vessel's masts, sails, etc.

right (rīt) *adj.* ⟦< OE *riht,* straight⟧ **1** with a straight line or plane perpendicular to a base *[a right angle]* **2** upright; virtuous **3** correct **4** fitting; suitable **5** desig-

THESAURUS

riches *n.* fortune, possessions, money; see WEALTH.

richness *n.* copiousness, bounty, abundance; see PLENTY.

rickety *a.* infirm, shaky, fragile; see WEAK 2.

ricochet *v.* bounce off, rebound, glance off; see BOUNCE.

rid *a.* relieved, freed, delivered; see FREE 2. —**be rid of** be freed from, be relieved of, have done with; see ESCAPE. —**get rid of 1** get free from, slough off, shed; see FREE. **2** eject, expel, remove; see ELIMINATE.

rid *v.* clear, relieve, disencumber; see FREE.

riddle[1] *n.* problem, question, knotty question, doubt, quandary, entanglement, dilemma, perplexity, enigma, confusion, complication, complexity, intricacy, strait, labyrinth, predicament, plight, distraction, bewilderment; see also PUZZLE 1.—*Ant.* SIMPLICITY, clarity, disentanglement.

ride *n.* drive, trip, transportation; see JOURNEY.

ride *v.* **1** [To be transported] be carried, travel in or on a vehicle, tour, journey, motor, drive, go for an airing, bicycle, go by automobile. **2** [To control a beast of burden by riding] manage, guide, handle; see DRIVE 1. **3** [To tease harshly] ridicule, bait, harass; see BOTHER 2.

rider *n.* **1** [One who rides] driver, fare, passenger, motorist, horseman, horsewoman, hitchhiker. **2** [An additional clause or provision, usually not connected with the main body of the document] amendment, appendix, supplement; see ADDITION 1.

ridge *n.* **1** [A long, straight, raised portion] raised strip, rib, seam; see RIM. **2** [A long, narrow elevation of land] mountain ridge, range, elevation; see HILL.

ridged *a.* crinkled, furrowed, ribbed, corrugated.

ridicule *n.* scorn, contempt, mockery, disdain, derision, jeer, leer, disparagement, sneer, flout, fleer, twit, taunt, burlesque, caricature, satire, parody, travesty, irony, sarcasm, persiflage, farce, buffoonery, horseplay, foolery, razz*, rib*, roast*, raspberry*, horselaugh.—*Ant.* PRAISE, commendation, approval.

ridicule *v.* scoff at, sneer at, laugh at, rail at, mock, taunt, banter, mimic, jeer, twit, disparage, flout, deride, scorn, make sport of, make fun of, rally, burlesque, caricature, satirize, parody, cartoon, travesty, run down, put down*, razz*, rib*, pull someone's leg*, roast*, pan*.—*Ant.* ENCOURAGE, approve, applaud.

ridiculous *a.* ludicrous, absurd, preposterous; see FUNNY 1, UNUSUAL 2.

rife *a.* **1** [Widespread] prevalent, extensive, common; see WIDESPREAD. **2** [Abundant] copious, abounding, profuse; see PLENTIFUL 1.

riffraff *n.* mob, masses, rabble; see PEOPLE 3.

rifle[1] *n.* repeating rifle, carbine, automatic rifle; see GUN, MACHINE GUN.

rift *n.* fissure, breach, rupture; see FRACTURE.

rig *n.* tackle, apparatus, gear; see EQUIPMENT.

right *a.* **1** [Correct] true, precise, exact, sure, certain, determined, proven, factual, correct; see also ACCURATE 2, VALID 1. **2** [Just] lawful, legitimate, honest; see FAIR 1. **3** [Suitable] apt, proper, appropriate; see FIT 1. **4** [Sane] reasonable, rational, sound; see SANE. **5** [Justly] fairly, evenly, equitably, honestly, decently, sincerely, legitimately, lawfully, conscientiously, squarely, impartially, objectively, reliably, dispassionately, without bias, without prejudice; see also JUSTLY 1. **6** [Straight] directly, unswervingly, immediately; see DIRECT 1. **7** [Opposite to left] dextral, dexter, right-handed, clockwise, on the right.—*Ant.* LEFT, sinistral, counterclockwise. —**right away** at once, directly, without delay; see IMMEDIATELY, NOW.

right *n.* **1** [Power or privilege] prerogative, immunity, exemption, license, benefit, advantage, favor, franchise, preference, priority; see also FREEDOM 2. **2** [Justice] equity, freedom, liberty, independence, emancipation, enfranchisement, self-determination; see also FAIRNESS. **3**

nating the side or surface meant to be seen **6** mentally or physically sound **7** *a*) designating or of that side of the body toward the east when one faces north *b*) designating or of the corresponding side of anything *c*) closer to the right side of one who is facing the thing mentioned —***n.*** **1** what is right, just, etc. **2** power, privilege, etc. belonging to one by law, nature, etc. **3** the right side **4** the right hand **5** [*often* **R-**] *Politics* a conservative or reactionary position, party, etc.: often with *the* —***adv.*** **1** straight; directly *[go right home]* **2** properly; fittingly **3** completely **4** exactly *[right here]* **5** according to law, justice, etc. **6** correctly **7** on or toward the right side **8** very: in certain titles *[the right reverend]* —***interj.*** agreed! OK! —***vt.*** **1** to put upright **2** to correct **3** to put in order —**right away** (or **off**) at once —**right on!** [Slang] that's right! —**right'ly** ***adv.*** —**right'ness** ***n.***

right'a·bout'-face' ***n.*** ABOUT-FACE

right angle an angle of 90 degrees

right·eous (rī'chəs) ***adj.*** **1** acting in a just, upright manner; virtuous **2** morally right or justifiable —**right'eous·ly** ***adv.*** —**right'eous·ness** ***n.***

right'ful ***adj.*** **1** fair and just; right **2** having a lawful claim —**right'ful·ly** ***adv.*** —**right'ful·ness** ***n.***

right'-hand' ***adj.*** **1** on or toward the right **2** of, for, or with the right hand **3** most helpful or reliable *[a right-hand man]*

right'-hand'ed ***adj.*** **1** using the right hand more skillfully than the left **2** done with or made for use with the right hand —***adv.*** **1** with the right hand **2** in such a way that the bat, club, etc. swings leftward —**right'-hand'ed·ness** ***n.***

right'ist ***n., adj.*** conservative or reactionary

right'-mind'ed ***adj.*** having sound principles

right of way **1** the right to move first at intersections **2** land over which a road, power line, etc. passes **3** right of passage, as over another's property Also **right'-of-way'**

right'-to-life' ***adj.*** designating any movement, party, etc. opposed to abortion —**right'-to-lif'er** ***n.***

right triangle a triangle with a right angle

right wing the more conservative or reactionary section of a political party or group —**right'-wing'** ***adj.*** —**right'-wing'er** ***n.***

rig·id (rij'id) ***adj.*** ⟦< L *rigere,* be stiff⟧ **1** not bending or flexible; stiff **2** not moving; fixed **3** severe; strict **4** having a rigid framework: said of a dirigible —**ri·gid·i·ty** (ri jid'ə tē) or **rig'id·ness** ***n.*** —**rig'id·ly** ***adv.***

rig·ma·role (rig'mə rōl') ***n.*** ⟦< ME *rageman rolle,* long list⟧ **1** nonsense **2** a foolishly complicated procedure

rig·or (rig'ər) ***n.*** ⟦< L *rigere:* see RIGID⟧ **1** severity; strictness **2** hardship Brit. sp. **rig'our** —**rig'or·ous** ***adj.*** —**rig'or·ous·ly** ***adv.***

rigor mor·tis (môr'tis) ⟦L, stiffness of death⟧ the stiffening of the muscles after death

rile (rīl) ***vt.*** **riled, ril'ing** ⟦var. of ROIL⟧ [Inf. or Dial.] to anger; irritate

rill (ril) ***n.*** ⟦< Du *ril*⟧ a rivulet

rim (rim) ***n.*** ⟦OE *rima*⟧ **1** an edge, border, or margin, esp. of something circular **2** the outer part of a wheel —***vt.*** **rimmed, rim'ming** to put a rim or rims on or around —**rim'less** ***adj.***

rime[1] (rīm) ***n., vi., vt.*** **rimed, rim'ing** RHYME

rime[2] (rīm) ***n.*** ⟦OE *hrim*⟧ FROST (sense 2)

rind (rīnd) ***n.*** ⟦OE⟧ a hard outer layer or covering

ring[1] (riŋ) ***vi.*** **rang** or [Now Chiefly Dial.] **rung, rung, ring'ing** ⟦OE *hringan*⟧ **1** to give forth a resonant sound, as a bell **2** to seem *[to ring true]* **3** to sound a bell, esp. as a summons **4** to resound *[to ring with laughter]* **5** to have a ringing sensation, as the ears —***vt.*** **1** to cause (a bell, etc.) to ring **2** to signal, announce, etc., as by ringing **3** to call by telephone —***n.*** **1** the sound of a bell **2** a characteristic quality *[the ring of truth]* **3** the act of ringing a bell **4** a telephone call —**ring a bell** to stir up a memory

ring[2] (riŋ) ***n.*** ⟦OE *hring*⟧ **1** an ornamental circular band worn on a finger **2** any similar band *[a key ring]* **3** a circular line, mark, figure, or course **4** a group of people or things in a circle **5** a group working to advance its own interests, esp. by dishonest means **6** an enclosed area for contests, exhibitions, etc. *[a circus ring]* **7** prizefighting: with *the* —***vt.*** **ringed, ring'ing** **1** to encircle **2** to form into a ring —**run rings around** **1** to run much faster than **2** to do much better than

ring'er[1] ***n.*** a horseshoe, etc. thrown so that it encircles the peg

ring'er[2] ***n.*** **1** one that rings a bell, etc. **2** [Slang] *a*) a person or thing closely resembling another *b*) a fraudulent substitute in a competition

ring'lead'er ***n.*** one who leads others, esp. in unlawful acts, etc.

ring'let (-lit) ***n.*** a long curl of hair

ring'mas'ter ***n.*** a person who directs the performances in a circus ring

ring'side' ***n.*** **1** the place just outside a boxing or circus ring **2** any place providing a close view

ring'worm' ***n.*** a contagious skin disease caused by a fungus

rink (riŋk) ***n.*** ⟦< OFr *renc,* a rank⟧ **1** an expanse of ice for skating **2** a smooth floor for roller-skating

rinse (rins) ***vt.*** **rinsed, rins'ing** ⟦ult. < L *recens,* fresh⟧ **1** to wash or flush lightly **2** to remove soap, etc. from with

THESAURUS

[The part opposite the left] right hand, right side, starboard, right part. —**by rights** properly, justly, suitably; see RIGHTLY. —**in one's own right** individually, acting as one's own agent, by one's own authority; see INDEPENDENTLY. —**in the right** correct, true, accurate; see VALID 1.

right ***v.*** **1** [To make upright] set up, make straight, balance; see STRAIGHTEN, TURN 2. **2** [To repair an injustice] adjust, correct, restore, vindicate, do justice, recompense, reward, remedy, rectify, mend, amend, set right; see also REPAIR.—*Ant.* WRONG, hurt, harm.

righteous ***a.*** **1** [Virtuous] just, upright, good, honorable, honest, worthy, exemplary, noble, right-minded, good-hearted, dutiful, trustworthy, equitable, scrupulous, conscientious, ethical, fair, impartial, fair-minded, commendable, praiseworthy, guiltless, blameless, sinless, peerless, sterling, matchless, deserving, laudable, creditable, charitable, philanthropic, having a clear conscience; see also RELIABLE.—*Ant.* CORRUPT, sinful, profligate. **2** [Religious] godly, devout, pious, saintly, humble, prayerful, God-fearing, observant, unworldly, angelic, devoted, reverent, reverential, faithful, fervent, strict, rigid, devotional, zealous, spiritual; see also HOLY 1, RELIGIOUS 2.—*Ant.* BAD, impious, irreligious. **3** [Conscious of one's own virtue] self-righteous, hypocritical, self-centered; see EGOTISTIC.

righteousness ***n.*** **1** [Justice] uprightness, nobility, fairness; see HONOR 1. **2** [Devotion to a sinless life] piety, saintliness, godliness; see DEVOTION.

rightful ***a.*** proper, just, honest; see FAIR 1, LEGAL, PERMITTED.

rightfully ***a.*** lawfully, justly, fairly, properly, truly, equitably, honestly, impartially, fittingly, legitimately, in all conscience, in equity, by right, by reason, objectively, fair and square*, on the level*, by rights; see also LEGALLY.

rightly ***a.*** justly, properly, correctly; see WELL 2.

right-wing ***a.*** traditional, reactionary, Tory; see CONSERVATIVE.

rigid ***a.*** **1** [Stiff] unyielding, inflexible, solid; see FIRM 1. **2** [Strict] exact, rigorous, firm; see SEVERE 1, 2. **3** [Fixed] set, unmoving, solid; see DEFINITE 1, DETERMINED.

rigorous ***a.*** harsh, austere, uncompromising; see SEVERE 1.

rile ***v.*** irritate, provoke, annoy; see BOTHER 2, ENRAGE.

rim ***n.*** edge, border, verge, brim, lip, brink, top, margin, line, outline, band, ring, strip, brow, curb, ledge, skirt, fringe, hem, limit, confines, end, terminus.—*Ant.* CENTER, interior, middle.

rind ***n.*** peel, hull, shell, surface, coating, crust, bark, cortex, integument; see also SKIN.—*Ant.* INSIDE, center, interior.

ring[1,2] ***n.*** **1** [A circle] circlet, girdle, brim; see CIRCLE 1, RIM. **2** [A circlet of metal] hoop, band, circle; see JEWELRY. *Rings include the following:* finger, wedding, engagement, signet, organization, class, friendship, graduation, pinkie, ankle, nose, key, harness, napkin; bracelet, earring, ear drop. **3** [A close association, often corrupt] cabal, combine, party, bloc, faction, group, gang, monopoly, cartel, junta, band, clique, pool, trust, syndicate, gang*, string; see also ORGANIZATION 2. **4** [Pugilism] prizefighting, boxing, professional fighting; see SPORT 3. **5** [A ringing sound] clank, clangor, jangle; see NOISE 1. —**give someone a ring** call, call up, phone; see TELEPHONE. —**run rings around*** excel, overtake, beat; see PASS 1.

ring[1,2] ***v.*** **1** [To encircle] circle, rim, surround, encompass, girdle, enclose, move around, loop, gird, belt, confine, hem in. **2** [To sound or cause to sound] clap, clang, bang, beat, toll, strike, pull, punch, buzz, play, resound, reverberate, peal, chime, tinkle, jingle, jangle, vibrate, clang, sound the brass*; see also SOUND. **3** [To call by ringing] give a ring, buzz, ring up; see SUMMON.

rinse ***v.*** clean, flush, dip in water; see SOAK 1, WASH 2.

clear water —*n.* **1** a rinsing or the liquid used **2** a solution used to rinse or tint hair

Ri·o de Ja·nei·ro (rē′ō dā′ zhə ner′ō) city & seaport in SE Brazil: pop. 5,093,000

Ri·o Gran·de (rē′ō grand′, -gran′dē) river flowing from S Colorado into the Gulf of Mexico: the S border of Texas

ri·ot (rī′ət) *n.* ⟦< OFr *riote,* dispute⟧ **1** wild or violent disorder, confusion, etc.; esp., a violent public disturbance **2** a brilliant display **3** [Inf.] something very funny —*vi.* to take part in a riot —**read the riot act to** to command to stop by threatening punishment —**run riot 1** to act wildly **2** to grow wild in abundance —**ri′ot·er** *n.* —**ri′ot·ous** *adj.*

rip (rip) *vt.* **ripped, rip′ping** ⟦ME *rippen*⟧ **1** *a)* to cut or tear apart roughly *b)* to remove in this way (with *off, out,* etc.) *c)* to sever the threads of (a seam) **2** to saw (wood) along the grain —*vi.* **1** to become ripped **2** [Inf.] to rush; speed —*n.* a ripped place —**rip into** [Inf.] to attack, esp. verbally —**rip off** [Slang] **1** to steal **2** to cheat or exploit —**rip′per** *n.*

R.I.P. or **RIP** *abbrev.* may he (she) rest in peace

rip cord a cord, etc. pulled to open a parachute during descent

ripe (rīp) *adj.* ⟦OE⟧ **1** ready to be harvested, as grain or fruit **2** of sufficient age, etc. to be used *[ripe* cheese*]* **3** fully developed; mature **4** fully prepared; ready *[ripe* for action*]* —**ripe′ly** *adv.* —**ripe′ness** *n.*

rip·en (rī′pən) *vi., vt.* to become or make ripe; mature, age, etc.

rip′-off′ *n.* [Slang] the act or an instance of stealing, cheating, etc.

ri·poste or **ri·post** (ri pōst′) *n.* ⟦Fr < L *respondere,* to answer⟧ a sharp, swift response; retort

rip·ple (rip′əl) *vi., vt.* **-pled, -pling** ⟦prob. < RIP⟧ to have or form little waves on the surface (of) —*n.* **1** a small wave **2** a rippling

ripple effect the spreading effects caused by a single event

rip′-roar′ing (-rôr′iŋ) *adj.* [Slang] boisterous; uproarious

rip′saw′ *n.* a saw with coarse teeth, for cutting wood along the grain

rip′tide′ *n.* a current opposing other currents, esp. along a seashore: also **rip tide**

rise (rīz) *vi.* **rose, ris·en** (riz′ən), **ris′ing** ⟦< OE *risan*⟧ **1** to stand or sit up after sitting, kneeling, or lying **2** to rebel; revolt **3** to go up; ascend **4** to appear above the horizon, as the sun **5** to attain a higher level, rank, etc. **6** to extend, slant, or move upward **7** to increase in amount, degree, etc. **8** to expand and swell, as dough with yeast **9** to originate; begin **10** *Theol.* to return to life —*n.* **1** upward movement; ascent **2** an advance in status, rank, etc. **3** a slope upward **4** an increase in degree, amount, etc. **5** beginning; origin —**give rise to** to bring about

ris′er *n.* **1** one that rises **2** a vertical piece between the steps in a stairway

ris·i·ble (riz′ə bəl) *adj.* ⟦< L *ridere,* to laugh⟧ causing laughter; funny —**ris′i·bil′i·ty,** *pl.* **-ties,** *n.*

ris′ing *n.* an uprising; revolt

risk (risk) *n.* ⟦< Fr < It *risco*⟧ the chance of injury, damage, or loss —*vt.* **1** to expose to risk *[to risk* one's life*]* **2** to incur the risk of *[to risk* a war*]* —**risk′y, -i·er, -i·est,** *adj.*

ris·qué (ris kā′) *adj.* ⟦Fr < *risquer,* to risk⟧ very close to being improper or indecent; suggestive

Rit·a·lin (rit′'l in) *trademark for* a stimulant drug used to treat depression, hyperactivity, etc.

rite (rīt) *n.* ⟦L *ritus*⟧ a ceremonial, solemn act, as in religious use

rite of passage a significant event, ceremony, etc. in a person's life

rit·u·al (rich′o͞o əl) *adj.* of, like, or done as a rite —*n.* a set form or system of rites, religious or otherwise —**rit′u·al·ism′** *n.* —**rit′u·al·ly** *adv.*

ri·val (rī′vəl) *n.* ⟦< L *rivalis*⟧ one who tries to get or do the same thing as another, or to equal or surpass another; competitor —*adj.* acting as a rival; competing —*vt.* **-valed** or **-valled, -val·ing** or **-val·ling 1** to try to equal or surpass **2** to equal in some way —**ri′val·rous** *adj.* —**ri′val·ry,** *pl.* **-ries,** *n.*

riv·en (riv′ən) *adj.* torn apart or split

riv·er (riv′ər) *n.* ⟦< L *ripa,* a bank⟧ a natural stream of water flowing into an ocean, a lake, etc.

river basin the area drained by a river and its tributaries

riv′er·side′ *n.* the bank of a river

Riv·er·side (riv′ər sīd′) city in S California: pop. 227,000

riv·et (riv′it) *n.* ⟦Fr < *river,* to clinch⟧ a metal bolt with a head and a plain end that is flattened after the bolt is

THESAURUS

riot *n.* confusion, uproar, tumult; see DISORDER, DISTURBANCE 2, PROTEST. —**run riot** revolt, riot, fight; see REBEL.

riot *v.* revolt, stir up trouble, fight in the streets; see REBEL.

rip *n.* rent, cleavage, split; see TEAR.

rip *v.* rend, split, cleave, rive, tear, shred; see also CUT 1.

ripe *a.* **1** [Ready to be harvested] fully grown, fully developed, ruddy, red, yellow, plump, filled out, matured, ready.—*Ant.* GREEN, undeveloped, half-grown. **2** [Improved by time and experience] mellow, wise, perfected; see MATURE. **3** [Ready] prepared, seasoned, consummate, perfected, finished, usable, fit, conditioned, prime, available, on the mark, complete; see also READY 2.—*Ant.* UNFIT, unready, unprepared.

ripen *v.* develop, evolve, advance; see GROW 2.

ripple *v.* undulate, curl, waver; see WAVE 1, 3.

rise *n.* **1** [The act of rising] ascent, mount, lift; see CLIMB. **2** [An increase] augmentation, growth, enlargement, multiplication, heightening, intensifying, stacking up, piling up, distention, addition, accession, inflation, acceleration, doubling, advance; see also INCREASE.—*Ant.* REDUCTION, lessening, decrease. **3** [Source] start, beginning, commencement; see ORIGIN 2. —**get a rise out of*** get a response from by teasing, provoke, annoy; see BOTHER 2. —**give rise to** initiate, begin, start; see CAUSE.

rise *v.* **1** [To move upward] ascend, mount, climb, scale, soar, tower, rocket, sweep upward, lift, bob up, move up, push up, reach up, come up, go up, surge, sprout, grow, rear, uprise, blast off, curl upward; see also FLY 1.—*Ant.* FALL, drop, come down. **2** [To get out of bed] get up, rise up, wake; see ARISE 1. **3** [To increase] grow, swell, intensify, mount, enlarge, spread, expand, extend, augment, heighten, enhance, distend, inflate, pile up, stack up, multiply, accelerate, speed up, add to, wax, advance, raise, double; see also INCREASE.—*Ant.* DECREASE, lessen, contract. **4** [To begin] spring, emanate, issue; see BEGIN 2. **5** [To improve one's station] prosper, flourish, thrive; see IMPROVE 1. **6** [To be built] stand, be placed, be located, be put up, go up, be founded, have foundation, be situated; see also STAND 1. **7** [To swell; *said usually of dough or batter*] inflate, billow, bulge; see SWELL.

rising *a.* climbing, ascending, going aloft, moving up, surging up, spiraling up, slanting up, inclining up, mounting, accelerating, on the rise, in ascension, upcoming, upswinging; see also GROWING.

risk *n.* **1** [Danger] hazard, peril, jeopardy; see DANGER. **2** [The basis of a chance] contingency, opportunity, prospect; see CHANCE 1, UNCERTAINTY 3. —**run a risk** take a chance, gamble, venture; see RISK, *v.*

risk *v.* gamble, hazard, venture, run the risk, do at one's own peril, hang by a thread, play with fire, go out of one's depth, go beyond one's depth, bell the cat*, make an investment, take the liberty, lay oneself open to, pour money into, go through fire and water, leave to luck, leap before one looks, fish in troubled waters, skate on thin ice*, defy danger, live in a glass house.

risky *a.* perilous, precarious, hazardous; see DANGEROUS, UNSAFE.

risqué *a.* indelicate, spicy, suggestive; see LEWD 2.

rite *n.* observance, service, ritual; see CEREMONY 2, CUSTOM.

ritual *n.* observance, rite, act; see CEREMONY 2, CUSTOM.

rival *a.* competing, striving, combatant, combatting, emulating, vying, opposing, disputing, contesting, contending, conflicting, battling, equal.—*Ant.* HELPFUL, aiding, assisting.

rival *n.* emulator, competitor, antagonist; see OPPONENT 1.

rival *v.* approach, match, compare with; see EQUAL.

rivalry *n.* competition, emulation, striving, contest, vying, struggle, battle, contention, opposition, dispute; see also FIGHT 1.—*Ant.* COOPERATION, combination, conspiracy.

river *n.* stream, flow, course, current, tributary, branch, estuary, waters, run, rivulet, river system, creek, brook, watercourse. *Famous rivers include the following:* Seine, Rhone, Thames, Po, Tiber, Rubicon, Danube, Rhine, Elbe, Don, Volga, Amur, Nile, Euphrates, Tigris, Jordan, Ganges, Indus, Congo, Zambezi, Niger, Mekong, Chang (Yangtze), Huang (Yellow), St. Lawrence, Yukon, Mackenzie, Mississippi, Missouri, Ohio, Platte, Delaware, Columbia, Colorado, Snake, Hudson, Rio Grande, Potomac, Tennessee, Brazos, Amazon, Orinoco.

riveting *a.* gripping, engrossing,

passed through parts to be held together —*vt.* to fasten with or as with rivets —**riv'et·er** *n.*

Riv·i·er·a (riv'ē er'ə) strip of the Mediterranean coast of SE France & NW Italy: a resort area

riv·u·let (riv'yo͞o lit) *n.* ⟦< L *rivus,* brook⟧ a little stream

rm *abbrev.* **1** ream **2** room

Rn *Chem. symbol for* radon

RN *abbrev.* Registered Nurse

RNA *n.* ⟦*r*(*ibo*)*n*(*ucleic*) *a*(*cid*)⟧ an essential component of all living matter: one form carries genetic information

roach[1] (rōch) *n. short for* COCKROACH

roach[2] (rōch) *n., pl.* **roach** or **roach'es** ⟦< OFr *roche*⟧ a freshwater fish of the carp family

road (rōd) *n.* ⟦OE *rad,* a ride⟧ **1** a way made for traveling; highway **2** a way; course *[*the *road* to fortune*]* **3** [*often pl.*] a place near shore where ships can ride at anchor —**on the road** traveling, as by a salesman or a touring troupe of actors

road'bed' *n.* the foundation laid for railroad tracks, a highway, etc.

road'block' *n.* **1** a blockade set up in a road as to prevent movement of vehicles **2** any hindrance

road'kill' *n.* [Slang] the body of an animal killed by a passing vehicle

road rage angry or violent behavior by motorists, as caused by stress in traffic

road'run'ner *n.* a long-tailed, swift-running desert bird of the SW U.S. and N Mexico: also **road runner**

road'show' *n.* a touring theatrical show

road'side' *n.* the side of a road —*adj.* on or at the side of a road

road'way' *n.* a road; specif., the part of a road used by vehicles

road'work' *n.* distance running or jogging as an exercise, esp. by a boxer

roam (rōm) *vi., vt.* ⟦ME *romen*⟧ to wander aimlessly (over or through) —**roam'er** *n.*

roan (rōn) *adj.* ⟦< OSp *roano*⟧ bay, black, etc. thickly sprinkled with white —*n.* a roan horse

roar (rôr) *vi.* ⟦OE *rarian*⟧ **1** to make a loud, deep, rumbling sound **2** to laugh boisterously —*vt.* to say loudly —*n.* a loud, deep, rumbling sound

roast (rōst) *vt.* ⟦< OFr *rostir*⟧ **1** to cook (meat, etc.) with little or no moisture, as in an oven or over an open fire **2** to process (coffee, etc.) by exposure to heat **3** to expose to great heat **4** [Inf.] to criticize severely —*vi.* **1** to undergo roasting **2** to be or become very hot —*n.* **1** roasted meat **2** a cut of meat for roasting **3** a picnic at which food is roasted —*adj.* roasted *[roast* pork*]* —**roast'er** *n.*

rob (räb) *vt.* **robbed, rob'bing** ⟦< OFr *rober*⟧ **1** to take money, etc. from unlawfully by force; steal from **2** to deprive *of* something unjustly or injuriously —*vi.* to be one who robs —**rob'ber** *n.* —**rob'ber·y,** *pl.* **-ies,** *n.*

robe (rōb) *n.* ⟦< OFr⟧ **1** a long, loose outer garment **2** such a garment worn to show rank or office, as by a judge **3** a bathrobe or dressing gown **4** a covering or wrap *[*a lap *robe]* —*vt., vi.* **robed, rob'ing** to dress in a robe

rob·in (räb'ən) *n.* ⟦< OFr dim. of *Robert*⟧ a North American thrush with a dull-red breast

Robin Hood *Eng. Legend* the leader of a band of outlaws who robs the rich to help the poor

Ro·bin·son Cru·soe (rä'bən sən kro͞o'sō') the title hero of Defoe's novel (1719) about a shipwrecked sailor

ro·bot (rō'bät') *n.* ⟦< Czech < OSlav *rabu,* servant⟧ **1** a mechanical device operating automatically, in a seemingly human way **2** a person acting like a robot

ro·bot'ics *n.* the science or technology of robots, their design, use, etc.

ro·bust (rō bust', rō'bust') *adj.* ⟦< L *robur,* oak⟧ strong and healthy —**ro·bust'ly** *adv.* —**ro·bust'ness** *n.*

Roch·es·ter (räch'əs tər) city in W New York: pop. 230,000

rock[1] (räk) *n.* ⟦< ML *rocca*⟧ **1** a large mass of stone **2** broken pieces of stone **3** mineral matter formed in masses in the earth's crust **4** anything like a rock; esp., a firm support —**on the rocks** [Inf.] **1** in trouble or near ruin **2** served over ice cubes: said of liquor, etc.

rock[2] (räk) *vt., vi.* ⟦OE *roccian*⟧ **1** to move back and forth or from side to side **2** to sway strongly; shake —*n.* **1** a rocking motion **2** ROCK-AND-ROLL

rock'a·bil'ly (-ə bil'ē) *n.* ⟦ROCK(-AND-ROLL) + *-a-* + (HILL)BILLY⟧ an early form of rock-and-roll with a strong country music influence

rock'-and-roll' *n.* a form of popular music that evolved from rhythm and blues, characterized by a strong rhythm with an accent on the offbeat

rock bottom the lowest level

rock'bound' *adj.* surrounded or covered by rocks

rock candy large, hard, clear crystals of sugar formed on a string

rock'er *n.* **1** either of the curved pieces on which a cradle, etc. rocks **2** a chair mounted on such pieces: also **rocking chair**

rocker panel any panel section below the doors of an automotive vehicle

THESAURUS

captivating; see INTERESTING.

road *n.* **1** [A strip prepared for travel] path, way, highway, roadway, street, avenue, thoroughfare, boulevard, high road, drive, terrace, parkway, byway, lane, alley, alleyway, crossroad, viaduct, subway, paving, slab, turnpike, trail, post road, secondary road, market road, national highway, state highway, county road, interstate, military road, Roman road, freeway, the main drag*. **2** [A course] scheme, way, plans; see PLAN 2. —**on the road** on tour, traveling, on the way; see EN ROUTE. —**one for the road*** cocktail, nightcap, toast; see DRINK 2.

roam *v.* ramble, range, stroll, rove, walk, traverse, stray, straggle, meander, prowl, tramp, saunter, knock around*, bat around*, scour, gallivant, struggle along, traipse*, hike; see also TRAVEL.

roar *n.* bellow, shout, boom, thunder, howl, bay, bawl, yell, bluster, uproar, din, clash, detonation, explosion, barrage, reverberation, rumble; see also CRY 1, 2, NOISE 1.—*Ant.* SILENCE, whisper, sigh.

roar *v.* bellow, shout, boom, thunder, howl, bay, bawl, yell, rumble, drum, detonate, explode, reverberate, resound, reecho; see also CRY 2, SOUND.

roast *v.* toast, broil, barbecue; see COOK.

rob *v.* thieve, take, burglarize, strip, plunder, deprive of, withhold from, defraud, cheat, swindle, pilfer, break into, hold up, stick up*, purloin, filch, lift*, abscond with, embezzle, pillage, sack, loot, snitch*, pinch*, swipe*, cop*; see also STEAL.

robber *n.* thief, burglar, cheat, plunderer, pillager, bandit, pirate, raider, thug, desperado, forger, holdup man*, second-story man*, privateer, buccaneer, swindler, highwayman, bank robber, pilferer, shoplifter, cattle thief, housebreaker, pickpocket, freebooter, marauder, brigand, pickpurse*, sharper, safecracker, fence, rustler*, crook*, con man*, clip artist*, chiseler*, paperhanger*, stickup man*; see also CRIMINAL, RASCAL.

robbery *n.* burglary, larceny, thievery; see CRIME.

robe *n.* gown, dress, garment, mantle, cloak, vestment, cassock, caftan, peignoir, wrapper, costume, covering, cape, dressing gown, bathrobe, negligee, tea gown, kimono, housecoat; see also CLOTHES.

robot *n.* **1** [A mechanical person] automaton, android, Frankenstein, mechanical monster, humanoid, thinking machine. **2** [A person who resembles a machine] slave, menial, scullion; see LABORER.

robust *a.* hale, hearty, sound; see HEALTHY.

rock[1,2] *n.* **1** [A solidified form of earth] stone, mineral mass, dike, mineral body, earth crust; see also METAL, MINERAL. *Rocks include the following:* igneous, sedimentary, metamorphic; gypsum, limestone, freestone, sandstone, conglomerate, marble, dolomite, chalk, soapstone, slate, shale, granite, pumice, basalt, obsidian, rhyolite, gneiss, tufa, schist, talc, chert, jasper, flint, tuff, coal, quartzite, salt, phyllite, amphibolite, diorite, gabbro, marl, puddingstone, breccia, travertine, peridotite, andesite. **2** [A piece of rock] stone, boulder, cobblestone, pebble, fieldstone, cliff, crag, promontory, scrap, escarpment, reef, chip, flake, sliver, building stone, paving block, slab. **3** [Anything firm or solid] defense, support, Rock of Gibraltar; see FOUNDATION. **4** [Lively dance music] rock-and-roll, popular music, rhythm and blues; see DANCE 1, MUSIC 1. —**on the rocks*** **1** bankrupt, poverty-stricken, impoverished; see POOR 1, RUINED 3. **2** over ice cubes, undiluted, straight; see STRONG 4.

rock[2] *v.* sway, vibrate, reel, totter, swing, move, push and pull, agitate, roll, shake, shove, jolt, jiggle, quake, convulse, tremble, undulate, oscillate, quiver, quaver, wobble; see also WAVE 3.

rock-bottom *a.* lowest, hopeless, way down; see POOR 2, WORST. —**hit rock bottom** drop, not succeed, plunge; see FAIL 1, FALL 1.

rock·et (räk′it) ***n.*** ⟦It *rocchetta,* spool⟧ any device driven forward by gases escaping through a rear vent, as a firework, a projectile weapon, or the propulsion mechanism of a spacecraft —***vi.*** to move in or like a rocket; soar

rock′et·ry (-ə trē) ***n.*** the science of building and launching rockets

rock garden a garden of flowers, etc. in ground studded with rocks

rocking horse a toy horse on rockers or springs, for a child to ride

rock lobster SPINY LOBSTER

rock′-ribbed′ ***adj.*** **1** having rocky ridges **2** firm; unyielding

rock salt common salt in rocklike masses

rock wool a fibrous material made from molten rock, used for insulation

rock·y[1] (räk′ē) ***adj.*** **-i·er, -i·est 1** full of rocks **2** consisting of rock **3** like a rock; firm, hard, etc. —**rock′i·ness *n.***

rock·y[2] (räk′ē) ***adj.*** **-i·er, -i·est** inclined to rock; unsteady —**rock′i·ness *n.***

Rocky Mountains mountain system in W North America, extending from New Mexico to N Alaska: also **Rock′ies**

Rocky Mountain sheep BIGHORN

ro·co·co (rə kō′kō) ***n.*** ⟦Fr < *rocaille,* shell work⟧ [*occas.* **R-**] a style of architecture, art, music, etc. marked by profuse and delicate ornamentation, etc. —***adj.*** **1** of or in rococo **2** too elaborate

rod (räd) ***n.*** ⟦< OE *rodd,* straight shoot or stem⟧ **1** a straight stick or bar **2** a stick for beating as punishment **3** a staff carried as a symbol of office; scepter **4** a pole for fishing **5** a measure of length equal to $5\frac{1}{2}$ yards **6** [Slang] a pistol

rode (rōd) ***vi., vt.*** *pt. & archaic pp. of* RIDE

ro·dent (rōd′'nt) ***n.*** ⟦< L *rodere*, gnaw⟧ any of an order of gnawing mammals, as rats or mice

ro·de·o (rō′dē ō′) ***n.,*** *pl.* **-os′** ⟦Sp < L *rotare*, to turn⟧ a public exhibition of the skills of cowboys, with contests in bull riding, lassoing, etc.

Ro·din (*rô* da*n*′), (**François**) **Au·guste** (**René**) (ô güst′) 1840-1917; Fr. sculptor

roe[1] (rō) ***n.*** ⟦ME *rowe*⟧ fish eggs

roe[2] (rō) ***n.,*** *pl.* **roe** or **roes** ⟦< OE *ra*⟧ a small, agile deer of Europe and Asia

roe′buck′ ***n.*** the male roe deer

roent·gen (rent′gən) ***n.*** ⟦after W. K. *Roentgen* (1845-1923), Ger physicist⟧ the unit for measuring the radiation of X-rays or gamma rays

Rog·er (räj′ər) ***interj.*** ⟦< name of signal flag for *R*⟧ [*also* **r-**] **1** received **2** [Inf.] right! OK!

rogue (rōg) ***n.*** ⟦< ?⟧ **1** a scoundrel **2** a mischievous person —**ro·guer·y** (rō′gər ē), *pl.* **-ies, *n.*** —**ro·guish** (rō′gish) ***adj.***

rogues′ gallery a police collection of photographs of criminals

roil (roil) ***vt.*** ⟦< L *robigo,* rust⟧ **1** to make (a liquid) cloudy, muddy, etc. by stirring up sediment **2** to vex

roist·er (rois′tər) ***vi.*** ⟦see RUSTIC⟧ to revel noisily —**roist′er·er *n.***

role (rōl) ***n.*** ⟦Fr⟧ **1** the part played by an actor **2** a function assumed by someone [an advisory *role*] Often **rôle**

role model a person so effective or inspiring as to be a model for others

role′-play′ing ***n.*** *Psychol.* a technique in which participants assume and act out roles so as to practice appropriate behavior, etc.

roll (rōl) ***vi.*** ⟦< L *rota*, a wheel⟧ **1** to move by turning around or over and over **2** to move on wheels **3** to pass [the years *roll* by] **4** to extend in gentle swells **5** to make a loud rising and falling sound [thunder *rolls*] **6** to rock from side to side —***vt.*** **1** to make move by turning around or over and over **2** to make move on wheels **3** to utter with full, flowing sound **4** to pronounce with a trill [to *roll* one's r's] **5** to give a swaying motion to **6** to move around or from side to side [to *roll* one's eyes] **7** to make into a ball or cylinder [*roll* up the rug] **8** to flatten or spread with a roller, etc. —***n.*** **1** a rolling **2** a scroll **3** a list of names **4** something rolled into a cylinder **5** a small portion of bread, etc. **6** a swaying motion **7** a loud, reverberating sound, as of thunder **8** a slight swell on a surface —**on a roll** [Slang] at a high point —**roll back** to reduce (prices) to a previous level —**strike off** (or **from**) **the rolls** to expel from membership

roll′back′ ***n.*** a rolling back, esp. of prices to a previous level

roll call the reading aloud of a roll to find out who is absent

roll·er (rōl′ər) ***n.*** **1** one that rolls **2** a cylinder of metal, wood, etc. on which something is rolled, or one used to crush, smooth, or spread something

roller bearing a bearing in which the shaft turns with rollers in a circular track

Roll′er·blade′ *trademark for* a kind of IN-LINE SKATE —***n.*** [r-] any IN-LINE SKATE —**roll′er·blad′ing *n.***

roller coaster an amusement ride in which small open cars move on tracks that dip and curve sharply

roller skate SKATE[1] (sense 2) —**roll′er-skate′, -skat′ed, -skat′ing, *vi.*** —**roller skater**

rol·lick (räl′ik) ***vi.*** ⟦< ? FROLIC⟧ to play or behave in a lively, carefree way —**rol′lick·ing *adj.***

rolling pin a smooth, heavy cylinder of wood, etc. used to roll out dough

roll′-top′ ***adj.*** having a sliding, flexible top of parallel slats [a *roll-top* desk]

Ro·lo·dex (rō′lə deks′) *trademark for* a kind of desktop

THESAURUS

rocket ***n.*** projectile, missile, retrorocket, flying missile. *Kinds of rockets include the following:* air-to-air, air-to-surface, ground-to-ground, surface-to-surface, air-to-ground, surface-to-air, ground-to-air, V-2, solid-fuel, liquid-fuel; guided missile, ballistic missile, cruise missile, intercontinental ballistic missile (ICBM), submarine-launched ballistic missile (SLBM), MIRV, heat-seeking missile, anti-tank missile, smart bomb*.

rocky[1] ***a.*** stony, flinty, hard, inflexible, solid, petrified, ragged, jagged, rugged; see also STONE.—*Ant.* SOFT, flexible, sandy.

rod ***n.*** **1** [A rodlike body] staff, bar, pole, wand, stave, baton, spike, pin, cylinder, bacillus, cylindrical object, scepter, twig, switch, whip, stock, stalk, trunk; see also STICK. **2** [A fishing rod] pole, rod and reel, tackle; see EQUIPMENT.

rodent ***n.*** *Common varieties of rodents include the following:* rat, mouse, squirrel, chipmunk, beaver, porcupine, muskrat, prairie dog, gopher, marmot, groundhog, woodchuck, ground squirrel, chinchilla, mole, guinea pig.

rodeo ***n.*** riding unbroken horses, rounding up cattle, roundup, features of a roundup. *Rodeo events include the following:* broncobusting, bulldogging, calf-roping, cutting out steers, Brahma bull riding.

rogue ***n.*** outlaw, problem, miscreant; see CRIMINAL.

roguish ***a.*** **1** [Dishonest] unscrupulous, sly, corrupt; see DISHONEST. **2** [Mischievous] playful, impish, arch; see NAUGHTY.

role ***n.*** function, task, part, character, title role, impersonation, leading man, leading woman, hero, heroine, ingénue, performance, presentation, acting, characterization, capacity, position, office, purpose.

roll ***n.*** **1** [The act of rolling] turn, turning over, revolution, rotation, wheeling, trundling, whirl, gyration. **2** [A relatively flat object rolled up on itself] scroll, volute, spiral, coil, whorl, convolution, fold, shell, cone, cornucopia, tube, cylinder. **3** [A long, heavy sound] thunder, roar, drumbeat; see NOISE 1. **4** [A small portion of bread] *Types of rolls include the following:* parkerhouse, hard, soft, dinner, crescent, sesame, poppy-seed, cloverleaf, rye, whole-wheat, sourdough, breakfast, sweet, cinnamon; popover, croissant, Danish, brioche, biscuit, hot cross bun, bagel, bun, English muffin; egg roll; see also BREAD, PASTRY. **5** [A list] register, table, schedule; see CATALOG, INDEX 2, LIST, RECORD 1.

roll ***v.*** **1** [To move by rotation, or in rotating numbers] rotate, come around, swing around, wheel, come in turn, circle, alternate, follow, succeed, be in sequence, follow in due course; see also MOVE 1, TURN 1. **2** [To revolve] turn, pivot, spin; see sense 1. **3** [To make into a roll] bend, curve, arch; see TWIST. **4** [To flatten or spread with a roller] press, level, flatten, spread, pulverize, grind.—*Ant.* CUT, roughen, toss up. **5** [To flow] run, billow, surge; see FLOW. **6** [To produce a relatively deep, continuous sound] reverberate, resound, echo; see ROAR, SOUND. **7** [To function] work, go, start production; see OPERATE 2.

rolled ***a.*** **1** [Made into a roll] twisted, folded, curved, bent, bowed, coiled, spiraled, arched, wound, convoluted.—*Ant.* SPREAD, unrolled, opened out. **2** [Flattened] pressed, leveled, evened; see FLAT 1, SMOOTH 1.

roller ***n.*** cylinder, rolling pin, hair roller; see ROLL 2.

rollicking ***a.*** high-spirited, jolly, exuberant; see HAPPY.

file holding cards containing names and addresses for ready reference

ro·ly-po·ly (rō′lē pō′lē) ***adj.*** ⟦< ROLL⟧ short and plump; pudgy

Rom *abbrev.* Roman

ROM (räm) ***n.*** ⟦*r(ead-)o(nly) m(emory)*⟧ computer memory whose contents can be read but not altered; also, a memory chip like this

ro·maine (rō mān′) ***n.*** ⟦Fr, ult. < L *Romanus*, Roman⟧ a type of lettuce with long leaves forming a slender head

Ro·man (rō′mən) ***adj.*** **1** of or characteristic of ancient or modern Rome or its people, etc. **2** of the Roman Catholic Church **3** [*usually* **r-**] designating or of the usual upright style of printing types; not italic —***n.*** **1** a person born or living in ancient or modern Rome **2** [*usually* **r-**] roman type or characters

Roman candle a firework consisting of a tube that sends out balls of fire, etc.

Roman Catholic **1** of the Christian church (**Roman Catholic Church**) headed by the pope **2** a member of this church

ro·mance (rō mans′, rō′mans′) ***adj.*** ⟦ult. < L *Romanicus*, Roman⟧ [**R-**] designating or of any of the languages derived from Vulgar Latin, as Italian, Spanish, or French —***n.*** **1** a long poem or tale, orig. written in a Romance dialect, about the adventures of knights **2** a novel of love, adventure, etc. **3** excitement, love, etc. of the kind found in such literature **4** a love affair —***vt.*** **-manced′**, **-manc′ing** to make love to; woo

Roman Empire empire of the ancient Romans (27 B.C.-A.D. 395), including W & S Europe, N Africa, & SW Asia

Ro·ma·ni·a (rō mā′nē ə) country in SE Europe: 91,699 sq. mi.; pop. 22,760,000 —**Ro·ma′ni·an** ***adj.***, ***n.***

Roman numerals Roman letters used as numerals: I = 1, V = 5, X = 10, L = 50, C = 100, D = 500, and M = 1,000

ro·man·tic (rō man′tik) ***adj.*** **1** of, like, or characterized by romance **2** fanciful or fictitious **3** not practical; visionary **4** full of thoughts, feelings, etc. of romance **5** suited for romance **6** [*often* **R-**] of a 19th-c. cultural movement characterized by freedom of form and spirit, emphasis on feeling and originality, etc. —***n.*** a romantic person —**ro·man′ti·cal·ly** ***adv.*** —**ro·man′ti·cism′** (-tə siz′ əm) ***n.***

ro·man′ti·cize′ (-tə sīz′) ***vt.*** **-cized′**, **-ciz′ing** to treat or regard romantically —***vi.*** to have romantic ideas, etc.

Rom·a·ny (räm′ə nē, rō′mə-) ***n.*** the language of the Gypsies

Rome (rōm) capital of Italy &, formerly, of the Roman Empire: pop. 2,605,000

Ro·me·o (rō′mē ō′) ***n.*** the hero of Shakespeare's *Romeo and Juliet* (c. 1595)

romp (rämp) ***n.*** ⟦prob. < OFr *ramper*, to climb⟧ boisterous, lively play —***vi.*** to play in a boisterous, lively way

romp′er ***n.*** **1** one who romps **2** [*pl.*] a loose, one-piece outer garment with pants like bloomers, for a small child

Rom·u·lus (räm′yoo ləs) ***n.*** *Rom. Myth.* founder and first king of Rome: he and his twin brother Remus are suckled by a female wolf

rood (ro͞od) ***n.*** ⟦OE *rod*⟧ **1** a crucifix **2** [Brit.] an old unit of area equal to ¼ acre

roof (ro͞of, roof) ***n.***, *pl.* **roofs** ⟦OE *hrof*⟧ **1** the outside top covering of a building **2** anything like this in position or use *[the roof of the mouth]* —***vt.*** to cover with or as with a roof —**roof′less** ***adj.***

roof′er ***n.*** a roof maker or repairer

roof′ing ***n.*** material for roofs

roof′top′ ***n.*** the roof of a building

rook[1] (rook) ***n.*** ⟦OE *hroc*⟧ a European crow —***vt.***, ***vi.*** to swindle; cheat

rook[2] (rook) ***n.*** ⟦< Pers *rukh*⟧ a chess piece that can move horizontally or vertically

rook′er·y ***n.***, *pl.* **-ies** a breeding place of rooks, or of seals, penguins, etc.

rook·ie (rook′ē) ***n.*** [Slang] **1** an inexperienced army recruit **2** [Inf.] any beginner

room (ro͞om, room) ***n.*** ⟦OE *rum*⟧ **1** space to contain something **2** suitable scope *[room for doubt]* **3** an interior space enclosed or set apart by walls **4** [*pl.*] living quarters **5** the people in a room —***vi.***, ***vt.*** to have or provide with lodgings —**room′ful′** ***n.*** —**room′y**, **-i·er**, **-i·est**, ***adj.*** —**room′i·ness** ***n.***

room and board lodging and meals

room′er ***n.*** one who rents a room or rooms to live in; lodger

room·ette (ro͞o met′) ***n.*** a small room in a railroad sleeping car

rooming house a house with furnished rooms for rent

room′mate′ ***n.*** a person with whom one shares a room or rooms

Roo·se·velt (rō′zə velt′) **1 Franklin Del·a·no** (del′ə nō′) 1882-1945; 32d president of the U.S. (1933-45) **2 Theodore** 1858-1919; 26th president of the U.S. (1901-09)

roost (ro͞ost) ***n.*** ⟦OE *hrost*⟧ **1** a perch on which birds, esp. domestic fowls, can rest **2** a place with perches for birds **3** a place for resting, sleeping, etc. —***vi.*** **1** to perch on a roost **2** to stay or settle down, as for the night

roost′er ***n.*** a male chicken

root[1] (ro͞ot, root) ***n.*** ⟦< ON *rot*⟧ **1** the part of a plant, usually underground, that anchors the plant, draws water from the soil, etc. **2** the embedded part of a tooth, a hair, etc. **3** a source or cause **4** a supporting or essential part **5** a quantity that, multiplied by itself a specified number of times, produces a given quantity **6** the basic element of a word or form, without affixes or phonetic changes —***vi.*** to take root —***vt.*** **1** to fix the roots of in the ground **2** to establish; settle —**root up** (or **out**) to pull up by the roots; destroy completely —**take root** **1** to begin growing by putting out roots **2** to become fixed, settled, etc.

root[2] (ro͞ot, root) ***vt.*** ⟦< OE *wrot*, snout⟧ to dig (*up* or *out*) with or as with the snout —***vi.*** **1** to search about; rummage **2** [Inf.] to encourage a team, etc.: usually with *for*

root beer a carbonated drink made or flavored with certain plant root extracts

root canal **1** a tubular channel in a tooth's root **2** a treatment involving opening, cleaning, filling, etc. such a channel

root′let (-lit) ***n.*** a little root

rope (rōp) ***n.*** ⟦OE *rap*⟧ **1** a thick, strong cord made of strands of fiber, etc. twisted together **2** a ropelike string, as of pearls —***vt.*** **roped**, **rop′ing** **1** to fasten or tie with a rope **2** to mark off or enclose with a rope **3** to catch with a lasso —**know the ropes** [Inf.] to be well acquainted with a procedure, etc. —**rope in** [Slang] to entice or trick into doing something

THESAURUS

Roman ***a.*** Latin, classic, classical, late classic, Augustan, ancient, Italic.

romance ***n.*** **1** [A love affair] affair, courtship, amour; see LOVE 1. **2** [A tale of love and adventure] historical romance, novel, fiction; see STORY.

romantic ***a.*** adventurous, novel, daring, charming, enchanting, lyric, poetic, fanciful, chivalrous, courtly, knightly.

romp ***v.*** gambol, celebrate, frolic; see PLAY 1, 2.

roof ***n.*** cover, shelter, tent, house, habitation, home.

roofing ***n.*** shingles, tiles, asphalt, thatch, roof.

room ***n.*** **1** [Space] vastness, reach, sweep; see EXTENT. **2** [An enclosure] chamber, apartment, cabin, cubicle, niche, vault. *Rooms include the following:* living room, dining room, sitting room, drawing room, bedroom, music room, playroom, bathroom, guest room, family room, waiting room, boardroom, conference room, foyer, vestibule, study, library, den, kitchen, hall, master bedroom, parlor, wardrobe, closet, pantry, basement, cellar, attic, garret, anteroom, dormitory, alcove, ward, office, breakfast nook, nursery, studio, schoolroom, loft. **3** [The possibility of admission] opening, place, opportunity; see VACANCY 2. **4** [A rented sleeping room] quarters, lodgings, digs*; see APARTMENT.

roomer ***n.*** lodger, occupant, dweller; see TENANT.

roommate ***n.*** roomie*, flatmate, bunkmate; see FRIEND.

roomy ***a.*** spacious, capacious, ample; see BIG 1, LARGE 1.

rooster ***n.*** cock, chanticleer*, chicken; see FOWL.

root[1] ***n.*** **1** [An underground portion of a plant] *Types of roots include the following:* conical, napiform, fusiform, fibrous, moniliform, nodulose, tuberous, adventitious, prop, aerial, tap. **2** [The cause or basis] source, reason, motive; see ORIGIN 2, 3. —**take root** begin growing, start, commence; see GROW 1.

rooted ***a.*** grounded, based, fixed; see FIRM 1.

rope ***n.*** cord, cordage, braiding, string, thread, strand, tape, cord, lace, cable, hawser, lariat, lasso, line, towline. —**at the end of one's rope** desperate, despairing, in despair; see EXTREME, HOPELESS. —**know the ropes*** be experienced, comprehend, understand; see KNOW 1. —**on the ropes*** near collapse, close to ruin, in danger; see ENDANGERED.

Roque·fort (rōk′fərt) ⟦after *Roquefort,* France, where made⟧ *trademark for* a strong French cheese with a bluish mold
Ror·schach test (rôr′shäk′) ⟦after H. *Rorschach* (1884-1922), Swiss psychiatrist⟧ *Psychol.* a personality test in which the subject's interpretations of standard inkblot designs are analyzed
ro·sa·ry (rō′zər ē) ***n.***, *pl.* **-ries** ⟦ML *rosarium*⟧ *R.C.Ch.* a string of groups of beads, used to keep count in saying prayers
rose[1] (rōz) ***n.*** ⟦< L *rosa* < Gr *rhodon*⟧ **1** a shrub with prickly stems and with flowers of red, pink, white, yellow, etc. **2** its flower **3** pinkish red or purplish red —***adj.*** of this color
rose[2] (rōz) ***vi.*** *pt. of* RISE
ro·sé (rō zā′) ***n.*** ⟦Fr, pink⟧ a pink wine, tinted by the grape skins early in fermentation
ro·se·ate (rō′zē it) ***adj.*** rose-colored
rose′bud′ ***n.*** the bud of a rose
rose′bush′ ***n.*** a shrub that bears roses
rose′-col′ored ***adj.*** **1** pinkish-red or purplish-red **2** optimistic —**through rose-colored glasses** with optimism, esp. undue optimism
rose·mar·y (rōz′mer′ē) ***n.*** ⟦< L *ros marinus*, sea dew⟧ an evergreen herb of the mint family, with fragrant leaves used in perfumes, in cooking, etc.
ro·sette (rō zet′) ***n.*** an ornament or arrangement, as of ribbons, resembling a rose
rose water a preparation of water and attar of roses, used as a perfume
rose window a circular window with a roselike pattern of tracery
rose′wood′ ***n.*** ⟦< its odor⟧ **1** a hard, reddish wood, used in furniture, etc. **2** a tropical tree yielding this wood
Rosh Ha·sha·na (rōsh′ hə shô′nə, -shä′-) the Jewish New Year
ros·in (räz′ən) ***n.*** ⟦see RESIN⟧ the hard resin left after the distillation of turpentine: it is rubbed on violin bows, used in making varnish, etc.
ros·ter (räs′tər) ***n.*** ⟦< Du *rooster*⟧ a list or roll, as of military personnel
ros·trum (räs′trəm) ***n.***, *pl.* **-trums** or **-tra** (-trə) ⟦L, beak⟧ a platform for public speaking
ros·y (rō′zē) ***adj.*** **-i·er, -i·est** ⟦ME⟧ **1** rose in color **2** bright, promising, etc. —**ros′i·ly** ***adv.*** —**ros′i·ness** ***n.***
rot (rät) ***vi., vt.*** **rot′ted, rot′ting** ⟦OE *rotian*⟧ to decompose; decay —***n.*** **1** a rotting or something rotten **2** a disease characterized by decay **3** [Slang] nonsense
ro·ta·ry (rōt′ər ē) ***adj.*** ⟦< L *rota,* wheel⟧ **1** turning around a central axis, as a wheel does **2** having rotating parts *[a rotary press]* —***n.***, *pl.* **-ries** **1** a rotary machine **2** TRAFFIC CIRCLE
ro·tate (rō′tāt′) ***vi., vt.*** **-tat′ed, -tat′ing** ⟦< L *rota,* wheel⟧ **1** to turn around an axis **2** to change or cause to change in regular succession —**ro·ta′tion** ***n.*** —**ro′ta′tor** ***n.***
ROTC *abbrev.* Reserve Officers' Training Corps
rote (rōt) ***n.*** ⟦ME⟧ a fixed, mechanical way of doing something —**by rote** by memory alone, without thought
rot·gut (rät′gut′) ***n.*** [Slang] raw, low-grade whiskey or other liquor
ro·tis·ser·ie (rō tis′ər ē) ***n.*** ⟦Fr < earlier Fr *rostir,* to roast⟧ a grill with an electrically turned spit
ro·to·gra·vure (rōt′ə grə vyoor′) ***n.*** ⟦< L *rota*, wheel + Fr *gravure*, engraving⟧ a printing process using a rotary press with cylinders etched from photographic plates
ro·tor (rōt′ər) ***n.*** **1** the rotating part of a motor, etc. **2** a system of rotating airfoils, as on a helicopter
ro·to·till·er (rōt′ə til′ər) ***n.*** a motorized machine with rotary blades, for loosening the earth around growing plants —**ro′to·till′** ***vt.***
rot·ten (rät′'n) ***adj.*** ⟦< ON *rotinn*⟧ **1** decayed; spoiled **2** foul-smelling **3** morally corrupt **4** unsound, as if decayed within **5** [Slang] very bad, unpleasant, etc. —**rot′ten·ness** ***n.***
Rot·ter·dam (rät′ər dam′) seaport in SW Netherlands: pop. 599,000
ro·tund (rō tund′) ***adj.*** ⟦L *rotundus*⟧ plump or stout —**ro·tun′di·ty** or **ro·tund′ness** ***n.***
ro·tun·da (rō tun′də) ***n.*** ⟦see prec.⟧ a round building, hall, or room, esp. one with a dome
rou·é (ro͞o ā′) ***n.*** ⟦Fr < L *rota,* wheel⟧ a dissipated man; rake
rouge (ro͞ozh) ***n.*** ⟦Fr, red⟧ **1** a reddish cosmetic powder or paste for adding color to the cheeks **2** a reddish powder for polishing jewelry, etc. —***vt.*** **rouged, roug′ing** to use cosmetic rouge on
rough (ruf) ***adj.*** ⟦OE *ruh*⟧ **1** not smooth or level; uneven **2** shaggy *[a rough coat]* **3** stormy *[rough weather]* **4** disorderly *[rough play]* **5** harsh or coarse **6** lacking comforts and conveniences **7** not polished or finished; crude **8** approximate *[a rough guess]* **9** [Inf.] difficult *[a rough time]* —***n.*** **1** rough ground, material, condition, etc. **2** *Golf* any part of the course with grass, etc. left uncut —***adv.*** in a rough way —***vt.*** **1** to roughen: often with *up* **2** to treat roughly: usually with *up* **3** to sketch, shape, etc. roughly: usually with *in* or *out* —**rough it** to live without customary comforts, etc. —**rough′ly** ***adv.*** —**rough′ness** ***n.***
rough′age ***n.*** rough or coarse food or fodder
rough′en ***vt., vi.*** to make or become rough
rough′-hew′ ***vt.*** **-hewed′, -hewed′** or **-hewn′, -hew′ing** **1** to hew (timber, stone, etc.) roughly, or without smoothing **2** to form roughly Also **rough′hew′**
rough′house′ [Inf.] ***n.*** rough, boisterous play, fighting, etc. —***vt., vi.*** **-housed′, -hous′ing** to treat or act roughly or boisterously
rough′neck′ ***n.*** **1** [Inf.] a rowdy **2** a worker on an oil rig —***vi.*** to work as a roughneck
rough′shod′ ***adj.*** shod with horseshoes having metal points —**ride roughshod over** to treat harshly and arrogantly
rou·lette (ro͞o let′) ***n.*** ⟦Fr < L *rota,* wheel⟧ a gambling game played by tossing a small ball into a whirling shallow bowl (**roulette wheel**) with numbered, red or black compartments

THESAURUS

rose[1] ***a.*** rose-colored, rosy, flushed; see PINK, RED.
rose[1] ***n.*** *Kinds of roses include the following:* wild, tea, hybrid tea, perpetual, multiflora, floribunda, musk, cabbage; eglantine, sweetbrier, rambler; see also FLOWER.
roster ***n.*** names, subscribers, program; see CATALOG, LIST, INDEX 2.
rostrum ***n.*** dais, pulpit, stage; see PLATFORM 1.
rosy ***a.*** **1** [Rose-colored] colored, deep pink, pale cardinal; see PINK, RED. **2** [Promising] optimistic, favorable, cheerful; see HOPEFUL 1, 2.
rot ***n.*** **1** [The process of rotting] decomposition, corruption, disintegration; see DECAY. **2** [*Nonsense] trash, silliness, foolishness; see NONSENSE 1.
rot ***v.*** decay, disintegrate, decompose; see SPOIL.
rotate ***v.*** twist, wheel, revolve; see MOVE 1, TURN 1.
rotation ***n.*** turn, circumrotation, circle; see REVOLUTION.
rotten ***a.*** **1** [Having rotted] bad, rotting, putrefying, decaying, putrefied, spoiled, decomposed, decayed, offensive, disgusting, rancid, fecal, rank, foul, corrupt, polluted, infected, loathsome, overripe, bad-smelling, putrid, crumbled, disintegrated, stale, noisome, smelling, fetid, noxious.—*Ant.* FRESH, unspoiled, good. **2** [Not sound] unsound, defective, impaired; see WEAK 2. **3** [Corrupt] contaminated, polluted, filthy, tainted, defiled, impure, sullied, unclean, soiled, debauched, blemished, morbid, infected, dirtied, depraved, tarnished; see also DIRTY.—*Ant.* PURE, clean, healthy.
rough ***a.*** **1** [Not smooth] unequal, broken, coarse, choppy, ruffled, uneven, ridged, rugged, irregular, not sanded, not finished, unfinished, not completed, needing the finishing touches, bumpy, rocky, stony, jagged, grinding, knobby, sharpening, cutting, sharp, crinkled, crumpled, rumpled, scraggly, straggly, hairy, shaggy, hirsute, bushy, tufted, bearded, woolly, nappy, unshaven, unshorn, gnarled, knotty, bristly.—*Ant.* LEVEL, flat, even. **2** [Not gentle] harsh, strict, stern; see SEVERE 2. **3** [Crude] boorish, uncivil, uncultivated; see RUDE 1. **4** [Not quiet] buffeting, stormy, tumultuous; see TURBULENT. **5** [Unfinished] incomplete, imperfect, uncompleted; see UNFINISHED. **6** [Approximate] inexact, unprecise, uncertain; see APPROXIMATE.
roughly ***a.*** **1** [Approximately] about, in round numbers, by guess; see APPROXIMATELY. **2** [In a brutal manner] coarsely, cruelly, inhumanly; see BRUTALLY.
roughness ***n.*** **1** [The quality of being rough on the surface] unevenness, coarseness, brokenness, bumpiness, irregularity, raggedness, jaggedness, wrinkledness, shagginess, bushiness, beardedness, hairiness, woolliness, bristling.—*Ant.* REGULARITY, smoothness, evenness. **2** [Things causing or exhibiting roughness] break, crack, ragged edge, scratch, abrasion, nick. **3** [The quality of being rough in conduct] harshness, severity, hardness; see RUDENESS.

round (round) ***adj.*** ⟦< L *rotundus*, rotund⟧ **1** shaped like a ball, circle, or cylinder **2** plump **3** full; complete *[a round dozen]* **4** expressed by a whole number or in tens, hundreds, etc. —***n.*** **1** something round, as the rung of a ladder **2** the part of a beef animal between the rump and the leg **3** a series or succession *[a round of parties]* **4** [*often pl.*] a regular, customary circuit, as by a watchman **5** a single shot from a gun, or from several guns together; also, the ammunition for this **6** a single outburst, as of applause **7** a single period of action, as in boxing **8** a short song which one group begins singing when another reaches the second phrase, etc. —***vt.*** **1** to make round **2** to express as a round number: with *off* **3** to finish: with *out* or *off* **4** to go around —***vi.*** **1** to turn; reverse direction **2** to become plump: often with *out* —***adv.*** **1** AROUND **2** through a recurring period of time *[to work the year round]* **3** for each of several **4** in a roundabout way —***prep.*** AROUND —**in the round** **1** in an arena theater **2** in full, rounded form: said of sculpture **3** in full detail —**round about** in or to the opposite direction —**round up** to collect in a herd, group, etc. —**round′ness** ***n.***

round′a·bout′ ***adj.*** indirect; circuitous

roun·de·lay (roun′də lā′) ***n.*** ⟦< OFr *rondel*, a short lyrical poem⟧ a simple song in which some phrase, line, etc. is continually repeated

round′house′ ***n.*** a circular building for storing and repairing locomotives

round′ly ***adv.*** **1** in a round form **2** vigorously **3** fully; completely and thoroughly

round′-shoul′dered ***adj.*** having the shoulders bent forward

round steak a steak cut from a round of beef

Round Table **1** in legend, the circular table around which King Arthur and his knights sit **2** [**r- t-**] a group gathered for an informal discussion

round′-the-clock′ ***adj.***, ***adv.*** throughout the day and night; continuous(ly)

round trip a trip to a place and back again —**round′-trip′** ***adj.***

round′-trip′per ***n.*** [Slang] *Baseball* a home run

round′up′ ***n.*** **1** a driving together of cattle, etc. on the range, as for branding **2** any similar collecting **3** a summary, as of news

round′worm′ ***n.*** NEMATODE

rouse (rouz) ***vt.***, ***vi.*** **roused**, **rous′ing** ⟦prob. < earlier Fr⟧ **1** to excite or become excited **2** to wake

Rous·seau (ro͞o sō′), **Jean Jacques** (zhän zhäk′) 1712-78; Fr. philosopher & writer, born in Switzerland

roust·a·bout (rous′tə bout′) ***n.*** ⟦< ROUSE + ABOUT⟧ an unskilled or transient laborer, as on a wharf or in an oil field

rout[1] (rout) ***n.*** ⟦< L *rupta*, broken⟧ **1** a disorderly flight **2** an overwhelming defeat —***vt.*** **1** to put to flight **2** to defeat overwhelmingly

rout[2] (rout) ***vt.*** ⟦< ROOT[2]⟧ to force out —**rout out** **1** to gouge out **2** to make (a person) get out

route (ro͞ot, rout) ***n.*** ⟦< L *rupta* (*via*), (path) broken through⟧ a road or course for traveling; often, a regular course, as in delivering mail —***vt.*** **rout′ed**, **rout′ing** **1** to send by a certain route **2** to arrange the route for

rou·tine (ro͞o tēn′) ***n.*** ⟦see prec.⟧ a regular procedure, customary or prescribed —***adj.*** like or using routine —**rou·tine′ly** ***adv.***

rou·tin′ize (-tē′nīz) ***vt.*** **-ized**, **-iz·ing** to make routine; reduce to a routine —**rou′tin·i·za′tion** ***n.***

rove (rōv) ***vi.***, ***vt.*** **roved**, **rov′ing** ⟦ME *roven*⟧ to roam —**rov′er** ***n.***

row[1] (rō) ***n.*** ⟦OE *ræw*⟧ **1** a number of people or things in a line **2** a line of seats in a theater, etc. —**in a row** in succession; consecutively

row[2] (rō) ***vt.***, ***vi.*** ⟦OE *rowan*⟧ **1** to propel (a boat) with oars **2** to carry in a rowboat —***n.*** a trip by rowboat

row[3] (rou) ***n.***, ***vi.*** ⟦< ? ROUSE⟧ quarrel or brawl

row·boat (rō′bōt′) ***n.*** a small boat made for rowing

row·dy (rou′dē) ***n.***, *pl.* **-dies** ⟦< ? ROW[3]⟧ a rough, quarrelsome, and disorderly person —***adj.*** **-di·er**, **-di·est** rough, quarrelsome, etc. —**row′di·ness** ***n.*** —**row′dy·ism′** ***n.***

row·el (rou′əl) ***n.*** ⟦ult. < L *rota*, wheel⟧ a small wheel with sharp points, at the end of a spur

row house (rō) any of a line of identical houses joined by common walls

roy·al (roi′əl) ***adj.*** ⟦< L *regalis*⟧ **1** of a king or queen **2** like, or fit for, a king or queen; magnificent, majestic, etc. **3** of a kingdom, its government, etc. —**roy′al·ly** ***adv.***

roy′al·ist ***n.*** one who supports a monarch or a monarchy

roy′al·ty ***n.***, *pl.* **-ties** **1** the rank or power of a king or queen **2** a royal person or persons **3** royal quality **4** a share of the proceeds from a patent, book, etc. paid to the owner, author, etc.

rpm *abbrev.* revolutions per minute

rps *abbrev.* revolutions per second

RR *abbrev.* **1** railroad **2** Rural Route: also **R.R.**

RSV *abbrev.* Revised Standard Version (of the Bible)

R.S.V.P. or **r.s.v.p.** *abbrev.* ⟦Fr, for *répondez s'il vous plaît*⟧ please reply: also **RSVP** or **rsvp**

rte *abbrev.* route

rub (rub) ***vt.*** **rubbed**, **rub′bing** ⟦ME *rubben*⟧ **1** to move (one's hand, a cloth, etc.) over (something) with pressure and friction **2** to apply (polish, etc.) in this way **3** to move (things) over each other with pressure and friction **4** to make sore by rubbing **5** to remove by rubbing (*out, off*, etc.) —***vi.*** **1** to move with pressure and friction (*on*, etc.) **2** to rub something —***n.*** **1** a rubbing **2** an obstacle, difficulty, or source of irritation —**rub down** **1** to massage **2** to smooth, polish, etc. by rubbing —**rub elbows**

THESAURUS

round ***a.*** **1** [Shaped like a globe or disk] spherical, spheroid, globular, orbicular, globe-shaped, ball-shaped, domical, circular, cylindrical, ringed, annular, oval, disk-shaped. **2** [Curved] arched, rounded, bowed, looped, recurved, incurved, coiled, curled. **3** [Approximate] rough, in tens, in hundreds; see APPROXIMATE.

round ***n.*** **1** [A round object] ring, orb, globe; see CIRCLE 1, RIM. **2** [A period of action] bout, course, whirl, cycle, circuit, routine, performance; see also SEQUENCE 1, SERIES. **3** [A unit of ammunition] cartridge, charge, load; see AMMUNITION, BULLET, SHOT 1.

round ***v.*** **1** [To turn] whirl, wheel, spin; see TURN 1. **2** [To make round] curve, convolute, bow, arch, bend, loop, whorl, shape, form, recurve, coil, fill out, curl, mold.—*Ant.* STRAIGHTEN, flatten, level. —**round off** approximate; round off by tens, hundreds, etc.; express as a round number; see also ESTIMATE. —**round out** expand, fill out, enlarge; see GROW 1.

round ***prep.*** about, near, in the neighborhood of, close to; see also ALMOST, APPROXIMATELY, AROUND.

roundabout ***a.*** circuitous, deviating, out-of-the-way; see INDIRECT.

roundness ***n.*** fullness, completeness, circularity, oneness, inclusiveness, wholeness.

roundup ***n.*** gathering, corralling, herding, wrangling, assembling.

rouse ***v.*** **1** [To waken] arouse, raise, awake; see AWAKEN, WAKE 1. **2** [To stimulate] urge, stir, provoke; see ANIMATE, EXCITE.

route ***n.*** **1** [A course being followed] way, course, path, track, beat, tack, divergence, detour, digression, meandering, rambling, wandering, circuit, round, rounds, range; see also ROAD 1. **2** [A projected course] map, plans, plot; see PLAN 2, PROGRAM 2.

routine ***a.*** usual, customary, methodical; see CONVENTIONAL 1, HABITUAL.

routine ***n.*** round, cycle, habit; see METHOD, SYSTEM.

rove ***v.*** walk, meander, wander; see ROAM.

row[1] ***n.*** series, order, file; see LINE 1. —**in a row** in succession, successively, in a line; see CONSECUTIVE.

rowdy ***a.*** rebellious, boisterous, mischievous; see LAWLESS 2, UNRULY.

royal ***a.*** **1** [Pertaining to a king or his family] high, elevated, highborn, monarchic, reigning, regnant, regal, ruling, dominant, absolute, imperial, sovereign, supreme, noble, of noble birth, of gentle birth; see also sense 2, NOBLE 3. **2** [Having qualities befitting royalty] great, grand, stately, lofty, illustrious, renowned, eminent, superior, worthy, honorable, dignified, chivalrous, courteous, kingly, greathearted, princely, princelike, majestic, magnificent, splendid, noble, courtly, impressive, commanding, aristocratic, lordly, august, imposing, superb, glorious, resplendent, gorgeous, sublime; see also sense 1, NOBLE 1, 2, WORTHY.

royalty ***n.*** kingship, sovereignty, nobility, authority, eminence, distinction, blood, birth, high descent, rank, greatness, power, supremacy, primacy, the crown, suzerainty; see also KING 1, QUEEN.

rub ***n.*** **1** [A rubbing action] brushing, stroke, massage, smoothing, scraping, scouring, grinding, rasping, friction, attrition; see also TOUCH 2. **2** [A difficulty] impediment, hindrance, dilemma; see DIFFICULTY 1, 2, PREDICAMENT.

rub ***v.*** **1** [To subject to friction] scrape, smooth, abrade, scour, grate, grind, wear away, graze, rasp, knead, fret, massage, polish, shine, burnish, scrub, erase, rub out, rub down, file, chafe, clean. **2** [To apply by rubbing; *usually with "on"*] brush, cover, finish; see PAINT 2. —**rub out** eradicate, erase, delete; see CANCEL, ELIMINATE.

with to associate or mingle with: also **rub shoulders with** —**rub it in** [Slang] to keep reminding someone of his or her mistake —**rub the wrong way** to annoy

ru·ba·to (ro͞o bät′ō) ***adj., adv.*** ⟦It, stolen⟧ *Music* intentionally and temporarily not in strict tempo

rub·ber (rub′ər) ***n.*** **1** one that rubs **2** ⟦< orig. use as an eraser⟧ an elastic substance made from the milky sap of various tropical plants or made synthetically **3** something made of this substance; specif., *a*) a low-cut overshoe *b*) [Slang] a condom —***adj.*** made of rubber —**rub′ber·y** ***adj.***

rubber band a narrow, continuous band of rubber as for holding small objects together

rubber cement an adhesive of unvulcanized rubber in a solvent that quickly evaporates when exposed to air

rubber check ⟦from the notion that it "bounces": see BOUNCE (*vi.* 3)⟧ [Slang] a check that is worthless because of insufficient funds in the writer's account

rubber game (rub′ər) ⟦< ?⟧ the deciding game in a series

rub′ber·ize′ (-īz′) ***vt.*** **-ized′, -iz′ing** to coat or impregnate with rubber

rub′ber·neck′ ***vi.*** to look at things or gaze about in curiosity by stretching the neck or turning the head, as a sightseer might do

rubber plant **1** any plant yielding latex **2** a house plant with large, glossy leaves

rubber stamp **1** a stamp of rubber, inked for printing dates, signatures, etc. **2** [Inf.] *a*) a person, bureau, etc. that gives routine or automatic approval *b*) such approval —**rub′ber-stamp′** ***vt.***

rub·bish (rub′ish) ***n.*** ⟦ME *robous*⟧ **1** any material thrown away as worthless; trash **2** nonsense

rub·ble (rub′əl) ***n.*** ⟦ME *robel*⟧ rough, broken pieces of stone, brick, etc.

rub′down′ ***n.*** a brisk rubbing of the body, as in massage

rube (ro͞ob) ***n.*** ⟦< name *Reuben*⟧ [Slang] an unsophisticated rustic

ru·bel·la (ro͞o bel′ə) ***n.*** ⟦< L *ruber,* red⟧ an infectious disease causing small red spots on the skin; German measles

Ru·bens (ro͞o′bənz), **Peter Paul** 1577-1640; Fl. painter

ru·bi·cund (ro͞o′bə kund′) ***adj.*** ⟦< L *ruber,* red⟧ reddish; ruddy

ru·ble (ro͞o′bəl) ***n.*** ⟦Russ *rubl′*⟧ the monetary unit of Russia, Belarus, & Tajikistan

ru·bric (ro͞o′brik) ***n.*** ⟦< L *ruber,* red⟧ **1** in early books, a section heading, letter, etc., often printed in red **2** any rule, explanatory comment, etc.

ru·by (ro͞o′bē) ***n.***, *pl.* **-bies** ⟦ult. < L *rubeus,* reddish⟧ **1** a clear, deep-red precious stone: a variety of corundum **2** deep red —***adj.*** deep-red

ruck·sack (ruk′sak′, ro͝ok′-) ***n.*** ⟦Ger, back sack⟧ a kind of knapsack

ruck·us (ruk′əs) ***n.*** ⟦prob. merging of RUMPUS & *ruction,* uproar⟧ [Inf.] noisy confusion; disturbance

rud·der (rud′ər) ***n.*** ⟦OE *rother*⟧ a broad, flat, movable piece hinged to the rear of a ship or aircraft, used for steering —**rud′der·less** ***adj.***

rud·dy (rud′ē) ***adj.*** **-di·er, -di·est** ⟦OE *rudig*⟧ **1** having a healthy red color **2** reddish —**rud′di·ness** ***n.***

rude (ro͞od) ***adj.*** **rud′er, rud′est** ⟦< L *rudis*⟧ **1** crude; rough **2** uncouth **3** discourteous **4** unskillful —**rude′ly** ***adv.*** —**rude′ness** ***n.***

ru·di·ment (ro͞o′də mənt) ***n.*** ⟦see RUDE⟧ [*usually pl.*] **1** a first principle as of a subject to be learned **2** a first slight beginning of something —**ru′di·men′ta·ry** (-men′ tər ē) ***adj.***

rue[1] (ro͞o) ***vt., vi.*** **rued, ru′ing** ⟦OE *hreowan*⟧ **1** to feel remorse for (a sin, fault, etc.) **2** to regret (an act, etc.) —***n.*** [Archaic] sorrow —**rue′ful** ***adj.*** —**rue′ful·ly** ***adv.***

rue[2] (ro͞o) ***n.*** ⟦< Gr *rhytē*⟧ a strong-scented shrub with bitter leaves

ruff (ruf) ***n.*** ⟦< RUFFLE⟧ **1** a high, frilled starched collar of the 16th and 17th c. **2** a band of colored or protruding feathers or fur about an animal's neck

ruf·fi·an (ruf′ē ən) ***n.*** ⟦< It *ruffiano,* a pimp⟧ a rowdy or hoodlum

ruf·fle (ruf′əl) ***vt.*** **-fled, -fling** ⟦< ON or LowG⟧ **1** to disturb the smoothness of **2** to make (feathers, etc.) stand up **3** to disturb or annoy —***vi.*** to become uneven —***n.*** a strip of cloth, lace, etc. gathered along one edge, used as a trimming

rug (rug) ***n.*** ⟦< Scand⟧ a piece of thick fabric used as a floor covering

rug·by (rug′bē) ***n.*** ⟦first played at *Rugby* School in England⟧ a game from which American football developed

rug·ged (rug′id) ***adj.*** ⟦ME⟧ **1** uneven; rough **2** severe; harsh **3** not refined **4** strong; robust —**rug′ged·ly** ***adv.*** —**rug′ged·ness** ***n.***

Ruhr (ro͝or) **1** river in WC Germany, flowing into the Rhine **2** major coal-mining & industrial region along this river: also called **Ruhr Basin**

ru·in (ro͞o′ən) ***n.*** ⟦< L *ruere,* to fall⟧ **1** [*pl.*] the remains of something destroyed, decayed, etc. **2** anything

THESAURUS

rubber ***a.*** elastic, rubbery, soft, stretchable, stretching, rebounding, flexible, ductile, lively, buoyant, resilient.

rubbish ***n.*** litter, debris, waste; see TRASH 1.

rude ***a.*** **1** [Boorish] rustic, ungainly, awkward, crude, coarse, gross, rough, harsh, blunt, rugged, common, barbarous, lumpish, ungraceful, hulking, loutish, antic, rowdy, disorderly, brutish, clownish, stupid, ill-proportioned, unpolished, uncultured, unrefined, untrained, indecorous, unknowing, untaught, uncouth, slovenly, ill-bred, inelegant, ignorant, inexpert, illiterate, clumsy, gawky, slouching, graceless, ungraceful, lumbering, green, unacquainted, unenlightened, uneducated, vulgar, indecent, ribald, homely, outlandish, disgraceful, inappropriate.—*Ant.* CULTURED, urbane, suave. **2** [Not polite] churlish, sullen, surly, sharp, harsh, gruff, snarling, ungracious, unkind, obstreperous, overbearing, sour, disdainful, unmannerly, ill-mannered, improper, shabby, ill-chosen, discourteous, ungentlemanly, fresh*, abusive, forward, loud, loud-mouthed, bold, brazen, audacious, brash, arrogant, supercilious, blustering, impudent, crass, raw, saucy, crusty, pert, unabashed, sharp-tongued, loose, mocking, barefaced, insolent, impertinent, offensive, naughty, impolite, hostile, insulting, disrespectful, scornful, flippant, presumptuous, sarcastic, defiant, outrageous, swaggering, disparaging, contemptuous, rebellious, disdainful, unfeeling, insensitive, scoffing, disagreeable, domineering, overbearing, highhanded, hypercritical, self-assertive, brutal, severe, hard, cocky, bullying, cheeky*, nervy*, assuming, dictatorial, magisterial, misbehaved, officious, meddling, intrusive, meddlesome, bitter, uncivilized, slandering, ill-tempered, bad-tempered, sassy*, snotty*, snooty*, uppity*.—*Ant.* POLITE, courteous, mannerly. **3** [Harsh] rough, violent, stormy; see TURBULENT. **4** [Approximate] surmised, guessed, imprecise; see APPROXIMATE. **5** [Coarse] rough, unrefined, unpolished; see CRUDE. **6** [Primitive] ignorant, uncivilized, barbarous; see PRIMITIVE 3.

rudely ***a.*** crudely, impudently, coarsely, impolitely, indecently, barbarously, roughly, harshly, bluntly, indecorously, insolently, contemptuously, brutally, dictatorially, churlishly, sullenly, gruffly, discourteously, loudly, brazenly, blusteringly, crassly, unabashedly, ribaldly, mockingly, snootily*.—*Ant.* KINDLY, politely, suavely.

rudeness ***n.*** discourtesy, bad manners, vulgarity, incivility, impoliteness, impudence, disrespect, misbehavior, barbarity, ungentlemanliness, unmannerliness, ill-breeding, crudity, brutality, barbarism, tactlessness, boorishness, unbecoming conduct, conduct not becoming a gentleman, crudeness, grossness, coarseness, bluntness, effrontery, impertinence, insolence, audacity, boldness, shamelessness, presumption, officiousness, intrusiveness, brazenness, sauciness, defiance, contempt, back talk, ill temper, irritability, disdain, bitterness, sharpness, unkindness, ungraciousness, harshness, gall*, sass*, lip*, nerve*, brass*, cheek*.

rudimentary ***a.*** **1** [Basic] elementary, primary, original; see FUNDAMENTAL. **2** [Immature] embryonic, undeveloped, simple; see UNFINISHED 1.

rudiments ***n.*** fundamentals, first principles, source; see ELEMENTS.

ruffle ***v.*** **1** [To disarrange] rumple, tousle, ripple; see CONFUSE, TANGLE. **2** [To anger] irritate, fret, anger; see BOTHER 1, 2.

rug ***n.*** carpet, carpeting, floor covering, Oriental rug, runner, scatter rug, throw rug, floor mat, drugget.

rugged ***a.*** **1** [Rough; *said especially of terrain*] hilly, broken, mountainous; see ROUGH 1. **2** [Strong; *said especially of persons*] hale, sturdy, hardy; see HEALTHY, STRONG 1.

ruin ***n.*** **1** [The act of destruction] extinction, demolition, overthrow; see DESTRUCTION 1, WRECK 1. **2** [A building fallen into decay; *often plural*] remains, traces, residue, foundation, vestiges, remnants, relics, wreck, walls, detritus, rubble; see also DESTRUCTION 2. **3** [The state of destruction] dilapidation, waste, wreck; see DESTRUCTION 2.

ruin ***v.*** **1** [To destroy] injure, overthrow, demolish; see DESTROY, RAVAGE. **2** [To cause to become bankrupt] impoverish, bankrupt, beggar;

destroyed, etc. **3** downfall, destruction, etc. **4** anything causing this —***vt.*** to bring to ruin; destroy, spoil, bankrupt, etc. —**ru'in·a'tion** ***n.*** —**ru'in·ous** ***adj.***

rule (ro͞ol) ***n.*** ⟦< L *regere,* to rule⟧ **1** an established regulation or guide for conduct, procedure, usage, etc. **2** custom **3** the customary course **4** government; reign **5** RULER (sense 2) —***vt., vi.*** **ruled, rul'ing 1** to have an influence (over); guide **2** to govern **3** to determine officially **4** to mark lines (on) as with a ruler —**as a rule** usually —**rule out** to exclude

rule of thumb a practical, though imprecise or unscientific, method

rul'er ***n.*** **1** one who governs **2** a strip of wood, etc. with a straight edge, used in drawing lines, measuring length, etc.

rul'ing ***adj.*** that rules —***n.*** an official decision, as of a court

rum (rum) ***n.*** ⟦< ?⟧ **1** an alcoholic liquor distilled from fermented sugar cane, etc. **2** any alcoholic liquor

Ru·ma·ni·a (ro͞o mā'nē ə) *var. of* ROMANIA —**Ru·ma'ni·an** ***adj., n.***

rum·ba (rum'bə, rum'-) ***n.*** ⟦AmSp⟧ a dance of Cuban origin, or music for it —***vi.*** to dance the rumba

rum·ble (rum'bəl) ***vi., vt.*** **-bled, -bling** ⟦ME *romblen*⟧ **1** to make or cause to make a continuous deep, rolling sound **2** to move with such a sound —***n.*** **1** a rumbling sound **2** [Slang] a fight between teenage gangs

ru·mi·nant (ro͞o'mə nənt) ***adj.*** ⟦see RUMINATE⟧ **1** of or belonging to the group of cud-chewing animals **2** meditative —***n.*** any of a group of cud-chewing mammals, as cattle, deer, or camels, having a stomach with three or four chambers

ru'mi·nate' (-nāt') ***vi.*** **-nat'ed, -nat'ing** ⟦< L *ruminare*⟧ **1** to chew a cud **2** to meditate —**ru'mi·na'tion** ***n.***

rum·mage (rum'ij) ***n.*** ⟦< Fr *rum,* ship's hold⟧ **1** odds and ends **2** a rummaging —***vt., vi.*** **-maged, -mag·ing** to search through (a place, etc.) thoroughly

rummage sale a sale of contributed miscellaneous articles, as for charity

rum·my (rum'ē) ***n.*** ⟦< ?⟧ a card game in which the object is to match cards into sets and sequences

ru·mor (ro͞o'mər) ***n.*** ⟦L, noise⟧ **1** general talk not based on definite knowledge **2** an unconfirmed report, story, etc. in general circulation —***vt.*** to tell or spread by rumor Brit. sp. **ru'mour**

rump (rump) ***n.*** ⟦< ON *rumpr*⟧ **1** the hind part of an animal, where the legs and back join **2** the buttocks

rum·ple (rum'pəl) ***n.*** ⟦< MDu *rompe*⟧ an uneven crease; wrinkle —***vt., vi.*** **-pled, -pling** to wrinkle; muss

rum·pus (rum'pəs) ***n.*** ⟦< ?⟧ [Inf.] an uproar or commotion

run (run) ***vi.*** **ran, run, run'ning** ⟦< ON & OE⟧ **1** to go by moving the legs faster than in walking **2** to go, move, etc. easily and freely **3** to flee **4** to make a quick trip (*up to, down to,* etc.) **5** to compete in a race, election, etc. **6** to ply between two points: said as of a train **7** to climb or creep, as a vine does **8** to ravel: said as of a stocking **9** to operate: said of a machine **10** to flow **11** to spread over cloth, etc. when moistened, as colors do **12** to discharge pus, etc. **13** to extend in time or space; continue **14** to pass into a specified condition, etc. *[to run into trouble]* **15** to be written, etc. in a specified way **16** to be at a specified size, price, etc. *[eggs run high]* —***vt.*** **1** to follow (a specified course) **2** to perform as by running *[to run a race]* **3** to incur (a risk) **4** to get past *[to run a blockade]* **5** to cause to run, move, compete, etc. **6** to drive into a specified condition, place, etc. **7** to drive (an object) into or against something **8** to make flow in a specified way, place, etc. **9** to manage (a business, etc.) **10** to undergo (a fever, etc.) **11** to publish (a story, etc.) in a newspaper —***n.*** **1** an act or period of running **2** the distance covered in running **3** a trip; journey **4** a route *[a delivery run]* **5** *a)* movement onward, progression, or trend *[the run of events]* *b)* a continuous period *[a run of good luck]* **6** a continuous course of performances, etc., as of a play **7** a continued series of demands, as on a bank **8** a brook **9** a kind or class; esp., the average kind **10** the output during a period of operation **11** an enclosed area for domestic animals **12** freedom to move about at will *[the run of the house]* **13** a large number of fish migrating together **14** a ravel, as in a stocking **15** *Baseball* a scoring point, made by a successful circuit of the bases —**in the long run** in the final outcome —**on the run** running or running away —**run across** to encounter by chance: also **run into** —**run down 1** to stop

THESAURUS

see WRECK.

ruined ***a.*** **1** [Destroyed] demolished, overthrown, torn down, razed, extinct, abolished, exterminated, annihilated, subverted, wrecked, desolated, ravaged, smashed, crushed, crashed, extinguished, dissolved, extirpated, totaled*; see also DESTROYED.—*Ant.* PROTECTED, saved, preserved. **2** [Spoiled] pillaged, harried, robbed, plundered, injured, hurt, impaired, defaced, harmed, marred, past hope, mutilated, broken, gone to the dogs*, done for*.—*Ant.* REPAIRED, restored, mended. **3** [Bankrupt] pauperized, poverty-stricken, beggared, reduced, left in penury, penniless, fleeced, in want, gone under*, under water*, through the mill*.—*Ant.* RICH, prosperous, well-off.

ruins ***n.*** remains, debris, wreckage; see DESTRUCTION 2, WRECK 2.

rule ***n.*** **1** [Government] control, dominion, jurisdiction; see GOVERNMENT 1. **2** [A regulation] edict, command, commandment; see LAW 3. **3** [The custom] habit, course, practice; see CUSTOM. —**as a rule** ordinarily, generally, usually; see REGULARLY.

rule ***v.*** **1** [To govern] conduct, control, dictate; see GOVERN. **2** [To regulate] order, decree, direct; see MANAGE 1. —**rule out** eliminate, not consider, preclude; see DENY, FORBID.

ruled ***a.*** administered, controlled, managed; see GOVERNED.

ruler ***n.*** **1** [One who governs] governor, commander, chief, manager, adjudicator, monarch, regent, director; see also DICTATOR, KING 1, LEADER 2. **2** [A straightedge] *Types of rulers include the following:* foot rule, yardstick, carpenter's rule, parallel rule, stationer's rule, T-square, try square, steel square, compositor's rule, compositor's ruler.

ruling ***n.*** order, decision, precept; see LAW 3.

rumble ***n.*** reverberation, thunder, roll; see NOISE 1.

rumble ***v.*** resound, growl, reverberate; see SOUND.

rummage ***v.*** search, ransack, search high and low, scour, turn inside out.

rumor ***n.*** report, news, tidings, intelligence, dispatch, hearsay, gossip, scandal, tattle, notoriety, noise, cry, popular report, fame, repute, grapevine, buzz*, breeze*, hoax, fabrication, suggestion, supposition, story, tale, invention, fiction, falsehood; see also LIE.

rumored ***a.*** reported, told, said, reputed, spread abroad, gossiped, given out, noised about, broadcast, as they say, all over town, current, circulating, in circulation, rife, prevailing, prevalent, persisting, general, going around, making the rounds.

rump ***n.*** posterior, buttocks, sacrum, hind end, tail end, posterior, butt end, bottom, croup, crupper, rear, rear end, derrière, backside, seat, breech, hunkers, fundament, butt*, buns*, duff*, bum*, tush*, keister*, can*.

rumple ***v.*** crumple, crush, fold; see WRINKLE.

run ***n.*** **1** [The act of running] sprint, pace, jog, bound, flow, amble, gallop, canter, lope, spring, trot, dart, rush, dash, flight, escape, break, charge, swoop, race, scamper, tear, whisk, flow, fall, drop. **2** [A series] continuity, succession, sequence; see SERIES. **3** [The average] par, norm, run of the mill; see AVERAGE. **4** [A course] way, route, field; see TRACK 1. —**in the long run** in the final outcome, finally, eventually; see ULTIMATELY. —**on the run 1** [Hurrying] busy, in a hurry, running; see HURRYING. **2** [Fleeing] retreating, defeated, routed; see BEATEN 1.

run ***v.*** **1** [To move, usually rapidly] flow in, flow over, chase along, fall, pour, tumble, drop, leap, spin, whirl, whiz, sail. **2** [To go swiftly by physical effort] rush, hurry, spring, bound, scurry, skitter, scramble, scoot, travel, run off, run away, dash ahead, dash on, put on a burst of speed, go on the double*, light out*, make tracks*, dart, dart ahead, gallop, canter, lope, spring, trot, single-foot, amble, pace, flee, speed, spurt, swoop, bolt, race, shoot, tear, whisk, scamper, scuttle. **3** [To function] move, work, go; see OPERATE 2. **4** [To cause to function] control, drive, govern; see MANAGE 1. **5** [To extend] encompass, cover, spread; see REACH 1, SURROUND 1. **6** [To continue] last, persevere, go on; see CONTINUE 1. **7** [To compete] oppose, contest, contend with; see COMPETE, RACE 2. —**run down 1** [To chase] hunt, seize, apprehend; see PURSUE 1. **2** [To ridicule] make fun of, belittle, depreciate; see RIDICULE. —**run into 1** [To collide with] bump into, crash into, have a collision with; see HIT 1. **2** [To encounter] come across, see, contact; see MEET 6. —**run out 1** [To stop] expire, finish, end; see STOP 2. **2** [To become exhausted] weaken, wear out, waste away; see TIRE 1. —**run out of** lose, dissipate, exhaust; see WASTE 2. —**run over** trample, drive over, run down; see HIT, KILL. —**run through** waste, squander, use up; see SPEND.

operating **2** to run against so as to knock down **3** to pursue and capture or kill **4** to speak of disparagingly —**run out** to come to an end; expire —**run out of** to use up —**run over** **1** to ride over **2** to overflow **3** to examine, rehearse, etc. rapidly —**run through** **1** to use up quickly or recklessly **2** to pierce —**run up** **1** to raise, rise, or accumulate rapidly **2** to sew rapidly

run'a·round' ***n.*** [Inf.] a series of evasions

run'a·way' ***n.*** **1** a fugitive **2** a horse, etc. that runs away —***adj.*** **1** escaping, fleeing, etc. **2** easily won: said as of a race **3** rising rapidly: said as of prices

run'down' ***n.*** a concise summary

run'-down' ***adj.*** **1** not wound and therefore not running, as a watch **2** in poor physical condition, as from overwork **3** fallen into disrepair

rune (ro͞on) ***n.*** ⟦OE *run*⟧ **1** any of the characters of an ancient Germanic alphabet **2** [*often pl.*] writing in these characters

rung[1] (ruŋ) ***n.*** ⟦OE *hrung,* staff⟧ a rod or bar forming a step of a ladder, a crosspiece on a chair, etc.

rung[2] (ruŋ) ***vi., vt.*** *pp. of* RING[1]

run'-in' ***n.*** [Inf.] a quarrel, fight, etc.

run·nel (run'əl) ***n.*** ⟦OE *rynel*⟧ a small stream

run'ner ***n.*** **1** *a)* one that runs, as a racer *b)* a messenger, etc. *c)* a smuggler **2** a long, narrow cloth or rug **3** a ravel, as in hosiery **4** a long, trailing stem, as of a strawberry **5** either of the long, narrow pieces on which a sled, etc. slides

run'ner-up' ***n., pl.*** **-ners-up'** a person or team that finishes second, etc. in a contest

run'ning ***n.*** the act of one that runs; racing, managing, etc. —***adj.*** **1** that runs (in various senses) **2** measured in a straight line **3** continuous *[a running commentary]* **4** current or concurrent —***adv.*** in succession *[for five days running]* —**in** (or **out of**) **the running** having a (or no) chance to win

running back *Football* an offensive back, responsible primarily for rushing the ball

running lights the lights that a ship or aircraft must display at night

running mate the candidate for the lesser of two closely associated offices, as for the vice-presidency

run'ny ***adj.*** **-ni·er, -ni·est** **1** flowing, esp. too freely **2** discharging mucus *[a runny nose]*

run'off' ***n.*** **1** something that runs off, as rain that is not absorbed into the ground **2** a deciding, final contest

run'-of-the-mill' ***adj.*** ordinary; average

runt (runt) ***n.*** ⟦< ?⟧ **1** a stunted animal, plant, or (contemptuously) person **2** the smallest animal of a litter —**runt'y, -i·er, -i·est,** ***adj.***

run'-through' ***n.*** a complete rehearsal, from beginning to end

run'way' ***n.*** a channel, track, etc. in, on, or along which something moves; esp., *a)* a strip of leveled ground for use by airplanes in taking off and landing *b)* a narrow platform extending from a stage into the audience

ru·pee (ro͞o'pē, ro͞o pē') ***n.*** ⟦< Sans *rūpyaḥ,* wrought silver⟧ the monetary unit of India, Nepal, Pakistan, Sri Lanka, etc.

rup·ture (rup'chər) ***n.*** ⟦< L *rumpere,* to break⟧ **1** a breaking apart or being broken apart; breach **2** a hernia —***vt., vi.*** **-tured, -tur·ing** to cause or suffer a rupture

ru·ral (roor'əl) ***adj.*** ⟦< L *rus,* the country⟧ of, like, or living in the country; rustic —**ru'ral·ism'** ***n.***

ruse (ro͞oz) ***n.*** ⟦< OFr *reuser,* deceive⟧ a stratagem, trick, or artifice

rush[1] (rush) ***vi., vt.*** ⟦< Fr *ruser,* repel⟧ **1** to move, push, drive, etc. swiftly or impetuously **2** to make a sudden attack (*on*) **3** to pass, go, send, act, do, etc. with unusual haste; hurry **4** *Football* to run with (the ball) on a running play —***n.*** **1** a rushing **2** an eager movement of many people to get to a place **3** busyness; haste *[the rush of modern life]* **4** a press, as of business, necessitating unusual haste **5** [Slang] a sudden thrill, etc.

rush[2] (rush) ***n.*** ⟦OE *risc*⟧ a grasslike marsh plant with round stems used in making mats, etc.

rush hour a time of the day when business, traffic, etc. is heavy

rusk (rusk) ***n.*** ⟦Sp *rosca,* twisted bread roll⟧ **1** sweet, raised bread or cake toasted until browned and crisp **2** a piece of this

Russ *abbrev.* **1** Russia **2** Russian

rus·set (rus'it) ***n.*** ⟦< L *russus,* reddish⟧ **1** yellowish brown or reddish brown **2** a winter apple with a mottled skin

Rus·sia (rush'ə) **1** former empire (1547-1917) in E Europe & N Asia: in full **Russian Empire** **2** loosely, the UNION OF SOVIET SOCIALIST REPUBLICS **3** country in E Europe and N Asia, stretching from the Baltic Sea to the Pacific: formerly a republic of the U.S.S.R.: 6,592,844 sq. mi.; pop. 148,022,000

Rus·sian (rush'ən) ***adj.*** of Russia or its people, language, etc. —***n.*** **1** a person born or living in Russia **2** the East Slavic language of the Russians

rust (rust) ***n.*** ⟦OE⟧ **1** the reddish-brown coating on iron or steel caused by oxidation during exposure to air and moisture **2** any stain resembling this **3** a reddish brown **4** a plant disease causing spotted stems and leaves —***vi., vt.*** **1** to form rust (on) **2** to deteriorate, as through disuse

rus·tic (rus'tik) ***adj.*** ⟦< L *rus,* the country⟧ **1** rural **2** simple or artless **3** rough or uncouth —***n.*** a country person —**rus'ti·cal·ly** ***adv.***

rus·ti·cate (rus'tə kāt') ***vi., vt.*** **-cat'ed, -cat'ing** **1** to go or send to live in the country **2** to become or make rustic —**rus'ti·ca'tion** ***n.***

rus·tle[1] (rus'əl) ***vi., vt.*** **-tled, -tling** ⟦ult. echoic⟧ to make or cause to make soft sounds, as of moving leaves, etc. —***n.*** a series of such sounds

rus·tle[2] (rus'əl) [Inf.] ***vi., vt.*** **-tled, -tling** ⟦< ?⟧ to steal (cattle, etc.) —**rustle up** to gather together —**rus'tler** ***n.***

rust'proof' ***vt., adj.*** (make) resistant to rust

rust·y (rus'tē) ***adj.*** **-i·er, -i·est** **1** coated with rust, as a metal **2** *a)* impaired by disuse, neglect, etc. *b)* having lost facility through lack of practice —**rust'i·ly** ***adv.*** —**rust'i·ness** ***n.***

rut[1] (rut) ***n.*** ⟦< ? Fr *route,* route⟧ **1** a groove, track, etc., as made by wheels **2** a fixed, routine course of action,

THESAURUS

runaway ***a.*** out of control, delinquent, wild; see DISORDERLY 1.

rundown ***n.*** report, outline, account; see SUMMARY.

run-down ***a.*** **1** [Exhausted] weak, debilitated, weary; see WEAK 1, 2, TIRED. **2** [Dilapidated] broken-down, shabby, beat-up*; see OLD 2, CRUMBLY.

runner ***n.*** racer, entrant, contestant, sprinter, dasher, distance runner, long-distance runner, middle-distance runner, miler, marathoner, cross-country runner, jogger, trackman, hurdler, messenger, courier, express, dispatch bearer; see also ATHLETE.

running ***a.*** **1** [In the act of running] pacing, racing, speeding, galloping, cantering, trotting, jogging, scampering, fleeing, bounding, whisking, sprinting, flowing, tumbling, falling, pouring. **2** [In the process of running] producing, operating, working, functioning, proceeding, moving, revolving, guiding, conducting, administering, going, in operation, in action, executing, promoting, achieving, transacting, determining, bringing about. **3** [Ranging] reaching, spreading, encompassing; see EXTENDING.

runoff ***n.*** spring runoff, drainage, surplus water; see FLOW, RIVER, WATER 1.

run-of-the-mill ***a.*** popular, mediocre, ordinary; see COMMON 1.

runt* ***n.*** shrimp*, twerp*, nobody, small fry*, little person.

rupture ***n.*** hole, separation, crack; see BREAK 1, TEAR.

rupture ***v.*** crack, tear, burst; see BREAK.

rural ***a.*** rustic, farm, agricultural, ranch, pastoral, bucolic, backwoods, country, agrarian, suburban.—*Ant.* URBAN, industrial, commercial.

ruse ***n.*** artifice, ploy, scam*; see DEVICE 2, TRICK 1.

rush[1] ***n.*** haste, dash, charge; see HURRY.

rush[1] ***v.*** hasten, speed, hurry up; see HURRY.

rushed ***a.*** hurried, pressed, pressured; see DRIVEN.

rushing ***a.*** being quick, bestirring oneself, losing no time; see HURRYING.

Russian ***a.*** Slavic, Slav, Muscovite, Siberian.

rust ***n.*** decomposition, corruption, corrosion, oxidation, decay, rot, dilapidation, breakup, wear.

rust ***v.*** oxidize, become rusty, degenerate, decay, rot, corrode.

rustic ***a.*** agricultural, pastoral, agrarian; see RURAL.

rustle[1] ***v.*** swish, stir, sough; see SOUND.

rusty ***a.*** **1** [Decayed] unused, neglected, worn; see OLD 2, WEAK 2. **2** [Unpracticed] out of practice, soft, out of shape; see WEAK 5.

rut[1] ***n.*** **1** [A deeply cut track] hollow, trench, furrow; see GROOVE. **2** [Habitual behavior] custom, habit, course, routine, practice, performance, round, circuit, circle, usage, procedure.—*Ant.* CHANGE, progress, variety.

thought, etc. —*vt.* **rut'ted, rut'ting** to make ruts in —**rut'ty, -ti·er, -ti·est,** *adj.*

rut[2] (rut) *n.* ⟦< L *rugire,* to roar⟧ the periodic sexual excitement of certain male mammals —*vi.* **rut'ted, rut'ting** to be in rut —**rut'tish** *adj.*

ru·ta·ba·ga (ro͞ot'ə bā'gə) *n.* ⟦Swed dial. *rotabagge*⟧ **1** a turniplike plant with a large, yellow root **2** this root

Ruth[1] (ro͞oth) *n. Bible* a woman devoted to her mother-in-law, for whom she left her own people

Ruth[2] (ro͞o*th*), **Babe** (bāb) (born *George Herman Ruth*) 1895-1948; U.S. baseball player

ruth'less (-lis) *adj.* ⟦OE *hreowan,* to rue⟧ without pity or compassion —**ruth'less·ly** *adv.* —**ruth'less·ness** *n.*

RV *n., pl.* **RVs** ⟦*R*(*ecreational*) *V*(*ehicle*)⟧ a camper, trailer, motor home, etc. outfitted for living in

Rwan·da (ro͞o än'də) country in EC Africa, east of Democratic Republic of the Congo: 10,169 sq. mi.; pop. 7,165,000

Rwy or **Ry** *abbrev.* Railway

Rx *symbol* PRESCRIPTION (sense 2)

-ry (rē) *suffix* -ERY *[foundry]*

rye (rī) *n.* ⟦OE *ryge*⟧ **1** a hardy cereal grass **2** its grain or seeds, used for making flour, etc. **3** whiskey distilled from this grain

THESAURUS

ruthless *a.* cruel, fierce, savage, brutal, merciless, inhuman, hard, cold, fiendish, unmerciful, pitiless, grim, unpitying, tigerish, ferocious, stonyhearted, coldblooded, remorseless, vindictive, vengeful, revengeful, rancorous, implacable, unforgiving, malevolent, hardhearted, hard, cold, unsympathetic, vicious, sadistic, surly, tyrannical, relentless, barbarous, inhuman, atrocious, flagrant, terrible, abominable, outrageous, oppressive, bloodthirsty, venomous, galling.—*Ant.* KIND, helpful, civilized.

S

s[1] or **S** (es) ***n.***, *pl.* **s's, S's** the 19th letter of the English alphabet —***adj.*** shaped like S
s[2] *abbrev.* **1** second(s) **2** shilling(s)
S[1] *abbrev.* **1** Saturday **2** small **3** south **4** southern **5** Sunday
S[2] *Chem. symbol for* sulfur
-s ⟦alt. of -ES⟧ *suffix* **1** forming the plural of most nouns *[hips]* **2** forming the 3d pers. sing., pres. indic., of certain verbs *[shouts]*
-'s[1] ⟦OE⟧ *suffix* forming the possessive singular of nouns and some pronouns, and the possessive plural of nouns not ending in *s [boy's, men's]*
-'s[2] *suffix* **1** is *[he's a sailor]* **2** has *[she's asked them both]* **3** [Inf.] does *[what's it matter?]* **4** us *[let's go]*
SA South America
Saar (sär, zär) rich coal-mining region in a river valley of SW Germany: also called **Saar Basin**
Sab·bath (sab'əth) ***n.*** ⟦< Heb *shabat*, to rest⟧ **1** the seventh day of the week (Saturday), set aside in Jewish scripture for rest and worship **2** Sunday as the usual Christian day of rest and worship
Sab·bat·i·cal (sə bat'i kəl) ***adj.*** **1** of the Sabbath **2** [**s-**] bringing a period of rest —***n.*** [**s-**] SABBATICAL LEAVE
sabbatical leave ⟦orig. given every seven years⟧ a period of absence with pay, for study, travel, etc., given as to teachers: also **sabbatical year**
sa·ber (sā'bər) ***n.*** ⟦< Hung *szablya*⟧ a heavy cavalry sword with a slightly curved blade: also **sa'bre**
Sa·bin vaccine (sā'bin) ⟦after Dr. A. B. *Sabin* (1906-93), its U.S. developer⟧ a polio vaccine taken orally
sa·ble (sā'bəl) ***n.*** ⟦< Russ *sobol'*⟧ **1** any marten **2** its costly fur pelt —***adj.*** black or dark brown
sa·bot (sa bō', sab'ō) ***n.*** ⟦Fr, ult. < Ar *sabbāṭ*, sandal⟧ a shoe shaped from a single piece of wood
sab·o·tage (sab'ə täzh') ***n.*** ⟦Fr < *sabot*, wooden shoe + -AGE: from damage done to machinery by sabots⟧ deliberate destruction or obstruction, as of railroads, bridges, etc. by enemy agents —***vt.***, ***vi.*** **-taged'**, **-tag'ing** to commit sabotage (on) —**sab'o·teur'** (-tur') ***n.***
sa·bra (sä'brə) ***n.*** ⟦Heb *sabra*, a native cactus fruit⟧ [*sometimes* **S-**] a native-born Israeli
sabre saw a portable electric saw with a narrow, oscillating blade
sac (sak) ***n.*** ⟦see SACK[1]⟧ a pouchlike part in a plant or animal
sac·cha·rin (sak'ə rin') ***n.*** ⟦< Gr *sakcharon*⟧ a white, crystalline coal-tar compound used as a sugar substitute
sac'cha·rine' (-rin') ***adj.*** **1** of or like sugar **2** too sweet *[a saccharine voice]*
sac·er·do·tal (sas'ər dōt''l; *occas.* sak'-) ***adj.*** ⟦< L *sacerdos*, priest⟧ of priests or the office of priest
sa·chem (sā'chəm) ***n.*** ⟦AmInd⟧ among some North American Indian tribes, the chief
sa·chet (sa shā') ***n.*** ⟦Fr⟧ a small perfumed packet used to scent clothes
sack[1] (sak) ***n.*** ⟦ult. < Heb *saq*⟧ **1** a bag, esp. a large one of coarse cloth **2** [Slang] dismissal from a job: with *the* **3** *Football* a sacking of a quarterback —***vt.*** **1** to put into sacks **2** [Slang] to fire (a person) **3** *Football* to tackle (a quarterback) behind the line of scrimmage —**hit the sack** [Slang] to go to bed: also **sack out**
sack[2] (sak) ***n.*** ⟦see prec.⟧ the plundering of a city, etc. —***vt.*** to plunder
sack[3] (sak) ***n.*** ⟦< Fr (*vin*)*sec*, dry (wine) < L⟧ a dry, white Spanish wine popular in England during the 16th and 17th c.
sack'cloth' ***n.*** **1** SACKING **2** [Historical] coarse cloth worn as a symbol of mourning
sack'ing ***n.*** a cheap, coarse cloth used for sacks
sac·ra·ment (sak'rə mənt) ***n.*** ⟦< L *sacer*, holy⟧ any of certain Christian rites, as baptism, the Eucharist, etc. —**sac'ra·men'tal** (-ment''l) ***adj.***
Sac·ra·men·to (sak'rə men'tō) capital of California: pop. 369,000
sa·cred (sā'krid) ***adj.*** ⟦< L *sacer*, holy⟧ **1** consecrated to a god or God; holy **2** having to do with religion **3** venerated; hallowed **4** inviolate —**sa'cred·ly** ***adv.*** —**sa'cred·ness** ***n.***
sac·ri·fice (sak'rə fīs') ***n.*** ⟦< L *sacrificium* < *sacer*, sacred + *facere*, make⟧ **1** an offering, as of a life or object, to a deity **2** a giving up of one thing for the sake of another —***vt.***, ***vi.*** **-ficed'**, **-fic'ing** **1** to offer as a sacrifice to a deity **2** to give up one thing for the sake of another **3** to sell at less than the supposed value —**sac'ri·fi'cial** (-fish'əl) ***adj.***
sac·ri·lege (sak'rə lij) ***n.*** ⟦< L *sacer*, sacred + *legere*, take away⟧ desecration of what is sacred —**sac'ri·le'gious** (-lij'əs, -lē'jəs) ***adj.***
sac·ris·tan (sak'ris tən) ***n.*** a person in charge of a sacristy
sac'ris·ty (-tē) ***n.***, *pl.* **-ties** ⟦ult. < L *sacer*, sacred⟧ a room in a church for sacred vessels, etc.
sac·ro·il·i·ac (sak'rō il'ē ak', sā'krō-) ***n.*** ⟦ModL, ult. < L *sacrum*, bone at bottom of spine + *ileum*, flank, groin⟧ the joint between the top part of the hipbone and the fused bottom vertebrae
sac·ro·sanct (sak'rō saŋkt') ***adj.*** ⟦< L *sacer*, sacred + *sanctus*, holy⟧ very sacred, holy, or inviolable
sad (sad) ***adj.*** **sad'der, sad'dest** ⟦OE *sæd*, sated⟧ **1** having or expressing low spirits; unhappy; sorrowful **2** causing dejection, sorrow, etc. **3** [Inf.] very bad; deplorable —**sad'ly** ***adv.*** —**sad'ness** ***n.***
sad'den ***vt.***, ***vi.*** to make or become sad
sad·dle (sad''l) ***n.*** ⟦OE *sadol*⟧ **1** a seat for a rider on a horse, bicycle, etc., usually padded and of leather **2** a cut of lamb, etc., including part of the backbone and the two loins —***vt.*** **-dled, -dling** **1** to put a saddle upon **2** to encumber or burden —**in the saddle** in control
sad'dle·bag' ***n.*** **1** a bag hung behind the saddle of a horse, etc. **2** a bag carried on a bicycle, etc.
saddle horse a horse for riding

THESAURUS

Sabbath ***n.*** day of rest, the Lord's Day, Saturday or Sunday; see WEEKEND.

sabotage ***n.*** demolition, overthrow, treason; see DESTRUCTION 1, REVOLUTION 2.

sabotage ***v.*** subvert, siege, undermine; see ATTACK 1, DESTROY.

sac ***n.*** welt, pouch, blister; see SORE.

sack[1] ***n.*** sac, pouch, pocket; see BAG, CONTAINER. —**hit the sack*** go to bed, go to sleep, retire; see SLEEP.

sacrament ***n.*** holy observance, ceremonial, ceremony, rite, ritual, liturgy, act of divine worship, mystery, the mysteries. *In the Roman Catholic and Eastern Orthodox churches, the seven sacraments are as follows:* baptism, confirmation or the laying on of hands, penance, Communion or the Eucharist, extreme unction or Anointing of the Sick, holy orders, matrimony.

sacramental ***a.*** sacred, pure, solemn; see HOLY 1, RELIGIOUS 1.

sacred ***a.*** **1** [Holy] pure, pious, saintly; see HOLY 1. **2** [Dedicated] consecrated, ordained, sanctioned; see DIVINE.

sacrifice ***n.*** **1** [An offering to a deity] offering, tribute, atonement; see CEREMONY. **2** [A loss] discount, deduction, reduction; see LOSS 1.

sacrifice ***v.*** **1** [To offer to a deity] consecrate, dedicate, give up; see BLESS. **2** [To give up as a means to an end] forfeit, forgo, relinquish, yield, suffer the loss of, renounce, spare, give up, let go, resign oneself to, sacrifice oneself, surrender, part with, go astray from. **3** [To sell at a loss] cut, reduce, sell out; see DECREASE 2, LOSE 2.

sad ***a.*** **1** [Afflicted with sorrow] unhappy, sorry, sorrowful, downcast, dismal, gloomy, glum, pensive, heavy-hearted, dispirited, dejected, desolate, depressed, troubled, melancholy, morose, grieved, pessimistic, crushed, brokenhearted, heartbroken, heartsick, despondent, careworn, disheartened, rueful, anguished, lamenting, mourning, grieving, weeping, bitter, woebegone, doleful, spiritless, joyless, heavy, crestfallen, discouraged, moody, low-spirited, despairing, hopeless, worried, downhearted, cast down, in heavy spirits, morbid, oppressed, blighted, grief-stricken, foreboding, apprehensive, horrified, anxious, wretched, miserable, mournful, disconsolate, forlorn, jaundiced, out of sorts*, distressed, afflicted, bereaved, repining, harassed, dreary, down in the dumps*, in bad humor, out of humor, cut up*, in the depths*, blue, stricken with grief, wearing a long face, in tears, feeling like hell*, down in the mouth*.—*Ant.* HAPPY, joyous, cheerful. **2** [Suggestive of sorrow] pitiable, unhappy, dejecting, saddening, disheartening, discouraging, joyless, dreary, dark, dismal, gloomy, moving, touching, mournful, disquieting, disturbing, somber, doleful, oppressive, funereal, lugubrious, pathetic, tragic, pitiful, piteous, woeful, rueful, sorry, unfortunate, hapless, heart-rending, dire, distressing, depressing, grievous.

sadden ***v.*** oppress, dishearten, discourage, cast down, deject, depress, break someone's heart.

saddle shoes white oxford shoes with a contrasting band across the instep

Sad·du·cee (saj′o͞o sē′) ***n.*** a member of an ancient Jewish party that accepted only the written law

sad·ism (sā′diz′əm, sad′iz′əm) ***n.*** ⟦after Marquis de *Sade* (1740-1814), Fr writer⟧ the getting of pleasure from mistreating others —**sad′ist** ***n.*** —**sa·dis′tic** ***adj.*** —**sa·dis′ti·cal·ly** ***adv.***

sad·o·mas·o·chism (sā′dō mas′ə kiz′əm, sad′ō-) ***n.*** the getting of sexual pleasure from sadism or masochism, or both —**sad′o·mas′o·chist** ***n.*** —**sad′o·mas′o·chis′tic** ***adj.***

sa·fa·ri (sə fär′ē) ***n.***, *pl.* **-ris** ⟦< Ar *safar*, to journey⟧ a journey or hunting expedition, esp. in Africa

safe (sāf) ***adj.*** **saf′er, saf′est** ⟦< L *salvus*⟧ **1** *a)* free from damage, danger, etc.; secure *b)* having escaped injury; unharmed **2** *a)* giving protection *b)* trustworthy —***n.*** a locking metal container for valuables —**safe′ly** ***adv.*** —**safe′ness** ***n.***

safe′-con′duct ***n.*** permission to travel safely through enemy regions

safe′-de·pos′it ***adj.*** designating or of a box or vault, as in a bank, for storing valuables: also **safe′ty-de·pos′it**

safe′guard′ ***n.*** a protection; precaution —***vt.*** to protect or guard

safe house a house, etc. used as a refuge or hiding place, as by an underground organization

safe′keep′ing ***n.*** protection or custody

safe sex sexual activity incorporating practices, as condom use, that reduce the risk of spreading sexually transmitted diseases

safe·ty (sāf′tē) ***n.***, *pl.* **-ties** **1** a being safe; security **2** any device for preventing an accident **3** *Football a)* a grounding of the ball by the offense behind its own goal line, that scores two points for the defense *b)* a defensive back responsible for covering pass receivers in the middle of the field —***adj.*** giving safety

safety glass shatterproof glass

safety match a match that lights when struck on a prepared surface

safety net **1** a net suspended as beneath aerialists **2** any protection against failure or loss

safety pin a pin bent back on itself and having the point held in a guard

safety razor a razor with a detachable blade held between guards

safety valve **1** an automatic valve that releases steam if the pressure in a boiler, etc. becomes excessive **2** any outlet for the release of strong emotion, etc.

saf·flow·er (saf′lou′ər) ***n.*** ⟦ult. < Ar *aṣfar*, yellow⟧ a thistlelike, annual plant with large, orange flowers and seeds yielding an edible oil

saf·fron (saf′rən) ***n.*** ⟦< Ar *za'farān*⟧ **1** a plant having orange stigmas **2** the dried stigmas, used as a dye and flavoring **3** orange yellow

sag (sag) ***vi.*** **sagged, sag′ging** ⟦prob. < Scand⟧ **1** to sink, esp. in the middle, from weight or pressure **2** to hang down unevenly **3** to weaken through weariness, age, etc. —***n.*** **1** a sagging **2** a sagging place —**sag′gy, -gi·er, -gi·est,** ***adj.***

sa·ga (sä′gə) ***n.*** ⟦ON, a tale⟧ **1** a medieval Scandinavian story relating the legendary history of a family **2** any long story of heroic deeds

sa·ga·cious (sə gā′shəs) ***adj.*** ⟦< L *sagax*, wise⟧ very wise; shrewd —**sa·gac′i·ty** (-gas′ə tē) ***n.***

sage[1] (sāj) ***adj.*** **sag′er, sag′est** ⟦ult. < L *sapere*, know⟧ **1** wise, discerning, etc. **2** showing wisdom —***n.*** a very wise man

sage[2] (sāj) ***n.*** ⟦< L *salvus*, safe: from its reputed healing powers⟧ **1** a plant of the mint family with leaves used for seasoning meats, etc. **2** SAGEBRUSH

sage′brush′ ***n.*** a plant with aromatic leaves, in the dry areas of the W U.S.

Sag·it·tar·i·us (saj′ə ter′ē əs) ***n.*** ⟦L, archer⟧ the ninth sign of the zodiac

sa·go (sā′gō) ***n.***, *pl.* **-gos** an edible starch from a Malayan palm tree, etc.

sa·gua·ro (sə gwär′ō) ***n.***, *pl.* **-ros** ⟦< native name⟧ a giant cactus of the SW U.S. and N Mexico

Sa·ha·ra (sə har′ə) vast desert region extending across N Africa

sa·hib (sä′ib′) ***n.*** ⟦Hindi < Ar⟧ sir; master: title used in colonial India when speaking to or of a European

said (sed) ***vt.***, ***vi.*** *pt. & pp. of* SAY —***adj.*** aforesaid

Sai·gon (sī gän′) *former name for* HO CHI MINH CITY

sail (sāl) ***n.*** ⟦OE *segl*⟧ **1** a sheet, as of canvas, spread to catch the wind, so as to drive a vessel forward **2** sails collectively **3** a trip in a ship or boat **4** anything like a sail —***vi.*** **1** to be moved forward by means of sails **2** to travel on water **3** to begin a trip by water **4** to manage a sailboat **5** to glide or move smoothly **6** [Inf.] to move quickly —***vt.*** **1** to move upon (a body of water) in a vessel **2** to manage or navigate (a vessel) —**set** (or **make**) **sail** to begin a trip by water —**under sail** sailing

sail′board′ ***n.*** a board used in windsurfing

sail′boat′ ***n.*** a boat propelled by a sail or sails

sail′cloth′ ***n.*** canvas or other cloth for making sails, tents, etc.

sail′fish′ ***n.***, *pl.* **-fish′** or (for different species) **-fish′es** a large marine fish with a sail-like dorsal fin

sail′or ***n.*** **1** a person whose work is sailing **2** an enlisted person in the navy

sail′plane′ ***n.*** a light glider

saint (sānt) ***n.*** ⟦< L *sanctus*, holy⟧ **1** a holy person **2** a person who is exceptionally charitable, patient, etc. **3** in certain Christian churches, a person officially recognized for having attained heaven after an exceptionally holy life —**saint′li·ness** ***n.*** —**saint′ly, -li·er, -li·est,** ***adj.***

THESAURUS

sadistic ***a.*** cruel, brutal, vicious; see CRUEL.

sadly ***a.*** unhappily, morosely, dejectedly, wistfully, sorrowfully, gloomily, joylessly, dismally, dolefully, mournfully, cheerlessly, in sorrow.

sadness ***n.*** sorrow, dejection, melancholy, depression, grief, despondency, oppression, gloom, the blues*.

safe ***a.*** **1** [Not in danger] out of danger, secure, in safety, in security, free from harm, free from danger, unharmed, safe and sound, protected, guarded, housed, screened from danger, unthreatened, unmolested, entrenched, impregnable, invulnerable, under the protection of, saved, safeguarded, secured, defended, supported, sustained, preserved, maintained, upheld, vindicated, shielded, nourished, sheltered, fostered, cared for, cherished, watched, impervious to, patrolled, looked after, supervised, tended, attended, kept in order, surveyed, regulated, with one's head above water, undercover, out of harm's way, on the safe side, on ice*, at anchor, in harbor, snug as a bug in a rug*, under lock and key.—*Ant.* DANGEROUS, unsafe, risky. **2** [Not dangerous] sound, secure, safety-inspected; see HARMLESS. **3** [Reliable] trustworthy, dependable, competent; see RELIABLE. —**keep safe** care for, escort, protect; see GUARD, WATCH.

safe ***n.*** strongbox, coffer, chest, repository, vault, case, lockbox, safe-deposit box.

safekeeping ***n.*** supervision, care, guardianship; see CUSTODY, PROTECTION 2.

safely ***a.*** securely, with impunity, without harm, without risk, without danger, harmlessly, carefully, cautiously, reliably.

safety ***n.*** **1** [Freedom from danger] security, protection, impregnability, surety, sanctuary, refuge, shelter, invulnerability. **2** [A lock] lock mechanism, safety catch, safety lock; see FASTENER, LOCK 1.

sag ***n.*** depression, dip, swale; see HOLE 1.

sag ***v.*** stoop, hang down, become warped; see BEND, LEAN 1.

said ***a.*** pronounced, aforesaid, aforementioned; see PRECEDING, SPOKEN.

sail ***n.*** **1** [Means of sailing a vessel] sheets, canvas, cloth; see GOODS. *Sails include the following:* mainsail, foresail, topsail, jib, spanker, flying jib, trysail, staysail, balloon sail, spinnaker, royal, topgallant. **2** [A journey by sailing vessel] voyage, cruise, trip; see JOURNEY. —**set sail** begin a voyage, shove off, weigh anchor; see LEAVE 1, SAIL 1.

sail ***v.*** **1** [To travel by sailing] cruise, voyage, go alongside, bear down on, bear for, direct one's course for, set sail, put to sea, sail away from, navigate, travel, make headway, lie in, make for, heave to, fetch up, bring to, bear off, close with, run in, put in. **2** [To fly] float, soar, ride the storm, skim, glide.

sailor ***n.*** seaman, mariner, seafarer, pirate, navigator, pilot, boatman, yachtsman, able-bodied seaman, Jack Tar*, tar*, sea dog*, limey*, salt*, swab*, swabbie*, bluejacket. *Kinds and ranks of sailors include the following—crew:* deck hand, stoker, cabin boy, yeoman, purser; ship's carpenter, cooper, tailor; steward, quartermaster, signalman, gunner, boatswain or bo's'n*; *officers:* captain or commander or skipper, navigating officer, deck officer; first, second, third mate.

saint ***n.*** a true Christian, child of God, son of God, paragon, salt of the earth, godly person, martyr, moral exemplar, canonized person, altruist, the pure in heart, a believer.

saintly ***a.*** angelic, pious, divine; see HOLY.

Saint Ber·nard (bər närd′) a large dog of a breed once used to rescue travelers lost in the snow
Saint Nich·o·las (nik′ə ləs) SANTA CLAUS: also **Saint Nick**
Saint Pat·rick's Day (pa′triks) March 17, observed by the Irish in honor of the patron saint of Ireland
Saint Valentine's Day Feb. 14, observed in honor of a martyr of the 3d c. and as a day for sending valentines
saith (seth) ***vt.***, ***vi.*** [Archaic] says
sake[1] (sāk) ***n.*** ⟦OE *sacu*, suit at law⟧ **1** motive; cause *[for* the *sake* of money*]* **2** behalf *[for* my *sake]*
sa·ke[2] (sä′kē) ***n.*** ⟦Jpn⟧ a Japanese alcoholic beverage made from rice: also sp. **sa′ki**
sa·laam (sə läm′) ***n.*** ⟦Ar *salām*, peace⟧ in India and the Near East, a greeting, etc. made by bowing low in respect or obeisance
sal·a·ble (sāl′ə bəl) ***adj.*** that can be sold; marketable: also sp. **sale′a·ble**
sa·la·cious (sə lā′shəs) ***adj.*** ⟦< L *salire*, to leap⟧ **1** lustful **2** obscene —**sa·la′cious·ly** ***adv.*** —**sa·la′cious·ness** ***n.***
sal·ad (sal′əd) ***n.*** ⟦< L *sal*, salt⟧ a dish, usually cold, of fruits, vegetables (esp. lettuce), meat, eggs, etc. usually mixed with salad dressing
salad bar a buffet in a restaurant, at which diners make their own salads
salad dressing oil, vinegar, spices, etc. put on a salad
sa·lade niçoise (sal′əd nē swäz′) a salad of tuna, tomatoes, etc. with a garlic vinaigrette
sal·a·man·der (sal′ə man′dər) ***n.*** ⟦< Gr *salamandra*⟧ **1** a mythological reptile said to live in fire **2** an amphibian with a tail and soft, moist skin
sa·la·mi (sə lä′mē) ***n.*** ⟦It < L *sal*, salt⟧ a spiced, salted sausage
sal·a·ry (sal′ə rē) ***n.***, *pl.* **-ries** ⟦< L *salarium*, orig. part of a soldier's pay for buying salt < *sal*, salt⟧ a fixed payment at regular intervals for work —**sal′a·ried** (-rēd) ***adj.***
sale (sāl) ***n.*** ⟦< ON *sala*⟧ **1** a selling **2** opportunity to sell; market **3** an auction **4** a special offering of goods at reduced prices **5** [*pl.*] receipts in business **6** [*pl.*] the work of, or a department involved in, selling *[a job in sales]* —**for sale** to be sold —**on sale** for sale, esp. at a reduced price
Sa·lem (sā′ləm) capital of Oregon, in the NW part: pop. 108,000
sales·clerk (sālz′klurk′) ***n.*** a person employed to sell goods in a store
sales′girl′ ***n.*** a girl or woman salesclerk
sales′la′dy ***n.***, *pl.* **-dies** [Inf.] a woman employed as a salesclerk
sales′man (-mən) ***n.***, *pl.* **-men** (-mən) **1** a man employed as a salesclerk **2** SALES REPRESENTATIVE
sales′man·ship′ ***n.*** the skill of selling
sales′per′son ***n.***, *pl.* **-peo′ple** a person employed to sell goods or services
sales representative a salesperson, esp. one employed as a traveling agent for a manufacturer, etc.
sales slip a receipt or bill of sale
sales tax a tax on sales
sales′wom′an ***n.***, *pl.* **-wom′en** a woman salesclerk or sales representative
sal·i·cyl·ic acid (sal′ə sil′ik) ⟦< L *salix*, willow⟧ a crystalline compound used to make aspirin, etc.
sa·lient (sāl′yənt) ***adj.*** ⟦< L *salire*, to leap⟧ **1** pointing outward; jutting **2** conspicuous; prominent —***n.*** a salient angle, part, etc. —**sa′lience** ***n.***
sa·line (sā′lēn′, -līn′) ***adj.*** ⟦< L *sal*, salt⟧ of, like, or containing salt —***n.*** a saline solution used in medicine, etc. —**sa·lin·i·ty** (sə lin′ə tē) ***n.***
sa·li·va (sə lī′və) ***n.*** ⟦L⟧ the watery fluid secreted by glands in the mouth: it aids in digestion —**sal·i·var·y** (sal′ə ver′ē) ***adj.***
sal·i·vate (sal′ə vāt′) ***vi.*** **-vat′ed**, **-vat′ing** ⟦< L *salivare*⟧ to secrete saliva —**sal′i·va′tion** ***n.***
sal·low (sal′ō) ***adj.*** ⟦ME *salou*⟧ of a sickly, pale-yellowish complexion
sal·ly (sal′ē) ***n.***, *pl.* **-lies** ⟦< L *salire*, to leap⟧ **1** a sudden rushing forth, as to attack **2** a witty remark; quip **3** an excursion —***vi.*** **-lied**, **-ly·ing** to rush or set (*forth* or *out*) on a sally
salm·on (sam′ən) ***n.***, *pl.* **-on** or **-ons** ⟦< L *salmo*⟧ **1** a game and food fish with yellowish pink flesh, that lives in salt water and spawns in fresh water **2** yellowish pink: also **salmon pink**
sal·mo·nel·la (sal′mə nel′ə) ***n.***, *pl.* **-nel′lae** (-ē), **-nel′la**, or **-nel′las** ⟦after D. E. *Salmon* (1850-1914), U.S. doctor⟧ any of a genus of bacilli that cause typhoid fever, food poisoning, etc.
sa·lon (sə län′) ***n.*** ⟦Fr: see fol.⟧ **1** a large reception hall or drawing room **2** a regular gathering of distinguished guests **3** a shop furnished to provide some personal service *[beauty salon]*
sa·loon (sə lo͞on′) ***n.*** ⟦< Fr < It *sala*⟧ **1** any large room or hall for receptions, etc. **2** [Old-fashioned] a place where alcoholic drinks are sold; bar
sal·sa (säl′sə) ***n.*** ⟦AmSp, sauce < L, salted food⟧ **1** a kind of Latin American dance music usually played at fast tempos **2** a hot sauce made with chilies, tomatoes, etc.
salt (sôlt) ***n.*** ⟦OE *sealt*⟧ **1** a white, crystalline substance, sodium chloride, found in natural beds, in sea water, etc., and used for seasoning food, etc. **2** a chemical compound derived from an acid by replacing hydrogen with a metal **3** piquancy; esp., pungent wit **4** [*pl.*] mineral salts used as a cathartic or restorative **5** [Inf.] a sailor —***adj.*** containing, preserved with, or tasting of salt —***vt.*** to sprinkle, season, or preserve with salt —**salt away** [Inf.] to store or save (money, etc.) —**salt of the earth** any person or persons regarded as the finest, etc. —**with a grain of salt** with allowance for exaggeration, etc.; skeptically —**salt′ed** ***adj.***
salt′cel′lar (-sel′ər) ***n.*** ⟦< prec. + Fr *salière*, saltcellar⟧ **1** a small dish for holding salt **2** a saltshaker
salt·ine (sôl tēn′) ***n.*** ⟦SALT + -INE[3]⟧ a flat, crisp, salted cracker
Salt Lake City capital of Utah: pop. 160,000
salt lick a natural deposit or a block of rock salt which animals lick
salt′pe′ter (-pēt′ər) ***n.*** ⟦< L *sal*, salt + *petra*, rock⟧ NITER
salt pork pork cured in salt
salt′shak′er ***n.*** a container for salt, with a perforated top
salt′wa′ter ***adj.*** of salt water or the sea

THESAURUS

sake[1] ***n.*** **1** [End] objective, consequence, final cause; see RESULT. **2** [Purpose] score, motive, principle; see PURPOSE 1. **3** [Welfare] benefit, interest, well-being; see ADVANTAGE, WELFARE 1.

salad ***n.*** salad greens, slaw, mixture, combination. *Common salads include the following:* green, tossed, vegetable, tomato, potato, macaroni, fruit, bean, taco, combination, chef's, tuna, shrimp, lobster, crab, chicken, ham, Waldorf, Caesar, Cobb, pineapple, banana, molded, frozen; cole slaw.

salary ***n.*** wages, compensation, remuneration; see PAY 2.

sale ***n.*** **1** [The act of selling; *used in the plural*] commerce, business, exchange, barter, merchandising, direct selling, mail-order selling, e-commerce, marketing, vending, trade. **2** [An individual instance of selling] deal, transaction, negotiation, turnover, trade, purchase, auction, disposal; see also BUYING, SELLING. **3** [An organized effort to promote selling] clearance, stock reduction, fire sale, unloading, dumping, closeout, liquidation, end-of-the-year clearance, remnant sale, going out of business sale, bankruptcy sale. —**for** (or **on** or **up for**) **sale** put on the market, to be sold, available, offered for purchase, not withheld. —**on sale** marked down, reduced, cut, at a bargain, at a cut rate, knocked down; see also REDUCED 2.

salesman ***n.*** **1** [A sales clerk] salesperson, seller, counterman; see CLERK. **2** [A commercial traveler] out-of-town representative, agent, canvasser, solicitor, seller, businessman, itinerant, fieldworker, traveler, traveling man, traveling salesman, sales representative, sales manager.

salesperson ***n.*** salesman, saleswoman, saleslady; see CLERK.

saliva ***n.*** water, spittle, salivation, excretion, phlegm, mucus, spit.

saloon ***n.*** bar, nightclub, cocktail lounge, pub*, brewpub*, gin mill*, beer joint*, hangout*, place; see also RESTAURANT.

salt ***a.*** alkaline, saline, briny; see SALTY.

salt ***n.*** **1** [A common seasoning and preservative] sodium chloride, common salt, table salt, savor, condiment, flavoring, spice, seasoning. *Common types of flavoring salts include the following:* garlic, sea, celery, onion, barbecue, salad, seasoning, hickory smoked; monosodium glutamate, MSG, poultry seasoning, salt substitute. **2** [Anything that provides savor] relish, pungency, smartness; see HUMOR 1, WIT. —**not worth one's salt** good-for-nothing, bad, worthless; see POOR 2. —**with a grain** (or **pinch**) **of salt** doubtingly, skeptically, dubiously; see SUSPICIOUSLY.

salt ***v.*** **1** [To flavor with salt] season, make tasty, make piquant; see FLAVOR. **2** [To scatter thickly] strew, spread, pepper; see DISTRIBUTE, SOW.

salt'y ***adj.*** **-i·er, -i·est 1** of or having salt **2** suggesting the sea **3** *a)* sharp; witty *b)* coarse *c)* cross or caustic

sa·lu·bri·ous (sə lo͞o'brē əs) ***adj.*** ⟦< L *salus*, health⟧ healthful; wholesome

sal·u·tar·y (sal'yo͞o ter'ē) ***adj.*** ⟦see prec.⟧ **1** healthful **2** beneficial

sal·u·ta·tion (sal'yo͞o tā'shən) ***n.*** ⟦see fol.⟧ **1** the act of greeting, addressing, etc. **2** a form of greeting, as the "Dear Sir" of a letter

sa·lute (sə lo͞ot') ***vt., vi.*** **-lut'ed, -lut'ing** ⟦< L *salus*, health⟧ **1** to greet with friendly words or ceremonial gesture **2** to honor by performing a prescribed act, such as raising the right hand to the head, in military and naval practice **3** to praise; commend —***n.*** an act or remark made in saluting

sal·vage (sal'vij) ***n.*** ⟦see SAVE[1]⟧ **1** *a)* the rescue of a ship and cargo from shipwreck, etc. *b)* compensation paid for such rescue **2** *a)* the rescue of any property from destruction or waste *b)* the property saved —***vt.*** **-vaged, -vag·ing** to save or rescue from shipwreck, fire, etc.

sal·va·tion (sal vā'shən) ***n.*** ⟦< L *salvare*, save⟧ **1** a saving or being saved **2** a person or thing that saves **3** *Theol.* deliverance from sin and from the penalties of sin; redemption

salve (sav) ***n.*** ⟦OE *sealf*⟧ **1** any soothing or healing ointment for wounds, burns, etc. **2** anything that soothes —***vt.*** **salved, salv'ing** to soothe

sal·ver (sal'vər) ***n.*** ⟦ult. < L *salvare*, save⟧ a tray

sal·vo (sal'vō) ***n.***, *pl.* **-vos** or **-voes** ⟦< It < L *salve*, hail!⟧ a discharge of a number of guns, in salute or at a target

SAM (sam) ***n.*** surface-to-air missile

sam·ba (sam'bə, säm'-) ***n.*** ⟦Port⟧ a Brazilian dance of African origin, or music for it

same (sām) ***adj.*** ⟦< ON *samr*⟧ **1** being the very one; identical **2** alike in kind, quality, amount, etc. **3** unchanged *[*to keep the *same* look*]* **4** before-mentioned Usually used with *the* —***pron.*** the same person or thing —***adv.*** in like manner: usually with *the* —**same'ness** ***n.***

sam·iz·dat (säm'iz dät') ***n.*** ⟦Russ, self-published⟧ in the U.S.S.R., a system by which writings officially disapproved of were circulated secretly

Sa·mo·a (sə mō'ə) country in the SW Pacific, consisting of two large islands & several small ones: 1,093 sq. mi.; pop. 160,000 —**Sa·mo'an** ***adj., n.***

sam·o·var (sam'ə vär') ***n.*** a Russian metal urn with a spigot, for heating water in making tea

sam·pan (sam'pan') ***n.*** ⟦< Chin dial.⟧ a small boat used in China and Japan, rowed with a scull from the stern

sam·ple (sam'pəl) ***n.*** ⟦see EXAMPLE⟧ **1** a part or item taken as representative of a whole thing, group, etc.; specimen **2** an example —***vt.*** **-pled, -pling** to take (and test) a sample of

sam'pler (-plər) ***n.*** **1** one who samples **2** a collection of representative selections **3** a cloth embroidered with designs, mottoes, etc. in different stitches

Sam·son (sam'sən) ***n.*** *Bible* an Israelite noted for his great strength

Sam·u·el (sam'yo͞o əl) ***n.*** *Bible* a Hebrew leader and prophet

sam·u·rai (sam'ə rī') ***n.***, *pl.* **-rai'** ⟦Jpn⟧ a member of a military class in feudal Japan

San An·to·ni·o (san' an tō'nē ō') city in SC Texas: site of the Alamo: pop. 935,000

san·a·to·ri·um (san'ə tôr'ē əm) ***n.***, *pl.* **-ri·ums** or **-ri·a** (-ə) *chiefly Brit. var. of* SANITARIUM

San Ber·nar·di·no (bur'nər dē'nō, -nə-) city in S California: pop. 164,000

sanc·ti·fy (saŋk'tə fī') ***vt.*** **-fied', -fy'ing** ⟦see SAINT & -FY⟧ **1** to set apart as holy; consecrate **2** to make free from sin —**sanc'ti·fi·ca'tion** ***n.***

sanc·ti·mo·ni·ous (saŋk'tə mō'nē əs) ***adj.*** pretending to be pious —**sanc'ti·mo'ni·ous·ly** ***adv.***

sanc'ti·mo'ny ***n.*** ⟦< L *sanctus*, holy⟧ pretended piety

sanc·tion (saŋk'shən) ***n.*** ⟦see SAINT⟧ **1** authorization **2** support; approval **3** a coercive measure, as an official trade boycott against a nation defying international law: *often used in pl.* —***vt.*** **1** to confirm; ratify **2** to authorize; permit

sanc·ti·ty (saŋk'tə tē) ***n.***, *pl.* **-ties** ⟦< L *sanctus*, holy⟧ **1** holiness **2** sacredness

sanc·tu·ar·y (saŋk'cho͞o er'ē) ***n.***, *pl.* **-ies** ⟦< L *sanctus*, sacred⟧ **1** a holy place; specif., *a)* a church, temple, etc. *b)* a particularly holy place within a church or temple **2** a place of refuge or protection

sanc·tum (saŋk'təm) ***n.*** ⟦L⟧ **1** a sacred place **2** a private room where one is not to be disturbed

sand (sand) ***n.*** ⟦OE⟧ **1** loose, gritty grains of eroded rock, as on beaches, in deserts, etc. **2** [*usually pl.*] a tract of sand —***vt.*** **1** to sprinkle with sand **2** to smooth or polish, as with sandpaper —**sand'er** ***n.***

san·dal (san'dəl) ***n.*** ⟦< Gr *sandalon*⟧ **1** a shoe made of a sole fastened to the foot by straps **2** any of various low slippers or shoes

san'dal·wood' ***n.*** ⟦ult. < Sans⟧ **1** the hard, sweet-smelling wood at the core of certain Asiatic trees **2** such a tree

sand'bag' ***n.*** a bag filled with sand, used for ballast, protecting levees, etc. —***vt.*** **-bagged', -bag'ging 1** to put sandbags in or around **2** [Inf.] to force into doing something

sand'bar' ***n.*** a ridge of sand, as one formed in a river or along a shore: also **sand bar** or **sand'bank'**

sand'blast' ***vt.*** to clean with a current of air or steam carrying sand at a high velocity,

sand'box' ***n.*** a box containing sand for children to play in

sand dollar any of various flat, round, disklike echinoderms that live on sandy ocean beds

S & H *abbrev.* shipping and handling

sand'hog' ***n.*** a laborer in underground or underwater construction

San Di·e·go (san' dē ā'gō) seaport in S California: pop. 1,111,000

S & L *abbrev.* savings and loan (association)

sand'lot' ***adj.*** of or having to do with baseball played by amateurs, orig. on a sandy lot

sand'man' ***n.*** a mythical person supposed to make children sleepy by dusting sand in their eyes

sand'pa'per ***n.*** paper coated on one side with sand, used for smoothing and polishing —***vt.*** to smooth or polish with sandpaper

sand'pip'er (-pī'pər) ***n.*** a small shorebird with a long, soft-tipped bill

sand'stone' ***n.*** a sedimentary rock composed of sand grains cemented together, as by silica

sand'storm' ***n.*** a windstorm in which large quantities of sand are blown about in the air

sand trap a hollow filled with sand, serving as a hazard on a golf course

sand·wich (sand'wich') ***n.*** ⟦after 4th Earl of *Sandwich* (1718-92)⟧ slices of bread with meat, cheese, etc.

THESAURUS

salty ***a.*** briny, brackish, pungent, alkaline, well-seasoned, flavored, well-flavored, highly flavored, sour, acrid.

salute ***v.*** snap to attention, dip the colors, touch one's cap, do honor to, recognize; see also PRAISE 1.

salvage ***v.*** retrieve, recover, regain; see SAVE 1.

salvation ***n.*** **1** [The act of preservation] deliverance, liberation, emancipation; see RESCUE. **2** [A means of preservation] buckler, safeguard, assurance; see PROTECTION 2.

salve ***n.*** ointment, unguent, lubricant, balm, medicine, emollient, unction, remedy, help, cure, cream.

same ***a.*** **1** [Like another in state] equivalent, identical, corresponding; see ALIKE, EQUAL. **2** [Like another in action] similarly, in the same manner, likewise; see ALIKE.

same ***pron.*** the very same, identical object, substitute, equivalent, similar thing.

sameness ***n.*** uniformity, unity, resemblance, analogy, similarity, alikeness, identity, standardization, equality, equivalence, no difference.

sample ***n.*** specimen, unit, individual; see EXAMPLE.

sample ***v.*** taste, test, inspect; see EXAMINE, EXPERIMENT.

sanction ***n.*** consent, acquiescence, assent; see PERMISSION.

sanction ***v.*** confirm, authorize, countenance; see APPROVE, ENDORSE 2.

sanctity ***n.*** holiness, sacredness, piety; see VIRTUE 1.

sanctuary ***n.*** **1** [A sacred place] shrine, church, temple; see CHURCH 1. **2** [A place to which one may retire] asylum, resort, haven; see SHELTER.

sand ***n.*** **1** [Rock particles] sandy soil, sandy loam, silt, dust, grit, powder, gravel, rock powder, rock flour, debris, dirt; see also EARTH 2. **2** [The beach] strand, seaside, seashore; see SHORE.

sandal ***n.*** slipper, thong, flip-flop; see SHOE.

sandwich ***n.*** lunch, light lunch, quick lunch. *Sandwiches include the following:* hamburger, burger*, cheeseburger, wiener, hot dog*, Denver, Western, club, tuna salad, ham, chicken, roast beef, ham and egg, cheese, deviled meat, steak, submarine, grilled cheese, BLT, egg salad,

between them —*vt.* to place or squeeze between other persons, things, etc.

sand·y (san′dē) *adj.* **-i·er, -i·est 1** of or like sand **2** pale reddish-yellow

sane (sān) *adj.* ⟦L *sanus*, healthy⟧ **1** mentally healthy; rational **2** sound; sensible —**sane′ly** *adv.*

San Fran·cis·co (san′ frən sis′kō) seaport on the coast of central California: pop. 724,000

San Francisco Bay an inlet of the Pacific in WC California: the harbor of San Francisco

sang (saŋ) *vi., vt. alt. pt. of* SING[1]

sang-froid (sän frwä′) *n.* ⟦Fr, lit., cold blood⟧ cool self-possession or composure

san·gri·a (san grē′ə, saŋ-) *n.* ⟦Sp < *sangre*, blood⟧ an iced punch made with red wine, fruit juice, pieces of fruit, etc.

san·gui·nar·y (saŋ′gwi ner′ē) *adj.* ⟦see fol.⟧ **1** accompanied by much bloodshed **2** bloodthirsty

san·guine (saŋ′gwin) *adj.* ⟦< L *sanguis*, blood⟧ **1** of the color of blood; ruddy **2** cheerful; confident

san·i·tar·i·um (san′ə ter′ē əm) *n., pl.* **-i·ums** or **-i·a** (-ə) ⟦ModL < L *sanitas*, health⟧ **1** a resort where people go to regain health **2** an institution for the care of invalids or convalescents

san·i·tar·y (san′ə ter′ē) *adj.* ⟦< L *sanitas*, health⟧ **1** of or bringing about health and healthful conditions **2** in a clean, healthy condition

sanitary napkin an absorbent pad worn by women during menstruation

san·i·ta·tion (san′ə tā′shən) *n.* **1** the science and practice of effecting hygienic conditions **2** drainage and disposal of sewage

san·i·tize (san′ə tīz′) *vt.* **-tized′, -tiz′ing 1** to make sanitary **2** to free from anything considered undesirable, damaging, etc.

san·i·ty (san′ə tē) *n.* **1** the state of being sane **2** soundness of judgment

San Jo·se (san′ hō zā′) city in WC California: pop. 782,000

San Juan (san′ hwän′) seaport & capital of Puerto Rico: pop. 438,000

sank (saŋk) *vi., vt. alt. pt. of* SINK

San Ma·ri·no (san′ mə rē′nō) independent country within E Italy: 24 sq. mi.; pop. 24,000

sans (sanz; *Fr* sän) *prep.* ⟦Fr < L *sine*⟧ without

San·skrit (san′skrit′) *n.* the classical literary language of ancient India: also **San′scrit**

San·ta An·a[1] (san′tə an′ə) hot desert wind from the east or northeast in S California

San·ta An·a[2] (san′tə an′ə) city in SW California: pop. 294,000

San·ta Claus (san′tə klôz′) ⟦< Du *Sant Nikolaas*, St. Nicholas⟧ *Folklore* a fat, white-bearded, jolly old man in a red suit, who distributes gifts at Christmas

San·ta Fe (san′tə fā′) capital of New Mexico: pop. 56,000

San·ti·a·go (sän′tē ä′gō, san′-) capital of Chile: pop. 4,100,000

São Pau·lo (soun pou′loo) city in SE Brazil: pop. 8,491,000

São To·mé and Prín·ci·pe (tô me′ and prin′sə pē′) country off the W coast of Africa, comprising two islands (**São Tomé** and **Príncipe**): 387 sq. mi.; pop. 120,000

sap[1] (sap) *n.* ⟦OE *sæp*⟧ **1** the juice that circulates through a plant, bearing water, food, etc. **2** vigor; energy **3** [Slang] a fool —**sap′less** *adj.*

sap[2] (sap) *vt.* **sapped, sap′ping** ⟦< Fr *sappe*, a hoe⟧ **1** to dig beneath; undermine **2** to weaken

sa·pi·ent (sā′pē ənt) *adj.* ⟦< L *sapere*, to taste, know⟧ wise —**sa′pi·ence** *n.*

sap·ling (sap′liŋ) *n.* a young tree

sap·phire (saf′īr) *n.* ⟦< Sans *śanipriya*⟧ a precious stone of a clear, deep-blue corundum

sap·py (sap′ē) *adj.* **-pi·er, -pi·est 1** full of sap; juicy **2** [Slang] foolish; silly —**sap′pi·ness** *n.*

sap·ro·phyte (sap′rə fīt′) *n.* ⟦< Gr *sapros*, rotten + *phyton*, a plant⟧ any plant that lives on dead or decaying organic matter, as some fungi —**sap′ro·phyt′ic** (-fit′ik) *adj.*

sap′suck′er *n.* an American woodpecker that often drills holes in trees for the sap

Sar·a·cen (sar′ə sən) *n.* any Arab or any Muslim, esp. at the time of the Crusades

Sar·ah (ser′ə) *n. Bible* the wife of Abraham and mother of Isaac

Sa·ra·je·vo (sar′ə yā′vō) capital of Bosnia and Herzegovina: pop. 416,000

sa·ran (sə ran′) *n.* ⟦arbitrary coinage⟧ a thermoplastic substance used in various fabrics, wrapping material, etc.

sar·casm (sär′kaz′əm) *n.* ⟦< Gr *sarkazein*, to tear flesh⟧ **1** a taunting or caustic remark, generally ironic **2** the making of such remarks

sar·cas·tic (sär kas′tik) *adj.* **1** of, like, or full of sarcasm **2** using sarcasm —**sar·cas′ti·cal·ly** *adv.*

sar·co·ma (sär kō′mə) *n., pl.* **-mas** or **-ma·ta** (-mə tə) ⟦< Gr *sarx*, flesh⟧ a malignant tumor in connective tissue

sar·coph·a·gus (sär käf′ə gəs) *n., pl.* **-gi′** (-jī′) or **-gus·es** ⟦< Gr *sarx*, flesh + *phagein*, to eat: limestone coffins hastened disintegration⟧ a stone coffin, esp. one exposed to view, as in a tomb

sar·dine (sär dēn′) *n.* ⟦< L *sarda*, a fish⟧ any of various small ocean fishes preserved in tightly packed cans for eating

sar·don·ic (sär dän′ik) *adj.* ⟦< Gr *sardonios*⟧ scornfully or bitterly sarcastic —**sar·don′i·cal·ly** *adv.*

sa·ri (sä′rē) *n.* ⟦< Sans⟧ the outer garment of a woman of India, Pakistan, etc., consisting of a long cloth wrapped around the body

sa·rong (sə rôŋ′, -räŋ′) *n.* ⟦Malay *sarung*⟧ a garment of men and women in the East Indies, etc., consisting of a cloth worn like a skirt

sar·sa·pa·ril·la (sas′ pə ril′ə) *n.* ⟦< Sp *zarza*, bramble + *parra*, vine⟧ **1** a tropical American vine with fragrant roots **2** a carbonated drink flavored with or as with the dried roots

sar·to·ri·al (sär tôr′ē əl) *adj.* ⟦< LL *sartor*, tailor⟧ **1** of tailors or their work **2** of men's dress

SASE *abbrev.* self-addressed, stamped envelope

sash[1] (sash) *n.* ⟦Ar *shāsh*, muslin⟧ an ornamental band, ribbon, etc. worn over the shoulder or around the waist

sash[2] (sash) *n.* ⟦< Fr *châssis*, a frame⟧ a frame for holding the glass pane of a window or door, esp. a sliding frame

sa·shay (sa shā′) *vi.* ⟦< Fr *chassé*, a dance step⟧ [Inf.] **1** to walk or go, esp. casually **2** to move, walk, etc. so as to attract attention

Sas·katch·e·wan (sas kach′ə wän′) province of SC Canada: 251,700 sq. mi.; pop. 990,000; cap. Regina: abbrev. *SK*

sass (sas) [Inf.] *n.* ⟦var. of SAUCE⟧ impudent talk —*vt.* to talk impudently to

sas·sa·fras (sas′ə fras′) *n.* ⟦Sp *sasafras*⟧ **1** a small tree having small, bluish fruits **2** its dried root bark, used for flavoring

sass·y (sas′ē) *adj.* **-i·er, -i·est** ⟦var. of SAUCY⟧ [Inf.] impudent; saucy

THESAURUS

open face, peanut butter and jelly, jelly.

sandy *a.* **1** [Containing sand; *said especially of soil*] light, loose, permeable, porous, easy to work, easily worked, granular, powdery, gritty. **2** [Suggestive of sand; *said especially of the hair*] fair-haired, fair, blond, light, light-haired, reddish, sandy-red, sun-bleached, flaxen, faded.

sane *a.* **1** [Sound in mind] rational, normal, lucid, right-minded, sober, in one's right mind, with a healthy mind, mentally sound, balanced, centered, healthy-minded, reasonable, in possession of one's faculties.—*Ant.* INSANE, irrational, delirious. **2** [Sensible] reasonable, practical, wise; see SENSIBLE.

sanitary *a.* hygienic, wholesome, sterile; see HEALTHFUL.

sanity *n.* sound mind, rationality, healthy mind, saneness, a clear mind, clearmindedness, wholesome outlook, common sense, intelligence, reason, reasonableness, prudence, good judgment, acumen, understanding, comprehension.

sap[1] *n.* **1** [The life fluid of a plant] fluid, secretion, essence; see LIQUID. **2** [*A dupe] dolt, gull, sucker*; see FOOL.

sapling *n.* scion, seedling, slip, sprig, young tree; see also TREE.

sappy *a.* **1** [Juicy] lush, succulent, watery; see JUICY. **2** [*Idiotic] foolish, silly, sentimental; see STUPID.

sarcasm *n.* satire, irony, banter, derision, contempt, scoffing, flouting, ridicule, burlesque, disparagement, criticism, cynicism, invective, censure, lampooning, aspersion, sneering, mockery.—*Ant.* FLATTERY, fawning, cajolery.

sarcastic *a.* scornful, mocking, ironical, satirical, taunting, severe, derisive, bitter, saucy, hostile, sneering, snickering, quizzical, arrogant, disrespectful, offensive, carping, cynical, disillusioned, snarling, unbelieving, corrosive, acid, cutting, scorching, captious, sharp, pert, brusque, caustic, biting, harsh, austere, grim.

sardonic *a.* sarcastic, cynical, scornful; see SARCASTIC.

sat (sat) ***vi., vt.*** *pt. & pp. of* SIT
Sat *abbrev.* Saturday
SAT *trademark for* Scholastic Assessment Tests
Sa·tan (sāt'n) ***n.*** ⟦< Heb *satan*, adversary⟧ the Devil
sa·tan·ic (sā tan'ik, sə-) ***adj.*** like Satan; wicked —**sa·tan'i·cal·ly *adv.***
satch·el (sach'əl) ***n.*** ⟦< L *saccus*, a bag⟧ a small bag for carrying clothes, books, etc.
sate (sāt) ***vt.* sat'ed, sat'ing** ⟦prob. < L *satiare*, fill full⟧ **1** to satisfy (an appetite, etc.) completely **2** to satiate
sa·teen (sa tēn') ***n.*** ⟦< SATIN⟧ a cotton cloth made to imitate satin
sat·el·lite (sat''l īt') ***n.*** ⟦< L *satelles*, an attendant⟧ **1** *a)* a celestial body revolving around a larger celestial body *b)* a man-made object rocketed into orbit around the earth, moon, etc. **2** a small state dependent on a larger one
sa·ti·ate (sā'shē āt') ***vt.* -at'ed, -at'ing** ⟦< L *satis*, enough⟧ to provide with more than enough, so as to weary or disgust; glut
sa·ti·e·ty (sə tī'ə tē) ***n.*** a being satiated
sat·in (sat''n) ***n.*** ⟦< Ar *zaitūnī*, of *Zaitūn*, former name of a Chinese seaport⟧ a fabric of silk, nylon, rayon, etc. with a smooth, glossy finish on one side —**sat'in·y *adj.***
sat'in·wood' ***n.*** **1** a smooth wood used in fine furniture **2** any of the trees yielding such a wood
sat·ire (sa'tīr') ***n.*** ⟦< L *satira*⟧ **1** a literary work in which vices, follies, etc. are held up to ridicule and contempt **2** the use of ridicule, sarcasm, etc. to attack vices, follies, etc. —**sa·tir·i·cal** (sə tir'i kəl) ***adj.*** —**sat·i·rist** (sat'ə rist) ***n.***
sat·i·rize (sat'ə rīz') ***vt.* -rized', -riz'ing** to attack with satire
sat·is·fac·tion (sat'is fak'shən) ***n.*** **1** a satisfying or being satisfied **2** something that satisfies; specif., *a)* anything that brings pleasure or contentment *b)* settlement of debt
sat'is·fac'to·ry (-tə rē) ***adj.*** good enough to fulfill a need, wish, etc.; satisfying or adequate —**sat'is·fac'to·ri·ly *adv.***
sat·is·fy (sat'is fī') ***vt.* -fied', -fy'ing** ⟦< L *satis*, enough + *facere*, make⟧ **1** to fulfill the needs or desires of; content **2** to fulfill the requirements of **3** to free from doubt; convince **4** *a)* to give what is due to *b)* to discharge (a debt, etc.)
sa·to·ri (sä tôr'ē) ***n.*** ⟦Jpn⟧ spiritual enlightenment: term in Zen Buddhism
sa·trap (sā'trap', sa'-) ***n.*** ⟦< Pers⟧ a petty tyrant
sat·u·rate (sach'ə rāt') ***vt.* -rat'ed, -rat'ing** ⟦< L *satur*, full⟧ **1** to make thoroughly soaked **2** to cause to be filled, charged, etc. with the most it can absorb —**sat'u·ra'tion *n.***
Sat·ur·day (sat'ər dā') ***n.*** ⟦< OE *Sæterdæg*, Saturn's day⟧ the seventh and last day of the week
Saturday night special ⟦from their use in weekend crimes⟧ [Slang] any small, cheap handgun
Sat·urn (sat'ərn) ***n.*** **1** the Roman god of agriculture **2** the second largest planet of the solar system, with thin, icy rings of particles around its equator: see PLANET
sat·ur·nine (sat'ər nīn') ***adj.*** ⟦< supposed influence of planet Saturn⟧ sluggish, gloomy, grave, etc.
sat·yr (sāt'ər, sat'-) ***n.*** ⟦< Gr *satyros*⟧ **1** *Gr. Myth.* a lecherous woodland deity represented as a man with a goat's legs, pointed ears, and short horns **2** a lecherous man
sat·y·ri·a·sis (sāt'ə rī'ə sis, sat'-) ***n.*** ⟦< Gr: see prec.⟧ uncontrollable desire by a man for sexual intercourse
sauce (sôs) ***n.*** ⟦< L *sal*, salt⟧ **1** a liquid or soft mixture served with food to add flavor **2** stewed or preserved fruit **3** [Inf.] impudence **4** [Slang] alcoholic liquor: with *the*
sauce'pan' ***n.*** a small pot with a projecting handle, used for cooking
sau·cer (sô'sər) ***n.*** ⟦see SAUCE⟧ **1** a small, round, shallow dish, esp. one designed to hold a cup **2** anything shaped like a saucer
sau·cy (sô'sē) ***adj.* -ci·er, -ci·est** ⟦SAUC(E) + -Y[2]⟧ **1** rude; impudent **2** pert; sprightly —**sau'ci·ly *adv.*** —**sau'ci·ness *n.***
Sa·u·di Arabia (sou'dē, sô'-) kingdom occupying most of Arabia: 849,400 sq. mi.; pop. 16,900,000
sau·er·bra·ten (sou'ər brät''n, zou'ər-) ***n.*** ⟦Ger *sauer*, sour + *braten*, roast⟧ beef marinated in vinegar with onions, spices, etc. before cooking
sau·er·kraut (sou'ər krout') ***n.*** ⟦Ger *sauer*, sour + *kraut*, cabbage⟧ chopped cabbage fermented in brine
Saul (sôl) ***n.*** *Bible* first king of Israel
sau·na (sô'nə, sä'-) ***n.*** ⟦Finnish⟧ a bath involving exposure to hot, dry air
saun·ter (sôn'tər) ***vi.*** ⟦ME *santren*, to muse⟧ to walk about idly; stroll —***n.*** a leisurely walk; stroll
sau·ri·an (sôr'ē ən) ***adj.*** ⟦< Gr *sauros*, lizard⟧ of or like lizards
sau·ro·pod (sôr'ə päd') ***n.*** ⟦< Gr *sauros*, lizard + -POD⟧ a gigantic dinosaur with a long neck and tail and a small head, as an apatosaurus
sau·sage (sô'sij) ***n.*** ⟦see SAUCE⟧ pork or other meat, chopped fine, seasoned, and often stuffed into a casing
sau·té (sô tā', sō-) ***vt.* -téed', -té'ing** ⟦Fr < *sauter*, to leap⟧ to fry quickly with a little fat
Sau·ternes (sō turn') ***n.*** ⟦after *Sauternes*, town in France⟧ [*often* **s-**] any of various white wines, of varying sweetness: also sp. **Sau·terne'**
sav·age (sav'ij) ***adj.*** ⟦< L *silva*, a wood⟧ **1** fierce; untamed [*a savage* tiger] **2** primitive; barbarous **3** cruel; pitiless —***n.*** **1** [Now Rare] a member of a preliterate, often tribal, culture **2** a brutal or crude person —**sav'age·ly *adv.*** —**sav'age·ry *n.***
sa·van·na or **sa·van·nah** (sə van'ə) ***n.*** ⟦Sp *sabana*⟧ a treeless plain or a grassland with scattered trees
Sa·van·nah (sə van'ə) seaport in SE Georgia: pop. 138,000
sa·vant (sə vänt', -vant'; sav'ənt) ***n.*** ⟦Fr < *savoir*, know⟧ a learned person
save[1] (sāv) ***vt.* saved, sav'ing** ⟦< L *salvus*, safe⟧ **1** to rescue or preserve from harm or danger **2** to preserve

THESAURUS

Satan ***n.*** Mephistopheles, Lucifer, Beelzebub; see DEVIL.
satanic ***a.*** malicious, evil, devilish; see SINISTER.
satellite ***n.*** **1** [A moon] planetoid, minor planet, secondary planet, inferior planet, asteroid. **2** [A man-made object put into orbit around a celestial body] artificial moon, spacecraft, moonlet, sputnik, space station, communications satellite, weather satellite, GPS satellite, geostationary satellite.
satire ***n.*** mockery, ridicule, caricature; see IRONY.
satisfaction ***n.*** **1** [The act of satisfying] gratification, fulfillment, achievement; see ACHIEVEMENT. **2** [The state or feeling of being satisfied] comfort, pleasure, well-being, content, contentment, gladness, delight, bliss, joy, happiness, relief, complacency, peace of mind, ease, heart's ease, serenity, contentedness, cheerfulness. **3** [Something that contributes to satisfaction] reward, prosperity, good fortune; see BLESSING 2. **4** [Settlement of a debt] reimbursement, repayment, compensation.
satisfactorily ***a.*** **1** [In a satisfactory manner] convincingly, suitably, competently; see ADEQUATELY. **2** [In a manner productive of satisfactory results] amply, abundantly, thoroughly; see AGREEABLY.
satisfactory ***a.*** adequate, satisfying, pleasing; see ENOUGH.
satisfied ***a.*** content, happy, contented, filled, supplied, fulfilled, paid, compensated, appeased, convinced, gratified, sated, at ease, with enough, without care, satiated.
satisfy ***v.*** **1** [To make content] comfort, cheer, elate, befriend, please, rejoice, delight, exhilarate, amuse, entertain, flatter, make merry, make cheerful, gladden, content, gratify, indulge, humor, conciliate, propitiate, capture, enthrall, enliven, animate, captivate, fascinate, fill, be of advantage, gorge. **2** [To pay] repay, clear up, disburse; see PAY 1, SETTLE 7. **3** [To fulfill] do, fill, serve the purpose, be enough, observe, perform, comply with, conform to, meet requirements, keep a promise, accomplish, complete, be adequate, be sufficient, provide, furnish, qualify, answer, serve, equip, meet, avail, suffice, fill the want, come up to, content one, appease one, fill the bill*, pass muster*, get by, do in a pinch*.—*Ant.* NEGLECT, leave open, fail to do.
satisfying ***a.*** pleasing, comforting, gratifying; see ENOUGH, PLEASANT 2.
saturate ***v.*** overfill, drench, steep; see IMMERSE, SOAK 1.
saturated ***a.*** drenched, full, soggy; see SOAKED, WET 1.
saturation ***n.*** fullness, soaking, overload; see EXCESS 1.
sauce ***n.*** topping, gravy, dressing; see FLAVORING, FOOD.
sausage ***n.*** link sausage, salami, liverwurst; see MEAT.
savage ***a.*** **1** [Primitive] crude, simple, original; see CRUDE. **2** [Cruel] barbarous, inhuman, brutal; see CRUEL. **3** [Wild] untamed, uncivilized, uncultured; see UNCONTROLLED.
savage ***n.*** primitive, ruffian, animal; see BEAST 2.
savagely ***a.*** cruelly, viciously, barbarically; see BRUTALLY.
save[1] ***v.*** **1** [To remove from danger]

for future use **3** to prevent loss or waste of *[to save time]* **4** to prevent or lessen *[to save expense]* **5** *Theol.* to deliver from sin —***vi.*** **1** to avoid expense, waste, etc. **2** to store (*up*) money or goods —***n.*** *Sports* an action that keeps an opponent from scoring or winning —**sav'er** ***n.***
save[2] (sāv) ***prep., conj.*** ⟦< OFr *sauf*, safe⟧ except; but
sav·ing (sā'viŋ) ***adj.*** that saves; specif., *a*) economizing or economical *b*) redeeming —***n.*** **1** [*often pl., with sing. v.*] any reduction in expense, time, etc. **2** [*pl.*] sums of money saved
sav·ior or **sav·iour** (sāv'yər) ***n.*** ⟦< L *salvare*, to save⟧ **1** one who saves **2** [**S-**] Jesus Christ
sa·voir-faire (sav'wär fer') ***n.*** ⟦Fr, to know (how) to do⟧ ready knowledge of what to do or say in any situation
sa·vor (sā'vər) ***n.*** ⟦< L *sapor*⟧ **1** a particular taste or smell **2** distinctive quality —***vi.*** to have the distinctive taste, smell, or quality (*of*) —***vt.*** to taste with delight Brit. sp. **sa'vour**
sa'vor·y ***adj.*** **-i·er, -i·est** **1** pleasing to the taste or smell **2** pleasant, agreeable, etc. Brit. sp. **sa'vour·y**
sav·vy (sav'ē) ***n.*** ⟦< Port *saber*, to know⟧ [Slang] shrewdness or understanding
saw[1] (sô) ***n.*** ⟦OE *sagu*⟧ a cutting tool consisting of a thin metal blade or disk with sharp teeth —***vt.*** to cut or shape with a saw —***vi.*** **1** to cut with or as with a saw **2** to be cut with a saw
saw[2] (sô) ***n.*** ⟦OE *sagu*⟧ a maxim; proverb
saw[3] (sô) ***vt., vi.*** *pt. of* SEE[1]
saw'dust' ***n.*** fine particles of wood formed in sawing wood
sawed'-off' ***adj.*** short or shortened
saw'horse' ***n.*** a rack on which wood is placed while being sawed
saw'mill' ***n.*** a factory where logs are sawed into boards
saw'-toothed' ***adj.*** having notches along the edge like the teeth of a saw: also **saw'tooth'**
saw·yer (sô'yər) ***n.*** one whose work is sawing wood
sax (saks) ***n.*** [Inf.] *short for* SAXOPHONE
Sax·on (sak'sən) ***n.*** **1** a member of an ancient Germanic people, some of whom settled in England **2** an Anglo-Saxon **3** any dialect of the Saxons
sax·o·phone (sak'sə fōn') ***n.*** ⟦Fr, after A. J. *Sax*, 19th-c. Belgian inventor + -PHONE⟧ a single-reed, keyed woodwind instrument with a metal body —**sax'o·phon'ist** (-fōn'ist) ***n.***
say (sā) ***vt.*** **said, say'ing** ⟦OE *secgan*⟧ **1** to utter or speak **2** to express in words; state **3** to state positively or as an opinion **4** to indicate or show *[the clock says one]* **5** to recite *[to say one's prayers]* **6** to estimate; assume *[he is, I'd say, forty]* —***n.*** **1** a chance to speak *[I had my say]* **2** authority, as to make a final decision: often with *the* —**that is to say** in other words
say'ing ***n.*** an adage, proverb, or maxim
say'-so' ***n.*** [Inf.] **1** one's word, assurance, etc. **2** right of decision
Sb ⟦L *stibium*⟧ *Chem. symbol for* antimony
sc *abbrev. Printing* small capitals
SC South Carolina
scab (skab) ***n.*** ⟦< ON *skabb*⟧ **1** a crust forming over a sore during healing **2** a worker who replaces a striking worker —***vi.*** **scabbed, scab'bing** to become covered with a scab —**scab'by, -bi·er, -bi·est,** ***adj.*** —**scab'bi·ness** ***n.***
scab·bard (skab'ərd) ***n.*** ⟦< ? OHG *scar*, sword⟧ a sheath for the blade of a sword, dagger, etc.
sca·bies (skā'bēz) ***n.*** ⟦L, the itch⟧ a contagious, itching skin disease caused by a mite
scab·rous (skab'rəs, skā'brəs) ***adj.*** ⟦< L *scabere*, to scratch⟧ **1** scaly or scabby **2** indecent, shocking, etc.
scads (skadz) ***pl.n.*** ⟦< ?⟧ [Inf.] a very large number or amount
scaf·fold (skaf'əld) ***n.*** ⟦< OFr *escafalt*⟧ **1** a temporary framework for supporting workers during the repairing, painting, etc. of a building, etc. **2** a raised platform on which criminals are executed
scaf'fold·ing ***n.*** **1** the materials forming a scaffold **2** a scaffold
scal·a·wag (skal'ə wag') ***n.*** ⟦< ?⟧ [Inf.] a scamp; rascal
scald (skôld) ***vt.*** ⟦< L *ex-*, intens. + *calidus*, hot⟧ **1** to burn with hot liquid or steam **2** to heat almost to the boiling point **3** to use boiling liquid on —***n.*** a burn caused by scalding
scale[1] (skāl) ***n.*** ⟦< L *scala*, ladder⟧ **1** *a*) a series of marks along a line used in measuring *[the scale of a thermometer]* *b*) any instrument so marked **2** the proportion that a map, etc. bears to the thing it represents *[a scale of one inch to a mile]* **3** *a*) a series of degrees classified by size, amount, etc. *[a wage scale]* *b*) any degree in such a series **4** *Music* a series of tones, rising or falling in pitch, according to a system of intervals —***vt.*** **scaled, scal'ing** **1** to climb up or over **2** to make according to a scale —**scale back** SCALE DOWN (see phrase below) —**scale down** (or **up**) to reduce (or increase) according to a fixed ratio
scale[2] (skāl) ***n.*** ⟦< OFr *escale*, shell⟧ **1** any of the thin, flat horny plates covering many fishes, reptiles, etc. **2** any thin, platelike layer or piece —***vt.*** **scaled, scal'ing** to scrape scales from —***vi.*** to flake or peel off in scales —**scal'y, -i·er, -i·est,** ***adj.***
scale[3] (skāl) ***n.*** ⟦< ON *skāl*, bowl⟧ **1** either pan of a balance **2** [*often pl.*] *a*) BALANCE (sense 1) *b*) any weighing machine —***vt.*** **scaled, scal'ing** to weigh —**turn the scales** to decide or settle
scale insect any of various small insects destructive to plants: the females secrete a waxy scale
sca·lene (skā'lēn', skā lēn') ***adj.*** ⟦< Gr *skalēnos*, uneven⟧ having unequal sides *[a scalene triangle]*
scal·lion (skal'yən) ***n.*** ⟦< L (*caepa*) *Ascalonia*, (onion of) Ascalon (Philistine city)⟧ any of various onions or onionlike plants, as the shallot, green onion, or leek
scal·lop (skäl'əp, skal'-) ***n.*** ⟦< OFr *escalope*⟧ **1** *a*) any of various edible mollusks with two curved, hinged shells *b*) one of the shells **2** any of a series of curves, etc. forming an ornamental edge —***vt.*** **1** to cut the edge of

THESAURUS

deliver, extricate, rescue, free, set free, liberate, release, emancipate, ransom, redeem, come to the rescue of, defend.—*Ant.* LEAVE, desert, condemn. **2** [To assure an afterlife] rescue from sin, reclaim, regenerate; see sense 1. **3** [To hoard] collect, store, invest, have on deposit, amass, accumulate, gather, treasure up, store up, pile up, hide away, cache, stow away, sock away*.—*Ant.* WASTE, spend, invest. **4** [To preserve] conserve, keep, put up; see PRESERVE 2.

saved ***a.*** **1** [Kept from danger] rescued, released, delivered, protected, defended, guarded, safeguarded, preserved, reclaimed, regenerated, cured, healed, conserved, maintained, safe, secure, freed, free from harm, unthreatened, free from danger.—*Ant.* RUINED, destroyed, lost. **2** [Not spent] kept, unspent, unused, untouched, accumulated, deposited, on deposit, retained, laid away, hoarded, invested, amassed, stored, spared.—*Ant.* WASTED, squandered, spent.

savings ***n.*** means, property, resources, funds, reserve, investment, provision, provisions, accumulation, store, riches, harvest, hoard, savings account, cache, nest egg, money in the bank, provision for a rainy day.

savior ***n.*** **1** [One who saves another] deliverer, rescuer, preserver; see PROTECTOR. **2** [Jesus Christ; *usually capital*] Redeemer, Messiah, Son of God; see CHRIST.

savor ***v.*** enjoy, relish, appreciate; see LIKE 1.

saw[1] ***n.*** power, circular, concave, mill, ice, crosscut, band, rip, hand, pruning, whip, buck, keyhole, back, butcher's, hack, jig, etc. saw; see also TOOL 1.

say ***v.*** tell, speak, relate, state, announce, declare, state positively, open one's mouth, have one's say, break silence, put forth, let out, assert, maintain, express oneself, answer, respond, suppose, assume. —**to say the least** at a minimum, at the very least, to put it mildly, minimally.

saying ***n.*** aphorism, adage, maxim, byword, motto, proverb, precept, dictum.

scab ***n.*** eschar, slough, crust.

scaffold ***n.*** framework, stage, structure; see BUILDING, PLATFORM 1.

scald ***v.*** char, blanch, parboil; see BURN.

scale[1,2,3] ***n.*** **1** [A series for measurement] rule, computation, system; see MEASURE 2. **2** [A flake or film] thin coating, covering, encrustation; see FLAKE, LAYER. **3** [A device for weighing; *often plural*] steelyard, analytical balance, balance, scale beam. *Varieties of scales include the following:* beam, automatic indicating, counter, cylinder, drum, barrel, platform, spring, computing, digital, household, miner's, assayer's, truck, jeweler's, butcher's, baker's. **4** [Musical tones] range, major scale, minor scale, harmonic scale, melodic scale; see also MUSIC. —**on a large scale** extensively, grandly, expansively; see GENEROUSLY. —**on a small scale** economically, in a limited way, with restrictions; see INADEQUATE, UNIMPORTANT.

scale[1,2,3] ***v.*** **1** [To climb] ascend, surmount, mount; see CLIMB. **2** [To peel] exfoliate, strip off, flake; see PEEL, SKIN. **3** [To measure] compare, balance, compute; see COMPARE 1.

in scallops 2 to bake until brown, usually with a creamy sauce and bread crumbs

scalp (skalp) ***n.*** ⟦< Scand⟧ the skin on the top and back of the head, usually covered with hair —***vt.*** **1** to cut or tear the scalp from **2** [Inf.] to buy (theater tickets, etc.) and resell them at higher prices —**scalp'er** ***n.***

scal·pel (skal'pəl) ***n.*** ⟦< L *scalprum*, a knife⟧ a small, sharp, straight knife used in surgery, etc.

scam (skam) ***n.*** ⟦prob. < *scheme*⟧ [Slang] a swindle or fraud, esp. a CONFIDENCE GAME —***vt.*** **scammed, scam'ming** [Slang] to cheat or swindle, as in a confidence game

scamp (skamp) ***n.*** ⟦< It *scampare*, to flee⟧ a mischievous fellow; rascal

scam·per (skam'pər) ***vi.*** ⟦see prec.⟧ to run or go quickly —***n.*** a scampering

scam·pi (skam'pē) ***n.***, *pl.* **-pi** or **-pies** ⟦It⟧ a large, edible shrimp

scan (skan) ***vt.*** **scanned, scan'ning** ⟦< L *scandere*, to climb⟧ **1** to analyze (verse) by marking the metrical feet **2** to look at closely **3** to glance at quickly **4** to examine the structure or condition of (an internal body organ) with ultrasound, etc. **5** to pass radar beams over (an area) —***vi.*** to conform to metrical principles: said of poetry —***n.*** the act or an instance of scanning

Scan or **Scand** *abbrev.* Scandinavia(n)

scan·dal (skan'dəl) ***n.*** ⟦< Gr *skandalon*, a snare⟧ **1** anything that offends moral feelings and leads to disgrace **2** shame, outrage, etc. caused by this **3** disgrace **4** malicious gossip

scan'dal·ize' (-də līz') ***vt.*** **-ized', -iz'ing** to outrage the moral feelings of by improper conduct

scan'dal·mon'ger (-dəl muŋ'gər, -mäŋ'-) ***n.*** one who spreads scandal or gossip

scan'dal·ous (-də ləs) ***adj.*** **1** causing scandal; shameful **2** spreading slander —**scan'dal·ous·ly** ***adv.***

Scan·di·na·vi·a (skan'də nā'vē ə) region in N Europe, including Norway, Sweden, & Denmark and, sometimes, Iceland

Scan·di·na·vi·an (skan'də nā'vē ən) ***adj.*** of Scandinavia or its peoples, languages, etc. —***n.*** **1** a person born or living in Scandinavia **2** the subbranch of the Germanic languages spoken by Scandinavians

scan·sion (skan'shən) ***n.*** ⟦Fr < L *scansio*⟧ the act of scanning, or analyzing, poetry

scant (skant) ***adj.*** ⟦< ON *skammr*, short⟧ **1** inadequate; meager **2** not quite up to full measure

scant'y ***adj.*** **-i·er, -i·est** **1** barely sufficient **2** insufficient; not enough —**scant'i·ly** ***adv.*** —**scant'i·ness** ***n.***

scape·goat (skāp'gōt') ***n.*** ⟦< ESCAPE + GOAT; see Lev. 16:7-26⟧ one who bears the blame for the mistakes of others —***vt.*** to make a scapegoat of

scape·grace (skāp'grās') ***n.*** ⟦< ESCAPE + GRACE⟧ a rogue; scamp

scap·u·la (skap'yə lə) ***n.***, *pl.* **-lae'** (-lē') or **-las** ⟦< L⟧ either of the two flat bones in the upper back; shoulder blade

scar (skär) ***n.*** ⟦< Gr *eschara*, orig., fireplace⟧ **1** a mark left after a wound, burn, etc. has healed **2** the lasting mental or emotional effects of suffering —***vt.*** **scarred, scar'ring** to mark as with a scar —***vi.*** to form a scar in healing

scar·ab (skar'əb) ***n.*** ⟦< L *scarabaeus*⟧ **1** a large, black beetle **2** a carved image of such a beetle

scarce (skers) ***adj.*** ⟦ult. < L *excerpere*, pick out⟧ **1** not common; rarely seen **2** not plentiful; hard to get —**make oneself scarce** [Inf.] to go or stay away —**scarce'ness** ***n.***

scarce'ly ***adv.*** **1** hardly; only just **2** probably not or certainly not

scar·ci·ty (sker'sə tē) ***n.***, *pl.* **-ties** **1** an inadequate supply; dearth **2** rarity; uncommonness

scare (sker) ***vt.*** **scared, scar'ing** ⟦< ON *skjarr*, timid⟧ to fill with sudden fear —***vi.*** to become frightened —***n.*** a sudden fear —**scare away** (or **off**) to drive away (or off) by frightening —**scare up** [Inf.] to produce or gather quickly

scare·crow (sker'krō') ***n.*** a human figure made with sticks, old clothes, etc., put in a field to scare birds away from crops

scarf (skärf) ***n.***, *pl.* **scarves** (skärvz) or sometimes **scarfs** ⟦< OFr *escharpe*, purse hung from the neck⟧ **1** a piece of cloth worn about the neck, head, etc. **2** a long, narrow covering for a table, etc.

scar·i·fy (skar'ə fī') ***vt.*** **-fied', -fy'ing** ⟦< L *scarifare*⟧ to make small cuts in (the skin, etc.) —**scar'i·fi·ca'tion** ***n.***

scar·let (skär'lit) ***n.*** ⟦< ML *scarlatum*⟧ very bright red —***adj.*** **1** of this color **2** sinful; specif., whorish

scarlet fever an acute contagious disease characterized by sore throat, fever, and a scarlet rash

scar·y (sker'ē) ***adj.*** **-i·er, -i·est** [Inf.] frightening —**scar'i·ness** ***n.***

scat[1] (skat) ***vi.*** **scat'ted, scat'ting** ⟦? short for SCATTER⟧ [Inf.] to go away: usually in the imperative

scat[2] (skat) ***adj.*** ⟦< ?⟧ *Jazz* using improvised, meaningless syllables in singing —***n.*** such singing —***vi.*** **scat'ted, scat'ting** to sing scat

scath·ing (skā'*th*iŋ) ***adj.*** ⟦< ON *skathi*, harm⟧ harsh or caustic *[scathing* remarks*]* —**scath'ing·ly** ***adv.***

sca·tol·o·gy (skə täl'ə jē) ***n.*** ⟦< Gr *skōr*, excrement⟧ obsession with excrement or excretion in literature —**scat·o·log·i·cal** (skat'ə läj'i kəl) ***adj.***

scat·ter (skat'ər) ***vt.*** ⟦ME *skateren*⟧ **1** to throw here and there; sprinkle **2** to separate and drive in many directions; disperse —***vi.*** to separate and go off in several directions

scat'ter·brain' ***n.*** one who is incapable of concentrated thinking

scatter rug a small rug

scav·eng·er (skav'in jər) ***n.*** ⟦< NormFr *escauwer*, to inspect⟧ **1** one who gathers things discarded by others **2** any animal that eats refuse and decaying matter —**scav'enge** (-inj), **-enged, -eng·ing,** ***vt., vi.***

sce·nar·i·o (sə ner'ē ō'; -när'-) ***n.***, *pl.* **-os'** ⟦see fol.⟧ **1** *a)* an outline of a play, etc. *b)* the script of a film **2** an outline for any planned series of events, real or imagined —**sce·nar'ist** ***n.***

scene (sēn) ***n.*** ⟦< Gr *skēnē*, stage⟧ **1** the place where an event occurs **2** the setting of a play, story, etc. **3** a division of a play, usually part of an act **4** a unit of action in a play, film, etc. **5** SCENERY (sense 1) **6** a display of

THESAURUS

scalpel ***n.*** dissecting instrument, surgical tool, blade; see KNIFE.

scamper ***v.*** hasten, scurry, hightail*; see HURRY 1, RUN 2.

scan ***v.*** browse, thumb through, consider; see LOOK 2.

scandal ***n.*** shame, disgrace, infamy, discredit, slander, disrepute, detraction, defamation, opprobrium, reproach, aspersion, backbiting, gossip, eavesdropping, rumor, hearsay.—*Ant.* PRAISE, adulation, flattery.

scandalize ***v.*** detract, defame, backbite; see SLANDER.

scandalous ***a.*** infamous, disreputable, ignominious; see SHAMEFUL 2.

scanty ***a.*** scarce, few, pinched, meager, little, small, bare, ragged, insufficient, inadequate, slender, narrow, thin, scrimp, scrimpy, tiny, wee, sparse, diminutive, short, stingy.—*Ant.* MUCH, large, many.

scar ***n.*** cicatrix, cicatrice, mark, blemish, discoloration, disfigurement, defect, flaw, hurt, wound, injury.

scar ***v.*** cut, disfigure, slash; see HURT 1.

scarce ***a.*** limited, infrequent, not plentiful; see RARE 2, UNCOMMON. —**make oneself scarce*** go, depart, run off; see LEAVE 1.

scarcely ***a.*** barely, only just, scantily; see HARDLY.

scarcity ***n.*** deficiency, inadequacy, insufficiency; see LACK 2, POVERTY 1.

scare ***n.*** fright, terror, alarm; see FEAR.

scare ***v.*** panic, terrify, alarm; see FRIGHTEN. —**scare off** (or **away**) drive off, drive out, drive away, get rid of, dispose of, disperse, scatter; see also FRIGHTEN.

scared ***a.*** startled, frightened, fearful; see AFRAID.

scarf ***n.*** throw, sash, muffler, shawl, comforter, ascot, stole, wrap; see also CLOTHES.

scarlet ***a.*** cardinal, royal red, vermilion; see RED.

scat[1]* ***v.*** be off, begone, get out of my way, get out from under my feet, out with you, be off with you, get out of my sight, scoot*, get out, beat it*, shoo*, scram*, get going.

scatter ***v.*** **1** [To become separated] run apart, run away, go one's own way, diverge, disperse, disband, migrate, spread widely, go in different directions, blow off, go in many directions, be strewn to the four winds.—*Ant.* ASSEMBLE, convene, congregate. **2** [To cause to separate] dispel, dissipate, diffuse, strew, divide, disband, shed, distribute, disseminate, separate, disunite, sunder, scatter to the wind, sever, put asunder.—*Ant.* UNITE, join, mix. **3** [To waste] expend, dissipate, fritter away; see SPEND, WASTE 2.

scattered ***a.*** spread, strewed, rambling, sowed, sown, sprinkled, spread abroad, separated, disseminated, dispersed, strung out, distributed, widespread, diffuse, all over the place, separate, shaken out.—*Ant.* GATHERED, condensed, concentrated.

scene ***n.*** spectacle, exhibition, display; see VIEW.

strong feeling *[to make a scene]* **7** [Inf.] the locale for a specified activity

sce·ner·y (sēn′ə rē) ***n.***, *pl.* **-ies 1** painted screens, backdrops, etc., used on the stage to represent places, as in a play, etc. **2** the features of a landscape

sce·nic (sē′nik) ***adj.*** **1** of stage scenery **2** *a)* of natural scenery *b)* having beautiful scenery

scent (sent) ***vt.*** ⟦ult. < L *sentire*, to feel⟧ **1** to smell **2** to get a hint of **3** to fill with an odor; perfume —***n.*** **1** an odor **2** the sense of smell **3** a perfume **4** an odor left by an animal, by which it is tracked —**scent′ed** ***adj.***

scep·ter (sep′tər) ***n.*** ⟦< Gr *skēptron*, staff⟧ a staff held by a ruler as a symbol of sovereignty: chiefly Brit. sp. **scep′tre**

scep·tic (skep′tik) ***n.***, ***adj.*** *chiefly Brit. sp. of* SKEPTIC —**scep′ti·cal** ***adj.*** —**scep′ti·cism′** ***n.***

sched·ule (ske′jo͞ol; *Brit & often Cdn* shej′o͞ol) ***n.*** ⟦< L *scheda*, a strip of papyrus⟧ **1** a list of details **2** a list of times of recurring events, projected operations, etc.; timetable **3** a timed plan for a project —***vt.*** **-uled**, **-ul·ing 1** to place in a schedule **2** to plan for a certain time

sche·mat·ic (skē mat′ik) ***adj.*** of or like a scheme, diagram, etc.

scheme (skēm) ***n.*** ⟦< Gr *schēma*, a form⟧ **1** *a)* a systematic program for attaining some end *b)* a secret plan; plot **2** an orderly combination of things on a definite plan **3** a diagram —***vt.***, ***vi.*** **schemed**, **schem′ing** to devise or plot —**schem′er** ***n.***

scher·zo (sker′tsō) ***n.***, *pl.* **-zos** or **-zi** (-tsē) ⟦It, a jest⟧ *Music* a lively composition, usually in 3/4 time, as the third movement of a symphony, etc.

schism (siz′əm, skiz′-) ***n.*** ⟦< Gr *schizein*, to cleave⟧ a split, as in a church, because of difference of opinion, doctrine, etc. —**schis·mat′ic** (-mat′ik) ***adj.***

schist (shist) ***n.*** ⟦< Gr *schistos*, easily cleft⟧ a crystalline rock easily split into layers

schiz·o·phre·ni·a (skit′sə frē′nē ə) ***n.*** ⟦< Gr *schizein*, cleave + *phrēn*, the mind⟧ a mental disorder characterized by separation between thought and emotions, by delusions, bizarre behavior, etc. —**schiz′oid** (-soid) or **schiz′o·phren′ic** (-ə fren′ik) ***adj.***, ***n.***

schle·miel (shlə mēl′) ***n.*** ⟦Yiddish⟧ [Slang] a bungling person who habitually fails or is easily victimized

schlep or **schlepp** (shlep) [Slang] ***vt.*** **schlepped**, **schlep′ping** ⟦via Yiddish < LowG *slepen*, to drag⟧ to carry, haul, etc. —***vi.*** to go or move with effort —***n.*** an ineffectual person

schlock (shläk) [Slang] ***n.*** ⟦< ? Ger *schlacke*, dregs⟧ anything cheap or inferior; trash —***adj.*** cheap; inferior: also **schlock′y**, **-i·er**, **-i·est**

schmaltz (shmälts, shmôlts) ***n.*** ⟦? via Yiddish < Ger *schmaltz*, rendered fat⟧ [Slang] highly sentimental music, literature, etc.

schnapps (shnäps) ***n.***, *pl.* **schnapps** ⟦Ger, a nip < Du *snaps*, a gulp⟧ a strong alcoholic liquor: also sp. **schnaps**

schnau·zer (shnou′zər) ***n.*** ⟦Ger < *schnauzen*, to snarl⟧ a sturdily built dog with a wiry coat and bushy eyebrows

schol·ar (skäl′ər) ***n.*** ⟦< L *schola*, a school⟧ **1** a learned person **2** a student or pupil —**schol′ar·ly** ***adj.***

schol′ar·ship′ ***n.*** **1** the quality of knowledge a student shows **2** the systematized knowledge of a scholar **3** a gift of money, etc. as by a foundation, to help a student

scho·las·tic (skə las′tik) ***adj.*** ⟦see fol.⟧ of schools, colleges, students, etc.; educational; academic

school[1] (sko͞ol) ***n.*** ⟦< Gr *scholē*, leisure⟧ **1** a place or institution, with its buildings, etc., for teaching and learning **2** all of its students and teachers **3** a regular session of teaching **4** formal education; schooling **5** a particular division of a university **6** a group following the same beliefs, methods, etc. —***vt.*** **1** to train; teach **2** to discipline or control —***adj.*** of a school or schools

school[2] (sko͞ol) ***n.*** ⟦Du, a crowd⟧ a group of fish, etc. swimming together

school board an elected or appointed group of people in charge of public or private schools

school′book′ ***n.*** a textbook

school′boy′ ***n.*** a boy attending school

school′girl′ ***n.*** a girl attending school

school′house′ ***n.*** a building used as a school

school′ing ***n.*** training or education; esp., formal instruction at school

school′marm′ (-märm′, -mäm′) ***n.*** **1** [Old-fashioned] a woman schoolteacher **2** [Inf.] any person who tends to be prudish, pedantic, etc.

school′mas′ter ***n.*** [Old-fashioned] a man who teaches in a school

school′mate′ ***n.*** a companion or acquaintance at school

school′mis′tress ***n.*** [Old-fashioned] a woman who teaches in a school

school′room′ ***n.*** a room in which pupils are taught, as in a school

school′teach′er ***n.*** one who teaches in a school

school′work′ ***n.*** lessons worked on in classes or done as homework

school′yard′ ***n.*** the ground around a school, used as a playground, etc.

school year the part of a year when school is in session, usually September to June

schoon·er (sko͞on′ər) ***n.*** ⟦< ?⟧ **1** a ship with two or more masts, rigged fore and aft **2** a large beer glass

Schu·bert (sho͞o′bərt), **Franz** (fränts) 1797-1828; Austrian composer

schuss (sho͝os) ***n.*** ⟦Ger, lit., shot⟧ a straight run down a hill in skiing —***vi.*** to do a schuss

schwa (shwä) ***n.*** ⟦Ger < Heb *sheva*⟧ **1** the neutral vowel sound of most unstressed syllables in English, as of *e* in *agent* **2** the symbol (ə) for this

sci·at·ic (sī at′ik) ***adj.*** ⟦see fol.⟧ of or in the hip or its nerves

sci·at·i·ca (sī at′i kə) ***n.*** ⟦< Gr *ischion*, the hip⟧ any painful condition in the hip or thigh; esp., neuritis of the long nerve (**sciatic nerve**) passing down the back of the thigh

sci·ence (sī′əns) ***n.*** ⟦< L *scire*, know⟧ **1** systematized knowledge derived from observation, study, etc. **2** a branch of knowledge, esp. one that systematizes facts,

THESAURUS

scenery ***n.*** landscape, prospect, spectacle; see VIEW.

scenic ***a.*** beautiful, spectacular, dramatic; see BEAUTIFUL.

scent ***n.*** odor, fragrance, redolence; see PERFUME, SMELL 1, 2.

schedule ***n.*** timetable, table of arrivals and departures, agenda, order of business, calendar, outline, program, plan, flowchart, game plan, catalogue, register; see also PLAN 2, PROGRAM 2. —**on schedule** on time, not delayed, prompt; see EARLY 2, PUNCTUAL.

schedule ***v.*** record, register, catalogue; see LIST 1.

scheduled ***a.*** listed, announced, arranged; see PLANNED, PROPOSED.

scheme ***n.*** project, course of action, purpose; see PLAN 2, SYSTEM.

scheme ***v.*** intrigue, contrive, plot; see PLAN 1.

scholar ***n.*** learned person, academic, authority, expert, professor, graduate student, fellow, scholar-in-residence, visiting scholar; see also STUDENT.

scholarly ***a.*** erudite, cultured, studious; see EDUCATED, LEARNED 1.

scholarship ***n.*** research, learning, pedantry; see KNOWLEDGE 1.

scholastic ***a.*** academic, literary, lettered; see LEARNED 1.

school[1] ***n.*** **1** [An institution of learning] *Varieties of schools include the following:* nursery school, elementary school, high school, secondary school, parochial school, preparatory school, private school, prep school, public school, boarding school, military school, academy, seminary, normal school, conservatory, trade school, technical school, graduate school, professional school, divinity school, art school, law school, college of arts and science, junior high school, middle school, senior high school, community college, junior college; see also COLLEGE, UNIVERSITY. **2** [Persons or products associated by common intellectual or artistic theories] party, following, circle; see FOLLOWING. **3** [A building housing a school] schoolhouse, establishment, institution; see BUILDING. —**attend school** undergo schooling, learn, go to school, get one's education, receive instruction, matriculate, study, take courses, be a student, enroll; see also LEARN, STUDY.

schoolbook ***n.*** primer, textbook, assigned reading; see BOOK.

schooling ***n.*** teaching, nurture, discipline; see EDUCATION 1.

schoolmate ***n.*** roommate, comrade, classmate; see FRIEND.

schoolteacher ***n.*** educator, lecturer, instructor; see TEACHER.

school year ***n.*** academic year, terms, semesters; see YEAR.

science ***n.*** **1** [An organized body of knowledge] department of learning, branch of knowledge, system of knowledge, body of fact; see also CHEMISTRY, MATHEMATICS, MEDICINE 3, SOCIAL SCIENCE, ZOOLOGY for commonly recognized sciences. **2** [A highly developed skill] craftsmanship, art, deftness; see ABILITY.

principles, and methods, as NATURAL SCIENCE **3** skill or technique

science fiction highly imaginative fiction typically involving some actual or projected scientific phenomenon

sci·en·tif·ic (sī'ən tif'ik) ***adj.*** **1** of or dealing with science **2** based on, or using, the principles and methods of science; systematic and exact —**sci'en·tif'i·cal·ly** ***adv.***

sci'en·tist ***n.*** a specialist in science, as in biology, chemistry, or physics

sci-fi (sī'fī') ***n.*** [Inf.] *short for* SCIENCE FICTION

scim·i·tar (sim'ə tər) ***n.*** ⟦It *scimitarra*⟧ a short, curved sword used chiefly by Turks and Arabs

scin·til·la (sin til'ə) ***n.*** ⟦L⟧ **1** a spark **2** a particle; the least trace: figurative only

scin·til·late (sint''l āt') ***vi.*** **-lat'ed**, **-lat'ing** ⟦< L *scintilla*, a spark⟧ **1** to sparkle or twinkle **2** to be brilliant and witty —**scin'til·la'tion** ***n.***

sci·on (sī'ən) ***n.*** ⟦< OFr *cion*⟧ **1** a shoot or bud of a plant, esp. one for grafting **2** a descendant; heir

scis·sor (siz'ər) ***vt.*** ⟦< fol.⟧ to cut, cut off, or cut out with scissors —***n.*** SCISSORS, esp. in adjectival use

scis·sors (siz'ərz) ***n.*** ⟦< LL *cisorium*, cutting tool⟧ [*also with pl. v.*] a cutting instrument with two opposing blades pivoted together so that they can work against each other as the instrument is closed on paper, etc.: also called **pair of scissors**

scle·ra (sklir'ə) ***n.***, *pl.* **-ras** or **-rae** (-ē) ⟦< Gr *sklēros*, hard⟧ the tough, white membrane covering all of the eyeball except the area covered by the cornea

scle·ro·sis (skli rō'sis) ***n.***, *pl.* **-ses** (-sēz') ⟦< Gr *sklēros*, hard⟧ an abnormal hardening of body tissues —**scle·rot'ic** (-rät'ik) ***adj.***

scoff (skäf, skôf) ***n.*** an expression of scorn or derision —***vt.***, ***vi.*** to mock or jeer (at) —**scoff'er** ***n.***

scoff'law' ***n.*** [Inf.] one who flouts traffic laws, liquor laws, etc.

scold (skōld) ***n.*** ⟦< ON *skald*, poet (prob. of satirical verses)⟧ a person, esp. a woman, who habitually uses abusive language —***vt.***, ***vi.*** to find fault (with) angrily; to rebuke —**scold'ing** ***adj.***, ***n.***

sco·li·o·sis (skō'lē ō'sis) ***n.*** ⟦< Gr *skolios*, crooked⟧ lateral curvature of the spine

sconce (skäns) ***n.*** ⟦ult. < L *abscondere*, to hide⟧ a wall bracket for candles

scone (skōn, skän) ***n.*** ⟦Scot⟧ a light cake resembling a biscuit and often quadrant-shaped

scooch (sko͞och) ***vi.*** **1** [Inf.] to scrunch (*down, through*, etc.) **2** to slide jerkily

scoop (sko͞op) ***n.*** ⟦< MDu *schope*, bailing vessel, *schoppe*, a shovel⟧ **1** any of various small, shovel-like utensils, as for taking up flour or ice cream **2** the deep shovel of a dredge, etc. **3** the act or motion of scooping **4** the amount scooped up at one time **5** [Inf.] *a*) the publication or broadcast of a news item before a competitor *b*) such a news item —***vt.*** **1** to take up or out with or as with a scoop **2** to hollow (*out*) **3** [Inf.] to publish news before (a competitor)

scoot (sko͞ot) ***vi.***, ***vt.*** ⟦prob. < ON *skjōta*, to shoot⟧ [Inf.] to go or move quickly; hurry (off)

scootch (sko͞och) ***vi.*** [Inf.] *alt. sp. of* SCOOCH

scoot'er ***n.*** ⟦< SCOOT⟧ **1** a child's two-wheeled vehicle moved by pushing one foot against the ground **2** a similar, motor-driven vehicle with a seat: in full **motor scooter**

scope (skōp) ***n.*** ⟦< Gr *skopos*, watcher⟧ **1** the extent of the mind's grasp **2** the range or extent of action, inclusion, inquiry, etc. **3** room or opportunity for freedom of action or thought

-scope (skōp) ⟦< Gr *skopein*, see⟧ *combining form* an instrument, etc. for seeing or observing *[telescope, kaleidoscope]*

scorch (skôrch) ***vt.*** ⟦< ? Scand⟧ **1** to burn slightly or superficially **2** to parch by intense heat —***vi.*** to become scorched —***n.*** a superficial burn

score (skôr) ***n.*** ⟦< ON *skor*⟧ **1** a scratch, mark, notch, incised line, etc. **2** an account or debt **3** a grievance one seeks to settle **4** a reason or motive **5** the number of points made, as in a game **6** a grade, as on a test **7** *a*) twenty people or things *b*) [*pl.*] very many **8** a copy of a musical composition showing all parts for the instruments or voices **9** [Inf.] the basic facts *[to know the score]* —***vt.*** **scored**, **scor'ing** **1** to mark with notches, cuts, lines, etc. **2** *a*) to make (runs, points, etc.) in a game *b*) to record the score of **3** to achieve *[score a success]* **4** to evaluate, as in testing **5** *Music* to arrange in a score —***vi.*** **1** to make points, as in a game **2** to keep the score of a game **3** to gain an advantage, a success, etc. —**scor'er** ***n.***

score'board' ***n.*** a large board for posting scores, etc., as in a stadium

score'less ***adj.*** with no points scored

scorn (skôrn) ***n.*** ⟦< OFr *escharnir*, to scorn⟧ extreme, often indignant, contempt —***vt.*** **1** to regard with scorn **2** to refuse or reject with scorn —**scorn'ful** ***adj.*** —**scorn'ful·ly** ***adv.***

Scor·pi·o (skôr'pē ō') ***n.*** ⟦L, scorpion⟧ the eighth sign of the zodiac

scor'pi·on (-ən) ***n.*** ⟦< Gr *skorpios*⟧ an arachnid with a long tail ending in a poisonous sting

Scot[1] (skät) ***n.*** a person born or living in Scotland

Scot[2] *abbrev.* **1** Scotland **2** Scottish

scotch (skäch) ***vt.*** ⟦prob. < OFr *coche*, a nick⟧ **1** to maim **2** to put an end to; stifle *[to scotch a rumor]*

Scotch (skäch) ***adj.*** of Scotland: cf. SCOTTISH —***n.*** **1** SCOTTISH **2** [*often* **s-**] whiskey distilled in Scotland from malted barley: in full **Scotch whisky**

Scotch'man (-mən) ***n.***, *pl.* **-men** (-mən) *var. of* SCOTSMAN

Scotch tape ⟦< *Scotch*, a trademark⟧ a thin, transparent adhesive tape

scot-free (skät'frē') ***adv.***, ***adj.*** ⟦< earlier *scot*, a tax⟧ without being punished or hurt

Scot·land (skät'lənd) division of the United Kingdom: the N half of Great Britain: 29,794 sq. mi.; pop. 4,962,000

Scotland Yard the London police headquarters, esp. its detective bureau

Scots (skäts) ***adj.***, ***n.*** SCOTTISH

Scots'man (-mən) ***n.***, *pl.* **-men** (-mən) a person born or living in Scotland, esp. a man: *Scotsman* or *Scot* is pre-

THESAURUS

scientific ***a.*** **1** [Objectively accurate] precise, exact, clear; see ACCURATE 2, OBJECTIVE 1. **2** [Concerning science] experimental, deductive, methodically sound; see LOGICAL.

scientist ***n.*** expert, specialist, investigator, laboratory technician, natural philosopher, student of natural history, explorer, research worker, research assistant, learned person, serious student, PhD, scientific thinker. *Scientists include the following:* anatomist, astronomer, botanist, biologist, chemist, biochemist, geneticist, geologist, mineralogist, metallurgist, geographer, mathematician, physicist, psychiatrist, psychologist, astrophysicist, ecologist, biophysicist, bacteriologist, marine biologist, oceanographer, pharmacist, chemical engineer, agronomist, entomologist, ornithologist, endocrinologist, radiologist, graphologist, geophysicist, neurologist, zoologist, paleontologist, anthropologist, ethnologist, archaeologist, sociologist, linguist; see also DOCTOR.

scissors ***n.*** shears, pair of scissors, blades, hair scissors, paper scissors, garden shears, cutting instrument.

scoff ***v.*** mock, deride, jeer, ridicule, put down, be dismissive, show contempt, scorn, tut-tut, dis*; see also RIDICULE.

scold ***v.*** admonish, chide, chew out*, bawl out*, get after, lay down the law*, jump on*, jump all over*, rebuke, censure, reprove, upbraid, reprimand, taunt, cavil, criticize, denounce, disparage, recriminate, rate, revile, rail, abuse, vilify, find fault with, nag, lecture, call on the carpet*, rake over the coals*, give one a talking to, chasten, preach, tell off*, keep after, light into*, put down; see also PUNISH.—*Ant.* PRAISE, commend, extol.

scoop ***v.*** ladle, shovel, bail; see DIP 2.

scoot ***v.*** dart, speed, rush; see HASTEN 2, HURRY 1.

scope ***n.*** reach, range, field; see EXTENT.

scorch ***v.*** roast, parch, shrivel; see BURN.

scorching ***a.*** fiery, searing, sweltering; see BURNING, HOT 1.

score ***n.*** **1** [A tally] reckoning, record, average, rate, account, count, number, summation, aggregate, sum, addition, summary, amount, final tally, final account; see also NUMBER, WHOLE. **2** [Written music] transcription, arrangement, orchestration; see MUSIC 1, COMPOSITION. —**know the score*** grasp, be aware of, comprehend; see KNOW 1, UNDERSTAND 1.

score ***v.*** **1** [To make a single score] make a goal, make a point, rack up*, chalk up, total, calculate, reckon, tally, enumerate, count, add. **2** [To compose a musical accompaniment] orchestrate, arrange, adapt; see COMPOSE 2.

scorn ***v.*** hold in contempt, despise, disdain; see HATE.

scornful ***a.*** contemptuous, disdainful, haughty; see EGOTISTIC.

ferred to *Scotchman* in Scotland —**Scots′wom′an**, *pl.* **-wom′en**, ***fem.n.***

Scot·tie or **Scot·ty** (skät′ē) ***n.***, *pl.* **-ties** SCOTTISH TERRIER

Scot·tish (skät′ish) ***adj.*** of Scotland or its people, variety of English, etc.: *Scottish* is formal usage, but with some words, *Scotch* is used (e.g., tweed, whisky), with others, *Scots* (e.g., law) —***n.*** the variety of English spoken in Scotland —**the Scottish** the Scottish people

Scottish terrier a short-legged terrier with a wiry coat

scoun·drel (skoun′drəl) ***n.*** ⟦prob. ult. < L *ab(s)-*, from + *condere*, to hide⟧ a mean, immoral, or wicked person

scour[1] (skour) ***vt.***, ***vi.*** ⟦< ? L *ex-*, intens. + *cura*, care⟧ **1** to clean by rubbing hard, as with abrasives **2** to clean or clear out as by a flow of water

scour[2] (skour) ***vt.*** ⟦< L *ex-*, out + *currere*, to run⟧ to pass over quickly, or range over, as in searching *[to scour a library for a book]*

scourge (skurj) ***n.*** ⟦< L *ex*, off + *corrigia*, a whip⟧ **1** a whip **2** any cause of serious affliction —***vt.*** **scourged**, **scourg′ing** **1** to whip or flog **2** to punish or afflict severely

scout (skout) ***n.*** ⟦< L *auscultare*, to listen⟧ **1** a soldier, plane, etc. sent to spy out the enemy's strength, actions, etc. **2** a person sent out to survey a competitor, find new talent, etc. **3** [**S-**] a Boy Scout or Girl Scout —***vt.***, ***vi.*** **1** to reconnoiter **2** to go in search of (something)

scout′ing ***n.*** **1** the act of one who scouts **2** [*often* **S-**] the activities of the Boy Scouts or Girl Scouts

scout′mas′ter ***n.*** the adult leader of a troop of Boy Scouts

scow (skou) ***n.*** ⟦Du *schouw*⟧ a large, flat-bottomed boat used for carrying loads, often towed by a tugboat

scowl (skoul) ***vi.*** ⟦prob. < Scand⟧ to look angry, sullen, etc., as by contracting the eyebrows —***n.*** a scowling look —**scowl′er** ***n.***

scrab·ble (skrab′əl) ***vi.*** **-bled**, **-bling** ⟦< Du *schrabben*, to scrape⟧ **1** to scratch, scrape, etc. as though looking for something **2** to struggle

scrag·gly (skrag′lē) ***adj.*** **-gli·er**, **-gli·est** ⟦prob. < ON⟧ uneven, ragged, etc. in growth or form

scram (skram) ***vi.*** **scrammed**, **scram′ming** ⟦< fol.⟧ [Slang] to get out, esp. in a hurry

scram·ble (skram′bəl) ***vi.*** **-bled**, **-bling** ⟦< ?⟧ **1** to climb, crawl, etc. hurriedly **2** to scuffle or struggle for something —***vt.*** **1** to mix haphazardly **2** to stir and cook (slightly beaten eggs) **3** to make (transmitted signals) unintelligible without special receiving equipment —***n.*** **1** a hard climb or advance **2** a disorderly struggle, as for something prized

scrap[1] (skrap) ***n.*** ⟦ult. < ON *skrapa*, to scrape⟧ **1** a small piece; fragment **2** discarded material **3** [*pl.*] bits of food —***adj.*** **1** in the form of pieces, leftovers, etc. **2** used and discarded —***vt.*** **scrapped**, **scrap′ping** **1** to make into scrap **2** to discard; junk —**scrap′per** ***n.***

scrap[2] (skrap) ***n.***, ***vi.*** **scrapped**, **scrap′ping** ⟦< ? SCRAPE⟧ [Inf.] fight or quarrel —**scrap′per** ***n.*** —**scrap′py**, **-pi·er**, **-pi·est**, ***adv.***

scrap′book′ ***n.*** a book in which to mount clippings, pictures, etc.

scrape (skrāp) ***vt.*** **scraped**, **scrap′ing** ⟦< ON *skrapa*⟧ **1** to make smooth or clean by rubbing with a tool or abrasive **2** to remove in this way: with *off, out*, etc. **3** to scratch or abrade **4** to gather slowly and with difficulty *[scrape up some cash]* —***vi.*** **1** to rub against something harshly; grate **2** to manage to get by: with *through, along, by* —***n.*** **1** a scraping **2** a scraped place **3** a grating sound **4** a predicament —**scrap′er** ***n.***

scrap′heap′ (-hēp′) ***n.*** a pile of discarded material, as of scrap iron —**throw** (or **toss, cast**, etc.) **on the scrapheap** to get rid of as useless

scratch (skrach) ***vt.*** ⟦ME *scracchen*⟧ **1** to mark, break, or cut the surface of slightly **2** to tear or dig with the nails or claws **3** to scrape lightly to relieve itching **4** to scrape with a grating noise **5** to write hurriedly or carelessly **6** to strike out (writing, etc.) **7** *Sports* to withdraw (a contestant, etc.) —***vi.*** **1** to use nails or claws in digging, wounding, etc. **2** to scrape —***n.*** **1** a scratching **2** a mark, tear, etc. made by scratching **3** a grating or scraping sound —***adj.*** used for hasty notes, figuring etc. *[scratch paper]* —**from scratch** from nothing; without resources, etc. —**up to scratch** [Inf.] up to standard —**scratch′y**, **-i·er**, **-i·est**, ***adj.*** —**scratch′i·ly** ***adv.*** —**scratch′i·ness** ***n.***

scratch′pad′ ***n.*** a pad of paper for jotting notes

scrawl (skrôl) ***vt.***, ***vi.*** ⟦< ?⟧ to write or draw hastily, carelessly, etc. —***n.*** sprawling, often illegible handwriting

scraw·ny (skrô′nē) ***adj.*** **-ni·er**, **-ni·est** ⟦prob. < Scand⟧ very thin; skinny —**scraw′ni·ness** ***n.***

scream (skrēm) ***vi.*** ⟦ME *screamen*⟧ **1** to utter a shrill, piercing cry in fright, pain, etc. **2** to shout, laugh, etc. wildly —***vt.*** to utter with or as with a scream —***n.*** **1** a sharp, piercing cry or sound **2** [Inf.] a very funny person or thing

screech (skrēch) ***vi.***, ***vt.*** ⟦< ON *skraekja*⟧ to utter (with) a shrill, high-pitched sound —***n.*** such a sound —**screech′y**, **-i·er**, **-i·est**, ***adj.***

screen (skrēn) ***n.*** ⟦< OFr *escren*⟧ **1** a partition, curtain, etc. used to separate, conceal, etc. **2** anything that shields, conceals, etc. **3** a coarse mesh of wire, etc., used as a sieve **4** a frame covered with a mesh *[a window screen]* **5** *a)* a surface on which films, slides, etc. are projected *b)* the film industry *c)* the surface of a TV set, computer, etc. on which images are formed —***vt.*** **1** to conceal or protect, as with a screen **2** to sift through a screen **3** to separate according to skills, etc. **4** to show (a film, etc.) to critics, the public, etc.

screen′play′ ***n.*** the script from which a film is produced

screen′writ′er ***n.*** the writer of a script for a film —**screen′writ′ing** ***n.***

screw (skro͞o) ***n.*** ⟦< Fr *escroue*, hole in which the screw turns⟧ **1** a cylindrical or conical piece of metal threaded in an advancing spiral, for fastening things: it penetrates when turned **2** any spiral thing like this **3** anything operating or threaded like a screw —***vt.*** **1** to twist; turn **2** to fasten, tighten, etc. as with a screw **3** to contort —***vi.*** **1** to go together or come apart by being turned like a screw *[the lid screws on]* **2** to twist or turn —**put the screws on** (or **to**) [Inf.] to subject to great pressure; coerce —**screw up** [Inf.] to bungle

THESAURUS

scoundrel ***n.*** rogue, scamp, villain; see RASCAL.

scour[1] ***v.*** scrub, cleanse, rub; see CLEAN, WASH 1, 2.

scout ***n.*** **1** [One who gathers information] explorer, pioneer, outpost, runner, advance guard, precursor, patrol, reconnoiterer. **2** [A Boy Scout or Girl Scout] *Degrees of scouts include the following:* Cub, Tenderfoot, Second Class, First Class, Star, Life, Eagle, Explorer, Queen's (British), bronze palm, gold palm, silver palm; Brownie, Junior, Cadette, Senior.

scowl ***v.*** glower, disapprove, grimace; see FROWN.

scramble ***v.*** **1** [To mix] combine, blend, interfuse; see MIX 1. **2** [To climb hastily] clamber, push, struggle; see CLIMB.

scrap[1,2] ***n.*** **1** [Junk metal] waste material, chips, cuttings; see TRASH 1. **2** [A bit] fragment, particle, portion; see BIT 1, PIECE 1. **3** [*A fight] quarrel, brawl, squabble; see FIGHT 1.

scrap[1,2] ***v.*** **1** [To discard] reject, forsake, dismiss; see ABANDON 1, DISCARD. **2** [*To fight] wrangle, battle, squabble; see FIGHT, QUARREL.

scrapbook ***n.*** portfolio, memorabilia, notebook; see ALBUM, COLLECTION.

scrape ***v.*** abrade, scour, rasp; see RUB 1.

scraper ***n.*** grater, rasp, abrasive; see TOOL 1.

scratch ***n.*** hurt, cut, mark; see INJURY, SCAR. —**from scratch** from the beginning, without preparation, from nothing; see ALONE, ORIGINAL 1.

scratch ***v.*** scrape, scarify, prick; see DAMAGE, HURT 1.

scratching ***a.*** grating, abrasive, rasping; see ROUGH 1.

scrawl ***v.*** scribble, scratch, doodle; see WRITE 2.

scrawled ***a.*** scribbled, scratched, inscribed; see WRITTEN 2.

scrawny ***a.*** lanky, gaunt, lean; see THIN 2.

scream ***n.*** screech, outcry, shriek; see CRY 1, YELL.

scream ***v.*** shriek, screech, squeal; see CRY 2, YELL.

screaming ***a.*** shrieking, screeching, squealing; see YELLING.

screen ***n.*** **1** [A concealment] cloak, cover, covering, curtain, shield, envelope, veil, mask, shade. **2** [A protection] shelter, guard, security; see COVER 1, PROTECTION 2.

screen ***v.*** **1** [To hide] veil, conceal, mask; see HIDE 1. **2** [To choose] select, eliminate, sift; see CHOOSE.

screw ***n.*** spiral, worm, bolt, pin; see also FASTENER. *Screws include the following:* jack, lead, double, drive, lag, right-handed, left-handed, metric, regulating, set, winged, thumb, spiral, triple, wood, machine, Phillips (trademark).

screw* ***v.*** cheat, swindle, beat; see DEFEAT, HURT 2, TRICK. —**screw up*** bungle, foul up*, mishandle; see BOTCH.

screw'ball' *n.* [Slang] an erratic, irrational or unconventional person
screw'driv'er *n.* a tool used for turning screws
screw'worm' *n.* the larva of an American blowfly that infests wounds, and the nostrils, navel, etc. of animals
screw·y (skro͞o'ē) *adj.* **-i·er, -i·est** [Slang] **1** crazy **2** peculiar, eccentric
scrib·ble (skrib'əl) *vt., vi.* **-bled, -bling** ⟦< L *scribere*, write⟧ **1** to write carelessly, hastily, etc. **2** to make meaningless or illegible marks (on) —*n.* scribbled writing —**scrib'bler** *n.*
scribe (skrīb) *n.* ⟦< L *scribere*, write⟧ **1** a person who copied manuscripts before the invention of printing **2** a writer
scrim (skrim) *n.* ⟦< ?⟧ **1** a light, sheer, loosely woven cotton or linen cloth **2** such a cloth used as a stage backdrop or semitransparent curtain
scrim·mage (skrim'ij) *n.* ⟦< SKIRMISH⟧ **1** *Football* play that follows the snap from center **2** a practice game —*vi.* **-maged, -mag·ing** to take part in a scrimmage
scrimp (skrimp) *vt., vi.* ⟦< ? Scand⟧ to be sparing or frugal (with)
scrim'shaw' (-shô') *n.* an intricate carving of bone, ivory, etc. done esp. by sailors
scrip (skrip) *n.* ⟦< fol.⟧ a certificate of a right to receive something, as money or goods
script (skript) *n.* ⟦< L *scribere*, to write⟧ **1** handwriting **2** a copy of the text of a play, film etc.
scrip·ture (skrip'chər) *n.* ⟦see prec.⟧ **1** any sacred writing **2** [**S-**] [*often pl.*] the sacred writings of the Jews; Old Testament **3** [**S-**] [*often pl.*] the Christian Bible; Old and New Testaments —**scrip'tur·al** *adj.*
script'writ'er *n.* one who writes scripts for films, TV, etc.
scrod (skräd) *n.* ⟦prob. < MDu *schrode*, piece cut off⟧ a young codfish or haddock, esp. one prepared for cooking
scrof·u·la (skräf'yə lə) *n.* ⟦< L *scrofa*, a sow⟧ tuberculosis of the lymphatic glands, esp. of the neck —**scrof'u·lous** *adj.*
scroll (skrōl) *n.* ⟦< ME *scrowle*⟧ **1** a roll of parchment, paper, etc., usually with writing on it **2** an ornamental design in coiled or spiral form —*vi.* to move lines of text, etc. vertically on a video screen
scro·tum (skrōt'əm) *n., pl.* **-ta** (-ə) or **-tums** ⟦L⟧ the pouch of skin holding the testicles
scrounge (skrounj) *vt.* **scrounged, scroung'ing** ⟦< ?⟧ [Inf.] **1** to get by begging or sponging; mooch **2** to pilfer —*vi.* [Inf.] to seek (*around*) for something —**scroung'er** *n.*
scroung'y *adj.* **-i·er, -i·est** [Slang] shabby, unkempt, dirty, etc. —**scroung'i·ness** *n.*
scrub[1] (skrub) *n.* ⟦ME, var. of *shrubbe*, shrub⟧ **1** a thick growth of stunted trees or bushes **2** any person or thing smaller than the usual, or inferior **3** *Sports* a substitute player —*adj.* small, stunted, inferior, etc. —**scrub'by, -bi·er, -bi·est,** *adj.*
scrub[2] (skrub) *vt., vi.* **scrubbed, scrub'bing** ⟦prob. < Scand⟧ **1** to clean or wash by rubbing hard **2** to rub hard —*n.* a scrubbing —**scrub'ber** *n.*
scrub'wom'an *n., pl.* **-wom'en** CHARWOMAN
scruff (skruf) *n.* ⟦< ON *skrufr*, a tuft of hair⟧ the nape of the neck
scruff·y (skruf'ē) *adj.* **-i·er, -i·est** ⟦< SCURF + -Y[2]⟧ shabby; unkempt
scrump·tious (skrump'shəs) *adj.* ⟦< SUMPTUOUS⟧ [Inf.] very pleasing, etc., esp. to the taste
scrunch (skrunch) *vt., vi.* ⟦< CRUNCH⟧ **1** to crunch, crush, etc. **2** to huddle, squeeze, etc. —*n.* a crunching or crumpling sound
scru·ple (skro͞o'pəl) *n.* ⟦< L *scrupulus*, small stone⟧ **1** a very small quantity **2** doubt arising from difficulty in deciding what is right —*vt., vi.* **-pled, -pling** to hesitate (at) from doubt
scru'pu·lous (-pyə ləs) *adj.* **1** having or showing scruples; conscientiously honest **2** careful of details; precise —**scru'pu·los'i·ty** (-läs'ət ē), *pl.* **-ties,** *n.* —**scru'pu·lous·ly** *adv.*
scru·ti·nize (skro͞ot''n īz') *vt.* **-nized', -niz'ing** to examine closely
scru·ti·ny (skro͞ot''n ē) *n., pl.* **-nies** ⟦< L *scrutari*, examine⟧ **1** a close examination or watch **2** a lengthy, searching look
scu·ba (sko͞o'bə) *n.* ⟦*s*(*elf-*)*c*(*ontained*) *u*(*nderwater*) *b*(*reathing*) *a*(*pparatus*)⟧ a diver's equipment with compressed-air tanks for breathing underwater
scud (skud) *vi.* **scud'ded, scud'ding** ⟦prob. < ON⟧ to move swiftly —*n.* a scudding
scuff (skuf) *vt., vi.* ⟦prob. < ON *skufa*, to shove⟧ **1** to wear or get a rough place on the surface (of) **2** to drag (the feet) —*n.* **1** a worn or rough spot **2** a flat-heeled house slipper with no back upper part
scuf·fle (skuf'əl) *vi.* **-fled, -fling** ⟦< prec.⟧ **1** to struggle or fight in rough confusion **2** to drag the feet —*n.* **1** a confused fight **2** a shuffling of feet
scull (skul) *n.* ⟦ME *skulle*⟧ **1** an oar worked from side to side over the stern of a boat **2** a light rowboat for racing —*vt., vi.* to propel with a scull
scul·ler·y (skul'ər ē) *n., pl.* **-ies** ⟦< L *scutella*, tray⟧ [Now Rare] a room near the kitchen, where pots, pans, etc. are cleaned and stored
scul·lion (skul'yən) *n.* ⟦ult. < L *scopa*, a broom⟧ [Archaic] a servant doing the rough kitchen work
sculpt (skulpt) *vt., vi.* SCULPTURE
sculp·tor (skulp'tər) *n.* an artist who creates works of sculpture
sculp·ture (skulp'chər) *n.* ⟦< L *sculpere*, to carve⟧ **1** the art of shaping stone, clay, wood, metal, etc. into statues, figures, etc. **2** a work or works of sculpture —*vt., vi.* **-tured, -tur·ing** **1** to cut, carve, chisel, etc. (statues, figures, etc.) **2** to make or form like sculpture —**sculp'tur·al** *adj.*
scum (skum) *n.* ⟦< MDu *schum*⟧ **1** a thin layer of impurities on the top of a liquid **2** refuse **3** [Inf.] a despicable person or persons —*vi.* to become covered with scum —**scum'my, -mi·er, -mi·est,** *adj.*
scup·per (skup'ər) *n.* ⟦< OFr *escopir*, to spit⟧ an opening in a ship's side to allow water to run off the deck
scurf (skurf) *n.* ⟦< ON⟧ **1** little, dry scales shed by the skin, as dandruff **2** any scaly coating —**scurf'y, -i·er, -i·est,** *adj.*
scur·ri·lous (skur'ə ləs) *adj.* ⟦< L *scurra*, buffoon⟧ vulgarly abusive —**scur·ril·i·ty** (skə ril'ə tē), *pl.* **-ties,** *n.* —**scur'ri·lous·ly** *adv.*
scur·ry (skur'ē) *vi.* **-ried, -ry·ing** ⟦< ?⟧ to run hastily; scamper —*n.* a scurrying
scur·vy (skur'vē) *adj.* **-vi·er, -vi·est** ⟦< SCURF⟧ low; mean —*n.* a disease resulting from a deficiency of vitamin C, characterized by weakness, anemia, spongy gums, etc. —**scur'vi·ly** *adv.*
scut·tle[1] (skut''l) *n.* ⟦< L *scutella*, tray⟧ a bucket for carrying coal
scut·tle[2] (skut''l) *vi.* **-tled, -tling** ⟦ME *scutlen*⟧ to scamper —*n.* a scamper
scut·tle[3] (skut''l) *n.* ⟦< Sp *escotilla*, an indentation⟧ an opening fitted with a cover, as in the hull or deck of a

THESAURUS

screwy* *a.* odd, crazy, nutty*; see INSANE, WRONG 2.
scribble *n.* scrawl, scratch, doodle; see HANDWRITING.
scribble *v.* scrawl, scratch, doodle; see WRITE 2.
scrimp *v.* limit, pinch, skimp; see ECONOMIZE.
script *n.* **1** [Handwriting] writing, characters, chirography; see HANDWRITING. **2** [Playbook] lines, text, dialogue, book, scenario.
scripture *n.* **1** [Truth] reality, verity, final word; see TRUTH. **2** [The Bible; *capital*] the Word, Holy Writ, the Book; see BIBLE.
scrub[1] *a.* second-rate, unimportant, mediocre; see POOR 2.
scrub[2] *v.* rub, cleanse, scour; see CLEAN, WASH 1, 2.
scrubbed *a.* cleaned, polished, immaculate; see CLEAN 1.
scruple *n.* compunction, qualm, uneasiness; see DOUBT.
scruples *n.* overconscientiousness, point of honor, scrupulousness; see ATTENTION, CARE 1.
scrupulous *a.* exact, punctilious, strict; see CAREFUL.
scrutinize *v.* view, study, stare; see EXAMINE, WATCH.
scrutiny *n.* analysis, investigation, inspection; see EXAMINATION 1.
scuffle *n.* struggle, shuffle, strife; see FIGHT 1.
sculptor *n.* artist, modeler, carver, stone carver, woodcarver, worker in bronze, worker in metal. *Major sculptors include the following:* Phidias, Praxiteles, Lorenzo Ghiberti, Donatello, Luca della Robbia, Michelangelo, Benvenuto Cellini, Gian Lorenzo Bernini, Auguste Rodin, Constantin Brancusi, Henry Moore, Alberto Giacometti, Claes Oldenburg, Louise Nevelson.
sculpture *n.* carving, modeling, carving in stone, modeling in clay, kinetic sculpture, mobile, op art, casting in bronze, woodcutting, stone carving, plastic art; see also ART, STATUE.
scum *n.* froth, film, impurities; see RESIDUE, TRASH 1.

ship —***vt.*** **-tled, -tling** to cut holes through the lower hull of (a ship, etc.) to sink it

scut·tle·butt (skut′'l but′) ***n.*** ⟦< *scuttled butt*, lidded cask⟧ [Inf.] rumor or gossip

scuz·zy (skuz′ē) ***adj.*** **-zi·er, -zi·est** ⟦< ?⟧ [Slang] dirty, shabby, etc.

scythe (sīth) ***n.*** ⟦OE *sithe*⟧ a tool with a long, single-edged blade on a long, curved handle, for cutting grass, grain, etc.

SD South Dakota

Se *Chem. symbol for* selenium

SE *abbrev.* **1** southeast **2** southeastern

sea (sē) ***n.*** ⟦OE *sæ*⟧ **1** the ocean **2** any of various smaller bodies of salt water *[*the Red *Sea]* **3** a large body of fresh water *[Sea* of Galilee*]* **4** the condition of the surface of the ocean *[*a calm *sea]* **5** a heavy wave **6** a very great amount *[*a *sea* of debt*]* —**at sea 1** on the open sea **2** uncertain; bewildered

sea anemone a sea polyp with a gelatinous body and petal-like tentacles

sea bass (bas) a saltwater food fish

sea′bed′ ***n.*** the mineral-rich ocean floor

sea′board′ ***n.*** ⟦SEA + BOARD⟧ land bordering on the sea —***adj.*** bordering on the sea

sea′coast′ ***n.*** land bordering on the sea

sea cow a large sea mammal with a cigar-shaped body and a blunt snout, as the manatee

sea′far′er (-fer′ər) ***n.*** a sea traveler; esp., a sailor —**sea′far′ing** ***adj.***, ***n.***

sea′floor′ ***n.*** the ground along the ocean bottom

sea′food′ ***n.*** food prepared from or consisting of saltwater fish or shellfish

sea′go′ing ***adj.*** **1** made for use on the open sea **2** SEAFARING

sea gull GULL[1]

sea horse a small semitropical fish with a head somewhat like that of a horse

seal[1] (sēl) ***n.*** ⟦< L *sigillum*⟧ **1** *a)* a design or initial impressed, often into wax, on a letter or document as a mark of authenticity *b)* a stamp or ring for making such an impression **2** a piece of paper, etc. bearing an impressed design recognized as official **3** something that seals or closes tightly **4** anything that guarantees; pledge **5** an ornamental paper stamp —***vt.*** **1** to mark with a seal, as to authenticate or certify **2** to close or shut tight as with a seal **3** to confirm the genuineness of (a promise, etc.) **4** to decide finally

seal[2] (sēl) ***n.*** ⟦OE *seolh*⟧ **1** a sea mammal with a torpedo-shaped body and four flippers **2** the fur of some seals —***vi.*** to hunt seals —**seal′er** ***n.***

seal·ant (sēl′ənt) ***n.*** a substance, as a wax or plastic, used for sealing

sea legs the ability to walk without loss of balance on board a ship at sea

sea level the mean level of the sea's surface: used in measuring heights

sea lion a seal of the N Pacific

seal′skin′ ***n.*** **1** the skin of the seal **2** a garment made of this

seam (sēm) ***n.*** ⟦OE⟧ **1** a line formed where two pieces of material are sewn together **2** a line that marks adjoining edges **3** a mark like this, as a scar or wrinkle **4** a layer of ore, coal, etc. —***vt.*** **1** to join together so as to form a seam **2** to mark with a seamlike line, etc. —**seam′less** ***adj.***

sea·man (sē′mən) ***n.***, *pl.* **-men** (-mən) **1** a sailor **2** *U.S. Navy* an enlisted person ranking below a petty officer —**sea′man·ship′** ***n.***

seam·stress (sēm′stris) ***n.*** a woman whose occupation is sewing

seam′y ***adj.*** **-i·er, -i·est** unpleasant or sordid *[*the *seamy* side of life*]*

sé·ance (sā′äns) ***n.*** ⟦Fr < L *sedere*, to sit⟧ a meeting at which a medium seeks to communicate with the spirits of the dead

sea′plane′ ***n.*** an airplane designed to land on and take off from water

sea′port′ ***n.*** a port or harbor used by ocean ships

sear (sir) ***vt.*** ⟦< OE *sear*, dry (adj.)⟧ **1** to wither **2** to burn the surface of **3** to brand

search (surch) ***vt.*** ⟦< LL *circare*, go about⟧ **1** to look through in order to find something **2** to examine (a person) for something concealed **3** to examine carefully; probe —***vi.*** to make a search —***n.*** a searching —**in search of** making a search for —**search′er** ***n.***

search engine software for locating documents, websites, etc. on a specified topic, etc.

search′ing ***adj.*** **1** examining thoroughly **2** piercing; penetrating

search′light′ ***n.*** **1** an apparatus on a swivel that projects a strong beam of light **2** such a beam

search warrant a legal document authorizing a police search

sea′scape′ (-skāp′) ***n.*** ⟦SEA + (LAND)SCAPE⟧ **1** a view of the sea **2** a drawing, painting, etc. of such a scene

sea′shell′ ***n.*** a saltwater mollusk shell

sea′shore′ ***n.*** land along the sea

sea′sick′ness ***n.*** nausea, dizziness, etc. caused by the rolling of a ship or boat —**sea′sick′** ***adj.***

sea′side′ ***n.*** SEASHORE

sea·son (sē′zən) ***n.*** ⟦< VL *satio*, season for sowing⟧ **1** any of the four divisions of the year; spring, summer, fall, or winter **2** the time when something takes place, is popular, is permitted, etc. **3** the suitable time —***vt.*** **1** to make (food) more tasty by adding salt, spices, etc. **2** to add zest to **3** to make more usable, as by aging **4** to make used to; accustom —***vi.*** to become seasoned

sea′son·a·ble ***adj.*** **1** suitable to the season **2** opportune; timely

sea′son·al ***adj.*** of or depending on the season —**sea′son·al·ly** ***adv.***

sea′son·ing ***n.*** anything that adds zest; esp., salt, spices, etc. added to food

THESAURUS

sea ***n.*** *Important seas include the following:* Barents, Ross, Weddell, Bering, Caribbean, Baltic, North, Irish, Mediterranean, Adriatic, Ionian, Aegean, Black, Caspian, Dead, Red, Tasman, Okhotsk, Japan, Yellow, South China, Arabian, East China, Java, Coral; Gulf of Mexico, Gulf of California, Persian Gulf, Hudson Bay, Baffin Bay, Bay of Bengal; see also OCEAN. —**at sea** confused, puzzled, upset; see BEWILDERED, UNCERTAIN. —**put (out) to sea** embark, go, start out; see LEAVE 1, SAIL 1.

sea bottom ***n.*** ocean floor, deep-sea floor, bottom of the sea, offshore lands, ocean bottom, ocean depths, continental shelf, undersea topography, marine farm, tidewater; see also OCEAN. *Terms for undersea topography include the following:* bank, sands, seamount, ridge, guyot, hill, tablemount, escarpment, plateau, reef, basin, canal, province, shoal, sill, channel, deep, depth, plain, trench, trough, fracture zone, rift.

seacoast ***n.*** seashore, seaboard, seaside; see SHORE.

seafood ***n.*** mollusk, lobster, oyster; see FISH, SHELLFISH.

seal[1] ***n.*** **1** [Approval] authorization, permit, allowance; see PERMISSION. **2** [Fastener] adhesive tape, sticker, tie; see FASTENER, TAPE.

sealed ***a.*** secured, fixed, held together; see FIRM 1, TIGHT 2.

seal off ***v.*** quarantine, close, segregate; see FORBID, RESTRICT.

seam ***n.*** joint, line of joining, union, stitching, line of stitching, closure, suture.

seamstress ***n.*** sewer, needleworker, designer; see TAILOR.

sear ***v.*** scorch, brown, toast; see COOK.

search ***n.*** exploration, research, quest; see HUNTING. —**in search of** looking for, seeking, on the lookout for; see SEARCHING.

search ***v.*** explore, examine, rummage, look up and down, track down, look for, go through, poke into, scrutinize, ransack; see also HUNT 1, SEEK.

searching ***a.*** hunting, looking for, seeking for, pursuing, in search of, ready for, in the market for, in need of, needing, wanting, on the lookout for, looking out for.

searchlight ***n.*** arc light, beam, ray; see LIGHT 3.

seashell ***n.*** *Common seashells include the following:* conch, periwinkle, abalone, ammonite, ram's horn, clam, mussel, oyster, starfish, sea urchin, sand dollar, sea snail, nautilus, scallop, cowrie, limpet, cockle, whelk; see also SHELL 3.

seashore ***n.*** seaboard, seaside, seacoast; see SHORE.

seasick ***a.*** nauseated, miserable, queasy; see SICK.

seaside ***n.*** seaboard, seashore, seacost; see SHORE.

season ***n.*** period, term, division of the year; see FALL 3, SPRING 2, SUMMER, WINTER. —**in season** legal to hunt, ready to pick, mature; see LEGAL, READY 2, RIPE 1, 3.

seasonal ***a.*** once a season, periodically, biennial; see ANNUAL, YEARLY.

seasoned ***a.*** **1** [Spicy] tangy, sharp, aromatic; see SPICY. **2** [Experienced] established, settled, mature; see ABLE, EXPERIENCED.

seasoning ***n.*** sauce, relish, herb, spice, pungency; see also FLAVORING.

season ticket a ticket or set of tickets for a series of concerts or baseball games
seat (sēt) ***n.*** ⟦ON *sæti*⟧ **1** *a)* a place to sit *b)* a thing to sit on; chair, etc. **2** *a)* the buttocks *b)* the part of a chair, garment, etc. that one sits on **3** the right to sit as a member *[*a *seat* on the council*]* **4** the center or the chief location *[*the *seat* of government*]* —***vt.*** **1** to set in or on a seat **2** to have seats for *[*the car *seats* six*]* **3** to put or fix in a place, position, etc. —**be seated** to sit down: also **take a seat**
seat belt straps across the hips, to protect a seated passenger: also **seat′belt′** ***n.***
Se·at·tle (sē at′'l) seaport in WC Washington: pop. 516,000
sea urchin a small sea animal with a round body in a shell covered with sharp spines
sea′ward ***adj.***, ***adv.*** toward the sea: also **sea′wards** ***adv.***
sea′way′ ***n.*** an inland waterway to the sea for ocean ships
sea′weed′ ***n.*** a sea plant, esp. an alga
sea′wor′thy (-wur′thē) ***adj.*** fit to travel on the sea: said of a ship
se·ba·ceous (sə bā′shəs) ***adj.*** ⟦< L *sebum*, tallow⟧ of, like, or secreting fat or a fatty substance *[sebaceous* glands*]*
seb·or·rhe·a or **seb·or·rhoe·a** (seb′ə rē′ə) ***n.*** ⟦ult. < L *sebum*, tallow + Gr *rheein*, flow⟧ an excessive discharge from the sebaceous glands, causing abnormally oily skin
sec *abbrev.* **1** second(s) **2** secondary **3** secretary **4** section(s)
SEC *abbrev.* Securities and Exchange Commission
se·cede (si sēd′) ***vi.*** **-ced′ed**, **-ced′ing** ⟦< L *se-*, apart + *cedere*, to go⟧ to withdraw formally from a group, organization, etc.
se·ces·sion (si sesh′ən) ***n.*** **1** a seceding **2** [*often* **S-**] the withdrawal of the Southern states from the federal Union at the start of the Civil War —**se·ces′sion·ist** ***n.***
se·clude (si klo͞od′) ***vt.*** **-clud′ed**, **-clud′ing** ⟦< L *se-*, apart + *claudere*, to close⟧ to shut off from others; isolate
se·clu·sion (si klo͞o′zhən) ***n.*** a secluding or being secluded; retirement; isolation
sec·ond[1] (sek′ənd) ***adj.*** ⟦< L *sequi*, follow⟧ **1** coming next after the first; 2d or 2nd **2** another of the same kind; other *[*a *second* chance*]* **3** next below the first in rank, value, etc. —***n.*** **1** one that is second **2** an article of merchandise not of first quality **3** an aide or assistant, as to a duelist or boxer **4** the gear next after first gear **5** [*pl.*] a second helping of food —***vt.*** **1** to assist **2** to indicate formal support of (a motion) before discussion or a vote —***adv.*** in the second place, group, etc.
sec·ond[2] (sek′ənd) ***n.*** ⟦< ML *(pars minuta) secunda*, second (small part): from being a further division⟧ **1** the sixtieth part of a minute of time or of angular measure **2** a moment; instant
sec·ond·ar·y (sek′ən der′ē) ***adj.*** **1** second in order, rank, importance, place, etc.; subordinate; minor **2** derived, not primary; derivative —***n.***, *pl.* **-ar′ies** **1** a secondary person or thing **2** *Football* the defensive backfield —**sec′ond·ar′i·ly** ***adv.***
secondary school a school, esp. a high school, coming after elementary school
secondary stress (or **accent**) a weaker stress (′) than the primary stress of a word
sec′ond-class′ ***adj.*** **1** of the class, rank, etc. next below the highest, best, etc. **2** of a cheaper mail class, as for periodicals **3** inferior, inadequate, etc. or treated as such —***adv.*** by second-class mail or travel accommodations
sec′ond-guess′ ***vt.***, ***vi.*** [Inf.] to use hindsight in criticizing (someone), remaking (a decision), etc.
sec′ond·hand′ ***adj.*** **1** not from the original source **2** used before; not new **3** of or dealing in used merchandise
second lieutenant *Mil.* a commissioned officer of the lowest rank
sec′ond·ly ***adv.*** in the second place
second nature an acquired habit, etc. deeply fixed in one's nature
second person the form of a pronoun or verb that refers to the person(s) spoken to
sec′ond-rate′ ***adj.*** **1** second in quality, rank, etc. **2** inferior
sec′ond-string′ ***adj.*** [Inf.] *Sports* that is a substitute player at a specified position —**sec′ond-string′er** ***n.***
second thought a change in thought after reconsidering —**on second thought** after reconsideration
second wind **1** the return of easy breathing after initial exhaustion, as while running **2** any fresh ability to continue
se·cre·cy (sē′krə sē) ***n.***, *pl.* **-cies** **1** a being secret **2** a tendency to keep things secret
se·cret (sē′krit) ***adj.*** ⟦< L *se-*, apart + *cernere*, sift⟧ **1** kept from the knowledge of others **2** beyond general understanding; mysterious **3** concealed from sight; hidden —***n.*** a secret fact, cause, process, etc. —**in secret** secretly —**se′cret·ly** ***adv.***
sec·re·tar·i·at (sek′rə ter′ē ət) ***n.*** a staff headed by a secretary; specif., an administrative staff, as in a government
sec·re·tar·y (sek′rə ter′ē) ***n.***, *pl.* **-tar′ies** ⟦< ML *secretarius*, one entrusted with secrets⟧ **1** one who keeps records, handles correspondence, etc. for an organization or person **2** [*often* **S-**] the head of a government department **3** a writing desk —**sec′re·tar′i·al** ***adj.***

THESAURUS

seat ***n.*** **1** [A structure on which one may sit] bench, chair, stool; see FURNITURE. **2** [Space in which one may sit] situation, chair, accommodation; see PLACE 2. **3** [The part of the body with which one sits] buttocks, rear, breech; see RUMP. —**have** (or **take**) **a seat** be seated, sit down, occupy a place; see SIT.

seated ***a.*** situated, located, settled, installed, established, rooted, set, fitted in place, placed, arranged, accommodated with seats.

seating ***n.*** places, reservations, chairs, seats, room, accommodation, arrangement, seating space.

seaward ***a.*** offshore, out to sea, over the sea; see MARITIME.

seaweed ***n.*** kelp, tangle, sea tangle, sea meadow, algae, marine meadow; see also PLANT. *Seaweed includes the following:* sea moss, Irish moss, Sargasso weed, rockweed, sea lettuce, kelp, giant kelp, gulfweed, sea cabbage.

seaworthy ***a.*** fit for sea, navigable, secure; see SAFE 1.

secede ***v.*** withdraw, retract, leave; see RETREAT.

secession ***n.*** departure, seceding, retraction; see WITHDRAWAL.

seclude ***v.*** screen out, conceal, cover; see HIDE 1.

secluded ***a.*** screened, isolated, sequestered; see WITHDRAWN.

seclusion ***n.*** solitude, aloofness, privacy; see RETIREMENT 2.

second[1] ***a.*** secondary, subordinate, subsidiary, junior, ancillary, auxiliary, inferior, next, next in order, following, next to the first, next in rank, another, other.

second[2] ***n.*** flash, trice, blink of an eye; see MOMENT 1.

secondary ***a.*** **1** [Derived] dependent, subsequent, subsidiary; see SUBORDINATE. **2** [Minor] inconsiderable, petty, small; see TRIVIAL, UNIMPORTANT.

secondhand ***a.*** used, not new, preowned, reclaimed, renewed, reused, old, worn, hand-me-down*, borrowed, derived, not original.

secondly ***a.*** in the second place, furthermore, also, besides, next, on the other hand, in the next place, for the next step, next in order, further, to continue; see also INCLUDING.

second-rate ***a.*** mediocre, inferior, common; see POOR 2.

secrecy ***n.*** concealment, confidence, hiding, seclusion, privacy, retirement, solitude, mystery, dark, darkness, isolation, reticence, stealth.

secret ***a.*** **1** [Not generally known] mysterious, ambiguous, hidden, unknown, arcane, cryptic, esoteric, occult, mystic, mystical, classified, dark, veiled, enigmatic, inscrutable, strange, deep, buried in mystery, obscure, clouded, shrouded, unenlightened, unintelligible, cabalistic.—*Ant.* KNOWN, revealed, exposed. **2** [Hidden] latent, secluded, concealed; see HIDDEN. **3** [Operating secretly] clandestine, underhand, underhanded, stealthy, sly, surreptitious, close, furtive, disguised, undercover, backdoor, confidential, classified, backstairs, incognito, camouflaged, enigmatic, under false pretenses, unrevealed, undisclosed, dissembled, dissimulated, under wraps; see also SECRETIVE.—*Ant.* OPEN, aboveboard, overt.

secret ***n.*** mystery, deep mystery, something veiled, something hidden, confidence, private matter, code, telegram, personal matter, privileged information, top secret, enigma, puzzle, something forbidden, classified information, confidential information, inside information, an unknown, the unknown. —**in secret** slyly, surreptitiously, quietly; see SECRET 3.

secretary ***n.*** **1** [A secondary executive officer] director, manager, superintendent; see EXECUTIVE. **2** [An assistant] clerk, typist, stenographer, copyist, amanuensis, recorder, confidential clerk, correspondent.

se·crete (si krēt′) ***vt.*** **-cret′ed, -cret′ing** ⟦see SECRET⟧ **1** to hide; conceal **2** to form and release (a substance) as a gland, etc. does
se·cre·tion (si krē′shən) ***n.*** **1** a secreting **2** a substance secreted by an animal or plant
se·cre·tive (sē′krə tiv) ***adj.*** concealing one's thoughts, etc.; not frank or open —**se′cre·tive·ly** ***adv.*** —**se′cre·tive·ness** ***n.***
se·cre·to·ry (si krēt′ər ē) ***adj.*** having the function of secreting, as a gland
Secret Service a division of the U.S. Treasury Department for uncovering counterfeiters, guarding the President, etc.
sect[1] (sekt) ***n.*** ⟦< L *sequi*, follow⟧ **1** a religious denomination **2** any group of people having a common philosophy, set of beliefs, etc.
sect[2] *abbrev.* section
sec·tar·i·an (sek ter′ē ən) ***adj.*** **1** of or devoted to some sect **2** narrow-minded —***n.*** a sectarian person —**sec·tar′i·an·ism′** ***n.***
sec·tion (sek′shən) ***n.*** ⟦< L *secare*, to cut⟧ **1** a cutting or cutting apart **2** a part cut off; portion **3** any distinct part, group, district, etc. **4** a drawing, etc. of a thing as it would appear if cut straight through —***vt.*** to divide into sections
sec′tion·al ***adj.*** **1** of or characteristic of a given section or district **2** made up of sections —**sec′tion·al·ism′** ***n.***
sec·tor (sek′tər) ***n.*** ⟦< L *secare*, to cut⟧ **1** part of a circle bounded by any two radii and the included arc **2** any of the districts into which an area is divided for military operations **3** a distinct part of society or of an economy, group, etc.
sec·u·lar (sek′yə lər) ***adj.*** ⟦< LL *saecularis*, worldly⟧ not religious; not connected with a church —**sec′u·lar·ism′** ***n.***
sec′u·lar·ize′ (-lə rīz′) ***vt.*** **-ized′, -iz′ing** to change from religious to civil use, control, influence, etc. —**sec′u·lar·i·za′tion** ***n.***
se·cure (si kyoor′) ***adj.*** ⟦< L *se-*, free from + *cura*, care⟧ **1** free from fear, care, etc. **2** free from danger, risk, etc.; safe **3** firm, stable, etc. *[make the knot secure]* —***vt.*** **-cured′, -cur′ing** **1** to make secure; protect **2** to make certain, as with a pledge **3** to make firm, fast, etc. **4** to obtain or bring about —**se·cure′ly** ***adv.***
se·cu·ri·ty (si kyoor′ə tē) ***n.***, *pl.* **-ties** **1** a feeling secure; freedom from fear, doubt, etc. **2** protection; safeguard **3** something given as a pledge of repayment, etc. **4** [*pl.*] bonds, stocks, etc. **5** a private police force
secy or **sec′y** *abbrev.* secretary
se·dan (si dan′) ***n.*** ⟦< ? L *sedere*, to sit⟧ an automobile with two or four doors, a permanent rigid top, and a full-sized rear seat
se·date[1] (si dāt′) ***adj.*** ⟦< L *sedare*, to settle⟧ calm or composed; esp., serious and unemotional —**se·date′ly** ***adv.***
se·date[2] (si dāt′) ***vt.*** **-dat′ed, -dat′ing** to dose with a sedative —**se·da′tion** ***n.***
sed·a·tive (sed′ə tiv) ***adj.*** ⟦see SEDATE[1]⟧ tending to soothe or quiet; lessening excitement, irritation, nervousness, etc. —***n.*** a sedative medicine
sed·en·tar·y (sed′′n ter′ē) ***adj.*** ⟦< L *sedere*, to sit⟧ marked by much sitting
Se·der (sā′dər) ***n.***, *pl.* **Se·dar·im** (sə där′im) or **Se′ders** ⟦Heb lit., arrangement⟧ [*also* **s-**] *Judaism* the feast of Passover as observed in the home on the eve of the first (by some also of the second) day of the holiday
sedge (sej) ***n.*** ⟦OE *secg*⟧ a coarse, grasslike plant growing in wet ground
sed·i·ment (sed′ə mənt) ***n.*** ⟦< L *sedere*, sit⟧ **1** matter that settles to the bottom of a liquid **2** *Geol.* matter deposited by water or wind
sed′i·men′ta·ry (-men′tər ē) ***adj.*** **1** of or containing sediment **2** formed by the deposit of sediment, as certain rocks
sed′i·men·ta′tion (-men tā′shən, -mən-) ***n.*** the depositing of sediment
se·di·tion (si dish′ən) ***n.*** ⟦< L *sed-*, apart + *itio*, a going⟧ a stirring up of rebellion against the government —**se·di′tion·ist** ***n.*** —**se·di′tious** ***adj.***
se·duce (si do͞os′) ***vt.*** **-duced′, -duc′ing** ⟦< L *se-*, apart + *ducere*, to lead⟧ **1** to tempt to wrongdoing **2** to entice into having, esp. for the first time, illicit sexual intercourse —**se·duc′er** ***n.*** —**se·duc′tion** (-duk′shən) ***n.*** —**se·duc′tive** ***adj.*** —**se·duc′tress** (-tris) ***fem.n.***
sed·u·lous (sej′oo ləs) ***adj.*** ⟦L *sedulus*⟧ diligent
se·dum (sē′dəm) ***n.*** ⟦< L⟧ a perennial plant found on rocks or walls, with white, yellow, or pink flowers
see[1] (sē) ***vt.*** **saw, seen, see′ing** ⟦OE *seon*⟧ **1** to get knowledge of through the eyes; look at **2** to understand **3** to learn; find out **4** to experience **5** to make sure *[see that he goes]* **6** to escort *[see her to her door]* **7** to encounter **8** to call on; consult **9** to receive *[too ill to see anyone]* —***vi.*** **1** to have the power of sight **2** to understand **3** to think *[let me see, who's next?]* —**see off** to accompany (someone) to the place from which that person is to depart, as on a journey —**see through** **1** to perceive the true nature of **2** to finish **3** to help through difficulty —**see to** to attend to
see[2] (sē) ***n.*** ⟦< L *sedes*, a seat⟧ the official seat or jurisdiction of a bishop
seed (sēd) ***n.***, *pl.* **seeds** or **seed** ⟦OE *sæd*⟧ **1** *a)* the part of a plant, containing the embryo, from which a new plant can grow *b)* such seeds collectively **2** the source of anything **3** [Archaic] descendants; posterity **4** sperm or semen **5** a seeded contestant —***vt.*** **1** to plant with seeds

THESAURUS

secrete ***v.*** **1** [To hide] conceal, cover, seclude; see DISGUISE, HIDE 1. **2** [To perspire] discharge, swelter, emit; see SWEAT.

secretion ***n.*** discharge, issue, movement; see EXCRETION, FLOW.

secretive ***a.*** reticent, taciturn, undercover, with bated breath, in private, in the dark, in chambers, by a side door, under one's breath, in the background, between ourselves, in privacy, in a corner, under the cloak of, reserved.

secretly ***a.*** privately, covertly, obscurely, darkly, surreptitiously, furtively, stealthily, underhandedly, slyly, behind one's back, intimately, personally, confidentially, between you and me, in strict confidence, in secret, behind the scenes, on the sly, behind closed doors, under the table*, quietly, hush-hush*.—*Ant.* OPENLY, obviously, publicly.

sect[1] ***n.*** denomination, following, order; see CHURCH 3, FACTION.

section ***n.*** **1** [A portion] subdivision, slice, segment; see PART 1, SHARE. **2** [An area] district, sector, locality; see REGION 1.

sector ***n.*** section, district, quarter; see AREA, DIVISION 2.

secure ***a.*** **1** [Firm] fastened, bound, adjusted; see FIRM 1, TIGHT 1. **2** [Safe] guarded, unharmed, defended; see SAFE 1. **3** [Self-confident] assured, stable, determined; see CONFIDENT.

secure ***v.*** **1** [To fasten] settle, lock, bind; see FASTEN, TIGHTEN 1. **2** [To obtain] achieve, acquire, grasp; see GET 1.

security ***n.*** **1** [Safety] protection, shelter, safety, refuge, retreat, defense, safeguard, preservation, sanctuary, ward, guard, immunity, freedom from harm, freedom from danger, redemption, salvation.—*Ant.* DANGER, risk, hazard. **2** [A guarantee] earnest, forfeit, token, pawn, pledge, surety, bond, collateral, assurance, bail, certainty, promise, warranty, pact, compact, contract, covenant, agreement, sponsor, bondsman, hostage; see also PROTECTION 2.—*Ant.* DOUBT, broken faith, unreliability.

sedative ***n.*** tranquilizer, medication, narcotic; see DRUG, MEDICINE 2.

sediment ***n.*** silt, dregs, grounds; see RESIDUE.

seduce ***v.*** decoy, allure, inveigle, entice, abduct, attract, tempt, bait, bribe, lure, fascinate, induce, stimulate, defile, deprave, lead astray, violate, prostitute, rape, deflower, ravish.—*Ant.* PRESERVE, protect, guide.

see[1] ***v.*** **1** [To perceive with the eye] observe, look at, behold, examine, inspect, regard, view, look out on, gaze, stare, eye, lay eyes on, mark, perceive, pay attention to, heed, mind, detect, take notice, discern, scrutinize, scan, spy, survey, contemplate, remark, clap eyes on*, make out, cast the eyes on, direct the eyes, catch sight of, cast the eyes over, get a load of*. **2** [To understand] perceive, comprehend, discern; see RECOGNIZE 1, UNDERSTAND 1. **3** [To witness] look on, be present, pay attention, notice, observe, regard, heed; see also WITNESS. **4** [To accompany] escort, attend, bear company; see ACCOMPANY. **5** [To have an appointment (with)] speak to, have a conference with, get advice from; see CONSULT, DISCUSS. —**see about** attend to, look after, provide for; see PERFORM 1. —**see through** **1** [To complete] finish up, bring to a successful conclusion, wind up; see COMPLETE, END 1. **2** [To understand] comprehend, penetrate, detect; see UNDERSTAND 1. —**see to** do, attend to, look after; see UNDERSTAND 1.

seed ***n.*** grain, bulbs, cuttings, ears, tubers, roots; seed corn, seed potatoes, etc. *Seeds and fruits commonly called seeds include the following:* grain, kernel, berry, ear, corn, nut. —**go** (or **run**) **to seed** decline, worsen, run out; see WASTE 3.

seed ***v.*** scatter, sow, broadcast; see PLANT.

seeding ***n.*** sowing, implanting, spreading; see FARMING.

2 to remove the seeds from 3 to distribute (contestants in a tournament) so that the best teams or players are not matched in early rounds —*vi.* to produce seeds —**go** (or **run**) **to seed** 1 to shed seeds after flowering 2 to deteriorate, weaken, etc. —**seed'less** *adj.*

seed'ling (-liŋ) *n.* 1 a plant grown from a seed 2 a young tree

seed money money to begin a long-term project

seed vessel any dry, hollow fruit containing seeds: also **seed'case'** *n.*

seed'y *adj.* **-i·er, -i·est** 1 full of seed 2 gone to seed 3 shabby, rundown, etc. —**seed'i·ness** *n.*

seek (sēk) *vt.* **sought, seek'ing** ⟦OE *secan*⟧ 1 to try to find; search for 2 to try to get 3 to aim at 4 to try; attempt *[to seek to please]* —**seek'er** *n.*

seem (sēm) *vi.* ⟦prob. < ON *sœma*, conform to⟧ 1 to appear to be *[to seem happy]* 2 to give the impression: usually with an infinitive *[she seems to know]*

seem'ing *adj.* that seems real, true, etc. without necessarily being so; apparent —**seem'ing·ly** *adv.*

seem'ly *adj.* **-li·er, -li·est** suitable, proper, etc. —**seem'li·ness** *n.*

seen (sēn) *vt., vi. pp. of* SEE[1]

seep (sēp) *vi.* ⟦OE *sipian*, to soak⟧ to leak through small openings; ooze —**seep'age** *n.*

seer (sir) *n.* one who supposedly foretells the future —**seer'ess** *fem.n.*

seer·suck·er (sir'suk'ər) *n.* ⟦< Pers *shir u shakar*, lit., milk and sugar⟧ a crinkled fabric of linen, cotton, etc.

see·saw (sē'sô') *n.* ⟦< SAW[1]⟧ 1 a plank balanced at the middle on which children at play, riding the ends, rise and fall alternately 2 any up-and-down or back-and-forth motion or change —*vt., vi.* to move up and down or back and forth

seethe (sē*th*) *vi.* **seethed, seeth'ing** 1 to boil, surge, or bubble 2 to be violently agitated

seg·ment (seg'mənt; *for v.,* -ment) *n.* ⟦< L *secare*, to cut⟧ any of the parts into which something is or can be separated; section —*vt., vi.* to divide into segments —**seg'men·ta'tion** *n.*

seg·re·gate (seg'rə gāt') *vt.* **-gat'ed, -gat'ing** ⟦< L *se-*, apart + *grex*, a flock⟧ to set apart from others; specif., to impose racial segregation on

seg're·ga'tion *n.* the policy of compelling racial groups to live apart and use separate schools, facilities, etc. —**seg're·ga'tion·ist** *n.*

se·gue (seg'wā, sā'gwā) *vi.* **-gued, -gue·ing** ⟦It, (it follows) < L sequi, to follow⟧ to continue without break (*to* or *into* the next part) —*n.* an immediate transition to the next part

sei·gnior (sān'yər, sān yôr') *n.* ⟦< OFr *seignor* < L *senior*⟧ a feudal lord

seine (sān) *n.* ⟦< Gr *sagēnē*⟧ a large fishing net weighted along the bottom —*vt., vi.* **seined, sein'ing** to fish with a seine —**sein'er** *n.*

Seine (sān; *Fr* sen) river in N France, flowing through Paris

seis·mic (sīz'mik) *adj.* ⟦< Gr *seismos*, earthquake⟧ of or caused by an earthquake —**seis'mi·cal·ly** *adv.*

seis'mo·graph' (-mə graf') *n.* ⟦see prec. & -GRAPH⟧ an instrument that records the intensity and duration of earthquakes

seis·mol·o·gy (sīz mäl'ə jē, sīs-) *n.* ⟦see SEISMIC & -LOGY⟧ the science dealing with earthquakes —**seis'mo·log'ic** (-mə läj'ik) or **seis'mo·log'i·cal** *adj.* —**seis·mol'o·gist** *n.*

seize (sēz) *vt.* **seized, seiz'ing** ⟦< ML *sacire*⟧ 1 *a)* to take legal possession of *b)* to capture; arrest 2 to take forcibly and quickly 3 to grasp suddenly 4 to attack or afflict suddenly *[seized with pain]* —*vi.* to stick or jam: said of a machine: often with *up*

sei·zure (sē'zhər) *n.* 1 a seizing or being seized 2 a sudden attack, as of epilepsy

sel·dom (sel'dəm) *adv.* ⟦OE *seldan*, strange⟧ rarely; infrequently

se·lect (sə lekt') *adj.* ⟦< L *se-*, apart + *legere*, to choose⟧ 1 chosen in preference to others 2 choice; excellent 3 exclusive —*vt., vi.* to choose or pick out —**se·lec'tor** *n.*

se·lec'tion (-lek'shən) *n.* 1 a selecting or being selected 2 that or those selected

se·lec'tive *adj.* 1 of selection 2 careful in choosing; discriminating —**se·lec'tiv'i·ty** *n.*

selective service compulsory military service set by age, fitness, etc.

se·lect'man (-mən) *n., pl.* **-men** (-mən) one of a board of governing officers in most New England towns

se·le·ni·um (sə lē'nē əm) *n.* ⟦ModL < Gr *selēnē*, the moon⟧ a nonmetallic chemical element, used in photoelectric devices

self (self) *n., pl.* **selves** ⟦OE⟧ 1 the identity, character, etc. of any person or thing 2 one's own person as distinct from all others 3 one's own welfare or interest —*adj.* of the same kind, color, material, etc. *[drapes with a self lining]*

self- *prefix* of, by, in, to, or with oneself or itself The following list includes some common compounds formed with *self-* that do not have special meanings:

self-abasement	**self-destructive**
self-advancement	**self-discipline**
self-appointed	**self-employed**
self-complacent	**self-examination**
self-criticism	**self-help**
self-deception	**self-imposed**
self-defeating	**self-improvement**
self-delusion	**self-incrimination**

THESAURUS

seeing *a.* observing, looking, regarding, viewing, noticing, surveying, looking at, observant, wide awake, alert, awake, perceiving, inspecting, witnessing.

seek *v.* search for, dig for, fish for, look around for, look up, hunt up, sniff out, dig out, hunt out, root out, smell around, go after, run after, see after, prowl after, go in pursuit of, go in search of, go gunning for.

seem *v.* appear to be, have the appearance, give the impression, take on the aspect, impress one, appear to one, look, look like, resemble, make a show of, show, have the features of, lead one to suppose something to be, have all the evidence of being, be suggestive of, give the effect of, sound like, make out to be, give the idea, have all the earmarks of, make a noise like.

seen *a.* observed, evident, viewed; see OBVIOUS 1.

seep *v.* leak, flow gently, trickle; see DRAIN 1, FLOW.

seepage *n.* drainage, infiltration, leakage; see FLOW.

seethe *v.* simmer, stew, burn; see BOIL, COOK.

segment *n.* section, portion, fragment; see DIVISION 2, PART 1.

segregate *v.* isolate, sever, split up; see DIVIDE, SEPARATE 2.

segregated *a.* divided along racial lines, isolated, excluded; see RACIAL, SEPARATED.

segregation *n.* dissociation, disconnection, separation; see DIVISION 1.

seize *v.* 1 [To grasp] take, take hold of, lay hold of, lay hands on, catch hold of, hang onto, catch, grip, clinch, clench, clasp, embrace, grab, clutch, grapple, snag, pluck, appropriate, snatch, swoop up, enclose, pinch, squeeze, hold fast, possess oneself of, envelop.—*Ant.* LEAVE, pass by, let alone. 2 [To take by force] capture, rape, occupy, win, take captive, pounce, conquer, take by storm, subdue, overwhelm, overrun, overpower, ambush, snatch, incorporate, exact, retake, carry off, apprehend, arrest, secure, commandeer, force, gain, take, recapture, appropriate, expropriate, take possession of, take over, hijack, skyjack, carjack, pounce on, usurp, overcome, impound, intercept, steal, abduct, snap up*, nab*, trap, throttle, lay hold of, lift, hook, collar*, fasten upon, wrench, claw, snare, bag, wring, get one's hands on, kidnap, rustle*, hold up, swipe*, scramble for, help oneself to. 3 [To comprehend] perceive, see, know; see UNDERSTAND 1.

seized *a.* confiscated, annexed, clutched; see BEATEN 1, CAPTURED.

seizure *n.* 1 [Capture] seizing, taking, apprehending; see CAPTURE. 2 [A spasm] spell, convulsion, breakdown; see FIT 1, ILLNESS 1.

seldom *a.* rarely, unusually, in a few cases, a few times, at times, seldom seen, usually, sporadically, irregularly, whimsically, sometimes, from time to time, on a few occasions, on rare occasions, infrequently, not often, not very often, occasionally, uncommonly, scarcely, hardly, hardly ever, scarcely ever, when the spirit moves, on and off, once in a while, once in a blue moon, once in a lifetime, every now and then, not in a month of Sundays*.—*Ant.* FREQUENTLY, often, frequent.

select *v.* decide, pick, elect; see CHOOSE.

selected *a.* picked, chosen, elected; see NAMED 2.

selection *n.* 1 [The act of selecting] choice, election, determination, choosing, preference, appropriation, adoption, reservation, separation. 2 [Anything selected] pick, preference, election; see CHOICE.

selective *a.* discriminating, judicious, particular; see CAREFUL.

self *a.* of one's self, by one's self, by one's own effort; see ALONE, INDIVIDUAL.

self *n.* oneself, one's being, inner nature; see CHARACTER 2.

self-induced
self-indulgence
self-indulgent
self-inflicted
self-knowledge
self-love
self-perpetuating
self-pity
self-pollination
self-preservation
self-protection
self-reproach
self-sealing
self-support
self-supporting
self-sustaining

self′-ad·dressed′ ***adj.*** addressed to oneself *[a self-addressed* envelope*]*
self′-ad·he′sive ***adj.*** made to stick without moistening
self′-as·ser′tion ***n.*** a demanding to be acknowledged or an insisting upon one's rights, etc.
self′-as·sur′ance ***n.*** confidence in oneself —**self′-as·sured′** ***adj.***
self′-cen′tered ***adj.*** **1** egocentric **2** selfish
self′-con′fi·dence ***n.*** confidence in one's own abilities, etc. —**self′-con′fi·dent** ***adj.***
self′-con′scious ***adj.*** unduly conscious of oneself as an object of notice; specif., ill at ease —**self′-con′scious·ly** ***adv.*** —**self′-con′scious·ness** ***n.***
self′-con·tained′ ***adj.*** **1** keeping one's affairs to oneself **2** showing self-control **3** complete within itself
self′-con′tra·dic′tion ***n.*** **1** contradiction of oneself or itself **2** any statement containing elements that contradict each other —**self′-con′tra·dic′to·ry** ***adj.***
self′-con·trol′ ***n.*** control of one's own emotions, desires, actions, etc. —**self′-con·trolled′** ***adj.***
self′-de·fense′ ***n.*** defense of oneself or of one's rights, beliefs, actions, etc.
self′-de·ni′al ***n.*** denial or sacrifice of one's own desires or pleasures
self′-de·scribed′ ***adj.*** described so by the person himself or herself *[a self-described* expert*]*
self′-de·struct′ ***vi.*** **1** to destroy itself automatically **2** to greatly harm oneself as the result of inherent flaws
self′-de·ter′mi·na′tion ***n.*** **1** a making up one's own mind **2** the right of a people to choose its own form of government —**self′-de·ter′mined** ***adj.***
self′-dis·cov′er·y ***n.*** a becoming aware of one's true potential, character, motives, etc.
self′-ed′u·cat′ed ***adj.*** educated by oneself, with little formal schooling
self′-ef·fac′ing ***adj.*** modest; retiring —**self′-ef·face′ment** ***n.***
self′-es·teem′ ***n.*** **1** self-respect **2** undue pride in oneself; conceit
self′-ev′i·dent ***adj.*** evident without need of proof
self′-ex·plan′a·to′ry ***adj.*** explaining itself; obvious
self′-ex·pres′sion ***n.*** expression of one's own personality or emotions, esp. in the arts
self′-ful·fill′ing ***adj.*** **1** bringing about one's personal goals **2** brought about chiefly as an effect of having been expected or predicted
self′-gov′ern·ment ***n.*** government of a group by its own members —**self′-gov′ern·ing** ***adj.***
self′-im′age ***n.*** one's conception of oneself and of one's own abilities, worth, etc.
self′-im·por′tant ***adj.*** having an exaggerated opinion of one's own importance —**self′-im·por′tance** ***n.***
self′-in′ter·est ***n.*** **1** one's own interest or advantage **2** an exaggerated regard for this
self′ish ***adj.*** having or showing too much concern for one's own interests, etc., with little concern for others —**self′ish·ly** ***adv.*** —**self′ish·ness** ***n.***
self′less ***adj.*** having or showing devotion to others' welfare; unselfish —**self′less·ly** ***adv.*** —**self′less·ness** ***n.***
self′-made′ ***adj.*** **1** made by oneself or itself **2** successful through one's own efforts
self′-por′trait ***n.*** a portrait of oneself, done by oneself
self′-pos·ses′sion ***n.*** full control of one's feelings, actions, etc. —**self′-pos·sessed′** ***adj.***
self′-pro·pelled′ ***adj.*** propelled by its own motor or power
self′-re·crim′i·na′tion ***n.*** a blaming of oneself
self′-reg′u·lat′ing ***adj.*** regulating oneself or itself, so as to function automatically or without outside control
self′-re·li′ance ***n.*** reliance on one's own judgment, abilities, etc. —**self′-re·li′ant** ***adj.***
self′-re·spect′ ***n.*** proper respect for oneself —**self′-re·spect′ing** ***adj.***
self′-re·straint′ ***n.*** restraint imposed on oneself by oneself; self-control
self′-right′eous ***adj.*** regarding oneself as being morally superior to others; smugly virtuous —**self′-right′eous·ly** ***adv.*** —**self′-right′eous·ness** ***n.***
self′-sac′ri·fice′ ***n.*** sacrifice of oneself or one's own interests for the benefit of others —**self′-sac′ri·fic′ing** ***adj.***
self′same′ ***adj.*** identical
self′-sat′is·fied′ ***adj.*** feeling or showing an often smug satisfaction with oneself —**self′-sat′is·fac′tion** ***n.***
self′-seek′er ***n.*** one who seeks mainly to further his or her own interests —**self′-seek′ing** ***n.***, ***adj.***
self′-serve′ ***adj.*** *short for* SELF-SERVICE
self′-serv′ice ***adj.*** of or being a store, cafeteria, etc. set up so that customers pay a cashier and serve themselves
self′-serv′ing ***adj.*** serving one's own selfish interests
self′-styled′ ***adj.*** so called only by oneself
self′-suf·fi′cient ***adj.*** able to get along without help; independent —**self′-suf·fi′cien·cy** ***n.***
self′-taught′ ***adj.*** having taught oneself through one's own efforts
self′-willed′ ***adj.*** stubborn; obstinate
self′-wind′ing (-wīn′diŋ) ***adj.*** wound automatically, as some wristwatches
sell (sel) ***vt.*** **sold**, **sell′ing** ⟦OE *sellan*, to give⟧ **1** to exchange (goods, services, etc.) for money, etc. **2** to offer for sale **3** to promote the sale of —***vi.*** **1** to engage in selling **2** to be sold (*for* or *at*) **3** to attract buyers —**sell out** **1** to get rid of completely by selling **2** [Inf.] to betray —**sell′er** ***n.***
sell′out′ ***n.*** [Inf.] **1** a selling out; betrayal **2** a show, game, etc. for which all seats have been sold

THESAURUS

self-assurance ***n.*** security, self-reliance, morale; see CONFIDENCE.
self-assured ***a.*** self-confident, assured, certain; see CONFIDENT.
self-centered ***a.*** self-indulgent, egotistical, self-conscious; see EGOTISTIC, SELFISH.
self-confidence ***n.*** assurance, courage, self-reliance; see CONFIDENCE.
self-confident ***a.*** fearless, secure, self-assured; see CONFIDENT.
self-conscious ***a.*** unsure, uncertain, shy; see DOUBTFUL, HUMBLE 1.
self-contained ***a.*** self-sustaining, complete, independent; see FREE 1, WHOLE 1.
self-control ***n.*** poise, self-restraint, reserve, self-government, restraint, discipline, self-discipline, discretion, balance, stability, sobriety, dignity, repression, constraint, self-regulation.—*Ant.* NERVOUSNESS, anger, talkativeness.
self-defense ***n.*** self-protection, self-preservation, putting up a fight; see FIGHT 1, PROTECTION 2.
self-esteem ***n.*** self-respect, self-confidence, confidence; see PRIDE 1, DIGNITY.
self-evident ***a.*** plain, apparent, visible; see OBVIOUS 2.
self-explanatory ***a.*** plain, clear, distinct; see OBVIOUS 2.
self-imposed ***a.*** accepted, self-determined, willingly adopted; see DELIBERATE, VOLUNTARILY.
selfish ***a.*** self-seeking, self-centered, self-indulgent, indulging oneself, wrapped up in oneself, narrow, narrow-minded, prejudiced, egotistical, egotistic, looking out for number one*; see also GREEDY.
selfishly ***a.*** egotistically, stingily, greedily, miserly, in one's own interest, meanly, wrongly, ungenerously, from selfish motives.
selfishness ***n.*** self-regard, self-indulgence, self-worship; see GREED.
self-made ***a.*** competent, self-reliant, capable; see ABLE, CONFIDENT.
self-reliant ***a.*** determined, resolute, independent; see ABLE, CONFIDENT.
self-respect ***n.*** self-esteem, worth, pride; see CONFIDENCE, DIGNITY.
self-restraint ***n.*** patience, endurance, self-control; see RESTRAINT 1.
self-sacrifice ***n.*** altruism, kind-heartedness, benevolence; see GENEROSITY, KINDNESS 1, 2.
self-satisfaction ***n.*** complacency, smugness, conceit; see EGOTISM.
self-satisfied ***a.*** smug, vain, conceited; see EGOTISTIC.
self-sufficient ***a.*** competent, self-confident, efficient; see CONFIDENT.
sell ***v.*** market, vend, auction, dispose of, put up for sale, put on the market, barter, exchange, transfer, liquidate, trade, bargain, peddle, retail, merchandise, sell over the counter, contract, wholesale, dump, clear out, have a sale, give title to, put in escrow.—*Ant.* BUY, obtain, get. —**sell out*** trick, turn in, betray, double-cross*; see also DECEIVE.
seller ***n.*** dealer, tradesman, salesman, saleswoman, saleslady, salesgirl, salesclerk, sales rep*, salesperson, retailer, agent, vendor, merchant, auctioneer, shopkeeper, marketer, peddler, trader, storekeeper; see also BUSINESSMAN, MERCHANT.
selling ***n.*** sale, auction, bartering, trading, vending, auctioning, transfer, transferring, commercial transaction, transacting, merchandising, disposal.—*Ant.* BUYING, purchasing, acquiring.
sellout* ***n.*** betrayal, deception, deal; see TRICK 1.

selt·zer (selt′sər) ***n.*** ⟦< *Niederselters*, Germany⟧ **1** [*often* **S-**] natural, effervescent mineral water **2** any carbonated water, often flavored
sel·vage or **sel·vedge** (sel′vij) ***n.*** ⟦< SELF + EDGE⟧ a specially woven edge that prevents cloth from raveling
selves (selvz) ***n.*** *pl. of* SELF
se·man·tics (sə man′tiks) ***pl.n.*** ⟦< Gr *sēmainein*, to show⟧ the study of the meanings of words —**se·man′tic** ***adj.***
sem·a·phore (sem′ə fôr′) ***n.*** ⟦< Gr *sēma*, sign + *pherein*, to bear⟧ any apparatus or system for signaling, as by lights, flags, etc.
sem·blance (sem′bləns) ***n.*** ⟦< L *similis*, like⟧ **1** outward appearance **2** a likeness or copy
se·men (sē′mən) ***n.*** ⟦L, seed⟧ the fluid secreted by the male reproductive organs
se·mes·ter (sə mes′tər) ***n.*** ⟦< L *sex*, six + *mensis*, month⟧ either of the two terms usually making up a school year
sem·i (sem′ī′) ***n.*** [Inf.] a semitrailer and its attached TRACTOR (sense 2)
semi- ⟦L⟧ *prefix* **1** half **2** partly, not fully **3** twice in a (specified period)
sem·i·an·nu·al (sem′ē an′yo͞o əl) ***adj.*** happening, coming, etc. every half year
sem′i·au′to·mat′ic ***adj.*** designating an automatic weapon requiring a trigger pull for each round fired —***n.*** a semiautomatic firearm
sem·i·cir·cle (sem′i sʉr′kəl) ***n.*** a half circle —**sem′i·cir′cu·lar** (-kyə lər) ***adj.***
sem′i·co′lon ***n.*** a mark of punctuation (;) indicating a degree of separation greater than that marked by the comma
sem′i·con·duc′tor ***n.*** a substance, as germanium, used as in transistors
sem′i·con′scious ***adj.*** not fully conscious or awake
sem·i·fi·nal (sem′i fīn′əl; *for n.*, sem′i fīn′əl) ***adj.*** coming just before the final match, as of a tournament —***n.*** a semifinal match, etc.
sem·i·month·ly (sem′i munth′lē) ***adj.*** done, happening, etc. twice a month —***adv.*** twice monthly
sem·i·nal (sem′ə nəl) ***adj.*** ⟦see SEMEN⟧ **1** of seed or semen **2** that is a source **3** of essential importance; specif., *a*) basic; central *b*) crucial
sem·i·nar (sem′ə när′) ***n.*** ⟦see fol.⟧ **1** a group of supervised students doing research **2** a course for such a group
sem·i·nar·y (sem′ə ner′ē) ***n.***, *pl.* **-nar′ies** ⟦< L *seminarium*, nursery⟧ a school where ministers, priests, or rabbis are trained —**sem′i·nar′i·an** ***n.***
Sem·i·nole (sem′ə nōl′) ***n.***, *pl.* **-noles′** or **-nole′** a member of a North American Indian people of S Florida & Oklahoma
se·mi·ot·ics (sē′mē ät′iks) ***n.*** ⟦< Gr *sēmeion*, sign⟧ *Philos.* a general theory of signs and symbols; esp., the analysis of signs in language
sem·i·pre·cious (sem′i presh′əs) ***adj.*** designating gems, as the garnet, turquoise, etc., of lower value than precious stones
sem′i·pri′vate ***adj.*** of a hospital room with two, three, or sometimes four beds
sem′i·pro·fes′sion·al ***n.*** one who engages in a sport for pay but not as a regular occupation: also **sem′i·pro′**
sem′i·skilled′ ***adj.*** of or doing manual work requiring only limited training
Sem·ite (sem′īt′) ***n.*** ⟦< Heb *Shem*, son of Noah⟧ a member of any of the peoples speaking a Semitic language
Se·mit·ic (sə mit′ik) ***n.*** a major group of African and Asian languages, including Hebrew, Arabic, etc. —***adj.*** designating or of the Semites or their languages, etc.
sem·i·tone (sem′i tōn′) ***n.*** *Music* the difference in pitch between any two immediately adjacent keys on the piano
sem′i·trail′er ***n.*** a detachable trailer designed to be attached to a coupling at the rear of a TRACTOR (sense 2)
sem′i·trop′i·cal ***adj.*** partly tropical
sem′i·week′ly ***adj.*** done, happening, etc. twice a week —***adv.*** twice weekly
sem·o·li·na (sem′ə lē′nə) ***n.*** ⟦It⟧ coarse flour from hard wheat
Sen *abbrev.* **1** Senate **2** Senator **3** [*also* **s-**] senior
sen·ate (sen′it) ***n.*** ⟦< L *senex*, old⟧ **1** a legislative assembly **2** [**S-**] the upper house of the U.S. Congress or of most of the U.S. state legislatures
sen·a·tor (sen′ət ər) ***n.*** a member of a senate —**sen·a·to·ri·al** (sen′ə tôr′ē əl) ***adj.***
send (send) ***vt.* sent, send′ing** ⟦OE *sendan*⟧ **1** to cause to go or be transmitted; dispatch; transmit **2** to cause (a person) to go **3** to impel; drive **4** to cause to happen, come, etc. —**send for** **1** to summon **2** to place an order for —**send′er** ***n.***
send′-off′ ***n.*** [Inf.] **1** a farewell demonstration for someone starting out on a trip, career, etc. **2** a start given to someone or something
Sen·e·gal (sen′i gôl′) country on the W coast of Africa: 76,124 sq. mi.; pop. 6,982,000
se·nile (sē′nīl′) ***adj.*** ⟦< L *senex*, old⟧ **1** of or resulting from old age **2** showing the deterioration accompanying old age, esp. confusion, memory loss, etc. —**se·nil·i·ty** (si nil′ə tē) ***n.***
sen·ior (sēn′yər) ***adj.*** ⟦< L *senex*, old⟧ **1** older: written *Sr.* after a father's name if his son's name is the same **2** of higher rank or longer service **3** of or for seniors —***n.*** **1** one who is older, of higher rank, etc. **2** a student in the last year of high school or college **3** *short for* SENIOR CITIZEN
senior citizen an elderly person, esp. one who is retired
senior high school high school, usually grades 10, 11, and 12
sen·ior·i·ty (sēn yôr′ə tē) ***n.***, *pl.* **-ties** **1** a being senior **2** status, priority, etc. achieved by length of service in a given job
sen·na (sen′ə) ***n.*** ⟦< Ar *sanā*, cassia plant⟧ the dried leaflets of a tropical cassia plant used, esp. formerly, as a laxative
se·ñor (se nyôr′) ***n.***, *pl.* ***se·ño′res*** (-nyô′res) ⟦Sp⟧ a man; gentleman: as a title, equivalent to *Mr.* or *Sir*
se·ño·ra (se nyô′rä) ***n.*** ⟦Sp⟧ a married woman: as a title, equivalent to *Mrs.* or *Madam*
se·ño·ri·ta (se′nyô rē′tä) ***n.*** ⟦Sp⟧ an unmarried woman or girl: as a title, equivalent to *Miss*
sen·sa·tion (sen sā′shən) ***n.*** ⟦< L *sensus*, sense⟧ **1** the receiving of sense impressions through hearing, seeing, etc. **2** a conscious sense impression **3** a generalized feeling *[a sensation of joy]* **4** *a*) a feeling of general excitement *b*) the cause of such a feeling
sen·sa′tion·al ***adj.*** **1** arousing intense interest **2** intended to shock, thrill, etc. —**sen·sa′tion·al·ism′** ***n.***
sense (sens) ***n.*** ⟦< L *sentire*, to feel⟧ **1** any faculty of receiving impressions through body organs; sight, touch,

THESAURUS

semester ***n.*** six-month period, eighteen weeks, four and one-half months; see TERM 2.
semifinal ***n.*** next to the last match, elimination round, final four; see ROUND 2.
seminary ***n.*** secondary school, institute, theological school; see SCHOOL 1.
senate ***n.*** legislative body, assembly, council; see LEGISLATURE.
Senate ***n.*** legislative body, upper branch of Congress, the Upper House; see LEGISLATURE.
senator ***n.*** statesman, politician, member of the senate; see REPRESENTATIVE 2.
send ***v.*** **1** [To dispatch] transmit, forward, convey, advance, express, ship, mail, send forth, send out, export, send in, delegate, expedite, hasten, accelerate, post, address, rush, rush off, hurry off, get under way, give papers, provide with credentials, send out for, address to, commission, consign, drop, convey, transfer, pack off, give, bestow, grant, confer, entrust, assign, impart, give out. **2** [To broadcast, usually electronically] transmit, relay, wire, cable, broadcast, televise, carry, conduct, communicate. **—send (away) for** order, request, write away for; see ASK, GET 1. **—send back** reject, mail back, decide against; see RETURN 2.
senile ***a.*** aged, infirm, feeble; see OLD 1, SICK.
senility ***n.*** old age, dotage, feebleness, growing old, aging, infirmity, decline, senile dementia, Alzheimer's disease, senescence, second childhood; see also AGE 2, WEAKNESS 1.
senior ***a.*** elder, older, higher in rank; see SUPERIOR.
seniority ***n.*** preferred standing, ranking, station; see ADVANTAGE.
sensation ***n.*** **1** [The sense of feeling] sensibility, consciousness, perception; see EMOTION, THOUGHT 1. **2** [A feeling] response, sentiment, passion; see FEELING 1.
sensational ***a.*** **1** [Fascinating] marvelous, exciting, incredible; see IMPRESSIVE, INTERESTING. **2** [Melodramatic] exaggerated, excessive, emotional; see EXCITING.
sense ***n.*** **1** [One of the powers of physical perception] kinesthesia, function, sensation; see HEARING 3, SIGHT 1, TASTE 1, TOUCH 1. **2** [Mental ability] intellect, understanding, reason, mind, spirit, soul, brains, judgment, wit, imagination, common sense, cleverness, reasoning, intellectual ability, mental capacity, savvy*, knowledge; see also THOUGHT 1.—

taste, smell, or hearing **2** *a)* feeling, perception, etc. through the senses *b)* a generalized feeling or awareness **3** an ability to understand some quality *[a sense of humor]* **4** sound judgment **5** [*pl.*] normal ability to reason *[to come to one's senses]* **6** meaning, as of a word —***vt.* sensed, sens'ing** **1** to perceive **2** to detect as by sensors —**in a sense** to a limited degree —**make sense** to be intelligible or logical

sense'less ***adj.*** **1** unconscious **2** stupid; foolish **3** meaningless

sen·si·bil·i·ty (sen'sə bil'ə tē) ***n.***, *pl.* **-ties** **1** the ability to respond to stimuli **2** [*often pl.*] (sensitive) awareness or responsiveness

sen'si·ble (-bəl) ***adj.*** **1** that can cause physical sensation **2** easily perceived **3** aware **4** having or showing good sense; wise —**sen'si·bly *adv.***

sen'si·tive (-tiv) ***adj.*** **1** keenly susceptible to stimuli **2** tender; raw **3** highly perceptive or responsive **4** easily offended; touchy **5** detecting or reacting to slight changes *[sensitive instruments]* **6** of delicate or secret matters —**sen'si·tiv'i·ty *n.***

sen'si·tize' (-tīz') ***vt.* -tized', -tiz'ing** to make sensitive

sen·sor (sen'sər) ***n.*** a device to detect, measure, or record physical phenomena, as radiation, heat, etc.

sen·so·ry (sen'sər ē) ***adj.*** of the senses or sensation

sen·su·al (sen'shoo əl) ***adj.*** ⟦< L *sensus*, sense⟧ **1** of the body and the senses as distinguished from the intellect or spirit **2** connected or preoccupied with sexual pleasure —**sen'su·al'i·ty** (-al'ə tē) ***n.*** —**sen'su·al·ly *adv.***

sen·su·ous (sen'shoo əs) ***adj.*** **1** of, derived from, or perceived by the senses **2** enjoying sensation

sent (sent) ***vt., vi. pt. & pp. of*** SEND

sen·tence (sen'təns) ***n.*** ⟦< L *sententia*, opinion⟧ **1** *a)* a decision as of a court; esp., the determination by a court of a punishment *b)* the punishment **2** a word or group of words, usually containing a subject and predicate, that states, asks, etc. —***vt.* -tenced, -tenc·ing** to pronounce punishment upon (a convicted person)

sen·ten·tious (sen ten'shəs) ***adj.*** characterized by pompous moralizing

sen·tient (sen'shənt) ***adj.*** ⟦see SENSE⟧ of or capable of perception; conscious

sen·ti·ment (sen'tə mənt) ***n.*** ⟦see SENSE⟧ **1** a complex combination of feelings and opinions **2** an opinion, etc., often, one colored by emotion: *often used in pl.* **3** tender feelings **4** appeal to the emotions in literature, etc. **5** maudlin emotion

sen·ti·men·tal (sen'tə ment''l) ***adj.*** **1** having or showing tender or delicate feelings **2** maudlin; mawkish **3** of or resulting from sentiment —**sen'ti·men'tal·ism' *n.*** —**sen'ti·men'tal·ist *n.*** —**sen'ti·men·tal'i·ty** (-tal'ə tē) ***n.*** —**sen'ti·men'tal·ly *adv.***

sen'ti·men'tal·ize' (-īz') ***vi., vt.* -ized', -iz'ing** to be sentimental or treat in a sentimental way

sen·ti·nel (sent''n əl) ***n.*** ⟦< L *sentire*, to sense⟧ a guard or sentry

sen·try (sen'trē) ***n.***, *pl.* **-tries** ⟦< ? obs. *centrinell*, var. of prec.⟧ a sentinel; esp., a soldier posted to guard against danger

Seoul (sōl) capital of South Korea: pop. 8,367,000

se·pal (sē'pəl) ***n.*** ⟦< Gr *skepē*, a covering + *petalon*, petal⟧ any of the leaflike parts of the calyx

sep·a·ra·ble (sep'ə rə bəl) ***adj.*** that can be separated —**sep'a·ra·bly *adv.***

sep·a·rate (sep'ə rāt'; *for adj.* sep'ə rit, sep'rit) ***vt.* -rat'ed, -rat'ing** ⟦< L *se-*, apart + *parare*, arrange⟧ **1** to set apart into sections, groups, etc.; divide **2** to keep apart by being between —***vi.*** **1** to withdraw **2** to part, become disconnected, etc. **3** to go in different directions **4** to stop living together without a divorce —***adj.*** **1** not joined, united, etc.; severed **2** distinct; individual **3** not shared —**sep'a·rate·ly *adv.*** —**sep'a·ra'tor *n.***

sep·a·ra·tion (sep'ə rā'shən) ***n.*** **1** a separating or being separated **2** the place this occurs; break; division **3** something that separates

sep'a·ra·tism' (-rə tiz'əm) ***n.*** advocacy of political, religious, or racial separation —**sep'a·ra·tist *n.***

se·pi·a (sē'pē ə) ***n., adj.*** ⟦< Gr *sēpia*, cuttlefish secreting inky fluid⟧ (of) a dark reddish-brown color

sep·sis (sep'sis) ***n.*** ⟦see SEPTIC⟧ a poisoning caused by the absorption of pathogenic microorganisms into the blood

Sep·tem·ber (sep tem'bər) ***n.*** ⟦< L *septem*, seven: seventh month in Roman calendar⟧ the ninth month of the year, having 30 days: abbrev. **Sept.**

sep·tet or **sep·tette** (sep tet') ***n.*** ⟦< L *septem*, seven⟧ *Music* **1** a composition for seven voices or instruments **2** the seven performers of this

sep·tic (sep'tik) ***adj.*** ⟦< Gr *sēpein*, to make putrid⟧ causing, or resulting from, sepsis or putrefaction

THESAURUS

Ant. DULLNESS, idiocy, ignorance. **3** [Reasonable and agreeable conduct] reasonableness, fair-mindedness, discretion; see FAIRNESS. **4** [Tact and understanding] insight, discernment, prudence; see FEELING 4, JUDGMENT 1. —**in a sense** in a way, to a degree, somewhat; see SOME, SOMEHOW. —**make sense** be reasonable, be intelligible, be clear, be understandable, be logical, be coherent, articulate, add up, follow, infer, deduce, hang together*, hold water*, put two and two together, seem, appear, stand to reason.

senseless *a.* ridiculous, silly, foolish; see ILLOGICAL, STUPID.

senses *n.* consciousness, mental faculties, sanity; see AWARENESS, LIFE 1, 2.

sensible *a.* **1** [Showing good sense] reasonable, prudent, perceptive, acute, shrewd, sharp, careful, aware, wise, cautious, capable, practical, judicious, having a head on one's shoulders*, endowed with reason, discerning, thoughtful; see also SANE 1, RATIONAL 1. **2** [Perceptive] aware, informed, attentive; see CONSCIOUS.

sensitive *a.* **1** [Tender] delicate, sore, painful; see SORE 1. **2** [Touchy] high-strung, tense, nervous; see IRRITABLE, UNSTABLE 2.

sensitivity *n.* **1** [Susceptibility] allergy, irritability, ticklishness; see FEELING 4. **2** [Emotional response or condition] delicacy, sensibility, sensitiveness, nervousness, acute awareness, consciousness, acuteness, subtlety, feeling, sympathetic response, sympathy, empathy.

sensory *a.* **1** [Neurological] sensible, relating to the senses, conscious; see SENSUAL 1. **2** [Conveyed by the senses] audible, perceptible, discernible; see OBVIOUS 1, 2, TANGIBLE.

sensual *a.* **1** [Sensory] tactile, sensuous, stimulating, sharpened, pleasing, dazzling, feeling, beautiful, heightened, enhanced, appealing, delightful, luxurious, emotional, fine, arousing, stirring, moving; see also EXCITING. **2** [Carnal] voluptuous, pleasure-loving, physical, lewd, hedonistic, lustful, lascivious, earthy, self-loving, self-indulgent, epicurean, intemperate, gluttonous, rakish, debauched, orgiastic, sensuous, piggish, hoggish, bestial.

sensuality *n.* sexuality, appetite, ardor; see DESIRE 2, EMOTION, LOVE 1.

sensuous *a.* passionate, physical, exciting; see SENSUAL 2.

sent *a.* shipped, mailed, commissioned, appointed, ordained, delegated, dispatched, directed, issued, transmitted, discharged, gone, on the road, in transit, uttered, sent forth, driven, impelled, forced to go, consigned, ordered, committed.—*Ant.* KEPT, restrained, held back.

sentence *n.* **1** [A pronounced judgment] edict, decree, order; see JUDGMENT 3, PUNISHMENT, VERDICT. **2** [An expressed thought] *Types of sentences include the following:* simple, complex, compound, compound-complex, kernel, cleft, conditional, complete, incomplete, declarative, interrogative, imperative, exclamatory; statement, question, command, exclamation.

sentence *v.* pronounce judgment, judge, send to prison; see CONDEMN, CONVICT, IMPRISON, PUNISH.

sentiment *n.* sensibility, predilection, tender feeling; see EMOTION, FEELING 4, THOUGHT 2.

sentimental *a.* emotional, romantic, silly, dreamy, idealistic, visionary, artificial, unrealistic, susceptible, overemotional, affected, mawkish, simpering, insincere, overacted, schoolgirlish, sappy*, corny*, gushy.

sentimentality *n.* sentimentalism, sentiment, melodramatics, bathos, mawkishness, melodrama, triteness, mush*, romance; see also EMOTION.

sentry *n.* sentinel, lookout, protector; see WATCHMAN.

separate *v.* **1** [To keep apart] isolate, insulate, single out, sequester, seclude, rope off, segregate, intervene, stand between, draw apart, split up, break up. **2** [To part company] take leave, go away, depart; see LEAVE 1.

separated *a.* divided, parted, apart, disconnected, partitioned, distinct, disunited, disjointed, sundered, disembodied, cut in two, cut apart, set apart, distant, removed, disassociated, distributed, scattered, put asunder, divorced, divergent, marked, severed, far between, in halves.—*Ant.* UNITED, together, whole.

separately *a.* singly, independently, distinctly; see CLEARLY 1, 2, INDIVIDUALLY.

separation *n.* **1** [The act of dividing] disconnection, severance, division, cut, detachment. **2** [The act of parting] coming apart, drawing apart, parting company, breaking up, departure, embarkation.

sep·ti·ce·mi·a (sep′tə sē′mē ə) ***n.*** ⟦see prec.⟧ a disease caused by infectious microorganisms in the blood

septic tank an underground tank in which waste matter is putrefied and decomposed by bacteria

sep·tu·a·ge·nar·i·an (sep′to͞o ə jə ner′ē ən) ***n.*** ⟦< L *septuaginta*, seventy⟧ a person between the ages of 70 and 80

Sep·tu·a·gint (sep′to͞o ə jint′) ***n.*** ⟦< L *septuaginta*, seventy: in tradition, done in 70 days⟧ a translation into Greek of the Hebrew Scriptures

sep·tum (sep′təm) ***n.***, *pl.* **-tums** or **-ta** (-tə) ⟦< L *saepire*, enclose, fence⟧ *Biol.* a wall or part that separates, as in the nose or in a fruit

sep·ul·cher (sep′əl kər) ***n.*** ⟦< L *sepelire*, bury⟧ a vault for burial; tomb

se·pul·chral (sə pul′krəl) ***adj.*** **1** of sepulchers, burial, etc. **2** suggestive of the grave or burial; gloomy **3** deep and melancholy: said of sound

seq. *abbrev.* ⟦L *sequentes*⟧ the following

se·quel (sē′kwəl) ***n.*** ⟦< L *sequi*, follow⟧ **1** something that follows; continuation **2** a result; consequence **3** any literary work, film, etc. continuing a story begun in an earlier one

se·quence (sē′kwəns) ***n.*** ⟦< L *sequi*, follow⟧ **1** *a*) the coming of one thing after another; succession *b*) the order in which this occurs **2** a series **3** a resulting event **4** *Film* a succession of scenes forming a single episode

se·quen·tial (si kwen′shəl) ***adj.*** of or occurring in a sequence —**se·quen′tial·ly** ***adv.***

se·ques·ter (si kwes′tər) ***vt.*** ⟦< L *sequester*, trustee⟧ **1** to set off or apart **2** to withdraw; isolate —**se·ques·tra·tion** (sē′kwə strā′shən) ***n.***

se·quin (sē′kwin) ***n.*** ⟦Fr; ult. < Ar *sikka*, a stamp, die⟧ a spangle, esp. one of many sewn on fabric for decoration —**se′quined** or **se′quinned** ***adj.***

se·quoi·a (si kwoi′ə) ***n.*** ⟦after *Sequoyah* (1760?-1843), Indian inventor of Cherokee writing system⟧ REDWOOD (sense 1)

se·ra (sir′ə) ***n.*** *alt. pl. of* SERUM

se·ra·glio (si ral′yō) ***n.***, *pl.* **-glios** ⟦< L *sera*, a lock⟧ HAREM (sense 1)

se·ra·pe (sə rä′pē) ***n.*** ⟦MexSp⟧ a bright-colored wool blanket used as a garment by men in Mexico, etc.

ser·aph (ser′əf) ***n.***, *pl.* **-aphs** or **-a·phim′** (-ə fim′) ⟦< Heb *serafim*, pl.⟧ *Theol.* a heavenly being, or any of the highest order of angels —**se·raph·ic** (sə raf′ik) ***adj.*** —**se·raph′i·cal·ly** ***adv.***

Serb (surb) ***n.*** a person born or living in Serbia; esp., a member of a Slavic people of Serbia and adjacent areas —***adj.*** SERBIAN

Ser·bi·a (sur′bē ə) the major constituent republic of Yugoslavia —**Ser′bi·an** ***adj.***, ***n.***

Ser·bo-Cro·a·tian (sur′bō krō ā′shən) ***n.*** the major Slavic language of Yugoslavia, Bosnia and Herzegovina, and Croatia

ser·e·nade (ser′ə nād′) ***n.*** ⟦ult. < L *serenus*, clear⟧ **1** music played or sung at night, esp. by a lover **2** a piece of music like this —***vt.***, ***vi.*** **-nad′ed**, **-nad′ing** to play or sing a serenade (to)

ser·en·dip·i·ty (ser′ən dip′ə tē) ***n.*** ⟦after Pers tale *The Three Princes of Serendip* (Sri Lanka)⟧ a seeming gift for finding good things accidentally —**ser′en·dip′i·tous** ***adj.***

se·rene (sə rēn′) ***adj.*** ⟦L *serenus*⟧ **1** clear; unclouded **2** undisturbed; calm —**se·rene′ly** ***adv.*** —**se·ren′i·ty** (-ren′ə tē) or **se·rene′ness** ***n.***

serf (surf) ***n.*** ⟦< L *servus*, a slave⟧ a person in feudal servitude, bound to a master's land and transferred with it to a new owner —**serf′dom** ***n.***

serge (surj) ***n.*** ⟦< L *sericus*, silken⟧ a strong twilled fabric

ser·geant (sär′jənt) ***n.*** ⟦< L *servire*, serve⟧ **1** a noncommissioned officer ranking above a corporal **2** a police officer ranking next below a captain or a lieutenant

ser′geant-at-arms′ ***n.***, *pl.* **ser′geants-at-arms′** an officer appointed to keep order, as in a court

sergeant major *pl.* **sergeants major** the highest ranking noncommissioned officer

se·ri·al (sir′ē əl) ***adj.*** ⟦< L *series*, a row, order⟧ appearing in a series of continuous parts at regular intervals —***n.*** a story, etc. presented in serial form —**se′ri·al·i·za′tion** ***n.*** —**se′ri·al·ize′**, **-ized′**, **-iz′ing**, ***vt.***

serial number one of a series of numbers given for identification

se·ries (sir′ēz) ***n.***, *pl.* **-ries** ⟦L < *serere*, join together⟧ a number of similar things or persons arranged in a row or coming one after another

se·ri·ous (sir′ē əs) ***adj.*** ⟦< L *serius*⟧ **1** earnest, grave, sober, etc. **2** not joking; sincere **3** requiring careful consideration **4** weighty **5** dangerous —**se′ri·ous·ly** ***adv.*** —**se′ri·ous·ness** ***n.***

ser·mon (sur′mən) ***n.*** ⟦< L *sermo*, a discourse⟧ **1** a speech on religion or morals, esp. by a member of the clergy **2** any serious talk on behavior, duty, etc., esp. a tedious one —**ser′mon·ize′**, **-ized′**, **-iz′ing**, ***vi.***

se·rous (sir′əs) ***adj.*** **1** of or containing serum **2** thin and watery

ser·pent (sur′pənt) ***n.*** ⟦< L *serpere*, to creep⟧ a snake

ser′pen·tine′ (-pən tēn′, -tīn′) ***adj.*** of or like a serpent; esp., *a*) cunning; treacherous *b*) coiled; winding

ser·rate (ser′āt′) ***adj.*** ⟦< L *serra*, a saw⟧ having sawlike notches along the edge: said of some leaves: also **ser′rat′ed** —**ser·ra′tion** ***n.***

ser·ried (ser′ēd) ***adj.*** ⟦< LL *serare*, to lock⟧ placed close together

se·rum (sir′əm) ***n.***, *pl.* **-rums** or **-ra** (-ə) ⟦L, whey⟧ **1** a clear, watery animal fluid, as the yellowish fluid (**blood serum**) separating from a blood clot after coagulation **2** blood serum used as an antitoxin, taken from an animal inoculated for a specific disease

serv·ant (sur′vənt) ***n.*** ⟦ult. < L *servire*, serve⟧ **1** a person employed by another, esp. to do household duties **2** a person devoted to another or to a cause, creed, etc.

serve (surv) ***vt.*** **served**, **serv′ing** ⟦< L *servus*, slave⟧ **1** to work for as a servant **2** to do services for; aid; help **3** to

THESAURUS

sequel ***n.*** consequence, continuation, progression; see SEQUENCE 1, SERIES.

sequence ***n.*** **1** [Succession] order, continuity, continuousness, continuance, successiveness, progression, graduation, consecutiveness, flow, perpetuity, unbrokenness, subsequence, course. **2** [Arrangement] placement, distribution, classification; see ORDER 3. **3** [A series] chain, string, array; see SERIES.

serenade ***n.*** melody, love song, nocturne; see MUSIC 1, SONG.

serene ***a.*** calm, clear, unruffled, peaceful, translucent, undisturbed, undimmed, tranquil, composed, cool, coolheaded, sedate, levelheaded, content, satisfied, patient, reconciled, easygoing, placid, limpid, comfortable, cheerful.—*Ant.* CONFUSED, disturbed, ruffled.

serenity ***n.*** quietness, calmness, tranquility; see PEACE 2, 3.

sergeant ***n.*** noncommissioned officer, top kick*, sarge*. *Types include the following:* master sergeant, staff sergeant, technical sergeant, first sergeant, top sergeant, platoon sergeant, drill sergeant, sergeant major, sergeant-at-arms, police sergeant; see also OFFICER 3, SOLDIER.

serial ***n.*** installment, series, continued story; see MOVIE.

series ***n.*** rank, file, line, row, set, train, range, list, string, chain, order, sequence, succession, group, procession, continuity, column, progression, category, classification, scale, array, gradation.

serious ***a.*** **1** [Involving danger] grave, severe, pressing; see DANGEROUS, IMPORTANT 1. **2** [Thoughtful] earnest, sober, reflective; see SOLEMN.

seriously ***a.*** **1** [In a manner fraught with danger] dangerously, precariously, perilously, in a risky way, threateningly, menacingly, grievously, severely, harmfully.—*Ant.* SAFELY, harmlessly, in no danger. **2** [In a manner that recognizes importance] gravely, soberly, earnestly, sedately, solemnly, thoughtfully, sternly, with great earnestness, all joking aside; see also SINCERELY.—*Ant.* LIGHTLY, thoughtlessly, airily. —**take seriously** consider, calculate on, work on; see BELIEVE, TRUST 1.

seriousness ***n.*** **1** [The quality of being dangerous] gravity, weight, enormity; see IMPORTANCE. **2** [The characteristic of being sober] earnestness, sobriety, solemnity, gravity, staidness, thoughtfulness, calmness, coolness, sedateness, sober-mindedness; see also SINCERITY.—*Ant.* FUN, gaiety, levity.

sermon ***n.*** lesson, doctrine, lecture; see SPEECH 3.

serpent ***n.*** reptile, viper, pit viper; see SNAKE.

servant ***n.*** attendant, retainer, helper, hireling, dependent, menial, lackey, domestic, drudge, slave; see also ASSISTANT. *Servants include the following:* butler, housekeeper, chef, cook, kitchenmaid, general maid, laundress, chambermaid, parlormaid, lady's maid, seamstress, nursemaid, nurse, valet, doorman, footman, squire, chauffeur, groom, gardener, yardman, kennelman.

serve ***v.*** **1** [To fulfill an obligation] hear duty's call, obey the call of one's country, carry out, discharge one's duty, assume one's responsibilities. **2** [To work for] be employed by, labor

do military or naval service for **4** to spend (a term of imprisonment, etc.) *[to serve ten years]* **5** to provide (customers, etc.) with goods or services **6** to set food, etc. before (a person) **7** to meet the needs of **8** to be used by *[this hospital serves the whole city]* **9** to function for *[if memory serves me well]* **10** to deliver (a summons, etc.) to (someone) **11** to hit (a tennis ball, etc.) in order to start play —***vi.*** **1** to work as a servant **2** to do service *[to serve in the navy]* **3** to carry out the duties of an office **4** to be of service **5** to meet needs **6** to provide guests with food or drink **7** to be favorable: said of weather, etc. —***n.*** a serving of the ball in tennis, etc. —**serve someone right** to be what someone deserves, for doing something wrong

serv'er ***n.*** **1** one who serves **2** a thing for serving, as a tray **3** *Comput.* the central computer in a network, on which shared files, etc. are stored

serv·ice (sur'vis) ***n.*** ⟦< L *servus*, slave⟧ **1** the occupation of a servant **2** *a)* public employment *[diplomatic service]* *b)* a branch of this; specif., the armed forces **3** work done for others *[repair service]* **4** any religious ceremony **5** *a)* benefit; advantage *b)* [*pl.*] friendly help; also, professional aid **6** the act or manner of serving food **7** a set of articles used in serving *[a tea service]* **8** a system of providing people with some utility, as water or gas **9** the act or manner of serving the ball in tennis, etc. —***vt.*** **-iced, -ic·ing** **1** to furnish with a service **2** to make fit for service, as by repairing —**at someone's service** **1** ready to serve someone **2** ready for someone's use —**in service** functioning —**of service** helpful

serv'ice·a·ble ***adj.*** **1** that can be of service; useful **2** that will give good service; durable

serv'ice·man' (-man', -mən) ***n.***, *pl.* **-men'** (-men', -mən) **1** a member of the armed forces **2** a person whose work is repairing something *[a TV serviceman]*: also **service man**

service mark a word, etc. used like a trademark by a supplier of a service

service station a place selling gasoline, oil, etc., for motor vehicles

ser·vile (sur'vəl, -vīl') ***adj.*** ⟦< L *servus*, slave⟧ **1** of slaves **2** like that of slaves or servants **3** humbly submissive —**ser·vil·i·ty** (sər vil'ə tē) ***n.***

ser·vi·tude (sur'və to͞od') ***n.*** ⟦see SERF⟧ **1** slavery or bondage **2** work imposed to punish a crime

ser·vo (sur'vō) ***n.***, *pl.* **-vos** *short for:* **1** SERVOMECHANISM **2** SERVOMOTOR

ser'vo·mech'a·nism ***n.*** an automatic control system of low power, used to exercise remote but accurate mechanical control

ser'vo·mo'tor ***n.*** a device, as an electric motor, for changing a small force into a large force, as in a servomechanism

ses·a·me (ses'ə mē') ***n.*** ⟦of Semitic origin⟧ **1** a plant whose edible seeds yield an oil **2** its seeds

ses·qui·cen·ten·ni·al (ses'kwi sen ten'ē əl) ***adj.*** ⟦< L *sesqui-*, more by a half + CENTENNIAL⟧ of a period of 150 years —***n.*** a 150th anniversary

ses·sion (sesh'ən) ***n.*** ⟦< L *sedere*, sit⟧ **1** *a)* the meeting of a court, legislature, etc. *b)* a series of such meetings *c)* the period of these **2** a school term **3** a period of activity of any kind

set (set) ***vt.*** **set, set'ting** ⟦OE *settan*⟧ **1** to cause to sit; seat **2** to put in a specified place, condition, etc. *[to set books on a shelf, set slaves free]* **3** to put in a proper condition; fix (a trap for animals), adjust (a clock or dial), arrange (a table for a meal), fix (hair) in a desired style, etc., put (a broken bone, etc.) into normal position, etc. **4** to make settled, rigid, or fixed *[pectin sets jelly]* **5** to mount (gems) **6** to direct; point **7** to appoint; establish; fix (boundaries, the time for an event, a rule, a quota, etc.) **8** to furnish (an example) for others **9** to fit (words *to* music or music *to* words) **10** to arrange (type) for printing —***vi.*** **1** to sit on eggs: said of a fowl **2** to become firm, hard, or fixed *[this cement sets quickly]* **3** to begin to move (*out, forth, off*, etc.) **4** to sink below the horizon *[the sun sets]* —***adj.*** **1** fixed; established *[a set time]* **2** intentional **3** fixed; rigid; firm **4** obstinate **5** ready *[get set]* —***n.*** **1** a setting or being set **2** the way or position in which a thing is set *[the set of his jaw]* **3** direction; tendency **4** the scenery for a play, etc. **5** a group of persons or things classed or belonging together **6** assembled equipment for radio or TV reception, etc. **7** *Tennis* a group of six or more games won by a margin of at least two —**set about** (or **in** or **to**) to begin —**set down** **1** to put in writing **2** to establish (rules, etc.) —**set forth** **1** to publish **2** to state —**set off** **1** to make prominent or enhance by contrast **2** to make explode —**set on** (or **upon**) to attack —**set up** **1** to erect **2** to establish; found

set'back' ***n.*** a reversal in progress

set'screw' ***n.*** a screw used in regulating the tension of a spring, etc.

set·tee (se tē') ***n.*** **1** a seat or bench with a back **2** a small sofa

set'ter ***n.*** a long-haired dog trained to hunt

set'ting ***n.*** **1** the act of one that sets **2** the position of a dial, etc. that has been set **3** a mounting, as of a gem **4** the time, place, etc., as of a story **5** actual physical surroundings

set·tle (set''l) ***vt.*** **-tled, -tling** ⟦< OE *setl*, a seat⟧ **1** to put in order; arrange *[to settle one's affairs]* **2** to set in place firmly or comfortably **3** to colonize **4** to cause to sink and become more compact **5** to free (the nerves, etc.) from disturbance **6** to decide (doubt) **7** to end (a dispute) **8** to pay (a debt, etc.) —***vi.*** **1** to stop moving and stay in one place **2** to descend, as fog does over a landscape, or gloom over a person **3** to become localized: said as of pain **4** to take up permanent residence **5** to sink *[the house settled]* **6** to become more dense by sinking,

THESAURUS

for, be in the employ of; see WORK 2. **3** [To help] give aid, assist, be of assistance; see HELP. **4** [To serve at table] wait on, attend, provide guests with food, help. —**serve someone right** deserve it, having it coming, get one's just deserts; see DESERVE.

served ***a.*** dressed, prepared, offered, apportioned, dealt, furnished, supplied, provided, dished up.

service ***n.*** **1** [Aid] cooperation, assistance, support; see HELP 1. **2** [Tableware] set, silver, setting; see DISH 1, POTTERY. **3** [A religious service] rite, worship, sermon; see CEREMONY 2. **4** [Military service] the armed forces, duty, active service, stint. —**at someone's service** zealous, anxious to help, obedient; see HELPFUL 1, READY 1, WILLING. —**of service** useful, handy, usable; see HELPFUL 1.

service ***v.*** maintain, work on, keep up; see REPAIR.

serviceable ***a.*** practical, advantageous, beneficial; see HELPFUL 1, USABLE.

serving ***n.*** plateful, course, portion; see MEAL 2.

session ***n.*** assembly, concourse, sitting; see GATHERING.

set ***a.*** **1** [Firm] stable, solid, settled; see FIRM 2. **2** [Determined] concluded, agreed upon, decided; see DETERMINED 1.

set ***n.*** **1** [Setting] attitude, position, bearing; see INCLINATION 1. **2** [A social group] clique, coterie, circle; see FACTION, ORGANIZATION 2. **3** [A collection of (like) items] kit, assemblage, assortment; see COLLECTION.

set ***v.*** **1** [To place] insert, settle, put, plant, store, situate, lay, deposit, arrange. **2** [To establish] anchor, fix, introduce; see ESTABLISH 2, INSTALL. **3** [To become firm] jell, solidify, congeal; see HARDEN, STIFFEN, THICKEN. —**set about** start, begin, start doing; see BEGIN 1. —**set off** **1** [To show by contrast] set in relief, enhance, intensify, make distinct. **2** [To explode] touch off, set the spark to, detonate; see EXPLODE. —**set up** **1** [To make arrangements] prearrange, inaugurate, work on; see ARRANGE 2. **2** [To finance] patronize, promote, support; see PAY 1.

setback ***n.*** hindrance, impediment, reversal; see DELAY, DIFFICULTY 1.

setting ***n.*** environment, surroundings, mounting, backdrop, frame, framework, background, context, perspective, horizon, shadow, shade, distance.—*Ant.* FRONT, foreground, focus.

settle ***v.*** **1** [To decide] reach a decision, form judgment on, come to a conclusion about; see DECIDE. **2** [To prove] establish, verify, make certain; see PROVE. **3** [To finish] end, make an end of, complete; see ACHIEVE. **4** [To sink] descend, fall, decline; see SINK 1. **5** [To establish residence] locate, lodge, become a citizen, reside, fix one's residence, abide, set up housekeeping, make one's home, establish a home, keep house; see also DWELL. **6** [To take up sedentary life; *often used with "down"*] follow regular habits, live an orderly life, become conventional, follow convention, buy a house, marry, marry and settle down, raise a family, get in a rut, hang up one's hat*. **7** [To satisfy a claim] pay, compensate, make an adjustment, reach a compromise, make payment, arrange a settlement, get squared away, pay damages, pay out, settle out of court, settle up, work out, settle the score*, even the score*, dispose of, resolve, rectify, reconcile.

settled ***a.*** decided, resolved, ended; see DETERMINED 1.

as sediment does **7** to become more stable **8** to reach an agreement or decision (*with* or *on*) —**set'tler** ***n.***

set'tle·ment ***n.*** **1** a settling or being settled **2** a new colony **3** a village **4** an agreement

set'-to' ***n.***, *pl.* **-tos'** [Inf.] **1** a fight **2** an argument

set'up' ***n.*** **1** *a)* the plan, makeup, or arrangement of equipment, an organization, etc. *b)* the details of a situation, plan, etc. **2** [Inf.] a contest, etc. arranged to result in an easy victory

sev·en (sev'ən) ***adj.***, ***n.*** ⟦OE *seofon*⟧ one more than six; 7; VII —**sev'enth** ***adj.***, ***n.***

sev'en·teen' (-tēn') ***adj.***, ***n.*** seven more than ten; 17; XVII —**sev'en·teenth'** (-tēnth') ***adj.***, ***n.***

seventeen-year locust a cicada which lives underground for 13-17 years before emerging as an adult

seventh heaven perfect happiness

sev·en·ty (sev'ən tē) ***adj.***, ***n.***, *pl.* **-ties** seven times ten; 70; LXX —**the seventies** the years, from 70 through 79, as of a century —**sev'en·ti·eth** (-ith) ***adj.***, ***n.***

sev·er (sev'ər) ***vt.***, ***vi.*** ⟦ult. < L *separare*⟧ to separate, divide, or divide off —**sev'er·ance** ***n.***

sev·er·al (sev'ər əl) ***adj.*** ⟦ult. < L *separ*⟧ **1** separate; distinct **2** different; respective **3** more than two but not many; few —***pl.n.*** a small number (*of*) —***pron.*** [*with pl. v.*] a few —**sev'er·al·ly** ***adv.***

se·vere (sə vir') ***adj.*** **-ver'er, -ver'est** ⟦< L *severus*⟧ **1** harsh or strict, as in treatment **2** serious or grave, as in expression **3** rigidly accurate or demanding **4** extremely plain *[a dress with severe lines]* **5** intense *[severe pain]* **6** rigorous; trying —**se·vere'ly** ***adv.*** —**se·vere'ness** or **se·ver'i·ty** (-ver'ə tē) ***n.***

Se·ville (sə vil') city in SW Spain: pop. 720,000

Sè·vres (sev'rə; *Fr* se'vr') ***n.*** ⟦after *Sèvres*, SW suburb of Paris, where made⟧ a type of fine French porcelain

sew (sō) ***vt.***, ***vi.*** **sewed, sewn** (sōn) or **sewed, sew'ing** ⟦OE *siwian*⟧ **1** to fasten with stitches made with needle and thread **2** to make, mend, etc. by sewing —**sew up 1** [Inf.] to get full control of **2** to make sure of success in —**sew'er** ***n.***

sew·age (so͞o'ij) ***n.*** the waste matter carried off by sewers or drains

sew·er (so͞o'ər) ***n.*** ⟦ult. < L *ex*, out + *aqua*, water⟧ a pipe or drain, usually underground, used to carry off water and waste matter

sew'er·age ***n.*** **1** a system of sewers **2** SEWAGE

sew'ing ***n.*** **1** the act of one who sews **2** something to be sewn

sewing machine a machine with a mechanically driven needle used for sewing

sex (seks) ***n.*** ⟦< L *sexus*⟧ **1** either of two divisions, male or female, into which persons, animals, or plants are divided **2** the character of being male or female **3** the attraction between the sexes **4** sexual intercourse —***adj.*** SEXUAL

sex- ⟦< L *sex*, six⟧ *combining form* six

sex·a·ge·nar·i·an (sek'sə ji ner'ē ən) ***n.*** ⟦< L⟧ a person between the ages of 60 and 70

sex appeal the physical charm that attracts members of the opposite sex

sex chromosome a sex-determining chromosome in the germ cells: eggs carry an X chromosome and spermatozoa either an X or a Y chromosome, with a female resulting from an XX pairing and a male from an XY

sex'ism' ***n.*** discrimination against people, esp. women, on the basis of sex —**sex'ist** ***adj.***, ***n.***

sex·tant (seks'tənt) ***n.*** ⟦< L *sextans*, a sixth part (of a circle)⟧ an instrument for measuring the angular distance of the sun, a star, etc. from the horizon, as to determine position at sea

sex·tet or **sex·tette** (seks tet') ***n.*** ⟦ult. < L *sex*, six⟧ **1** a group of six **2** *Music* a composition for six voices or instruments, or its six performers

sex·ton (seks'tən) ***n.*** ⟦ult. < L *sacer*, sacred⟧ a church official who maintains church property

sex·u·al (sek'sho͞o əl) ***adj.*** of or involving sex, the sexes, the sex organs, etc. —**sex'u·al·ly** ***adv.*** —**sex'u·al'i·ty** (-al'ə tē) ***n.***

sexual harassment inappropriate, unwelcome behavior by an employer or colleague that is sexual in nature

sexual intercourse a joining of the sexual organs of a male and a female human being

sex'y ***adj.*** **-i·er, -i·est 1** [Inf.] exciting or intended to excite sexual desire **2** [Slang] exciting, glamorous, etc. —**sex'i·ly** ***adv.*** —**sex'i·ness** ***n.***

Sey·chelles (sā shel', -shelz') country on a group of islands in the Indian Ocean, northeast of Madagascar: 175 sq. mi.; pop. 67,000

sf or **SF** *abbrev.* science fiction

Sgt *abbrev.* Sergeant

sh (sh) ***interj.*** used to ask for silence

shab·by (shab'ē) ***adj.*** **-bi·er, -bi·est** ⟦OE *sceabb*, scab⟧ **1** rundown; dilapidated **2** *a)* ragged; worn *b)* wearing worn clothing **3** mean; shameful *[shabby treatment]* —**shab'bi·ly** ***adv.*** —**shab'bi·ness** ***n.***

shack (shak) ***n.*** ⟦< ?⟧ a small, crudely built house or cabin; shanty

shack·le (shak'əl) ***n.*** ⟦OE *sceacel*⟧ **1** a metal fastening, usually in pairs, for the wrist or ankle of a prisoner; fetter **2** anything that restrains freedom, as of expression **3** a device for fastening or coupling —***vt.*** **-led, -ling 1** to put shackles on **2** to restrain in freedom of expression or action

shad (shad) ***n.***, *pl.* **shad** or **shads** ⟦OE *sceadd*⟧ an American coastal food fish

shade (shād) ***n.*** ⟦OE *sceadu*⟧ **1** comparative darkness caused by an object cutting off rays of light **2** an area

THESAURUS

settlement ***n.*** **1** [An agreement] covenant, arrangement, compact; see AGREEMENT 1, CONTRACT. **2** [A payment] compensation, remuneration, reimbursement; see ADJUSTMENT, PAY 1. **3** [A colony] principality, plantation, establishment; see COLONY.

settler ***n.*** planter, immigrant, homesteader; see PIONEER 2.

setup ***n.*** structure, composition, plan; see ORDER 3, ORGANIZATION 2.

sever ***v.*** part, split, cleave; see CUT 1, DIVIDE.

several ***a.*** **1** [Few] some, any, a few, quite a few, not many, sundry, two or three, a small number of, scarce, sparse, hardly any, scarcely any, half a dozen, only a few, scant, scanty, rare, infrequent, in a minority, a handful, more or less, not too many.—*Ant.* many, large numbers of, none. **2** [Various] plural, a number of, numerous; see MANY, VARIOUS.

several ***n.*** various ones, a small number, quite a few; see FEW.

severe ***a.*** **1** [Stern] exacting, uncompromising, unbending, inflexible, unchanging, unalterable, harsh, cruel, oppressive, close, grinding, obdurate, resolute, austere, rigid, grim, earnest, stiff, forbidding, resolved, relentless, determined, unfeeling, with an iron will, strict, inconsiderate, firm, unsparing, immovable, unyielding, adamant. **2** [Difficult or rigorous] overbearing, tyrannical, sharp, exacting, drastic, domineering, rigid, oppressive, despotic, intractable, unmerciful, bullying, uncompromising, relentless, unrelenting, hard, rigorous, austere, grinding, grim, implacable, cruel, pitiless, critical, unjust, barbarous, crusty, gruff, stubborn, autocratic, hidebound; see also DIFFICULT 1.—*Ant.* EASY, easygoing, indulgent.

severely ***a.*** critically, harshly, rigorously; see FIRMLY 2, SERIOUSLY 1.

severity ***n.*** hardness, hardheartedness, strictness; see CRUELTY.

sew ***v.*** stitch, seam, fasten, work with needle and thread, tailor, tack, embroider, bind, piece, baste.

sewage ***n.*** excrement, offal, waste matter; see RESIDUE.

sewer ***n.*** drain, drainpipe, drainage tube, conduit, gutter, disposal system, sewage system, septic tank, dry well, trench, leach field, leach bed, leach ditches, sewage disposal, sanitary sewer, sanitary facilities.

sewing ***n.*** stitching, seaming, tailoring, embroidering, darning, mending, piecing, patching, dressmaking.

sex ***n.*** **1** [Ideas associated with sexual relationships] sex attraction, sex appeal, magnetism, sensuality, affinity, love, courtship, marriage, generation, reproduction. **2** [A group, either male or female] men, women, males, females, the feminine world, the masculine world. **3** [Gender] sexuality, masculinity, femininity, womanliness, manhood, manliness. **4** [Sexual intercourse] making love, the sexual act, going to bed with someone; see COPULATION, FORNICATION.

sexual ***a.*** **1** [Reproductive] generative, reproductive, procreative; see ORIGINAL 1. **2** [Intimate] carnal, wanton, passionate; see SENSUAL 2.

sexuality ***n.*** lust, sensuality, passion; see DESIRE 2.

shabby ***a.*** ragged, threadbare, faded, ill-dressed, dilapidated, decayed, deteriorated, poor, pitiful, worn, meager, miserable, wretched, poverty-stricken, scrubby, seedy, gone to seed, down at the heel, grubby, in bad repair.—*Ant.* NEAT, new, well-kept.

shack ***n.*** hut, shed, hovel, cabin, shanty, cottage.

shade ***n.*** **1** [Lack of light] blackness, shadow, dimness; see DARKNESS 1. **2** [A degree of color] brilliance, saturation, hue; see COLOR, TINT. **3** [A slight difference] variation, trace, hint; see SUGGESTION 1. **4** [An obstruction to light] covering, blind, screen; see CURTAIN.

shade ***v.*** **1** [To intercept direct

with less light than its surroundings **3** degree of darkness of a color *[shades* of blue*]* **4** *a)* a small difference *[shades* of opinion*]* *b)* a slight amount or degree **5** [Chiefly Literary] a ghost **6** a device used to screen from light *[*a window *shade]* **7** [*pl.*] [Slang] sunglasses —***vt.*** **shad'ed, shad'ing** **1** to screen from light **2** to darken; dim **3** to represent shade in (a painting, etc.) —***vi.*** to change slightly or by degrees —**shades of** *exclamation used to refer to* a reminder of the past

shad'ing ***n.*** **1** a shielding against light **2** shade in a picture **3** a small variation

shad·ow (shad'ō) ***n.*** ⟦< OE *sceadu*, shade⟧ **1** (a) shade cast by a body intercepting light rays **2** gloom or that which causes gloom **3** a shaded area in a picture **4** a ghost **5** a remnant; trace —***vt.*** **1** to throw a shadow upon **2** to follow closely, esp. in secret —**shad'ow·y** ***adj.***

shad'ow·box' ***vi.*** *Boxing* to spar with an imaginary opponent in training

shad·y (shā'dē) ***adj.*** **-i·er, -i·est** **1** giving shade **2** shaded; full of shade **3** [Inf.] of questionable character —**on the shady side of** beyond (a given age) —**shad'i·ness** ***n.***

shaft (shaft) ***n.*** ⟦OE *sceaft*⟧ **1** an arrow or spear, or its stem **2** anything hurled like a missile *[shafts* of wit*]* **3** a long, slender part or object, as a pillar, a bar transmitting motion to a mechanical part, or either of the poles between which an animal is harnessed to a vehicle **4** a long, narrow passage sunk into the earth **5** a vertical opening passing through a building, as for an elevator —***vt.*** [Slang] to cheat, trick, exploit, etc.

shag[1] (shag) ***n.*** ⟦< OE *sceacga*, rough hair⟧ a rough, heavy nap, as on some cloth

shag[2] (shag) ***vt.*** **shagged, shag'ging** to chase after and retrieve (baseballs hit in batting practice)

shag'gy ***adj.*** **-gi·er, -gi·est** **1** covered with long, coarse hair or wool **2** unkempt, straggly, etc. **3** having a rough nap

shah (shä) ***n.*** ⟦Pers *šāh*⟧ the title of any of the former rulers of Iran

shake (shāk) ***vt., vi.*** **shook, shak'en, shak'ing** ⟦OE *sceacan*⟧ **1** to move quickly up and down, back and forth, etc. **2** to bring, force, mix, etc. by brisk movements **3** to tremble or cause to tremble **4** *a)* to become or cause to become unsteady *b)* to unnerve or become unnerved **5** to clasp (another's hand), as in greeting —***n.*** **1** an act of shaking **2** a wood shingle **3** *short for* MILKSHAKE **4** [*pl.*] [Inf.] a convulsive trembling: usually with *the* —**no great shakes** [Inf.] not outstanding —**shake down** **1** to cause to fall by shaking **2** [Slang] to extort money from —**shake off** to get rid of

shake'down' ***n.*** **1** [Slang] an extortion of money, as by blackmail **2** a thorough search —***adj.*** for testing new equipment, etc. *[*a *shakedown* cruise*]*

shake'out' ***n.*** a drop in economic activity that eliminates unprofitable businesses, etc.

shak'er ***n.*** **1** one that shakes **2** a device used in shaking **3** [**S-**] a member of a religious sect that lived in celibate communities in the U.S.

Shake·speare (shāk'spir), **William** 1564-1616; Eng. poet & dramatist —**Shake·spear'e·an** or **Shake·spear'i·an** ***adj., n.***

shake'-up' ***n.*** a shaking up; specif., an extensive reorganization

shak'y ***adj.*** **-i·er, -i·est** **1** not firm; weak or unsteady **2** *a)* trembling *b)* nervous **3** not reliable; questionable —**shak'i·ness** ***n.***

shale (shāl) ***n.*** ⟦< OE *scealu*, shell⟧ a rock formed of hard clay: it splits easily into thin layers

shale oil oil distilled from a hard shale containing veins of a greasy organic solid

shall (shal) ***v.aux.*** *pt.* **should** ⟦OE *sceal*⟧ **1** used in the first person to indicate simple future time **2** used in the second or third person, esp. in formal speech or writing, to express determination, compulsion, obligation, or necessity See usage note at WILL[2]

shal·lot (shə lät', shal'ət) ***n.*** ⟦< OFr *eschaloigne*, scallion⟧ **1** a small onion whose clustered bulbs are used for flavoring **2** GREEN ONION

shal·low (shal'ō) ***adj.*** ⟦ME *shalow*⟧ **1** not deep **2** lacking depth of character, intellect, etc. —***n.*** [*usually pl., often with sing. v.*] SHOAL[2] (sense 1)

shalt (shalt) ***v.aux.*** *archaic 2d pers. sing., pres. indic., of* SHALL: used with *thou*

sham (sham) ***n.*** ⟦< ? shame⟧ something false or fake; person or thing that is a fraud —***adj.*** false or fake —***vt., vi.*** **shammed, sham'ming** to pretend; feign

sham·ble (sham'bəl) ***vi.*** **-bled, -bling** ⟦< obs. use in *shamble legs*, bench legs⟧ to walk clumsily; shuffle —***n.*** a shambling walk

sham'bles ***n.*** ⟦ME *schamel*, butcher's bench; ult. < L⟧ **1** a slaughterhouse **2** a scene of great slaughter, destruction, or disorder

shame (shām) ***n.*** ⟦OE *scamu*⟧ **1** a painful feeling of guilt for improper behavior, etc. **2** dishonor or disgrace **3** something regrettable or outrageous —***vt.*** **shamed, sham'ing** **1** to cause to feel shame **2** to dishonor or disgrace **3** to force by a sense of shame —**put to shame** **1** to cause to feel shame **2** to surpass; outdo —**shame'ful** ***adj.*** —**shame'ful·ly** ***adv.*** —**shame'ful·ness** ***n.***

shame'faced' ***adj.*** showing shame; ashamed

shame'less ***adj.*** having or showing no shame, modesty, or decency; brazen —**shame'less·ly** ***adv.***

sham·poo (sham po͞o') ***vt.*** **-pooed', -poo'ing** ⟦Hindi *chāmpnā*, to press⟧ **1** to wash (the hair) **2** to wash (a rug, sofa, etc.) —***n.*** **1** a shampooing **2** a liquid soap, etc. used for this

sham·rock (sham'räk') ***n.*** ⟦Ir *seamar*, clover⟧ a plant, esp. a clover, with leaflets in groups of three: the emblem of Ireland

shang·hai (shaŋ'hī') ***vt.*** ⟦< such kidnapping for crews on the China run⟧ to kidnap, usually by drugging, for service aboard ship

THESAURUS

rays] screen, cover, shadow; see SHELTER. **2** [To make darker] darken, blacken, obscure, cloud, shadow, make dim, tone down, black out, make dusky, deepen the shade, overshadow, make gloomy, screen, shut out the light, keep out the light. **3** [To become darker] grow dark, grow black, become dark, grow dim, blacken, turn to twilight, deepen into night, become gloomy, be overcast, grow dusky, cloud up, cloud over, overcloud, grow shadowy.

shadow ***n.*** umbra, murkiness, gloom; see DARKNESS 1.

shadow ***v.*** **1** [To shade] dim, veil, screen; see SHADE 1, 2, SHELTER. **2** [To follow secretly] trail, watch, keep in sight; see PURSUE 1.

shady ***a.*** **1** [Shaded] dusky, shadowy, murky, gloomy, overcast, in the shade, sheltered, out of the sun, dim, cloudy, under a cloud, cool, indistinct, vague; see also DARK 1. **2** [*Questionable] suspicious, disreputable, dubious, dishonest, fishy*, underhanded.

shaft ***n.*** **1** [Rod] stem, bar, pole; see ROD 1. **2** [Light ray] wave, streak, beam of light; see RAY.

shake ***n.*** tremor, shiver, pulsation; see MOVEMENT 1, 2.

shake ***v.*** **1** [To vibrate] tremble, quiver, quake, shiver, shudder, palpitate, wave, waver, fluctuate, reel, flap, flutter, totter, wobble, stagger, waggle. **2** [To cause to vibrate] agitate, rock, sway, swing, joggle, jolt, bounce, jar, move, set in motion, convulse.

shaken ***a.*** unnerved, upset, overcome; see EXCITED.

shaky ***a.*** **1** [Not firm] quivery, trembling, jellylike, unsettled, not set, yielding, unsteady, tottering, insecure, unsound, unstable, infirm, jittery, nervous.—*Ant.* FIRM, settled, rigid. **2** [Not reliable] uncertain, not dependable, questionable; see UNRELIABLE, UNSTABLE 2.

shall ***v.*** intend, want to, must; see WILL 3.

shallow ***a.*** **1** [Lacking physical depth] slight, inconsiderable, superficial, with the bottom in plain sight, with no depth, with little depth, not deep, one-dimensional.—*Ant.* DEEP, bottomless, unfathomable. **2** [Lacking intellectual depth] simple, silly, trifling, frivolous, superficial, petty, foolish, idle, unintelligent, dull, piddling, wishy-washy*; see also STUPID.

sham ***a.*** not genuine, counterfeit, misleading; see FALSE 3.

sham ***n.*** pretense, deception, counterfeit; see FAKE.

shame ***n.*** **1** [A disgrace] embarrassment, stigma, blot; see DISGRACE. **2** [A sense of wrongdoing] bad conscience, mortification, confusion, humiliation, compunction, regret, chagrin, discomposure, irritation, remorse, embarrassment, abashment, self-reproach, self-disgust; see also GUILT. **3** [A condition of disgrace] humiliation, dishonor, degradation; see DISGRACE, SCANDAL.

shame ***v.*** humiliate, mortify, dishonor; see DISGRACE, HUMBLE.

shameful ***a.*** **1** [Offensive] immodest, corrupt, immoral, intemperate, debauched, drunken, villainous, knavish, degraded, reprobate, diabolical, indecent, indelicate, lewd, vulgar, impure, unclean, carnal, sinful, wicked. **2** [Disgraceful] dishonorable, scandalous, flagrant, obscene, ribald, infamous, opprobrious, outrageous, gross, infernal, disgusting, too bad, unworthy, evil, foul, hellish, disreputable, corrupt, dishonest, despicable; see also WRONG.—*Ant.* WORTHY, admirable, creditable.

shameless ***a.*** brazen, bold, forward; see RUDE 2, LEWD 2.

Shang·hai (shaŋ′hī′) seaport in E China: pop. 6,293,000

shank (shaŋk) ***n.*** ⟦OE *scanca*⟧ **1** the part of the leg between the knee and ankle in humans, or a corresponding part in animals **2** the whole leg **3** the part between the handle and the working part of a tool, etc. —**shank of the evening** early evening

shan't (shant) *contr.* shall not

Shan·tung (shan′tuŋ′) ***n.*** ⟦< Chin province⟧ [*sometimes* **s-**] a silk or silky fabric with an uneven surface

shan·ty (shan′tē) ***n.***, *pl.* **-ties** ⟦< CdnFr *chantier*, workshop⟧ a small, shabby dwelling; shack; hut

shape (shāp) ***n.*** ⟦< OE (*ge*)*sceap*, a form⟧ **1** that quality of a thing which depends on the relative position of all the points on its surface; physical form **2** the contour of the body **3** definite or regular form *[*to begin to take *shape]* **4** good physical condition —***vt.*** **shaped, shap′ing 1** to give definite shape to **2** to arrange, express, etc. (a plan, etc.) in definite form **3** to adapt *[shaped* to our needs*]* —**shape up** [Inf.] **1** to develop to a definite form, satisfactorily, etc. **2** to behave as required —**take shape** to begin to have definite form —**shape′less** ***adj.*** —**shape′less·ness** ***n.***

shape′ly ***adj.*** **-li·er, -li·est** having a pleasing figure: used esp. of a woman

shard (shärd) ***n.*** ⟦OE *sceard*⟧ a broken piece, esp. of pottery

share[1] (sher) ***n.*** ⟦OE *scearu*⟧ **1** a portion that belongs to an individual **2** any of the equal parts of capital stock of a corporation —***vt.*** **shared, shar′ing 1** to distribute in shares **2** to receive, use, etc. in common with others —***vi.*** to have a share (*in*)

share[2] (sher) ***n.*** ⟦OE *scear*⟧ a plowshare

share′crop′ ***vi.***, ***vt.*** **-cropped′, -crop′ping** to work (land) for a share of the crop, esp. as a tenant farmer —**share′crop′per** ***n.***

share′hold′er ***n.*** a person who owns shares of stock in a corporation

shark[1] (shärk) ***n.*** ⟦prob. < Ger *schurke*, scoundrel⟧ **1** a swindler **2** [Slang] an expert in an activity

shark[2] (shärk) ***n.*** ⟦< ?⟧ a large, predatory sea fish with a tough, gray skin

shark′skin′ ***n.*** a smooth, silky cloth of cotton, wool, rayon, etc.

sharp (shärp) ***adj.*** ⟦OE *scearp*⟧ **1** having a fine edge or point for cutting or piercing **2** having a point or edge; not rounded **3** not gradual; abrupt **4** clearly defined; distinct *[*a *sharp* contrast*]* **5** quick in perception; clever **6** attentive; vigilant **7** crafty; underhanded **8** harsh; severe *[*a *sharp* temper*]* **9** violent *[*a *sharp* attack*]* **10** brisk; active **11** intense *[*a *sharp* pain*]* **12** pungent **13** nippy *[*a *sharp* wind*]* **14** [Slang] stylishly dressed **15** *Music* above the true pitch —***adv.*** **1** in a sharp manner; specif., *a*) abruptly or briskly *b*) attentively or alertly *c*) *Music* above the true pitch **2** precisely *[*one o'clock *sharp]* —***n.*** **1** [Inf.] an expert or adept **2** *Music a*) a tone one half step above another *b*) the symbol (♯) for such a note —***vt.***, ***vi.*** *Music* to make, sing, or play sharp —**sharp′ly** ***adv.*** —**sharp′ness** ***n.***

sharp′en ***vt.***, ***vi.*** to make or become sharp or sharper —**sharp′en·er** ***n.***

sharp′er ***n.*** a swindler or cheat

sharp′-eyed′ ***adj.*** having keen sight or perception: also **sharp′-sight′ed** ***adj.***

sharp·ie (shär′pē) ***n.*** [Inf.] a shrewd, cunning person, esp. a sharper

sharp′shoot′er ***n.*** a good marksman

sharp′-tongued′ ***adj.*** using sharp or harshly critical language

sharp′-wit′ted (-wit′id) ***adj.*** thinking quickly and effectively

shat·ter (shat′ər) ***vt.*** ⟦ME *schateren*, scatter⟧ **1** to break or burst into pieces suddenly, as with a blow **2** to damage or be damaged severely

shat′ter·proof′ ***adj.*** that will resist shattering

shave (shāv) ***vt.*** **shaved**, **shaved** or **shav′en**, **shav′ing** ⟦OE *sceafan*⟧ **1** to cut away thin slices or sections from **2** *a*) to cut off (hair) at the surface of the skin *b*) to cut the hair to the surface of (the face, etc.) *c*) to cut the beard of (a person) **3** to barely touch in passing; graze —***vi.*** to cut off a beard with a razor, etc. —***n.*** the act or an instance of shaving

shav′er ***n.*** **1** a person who shaves **2** an instrument used in shaving, esp. one with electrically operated cutters **3** [Inf.] a boy; lad

shav′ing ***n.*** **1** the act of one who shaves **2** a thin piece of wood, metal, etc. shaved off

Shaw (shô), **George Ber·nard** (bər närd′, bur′nərd) 1856-1950; Brit. dramatist & critic, born in Ireland —**Sha·vi·an** (shā′vē ən) ***adj.***, ***n.***

shawl (shôl) ***n.*** ⟦prob. < Pers *shāl*⟧ a cloth worn as a covering for the head or shoulders

shay (shā) ***n.*** ⟦< CHAISE, assumed as pl.⟧ [Dial.] a light carriage; chaise

she (shē) ***pron.***, *pl. see* THEY ⟦< OE *seo*⟧ the woman, girl, or female animal previously mentioned —***n.***, *pl.* **shes** a female

sheaf (shēf) ***n.***, *pl.* **sheaves** ⟦OE *sceaf*⟧ **1** a bundle of cut stalks of grain, etc. **2** a collection, as of papers, bound in a bundle

shear (shir) ***vt.*** **sheared**, **sheared** or **shorn**, **shear′ing** ⟦OE *scieran*⟧ **1** to cut with or as with shears **2** to clip (hair) from (the head), (wool) from (sheep), etc. **3** to divest (someone) *of* a power, etc. —***n.*** a shearing —**shear′er** ***n.***

shears ***pl.n.*** **1** a large pair of scissors **2** a large cutting tool or machine with two opposed blades

sheath (shēth) ***n.***, *pl.* **sheaths** (shēthz, shēths) ⟦OE *sceath*⟧ **1** a case for the blade of a knife, sword, etc. **2** a covering resembling this, as the membrane around a muscle **3** a woman's closefitting dress

THESAURUS

shape ***n.*** **1** [Form] contour, aspect, configuration; see FORM 1, LOOKS. **2** [An actual form] pattern, stamp, frame; see MOLD 1. **3** [Condition] fitness, physical state, health; see STATE 2. —**out of shape** distorted, misshapen, battered; see BENT, BROKEN 1, FLAT 1, RUINED 1, 2, TWISTED 1. —**take shape** take on form, mature, fill out; see DEVELOP 1, IMPROVE 2.

shape ***v.*** **1** [To give shape] mold, cast, fashion; see FORM 1. **2** [*To take shape] become, develop, take form; see FORM 4, GROW 2. —**shape up*** **1** [To obey] mind, observe the rules, conform; see BEHAVE, OBEY, IMPROVE 2. **2** [To develop] enlarge, expand, advance; see DEVELOP 1.

shaped ***a.*** made, fashioned, created; see FORMED.

shapeless ***a.*** **1** [Formless] indistinct, indefinite, invisible, vague, without form, without shape, amorphous, lacking form, unformed, unmade, not formed, with no definite outline; see also UNCERTAIN. **2** [Deformed] misshapen, irregular, unshapely, unsymmetrical, mutilated, disfigured, malformed, ill-formed, warped, abnormal; see also DEFORMED.—*Ant.* REGULAR, symmetrical, shapely.

shapely ***a.*** symmetrical, comely, proportioned; see TRIM 2.

share[1] ***n.*** division, apportionment, part, portion, helping, serving, piece, ration, slice, allotment, parcel, dose, fraction, fragment, allowance, dividend, percentage, commission, cut*.

share[1] ***v.*** **1** [To divide] allot, distribute, apportion, part, deal, dispense, assign, administer.—*Ant.* UNITE, combine, withhold. **2** [To partake] participate, share in, experience, take part in, receive, have a portion of, have a share in, go in with, take a part of, take a share of.—*Ant.* AVOID, have no share in, take no part in. **3** [To give] grant, bestow, contribute; see GIVE 1.

sharp ***a.*** **1** [Having a keen edge] acute, edged, razor-edged, sharpened, ground fine, honed, razor-sharp, sharp-edged, fine, cutting, knifelike, knife-edged.—*Ant.* DULL, unsharpened, blunt. **2** [Having a keen point] pointed, sharp-pointed, spiked, spiky, peaked, salient, needlepointed, keen, fine, spiny, thorny, prickly, barbed, needlelike, stinging, sharp as a needle, pronged, tapered, tapering, horned. **3** [Having a keen mind] clever, astute, bright; see INTELLIGENT. **4** [Distinct] audible, visible, explicit; see CLEAR 2, DEFINITE 2, OBVIOUS 1. **5** [Intense] cutting, biting, piercing; see INTENSE. **6** [*Stylish] dressy, chic, in style; see FASHIONABLE.

sharpen ***v.*** **1** [To make keen] grind, file, hone, put an edge on, grind to a fine edge, make sharp, make acute, whet, give an edge to, put a point on, give a fine point to.—*Ant.* FLATTEN, thicken, dull. **2** [To make more exact] focus, bring into focus, intensify, make clear, make clearer, clarify, outline distinctly, make more distinct.—*Ant.* CONFUSE, cloud, obscure.

sharply ***a.*** piercingly, pointedly, distinctly; see CLEARLY 1, 2.

shatter ***v.*** smash, split, burst; see BREAK 2.

shattered ***a.*** splintered, crushed, destroyed; see BROKEN 1.

shave ***v.*** shear, graze, barber, cut, use a razor, clip closely, strip, strip the hair from, tonsure, make bare, peel, skin, remove, slice thin.

she ***pron.*** this one, this girl, this woman, that girl, that woman, a female animal; see also WOMAN 1.

shears ***n.*** cutters, clippers, snips; see SCISSORS.

sheathe (shēth) ***vt.* sheathed, sheath′ing** **1** to put into a sheath **2** to enclose in a case or covering

sheath·ing (shē′thiŋ) ***n.*** something that sheathes, as boards, etc. forming the base for roofing or siding

she·bang (shə baŋ′) ***n.*** [Inf.] an affair, business, contrivance, etc.: chiefly in **the whole shebang**

shed[1] (shed) ***n.*** ⟦OE *scead*⟧ a small structure for shelter or storage

shed[2] (shed) ***vt.* shed, shed′ding** ⟦< OE *sceadan*, to separate⟧ **1** to pour out; emit **2** to cause to flow *[to shed tears]* **3** to cause to flow off *[oilskin sheds water]* **4** to cast off or lose (a natural growth, as hair, etc.) **5** to get rid of (something unwanted) *[to shed a few pounds]* —***vi.*** to shed hair, etc. —**shed blood** to kill violently

sheen (shēn) ***n.*** ⟦< OE *sciene*, beautiful⟧ brightness; luster

sheep (shēp) ***n.***, *pl.* **sheep** ⟦< OE *sceap*⟧ **1** a cud-chewing mammal with heavy wool and edible flesh called *mutton*, closely related to goats, antelope, etc. **2** one who is meek, timid, etc.

sheep′dog′ ***n.*** a dog trained to herd sheep

sheep′fold′ ***n.*** a pen or enclosure for sheep: also, chiefly Brit., **sheep′cote′** (-kōt′) ***n.***

sheep′ish ***adj.*** **1** embarrassed or chagrined **2** shy or bashful —**sheep′ish·ly** ***adv.*** —**sheep′ish·ness** ***n.***

sheep′skin′ ***n.*** **1** the skin of a sheep **2** parchment or leather made from it **3** [Inf.] a diploma

sheer[1] (shir) ***vi.***, ***vt.*** ⟦var. of SHEAR⟧ to turn aside or cause to turn aside from a course; swerve

sheer[2] (shir) ***adj.*** ⟦< ON *skærr*, bright⟧ **1** very thin; transparent: said of textiles **2** absolute; utter *[sheer folly]* **3** extremely steep **4** not mixed with anything; pure *[sheer ice]* —***adv.*** very steeply

sheet[1] (shēt) ***n.*** ⟦OE *sceat*⟧ **1** a large piece of cotton, linen, etc., used on a bed **2** *a)* a single piece of paper *b)* [Inf.] a newspaper **3** a broad, continuous surface or expanse, as of flame or ice **4** a broad, thin piece of any material, as glass, plywood, or metal

sheet[2] (shēt) ***n.*** ⟦short for OE *sceatline*⟧ a rope for controlling the set of a sail

sheet′ing ***n.*** **1** cotton or linen material used for making sheets **2** material used to cover or line a surface *[copper sheeting]*

sheet metal metal rolled thin in the form of a sheet

sheet music music printed on unbound sheets of paper

sheik or **sheikh** (shēk, shāk) ***n.*** ⟦Ar *shaikh*, lit., old man⟧ the chief of an Arab family, tribe, or village

shek·el (shek′əl) ***n.*** ⟦Heb < *shakal*, weigh⟧ **1** a gold or silver coin of the ancient Hebrews **2** the monetary unit of Israel **3** [*pl.*] [Slang] money

shelf (shelf) ***n.***, *pl.* **shelves** ⟦prob. < MLowG *schelf*⟧ **1** a thin, flat board fixed horizontally to a wall, used for holding things **2** something like a shelf; specif., *a)* a ledge *b)* a sandy reef —**on the shelf** out of use, activity, etc.

shelf life the length of time a packaged food, etc. can be stored without deteriorating

shell (shel) ***n.*** ⟦OE *sciel*⟧ **1** a hard outer covering, as of a turtle, egg, nut, etc. **2** something like a shell in being hollow, empty, a covering, etc. **3** a light, narrow racing boat rowed by a team **4** an explosive artillery projectile **5** a small-arms cartridge —***vt.*** **1** to remove the shell or covering from *[to shell peas]* **2** to bombard with shells from a large gun —**shell out** [Inf.] to pay out (money)

shel·lac or **shel·lack** (shə lak′) ***n.*** ⟦< SHELL & LAC⟧ **2** a thin varnish containing lac and alcohol —***vt.* -lacked′, -lack′ing** **1** to apply shellac to **2** [Slang] *a)* to beat *b)* to defeat decisively

-shelled (sheld) *combining form* having a (specified kind of) shell

Shel·ley (shel′ē) **1 Mary Woll·stone·craft** (wool′stən kraft′) 1797-1851; Eng. novelist: second wife of Percy **2 Per·cy Bysshe** (pur′sē bish) 1792-1822; Eng. poet

shell′fire′ ***n.*** the firing of artillery shells

shell′fish′ ***n.***, *pl.* **-fish′** or (for different species) **-fish′es** any aquatic animal with a shell, esp. an edible one, as the clam or lobster

shel·ter (shel′tər) ***n.*** ⟦< ? OE *scield*, shield + *truma*, a troop⟧ **1** something that protects, as from the elements, danger, etc. **2** a being covered, protected, etc.; protection **3** a place that provides food and lodging on a temporary basis —***vt.*** to provide shelter for; protect —***vi.*** to find shelter

shelve (shelv) ***vt.* shelved, shelv′ing** **1** to equip with shelves **2** to put on a shelf **3** to put aside; defer

shelves (shelvz) ***n.*** *pl. of* SHELF

shelv·ing (shel′viŋ) ***n.*** **1** material for shelves **2** shelves collectively

she·nan·i·gan (shi nan′i gən) ***n.*** ⟦altered < ? Ir *sionnachuighim*, I play the fox⟧ [Inf.] a deceitful or mischievous trick: *usually used in pl.*

shep·herd (shep′ərd) ***n.*** ⟦see SHEEP & HERD⟧ **1** one who herds sheep **2** a religious leader **3** GERMAN SHEPHERD —***vt.*** to herd, lead, etc. as a shepherd —**shep′herd·ess** ***fem.n.***

sher·bet (shur′bət) ***n.*** ⟦< Ar *sharba(t)*, a drink⟧ a frozen dessert like an ice but with gelatin and, often, milk added: also, erroneously, **sher′bert** (-bərt)

sher·iff (sher′if) ***n.*** ⟦< OE *scir*, shire + *gerefa*, chief officer⟧ the chief law-enforcement officer of a county

Sher·pa (shur′pə, sher′-) ***n.*** *pl.* **-pas** or **-pa** a member of a Tibetan people of Nepal, famous as mountain climbers

sher·ry (sher′ē) ***n.***, *pl.* **-ries** ⟦after *Jerez*, Spain⟧ **1** a yellow or brown Spanish fortified wine **2** any similar wine

shib·bo·leth (shib′ə leth′, -ləth) ***n.*** ⟦< Heb *shibolet*, a stream⟧ **1** *Bible* the test word used to distinguish the enemy: Judg. 12:4-6 **2** any phrase, custom, etc. peculiar to a certain party, class, etc.

shied (shīd) ***vi.***, ***vt.*** *pt. & pp. of* SHY[1], SHY[2]

shield (shēld) ***n.*** ⟦OE *scield*⟧ **1** a flat piece of metal, etc. worn on the forearm to ward off blows, etc. **2** one that guards, protects, etc. **3** anything shaped like a triangular shield with curved sides —***vt.***, ***vi.*** to defend; protect

shift (shift) ***vt.*** ⟦OE *sciftan*, divide⟧ **1** to move from one person or place to another **2** to replace by another or others **3** to change the arrangement of (gears) —***vi.*** **1** to change position, direction, etc. **2** to get along; manage *[to shift for oneself]* —***n.*** **1** a shifting; transfer **2** a plan of conduct, esp. for an emergency **3** an evasion; trick **4** a gearshift **5** *a)* a group of people working in relay with another *b)* their regular work period

shift′less ***adj.*** incapable, inefficient, lazy, etc. —**shift′less·ness** ***n.***

THESAURUS

shed[1] ***n.*** shelter, outbuilding, hut, lean-to, woodshed.

shed[2] ***v.*** drop, let fall, give forth, shower down, cast, molt, slough, discard, exude, emit, scatter, sprinkle.

sheep ***n.*** lamb, ewe, ram; see ANIMAL, GOAT.

sheer[2] ***a.*** **1** [Abrupt] perpendicular, very steep, precipitous; see STEEP. **2** [Thin] transparent, delicate, fine; see THIN 1.

sheet[1] ***n.*** **1** [A bed cover] covering, bed sheet, bedding; see CLOTH, COVER 1. **2** [A thin, flat object] lamina, leaf, foil, veneer, layer, stratum, coat, film, ply, covering, expanse.

shelf ***n.*** **1** [A ledge] rock, reef, shoal; see LEDGE. **2** [A cupboard rack] counter, cupboard, mantelpiece, rack, bookshelf.

shell ***n.*** **1** [A shell-like cover or structure] husk, crust, nut, pod, case, casing, scale, shard, integument, eggshell, carapace, plastron. **2** [An explosive projectile] bullet, cartridge, ammo*; see WEAPON. **3** [A crustaceous covering] *Varieties include the following:* tortoise, crustacean, bivalve, mollusk, clam, mussel, conch, snail; see also SEASHELL.

shell ***v.*** shuck, strip, peel off; see SKIN.

shellfish ***n.*** crustacean, mollusk, crustaceous animal, invertebrate, marine animal, arthropod, gastropod, bivalve. *Creatures often called shellfish include the following:* crab, lobster, clam, shrimp, prawn, crawfish, crayfish, mussel, whelk, cockle, abalone, snail.

shelter ***n.*** refuge, harbor, haven, sanctuary, asylum, retreat, shield, screen, defense, security, safety, guardian, protector, house, roof, tent, shack, shed, hut, shade.

shelter ***v.*** screen, cover, hide, conceal, guard, take in, ward, harbor, defend, protect, shield, watch over, take care of, secure, preserve, safeguard, surround, enclose, lodge, house.—*Ant.* EXPOSE, turn out, evict.

sheltered ***a.*** **1** [Shaded] screened, protected, shady, veiled, covered, protective, curtained. **2** [Protected] guarded, supervised, shielded; see SAFE, WATCHED.

sheriff ***n.*** county officer, county administrator, peace officer; see POLICE OFFICER.

shield ***n.*** bumper, protection, guard; see COVER 1.

shift ***n.*** **1** [A change] transfer, transformation, substitution, displacement, fault, alteration, variation; see also CHANGE 1. **2** [A working period] turn, shift, stint; see TIME 1.

shift ***v.*** **1** [To change position] move, turn, stir; see CHANGE 2. **2** [To cause to shift] displace, remove, substitute; see EXCHANGE 1. **3** [To put in gear] change gears, downshift, put in drive; see DRIVE 2.

shift'y ***adj.*** **-i·er, -i·est** of a tricky or deceitful nature; evasive —**shift'i·ly** ***adv.*** —**shift'i·ness** ***n.***

Shih Tzu (shēd'zo͞o', shēt'so͞o') *pl.* **Shih Tzus** or **Shih Tzu** ⟦Mandarin *shihtzu*, lion⟧ a small dog with long, silky hair and short legs

shii·ta·ke (shē tä'kē) ***n.*** ⟦Jpn⟧ an edible Japanese mushroom

shill (shil) [Slang] ***n.*** a confederate of a gambler, auctioneer, etc. who pretends to bet, bid, etc. so as to lure others —***vi.*** to act as a shill

shil·le·lagh or **shil·la·lah** (shi lā'lē, -lə) ***n.*** ⟦after *Shillelagh*, Ir village⟧ a club or cudgel: used chiefly of or by the Irish

shil·ling (shil'iŋ) ***n.*** ⟦OE *scylling*⟧ **1** a former British monetary unit and coin, equal to $\frac{1}{20}$ of a pound **2** the basic monetary unit of various countries

shil·ly-shal·ly (shil'ē shal'ē) ***vi.*** **-lied, -ly·ing** ⟦< *shall I?*⟧ to vacillate, esp. over trifles

shim (shim) ***n.*** ⟦< ?⟧ a thin wedge of wood, metal, etc. used as for filling space

shim·mer (shim'ər) ***vi.*** ⟦OE *scymrian*⟧ to shine with an unsteady light; glimmer —***n.*** a shimmering light

shim·my (shim'ē) ***n.*** ⟦< a jazz dance < CHEMISE⟧ a marked vibration or wobble, as in a car's front wheels —***vi.*** **-mied, -my·ing** to vibrate or wobble

shin (shin) ***n.*** ⟦OE *scinu*⟧ the front part of the leg between the knee and the ankle —***vi.*** **shinned, shin'ning** to climb a pole, etc. by gripping with hands and legs: also **shin'ny**: with *up* or *down*

shin'bone' ***n.*** TIBIA

shin·dig (shin'dig') ***n.*** ⟦< old informal *shindy*, commotion⟧ [Inf.] a dance, party, or other informal gathering

shine (shīn) ***vi.*** **shone** or, esp. for *vt.* 2, **shined, shin'ing** ⟦OE *scinan*⟧ **1** to emit or reflect light **2** to stand out; excel **3** to exhibit itself clearly *[love shining from her face]* —***vt.*** **1** to direct the light of **2** to make shiny by polishing *[to shine shoes]* —***n.*** **1** brightness **2** luster; gloss **3** *short for* SHOESHINE

shin·er (shī'nər) ***n.*** [Slang] BLACK EYE

shin·gle (shiŋ'gəl) ***n.*** ⟦OE *scindel*⟧ **1** a thin, wedge-shaped piece of wood, slate, etc. laid with others in overlapping rows, as in covering roofs **2** a small signboard, as that of a doctor —***vt.*** **-gled, -gling** to cover (a roof, etc.) with shingles

shin·gles (shiŋ'gəlz) ***n.*** ⟦< L *cingere*, to gird⟧ *nontechnical name for* HERPES ZOSTER

shin·guard (shin'gärd') ***n.*** a padded guard worn to protect the shins in some sports

shin'splints' ***pl.n.*** ⟦< SHIN & *splint*, growth on bone of a horse's leg⟧ *[with sing. or pl. v.]* painful strain of muscles of the lower leg

Shin·to (shin'tō) ***n.*** ⟦Jpn < Chin *shen*, god + *tō*, *dō*, way⟧ a religion of Japan, emphasizing ancestor worship —**Shin'to·ism'** ***n.***

shin·y (shī'nē) ***adj.*** **-i·er, -i·est** **1** bright; shining **2** highly polished —**shin'i·ness** ***n.***

ship (ship) ***n.*** ⟦OE *scip*⟧ **1** any large vessel for traveling on deep water **2** an aircraft —***vt.*** **shipped, ship'ping** **1** to put or take on board a ship **2** to send or transport by any carrier *[to ship coal by rail]* **3** to take in (water) over the side, as in a stormy sea **4** to put (an object) in place on a vessel **5** [Inf.] to send (*away*, *out*, etc.); get rid of —***vi.*** to go aboard, or travel by, ship —**ship'per** ***n.***

-ship (ship) ⟦OE *-scipe*⟧ *suffix* **1** the quality or state of being *[friendship]* **2** *a)* the rank or office of *[professorship]* *b)* one having the rank of *[lordship]* **3** skill as *[leadership]* **4** all persons (of a specified group) collectively *[readership]*

ship'board' ***n.*** used chiefly in **on shipboard**, aboard a ship

ship'build'er ***n.*** one whose business is building ships —**ship'build'ing** ***n.***

ship'mate' ***n.*** a fellow sailor on the same ship

ship'ment ***n.*** **1** the shipping of goods **2** goods shipped

ship'ping ***n.*** **1** the act or business of transporting goods **2** ships collectively, as of a nation or port

shipping clerk an employee who prepares goods for shipment, and keeps records of shipments made

ship'shape' ***adj.*** having everything neatly in place; trim

ship'wreck' ***n.*** **1** the remains of a wrecked ship **2** the loss of a ship through storm, etc. **3** ruin; failure —***vt.*** to cause to undergo shipwreck

ship'yard' ***n.*** a place where ships are built and repaired

shire (shīr) ***n.*** ⟦OE *scir*, office⟧ in England, a county

shirk (shurk) ***vt.***, ***vi.*** ⟦< ?⟧ to neglect or evade (a duty, etc.) —**shirk'er** ***n.***

shirr (shur) ***vt.*** ⟦< ?⟧ **1** to make shirring in (cloth) **2** to bake (eggs) in buttered dishes

shirr'ing ***n.*** a gathering made in cloth by drawing the material up on parallel rows of short stiches

shirt (shurt) ***n.*** ⟦OE *scyrte*⟧ **1** a garment worn on the upper part of the body, usually with a collar and a buttoned front **2** an undershirt —**keep one's shirt on** [Slang] to remain patient or calm

shirt'tail' ***n.*** the part of a shirt extending below the waist

shirt'waist' ***n.*** **1** [Archaic] a woman's blouse tailored like a shirt **2** a dress with a bodice like this: in full **shirt-waist dress**

shish ke·bab (shish' kə bäb') ⟦< Ar *shīsh*, skewer + *kabāb*, kebab⟧ a dish of kebabs, esp. lamb, stuck on a skewer, often with vegetables, and broiled

shiv (shiv) ***n.*** ⟦prob. < Romany *chiv*, blade⟧ [Slang] a knife

shiv·er[1] (shiv'ər) ***n.*** ⟦ME *schievere*⟧ a fragment —***vt.***, ***vi.*** to break into fragments; shatter

shiv·er[2] (shiv'ər) ***vi.*** ⟦< ? OE *ceafl*, jaw⟧ to shake or tremble, as from fear or cold —***n.*** a shaking, trembling, etc. —**shiv'er·y** ***adj.***

shlep or **shlepp** (shlep) ***n.***, ***vt.***, ***vi.*** **shlepped, shlep'ping** [Slang] *alt. sp. of* SCHLEP

shmaltz (shmôlts, shmälts) ***n.*** [Slang] *alt. sp. of* SCHMALTZ

shoal[1] (shōl) ***n.*** ⟦OE *scolu*⟧ a school of fish

shoal[2] (shōl) ***n.*** ⟦< OE *sceald*, shallow⟧ **1** a shallow place in a river, sea, etc. **2** a sandbar forming a shallow place

shoat (shōt) ***n.*** ⟦ME *schote*⟧ a young, weaned pig

shock[1] (shäk) ***n.*** ⟦< MFr *choquer*, to collide⟧ **1** a sudden, powerful blow, shake, etc. **2** *a)* a sudden emotional disturbance *b)* the cause of this **3** an extreme stimulation of the nerves by the passage of electric current through the body **4** [Inf.] *short for* SHOCK ABSORBER **5** a disorder of the blood circulation produced by hemorrhage, disturbance of heart function, etc. —***vt.*** **1** to astonish, horrify, etc. **2** to produce electrical shock in —**shock'er** ***n.***

THESAURUS

shin ***n.*** tibia, leg, limb; see BONE, LEG.

shindig* ***n.*** banquet, dance, dinner; see PARTY 1.

shine ***v.*** **1** [To give forth light] radiate, beam, scintillate, glitter, sparkle, twinkle, glimmer, glare, glow, flash, blaze, shimmer, illuminate, blink, shoot out beams, irradiate, dazzle, bedazzle, flash, flicker, luminesce, light. **2** [To reflect light] glisten, gleam, glow, look good, grow bright, give back, give light, deflect, mirror; see also REFLECT 3. **3** [To cause to shine, usually by polishing] scour, brush, polish, put a gloss on, put a finish on, finish, burnish, wax, buff, polish up, make brilliant, make glitter, glaze; see also CLEAN, PAINT 2.

shining ***a.*** radiant, gleaming, luminous; see BRIGHT 1.

shiny ***a.*** polished, sparkling, glistening; see BRIGHT 1.

ship ***n.*** *Types of ships include the following:* steamer, steamship, liner, freighter, landing barge, dredge, trawler, floating cannery, factory ship, supply ship, ferry, clipper, square-rigged vessel, sailing ship, transport, tanker, pilot boat, junk, galleon, sampan, battleship, cruiser, destroyer, aircraft carrier, submarine, whaling vessel, bark, schooner, windjammer, yacht, cutter, sloop, tug, cruise ship, paddle-wheeler; see also BOAT.

ship ***v.*** send, consign, ship out; see SEND 1.

shipment ***n.*** cargo, carload, purchase; see FREIGHT.

shipped ***a.*** transported, exported, delivered; see SENT.

shirk ***v.*** elude, cheat, malinger; see AVOID, EVADE.

shirt ***n.*** *Shirts include the following:* dress, undershirt, sport, work, cowboy, Western, long-sleeved, short-sleeved, cotton, silk, flannel, polo, button-down, T-shirt, tank top, blouse, jersey, pull-over, turtleneck; see also CLOTHES.

shiver[2] ***v.*** be cold, vibrate, quiver; see SHAKE 1, WAVE 3.

shock[1] ***n.*** **1** [The effect of physical impact] crash, clash, wreck; see COLLISION. **2** [The effect of a mental blow] excitement, hysteria, emotional upset; see CONFUSION. **3** [The aftereffect of physical harm] concussion, stupor, collapse; see ILLNESS 1, INJURY.

shock[1] ***v.*** **1** [To disturb one's self-control] startle, agitate, astound; see DISTURB. **2** [To disturb one's sense of propriety] insult, outrage, horrify, revolt, offend, appall, abash, astound, anger, floor, shake up, disquiet, dismay. **3** [To jar] rock, agitate, jolt; see SHAKE 2.

shocked ***a.*** startled, aghast, upset, astounded, offended, appalled, dismayed; see also TROUBLED.

shock[2] (shäk) ***n.*** ⟦ME *schokke*⟧ a number of grain sheaves stacked together
shock[3] (shäk) ***n.*** ⟦< ? prec.⟧ a thick, bushy mass of hair
shock absorber a device, as on a motor vehicle, that absorbs the force of bumps and jarring
shock'ing ***adj.*** **1** causing great surprise and distress **2** disgusting —**shock'ing·ly** ***adv.***
shock'proof' ***adj.*** able to absorb shock without being damaged
shock therapy the treatment of certain mental disorders by using electricity or drugs to produce convulsions or coma
shock troops troops trained to lead an attack
shod (shäd) ***vt.*** *alt. pt. & pp. of* SHOE
shod·dy (shäd'ē) ***n.***, *pl.* **-dies** ⟦< ?⟧ an inferior woolen cloth made from used fabrics —***adj.*** **-di·er, -di·est 1** made of inferior material **2** poorly done or made **3** contemptible; low —**shod'di·ly** ***adv.*** —**shod'di·ness** ***n.***
shoe (sho͞o) ***n.*** ⟦OE *sceoh*⟧ **1** an outer covering for the foot **2** *short for* HORSESHOE **3** the part of a brake that presses against a wheel —***vt.*** **shod** or **shoed, shoe'ing** to furnish with shoes —**fill someone's shoes** to take someone's place
shoe'horn' ***n.*** an implement used to help slip the heel of a foot into a shoe —***vt.*** to force or squeeze into a narrow space
shoe'lace' ***n.*** a length of cord, etc. used for lacing and fastening a shoe
shoe'mak'er ***n.*** one whose business is making or repairing shoes
shoe'shine' ***n.*** the cleaning and polishing of a pair of shoes
shoe'string' ***n.*** **1** a shoelace **2** a small amount of capital *[a business started on a shoestring]* —***adj.*** **1** like a shoestring; long and narrow **2** of or characterized by a small amount of money **3** at or near the ankles *[a shoestring catch]*
shoe tree a form made of wood, etc. inserted in a shoe to stretch it or preserve its shape
sho·gun (shō'gun') ***n.*** ⟦< Chin *chiang-chun*⟧ any of the hereditary governors of Japan who, until 1867, were absolute rulers —**sho'gun·ate** (-gə nit) ***n.***
shone (shōn) ***vi.***, ***vt.*** *alt. pt. & pp. of* SHINE
shoo (sho͞o) ***interj.*** go away! get out! —***vt.*** **shooed, shoo'ing** to drive away, as by crying "shoo"
shoo'-in' ***n.*** [Inf.] one expected to win easily in a race, etc.
shook (sho͝ok) ***vt.***, ***vi.*** *pt. and dial. pp. of* SHAKE —**shook up** [Inf.] upset; agitated
shoot (sho͞ot) ***vt.*** **shot, shoot'ing** ⟦OE *sceotan*⟧ **1** to move swiftly over, by, etc. *[to shoot the rapids]* **2** to streak or vary (*with* another color, etc.) **3** to thrust or put forth **4** to discharge or fire (a bullet, arrow, etc.) **5** to send forth swiftly or with force **6** to hit, wound, etc. with a bullet, arrow, etc. **7** to photograph **8** *Sports a)* to throw or drive (a ball, etc.) toward the objective *b)* to score (a goal, points, etc.) —***vi.*** **1** to move swiftly **2** to be felt suddenly, as pain **3** to grow rapidly **4** to jut out **5** to send forth a missile; discharge bullets, etc. **6** to use guns, etc. as in hunting —***n.*** **1** a shooting trip, contest, etc. **2** a new growth; sprout —**shoot at** (or **for**) [Inf.] to strive for —**shoot'er** ***n.***
shooting star METEOR (sense 1)
shoot'out' or **shoot'-out'** ***n.*** **1** a battle with handguns, etc., as between police and criminals **2** *Sports* a procedure used to break a tie at the end of a game, esp. in soccer
shop (shäp) ***n.*** ⟦OE *sceoppa*, booth⟧ **1** a place where certain things are offered for sale; esp., a small store **2** a place where a particular kind of work is done —***vi.*** **shopped, shop'ping** to visit shops to examine or buy goods —**talk shop** to discuss one's work
shop'keep'er ***n.*** one who owns or operates a shop, or small store
shop'lift' ***vt.***, ***vi.*** to steal (articles) from a store during shopping hours —**shop'lift'er** ***n.***
shoppe (shäp) ***n.*** *alt. sp. of* SHOP (*n.* 1): now used only in shop names
shop'per ***n.*** **1** one who shops **2** one hired by a store to shop for others **3** one hired by a store to compare competitors' prices, etc.
shopping center a complex of stores, restaurants, etc. with a common parking area
shop'talk' ***n.*** **1** the specialized words and idioms of those in the same work **2** talk about work, esp. after hours
shop'worn' ***adj.*** soiled, faded, etc. from having been displayed in a shop
shore[1] (shôr) ***n.*** ⟦ME *schore*⟧ land at the edge of a body of water
shore[2] (shôr) ***n.*** ⟦ME *schore*⟧ a prop, beam, etc. used for support, etc. —***vt.*** **shored, shor'ing** to support as with shores; prop (*up*)
shore'bird' ***n.*** a bird that lives or feeds near the shore
shore'line' ***n.*** the edge of a body of water
shore patrol a detail of the U.S. Navy, Coast Guard, or Marine Corps acting as military police on shore
shorn (shôrn) ***vt.***, ***vi.*** *alt. pp. of* SHEAR
short (shôrt) ***adj.*** ⟦OE *scort*⟧ **1** not measuring much from end to end in space or time **2** not great in range or scope **3** not tall **4** brief; concise **5** not retentive *[a short memory]* **6** curt; abrupt **7** less than a sufficient or correct amount **8** crisp or flaky, as pastry rich in shortening **9** designating a sale of securities, etc. which the seller does not yet own but expects to buy later at a lower price —***n.*** **1** something short **2** [*pl.*] *a)* short trousers *b)* a man's undergarment like these **3** *short for a)* SHORTSTOP *b)* SHORT CIRCUIT —***adv.*** **1** abruptly; suddenly **2** briefly; concisely **3** so as to be short in length **4** by surprise *[caught short]* —***vt.***, ***vi.*** **1** to give less than what is needed or usual **2** *short for a)* SHORTCHANGE *b)* SHORT-CIRCUIT —**in short** briefly —**run short** to have less than enough —**short of 1** less than or lacking **2** without actually resorting to —**short'ness** ***n.***
short'age ***n.*** a deficiency in the amount needed or expected; deficit
short'bread' ***n.*** a rich, crumbly cake or cookie made with much shortening
short'cake' ***n.*** a light biscuit or a sweet cake served with fruit, etc.

THESAURUS

shocking ***a.*** repulsive, hateful, revolting; see OFFENSIVE 2.

shoe ***n.*** footwear, boot, slipper, sandal, pump, moccasin, Oxford, saddle shoe, high-top, wingtip, brogue, hush puppy, flat, clog, galosh, tennis shoe, cleat, jogging shoe, running shoe, cross-training shoe, gym shoe, walking shoe, ski boot, track shoe, sneaker, loafer, heels, wedgie. —**in another's shoes** in the place of another, in other circumstances, reversal of roles; see SYMPATHETIC, UNDERSTOOD 1.

shoo ***interj.*** get away, begone, leave.

shoot ***v.*** **1** [To discharge] fire, shoot off, expel, pull the trigger, set off, torpedo, explode, ignite, blast, sharpshoot, open fire, rake, pump full of lead*. **2** [To move rapidly] dart, spurt, rush; see HURRY 1. **3** [To kill by shooting] dispatch, murder, execute; see KILL 1. —**shoot at 1** [To fire a weapon at] shoot, fire at, take a shot at; see ATTACK 1. **2** [*To strive for] aim, endeavor, strive; see TRY 1.

shop ***n.*** store, department store, retail store, thrift shop, drugstore, discount house, novelty shop. —**set up shop** go into business, start, open a business; see BEGIN 1, 2. —**shut up shop** close up, go out of business, cease functioning; see CLOSE 4, STOP 2. —**talk shop** talk business, exchange views, discuss one's specialty; see GOSSIP, TALK 1.

shop ***v.*** shop for, look for, try to buy; see BUY.

shopkeeper ***n.*** manager, merchant, storekeeper; see BUSINESSMAN.

shopper ***n.*** bargain hunter, professional shopper, purchaser; see BUYER.

shopping ***n.*** purchasing, hunting, looking; see BUYING.

shopping center ***n.*** shops, mall, shopping mall; see BUSINESS 4, PARKING LOT.

shore[1] ***n.*** beach, strand, seaside, sand, coast, seacoast, seashore, bank, border, seaboard, margin, lakeside, lakeshore, riverbank, riverside.

short ***a.*** **1** [Not long in space] low, skimpy, slight, not tall, not long, undersized, little, abbreviated, dwarfish, stubby, stunted, stocky, diminutive, tiny, small, dwarf, dwarfed, close to the ground, dumpy, chunky, compact, squat, thickset, pint-size, stumpy, sawed-off*, runty. **2** [Not long in time] brief, curtailed, cut short, fleeting, not protracted, concise, unprolonged, unsustained, condensed, terse, succinct, pithy, summary, pointed, precise, bare, abridged, summarized, abbreviated, hasty, compressed, short-term, short-lived. **3** [Inadequate] deficient, insufficient, meager; see INADEQUATE. —**be** (or **run**) **short** (**of**) lack, want, run out of; see NEED. —**fall short** not reach, be inadequate, fall down; see FAIL 1, MISS 3. —**for short** as a nickname, familiarly, commonly; see NAMED 1, SO-CALLED. —**in short** that is, in summary, to make a long story short; see BRIEFLY, FINALLY 1.

shortage ***n.*** short fall, scant supply, curtailment; see LACK 1.

short'change' *vt., vi.* **-changed', -chang'ing** [Inf.] **1** to give less money than is due in change **2** to cheat by depriving of something due
short circuit **1** a usually accidental connection between two points in an electric circuit, resulting in excessive current flow that causes damage **2** popularly, a disrupted electric circuit caused by this —**short'-cir'cuit** *vt., vi.*
short'com'ing *n.* a defect or deficiency
short'cut' *n.* **1** a shorter route **2** any way of saving time, effort, etc.
short'en *vt., vi.* to make or become short or shorter
short·en·ing (shôrt''n iŋ, shôrt'niŋ) *n.* edible fat used to make pastry, etc. crisp or flaky
short'fall' *n.* a falling short, or the amount of the shortage
short'hand' *n.* any system of speed writing using symbols for words
short'-hand'ed *adj.* short of workers
short'-lived' (-līvd', -livd') *adj.* having a short life span or existence
short'ly *adv.* **1** briefly **2** soon **3** abruptly and rudely; curtly
short order any food that can be cooked or served quickly when ordered
short'-range' *adj.* reaching over a short distance or period of time
short ribs the rib ends from the front half of a side of beef
short shrift very little care or attention —**make short shrift of** to dispose of quickly and impatiently
short'sight'ed *adj.* **1** NEARSIGHTED **2** lacking in foresight —**short'sight'ed·ly** *adv.* —**short'sight'ed·ness** *n.*
short'-spo'ken *adj.* using few words, esp. to the point of rudeness; curt
short'stop' *n. Baseball* the infielder usually positioned to the left of second base
short story a piece of prose fiction shorter than a short novel
short subject a short film, as that shown with a film feature
short'-tem'pered *adj.* easily or quickly angered
short'-term' *adj.* for or extending over a short time
short ton 2,000 pounds: see TON
short'-waist'ed (-wās'tid) *adj.* unusually short between shoulders and waistline
short'wave' *n.* **1** a radio wave 60 meters or less in length: shorter than the waves used in commercial broadcasting **2** a radio or radio band for broadcasting or receiving shortwaves: in full **shortwave radio**
short'-wind'ed (-win'did) *adj.* easily put out of breath by exertion
shot[1] (shät) *n.* ⟦OE *sceot*⟧ **1** the act of shooting **2** range; scope **3** an attempt or try **4** a pointed, critical remark **5** the path of an object thrown, etc. **6** *a*) a projectile for a gun *b*) projectiles collectively **7** small pellets of lead or steel for a shotgun **8** the heavy metal ball used in the shot put **9** a marksman **10** a photograph or a film sequence **11** a hypodermic injection **12** a drink of liquor —**call the shots** [Inf.] to direct or control what is done
shot[2] (shät) *vt., vi. pt. & pp. of* SHOOT —*adj.* [Inf.] ruined or worn out
shot'gun' *n.* **1** a gun for firing a charge of shot at short range **2** *Football* a formation in which the quarterback stands several yards behind the line of scrimmage to receive the ball
shot put a contest in which a heavy metal ball is propelled with an overhand thrust from the shoulder —**shot'-put'ter** *n.* —**shot'-put'ting** *n.*
should (shood) *v.aux.* ⟦OE *sceolde*⟧ **1** *pt. of* SHALL **2** used to express: *a*) obligation, duty, etc. *[you should help]* *b*) expectation or probability *[he should be here soon]* *c*) a future condition *[if I should die tomorrow]*
shoul·der (shōl'dər) *n.* ⟦OE *sculdor*⟧ **1** *a*) the joint connecting the arm or forelimb with the body *b*) the part of the body including this joint **2** [*pl.*] the two shoulders and the part of the back between them **3** a shoulderlike projection **4** the land along the edge of a paved road —*vt.* **1** to push along or through, as with the shoulder **2** to carry upon the shoulder **3** to assume the burden of —**straight from the shoulder** without reserve; frankly —**turn** (or **give**) **a cold shoulder to** to snub or shun
shoulder blade SCAPULA
shoulder harness an anchored strap passing across the chest, used with a seat belt, as in a car: also called **shoulder belt**
shout (shout) *n.* ⟦ME *schoute*⟧ a loud cry or call —*vt., vi.* to utter or cry out in a shout —**shout'er** *n.*
shove (shuv) *vt., vi.* **shoved, shov'ing** ⟦OE *scufan*⟧ **1** to push, as along a surface **2** to push roughly —*n.* a push —**shove off** **1** to push (a boat) away from shore **2** [Inf.] to leave
shov·el (shuv'əl) *n.* ⟦OE *scofl*⟧ a tool with a broad scoop or blade and a long handle, for lifting and moving loose material —*vt.* **-eled** or **-elled, -el·ing** or **-el·ling** **1** to move with a shovel **2** to dig out with a shovel
shov'el·ful' *n., pl.* **-fuls'** as much as a shovel will hold
show (shō) *vt.* **showed, shown** or **showed, show'ing** ⟦< OE *sceawian*⟧ **1** to bring or put in sight **2** to guide; conduct **3** to point out **4** to reveal, as by behavior **5** to prove; demonstrate **6** to bestow (favor, mercy, etc.) —*vi.* **1** to be or become seen; appear **2** to be noticeable **3** to finish third or better in a horse race —*n.* **1** a showing or demonstration **2** pompous display **3** pretense *[sorrow that was mere show]* **4** a public display or exhibition **5** a presentation of entertainment —**show off** **1** to make a display of **2** to attract attention to oneself —**show up** **1** to expose **2** to be seen **3** to arrive
show'biz' (-biz') *n.* [Inf.] SHOW BUSINESS
show'boat' *n.* **1** a boat with a theater and actors who play river towns **2** [Slang] a showoff —*vi.* [Slang] to show off
show business the theater, films, TV, etc. as a business or industry

THESAURUS

shortcoming *n.* fault, deficiency, lapse; see WEAKNESS 1.
shortcut *n.* bypass, alternative, timesaver; see MEANS 1, WHY.
shorten *v.* curtail, abridge, abbreviate; see DECREASE 2.
shorter *a.* smaller, lower, not so long, briefer, more limited, more concise, more abrupt, lessened, diminished, reduced, curtailed.—*Ant.* HIGHER, longer, taller.
short-lived *a.* brief, momentary, temporary; see SHORT 2.
shortly *a.* presently, quickly, right away; see SOON.
shortness *n.* brevity, briefness, conciseness; see LENGTH 1.
shortsighted *a.* unthinking, foolish, unwary; see RASH, STUPID.
shot[1] *n.* **1** [A flying missile] bullet, dumdum, slug, ball, pellet, lead, projectile, buckshot, grapeshot. **2** [An opportunity to shoot] occasion, chance, turn; see OPPORTUNITY 1. **3** [One who shoots] gunner, rifleman, marksman; see HUNTER. —**call the shots** direct, command, supervise; see CONTROL. —**have** (or **take**) **a shot at*** endeavor, attempt, do one's best at; see TRY 1. —**like a shot** rapidly, speedily, like a bat out of hell*; see FAST 1, QUICKLY. —**shot in the arm** help, boost, assistance; see ENCOURAGEMENT.
shoulder *n.* upper arm, shoulder cut, shoulder joint; see ARM 1, 2, JOINT 1. —**cry on someone's shoulder** weep, object, shed tears; see CRY 1, COMPLAIN. —**turn** (or **give**) **a cold shoulder to** ignore, neglect, pass over; see INSULT.
shout *n.* roar, bellow, scream; see CRY 1, YELL.
shout *v.* screech, roar, scream; see YELL.
shouting *n.* cries, yelling, jeering; see CRY 1.
shove *v.* jostle, push out of one's way, shoulder; see PUSH 1.
shovel *n. Shovels include the following:* coal, snow, fire, miner's, irrigating, split, twisted, pronged, scoop, spade, round-pointed; see also TOOL 1.
shovel *v.* take up, pick up, take up with a shovel, clean out, throw, lift out, move, pass, shift; see also DIG 1, LOAD 1.
show *n.* **1** [An exhibition] presentation, exhibit, showing, exposition, expo*, display, occurrence, sight, appearance, program, flower show, boat show, home show, dog show, carnival, representation, burlesque, production, concert, act, pageant, spectacle, light show, entertainment; see also COMEDY, DRAMA, MOVIE. **2** [Pretense] sham, make-believe, semblance; see PRETENSE 1, 2. —**for show** for sake of appearances, ostensibly, ostentatiously; see APPARENTLY. —**get** (or **put**) **the show on the road*** start, open, get started; see BEGIN 1. —**steal the show** triumph, get the best of it, win out; see DEFEAT, WIN 1.
show *v.* **1** [To display] exhibit, manifest, present; see DISPLAY. **2** [To explain] reveal, tell, explicate; see EXPLAIN. **3** [To demonstrate] attest, determine, confirm; see PROVE. **4** [To convince] teach, prove to, persuade; see CONVINCE. **5** [To indicate] register, note, point; see RECORD 1. —**show off** brag, swagger, make a spectacle of oneself; see BOAST. —**show up** **1** [To arrive] appear, come, turn up; see ARRIVE. **2** [To expose] discredit, defeat, belittle; see EXPOSE 1.

show'case' *n.* a glass-enclosed case for displaying things, as in a store —*vt.* **-cased', -cas'ing** to display to good advantage

show'down' *n.* [Inf.] an action that brings matters to a climax or settles them

show·er (shou'ər) *n.* ⟦OE *scur*⟧ **1** a brief fall of rain, etc. **2** a sudden, abundant fall or flow, as of sparks **3** a party at which gifts are presented to the guest of honor **4** a bath in which the body is sprayed from overhead with fine streams of water —*vt.* **1** to spray with water, etc. **2** to pour forth as in a shower —*vi.* **1** to fall or come as a shower **2** to bathe under a shower —**show'er·y** *adj.*

show·ing (shō'iŋ) *n.* **1** a bringing to view or notice; exhibition **2** a performance, appearance, etc. *[a good showing in the contest]*

show·man (shō'mən) *n., pl.* **-men** (-mən) **1** one whose business is producing shows **2** a person skilled at presenting anything in a striking manner —**show'man·ship'** *n.*

shown (shōn) *vt., vi. alt. pp. of* SHOW

show'off' *n.* one who shows off

show of hands a raising of hands, as in voting or volunteering

show'piece' *n.* **1** something displayed or exhibited **2** something that is a fine example of its kind

show'place' *n.* **1** a place displayed to the public for its beauty, etc. **2** any beautiful place

show'room' *n.* a room where merchandise is displayed for advertising or sale

show'time' *n.* the time when a show begins

show window a store window in which merchandise is displayed

show'y *adj.* **-i·er, -i·est** **1** of striking appearance **2** attracting attention in a gaudy way —**show'i·ness** *n.*

shpt *abbrev.* shipment

shrank (shraŋk) *vt., vi. alt. pt. of* SHRINK

shrap·nel (shrap'nəl) *n.* ⟦after Gen. H. *Shrapnel* (1761-1842), its Brit inventor⟧ **1** an artillery shell filled with an explosive charge and small metal balls **2** these balls **3** any fragments scattered by an exploding shell, bomb, etc.

shred (shred) *n.* ⟦OE *screade*⟧ **1** a narrow strip cut, torn off, etc. **2** a fragment —*vt.* **shred'ded** or **shred, shred'ding** to cut or tear into shreds —**shred'da·ble** *adj.* —**shred'der** *n.*

Shreve·port (shrēv'pôrt') city in NW Louisiana: pop. 199,000

shrew (shro͞o) *n.* ⟦< OE *screawa*⟧ **1** a small, mouselike mammal with a long snout **2** a nagging, bad-tempered woman —**shrew'ish** *adj.*

shrewd (shro͞od) *adj.* ⟦see prec.⟧ clever or sharp in practical affairs; astute —**shrewd'ly** *adv.* —**shrewd'ness** *n.*

shriek (shrēk) *vi., vt.* ⟦ME *schriken*⟧ to make or utter with a loud, piercing cry —*n.* such a cry

shrift (shrift) *n.* ⟦ult. < L *scribere*, write⟧ [Archaic] confession to and absolution by a priest: see also SHORT SHRIFT

shrike (shrīk) *n.* ⟦OE *scric*⟧ a shrill-voiced, predatory songbird with a hooked beak

shrill (shril) *adj.* ⟦echoic⟧ producing a high, thin, piercing sound —*vi., vt.* to utter (with) a shrill sound —**shril'ly** *adv.* —**shrill'ness** *n.*

shrimp (shrimp) *n.* ⟦OE *scrimman*, to shrink⟧ **1** a small, long-tailed crustacean, valued as food **2** [Inf.] a small or insignificant person

shrine (shrīn) *n.* ⟦< L *scrinium*, box⟧ **1** a container holding sacred relics **2** a saint's tomb **3** a place of worship **4** any hallowed place

shrink (shriŋk) *vi.* **shrank** or **shrunk, shrunk** or **shrunk'en, shrink'ing** ⟦OE *scrincan*⟧ **1** to contract, as from heat, cold, moisture, etc. **2** to lessen, as in amount **3** to draw back; flinch —*vt.* to make shrink —**shrink'a·ble** *adj.*

shrink'age *n.* **1** a shrinking **2** the amount of shrinking

shrinking violet a very shy person

shrink'-wrap' *vt.* **-wrapped', -wrap'ping** to wrap in a plastic material that is then shrunk by heating to fit tightly —*n.* a wrapping of such material

shrive (shrīv) *vt.* **shrived** or **shrove, shriv·en** (shriv'ən) or **shrived, shriv'ing** ⟦OE *scrifan*⟧ [Archaic] to hear the confession of and absolve

shriv·el (shriv'əl) *vt., vi.* **-eled** or **-elled, -el·ing** or **-el·ling** ⟦prob. < Scand⟧ to shrink and wrinkle or wither

shroud (shroud) *n.* ⟦OE *scrud*⟧ **1** a cloth used to wrap a corpse for burial **2** something that covers, veils, etc. **3** any of the ropes from a ship's side to a masthead —*vt.* to hide; cover

Shrove Tuesday ⟦see SHRIVE⟧ the last day before Lent

shrub (shrub) *n.* ⟦OE *scrybb*, brushwood⟧ a low, woody plant with several stems; bush —**shrub'by** *adj.*

shrub'ber·y (-ər ē) *n.* shrubs collectively

shrug (shrug) *vt., vi.* **shrugged, shrug'ging** ⟦ME *schruggen*⟧ to draw up (the shoulders), as in indifference, doubt, etc. —*n.* the gesture so made —**shrug off** to dismiss or disregard in a carefree way

shrunk (shruŋk) *vi., vt. alt. pt. & pp. of* SHRINK

shrunk'en *vi., vt. alt. pp. of* SHRINK —*adj.* contracted in size; shriveled

shtick (shtik) *n.* ⟦Yiddish⟧ **1** a comic scene or gimmick **2** an attention-getting device

shuck (shuk) *n.* ⟦< ?⟧ a shell, pod, or husk —*vt.* to remove shucks from

shucks (shuks) *interj.* used to express mild disappointment, embarrassment, etc.

shud·der (shud'ər) *vi.* ⟦ME *schoderen*⟧ to shake or tremble, as in horror —*n.* a shuddering

shuf·fle (shuf'əl) *vt., vi.* **-fled, -fling** ⟦prob. < LowG *schuffeln*⟧ **1** to move (the feet) with a dragging gait **2** to mix (playing cards) **3** to mix together in a jumble —*n.* a shuffling —**shuf'fler** *n.*

shuf'fle·board' *n.* ⟦< earlier *shovel board*⟧ a game in which disks are pushed with a cue toward numbered squares on a diagram

shun (shun) *vt.* **shunned, shun'ning** ⟦OE *scunian*⟧ to keep away from; avoid scrupulously

shunt (shunt) *vt., vi.* ⟦ME *schunten*⟧ **1** to move or turn to one side **2** to switch from one track to another: said as of a train —*n.* **1** a shunting **2** a railroad switch **3** a surgically created channel allowing flow from one organ, etc. to another

shush (shush) *interj.* ⟦echoic⟧ hush! be quiet! —*vt.* to say "shush" to

shut (shut) *vt.* **shut, shut'ting** ⟦OE *scyttan*⟧ **1** to move (a door, lid, etc.) so as to close (an opening, container, etc.)

THESAURUS

showdown *n.* crisis, turning point, culmination; see CLIMAX.

shower *n.* **1** [Water falling in drops] drizzle, mist, rainfall; see RAIN 1. **2** [Act of cleansing the body] bathing, washing, sponging; see BATH 1.

shown *a.* **1** [Put on display] displayed, demonstrated, advertised, exposed, set out, presented, delineated, exhibited, laid out, put up for sale, put up, put on the block.—*Ant.* WITHDRAWN, concealed, held back. **2** [Proved] demonstrated, determined, made clear; see OBVIOUS 2.

showoff *n.* boaster, exhibitionist, egotist; see BRAGGART.

showpiece *n.* masterpiece, prize, work of art; see MASTERPIECE.

show window *n.* display window, store window, picture window; see DISPLAY.

showy *a.* flashy, glaring, gaudy; see ORNATE.

shred *n.* fragment, piece, tatter; see BIT 1.

shred *v.* slice, strip, cut into small pieces; see TEAR.

shrewd *a.* astute, ingenious, sharp; see INTELLIGENT.

shrewdly *a.* knowingly, cleverly, trickily, sagaciously, astutely, skillfully, ably, slyly, foxily, guilefully, smartly, deceptively, cunningly, intelligently, judiciously, neatly, coolly, handily, facilely, adroitly, deftly, with skill, in a crafty manner, in a cunning manner, with consummate skill, knowing one's way around; see also CAREFULLY 1, DELIBERATELY.

shriek *n.* scream, screech, howl; see CRY 1, 3, YELL 1.

shriek *v.* scream, screech, squawk; see CRY 1, 2, YELL.

shrill *a.* high-pitched, piercing, penetrating, sharp, screeching, deafening, earsplitting, blatant, noisy, clanging, harsh, blaring, raucous, metallic, discordant, cacophonous, acute; see also LOUD 1.—*Ant.* SOFT, low, faint.

shrine *n.* sacred place, hallowed place, altar; see CHURCH 1.

shrink *v.* withdraw, recoil, flinch; see CONTRACT 1.

shrinkage *n.* lessening, reduction, depreciation; see LOSS 1, 3.

shrivel *v.* parch, dry up, shrink; see CONTRACT 1, DRY 1.

shrub *n.* bush, fern, hedge; see PLANT.

shrubbery *n.* shrubs, bushes, hedge; see BRUSH 3.

shrunken *a.* withdrawn, withered, contracted; see DRY 1, WRINKLED.

shudder *n.* tremor, shuddering, shaking, trembling.

shudder *v.* quiver, quake, shiver; see SHAKE 1, WAVE 1.

shun *v.* dodge, evade, keep away from; see AVOID.

shut *a.* stopped, locked, fastened; see TIGHT 2.

shut *v.* close up, lock, seal; see CLOSE 4. —**shut down** close down, shut up, abandon; see STOP 1. —**shut off** turn off, discontinue, put a stop to; see CLOSE 4, STOP 1. —**shut out**

2 *a)* to prevent entrance to or exit from *b)* to confine *in* a room, etc. 3 to bring together the parts of (a book, the eyes, etc.) —***vi.*** to be or become shut —***adj.*** closed, fastened, etc. —**shut down** to cease operating —**shut off** to prevent passage of or through —**shut out** 1 to deny entrance to 2 to prevent from scoring —**shut up** 1 to confine 2 [Inf.] to stop or cause to stop talking

shut'down' ***n.*** a stoppage of work or activity, as in a factory

shut'-eye' ***n.*** [Slang] sleep

shut'-in' ***adj.*** confined indoors by illness —***n.*** an invalid who is shut-in

shut'out' ***n.*** a game in which a team is kept from scoring

shut·ter (shut'ər) ***n.*** 1 a person or thing that shuts 2 a movable cover for a window 3 a device for opening and closing the aperture of a camera lens —***vt.*** to close or furnish with a shutter

shut·tle (shut''l) ***n.*** ⟦< OE *scytel*, missile⟧ 1 a device that carries thread back and forth, as in weaving 2 *a)* a traveling back and forth over a short route *b)* an airplane, bus, etc. used in a shuttle —***vt.***, ***vi.*** **-tled**, **-tling** to move back and forth rapidly

shut'tle·cock' (-käk') ***n.*** in badminton, a rounded piece of cork having a flat end stuck with feathers, or a similar plastic device

shy[1] (shī) ***adj.*** **shy'er** or **shi'er**, **shy'est** or **shi'est** ⟦OE *sceoh*⟧ 1 easily frightened; timid 2 not at ease with others; bashful 3 distrustful; wary 4 [Slang] lacking —***vi.*** **shied**, **shy'ing** 1 to move suddenly as when startled 2 to be or become cautious, etc. —**shy'ly** ***adv.*** —**shy'ness** ***n.***

shy[2] (shī) ***vt.***, ***vi.*** **shied**, **shy'ing** ⟦< ?⟧ to fling, esp. sideways

shy·ster (shī'stər) ***n.*** ⟦prob. < Ger *scheisser*, one who defecates⟧ [Slang] a lawyer who uses unethical or tricky methods

Si *Chem. symbol for* silicon

Si·am (sī am') *former name for* THAILAND

Si·a·mese (sī'ə mēz') ***n.***, *pl.* **-mese'** 1 *former name for* THAI 2 a domestic cat with blue eyes and a light-colored coat —***adj.*** *former term for* THAI

Siamese twins ⟦after such a pair born in *Siam*⟧ any pair of twins born with bodies joined together

Si·ber·i·a (sī bir'ē ə) region in N Asia, between the Urals & the Pacific: Asian section of Russia —**Si·ber'i·an** ***adj.***, ***n.***

sib·i·lant (sib'ə lənt) ***adj.*** ⟦< L *sibilare*, to hiss⟧ having or making a hissing sound —***n.*** a sibilant consonant, as (s) or (z)

sib·ling (sib'liŋ) ***n.*** ⟦< OE *sib*, kinsman + -LING⟧ a brother or sister

sib·yl (sib'əl) ***n.*** ⟦< Gr *sibylla*⟧ ancient Greek or Roman prophetess —**sib'yl·line'** (-īn', -ēn') ***adj.***

sic (sik) ***vt.*** **sicced** or **sicked**, **sic'cing** or **sick'ing** ⟦< SEEK⟧ to incite (a dog) to attack

sic (sik, sēk) ***adv.*** ⟦L⟧ thus; so: used within brackets, [*sic*], to show that a quoted passage, esp. one containing an error, is reproduced accurately

Sic·i·ly (sis'ə lē) island of Italy, off its S tip —**Si·cil·i·an** (si sil'yən) ***adj.***, ***n.***

sick[1] (sik) ***adj.*** ⟦OE *seoc*⟧ 1 suffering from disease; ill 2 having nausea 3 of or for sick people *[sick* leave*]* 4 deeply disturbed, as by grief 5 disgusted by an excess *[sick* of excuses*]* 6 [Inf.] sadistic, morbid, etc. *[a sick* joke*]* —**the sick** sick people —**sick'ish** ***adj.***

sick[2] (sik) ***vt.*** *alt. sp. of* SIC (incite)

sick bay a hospital and dispensary on a ship

sick'bed' ***n.*** the bed of a sick person

sick'en ***vt.***, ***vi.*** to make or become ill, disgusted, etc. —**sick'en·ing** ***adj.***

sick'ie (-ē) ***n.*** [Slang] a sick person, esp. one who is emotionally disturbed, sadistic, etc.

sick·le (sik'əl) ***n.*** ⟦ult. < L *secare*, to cut⟧ a tool having a crescent-shaped blade on a short handle, for cutting tall grasses and weeds

sickle cell anemia an inherited chronic anemia found chiefly among black people, in which defective hemoglobin causes sickle-shaped red blood cells

sick'ly ***adj.*** **-li·er**, **-li·est** 1 in poor health 2 produced by sickness *[a sickly* pallor*]* 3 faint 4 weak

sick'ness ***n.*** 1 a being sick or diseased 2 a malady 3 nausea

sick'out' ***n.*** a staying out of work on the claim of illness, as by a group of employees trying to win demands but forbidden to strike

sick'room' ***n.*** the room of a sick person

side (sīd) ***n.*** ⟦OE⟧ 1 the right or left half, as of the body 2 a position beside one 3 *a)* any of the lines or surfaces that bound something *b)* either of the two bounding surfaces of an object that are not the front, back, top, or bottom 4 either of the two surfaces of paper, cloth, etc. 5 an aspect *[his cruel side]* 6 any location, etc. with reference to a central point 7 the position or attitude of one person or faction opposing another 8 one of the parties in a contest, conflict, etc. 9 a line of descent —***adj.*** 1 of, at, or on a side 2 to or from one side *[a side* glance*]* 3 secondary *[a side* issue*]* —***vi.*** to align oneself (*with* a faction, etc.) —**side by side** together —**take sides** to support a faction

side'arm' ***adj.***, ***adv.*** with a forward arm motion at or below shoulder level

side arm a weapon worn at the side or waist, as a sword or pistol: *often used in pl.*

side'bar' ***n.*** a short article about a sidelight of a major news story and printed alongside it

side'board' ***n.*** a piece of furniture for holding linen, china, silverware, etc.

side'burns' ***pl.n.*** ⟦< *burnsides*, side whiskers worn by A. E. *Burnside*, Civil War general⟧ the hair growing on the sides of a man's face, just in front of the ears

side'car' ***n.*** a small car attached to the side of a motorcycle

side dish any food served along with the main course, usually in a separate dish

side effect an incidental effect, as an unrelated symptom produced by a drug

side'kick' ***n.*** [Slang] 1 a close friend 2 a partner; confederate

side'light' ***n.*** a bit of incidental knowledge or information

side'line' ***n.*** 1 either of two lines marking the side limits of a playing area, as in football 2 a secondary line of merchandise, work, etc.

side'long' ***adv.*** toward the side —***adj.*** directed to the side: said as of a glance

THESAURUS

keep out, evict, fence out; see REFUSE. —**shut up** 1 [To cease speaking] be quiet, stop talking, quiet, hush, quit chattering, silence. 2 [To close] padlock, close up, stop; see CLOSE 4.

shutter ***n.*** blind, cover, shade; see CURTAIN, SCREEN 1.

shy[1] ***a.*** retiring, bashful, modest, diffident, submissive, timid, passive, reticent, fearful, tentative, subservient, docile, compliant, humble, coy, restrained, timorous, demure.

shyness ***n.*** bashfulness, reserve, timidity, modesty, timidness, coyness, demureness, sheepishness, diffidence, apprehension, backwardness, nervousness, insecurity, reticence, stage fright; see also RESTRAINT 1.

sick[1] ***a.*** ill, ailing, unwell, disordered, diseased, feeble, frail, impaired, weak, suffering, feverish, sickly, declining, unhealthy, rabid, indisposed, distempered, infected, invalid, delicate, infirm, rickety, peaked, broken-down, physically rundown, confined, laid up, under medication, bedridden, in poor health, nauseated, nauseous, at death's door, hospitalized, quarantined, incurable, out of kilter*, feeling poorly, sick as a dog*, in a bad way, not so hot*, under the weather*.—*Ant.* HEALTHY, hearty, well. —**get sick** become sick or ill, contract a disease, take sick; see SICKEN 1. —**sick of** tired of, disgusted, fed up; see DISGUSTED.

sicken ***v.*** 1 [To contract a disease] become ill, become infected, take sick, fall ill, become diseased, fall victim to a disease, be stricken, run a temperature, run a fever, be taken with, come down with, catch a disease, acquire, waste away, languish, suffer a relapse, break out with, catch one's death*, pick up a bug*. 2 [To offend] repel, nauseate, revolt; see DISGUST.

sickening ***a.*** 1 [Contaminated] sickly, tainted, diseased; see SICK. 2 [Disgusting] revolting, nauseous, putrid; see OFFENSIVE 2.

sickly ***a.*** ailing, weakly, feeble; see SICK.

sickness ***n.*** ill health, ailment, infirmity; see ILLNESS 1.

side ***a.*** to the side, indirect, roundabout; see OBLIQUE.

side ***n.*** 1 [One of two opponents] party, contestant, combatant; see FACTION. 2 [A face] facet, front, front side, rear, surface, outer surface, inner surface, top, bottom, elevation, view; see also PLANE 1. —**from side to side** back and forth, wobbly, unstable; see IRREGULAR 1. —**on the side** in addition to, as a bonus, additionally; see EXTRA. —**side by side** adjacent, nearby, faithfully; see LOYALLY, NEAR 1. —**take sides** join, fight for, declare oneself; see HELP, SUPPORT 2.

sideline ***n.*** avocation, interest, trade; see HOBBY.

side′man′ (-man′) ***n.***, *pl.* **-men′** (-men′) a band member other than the leader or soloist
side′piece′ ***n.*** a piece on the side of something
si·de·re·al (sī dir′ē əl) ***adj.*** ⟦< L *sidus*, star⟧ with reference to the stars
side′sad′dle ***n.*** a saddle designed for a rider sitting with both legs on the same side of the animal —***adv.*** on or as if on a sidesaddle
side′show′ ***n.*** a small show in connection with the main show, as of a circus
side′slip′ ***vi.*** **-slipped′**, **-slip′ping** to slip or skid sideways —***vt.*** to cause to sideslip —***n.*** a slip or skid to the side
side′split′ting ***adj.*** **1** very hearty: said of laughter **2** very funny
side′step′ ***vt.***, ***vi.*** **-stepped′**, **-step′ping** to dodge as by stepping aside
side′swipe′ ***vt.*** **-swiped′**, **-swip′ing** to hit along the side in passing —***n.*** such a glancing blow
side′track′ ***vt.***, ***vi.*** **1** to switch (a train) to a siding **2** to turn away from the main issue
side′walk′ ***n.*** a path for pedestrians, usually paved, along the side of a street
side′wall′ ***n.*** the side of a tire between the tread and the wheel rim
side′ways′ (-wāz′) ***adv.***, ***adj.*** **1** toward or from one side **2** with one side forward Also **side′wise′** (-wīz′)
sid·ing (sīd′iŋ) ***n.*** **1** a covering, as of overlapping boards, for the outside of a frame building **2** a short railroad track connected with a main track by a switch and used for unloading, etc.
si·dle (sīd′'l) ***vi.*** **-dled**, **-dling** ⟦< *sideling*, sideways⟧ to move sideways, esp. shyly or stealthily
SIDS (sidz) *abbrev.* SUDDEN INFANT DEATH SYNDROME
siege (sēj) ***n.*** ⟦ult. < L *sedere*, sit⟧ **1** the encirclement of a fortified place by an enemy intending to take it **2** any persistent attempt to gain control, etc. —**lay siege to** to subject to a siege
si·en·na (sē en′ə) ***n.*** ⟦It⟧ yellowish brown or reddish brown
si·er·ra (sē er′ə) ***n.*** ⟦Sp < L *serra*, a saw⟧ a range of hills or mountains with a saw-toothed appearance
Si·er·ra Le·one (sē er′ə lē ōn′) country in W Africa, on the Atlantic: 27,925 sq. mi.; pop. 3,518,000
si·es·ta (sē es′tə) ***n.*** ⟦Sp < L *sexta* (*hora*), sixth (hour), noon⟧ a brief nap or rest after the noon meal
sieve (siv) ***n.*** ⟦OE *sife*⟧ a utensil with many small holes for straining liquids, etc.; strainer
sift (sift) ***vt.*** ⟦OE *siftan*⟧ **1** to pass (flour, etc.) through a sieve **2** to examine (evidence, etc.) with care **3** to separate *[to sift fact from fable]* —***vi.*** to pass as through a sieve —**sift′er** ***n.***
sigh (sī) ***vi.*** ⟦< OE *sican*⟧ **1** to take in and let out a long, deep, audible breath, as in sorrow, relief, or longing **2** to feel longing or grief (*for*) —***n.*** the act or sound of sighing
sight (sīt) ***n.*** ⟦< OE *seon*, to see⟧ **1** something seen or worth seeing **2** the act of seeing **3** a device to aid the eyes in aiming a gun, etc. **4** aim or an observation taken, as on a sextant **5** the power or range of seeing; eyesight **6** [Inf.] anything that looks unpleasant, odd, etc. —***vt.*** **1** to observe **2** to glimpse; see **3** to aim at **4** to adjust the sights of —***vi.*** to look carefully *[sight along the line]* —**at** (or **on**) **sight** as soon as seen —**by sight** by appearance —**not by a long sight** **1** not nearly **2** not at all —**out of sight** **1** not in sight **2** far off **3** [Inf.] beyond reach **4** [Slang] excellent; wonderful
sight′ed ***adj.*** **1** having sight; not blind **2** having (a specified kind of) sight *[farsighted]*
sight′ing ***n.*** an observation, as of something rare
sight′less ***adj.*** blind
sight′ly ***adj.*** **-li·er**, **-li·est** pleasant to the sight —**sight′li·ness** ***n.***
sight reading the skill of performing written music on first sight —**sight′-read′** ***vt.***, ***vi.***
sight′see′ing ***n.*** the visiting of places of interest —**sight′seer** (-sē′ər) ***n.***
sig·ma (sig′mə) ***n.*** the eighteenth letter of the Greek alphabet (Σ, σ, ς)
sign (sīn) ***n.*** ⟦< L *signum*⟧ **1** something that indicates a fact, quality, etc.; token **2** a gesture that conveys information, etc. **3** a mark or symbol having a specific meaning *[a dollar sign ($)]* **4** a placard, etc. bearing information, advertising, etc. **5** any trace or indication —***vt.*** **1** to write (one's name) on (a letter, check, contract, etc.) **2** to engage by written contract —***vi.*** to write one's signature —**sign in** (or **out**) to sign a register on arrival (or departure) —**sign off** to stop broadcasting, as for the day —**sign off on** to approve
sign′age ***n.*** public signs collectively, often, specif., when graphically coordinated
sig·nal (sig′nəl) ***n.*** ⟦< L *signum*, a sign⟧ **1** a sign or event that initiates action *[a bugle signal to attack]* **2** a gesture, device, etc. that conveys command, warning, etc. **3** in radio, etc., the electrical impulses transmitted or received —***adj.*** **1** remarkable; notable **2** used as a signal —***vt.***, ***vi.*** **-naled** or **-nalled**, **-nal·ing** or **-nal·ling** **1** to make a signal or signals (to) **2** to communicate by signals
sig′nal·ize′ (-nə līz′) ***vt.*** **-ized′**, **-iz′ing** to make known or draw attention to
sig′nal·ly ***adv.*** in a signal way; notably
sig·na·to·ry (sig′nə tôr′ē) ***adj.*** having joined in signing something —***n.***, *pl.* **-ries** a signatory person, nation, etc.
sig·na·ture (sig′nə chər) ***n.*** ⟦< L *signare*, to sign⟧ **1** a person's name written by that person **2** *Music* a staff sign showing key or time
sign·board (sīn′bôrd′) ***n.*** a board bearing a sign or advertisement
sig·net (sig′nit) ***n.*** ⟦< Fr *signe*, a sign⟧ a seal, as on a ring, used in marking documents as official, etc.
sig·nif·i·cance (sig nif′ə kəns) ***n.*** **1** that which is signified; meaning **2** the quality of being significant; expressiveness **3** importance

THESAURUS

sidestep ***v.*** evade, elude, shun; see AVOID.
sidewalk ***n.*** footpath, pavement, walkway; see PATH.
sideways ***a.*** indirectly, sloping, sidelong; see OBLIQUE.
siege ***n.*** offense, onslaught, assault; see ATTACK.
sieve ***n.*** strainer, sifter, colander, screen, bolter, mesh, hair sieve, drum sieve, flat sieve, gravel sieve, flour sieve.
sift ***v.*** **1** [To evaluate] investigate, scrutinize, probe; see EXAMINE. **2** [To put through a sieve] bolt, screen, winnow, grade, sort, colander, size, strain; see also CLEAN, FILTER 2, PURIFY.
sigh ***n.*** deep breath, sigh of relief, expression of sorrow; see CRY 1.
sigh ***v.*** groan, moan, lament; see CRY 1, GASP.
sight ***n.*** **1** [The power of seeing] perception, eyesight, eyes for, range of vision, apprehension, keen sight, clear sight; see also VISION 1. **2** [Something worth seeing; *often plural*] show, view, spectacle, display, scene, point of interest, local scene, landmark. **3** [*An unsightly person] eyesore, hag, ogre; see SLOB. —**a sight for sore eyes*** beauty, welcome sight, delight; see BLESSING 2, FRIEND, VIEW. —**at first sight** hastily, without much consideration, provisionally; see QUICKLY. —**by sight** somewhat acquainted, not intimately, superficially; see UNFAMILIAR 1. —**catch sight of** glimpse, notice, see momentarily; see SEE 1. —**lose sight of** miss, fail to follow, slip up on; see FORGET, NEGLECT 1. —**on sight** at once, without hesitation, precipitately; see IMMEDIATELY, QUICKLY. —**out of sight (of)** disappeared, vanished, indiscernible; see GONE 1, INVISIBLE.
sightseeing ***n.*** vacationing, excursion, tour; see TRAVEL.
sightseer ***n.*** observer, tourist, voyager; see TRAVELER.
sign ***n.*** **1** [A signal] indication, clue, omen, divination, premonition, handwriting on the wall, foreshadowing, manifestation, foreboding, foreknowledge, token, harbinger, herald, hint, symptom, assurance, prediction, portent, prophecy, mark, badge, symbol, caution, warning, beacon, flag, hand signal, gesture, wave of the arm, flash, whistle, warning bell, signal bell, signal light, high sign*. **2** [An emblem] insignia, badge, crest; see EMBLEM. **3** [A symbol] type, visible sign, token; see sense 1.
sign ***v.*** **1** [Authorize] endorse, confirm, acknowledge; see APPROVE. **2** [Indicate] express, signify, signal; see MEAN 1. **3** [Hire] engage, contract, employ; see HIRE.
signal ***n.*** beacon, flag, gesture; see SIGN 1.
signal ***v.*** give a sign to, flag, wave, gesture, motion, nod, beckon, warn, indicate.
signature ***n.*** sign, stamp, mark, name, written name, subscription, autograph, impression, indication, designation, trademark, one's John Hancock*.
signed ***a.*** autographed, endorsed, marked, written, undersigned, countersigned, sealed, witnessed, notarized, registered, enlisted, signed on the dotted line*.
signer ***n.*** cosigner, underwriter, endorser; see WITNESS.
significance ***n.*** weight, consequence, point; see IMPORTANCE.

sig·nif'i·cant (-kənt) ***adj.*** ⟦< L *significare*, signify⟧ **1** having or expressing a meaning, esp. a special or hidden one **2** full of meaning **3** important —**sig·nif'i·cant·ly** ***adv.***
sig·ni·fy (sig'nə fī') ***vt.*** **-fied', -fy'ing** ⟦< L *signum*, a sign + *facere*, make⟧ **1** to be an indication of; mean **2** to make known by a sign, words, etc. —***vi.*** to be important —**sig'ni·fi·ca'tion** ***n.***
sign language hand signals and gestures used, as by the deaf, as a language
sign of the cross an outline of a CROSS (sense 2) made symbolically by moving the hand or fingers
sign of the zodiac any of the twelve divisions of the zodiac, each represented by a symbol
si·gnor (sē nyôr') ***n.***, *pl.* ***-gno'ri*** (-nyô'rē) ⟦It⟧ **1** [**S-**] Mr.: Italian title **2** a man; gentleman
si·gno·ra (sē nyô'rä) ***n.***, *pl.* ***-gno're*** (-re) ⟦It⟧ **1** [**S-**] Mrs.; Madam: Italian title **2** a married woman
si·gno·ri·na (sē'nyô rē'nä) ***n.***, *pl.* ***-ri'ne*** (-ne) ⟦It⟧ **1** [**S-**] Miss: Italian title **2** an unmarried woman or a girl
sign'post' ***n.*** **1** a post bearing a sign **2** an obvious clue, symptom, etc.
Sikh (sēk, sik) ***n.*** ⟦Hindi, disciple⟧ a member of a monotheistic religion founded in N India
si·lage (sī'lij) ***n.*** green fodder preserved in a silo
si·lence (sī'ləns) ***n.*** **1** a keeping silent **2** absence of sound **3** an omission of mention —***vt.*** **-lenced, -lenc·ing** **1** to make silent **2** to put down; repress —***interj.*** be silent!
si'lenc·er ***n.*** **1** one that silences **2** a device to muffle the sound of a gun
si·lent (sī'lənt) ***adj.*** ⟦< L *silere*, be silent⟧ **1** making no vocal sound; mute **2** not talkative **3** still; noiseless **4** not expressed; tacit **5** not active *[*a *silent* partner*]* —**si'lent·ly** ***adv.***
sil·hou·ette (sil'ə wet') ***n.*** ⟦Fr, after E. de *Silhouette*, 18th-c. Fr statesman⟧ **1** a solid, usually black, outline drawing, esp. a profile **2** any dark shape seen against a light background —***vt.*** **-et'ted, -et'ting** to show in silhouette
sil·i·ca (sil'i kə) ***n.*** ⟦< L *silex*, flint⟧ a hard, glassy mineral found in a variety of forms, as in quartz, opal, or sand —**si·li·ceous** (sə lish'əs) ***adj.***
sil'i·cate (-kit, -kāt') ***n.*** a salt or ester derived from silica
sil'i·con (-kän', -kən) ***n.*** ⟦ult. < L *silex*, flint⟧ a nonmetallic chemical element found always in combination
sil'i·cone' (-kōn') ***n.*** an organic silicon compound highly resistant to heat, water, etc.
Silicon Valley ⟦after the material used for electronic chips⟧ *name for* an area near San Francisco: a center of high-technology activities
sil'i·co'sis (-kō'sis) ***n.*** ⟦see SILICON & -OSIS⟧ a chronic lung disease from inhaling silica dust
silk (silk) ***n.*** ⟦ult. < ? L *sericus*, (fabric) of the *Seres*, prob. the Chinese⟧ **1** *a)* the fine, soft fiber produced by silkworms *b)* thread or fabric made from this **2** any silklike filament or substance —**silk'en** ***adj.*** —**silk·y** (sil'kē), **-i·er, -i·est,** ***adj.*** —**silk'i·ness** ***n.***
silk-screen process a stencil method of printing a color design through a piece of silk or other fine cloth on which parts of the design not to be printed have been blocked out —**silk'-screen'** ***vt.***
silk'worm' ***n.*** any of certain moth caterpillars that produce cocoons of silk fiber
sill (sil) ***n.*** **1** a heavy horizontal timber or line of masonry supporting a house wall, etc. **2** a horizontal piece forming the bottom frame of a window or door opening
sil·ly (sil'ē) ***adj.*** **-li·er, -li·est** ⟦< OE *sælig*, happy⟧ having or showing little sense, judgment, or sobriety; foolish, absurd, etc. —**sil'li·ness** ***n.***
si·lo (sī'lō) ***n.***, *pl.* **-los** ⟦< Gr *siros*⟧ **1** an airtight pit or tower in which green fodder is preserved **2** an underground facility for a long-range ballistic missile
silt (silt) ***n.*** ⟦prob. < Scand⟧ a fine-grained, sandy sediment carried or deposited by water —***vt.***, ***vi.*** to fill or choke up with silt
sil·ver (sil'vər) ***n.*** ⟦< OE *seolfer*⟧ **1** a white metallic chemical element that is very ductile and malleable: a precious metal **2** *a)* silver coin *b)* money; riches **3** silverware **4** a lustrous, grayish white —***adj.*** **1** of, containing, or plated with silver **2** silvery **3** marking a 25th anniversary —***vt.*** to cover with or as with silver
sil'ver·fish' ***n.***, *pl.* **-fish'** a wingless insect with silvery scales and long feelers, found in damp places
silver lining some basis for hope or comfort in the midst of despair
silver nitrate a colorless crystalline salt, used in photography, as an antiseptic, etc.
sil'ver·smith' ***n.*** an artisan who makes and repairs silver articles
sil'ver-tongued' (-tuŋd') ***adj.*** eloquent
sil'ver·ware' ***n.*** **1** articles, esp. tableware, made of or plated with silver **2** any metal tableware
sil'ver·y ***adj.*** **1** of, like, or containing silver **2** soft and clear in tone
sim·i·an (sim'ē ən) ***adj.***, ***n.*** ⟦< L *simia*, an ape⟧ (of or like) an ape or monkey
sim·i·lar (sim'ə lər) ***adj.*** ⟦< L *similis*⟧ nearly but not exactly the same or alike —**sim'i·lar'i·ty** (-ler'ə tē), *pl.* **-ties,** ***n.*** —**sim'i·lar·ly** ***adv.***
sim·i·le (sim'ə lē') ***n.*** ⟦< L, a likeness⟧ a figure of speech likening one thing to another by the use of *like, as,* etc. (Ex.: tears flowed like wine)
si·mil·i·tude (sə mil'ə to͞od') ***n.*** ⟦< L *similitudo*⟧ likeness; resemblance
sim·mer (sim'ər) ***vi.*** ⟦echoic⟧ **1** to remain at or just below the boiling point **2** to be about to break out, as in anger or revolt —***vt.*** to keep at or just below the boiling point —***n.*** a simmering
si·mon-pure (sī'mən pyoor') ***adj.*** ⟦after *Simon Pure*, a character in an 18th-c. play⟧ genuine; authentic
si·mo·ny (sī'mə nē, sim'ə-) ***n.*** ⟦after *Simon* Magus: Acts 8:9-24⟧ the buying or selling of sacraments or benefices
sim·pa·ti·co (sim pät'i kō, -pat'-) ***adj.*** ⟦< It or Sp⟧ compatible or congenial
sim·per (sim'pər) ***vi.*** ⟦early Modern Eng⟧ to smile in a silly or affected way —***n.*** such a smile

THESAURUS

significant ***a.*** meaningful, notable, vital; see IMPORTANT 1.
signify ***v.*** imply, import, purport; see MEAN 1.
silence ***n.*** **1** [Absence of sound] quietness, stillness, hush, utter stillness, absolute quiet, quietude, calm, noiselessness, quiet, deep stillness, soundlessness, loss of signal, radio silence, security silence, security blackout, censorship, hush of early dawn.—*Ant.* NOISE, din, uproar. **2** [Absence of speech] muteness, secrecy, reserve, reticence, inarticulateness, golden silence, respectful silence.
silence ***v.*** hush, quell, still; see QUIET 2.
silenced ***a.*** quieted, calmed, stilled, restrained, repressed, held down, held back, restricted, subdued, gagged, inhibited, coerced, suppressed, under duress, under compulsion, murdered*; see also INTERRUPTED.
silent ***a.*** **1** [Without noise] still, hushed, soundless; see CALM 2, QUIET. **2** [Without speech] reserved, mute, speechless; see DUMB 1.
silently ***a.*** without noise, without a sound, as still as a mouse, like a shadow, in utter stillness, noiselessly, calmly, quietly, soundlessly, mutely, dumbly, secretly, sneakily, in deathlike silence, like one struck dumb, speechlessly, wordlessly, as silently as falling snow.
silhouette ***n.*** contour, shape, profile; see FORM 1, OUTLINE 3.
sill ***n.*** threshold, beam, bottom of the frame; see LEDGE.
silly ***a.*** senseless, ridiculous, nonsensical, absurd, brainless, simpleminded, unreasonable, foolish, irrational, inconsistent, stupid, illogical, vacuous, inane, frivolous, ludicrous, preposterous; see also CHILDISH.
silver ***a.*** silvery, pale, white, lustrous, bright, shiny, silvery white, silverlike, shimmering, glittering, resplendent, white as silver.
silverware ***n.*** silver, service, cutlery, flatware, silver plate, holloware. *Common pieces of silverware include the following:* knife, dinner knife, butter knife, steak knife, fork, salad fork, cold meat fork, tablespoon, soup spoon, dessert spoon, grapefruit spoon, ice-cream spoon, iced-tea spoon, coffee spoon, teaspoon, soup ladle, gravy ladle, sugar spoon, spatula.
silvery ***a.*** shiny, glittering, brilliant; see BRIGHT 1.
similar ***a.*** much the same, comparable, related; see ALIKE.
similarity ***n.*** correspondence, likeness, resemblance, parallelism, semblance, agreement, affinity, kinship, analogy, closeness, approximation, conformity, concordance, concurrence, coincidence, congruity, parity, harmony, comparability, identity, community, relation, correlation, relationship, proportion, comparison, simile, interrelation, association, connection, similar form, like quality, point of likeness, similar appearance.—*Ant.* DIFFERENCE, variance, dissimilarity.
similarly ***a.*** likewise, thus, furthermore, in a like manner, correspondingly, by the same token, in addition, then, as well, too; see also SO.
simmer ***v.*** seethe, stew, warm; see BOIL, COOK.
simmering ***a.*** broiling, heated, boiling; see HOT 1.

sim·ple (sim′pəl) ***adj.*** **-pler, -plest** ⟦< L *simplus*⟧ **1** having only one or a few parts; uncomplicated **2** easy to do or understand **3** without additions *[the simple facts]* **4** not ornate or luxurious; plain **5** without guile or deceit **6** without ostentation; natural **7** of low rank or position **8** stupid or foolish —**sim′ple·ness** ***n.***

simple interest interest computed on principal alone, and not on principal plus interest

sim′ple-mind′ed ***adj.*** **1** artless; unsophisticated **2** foolish **3** mentally retarded

sim′ple·ton (-tən) ***n.*** a fool

sim·plic·i·ty (sim plis′ə tē) ***n.***, *pl.* **-ties** **1** a simple state or quality; freedom from complexity **2** absence of elegance, luxury, etc.; plainness

sim·pli·fy (sim′plə fī′) ***vt.*** **-fied′, -fy′ing** to make simpler or less complex —**sim′pli·fi·ca′tion** ***n.***

sim·plis·tic (sim plis′tik) ***adj.*** making complex problems unrealistically simple —**sim·plis′ti·cal·ly** ***adv.***

sim·ply (sim′plē) ***adv.*** **1** in a simple way **2** merely *[simply trying]* **3** completely *[simply furious]*

sim·u·late (sim′yoo lāt′) ***vt.*** **-lat′ed, -lat′ing** ⟦< L *simulare*⟧ **1** to give a false appearance of; feign **2** to look or act like —**sim′u·la′tion** ***n.*** —**sim′u·la′tor** ***n.***

si·mul·cast (sī′məl kast′) ***vt.*** **-cast′** or **-cast′ed, -cast′ing** to broadcast (a program) simultaneously by radio and television —***n.*** a program so broadcast

si·mul·ta·ne·ous (sī′məl tā′nē əs) ***adj.*** ⟦< L *simul*, together⟧ occurring, done, etc. at the same time —**si′mul·ta·ne′i·ty** (-tə nē′ə tē, -nā′-) ***n.*** —**si′mul·ta′ne·ous·ly** ***adv.***

sin (sin) ***n.*** ⟦OE *synne*⟧ **1** the willful breaking of religious or moral law **2** any offense or fault —***vi.*** **sinned, sin′ning** to commit a sin

Si·nai (sī′nī′), **Mount** *Bible* the mountain where Moses received the law from God: Exodus 19

since (sins) ***adv.*** ⟦ult. < OE *sith*, after + *thæt*, that⟧ **1** from then until now *[I've been here ever since]* **2** at some time between then and now *[he has since recovered]* **3** before now; ago *[long since gone]* —***prep.*** **1** continuously from (then) until now *[since noon]* **2** during the period between (then) and now *[twice since May]* —***conj.*** **1** after the time that *[two years since they met]* **2** continuously from the time when *[lonely ever since she left]* **3** because *[since you're done, let's go]*

sin·cere (sin sir′) ***adj.*** **-cer′er, -cer′est** ⟦< L *sincerus*, pure⟧ **1** truthful; honest **2** genuine *[sincere grief]* —**sin·cere′ly** ***adv.*** —**sin·cer′i·ty** (-ser′ə tē) ***n.***

si·ne·cure (sī′nə kyoor′, sin′ə-) ***n.*** ⟦< L *sine*, without + *cura*, care⟧ any position providing an income but requiring little or no work

si·ne di·e (sī′nē dī′ē) ⟦LL, without a day⟧ for an indefinite period

si·ne qua non (sī′nē kwā nän′, sin′ā kwä nōn′) ⟦L, without which not⟧ an indispensable condition or thing

sin·ew (sin′yoo) ***n.*** ⟦OE *seonwe*⟧ **1** a tendon **2** muscular power; strength —**sin′ew·y** ***adj.***

sin′ful ***adj.*** wicked; immoral —**sin′ful·ly** ***adv.***

sing[1] (siŋ) ***vi.*** **sang, sung, sing′ing** ⟦OE *singan*⟧ **1** to produce musical sounds with the voice **2** to use song or verse in praise, etc. *[of thee I sing]* **3** to make musical sounds, as a songbird does **4** to hum, buzz, etc., as a bee does —***vt.*** **1** to render (a song, etc.) by singing **2** to extol, etc. in song **3** to bring or put by singing *[to sing a baby to sleep]* —***n.*** [Inf.] group singing —**sing′er** ***n.***

sing[2] *abbrev.* singular

sing′a·long′ ***n.*** an informal gathering of people to sing songs

Sin·ga·pore (siŋ′ə pôr′) **1** island country off the S tip of the Malay Peninsula: 248 sq. mi.; pop. 2,930,000 **2** its capital, a seaport on the S coast: pop. 2,756,000

singe (sinj) ***vt.*** **singed, singe′ing** ⟦OE *sengan*⟧ **1** to burn superficially **2** to expose (an animal carcass) to flame in removing feathers, etc. —***n.*** **1** a singeing **2** a superficial burn

sin·gle (siŋ′gəl) ***adj.*** ⟦< L *singulus*⟧ **1** *a)* one only *b)* separate and distinct *[every single time]* **2** solitary **3** of or for one person or family **4** between two persons only *[single combat]* **5** unmarried **6** having only one part; not multiple, etc. **7** whole; unbroken *[a single front]* —***vt.*** **-gled, -gling** to select from others: usually with *out* —***vi.*** *Baseball* to hit a single —***n.*** **1** a single person or thing **2** *Baseball* a hit on which the batter reaches first base **3** [*pl.*] *Racket Sports* a match with only one player on each side —**sin′gle·ness** ***n.***

sin′gle-breast′ed (-bres′tid) ***adj.*** overlapping in front enough to fasten *[a single-breasted coat]*

single file **1** a single line of people or things, one behind another **2** in such a line

sin′gle-hand′ed ***adj.***, ***adv.*** **1** using only one hand **2** without help —**sin′gle-hand′ed·ly** ***adv.***

sin′gle-mind′ed ***adj.*** with only one aim or purpose —**sin′gle-mind′ed·ly** ***adv.***

sin′gle·ton (-tən) ***n.*** **1** a playing card that is the only one of its suit held by a player **2** a single person or thing

THESAURUS

simple ***a.*** **1** [Not complicated] single, unmixed, unblended, mere, unadulterated, not complex, simplistic, not confusing, obvious, direct, pure. **2** [Plain] homely, unaffected, unadorned; see MODEST 2. **3** [Easy] not difficult, effortless, done with ease; see EASY 2.

simple-minded ***a.*** unintelligent, childish, mindless; see DULL 3, NAIVE, STUPID.

simpleton ***n.*** clod, idiot, bungler; see FOOL.

simplicity ***n.*** **1** [The quality of being plain] plainness, stark reality, lack of ornament, lack of sophistication, bareness, monotony, homeliness, severity. **2** [Artlessness] naiveté, plainness, primitiveness; see INNOCENCE 2.

simplified ***a.*** made easy, made plain, uncomplicated, clear, interpreted, broken down, cleared up, reduced, abridged; see also OBVIOUS 2.

simplify ***v.*** clear up, clarify, interpret; see EXPLAIN.

simplistic ***a.*** simplest, naive, oversimplified; see CHILDISH, SIMPLE 1.

simply ***a.*** **1** [With simplicity] clearly, plainly, intelligibly, directly, candidly, sincerely, modestly, easily, quietly, naturally, honestly, frankly, unaffectedly, artlessly, ingenuously, without self-consciousness, commonly, ordinarily, matter-of-factly, unpretentiously, openly, guilelessly. **2** [Merely] utterly, just, solely; see ONLY 2.

simulate ***v.*** imitate, feign, lie; see PRETEND 1.

simultaneous ***a.*** coincident, at the same time, concurrent, in concert, in the same breath, in chorus, at the same instant, in sync; see also EQUALLY.

simultaneously ***a.*** at the same time, as one, concurrently; see TOGETHER 2.

sin ***n.*** error, wrongdoing, trespass, wickedness, evildoing, iniquity, immorality, transgression, ungodliness, unrighteousness, veniality, disobedience to the divine will, transgression of the divine law, violation of God's law; see also CRIME. *Sins recognized as deadly include the following:* pride, covetousness, lust, anger, gluttony, envy, sloth.

sin ***v.*** err, do wrong, commit a crime, offend, break the moral law, break one of the Commandments, trespass, transgress, misbehave, go astray, fall, lapse, fall from grace, wander from the straight and narrow*, backslide.

since ***a.***, ***prep.***, ***conj.*** **1** [Because] for, as, inasmuch as, considering, in consideration of, after all, seeing that, in view of, for the reason that, by reason of, on account of, in view of; see also BECAUSE. **2** [Between the present and a previous time] ago, from the time of, subsequent to, after, following, more recently than, until now.

sincere ***a.*** truthful, faithful, trustworthy; see HONEST 1, RELIABLE.

sincerely ***a.*** truthfully, truly, really, genuinely, earnestly, aboveboard, seriously, naturally, candidly, frankly, profoundly, deeply, to the bottom of one's heart.

sincerity ***n.*** openness, frankness, truthfulness; see HONESTY, RELIABILITY.

sinful ***a.*** wicked, erring, immoral; see BAD 1, WRONG 1.

sinfully ***a.*** wickedly, immorally, unjustly; see WRONGLY.

sing[1] ***v.*** chant, carol, warble, vocalize, hum, harmonize, trill, croon, twitter, chirp, raise a song, lift up the voice in song, burst into song.

singe ***v.*** brand, sear, scorch; see BURN.

singer ***n.*** vocalist, songster, chorister, choirmaster, soloist, minstrel, chanter, entertainer; see also MUSICIAN.

singing ***n.*** warbling, crooning, chanting; see MUSIC 1.

single ***a.*** **1** [Unique] sole, original, exceptional, singular, only, without equal, unequaled, peerless, unrivaled; see also RARE 2, UNIQUE, UNUSUAL 1.—*Ant.* MANY, numerous, widespread. **2** [Individual] particular, separate, indivisible; see INDIVIDUAL, PRIVATE. **3** [Unmarried] unwed, divorced, celibate, eligible, virginal, living alone, companionless, unattached, available, free, footloose, unfettered*.—*Ant.* MARRIED, UNITED, wed.

single-handed ***a.*** without assistance, courageously, self-reliantly; see ALONE, BRAVELY.

single-minded ***a.*** stubborn, self-reliant, bigoted; see SELFISH.

sin′gle-track′ *adj.* ONE-TRACK
sin′gle·tree′ (-trē′) *n.* ⟦< ME *swingle*, rod + *tre*, tree⟧ the crossbar on the hitch of a wagon, etc. to which the traces of a horse's harness are hooked
sin·gly (siŋ′glē) *adv.* **1** alone **2** one by one **3** unaided
sing′song′ *n.* a monotonous rise and fall of tone, as in speaking
sin·gu·lar (siŋ′gyə lər) *adj.* ⟦< L *singulus*, single⟧ **1** unique **2** extraordinary; remarkable **3** peculiar; odd **4** *Gram.* designating only one —*n. Gram.* the singular form of a word —**sin′gu·lar′i·ty** (-ler′ə tē) *n.* —**sin′gu·lar·ly** *adv.*
Sin·ha·lese (sin′hə lēz′, -lēs′) *adj.* of Sri Lanka (island country of S Asia) or its principal people, language, etc. —*n.* **1** *pl.* **-lese′** a member of the Sinhalese people **2** the language of this people
sin·is·ter (sin′is tər) *adj.* ⟦< L *sinister*, left-hand (side)⟧ **1** [Archaic] on or to the left-hand side **2** threatening harm, evil, etc. **3** wicked; evil
sink (siŋk) *vi.* **sank** or **sunk**, **sunk**, **sink′ing** ⟦OE *sincan*⟧ **1** to go beneath the surface of water, etc. **2** to go down slowly **3** to appear to descend, as the sun does **4** to become lower, as in level, value, or rank **5** to subside: said as of wind or sound **6** to become hollow: said as of the cheeks **7** to pass gradually (*into* sleep, etc.) **8** to approach death —*vt.* **1** to cause to sink **2** to make (a mine, engraving, etc.) by digging, cutting, etc. **3** to invest **4** to defeat; undo —*n.* **1** a cesspool or sewer **2** a basin, as in a kitchen, with a drainpipe **3** an area of sunken land —**sink in** [Inf.] to be understood in full —**sink′a·ble** *adj.*
sink′er *n.* **1** one that sinks **2** a lead weight used in fishing
sink′hole′ *n.* a surface depression resulting when ground collapses
sinking fund a fund built up over time to pay off a future debt, as of a corporation
sin′ner *n.* a person who sins
Sino- ⟦< Gr *Sinai*⟧ *combining form* Chinese and
sin tax a tax on something seen as sinful or harmful, as on liquor, tobacco, or gambling
sin·u·ous (sin′yo͞o əs) *adj.* ⟦< L *sinus*, a bend⟧ bending or winding in and out; wavy —**sin′u·os′i·ty** (-äs′ə tē) *n.* —**sin′u·ous·ly** *adv.*
si·nus (sī′nəs) *n.* ⟦L, a bend⟧ a cavity, hollow, etc.; specif., any of the air cavities in the skull opening into the nasal cavities
si′nus·i′tis (-īt′is) *n.* inflammation of the sinuses, esp. those of the skull
Sioux (so͞o) *n.*, *pl.* **Sioux** (so͞o, so͞oz) a member of a group of Indian tribes of the N U.S. and S Canada —*adj.* of these tribes
sip (sip) *vt.*, *vi.* **sipped**, **sip′ping** ⟦ME *sippen*⟧ to drink a little at a time —*n.* **1** the act of sipping **2** a quantity sipped —**sip′per** *n.*
si·phon (sī′fən) *n.* ⟦< Gr *siphōn*, tube⟧ a bent tube for carrying liquid out over the edge of a container to a lower level —*vt.* to draw off through or as through a siphon
sir (sʉr) *n.* ⟦ME < *sire*, SIRE⟧ **1** [*sometimes* **S-**] a respectful term of address used to a man: not followed by the name **2** [**S-**] the title used before the name of a knight or baronet
sire (sīr) *n.* ⟦< OFr < L *senior*, compar. of *senex*, old⟧ **1** [**S-**] a title of respect used in addressing a king **2** [Old Poet.] a father or forefather **3** the male parent of a four-legged mammal —*vt.* **sired**, **sir′ing** to beget: said esp. of animals
si·ren (sī′rən) *n.* ⟦< Gr *Seirēn*⟧ **1** *Gr. & Rom. Myth.* any of several sea nymphs whose singing lures sailors to their death on rocky coasts **2** a woman considered seductive **3** a warning device producing a loud, wailing sound
sir·loin (sʉr′loin′) *n.* ⟦< OFr *sur*, over + *loigne*, loin⟧ a choice cut of beef from the loin end in front of the rump
si·roc·co (sə räk′ō) *n.*, *pl.* **-cos** ⟦It < Ar *sharq*, the east⟧ a hot, oppressive wind blowing from the deserts of N Africa into S Europe
sir·ree or **sir·ee** (sə rē′) *interj.* ⟦< SIR⟧ used to provide emphasis after *yes* or *no*
sir·up (sʉr′əp, sir′-) *n. alt. sp. of* SYRUP
sis (sis) *n.* [Inf.] *short for* SISTER (senses 1-3)
si·sal (sī′səl, sis′əl) *n.* ⟦after *Sisal*, in SE Mexico⟧ a strong fiber obtained from the leaves of an agave
sis·sy (sis′ē) *n.*, *pl.* **-sies** ⟦dim. of SIS⟧ [Inf.] **1** an effeminate boy or man **2** a timid person —**sis′si·fied′** (-ə fīd′) *adj.*
sis·ter (sis′tər) *n.* ⟦< ON *systir*⟧ **1** a woman or girl as she is related to the other children of her parents **2** a half sister or stepsister **3** a female friend who is like a sister **4** a female fellow member of the same race, organization, etc. **5** [*often* **S-**] a nun **6** something of the same kind, model, etc. —**sis′ter·hood′** *n.* —**sis′ter·ly** *adj.*
sis′ter-in-law′ *n.*, *pl.* **sis′ters-in-law′** **1** the sister of one's spouse **2** the wife of one's brother **3** the wife of the brother of one's spouse
Sis·y·phus (sis′ə fəs) *Gr. Myth.* a greedy king doomed in Hades to roll uphill a stone which always rolls down again
sit (sit) *vi.* **sat**, **sit′ting** ⟦OE *sittan*⟧ **1** *a*) to rest oneself upon the buttocks, as on a chair *b*) to rest on the haunches with the forelegs braced (said of a dog, etc.) *c*) to perch (said of a bird) **2** to cover and warm eggs for hatching; brood **3** *a*) to occupy a seat as a judge, legislator, etc. *b*) to be in session (said as of court) **4** to pose, as for a portrait **5** to be located **6** to rest or lie as specified *[cares sit lightly on him]* **7** BABY-SIT —*vt.* **1** to cause to sit; seat **2** to keep one's seat on (a horse, etc.) —**sit down** to take a seat —**sit in** to attend: often with *on* —**sit out** to take no part in (a dance, etc.) —**sit up** **1** to sit erect **2** to postpone going to bed **3** [Inf.] to become suddenly alert —**sit′ter** *n.*
si·tar (si tär′, si′tär′) *n.* ⟦Hindi *sitār*⟧ a lutelike instrument of India with a long, fretted neck
sit·com (sit′käm′) *n.* [Inf.] *short for* SITUATION COMEDY
sit′-down′ (strike) a strike in which the strikers refuse to leave the premises
site (sīt) *n.* ⟦< L *situs*, position⟧ a location or scene
sit′-in′ *n.* a method of protest in which demonstrators sit in, and refuse to leave, a public place
sit′ting *n.* **1** the act or position of one that sits **2** a session, as of a court **3** a period of being seated
sitting duck [Inf.] a person or thing especially vulnerable to attack; easy target
sit·u·ate (sich′o͞o āt′) *vt.* **-at′ed**, **-at′ing** ⟦see SITE⟧ to put in a certain place or position; place; locate
sit′u·a′tion *n.* **1** location; position **2** condition with regard to circumstances **3** state of affairs **4** a position of employment

THESAURUS

singly *a.* alone, by itself, by oneself, separately, only, solely, one by one, privately, individually, once.
singular *a.* sole, one only, single; see UNIQUE.
sinister *a.* evil, inauspicious, wicked, bad, corrupt, perverse, dishonest, foreboding, disastrous, malignant, hurtful, harmful, injurious, dire, poisonous, adverse, unlucky, woeful, ominous, unfortunate, unfavorable; see also BAD 1.
sink *n.* sewer, basin, cesspool, washbasin, tub, pan, bowl.
sink *v.* **1** [To go downward] descend, decline, fall, crash, subside, drop, droop, slump, go under, immerse, go to the bottom, be submerged, settle, go to Davy Jones's locker, touch bottom, go down with the ship.—*Ant.* RISE, float, come up. **2** [To cause to sink] submerge, scuttle, depress, immerse, engulf, overwhelm, swamp, lower, bring down, force down, cast down, let down; see also IMMERSE. **3** [To weaken] decline, fail, fade; see WEAKEN 1. **4** [To decrease] lessen, diminish, wane; see DECREASE 1. —**sink in*** impress, take hold, make an impression; see INFLUENCE.
sinner *n.* wrongdoer, terrorist, lawbreaker; see CRIMINAL.
sip *v.* taste, drink in, extract; see DRINK 1.
siren *n.* horn, whistle, signal; see ALARM.
sister *n.* **1** [A female sibling] blood relative, member of the family, stepsister, half sister, big sister, little sister, kid sister*, sis*; see also RELATIVE. **2** [A female member of a group] associate, co-worker, companion.
sit *v.* be seated, seat oneself, take a seat, sit down, sit up, squat, perch, take a load off one's feet*, have a place, have a chair, sit in, take a chair, take a seat, take a place.—*Ant.* RISE, stand up, get up. —**sit in** sit in on, take part in, be a part of; see COOPERATE, JOIN 2. —**sit out** ignore, abstain from, hold back; see NEGLECT 1, 2.
site *n.* locality, section, situation; see PLACE 3, POSITION 1.
sit-in *n.* demonstration, march, display; see PROTEST, STRIKE 1.
sitter *n.* baby sitter, attendant, daycare provider; see SERVANT.
situated *a.* established, fixed, located; see PLACED.
situation *n.* **1** [Circumstance] condition, state, state of one's affairs; see CIRCUMSTANCES 1, 2. **2** [A physical position] location, site, spot; see PLACE 3, POSITION 1.

situation comedy a comic TV series made up of episodes involving the same group of characters

sit'-up' or **sit'up'** ***n.*** an exercise in which a person lying supine rises to a sitting position without using the hands

sitz bath (sits, zits) ⟦< Ger⟧ a therapeutic bath in which only the hips and buttocks are immersed

Si·va (sē'və, shē'-) ***n.*** Hindu god of destruction and reproduction

six (siks) ***adj.***, ***n.*** ⟦OE *sex*⟧ one more than five; 6; VI —**sixth** ***adj.***, ***n.***

six'-pack' ***n.*** a package of six units, as one with six cans of beer

six'-shoot'er ***n.*** [Inf.] a revolver having a cylinder that holds six cartridges: also **six'-gun'**

six'teen' (-tēn') ***adj.*** ⟦OE *syxtene*⟧ six more than ten; 16; XVI —**six'teenth'** ***adj.***, ***n.***

sixth sense intuitive power

six·ty (siks'tē) ***adj.***, ***n.***, *pl.* **-ties** ⟦OE *sixtig*⟧ six times ten; 60; LX —**the sixties** the numbers or years, as of a century, from 60 through 69 —**six'ti·eth** (-ith) ***adj.***, ***n.***

siz·a·ble (sī'zə bəl) ***adj.*** quite large or bulky: also sp. **size'a·ble**

size[1] (sīz) ***n.*** ⟦ult. < L *sedere*, sit⟧ **1** that quality of a thing which determines how much space it occupies; dimensions or magnitude **2** any of a series of graded classifications of measure into which merchandise is divided —***vt.*** **sized, siz'ing** to make or grade according to size —**size up** [Inf.] **1** to make an estimate or judgment of **2** to meet requirements

size[2] (sīz) ***n.*** ⟦ME *syse*⟧ a pasty substance used as a glaze or filler on plaster, paper, cloth, etc. —***vt.*** **sized, siz'ing** to fill, stiffen, or glaze with size

-sized (sīzd) *combining form* having a (specified) size *[medium-sized]*: also **-size**

siz'ing ***n.*** **1** SIZE[2] **2** the act of applying SIZE[2]

siz·zle (siz'əl) ***vi.*** **-zled, -zling** ⟦echoic⟧ **1** to make a hissing sound when in contact with heat **2** to be extremely hot —***n.*** a sizzling sound

S.J. *abbrev.* Society of Jesus

SK Saskatchewan

skate[1] (skāt) ***n.*** ⟦< OFr *eschace*, stilt⟧ **1** a metal runner in a frame, fastened to a shoe for gliding on ice **2** a similar frame or shoe with wheels, for gliding on a floor, sidewalk, etc. —***vi.*** **skat'ed, skat'ing** to glide or roll on or as on skates —**skat'er** ***n.***

skate[2] (skāt) ***n.*** ⟦< ON *skata*⟧ any ray fish

skate'board' ***n.*** a short, oblong board with two wheels at each end, ridden standing up, as down an incline —***vi.*** to ride on a skateboard

ske·dad·dle (ski dad''l) ***vi.*** **-dled, -dling** ⟦< ?⟧ [Inf.] to run away

skeet (skēt) ***n.*** ⟦< ON *skeyti*, projectile⟧ trapshooting in which the shooter fires from different angles

skein (skān) ***n.*** ⟦< MFr *escaigne*⟧ a quantity of thread or yarn in a coil

skel·e·ton (skel'ə tən) ***n.*** ⟦< Gr *skeletos*, dried up⟧ **1** the hard framework of bones of an animal body **2** a supporting framework **3** an outline, as of a book —***adj.*** greatly reduced *[a skeleton crew]* —**skel'e·tal** ***adj.***

skeleton key a key that can open many simple locks

skep·tic (skep'tik) ***n.*** ⟦L < Gr *skeptikos*, inquiring⟧ **1** an adherent of skepticism **2** one who habitually questions matters generally accepted **3** one who doubts religious doctrines

skep'ti·cal (-ti kəl) ***adj.*** doubting; questioning —**skep'ti·cal·ly** ***adv.***

skep'ti·cism' (-tə siz'əm) ***n.*** **1** the doctrine that the truth of all knowledge must always be in question **2** skeptical attitude **3** doubt about religious doctrines

sketch (skech) ***n.*** ⟦ult. < Gr *schedios*, extempore⟧ **1** a rough drawing or design, done rapidly **2** a brief outline **3** a short, light story, play, etc. —***vt.***, ***vi.*** make a sketch or sketches (of) —**sketch'y, -i·er, -i·est,** ***adj.***

skew (skyo͞o) ***vi.***, ***vt.*** ⟦< OFr *eschiver*, shun < OHG⟧ **1** to slant or set at a slant **2** to distort —***adj.*** slanting —***n.*** a slant or twist

skew·er (skyo͞o'ər) ***n.*** ⟦< ON *skifa*, a slice⟧ a long pin used to hold meat together while cooking —***vt.*** to fasten or pierce with or as with skewers

ski (skē) ***n.***, *pl.* **skis** ⟦Norw < ON *skith*, snowshoe⟧ either of a pair of long runners of wood, etc. fastened to shoes for gliding over snow —***vi.*** **skied, ski'ing** to glide on skis —**ski'er** ***n.***

skid (skid) ***n.*** ⟦prob. < ON *skith*, snowshoe⟧ **1** a plank, log, etc., often used as a track upon which to slide a heavy object **2** a low, wooden platform for holding loads **3** a runner on aircraft landing gear **4** a sliding wedge used to brake a wheel **5** the act of skidding —***vt.***, ***vi.*** **skid'ded, skid'ding** to slide or slip, as a vehicle on ice —**be on** (or **hit**) **the skids** [Slang] to be on the decline, or to fail

skid row ⟦altered < *skid road*, trail to skid logs along⟧ a section of a city frequented by vagrants, derelicts, etc.

skiff (skif) ***n.*** ⟦< It *schifo*⟧ any light, open boat propelled by oars, motor, or sail

ski lift an endless cable with seats, for carrying skiers up a slope

skill (skil) ***n.*** ⟦< ON *skil*, distinction⟧ **1** great ability or proficiency **2** *a)* an art, craft, etc., esp. one involving the hands or body *b)* ability in such an art, etc. —**skilled** ***adj.*** —**skill'ful** or **skil'ful** ***adj.***

skil·let (skil'it) ***n.*** ⟦< ? L *scutra*, dish⟧ a pan for frying

skim (skim) ***vt.***, ***vi.*** **skimmed, skim'ming** ⟦ME *skimen*⟧ **1** to remove (floating matter) from (a liquid) **2** to glance through (a book, etc.) without reading word for word **3** to glide lightly (over)

skim milk milk with the cream removed: also **skimmed milk**

skimp (skimp) ***vi.***, ***vt.*** SCRIMP

skimp'y ***adj.*** **-i·er, -i·est** [Inf.] barely enough; scanty

skin (skin) ***n.*** ⟦< ON *skinn*⟧ **1** the outer covering of the animal body **2** a pelt **3** something like skin, as fruit rind, etc. —***vt.*** **skinned, skin'ning** **1** to remove skin from **2** to injure by scraping (one's knee, etc.) **3** [Inf.] to swindle

skin diving underwater swimming with such gear as a face mask, flippers, scuba equipment, etc. —**skin'-dive', -dived', -div'ing,** ***vi.*** —**skin diver**

skin'flick' ***n.*** [Slang] a film emphasizing nudity or explicit sexual activity

THESAURUS

size[1] ***n.*** **1** [Measurement] extent, area, dimension; see MEASUREMENT 2. **2** [Magnitude] bulk, largeness, greatness, extent, vastness, scope, immensity, enormity, stature, hugeness, breadth, substance, volume, mass, extension, intensity, capacity, proportion; see also EXTENT, QUANTITY.

size up* ***v.*** judge, survey, scrutinize; see EXAMINE.

sizzle ***n.*** hiss, hissing, sputtering; see NOISE 1.

sizzle ***v.*** brown, grill, broil; see COOK, FRY.

skate[1] ***v.*** slide, glide, skim, slip, skid, go quickly, race, ice-skate, roller-skate, skateboard, rollerblade, board*, blade*.

skeleton ***n.*** **1** [Bony structure] skeletal frame, bone, support; see BONE. **2** [Framework] design, outline, sketch; see FRAME 1.

skeptic ***n.*** doubter, unbeliever, cynic; see CYNIC.

skeptical ***a.*** cynical, dubious, unbelieving; see DOUBTFUL, SUSPICIOUS 1.

sketch ***n.*** portrayal, picture, draft, design, outline, drawing, representation, painting, skeleton, figure, illustration, copy, likeness, depiction; see also PICTURE 2, PLAN 1.

sketch ***v.*** paint, etch, depict; see DRAW 2.

sketchy ***a.*** coarse, crude, preliminary; see UNFINISHED 1.

skid ***v.*** slip, glide, move; see SLIDE.

skill ***n.*** dexterity, facility, craft; see ABILITY.

skilled ***a.*** skillful, a good hand at, proficient; see ABLE, EXPERIENCED.

skillful ***a.*** skilled, practiced, accomplished; see ABLE, EXPERIENCED.

skim ***v.*** **1** [To pass lightly and swiftly] soar, float, sail, dart; see also FLY 1. **2** [To remove the top; especially, to remove cream] brush, scoop, separate; see DIP 2, REMOVE 1. **3** [To read swiftly] look through, speed-read, scan; see EXAMINE, READ 1.

skimp ***v.*** pinch pennies, cut corners, scrimp; see SACRIFICE 2, SAVE 3.

skimpy ***a.*** short, scanty, insufficient; see INADEQUATE.

skin ***n.*** epidermis, derma, cuticle, bark, peel, husk, rind, hide, coat, pelt, fur, covering, surface, parchment. —**be no skin off one's back** (or **nose**)* not hurt one, do no harm, not affect one; see SURVIVE 1. —**by the skin of one's teeth** barely, scarcely, narrowly; see HARDLY. —**get under someone's skin** irritate, disturb, upset; see ENRAGE. —**save one's skin*** get away, evade, leave just in time; see ESCAPE, SURVIVE 1.

skin ***v.*** peel, pare, flay, scalp, strip, strip off, pull off, remove the surface from, skin alive, husk, shuck, lay bare, bare.

skin diver ***n.*** scuba diver, submarine diver, deep-sea diver, pearl diver, aquanaut, frogman; see also DIVER.

skin'flint' ***n.*** ⟦lit., one who would skin a flint for economy⟧ a miser
-skinned *combining form* having (a specified kind of) skin *[*dark-*skinned]*
skin'ny ***adj.*** **-ni·er, -ni·est** without much flesh; very thin —**skin'ni·ness** ***n.***
skin'ny-dip' ***vi.*** **-dipped', -dip'ping** [Inf.] to swim nude — ***n.*** [Inf.] a swim in the nude
skin'tight' ***adj.*** tightfitting *[skintight* jeans*]*
skip (skip) ***vi., vt.*** **skipped, skip'ping** ⟦ME *skippen*⟧ **1** to move along by hopping on first one foot and then the other **2** to ricochet or bounce **3** to pass from one point to another, omitting or ignoring (what lies between) **4** [Inf.] to leave (town, etc.) hurriedly —***n.*** a skipping — **skip it!** [Inf.] it doesn't matter
skip·per (skip'ər) ***n.*** ⟦< MDu *schip*, a ship⟧ the captain of a ship
skir·mish (skur'mish) ***n.*** ⟦< It *schermire* < Gmc⟧ **1** a brief fight between small groups, as in a battle **2** any slight, unimportant conflict —***vi.*** to take part in a skirmish
skirt (skurt) ***n.*** ⟦< ON *skyrt*, shirt⟧ **1** that part of a dress, coat, etc. that hangs below the waist **2** a woman's garment that hangs from the waist **3** something like a skirt —***vt., vi.*** to be on, or move along, the edge (of)
ski run a slope or course for skiing
skit (skit) ***n.*** ⟦prob. ult. < ON *skjōta*, to shoot⟧ a short, humorous sketch, as in the theater
ski tow a kind of ski lift for pulling skiers up a slope on their skis
skit·ter (skit'ər) ***vi.*** ⟦< Scand⟧ to move along quickly and lightly
skit·tish (skit'ish) ***adj.*** ⟦see SKIT & -ISH⟧ **1** lively; playful **2** easily frightened; jumpy **3** fickle
skiv·vy (skiv'ē) ***n., pl.*** **-vies** ⟦< ?⟧ [Slang] **1** a man's, esp. a sailor's, short-sleeved undershirt: usually **skivvy shirt** **2** [*pl.*] men's underwear
skoal (skōl) ***interj.*** ⟦< ON *skāl*, a bowl⟧ to your health!: used as a toast
skul·dug·ger·y or **skull·dug·ger·y** (skul dug'ər ē) ***n.*** ⟦< obs. Scot⟧ [Inf.] sneaky, dishonest behavior; trickery
skulk (skulk) ***vi.*** ⟦ME *sculken*⟧ to move in a stealthy manner; slink
skull (skul) ***n.*** ⟦< Scand⟧ **1** the bony framework of the head, enclosing the brain **2** the head; mind
skull'cap' ***n.*** a light, closefitting, brimless cap, usually worn indoors
skunk (skuŋk) ***n.*** ⟦< AmInd⟧ **1** a small, bushy-tailed mammal having black fur with white stripes down the back: it ejects a foul-smelling liquid when disturbed or frightened **2** its fur **3** [Inf.] a despicable person
sky (skī) ***n., pl.*** **skies** ⟦< ON, a cloud⟧ **1** [*often pl.*] the upper atmosphere *[*blue *skies*, a cloudy *sky]* **2** the firmament **3** heaven
sky'box' ***n.*** a private section of seats, often luxurious and usually elevated, in a stadium, etc.
sky'cap' ***n.*** a porter at an airport terminal
sky diving parachute jumping involving free-fall maneuvers
sky'-high' ***adj.*** very high —***adv.*** **1** very high **2** in or to pieces
sky'jack' ***vt.*** to hijack (an aircraft) —**sky'jack'er** ***n.***
sky'lark' ***n.*** a Eurasian lark famous for the song it utters as it soars —***vi.*** to romp or frolic
sky'light' ***n.*** a window in a roof or ceiling
sky'line' ***n.*** **1** the visible horizon **2** the outline, as of a city, seen against the sky
sky'rock'et ***n.*** a fireworks rocket that explodes aloft — ***vi., vt.*** to rise or cause to rise rapidly
sky'scrap'er ***n.*** a very tall building
sky'ward ***adv., adj.*** toward the sky: also **sky'wards** ***adv.***
sky'way' ***n.*** **1** AIR LANE **2** an elevated highway or walkway
sky'writ'ing ***n.*** the tracing of words, etc. in the sky by trailing smoke from an airplane —**sky'writ'er** ***n.***
slab (slab) ***n.*** ⟦ME *sclabbe*⟧ a flat, broad, and fairly thick piece
slack[1] (slak) ***adj.*** ⟦< OE *slæc*⟧ **1** slow; sluggish **2** not busy; dull *[*a *slack* period*]* **3** loose; not tight **4** careless *[*a *slack* worker*]* —***vt., vi.*** to slacken —***n.*** **1** a part that hangs loose **2** a lack of tension **3** a dull period; lull — **cut someone some slack** [Slang] to demand less of someone —**slack off** to slacken —**slack'ness** ***n.***
slack[2] (slak) ***n.*** ⟦ME *sleck*⟧ a mixture of small pieces of coal, coal dust, etc. left from screening coal
slack·en (slak'ən) ***vt., vi.*** **1** to make or become less active, brisk, etc. **2** to loosen or relax, as rope
slack'er ***n.*** one who shirks
slacks (slaks) ***pl.n.*** trousers for men or women
slag (slag) ***n.*** ⟦< earlier LowG *slagge*⟧ the fused refuse separated from metal in smelting
slain (slān) ***vt.*** *pp. of* SLAY
slake (slāk) ***vt.*** **slaked, slak'ing** ⟦< OE *slæc*, SLACK[1]⟧ **1** to satisfy (thirst, etc.) **2** to produce a chemical change in (lime) by mixing with water
sla·lom (slä'ləm) ***n.*** ⟦Norw⟧ a downhill ski race over a zigzag course —***vi.*** to take part in a slalom
slam (slam) ***vt.*** **slammed, slam'ming** ⟦prob. < Scand⟧ **1** to shut, hit, throw, or put with force and noise **2** [Inf.] to criticize severely —***n.*** **1** a slamming **2** [Inf.] a severe criticism
slam'-bang' [Inf.] ***adv.*** **1** swiftly or abruptly and recklessly **2** noisily —***adj.*** lively, noisy, etc.
slam'-dunk' ***n.*** *Basketball* a forceful shot from directly above the basket
slam·mer (slam'ər) ***n.*** [Slang] a prison or jail
slan·der (slan'dər) ***n.*** ⟦see SCANDAL⟧ **1** the utterance of a falsehood that damages another's reputation **2** such a spoken statement —***vt.*** to utter a slander about — **slan'der·er** ***n.*** —**slan'der·ous** ***adj.***
slang (slaŋ) ***n.*** ⟦< ?⟧ highly informal speech that is outside standard usage and consists both of coined words and phrases and of new meanings given to established terms —**slang'y, -i·er, -i·est,** ***adj.***
slant (slant) ***vt., vi.*** ⟦< Scand⟧ **1** to incline; slope **2** to tell so as to express a particular bias —***n.*** **1** an oblique surface, line, etc. **2** a point of view or attitude —***adj.*** sloping
slap (slap) ***n.*** ⟦echoic⟧ **1** a blow with something flat, as the palm of the hand **2** an insult or rebuff —***vt.*** **slapped, slap'ping** **1** to strike with something flat **2** to put, hit, etc. with force
slap'dash' ***adj., adv.*** hurried(ly), careless(ly), haphazard(ly), etc.
slap'-hap'py ***adj.*** [Slang] **1** dazed, as by blows **2** silly or giddy
slap'stick' ***n.*** crude comedy full of horseplay —***adj.*** characterized by such comedy
slash (slash) ***vt.*** ⟦< ? OFr *esclachier*, to break⟧ **1** to cut with sweeping strokes, as of a knife **2** to cut slits in **3** to reduce drastically *[slash* prices*]* —***vi.*** to make a sweeping stroke as with a knife —***n.*** **1** a slashing **2** a cut made by slashing **3** a virgule —**slash'er** ***n.***
slash'-and-burn' ***adj.*** **1** of a method of clearing fields by

THESAURUS

skinflint ***n.*** scrimper, tightwad*, hoarder; see MISER.
skinny ***a.*** lean, gaunt, slender; see THIN 2.
skip ***v.*** hop, spring, leap; see JUMP 1.
skirmish ***n.*** engagement, encounter, conflict; see BATTLE, FIGHT 1.
skirt ***n.*** kilt, petticoat, miniskirt; see CLOTHES, DRESS 2.
skull ***n.*** scalp, cranium, brain case; see HEAD 1.
sky ***n.*** firmament, atmosphere, the blue yonder; see AIR 1, HEAVEN. —**out of a clear blue sky** without warning, suddenly, abruptly; see QUICKLY, SOON.
skyscraper ***n.*** tall building, high-rise building, high-rise; see BUILDING.
slab ***n.*** slice, chunk, lump; see PART 1.
slack[1] ***a.*** relaxed, lax, limp; see LOOSE 1.
slack off (or **up**) ***v.*** decline, lessen, become slower; see DECREASE 1, SLOW 1.
slam ***v.*** **1** [To throw with a slam] thump, fling, hurl; see THROW 1. **2** [To shut with a slam] bang, crash, push; see CLOSE 2, 4.
slander ***n.*** defamation, calumny, scandal; see LIE.
slander ***v.*** defame, libel, defile, detract, depreciate, disparage, revile, dishonor, blaspheme, curse, attack, sully, tarnish, vilify, blot, cast a slur on, scandalize, belittle, backbite, malign, speak evil of, give a bad name, sling mud.—*Ant.* PRAISE, applaud, eulogize.
slang ***n.*** cant, argot, colloquialism, pidgin English, vulgarism, lingo, shoptalk, vulgarity; see also JARGON 1, 2.
slant ***v.*** veer, lie obliquely, incline; see BEND, LEAN 1, TILT.
slanting ***a.*** inclining, sloping, tilting; see BENT.
slap ***v.*** strike, pat, spank; see HIT 1.
slapdash ***a.*** hasty, haphazard, impetuous; see CARELESS.
slap-happy* ***a.*** punch-drunk, dazed, dizzy; see BEATEN 1, SILLY.
slapstick ***a.*** absurd, droll, comical; see FUNNY 1.
slash ***v.*** slit, gash, sever; see CUT 1.

cutting down and burning vegetation **2** indiscriminately destructive

slash pocket a pocket (in a garment) with a finished diagonal opening

slat (slat) ***n.*** ⟦< OFr *esclat,* fragment⟧ a narrow strip of wood, metal, etc.

slate (slāt) ***n.*** ⟦see prec.⟧ **1** a hard, fine-grained rock that cleaves into thin, smooth layers **2** a thin piece of slate or slatelike material, as a roofing tile or writing tablet **3** the bluish-gray color of most slate: also **slate blue** —***vt.*** **slat'ed, slat'ing 1** to cover with slate **2** to designate, as for candidacy —**a clean slate** a record showing no marks of discredit, dishonor, etc.

slath·er (sla*th*'ər) ***vt.*** ⟦< ?⟧ [Inf. or Dial.] to cover or spread on thickly

slat·tern (slat'ərn) ***n.*** ⟦< dial. *slatter,* to slop⟧ a slovenly or sluttish woman —**slat'tern·ly *adj.***

slaugh·ter (slôt'ər) ***n.*** ⟦< ON *slātr,* lit., slain flesh⟧ **1** the killing of animals for food; butchering **2** the brutal killing of a person **3** the killing of many people, as in battle —***vt.*** **1** to kill (animals) for food; butcher **2** to kill (people) brutally or in large numbers —**slaugh'ter·er *n.***

slaugh'ter·house' ***n.*** a place where animals are butchered for food

Slav (släv, slav) ***n.*** a member of a group of peoples of E and SE Europe, including Russians, Serbs, Czechs, Poles, etc. —***adj.*** *var. of* SLAVIC

slave (slāv) ***n.*** ⟦< Gr *Sklabos,* ult. < OSlav *Slovēne,* first used of captive Slavs⟧ **1** a human being who is owned as property by another **2** one dominated by some influence, etc. **3** one who slaves —***vi.*** **slaved, slav'ing** to work like a slave; drudge

slave driver 1 one who oversees slaves **2** any merciless taskmaster

slav·er (slav'ər) ***vi.*** ⟦< Scand⟧ to drool

slav·er·y (slā'vər ē) ***n.*** **1** the owning of slaves as a practice **2** the condition of a slave; bondage **3** drudgery; toil

Slav·ic (släv'ik, slav'-) ***adj.*** of the Slavs, their languages, etc. —***n.*** a family of languages, including Russian, Polish, Czech, Bulgarian, etc.

slav·ish (slā'vish) ***adj.*** **1** of or like slaves; servile **2** blindly dependent or imitative —**slav'ish·ly *adv.***

slaw (slô) ***n.*** ⟦Du *sla* < Fr *salade,* salad⟧ *short for* COLESLAW

slay (slā) ***vt.*** **slew, slain, slay'ing** ⟦OE *slean*⟧ to kill in a violent way —**slay'er *n.***

sleaze (slēz) ***n.*** ⟦< SLEAZY⟧ [Slang] **1** sleaziness **2** someone or something sleazy

slea·zoid (slē'zoid') [Slang] ***adj.*** SLEAZY (sense 2) —***n.*** a coarse or immoral person

slea·zy (slē'zē) ***adj.*** **-zi·er, -zi·est** ⟦< *silesia,* orig. cloth made in central Europe⟧ **1** flimsy or thin in substance **2** shoddy, shabby, immoral, etc. —**slea'zi·ly *adv.*** —**slea'zi·ness *n.***

sled (sled) ***n.*** ⟦ME *sledde*⟧ a vehicle on runners for moving over snow, ice, etc. —***vt., vi.*** **sled'ded, sled'ding** to carry or ride on a sled —**sled'der *n.***

sledge[1] (slej) ***n.*** ⟦OE *slecge*⟧ SLEDGEHAMMER

sledge[2] (slej) ***n.*** ⟦MDu *sleedse*⟧ a sled or sleigh

sledge'ham'mer ***n.*** ⟦see SLEDGE[1]⟧ a long, heavy hammer, usually held with both hands

sleek (slēk) ***adj.*** ⟦var. of SLICK⟧ **1** smooth and shiny; glossy **2** of well-fed or well-groomed appearance **3** suave, elegant, etc. —***vt.*** to make sleek —**sleek'ly *adv.*** —**sleek'ness *n.***

sleep (slēp) ***n.*** ⟦OE *slæp*⟧ **1** the natural, regularly recurring rest for the body, during which there is little or no conscious thought **2** any state like this —***vi.*** **slept, sleep'ing** to be in a state of or like sleep —**sleep off** to rid oneself of by sleeping —**sleep'less *adj.*** —**sleep'less·ness *n.***

sleep'er ***n.*** **1** one who sleeps **2** a railroad car with berths for sleeping: also **sleeping car 3** a beam laid flat to support something **4** something that achieves an unexpected success

sleeping bag a warmly lined, zippered bag for sleeping in outdoors

sleeping sickness an infectious disease, esp. of Africa, transmitted by the tsetse fly and characterized by lethargy, prolonged coma, etc.

sleep'o'ver ***n.*** a spending the night at another's home, as by a group of young people for fun

sleep'walk'ing ***n.*** the act of walking while asleep —**sleep'walk'er *n.***

sleep'wear' ***n.*** NIGHTCLOTHES

sleep'y ***adj.*** **-i·er, -i·est 1** ready or inclined to sleep; drowsy **2** dull; idle *[*a *sleepy* town*]* —**sleep'i·ly *adv.*** —**sleep'i·ness *n.***

sleet (slēt) ***n.*** ⟦ME *slete*⟧ **1** partly frozen rain **2** the icy coating formed when rain freezes on trees, etc. —***vi.*** to fall as sleet —**sleet'y *adj.***

sleeve (slēv) ***n.*** ⟦OE *sliefe*⟧ **1** that part of a garment that covers the arm **2** a tubelike part fitting over or around another part —**up one's sleeve** hidden but ready at hand —**sleeve'less *adj.***

sleigh (slā) ***n.*** ⟦Du *slee*⟧ a vehicle on runners, usually horse-drawn, for moving over snow, ice, etc.

sleight of hand (slīt) ⟦< ON *slœgr,* crafty⟧ **1** skill with the hands, esp. in deceiving onlookers, as in magic **2** a trick thus performed

slen·der (slen'dər) ***adj.*** ⟦ME *s(c)lendre* < ?⟧ **1** long and thin **2** slim of figure **3** small in amount, size, force, etc. —**slen'der·ness *n.***

slen'der·ize' ***vt., vi.*** **-ized', -iz'ing** to make or become slender

slept (slept) ***vi., vt.*** *pt. & pp. of* SLEEP

sleuth (slo͞oth) ***n.*** ⟦< ON *slóth,* a trail⟧ [Inf.] a detective

slew[1] (slo͞o) ***n.*** ⟦Ir *sluagh,* a host⟧ [Inf.] a large number or amount

slew[2] (slo͞o) ***vt.*** *pt. of* SLAY

slice (slīs) ***n.*** ⟦< OFr *esclicier*⟧ **1** a relatively thin, broad piece cut from something **2** a part or share —***vt.*** **sliced, slic'ing 1** to cut into slices **2** to cut off as in a slice or slices: often with *off, from, away,* etc. **3** to hit (a ball) so that it curves to the right if right-handed or the left if left-handed —**slic'er *n.***

slick (slik) ***vt.*** ⟦OE *slician*⟧ **1** to make smooth **2** [Inf.] to make smart, neat, etc.: usually with *up* —***adj.*** **1** sleek; smooth **2** slippery **3** adept; clever **4** [Inf.] smooth but superficial, tricky, etc. —***n.*** **1** a smooth area on the water, as from a layer of oil **2** a slippery, oily area on the surface of a road —**slick'ly *adv.*** —**slick'ness *n.***

slick'er ***n.*** **1** a loose, waterproof coat **2** [Inf.] a tricky person

slide (slīd) ***vi.*** **slid** (slid), **slid'ing** ⟦OE *slidan*⟧ **1** to move along in constant contact with a smooth surface, as on ice **2** to glide **3** to slip *[*it *slid* from his hand*]* —***vt.*** **1** to cause to slide **2** to place quietly or deftly (*in* or *into*) —

THESAURUS

slaughter ***n.*** butchery, killing, massacre; see MURDER.

slaughter ***v.*** slay, murder, massacre; see BUTCHER 1, KILL.

Slav ***n.*** *Slavs include the following:* Russian, Belorussian, Yugoslav, Bosnian, Montenegrin, Macedonian, Bulgarian, Pole, Slovene, Slovak, Ukrainian, Bohemian, Czech, Serb, Croat, Lusatian.

slave ***n.*** bondsman, bondservant, chattel, serf, toiler, menial, drudge, thrall, drone, laborer, captive, bondmaid, bondwoman, victim of tyranny, one of a subject people.

slavery ***n.*** **1** [Bondage] subjugation, restraint, involuntary servitude; see CAPTIVITY. **2** [Drudgery] toil, menial labor, grind; see WORK 2.

Slavic ***a.*** Slav, Slavonic, Old Church Slavonic. *Words referring to Slavic peoples languages, etc. include the following:* Cyrillic, Glagolitic, Russian, Polish, Bulgarian, Czech or Bohemian, Serbian, Croatian or Croat, Bosnian, Montenegrin, Yugoslav, Ukrainian, Serbo-Croatian, Slovenian, Belorussian, Lusatian, Macedonian, Slovak.

slay ***v.*** murder, slaughter, assassinate; see KILL 1.

sleazy ***a.*** shoddy, flimsy, cheap; see SHABBY, POOR 2.

sled ***n.*** hand sled, bobsled, sleigh, coasting sled, child's sled, toboggan, coaster.

sleek ***a.*** silken, silky, satin; see SMOOTH 1.

sleep ***n.*** slumber, doze, nap, rest, sound sleep, deep sleep, siesta, catnap, dream, hibernation, the sandman*, snooze*, shut-eye*.

sleep ***v.*** slumber, doze, drowse, rest, nap, snooze*, hibernate, dream, snore, nod, yawn, relax, go to bed, fall asleep, take forty winks*, catnap, turn in, hit the hay*, saw logs*, sack out*. —**sleep (something) off** get over it, improve, sober up; see RECOVER 3.

sleeping ***a.*** dormant, inert, inactive; see ASLEEP.

sleepy ***a.*** dozy, somnolent, drowsy; see TIRED.

slender ***a.*** slim, slight, spare; see THIN 1, 2.

slice ***n.*** thin piece, chop, chunk; see PART 1.

slick ***a.*** sleek, slippery, glossy; see OILY 2, SMOOTH 1.

slide ***v.*** glide, skate, skim, slip, coast, skid, move along, move over, move past, pass along. —**let slide** ignore, pass over, allow to decline; see NEGLECT 1, 2.

n. 1 a sliding 2 a smooth, often inclined surface for sliding down 3 something that works by sliding 4 a photographic transparency for use with a viewer or projector 5 a small glass plate on which objects are mounted for microscopic study 6 the fall of a mass of rock, snow, etc. down a slope —**let slide** to fail to attend to properly

slide fastener a zipper or a zipperlike device with two grooved plastic edges joined or separated by a sliding tab

slid'er *n.* 1 one that slides 2 *Baseball* a fast pitch that curves

sliding scale a schedule, as of fees, wages, etc., that varies with given conditions, as cost of living, etc.

slight (slīt) *adj.* ⟦OE *sliht*⟧ 1 *a)* light in build; slender *b)* frail; fragile 2 lacking strength, importance, etc. 3 small in amount or extent —*vt.* 1 to neglect 2 to treat with disrespect 3 to treat as unimportant —*n.* a slighting or being slighted —**slight'ly** *adv.* —**slight'ness** *n.*

slim (slim) *adj.* **slim'mer, slim'mest** ⟦< Du, bad⟧ 1 small in girth; slender 2 small in amount, degree, etc. —*vt., vi.* **slimmed, slim'ming** to make or become slim —**slim'ness** *n.*

slime (slīm) *n.* ⟦OE *slim*⟧ any soft, moist, slippery, often sticky matter —**slim'y, -i·er, -i·est,** *adj.*

sling (sliŋ) *n.* ⟦prob. < ON *slyngua*, to throw⟧ 1 a primitive instrument whirled by hand for throwing stones 2 a cast; throw; fling 3 *a)* a supporting band, etc. as for raising a heavy object *b)* a cloth looped from the neck under an injured arm for support —*vt.* **slung, sling'ing** 1 to throw as with a sling 2 to suspend

sling'shot' *n.* a Y-shaped piece of wood, etc. with an elastic band attached to it for shooting stones, etc.

slink (sliŋk) *vi.* **slunk, slink'ing** ⟦OE *slincan*, to creep⟧ to move in a furtive or sneaking way

slink'y *adj.* **-i·er, -i·est** 1 furtive; sneaking 2 [Slang] sinuous in movement or line

slip[1] (slip) *vi.* **slipped, slip'ping** ⟦ME *slippen*, ult. < Ger⟧ 1 to go quietly or secretly [to *slip* out of a room] 2 to pass smoothly or easily 3 to escape from one's memory, grasp, etc. 4 to slide, lose footing, etc. 5 to make a mistake; err 6 to become worse —*vt.* 1 to cause to slip 2 to put, pass, etc. deftly or stealthily 3 to escape from (the memory) —*n.* 1 a space between piers for docking ships 2 a woman's undergarment the length of a skirt 3 a pillow case 4 a slipping or falling down 5 an error or mistake —**let slip** to say without intending to —**slip up** to make a mistake

slip[2] (slip) *n.* ⟦< MDu *slippen*, to cut⟧ 1 a stem, root, etc. of a plant, used for planting or grafting 2 a young, slim person 3 a small piece of paper

slip'case' *n.* a boxlike container for a book or books, open at one end

slip'cov'er *n.* a removable, fitted cloth cover for a chair, sofa, etc.

slip'knot' *n.* a knot that will slip along the rope around which it is tied

slip·page (slip'ij) *n.* a slipping, as of one gear past another

slipped disk a ruptured cartilaginous disk between vertebrae

slip·per (slip'ər) *n.* a light, low shoe easily slipped on the foot, esp. one for indoor wear —**slip'pered** *adj.*

slip·per·y (slip'ər ē, slip'rē) *adj.* **-i·er, -i·est** 1 liable to cause slipping, as a wet surface 2 tending to slip away, as from a grasp 3 unreliable; deceitful

slip'shod' (-shäd') *adj.* ⟦< obs. *slip-shoe*, a slipper⟧ careless, as in workmanship

slip'-up' *n.* [Inf.] an error: also **slip'up'**

slit (slit) *vt.* **slit, slit'ting** ⟦ME *slitten*⟧ 1 to cut or split open, esp. lengthwise 2 to cut into strips —*n.* a straight, narrow cut, opening, etc.

slith·er (sli*th*'ər) *vi.* ⟦< OE *slidan*, to slide⟧ to slip, slide, or glide along —**slith'er·y** *adj.*

sliv·er (sliv'ər) *n.* ⟦< OE *slifan*, to split⟧ a thin, sharp piece cut or split off; splinter —*vt., vi.* to cut or break into slivers

slob (släb) *n.* ⟦Ir *slab*, mud⟧ [Inf.] a sloppy or coarse person

slob·ber (släb'ər) *vi.* ⟦prob. < LowG *slubberen*, to swig⟧ to drool

sloe (slō) *n.* ⟦OE *sla*⟧ 1 the blackthorn 2 its small, plumlike fruit

sloe'-eyed' *adj.* 1 having large, dark eyes 2 having almond-shaped eyes

sloe gin a liqueur of gin flavored with sloes

slog (släg) *vt., vi.* **slogged, slog'ging** ⟦ME *sluggen*, go slowly⟧ 1 to make (one's way) with great effort; plod 2 to toil (at) —*n.* an arduous trip, task, etc. —**slog'ger** *n.*

slo·gan (slō'gən) *n.* ⟦< Gael *sluagh*, a host + *gairm*, a call: orig., a battle cry⟧ 1 a motto associated with a political party, etc. 2 a catchy phrase used in advertising

sloop (slo͞op) *n.* ⟦< LowG *slupen*, to glide⟧ a sailing vessel having a single mast with a mainsail and a jib

slop (släp) *n.* ⟦OE *sloppe*⟧ 1 watery snow or mud; slush 2 a puddle of spilled liquid 3 unappetizing, watery food 4 [*often pl.*] liquid waste —*vi., vt.* **slopped, slop'ping** to spill or splash

slope (slōp) *n.* ⟦< OE *slupan*, to glide⟧ 1 rising or falling ground 2 any inclined line, surface, etc.; slant 3 the amount or degree of deviation from the horizontal or vertical —*vi.* **sloped, slop'ing** to have an upward or downward inclination; incline; slant —*vt.* to cause to slope

slop·py (släp'ē) *adj.* **-pi·er, -pi·est** 1 splashy; slushy 2 *a)* slovenly *b)* slipshod 3 [Inf.] gushingly sentimental —**slop'pi·ness** *n.*

sloppy Joe (jō) ground meat cooked with tomato sauce, spices, etc. and served on a bun

slosh (släsh) *vi.* ⟦var. of SLUSH⟧ 1 to splash through water, mud, etc. 2 to splash about: said of a liquid —*n.* the sound of sloshing liquid —**slosh'y** *adj.*

slot (slät) *n.* ⟦< OFr *esclot*, hollow between the breasts⟧ 1 a narrow opening, as for a coin in a vending machine 2 [Inf.] a position in a group, etc. —*vt.* **slot'ted, slot'ting** 1 to make a slot in 2 [Inf.] to place in a series or sequence

sloth (slôth, släth; *also* slōth) *n.* ⟦< OE *slaw*, slow⟧ 1 laziness; idleness 2 a slow-moving, tree-dwelling mammal of tropical America that hangs, back down, from branches —**sloth'ful** *adj.* —**sloth'ful·ness** *n.*

slot machine a machine, specif. a gambling device, activated by the insertion of a coin in a slot

slouch (slouch) *n.* ⟦< ON *slōka*, to droop⟧ 1 a lazy or incompetent person 2 a drooping or slovenly posture —*vi.* to sit, stand, walk, etc. in a slouch —**slouch'y, -i·er, -i·est,** *adj.*

slough[1] (sluf) *n.* ⟦ME *slouh*, a skin⟧ a castoff layer or covering, as the skin of a snake —*vt.* to throw off; discard

THESAURUS

slight *a.* 1 [Trifling] insignificant, petty, piddling; see TRIVIAL, UNIMPORTANT. 2 [Inconsiderable] small, sparse, scanty; see INADEQUATE. 3 [Delicate] frail, slender, flimsy; see DAINTY.

slightly *a.* a little, to some extent, hardly at all, scarcely any, not noticeably, unimportantly, inconsiderably, insignificantly, lightly, somewhat.

slim *a.* slender, narrow, lank; see THIN 2.

slime *n.* fungus, mire, ooze; see MUD.

slimy *a.* oozy, slippery, mucky; see MUDDY 1, 2.

sling *v.* hurl, send, catapult; see THROW 1.

slink *v.* prowl, cower, lurk; see SNEAK.

slip[1] *n.* 1 [Error] lapse, misdeed, indiscretion; see ERROR. 2 [Misstep] slide, skid, stumble; see FALL 1. 3 [Undergarment] underclothing, chemise, half slip; see CLOTHES, UNDERWEAR. —**give someone the slip** get away, slip away, escape from; see LEAVE 1. —**slip up** make a mistake, err, bungle; see FAIL 1.

slipper *n.* house shoe, sandal, light shoe; see SHOE.

slippery *a.* glassy, smooth, glazed, polished, oily, waxy, soapy, greasy, slimy, icy, sleek, glistening, wet, unsafe, insecure, uncertain, tricky, shifty, slithery, slippery as an eel*.

slip-up* *n.* oversight, mishap, omission; see ERROR.

slit *n.* split, cleavage, crevice; see HOLE 1, TEAR.

slit *v.* tear, slice, split; see CUT 1.

sliver *n.* splinter, slice, fragment; see BIT 1, FLAKE.

slob* *n.* pig, hog, slattern, tramp, bum, yokel, ragamuffin.

slobber *v.* drip, salivate, dribble; see DROOL.

slogan *n.* catchword, rallying cry, trademark; see MOTTO, PROVERB.

slop *v.* slosh, wallow, splash, drip, spill, run over; see also DROP 1, EMPTY 1.

slope *n.* rising ground, incline, grade; see HILL.

sloppy *a.* clumsy, amateurish, mediocre; see AWKWARD, CARELESS.

slot *n.* aperture, opening, cut; see HOLE 1.

slough[2] (slou) ***n.*** ⟦OE *sloh*⟧ **1** a place full of soft, deep mud **2** deep, hopeless dejection

Slo·vak (slō′väk′, -vak′) ***n.*** **1** a member of a Slavic people living chiefly in Slovakia **2** the language of this people —***adj.*** of the Slovaks

Slo·va·ki·a (slō vä′kē ə) country in central Europe: formerly the E republic of Czechoslovakia: 18,933 sq. mi.; pop. 5,297,000

slov·en (sluv′ən) ***n.*** ⟦prob. < MDu *slof*, lax⟧ a careless, untidy person —**slov′en·ly, -li·er, -li·est, *adj.***

Slo·ve·ni·a (slō vē′nē ə) country in SE Europe: 7,819 sq. mi.; pop. 1,966,000 —**Slo·ve′ni·an** or **Slo′vene′ *adj., n.***

slow (slō) ***adj.*** ⟦OE *slaw*⟧ **1** not quick in understanding **2** taking a longer time than is usual **3** marked by low speed, etc.; not fast **4** behind the correct time, as a clock **5** passing tediously; dull —***vt., vi.*** to make or become slow or slower: often with *up* or *down* —***adv.*** in a slow manner —**slow′ly *adv.*** —**slow′ness *n.***

slow′down′ ***n.*** a slowing down, as of production

slow′-mo′tion ***adj.*** **1** moving slowly **2** designating a film or taped TV sequence showing the action slowed down

slow′poke′ (-pōk′) ***n.*** [Slang] a person who acts or moves slowly

slow′-wit′ted ***adj.*** mentally slow; dull

SLR ***n.*** ⟦*s(ingle) l(ens) r(eflex)*⟧ a camera allowing the photographer to see the subject through the same lens that brings the image to the film

slub (slub) ***n.*** ⟦< ?⟧ a soft, thick lump or irregularity in yarn or fabric

sludge (sluj) ***n.*** ⟦var. of *slutch*, mud⟧ any heavy, slimy deposit, sediment, etc.

slue (slo͞o) ***vt., vi.*** **slued, slu′ing** ⟦< ?⟧ to turn or swing around, as on a pivot

slug[1] (slug) ***n.*** ⟦ME *slugge*, clumsy one⟧ a small mollusk like a shell-less snail

slug[2] (slug) ***n.*** ⟦prob. < prec.⟧ a small piece of metal; specif., a bullet or counterfeit coin

slug[3] (slug) ***n.*** ⟦prob. < Dan *sluge*, to gulp⟧ [Slang] a drink of liquor

slug[4] (slug) [Inf.] ***vt.*** **slugged, slug′ging** ⟦< ON *slag*⟧ to hit hard, esp. with the fist or a bat —***n.*** a hard blow or hit —**slug′ger *n.***

slug·gard (slug′ərd) ***n.*** ⟦< ME *sluggen*, be lazy⟧ a lazy person

slug′gish (-ish) ***adj.*** ⟦< SLUG[1]⟧ **1** lacking energy or alertness **2** slow or slow-moving **3** not functioning with normal vigor —**slug′gish·ness *n.***

sluice (slo͞os) ***n.*** ⟦< L *excludere*, to shut out⟧ **1** an artificial channel for water, with a gate to regulate the flow **2** such a gate: also **sluice gate** **3** any channel for excess water **4** a sloping trough, as for washing gold ore —***vt.*** **sluiced, sluic′ing** **1** to draw off through a sluice **2** to wash with water from a sluice

slum (slum) ***n.*** ⟦< ?⟧ a populous area characterized by poverty, poor housing, etc. —***vi.*** **slummed, slum′ming** to visit a slum, etc. for reasons held to be condescending —**slum′my, -mi·er, -mi·est, *adj.***

slum·ber (slum′bər) ***vi.*** ⟦OE *sluma*⟧ **1** to sleep **2** to be inactive —***n.*** **1** sleep **2** an inactive state

slum′lord′ ***n.*** [Slang] an absentee landlord who exploits slum property

slump (slump) ***vi.*** ⟦prob. < Ger⟧ **1** to fall or sink suddenly **2** to slouch —***n.*** a decline in activity, prices, performance, etc.

slung (sluŋ) ***vt.*** *pt. & pp. of* SLING

slunk (sluŋk) ***vi.*** *pt. & pp. of* SLINK

slur (slur) ***vt.*** **slurred, slur′ring** ⟦prob. < MDu *sleuren*, to drag⟧ **1** to pass over lightly: often with *over* **2** to pronounce indistinctly **3** to disparage **4** *Music* to produce (successive notes) by gliding without a break —***n.*** **1** a slurring **2** an aspersion **3** *Music* a curved line connecting notes to be slurred

slurp (slurp) [Slang] ***vt., vi.*** ⟦Du *slurpen*, to sip⟧ to drink or eat noisily —***n.*** a loud sipping or sucking sound

slur·ry (slur′ē) ***n., pl.*** **-ries** ⟦< MDu *slore*, thin mud⟧ a thin, watery mixture of clay, cement, etc.

slush (slush) ***n.*** ⟦prob. < Scand⟧ **1** partly melted snow or ice **2** soft mud **3** sentimentality; drivel —**slush′y, -i·er, -i·est, *adj.***

slush fund money used for bribery, political pressure, etc.

slut (slut) ***n.*** ⟦ME *slutte*⟧ **1** a dirty, slovenly woman **2** a sexually promiscuous woman: a derogatory term —**slut′tish *adj.***

sly (slī) ***adj.*** **sli′er** or **sly′er, sli′est** or **sly′est** ⟦< ON *slœgr*⟧ **1** skillful at trickery; crafty **2** cunningly underhanded **3** playfully mischievous —**on the sly** secretly —**sly′ly** or **sli′ly *adv.*** —**sly′ness *n.***

smack[1] (smak) ***n.*** ⟦OE *smæc*⟧ **1** a slight taste or flavor **2** a small amount; trace —***vi.*** to have a smack (*of*)

smack[2] (smak) ***n.*** ⟦< ?⟧ **1** a sharp noise made by parting the lips suddenly **2** a loud kiss **3** a slap —***vt.*** **1** to part (the lips) with a smack **2** to slap loudly —***adv.*** **1** with a smack **2** directly

smack[3] (smak) ***n.*** ⟦prob. < Du *smak*⟧ a fishing boat with a well for keeping fish alive

smack[4] (smak) ***n.*** ⟦< ?⟧ [Slang] heroin

smack′er ***n.*** [Old Slang] a dollar

small (smôl) ***adj.*** ⟦OE *smæl*⟧ **1** comparatively little in size; not big **2** little in quantity, extent, duration, etc. **3** of little importance; trivial **4** young *[small* children*]* **5** mean; petty **6** lowercase —***n.*** the small part *[*the *small* of the back*]*

small arms firearms of small caliber, as pistols, rifles, etc.

small fry ⟦see FRY[2]⟧ **1** children **2** persons considered insignificant

small intestine the narrow section of the intestines, extending from the stomach to the large intestine

small′-mind′ed ***adj.*** mean, narrow-minded, or selfish

small′pox′ ***n.*** an acute, contagious viral disease characterized by fever and pustules

small talk light conversation about common, everyday things; chitchat

small′-time′ ***adj.*** [Inf.] minor or petty

smarm·y (smär′mē) ***adj.*** **-i·er, -i·est** ⟦< *smarm*, to smear⟧ [Inf., Chiefly Brit.] flattering in an insincere way

THESAURUS

slow *a.* **1** [Slow in motion] sluggish, laggard, deliberate, gradual, loitering, leaden, creeping, inactive, slow-moving, crawling, slow-paced, leisurely, as slow as molasses in January*.—*Ant.* FAST, swift, rapid. **2** [Slow in starting] dilatory, procrastinating, delaying, postponing, idle, indolent, tardy, lazy, apathetic, phlegmatic, inactive, sluggish, heavy, quiet, drowsy, inert, sleepy, lethargic, stagnant, negligent, listless, dormant, potential, latent; see also LATE 1.—*Ant.* IMMEDIATE, alert, instant. **3** [Slow in producing an effect] belated, behindhand, backward, overdue, delayed, long-delayed, retarded, detained, hindered.—*Ant.* BUSY, diligent, industrious. **4** [Dull or stupid] stolid, not lively, uninteresting; see DULL 3.

slow *v.* **1** [To become slower] slacken, slow up, slow down, lag, loiter, relax, procrastinate, stall, let up, wind down, ease up. **2** [To cause to become slower] delay, postpone, moderate, reduce, retard, detain, decrease, diminish, hinder, hold back, keep waiting, brake, curtail, check, curb, cut down, rein in, cut back.

slowly *a.* moderately, gradually, nonchalantly, gently, leisurely, at one's leisure, taking one's own sweet time*.

slowness *n.* sluggishness, apathy, lethargy; see INDIFFERENCE.

sluggish *a.* inactive, torpid, indolent; see LAZY 1, SLOW 1, 2.

sluggishness *n.* apathy, drowsiness, lethargy; see FATIGUE, LAZINESS.

slum *n.* cheap housing, poor district, tenement neighborhood, skid row, the wrong side of the tracks*.

slump *n.* depreciation, slip, descent; see DROP 2.

slump *v.* decline, depreciate, decay; see SINK 1.

slush *n.* melting snow, mire, refuse; see MUD.

slut *n.* wench, whore, hooker*; see PROSTITUTE.

sly *a.* wily, tricky, foxy, shifty, crafty, shrewd, designing, deceitful, scheming, deceiving, intriguing, cunning, unscrupulous, deceptive, conniving, calculating, plotting, dishonest, treacherous, underhanded, sneaking, double-dealing, faithless, traitorous, sharp, smart, ingenious, cagey*, dishonorable, crooked, mean, dirty, double-crossing*, slick*, smooth*, slippery, shady*.

slyly *a.* secretly, cunningly, furtively; see CLEVERLY.

small *a.* **1** [Little in size] tiny, diminutive, miniature; see LITTLE 1. **2** [Little in quantity] scanty, short, meager; see INADEQUATE. **3** [Unimportant] trivial, inessential, insignificant; see SHALLOW 2, UNIMPORTANT.

smaller *a.* tinier, lesser, petite; see LESS, SHORTER.

smallness *n.* littleness, narrowness, diminutive size, shortness, brevity, slightness, scantiness, tininess.

small talk *n.* chitchat, light conversation, banter, table talk, badinage, babble.

smart (smärt) ***vi.*** ⟦OE *smeortan*⟧ **1** *a)* to cause sharp, stinging pain, as a slap does *b)* to feel such pain **2** to feel mental distress or irritation —***n.*** **1** a stinging sensation **2** [*pl.*] [Slang] intelligence —***adj.*** **1** causing sharp pain **2** sharp, as pain **3** brisk; lively *[a smart pace]* **4** intelligent **5** neat; trim **6** stylish **7** [Inf.] insolent **8** *Comput. a)* working by means of a computer or microchip *b)* programmed in advance —**smart'ly** ***adv.*** —**smart'ness** ***n.***

smart al·eck or **smart al·ec** (al'ik) ⟦prec. + *Aleck*, dim. of *Alexander*⟧ [Inf.] an offensively conceited person

smart bomb [Mil. Slang] a guided missile directed to its target by electronic means

smart'en ***vt., vi.*** to make or become smart or smarter: usually with *up*

smash (smash) ***vt., vi.*** ⟦prob. < MASH⟧ **1** to break into pieces with noise or violence **2** to hit, collide, or move with force **3** to destroy or be destroyed —***n.*** **1** a hard, heavy hit **2** a violent, noisy breaking **3** a violent collision **4** a popular success

smash'ing ***adj.*** [Inf.] extraordinary

smash'up' ***n.*** **1** a violent wreck or collision **2** total failure; ruin

smat·ter·ing (smat'ər iŋ) ***n.*** ⟦ME *smateren*, to chatter⟧ **1** a slight knowledge **2** a small number or limited amount

smear (smir) ***vt.*** ⟦< OE *smerian*, to anoint⟧ **1** to cover or soil with something greasy, sticky, etc. **2** to apply (something greasy, etc.) **3** to streak by rubbing **4** to slander —***vi.*** to be or become smeared —***n.*** **1** a mark made by smearing **2** slander —**smear'y**, **-i·er**, **-i·est**, ***adj.***

smell (smel) ***vt.*** **smelled** or [Chiefly Brit.] **smelt**, **smell'ing** ⟦ME *smellen*⟧ **1** to be aware of through the nose; detect the odor of **2** to sense the presence of *[to smell trouble]* —***vi.*** **1** to use the sense of smell; sniff **2** to have an odor **3** to stink —***n.*** **1** the sense by which odors are perceived **2** odor; scent **3** a smelling

smelling salts an ammonia compound sniffed to relieve faintness

smell'y ***adj.*** **-i·er**, **-i·est** having an unpleasant smell

smelt[1] (smelt) ***n.*** ⟦OE⟧ a small, silvery food fish found esp. in northern seas

smelt[2] (smelt) ***vt.*** ⟦< MDu *smelten*⟧ **1** to melt (ore, etc.) so as to extract the pure metal **2** to refine (metal) in this way

smelt[3] (smelt) ***vt., vi.*** *chiefly Brit. pt. & pp. of* SMELL

smelt'er ***n.*** **1** one whose work is smelting **2** a place for smelting

smidg·en (smij'ən) ***n.*** ⟦prob. < dial. *smidge*, particle⟧ [Inf.] a small amount; bit: also **smidg'in** or **smidge**

smile (smīl) ***vi.*** **smiled**, **smil'ing** ⟦ME *smilen*⟧ to show pleasure, amusement, affection, etc. by an upward curving of the mouth —***vt.*** to express with a smile —***n.*** the act or expression of smiling —**smil'ing·ly** ***adv.***

smirch (smurch) ***vt.*** ⟦prob. < OFr *esmorcher*, to hurt⟧ **1** to soil or stain **2** to dishonor —***n.*** **1** a smudge; smear **2** a stain on reputation, etc.

smirk (smurk) ***vi.*** ⟦< OE *smearcian*, to smile⟧ to smile in a conceited or complacent way —***n.*** such a smile

smite (smīt) ***vt.*** **smote**, **smit'ten** or **smote**, **smit'ing** ⟦OE *smitan*⟧ **1** to strike with powerful effect **2** to affect or impress strongly

smith (smith) ***n.*** **1** one who makes or repairs metal objects **2** *short for* BLACKSMITH

Smith (smith), Captain **John** 1580?-1631; Eng. colonist in America

smith·er·eens (smi*th*'ər ēnz') ***pl.n.*** ⟦Ir *smidirīn*⟧ [Inf.] fragments; bits

smith·y (smith'ē) ***n.***, *pl.* **-ies** the workshop of a smith, esp. a blacksmith

smock (smäk) ***n.*** ⟦OE *smoc*⟧ a loose, shirtlike outer garment worn to protect the clothes

smock'ing ***n.*** decorative stitching used to gather cloth and make it hang in folds

smog (smäg, smôg) ***n.*** ⟦SM(OKE) + (F)OG⟧ a low-lying, perceptible layer of polluted air —**smog'gy**, **-gi·er**, **-gi·est**, ***adj.***

smoke (smōk) ***n.*** ⟦OE *smoca*⟧ **1** the vaporous matter arising from something burning **2** any vapor, etc. like this **3** an act of smoking tobacco, etc. **4** a cigarette, cigar, etc. —***vi.*** **smoked**, **smok'ing** **1** to give off smoke **2** *a)* to draw in and exhale the smoke of tobacco, etc. *b)* to be a habitual user of cigarettes, etc. —***vt.*** **1** to cure (meat, etc.) with smoke **2** to use (a pipe, cigarette, etc.) in smoking **3** to drive out as with smoke —**smoke out** to force out of hiding —**smoke'less** ***adj.*** —**smok'er** ***n.***

smoke detector a warning device that sets off a loud signal when excessive smoke or heat is detected

smoke'house' ***n.*** a building where meats, fish, etc. are cured with smoke

smoke screen **1** a cloud of smoke for hiding troop movements, etc. **2** anything said or done to conceal or mislead

smoke'stack' ***n.*** a pipe for discharging smoke from a factory, etc.

smok·y (smō'kē) ***adj.*** **-i·er**, **-i·est** **1** giving off smoke **2** of or like smoke **3** filled with smoke —**smok'i·ness** ***n.***

smol·der (smōl'dər) ***vi.*** ⟦ME *smoldren*⟧ **1** to burn and smoke without flame **2** to exist in a suppressed state —***n.*** a smoldering

smooch (smōōch) ***n., vt., vi.*** [Slang] kiss

smoosh (smoosh) ***vt.*** [Inf.] *alt. sp. of* SMUSH

smooth (smōō*th*) ***adj.*** ⟦OE *smoth*⟧ **1** having an even surface, with no roughness **2** without lumps **3** even or gentle in movement *[a smooth voyage]* **4** free from interruptions, obstacles, etc. **5** pleasing to the taste; not harsh or bitter **6** having an easy, flowing rhythm or sound **7** polished or ingratiating, esp. in an insincere way —***vt.*** **1** to make level or even **2** to remove lumps or wrinkles from **3** to free from difficulties, etc.; make easy **4** to make calm; soothe **5** to polish or refine —***adv.*** in a smooth manner —**smooth'ly** ***adv.*** —**smooth'ness** ***n.***

THESAURUS

smart ***v.*** sting, be painful, burn; see HURT 1.

smart ***a.*** **1** [Intelligent] clever, bright, quick; see INTELLIGENT. **2** [*Impudent] bold, brazen, forward; see RUDE 2.

smart aleck* ***n.*** showoff, boaster, life of the party; see BRAGGART.

smash ***n.*** crash, shattering, breaking; see BLOW.

smash ***v.*** crack, shatter, crush, burst, shiver, fracture, break, demolish, dash to pieces, destroy, batter, crash, wreck, break up, overturn, overthrow, lay in ruins, raze, topple, tumble.

smashed ***a.*** wrecked, crushed, mashed; see BROKEN 1.

smear ***v.*** **1** [To spread] cover, coat, apply; see PAINT 2, SPREAD 3. **2** [To slander] defame, vilify, libel; see INSULT, SLANDER.

smell ***n.*** **1** [A pleasant smell] fragrance, odor, scent, perfume, essence, aroma, bouquet. **2** [An unpleasant smell] malodor, stench, stink, reek, mustiness, foulness, uncleanness, fume. **3** [The sense of smell] smelling, olfactory perception, olfaction; see AWARENESS.

smell ***v.*** **1** [To give off odor] perfume, scent, exhale, reek, stink. **2** [To use the sense of smell] scent, sniff, inhale, snuff, nose out, get a whiff of; see also BREATHE.

smelly ***a.*** stinking, foul, fetid; see RANK 2.

smile ***n.*** grin, smirk, tender look, friendly expression, delighted look, joyous look; see also LAUGH.

smile ***v.*** beam, be gracious, look happy, look delighted, look pleased, break into a smile, look amused, smirk, grin; see also LAUGH.

smiling ***a.*** bright, with a smile, sunny, beaming; see also HAPPY.

smirk ***n.*** leer, grin, smile; see SNEER.

smith ***n.*** metalworker, forger, blacksmith; see CRAFTSMAN, WORKMAN.

smog ***n.*** pollution, smaze, fog, fumes, dirty fog, haze, mist, air pollution; see also SMOKE.

smoke ***n.*** vapor, fume, gas, soot, reek, haze, smudge, smog.

smoke ***v.*** **1** [To give off smoke] burn, fume, smudge, smoke up, smolder, reek. **2** [To use smoke, especially from tobacco] puff, inhale, smoke a pipe, smoke cigarettes, smoke cigars. —**smoke out** uncover, reveal, find; see DISCOVER.

smoked ***a.*** cured, dried, kippered; see PRESERVED 2.

smoky ***a.*** smoking, smoldering, reeking; see BURNING.

smolder ***v.*** fume, give off smoke, steam; see BURN, SMOKE 1.

smooth ***a.*** **1** [Without bumps] flat, plane, flush, horizontal, unwrinkled, level, monotonous, unrelieved, unruffled, mirrorlike, quiet, still, tranquil, glossy, glassy, lustrous, smooth as glass.—*Ant.* ROUGH, steep, broken. **2** [Without jerks] uniform, regular, even, invariable, steady, stable, fluid, flowing, rhythmic, constant, continuous. **3** [Without hair] shaven, beardless, whiskerless, cleanshaven, smooth-faced, smooth-chinned; see also BALD.—*Ant.* HAIRY, bearded, unshaven.

smooth ***v.*** even, level, flatten, grade, iron, polish, varnish, gloss, clear the way, smooth the path.

smoothly ***a.*** flatly, sleekly, placidly; see EASILY, EVENLY 1.

smooth muscle involuntary muscle tissue occurring in the uterus, stomach, blood vessels, etc.
smooth'-spo'ken ***adj.*** speaking in a pleasing, persuasive, or polished manner
smor·gas·bord or **smör·gås·bord** (smôr'gəs bôrd', smur'-) ***n.*** ⟦Swed⟧ a wide variety of appetizers, cheeses, meats, etc., served buffet style
smote (smōt) ***vt., vi.*** *pt. & alt. pp. of* SMITE
smoth·er (smuth'ər) ***vt.*** ⟦< ME *smorther*, dense smoke⟧ **1** to keep from getting air; suffocate **2** to cover over thickly **3** to stifle *[to smother a yawn]* **—*vi.*** to be suffocated
smoul·der (smōl'dər) ***vi., n.*** *Brit. sp. of* SMOLDER
smudge (smuj) ***vt., vi.*** **smudged, smudg'ing** ⟦ME *smogen*⟧ to make or become dirty; smear **—*n.*** **1** a dirty spot **2** a fire made to produce dense smoke **—smudg'y, -i·er, -i·est,** ***adj.***
smug (smug) ***adj.*** **smug'ger, smug'gest** ⟦prob. < LowG *smuk*, trim, neat⟧ annoyingly self-satisfied; complacent **—smug'ly** ***adv.*** **—smug'ness** ***n.***
smug·gle (smug'əl) ***vt.*** **-gled, -gling** ⟦< LowG *smuggeln*⟧ **1** to bring into or take out of a country secretly or illegally **2** to bring, take, etc. secretly **—*vi.*** to practice smuggling **—smug'gler** ***n.***
smush (smoosh) ***vt.*** [Inf.] to smash, squeeze, etc.
smut (smut) ***n.*** ⟦< LowG *smutt*⟧ **1** a particle of soot **3** indecent talk, writing, etc. **4** a fungal disease of plants **—smut'ty, -ti·er, -ti·est,** ***adj.***
Sn ⟦L *stannum*⟧ *Chem. symbol for* tin
snack (snak) ***n.*** ⟦< ME *snaken*, to bite⟧ a light meal between regular meals **—*vi.*** to eat a snack
snack bar a counter for serving snacks
snag (snag) ***n.*** ⟦< Scand⟧ **1** a sharp point or projection **2** an underwater tree stump or branch **3** a tear, as in cloth, made by a snag, etc. **4** an unexpected or hidden difficulty, etc. **—*vt.*** **snagged, snag'ging** **1** to catch, tear, etc. on a snag **2** to impede with a snag
snail (snāl) ***n.*** ⟦OE *snægl*⟧ a slow-moving mollusk having a wormlike body and a spiral protective shell
snake (snāk) ***n.*** ⟦OE *snaca*⟧ **1** a long, scaly, limbless reptile with a tapering tail **2** a treacherous or deceitful person **3** a plumber's tool for clearing pipes **—*vi.*** **snaked, snak'ing** to move, twist, etc. like a snake **—snake'like'** ***adj.***
snak·y (snā'kē) ***adj.*** **-i·er, -i·est** **1** of or like a snake or snakes **2** winding; twisting **3** cunningly treacherous or evil
snap (snap) ***vi., vt.*** **snapped, snap'ping** ⟦< MDu *snappen*⟧ **1** to bite or grasp suddenly: with *at* **2** to speak or utter sharply: often with *at* **3** to break suddenly **4** to make or cause to make a sudden, cracking sound **5** to close, fasten, etc. with this sound **6** to move or cause to move suddenly and smartly *[to snap to attention]* **7** to take a snapshot (of) **—*n.*** **1** a sudden bite, grasp, etc. **2** a sharp cracking sound *[the snap of a whip]* **3** a short, angry way of speaking **4** a brief period of cold weather **5** a fastening that closes with a click **6** a hard, thin cookie **7** *short for* SNAPSHOT **8** [Inf.] alertness or vigor **9** [Slang] an easy job, problem, etc. **—*adj.*** **1** made or done quickly *[a snap decision]* **2** that fastens with a snap **3** [Slang] easy **—snap back** to recover quickly **—snap out of it** to improve or recover quickly **—snap'per** ***n.***
snap bean a green bean or wax bean
snap'drag'on ***n.*** ⟦SNAP + DRAGON: from the mouth-shaped flowers⟧ a plant with saclike, two-lipped flowers
snap'pish ***adj.*** **1** likely to bite **2** irritable
snap'py ***adj.*** **-pi·er, -pi·est** **1** cross; irritable **2** that snaps **3** [Inf.] *a)* brisk or lively *b)* sharply chilly **4** [Inf.] stylish
snap'shot' ***n.*** an informal photograph taken with a hand camera
snare (sner) ***n.*** ⟦< ON *snara*⟧ **1** a trap for small animals **2** anything dangerous, etc. that tempts or attracts **3** a length of wire or gut across the bottom of a drum **—*vt.*** **snared, snar'ing** to catch as in a snare; trap
snarl[1] (snärl) ***vi.*** ⟦< earlier *snar*, to growl⟧ **1** to growl, baring the teeth, as a dog does **2** to speak sharply, as in anger **—*vt.*** to utter with a snarl **—*n.*** a fierce growl **—snarl'ing·ly** ***adv.***
snarl[2] (snärl) ***n., vt., vi.*** ⟦< SNARE⟧ tangle **—snarl'y, -i·er, -i·est,** ***adj.***
snatch (snach) ***vt.*** ⟦ME *snacchen*⟧ to take suddenly, specif. without right or warning **—*vi.*** **1** to try to seize; grab (*at*) **2** to take advantage of a chance, etc. eagerly: with *at* **—*n.*** **1** a snatching **2** a brief period **3** a fragment; bit
sneak (snēk) ***vt., vi.*** **sneaked** or [Inf.] **snuck, sneak'ing** ⟦prob. < OE *snican*, to crawl⟧ to move, act, give, put, take, etc. secretly or stealthily **—*n.*** **1** one who sneaks **2** a sneaking **—*adj.*** without warning *[a sneak attack]* **—sneak'y, -i·er, -i·est,** ***adj.***
sneak'er ***n.*** a shoe with a canvas upper and a soft rubber sole
sneak preview an advance showing of a film, as for evaluating audience reaction
sneer (snir) ***vi.*** ⟦ME *sneren*⟧ **1** to show scorn as by curling the upper lip **2** to express derision, etc. in speech or writing **—*n.*** a sneering
sneeze (snēz) ***vi.*** **sneezed, sneez'ing** ⟦ME *snesen*⟧ to exhale breath from the nose and mouth in an involuntary, explosive action **—*n.*** a sneezing
snick·er (snik'ər) ***vi.*** ⟦echoic⟧ to laugh in a sly, partly stifled way **—*n.*** a snickering
snide (snīd) ***adj.*** ⟦prob. < Du dial.⟧ slyly malicious or derisive
sniff (snif) ***vi., vt.*** ⟦ME *sniffen*⟧ **1** to draw in (air) forcibly through the nose **2** to express (disdain, etc.) by sniffing **3** to smell by sniffing **—*n.*** **1** an act or sound of sniffing **2** something sniffed
snif·fle (snif'əl) ***vi.*** **-fled, -fling** to sniff repeatedly, as in checking mucus running from the nose **—*n.*** an act or sound of sniffling **—the sniffles** [Inf.] a head cold
snif·ter (snif'tər) ***n.*** ⟦< *snift*, var. of SNIFF⟧ a goblet tapering to a small opening to concentrate the aroma, as of brandy
snig·ger (snig'ər) ***vi., n.*** ⟦echoic⟧ SNICKER
snip (snip) ***vt., vi.*** **snipped, snip'ping** ⟦Du *snippen*⟧ to cut or cut off in a short, quick stroke, as with scissors **—*n.*** **1** a small piece cut off **2** [Inf.] a young or insignificant person
snipe (snīp) ***n.*** ⟦< ON *snipa*⟧ a long-billed wading bird **—*vi.*** **sniped, snip'ing** to shoot from a hidden position, as at individuals **—snip'er** ***n.***

THESAURUS

smorgasbord ***n.*** buffet, appetizers, salad bar; see FOOD, LUNCH, MEAL 2.
smother ***v.*** stifle, suffocate, suppress; see CHOKE, EXTINGUISH.
smothered ***a.*** **1** [Extinguished] drenched, consumed, drowned, put out, not burning, quenched, snuffed. **2** [Strangled] choked, asphyxiated, breathless; see DEAD 1.
smudge ***n.*** smirch, spot, soiled spot; see BLEMISH.
smug ***a.*** self-satisfied, complacent, conceited, pleased with oneself, snobbish, egotistical, self-righteous, stuck up*, stuck on oneself*.
snack ***n.*** luncheon, slight meal, bite; see LUNCH, MEAL 2.
snack bar ***n.*** cafeteria, lunchroom, cafe; see RESTAURANT.
snag ***n.*** obstacle, hindrance, knot; see BARRIER, DIFFICULTY 1.
snake ***n.*** reptile, serpent, legless reptile. *Common snakes include the following:* viper, pit viper, water moccasin, copperhead, blacksnake, bullsnake, rattlesnake, python, cobra, coral snake, blue racer, garter snake, gopher snake, kingsnake, milk snake, water snake, boa constrictor, adder, puff adder, anaconda, asp, garden snake, cottonmouth, sidewinder, green snake, rat snake.
snap ***n.*** clasp, fastening, catch; see FASTENER.
snap ***v.*** catch, clasp, lock; see CLOSE 4, FASTEN. **—snap at** vent one's anger at, jump down someone's throat*, take it out on; see GET ANGRY. **—snap out of it** pull through, get over, revive; see RECOVER 3.
snapshot ***n.*** snap, photo, action shot; see PHOTOGRAPH, PICTURE 2, 3.
snare ***n.*** trap, lure, decoy; see TRICK 1.
snarl[1] ***v.*** growl, grumble, mutter, threaten, bark, yelp, snap, gnash the teeth, bully, quarrel.
snarl[1,2] ***n.*** **1** [Confusion] tangle, entanglement, complication; see CONFUSION. **2** [A snarling sound] grumble, gruffness, angry words; see GROWL.
snatch ***v.*** jerk, grasp, steal; see SEIZE 1, 2.
sneak ***v.*** skulk, slink, creep, slip away, move secretly, hide, prowl, lurk; see also EVADE.
sneaky ***a.*** tricky, deceitful, unreliable; see DISHONEST.
sneer ***v.*** mock, scoff, jeer, taunt, slight, scorn, decry, belittle, detract, lampoon, ridicule, deride, caricature, laugh at, look down, insult, disdain, satirize, condemn, give the raspberry*, give the Bronx cheer*.
sneeze ***n.*** explosive exhalation, cough, fit of sneezing; see COLD 2, FIT 1.
snicker ***v.*** giggle, titter, chuckle; see LAUGH.
sniff ***v.*** detect, scent, inhale; see SMELL 2.
snip ***v.*** clip, slice, nip; see CUT 1.

snip·pet (snip′it) ***n.*** ⟦dim. of SNIP⟧ a small piece or scrap, specif. of information

snip′py ***adj.*** **-pi·er, -pi·est** [Inf.] insolently curt, sharp, etc.

snit (snit) ***n.*** ⟦< ? prec. + (F)IT²⟧ a fit of anger, resentment, etc.: usually **in** (or **into**) **a snit**

snitch (snich) [Slang] ***vt.*** to steal; pilfer —***vi.*** to tattle (*on*) —***n.*** an informer

sniv·el (sniv′əl) ***vi.*** **-eled** or **-elled, -el·ing** or **-el·ling** ⟦ME *snivelen*⟧ **1** to cry and sniffle **2** to complain and whine **3** to make a tearful, often false display of grief, etc. —**sniv′el·er** ***n.***

snob (snäb) ***n.*** ⟦< ?⟧ one who disdains supposed inferiors —**snob′bish** ***adj.*** —**snob′bish·ness** or **snob′ber·y** ***n.***

snood (sno͞od) ***n.*** ⟦OE *snod*⟧ a baglike net worn at the back of a woman's head to hold the hair

snook·er (sno͝ok′ər) ***n.*** a variety of the game of pool —***vt.*** [Slang] to deceive

snoop (sno͞op) [Inf.] ***vi.*** ⟦Du *snoepen*, eat on the sly⟧ to pry about in a sneaking way —***n.*** one who snoops: also **snoop′er** —**snoop′y, -i·er, -i·est,** ***adj.***

snoot (sno͞ot) ***n.*** ⟦see SNOUT⟧ [Inf.] the nose

snoot′y ***adj.*** **-i·er, -i·est** [Inf.] haughty; snobbish —**snoot′i·ness** ***n.***

snooze (sno͞oz) ***n., vi.*** ⟦< LowG *snusen*, to snore⟧ **snoozed, snooz′ing** [Inf.] nap; doze —**snooz′er** ***n.***

snore (snôr) ***vi.*** **snored, snor′ing** ⟦see SNARL¹⟧ to breathe, while asleep, with harsh sounds —***n.*** the act or sound of snoring —**snor′er** ***n.***

snor·kel (snôr′kəl) ***n.*** ⟦Ger *schnorchel*, inlet⟧ a breathing tube extending above the water, used in swimming just below the surface —***vi.*** **-keled, -kel·ing** to swim underwater using a snorkel —**snor′kel·er** ***n.***

snort (snôrt) ***vi.*** **1** to force breath audibly through the nostrils **2** to express contempt, etc. by a snort —***vt.*** **1** to express with a snort **2** [Slang] to inhale (a drug) through the nose —***n.*** **1** a snorting **2** [Slang] a quick drink of liquor

snot (snät) ***n.*** ⟦OE *(ge)snot*, mucus⟧ [Slang] **1** nasal mucus: considered mildly vulgar **2** an impudent young person —**snot′ty, -ti·er, -ti·est,** ***adj.***

snout (snout) ***n.*** ⟦prob. < MDu *snute*⟧ the projecting nose and jaws of an animal

snow (snō) ***n.*** ⟦OE *snaw*⟧ **1** frozen particles of water vapor that fall to earth as soft, white flakes **2** a falling of snow —***vi.*** to fall as or like snow —***vt.*** **1** to cover or obstruct with snow: with *in, up, under*, etc. **2** [Slang] to deceive or mislead —**snow under 1** to overwhelm with work, etc. **2** to defeat decisively —**snow′y, -i·er, -i·est,** ***adj.***

snow′ball′ ***n.*** a mass of snow packed into a ball —***vi.*** to grow rapidly like a ball of snow rolling downhill

snow′bank′ ***n.*** a large mass of snow

Snow′belt′ the NE and Midwestern U.S., characterized by cold, snowy winters: also **Snow Belt**

snow′board′ ***n.*** a board somewhat like a small surfboard, for sliding down snowy hills for sport —***vi.*** to use a snowboard —**snow′board′er** ***n.***

snow′bound′ ***adj.*** shut in or blocked off by snow

snow′cone′ ***n.*** crushed ice mixed with a flavored syrup, served in a paper cone

snow′drift′ ***n.*** a heap of snow piled up by the wind

snow′drop′ ***n.*** a small plant with small, bell-shaped, white flowers

snow′fall′ ***n.*** a fall of snow or the amount of this in a given area or time

snow fence a light fence of lath and wire to control the drifting of snow

snow′flake′ ***n.*** a single snow crystal

snow′man′ (-man′) ***n.,*** *pl.* **-men′** (-men′) a crude human figure made of snow packed together

snow′mo·bile′ ***n.*** a motor vehicle with steerable runners at the front and tractor treads at the rear —***vi.*** **-biled′, -bil′ing** to travel by snowmobile

snow′plow′ ***n.*** a plowlike machine used to clear snow off a road, etc.

snow′shoe′ ***n.*** one of a pair of racket-shaped wooden frames crisscrossed with leather strips, etc., worn on the feet to prevent sinking in deep snow

snow′storm′ ***n.*** a storm with a heavy snowfall

snow′suit′ ***n.*** a child's heavily lined, hooded garment, for cold weather

snow tire a tire with a deep tread for added traction on snow or ice

snub (snub) ***vt.*** **snubbed, snub′bing** ⟦< ON *snubba*, chide⟧ **1** to treat with scorn, disdain, etc. **2** to check suddenly the movement of (a rope, etc.) —***n.*** scornful treatment —***adj.*** short and turned up: said of a nose

snub′-nosed′ ***adj.*** **1** having a snub nose **2** having a short barrel: said of a handgun

snuck (snuk) ***vi., vt.*** [Inf.] *alt. pt. & pp. of* SNEAK

snuff¹ (snuf) ***vt.*** ⟦ME⟧ **1** to trim off the charred end of (a wick) **2** to put out (a candle) —**snuff out 1** to extinguish **2** to destroy —**snuff′er** ***n.***

snuff² (snuf) ***vt., vi.*** ⟦< MDu *snuffen*⟧ to sniff or smell —***n.*** **1** a sniff **2** powdered tobacco taken up into the nose or put on the gums —**up to snuff** [Inf.] up to the usual standard

snuff′box′ ***n.*** a small box for snuff

snuf·fle (snuf′əl) ***n., vi.*** **-fled, -fling** ⟦< SNUFF²⟧ SNIFFLE

snug (snug) ***adj.*** **snug′ger, snug′gest** ⟦prob. < Scand⟧ **1** warm and cozy **2** neat; trim *[a snug cottage]* **3** tight in fit —**snug′ly** ***adv.***

snug′gle (-əl) ***vi., vt.*** **-gled, -gling** ⟦< prec.⟧ to nestle; cuddle

so (sō) ***adv.*** ⟦OE *swa*⟧ **1** as shown or described *[hold the bat just so]* **2** *a)* to such an extent *[why are you so late?]* *b)* very *[they are so happy]* *c)* [Inf.] very much *[she so wants to go]* **3** therefore *[they were tired, and so left]* **4** more or less *[fifty dollars or so]* **5** also; likewise *[I am going, and so are you]* **6** then *[and so to bed]* —***conj.*** **1** in order (*that*) **2** with the result that —***pron.*** that which has been specified or named *[he is a friend and will remain so]* —***interj.*** used to express surprise, triumph, etc. —***adj.*** true *[that's so]* —**and so on** (or **forth**) and the rest; et cetera —**so as** with the purpose or result —**so what?** [Inf.] even if so, what then?

soak (sōk) ***vt.*** ⟦OE *socian*⟧ **1** to make thoroughly wet **2** to take in; absorb: usually with *up* **3** [Inf.] to overcharge —***vi.*** **1** to stay in a liquid for wetting, softening, etc. **2** to penetrate —***n.*** **1** a soaking or being soaked **2** [Slang] a drunkard

so′-and-so′ ***n.,*** *pl.* **so′-and-sos′** [Inf.] an unspecified person or thing: often used euphemistically

soap (sōp) ***n.*** ⟦OE *sape*⟧ **1** a substance, usually a salt derived from fatty acids, used with water to produce suds for washing **2** [Slang] SOAP OPERA —***vt.*** to lather, etc. with soap —**no soap** [Slang] (it is) not acceptable —**soap′y, -i·er, -i·est,** ***adj.***

soap′box′ ***n.*** any improvised platform used in speaking to a street audience

soap opera [Inf.] a radio or television serial melodrama

soap′stone′ ***n.*** a soft, impure talc in rock form, used as an insulator, etc.

THESAURUS

snob ***n.*** elitist, highbrow, stuffed shirt*; see BRAGGART.

snobbish ***a.*** ostentatious, pretentious, overbearing; see EGOTISTIC.

snooty* ***a.*** conceited, nasty, egotistical; see EGOTISTIC.

snore ***v.*** snort, wheeze, sleep; see BREATHE.

snotty* ***a.*** impudent, like a spoiled brat, nasty; see RUDE 2.

snout ***n.*** muzzle, proboscis, nozzle; see NOSE 1.

snow ***n.*** **1** [A snowstorm] blizzard, snowfall, snow flurries; see STORM. **2** [Frozen vapor] snow crystal, snowflake, slush, sleet, snowdrift, snowbank, powder snow, snowpack, snowfall, fall of snow.

snow ***v.*** storm, squall, howl, blow, cover, pelt, shower, sleet.

snub ***v.*** ignore, disregard, disdain; see NEGLECT 1.

snug ***a.*** **1** [Cozy] homelike, secure, sheltered; see COMFORTABLE 1, WARM 1. **2** [Close in fit] trim, well-built, close; see TIGHT 3.

so ***a.*** **1** [To a degree] very, this much, so large, vaguely, indefinitely, extremely, infinitely, remarkably, unusually, so much, extremely, in great measure, in some measure; see also SUCH. **2** [Thus] and so on, and so forth, in such manner, in this way, in this degree, to this extent; see also THUS. **3** [Accordingly] then, therefore, consequently; see ACCORDINGLY.

soak ***v.*** **1** [To drench] wet, immerse, dip, immerge*, water, percolate, permeate, drown, saturate, pour into, pour on, wash over, flood; see also MOISTEN. **2** [To remain in liquid] steep, soften, be saturated, be waterlogged, be permeated. **3** [To absorb] dry up, sop up, mop up; see ABSORB.

soaked ***a.*** sodden, saturated, wet, wet through, drenched, soggy, dripping, seeping, immersed, steeped, dipped, flooded, drowned, waterlogged.

soap ***n.*** solvent, softener, cleanser, cleaner, soapsuds. *Varieties and forms of soap include the following:* bar, liquid, glycerine, saddle, powdered, perfumed, bath, laundry, dish; soap flakes; see also CLEANSER.

soap'suds' ***pl.n.*** foamy, soapy water
soar (sôr) ***vi.*** ⟦ult. < L *ex-*, out + *aura*, air⟧ **1** to rise or fly high into the air **2** to glide along high in the air **3** to rise above the usual level
So·a·ve (sə wä′vā, swä′vā) ***n.*** ⟦It⟧ an Italian dry white wine
sob (säb) ***vi.*** **sobbed, sob'bing** ⟦ME *sobben*⟧ to weep aloud with short, gasping breaths —***vt.*** to utter with sobs —***n.*** the act or sound of sobbing
so·ber (sō′bər) ***adj.*** ⟦< L *sobrius*⟧ **1** temperate, esp. in the use of liquor **2** not drunk **3** serious, reasonable, sedate, etc. **4** not flashy; plain —***vt.***, ***vi.*** to make or become sober: often with *up* —**so'ber·ly** ***adv.*** —**so'ber·ness** ***n.***
so·bri·e·ty (sə brī′ə tē) ***n.*** a being sober; specif., *a*) temperance, esp. in the use of liquor *b*) seriousness
so·bri·quet (sō′brə kā′, -ket′) ***n.*** ⟦Fr⟧ **1** a nickname **2** an assumed name
soc *abbrev.* **1** social **2** socialist **3** society
so'-called' ***adj.*** **1** known by this term **2** inaccurately or questionably designated as such *[a so-called liberal]*
soc·cer (säk′ər) ***n.*** ⟦alt. < (*as*)*soc*(*iation football*)⟧ a team game played by kicking a round ball
so·cia·ble (sō′shə bəl) ***adj.*** ⟦see fol.⟧ **1** friendly; gregarious **2** characterized by informal conversation and companionship —**so'cia·bil'i·ty** ***n.*** —**so'cia·bly** ***adv.***
so·cial (sō′shəl) ***adj.*** ⟦< L *socius*, companion⟧ **1** of or having to do with human beings, etc. in their living together **2** living with others; gregarious *[man as a social being]* **3** of or having to do with society, esp. fashionable society **4** sociable **5** of or for companionship **6** of or doing welfare work —***n.*** an informal gathering —**so'cial·ly** ***adv.***
social disease any venereal disease
so'cial·ism' ***n.*** **1** a theory or system of ownership of the means of production and distribution by society rather than by individuals **2** [*often* **S-**] a political movement for establishing such a system —**so'cial·ist** ***n.***, ***adj.*** —**so'cial·is'tic** ***adj.***
so·cial·ite (so′shə līt′) ***n.*** a person prominent in fashionable society
so'cial·ize' (-shə līz′) ***vt.*** **-ized′**, **-iz'ing** **1** to make fit for living in a group **2** to subject to governmental ownership or control —***vi.*** to take part in social activity —**so'cial·i·za'tion** ***n.***
socialized medicine a system supplying complete medical and hospital care to all through public funds
social science a field of study, as economics or anthropology, dealing with the structure, etc. of society —**social scientist**
Social Security [*sometimes* **s- s-**] a federal system of old-age, unemployment, or disability insurance
social studies a course of study including history, geography, etc.
social work any service or activity promoting the welfare of the community and the individual, as through counseling services, etc. —**social worker**
so·ci·e·ty (sə sī′ə tē) ***n.***, *pl.* **-ties** ⟦< L *socius*, companion⟧ **1** a group of persons, etc. forming a single community **2** the system of living together in such a group **3** all people, collectively **4** companionship **5** an organized group with some interest in common **6** the wealthy, dominant class —**so·ci'e·tal** (-təl) ***adj.***
Society of Friends a Christian denomination that believes in plain worship, pacifism, etc.: see also QUAKER
so·ci·o·e·co·nom·ic (sō′sē ō ē′kə näm′ik, -shē-; -ek′ə-) ***adj.*** of or involving both social and economic factors
so·ci·ol·o·gy (sō′sē äl′ə jē, -shē-) ***n.*** ⟦see SOCIAL & -LOGY⟧ the science of social relations, organization, and change —**so'ci·o·log'i·cal** (-ə lä′ji kəl) ***adj.*** —**so'ci·ol'o·gist** ***n.***
so·ci·o·path (sō′sē ə path′, -shē-) ***n.*** an aggressively antisocial psychopath
sock[1] (säk) ***n.***, *pl.* **socks** or **sox** ⟦< L *soccus*, type of light shoe⟧ a short stocking —**sock away** [Inf.] to set aside (money) as savings
sock[2] (säk) [Slang] ***vt.*** to hit with force —***n.*** a blow
sock·et (säk′it) ***n.*** ⟦< OFr *soc*, plowshare⟧ a hollow part into which something fits *[an eye socket]*
sock·eye salmon (säk′ī′) a red-fleshed salmon of the N Pacific
Soc·ra·tes (säk′rə tēz′) 470?-399 B.C.; Athenian philosopher & teacher —**So·crat·ic** (sə krat′ik) ***adj.***, ***n.***
sod (säd) ***n.*** ⟦prob. < MDu *sode*⟧ **1** a surface layer of earth containing grass with its roots; turf **2** a piece of this —***vt.*** **sod'ded, sod'ding** to cover with sod
so·da (sō′də) ***n.*** ⟦ML⟧ **1** *a*) SODIUM BICARBONATE *b*) SODA WATER *c*) SODA POP **2** a confection of soda water mixed with syrup and having ice cream in it
soda cracker a light, crisp cracker made from flour, water, and leavening, orig. baking soda
soda fountain a counter for making and serving soft drinks, sodas, etc.
soda pop a flavored, carbonated soft drink
soda water **1** water charged under pressure with carbon dioxide gas **2** SODA POP
sod·den (säd′′n) ***adj.*** **1** soaked through **2** soggy from improper cooking **3** dull or stupefied, as from liquor —**sod'den·ly** ***adv.***
so·di·um (sō′dē əm) ***n.*** ⟦< *soda*⟧ an alkaline, metallic chemical element
sodium bicarbonate a white powder, used in baking powder, as an antacid, etc.
sodium chloride common salt
sodium hydroxide a caustic base used in oil refining, etc.
sodium nitrate a clear, crystalline salt used in explosives, fertilizers, etc.
sodium pen·to·thal (pen′tə thôl′) a yellowish powder injected in solution as a general anesthetic
Sod·om and Go·mor·rah (säd′əm and gə môr′ə) *Bible* two sinful cities destroyed by fire
sod·om·y (säd′ə mē) ***n.*** ⟦after *Sodom*⟧ any sexual intercourse held to be abnormal —**sod'om·ite'** (-mīt′) ***n.***
so·fa (sō′fə) ***n.*** ⟦< Ar *ṣuffa*, a platform⟧ an upholstered couch with fixed back and arms
sofa bed a sofa that can be opened into a bed
So·fi·a (sō′fē ə, sō fē′ə) capital of Bulgaria: pop. 1,116,000
soft (sôft) ***adj.*** ⟦OE *softe*, gentle⟧ **1** giving way easily under pressure **2** easily cut, marked, shaped, etc. *[a soft metal]* **3** not as hard as is normal, desirable, etc. *[soft butter]* **4** smooth to the touch **5** easy to digest: said of a

THESAURUS

sob ***n.*** weeping, bewailing, convulsive sigh; see CRY 3.
sob ***v.*** lament, sigh convulsively, weep; see CRY 1.
sober ***a.*** solemn, serious, sedate, clearheaded, not drunk, calm, grave, temperate, abstemious, abstinent, teetotaling, abstaining, steady; see also MODERATE 4.
soberly ***a.*** moderately, temperately, abstemiously, solemnly, gravely, sedately, in a subdued manner, quietly, regularly, steadily, calmly, coolly, seriously, somberly, staidly, earnestly, dispassionately, fairly, justly.
so-called ***a.*** commonly named, nominal, professed, doubtfully called, allegedly, thus termed, wrongly named, popularly supposed, erroneously accepted as, supposed, also know as.
sociable ***a.*** affable, genial, companionable; see FRIENDLY.
social ***a.*** genial, amusing, entertaining, companionable, pleasurable, civil, polite, polished, mannerly, pleasure-seeking, hospitable, pleasant.
socialist ***n.*** Marxist, communist, populist; see RADICAL.
socialistic ***a.*** Marxist, communistic, social-democrat, noncapitalistic; see also DEMOCRATIC, RADICAL.
socially ***a.*** politely, civilly, courteously, hospitably, companionably, entertainingly, amusingly, cordially, genially, sociably.
social science ***n.*** study of people and social phenomena, study of human society, political science, anthropology, social studies; see also ECONOMICS, GEOGRAPHY, HISTORY, POLITICS, PSYCHOLOGY, SCIENCE 1, SOCIOLOGY.
social security ***n.*** social insurance, old-age insurance, disability insurance, unemployment insurance, social security payments, retirement.
social service ***n.*** social work, welfare, aid for the needy, charity, philanthropy.
society ***n.*** **1** [Friendly association] friendship, social intercourse, fellowship; see ORGANIZATION 2. **2** [Organized humanity] culture, the public, civilization, nation, community, human groupings, the people, the world at large, social life.
sociology ***n.*** study of society, cultural anthropology, social psychology, analysis of human institutions, study of human groups; see also SOCIAL SCIENCE.
sock[1] ***n.*** stocking, hose, short stocking; see HOSIERY.
socket ***n.*** holder, opening, cavity; see JOINT 1.
soda ***n.*** soda water, carbonated water, mineral water; see DRINK 2.
sofa ***n.*** couch, divan, love seat; see FURNITURE.
soft ***a.*** **1** [Soft to the touch] smooth, satiny, velvety, silky, delicate, fine, thin, flimsy, limp, fluffy, feathery, downy, woolly, doughy, spongy, mushy.—*Ant.* HARSH, rough, flinty. **2** [Soft to the eye] dull, dim, quiet, shaded, pale, light, pastel, faint, blond, misty, hazy, dusky, delicate, pallid, ashen, tinted; see also

diet **6** nonalcoholic: said of drinks **7** having few of the mineral salts that keep soap from lathering **8** mild, as a breeze **9** weak; not vigorous **10** easy *[a soft job]* **11** kind or gentle **12** not bright: said of color or light **13** gentle; low: said of sound —***adv.*** gently; quietly —**soft'ly** ***adv.*** —**soft'ness** ***n.***

soft'ball' ***n.*** **1** a kind of baseball played with a larger ball **2** this ball

soft'-boiled' ***adj.*** boiled a short time to keep the yolk soft: said of an egg

soft coal BITUMINOUS COAL

soft drink a nonalcoholic drink, esp. one that is carbonated

soft·en (sôf'ən) ***vt.***, ***vi.*** to make or become soft or softer —**soft'en·er** ***n.***

soft'heart'ed ***adj.*** **1** full of compassion **2** not strict or severe; lenient

soft landing a landing of a spacecraft without damage to the craft or its contents

soft money money donated to a political party but not for a particular candidate

soft palate the soft, fleshy part at the rear of the roof of the mouth; velum

soft'-ped'al ***vt.*** **-aled** or **-alled**, **-al·ing** or **-al·ling** ⟦from pedal to soften an instrument's tone⟧ [Inf.] to make less emphatic; tone down; play down

soft sell selling that relies on subtle inducement or suggestion

soft soap [Inf.] flattery or smooth talk —**soft'-soap'** ***vt.***

soft'ware' ***n.*** the programs, routines, etc. for a computer

soft'wood' ***n.*** **1** any light, easily cut wood **2** the wood of any tree bearing cones, as the pine

soft'y ***n.***, *pl.* **soft'ies** [Inf.] one who is too sentimental or trusting

sog·gy (säg'ē, sôg'ē) ***adj.*** **-gi·er**, **-gi·est** ⟦prob. < ON *sea*, a sucking⟧ soaked; moist and heavy —**sog'gi·ness** ***n.***

soil[1] (soil) ***n.*** ⟦< L *solum*⟧ **1** the surface layer of earth, supporting plant life **2** land; country *[native soil]* **3** ground or earth *[barren soil]*

soil[2] (soil) ***vt.*** ⟦ult. < L *sus*, pig⟧ **1** to make dirty; stain **2** to disgrace —***vi.*** to become soiled or dirty —***n.*** a soiled spot; stain

soi·ree or **soi·rée** (swä rā') ***n.*** ⟦< Fr *soir*, evening⟧ an evening party

so·journ (sō'jurn; *also, for v.,* sō jurn') ***vi.*** ⟦< L *sub-*, under + *diurnus*, of a day⟧ to live somewhere temporarily —***n.*** a brief stay; visit

sol (sōl) ***n.*** ⟦< ML⟧ *Music* the fifth tone of the diatonic scale

Sol (säl) ***n.*** ⟦L⟧ **1** *Rom. Myth.* the sun god **2** the sun personified

sol·ace (säl'is) ***n.*** ⟦< L *solacium*⟧ **1** an easing of grief, loneliness, etc. **2** a comfort or consolation —***vt.*** **-aced**, **-ac·ing** to comfort; console

so·lar (sō'lər) ***adj.*** ⟦< L *sol*, the sun⟧ **1** of or having to do with the sun **2** produced by or coming from the sun

solar battery an assembly of cells (**solar cells**) used to convert solar energy into electric power

so·lar·i·um (sō ler'ē əm) ***n.***, *pl.* **-i·a** (-ē ə) ⟦< L *sol*, sun⟧ a glassed-in porch, etc. to sun oneself

solar plexus a network of nerves in the abdomen behind the stomach

solar system that portion of our galaxy subject to the sun's gravity; esp., the sun and its planets

sold (sōld) ***vt.***, ***vi.*** *pt. & pp. of* SELL

sol·der (säd'ər) ***n.*** ⟦ult. < L *solidus*, solid⟧ a metal alloy heated and used to join or patch metal parts, etc. —***vt.***, ***vi.*** to join with solder

sol·dier (sōl'jər) ***n.*** ⟦< LL *solidus*, a coin⟧ **1** a member of an army **2** an enlisted person, as distinguished from an officer **3** one who works for a specified cause —***vi.*** **1** to serve as a soldier **2** to proceed stubbornly (*on*) —**sol'dier·ly** ***adj.***

soldier of fortune a mercenary or any adventurer

sole[1] (sōl) ***n.*** ⟦< L *solum*, a base⟧ **1** the bottom surface of the foot **2** the part of a shoe, etc. corresponding to this —***vt.*** **soled**, **sol'ing** to furnish (a shoe, etc.) with a sole

sole[2] (sōl) ***adj.*** ⟦< L *solus*⟧ without another; single; one and only

sole[3] (sōl) ***n.***, *pl.* **sole** or **soles** ⟦< L *solea*, SOLE[1]: from its shape⟧ a sea flatfish valued as food

sol·e·cism (säl'ə siz'əm) ***n.*** ⟦< Gr *soloikos*, speaking incorrectly⟧ a violation of the conventional usage, grammar, etc. of a language

sole·ly (sōl'lē) ***adv.*** **1** alone **2** only, exclusively, or merely

sol·emn (säl'əm) ***adj.*** ⟦< L *sollemnis*, annual, hence religious: said of festivals⟧ **1** sacred **2** formal **3** serious; grave; earnest —**sol'emn·ly** ***adv.***

so·lem·ni·ty (sə lem'nə tē) ***n.***, *pl.* **-ties** **1** solemn ceremony, ritual, etc. **2** seriousness; gravity

sol·em·nize (säl'əm nīz') ***vt.*** **-nized'**, **-niz'ing** **1** to celebrate formally or according to ritual **2** to perform the ceremony of (marriage, etc.)

so·le·noid (sō'lə noid', sä'-) ***n.*** ⟦< Gr *sōlēn*, channel + *eidos*, a form⟧ a coil of wire with a movable iron core, used as an electromagnetic switch

so·lic·it (sə lis'it) ***vt.***, ***vi.*** ⟦see SOLICITOUS⟧ **1** to appeal to (persons) for (aid, donations, etc.) **2** to entice or lure —**so·lic'i·ta'tion** ***n.***

so·lic'i·tor ***n.*** **1** one who solicits trade, contributions, etc. **2** in England, a lawyer other than a barrister **3** the law officer for a city, etc.

so·lic·i·tous (sə lis'ə təs) ***adj.*** ⟦< L *sollus*, whole + *ciere*, set in motion⟧ **1** showing care or concern *[solicitous for her welfare]* **2** desirous; eager

so·lic'i·tude' (-to͞od') ***n.*** a being solicitous; care, concern, etc.

sol·id (säl'id) ***adj.*** ⟦< L *solidus*⟧ **1** relatively firm or compact; neither liquid nor gaseous **2** not hollow **3** having three dimensions **4** firm; strong; substantial **5** having no breaks or divisions **6** of one color, material, etc. throughout **7** showing unity; unanimous **8** reliable or dependable —***n.*** **1** a solid substance, not a liquid or gas **2** an object having length, breadth, and thickness —**sol'id·ly** ***adv.*** —**sol'id·ness** ***n.***

sol·i·dar·i·ty (säl'ə dar'ə tē) ***n.*** complete unity, as of opinion or feeling

so·lid·i·fy (sə lid'ə fī') ***vt.***, ***vi.*** **-fied'**, **-fy'ing** to make or become solid, hard, etc. —**so·lid'i·fi·ca'tion** ***n.***

so·lid'i·ty (-tē) ***n.*** a being solid

sol'id-state' ***adj.*** **1** of the branch of physics dealing with the structure, properties, etc. of solids **2** equipped with transistors, etc.

so·lil·o·quy (sə lil'ə kwē) ***n.***, *pl.* **-quies** ⟦< L *solus*, alone +

THESAURUS

SHADY.—*Ant.* BRIGHT, glaring, brilliant. **3** [Soft to the ear] low, melodious, faraway; see FAINT 3. —**be soft on** treat lightly, not condemn, fail to attack; see FAVOR, NEGLECT 1.

soften ***v.*** dissolve, lessen, diminish, disintegrate, become tender, become mellow, thaw, melt, moderate, bend, give, yield, relax, relent, mellow, modify, mollify, appease, mash, knead, temper, tone down, qualify, tenderize, enfeeble, weaken.—*Ant.* STRENGTHEN, increase, tone up.

softhearted ***a.*** tender, kind-hearted, humane; see KIND.

softness ***n.*** mellowness, impressibility, plasticity; see FLEXIBILITY.

soggy ***a.*** mushy, spongy, saturated; see SOAKED, WET 1.

soil[1] ***n.*** dirt, loam, clay; see EARTH 2.

soil[2] ***v.*** stain, sully, spoil; see DIRTY.

soiled ***a.*** stained, tainted, ruined; see DIRTY 1.

sold ***a.*** **1** [Sold out] disposed of, gone, taken; see SOLD OUT. **2** [*Convinced] persuaded, impressed, taken with; see SATISFIED. —**sold out** out of, all sold, out of stock, not in stock, gone, depleted.

soldier ***n.*** warrior, fighter, private, enlisted man, enlisted woman, officer, fighting man, rank and file, foot soldier, draftee, volunteer, conscript, commando, mercenary, cadet, commissioned officer, noncommissioned officer, recruit, selectee, ranker*, veteran, militant, marine, infantryman, guerrilla, guardsman, scout, sharpshooter, artilleryman, gunner, engineer, airman, bomber pilot, fighter pilot, paratrooper, machine-gunner, G.I. Joe*, grunt*.

sole[2] ***a.*** only, no more than one, remaining; see INDIVIDUAL, SINGLE 1.

solely ***a.*** singly, undividedly, singularly; see INDIVIDUALLY, ONLY 1.

solemn ***a.*** grave, serious, sober, earnest, intense, deliberate, heavy, austere, somber, dignified, staid, sedate, moody, pensive, brooding, grim, stern, thoughtful, reflective.

solemnly ***a.*** sedately, gravely, impressively; see SERIOUSLY 2.

solid ***a.*** **1** [Firm in position] stable, fixed, rooted; see FIRM 1. **2** [Firm or close in texture] compact, hard, dense; see FIRM 2, THICK 1. **3** [Reliable] dependable, trustworthy, steadfast; see RELIABLE. **4** [Continuous] uninterrupted, continued, unbroken; see CONSECUTIVE, REGULAR 3.

solid ***n.*** cube, cone, pyramid, cylinder, block, prism, sphere.

solidification ***n.*** hardening, freezing, calcification, ossification, stiffening, setting, crystallization, fossilization, compression, coagulation, concentration.

solidify ***v.*** set, fix, crystallize; see COMPRESS, HARDEN, THICKEN.

loqui, speak⟧ **1** a talking to oneself **2** lines in a drama spoken by a character as if to himself or herself —**so·lil'o·quize'** (-kwīz'), **-quized'**, **-quiz'ing**, ***vi.***, ***vt.***

sol·i·taire (säl'ə ter') ***n.*** ⟦Fr: see fol.⟧ **1** a diamond or other gem set by itself **2** a card game for one player

sol'i·tar'y (-ter'ē) ***adj.*** ⟦< L *solus*, alone⟧ **1** living or being alone **2** single; only *[a solitary example]* **3** lonely; remote **4** done in solitude

sol'i·tude' (-to͞od') ***n.*** ⟦see prec.⟧ **1** a being solitary, or alone; seclusion **2** a secluded place

so·lo (sō'lō) ***n.***, *pl.* **-los** or **-li** (-lē) ⟦It < L *solus*, alone⟧ **1** a musical piece or passage to be performed by one person **2** any performance by one person alone —***adj.*** for or by a single person —***adv.*** alone —***vi.*** **-loed**, **-lo·ing** to perform a solo —**so'lo·ist** ***n.***

Sol·o·mon (säl'ə mən) ***n.*** *Bible* king of Israel noted for his wisdom

Solomon Islands country on a group of islands in the SW Pacific, east of New Guinea: 10,954 sq. mi.; pop. 286,000

So·lon (sō'lən, -län') 640?-559? B.C.; Athenian statesman & lawgiver

so long [Inf.] GOODBYE

sol·stice (säl'stis, sōl'-) ***n.*** ⟦< L *sol*, sun + *sistere*, to stand⟧ the time of the year when the sun reaches the point farthest north (about June 21) or farthest south (about Dec. 21) of the equator: in the Northern Hemisphere, the **summer solstice** and **winter solstice**, respectively

sol·u·ble (säl'yə bəl) ***adj.*** ⟦see SOLVE⟧ **1** that can be dissolved **2** capable of being solved

sol·ute (säl'yo͞ot') ***n.*** the substance dissolved in a solution

so·lu·tion (sə lo͞o'shən) ***n.*** ⟦see fol.⟧ **1** the solving of a problem **2** an answer, explanation, etc. **3** the dispersion of one substance in another, usually a liquid, so as to form a homogeneous mixture **4** the mixture so produced

solve (sälv, sôlv) ***vt.*** **solved**, **solv'ing** ⟦< L *se-*, apart + *luere*, let go⟧ to find the answer to (a problem, etc.) —**solv'a·ble** ***adj.*** —**solv'er** ***n.***

sol·vent (säl'vənt, sôl'-) ***adj.*** ⟦see prec.⟧ **1** able to pay all one's debts **2** that can dissolve another substance —***n.*** a substance that can dissolve another substance —**sol'ven·cy** ***n.***

So·ma·li·a (sō mä'lē ə) country of E Africa, on the Indian Ocean: 246,201 sq. mi.; pop. 9,200,000

so·mat·ic (sō mat'ik) ***adj.*** ⟦< Gr *sōma*, body⟧ of the body; physical

somatic cell any of the cells that form the tissues and organs of the body: opposed to GERM CELL

som·ber (säm'bər) ***adj.*** ⟦< L *sub*, under + *umbra*, shade⟧ **1** dark and gloomy **2** melancholy **3** solemn Also [Chiefly Brit.] **som'bre** —**som'ber·ly** ***adv.***

som·bre·ro (säm brer'ō) ***n.***, *pl.* **-ros** ⟦Sp < *sombra*, shade: see prec.⟧ a broad-brimmed, tall-crowned hat worn in Mexico, the Southwest, etc.

some (sum) ***adj.*** ⟦OE *sum*⟧ **1** certain but not specified or known *[open some evenings]* **2** of a certain unspecified quantity, degree, etc. *[have some candy]* **3** about *[some ten of them]* **4** [Inf.] remarkable, striking, etc. *[it was some fight]* —***pron.*** a certain unspecified number, quantity, etc. *[some of them agree]* —***adv.*** **1** approximately *[some ten men]* **2** [Inf.] to some extent; somewhat *[slept some]* **3** [Inf.] to a great extent or at a great rate *[must run some to catch up]* —**and then some** [Inf.] and more than that

-some[1] (səm) ⟦OE *-sum*⟧ *suffix* tending to (be) *[tiresome]*

-some[2] (sōm) ⟦< Gr *sōma*, body⟧ *combining form* body *[chromosome]*

some·bod·y (sum'bäd'ē, -bud'ē) ***pron.*** a person unknown or not named; some person; someone —***n.***, *pl.* **-bod'ies** a person of importance

some'day' ***adv.*** at some future day or time

some'how' ***adv.*** in a way or by a method not known or stated: often in **somehow or other**

some'one' ***pron.*** SOMEBODY

som·er·sault (sum'ər sôlt') ***n.*** ⟦< L *supra*, over + *saltus*, a leap⟧ an acrobatic stunt performed by turning the body one full revolution, heels over head —***vi.*** to perform a somersault

some'thing ***pron.*** **1** a thing not definitely known, understood, etc. *[something went wrong]* **2** a definite but unspecified thing *[have something to eat]* **3** a bit; a little —***n.*** [Inf.] an important or remarkable person or thing —***adv.*** **1** somewhat *[looks something like me]* **2** [Inf.] really; quite *[sounds something awful]* —**something else** [Slang] one that is quite remarkable

some'time' ***adv.*** at some unspecified or future time —***adj.*** **1** former **2** occasional

some'times' ***adv.*** occasionally

some'way' ***adv.*** in some way: also **some'ways'**

some'what' ***pron.*** some degree, amount, part, etc. —***adv.*** to some extent or degree; a little

some'where' ***adv.*** **1** in, to, or at some place not known or specified **2** at some time, degree, age, etc. (with *about, around, near, in, between*, etc.)

som·nam·bu·lism (säm nam'byo͞o liz'əm) ***n.*** ⟦< L *somnus*, sleep + *ambulare*, to walk⟧ sleepwalking —**som·nam'bu·list** ***n.***

som·no·lent (säm'nə lənt) ***adj.*** ⟦< L *somnus*, sleep⟧ **1** sleepy **2** inducing drowsiness —**som'no·lence** ***n.***

son (sun) ***n.*** ⟦OE *sunu*⟧ **1** a boy or man as he is related to his parents **2** a male descendant —**the Son** Jesus Christ

so·nar (sō'när') ***n.*** ⟦*so(und) n(avigation) a(nd) r(anging)*⟧ an apparatus that transmits sound waves in water, used to find depths, etc.

so·na·ta (sə nät'ə) ***n.*** ⟦It < L *sonare*, to sound⟧ a musical composition for one or two instruments, usually consisting of several movements

song (sôŋ) ***n.*** ⟦OE *sang*⟧ **1** the act or art of singing **2** a piece of music for singing **3** *a)* [Old Poet.] poetry *b)* a lyric set to music **4** a sound like singing —**for a song** [Inf.] for a small sum; cheap

song'bird' ***n.*** a bird that makes vocal sounds that are like music

song'fest' ***n.*** ⟦SONG + -FEST⟧ an informal gathering of people for singing, esp. folk songs

song'ster (-stər) ***n.*** a singer —**song'stress** (-stris) ***fem.n.***

son·ic (sän'ik) ***adj.*** ⟦< L *sonus*, a sound⟧ of or having to do with sound or the speed of sound

sonic boom the explosive sound of a supersonic jet passing overhead

son'-in-law' ***n.***, *pl.* **sons'-in-law'** the husband of one's daughter

son·net (sän'it) ***n.*** ⟦ult. < L *sonus*, a sound⟧ a poem normally of fourteen lines in any of several rhyme schemes

son·ny (sun'ē) ***n.***, *pl.* **-nies** little son: used as a familiar term of address to a young boy

So·no·ra (sô nô'rä) state of NW Mexico: 71,403 sq. mi.; pop. 1,824,000

THESAURUS

solitary ***a.*** sole, only, alone, single, secluded, companionless, lonely, separate, individual, isolated, singular.—*Ant.* ACCOMPANIED, social, attended.

solitude ***n.*** isolation, seclusion, retirement; see SILENCE 1.

soluble ***a.*** dissolvable, emulsifiable, dispersible, water-soluble, fat-soluble.

solution ***n.*** **1** [Explanation] interpretation, resolution, clarification; see ANSWER. **2** [Fluid] suspension, fluid, fluid mixture; see LIQUID.

solve ***v.*** figure out, work out, reason out, think out, find out, puzzle out, decipher, unravel, interpret, explain, resolve, answer, decode, get to the bottom of, get right, hit upon a solution, work, do, settle, clear up, untangle, elucidate, fathom, unlock, determine, hit the nail on the head*, put two and two together, have it.

somber ***a.*** melancholy, dreary, gloomy; see DISMAL.

some ***a.*** few, a few, a little, a bit, part of, more than a few, more than a little, any.

some ***pron.*** any, a few, a number, an amount, a part, a portion.

somebody ***pron.*** someone, some person, a person, one, anybody, he, she, a certain person, this person, so-and-so, whoever.

someday ***a.*** sometime, one time, one time or another, at a future time, anytime, one day, one of these days, after a while, subsequently, finally, eventually.

somehow ***a.*** in some way, in one way or another, by some means, somehow or other, by hook or by crook, anyhow, after a fashion, with any means at one's disposal.

someone ***pron.*** some person, one, anyone; see SOMEBODY.

something ***pron.*** event, object, portion, anything, being; see also THING 1, 8.

sometime ***a.*** one day, in a time to come, in the future; see SOMEDAY.

sometimes ***a.*** at times, at intervals, now and then; see SELDOM.

somewhat ***a.*** a little, to a degree, to some extent; see MODERATELY, SLIGHTLY.

somewhere ***a.*** in some place, here and there, around, in one place or another, someplace, about, kicking around*, any old place*.

son ***n.*** male child, male offspring, descendant, stepson, heir, junior; see also CHILD, BOY.

song ***n.*** melody, lyric, strain, verse, poem, tune; see also MUSIC 1. —**for a song*** cheaply, at a bargain, for almost nothing; see CHEAPLY. —**song and dance*** drivel, boasting, pretense; see NONSENSE 1, 2.

so·no·rous (sə nôr′əs, sän′ər əs) ***adj.*** ⟦< L *sonor*, a sound⟧ **1** producing sound; resonant **2** full, deep, or rich in sound —**so·nor′i·ty** (-ə tē), *pl.* **-ties**, ***n.***

soon (so͞on) ***adv.*** ⟦OE *sona*, at once⟧ **1** in a short time *[will soon be there]* **2** promptly; quickly *[as soon as possible]* **3** ahead of time; early *[we left too soon]* **4** readily; willingly *[as soon go as stay]* —**sooner or later** inevitably; eventually

soot (soot) ***n.*** ⟦OE *sot*⟧ a black substance consisting chiefly of carbon particles, in the smoke of burning matter —**soot′y**, **-i·er**, **-i·est**, ***adj.***

sooth (so͞oth) ***n.*** ⟦OE *soth*⟧ [Archaic] truth

soothe (so͞o*th*) ***vt.*** **soothed**, **sooth′ing** ⟦OE *sothian*, prove true⟧ **1** to make calm or composed, as by gentleness or flattery **2** to relieve (pain, etc.) —**sooth′er** ***n.*** —**sooth′ing** ***adj.***

sooth·say·er (so͞oth′sā′ər) ***n.*** ⟦ME *sothseyere*, one who speaks the truth⟧ [Historical] a person who professes to predict the future —**sooth′say′ing** ***n.***

sop (säp) ***n.*** ⟦OE *sopp*⟧ **1** a piece of food, as bread, soaked in milk, etc. **2** *a)* something given to appease *b)* a bribe —***vt.***, ***vi.*** **sopped**, **sop′ping** **1** to soak, steep, etc. **2** to take up (liquid) by absorption: usually with *up*

SOP *abbrev.* standard operating procedure

soph·ism (säf′iz′əm) ***n.*** ⟦< Gr *sophos*, clever⟧ a clever and plausible but fallacious argument

soph′ist ***n.*** one who uses clever, specious reasoning —**so·phis·ti·cal** (sə fis′ti kəl) ***adj.***

so·phis·ti·cate (sə fis′tə kāt′; *for n., usually*, -kit) ***vt.*** **-cat′ed**, **-cat′ing** ⟦ult. < Gr *sophistēs*, wise man⟧ to change from a natural or simple state; make worldly-wise —***n.*** a sophisticated person

so·phis′ti·cat′ed ***adj.*** **1** not simple, naive, etc.; worldly-wise or knowledgeable, subtle, etc. **2** for sophisticated people **3** highly complex or developed —**so·phis′ti·ca′tion** ***n.***

soph·ist·ry (säf′is trē) ***n.*** misleading but clever reasoning

Soph·o·cles (säf′ə klēz′) 496?-406 B.C.; Gr. writer of tragic dramas

soph·o·more (säf′môr′, säf′ə môr′) ***n.*** ⟦< obs. *sophumer*, sophism⟧ a student in the second year of college or the tenth grade in high school —***adj.*** of or for sophomores

soph′o·mor′ic ***adj.*** of or like sophomores; seen as opinionated, immature, etc.

-so·phy (sə fē) ⟦< Gr *sophia*, wisdom⟧ *combining form* knowledge

sop·o·rif·ic (säp′ə rif′ik, sō′pə-) ***adj.*** ⟦< L *sopor*, sleep + -FIC⟧ causing sleep —***n.*** a soporific drug, etc.

sop·py (säp′ē) ***adj.*** **-pi·er**, **-pi·est** **1** very wet: also **sop′ping** **2** [Inf.] sentimental

so·pra·no (sə pran′ō, -prä′nō) ***n.***, *pl.* **-nos** or **-ni** ⟦It < *sopra*, above⟧ **1** the range of the highest voice of women or boys **2** a voice, singer, or instrument with such a range **3** a part for a soprano —***adj.*** of or for a soprano

sor·bet (sôr bā′, sôr′bət) ***n.*** ⟦Fr < Ar *sharba(t)*, a drink⟧ a tart ice, as of fruit juice

sor·cer·y (sôr′sər ē) ***n.***, *pl.* **-ies** ⟦< L *sors*, lot, chance⟧ **1** in the belief of some, the use of an evil supernatural power over people **2** charm, influence, etc. —**sor′cer·er** ***n.*** —**sor′cer·ess** ***fem.n.***

sor·did (sôr′did) ***adj.*** ⟦< L *sordes*, filth⟧ **1** dirty; filthy **2** squalid; wretched **3** base; ignoble; mean —**sor′did·ly** ***adv.*** —**sor′did·ness** ***n.***

sore (sôr) ***adj.*** **sor′er**, **sor′est** ⟦OE *sar*⟧ **1** giving or feeling pain; painful **2** filled with grief **3** causing irritation *[a sore point]* **4** [Inf.] angry; offended —***n.*** a sore, usually infected spot on the body —***adv.*** [Archaic] greatly —**sore′ness** ***n.***

sore′head′ ***n.*** [Inf.] a person easily angered, made resentful, etc.

sore′ly ***adv.*** **1** grievously; painfully **2** urgently *[sorely needed]*

sor·ghum (sôr′gəm) ***n.*** ⟦< It *sorgo*⟧ **1** a cereal grass grown for grain, syrup, fodder, etc. **2** syrup made from its juices

so·ror·i·ty (sə rôr′ə tē) ***n.***, *pl.* **-ties** ⟦< L *soror*, sister⟧ a group of women or girls joined together for fellowship, etc., as in some colleges

sor·rel[1] (sôr′əl, sär′-) ***n.*** ⟦< OFr *surele*⟧ any of various plants with edible sour leaves

sor·rel[2] (sôr′əl, sär′-) ***n.*** ⟦< OFr *sor*, light brown⟧ **1** light reddish brown **2** a horse, etc. of this color

sor·row (sär′ō, sôr′ō) ***n.*** ⟦OE *sorg*⟧ **1** mental suffering caused by loss, disappointment, etc.; grief **2** that which causes such suffering —***vi.*** to grieve —**sor′row·ful** ***adj.*** —**sor′row·ful·ly** ***adv.***

sor·ry (sär′ē, sôr′ē) ***adj.*** **-ri·er**, **-ri·est** ⟦< OE *sar*, sore⟧ **1** full of sorrow, pity, or regret **2** inferior; poor **3** wretched —**sor′ri·ly** ***adv.*** —**sor′ri·ness** ***n.***

sort (sôrt) ***n.*** ⟦< L *sors*, lot, chance⟧ **1** any group of related things; kind; class **2** quality or type —***vt.*** to arrange according to class or kind —**of sorts** of an inferior kind: also **of a sort** —**out of sorts** [Inf.] not in good humor or health —**sort of** [Inf.] somewhat

sor·tie (sôrt′ē) ***n.*** ⟦Fr < *sortir*, go out⟧ **1** a quick raid by forces from a besieged place **2** one mission by a single military plane

SOS (es′ō′es′) ***n.*** a signal of distress, as in wireless telegraphy

so′-so′ ***adv.***, ***adj.*** just passably or passable; fair

sot (sät) ***n.*** ⟦< ML *sottus*, a fool⟧ a drunkard —**sot′tish** ***adj.***

sot·to vo·ce (sät′ō vō′chē) ⟦It, under the voice⟧ in a low voice, so as not to be overheard

souf·flé (so͞o flā′) ***n.*** ⟦Fr < L *sufflare*, puff out⟧ a baked food made light and puffy by beaten egg whites added before baking

sough (sou, suf) ***n.*** ⟦OE *swogan*, to sound⟧ a soft sighing or rustling sound —***vi.*** to make a sough

sought (sôt) ***vt.***, ***vi.*** *pt. & pp. of* SEEK

soul (sōl) ***n.*** ⟦OE *sawol*⟧ **1** an entity without material reality, regarded as the spiritual part of a person **2** the moral or emotional nature of a person **3** spiritual or emotional warmth, force, etc. **4** vital or essential part, quality, etc. **5** a person *[I didn't see a soul]* **6** the deep spiritual and emotional quality of black American culture; also, the expression of this, as in music —***adj.*** of, for, or like black Americans

THESAURUS

soon ***a.*** before long, in a short time, presently, in due time, shortly, forthwith, quickly, in a minute, in a second, in short order, anon*; see also SOMEDAY.

sooner or later ***a.*** eventually, certainly, inevitably; see SOMEDAY, SURELY.

soot ***n.*** carbon, smoke, grit; see RESIDUE.

soothe ***v.*** quiet, tranquilize, alleviate, calm, relax, mollify, help, pacify, lighten, unburden, console, cheer; see also COMFORT 1, EASE 1, 2, RELIEVE.

sophisticated ***a.*** refined, adult, well-bred; see CULTURED, MATURE.

sophistication ***n.*** elegance, refinement, finesse; see COMPOSURE.

soppy ***a.*** soaked, drippy, damp; see WET 1, 2.

sorcerer ***n.*** sorceress, wizard, witch, alchemist; see also MAGICIAN.

sorcery ***n.*** enchantment, divination, alchemy; see MAGIC 1, WITCHCRAFT.

sore ***a.*** **1** [Tender] painful, hurtful, raw, aching, sensitive, irritated, irritable, bruised, inflamed, burned, unpleasant, ulcerated, abscessed, uncomfortable. **2** [*Angry] irked, resentful, irritated; see ANGRY.

sore ***n.*** cut, bruise, wound, boil, lesion, ulcer, hurt, abscess, gash, sting, soreness, discomfort, injury; see also PAIN 2.

sorely ***a.*** extremely, painfully, badly; see SO 1, VERY.

sorrow ***n.*** sadness, anguish, pain; see GRIEF.

sorrow ***v.*** bemoan, lament, be sad; see MOURN.

sorrowful ***a.*** grieved, afflicted, in sorrow, in mourning, depressed, dejected; see also SAD 1.

sorrowfully ***a.*** regretfully, weeping, in sadness; see SADLY.

sorry ***a.*** **1** [Penitent] contrite, repentant, softened, remorseful, regretful, conscience-stricken, sorrowful, touched, apologetic. **2** [Inadequate in quantity or quality] poor, paltry, trifling, cheap, mean, shabby, stunted, beggarly, scrubby, small, trivial, unimportant, insignificant, worthless, dismal, pitiful, despicable; see also INADEQUATE.—*Ant.* ENOUGH, plentiful, adequate.

sort ***n.*** species, description, class; see KIND 2, VARIETY 2. —**out of sorts*** irritated, upset, in a bad mood; see ANGRY, TROUBLED.

sort ***v.*** file, arrange, class; see CLASSIFY, DISTRIBUTE, ORDER 3.

sort of* ***a.*** somewhat, to a degree, kind of*; see MODERATELY, SLIGHTLY.

so-so ***a.*** ordinary, mediocre, average; see COMMON 1, DULL 4, FAIR 2.

sought ***a.*** wanted, needed, desired; see HUNTED.

soul ***n.*** **1** [Essential nature] spiritual being, heart, substance, individuality, disposition, cause, personality, force, essence, genius, principle, ego, psyche, life. **2** [The more lofty human qualities] courage, love, honor, duty, idealism, heroism, art, poetry, sense of beauty. **3** [A person] human being, person, being; see PERSON 1.

soul food [Inf.] food items, as chitterlings, popular orig. in the South, esp. among blacks
soul'ful *adj.* full of deep feeling —**soul'ful·ly** *adv.* — **soul'ful·ness** *n.*
soul mate [Inf.] a person, esp. of the opposite sex, with whom one has a deeply personal relationship
sound[1] (sound) *n.* ⟦< L *sonus*⟧ **1** that which is heard, resulting from stimulation of auditory nerves by vibrations (**sound waves**) in the air; also the vibrations **2** the distance within which a sound may be heard; earshot **3** the mental impression produced *[*the *sound* of his report*]* —*vi.* **1** to make a sound **2** to seem upon being heard *[*to *sound* troubled*]* —*vt.* **1** to cause to sound **2** to signal, express, etc. **3** to utter distinctly *[*to *sound* one's r's*]* —**sound'less** *adj.*
sound[2] (sound) *adj.* ⟦OE (*ge*)*sund*⟧ **1** free from defect, damage, or decay **2** healthy *[*a *sound* body*]* **3** safe; stable *[*a *sound* bank*]* **4** based on valid reasoning; sensible **5** thorough; forceful *[*a *sound* defeat*]* **6** deep and undisturbed: said of sleep **7** honest, loyal, etc. —*adv.* deeply *[sound* asleep*]* —**sound'ly** *adv.* —**sound'ness** *n.*
sound[3] (sound) *n.* ⟦< OE & ON *sund*⟧ **1** a wide channel linking two large bodies of water or separating an island from the mainland **2** a long inlet or arm of the sea
sound[4] (sound) *vt., vi.* ⟦< L *sub,* under + *unda,* a wave⟧ **1** to measure the depth of (water), esp. with a weighted line **2** to try to find out the opinions of (a person), usually subtly: often with *out* —**sound'ing** *n.*
sound barrier the large increase of air resistance of some aircraft flying near the speed of sound
sound bite a brief, quotable remark, as by a politician, suitable for use in radio or TV news
sounding board **1** something to increase resonance or reflect sound: often **sound'board'** *n.* **2** a person on whom one tests one's ideas, etc.
sound'proof' *adj.* that keeps sound from coming through —*vt.* to make soundproof
sound'stage' *n.* an enclosed soundproof area for producing films or TV shows
sound'track' *n.* the sound portion of a film
soup (so͞op) *n.* ⟦Fr *soupe*⟧ a liquid food made by cooking meat, vegetables, etc. in water, milk, etc. —**soup up** [Slang] to increase the capacity for speed of (an engine, etc.)
soup·çon (so͞op sōn') *n.* ⟦Fr < L *suspicio,* suspicion⟧ **1** a slight trace, as of a flavor **2** a tiny bit
soup·y (so͞o'pē) *adj.* **-i·er, -i·est** **1** watery like soup **2** [Inf.] foggy
sour (sour) *adj.* ⟦OE *sur*⟧ **1** having the sharp, acid taste of vinegar, etc. **2** made acid or rank by fermentation **3** cross; bad-tempered **4** distasteful or unpleasant —*vt., vi.* to make or become sour —**sour'ly** *adv.* —**sour'ness** *n.*
source (sôrs) *n.* ⟦< L *surgere,* to rise⟧ **1** a spring, etc. from which a stream arises **2** a place or thing from which something originates or develops **3** a person, book, etc. that provides information
sour cream thickened and soured cream
sour·dough (sour'dō') *n.* **1** bread made from fermented dough **2** a lone prospector for gold, etc., as in the W U.S.
sour grapes a scorning of something only because it cannot be had or done
sour'puss' (-poos') *n.* [Slang] a gloomy or disagreeable person
souse (sous) *n.* ⟦< OHG *sulza,* brine⟧ **1** a pickled food, as pigs' feet **2** liquid for pickling; brine **3** a plunging into a liquid **4** [Slang] a drunkard —*vt., vi.* **soused, sous'ing** **1** to pickle **2** to plunge into a liquid **3** to make or become soaking wet
soused *adj.* [Slang] drunk
south (south) *n.* ⟦OE *suth*⟧ **1** the direction to the left of one facing the sunset (180° on the compass) **2** a region in or toward this direction —*adj.* **1** in, of, or toward the south **2** from the south —*adv.* in or toward the south — **go south** [Inf.] to decline, deteriorate, fail, etc. —**the South** that part of the U.S. south of Pennsylvania and the Ohio River, and generally east of the Mississippi; specif., the states that formed the Confederacy
South Africa country in southernmost Africa: 472,855 sq. mi.; pop. 37,714,000
South America S continent in the Western Hemisphere: *c.* 6,900,000 sq. mi.; pop. *c.* 318,000,000 —**South American**
South Bend city in N Indiana: pop. 106,000
South Car·o·li·na (kar'ə lī'nə) state of the SE U.S.: 30,111 sq. mi.; pop. 3,487,000; cap. Columbia: abbrev. *SC* —**South Car'o·lin'i·an** (-lin'ē ən)
South China Sea arm of the W Pacific, between SE Asia & the Philippines
South Da·ko·ta (də kōt'ə) Midwestern state of the U.S.: 75,898 sq. mi.; pop. 696,000; cap. Pierre: abbrev. *SD* — **South Da·ko'tan**
south'east' *n.* **1** the direction halfway between south and east **2** a region in or toward this direction —*adj.* **1** in, of, or toward the southeast **2** from the southeast — *adv.* in or toward the southeast —**south'east'er·ly** *adj., adv.* —**south'east'ern** *adj.* —**south'east'ward** *adv., adj.* —**south'east'wards** *adv.*
south·er·ly (su*th*'ər lē) *adj., adv.* **1** toward the south **2** from the south
south·ern (su*th*'ərn) *adj.* **1** in, of, or toward the south **2** from the south **3** of the south
south'ern·er *n.* a person born or living in the south

THESAURUS

sound[1] *v.* vibrate, echo, resound, reverberate, shout, sing, whisper, murmur, clatter, clank, rattle, blow, blare, bark, ring out, explode, thunder, buzz, rumble, hum, jabber, jangle, whine, crash, bang, boom, burst, chatter, creak, clang, roar, babble, clap, patter, prattle, clink, toot, cackle, clack, thud, slam, smash, thump, snort, shriek, moan, quaver, trumpet, croak, caw, quack, squawk.

sound[1,3] *n.* **1** [Something audible] vibration, din, racket; see NOISE 1. **2** [The quality of something audible] tonality, resonance, note, timbre, tone, pitch, intonation, accent, character, quality, softness, lightness, loudness, reverberation, ringing, vibration, modulation, discord, consonance, harmony. **3** [Water between an island and the mainland] strait, bay, bight; see CHANNEL.

sound[2] *a.* **1** [Healthy] hale, hearty, well; see HEALTHY. **2** [Firm] solid, stable, safe; see RELIABLE. **3** [Sensible] reasonable, rational, prudent; see SENSIBLE. **4** [Free from defect] flawless, unimpaired, undecayed; see WHOLE 2.

sounding *a.* ringing, thudding, bumping, roaring, calling, thundering, booming, crashing, clattering, clinking, clanging, tinkling, whispering, pinging, rattling, rumbling, ticking, crying, clicking, echoing, pattering, clucking, chirping, peeping, growling, grunting, bellowing, murmuring, whirring, making noise, making a sound, screeching, screaming, squealing.

sound out *v.* probe, feel out, feel, put out a feeler, send up a trial balloon, see how the land lies, get the lay of the land, see which way the wind blows; see also EXAMINE, EXPERIMENT.

soundproof *a.* soundproofed, insulated from noise, soundless; see QUIET.

soup *n.* *Soups include the following:* broth, bouillon, consommé, purée, bisque, chowder, gumbo, pottage, *potage* (French); chicken, beef, vegetable, tomato, potato, celery, lentil, mushroom, navy bean, barley, cheese, split pea, French onion, oxtail, mock turtle, wonton, egg-drop, matzo ball, etc. soup; minestrone, clam chowder, oyster stew, vichyssoise, bouillabaisse, borscht, gazpacho, mulligatawny, corn chowder, pepper pot, cock-a-leekie, Scotch broth; see also FOOD, STEW.

soupçon *n.* trace, drop, hint; see DASH 3.

sour *a.* acid, tart, vinegary, fermented, rancid, musty, turned, acrid, salty, bitter, caustic, cutting, stinging, acrid, harsh, irritating, unsavory, tangy, briny, brackish, sharp, keen, biting, pungent, curdled, unripe. — **turn sour** putrefy, rot, decay; see SPOIL.

sour *v.* turn, ferment, spoil, make sour, curdle.

source *n.* beginning, cause, root; see ORIGIN 2, 3.

south *a.* **1** [Situated to the south] southern, southward, on the south side of, in the south, toward the equator, southernmost, toward the South Pole, southerly, tropical, equatorial, in the torrid zone. **2** [Moving toward the south] southward, to the south, southbound, headed south, southerly, in a southerly direction, toward the equator. **3** [Coming from the south] southerly, headed north, northbound, out of the south, from the south, toward the North Pole.

south *n.* southland, southern section, southern region, tropics, tropical region, equatorial region, Southern Hemisphere.

South *n.* South Atlantic States, the Confederacy, the Old South, antebellum South, Southern United States, the New South, the Deep South, Sunbelt, way down south, Dixie, southland.

southeast *a.* SE, southeastern, southeasterly, southeastward, south-southeast, southeast by south, southeast by east; see also DIRECTION.

southern *a.* in the south, of the south, from the south, toward the south, southerly; see also SOUTH 1.

Southern Hemisphere that half of the earth south of the equator
southern lights [*also* **S- L-**] aurora australis
south·paw (south'pô') ***n.*** [Slang] a left-handed person; esp., a left-handed baseball pitcher
South Pole the southern end of the earth's axis
South Sea Islands the islands in the S Pacific
south'ward ***adv., adj.*** toward the south: also **south'wards** ***adv.***
south'west' ***n.*** **1** the direction halfway between south and west **2** a region in or toward this direction —***adj.*** **1** in, of, or toward the southwest **2** from the southwest —***adv.*** in or toward the southwest —**south'west'er·ly** ***adj., adv.*** —**south'west'ern** ***adj.*** —**south'west'ward** ***adv., adj.*** —**south'west'wards** ***adv.***
sou·ve·nir (sōō'və nir') ***n.*** ⟦< Fr < L *subvenire*, come to mind⟧ something kept as a reminder
sov·er·eign (säv'rən, -ər in) ***adj.*** ⟦< L *super*, above⟧ **1** above all others; chief; supreme **2** supreme in power, rank, etc. **3** independent of all others *[a sovereign state]* —***n.*** **1** a monarch or ruler **2** a British gold coin worth one pound: no longer minted
sov'er·eign·ty ***n.*** **1** the status, rule, etc. of a sovereign **2** supreme and independent political authority
so·vi·et (sō'vē et') ***n.*** ⟦Russ *sovyet*, council⟧ **1** in Russia, Uzbekistan, and, formerly, the Soviet Union, any of the various elected governing councils, local, intermediate, and national **2** any similar council in a socialist governing system —***adj.*** **[S-]** of or connected with the Soviet Union
Soviet Union UNION OF SOVIET SOCIALIST REPUBLICS
sow[1] (sou) ***n.*** ⟦OE *sugu*⟧ an adult female pig
sow[2] (sō) ***vt.*** **sowed, sown** (sōn) or **sowed, sow'ing** ⟦OE *sawan*⟧ **1** to scatter (seed) for growing **2** to plant seed in (a field, etc.) **3** to spread or scatter —***vi.*** to sow seed —**sow'er** ***n.***
sox (säks) ***n.*** *alt. pl. of* SOCK[1]
soy (soi) ***n.*** ⟦Jpn⟧ **1** a dark, salty sauce made from fermented soybeans: in full **soy sauce** **2** the soybean plant or its seeds Also [Chiefly Brit.] **soy·a** (soi'ə)
soy'bean' ***n.*** **1** a plant widely grown for its seeds, which contain much protein and oil **2** its seed
sp *abbrev.* **1** special **2** spelling
Sp *abbrev.* **1** Spain **2** Spanish
spa (spä) ***n.*** ⟦after *Spa*, resort in Belgium⟧ **1** a health resort having a mineral spring **2** a commercial establishment with exercise rooms, sauna baths, etc.
space (spās) ***n.*** ⟦< L *spatium*⟧ **1** *a)* the continuous, three-dimensional expanse in which all things are contained *b)* OUTER SPACE **2** *a)* the distance, area, etc. between or within things *b)* room for something *[a parking space]* **3** an interval of time —***vt.*** **spaced, spac'ing** to arrange with space or spaces between
space'craft' ***n., pl.*** **-craft'** any vehicle or satellite for orbiting the earth, space travel, etc.
spaced'-out' ***adj.*** [Slang] under or as if under the influence of a drug: also **spaced**
space'flight' ***n.*** flight in a spacecraft
space heater a small heating unit for a room or other confined area
space'man' (-man', -mən) ***n., pl.*** **-men'** (-men', -mən) an astronaut or any of the crew of a spaceship
space'port' ***n.*** a center for assembling, testing, and launching spacecraft
space'ship' ***n.*** a spacecraft, esp. if manned
space shuttle an airplanelike spacecraft designed to carry personnel and equipment between earth and a space station
space station (or **platform**) a spacecraft in long-term orbit serving as a launch pad, research center, etc.
space'suit' ***n.*** a garment pressurized for use by astronauts
space'walk' ***n.*** the act of an astronaut in moving about in space outside a spacecraft
space·y or **spac·y** (spā'sē) ***adj.*** **-i·er, -i·est** [Slang] **1** SPACED-OUT **2** *a)* eccentric or unconventional *b)* flighty, irresponsible, neurotic, etc. —**spac'i·ness** ***n.***
spa·cious (spā'shəs) ***adj.*** having more than enough space; vast —**spa'cious·ly** ***adv.*** —**spa'cious·ness** ***n.***
Spack·le (spak'əl) ⟦prob. < Ger *spachtel*, spatula⟧ *trademark for* a powder mixed with water to form a paste that dries hard, used to fill holes, cracks, etc. in wallboard, wood, etc. —***n.*** **[s-]** this substance —***vt.*** **-led, -ling** **[s-]** to fill or cover with spackle
spade[1] (spād) ***n.*** ⟦OE *spadu*⟧ a flat-bladed, long-handled digging tool, like a shovel —***vt., vi.*** **spad'ed, spad'ing** to dig with or as with a spade —**spade'ful** ***n.***
spade[2] (spād) ***n.*** ⟦ult. < Gr *spathē*, flat blade⟧ **1** any of a suit of playing cards marked with black figures like this ♠ **2** [*pl.*] this suit
spade'work' ***n.*** preparatory work for some main project, esp. when tiresome
spa·dix (spā'diks) ***n., pl.*** **-dix·es** or **-di·ces'** (-də sēz') ⟦ult. < Gr⟧ a spike of tiny flowers, usually enclosed in a spathe
spa·ghet·ti (spə get'ē) ***n.*** ⟦It < *spago*, small cord⟧ pasta in long, thin strings, boiled or steamed
Spain (spān) country in SW Europe: 190,191 sq. mi.; pop. 38,872,000
spake (spāk) ***vi., vt.*** *archaic pt. of* SPEAK
span (span) ***n.*** ⟦OE *sponn*⟧ **1** the distance (about 9 in.) between the tips of the thumb and little finger **2** *a)* the full extent between any two limits *b)* the distance between ends or supports *[the span of an arch]* *c)* the full duration (*of*) *[span of attention]* **3** a part between two supports —***vt.*** **spanned, span'ning** **1** to measure, esp. by the span of the hand **2** to extend over
Span *abbrev.* Spanish
span·dex (span'deks') ***n.*** ⟦< EXPAND⟧ an elastic synthetic fiber used in girdles, etc.
span·gle (spaŋ'gəl) ***n.*** ⟦< OE *spang*, a clasp⟧ a small piece of bright metal sewn on fabric for decoration —***vt.*** **-gled, -gling** to decorate as with spangles
Span·iard (span'yərd) ***n.*** a person born or living in Spain
span·iel (span'yəl) ***n.*** ⟦< MFr *espagnol*, lit., Spanish⟧ any of several breeds of dog with large, drooping ears and a dense, wavy coat
Span·ish (span'ish) ***adj.*** of Spain or its people, language, etc. —***n.*** the language of Spain and Spanish America —**the Spanish** the people of Spain
Spanish America those countries south of the U.S. in which Spanish is the chief language —**Span'ish-A·mer'i·can** ***adj., n.***
Spanish moss a rootless plant that grows in long, graceful strands from tree branches in the SE U.S.
spank (spaŋk) ***vt.*** ⟦echoic⟧ to strike with the open hand, etc., esp. on the buttocks, as in punishment —***n.*** a smack given in spanking
spank'ing ***adj.*** **1** swiftly moving **2** brisk: said of a breeze —***adv.*** [Inf.] completely *[spanking new]*
spar[1] (spär) ***n.*** ⟦< ON *sparri* or MDu *sparre*⟧ any pole, as a mast or yard, supporting a sail of a ship
spar[2] (spär) ***vi.*** **sparred, spar'ring** ⟦prob. < It *parare*, to parry⟧ **1** to box with feinting movements, landing few heavy blows **2** to wrangle
spare (sper) ***vt.*** **spared, spar'ing** ⟦OE *sparian*⟧ **1** to refrain from killing, hurting, etc. **2** to save or free (a person) from something **3** to avoid using or use frugally **4** to part with or give up conveniently *[can you spare a dime?]* —***adj.*** **1** not in regular use; extra **2** free *[spare*

THESAURUS

southwest ***a.*** SW, southwestern, southwesterly, southwestward, south-southwest, southwest by south, southwest by west; see also DIRECTION.
souvenir ***n.*** memento, keepsake, relic; see MEMORIAL.
sow[2] ***v.*** seed, scatter, plant, broadcast, drill in, drill, strew, put in small grain, do the seeding.
sowed ***a.*** scattered, cast, broadcast, spread, distributed, strewn, dispersed, planted.
spa ***n.*** baths, spring, health resort; see RESORT 2.
space ***n.*** **1** [The infinite regions] outer space, infinite distance, infinity, interstellar space, interplanetary space, the universe, cosmos, solar system, galaxy, the beyond; see also EXPANSE.—*Ant.* BOUNDARY, measure, definite area. **2** [Room] expanse, scope, range; see EXTENT. **3** [A place] area, location, reservation; see PLACE 2.
spacecraft ***n.*** rocket, spaceship, space shuttle, capsule, orbiter, space station, weather satellite, spy satellite, lunar module, UFO, unidentified flying object, flying saucer; see also SATELLITE 2.
spaced ***a.*** divided, distributed, dispersed; see SEPARATED.
spacious ***a.*** capacious, roomy, vast; see BIG 1.
spade[1] ***n.*** shovel, garden tool, digging tool; see TOOL 1.
Spanish ***a.*** Spanish-speaking, Iberian, Romance, Hispanic, Latino, Central American, South American, Spanish-American, Mexican, Latin American.
spank ***v.*** whip, chastise, thrash; see BEAT 1, PUNISH.
spare ***a.*** superfluous, auxiliary, additional; see EXTRA.
spare ***v.*** pardon, forgive, be merciful; see PITY, SAVE 1.

time] **3** meager; scanty **4** lean; thin —***n.*** **1** a spare, or extra, thing **2** *Bowling* a knocking down of all the pins with two rolls of the ball —**spare'ly** ***adv.***

spare'ribs' ***pl.n.*** a cut of meat, esp. pork, consisting of the thin end of the ribs

spar'ing ***adj.*** careful; frugal —**spar'ing·ly** ***adv.***

spark (spärk) ***n.*** ⟦OE *spearca*⟧ **1** a glowing bit of matter, esp. one thrown off by a fire **2** any flash or sparkle **3** a particle or trace **4** a brief flash of light accompanying an electric discharge as through air —***vi.*** to make sparks —***vt.*** to stir up; activate

spar·kle (spär'kəl) ***vi.*** **-kled**, **-kling** **1** to throw off sparks **2** to glitter **3** to effervesce or bubble **4** to be brilliant and lively —***n.*** **1** a sparkling **2** brilliance; liveliness —**spar'kler** (-klər) ***n.***

spark plug an electrical device fitted into a cylinder of an engine to ignite the fuel mixture by making sparks

spar·row (spar'ō) ***n.*** ⟦OE *spearwa*⟧ any of numerous small, perching songbirds

sparse (spärs) ***adj.*** ⟦< L *spargere,* scatter⟧ thinly spread; not dense —**sparse'ly** ***adv.*** —**sparse'ness** or **spar'si·ty** (-sə tē) ***n.***

Spar·ta (spärt'ə) ancient city in S Greece: a military power

Spar·tan (spärt''n) ***adj.*** **1** of ancient Sparta or its people or culture **2** like the Spartans; warlike, hardy, disciplined, etc. —***n.*** a Spartan person

spasm (spaz'əm) ***n.*** ⟦< Gr *spasmos*⟧ **1** a sudden, involuntary muscular contraction **2** any sudden, violent, temporary activity, feeling, etc. —***vi.*** to undergo a spasm

spas·mod·ic (spaz mäd'ik) ***adj.*** ⟦see prec. & -OID⟧ of or like spasms; fitful —**spas·mod'i·cal·ly** ***adv.***

spas·tic (spas'tik) ***adj.*** of or characterized by muscular spasms —***n.*** one having spastic paralysis

spat[1] (spat) [Inf.] ***n.*** ⟦prob. echoic⟧ a brief, petty quarrel —***vi.*** **spat'ted**, **spat'ting** to engage in a spat

spat[2] (spat) ***n.*** ⟦< *spatterdash,* a legging⟧ a gaiterlike covering for the instep and ankle

spat[3] (spat) ***vt.***, ***vi.*** *alt. pt. & pp. of* SPIT[2]

spate (spāt) ***n.*** ⟦< ?⟧ an unusually large flow, as of words

spathe (spā*th*) ***n.*** ⟦< L *spatha,* a flat blade⟧ a large, leaflike part enclosing a flower cluster

spa·tial (spā'shəl) ***adj.*** ⟦< L *spatium,* space⟧ of, or existing in, space

spat·ter (spat'ər) ***vt.***, ***vi.*** ⟦< ?⟧ **1** to scatter or spurt out in drops **2** to splash —***n.*** **1** a spattering **2** a mark caused by spattering

spat·u·la (spach'ə lə) ***n.*** ⟦L < Gr *spathē,* flat blade⟧ an implement with a broad, flat, flexible blade for spreading or blending foods, paints, etc.

spat'u·late' (-lāt') ***adj.*** shaped like a spatula

spav·in (spav'in) ***n.*** ⟦< MFr *esparvain*⟧ a disease that lames horses in the hock joint —**spav'ined** ***adj.***

spawn (spôn) ***vt.***, ***vi.*** ⟦< L *expandere:* see EXPAND⟧ **1** to produce or deposit (eggs, sperm, or young) **2** to bring forth or produce prolifically —***n.*** **1** the mass of eggs or young produced by fish, mollusks, etc. **2** something produced, esp. in great quantity, as offspring

spay (spā) ***vt.*** ⟦< Gr *spathē,* flat blade⟧ to sterilize (a female animal) by removing the ovaries

speak (spēk) ***vi.*** **spoke**, **spo'ken**, **speak'ing** ⟦OE *sp(r)ecan*⟧ **1** to utter words; talk **2** to communicate as by talking **3** to make a request (*for*) **4** to make a speech —***vt.*** **1** to make known as by speaking **2** to use (a given language) in speaking **3** to utter (words) —**so to speak** that is to say — **speak out** (or **up**) to speak clearly or freely —**speak to** to respond to, deal with, etc. —**speak well for** to say or indicate something favorable about

speak'-eas'y (-ē'zē) ***n.***, *pl.* **-ies** [Old Slang] a place where alcoholic drinks are sold illegally

speak'er ***n.*** **1** one who speaks; esp., *a)* an orator *b)* the presiding officer of various lawmaking bodies *c)* [**S-**] the presiding officer of the U.S. House of Representatives **2** a device for converting electrical signals to audible sound waves

spear (spir) ***n.*** ⟦OE *spere*⟧ **1** a weapon with a long shaft and a sharp point, for thrusting or throwing **2** ⟦var. of SPIRE⟧ a long blade or shoot, as of grass —***vt.*** **1** to pierce or stab with or as with a spear **2** [Inf.] to reach out and catch (a baseball, etc.)

spear'fish' ***n.***, *pl.* **-fish'** or (for different species) **-fish'es** any of a group of large food and game fishes of the open seas —***vi.*** to fish with a spear, etc.

spear'head' ***n.*** **1** the pointed head of a spear **2** the leading person or group, as in an attack —***vt.*** to take the lead in (an attack, etc.)

spear'mint' ***n.*** ⟦prob. from the shape of its flowers⟧ a fragrant plant of the mint family, used for flavoring

spec[1] (spek) [Inf.] ***n.*** *short for:* **1** SPECIFICATION (sense 1) **2** SPECULATION —**on spec** **1** according to specification(s) **2** as a speculation or gamble

spec[2] *abbrev.* **1** special **2** specifically

spe·cial (spesh'əl) ***adj.*** ⟦< L *species,* kind⟧ **1** distinctive or unique **2** exceptional; unusual **3** highly valued **4** of or for a particular purpose, etc. **5** not general; specific —***n.*** a special thing, as, specif., a sale item —**spe'cial·ly** ***adv.***

special delivery mail delivery by a special messenger, for a special fee

spe'cial·ist ***n.*** one who specializes in a particular field of study, work, etc.

spe'cial·ize' ***vi.*** **-ized'**, **-iz'ing** to concentrate on a particular branch of study, work, etc. —**spe'cial·i·za'tion** ***n.***

spe'cial·ty ***n.***, *pl.* **-ties** **1** a special quality, feature, etc. **2** a special interest, study, etc.

spe·cie (spē'shē, -sē) ***n.*** ⟦< L *species,* kind⟧ coin, rather than paper money

spe·cies (spē'shēz, -sēz) ***n.***, *pl.* **-cies** ⟦L, appearance, kind⟧ **1** a distinct kind; sort **2** any of the groups of related plants or animals that usually breed only among themselves: similar species form a genus

specif *abbrev.* specifically

spe·cif·ic (spə sif'ik) ***adj.*** ⟦< L *species,* kind + *-ficus,* -FIC⟧ **1** definite; explicit **2** peculiar to or characteristic of something **3** of a particular kind **4** specially indicated as a cure for some disease —***n.*** **1** a specific cure **2** a distinct item or detail; particular —**spe·cif'i·cal·ly** ***adv.***

-spe·cif'ic *combining form* limited or specific to

spec·i·fi·ca·tion (spes'ə fi kā'shən) ***n.*** **1** [*usually pl.*] a statement or enumeration of particulars, as to size, quality, or terms **2** something specified

specific gravity the ratio of the weight or mass of a given volume of a substance to that of an equal volume of another substance (as water) used as a standard

spec·i·fy (spes'ə fī') ***vt.*** **-fied'**, **-fy'ing** ⟦< LL *specificus,* specific⟧ **1** to state definitely **2** to include in a set of specifications

THESAURUS

spark ***n.*** glitter, flash, sparkle; see FIRE 1.

sparkle ***v.*** glitter, glisten, twinkle; see SHINE 1.

sparse ***a.*** scattered, scanty, meager; see INADEQUATE, RARE 1.

spasm ***n.*** convulsion, seizure, contraction; see FIT 1.

spatter ***v.*** splash, spot, wet, sprinkle, soil, scatter, stain, dash, dot, speckle, shower, dribble, spray.

speak ***v.*** **1** [To utter] vocalize, say, express; see UTTER. **2** [To communicate] converse, discourse, chat; see TALK 1. **3** [To deliver a speech] lecture, declaim, deliver; see ADDRESS 2. —**so to speak** that is to say, in a manner of speaking, as the saying goes; see ACCORDINGLY. —**speak out** insist, assert, make oneself heard; see DECLARE. —**speak well for** commend, recommend, support; see PRAISE 1. —**to speak of** worth mentioning, significant, noteworthy.

speaker ***n.*** speechmaker, orator, lecturer, public speaker, preacher, spokesman, spokeswoman, spokesperson, spellbinder, talker.

speaking ***a.*** oral, verbal, vocal; see TALKING.

spear ***n.*** lance, javelin, bayonet; see WEAPON.

special ***a.*** specific, particular, appropriate, peculiar, proper, individual, unique, restricted, exclusive, defined, limited, reserved, specialized, determinate, distinct, select, choice, definite, marked, designated, earmarked; see also UNUSUAL 1, 2.

special* ***n.*** sale item, feature, prepared dish; see MEAL 2, SALE 1, 2.

specialist ***n.*** expert, devotee, master, ace, virtuoso, veteran, scholar, professional, authority, connoisseur, maven*.—*Ant.* AMATEUR, beginner, novice.

specialize ***v.*** work in exclusively, go in for*, limit oneself to; see PRACTICE 2.

specialized ***a.*** specific, for a particular purpose, functional; see SPECIAL.

specialty ***n.*** pursuit, specialization, special interest; see HOBBY, JOB 1.

species ***n.*** group, type, sort; see DIVISION 2, KIND 2.

specific ***a.*** particular, distinct, precise; see DEFINITE 1, 2, SPECIAL.

specifically ***a.*** particularly, individually, characteristically; see ESPECIALLY.

specification ***n.*** designation, stipulation, written requirement; see PLAN 1, 2, REQUIREMENT 1.

specified ***a.*** particularized, precise, detailed; see NECESSARY.

specify ***v.*** name, designate, stipulate; see CHOOSE.

spec·i·men (spes′ə mən) ***n.*** ⟦L < *specere,* see⟧ **1** a part or individual used as a sample of a whole or group **2** *Med.* a sample, as of urine, for analysis

spe·cious (spē′shəs) ***adj.*** ⟦< L *species,* appearance⟧ seeming to be good, sound, correct, etc. without really being so —**spe′cious·ly** ***adv.***

speck (spek) ***n.*** ⟦OE *specca*⟧ **1** a small spot, mark, etc. **2** a very small bit —***vt.*** to mark with specks

speck·le (spek′əl) ***n.*** a small speck —***vt.*** **-led**, **-ling** to mark with speckles

specs (speks) ***pl.n.*** [Inf.] **1** spectacles; eyeglasses **2** specifications

spec·ta·cle (spek′tə kəl) ***n.*** ⟦< L *specere,* see⟧ **1** a remarkable sight **2** a large public show **3** [*pl.*] [Old-fashioned] a pair of eyeglasses

spec·tac·u·lar (spek tak′yə lər) ***adj.*** unusual to a striking degree —***n.*** an elaborate show or display —**spec·tac′u·lar·ly** ***adv.***

spec·ta·tor (spek′tāt′ər) ***n.*** ⟦L < *spectare,* behold⟧ one who watches without taking an active part

spec·ter (spek′tər) ***n.*** ⟦< L *spectare,* behold⟧ a ghost; apparition: Brit. sp. **spec′tre**

spec′tral (-trəl) ***adj.*** **1** of or like a specter **2** of a spectrum

spec·tro·scope (spek′trə skōp′) ***n.*** ⟦< Ger, ult. < L *spectare*, behold⟧ an optical instrument used for forming spectra for study —**spec′tro·scop′ic** (-skäp′ik) ***adj.*** —**spec·tros′co·py** (-träs′kə pē) ***n.***

spec·trum (spek′trəm) ***n.***, *pl.* **-tra** (-trə) or **-trums** ⟦< L: see SPECTER⟧ **1** the series of colored bands separated and arranged in order of their respective wavelengths by the passage of white light through a prism, etc. **2** a continuous range or entire extent

spec·u·late (spek′yə lāt′) ***vi.*** **-lat′ed**, **-lat′ing** ⟦< L *specere,* see⟧ **1** to ponder; esp., to conjecture **2** to take part in any risky venture (as buying or selling certain stocks, etc.) on the chance of making huge profits —**spec′u·la′tion** ***n.*** —**spec′u·la′tive** (-lāt′iv, -lə tiv) ***adj.*** —**spec′u·la′tor** ***n.***

speech (spēch) ***n.*** ⟦< OE *sprecan,* speak⟧ **1** the act of speaking **2** the power to speak **3** that which is spoken; utterance, remark, etc. **4** a talk given to an audience **5** the language of a certain people

speech′less ***adj.*** **1** incapable of speech **2** silent, as from shock

speed (spēd) ***n.*** ⟦OE *spæd,* success⟧ **1** swiftness; quick motion **2** rate of movement; velocity **3** an arrangement of gears, as for the drive of an engine **4** [Inf.] one's kind of taste, capability, etc. **5** [Slang] any of various amphetamine compounds —***vi.*** **sped** (sped) or **speed′ed**, **speed′ing** to move rapidly, esp. too rapidly —***vt.*** **1** to help to succeed; aid **2** to cause to speed —**speed up** to increase in speed —**up to speed** **1** working, etc. at full speed **2** [Inf.] fully informed —**speed′er** ***n.***

speed′boat′ ***n.*** a fast motorboat

speed·om·e·ter (spi däm′ət ər) ***n.*** a device attached to a motor vehicle, etc. to indicate speed

speed·ster (spēd′stər) ***n.*** a very fast driver, runner, etc.

speed′way′ ***n.*** a track for racing automobiles or motorcycles

speed′y ***adj.*** **-i·er**, **-i·est** **1** rapid; fast; swift **2** without delay; prompt —**speed′i·ly** ***adv.***

spe·le·ol·o·gy (spē′lē äl′ə jē) ***n.*** ⟦< Gr *spēlaion*, a cave⟧ the scientific study and exploration of caves —**spe′le·ol′o·gist** ***n.***

spell[1] (spel) ***n.*** ⟦OE, a saying⟧ **1** a word or formula thought to have some magic power **2** irresistible influence; charm; fascination

spell[2] (spel) ***vt.*** **spelled** or **spelt**, **spell′ing** ⟦< OFr *espeller*, explain⟧ **1** to name, write, etc. in order the letters of (a word) **2** to make up (a word, etc.): said of specified letters **3** to mean *[*red *spells* danger*]* —***vi.*** to spell words —**spell out** to explain in detail

spell[3] (spel) ***vt.*** **spelled**, **spell′ing** ⟦OE *spelian*⟧ [Inf.] to work in place of (another) for an interval; relieve —***n.*** **1** a period of work, duty, etc. **2** a period of anything *[*a *spell* of brooding*]* **3** [Inf.] a fit of illness

spell′bind′ ***vt.*** **-bound′**, **-bind′ing** to cause to be spellbound; fascinate —**spell′bind′er** ***n.***

spell′bound′ ***adj.*** held by or as by a spell; fascinated

spell′-check′er ***n.*** a word-processing program used to check the spelling of words in a document

spell′down′ ***n.*** SPELLING BEE

spell′er ***n.*** **1** one who spells words **2** a textbook for teaching spelling

spell′ing ***n.*** **1** the act of one who spells words **2** the way a word is spelled; orthography

spelling bee a spelling contest, esp. one in which a contestant is eliminated after misspelling a word

spe·lunk·er (spi luŋ′kər) ***n.*** ⟦< Gr *spēlynx*, a cave⟧ a cave explorer —**spe·lunk′ing** ***n.***

spend (spend) ***vt.*** **spent**, **spend′ing** ⟦< L *expendere:* see EXPEND⟧ **1** to use up, exhaust, etc. *[*his fury was *spent]* **2** to pay out (money) **3** to devote (time, labor, etc.) to something **4** to pass (time) —***vi.*** to pay out or use up money, etc. —**spend′a·ble** ***adj.*** —**spend′er** ***n.***

spend′thrift′ ***n.*** one who wastes money —***adj.*** wasteful

spent (spent) ***vt.***, ***vi.*** *pt. & pp. of* SPEND —***adj.*** **1** tired out; exhausted **2** used up; worn out

sperm (spurm) ***n.*** ⟦< Gr *sperma*, seed⟧ **1** the male generative fluid; semen **2** *pl.* **sperm** or **sperms** a male germ cell, esp. a spermatozoon

sper·ma·to·zo·on (spur′mə tə zō′än′, -ən) ***n.***, *pl.* **-zo′a** (-zō′ə) ⟦< Gr *sperma*, seed + *zōion*, animal⟧ the male germ cell, found in semen, which penetrates the egg of the female to fertilize it

sperm·i·cide (spur′mə sīd′) ***n.*** ⟦SPERM + *-i-* + -CIDE⟧ an agent that kills spermatozoa —**sperm′i·cid′al** ***adj.***

sperm whale a large toothed whale found in warm seas: its head contains a valuable lubricating oil (**sperm oil**)

spew (spyo͞o) ***vt.***, ***vi.*** ⟦OE *spiwan*⟧ **1** to throw up (something) from or as from the stomach; vomit **2** to flow or cause to flow or gush forth —***n.*** something spewed

sp gr *abbrev.* specific gravity

sphere (sfir) ***n.*** ⟦< Gr *sphaira*⟧ **1** any round body having the surface equally distant from the center at all points; globe; ball **2** the place, range, or extent of action, existence, knowledge, experience, etc. —**spher·i·cal** (sfer′i kəl, sfir′-) ***adj.***

THESAURUS

specimen ***n.*** individual, part, unit; see EXAMPLE.

speck ***n.*** spot, dot, mark; see BIT 1.

speckled ***a.*** specked, dotted, motley; see SPOTTED 1.

spectacle ***n.*** scene, representation, exhibition; see DISPLAY, VIEW. —**make a spectacle of oneself** show off, act ridiculously, play the fool; see MISBEHAVE.

spectacular ***a.*** striking, magnificent, dramatic; see IMPRESSIVE.

spectator ***n.*** beholder, viewer, onlooker; see OBSERVER.

speculate ***v.*** reflect, meditate, theorize; see THINK 1.

speech ***n.*** **1** [Language] tongue, mother tongue, native tongue; see LANGUAGE 1. **2** [The power of audible expression] talk, utterance, articulation, diction, pronunciation, expression, locution, vocalization, discourse, oral expression, parlance, enunciation, communication, prattle, conversation, chatter. **3** [An address] lecture, discourse, oration, pep talk*, harangue, sermon, dissertation, homily, exhortation, eulogy, recitation, talk, rhetoric, tirade, bombast, diatribe, commentary, appeal, invocation, valedictory, paper, stump speech, panegyric, keynote address, spiel*; see also COMMUNICATION.

speechless ***a.*** silent, inarticulate, mum; see DUMB 1, MUTE.

speed ***n.*** swiftness, briskness, activity, eagerness, haste, hurry, acceleration, dispatch, velocity, readiness, agility, liveliness, quickness, momentum, rate, pace, alacrity, promptness, expedition, rapidity, rush, urgency, headway, fleetness, good clip, lively clip, steam*.

speed ***v.*** move rapidly, hurry, rush, go fast, cover ground, roll, sail, hasten, gear up, ride hard, breeze*, go like the wind, go all out, gun the motor*, give it the gun*, step on the gas*, break the sound barrier; see also RACE 1. —**speed up** **1** [To accelerate] go faster, increase speed, move into a higher speed; see RACE 1. **2** [To cause to accelerate] promote, further, get things going; see URGE 3.

speedy ***a.*** quick, nimble, expeditious; see FAST 1.

spell[1,3] ***n.*** **1** [A charm] abracadabra, talisman, amulet; see CHARM 1. **2** [A period of time] term, interval, season; see TIME 1. —**cast a spell on** (or **over**) enchant, bewitch, beguile; see CHARM. —**under a spell** enchanted, mesmerized, bewitched; see CHARMED.

spell out ***v.*** make clear, go into detail, simplify; see EXPLAIN.

spend ***v.*** consume, deplete, waste, dispense, contribute, donate, give, liquidate, exhaust, squander, disburse, allocate, misspend, pay, discharge, lay out, pay up, settle, use up, throw away, foot the bill*, fork out*, fork over*, pony up*, ante up*, open the purse, shell out*, blow*.—*Ant.* SAVE, keep, conserve.

spent ***a.*** used, consumed, disbursed; see FINISHED 1.

sphere ***n.*** ball, globe, orb; see CIRCLE 1.

sphe·roid (sfir′ɔid) ***n.*** a body that is almost but not quite a sphere —**sphe·roi′dal** ***adj.***
sphinc·ter (sfiŋk′tər) ***n.*** ⟦< Gr *sphingein,* to draw close⟧ a ring-shaped muscle at a body orifice
sphinx (sfiŋks) ***n.*** ⟦< Gr, strangler⟧ **1** *Gr. Myth.* a winged monster with a lion's body and a woman's head **2** [**S-**] a statue with a lion's body and a man's head, near Cairo, Egypt **3** one who is difficult to know or understand
spice (spīs) ***n.*** ⟦< L *species,* kind⟧ **1** an aromatic vegetable substance, as nutmeg or pepper, used to season food **2** that which adds zest or interest —***vt.*** **spiced**, **spic′ing** **1** to season with spice **2** to add zest to —**spic′y**, **-i·er**, **-i·est**, ***adj.***
spick-and-span (spik′′n span′) ***adj.*** ⟦< *spike,* nail + ON *spānn,* a chip⟧ **1** new or fresh **2** neat and clean
spic·ule (spik′yo͞ol′) ***n.*** ⟦< L *spica,* a point⟧ a hard, needle-like part
spi·der (spī′dər) ***n.*** ⟦< OE *spinnan,* to spin⟧ any of various arachnids that spin webs
spi′der·y ***adj.*** like a spider
spiel (spēl) ***n.*** ⟦Ger, play⟧ [Slang] a talk or harangue, as in selling
spiff·y (spif′ē) ***adj.*** **-i·er**, **-i·est** ⟦< dial. *spiff,* well-dressed person⟧ [Slang] spruce, smart, or dapper
spig·ot (spig′ət) ***n.*** ⟦ME *spigote*⟧ **1** a plug to stop the vent in a barrel, etc. **2** a faucet
spike[1] (spīk) ***n.*** ⟦< ON *spīkr* or MDu *spīker*⟧ **1** a long, heavy nail **2** a sharp-pointed projection, as on the sole of a shoe to prevent slipping —***vt.*** **spiked**, **spik′ing** **1** to fasten or fit as with spikes **2** to pierce with, or impale on, a spike **3** to thwart (a scheme, etc.) **4** [Slang] to add alcoholic liquor to (a drink) —***vi.*** to rise suddenly and rapidly
spike[2] (spīk) ***n.*** ⟦L *spica*⟧ **1** an ear of grain **2** a long flower cluster
spill (spil) ***vt.*** **spilled** or **spilt** (spilt), **spill′ing** ⟦OE *spillan,* destroy⟧ **1** to allow or cause, esp. unintentionally, to run, scatter, or flow over from a container **2** to shed (blood) **3** to throw off (a rider, etc.) **4** [Inf.] to let (a secret) become known —***vi.*** to be spilled; overflow —***n.*** **1** a spilling **2** a fall or tumble —**spill′age** ***n.***
spill′way′ ***n.*** a channel to carry off excess water, as around a dam
spin (spin) ***vt.*** **spun**, **spin′ning** ⟦OE *spinnan*⟧ **1** *a)* to draw out and twist fibers of (wool, cotton, etc.) into thread *b)* to make (thread, etc.) thus **2** to make (a web, cocoon, etc.), as a spider does **3** to draw *out* (a story) to a great length **4** to rotate swiftly —***vi.*** **1** to spin thread or yarn **2** to form a web, cocoon, etc. **3** to whirl **4** to seem to be spinning from dizziness **5** to move along swiftly and smoothly —***n.*** **1** a spinning or rotating movement **2** a ride in a motor vehicle **3** a descent of an airplane, nose first along a spiral path **4** a particular emphasis or slant given to news, etc. —**spin off** to produce as an outgrowth or secondary development, etc. —**spin′ner** ***n.***
spi·na bi·fi·da (spī′nə bif′i də) a congenital defect in which part of the spinal column is exposed, causing paralysis, etc.
spin·ach (spin′ich) ***n.*** ⟦ult. < Pers *aspanākh*⟧ **1** a plant with dark-green, juicy, edible leaves **2** these leaves
spi·nal (spī′nəl) ***adj.*** of or having to do with the spine or spinal cord —***n.*** a spinal anesthetic
spinal column the series of joined vertebrae forming the axial support for the skeleton; spine; backbone
spinal cord the thick cord of nerve tissue in the spinal column
spin·dle (spin′dəl) ***n.*** ⟦< OE *spinnan,* to spin⟧ **1** a slender rod used in spinning for twisting, winding, or holding thread **2** a spindlelike thing **3** any rod or pin that revolves or serves as an axis for a revolving part
spin·dly (spind′lē) ***adj.*** **-dli·er**, **-dli·est** long or tall and very thin
spin doctor [Slang] a person employed as by a politician to use spin in presenting information in a favorable light
spine (spīn) ***n.*** ⟦< L *spina,* thorn⟧ **1** *a)* a sharp, stiff projection, as on a cactus *b)* anything like this **2** *a)* SPINAL COLUMN *b)* anything like this, as the back of a book —**spin′y**, **-i·er**, **-i·est**, ***adj.***
spine′less ***adj.*** **1** having no spine or spines **2** lacking courage or willpower
spin·et (spin′it) ***n.*** ⟦< It *spinetta*⟧ a small upright piano
spine′-tin′gling ***adj.*** very thrilling, terrifying, etc.
spin·ner·et (spin′ə ret′) ***n.*** the organ in spiders, caterpillars, etc., that spins thread for webs or cocoons
spinning wheel a simple machine for spinning thread with a spindle driven by a large wheel spun as by a treadle
spin·off (spin′ôf′) ***n.*** a secondary benefit, product, development, etc.
spin·ster (spin′stər) ***n.*** ⟦ME < *spinnen,* to spin⟧ an unmarried woman, esp. an elderly one —**spin′ster·hood′** ***n.***
spiny lobster a type of lobster with a spiny shell and no pincers
spi·ra·cle (spir′ə kəl) ***n.*** ⟦< L < *spirare,* breathe⟧ an opening for breathing, as on the sides of an insect's body or on the top of a whale's head
spi·ral (spī′rəl) ***adj.*** ⟦< Gr *speira,* a coil⟧ circling around a point in constantly increasing (or decreasing) curves, or in constantly changing planes —***n.*** **1** a spiral curve, coil, path, etc. **2** a continuous, widening decrease or increase *[an inflationary spiral]* —***vi.***, ***vt.*** **-raled** or **-ralled**, **-ral·ing** or **-ral·ling** to move in or form a spiral
spire (spīr) ***n.*** ⟦OE *spir*⟧ **1** the top part of a pointed, tapering object **2** anything tapering to a point, as a steeple
spi·re·a (spī rē′ə) ***n.*** ⟦< Gr *speira,* a coil⟧ a plant of the rose family, with dense clusters of small, pink or white flowers: also sp. **spi·rae′a**
spir·it (spir′it) ***n.*** ⟦< L *spirare,* breathe⟧ **1** *a)* the life principle, esp. in human beings *b)* SOUL (sense 1) **2** [*also* **S-**] life, will, thought, etc., regarded as separate from matter **3** a supernatural being, as a ghost or angel **4** an individual *[a brave spirit]* **5** [*usually pl.*] disposition; mood *[high spirits]* **6** vivacity, courage, etc. **7** enthusiastic loyalty *[school spirit]* **8** real meaning *[the spirit of the law]* **9** a pervading animating principle or characteristic quality *[the spirit of the times]* **10** [*usually pl.*] distilled alcoholic liquor —***vt.*** to carry (*away, off,* etc.) secretly and swiftly —**spir′it·less** ***adj.***
spir′it·ed ***adj.*** lively; animated
spir·it·u·al (spir′i cho͞o əl) ***adj.*** **1** of the spirit or the soul **2** of or consisting of spirit; not corporeal **3** of religion; sacred —***n.*** a folk hymn, specif. one originating among S U.S. blacks —**spir′it·u·al′i·ty** (-al′ə tē) ***n.*** —**spir′it·u·al·ly** ***adv.***
spir′it·u·al·ism′ ***n.*** the belief that the dead survive as spirits that can communicate with the living —**spir′it·u·al·ist** ***n.*** —**spir′it·u·al·is′tic** ***adj.***
spir·it·u·ous (spir′i cho͞o əs) ***adj.*** of or containing distilled alcohol

THESAURUS

spice ***n.*** seasoning, herb, pepper, cinnamon, nutmeg, ginger, cloves, salt, paprika, oregano, anise, coriander, allspice, savor, relish; see also FLAVORING.

spicy ***a.*** **1** [Suggestive of spice] pungent, piquant, keen, hot, fresh, aromatic, fragrant, seasoned, tangy, savory, flavorful, tasty; see also SALTY, SOUR. **2** [Risqué] racy, suggestive, daring, indelicate; see also LEWD 2, SENSUAL 2.

spider ***n.*** *Common spiders include the following:* black widow, trapdoor, wolf, jumping, brown, brown recluse; daddy longlegs, tarantula.

spigot ***n.*** plug, valve, tap; see FAUCET.

spill ***v.*** lose, scatter, drop, spill over, pour out, run out; see also EMPTY 2.

spilled ***a.*** poured out, lost, run out; see EMPTY.

spin ***n.*** circuit, rotation, gyration; see REVOLUTION 1, TURN 1.

spin ***v.*** revolve, twirl, rotate; see TURN 1.

spine ***n.*** **1** [A spikelike protrusion] thorn, prickle, spike, barb, quill, ray, thistle, needle; see also POINT 2. **2** [A column of vertebrae] spinal column, ridge, backbone, vertebrae; see also BONE.

spineless ***a.*** timid, fearful, frightened; see COWARDLY, WEAK 3.

spinster ***n.*** unmarried woman, virgin, single woman, old maid*, bachelor girl*; see also WOMAN 1.

spiny ***a.*** pointed, barbed, spiked; see SHARP 1.

spiral ***a.*** winding, circling, coiled, whorled, radial, curled, rolled, scrolled, helical, screw-shaped, wound.

spirit ***n.*** **1** [Life] breath, vitality, animation; see LIFE 1. **2** [Soul] psyche, essence, substance; see SOUL 2. **3** [A supernatural being] vision, apparition, specter; see GHOST, GOD. **4** [Courage] boldness, ardor, enthusiasm; see COURAGE. **5** [Feeling; *often plural*] humor, frame of mind, temper; see FEELING 4, MOOD 1.

spirited ***a.*** lively, vivacious, animated; see ACTIVE.

spiritless ***a.*** dull, apathetic, unconcerned; see INDIFFERENT.

spiritual ***a.*** refined, pure, holy; see RELIGIOUS 1.

spi·ro·chete (spī′rō kēt′) ***n.*** ⟦< Gr *speira,* a coil + *chaitē,* hair⟧ any of various spiral-shaped bacteria

spit[1] (spit) ***n.*** ⟦OE *spitu*⟧ **1** a thin, pointed rod on which meat is roasted over a fire, etc. **2** a narrow point of land extending into the water —***vt.*** **spit′ted, spit′ting** to fix as on a spit

spit[2] (spit) ***vt.*** **spit** or **spat, spit′ting** ⟦OE *spittan*⟧ **1** to eject from the mouth **2** to eject explosively —***vi.*** to eject saliva from the mouth —***n.*** **1** a spitting **2** saliva —**spit and image** [Inf.] perfect likeness: also **spitting image**

spit′ball′ ***n.*** **1** paper chewed up into a wad for throwing **2** *Baseball* a pitch, now illegal, made to curve by wetting one side of the ball as with spit

spite (spīt) ***n.*** ⟦see DESPITE⟧ ill will; malice —***vt.*** **spit′ed, spit′ing** to vent one's spite upon by hurting, frustrating, etc. —**in spite of** regardless of —**spite′ful** ***adj.***

spit′fire′ ***n.*** a woman or girl easily aroused to violent anger

spit·tle (spit′'l) ***n.*** saliva; spit

spit·toon (spi to͞on′) ***n.*** a container to spit into

splash (splash) ***vt.*** ⟦echoic⟧ **1** to cause (a liquid) to scatter **2** to dash a liquid, mud, etc. on, so as to wet or soil —***vi.*** to move, strike, etc. with a splash —***n.*** **1** a splashing **2** a spot made by splashing —**make a splash** [Inf.] to attract great attention

splash′down′ ***n.*** a spacecraft's soft landing on the sea

splash′y ***adj.*** **-i·er, -i·est** **1** splashing or apt to splash; wet, muddy, etc. **2** [Inf.] spectacular —**splash′i·ly** ***adv.*** —**splash′i·ness** ***n.***

splat[1] (splat) ***n.*** ⟦< SPLIT⟧ a thin slat of wood, as in a chair back

splat[2] (splat) ***n., interj.*** ⟦echoic⟧ (used to suggest) a splattering or wet, slapping sound —***vi.*** **1** to make such a sound **2** to flatten on impact

splat·ter (splat′ər) ***n., vt., vi.*** spatter or splash

splay (splā) ***vt., vi.*** ⟦ME *splaien*⟧ to spread out or apart: often with *out* —***adj.*** spreading outward

splay′foot′ ***n., pl.*** **-feet′** a foot that is flat and turned outward —**splay′foot′ed** ***adj.***

spleen (splēn) ***n.*** ⟦< Gr *splēn*⟧ **1** a large lymphatic organ in the upper left part of the abdomen: it modifies the blood structure **2** malice; spite

splen·did (splen′did) ***adj.*** ⟦< L *splendere,* to shine⟧ **1** shining; brilliant **2** magnificent; gorgeous **3** grand; illustrious **4** [Inf.] very good; fine —**splen′did·ly** ***adv.***

splen·dor (splen′dər) ***n.*** ⟦see prec.⟧ **1** great luster; brilliance **2** pomp; grandeur Brit. sp. **splen′dour**

sple·net·ic (spli net′ik) ***adj.*** **1** of the spleen **2** bad-tempered; irritable

splice (splīs) ***vt.*** **spliced, splic′ing** ⟦MDu *splissen*⟧ **1** to join (ropes) by weaving together the end strands **2** to join the ends of (timbers) by overlapping **3** to fasten the ends of (wire, film, etc.) together, as by soldering or twisting —***n.*** a joint made by splicing —**splic′er** ***n.***

splint (splint) ***n.*** ⟦prob. < MDu *splinte*⟧ **1** a thin strip of wood, etc. woven with others to make baskets, etc. **2** a thin, rigid strip of wood, etc. used to hold a broken bone in place

splin·ter (splin′tər) ***vt., vi.*** ⟦see prec.⟧ to break or split into thin, sharp pieces —***n.*** a thin, sharp piece, as of wood, made by splitting, etc.; sliver

split (split) ***vt., vi.*** **split, split′ting** ⟦MDu *splitten*⟧ **1** to separate lengthwise into two or more parts **2** to break or tear apart **3** to divide into shares **4** to disunite **5** *a)* to break (a molecule) into atoms *b)* to produce nuclear fission in (an atom) **6** *Finance* to divide (stock) by converting each share into two for more shares with the same overall value —***n.*** **1** a splitting **2** a break; crack **3** a division in a group, etc. **4** [*often pl.*] the feat of spreading the legs apart on the floor until they lie flat —***adj.*** divided; separated

split′-lev′el ***adj.*** having floor levels staggered about a half story apart

split pea a green or yellow pea shelled, dried, and split: used esp. for soup

split′ting ***adj.*** severe, as a headache

splotch (spläch) ***n.*** ⟦prob. < SPOT + BLOTCH⟧ an irregular spot, splash, or stain —***vt., vi.*** to mark or be marked with splotches —**splotch′y, -i·er, -i·est,** ***adj.***

splurge (splurj) [Inf.] ***n.*** ⟦echoic⟧ a spell of extravagant spending —***vi.*** **splurged, splurg′ing** to spend money freely

splut·ter (splut′ər) ***vi.*** ⟦var. of SPUTTER⟧ **1** to make hissing or spitting sounds **2** to speak hurriedly and confusedly —***n.*** a spluttering

spoil (spoil) ***vt.*** **spoiled** or [Brit.] **spoilt, spoil′ing** ⟦< L *spolium,* plunder⟧ **1** to damage so as to make useless, etc. **2** to impair the enjoyment, etc. of **3** to cause to expect too much by overindulgence —***vi.*** to become spoiled; decay, etc., as food does —***n.*** [*usually pl.*] plunder; booty —**spoil′age** ***n.*** —**spoil′er** ***n.***

spoil′sport′ ***n.*** one whose actions ruin the pleasure of others

spoils system the treating of public offices as the booty of a successful political party

Spo·kane (spō kan′) city in E Washington: pop. 177,000

spoke[1] (spōk) ***n.*** ⟦OE *spaca*⟧ any of the braces or bars extending from the hub to the rim of a wheel

spoke[2] (spōk) ***vi., vt.*** *pt. & archaic pp. of* SPEAK

spo·ken (spō′kən) ***vi., vt.*** *pp. of* SPEAK —***adj.*** **1** uttered; oral **2** having a (specified) kind of voice *[soft-spoken]*

spokes·man (spōks′mən) ***n., pl.*** **-men** (-mən) one who speaks for another or for a group —**spokes′wom′an,** *pl.* **-wom′en,** ***fem.n.***

spokes′per′son ***n.*** SPOKESMAN: used to avoid the masculine implication of *spokesman*

spo·li·a·tion (spō′lē ā′shən) ***n.*** ⟦< L *spoliatio*⟧ robbery; plundering

sponge (spunj) ***n.*** ⟦< Gr *spongia*⟧ **1** a stationary aquatic animal with a porous structure **2** the highly absorbent skeleton of such animals, used for washing surfaces, etc. **3** any substance like this, as a piece of light, porous rubber, etc. —***vt.*** **sponged, spong′ing** **1** to dampen, wipe, absorb, etc. as with a sponge **2** [Inf.] to get as by begging, imposition, etc. —***vi.*** [Inf.] to live as a parasite upon other people —**spong′er** ***n.*** —**spon′gy, -gi·er, -gi·est,** ***adj.***

sponge bath a bath taken by using a wet sponge or cloth without getting into water

sponge′cake′ ***n.*** a light, spongy cake without shortening: also **sponge cake**

spon·sor (spän′sər) ***n.*** ⟦L < *spondere,* promise solemnly⟧ **1** one who assumes responsibility for something; proponent, underwriter, endorser, etc. **2** a godparent **3** a business firm, etc. that pays for a radio or TV program advertising its product —***vt.*** to act as sponsor for —**spon′sor·ship′** ***n.***

spon·ta·ne·i·ty (spän′tə nē′ə tē, -nā′-) ***n.*** **1** a being spontaneous **2** *pl.* **-ties** spontaneous behavior, action, etc.

spon·ta·ne·ous (spän tā′nē əs) ***adj.*** ⟦< L *sponte,* of free will⟧ **1** acting or resulting from a natural feeling or impulse, without constraint, effort, etc. **2** occurring through internal causes

THESAURUS

spit[2] ***v.*** splutter, eject, expectorate, drivel, slobber, drool.

spite ***n.*** malice, resentment, hatred; see HATE. —**in spite of** regardless of, in defiance of, despite; see REGARDLESS 2.

splash ***n.*** plash, plop, dash, spatter, sprinkle, spray, slosh, slop.

splash ***v.*** splatter, dabble, get wet; see MOISTEN.

splendid ***a.*** grand, great, fine; see BEAUTIFUL, EXCELLENT, GLORIOUS.

splendor ***n.*** luster, brilliance, brightness; see GLORY 2.

splice ***v.*** knit, graft, mesh; see JOIN 1, WEAVE 1.

splint ***n.*** prop, rib, reinforcement; see BRACE, SUPPORT 2.

splinter ***n.*** sliver, flake, chip; see BIT 1.

split ***n.*** **1** [A dividing] separation, breaking up, severing; see DIVISION 1. **2** [An opening] crack, fissure, rent; see HOLE 1.

split ***v.*** burst, rend, cleave; see BREAK 1, CUT 1, DIVIDE. —**split up** part, break up, separate; see DIVIDE, DIVORCE.

spoil ***v.*** **1** [To decay] rot, blight, fade, wither, molder, crumble, mold, mildew, corrode, decompose, putrefy, degenerate, weaken, become tainted. **2** [To ruin] damage, defile, plunder; see DESTROY.

spoiled ***a.*** damaged, marred, injured; see RUINED 2, WASTED.

spoiling ***a.*** rotting, breaking up, wasting away; see DECAYING.

spoils ***n.*** plunder, pillage, prize; see BOOTY.

spoke[1] ***n.*** bar, brace, crosspiece; see ROD 1.

spoken ***a.*** uttered, expressed, told, announced, mentioned, communicated, oral, verbal, phonetic, voiced, unwritten.

spokesman ***n.*** deputy, mediator, substitute, spokesperson, spokeswoman; see also AGENT, SPEAKER.

sponsor ***n.*** advocate, backer, supporter, champion; see also PATRON.

spontaneous ***a.*** involuntary, instinctive, unplanned, impromptu, ad-lib*, casual, unintentional, impulsive, automatic, unforced, natural, unavoidable, unconscious, uncontrollable.—*Ant.* DELIBERATE, willful, intended.

spontaneous combustion the process of catching fire through heat generated by internal chemical action

spoof (spo͞of) ***n.*** **1** a hoax or joke **2** a light satire —***vt., vi.*** **1** to fool; deceive **2** to satirize playfully

spook (spo͝ok) [Inf.] ***n.*** ⟦Du⟧ a ghost —***vt., vi.*** to frighten or become frightened

spook'y ***adj.*** **-i·er, -i·est** [Inf.] **1** weird; eerie **2** easily frightened; nervous, jumpy, etc.

spool (spo͞ol) ***n.*** ⟦< MDu *spoele*⟧ **1** a cylinder on which thread, wire, etc. is wound **2** the material wound on a spool

spoon (spo͞on) ***n.*** ⟦< OE *spon*, a chip⟧ **1** a utensil consisting of a small, shallow bowl and a handle, used for eating, stirring, etc. **2** something shaped like a spoon, as a shiny, curved fishing lure —***vt.*** to take up with a spoon —**spoon'ful'**, *pl.* **-fuls'**, ***n.***

spoon'bill' ***n.*** a wading bird whose flat bill is spoon-shaped at the tip

spoon·er·ism (spo͞on'ər iz'əm) ***n.*** ⟦after Rev. W. A. *Spooner* (1844-1930), of England, who made such slips⟧ an unintentional interchange of the initial sounds of words (Ex.: "a well-boiled icicle" for "a well-oiled bicycle")

spoon'-feed' ***vt.*** **-fed', -feed'ing** **1** to feed with a spoon **2** to pamper; coddle

spoor (spoor) ***n.*** ⟦Afrik⟧ the track or trail of a wild animal

spo·rad·ic (spə rad'ik) ***adj.*** ⟦< Gr *sporas*, scattered⟧ happening or appearing in isolated instances *[sporadic* storms*]* —**spo·rad'i·cal·ly** ***adv.***

spore (spôr) ***n.*** ⟦< Gr *spora*, a seed⟧ a small reproductive body produced by algae, ferns, etc. and capable of giving rise to a new individual

sport (spôrt) ***n.*** ⟦< DISPORT⟧ **1** any recreational activity; specif., a game, competition, etc. requiring bodily exertion **2** fun or play **3** [Inf.] a sportsmanlike person **4** [Inf.] a showy, flashy fellow **5** *Biol.* a plant or animal markedly different from the normal type —***vt.*** [Inf.] to display *[*to *sport* a loud tie*]* —***vi.*** to play —***adj.*** **1** of or for sports **2** suitable for casual wear *[*a *sport* coat*]* Also, for adj., **sports** —**in** (or **for**) **sport** in jest —**make sport of** to mock or ridicule

sport'ing ***adj.*** **1** of or interested in sports **2** sportsmanlike; fair **3** of games, races, etc. involving gambling or betting

spor·tive (spôrt'iv) ***adj.*** **1** full of sport or fun **2** done in fun —**spor'tive·ly** ***adv.***

sports car a small car characterized by above-average speed and handling

sports'cast' ***n.*** a broadcast of sports news on radio or TV —**sports'cast'er** ***n.***

sports'man (-mən) ***n.***, *pl.* **-men** (-mən) **1** a man who takes part in sports, esp. hunting, fishing, etc. **2** one who plays fair and can lose without complaint or win without gloating —**sports'man·like'** ***adj.*** —**sports'man·ship'** ***n.***

sport utility vehicle a vehicle like a station wagon, but with a small-truck chassis and, usually, four-wheel drive

sport'y ***adj.*** **-i·er, -i·est** [Inf.] **1** sporting or sportsmanlike **2** flashy or showy —**sport'i·ness** ***n.***

spot (spät) ***n.*** ⟦prob. < MDu *spotte*⟧ **1** *a)* a small area differing in color, etc. from the surrounding area *b)* a stain, speck, etc. **2** a flaw or defect **3** a locality; place —***vt.*** **spot'ted, spot'ting** **1** to mark with spots **2** to stain; blemish **3** to place; locate **4** to see; recognize **5** [Inf.] to allow as a handicap *[*to *spot* an opponent points*]* —***vi.*** **1** to become marked with spots **2** to make a stain —***adj.*** **1** ready *[spot* cash*]* **2** made at random *[*a *spot* survey*]* —**hit the spot** [Inf.] to satisfy a craving or need —**in a (bad) spot** [Slang] in trouble —**on the spot** [Slang] in a bad or demanding situation —**spot'less** ***adj.*** —**spot'less·ly** ***adv.*** —**spot'ted** ***adj.***

spot'-check' ***vt.*** to check or examine at random or by sampling —***n.*** such a checking

spot'light' ***n.*** **1** *a)* a strong beam of light focused on a particular person, thing, etc. *b)* a lamp used to project such a beam **2** public notice or prominence —***vt.*** to light or draw attention to, by or as by a spotlight

spot'ty ***adj.*** **-ti·er, -ti·est** **1** having, occurring in, or marked with spots **2** not uniform or consistent —**spot'ti·ly** ***adv.***

spouse (spous) ***n.*** ⟦< L *sponsus*, betrothed⟧ (one's) husband or wife —**spous·al** (spou'zəl) ***adj.***

spout (spout) ***n.*** ⟦< ME *spouten*, to spout⟧ **1** a lip, orifice, or projecting tube by which a liquid is poured or discharged **2** a stream, etc. as of liquid from a spout —***vt., vi.*** **1** to shoot out (liquid, etc.) as from a spout **2** to speak or utter (words, etc.) in a loud, pompous manner

sprain (sprān) ***vt.*** ⟦< ? L *ex-*, out + *premere*, to press⟧ to wrench a ligament or muscle of (a joint) without dislocating the bones —***n.*** an injury resulting from this

sprang (spraŋ) ***vi., vt.*** *alt. pt. of* SPRING

sprat (sprat) ***n.*** ⟦OE *sprott*⟧ a small European herring

sprawl (sprôl) ***vi.*** ⟦< OE *spreawlian*, move convulsively⟧ **1** to sit or lie with the limbs in a relaxed or awkward position **2** to spread out awkwardly or unevenly —***n.*** **1** a sprawling movement or position **2** the uncontrolled spread of real-estate development into areas around a city

spray[1] (sprā) ***n.*** ⟦prob. < MDu *spraeien*⟧ **1** a mist of fine liquid particles **2** *a)* a jet of such particles, as from a spray gun *b)* a device for spraying **3** something likened to a spray —***vt., vi.*** **1** to direct a spray (on) **2** to shoot out in a spray —**spray'er** ***n.***

spray[2] (sprā) ***n.*** ⟦ME⟧ a small branch of a tree or plant, with leaves, flowers, etc.

spray can a can from which gas under pressure sprays out the contents

spray gun a device that shoots out a spray of liquid, as paint or insecticide

spread (spred) ***vt., vi.*** **spread, spread'ing** ⟦OE *sprædan*⟧ **1** to open or stretch out; unfold **2** to move (the fingers, wings, etc.) apart **3** to distribute or be distributed over an area or surface **4** to extend in time **5** to make or be

THESAURUS

spontaneously ***a.*** instinctively, impulsively, automatically; see UNCONSCIOUSLY.

spoof ***n.*** joke, put-on*, satire; see DECEPTION.

spoof ***v.*** fool, play a trick on, kid*; see TRICK.

spooky* ***a.*** weird, eerie, ominous; see MYSTERIOUS 2, UNCANNY.

spoon ***n.*** teaspoon, tablespoon, ladle; see SILVERWARE.

sport ***n.*** **1** [Entertainment] diversion, recreation, play, amusement, merrymaking, festivity, revelry, pastime, pleasure, enjoyment; see also ENTERTAINMENT, FUN, GAME 1. **2** [A joke] pleasantry, mockery, jest, mirth, joke, joking, antics, tomfoolery, nonsense, laughter, practical joke. **3** [Athletic or competitive amusement] *Sports include the following:* hunting, shooting, (the) Olympics, horse racing, automobile racing, running, fishing, basketball, golf, tennis, squash, handball, volleyball, soccer, gymnastics, football, baseball, track, cricket, lacrosse, ice hockey, skating, skiing, fencing, cycling, bowling, field hockey, swimming, diving, windsurfing, polo, billiards, mountain climbing, boxing, wrestling.

sporting ***a.*** considerate, sportsmanlike, gentlemanly; see GENEROUS, REASONABLE 1.

sportsman ***n.*** huntsman, big game hunter, woodsman; see FISHERMAN, HUNTER.

sportsmanship ***n.*** **1** [Skill] facility, dexterity, cunning; see ABILITY. **2** [Honor] justice, integrity, truthfulness; see HONESTY.

spot ***n.*** **1** [A dot] speck, flaw, pimple; see BIT 1, BLEMISH. **2** [A place] point, location, scene; see PLACE 3. —**hit the high spots*** treat hastily, go over lightly, touch up; see NEGLECT 1, 2. —**hit the spot*** please, delight, be just right; see SATISFY 1. —**in a bad spot*** in danger, threatened, on the spot*; see DANGEROUS.

spot ***v.*** blemish, blotch, spatter; see DIRTY.

spotless ***a.*** stainless, immaculate, without spot or blemish; see CLEAN, PURE 2.

spotted ***a.*** **1** [Dotted] marked, dappled, mottled, dotted, speckled, motley, blotchy. **2** [Blemished] soiled, smudged, smeared; see DIRTY 1.

spouse ***n.*** marriage partner, groom, bride; see HUSBAND, MATE 3, WIFE.

sprain ***n.*** twist, overstrain, strain; see INJURY.

sprained ***a.*** wrenched, strained, pulled out of place; see HURT, TWISTED 1.

sprawl ***v.*** slouch, relax, lounge; see LIE 3.

spray[1] ***n.*** splash, steam, fine mist; see FOG.

spray[1] ***v.*** scatter, diffuse, sprinkle; see SPATTER.

spread ***a.*** expanded, dispersed, extended, opened, unfurled, sown, scattered, diffused, strewn, spread thin, disseminated, broadcast; see also DISTRIBUTED.—*Ant.* RESTRICTED, narrowed, restrained.

spread ***n.*** **1** [Extent] scope, range, expanse; see EXTENT, MEASURE 1. **2** [A spread cloth] bedspread, coverlet, counterpane; see COVER 1. **3** [A spread food] preserves, peanut butter, pâté; see BUTTER, CHEESE. **4** [*A meal] feast, banquet, elaborate meal; see DINNER, LUNCH, MEAL 2.

made widely known, felt, etc. **6** to set (a table) for a meal **7** to push or be pushed apart —*n.* **1** the act or extent of spreading **2** an expanse **3** a cloth cover for a table, bed, etc. **4** jam, butter, etc. used on bread **5** [Inf.] a meal with many different foods —**spread′er** *n.*

spread′-ea′gle *adj.* having the figure of an eagle with wings and legs spread —*vt.* **-gled, -gling** to stretch out in this form, as for a flogging

spread′sheet′ *n.* a computer program that organizes numerical data into rows and columns on a video screen

spree (sprē) *n.* ⟦< earlier *spray*⟧ **1** a noisy frolic **2** a period of drunkenness **3** a period of uninhibited activity *[a shopping spree]*

sprig (sprig) *n.* ⟦ME *sprigge*⟧ a little twig or spray

spright·ly (sprīt′lē) *adj.* **-li·er, -li·est** ⟦< *spright,* var. of SPRITE⟧ full of energy and spirit; lively —*adv.* in a sprightly manner —**spright′li·ness** *n.*

spring (spriŋ) *vi.* **sprang** or **sprung, sprung, spring′ing** ⟦OE *springan*⟧ **1** to leap; bound **2** to come, appear, etc. suddenly **3** to bounce **4** to arise as from some source; grow or develop **5** to become warped, split, etc. Often followed by *up* —*vt.* **1** to cause (a trap, etc.) to snap shut **2** to cause to warp, split, etc. **3** to make known suddenly **4** [Slang] to get (someone) released from jail —*n.* **1** a leap, or the distance so covered **2** elasticity; resilience **3** a device, as a coil of wire, that returns to its original form after being forced out of shape **4** a flow of water from the ground **5** a source or origin **6** *a)* the season of the year following winter, when plants begin to grow *b)* any period of beginning —*adj.* **1** of, for, appearing in, or planted in the spring **2** having, or supported on, springs **3** coming from a spring *[spring water]* —**spring a leak** to begin unexpectedly to leak —**spring for** [Inf.] to bear the cost of for someone else

spring′board′ *n.* a springy board used as a takeoff in leaping or diving

spring fever the laziness or restlessness that many people feel in the early days of spring

Spring·field (spriŋ′fēld′) **1** city in SW Missouri: pop. 140,000 **2** capital of Illinois: pop. 105,000

spring′time′ *n.* the season of spring

spring′y *adj.* **-i·er, -i·est** having spring; elastic, resilient, etc. —**spring′i·ness** *n.*

sprin·kle (spriŋ′kəl) *vt., vi.* **-kled, -kling** ⟦ME *sprinklen*⟧ **1** to scatter or fall in drops or particles **2** to scatter drops or particles (upon) **3** to rain lightly —*n.* **1** a sprinkling **2** a light rain —**sprin′kler** *n.*

sprin′kling (-kliŋ) *n.* a small number or amount, esp. when scattered thinly

sprint (sprint) *vi., n.* ⟦ME *sprenten*⟧ run or race at full speed for a short distance —**sprint′er** *n.*

sprite (sprīt) *n.* ⟦< L *spiritus,* spirit⟧ *Folklore* an imaginary being, as an elf

spritz (sprits, shprits) *vt., vi., n.* ⟦< Ger *spritzen* & Yiddish *shprits*⟧ squirt or spray

spritz′er *n.* a drink consisting of white wine and soda water

sprock·et (spräk′it) *n.* ⟦< ?⟧ **1** any of the teeth, as on the rim of a wheel, arranged to fit the links of a chain **2** a wheel fitted with such teeth: in full **sprocket wheel**

sprout (sprout) *vi.* ⟦OE *sprutan*⟧ to begin to grow; give off shoots —*vt.* to cause to sprout or grow —*n.* **1** a young growth on a plant; shoot **2** a new growth from a bud, etc. **3** a new growth from a seed of alfalfa, etc., used as in salads

spruce[1] (sproos) *n.* ⟦ME *Spruce,* Prussia⟧ **1** an evergreen tree with slender needles **2** its wood

spruce[2] (sproos) *adj.* **spruc′er, spruc′est** ⟦< *Spruce leather* (see prec.)⟧ neat and trim in a smart way —*vt., vi.* **spruced, spruc′ing** to make (oneself) spruce: usually with *up*

sprung (spruŋ) *vi., vt. pp. & alt. pt. of* SPRING

spry (sprī) *adj.* **spri′er** or **spry′er, spri′est** or **spry′est** ⟦< Scand⟧ full of life; active, esp. though elderly —**spry′ly** *adv.* —**spry′ness** *n.*

spud (spud) *n.* [Inf.] a potato

spume (spyoom) *n.* ⟦< L *spuma*⟧ foam, froth, or scum —*vi.* **spumed, spum′ing** to foam; froth

spu·mo·ni (spə mō′nē) *n.* ⟦It < L *spuma,* foam⟧ Italian ice cream in variously flavored and colored layers

spun (spun) *vt., vi. pt. & pp. of* SPIN

spunk (spuŋk) *n.* ⟦Ir *sponc,* tinder⟧ [Inf.] courage; spirit —**spunk′y, -i·er, -i·est,** *adj.*

spur (spur) *n.* ⟦OE *spura*⟧ **1** a pointed device worn on the heel by a rider, used to urge a horse forward **2** anything that urges; stimulus **3** any spurlike projection **4** a short railroad track connected with the main track —*vt.* **spurred, spur′ring** **1** to prick with spurs **2** to urge or incite —**on the spur of the moment** abruptly and impulsively

spurge (spurj) *n.* ⟦< earlier Fr *espurger,* to purge⟧ any of a group of plants with milky juice and tiny flowers

spu·ri·ous (spyoor′ē əs, spur′-) *adj.* ⟦L *spurius,* illegitimate⟧ not genuine; false —**spu′ri·ous·ly** *adv.* —**spu′ri·ous·ness** *n.*

spurn (spurn) *vt.* ⟦OE *spurnan*⟧ to reject with contempt; scorn

spurt (spurt) *vt.* ⟦prob. < OE *sprutan,* to sprout⟧ to expel in a stream or jet —*vi.* **1** to gush forth in a stream or jet **2** to show a sudden, brief burst of energy, etc. —*n.* **1** a sudden shooting forth; jet **2** a sudden, brief burst of energy, etc.

sput·nik (spoot′nik, sput′-) *n.* ⟦Russ, lit., co-traveler⟧ any of a series of man-made satellites launched by the U.S.S.R. starting in 1957

sput·ter (sput′ər) *vi., vt.* ⟦< MDu *spotten,* to spit⟧ **1** to spit out (bits, drops, etc.) explosively, as when talking excitedly **2** to speak or utter in a confused, explosive way **3** to make sharp, sizzling sounds, as frying fat does —*n.* a sputtering

spu·tum (spyoot′əm) *n., pl.* **-ta** (-ə) ⟦< L *spuere,* to spit⟧ saliva, usually mixed with mucus, ejected from the mouth

spy (spī) *vt.* **spied, spy′ing** ⟦< OHG *spehōn,* examine⟧ **1** to watch closely and secretly: often with *out* **2** to catch sight of; see —*vi.* to watch closely and secretly; act as a spy —*n., pl.* **spies** **1** one who keeps close and secret watch on others **2** one employed by a government to get secret information about another government

spy′glass′ *n.* a small telescope

sq *abbrev.* **1** sequence **2** squadron **3** square

sqq. *abbrev.* ⟦L *sequentes; sequentia*⟧ the following ones; what follows

squab (skwäb) *n.* ⟦prob. < Scand⟧ a nestling pigeon

squab·ble (skwäb′əl) *vi.* **-bled, -bling** ⟦< Scand⟧ to quarrel noisily over a small matter; wrangle —*n.* a noisy, petty quarrel —**squab′bler** *n.*

squad (skwäd) *n.* ⟦< Sp *escuadra* or It *squadra,* a square⟧ **1** a small group of soldiers, often a subdivision of a platoon **2** any small group of people working together

squad car PATROL CAR

THESAURUS

spread *v.* **1** [To distribute] cast, diffuse, disseminate; see RADIATE 1, SCATTER 2, SOW. **2** [To extend] open, unfurl, roll out, unroll, unfold, reach, circulate, lengthen, widen, expand, untwist, unwind, uncoil, enlarge, increase, develop, branch off, radiate, diverge, expand; see also FLOW, REACH 1.—*Ant.* CLOSE, shorten, shrink. **3** [To apply over a surface] cover, coat, smear, daub, plate, gloss, enamel, paint, spray, plaster, pave, wax, spatter, gild, varnish. **4** [To separate] part, sever, disperse; see DIVIDE, SEPARATE 1.

spreading *a.* extending, extensive, spread out, growing, widening.

spree *n.* revel, frolic, binge*; see CELEBRATION.

sprightly *a.* lively, quick, alert; see AGILE.

spring *n.* **1** [A fountain] flowing water, artesian well, sweet water; see ORIGIN 2. **2** [The season between winter and summer] springtime, seedtime, flowering, budding, vernal equinox, blackberry winter*; see also SEASON.

sprinkle *v.* dampen, bedew, spray; see MOISTEN.

sprout *v.* germinate, take root, shoot up, bud, burgeon; see also GROW 1.

spry *a.* nimble, fleet, vigorous; see AGILE.

spunk* *n.* spirit, courage, nerve; see COURAGE.

spurn *v.* despise, reject, look down on; see EVADE.

spurt *n.* squirt, jet, stream; see WATER 2.

spurt *v.* spout, jet, burst; see FLOW.

sputter *v.* stumble, stutter, falter; see STAMMER.

spy *n.* secret agent, foreign agent, scout, detective, undercover man, CIA operative, observer, watcher, mole, counterspy, double agent, spook*.

spy *v.* scout, observe, watch, examine, bug*, tap, scrutinize, take note, search, discover, look for, hunt, peer, pry, spy upon, set a watch on, hound, trail, tail*, follow; see also MEDDLE 1, 2.

squabble *n.* spat, quarrel, feud; see DISPUTE.

squabble *v.* argue, disagree, fight; see QUARREL.

squad *n.* company, unit, crew; see TEAM 1.

squad′ron (-rən) ***n.*** ⟦< It *squadra,* a square⟧ a unit of warships, military aircraft, etc.

squal·id (skwäl′id, skwôl′id) ***adj.*** ⟦< L *squalere,* be foul⟧ **1** foul or unclean **2** wretched

squall[1] (skwôl) ***n.*** ⟦< Scand⟧ a brief, violent windstorm, usually with rain or snow —**squall′y, -i·er, -i·est,** ***adj.***

squall[2] (skwôl) ***vi., vt.*** ⟦< ON *skvala*⟧ to cry or scream loudly and harshly —***n.*** a harsh cry or loud scream

squal·or (skwäl′ər, skwôl′ər) ***n.*** a being squalid; filth and wretchedness

squa·mous (skwā′məs) ***adj.*** ⟦< L *squama,* a scale⟧ like, formed of, or covered with scales

squan·der (skwän′dər) ***vt.*** ⟦prob. < dial. *squander,* to scatter⟧ to spend or use wastefully or extravagantly

square (skwer) ***n.*** ⟦< L *ex,* out + *quadrare,* to square⟧ **1** *a)* a plane figure having four equal sides and four right angles *b)* anything of or approximating this shape **2** an open area bounded by several streets, used as a park, etc. **3** an instrument for drawing or testing right angles **4** the product of a number multiplied by itself **5** [Slang] a person who is SQUARE (*adj.* 10) —***vt.* squared, squar′ing 1** to make square **2** to make straight, even, right-angled, etc. **3** to settle; adjust *[to square accounts]* **4** to make conform *[to square a statement with the facts]* **5** to multiply (a quantity) by itself —***vi.*** to fit; agree; accord (*with*) —***adj.* squar′er, squar′est 1** having four equal sides and four right angles **2** forming a right angle **3** straight, level, even, etc. **4** leaving no balance; even **5** just; fair **6** direct; straightforward **7** designating a unit of surface measure in the form of a square *[a square foot]* **8** sturdy and somewhat rectangular *[a square jaw]* **9** [Inf.] substantial *[a square meal]* **10** [Slang] old-fashioned, unsophisticated, etc. —***adv.*** in a square manner —**square off** to assume a posture of attack or self-defense —**square oneself** [Inf.] to make amends —**square′ly** ***adv.*** —**square′ness** ***n.*** —**squar′ish** ***adj.***

square dance a dance with various steps, in which couples are grouped in a given form, as a square —**square′-dance′, -danced′, -danc′ing,** ***vi.***

square′-rigged′ ***adj.*** rigged with square sails as the principal sails

square root the number or quantity which when squared will produce a given number or quantity *[3 is the square root of 9]*

squash[1] (skwôsh, skwäsh) ***vt.*** ⟦< L *ex-,* intens. + *quatere,* to shake⟧ **1** to crush into a soft or flat mass; press **2** to suppress; quash —***vi.* 1** to be squashed **2** to make a sound of squashing —***n.* 1** the act or sound of squashing **2** a game played in a walled court with rackets and a rubber ball —**squash′y, -i·er, -i·est,** ***adj.***

squash[2] (skwôsh, skwäsh) ***n.*** ⟦< AmInd⟧ the fleshy fruit of various plants of the gourd family, eaten as a vegetable

squat (skwät) ***vi.* squat′ted, squat′ting** ⟦ult. < L *ex-,* intens. + *cogere,* to force⟧ **1** to crouch so as to sit on the heels with knees bent and weight resting on the balls of the feet **2** to crouch close to the ground **3** to settle on land without right or title **4** to settle on public land in order to get title to it —***adj.* -ter, -test** short and heavy or thick: also **squat′ty, -ti·er, -ti·est** —***n.*** the act or position of squatting —**squat′ness** ***n.*** —**squat′ter** ***n.***

squaw (skwô) ***n.*** ⟦< AmInd⟧ [Now Rare] a North American Indian woman or wife: term now considered offensive

squawk (skwôk) ***vi.*** ⟦echoic⟧ **1** to utter a loud, harsh cry **2** [Inf.] to complain loudly —***n.* 1** a loud, harsh cry **2** [Inf.] a loud complaint

squeak (skwēk) ***vi.*** ⟦ME *squeken*⟧ to make or utter a sharp, high-pitched sound or cry —***vt.*** to say in a squeak —***n.*** a thin, sharp sound or cry —**narrow** (or **close**) **squeak** [Inf.] a narrow escape —**squeak through** (or **by,** etc.) [Inf.] to succeed, survive, etc. with difficulty —**squeak′y, -i·er, -i·est,** ***adj.***

squeak′er ***n.*** [Inf.] a narrow escape, victory, etc.

squeal (skwēl) ***vi.*** ⟦ME *squelen*⟧ **1** to utter or make a long, shrill cry or sound **2** [Slang] to act as an informer —***vt.*** to utter in a squeal —***n.*** a squealing —**squeal′er** ***n.***

squeam·ish (skwē′mish) ***adj.*** ⟦ME *squaimous*⟧ **1** easily nauseated **2** easily shocked **3** fastidious —**squeam′ish·ly** ***adv.*** —**squeam′ish·ness** ***n.***

squee·gee (skwē′jē) ***n.*** ⟦prob. < fol.⟧ a rubber-edged tool for scraping water from a flat surface

squeeze (skwēz) ***vt.* squeezed, squeez′ing** ⟦< OE *cwysan*⟧ **1** to press hard, esp. from two or more sides **2** to extract (juice, etc.) from (fruit, etc.) **3** to force (*into, out,* etc.) by pressing **4** to embrace closely; hug —***vi.* 1** to yield to pressure **2** to exert pressure **3** to force one's way by pushing (*in, out,* etc.) —***n.* 1** a squeezing or being squeezed **2** a close embrace; hug **3** the state of being closely pressed or packed; crush **4** a period of scarcity, hardship, etc.

squeeze bottle a plastic bottle that is squeezed to eject its contents

squelch (skwelch) [Inf.] ***n.*** ⟦prob. echoic⟧ a crushing retort, rebuke, etc. —***vt.*** to suppress or silence completely

squib (skwib) ***n.*** ⟦prob. echoic⟧ **1** a firecracker that burns with a hissing noise before exploding **2** a short, witty attack in words; lampoon **3** a short news item

squid (skwid) ***n.*** ⟦prob. < *squit,* dial. for SQUIRT⟧ a long, slender sea mollusk with eight arms and two long tentacles

squig·gle (skwig′əl) ***n.*** ⟦SQU(IRM) + (W)IGGLE⟧ a short, wavy line or illegible scrawl —***vt., vi.* -gled, -gling** to write as, or make, a squiggle or squiggles

squint (skwint) ***vi.*** ⟦< (*a*)*squint,* with a squint < ME *on skwyn,* sideways⟧ **1** to peer with the eyes partly closed **2** to be cross-eyed —***n.* 1** a squinting **2** a being cross-eyed **3** [Inf.] a quick look

squire (skwīr) ***n.*** ⟦see ESQUIRE⟧ **1** in England, the owner of a large, rural estate **2** a man escorting a woman —***vt.* squired, squir′ing** to escort

squirm (skwʉrm) ***vi.*** ⟦prob. echoic, infl. by WORM⟧ **1** to twist and turn the body; wriggle **2** to show or feel shame or embarrassment —***n.*** a squirming —**squirm′y, -i·er, -i·est,** ***adj.***

squir·rel (skwʉr′əl, skwʉrl) ***n.*** ⟦< Gr *skia,* shadow + *oura,* tail⟧ **1** a small, tree-dwelling rodent with heavy fur and a long, bushy tail **2** its fur

squirt (skwʉrt) ***vt.*** ⟦prob. < LowG *swirtjen*⟧ **1** to shoot out (a liquid) in a jet; spurt **2** to wet with liquid so shot out —***n.* 1** a jet of liquid **2** [Inf.] a small or young person, esp. an impudent one

squish (skwish) ***vi.*** ⟦echoic var. of SQUASH[1]⟧ to make a soft, splashing sound when squeezed, etc. —***vt.*** [Inf.] to squash —***n.* 1** a squishing sound **2** [Inf.] a squashing —**squish′y, -i·er, -i·est,** ***adj.***

Sr[1] *abbrev.* **1** Senior **2** Sister

Sr[2] *Chem. symbol for* strontium

Sri Lan·ka (srē läŋ′kə) country coextensive with an island off the SE tip of India: 25,332 sq. mi.; pop. 14,847,000 —**Sri Lan′kan**

SRO *abbrev.* **1** single room occupancy **2** standing room only

SS *abbrev.* **1** Social Security **2** steamship

SST *abbrev.* supersonic transport

St *abbrev.* **1** Saint **2** Strait **3** Street

stab (stab) ***n.*** ⟦prob. < ME *stubbe,* stub⟧ **1** a wound made by stabbing **2** a thrust, as with a knife **3** a sudden,

THESAURUS

squalid ***a.*** filthy, sordid, foul; see DIRTY 1.

squall[1] ***n.*** blast, gust, gale; see STORM.

squalor ***n.*** ugliness, disorder, uncleanness; see FILTH.

squander ***v.*** use wastefully, spend lavishly, throw away; see WASTE 2.

square ***a.*** **1** [Having right angles] right-angled, four-sided, equal-sided, squared, equilateral, rectangular, rectilinear. **2** [*Old-fashioned] dated, stuffy, conventional; see CONSERVATIVE, OLD-FASHIONED.

square ***n.*** **1** [A rectangle] equal-sided rectangle, plane figure, four-sided figure; see RECTANGLE. **2** [A park] city center, town square, plaza, recreational area; see also PARK 1.

squat ***v.*** stoop, hunch, cower; see SIT.

squawk ***v.*** cackle, crow, yap; see CRY 2.

squeak ***n.*** peep, squeal, screech; see CRY 2, NOISE 1.

squeak ***v.*** creak, peep, squeal; see CRY 2, SOUND. —**squeak through*** manage, survive, get by*; see ENDURE 2, SUCCEED 1.

squeal ***v.*** shout, yell, screech; see CRY 1, 2.

squeamish ***a.*** finicky, fussy, delicate, hard to please, fastidious, particular, exacting, prim, prudish, queasy, qualmish, easily nauseated, persnickety*, prissy*.

squeeze* ***n.*** influence, restraint, force; see PRESSURE 1, 2. —**put the squeeze on*** compel, urge, use force with; see FORCE, INFLUENCE.

squeeze ***v.*** clasp, pinch, clutch; see HUG, PRESS 1.

squint ***v.*** narrow the eyes, peek, peep; see LOOK 2.

squirm ***v.*** wriggle, twist, fidget; see WIGGLE.

squirt ***v.*** spurt, spit, eject; see EMIT.

stab ***n.*** thrust, wound, puncture;

sharp pain —*vt., vi.* **stabbed, stab'bing** **1** to pierce or wound as with a knife **2** to thrust (a knife, etc.) into something **3** to pain sharply —**make** (or **take**) **a stab at** [Inf.] to make an attempt at

sta·bil·i·ty (stə bil'ə tē) ***n.*** **1** a being stable; steadiness **2** firmness of character, purpose, etc. **3** permanence

sta·bi·lize (stā'bə līz') ***vt.*** **-lized', -liz'ing** **1** to make stable **2** to keep from changing **3** to give stability to (a plane or ship) —*vi.* to become stabilized —**sta'bi·li·za'tion** ***n.*** —**sta'bi·liz'er** ***n.***

sta·ble[1] (stā'bəl) ***adj.*** **-bler, -blest** ⟦< L *stare,* to stand⟧ **1** not likely to give way; firm; fixed **2** firm in character, purpose, etc.; steadfast **3** not likely to change; lasting

sta·ble[2] (stā'bəl) ***n.*** ⟦see prec.⟧ **1** a building in which horses or cattle are sheltered and fed **2** all the race-horses belonging to one owner —*vt., vi.* **-bled, -bling** to lodge, keep, or be kept in or as in a stable

stac·ca·to (stə kät'ō) ***adj., adv.*** ⟦It < *distaccare,* detach⟧ *Music* with distinct breaks between successive tones

stack (stak) ***n.*** ⟦< ON *stakkr*⟧ **1** a large, neatly arranged pile of straw, hay, etc. **2** any orderly pile **3** SMOKESTACK **4** [*pl.*] a series of bookshelves, as in a library —*vt.* **1** to arrange in a stack **2** to rig so as to predetermine the outcome —**stack up** to stand in comparison (*with* or *against*)

stack'up' ***n.*** an arrangement of circling aircraft at various altitudes awaiting their turn to land

sta·di·um (stā'dē əm) ***n.*** ⟦< Gr *stadion,* ancient unit of length, *c.* 607 feet⟧ a large structure as for sports events, with tiers of seats for spectators

staff (staf) ***n.,*** *pl.* **staffs**; also, for 1 & 4, **staves** ⟦OE *stæf*⟧ **1** a stick or rod used as a support, a symbol of authority, etc. **2** a group of people assisting a leader **3** a specific group of workers *[a teaching staff]* **4** *Music* the horizontal lines on and between which notes are written —*vt.* to provide with a staff, as of workers

staff'er ***n.*** a member of a staff, as of a newspaper

stag (stag) ***n.*** ⟦OE *stagga*⟧ a full-grown male deer —*adj.* for men only *[a stag dinner]*

stage (stāj) ***n.*** ⟦< L *stare,* to stand⟧ **1** a platform **2** *a)* an area or platform on which plays, etc. are presented *b)* the theater, or acting as a profession (with *the*) **3** the scene of an event **4** a stopping place, or the distance between stops, on a journey **5** *short for* STAGECOACH **6** a period or level in a process of development *[the larval stage]* **7** any of the propulsion units used in sequence to launch a missile, spacecraft, etc. —*vt.* **staged, stag'ing** **1** to present as on a stage **2** to plan and carry out *[to stage an attack]*

stage'coach' ***n.*** a horse-drawn public coach that, formerly, traveled a regular route

stage'hand' ***n.*** one who sets up scenery, furniture, lights, etc. for a stage play

stage'-struck' ***adj.*** having an intense desire to become an actor or actress

stag·ger (stag'ər) ***vi.*** ⟦< ON *stakra,* totter⟧ to totter, reel, etc. as from a blow or fatigue —*vt.* **1** to cause to stagger, as with a blow **2** to affect strongly with astonishment, grief, etc. **3** to set or arrange alternately, as on either side of a line; make zigzag **4** to arrange so as to come at different times *[to stagger employees' vacations]* —*n.* **1** a staggering **2** [*pl., with sing. or pl. v.*] a nervous disease of horses, etc. causing this

stag·nant (stag'nənt) ***adj.*** ⟦see fol.⟧ **1** not flowing or moving **2** foul from lack of movement: said of water **3** dull; sluggish

stag'nate' (-nāt') ***vi., vt.*** **-nat'ed, -nat'ing** ⟦< L *stagnare*⟧ to become or make stagnant —**stag·na'tion** ***n.***

staid (stād) ***vi., vt.*** *archaic pt. & pp. of* STAY[3] —*adj.* sober; sedate —**staid'ly** ***adv.***

stain (stān) ***vt.*** ⟦ult. < L *dis-,* from + *tingere,* to tinge⟧ **1** to spoil by discoloring or spotting **2** to disgrace; dishonor **3** to color (wood, etc.) with a dye —*n.* **1** a color or spot resulting from staining **2** a moral blemish **3** a dye for staining wood, etc.

stain'less steel steel alloyed with chromium, etc., virtually immune to rust and corrosion

stair (ster) ***n.*** ⟦OE *stæger*⟧ **1** [*usually pl.*] a stairway **2** a single step, as of a stairway

stair'case' ***n.*** a stairway in a building, usually with a handrail

stair'way' ***n.*** a means of access, as from one level of a building to another, consisting of a series of stairs

stair'well' ***n.*** a vertical shaft (in a building) containing a staircase

stake (stāk) ***n.*** ⟦OE *staca*⟧ **1** a pointed length of wood or metal for driving into the ground **2** the post to which a person was tied for execution by burning **3** [*often pl.*] money risked, as in a wager or business venture **4** [*often pl.*] the winner's prize in a race, etc. —*vt.* **staked, stak'ing** **1** to mark the boundaries of *[to stake out a claim]* **2** to fasten to a stake or stakes **3** to gamble **4** [Inf.] to furnish with money or resources —**at stake** being risked —**pull up stakes** [Inf.] to change one's residence, etc. —**stake out** to put under police surveillance

stake'out' ***n.*** **1** the putting of a suspect or a place under police surveillance **2** an area under such surveillance

sta·lac·tite (stə lak'tīt) ***n.*** ⟦< Gr *stalaktos,* trickling⟧ an icicle-shaped mineral deposit hanging from a cave roof

sta·lag (shtä'läk; *E* stä'läg) ***n.*** ⟦Ger⟧ a German prisoner-of-war camp, esp. in WWII

sta·lag·mite (stə lag'mīt') ***n.*** ⟦< Gr *stalagmos,* a dropping⟧ a cone-shaped mineral deposit built up on a cave floor by dripping water

stale (stāl) ***adj.*** **stal'er, stal'est** ⟦prob. < OFr *estale,* quiet⟧ **1** no longer fresh; flat, dry, etc. **2** trite *[a stale joke]* **3** out of condition, bored, etc.

stale'mate' ***n.*** ⟦< OFr *estal,* fixed location⟧ **1** *Chess* any situation in which a player cannot move: it results in a draw **2** any deadlock —*vt.* **-mat'ed, -mat'ing** to bring into a stalemate

Sta·lin (stä'lin), **Joseph** 1879-1953; Soviet premier (1941-53) —**Sta'lin·ism'** ***n.*** —**Sta'lin·ist** ***adj., n.***

stalk[1] (stôk) ***vi., vt.*** ⟦OE *stealcian*⟧ **1** to walk (through) in a stiff, haughty manner **2** to advance grimly **3** *a)* to pursue (game, etc.) stealthily *b)* to pursue (a person) in a persistent, harassing, obsessive way —*n.* **1** a slow, stiff, haughty stride **2** a stalking

stalk[2] (stôk) ***n.*** ⟦ME *stalke*⟧ **1** any stem or stemlike part **2** the main stem of a plant

stall[1] (stôl) ***n.*** ⟦OE *steall*⟧ **1** a section for one animal in a stable **2** *a)* a booth, etc. as at a market *b)* a pew in a

THESAURUS

see CUT. —**make (or take) a stab at** endeavor, try to, do one's best to; see TRY 1.

stab ***v.*** pierce, wound, stick, cut, hurt, run through, thrust, prick, drive, puncture, hit, bayonet, knife; see also KILL 1.

stability ***n.*** **1** [Firmness of position] steadiness, durability, solidity, endurance, immobility, suspension, balance, permanence. **2** [Steadfastness of character] stableness, aplomb, security, endurance, maturity, resoluteness, determination, perseverance, adherence, backbone, assurance, resistance; see also CONFIDENCE.

stable[1] ***a.*** **1** [Fixed] steady, stationary, solid; see FIRM 1. **2** [Steadfast] calm, firm, consistent; see CONSTANT.

stable[2] ***n.*** barn, coop, corral; see PEN 1.

stack ***n.*** pile, heap, mound; see BUNCH.

stack ***v.*** heap, pile up, accumulate; see LOAD 1. —**stack up** compare, measure up, match; see EQUAL.

stadium ***n.*** gymnasium, stands, amphitheater; see ARENA.

staff ***n.*** **1** [A stick] wand, pole, stave; see STICK. **2** [A corps of employees] personnel, assistants, men, women, force, help, workers, crew, team, faculty, cadre, cast, factotums, organization, agents, operatives, deputies, servants.

stage ***n.*** **1** [The theater] theater, limelight, spotlight; see DRAMA. **2** [A platform] frame, scaffold, staging; see PLATFORM 1. **3** [A level, period, or degree] grade, plane, step; see DEGREE 1. —**by easy stages** easily, gently, taking one's time; see SLOWLY.

stagger ***v.*** totter, waver, sway, weave, bob, careen, vacillate.

staggering ***a.*** monstrous, huge, tremendous; see LARGE 1, UNBELIEVABLE.

stagnant ***a.*** inert, dead, inactive; see IDLE.

stagnate ***v.*** deteriorate, putrefy, rot; see DECAY.

staid ***a.*** sober, grave, steady; see DIGNIFIED.

stain ***n.*** blot, blemish, spot, splotch, stained spot, smudge, stigma, brand, blotch, ink spot, spatter, drip, speck.

stain ***v.*** spot, discolor, taint; see DIRTY.

stairs ***n.*** stairway, staircase, flight, steps, stair, fire escape, escalator, ascent.

stake ***n.*** rod, paling, pale; see STICK. —**at stake** in danger, at risk, involved, implicated, in jeopardy, in question, hazarded, concerned*, endangered. —**pull up stakes*** depart, move, decamp; see LEAVE 1.

stale ***a.*** spoiled, dried, smelly; see OLD 2.

stalk[1] ***v.*** shadow, track, chase; see HUNT 1, PURSUE 1.

stalk[2] ***n.*** stem, support, upright, spire, shaft, spike, straw, stock, trunk.

stall[1,2] ***v.*** **1** [To break down] not

church 3 the state of being in a stop or standstill, as a result of some malfunction —*vt.*, *vi.* 1 to keep or be kept in a stall 2 to bring or be brought to a standstill, esp. unintentionally

stall[2] (stôl) *vi.*, *vt.* ⟦< *stall,* a decoy⟧ to act evasively so as to deceive or delay —*n.* any action used in stalling

stal·lion (stal′yən) *n.* ⟦< OFr *estalon*⟧ an uncastrated male horse

stal·wart (stôl′wərt) *adj.* ⟦< OE *stathol,* foundation + *wyrthe,* worth⟧ 1 strong; sturdy 2 brave; valiant 3 resolute; firm —*n.* a stalwart person

sta·men (stā′mən) *n.* ⟦< L, thread⟧ the pollen-bearing organ in a flower

Stam·ford (stam′fərd) city in SW Connecticut: pop. 108,000

stam·i·na (stam′ə nə) *n.* ⟦L, pl. of STAMEN⟧ resistance to fatigue, illness, hardship, etc.; endurance

stam·mer (stam′ər) *vt.*, *vi.* ⟦OE *stamerian*⟧ to speak or say with involuntary pauses and rapid repetitions of some sounds —*n.* a stammering —**stam′mer·er** *n.*

stamp (stamp) *vt.* ⟦ME *stampen*⟧ 1 to bring (the foot) down forcibly 2 to crush or pound with the foot 3 to imprint or cut out (a design, etc.) 4 to cut (*out*) by pressing with a die 5 to put a stamp on —*vi.* 1 to bring the foot down forcibly 2 to walk with loud, heavy steps, as in anger —*n.* 1 a stamping 2 *a*) a machine, tool, or die for stamping *b*) a mark or form made by stamping 3 any of various seals, gummed pieces of paper, etc. used to show that a fee, as for postage, has been paid 4 any similar stamp 5 class; kind —**stamp out** 1 to crush by treading on forcibly 2 to suppress, or put down —**stamp′er** *n.*

stam·pede (stam pēd′) *n.* ⟦< Sp *estampar,* to stamp⟧ a sudden, headlong rush or flight, as of a herd of cattle —*vi.* **-ped′ed, -ped′ing** to move, or take part, in a stampede

stamping ground [Inf.] a regular or favorite gathering place: *also used in pl.*

stance (stans) *n.* ⟦< L *stare,* to stand⟧ 1 the way one stands, esp. the placement of the feet 2 the attitude taken in a given situation

stanch *vt.*, *vi.*, *adj. see* STAUNCH

stan·chion (stan′chən) *n.* ⟦see STANCE⟧ 1 an upright post or support 2 a device for confining a cow, fitted loosely around the neck

stand (stand) *vi.* **stood, stand′ing** ⟦OE *standan*⟧ 1 to be in, or assume, an upright position on the feet 2 to be supported on a base, pedestal, etc. 3 to take or be in a (specified) position, attitude, etc. 4 to have a (specified) height when standing 5 to be placed or situated 6 to gather and remain: said as of water 7 to remain unchanged 8 to make resistance 9 *a*) to halt *b*) to be stationary —*vt.* 1 to place upright 2 to endure 3 to withstand 4 to undergo *[to stand trial]* —*n.* 1 a standing; esp., a halt or stop 2 a position; station 3 a view, opinion, etc. 4 a structure to stand or sit on 5 a place of business, esp. a stall, etc. where goods are sold 6 a rack, small table, etc. for holding things 7 a growth of trees, etc. —**stand a chance** to have a chance (*of* winning, surviving, etc.) —**stand by** 1 to be ready if needed 2 to aid —**stand for** 1 to represent; mean 2 [Inf.] to tolerate —**stand on** 1 to be founded on 2 to insist upon —**stand out** 1 to project 2 to be distinct, prominent, etc. —**stand up** 1 to rise to a standing position 2 to prove valid, durable, etc. 3 [Slang] to fail to keep a date with —**take the stand** to testify in court

stand·ard (stan′dərd) *n.* ⟦< OFr *estendard*⟧ 1 a flag or banner used as an emblem of a military unit, etc. 2 something established for use as a rule or basis of comparison in measuring quantity, quality, etc. 3 an upright support —*adj.* 1 used as, or conforming to, a standard, rule, model, etc. 2 generally accepted as reliable or authoritative 3 typical; ordinary

stand′ard-bear′er *n.* 1 one who carries the flag 2 the leader of a movement, political party, etc.

stand′ard·ize′ *vt.* **-ized′, -iz′ing** to make standard or uniform —**stand′ard·i·za′tion** *n.*

standard time the time in any of the 24 time zones, each an hour apart, into which the earth is divided, based on distance east or west of Greenwich, England

stand′by′ *n., pl.* **-bys′** a person or thing that is dependable or is a possible substitute

stand·ee (stan dē′) *n.* one who stands, as in a theater or bus

stand′-in′ *n.* a temporary substitute, as for an actor at rehearsals

stand′ing *n.* 1 status or reputation *[in good standing]* 2 duration *[a rule of long standing]* —*adj.* 1 upright or erect 2 from a standing position *[a standing jump]* 3 stagnant: said as of water 4 lasting; permanent *[a standing order]*

stand′off′ *n.* a tie in a game or contest

stand′off′ish *adj.* reserved; aloof

stand′out′ *n.* [Inf.] a person or thing outstanding in performance, quality, etc.

stand′pipe′ *n.* a high vertical pipe or cylindrical tank, as in a town's water-supply system, for storing water at a desired pressure

stand′point′ *n.* point of view

stand′still′ *n.* a stop or halt

stand′-up′ *adj.* 1 in a standing position 2 designating a comedian who delivers monologues, tells jokes, etc., as in a nightclub

stank (staŋk) *vi. alt. pt. of* STINK

stan·za (stan′zə) *n.* ⟦It: ult. < L *stare*, to stand⟧ a group of lines of verse forming a division of a poem or song

staph (staf) *n. short for* STAPHYLOCOCCUS

staph·y·lo·coc·cus (staf′ə lō käk′əs) *n., pl.* **-coc′ci′** (-käk′sī′) ⟦< Gr *staphylē*, bunch of grapes + *kokkos*, kernel⟧ any of certain spherical bacteria, a common source of infection

sta·ple[1] (stā′pəl) *n.* ⟦< MDu *stapel*, mart⟧ 1 a chief commodity made or grown in a particular place 2 a chief part or element in anything 3 a regularly stocked item of trade, as flour, salt, etc. 4 the fiber of cotton, wool, etc. —*adj.* 1 regularly stocked, produced, or used 2 most important; principal

sta·ple[2] (stā′pəl) *n.* ⟦OE *stapol,* a post⟧ a U-shaped piece of metal with sharp ends, driven into wood, etc. as to hold a hook, wire, etc., or through papers as a binding —*vt.* **-pled, -pling** to fasten or bind with a staple or staples —**sta′pler** *n.*

star (stär) *n.* ⟦OE *steorra*⟧ 1 any of the luminous celestial objects seen as points of light in the sky; esp., any far-

THESAURUS

start, conk out*, die; see BREAK DOWN 2. 2 [To delay] postpone, hamper, hinder; see DELAY.

stamina *n.* strength, vigor, vitality; see ENDURANCE.

stammer *v.* stutter, repeat oneself, hem and haw, falter, stop, stumble, hesitate, pause; see also SPEAK 1.

stamp *n.* emblem, brand, cast; see MARK 1.

stamp *v.* impress, imprint, brand; see MARK 1. —**stamp out** eliminate, kill off, dispatch; see DESTROY.

stamped *a.* marked, branded, okayed*; see APPROVED.

stampede *n.* rush, dash, flight; see RUN 1.

stampede *v.* bolt, rush, panic; see RUN 2.

stand *n.* notion, view, belief; see ATTITUDE, OPINION 1. —**make** (or **take**) **a stand** insist, assert, take a position; see DECLARE.

stand *v.* 1 [To be in an upright position] be erect, be on one's feet, stand up, come to one's feet, rise, jump up. 2 [To endure] last, hold, abide; see ENDURE 1. 3 [To be of a certain height] be, attain, come to; see REACH 1. —**stand a chance** have a chance, be a possibility, have something in one's favor, have something on one's side, be preferred. —**stand by** 1 [To defend or help] befriend, second, abet; see DEFEND 2, HELP. 2 [To wait] be prepared, be ready, be near; see WAIT 1. —**stand for** 1 [To mean] represent, suggest, imply; see MEAN 1. 2 [To allow] permit, suffer, endure; see ALLOW. —**stand out** be prominent, be conspicuous, emerge; see LOOM 2.

standard *a.* regular, regulation, typical; see APPROVED.

standard *n.* pattern, type, example; see MODEL 2.

standardization *n.* uniformity, sameness, likeness, evenness, levelness, monotony; see also REGULARITY.

standardize *v.* regulate, institute, normalize; see ORDER 3, SYSTEMATIZE.

standardized *a.* patterned, regularized, made alike; see REGULATED.

standby *n.* supporter, stand-in, proxy; see SUBSTITUTE.

stand-in *n.* proxy, second, understudy; see SUBSTITUTE.

standing *n.* position, status, reputation; see RANK 3.

standoff *n.* stalemate, deadlock, dead end; see DELAY.

standoffish *a.* cool, aloof, distant; see INDIFFERENT.

standpoint *n.* attitude, point of view, view; see OPINION 1.

standstill *n.* stop, halt, cessation; see DELAY.

star *n.* 1 [A luminous heavenly body] sun, astral body, pulsar, quasar, fixed star, variable star. *Familiar stars include the following—individual stars*: Betelgeuse, Sirius, Vega,

off, self-luminous one **2** such an object regarded as influencing one's fate: *often used in pl.* **3** a conventionalized figure with five or six points, or anything like this **4** ASTERISK **5** one who excels, as in a sport **6** a leading actor or actress —***vt.* starred, star′ring 1** to mark with stars as a decoration, etc. **2** to feature (an actor or actress) in a leading role —***vi.* 1** to perform brilliantly **2** to perform as a star, as in films —***adj.* 1** having great skill; outstanding **2** of a star

star·board (stär′bərd, -bôrd′) ***n.*** ⟦< OE *steoran,* to steer (rudder formerly on right side) + *bord,* side (of ship)⟧ the right-hand side of a ship, etc. as one faces forward —***adj.*** of or on this side

starch (stärch) ***n.*** ⟦< OE *stearc,* stiff⟧ **1** a white, tasteless, odorless food substance found in potatoes, cereals, etc. **2** a powdered form of this, used in laundering for stiffening cloth, etc. —***vt.*** to stiffen as with starch —**starch′y, -i·er, -i·est,** ***adj.***

star′-crossed′ ***adj.*** ⟦see STAR, *n.* 2⟧ ill-fated

star·dom (stär′dəm) ***n.*** the status of a star, as of films

stare (ster) ***vi.* stared, star′ing** ⟦OE *starian*⟧ to gaze steadily and intently —***vt.*** to look fixedly at —***n.*** a steady, intent look —**star′er** ***n.***

star′fish′ ***n.***, *pl.* **-fish′** or (for different species) **-fish′es** a small, star-shaped sea animal

star′gaze′ ***vi.* -gazed′, -gaz′ing 1** to gaze at the stars **2** to indulge in dreamy thought —**star′gaz′er** ***n.***

stark (stärk) ***adj.*** ⟦OE *stearc*⟧ **1** rigorous; severe **2** sharply outlined **3** bleak; desolate **4** sheer; downright —***adv.*** utterly; wholly

star′less ***adj.*** with no stars visible

star·let (stär′lit) ***n.*** a young actress being promoted as a future star

star′light′ ***n.*** light given by the stars —**star′lit′** ***adj.***

star·ling (stär′liŋ) ***n.*** ⟦OE *stær*⟧ any of an Old World family of birds; esp., the **common starling** with iridescent plumage, introduced into the U.S.

Star of David a six-pointed star, Judaic symbol

star′ry ***adj.* -ri·er, -ri·est 1** shining; bright **2** lighted by or full of stars

star′ry-eyed′ ***adj.* 1** with sparkling eyes **2** overly optimistic

Stars and Stripes *name for* the U.S. flag

star′-span′gled ***adj.*** studded with stars

Star-Spangled Banner the U.S. national anthem

star′-struck′ or **star′struck′** ***adj.*** fascinated by celebrities, esp. by stars of movies, etc.

start (stärt) ***vi.*** ⟦OE *styrtan*⟧ **1** to make a sudden or involuntary move **2** to go into action or motion; begin; commence **3** to spring into being, activity, etc. —***vt.* 1** to flush (game) **2** to displace, loosen, etc. *[to start a seam]* **3** *a)* to begin to play, do, etc. *b)* to set into motion, action, etc. **4** to cause to be an entrant in a race, etc. **5** to play in (a game) at the beginning —***n.* 1** a sudden, startled reaction or movement **2** a starting, or beginning **3** *a)* a place or time of beginning *b)* a lead or other advantage **4** an opportunity of beginning a career —**start out** (or **off**) to start a journey, project, etc. —**start′er** ***n.***

star·tle (stärt′'l) ***vt.* -tled, -tling** ⟦< ME *sterten,* to start⟧ to surprise, frighten, or alarm suddenly; esp., to cause to start —***vi.*** to be startled

start′-up′ ***adj., n.*** (of) a new business venture

starve (stärv) ***vi.* starved, starv′ing** ⟦< OE *steorfan,* to die⟧ **1** to die from lack of food **2** to suffer from hunger **3** to suffer great need: with *for* —***vt.* 1** to cause to starve **2** to force by starvation —**star·va·tion** (stär vā′shən) ***n.***

starve′ling (-liŋ) ***n.*** a person or animal that is weak from lack of food

Star Wars ⟦from a film title⟧ [Inf.] a proposed defense system of space-based weapons for destroying missiles

stash (stash) [Inf.] ***vt.*** ⟦< ?⟧ to put or hide away (money, etc.) —***n.* 1** a place for hiding things **2** something hidden away

-stat (stat) *combining form* a device or agent that keeps something (specified) stable *[thermostat]*

state (stāt) ***n.*** ⟦< L *stare,* to stand⟧ **1** a set of circumstances, etc. characterizing a person or thing; condition **2** condition as regards structure, form, etc. **3** rich display; pomp **4** [*sometimes* **S-**] a body of people politically organized under one government; nation **5** [*often* **S-**] any of the political units forming a federal government, as in the U.S. **6** civil government *[church and state]* —***adj.* 1** formal; ceremonial **2** [*sometimes* **S-**] of the government or of a state —***vt.* stat′ed, stat′ing 1** to establish by specifying **2** *a)* to set forth in words *b)* to express nonverbally —**in a state** [Inf.] in an excited condition —**lie in state** to be displayed formally before burial —**the States** the United States

state′hood′ ***n.*** the condition of being a state

state′house′ ***n.*** [*often* **S-**] the official legislative meeting place of each U.S. state

state′less ***adj.*** having no state or nationality

state′ly ***adj.* -li·er, -li·est 1** imposing; majestic **2** slow, dignified, etc. —**state′li·ness** ***n.***

state′ment ***n.* 1** *a)* a stating *b)* a declaration, assertion, etc. **2** *a)* a financial account *b)* a bill; invoice

Stat·en Island (stat′'n) island borough of New York City: pop. 379,000

state of the art the current level of sophistication, as of technology —**state′-of-the-art′** ***adj.***

state′room′ ***n.*** a private room on a ship or train

state′side′ [Inf.] ***adj.*** of or in the U.S. (as viewed from abroad) —***adv.*** in or to the U.S.

states·man (stāts′mən) ***n.***, *pl.* **-men** (-mən) one who is wise or experienced in the business of government —**states′man·ship′** ***n.***

stat·ic (stat′ik) ***adj.*** ⟦< Gr *statikos,* causing to stand⟧ **1** of masses, forces, etc. at rest or in equilibrium **2** at rest; inactive **3** of or producing stationary electrical charges, as from friction **4** of or having to do with static —***n.* 1** noise in radio or TV reception, caused by atmospheric electrical discharges **2** [Slang] adverse criticism —**stat′i·cal·ly** ***adv.***

sta·tion (stā′shən) ***n.*** ⟦< L *stare,* to stand⟧ **1** the place where a person or thing stands or is located; esp., an

THESAURUS

Spica, Arcturus, Aldebaran, Antares, Alpha Centauri or Rigil Kent, Deneb, Rigel, Canopus, Procyon, Castor, Pollux, Capella, Algol, North Star or Polaris; *constellations:* Ursa Major or the Great Bear, Ursa Minor or the Little Bear, Big Dipper, Little Dipper, Orion or the Hunter, Coma Berenices or Berenice's Hair, Gemini or the Twins, Cassiopeia, Pleiades, Taurus or the Bull, Canis Major or the Greater Dog, Canis Minor or the Lesser Dog, Scorpius or the Scorpion, Sagittarius or the Archer, Corona Borealis or the Northern Crown, Pegasus, Leo or the Lion, Hercules, Boötes or the Herdsman, Cetus or the Whale, Aquila or the Eagle, Cygnus or the Swan, Corona Australis or the Southern Crown, Crux or the Southern Cross, Cancer or the Crab, Virgo or the Virgin, Libra or the Scales, Capricornus or the Sea Goat, Aquarius or the Water Bearer, Pisces or the Fishes, Aries or the Ram. **2** [A conventional figure] asterisk, Star of David, five-pointed star; see FORM 1. **3** [A superior performer] headliner, leading lady, leading man, movie actor, movie actress, actor, actress, matinee idol, chief attraction, superstar.

stare ***v.*** gaze, gawk, ogle; see LOOK 2, WATCH.

stark-naked ***a.*** nude, without a stitch of clothing, in the altogether*; see NAKED 1.

start ***n.*** inception, commencement, beginning; see ORIGIN 2.

start ***v.*** commence, begin, initiate, originate, inaugurate, launch, create, kick off*, turn on, switch on, fire up, power up, set off; see also BEGIN 1, 2.

started ***a.*** evoked, initiated, instituted; see BEGUN.

startle ***v.*** alarm, shock, astonish; see SURPRISE.

starvation ***n.*** deprivation, need, want; see HUNGER.

starve ***v.*** famish, crave, perish; see DIE.

starving ***a.*** famished, weakening, dying; see HUNGRY.

state ***n.* 1** [A sovereign unit] republic, body politic, kingdom; see NATION 1. **2** [A condition] circumstance, situation, welfare, phase, case, station, nature, estate, footing, status, standing, occurrence, occasion, eventuality, element, requirement, category, standing, reputation, environment, chances, outlook, position. —**in a state*** disturbed, upset, badly off; see TROUBLED.

state ***v.*** pronounce, assert, affirm; see DECLARE.

stately ***a.* 1** [*Said of persons*] dignified, haughty, noble; see PROUD 1. **2** [*Said of objects*] large, imposing, magnificent; see GRAND.

statement ***n.* 1** [The act of stating] allegation, declaration, assertion, profession, acknowledgment, assurance, affirmation; see also ANNOUNCEMENT. **2** [A statement of account] bill, charge, reckoning, invoice, account, record, report, budget, audit, balance sheet, tab*, check.

statesman ***n.*** legislator, lawgiver, administrator, executive, minister, official, politician, diplomat, representative, elder statesman, veteran lawmaker.

station ***n.* 1** [Place] situation, site,

assigned post **2** a building, etc. at which a service, etc. is provided *[police station]* **3** a regular stopping place, as on a railroad **4** social standing **5** *a)* a place equipped for radio or TV transmission *b)* its assigned frequency or channel —***vt.*** to assign to a station

sta·tion·ar·y (stā′shə ner′ē) ***adj.*** **1** not moving; fixed **2** unchanging

station break a pause in radio or TV programs for station identification

sta·tion·er (stā′shə nər) ***n.*** ⟦< ML *stationarius,* shopkeeper⟧ a dealer in office supplies, etc.

sta′tion·er′y (-ner′ē) ***n.*** writing materials; specif., paper and envelopes

station wagon an automobile with extra space for cargo or seating and a rear door for loading

sta·tis·tics (stə tis′tiks) ***pl.n.*** ⟦< L *status,* standing⟧ numerical data assembled and classified so as to present significant information —***n.*** the science of compiling such data —**sta·tis′ti·cal** ***adj.*** —**stat·is·ti·cian** (stat′is tish′ ən) ***n.***

stats (stats) ***pl.n.*** [Inf.] *short for* STATISTICS

stat·u·ar·y (stach′o͞o er′ē) ***n.*** statues collectively

stat·ue (stach′o͞o) ***n.*** ⟦< L *statuere,* to set⟧ a figure, as of a person, or an abstract form carved in stone, cast in bronze, etc.

stat′u·esque′ (-esk′) ***adj.*** tall and stately

stat′u·ette′ (-et′) ***n.*** a small statue

stat·ure (stach′ər) ***n.*** ⟦< L *statura*⟧ **1** standing height, esp. of a person **2** level of attainment *[moral stature]*

sta·tus (stat′əs, stāt′-) ***n., pl.*** **-tus·es** ⟦L, standing⟧ **1** legal condition *[the status of a minor]* **2** *a)* position; rank *b)* prestige **3** state, as of affairs

status quo (kwō′) ⟦L, the state in which⟧ the existing state of affairs

status symbol a possession regarded as a mark of high social status

stat·ute (stach′o͞ot) ***n.*** ⟦see STATUE⟧ **1** an established rule **2** a law passed by a legislative body

statute of limitations a statute limiting the time for legal action

stat·u·to·ry (stach′o͞o tôr′ē) ***adj.*** **1** fixed or authorized by statute **2** punishable by statute

St. Au·gus·tine (ô′gəs tēn′) seaport in NE Florida: oldest city (founded 1565) in the U.S.: pop. 12,000

staunch (stônch, stänch) ***vt.*** ⟦< L *stare,* to stand⟧ to check the flow of (blood, etc.) from (a cut, etc.) —***vi.*** to stop flowing —***adj.*** **1** seaworthy **2** steadfast; loyal **3** strong; solid Also, esp. for v., **stanch** (stänch, stanch) —**staunch′ly** ***adv.***

stave (stāv) ***n.*** ⟦< *staves,* pl. of STAFF⟧ **1** any of the shaped strips of wood forming the wall of a barrel, bucket, etc. **2** a stick or staff **3** a stanza —***vt.*** **staved** or **stove, stav′ing** to smash or break *(in)* —**stave off** to hold off or put off

staves (stāvz) ***n.*** **1** *alt. pl. of* STAFF **2** *pl. of* STAVE

stay[1] (stā) ***n.*** ⟦OE *stæg*⟧ a heavy rope or cable, used as a brace or support

stay[2] (stā) ***n.*** ⟦Fr *estaie*⟧ **1** a support or prop **2** a strip of stiffening material used in a corset, shirt collar, etc. —***vt.*** to support, or prop up

stay[3] (stā) ***vi.*** **stayed, stay′ing** ⟦< L *stare,* to stand⟧ **1** to continue in the place or condition specified; remain **2** to live; dwell **3** to stop; halt **4** to pause; delay **5** [Inf.] to continue; last —***vt.*** **1** to stop or check **2** to hinder or detain **3** to postpone (legal action) **4** to satisfy (thirst, etc.) for a time **5** *a)* to remain to the end of *b)* to be able to last through —***n.*** **1** *a)* a stopping or being stopped *b)* a halt or pause **2** a postponement in legal action **3** the action of remaining, or the time spent, in a place —**stay put** [Inf.] to remain in place or unchanged

staying power endurance

St. Cath·ar·ines (kath′ər inz) city in SE Ontario, Canada: pop. 131,000

St. Chris·to·pher (kris′tə fər) St. Kitts: see ST. KITTS AND NEVIS

STD *abbrev.* sexually transmitted disease

Ste ⟦Fr *Sainte*⟧ *abbrev.* **1** Saint (female) **2** Suite

stead (sted) ***n.*** ⟦OE *stede*⟧ the place of a person or thing as filled by a substitute —**stand someone in good stead** to give someone good service

stead′fast′ ***adj.*** ⟦OE *stedefæste*⟧ **1** firm; fixed **2** constant —**stead′fast′ly** ***adv.***

stead′y ***adj.*** **-i·er, -i·est** ⟦STEAD + -Y[2]⟧ **1** firm; stable; not shaky **2** constant, regular, or uniform *[a steady gaze]* **3** constant in behavior, loyalty, etc. **4** habitual or regular; by habit *[a steady customer]* **5** calm and controlled *[steady nerves]* **6** sober; reliable —***vt., vi.*** **-ied, -y·ing** to make or become steady —***n.*** [Inf.] a person one dates regularly —***adv.*** in a steady manner —**go steady** [Inf.] to date someone (or each other) exclusively —**stead′i·ly** ***adv.*** —**stead′i·ness** ***n.***

steak (stāk) ***n.*** ⟦< ON *steikja,* to roast on a spit⟧ a slice of beef, fish, etc. for broiling or frying

steal (stēl) ***vt.*** **stole, stol′en, steal′ing** ⟦OE *stælan*⟧ **1** to take (another's property, etc.) dishonestly or unlawfully, esp. in a secret manner **2** to take (a look, etc.) slyly **3** to gain insidiously or artfully *[he stole her heart]* **4** to move, put, etc. stealthily *(in, from,* etc.) **5** *Baseball* to gain (a base), as by running to it from another base while the pitch is being delivered —***vi.*** **1** to be a thief **2** to move, etc. stealthily —***n.*** [Inf.] an extraordinary bargain

stealth (stelth) ***n.*** ⟦< ME *stelen,* to steal⟧ secret or furtive action —***adj.*** of or using technology that prevents detection by enemy radar —**stealth′y** ***adj.*** —**stealth′i·ly** ***adv.***

steam (stēm) ***n.*** ⟦OE⟧ **1** water as converted into a vapor by being heated to the boiling point **2** the power of steam under pressure **3** condensed water vapor **4** [Inf.] vigor; energy —***adj.*** using, conveying, or operated by, steam —***vi.*** **1** to give off steam **2** to become covered or coated with condensed steam: usually with *up* **3** to move by steam power —***vt.*** to cook, remove, etc. with steam —**steam′y, -i·er, -i·est,** ***adj.***

steam′boat′ ***n.*** a small steamship

steam engine an engine using steam under pressure to supply mechanical energy

steam′er ***n.*** **1** something operated by steam, as a steamship **2** a container for cooking, cleaning, etc. with steam

steam′fit′ter ***n.*** one whose work is installing boilers, pipes, etc. in steam-pressure systems

steam′roll′er ***n.*** a construction machine or vehicle with a heavy roller —***vt., vi.*** to move, crush, override, etc. as (with) a steamroller: also **steam′roll′**

steam′ship′ ***n.*** a ship driven by steam power

THESAURUS

location; see POSITION 1. **2** [Depot] terminal, stop, stopping place; see DEPOT. **3** [Social position] order, standing, state; see RANK 3. **4** [An establishment to vend petroleum products] gas station, gasoline station, service station, filling station, petrol station, pumps, petroleum retailer; see also GARAGE. **5** [A broadcasting establishment] television station, radio station, television transmission, radio transmission, microwave transmitter, radio transmitter, television transmitter, broadcasting station, studios, channel; see also COMMUNICATIONS, RADIO, TELEVISION.

station ***v.*** place, commission, post; see ASSIGN.

stationary ***a.*** fixed, stable, permanent; see MOTIONLESS 1.

stationery ***n.*** writing materials, office supplies, school supplies; see PAPER 4.

statue ***n.*** statuette, cast, figure, bust, representation, likeness, image, sculpture, statuary, marble, bronze, ivory, icon.

statuesque ***a.*** stately, beautiful, grand; see GRACEFUL 2.

stature ***n.*** development, growth, tallness; see HEIGHT, SIZE 2.

status ***n.*** situation, standing, station; see RANK 3.

staunch ***a.*** steadfast, strong, constant; see FAITHFUL.

stay[1,2,3] ***n.*** **1** [A support] prop, hold, truss; see SUPPORT 2. **2** [A visit] stop, sojourn, halt; see VISIT.

stay[3] ***v.*** tarry, linger, sojourn; see VISIT. —**stay put*** remain, stand still, persist; see WAIT 1.

steadfast ***a.*** staunch, stable, constant; see FAITHFUL.

steadily ***a.*** firmly, unwaveringly, undeviatingly; see REGULARLY.

steady ***a.*** uniform, unvarying, patterned; see CONSTANT, REGULAR 3. —**go steady** (**with**)* keep company with, court, go together*; see COURT, LOVE 1, 2.

steak ***n.*** filet mignon, sirloin, T-bone; see FOOD, MEAT.

steal ***v.*** take, filch, pilfer, thieve, loot, rob, purloin, embezzle, defraud, keep, carry off, shoplift, appropriate, take possession of, lift, remove, impress, abduct, shanghai, kidnap, run off with, hold up, strip, poach, swindle, plagiarize, misappropriate, burglarize, blackmail, fleece, plunder, pillage, ransack, burgle*, stick up*, hijack, rip off*, pinch*, mooch*, gyp*; see also SEIZE 2.

stealing ***n.*** piracy, embezzlement, shoplifting; see CRIME, THEFT.

steam ***n.*** vaporized water, fumes, fog; see VAPOR.

steam ***v.*** heat, brew, pressure-cook; see COOK.

steamboat ***n.*** steamer, steamship, riverboat; see BOAT, SHIP.

steam shovel a large, mechanically operated digger
steed (stēd) *n.* ⟦OE *steda*⟧ a horse for riding
steel (stēl) *n.* ⟦OE *stiele*⟧ **1** a hard, tough alloy of iron with carbon **2** a thing of steel **3** great strength or hardness —*adj.* of or like steel —*vt.* to make hard, tough, etc. —**steel'y, -i·er, -i·est,** *adj.*
steel wool long, thin shavings of steel in a pad, used for scouring, polishing, etc.
steel'yard' *n.* ⟦STEEL + obs. *yard*, rod⟧ a scale consisting of a metal arm suspended from above
steep[1] (stēp) *adj.* ⟦OE *steap,* lofty⟧ **1** having a sharp rise or slope; precipitous **2** [Inf.] excessive; extreme —**steep'ly** *adv.* —**steep'ness** *n.*
steep[2] (stēp) *vt.* ⟦ME *stepen*⟧ to soak, saturate, imbue, etc.
stee·ple (stē'pəl) *n.* ⟦OE *stepel*⟧ **1** a tower rising above the main structure, as of a church **2** a spire
stee'ple·chase' *n.* a horse race run over a course obstructed with ditches, hedges, etc.
stee'ple·jack' *n.* one who builds or repairs steeples, smokestacks, etc.
steer[1] (stir) *vt., vi.* ⟦OE *stieran*⟧ **1** to guide (a ship, etc.) with a rudder **2** to direct the course of (an automobile, etc.) **3** to follow (a course) —**steer clear of** to avoid —**steer'a·ble** *adj.*
steer[2] (stir) *n.* ⟦OE *steor*⟧ a castrated male ox, esp. one raised for beef
steer·age (stir'ij) *n.* **1** a steering **2** [Historical] a section in a ship for the passengers paying the lowest fare
steg·o·sau·rus (steg'ə sôr'əs) *n., pl.* **-ri** (-ī) ⟦< Gr *stegos,* roof + *sauros,* lizard⟧ a large dinosaur with pointed, bony plates along the backbone
stein (stīn) *n.* ⟦Ger⟧ a beer mug
stein'bok' (-bäk') *n.* ⟦Ger⟧ an African antelope
stel·lar (stel'ər) *adj.* ⟦< L *stella,* a star⟧ **1** of a star **2** excellent **3** leading; chief *[a stellar role]*
stem[1] (stem) *n.* ⟦OE *stemn*⟧ **1** the main stalk of a plant **2** any stalk or part supporting leaves, flowers, or fruit **3** a stemlike part, as of a pipe, goblet, etc. **4** the prow of a ship; bow **5** the part of a word to which inflectional endings are added —*vt.* **stemmed, stem'ming** to make headway against *[to stem the tide]* —*vi.* to derive
stem[2] (stem) *vt.* **stemmed, stem'ming** ⟦< ON *stemma*⟧ to stop or check by or as if by damming up
stem'ware' *n.* goblets, wineglasses, etc. having stems
stench (stench) *n.* ⟦< OE *stincan,* to stink⟧ an offensive smell; stink
sten·cil (sten'səl) *vt.* **-ciled** or **-cilled, -cil·ing** or **-cil·ling** ⟦ult. < L *scintilla,* a spark⟧ to make or mark with a stencil —*n.* **1** a thin sheet, as of paper, cut through so that when ink, etc. is applied, designs, letters, etc. form on the surface beneath **2** a design, etc. so made
ste·nog·ra·phy (stə näg'rə fē) *n.* shorthand writing, as of dictation, testimony, etc., for later transcription —**ste·nog'ra·pher** *n.* —**sten·o·graph·ic** (sten'ə graf'ik) *adj.*
stent (stent) *n.* ⟦after C.R. *Stent*, Brit dentist⟧ a surgical device used to hold tissue in place, as inside a blood vessel to keep the vessel open
sten·to·ri·an (sten tôr'ē ən) *adj.* ⟦after *Stentor*, Gr herald in the *Iliad*⟧ very loud
step (step) *n.* ⟦OE *stepe*⟧ **1** a single movement of the foot, as in walking **2** the distance covered by such a movement **3** a short distance **4** a manner of stepping **5** the sound of stepping **6** a rest for the foot in climbing, as a stair **7** a degree; level; stage **8** any of a series of acts, processes, etc. —*vi.* **stepped, step'ping** **1** to move by executing a step **2** to walk a short distance **3** to move briskly (*along*) **4** to enter (*into* a situation, etc.) **5** to press the foot down (*on*) —*vt.* to measure by taking steps: with *off* —**in** (or **out of**) **step** conforming (or not conforming) to a rhythm, a regular procedure, etc. —**step by step** **1** gradually **2** by noting each stage in a process —**step down** to resign —**step up** **1** to advance **2** to increase, as in rate —**take steps** to do the things needed —**step'per** *n.*
step'broth'er *n.* one's stepparent's son by a former marriage
step'child' *n., pl.* **-chil'dren** ⟦< OE *steop-*, orphaned + *cild,* child⟧ one's spouse's child (**step'daugh'ter** or **step'son'**) by a former marriage
step'-down' *n.* a decrease, as in amount, intensity, etc.
step'lad'der *n.* a four-legged ladder with broad, flat steps
step'par'ent *n.* the person (**step'fa'ther** or **step'moth'er**) who has married one's parent after the death of or divorce from the other parent
steppe (step) *n.* ⟦Russ *styep'*⟧ any of the great plains of SE Europe and Asia, having few trees
step'ping·stone' *n.* **1** a stone to step on, as in crossing a stream **2** a means of bettering oneself
step'sis'ter *n.* one's stepparent's daughter by a former marriage
step'-up' *n.* an increase, as in amount, intensity, etc.
-ster (stər) ⟦OE *-estre*⟧ *suffix* one who is, does, creates, or is associated with (something specified) *[trickster, gangster]*
ster·e·o (ster'ē ō') *n., pl.* **-os'** a stereophonic device, system, effect, etc. —*adj. short for* STEREOPHONIC
stereo- ⟦< Gr *stereos,* solid⟧ *combining form* solid, firm, three-dimensional *[stereoscope]*
ster·e·o·phon·ic (ster'ē ə fän'ik) *adj.* designating or of sound reproduction using two or more channels to carry a blend of sounds from separate sources through separate speakers
ster'e·o·scop'ic (-skäp'ik) *adj.* appearing three-dimensional
ster'e·o·type' (-tīp') *n.* ⟦see STEREO- & -TYPE⟧ **1** a printing plate cast from a mold, as a page of set type **2** a fixed or conventional notion or conception —*vt.* **-typed', -typ'ing** to make a stereotype of —**ster'e·o·typed'** *adj.*
ster'e·o·typ'i·cal (-tip'i kəl) *adj.* **1** stereotyped **2** hackneyed
ster·ile (ster'əl) *adj.* ⟦L *sterilis*⟧ **1** incapable of producing offspring, fruit, etc.; barren **2** free from living microorganisms —**ste·ril·i·ty** (stə ril' ə tē) *n.*
ster'i·lize' (-ə līz') *vt.* **-lized', -liz'ing** to make sterile; specif., *a)* to make incapable of reproduction *b)* to make free of germs, etc. —**ster'i·li·za'tion** *n.* —**ster'i·liz'er** *n.*
ster·ling (stur'liŋ) *n.* ⟦ME *sterlinge,* Norman coin⟧ **1** sterling silver **2** British money —*adj.* **1** of silver that is at least 92.5 percent pure **2** of British money **3** made of sterling silver **4** excellent *[a sterling reputation]*
stern[1] (sturn) *adj.* ⟦OE *styrne*⟧ **1** severe; strict *[stern measures]* **2** grim *[a stern face]* **3** relentless or firm —**stern'ly** *adv.* —**stern'ness** *n.*
stern[2] (sturn) *n.* ⟦< ON *styra,* to steer⟧ the rear end of a ship, etc.
ster·num (stur'nəm) *n., pl.* **-nums** or **-na** (-nə) ⟦< Gr

THESAURUS

steep[1] *a.* precipitous, sudden, sharp, angular, craggy, rough, rugged, irregular, vertical, uphill, downhill, abrupt, sheer, perpendicular.

steer[1] *v.* point, head for, direct; see DRIVE 2. —**steer clear of** stay away from, miss, evade; see AVOID.

stem[1] *n.* peduncle, petiole, trunk; see STALK. —**from stem to stern** the full length, completely, entirely; see EVERYWHERE, THROUGHOUT.

stench *n.* odor, stink, foulness; see SMELL 2.

step *n.* **1** [A movement of the foot] pace, stride, gait, footfall, tread, stepping. **2** [One degree in a graded rise] rest, run, tread, round, rung, level. **3** [The print of a foot] footprint, footmark, print, imprint, impression, footstep, spoor, trail, trace, mark; see also TRACK 2. —**in step (with)** in agreement with, coinciding with, similar to; see ALIKE, SIMILARLY. —**out of step** inappropriate, behind the times, inaccurate; see WRONG 2, WRONGLY. —**step by step** by degrees, cautiously, tentatively; see SLOWLY. —**take steps** do something, start, intervene; see ACT 1. —**watch one's step** be careful, take precautions, look out; see WATCH OUT.

step *v.* pace, stride, advance, recede, go forward, go backward, go up, go down, ascend, descend, pass, walk, march, move, hurry, hop; see also CLIMB, RISE 1. —**step up** augment, improve, intensify; see INCREASE.

steppingstone *n.* help, agent, factor; see MEANS 1.

stereotype *n.* convention, prejudgment, institution; see AVERAGE, PREJUDICE.

stereotype *v.* conventionalize, prejudge, pigeonhole, categorize.

stereotyped *a.* hackneyed, trite, ordinary; see CONVENTIONAL 1, 3, DULL 4.

sterile *a.* **1** [Incapable of producing young] infertile, impotent, childless, nulliparous, barren.—*Ant.* FERTILE, productive, potent. **2** [Incapable of producing vegetation] desolate, fallow, waste, desert, arid, dry, barren, unproductive, fruitless, bleak; see also EMPTY. **3** [Scrupulously clean] antiseptic, disinfected, decontaminated, germ-free, sterilized, uninfected, sanitary, pasteurized; see also PURE 2.

sterilize *v.* antisepticize, disinfect, pasteurize; see CLEAN, PURIFY.

stern[1] *a.* rigid, austere, strict; see SEVERE 1.

sternon⟧ the flat, bony structure to which most of the ribs are attached in the front of the chest; breastbone

ster·oid (stir′oid′, ster′-) ***n.*** ⟦< (CHOLE)STER(OL) + -OID⟧ any of a group of compounds including the bile acids, sex hormones, etc. —**ste·roi′dal** ***adj.***

stet (stet) ***v.*** *imper.* ⟦L⟧ let it stand: printer's term indicating that matter marked for deletion or change is to remain —***vt.*** **stet′ted, stet′ting** to mark with "stet"

steth·o·scope (steth′ə skōp′) ***n.*** ⟦< Gr *stēthos,* chest + -SCOPE⟧ *Med.* an instrument used to examine the heart, lungs, etc. by listening to the sounds they make

ste·ve·dore (stē′və dôr′) ***n.*** ⟦ult. < L *stipare,* cram⟧ LONGSHOREMAN

Ste·ven·son (stē′vən sən), **Rob·ert Lou·is** (rä′bərt lo͞o′is) 1850-94; Scot. writer

stew (sto͞o) ***vt., vi.*** ⟦ult. < L *ex-,* out + Gr *typhos,* steam⟧ **1** to cook by simmering or boiling slowly **2** to worry —***n.*** **1** a dish, esp. of meat and vegetables, cooked by stewing **2** a state of worry

stew·ard (sto͞o′ərd) ***n.*** ⟦< OE *stig,* hall + *weard,* keeper⟧ **1** a person put in charge of a large estate **2** an administrator, as of finances and property **3** one responsible for the food and drink, etc. in a club, etc. **4** an attendant, as on a ship or airplane **5** a union representative —**stew′ard·ship′** ***n.***

stew′ard·ess (-ər dis) ***n.*** a woman flight attendant

stick (stik) ***n.*** ⟦OE *sticca*⟧ **1** a twig or small branch broken or cut off **2** a long, slender piece of wood, as a club, cane, etc. **3** any sticklike piece *[a stick of gum]* —***vt.*** **stuck, stick′ing 1** to pierce, as with a pointed instrument **2** to pierce with (a knife, pin, etc.) **3** to thrust (*in, into, out,* etc.) **4** to attach as by gluing, pinning, etc. **5** to obstruct, detain, etc. *[the wheels were stuck]* **6** [Inf.] to place; put; set **7** [Inf.] to puzzle; baffle **8** [Slang] *a)* to impose a burden, etc. upon *b)* to defraud —***vi.*** **1** to be fixed by a pointed end, as a nail **2** to adhere; cling; remain **3** to persevere *[to stick at a job]* **4** to remain firm and resolute *[he stuck with us]* **5** to become embedded, jammed, etc. **6** to become stopped or delayed **7** to hesitate; scruple *[he'll stick at nothing]* **8** to protrude or project (*out, up,* etc.) —**stick by** to remain loyal to —**stick up for** [Inf.] to uphold; defend —**the sticks** [Inf.] the rural districts

stick′er ***n.*** a person or thing that sticks; specif., a gummed label

stick′-in-the-mud′ ***n.*** [Inf.] one who resists change, new ideas, etc.

stick·le·back (stik′əl bak′) ***n.*** a small, bony-plated fish with sharp dorsal spines: the male builds a nest for the female's eggs

stick·ler (stik′lər) ***n.*** ⟦prob. < ME *stightlen,* to order⟧ **1** one who insists on a certain way of doing things *[a stickler for discipline]* **2** [Inf.] something difficult to solve

stick′pin′ ***n.*** an ornamental pin worn in a necktie, on a lapel, etc.

stick shift a gearshift, as on a car, operated manually

stick′um (-əm) ***n.*** ⟦STICK + *'em,* short for THEM⟧ [Inf.] any sticky, or adhesive, substance

stick′up′ ***n.*** *slang term for* HOLDUP (sense 2)

stick′y ***adj.*** **-i·er, -i·est 1** that sticks; adhesive **2** [Inf.] hot and humid **3** [Inf.] troublesome —**stick′i·ness** ***n.***

stiff (stif) ***adj.*** ⟦OE *stif*⟧ **1** hard to bend or move; rigid; firm **2** sore or limited in movement: said of joints and muscles **3** not fluid; thick **4** strong; powerful *[a stiff wind]* **5** harsh *[stiff punishment]* **6** difficult *[a stiff climb]* **7** very formal or awkward **8** [Inf.] excessive *[a stiff price]* —***vt.*** **stiffed, stiff′ing** [Slang] to cheat —**stiff′ly** ***adv.*** —**stiff′ness** ***n.***

stiff′-arm′ ***vt.*** to push (someone) away with one's arm out straight

stiff′en ***vt., vi.*** to make or become stiff or stiffer —**stiff′en·er** ***n.***

stiff′-necked′ (-nekt′) ***adj.*** stubborn

sti·fle (stī′fəl) ***vt.*** **-fled, -fling** ⟦< Fr *estouffer*⟧ **1** to suffocate; smother **2** to suppress; hold back; stop *[to stifle a sob]* —***vi.*** to die or suffer from lack of air —**sti′fling·ly** ***adv.***

stig·ma (stig′mə) ***n.,*** *pl.* **-mas** or **stig·ma′ta** (-mät′ə) ⟦< Gr, lit., a puncture made with a sharp instrument⟧ **1** a mark of disgrace or reproach **2** a spot on the skin, esp. one that bleeds **3** the upper tip of the pistil of a flower, on which pollen falls and develops —**stig·mat′ic** (-mat′ik) ***adj.***

stig′ma·tize′ (-tīz′) ***vt.*** **-tized′, -tiz′ing** to mark or characterize as disgraceful

stile (stīl) ***n.*** ⟦< OE *stigan,* to climb⟧ a set of steps for climbing over a fence or wall

sti·let·to (sti let′ō) ***n.,*** *pl.* **-tos** or **-toes** ⟦It < L *stilus,* pointed tool⟧ a small dagger with a slender blade

still[1] (stil) ***adj.*** ⟦OE *stille*⟧ **1** noiseless; silent **2** stationary **3** tranquil; calm **4** designating or of a single photograph taken from a film —***n.*** **1** silence; quiet **2** a still photograph —***adv.*** **1** at or up to the time indicated **2** even; yet *[still colder]* **3** nevertheless; yet *[rich but still unhappy]* —***conj.*** nevertheless; yet —***vt., vi.*** to make or become still —**still′ness** ***n.***

still[2] (stil) ***n.*** ⟦< obs. *still,* to distill⟧ an apparatus used for distilling liquids, esp. alcoholic liquors

still′birth′ ***n.*** **1** the birth of a stillborn fetus **2** such a fetus

still′born′ ***adj.*** **1** dead when delivered from the uterus **2** unsuccessful from the start

still life *pl.* **still lifes** a picture of inanimate objects, as fruit, flowers, etc.

stilt (stilt) ***n.*** ⟦ME *stilte*⟧ **1** either of a pair of poles, each with a footrest, used for walking high off the ground **2** any of a number of long posts used to hold a building, etc. above ground or out of water **3** a bird with a long, slender bill and long legs

stilt·ed (stil′tid) ***adj.*** pompous, affected, etc.

stim·u·lant (stim′yə lənt) ***n.*** anything, as a drug, that stimulates

stim′u·late′ (-lāt′) ***vt.*** **-lat′ed, -lat′ing** ⟦see fol.⟧ to rouse or excite to activity or increased activity —**stim′u·la′tion** ***n.***

stim′u·lus (-ləs) ***n.,*** *pl.* **-li′** (-lī′) ⟦L, a goad⟧ **1** an incentive **2** any action or agent that causes an activity in an organism, organ, etc.

sting (stiŋ) ***vt.*** **stung, sting′ing** ⟦OE *stingan*⟧ **1** to prick or wound with a sting **2** to cause sudden, pricking pain to **3** to make unhappy **4** to stimulate suddenly and sharply **5** [Slang] to cheat —***vi.*** to cause or feel sharp, smarting pain —***n.*** **1** a stinging **2** a pain or wound resulting from stinging **3** a sharp-pointed organ, as in insects and plants, that pricks, wounds, etc. **4** [Slang] *a)* a swindling, as in a confidence game *b)* a scheme by police, etc. for entrapping lawbreakers

THESAURUS

stew ***n.*** ragout, goulash, Hungarian goulash, chowder, beef stew, Irish stew, mulligan stew, ratatouille, bouillabaisse, casserole; see also FOOD, SOUP.

stick ***n.*** shoot, twig, branch, stem, stalk, rod, wand, staff, stave, walking stick, cane, matchstick, club, baton, drumstick, pole, bludgeon, bat, ruler, stock, cue, mast. **—the sticks*** rural areas, the backcountry, outlying districts; see COUNTRY 1.

stick ***v.*** **1** [To remain fastened] adhere, cling, fasten, attach, unite, cohere, hold, stick together, hug, clasp, hold fast.—*Ant.* LOOSEN, let go, fall, come away. **2** [To penetrate with a point] prick, impale, pierce; see PENETRATE. **—stick by (someone)** be loyal to, stand by, believe in; see SUPPORT 2. **—stick out** jut, show, come through; see PROJECT 1. **—stick up for*** support, aid, fight for; see SUPPORT 2.

stickup* ***n.*** holdup, robbery, stealing; see CRIME, THEFT.

sticky ***a.*** ropy, viscous, tacky, sticking, gummy, waxy, pasty, gluey.

stiff ***a.*** **1** [Not easily bent] solid, rigid, petrified, firm, tense, unyielding, inflexible, hard, hardened, starched, taut, thick, stubborn, obstinate, unbending, thickened, wooden, steely, frozen, solidified.—*Ant.* SOFT, flexible, softened. **2** [Formal] ungainly, ungraceful, unnatural; see AWKWARD. **3** [Severe] strict, rigorous, exact; see SEVERE 1, 2. **4** [Potent] hard, potent, powerful; see STRONG 4.

stiffen ***v.*** gel, harden, starch, petrify, brace, prop, cement, strengthen, thicken, clot, coagulate, solidify, congeal, condense, set, curdle, freeze, cake, crystallize.

stifle ***v.*** smother, suffocate, extinguish; see CHOKE.

still[1] ***a.*** **1** [Silent] calm, tranquil, noiseless; see QUIET. **2** [Yet] nevertheless, furthermore, however; see BESIDES, BUT 1, YET 1.

stimulant ***n.*** tonic, bracer, energizer; see DRUG.

stimulate ***v.*** excite, incite, rouse, spur on, foster, induce, jolt, provoke, key up, fire up; see also URGE 2.

stimulated ***a.*** keyed up, speeded up, aroused; see EXCITED.

stimulating ***a.*** intriguing, enlivening, arousing, high-spirited, bracing, rousing, energetic, refreshing, exhilarating, enjoyable, refreshing, provocative, sharp, evocative, exciting, inspiring, provoking, animating.—*Ant.* DULL, dreary, humdrum.

sting ***n.*** **1** [An injury] wound, swelling, sore; see INJURY. **2** [Pain] prick, bite, burn; see PAIN 2.

sting ***v.*** prick, prickle, tingle; see HURT 1.

sting′er ***n.*** one that stings, specif., a STING (*n.* 3)
sting′ray′ ***n.*** a large ray with one or more poisonous spines that can inflict painful wounds
stin·gy (stin′jē) ***adj.*** **-gi·er, -gi·est** ⟦< dial. form of STING⟧ **1** giving or spending grudgingly; miserly **2** less than needed; scanty —**stin′gi·ly** ***adv.*** —**stin′gi·ness** ***n.***
stink (stiŋk) ***vi.*** **stank** or **stunk, stunk, stink′ing** ⟦OE *stincan*⟧ to give off a strong, unpleasant smell —***n.*** a strong, unpleasant smell; stench —**stink′er** ***n.*** —**stink′y, -i·er, -i·est,** ***adj.***
stint (stint) ***vt.*** ⟦< OE *styntan,* to blunt⟧ to restrict to a certain quantity, often small —***vi.*** to be sparing in giving or using —***n.*** **1** restriction; limit **2** an assigned task or period of work —**stint′er** ***n.***
sti·pend (stī′pənd) ***n.*** ⟦< L *stips,* coin + *pendere,* to pay⟧ a regular or fixed payment, as a salary
stip·ple (stip′əl) ***vt.*** **-pled, -pling** ⟦< Du *stippel,* a speckle⟧ to paint, draw, or engrave in small dots
stip·u·late (stip′yə lāt′) ***vt.*** **-lat′ed, -lat′ing** ⟦< L *stipulari,* to bargain⟧ **1** to arrange definitely **2** to specify as an essential condition of an agreement —**stip′u·la′tion** ***n.***
stir[1] (stʉr) ***vt., vi.*** **stirred, stir′ring** ⟦OE *styrian*⟧ **1** to move, esp. slightly **2** to make or be active **3** to mix (a liquid, etc.) as by agitating with a spoon **4** to excite the feelings (of) **5** to incite: often with *up* —***n.*** **1** a stirring **2** movement; activity **3** excitement; tumult —**stir′rer** ***n.***
stir[2] (stʉr) ***n.*** ⟦19th-c. thieves' slang⟧ [Slang] a prison
stir′-cra′zy ***adj.*** [Slang] anxious, tense, etc. from long, close confinement, specif. in prison
stir′-fry′ ***vt.*** **-fried′, -fry′ing** to fry (diced or sliced vegetables, meat, etc.) quickly in a wok while stirring constantly
stir′ring ***adj.*** **1** active; busy **2** rousing; exciting
stir·rup (stʉr′əp) ***n.*** ⟦OE *stigrap*⟧ **1** a flat-bottomed ring hung from a saddle and used as a footrest **2** one of the three small bones in the middle ear
stitch (stich) ***n.*** ⟦OE *stice,* a puncture⟧ **1** *a)* a single complete in-and-out movement of a needle in sewing, etc. *b)* a suture **2** a loop, knot, etc. made by stitching **3** a particular kind of stitch or style of stitching **4** a sudden, sharp pain **5** a bit or piece —***vi., vt.*** to make stitches (in); sew —**in stitches** in a state of uproarious laughter
stitch′er·y (-ər ē) ***n.*** ornamental needlework
St. John's seaport & capital of Newfoundland: pop. 102,000
St. Kitts and Nevis (kits) country in the Leeward Islands, consisting of two islands, St. Kitts & Nevis: *c.* 101 sq. mi.; pop. 41,000
St. Lawrence river flowing from Lake Ontario into the Atlantic: the main section of an inland waterway (**St. Lawrence Seaway**) connecting the Great Lakes with the Atlantic
St. Lou·is (lo͞o′is, lo͞o′ē) city & port in E Missouri, on the Mississippi: pop. 397,000
St. Lu·ci·a (lo͞o′shē ə, lo͞o sē′ə) island country of the West Indies: 238 sq. mi.; pop. 133,000
stoat (stōt) ***n.*** ⟦ME *stote*⟧ a large European ermine, esp. in its brown summer coat
stock (stäk) ***n.*** ⟦OE *stocc*⟧ **1** the trunk of a tree **2** *a)* descent; lineage *b)* a strain, race, etc. of animals or plants **3** a supporting or main part of an implement, etc., as the wooden handle to which the barrel of a rifle is attached **4** [*pl.*] a wooden frame with holes for confining the ankles or wrists, formerly used for punishment **5** raw material **6** water in which meat, fish, etc. has been boiled, used in soups **7** livestock **8** a supply of goods on hand in a store, etc. **9** (a certificate for) a share or shares of corporate ownership **10** a stock company or its repertoire —***vt.*** **1** to furnish (a farm, shop, etc.) with stock **2** to keep a supply of, as for sale or for future use —***vi.*** to put in a stock, or supply: with *up* —***adj.*** **1** kept in stock *[stock sizes]* **2** common or trite *[a stock excuse]* **3** that deals with stock **4** relating to a stock company —**in** (or **out of**) **stock** (not) available for sale or use —**take stock 1** to inventory the stock on hand **2** to make an appraisal —**take** (or **put**) **stock in** to have faith in
stock·ade (stä kād′) ***n.*** ⟦< Prov *estaca,* a stake⟧ **1** a barrier of stakes driven into the ground side by side, for defense **2** an enclosure, as a fort, made with such stakes **3** an enclosure for military prisoners
stock′bro′ker ***n.*** one who acts as an agent in buying and selling stocks, bonds, etc.
stock car a standard automobile, modified for racing
stock company a theatrical company presenting a repertoire of plays
stock exchange 1 a place where stocks and bonds are bought and sold **2** an association of stockbrokers Also **stock market**
stock′hold′er ***n.*** one owning stock in a given company
Stock·holm (stäk′hōm′, -hōlm′) seaport & capital of Sweden: pop. 704,000
stock′ing ***n.*** ⟦< obs. sense of *stock*⟧ a closefitting covering, usually knitted, for the foot and leg
stocking cap a long, tapered knitted cap, often with a tassel at the end
stock′pile′ ***n.*** a reserve supply of goods, raw material, etc. —***vt., vi.*** **-piled′, -pil′ing** to accumulate a stockpile (of)
stock′-still′ ***adj.*** motionless
Stock·ton (stäk′tən) city in central California: pop. 211,000
stock′y ***adj.*** **-i·er, -i·est** heavily built; short and thickset —**stock′i·ness** ***n.***
stock′yard′ ***n.*** an enclosure where cattle, hogs, etc. are kept before slaughtering
stodg·y (stä′jē) ***adj.*** **-i·er, -i·est** ⟦< *stodge,* heavy food⟧ **1** dull; uninteresting **2** old-fashioned; conventional —**stodg′i·ness** ***n.***
sto·gie or **sto·gy** (stō′gē) ***n.,*** *pl.* **-gies** ⟦after *Conestoga* Valley, PA⟧ a cigar, esp. one that is long, thin, and, usually, inexpensive
Sto·ic (stō′ik) ***n.*** ⟦< Gr *stoa,* a colonnade: where first Stoics met⟧ **1** a member of an ancient Greek school of philosophy **2** [**s-**] a stoical person —***adj.*** [**s-**] STOICAL —**sto′i·cism′** (-i siz′əm) ***n.***
sto′i·cal (-i kəl) ***adj.*** showing indifference to joy, grief, pleasure, or pain; impassive —**sto′i·cal·ly** ***adv.***
stoke (stōk) ***vt., vi.*** **stoked, stok′ing** ⟦< Du *stoken,* to poke⟧ **1** to stir up and feed fuel to (a fire) **2** to tend (a furnace, boiler, etc.) —**stok′er** ***n.***
STOL *abbrev.* short takeoff and landing
stole[1] (stōl) ***n.*** ⟦< Gr *stolē,* garment⟧ **1** a long strip of cloth worn about the neck by members of the clergy at various rites **2** a woman's long scarf of cloth or fur worn around the shoulders
stole[2] (stōl) ***vt., vi.*** *pt. of* STEAL
stol·en (stō′lən) ***vt., vi.*** *pp. of* STEAL
stol·id (stäl′id) ***adj.*** ⟦L *stolidus,* slow⟧ having or showing little or no emotion; unexcitable —**sto·lid·i·ty** (stə lid′ə tē) ***n.*** —**stol′id·ly** ***adv.***
sto·lon (stō′län′) ***n.*** ⟦< L *stolo,* a shoot⟧ a creeping stem lying above the soil surface and bearing leaves, as in the strawberry
stom·ach (stum′ək) ***n.*** ⟦ult. < Gr *stoma,* mouth⟧ **1** the saclike digestive organ into which food passes from the esophagus **2** the abdomen, or belly **3** appetite for food **4** desire or inclination —***vt.*** **1** to be able to eat or digest **2** to tolerate; bear

THESAURUS

stingy ***a.*** parsimonious, niggardly, miserly, penurious, close, closefisted, greedy, covetous, tightfisted, tight*, grasping, penny-pinching, cheap*, selfish, mean, cheeseparing.—*Ant.* GENEROUS, bountiful, liberal.
stink ***n.*** stench, fetor, offensive odor; see SMELL 2.
stink ***v.*** smell bad, emit a stench, be offensive; see SMELL 1.
stir[1] ***v.*** move, beat, agitate; see MIX 1. —**stir up trouble** cause difficulty, foment, agitate; see BOTHER 2, DISTURB.
stitch ***v.*** join, make a seam, baste; see SEW.
stock ***a.*** trite, hackneyed, stereotyped; see COMMON 1, DULL 4.
stock ***n.*** **1** [Goods] merchandise, produce, accumulation; see PRODUCE. **2** [Livestock] domestic animals, barnyard animals, farm animals; see CATTLE. **3** [A stalk] stem, plant, trunk; see STALK. —**in stock** not sold out, stocked, not difficult to get; see AVAILABLE. —**out of stock** sold out, gone, not available; see SOLD OUT. —**take stock (of) 1** [To inventory] enumerate, audit, take account of; see EXAMINE. **2** [To consider] examine, study, review; see CONSIDER, THINK 1. —**take stock in** believe in, put faith in, rely on; see TRUST 1.
stockings ***n.*** hose, pantyhose, nylons; see HOSIERY.
stock-still ***a.*** frozen, stagnant, inactive; see MOTIONLESS 1.
stock (up) ***v.*** replenish, supply, furnish; see BUY.
stolen ***a.*** taken, kept, robbed, filched, pilfered, purloined, appropriated, lifted*, abducted, kidnapped, snatched*, run off with, poached, copped*, plagiarized, misappropriated, embezzled, converted.
stomach ***n.*** paunch, belly, midsection, solar plexus, bowels, intestines, viscera, entrails, insides*, guts, gut*, tummy, pot*, middle, breadbasket*, corporation*.

stom′ach·ache′ ***n.*** pain in the stomach or abdomen
stom′ach·er ***n.*** an ornamented piece of cloth formerly worn over the chest and abdomen, esp. by women
stomp (stämp) ***vt., vi.*** *var. of* STAMP (*vt.* 1, 2; *vi.* 1, 2)
stomping ground [Inf.] STAMPING GROUND: *also used in pl.*
stone (stōn) ***n.*** ⟦OE *stan*⟧ **1** the hard, solid, nonmetallic mineral matter of which rock is composed **2** a piece of rock **3** the seed of certain fruits **4** *short for* PRECIOUS STONE **5** *pl.* **stone** [Brit.] 14 pounds avoirdupois **6** an abnormal stony mass formed in the kidney, gall bladder, etc. —***vt.*** **stoned, ston′ing** **1** to pelt or kill with stones **2** to remove the stone from (a peach, etc.) —***adv.*** completely
stone- ⟦< prec.⟧ *combining form* completely *[stone-*blind*]*
Stone Age the period in human culture when stone tools were used
stoned ***adj.*** [Slang] drunk or under the influence of a drug
stone's throw a short distance
stone′wall′ ***vi.*** [Inf.] to behave in an obstructive manner, as by withholding information, etc.
stone′ware′ ***n.*** a dense, opaque, glazed or unglazed pottery
ston′y ***adj.*** **-i·er, -i·est** **1** full of stones **2** of or like stone; specif., unfeeling; pitiless —**ston′i·ness** ***n.***
stood (stood) ***vi., vt.*** *pt. & pp. of* STAND
stooge (stōōj) ***n.*** ⟦< ?⟧ [Inf.] **1** an actor who serves as the victim of a comedian's jokes, pranks, etc. **2** anyone who acts as a foil or underling
stool (stōōl) ***n.*** ⟦OE *stol*⟧ **1** a single seat having no back or arms **2** feces
stool pigeon [Inf.] a spy or informer, esp. for the police
stoop[1] (stōōp) ***vi.*** ⟦OE *stupian*⟧ **1** to bend the body forward **2** to carry the head and shoulders habitually bent forward **3** to degrade oneself —***n.*** the act or position of stooping
stoop[2] (stōōp) ***n.*** ⟦Du *stoep*⟧ a small porch at the door of a house
stop (stäp) ***vt.*** **stopped, stop′ping** ⟦< L *stuppa*, a kind of stuffing material⟧ **1** to close by filling, shutting off, etc. **2** to cause to cease motion, activity, etc. **3** to block; intercept; prevent **4** to cease; desist from *[stop* talking*]* —***vi.*** **1** to cease moving, etc.; halt **2** to leave off doing something **3** to cease operating **4** to become clogged **5** to tarry or stay —***n.*** **1** a stopping or being stopped **2** a finish; end **3** a stay or sojourn **4** a place stopped at, as on a bus route **5** an obstruction, plug, etc. **6** a finger hole in a wind instrument, closed to produce a desired tone **7** a pull, lever, etc. for controlling a set of organ pipes —**stop off** to stop for a while en route to a place —**stop over** to visit for a while: also **stop in** (or **by**)
stop′cock′ ***n.*** a cock or valve to stop or regulate the flow of a fluid
stop′gap′ ***n.*** a person or thing serving as a temporary substitute
stop′light′ ***n.*** a traffic light, esp. when red to signal vehicles to stop
stop′o′ver ***n.*** a brief stop or stay at a place in the course of a journey
stop′page ***n.*** **1** a stopping or being stopped **2** an obstructed condition; block
stop′per ***n.*** something inserted to close an opening; plug
stop′watch′ ***n.*** a watch that can be started and stopped instantly, as for timing races
stor·age (stôr′ij) ***n.*** **1** a storing or being stored **2** a place for, or the cost of, storing goods **3** computer memory
storage battery a battery for producing electric current, with cells that can be recharged
store (stôr) ***vt.*** **stored, stor′ing** ⟦< L *instaurare*, restore⟧ **1** to put aside for use when needed **2** to furnish with a supply **3** to put, as in a warehouse, for safekeeping —***n.*** **1** a supply (*of* something) for use when needed; stock **2** [*pl.*] supplies, esp. of food, clothing, etc. **3** a retail establishment where goods are offered for sale —**in store** set aside for the future; in reserve —**set** (or **put** or **lay**) **store by** to value
store′front′ ***n.*** a front room on the ground floor of a building, designed for use as a retail store
store′house′ ***n.*** a place where things are stored; esp., a warehouse
store′keep′er ***n.*** **1** a person in charge of military or naval stores **2** a retail merchant
store′room′ ***n.*** a room where things are stored
sto·rey (stôr′ē) ***n.***, *pl.* **-reys** *Brit., etc. sp. of* STORY[2]
sto·ried (stôr′ēd) ***adj.*** famous in story or history
stork (stôrk) ***n.*** ⟦OE *storc*⟧ a large, long-legged wading bird with a long neck and bill
storm (stôrm) ***n.*** ⟦OE⟧ **1** a strong wind, with rain, snow, thunder, etc. **2** any heavy fall of snow, rain, etc. **3** a strong emotional outburst **4** any strong disturbance **5** a sudden, strong attack on a fortified place —***vi.*** **1** to blow rain, snow, etc. violently **2** to rage; rant **3** to rush violently *[to storm* into a room*]* —***vt.*** to attack vigorously
storm door (or **window**) a door (or window) placed outside the regular one as added protection
storm′y ***adj.*** **-i·er, -i·est** **1** of or characterized by storms **2** violent, raging, etc. —**storm′i·ly** ***adv.*** —**storm′i·ness** ***n.***
sto·ry[1] (stôr′ē) ***n.***, *pl.* **-ries** ⟦< Gr *historia*, narrative⟧ **1** the telling of an event or events; account; narration **2** a fictional prose narrative shorter than a novel **3** the plot of a novel, play, etc. **4** [Inf.] a falsehood **5** a news report
sto·ry[2] (stôr′ē) ***n.***, *pl.* **-ries** ⟦< prec.⟧ a horizontal division of a building, from a floor to the ceiling above it
sto′ry·board′ ***n.*** a large board on which sketches, etc. for

THESAURUS

stomachache ***n.*** indigestion, dyspepsia, gastric upset; see ILLNESS 1, 2.
stone ***a.*** rock, stony, rocky, hard, rough, craggy, petrified, marble, granite.
stone ***n.*** mass, crag, cobblestone, boulder, gravel, pebble, rock, sand, grain, granite, marble, flint, gem, jewel. —**cast the first stone** criticize, blame, reprimand; see ATTACK, SCOLD. —**leave no stone unturned** take great pains, be scrupulous, try hard; see PURSUE 1, WORK 1.
stoned* ***a.*** drugged, high*, intoxicated; see DRUNK.
stony ***a.*** inflexible, cruel, pitiless; see FIRM 2, ROUGH 1.
stool ***n.*** seat, footstool, footrest; see FURNITURE.
stoop[1] ***v.*** bend forward, incline, crouch; see LEAN 1.
stop ***n.*** **1** [A pause] halt, stay, standstill; see END 2, PAUSE. **2** [A stopping place] station, platform, bus stop; see DEPOT. —**put a stop to** halt, interrupt, interdict; see STOP 1.
stop ***v.*** **1** [To halt] pause, stay, stand still, lay over, stay over, break the journey, shut down, rest, discontinue, curtail, pull up, reach a standstill, hold, stop dead in one's tracks*, stop short, freeze, call it a day*, cut short; see also END 1. **2** [To cease] terminate, finish, conclude, withdraw, leave off, let up, pull up, fetch up, wind up, relinquish, have done, desist, refrain, settle, discontinue, end, close, tie up, give up, call off, bring up, close down, break up, hold up, pull up, lapse, be at an end, cut out, die away, go out, defect, surrender, close, peter out*, call it a day*, knock off*, lay off*, throw in the towel*, melt away, drop it, run out, write off, run its course.—*Ant.* BEGIN, start, commence. **3** [To prevent] hinder, obstruct, arrest; see PREVENT.
stopover ***n.*** layover, overnight, pause; see DELAY.
stopped ***a.*** at a halt, cancelled, cut short; see INTERRUPTED.
storage ***n.*** warehouse, repository, accommodation; see STOREHOUSE.
store ***n.*** shop, mart, shopping mall, mall, strip mall, retail establishment, sales outlet, market, department store, specialty shop, chain store, drygoods store, boutique, emporium, grocery store, convenience store, warehouse club, superstore, drugstore.
store ***v.*** put, deposit, cache, stock, store away, stow away, lay by, lay in, lay up, put by, put away, put aside, lock away, bank, warehouse, stockpile, hoard, collect, pack away, set aside, set apart, amass, file, stash*, salt away*, put in mothballs*; see also SAVE 3.—*Ant.* SPEND, draw out, withdraw.
stored ***a.*** stocked, reserved, hoarded; see SAVED 2.
storehouse ***n.*** depository, warehouse, granary, silo, store, storage space, corncrib, barn, depot, cache, cellar, grain elevator, safe-deposit vault, armory, arsenal, repository.
storekeeper ***n.*** small businessman, purveyor, grocer; see MERCHANT.
storm ***n.*** tempest, downpour, thunderstorm, cloudburst, disturbance, waterspout, blizzard, snowstorm, squall, hurricane, cyclone, tornado, twister*, gust, blast, gale, blow, monsoon, typhoon.
storm ***v.*** blow violently, howl, blow a gale, roar, set in, squall, pour, drizzle, rain, rain cats and dogs*.
stormy ***a.*** rainy, wet, damp, cold, bitter, raging, roaring, frigid, windy, blustery, pouring, turbulent, storming, wild, boisterous, rough, squally, dark, violent, threatening, menacing.
story[1] ***n.*** imaginative writing, fable, narrative, tale, tall tale, myth, fairy tale, anecdote, legend, account, satire, burlesque, memoir, parable, fiction, novel, romance, allegory, epic, saga, fantasy; see also LITERATURE 1.

shots or scenes of a film are arranged in sequence —*vt.* to make a storyboard of (a shot or scene) for (a film)
sto'ry·book' *n.* a book of stories, esp. one for children
sto'ry·tell'er *n.* one who narrates stories —**sto'ry·tell'ing** *n.*
stoup (stōōp) *n.* ⟦< ON *staup*, cup⟧ a font for holy water
stout (stout) *adj.* ⟦< OFr *estout*, bold⟧ **1** courageous **2** strong; sturdy; firm **3** powerful; forceful **4** fat; thickset —*n.* a heavy, dark-brown beer —**stout'ly** *adv.* —**stout'ness** *n.*
stout'heart'ed *adj.* courageous; brave
stove[1] (stōv) *n.* ⟦< MDu, heated room⟧ an apparatus for heating, cooking, etc.
stove[2] (stōv) *vt., vi. alt. pt. & pp. of* STAVE
stove'pipe' *n.* a metal pipe used to carry off smoke from a stove
stow (stō) *vt.* ⟦< OE *stowe,* a place⟧ to pack in an orderly way —**stow away 1** to put or hide away **2** to be a stowaway —**stow'age** *n.*
stow'a·way' *n.* one who hides aboard a ship, airplane, etc. as to get free passage
St. Paul capital of Minnesota: pop. 272,000
St. Pe·ters·burg (pēt'ərz burg') **1** seaport in NW Russia: pop. 4,456,000 **2** city in WC Florida: pop. 240,000
strad·dle (strad''l) *vt.* **-dled, -dling** ⟦< STRIDE⟧ **1** to stand or sit astride of **2** to take or appear to take both sides of (an issue) —*n.* a straddling —**strad'dler** *n.*
strafe (strāf) *vt.* **strafed, straf'ing** ⟦< Ger *Gott strafe England* (God punish England)⟧ to attack with machine-gun fire from low-flying aircraft
strag·gle (strag'əl) *vi.* **-gled, -gling** ⟦prob. < ME *straken,* roam⟧ **1** to wander from the main group **2** to be scattered over a wide area; ramble **3** to hang in an unkempt way, as hair —**strag'gler** *n.* —**strag'gly** *adj.*
straight (strāt) *adj.* ⟦< ME *strecchen,* to stretch⟧ **1** having the same direction throughout its length; not crooked, bent, etc. **2** direct; undeviating, etc. **3** in order; properly arranged, etc. **4** honest; sincere **5** undiluted **6** [Slang] normal or conventional **7** [Slang] heterosexual —*adv.* **1** in a straight line **2** upright; erectly **3** without detour, delay, etc. —*n. Poker* a hand of five cards in sequence —**straight away** (or **off**) without delay —**straight'ness** *n.*
straight arrow [Inf.] one who is proper, righteous, conscientious, etc. and often regarded as stodgy, dull, etc. —**straight'-ar'row** *adj.*
straight'a·way' *n.* a straight section of a racetrack, highway, etc. —*adv.* without delay
straight'edge' *n.* a strip of wood, etc. having a perfectly straight edge, used in drawing straight lines, etc.
straight'en *vt., vi.* to make or become straight —**straighten out 1** to make or become less confused, easier to deal with, etc. **2** to reform —**straight'en·er** *n.*
straight face a facial expression showing no amusement or other emotion —**straight'-faced'** *adj.*
straight'for'ward *adj.* **1** moving or leading straight ahead; direct **2** honest; frank —*adv.* in a straightforward manner: also **straight'for'wards**
straight man an actor whose remarks a comedian answers with a quip
straight shooter [Inf.] a person who is honest, sincere, etc.
straight ticket a ballot cast for candidates of only one party
straight time 1 the standard number of working hours, as per week **2** the rate of pay for these hours
straight'way' *adv.* [Now Chiefly Literary] at once
strain[1] (strān) *vt.* ⟦< L *stringere*⟧ **1** to stretch tight **2** to exert to the utmost **3** to injure by overexertion *[to strain a muscle]* **4** to stretch beyond normal limits **5** to pass through a screen, sieve, etc.; filter —*vi.* **1** to strive hard **2** to filter, ooze, etc. —*n.* **1** a straining or being strained **2** great effort, exertion, etc. **3** a bodily injury from overexertion **4** stress or force **5** a great demand on one's emotions, resources, etc.
strain[2] (strān) *n.* ⟦< OE *strynan*, to produce⟧ **1** ancestry; lineage **2** race; stock; line **3** a line of individuals differentiated from its species or race **4** an inherited tendency **5** a musical tune
strained *adj.* not natural or relaxed
strain'er *n.* a device for straining, sifting, or filtering; sieve, filter, etc.
strait (strāt) *adj.* ⟦< L *stringere*, draw tight⟧ [Archaic] narrow or strict —*n.* **1** [*often pl.*] a narrow waterway connecting two large bodies of water **2** [*usually pl.*] difficulty; distress
strait'en *vt.* to bring into difficulties: usually in **in straitened circumstances**, lacking enough money
strait'jack'et *n.* a coatlike device for restraining violent persons
strait'-laced' *adj.* narrowly strict in behavior or moral views
strand[1] (strand) *n.* ⟦OE⟧ shore, esp. ocean shore —*vt., vi.* **1** to run or drive aground, as a ship **2** to put or be put into a helpless position *[stranded* abroad with no money*]*
strand[2] (strand) *n.* ⟦ME *stronde*⟧ **1** any one of the threads, wires, etc. that are twisted together to form a string, cable, etc. **2** a ropelike length of anything *[a strand* of pearls*]*
strange (strānj) *adj.* **strang'er, strang'est** ⟦< L *extraneus*, foreign⟧ **1** not previously known, seen, etc.; unfamiliar **2** unusual; extraordinary **3** peculiar; odd —**strange'ly** *adv.* —**strange'ness** *n.*
stran·ger (strān'jər) *n.* **1** a newcomer **2** a person not known to one
stran·gle (straŋ'gəl) *vt., vi.* **-gled, -gling** ⟦< Gr *strangos*, twisted⟧ **1** to choke to death **2** to suppress, stifle, or repress —**stran'gler** *n.*
stran'gle·hold' *n.* **1** an illegal wrestling hold that chokes an opponent **2** a force or action that suppresses freedom
stran·gu·late (straŋ'gyə lāt') *vt.* **-lat'ed, -lat'ing 1** STRANGLE **2** *Med.* to block (a tube, etc.) by constricting —**stran'gu·la'tion** *n.*
strap (strap) *n.* ⟦dial. form of STROP⟧ a narrow strip of leather, etc., as for securing things —*vt.* **strapped, strap'ping** to fasten with a strap
strap'less *adj.* having no shoulder straps
strapped *adj.* [Inf.] in great need of money
strap'ping *adj.* [Inf.] tall and well-built; robust
stra·ta (strāt'ə, strat'ə) *n. alt. pl. of* STRATUM
strat·a·gem (strat'ə jəm) *n.* ⟦< Gr *stratos,* army + *agein,* to lead⟧ **1** a trick, plan, etc. for deceiving an enemy in war **2** any tricky scheme
strat·e·gy (strat'ə jē) *n., pl.* **-gies 1** the science of planning and directing military operations **2** skill in managing or planning **3** a stratagem, plan, etc. —**stra·te·gic** (strə tē'jik) *adj.* —**stra·te'gi·cal·ly** *adv.* —**strat'e·gist** *n.*

THESAURUS

stout *a.* corpulent, fleshy, portly; see FAT.
stove[1] *n.* range, heater, cookstove, oven, furnace; see also APPLIANCE.
straight *a.* **1** [Not curved or twisted] rectilinear, linear, vertical, perpendicular, plumb, upright, erect, in line, unbent, in a row, on a line, even, level.—*Ant.* BENT, curved, curving. **2** [Direct] uninterrupted, continuous, through; see DIRECT 1.
straighten *v.* order, compose, make straight, untwist, unsnarl, unbend, uncoil, unravel, uncurl, unfold, put straight, level, arrange, arrange on a line, align.—*Ant.* BEND, twist, curl. —**straighten out** put in order, clarify, make less confused, clean up, arrange.
straightforward *a.* sincere, candid, outspoken; see FRANK, HONEST 1.
strain[1] *n.* **1** [Effort] exertion, struggle, endeavor; see EFFORT. **2** [Mental tension] anxiety, tension, pressure; see STRESS 2.
strain[1] *v.* **1** [To exert] endeavor, strive, labor; see TRY 1. **2** [To filter] refine, purify, screen; see SIFT 2.
strained *a.* forced, constrained, tense; see DIFFICULT 1.
strainer *n.* mesh, filter, colander; see SIEVE.
strait-laced *a.* strict, severe, stiff; see PRUDISH.
stranded *a.* deserted, left behind, marooned; see ABANDONED.
strange *a.* foreign, rare, unusual, uncommon, external, outside, without, detached, apart, faraway, remote, alien, unexplored, isolated, unrelated, irrelevant; see also UNFAMILIAR 2, UNKNOWN 1, 2, 3, UNNATURAL 1.—*Ant.* familiar, present, close.
strangely *a.* oddly, queerly, unfamiliarly, unnaturally, uncommonly, exceptionally, remarkably, rarely, fantastically, amazingly, surprisingly, singularly, peculiarly, unusually.—*Ant.* REGULARLY, commonly, usually.
strangeness *n.* newness, unfamiliarity, novelty, abnormality, eccentricity, remoteness.
stranger *n.* foreigner, outsider, unknown person, uninvited person, visitor, guest, immigrant, intruder, alien, interloper, new kid in town*, new kid on the block*, drifter, squatter, perfect stranger, complete stranger.
strangle *v.* asphyxiate, suffocate, garrote; see CHOKE.
strap *n.* thong, strop, leash; see BAND 1.
strategy *n.* approach, method, procedure; see TACTICS.

strat·i·fy (strat′ə fī′) ***vt.***, ***vi.*** **-fied′**, **-fy′ing** ⟦< L *stratum,* layer + *facere,* make⟧ to form in layers or strata —**strat′i·fi·ca′tion** ***n.***

strat′o·sphere′ (-ə sfir′) ***n.*** ⟦< ModL *stratum*, stratum + Fr *sphère,* sphere⟧ **1** the atmospheric zone at an altitude of *c.* 20 to 50 km **2** an extremely high point, level, etc. —**strat′o·spher′ic** (-sfer′ik, -sfir′-) ***adj.***

stra·tum (strāt′əm, strat′-) ***n.***, *pl.* **-ta** (-ə) or **-tums** ⟦ModL < L *stratus,* a spreading⟧ **1** a horizontal layer of matter, as of sedimentary rock **2** any of the socioeconomic groups of a society

stra′tus (-əs) ***n.***, *pl.* **-ti** (-ī) ⟦see prec.⟧ a uniform, low, gray cloud layer

Strauss (strous), **Jo·hann** (yō′hän′) 1825-99; Austrian composer, esp. of waltzes

Stra·vin·sky (strə vin′skē), **I·gor** (ē′gôr) 1882-1971; Russ. composer & conductor, in the U.S. after 1940

straw (strô) ***n.*** ⟦OE *streaw*⟧ **1** hollow stalks of grain after threshing **2** a single one of these **3** a tube used for sucking beverages **4** a trifle —***adj.*** **1** straw-colored; yellowish **2** made of straw

straw′ber′ry (-ber′ē, -bər ē) ***n.***, *pl.* **-ries** ⟦prob. from the strawlike particles on the fruit⟧ **1** the small, red, fleshy fruit of a vinelike plant of the rose family **2** this plant

straw boss [Inf.] one having subordinate authority

straw vote (or **poll**) an unofficial vote taken to determine general group opinion

stray (strā) ***vi.*** ⟦< LL *strata,* street⟧ **1** to wander from a given place, course, etc. **2** to deviate (*from* what is right) —***n.*** one that strays; esp., a lost domestic animal —***adj.*** **1** having strayed; lost **2** isolated or incidental *[*a few *stray* words*]*

streak (strēk) ***n.*** ⟦< OE *strica*⟧ **1** a long, thin mark or stripe **2** a layer, as of fat in meat **3** a tendency in behavior, etc. *[*a nervous *streak]* **4** a period, as of luck —***vt.*** to make streaks on or in —***vi.*** **1** to become streaked **2** to go fast **3** to dash naked in public as a prank —**streak′er** ***n.*** —**streak′y**, **-i·er**, **-i·est**, ***adj.***

stream (strēm) ***n.*** ⟦OE⟧ **1** a current of water; specif., a small river **2** a steady flow, as of air, light, etc. **3** a continuous series *[*a *stream* of cars*]* —***vi.*** **1** to flow as in a stream **2** to move swiftly

stream′er ***n.*** **1** a long, narrow flag **2** any long, narrow strip hanging loose at one end

stream′line′ ***vt.*** **-lined′**, **-lin′ing** to make streamlined —***adj.*** STREAMLINED

stream′lined′ ***adj.*** **1** having a contour designed to offer the least resistance in moving through air, water, etc. **2** efficient, trim, simplified, etc.

street (strēt) ***n.*** ⟦< L *strata* (*via*), paved (road)⟧ **1** a public road in a town or city, esp. a paved one **2** such a road with its sidewalks, buildings, etc. **3** the people living, working, etc. along a given street

street′car′ ***n.*** a car on rails for public transportation along certain streets

street′light′ ***n.*** a lamp on a post for lighting a street: also **street′lamp′**

street′-smart′ ***adj.*** [Inf.] STREETWISE

street smarts [Inf.] cunning or shrewdness needed to live in an urban environment characterized by poverty, crime, etc.

street′walk′er ***n.*** a prostitute

street′wise′ ***adj.*** [Inf.] experienced in dealing with the people in urban poverty areas where vice and crime are common

strength (streŋkth) ***n.*** ⟦OE *strengthu*⟧ **1** the state or quality of being strong; force; power **2** toughness; durability **3** the power to resist attack **4** potency or concentration, as of drugs, etc. **5** intensity, as of sound, etc. **6** force of an army, etc., as measured in numbers —**on the strength of** based or relying on

strength′en ***vt.***, ***vi.*** to make or become stronger —**strength′en·er** ***n.***

stren·u·ous (stren′yoo̅ əs) ***adj.*** ⟦L *strenuus*⟧ requiring or characterized by great effort or energy —**stren′u·ous·ly** ***adv.*** —**stren′u·ous·ness** ***n.***

strep (strep) ***n.*** *short for:* **1** STREPTOCOCCUS **2** STREP THROAT

strep throat (strep) a sore throat caused by a streptococcus, with inflammation and fever

strep·to·coc·cus (strep′tə käk′əs) ***n.***, *pl.* **-coc′ci′** (-käk′sī′) ⟦< Gr *streptos,* twisted + COCCUS⟧ any of various spherical bacteria that occur in chains: some cause serious diseases

strep′to·my′cin (-mī′sin) ***n.*** ⟦< Gr *streptos*, bent + *mykēs*, fungus⟧ an antibiotic drug used in treating various diseases

stress (stres) ***n.*** ⟦< L *strictus,* strict⟧ **1** strain; specif., force that strains or deforms **2** emphasis; importance **3** *a*) mental or physical tension *b*) urgency, pressure, etc. causing this **4** the relative force of utterance given a syllable or word; accent —***vt.*** **1** to put stress or pressure on **2** to accent **3** to emphasize

stressed′-out′ ***adj.*** tired, nervous, etc. as from overwork, mental pressure, etc.

stress fracture a leg fracture caused by repetitive stress, as in marathon running

stretch (strech) ***vt.*** ⟦OE *streccan*⟧ **1** to reach out; extend **2** to draw out to full extent or to greater size **3** to cause to extend too far; strain **4** to strain in interpretation, scope, etc. —***vi.*** **1** *a*) to spread out to full extent or beyond normal limits *b*) to extend over a given distance or time **2** *a*) to extend the body or limbs to full length *b*) to lie down (usually with *out*) **3** to become stretched —***n.*** **1** a stretching or being stretched **2** an unbroken period *[*a ten-day *stretch]* **3** an unbroken length, tract, etc. **4** *short for* HOMESTRETCH **5** an action that exceeds someone's normal powers —***adj.*** **1** made of elasticized fabric so as to stretch easily **2** designating a vehicle built extra long to enlarge seating capacity *[*a *stretch* limousine*]* —**stretch′a·ble** ***adj.*** —**stretch′y**, **-i·er**, **-i·est**, ***adj.***

stretch′er ***n.*** **1** one that stretches **2** a canvas-covered frame for carrying the sick or injured

strew (stroo̅) ***vt.*** **strewed**, **strewed** or **strewn**, **strew′ing** ⟦OE *streawian*⟧ **1** to spread here and there; scatter **2** to cover as by scattering

stri·at·ed (strī′āt′id) ***adj.*** ⟦< L *striare*, to groove⟧ marked with parallel lines, bands, furrows, etc.

THESAURUS

straw ***n.*** *Straws and strawlike fibers include the following:* oat, wheat, barley, rye, rice, buckwheat, bean; see also HAY. —**a straw in the wind** evidence, indication, signal; see SIGN 1. —**grasp at straws** (or **a straw**) try any expedient, panic, show desperation; see FEAR, TRY 1.

straw vote ***n.*** opinion poll, unofficial ballot, dry run*; see OPINION 1, VOTE 1, 2.

stray ***v.*** rove, roam, go astray; see WALK 1.

streak ***n.*** stripe, strip, ridge; see BAND 1.

stream ***n.*** current, rivulet, brook; see RIVER, WATER 2.

stream ***v.*** gush, run, flow; see FLOW.

street ***n.*** highway, way, lane, path, avenue, thoroughfare, boulevard, terrace, drive, place, road, route, artery, parkway, court, cross street, alley, circle, dead end, passage.

streetcar ***n.*** tram, trolley, bus; see VEHICLE.

streetwalker ***n.*** whore, hustler*, hooker*; see PROSTITUTE.

strength ***n.*** vigor, brawn, energy, nerve, vitality, muscle, stoutness, health, toughness, sturdiness, hardiness, tenacity, soundness.—*Ant.* WEAKNESS, feebleness, loss of energy.

strengthen ***v.*** intensify, add, invigorate, fortify, reinforce, confirm, encourage, increase, multiply, arm, empower, harden, steel, brace, buttress, stimulate, sustain, nerve, animate, reanimate, restore, refresh, recover, hearten, establish, toughen, temper, rejuvenate, tone up, build up, make firm, stiffen, brace up, rally, sharpen, enliven, substantiate, uphold, back, augment, enlarge, extend, mount, rise, ascend, wax, grow, back up, beef up*.—*Ant.* WEAKEN, cripple, tear down.

strenuous ***a.*** vigorous, arduous, zealous; see DIFFICULT 1.

strenuously ***a.*** hard, laboriously, energetically; see VIGOROUSLY.

stress ***n.*** **1** [Importance] significance, weight, import; see IMPORTANCE. **2** [Pressure] strain, tension, force, burden, trial, fear, tenseness, stretch, tautness, pull, draw, extension, protraction, intensity, tightness, spring; see also PRESSURE 1.

stress ***v.*** accent, underline, accentuate; see EMPHASIZE.

stretch ***n.*** compass, range, reach; see EXTENT.

stretch ***v.*** **1** [To spread out] grow, expand, extend, spread, unfold, radiate, increase, swell, spring up, shoot up, open.—*Ant.* CONTRACT, shrink, wane. **2** [To cause to become longer, spread out, etc.] tighten, strain, make tense, draw, draw out, elongate, extend, develop, distend, inflate, lengthen, magnify, amplify, widen, draw tight.—*Ant.* RELAX, let go, slacken.

stretcher ***n.*** litter, cot, gurney; see BED 1.

strew ***v.*** spread, toss, cover; see SCATTER 2.

strick·en (strik′ən) ***vt.***, ***vi.*** *alt. pp. of* STRIKE —***adj.*** **1** struck or wounded **2** afflicted, as by something painful

strict (strikt) ***adj.*** ⟦< L *stringere,* draw tight⟧ **1** exact or precise **2** *a)* enforcing rules carefully *b)* closely enforced —**strict′ly** ***adv.*** —**strict′ness** ***n.***

stric·ture (strik′chər) ***n.*** ⟦see prec.⟧ **1** adverse criticism **2** a limiting; restriction **3** an abnormal narrowing of a passage in the body

stride (strīd) ***vi.*** **strode**, **strid′den**, **strid′ing** ⟦OE *stridan*⟧ **1** to walk with long steps **2** to take a single, long step (esp. *over* something) —***n.*** **1** a long step **2** the distance covered by such a step **3** [*usually pl.*] progress *[*to make *strides]*

stri·dent (strīd′'nt) ***adj.*** ⟦< L *stridere,* to rasp⟧ harsh-sounding; shrill; grating —**stri′dent·ly** ***adv.***

strife (strīf) ***n.*** ⟦< OFr *estrif*⟧ **1** contention **2** fighting or quarreling; struggle

strike (strīk) ***vt.*** **struck**, **struck** or, esp. for *vt.* 7 & 10, **strick′en**, **strik′ing** ⟦OE *strican,* to go, advance⟧ **1** to hit with the hand, a tool, etc. **2** to make by stamping, etc. *[*to *strike* coins*]* **3** to announce (time), as with a bell: said of clocks, etc. **4** to ignite (a match) or produce (a light, etc.) by friction **5** to collide with or cause to collide *[*he *struck* his head on a beam*]* **6** to attack **7** to afflict, as with disease, pain, etc. **8** to come upon; notice, find, etc. **9** to affect as if by contact, etc.; occur to *[*an idea *struck* me*]* **10** to remove (*from* a list, record, etc.) **11** to make (a bargain, truce, etc.) **12** to lower (a sail, flag, etc.) **13** to assume (an attitude, pose, etc.) —***vi.*** **1** to hit (*at*) **2** to attack **3** to make sounds as by being struck: said of a bell, clock, etc. **4** to collide; hit (*against, on,* or *upon*) **5** to seize bait: said of a fish **6** to come suddenly (*on* or *upon*) **7** to refuse to continue to work until certain demands are met **8** to proceed, esp. in a new direction —***n.*** **1** the act of striking; specif., a military attack **2** a refusal by employees to go on working, in an attempt to gain better working conditions, etc. **3** the discovery of a rich deposit of oil, etc. **4** *Baseball* a pitched ball missed, or fouled off, by the batter or called a good pitch by the umpire **5** *Bowling* a knocking down of all the pins on the first roll —**strike out** **1** to erase **2** to start out **3** *Baseball* to put out, or be put out, on three strikes —**strike up** to begin —**strik′er** ***n.***

strike′out′ ***n.*** *Baseball* an out made by a batter charged with three strikes

strik′ing ***adj.*** very impressive, attractive, etc.

string (striŋ) ***n.*** ⟦OE *streng*⟧ **1** a thin line of fiber, leather, etc. used for tying, pulling, etc. **2** a group of like things on a string *[*a *string* of pearls*]* **3** a row, series, etc. of like things *[*a *string* of houses*]* **4** *a)* a slender cord of wire, gut, etc. bowed, plucked, or struck to make a musical sound *b)* [*pl.*] all the stringed instruments of an orchestra **5** a fiber of a plant **6** [Inf.] a condition attached to a plan, offer, etc.: *usually used in pl.* —***vt.*** **strung**, **string′ing** **1** to provide with strings **2** to thread on a string **3** to tie, hang, etc. with a string **4** to remove the strings from (beans, etc.) **5** to arrange in a row **6** to extend *[string* a cable*]* —**pull strings** to get someone to use influence in one's behalf, often secretly —**string′y**, **-i·er**, **-i·est**, ***adj.***

string bean SNAP BEAN

stringed instrument (striŋd) an instrument with vibrating strings, as a violin or guitar

strin·gent (strin′jənt) ***adj.*** ⟦see STRICT⟧ strict; severe —**strin′gen·cy** ***n.***

string′er ***n.*** **1** a long horizontal piece in a structure **2** a part-time, local correspondent for a newspaper, magazine, etc.

strip[1] (strip) ***vt.*** **stripped**, **strip′ping** ⟦OE *stripan*⟧ **1** to remove (the clothing, etc.) from (a person) **2** to dispossess of (honors, titles, etc.) **3** to plunder; rob **4** to take off (a covering, etc.) from (a person or thing) **5** to make bare by taking away removable parts, etc. **6** to break the thread of (a nut, bolt, etc.) or the teeth of (a gear) —***vi.*** to take off all clothing

strip[2] (strip) ***n.*** ⟦< STRIPE⟧ **1** a long, narrow piece, as of land, tape, etc. **2** *short for* AIRSTRIP

strip cropping crop planting in alternate rows to lessen erosion, as on a hillside

stripe (strīp) ***n.*** ⟦< MDu *strīp*⟧ **1** a long, narrow band differing from the surrounding area **2** a strip of cloth on a uniform to show rank, years served, etc. **3** kind; sort *[*a man of his *stripe]* —***vt.*** **striped**, **strip′ing** to mark with stripes

strip·ling (strip′liŋ) ***n.*** a grown boy

strip mall a shopping center of connected storefronts with a parking area in front

strip mining mining, esp. for coal, by laying bare a mineral deposit near the surface of the earth

stripped′-down′ ***adj.*** reduced to essentials

strip′-search′ ***vt.*** to search (a person) by requiring removal of the clothes —***n.*** such a search Also **strip search**

strip′tease′ ***n.*** an entertainment in which the performer undresses slowly, usually to musical accompaniment

strive (strīv) ***vi.*** **strove** or **strived**, **striv·en** (striv′ ən) or **strived**, **striv′ing** ⟦< OFr *estrif,* effort⟧ **1** to make great efforts; try very hard **2** to struggle

strobe (light) (strōb) ⟦< Gr *strobus,* a twisting around⟧ an electronic tube emitting rapid, brief, and brilliant flashes of light

strode (strōd) ***vi.***, ***vt.*** *pt. of* STRIDE

stroke (strōk) ***n.*** ⟦ME⟧ **1** a blow of an ax, whip, etc. **2** a sudden action or event *[*a *stroke* of luck*]* **3** an interruption of normal blood flow to the brain, as from a hemorrhage, blood clot, etc., causing paralysis, etc. **4** a single strong effort **5** the sound of striking, as of a clock **6** *a)* a single movement, as with a tool, racket, etc. *b)* any of a series of repeated motions made in rowing, swimming, etc. **7** a mark made by a pen, etc. —***vt.*** **stroked**, **strok′ing** to draw one's hand, a tool, etc. gently over the surface of

stroll (strōl) ***vi.*** ⟦prob. < Ger *strolch,* vagabond⟧ **1** to walk about leisurely; saunter **2** to wander —***vt.*** to stroll along or through —***n.*** a leisurely walk

stroll′er ***n.*** **1** one who strolls **2** a light, chairlike baby carriage

strong (strôŋ) ***adj.*** ⟦OE *strang*⟧ **1** *a)* physically powerful *b)* healthy; hearty **2** morally or intellectually powerful

THESAURUS

stricken ***a.*** wounded, injured, harmed; see HURT.

strict ***a.*** stringent, stern, austere; see SEVERE 2.

strictly ***a.*** rigidly, rigorously, stringently; see SURELY.

stride ***n.*** step, pace, long step; see GAIT. —**take in one's stride** handle, do easily, deal with; see MANAGE 1.

strife ***n.*** quarrel, struggle, conflict; see FIGHT 1.

strike ***n.*** **1** [An organized refusal] walkout, deadlock, work stoppage, quitting, sit-down strike, wildcat strike, moratorium, embargo, tie-up, slowdown, confrontation, sit-in; see also REVOLUTION 2. **2** [A blow] hit, stroke, punch; see BLOW. —**(out) on strike** striking, protesting, on the picket line; see UNEMPLOYED.

strike ***v.*** **1** [To hit] box, punch, thump; see BEAT 1, HIT 1. **2** [To refuse to work] walk out, tie up, sit down, slow down, go out, be on strike, sit in, arbitrate, negotiate a contract, picket, boycott, stop, quit, resist, hold out; see also OPPOSE 1, 2. **3** [To light] kindle, ignite, scratch; see IGNITE. —**strike out** **1** [To begin something new] start out, initiate, find a new approach; see BEGIN 1. **2** [To cancel] obliterate, invalidate, expunge; see CANCEL. **3** [In baseball, to be out on strikes] fan, whiff*, go down swinging*, go down on strikes, take a called third strike.

striking ***a.*** attractive, stunning, dazzling; see BEAUTIFUL, HANDSOME.

string ***n.*** **1** [A sequence] chain, succession, procession; see SEQUENCE 1, SERIES. **2** [Twine] cord, twist, strand; see ROPE. —**string along*** accede, go along, agree; see FOLLOW 2.

stringy ***a.*** wiry, ropy, woody, pulpy, hairy, veined, coarse, threadlike.

strip[1] ***v.*** **1** [Undress] divest, disrobe, become naked; see UNDRESS. **2** [Remove] pull off, tear off, lift off; see PEEL.

strip[2] ***n.*** tape, slip, shred; see BAND 1, LAYER.

stripe ***n.*** line, division, strip, contrasting color, band, border, ribbon, zigzag; see also LAYER.

striped ***a.*** lined, marked, streaked, veined, ribbed; see also BARRED 1.

strive ***v.*** endeavor, aim, attempt; see TRY 1.

stroll ***v.*** ramble, saunter, roam; see WALK 1.

strong ***a.*** **1** [Physically strong; *said especially of persons*] robust, sturdy, firm, muscular, sinewy, vigorous, stout, hardy, big, heavy, husky, lusty, active, energetic, tough, virile, mighty, athletic, able-bodied, powerful, manly, brawny, burly, wiry, strapping, made of iron.—*Ant.* WEAK, emaciated, feeble. **2** [Physically strong; *said especially of things*] solid, firm, staunch, well-built, secure, tough, durable, unyielding, steady, stable, fixed, sound, powerful, mighty, rugged, substantial.—*Ant.* UNSTABLE, insecure, tottering. **3** [Wielding power] great, mighty, influential; see POWERFUL 1. **4** [Potent in effect] powerful, potent, high-pow-

[a *strong* will] **3** firm; durable **4** powerful in wealth, numbers, etc. **5** of a specified number [troops 6,000 *strong*] **6** having a powerful effect **7** intense in degree or quality **8** forceful; vigorous, etc. —**strong'ly** ***adv.***

strong'-arm' [Inf.] ***adj.*** using physical force —***vt.*** to use force upon

strong'box' ***n.*** a heavily made box or safe for storing valuables

strong'hold' ***n.*** a place having strong defenses; fortress

strong'-mind'ed ***adj.*** unyielding; determined: also **strong'-willed'**

stron·ti·um (strän'shəm, -shē əm; stränt'ē əm) ***n.*** ⟦ult. after *Strontian,* Scotland, where first found⟧ a metallic chemical element resembling calcium in properties

strop (sträp) ***n.*** ⟦OE⟧ a leather band for sharpening razors —***vt.*** **stropped, strop'ping** to sharpen on a strop

stro·phe (strō'fē) ***n.*** ⟦Gr *strophē,* a turning⟧ a stanza of a poem

strove (strōv) ***vi.*** *alt. pt. of* STRIVE

struck (struk) ***vt., vi.*** *pt. & pp. of* STRIKE

struc·ture (struk'chər) ***n.*** ⟦< L *struere,* arrange⟧ **1** something built or constructed, as a building or dam **2** the arrangement of all the parts of a whole **3** something composed of related parts —***vt.*** **-tured, -tur·ing** to put together systematically —**struc'tur·al** ***adj.***

stru·del (strōōd''l) ***n.*** ⟦Ger⟧ a pastry made of a thin sheet of dough filled with apples, etc., rolled up, and baked

strug·gle (strug'əl) ***vi.*** **-gled, -gling** ⟦ME *strogelen*⟧ **1** to fight violently with an opponent **2** to make great efforts; strive; labor —***n.*** **1** great effort **2** conflict; strife

strum (strum) ***vt., vi.*** **strummed, strum'ming** ⟦echoic⟧ to play (a guitar, etc.) with long strokes across the strings, often casually

strum·pet (strum'pit) ***n.*** ⟦ME⟧ a prostitute

strung (struŋ) ***vt., vi.*** *pt. & alt. pp. of* STRING

strut (strut) ***vi.*** **strut'ted, strut'ting** ⟦OE *strutian,* stand rigid⟧ to walk in a swaggering manner —***n.*** **1** a swaggering walk **2** a brace fitted into a framework to stabilize the structure

strych·nine (strik'nin, -nēn', -nīn') ***n.*** ⟦< Gr *strychnos,* nightshade⟧ a colorless, highly poisonous, crystalline alkaloid

stub (stub) ***n.*** ⟦OE *stybb*⟧ **1** a tree or plant stump **2** a short piece left over [a pencil *stub*] **3** any short or blunt projection **4** the part of a ticket, bank check, etc. kept as a record —***vt.*** **stubbed, stub'bing** **1** to strike (one's toe, etc.) against something **2** to put out (a cigarette, etc.) by pressing the end against a surface: often with *out*

stub·ble (stub'əl) ***n.*** ⟦< L *stipula,* a stalk⟧ **1** short stumps of grain, corn, etc., left after harvesting **2** any short, bristly growth, as of a beard

stub·born (stub'ərn) ***adj.*** ⟦ME *stoburn*⟧ **1** refusing to yield or comply; obstinate **2** done in an obstinate or persistent way **3** hard to handle or deal with —**stub'born·ly** ***adv.*** —**stub'born·ness** ***n.***

stub·by (stub'ē) ***adj.*** **-bi·er, -bi·est** **1** covered with stubs or stubble **2** short and dense **3** short and thickset

stuc·co (stuk'ō) ***n., pl.*** **-coes** or **-cos** ⟦It⟧ plaster or cement for surfacing walls, etc. —***vt.*** **-coed, -co·ing** to cover with stucco

stuck (stuk) ***vt., vi.*** *pt. & pp. of* STICK

stuck'-up' ***adj.*** [Inf.] snobbish; conceited

stud[1] (stud) ***n.*** ⟦OE *studu,* a post⟧ **1** any of a series of small knobs, etc. used to ornament a surface **2** a small, buttonlike device for fastening a shirt front, etc. **3** an upright piece in the wall of a building, to which panels, laths, etc. are nailed —***vt.*** **stud'ded, stud'ding** **1** to set or decorate with studs, etc. **2** to be set thickly on [rocks *stud* the hill]

stud[2] (stud) ***n.*** ⟦OE⟧ a male animal, esp. a horse (**stud'horse'**), kept for breeding

stud'book' ***n.*** a register of purebred animals, esp. racehorses: also **stud book**

stud'ding ***n.*** studs, esp. for walls

stu·dent (stōōd''nt) ***n.*** ⟦< L *studere,* to study⟧ **1** one who studies, or investigates **2** one who is enrolled for study at a school, college, etc.

stud·ied (stud'ēd) ***adj.*** **1** prepared by careful study **2** deliberate

stu·di·o (stōō'dē ō') ***n., pl.*** **-os'** ⟦It⟧ **1** a place where an artist, etc. works or where music or dancing lessons, etc. are given **2** a place where films, radio or TV programs, etc. are produced

studio apartment a one-room apartment with a kitchen area and a bathroom

studio couch a couch that can be opened into a full-sized bed

stu·di·ous (stōō'dē əs) ***adj.*** ⟦< L *studiosus*⟧ **1** fond of study **2** zealous or attentive

stud·y (stud'ē) ***n., pl.*** **-ies** ⟦< L *studere,* to study⟧ **1** the acquiring of knowledge, as by reading or investigating **2** careful examination of a subject, event, etc. **3** a branch of learning **4** [*pl.*] formal education; schooling **5** an essay, thesis, etc. containing the results of an investigation **6** an earnest effort **7** deep thought **8** a room for study, etc. —***vt.*** **-ied, -y·ing** **1** to try to learn or understand by reading, thinking, etc. **2** to investigate carefully **3** to read (a book, etc.) intently **4** to take a course in, as at a school —***vi.*** **1** to study something **2** to be a student **3** to meditate

stuff (stuf) ***n.*** ⟦< OFr *estoffe*⟧ **1** the material out of which anything is made **2** essence; character **3** matter of an unspecified kind **4** cloth, esp. woolen cloth **5** objects; things **6** worthless objects; junk **7** [Inf.] ability, skill, etc. —***vt.*** **1** to fill or pack; specif., *a*) to fill the skin of (a dead animal) in taxidermy *b*) to fill (a turkey, etc.) with seasoning, bread crumbs, etc. before roasting **2** to fill too full; cram **3** to plug; block —***vi.*** to eat too much

stuffed shirt [Slang] a pompous, pretentious person

stuff'ing ***n.*** something used to stuff, as padding in cushions or a seasoned mixture for stuffing fowl

stuff'y ***adj.*** **-i·er, -i·est** **1** poorly ventilated; close **2** having the nasal passages stopped up, as from a cold **3** [Inf.] dull, conventional, or pompous —**stuff'i·ness** ***n.***

stul·ti·fy (stul'tə fī') ***vt.*** **-fied', -fy'ing** ⟦< L *stultus,* foolish + *facere,* make⟧ **1** to make seem foolish, stupid, etc. **2** to make worthless, etc.

stum·ble (stum'bəl) ***vi.*** **-bled, -bling** ⟦ME *stumblen*⟧ **1** to trip in walking, running, etc. **2** to walk unsteadily **3** to speak, act, etc. in a blundering way **4** to do wrong **5** to come by chance —***n.*** a stumbling —**stum'bler** ***n.***

stumbling block a difficulty or obstacle

stump (stump) ***n.*** ⟦ME *stumpfe*⟧ **1** the end of a tree or plant left in the ground after the upper part has been

THESAURUS

ered, stiff, effective, hard, high-potency, stimulating, inebriating, intoxicating. **5** [Intense] sharp, acute, keen; see INTENSE. **6** [Financially sound] stable, solid, safe; see RELIABLE.

strongest ***a.*** mightiest, stoutest, firmest, hardiest, healthiest, most vigorous, most active, most intense, most capable, most masterful, sturdiest, most courageous, strongest-willed, most efficient.—*Ant.* WEAK, feeblest, most timid.

strongly ***a.*** stoutly, vigorously, actively, heavily, fully, completely, sturdily, robustly, firmly, solidly, securely, immovably, steadily, heartily, forcibly, resolutely, capably, powerfully.

structure ***n.*** arrangement, composition, framework; see BUILDING.

struggle ***n.*** conflict, contest, strife; see FIGHT 1.

struggle ***v.*** strive, grapple, contend; see FIGHT.

stub ***n.*** stump, short end, snag, root, remainder, remnant.

stubborn ***a.*** unreasonable, obstinate, firm, dogged, opinionated, contradictory, contrary, determined, resolved, bullheaded, mulish, fixed, hard, willful, dogmatic, prejudiced, tenacious, unyielding, headstrong.

stubbornly ***a.*** persistently, resolutely, willfully, doggedly, tenaciously; see also FIRMLY 2.

stubbornness ***n.*** obstinacy, doggedness, inflexibility, pertinacity, tenacity, perverseness, bullheadedness, pigheadedness; see also DETERMINATION.

stuck ***a.*** [Tight] fast, fastened, cemented; see TIGHT 2.

student ***n.*** learner, undergraduate, novice, high-school student, high schooler, coed*, college student, graduate student, pupil, docent, apprentice; see also SCHOLAR.

studious ***a.*** thoughtful, well-read, well-informed, scholarly, lettered, learned, bookish, erudite, earnest, industrious, diligent, attentive.

study ***n.*** research, investigation, scholarship; see EDUCATION 1.

study ***v.*** read, go into, refresh the memory, read up on, burn the midnight oil, bone up*, go over, cram, think, inquire, investigate, research, analyze, bury oneself in, plunge into.

stuff ***v.*** ram, pad, wad; see FILL 1, PACK 2.

stuffed ***a.*** crowded, packed, crammed; see FULL 1.

stuffed shirt* ***n.*** phony*, pompous person, blowhard*; see FAKE.

stuffing ***n.*** packing, wadding, padding, quilting, filler, packing material.

stuffy ***a.*** confined, stagnant, muggy; see CLOSE 5.

stumble ***v.*** trip, lurch, shamble; see FALL 1, TRIP 1.

stump ***n.*** butt, piece, projection; see END 4.

stumped* ***a.*** puzzled, baffled, at a

cut off **2** the part of a limb, tooth, etc. left after the rest has been removed **3** the place where a political speech is made —***vt.*** **1** to travel over (a district), making political speeches **2** [Inf.] to puzzle or perplex —***vi.*** **1** to walk with a heavy step **2** to travel about, making political speeches —**stump′y, -i·er, -i·est,** ***adj.***

stun (stun) ***vt.*** **stunned, stun′ning** ⟦ult. < L *ex-*, intens. + *tonare*, to thunder⟧ **1** to make unconscious, as by a blow **2** to daze; shock

stung (stuŋ) ***vt., vi.*** *pt. & pp. of* STING

stunk (stuŋk) ***vi.*** *pp. & alt. pt. of* STINK

stun·ning (stun′iŋ) ***adj.*** [Inf.] remarkably attractive, excellent, etc.

stunt[1] (stunt) ***vt.*** ⟦< OE, stupid⟧ **1** to check the growth or development of **2** to hinder (growth, etc.)

stunt[2] (stunt) ***n.*** ⟦< ?⟧ something done to show one's skill or daring, get attention, etc. —***vi.*** to do a stunt

stu·pe·fy (sto͞o′pə fī′) ***vt.*** ⟦< L *stupere*, be stunned + *facere*, make⟧ **1** to produce stupor in; stun **2** to astound; bewilder —**stu′pe·fac′tion** (-fak′shən) ***n.***

stu·pen·dous (sto͞o pen′dəs) ***adj.*** ⟦< L *stupere*, be stunned⟧ **1** astonishing **2** astonishingly great

stu·pid (sto͞o′pid) ***adj.*** ⟦see prec.⟧ **1** lacking normal intelligence **2** foolish; silly *[a stupid idea]* **3** dull and boring —**stu·pid′i·ty,** *pl.* **-ties,** ***n.***

stu·por (sto͞o′pər) ***n.*** ⟦see STUPENDOUS⟧ a state in which the mind and senses are dulled; loss of sensibility

stur·dy (stʉr′dē) ***adj.*** **-di·er, -di·est** ⟦< OFr *estourdi*, hard to control⟧ **1** firm; resolute **2** strong; vigorous **3** strongly constructed —**stur′di·ly** ***adv.*** —**stur′di·ness** ***n.***

stur·geon (stʉr′jən) ***n.*** ⟦< OFr *esturjon*⟧ a large food fish valuable as a source of caviar

stut·ter (stut′ər) ***vt., vi., n.*** ⟦< ME *stutten*⟧ STAMMER

Stutt·gart (sto͝ot′gärt′; *Ger* shto͝ot′gärt′) city in SW Germany: pop. 592,000

St. Vin·cent and the Gren·a·dines (sānt vin′sənt and *th*ə gren′ə dēnz′) country consisting of the island of St. Vincent and the N Grenadines, in the West Indies: 150 sq. mi.; pop. 106,000

sty[1] (stī) ***n.***, *pl.* **sties** ⟦< OE *sti*, hall, enclosure⟧ **1** a pen for pigs **2** any foul place

sty[2] or **stye** (stī) ***n.***, *pl.* **sties** or **styes** ⟦ult. < OE *stigan*, to rise⟧ a small, inflamed swelling on the rim of an eyelid

Styg·i·an (stij′ē ən, stij′ən) ***adj.*** **1** of the Styx **2** [*also* **s-**] *a)* infernal *b)* dark or gloomy

style (stīl) ***n.*** ⟦< L *stilus*, pointed writing tool⟧ **1** a stylus **2** *a)* manner of expression in language *b)* characteristic manner of expression, design, etc. in any art, period, etc. *c)* excellence of artistic expression **3** *a)* fashion *b)* something stylish —***vt.*** **styled, styl′ing** **1** to name; call **2** to design the style of **3** to arrange (hair) by cutting, etc.

styl·ish (stī′lish) ***adj.*** conforming to current style, as in dress; fashionable

styl′ist (-list) ***n.*** **1** a writer, etc. whose work has style and distinction **2** a person who styles hair —**sty·lis′tic** ***adj.*** —**sty·lis′ti·cal·ly** ***adv.***

styl′ize′ (-līz′) ***vt.*** **-ized′, -iz′ing** to design or represent according to a style rather than nature

sty·lus (stī′ləs) ***n.***, *pl.* **-lus·es** or **-li** (-lī) ⟦L, for *stilus*, pointed instrument⟧ **1** a sharp, pointed marking device **2** *a)* a sharp, pointed device for cutting the grooves of a phonograph record *b)* the short, pointed piece moving in such grooves, that transmits vibrations

sty·mie (stī′mē) ***n.*** ⟦prob. < Scot, person partially blind⟧ *Golf* a situation in which a ball to be putted has another ball between it and the hole —***vt.*** **-mied, -mie·ing** to block; impede

sty′my ***n.*** *pl.* **-mies,** ***vt.*** **-mied, -my·ing** *alt. sp. of* STYMIE

styp·tic pencil (stip′tik) a piece of astringent, used to stop minor bleeding

Sty·ro·foam (stī′rə fōm′) *trademark for* a rigid, lightweight, spongelike polystyrene —***n.*** [*also* **s-**] this substance

Styx (stiks) ***n.*** *Gr. Myth.* the river crossed by dead souls entering Hades

sua·sion (swā′zhən) ***n.*** ⟦< L *suadere*, to persuade⟧ PERSUASION: now chiefly in **moral suasion**, a persuading by appealing to one's sense of morality

suave (swäv) ***adj.*** ⟦< L *suavis*, sweet⟧ smoothly gracious or polite; polished —**suave′ly** ***adv.*** —**suav′i·ty** ***n.***

sub[1] (sub) ***n.*** *short for:* **1** SUBMARINE **2** SUBSTITUTE **3** SUBMARINE SANDWICH —***vi.*** **subbed, sub′bing** [Inf.] to be a substitute (*for* someone)

sub[2] *abbrev.* **1** substitute(s) **2** suburb(an)

sub- ⟦< L *sub*, under⟧ *prefix* **1** under *[submarine]* **2** lower than; inferior to *[subhead]* **3** to a lesser degree than *[subhuman]*

sub·a·tom·ic (sub′ə täm′ik) ***adj.*** of the inner part of or a particle smaller than an atom

sub′branch′ ***n.*** a division of a branch

sub′com·mit′tee ***n.*** a small committee chosen from a main committee

sub·com′pact′ ***n.*** an automobile model smaller than a compact

sub′con′scious ***adj.*** occurring with little or no conscious perception on the part of the individual: said of mental processes and reactions —**the subconscious** subconscious mental activity —**sub·con′scious·ly** ***adv.***

sub′con′ti·nent ***n.*** a large land mass smaller than a continent

sub′con′tract′ ***n.*** a secondary contract undertaking some or all obligations of another contract —***vt., vi.*** to make a subcontract (for) —**sub′con′trac′tor** ***n.***

sub′cul′ture ***n.*** **1** a distinctive social group within a larger social group **2** its cultural patterns

sub′cu·ta′ne·ous ***adj.*** beneath the skin

sub′dea′con ***n.*** a cleric ranking below a deacon

sub′dis′trict ***n.*** a subdivision of a district

sub′di·vide′ ***vt., vi.*** **-vid′ed, -vid′ing** **1** to divide further **2** to divide (land) into small parcels —**sub′di·vi′sion** ***n.***

sub·due (səb do͞o′) ***vt.*** **-dued′, -du′ing** ⟦< L *subducere*, take away⟧ **1** to conquer **2** to overcome; control **3** to make less intense; diminish

sub′fam′i·ly ***n.***, *pl.* **-lies** a main subdivision of a family, as of plants or of languages

sub′head′ ***n.*** a subordinate heading or title, as of a magazine article

subj *abbrev.* **1** subject **2** subjunctive

sub·ject (sub′jikt, -jekt′; *for v.* səb jekt′) ***adj.*** ⟦< L *sub-*, under + *jacere*, to throw⟧ **1** under the authority or con-

THESAURUS

loss; see UNCERTAIN.

stun ***v.*** **1** [To render unconscious] daze, put to sleep, knock out; see DEADEN. **2** [To astound] astonish, amaze, bewilder; see SURPRISE.

stunned ***a.*** dazed, astonished, nonplussed; see SHOCKED.

stunning ***a.*** striking, marvelous, remarkable; see BEAUTIFUL, HANDSOME.

stunt[2] ***n.*** feat, trick, prank; see ACHIEVEMENT, JOKE.

stupid ***a.*** senseless, brainless, idiotic, simple, shallow, dense, imprudent, witless, irrational, inane, ridiculous, mindless, ludicrous, muddled, absurd, half-witted, funny, comical, silly, laughable, nonsensical, illogical, indiscreet, unintelligent, irresponsible, scatterbrained, crackbrained, addled, foolish, unwary, incautious, misguided, wild, injudicious, imbecile, addlebrained, addleheaded, addlepated, lunatic, insane, mad, crazy, moronic, touched, freakish, comic, narrow-minded, incoherent, childish, senile, far-fetched, preposterous, unreasonable, asinine, unwise, thoughtless, careless, fatuous, light, lightheaded, flighty, madcap, giddy, cuckoo*, boneheaded*, cracked*, dumb*, goofy*, half-baked, in a daze, wacky*, harebrained, screwy*, cockeyed*, loony*, batty*, dopey*, nutty*.—*Ant.* SANE, wise, judicious.

stupidity ***n.*** **1** [Dullness of mind] stupor, slowness, heaviness, obtuseness, sluggishness, feeblemindedness, weakness, silliness, nonsense, folly, absurdity, imbecility, brainlessness, imprudence, lunacy, idiocy, shallowness, weakmindedness, impracticality, senility, giddiness, thickheadedness, asininity, slowness, lack of judgment.—*Ant.* INTELLIGENCE, wisdom, judgment. **2** [Extreme folly] nonsense, absurdity, silliness; see CARELESSNESS, NONSENSE 2.

stupidly ***a.*** imprudently, stubbornly, obtusely; see FOOLISHLY.

sturdy ***a.*** firm, resolute, unyielding; see STRONG 1, 2.

stutter ***v.*** stumble, falter, sputter; see STAMMER.

style ***n.*** **1** [Distinctive manner] way, form, technique; see METHOD. **2** [Fashion] vogue, habit, custom; see FASHION 2. —**in style** current, chic, stylish; see FASHIONABLE, POPULAR 1.

stylish ***a.*** chic, smart, in fashion; see FASHIONABLE.

suave ***a.*** sophisticated, ingratiating, urbane; see CULTURED.

subconscious ***a.*** subliminal, innermost, unconscious; see MENTAL 2.

subconscious ***n.*** the unconscious, psyche, mind; see SOUL 2.

subject ***a.*** governed, ruled, controlled, directed, obedient, submissive, servile, slavish, subservient, subjected, at someone's feet, at the mercy of.

subject ***n.*** substance, matter, theme, material, topic, question, problem, point, case, matter for discussion, matter in hand, item on the agenda, topic under consideration, field of inquiry, head, chapter, argument, thought, discussion.

subject ***v.*** cause to experience

trol of another **2** having a tendency *[subject* to anger*]* **3** exposed *[subject* to censure*]* **4** contingent upon: with *to [subject* to approval*]* —*n.* **1** one under the authority or control of another **2** one made to undergo a treatment, experiment, etc. **3** something dealt with in discussion, study, etc.; theme **4** a course of study in a school or college **5** *Gram.* the noun, etc. in a sentence about which something is said —*vt.* **1** to bring under the authority or control of **2** to cause to undergo something *[to subject* someone to questioning*]* —**sub·jec'tion** *n.*

sub·jec·tive (səb jek'tiv) *adj.* of or resulting from the feelings of the person thinking; not objective; personal —**sub·jec·tiv·i·ty** (sub'jek tiv'ə tē) *n.*

sub·join (səb join') *vt.* ⟦see SUB- & JOIN⟧ to append

sub·ju·gate (sub'jə gāt') *vt.* **-gat'ed**, **-gat'ing** ⟦< L *sub-*, under + *jugum,* a yoke⟧ to bring under control; conquer —**sub'ju·ga'tion** *n.*

sub·junc·tive (səb juŋk'tiv) *adj.* ⟦< L *subjungere,* subjoin⟧ designating or of the mood of a verb that is used to express supposition, desire, possibility, etc., rather than to state an actual fact

sub·lease (sub'lēs'; *for v.* sub lēs') *n.* a lease granted by a lessee —*vt.* **-leased'**, **-leas'ing** to grant or hold a sublease of

sub·let (sub let') *vt.* **-let'**, **-let'ting** **1** to let to another (property which one is renting) **2** to let out (work) to a subcontractor

sub·li·mate (sub'lə māt') *vt.* **-mat'ed**, **-mat'ing** **1** to change (a solid) to a gas, or (a gas) to a solid, without becoming a liquid **2** to express (unacceptable impulses) in acceptable forms, often unconsciously —**sub'li·ma'tion** *n.*

sub·lime (sə blīm') *adj.* ⟦< L *sub-*, up to + *limen,* lintel⟧ **1** noble; exalted **2** inspiring awe or admiration —*vt.* **-limed'**, **-lim'ing** SUBLIMATE (*vt.* 1) —**sub·lim·i·ty** (sə blim'ə tē) *n.*

sub·lim·i·nal (sub lim'ə nəl) *adj.* ⟦< SUB- + L *limen,* threshold + -AL⟧ below the threshold of consciousness

sub'ma·chine' gun a portable automatic firearm

sub·mar·gin·al (sub mär'jə nəl) *adj.* below minimum requirements or standards

sub·ma·rine (sub'mə rēn', sub'mə rēn') *adj.* being, living, etc. underwater —*n.* a ship, esp. a warship, that can operate under water

submarine sandwich HERO SANDWICH

sub·merge (səb murj') *vt.*, *vi.* **-merged'**, **-merg'ing** ⟦< L *sub-*, under + *mergere,* to plunge⟧ to place or sink beneath the surface, as of water —**sub·mer'gence** (-mur'jəns) *n.*

sub·merse' (-murs') *vt.* **-mersed'**, **-mers'ing** SUBMERGE —**sub·mers'i·ble** *adj.* —**sub·mer'sion** *n.*

sub·mis·sion (səb mish'ən) *n.* **1** a submitting or surrendering **2** obedience; resignation **3** *a)* the submitting of something to another *b)* the thing submitted, as a manuscript —**sub·mis'sive** *adj.*

sub·mit' (-mit') *vt.* **-mit'ted**, **-mit'ting** ⟦< L *sub-*, down + *mittere,* send⟧ **1** to present to others for consideration, etc. **2** to yield to the control or power of another **3** to offer as an opinion —*vi.* to yield; give in

sub·nor·mal (sub nôr'məl) *adj.* below normal, esp. in intelligence

sub·or'bit·al (-ôr'bit'l) *adj.* designating a flight in which a rocket, spacecraft, etc. follows a trajectory of less than one orbit

sub·or·di·nate (sə bôrd''n it; *for v.*, -bôr'də nāt') *adj.* ⟦< L *sub-*, under + *ordinare,* to order⟧ **1** below another in rank, importance, etc. **2** under the authority of another **3** *Gram.* having the function of a noun, adjective, or adverb within a sentence *[a subordinate* clause*]* —*n.* one that is subordinate —*vt.* **-nat'ed**, **-nat'ing** to place in a subordinate position —**sub·or'di·na'tion** *n.*

subordinate clause *Gram.* DEPENDENT CLAUSE

sub·orn (sə bôrn') *vt.* ⟦< L *sub-*, under + *ornare,* furnish⟧ to induce (another) to commit perjury —**sub·or·na·tion** (sub'ôr nā'shən) *n.*

sub'plot' *n.* a secondary plot in a play, novel, etc.

sub·poe·na (sə pē'nə) *n.* ⟦< L *sub poena,* under penalty⟧ a written legal order directing a person to appear in court to testify, etc. —*vt.* **-naed**, **-na·ing** to summon with such an order Also **sub·pe'na**

sub ro·sa (sub rō'zə) ⟦L, under the rose, ancient symbol of secrecy⟧ secretly; privately

sub·scribe (səb skrīb') *vt.*, *vi.* **-scribed'**, **-scrib'ing** ⟦< L *sub-*, under + *scribere,* write⟧ **1** to sign (one's name) at the end of a document, etc. **2** to give support or consent (to) **3** to promise to contribute (money) **4** to agree to receive and pay for a periodical, service, etc. (with *to*) —**sub·scrib'er** *n.*

sub·script (sub'skript') *n.* ⟦see prec.⟧ a figure, letter, or symbol written below and to the side of another

sub·scrip·tion (səb skrip'shən) *n.* **1** a subscribing **2** money subscribed **3** a formal agreement to receive and pay for a periodical, etc.

sub·se·quent (sub'si kwənt) *adj.* ⟦< L *sub-*, after + *sequi,* follow⟧ coming after; following —**subsequent to** after —**sub'se·quent·ly** *adv.*

sub·ser·vi·ent (səb sur'vē ənt) *adj.* ⟦< L *sub-*, under + *servire,* to serve⟧ **1** that is of service, esp. in a subordinate capacity **2** submissive —**sub·ser'vi·ence** *n.*

sub·set (sub'set') *n.* a mathematical set containing some or all of the elements of a given set

sub·side (səb sīd') *vi.* **-sid'ed**, **-sid'ing** ⟦< L *sub-*, under + *sidere,* to settle⟧ **1** to sink to the bottom or to a lower level **2** to become less active, intense, etc. —**sub·sid'ence** *n.*

sub·sid·i·ar·y (səb sid'ē er'ē) *adj.* ⟦see SUBSIDY⟧ **1** giving aid, service, etc.; auxiliary **2** being in a subordinate relationship —*n.*, *pl.* **-ies** one that is subsidiary; specif., a company controlled by another company

sub·si·dize (sub'sə dīz') *vt.* **-dized'**, **-diz'ing** to support with a subsidy —**sub'si·di·za'tion** *n.*

sub·si·dy (sub'sə dē) *n.*, *pl.* **-dies** ⟦< L *subsidium,* auxiliary forces⟧ a grant of money, as from a government to a private enterprise

sub·sist (səb sist') *vi.* ⟦< L *sub-*, under + *sistere,* to stand⟧ **1** to continue to be or exist **2** to continue to live; remain alive (*on* or *by*)

sub·sist'ence *n.* **1** existence **2** the act of providing sustenance **3** means of support or livelihood, esp. the barest means

sub·soil (sub'soil') *n.* the layer of soil beneath the topsoil

sub·son·ic (sub sän'ik) *adj.* designating, of, or moving at a speed less than that of sound

sub·stance (sub'stəns) *n.* ⟦< L *substare,* be present⟧ **1** the real or essential part of anything; essence **2** the physical matter of which a thing consists **3** *a)* solid or substantial quality *b)* consistency; body **4** the real meaning; gist **5** wealth **6** a drug: see CONTROLLED SUBSTANCE

THESAURUS

something, lay open, expose, submit.

subjective *a.* nonobjective, introspective, arbitrary; see INTERNAL 1.

subjectively *a.* internally, intrinsically, individually, egocentrically, mentally, nonobjectively, emotionally, introspectively, inherently; see also PERSONALLY 2.

sublime *a.* exalted, lofty, stately; see GRAND.

submarine *n.* U-boat, submersible, sub; see SHIP.

submerge *v.* submerse, engulf, swamp; see IMMERSE, SINK 2.

submission *n.* **1** [A yielding] obedience, meekness, assent; see RESIGNATION 1. **2** [Something submitted] report, memorandum, account; see RECORD 1.

submissive *a.* passive, tractable, yielding; see DOCILE.

submit *v.* **1** [To offer] tender, proffer, present; see OFFER 1. **2** [To surrender] capitulate, yield, give in; see OBEY.

subordinate *a.* inferior, junior, smaller, low, insignificant, subnormal, paltry, not up to snuff*, below par, unequal to, not comparable to, lower, minor, depending on, lower in rank, subject, subservient, submissive, subsidiary, auxiliary, ancillary; see also UNDER 2.—*Ant.* superior, higher, excellent.

subordinate *n.* assistant, helper, aide; see ASSISTANT.

subsequent *a.* succeeding, consequent, coming after; see FOLLOWING.

subsequently *a.* afterward, consequently, in the end; see FINALLY 2.

subside *v.* recede, sink, dwindle; see FALL 1.

subsidiary *a.* secondary, auxiliary, supplementary; see SUBORDINATE.

subsidize *v.* support, finance, back; see PROMOTE 1.

subsidy *n.* allowance, support, grant; see PAYMENT 1.

subsist *v.* stay alive, remain alive, live on; see LIVE 4.

subsistence *n.* **1** [The supporting of life] living, sustenance, maintenance, support, keep, necessities of life. **2** [The means of supporting life] means, circumstances, resources, property, money, riches, wealth, capital, substance, affluence, independence, gratuity, fortune, dowry, legacy, earnings, wages, salary, tips, income, pension; see also FUNDS.—*Ant.* POVERTY, penury, pennilessness.

substance *n.* matter, material, being, object, item, person, animal, something, element; see also THING 1.

sub·stand'ard *adj.* below standard
sub·stan·tial (səb stan'shəl) *adj.* **1** having substance **2** real; true **3** strong; solid **4** ample; large **5** important **6** wealthy **7** with regard to essential elements —**sub·stan'tial·ly** *adv.*
sub·stan'ti·ate' (-shē āt') *vt.* **-at'ed, -at'ing** ⟦see SUBSTANCE⟧ to show to be true or real by giving evidence —**sub·stan'ti·a'tion** *n.*
sub·stan·tive (sub'stən tiv) *adj.* ⟦see SUBSTANCE⟧ of or dealing with essentials —*n. Gram.* a noun or any other word or group of words used as a noun
sub'sta'tion *n.* a small post-office station, as in a store
sub·sti·tute (sub'stə to͞ot') *n.* ⟦< L *sub-*, under + *statuere*, put⟧ a person or thing serving or used in place of another —*vt., vi.* **-tut'ed, -tut'ing** to put, use, or serve in place of (another) —**sub'sti·tu'tion** *n.*
sub·stra·tum (sub'strāt'əm, -strat'-) *n., pl.* **-ta** (-ə) or **-tums** a part, substance, etc. which lies beneath and supports another
sub'struc'ture *n.* a part or structure that is a support, base, etc.
sub·sume (sub so͞om') *vt.* **-sumed', -sum'ing** ⟦< L *sub-*, under + *sumere*, take⟧ to include within a larger class
sub'teen' *n.* a child nearly a teenager
sub'ten'ant *n.* a person who rents from a tenant —**sub·ten'an·cy** *n.*
sub·ter·fuge (sub'tər fyo͞oj') *n.* ⟦< L *subter*, secretly + *fugere*, flee⟧ any plan or action used to hide or evade something
sub·ter·ra·ne·an (sub'tə rā'nē ən) *adj.* ⟦< L *sub-*, under + *terra*, earth⟧ **1** underground **2** secret; hidden
sub·text (sub'tekst') *n.* an underlying meaning, theme, etc.
sub'ti'tle *n.* **1** a secondary or explanatory title **2** one or more lines of translated dialogue, etc. at the bottom of a film or video image —*vt.* **-ti'tled, -ti'tling** to add a subtitle or subtitles to
sub·tle (sut''l) *adj.* **-tler** (-lər, -'l ər), **-tlest** ⟦< L *subtilis*, fine, thin⟧ **1** thin; not dense **2** mentally keen **3** delicately skillful **4** crafty **5** not obvious —**sub'tle·ty**, *pl.* **-ties**, *n.* —**sub'tly** *adv.*
sub'to'tal *n.* a total that is part of a complete total —*vt., vi.* **-taled** or **-talled, -tal·ing** or **-tal·ling** to add up so as to form a subtotal
sub·tract (səb trakt') *vt., vi.* ⟦< L *sub-*, under + *trahere*, to draw⟧ to take away or deduct (one quantity from another) —**sub·trac'tion** *n.*
sub·tra·hend (sub'trə hend') *n.* a quantity to be subtracted from another (the *minuend*)
sub·trop·i·cal (sub trä'pi kəl) *adj.* **1** of regions bordering on the tropics **2** characteristic of such regions Also **sub·trop'ic**
sub·urb (sub'ərb) *n.* ⟦< L *sub-*, near + *urbs*, town⟧ a district, town, etc. on the outskirts of a city —**sub·ur·ban** (sə bʉr'bən) *adj.*
sub·ur·ban·ite (sə bʉr'bən īt') *n.* a person living in a suburb
sub·ur'bi·a (-bē ə) *n.* the suburbs or suburbanites collectively
sub·ven·tion (səb ven'shən) *n.* ⟦< LL *subventio*, aid⟧ a subsidy
sub·ver·sive (səb vʉr'siv) *adj.* tending to subvert —*n.* a person seen as being subversive
sub·vert (səb vʉrt') *vt.* ⟦< L *sub-*, under + *vertere*, to turn⟧ **1** to overthrow or destroy (something established) **2** to corrupt, as in morals —**sub·ver'sion** (-vʉr'zhən) *n.*
sub'way' *n.* an underground, electric metropolitan railway
suc- *prefix* SUB-: used before *c [succumb]*
suc·ceed (sək sēd') *vi.* ⟦< L *sub-*, under + *cedere*, go⟧ **1** to follow, as into office **2** to be successful —*vt.* to come after; follow
suc·cess (sək ses') *n.* **1** a favorable result **2** the gaining of wealth, fame, etc. **3** a successful person or thing
suc·cess'ful *adj.* **1** turning out as was hoped for **2** having gained wealth, fame, etc. —**suc·cess'ful·ly** *adv.*
suc·ces·sion (sək sesh'ən) *n.* **1** *a*) the act of succeeding another, as to an office *b*) the right to do this **2** a number of persons or things coming one after another
suc·ces'sive (-ses'iv) *adj.* coming one after another —**suc·ces'sive·ly** *adv.*
suc·ces'sor *n.* one that succeeds another, as to an office
suc·cinct (sək siŋkt') *adj.* ⟦< L *sub-*, under + *cingere*, gird⟧ clear and brief; terse —**suc·cinct'ly** *adv.* —**suc·cinct'ness** *n.*
suc·cor (suk'ər) *vt.* ⟦< L *sub-*, under + *currere*, to run⟧ to help in time of need or distress —*n.* aid; relief
suc·co·tash (suk'ə tash') *n.* ⟦< AmInd⟧ a dish of lima beans and corn kernels cooked together
suc·cu·lent (suk'yo͞o lənt) *adj.* ⟦< L *sucus*, juice⟧ full of juice —**suc'cu·lence** or **suc'cu·len·cy** *n.*

THESAURUS

substantial *a.* **1** [Real] material, actual, visible; see TANGIBLE. **2** [Considerable] ample, abundant, plentiful; see LARGE 1, MUCH 2.
substantially *a.* extensively, considerably, largely; see MUCH 1, 2.
substitute *n.* deputy, double, dummy, relief, stand-in, standby, understudy, proxy, replacement, ringer*, sub*, pinch-hitter*, designated hitter*; see also DELEGATE.
substitute *v.* act for, do the work of, replace, supplant, displace, take another's place, double for, answer for, pass for, go for, go as, fill in for, pinch-hit for, take the rap for*, go to bat for*, front for, be in someone's shoes.
substitution *n.* change, swap, replacement; see EXCHANGE 3.
subterranean *a.* subsurface, sunken, subterraneous; see UNDERGROUND.
subtle *a.* indirect, implied, insinuated; see MENTAL 2.
subtlety *n.* fine distinction, nuance, innuendo; see SUGGESTION 1.
subtract *v.* deduct, take away, withhold; see DECREASE 2.
subtraction *n.* deducting, deduction, diminution; see DISCOUNT, REDUCTION 1.
suburb *n.* outlying district, residential district, bedroom community; see AREA.
suburban *a.* residential, rural, exurban; see DISTRICT, LOCAL 1, RURAL.
subversion *n.* overthrow, undermining, sabotage; see DEFEAT, REVOLUTION 2.
subversive *a.* ruinous, riotous, insurgent; see REBELLIOUS.
subway *n.* underground (British), tube (British), rapid transit; see RAILROAD, TRAIN.
succeed *v.* **1** [To attain success] achieve, accomplish, get, prosper, attain, reach, be successful, fulfill, earn, do well, secure, succeed in, score, obtain, thrive, profit, realize, acquire, flourish, be victorious, capture, reap, benefit, recover, retrieve, gain, receive, master, triumph, possess, overcome, win, win out, work out, carry out, surmount, prevail, conquer, vanquish, distance, outdistance, reduce, suppress, worst, work, outwit, outmaneuver, score a point, be accepted, be well-known, grow famous, carry off, pull off, come off, come through, make one's way, make one's fortune, satisfy one's ambition, make one's mark, hit the mark, live high, come through with flying colors, beat the game*, work well, overcome all obstacles, play one's cards well, crown, top, do oneself proud*, make it*, make good, do all right by oneself, be on top of the heap*, go places*, click*, set the world on fire*, cut the mustard*, make a killing*, put across*.—*Ant.* FAIL, give up, go amiss. **2** [To follow in time] follow after, come after, take the place of, ensue, supervene, supplant, supersede, succeed, replace, postdate, displace, come next, become heir to, result, be subsequent to, follow in order, bring up the rear.
succeeding *a.* ensuing, following after, next in order; see FOLLOWING.
success *n.* **1** [The fact of having succeeded to a high degree] fortune, good luck, achievement, accomplishment, gain, benefit, prosperity, victory, advance, attainment, progress, profit, end, completion, triumph, conclusion, the life of Riley*, bed of roses*, easy street*, favorable outcome.—*Ant.* DEFEAT, loss, disaster. **2** [A successful person or thing] celebrity, famous person, leader, authority, master, expert, somebody, star, superstar, VIP*, tops.—*Ant.* FAILURE, loser, nonentity.
successful *a.* prosperous, fortunate, lucky, victorious, triumphant, auspicious, happy, unbeaten, favorable, strong, propitious, advantageous, encouraging, contented, satisfied, thriving, flourishing, wealthy, ahead of the game*, sitting pretty*, on easy street*, at the top of the ladder, out in front, on the track*, over the hump*.—*Ant.* UNSUCCESSFUL, poor, failing.
successfully *a.* fortunately, triumphantly, luckily, victoriously, happily, favorably, strongly, thrivingly, flourishingly, famously, propitiously, auspiciously, prosperously, contentedly, beyond all expectation.
succession *n.* continuation, suite, set; see SEQUENCE 1, SERIES.
successive *a.* serial, succeeding, in line; see CONSECUTIVE.
successor *n.* heir, follower, replacement; see CANDIDATE.

suc·cumb (sə kum′) ***vi.*** ⟦< L *sub-,* under + *cumbere,* to lie⟧ **1** to give way (*to*); yield **2** to die

such (such) ***adj.*** ⟦OE *swilc*⟧ **1** *a*) of the kind mentioned *b*) of the same or a similar kind **2** whatever *[at such time as you go]* **3** so extreme, so much, etc. *[such an honor]* —***adv.*** to so great a degree *[such good news]* —***pron.*** **1** such a person or thing **2** the person or thing mentioned *[such was her nature]* —**as such 1** as being what is indicated **2** in itself —**such as** for example

such and such (being) something particular but not named or specified *[such and such a place]*

such′like′ ***adj.*** of such a kind —***pron.*** persons or things of such a kind

suck (suk) ***vt.*** ⟦< OE *sucan*⟧ **1** to draw (liquid) into the mouth **2** to take in by or as by sucking **3** to suck liquid from (fruit, etc.) **4** to hold (ice, etc.) in the mouth and lick so as to dissolve **5** to place (the thumb, etc.) in the mouth and draw on —***vi.*** to suck something —***n.*** the act of sucking

suck′er ***n.*** **1** one that sucks **2** a freshwater bony fish with a mouth adapted for sucking **3** a part used for sucking or for holding fast by suction **4** LOLLIPOP **5** [Slang] one easily cheated **6** *Bot.* a subordinate shoot on the root or stem of a plant

suck·le (suk′əl) ***vt.*** **-led, -ling** ⟦ME *sokelen*⟧ **1** to cause to suck at the breast or udder; nurse **2** to bring up; rear —***vi.*** to suck at the breast or udder

suck′ling ***n.*** an unweaned child or young animal

su·crose (so͞o′krōs′) ***n.*** ⟦< Fr *sucre,* sugar + -OSE[1]⟧ a sugar extracted from sugar cane or sugar beets

suc·tion (suk′shən) ***n.*** ⟦< L *sugere,* to suck⟧ **1** a sucking **2** the production of a vacuum in a cavity or over a surface so that external atmospheric pressure forces fluid in or causes something to adhere to the surface

Su·dan (so͞o dan′) country in NE Africa: 967,500 sq. mi.; pop. 20,564,000: often preceded by *the* —**Su·da·nese** (so͞o′ də nēz′), *pl.* **-nese′**, ***adj.***, ***n.***

sud·den (sud′′n) ***adj.*** ⟦< L *sub-,* under + *ire,* go⟧ **1** *a*) happening or coming unexpectedly *b*) sharp or abrupt **2** quick or hasty —**all of a sudden** unexpectedly —**sud′den·ly** ***adv.*** —**sud′den·ness** ***n.***

sudden death *Sports* an extra period added to a tied game: the game ends when one side scores

sudden infant death syndrome the sudden death of an apparently healthy infant, possibly caused by a breathing problem

suds (sudz) ***pl.n.*** ⟦prob. < MDu *sudse,* marsh water⟧ **1** soapy, frothy water **2** foam —**suds′y, -i·er, -i·est,** ***adj.***

sue (so͞o) ***vt.***, ***vi.*** **sued, su′ing** ⟦< L *sequi,* follow⟧ **1** to appeal (to); petition **2** to prosecute in a court in seeking justice, etc.

suede or **suède** (swād) ***n.*** ⟦< Fr *gants de Suède,* Swedish gloves⟧ **1** tanned leather with the flesh side buffed into a nap **2** a kind of cloth like this

su·et (so͞o′it) ***n.*** ⟦ult. < L *sebum,* tallow⟧ the hard fat of cattle and sheep: used in cooking, etc.

Su·ez Canal (so͞o ez′) ship canal joining the Mediterranean & Red seas

suf or **suff** *abbrev.* suffix

suf- *prefix* SUB-: used before *f*

suf·fer (suf′ər) ***vt.***, ***vi.*** ⟦< L *sub-,* under + *ferre,* to bear⟧ **1** to undergo (pain, injury, grief, etc.) **2** to experience (any process) **3** to permit; tolerate —**suf′fer·er** ***n.***

suf·fer·ance (suf′ər əns, suf′rəns) ***n.*** **1** the capacity to endure pain, etc. **2** consent, permission, etc. implied by failure to prohibit

suf′fer·ing (-ər iŋ, -riŋ) ***n.*** **1** the bearing of pain, distress, etc. **2** something suffered

suf·fice (sə fīs′) ***vi.*** **-ficed′, -fic′ing** ⟦< L *sub-,* under + *facere,* make⟧ to be enough or adequate

suf·fi·cient (sə fish′ənt) ***adj.*** as much as is needed; enough —**suf·fi′cien·cy** ***n.*** —**suf·fi′cient·ly** ***adv.***

suf·fix (suf′iks) ***n.*** ⟦< L *sub-,* under + *figere,* fix⟧ a syllable or syllables joined to the end of a word to alter its meaning, etc. (Ex.: *-ness* in *darkness*)

suf·fo·cate (suf′ə kāt′) ***vt.*** **-cat′ed, -cat′ing** ⟦< L *sub-,* under + *fauces,* throat⟧ **1** to kill by cutting off the supply of air for breathing **2** to smother, suppress, etc. —***vi.*** **1** to die by being suffocated **2** to choke; stifle —**suf′fo·ca′tion** ***n.***

suf·frage (suf′rij) ***n.*** ⟦< L *suffragium,* a ballot⟧ **1** a vote or voting **2** the right to vote; franchise

suf·fra·gette (suf′rə jet′) ***n.*** ⟦< prec. + -ETTE⟧ a woman who advocates female suffrage: term objected to by some, who prefer *suffragist*

suf′fra·gist ***n.*** one who believes in extending the right to vote, esp. to women

suf·fuse (sə fyo͞oz′) ***vt.*** **-fused′, -fus′ing** ⟦< L *sub-,* under + *fundere,* pour⟧ to overspread so as to fill with a glow, etc. —**suf·fu′sion** ***n.***

sug- *prefix* SUB-: used before *g*

sug·ar (sho͝og′ər) ***n.*** ⟦< Sans *śárkarâ*⟧ any of a class of sweet, soluble carbohydrates, as sucrose or glucose; specif., sucrose used as a food and sweetening agent —***vt.*** to sweeten, etc. with sugar —***vi.*** to form sugar —**sug′ar·less** ***adj.*** —**sug′ar·y** ***adj.***

sugar beet a beet having a white root with a high sugar content

sugar cane a very tall tropical grass cultivated as the main source of sugar

sug′ar·coat′ ***vt.*** **1** to coat with sugar **2** to make (something disagreeable) seem more pleasant

sug′ar·plum′ ***n.*** a round piece of sugary candy

sug·gest (səg jest′) ***vt.*** ⟦< L *sub-,* under + *gerere,* carry⟧ **1** to bring to the mind for consideration **2** to call to mind by association of ideas **3** to propose as a possibility **4** to show indirectly; imply

sug·gest′i·ble ***adj.*** readily influenced by suggestion —**sug·gest′i·bil′i·ty** ***n.***

sug·ges′tion (-jes′chən) ***n.*** **1** a suggesting or being suggested **2** something suggested **3** a hint or trace

sug·ges′tive ***adj.*** **1** that tends to suggest ideas **2** tending to suggest something considered improper or indecent —**sug·ges′tive·ly** ***adv.***

THESAURUS

such ***a.*** so, so very, of this kind, of that kind, of the sort, of the degree, so much, before-mentioned.

such ***pron.*** this, that, such a one, such a person, such a thing. **—as such** in and of itself, by its own nature, more than in name only; see ACCORDINGLY, ESSENTIALLY.

such as ***conj.***, ***prep.*** for example, for instance, to give an example; see INCLUDING, SIMILARLY, THUS.

suck ***v.*** absorb, take up, swallow up; see SWALLOW.

sucker ***n.*** **1** [*A victim] dupe, fool, cat's-paw; see VICTIM. **2** [Candy] lollipop, sweet, confectionary; see CANDY.

suction ***n.*** sucking, vacuum, drawing power; see ATTRACTION, POWER 2, PULL 1.

sudden ***a.*** precipitate, impromptu, swift; see IMMEDIATE, UNEXPECTED. **—all of a sudden** unexpectedly, suddenly, precipitously; see QUICKLY.

suddenly ***a.*** without any warning, abruptly, swiftly; see QUICKLY.

suds ***n.*** foam, bubbles, lather; see FROTH, SOAP.

sue ***v.*** prosecute, follow up, claim, demand, indict, litigate, contest, pray, entreat, plead, petition, appeal, accuse, file a plea, claim damages, go to court, file suit, prefer a claim, enter a lawsuit, take to court, file a claim, have the law on, haul into court*.

suffer ***v.*** **1** [To feel pain] undergo, experience, ache, smart, be in pain, be wounded, agonize, grieve, be racked, be convulsed, droop, flag, sicken, torture oneself, get it in the neck*, look green about the gills, complain of, be affected with, go hard with, match it, flinch at, not feel like anything, labor under.—*Ant.* RECOVER, be relieved, be restored. **2** [To endure] bear, sustain, put up with; see ENDURE 2. **3** [To permit] admit, let, submit; see ALLOW.

suffering ***n.*** distress, misery, affliction; see DIFFICULTY 1, 2, PAIN 2.

sufficient ***a.*** adequate, ample, satisfactory; see ENOUGH 1.

sufficiently ***a.*** to one's satisfaction, enough, amply; see ADEQUATELY.

suffocate ***v.*** stifle, smother, strangle; see CHOKE.

sugar ***n.*** *Common varieties and forms of sugar include the following:* sucrose, cane sugar, brown sugar, beet sugar, grape sugar, dextrose, fructose, fruit sugar, maltose, malt sugar, lactose, maple sugar; see also FOOD.

sugary ***a.*** saccharine, treacly, candied; see SWEET 1.

suggest ***v.*** **1** [To make a suggestion] submit, advise, recommend; see PROPOSE 1. **2** [To bring to mind] imply, infer, intimate; see HINT.

suggested ***a.*** submitted, advanced, proposed, propounded, advised, recommended, counseled, tendered, reminded, prompted, summoned up, called up, offered, laid before, put forward.

suggestion ***n.*** **1** [A suggested detail] hint, allusion, suspicion, intimation, implication, innuendo, insinuation, opinion, proposal, advice, recommendation, injunction, charge, instruction, submission, reminder, approach, advance, bid, idea, tentative statement, presentation, proposition, tip. **2** [A suggested plan] scheme, idea, outline; see PLAN 2. **3** [A very small quantity] trace, touch, taste; see BIT 1.

su·i·cide (so͞o′ə sīd′) ***n.*** ⟦L *sui,* of oneself + -CIDE⟧ **1** the act of killing oneself intentionally **2** one who commits suicide —**su′i·ci′dal** ***adj.***

su·i ge·ne·ris (so͞o′ē jen′ər is) ⟦L, of his (or her or its) own kind⟧ without equal; unique

suit (so͞ot) ***n.*** ⟦< L *sequi,* follow⟧ **1** a set of clothes; esp., a coat and trousers (or skirt) **2** any of the four sets of playing cards **3** action to secure justice in a court of law **4** an act of suing, pleading, etc. **5** courtship —***vt.*** **1** to be appropriate to **2** to make right or appropriate; fit **3** to please; satisfy *[nothing suits him]* —**follow suit** to follow the example set —**suit oneself** to act according to one's own wishes —**suit up** to put on an athletic uniform, spacesuit, etc. in preparation for a particular activity

suit′a·ble ***adj.*** that suits a given purpose, etc.; appropriate —**suit′a·bil′i·ty** ***n.*** —**suit′a·bly** ***adv.***

suit′case′ ***n.*** a travel case for clothes, etc.

suite (swēt; *for 3, also* so͞ot) ***n.*** ⟦Fr: see SUIT⟧ **1** a group of attendants; staff **2** a set of connected rooms, as an apartment **3** a set of matched furniture for a given room

suit′ing ***n.*** cloth for making suits

suit′or ***n.*** a man courting a woman

su·ki·ya·ki (so͞o′kē yä′kē) ***n.*** ⟦Jpn⟧ a Japanese dish of thinly sliced meat and vegetables, cooked quickly with soy sauce, sake, etc.

Suk·kot or **Suk·koth** (so͝ok′ōt, so͝ok′ōs) ***n.*** ⟦Heb, lit., tabernacles⟧ a Jewish fall festival commemorating the wandering of the Hebrews during the Exodus

sul·fa (sul′fə) ***adj.*** of a family of drugs used in combating certain bacterial infections

sul·fate (sul′fāt′) ***n.*** a salt or ester of sulfuric acid

sul′fide′ (-fīd′) ***n.*** a compound of sulfur with another element or a radical

sul·fur (sul′fər) ***n.*** ⟦< L *sulphur*⟧ a pale-yellow, nonmetallic chemical element: it burns with a blue flame and a stifling odor

sul·fu·ric (sul fyo͝or′ik) ***adj.*** of or containing sulfur

sulfuric acid an oily, colorless, corrosive liquid used in making dyes, explosives, fertilizers, etc.

sul·fu·rous (sul′fər əs, sul fyo͝or′əs) ***adj.*** **1** of or containing sulfur **2** like burning sulfur in odor, color, etc.

sulk (sulk) ***vi.*** ⟦< fol.⟧ to be sulky —***n.*** a sulky mood: also **the sulks**

sulk·y (sul′kē) ***adj.*** **-i·er, -i·est** ⟦prob. < OE *-seolcan,* become slack⟧ showing resentment by petulant withdrawal —***n.***, *pl.* **-ies** a light, two-wheeled carriage for one person —**sulk′i·ly** ***adv.*** —**sulk′i·ness** ***n.***

sul·len (sul′ən) ***adj.*** ⟦< L *solus,* alone⟧ **1** showing resentment and ill humor by morose, unsociable withdrawal **2** gloomy; sad —**sul′len·ly** ***adv.*** —**sul′len·ness** ***n.***

sul·ly (sul′ē) ***vt.*** **-lied, -ly·ing** ⟦prob. < OFr *soillier*⟧ to soil, tarnish, etc., esp. by disgracing

sul·phur (sul′fər) ***n.*** *chiefly Brit. sp. of* SULFUR

sul·tan (sult′'n) ***n.*** ⟦Fr < Ar *sulṭān*⟧ a Muslim ruler

sul·tan·a (sul tan′ə) ***n.*** **1** a sultan's wife, mother, sister, or daughter **2** a small, white, seedless grape used for raisins

sul·tan·ate (sult′'n it, -āt′) ***n.*** a sultan's authority, office, or domain

sul·try (sul′trē) ***adj.*** **-tri·er, -tri·est** ⟦< SWELTER⟧ **1** oppressively hot and moist **2** suggesting or showing passion, lust, etc.

sum (sum) ***n.*** ⟦< L *summus,* highest⟧ **1** an amount of money **2** gist; summary **3** the result obtained by adding quantities; total —**sum up** to summarize

su·mac or **su·mach** (so͞o′mak′, sho͞o′-) ***n.*** ⟦< Ar *summāq*⟧ any of numerous poisonous and nonpoisonous trees and shrubs of the cashew family

Su·ma·tra (so͞o mä′trə) large island of Indonesia

sum·ma·rize (sum′ə rīz′) ***vt.*** **-rized′, -riz′ing** to make or be a summary of

sum′ma·ry (-rē) ***adj.*** ⟦< L *summa,* a sum⟧ **1** summarizing; concise **2** prompt and without formality **3** hasty and arbitrary —***n.***, *pl.* **-ries** a brief statement covering the main points; digest —**sum·mar·i·ly** (sə mer′ə lē) ***adv.***

sum·ma·tion (sə mā′shən) ***n.*** a final summary of arguments, as in a trial

sum·mer (sum′ər) ***n.*** ⟦< OE *sumor*⟧ the warmest season of the year, following spring —***adj.*** of or typical of summer —***vi.*** to pass the summer —**sum′mer·y** ***adj.***

sum′mer·house′ ***n.*** a small, open structure in a garden, park, etc.

summer sausage a type of hard, dried or smoked sausage

sum′mer·time′ ***n.*** the summer season

sum·mit (sum′it) ***n.*** ⟦< L *summus,* highest⟧ the highest or utmost point; top; apex —***adj.*** of the heads of state *[a summit conference]*

sum·mit·ry (sum′i trē) ***n.***, *pl.* **-ries** the use of conferences between heads of state to resolve problems of diplomacy

sum·mon (sum′ən) ***vt.*** ⟦< L *sub-,* under + *monere,* warn⟧ **1** to call together; order to meet **2** to call or send for with authority **3** to rouse *[summon up one's strength]* —**sum′mon·er** ***n.***

sum′mons (-ənz) ***n.***, *pl.* **-mons·es** ⟦see prec.⟧ **1** an order or command to come, attend, etc. **2** *Law* an official order to appear in court

su·mo (wrestling) (so͞o′mō) ⟦Jpn *sumō,* compete⟧ *[sometimes* **S- w-***]* Japanese wrestling by large, extremely heavy men

sump (sump) ***n.*** ⟦ME *sompe,* swamp⟧ a pit, cistern, cesspool, etc. for draining, collecting, or storing liquids

sump·tu·ous (sump′cho͞o əs) ***adj.*** ⟦< L *sumptus,* expense⟧ **1** costly; lavish **2** magnificent

sun (sun) ***n.*** ⟦OE *sunne*⟧ **1** the gaseous, self-luminous central star of the solar system **2** the heat or light of the sun **3** any star that is the center of a planetary system —***vt.***, ***vi.*** **sunned, sun′ning** to expose (oneself) to direct sunlight

Sun *abbrev.* Sunday

sun′bathe′ ***vi.*** **-bathed′, -bath′ing** to expose the body to direct sunlight —**sun bath** —**sun′bath′er** ***n.***

sun′beam′ ***n.*** a beam of sunlight

Sun′belt′ in the U.S., the S and SW states having a sunny climate and an expanding economy: also **Sun Belt**

sun′block′ ***n.*** SUNSCREEN

sun′bon′net ***n.*** a bonnet for shading the face and neck from the sun

sun′burn′ ***n.*** an inflammation of the skin from exposure

THESAURUS

suicide ***n.*** self-murder, self-destruction, hara-kiri; see DEATH. —**commit suicide** kill oneself, take an overdose, slash one's wrists, take one's own life, end it all*, commit hara-kiri, poison oneself, jump off a bridge, blow one's brains out*.

suit ***n.*** **1** [A series] suite, set, group; see SERIES. **2** [A case at law] lawsuit, action, litigation; see TRIAL 2. **3** [Clothes to be worn together] costume, ensemble, outfit, livery, uniform; see also CLOTHES. *Kinds of suits include the following— women:* sport suit, tailored suit, pantsuit, suit, jumpsuit, evening suit, bathing suit, sunsuit, play suit; *men:* sport suit, business suit, full dress, tails*, monkey suit*, dinner jacket, tuxedo, tux*, bathing suit. —**bring suit** prosecute, start legal proceedings, litigate; see SUE.

suit ***v.*** **1** [To be in accord with] befit, be agreeable, be appropriate to; see AGREE. **2** [To please] amuse, fill, gratify; see ENTERTAIN 1, SATISFY 1. **3** [To adapt] accommodate, revise, readjust; see ALTER 1.

suitable ***a.*** fitting, becoming, proper; see FIT 1.

suitably ***a.*** well, all to the good, fittingly; see FIT 1.

suitcase ***n.*** grip, satchel, luggage; see BAG.

suited ***a.*** adapted, satisfactory, fit; see FIT 1.

sullen ***a.*** unsociable, silent, morose, glum, sulky, sour, cross, ill-humored, petulant, moody, grouchy, fretful, ill-natured, peevish, gloomy, gruff, churlish; see also IRRITABLE.—*Ant.* FRIENDLY, sociable, jolly.

sullenly ***a.*** morosely, glumly, sourly; see ANGRILY, SILENTLY.

sum ***n.*** amount, value, total; see WHOLE.

summarily ***a.*** promptly, readily, speedily; see IMMEDIATELY.

summarize ***v.*** review, condense, shorten; see DECREASE 2.

summary ***n.*** outline, digest, synopsis, recap, analysis, abstract, abbreviation, résumé, précis, skeleton, brief, case, reduction, version, core, report, survey, sketch, syllabus, condensation, sum and substance, wrap-up*.

summer ***n.*** summertime, summer season, dog days, sunny season, harvest, haying time, vacation time; see also SEASON.

summit ***n.*** apex, zenith, crown; see TOP 1.

summon ***v.*** request, beckon, send for, invoke, bid, ask, draft, petition, signal, motion, sign, order, command, direct, enjoin, conjure up, ring, charge, recall, call in, call for, call out, call forth, call up, call away, call down, call together, volunteer.

sun ***n.*** day-star, solar disk, eye of heaven*, light of the day, solar energy, source of light; see also STAR 1. —**under the sun** on earth, terrestrial, mundane; see EARTHLY.

to the sun's rays or to a sunlamp —***vi.***, ***vt.*** **-burned′** or **-burnt′**, **-burn′ing** to get or cause to get a sunburn

sun′burst′ ***n.*** **1** sudden sunlight **2** a decorative device representing the sun with spreading rays

sun·dae (sun′dā, -dē) ***n.*** ⟦prob. < fol.⟧ a serving of ice cream covered with a syrup, fruit, nuts, etc.

Sun·day (sun′dā) ***n.*** ⟦OE *sunnandæg,* sun day⟧ the first day of the week: it is the Sabbath for most Christians: abbrev. **Sun**

sun·der (sun′dər) ***vt.***, ***vi.*** ⟦< OE *sundor,* asunder⟧ to break apart; split

sun′di′al ***n.*** an instrument that shows time by the shadow of a pointer cast by the sun onto a dial

sun′down′ ***n.*** SUNSET

sun′dries (-drēz) ***pl.n.*** sundry items

sun′dry (-drē) ***adj.*** ⟦< OE *sundor,* apart⟧ miscellaneous

sun′fish′ ***n.***, *pl.* **-fish′** or (for different species) **-fish′es** **1** any of a family of North American freshwater fishes **2** a large, sluggish ocean fish

sun′flow′er ***n.*** a tall plant having large, yellow, daisylike flowers

sung (suŋ) ***vi.***, ***vt.*** *pp. & rare pt. of* SING[1]

sun′glass′es ***pl.n.*** eyeglasses with tinted lenses to shade the eyes

sunk (suŋk) ***vi.***, ***vt.*** *pp. & alt. pt. of* SINK

sunk′en (-ən) ***adj.*** **1** submerged **2** below the general level *[a sunken patio]* **3** deeply set; hollow *[sunken cheeks]*

sun′lamp′ ***n.*** an ultraviolet-ray lamp, used for tanning the body, etc.

sun′light′ ***n.*** the light of the sun

sun′lit′ ***adj.*** lighted by the sun

sun′ny (-ē) ***adj.*** **-ni·er**, **-ni·est** **1** full of sunshine **2** bright; cheerful —**sun′ni·ness** ***n.***

sunny side **1** the sunlit side **2** the brighter aspect —**sunny side up** fried upturned and with unbroken yolk *[two eggs sunny side up]*

sun′rise′ ***n.*** **1** the daily appearance of the sun above the E horizon **2** the varying time of this

sun′roof′ ***n.*** a panel in a car roof, that opens to let in light and air: also **sun roof**

sun′room′ ***n.*** a room with large windows to let in sunlight

sun′screen′ ***n.*** a chemical used in lotions, creams, etc. to block certain ultraviolet rays of the sun and reduce the danger of sunburn

sun′set′ ***n.*** **1** the daily disappearance of the sun below the W horizon **2** the varying time of this

sun′shine′ ***n.*** **1** the shining of the sun **2** the light and heat from the sun **3** a sunny place **4** cheerfulness, happiness, etc. —**sun′shin′y** ***adj.***

sun′spot′ ***n.*** any of the temporarily cooler regions appearing cyclically as dark spots on the sun

sun′stroke′ ***n.*** a form of heatstroke caused by excessive exposure to the sun

sun′suit′ ***n.*** short pants with a bib and shoulder straps, worn by babies and young children

sun′tan′ ***n.*** a darkened condition of the skin resulting from exposure to the sun

sun′up′ ***n.*** SUNRISE

sup (sup) ***vi.*** **supped**, **sup′ping** ⟦< OFr *soupe,* soup⟧ to have supper

sup- *prefix* SUB-: used before *p*

su·per (sōō′pər) ***n.*** ⟦< fol.⟧ *short for:* **1** SUPERNUMERARY (sense 2) **2** SUPERINTENDENT (sense 2) —***adj.*** **1** [Inf.] outstanding; exceptionally fine **2** great, extreme, or excessive

super- ⟦L < *super,* above⟧ *prefix* **1** over, above *[superstructure]* **2** *a)* surpassing *[superabundant]* *b)* greater than others of its kind *[supermarket]* **3** additional *[supertax]*

su′per·a·bun′dant ***adj.*** being more than enough —**su′per·a·bun′dance** ***n.***

su·per·an·nu·at·ed (sōō′pər an′yōō āt′id) ***adj.*** ⟦< L *super,* above + *annus,* year⟧ **1** too old for service **2** retired, esp. with a pension, because of old age **3** obsolete; old-fashioned

su·perb (sə purb′, sōō-) ***adj.*** ⟦see SUPER-⟧ **1** noble or majestic **2** rich or magnificent **3** extremely fine; excellent —**su·perb′ly** ***adv.***

su′per·car′go ***n.***, *pl.* **-goes** or **-gos** an officer on a merchant ship in charge of the cargo

su′per·charge′ ***vt.*** **-charged′**, **-charg′ing** to increase the power of (an engine), as with a device (**su′per·charg′er**) that forces extra air and fuel into the cylinders

su·per·cil·i·ous (sōō′pər sil′ē əs) ***adj.*** ⟦< L *super-*, above + *cilium,* eyelid, hence (in allusion to raised eyebrows) haughtiness⟧ disdainful or contemptuous; haughty

su′per·con′duc·tiv′i·ty ***n.*** *Physics* the lack of resistance to electrical current in certain metals, etc. when cooled to low temperatures

su′per·con·duc′tor ***n.*** any material that exhibits superconductivity

su′per·e′go ***n.***, *pl.* **-gos** *Psychoanalysis* that part of the psyche that enforces moral standards

su′per·er′o·ga′tion (-er′ə gā′shən) ***n.*** ⟦< L *super-*, above + *erogare,* pay out⟧ a doing more than is needed or expected —**su′per·e·rog′a·to′ry** (-i räg′ə tôr′ē) ***adj.***

su′per·fi′cial (-fish′əl) ***adj.*** ⟦< L *super-*, above + *facies,* face⟧ **1** of or being on the surface **2** concerned with and understanding only the obvious; shallow **3** quick and cursory **4** seeming such only at first glance —**su′per·fi′ci·al′i·ty** (-fish′ē al′ə tē), *pl.* **-ties**, ***n.*** —**su′per·fi′cial·ly** ***adv.***

su·per·flu·ous (sə pur′flōō əs, sōō-) ***adj.*** ⟦< L *super-*, above + *fluere,* to flow⟧ excessive or unnecessary —**su·per·flu·i·ty** (sōō′pər flōō′ə tē), *pl.* **-ties**, ***n.***

su′per·he′ro ***n.***, *pl.* **-roes** a nearly invincible hero, as in comic books

su′per·high′way′ ***n.*** EXPRESSWAY

su′per·hu′man ***adj.*** **1** having a nature above that of man; divine **2** greater than that of a normal human being

su′per·im·pose′ ***vt.*** **-posed′**, **-pos′ing** to put, lay, or stack on top of something else

su·per·in·tend (sōō′pər in tend′) ***vt.*** to act as superintendent of; supervise —**su′per·in·tend′ence** or **su′per·in·tend′en·cy** ***n.***

su′per·in·tend′ent (-ten′dənt) ***n.*** ⟦< LL *superintendere,* superintend⟧ **1** a person in charge of a department, institution, etc.; director **2** a person responsible for the maintenance of a building

su·pe·ri·or (sə pir′ē ər) ***adj.*** ⟦see SUPER-⟧ **1** higher in space, order, rank, etc. **2** greater in quality or value than: with *to* **3** above average in quality; excellent **4** refusing to give in to or be affected by: with *to* **5** showing a feeling of being better than others; haughty —***n.*** **1** a superior person or thing **2** the head of a religious community —**su·pe′ri·or′i·ty** (-ôr′ə tē) ***n.***

Su·pe·ri·or (sə pir′ē ər), **Lake** largest of the Great Lakes, between Michigan & Ontario, Canada

superl *abbrev.* superlative

su·per·la·tive (sə pur′lə tiv, sōō-) ***adj.*** ⟦< L *super-*, above + *latus,* pp. of *ferre,* to bear, carry⟧ **1** superior to all others; supreme **2** *Gram.* designating the extreme degree of comparison of adjectives and adverbs —***n.*** **1** the highest degree; peak **2** *Gram.* the superlative degree *[*"finest" is the *superlative* of "fine"*]* —**su·per′la·tive·ly** ***adv.***

su′per·ma·jor′i·ty ***n.*** the quantity of votes, above a mere majority, required to pass certain bills, etc.

su′per·man′ (-man′) ***n.***, *pl.* **-men′** (-men′) an apparently superhuman man

THESAURUS

sunburned ***a.*** tanned, burned, sunburnt, brown, suntanned, bronzed, ruddy.—*Ant.* PALE, white-skinned, pallid.

Sunday ***n.*** first day of the week, Sabbath, day of rest; see WEEKEND.

sunken ***a.*** lowered, depressed, down; see UNDER 1.

sunlight ***n.*** daylight, sunshine, light of day; see LIGHT 1.

sunny ***a.*** shining, brilliant, sunshiny; see BRIGHT 1.

sunrise ***n.*** dawn, daybreak, aurora; see MORNING 1.

sunset ***n.*** sundown, evening, end of the day, close of the day, nightfall, twilight, dusk; see also NIGHT 1.—*Ant.* MORNING, dawn, sunrise.

sunshine ***n.*** sunlight, the sun, sunbeams; see LIGHT 1.

superb ***a.*** magnificent, splendid, elegant; see EXCELLENT, GRAND.

superficial ***a.*** flimsy, cursory, hasty, shallow, shortsighted, ignorant, narrow-minded, prejudiced, partial, external, unenlightened.—*Ant.* LEARNED, deep, profound.

superficially ***a.*** lightly, on the surface, frivolously; see CARELESSLY.—*Ant.* CAREFULLY, thoughtfully, thoroughly.

superfluous ***a.*** unnecessary, excessive, extra; see EXTREME.

superintendent ***n.*** supervisor, inspector, director; see EXECUTIVE.

superior ***a.*** higher, better, preferred, above, finer, of higher rank, a cut above*, more exalted; see also EXCELLENT.

superiority ***n.*** supremacy, preponderance, advantage; see PERFECTION.

su'per·mar'ket *n.* a large, self-service, retail food store or market
su·per·nal (so͞o pʉrn'əl) *adj.* ⟦< L *supernus,* upper⟧ celestial or divine
su'per·nat'u·ral *adj.* not explainable by the known forces or laws of nature; specif., of or involving God, ghosts, spirits, etc.
su'per·no'va *n., pl.* **-vas** or **-vae** (-vē) a rare, extremely bright nova
su·per·nu·mer·ar·y (so͞o'pər no͞o'mə rer'ē) *n., pl.* **-ies** ⟦< L *super,* above + *numerus,* number⟧ **1** an extra person or thing **2** *Theater* a person with a small, nonspeaking part
su'per·pose' *vt.* **-posed', -pos'ing** ⟦see SUPER- & POSE⟧ to place on or above something else —**su'per·pos'a·ble** *adj.* —**su'per·po·si'tion** *n.*
su'per·pow'er *n.* an extremely powerful, influential nation
su'per·sat'u·rate' *vt.* **-rat'ed, -rat'ing** to make more highly concentrated than in normal saturation —**su'per·sat'u·ra'tion** *n.*
su'per·script' *n.* ⟦see SUPER- & SCRIPT⟧ a figure, letter, or symbol written above and to the side of another
su·per·sede (so͞o'pər sēd') *vt.* **-sed'ed, -sed'ing** ⟦< L *supersedere,* sit over⟧ to replace or succeed
su'per·son'ic *adj.* ⟦SUPER- + SONIC⟧ **1** designating, of, or moving at a speed greater than that of sound **2** ULTRASONIC
su'per·star' *n.* a star performer, as in sports or entertainment
su·per·sti·tion (so͞o'pər stish'ən) *n.* ⟦< L *superstitio,* lit., a standing (in awe) over⟧ **1** any belief that is inconsistent with known facts or rational thought, esp. such a belief in omens, the supernatural, etc. **2** any action or practice based on such a belief —**su'per·sti'tious** *adj.*
su'per·store' *n.* a very large retail store with a wide variety of goods
su'per·struc'ture *n.* **1** a structure built on top of another **2** that part of a building above the foundation **3** that part of a ship above the main deck
su'per·tank'er *n.* an extremely large tanker, of 300,000 tons or more
su·per·vene (so͞o'pər vēn') *vi.* **-vened', -ven'ing** ⟦< L *super-,* over + *venire,* come⟧ to come or happen as something extraneous or unexpected
su·per·vise (so͞o'pər vīz') *vt., vi.* **-vised', -vis'ing** ⟦< L *super-,* over + *videre,* see⟧ to oversee or direct (work, workers, etc.) —**su'per·vi'sion** (-vizh'ən) *n.* —**su'per·vi'sor** *n.* —**su'per·vi'so·ry** *adj.*
su·pine (so͞o pīn') *adj.* ⟦L *supinus*⟧ **1** lying on the back, face upward **2** inactive; sluggish; listless
supp or **suppl** *abbrev.* **1** supplement **2** supplementary
sup·per (sup'ər) *n.* ⟦see SUP⟧ an evening meal
supper club an expensive nightclub
sup·plant (sə plant') *vt.* ⟦< L *sub-,* under + *planta,* sole of the foot⟧ **1** to take the place of, esp. by force or plotting **2** to remove in order to replace with something else
sup·ple (sup'əl) *adj.* **-pler, -plest** ⟦< L *supplex,* submissive⟧ **1** easily bent; flexible **2** lithe; limber **3** adaptable
sup·ple·ment (sup'lə mənt; *for v.,* -ment') *n.* ⟦see SUPPLY⟧ **1** something added, esp. to make up for a lack **2** a section of additional material in a book, newspaper, etc. —*vt.* to provide a supplement to —**sup'ple·men'tal** or **sup'ple·men'ta·ry** *adj.*
sup·pli·ant (sup'lē ənt) *n.* one who supplicates —*adj.* supplicating
sup'pli·cant (-lə kənt) *adj., n.* SUPPLIANT
sup·pli·cate (sup'lə kāt') *vt., vi.* **-cat'ed, -cat'ing** ⟦< L *sub-,* under + *plicare,* to fold⟧ **1** to ask for (something) humbly **2** to make a humble request (of) —**sup'pli·ca'tion** *n.*
sup·ply (sə plī') *vt.* **-plied', -ply'ing** ⟦< L *sub-,* under + *plere,* fill⟧ **1** to furnish or provide (what is needed) to (someone) **2** to compensate for (a deficiency, etc.); make good —*n., pl.* **-plies'** **1** the amount available for use or sale; stock **2** [*pl.*] needed materials, provisions, etc. —**sup·pli'er** *n.*
sup·ply'-side' *adj.* designating or of an economic theory that an increase in money for investment, as supplied by lowering taxes, will stimulate economic growth
sup·port (sə pôrt') *vt.* ⟦< L *sub-,* under + *portare,* carry⟧ **1** to carry the weight of; hold up **2** to encourage; help **3** to advocate; uphold **4** to maintain (a person, institution, etc.) with money or subsistence **5** to help prove, vindicate, etc. **6** to bear; endure **7** to keep up; maintain **8** to have a role subordinate to (a star) in a play —*n.* **1** a supporting or being supported **2** a person or thing that supports **3** a means of maintaining a livelihood —**sup·port'a·ble** *adj.* —**sup·port'er** *n.*
sup·port'ive *adj.* giving support or help
sup·pose (sə pōz') *vt.* **-posed', -pos'ing** ⟦< L *sub-,* under + *ponere,* put⟧ **1** to assume to be true, as for argument's sake **2** to believe, think, etc. **3** to consider as a possibility *[suppose* I go*]* **4** to expect *[*I'm *supposed* to sing*]* —*vi.* to conjecture —**sup·posed'** *adj.* —**sup·pos'ed·ly** *adv.*
sup·po·si·tion (sup'ə zish'ən) *n.* **1** a supposing **2** something supposed
sup·pos·i·to·ry (sə päz'ə tôr'ē) *n., pl.* **-ries** ⟦see SUPPOSE⟧ a small piece of medicated substance placed in the rectum or vagina, where it melts
sup·press (sə pres') *vt.* ⟦< L *sub-,* under + *premere,* to press⟧ **1** to put down by force; quell **2** to keep from being known, published, etc. **3** to keep back; restrain —**sup·pres'sion** (-presh'ən) *n.*
sup·pres'sant (-ənt) *n.* a drug, etc. that tends to suppress an action, condition, etc.

THESAURUS

supernatural *a.* preternatural, superhuman, spectral, ghostly, occult, metaphysical, hidden, mysterious, secret, unknown, unrevealed, dark, mystic, mythical, mythological, fabulous, legendary, unintelligible, unfathomable, inscrutable, incomprehensible, undiscernible, transcendental, obscure, unknowable, impenetrable, invisible, concealed.—*Ant.* NATURAL, plain, common.
superstition *n.* irrational belief, fear, old wives' tale; see FEAR.
superstitious *a.* fearful, apprehensive, credulous; see AFRAID.
supervise *v.* oversee, conduct, control; see MANAGE 1.
supervised *a.* directed, administered, superintended; see MANAGED 2.
supervision *n.* guidance, surveillance, direction; see MANAGEMENT 1.
supervisor *n.* director, superintendent, administrator; see EXECUTIVE.
supper *n.* evening meal, high tea (British), midnight snack; see DINNER.
supplement *n.* sequel, continuation, complement; see ADDITION 1.
supplement *v.* add to, reinforce, strengthen; see INCREASE.
supplementary *a.* additional, completing, supplemental; see EXTRA.
supply *n.* stock, amount, reserve; see QUANTITY.
supply *v.* furnish, fulfill, outfit; see SATISFY 3.
support *n.* **1** [Aid] care, assistance, comfort; see HELP 1. **2** [A reinforcement] lining, coating, rib, stilt, stay, supporter, buttress, pole, post, prop, guide, backing, stiffener, rampart, stave, stake, rod, pillar, timber; see also BRACE. **3** [Financial aid] maintenance, livelihood, sustenance; see PAYMENT 1. —**in support of** for, condoning, approving; see FOR.
support *v.* **1** [To hold up from beneath] prop, hold up, buoy up, keep up, shore up, bear up, bolster, buttress, brace, sustain, stay, keep from falling, shoulder, carry, bear.—*Ant.* DROP, let fall, break down. **2** [To uphold] maintain, sustain, back up, abet, aid, assist, help, bolster, comfort, carry, bear out, hold, foster, shoulder, corroborate, cheer, establish, promote, advance, champion, advocate, approve, stick by, stand by, stand behind, substantiate, verify, get back of, confirm, further, encourage, hearten, strengthen, recommend, take care of, pull for, agree with, stand up for, keep up, stand back of, take the part of, rally round, give a lift to, stick up for*, go to bat for*, boost. **3** [To provide for] take care of, keep an eye on, care for, attend to, look after, back, bring up, sponsor, put up the money for, finance, pay for, subsidize, nurse, pay the expenses of, grubstake*, stake*, raise.—*Ant.* ABANDON, ignore, fail.
supported *a.* **1** [Backed personally] financed, promoted, sustained; see BACKED 2. **2** [Supported physically] held up, propped up, braced, bolstered, borne up, floating on, floated, buoyed up, based on, founded on, raised up, having a sufficient base, having an adequate foundation; see also FIRM 1.
supporter *n.* advocate, sponsor, helper; see PATRON.
suppose *v.* conjecture, surmise, deem; see GUESS.
supposed *a.* assumed, presumed, presupposed; see LIKELY 1.
supposedly *a.* seemingly, supposably, believably; see PROBABLY.
supposing *conj., a.* if, in case that, in these circumstances, under these conditions, let us suppose, allowing that, presuming, assuming, taking for granted that.
suppress *v.* crush, overpower, subdue; see DEFEAT.
suppression *n.* abolition, suppressing, overthrow; see DEFEAT.

sup·pu·rate (sup′yoo rāt′) *vi.* **-rat′ed, -rat′ing** ⟦< L *sub-*, under + *pus*, pus⟧ to form or discharge pus
supra- ⟦< L *supra*, above⟧ *prefix* above, over, beyond
su·pra·na·tion·al (soo′prə nash′ə nəl) *adj.* of, for, or above all or a number of nations
su·prem·a·cist (sə prem′ə sist, soo-) *n.* one who believes in the supremacy of a particular group
su·prem′a·cy (-sē) *n.*, *pl.* **-cies** supreme condition or power
su·preme′ (-prēm′) *adj.* ⟦< L *superus*, that is above⟧ **1** highest in rank, power, etc. **2** highest in quality, achievement, etc. **3** highest in degree **4** final; ultimate —**su·preme′ly** *adv.*
Supreme Being God
Supreme Court **1** the highest U.S. federal court **2** the highest court in most U.S. states
Supreme Soviet **1** a part of the legislature of Russia **2** formerly, the parliament of the U.S.S.R.
Supt *abbrev.* Superintendent
sur- ⟦< L *super*, over⟧ *prefix* over, upon, above, beyond
sur·cease (sur′sēs′) *n.* ⟦< L *supersedere*, refrain from⟧ an end, or cessation
sur·charge (sur′chärj′) *vt.* **-charged′, -charg′ing** ⟦see SUR- & CHARGE⟧ **1** to overcharge **2** to mark (a postage stamp) with a surcharge —*n.* **1** an additional charge **2** a new valuation printed over the original valuation on a postage stamp
sur·cin·gle (sur′siŋ′gəl) *n.* ⟦< OFr *sur-*, over + L *cingulum*, a belt⟧ a strap passed around a horse's body to bind on a saddle, pack, etc.
sure (shoor) *adj.* **sur′er, sur′est** ⟦< L *securus*⟧ **1** that will not fail *[a sure method]* **2** that cannot be doubted or questioned **3** having no doubt; confident *[sure of the facts]* **4** that can be counted on to be or happen *[a sure defeat]* **5** certain (to do, be, etc.) *[sure to lose]* —*adv.* [Inf.] certainly; indeed —**for sure** certain(ly) —**sure enough** [Inf.] without doubt —**sure′ness** *n.*
sure′fire′ or **sure′-fire′** *adj.* [Inf.] sure to be successful or as expected
sure′-foot′ed *adj.* not likely to stumble, slip, fall, or err —**sure′-foot′ed·ness** *n.*
sure′ly *adv.* **1** with confidence **2** without a doubt; certainly
sur·e·ty (shoor′ə tē, shoor′tē) *n.*, *pl.* **-ties** **1** something that gives assurance, as against loss, etc. **2** one who takes responsibility for another
surf (surf) *n.* ⟦prob. var. of SOUGH⟧ the waves of the sea breaking on the shore or a reef —*vi.* to engage in surfing —*vt.* [Inf.] to browse a succession of (TV channels, websites, etc.) on (a TV, computer network, etc.) —**surf′er** *n.*
sur·face (sur′fis) *n.* ⟦< Fr *sur-*, over + *face*, a face⟧ **1** *a)* the exterior of an object *b)* any of the faces of a solid **2** superficial features or outward appearance —*adj.* **1** of, on, or at the surface **2** external; superficial —*vt.* **-faced, -fac·ing** to give a surface to, as in paving —*vi.* **1** to rise to the surface of the water **2** to become known
surf′board′ *n.* a long, narrow board used in the sport of surfing
surf′-cast′ *vi.* **-cast′, -cast′ing** to fish by casting into the surf from or near the shore
sur·feit (sur′fit) *n.* ⟦< OFr *sorfaire*, overdo⟧ **1** too great an amount **2** overindulgence, esp. in food or drink **3** disgust, nausea, etc. resulting from excess —*vt.* to feed or supply to excess
surf·ing (surf′iŋ) *n.* the sport of riding in toward shore on the crest of a wave, esp. on a surfboard
surge (surj) *n.* ⟦< L *surgere*, to rise⟧ **1** a large wave of water, or its motion **2** a sudden, strong increase, as of power —*vi.* **surged, surg′ing** **1** to move in or as in a surge **2** to increase suddenly
sur·geon (sur′jən) *n.* a doctor who specializes in surgery
sur·ger·y (sur′jər ē) *n.*, *pl.* **-ger·ies** ⟦< Gr *cheir*, the hand + *ergein*, to work⟧ **1** the treatment of disease, injury, etc. by manual or instrumental operations **2** a room used for this
sur′gi·cal (-ji kəl) *adj.* **1** of surgeons or surgery **2** very accurate, precisely targeted, etc. —**sur′gi·cal·ly** *adv.*
sur·gi·cen·ter (sur′jə sent′ər) *n.* ⟦< *Surgicenter*, a service mark⟧ a facility for performing minor surgery on outpatients
Su·ri·name (soor′i näm′) country in NE South America: 63,251 sq. mi.; pop. 355,000: formerly **Su′ri·nam′**
sur·ly (sur′lē) *adj.* **-li·er, -li·est** ⟦earlier *sirly*, imperious < *sir*, sir⟧ bad-tempered; sullenly rude
sur·mise (sər mīz′) *n.* ⟦OFr *sur-*, upon + *mettre*, put⟧ a conjecture —*vt., vi.* **-mised′, -mis′ing** to guess
sur·mount (sər mount′) *vt.* ⟦SUR- & MOUNT[2]⟧ **1** to overcome (a difficulty) **2** to be at the top of; rise above **3** to climb up and across (a height, etc.) —**sur·mount′a·ble** *adj.*
sur·name (sur′nām′) *n.* ⟦< OFr *sur-* (see SUR-) + *nom*, name⟧ the family name, or last name
sur·pass (sər pas′) *vt.* ⟦< Fr *sur-* (see SUR-) + *passer*, to pass⟧ **1** to excel or be superior to **2** to go beyond the limit, capacity, etc. of
sur·plice (sur′plis) *n.* ⟦< L *super-*, above + *pelliceum*, fur robe⟧ a loose, white outer ecclesiastical vestment
sur·plus (sur′plus′) *n.* ⟦< OFr *sur-*, above (see SUR-) + L *plus*, more⟧ a quantity over and above what is needed or used —*adj.* excess; extra
sur·prise (sər prīz′) *vt.* **-prised′, -pris′ing** ⟦< OFr *sur-* (see SUR-) + *prendre*, to take⟧ **1** to come upon suddenly or unexpectedly; take unawares **2** to amaze; astonish —*n.* **1** a being surprised **2** something that surprises
sur·re·al (sə rē′əl) *adj.* **1** of or like surrealism **2** bizarre; fantastic
sur·re′al·ism′ *n.* ⟦see SUR- & REAL⟧ a modern movement in the arts in which the workings of the unconscious are depicted —**sur·re′al·is′tic** *adj.* —**sur·re′al·ist** *adj.*, *n.*
sur·ren·der (sə ren′dər) *vt.* ⟦< Fr *sur-*, up + *rendre*, render⟧ **1** to give up possession of; yield to another on compulsion **2** to give up or abandon —*vi.* to give oneself up, esp. as a prisoner —*n.* the act of surrendering
sur·rep·ti·tious (sur′əp tish′əs) *adj.* ⟦< L *sub-*, under + *rapere*, seize⟧ done, gotten, acting, etc. in a stealthy way
sur·rey (sur′ē) *n.*, *pl.* **-reys** ⟦after *Surrey*, county in England⟧ a light, four-wheeled carriage with two seats and a flat top

THESAURUS

supremacy *n.* domination, mastery, supreme authority; see POWER 2.
supreme *a.* highest, greatest, paramount, chief; see also BEST.
sure *a.*, *interj.* **1** [Confident] positive, assured, convinced; see CERTAIN 1. **2** [*Certainly] of course, by all means, positively, absolutely, definitely; see also SURELY. —**for sure** certainly, for certain, without doubt; see SURELY. —**make sure** make certain, determine, establish; see GUARANTEE. —**to be sure** of course, certainly, obviously; see SURELY.
surefire* *a.* dependable, certain, infallible; see EXCELLENT, RELIABLE.
surely *a.* doubtlessly, certainly, undoubtedly, definitely, absolutely, evidently, explicitly, without doubt, beyond doubt, beyond question, plainly, infallibly, most assuredly, decidedly, inevitably, indisputably, positively, unquestionably, without any doubt, admittedly, clearly, with assurance, beyond the shadow of a doubt, nothing else but, precisely, conclusively, distinctly, by all means, at any rate, with certainty, unerringly, unmistakably, at all events, undeniably, with confidence, as a matter of course, rain or shine*.
surf *n.* breakers, rollers, combers; see WAVE 1.
surface *n.* exterior, covering, facade; see COVER 1, OUTSIDE 1.
surgeon *n.* specialist, operator, sawbones*; see DOCTOR.
surgery *n.* surgical procedure, arthroscopic surgery, the knife*; see MEDICINE 3, OPERATION 4.
surname *n.* cognomen, last name, patronymic; see NAME 1.
surpass *v.* excel, outdo, better; see EXCEED.
surplus *n.* residue, leftover, something extra; see EXCESS 1, REMAINDER.
surprise *n.* **1** [A feeling] astonishment, wonderment, shock; see WONDER 1. **2** [The cause of a feeling] something unexpected, blow, sudden attack, unexpected good fortune, sudden misfortune, unawaited event, unsuspected plot. —**take by surprise** startle, assault, sneak up on; see SURPRISE *v.*
surprise *v.* astonish, astound, bewilder, confound, shock, amaze, overwhelm, dumbfound, unsettle, stun, electrify, petrify, startle, stupefy, stagger, take aback, cause wonder, awe, dazzle, daze, perplex, leave aghast, flabbergast, floor*, bowl over*, jar, take one's breath away, strike dumb, beggar belief, creep up on, catch unawares.
surprised *a.* upset, taken by surprise, taken unawares, astounded, caught napping, astonished, bewildered, caught off guard, shocked, confounded, startled.
surprising *a.* shocking, extraordinary, remarkable; see UNUSUAL 1, 2, UNEXPECTED.
surrender *n.* capitulation, yielding, giving up, submission, giving way, unconditional surrender, abdication, resignation, delivery.
surrender *v.* **1** [To accept defeat] capitulate, yield, raise the white flag; see QUIT 2. **2** [To relinquish possession] give up, let go, resign; see ABANDON 1.

sur·ro·gate (sur'ə git, -gāt') ***n.*** ⟦< L *sub-*, in place of + *rogare,* ask⟧ **1** a deputy or substitute **2** in some U.S. states, a probate court judge **3** a woman who bears a child for another woman, who will raise it —**sur'ro·ga·cy,** *pl.* **-cies,** ***n.***
sur·round (sə round') ***vt.*** ⟦< L *super-*, over + *undare,* to rise⟧ to encircle on all or nearly all sides
sur·round'ings ***pl.n.*** the things, conditions, etc. around a person or thing
sur·tax (sur'taks') ***n.*** an extra tax on top of the regular tax
sur·veil·lance (sər vā'ləns) ***n.*** ⟦Fr < *sur-* (see SUR-) + *veiller,* to watch⟧ close watch kept over someone, esp. a suspect
sur·vey (sər vā'; *for n.* sur'vā') ***vt.*** ⟦< OFr *sur-* (see SUR-) + *veoir,* see⟧ **1** to examine or consider in detail or comprehensively **2** to determine the location, form, or boundaries of (a tract of land) —***n.,*** *pl.* **-veys** **1** a detailed study, as by gathering information and analyzing it **2** a general view **3** *a)* the process of surveying a tract of land *b)* a written description of this —**sur·vey'or** ***n.***
sur·vey'ing ***n.*** the science or work of making land surveys
sur·viv·al·ist (sər vī'vəl ist) ***n.*** one who takes measures, as storing food and weapons, to ensure survival after an economic collapse, nuclear war, etc.
sur·vive (sər vīv') ***vt.*** **-vived', -viv'ing** ⟦< L *super-*, above + *vivere,* to live⟧ to remain alive or in existence after —***vi.*** to continue living or existing —**sur·viv'al** ***n.***
sur·vi'vor (-ər) ***n.*** **1** one that survives **2** someone regarded as capable of surviving changing conditions, misfortune, etc.
sus·cep·ti·ble (sə sep'tə bəl) ***adj.*** ⟦< L *sus-*, under + *capere,* take⟧ easily affected emotionally —**susceptible of** admitting; allowing *[*testimony *susceptible of* error*]* —**susceptible to** easily influenced or affected by —**sus·cep'ti·bil'i·ty** ***n.***
su·shi (sōō'shē) ***n.*** ⟦Jpn⟧ a dish consisting of small cakes of cold rice garnished with raw or cooked fish, vegetables, etc.
sus·pect (sə spekt'; *for adj. & n.* sus'pekt') ***vt.*** ⟦< L *sus-*, under + *spicere,* to look⟧ **1** to believe to be guilty on little or no evidence **2** to believe to be bad, wrong, etc.; distrust **3** to guess; surmise —***adj.*** suspected —***n.*** one suspected of a crime, etc.
sus·pend (sə spend') ***vt.*** ⟦< L *sus-*, under + *pendere,* hang⟧ **1** to exclude as a penalty from an office, school, etc., for a time **2** to stop temporarily **3** to hold back (judgment, etc.) **4** to hang by a support from above **5** to hold in place as though hanging *[*dust particles *suspended* in the air*]*
suspended animation a temporary cessation of the vital functions, resembling death
sus·pend'ers ***pl.n.*** a pair of straps passed over the shoulders to hold up trousers
sus·pense (sə spens') ***n.*** ⟦< L *suspendere,* suspend⟧ **1** a state of uncertainty **2** the growing excitement felt while awaiting a climax of a novel, play, etc. —**sus·pense'ful** ***adj.***
sus·pen·sion (sə spen'shən) ***n.*** **1** a suspending or being suspended **2** the system of springs, etc. supporting a vehicle upon its undercarriage or axles **3** a substance whose particles are dispersed through a fluid but not dissolved in it
suspension bridge a bridge suspended from cables anchored at either end and supported by towers at intervals
sus·pi·cion (sə spish'ən) ***n.*** ⟦< L *suspicere,* suspect⟧ **1** a suspecting **2** the feeling or state of mind of one who suspects **3** a very small amount; trace —***vt.*** [Inf. or Dial.] to suspect
sus·pi'cious ***adj.*** **1** arousing suspicion **2** showing or feeling suspicion —**sus·pi'cious·ly** ***adv.***
sus·tain (sə stān') ***vt.*** ⟦< L *sus-*, under + *tenere,* to hold⟧ **1** to keep in existence; maintain or prolong **2** to provide sustenance for **3** to carry the weight of; support **4** to endure; withstand **5** to comfort or encourage **6** to suffer (an injury, loss, etc.) **7** to uphold the validity of **8** to confirm; corroborate
sus·te·nance (sus'tə nəns) ***n.*** **1** a sustaining **2** means of livelihood **3** nourishment; food
sut·ler (sut'lər) ***n.*** ⟦< 16th-c. Du *soeteler*⟧ [Historical] a person following an army to sell things to its soldiers
su·ture (sōō'chər) ***n.*** ⟦< L *suere,* sew⟧ **1** the line of junction of two parts, esp. of bones of the skull **2** *a)* the stitching together of the two edges of a wound or incision *b)* the thread, etc. used or any of the stitches so made
SUV *abbrev.* SPORT UTILITY VEHICLE
su·ze·rain (sōō'zə rin', -rān') ***n.*** ⟦Fr < L *sursum,* above⟧ **1** a feudal lord **2** a state in relation to another over which it has some political control
svelte (svelt) ***adj.*** ⟦Fr⟧ **1** slender; lithe **2** suave
Sw *abbrev.* **1** Sweden **2** Swedish
SW *abbrev.* **1** southwest **2** southwestern
swab (swäb) ***n.*** ⟦< Du *zwabben,* do dirty work⟧ **1** a yarn mop **2** a small piece of cotton, etc. used to medicate or cleanse a bodily orifice or a wound —***vt.*** **swabbed, swab'bing** to use a swab on
swad·dle (swäd''l) ***vt.*** **-dled, -dling** ⟦prob. < OE *swathian,* swathe⟧ to wrap (a newborn baby) in a blanket or, formerly, in long, narrow bands of cloth (**swaddling clothes**)
swag (swag) ***vt.*** **swagged, swag'ging** ⟦see SWAGGER⟧ to hang in a swag —***n.*** **1** a valance, garland, etc. hanging decoratively in a curve **2** [Slang] loot
swage (swāj) ***n.*** a tool for bending or shaping metal
swag·ger (swag'ər) ***vi.*** ⟦prob. < Norw *svagga,* sway⟧ **1** to walk with a bold, arrogant stride **2** to boast or brag loudly —***n.*** swaggering walk or manner
Swa·hi·li (swä hē'lē) ***n.*** ⟦< Ar *sawāḥil,* the coasts⟧ a Bantu language of E Africa

THESAURUS

surround ***v.*** **1** [To be on all sides] girdle, circle, environ, enclose, close in, close around, circle about, envelop, hem in, wall in. **2** [To take a position on all sides] encompass, encircle, inundate, flow around, close in, close around, hem in, go around, beleaguer, blockade.—*Ant.* ABANDON, flee from, desert.
surrounded ***a.*** girdled, encompassed, encircled, hemmed in, fenced in, hedged in, circled about, enclosed, fenced about, enveloped.—*Ant.* FREE, unfenced, agape.
surrounding ***a.*** enclosing, encircling, encompassing; see AROUND.
surroundings ***n.*** setting, environs, vicinity; see ENVIRONMENT.
survey ***n.*** study, critique, outline; see EXAMINATION 1.
survey ***v.*** **1** [To look upon] look over, take a view of, view; see SEE 1. **2** [To examine or summarize] study, scan, inspect; see EXAMINE.
survival ***n.*** endurance, durability, continuance; see CONTINUATION.
survive ***v.*** **1** [To live on] outlive, outlast, outwear, live down, live out, weather the storm, make out, persist, persevere, last, remain, pull through, come through, keep afloat, get on; see also ENDURE 1. **2** [To endure] suffer through, withstand, sustain; see ENDURE 2.
survivor ***n.*** heir, widow, widower, descendant, orphan.
suspect ***a.*** dubious, questionable, suspected; see UNLIKELY, SUSPICIOUS 2.
suspect ***v.*** **1** [To doubt someone] distrust, disbelieve, mistrust; see DOUBT. **2** [To suppose] presume, surmise, speculate; see ASSUME.
suspected ***a.*** doubtful, imagined, fancied; see SUSPICIOUS 2.
suspend ***v.*** **1** [To exclude temporarily] reject, exclude, drop, remove; see also BAR 2, EJECT, REFUSE. **2** [To cease temporarily] postpone, defer, put off, discontinue, adjourn, interrupt, delay, procrastinate, shelve, waive, retard, protract, lay on the table, file, lay aside, break up, restrain, desist, break off, halt, put a stop to, check, put an end to.—*Ant.* CONTINUE, carry on, proceed.
suspended ***a.*** pensile, in midair, pendulous; see HANGING.
suspense ***n.*** apprehension, uncertainty, anxiety; see DOUBT.
suspicion ***n.*** misgiving, mistrust, surmise; see DOUBT. —**above suspicion** honorable, cleared, unassailable; see HONEST 1, INNOCENT 1. —**under suspicion** suspected, held for questioning, dubious; see SUSPICIOUS 2.
suspicious ***a.*** **1** [Entertaining suspicion] jealous, distrustful, suspecting, doubting, questioning, doubtful, dubious, in doubt, skeptical, unbelieving, wondering.—*Ant.* TRUSTING, trustful, without any doubt. **2** [Arousing suspicion] not quite trustworthy, questionable, queer*, suspect, irregular, unusual, peculiar, out of line, debatable, disputable.—*Ant.* REGULAR, usual, common.
suspiciously ***a.*** doubtingly, doubtfully, skeptically, dubiously, uncertainly, unbelievingly, questioningly, in doubt, having doubt, causing suspicion, with caution, with reservations, with a grain of salt.
sustain ***v.*** **1** [To carry] bear, transport, pack; see CARRY 1, SUPPORT 1, 2. **2** [To nourish] maintain, provide for, nurse; see PROVIDE 1, SUPPORT 2.

swain (swān) ***n.*** ⟦< ON *sveinn,* boy⟧ [Archaic] **1** a country youth **2** a lover

swal·low[1] (swä′lō) ***n.*** ⟦OE *swealwe*⟧ a small, swift-flying bird with long, pointed wings and a forked tail

swal·low[2] (swä′lō) ***vt.*** ⟦OE *swelgan*⟧ **1** to pass (food, etc.) from the mouth into the stomach **2** to take in; absorb: often with *up* **3** to retract (words said) **4** to put up with *[to swallow insults]* **5** to suppress *[to swallow one's pride]* **6** [Inf.] to accept as true without question —***vi.*** to perform the actions of swallowing something, esp. as a result of emotion —***n.*** **1** a swallowing **2** the amount swallowed at one time

swam (swam) ***vi., vt.*** *pt. of* SWIM[1] & SWIM[2]

swa·mi (swä′mē) ***n.,*** *pl.* **-mis** ⟦< Sans *svāmin,* lord⟧ **1** lord; master: title of respect for a Hindu religious teacher **2** a learned man; pundit

swamp (swämp, swômp) ***n.*** ⟦prob. < LowG⟧ a piece of wet, spongy land; marsh; bog —***vt.*** **1** to plunge or sink in a swamp, water, etc. **2** to flood as with water **3** to overwhelm *[swamped by debts]* **4** to sink (a boat) by filling with water —**swamp′y, -i·er, -i·est,** ***adj.***

swan (swän, swôn) ***n.*** ⟦OE⟧ a large waterfowl, usually white, with a long, graceful neck

swank (swaŋk) [Inf.] ***n.*** ⟦akin to OE *swancor,* pliant⟧ ostentatious display —***adj.*** ostentatiously stylish

swank′y ***adj.*** **-i·er, -i·est** [Inf.] ostentatiously stylish

swan's′-down′ ***n.*** **1** the soft down of the swan, used for trimming clothes, etc. **2** a soft, thick flannel Also **swans′down′**

swan song ⟦after the song sung, in ancient fable, by a dying swan⟧ the last act, final creative work, etc. of a person

swap (swäp, swôp) [Inf.] ***vt., vi.*** **swapped, swap′ping,** ***n.*** ⟦ME *swappen,* to strike⟧ trade; barter

sward (swôrd) ***n.*** ⟦< OE *sweard,* a skin⟧ grass-covered soil; turf

swarm (swôrm) ***n.*** ⟦OE *swearm*⟧ **1** a large number of bees, led by a queen, leaving a hive to start a new colony **2** a colony of bees in a hive **3** a moving mass, crowd, or throng —***vi.*** **1** to fly off in a swarm: said of bees **2** to move, be present, etc. in large numbers **3** to be crowded

swarth·y (swôr′*th*ē, -thē) ***adj.*** **-i·er, -i·est** ⟦< OE *sweart*⟧ having a dark complexion

swash′buck′ler (-buk′lər) ***n.*** ⟦< *swash,* to swagger + *buckler,* a shield⟧ a blustering, swaggering fighting man —**swash′buck′ling** ***n., adj.***

swas·ti·ka (swäs′ti kə) ***n.*** ⟦< Sans *svasti,* well-being⟧ **1** an ancient design and mystic symbol in the form of a cross with four equal arms, each bent in a right angle **2** this design with the arms bent clockwise, used as an emblem of Nazism and anti-Semitism

swat (swät) ***vt.*** **swat′ted, swat′ting** ⟦echoic⟧ to hit with a quick, sharp blow —***n.*** a quick, sharp blow —**swat′ter** ***n.***

SWAT (swät) ***n.*** ⟦S*(pecial)* W*(eapons)* a*(nd)* T*(actics)*⟧ a special police unit trained to deal with violence, riots, terrorism, etc.: in full **SWAT team**

swatch (swäch) ***n.*** ⟦orig., a cloth tag or label⟧ a sample piece of cloth, etc.

swath (swäth, swôth) ***n.*** ⟦OE *swathu,* a track⟧ **1** the width covered with one cut of a scythe or other mowing device **2** a strip, row, etc. that has been mowed

swathe (swā*th,* swä*th*) ***vt.*** **swathed, swath′ing** ⟦OE *swathian*⟧ **1** to wrap up in a long strip of cloth **2** to envelop; enclose

sway (swā) ***vi.*** ⟦< ON *sveigja,* to turn, bend⟧ **1** to swing or move from side to side or to and fro **2** to lean or go to one side —***vt.*** **1** to cause to sway **2** to influence —***n.*** **1** a swaying or being swayed **2** influence *[the sway of passion]* —**hold sway** to reign or prevail

sway′backed′ (-bakt′) ***adj.*** having a sagging spine: said as of some horses

Swa·zi·land (swä′zē land′) country in SE Africa: 6,705 sq. mi.; pop. 681,000

swear (swer) ***vi.*** **swore, sworn, swear′ing** ⟦OE *swerian*⟧ **1** to make a solemn declaration with an appeal to God to confirm it **2** to make a solemn promise; vow **3** to use profane language; curse —***vt.*** to declare, pledge, or vow on oath —**swear in** to administer an oath to (a person taking office, a witness, etc.) —**swear off** to renounce —**swear out** to obtain (a warrant for arrest) by making a charge under oath —**swear′er** ***n.***

swear′word′ ***n.*** a profane word or phrase

sweat (swet) ***vi., vt.*** **sweat** or **sweat′ed, sweat′ing** ⟦< OE *swat,* sweat⟧ **1** to give forth or cause to give forth a salty moisture through the pores of the skin; perspire **2** to give forth or condense (moisture) on its surface **3** to work hard enough to cause sweating —***n.*** **1** the salty liquid given forth in perspiration **2** moisture collected in droplets on a surface **3** a sweating or being sweated **4** a condition of eagerness, anxiety, etc. **5** [*pl.*] clothes worn for exercising, etc.; specif., a sweat suit —**sweat out** [Inf.] **1** to get rid of by sweating *[to sweat out a cold]* **2** to wait anxiously for or through —**sweat′y, -i·er, -i·est,** ***adj.***

sweat′er ***n.*** a knitted or crocheted outer garment for the upper body

sweat shirt a heavy, long-sleeved pullover of cotton jersey worn to absorb sweat during or after exercise, sometimes with matching loose trousers (**sweat pants**) in an ensemble (**sweat suit**)

sweat′shop′ ***n.*** a shop where employees work long hours at low wages under poor conditions

Swed *abbrev.* **1** Sweden **2** Swedish

Swede (swēd) ***n.*** a person born or living in Sweden

Swe·den (swēd′′n) country in N Europe: 173,732 sq. mi.; pop. 8,587,000

Swed·ish (swē′dish) ***adj.*** of Sweden or its people, language, etc. —***n.*** the Germanic language of Sweden

sweep (swēp) ***vt.*** **swept, sweep′ing** ⟦OE *swapan*⟧ **1** to clean (a floor, etc.) as by brushing with a broom **2** to remove (dirt, etc.) as with a broom **3** to strip, carry away, or destroy with a forceful movement **4** to touch in moving across *[hands sweeping the keyboard]* **5** to pass swiftly over or across **6** *a)* to win all the games of (a series, etc.) *b)* to win overwhelmingly —***vi.*** **1** to clean a floor, etc. as with a broom **2** to move steadily with speed or grace **3** to extend in a long curve or line *[a road sweeping up the hill]* —***n.*** **1** the act of sweeping **2** a steady sweeping movement **3** range or scope **4** extent, as of land; stretch **5** a line, curve, etc. that seems to flow or move **6** one whose work is sweeping *[a chimney sweep]* —**sweep′er** ***n.*** —**sweep′ing** ***adj.*** —**sweep′ing·ly** ***adv.***

sweep′ings ***pl.n.*** things swept up, as litter from a floor

sweep′stakes′ ***n.,*** *pl.* **-stakes′** a lottery in which each participant puts up money in a common fund that is given as the prize to the winner or winners, as determined by the result of a horse race or other contest: also **sweep′stake′**

sweet (swēt) ***adj.*** ⟦OE *swete*⟧ **1** having a taste of, or like that of, sugar **2** *a)* having an agreeable taste, smell, sound, etc. *b)* gratifying *c)* friendly, kind, etc. **3** *a)* not

THESAURUS

swallow[2] ***v.*** consume, engulf, gulp, take, wash down, pour, swill, bolt, swig, choke down, swallow up, toss off, chug*, chug-a-lug*; see also DRINK 1, EAT 1.

swamp ***n.*** bog, fen, quagmire, morass, marsh, slough, soft ground, wet ground, mire, peat bog, bottoms, river bottoms, lowland, bottomland, muskeg.

swampy ***a.*** boggy, wet, miry; see MUDDY 2.

swanky ***a.*** showy, elegant, fancy, ritzy*; see also EXCELLENT, EXPENSIVE, ORNATE.

swap* ***v.*** interchange, trade, barter; see EXCHANGE.

swarm ***n.*** throng, crowd, multitude, horde, pack, troop, school, hive, mass, flock.

swarm ***v.*** rush together, crowd, throng; see GATHER, RUN.

swarthy ***a.*** dark-skinned, tawny, dark-hued, dark-complexioned.

swat ***v.*** beat, knock, slap; see HIT 1.

sway ***n.*** swaying, swinging, swing, oscillation, vibration, undulation, wave.

sway ***v.*** bend, oscillate, swagger; see WAVE 3.

swear ***v.*** **1** [To curse] blaspheme, utter profanity, cuss*; see CURSE. **2** [To take an oath] avow, affirm, testify, state, vow, attest, warrant, vouch, assert, swear by, bear witness, cross one's heart.

sweat ***n.*** perspiration, beads of sweat, sweating, steam.

sweat ***v.*** perspire, secrete, swelter, wilt, exude, break out in a sweat.

sweater ***n.*** *Types of sweaters include the following:* coat, twin, evening, sport, long-sleeved, short-sleeved, sleeveless, crew-neck, turtleneck, V-neck, pullover, cardigan; see also CLOTHES.

sweaty ***a.*** perspiring, moist, wet with perspiration, glowing, bathed in sweat; see also HOT 1.

sweep ***v.*** brush up, clear, clear up; see CLEAN, MOP.

sweepings ***n.*** dirt, litter, refuse; see FILTH, TRASH 1.

sweet ***a.*** **1** [Sweet in taste] toothsome, sugary, luscious, candied, honeyed, saccharine, cloying, like nectar, delicious; see also RICH 4.—*Ant.* SOUR, bitter, sharp. **2** [Sweet in disposition] agreeable, pleasing, engaging, winning, delightful, reasonable, gentle, kind, generous, unselfish, even-tem-

rancid or sour *b*) not salty or salted —*n.* [*pl.*] sweet foods —**sweet'ish** *adj.* —**sweet'ly** *adv.* —**sweet'ness** *n.*

sweet'bread' (-bred') *n.* the thymus or sometimes the pancreas of a calf, lamb, etc., when used as food: *usually used in pl.*

sweet'bri'er or **sweet'bri'ar** (-brī'ər) *n.* EGLANTINE

sweet corn a variety of Indian corn eaten unripe as a table vegetable

sweet'en *vt.* **1** to make sweet **2** to make pleasant or agreeable **3** [Inf.] to increase the value of (collateral, an offer, etc.)

sweet'en·er *n.* a sweetening agent, esp. a synthetic one, as saccharin

sweet'heart' *n.* a loved one; lover

sweetheart contract a contract arranged by collusion between union officials and an employer with terms disadvantageous to union members

sweet'meat' *n.* a candy

sweet pea a climbing plant with butterfly-shaped flowers

sweet pepper **1** a red pepper plant producing a large, mild fruit **2** the fruit

sweet potato **1** a tropical plant with a fleshy, brownish root used as a vegetable **2** its root

sweet'-talk' *vt., vi.* [Inf.] to talk in a flattering way (to)

sweet tooth [Inf.] a fondness or craving for sweets

swell (swel) *vi., vt.* **swelled, swelled** or **swol'len, swell'ing** ⟦OE *swellan*⟧ **1** to expand as a result of pressure from within **2** to curve out; bulge **3** to fill (*with* pride, etc.) **4** to increase in size, force, intensity, loudness, etc. —*n.* **1** a part that swells; specif., a large, rolling wave **2** an increase in size, amount, degree, etc. **3** a crescendo —*adj.* [Slang] excellent

swell'head' *n.* [Inf.] a conceited person —**swell'head'ed** *adj.*

swell'ing *n.* **1** an increase in size, volume, etc. **2** a swollen part

swel·ter (swel'tər) *vi.* ⟦< OE *sweltan,* to die, faint⟧ to feel uncomfortably hot; sweat, feel weak, etc. from great heat

swel'ter·ing *adj.* very hot; sultry

swept (swept) *vt., vi. pt. & pp. of* SWEEP

swept'back' *adj.* having a backward slant: said of the wings of an aircraft

swerve (swʉrv) *vi., vt.* **swerved, swerv'ing** ⟦< OE *sweorfan,* to scour⟧ to turn aside from a straight line, course, etc. —*n.* a swerving

swift (swift) *adj.* ⟦OE⟧ **1** moving with great speed; fast **2** coming, acting, etc. quickly —*n.* a swift-flying, swallow-like bird —**swift'ly** *adv.* —**swift'ness** *n.*

Swift (swift), **Jon·a·than** (jän'ə thən) 1667-1745; Eng. satirist, born in Ireland

swig (swig) [Inf.] *vt., vi.* **swigged, swig'ging** ⟦< ?⟧ to drink in gulps —*n.* a big gulp, as of liquor

swill (swil) *vt., vi.* ⟦OE *swilian*⟧ **1** to drink greedily **2** to feed swill to (pigs, etc.) —*n.* **1** liquid garbage fed to pigs **2** garbage

swim[1] (swim) *vi.* **swam, swum, swim'ming** ⟦OE *swimman*⟧ **1** to move through water by moving arms, legs, fins, etc. **2** to move along smoothly **3** to float on or in a liquid **4** to overflow [*eyes swimming* with tears] —*vt.* to swim in or across —*n.* the act of swimming —*adj.* [Inf.] of or for swimming [*swim* trunks] —**in the swim** active in what is popular at the moment —**swim'mer** *n.*

swim[2] (swim) *n.* ⟦OE *swima*⟧ a dizzy spell —*vi.* **swam, swum, swim'ming** **1** to be dizzy **2** to seem to whirl [the room *swam* before me]

swimming hole a deep place in a river, creek, etc. used for swimming

swim'ming·ly *adv.* easily and with success

swim'suit' *n.* a garment worn for swimming

swin·dle (swin'dəl) *vt., vi.* **-dled, -dling** ⟦< Ger *schwindeln*⟧ to defraud (another) of money or property; cheat —*n.* an act of swindling; trick; fraud —**swin'dler** *n.*

swine (swīn) *n., pl.* **swine** ⟦OE *swin*⟧ **1** a pig or hog: usually used collectively **2** a vicious, contemptible person

swing (swiŋ) *vi.* **swung, swing'ing** ⟦OE *swingan*⟧ **1** to sway or move backward and forward **2** to walk, trot, etc. with relaxed movements **3** to strike (*at*) **4** to turn, as on a hinge **5** to move in a curve **6** to hang; be suspended **7** [Slang] *a*) to be ultra-fashionable, esp. in seeking pleasure *b*) to engage in casual sexual relations —*vt.* **1** to move, lift, etc. with a sweeping motion **2** to cause to move backward and forward **3** to cause to turn, as on a hinge **4** to cause to move in a curve [*swing* the car around] **5** [Inf.] to cause to come about successfully [to *swing* an election] —*n.* **1** a swinging **2** the arc through which something swings **3** the manner of swinging a golf club, etc. **4** a relaxed motion, as in walking **5** a sweeping blow **6** the course of some activity, etc. **7** rhythm, as of music **8** a seat hanging from ropes, etc. on which one can swing **9** a trip or tour **10** jazz (*c.* 1935-45) characterized by large bands and written arrangements —*adj.* having decisive power, as in determining an election [the *swing* vote]

swing'er *n.* [Slang] a sophisticated, uninhibited, pleasure-seeking person

swing shift [Inf.] the evening work shift, commonly from 4:00 P.M. to midnight

swipe (swīp) *n.* ⟦prob. var. of SWEEP⟧ [Inf.] **1** a hard, sweeping blow **2** a sweeping motion —*vt.* **swiped, swip'ing** **1** [Inf.] to hit with a swipe **2** [Inf.] to pass across or through with a sweeping motion **3** [Slang] to steal

swirl (swʉrl) *vi., vt.* ⟦ME (Scot) *swyrl*⟧ to move or cause to move with a whirling motion —*n.* **1** a whirl; eddy **2** a twist; curl —**swirl'y** *adj.*

swish (swish) *vi.* ⟦echoic⟧ **1** to move with a sharp, hissing sound: said as of a cane swung through the air **2** to move with a light, brushing sound: said as of skirts in walking —*vt.* **1** to cause to swish **2** to move (liquid), esp. in the mouth, with a hissing or gurgling sound —*n.* a swishing sound or movement

Swiss (swis) *adj.* of Switzerland or its people, etc. —*n., pl.* **Swiss** a person born or living in Switzerland

Swiss chard CHARD

Swiss (cheese) a hard, pale-yellow cheese with many large holes

Swiss steak a thick cut of round steak pounded with flour and braised with vegetables

switch (swich) *n.* ⟦Early Modern Eng *swits*⟧ **1** a thin, flexible stick used for whipping **2** a separate tress of hair, used as part of a coiffure **3** a device used to open,

THESAURUS

pered, good-humored, considerate, thoughtful, companionable; see also FRIENDLY.—*Ant.* SELFISH, repulsive, inconsiderate. **3** [Sweet in smell] fragrant, sweet-smelling, fresh, delicate, delicious, spicy, rich, perfumed, clean.

sweeten *v.* add sugar, make sweet, mull; see FLAVOR.

sweetheart *n.* beloved, dear, loved one; see LOVER 1.

sweetly *a.* agreeably, pleasantly, comfortably, gently, gratefully, softly, smoothly, kindly, in a winning manner, charmingly.

sweets *n.* bonbons, candy, confections, desserts, sugar, sweetmeats, preserves, candied fruit; see also CANDY.

swell* *a.* just what one wants, desirable, fine; see EXCELLENT.

swell *v.* dilate, expand, distend, increase, enlarge, grow, grow larger, puff up, be inflated, become larger, bulge, puff, inflate, bulge out, blister, round out, fill out.

swelling *n.* welt, wart, pimple, carbuncle, boil, pock, pustule, inflammation, growth, corn, lump, bunion, tumor, blister, abscess; see also INJURY.

swerve *v.* move, bend, turn aside; see TURN 6.

swift *a.* flying, sudden, speedy; see FAST 1.

swiftly *a.* speedily, rapidly, fast; see QUICKLY.

swim[1] *n.* bath, dip, plunge, dive, jump, splash.

swim[1] *v.* bathe, float, glide, slip through the water, stroke, paddle, go for a swim, take a dip, train for the swimming team, swim freestyle.

swimming *n.* diving, aquatics, bathing; see SPORT 3.

swindle *n.* imposition, deception, knavery; see TRICK 1.

swindle *v.* dupe, victimize, defraud; see DECEIVE.

swindler *n.* cheat, cheater, thief, impostor, charlatan, deceiver, trickster, falsifier, counterfeiter, card shark*, cardsharp*, forger, fraud, con man*, con artist*, four-flusher*, sharper, gypster*; see also CRIMINAL.

swing *n.* sway, motion, fluctuation, stroke, vibration, oscillation, lilt, beat, rhythm; see also WAVE 2. —**in full swing** lively, vigorous, animated; see ACTIVE, EXCITING.

swing *v.* sway, pivot, rotate, turn, turn about, revolve, fluctuate, waver, vibrate, turn on an axis; see also WAVE 3.

swinger* *n.* pleasure seeker, libertine, sophisticated person, life of the party*, cohabitant.

switch *n.* dial, knob, lever; see CONTROL 2.

switch *v.* change, shift, rearrange; see ALTER 1, TURN 2.

close, or divert an electric circuit **4** a device used to transfer a train from one track to another **5** a shift; change —*vt.* **1** to whip as with a switch **2** to jerk sharply *[the cow switched its tail]* **3** to shift; change **4** to turn (an electric light, etc.) *on* or *off* **5** to transfer (a train, etc.) to another track **6** [Inf.] to change or exchange —*vi.* to shift —**switch'er** *n.*

switch'back' *n.* a road or railroad following a zigzag course up a steep grade

switch'blade' (knife) a large jackknife that snaps open when a release button is pressed

switch'board' *n.* a panel for controlling a system of electric circuits, as in a telephone exchange

switch'-hit'ter *n.* a baseball player who can bat right-handed and left-handed

Swit·zer·land (swit'sər lənd) country in WC Europe: 15,880 sq. mi.; pop. 6,366,000

swiv·el (swiv'əl) *n.* ⟦< OE *swifan,* to revolve⟧ a coupling device that allows free turning of the parts attached to it —*vi., vt.* **-eled** or **-elled**, **-el·ing** or **-el·ling** to turn or cause to turn on or as on a swivel or pivot

swiz·zle stick (swiz'əl) ⟦< ?⟧ a small rod for stirring mixed drinks

swob (swäb) *n., vt.* **swobbed**, **swob'bing** *alt. sp. of* SWAB

swol·len (swōl'ən) *vi., vt. alt. pp. of* SWELL —*adj.* blown up; distended; bulging

swoon (swo͞on) *vi., n.* ⟦< OE *geswogen,* unconscious⟧ FAINT

swoop (swo͞op) *vi.* ⟦< OE *swapan,* sweep along⟧ to pounce or sweep (*down* or *upon*), as a bird does in hunting —*n.* the act of swooping

swop (swäp) *vt., vi.* **swopped**, **swop'ping**, *n.* [Chiefly Brit.] *alt. sp. of* SWAP

sword (sôrd) *n.* ⟦OE *sweord*⟧ a hand weapon with a long, sharp-pointed blade set in a hilt —**at swords' points** ready to quarrel or fight

sword'fish' *n., pl.* **-fish'** a large marine food fish with an upper jawbone extending in a swordlike point

sword'play' *n.* the act or skill of using a sword, as in fencing

swords·man (sôrdz'mən) *n., pl.* **-men** one skilled in using a sword

swore (swôr) *vi., vt. pt. of* SWEAR

sworn (swôrn) *vi., vt. pp. of* SWEAR —*adj.* bound, pledged, etc. by or as by an oath

swum (swum) *vi., vt. pp. of* SWIM[1] & SWIM[2]

swung (swuŋ) *vi., vt. pp. & pt. of* SWING

syb·a·rite (sib'ə rīt') *n.* ⟦after *Sybaris,* ancient Gr city in Italy⟧ anyone very fond of luxury and pleasure —**syb'a·rit'ic** (-rit'ik) *adj.*

syc·a·more (sik'ə môr') *n.* ⟦< Gr *sykomoros,* a fig tree mentioned in the Bible⟧ **1** a maple tree of Europe and Asia **2** an American tree with bark that sheds in patches

syc·o·phant (sik'ə fənt) *n.* ⟦< Gr *sykophantēs,* informer⟧ one who seeks favor by flattering people of wealth or influence —**syc'o·phan·cy** *n.*

Syd·ney (sid'nē) seaport in SE Australia: pop. 3,365,000

syl·lab·i·cate (si lab'i kāt') *vt.* **-cat'ed**, **-cat'ing** SYLLABIFY —**syl·lab'i·ca'tion** *n.*

syl·lab·i·fy (si lab'ə fī') *vt.* **-fied'**, **-fy'ing** ⟦ult. < L *syllaba,* syllable + *facere,* make⟧ to form or divide into syllables —**syl·lab'i·fi·ca'tion** *n.*

syl·la·ble (sil'ə bəl) *n.* ⟦< Gr *syn-,* together + *lambanein,* to hold⟧ **1** a word or part of a word pronounced with a single, uninterrupted sounding of the voice **2** one or more letters written to represent a spoken syllable —**syl·lab·ic** (si lab'ik) *adj.*

syl·la·bus (sil'ə bəs) *n., pl.* **-bus·es** or **-bi'** (-bī') ⟦ult. < Gr *sittybos,* strip of leather⟧ a summary or outline, esp. of a course of study

syl·lo·gism (sil'ə jiz'əm) *n.* ⟦< Gr *syn-,* together + *logizesthai,* to reason⟧ a form of reasoning in which two premises are made and a logical conclusion is drawn from them

sylph (silf) *n.* ⟦Mod L *sylphus,* a spirit⟧ **1** an imaginary being supposed to inhabit the air **2** a slender, graceful woman or girl —**sylph'like'** *adj.*

syl·van (sil'vən) *adj.* ⟦< L *silva,* forest⟧ **1** of, characteristic of, or living in the woods or forest **2** covered with trees; wooded

sym·bi·o·sis (sim'bī ō'sis, -bē-) *n.* ⟦< Gr *symbioun,* to live together⟧ the living together of two kinds of organisms to their mutual advantage —**sym'bi·ot'ic** (-ät'ik) *adj.*

sym·bol (sim'bəl) *n.* ⟦< Gr *syn-,* together + *ballein,* to throw⟧ **1** an object used to represent something abstract *[the dove is a peace symbol]* **2** a mark, letter, etc. standing for an object, quality, quantity, process, etc., as in music or chemistry —**sym·bol'ic** (-bäl'ik) or **sym·bol'i·cal** *adj.* —**sym·bol'i·cal·ly** *adv.*

sym'bol·ism' *n.* **1** representation by symbols **2** a system of symbols **3** symbolic meaning

sym'bol·ize' *vt.* **-ized'**, **-iz'ing** **1** to be a symbol of; stand for **2** to represent by a symbol or symbols

sym·me·try (sim'ə trē) *n., pl.* **-tries** ⟦< Gr *syn-,* together + *metron,* a measure⟧ **1** correspondence of opposite parts in size, shape, and position **2** balance or beauty of form resulting from this —**sym·met·ri·cal** (si me'tri kəl) *adj.* —**sym·met'ri·cal·ly** *adv.*

sym·pa·thet·ic (sim'pə thet'ik) *adj.* **1** of, feeling, or showing sympathy **2** in agreement with one's tastes, mood, etc. **3** *Physiology* designating the part of the autonomic nervous system involved esp. in communicating the involuntary response to alarm, as by speeding the heart rate —**sym'pa·thet'i·cal·ly** *adv.*

sym'pa·thize' (-thīz') *vi.* **-thized'**, **-thiz'ing** **1** to share the feelings or ideas of another **2** to feel or express sympathy —**sym'pa·thiz'er** *n.*

sym'pa·thy (-thē) *n., pl.* **-thies** ⟦< Gr *syn-,* together + *pathos,* feeling⟧ **1** sameness of feeling **2** mutual liking or understanding **3** *a)* ability to share another's ideas, emotions, etc. *b)* pity or compassion for another's trouble or suffering

sym·pho·ny (sim'fə nē) *n., pl.* **-nies** ⟦< Gr *syn-,* together + *phōnē,* a sound⟧ **1** harmony of sounds, color, etc. **2** an extended musical composition in several movements, for full orchestra **3** SYMPHONY ORCHESTRA **4** [Inf.] a concert by a symphony orchestra —**sym·phon'ic** (-fän'ik) *adj.*

symphony orchestra a large orchestra for playing symphonic works

sym·po·si·um (sim pō'zē əm) *n., pl.* **-si·ums** or **-si·a** (-ə) ⟦< Gr *syn-,* together + *posis,* a drinking⟧ **1** a conference to discuss a topic **2** a published group of opinions on a topic

symp·tom (simp'təm) *n.* ⟦< Gr *syn-,* together + *piptein,* to fall⟧ any circumstance or condition that indicates the existence of something, as a particular disease —**symp'to·mat'ic** (-tə mat'ik) *adj.*

syn *abbrev.* synonym

syn- ⟦Gr⟧ *prefix* with, together, at the same time

syn·a·gogue (sin'ə gäg', -gôg') *n.* ⟦< Gr *syn-,* together + *agein,* do⟧ **1** an assembly of Jews for worship and religious study **2** a building or place for such assembly —**syn'a·gog'al** *adj.*

syn·apse (sin'aps') *n.* ⟦< Gr *syn-,* together + *apsis,* a joining⟧ the space between nerve cells through which nerve impulses are transmitted

sync or **synch** (siŋk) *vi., vt.* **synced** or **synched**, **sync'ing** or **synch'ing** *short for* SYNCHRONIZE —*n. short for* SYN-

THESAURUS

swivel *v.* rotate, spin, revolve; see TURN 1.

swollen *a.* distended, puffed, swelled; see ENLARGED.

swoop *n.* plunge, fall, drop; see DESCENT 2, DIVE 1.

swoop *v.* slide, plummet, plunge; see DESCEND, DIVE, FALL 1.

sword *n.* saber, rapier, weapon; see KNIFE.

syllabus *n.* summary, outline, course plan; see PLAN 1, PROGRAM 2.

sylvan *a.* wooded, shady, forestlike; see RURAL.

symbol *n.* representation, token, figure; see SIGN 1.

symbolic *a.* representative, typical, indicative, suggestive, symptomatic, characteristic.

symbolize *v.* typify, signify, express; see MEAN 1.

symmetry *n.* proportion, arrangement, order, equality, regularity, harmony, agreement, equivalence, equipoise, evenness, balance, equilibrium, similarity.

sympathetic *a.* compassionate, loving, considerate; see THOUGHTFUL 2.

sympathetically *a.* sensitively, perceptively, responsively, harmoniously, in accord, in harmony, in concert, understandingly, appreciatively, with feeling, warmly, heartily, cordially, kindheartedly, warmheartedly, softheartedly, humanely, in tune with others*.

sympathize *v.* pity, show mercy, comfort, understand, be understanding, love, be kind to, commiserate, express sympathy.

sympathy *n.* **1** [Fellow feeling] understanding, commiseration, compassion; see PITY. **2** [An expression of sympathy] condolence, consolation, solace, comfort, cheer, encouragement, reassurance; see also HELP 1, ENCOURAGEMENT.

symptom *n.* mark, sign, token; see CHARACTERISTIC.

CHRONIZATION —**in** (or **out of**) **sync** in (or out of) synchronization or harmony (*with*)

syn·chro·nize (siŋ′krə nīz′) *vi.* **-nized′**, **-niz′ing** ⟦< Gr *syn-*, together + *chronos,* time⟧ to move or occur at the same time or rate —*vt.* to cause to agree in time or rate of speed —**syn′chro·ni·za′tion** *n.*

syn′chro·nous *adj.* happening at the same time or at the same rate

syn·co·pate (siŋ′kə pāt′) *vt.* **-pat′ed**, **-pat′ing** ⟦< Gr *syn-*, together + *koptein,* to cut⟧ *Music* to begin a tone on an unaccented beat and continue it through the next accented beat —**syn′co·pa′tion** *n.*

syn·di·cate (sin′də kit; *for v.,* -kāt′) *n.* ⟦< Gr *syn-*, together + *dikē,* justice⟧ **1** an association of individuals or corporations formed to carry out a project requiring much capital **2** any group, as of criminals, organized for some undertaking **3** an organization selling articles or features to many newspapers, etc. —*vt.* **-cat′ed**, **-cat′ing** **1** to manage as or form into a syndicate **2** *a)* to sell (an article, etc.) through a syndicate *b)* to sell (a program, etc.) to a number of radio or TV stations —*vi.* to form a syndicate —**syn′di·ca′tion** *n.*

syn·drome (sin′drōm′) *n.* ⟦< Gr *syn-*, with + *dramein,* to run⟧ a set of symptoms characterizing a disease or condition

syn·er·gism (sin′ər jiz′əm) *n.* ⟦< Gr *syn-*, together + *ergon,* work⟧ an interaction of several things that results in a greater effect than the sum of the things' individual effects: said esp. of drugs —**syn′er·gis′tic** *adj.*

syn·fu·el (sin′fyo͞o′əl) *n.* ⟦SYN(THETIC) + FUEL⟧ a fuel, as oil or gas made from coal, used as a substitute for petroleum or natural gas

syn·od (sin′əd) *n.* ⟦< Gr *syn-*, together + *hodos,* way⟧ **1** an ecclesiastical council **2** a high governing body in certain Christian churches

syn·o·nym (sin′ə nim) *n.* ⟦< Gr *syn-*, together + *onyma,* a name⟧ a word having the same or nearly the same meaning as another in the same language —**syn·on·y·mous** (si nän′ə məs) *adj.*

syn·on·y·my (si nän′ə mē) *n.* a list of synonyms

syn·op·sis (si näp′sis) *n., pl.* **-ses′** (-sēz′) ⟦< Gr *syn-*, together + *opsis,* a seeing⟧ a brief, general review or condensation; summary

syn·tax (sin′taks′) *n.* ⟦< Gr *syn-*, together + *tassein,* arrange⟧ the arrangement of and relationships among words, phrases, and clauses forming sentences —**syn·tac′tic** (-tak′tik) or **syn·tac′ti·cal** *adj.*

syn·the·sis (sin′thə sis) *n., pl.* **-ses′** (-sēz′) ⟦< Gr *syn-*, together + *tithenai,* to place⟧ the combining of parts or elements so as to form a whole, a compound, etc. —**syn′the·size′** (-sīz′), **-sized′**, **-siz′ing**, *vt.*

syn′the·siz′er *n.* an electronic device producing sounds unobtainable from ordinary musical instruments or imitating instruments and voices

syn·thet′ic (-thet′ik) *adj.* **1** of or involving synthesis **2** produced by chemical synthesis, rather than of natural origin **3** not real; artificial —*n.* something synthetic —**syn·thet′i·cal·ly** *adv.*

syph·i·lis (sif′ə lis) *n.* ⟦after *Syphilus,* hero of a L poem (1530)⟧ a sexually transmitted disease caused by a spirochete —**syph′i·lit′ic** *adj., n.*

Syr·i·a (sir′ē ə) country in SW Asia, at the E end of the Mediterranean: 71,498 sq. mi.; pop. 9,046,000 —**Syr′i·an** *adj., n.*

sy·ringe (sə rinj′, sir′inj) *n.* ⟦< Gr *syrinx,* a pipe⟧ **1** a device consisting of a tube with a rubber bulb or piston at one end, for drawing in a liquid and then ejecting it in a stream: used to inject fluids into body cavities, etc. **2** HYPODERMIC SYRINGE —*vt.* **-ringed′**, **-ring′ing** to cleanse, inject, etc. by using a syringe

syr·up (sʉr′əp, sir′-) *n.* ⟦< OFr *sirop* < ML *sirupus* < Ar *sharāb,* a drink⟧ any thick, sweet liquid; specif., a solution of sugar and water boiled together

syr′up·y *adj.* **1** like syrup **2** overly sentimental

sys·tem (sis′təm) *n.* ⟦< Gr *syn-*, together + *histanai,* to set⟧ **1** a set or arrangement of things related so as to form a whole *[*a solar *system,* a school *system]* **2** a set of facts, rules, etc. arranged to show a logical plan linking them **3** a method or plan **4** an established, orderly way of doing something **5** the body, or a number of bodily organs, functioning as a unit

sys′tem·at′ic (-tə mat′ik) *adj.* **1** constituting or based on a system **2** according to a system; orderly —**sys′tem·at′i·cal·ly** *adv.*

sys′tem·a·tize′ (-tə mə tīz′) *vt.* **-tized′**, **-tiz′ing** to arrange according to a system; make systematic —**sys′tem·a·ti·za′tion** *n.*

sys·tem·ic (sis tem′ik) *adj.* of or affecting the body as a whole

sys·to·le (sis′tə lē′) *n.* ⟦< Gr *syn-*, together + *stellein,* to set up⟧ the usual rhythmic contraction of the heart —**sys·tol′ic** (-täl′ik) *adj.*

THESAURUS

synonymous *a.* same, like, similar, equivalent, identical, correspondent, corresponding, alike, interchangeable, convertible, compatible; see also EQUAL.—*Ant.* OPPOSITE, divergent, contrary.

synopsis *n.* outline, digest, brief; see SUMMARY.

syntax *n.* order of words, arrangement, grammatical rules; see GRAMMAR, LANGUAGE 2.

synthetic *a.* artificial, counterfeit, plastic; see FALSE 3.

syrup *n.* sugar solution, sweet liquid, glucose; see SUGAR. *Kinds of syrup include the following:* cane, corn, maple, simple, sugar; molasses, honey, treacle, sorghum.

system *n.* orderliness, regularity, conformity, logical order, definite plan, arrangement, rule, systematic order, systematic procedure, logical process; see also ORDER 3.

systematic *a.* orderly, methodical, precise; see REGULAR 3.

systematize *v.* plan, arrange, organize; see ORDER 3.

T

t[1] or **T** (tē) ***n.**, pl.* **t's, T's** the 20th letter of the English alphabet —**to a T** to perfection; exactly

t[2] *abbrev.* **1** teaspoon(s) **2** temperature **3** tense **4** ton(s) **5** transitive

T *abbrev.* **1** tablespoon(s) **2** temperature **3** Thursday **4** Tuesday

't- *prefix* it: used chiefly in poetry *['twas]*

tab[1] (tab) ***n.*** ⟦< ?⟧ **1** a small, flat loop or strap fastened to something **2** a projecting piece as of a file folder, used in filing

tab[2] (tab) ***n.*** ⟦prob. < TABULATION⟧ [Inf.] **1** a bill, as for expenses **2** total cost —**keep tabs** (or **a tab**) **on** [Inf.] to keep a check on

Ta·bas·co (tə bas′kō) *trademark for* a very hot sauce made from a tropical American hot red pepper

tab·bou·leh (tə bo͞o′lē, -le) ***n.*** ⟦Ar⟧ a salad of coarsely ground wheat with chopped parsley, tomatoes, scallions, etc.

tab·by (tab′ē) ***n.**, pl.* **-bies** ⟦ult. < Ar⟧ a domestic cat, esp. a female

tab·er·nac·le (tab′ər nak′əl) ***n.*** ⟦< L *taberna,* hut⟧ **1** a large place of worship **2** [T-] the portable sanctuary carried by the Jews during the Exodus

tab·la (täb′lä) ***n.*** ⟦< Ar *ṭabla,* a drum⟧ a set of two small drums whose pitch can be varied, used esp. in India and played with the hands

ta·ble (tā′bəl) ***n.*** ⟦< L *tabula,* a board⟧ **1** [Obs.] a thin slab of metal, stone, etc. **2** *a)* a piece of furniture having a flat top set on legs *b)* such a table set with food *c)* food served *d)* the people seated at a table **3** *a)* a systematic list of details, contents, etc. *b)* an orderly arrangement of facts, figures, etc. **4** any flat, horizontal surface, piece, etc. —***vt.*** **-bled, -bling** to postpone indefinitely the consideration of (a legislative bill, etc.) —**at table** at a meal —**turn the tables** to reverse a situation

tab·leau (tab′lō′, ta blō′) ***n.**, pl.* **-leaux′** (-lōz′) or **-leaus′** ⟦Fr < OFr, dim. of *table*⟧ a striking, dramatic scene or picture

ta′ble·cloth′ ***n.*** a cloth for covering a table, esp. at meals

ta·ble d'hôte (tä′bəl dōt′) ⟦Fr, table of the host⟧ a complete meal served at a restaurant for a set price

ta′ble-hop′ ***vi.*** **-hopped′, -hop′ping** to leave one's table, as at a restaurant, and visit at other tables

ta′ble·land′ ***n.*** a plateau

ta′ble·spoon′ ***n.*** **1** a large spoon for serving or for eating soup **2** a measuring spoon holding ½ fluid ounce —**ta′ble·spoon′ful**, *pl.* **-fuls**, ***n.***

tab·let (tab′lit) ***n.*** ⟦see TABLE⟧ **1** a thin, flat piece of stone, metal, etc. with an inscription **2** a writing pad of paper sheets glued together at one edge **3** a small, flat piece of compressed material, as of medicine

table tennis a game somewhat like tennis, played on a table with a small, hollow celluloid ball

ta′ble·ware′ (-wer′) ***n.*** dishes, glassware, silverware, etc. for use at a meal

tab·loid (tab′loid′) ***n.*** ⟦TABL(ET) + -OID⟧ a newspaper, usually half size, with many pictures and short, often sensational, news stories

ta·boo (tə bo͞o′, ta-) ***n.*** ⟦< a Polynesian language⟧ **1** among some Polynesian peoples, a sacred prohibition making certain people or things untouchable, etc. **2** any conventional social restriction —***adj.*** prohibited by taboo —***vt.*** **-booed′, -boo′ing** **1** to put under taboo **2** to prohibit or forbid Also **ta·bu′**

ta·bou·li (tə bo͞o′lē) ***n.*** *var. of* TABBOULEH

tab·u·lar (tab′yə lər) ***adj.*** ⟦see TABLE⟧ **1** flat **2** of, arranged in, or computed from a table or list

tab′u·late′ (-lāt′) ***vt.*** **-lat′ed, -lat′ing** to put (facts, statistics, etc.) in a table —**tab′u·la′tion** ***n.*** —**tab′u·la′tor** ***n.***

ta·chom·e·ter (ta käm′ət ər) ***n.*** ⟦< Gr *tachos,* speed + -METER⟧ a device that measures the rate of rotation of a revolving shaft

tach·y·car·di·a (tak′i kär′dē ə) ***n.*** ⟦< Gr *tachys,* swift + *kardia,* heart⟧ an abnormally fast heartbeat

tac·it (tas′it) ***adj.*** ⟦< L *tacere,* be silent⟧ **1** unspoken **2** not expressed openly, but implied or understood —**tac′it·ly** ***adv.*** —**tac′it·ness** ***n.***

tac·i·turn (tas′ə tʉrn′) ***adj.*** ⟦see prec.⟧ almost always silent; not liking to talk —**tac′i·tur′ni·ty** ***n.***

tack (tak) ***n.*** ⟦< MDu *tacke,* twig, point⟧ **1** a short nail or pin with a sharp point and a large, flat head **2** a temporary stitch **3** a course of action **4** *a)* the direction a ship goes in relation to the position of the sails *b)* a change of a ship's direction —***vt.*** **1** to fasten with tacks **2** to attach or add **3** to change the course of (a ship) —***vi.*** to change course suddenly

tack·le (tak′əl) ***n.*** ⟦< MDu *takel*⟧ **1** equipment; gear **2** a system of ropes and pulleys for moving weights **3** a tackling, as in football **4** *Football* a lineman next to the end —***vt.*** **tack′led, tack′ling** **1** to take hold of; seize **2** to try to do; undertake **3** *Football* to throw (the ball carrier) to the ground —**tack′ler** ***n.***

tack·y (tak′ē) ***adj.*** **-i·er, -i·est** **1** sticky: said as of drying varnish **2** dowdy or shabby **3** in poor taste —**tack′i·ness** ***n.***

ta·co (tä′kō) ***n.**, pl.* **-cos** ⟦Sp, light lunch⟧ a fried tortilla filled with chopped meat, lettuce, etc.

Ta·co·ma (tə kō′mə) seaport in W Washington: pop. 177,000

tact (takt) ***n.*** ⟦< L *tangere,* to touch⟧ delicate perception of the right thing to say or do without offending —**tact′ful** ***adj.*** —**tact′less** ***adj.***

tac·tics (tak′tiks) ***pl.n.*** ⟦< Gr *tassein,* arrange⟧ **1** [*with sing. v.*] the science of maneuvering military and naval

THESAURUS

tab[1] ***n.*** loop, stop, clip; see LABEL, MARKER, TAG 2.

table ***n.*** **1** [A piece of furniture] desk, pulpit, stand, board, counter, slab, dresser, bureau, lectern, sideboard, washstand; see also FURNITURE. *Tables include the following:* writing, dining, kitchen, card, folding, drafting, vanity, gateleg, dressing, drop-leaf, operating, end, laboratory, refectory, coffee, picnic, butcher-block, Parsons, work, typing, round, conference; secretary, computer stand, altar, workbench, TV tray. **2** [A statement in tabulated form] synopsis, report, record; see SUMMARY. —**turn the tables** reverse, change, switch; see ALTER 1. —**under the table*** covertly, surreptitiously, not obviously; see SECRETLY.

tableau ***n.*** scene, picture, illustration; see VIEW.

tablecloth ***n.*** covering, spread, place mats; see COVER 1.

tablet ***n.*** **1** [A thin piece of material bearing a legend] slab, stone, monument; see MEMORIAL. **2** [Writing paper] folder, pad, sheets; see PAPER 4. **3** [A pharmaceutical preparation] pill, dose, capsule; see MEDICINE 2.

taboo ***a.*** forbidden, out of bounds, reserved; see ILLEGAL, RESTRICTED.

taboo ***n.*** restriction, reservation, prohibition; see RESTRAINT 2.

taboo ***v.*** inhibit, forbid, prevent; see HINDER, RESTRAIN.

tabulate ***v.*** systematize, arrange, index; see LIST 1, RECORD 1.

tack ***n.*** **1** [A short, broad-headed nail] thumbtack, pushpin, carpet tack, copper tack; see also NAIL, PIN 1. **2** [An oblique course] digression, tangent, deviation; see TURN 6.

tack ***v.*** **1** [To fasten lightly] pin, nail, stitch; see FASTEN. **2** [To steer an oblique course] go in zigzags, zigzag, change course; see TURN 6.

tackle ***n.*** **1** [Equipment] rigging, ropes and pulleys, apparatus; see EQUIPMENT. **2** [A contrivance having mechanical advantage] pulleys, block and tackle, movable pulley; see TOOL 1. **3** [In football, an attempt to down a ballcarrier] flying, running, shoulder, etc. tackle; sack, hit; see DEFENSE 1, JUMP. **4** [In football, one who plays between end and guard] linesman, right tackle, left tackle; see FOOTBALL PLAYER. **5** [In fishing, equipment] gear, sporting goods, fishing outfit; see EQUIPMENT. *Fishing tackle includes the following:* hook, line, fly, casting rod, casting reel, cut bait, live bait, minnow, grasshopper, fish eggs, worm, lure, spinner, fish net, landing net, pole, float, cork, sinker, creel, tackle box, deep-sea tackle, leader, stringer, fish sack, basket.

tackle ***v.*** **1** [To undertake] begin, turn to, make an attempt at; see TRY 1, UNDERTAKE. **2** [In football, to endeavor to down an opponent] seize, throw down, grab; see UPSET 1.

tact ***n.*** perception, discrimination, judgment, acuteness, penetration, intelligence, acumen, common sense, subtlety, discernment, prudence, aptness, good taste, refinement, delicacy, the ability to get along with others, finesse, horse sense*.—*Ant.* RUDENESS, coarseness, misconduct.

tactful ***a.*** diplomatic, civil, considerate; see THOUGHTFUL 2.

tactics ***n.*** strategy, maneuvering, military art, generalship, plan of attack, plan of defense, procedure, stratagem, approach, disposition, map work, chalk work.

forces **2** any skillful methods to gain an end —**tac'ti·cal** *adj.* —**tac·ti'cian** (-tish'ən) *n.*

tac·tile (tak'təl) *adj.* ⟦< L *tangere,* to touch⟧ of, having, or perceived by the sense of touch

tad (tad) *n.* ⟦prob. < TADPOLE⟧ a small amount or degree: often used adverbially *[a tad tired]*

tad·pole (tad'pōl') *n.* ⟦ME *tadde,* toad + *poll,* head⟧ the larva of a frog or toad, having gills and a tail and living in water

taf·fe·ta (taf'i tə) *n.* ⟦< Pers *tāftan,* to weave⟧ a fine, stiff fabric of silk, nylon, etc., with a sheen

taff·rail (taf'rāl') *n.* ⟦< Du⟧ the rail around the stern of a ship

taf·fy (taf'ē) *n.* ⟦< ?⟧ a chewy candy made of sugar or molasses

Taft (taft), **Wil·liam How·ard** (wil'yəm hou'ərd) 1857-1930; 27th president of the U.S. (1909-13): chief justice of the U.S. (1921-30)

tag (tag) *n.* ⟦prob. < Scand⟧ **1** a hanging end or part **2** a hard-tipped end on a cord or lace **3** a card, etc. attached as a label **4** an epithet **5** ending for a story, etc. **6** TAG LINE **7** a children's game in which one player chases the others with the object of touching one of them —*vt.* **tagged, tag'ging 1** to provide with a tag; label **2** to choose or select **3** to touch in playing tag **4** [Inf.] to strike or hit hard —*vi.* [Inf.] to follow closely: with *along, after,* etc. —**tag'ger** *n.*

Ta·ga·log (tä gä'lôg') *n.* **1** *pl.* **-logs'** or **-log'** a member of the ethnic group native to the Manila region in the Philippines **2** the language of this group, an official language of the Republic of the Philippines

tag line the last line or lines of a speech, etc.

Ta·hi·ti (tə hēt'ē) French island in the S Pacific —**Ta·hi'ti·an** (-hēsh'ən) *adj., n.*

Tai (tī) *n.* **1** a group of languages spoken in central and SE Asia **2** a member of a group of peoples of SE Asia that speak these languages —*adj.* of these languages or peoples

tai chi (tī' jē', tī chē') ⟦Mandarin⟧ a Chinese exercise system consisting of a series of slow, relaxed movements: in full **t'ai chi ch'uan** (chwän)

tai·ga (tī'gə) *n.* ⟦Russ⟧ a type of plant community in the far north, having scattered trees

tail (tāl) *n.* ⟦OE *tægel*⟧ **1** the rear end of an animal's body, esp. when a distinct appendage **2** anything like an animal's tail in form or position **3** the hind, bottom, last, or inferior part of anything **4** [*often pl.*] the reverse side of a coin **5** [*pl.*] full-dress attire for men **6** [Inf.] one that follows another, esp. in surveillance —*adj.* **1** at the rear or end **2** from the rear *[a tail wind]* —*vt.* [Slang] to follow stealthily —*vi.* [Inf.] to follow close behind

tail'back' *n. Football* the offensive back farthest from the line

tail'gate' *n.* the hinged or removable gate at the back of a wagon, truck, etc. —*vi., vt.* **-gat'ed, -gat'ing** to drive too closely behind (another vehicle) —**tail'gat'er** *n.*

tail'ings *pl.n.* waste or refuse left in various processes of milling, mining, etc.

tail'light' *n.* a light, usually red, at the rear of a vehicle to warn vehicles coming from behind

tai·lor (tā'lər) *n.* ⟦< VL *taliare,* to cut⟧ one who makes, repairs, or alters clothes —*vt.* **1** to make by tailor's work **2** to form, alter, etc. for a certain purpose

tail'pipe' *n.* the exhaust pipe coming from the muffler of a motor vehicle

tail'spin' *n.* SPIN (*n.* 3)

taint (tānt) *vt.* ⟦< ?⟧ **1** to affect with something injurious, unpleasant, etc.; infect, spoil, etc. **2** to make morally corrupt —*n.* a trace of contamination, corruption, etc.

Tai·pei (tī'pā') capital of Taiwan: pop. 2,108,000

Tai·wan (tī'wän') island province of China, off the SE coast: together with nearby islands it forms the *Republic of China*: 13,970 sq. mi.; pop. 21,000,000

Ta·jik·i·stan (tä jik'i stan') country in WC Asia: formerly a republic of the U.S.S.R.: 55,240 sq. mi.; pop. 5,093,000

take (tāk) *vt.* **took, tak'en, tak'ing** ⟦< ON *taka*⟧ **1** to get possession of; capture, seize, etc. **2** to get hold of **3** to capture the fancy of; charm **4** to obtain, acquire,

THESAURUS

tactile *a.* palpable, physical, tactual; see REAL 2, TANGIBLE.

tactless *a.* unperceptive, inconsiderate, rude, discourteous, unsympathetic, unthoughtful, insensitive, boorish, misunderstanding, impolite, rash, hasty, awkward, clumsy, imprudent, rough, crude, unpolished, gruff, uncivil, vulgar.

tag *n.* **1** [A remnant or scrap] rag, piece, patch; see REMNANTS. **2** [A mark of identification] ticket, badge, card, tab, trademark, stamp, stub, voucher, slip, label, emblem, insignia, tally, motto, sticker, inscription, laundry mark, price tag, bar code, identification number, button, pin. **3** [A children's game] hide-and-seek, freeze tag, capture the flag; see GAME 1.

tag *v.* **1** [To fit with a tag] designate, denote, earmark; see MARK 2. **2** [*To follow closely] chase, dog, trail; see PURSUE 1.

tail *n.* rear end, rear appendage, extremity, hind part, butt*, coccyx; see also REAR. —**on someone's tail** behind, shadowing, trailing; see FOLLOWING. —**with one's tail between one's legs** in defeat, humbly, dejectedly; see FEARFULLY.

tailor *n.* garment maker, clothier, dressmaker, seamstress, designer, one who alters and repairs clothing.

tainted *a.* contaminated, polluted, impaired; see SPOILED.

take *n.* **1** [Something that is taken] part, cut, proceeds; see PROFIT 2, SHARE. **2** [Scene filmed or televised] film, shot, motion picture; see PHOTOGRAPH. **3** [*Something that is seized] holdings, catch, haul*; see BOOTY.

take *v.* **1** [To seize] appropriate, take hold of, catch, grip, grab, pluck, pocket, carry off; see also SEIZE 1, 2. **2** [To collect] gather up, accept, reap; see RECEIVE 1. **3** [To catch] capture, grab, get hold of; see CATCH 1. **4** [To choose] select, settle on, opt for, make a selection, pick, decide on, prefer; see also CHOOSE, DECIDE. **5** [To acquire] win, procure, gain, achieve, receive, attain, obtain, secure; see also EARN 2, GET 1. **6** [To require] necessitate, demand, call for; see NEED. **7** [To contract; *said of a disease*] get, come down with, be seized with; see CATCH 4. **8** [To record] note, register, take notes; see RECORD 1. **9** [To transport] move, drive, bear; see CARRY 1. **10** [To captivate] charm, delight, overwhelm; see ENTERTAIN 1, FASCINATE. **11** [To win] prevail in, triumph over, beat; see DEFEAT 2, 3. **12** [To buy] pay for, select, procure; see BUY. **13** [To rent] lease, hire, charter; see RENT 2. **14** [To steal] misappropriate, loot, rob; see STEAL. **15** [To undergo] tolerate, suffer, bear; see ENDURE 2, UNDERGO. **16** [To lead] guide, steer, pilot; see LEAD 1. **17** [To escort] conduct, attend, go with; see ACCOMPANY. **18** [To admit] let in, accommodate, give access to; see RECEIVE 4. **19** [To adopt] utilize, assume, appropriate; see ADOPT 2. **20** [To apply] put in practice, exert, exercise; see PRACTICE 1, USE 1. **21** [To experience] sense, observe, be aware of; see FEEL 2. **22** [*To cheat] defraud, trick, swindle; see DECEIVE. **23** [To begin to grow] germinate, take root, develop; see BECOME. —**take after** [To resemble] look like, be like, seem like; see RESEMBLE. —**take away 1** [To subtract] deduct, take from, minus*; see DECREASE 2. **2** [To carry off] transport, cart off, carry away; see REMOVE 1. —**take back 1** [To regain] retrieve, get back, reclaim; see RECOVER 1. **2** [To restrict] draw in, retire, pull in; see REMOVE 1, WITHDRAW. **3** [To disavow] retract, recant, recall; see DENY, WITHDRAW. —**take down 1** [To dismantle] disassemble, take apart, undo; see DISMANTLE. **2** [To write down] inscribe, jot down, note down; see RECORD 1, WRITE 2. —**take for 1** [To mistake for] misapprehend as, misidentify as, believe to be; see MISTAKE. **2** [To assume] presuppose, infer, accept; see ASSUME. —**take in 1** [To include] embrace, comprise, incorporate; see INCLUDE 1. **2** [To understand] comprehend, apprehend, perceive; see UNDERSTAND 1. **3** [To cheat] swindle, lie, defraud; see DECEIVE. **4** [To give hospitality to] welcome, shelter, accept; see RECEIVE 1, 4. **5** [To shorten] reduce, lessen, cut down; see DECREASE 2. —**take off 1** [To remove] strip off, take one's clothes off, disrobe; see UNDRESS. **2** [To deduct] lessen by, subtract, take away; see DECREASE 2. **3** [To leave the earth] blast off, ascend, soar; see FLY 1, 4, RISE 1. **4** [To leave] go away, depart, shove off*; see LEAVE 1. —**take on 1** [To hire] employ, engage, give work to; see HIRE. **2** [To acquire an appearance] emerge as, develop, acquire; see BECOME, SEEM. **3** [To undertake] attempt, handle, endeavor; see TRY 1, UNDERTAKE. **4** [To meet in fight or sport] engage, battle, contest; see ATTACK 1, COMPETE. —**take over 1** [To take control] take charge, take command, assume control; see LEAD 1. **2** [To seize control of] take the reins of, take the helm of, overthrow; see SEIZE 2. **3** [To convey] transport, bear, move; see CARRY 1, SEND 1. —**take to** enjoy, be fond of, admire; see FAVOR, LIKE 1, 2. —**take up 1** [To begin] start, initiate, commence; see BEGIN 1. **2** [To raise] lift, elevate, hoist; see RAISE 1. **3** [To shorten] tighten, reduce, lessen; see DECREASE 2. **4** [To occupy] consume, engage, fill; see OCCUPY 2, USE 1. **5** [To adopt as a cause] appropriate,

assume, etc. **5** to use, consume, etc. **6** to buy, rent, subscribe to, etc. **7** to join with (one side in a disagreement, etc.) **8** to choose; select **9** to travel by [to *take* a bus] **10** to deal with; consider **11** to occupy [*take* a chair] **12** to require; demand [it *takes* money] **13** to derive (a name, quality, etc.) from **14** to excerpt; extract **15** to study **16** to write down [*take* notes] **17** to make by photographing **18** to win (a prize, etc.) **19** to undergo [*take* punishment] **20** to occupy oneself in; enjoy [*take* a nap] **21** to accept (an offer, bet, etc.) **22** to react to [*take* a joke in earnest] **23** to contract (a disease, etc.) **24** to understand **25** to suppose; presume **26** to feel [*take* pity] **27** to lead, escort, etc. **28** to carry **29** to remove, as by stealing **30** to subtract **31** [Slang] to cheat; trick **32** *Gram.* to be used with [the verb "hit" *takes* an object] —***vi.*** **1** to take root: said of a plant **2** to catch [the fire *took*] **3** to gain favor, success, etc. **4** to be effective [the vaccination *took*] **5** [Inf. or Dial.] to become (sick) —***n.*** **1** a taking **2** *a*) the amount taken *b*) [Slang] receipts or profit —**on the take** [Slang] taking bribes, etc. —**take after** to be, act, or look like —**take back** to retract (something said, etc.) —**take down** to put in writing; record —**take for** **1** to regard as **2** to mistake for —**take in** **1** to admit; receive **2** to make smaller **3** to understand **4** to cheat; trick —**take off** **1** to leave the ground, etc. in flight **2** [Inf.] to start **3** [Inf.] to imitate in a burlesque manner: with *on* —**take on** **1** to acquire; assume **2** to employ **3** to undertake (a task, etc.) —**take over** to assume control or possession of —**take to** **1** to become fond of **2** to go to or withdraw to [to *take to* the hills] —**take up** **1** to make tighter or shorter **2** to become interested in (an occupation, study, etc.) —**tak'er** ***n.***

take'off' ***n.*** **1** the act or place of leaving the ground, as in jumping or flight **2** [Inf.] a mocking imitation; caricature

take'out' ***n.*** prepared food bought to be taken away —***adj.*** designating or of such food

take'o'ver ***n.*** **1** the usurpation of power in a nation, organization, etc. **2** the assumption of management in acquiring a corporation

tak·ing (tāk'iŋ) ***adj.*** attractive; winning —***n.*** **1** the act of one that takes **2** [*pl.*] earnings; profits

talc (talk) ***n.*** ⟦< Ar *ṭalq*⟧ **1** a soft mineral used to make talcum powder, etc. **2** *short for* TALCUM (POWDER)

tal·cum (powder) (tal'kəm) a powder for the body made of purified talc

tale (tāl) ***n.*** ⟦OE *talu*⟧ **1** a story; narrative **2** idle or malicious gossip **3** a fiction; lie

tale'bear'er (-ber'ər) ***n.*** a gossip

tal·ent (tal'ənt) ***n.*** ⟦< Gr *talanton,* a weight⟧ **1** an ancient unit of weight or money **2** any natural ability or power **3** a superior ability in an art, etc. **4** people, or a person, with talent —**tal'ent·ed** ***adj.***

tal·is·man (tal'is mən, -iz-) ***n.***, *pl.* **-mans** ⟦< 5th-c. medieval Gr *telesma,* religious rite⟧ **1** a ring, stone, etc. bearing engraved figures thought to bring good luck, avert evil, etc. **2** a charm

talk (tôk) ***vi.*** ⟦prob. < OE *talian,* reckon⟧ **1** to put ideas into words; speak **2** to express ideas by speech substitutes [*talk* by signs] **3** to chatter; gossip **4** to confer; consult **5** to confess or inform on someone —***vt.*** **1** to use in speaking [to *talk* French] **2** to discuss **3** to put into a specified condition, etc. by talking —***n.*** **1** the act of talking **2** conversation **3** a speech **4** a conference **5** gossip **6** the subject of conversation, gossip, etc. **7** speech; dialect —**talk back** to answer impertinently —**talk down to** to talk patronizingly to, as by simple speech —**talk up** to promote in discussion —**talk'er** ***n.***

talk'a·tive (-ə tiv) ***adj.*** talking a great deal; loquacious

talking book a recording of a reading of a book, etc. for use esp. by the blind

talk·ing-to (tôk'iŋ to͞o') ***n.*** [Inf.] a scolding

talk show *Radio, TV* a program in which a host talks with guest celebrities, experts, etc.

talk'y ***adj.*** **-i·er, -i·est** **1** talkative **2** containing too much talk, or dialogue

tall (tôl) ***adj.*** ⟦< OE (*ge*)*tæl,* swift⟧ **1** higher in stature than the average **2** having a specified height **3** [Inf.] exaggerated [a *tall* tale] **4** [Inf.] large [a *tall* drink] —***adv.*** in an upright, dignified manner [to stand *tall*] —**tall'ness** ***n.***

Tal·la·has·see (tal'ə has'ē) capital of Florida: pop. 125,000

tal·low (tal'ō) ***n.*** ⟦prob. < LowG *talg*⟧ the solid fat of cattle, sheep, etc., used in candles, soaps, etc.

tal·ly (tal'ē) ***n.***, *pl.* **-lies** ⟦< L *talea,* a stick (notched to keep accounts)⟧ **1** anything used as a record for an account or score **2** an account, score, etc. **3** a tag or label —***vt.*** **-lied, -ly·ing** **1** to put on or as on a tally **2** to add (*up*) —***vi.*** **1** to score a point **2** to agree; correspond

tal·ly·ho (tal'ē hō') ***interj.*** the cry of a hunter on sighting the fox

Tal·mud (täl'mood, tal'məd) ***n.*** ⟦Heb, learning⟧ the body of early Jewish civil and religious law

tal·on (tal'ən) ***n.*** ⟦< L *talus,* an ankle⟧ the claw of a bird of prey

tam (tam) ***n.*** *short for* TAM-O'-SHANTER

ta·ma·le (tə mä'lē) ***n.*** ⟦< MexSp⟧ spicy minced meat wrapped in a dough of corn meal

tam·a·rack (tam'ə rak') ***n.*** ⟦< AmInd⟧ **1** an American larch tree usually found in swamps **2** its wood

tam·a·rind (tam'ə rind') ***n.*** ⟦< Ar *tamr hindī,* date of India⟧ **1** a tropical tree with yellow flowers and brown pods **2** its sharp-tasting, edible fruit

tam·bou·rine (tam'bə rēn') ***n.*** ⟦prob. < Ar *ṭanbūr,* stringed instrument⟧ a shallow, single-headed hand drum with jingling metal disks in the rim: played by shaking, hitting, etc.

tame (tām) ***adj.*** **tam'er, tam'est** ⟦OE *tam*⟧ **1** changed from a wild state and trained for human use **2** gentle; docile **3** without spirit or force; dull —***vt.*** **tamed,**

THESAURUS

become involved with, assume; see ADOPT 2.

taken ***a.*** **1** [Captured] arrested, seized, appropriated; see CAPTURED. **2** [Employed or rented] occupied, reserved, held; see RENTED.

takeoff ***v.*** ascent, upward flight, flyoff, climb, hop, jump, vertical takeoff; see also RISE 1.

tale ***n.*** **1** [A story] anecdote, fairy tale, folk tale; see STORY. **2** [A lie] tall tale, fiction, exaggeration; see LIE.

talent ***n.*** aptitude, faculty, gift; see ABILITY.

talented ***a.*** gifted, capable, skilled; see ABLE.

talk ***n.*** **1** [Human speech] utterance, locution, parlance; see COMMUNICATION, SPEECH 2. **2** [A conference] symposium, parley, consultation; see CONVERSATION, DISCUSSION. **3** [An address] lecture, oration, sermon; see SPEECH 3. **4** [Gossip] report, hearsay, chatter; see GOSSIP 1, RUMOR. **5** [Nonsense] noise, rubbish, jive; see JARGON 1, NONSENSE 1.

talk ***v.*** **1** [To converse] discuss, confer, chat, interview, speak, communicate, talk together, engage in a dialogue, have a meeting of the minds, chatter, gossip, yammer, remark, be on the phone with, be in contact with, talk over, reason with, visit with, parley, read, hold a discussion, confide in, argue, observe, notice, inform, rehearse, debate, have an exchange, exchange opinions, have a conference with, talk away, go on*, gab*, chew the fat*, compare notes with, talk someone's leg off*, shoot off one's mouth*, spit it out*, shoot the breeze*, pass the time of day, engage in conversation. **2** [To lecture] speak, give a talk, deliver a speech; see ADDRESS 2. **3** [To inform] reveal to, divulge to, notify; see TELL 2. **4** [To utter] pronounce, express, speak; see UTTER. —**talk about** treat, take under consideration, deal with; see CONSIDER, DISCUSS. —**talk back** sass, retort, defy; see ANSWER 1. —**talk down to** stoop, snub, be overbearing; see HUMILIATE, PATRONIZE 2. —**talk someone into** win over, sway, affect; see CONVINCE, INFLUENCE, PERSUADE.

talkative ***a.*** wordy, verbal, long-winded; see FLUENT.

talker ***n.*** speaker, orator, speechmaker, mouthpiece, spokesman, spokeswoman, lecturer, actor, performer, debater, storyteller, gossip, conversationalist, barker, announcer, preacher, lawyer, reader, after-dinner speaker, windbag*.

talking ***a.*** eloquent, chattering, mouthing, repeating, echoing, pronouncing, fluent, articulating, expressing, enunciating, ranting, spouting, haranguing, speaking, vocalizing, verbalizing, orating, verbose, conversing, discussing, holding forth.

tall ***a.*** **1** [Lofty] big, great, towering; see HIGH 1. **2** [Exaggerated] far-fetched, outlandish, unbelievable; see EXAGGERATED.

tally ***n.*** reckoning, account, poll; see SCORE 1.

tally ***v.*** record, write down, register, mark down, count, total, add up, sum up, correspond, match, jibe*; see also RECORD 1, COUNT, AGREE.

tame ***a.*** **1** [Domesticated] subdued, submissive, housebroken, harmless, trained, overcome, mastered, civilized, broken in, harnessed, yoked, acclimated, muzzled, bridled.—*Ant.* WILD, untamed, undomesticated. **2** [Gentle] tractable, obedient, kindly; see GENTLE 3. **3** [Uninteresting] insipid, monotonous, routine; see CONVENTIONAL 3, DULL 4, UNINTERESTING.

tam′ing 1 to make tame 2 to make gentle; subdue — **tam′a·ble** or **tame′a·ble** *adj.* —**tame′ly** *adv.* — **tame′ness** *n.* —**tam′er** *n.*

Tam·il (tam′əl) *n.* the language of the Tamils, a people of S India and N Sri Lanka

tam-o′-shan·ter (tam′ə shan′tər) *n.* ⟦< title character of Robert Burns's poem⟧ a Scottish cap with a round, flat top

tamp (tamp) *vt.* ⟦< ? Fr *tampon*, a plug⟧ to pack firmly or pound (*down*) by a series of blows or taps

Tam·pa (tam′pə) seaport in WC Florida, on the Gulf of Mexico: pop. 280,000

tam·per (tam′pər) *vi.* ⟦< TEMPER⟧ 1 to make secret, illegal arrangements (*with*) 2 to interfere (*with*) or meddle (*with*)

tam·pon (tam′pän′) *n.* ⟦Fr⟧ a plug of cotton, etc. put into a body cavity, etc., as to stop bleeding

tan (tan) *n.* ⟦< ML *tanum*, a bark used to tan hides⟧ 1 a yellowish-brown color 2 a darkening of the skin as by exposure to the sun, etc. —***adj.* tan′ner, tan′nest** yellowish-brown —***vt.* tanned, tan′ning** 1 to change (hide) into leather by soaking in tannin 2 to produce a suntan in 3 [Inf.] to whip severely —***vi.*** to become tanned

tan·a·ger (tan′ə jər) *n.* ⟦< AmInd (Brazil) *tangara*⟧ any of various small, American songbirds: the males usually are brightly colored

tan·bark (tan′bärk′) *n.* any bark containing tannin, used to tan hides, etc.

tan·dem (tan′dəm) *adv.* ⟦< punning use of L *tandem*, at length⟧ one behind another; in single file —*n.* teamwork between two persons, etc. *[to work in tandem]*

tang (taŋ) *n.* ⟦< ON *tangi*, a sting⟧ 1 a prong on a file, etc., that fits into the handle 2 a strong, penetrating taste or odor —**tang′y, -i·er, -i·est,** *adj.*

tan·ge·lo (tan′jə lō′) *n., pl.* **-los′** ⟦TANG(ERINE) + (*pom*)*elo*, grapefruit⟧ a fruit produced by crossing a tangerine with a grapefruit

tan·gent (tan′jənt) *adj.* ⟦< L *tangere*, to touch⟧ 1 touching 2 *Geom.* touching a curved surface at one point but not intersecting it —*n.* a tangent line, curve, or surface —**go off at** (or **on**) **a tangent** to change suddenly to another line of action, etc. —**tan·gen′tial** (-jen′shəl) *adj.*

tan·ge·rine (tan′jə rēn′) *n.* ⟦after *Tangier*, city in N Africa⟧ a small, loose-skinned, reddish-yellow orange with easily separated segments

tan·gi·ble (tan′jə bəl) *adj.* ⟦< L *tangere*, to touch⟧ 1 that can be touched or felt 2 definite; objective —*n.* [*pl.*] assets having real substance and able to be appraised for value —**tan′gi·bil′i·ty** *n.*

tan·gle (taŋ′gəl) *vt.* **-gled, -gling** ⟦< ? Swed⟧ 1 to catch as in a snare; trap 2 to make a snarl of; intertwine —*vi.* 1 to become tangled 2 [Inf.] to argue —*n.* 1 an intertwined, confused mass 2 a confused condition or state

tan·go (taŋ′gō) *n., pl.* **-gos** ⟦AmSp⟧ 1 a South American dance for couples with long gliding steps and dips 2 music for this dance in 2/4 or 4/4 time —*vi.* to dance the tango

tank (taŋk) *n.* ⟦in sense 1 < Sans⟧ 1 any large container for liquid or gas 2 an armored combat vehicle with tractor treads —*vi.* [Slang] to fail

tank·ard (taŋ′kərd) *n.* ⟦< OFr *tanquart*⟧ a large drinking cup with a handle

tank·er (taŋ′kər) *n.* 1 a ship equipped to transport oil or other liquids 2 a plane designed to carry liquids, as for refueling another plane in flight 3 a truck, etc. equipped to transport liquids or dry commodities in bulk

tank top ⟦orig. worn in swimming tanks⟧ a sleeveless casual shirt with shoulder straps

tank truck a motor truck built to transport gasoline, oil, etc.

tan·ner (tan′ər) *n.* a person whose work is making leather by tanning hides

tan′ner·y *n., pl.* **-ner·ies** a place where leather is made by tanning hides

tan·nic acid (tan′ik) a yellowish, astringent substance used in tanning hides, dyeing, etc.

tan′nin (-in) *n.* ⟦< *tan*, TAN + *-in*, -INE[3]⟧ any of a group of compounds, as tannic acid, that convert hide into leather

tan·sy (tan′zē) *n., pl.* **-sies** ⟦< LL *tanacetum*⟧ a plant with a strong smell and small, yellow flowers

tan·ta·lize (tan′tə līz′) *vt.* **-lized′, -liz′ing** ⟦after *Tantalus*, in Gr myth, a king doomed in Hades to stand in water that always recedes when he wishes to drink and under fruit he cannot reach⟧ to promise or show something desirable and then withhold it; tease

tan·ta·mount (tant′ə mount′) *adj.* ⟦< OFr *tant*, so much + *amont*, upward⟧ equal (*to*) in value, effect, etc.

tan·tra (tun′trə, tän′-) *n.* ⟦Sans⟧ [*often* **T-**] a form of yoga teaching attainment of ecstasy —**tan′tric** *adj.*

tan·trum (tan′trəm) *n.* ⟦< ?⟧ a violent, willful outburst of rage, etc.

Tan·za·ni·a (tan′zə nē′ə) country in E Africa: 364,881 sq. mi.; pop. 23,174,000 —**Tan′za·ni′an** *adj., n.*

Tao·ism (dou′iz′əm, tou′-) *n.* ⟦Chin *tao*, the way⟧ a Chinese religion and philosophy advocating simplicity, selflessness, etc. —**Tao′ist** *n., adj.*

tap[1] (tap) *vt., vi.* **tapped, tap′ping** ⟦echoic⟧ 1 to strike lightly 2 to make or do by tapping *[to tap a message]* 3 to choose, as for membership in a club —*n.* a light, rapid blow

tap[2] (tap) *n.* ⟦OE *tæppa*⟧ 1 a faucet or spigot 2 a plug, cork, etc. for stopping a hole in a cask, etc. 3 a tool used to cut threads inside a nut, pipe, etc. 4 the act or an instance of wiretapping 5 *Elec.* a place in a circuit where a connection can be made —***vt.* tapped, tap′ping** 1 to put a tap or spigot on 2 to make a hole in, or pull the plug from, for drawing off liquid 3 to draw off (liquid) 4 to make use of *[to tap new resources]* 5 to make a connection with (a pipe, circuit, etc.); specif., to wiretap

tap dance a dance done with sharp, loud taps of the foot, toe, or heel at each step —**tap′-dance′, -danced′, -danc′ing,** *vi.* —**tap′-danc′er** *n.*

tape (tāp) *n.* ⟦OE *tæppe*, a fillet⟧ 1 a strong, narrow strip of cloth, paper, etc. used for binding, tying, etc. 2 *short for* MAGNETIC TAPE 3 *short for* TAPE MEASURE —***vt.* taped, tap′ing** 1 to bind, tie, etc. with tape 2 to record on magnetic tape

tape deck a component of an audio system, that records and plays back magnetic tapes

tape measure a tape with marks in inches, feet, etc. for measuring

ta·per (tā′pər) *n.* ⟦OE *tapur*⟧ 1 a slender candle 2 a gradual decrease in width or thickness —*vt., vi.* 1 to decrease gradually in width or thickness 2 to lessen; diminish Often with *off*

tape recorder a device for recording on magnetic tape and for playing back what has been recorded

THESAURUS

tamper with *v.* interfere with, change, meddle with; see ALTER 1, DESTROY.

tan *a.* brownish, suntanned, weathered; see BROWN.

tan *n.* light brown, beige, neutral color; see BROWN, GOLD, YELLOW.

tang *n.* zest, flavor, savor; see TASTE 2.

tangible *a.* perceptible, palpable, material, real, substantial, sensible, touchable, verifiable, physical, corporeal, solid, visible, stable, well-grounded, incarnated, embodied, manifest, factual, objective, tactile.—*Ant.* SPIRITUAL, ethereal, intangible.

tangle *n.* snarl, snag, muddle; see CONFUSION, KNOT 2.

tangle *v.* involve, complicate, confuse, obstruct, hamper, derange, mix up, disorganize, upset, unbalance, unhinge, perplex, tie up, trap, mess up.—*Ant.* ORDER, fix, unravel.

tangled *a.* tied up, confused, knit together, disordered, chaotic, out of place, mixed up, snarled, trapped, entangled, twisted, muddled, messed up, balled up*, screwy*, with wires crossed*.

tank *n.* 1 [A large container for liquids] tub, basin, vat; see CONTAINER. 2 [An armored vehicle on a roller belt with cogged wheels] armored tank, armored personnel carrier, armored car; see WEAPON.

tantrum *n.* rage, outburst, spell; see ANGER, FIT 2.

tap[1,2] *n.* 1 [A light blow] pat, rap, dab; see BLOW. 2 [A spigot] faucet, petcock, drain; see FAUCET.

tap[1,2] *v.* 1 [To strike lightly] pat, touch, rap; see HIT 1. 2 [To puncture in order to draw liquid] open, pierce, bore; see PENETRATE.

tape *n.* ribbon, line, rope. *Tapes include the following:* recording tape, cartridge, cassette, edging, tapeline, tape measure, steel tape, surveyor's chain, adhesive tape, gummed tape, duct tape, electrical tape, draftsman's tape, Scotch tape, masking tape, packing tape, transparent tape, audiotape, videotape, mending tape, bias tape, seam binding.

tape *v.* 1 [To fasten] tie up, bind, bond; see FASTEN. 2 [To record] register, make a recording, put on tape; see RECORD 3. 3 [To bandage] tie, bind up, dress; see BIND 1, FASTEN.

taper *v.* narrow, lessen, thin out; see DECREASE 1, 2. —**taper off** recede, peter out*, diminish; see DECREASE 2.

tape recorder *n.* recording equipment, stereo, stereophonic recorder,

tap·es·try (tap′əs trē) ***n.***, *pl.* **-tries** ⟦< Gr *tapes*, a carpet⟧ a heavy woven cloth with decorative designs and pictures, used as a wall hanging, etc.
tape′worm′ ***n.*** a long, tapelike flatworm that lives as a parasite in the intestines
tap·i·o·ca (tap′ē ō′kə) ***n.*** ⟦< AmInd (Brazil)⟧ a starchy substance from cassava roots, used for puddings, etc.
ta·pir (tā′pər) ***n.*** ⟦< AmInd (Brazil)⟧ a large, hoglike mammal of tropical America and the Malay Peninsula
tapped out [Slang] **1** having no money; broke **2** exhausted or depleted
tap′room′ ***n.*** BARROOM
tap′root′ ***n.*** ⟦TAP² + ROOT¹⟧ a main root, growing downward, from which small branch roots spread out
taps (taps) ***n.*** ⟦< TAP¹, because orig. a drum signal⟧ [*with sing. or pl. v.*] a bugle call to put out lights in retiring for the night
tar¹ (tär) ***n.*** ⟦OE *teru*⟧ a thick, sticky, black liquid formed when hot coal, wood, etc. decomposes in the absence of air —***vt.*** **tarred**, **tar′ring** to cover or smear with tar —**tar′ry**, **-ri·er**, **-ri·est**, ***adj.***
tar² (tär) ***n.*** ⟦< TAR(PAULIN)⟧ [Inf.] a sailor
ta·ran·tu·la (tə ran′choo lə) ***n.*** ⟦after *Taranto*, city in S Italy⟧ any of several large, hairy, somewhat poisonous spiders of S Europe and tropical America
tar·dy (tär′dē) ***adj.*** **-di·er**, **-di·est** ⟦< L *tardus*, slow⟧ **1** slow in moving, acting, etc. **2** late, delayed, etc. —**tar′di·ly** ***adv.*** —**tar′di·ness** ***n.***
tare¹ (ter) ***n.*** ⟦ME⟧ **1** any of various vetches **2** *Bible* an undesirable weed
tare² (ter) ***n.*** ⟦< Ar *ṭaraḥa*, to reject⟧ the weight of a container, etc. deducted from the total weight to determine the weight of the contents or load
tar·get (tär′git) ***n.*** ⟦< medieval Fr *targe*, a shield⟧ **1** a board, etc. marked as with concentric circles, aimed at in archery, rifle practice, etc. **2** any object that is shot at **3** an objective; goal **4** an object of attack, criticism, etc. —***vt.*** to establish as a target, goal, etc.
tar·iff (tar′if) ***n.*** ⟦< Ar *ta'rīf*, information⟧ **1** a list or system of taxes upon exports or, esp., imports **2** such a tax, or its rate **3** a list or scale of prices, charges, etc. **4** [Inf.] any bill, charge, etc.
tar·mac (tär′mak′) ***n.*** ⟦ult. < TAR¹ + MAC(ADAM)⟧ [Chiefly Brit.] an airport runway or apron
tar·nish (tär′nish) ***vt.*** ⟦< Fr *ternir*, make dim⟧ **1** to dull the luster of **2** to sully or mar —***vi.*** **1** to lose luster **2** to become sullied —***n.*** **1** dullness **2** a stain —**tar′nish·a·ble** ***adj.***
ta·ro (ter′ō, tär′ō) ***n.***, *pl.* **-ros** ⟦< a Polynesian language⟧ a tropical Asiatic plant with a starchy, edible root
tar·ot (tar′ō, -ət; ta rō′) ***n.*** ⟦Fr < Ar *ṭaraḥa*, to reject⟧ [*often* **T-**] any of a set of 22 cards with pictures, used in fortunetelling
tarp (tärp) ***n.*** [Inf.] *short for* TARPAULIN
tar·pau·lin (tär pô′lin, tär′pə-) ***n.*** ⟦< TAR¹ + PALL², a covering⟧ **1** canvas coated with a waterproofing compound **2** a sheet of this
tar·pon (tär′pən) ***n.*** ⟦< ?⟧ a large, silvery game fish of the W Atlantic
tar·ra·gon (tar′ə gän′) ***n.*** ⟦< Sp < Ar < Gr *drakōn*, a dragon⟧ an Old World plant with fragrant leaves used for seasoning
tar·ry (tar′ē) ***vi.*** **-ried**, **-ry·ing** ⟦< OE *tergan*, to vex & prob. OFr *targer*, to delay⟧ **1** to delay; linger **2** to stay for a time **3** to wait
tart¹ (tärt) ***adj.*** ⟦OE *teart*⟧ **1** sharp in taste; sour; acid **2** sharp in meaning; cutting *[a tart answer]* —**tart′ly** ***adv.*** —**tart′ness** ***n.***
tart² (tärt) ***n.*** ⟦< OFr *tarte*⟧ a small pastry shell filled with jam, jelly, etc.
tart³ (tärt) ***n.*** ⟦< prec., orig., slang term of endearment⟧ [Inf.] a prostitute
tar·tan (tärt′'n) ***n.*** ⟦prob. < medieval Fr *tiretaine*, a cloth of mixed fibers⟧ a woolen cloth in any of various woven plaid patterns, worn esp. in the Scottish Highlands
tar·tar (tärt′ər) ***n.*** ⟦< medieval Gr *tartaron*⟧ **1** cream of tartar, esp. the crude form present in grape juice and forming a crustlike deposit in wine casks **2** a hard deposit on the teeth
Tar·tar (tärt′ər) ***n.*** TATAR
tar·tar sauce (tärt′ər) ⟦Fr⟧ a sauce of mayonnaise with chopped pickles, olives, capers, etc.: also **tar′tare sauce**
task (task) ***n.*** ⟦ult. < L *taxare*, to rate⟧ **1** a piece of work to be done **2** any difficult undertaking —***vt.*** to burden; strain —**take to task** to scold
task force a group, esp. a military unit, assigned a specific task
task′mas′ter ***n.*** one who assigns tasks to others, esp. when severe
Tas·ma·ni·a (taz mā′nē ə) island of Australia, off its SE coast —**Tas·ma′ni·an** ***adj.***, ***n.***
tas·sel (tas′əl) ***n.*** ⟦OFr, knob⟧ **1** an ornamental tuft of threads, etc. hanging loosely from a knob **2** something resembling this, as a tuft of corn silk
taste (tāst) ***vt.*** **tast′ed**, **tast′ing** ⟦< OFr *taster*⟧ **1** to test the flavor of by putting a little in one's mouth **2** to detect the flavor of by the sense of taste **3** to eat or drink a small amount of **4** to experience *[to taste success]* —***vi.*** to have a specific flavor —***n.*** **1** the sense by which flavor is perceived through the taste buds on the tongue **2** the quality so perceived; flavor **3** a small amount tasted as a sample **4** a bit; trace **5** the ability to appreciate what is beautiful, appropriate, etc. **6** a specific preference **7** a liking; inclination —**in bad** (or **good**) **taste** in a style showing a bad (or good) sense of beauty, fitness, etc. —**taste′less** ***adj.*** —**tast′er** ***n.***
taste bud any of the cells, esp. in the tongue, that are the organs of taste
taste′ful ***adj.*** having or showing good TASTE (*n.* 5) —**taste′ful·ly** ***adv.***
tast·y (tās′tē) ***adj.*** **-i·er**, **-i·est** that tastes good; flavorful —**tast′i·ness** ***n.***
tat (tat) ***vt.*** **tat′ted**, **tat′ting** to make by tatting —***vi.*** to do tatting
ta·ta·mi (tə tä′mē) ***n.***, *pl.* **-mi** or **-mis** ⟦Jpn⟧ a floor mat of rice straw, used traditionally in Japanese homes for sitting on
Ta·tar (tät′ər) ***n.*** **1** a member of any of the E Asian peoples that invaded W Asia and E Europe in the Middle Ages **2** a Turkic language
tat·ter (tat′ər) ***n.*** ⟦< ON *töturr*, rags⟧ **1** a torn and hanging piece, as of a garment **2** [*pl.*] torn, ragged clothes —***vt.***, ***vi.*** to make or become ragged —**tat′tered** ***adj.***
tat′ter·de·mal′ion (-di māl′yən) ***n.*** ⟦< prec. + ?⟧ a person in torn, ragged clothes

THESAURUS

cassette recorder, cassette deck, cassette player, dictaphone, VCR, videotape machine, videocassette recorder.
tapestry ***n.*** hanging, fabric, weaving; see CLOTH, CURTAIN, DECORATION 2.
tar¹ ***n.*** pitch, asphalt, coal tar; see GUM.
tardy ***a.*** overdue, too late, delayed; see LATE 1, SLOW 2, 3.
target ***n.*** **1** [A goal] objective, aim, purpose, end, destination, mark. **2** [Bull's-eye] point, spot, butt, mark, dummy. **3** [A prey] quarry, game, scapegoat; see VICTIM.
tarnish ***v.*** soil, turn dark, lose luster; see DIRTY.
tart¹ ***a.*** bitter, pungent, sharp; see SOUR.
tartly ***a.*** aciduously, sharply, curtly; see ANGRILY.
tartness ***n.*** sourness, acidity, acridity; see BITTERNESS.
task ***n.*** chore, responsibility, business; see DUTY 1.
taste ***n.*** **1** [The sense that detects flavor] tongue, taste buds, palate, senses. **2** [The quality detected by taste] flavor, savor, savoriness, aftertaste, tang, suggestion, zip*, wallop*, kick*, smack, jolt, zing*, punch*. **3** [Judgment, especially aesthetic judgment] discrimination, susceptibility, appreciation, good taste, discernment, acumen, sensibilities, penetration, acuteness, feeling, refinement, appreciation; see also JUDGMENT 1. **4** [Preference] tendency, leaning, attachment; see INCLINATION 1. —**in bad taste** pretentious, rude, crass; see TASTELESS 3. —**in good taste** elegant, pleasing, refined; see ARTISTIC, DAINTY. —**to someone's taste** pleasing, satisfying, appealing; see PLEASANT 2.
taste ***v.*** **1** [To test by the tongue] sip, try, touch, sample, lick, suck, roll over in the mouth, partake of. **2** [To recognize by flavor] sense, discern, distinguish; see KNOW 3. **3** [To experience] feel, perceive, know; see UNDERGO.
tasteful ***a.*** delicate, elegant, fine; see DAINTY.
tasteless ***a.*** **1** [Lacking flavor] unsavory, bland, unseasoned, vapid, flat, watery, flavorless, without spice; see also DULL 4, ORDINARY 2.—*Ant.* DELICIOUS, seasoned, spicy. **2** [Plain] homely, insipid, trite; see COMMON 1. **3** [Lacking good taste] pretentious, ornate, showy, trivial, artificial, florid, ostentatious, clumsy, makeshift, coarse, useless, rude, uncouth, ugly, unsightly, unlovely, hideous, foolish, stupid, crass.—*Ant.* REFINED, civilized, cultivated.
tasty ***a.*** savory, palatable, appetizing; see DELICIOUS.

tat·ting (tat′iŋ) ***n.*** ⟦prob. < Brit dial. *tat*, to tangle⟧ **1** a fine lace made by looping and knotting thread **2** the act or process of making this

tat·tle (tat′'l) ***vi.* -tled, -tling** ⟦prob. < MDu *tatelen*⟧ **1** to talk idly **2** to reveal others' secrets —***vt.*** to reveal (a secret) by gossiping —**tat′tler** ***n.***

tat′tle·tale′ ***n.*** an informer; a gossip

tat·too[1] (ta to͞o′) ***vt.* -tooed′, -too′ing** ⟦< a Polynesian language⟧ to make (permanent designs) on (the skin) by puncturing and inserting indelible color —***n.***, *pl.* **-toos′** a tattooed design

tat·too[2] (ta to͞o′) ***n.***, *pl.* **-toos′** ⟦< Du *tap toe*, tap to (shut): a signal for closing barrooms⟧ **1** a signal on a drum or bugle, summoning military personnel to their quarters at night **2** a drumming, rapping, etc.

tau (tou, tô) ***n.*** the 19th letter of the Greek alphabet (Τ, τ)

taught (tôt) ***vt.***, ***vi.*** *pt. & pp. of* TEACH

taunt (tônt, tänt) ***vt.*** ⟦< ? Fr *tant pour tant*, tit for tat⟧ to reproach scornfully or sarcastically; mock —***n.*** a scornful or jeering remark

taupe (tōp) ***n.*** ⟦Fr < L *talpa*, mole⟧ a dark, brownish gray

Tau·rus (tôr′əs) ***n.*** ⟦L, a bull⟧ the second sign of the zodiac

taut (tôt) ***adj.*** ⟦ME *toght*, tight⟧ **1** tightly stretched, as a rope **2** tense *[a taut* smile*]* **3** trim, tidy, etc. —**taut′ly** ***adv.*** —**taut′ness** ***n.***

tau·tol·o·gy (tô täl′ə jē) ***n.***, *pl.* **-gies** ⟦< Gr < *to auto*, the same + -LOGY⟧ needless repetition of an idea in a different word, phrase, etc.; redundancy —**tau′to·log′i·cal** ***adj.***

tav·ern (tav′ərn) ***n.*** ⟦< L *taberna*⟧ **1** a saloon; bar **2** an inn

taw·dry (tô′drē) ***adj.* -dri·er, -dri·est** ⟦after *St. Audrey laces,* sold at St. Audrey's fair in Norwich, England⟧ cheap and showy; gaudy

taw·ny (tô′nē) ***adj.* -ni·er, -ni·est** ⟦< OFr *tanner*, to tan⟧ brownish-yellow; tan —**taw′ni·ness** ***n.***

tax (taks) ***vt.*** ⟦< L *taxare*, appraise⟧ **1** to require to pay a tax **2** to assess a tax on (income, purchases, etc.) **3** to put a strain on **4** to accuse; charge —***n.*** **1** a compulsory payment of a percentage of income, property value, etc. for the support of a government **2** a heavy demand; burden —**tax′a·ble** ***adj.*** —**tax·a′tion** ***n.***

tax·i (tak′sē) ***n.***, *pl.* **-is** *short for* TAXICAB —***vi.* -ied, -i·ing** or **-y·ing** **1** to go in a taxicab **2** to move along the ground or on the water as after landing: said of an airplane

tax′i·cab′ ***n.*** ⟦< *taxi(meter) cab*⟧ an automobile in which passengers are carried for a fare

tax·i·der·my (tak′si dur′mē) ***n.*** ⟦< Gr *taxis*, arrangement + *derma*, skin⟧ the art of preparing, stuffing, etc. the skins of animals to make them appear lifelike —**tax′i·der′mist** ***n.***

tax·i·me·ter (tak′sē mēt′ər) ***n.*** ⟦< Fr, ult. < ML *taxa*, tax + *-meter*, -METER⟧ an automatic device in taxicabs that registers the fare due

tax·on·o·my (tak sän′ə mē) ***n.***, *pl.* **-mies** ⟦< Gr *taxis*, arrangement + *nomos*, law⟧ classification, esp. of animals and plants —**tax·on′o·mist** ***n.***

tax′pay′er ***n.*** one who pays a tax

tax shelter an investment made to reduce one's income tax

tax·us (tak′səs) ***n.*** ⟦ModL⟧ YEW (*n.* 1)

Tay·lor (tā′lər), **Zach·a·ry** (zak′ə rē) 1784-1850; U.S. general: 12th president of the U.S. (1849-50)

TB (tē′bē′) ***n.*** tuberculosis

TBA, t.b.a., or **tba** *abbrev.* to be announced

T-ball (tē′bôl′) ***n.*** a baseball game for young children in which the ball is placed on and struck from a tall TEE (*n.* 1)

T-bone steak (tē′bōn′) a beefsteak with a T-shaped bone, containing some tenderloin

tbs or **tbsp** *abbrev.* **1** tablespoon(s) **2** tablespoonful(s)

T cell any of the lymphocytes affected by the thymus, that regulate immunity, reject foreign tissue, etc.: cf. B CELL

Tchai·kov·sky (chī kôf′skē), **Peter** 1840-93; Russ. composer

TD *abbrev.* touchdown: sometimes **td**

tea (tē) ***n.*** ⟦< Chin dial. *t'e*⟧ **1** an evergreen plant grown in Asia **2** its dried leaves, used to make a beverage **3** the beverage made by soaking such leaves in boiling water **4** a tealike beverage made from other plants or from a meat extract **5** [Chiefly Brit.] a meal in the late afternoon at which tea is the drink **6** an afternoon party at which tea, etc. is served

tea·ber·ry (tē′ber′ē) ***n.***, *pl.* **-ries** **1** WINTERGREEN (sense 1) **2** the berry of the wintergreen

teach (tēch) ***vt.* taught, teach′ing** ⟦OE *tæcan*⟧ **1** to show or help (a person) to learn (*how*) to do something **2** to give lessons to (a student, etc.) **3** to give lessons in (a subject) **4** to provide with knowledge, insight, etc. —***vi.*** to give lessons or instruction —**teach′a·ble** ***adj.***

teach′er ***n.*** one who teaches, esp. as a profession

teach′ing ***n.*** **1** the profession of a teacher **2** something taught; precept, doctrine, etc.: *usually used in pl.*

tea′cup′ ***n.*** a cup for drinking tea, etc. —**tea′cup·ful′**, *pl.* **-fuls′**, ***n.***

teak (tēk) ***n.*** ⟦< Malayalam *tēkka*⟧ **1** a tall SE Asian tree with hard, yellowish-brown wood **2** its wood: also **teak′wood′**

tea′ket′tle ***n.*** a kettle with a spout, for boiling water to make tea, etc.

teal (tēl) ***n.*** ⟦ME *tele*⟧ **1** a small, short-necked, freshwater wild duck **2** a dark grayish or greenish blue: also **teal blue**

team (tēm) ***n.*** ⟦OE, offspring⟧ **1** two or more horses, oxen, etc. harnessed to the same plow, etc. **2** a group of people working or playing together —***vi.*** to join in cooperative activity: often with *up* —***adj.*** of or done by a team

team′mate′ ***n.*** one on the same team

team′ster (-stər) ***n.*** one whose work is hauling loads with a team or truck

team′work′ ***n.*** joint action by a group of people

tea′pot′ ***n.*** a pot with a spout and handle, for brewing and pouring tea

THESAURUS

tattle ***v.*** blab, tell on, report; see GOSSIP.

tattler ***n.*** busybody, tattletale, snoop; see GOSSIP 2, TRAITOR.

tattletale ***n.*** informer, tattler, busybody, snitch*, fink*, squealer*, stool pigeon*, stoolie*, rat*.

taught ***a.*** instructed, informed, directed; see EDUCATED, LEARNED 1.

taunt ***n.*** insult, mockery, jibe; see RIDICULE.

tavern ***n.*** taproom, alehouse, roadhouse; see BAR 2.

tax ***n.*** **1** [A pecuniary levy] fine, charge, rate, toll, levy, impost, duty, assessment, tariff, tribute, obligation, price, cost, contribution, expense; see also DUES. **2** [A burden] strain, task, demand; see BURDEN 2.

tax ***v.*** **1** [To cause to pay a tax] assess, exact from, demand, exact tribute, charge duty, demand toll, require a contribution, enact a tax. **2** [To burden] encumber, weigh down, overload; see BURDEN.

taxation ***n.*** levying, assessment, money-gathering; see DUES, TAX 1.

taxed ***a.*** **1** [Paying taxes] levied upon, demanded to pay, required to pay, assessed, subject to tax. **2** [Burdened] overtaxed, strained, harassed, fatigued; see also TIRED.

taxicab ***n.*** taxi, cab, hack*; see AUTOMOBILE.

tea ***n.*** **1** [An infusion made from tea leaves] beverage, brew, infusion, decoction; see also DRINK 2. *Tea and tealike drinks include the following:* black, green, Lapsang souchong, oolong, Darjeeling, orange pekoe, pekoe, gunpowder, Earl Grey, English breakfast, rose hip, spiced, jasmine, blended, sassafras, sage, mint, camomile, herb; iced tea or ice tea, cambric tea. **2** [A light afternoon or evening meal] snack, refreshment, tea party; see LUNCH, MEAL 2.

teach ***v.*** instruct, tutor, coach, educate, profess, explain, expound, lecture, direct, give a briefing, edify, enlighten, guide, show, give lessons in, ground, rear, prepare, fit, interpret, bring up, instill, inculcate, indoctrinate, brainwash*, develop, form, address to, initiate, inform, nurture, illustrate, imbue, implant, break in, give the facts, give an idea of, improve someone's mind, open one's eyes, knock into someone's head*, bring home to*, cram, stuff; see also INFLUENCE, MOTIVATE.—*Ant.* LEARN, gain, acquire.

teacher ***n.*** schoolmaster, schoolmistress, schoolman, educator, public school teacher, high-school teacher, tutor, mentor, pedagogue, master, guru, swami, mistress, kindergarten teacher, teacher-in-training, substitute teacher, professor, lecturer, instructor, faculty member, graduate assistant.

teaching ***n.*** pedagogy, instruction, training; see EDUCATION 1, 3.

team ***n.*** **1** [A group of people working together, as on the stage] partners, combo, troupe, company, duo, trio; see also ORGANIZATION 2. **2** [An organization, especially in sport] squad, crew, club; see ORGANIZATION 2.

team up with ***v.*** attach oneself to, collaborate with, join; see ACCOMPANY, COOPERATE, HELP.

teamwork ***n.*** partisanship, collaboration, union; see ALLIANCE 1, COOPERATION, PARTNERSHIP.

tear[1] (ter) ***vt.*** **tore, torn, tear'ing** ⟦OE *teran,* rend⟧ **1** to pull apart into pieces by force; rip **2** to make by tearing *[to tear a hole]* **3** to lacerate **4** to disrupt; split *[ranks torn by dissensions]* **5** to divide with doubt, etc. **6** to pull with force: with *up, out, away, off,* etc. —***vi.*** **1** to be torn **2** to move with force or speed —***n.*** **1** a tearing **2** a torn place; rent —**tear down** **1** to wreck **2** to dismantle

tear[2] (tir) ***n.*** ⟦OE *tēar*⟧ a drop of the salty fluid which flows from the eye, as in weeping —**in tears** crying; weeping —**tear'ful** ***adj.*** —**tear'ful·ly** ***adv.*** —**tear'y, -i·er, -i·est,** ***adj.***

tear·drop (tir'dräp') ***n.*** a tear

tear gas (tir) a liquid or gas that causes irritation of the eyes, used as by the police to disperse rioters —**tear'-gas', -gassed', -gas'sing,** ***vt.***

tear·jerk·er (tir'jur'kər) ***n.*** [Slang] a sad, overly sentimental film, play, etc.

tea'room' ***n.*** a restaurant that serves tea, coffee, light lunches, etc.

tease (tēz) ***vt.*** **teased, teas'ing** ⟦OE *tæsan*⟧ **1** *a)* to card or comb (flax, wool, etc.) *b)* to fluff (the hair) by combing toward the scalp **2** to annoy by mocking, poking fun, etc. **3** to beg; importune **4** to tantalize —***vi.*** to indulge in teasing —***n.*** one who teases

tea·sel (tē'zəl) ***n.*** ⟦see prec.⟧ a bristly plant with prickly flowers

teas·er (tē'zər) ***n.*** **1** a person or thing that teases **2** a puzzling problem

tea'spoon' ***n.*** **1** a spoon for stirring tea, etc. **2** a spoon for measuring ⅓ tablespoon —**tea'spoon·ful',** *pl.* **-fuls',** ***n.***

teat (tēt) ***n.*** ⟦< OFr *tete*⟧ the nipple on a breast or udder

tech *abbrev.* **1** technical(ly) **2** technology

tech·ie (tek'ē) ***n.*** [Inf.] an expert in computer technology

tech·ni·cal (tek'ni kəl) ***adj.*** ⟦< Gr *technē,* an art⟧ **1** dealing with the industrial or mechanical arts or the applied sciences **2** of a specific science, art, craft, etc. **3** of, in or showing technique **4** concerned with minute details —**tech'ni·cal·ly** ***adv.***

tech'ni·cal'i·ty (-kal'ə tē) ***n.,*** *pl.* **-ties** **1** the state or quality of being technical **2** a technical point, detail, etc. **3** a minute point, detail, etc. brought to bear upon a main issue

tech·ni·cian (tek nish'ən) ***n.*** one skilled in the technique of some art, craft, or science

Tech·ni·col·or (tek'ni kul'ər) *trademark for* a process of making color movies —***n.*** [**t-**] this process

tech·nique (tek nēk') ***n.*** ⟦Fr⟧ **1** the method of procedure in artistic work, scientific activity, etc. **2** the degree of expertness in following this

tech·noc·ra·cy (tek näk'rə sē) ***n.*** ⟦< Gr *technē,* an art + -CRACY⟧ government by scientists and engineers —**tech'no·crat'** (-nə krat') ***n.***

tech·nol·o·gy (tek näl'ə jē) ***n.*** ⟦Gr *technologia,* systematic treatment⟧ **1** the science of the practical or industrial arts **2** applied science —**tech'no·log'i·cal** (-nə läj'i kəl) ***adj.***

tech·no·phile (tek'nə fīl') ***n.*** one who is enthusiastic about advanced technology

tech'no·pho'bi·a ***n.*** dislike or fear of advanced technology —**tech'no·phobe'** ***n.***

ted·dy bear (ted'ē) ⟦after *Teddy* (Theodore) Roosevelt⟧ a child's stuffed toy made to look like a bear cub

te·di·ous (tē'dē əs) ***adj.*** full of tedium; long and dull —**te'di·ous·ly** ***adv.***

te'di·um (-əm) ***n.*** ⟦< L *taedet,* it offends⟧ the condition or quality of being tiresome, boring, etc.

tee (tē) ***n.*** ⟦prob. < Scot dial. *teaz*⟧ *Golf* **1** a small peg from which the ball is driven **2** the place from which a player makes the first stroke on each hole —***vt., vi.*** **teed, tee'ing** to place (a ball) on a tee —**tee off** **1** to play a golf ball from a tee **2** [Slang] to make angry or disgusted

teem (tēm) ***vi.*** ⟦< OE *team,* progeny⟧ to be prolific; abound; swarm

teen (tēn) ***n.*** ⟦OE *tien,* ten⟧ **1** [*pl.*] the years from 13 through 19, as of a person's age **2** TEENAGER

teen·age (tēn'āj') ***adj.*** **1** in one's teens **2** of or for people in their teens —**teen'ag'er** ***n.***

tee·ny (tē'nē) ***adj.*** **-ni·er, -ni·est** *inf. var. of* TINY: also **teen·sy** (tēn'zē, -sē), **-si·er, -si·est**

tee·ny-wee·ny (tē'nē wē'nē) ***adj.*** [Inf.] tiny: also **teen·sy-ween·sy** (tēn'zē wēn'zē, tēn'sē wēn'sē)

tee·pee (tē'pē) ***n.*** *alt. sp. of* TEPEE

tee shirt *var. of* T-SHIRT

tee·ter (tēt'ər) ***vi.*** ⟦< ON *titra,* to tremble⟧ to totter, wobble, etc.

tee'ter-tot'ter (-tôt'ər, -tät'-) ***n., vi.*** SEESAW

teeth (tēth) ***n.*** *pl. of* TOOTH —**in the teeth of** **1** directly against **2** defying

teethe (tē*th*) ***vi.*** **teethed, teeth'ing** to grow teeth; cut one's teeth

tee·to·tal·er or **tee·to·tal·ler** (tē tōt''l ər) ***n.*** ⟦< doubling of initial *t* in *total*⟧ one who practices total abstinence from alcoholic liquor

te·fil·lin (tə fil'in) ***n.*** either of two small, leather cases holding Scripture texts, worn in prayer on the forehead and arm by orthodox Jewish men

Tef·lon (tef'län') *trademark for* a tough polymer, used for nonsticking coatings as for cookware —***n.*** [**t-**] this substance

Teh·ran (te rän') capital of Iran: pop. 6,043,000: also **Te·he·ran'**

tek·tite (tek'tīt') ***n.*** ⟦< Gr *tēktos,* molten⟧ a small, dark, glassy body thought to have originated as a meteorite: also sp. **tec'tite'**

tel *abbrev.* **1** telegram **2** telephone

Tel A·viv (tel' ə vēv') seaport in W Israel: pop. 356,000

tele- *combining form* **1** ⟦< Gr *tēle,* far off⟧ at, over, etc. a distance *[telegraph]* **2** ⟦< TELE(VISION)⟧ of, in, or by television *[telecast]*

tel·e·cast (tel'ə kast') ***vt., vi.*** **-cast'** or **-cast'ed, -cast'ing** to broadcast by television —***n.*** a television broadcast —**tel'e·cast'er** ***n.***

tel'e·com·mu'ni·ca'tion ***n.*** [*also pl., with sing. or pl. v.*] communication by electronic or electrical means, as through radio, TV, computers, etc.: also **tel'e·com'** (-käm')

tel'e·com·mute' ***vi.*** to do office work at home using a computer

tel'e·con'fer·ence ***n.*** a conference of persons in different locations, as by telephone, TV, etc.

tel'e·gram' ***n.*** a message transmitted by telegraph

tel'e·graph' ***n.*** ⟦see TELE- & -GRAPH⟧ an apparatus or system that transmits messages by electrical impulses sent by wire or radio —***vt., vi.*** to send (a message) to (a person) by telegraph —**tel'e·graph'ic** ***adj.***

te·leg·ra·phy (tə leg'rə fē) ***n.*** the operation of telegraph apparatus —**te·leg'ra·pher** ***n.***

tel·e·ki·ne·sis (tel'ə ki nē'sis) ***n.*** ⟦see TELE- & KINETIC⟧ *Parapsychology* the causing of an object to move by psychic, rather than physical, force

THESAURUS

tear[1] ***n.*** rent, rip, hole, slit, laceration, split, break, gash, rupture, fissure, crack, cut, breach, damage, imperfection.—*Ant.* REPAIR, patch, renovation.

tear[1] ***v.*** rend, rip, shred, mangle, rive, rip up, split, lacerate; see also CUT 1.

tear[2] ***n.*** teardrop, droplet, eyewash; see DROP 1.

tearful ***a.*** weeping, mournful, lamenting, teary, weepy, on the edge of tears.

tears ***n.*** sobbing, sob, crying, cry, weeping, lamenting, whimpering, grieving, mourning, waterworks*; see also GRIEF.

tease ***v.*** taunt, tantalize, torment; see BOTHER 2, RIDICULE.

teaspoon ***n.*** kitchen utensil, measuring spoon, 1/3 of a tablespoon, stirrer; see also UTENSILS.

technical ***a.*** specialized, special, scientific, professional, scholarly, mechanical, restricted, methodological, technological, industrial.—*Ant.* ARTISTIC, nontechnical, simplified.

technician ***n.*** practitioner, professional, engineer; see CRAFTSMAN, SPECIALIST.

technique ***n.*** procedure, system, routine; see METHOD.

tedious ***a.*** slow, wearisome, tiresome; see DULL 4.

tedium ***n.*** boredom, tediousness, dullness; see MONOTONY.

teenage ***a.*** immature, youthful, adolescent; see YOUNG 1, 2.

teens ***n.*** boyhood, girlhood, adolescence, early adolescence, late adolescence, awkward age*; see also YOUTH 1.

teeter ***v.*** seesaw, totter, wobble; see SHAKE 1.

teeth ***n.*** dentition, fangs, tusks; see TOOTH.

teetotaler ***n.*** nondrinker, prohibitionist, prude, abstainer.

telegram ***n.*** wire, cable, cablegram, message, teletype copy, radiogram, call, report, summons, night message, night letter, day letter, news message, code message, signal, flash; see also COMMUNICATION.

telegraph ***n.*** Morse telegraph, wireless, transmitter; see COMMUNICATION, RADIO 2.

telegraph ***v.*** wire, send a wire, send a cable; see COMMUNICATE 2.

tel'e·mar'ket·ing ***n.*** the use of the telephone in selling, market research, promotion, etc. —**tel'e·mar'ket·er** ***n.***

tel·e·me·ter (tel'ə mēt'ər, tə lem'ət ər) ***n.*** a device for measuring and transmitting data about radiation, temperature, etc. from a remote point —**te·lem'e·try** ***n.***

te·lep·a·thy (tə lep'ə thē) ***n.*** ⟦TELE- + -PATHY⟧ *Parapsychology* extrasensory communication between minds —**tel·e·path·ic** (tel'ə path'ik) ***adj.***

tel·e·phone (tel'ə fōn') ***n.*** ⟦TELE- + -PHONE⟧ an instrument or system for conveying speech or computerized information over distances, usually by converting sound into electrical impulses sent through a wire —***vt.***, ***vi.*** **-phoned'**, **-phon'ing** to convey (a message) to (a person) by telephone —**tel'e·phon'ic** (-fän'ik) ***adj.***

te·leph·o·ny (tə lef'ə nē) ***n.*** the making or operation of telephones

tel·e·pho·to (tel'ə fōt'ō) ***adj.*** designating or of a camera lens that produces a large image of a distant object

tel'e·proc'ess·ing ***n.*** computerized data processing, over communication lines

tel'e·promp'ter (-prämp'tər) ***n.*** ⟦< *TelePrompTer*, a former trademark⟧ an electronic device that unrolls a speech, script, etc. line by line, as an aid to a speaker, etc. on TV

tel·e·scope (tel'ə skōp') ***n.*** ⟦see TELE- & -SCOPE⟧ an optical instrument for making distant objects appear nearer and larger —***vi.***, ***vt.*** **-scoped'**, **-scop'ing** to slide one into another like the tubes of a collapsible telescope —**tel'e·scop'ic** (-skäp'ik) ***adj.***

tel'e·thon' (-thän') ***n.*** ⟦TELE(VISION) + (MARA)THON⟧ a campaign, as on a lengthy telecast, seeking donations

Tel·e·type (tel'ə tīp') ***n.*** *trademark for* a former kind of telegraphic apparatus for transmitting typed messages —**tel'e·type'writ'er** ***n.***

tel·e·vise (tel'ə vīz') ***vt.***, ***vi.*** **-vised'**, **-vis'ing** to transmit by television

tel'e·vi'sion (-vizh'ən) ***n.*** **1** the process of transmitting images by converting light rays into electrical signals: the receiver reconverts the signals to reproduce the images on a screen **2** television broadcasting **3** a television receiving set **4** a television program or programs

tel·ex (tel'eks') ***n.*** ⟦TEL(ETYPEWRITER) + EX(CHANGE)⟧ **1** a teletypewriter which sends messages over telephone lines **2** a message sent in this way —***vt.*** to send by telex

tell (tel) ***vt.*** **told**, **tell'ing** ⟦OE *tellan,* calculate⟧ **1** to count; reckon *[to tell time]* **2** to narrate; relate *[to tell a story]* **3** to express in words; say *[to tell the truth]* **4** to reveal; disclose **5** to recognize; distinguish *[to tell twins apart]* **6** to inform *[tell me later]* **7** to order *[tell him to go]* —***vi.*** **1** to give an account or evidence (*of* something) **2** to be effective *[each blow told]* —**tell off** [Inf.] to rebuke severely —**tell on** **1** to have an adverse effect on **2** [Inf.] to inform against

tell'er ***n.*** **1** one who tells (a story, etc.) **2** a bank clerk who pays out or receives money

tell'ing ***adj.*** **1** forceful; striking **2** that reveals much —**tell'ing·ly** ***adv.***

tell'tale' ***adj.*** revealing what is meant to be kept secret or hidden

tel·ly (tel'ē) ***n.***, *pl.* **-lies** *Brit. inf. term for* TELEVISION

tem·blor (tem'blôr', -blər) ***n.*** ⟦Sp < *temblar,* to tremble⟧ EARTHQUAKE

te·mer·i·ty (tə mer'ə tē) ***n.*** ⟦< L *temere,* rashly⟧ foolish or rash boldness

temp[1] (temp) ***n.*** [Inf.] one who works at a place on a temporary basis

temp[2] *abbrev.* **1** temperature **2** temporary

tem·per (tem'pər) ***vt.*** ⟦< L *temperare,* regulate⟧ **1** to moderate, as by mingling with something else *[to temper blame with praise]* **2** to bring to the proper condition by some treatment *[to temper steel]* **3** to toughen —***n.*** **1** the degree of hardness and resiliency of a metal **2** frame of mind; disposition **3** calmness of mind: in **lose** (or **keep**) **one's temper** **4** a tendency to become angry **5** anger; rage

tem·per·a (tem'pər ə) ***n.*** ⟦It: see prec.⟧ a process of painting with pigments mixed with size, casein, or egg

tem·per·a·ment (tem'pər ə mənt, -prə mənt) ***n.*** ⟦see TEMPER⟧ **1** one's natural disposition; nature **2** a nature that is excitable, moody, etc. —**tem'per·a·men'tal** ***adj.***

tem·per·ance (tem'pər əns, -prəns) ***n.*** **1** self-restraint in conduct, indulgence of the appetites, etc.; moderation **2** moderation in drinking alcoholic liquors or total abstinence from them

tem·per·ate (tem'pər it, -prit) ***adj.*** ⟦see TEMPER⟧ **1** moderate, as in one's appetites, behavior, etc. **2** neither very hot nor very cold: said of climate, etc.

Temperate Zone either of the two zones of the earth (**North Temperate Zone** and **South Temperate Zone**) between the tropics and the polar circles

tem·per·a·ture (tem'pər ə chər, -prə chər) ***n.*** ⟦< L *temperatus,* temperate⟧ **1** the degree of hotness or coldness of anything **2** an excess of body heat over the normal; fever

tem·pered (tem'pərd) ***adj.*** **1** having been given the desired TEMPER (*n.* 1) **2** having a (specified) TEMPER (*n.* 2)

tem·pest (tem'pist) ***n.*** ⟦< L *tempus,* time⟧ a violent storm with high winds, esp. one accompanied by rain, hail, etc.

tem·pes·tu·ous (tem pes'cho͞o əs) ***adj.*** of or like a tempest; violent

tem·plate (tem'plit) ***n.*** ⟦< L *templum,* small timber⟧ a pattern, as a thin metal plate, for making an exact copy

THESAURUS

telepathy ***n.*** insight, premonition, extrasensory perception; see COMMUNICATION.

telephone ***n.*** phone, private phone, extension phone, radiophone, radiotelephone, car phone, cellular phone, cellphone, cordless phone, wireless phone, fax machine, mouthpiece, line, party line, long distance, extension, pay phone.

telephone ***v.*** call, call up, phone, ring, ring up, make a call to, dial, call on the phone, fax, put in a call to, phone up*, give a ring, give a buzz.

telephoned ***a.*** phoned, called, phoned in, rang, buzzed, faxed, reached by phone.

telescope ***n.*** field glasses, binoculars, opera glasses, glass, optical instrument, reflecting telescope, refracting telescope, radio telescope; see also GLASSES.

television ***n.*** TV, video, color television, home entertainment center, boob tube*, the tube*, the box*; see also STATION 5.

tell ***v.*** **1** [To inform] communicate, explain, instruct, direct, order, divulge, reveal, make known, utter, speak, report, recite, reel off, spit out, put before, let in on, open up to, give the facts, lay open, fill someone in, let on, let slip, level with, leave word, hand it to, lay before, break it to, break the news, add up, keep someone posted, let know, give out, leak, give notice, declare, acquaint with, advise, confess, impart, notify, represent, assert, mention, tell all, break down, give away, cough up*, come across with*, shoot*, come clean*, make a clean breast of; see also DISCUSS, SAY.—*Ant.* HIDE, keep secret, be silent. **2** [To deduce] know, understand, make out, perceive, ascertain, find out, recognize, be sure, differentiate, discriminate, determine, know for certain. —**tell off** rebuke, reprimand, chide; see SCOLD.

teller ***n.*** cashier, clerk, bank clerk; see WORKMAN.

telling ***a.*** crucial, conspicuous, significant; see EFFECTIVE, IMPORTANT 1.

temper ***n.*** **1** [State of mind] disposition, frame of mind, humor; see MOOD 1. **2** [An angry state of mind] furor, ire, passion; see ANGER, RAGE 1. **3** [The quality of being easily angered] impatience, excitability, touchiness, sourness, sensitivity, fretfulness, peevishness, irritability, ill humor, petulance, irascibility, crossness, churlishness, pugnacity, sullenness, grouchiness, huffiness.—*Ant.* PATIENCE, calmness, equanimity. **4** [The quality of induced hardness or toughness in materials] tensile strength, sturdiness, hardness; see FIRMNESS, STRENGTH. —**lose one's temper** become angry, get mad, fly off the handle*; see RAGE 1.

temper ***v.*** **1** [To soften or qualify] mitigate, pacify, moderate; see EASE 1, 2, SOFTEN. **2** [To toughen or harden] steel, stiffen, solidify, heat-treat; see also STRENGTHEN.

temperament ***n.*** character, disposition, constitution, nature, inner nature, quality, temper, spirit, mood, attitude, type, structure, makeup, humor, outlook, peculiarity, individuality, idiosyncrasy, distinctiveness, psychological habits, mentality, intellect, susceptibility, ego, inclination, tendency, turn of mind, frame of mind.

temperamental ***a.*** moody, sensitive, touchy; see IRRITABLE.

temperance ***n.*** moderation, abstinence, self-control; see RESTRAINT 1.

temperate ***a.*** **1** [Moderate] regulated, reasonable, fair; see MODERATE 4. **2** [Neither hot nor cold] medium, warm, balmy; see FAIR 3, MILD 2. **3** [Not given to drinking] abstemious, abstinent, restrained; see MODERATE 5.

temperature ***n.*** heat, warmth, cold, coolness, degrees above or below zero, sensation, comfort level, body heat, weather condition, climatic characteristic, thermal reading.

tempestuous ***a.*** raging, tumultuous, furious; see STORMY, TURBULENT.

tem·ple[1] (tem′pəl) ***n.*** ⟦< L *templum*⟧ **1** a building for the worship of God or gods **2** a large building for some special purpose *[a temple* of art*]*

tem·ple[2] (tem′pəl) ***n.*** ⟦< L *tempus*⟧ **1** the flat surface alongside the forehead, in front of each ear **2** either of the sidepieces of a pair of glasses

tem·po (tem′pō) ***n.***, *pl.* **-pos** or **-pi** (-pē) ⟦It < L *tempus,* time⟧ **1** the speed at which a musical composition is performed **2** rate of activity

tem·po·ral[1] (tem′pə rəl) ***adj.*** ⟦< L *tempus,* time⟧ **1** worldly; not spiritual **2** secular **3** of or limited by time

tem·po·ral[2] (tem′pə rəl) ***adj.*** of or near the temples (of the head)

tem′po·rar′y (-rer′ē) ***adj.*** ⟦< L *tempus,* time⟧ lasting only a while; not permanent —**tem′po·rar′i·ly** ***adv.***

tem′po·rize′ (-rīz′) ***vi.*** **-rized′**, **-riz′ing** to give temporary compliance, evade decision, etc., so as to gain time or avoid argument

tempt (tempt) ***vt.*** ⟦< L *temptare,* to test⟧ **1** to induce or entice, as to something immoral **2** to be inviting to; attract **3** to provoke or risk provoking (fate, etc.) **4** to incline strongly *[to be tempted* to accept*]* —**temp·ta·tion** (temp tā′shən) ***n.***

tempt·ress (temp′tris) ***n.*** a woman who tempts, esp. sexually

tem·pu·ra (tem′po͞o rä′, tem po͞or′ə) ***n.*** ⟦Jpn⟧ a Japanese dish of deep-fried shrimp, fish, vegetables, etc.

ten (ten) ***adj.***, ***n.*** ⟦OE⟧ one more than nine; 10; X

ten·a·ble (ten′ə bəl) ***adj.*** ⟦< L *tenere,* to hold⟧ that can be defended or believed —**ten′a·bil′i·ty** ***n.***

te·na·cious (tə nā′shəs) ***adj.*** ⟦< L *tenere,* to hold⟧ **1** holding firmly *[a tenacious* grip*]* **2** retentive *[a tenacious* memory*]* **3** strongly cohesive or adhesive **4** persistent; stubborn *[tenacious* courage*]* —**te·na′cious·ly** ***adv.*** —**te·nac·i·ty** (tə nas′ə tē) ***n.***

ten·ant (ten′ənt) ***n.*** ⟦see prec.⟧ **1** one who pays rent to occupy land, a building, etc. **2** an occupant —***vt.*** to hold as a tenant; occupy —**ten′an·cy**, *pl.* **-cies**, ***n.***

tenant farmer one who farms land owned by another and pays rent

Ten Commandments *Bible* the ten laws of moral and religious conduct given to Moses by God: Exodus 20:2-17

tend[1] (tend) ***vt.*** ⟦see ATTEND⟧ **1** to take care of **2** to manage or operate

tend[2] (tend) ***vi.*** ⟦< L *tendere,* to stretch⟧ **1** to be inclined, disposed, etc. (*to*) **2** to be directed (*to* or *toward*)

tend·en·cy (ten′dən sē) ***n.***, *pl.* **-cies** ⟦see prec.⟧ **1** an inclination to move or act in a particular direction or way **2** a course toward some object

ten·den·tious (ten den′shəs) ***adj.*** ⟦< Ger *tendenz,* TENDENCY⟧ advancing a definite point of view *[tendentious* writings*]* —**ten·den′tious·ly** ***adv.***

ten·der[1] (ten′dər) ***adj.*** ⟦< L *tener,* soft⟧ **1** soft and easily chewed, broken, cut, etc. **2** physically weak **3** immature **4** that requires careful handling **5** gentle or light **6** acutely sensitive, as to pain **7** sensitive to emotions, others' feelings, etc. —**ten′der·ly** ***adv.*** —**ten′der·ness** ***n.***

ten·der[2] (ten′dər) ***vt.*** ⟦see TEND[2]⟧ to offer formally —***n.*** **1** a formal offer **2** money, etc. offered in payment

tend·er[3] (ten′dər) ***n.*** **1** one who tends something **2** a small ship for supplying a larger one **3** a railroad car attached behind, and carrying fuel and water for, a steam locomotive

ten′der·foot′ ***n.***, *pl.* **-foots′** or **-feet′** **1** a newcomer to ranching in the West, unused to hardships **2** any novice

ten′der·heart′ed ***adj.*** quick to feel pity or compassion

ten·der·ize (ten′dər īz′) ***vt.*** **-ized′**, **-iz′ing** to make (meat) tender

ten′der·loin′ ***n.*** the tenderest part of a loin of beef, pork, etc.

ten·di·ni·tis (ten′də nīt′is) ***n.*** inflammation of a tendon

ten·don (ten′dən) ***n.*** ⟦< Gr *teinein,* to stretch⟧ any of the inelastic cords of tough, connective tissue by which muscles are attached to bones, etc.

ten·dril (ten′drəl) ***n.*** ⟦prob. ult. < L *tener,* delicate⟧ a threadlike, clinging part of a climbing plant

ten·e·ment (ten′ə mənt) ***n.*** ⟦< L *tenere,* to hold⟧ a building divided into tenements; now specif., one that is rundown, overcrowded, etc.: in full **tenement house**

ten·et (ten′it) ***n.*** ⟦L, he holds⟧ a principle, doctrine, or belief held as a truth, as by some group

Ten·nes·see (ten′ə sē′) state of the EC U.S.: 41,220 sq. mi.; pop. 4,877,000; cap. Nashville: abbrev. *TN* —**Ten′nes·se′an** ***adj.***, ***n.***

ten·nis (ten′is) ***n.*** ⟦prob. < OFr *tener,* hold (imperative)⟧ a game in which players in a marked area (**tennis court**) hit a ball back and forth with rackets over a net

tennis elbow inflammation of the elbow tendons, caused by strain

tennis shoe a sneaker

Ten·ny·son (ten′i sən), **Al·fred** (al′frəd) 1809-92; Eng. poet: called *Alfred, Lord Tennyson*

ten·on (ten′ən) ***n.*** ⟦ult. < L *tenere,* to hold⟧ a projecting part cut on the end of a piece of wood for insertion into a mortise to make a joint

ten·or (ten′ər) ***n.*** ⟦< L *tenere,* to hold⟧ **1** general tendency **2** general meaning; drift **3** *a)* the range of the highest regular adult male voice *b)* a voice, singer, or instrument with such a range *c)* a part for a tenor —***adj.*** of or for a tenor

ten′pins′ ***n.*** the game of bowling in which ten pins are used

tense[1] (tens) ***adj.*** **tens′er**, **tens′est** ⟦< L *tendere,* to stretch⟧ **1** stretched tight; taut **2** feeling or showing tension —***vt.***, ***vi.*** **tensed**, **tens′ing** to make or become tense

tense[2] (tens) ***n.*** ⟦< L *tempus,* time⟧ any of the forms of a verb that show the time of its action or existence

ten·sile (ten′səl) ***adj.*** **1** of, undergoing, or exerting tension **2** capable of being stretched

THESAURUS

temple[1] ***n.*** house of prayer, synagogue, pagoda; see CHURCH 1.

tempo ***n.*** pace, rate, meter; see SPEED.

temporal[1] ***a.*** **1** [Transitory] fleeting, transient, ephemeral; see TEMPORARY. **2** [Worldly] secular, earthly, mundane; see WORLDLY.

temporarily ***a.*** momentarily, briefly, tentatively, for a while, for the moment, for a time, provisionally, transitorily, for the time being, pro tempore, pro tem.—*Ant.* FOREVER, perpetually, perennially.

temporary ***a.*** transitory, transient, fleeting, short, brief, ephemeral, fugitive, volatile, shifting, momentary, passing, summary, stopgap, makeshift, substitute, for the time being, overnight, ad hoc, impermanent, irregular, changeable, unenduring, unfixed, unstable, perishable, provisional, short-lived, mortal, pro tem, on the fly*, on the wing, here today and gone tomorrow*.—*Ant.* PERMANENT, fixed, eternal.

tempt ***v.*** lure, fascinate, seduce, appeal to, induce, intrigue, incite, provoke, allure, charm, captivate, entice, draw out, bait, stimulate, move, motivate, rouse, instigate, wheedle, coax, inveigle, vamp, make a play for*, make someone's mouth water.

temptation ***n.*** lure, attraction, fascination; see APPEAL 2.

tempted ***a.*** desiring, inclined, enticed; see CHARMED.

tempting ***a.*** appetizing, attractive, fascinating; see CHARMING.

ten ***a.*** tenth, tenfold, decuple, denary, decimal.

tenant ***n.*** renter, lessee, householder, rent payer, dweller, inhabitant, occupant, resident, roomer, lodger, holder, possessor, leaseholder, tenant farmer; see also RESIDENT.—*Ant.* OWNER, proprietor, landlord.

tend[1,2] ***v.*** **1** [To watch over] care for, direct, superintend, do, perform, accomplish, guard, administer, minister to, oversee, wait upon, attend, serve, nurse, mind; see also MANAGE 1. **2** [To have a tendency (toward)] lead, point, direct, make for, result in, serve to, be in the habit of, favor, be predisposed to, be prejudiced in favor of, be apt to, gravitate toward, incline to, verge on.

tendency ***n.*** **1** [Direction] aim, bent, trend; see DRIFT 1. **2** [Inclination] leaning, bias, bent; see INCLINATION 1.

tender[1] ***a.*** **1** [Soft] delicate, fragile, supple; see SOFT 2. **2** [Kind] loving, solicitous, compassionate; see KIND. **3** [Touching] moving, pathetic, affecting; see PITIFUL. **4** [Sensitive] touchy, ticklish, oversensitive; see RAW 5, SORE 1.

tenderhearted ***a.*** softhearted, tender, sensitive; see HUMANE, KIND, MERCIFUL.

tenderly ***a.*** **1** [Softly] gently, carefully, delicately; see LIGHTLY. **2** [Lovingly] fondly, affectionately, appreciatively; see LOVINGLY.

tenderness ***n.*** fondness, consideration, care; see FRIENDSHIP, KINDNESS 1.

tennis ***n.*** lawn tennis, court tennis, tennis tournament; see SPORT 3.

tennis shoes ***n.*** sneakers, gym shoes, canvas shoes, tennies*, cross-training shoes, high-tops, athletic shoes, trainers, running shoes; see also SHOE.

tense[1] ***a.*** **1** [Nervous] agitated, anxious, high-strung, on edge, fluttery, jumpy, jittery; see also EXCITED.—*Ant.* CALM, unconcerned, indifferent. **2** [Stretched tight] rigid, stiff, firm; see TIGHT 1.

ten·sion (ten′shən) ***n.*** **1** a tensing or being tensed **2** mental or nervous strain **3** a state of strained relations due to mutual hostility **4** VOLTAGE **5** stress on a material produced by the pull of forces causing extension

tent (tent) ***n.*** ⟦< L *tendere,* to stretch⟧ a portable shelter made of canvas, etc. stretched over poles —***vi., vt.*** to lodge in a tent or tents

ten·ta·cle (ten′tə kəl) ***n.*** ⟦< L *tentare,* to touch⟧ a long, slender, flexible growth on the head of some invertebrates, used to grasp, feel, etc.

ten·ta·tive (ten′tə tiv) ***adj.*** ⟦< L *tentare,* to try⟧ **1** made, done, etc. provisionally; not final **2** indicating timidity or uncertainty —**ten′ta·tive·ly** ***adv.***

ten·ter·hook (ten′tər ho͝ok′) ***n.*** ⟦< L *tendere,* to stretch + HOOK⟧ a kind of hooked nail —**on tenterhooks** in anxious suspense

tenth (tenth) ***adj.*** ⟦OE *teogotha*⟧ preceded by nine others in a series; 10th —***n.*** **1** the one following the ninth **2** any of the ten equal parts of something; $\frac{1}{10}$

ten·u·ous (ten′yo͞o əs) ***adj.*** ⟦< L *tenuis,* thin⟧ **1** slender or fine, as a fiber **2** rare, as air at high altitudes **3** flimsy *[tenuous evidence]*

ten·ure (ten′yər) ***n.*** ⟦< medieval Fr < *tenir,* to hold⟧ **1** the act or right of holding property, an office, etc. **2** the length of time, or the conditions under which, something is held **3** the status of holding one's position on a permanent basis, granted to teachers, etc.

te·pee (tē′pē) ***n.*** ⟦< AmInd *tʰipi,* dwelling⟧ a cone-shaped tent used by some North American Indians

tep·id (tep′id) ***adj.*** ⟦< L *tepidus*⟧ **1** lukewarm **2** lacking enthusiasm

te·qui·la (tə kē′lə) ***n.*** ⟦< AmInd (Mexico) *Tuiquila,* region in Mexico⟧ an alcoholic liquor of Mexico, distilled from an agave mash

ter·cen·te·nar·y (tʉr′sen ten′ər ē, tər sen′tə ner′ē) ***adj., n.***, *pl.* **-ies** ⟦L *ter,* three times + CENTENARY⟧ TRICENTENNIAL

term (tʉrm) ***n.*** ⟦< L *terminus,* a limit⟧ **1** a set date, as for payment, etc. **2** a set period of time *[school term, term of office]* **3** [*pl.*] conditions of a contract, etc. **4** [*pl.*] mutual relationship between persons *[on speaking terms]* **5** a word or phrase, esp. as used in some science, art, etc. **6** [*pl.*] words; speech *[unkind terms]* **7** *Math. a*) either quantity of a fraction or a ratio *b*) each quantity in a series or algebraic expression —***vt.*** to call by a term; name —**bring** (or **come**) **to terms** to force into (or arrive at) an agreement

ter·ma·gant (tʉr′mə gənt) ***n.*** ⟦< OFr *Tervagant,* imaginary Muslim deity⟧ a quarrelsome, scolding woman

ter·mi·na·ble (tʉr′mi nə bəl) ***adj.*** that can be, or is, terminated

ter·mi·nal (tʉr′mə nəl) ***adj.*** ⟦L *terminalis*⟧ **1** of, at, or forming the end or extremity **2** concluding; final **3** close to causing death *[terminal cancer]* **4** of or at the end of a transportation line —***n.*** **1** an end; extremity **2** a connective point on an electric circuit **3** either end of a transportation line, or a main station on it **4** a device, usually with a keyboard and video display, for putting data in, or getting it from, a computer

ter·mi·nate (tʉr′mə nāt′) ***vt.*** **-nat′ed, -nat′ing** ⟦< L *terminus,* a limit⟧ **1** to form the end of **2** to put an end to; stop **3** to dismiss from employment; fire —***vi.*** **1** to come to an end **2** to have its end (*in* something) —**ter′mi·na′tion** ***n.***

ter·mi·nol·o·gy (tʉr′mə näl′ə jē) ***n.***, *pl.* **-gies** the terms used in a specific science, art, etc.

term insurance life insurance that expires after a specified period

ter·mi·nus (tʉr′mə nəs) ***n.***, *pl.* **-ni′** (-nī′) or **-nus·es** ⟦L, a limit⟧ **1** a limit **2** an end; extremity or goal **3** [Chiefly Brit.] either end of a transportation line

ter·mite (tʉr′mīt′) ***n.*** ⟦< L *tarmes,* wood-boring worm⟧ a social insect that is very destructive to wooden structures

tern (tʉrn) ***n.*** ⟦< ON *therna*⟧ a gull-like seabird with webbed feet and a straight bill

ter·race (ter′əs) ***n.*** ⟦< L *terra,* earth⟧ **1** a raised, flat mound of earth with sloping sides, esp. one in a series on a hillside **2** an unroofed, paved area, between a house and lawn **3** a row of houses on ground above street level **4** a small, usually roofed balcony, as outside an apartment —***vt.*** **-raced, -rac·ing** to form into a terrace or terraces

ter·ra cot·ta (ter′ə kät′ə) ⟦It, lit., baked earth⟧ a hard, brown-red earthenware, or its color

ter·ra fir·ma (ter′ə fʉr′mə) ⟦L⟧ firm earth

ter·rain (tə rān′) ***n.*** ⟦< L *terra,* earth⟧ a tract of ground, as with regard to its features

ter·ra·pin (ter′ə pin) ***n.*** ⟦< Algonquian⟧ **1** any of various terrestrial, freshwater or tidewater turtles **2** its edible flesh

ter·rar·i·um (tə rer′ē əm) ***n.***, *pl.* **-i·ums** or **-i·a** (-ə) ⟦< L *terra,* earth + *-arium,* as in *aquarium*⟧ an enclosure, as of glass, in which small plants are grown or small land animals are kept

ter·raz·zo (tə raz′ō, tə rät′sō) ***n.*** ⟦It⟧ flooring of small chips of marble set in cement and polished

ter·res·tri·al (tə res′trē əl) ***adj.*** ⟦< L *terra,* earth⟧ **1** worldly; mundane **2** of the earth **3** consisting of land, not water **4** living on land

ter·ri·ble (ter′ə bəl) ***adj.*** ⟦< L *terrere,* frighten⟧ **1** causing terror; dreadful **2** extreme; intense **3** [Inf.] very unpleasant, etc. —**ter′ri·bly** ***adv.***

ter·ri·er (ter′ē ər) ***n.*** ⟦< medieval Fr *(chien) terrier,* hunting (dog)⟧ any of several breeds of small and typically aggressive dog

ter·rif·ic (tə rif′ik) ***adj.*** ⟦< L *terrere,* frighten⟧ **1** causing great fear **2** [Inf.] *a*) very great, intense, etc. *b*) unusually fine, admirable, etc.

ter·ri·fy (ter′ə fī′) ***vt.*** **-fied′, -fy′ing** to fill with terror; frighten greatly

ter·ri·to·ry (ter′ə tôr′ē) ***n.***, *pl.* **-ries** ⟦< L *terra,* earth⟧ **1** an area under the jurisdiction of a nation, ruler, etc. **2** a part of a country or empire that does not have full status **3** any large tract of land **4** an assigned area **5** a sphere of action, thought, etc. —**ter′ri·to′ri·al** ***adj.***

THESAURUS

tension ***n.*** **1** [Stress] tautness, force, tightness; see BALANCE 2, STRESS 2. **2** [Mental stress] pressure, strain, anxiety; see STRESS 2.

tent ***n.*** shelter, canvas, canopy, tarpaulin, covering; see also COVER 1. *Tentlike coverings include the following:* umbrella tent, awning, marquee, wigwam, tepee, booth, pavilion, pup tent, fly tent, lean-to tent, circus tent, big top*.

tentative ***a.*** provisional, probationary, makeshift; see EXPERIMENTAL.

tentatively ***a.*** experimentally, conditionally, provisionally; see TEMPORARILY.

tepee ***n.*** Indian tent, wigwam, wickiup; see TENT.

term ***n.*** **1** [A name] expression, terminology, phrase, word, locution, indication, denomination, article, appellation, designation, title, head, caption, nomenclature, moniker*; see also NAME 1. **2** [A period of time] span, interval, course, cycle, season, duration, phase, quarter, course of time, semester, school period, session, period of confinement; see also TIME 2. —**come to terms** compromise, arrive at an agreement, arbitrate; see AGREE. —**in terms of** in reference to, about, concerning; see REGARDING.

terminal ***a.*** final, concluding, ending; see LAST 1.

terminal ***n.*** **1** [An end] limit, extremity, terminus; see END 4. **2** [Part of a computer] PC, workstation, personal computer; see COMPUTER.

terminate ***v.*** complete, end, perfect; see ACHIEVE.

terminology ***n.*** nomenclature, vocabulary, argot; see JARGON 2, LANGUAGE 1.

terms ***n.*** **1** [Conditions] details, items, points, particulars; see also CIRCUMSTANCES 2. **2** [An agreement] understanding, treaty, conclusion; see AGREEMENT 1.

terrace ***n.*** patio, garden, lawn; see GARDEN, YARD 1.

terra firma ***n.*** solid ground, land, soil; see EARTH 2.

terrain ***n.*** ground, region, territory; see AREA.

terrible ***a.*** **1** [Inspiring terror] terrifying, appalling, fearful, awesome, horrifying, ghastly, awe-inspiring, petrifying, revolting, gruesome, shocking, unnerving; see also FRIGHTFUL.—*Ant.* HAPPY, joyful, pleasant. **2** [*Unpleasant] disastrous, inconvenient, disturbing, awful, horrible*, atrocious*, lousy*; see also OFFENSIVE 2.—*Ant.* WELCOME, good, attractive.

terribly* ***a.*** horribly, frightfully, drastically; see BADLY 1, VERY.

terrific ***a.*** shocking, immense, tremendous; see GREAT 1, LARGE 1.

terrify ***v.*** shock, horrify, terrorize; see FRIGHTEN.

territorial ***a.*** regional, sectional, provincial; see NATIONAL 1.

territory ***n.*** **1** [A specified area] region, township, empire; see AREA. **2** [An area organized politically under the central government] commonwealth, colony, protectorate; see NATION 1. **3** [An indefinite area] section, area, boundary; see REGION 1.

ter·ror (ter′ər) ***n.*** ⟦< L *terrere,* frighten⟧ **1** intense fear **2** *a)* one that causes intense fear *b)* the quality of causing such fear **3** [Inf.] one who is very annoying or unmanageable, esp. a child

ter′ror·ism′ ***n.*** the use of force or threats to intimidate, etc., esp. as a political policy —**ter′ror·ist** ***n., adj.***

ter′ror·ize′ (-īz′) ***vt.*** **-ized′, -iz′ing** **1** to terrify **2** to coerce, make submit, etc. by filling with terror

ter·ry (ter′ē) ***n.*** ⟦prob. < Fr *tirer,* to draw⟧ cloth having a pile of uncut loops, esp. cotton cloth used for toweling: also **terry cloth**

terse (tʉrs) ***adj.*** **ters′er, ters′est** ⟦L *tersus,* wiped off⟧ free of superfluous words; concise; succinct —**terse′ly** ***adv.*** —**terse′ness** ***n.***

ter·ti·ar·y (tʉr′shē er′ē) ***adj.*** ⟦< L *tertius,* third⟧ third in order

tes·sel·late (tes′ə lāt′) ***vt.*** **-lat′ed, -lat′ing** ⟦< L *tessella,* little square stone⟧ to lay out in a mosaic pattern of small, square blocks

test (test) ***n.*** ⟦< OFr, assaying cup⟧ **1** *a)* an examination or trial, as of something's value *b)* the method or a criterion used in this **2** an event, etc. that tries one's qualities **3** a set of questions, etc. for determining one's knowledge, etc. **4** *Chem.* a trial or reaction for identifying a substance —***vt.*** to subject to a test; try —***vi.*** to be rated by a test

tes·ta·ment (tes′tə mənt) ***n.*** ⟦< L *testis,* a witness⟧ **1** [T-] either of the two parts of the Bible, the *Old Testament* and the *New Testament* **2** *a)* a testimonial *b)* an affirmation of beliefs **3** *Law* a will —**tes′ta·men′ta·ry** (-men′tə rē) ***adj.***

tes·tate (tes′tāt′) ***adj.*** ⟦< L *testari,* make a will⟧ having left a legally valid will

tes·ta·tor (tes′tāt′ər, tes tāt′-) ***n.*** one who has made a will

tes·ti·cle (tes′ti kəl) ***n.*** ⟦< L *testis*⟧ either of two male sex glands

tes·ti·fy (tes′tə fī′) ***vi.*** **-fied′, -fy′ing** ⟦< L *testis,* a witness + *facere,* to make⟧ **1** to give evidence, esp. under oath in court **2** to serve as evidence —***vt.*** to affirm; declare, esp. under oath in court

tes·ti·mo·ni·al (tes′tə mō′nē əl) ***n.*** **1** a statement recommending a person or thing **2** something given or done to show gratitude or appreciation

tes·ti·mo·ny (tes′tə mō′nē) ***n.,*** *pl.* **-nies** ⟦< L *testis,* a witness⟧ **1** a statement made under oath to establish a fact **2** any declaration **3** any form of evidence; proof

tes·tis (tes′tis) ***n.,*** *pl.* **-tes′** (-tēz′) ⟦L⟧ TESTICLE

tes·tos·ter·one (tes täs′tər ōn′) ***n.*** ⟦see TESTICLE⟧ a male sex hormone

test tube a tube of thin, transparent glass closed at one end, used in chemical experiments, etc.

tes·ty (tes′tē) ***adj.*** **-ti·er, -ti·est** ⟦< L *testa,* the head⟧ irritable; touchy

tet·a·nus (tet′'n əs, tet′nəs) ***n.*** ⟦< Gr *tetanos,* spasm⟧ an acute infectious disease, often fatal, caused by a toxin and characterized by spasmodic contractions and rigidity of muscles

tête-à-tête (tāt′ə tāt′) ***n.*** ⟦Fr, lit., head-to-head⟧ a private conversation between two people

teth·er (te*th*′ər) ***n.*** ⟦< ON *tjōthr*⟧ **1** a rope or chain fastened to an animal to keep it from roaming **2** the limit of one's abilities, resources, etc. —***vt.*** to fasten with a tether

tet·ra (te′trə) ***n.*** ⟦< ModL⟧ a brightly colored, tropical American fish

tetra- ⟦Gr < *tettares,* four⟧ *combining form* four

tet·ra·cy·cline (te′trə sī′klin) ***n.*** a yellow, crystalline compound, used as an antibiotic

tet·ra·he·dron (te′trə hē′drən) ***n.,*** *pl.* **-drons** or **-dra** (-drə) ⟦see TETRA- & -HEDRON⟧ a solid figure with four triangular faces

te·tram·e·ter (te tram′ət ər) ***n.*** ⟦see TETRA- & METER[1]⟧ **1** a line of verse containing four metrical feet **2** verse consisting of tetrameters

Teu·ton·ic (to͞o tän′ik) ***adj.*** designating or of a group of north European peoples, esp. the Germans —**Teu·ton** (to͞ot′'n) ***n.***

Tex·as (tek′səs) state of the SW U.S.: 261,914 sq. mi.; pop. 16,987,000; cap. Austin: abbrev. *TX* —**Tex′an** ***adj., n.***

text (tekst) ***n.*** ⟦< L *texere,* to weave⟧ **1** the actual words of an author, as distinguished from notes, etc. **2** any form in which a written work exists **3** the principal matter on a printed page, as distinguished from notes, headings, etc. **4** *a)* a Biblical passage used as the topic of a sermon, etc. *b)* any topic or subject **5** *short for* TEXTBOOK —**tex·tu·al** (teks′cho͞o əl) ***adj.***

text′book′ ***n.*** a book giving instructions in a subject of study —***adj.*** so typical as to be a classic example or model of its kind

tex·tile (teks′tīl′, -təl) ***adj.*** ⟦see TEXT⟧ **1** having to do with weaving **2** that has been or can be woven —***n.*** **1** a woven or knitted fabric; cloth **2** raw material suitable for this

tex·ture (teks′chər) ***n.*** ⟦< L *texere,* to weave⟧ **1** the character of a fabric, determined by the arrangement, size, etc. of its threads **2** the arrangement of the constituent parts of anything —**tex′tur·al** ***adj.***

tex′tured ***adj.*** having an uneven surface; not smooth *[textured* wallpaper*]*

-th[1] ⟦OE⟧ *suffix* **1** the act of ___ing *[growth]* **2** the state or quality of being or having *[wealth]*

-th[2] ⟦< OE⟧ *suffix* forming ordinal numerals *[fourth, ninth]*

Th *Chem. symbol for* thorium

Thai (tī) ***n.*** **1** *pl.* **Thais** or **Thai** a person born or living in Thailand **2** the language of Thailand **3** *alt. sp. of* TAI —***adj.*** of Thailand or its people, culture, etc.

Thai·land (tī′land′) country in SE Asia: 198,114 sq. mi.; pop. 54,532,000

thal·a·mus (thal′ə məs) ***n.,*** *pl.* **-mi′** (-mī′) ⟦< Gr *thalamos,* inner chamber⟧ a mass of gray matter at the base of the brain, involved in the transmission of certain sensations

tha·lid·o·mide (thə lid′ə mīd′) ***n.*** a drug formerly used as a sedative, but found to cause severe birth deformities when taken in pregnancy

thal·lo·phyte (thal′ə fīt′) ***n.*** ⟦< Gr *thallos,* young shoot + *phyton,* a plant⟧ any of a large group of plants lacking true roots, leaves, or stems, as the fungi, the lichens, and most algae

Thames (temz) river in S England, flowing through London into the North Sea

than (*th*an) ***conj.*** ⟦OE *thenne*⟧ introducing the second element in a comparison *[*A is taller *than* B*]*

thank (thaŋk) ***vt.*** ⟦OE *thancian*⟧ **1** to express gratitude to, as by saying "thank you" **2** to blame: an ironic use —**thank you** *short for* I thank you

THESAURUS

terror ***n.*** fright, horror, panic; see FEAR.

terrorist ***n.*** subversive, revolutionary, incendiary; see REBEL.

terrorize ***v.*** coerce, intimidate, browbeat; see THREATEN.

test ***n.*** **1** [A check for adequacy] inspection, analysis, countdown, probing, inquiry, inquest, elimination, proving grounds, search, dry run*; see also EXAMINATION 1, EXPERIMENT. *Tests include the following:* technical, structural, mechanical, chemical, psychological, mental, intelligence, IQ, intelligence quotient, aptitude, vocational, qualifying, comprehensive, written, true-false, multiple-choice, objective, diagnostic, semester, term, psychiatric. **2** [A formal examination] quiz, questionnaire, essay; see EXAMINATION 2.

test ***v.*** inquire, question, try out; see EXAMINE, EXPERIMENT.

tested ***a.*** examined, tried, proven; see ESTABLISHED 2, RELIABLE.

tester ***n.*** validator, examiner, lab assistant; see INSPECTOR.

testify ***v.*** **1** [To demonstrate] indicate, show, make evident; see PROVE. **2** [To bear witness] affirm, give evidence, swear, swear to, attest, witness, bear witness, give one's word, certify, warrant, depose, vouch, give the facts, stand up for, say a good word for. **3** [To declare] assert, attest, claim; see DECLARE.

testimony ***n.*** **1** [The act of stating] attestation, statement, assertion; see DECLARATION. **2** [Evidence] grounds, facts, data; see PROOF. **3** [Statement] deposition, affidavit, affirmation; see DECLARATION.

text ***n.*** **1** [A textbook] required reading, manual, handbook; see BOOK. **2** [A subject, expecially a verse from the Bible] quotation, stanza, passage; see SUBJECT. **3** [Writing, considered for its authenticity] lines, textual evidence, document; see MANUSCRIPT, WRITING 2.

texture ***n.*** **1** [Quality] character, disposition, fineness, roughness, coarseness, feeling, feel, sense, flexibility, stiffness, smoothness, taste; see also FIBER. **2** [Structure] composition, organization, arrangement; see CONSTRUCTION 2, FORM 2.

thank ***v.*** be obliged, show gratitude, give thanks, acknowledge, show appreciation, be obligated to, be indebted to, bless, praise, smile on, show courtesy, express one's obligation to; see also APPRECIATE 1.—*Ant.* NEGLECT, ignore, show indifference.

thanked ***a.*** blessed, applauded, appreciated; see PRAISED.

thank'ful *adj.* feeling or expressing thanks —**thank'ful·ly** *adv.*
thank'less *adj.* **1** not feeling or expressing thanks; ungrateful **2** unappreciated
thanks (thaŋks) *pl.n.* an expression of gratitude —*interj.* I thank you —**thanks to 1** let thanks be given to **2** on account of; because of
thanks'giv'ing *n.* **1** a formal public expression of thanks to God **2** [T-] an annual U.S. holiday observed on the fourth Thursday of November
that (*th*at) *pron.*, *pl.* **those** ⟦OE *thæt*⟧ **1** the person or thing mentioned *[that* is John*]* **2** the farther one or the other one *[*this is better than *that]* **3** who, whom, or which *[*the road *that* we took*]* **4** where *[*the place *that* I saw her*]* **5** when *[*the year *that* I was born*]* —*adj.*, *pl.* **those 1** designating the one mentioned *[that* man is John*]* **2** designating the farther one or the other one *[*this house is larger than *that* one*]* —*conj.* subordinating conjunction used to introduce: *a)* a noun clause *[that* she's gone is obvious*]* *b)* an adverbial clause expressing purpose *[*they died *that* we might live*]*, result *[*I ran so fast *that* I won*]*, or cause *[*I'm glad *that* I won*]* *c)* an elliptical sentence expressing surprise, desire, etc. *[*oh, *that* she were here!*]* —*adv.* to that extent *[*I can't see *that* far*]* —**at that** [Inf.] **1** at that point: also **with that 2** even so —**that is 1** to be specific **2** in other words
thatch (thach) *n.* ⟦OE *thæc*⟧ **1** a roof of straw, rushes, etc. **2** material for such a roof: also **thatch'ing 3** a layer of tangled, partly decayed leaves, stems, etc. lying on top of the soil —*vt.* to cover as with thatch
thaw (thô) *vi.* ⟦OE *thawian*⟧ **1** *a)* to melt (said of ice, snow, etc.) *b)* to pass to an unfrozen state (said of frozen foods) **2** to become warmer so that snow, etc. melts **3** to lose one's coldness of manner —*vt.* to cause to thaw —*n.* **1** a thawing **2** a spell of weather warm enough to allow thawing
THC *n.* ⟦*t(etra)h(ydro)c(annabinol)*⟧ the principal and most active chemical in marijuana
ThD or **Th.D.** *abbrev.* ⟦L *Theologiae Doctor*⟧ Doctor of Theology
the (*th*ə; *before vowels th*ē, *th*i) *adj.*, *definite article* ⟦< OE *se* with *th-* from other forms⟧ *the* (as opposed to *a, an*) refers to: **1** a particular person, thing, or group *[the* story ended; *the* President*]* **2** a person or thing considered generically *[the* cow is a domestic animal; *the* poor*]* —*adv.* **1** that much *[the* better to see you with*]* **2** by how much . . . by that much *[the* sooner *the* better*]*
the·a·ter or **the·a·tre** (thē'ə tər) *n.* ⟦< Gr *theasthai,* to view⟧ **1** a place, esp. a building, where plays, operas, films, etc. are presented **2** any similar place with banked rows of seats **3** any place where events occur **4** *a)* the dramatic art *b)* the theatrical world
the·at·ri·cal (thē a'tri kəl) *adj.* **1** having to do with the theater **2** dramatic; esp. (in disparagement), melodramatic —**the·at'ri·cal·ly** *adv.*
thee (*th*ē) *pron.* ⟦OE *the*⟧ [Archaic] *objective form of* THOU
theft (theft) *n.* ⟦OE *thiefth*⟧ the act or an instance of stealing; larceny
their (*th*er) *poss. pronominal adj.* ⟦< ON *theirra*⟧ of, belonging to, or done by them
theirs (*th*erz) *pron.* that or those belonging to them: poss. form of THEY *[*that book is *theirs*; *theirs* are better*]*
the·ism (thē'iz'əm) *n.* ⟦< Gr *theos,* god⟧ **1** belief in a god or gods **2** MONOTHEISM —**the'ist** *n., adj.* —**the·is'tic** *adj.*
them (*th*em) *pron.* ⟦< ON *theim*⟧ *objective form of* THEY
theme (thēm) *n.* ⟦< Gr *thema,* what is laid down⟧ **1** a topic, as of an essay **2** a short essay **3** a short melody used as the subject of a musical composition **4** a recurring or identifying song in a film, musical, radio or TV series, etc.: in full **theme song** —**the·mat·ic** (thē mat'ik) *adj.*
them·selves (*th*em selvz') *pron.* a form of THEY, used as an intensive *[*they went *themselves]*, as a reflexive *[*they hurt *themselves]*, or with the meaning "their true selves" *[*they are not *themselves* when they are sick*]*
then (*th*en) *adv.* ⟦see THAN⟧ **1** at that time *[*he was young *then]* **2** next in time or order *[*he took his hat and *then* left*]* **3** in that case; accordingly *[*if she read it, *then* she knows*]* **4** besides; moreover *[*he likes to walk, and *then* it's good exercise*]* **5** at another time *[*now it's warm, *then* freezing*]* —*adj.* being such at that time *[*the *then* director*]* —*n.* that time *[*by *then*, they were gone*]*
thence (*th*ens) *adv.* ⟦OE *thanan*⟧ **1** from that place **2** from that time; thenceforth
thence'forth' *adv.* from that time onward; thereafter: also **thence·for'ward**
the·oc·ra·cy (thē äk'rə sē) *n., pl.* **-cies** ⟦< Gr *theos*, god + *kratos*, rule, power⟧ **1** government by a person or persons claiming divine authority **2** a country with this form of government
the·o·lo·gi·an (thē'ə lō'jən) *n.* a student of or specialist in theology
the·ol·o·gy (thē äl'ə jē) *n.* ⟦< Gr *theos*, god + *logos*, word⟧ the study of God and of religious doctrines and matters of divinity —**the'o·log'i·cal** (-ə läj'i kəl) *adj.*
the·o·rem (thē'ə rəm, thir'əm) *n.* ⟦< Gr *theōrein,* to view⟧ **1** a proposition that can be proved from accepted premises; law or principle **2** *Math., Physics* a proposition embodying something to be proved
the·o·ret·i·cal (thē'ə ret'i kəl) *adj.* **1** limited to or based on theory; hypothetical **2** tending to theorize; speculative Also **the'o·ret'ic** —**the'o·ret'i·cal·ly** *adv.*

THESAURUS

thankful *a.* obliged, grateful, gratified, contented, satisfied, indebted, pleased, kindly disposed, appreciative, giving thanks, overwhelmed.
thankless *a.* **1** [Not returning thanks] unappreciative, ungrateful, self-centered; see CRUEL, RUDE 2. **2** [Not eliciting thanks] poorly paid, unappreciated, unrewarded; see USELESS 1.
thanks *n.* appreciation, thankfulness, acknowledgment, recognition, gratitude, gratefulness.—*Ant.* BLAME, censure, criticism.
thanks *interj.* thank you, I thank you, much obliged, I appreciate it*.
Thanksgiving *n.* harvest festival, last Thursday in November, day of gratitude; see CELEBRATION, FEAST, HOLIDAY.
that *conj.* in that, so, so that, in order that, to the end that, for the reason that; see also BECAUSE.
that *a.* the, this, one, a certain, the indicated, the past, the future, the previously mentioned, a certain, a particular, not this.
that *pron.* the one, that one, this one, the one in question, that fact, that person, the thing indicated, the aforementioned one, who, which. —**at that*** even so, all things considered, anyway; see ANYHOW. —**not all that*** not so very, not so, rather less; see NOT.
thaw *v.* liquefy, flow, run, liquate, fuse, become liquid; see also DISSOLVE, MELT 1.—*Ant.* FREEZE, congeal, refrigerate.
the *a., definite article* **1** [The definite article] some, a few, a particular, a special, a specific, a certain, an individual, this, that, each, every, these, those, the whole, the entire. **2** [Special or unique; *often italics*] preeminent, outstanding, particular, supreme, unparalleled, unequaled, unsurpassed, unusual, uncommon, rare, singular, unprecedented, exceptional, one, sole, single, significant, distinguished, specific, choice, individual, peculiar, exceptional, occasional, unfamiliar, strange, spectacular, phenomenal, unheard-of, unknown, unattainable, invincible, almighty, all-powerful; see also SPECIAL, UNIQUE.—*Ant.* COMMON, USUAL, ordinary.
theater *n.* **1** [A building intended for theatrical productions] playhouse, concert hall, coliseum; see AUDITORIUM. **2** [The legitimate stage] stage, drama, Broadway; see COMEDY, MOVIES 2.
theatrical *a.* ceremonious, meretricious, superficial; see AFFECTED 2.
theft *n.* robbery, racket, thievery, larceny, stealing, swindling, swindle, cheating, defrauding, fraud, piracy, burglary, pillage, pilfering, plunder, vandalism, holdup, pocket-picking, safecracking, extortion, embezzlement, looting, appropriation, shoplifting, fleecing, mugging, stickup*; see also CRIME.
their *poss. pronominal adj.* belonging to them, belonging to others, their own, of them.
them *pron.* these persons, these things, those persons, those things, the others, the above, some people, him and her; see also EVERYBODY.
theme *n.* **1** [A subject] topic, proposition, argument, thesis, text, subject matter, matter at hand, problem, question, point at issue, affair, business, point, case, thought, idea, line; see also SUBJECT. **2** [A recurrent melody] melody, motif, strain; see SONG. **3** [A short composition] essay, report, paper; see WRITING 2, STATEMENT 1.
then *a.* at that time, formerly, before, years ago, at that point, suddenly, all at once, soon after, before long, next, later, thereupon; see also WHEN 2, 3. —**but then** but at the same time, on the other hand, however; see BUT 1, 2. —**what then?** what would happen in that case?, and then?, what would the result be?; see WHAT 1.
theology *n.* dogma, creed, theism; see BELIEF, FAITH 2.
theoretical *a.* ideal, analytical, academic; see ASSUMED.

the·o·rize (thē′ə rīz′) ***vi.*** **-rized′**, **-riz′ing** to form a theory or theories; speculate —**the′o·re·ti′cian** (-rə tish′ən) or **the′o·rist** (-rist) ***n.***

the·o·ry (thē′ə rē, thir′ē) ***n.***, *pl.* **-ries** ⟦< Gr *theōrein,* to view⟧ **1** a speculative plan **2** a formulation of underlying principles of certain observed phenomena that has been verified to some degree **3** the principles of an art or science, rather than its practice **4** a conjecture or guess

the·os·o·phy (thē äs′ə fē) ***n.*** ⟦< Gr *theos,* god + *sophia,* wisdom⟧ [*also* **T-**] a religious or semireligious set of occult beliefs rejecting Christian theology and held to be based on a special mystical insight —**the′o·soph′ic** (-ə säf′ik) or **the′o·soph′i·cal** ***adj.*** —**the·os′o·phist** ***n.***

ther·a·peu·tic (ther′ə pyo͞ot′ik) ***adj.*** ⟦< Gr *therapeuein,* to nurse⟧ serving to cure or heal or to preserve health

ther′a·peu′tics ***n.*** the branch of medicine that deals with the treatment of diseases; therapy

ther′a·py (-pē) ***n.***, *pl.* **-pies** ⟦see THERAPEUTIC⟧ **1** the treatment of any physical or mental disorder by medical or physical means, usually excluding surgery **2** *short for* PSYCHOTHERAPY —**ther′a·pist** ***n.***

there (*th*er) ***adv.*** ⟦OE *ther*⟧ **1** at, in, or to that place **2** at that point; then *[there* I paused*]* **3** in that respect *[there* you are wrong*]* *There* is also used in impersonal constructions in which the real subject follows the verb *[there* is little time*]* —***n.*** that place —***interj.*** used to express defiance, satisfaction, sympathy, etc. —**(not) all there** [Inf.] (not) mentally sound

there′a·bouts′ (-ə bouts′) ***adv.*** **1** near that place **2** near that time, number, degree, etc. Also **there′a·bout′**

there·af′ter ***adv.*** from then on

there·at′ ***adv.*** **1** at that place; there **2** at that time **3** for that reason

there·by′ ***adv.*** **1** by that means **2** connected with that

there·for′ ***adv.*** for this; for that; for it

there′fore′ (-fôr′) ***adv.*** for this or that reason; hence

there·in′ ***adv.*** **1** in or into that place **2** in that matter, detail, etc.

there·of′ ***adv.*** **1** of that **2** from that as a cause, reason, etc.

there·on′ ***adv.*** **1** on that or it **2** THEREUPON

there·to′ ***adv.*** to that place, thing, etc.: also **there·un·to** (*th*er un′to͞o, *th*er′un to͞o′)

there′to·fore′ ***adv.*** until that time

there′up·on′ ***adv.*** **1** immediately following that **2** as a consequence of that **3** on that subject, etc.

there·with′ ***adv.*** **1** along with that **2** immediately thereafter

ther·mal (thur′məl) ***adj.*** ⟦< Gr *thermē,* heat⟧ **1** having to do with heat **2** designating a loosely knitted material with air spaces for insulation —***n.*** *Meteorol.* a rising column of warm air

thermal pollution the harmful discharge of heated liquid or air into lakes, rivers, etc.

thermo- ⟦< Gr *thermē,* heat⟧ *combining form* heat

ther·mo·dy·nam·ics (thur′mō dī nam′iks) ***n.*** the branch of physics dealing with the transformation of heat to and from other forms of energy —**ther′mo·dy·nam′ic** ***adj.***

ther·mom·e·ter (thər mäm′ət ər) ***n.*** ⟦see THERMO- & -METER⟧ an instrument for measuring temperatures, as a graduated glass tube in which mercury, etc. rises or falls as it expands or contracts with changes in temperature

ther·mo·nu·cle·ar (thur′mō no͞o′klē ər) ***adj.*** *Physics* **1** designating a reaction in which isotopes of a light element fuse, at extremely high heat, into heavier nuclei **2** of or using the heat energy released in nuclear fusion

ther·mo·plas·tic (thur′mə plas′tik) ***adj.*** soft and moldable when subjected to heat: said of certain plastics —***n.*** a thermoplastic substance

Ther·mos (thur′məs) ⟦< Gr *thermos,* hot⟧ *trademark for* a vacuum-insulated container for keeping liquids at almost their original temperature —***n.*** [*usually* **t-**] such a container

ther·mo·stat (thur′mə stat′) ***n.*** ⟦THERMO- + -STAT⟧ an apparatus for regulating temperature, esp. one that automatically controls a heating or cooling unit

the·sau·rus (thi sô′rəs) ***n.***, *pl.* **-ri′** (-rī′) or **-rus·es** ⟦< Gr *thēsauros,* a treasure⟧ a book of synonyms and antonyms

these (*th*ēz) ***pron.***, ***adj.*** *pl. of* THIS

The·seus (thē′so͞os′, thē′sē əs) ***n.*** *Gr. Legend* the king of Athens who kills the Minotaur

the·sis (thē′sis) ***n.***, *pl.* **-ses′** (-sēz′) ⟦< Gr *tithenai,* to put⟧ **1** a proposition to be defended in argument **2** a long research paper, esp. one written by a candidate for a master's degree

Thes·pi·an (thes′pē ən) ***adj.*** ⟦after *Thespis,* ancient Gr poet⟧ [*often* **t-**] having to do with the drama; dramatic —***n.*** [*often* **t-**] an actor or actress

the·ta (thāt′ə, thēt′-) ***n.*** the eighth letter of the Greek alphabet (Θ, θ, ϑ)

thews (thyo͞oz) ***pl.n.***, *sing.* **thew** ⟦< OE *theaw,* habit⟧ muscles or sinews

they (*th*ā) ***pron.***, *sing.* **he**, **she**, or **it** ⟦< ON *thei-r*⟧ **1** the persons, animals, or things previously mentioned **2** people generally *[they* say it's so*]*

thi·a·mine (thī′ə min, -mēn′) ***n.*** ⟦ult. < Gr *theion,* brimstone + (VIT)AMIN⟧ a white, crystalline B vitamin, found in cereals, egg yolk, liver, etc.; vitamin B_1: also **thi′a·min** (-min)

thick (thik) ***adj.*** ⟦OE *thicce*⟧ **1** of relatively great extent from side to side **2** as measured between opposite surfaces *[*one inch *thick]* **3** close and abundant *[thick* hair*]* **4** viscous **5** dense *[thick* smoke*]* **6** husky; blurred *[thick* speech*]* **7** [Inf.] stupid **8** [Inf.] close in friendship —***n.*** the thickest part —**thick′ly** ***adv.*** —**thick′ness** ***n.***

thick′en ***vt.***, ***vi.*** **1** to make or become thick or thicker **2** to make or become more complex —**thick′en·ing** ***n.***

thick·et (thik′it) ***n.*** ⟦see THICK⟧ a thick growth of shrubs or small trees

thick′set′ ***adj.*** **1** planted thickly or closely **2** thick in body; stocky

thick′-skinned′ ***adj.*** insensitive, as to insult

thief (thēf) ***n.***, *pl.* **thieves** (thēvz) ⟦OE *theof*⟧ one who steals

thieve (thēv) ***vt.***, ***vi.*** **thieved**, **thiev′ing** to steal —**thiev′ish** ***adj.***

thiev′er·y (-ər ē) ***n.***, *pl.* **-ies** the act or an instance of stealing; theft

THESAURUS

theory ***n.*** **1** [Principles] method, approach, philosophy; see LAW 4. **2** [Something to be proved] hypothesis, conjecture, speculation; see OPINION 1.

therapeutic ***a.*** curative, healing, corrective, remedial.

therapy ***n.*** remedy, healing, cure; see MEDICINE 3.

there ***a.*** in that place, not here, beyond, over there, yonder, in the distance, at a distance, over yonder, in that spot, at that point; see also WHERE 2. **—not all there*** crazy, eccentric, demented; see INSANE.

thereafter ***a.*** from then on, from that day on, after that; see FOLLOWING, HEREAFTER.

thereby ***a.*** by way of, that, by that means, by which; see also THROUGH 4, WHEREBY.

therefore ***a.***, ***conj.*** accordingly, consequently, hence, wherefore, for, since, inasmuch as, for this reason, on account of, to that end, in that event, in consequence, as a result.

thermometer ***n.*** mercury, thermostat, thermoregulator; see MEASURE 2.

these ***a.*** those, the, the indicated, the present, the previously mentioned, the above, certain, not those.

these ***pron.*** those, the ones here, they, them, not those.

they ***pron.*** people, men, women, men and women, these people, everyone, those people, all, others, he and she, both; see also EVERYBODY.

thick ***a.*** **1** [Dense] compact, impervious, condensed, compressed, multitudinous, numerous, rank, crowded, close, solid, packed, populous, profuse, populated, swarming, heaped, abundant, impenetrable, concentrated, crammed, packed together, closely packed, like a can of sardines*, jam-packed*.—*Ant.* SCATTERED, spacious, wide-open. **2** [Deep] in depth, edgewise, third-dimensional; see DEEP 2. **3** [Of heavy consistency] compact, heavy, viscous, viscid, dense, syrupy, ropy, coagulated, curdled, turbid, gelatinous, glutinous, gummy, clotted, opaque; see also STRINGY.—*Ant.* LIGHT, porous, filmy. **4** [Not clear] cloudy, turbid, indistinct; see DULL 2, MUDDY 1, OBSCURE 1. **5** [*Stupid] obtuse, ignorant, doltish; see DULL 3. **6** [*Intimate] cordial, familiar, fraternal; see FRIENDLY. **—through thick and thin** faithfully, devotedly, in good and bad times; see LOYALLY.

thicken ***v.*** coagulate, curdle, petrify, ossify, solidify, freeze, clot, set, congeal, jell, grow thick; see also HARDEN, STIFFEN.

thickness ***n.*** density, compactness, solidity, closeness, heaviness, stiffness, condensation, concentration, clot.—*Ant.* FRAILTY, thinness, slimness.

thief ***n.*** burglar, highwayman, robber; see CRIMINAL.

thieve ***v.*** loot, rob, filch; see STEAL.

thievery ***n.*** burglary, robbery, pilfering; see CRIME, THEFT.

thigh (thī) ***n.*** ⟦OE *theoh*⟧ that part of the leg between the knee and the hip
thigh'bone' ***n.*** FEMUR
thim·ble (thim'bəl) ***n.*** ⟦< OE *thuma,* a thumb⟧ a small cap worn to protect the finger that pushes the needle in sewing —**thim'ble·ful'**, *pl.* **-fuls'**, ***n.***
thin (thin) ***adj.*** **thin'ner, thin'nest** ⟦OE *thynne*⟧ **1** of relatively little extent from side to side **2** lean; slender **3** not dense or compact *[thin* hair*]* **4** very fluid or watery *[thin* soup*]* **5** high-pitched and weak *[*a *thin* voice*]* **6** sheer: said as of fabric **7** flimsy or unconvincing *[*a *thin* excuse*]* **8** lacking substance, depth, etc.; weak —***vt., vi.*** **thinned, thin'ning** to make or become thin or thinner —**thin'ly** ***adv.*** —**thin'ness** ***n.***
thine (*th*īn) [Archaic] ***pron.*** ⟦OE *thin*⟧ that or those belonging to thee: poss. form of THOU —***poss. pronominal adj.*** thy: used esp. before a vowel
thing (thiŋ) ***n.*** ⟦OE, council⟧ **1** any matter, affair, or concern **2** a happening, act, incident, event, etc. **3** *a)* a tangible object *b)* an inanimate object **4** an item, detail, etc. **5** *a)* [*pl.*] personal belongings *b)* a garment **6** [Inf.] a person *[*poor *thing]* **7** [Inf.] a point of contention; issue **8** [Inf.] an irrational liking, fear, etc. **9** [Inf.] what one wants to do or is adept at *[*to do one's own *thing]* —**see things** [Inf.] to have hallucinations
think (thiŋk) ***vt.*** **thought, think'ing** ⟦OE *thencan*⟧ **1** to form or have in the mind *[thinking* good thoughts*]* **2** to judge; consider *[*many *think* her charming*]* **3** to believe *[*I *think* I can come*]* —***vi.*** **1** to use the mind; reason **2** to have an opinion, etc.: with *of* or *about* **3** to remember or consider: with *of* or *about* **4** to conceive (*of*) —**think up** to invent, plan, etc. by thinking —**think'er** ***n.***
think tank a group or center organized to do intensive research and problem-solving
thin·ner (thin'ər) ***n.*** a substance added to paint, shellac, etc. to thin it
thin'-skinned' ***adj.*** sensitive, as to insult
Thin·su·late (thin'sə lāt') *trademark for* thermal insulation made of synthetic fibers, for lining clothing
third (thurd) ***adj.*** ⟦OE *thridda*⟧ preceded by two others in a series; 3d or 3rd —***adv.*** in the third place, etc.: also **third'ly** —***n.*** **1** the one following the second **2** any of the three equal parts of something; $\frac{1}{3}$ **3** the third forward gear of a transmission, providing more speed than second
third'-class' ***adj.*** **1** of the class, rank, etc. next below the second **2** of a low-cost mail class, as for advertisements —***adv.*** by third-class mail or travel accommodations
third degree [Inf.] cruel treatment and questioning to force a confession: with *the*
third dimension **1** *a)* depth *b)* solidity **2** the quality of seeming real
third person the form of a pronoun or verb that refers to the person or thing spoken of
third'-rate' ***adj.*** **1** third in quality or other rating **2** inferior; very poor
Third World [*also* **t- w-**] the economically underdeveloped countries of the world
thirst (thurst) ***n.*** ⟦OE *thurst*⟧ **1** the discomfort caused by a need for water **2** a strong desire; craving —***vi.*** **1** to feel thirst **2** to have a strong desire or craving —**thirst'y, -i·er, -i·est,** ***adj.*** —**thirst'i·ly** ***adv.***
thir·teen (thur'tēn') ***adj., n.*** ⟦OE *threotyne*⟧ three more than ten; 13; XIII —**thir'teenth'** ***adj., n.***
thir·ty (thurt'ē) ***adj., n., pl.*** **-ties** ⟦OE *thritig*⟧ three times ten; 30; XXX —**the thirties** the numbers or years, as of a century, from 30 through 39 —**thir'ti·eth** (-ith) ***adj., n.***
this (*th*is) ***pron.,*** *pl.* **these** ⟦OE *thes*⟧ **1** the person or thing mentioned *[this* is John*]* **2** the nearer one or another one *[this* is older than that*]* **3** something about to be presented *[*listen to *this]* —***adj.,*** *pl.* **these** **1** designating the person or thing mentioned *[this* man is John*]* **2** designating the nearer one or another one *[this* desk is older than that one*]* **3** designating something about to be presented *[*hear *this* news*]* —***adv.*** to this extent *[*it was *this* big*]*
this·tle (this'əl) ***n.*** ⟦OE *thistel*⟧ a plant with prickly leaves and white, purple, etc. flowers
this'tle·down' ***n.*** the down growing from the flowers of a thistle
thith·er (*th*i*th*'ər, thi*th*'-) ***adv.*** ⟦OE *thider*⟧ to or toward that place; there
tho or **tho'** (*th*ō) ***conj., adv.*** *phonetic sp. of* THOUGH
thole (thōl) ***n.*** ⟦OE *thol*⟧ one of a pair of pins set as an oarlock into the gunwale of a boat: also **thole'pin'**
-thon (thän) *suffix* -ATHON: used after a vowel *[radiothon]*
thong (thôŋ) ***n.*** ⟦OE *thwang*⟧ a narrow strip of leather, etc. used as a lace, strap, etc.
Thor (thôr) ***n.*** *Norse Myth.* the god of thunder, war, and strength
tho·rax (thôr'aks') ***n., pl.*** **-rax'es** or **-ra·ces'** (-ə sēz') ⟦< Gr⟧ **1** the part of the body between the neck and the abdomen; chest **2** the middle segment of an insect's body —**tho·rac·ic** (thō ras'ik, thô-) ***adj.***
Tho·reau (thôr'ō, thə rō'), **Henry David** 1817-62; U.S. writer
tho·ri·um (thôr'ē əm) ***n.*** ⟦< THOR⟧ a rare, grayish, radioactive, metallic chemical element, used as a nuclear fuel
thorn (thôrn) ***n.*** ⟦OE⟧ **1** *a)* a very short, hard, leafless stem with a sharp point *b)* any small tree or shrub

THESAURUS

thigh ***n.*** thighbone, femur, ham; see LEG.
thin ***a.*** **1** [Of little thickness] flimsy, slim, slight, diaphanous, sheer, rare, sleazy, permeable, paper-thin, wafer-thin.—*Ant.* THICK, heavy, coarse. **2** [Slender] slim, lean, skinny, scraggy, lank, spare, gaunt, bony, wan, rangy, skeletal, scrawny, lanky, delicate, wasted, haggard, emaciated, rawboned, shriveled, wizened, rickety, spindly, pinched, starved.—*Ant.* FAT, obese, heavy. **3** [Sparse] scarce, insufficient, deficient; see INADEQUATE. **4** [Having little content] sketchy, slight, insubstantial; see SHALLOW 1, 2. **5** [Having little volume] faint, shrill, weak; see LIGHT 7.
thin ***v.*** thin out, weed out, dilute; see DECREASE 2, WEAKEN 2.
thing ***n.*** **1** [An object] article, object, item, lifeless object, commodity, device, gadget, material object, being, entity, body, person, something, anything, everything, element, substance, piece, shape, form, figure, configuration, creature, stuff, goods, matter, thingamajig*, doohickey*, thingamabob*. **2** [A circumstance] matter, condition, situation; see CIRCUMSTANCE 1. **3** [An act] deed, feat, movement; see ACTION 2. **4** [A characteristic] quality, trait, attribute; see CHARACTERISTIC. **5** [An idea] notion, opinion, impression; see THOUGHT 2. **6** [A pitiable person] wretch, poor person, sufferer, urchin; see also PATIENT, REFUGEE. **7** [Belongings; *usually pl.*] possessions, clothes, luggage; see PROPERTY 1, BAGGAGE. **8** [Something so vague as to be nameless] affair, matter, concern, business, occurrence, anything, everything, something, stuff, point, information, subject, idea, question, indication, intimation, contrivance, word, name, shape, form, entity. **9** [Something to be done] task, obligation, duty; see JOB 2. —**do one's own thing*** live according to one's own principles, do what one likes, live fully; see LIVE 1.
things ***n.*** possessions, luggage, belongings; see BAGGAGE, PROPERTY 1.
think ***v.*** **1** [To examine something with the mind] cogitate, muse, ponder, consider, contemplate, deliberate, stop to consider, study, reflect, examine, think twice, estimate, evaluate, appraise, resolve, ruminate, scan, confer, consult, meditate, meditate upon, take under consideration, have on one's mind, brood over, speculate, weigh, have in mind, keep in mind, bear in mind, mull over, turn over, sweat over*, stew, bone up*, beat one's brains, rack one's brains, use the old bean*, figure out, put on one's thinking cap, use one's head, hammer away at, hammer out, bury oneself in.—*Ant.* NEGLECT, take for granted, accept. **2** [To believe] be convinced, deem, hold; see BELIEVE. **3** [To suppose] imagine, guess, presume; see ASSUME. **4** [To form in the mind] conceive, invent, create; see IMAGINE. **5** [To remember] recollect, recall, reminisce; see REMEMBER 1, 2.
thinking ***a.*** pensive, introspective, reflective; see THOUGHTFUL 1. —**put on one's thinking cap** begin thinking, study, examine; see THINK 1.
thinking ***n.*** reasoning, reason, contemplation; see THOUGHT 1.
thinness ***n.*** slenderness, slimness, shallowness; see LIGHTNESS 2.
thin-skinned ***a.*** sensitive, touchy, moody; see IRRITABLE.
third ***a.*** part, after the second, next but one; see THREE.
thirst ***n.*** dryness, need for liquid, longing, craving.
thirsty ***a.*** dry, parched, arid, eager, hankering for, burning for, craving, longing for, partial to, hungry for, itching for, inclined to, bone-dry*, crazy for*, wild for; see also HUNGRY.—*Ant.* SATISFIED, full, replete.
this ***a.*** the, that, the indicated, the present, one, the previously mentioned, a certain, not that, a particular.
this ***pron.*** the one, this one, that one, the one in question, the aforementioned one, this person, the thing indicated, this fact, who, which.
thorn ***n.*** spine, briar, neetle; see

bearing thorns **2** a source of constant trouble or irritation —**thorn′y, -i·er, -i·est,** ***adj.***

thor·ough (thʉr′ō) ***adj.*** ⟦var. of THROUGH⟧ **1** omitting nothing; complete **2** absolute *[a thorough rascal]* **3** very exact, accurate, or painstaking —**thor′ough·ly** ***adv.*** —**thor′ough·ness** ***n.***

thor·ough·bred (thʉr′ō bred′, thʉr′ə-) ***adj.*** of pure stock; pedigreed —***n.*** **[T-]** any of a breed of light horse developed primarily for racing

thor′ough·fare′ (-fer′) ***n.*** a public street open at both ends, esp. a main highway

thor′ough·go′ing ***adj.*** very thorough

those (thōz) ***pron., adj. pl. of*** THAT

thou (thou) ***pron., pl.*** **you** or **ye** ⟦OE *thu*⟧ [Archaic] you: in poetic or religious use

though (thō) ***conj.*** ⟦OE *theah*⟧ **1** in spite of the fact that *[though it rained, he went]* **2** and yet *[they can win, though no one thinks so]* **3** even if *[though he may fail, he will have tried]* —***adv.*** however; nevertheless *[she sings well, though]*

thought[1] (thôt) ***n.*** ⟦OE *thoht*⟧ **1** the act or process of thinking **2** the power of reasoning **3** an idea, concept, etc. **4** attention; consideration **5** mental concentration *[deep in thought]*

thought[2] (thôt) ***vt., vi. pt. & pp. of*** THINK

thought′ful ***adj.*** **1** full of thought; meditative **2** considerate of others —**thought′ful·ly** ***adv.*** —**thought′ful·ness** ***n.***

thought′less ***adj.*** **1** not stopping to think; careless **2** ill-considered; rash **3** inconsiderate —**thought′less·ly** ***adv.*** —**thought′less·ness** ***n.***

thou·sand (thou′zənd) ***n., adj.*** ⟦OE *thusend*⟧ ten hundred; 1,000; M —**thou′sandth** (-zəndth) ***adj., n.***

thrall (thrôl) ***n.*** ⟦< ON *thræll*⟧ **1** [Now Chiefly Literary] a slave **2** the condition of being dominated or enslaved, esp. psychologically: now used chiefly in **hold in thrall** —**thrall′dom** or **thral′dom** (-dəm) ***n.***

thrash (thrash) ***vt., vi.*** ⟦OE *therscan*⟧ **1** THRESH **2** to beat; flog **3** to toss about violently **4** to defeat overwhelmingly —**thrash out** to settle by detailed discussion

thrash′er ***n.*** ⟦E dial. *thresher*⟧ a thrushlike American songbird

thread (thred) ***n.*** ⟦OE *thræd*⟧ **1** a fine, stringlike length of spun cotton, silk, nylon, etc. used in sewing **2** any thin line, vein, etc. **3** something like a thread in its length, sequence, etc. *[the thread of a story]* **4** the spiral ridge of a screw, nut, etc. —***vt.*** **1** to put a thread through (a needle, etc.) **2** to make (one's way) by twisting, weaving, etc. **3** to fashion a THREAD (sense 4) on or in (a screw, pipe, etc.)

thread′bare′ ***adj.*** **1** worn down so that the threads show *[a threadbare rug]* **2** wearing worn clothes; shabby **3** stale; trite

threat (thret) ***n.*** ⟦OE *threat,* pressure⟧ **1** an expression of intention to hurt, destroy, punish, etc. **2** an indication of, or a source of, imminent danger, harm, etc.

threat′en ***vt., vi.*** **1** to make threats, as of injury (against) **2** to indicate the likely occurrence of (something dangerous, unpleasant, etc.) **3** to be a source of danger (to)

three (thrē) ***adj., n.*** ⟦OE *threo*⟧ one more than two; 3; III

three′-deck′er (-dek′ər) ***n.*** anything having three levels, layers, etc.

three′-di·men′sion·al ***adj.*** having or seeming to have depth or thickness

three′fold′ ***adj.*** **1** having three parts **2** having three times as much or as many —***adv.*** three times as much or as many

three R's reading, writing, and arithmetic, regarded as the fundamentals of an education: with *the*

three·score (thrē′skôr′) ***adj., n.*** sixty

thren·o·dy (thren′ə dē) ***n., pl.*** **-dies** ⟦< Gr *thrēnos,* lamentation + *ōidē,* song⟧ a song of lamentation; dirge

thresh (thresh) ***vt., vi.*** ⟦ME *threschen*: see THRASH⟧ **1** to beat out (grain) from (husks), as with a flail **2** THRASH —**thresh′er** ***n.***

thresh·old (thresh′ōld′, -hōld′) ***n.*** ⟦OE *therscwold*⟧ **1** a length of wood, stone, etc. along the bottom of a doorway **2** the beginning point

threw (thro͞o) ***vt., vi. pt. of*** THROW

thrice (thrīs) ***adv.*** ⟦OE *thriwa*⟧ **1** three times **2** threefold

thrift (thrift) ***n.*** ⟦< ON *thrifa,* to grasp⟧ economy; frugality —**thrift′less** ***adj.*** —**thrift′y, -i·er, -i·est,** ***adj.*** —**thrift′i·ly** ***adv.*** —**thrift′i·ness** ***n.***

thrift shop a store where castoff clothes, etc. are sold to raise money for charity

THESAURUS

POINT 2.

thorny ***a.*** bothersome, perplexing, formidable; see DIFFICULT 1, 2.

thorough ***a.*** **1** [Painstaking] exact, meticulous, precise; see ACCURATE 2, CAREFUL. **2** [Complete] thoroughgoing, out-and-out, total; see ABSOLUTE 1.

thoroughly ***a.*** fully, wholly, in detail; see COMPLETELY.

those ***a.*** the, the previously mentioned, the past, the future, certain, not these, these, the above-mentioned, the indicated.

those ***pron.*** these, the others, they, them, not these.

though ***conj.*** despite the fact that, even if, if; see ALTHOUGH, BUT 1.

thought[1] ***n.*** **1** [Mental activity] speculation, reflection, deliberation, meditation, rumination, perceiving, apprehending, seeing, consideration, reasoning, intuition, logical process, perception, insight, understanding, viewpoint, concept, brain work, thinking, knowing, realizing, discerning, rationalizing, concluding, drawing conclusions, inferring, deducing, deriving, deduction, inducing, logic, judging, rationalization, judgment, argumentation, cogitation, contemplation, cognition, intellection, brainstorm. **2** [The result of mental activity] idea, plan, view, fancy, notion, impression, image, understanding, appreciation, conception, observation, belief, feeling, opinion, guess, inference, theory, hypothesis, supposition, assumption, intuition, conjecture, deduction, postulate, premise, knowledge, evaluation, appraisal, assessment, estimate, verdict, finding, decision, determination, reflection, consideration, abstraction, conviction, tenet, presumption, surmise, doctrine, principle, drift, calculation, caprice, reverie, sentiment, care, worry, anxiety, uneasiness, dream. **3** [Care or attention] heed, thoughtfulness, solicitude; see ATTENTION.

thoughtful ***a.*** **1** [Notable for thought] thinking, meditative, engrossed, absorbed, rapt in, pensive, considered, seasoned, matured, studied, philosophic, contemplative, studious, cogitative, examined, pondered, speculative, deliberative, reflective, introspective, clearheaded, levelheaded, keen, wise, farsighted, rational, calculating, discerning, penetrating, politic, shrewd, careful, sensible, retrospective, intellectual, brainy*, deep.—*Ant.* THOUGHTLESS, unthinking, irrational. **2** [Considerate] heedful, polite, courteous, solicitous, friendly, kind, kindly, unselfish, concerned, anxious, neighborly, regardful, social, cooperative, responsive, aware, sensitive, benign, indulgent, obliging, careful, attentive, gallant, chivalrous, charitable.—*Ant.* SELFISH, boorish, inconsiderate.

thoughtfulness ***n.*** understanding, helpfulness, indulgence; see KINDNESS 1.

thoughtless ***a.*** **1** [Destitute of thought] irrational, unreasoning, unreasonable, inane, incomprehensible, witless, undiscerning, foolish, doltish, babbling, bewildered, confused, puerile, senseless, driveling, inept, dull, heavy-handed, obtuse, flighty; see also STUPID. **2** [Inconsiderate] heedless, negligent, inattentive, neglectful, careless, self-centered, egocentric, selfish, asocial, antisocial, unmindful, unheeding, indifferent, unconcerned, listless, apathetic, boorish, discourteous, unrefined; see also RUDE 2.—*Ant.* CAREFUL, thoughtful, unselfish.

thoughtlessness ***n.*** inattention, oversight, heedlessness; see CARELESSNESS, NEGLECT 1.

thousand ***a.*** ten hundred, millenary, thousandfold; see MANY.

thrash ***v.*** trounce, whip, chasten; see BEAT 1, PUNISH.

thread ***n.*** yarn, string, strand; see FIBER.

thread ***v.*** attach, weave together, string together; see JOIN 1.

threat ***n.*** menace, fulmination, intimidation; see WARNING.

threaten ***v.*** intimidate, caution, admonish, scare, torment, push around, forewarn, bully, abuse, bluster, endanger, be dangerous, be gathering, be in the offing, imperil, be brewing, approach, come on, advance; see also FRIGHTEN, WARN.—*Ant.* HELP, mollify, placate.

threatened ***a.*** warned, endangered, imperiled, jeopardized, in bad straits, insecure, unsafe, unprotected, vulnerable, exposed, in a crucial state, in danger, besieged, surrounded, under attack, set upon, in a bad way.—*Ant.* SAFE, invulnerable, protected.

threatening ***a.*** alarming, dangerous, aggressive; see OMINOUS, SINISTER, UNSAFE.

three ***a.*** triple, treble, threefold, third, triform, triune, tertiary, thrice, triply.

threshold ***n.*** sill, gate, door; see ENTRANCE 1.

thrift ***n.*** saving, parsimony, frugality; see ECONOMY.

thrifty ***a.*** parsimonious, careful, frugal; see ECONOMICAL 1.

thrill (thril) ***vi., vt.*** ⟦< OE *thurh,* through⟧ **1** to feel or cause to feel emotional excitement **2** to quiver or cause to quiver —***n.*** a thrilling or being thrilled —**thrill'er** ***n.***

thrive (thrīv) ***vi.*** **thrived** or **throve, thrived** or **thriv·en** (thriv'ən), **thriv'ing** ⟦< ON *thrifa,* to grasp⟧ **1** to prosper or flourish; be successful **2** to grow vigorously or luxuriantly

throat (thrōt) ***n.*** ⟦OE *throte*⟧ **1** the front part of the neck **2** the upper part of the passage from the mouth and nose to the stomach and lungs **3** any narrow passage

throat'y ***adj.*** **-i·er, -i·est** **1** produced in the throat: said of some sounds **2** husky; hoarse

throb (thräb) ***vi.*** **throbbed, throb'bing** ⟦ME *throbben*⟧ **1** to beat, pulsate, vibrate, etc., esp. strongly or fast **2** to feel excitement —***n.*** **1** a throbbing **2** a strong beat or pulsation

throe (thrō) ***n.*** ⟦prob. < OE *thrawu,* pain⟧ a spasm or pang of pain: *usually used in pl.* [the *throes* of childbirth, death *throes]* —**in the throes of** in the act of struggling with (a problem, task, etc.)

throm·bose (thräm'bōs', -bōz') ***vt., vi.*** **-bosed', -bos'ing** to clot or become clotted with a thrombus

throm·bo·sis (thräm bō'sis) ***n.*** ⟦< Gr *thrombos,* a clot⟧ coagulation of the blood in the heart or a blood vessel, forming a clot

throm·bus (thräm'bəs) ***n.*** **-bi'** (-bī') ⟦see prec.⟧ the clot attached at the site of thrombosis

throne (thrōn) ***n.*** ⟦< Gr *thronos,* a seat⟧ **1** the chair on which a king, cardinal, etc. sits on formal occasions **2** the power or rank of a king, etc.

throng (thrôŋ) ***n.*** ⟦OE *thringan,* to crowd⟧ **1** a crowd **2** any great number of things considered together —***vi.*** to gather together in a throng —***vt.*** to crowd into

throt·tle (thrät''l) ***n.*** ⟦prob. dim. of THROAT⟧ the valve, or its control lever or pedal, that regulates the amount of fuel vapor entering an engine —***vt.*** **-tled, -tling** **1** to choke; strangle **2** to censor or suppress **3** to slow by means of a throttle

through (thro͞o) ***prep.*** ⟦OE *thurh*⟧ **1** in one side and out the other side of **2** in the midst of; among **3** by way of **4** around [touring *through* France] **5** *a)* from the beginning to the end of *b)* up to and including **6** by means of **7** as a result of [done *through* error] —***adv.*** **1** in one side and out the other **2** from the beginning to the end **3** completely to the end [to see something *through]* **4** completely [soaked *through]*: also **through and through** —***adj.*** **1** extending from one place to another [a *through* street] **2** traveling to the destination without stops [a *through* train] **3** finished [*through* with the job]

through·out' ***prep.*** all the way through —***adv.*** in every part; everywhere

through'way' ***n.*** *alt. sp. of* THRUWAY: see EXPRESSWAY

throve (thrōv) ***vi.*** *alt. pt. of* THRIVE

throw (thrō) ***vt.*** **threw, thrown, throw'ing** ⟦OE *thrawan,* to twist⟧ **1** to send through the air by a rapid motion of the arm, etc. **2** to cause to fall; upset **3** to send rapidly [to *throw* troops into battle] **4** to put suddenly into a specified state, etc. [*throw* into confusion] **5** to move (a switch, etc.) so as to connect, disconnect, etc. **6** to direct, cast, etc. [*throw* a glance] **7** [Inf.] to lose (a game, etc.) deliberately **8** [Inf.] to give (a party, etc.) **9** [Inf.] to confuse or disconcert [the question *threw* him] **10** [Inf.] to have (a tantrum, etc.) —***vi.*** to cast or hurl something —***n.*** **1** the act of one who throws **2** the distance something is or can be thrown [a stone's *throw]* **3** a spread for a bed, etc. —**throw away** **1** to discard **2** to waste —**throw in** to add on free or add to others —**throw off** **1** to rid oneself of **2** to mislead or confuse **3** to expel, emit, etc. —**throw oneself at** to try very hard to win the love of —**throw out** **1** to discard **2** to reject or remove —**throw over** **1** to give up; abandon **2** to jilt —**throw together** to assemble hurriedly —**throw up** to vomit —**throw'er** ***n.***

throw'a·way' ***n.*** a leaflet, handbill, etc. given out on the streets, from house to house, etc. —***adj.*** for discarding after use

throw'back' ***n.*** (a) reversion to an earlier or more primitive type

throw rug SCATTER RUG

thru (thro͞o) ***prep., adv., adj.*** *informal sp. of* THROUGH

thrush (thrush) ***n.*** ⟦OE *thrysce*⟧ any of a family of songbirds, including the robin

thrust (thrust) ***vt., vi.*** **thrust, thrust'ing** ⟦< ON *thrysta*⟧ **1** to push with sudden force **2** to stab **3** to force or impose —***n.*** **1** a sudden, forceful push **2** a stab **3** continuous pressure, as of a rafter against a wall **4** *a)* the driving force of a propeller *b)* the forward force produced by a jet or rocket engine **5** forward movement **6** the basic meaning; point

thru·way (thro͞o'wā') ***n.*** EXPRESSWAY

Thu·cyd·i·des (tho͞o sid'i dēz') 460?-400? B.C.; Athenian historian

thud (thud) ***vi.*** **thud'ded, thud'ding** ⟦prob. < OE *thyddan,* to strike⟧ to hit or fall with a dull sound —***n.*** a dull sound, as of an object dropping on a soft surface

thug (thug) ***n.*** ⟦Hindi *ṭhag,* swindler⟧ a brutal hoodlum, gangster, etc. —**thug'gish** ***adj.***

thumb (thum) ***n.*** ⟦OE *thuma*⟧ the short, thick digit of the hand —***vt.*** **1** to handle, soil, etc. as with the thumb **2** [Inf.] to solicit or get (a ride) in hitchhiking by signaling

THESAURUS

thrill ***n.*** pleasant sensation, stimulation, tingle; see EXCITEMENT, FUN.

thrill ***v.*** animate, inspire, rouse; see EXCITE.

thrilled ***a.*** inspired, moved, electrified; see EXCITED, HAPPY.

thrilling ***a.*** overwhelming, exciting, breathtaking; see STIMULATING.

thrive ***v.*** flourish, increase, succeed; see GROW 1.

throat ***n.*** neck, windpipe, larynx, trachea, esophagus, jugular region, gullet, gorge. —**cut each other's throats*** ruin each other, fight, feud; see DESTROY. —**cut one's own throat*** ruin oneself, cause one's own destruction, act contrary to one's best interests; see COMMIT SUICIDE, DAMAGE. —**ram down someone's throat*** impose, pressure, coerce; see FORCE. —**stick in someone's throat*** be difficult to say, not come easily, be disturbing; see DISTURB.

throaty ***a.*** husky, hoarse, deep; see HOARSE.

throb ***n.*** pulse, pulsation, palpitation; see BEAT 1.

throb ***v.*** vibrate, pulsate, palpitate; see BEAT 2.

throne ***n.*** authority, sway, dominion, royal power, sovereignty, the crown, Royal Majesty or Highness; see also CHAIR 2, ROYALTY.

throng ***n.*** multitude, mass, concourse; see CROWD, GATHERING.

throttle ***v.*** strangle, stifle, silence; see CHOKE.

through ***a., prep.*** **1** [Finished] completed, over, ended; see DONE 1, FINISHED 1. **2** [From one side to the other] straight through, through and through, clear through; see IN 2, INTO, WITHIN. **3** [During] throughout, for the period of, from beginning to end; see DURING. **4** [By means of] by, by way of, by reason of, in virtue of, in consequence of, for, by the agency of, at the hand of. **5** [Referring to continuous passage] nonstop, unbroken, one-way; see CONSECUTIVE, CONSTANT, REGULAR 3. —**through and through** permeating, pervasive, enduring; see THROUGHOUT, COMPLETELY.

throughout ***a., prep.*** all through, during, from beginning to end, from one end to the other, everywhere, all over, in everything, in every place, up and down, on all accounts, in all respects, inside and out, at full length, every bit, to the end, from the word go, to the brim*; see also COMPLETELY.

throw ***v.*** **1** [To hurl] fling, butt, bunt, pitch, fire, let go, sling, toss, heave, lob, dash, launch, chuck, bowl, cast, hurl at, let fly, deliver, cast off.—*Ant.* CATCH, receive, grab. **2** [To use a switch to connect or disconnect power] flip a switch, turn a knob, push a button; see TURN OFF, TURN ON 1. **3** [To force to the ground] pin, nail*, flatten; see DEFEAT 3. **4** [*To lose by allowing an opponent to succeed] lose deliberately, lose as planned, give over; see LOSE 3. —**throw away** reject, refuse, turn down; see DISCARD. —**throw in** add, expend, give; see INCREASE. —**throw out** discharge, throw away, reject; see DISCARD. —**throw together** make quickly, do in a hurry, do a rush job; see BUILD, MANUFACTURE. —**throw up** **1** [To vomit] regurgitate, retch, barf*; see VOMIT. **2** [To quit] give up, cease, terminate; see STOP 2. **3** [To construct, usually hastily] build overnight, patch up, knock together; see BUILD.

thrown ***a.*** **1** [Hurled] pitched, tossed, heaved; see SENT. **2** [Beaten] knocked over, sent sprawling, heaved; see BEATEN 1.

thrust ***n.*** **1** [A jab] punch, stab, poke; see BLOW. **2** [An attack] onset, onslaught, advance; see ATTACK. **3** [A strong push] drive, impetus, pressure; see PUSH.

thrust ***v.*** poke, push, shove; see HIT 1.

thud ***n.*** thump, dull sound, plop; see NOISE 1.

thumb ***n.*** opposable digit, first digit, preaxial digit; see FINGER. —**all thumbs** fumbling, clumsy, inept; see AWKWARD. —**under someone's thumb** under someone's control, controlled, governed; see MANAGED.

with the thumb —**all thumbs** clumsy —**under someone's thumb** under someone's influence

thumb'nail' *n.* the nail of the thumb —*adj.* very small, brief, or concise

thumb'screw' *n.* **1** a screw that can be turned by the thumb and forefinger **2** a former instrument of torture for squeezing the thumbs

thumb'tack' *n.* a tack with a wide, flat head that can be pressed into a board, etc. with the thumb

thump (thump) *n.* ⟦echoic⟧ **1** a blow with something heavy and blunt **2** the dull sound made by such a blow —*vt.* to strike with a thump —*vi.* **1** to hit or fall with a thump **2** to make a dull, heavy sound

thump'ing *adj.* **1** that thumps **2** [Inf.] very large; whopping

thun·der (thun'dər) *n.* ⟦OE *thunor*⟧ **1** the sound following a flash of lightning **2** any similar sound —*vi.* to produce thunder or a sound like this —*vt.* to say very loudly —**thun'der·ous** *adj.*

thun'der·bolt' *n.* **1** a flash of lightning and the accompanying thunder **2** something sudden and shocking, as bad news

thun'der·clap' *n.* a clap, or loud crash, of thunder

thun'der·cloud' *n.* a storm cloud charged with electricity and producing lightning and thunder

thun'der·head' *n.* a round mass of cumulus clouds appearing before a thunderstorm

thun'der·show'er *n.* a shower accompanied by thunder and lightning

thun'der·storm' *n.* a storm accompanied by thunder and lightning

thun'der·struck' *adj.* struck with amazement, terror, etc.: also **thun'der·strick'en** (-strik'ən)

Thurs·day (thurz'dā) *n.* ⟦< ON *Thorsdagr,* Thor's day⟧ the fifth day of the week: abbrev. **Thur** or **Thurs**

thus (*th*us) *adv.* ⟦OE⟧ **1** in this or that manner **2** to this or that degree or extent **3** therefore **4** for example

thwack (thwak) *vt., n.* ⟦prob. echoic⟧ WHACK

thwart (thwôrt) *n.* ⟦< ON *thvert,* transverse⟧ a seat across a boat —*vt.* to obstruct, frustrate, or defeat (a person, plans, etc.)

thy (*th*ī) *poss. pronominal adj.* ⟦< ME *thin*⟧ *archaic or poet. var. of* YOUR

thyme (tīm) *n.* ⟦< Gr *thymon*⟧ an herb of the mint family, with leaves used for seasoning

thy·mo·sin (thī'mə sin) *n.* ⟦< Gr *thymos,* thymus⟧ a hormone secreted by the thymus that stimulates the immune system

thy·mus (thī'məs) *n.* ⟦Gr *thymos*⟧ an endocrine gland situated near the throat: also **thymus gland**

thy·roid (thī'roid') *adj.* ⟦< Gr *thyreos,* large shield⟧ designating or of a large endocrine gland near the trachea, secreting a hormone that regulates growth —*n.* **1** the thyroid gland **2** an animal extract of this gland, used in treating goiter

thy·self (*th*ī self') *pron.* [Archaic] *reflexive or intensive form of* THOU

ti (tē) *n. Music* the seventh tone of the diatonic scale

Ti *Chem. symbol for* titanium

Ti·a Jua·na (tē'ə wä'nə) *former name for* TIJUANA

Tian·jin (tyen'jin') seaport in NE China: pop. 5,152,000

ti·ar·a (tē er'ə, -ar'-, -är'-) *n.* ⟦< Gr⟧ **1** the pope's triple crown **2** a woman's crownlike headdress

Ti·ber (tī'bər) river in central Italy, flowing through Rome

Ti·bet (ti bet') plateau region of SW China, north of the Himalayas —**Ti·bet'an** *adj., n.*

tib·i·a (tib'ē ə) *n., pl.* **-i·ae'** (-ē ē') or **-i·as** ⟦L⟧ the inner and thicker of the bones of the lower leg

tic (tik) *n.* ⟦Fr < ?⟧ any involuntary, regularly repeated, spasmodic contraction of a muscle

tick[1] (tik) *n.* ⟦prob. echoic⟧ **1** a light clicking sound, as of a clock **2** a mark made to check off items —*vi.* to make a tick or ticks —*vt.* to record, mark, or check by ticks —**tick off** [Slang] to make angry

tick[2] (tik) *n.* ⟦OE *ticia*⟧ a wingless, bloodsucking mite that infests humans, cattle, etc.

tick[3] (tik) *n.* ⟦< ? L *theca,* a cover⟧ the cloth case of a mattress or pillow

ticked (tikt) *adj.* ⟦< TICK OFF⟧ [Slang] angry

tick'er *n.* **1** one that ticks **2** a telegraphic device for recording stock market quotations, etc. on a paper tape (**ticker tape**) **3** [Slang] the heart

tick·et (tik'it) *n.* ⟦< obs. Fr *etiquet,* etiquette⟧ **1** a printed card, etc. that gives one a right, as to attend a theater **2** a license or certificate **3** a label on merchandise giving size, price, etc. **4** the list of candidates nominated by a political party **5** [Inf.] a summons to court for a traffic violation —*vt.* **1** to label with a ticket **2** to give a ticket to

tick'ing *n.* strong cloth, often striped, used for casings of pillows, etc.

tick·le (tik'əl) *vt.* **-led, -ling** ⟦ME *tikelen*⟧ **1** to please, gratify, delight, etc. **2** to stroke lightly so as to cause involuntary twitching, laughter, etc. —*vi.* to have or cause an itching or tingling sensation —*n.* a sensation of being tickled

tick·ler (tik'lər) *n.* a pad, file, etc. for noting matters to be remembered

tick'lish (-lish) *adj.* **1** sensitive to tickling **2** needing careful handling; precarious; delicate

tick-tack-toe or **tic-tac-toe** (tik'tak tō') *n.* a game for two, each marking X (or O) in turn in a nine-square block so as to complete any one row before the other can

tick·tock (tik'täk') *n.* the sound made by a clock or watch

tid·al (tīd''l) *adj.* of, having, or caused by, a tide or tides

tidal wave **1** *nontechnical term for* a tsunami or a similar huge wave caused by strong winds **2** any widespread movement, feeling, etc.

tid·bit (tid'bit') *n.* ⟦dial. *tid,* small object⟧ a choice bit of food, gossip, etc.

tid·dly·winks (tid'lē wiŋks') *n.* ⟦< ?⟧ a game in which little disks are snapped into a cup by pressing their edges with a larger disk

tide (tīd) *n.* ⟦OE *tid,* time⟧ **1** a period of time: now only in combination *[Eastertide]* **2** the alternate rise and fall, about twice a day, of the surface of oceans, seas, etc., caused by the attraction of the moon and sun **3** something that rises and falls like the tide **4** a stream, trend, etc. —*vi.* **tid'ed, tid'ing** to help along temporarily: with *over*

tide'land' *n.* **1** land uncovered at low tide **2** [*pl.*] loosely, land under the sea within territorial waters of a country

tide'wa'ter *n.* **1** water that is affected by the tide **2** land that is affected by the tide —*adj.* of or along a tidewater

ti·dings (tī'diŋz) *pl.n.* ⟦OE *tidung*⟧ news; information

ti·dy (tī'dē) *adj.* **-di·er, -di·est** ⟦<OE *tid,* time⟧ **1** neat in appearance, arrangement, etc.; orderly **2** [Inf.] rather large *[a tidy sum]* —*vt., vi.* **-died, -dy·ing** to make tidy: often with *up* —**ti'di·ness** *n.*

tie (tī) *vt.* **tied, ty'ing** or **tie'ing** ⟦< OE *teag,* a rope⟧ **1** to bind, as with string, rope, etc. **2** to knot the laces, etc. of

THESAURUS

thump *n.* thud, knock, rap; see NOISE 1, BLOW.

thump *v.* pound, knock, rap, wallop, slap, strike, whack, hit; see also BEAT 1, HIT 1.

thunder *n.* crash, peal, outburst, explosion, boom, booming, roar, rumble, clap, crack, discharge, thunderbolt, uproar, blast; see also NOISE 1.

thunder *v.* peal, boom, rumble, resound, roll, crash, clamor, clash; see also SOUND, STORM.

thunderous *a.* booming, roaring, crashing; see LOUD 1, 2.

thunderstorm *n.* electrical storm, squall, downpour; see THUNDER, STORM.

thunderstruck *a.* astonished, confounded, astounded, dumbfounded; see also BEWILDERED.

thus *a.* in this manner, so, consequently, hence, in such a way, just like that, in kind, along these lines; see also THEREFORE.

thwart *v.* stop, impede, frustrate; see CONFUSE, PREVENT.

tick[1,2] *n.* **1** [A light beat] beat, tap, click, ticktock; see also BEAT 1, 2. **2** [An insect] parasite, louse, mite; see INSECT, PEST 1.

ticket *n.* **1** [A valid token] check, tag, slip, pass, note, card, badge, label, voucher, rain check, stub, receipt, record, license, permit, passage, credential, visa, passport, document. **2** [Candidates representing a political party] party list, choice, ballot; see CANDIDATE, FACTION, PARTY 3.

tickle *v.* rub, caress, stroke; see TOUCH 1.

ticklish *a.* sensitive, unsteady, touchy; see IRRITABLE, UNSTABLE 2.

tidbit *n.* morsel, mouthful, bite; see BIT 1.

tide *n.* current, flow, flux, stream, course, sluice, undercurrent, undertow, drag, whirlpool, eddy, vortex, torrent, wave, tidal wave, tsunami. *Tides of the sea include the following:* low, neap, ebb, spring, full, high, flood.

tidiness *n.* neatness, orderliness, uniformity; see CLEANLINESS.

tidy *a.* orderly, trim, spruce; see NEAT 1.

tie *n.* **1** [A fastening] band, bond, strap, brace, yoke, bandage, zipper; see also FASTENER. **2** [A necktie] cravat, neckerchief, bow tie, Windsor tie, ascot, four-in-hand, scarf, neckcloth, choker. **3** [Affection] bond, relation,

3 to make (a knot) in **4** to bind in any way **5** to equal the score of, as in a contest —***vi.*** to make an equal score, as in a contest —***n.*** **1** a string, cord, etc. used to tie things **2** something that connects, binds, etc. **3** a necktie **4** a beam, rod, etc. that holds parts together **5** any of the crossbeams to which the rails of a railroad are fastened **6** *a)* an equality of scores, etc. *b)* a contest in which this occurs —***adj.*** that has been made equal *[a tie score]* —**tie down** to confine; restrict —**tie up** **1** to wrap up and tie **2** to moor to a dock **3** to obstruct; hinder **4** to cause to be already in use, committed, etc.

tie'back' ***n.*** a band or ribbon used to tie curtains, etc. to one side

tie'break'er ***n.*** an additional game, period of play, etc. used to establish a winner from among those tied at the end of a contest

tie clasp a decorative clasp for fastening a necktie to the shirt: also **tie clip**

tie'-dye' ***n.*** a method of dyeing designs on cloth by tying bunches of it so that the dye affects only exposed parts —***vt.*** **-dyed', -dye'ing** to dye in this way

tie'-in' ***n.*** a connection or relationship

Tien·tsin (tyen'tsin') *a former transliteration of* TIANJIN

tier (tir) ***n.*** ⟦< OFr *tire*, order⟧ any of a series of rows arranged one above or behind another

tie rod a rod connecting certain parts in the steering linkage of a motor vehicle

tie tack or **tie tac** a decorative pin fitted into a snap to fasten a necktie to a shirt

tie-up (tī'up') ***n.*** **1** a temporary stoppage of production, traffic, etc. **2** connection or relation

tiff (tif) ***n.*** ⟦< ?⟧ a slight quarrel; spat

Tif·fa·ny (tif'ə nē) ***adj.*** ⟦after L. C. *Tiffany* (1848-1933), U.S. designer⟧ of a style in stained glass

ti·ger (tī'gər) ***n.*** ⟦< Gr *tigris*⟧ **1** a large, fierce Asian cat, having a tawny coat striped with black **2** one who is dynamic, fierce, etc.

tight (tīt) ***adj.*** ⟦< OE *-thight*, strong⟧ **1** so compact in structure that water, air, etc. cannot pass through **2** drawn, packed, etc. closely together **3** fixed securely; firm **4** fully stretched; taut **5** fitting so closely as to be uncomfortable **6** difficult: esp. in **a tight corner** (or **squeeze**, etc.), a difficult situation **7** showing tension, etc. *[a tight smile]* **8** almost tied *[a tight race]* **9** sharp; abrupt *[a tight turn in the road]* **10** difficult to get; scarce **11** [Inf.] stingy **12** [Slang] drunk **13** [Slang] very familiar —***adv.*** **1** securely **2** [Inf.] soundly *[sleep tight]* —**sit tight** to keep one's opinion or position and wait —**tight'ly** ***adv.*** —**tight'ness** ***n.***

tight'en ***vt., vi.*** to make or become tight or tighter —**tight'en·er** ***n.***

tight'fist'ed ***adj.*** stingy

tight'fit'ting ***adj.*** fitting very tight

tight'-lipped' ***adj.*** secretive

tight'rope' ***n.*** a tightly stretched rope on which acrobats perform

tights ***pl.n.*** a tightly fitting garment for the lower half of the body, as worn by acrobats or dancers

tight ship [Inf.] an organization as efficient as a well-run ship

tight'wad' ***n.*** ⟦TIGHT + *wad*, roll of money⟧ [Slang] a stingy person

ti·gress (tī'gris) ***n.*** a female tiger

Ti·gris (tī'gris) river flowing from EC Turkey to a juncture with the Euphrates in SE Iraq

Ti·jua·na (tē'ə wä'nə) city in Baja California, NW Mexico, on the U.S. border: official pop. 747,000; actual pop. between 1,000,000 and 2,000,000

til·de (til'də) ***n.*** ⟦Sp < L *titulus*, a sign⟧ a diacritical mark (~)

tile (tīl) ***n.*** ⟦< L *tegula*⟧ **1** a thin piece of stone, fired clay, etc. used for roofing, flooring, etc. **2** a similar piece of plastic, etc. **3** a drain of earthenware pipe —***vt.*** **tiled, til'ing** to cover with tiles

til'ing ***n.*** tiles collectively

till[1] (til) ***prep., conj.*** ⟦OE *til*⟧ UNTIL

till[2] (til) ***vt., vi.*** ⟦< OE *tilian*, lit., strive for⟧ to prepare (land) for raising crops, as by plowing

till[3] (til) ***n.*** ⟦< ? ME *tillen*, to draw⟧ a drawer for keeping money

till'age ***n.*** **1** the tilling of land **2** land that is tilled

till·er (til'ər) ***n.*** ⟦< ML *telarium*, weaver's beam⟧ a bar or handle for turning a boat's rudder

tilt (tilt) ***vt.*** ⟦ME *tilten*, totter⟧ to cause to slant; tip —***vi.*** **1** to slope; incline **2** to charge (*at* an opponent) **3** to take part in a tilt —***n.*** **1** a medieval contest in which two horsemen fight with lances **2** any spirited contest **3** a slope —**(at) full tilt** at full speed

tilt'-top' ***adj.*** of a table with a hinged top that can be tipped vertically

tim·bale (tim'bəl) ***n.*** ⟦Fr⟧ **1** chicken, lobster, etc. in a cream sauce, baked in a drum-shaped mold **2** a pastry shell, filled with a cooked food

tim·ber (tim'bər) ***n.*** ⟦OE⟧ **1** wood for building houses, ships, etc. **2** a wooden beam used in building **3** trees collectively —**tim'bered** ***adj.***

tim'ber·line' ***n.*** the line above or beyond which trees do not grow, as on mountains

tim·bre (tam'bər, tim'-) ***n.*** ⟦< OFr, kind of drum⟧ the quality of sound that distinguishes one voice or musical instrument from another

time (tīm) ***n.*** ⟦OE *tima*⟧ **1** every moment there has ever been or ever will be **2** a system of measuring duration *[standard time]* **3** the period during which something

THESAURUS

kinship; see AFFECTION, LOVE 1. **4** [An equal score, or a contest having that score] deadlock, draw, even game, dead heat, drawn battle, neck-and-neck contest, even-steven*, stalemate, standoff, wash*.

tie ***v.*** **1** [To fasten] bind, make fast, attach; see FASTEN, JOIN 1. **2** [To tie a knot in] knot, make a bow, make a tie, make a knot, do up, fix a tie, make a hitch; see also sense 1. **3** [To equal] match, keep up with, parallel; see EQUAL. —**tie up** **1** [To fasten] wrap, package, secure; see CLOSE 4, ENCLOSE. **2** [To obstruct] hinder, stop, delay; see HINDER.

tied ***a.*** **1** [Firm] fixed, bound, made firm; see FIRM 1. **2** [Even] evenly matched, running neck and neck, in a dead heat; see ALIKE, EQUAL.

tight ***a.*** **1** [Firm] taut, secure, fast, bound up, close, clasped, fixed, steady, stretched thin, established, compact, strong, stable, enduring, steadfast, unyielding, unbending, set, stuck hard, hidebound, invulnerable, snug, sturdy; see also FIRM 1.—*Ant.* LOOSE, tottery, shaky. **2** [Closed] sealed, airtight, impenetrable, impermeable, impervious, watertight, waterproof, hermetically sealed, padlocked, bolted, locked, fastened, shut tight, clamped, fixed, tied, snapped, swung to, tied up, nailed, spiked, slammed, obstructed, blocked, blind, shut, stopped up, plugged.—*Ant.* OPEN, penetrable, unprotected. **3** [Closefitting] pinching, shrunken, snug, uncomfortable, cramping, skintight, short, crushing, choking, smothering, cutting.—*Ant.* LOOSE, ample, wide. **4** [*Intoxicated] inebriated, drunken, tipsy; see DRUNK. **5** [*Stingy] parsimonious, miserly, cheap*; see STINGY. **6** [Difficult to obtain; *said especially of money*] scarce, frozen, tied up; see RARE 2. —**sit tight** do nothing, refrain from action, stay put; see WAIT 1.

tighten ***v.*** **1** [To make tight] compress, condense, squeeze, bind, contract, strangle, constrict, crush, cramp, pinch, grip more tightly, clench, screw down, add pressure; see also STRETCH 2.—*Ant.* LOOSEN, relax, unloose. **2** [To become tight] contract, harden, congeal, stiffen, toughen, become more disciplined.—*Ant.* SOFTEN, melt, liquefy.

tightfisted ***a.*** thrifty, niggardly, frugal; see STINGY.

tile ***n.*** baked clay, flooring, roofing; see CLAY, FLOORING.

till[2] ***v.*** cultivate, work, raise crops from; see FARM.

tilt ***n.*** slant, slope, incline; see INCLINATION 2.

tilt ***v.*** slant, tip, turn, set at an angle, lean, slope, slouch, shift, dip, sway, make oblique, deviate, turn edgewise; see also BEND.—*Ant.* STRAIGHTEN, level, bring into line.

timber ***n.*** **1** [Standing trees] wood, lumber, timberland; see FOREST. **2** [A beam] stake, pole, club; see BEAM 1, LUMBER.

time ***n.*** **1** [Duration] continuance, lastingness, extent, past, present, future, infinity, space-time, chronology; see also TODAY. *Units of measuring time include the following:* second, minute, hour, day, term, millisecond, nanosecond, week, month, year, decade, generation, lifetime, century, millennium, eon, epoch, era, period. **2** [A point in time] incident, event, occurrence, occasion, moment, instant, term, season, tide, course, sequence, point, generation. **3** [A period of time] season, era, interval; see AGE 3. **4** [Experience] background, living, participation; see EXPERIENCE. **5** [Leisure] opportunity, free moment, chance; see FREEDOM 2. **6** [Circumstances; *usually plural; used with "the"*] condition, the present, nowadays; see CIRCUMSTANCE 1, CIRCUMSTANCES 2. **7** [A measure of speed] tempo, rate, meter; see BEAT 2. —**ahead of time** ahead of schedule, fast, earlier than expected; see EARLY 2. —**at one time** simultaneously, concurrently, at once; see

exists, happens, etc. **4** [*often pl.*] a period of history; age, era, etc. **5** [*usually pl.*] prevailing conditions [*times* are good] **6** a set period or term, as of work, confinement, etc. **7** standard rate of pay **8** rate of speed in marching, driving, etc. **9** a precise or designated instant, moment, day, etc. **10** an occasion or repeated occasion [the fifth *time* it's been on TV] **11** *Music a*) rhythm as determined by the grouping of beats into measures *b*) tempo **12** *Sports* TIMEOUT —***vt.* timed, tim'ing** **1** to arrange the time of so as to be suitable, opportune, etc. **2** to adjust, set, etc. so as to coincide in time [*time* our watches] **3** to calculate the pace, speed, etc. of —***adj.*** **1** having to do with time **2** set to explode, open, etc. at a given time [a *time* bomb] **3** having to do with paying in installments —**ahead of time** early —**at the same time** however —**at times** occasionally —**do time** [Inf.] to serve a prison term —**for the time being** temporarily —**from time to time** now and then —**in time** **1** eventually **2** before it is too late **3** keeping the set tempo, pace, etc. —**make time** to travel, work, etc. rapidly —**on time** **1** at the appointed time **2** for or by payment by installments —**time after time** again and again: also **time and again**

time clock a clock with a mechanism for recording the time an employee begins and ends a work period

time exposure a photograph taken by exposure of a film or plate for a relatively long period

time frame a given period of time

time'-hon'ored ***adj.*** honored because of long existence or usage

time'keep'er ***n.*** one who keeps account of hours worked by employees or of the elapsed time in races, games, etc.

time'-lapse' ***adj.*** of filming a slow process by exposing single frames at long intervals: the film is projected at regular speed, showing the process greatly speeded up

time'less ***adj.*** **1** eternal **2** always valid or true

time'line' ***n.*** a chronological chart or list of events, dates, plans, etc.

time'ly ***adj.*** **-li·er, -li·est** well-timed; opportune —**time'li·ness** ***n.***

time'out' ***n.*** *Sports* any temporary suspension of play

time'piece' ***n.*** any device for measuring and recording time, as a clock or watch

tim·er (tīm'ər) ***n.*** a device for controlling the timing of some mechanism

time'-re·lease' ***adj.*** releasing active ingredients gradually

times (tīmz) ***prep.*** multiplied by

time sharing **1** a system for simultaneous computer use at many remote sites **2** a system for sharing ownership of a vacation home, etc., with each joint purchaser occupying the unit at a specific time each year: also **time share**

time sheet a sheet on which are recorded the hours an employee works

time'ta'ble ***n.*** a schedule of the times of arrival and departure of airplanes, trains, buses, etc.

time'-test'ed ***adj.*** having value proved by long use or experience

time warp displacement from one point in time to another, as in science fiction

time'worn' ***adj.*** **1** worn out by long use **2** hackneyed; trite

time zone *see* STANDARD TIME

tim·id (tim'id) ***adj.*** ⟦< L *timere*, to fear⟧ lacking self-confidence; shy; fearful; hesitant —**ti·mid·i·ty** (tə mid'ə tē) ***n.*** —**tim'id·ly** ***adv.***

tim·ing (tīm'iŋ) ***n.*** the regulation of pace or speed as it affects performance

tim·or·ous (tim'ər əs) ***adj.*** ⟦< L *timor*, fear⟧ full of fear; timid; afraid

tim·o·thy (tim'ə thē) ***n.*** ⟦after a *Timothy* Hanson, c. 1720⟧ a perennial grass with dense spikes, grown for hay

tim·pa·ni (tim'pə nē) ***pl.n.***, *sing.* **-no'** (-nō') ⟦It: see TYMPANUM⟧ [*often with sing. v.*] kettledrums; esp., a set of them played by one performer —**tim'pa·nist** ***n.***

tin (tin) ***n.*** ⟦OE⟧ **1** a soft, silver-white, metallic chemical element **2** TIN PLATE **3** *a*) a pan, box, etc. made of tin plate *b*) [Chiefly Brit.] CAN[2] (*n.* 2, 3) Variously used to connote cheapness, etc. of something —***vt.* tinned, tin'ning** **1** to plate with tin **2** [Chiefly Brit.] CAN[2] (*vt.* 1)

tin can CAN[2] (*n.* 2)

tinc·ture (tiŋk'chər) ***n.*** ⟦< L *tingere*, to dye⟧ **1** a light color; tinge **2** a slight trace **3** a dilute solution of a medicinal substance in alcohol —***vt.* -tured, -tur·ing** to tinge

tin·der (tin'dər) ***n.*** ⟦OE *tynder*⟧ any dry, easily flammable material

tin'der·box' ***n.*** **1** [Obs.] a box to hold tinder **2** a highly flammable building, etc. **3** a potential source of war, rebellion, etc.

tine (tīn) ***n.*** ⟦OE *tind*⟧ a slender, projecting point; prong [fork *tines*]

tin'foil' ***n.*** **1** tin in thin sheets **2** aluminum in thin sheets, used for wrapping food, etc.

tinge (tinj) ***n.*** ⟦see TINT⟧ **1** a slight coloring; tint **2** a slight trace, flavor, etc. —***vt.* tinged, tinge'ing** or **ting'ing** to give a tinge to

tin·gle (tiŋ'gəl) ***vi.*** **-gled, -gling** ⟦var. of TINKLE⟧ to have a prickling or stinging feeling, as from cold, excitement, etc. —***n.*** this feeling —**tin'gly** ***adj.***

tin·ker (tiŋk'ər) ***n.*** ⟦ME *tinkere*⟧ **1** one who mends pots, pans, etc. **2** a bungler —***vi.*** **1** to attempt clumsily to mend something **2** to putter

tin·kle (tiŋk'əl) ***vi.*** **-kled, -kling** ⟦echoic⟧ to make a series of light sounds as of a tiny bell —***vt.*** to cause to tinkle —***n.*** a tinkling sound

tin·ny (tin'ē) ***adj.*** **-ni·er, -ni·est** **1** of or like tin **2** not well-made **3** high-pitched and lacking resonance [*tinny* music] —**tin'ni·ness** ***n.***

tin plate thin sheets of iron or steel plated with tin

tin·sel (tin'səl) ***n.*** ⟦< L *scintilla*, a spark⟧ **1** thin strips of tin, metal foil, etc., as for decoration **2** something of little worth that glitters

tin'smith' ***n.*** one who works in tin or tin plate

tint (tint) ***n.*** ⟦< L *tingere*, to dye⟧ **1** a pale color **2** a gradation of a color; shade **3** a hair dye —***vt.*** to give a tint to

tin·tin·nab·u·la·tion (tin'ti nab'yoo lā'shən) ***n.*** ⟦< L *tintinnabulum*, little bell⟧ the ringing sound of bells

tin·type (tin'tīp') ***n.*** an old kind of photograph taken directly as a positive print on a treated plate of tin or iron

THESAURUS

TOGETHER 2. —**at the same time** simultaneously, concurrently, at once; see TOGETHER 2. —**at times** occasionally, sometimes, once in a while; see SELDOM. —**behind the times** out of date, archaic, obsolete; see OLD-FASHIONED. —**behind time** tardy, delayed, coming later; see LATE 1. —**do time*** serve a prison term, go to jail, be imprisoned; see SERVE TIME. —**for the time being** for the present, for now, under consideration; see TEMPORARILY. —**from time to time** occasionally, sometimes, once in a while; see FREQUENTLY. —**in due time** eventually, at an appropriate time, in the natural course of events; see FINALLY 2, ULTIMATELY. —**in no time** instantly, rapidly, without delay; see QUICKLY, SOON. —**in time** eventually, after the proper time, inevitably; see FINALLY 2. —**lose time** go too slow, tarry, cause a delay; see DELAY. —**make time** gain time, act hastily, hasten; see HURRY 1. —**many a time** often, regularly, consistently; see FREQUENTLY. —**on time** **1** at the appointed time, punctually, correct; see PUNCTUAL. **2** by credit, in installments, on account; see UNPAID 1. —**pass the time of day** exchange greetings, chat, converse; see GREET. —**serve time** serve a jail sentence, be incarcerated, be in jail, pay one's debt to society, go to jail, do time*, be sent up*. —**take one's time** dawdle, slow down, dillydally; see DELAY, LOITER. —**waste time** malinger, dawdle, drift; see LOAF.

time ***v.*** register distance, clock, measure time; see MEASURE 1.

time-honored ***a.*** revered, eminent, noble; see VENERABLE.

timely ***a.*** opportune, seasonable, in good time, fitting the times, suitable, appropriate, convenient, propitious, well-timed, modern, up-to-date, newsworthy, fit.—*Ant.* UNTIMELY, ill-timed, inappropriate.

timepiece ***n.*** timekeeper, chronometer, stopwatch; see CLOCK, WATCH 1.

timid ***a.*** **1** [Irresolute] indecisive, vacillating, wavering; see IRRESPONSIBLE. **2** [Cowardly] fainthearted, spiritless, weak; see AFRAID, COWARDLY. **3** [Reticent] shy, withdrawn, modest; see HUMBLE 1.

tinge ***n.*** tint, shade, hint; see TRACE 1, TINT.

tingle ***v.*** shiver, prickle, sting, itch, creep, grow excited, thrill, get goose pimples all over*.

tinker ***v.*** try to mend, play with, take apart; see REPAIR.

tint ***n.*** tinge, hue, shade, color value, cast, flush, dye, tinct, taint, coloring, glow, pastel color, luminous color, pale hue, tone, tincture, dash, touch, luminosity, color tone, coloration, pigmentation, ground color, complexion; see also COLOR.

tinted ***a.*** tinged, painted, touched up; see COLORED.

ti·ny (tī′nē) ***adj.*** **-ni·er, -ni·est** ⟦< ME *tine, n.*, a little⟧ very small

-tion (shən) ⟦< Fr < L⟧ *suffix* **1** the act of ___ing **2** the state of being ___ed **3** the thing that is ___ed

-tious (shəs) *suffix* of, having, or characterized by

tip[1] (tip) ***n.*** ⟦ME *tippe*⟧ **1** the point or end of something **2** something attached to the end, as a cap, etc. —***vt.*** **tipped, tip′ping 1** to form a tip on **2** to cover the tip of

tip[2] (tip) ***vt.*** **tipped, tip′ping** ⟦< ?⟧ **1** to strike lightly and sharply **2** to give a gratuity to (a waiter, etc.) **3** [Inf.] to give secret information to: often with *off* —***vi.*** to give a tip or tips —***n.*** **1** a light, sharp blow **2** a piece of confidential information **3** a hint, warning, etc. **4** a gratuity —**tip one's hand** [Slang] to reveal a secret, one's plans, etc., often without meaning to —**tip′per** ***n.***

tip[3] (tip) ***vt.***, ***vi.*** **tipped, tip′ping** ⟦ME *tipen*⟧ **1** to overturn or upset: often with *over* **2** to tilt or slant —***n.*** a tilt; slant

tip′-off′ ***n.*** a tip; confidential disclosure, hint, or warning

tip·ple (tip′əl) ***vi.***, ***vt.*** **-pled, -pling** ⟦< ?⟧ to drink (alcoholic liquor) habitually —**tip′pler** ***n.***

tip·ster (tip′stər) ***n.*** [Inf.] one who sells tips, as on horse races or the stock market

tip·sy (tip′sē) ***adj.*** **-si·er, -si·est 1** that tips easily; not steady **2** somewhat drunk —**tip′si·ly** ***adv.***

tip′toe′ ***vi.*** **-toed′, -toe′ing** to walk carefully, with the heels raised —**on tiptoe 1** standing with the heels raised **2** excited, alert, etc. **3** silently and stealthily

tip′top′ ***n.*** ⟦TIP[1] + TOP[1]⟧ the highest point —***adj.***, ***adv.*** **1** at the highest point **2** [Inf.] at the highest point of excellence, health, etc.

ti·rade (tī′rād′) ***n.*** ⟦< It *tirare*, to fire⟧ a long, vehement speech or denunciation; harangue

tire[1] (tīr) ***vt.***, ***vi.*** **tired, tir′ing** ⟦OE *tiorian*⟧ to make or become weary, exhausted, bored, etc.

tire[2] (tīr) ***n.*** ⟦ME *tyre*⟧ **1** a hoop of iron or rubber around the wheel of a vehicle **2** an inflatable, vulcanized rubber or synthetic casing sealed to a wheel rim by air pressure

tired (tīrd) ***adj.*** **1** weary **2** hackneyed —**tired′ly** ***adv.*** —**tired′ness** ***n.***

tire iron a crowbar with a built-in wrench, for changing automobile tires

tire′less ***adj.*** persistent, unwavering, etc. —**tire′less·ly** ***adv.*** —**tire′less·ness** ***n.***

tire′some (-səm) ***adj.*** **1** tiring; boring **2** annoying —**tire′some·ly** ***adv.*** —**tire′some·ness** ***n.***

Ti·rol (ti rōl′, -räl′) E Alpine region in W Austria & N Italy —**Ti·ro·le·an** (ti rō′lē ən, tī-) ***adj.***, ***n.***

'tis (tiz) *contr.* [Old Poet.] it is

tis·sue (tish′o͞o) ***n.*** ⟦< L *texere*, to weave⟧ **1** light, thin cloth **2** an interwoven mass; mesh; web **3** a piece of soft, absorbent paper, used as a disposable handkerchief, etc. **4** TISSUE PAPER **5** the substance of an organic body, consisting of cells and intercellular material

tissue paper very thin wrapping paper

tit[1] (tit) ***n.*** a titmouse

tit[2] (tit) ***n.*** ⟦OE⟧ **1** NIPPLE (sense 1) **2** a breast: in this sense now vulgar

ti·tan (tīt′′n) ***n.*** ⟦< Gr *Titan*, a giant deity⟧ any person or thing of great size or power

ti·tan·ic (tī tan′ik) ***adj.*** of great size, strength, or power

ti·ta·ni·um (tī tā′nē əm) ***n.*** ⟦see TITAN⟧ a silvery or dark-gray, metallic chemical element used in manufacturing

tit for tat ⟦var. of earlier *tip for tap*⟧ this for that: phrase indicating retribution

tithe (tīth) ***n.*** ⟦OE *teothe*, a tenth⟧ a tenth of one's income paid to a church —***vi.*** **tithed, tith′ing** to pay a tithe

ti·tian (tish′ən) ***n.*** ⟦after *Titian* (1490?-1576), Venetian painter⟧ reddish gold

tit·il·late (tit′′l āt′) ***vt.*** **-lat′ed, -lat′ing** ⟦< L *titillare*, tickle⟧ to excite pleasurably —**tit′il·la′tion** ***n.***

ti·tle (tīt′′l) ***n.*** ⟦< L *titulus*⟧ **1** the name of a book, poem, picture, etc. **2** an epithet **3** an appellation indicating one's rank, profession, etc. **4** a claim **5** *Film, TV* a subtitle, credit, etc. **6** *Law a)* a right to ownership, esp. of real estate *b)* a deed **7** *Sports, etc.* a championship —***vt.*** **-tled, -tling** to give a title to

ti′tled ***adj.*** having a title, esp. of nobility

ti′tle·hold′er ***n.*** the holder of a title; specif., the champion in some sport

title role (or **character**) the character in a play, film, etc. whose name is used as or in its title

ti·tlist (tīt′′l ist) ***n.*** a champion in some sport

tit·mouse (tit′mous′) ***n.***, *pl.* **-mice′** (-mīs′) ⟦ME *titemose*⟧ a small bird with ashy-gray feathers

tit·ter (tit′ər) ***vi.*** ⟦echoic⟧ to laugh in a half-suppressed way; giggle —***n.*** a tittering

tit·tle (tit′′l) ***n.*** ⟦ME *title*⟧ a very small particle; jot

tit·u·lar (tich′ə lər, tit′yə-) ***adj.*** ⟦see TITLE⟧ **1** of a title **2** having a title **3** in name only *[a titular sovereign]*

tiz·zy (tiz′ē) ***n.***, *pl.* **-zies** ⟦< ?⟧ [Inf.] a state of frenzied excitement

tko or **TKO** ***n.*** *Boxing* a technical knockout

TLC *abbrev.* tender, loving care

TM *abbrev.* trademark

tn *abbrev.* ton(s)

TN Tennessee

TNT ***n.*** ⟦*t(ri)n(itro)t(oluene)*⟧ a high explosive used for blasting, etc.

to (to͞o, too, tə) ***prep.*** ⟦OE⟧ **1** toward *[turn to the left]* **2** so as to reach *[she went to Boston]* **3** as far as *[wet to the skin]* **4** into a condition of *[a rise to fame]* **5** *a)* on, onto, against, at, etc. *[tied to a post]* *b)* in front of *[face to face]* **6** *a)* until *[from noon to night]* *b)* before *[the time is ten to six]* **7** for the purpose of *[come to dinner]* **8** in regard to *[open to attack]* **9** with the result of producing

THESAURUS

tiny ***a.*** small, miniature, diminutive; see LITTLE 1.

tip[1,2] ***n.*** **1** [The point] apex, peak, top; see POINT 2. **2** [A gratuity] reward, gift, compensation, fee, small change, money, lagniappe, handout; see also PAY 2. **3** [*A bit of information] hint, clue, warning; see KNOWLEDGE 1, NEWS 1.

tip[3] ***v.*** slant, incline, shift; see BEND, LEAN 1, TILT.

tiptop* ***a.*** superior, prime, choice; see BEST, EXCELLENT.

tire[1] ***v.*** **1** [To become exhausted] grow weary, break down, droop, flag, pall, faint, drop, huff and puff*, jade, sink, yawn, collapse, give out, wilt, go stale, poop out*, burn out.—*Ant.* REST, awake, relax. **2** [To make a person exhausted] tax, overtax, harass, fatigue, exhaust, overwork, strain, drain, overstrain, overburden, prostrate, depress, dispirit, pain, vex, worry, distress, deject, dishearten, wear out, run a person ragged, do in*.

tire[2] ***n.*** *Terms for types of tires include the following:* tubeless, belted, radial, snow, mud, puncture-proof, steel-belted, all-weather, all-terrain, recapped, synthetic, low-pressure, natural rubber, solid rubber, pneumatic, oversize, airplane, motorcycle, bicycle, recap.

tired ***a.*** fatigued, weary, run-down, exhausted, overworked, overtaxed, wearied, worn, spent, burned out, jaded, wasted, worn-out, drooping, distressed, drowsy, droopy, sleepy, haggard, faint, prostrated, broken-down, drained, consumed, empty, collapsing, all in*, finished, stale, fagged, dog-tired*, dead on one's feet*, pooped*, done in*, done for*, worn to a frazzle*, played out*, tuckered out*, fed up*.—*Ant.* ACTIVE, lively, energetic.

tireless ***a.*** unwearied, energetic, untiring; see ACTIVE.

tiresome ***a.*** irksome, wearying, monotonous; see DULL 4.

tissue ***n.*** **1** [A network] web, mesh, filigree; see NETWORK 2. **2** [Thin fabric] gauze, gossamer, lace; see VEIL, WEB. **3** [Protective layer, especially in living organisms] film, membrane, intercellular substance; see MUSCLE.

title ***n.*** **1** [A designation] indication, inscription, sign; see NAME 1. **2** [Ownership or evidence of ownship] right, claim, license; see OWNERSHIP. **3** [Mark of rank or dignity] commission, decoration, medal, ribbon, coat of arms, crest, order, authority, privilege, degree; see also EMBLEM. *Titles include the following:* Sir, Madam, Ma'am*, Doctor, Mr., Ms., Mrs., Miss, Reverend, Pastor, Father, Brother, Sister, Monsignor, Bishop, Archbishop, His Holiness, Pope, Cardinal, Patriarch, Rabbi, Imam, Swami, King, Queen, Prince, Princess, Duke, Duchess, Grand Duke, Marquis, Marquess, Marquise, Count, Earl, Countess, Viscount, Viscountess, Baron, Baroness, Dame, Lord, Lady, Sultan, Emperor, Empress, Monsieur, Madame, Mademoiselle, Don, Doña, Herr, Frau, Fräulein, Señor, Señora, Señorita, Signor, Signora, Signorina, General, Colonel, Major, Captain, Lieutenant, Admiral, Commander, Ensign, President, Vice President, Senator, Representative, Congressman, Congresswoman, Congressperson, Speaker, Secretary, Justice, Judge, Governor, Mayor, Professor, Esquire.

to ***prep.*** **1** [In the direction of] toward, via, into, facing, through, directed toward, traveling to, along the line of. **2** [Indicating position] over, upon, in front of; see ON 1. **3** [Until] till, up to, stopping at; see UNTIL. **4** [So that] in order to, intending to, that one may, for the purpose of. **5** [Indicating degree] up to, down to, as far as, in that degree, to this extent. **6** [Indicating result] becoming, until, back, ending with.

[torn *to* bits] **10** along with [add this *to* the rest] **11** belonging with [a key *to* the house] **12** as compared with [a score of 10 *to* 0] **13** in agreement with [not *to* my taste] **14** constituting [four quarts *to* a gallon] **15** with (a specified person or thing) as the recipient of the action [give it *to* me] **16** in honor of [a toast *to* you] **17** by [known *to* me] *To* is also a sign of the infinitive (Ex.: I want *to* stay) —***adv.*** **1** forward [wrong side *to*] **2** shut; closed [pull the door *to*] **3** into a state of consciousness [the boxer came *to*] **4** at hand [we were close *to* when it happened] —**to and fro** first in one direction and then in the opposite

toad (tōd) ***n.*** ⟦OE *tadde*⟧ a froglike amphibian that lives on moist land

toad'stool' (-sto͞ol') ***n.*** a mushroom; esp., any poisonous mushroom

toad·y (tō'dē) ***n.***, *pl.* **-ies** ⟦short for *toadeater*, quack doctor's assistant⟧ a servile flatterer —***vt.***, ***vi.*** **-ied**, **-y·ing** to be a toady (to)

toast[1] (tōst) ***vt.*** ⟦< L *torrere*, parch⟧ **1** to brown the surface of (bread, etc.) by heating **2** to warm thoroughly —***vi.*** to become toasted —***n.*** sliced bread made brown and crisp by heat —**toast'er** ***n.***

toast[2] (tōst) ***n.*** ⟦from the use of toasted spiced bread to flavor the wine⟧ **1** a drink, or a proposal to drink, in honor of some person, etc. **2** someone greatly admired or acclaimed [the *toast* of Broadway] —***vt.***, ***vi.*** to propose or drink a toast (to)

toast'mas'ter ***n.*** the person at a banquet who proposes toasts, introduces after-dinner speakers, etc.

toast'y ***adj.*** **-i·er**, **-i·est** warm and comfortable or cozy

to·bac·co (tə bak'ō) ***n.***, *pl.* **-cos** ⟦Sp *tabaco* < ?⟧ **1** a plant with large leaves that are prepared for smoking, chewing, etc. **2** cigars, cigarettes, etc.

to·bac·co·nist (tə bak'ə nist) ***n.*** [Chiefly Brit.] a dealer in tobacco

to·bog·gan (tə bäg'ən) ***n.*** ⟦< AmInd⟧ a long, flat sled without runners, for coasting downhill —***vi.*** **1** to coast on a toboggan **2** to decline rapidly

toc·sin (täk'sin) ***n.*** ⟦Fr < Prov *toc*, a stroke + *senh*, a bell⟧ an alarm bell or its sound

to·day (tə dā') ***adv.*** ⟦OE *to dæg*⟧ **1** on or during the present day **2** in the present time —***n.*** **1** the present day **2** the present time

tod·dle (täd''l) ***vi.*** **-dled**, **-dling** ⟦? < *totter*⟧ to walk with short, uncertain steps

tod'dler ***n.*** a very young child

tod·dy (täd'ē) ***n.***, *pl.* **-dies** ⟦< Hindi⟧ a drink of whiskey, etc. mixed with hot water, sugar, etc.: also **hot toddy**

to-do (tə do͞o') ***n.***, *pl.* **-dos'** [Inf.] a commotion; fuss

toe (tō) ***n.*** ⟦OE *ta*⟧ **1** *a)* any of the digits of the foot *b)* the forepart of the foot **2** anything like a toe in location, shape, or use —***vt.*** **toed**, **toe'ing** to touch, kick, etc. with the toes —***vi.*** to stand, walk, etc. with the toes in a specified position [he *toes* in] —**on one's toes** [Inf.] alert —**toe the line** (or **mark**) to follow orders, rules, etc. strictly

toed (tōd) ***adj.*** having (a specified kind or number of) toes: usually in compounds [two-*toed*]

toe dance a dance performed on the tips of the toes, as in ballet —**toe'-dance'**, **-danced'**, **-danc'ing**, ***vi.*** —**toe'-danc'er** ***n.***

toe'hold' ***n.*** **1** a small space to support the toe in climbing, etc. **2** a slight footing or advantage

toe'less ***adj.*** having the toe open or uncovered [a *toeless* shoe]

toe'nail' ***n.*** the nail of a toe

tof·fee or **tof·fy** (tôf'ē, täf'ē) ***n.*** ⟦< TAFFY⟧ a hard, chewy candy, a kind of taffy

to·fu (tō'fo͞o) ***n.*** ⟦Jpn⟧ a cheeselike food made from soybeans

to·ga (tō'gə) ***n.***, *pl.* **-gas** or **-gae** (-jē, -gē) ⟦L < *tegere*, to cover⟧ in ancient Rome, a loose outer garment worn in public by citizens

to·geth·er (tə ge*th*'ər) ***adv.*** ⟦< OE *to*, to + *gædre*, together⟧ **1** in or into one group, place, etc. [we ate *together*] **2** in or into contact, union, etc. [the cars skidded *together*] **3** considered collectively [he lost more than all of us *together*] **4** at the same time [shots fired *together*] **5** in succession [sulking for three whole days *together*] **6** in or into agreement, cooperation, etc. [to get *together* on a deal] —***adj.*** **1** with one another; not apart **2** [Slang] having a harmoniously organized personality

to·geth'er·ness ***n.*** the spending of much time together, as by family members, resulting in a more unified relationship

tog·gle switch (täg'əl) a switch consisting of a lever moved back and forth to open or close an electric circuit

To·go (tō'gō) country on the W coast of Africa: 21,925 sq. mi.; pop. 2,701,000

togs (tägz, tôgz) ***pl.n.*** ⟦ult. < L *toga*, toga⟧ [Inf.] clothes

toil (toil) ***vi.*** ⟦< L *tudiculare*, to stir about⟧ **1** to work hard and continuously **2** to proceed laboriously —***n.*** hard, tiring work —**toil'er** ***n.***

toi·let (toi'lit) ***n.*** ⟦< OFr *toile*, cloth < L *tela*, a web⟧ **1** TOILETTE **2** (a room with) a bowl-shaped fixture for defecation or urination

toilet paper (or **tissue**) soft paper for cleaning oneself after evacuation

toi'let·ry (-lə trē) ***n.***, *pl.* **-ries** soap, lotion, etc. used in grooming oneself

toi·lette (twä let', toi-) ***n.*** ⟦Fr⟧ **1** the process of grooming oneself **2** dress; attire

toilet water a lightly scented liquid containing alcohol, applied to the skin after bathing, etc.

toils (toilz) ***pl.n.*** ⟦< L *tela*, web⟧ any snare suggestive of a net

toil·some (toil'səm) ***adj.*** laborious

toke (tōk) [Slang] ***n.*** ⟦? < fol.⟧ a puff on a cigarette, esp. one of marijuana or hashish —***vi.*** **toked**, **tok'ing** to take such a puff

to·ken (tō'kən) ***n.*** ⟦OE *tacn*⟧ **1** a sign, indication, symbol, etc. [a *token* of one's affection] **2** a keepsake **3** a metal disk to be used in place of currency, as for transportation fares —***adj.*** **1** symbolic **2** merely simulated; slight [*token* resistance] —**by the same token** for the same reason

to'ken·ism' ***n.*** the making of small, often merely formal concessions to a demand, etc.; specif., token integration of blacks, as in jobs

To·ky·o (tō'kē ō') capital of Japan, on S Honshu: pop. 8,352,000

told (tōld) ***vt.***, ***vi.*** *pt. & pp. of* TELL —**all told** all things considered

tole (tōl) ***n.*** ⟦Fr *tôle*, sheet iron⟧ a type of lacquered or

THESAURUS

to and fro ***a.*** seesaw, zigzag, back and forth, backwards and forwards, in and out, up and down, from side to side, off and on, round and round, forward and back.

toast[1,2] ***n.*** **1** [A sentiment or person drunk to] pledge, salute, acknowledgment; see HONOR 1. *Invitations for toasts include the following:* here's to you, good luck, lest we forget, your health, *prosit* (German), *skoal* (Scandinavian), *salud* (Spanish), *a votre sante* (French), down the hatch*, here's how*, here's mud in your eye*, here's looking at you*, cheers. **2** [Browned bread] *Varieties of toast include the following:* zwieback Melba, French, milk, cinnamon; see also BREAD.

toast[1,2] ***v.*** **1** [To honor by drinking liquor] drink to, compliment, propose a toast; see DRINK 2, PRAISE 1. **2** [To brown bread] put in a toaster, heat, crisp; see COOK.

tobacco ***n.*** *Forms of tobacco include the following:* cigarette, cigar, chewing tobacco, pipe tobacco, snuff, shag, flake, plug, crimp cut, navy cut, cavendish, aromatic, maduro, claro, natural. *Types of tobacco include the following:* Turkish, Oriental, Virginia, Burley, Perique, Latakia, Olor, Cubano, Connecticut Shade.

today ***n.*** this day, the present, our time, this moment; see also NOW 1.

to-do* ***n.*** commotion, stir, fuss; see DISORDER, FIGHT 1.

toe ***n.*** digit, front of the foot, tip of a shoe; see FOOT 2. —**on one's toes*** alert, aware, attentive; see CAREFUL. —**step** (or **tread**) **on someone's toes** annoy, offend, disturb; see ANGER.

together ***a.*** **1** [Jointly] collectively, unitedly, commonly; see sense 2. **2** [Simultaneously] at the same time, concurrently, coincidentally, concomitantly, contemporaneously, at once, in connection with, at a blow, in unison, at one jump, in sync.

togs* ***n.*** clothing, outfit, attire; see CLOTHES.

toil ***n.*** labor, occupation, drudgery; see WORK 2.

toil ***v.*** sweat, labor, slave; see WORK.

toilet ***n.*** lavatory, washroom, rest room, men's room, women's room, powder room, gentlemen's room, ladies' room, comfort station, bathroom, bath, latrine, privy, outhouse, little boy's room*, little girl's room*, head*, potty*, can*, pot*, john*.

token ***n.*** mark, favor, sample; see GIFT 1. —**by the same token** following from this, similarly, thus; see THEREFORE. —**in token of** as evidence of, by way of, as a gesture; see BY 2.

told ***a.*** recounted, recorded, set down, reported, known, made known, chronicled, revealed, exposed, said, published, printed, announced, released, described, stated, set forth,

enameled metalware, usually dark-green, ivory, or black, used for lamps, trays, etc.

To·le·do (tə lē′dō) city & port in NW Ohio: pop. 333,000

tol·er·a·ble (täl′ər ə bəl) ***adj.*** **1** endurable **2** fairly good; passable —**tol′er·a·bly** ***adv.***

tol′er·ance (-əns) ***n.*** **1** a being tolerant of others' views, beliefs, practices, etc. **2** the amount of variation allowed from a standard **3** *Med.* the (developed) ability to resist the effects of a drug, etc.

tol′er·ant (-ənt) ***adj.*** having or showing tolerance of others' beliefs, etc.

tol′er·ate′ (-āt′) ***vt.*** **-at′ed, -at′ing** ⟦< L *tolerare*, to bear⟧ **1** to allow **2** to respect (others' beliefs, practices, etc.) without sharing them **3** to bear (someone or something disliked); put up with **4** *Med.* to have tolerance for —**tol′er·a′tion** ***n.***

toll[1] (tōl) ***n.*** ⟦ult. < Gr *telos*, tax⟧ **1** a tax or charge for a privilege, as for the use of a turnpike **2** a charge for service, as for a long-distance telephone call **3** the number lost, etc. *[the tornado took a heavy toll of lives]*

toll[2] (tōl) ***vt.*** ⟦ME *tollen*, to pull⟧ **1** to ring (a church bell, etc.) with slow, regular strokes **2** to announce, summon, etc. by this —***vi.*** to ring slowly: said of a bell —***n.*** the sound of a bell tolling

toll′booth′ ***n.*** a booth at which a toll is collected, as before entering a toll road

toll′gate′ ***n.*** a gate for stopping travel at a point where a toll is collected

toll road a road on which a toll must be paid: also **toll′way′** (-wā′) ***n.***

Tol·stoy or **Tol·stoi** (tōl′stoi′), Count **Le·o** (lē′ō) 1828-1910; Russ. novelist

tol·u·ene (täl′yo͞o ēn′) ***n.*** ⟦Sp *tolu*, after *Tolú*, seaport in Colombia + (BENZ)ENE⟧ a colorless, poisonous liquid obtained from coal tar or petroleum and used in making dyes, explosives, etc.

tom (täm) ***adj.*** ⟦after the name *Tom*⟧ male *[a tomcat, a tom turkey]*

tom·a·hawk (täm′ə hôk′) ***n.*** ⟦< AmInd⟧ a light ax used by North American Indians as a tool and a weapon

to·ma·to (tə māt′ō, -mät′ō) ***n.***, *pl.* **-toes** ⟦< AmInd (Mexico)⟧ **1** a red or yellowish fruit with a juicy pulp, used as a vegetable **2** the plant it grows on

tomb (to͞om) ***n.*** ⟦< Gr *tymbos*⟧ a vault or grave for the dead

tom·boy (täm′boi′) ***n.*** a girl who behaves like an active boy

tomb·stone (to͞om′stōn′) ***n.*** a stone or monument marking a tomb or grave

tom·cat (täm′kat′) ***n.*** a male cat

tome (tōm) ***n.*** ⟦< Gr *tomos*, piece cut off⟧ a book, esp. a large one

tom·fool·er·y (täm′fo͞ol′ər ē) ***n.***, *pl.* **-ies** foolish behavior; silliness

tom·my gun (täm′ē) *[sometimes* **T- g-***]* a submachine gun

to·mog·ra·phy (tə mäg′rə fē) ***n.*** ⟦< Gr *temnein*, to cut + -GRAPHY⟧ an X-ray process for producing an image of a single plane of an object, used in medical diagnosis

to·mor·row (tə mär′ō, -môr′-) ***adv.*** ⟦OE *to morgen*⟧ on the day after today —***n.*** the day after today

tom·tit (täm tit′, täm′tit′) ***n.*** [Chiefly Brit.] a titmouse or other small bird

tom-tom (täm′täm′) ***n.*** ⟦Hindi *ṭamṭam*⟧ a simple kind of drum, usually beaten with the hands

-to·my (tə mē) ⟦< Gr < *tomē*, a cutting⟧ *combining form* a surgical operation

ton (tun) ***n.*** ⟦var. of TUN⟧ **1** a unit of weight equal to 2,000 pounds **2** in Great Britain, a unit of weight equal to 2,240 pounds

ton·al (tō′nəl) ***adj.*** of a tone —**ton′al·ly** ***adv.***

to·nal·i·ty (tō nal′ə tē) ***n.***, *pl.* **-ties** *Music* **1** KEY[1] (*n.* 6) **2** tonal character, as determined by the relationship of the tones to the keynote

tone (tōn) ***n.*** ⟦< Gr *teinein*, to stretch⟧ **1** a vocal or musical sound, or its quality as to pitch, intensity, etc. **2** a manner of expression showing a certain attitude *[a friendly tone]* **3** style, character, spirit, etc. **4** elegance **5** a quality of color; shade **6** normal, healthy condition of a muscle, organ, etc. **7** *Music a)* a sound of distinct pitch *b)* any of the full intervals of a diatonic scale —***vt.*** **toned, ton′ing** to give a tone to —**tone down** (or **up**) to give a less (or more) intense tone to —**tone′less** ***adj.***

tone′arm′ ***n.*** the pivoted arm beside a phonograph turntable, holding the stylus

tone′-deaf′ ***adj.*** not able to distinguish differences in musical pitch

ton·er (tō′nər) ***n.*** **1** the black or colored powder used to form images in xerography **2** a facial cleanser

tone row (or **series**) see TWELVE-TONE

tong (tôŋ, täŋ) ***n.*** ⟦Mandarin *t'ang*, meeting place⟧ a Chinese association, society, etc.

Ton·ga (täŋ′gə) kingdom on a group of islands (**Tonga Islands**) in the SW Pacific, east of Fiji: 289 sq. mi.; pop. 95,000 —**Ton′gan** ***n.***

tongs (tôŋz, täŋz) ***pl.n.*** ⟦OE *tange*⟧ *[sometimes with sing. v.]* a device for seizing or lifting objects, having two long arms pivoted or hinged together

tongue (tuŋ) ***n.*** ⟦OE *tunge*⟧ **1** the movable, muscular structure in the mouth, used in eating, tasting, and (in humans) speaking **2** talk; speech **3** the act, power, or manner of speaking **4** a language or dialect **5** something like a tongue in shape, position, use, etc., as the flap under the laces of a shoe —**hold one's tongue** to keep from speaking —**speak in tongues** to utter unintelligible sounds, as while in a religious trance —**(with) tongue in cheek** in a humorously ironic or insincere way —**tongue′less** ***adj.***

tongue′-and-groove′ joint a kind of joint in which a projection on one board fits into a groove in another

tongue′-lash′ing ***n.*** [Inf.] a harsh scolding or reproving; reprimand

tongue′-tied′ ***adj.*** speechless from amazement, embarrassment, etc.

tongue twister a phrase or sentence hard to say fast (Ex: six sick sheiks)

ton·ic (tän′ik) ***adj.*** ⟦see TONE⟧ **1** of or producing good muscular tone **2** *Music* designating or based on a keynote —***n.*** **1** anything that invigorates, as a drug or medicine **2** a quinine-flavored beverage served with gin, vodka, etc. **3** *Music* a keynote

THESAURUS

included in the official statement, made public property, become common knowledge, related, depicted, enunciated, pronounced, given out, handed down, telegraphed, broadcast, telecast, confessed, admitted, well-known, discovered; see also SPOKEN.—*Ant.* SECRET, concealed, unknown. —**all told** in all, in toto, on the whole; see ALTOGETHER.

tolerable ***a.*** endurable, sufferable, sustainable; see BEARABLE.

tolerance ***n.*** **1** [Open-mindedness] concession, liberality, permission, forbearance, indulgence, mercy, compassion, sympathy, empathy, license, sufferance, grace, understanding, sensitivity, charity, altruism, benevolence, humanity, endurance, patience, goodwill; see also KINDNESS 1. **2** [Saturation point] threshold, tolerance level, end; see LIMIT 2.

tolerant ***a.*** understanding, receptive, sympathetic; see LIBERAL, PATIENT 1.

tolerate ***v.*** **1** [To allow] permit, consent to, put up with; see ALLOW. **2** [To endure] bear, undergo, abide; see ENDURE 2.

toll[1] ***n.*** **1** [Charges] duty, fee, customs, exaction, tollage; see also PRICE, TAX. **2** [Loss] casualties, deaths, losses; see DAMAGE 2.

tomb ***n.*** vault, crypt, mausoleum; see GRAVE.

tombstone ***n.*** monument, gravestone, headstone, footstone, stone, marker, cross, funerary statue.

tomorrow ***n.*** the morrow, next day in the course of time, the future, *mañana* (Spanish); see also DAY 1.

ton ***n.*** two thousand pounds, short ton, metric ton, long ton, shipping ton, displacement ton, measurement ton, freight ton; see also WEIGHT 1, 2.

tone ***n.*** **1** [A musical sound] pitch, timbre, resonance; see SOUND 2. **2** [Quality] nature, trend, temper; see CHARACTER 1. **3** [Manner] expression, condition, aspect; see MOOD 1. **4** [A degree of color] hue, tint, coloration; see COLOR.

tone down ***v.*** subdue, moderate, temper; see SOFTEN.

tongs ***n.*** pinchers, pliers, tweezers; see UTENSILS.

tongue ***n.*** **1** [The movable muscle in the mouth] organ of taste, organ of speech, lingua; see MUSCLE, ORGAN 2. *Parts of the tongue used in speech are:* tip, apex, front, center, back. **2** [Speech] talk, utterance, discourse; see LANGUAGE 1. —**hold one's tongue** refrain from speaking, hold back, keep silent; see RESTRAIN. —**on the tip of someone's tongue** forgotten, not quite remembered, not readily recalled; see FAMILIAR, FORGOTTEN.

tongue-tied ***a.*** **1** [Mute] silent, speechless, voiceless; see DUMB 1, MUTE 1. **2** [Inarticulate] reticent, nervous, inarticulate; see RESERVED 3.

to·night (tə nīt′) ***adv.*** ⟦OE *to niht*⟧ on or during the present or coming night —***n.*** the present or coming night

ton·nage (tun′ij) ***n.*** **1** the total amount of shipping of a country or port, calculated in tons **2** the carrying capacity of a ship, calculated in tons

ton·sil (tän′səl) ***n.*** ⟦L *tonsillae*, pl.⟧ either of a pair of oval masses of tissue at the back of the mouth

ton·sil·lec·to·my (tän′sə lek′tə mē) ***n.***, *pl.* **-mies** ⟦prec. + -ECTOMY⟧ the surgical removal of the tonsils

ton′sil·li′tis (-līt′is) ***n.*** ⟦ModL < L *tonsillae*, tonsils + -ITIS⟧ inflammation of the tonsils

ton·so·ri·al (tän sôr′ē əl) ***adj.*** ⟦see fol.⟧ of a barber or barbering: often humorous *[a tonsorial artist]*

ton·sure (tän′shər) ***n.*** ⟦< L *tondere*, to clip⟧ **1** a shaving off of part of the hair of the head, done as a sign of entrance into the clerical or monastic state **2** the head area so shaved

to·nus (tō′nəs) ***n.*** ⟦ModL, ult. < Gr *teinein*, to stretch⟧ the slight, continuous contraction characteristic of a normal relaxed muscle

ton·y (tō′nē) ***adj.*** **-i·er, -i·est** [Slang] very elegant

too (to͞o) ***adv.*** ⟦stressed form of TO⟧ **1** in addition; also **2** more than enough *[the hat is too big]* **3** extremely; very *[it was just too delicious!]*

took (to͝ok) ***vt.***, ***vi.*** *pt. of* TAKE

tool (to͞ol) ***n.*** ⟦OE *tol*⟧ **1** any hand implement, instrument, etc. used for some work **2** any similar instrument that is the working part of a machine, as a drill **3** anything that serves as a means **4** a stooge —***vt.*** to impress designs on (leather, etc.) with a tool —***vi.*** to install the tools, equipment, etc. needed: often with *up*

toot (to͞ot) ***vi.***, ***vt.*** ⟦echoic⟧ to sound (a horn, whistle, etc.) in short blasts —***n.*** a short blast of a horn, whistle, etc.

tooth (to͞oth) ***n.***, *pl.* **teeth** (tēth) ⟦OE *toth*⟧ **1** any of the hard, bonelike structures in the jaws, used for biting, chewing, etc. **2** a toothlike part, as on a saw, comb, gearwheel, etc.; tine, prong, cog, etc. **3** [*pl.*] effective means of enforcement *[a law with teeth]* —**tooth and nail** with all one's strength —**toothed** ***adj.*** —**tooth′less** ***adj.***

tooth′ache′ ***n.*** pain in a tooth

tooth′brush′ ***n.*** a small brush for cleaning the teeth

tooth′paste′ ***n.*** a paste used for brushing the teeth

tooth′pick′ ***n.*** a very small, pointed stick for getting bits of food free from between the teeth

tooth powder a powder used like toothpaste

tooth′some (-səm) ***adj.*** tasty; savory

tooth′y ***adj.*** **-i·er, -i·est** having or exposing teeth that show prominently —**tooth′i·ly** ***adv.***

top[1] (täp) ***n.*** ⟦OE⟧ **1** the head or crown **2** the highest point or surface of anything **3** the part of a plant above ground **4** the uppermost part or covering, as a lid, cap, etc. **5** the highest degree *[at the top of his voice]* **6** the highest rank *[the top of the class]* —***adj.*** of, at, or being the top; highest or foremost —***vt.*** **topped, top′ping** **1** to take off the top of (a plant, etc.) **2** to provide with a top **3** to be a top for **4** to reach the top of **5** to exceed in amount, etc. **6** to surpass; outdo —**blow one's top** [Slang] to lose one's temper —**on top** successful —**on top of** **1** resting upon **2** besides **3** controlling successfully —**top off** to complete by adding a finishing touch —**top′per** ***n.***

top[2] (täp) ***n.*** ⟦OE⟧ a cone-shaped toy with a point upon which it is spun

to·paz (tō′paz′) ***n.*** ⟦< Gr *topazos*⟧ any of various yellow gems, esp. a variety of aluminum silicate

top brass [Slang] important officials

top′coat′ ***n.*** a lightweight overcoat

top′-drawer′ (-drôr′) ***adj.*** of first importance

top′-dress′ing ***n.*** material applied to a surface, as fertilizer on land

To·pe·ka (tə pē′kə) capital of Kansas: pop. 120,000

top·er (tō′pər) ***n.*** ⟦< archaic *tope*, to drink (much liquor)⟧ a drunkard

top′-flight′ ***adj.*** [Inf.] first-rate

top hat a man's tall, black, cylindrical silk hat, worn in formal dress

top′-heav′y ***adj.*** too heavy at the top, so as to be unstable

top·ic (täp′ik) ***n.*** ⟦ult. < Gr *topos*, place⟧ the subject of an essay, speech, discussion, etc.

top′i·cal ***adj.*** dealing with topics of the day; of current or local interest

top′knot′ ***n.*** a tuft of hair or feathers on the top of the head

top′less ***adj.*** without a top: said as of a costume exposing the breasts

top-lev·el (täp′lev′əl) ***adj.*** of or by persons of the highest office or rank

top′mast′ ***n.*** the second mast above the deck of a sailing ship, supported by the lower mast

top′most′ ***adj.*** at the very top

top′-notch′ ***adj.*** [Inf.] first-rate; excellent

to·pog·ra·phy (tə päg′rə fē) ***n.***, *pl.* **-phies** ⟦see TOPIC & -GRAPHY⟧ **1** the science of representing surface features of a region on maps and charts **2** these surface features —**top·o·graph·ic** (täp′ə graf′ik) or **top′o·graph′i·cal** ***adj.***

top·ping (täp′iŋ) ***n.*** something put on top of something else, as a sauce on food

top·ple (täp′əl) ***vi.*** **-pled, -pling** ⟦< TOP[1]⟧ to fall top forward; fall (*over*) because top-heavy, etc. —***vt.*** to cause to topple; overturn

top·sail (täp′sāl′; *naut.*, -səl) ***n.*** in a square-rigged vessel, the square sail next above the lowest sail on a mast

top′-se′cret ***adj.*** designating or of the most secret information

top·side (täp′sīd′) ***adv.*** on or to an upper deck or the main deck of a ship

top′soil′ ***n.*** the upper layer of soil, usually richer than the subsoil

top·sy-tur·vy (täp′sē tur′vē) ***adv.***, ***adj.*** ⟦prob. < *top*, highest part + ME *terven*, to roll⟧ **1** upside down; in a reversed condition **2** in disorder

toque (tōk) ***n.*** ⟦Fr⟧ a woman's small, round, usually brimless hat

THESAURUS

tonight ***n.*** this evening, this night, later; see NIGHT 1.

too ***a.*** **1** [Also] as well, likewise, in addition, additionally, moreover, futhermore, further, besides; see also ALSO. **2** [In excess] extremely, excessively, over and above; see BESIDES.

tool ***n.*** **1** [An implement] utensil, machine, instrument, mechanism, weapon, apparatus, appliance, engine, means, contrivance, gadget; see also DEVICE 1. *Common tools include the following:* can opener, hammer, knife, jack, crank, pulley, wheel, bar, crowbar, lever, sledge, winch, grinder, stapler, clamp, vise, plumb, vise-grip, hex key, Allen wrench, utility knife, box cutter, chisel, plane, screw, brace, bit, file, saw, screwdriver, ax, corkscrew, hatchet, wrench, pliers, drill, sander, router, jimmy. **2** [One who permits himself to be used] accomplice, hireling, dupe; see SERVANT.

tooth ***n.*** **1** [A dental process] fang, tusk, saber-tooth, ivory, artificial tooth, false tooth, bony appendage. *Human teeth include the following:* incisor, canine, cuspid, eyetooth, bicuspid, premolar, molar, grinder, wisdom tooth; deciduous teeth, baby teeth, milk teeth, permanent teeth. **2** [A toothlike or tooth-shaped object] point, stub, projection; see ROOT 1. —**get (or sink) one's teeth into** become occupied with, involve oneself in, be busy at; see ACT 1. —**tooth and nail** energetically, fervently, forcefully; see EAGERLY, FIERCELY.

toothache ***n.*** swollen gums, abscessed tooth, decayed tooth; see PAIN 2.

top[1] ***a.*** **1** [Highest] topmost, uppermost, highest, on the upper end; see also HIGHEST. **2** [Best] prime, head, first, among the first; see also BEST 1.

top[1] ***v.*** **1** [To remove the top] prune, lop off, trim; see CUT 1. **2** [To exceed] better, beat, excel; see EXCEED. **3** [To apply topping] cover, screen, coat; see PAINT 2. —**top off** finish, end, bring to a conclusion; see COMPLETE.

top[1,2] ***n.*** **1** [The uppermost portion] peak, summit, crown, head, crest, tip, apex, acme, cap, crowning point, headpiece, capital, pinnacle, zenith, spire; see also HEIGHT.—*Ant.* BOTTOM, lower end, nadir. **2** [A cover] lid, roof, ceiling; see COVER 1. **3** [A spinning toy] spinner, musical top, whistling top; see TOY 1. **4** [The leader] head, captain, chief; see LEADER 2. —**blow one's top*** lose one's temper, become angry, be enraged; see RAGE 1. —**off the top of one's head** speaking offhand, chatting casually, spontaneous; see SPONTANEOUS. —**on top** prosperous, thriving, superior; see SUCCESSFUL.

top-heavy ***a.*** overweight, unstable, unbalanced; see SHAKY 1.

topic ***n.*** question, theme, material; see SUBJECT.

topless ***a.*** almost nude, bare to the waist, exposed; see NAKED 1.

top-level ***a.*** leading, superior, supreme; see EXCELLENT, IMPORTANT 1.

top-secret ***a.*** restricted, kept quiet, hush-hush*; see SECRET 1.

topsy-turvy ***a.*** confused, upside down, disordered; see DISORDERLY 1.

To·rah or **To·ra** (tō′rə, tôr′ə) [*occas.* **t-**] ***n.*** ⟦< Heb, law⟧ **1** the body of Jewish religious literature **2** the Pentateuch
torch (tôrch) ***n.*** ⟦see TORQUE⟧ **1** a portable flaming light **2** a device for producing a very hot flame, as in welding **3** [Brit.] a flashlight —***vt.*** [Slang] to set fire to, as in arson
torch′bear′er ***n.*** **1** one who carries a torch **2** *a)* one who brings enlightenment, truth, etc. *b)* an inspirational leader, as in some movement
torch′light′ ***n.*** the light of a torch or torches —***adj.*** done by torchlight
torch song a sentimental song of unrequited love —**torch singer**
tore (tôr) ***vt.***, ***vi.*** *pt. of* TEAR[1]
tor·e·a·dor (tôr′ē ə dôr′) ***n.*** ⟦Sp < L *taurus*, a bull⟧ a bullfighter
tor·ment (tôr′ment′; *for v.* tôr ment′) ***n.*** ⟦OFr < L: see TORQUE⟧ **1** great pain or anguish **2** a source of pain, anxiety, etc. —***vt.*** **1** to cause great physical pain or mental anguish in **2** to annoy; harass —**tor·ment′ing·ly** ***adv.*** —**tor·men′tor** or **tor·ment′er** ***n.***
torn (tôrn) ***vt.***, ***vi.*** *pp. of* TEAR[1]
tor·na·do (tôr nā′dō) ***n.***, *pl.* **-does** or **-dos** ⟦< Sp < L *tonare*, to thunder⟧ a violently whirling column of air seen as a funnel-shaped cloud that usually destroys everything in its narrow path
To·ron·to (tə ränt′ō) capital of Ontario, Canada: pop. 654,000 (met. area, 4,264,000)
tor·pe·do (tôr pē′dō) ***n.***, *pl.* **-does** ⟦< L: see fol.⟧ **1** a large, cigar-shaped, self-propelled underwater projectile containing explosives **2** any of various explosive devices —***vt.*** **-doed**, **-do·ing** to attack, destroy, etc. as with a torpedo
tor·pid (tôr′pid) ***adj.*** ⟦< L *torpere*, be numb⟧ **1** dormant or inactive **2** dull; sluggish
tor′por (-pər) ***n.*** ⟦L⟧ **1** a torpid state; sluggishness; stupor **2** dullness; apathy
torque (tôrk) ***n.*** ⟦< L *torquere*, to twist⟧ **1** *Physics* a measure of the tendency of a force to cause rotation **2** popularly, the force that acts to produce rotation, as in an automotive vehicle
tor·rent (tôr′ənt, tär′-) ***n.*** ⟦< L *torrens*, rushing⟧ **1** a swift, violent stream, esp. of water **2** a flood or rush of words, mail, etc. —**tor·ren·tial** (tô ren′shəl) ***adj.***
tor·rid (tôr′id, tär′-) ***adj.*** ⟦< L *torrere*, to dry⟧ **1** subjected to intense heat, esp. of the sun; parched **2** very hot; scorching **3** passionate; ardent
Torrid Zone the area of the earth's surface between the Tropic of Cancer & the Tropic of Capricorn and divided by the equator
tor·sion (tôr′shən) ***n.*** ⟦see TORQUE⟧ **1** a twisting or being twisted **2** the stress produced in a rod, wire, etc. by twisting along a longitudinal axis
tor·so (tôr′sō) ***n.***, *pl.* **-sos** or **-si** (-sē) ⟦< Gr *thyrsos*, a stem⟧ the trunk of the human body
tort (tôrt) ***n.*** ⟦< L *torquere*, to twist⟧ *Law* a wrongful act or damage (not involving a breach of contract), for which a civil action can be brought
torte (tôrt; *Ger* tôr′tə) ***n.***, *pl.* **tortes** or Ger. ***tor·ten*** (tôr′tən) ⟦Ger < It < LL *torta*, a twisted bread⟧ a rich cake, as one made of eggs, finely chopped nuts, crumbs, etc.
tor·tel·li·ni (tôrt′ə lē′nē) ***n.*** ⟦It⟧ pasta in tiny ring-shaped pieces, filled with meat, etc.
tor·til·la (tôr tē′ə) ***n.*** ⟦Sp, dim. of *torta*, a cake⟧ a flat cake of unleavened cornmeal, or of flour
tor·toise (tôrt′əs) ***n.*** ⟦< ? *c.* 4th-c. Gr *tartarouchos*, evil demon⟧ a turtle, esp. one that lives on land
tor′toise·shell′ ***n.*** **1** the hard, mottled, yellow-and-brown shell of some turtles **2** a synthetic substance resembling this
tor·to·ni (tôr tō′nē) ***n.*** ⟦prob. alt. < It *tortone*, lit., big pastry tart⟧ an ice cream made with heavy cream, maraschino cherries, almonds, etc.
tor·tu·ous (tôr′cho̅o̅ əs) ***adj.*** ⟦see TORQUE⟧ **1** full of twists, turns, etc.; crooked **2** deceitful or tricky
tor·ture (tôr′chər) ***n.*** ⟦see TORQUE⟧ **1** the inflicting of severe pain, as to elicit information or force a confession **2** any severe physical or mental pain; agony —***vt.*** **-tured**, **-tur·ing** **1** to subject to torture **2** to twist or distort (meaning, etc.) —**tor′tur·er** ***n.***
To·ry (tôr′ē) ***n.***, *pl.* **-ries** ⟦Ir *tōruidhe*, robber⟧ **1** after 1689, a member of the major conservative party of England **2** in the American Revolution, one loyal to Great Britain **3** [*often* **t-**] any extreme conservative
toss (tôs, täs) ***vt.*** ⟦prob. < Scand⟧ **1** to throw about *[waves tossed the boat]* **2** to throw lightly from the hand **3** to jerk upward *[to toss one's head]* —***vi.*** **1** to be thrown about **2** to fling oneself about in sleep, etc. —***n.*** a tossing or being tossed
toss′up′ ***n.*** **1** the flipping of a coin to decide something **2** an even chance
tot[1] (tät) ***n.*** ⟦prob. < ON⟧ **1** a young child **2** [Chiefly Brit.] a small drink of alcoholic liquor
tot[2] (tät) ***vt.***, ***vi.*** **tot′ted**, **tot′ting** [Inf., Chiefly Brit.] to total: with *up*
to·tal (tōt′'l) ***adj.*** ⟦< L *totus*, all⟧ **1** constituting a whole **2** complete; utter *[a total loss]* —***n.*** the whole amount; sum —***vt.*** **-taled** or **-talled**, **-tal·ing** or **-tal·ling** **1** to find the total of **2** to add up to **3** [Slang] to demolish —**to′tal·ly** ***adv.***
to·tal·i·tar·i·an (tō tal′ə ter′ē ən) ***adj.*** ⟦prec. + (AUTHOR)ITARIAN⟧ designating or of a government in which one political group maintains complete control, esp. under a dictator —***n.*** one who favors such a government —**to·tal′i·tar′i·an·ism′** ***n.***
to·tal·i·ty (tō tal′ə tē) ***n.***, *pl.* **-ties** the total amount or sum
to·tal·i·za·tor (tōt′'l i zāt′ər) ***n.*** a machine for registering bets and computing the odds and payoffs, as at a horse race: also **to′tal·iz′er** (-ī′zər) ***n.***
tote (tōt) ***vt.*** **tot′ed**, **tot′ing** ⟦< ?⟧ [Inf.] to carry or haul —***n.*** **1** a small piece of luggage **2** a large, open handbag: in full **tote bag**
to·tem (tōt′əm) ***n.*** ⟦< Algonquian⟧ **1** among some peoples, an animal or natural object taken as the symbol of a family or clan **2** an image of this
totem pole a pole carved and painted with totems by Indian tribes of NW North America
tot·ter (tät′ər) ***vi.*** ⟦prob. < Scand⟧ **1** to rock as if about to fall **2** to be unsteady on one's feet; stagger
tou·can (to̅o̅′kan′) ***n.*** ⟦< AmInd (Brazil)⟧ a brightly colored bird of tropical America, with a very large beak
touch (tuch) ***vt.*** ⟦< OFr *tochier*⟧ **1** to put the hand, etc. on, so as to feel **2** to bring (something), or come, into contact with (something else) **3** to border on **4** to strike

THESAURUS

torch ***n.*** beacon, light, flare; see LIGHT 3.
torment ***n.*** agony, suffering, misery; see PAIN 1, 2, TORTURE.
torment ***v.*** mistreat, torture, irritate; see HURT 1.
tormentor ***n.*** oppressor, persecutor, antagonist; see ENEMY.
torn ***a.*** ripped, slit, split, severed, lacerated, mutilated, broken, rent, fractured, cracked, slashed, gashed, ruptured, snapped, sliced, burst, cleaved, wrenched, divided, riven, pulled out, impaired, damaged, spoiled; see also RUINED 1.—*Ant.* WHOLE, repaired, fixed.
torrent ***n.*** overflow, deluge, downpour; see FLOOD, FLOW, STORM.
torrid ***a.*** blazing, fiery, sweltering; see HOT 1.
torture ***n.*** pain, anguish, agony, torment, crucifixion, martyrdom, pang, ache, twinge, physical suffering, mental suffering, tribulation; see also CRUELTY.—*Ant.* COMFORT, enjoyment, delight.
torture ***v.*** annoy, irritate, disturb; see ABUSE, BOTHER 2.
Tory ***n.*** traditionalist, reactionary, extreme conservative; see CONSERVATIVE.
toss ***v.*** **1** [To throw easily] hurl, fling, cast; see THROW 1. **2** [To move up and down] bob, buffet, stir, move restlessly, tumble, pitch, roll, heave, sway, flounder, rock, wobble, undulate, swing, rise and fall; see also WAVE 3.
tossup ***n.*** deadlock, stalemate, draw; see TIE 4.
tot[1] ***n.*** child, infant, youngster; see BABY.
total ***a.*** **1** [Whole] entire, inclusive, every; see WHOLE 1. **2** [Complete] utter, gross, thorough; see ABSOLUTE 1.
total ***n.*** sum, entirety, result; see WHOLE.
total ***v.*** **1** [To add] figure, calculate, count up, ring up, tag up, sum up, add up; see also ADD 1. **2** [To amount to] consist of, come to, add up to; see AMOUNT TO, EQUAL.
totality ***n.*** everything, oneness, collectivity; see WHOLE.
totally ***a.*** entirely, wholly, exclusively; see COMPLETELY.
totem ***n.*** figure, symbol, crest; see EMBLEM.
totter ***v.*** shake, rock, careen, quake, tremble, stumble, lurch, stagger, falter, trip, weave, zigzag, reel, rock, roll, walk drunkenly, wobble, waver, hesitate, seesaw, teeter, dodder, crumple, sway, be loose, be weak; see also WAVE 3.
touch ***n.*** **1** [The tactile sense] feeling, touching, feel, perception, tactility. **2** [Contact] rub, stroke, pat, fondling, rubbing, petting, stroking, licking, handling, graze, scratch, brush, taste, nudge, kiss, peck, embrace, hug,

lightly **5** to give a light tint, aspect, etc. to *[touched* with pink*]* **6** to handle; use **7** to come up to; reach **8** to compare with; equal **9** to affect; concern **10** to arouse sympathy, gratitude, etc. in **11** [Slang] to seek a loan or gift of money from —***vi.*** **1** to touch a person or thing **2** to be or come in contact **3** to verge (*on* or *upon*) **4** to pertain; bear (*on* or *upon*) **5** to treat in passing: with *on* or *upon* —***n.*** **1** a touching or being touched; specif., a light tap **2** the sense by which physical objects are felt **3** a special quality or skill **4** a subtle change or addition in a painting, story, etc. **5** a trace, tinge, etc. **6** a slight attack *[a touch* of the flu*]* **7** contact or communication *[*keep in *touch]* **8** [Slang] the act of seeking or getting a loan or gift of money **9** *Music* the manner of striking the keys of a piano, etc. —**touch down** to land: said of an aircraft or spacecraft —**touch up** to improve by minor changes

touch'-and-go' ***adj.*** uncertain, risky, etc.

touch'down' ***n.*** **1** the moment at which an aircraft or spacecraft lands **2** *Football* a play, scoring six points, in which a player carries, catches, or recovers the ball past the opponent's goal line

tou·ché (too͞ shā') ***interj.*** ⟦Fr⟧ touched: said when one's opponent in fencing scores a point, or as to acknowledge a clever retort

touched (tucht) ***adj.*** **1** emotionally affected; moved **2** slightly demented

touch'ing ***adj.*** arousing tender emotions; moving

touch'stone' ***n.*** **1** a stone formerly used to test the purity of gold or silver **2** any test of genuineness

touch'-type' ***vi.*** **-typed', -typ'ing** to type without looking at the keyboard by regularly touching a given key with a specific finger

touch'y ***adj.*** **-i·er, -i·est** **1** easily offended; oversensitive; irritable **2** very risky or precarious

touch'y-feel'y (-fē'lē) ***adj.*** [Inf.] having or showing too much affection, compassion, etc.

tough (tuf) ***adj.*** ⟦OE *toh*⟧ **1** that will bend, etc. without tearing or breaking **2** not easily cut or chewed *[tough* steak*]* **3** strong; hardy **4** stubborn **5** brutal or rough **6** very difficult; laborious —***n.*** a tough person; thug

tough'en ***vt., vi.*** to make or become tough or tougher —**tough'en·er** ***n.***

tou·pee (too͞ pā') ***n.*** ⟦< Fr < OFr *toup*, tuft of hair⟧ a man's small wig

tour (toor) ***n.*** ⟦< OFr *tourner*, to turn⟧ **1** a turn, period, etc., as of military duty **2** a long trip, as for sightseeing **3** any trip, as for inspection, for giving performances, etc. —***vt., vi.*** to go on a tour (through)

tour de force (toor' də fôrs') *pl.* **tours de force** (toor') ⟦Fr⟧ an unusually skillful or ingenious creation or performance, sometimes a merely clever one

Tou·rette's syndrome (too rets') ⟦after G. de la *Tourette*, 19th-c. Fr doctor⟧ a nervous disorder characterized by involuntary movements, obscene utterances, etc.

tour'ism' ***n.*** tourist travel

tour'ist ***n.*** one who tours, esp. for pleasure —***adj.*** of or for tourists

tour·ma·line (toor'mə lin, -lēn') ***n.*** ⟦Fr⟧ a crystalline mineral used as a gemstone, etc.

tour·na·ment (toor'nə mənt, tur'-) ***n.*** ⟦< OFr *tourner*, to turn⟧ **1** in the Middle Ages, a contest between knights on horseback who tried to unseat one another with lances **2** a series of contests in competition for a championship Also **tour'ney** (-nē) ***n.***, *pl.* **-neys**

tour'ni·quet (toor'ni kit, tur'-) ***n.*** ⟦Fr < L *tunica*, tunic⟧ a device for compressing a blood vessel to stop bleeding, as a bandage twisted about a limb and released at intervals

tou·sle (tou'zəl) ***vt.*** **-sled, -sling** ⟦< ME *tusen*, to pull⟧ to disorder, dishevel, muss, etc.

tout (tout) [Inf.] ***vi., vt.*** ⟦OE *totian*, to peep⟧ **1** to praise highly **2** to sell betting tips on (racehorses) —***n.*** one who touts

tow (tō) ***vt.*** ⟦OE *togian*⟧ to pull, as by a rope or chain —***n.*** **1** a towing or being towed **2** something towed **3** TOWLINE —**in tow** **1** being towed **2** in one's company or charge

toward (tôrd, twôrd) ***prep.*** ⟦see TO & -WARD⟧ **1** in the direction of **2** facing **3** along a likely course to *[*steps *toward* peace*]* **4** concerning **5** just before *[toward* noon*]* **6** for *[*save *toward* a car*]* Also **towards**

tow·el (tou'əl) ***n.*** ⟦< OFr *toaille*⟧ a piece of cloth or paper for wiping or drying things —***vt.*** **-eled** or **-elled, -el·ing** or **-el·ling** to wipe or dry with a towel —**throw** (or **toss,** etc.) **in the towel** [Inf.] to admit defeat

tow'el·ing or **tow'el·ling** ***n.*** material for making towels

tow·er (tou'ər) ***n.*** ⟦< L *turris*⟧ **1** a high structure, often part of a building **2** such a structure used as a fortress, etc. —***vi.*** to rise high like a tower —**tow'er·ing** ***adj.***

tow·head (tō'hed') ***n.*** ⟦< *tow*, fibers of flax, etc.⟧ a person with pale-yellow hair —**tow'head'ed** ***adj.***

tow·hee (tō'hē, -ē) ***n.*** ⟦echoic⟧ any of various small North American sparrows

tow·line (tō'līn') ***n.*** a rope, etc. used for towing

town (toun) ***n.*** ⟦OE *tun*⟧ **1** a concentration of houses, etc. somewhat larger than a village **2** a city **3** a township **4** the business center of a city **5** the people of a town —**on the town** [Inf.] out for a good time

town crier one who, formerly, cried public announcements through the streets of a village or town

town hall a building in a town, housing the offices of officials, etc.

THESAURUS

cuddling, caress. **3** [A sensation] sense, impression, pressure; see FEELING 2. **4** [Skill] knack, technique, talent; see ABILITY, METHOD. **5** [A trace] suggestion, scent, inkling; see BIT 1. **—get in touch (with)** call, telephone, write to, contact, wire, telegraph, correspond with, communicate with, reach, keep in contact with, make overtures.

touch ***v.*** **1** [To be in contact] stroke, graze, rub, nudge, thumb, finger, paw, pat, pet, caress, lick, taste, brush, kiss, glance, sweep, fondle, smooth, massage, sip, partake; see also FEEL 1. **2** [To come into contact with] meet, encounter, reach; see MEET 1. **3** [To relate to] refer to, regard, affect; see CONCERN 1. **—touch on** treat, refer to, mention; see DISCUSS. **—touch up** renew, modify, rework; see REMODEL, REPAIR.

touch-and-go ***a.*** **1** [Hasty] rapid, casual, superficial; see SHALLOW 2. **2** [Risky] ticklish, hazardous, tricky; see DANGEROUS, UNCERTAIN.

touched ***a.*** **1** [Having been in slight contact] fingered, nudged, used, brushed, bumped, handled, rubbed, stroked, rearranged, kissed, grazed, licked, tasted, fondled. **2** [Affected] moved, impressed, stirred; see AFFECTED 1.

touching ***a., prep.*** **1** [Referring to] regarding, in regard to, in reference to; see ABOUT 2. **2** [Affecting] moving, pathetic, tender; see PITIFUL. **3** [Adjacent] tangent, in contact, against; see NEAR 1, NEXT 2.

touchy ***a.*** **1** [Irritable] ill-humored, testy, sensitive; see IRRITABLE. **2** [Dangerous] harmful, hazardous, risky; see UNSAFE.

tough ***a.*** **1** [Strong] robust, wiry, mighty; see STRONG 1, 2. **2** [Cohesive] solid, firm, sturdy, hard, hardened, adhesive, leathery, coherent, inseparable, molded, tight, cemented, unbreakable, in one piece, dense, closely packed.—*Ant.* WEAK, fragile, brittle. **3** [Difficult to chew] half-cooked, uncooked, sinewy, indigestible, inedible, fibrous, old, hard as nails, tough as shoeleather*.—*Ant.* SOFT, tender, overcooked. **4** [Difficult] hard, troublesome, laborious; see DIFFICULT 1, SEVERE 1. **5** [Hardy] robust, sound, capable; see HEALTHY. **6** [Rough and cruel] savage, fierce, ferocious; see CRUEL. **7** [*Unfavorable] bad, unfortunate, untimely; see UNFAVORABLE. **8** [*Excellent] fine, terrific*, first-class; see EXCELLENT. **—tough it out*** persevere, persist, endure; see ENDURE 1.

tour ***n.*** trip, voyage, travel; see JOURNEY.

tour ***v.*** voyage, vacation, take a trip; see TRAVEL.

tourist ***n.*** sightseer, vacationist, visitor; see TRAVELER.

tournament ***n.*** meet, tourney, match; see SPORT 3.

tout* ***v.*** praise highly, laud, puff; see PROMOTE 1.

tow ***v.*** haul, pull, drag; see DRAW 1.

toward ***a., prep.*** to, in the direction of, pointing to, via, on the way to, proceeding, moving, approaching, in relation to, close to, headed for, on the road to; see also NEAR 1.

towel ***n.*** wiper, drier, absorbent paper, sheet, toweling, napkin, cloth, rag. *Towels include the following:* linen, cotton, terry, terry cloth, guest, face, Turkish, hand, bath, beach, dish, tea, paper. **—throw in the towel*** admit defeat, give in, surrender; see QUIT 2.

tower ***n.*** spire, mast, steeple, bell tower, lookout tower, keep, belfry, campanile, turret, radio tower, skyscraper, obelisk, pillar, column, minaret.

tower ***v.*** look over, extend above, surmount; see OVERLOOK.

town ***a.*** civic, community, civil; see MUNICIPAL, URBAN.

town ***n.*** **1** [In the United States, a small collection of dwellings] township, village, hamlet, county seat, municipality, borough, small town, burg*, hick town*. **2** [The people in a city, especially the prominent people] townspeople, inhabitants, society; see POPULATION.

town house a two-story or three-story dwelling, a unit in a complex of such dwellings

town meeting a meeting of the voters of a town, as in New England

town'ship *n.* a division of a county, constituting a unit of local government

towns'peo'ple *pl.n.* the people of a town: also **towns'folk'**

tow·path (tō'path') *n.* a path along a canal, used by men or animals towing freight-carrying boats

tow'rope' *n.* a rope used in towing

tox·e·mi·a (täk sē'mē ə) *n.* ⟦see fol. & -EMIA⟧ a condition in which the blood contains poisonous substances, esp. toxins produced by pathogenic bacteria

tox·ic (täk'sik) *adj.* ⟦< Gr *toxicon*, a poison⟧ **1** of, affected by, or caused by a toxin **2** poisonous

tox·i·col·o·gy (täk'si käl'ə jē) *n.* ⟦see prec. & -LOGY⟧ the science of poisons and their effects, antidotes, etc. —**tox'i·col'o·gist** *n.*

tox·in (täk'sin) *n.* ⟦< TOXIC⟧ **1** any of various poisons produced by microorganisms and causing certain diseases **2** any poison secreted by plants or animals

toy (toi) *n.* ⟦< ? MDu *toi*, finery⟧ **1** a trifle **2** a plaything for children —*adj.* **1** like a plaything in size, use, etc. **2** made as a toy —*vi.* to trifle (*with* a thing, an idea, etc.)

tr *abbrev.* **1** translated **2** translation **3** translator **4** transpose

trace[1] (trās) *n.* ⟦< L *trahere*, to draw⟧ **1** a mark, track, sign, etc. left by a person, animal, or thing **2** a barely perceptible amount —*vt.* **traced, trac'ing 1** to follow the trail of; track **2** *a)* to follow the development or history of *b)* to determine (a source, etc.) by this procedure **3** to draw, outline, etc. **4** to copy (a drawing, etc.) by following its lines on a superimposed transparent sheet —**trace'a·ble** *adj.* —**trac'er** *n.*

trace[2] (trās) *n.* ⟦see TRAIT⟧ either of two straps, etc. connecting a draft animal's harness to the vehicle drawn

trace element a chemical element, as copper, zinc, etc., essential in nutrition, but only in minute amounts

trac·er·y (trās'ər ē) *n., pl.* **-ies** ⟦< TRACE[1] + -ERY⟧ ornamental work of interlacing or branching lines

tra·che·a (trā'kē ə) *n., pl.* **-che·ae'** (-ē') or **-che·as** ⟦< Gr *tracheia* (*arteria*), rough (windpipe)⟧ the passage that conveys air from the larynx to the bronchi; windpipe —**tra'che·al** *adj.*

tra·che·ot·o·my (trā'kē ät'ə mē) *n., pl.* **-mies** ⟦see prec. & -TOMY⟧ an incision of the trachea to aid breathing in an emergency

trac·ing (trās'iŋ) *n.* something traced; specif., *a)* a copy of a drawing, etc. *b)* a traced line made by a recording instrument

track (trak) *n.* ⟦< Fr *trac*⟧ **1** a mark left in passing, as a footprint, wheel rut, etc. **2** a path or trail **3** a sequence of ideas, events, etc. **4** a path or circuit laid out for racing, etc. **5** a pair of parallel metal rails on which trains, etc. run **6** *a)* sports performed on a track, as running, hurdling, etc. *b)* these sports along with other contests in jumping, throwing, etc. **7** *a)* a band on a phonograph record, compact disc, etc. *b)* any of the separate, parallel recording surfaces along a magnetic tape —*vt.* **1** to follow the track of **2** to trace by means of evidence, etc. **3** to plot the path of, as with radar **4** to leave tracks of (mud, etc.) on: often with *up* —**in one's tracks** where one is at the moment —**keep** (or **lose**) **track of** to stay (or fail to stay) informed about —**track'less** *adj.*

track lighting a method of lighting a room with spotlights inserted along a narrow, wired track

track record [Inf.] the record of the performance of a person, etc. as in some activity

tract[1] (trakt) *n.* ⟦< L *trahere*, to draw⟧ **1** a continuous expanse of land **2** a system of organs having some special function [the digestive *tract*]

tract[2] (trakt) *n.* ⟦< LL *tractatus*, treatise⟧ a propagandizing pamphlet

trac·ta·ble (trak'tə bəl) *adj.* ⟦< L *trahere*, to draw⟧ easily managed; docile; compliant

tract house a house built to a design that is used many times throughout a housing development

trac·tion (trak'shən) *n.* ⟦< L *trahere*, to draw⟧ **1** *a)* a pulling or drawing *b)* a being pulled or drawn *c)* the kind of power used for pulling [electric *traction*] **2** the power, as of tires on pavement, to hold to a surface without slipping

trac·tor (trak'tər) *n.* ⟦see prec.⟧ **1** a powerful, motor-driven vehicle for pulling farm machinery, etc. **2** a truck with a driver's cab and no body, for hauling large trailers

trac'tor-trail'er *n.* a TRACTOR (sense 2) combined with a trailer or semitrailer, used for transporting goods

trade (trād) *n.* ⟦< LowG, a track⟧ **1** occupation; esp., skilled work **2** all the persons in a particular business **3** buying and selling; commerce **4** customers **5** an exchange; swap —*vi.* **trad'ed, trad'ing 1** to carry on a business **2** to have business dealings (*with*) **3** to make an exchange (*with*) **4** [Inf.] to be a customer (*at* a certain store) —*vt.* to exchange; barter —**trade on** (or **upon**) to take advantage of

trade'-in' *n.* a thing given or taken as part payment for something else

trade journal (or **magazine**) a magazine devoted to a specific trade or industry

trade'mark' *n.* **1** a symbol, word, etc. used by a manufacturer or dealer to distinguish a product: usually protected by law **2** [Inf.] a distinctive, identifying feature or characteristic

trade name 1 the name by which a commodity is commonly known by those who deal in it **2** a name used as a trademark **3** the business name of a company

trade'-off' *n.* an exchange in which one benefit is given up for another considered more desirable: also **trade'off'**

trad'er *n.* **1** one who trades; merchant **2** a ship used in trade

THESAURUS

toxic *a.* noxious, virulent, lethal; see DEADLY, POISONOUS.

toy *a.* childish, miniature, small; see LITTLE 1.

toy *n.* **1** [Something designed for amusement] game, plaything, pastime; see DOLL, GAME 1. *Toys include the following:* dolls, games, board games, balls, toy weapons, blocks, jacks, tops, puzzles, models, jump ropes, scooters, wagons, kites, sporting goods, electronic devices, electronic games, bicycles, tricycles, roller skates, rollerblades, marbles, skateboards, hobby horses. **2** [Anything trivial] trifle, bauble, gadget; see KNICKKNACK.

trace[1] *n.* **1** [A very small quantity] indication, fragment, dash, dab, sprinkling, tinge, pinch, taste, crumb, trifle, shred, drop, speck, shade, hint, shadow, nuance, iota, scintilla, particle, jot, suggestion, touch, tittle, suspicion, minimum, smidgen*, snippet, tad, smell, spot; see also BIT 1. **2** [A track] evidence, trail, footprint; see TRACK 2.

trace[1] *v.* **1** [To track] smell out, track down, run down; see TRACK 1. **2** [To draw] sketch, outline, copy; see DRAW 2.

tracing *n.* imitation, reproduction, duplicate; see COPY.

track *n.* **1** [A prepared way] path, course, road; see RAILROAD. **2** [Evidence left in passage] footprint, step, trace, vestige, impression, tire track, mark, footmark, footstep, trail, fingerprint, blood stain, imprint, remnant, record, indication, print, sign, remains, token, symbol, clue, scent, wake. —**keep track of** keep an account of, stay informed about, maintain contact with; see TRACK 1, WATCH. —**lose track of** lose sight of, lose contact with, abandon; see FORGET. —**make tracks*** run away, abandon, depart quickly; see LEAVE 1. —**off the track** deviant, variant, deviating; see MISTAKEN 1. —**the wrong side of the tracks** ghetto, poor side of town, lower class neighborhood; see SLUM.

track *v.* **1** [To follow by evidence] hunt, pursue, smell out, add up, put together, trail, follow, watch, trace, follow the scent, follow a clue, follow footprints, draw an inference, piece together, dog, be hot on the trail of, tail*, shadow. **2** [To dirty with tracks] leave footprints, leave mud, muddy, stain, soil, besmear, spatter, leave a trail of dirt; see also DIRTY.

trade *n.* **1** [Business] commerce, sales, enterprise; see BUSINESS 1. **2** [A craft] occupation, profession, position; see JOB 1. *Common trades include the following:* auto mechanic, boilermaker, baker, barber, butcher, bookbinder, bricklayer, carpenter, construction worker, cook, cabinetmaker, cameraman, dressmaker, electrician, embalmer, engraver, jeweler, locksmith, metallurgist, miner, machinist, optician, painter, plumber, printer, seamstress, shoemaker, tailor, textile worker, technician, toolmaker, welder. **3** [An individual business transaction] deal, barter, contract; see SALE 2.

trade *v.* **1** [To do business] patronize, shop, purchase; see BUY, SELL. **2** [To give one thing for another] barter, swap, give in exchange; see EXCHANGE. —**trade in** turn in, make part of a deal, get rid of; see SELL.

trademark *n.* brand, tag, commercial stamp; see LABEL.

trader *n.* salesman, dealer, mer-

trades·man (trādz′mən) ***n.***, *pl.* **-men** (-mən) [Chiefly Brit.] a storekeeper —**trades′wom′an**, *pl.* **-wom′en**, ***fem.n.***

trade union LABOR UNION

trade wind a wind that blows toward the equator from either side of it

trading post a store in an outpost, settlement, etc., where trading is done

tra·di·tion (trə dish′ən) ***n.*** ⟦< L *tradere*, deliver⟧ **1** the handing down orally of beliefs, customs, etc. from generation to generation **2** a story, belief, custom, etc. handed down in this way

tra·di′tion·al ***adj.*** of, handed down by, or conforming to tradition

tra·di′tion·al·ism′ ***n.*** adherence to tradition; sometimes, specif., excessive devotion to tradition —**tra·di′tion·al·ist** ***n.***

tra·duce (trə do͞os′, -dyo͞os′) ***vt.*** **-duced′**, **-duc′ing** ⟦< L *trans*, across + *ducere*, to lead⟧ to slander

traf·fic (traf′ik) ***n.*** ⟦< It *traffico* < L *trans*, across +It *ficcare*, bring⟧ **1** buying and selling; trade **2** dealings (*with* someone) **3** the movement or number of automobiles, pedestrians, etc. along a street, etc. **4** the business done by a transportation company —***adj.*** of or having to do with traffic —***vi.*** **-ficked**, **-fick·ing** **1** to carry on traffic (*in* a commodity) **2** to have dealings (*with* someone)

traffic circle a circular road at the intersection of several streets: vehicles move on it in one direction only

traffic light (or **signal**) a set of signal lights at a street intersection for regulating traffic

tra·ge·di·an (trə jē′dē ən) ***n.*** **1** a writer of tragedy **2** an actor in tragedies

trag·e·dy (traj′ə dē) ***n.***, *pl.* **-dies** ⟦< Gr *tragos*, goat + *ōidē*, song⟧ **1** a serious play with an unhappy ending **2** a very sad or tragic event; disaster

trag·ic (traj′ik) ***adj.*** **1** of or like a tragedy **2** disastrous, fatal, etc. —**trag′i·cal·ly** ***adv.***

trail (trāl) ***vt.*** ⟦< L *trahere*, to draw⟧ **1** to drag or let drag behind one **2** to follow the tracks of; track **3** to hunt by tracking **4** to follow behind —***vi.*** **1** to drag along on the ground, etc. **2** to grow along the ground, etc., as some plants do **3** to flow behind: said as of smoke **4** to follow or lag behind; straggle **5** to grow weaker, dimmer, etc.: with *off* or *away* —***n.*** **1** something that trails behind **2** a mark, scent, etc. left by a person, animal, or thing that has passed **3** a beaten path

trail bike a small motorcycle for off-road riding

trail′blaz′er ***n.*** **1** one who blazes a trail **2** a pioneer in any field

trail′er ***n.*** **1** one that trails **2** *a*) a wagon, van, etc. designed to be pulled by an automobile, truck, etc. *b*) such a vehicle designed to be lived in

trailer park an area, usually with piped water, electricity, etc., for trailers, esp. mobile homes

trail mix GORP

train (trān) ***n.*** ⟦< L *trahere*, to pull⟧ **1** something that drags along behind, as a trailing skirt **2** a group of followers; retinue **3** a procession; caravan **4** any connected order; sequence *[a train of thought]* **5** a line of connected railroad cars pulled by a locomotive —***vt.*** **1** to guide the growth of (a plant) **2** to guide the mental, moral, etc. development of; rear **3** to instruct so as to make proficient **4** to make fit for an athletic contest, etc. **5** to aim (a gun, etc.) —***vi.*** to undergo training —**train·ee** (trān ē′) ***n.*** —**train′er** ***n.***

traipse (trāps) ***vi.***, ***vt.*** **traipsed**, **traips′ing** ⟦< ?⟧ [Inf. or Dial.] to walk, wander, or tramp

trait (trāt) ***n.*** ⟦< L *trahere*, to draw⟧ a distinguishing quality or characteristic

trai·tor (trāt′ər) ***n.*** ⟦< L *tradere*, betray⟧ one who betrays one's country, cause, friends, etc. —**trai′tor·ous** ***adj.***

tra·jec·to·ry (trə jek′tə rē) ***n.***, *pl.* **-ries** ⟦ult. < L *trans*, across + *jacere*, to throw⟧ the curved path of something hurtling through space

tram (tram) ***n.*** ⟦prob. < LowG *traam*, a beam⟧ [Brit.] a streetcar

tram·mel (tram′əl) ***n.*** ⟦< L *tres*, three + *macula*, a mesh⟧ [*usually pl.*] something that confines or restrains —***vt.*** **-meled** or **-melled**, **-mel·ing** or **-mel·ling** to confine, restrain, etc.

tramp (tramp) ***vi.*** ⟦ME *trampen*⟧ **1** to walk or step heavily **2** to travel about on foot —***vt.*** **1** to step on heavily **2** to walk through —***n.*** **1** a vagrant; hobo **2** the sound of heavy steps **3** a journey on foot; hike **4** a freight ship with no schedule, that picks up cargo, etc. as it goes along **5** [Slang] a sexually promiscuous woman

tram·ple (tram′pəl) ***vi.*** **-pled**, **-pling** ⟦see prec.⟧ to tread heavily —***vt.*** to crush, destroy, etc. by or as by treading heavily on

tram·po·line (tram′pə lēn′, -lin) ***n.*** ⟦< It⟧ a sheet of strong canvas stretched tightly on a frame with springs, used in acrobatic tumbling and jumping

trance (trans) ***n.*** ⟦< L *transire*, go across, die⟧ **1** a state of altered consciousness, resembling sleep, as in hypnosis **2** a daze; stupor **3** a state of great mental abstraction

THESAURUS

chant; see BUSINESSMAN.

tradesman ***n.*** storekeeper, retailer, merchant; see BUSINESSMAN.

trade union ***n.*** union, organized labor, guild; see LABOR 4.

tradition ***n.*** **1** [The process of preserving orally] folklore, legend, fable; see STORY. **2** [Cultural heritage] ritual, mores, law; see CULTURE 2, CUSTOM.

traditional ***a.*** folkloric, legendary, mythical, epical, ancestral, unwritten, balladic, told, handed down, anecdotal, proverbial, inherited, folkloristic, old, acknowledged, customary, generally accepted, habitual, widespread, usual, widely used, popular, acceptable, established, fixed, sanctioned, universal, taken for granted, rooted, classical, prescribed, doctrinal, conventional; see also COMMON 1, REGULAR 3.

traffic ***n.*** **1** [The flow of transport] travel, passage, transportation, flux, movement, transfer, transit, passenger service, freight shipment, influx. **2** [Dealings] commerce, transactions, exchange; see BUSINESS.

tragedy ***n.*** **1** [Unhappy fate] lot, bad fortune, misfortune, doom, problem, error, mistake.—*Ant.* HAPPINESS, fortune, success. **2** [A series of tragic events] adversity, affliction, hardship; see DIFFICULTY 1, 2.—*Ant.* SUCCESS, prosperity, good fortune. **3** [An artistic creation climaxed by catastrophe] play, tragic drama, melodrama; see DRAMA, MOVIE, NOVEL.

tragic ***a.*** catastrophic, fatal, disastrous; see UNFORTUNATE.

trail ***n.*** trace, tracks, path; see WAY 2.

trail ***v.*** **1** [To follow] track, trace, follow a scent; see HUNT 1, PURSUE 1. **2** [To lag behind] fall back, loiter, tarry; see WAIT 1.

trailer ***n.*** house trailer, recreational vehicle, mobile home; see HOME 1.

train ***n.*** **1** [A sequence] string, chain, succession; see SERIES. **2** [A locomotive and attached cars] transport train, passenger train, freight train, local train, limited, supply train, express train, excursion train, commuter train, troop train, boat train, mail train, bullet train, subway, rapid transit, underground, elevated, el*, electric, diesel, choo-choo*; see also RAILROAD.

train ***v.*** **1** [To drill] practice, exercise, discipline; see REACH 2. **2** [To educate] instruct, tutor, enlighten; see TEACH. **3** [To toughen oneself] prepare, grow strong, get into practice, reduce, make ready, fit out, equip, qualify, bring up to standard, whip into shape*, work out, get a workout.—*Ant.* WEAKEN, break training, be unfit. **4** [To direct the growth of] rear, lead, discipline, mold, bend, implant, guide, shape, care for, encourage, infuse, imbue, order, bring up, nurture, nurse, prune, weed; see also RAISE 1.—*Ant.* NEGLECT, ignore, disdain. **5** [To aim] bring to bear, level, draw a bead; see AIM.

trained ***a.*** prepared, qualified, cultured, initiated, skilled, informed, schooled, primed, graduated, disciplined, enlightened; see also EDUCATED.—*Ant.* INEXPERIENCED, raw, untrained.

trainer ***n.*** teacher, tutor, instructor, coach, manager, mentor, officer, master, boss, handler, pilot, guide, leader.

training ***n.*** drill, practice, exercise, preparation, instruction, foundation, schooling, discipline, basic principles, groundwork, basic training, coaching, indoctrination, preliminaries, tuneup, buildup*; see also EDUCATION.

trait ***n.*** habit, manner, peculiarity; see CHARACTERISTIC.

traitor ***n.*** betrayer, deserter, renegade, Judas, Benedict Arnold, informant, informer, spy, counterspy, agent, double agent, hypocrite, quisling, impostor, plotter, conspirator, turncoat, sneak, double-crosser*, fink*, rat*, rat fink*, stool pigeon*, two-timer*; see also REBEL.—*Ant.* SUPPORTER, follower, partisan.

traitorous ***a.*** seditious, disloyal, treacherous; see FALSE 1.

tramp ***n.*** **1** [Vagrant] hobo, wanderer, bum*; see BEGGAR. **2** [A long walk, often in rough country] hike, excursion, stroll; see WALK 3. **3** [*Prostitute] whore, harlot, slut; see PROSTITUTE.

trample ***v.*** stamp on, crush, tread on, grind underfoot, injure, squash, bruise, tramp over, overwhelm, defeat.

trance ***n.*** coma, daze, stupor; see

tran·quil (traŋ′kwəl) ***adj.*** **-quil·er** or **-quil·ler, -quil·est** or **-quil·lest** ⟦L *tranquillus*⟧ calm, serene, placid, etc. —**tran·quil′li·ty** or **tran·quil′i·ty** (-kwil′ə tē) ***n.*** —**tran′quil·ly *adv.***

tran′quil·ize′ or **tran′quil·lize′** (-kwə līz′) ***vt., vi.*** **-ized′** or **-lized′, -iz′ing** or **-liz′ing** to make or become tranquil

tran′quil·iz′er or **tran′quil·liz′er *n.*** a drug used as a calming agent in treating various emotional disturbances, etc.

trans *abbrev.* **1** translated **2** translation **3** translator **4** transportation

trans- ⟦L < *trans*, across⟧ *prefix* over, across, beyond, through

trans·act (tran zakt′, -sakt′) ***vt.*** ⟦< L *trans-*, over + *agere*, to drive⟧ to carry on or complete (business, etc.)

trans·ac′tion *n.* **1** a transacting **2** something transacted; specif., *a*) a business deal *b*) [*pl.*] a record of the proceedings of a society, etc.

trans·at·lan·tic (trans′at lan′tik, tranz′-) ***adj.*** **1** crossing the Atlantic **2** on the other side of the Atlantic

trans·ceiv·er (tran sē′vər) ***n.*** a radio transmitter and receiver in a single housing

tran·scend (tran send′) ***vt.*** ⟦< L *trans-*, over + *scandere*, climb⟧ **1** to go beyond the limits of; exceed **2** to surpass; excel —**tran·scend′ent *adj.***

tran·scen·den·tal (tran′sen dent′′l) ***adj.*** **1** supernatural **2** abstract —**tran′scen·den′tal·ly *adv.***

tran′scen·den′tal·ism′ *n.* [*often* **T-**] a philosophy based on a search for reality through spiritual intuition

trans·con·ti·nen·tal (trans′kän tə nent′′l, tranz′-) ***adj.*** **1** that crosses a continent **2** on the other side of a continent

tran·scribe (tran skrīb′) ***vt.*** **-scribed′, -scrib′ing** **1** to write out or type out in full (shorthand notes, etc.) **2** to represent (speech sounds) in symbols

tran·script (tran′skript′) ***n.*** **1** a written, typewritten, or printed copy **2** a copy, esp. an official copy, as of a student's record

tran·scrip′tion (-skrip′shən) ***n.*** **1** a transcribing **2** a transcript; copy **3** an arrangement of a piece of music for an instrument or voice other than that for which it was written

trans·duc·er (trans dōō′sər, tranz-) ***n.*** ⟦< L *trans-*, over + *ducere*, to lead⟧ a device that transmits energy from one system to another, sometimes converting the energy to a different form

tran·sept (tran′sept′) ***n.*** ⟦< L *trans-*, across + *septum*, enclosure⟧ the part of a cross-shaped church at right angles to the nave, or either of its arms

trans·fer (trans′fər) ***vt.*** **-ferred, -fer·ring** ⟦< L *trans-*, across + *ferre*, to bear⟧ **1** to carry, send, etc. to another person or place **2** to make over (property, etc.) to another **3** to convey (a picture, etc.) from one surface to another —***vi.*** **1** to transfer oneself or be transferred **2** to change as to another school or another bus —***n.*** **1** a transferring or being transferred **2** one that is transferred **3** a ticket entitling the bearer to change to another bus, etc. —**trans·fer′ral** (-fur′-) ***n.***

trans·fer·ence (trans′fər əns, trans fur′-) ***n.*** a transferring or being transferred

trans·fig·ure (trans fig′yər) ***vt.*** **-ured, -ur·ing** ⟦< L *trans-*, across + *figura*, figure⟧ **1** to change the form or appearance of **2** to transform so as to glorify —**trans·fig′u·ra′tion *n.***

trans·fix (trans fiks′) ***vt.*** ⟦< L *trans-*, through + *figere*, to fix⟧ **1** to pierce through; impale **2** to make motionless, as if impaled

trans·form (trans fôrm′) ***vt.*** ⟦< L *trans-*, over + *forma*, a form⟧ **1** to change the form or appearance of **2** to change the condition, nature, or function of —**trans′for·ma′tion *n.***

trans·form′er *n.* a device for changing electrical energy to a different voltage

trans·fuse′ (-fyōōz′) ***vt.*** **-fused′, -fus′ing** ⟦< L *trans-*, across + *fundere*, pour⟧ **1** to instill; imbue **2** to transfer (blood, etc.) into a blood vessel —**trans·fu′sion *n.***

trans·gress (trans gres′, tranz-) ***vt., vi.*** ⟦< L *trans-*, over + *gradi*, to step⟧ **1** to break (a law, command, etc.); sin (against) **2** to go beyond (a limit, etc.) —**trans·gres′sion** (-gresh′ən) ***n.*** —**trans·gres′sor *n.***

tran·sient (tran′shənt, -zē ənt) ***adj.*** ⟦< L *trans-*, over + *ire*, to go⟧ **1** passing away with time; temporary **2** passing quickly; fleeting **3** staying only a short time —***n.*** a transient person —**tran′sience** or **tran′sien·cy *n.***

tran·sis·tor (tran zis′tər, -sis′-) ***n.*** ⟦TRAN(SFER) + (RE)SISTOR⟧ a compact electronic device, composed of semiconductor material, that controls current flow —**tran·sis′tor·ize′, -ized′, -iz′ing, *vt.***

trans·it (tran′sit, -zit) ***n.*** ⟦< L *trans-*, over + *ire*, to go⟧ **1** passage through or across **2** *a*) a carrying through or across; conveyance *b*) a system of urban public transportation **3** a surveying instrument for measuring horizontal angles

tran·si·tion (tran zish′ən) ***n.*** a passing from one condition, place, etc. to another —**tran·si′tion·al *adj.***

tran·si·tive (tran′sə tiv, -zə-) ***adj.*** designating a verb that takes a direct object

tran·si·to·ry (tran′sə tôr′ē, -zə-) ***adj.*** not enduring; temporary; fleeting

transl *abbrev.* **1** translated **2** translation

trans·late (trans lāt′, tranz-) ***vt.*** **-lat′ed, -lat′ing** ⟦< L *translatus*, transferred⟧ **1** to move from one place or condition to another **2** to put into the words of a different language **3** to put into different words —**trans·la′tor *n.***

trans·la′tion *n.* **1** a translating **2** writing or speech translated into another language

trans·lit·er·ate (trans lit′ər āt′, tranz-) ***vt.*** **-at′ed, -at′ing** ⟦< TRANS- + L *litera*, letter⟧ to write (words, etc.) in the characters of another alphabet —**trans·lit′er·a′tion *n.***

trans·lu′cent (-lōō′sənt) ***adj.*** ⟦< L *trans-*, through + *lucere*, to shine⟧ letting light pass through, but not transparent

trans·mi′grate′ (-mī′grāt′) ***vi.*** **-grat′ed, -grat′ing** ⟦see TRANS- & MIGRATE⟧ to pass into another body at death:

THESAURUS

CONFUSION.

tranquil *a.* composed, agreeable, gentle; see SERENE.

tranquilize *v.* calm, pacify, quell; see CALM DOWN, QUIET 1, SOOTHE.

tranquilizer *n.* sleeping pill, depressant, alleviator, palliative, soother, mollifier, calmative, sedative, placebo, pacifier, downer*; see also DRUG, MEDICINE 2.

tranquillity *n.* calmness, peacefulness, serenity; see PEACE 2, 3.

transact *v.* accomplish, carry on, conclude; see BUY, SELL.

transaction *n.* sale, proceeding, deal; see BUSINESS 4.

transcend *v.* rise above, transform, excel; see EXCEED.

transcontinental *a.* trans-American, trans-Siberian, trans-Canadian, trans-European, intracontinental, cross-country.

transcribe *v.* reprint, reproduce, decipher; see COPY.

transcript *n.* record, reprint, reproduction; see COPY.

transfer *n.* **1** [Ticket] token, fare, check; see TICKET 1. **2** [A document providing for a change] new orders, instructions, new assignment; see COMMAND, DIRECTIONS.

transfer *v.* **1** [To carry] transport, convey, shift; see CARRY 1. **2** [To assign] sell, hand over, deliver; see ASSIGN, GIVE 1.

transferred *a.* moved, removed, shifted, transported, relocated, transmitted, turned over, sent, relayed, shipped, mailed, faxed, transplanted, reassigned, transposed, restationed, conveyed, delivered, transmuted; see also SENT.—*Ant.* FIXED, retained, kept.

transform *v.* convert, metamorphose, reconstruct; see ALTER 1.

transformation *n.* **1** [A change] alteration, transmutation, conversion; see CHANGE 1. **2** [A grammatical construction] transform, transformed construction, equivalent grammatical sequence; see ADJECTIVE, PHRASE, SENTENCE 2.

transfusion *n.* dialysis, blood transfusion, transfer; see EXCHANGE 1.

transgress *v.* overstep, rebel, infringe; see DISOBEY.

transgression *n.* misbehavior, trespass, infraction; see CRIME, SIN, VIOLATION.

transgressor *n.* offender, sinner, rebel; see CRIMINAL.

transient *a.* provisional, ephemeral, transitory; see TEMPORARY.

transient *n.* tourist, traveler, visitor, migrant, migrant worker.

transistor *n.* portable radio, pocket radio, receiver; see RADIO 2.

transition *n.* shift, passage, flux, alteration, modification, switch, variation, passing, development, transformation, turn, realignment; see also CHANGE 2.—*Ant.* STABILITY, constancy, durability.

translate *v.* decode, transliterate, interpret, decipher, paraphrase, render, transpose, turn, gloss, put in equivalent terms.

translated *a.* interpreted, adapted, rendered, transliterated, glossed, paraphrased, transposed, reworded, reworked, transferred, rewritten.

translation *n.* transliteration, version, adaptation, rendition, rendering, interpretation, paraphrase, rewording, gloss, reading.

said of the soul, as in Hindu religious belief —**trans′mi·gra′tion** ***n.***

trans·mis′sion (-mish′ən) ***n.*** **1** a transmitting **2** something transmitted **3** the part of a motor vehicle that transmits power to the wheels

trans·mit′ (-mit′) ***vt.*** **-mit′ted, -mit′ting** ⟦< L *trans-*, over + *mittere*, send⟧ **1** to cause to go to another person or place; transfer **2** to hand down by heredity, inheritance, etc. **3** *a)* to pass (light, heat, etc.) through some medium *b)* to conduct *[water transmits sound]* **4** to convey (force, movement, etc.) to **5** to send out (radio or television broadcasts) —**trans·mis′si·ble** (-mis′ə bəl) ***adj.*** —**trans·mit′ta·ble** ***adj.*** —**trans·mit′tal** ***n.***

trans·mit′ter ***n.*** the apparatus that transmits signals in telephony, radio, etc.

trans·mute′ (-myo͞ot′) ***vt., vi.*** **-mut′ed, -mut′ing** ⟦< L *trans-*, over + *mutare*, to change⟧ to change from one form, nature, substance, etc. into another; transform —**trans′mu·ta′tion** ***n.***

trans·na′tion·al (-nash′ə nəl) ***adj.*** transcending the limits, interests, etc. of a single nation

trans′o′ce·an′ic (-ō′shē an′ik) ***adj.*** crossing the ocean

tran·som (tran′səm) ***n.*** ⟦prob. < L *transtrum*, crossbeam⟧ **1** a horizontal crossbar, as across the top of a door or window **2** a small window just above a door or window

trans·pa·cif·ic (trans′pə sif′ik) ***adj.*** **1** crossing the Pacific **2** on the other side of the Pacific

trans·par·en·cy (trans per′ən sē) ***n., pl.*** **-cies** a transparent film or slide having an image that can be projected on a screen

trans·par′ent ***adj.*** ⟦< L *trans-*, through + *parere*, appear⟧ **1** transmitting light rays so that objects on the other side can be seen clearly **2** so fine in texture as to be seen through **3** easily understood or detected; clear; obvious —**trans·par′ent·ly** ***adv.***

tran·spire (tran spīr′) ***vi.*** **-spired′, -spir′ing** ⟦< L *trans-*, through + *spirare*, breathe⟧ **1** to give off vapor, moisture, etc., as through pores **2** to become known **3** to happen

trans·plant (trans plant′; *also, and for n. always,* trans′plant′) ***vt.*** **1** to remove from one place and plant, resettle, etc. in another **2** *Surgery* to transfer (tissue or an organ) from one to another; graft —***n.*** a transplanting or something transplanted, as a body organ or a seedling —**trans′plan·ta′tion** (-plan tā′shən) ***n.***

tran·spon·der (tran spän′dər) ***n.*** ⟦< TRAN(SMITTER) & RESPOND⟧ a transceiver that automatically transmits signals

trans·port (trans pôrt′; *for n.* trans′pôrt′) ***vt.*** ⟦< L *trans-*, over + *portare*, carry⟧ **1** to carry from one place to another **2** to carry away with emotion —***n.*** **1** a transporting; transportation **2** strong emotion, esp. joy **3** a vehicle for transporting

trans′por·ta′tion (-pər tā′shən) ***n.*** **1** a transporting or being transported **2** a means of conveyance **3** fare or a ticket for being transported

trans·pose (trans pōz′) ***vt., vi.*** **-posed′, -pos′ing** ⟦see TRANS- & POSE⟧ **1** to change the usual order or position of; interchange **2** to rewrite or play (a musical composition) in a different key —**trans′po·si′tion** (-pə zish′ən) ***n.***

trans·sex·u·al (trans sek′sho͞o əl) ***n.*** a person who identifies with the opposite sex, sometimes so strongly as to undergo sex-change surgery

trans·ship (trans ship′) ***vt., vi.*** **-shipped′, -ship′ping** to transfer from one ship, train, truck, etc. to another for further shipment —**trans·ship′ment** ***n.***

trans·verse (trans vurs′, tranz-; *also, and for n. usually,* trans′vurs′, tranz′-) ***adj.*** ⟦< L *trans-*, across + *vertere*, to turn⟧ situated across; crosswise —***n.*** a transverse part, etc.

trans·ves·tite (trans ves′tīt′, tranz-) ***n.*** ⟦< TRANS- + L *vestire*, to dress⟧ a person who gets sexual pleasure from dressing in the clothes of the opposite sex

trap (trap) ***n.*** ⟦< OE *træppe*⟧ **1** a device for catching animals, as one that snaps shut tightly when stepped on **2** any stratagem designed to catch or trick **3** a device, as in a drainpipe, for preventing the escape of gas, etc. —***vt.*** **trapped, trap′ping** to catch in or as in a trap —***vi.*** to trap animals, esp. for their furs —**trap′per** ***n.***

trap′door′ ***n.*** a hinged or sliding door in a roof, ceiling, or floor

tra·peze (tra pēz′) ***n.*** ⟦see fol.⟧ a short horizontal bar, hung high by two ropes, on which gymnasts, etc. swing

tra·pe·zi·um (trə pē′zē əm) ***n., pl.*** **-zi·ums** or **-zi·a** (-ə) ⟦< Gr *trapeza*, table⟧ a plane figure with four sides, no two of which are parallel

trap·e·zoid (trap′i zoid′) ***n.*** ⟦see prec.⟧ a plane figure with four sides, only two of which are parallel —**trap′e·zoi′dal** ***adj.***

trap′pings ***pl.n.*** ⟦< OFr *drap,* cloth⟧ **1** an ornamental covering for a horse **2** adornments

trap′shoot′ing ***n.*** the sport of shooting at clay disks sprung into the air from throwing devices

trash (trash) ***n.*** ⟦prob. < Scand⟧ **1** broken, discarded, or worthless things; rubbish **2** a person or people regarded as disreputable, etc. —***vt.*** [Slang] **1** to destroy (property) as by vandalism **2** to criticize or insult (a person, etc.) sharply or maliciously —**trash′y, -i·er, -i·est,** ***adj.***

trau·ma (trô′mə, trä′-) ***n., pl.*** **-mas** or **-ma·ta** (-mə tə) ⟦Gr⟧ **1** a bodily injury or shock **2** an emotional shock, often having a lasting psychic effect —**trau·mat·ic** (trô mat′ik) ***adj.***

trau′ma·tize′ (-tīz′) ***vt.*** **-tized′, -tiz′ing** to subject to a physical or mental trauma

trav·ail (trə vāl′, trav′āl′) ***n.*** ⟦< L *tri-*, three + *palus*, stake: referring to a torture device⟧ **1** very hard work **2** intense pain; agony

trav·el (trav′əl) ***vi.*** **-eled** or **-elled, -el·ing** or **-el·ling** ⟦var. of prec.⟧ **1** to go from one place to another **2** to move, pass, or be transmitted —***vt.*** to make a journey over or through —***n.*** **1** a traveling **2** [pl.] trips, journeys, etc. —**trav′el·er** or **trav′el·ler** ***n.***

THESAURUS

transmission ***n.*** **1** [The act of transporting] transference, conveyance, carrying; see DELIVERY 1, TRANSPORTATION. **2** [The carrying of sound on radio waves] broadcast, telecast, radiocast; see BROADCASTING. **3** [A mechanism for adapting power] gears, gear box, automatic transmission; see DEVICE 1.

transmit ***v.*** **1** [To send] dispatch, forward, convey; see SEND 1, 2. **2** [To carry] pass on, transfer, communicate; see SEND 2.

transmitter ***n.*** antenna, radio tower, wire; see COMMUNICATION, ELECTRONICS.

transparent ***a.*** **1** [Allowing light to pass through] translucent, lucid, crystalline, gauzy, thin, permeable, pellucid, sheer, see-through, diaphanous, glassy; see also CLEAR 2.—*Ant.* DARK, black, smoky. **2** [Obvious] easily seen, plain, clear; see OBVIOUS 1.

transplant ***n.*** transplanting, transplantation, graft; see OPERATION 4.

transplant ***v.*** reset, graft, remove; see ALTER 1.

transport ***v.*** convey, move, bring; see CARRY 1.

transportation ***n.*** conveying, conveyance, carrying, hauling, shipping, carting, moving, transferring, truckage, freightage, airlift, transference, transit, passage, a ride, a lift.

transported ***a.*** conveyed, forwarded, transferred; see MOVED 1.

trap ***n.*** **1** [A device to catch game or persons] net, box trap, steel trap, spring trap, snare, mousetrap, pit, blind, pitfall, cul-de-sac, deadfall. **2** [A trick] prank, practical joke, snare; see TRICK 1.

trap ***v.*** ensnare, seduce, fool; see AMBUSH, DECEIVE.

trapped ***a.*** ambushed, cornered, with one's back to the wall; see CAPTURED.

trash ***n.*** **1** [Rubbish] garbage, waste, refuse, dregs, filth, litter, debris, dross, sweepings, rubble, odds and ends, stuff, rags, scraps, scrap, excess, scourings, fragments, pieces, shavings, loppings, slash, rakings, slag, parings, rinsings, residue, offal, junk, sediment, leavings, droppings.—*Ant.* MONEY, goods, riches. **2** [Nonsense] drivel, rubbish, senselessness; see NONSENSE 1.

travel ***n.*** riding, roving, wandering, visiting, rambling, sailing, boating, busing, touring, biking, hiking, cruising, driving, wayfaring, going abroad, seeing the world, sightseeing, voyaging, journeying, trekking, flying, globe-trotting, space travel, rocketing.

travel ***v.*** tour, cruise, voyage, roam, explore, jet to, rocket to, orbit, go into orbit, take a jet, go by jet, migrate, trek, vacation, motor, visit, traverse, jaunt, wander, junket, journey, adventure, quest, trip, rove, inspect, make an expedition, cross the continent, cross the ocean, encircle the globe, make the grand tour, sail, see the country, go camping, go abroad, take a trip, cover, go walking, go riding, go bicycling, make a train trip, drive, fly, set out, set forth, sightsee; see also WALK 1.

traveled ***a.*** **1** [*Said of persons*] worldly, cosmopolitan, experienced; see CULTURED. **2** [*Said of roads*] well-used, busy, operating, in use, frequented, widely known, sure, safe, well-trodden, accepted.—*Ant.* ABANDONED, little-used, unexplored.

traveler ***n.*** voyager, adventurer, tourist, explorer, nomad, wanderer, truant, peddler, roamer, rambler, wayfarer, migrant, excursionist, junketeer, sightseer, straggler, vagabond, vagrant, hobo, tramp, gypsy, gad-

traveler's check a check, issued by a bank, etc., sold to a traveler who signs it at issuance and again when cashing it

trav·e·logue or **trav·e·log** (trav'ə lôg') ***n.*** **1** an illustrated lecture on travels **2** a short film about a place, esp. one that is foreign, unusual, etc.

tra·verse (trə vurs'; *for n. & adj.* trav'ərs) ***vt.* -versed', -vers'ing** ⟦< L *trans-*, across + *vertere*, to turn⟧ to pass over, across, or through —***n.* trav'erse** **1** something that traverses or crosses, as a crossbar **2** a traversing —***adj.* trav'erse** **1** extending across **2** designating or of draperies drawn by pulling a cord at the side

trav·es·ty (trav'is tē) ***n.***, *pl.* **-ties** ⟦< L *trans-*, over + *vestire*, to dress⟧ **1** a farcical imitation in ridicule **2** a ridiculous representation *[a travesty of justice]* —***vt.* -tied, -ty·ing** to make a travesty of

trawl (trôl) ***n.*** ⟦< ? MDu *traghel*, dragnet⟧ **1** a large dragnet for fishing **2** a long line supported by buoys, from which fishing lines are hung —***vi.***, ***vt.*** to fish or catch with a trawl

trawl'er ***n.*** a boat used in trawling

tray (trā) ***n.*** ⟦< OE *treg*, wooden board⟧ a flat receptacle with raised edges, for holding or carrying things

treach·er·ous (trech'ər əs) ***adj.*** **1** characterized by treachery; disloyal **2** untrustworthy or insecure —**treach'er·ous·ly *adv.***

treach·er·y (trech'ər ē) ***n.***, *pl.* **-ies** ⟦< OFr *trichier*, to cheat⟧ **1** betrayal of trust; disloyalty **2** treason

trea·cle (trē'kəl) ***n.*** ⟦< Gr *(antidotos) thēriakē*, (remedy) for venom⟧ [Brit.] **1** molasses **2** anything very sweet or cloying —**trea'cly** (-klē) ***adj.***

tread (tred) ***vt.* trod, trod'den** or **trod, tread'ing** ⟦OE *tredan*⟧ **1** to walk on, in, along, etc. **2** to do or follow by walking, dancing, etc. **3** to press or beat with the feet —***vi.*** **1** to walk **2** to set one's foot (*on, across,* etc.) **3** to trample (*on* or *upon*) —***n.*** **1** the manner or sound of treading **2** something for treading or moving on, as a shoe sole or surface of a stair **3** the thick outer layer of an automotive tire —**tread water** *pt. & pp. usually* **tread'ed** to stay upright in swimming by moving the legs and arms back and forth

trea·dle (tred''l) ***n.*** ⟦< OE *tredan*, to tread⟧ a lever moved by the foot as to turn a wheel

tread'mill' ***n.*** **1** a mill wheel turned by an animal treading an endless belt **2** any monotonous work in which one seems to make no progress **3** an exercise machine with an endless belt on which one walks or runs

treas *abbrev.* **1** treasurer **2** treasury

trea·son (trē'zən) ***n.*** ⟦< L *trans-*, over + *dare*, give⟧ betrayal of one's country to an enemy —**trea'son·a·ble** or **trea'son·ous *adj.***

treas·ure (trezh'ər) ***n.*** ⟦< Gr *thēsauros*⟧ **1** accumulated wealth, as money or jewels **2** any person or thing considered valuable —***vt.* -ured, -ur·ing** **1** to save up for future use **2** to value greatly

treas·ur·er (trezh'ər ər) ***n.*** one in charge of a treasury, as of a government or club

treas'ure-trove' (-trōv') ***n.*** ⟦*trove* < OFr *trover*, find⟧ **1** treasure found hidden, the original owner of which is unknown **2** a valuable source or collection

treas·ur·y (trezh'ər ē) ***n.***, *pl.* **-ies** **1** a place where treasure or funds are kept **2** the funds or revenues of a state, corporation, etc. **3** [T-] the department of government in charge of revenue, taxation, and public finances

treat (trēt) ***vi.*** ⟦ult. < L *trahere*, to draw⟧ **1** to discuss terms (*with*) **2** to speak or write (*of*) —***vt.*** **1** to deal with (a subject) in writing, music, etc. in a specified manner **2** to act toward (someone or something) in a specified manner **3** to pay for the food, etc. of (another) **4** to subject to some process, chemical, etc. **5** to give medical care to —***n.*** **1** a meal, drink, etc. paid for by another **2** anything that gives great pleasure

trea·tise (trēt'is) ***n.*** ⟦see prec.⟧ a formal article or book on some subject

treat·ment (trēt'mənt) ***n.*** **1** act, manner, method, etc. of treating **2** medical or surgical care

trea·ty (trēt'ē) ***n.***, *pl.* **-ties** ⟦< L *trahere*, to draw⟧ a formal agreement between two or more nations

tre·ble (treb'əl) ***adj.*** ⟦< L *triplus*, triple⟧ **1** threefold; triple **2** of, for, or performing the treble —***n.*** **1** the highest part in musical harmony; soprano **2** a high-pitched voice or sound —***vt.***, ***vi.* -bled, -bling** to make or become threefold

tree (trē) ***n.*** ⟦OE *trēow*⟧ **1** a large, woody perennial plant with one main trunk and many branches **2** *a)* anything resembling a tree *b)* FAMILY TREE —***vt.* treed, tree'ing** to chase up a tree —**tree'less *adj.*** —**tree'like' *adj.***

tre·foil (trē'foil') ***n.*** ⟦< L *tri-*, three + *folium*, leaf⟧ **1** a plant with leaves divided into three leaflets, as the clover **2** a design, etc. shaped like such a leaf

trek (trek) ***vi.* trekked, trek'king** ⟦Afrik < Du *trekken*, to pull⟧ **1** to travel slowly or laboriously **2** [Inf.] to go on foot —***n.*** **1** a journey **2** a migration

trel·lis (trel'is) ***n.*** ⟦< L *trilix*, triple-twilled⟧ a lattice on which vines are trained

trem·a·tode (trem'ə tōd', trē'mə-) ***n.*** ⟦< Gr *trēmatōdēs*, perforated⟧ a parasitic flatworm with muscular suckers; fluke

trem·ble (trem'bəl) ***vi.* -bled, -bling** ⟦< L *tremere*⟧ **1** to shake or shiver from cold, fear, etc. **2** to feel great anxiety **3** to quiver, vibrate, etc. —***n.*** **1** a trembling **2** [*sometimes pl.*] a fit of trembling

tre·men·dous (tri men'dəs) ***adj.*** ⟦< L *tremere*, to tremble⟧ **1** very large; great **2** [Inf.] wonderful, amazing, etc. —**tre·men'dous·ly *adv.***

trem·o·lo (trem'ə lō') ***n.***, *pl.* **-los'** ⟦It⟧ *Music* a tremulous effect produced by rapid reiteration of the same tone

THESAURUS

about, itinerant, pilgrim, rover, passenger, commuter, globe-trotter.

traveling ***a.*** passing, en route, on board, shipped, freighted, transported, moving, carried, conveyed, consigned, wandering, touring, roving, on tour, vagrant, migrant, nomadic, wayfaring, itinerant, cruising, excursioning, commuting, driving, flying, sailing, riding, on vacation, migrating, voyaging; see also MOVING 2.

travesty ***n.*** burlesque, spoof, caricature; see PARODY.

tray ***n.*** platter, plate, salver; see DISH 1.

treacherous ***a.*** deceptive, undependable, dangerous, risky, misleading, tricky, false, deceitful, ensnaring, faulty, precarious, unstable, insecure, shaky, slippery, ticklish, difficult, ominous, alarming, menacing.—*Ant.* RELIABLE, dependable, steady.

treachery ***n.*** faithlessness, disloyalty, betrayal; see DISHONESTY, TREASON.

tread ***v.*** walk, step, step on; see TRAMPLE.

treason ***n.*** sedition, seditiousness, disloyalty, perfidy, treachery, seditionary act, seditious act, aid and comfort to the enemy; see also DISHONESTY, DECEPTION, REVOLUTION 2.

treasure ***n.*** richness, riches, nest egg; see WEALTH.

treasure ***v.*** prize, value, appreciate, guard, cherish, adore, fancy, like; see also LOVE 1.

treasurer ***n.*** bursar, cashier, banker; see CLERK.

treasury ***n.*** exchequer, safe, depository; see BANK 2.

treat ***n.*** entertainment, surprise, amusement, feast, source of gratification, gift, special dish.

treat ***v.*** **1** [To deal with a person or thing] negotiate, manage, have to do with, have business with, behave toward, handle, make terms with, act toward, react toward, use, employ, have recourse to.—*Ant.* NEGLECT, ignore, have nothing to do with. **2** [To assist toward a cure] attend, administer, prescribe, dose, operate, nurse, dress, minister to, apply therapy, care for, doctor*; see also HEAL. **3** [To pay for another's entertainment] entertain, indulge, satisfy, amuse, divert, play host to, escort, take, pick up the check*.

treatise ***n.*** tract, paper, monograph, thesis, study, report, essay.

treatment ***n.*** **1** [Usage] handling, processing, dealing, approach, execution, procedure, method, manner, proceeding, way, strategy, custom, habit, employment, practice, mode, line, angle. **2** [Assistance toward a cure] diet, operation, medical care, surgery, therapy, remedy, prescription, regimen, hospitalization, doctoring*; see also MEDICINE 2.

treaty ***n.*** agreement, pact, settlement, covenant, compact, convention, alliance, charter, sanction, bond, understanding, arrangement, bargain, negotiation, truce, cease-fire, deal.

tree ***n.*** *Trees include the following:* ash, elm, oak, maple, evergreen, birch, tulip, fir, cypress, juniper, spruce, larch, tamarack, pine, cedar, beech, chestnut, buckeye, eucalyptus, hickory, walnut, sycamore, palm, willow, locust, sequoia, redwood, poplar, acacia, cottonwood, dogwood, box elder, apple, cherry, peach, plum, pear, olive, banyan, mahogany, bamboo, ebony, ironwood, bottletree; see also WOOD 1. —**up a tree*** cornered, in difficulty, trapped; see IN TROUBLE.

trees ***n.*** wood, woods, windbreak; see FOREST.

trek ***v.*** hike, migrate, journey; see TRAVEL.

tremble ***v.*** quiver, shiver, vibrate; see SHAKE 1.

tremendous ***a.*** huge, great, colossal; see LARGE 1.

trem·or (trem′ər) ***n.*** ⟦< L *tremere,* to tremble⟧ **1** a trembling, shaking, etc. **2** a trembling sensation

trem·u·lous (trem′yo͞o ləs) ***adj.*** ⟦< L *tremere,* to tremble⟧ **1** trembling; quivering **2** fearful; timid

trench (trench) ***vt.*** ⟦< OFr *trenchier,* to cut⟧ to dig a ditch or ditches in —***n.*** **1** a deep furrow **2** a long, narrow ditch dug by soldiers for cover, with earth heaped up in front

trench·ant (tren′chənt) ***adj.*** ⟦see prec.⟧ **1** sharp; incisive *[trenchant* words*]* **2** forceful; effective *[*a *trenchant* argument*]* —**trench′ant·ly** ***adv.***

trench coat a belted raincoat in a military style

trench′er ***n.*** ⟦see TRENCH⟧ [Archaic] a wooden platter for meat

trench′er·man (-mən) ***n.***, *pl.* **-men** (-mən) an eater; esp., one who eats much

trench foot a diseased condition of the feet from prolonged exposure to wet and cold

trench mouth an infectious disease of the mucous membranes of the mouth and throat

trend (trend) ***vi.*** ⟦OE *trendan*⟧ to have a general direction or tendency —***n.*** **1** a general tendency or course; drift **2** a current style

trend·y (tren′dē) ***adj.*** **-i·er, -i·est** [Inf.] of or in the latest style, or trend

Tren·ton (trent′′n) capital of New Jersey: pop. 89,000

trep·i·da·tion (trep′ə dā′shən) ***n.*** ⟦< L *trepidus,* disturbed⟧ fearful uncertainty; anxiety

tres·pass (tres′pəs, -pas′) ***vi.*** ⟦< L *trans-,* across + *passus,* a step⟧ **1** to go beyond the limits of what is considered right; do wrong; transgress **2** to enter another's property without permission or right —***n.*** a trespassing; specif., a moral offense —**tres′pass·er** ***n.***

tress (tres) ***n.*** ⟦< OFr *tresse,* braid of hair⟧ **1** a lock of human hair **2** [*pl.*] a woman's or girl's hair, esp. when long

tres·tle (tres′əl) ***n.*** ⟦< L *transtrum,* a beam⟧ **1** a horizontal beam fastened to two pairs of spreading legs, used as a support **2** a framework of uprights and crosspieces, supporting a bridge, etc.

trey (trā) ***n.*** ⟦< L *tres,* three⟧ a playing card with three spots

tri- ⟦< Fr, L, or Gr⟧ *prefix* **1** having or involving three **2** three times, into three **3** every third

tri·ad (trī′ad′) ***n.*** ⟦< Gr *treis,* three⟧ a group of three

tri·age (trē äzh′, trē′äzh′) ***n.*** ⟦< Fr *trier,* sift⟧ a system of establishing the order in which acts are to be carried out in an emergency, esp. acts of medical assistance —***vt.*** **-aged′, -ag′ing** to prioritize (patients, problems, etc.)

tri·al (trī′əl) ***n.*** ⟦see TRY⟧ **1** the act or process of trying, testing, etc.; test; probation **2** a hardship, suffering, etc. **3** a source of annoyance **4** a hearing and deciding of a case in a court of law **5** an attempt; effort —***adj.*** **1** of a trial **2** for the purpose of trying, testing, etc. —**on trial** in the process of being tried

trial and error the process of making repeated trials, tests, and adjustments until the right result is found

trial balloon something said or done to test public opinion on an issue

tri·an·gle (trī′aŋ′gəl) ***n.*** ⟦see TRI- & ANGLE[1]⟧ **1** a plane figure having three angles and three sides **2** anything with three sides or three corners **3** a situation involving three persons *[*a love *triangle]* —**tri·an′gu·lar** (-gyo͞o lər) ***adj.***

tri·an′gu·late′ (-gyə lāt′) ***vt.*** **-lat′ed, -lat′ing** to divide (an area) into triangles in order to determine distance or relative positions —**tri·an′gu·la′tion** ***n.***

tri·ath·lon (trī ath′län′, -lən) ***n.*** ⟦TRI- + Gr *athlon,* a contest⟧ an endurance race combining events in swimming, bicycling, and running

tribe (trīb) ***n.*** ⟦< L *tribus*⟧ **1** a group of persons or clans descended from a common ancestor and living under a leader or chief **2** a natural group of related plants or animals —**trib′al** ***adj.*** —**trib′al·ly** ***adv.*** —**tribes′man** (-mən), *pl.* **-men,** ***n.***

trib·u·la·tion (trib′yə lā′shən) ***n.*** ⟦< L *tribulare,* to press⟧ great misery or distress, or the cause of it

tri·bu·nal (trī byo͞o′nəl, tri-) ***n.*** ⟦see fol.⟧ **1** a seat for a judge in a court **2** a court of justice

trib·une (trib′yo͞on′; *for 2, often* tri byo͞on′) ***n.*** ⟦< L *tribus,* tribe⟧ **1** in ancient Rome, a magistrate appointed to protect the rights of plebeians **2** a champion of the people: often used in newspaper names

trib·u·tar·y (trib′yo͞o ter′ē) ***adj.*** **1** paying tribute **2** subject *[*a *tributary* nation*]* **3** flowing into a larger one *[*a *tributary* stream*]* —***n.***, *pl.* **-ies** **1** a tributary nation **2** a tributary river

trib·ute (trib′yo͞ot) ***n.*** ⟦< L *tribuere,* allot⟧ **1** money paid regularly by one nation to another as acknowledgment of subjugation, for protection, etc. **2** any forced payment **3** something given, done, or said to show gratitude, honor, or praise

trice (trīs) ***n.*** ⟦< MDu *trisen,* to pull⟧ an instant; moment: now only in **in a trice**

tri·cen·ten·ni·al (trī′sen ten′ē əl) ***adj.*** happening once every 300 years —***n.*** a 300th anniversary

tri·ceps (trī′seps′) ***n.***, *pl.* **-ceps′** or **-ceps′es** ⟦L < *tri-,* three + *caput,* head⟧ a muscle with three points of origin, esp. the muscle on the back of the upper arm

tri·cer·a·tops (trī ser′ə täps′) ***n.*** ⟦< TRI- + Gr *keras,* horn + *ōps,* eye⟧ a plant-eating dinosaur with three horns

tri·chi·na (tri kī′nə) ***n.***, *pl.* **-nae** (-nē) ⟦< Gr *trichinos,* hairy⟧ a very small worm that causes trichinosis

trich·i·no·sis (trik′i nō′sis) ***n.*** ⟦< Gr *trichinos,* hairy⟧ a disease caused by intestinal worms, and acquired by eating insufficiently cooked pork from an infested hog

trick (trik) ***n.*** ⟦< OFr *trichier,* to cheat⟧ **1** something designed to deceive, cheat, etc. **2** a practical joke; prank **3** a clever act intended to amuse **4** any feat requiring skill **5** a personal mannerism **6** a round of duty; shift **7** *Card Games* the cards won in a single round —***vt.*** to deceive or swindle —***adj.*** apt to malfunction *[*a *trick* knee*]* —**do** (or **turn**) **the trick** [Inf.] to produce the desired result —**trick′er·y,** *pl.* **-ies,** ***n.***

trick·le (trik′əl) ***vi.*** **-led, -ling** ⟦ME *triklen* < ?⟧ **1** to flow slowly in a thin stream or fall in drops **2** to move slowly *[*the crowd *trickled* away*]* —***n.*** a slow, small flow

THESAURUS

tremor ***n.*** trembling, shaking, shivering; see EARTHQUAKE.

trench ***n.*** rut, hollow, gully, ravine, depression, gutter, furrow, drainage canal, creek, moat, dike, drain, channel, gorge, gulch, arroyo. *Military trenches include the following:* dugout, earthwork, entrenchment, fortification, breastwork, pillbox, excavation, bunker, machine-gun nest, foxhole, slit trench, moat, tank-trap.

trend ***n.*** bias, bent, leaning; see INCLINATION 1.

trendy* ***a.*** stylish, popular, contemporary; see FASHIONABLE.

trespass ***v.*** encroach, invade, infringe; see MEDDLE 1.

trespasser ***n.*** encroacher, invader, infringer; see INTRUDER.

trial ***a.*** tentative, test, preliminary; see EXPERIMENTAL.

trial ***n.*** **1** [An effort to learn the truth] analysis, test, examination; see EXPERIMENT. **2** [A case at law] suit, lawsuit, fair hearing, hearing, action, case, contest, indictment, legal proceedings, claim, cross-examination, litigation, counterclaim, arraignment, prosecution, citation, court action, judicial contest, seizure, bill of divorce, habeas corpus, court-martial, impeachment. **3** [An ordeal] suffering, misfortune, heavy blow; see DIFFICULTY 1, 2. —**on trial** **1** [In court] in litigation, up for investigation, at the bar, before the bar, before a judge, before a jury, being tried, contested, appealed, indicted; see also ACCUSED. **2** [Experimental] on a trial basis, for a trial period, on approval; see UNCERTAIN.

triangle ***n.*** *Triangles include the following:* equilateral, isosceles, right-angled, obtuse-angled, scalene, acute-angled.

triangular ***a.*** three-cornered, three-sided, triagonal; see ANGULAR.

tribal ***a.*** tribalistic, group, kindred; see RACIAL.

tribe ***n.*** primitive group, ethnic group, clan; see RACE 2.

tributary ***n.*** stream, branch, sidestream; see RIVER.

tribute ***n.*** applause, recognition, eulogy; see PRAISE 2.

trick ***n.*** **1** [A deceit] wile, fraud, deception, ruse, cheat, cover, feint, hoax, artifice, decoy, trap, stratagem, intrigue, fabrication, double-dealing, forgery, fake, illusion, invention, subterfuge, distortion, delusion, ambush, snare, blind, evasion, plot, equivocation, concealment, treachery, swindle, feigning, impersonation, pretense, duplicity, falsehood, falsification, perjury, disguise, conspiracy, circumvention, quibble, trickery, beguiling, chicanery, humbug, maneuver, sham, counterfeit, scam*, gyp*, touch*, phoney*, come-on*, fast one*, dodge*, plant*, clip*, sucker deal*, con game*, bluff, shakedown*, sell-out*, con*, funny business*, dirty work*, crooked deal, front*, gimmick*; see also LIE.—*Ant.* HONESTY, truth, veracity. **2** [A prank] jest, sport, practical joke; see JOKE. **3** [A practical method or expedient] skill, facility, know-how*; see ABILITY, METHOD.

trick ***v.*** dupe, outwit, fool; see DECEIVE.

trickle ***v.*** drip, leak, run; see FLOW.

trick′le·down′ *adj.* of an economic theory holding that government aid to the largest businesses will ultimately benefit the poor

trick′ster (-stər) *n.* a person who tricks; cheat

trick′y *adj.* **-i·er, -i·est 1** given to or characterized by trickery **2** like a trick in deceptiveness or intricacy

tri·col·or (trī′kul′ər) *n.* a flag having three colors in large areas; esp., the flag of France

tri·cy·cle (trī′sə kəl) *n.* ⟦Fr: see TRI- & CYCLE⟧ a child's three-wheeled vehicle operated by pedals

tri·dent (trīd′′nt) *n.* ⟦< L *tri-,* three + *dens,* tooth⟧ a three-pronged spear

tried (trīd) *vt., vi. pt. & pp. of* TRY —*adj.* **1** tested; proved **2** trustworthy

tri·en·ni·al (trī en′ē əl) *adj.* ⟦< L *tri-,* three + *annus,* year⟧ **1** happening every three years **2** lasting three years —**tri·en′ni·al·ly** *adv.*

Tri·este (trē est′) seaport in NE Italy: pop. 228,000

tri·fle (trī′fəl) *n.* ⟦< OFr *truffe,* deception⟧ **1** something of little value or importance **2** a small amount of money —*vi.* **-fled, -fling 1** to talk or act jokingly **2** to toy (*with*) —*vt.* to waste *[to trifle the hours away]* —**tri′fler** *n.*

tri′fling (-fliŋ) *adj.* **1** frivolous; shallow **2** of little importance; trivial

tri·fo·cals (trī′fō′kəlz) *pl.n.* eyeglasses like bifocals, but with a third area in the lens ground for viewing objects at an intermediate distance

trig (trig) *n. short for* TRIGONOMETRY

trig·ger (trig′ər) *n.* ⟦< Du *trekken,* to pull⟧ a lever pulled to release a catch, etc., esp. one pressed to activate the firing mechanism on a firearm —*vt.* to initiate (an action)

trig′ger-hap′py *adj.* **1** tending to resort to force rashly or irresponsibly **2** ready to start a war for the slightest cause

tri·glyc·er·ide (trī glis′ər īd′) *n.* ⟦TRI- + Gr *glykeros,* sweet⟧ an ester derived from glycerol: the chief component of fats and oils

trig·o·nom·e·try (trig′ə näm′ə trē) *n.* ⟦< Gr *trigōnon,* triangle + *-metria,* measurement⟧ the branch of mathematics analyzing, and making calculations from, relations between the sides of right triangles with reference to their angles —**trig′o·no·met′ric** (-nə me′trik) *adj.*

trill (tril) *n.* ⟦ult. echoic⟧ **1** a rapid alternation of a musical tone with a slightly higher tone **2** a warble **3** a rapid vibration of the tongue or uvula —*vt., vi.* to sound, speak, or play with a trill

tril·lion (tril′yən) *n.* **1** 1 followed by 12 zeros **2** [Brit.] 1 followed by 18 zeros —**tril′lionth** *adj., n.*

tril·li·um (tril′ē əm) *n.* ⟦ModL < L *tri-,* three⟧ a woodland plant having a single flower with three petals and three sepals

tril·o·gy (tril′ə jē) *n., pl.* **-gies** ⟦see TRI- & -LOGY⟧ a set of three related plays, novels, etc.

trim (trim) *vt.* **trimmed, trim′ming** ⟦< OE *trymman,* make firm⟧ **1** to put in proper order; make neat or tidy *[to trim hair]* **2** to clip, lop, cut, etc. **3** to decorate, as by adding ornaments, etc. **4** *a)* to balance (a ship) by ballasting, etc. *b)* to put (sails) in order for sailing **5** to balance (a flying aircraft) **6** [Inf.] to beat, punish, defeat, cheat, etc. —*vi.* to adjust according to expediency —*n.* **1** order; arrangement **2** good condition **3** a trimming, as by clipping **4** decorative parts or borders —*adj.* **trim′mer, trim′mest 1** orderly; neat **2** well-proportioned **3** in good condition —**trim′ly** *adv.* —**trim′mer** *n.* —**trim′ness** *n.*

tri·ma·ran (trī′mə ran′) *n.* a boat like a catamaran, but with three parallel hulls

tri·mes·ter (trī mes′tər, trī′mes′-) *n.* ⟦< L *tri-,* three + *mensis,* month⟧ **1** a three-month period, as of pregnancy **2** in some colleges, any of the three periods of the academic year

trim·ming (trim′iŋ) *n.* **1** decoration; ornament **2** [*pl.*] *a)* the side dishes of a meal *b)* parts trimmed off **3** [Inf.] a beating, defeat, cheating, etc.

Trin·i·dad and To·ba·go (trin′i dad′ and tə bā′gō) island country in the West Indies: 1,980 sq. mi.; pop. 1,260,000

trin·i·ty (trin′i tē) *n., pl.* **-ties** ⟦< L *trinitas*⟧ a set of three —**the Trinity** *Christian Theol.* the union of Father, Son, and Holy Spirit in one Godhead

trin·ket (triŋ′kit) *n.* ⟦ME *trenket*⟧ **1** a small, cheap ornament, piece of jewelry, etc. **2** a trifle or toy

tri·o (trē′ō) *n., pl.* **-os** ⟦< L *tres,* three⟧ **1** a group of three **2** *Music a)* a composition for three voices or three instruments *b)* the three performers of such a composition

trip (trip) *vi., vt.* **tripped, trip′ping** ⟦< OFr *treper*⟧ **1** to move or perform with light, rapid steps; skip **2** to stumble or cause to stumble **3** to make or cause to make a mistake **4** to run past or release (a spring, wheel, etc.) —*n.* **1** a light, quick tread **2** a journey, jaunt, etc. **3** a stumble or a causing to stumble **4** [Slang] *a)* an experience induced by a psychedelic drug, esp. LSD *b)* an experience that is pleasing, exciting, etc. —**trip up** to catch in a lie, error, etc. —**trip′per** *n.*

tri·par·tite (trī pär′tīt′) *adj.* ⟦< L *tri-,* three + *partire,* to part⟧ **1** having three parts **2** made between three parties, as an agreement

tripe (trīp) *n.* ⟦prob. ult. < Ar *tharb,* layer of fat lining the intestines⟧ **1** part of the stomach of an ox, etc., used as food **2** [Slang] anything worthless, etc.; nonsense

trip′ham′mer *n.* a heavy, power-driven hammer, alternately raised and allowed to fall by a tripping device: also **trip hammer**

tri·ple (trip′əl) *adj.* ⟦< L *triplus*⟧ **1** consisting of three; threefold **2** three times as much or as many —*n.* **1** an amount three times as much or as many **2** *Baseball* a hit on which the batter reaches third base —*vt., vi.* **tri′pled, tri′pling 1** to make or become three times as much or as many **2** *Baseball* to hit a triple —**tri′ply** *adv.*

tri·plet (trip′lit) *n.* **1** a group of three, as three successive lines of poetry **2** any of three offspring from the same pregnancy

trip·li·cate (trip′li kit; *for v.,* -kāt′) *adj.* ⟦< L *triplex*⟧ **1** threefold **2** being the last of three identical copies —*n.* any one of such copies —*vt.* **-cat′ed, -cat′ing** to make three identical copies of —**in triplicate** in three identical copies

tri·pod (trī′päd′) *n.* ⟦< Gr *tri-,* three + *pous,* foot⟧ a three-legged caldron, stool, support, etc.

trip·tych (trip′tik) *n.* ⟦< Gr *tri-,* three + *ptychē,* a fold⟧ a set of three hinged panels with pictures, etc., commonly placed above and behind an altar

THESAURUS

tricky *a.* **1** [Shrewd] clever, sharp, keen-witted; see INTELLIGENT. **2** [Delicate or difficult] complicated, intricate, critical, touchy, involved, dangerous, demanding, exacting, perplexing, knotty, thorny, complex, unstable, ticklish, catchy, likely to go wrong, hanging by a thread*; see also DIFFICULT 1, 2.—*Ant.* EASY, clearcut, simple.

tricycle *n.* velocipede, trike*, three-wheeler; see VEHICLE.

tried *a.* dependable, proved, used; see USED 1.

trifle *n.* **1** [A small quantity] particle, piece, speck; see BIT 1. **2** [A small degree] jot, eyelash, fraction; see BIT 2. **3** [Something of little importance] triviality, small matter, nothing; see INSIGNIFICANCE.

trifling *a.* petty, small, insignificant; see TRIVIAL, UNIMPORTANT.

trill *n.* warble, quaver, vibrato, tremolo.

trill *v.* quaver, warble, whistle, chirp, twitter; see also SOUND.

trim *a.* **1** [Neat] orderly, tidy, spruce; see CLEAN 1, NEAT 1. **2** [Well-proportioned] shapely, well-designed, streamlined, clean, slim, shipshape, delicate, fit, comely, well-formed, symmetrical, well-made, clean-cut, well-balanced, graceful, well-molded, harmonious, beautiful, classical, compact, smart, built*, buff*; see also HANDSOME.—*Ant.* DISORDERED, shapeless, overweight.

trim *v.* **1** [To cut off excess] prune, shave, lop; see CUT 1. **2** [To adorn] ornament, embellish, deck; see DECORATE. **3** [To prepare for sailing] ballast, rig, outfit; see SAIL 1.

trimming *n.* **1** [Ornamentation] accessory, frill, tassel; see DECORATION 2. **2** [The act of cutting off excess] shearing, lopping off, shaving off; see REDUCTION 1.

trinity *n.* trio, trilogy, triplet, triplicate, threesome, triad, troika, the Godhead; Father, Son, and Holy Spirit; the Triune God, Trinity; see also GOD 1.

trinket *n.* gadget, novelty, bauble; see JEWEL, JEWELRY.

trio *n.* **1** [A combination of three] threesome, triangle, triplet; see TRINITY. **2** [Three musicians performing together] string trio, vocal trio, piano trio; see BAND 3.

trip *n.* **1** [A journey] voyage, excursion, tour; see JOURNEY. **2** [A psychedelic experience] hallucinations, LSD trip, being turned on*; see DRUG.

trip *v.* **1** [To stumble] tumble, slip, lurch, slide, founder, fall, pitch, fall over, slip upon, plunge, sprawl, topple, go head over heels.—*Ant.* ARISE, ascend, get up. **2** [To cause to stumble] block, hinder, bind, tackle, overthrow, push, send headlong, kick, shove, mislead.—*Ant.* HELP, pick up, give a helping hand.

triple *a.* in triplicate, by three, threefold; see THREE.

tri·sect (trī sekt′, trī′sekt′) ***vt.*** ⟦< TRI- + L *secare,* to cut⟧ to cut or divide into three equal parts

trite (trīt) ***adj.*** **trit′er, trit′est** ⟦< L *terere,* wear out⟧ worn out by constant use; stale —**trite′ness** ***n.***

trit·i·um (trit′ē əm) ***n.*** a radioactive isotope of hydrogen having an atomic weight of 3

tri·umph (trī′əmf) ***n.*** ⟦< L *triumphus*⟧ **1** a victory; success **2** exultation or joy over a victory, etc. —***vi.*** **1** to gain victory or success **2** to rejoice over victory, etc. —**tri·um′phal** (-um′fəl) ***adj.***

tri·um′phal·ism′ ***n.*** an arrogant confidence in a set of beliefs —**tri·um′phal·ist** ***adj., n.***

tri·um′phant (-fənt) ***adj.*** **1** successful; victorious **2** rejoicing for victory —**tri·um′phant·ly** ***adv.***

tri·um·vir (trī um′vir′) ***n.,*** *pl.* **-virs′** or **-vi·ri′** (-vi rī′) ⟦L: see fol.⟧ in ancient Rome, any of three administrators sharing authority

tri·um·vi·rate (trī um′və rit) ***n.*** ⟦< L *trium virum,* of three men⟧ government by three persons or parties

tri·va·lent (trī vā′lənt) ***adj.*** *Chem.* having three valences or a valence of three

triv·et (triv′it) ***n.*** ⟦< L *tripes,* tripod⟧ **1** a three-legged stand for holding pots, etc. near a fire **2** a short-legged stand for hot dishes to rest on

triv·i·a (triv′ē ə) ***pl.n.*** [*usually with sing. v.*] unimportant matters

triv·i·al (triv′ē əl) ***adj.*** ⟦< L *trivialis,* commonplace⟧ unimportant; insignificant —**triv′i·al′i·ty** (-al′ə tē) ***n.***

triv′i·al·ize′ (-īz′) ***vt.*** **-ized′, -iz′ing** to regard or treat as trivial; make seem unimportant

-trix (triks) ⟦L⟧ *suffix* forming feminine nouns of agency

tro·chee (trō′kē) ***n.*** ⟦< Gr *trechein,* to run⟧ a metrical foot of one accented syllable followed by one unaccented syllable —**tro·cha′ic** (-kā′ik) ***adj.***

trod (träd) ***vt., vi.*** *pt. & alt. pp. of* TREAD

trod·den (träd′'n) ***vt., vi.*** *alt. pp. of* TREAD

trog·lo·dyte (träg′lə dīt′) ***n.*** ⟦< Gr *trōglē,* hole + *dyein,* enter⟧ **1** any of the prehistoric people who lived in caves **2** a recluse

troi·ka (trơi′kə) ***n.*** ⟦Russ⟧ **1** a vehicle drawn by three horses abreast **2** an association of three in authority

Tro·jan (trō′jən) ***adj.*** of ancient Troy or its people or culture —***n.*** **1** a person born or living in ancient Troy **2** a strong, hard-working, determined person

Trojan horse **1** *Gr. Legend* a huge, hollow wooden horse with Greek soldiers inside: it is brought into Troy, the soldiers creep out and open the gates, and the Greek army destroys the city **2** one that subverts a nation, etc. from within

troll[1] (trōl) ***vt., vi.*** ⟦ME *trollen,* to roll⟧ **1** to sing the parts of (a round, etc.) in succession **2** to sing in a full voice **3** to fish (in) with a baited line trailed behind a slowly moving boat —**troll′er** ***n.***

troll[2] (trōl) ***n.*** ⟦ON⟧ *Scand. Folklore* a supernatural being, as a giant or dwarf, living in a cave

trol·ley (trä′lē) ***n.,*** *pl.* **-leys** ⟦< TROLL[1]⟧ **1** a wheeled basket, etc. that runs suspended from an overhead track **2** a grooved wheel at the end of a pole, for transmitting electric current from an overhead wire to a streetcar, etc. **3** a trolley car

trolley bus an electric bus powered by trolleys

trolley car an electric streetcar that gets its power from a trolley

trol·lop (trä′ləp) ***n.*** ⟦prob. < Ger *trolle,* wench⟧ a prostitute

trom·bone (träm bōn′) ***n.*** ⟦It < *tromba,* a trumpet⟧ a large brass instrument, usually with a slide, or movable section —**trom·bon′ist** ***n.***

troop (tro͞op) ***n.*** ⟦< ML *troppus,* flock⟧ **1** a group of persons or animals **2** [*pl.*] soldiers **3** a subdivision of a cavalry regiment **4** a unit of Boy Scouts or Girl Scouts —***vi.*** **1** to gather or go together in a group **2** to walk or go

troop′er ***n.*** ⟦prec. + -ER⟧ **1** a soldier in the mounted cavalry **2** a mounted police officer **3** in the U.S., a state police officer

trope (trōp) ***n.*** ⟦< Gr *tropos,* a turning⟧ figurative language or a word used in a figurative sense

tro·phy (trō′fē) ***n.,*** *pl.* **-phies** ⟦< Gr *tropaion*⟧ a memorial of victory in war, sports competition, etc.; prize

trop·ic (träp′ik) ***n.*** ⟦< Gr *tropikos,* of a turn (of the sun at the solstices)⟧ **1** either of two parallels of latitude, one, the **Tropic of Cancer,** *c.* 23° 26′ north, and the other, the **Tropic of Capricorn,** *c.* 23° 26′ south **2** [*also* **T-**] [*pl.*] the region between these latitudes —***adj.*** of the tropics; tropical

trop′i·cal (-i kəl) ***adj.*** **1** of, in, characteristic of, or suitable for the tropics **2** very hot; sultry; torrid

tro·pism (trō′piz′əm) ***n.*** ⟦< Gr *tropē,* a turn⟧ the tendency of a plant or animal to grow or turn toward, or away from, a stimulus, as light

tro·po·sphere (trō′pə sfir′, träp′ə-) ***n.*** ⟦Fr < Gr *tropos,* a turning + Fr *sphère,* sphere⟧ the atmospheric zone characterized by water vapor, weather, and decreasing temperatures with increasing altitude

trot (trät) ***vt., vi.*** **trot′ted, trot′ting** ⟦< OHG *trottōn,* to tread⟧ **1** to move, ride, go, etc. at a trot **2** to hurry; run —***n.*** **1** a gait, as of a horse, in which a front leg and the opposite hind leg are lifted at the same time **2** a jogging gait of a person —**trot′ter** ***n.***

troth (trôth, trōth) ***n.*** ⟦ME *trouthe*⟧ [Archaic] **1** faithfulness; loyalty **2** truth **3** a promise, esp. to marry

trou·ba·dour (tro͞o′bə dôr′) ***n.*** ⟦Fr < Prov *trobar,* compose⟧ **1** any of a class of lyric poets and poet-musicians in S France and N Spain and Italy in the 11th to 13th c. **2** a minstrel or singer

trou·ble (trub′əl) ***vt.*** **-bled, -bling** ⟦< L *turba,* crowd⟧ **1** to disturb or agitate **2** to worry; harass **3** to cause inconvenience to *[don't trouble yourself]* —***vi.*** to take pains;

THESAURUS

trite ***a.*** hackneyed, typical, stereotyped; see COMMON 1, DULL 4.

triumph ***n.*** conquest, achievement, success; see VICTORY.

triumphant ***a.*** victorious, successful, lucky, winning, conquering, in the lead, triumphal, jubilant, dominant, laurel-crowned, champion, championship, prize-winning, unbeaten, top-seeded, out front, triumphing, elated, in the ascendancy, with flying colors.—*Ant.* BEATEN, defeated, overwhelmed.

trivial ***a.*** petty, trifling, small, superficial, piddling, wee, little, frivolous, insignificant, irrelevant, unimportant, nugatory, skin-deep, meaningless, mean, diminutive, slight, of no account, of no consequence, scanty, meager, inappreciable, microscopic, dribbling, nonessential, flimsy, inconsiderable, vanishing, momentary, immaterial, indifferent, beside the point, minute, inessential, paltry, inferior, minor, small-minded, beggarly, useless, inconsequential, worthless, mangy, trashy, pitiful, of little moment, dinky*, small-town*, cutting no ice*, cut and dried; see also SHALLOW 2.—*Ant.* IMPORTANT, great, serious.

troop ***n.*** flock, collection, company, troupe, band, assemblage; see also GATHERING.

troops ***n.*** soldiers, armed forces, fighting men; see ARMY 1.

trophy ***n.*** citation, medal, cup; see PRIZE.

tropic ***a.*** **1** [Related to the tropics] tropical, equatorial, jungle; see HOT 1. **2** [Hot] thermal, torrid, burning; see HOT 1.

tropics ***n.*** torrid zone, equator, Equatorial Africa; South America, Latin America, Caribbean, Amazon, the Congo, the Pacific Islands, jungles; see also JUNGLE.

trot ***v.*** lope, jog, amble; see RUN 2.

trouble ***n.*** **1** [A person or thing causing trouble] annoyance, difficult situation, bother, bind, hindrance, difficulty, task, puzzle, predicament, plight, problem, fear, worry, concern, inconvenience, nuisance, disturbance, calamity, catastrophe, disaster, crisis, delay, quarrel, dispute, bad news, affliction, intrusion, irritation, trial, pain, ordeal, discomfort, injury, adversity, hang-up*, case, gossip, problem child, meddler, pest, tease, tiresome person, inconsiderate person, intruder, troublemaker, fly in the ointment, headache*, brat, holy terror*, peck of trouble*, hassle*.—*Ant.* HELP, aid, comfort. **2** [Illness] ailment, malady, affliction; see ILLNESS 1, 2. **3** [Civil disorder] riot, turmoil, strife; see DISTURBANCE 2. **4** [A quarrel] argument, feud, bickering; see DISPUTE, FIGHT 1. —**in trouble** in a quandary, in difficulty, in a predicament, in bad*, in hot water*, in for it*, in the doghouse*, in a jam*, out on a limb*; see also TROUBLED.

trouble ***v.*** **1** [To disturb] disconcert, annoy, irritate; see BOTHER 2, DISTURB. **2** [To take care] be concerned with, make an effort, take pains; see BOTHER 1.

troubled ***a.*** disturbed, agitated, grieved, apprehensive, pained, anxious, perplexed, afflicted, confused, puzzled, overwrought, aggravated*, uptight*, bothered, harassed, vexed, plagued, teased, annoyed, concerned, uneasy, discomposed, harried, careworn, mortified, badgered, baited, inconvenienced, put out, upset, flustered, tortured, goaded, irritated, displeased, unhappy, tried, roused, disconcerted, pursued, chafed, ragged, galled, rubbed the wrong way, tired, molested, crossed, thwarted, distressed, wounded, sickened, restless, irked, pestered, heckled, persecuted, frightened, alarmed, terrified, scared, anguished, harrowed, tormented, provoked, stung, ruffled, fretting, perturbed, afraid, shaky, shaken, fearful,

bother —*n.* **1** a state of mental distress; worry **2** a misfortune; calamity **3** a person, event, etc. causing annoyance, distress, etc. **4** public disturbance **5** effort; bother *[take the trouble to listen]*

trou'ble·mak'er *n.* one who incites others to quarrel, rebel, etc.

trou'ble·shoot'er *n.* one whose work is to locate and fix breakdowns, eliminate the source of trouble in work flow, etc. —**trou'ble·shoot'ing** *n.*

trou'ble·some (-səm) *adj.* characterized by or causing trouble

trough (trôf, träf) *n.* ⟦OE *trog*⟧ **1** a long, narrow, open container, esp. one to hold water or food for animals **2** a channel or gutter for carrying off rainwater **3** a long, narrow hollow, as between waves **4** a low in an economic cycle **5** a long, narrow area of low barometric pressure

trounce (trouns) *vt.* **trounced, trounc'ing** ⟦< ?⟧ **1** to beat; flog **2** [Inf.] to defeat —**trounc'er** *n.*

troupe (tro͞op) *n.* ⟦Fr⟧ a group of actors, singers, etc. —*vi.* **trouped, troup'ing** to travel as a member of a troupe

troup'er *n.* **1** a troupe member **2** [Inf.] one who is steady, dependable, etc., during trying times

trou·sers (trou'zərz) *pl.n.* ⟦< Gael *triubhas*⟧ a two-legged outer garment, esp. for men and boys, extending from the waist to the ankles

trous·seau (tro͞o sō', tro͞o'sō) *n., pl.* **-seaux'** (-sōz') or **-seaus'** ⟦Fr < OFr *trousse,* a bundle⟧ a bride's clothes, linens, etc.

trout (trout) *n., pl.* **trout** or **trouts** ⟦< Gr *trōgein,* gnaw⟧ a food and game fish, related to the salmon, found chiefly in fresh water

trow (trō, trou) *vi., vt.* ⟦< OE *treow,* faith⟧ [Archaic] to believe

trow·el (trou'əl) *n.* ⟦< L *trua,* ladle⟧ **1** a flat hand tool for smoothing plaster or applying mortar **2** a scooplike tool for loosening soil, etc. —*vt.* **-eled** or **-elled, -el·ing** or **-el·ling** to spread, smooth, dig, etc. with a trowel

troy (troi) *adj.* ⟦after *Troyes,* city in France, where first used⟧ of or by a system of weights (**troy weight**) for gold, silver, gems, etc.

Troy (troi) ancient city in NW Asia Minor

tru·ant (tro͞o'ənt) *n.* ⟦< OFr, beggar⟧ **1** a pupil who stays away from school without permission **2** one who neglects duties —*adj.* **1** that is a truant **2** errant; straying —**tru'an·cy,** *pl.* **-cies,** *n.*

truce (tro͞os) *n.* ⟦< OE *treow,* faith⟧ **1** a temporary cessation of warfare by agreement between the belligerents **2** respite from conflict, trouble, etc.

truck[1] (truk) *n.* ⟦< Gr *trochos,* wheel⟧ **1** a two-wheeled barrow or low, wheeled frame for carrying heavy articles **2** an automotive vehicle for hauling loads **3** a swiveling, wheeled frame under each end of a railroad car, etc. —*vt.* to carry on a truck —*vi.* to drive a truck —**truck'er** *n.*

truck[2] (truk) *vt., vi.* ⟦< Fr *troquer*⟧ to exchange; barter —*n.* **1** small articles of little value **2** vegetables raised for market **3** [Inf.] dealings **4** [Inf.] trash; rubbish

truck farm a farm where vegetables are grown to be marketed

truck·le (truk'əl) *n.* ⟦< Gr *trochos,* wheel⟧ TRUNDLE BED: in full **truckle bed** —*vi.* **-led, -ling** to be servile; submit (*to*)

truc·u·lent (truk'yo͞o lənt, -yə-) *adj.* ⟦< L *trux*⟧ **1** fierce; cruel; savage **2** pugnacious —**truc'u·lence** *n.* —**truc'u·lent·ly** *adv.*

trudge (truj) *vi.* **trudged, trudg'ing** ⟦< ?⟧ to walk, esp. wearily or laboriously —*n.* a wearying walk

true (tro͞o) *adj.* **tru'er, tru'est** ⟦OE *treowe*⟧ **1** faithful; loyal **2** in accordance with fact; not false **3** conforming to standard, etc.; correct **4** rightful; lawful **5** accurately fitted, shaped, etc. **6** real; genuine —*adv.* **1** truly **2** *Biol.* without variation from type —*vt.* **trued, tru'ing** or **true'ing** to fit, place, or shape accurately: often with *up* —*n.* that which is true: with *the*

true believer a dedicated follower or disciple, esp. one who follows without doubts or questions

true bill a bill of indictment endorsed by a grand jury

true'-blue' *adj.* very loyal; staunch

truf·fle (truf'əl) *n.* ⟦ult. < L *tuber,* knob⟧ a fleshy, edible underground fungus

tru·ism (tro͞o'iz'əm) *n.* a statement the truth of which is obvious

tru'ly *adv.* **1** in a true manner; accurately, genuinely, etc. **2** really; indeed **3** sincerely

Tru·man (tro͞o'mən), **Har·ry S** (har'ē) 1884-1972; 33d president of the U.S. (1945-53)

trump (trump) *n.* ⟦< TRIUMPH⟧ **1** any playing card of a suit ranked higher than any other suit for a given hand **2** such a suit **3** any advantage held in reserve —*vt., vi.* to play a trump on (a trick, etc.) —**trump up** to devise fraudulently

trump·er·y (trump'ər ē) *n., pl.* **-ies** ⟦< Fr *tromper,* deceive⟧ **1** something showy but worthless **2** nonsense

trum·pet (trum'pit) *n.* ⟦< OFr *trompe*⟧ **1** a brass instrument consisting of a looped tube with a flared bell and three valves **2** a trumpetlike device for channeling sound, as an early kind of hearing aid **3** a sound like that of a trumpet —*vi.* to make the sound of a trumpet —*vt.* to proclaim loudly —**trum'pet·er** *n.*

trun·cate (truŋ'kāt') *vt.* **-cat'ed, -cat'ing** ⟦< L *truncus,* stem⟧ to cut off a part of —**trun·ca'tion** *n.*

trun·cheon (trun'chən) *n.* ⟦< L *truncus,* stem⟧ [Chiefly Brit.] a policeman's stick or billy

trun·dle (trun'dəl) *vt., vi.* **-dled, -dling** ⟦< OE *trendan,* to roll⟧ to roll along —**trun'dler** *n.*

trundle bed a low bed on small wheels, that can be rolled under another bed when not in use

trunk (truŋk) *n.* ⟦< L *truncus*⟧ **1** the main stem of a tree **2** a human or animal body, not including the head and limbs **3** a long snout, as of an elephant **4** a large, reinforced box to hold clothes, etc. in travel **5** [*pl.*] shorts worn by men for athletics **6** a compartment in a car, usually in the rear, for luggage, etc.

trunk line a main line of a railroad, telephone system, etc.

THESAURUS

unsettled, suspicious, in turmoil, full of misgivings, dreading, bugged*, in a quandary, in a stew, on pins and needles*, all hot and bothered*, worried stiff*, in a tizzy*, burned up*, miffed*, peeved*, riled*, floored*, up a tree*, hung-up*, up the creek without a paddle*.—*Ant.* CALM, at ease, settled.

troublemaker *n.* rogue, knave, recreant; see CRIMINAL.

troublesome *a.* bothersome, difficult, annoying, irritating, oppressive, repressive, distressing, upsetting, painful, dangerous, damaging, disturbing, alarming, vexing.

trough *n.* dip, channel, hollow; see HOLE 2.

trousers *n.* slacks, breeches, pants; see CLOTHES.

trout *n.* *Trout include the following:* speckled, brook, rainbow, cutthroat, lake, steelhead, brown, golden, tiger, bull, Apache; see also FISH.

trowel *n.* blade, scoop, implement; see TOOL 1.

truant *a.* missing, straying, playing hooky*; see ABSENT.

truce *n.* armistice, cease-fire, lull; see PEACE 1.

truck[1] *n.* carriage, van, lorry, motor vehicle; see also VEHICLE. *Types of trucks include the following:* moving van, police van, laundry truck, pickup truck, delivery truck, freight truck, logging truck, trailer, piggyback trailer, tractor trailer, truck train, cement mixer, refrigerator truck, refrigerated truck, four-wheel drive truck, garbage truck, dump truck, rig, semi*, halftrack, armored personnel carrier, APC.

trudge *v.* plod, step, tread; see WALK 1.

true *a.* **1** [Accurate] precise, verified, proved, certain, certified, definite, checked, exact, correct; see also VALID 1. **2** [Loyal] sure, reliable, trustworthy, faithful, dependable, sincere; see also FAITHFUL, RELIABLE. **3** [Genuine] authentic, virtual, substantial, tangible, actual, pure; see also REAL 2, VALID 2. **—come true** become a fact, be actualized, come about; see DEVELOP 1, HAPPEN 2.

truism *n.* commonplace, self-evident truth, adage; see CLICHÉ, MOTTO, PROVERB.

truly *a.* honestly, exactly, definitely, factually, correctly, accurately, unequivocally, reliably, sincerely, scrupulously, fairly, justly, validly, scientifically, rightfully, righteously, faithfully, worthily, without bias, without prejudice, fairly and squarely*.—*Ant.* WRONGLY, dishonestly, deceptively.

trumped up *a.* falsified, concocted, magnified; see EXAGGERATED, FALSE 2.

trumpet *n.* horn, bugle, cornet; see MUSICAL INSTRUMENT.

trump up *v.* think up, devise, concoct, falsify, present fraudulent evidence, misrepresent; see also LIE 1, DECEIVE.

trunk *n.* **1** [A container for goods] chest, case, foot locker; see CONTAINER. **2** [The torso] body, abdomen, thorax; see BACK 1, STOMACH. **3** [The stem of a tree] column, stock, log; see STALK. **4** [A proboscis] prow, snoot, snout; see NOSE 1.

truss (trus) ***vt.*** ⟦< OFr *trousser*⟧ **1** to tie, bind, or bundle: often with *up* **2** to support with a truss —***n.*** **1** a bundle or pack **2** a framework for supporting a roof, bridge, etc. **3** a padded device for giving support in cases of rupture or hernia

trust (trust) ***n.*** ⟦< ON *traust*⟧ **1** *a)* firm belief in the honesty, reliability, etc. of another; faith *b)* the one trusted **2** confident expectation, hope, etc. **3** responsibility resulting from confidence placed in one **4** care; custody **5** something entrusted to one **6** faith in a buyer's ability to pay; credit **7** a combination of corporations to establish a monopoly **8** *Law a)* the fact of having nominal ownership of property to keep, use, or administer for another *b)* such property —***vi.*** to be confident —***vt.*** **1** to have confidence in **2** to commit (something) *to* a person's care **3** to allow to do something without misgivings **4** to believe **5** to hope; expect **6** to grant business credit to —***adj.*** **1** relating to a trust **2** acting as trustee —**in trust** entrusted to another's care

trust·ee (trus tē′) ***n.*** **1** one to whom another's property or its management is entrusted **2** a member of a board managing the affairs of a college, hospital, etc. —**trust·ee′ship** ***n.***

trust′ful ***adj.*** full of trust; ready to confide; trusting —**trust′ful·ly** ***adv.*** —**trust′ful·ness** ***n.***

trust fund money, securities, etc. held in trust

trust′ing ***adj.*** that trusts; trustful

trust territory a territory placed under the administrative authority of a country by the United Nations

trust′wor′thy ***adj.*** **-thi·er, -thi·est** worthy of trust; reliable —**trust′wor′thi·ness** ***n.***

trust′y ***adj.*** **-i·er, -i·est** dependable; trustworthy —***n.***, *pl.* **-ies** a convict granted special privileges as a trustworthy person

truth (tro͞oth) ***n.***, *pl.* **truths** (tro͞o*th*z, tro͞oths) ⟦OE *treowth*⟧ **1** a being true; specif., *a)* sincerity; honesty *b)* conformity with fact *c)* reality; actual existence *d)* correctness; accuracy **2** that which is true **3** an established fact —**in truth** truly

truth′ful ***adj.*** **1** telling the truth; honest **2** corresponding with fact or reality —**truth′ful·ly** ***adv.*** —**truth′ful·ness** ***n.***

try (trī) ***vt.*** **tried**, **try′ing** ⟦< OFr *trier*⟧ **1** to melt out or render (fat, etc.) **2** to conduct the trial of in a law court **3** to put to the proof; test **4** to subject to trials, etc.; afflict **5** to experiment with *[to try a recipe]* **6** to attempt; endeavor —***vi.*** to make an effort, attempt, etc. —***n.***, *pl.* **tries** an attempt; effort; trial —**try on** to test the fit of (something to wear) by putting it on —**try out** **1** to test by putting into use **2** to test one's fitness, as for a place on a team

try′ing ***adj.*** that tries one's patience; annoying; irksome —**try′ing·ly** ***adv.***

try′out′ ***n.*** [Inf.] a test to determine fitness, etc.

tryst (trist) ***n.*** ⟦< OFr *triste*, hunting station⟧ **1** an appointment to meet, esp. one made by lovers **2** an appointed meeting or meeting place

tsar (tsär, zär) ***n.*** *alt. sp. of* CZAR (sense 1) —**tsa·ri·na** (tsä rē′nə, zä-) ***fem.n.***

tset·se fly (tset′sē, tsēt′-) ⟦< Bantu name⟧ a small fly of central and S Africa: one kind carries sleeping sickness

T′-shirt′ ***n.*** a collarless pullover knit shirt with short sleeves: also **t′-shirt′**

tsp *abbrev.* **1** teaspoon(s) **2** teaspoonful(s)

T square a T-shaped ruler for drawing parallel lines

tsu·na·mi (tso͞o nä′mē) ***n.***, *pl.* **-mis** or **-mi** ⟦Jpn < *tsu*, a harbor + *nami*, a wave⟧ a huge sea wave caused by an undersea earthquake, volcanic eruption, etc.

tub (tub) ***n.*** ⟦< MDu *tubbe*⟧ **1** a round, wooden container, usually with staves and hoops **2** any large, open container, as of metal **3** a bathtub

tu·ba (to͞o′bə) ***n.*** ⟦L, trumpet⟧ a large, low-pitched brass musical instrument

tub·al (to͞o′bəl) ***adj.*** of or in a tube, esp. a fallopian tube *[a tubal pregnancy]*

tub·by (tub′ē) ***adj.*** **-bi·er, -bi·est** **1** shaped like a tub **2** fat and short

tube (to͞ob) ***n.*** ⟦< L *tubus*, pipe⟧ **1** a slender pipe of metal, glass, etc. for conveying fluids **2** a tubelike part, organ, etc. **3** a pliable cylinder with a screw cap, for holding paste, etc. **4** *short for*: *a)* ELECTRON TUBE *b)* VACUUM TUBE **5** [Brit.] a subway —**the tube** [Inf.] television —**tube′less** ***adj.***

tu·ber (to͞o′bər) ***n.*** ⟦L, lit., a swelling⟧ a short, thick part of an underground stem, as a potato —**tu′ber·ous** ***adj.***

tu′ber·cle (-kəl) ***n.*** ⟦see prec.⟧ **1** a small, rounded projection, as on a bone or a plant root **2** any abnormal hard nodule or swelling; specif., the typical lesion of tuberculosis

tu·ber·cu·lin (to͞o bur′kyə lin) ***n.*** a solution injected into the skin as a test for tuberculosis

tu·ber′cu·lo′sis (-lō′sis) ***n.*** ⟦see TUBERCLE & -OSIS⟧ an infectious disease characterized by the formation of

THESAURUS

trust ***n.*** **1** [Reliance] confidence, dependence, credence; see FAITH 1. **2** [Responsibility] guardianship, liability, account; see DUTY 1. **3** [A large company] monopoly, corporation, institution; see BUSINESS 4. —**in trust** in another's care, held for, reserved; see SAVED 2.

trust ***v.*** **1** [To believe in] swear by, place confidence in, confide in, esteem, depend upon, expect help from, presume upon, lean on, fall back on, have no doubt, rest assured, be sure about, have no reservations, rely on, put faith in, look to, count on, assume that, presume that, be persuaded by, be convinced, put great stock in, set great store by, bank on*, take at one's word; see also BELIEVE.—*Ant.* DOUBT, mistrust, disbelieve. **2** [To hope] presume, take, imagine; see ASSUME, HOPE. **3** [To place in the protection of another] lend, put in safekeeping, entrust; see sense 1. **4** [To give credit to] advance, lend, loan, let out, grant, confer, let, patronize, aid, give financial aid to.—*Ant.* BORROW, raise money, pawn.

trusted ***a.*** trustworthy, dependable, reliable, trusty, tried, proved, intimate, close, faithful, loyal, true, staunch, constant, devoted, incorruptible, safe, honorable, honored, inviolable, on the level*, regular*, right, sure-fire*.—*Ant.* DISHONEST, questionable, unreliable.

trustee ***n.*** guardian, custodian, controller, lawyer, stockholder, guarantor, regent, board member, appointee, administrator, member of the directorate.

trusting ***a.*** trustful, credulous, confiding, gullible, unsuspecting, easygoing, open, candid, indulgent, obliging, well-meaning, good-natured, tenderhearted, green; see also NAIVE.—*Ant.* SUSPICIOUS, skeptical, critical.

trustworthiness ***n.*** integrity, uprightness, loyalty; see HONESTY.

trustworthy ***a.*** accurate, honest, true; see RELIABLE.

trusty ***n.*** trusted person, trustworthy convict, prison attendant, privileged prisoner; see also PRISONER.

truth ***n.*** **1** [Conformity to reality] truthfulness, correctness, sincerity, verity, candor, openness, honesty, fidelity, frankness, revelation, authenticity, exactness, infallibility, precision, perfection, certainty, genuineness, accuracy, fact, the gospel truth*, straight dope*, inside track*, the nitty-gritty*, the facts, the case.—*Ant.* LIE, deception, falsehood. **2** [Integrity] trustworthiness, honor, veracity; see HONESTY. —**in truth** in fact, indeed, really; see TRULY.

truthful ***a.*** correct, frank, just; see HONEST 1.

truthfully ***a.*** honestly, honorably, veraciously; see SINCERELY, TRULY.

truthfulness ***n.*** integrity, frankness, accuracy; see HONESTY.

try ***v.*** **1** [To endeavor] attempt, undertake, exert oneself, contend, strive, make an effort, risk, have a try at, contest, wrangle, labor, work, aspire, propose, try to reach, do what one can, tackle, venture, struggle for, compete for, speculate, make every effort, put oneself out, vie for, aspire to, attack, make a bid for, beat one's brains*, bear down, shoot at*, shoot for*, drive for, chip away at*, do one's best, make a pass at, go after, go out of the way, do all in one's power, buckle down, lift a finger, break an arm*, lay out, do oneself justice, have a go at*, make a go of it*, go all out, leave no stone unturned, move heaven and earth, knock oneself out*, break one's neck*, bust a gut*, take a crack at*, give it a whirl*, fight the good fight*. **2** [To test] assay, investigate, put to the proof; see ANALYZE, EXAMINE. **3** [To conduct a trial] hear a case, examine, decide; see JUDGE. —**try on** fit, have a fitting, try on for size; see WEAR 1. —**try out for** go out for, audition for, compete; see REHEARSE 3.

trying ***a.*** troublesome, bothersome, irritating; see DIFFICULT 1, 2.

tryout ***n.*** test, demonstration, rehearsal; see EXAMINATION 1.

tryst ***n.*** rendezvous, assignation, union; see APPOINTMENT 2, MEETING 1.

tub ***n.*** keg, bucket, tank; see CONTAINER.

tubby ***a.*** plump, beefy, stout; see FAT, SHORT 1.

tube ***n.*** **1** [A pipe] conduit, hose, test tube, tubing, tunnel, subway; see also PIPE 1. **2** [A metal container] package, holder, squeeze tube; see CONTAINER. **3** [An electronic device] cathode ray tube, picture tube, fluorescent tube; see DEVICE 1, MACHINE.

tubercles in body tissue; specif., tuberculosis of the lungs —**tu·ber'cu·lar** or **tu·ber'cu·lous** ***adj.***
tube sock a stretchable sock in the form of a long tube with no shaped heel
tube top a tight-fitting, one-piece, sleeveless and strapless women's garment for the upper body
tub·ing (to͞o'biŋ) ***n.*** **1** a series or system of tubes **2** material in the form of a tube **3** a piece of tube
tu·bu·lar (to͞o'byə lər) ***adj.*** ⟦< L *tubus*, pipe⟧ **1** of or like a tube **2** made with a tube or tubes
tu'bule' (-byo͞ol') ***n.*** a small tube
tuck (tuk) ***vt.*** ⟦< MDu *tucken*⟧ **1** to pull or gather (*up*) in a fold or folds **2** to sew a fold or folds in (a garment) **3** to fold the edges of (a sheet, etc.) under or in, to make secure **4** to press snugly into a small space —***n.*** **1** a sewed fold in a garment **2** [Inf.] cosmetic plastic surgery to remove fat
tuck·er (tuk'ər) ***vt.*** ⟦prob. < prec., in obs. sense "to punish, rebuke"⟧ [Inf.] to tire (*out*); weary
Tuc·son (to͞o'sän') city in S Arizona: pop. 405,000
-tude (to͞od, tyo͞od) ⟦< L *-tudo*⟧ *suffix* state, quality, or instance of being
Tues·day (to͞oz'dā) ***n.*** ⟦OE *Tiwes dæg*, day of the god of war *Tiu*⟧ the third day of the week: abbrev. **Tue, Tues**
tuft (tuft) ***n.*** ⟦< OFr *tufe*⟧ **1** a bunch of hairs, grass, etc. growing closely together **2** any cluster, as the fluffy ball forming the end of a cluster of threads drawn through a mattress —***vt.*** **1** to provide with tufts **2** to secure the padding of (a mattress, etc.) with tufts —**tuft'ed** ***adj.*** —**tuft'er** ***n.***
tug (tug) ***vi.***, ***vt.*** **tugged, tug'ging** ⟦prob. < ON *toga*, to pull⟧ **1** to pull hard; drag; haul **2** to tow with a tugboat —***n.*** **1** a hard pull **2** a tugboat
tug·boat (tug'bōt') ***n.*** a sturdy, powerful boat for towing or pushing ships, barges, etc.
tug of war **1** a contest in which two teams pull at opposite ends of a rope **2** a power struggle
tu·i·tion (to͞o ish'ən) ***n.*** ⟦< L *tueri*, protect⟧ the charge for instruction, as at a college
tu·la·re·mi·a (to͞o'lə rē'mē ə) ***n.*** ⟦after *Tulare* County, CA⟧ an infectious disease of rodents, esp. rabbits, transmissible to humans
tu·lip (to͞o'lip) ***n.*** ⟦< Turk *tülbend*, turban: from its shape⟧ **1** a bulb plant with a large, cup-shaped flower **2** the flower
tulle (to͞ol) ***n.*** ⟦after *Tulle*, city in France⟧ a fine netting of silk, rayon, nylon, etc., used as for veils and scarves
Tul·sa (tul'sə) city in NE Oklahoma: pop. 367,000
tum·ble (tum'bəl) ***vi.*** **-bled, -bling** ⟦< OE *tumbian*, to jump⟧ **1** to do somersaults or similar acrobatic feats **2** to fall suddenly or helplessly **3** to toss or roll about **4** to move in a hasty, disorderly manner —***vt.*** **1** to cause to tumble **2** to put into disorder; disarrange —***n.*** **1** a fall **2** disorder
tum'ble·down' ***adj.*** dilapidated
tum'bler (-blər) ***n.*** **1** an acrobat who does somersaults, etc. **2** a drinking glass **3** a part of a lock whose position must be changed by a key in order to release the bolt
tum'ble·weed' ***n.*** a plant that breaks off near the ground in autumn and is blown about by the wind
tum·brel or **tum·bril** (tum'brəl) ***n.*** ⟦< Fr *tomber*, to fall⟧ a cart that can be tilted for emptying
tu·mes·cence (to͞o mes'əns) ***n.*** ⟦see fol.⟧ **1** a swelling; distention **2** a swollen or distended part —**tu·mes'cent** ***adj.***
tu·mid (to͞o'mid) ***adj.*** ⟦< L *tumere*, to swell⟧ **1** swollen; bulging **2** inflated or pompous —**tu·mid'i·ty** ***n.***
tum·my (tum'ē) ***n.***, *pl.* **-mies** [Inf.] the stomach or abdomen
tu·mor (to͞o'mər) ***n.*** ⟦L, a swelling⟧ an abnormal growth of new tissue, independent of its surrounding structures; neoplasm: Brit. sp. **tu'mour**
tu·mult (to͞o'mult') ***n.*** ⟦< L *tumere*, to swell⟧ **1** noisy commotion **2** confusion; disturbance
tu·mul·tu·ous (to͞o mul'cho͞o əs) ***adj.*** full of tumult, uproar, etc.
tun (tun) ***n.*** ⟦OE *tunne*⟧ a large cask
tu·na (to͞o'nə) ***n.***, *pl.* **-na** or **-nas** ⟦AmSp⟧ **1** a large, edible ocean fish, as the albacore **2** the flesh of the tuna, canned for food: also **tuna fish**
tun·dra (tun'drə) ***n.*** ⟦Russ⟧ a vast, treeless arctic plain
tune (to͞on) ***n.*** ⟦ME, var. of *tone*, tone⟧ **1** a rhythmic succession of musical tones; melody **2** *a)* correct musical pitch *b)* agreement; concord: now used chiefly in the phrases **in tune** and **out of tune** —***vt.*** **tuned, tun'ing** **1** to adjust (a musical instrument) to some standard of pitch **2** to adapt to some condition, mood, etc. **3** to adjust (a motor, circuit, etc.) for proper performance —**to the tune of** [Inf.] to the sum, price, or extent of —**tune in** to adjust a radio or TV receiver so as to receive (a station, etc.) —**tun'er** ***n.***
tune'ful ***adj.*** full of music; melodious
tune'less ***adj.*** **1** not melodious **2** not producing music —**tune'less·ly** ***adv.*** —**tune'less·ness** ***n.***
tune'up' or **tune'-up'** ***n.*** an adjusting, as of an engine, to the proper condition
tung·sten (tuŋ'stən) ***n.*** ⟦Swed < *tung*, heavy + *sten*, stone⟧ a hard, heavy metallic chemical element, used in steel, etc.
tu·nic (to͞o'nik, tyo͞o'-) ***n.*** ⟦L *tunica*⟧ **1** a loose, gownlike garment worn by men and women in ancient Greece and Rome **2** a blouselike garment extending to the hips, often belted
tuning fork a two-pronged steel instrument which when struck sounds a certain fixed tone in perfect pitch
Tu·nis (to͞o'nis) seaport & capital of Tunisia: pop. 674,000
Tu·ni·si·a (to͞o nē'zhə) country in N Africa, on the Mediterranean: 63,378 sq. mi.; pop. 6,966,000 —**Tu·ni'si·an** ***adj.***, ***n.***
tun·nel (tun'əl) ***n.*** ⟦< Fr *tonnelle*, a vault⟧ **1** an underground passageway, as for autos, etc. **2** any tunnel-like passage, as in a mine —***vt.***, ***vi.*** **-neled** or **-nelled**, **-nel·ing** or **-nel·ling** to make a tunnel (through or under) —**tun'nel·er** or **tun'nel·ler** ***n.***
tunnel vision a narrow outlook, as on a particular problem
tun·ny (tun'ē) ***n.***, *pl.* **-nies** TUNA (sense 1)
tur·ban (tʉr'bən) ***n.*** ⟦< Pers *dulbänd*⟧ **1** a headdress worn by men in parts of Asia, consisting of cloth wound in folds about the head **2** any similar headdress
tur·bid (tʉr'bid) ***adj.*** ⟦< L *turba*, a crowd⟧ **1** muddy or cloudy from stirring sediment **2** thick, dense, or dark, as clouds **3** confused
tur·bine (tʉr'bin, -bīn') ***n.*** ⟦< L *turbo*, a whirl⟧ an engine driven as by the pressure of steam, water, or air against the curved vanes of a wheel
tur·bo·charge (tʉr'bō chärj') ***vt.*** **-charged', -charg'ing** to increase the power of (an engine) by the use of a type of compressor (**tur'bo·charg'er**) driven by a turbine powered by exhaust gases
tur'bo·fan' (-fan') ***n.*** a turbojet engine developing extra thrust from air that bypasses the combustion chamber and is accelerated by a fan: in full **turbofan engine**
tur'bo·jet' (-jet') ***n.*** **1** a jet engine in which the energy of the jet spins a turbine which drives the air compressor: in full **turbojet engine** **2** an aircraft with such an engine
tur'bo·prop' (-präp') ***n.*** **1** a turbojet engine whose turbine shaft drives a propeller: in full **turboprop engine** **2** an aircraft with such an engine
tur·bot (tʉr'bət) ***n.***, *pl.* **-bot** or **-bots** ⟦< OFr *tourbout*⟧ any of various flounders highly regarded as food
tur·bu·lent (tʉr'byə lənt) ***adj.*** ⟦< L *turba*, a crowd⟧ **1** wild or disorderly **2** full of violent motion —**tur'bu·lence** ***n.*** —**tur'bu·lent·ly** ***adv.***

THESAURUS

tuck ***n.*** crease, folding, pleat; see FOLD.
tuft ***n.*** clump, cluster, group; see BUNCH.
tug ***v.*** pull, haul, tow; see DRAW 1.
tuition ***n.*** fee, cost, expenditure; see PRICE.
tumble ***v.*** drop, plunge, descend; see FALL 1, TRIP 1.
tumbler ***n.*** **1** [An acrobat] equilibrist, gymnast, trampolinist; see ACROBAT, ATHLETE. **2** [A glass] goblet, cup, mug; see GLASS.
tumor ***n.*** neoplasm, growth, cyst; see SWELLING.
tumult ***n.*** agitation, uproar, turbulence; see CONFUSION, DISTURBANCE 2, FIGHT 1.
tune ***n.*** melody, ballad, strain; see SONG. —**change one's tune** change one's mind, alter one's actions, be transformed; see ALTER 1. —**sing a different tune** change one's mind, alter one's actions, be transformed; see ALTER 1.
tune ***v.*** adjust the pitch, attune, put in tune, tune up, tighten the strings, use the tuning fork, set the tune; see also HARMONIZE.
tunnel ***n.*** hole, burrow, underground passage, cave, passageway, subway, tube, crawl space, crawlway, shaft, mine, pit.
turbulence ***n.*** disorder, commotion, fracas; see CONFUSION, DISTURBANCE 2, FIGHT 1.
turbulent ***a.*** riotous, violent, stormy, disturbed, noisy, restless, raging, howling, buffeting, thunderous,

tu·reen (too rēn′) ***n.*** ⟦< Fr *terrine*, earthen vessel⟧ a large, deep dish with a lid, for soups, etc.

turf (turf) ***n.*** ⟦OE⟧ **1** *a)* a top layer of earth containing grass with its roots; sod *b)* [Chiefly Brit.] a piece of this **2** peat **3** a track for horse racing; also, horse racing: usually with *the* **4** [Slang] *a)* an area seen by a street gang as its territory to be defended *b)* one's own territory —***vt.*** to cover with turf —**turf′y *adj.***

tur·gid (tur′jid) ***adj.*** ⟦< L *turgere*, to swell⟧ **1** swollen; distended **2** bombastic; pompous —**tur·gid′i·ty** or **tur′gid·ness *n.*** —**tur′gid·ly *adv.***

Tu·rin (toor′in) city in NW Italy: pop. 953,000

Turk[1] (turk) ***n.*** a person born or living in Turkey

Turk[2] *abbrev.* **1** Turkey **2** Turkish

tur·key (tur′kē) ***n.*** ⟦< similarity to a fowl formerly imported through *Turkey*⟧ **1** a large North American bird with a spreading tail **2** its flesh, used as food

Tur·key (tur′kē) country occupying Asia Minor & a SE part of the Balkan Peninsula: 300,947 sq. mi.; pop. 56,473,000

turkey vulture a dark-colored vulture of temperate and tropical America: also **turkey buzzard**

Turk·ic (tur′kik) ***adj.*** designating or of a family of languages including Turkish, Tatar, etc.

Turk·ish (tur′kish) ***adj.*** of Turkey or its people, language, etc. —***n.*** the language of Turkey

Turkish bath a bathhouse with steam rooms, showers, massage, etc.

Turk·men·i·stan (tərk men′i stan′) country in central Asia: formerly a republic of the U.S.S.R.: 186,400 sq. mi.; pop. 3,523,000

tur·mer·ic (tur′mər ik) ***n.*** ⟦< ML *terra merita*, deserved earth⟧ an East Indian plant whose powdered root is used as a yellow dye or a seasoning

tur·moil (tur′moil′) ***n.*** ⟦< ?⟧ tumult; commotion

turn (turn) ***vt.*** ⟦ult. < Gr *tornos*, a lathe⟧ **1** to rotate (a wheel, etc.) **2** to move around or partly around */turn* the key*/* **3** to give form to, as in a lathe **4** to change the position or direction of **5** to reverse the position or sides of **6** to wrench */turn* one's ankle*/* **7** to upset (the stomach) **8** to deflect; divert **9** to cause to change actions, beliefs, aims, etc. **10** to go around (a corner, etc.) **11** to reach or pass (a certain age, amount, etc.) **12** to drive, set, let go, etc. */turn* the dog loose*/* **13** to direct, point, aim, etc. **14** to change */*to *turn* cream into butter*/* **15** to make sour **16** to affect in some way —***vi.*** **1** to rotate or revolve; pivot **2** to move around or partly around **3** to reel; whirl **4** to become upset: said of the stomach **5** to change or reverse course, direction, etc., or one's feelings, allegiance, etc. **6** to refer (*to*) **7** to apply (*to*) for help **8** to shift one's attention */*he *turned* to music*/* **9** to make a sudden attack (*on*) **10** to be contingent or depend (*on* or *upon*) **11** to become */*to *turn* cold*/* **12** to change to another form */*the rain *turned* to snow*/* **13** to become rancid, sour, etc. —***n.*** **1** a turning around; rotation; revolution **2** a single twist, winding, etc. **3** a change or reversal of course or direction **4** a short walk, ride, etc. **5** a bend; curve */*a *turn* in the road*/* **6** a change in trend, events, etc. **7** a sudden shock or fright **8** an action or deed */*a good *turn/* **9** the right, duty, or chance to do something in regular order */*my *turn* to go*/* **10** a distinctive form, detail, etc. */*an odd *turn* of speech*/* **11** natural inclination */*a curious *turn* of mind*/* —**in** (or **out of**) **turn** (not) in proper sequence —**turn down** to reject (a request, etc.) —**turn in 1** to deliver; hand in **2** [Inf.] to go to bed —**turn off 1** to stop the flow of (water, gas, etc.) **2** to make (an electrical device) stop functioning **3** [Slang] to cause to be bored, depressed, etc. —**turn on 1** to start the flow of **2** to make (an electrical device) start functioning **3** [Slang] to make or become elated, enthusiastic, etc. —**turn out 1** to put out (a light, etc.) **2** to dismiss **3** to come out or assemble **4** to produce **5** to result **6** to prove to be **7** [Inf.] to get out of bed —**turn over 1** to ponder **2** to hand over; transfer —**turn up** to happen, appear, arrive, etc. —**turn′er *n.***

turn′a·bout′ ***n.*** a shift or reversal of position, allegiance, opinion, etc.

turn′a·round′ ***n.*** **1** TURNABOUT **2** a wide area, as in a driveway, for turning a vehicle around

turn′buck′le (-buk′əl) ***n.*** an adjustable coupling for two

THESAURUS

tumultuous, excited, passionate, uncontrolled, vehement, roaring, tempestuous, rampant, rowdy, lawless, disorderly, untamed, disordered, chaotic, agitated, fierce, wild, rude, rough, blustering, angry, storming, uproarious, clamorous, mutinous, rebellious, destructive, hard, stern, intense, bitter, fiery, boisterous, perturbed, foaming, shaking, vociferous, demonstrative.—*Ant.* PEACEFUL, tranquil, at ease.

turf *n.* earth, peat, lawn; see GRASS 1.

turkey *n.* turkey cock, turkey hen, tom, tom turkey, bird, fowl, Thanksgiving bird, Christmas bird, gobbler, turkey gobbler, wild turkey, domestic turkey.

turmoil *n.* agitation, turbulence, riot; see CONFUSION, DISTURBANCE 2.

turn *n.* **1** [A revolution] rotation, cycle, circle, round, circulation, pirouette, barrel roll, gyre, gyration, spin, about-face, roll, forward roll, backward roll, somersault, flip, back flip, cartwheel, aerial, turning, circumrotation, spiral; see also REVOLUTION 1. **2** [A bend] curve, winding, twist, wind, hook, shift, angle, corner, fork, branch. **3** [A turning point] climax, crisis, juncture, emergency, critical period, crossing, change, new development, shift, twist. **4** [A shock] fright, jolt, blow; see SURPRISE 2. **5** [An action] deed, accomplishment, service; see HELP 1. **6** [A change in course] curve, detour, deviation, correction, course correction, corner, loop, stem turn, jump turn, telemark, kick turn, spiral, dodge, cut back, zigzag. **—at every turn** in every instance, constantly, consistently; see REGULARLY. **—by turns** taking turns, in succession, alternately; see CONSECUTIVE. **—call the turn** anticipate, predict, foretell; see EXPECT 1. **—take turns** do by turns, do in succession, share; see ALTERNATE 1. **—to a turn** correctly, properly, to the right degree; see PERFECTLY.

turn *v.* **1** [To pivot] revolve, rotate, roll, spin, wheel, whirl, circulate, go around, swivel, round, twist, twirl, gyrate, loop; see also SWING. **2** [To reverse] go back, recoil, change, upset, retrace, face about, turn around, flip, capsize, shift, alter, vary, convert, transform, invert, subvert, return, alternate. **3** [To divert] deflect, veer, turn aside, turn away, sidetrack, swerve, put off, call off, turn off, deviate, dodge, twist, avoid, shift, switch, avert, shy away, redirect, draw aside. **4** [To become] grow into, change into, pass into; see BECOME. **5** [To sour] curdle, acidify, become rancid; see SOUR. **6** [To change direction] swerve, swing, bend, veer, tack, round to, incline, deviate, detour, loop, curve, dodge, cut back, zigzag. **7** [To incline] prefer, be predisposed to, favor; see LEAN 1, TEND 2. **8** [To sprain] strain, bruise, dislocate; see HURT 1. **9** [To nauseate] sicken, make one sick, revolt; see DISGUST. **10** [To bend] curve, twist, fold; see BEND. **11** [To transform] transmute, remake, transpose; see ALTER 1. **12** [To make use of] apply, adapt, utilize; see USE 1. **13** [To point] direct, set, train; see AIM. **14** [To repel] repulse, push back, throw back; see REPEL 1. **—turn about** turn around, pivot, reverse; see TURN 1. **—turn against** revolt, disobey, defy; see OPPOSE 1, 2, REBEL. **—turn aside** avert, deflect, divert; see TURN 3. **—turn back** retrogress, retrograde, revert; see RETURN 1, 2. **—turn down 1** [To decrease in volume, etc.] hush, lower, curb; see DECREASE 2. **2** [To refuse] reject, decline, rebuff; see REFUSE. **—turn in 1** [To deliver] hand over, transfer, give up; see GIVE 1. **2** [*To go to bed] lie down, retire, hit the hay*; see REST 1. **—turn into 1** [To change] transform, alter, transmute; see ALTER 1. **2** [To become changed] be converted, transform, modify; see CHANGE 2. **—turn off** stop, shut off, douse, turn out, log off, halt, close, shut, extinguish, shut down, kill the light*, turn off the juice*, cut the motor*, hit the switch*. **—turn on 1** [To start the operation of] set going, switch on, set in motion, log on, put in gear; see also BEGIN 1. **2** [To attack] strike, assail, assault; see ATTACK. **3** [*To take drugs] smoke marijuana, get high*, take a trip*, smoke pot*, get stoned*, freak out*, blow pot*, trip out*, get wasted*. **4** [*To arouse] titillate, stimulate, stir up; see EXCITE. **5** [To depend on or upon] hinge on, be dependent on, be based on; see DEPEND ON 2. **—turn out 1** [To stop the operation of] extinguish, shut off, stop; see TURN OFF. **2** [To dismiss] discharge, evict, send away; see DISMISS, OUST. **3** [To produce] make, put out, build; see MANUFACTURE, PRODUCE 2. **4** [To finish] end, complete, perfect; see ACHIEVE. **—turn over 1** [To invert] overturn, reverse, subvert; see UPSET 1. **2** [To transfer] hand over, give over, deliver; see ASSIGN, GIVE 1. **—turn to 1** [To rely upon] confide, appeal to, depend upon; see TRUST 1. **2** [To start] start to work, become interested in, take up; see BEGIN 1. **—turn up 1** [To find] bring to light, detect, come across; see DISCOVER, FIND. **2** [To arrive] enter, come, roll in; see ARRIVE. **3** [To increase the volume, etc.] amplify, augment, boost; see INCREASE, STRENGTHEN.

rods, etc., consisting of a metal sleeve with opposite internal threads at each end
turn′coat′ *n.* a renegade; traitor
turn′ing *n.* **1** the action of one that turns **2** a place where a road, etc. turns
turning point a point in time when a decisive change occurs
tur·nip (tur′nip) *n.* ⟦prob. < Fr *tour*, round + ME *nepe*, turnip⟧ **1** a plant related to cabbage and broccoli, with a light-colored, roundish, edible root **2** the root
turn′key′ *n., pl.* **-keys′** a jailer
turn′off′ *n.* **1** a turning off **2** a place to turn off, as a road ramp **3** [Slang] someone or something regarded as being boring, distasteful, etc.
turn′-on′ *n.* [Slang] someone or something regarded as being interesting, exciting, etc.
turn′out′ *n.* **1** a gathering of people, as for a meeting **2** a wider part of a narrow road, enabling vehicles to pass each other
turn′o′ver *n.* **1** a small pie with half the crust folded back over the other half **2** *a)* the number of times a stock of goods is sold and replaced in a given period *b)* the amount of business done during a given period **3** the rate of replacement of workers
turn′pike′ (-pīk′) *n.* ⟦ME *turnpyke*, a spiked road barrier⟧ a toll road, esp. one that is an expressway
turn′stile′ (-stīl′) *n.* a device, as a post with revolving horizontal bars, placed in an entrance to allow the passage of persons one at a time
turn′ta′ble *n.* a circular rotating platform, as for supporting a phonograph record being played
tur·pen·tine (tur′pən tīn′) *n.* ⟦< Gr *terebinthos*, tree yielding this substance⟧ a colorless, volatile oil distilled from a substance extracted from various coniferous trees: used in paints, etc.
tur·pi·tude (tur′pi to͞od′) *n.* ⟦< L *turpis*, vile⟧ baseness; vileness
tur·quoise (tur′koiz′, -kwoiz′) *n.* ⟦< OFr *turqueis*, Turkish⟧ **1** a greenish-blue semiprecious stone **2** its color
tur·ret (tur′it) *n.* ⟦see TOWER⟧ **1** a small tower projecting from a building, usually at a corner **2** a dome or revolving structure for guns, as on a warship, tank, or airplane **3** a rotating attachment for a lathe, etc. holding cutting tools
tur·tle (turt′'l) *n.* ⟦< Fr *tortue*, tortoise⟧ any of various land or water reptiles having a soft body encased in a tough shell —**turn turtle** to turn upside down
tur′tle·dove′ *n.* ⟦< L echoic *turtur*⟧ a wild dove with a plaintive call
tur′tle·neck′ *n.* **1** a high, snug, turned-down collar, as on a pullover sweater **2** a sweater, etc. with such a collar
tusk (tusk) *n.* ⟦OE *tucs*⟧ a very long, large, pointed tooth projecting outside the mouth
tus·sle (tus′əl) *vi.* **-sled, -sling,** *n.* ⟦< ME *tusen*, to pull⟧ struggle; scuffle
tus·sock (tus′ək) *n.* ⟦< ?⟧ a thick tuft or clump of grass, sedge, etc.
tu·te·lage (to͞ot′'l ij) *n.* ⟦< L *tutela*, protection⟧ **1** guardianship; care, protection, etc. **2** instruction —**tu′te·lar′y** (-er′ē) *adj.*
tu·tor (to͞ot′ər) *n.* ⟦< L *tueri*, to guard⟧ a private teacher —*vt., vi.* to act as a tutor (to); teach —**tu·to·ri·al** (to͞o tôr′ē əl, tyo͞o-) *adj., n.*
tut·ti-frut·ti (to͞ot′ē fro͞ot′ē) *n.* ⟦It, all fruits⟧ ice cream, etc. made with mixed fruits
tu·tu (to͞o′to͞o′) *n.* ⟦Fr⟧ a very short, full, projecting skirt worn by ballerinas
Tu·va·lu (to͞o′və lo͞o′) country on a group of islands in the WC Pacific, north of Fiji: 10 sq. mi.; pop. 10,000
tux (tuks) *n., pl.* **tux′es** *short for* TUXEDO
tux·e·do (tuk sē′dō) *n., pl.* **-dos** ⟦after a country club near *Tuxedo* Lake, NY⟧ a man's semiformal suit with a tailless jacket
TV *n.* **1** television **2** *pl.* **TVs** or **TV's** a television receiving set
TVA *abbrev.* Tennessee Valley Authority
TV dinner a frozen, precooked dinner packaged in a divided tray for heating and serving
twad·dle (twäd′'l) *n.* ⟦prob. var. of TATTLE⟧ foolish, empty talk or writing; nonsense
twain (twān) *adj., n.* ⟦OE *twegen*, two⟧ *archaic var. of* TWO
Twain (twān), **Mark** *pseud. for* Samuel Langhorne CLEMENS
twang (twaŋ) *n.* ⟦echoic⟧ **1** a sharp, vibrating sound, as of a plucked string **2** a sharply nasal way of speaking —*vi., vt.* to make or cause to make a twang —**twang′y, -i·er, -i·est,** *adj.*
'twas (twuz, twäz) *contr.* [Old Poet.] it was
tweak (twēk) *vt.* ⟦OE *twiccan*, to twitch⟧ **1** to give a twisting pinch to (someone's nose, ear, etc.) **2** to adjust slightly —*n.* such a pinch
tweed (twēd) *n.* ⟦< misreading of *tweel*, Scot form of TWILL⟧ **1** a rough wool fabric in a weave of two or more colors **2** [*pl.*] clothes of tweed
tweed′y *adj.* **-i·er, -i·est** **1** of, like, or wearing tweeds **2** having an informal style, a fondness for the outdoors, etc.
'tween (twēn) *contr. prep.* ⟦ME *twene*⟧ [Old Poet.] between
tweet (twēt) *interj., n.* ⟦echoic⟧ (used to signify or imitate) the thin, chirping sound of a small bird —*vi.* to make this sound
tweet′er *n.* a small, high-fidelity speaker for reproducing high-frequency sounds
tweez·ers (twē′zərz) *pl.n.* ⟦< obs. *tweeze*, surgical set⟧ [*also with sing. v.*] a small tool having two arms joined at one end, for plucking out hairs, etc.
twelfth (twelfth) *adj.* ⟦OE *twelfta*⟧ preceded by eleven others; 12th —*n.* **1** the one following the eleventh **2** any of the twelve equal parts of something; 1/12
Twelfth Day Epiphany, the twelfth day after Christmas: **Twelfth Night** is the evening before, or of, Epiphany
twelve (twelv) *adj., n.* ⟦OE *twelf*⟧ two more than ten; 12; XII
12-step or **twelve-step** (twelv′step′) *adj.* designating or of any rehabilitation program modeled on that of AA
twelve′-tone′ *adj. Music* of composition in which the twelve tones of the chromatic scale are fixed in some arbitrary succession (*tone row*)
twen·ty (twent′ē) *adj., n., pl.* **-ties** ⟦OE *twegentig*⟧ two times ten; 20; XX —**the twenties** the numbers or years, as of a century, from 20 through 29 —**twen′ti·eth** (-ith) *adj., n.*
twen′ty-one′ *n.* BLACKJACK (*n.* 2)
twen′ty-twen′ty (or **20/20**) **vision** normal visual ability, i.e., seeing clearly at 20 feet what the normal eye sees at 20 feet
twerp (twurp) *n.* ⟦ult. < ? Dan *tver*, perverse⟧ [Slang] a person regarded as insignificant, contemptible, etc.
twice (twīs) *adv.* ⟦OE *twiga*⟧ **1** two times **2** two times as much or as many
twid·dle (twid′'l) *vt., vi.* **-dled, -dling** ⟦prob. < TW(IST) + (*d*)*iddle*, move back and forth rapidly⟧ to twirl or play with (something) lightly or idly —**twiddle one's thumbs** to be idle
twig (twig) *n.* ⟦OE *twigge*⟧ a small branch of a tree or shrub

THESAURUS

turncoat *n.* traitor, renegade, betrayer, defector; see also DESERTER, TRAITOR.
turned *a.* **1** [Revolved] rotated, rounded, circled, circulated, spun, rolled, whirled, gyrated, set going. **2** [Deflected] switched, twisted, dodged, avoided, shied away from, shifted, shunted, changed.
turning *a.* spinning, twisting, shifting, whirling, rotating, revolving, bending, curving, shunting; see also GROWING, CHANGING.—*Ant.* PERMANENT, static, fixed.
turning *n.* whirling, revolving, rotating; see REVOLUTION 1.
turning point *n.* peak, juncture, culmination; see CLIMAX, CRISIS.
turnout *n.* **1** [Production] output, result, volume; see PRODUCTION 1. **2** [A gathering] assembly, attendance, group; see GATHERING.
tusk *n.* canine tooth, fang, incisor; see TOOTH 1.
tussle *n.* scuffle, struggle, scrap; see FIGHT 1.
tutelage *n.* **1** [Instruction] teaching, tutoring, tutorship, schooling; see also EDUCATION 1. **2** [Care] guardianship, charge, protection; see CUSTODY.
tutor *n.* instructor, tutorial assistant, private tutor; see TEACHER.
tutoring *n.* coaching, training, instruction; see EDUCATION 1.
TV *n.* video, cable, idiot box*; see TELEVISION.
tweak *v.* twitch, squeeze, jerk; see PINCH.
tweezers *n.* forceps, nippers, tongs; see TOOL 1.
twelve *a.* dozen, twelvefold, twelfth; see NUMBER.
twenty *a.* twentieth, vicenary, twentyfold, vicennial.
twice *a.* double, doubly, once and again, over again, once over.
twig *n.* offshoot, limb, sprig; see BRANCH 2.

twi·light (twī′līt′) ***n.*** ⟦ME⟧ **1** the subdued light just after sunset **2** the period from sunset to dark **3** a gradual decline —***adj.*** of twilight

twill (twil) ***n.*** ⟦OE *twilic*, woven of double thread⟧ a kind of cloth woven in parallel diagonal lines —**twilled** ***adj.***

twin (twin) ***adj.*** ⟦OE *twinn*, double⟧ **1** consisting of, or being one of a pair of, two similar things **2** being a twin or twins —***n.*** **1** either of two offspring from the same pregnancy **2** either of two persons or things that are very much alike

twin bed either of a pair of single beds

twine (twīn) ***n.*** ⟦OE *twin*⟧ strong thread, string, etc. of strands twisted together —***vt.***, ***vi.*** **twined, twin′ing** **1** to twist together **2** to wind (around)

twinge (twinj) ***vt.***, ***vi.*** **twinged, twing′ing** ⟦OE *twengan*, to squeeze⟧ to (cause to) have a sudden, sharp pain, qualm, etc. —***n.*** such a pain, etc.

twi-night or **twi·night** (twī′nīt′) ***adj.*** ⟦TWI(LIGHT) + NIGHT⟧ *Baseball* designating a double-header starting in late afternoon and going into evening

twin·kle (twiŋ′kəl) ***vi.*** **-kled, -kling** ⟦OE *twinclian*⟧ **1** to shine with quick, intermittent gleams **2** to light up, as with amusement: said of the eyes **3** to move to and fro quickly: said as of a dancer's feet —***n.*** **1** a glint in the eye **2** a gleam; sparkle

twin′kling ***n.*** an instant

twin′-size′ ***adj.*** of or being the standard size of a twin bed: also **twin′-sized′**

twirl (twurl) ***vt.***, ***vi.*** ⟦prob. < Scand⟧ **1** to rotate rapidly; spin **2** to whirl in a circle —***n.*** **1** a twirling **2** a twist, coil, etc. —**twirl′er** ***n.***

twist (twist) ***vt.*** ⟦< OE *-twist*, a rope⟧ **1** to wind (strands, etc.) around one another **2** to wind (rope, etc.) around something **3** to give spiral shape to **4** *a*) to subject to torsion *b*) to wrench; sprain **5** to contort or distort **6** to confuse **7** to pervert the meaning of **8** to cause to rotate **9** to break (*off*) by turning the end —***vi.*** **1** to undergo twisting **2** to spiral, twine, etc. (*around* or *about*) **3** to revolve or rotate **4** to wind, as a path does **5** to squirm; writhe —***n.*** **1** something twisted **2** a twisting or being twisted **3** stress produced by twisting **4** a contortion **5** a wrench or sprain **6** a turn; bend **7** distortion, as of meaning **8** an unexpected or different direction, method, slant, etc.

twist′er ***n.*** **1** a person or thing that twists **2** [Inf.] a tornado or cyclone

twist′-tie′ ***n.*** a short wire covered with paper or plastic, twisted to tie closed a plastic bag, etc.

twit[1] (twit) ***vt.*** **twit′ted, twit′ting** ⟦< OE *æt*, at + *witan*, accuse⟧ to reproach, taunt, etc.

twit[2] (twit) ***n.*** ⟦< ?⟧ [Inf.] a foolish, contemptible person

twitch (twich) ***vt.***, ***vi.*** ⟦< OE *twiccian*, to pluck⟧ to pull (at) or move with a quick, slight jerk —***n.*** **1** a twitching **2** a sudden, quick motion, esp. a spasmodic one

twitch′y ***adj.*** **-i·er, -i·est** [Inf.] nervous; jittery

twit·ter (twit′ər) ***vi.*** ⟦ME *twiteren*⟧ **1** to chirp rapidly **2** *a*) to chatter *b*) to giggle **3** to tremble with excitement —***n.*** **1** a twittering **2** a condition of trembling excitement

′twixt (twikst) ***prep.*** [Old Poet.] betwixt; between

two (to͞o) ***adj.***, ***n.*** ⟦OE *twa*⟧ one more than one; 2; II —**in two** in two parts

two′-bit′ ***adj.*** [Slang] cheap, inferior, etc.

two bits [Inf.] twenty-five cents

two′-by-four′ ***n.*** a piece of lumber two inches thick and four inches wide when untrimmed ($1\frac{1}{2}$ by $3\frac{1}{2}$ inches trimmed)

two′-edged′ ***adj.*** **1** having two cutting edges **2** that can be taken two ways *[a two-edged remark]*

two′-faced′ ***adj.*** **1** having two faces, surfaces, etc. **2** deceitful; hypocritical

two·fer (to͞o′fər) ***n.*** ⟦altered < *two for*⟧ [Inf.] a pair, as of theater tickets, sold for the price of one

two′-fist′ed ***adj.*** [Inf.] **1** able to use both fists **2** vigorous; virile

two′fold′ ***adj.*** **1** having two parts **2** having twice as much or as many —***adv.*** twice as much or as many

two′-hand′ed ***adj.*** **1** requiring the use of both hands **2** operated, played, etc. by two persons

two·pence (tup′əns) ***n.*** two pence

two′-ply′ ***adj.*** having two layers, strands, etc.

two′some (-səm) ***n.*** two people; a couple

two′-time′ ***vt.*** **-timed′, -tim′ing** [Slang] to be unfaithful to —**two′-tim′er** ***n.***

two′-way′ ***adj.*** **1** allowing passage in either direction **2** involving two or used in two ways

Twp *abbrev.* township

TX Texas

-ty (tē, ti) ⟦< L *-tas*⟧ *suffix* quality of, condition of

ty·coon (tī ko͞on′) ***n.*** ⟦< Jpn < Chin *tai*, great + *kuan*, official⟧ a wealthy, powerful industrialist, financier, etc.

ty·ing (tī′iŋ) ***vt.***, ***vi.*** *prp. of* TIE

tyke (tīk) ***n.*** ⟦< ON *tik*, a bitch⟧ [Inf.] a small child

Ty·ler (tī′lər), **John** 1790-1862; 10th president of the U.S. (1841-45)

tym·pa·ni (tim′pə nē) ***pl.n.***, *sing.* **-no′** (-nō′) *alt. sp. of* TIMPANI —**tym′pa·nist** ***n.***

tym·pan·ic membrane (tim pan′ik) a thin membrane inside the ear that vibrates when struck by sound waves

tym·pa·num (tim′pə nəm) ***n.***, *pl.* **-nums** or **-na** (-nə) ⟦L, a drum⟧ **1** MIDDLE EAR **2** TYMPANIC MEMBRANE

type (tīp) ***n.*** ⟦< Gr *typos*, a mark⟧ **1** the characteristic form, plan, style, etc. of a class or group **2** a class, group, etc. with characteristics in common **3** a person, animal, or thing representative of a class **4** a perfect example; model **5** *a*) a piece of metal or wood with a raised letter, etc. in reverse on its top, used in printing *b*) such pieces collectively *c*) a printed or photographically reproduced character or characters —***vt.*** **typed, typ′ing** **1** to classify **2** to write using the keyboard of a typewriter or computer —***vi.*** to use the keyboard of a typewriter or computer

THESAURUS

twilight ***n.*** dusk, nightfall, gloaming, late afternoon, early evening, sunset, dawn, break of day; see also NIGHT 1.

twin ***a.*** identical, fellow, twofold, second, accompanying, joint, coupled, matched, copied, duplicating; see also SECOND, TWO.—*Ant.* SINGLE, lone, solitary.

twin ***n.*** identical twin, fraternal twin, look-alike, double, counterpart, duplicate, copy, doppelgänger.

twine ***n.*** braid, cord, string; see ROPE.

twinge ***v.*** twitch, shiver, smart; see TINGLE.

twinkle ***v.*** shimmer, flicker, sparkle; see SHINE 1.

twinkling ***a.*** sparkling, glimmering, flashing; see BRIGHT 1.

twirl ***v.*** spin, rotate, twist; see TURN 1.

twist ***v.*** wring, wrap, twine, twirl, spin, turn around, wrap around; see also TURN 1.

twisted ***a.*** **1** [Crooked] contorted, wrenched, bent, knotted, braided, twined, wound, wreathed, writhing, convolute, twisting.—*Ant.* STRAIGHT, even, regular. **2** [Confused] erroneous, perplexing, wrongheaded, awry, puzzling, unintelligible, disorganized, tangled, perverted; see also WRONG 2.—*Ant.* CLEAR, simple, logical.

twitch ***v.*** **1** [To pluck] pull, tug, snatch; see PULL 2. **2** [To jerk] shiver, shudder, have a fit, kick, work, palpitate, beat, twinge, pain.

twitter ***n.*** sing, chirp, whistle, peep, cheep, coo.

two ***a.*** twin, dual, binary, both, double, forked, bifid.

two ***n.*** two of a kind, twins, couple; see PAIR. **—in two** halved, divided, split; see SEPARATED. **—put two and two together*** reason, figure out, see the light; see DECIDE.

two-faced ***a.*** deceitful, hypocritical, Janus-faced; see FALSE 1.

tycoon ***n.*** magnate, mogul, director; see BUSINESSMAN, EXECUTIVE.

type ***n.*** **1** [Kind] sort, nature, character; see KIND 2, VARIETY 2. **2** [Representive] representation, sample, example; see MODEL 1, 2. **3** [Letter] symbol, emblem, figure, character, sign; see also LETTER 1. *Styles of types include the following:* Times Roman, Courier, Gothic, Helvetica, Caslon, Goudy, Bembo, Bodoni, Old Style, Century Gothic, Granjon, Garamond, Plantin, Optima, Futura, Perpetua, Frutiger, Gill Sans, Century Schoolbook, Baskerville. *Font types include the following:* standard, lightface, boldface, extrabold, serif, sans serif, roman, italic, oblique, upright, small caps, black letter, monospace, slab serif, cursive, open, extended, condensed, shaded, wide, expanded.

type ***v.*** **1** [To write using a keyboard] typewrite, copy, transcribe, teletype, input, touchtype, keyboard, input, hunt and peck*. **2** [To classify] categorize, normalize, standardize; see CLASSIFY.

typed ***a.*** **1** [In typewritten format] typewritten, copied, typed-up, keyboarded, formatted, transcribed; see also PRINTED. **2** [Classified] labeled, characterized, analyzed, symbolized, classed, prefigured, sampled, marked, regulated, exemplified, made out to be, patterned, standardized, stylized, cast, formalized.

-type (tīp) *combining form* **1** type, representative form, example *[stereotype]* **2** print, printing type
type′cast′ *vt.* **-cast′**, **-cast′ing** to cast (an actor) repeatedly in the same type of part
type′script′ *n.* typewritten matter
type′set′ *vt.* **-set′**, **-set′ting** to set in type; compose
type′set′ter *n.* **1** a person who sets type **2** a machine for setting type
type′write′ *vt.*, *vi.* **-wrote′**, **-writ′ten**, **-writ′ing** to write with a typewriter: now usually *type*
type′writ′er *n.* a writing machine with a keyboard, for reproducing letters resembling printed ones
ty·phoid (tī′foid′) *n.* ⟦TYPH(US) + -OID⟧ an acute infectious disease caused by a bacillus and acquired by ingesting contaminated food or water: characterized by fever, intestinal disorders, etc.: in full **typhoid fever**
ty·phoon (tī fo͞on′) *n.* ⟦< Chin *tai-fung*, great wind⟧ a violent tropical cyclone originating in the W Pacific
ty·phus (tī′fəs) *n.* ⟦< Gr *typhos*, fever⟧ an acute infectious disease caused by certain bacteria, transmitted by fleas, lice, etc., and characterized by fever, skin rash, etc.: in full **typhus fever**
typ·i·cal (tip′i kəl) *adj.* **1** serving as a type **2** having the distinguishing characteristics of a class, group, etc.; representative **3** belonging to a type; characteristic —**typ′i·cal·ly** *adv.*
typ·i·fy (tip′i fī′) *vt.* **-fied′**, **-fy′ing** to have the characteristics of; be typical of; exemplify —**typ′i·fi·ca′tion** *n.*
typ·ist (tīp′ist) *n.* a person who operates a typewriter
ty·po (tī′pō) *n.*, *pl.* **-pos** [Inf.] an error made in setting type or in typing
ty·pog·ra·phy (tī päg′rə fē) *n.* ⟦see TYPE & -GRAPHY⟧ **1** setting, and printing with, type **2** the arrangement, style, etc. of matter printed from type —**ty·pog′ra·pher** *n.* —**ty′po·graph′i·cal** (-pə graf′i kəl) *adj.*
ty·ran·ni·cal (tə ran′i kəl, tī-) *adj.* **1** of or suited to a tyrant **2** harsh, cruel, unjust, etc. Also **ty·ran′nic** —**ty·ran′ni·cal·ly** *adv.*
tyr·an·nize (tir′ə nīz′) *vi.* **-nized′**, **-niz′ing** **1** to govern as a tyrant **2** to govern or use authority harshly or cruelly —*vt.* to treat tyrannically; oppress
ty·ran·no·saur (tə ran′ə sôr′) *n.* ⟦< Gr *tyrannos*, tyrant + *sauros*, lizard⟧ a huge, two-footed, flesh-eating dinosaur: also **ty·ran′no·saur′us** (-əs)
tyr·an·ny (tir′ə nē) *n.*, *pl.* **-nies** **1** the authority, government, etc. of a tyrant **2** cruel and unjust use of power **3** a tyrannical act —**tyr′an·nous** *adj.*
ty·rant (tī′rənt) *n.* ⟦< Gr *tyrannos*⟧ **1** an absolute ruler **2** a cruel, oppressive ruler, master, etc.
ty·ro (tī′rō) *n.*, *pl.* **-ros** ⟦< L *tiro*, young soldier⟧ a beginner in learning something; novice
Ty·rol (ti rōl′, -räl′) *alt. sp. of* TIROL
tzar (tsär, zär) *n.* *var. of* CZAR —**tza·ri·na** (tsä rē′nə, zä-) *fem.n.*

THESAURUS

typewritten *a.* written on a typewriter, transcribed, copied; see PRINTED.
typical *a.* characteristic, habitual, usual, representative, symbolic, normal, illustrative, conventional, archetypical, prototypical, stereotypical, ideal, expected, suggestive, standardized, standard, patterned, common, ordinary, average, everyday, regular.—*Ant.* SUPERIOR, exceptional, extraordinary.
typify *v.* exemplify, symbolize, embody; see MEAN 1.
typist *n.* secretary, typewriter operator, office girl, inputter, clerk, clerical worker.
tyrannical *a.* dictatorial, domineering, totalitarian; see ABSOLUTE 2.
tyranny *n.* oppression, cruelty, severity, reign of terror, despotism, absolutism.
tyrant *n.* despot, absolute ruler, dictator; see DICTATOR.

U

u[1] or **U** (yo͞o) ***n.**, pl.* **u's, U's** the 21st letter of the English alphabet
u[2] *abbrev.* unit(s)
U[1] *abbrev.* **1** Union **2** United **3** University
U[2] *Chem. symbol for* uranium
UAW *abbrev.* United Automobile Workers (of America)
u·biq·ui·tous (yo͞o bik′wə təs) ***adj.*** ⟦< L *ubique,* everywhere⟧ (seemingly) present everywhere at the same time —**u·biq′ui·ty *n.***
U′-boat′ *n.* ⟦< Ger *Unterseeboot,* undersea boat⟧ a German submarine
U bolt a U-shaped bolt with threads and a nut at each end
ud·der (ud′ər) ***n.*** ⟦OE *udr*⟧ a baglike, milk-secreting organ with two or more teats, as in cows
UFO *n., pl.* **UFOs** or **UFO's** an unidentified flying object
u·fol·o·gy (yo͞o fäl′ə jē) ***n.*** the study of UFOs, esp. when regarded as spacecraft from another planet —**u·fol′o·gist *n.***
U·gan·da (yo͞o gan′də, -gän′-) country in EC Africa: 93,065 sq. mi.; pop. 16,583,000 —**U·gan′dan *adj., n.***
ugh (ookh, oo, ug, *etc.*) ***interj.*** used to express disgust, horror, etc.
ug·ly (ug′lē) ***adj.* -li·er, -li·est** ⟦< ON *uggr,* fear⟧ **1** unpleasing to look at **2** bad, disgusting, etc. *[an ugly lie]* **3** ominous *[ugly storm clouds]* **4** [Inf.] cross; quarrelsome *[an ugly mood]* —**ug′li·ness *n.***
uh (u, un) ***interj.*** **1** HUH **2** used when hesitating in speaking
UHF or **uhf** *abbrev.* ultrahigh frequency
UK United Kingdom
u·kase (yo͞o′kās′, -kāz′) ***n.*** ⟦Russ *ukaz,* edict⟧ an official decree
U·kraine (yo͞o krān′) country in SE Europe: formerly a republic of the U.S.S.R.: 231,990 sq. mi.; pop. 51,452,000 —**U·krain′i·an *n., adj.***
u·ku·le·le (yo͞o′kə lā′lē) ***n.*** ⟦Haw, leaping flea⟧ a small, four-stringed, guitarlike musical instrument
UL *trademark for* Underwriters Laboratories
ul·cer (ul′sər) ***n.*** ⟦L *ulcus*⟧ **1** an open sore, often one discharging pus, on the skin or some mucous membrane **2** any corrupt condition —**ul′cer·ous *adj.***
ul′cer·ate′ (-āt′) ***vt., vi.* -at′ed, -at′ing** to make or become ulcerous —**ul′cer·a′tion *n.***
ul·na (ul′nə) ***n.**, pl.* **-nae** (-nē) or **-nas** ⟦L, the elbow⟧ the larger of the two bones of the forearm —**ul′nar *adj.***
ul·ster (ul′stər) ***n.*** ⟦after *Ulster,* in N Ireland⟧ a long, loose, heavy overcoat
ult *abbrev.* ultimate(ly)
ul·te·ri·or (ul tir′ē ər) ***adj.*** ⟦L: see ULTRA-⟧ **1** lying beyond or on the farther side **2** beyond what is expressed or implied; undisclosed
ul·ti·mate (ul′tə mit) ***adj.*** ⟦< L *ultimus,* last⟧ **1** beyond which it is impossible to go **2** final; conclusive **3** basic **4** greatest possible —***n.*** a final point or result —**ul′ti·mate·ly *adv.***
ul·ti·ma·tum (ul′tə māt′əm) ***n.**, pl.* **-tums** or **-ta** (-ə) ⟦see prec.⟧ a final offer or demand, as in negotiations
ul·tra (ul′trə) ***adj.*** ⟦< fol.⟧ going beyond the usual limit; extreme
ultra- ⟦L < *ultra,* beyond⟧ *prefix* **1** beyond *[ultrasonic]* **2** extremely *[ultraconservative]*
ul·tra·con·serv·a·tive (ul′trə kən sur′və tiv) ***adj.*** extremely conservative
ul·tra·high frequency (ul′trə hī′) any radio frequency between 300 and 3,000 megahertz
ul′tra·ma·rine′ (-mə rēn′) ***adj.*** deep-blue —***n.*** deep blue
ul′tra·son′ic (-sän′ik) ***adj.*** above the range of sound audible to the human ear —**ul′tra·son′i·cal·ly *adv.***
ul′tra·sound′ (-sound′) ***n.*** ultrasonic waves, used in medical diagnosis and therapy, etc.
ul′tra·vi′o·let (-vī′ə lit) ***adj.*** of or designating those rays that are just beyond the violet end of the visible spectrum
ul·u·late (yo͞ol′yoo lāt′, ul′-) ***vi.* -lat′ed, -lat′ing** ⟦< L *ululare,* to howl⟧ to howl, hoot, or wail loudly —**ul′u·la′tion *n.***
U·lys·ses (yoo lis′ēz′) ***n.*** ⟦ML⟧ ODYSSEUS
um·bel (um′bəl) ***n.*** ⟦L *umbella,* parasol: see UMBRELLA⟧ a cluster of flowers with stalks of similar length springing from the same point
um·ber (um′bər) ***n.*** ⟦< It *(terra d')ombra,* (earth of) shade⟧ **1** a kind of earth used as a yellowish-brown or reddish-brown pigment **2** a yellowish-brown or reddish-brown color
um·bil·i·cal (um bil′i kəl) ***adj.*** ⟦< L *umbilicus,* navel⟧ of a cordlike structure (**umbilical cord**) connecting a fetus's navel to the placenta, for conveying nourishment to, and removing waste from, the fetus
um·bil·i·cus (um bil′i kəs) ***n.**, pl.* **-ci′** (-sī′) ⟦L⟧ NAVEL
um·bra (um′brə) ***n.**, pl.* **-brae** (-brē) or **-bras** ⟦L, a shade⟧ **1** shade or a shadow **2** the dark cone of shadow from a planet or satellite on the side opposite the sun
um·brage (um′brij) ***n.*** ⟦< L *umbra,* a shade⟧ **1** [Obs.] shade **2** offense or resentment
um·brel·la (um brel′ə) ***n.*** ⟦< L *umbra,* a shade⟧ **1** a screen, usually of cloth on a folding frame, carried for protection against rain or sun **2** any comprehensive, protective alliance, strategy, device, etc.
u·mi·ak (o͞o′mē ak′) ***n.*** ⟦Esk⟧ a large, open boat made of skins on a wooden frame, used by Eskimos
um·laut (oom′lout) ***n.*** ⟦Ger < *um,* about + *laut,* a sound⟧ *Linguistics* **1** a vowel changed in sound by its assimilation to another vowel **2** the mark (¨) placed over such a vowel
ump (ump) ***n., vt., vi.*** *short for* UMPIRE
um·pire (um′pīr′) ***n.*** ⟦< Fr *nomper,* uneven, hence a third person⟧ **1** a person chosen to judge a dispute **2** an official who administers the rules in certain sports —***vt., vi.* -pired′, -pir′ing** to act as umpire (in or of)
ump·teen (ump′tēn′) ***adj.*** [Slang] a great number of; very many —**ump′teenth′ *adj.***
UN *abbrev.* United Nations
un- *prefix* **1** ⟦OE⟧ not, lack of, the opposite of *[unconcern]* **2** ⟦OE *un-, on-*⟧ back: indicating a reversal of action *[unfold]* The following list includes some common compounds formed with *un-* (either sense) that do not have special meanings:

unabashed
unable
unabridged
unaccented
unacceptable
unaccompanied
unacquainted
unadorned
unadulterated
unafraid
unaided
unaltered
unambiguous
unannounced
unanswered
unashamed
unasked
unassailable
unassisted
unattainable
unattractive
unauthorized
unavailable
unavoidable
unbearable
unbeaten
unbiased
unbleached
unblemished
unbound

THESAURUS

ubiquitous *a.* omnipresent, universal, allover; see EVERYWHERE.
ugliness *n.* unsightliness, homeliness, hideousness, repulsiveness, loathsomeness, unseemliness, offensiveness, deformity, bad looks, ill looks, ill-favored countenance, plainness, disfigurement, grim aspect, foulness, horridness, monstrousness, inelegance, frightfulness, fearfulness.—*Ant.* BEAUTY, fairness, attractiveness.
ugly *a.* **1** [Ill-favored] unsightly, loathsome, hideous, homely, repulsive, unseemly, uncomely, deformed, bad-looking, plain, disfigured, monstrous, foul, horrid, frightful, revolting, repellent, unlovely, appalling, haggish, misshapen, misbegotten, grisly, looking a mess*, looking like the devil*, not fit to be seen*.—*Ant.* BEAUTIFUL, handsome, graceful. **2** [Dangerous] pugnacious, quarrelsome, bellicose, rough, cantankerous, violent, vicious, evil, sinister, treacherous, wicked, formidable.—*Ant.* REASONABLE, mild, complaisant.
ukase *n.* decree, proclamation, edict; see JUDGMENT.
ulcer *n.* boil, abscess, infection; see SORE.
ulterior *a.* unstated, undisclosed, not explicit, having a hidden agenda, implied, veiled.
ultimate *a.* final, terminal, latest; see LAST 1.
ultimately *a.* eventually, at last, in the end, sooner or later, as a conclusion, to cap the climax, sequentially, after all, at long last, climactically, at the close, in conclusion, conclusively, in due time, after a while, in after days, presently, by and by; see also FINALLY.—*Ant.* EARLY, in the beginning, at present.
ultimatum *n.* demands, requirements, deadline.
umbrella *n.* parasol, sunshade, beach umbrella; see HAT.
umpire *n.* referee, moderator, mediator; see JUDGE 1.

unbreakable
unbroken
unbuckle
unbutton
uncap
unceasing
uncensored
unchallenged
unchanged
unchanging
unchecked
uncivilized
unclassified
unclean
unclear
uncomplaining
uncompleted
uncomplimentary
unconcealed
unconfirmed
unconnected
uncontaminated
uncontrollable
uncontrolled
uncontroversial
unconventional
unconvinced
uncooked
uncooperative
uncoordinated
uncultivated
undamaged
undefeated
undemocratic
undependable
undeserved
undesirable
undeveloped
undifferentiated
undiminished
undisciplined
undiscovered
undiscriminating
undisguised
undisputed
undistinguished
undisturbed
undivided
uneducated
unemotional
unending
unenlightened
unenviable
unethical
uneventful
unexpired
unexplained
unexplored
unexpressed
unexpurgated
unfair
unfashionable
unfasten
unfavorable
unfit
unflattering
unfocused
unforeseen
unforgivable
unforgotten
unfulfilled
unfurnished
ungrammatical
ungrateful
unhampered
unhandy
unharmed
unhealthful
unheeded
unhesitating
unhitch
unhook
unhurried
unhurt
unidentified
unimaginable
unimaginative
unimpaired
unimportant
unimproved
unincorporated
uninformed
uninhabited
uninjured
uninspired
uninsured
unintelligent
unintelligible
unintentional
uninteresting
uninterrupted
uninvited
uninviting
unjustifiable
unjustified
unknowing
unlace
unlatch
unleavened
unlicensed
unlined
unlisted
unloved
unmanageable
unmannerly
unmarked
unmarried
unmatched
unmerited
unmoved
unnamed
unnoticed
unobserved
unobstructed
unobtainable
unobtrusive
unoccupied
unofficial
unopened
unopposed
unorthodox
unpaid
unpalatable
unpardonable
unpaved
unpin
unplanned
unpolished
unpolluted
unpredictable
unprejudiced
unpremeditated
unprepared
unpretentious
unprofitable
unpromising
unprotected
unproved
unproven
unprovoked
unpunished
unquenchable
unquestioned
unquestioning
unreadable
unrealistic
unrealized
unrecognizable
unrecognized
unrecorded
unrefined
unregulated
unrelated
unreliable
unrelieved
unrepentant
unresponsive
unrestricted
unsafe
unsanitary
unsatisfactory
unsatisfied
unsaturated
unscientific
unseasoned
unseeing
unseen
unsegmented
unselfish
unshackle
unshakable
unshaken
unshaven
unsociable
unsold
unsolicited
unsought
unspoiled
unspoken
unsportsmanlike
unsuccessful
unsuitable
unsullied
unsupervised
unsure
unsurpassed
unsuspecting
unsweetened
unsympathetic
untainted
untamed
untarnished
untasted
untenable
untiring
untouched
untrained
untried
untroubled
untrue
untrustworthy
unvarying
unverified
unwanted
unwarranted
unwavering
unwed
unworkable
unyielding
unzip

un·ac·count·a·ble (un'ə kount'ə bəl) ***adj.*** **1** that cannot be explained; strange **2** not responsible

un'ac·cus'tomed ***adj.*** **1** not accustomed (*to*) **2** not usual; strange

un'ad·vised' ***adj.*** **1** without counsel or advice **2** indiscreet; rash

un'af·fect'ed ***adj.*** **1** not affected or influenced **2** without affectation; simple; sincere

un'-A·mer'i·can ***adj.*** regarded as not properly American; esp., regarded as opposed to the U.S., its institutions, etc.

u·nan·i·mous (yo͞o nan'ə məs) ***adj.*** ⟦< L *unus*, one + *animus*, the mind⟧ agreeing completely; without dissent —**u·nan·im·i·ty** (yo͞o'nə nim'ə tē) ***n.*** —**u·nan'i·mous·ly** ***adv.***

un'ap·proach'a·ble ***adj.*** **1** not to be approached; inaccessible; aloof **2** having no equal; unmatched

un·armed' ***adj.*** having no weapons

un'as·sum'ing ***adj.*** not forward; modest

un'at·tached' ***adj.*** **1** not attached **2** not engaged or married

un'at·tend'ed ***adj.*** **1** not waited on **2** not accompanied (*by*) **3** neglected

un'a·vail'ing (-ə vāl'iŋ) ***adj.*** futile; useless

un'a·ware' ***adj.*** not aware or conscious —***adv.*** UNAWARES

un'a·wares' ***adv.*** **1** unintentionally **2** unexpectedly

un·backed' ***adj.*** not backed, supported, etc.

un·bal'anced ***adj.*** **1** not in balance **2** *a*) mentally deranged *b*) erratic or unstable

THESAURUS

unable ***a.*** incapable, powerless, weak, incompetent, unskilled, impotent, not able, inept, incapacitated, inefficacious, helpless, unfitted, inefficient, unqualified, inadequate, ineffectual, inoperative.—*Ant.* ABLE, capable, effective.

unaccompanied ***a.*** sole, solitary, deserted; see ALONE.

unaccustomed ***a.*** **1** [Unfamiliar] strange, unknown, unusual; see UNFAMILIAR 1. **2** [Unpracticed] incompetent, unskilled, untrained; see NAIVE.

unacquainted ***a.*** ignorant, out of touch, unknown; see UNFAMILIAR 1.

unadulterated ***a.*** uncorrupted, unalloyed, undiluted; see PURE 1.

unaffected ***a.*** **1** [Genuine] spontaneous, candid, simple; see NATURAL 3. **2** [Uninfluenced] steady, unmoved, unchanged; see CALM 1.

unanimous ***a.*** united, single, collective, combined, unified, concerted, harmonious, concordant, concurrent, public, popular, undivided, of one accord, agreed, common, communal, shared, universal, accepted, unquestioned, undisputed, uncontested, consonant, consistent, with one voice, homogeneous, accordant, assenting.—*Ant.* DIFFERENT, dissenting, irreconcilable.

unanimously ***a.*** with one voice, harmoniously, all together, by acclamation, universally, unitedly, singly, collectively, without a dissenting voice, by common consent, by vote, in unison, cooperatively, concurrently, popularly, commonly, undisputedly, consonantly, consistently, in agreement.

unanswered ***a.*** without reply, unrefuted, not responded to, unnoticed, unchallenged, unquestioned, demanding an answer, filed, ignored, unsettled, undecided, in doubt, disputed, moot, debatable, vexed, open, pending, under consideration, undetermined, tabled, up in the air.—*Ant.* DETERMINED, answered, responded to.

unapproachable ***a.*** withdrawn, hesitant, aloof; see DISTANT.

unarmed ***a.*** weaponless, defenseless, peaceable; see WEAK 5.

unasked ***a.*** uninvited, not asked, unwelcome; see UNPOPULAR.

unattached ***a.*** unbound, independent, ungoverned; see FREE 1, 2, 3.

unauthorized ***a.*** unofficial, unapproved, unlawful; see ILLEGAL.

unavoidable ***a.*** inescapable, impending, sure; see CERTAIN 2.

unaware ***a.*** uninformed, oblivious, ignorant, not cognizant, unmindful, unconscious, unknowing, heedless, negligent, careless, insensible, forgetful, unconcerned, blind, deaf, inattentive, without notice, deaf to, caught napping, in a daze, out of it*, not seeing the forest for the trees*.—*Ant.* CONSCIOUS, aware, cognizant.

unbalanced ***a.*** **1** [Deranged] crazy, unsound, psychotic; see INSANE,

un·bar′ *vt.* **-barred′**, **-bar′ring** to remove the bar or bars from; open

un′be·com′ing *adj.* not appropriate or suited to one's appearance, character, etc.; unattractive, indecorous, etc.

un·be·known (un′bē nōn′) *adj.* without one's knowledge; unknown: usually with *to*: also **un′be·knownst′** (-nōnst′)

un′be·lief′ *n.* lack of belief, esp. in religion

un′be·liev′a·ble *adj.* beyond belief; astounding; incredible

un′be·liev′er *n.* **1** one who does not believe **2** one who does not accept any, or any particular, religious belief

un·bend′ *vt.*, *vi.* **-bent′** or **-bend′ed**, **-bend′ing** **1** to relax, as from formality **2** to straighten

un·bend′ing *adj.* **1** rigid; stiff **2** firm; resolute **3** aloof; austere

un·bid′den *adj.* **1** not commanded **2** not invited

un·blush′ing *adj.* **1** not blushing **2** shameless —**un·blush′ing·ly** *adv.*

un·bolt′ *vt.*, *vi.* to withdraw the bolt or bolts of (a door, etc.); open

un·born′ *adj.* **1** not born **2** still in the mother's uterus **3** yet to be

un·bos′om (-booz′əm) *vt.*, *vi.* to tell or reveal (feelings, secrets, etc.) —**unbosom oneself** to reveal one's feelings, secrets, etc.

un·bound′ed *adj.* **1** without bounds or limits **2** not restrained

un′bowed′ (-boud′) *adj.* not yielding or giving in

un·bri′dled *adj.* **1** having no bridle on: said of a horse, etc. **2** uncontrolled

un·bur′den *vt.* **1** to free from a burden **2** to relieve (oneself, one's mind, etc.) by disclosing (guilt, etc.)

un′but′toned *adj.* **1** with buttons unfastened **2** free and easy; casual

un·called′-for′ *adj.* **1** not needed **2** unnecessary and out of place

un·can·ny (un kan′ē) *adj.* **1** mysterious and eerie; weird **2** so good, acute, etc. as to seem preternatural —**un·can′ni·ly** *adv.*

un·cared′-for′ *adj.* not cared for or looked after; neglected

un′cer·e·mo′ni·ous *adj.* **1** not ceremonious; informal **2** curt; abrupt

un·cer′tain *adj.* **1** *a)* not surely or certainly known *b)* not sure or certain in knowledge; doubtful **2** vague **3** not dependable or reliable **4** varying —**un·cer′tain·ty**, *pl.* **-ties**, *n.*

un·char′i·ta·ble *adj.* harsh or severe, as in opinion —**un·char′i·ta·bly** *adv.*

un·chart′ed *adj.* not marked on a chart or map; unexplored or unknown

un·chris′tian *adj.* **1** not Christian **2** [Inf.] outrageous; dreadful

un·ci·al (un′shē əl, -shəl) *adj.* ⟦L *uncialis,* inch-high⟧ designating or of the large, rounded letters of Greek and Latin manuscripts between A.D. 300 and 900 —*n.* uncial script or an uncial letter

un·cir′cum·cised′ *adj.* **1** not circumcised; specif., not Jewish; gentile **2** [Archaic] heathen

un·clasp′ *vt.* **1** to unfasten the clasp of **2** to release from a clasp or grasp

un·cle (uŋ′kəl) *n.* ⟦< L *avunculus*⟧ **1** the brother of one's father or mother **2** the husband of one's aunt

Uncle Sam ⟦< abbrev. *U.S.*⟧ [Inf.] the U.S. (government or people), personified as a tall man with whiskers, dressed in red, white, and blue

Uncle Tom ⟦after main character in novel *Uncle Tom's Cabin* (1852)⟧ [Inf.] a black person regarded as servile toward whites: a term of contempt

un·cloak′ *vt.* to reveal; expose

un·clothe′ *vt.* **-clothed′** or **-clad′**, **-cloth′ing** to undress, uncover, etc.

un·coil′ *vt.*, *vi.* to unwind

un·com′fort·a·ble *adj.* **1** feeling discomfort **2** causing discomfort **3** ill at ease —**un·com′fort·a·bly** *adv.*

THESAURUS

TROUBLED. **2** [Unsteady] wobbly, shaky, treacherous; see UNSTABLE 1.

unbearable *a.* intolerable, unacceptable, too much*; see TERRIBLE 2.

unbeaten *a.* victorious, triumphant, winning; see SUCCESSFUL.

unbecoming *a.* unsuitable, unfitted, awkward; see IMPROPER.

unbelievable *a.* beyond belief, incredible, inconceivable, staggering, unimaginable, not to be credited, dubious, doubtful, improbable, questionable, implausible, open to doubt, a bit thick*; see also UNLIKELY.—*Ant.* LIKELY, believable, probable.

unbeliever *n.* atheist, agnostic, heathen; see SKEPTIC.

unbend *v.* become more casual, be informal, relax; see REST 1.

unblemished *a.* spotless, flawless, unmarked; see PERFECT 2.

unborn *a.* embryonic, incipient, expected, future, prospective, potential, latent, anticipated, awaited.

unbound *a.* loose, untied, unfastened; see FREE 1, 2, 3.—*Ant.* BOUND, stapled, tied.

unbreakable *a.* indestructible, durable, everlasting, cast-iron, lasting, unshakeable, solid, firm, unchangeable, invulnerable, incorruptible, resistant, rugged, tight, unyielding.—*Ant.* DAINTY, fragile, brittle.

unbridled *a.* unrestrained, uncontrolled, unchecked; see UNRULY.

unbroken *a.* **1** [Whole] entire, intact, unimpaired; see WHOLE 2. **2** [Continuous] uninterrupted, continuous, even; see REGULAR 3, SMOOTH 1, 2.

unburden *v.* **1** [To unload] dump, dispose of, relinquish; see LIGHTEN, RELIEVE. **2** [To reveal] disclose, confess, divulge; see ADMIT 2.

unbutton *v.* undo, open up, unfasten; see OPEN 2.

uncalled-for *a.* unjustified, redundant, not needed; see UNNECESSARY.

uncanny *a.* weird, unnatural, supernatural, preternatural, superhuman, ghostly, inexplicable, strange, odd, mystifying, incredible, mysterious, magical, devilish; see also MAGIC.

uncertain *a.* undecided, undetermined, unsettled, doubtful, changeable, unpredictable, improbable, unlikely, unfixed, unsure, indeterminate, haphazard, random, chance, casual, provisional, contingent, alterable, subject to change, possible, vague, conjectural, questionable, problematic, suppositional, hypothetical, theoretical, open to question, equivocal, perplexing, debatable, dubious, indefinite, unascertained, ambiguous, unresolved, debated, conjecturable, unknown, unannounced, imprecise, in abeyance, up in the air, in doubt.

uncertainty *n.* **1** [The mental state of being uncertain] perplexity, doubt, puzzlement, quandary, mystification, indecision, ambivalence.—*Ant.* BELIEF, certainty, decision. **2** [The state of being undetermined or unknown] questionableness, contingency, obscurity, vagueness, ambiguity, difficulty, incoherence, intricacy, involvement, darkness, inconclusiveness, indeterminateness, improbability, unlikelihood, low probability, conjecturability; see also DOUBT.—*Ant.* DETERMINATION, sureness, necessity. **3** [That which is not determined or not known] chance, mutability, change, unpredictability, possibility, emergence, contingency, blind spot, puzzle, enigma, question, guesswork, conjecture, dilemma, blank, vacancy, maze, theory, risk, leap in the dark.—*Ant.* TRUTH, fact, matter of record.

unchanged *a.* unaltered, the same, unmoved, constant, steady, fixed, continuing, stable, permanent, durable, unvarying, eternal, invariable, consistent, persistent, firm, unvaried, resolute, perpetual, continuous, maintained, uninterrupted, fast.—*Ant.* CHANGED, altered, modified.

uncivilized *a.* barbarous, uncontrolled, barbarian; see PRIMITIVE 3.

unclassified *a.* not classified, disordered, out of order; see CONFUSED 2, UNKNOWN 1.

uncle *n.* father's brother, mother's brother, elder; see RELATIVE.

unclean *a.* soiled, sullied, stained, spotted, filthy, bedraggled, smeared, befouled, nasty, grimy, polluted, rank, unhealthful, defiled, muddy, stinking, fetid, rotten, vile, decayed, contaminated, tainted, rancid, putrid, putrescent, moldy, germy, musty, mildewed, besmirched, smirched, filmed over, bleary, dusty, sooty, smudgy, scurvy, scurfy, clogged, slimy, mucky, tarnished, murky, smudged, daubed, blurred, spattered; see also DIRTY 1, IMPURE 1.—*Ant.* CLEAN, pure, white.

uncomfortable *a.* **1** [Troubled in body or mind] distressed, ill at ease, uneasy, nervous, disturbed, pained, miserable, wretched, restless, annoyed, angry, in pain, smarting, suffering, upset, vexed, on pins and needles, weary, tired, fatigued, exhausted, strained, worn, aching, sore, galled, stiff, chafed, cramped, agonized, hurt, anguished.—*Ant.* QUIET, rested, happy. **2** [Causing discomfort] ill-fitting, tight, constrictive, binding, chafing, abrasive, piercing, awkward, annoying, irritating, distressful, galling, wearisome, difficult, hard, thorny, troublesome, harsh, grievous, dolorous, bitter, excruciating, afflictive, distressing, torturing, painful, agonizing, disagreeable.—*Ant.* EASY, pleasant, grateful.

uncomfortably *a.* distressfully, uneasily, dolefully, agonizingly, painfully, miserably, wretchedly, restlessly, sadly, fretfully, annoyingly,

un'com·mit'ted ***adj.*** **1** not committed or pledged **2** not taking a stand
un·com'mon ***adj.*** **1** rare; not common or usual **2** strange; remarkable
un'com·mu'ni·ca'tive ***adj.*** not communicative; reserved; taciturn
un·com'pro·mis'ing ***adj.*** not yielding; firm; inflexible
un'con·cern' ***n.*** **1** apathy; indifference **2** lack of concern, or worry
un'con·cerned' ***adj.*** **1** indifferent **2** not solicitous or anxious —**un'con·cern'ed·ly** ***adv.***
un'con·di'tion·al ***adj.*** without conditions or reservations; absolute
un·con·scion·a·ble (un kän'shən ə bəl) ***adj.*** **1** not guided or restrained by conscience **2** unreasonable or excessive **3** not fair or just —**un·con'scion·a·bly** ***adv.***
un·con'scious ***adj.*** **1** deprived of consciousness **2** not aware *(of)* **3** not doing or done on purpose *[an unconscious habit]* —**the unconscious** *Psychoanalysis* the sum of all thoughts, impulses, etc. of which the individual is not conscious but which influence the emotions and behavior —**un·con'scious·ly** ***adv.***
un'con·sti·tu'tion·al ***adj.*** not in accordance with a constitution, specif. the U.S. constitution
un·cool' ***adj.*** [Slang] **1** unsophisticated **2** unfashionable, unacceptable, etc.
un·cork' ***vt.*** to pull the cork out of
un·count'ed ***adj.*** **1** not counted **2** inconceivably numerous
un·cou'ple ***vt.*** **-pled**, **-pling** to unfasten (things coupled together)
un·couth (un ko͞oth') ***adj.*** ⟦OE < *un-*, not + *cunnan*, know⟧ **1** awkward; ungainly **2** not cultured; crude
un·cov'er ***vt.*** **1** to disclose **2** to remove the cover from **3** to remove the hat, etc. from (the head) —***vi.*** to bare the head, as in respect
unc·tion (uŋk'shən) ***n.*** ⟦< L *ungere*, anoint⟧ **1** *a)* the act of anointing, as for medical or religious purposes *b)* the oil, ointment, etc. used for this **2** anything that soothes or comforts
unc·tu·ous (uŋk'cho͞o əs) ***adj.*** ⟦see prec.⟧ **1** oily or greasy **2** characterized by a smooth but insincere show of deep or earnest feeling
un·cut' ***adj.*** not cut; specif., *a)* not ground to shape (said of a gem) *b)* not abridged or shortened
un·daunt'ed ***adj.*** not daunted; not hesitating because of fear or discouragement
un'de·ceive' ***vt.*** **-ceived'**, **-ceiv'ing** to cause to be no longer deceived or misled
un'de·cid'ed ***adj.*** **1** not decided **2** not having come to a decision
un'de·mon'stra·tive ***adj.*** not demonstrative; not showing feelings openly; reserved
un'de·ni'a·ble ***adj.*** that cannot be denied; indisputable —**un'de·ni'a·bly** ***adv.***
un·der (un'dər) ***prep.*** ⟦OE⟧ **1** in, at, or to a position down from; below **2** beneath the surface of **3** below and to the other side of *[drive under the bridge]* **4** covered by *[a vest under his coat]* **5** *a)* lower in rank, position, amount, etc. than *b)* lower than the required degree of *[under age]* **6** subject to the control, limitations, etc. of *[under oath]* **7** undergoing *[under repair]* **8** with the disguise of *[under an alias]* **9** in (the designated category) **10** during the rule of *[under Elizabeth I]* **11** being the subject of *[under discussion]* **12** because of *[under the circumstances]* **13** authorized by —***adv.*** **1** in or to a lower position or state **2** so as to be covered, concealed, etc. —***adj.*** lower in position, authority, amount, etc.
under- *prefix* **1** in, on, to, or from a lower place; beneath *[undertow]* **2** in a subordinate position *[undersecretary]* **3** too little; insufficiently *[underdeveloped]*
un·der·a·chieve (un'dər ə chēv') ***vi.*** **-chieved'**, **-chiev'ing** to fail to do as well in school as might be expected from intelligence tests —**un'der·a·chiev'er** ***n.***
un'der·act' ***vt.***, ***vi.*** to act (a theatrical role) with insufficient emphasis or too great restraint
un'der·age' ***adj.*** below the age required by law
un'der·arm' ***adj.*** **1** of, for, in, or used on the area under the arm, or the armpit **2** UNDERHAND (sense 1) —***adv.*** UNDERHAND
un'der·bel'ly ***n.*** **1** the lower, posterior part of an animal's belly **2** any vulnerable area, point, etc.
un'der·bid' ***vt.***, ***vi.*** **-bid'**, **-bid'ding** **1** to bid lower than

THESAURUS

disturbingly, awkwardly, irritatingly, troublesomely, harshly, grievously, bitterly, poignantly, sharply, keenly, excruciatingly, disagreeably, unhappily, dismally, in anguish.

uncommitted ***a.*** **1** [Neutral] unpledged, unaffiliated, free; see NEUTRAL 1. **2** [Reserved] evasive, reticent, shy; see WITHDRAWN.

uncommon ***a.*** unusual, out of the ordinary, different, extraordinary, unheard of, unique, rare, exceptional, out-of-the-way, strange, exotic, arcane, remarkable, startling, surprising, fantastic, unaccustomed, unfamiliar, freakish, irregular, uncustomary, unconventional, unorthodox, abnormal, aberrant, peculiar, odd, bizarre, eccentric, original, prodigious, fabulous, monstrous, wonderful, unaccountable, noteworthy, curious, queer, unparalleled, outlandish, extreme.—*Ant.* COMMON, usual, ordinary.

uncommunicative ***a.*** reticent, silent, evasive; see QUIET, RESERVED.

uncompromising ***a.*** strong, inflexible, determined; see FIRM 1.

unconcern ***n.*** apathy, aloofness, coldness; see INDIFFERENCE.

unconcerned ***a.*** careless, apathetic, inattentive; see NONCHALANT, INDIFFERENT.

unconditional ***a.*** positive, definite, absolute, unconstrained, without reserve, outright, final, certain, complete, entire, whole, total, unrestricted, unqualified, unlimited, actual, thorough, thoroughgoing, genuine, indubitable, assured, determinate, unequivocal, full, categorical, decisive, unmistakable, clear, unquestionable.

unconnected ***a.*** **1** [Separate] divided, detached, disconnected; see SEPARATED. **2** [Irrelevant] discrete, unrelated, inapplicable; see IRRELEVANT.

unconscious ***a.*** insensible, swooning, in a state of suspended animation, torpid, lethargic, inanimate, senseless, drowsy, motionless, benumbed, stupefied, numb, inert, paralyzed, palsied, entranced, in a stupor, in a coma, in a trance, raving, out of one's head, out like a light*, knocked out, zonked*, unaware, blind, oblivious.—*Ant.* CONSCIOUS, vivacious, awake.

unconscious ***n.*** [*Usually used with "the"*] psyche, instinct, motive force; see MEMORY 1, MIND 1.

unconsciously ***a.*** abstractedly, mechanically, carelessly, automatically, habitually, by rote, unintentionally, inattentively, heedlessly, without reflection, negligently, disregardfully, thoughtlessly, neglectfully, hurriedly, unthinkingly, without calculation, unguardedly.—*Ant.* DELIBERATELY, intentionally, willfully.

unconstitutional ***a.*** unjust, undemocratic, lawless; see ILLEGAL.

uncontrollable ***a.*** ungovernable, stubborn, insurgent; see UNRULY.

uncontrolled ***a.*** open, clear, free, unchecked, unhindered, boundless, ungoverned, unregulated, unsuppressed, limitless, unbridled, unfettered, unobstructed, independent, unburdened, unlimited, unbounded, unhampered, uncurbed, unconstrained, unconfined.

unconventional ***a.*** novel, individual, different; see UNIQUE, UNUSUAL 2.

uncouth ***a.*** awkward, clumsy, crude; see RUDE 1, 2.

uncover ***v.*** unseal, uncork, unscrew, pry open, lift the lid, dig up, reveal, tap, lay open, lay bare, bring to light, flush out, ferret out, unclose, fish out, fish up, take the wraps off of; see also OPEN 2.—*Ant.* CLOSE, cover, seal up.

undamaged ***a.*** uninjured, safe, unharmed; see WHOLE 2.

undecided ***a.*** undetermined, in the balance, unsettled; see DOUBTFUL, UNCERTAIN.

undefeated ***a.*** unbeaten, victorious, winning; see SUCCESSFUL.

undefined ***a.*** **1** [Infinite] limitless, boundless, forever; see INFINITE. **2** [Vague] dim, unclear, indistinct; see IRREGULAR 4, OBSCURE 1.

undemonstrative ***a.*** restrained, distant, stoic; see RESERVED, WITHDRAWN.

undeniable ***a.*** proven, sound, sure; see ACCURATE 1.

undependable ***a.*** unsound, careless, inconstant; see IRRESPONSIBLE, UNRELIABLE.

under ***a.***, ***prep.*** **1** [Referring to physical position] on the bottom of, below, covered by, 'neath*, concealed by, held down by, supporting, pinned beneath, on the underside of, pressed down by, beneath.—*Ant.* ABOVE, over, on top of. **2** [Subject to authority] governed by, in the power of, obedient to; see SUBORDINATE. **3** [Included within] belonging to, subsequent to, following; see BELOW 3.

underachiever ***n.*** slow learner, retarded child, underprivileged person, backward child, misfit, problem child, foreigner, nonnative speaker, foreign-born pupil; see also FOOL.

underage ***a.*** juvenile, youthful, minor; see YOUNG 1.

(another person) **2** to bid less than the worth of (a thing, as one's hand in bridge)

un′der·brush′ ***n.*** small trees, shrubs, etc. growing in woods or forests

un′der·car′riage ***n.*** a supporting frame, as of an automobile

un′der·charge′ ***vt.***, ***vi.*** **-charged′, -charg′ing** **1** to charge too low a price (to) **2** to provide with too small or low a charge

un′der·class′ ***n.*** the socioeconomic class with incomes below subsistence level, including esp. the underprivileged

un′der·class′man (-mən) ***n.***, *pl.* **-men** (-mən) a freshman or sophomore in high school or college

un′der·clothes′ ***pl.n.*** UNDERWEAR: also **un′der·cloth′ing** ***sing.n.***

un′der·coat′ ***n.*** **1** a tarlike coating applied to the underside of a motor vehicle to retard rust, etc. **2** a coat of paint, etc. applied before the final coat Also **un′der·coat′ing** —***vt.*** to apply an undercoat to

un′der·cov′er ***adj.*** acting or carried out in secret

un′der·cur′rent ***n.*** **1** a current flowing beneath the surface **2** an underlying tendency, opinion, etc.

un′der·cut′ ***vt.*** **-cut′, -cut′ting** **1** to make a cut below or under **2** to undersell or work for lower wages than **3** to weaken or undermine

un′der·de·vel′oped ***adj.*** inadequately developed, esp. economically and industrially

un′der·dog′ ***n.*** **1** a person or team that is losing or expected to lose **2** a person at a disadvantage because of injustice, prejudice, etc.

un′der·done′ ***adj.*** not cooked enough

un′der·em·ployed′ ***adj.*** **1** working less than full time **2** working at low-skilled, poorly paid jobs when capable of doing more highly skilled work

un′der·es′ti·mate′ ***vt.*** **-mat′ed, -mat′ing** to set too low an estimate on or for —**un′der·es′ti·ma′tion** ***n.***

un′der·ex·pose′ ***vt.*** **-posed′, -pos′ing** to expose (photographic film, etc.) to inadequate light or for too short a time

un′der·foot′ ***adv.***, ***adj.*** **1** under the foot or feet **2** in the way

un′der·gar′ment ***n.*** a piece of underwear

un′der·go′ ***vt.*** **-went′, -gone′, -go′ing** to experience; go through

un′der·grad′u·ate ***n.*** a college student who has not yet earned a degree

un′der·ground′ ***adj.*** **1** under the earth's surface **2** secret; hidden **3** of newspapers, movies, etc. that are unconventional, radical, etc. —***adv.*** **1** under the earth's surface **2** in or into secrecy —***n.*** **1** the region under the earth's surface **2** a secret movement in a country to oppose the government or enemy occupation forces **3** [Brit.] a subway

un′der·growth′ ***n.*** UNDERBRUSH

un′der·hand′ ***adj.*** **1** done with the hand below the level of the elbow or shoulder **2** UNDERHANDED —***adv.*** with an underhand motion

un′der·hand′ed ***adj.*** sly, deceitful, etc. —**un′der·hand′ed·ly** ***adv.***

un′der·lie′ ***vt.*** **-lay′, -lain′, -ly′ing** **1** to lie beneath **2** to be the basis for; form the foundation of

un′der·line′ ***vt.*** **-lined′, -lin′ing** **1** to draw a line beneath **2** to stress

un·der·ling (un′dər liŋ) ***n.*** ⟦OE: see UNDER- & -LING⟧ a person in a subordinate position; inferior: usually a contemptuous term

un′der·ly′ing ***adj.*** **1** lying under **2** fundamental; basic

un′der·mine′ ***vt.*** **-mined′, -min′ing** **1** to dig beneath, so as to form a tunnel or mine **2** to wear away and weaken the supports of **3** to injure or weaken, esp. by subtle or insidious means

un′der·most′ ***adj.***, ***adv.*** lowest in place, position, rank, etc.

un·der·neath (un′dər nēth′) ***adv.***, ***prep.*** ⟦< OE *under,* UNDER + *neothan,* below⟧ under; below

un′der·nour′ished ***adj.*** not getting the food needed for health and growth

un′der·pants′ ***pl.n.*** an undergarment, long or short, for the lower part of the body

un′der·pass′ ***n.*** a passage under something; esp., a passageway under a railway

un′der·per·form′ ***vi.*** to be less successful than expected or needed —***vt.*** to produce a smaller return than: said of stocks, etc.

un′der·pin′ning (-pin′iŋ) ***n.*** **1** a support or prop **2** [*pl.*] [Inf.] the legs

un′der·play′ ***vt.***, ***vi.*** **1** UNDERACT **2** to make seem less important

un′der·priv′i·leged ***adj.*** deprived of a decent standard of living and economic security through poverty, discrimination, etc.

un′der·pro·duce′ ***vt.***, ***vi.*** **-duced′, -duc′ing** to produce less than is needed or wanted

un′der·rate′ ***vt.*** **-rat′ed, -rat′ing** to rate or estimate too low

un′der·score′ ***vt.*** **-scored′, -scor′ing** UNDERLINE

un′der·sea′ ***adj.***, ***adv.*** beneath the surface of the sea: also **un′der·seas′** ***adv.***

un′der·sec′re·tar′y ***n.***, *pl.* **-ies** an assistant secretary

un′der·sell′ ***vt.*** **-sold′, -sell′ing** **1** to sell at a lower price than **2** to publicize or promote in a restrained or inadequate manner

un′der·shirt′ ***n.*** a collarless undergarment worn under an outer shirt

un′der·shorts′ ***pl.n.*** short underpants worn by men and boys

un′der·shot′ ***adj.*** **1** with the lower part extending past the upper [an *undershot* jaw] **2** driven by water flowing along the lower part [an *undershot* water wheel]

un′der·side′ ***n.*** the side or surface that is underneath

un′der·signed′ ***adj.*** whose name is signed at the end —**the undersigned** the person or persons having signed at the end

un′der·skirt′ ***n.*** a skirt worn under another

un′der·staffed′ ***adj.*** having fewer workers on the staff than are needed

THESAURUS

underbrush ***n.*** thicket, brush, brushwood, jungle, second growth, tangle, hedge, cover, scrub, bush; see also FOREST.

underclothes ***n.*** lingerie, intimate apparel, undies*; see CLOTHES, UNDERWEAR.

undercover ***a.*** **1** [Secret] hidden, surreptitious, clandestine; see SECRET 3. **2** [Secretly] privately, surreptitiously, stealthily; see SECRETLY.

underdeveloped ***a.*** backward, retarded, third-world; see WEAK 1, 2, 3, 5.

underdog ***n.*** loser, underling, low man on the totem pole*; see FAILURE 2, VICTIM.

underestimate ***v.*** miscalculate, come short of, undervalue, depreciate, underrate, disparage, slight, minimize, think too little of, hold too lightly, not give someone enough credit, make light of, deprecate.

underfoot ***a.*** **1** [Beneath] down, at bottom, below; see UNDER 1. **2** [In the way] annoying, tiresome, impeding; see DISTURBING.

undergo ***v.*** sustain, submit to, support, experience, feel, know, be subject to, bear, meet with, endure, go through, encounter, bear up under, put up with, share, withstand.—*Ant.* AVOID, ESCAPE, RESIST.

undergone ***a.*** sustained, submitted to, supported, experienced, felt, suffered, borne, met with, known, endured, gone through, encountered, put up with, shared, seen, withstood.

underground ***a.*** **1** [Subterranean] buried, covered, earthed over, under the sod, in the recesses of the earth, hidden from the light of day, gone to earth; see also UNDER 1. **2** [Secret] hidden, undercover, clandestine; see SECRET 3. **3** [Unconventional] experimental, radical, avant-garde; see UNUSUAL 2.

undergrowth ***n.*** underwood, tangle, scrub; see BRUSH 3.

underhanded ***a.*** deceptive, sneaky, secretive; see SLY.

underlie ***v.*** carry, bear, hold up; see HOLD 7.

underline ***v.*** **1** [Emphasize] stress, mark, indicate; see EMPHASIZE. **2** [To make a line under] underscore, mark, interline, bracket, check off, italicize.

underling ***n.*** subordinate, hireling, servant, menial, minion, flunky*; see also ASSISTANT.

undermine ***v.*** impair, threaten, ruin; see WEAKEN 2.

underneath ***a.***, ***prep.*** beneath, below, lower than; see UNDER 1.

undernourished ***a.*** underfed, mistreated, afflicted with malnutrition; see HUNGRY.

underpass ***n.*** bridge, culvert, cave; see TUNNEL.

underprivileged ***a.*** indigent, destitute, educationally handicapped; see POOR 1.

underrate ***v.*** undervalue, discount, disparage; see UNDERESTIMATE.

undershirt ***n.*** shirt, T-shirt, turtleneck; see CLOTHES, UNDERWEAR.

underside ***n.*** underneath, base, root; see BOTTOM, FOUNDATION 2.

un'der·stand' *vt.* **-stood', -stand'ing** ⟦< OE *understandan,* lit., to stand among⟧ **1** to perceive the meaning of **2** to assume from what is heard, etc.; infer **3** to take as meant; interpret **4** to take as a fact **5** to know the nature, character, etc. of **6** to have a sympathetic rapport with —*vi.* **1** to have understanding, comprehension, etc. **2** to be informed; believe —**un'der·stand'a·ble** *adj.* —**un'der·stand'a·bly** *adv.*

un'der·stand'ing *n.* **1** comprehension **2** the power to think and learn; intelligence **3** a specific interpretation **4** mutual agreement, esp. one that settles differences —*adj.* that understands; sympathetic

un'der·state' *vt.* **-stat'ed, -stat'ing** **1** to state too weakly **2** to state in a restrained style —**un'der·state'ment** *n.*

un'der·stud'y *n., pl.* **-ies** an actor prepared to substitute for another —*vt., vi.* **-ied, -y·ing** to learn (a part) as an understudy (to)

un'der·take' *vt.* **-took', -tak'en, -tak'ing** **1** to take upon oneself (a task, etc.) **2** to promise; guarantee

un'der·tak'er *n.* FUNERAL DIRECTOR: a somewhat old-fashioned usage

un'der·tak'ing *n.* **1** something undertaken; task; enterprise **2** a promise; guarantee

un'der-the-count'er *adj.* [Inf.] done secretly in an unlawful way: also **un'der-the-ta'ble**

un'der·things' *pl.n.* women's or girls' underwear

un'der·tone' *n.* **1** a low tone of voice **2** a subdued color **3** an underlying quality, factor, etc.

un'der·tow' *n.* a current of water moving beneath the surface water and in a different direction

un'der·wa'ter *adj.* being, done, etc. beneath the surface of the water

un'der·way' *adj.* **1** moving; making progress **2** *Naut.* not anchored or moored or aground

un'der·wear' *n.* clothing worn under one's outer clothes, usually next to the skin, as undershirts

un·der·weight (un'dər wāt', un'dər wāt') *adj.* below the normal, desirable, or allowed weight

un'der·world' *n.* **1** the mythical world of the dead; Hades **2** criminals regarded as a group

un'der·write' *vt.* **-wrote', -writ'ten, -writ'ing** **1** to agree to market (an issue of securities), guaranteeing to buy any part remaining unsubscribed **2** to agree to pay the cost of or cover the losses of (an undertaking, etc.) **3** to sign one's name to (an insurance policy), thus assuming liability —**un'der·writ'er** *n.*

un·dies (un'dēz') *pl.n.* [Inf.] women's or girls' underwear

un·do' *vt.* **-did', -done', -do'ing** **1** to untie, open, etc. **2** to do away with; cancel **3** to bring to ruin

un·doc'u·ment'ed *adj.* not having a proper visa for U.S. residence *[*an *undocumented* alien*]*

un·do'ing *n.* **1** an annulling **2** a bringing to ruin **3** the cause of ruin

un·done' *adj.* **1** not done; not performed, accomplished, etc. **2** ruined **3** emotionally upset

un·doubt'ed *adj.* not doubted or disputed; certain —**un·doubt'ed·ly** *adv.*

THESAURUS

understand *v.* **1** [To comprehend] apprehend, fathom, take in, grasp, figure out, seize, identify with, know, perceive, appreciate, follow, master, conceive, be aware of, sense, recognize, grow aware, explain, interpret, see through, learn, find out, see into, catch, note, be conscious of, have cognizance of, realize, discern, read, distinguish, infer, deduce, induce, make out, become alive to, have been around*, experience, have knowledge of, be instructed in, get to the bottom of, get at the root of, penetrate, possess, be informed of, come to one's senses, see the light, make out, register*, savvy*, get the gist of, catch on, get the point of, dig*, read between the lines, be with it*, get the idea, get it*. **2** [To suppose] guess, conjecture, surmise; see ASSUME. **3** [To accept] concede, take for granted, count on; see AGREE.

understandable *a.* comprehensible, conceivable, appreciable, expected, to be expected, natural, normal, regular, making sense, intelligible, in harmony with, readable, reasonable, logical, right, customary, recognizable, justifiable, imaginable, acceptable, apprehensible, credible.

understanding *n.* **1** [The power to understand] sharpness, intelligence, comprehension; see JUDGMENT 1. **2** [The act of comprehending] recognition, knowing, perception; see JUDGMENT 2, THOUGHT 1. **3** [That which comes from understanding] conclusion, knowledge, perception; see BELIEF, OPINION 1. **4** [Informal agreement] meeting of minds, common view, harmony; see AGREEMENT 1. **5** [The intellect] head, brain, mentality; see MIND 1.

understate *v.* undervalue, minimize, lessen; see DECREASE 2, UNDERESTIMATE.

understood *a.* **1** [Comprehended] penetrated, realized, appreciated, known, discovered, grasped, reasoned out, rationalized, explained, experienced, discerned, distinguished, made out, learned, fathomed, searched, explored, analyzed, mastered, conned, taken to heart.—*Ant.* UNKNOWN, overlooked, uncomprehended. **2** [Agreed upon] concerted, ratified, assumed, stipulated, pledged, tacitly agreed upon, engaged for, settled, concluded, fixed upon, endorsed, subscribed to, accepted.

undertake *v.* endeavor, engage, set out, promise, try out, try, begin, offer, set in motion, volunteer, initiate, commit oneself to, embark upon, venture, take upon oneself, answer for, hazard, stake, move, devote oneself to, take up for, take on, set about, go in for, put one's hand to, have one's hands in, have in hand, launch into, address oneself to, enter upon, busy oneself with, tackle, pitch into*, fall into, buckle down, take on, take the plunge, fall to, have a try at, go for in a big way.

undertaken *a.* set in motion, begun, launched, embarked upon, initiated, pushed forward, ventured, started, endeavored, assumed, taken up, promised, offered, volunteered, hazarded, chanced, risked, pledged, tackled, essayed, tried, aimed at, attempted, striven for, engaged for.

undertaker *n.* mortician, funeral director, embalmer, mortuary director.

undertaking *n.* engagement, enterprise, attempt; see ACTION 1, 2.

undertone *n.* buzz, murmur, hum; see WHISPER 1.

undertow *n.* whirlpool, undercurrent, riptide; see FLOW, TIDE.

underwater *a.* submarine, sunken, marine; see UNDER 1.

underwear *n.* undergarments, underclothing, unmentionables*, lingerie, intimate apparel, underlinen, underclothes, skivvies*; see also CLOTHES. *Types of underwear include the following—men*: shirt, shorts, briefs, drawers, red flannels, union suit, jockey shorts, T-shirt, boxer shorts, long underwear; *women*: underskirt, slip, petticoat, girdle, brassiere, garter belt, bra-slip, bra, halfslip, corset, corselet, bodice, camisole, *cache-sexe* (French), vest, briefs, foundation garment, panty girdle, panties, pantyhose, shorts, knickers (British), falsies*; *infants*: shirt, drawers, pants, diaper, slip, rubber pants.

underweight *a.* skinny, undersized, puny; see THIN 2.

underworld *n.* **1** [Hell] Hades, Inferno, netherworld; see HELL. **2** [Crime] gangdom, rackets, organized crime; see CRIME.

undesirable *a.* objectionable, shunned, disliked, to be avoided, unwanted, outcast, rejected, defective, disadvantageous, inexpedient, inconvenient, troublesome, unwished for, repellent, loathed, unsought, dreaded, annoying, insufferable, unacceptable, scorned, displeasing, distasteful, loathsome, abominable, obnoxious, unpopular, bothersome, unlikable, unwelcome, unapprovable, useless, inadmissible, unsatisfactory, disagreeable, awkward, embarrassing, unfit.—*Ant.* WELCOME, proper, suitable.

undeveloped *a.* potential, incipient, nascent; see HIDDEN.

undisputed *a.* unchallenged, unquestioned, assured; see CERTAIN 2.

undistinguished *a.* ordinary, commonplace, plain; see COMMON 1, CONVENTIONAL 3, DULL 4.

undisturbed *a.* settled, unruffled, untroubled; see CALM 1, 2.

undivided *a.* **1** [Unified] united, full, collective; see WHOLE. **2** [Undistracted] exclusive, complete, entire; see WHOLE 1.

undo *v.* **1** [To bring to ruin] mar, destroy, ruin, wreck, break, bring to naught, subvert, injure, overthrow, unsettle, turn topsy-turvy, upset, defeat. **2** [To open] untie, unfasten, unbuckle, untangle, unwind, unhook, disengage, loosen.

undoing *n.* ruination, downfall, reversal, destruction, misfortune, calamity, overthrow, trouble, grief, catastrophe, defeat, shipwreck, smash, wrack, subversion, collapse, casualty, accident, mishap, misadventure, misstep, mischance, bad luck, adversity, reverse, blow, trial, affliction, stroke of fate, slip, blunder, fault, omission, difficulty, failure, error, miscalculation, trip, stumble, fumble, blunder, repulse, discouragement, deathblow, last straw.—*Ant.* ADVANTAGE, good omen, godsend.

undone *a.* **1** [Unfinished] left, incomplete, unperformed; see UNFINISHED 1. **2** [Distraught] upset, disturbed, agitated; see TROUBLED. **3** [Ruined] betrayed, destroyed, killed; see DEAD 1, RUINED 1, 2.

undoubtedly *a.* assuredly, without

un·dreamed′ *adj.* not even dreamed (*of*) or imagined: also **un·dreamt′** (-dremt′)
un·dress′ *vt.* to take off the clothing of —*vi.* to take off one's clothes
un·due′ *adj.* **1** not appropriate; improper **2** excessive; immoderate
un·du·lant (un′jə lənt, -dyə-) *adj.* undulating
un′du·late′ (-lāt′) *vi., vt.* ⟦< L *unda*, a wave⟧ **1** to move or cause to move in waves **2** to have or cause to have a wavy form or surface —**un′du·la′tion** *n.*
un·du′ly *adv.* **1** improperly **2** excessively
un·dy′ing *adj.* immortal or eternal
un·earned′ *adj.* not earned by work or service; specif., obtained as a return on an investment *[unearned income]*
un·earth′ *vt.* **1** to dig up from the earth **2** to bring to light; disclose
un·earth′ly *adj.* **1** supernatural **2** weird; mysterious **3** [Inf.] fantastic, outlandish, etc.
un·eas′y *adj.* **-i·er, -i·est** **1** having, showing, or allowing no ease of body or mind; uncomfortable **2** awkward; constrained **3** anxious; apprehensive —**un·eas′i·ly** *adv.* —**un·eas′i·ness** *n.*
un′em·ploy′a·ble *adj.* not employable, specif. because of severe physical or mental handicaps, outmoded skills, etc.
un′em·ployed′ *adj.* **1** not employed; without work **2** not being used —**un′em·ploy′ment** *n.*
un·e′qual *adj.* **1** not equal, as in size, strength, ability, or value **2** not balanced, even, regular, etc. **3** not adequate (*to*)
un·e′qualed or **un·e′qualled** *adj.* not equaled; unmatched; unrivaled
un′e·quiv′o·cal *adj.* not equivocal; plain; clear
un·err·ing (un ʉr′iŋ, -er′-) *adj.* **1** free from error **2** not missing or failing; sure; exact
UNESCO (yo͞o nes′kō) *n.* United Nations Educational, Scientific, and Cultural Organization
un·e′ven *adj.* **1** not even, level, smooth, regular, etc. **2** unequal **3** *Math.* odd —**un·e′ven·ly** *adv.*
un′ex·am′pled *adj.* having no parallel or precedent; unprecedented
un′ex·cep′tion·a·ble *adj.* not exceptionable; without fault; beyond criticism
un′ex·cep′tion·al *adj.* ordinary
un′ex·pect′ed *adj.* not expected; unforeseen —**un′ex·pect′ed·ly** *adv.*
un·fail′ing *adj.* **1** not failing **2** never ceasing or falling short; inexhaustible **3** always reliable
un·faith′ful *adj.* **1** lacking or breaking faith or loyalty **2** not true, accurate, etc. **3** adulterous —**un·faith′ful·ness** *n.*
un′fa·mil′iar *adj.* **1** not well-known; strange **2** not acquainted (*with*) —**un′fa·mil′i·ar′i·ty** *n.*
un·feel′ing *adj.* **1** incapable of feeling; insensible **2** hardhearted; cruel —**un·feel′ing·ly** *adv.*
un·feigned (un fānd′) *adj.* genuine
un·fin′ished *adj.* **1** not finished; incomplete **2** not painted, varnished, etc.

THESAURUS

doubt, of course; see UNQUESTIONABLY.

undress *v.* strip, take off one's clothes, disrobe, dismantle, divest, become naked, peel*, pile out of one's clothes*.—*Ant.* DRESS, put on one's clothes, attire oneself.

undue *a.* improper, illegal, indecorous, unfair, unseemly, unjust, underhanded, sinister, forbidden, excessive, unnecessary, extreme, extravagant, disproportionate, immoderate.—*Ant.* NECESSARY, proper, requisite.

unduly *a.* improperly, excessively, extremely; see UNNECESSARILY.

undying *a.* everlasting, perpetual, deathless; see ETERNAL.

unearned *a.* won, accrued, unmerited; see FREE 4.

unearth *v.* **1** [To disclose] reveal, find, uncover; see LEARN. **2** [To dig up] excavate, exhume, mine; see DIG 1.

unearthly *a.* frightening, ghostly, supernatural; see UNNATURAL 1.

uneasiness *n.* disquiet, restlessness, agitation; see FEAR.

uneasy *a.* unquiet, anxious, fearful, irascible, troubled, harassed, vexed, perturbed, alarmed, upset, afraid, apprehensive, nervous, frightened, shaky, perplexed, agitated, unsettled, suspicious, peevish, irritable, fretful, worried, anguished, in turmoil, disquieted, shaken, full of misgivings, fidgety, jittery, on edge, all nerves, jumpy, snappish, uncomfortable, molested, tormented, in distress.—*Ant.* QUIET, placid, soothed.

uneducated *a.* unschooled, illiterate, untaught; see IGNORANT 2.

unemotional *a.* reticent, apathetic, insensitive; see INDIFFERENT, QUIET.

unemployed *a.* out of work, in the unemployment line, on welfare, receiving charity, jobless, idle, inactive, laid off, loafing, unoccupied, without gainful employment, on the dole, cooling one's heels*, on the shelf.—*Ant.* BUSY, employed, at work.

unending *a.* everlasting, infinite, neverending; see ETERNAL.

unequal *a.* **1** [Not alike] odd, ill-matched, dissimilar; see UNLIKE. **2** [One-sided] uneven, unbalanced, inequitable; see IRREGULAR 1.

unequaled *a.* unmatched, unrivaled, supreme; see UNIQUE.

unethical *a.* sneaky, immoral, unfair; see DISHONEST, WRONG 1.

uneven *a.* **1** [Rough] bumpy, rugged, jagged; see ROUGH 1. **2** [Irregular] notched, jagged, serrate; see IRREGULAR 4. **3** [Variable] intermittent, spasmodic, fitful; see IRREGULAR 1. **4** [Odd] remaining, leftover, additional; see ODD 4.

unevenly *a.* roughly, intermittently, irregularly, spottily, bumpily, with friction, haphazardly, jumpily, all up and down, fitfully, off an on.

uneventful *a.* routine, monotonous, unexciting, quiet; see also DULL 4, 6.

unexampled *a.* unprecedented, singular, unequaled; see UNIQUE, UNUSUAL 1.

unexpected *a.* unforeseen, surprising, unlooked for, sudden, startling, unpredicted, coming unaware, astonishing, staggering, stunning, electrifying, amazing, not in the cards, not on the books, unanticipated, not bargained for, left out of calculation, wonderful, unprepared for, instantaneous, eye-opening, like a bolt from the blue.—*Ant.* EXPECTED, predicted, foreseen.

unexpectedly *a.* surprisingly, instantaneously, suddenly, startlingly, without warning, like a bolt from the blue; see also QUICKLY.—*Ant.* REGULARLY, according to prediction, as anticipated.

unfair *a.* **1** [Unjust] wrongful, wrong, low, base, injurious, unethical, bad, wicked, culpable, blamable, blameworthy, foul, illegal, inequitable, improper, unsporting, shameful, cruel, shameless, dishonorable, unreasonable, grievous, vicious, vile, undue, unlawful, petty, mean, inexcusable, unjustifiable, immoral, criminal, forbidden, irregular.—*Ant.* FAIR, proper, sporting. **2** [Not in accord with approved trade practices] unethical, criminal, discriminatory; see sense 1.

unfaithful *a.* **1** [Not faithful] false, untrue, deceitful; see UNRELIABLE. **2** [Having broken the marriage vow] adulterous, incontinent, unchaste; see BAD 1.

unfamiliar *a.* **1** [Unacquainted] not introduced, not associated, unknown, not on speaking terms, not versed in, not in the habit of, out of contact with.—*Ant.* FRIENDLY, intimate, acquainted. **2** [Strange] alien, outlandish, exotic, remote, novel, original, different, unusual, extraordinary, unaccustomed, unexplored, uncommon.—*Ant.* COMMON, ordinary, usual.

unfashionable *a.* outmoded, antiquated, obsolete; see OLD-FASHIONED.

unfasten *v.* unsnap, untie, unlock; see LOOSEN 1.

unfavorable *a.* untimely, inopportune, unseasonable, adverse, calamitous, unpropitious, inexpedient, bad, ill-chosen, ill-fated, ill-suited, ill-timed, unsuitable, improper, wrong, abortive, untoward, inauspicious, unlucky, ill, unfortunate, regrettable, premature, tardy, late, unfit, inadvisable, objectionable, inconvenient, disadvantageous, damaging, destructive, unseemly, ill-advised, obstructive, troublesome, embarrassing, unpromising, awkward.

unfavorably *a.* adversely, negatively, opposingly, oppositely, antagonistically, conflictingly, obstructively, malignantly, on the contrary, counteractively, contrarily, in opposition, in the negative, by turning thumbs down, by giving the red light; see also AGAINST 3.

unfinished *a.* **1** [Not completed] uncompleted, undone, half done, incomplete, under construction, unperformed, imperfect, unconcluded, deficient, unexecuted, unaccomplished, in preparation, in the making, not done, in the rough, sketchy, tentative, partial, shapeless, formless, unperfected, unfulfilled, undeveloped, unassembled, defective, found wanting, cut short, immature, faulty, crude, rough.—*Ant.* DONE, completed, perfected. **2** [Without a finish] unpainted, unvarnished, bare, raw, rough, crude, unprotected, uncovered, plain, undecorated, unadorned.

unfit *a.* **1** [Incompetent] unqualified, feeble, unpracticed, inexperienced, weak, impotent, inept, clumsy, debilitated, incapacitated, badly qualified, incompetent, unable, unprepared, ineffective, unapt.—*Ant.* ABLE, fit, effective. **2** [Unsuitable] ill-

un·flap'pa·ble (-flap'ə bəl) ***adj.*** ⟦< UN- + FLAP, *n.* 3 + -ABLE⟧ [Inf.] not easily excited; imperturbable
un·flinch'ing ***adj.*** steadfast; firm
un·fold' ***vt.*** **1** to open and spread out (something folded) **2** to lay open to view; reveal, explain, etc. —***vi.*** **1** to become unfolded **2** to develop fully
un'for·get'ta·ble ***adj.*** so important, beautiful, shocking, etc. as never to be forgotten
un'for·giv'ing ***adj.*** not willing or not able to forgive
un·for'tu·nate ***adj.*** **1** having or bringing bad luck; unlucky **2** not suitable or successful —***n.*** an unfortunate person —**un·for'tu·nate·ly** ***adv.***
un·found'ed ***adj.*** not founded on fact or truth
un·friend'ly ***adj.*** **-li·er, -li·est 1** not friendly or kind **2** not favorable —**un·friend'li·ness** ***n.***
un·frock' ***vt.*** to deprive of the rank of priest or minister
un·furl' ***vt., vi.*** to open or spread out from a furled state
un·gain·ly (un gān'lē) ***adj.*** ⟦< ME *un-,* not + ON *gegn,* ready⟧ awkward; clumsy
un·god'ly ***adj.*** **1** not godly or religious **2** [Inf.] outrageous —**un·god'li·ness** ***n.***
un·gov'ern·a·ble ***adj.*** that cannot be governed or controlled; unruly
un·gra'cious ***adj.*** **1** not gracious; rude **2** unpleasant; unattractive
un·guard'ed ***adj.*** **1** unprotected **2** without guile or cunning **3** careless; imprudent
un·guent (uŋ'gwənt) ***n.*** ⟦< L *unguere,* anoint⟧ a salve or ointment
un·gu·late (uŋ'gyōō lit, -lāt') ***adj.*** ⟦< L *unguis,* a nail⟧ having hoofs —***n.*** a mammal having hoofs
un·hand' ***vt.*** to release from the hand or hands; let go of
un·hap'py ***adj.*** **-pi·er, -pi·est 1** unfortunate **2** sad; wretched **3** not suitable —**un·hap'pi·ly** ***adv.*** —**un·hap'pi·ness** ***n.***
un·health'y ***adj.*** **-i·er, -i·est 1** sickly; not well **2** harmful to health **3** harmful to morals **4** dangerous or risky —**un·health'i·ness** ***n.***
un·heard' ***adj.*** **1** not perceived by the ear **2** not given a hearing
un·heard'-of' ***adj.*** **1** not heard of before; unprecedented or unknown **2** unacceptable or outrageous
un·hinge' ***vt.*** **-hinged', -hing'ing 1** to remove from the hinges **2** to unbalance (the mind) of (someone)
un·ho'ly ***adj.*** **-li·er, -li·est 1** not sacred, hallowed, etc. **2** wicked; profane **3** [Inf.] outrageous
un·horse' ***vt.*** **-horsed', -hors'ing** to throw (a rider) from a horse
uni- ⟦L < *unus,* one⟧ *prefix* one; having only one
u·ni·bod·y (yōō'nə bäd'ē) ***adj.*** designating automobile construction in which roof, floor, panels, etc. are welded together into a single unit
u'ni·cam'er·al (-kam'ər əl) ***adj.*** ⟦< UNI- + L *camera,* chamber⟧ of or having a single legislative chamber
UNICEF (yōō'nə sef') ***n.*** United Nations Children's Fund: formerly, *United Nations International Children's Emergency Fund*
u·ni·corn (yōō'nə kôrn') ***n.*** ⟦< L *unus,* one + *cornu,* horn⟧ a mythical horselike animal with a single horn growing from its forehead
u·ni·cy·cle (yōō'nə sī'kəl) ***n.*** ⟦UNI- + (BI)CYCLE⟧ a one-wheeled vehicle straddled by the rider who pushes its pedals —**u'ni·cy'clist** ***n.***
u·ni·form (yōō'nə fôrm') ***adj.*** ⟦< L *unus,* one + *-formis,* -FORM⟧ **1** not varying in form, rate, degree, etc. **2** like others of the same class —***n.*** the distinctive clothes of a particular group, as of soldiers —***vt.*** to supply with a uniform —**u'ni·form'i·ty** ***n.*** —**u'ni·form'ly** ***adv.***
u·ni·fy (yōō'nə fī') ***vt., vi.*** **-fied', -fy'ing** ⟦see UNI- & -FY⟧ to become or make united —**u'ni·fi·ca'tion** ***n.***
u·ni·lat·er·al (yōō'nə lat'ər əl) ***adj.*** **1** of, occurring on, or affecting one side only **2** involving only one of several parties; not reciprocal
un·im·peach·a·ble (un'im pēch'ə bəl) ***adj.*** that cannot be doubted or discredited; irreproachable

THESAURUS

adapted, improper, wrong, ill-advised, unlikely, unpromising, inexpedient, inappropriate, inapplicable, useless, valueless, mistaken, incorrect, inadequate, flimsy.—*Ant.* FIT, suitable, correct.

unfold ***v.*** shake out, straighten, release, display, unwind, spread out, uncurl, unwrap, reel out, unbend, open, flatten, loosen, unroll.—*Ant.* FOLD, roll, lap.

unforeseen ***a.*** surprising, abrupt, sudden; see UNEXPECTED.

unforgettable ***a.*** notable, exceptional, extraordinary; see IMPRESSIVE.

unforgivable ***a.*** inexcusable, unpardonable, unjustifiable, indefensible, inexpiable; see also WRONG 1.

unfortunate ***a.*** unlucky, luckless, unhappy, afflicted, troubled, stricken, unsuccessful, without success, burdened, pained, not prosperous, in adverse circumstances, broken, shattered, ill-fated, on the road to ruin, in a desperate plight, ruined, out of luck, in a bad way, jinxed*, snakebit*, behind the eight ball*, gone to the dogs*, down on one's luck; see also SAD 1.—*Ant.* HAPPY, lucky, prosperous.

unfortunately ***a.*** unluckily, unhappily, miserably, sadly, grievously, disastrously, dismally, calamitously, badly, sickeningly, discouragingly, catastrophically, horribly, if worst comes to worst.—*Ant.* HAPPILY, favorably, prosperously.

unfounded ***a.*** baseless, unproven, groundless; see UNTRUE.

unfriendly ***a.*** **1** [Hostile] opposed, alienated, ill-disposed, against, opposite, contrary, warlike, bellicose, competitive, conflicting, antagonistic, estranged, at variance, irreconcilable, not on speaking terms, turned against, with a chip on one's shoulder*.—*Ant.* FRIENDLY, intimate, approving. **2** [Lacking friendly qualities] grouchy, bearish, surly, misanthropic, gruff, ill-disposed, envious, uncharitable, faultfinding, combative, quarrelsome, grudging, malignant, spiteful, malicious, vengeful, resentful, hateful, peevish, aloof, unsociable, querulous, suspicious, sour.—*Ant.* GENEROUS, frank, open.

ungainly ***a.*** clumsy, gawky, inexpert; see AWKWARD, RUDE 1.

ungodly* ***a.*** dreadful, atrocious, immoral; see BAD 1.

ungovernable ***a.*** unmanageable, wild, uncontrollable; see UNRULY.

ungracious ***a.*** unpleasant, discourteous, impolite; see RUDE 1, 2.

ungrateful ***a.*** thankless, selfish, lacking in appreciation, grasping, demanding, forgetful, unmindful, heedless, careless, insensible, dissatisfied, grumbling, looking a gift horse in the mouth, faultfinding, oblivious.—*Ant.* THANKFUL, grateful, obliged.

unguarded ***a.*** thoughtless, frank, careless; see CARELESS.

unhandy ***a.*** awkward, ill-arranged, unwieldy, ill-contrived, clumsy; see also TROUBLESOME.

unhappily ***a.*** regrettably, lamentably, unluckily; see UNFORTUNATELY.

unhappiness ***n.*** sorrow, woe, sadness; see DEPRESSION 2, GRIEF.

unhappy ***a.*** **1** [Sad] miserable, sorrowful, wretched; see TROUBLED. **2** [Unfortunate] afflicted, troubled, in a desperate plight; see UNFORTUNATE.

unharmed ***a.*** unhurt, uninjured, intact; see SAFE 1, WHOLE 2.

unhealthy ***a.*** sickly, sick, in a decline, in ill health, infirm, delicate, feeble, shaky, undernourished, rickety, spindling, ailing, weak, rundown, debilitated.—*Ant.* HEALTHY, robust, hale.

unheard ***a.*** noiseless, soundless, hushed; see QUIET.

unheard-of ***a.*** unprecedented, unique, new; see UNKNOWN 1.

unhinge ***v.*** **1** [To detach] dislodge, disjoint, disunite; see REMOVE 1. **2** [To upset] unbalance, disorder, derange; see UPSET 1.

unhurried ***a.*** leisurely, deliberate, nonchalant; see SLOW 1.

unhurt ***a.*** uninjured, all right, whole; see SAFE 1.

unidentified ***a.*** unnamed, nameless, not known; see UNKNOWN 1, 2.

unified ***a.*** made one, united, joined, combined, concerted, synthesized, amalgamated, conjoined, incorporated, blended, identified, coalesced, federated, centralized, intertwined, consolidated, associated, cemented, coupled, allied, wedded, married, merged, confederated.—*Ant.* SEPARATED, distinct, disjoined.

uniform ***a.*** **1** [Even] symmetrical, smooth, straight; see REGULAR 3. **2** [Alike] equal, well-matched, similar; see ALIKE.

uniform ***n.*** costume, suit, dress; see CLOTHES.

uniformity ***n.*** **1** [Regularity] sameness, steadiness, evenness; see REGULARITY. **2** [Harmony] unity, accord, concord; see AGREEMENT 1.

uniformly ***a.*** without exception, with great regularity, consistently; see EVENLY 2, REGULARLY.

unify ***v.*** consolidate, ally, conjoin; see UNITE.

unimaginable ***a.*** inconceivable, incomprehensible, incredible, unbelievable, unheard-of, indescribable, unthinkable, improbable; see also IMPOSSIBLE.

unimaginative ***a.*** barren, tedious, usual; see COMMON 1, DULL 4.

unimpeachable ***a.*** blameless, irreproachable, faultless; see INNOCENT 1, 2, UPRIGHT 2.

unimportant ***a.*** trifling, inconsiderable, slight, worthless, inconsequential, insignificant, unnecessary, imma-

un'in·hib'it·ed *adj.* without inhibition; esp., free of the usual social or psychological restraints on one's behavior

un·in'ter·est·ed *adj.* not interested; indifferent

un·ion (yo͞on'yən) *n.* ⟦< L *unus,* one⟧ **1** a uniting or being united; combination **2** a grouping together of nations, etc. for some specific purpose **3** marriage **4** something united **5** *short for* LABOR UNION **6** a design symbolizing political union, used as in a flag **7** a device for joining parts, as of a machine —**the Union 1** the United States **2** the North in the Civil War

un'ion·ize' (-īz') *vt., vi.* **-ized', -iz'ing** to organize into a labor union —**un'ion·i·za'tion** *n.*

union jack 1 a flag, esp. a national flag, consisting only of a UNION (sense 6) **2 [U- J-]** the flag of the United Kingdom

Union of Soviet Socialist Republics former country in E Europe & N Asia: formed as a union of 15 constituent republics, it was disbanded in 1991

u·nique (yo͞o nēk') *adj.* ⟦< L *unus,* one⟧ **1** one and only; sole **2** without like or equal **3** very unusual: a usage still objected to by some

u·ni·sex (yo͞o'nə seks') *adj.* of or involving a fashion, as in haircuts, that is not differentiated for the sexes

u·ni·son (yo͞o'nə sən, -zən) *n.* ⟦< L *unus,* one + *sonus,* a sound⟧ **1** a musical interval consisting of two identical pitches **2** agreement —**in unison** with all the voices or instruments performing the same part

u·nit (yo͞o'nit) *n.* ⟦< UNITY⟧ **1** the smallest whole number; one **2** a standard basic quantity, measure, etc. **3** a single person or group, esp. as a part of a whole **4** a distinct part or object with a specific purpose

U·ni·tar·i·an (yo͞o'nə ter'ē ən) *n.* a member of a religious denomination accepting the moral teachings of Jesus, but holding that God is a single being

u·ni·tar·y (yo͞o'nə ter'ē) *adj.* **1** of a unit or units **2** of or based on unity

u·nite (yo͞o nīt') *vt., vi.* **-nit'ed, -nit'ing** ⟦< L *unus,* one⟧ **1** to put or join together so as to make one; combine **2** to bring or come together in common cause, action, etc.

United Arab E·mir·ates (em'ər əts) country in E Arabia, on the Persian Gulf: 32,300 sq. mi.; pop. 1,622,000

United Arab Republic *former name for* Egypt (1961-71)

United Kingdom country in W Europe, consisting of Great Britain & Northern Ireland: 93,636 sq. mi.; pop. 55,734,000

United Nations an international organization of nations for world peace and security: formed in 1945 and having, in 2001, a membership of 189

United States of America country including 49 states in North America, & Hawaii: 3,787,318 sq. mi.; pop. 248,710,000; cap. Washington, DC: also called **United States**

u·nit·ize (yo͞o'nə tīz') *vt.* **-ized', -iz'ing** to make into a single unit

unit pricing a system of showing prices, as of foods, in terms of standard units

u·ni·ty (yo͞o'nə tē) *n., pl.* **-ties** ⟦< L *unus,* one⟧ **1** a being united; oneness **2** a single, separate thing **3** harmony; agreement **4** a complex that is a union of related parts **5** a harmonious, unified arrangement of parts in an artistic work **6** continuity of purpose, action, etc. **7** *Math.* any quantity, etc. identified as a unit, or 1

univ *abbrev.* university

u·ni·va·lent (yo͞o'nə vā'lənt) *adj. Chem.* **1** having one valence **2** having a valence of one

u·ni·valve (yo͞o'nə valv') *n.* a mollusk with a one-piece shell, as a snail

u·ni·ver·sal (yo͞o'nə vʉr'səl) *adj.* **1** of the universe; present everywhere **2** of, for, or including all or the whole **3** used, or intended to be used, for all kinds, sizes, etc. or by all people —**u'ni·ver·sal'i·ty** (-vər sal'ə tē) *n.*

u'ni·ver'sal·ize' *vt.* **-ized', -iz'ing** to make universal

universal joint (or **coupling**) a joint or coupling that permits a swing of limited angle in any direction, esp. one for transmitting rotary motion from one shaft to another not in line with it

u'ni·ver'sal·ly *adv.* **1** in every instance **2** in every part or place

Universal Product Code a patterned series of vertical bars printed on consumer products: it can be read by computerized scanners for pricing, etc.

u·ni·verse (yo͞o'nə vʉrs') *n.* ⟦< L *unus,* one + *vertere,* to turn⟧ **1** the totality of all things that exist **2** the world

u·ni·ver·si·ty (yo͞o'nə vʉr'sə tē) *n., pl.* **-ties** ⟦see prec.⟧ **1** an educational institution offering bachelor's and

THESAURUS

terial, indifferent, beside the point, frivolous, useless, of no account, worthless, trivial, paltry, superfluous, fleeting, ephemeral.—*Ant.* IMPORTANT, weighty, great.

uninformed *a.* unenlightened, naive, unacquainted; see IGNORANT 1, 2.

unintentional *a.* unthinking, involuntary, erratic; see AIMLESS.

uninterested *a.* apathetic, impassive, detached; see INDIFFERENT.

uninteresting *a.* tedious, boring, tiresome, dreary, wearisome, prosaic, fatiguing, monotonous, dull, stale, trite, commonplace, irksome, stupid, humdrum, prosy, flat, mundane, insipid, unentertaining, soporific, banal.—*Ant.* INTERESTING, exciting, lively.

uninterrupted *a.* unending, continuous, unbroken; see CONSECUTIVE, CONSTANT.

uninvited *a.* unasked, unwanted, not invited; see UNPOPULAR.

union *n.* **1** [The act of joining] unification, junction, meeting, uniting, joining, coupling, embracing, coming together, merging, fusion, mingling, concurrence, symbiosis, amalgamation, confluence, congregation, reconciliation, conciliation, correlation, combination, connection, linking, attachment, coalition, conjunction, consolidation, incorporation, centralization, affiliation, confederation, copulation, coition.—*Ant.* DIVORCE, separation, severance. **2** [A closely knit group] association, federation, society; see ORGANIZATION 2. **3** [A marriage] wedlock, conjugal ties, matrimony, cohabitation, nuptial connection, match, matrimonial affiliation. **4** [A labor union] labor federation, brotherhood, local; see LABOR 4.

Union *n.* [The North in the American Civil War] the Free States, Antislavery States, the Northern States.

unique *a.* single, peerless, matchless, unprecedented, unparalleled, sui generis, novel, individual, sole, unexampled, lone, different, unequaled.—*Ant.* COMMON, frequent, many.

unison *n.* concert, unity, harmony; see UNITY 1.

unit *n.* **1** [A whole] entirety, complement, total, totality, assemblage, assembly, system. **2** [A detail] section, segment, part, fraction, piece, joint, block, square, layer, link, length, digit, member, factor.

unite *v.* join, meet, ally, combine, solidify, harden, strengthen, condense, confederate, couple, affiliate, merge, band together, blend, mix, become one, concentrate, consolidate, entwine, intertwine, grapple, amalgamate, league, band, embody, embrace, copulate, associate, assemble, gather together, conjoin, keep together, tie in, pull together, hang together, join forces, coalesce, fuse, wed, marry, merge, mingle, stick together, stay together.—*Ant.* DIVIDE, separate, part.

united *a.* unified, leagued, combined, affiliated, federal, confederated, integrated, amalgamated, as one, singular, cooperative, consolidated, concerted, congruent, associated, assembled, linked, banded, in partnership; see also ORGANIZED.—*Ant.* SEPARATED, distinct, individual.

United Nations *n.* UN, peace-keeping force, international society, community of nations. *Principal bodies of the United Nations are:* General Assembly, Security Council, Economic and Social Council, Trusteeship Council, International Court of Justice, Secretariat.

unity *n.* **1** [The quality of oneness] homogeneity, homogeneousness, sameness, indivisibility, identity, inseparability, singleness, similarity, uniqueness, integration, universality, all-togetherness, ensemble, uniformity, wholeness; see also WHOLE.—*Ant.* DIFFERENCE, diversity, divorce. **2** [Union] federation, confederation, compact, combination, correspondence, alliance, agreement, concord, identity of purpose, unification, aggregation; see also ORGANIZATION 2. **3** [Harmony] concord, agreement, accord; see HARMONY 1.

universal *a.* **1** [Concerning the universe] cosmic, stellar, celestial, sidereal, astronomical, cosmogonic. **2** [Worldwide] mundane, earthly, terrestrial, sublunary, terrene, human, worldly.—*Ant.* LOCAL, restricted, district. **3** [General] entire, all-embracing, prevalent, customary, usual, whole, sweeping, extensive, comprehensive, total, unlimited, limitless, endless, vast, widespread, catholic, common, regular, undisputed, accepted, unrestricted.—*Ant.* SPECIAL, limited, peculiar.

universally *a.* entirely, prevailingly, comprehensively; see COMPLETELY.

universe *n.* cosmos, creation, the visible world, astral system, universal frame, all created things, everything, nature, the natural world.

university *a.* professional, college, collegiate, advanced, graduate, undergraduate, freshman, sophomore, junior, senior, learned, academic, educa-

advanced degrees **2** the grounds, buildings, etc. of a university
un·just (un just′) ***adj.*** not just or right; unfair —**un·just′ly *adv.***
un·kempt′ (-kempt′) ***adj.*** ⟦UN- + *kempt* < dial. *kemben,* to comb⟧ **1** tangled, disheveled, etc. **2** not tidy; slovenly
un·kind′ ***adj.*** not kind; specif., *a)* not considerate of others *b)* harsh, severe, cruel, etc. —**un·kind′ness *n.***
un·kind′ly ***adj.*** UNKIND —***adv.*** in an unkind way
un·known′ ***adj.*** not known; specif., *a)* unfamiliar (*to*) *b)* not identified, etc. —***n.*** an unknown person or thing
un·law′ful ***adj.*** **1** against the law; illegal **2** immoral —**un·law′ful·ly *adv.*** —**un·law′ful·ness *n.***
un·lead′ed ***adj.*** not containing lead compounds: said of gasoline
un·learn′ ***vt., vi.*** to forget or try to forget (something learned)
un·learn′ed (-lur′nid; *for 2,* -lurnd′) ***adj.*** **1** not having much learning; uneducated **2** not learned or memorized *[unlearned* lessons*]*
un·leash′ ***vt.*** to release from or as from a leash
un·less (un les′) ***conj.*** ⟦< ME *on lesse that,* at less than⟧ except if; except that
un·let′tered ***adj.*** **1** ignorant; uneducated **2** illiterate
un·like′ ***adj.*** not alike; different —***prep.*** **1** not like; different from **2** not characteristic of
un·like′ly ***adj.*** **1** not likely; improbable **2** not likely to succeed —**un·like′li·hood′ *n.***
un·lim′ber ***vt., vi.*** to get ready for use or action
un·lim′it·ed ***adj.*** **1** without limits or restrictions **2** vast; immeasurable
un·load′ ***vt., vi.*** **1** *a)* to remove (a load) *b)* to take a load from **2** *a)* to tell (one's troubles, etc.) without restraint *b)* to relieve of something that troubles **3** to remove the charge from (a gun) **4** to get rid of
un·lock′ ***vt.*** **1** *a)* to open (a lock) *b)* to open the lock of (a door, etc.) **2** to let loose; release **3** to reveal
un·looked′-for′ ***adj.*** not expected
un·loose′ ***vt.*** **-loosed′, -loos′ing** to set loose; loosen, release, etc.: also **un·loos′en**
un·luck′y ***adj.*** **-i·er, -i·est** having or bringing bad luck; unfortunate
un·make′ ***vt.*** **-made′, -mak′ing** **1** to cause to be as before; undo **2** to ruin; destroy **3** to depose from a position or rank
un·man′ ***vt.*** **-manned′, -man′ning** to deprive of manly courage, nerve, etc.
un·man′ly ***adj.*** **-li·er, -li·est** not manly; specif., *a)* cowardly, weak, etc. *b)* effeminate; womanish
un·manned′ ***adj.*** without people aboard and operating by remote control
un·mask′ ***vi., vt.*** **1** to remove a mask or disguise (from) **2** to disclose the true nature or character (of)
un·mean′ing ***adj.*** lacking in meaning or sense
un·men′tion·a·ble ***adj.*** not fit to be mentioned
un·mer′ci·ful ***adj.*** having or showing no mercy; cruel; pitiless
un′mis·tak′a·ble ***adj.*** that cannot be mistaken or misinterpreted; clear —**un′mis·tak′a·bly *adv.***
un·mit′i·gat′ed ***adj.*** **1** not lessened or eased **2** out-and-out; absolute
un·mor′al ***adj.*** AMORAL
un·nat′u·ral ***adj.*** **1** contrary to nature; abnormal **2** artificial **3** very cruel —**un·nat′u·ral·ly *adv.***
un·nec′es·sar′y ***adj.*** not necessary; needless —**un·nec′es·sar′i·ly *adv.***
un·nerve′ ***vt.*** **-nerved′, -nerv′ing** to cause to lose one's self-confidence, courage, etc.

THESAURUS

tional.
university ***n.*** educational institution, institution of higher learning, multiversity, normal school, state university; see also COLLEGE, SCHOOL 1.
unjust ***a.*** wrong, inequitable, wrongful; see UNFAIR.
unjustifiable ***a.*** unallowable, unforgivable, unjust; see WRONG 1.
unjustly ***a.*** unfairly, dishonestly, unrighteously; see WRONGLY.
unkind ***a.*** malignant, spiteful, mean, malicious, cruel, curt, indifferent, uncharitable, ungracious, inconsiderate, boorish; see also RUDE 1, 2.—*Ant.* KIND, benevolent, helpful.
unknown ***a.*** **1** [Not known; *said of information*] uncomprehended, unapprehended, undiscovered, untold, unexplained, uninvestigated, unexplored, unheard-of, unperceived, concealed, hidden, unrevealed.—*Ant.* KNOWN, established, understood. **2** [Not known; *said of people*] alien, unfamiliar, not introduced, unheard-of, obscure, foreign, strange, friendless, private, retired, aloof, anonymous, reclusive, secretive, forgotten. **3** [Not known; *said of terrain*] unexplored, far-off, remote, far, distant, foreign, undiscovered, exotic, transoceanic, transmarine, at the far corners of the earth, faraway, unfrequented, untraveled, desolate, desert, unvisited, legendary, strange.
unlawful ***a.*** forbidden, illicit, outlawed; see ILLEGAL.
unlawfully ***a.*** illegally, unjustly, unjustifiably; see WRONGLY.
unlearned ***a.*** unlettered, rude, boorish, uneducated, ignorant, illiterate, clownish, untutored, untaught, unread, doltish, crass, half-taught, ill-bred, half-educated, uninitiated, unversed, uninstructed, unguided, unenlightened, dull, misguided, empty, unaccomplished, backward, lowbrow*.—*Ant.* LEARNED, educated, adept.
unleash ***v.*** release, unfetter, set free; see FREE.
unless ***prep., conj.*** saving, without the provision that, if not, except, except that, excepting that.
unlike ***a.*** dissimilar, different, incongruous, contradictory, hostile, opposed, inconsistent, heterogeneous, diverse, contrasted, conflicting, contrary, disparate, dissonant, discordant, clashing, separate, opposite, divergent, various, variant.—*Ant.* LIKE, similar, correspondent.
unlikely ***a.*** improbable, unheard-of, incredible, implausible, against the odds, unbelievable, absurd, unconvincing, not likely, scarcely possible, apparently false, contrary to expectation, inconceivable, doubtful, dubious, questionable, extraordinary, marvelous, out of the ordinary, strange.—*Ant.* LIKELY, probable, credible.
unlimited ***a.*** infinite, limitless, boundless, unending, extensive, universal, unrestricted, unconditional, unfathomable, inexhaustible, unconfined, immense, illimitable, measureless, incalculable, interminable, without number, unfathomed, unsounded, untold, countless, numberless, incomprehensible, immeasurable, endless.
unload ***v.*** disburden, discharge, dump, slough, lighten, cast, unpack, relieve, remove cargo, disgorge, empty, deplane, unburden, break bulk.—*Ant.* FILL, load, pack.
unlock ***v.*** unbar, unfasten, open the lock; see OPEN 2.
unloved ***a.*** disliked, detested, despised; see HATED.
unlucky ***a.*** **1** [Unfortunate] luckless, hapless, ill-starred; see UNFORTUNATE. **2** [Unpropitious] ill-chosen, ill-fated, untimely; see UNFAVORABLE.
unmanageable ***a.*** uncontrollable, irrepressible, ungovernable; see UNRULY.
unmarried ***a.*** celibate, unwed, single, virgin, maiden, eligible, chaste, unwedded, spouseless, footloose and fancy-free.—*Ant.* MARRIED, wed, wedded.
unmistakable ***a.*** conspicuous, distinct, evident; see CLEAR 2, OBVIOUS 1.
unmitigated ***a.*** out-and-out, complete, unabridged; see ABSOLUTE 1.
unmoved ***a.*** **1** [Not moved physically] firm, stable, motionless, static, solid, durable, immovable, firm as a rock, staunch, fast, moveless, statuelike, rooted, steady, immobile, unshaken, changeless, unwavering. **2** [Not moved emotionally] impasssive, stoic, quiet, cold, cool, calm, collected, deliberate, resolute, dispassionate, calculating, unaffected, unemotional, indifferent, judicious, unflinching, nerveless, cool as a cucumber.
unnatural ***a.*** **1** [Contrary to nature] monstrous, phenomenal, malformed, unaccountable, abnormal, perverted, abominable, preposterous, marvelous, uncanny, wonderful, strange, incredible, sublime, freakish, unconforming, inhuman, outrageous, unorthodox, miraculous, contrary to known laws.—*Ant.* COMMON, ordinary, usual. **2** [Artificial] synthetic, imitation, manufactured, ersatz, concocted, made-up, fabricated, false, pseudo, mock, spurious, phony*.—*Ant.* NATURAL, occurring, naturally.
unnecessarily ***a.*** needlessly, by chance, carelessly, fortuitously, casually, haphazardly, wantonly, accidentally, unessentially, redundantly, inexpediently, uselessly, exorbitantly, superfluously, undesirably, objectionably, disadvantageously, optionally, avoidably, without cause, without reason, gratuitously; see also FOOLISHLY.—*Ant.* NECESSARILY, indispensably, unavoidably.
unnecessary ***a.*** needless, fortuitous, casual, chance, haphazard, wanton, accidental, unessential, nonessential, beside the point, irrelevant, futile, extraneous, additional, redundant, useless, exorbitant, superfluous, worthless, undesirable, optional, avoidable, objectionable, disadvantageous, random, noncompulsory, dispensable, adventitious, without compulsion, uncalled-for, gratuitous.—*Ant.* NECESSARY, essential, required.
unnoticed ***a.*** unobserved, unseen, unheeded, overlooked, inconspicuous, secret, hidden, passed by, unobtrusive, disregarded, unconsidered, unattended, neglected, unmarked, unre-

un·num'bered *adj.* **1** not counted **2** innumerable **3** having no identifying number
un·or'gan·ized' *adj.* not organized; specif., not belonging to a labor union
un·pack' *vt., vi.* **1** to remove (the contents of a trunk, suitcase, etc.) **2** to take things out of (a trunk, etc.)
un·par'al·leled' *adj.* that has no parallel, equal, or counterpart
un·pleas'ant *adj.* offensive; disagreeable —**un·pleas'ant·ly** *adv.* —**un·pleas'ant·ness** *n.*
un·plumbed' *adj.* not fully understood
un·pop'u·lar *adj.* not liked by the public or by the majority —**un'pop·u·lar'i·ty** (-lar'ə tē) *n.*
un·prac'ticed *adj.* **1** not habitually or repeatedly done, etc. **2** not skilled or experienced
un·prec'e·dent'ed *adj.* having no precedent or parallel; unheard-of
un·prin'ci·pled *adj.* lacking moral principles; unscrupulous
un·print'a·ble *adj.* not fit to be printed, as because of obscenity
un'pro·fes'sion·al *adj.* not professional; esp., violating the ethical code of a given profession
un·qual'i·fied' *adj.* **1** lacking the necessary qualifications **2** not limited; absolute
un·ques'tion·a·ble *adj.* not to be questioned, doubted, or disputed; certain —**un·ques'tion·a·bly** *adv.*
un'quote' *interj.* I end the quotation
un·rav'el *vt.* **-eled** or **-elled**, **-el·ing** or **-el·ling** **1** to separate the threads of (something woven, tangled, etc.) **2** to make clear; solve —*vi.* to become unraveled
un·read' (-red') *adj.* **1** not read, as a book **2** having read little or nothing
un·re'al *adj.* not real or actual; imaginary, fanciful, false, etc.
un·rea'son·a·ble *adj.* **1** not reasonable or rational **2** excessive; immoderate —**un·rea'son·a·bly** *adv.*
un·rea'son·ing *adj.* not reasoning or reasoned; irrational
un're·con·struct'ed *adj.* holding to an earlier, outmoded practice or point of view
un're·gen'er·ate *adj.* stubbornly defiant
un're·lent'ing *adj.* **1** inflexible; relentless **2** without mercy; cruel **3** not relaxing in effort, speed, etc.
un're·mit'ting *adj.* not stopping, relaxing, etc.; incessant; persistent
un're·quit'ed *adj.* not reciprocated
un're·served' *adj.* not reserved; specif., *a*) frank or open in speech *b*) not restricted; unlimited —**un're·serv'ed·ly** *adv.*
un·rest' *n.* restlessness; disquiet; specif., angry discontent verging on revolt
un·ripe' *adj.* not ripe or mature; green
un·ri'valed or **un·ri'valled** *adj.* having no rival, equal, or competitor
un·roll' *vt.* **1** to open (something rolled up) **2** to display —*vi.* to become unrolled
un·ruf'fled *adj.* not ruffled or disturbed; calm; smooth; serene
un·ru'ly (un ro͞o'lē) *adj.* **-i·er**, **-i·est** hard to control, restrain, or keep in order —**un·rul'i·ness** *n.*
un·sad'dle *vt.* **-dled**, **-dling** to take the saddle off (a horse, etc.)

THESAURUS

membered, unscrutinized, unremarked, unrecognized, slurred over, uninspected, winked at, glossed over, lost sight of, ignored, shoved into the background, undistinguished, unexamined, unwatched, unlooked at.—*Ant.* SEEN, watched, noticed.

unoccupied *a.* **1** [Vacant] uninhabited, empty, deserted, unfurnished, void, voided, untenanted.—*Ant.* FULL, inhabited, tenanted. **2** [Idle] loitering, inactive, unemployed; see IDLE.

unofficial *a.* unsanctioned, off-the-record, without legal force; see INFORMAL.

unopposed *a.* unchallenged, unrestricted, unhampered; see FREE 1, 2, 3.

unorganized *a.* chaotic, random, disorganized; see CONFUSED 2.

unorthodox *a.* unconventional, irregular, eccentric; see UNUSUAL 2.

unpack *v.* unload, uncrate, unwrap; see REMOVE 1.

unpaid *a.* **1** [Owed; *said of debts*] due, payable, not discharged, past due, overdue, delinquent, unsettled, unliquidated, undefrayed, outstanding.—*Ant.* PAID, defrayed, discharged. **2** [Working without salary] voluntary, unsalaried, amateur, freewill, donated, contributed.

unpleasant *a.* **1** [Not pleasing in society] disagreeable, obnoxious, boring; see RUDE 2. **2** [Not pleasing to the senses] repulsive, obnoxious, abhorrent; see OFFENSIVE 2.

unpleasantness *n.* disturbance, nuisance, bother; see DIFFICULTY 1, 2, TROUBLE 1.

unpopular *a.* disliked, despised, out of favor, abhorred, loathed, shunned, avoided, ostracized, scorned, detested, unloved, unvalued, uncared-for, obnoxious.—*Ant.* POPULAR, liked, agreeable.

unprecedented *a.* unparalleled, novel, original; see UNIQUE.

unpredictable *a.* random, inconstant, variable; see IRREGULAR 1.

unprepared *a.* unready, unwarned, unwary, unexpectant, surprised, taken aback, unguarded, unnotified, unadvised, unaware, unsuspecting, taken off guard, napping, in the dark, going off half-cocked.

unproductive *a.* unprolific, impotent, barren; see STERILE 1, 2.

unprofitable *a.* losing, loss-making, in the red, not worth the effort, profitless, costly, unlucrative, unremunerative.—*Ant.* PROFITABLE, gainful, productive.

unpromising *a.* discouraging, unfavorable, adverse; see UNLIKELY.

unprotected *a.* defenseless, unarmed, unguarded; see UNSAFE.

unpublished *a.* unprinted, in manuscript, circulated privately; see UNKNOWN 1.

unqualified *a.* **1** [Absolute] downright, utter, outright; see CERTAIN 2. **2** [Incompetent] inexperienced, unprepared, incapable; see UNFIT.

unquestionable *a.* **1** [Certain] sure, obvious, clear; see CERTAIN 2. **2** [Faultless] superior, unexceptionable, flawless; see EXCELLENT.

unquestionably *a.* certainly, without a doubt, surely, indubitably, indisputably, definitely, reliably, absolutely, positively, incontrovertibly, indeed, assuredly, of course, undoubtedly, undeniably, beyond doubt, beyond a shadow of a doubt, beyond dispute.

unravel *v.* unwind, disengage, undo; see FREE.

unreal *a.* visionary, delusive, deceptive, illusory, imagined, hallucinatory, ideal, dreamlike, insubstantial, nonexistent, fanciful, misleading, fictitious, theoretical, hypothetical, fabulous, notional, whimsical, fantastic; see also UNBELIEVABLE.—*Ant.* REAL, substantial, genuine.

unrealistic *a.* unworkable, not practical, nonsensical; see UNRELIABLE.

unreasonable *a.* **1** [Illogical] irrational, biased, fatuous; see ILLOGICAL. **2** [Immoderate] exorbitant, extravagant, inordinate; see EXTREME. **3** [Senseless] foolish, silly, thoughtless; see STUPID.

unreasonably *a.* illogically, irrationally, stupidly; see FOOLISHLY.

unregulated *a.* uncontrollable, unchecked, chaotic; see UNCONTROLLED.

unrelated *a.* independent, unattached, irrelevant; see SEPARATE.

unrelenting *a.* cruel, merciless, pitiless; see RUTHLESS.

unreliable *a.* undependable, unstable, wavering, deceitful, tricky, shifty, furtive, underhanded, untrue, fickle, giddy, untrustworthy, vacillating, fallible, weak, unpredictable; see also DISHONEST.

unrest *n.* **1** [Lack of mental calm] malaise, distress, discomfort, perturbation, agitation, worry, sorrow, anxiety, grief, trouble, annoyance, tension, ennui, disquiet, soul-searching, irritation, harassment, upset, vexation, chagrin, mortification, perplexity, unease, disease, moodiness, disturbance, bother, dither, tizzy*. **2** [Social or political restlessness] disquiet, agitation, turmoil, strife, disturbance, uproar, debate, contention, bickering, change, altercation, crisis, confusion, disputation, contest, controversy, quarrel, sparring, uncertainty, insurrection, suspicion, dissatisfaction.

unrestricted *a.* allowable, not forbidden, free; see OPEN 3.

unripe *a.* green, tart, immature; see RAW 1.

unrivaled *a.* matchless, unequaled, without peer; see UNIQUE, UNUSUAL 1.

unroll *v.* display, uncover, present; see EXPOSE 1.

unruffled *a.* collected, smooth, serene; see CALM 1, 2.

unruly *a.* uncontrollable, willful, headstrong, forward, violent, impulsive, uncurbed, impetuous, ill-advised, rash, reckless, dashing, heedless, perverse, intractable, recalcitrant, self-assertive, refractory, rebellious, wayward, inexorable, restive, impervious, hidebound, unyielding, incorrigible, intemperate, drunken, lawless, vicious, brawling, unlicensed, rowdy, bawdy, quarrelsome, immovable, unwieldy, resolute, inflexible, forceful, dogged, mulish, fanatic, irrational, unreasonable, irrepressible, high-spirited, impudent, abandoned, profligate, stubborn, obstinate, turbulent, disorderly, self-willed, opinionated, bullheaded, ungovernable, stiff-necked, ornery*, mean, skittish, dangerous.

unsafe *a.* hazardous, perilous,

un·said′ *adj.* not expressed
un·sa′vor·y *adj.* **1** unpleasant to taste or smell **2** morally offensive
un·scathed′ (-skāthd′) *adj.* ⟦< *un-* + ON *skathi*, harm⟧ unharmed
un·schooled′ *adj.* not educated or trained, esp. by formal schooling
un·scram′ble *vt.* **-bled, -bling** to cause to be no longer scrambled, mixed up, or unintelligible
un·screw′ *vt.* to detach or loosen by removing screws, or by turning
un·script′ed *adj.* without or not in a prepared script
un·scru′pu·lous *adj.* not restrained by ideas of right and wrong; unprincipled
un·seal′ *vt.* **1** to break the seal of **2** to open
un·sea′son·a·ble *adj.* **1** not usual for the season **2** at the wrong time
un·seat′ *vt.* **1** to dislodge from a seat **2** to remove from office
un·seem′ly *adj.* not seemly; not decent or proper; unbecoming
un·set′tle *vt., vi.* **-tled, -tling** to make or become unstable; disturb or displace
un·set′tled *adj.* **1** not settled; not fixed, orderly, stable, calm, decided, etc. **2** not paid **3** having no settlers
un·sheathe′ (-shēth′) *vt.* **-sheathed′, -sheath′ing** to remove (a sword, etc.) from a sheath
un·sight′ly *adj.* not sightly or pleasant to look at; ugly —**un·sight′li·ness** *n.*
un·skilled′ *adj.* having or requiring no special skill or training
un·skill′ful *adj.* having little or no skill; awkward
un·snap′ *vt.* **-snapped′, -snap′ping** to undo the snaps of, so as to loosen or detach
un·snarl′ *vt.* to untangle
un′so·phis′ti·cat′ed *adj.* not sophisticated; simple, ingenuous, etc.
un·sound′ *adj.* not sound; specif., *a*) not healthy, safe, firm, etc. *b*) not reliable, sensible, etc.
un·spar′ing *adj.* **1** not sparing; lavish **2** not merciful; severe
un·speak′a·ble *adj.* **1** that cannot be spoken **2** so bad, foul, evil, etc. as to defy description or be unfit for discussion *[unspeakable* depravity*]* —**un·speak′a·bly** *adv.*
un·sta′ble *adj.* not stable; specif., *a*) easily upset *b*) changeable *c*) unreliable *d*) emotionally or psychologically unsettled *e*) *Chem.* tending to decompose
un·stead′y *adj.* not steady; specif., *a*) not firm; shaky *b*) changeable; inconstant *c*) erratic in habits, purpose, etc.
un·stop′ *vt.* **-stopped′, -stop′ping** **1** to remove the stopper from **2** to clear (a pipe, etc.) of an obstruction
un·struc′tured *adj.* not formally organized; loose, free, open, etc.
un·strung′ *adj.* **1** nervous or upset **2** with the strings loosened or detached, as a bow or racket
un·stuck′ *adj.* loosened or freed from being stuck
un·stud′ied *adj.* not gotten by study or conscious effort; spontaneous; natural
un′sub·stan′tial *adj.* **1** having no material substance **2** not solid; flimsy **3** unreal; visionary
un·sung′ *adj.* not honored or celebrated, as in song or poetry
unsure
un·tan′gle *vt.* **-gled, -gling** **1** to free from a snarl or tangle **2** to free from confusion; put in order
un·taught′ *adj.* **1** not taught; uneducated **2** acquired without being taught

THESAURUS

risky, threatening, treacherous, fearsome, unreliable, insecure, venturesome, unstable, alarming, precarious, ticklish, giddy, dizzy, slippery, uncertain, unpromising, shaky, explosive.—*Ant.* SAFE, harmless, proof.

unsaid *a.* unspoken, not expressed, unstated; see QUIET.

unsatisfactory *a.* disappointing, below expectation, displeasing, undesirable, regrettable, disconcerting, disquieting, vexing, distressing, upsetting, disturbing, offensive, unacceptable, disagreeable, unwelcome, shocking, deficient; see also POOR 2.—*Ant.* EXCELLENT, satisfactory, gratifying.

unsavory *a.* disagreeable, unpleasant, revolting; see OFFENSIVE 2.

unscientific *a.* irrational, impulsive, inconclusive; see ILLOGICAL.

unscrew *v.* screw out, unfasten, untwist; see LOOSEN 1.

unscrupulous *a.* unprincipled, dishonest, wicked; see DISHONEST.

unseal *v.* free, remove, crack; see OPEN 2.

unseemly *a.* **1** [In bad taste; *said of conduct*] improper, unbecoming, inept; see RUDE 1. **2** [In bad taste; *said of things*] vulgar, tawdry, cheap; see POOR 2.

unseen *a.* imagined, imaginary, hidden, obscure, unobserved, veiled, occult, sensed, unperceived, unnoticed, unsuspected, curtained, unobtrusive, viewless, invisible, sightless, dark, shrouded, impalpable, imperceptible, inconspicuous, undiscovered, impenetrable, dense.

unselfish *a.* disinterested, selfless, charitable; see KIND.

unsettle *v.* disrupt, displace, disarrange; see BOTHER 2, DISTURB.

unsettled *a.* **1** [Undetermined] undecided, unfixed, unresolved; see UNCERTAIN. **2** [Unstable] confused, agitated, troubled, changing, explosive, shifting, precarious, ticklish, unpredictable, uneasy, unbalanced, perilous, complex, complicated, fluid, kinetic, active, busy, critical.—*Ant.* SIMPLE, stable, solid.

unshaken *a.* unmoved, unaffected, undaunted; see FIRM 1.

unsightly *a.* hideous, deformed, homely; see REPULSIVE 1, UGLY 1.

unskilled *a.* untrained, uneducated, amateur; see IGNORANT 2.

unsophisticated *a.* ingenuous, innocent, simple; see INEXPERIENCED, NAIVE.

unsound *a.* **1** [False] ill-founded, erroneous, incongruous; see ILLOGICAL. **2** [Insecure] weak, unreliable, unbacked; see UNSTABLE 2.

unspeakable *a.* horrid, unutterable, abominable, horrible, fearful, inexpressible, unimaginable, dreadful, dire, shocking, appalling, frightful, frightening, alarming, beastly, inhuman, calamitous.

unspeakably *a.* greatly, unbelievably, terribly; see MUCH 1, 2.

unspoiled *a.* unblemished, spotless, faultless; see PERFECT 2, PURE 2.

unspoken *a.* tacit, implicit, inferred; see UNDERSTOOD 1.

unstable *a.* **1** [Having a high center of gravity] unsteady, wavering, unbalanced, giddy, wobbly, wiggly, weaving, shifty, precarious, top-heavy, teetering, shifting, uncertain, rattletrap, beetling, jutting, lightly balanced.—*Ant.* FIRM, steady, solid. **2** [Easily disturbed] variable, changeable, giddy, capricious, fluctuating, shifty, volatile, rootless, dizzy, unpredictable, uncertain, sensitive, oversensitive, thin-skinned, timid, delicate.

unsteady *a.* **1** [Wobbly] wiggly, wavering, shaky, treacherous, unbalanced, top-heavy, leaning, ramshackle, giddy, weaving, heaving, precarious, teetering, uncertain; see also IRREGULAR 1. **2** [Inconstant] changeable, fluctuating, vacillating, variable, uncertain, unfixed, capricious, volatile, unreliable, tricky, shifty, shaky, jerky, fluttering.

unstuck *a.* unfastened, unglued, rattling; see LOOSE 1.

unsuccessful *a.* defeated, disappointed, frustrated, aborted, disastrous, unprosperous, unfortunate, unlucky, futile, failing, fruitless, worthless, sterile, bootless, unavailing, ineffectual, ineffective, immature, useless, foiled, shipwrecked, overwhelmed, overpowered, broken, ruined, destroyed, thwarted, crossed, disconcerted, dashed, circumvented, premature, inoperative, of no effect, balked, left holding the sack*, skunked*, stymied, jinxed*, out of luck, stuck*.—*Ant.* SUCCESSFUL, fortunate, lucky.

unsuitable *a.* inapt, inadequate, improper, malapropos, disagreeable, discordant, incongruous, inharmonious, incompatible, clashing, out of place, jarring, dissonant, discrepant, irrelevant, uncalled-for, dissident, inappropriate, ill-suited, unseemly, conflicting, opposite, contrary, unbecoming, unfitting, unfit, disparate, disturbing, mismatched, disproportionate, divergent, mismated, inapplicable, unassimilable, inconsistent, intrusive, amiss, interfering, disagreeing, inept, unbefitting, inadmissible, absurd, unseasonable, ill-timed, unfortunate, unsympathetic, not in keeping, out of joint, at odds, at variance, repugnant, out of kilter*, cockeyed*.—*Ant.* FIT, suitable, proper.

unsung *a.* slighted, disregarded, unacknowledged; see NEGLECTED.

unsure *a.* unreliable, hesitant, doubtful; see UNCERTAIN.

unsurpassed *a.* unequaled, unexcelled, matchless; see UNIQUE.

unsuspecting *a.* **1** [Gullible] confiding, undoubting, credulous; see TRUSTING. **2** [Naive] innocent, inexperienced, simple; see NAIVE.

unsympathetic *a.* unmoved, apathetic, cold; see INDIFFERENT.

untangle *v.* clear up, put in order, disentangle; see ORDER 3.

untaught *a.* artless, instinctive, innate; see NATURAL 1.

un·think′a·ble ***adj.*** **1** that cannot be imagined; inconceivable **2** so foul, etc. as to be unfit to be considered *[unthinkable* war crimes*]*
un·think′ing ***adj.*** **1** thoughtless; heedless **2** unable to think
un·ti′dy ***adj.*** **-di·er, -di·est** not neat; messy
un·tie′ ***vt.*** **-tied′, -ty′ing** or **-tie′ing** **1** to unfasten (a thing tied or knotted) **2** to free, as from restraint
un·til (un til′) ***prep.*** ⟦ME *untill*⟧ **1** up to the time of *[until* death*]* **2** before *[*not *until* tomorrow*]* —***conj.*** **1** up to the time when or that *[until* you leave*]* **2** to the point, degree, etc. that *[*cook *until* it is done*]* **3** before *[*not *until* I die*]*
un·time′ly ***adj., adv.*** **1** before the proper time; premature(ly) **2** at the wrong time —**un·time′li·ness** ***n.***
un·to (un′to͞o, -too) ***prep.*** ⟦ME⟧ *old poet. var. of:* **1** TO **2** UNTIL
un·told′ ***adj.*** **1** not told or revealed **2** too many to be counted **3** indescribably great *[untold* misery*]*
un·touch′a·ble ***adj.*** that cannot or should not be touched —***n.*** in India, a member of the lowest castes (now called *Scheduled castes*)
un·to·ward (un tō′ərd, -tôrd′) ***adj.*** **1** improper, unseemly, etc. **2** not favorable; adverse
un·trav′eled or **un·trav′elled** ***adj.*** **1** not used or frequented by travelers **2** not having done much traveling
un·truth′ ***n.*** **1** falsity **2** a falsehood; lie —**un·truth′ful** ***adj.***
un·tu′tored ***adj.*** uneducated
un·twist′ ***vt., vi.*** to loosen or separate, as something twisted together; unwind
un·used′ ***adj.*** **1** not in use **2** never used before **3** unaccustomed (*to*)
un·u′su·al ***adj.*** not usual or common; rare —**un·u′su·al·ly** ***adv.***
un·ut′ter·a·ble ***adj.*** inexpressible
un·var′nished ***adj.*** **1** not varnished **2** plain; simple; unadorned
un·veil′ ***vt.*** to reveal as by removing a veil from —***vi.*** to take off one's veil
un·voiced′ ***adj.*** not expressed; not spoken
un·war′y ***adj.*** not wary or cautious
un′wea′ried (-wir′ēd) ***adj.*** ⟦ME *unweried* (see UN- & WEARY)⟧ never wearying; tireless; indefatigable
un·well′ ***adj.*** not well; sick
un·whole′some ***adj.*** **1** harmful to body or mind **2** of unsound health or unhealthy appearance **3** morally harmful —**un·whole′some·ness** ***n.***
un·wield′y ***adj.*** hard to wield, manage, etc., as because of large size
un·will′ing ***adj.*** **1** not willing; reluctant **2** done, said, etc. reluctantly —**un·will′ing·ly** ***adv.***
un·wind′ (-wīnd′) ***vt.*** **-wound′, -wind′ing** **1** to wind off or undo (something wound) **2** to untangle (something involved) —***vi.*** **1** to become unwound **2** to become relaxed
un·wise′ ***adj.*** having or showing a lack of wisdom or sound judgment
un·wit′ting ***adj.*** **1** not knowing; unaware **2** unintentional
un·wont′ed ***adj.*** not common, usual, or habitual
un·wor′thy ***adj.*** **-thi·er, -thi·est** **1** lacking merit or value; worthless **2** not deserving (*of*) **3** not fit or becoming: usually with *of* —**un·wor′thi·ness** ***n.***

THESAURUS

unthinkable ***a.*** inconceivable, unimaginable, improbable; see UNLIKELY.
unthinking ***a.*** heedless, rude, inconsiderate; see CARELESS.
untidy ***a.*** slovenly, unkempt, disorderly; see DIRTY 1.
untie ***v.*** unlace, unknot, loosen, unfasten; see also LOOSEN 1.
untied ***a.*** unfastened, slack, unbound; see FREE 2, 3, LOOSE 1.
until ***prep.*** till, to, between the present and, in anticipation of, prior to, during the time preceding, down to, continuously, before the coming of, in expectation of, as far as; see also UNTO.
untimely ***a.*** unseasonable, awkward, ill-timed, inauspicious, badly timed, too early, abortive, too late, unpromising, ill-chosen, improper, unseemly, inappropriate, wrong, unfit, disagreeable, mistimed, intrusive, badly calculated, inopportune, out-of-date, malapropos, premature, unlucky, unfavorable, unfortunate, inexpedient, anachronistic.—*Ant.* EARLY, timely, seasonable.
untiring ***a.*** inexhaustible, powerful, persevering; see STRONG 1.
unto ***prep.*** to, toward, till, until, contiguous to, against, up to, next to, beside, in the direction of, to the degree of, to the extreme of.
untold ***a.*** uncounted, countless, unnumbered, many, innumerable, beyond measure, inexpressible, incalculable, undreamed of, staggering, unimaginable, multitudinous, manifold, multiple.
untouchable ***a.*** taboo, forbidden, denied; see ILLEGAL.
untouched ***a.*** **1** [Not harmed] intact, whole, secure, unbroken, in good order, unharmed, in good condition, in a good state of preservation, safe and sound, out of danger, shipshape. **2** [Not contaminated] virgin, clear, pure; see CLEAN 1.
untrained ***a.*** green, raw, novice; see INEXPERIENCED.
untried ***a.*** untested, uninitiated, new; see INEXPERIENCED.
untroubled ***a.*** composed, serene, placid; see CALM 1, 2.
untrue ***a.*** false, misleading, specious, lying, hollow, deceptive, delusive, untrustworthy, deceitful, sham, spurious, incorrect, prevaricating, wrong.
untruth ***n.*** falsehood, misrepresentation, evasion; see LIE.
untruthful ***a.*** insincere, crooked, deceitful; see DISHONEST.
untutored ***a.*** unlearned, uneducated, illiterate; see IGNORANT 2.
unused ***a.*** **1** [Not used] fresh, available, usable; see NEW 1. **2** [Surplus] additional, remaining, superfluous; see EXTRA.
unusual ***a.*** **1** [Remarkable] rare, extraordinary, strange, outstanding, great, uncommon, special, distinguished, prominent, important, noteworthy, awe-inspiring, awesome, unique, fine, unheard-of, unexpected, seldom met with, surprising, superior, astonishing, amazing, prodigious, incredible, inconceivable, atypical, conspicuous, exceptional, eminent, significant, memorable, renowned, refreshing, singular, fabulous, unprecedented, unparalleled, unexampled, unaccountable, stupendous, unaccustomed, wonderful, notable, superior, marvelous, striking, overpowering, electrifying, dazing, fantastic, startling, astounding, indescribable, appalling, stupefying, ineffable, out of sight*.—*Ant.* COMMON, familiar, customary. **2** [Different] unique, extreme, uncommon, particular, exaggerated, distinctive, choice, little-known, out of the ordinary, marked, forward, unconventional, radical, exceptional, peculiar, strange, foreign, unnatural, puzzling, perplexing, confounding, disturbing, novel, advanced, startling, shocking, staggering, uncustomary, breaking with tradition, infrequent, mysterious, mystifying, surprising, extraordinary, unparalleled, deep, profound, aberrant, singular, unorthodox, unconformable, not to be expected, eccentric, unbalanced, unprecedented, inconsistent, individual, original, refreshing, newfangled, new, modern, recent, late, fresh, curious, unfamiliar, irregular, odd, unaccountable, alien, queer, quaint, freakish, bizarre, far-fetched, neurotic, exotic, outlandish, old-fashioned, out-of-the-way, abnormal, irrational, monstrous, anomalous, fearful.—*Ant.* COMMON, ordinary, normal.
unusually ***a.*** **1** [Not usually] oddly, curiously, peculiarly; see ESPECIALLY 1. **2** [To a marked degree] extraordinarily, remarkably, surprisingly; see VERY.
unveil ***v.*** uncover, reveal, make known; see EXPOSE 1.
unwanted ***a.*** undesired, rejected, outcast; see HATED, UNPOPULAR.
unwarranted ***a.*** unjust, wrong, groundless; see UNFAIR 1.
unwell ***a.*** ailing, ill, diseased; see SICK.
unwholesome ***a.*** unhealthful, toxic, dangerous; see POISONOUS.
unwieldy ***a.*** awkward, clumsy, cumbersome; see HEAVY 1.
unwilling ***a.*** backward, resistant, reluctant, recalcitrant, unenthusiastic, doubtful, wayward, unready, indisposed, disinclined, averse, opposed, against, contrary, indifferent, indocile, intractable, demurring, shrinking, flinching, hesitating, shy, slack, evasive, loath, shy of, malcontent, slow, remiss, grudging, uncooperative, contrary, against the grain.—*Ant.* READY, willing, eager.
unwillingly ***a.*** grudgingly, resentfully, involuntarily; see ANGRILY.
unwind ***v.*** **1** [To undo] separate, loose, undo; see UNWRAP. **2** [To uncoil] untwist, unravel, untwine; see FREE, LOOSEN 2. **3** [To relax] recline, get rid of one's tensions, calm down; see RELAX.
unwise ***a.*** ill-considered, ill-advised, rash; see STUPID.
unwitting ***a.*** chance, inadvertent, accidental; see AIMLESS.
unworthy ***a.*** undeserving, reprehensible, contemptible; see OFFENSIVE 2.

un·wrap' *vt.* **-wrapped', -wrap'ping** to take off the wrapping of

un·writ'ten *adj.* **1** not in writing **2** operating only through custom or tradition *[an unwritten rule]*

up[1] (up) *adv.* ⟦OE⟧ **1** to, in, or on a higher place or level **2** to a later period **3** to or into a higher condition, amount, etc. **4** *a)* in or into a standing or upright position *b)* out of bed **5** in or into action, view, consideration, etc. **6** aside; away *[lay up wealth]* **7** so as to be even with in time, degree, etc. **8** completely; thoroughly *[eat up the cake]* **9** *Baseball* to one's turn at batting **10** used with verbs: *a)* to form idioms with meanings different from the simple verb *[look up this word]* *b)* as an intensive *[dress up]* —*prep.* up to, toward, along, through, into, or upon —*adj.* **1** directed toward a higher position **2** in a higher place or position **3** advanced in amount, degree, etc. *[rents are up]* **4** in a standing or upright position **5** in an active or excited state **6** at an end; over *[time's up]* **7** available for use, as a computer **8** [Inf.] going on *[what's up]* **9** *Baseball* at bat —*n.* **1** an upward slope **2** an upward movement, etc. —*vi.* **upped, up'ping** [Inf.] to get up; rise —*vt.* [Inf.] **1** to put up, lift up, etc. **2** to cause to rise *[to up prices]* —**on the up and up** [Slang] honest —**up against** [Inf.] confronted with —**up on** (or **in**) [Inf.] well-informed concerning —**ups and downs** good periods and bad periods —**up to 1** doing or scheming **2** capable of (doing, etc.) **3** as many as **4** as far as **5** dependent upon —**up with!** give or restore power, favor, etc. to!

up[2] (up) *adv.* ⟦phonetic respelling of *ap(iece)*⟧ apiece *[a score of ten up]*

up- *combining form* up

up'-and-com'ing *adj.* **1** enterprising, promising, etc. **2** gaining in prominence

up'beat' *n. Music* an unaccented beat, esp. when on the last note of a bar —*adj.* [Inf.] cheerful; optimistic

up·braid (up brād') *vt.* ⟦< OE *up-*, up + *bregdan,* to pull⟧ to rebuke severely; censure; scold

up'bring'ing *n.* the training and education received while growing up

UPC *abbrev.* Universal Product Code

up'chuck' *vi., vt., n.* [Slang] VOMIT

up'com'ing *adj.* coming soon

up'coun'try *adj., adv.* in or toward the interior of a country

up·date (up dāt'; *also, and for n. always,* up'dāt') *vt.* **-dat'ed, -dat'ing** to make up-to-date; make conform to the most recent facts, methods, etc. —*n.* **1** an updating **2** an updated report, etc.

up·end' *vt., vi.* **1** to set, turn, or stand on end **2** to topple

up'front' [Inf.] *adj.* **1** forthright **2** in advance *[upfront money]* —*adv.* in advance Also **up'-front'**

up·grade (up'grād'; *also, and for v. usually,* up grād') *n.* **1** an upward slope **2** an improvement —*adj., adv.* uphill; upward —*vt., vi.* **-grad'ed, -grad'ing** to raise or improve in value, grade, rank, quality, etc.

up·heav·al (up hē'vəl) *n.* **1** a heaving up **2** a sudden, violent change

up'hill' *adv.* **1** toward the top of a hill; upward **2** with difficulty —*adj.* **1** going or sloping up **2** laborious; tiring

up·hold' *vt.* **-held', -hold'ing 1** to hold up **2** to keep from falling; support **3** to confirm; sustain

up·hol·ster (up hōl'stər) *vt.* ⟦ult. < ME *upholder,* tradesman⟧ to fit out (furniture, etc.) with coverings, padding, springs, etc. —**up·hol'ster·er** *n.*

up·hol'ster·y *n., pl.* **-ies 1** the material used in upholstering **2** the work of an upholsterer

up'keep' *n.* **1** maintenance **2** state of repair **3** the cost of maintenance

up'land (-lənd, -land') *n.* land elevated above other land —*adj.* of or situated in upland

up·lift (up lift'; *also, and for n. always,* up'lift') *vt.* **1** to lift up **2** to raise to a higher moral, social, or cultural level —*n.* **1** a lifting up **2** a movement for moral, social, or cultural betterment

up'load' *vt., vi.* to transfer (information) as from a personal computer to a main computer

up'-mark'et *adj.* UPSCALE

up·on (ə pän', ə pôn') *prep.* on, or up and on: used interchangeably with *on* —*adv.* on

up·per (up'ər) *adj.* **1** higher in place **2** higher in rank, etc. **3** farther north —*n.* **1** the part of a shoe above the sole **2** [Slang] any drug that is a stimulant —**on one's uppers** [Inf.] in need

up·per·case (up'ər kās') *n.* capital-letter type used in printing, as distinguished from small letters —*adj.* of or in uppercase

upper class the rich or aristocratic social class —**up'per-class'** *adj.*

up'per·class'man (-mən) *n., pl.* **-men** (-mən) a junior or senior in high school or college

up'per·cut' *n. Boxing* a short, swinging blow directed upward

upper hand the position of advantage or control

up'per·most' *adj.* highest in place, authority, etc. —*adv.* in the highest place, rank, etc.

Upper Vol·ta (väl'tə) *former name for* BURKINA FASO

up·pi·ty (up'ə tē) *adj.* [Inf.] haughty, arrogant, snobbish, etc.: also [Brit. Inf.] **up'pish**

up·raise' *vt.* **-raised', -rais'ing** to raise up; lift

up·rear' *vt.* to lift up —*vi.* to rise up

up·right (up'rīt'; *for adj. and adv., also* up rīt') *adj.* **1** standing, pointing, etc. straight up; erect **2** honest and just —*adv.* in an upright position or direction —*n.* something in an upright position

upright piano a piano with a vertical, rectangular body

up'ris'ing *n.* a revolt

up'riv'er *adv., adj.* in the direction against the current of a river

THESAURUS

unwrap *v.* untie, undo, unpack, take out of wrappings, unroll, disclose, free, uncover, strip, lay bare, divest, dismantle, peel, husk, shuck, flay, expose, lay open, unclothe, denude.—*Ant.* COVER, wrap, pack.

unwritten *a.* **1** [Oral] unrecorded, vocal, word-of-mouth; see SPOKEN. **2** [Traditional] unsaid, customary, unspoken, generally accepted; see also TRADITIONAL, UNDERSTOOD 2.

unzip *v.* unfasten, undo, free; see OPEN 3.

up[1] *a., prep.* **1** [Situated above] at the top of, at the crest of, at the summit of, at the apex of, nearer the top of, nearer the head of, nearer the source of.—*Ant.* DOWN, nearer the bottom of, farther from the head of. **2** [Moving from the earth] upward, uphill, skyward, heavenward, away from the center of gravity, perpendicularly, into the air, higher, away from the earth. **3** [Expired] lapsed, elapsed, run out, terminated, invalid, ended, come to a term, outdated, exhausted, finished, done. **4** [Happening] under consideration, being scrutinized, moot, live, current, pertinent, timely, relevant, pressing, urgent. **5** [Next] after, in order, prospective; see FOLLOWING. —**up to 1** [Until] before, preceding, previous to; see UNTIL. **2** [*Doing] occupied with, engaged in, carrying out, dealing with. **3** [*Dependent upon] assigned to, expected of, delegated to, enjoined upon.

up[1]* *v.* elevate, raise up, boost; see INCREASE.

up-and-coming *a.* industrious, prospering, alert; see ACTIVE.

upbringing *n.* rearing, bringing up, instruction; see CHILDHOOD, TRAINING.

upchuck* *v.* vomit, puke*, toss one's cookies*, barf*, lose one's lunch*.

upcoming *a.* expected, future, imminent; see FORTHCOMING.

update *v.* modernize, bring up to date, refresh; see RENEW 1.

upheaval *n.* outburst, explosion, eruption; see OUTBREAK 1.

upheld *a.* supported, maintained, advanced; see BACKED 2.

uphill *a.* up, toward the summit, toward the crest, skyward, ascending, climbing.—*Ant.* DOWN, downhill, descending.

uphold *v.* **1** [To hold up] brace, buttress, prop; see SUPPORT 1. **2** [To maintain] confirm, sustain, back up; see SUPPORT 2.

upholstery *n.* padding, stuffing, cushioning, pillows, filling.

upkeep *n.* **1** [Maintenance] conservation, subsistence, repair; see CARE 1. **2** [Cost of maintenance] expenses, outlay, expenditure; see PRICE.

upon *a., prep.* **1** [On] on top of, in, attached to, visible on, against, affixed to, above, next to, located at, superimposed on. **2** [At the time of] consequent to, beginning with, at the occurrence of; see SIMULTANEOUS.

upper *a.* top, topmost, uppermost, above, higher, more elevated, loftier, overhead.—*Ant.* UNDER, lower, bottom.

upper-class *a.* well-born, cultivated, genteel; see NOBLE 3.

upper hand *n.* sway, dominion, superiority; see ADVANTAGE.

upright *a.* **1** [Vertical] erect, perpendicular, on end; see STRAIGHT 1. **2** [Honorable] straightforward, honest, fair; see HONEST 1.

uprising *n.* rebellion, upheaval, riot; see REVOLUTION 2.

up·roar (up′rôr′) ***n.*** ⟦Du *oproer,* a stirring up⟧ **1** violent disturbance; tumult **2** loud, confused noise
up·roar·i·ous (up rôr′ē əs) ***adj.*** **1** making an uproar **2** boisterous **3** causing loud laughter
up·root′ ***vt.*** **1** to tear up by the roots **2** to destroy or remove utterly
UPS *service mark for* United Parcel Service
up′scale′ ***adj.*** of or for people who are affluent, stylish, etc.
up·set (up set′; *for n.,* up′set′) ***vt.*** **-set′, -set′ting** **1** *a)* to tip over; overturn *b)* to defeat unexpectedly **2** *a)* to disturb the functioning of *[to upset a schedule]* *b)* to disturb emotionally or physically —***vi.*** to become overturned or upset —***n.*** **1** an upsetting **2** an unexpected victory or defeat **3** a disturbance —***adj.*** **1** tipped over **2** overthrown or defeated **3** disturbed or disordered
up′shot′ ***n.*** ⟦orig., final shot in an archery match⟧ the conclusion; result
up′side′[1] ***prep.*** [Chiefly Dial.] on or against the side of *[struck upside the head]*
up′side′[2] ***n.*** **1** the upper side or part **2** appreciation or gain, as on an investment
upside down **1** with the top side or part underneath or turned over; inverted **2** in disorder —**up′side′-down′** ***adj.***
up·si·lon (o͞op′sə län′, up′-) ***n.*** the twentieth letter of the Greek alphabet (Υ, υ)
up·stage (up′stāj′; *for v.,* up stāj′) ***adv., adj.*** toward or at the rear of a stage —***vt.*** **-staged′, -stag′ing** to draw attention away from another, as by moving upstage
up′stairs′ ***adv.*** **1** up the stairs **2** on or to an upper floor or higher level **3** [Inf.] in the mind —***adj.*** on an upper floor —***n.*** an upper floor
up′stand′ing ***adj.*** **1** erect **2** upright in character; honorable
up′start′ ***n.*** one who has recently come into wealth, power, etc., esp. one who is presumptuous, aggressive, etc. —***adj.*** of or like an upstart
up′state′ ***adj., adv.*** in, to, or from the northerly part of a U.S. state
up′stream′ ***adv., adj.*** in the direction against the current of a stream
up′surge′ ***n.*** a surge upward
up′swing′ ***n.*** a swing, trend, or movement upward
up′take′ ***n.*** a taking up —**quick** (or **slow**) **on the uptake** [Inf.] quick (or slow) to comprehend
up′tight′ ***adj.*** [Slang] very tense, nervous, etc.: also **uptight**
up′-to-date′ ***adj.*** **1** extending to the present time **2** keeping up with what is most recent
up′town′ ***adj., adv.*** in or toward the residential part of a city —***n.*** the uptown section of a city
up·turn′ (-turn′; *for n.,* up′turn′) ***vt., vi.*** to turn up or over —***n.*** an upward turn or trend —**up′turned′** ***adj.***
up′ward ***adv., adj.*** toward a higher place, position, etc.: also **up′wards** ***adv.*** —**upwards** (or **upward**) **of** more than —**up′ward·ly** ***adv.***
upward mobility movement to a higher social and economic status
up′wind′ ***adv., adj.*** in the direction from which the wind is blowing or usually blows
Ur (o͝or, ur) ancient city on the Euphrates River
u·ra·cil (yo͝or′ə sil′) ***n.*** a colorless, crystalline base that is a constituent of RNA
U·ral Mountains (yo͝or′əl) mountain system in Russia, regarded as the boundary between Europe & Asia: also **Urals**
u·ra·ni·um (yo͞o rā′nē əm) ***n.*** ⟦after fol.⟧ a very hard, heavy, silver-colored, radioactive, metallic chemical element: used in work on atomic energy
U·ra·nus (yo͝or′ə nəs, yo͞o rā′nəs) ***n.*** ⟦< Gr *Ouranos,* heaven⟧ the planet seventh in distance from the sun: see PLANET
ur·ban (ur′bən) ***adj.*** ⟦< L *urbs,* city⟧ **1** of, in, or constituting a city **2** characteristic of cities
ur·bane (ur bān′) ***adj.*** ⟦see prec.⟧ polite in a smooth, polished way; refined —**ur·ban′i·ty** (-ban′ə tē) ***n.***
ur·ban·ize (ur′bə nīz′) ***vt.*** **-ized′, -iz′ing** to change from rural to urban —**ur′ban·i·za′tion** ***n.***
urban legend (or **myth**) a widely circulating secondhand report of a purportedly true incident
urban renewal rehabilitation of deteriorated urban areas, as by slum clearance and housing construction
urban sprawl the spread of urban congestion into surrounding areas
ur·chin (ur′chin) ***n.*** ⟦< L *ericius,* hedgehog⟧ a small child; esp., a mischievous boy
-ure (ər) ⟦Fr < L *-ura*⟧ *suffix* **1** act, process, or result *[exposure]* **2** agent of **3** state of being ___ed *[composure]* **4** office, rank, or collective body *[legislature]*
u·re·a (yo͞o rē′ə) ***n.*** ⟦< Gr *ouron,* urine⟧ a soluble, crystalline solid found in urine or made synthetically
u·re·mi·a (yo͞o rē′mē ə) ***n.*** ⟦< Gr *ouron,* urine + *haima,* blood⟧ a toxic condition caused by the presence in the blood of waste products normally eliminated in the urine —**u·re′mic** ***adj.***
u·re·ter (yo͞o rēt′ər) ***n.*** ⟦< Gr *ourein,* urinate⟧ a tube carrying urine from a kidney to the bladder
u·re·thane (yo͝or′ə thān′) ***n.*** ⟦< Fr⟧ a white, crystalline compound used as a hypnotic and sedative, a solvent, etc.
u·re·thra (yo͞o rē′thrə) ***n.,*** *pl.* **-thrae** (-thrē′) or **-thras** ⟦< Gr *ouron,* urine⟧ the duct through which urine is discharged from the bladder: in males, also the duct for semen
urge (urj) ***vt.*** **urged, urg′ing** ⟦L *urgere,* press hard⟧ **1** *a)* to press upon the attention; advocate *b)* to plead with;

THESAURUS

uproar ***n.*** babble, confusion, turmoil, ado, hassle, commotion, clamor, disturbance, tumult, din, racket, clatter, hubbub, fracas, clangor, jangle, bustle, bickering, discord, row.
uproarious ***a.*** noisy, confused, disorderly; see LOUD 2.
uproot ***v.*** deracinate, pull up, weed out; see REMOVE 1.
upset ***a.*** disconcerted, amazed, shocked; see CONFUSED 2.
upset ***n.*** overthrow, destruction, subversion; see DEFEAT.
upset ***v.*** **1** [To turn over] overturn, upturn, subvert, turn bottom-side up, turn inside out, upend, reverse, keel over, overset, topple, tip over, turn topsy-turvy, overbalance, invert, capsize, tilt, pitch over, overthrow.—*Ant.* STAND, erect, elevate. **2** [To disturb] agitate, fluster, perturb; see BOTHER 2. **3** [To beat] conquer, outplay, overpower; see DEFEAT 2, 3.
upside-down ***a.*** topsy-turvy, tangled, bottomside up, inverted, rearend foremost, backward, the wrong way, wrongside uppermost, cart-before-the-horse, head over heels.—*Ant.* STEADY, upright, right side up.
upstairs ***a.*** in the upper story, above, up the steps; see UPPER.
upstairs ***n.*** the upper story, the penthouse, the rooms above the ground floor; see FLOOR 2.
upstanding ***a.*** honorable, upright, straightforward; see HONEST 1.
upswing ***n.*** growth, boom, acceleration; see INCREASE.
uptight* ***a.*** **1** [Troubled] worried, concerned, apprehensive; see TROUBLED. **2** [Cautious] conventional, old-fashioned, strict; see CONSERVATIVE.
up-to-date ***a.*** in vogue, in fashion, fashionable, conventional, stylish, modern, modernistic, streamlined, popular, faddish, brand-new, current, up-to-the-minute, au courant, according to the prevailing taste, modish, the latest, all the rage, hip*, trendy*, in*, with-it*.
upturn ***n.*** upswing, upsurge, recuperation; see IMPROVEMENT 1, RECOVERY 1, 2.
upturned ***a.*** tilted, tipped, upside-down, inclined, sloped, slanted, oblique, expectant, upward-looking, turned up, extended.
upward ***a.*** up, higher, skyward, in the air, uphill, away from the earth, up the slope, on an incline, up north.
urban ***a.*** **1** [Concerning city government] city, municipal, metropolitan; see PUBLIC 2. **2** [Concerning city living] big-city, civic, municipal, metropolitan, within the city limits, inner-city, central-city, downtown, zoned, planned, business-district, civil, nonrural, ghetto, shopping, residential, apartment-dwelling.
urbane ***a.*** suave, smooth, refined; see POLITE, CULTURED.
urge ***v.*** **1** [To present favorably] favor, further, support; see APPROVE. **2** [To induce] charge, beg, plead, adjure, influence, beseech, implore, ask, command, entreat, desire, request, press, inveigle, talk into, incite, spur, move, allure, tempt, attract, influence, prompt, instigate, exhort, advise, solicit, inspire, stimulate, conjure, coax, wheedle, maneuver, draw, put up to*, prevail upon.—*Ant.* RESTRAIN, deter, discourage. **3** [To drive] compel, drive, propel, impel, force, coerce, constrain, press, push, make, oblige, goad, prod, spur.—*Ant.* DENY, block, withhold.
urged ***a.*** **1** [Supported] favored, furthered, proposed; see BACKED 2. **2** [Pressed] begged, charged, implored, asked, commanded, entreated, desired, requested, inveigled, talked into, incited, moved, motivated, allured, lured, tempted, seduced, attracted, influenced, prompted, instigated, exhorted, advised, solicited, inspired, whipped up, stimulated, coaxed, wheedled, maneuvered,

ask earnestly **2** to incite; provoke **3** to drive or force onward —***n.*** **1** an urging **2** an impulse

ur·gent (ʉr′jənt) ***adj.*** ⟦see URGE⟧ **1** calling for haste, immediate action, etc. **2** insistent —**ur′gen·cy**, *pl.* **-cies**, ***n.*** —**ur′gent·ly** ***adv.***

-ur·gy (ʉr′jē) ⟦< Gr *ergon*, work⟧ *combining form* a working with or by means of (something specified) *[chemurgy]*

u·ric (yoor′ik) ***adj.*** of, in, or from urine

u·ri·nal (yoor′ə nəl) ***n.*** **1** a receptacle or fixture for urinating **2** a place for urinating

u·ri·nal·y·sis (yoor′ə nal′ə sis) ***n.***, *pl.* **-ses′** (-sēz′) chemical or microscopic analysis of urine

u·ri·nar·y (yoor′ə ner′ē) ***adj.*** **1** of urine **2** of the organs that secrete and discharge urine

u·ri·nate (yoor′ə nāt′) ***vi.*** **-nat′ed**, **-nat′ing** to discharge urine from the body —**u′ri·na′tion** ***n.***

u·rine (yoor′in) ***n.*** ⟦< L *urina*⟧ the yellowish liquid, containing waste products, secreted by the kidneys and discharged through the urethra

URL ***n.*** ⟦*u(niform) r(esource) l(ocator)*⟧ an address on the World Wide Web

urn (ʉrn) ***n.*** ⟦< L *urna*⟧ **1** *a)* a vase with a pedestal *b)* such a vase used to hold ashes after cremation **2** a metal container with a faucet, for making or serving hot coffee, tea, etc.

u·ro·gen·i·tal (yoor′ō jen′i təl) ***adj.*** of the urinary and genital organs

u·rol·o·gy (yoo räl′ə jē) ***n.*** ⟦< Gr *ouron*, urine + -LOGY⟧ the branch of medicine dealing with the urinary and genital organs and their diseases —**u·rol′o·gist** ***n.***

Ur·sa Major (ʉr′sə) ⟦L, lit., Great Bear⟧ a prominent N constellation

Ursa Minor ⟦L, lit., Little Bear⟧ a N constellation, containing Polaris

ur·sine (ʉr′sīn′, -sin) ***adj.*** ⟦< L *ursus*, a bear⟧ of or like a bear

ur·ti·car·i·a (ʉrt′i ker′ē ə) ***n.*** ⟦< L *urtica*, a nettle⟧ HIVES

U·ru·guay (yoor′ə gwā′, oor′-; -gwī′) country in SE South America: 68,037 sq. mi.; pop. 2,940,000 —**Ur′u·guay′an** ***adj.***, ***n.***

us (us) ***pron.*** ⟦OE⟧ *objective form of* WE

US or **U.S.** United States

USA *abbrev.* **1** United States of America: also **U.S.A.** **2** United States Army

us·a·ble or **use·a·ble** (yo͞o′zə bəl) ***adj.*** that can be used; fit for use —**us′a·bil′i·ty** (-bil′ə tē) or **use′a·bil′i·ty** ***n.***

USAF *abbrev.* United States Air Force

us·age (yo͞o′sij) ***n.*** **1** the act, way, or extent of using; treatment **2** established practice; custom; habit **3** the way in which a word, phrase, etc. is used to express a particular idea

USCG *abbrev.* United States Coast Guard

USDA *abbrev.* United States Department of Agriculture

use (yo͞oz; *for n.*, yo͞os) ***vt.*** **used**, **us′ing** ⟦< L *uti*⟧ **1** to put into action or service **2** to exercise *[use* your judgment*]* **3** to deal with; treat *[*to *use* a friend badly*]* **4** to consume, expend: often with *up* **5** to consume habitually *[*to *use* drugs*]* **6** to exploit (someone) —***n.*** **1** a using or being used **2** the ability to use **3** the right to use **4** the need or opportunity to use **5** a way of using **6** usefulness **7** the purpose for which something is used **8** function —**used to** (yo͞os′tə, -to͞o) **1** did at one time *[*I *used to* live here*]* **2** accustomed to

used (yo͞ozd) ***vt.*** *pt. & pp. of* USE —***adj.*** not new; secondhand

use·ful (yo͞os′fəl) ***adj.*** that can be used; serviceable; helpful —**use′ful·ly** ***adv.*** —**use′ful·ness** ***n.***

use′less (-lis) ***adj.*** **1** having no use **2** to no purpose —**use′less·ly** ***adv.*** —**use′less·ness** ***n.***

us·er (yo͞o′zər) ***n.*** one that uses something; specif., one who uses drugs habitually, a computer, etc.

us′er-friend′ly ***adj.*** easy to use or understand: said esp. of computer hardware, programs, etc.

ush·er (ush′ər) ***n.*** ⟦< L *ostiarius*, doorkeeper⟧ **1** one who shows people to their seats in a theater, church, etc. **2** a bridegroom's attendant —***vt.*** **1** to escort (others) to seats, etc. **2** to be a forerunner of: often with *in*

USMC *abbrev.* United States Marine Corps

USN *abbrev.* United States Navy

USO *abbrev.* United Service Organizations

USP *abbrev.* United States Pharmacopoeia

USPS *abbrev.* United States Postal Service

USS *abbrev.* United States Ship

USSR or **U.S.S.R.** Union of Soviet Socialist Republics

THESAURUS

put up to*, prevailed upon, compelled, obliged, propelled, driven, induced, impelled, coerced, forced, constrained.

urgency ***n.*** import, need, seriousness; see IMPORTANCE, NECESSITY 3.

urgent ***a.*** **1** [Of immediate importance] pressing, critical, necessary, compelling, imperative, important, indispensable, momentous, wanted, required, called for, demanded, salient, chief, paramount, essential, primary, vital, principal, absorbing, all-absorbing, not to be delayed, crucial, instant, leading, capital, overruling, foremost, exigent, crying. **2** [Insistent] compelling, persuasive, imperious, solemn, grave, weighty, impressive, earnest, importunate, clamorous, hasty, breathless, precipitate, frantic, impetuous, imperative, convincing, beseeching, seductive, commanding, imploring, eager, zealous, anxious, enthusiastic, moving, excited, impulsive, vigorous, overpowering, masterful.

urgently ***a.*** **1** [Critically] pressingly, instantly, imperatively, necessarily, indispensably, crucially, requisitely, essentially, primarily, capitally. **2** [Insistently] compellingly, persuasively, solemnly, gravely, weightily, impressively, earnestly, importunately, clamorously, hastily, breathlessly, precipitately, frantically, impetuously, convincingly, beseechingly, seductively, commandingly, imploringly, eagerly, anxiously, zealously, movingly, emotionally, excitedly, impulsively, compulsively, vigorously, irresistibly, overpoweringly, enthusiastically, masterfully.

urinate ***v.*** go to the restroom, go to the bathroom, go to the lavatory, have to go*, excrete, micturate, use the urinal, use the bedpan, make water, tinkle*, wizz*, pee*, take a leak*, piss*.

urn ***n.*** vessel, jar, amphora, pot, container, funerary urn.

usable ***a.*** available, at hand, useful, employable, unused, good, serviceable, applicable, ready, subservient, helpful, valuable, beneficial, profitable, advantageous, fit, desirable, efficacious, instrumental, fitting, conformable, suitable, proper, practical, convenient.—*Ant.* USELESS, worthless, no good.

usage ***n.*** **1** [Custom] practice, rule, habit; see USE 1. **2** [Accepted language] good usage, grammatical usage, approved diction; see GRAMMAR, LANGUAGE.

use ***n.*** **1** [The act of using] practice, employment, application, usage, appliance, effecting, manner, adoption, utilization, manipulation, bringing to bear, management, handling, performance, conduct, recourse, resort, exercise, treatment, method, technique, control, resolution, realization, association.—*Ant.* NEGLECT, disuse, dismissal. **2** [The state of being useful] utility, usefulness, usability, employment, application, value, advantage, excellence, helpfulness, convenience, suitability, expedience, aid, serviceability, merit, profit, practicability, practicality, fitness, subservience, effectiveness, applicability.

use ***v.*** **1** [To make use of] avail oneself of, employ, put to use, exercise, exert, put forth, utilize, apply, bring to bear, practice, play on, do with, draw on, adopt, take advantage of, make do, accept, work, put in practice, relate, make with, put to work, make shift with.—*Ant.* DISCARD, reject, refuse. **2** [To make a practice of; *now used principally in the past tense*] be accustomed to, practice, adapt, conform, habituate, regulate, suit, familiarize, attune. **3** [To behave toward] deal with, handle, bear oneself toward; see MANAGE 1. —**use up** consume, exhaust, squander; see SPEND, WASTE 1, 2.

used ***a.*** **1** [Employed] put to use, utilized, applied, adopted, adapted, accepted, put in service, practiced, turned to account.—*Ant.* DISCARDED, rejected, unused. **2** [Accustomed] practiced, customary, suited; see HABITUAL. **3** [Secondhand] castoff, depreciated, reconditioned; see OLD 2.

useful ***a.*** valuable, beneficial, serviceable; see HELPFUL 1.

usefulness ***n.*** application, value, advantage, excellence, convenience, suitability, usability, range, versatility, helpfulness, utility, serviceability, merit, profitableness, fitness, practicality, practicability, propriety, adaptability; see also USE 2.

useless ***a.*** **1** [Unserviceable] worthless, unusable, ineffectual, expendable, incompetent, of no use, ineffective, inoperate, dysfunctional, counterproductive, inefficient, unprofitable, broken, shot*.—*Ant.* EFFICIENT, usable, operative. **2** [Futile] vain, pointless, fruitless; see HOPELESS.

using ***a.*** employing, utilizing, applying, adopting, running, working, accepting, practicing, manipulating, controlling, putting in service, trying out, testing, proving, wearing out.

u·su·al (yo͞o′zhə wəl) ***adj.*** ⟦see USE⟧ such as is most often seen, used, etc.; common; customary —**u′su·al·ly** ***adv.***

u·surp (yo͞o surp′, -zurp′) ***vt., vi.*** ⟦< L *usus*, a use + *rapere*, to seize⟧ to take (power, a position, etc.) by force —**u·sur·pa·tion** (yo͞o′zər pā′shən, -sər-) ***n.*** —**u·surp′er** ***n.***

u·su·ry (yo͞o′zhə rē) ***n.***, *pl.* **-ries** ⟦see USE⟧ **1** the lending of money at an excessive rate of interest **2** an excessive interest rate —**u′su·rer** ***n.*** —**u·su·ri·ous** (yo͞o zhoor′ē əs) ***adj.***

U·tah (yo͞o′tô′, -tä′) Mountain State of the W U.S.: 82,168 sq. mi.; pop. 1,723,000; cap. Salt Lake City: abbrev. **UT** —**U′tah′an** or (local usage) **U·tahn** (yo͞o′tôn′, -tän′) ***adj., n.***

u·ten·sil (yo͞o ten′səl) ***n.*** ⟦< L *uti*, to use⟧ an implement or container, esp. one for use in a kitchen

u·ter·us (yo͞ot′ə rəs) ***n.***, *pl.* **-ter·i′** (-ī′) ⟦L⟧ a hollow organ of female mammals in which the embryo and fetus are developed; womb —**u′ter·ine** (-rin, -rīn′) ***adj.***

u·til·i·tar·i·an (yo͞o til′ə ter′ē ən) ***adj.*** **1** of or having to do with utility **2** stressing usefulness over beauty or other considerations

u·til′i·tar′i·an·ism′ ***n.*** **1** the doctrine that worth or value is determined solely by utility **2** the doctrine that the purpose of all action should be to bring about the greatest happiness of the greatest number

u·til·i·ty (yo͞o til′ə tē) ***n.***, *pl.* **-ties** ⟦< L *uti*, to use⟧ **1** usefulness **2** something useful, as the service to the public of gas, water, etc. **3** a company providing such a service

utility room a room containing laundry appliances, heating equipment, etc.

u·ti·lize (yo͞ot′'l īz′) ***vt.*** **-lized′**, **-liz′ing** to put to profitable use; make use of —**u′ti·li·za′tion** ***n.***

ut·most (ut′mōst′) ***adj.*** ⟦< OE superl. of *ut*, out⟧ **1** farthest **2** of the greatest degree, amount, etc. —***n.*** the most that is possible

U·to·pi·a (yo͞o tō′pē ə) ***n.*** ⟦< Gr *ou*, not + *topos*, a place⟧ **1** an imaginary island with a perfect political and social system, described in *Utopia* (1516) by Sir Thomas More, Eng. statesman **2** [*often* **u-**] *a*) any idealized place of perfection *b*) any visionary scheme for a perfect society —**U·to′pi·an** or **u·to′pi·an** ***adj., n.***

ut·ter[1] (ut′ər) ***adj.*** ⟦< OE compar. of *ut*, out⟧ **1** complete; total **2** unqualified; absolute; unconditional —**ut′ter·ly** ***adv.***

ut·ter[2] (ut′ər) ***vt.*** ⟦< ME *utter*, outward⟧ to speak or express audibly (sounds, words, etc.)

ut′ter·ance ***n.*** **1** an uttering **2** the power or style of speaking **3** that which is uttered

ut′ter·most′ ***adj., n.*** UTMOST

U′-turn′ ***n.*** **1** a turn by a car made so as to head in the opposite direction **2** a reversal of opinion, strategy, etc.

UV or **uv** *abbrev.* ultraviolet

u·vu·la (yo͞o′vyə lə) ***n.***, *pl.* **-las** or **-lae′** (-lē′) ⟦< L *uva*, grape⟧ the small, fleshy part hanging down from the soft palate above the back of the tongue —**u′vu·lar** ***adj.***

ux·o·ri·ous (uk sôr′ē əs, -zôr′-) ***adj.*** ⟦< L < *uxor*, wife⟧ dotingly fond of or submissive to one's wife

Uz·bek·i·stan (o͝oz bek′i stan′) country in central Asia: formerly a republic of the U.S.S.R.: 172,741 sq. mi.; pop. 19,810,000

U·zi (o͞o′zē) *trademark for* a small submachine gun

THESAURUS

usual ***a.*** **1** [Ordinary] general, frequent, normal; see COMMON 1. **2** [Habitual] prevailing, accustomed, customary; see CONVENTIONAL 1.

usually ***a.*** ordinarily, customarily, habitually; see REGULARLY.

usurp ***v.*** assume, appropriate, expropriate, commandeer, lay hold of; see also SEIZE 2.

utensils ***n.*** [Implements; *especially for the kitchen*] equipment, tools, appliances, conveniences, wares; see also TOOL 1. *Kitchen utensils include the following:* sieve, egg beater, knife, fork, spoon, measuring cup, grater, spatula, skewer, pancake turner, can opener, egg slicer, meat grinder, butcher knife, peeler, paring knife, pastry cutter, squeezer, knife sharpener, coffee grinder, blender, food processor, mixer, vegetable brush, pan scourer, frying pan, saucepan, cake pan, pie pan, roaster, bottle brush, dishpan, draining pan, sink strainer, dishmop, mixing bowl, pan lid, rolling pin, pastry board, coffee pot, bread pan, cookie sheet.

utilities ***n.*** *Public utilities' services include the following:* phone service, cable, electricity, electric power, light and power, nuclear energy, steam generation, cogeneration, natural gas transmission, energy supply, water filtration, wastewater treatment, sewerage, recycling, refuse collection, rubbish removal.

utility ***n.*** [Usefulness] service, advantage, convenience; see USE 2.

utilize ***v.*** employ, appropriate, turn to account; see USE 1.

utmost ***a.*** ultimate, chief, entire, whole, full, unreserved, complete, unstinted, total, absolute, unlimited, unsparing, thorough, exhaustive, highest, maximum, most, top, undiminished, undivided, thoroughgoing, unmitigated, sheer, unqualified, unconditional, all-out.

utopian ***a.*** visionary, idealistic, quixotic; see IMPRACTICAL.

utter[1] ***a.*** complete, total, thorough; see ABSOLUTE 1.

utter[2] ***v.*** pronounce, talk, express, articulate, voice, whisper, mutter, shout, exclaim, enunciate, air, speak, tell, disclose, declare, say, assert, affirm, ejaculate, vocalize, proclaim, give tongue to, recite, blurt out, let fall, announce, come out with.

utterance ***n.*** declaration, saying, assertion, announcement, pronouncement, ejaculation, vociferation, talk, speech, statement, query, expression, sentence, proclamation, recitation, spiel*, rant, response, reply, oration.

uttered ***a.*** asserted, expressed, announced; see ORAL.

utterly ***a.*** entirely, thoroughly, wholly; see COMPLETELY.

V

v[1] or **V** (vē) ***n.***, *pl.* **v's, V's** the 22d letter of the English alphabet
v[2] *abbrev.* **1** ⟦L *vide*⟧ see **2** velocity **3** verb **4** versus **5** volt(s) **6** volume
V[1] (vē) ***n.*** a Roman numeral for 5
V[2] *abbrev.* **1** velocity **2** volt(s) **3** volume
V[3] *Chem. symbol for* vanadium
VA *abbrev.* **1** Veterans Administration **2** Virginia
va·can·cy (vā′kən sē) ***n.***, *pl.* **-cies** **1** a being vacant **2** empty or vacant space **3** an unoccupied position, office, quarters, etc.
va·cant (vā′kənt) ***adj.*** ⟦< L *vacare,* be empty⟧ **1** having nothing in it **2** not held, occupied, etc., as a seat or house **3** free from work; leisure *[vacant* time*]* **4** without thought, interest, etc.
va′cate′ (-kāt′) ***vt.*** **-cat′ed, -cat′ing** **1** to cause (an office, house, etc.) to be vacant **2** *Law* to make void; annul
va·ca·tion (vā kā′shən, və-) ***n.*** ⟦< L *vacatio*⟧ a period of rest from work, study, etc. —***vi.*** to take one's vacation —**va·ca′tion·er** or **va·ca′tion·ist** ***n.***
vac·ci·nate (vak′sə nāt′) ***vt.***, ***vi.*** **-nat′ed, -nat′ing** to inoculate with a vaccine to prevent disease —**vac′ci·na′tion** ***n.***
vac·cine (vak sēn′) ***n.*** ⟦< L *vacca,* cow: from use of cowpox virus in smallpox vaccine⟧ any preparation introduced into the body to produce immunity to a specific disease
vac·il·late (vas′ə lāt′) ***vi.*** **-lat′ed, -lat′ing** ⟦< L *vacillare*⟧ **1** to sway to and fro; waver **2** to fluctuate **3** to show indecision —**vac′il·la′tion** ***n.***
va·cu·i·ty (va kyōō′ə tē) ***n.***, *pl.* **-ties** ⟦< L *vacuus,* empty⟧ **1** emptiness **2** an empty space **3** emptiness of mind **4** something senseless or silly
vac·u·ous (vak′yōō əs) ***adj.*** ⟦L *vacuus*⟧ **1** empty **2** stupid; senseless —**vac′u·ous·ly** ***adv.***
vac·uum (vak′yōōm) ***n.***, *pl.* **-ums** or **-u·a** (-yōō ə) ⟦L⟧ **1** space with nothing at all in it **2** a space from which most of the air or gas has been taken **3** any void —***adj.*** **1** of or used to make a vacuum **2** having or working by a vacuum —***vt.***, ***vi.*** to clean with a vacuum cleaner
vacuum cleaner a machine for cleaning carpets, floors, etc. by suction
vac′uum-packed′ ***adj.*** packed in an airtight container to maintain freshness
vacuum tube an electron tube from which most of the air has been evacuated, containing one or more grids, used as an amplifier, etc.
vag·a·bond (vag′ə bänd′) ***adj.*** ⟦< L *vagari,* wander⟧ **1** wandering **2** living a drifting or irresponsible life; shiftless —***n.*** **1** one who wanders from place to place **2** a wandering beggar **3** an idle or shiftless person —**vag′a·bond′age** ***n.***
va·gar·y (vā′gə rē, və ger′ē) ***n.***, *pl.* **-ies** ⟦see prec.⟧ **1** an odd or eccentric action **2** a whimsical or freakish notion; caprice —**va·gar′i·ous** ***adj.***
va·gi·na (və jī′nə) ***n.***, *pl.* **-nas** or **-nae** (-nē) ⟦L, sheath⟧ in female mammals, the canal from the vulva to the uterus —**vag·i·nal** (vaj′ə nəl) ***adj.***
va·grant (vā′grənt) ***n.*** ⟦prob. < OFr *walcrer,* wander⟧ one who wanders from place to place supporting oneself by begging, etc. —***adj.*** **1** nomadic **2** of or like a vagrant **3** wayward, erratic, etc. —**va′gran·cy,** *pl.* **-cies,** ***n.***
vague (vāg) ***adj.*** **va′guer, va′guest** ⟦< L *vagus,* wandering⟧ **1** indefinite in shape or form **2** not sharp, certain, or precise in thought or expression —**vague′ly** ***adv.*** —**vague′ness** ***n.***
vain (vān) ***adj.*** ⟦< L *vanus,* empty⟧ **1** having no real value; worthless *[vain* pomp*]* **2** without effect; futile *[a vain* endeavor*]* **3** having an excessively high regard for one's self, looks, etc.; conceited —**in vain** **1** fruitlessly **2** profanely
vain′glo′ry (-glôr′ē) ***n.*** ⟦< L *vana gloria,* empty boasting⟧ excessive vanity —**vain′glo′ri·ous** ***adj.***
val *abbrev.* **1** valuation **2** value
val·ance (val′əns, vā′ləns) ***n.*** ⟦ME < ?⟧ a short curtain forming a border, esp. across the top of a window
vale (vāl) ***n.*** [Old Poet.] VALLEY
val·e·dic·to·ri·an (val′ə dik tôr′ē ən) ***n.*** the student, usually the one with the highest grades, who delivers the valedictory at graduation
val′e·dic′to·ry (-tər ē) ***n.***, *pl.* **-ries** ⟦< L *vale,* farewell + *dicere,* to say⟧ a farewell speech, esp. at graduation
va·lence (vā′ləns) ***n.*** ⟦< L *valere,* be strong⟧ *Chem.* the combining capacity of an element or radical as measured by the number of hydrogen or chlorine atoms which one radical or atom of the element will combine with or replace: also **va′len·cy,** *pl.* **-cies**
Va·len·ci·a (və len′shē ə, -shə) seaport in E Spain: pop. 763,000
val·en·tine (val′ən tīn′) ***n.*** **1** a sweetheart chosen or greeted on Saint Valentine's Day **2** a greeting card or gift sent on this day
val·et (va lā′; *also, but now rarely* val′it) ***n.*** ⟦Fr, a groom⟧ **1** a personal manservant who takes care of a man's clothes, helps him dress, etc. **2** an employee, as of a hotel, who cleans or presses clothes, etc.
val·e·tu·di·nar·i·an (val′ə tōō′də ner′ē ən) ***n.*** ⟦< L *valetudo,* state of health, sickness⟧ **1** a person in poor health **2** one who worries about one's health
Val·hal·la (val hal′ə, väl häl′ə) ***n.*** *Norse Myth.* the great hall where Odin feasts the souls of heroes slain in battle
val·iant (val′yənt) ***adj.*** ⟦< L *valere,* be strong⟧ brave; courageous —**val′iance** ***n.*** —**val′iant·ly** ***adv.***
val·id (val′id) ***adj.*** ⟦< L *valere,* be strong⟧ **1** having legal force **2** based on evidence or sound reasoning —**val′id·ly** ***adv.*** —**val′id·ness** ***n.***

THESAURUS

vacancy ***n.*** **1** [A vacated position] opening, vacated post, post without an incumbent, unfilled position, unheld office, job. **2** [A vacated residence] empty apartment, tenantless house, uninhabited house, vacant house, unoccupied house, deserted house, house for rent, house for sale.

vacant ***a.*** **1** [Without contents] devoid, void, unfilled; see EMPTY. **2** [Without an occupant] unoccupied, untenanted, tenantless, uninhabited, idle, free, deserted, abandoned, without a resident, not lived in.—*Ant.* INHABITED, occupied, tenanted.

vacate ***v.*** go away, relinquish, depart; see LEAVE 1.

vacation ***n.*** respite, rest, recreation time, intermission, recess, holiday, leave of absence, sabbatical, time off*.

vaccinate ***v.*** inoculate, immunize, prevent, treat, mitigate, protect, inject, shoot.

vaccinated ***a.*** immunized, inoculated, given injections; see PROTECTED.

vaccination ***n.*** **1** [The act of administering a vaccine] injection, inoculation, shots; see TREATMENT 2. **2** [A result of vaccination] protection, immunization, inoculation; see IMMUNITY 2.

vacuous ***a.*** inane, senseless, empty-headed; see STUPID.

vacuum ***n.*** space, void, hollowness, emptiness.

vacuum cleaner ***n.*** vacuum, carpet sweeper, vacuum sweeper; see APPLIANCE.

vagrant ***a.*** **1** [Having no home] roaming, itinerant, nomadic; see TRAVELING. **2** [Having no occupation] begging, mendicant, profligate, idling, prodigal, loafing, beachcombing, panhandling*, bumming*, mooching*. **3** [Having no fixed course] wayward, capricious, erratic; see AIMLESS.

vagrant ***n.*** beggar, idler, loafer, tramp, bum*, street person, bag lady*, wino*, slacker*.

vague ***a.*** **1** [Not clearly expressed] indefinite, unintelligible, superficial; see OBSCURE 1. **2** [Not clearly understood] uncertain, undetermined, unsure, doubtful, dubious, questionable, misunderstood, enigmatic, puzzling, nebulous, inexplicable, unsettled, bewildering, perplexing, problematic.—*Ant.* CERTAIN, sure, positive. **3** [Not clearly visible] dim, nebulous, dark; see HAZY.

vaguely ***a.*** uncertainly, unclearly, hazily, foggily, confusedly, mistily, shiftily, unreliably, dubiously, eccentrically, unsurely, illegally, evasively, unpredictably, obscurely, indefinitely, without clear outlines, incapable of being determined.

vagueness ***n.*** ambiguity, obscurity, difficulty; see CONFUSION, UNCERTAINTY 1, 2.

vain ***a.*** **1** [Possessing unwarranted self-esteem] proud, haughty, arrogant; see EGOTISTIC. **2** [Useless] worthless, hopeless, profitless; see FUTILE, USELESS 1. —**in vain** futilely, purposelessly, unprofitably; see USELESS.

valentine ***n.*** sentimental letter, St. Valentine's Day greeting, love verse; see LETTER 2.

valet ***n.*** manservant, body servant, attendant, gentleman's gentleman; see also SERVANT.

valiant ***a.*** courageous, unafraid, dauntless; see BRAVE.

valiantly ***a.*** courageously, boldly, fearlessly; see BRAVELY.

valid ***a.*** **1** [Capable of proof] sound, cogent, logical, conclusive, solid, well-grounded, well-founded, tested, accurate, convincing, telling, correct,

val·i·date (val′ə dāt′) ***vt.*** **-dat′ed, -dat′ing 1** to make legally valid **2** to prove to be valid
va·lid·i·ty (və lid′ə tē) ***n.***, *pl.* **-ties** the quality or fact of being valid
va·lise (və lēs′) ***n.*** ⟦Fr < L *valesium* < ?⟧ [Old-fashioned] a piece of hand luggage
Val·i·um (val′ē əm) *trademark for* a tranquilizing drug
Val·kyr·ie (val kir′ē, val′ki rē) ***n.*** *Norse Myth.* any of the maidens of Odin who conduct the souls of heroes slain in battle to Valhalla
val·ley (val′ē) ***n.***, *pl.* **-leys** ⟦< L *vallis*⟧ **1** low land lying between hills or mountains **2** the land drained by a river system **3** any valleylike dip
Valley Forge village in SE Pennsylvania: scene of Washington's winter encampment (1777-78)
val·or (val′ər) ***n.*** ⟦< L *valere,* be strong⟧ courage or bravery: Brit. sp. **val′our** —**val′or·ous *adj.***
Val·pa·rai·so (val′pə rā′zō, -rī′sō) seaport in central Chile: pop. 277,000
val·u·a·ble (val′yə bəl, -yoo͞ ə bəl) ***adj.*** **1** having value, esp. great monetary value **2** highly important, esteemed, etc. —***n.*** an article of value: *usually used in pl.*
val·u·a·tion (val′yoo͞ ā′shən) ***n.*** **1** the determining of the value of anything **2** determined or estimated value
val·ue (val′yoo͞) ***n.*** ⟦< L *valere* be worth⟧ **1** the worth of a thing in money or goods **2** estimated worth **3** purchasing power **4** that quality of a thing which makes it more or less desirable, useful, etc. **5** a thing or quality having intrinsic worth **6** [*pl.*] beliefs or standards **7** relative duration, intensity, etc. —***vt.*** **val′ued, val′u·ing 1** to estimate the value of; appraise **2** to place a certain estimate of worth on [*to value* health above wealth] **3** to think highly of —**val′ue·less *adj.***
val′ue-add′ed tax a tax based and paid on products, etc. at each stage of production or distribution, and included in the cost to the consumer
val′ued *adj.* highly thought of
value judgment an estimate made of the worth, goodness, etc. of a person, action, etc., esp. when such a judgment is not called for or desired
valve (valv) ***n.*** ⟦< L *valva,* leaf of a folding door⟧ **1** *Anat.* a membranous structure which permits body fluids to flow in one direction only, or opens and closes a tube, etc. **2** any device in a pipe, etc. that regulates the flow by means of a flap, lid, etc. **3** *Music* a device, as in the trumpet, that changes the tube length so as to change the pitch **4** *Zoology* one of the parts making up the shell of a mollusk, clam, etc.
va·moose (va moo͞s′) ***vi.***, ***vt.*** **-moosed′, -moos′ing** ⟦< Sp *vamos,* let us go⟧ [Old Slang] to leave quickly
vamp (vamp) ***n.*** ⟦< OFr *avant,* before + *pié,* foot⟧ **1** the part of a boot or shoe covering the instep **2** *Music* a simple, improvised introduction or interlude —***vi.*** *Music* to play a vamp
vam·pire (vam′pīr′) ***n.*** ⟦< Slavic⟧ **1** in folklore, a reanimated corpse that sucks the blood of sleeping persons **2** one who preys ruthlessly on others
vampire bat a tropical American bat that lives on the blood of animals
van[1] (van) ***n.*** *short for* VANGUARD
van[2] (van) ***n.*** ⟦< CARAVAN⟧ a large, closed truck used as for moving, or a small one used for deliveries, fitted out as an RV, etc.
va·na·di·um (və nā′dē əm) ***n.*** ⟦< ON *Vanadis,* goddess of love⟧ a ductile, metallic chemical element used in steel alloys, etc.
Van Al·len radiation belt (van al′ən) ⟦after J. *Van Allen* (1914-), U.S. physicist⟧ a broad belt of radiation encircling the earth at varying levels
Van Bu·ren (van byoor′ən), **Mar·tin** (märt′′n) 1782-1862; 8th president of the U.S. (1837-41)
Van·cou·ver (van koo͞′vər) seaport in SW British Columbia, Canada: pop. 514,000
Van·dal (van′dəl) ***n.*** **1** a member of a Germanic people that sacked Rome (A.D. 455) **2** [**v-**] one who maliciously destroys property
van·dal·ize (van′də līz′) ***vt.*** **-ized′, -iz′ing** to destroy or damage (property) maliciously —**van′dal·ism′ *n.***
Van·dyke (beard) (van dīk′) a closely trimmed, pointed beard
vane (vān) ***n.*** ⟦< OE *fana,* a flag⟧ **1** a free-swinging piece of metal, etc. that shows which way the wind is blowing; weather vane **2** any of the flat pieces set around an axle and rotated about it by moving air, water, etc. or rotated to move the air or water
van Gogh (van gō′, -gôkh′), **Vin·cent** (vin′sənt) 1853-90; Du. painter
van·guard (van′gärd′) ***n.*** ⟦< OFr *avant,* before + *garde,* guard⟧ **1** the part of an army which goes ahead of the main body **2** the leading position or persons in a movement
va·nil·la (və nil′ə) ***n.*** ⟦< Sp *vaina,* pod⟧ **1** a climbing orchid with podlike capsules (**vanilla beans**) **2** a flavoring made from these capsules —***adj.*** **1** of or flavored with vanilla **2** ⟦in allusion to the commonness of *vanilla* ice cream⟧ [Inf.] bland, plain, or basic
van·ish (van′ish) ***vi.*** ⟦see EVANESCENT⟧ **1** to pass suddenly from sight; disappear **2** to cease to exist
van·i·ty (van′ə tē) ***n.***, *pl.* **-ties** ⟦< L *vanus,* vain⟧ **1** anything vain or futile **2** worthlessness; futility **3** a being vain, or too proud of oneself **4** a small table with a mirror for use while putting on cosmetics, etc. **5** a bathroom cabinet containing a washbowl
vanity case a woman's small traveling case for carrying cosmetics, toilet articles, etc.
van·quish (vaŋ′kwish, van′-) ***vt.*** ⟦< L *vincere*⟧ to conquer or defeat
van·tage (van′tij) ***n.*** ⟦see ADVANTAGE⟧ **1** a favorable position **2** a position allowing a clear view, understanding, etc.: also **vantage point**
Va·nua·tu (van′wä too͞′) country on a group of islands in the SW Pacific, west of Fiji: 4,706 sq. mi.; pop. 143,000
vap·id (vap′id) ***adj.*** ⟦L *vapidus*⟧ tasteless; dull —**va·pid·i·ty** (va pid′ə tē) or **vap′id·ness *n.***
va·por (vā′pər) ***n.*** ⟦L⟧ **1** *a*) visible particles of moisture floating in the air, as fog or steam *b*) smoke, fumes, etc.

THESAURUS

determinative, compelling, persuasive, potent, stringent, strong, ultimate, unanswerable, irrefutable.—*Ant.* WRONG, erring, misleading. **2** [Genuine] true, original, factual, real, actual, pure, uncorrupted, authentic, confirmed, authoritative, trustworthy, credible, attested, efficient, legitimate, adequate, substantial, proven, unadulterated.—*Ant.* FALSE, fictitious, counterfeit.

validate *v.* confirm, sanction, legalize; see APPROVE.

validity *n.* soundness, advantage, value; see USEFULNESS.

valley *n.* vale, glen, canyon, depression, trough, notch, channel, lowland, river valley, stream valley, hollow, plain, dell, valley floor, coulee, dale, river bottom; see also GAP, RAVINE.—*Ant.* MOUNTAIN, ridge, hilltop.

valor *n.* bravery, heroism, boldness; see COURAGE.

valuable *a.* salable, marketable, in demand, high-priced, commanding a good price, costly, expensive, dear, priceless, precious, of value, in great demand, hardly obtainable, scarce, without price, good as good*.—*Ant.* CHEAP, unsalable, unmarketable.

valuation *n.* cost, appraisal, judgment; see ESTIMATE.

value *n.* **1** [Monetary value] price, expense, cost, profit, value in exhange, equivalent, rate, amount, market price, charge, face value, assessment, appraisal. **2** [The quality of being desirable] use, benefit, advantage; see sense 3. **3** [Quality] worth, merit, significance, consequence, goodness, condition, state, excellence, distinction, desirability, grade, finish, perfection, eminence, superiority, advantage, power, regard, importance, mark, caliber, repute. **4** [Precise signification] significance, force, sense; see MEANING.

value *v.* **1** [To believe to be valuable] esteem, prize, appreciate; see ADMIRE. **2** [To set a price upon] estimate, reckon, assess, appraise, fix the price of, place a value on, assay, rate, figure, compute, evaluate, judge, repute, consider, enumerate, account, charge, levy, ascertain, price.

valued *a.* evaluated, appraised, charged; see MARKED 2.

valve *n.* flap, lid, plug; see PIPE 1. *Valves include the following:* automatic, alarm, check, cutoff, side, overhead, dry-pipe, gate, lift, piston, rocking, safety, slide, throttle, sleeve, intake, exhaust, butterfly.

vandal *n.* despoiler, looter, hooligan*; see PIRATE.

vandalism *n.* piracy, demolition, wreckage; see DESTRUCTION 1.

vanguard *n.* advance guard, forerunners, precursors, front line, avant-garde.

vanish *v.* fade out, go away, dissolve; see DISAPPEAR.

vanishing *a.* disappearing, going, fading; see HAZY.

vanity *n.* ostentation, display, conceit, show, self-love, narcissism, self-glorification, self-applause, pretension, vainglory, conceitedness, affectation, complacency, smugness.

vanquish *v.* conquer, overcome, subdue; see DEFEAT 2, 3.

vapid *a.* flat, boring, uninteresting; see DULL 3, 4.

vapor *n.* mist, steam, condensation,

2 the gaseous form of any substance normally a liquid or solid Brit. sp. **va'pour**
va'por·ize' (-pə rīz') ***vt.***, ***vi.*** **-ized'**, **-iz'ing** to change into vapor —**va'por·i·za'tion** ***n.*** —**va'por·iz'er** ***n.***
va·por·ous (vā'pər əs) ***adj.*** **1** forming or full of vapor; foggy; misty **2** like vapor
vapor trail CONTRAIL
va·que·ro (vä ker'ō) ***n.***, *pl.* **-ros** ⟦Sp < *vaca,* cow⟧ [Southwest] a man who herds cattle; cowboy
var *abbrev.* **1** variant(s) **2** various
var·i·a·ble (ver'ē ə bəl, var'-) ***adj.*** **1** apt to change or vary; changeable, inconstant, etc. **2** that can be changed or varied —***n.*** anything changeable; a thing that varies —**var'i·a·bil'i·ty** ***n.***
var'i·ance (-əns) ***n.*** **1** a varying or being variant **2** degree of change or difference; discrepancy **3** official permission to bypass regulations —**at variance** not in agreement or accord
var'i·ant (-ənt) ***adj.*** varying; different in some way from others of the same kind —***n.*** anything variant, as a different spelling of the same word
var'i·a'tion (-ā'shən) ***n.*** **1** a varying; change in form, extent, etc. **2** the degree of such change **3** a thing somewhat different from another of the same kind **4** *Music* the repetition of a theme with changes in rhythm, key, etc.
var·i·col·ored (ver'i kul'ərd, var'-) ***adj.*** of several or many colors
var·i·cose (var'ə kōs') ***adj.*** ⟦< L *varix,* enlarged vein⟧ abnormally and irregularly swollen *[varicose* veins*]*
var·ied (ver'ēd, var'-) ***adj.*** **1** of different kinds; various **2** changed; altered
var·i·e·gat·ed (ver'ē ə gāt'id, var'-) ***adj.*** ⟦< L *varius,* various⟧ **1** marked with different colors in spots, streaks, etc. **2** having variety; varied
va·ri·e·tal (və rī'ə təl) ***adj.*** **1** of or being a variety **2** designating a wine named after the kind of grape from which it is made —***n.*** a varietal wine
va·ri'e·ty (-tē) ***n.***, *pl.* **-ties** **1** a being various or varied **2** a different form of some thing, condition, etc.; kind **3** a collection of different things
variety store a retail store selling many small, inexpensive items
var·i·ous (ver'ē əs, var'-) ***adj.*** ⟦L *varius,* diverse⟧ **1** differing one from another; of several kinds **2** several or many —**var'i·ous·ly** ***adv.***
var·let (vär'lit) ***n.*** ⟦OFr, a page⟧ [Archaic] a scoundrel; knave
var·mint or **var·ment** (vär'mənt) ***n.*** ⟦var. of VERMIN⟧ [Inf. or Dial.] a person or animal regarded as objectionable
var·nish (vär'nish) ***n.*** ⟦< ML *veronix,* resin⟧ **1** a preparation of resinous substances dissolved in oil, alcohol, etc., used to give a hard, glossy surface to wood, metal, etc. **2** this surface **3** a surface smoothness, as of manner —***vt.*** **1** to cover with varnish **2** to make superficially attractive
var·si·ty (vär'sə tē) ***n.***, *pl.* **-ties** ⟦< UNIVERSITY⟧ the main team representing a university, school, etc., as in a sport
var·y (ver'ē, var'ē) ***vt.*** **var'ied**, **var'y·ing** ⟦< L *varius,* various⟧ **1** to change; alter **2** to make different from one another **3** to give variety to *[to vary one's reading]* —***vi.*** **1** to undergo change **2** to be different **3** to deviate or depart *(from)*
vas·cu·lar (vas'kyə lər) ***adj.*** ⟦< L *vas,* vessel⟧ of or having vessels or ducts for conveying blood, sap, etc.
vase (vās, vāz) ***n.*** ⟦< L *vas,* vessel⟧ an open container used for decoration, displaying flowers, etc.
vas·ec·to·my (va sek'tə mē) ***n.***, *pl.* **-mies** ⟦< L *vas,* vessel + -ECTOMY⟧ the surgical removal or tying of the duct carrying sperm from the testicle
Vas·e·line (vas'ə lēn') ⟦< Ger *was(ser),* water + Gr *el(aion),* oil⟧ *trademark for* petrolatum —***n.*** [**v-**] petrolatum
vas·o·mo·tor (vas'ō mōt'ər, vā'zō-) ***adj.*** ⟦< L *vas,* vessel + MOTOR⟧ regulating the diameter of blood vessels: said of a nerve, drug, etc.
vas·sal (vas'əl) ***n.*** ⟦< ML *vassus,* servant⟧ **1** under feudalism, one who held land, owing fealty to an overlord **2** a subordinate, servant, slave, etc. —**vas'sal·age** (-ij) ***n.***
vast (vast) ***adj.*** ⟦L *vastus*⟧ very great in size, degree, etc. —**vast'ly** ***adv.*** —**vast'ness** ***n.***
vat (vat) ***n.*** ⟦< OE *fæt,* cask⟧ a large container for holding liquids
VAT (vē'ā'tē', vat) *abbrev.* value-added tax
Vat·i·can (vat'i kən) ***n.*** **1** the papal palace in Vatican City **2** the papal government
Vatican City independent papal state, an enclave in Rome (Italy), including the Vatican: 108 acres or 0.17 sq. mi.; pop. *c.* 1,000
vaude·ville (vôd'vil) ***n.*** ⟦Fr, after *Vau-de-Vire,* a valley in Normandy, famous for convivial songs⟧ a stage show consisting of various acts
vault[1] (vôlt) ***n.*** ⟦< L *volvere,* to roll⟧ **1** an arched roof or ceiling **2** an arched chamber or space **3** a cellar room used for storage **4** a burial chamber **5** a room for the safekeeping of valuables, as in a bank —***vt.*** to cover with, or build as, a vault —***vi.*** to curve like a vault
vault[2] (vôlt) ***vi.***, ***vt.*** ⟦< earlier It *voltare*⟧ to jump over (a barrier), esp. with the hands supported on the barrier or holding a long pole —***n.*** a vaulting —**vault'er** ***n.***
vault'ing ***adj.*** **1** leaping **2** unduly confident *[vaulting* ambition*]* **3** used in vaulting
vaunt (vônt) ***vi.***, ***n.*** ⟦< L *vanus,* vain⟧ boast —**vaunt'ed** ***adj.***
VCR ***n.*** VIDEOCASSETTE RECORDER
VD *abbrev.* venereal disease
VDT ***n.*** a video display terminal
-'ve (v, əv) *suffix* have: used in contractions *[we've* seen it*]*
veal (vēl) ***n.*** ⟦< L *vitulus,* calf⟧ the flesh of a young calf, used as food
vec·tor (vek'tər) ***n.*** ⟦< L *vehere,* to carry⟧ **1** an animal that transmits a disease-producing organism **2** *Math. a)*

THESAURUS

smog, exhalation, breath, fog, gas, haze, smoke.

vaporize ***v.*** diffuse, vanish, dissipate; see EVAPORATE.

vaporous ***a.*** fleeting, wispy, without substance; see IMAGINARY.

variable ***a.*** inconstant, shifting, unsteady; see IRREGULAR 1, 4.

variance ***n.*** change, fluctuation, deviation; see VARIATION 2.

variation ***n.*** **1** [Change] modification, alteration, mutation; see CHANGE 1. **2** [Disparity] inequality, difference, dissimilarity, distinction, disproportion, exception, contrast, irregularity, aberration, abnormality, disparity.—*Ant.* SIMILARITY, conformity, likeness.

varied ***a.*** discrete, different, diverse; see MIXED 1, VARIOUS.

variety ***n.*** **1** [Quality or state of being diverse] diversity, change, diversification, difference, variance, medley, mixture, miscellany, disparateness, divergency, variation, incongruity, fluctuation, departure, shift, change, modification, departure, many-sidedness. **2** [Sort] kind, class, division, species, genus, race, tribe, family, assortment, type, stripe, nature, ilk, character, description, rank, grade, category, classification, quality.—*Ant.* EQUALITY, equalness, similarity.

various ***a.*** different, disparate, dissimilar, diverse, diversified, variegated, varicolored, many-sided, several, manifold, numerous, unlike, many, sundry, variable, changeable, inconstant, uncertain, of any kind, all manner of, of every description, distinct; see also MULTIPLE 1.—*Ant.* ALIKE, undiversified, identical.

variously ***a.*** varyingly, inconsistently, unpredictably; see DIFFERENTLY, UNEVENLY.

varnish ***v.*** finish, paint, shellac, lacquer, wax, size, enamel, japan, surface, coat, luster, polish, gloss, adorn, refinish, glaze, gloss over.—*Ant.* EXPOSE, remove the finish, strip.

vary ***v.*** diverge, differ, deviate, digress, swerve, depart, fluctuate, alternate, diverge from, be distinguished from, range, be inconstant, mutate, be uncertain.—*Ant.* REMAIN, be steady, hold.

varying ***a.*** diverse, differing, diverging; see CHANGING.

vase ***n.*** vessel, urn, jar, pottery, porcelain, receptacle, flower holder, ornament.

vast ***a.*** **1** [Large] huge, enormous, immense; see LARGE 1. **2** [Extensive] broad, far-flung, wide, spacious, expansive, spread-out, ample, far-reaching, widespread, comprehensive, detailed, all-inclusive, astronomical, prolonged, stretched out, expanded.—*Ant.* NARROW, limited, confined.

vastness ***n.*** hugeness, extent, enormity; see EXPANSE, SIZE 2.

vat ***n.*** vessel, tub, barrel; see CONTAINER.

vault[1] ***n.*** **1** [A place for the dead] tomb, crypt, grave; see MONUMENT 1. **2** [A place for preserving valuables] safe-deposit box, safety-deposit box, burglar-proof safe; see SAFE.

vault[2] ***v.*** jump over, hurdle, clear; see JUMP 1.

veal ***n.*** calf, beef, baby beef; see MEAT. *Cuts of veal include the following:* chops, leg, loin, rack, shank, neck, breast, chuck. *Veal dishes include the following:* breaded veal cutlet, veal stew, calf's liver, Wiener schnitzel, veal parmigiana, veal scaloppine.

an expression that denotes magnitude and direction, as velocity *b)* a line segment representing such an expression **3** the compass heading of an aircraft, etc.

Ve·da (vā′də, vē′-) ***n.*** ⟦Sans *veda,* knowledge⟧ any of four ancient sacred books of Hinduism —**Ve′dic** ***adj.***

Veep (vēp) ***n.*** [*sometimes* **v-**] [Inf.] a vice-president

veer (vir) ***vi., vt.*** ⟦< Fr *virer,* turn around⟧ to change in direction; shift; turn —***n.*** a change of direction

veg·e·ta·ble (vej′tə bəl, vej′ə tə-) ***adj.*** ⟦see VEGETATE⟧ **1** of plants in general **2** of, from, or like edible vegetables —***n.*** **1** any plant, as distinguished from animal or inorganic matter **2** a plant eaten whole or in part, raw or cooked **3** a person thought of as like a vegetable, as a person in a coma

veg·e·tar·i·an (vej′ə ter′ē ən) ***n.*** one who eats no meat —***adj.*** **1** of vegetarians **2** consisting only of vegetables

veg·e·tate (vej′ə tāt′) ***vi.*** **-tat′ed, -tat′ing** ⟦< L *vegere,* quicken⟧ **1** to grow as plants **2** to lead a dull, inactive life —**veg′e·ta′tive** ***adj.***

veg′e·ta′tion (-tā′shən) ***n.*** **1** a vegetating **2** plant life in general

veg·gie (vej′ē) [Slang] ***n.*** **1** a vegetable **2** a vegetarian —***adj.*** vegetarian Also **veg′ie**

ve·he·ment (vē′ə mənt) ***adj.*** ⟦< L *vehere,* carry⟧ **1** violent; impetuous **2** full of intense or strong passion —**ve′he·mence** or **ve′he·men·cy** ***n.*** —**ve′he·ment·ly** ***adv.***

ve·hi·cle (vē′ə kəl) ***n.*** ⟦< L *vehere,* to carry⟧ **1** any device for carrying or conveying persons or objects **2** a means of expressing thoughts, etc. —**ve·hic′u·lar** (-hik′yoo lər) ***adj.***

veil (vāl) ***n.*** ⟦< L *velum,* cloth⟧ **1** a piece of light fabric, as of net, worn, esp. by women, over the face or head **2** anything used to conceal, cover, separate, etc. *[a veil of silence]* **3** a part of a nun's headdress —***vt.*** **1** to cover with a veil **2** to hide or disguise —**take the veil** to become a nun

veiled (vāld) ***adj.*** **1** wearing a veil **2** concealed, hidden, etc. **3** not openly expressed

vein (vān) ***n.*** ⟦< L *vena*⟧ **1** any blood vessel carrying blood to the heart **2** any of the ribs of an insect's wing or of a leaf blade **3** a body of minerals occupying a fissure in rock **4** a lode **5** a streak of a different color, etc., as in marble **6** a distinctive quality in one's character, speech, etc. **7** a mood —***vt.*** to mark as with veins

Vel·cro (vel′krō) *trademark for* a nylon material for fastenings, made up of matching strips with tiny hooks and adhesive pile, that can be easily pressed together or pulled apart —***n.*** [*occas.* **v-**] this material

veld or **veldt** (velt) ***n.*** ⟦Afrik < MDu *veld,* field⟧ in S & E Africa, open, grassy country, with few bushes or trees

vel·lum (vel′əm) ***n.*** ⟦< L *vitulus,* calf⟧ **1** a fine parchment prepared from calfskin, lambskin, etc. used for writing on or for binding books **2** a strong paper made to resemble this

ve·loc·i·ty (və läs′ə tē) ***n., pl.*** **-ties** ⟦< L *velox,* swift⟧ **1** quickness of motion; swiftness **2** rate of change of position, in relation to time; speed

ve·lour or **ve·lours** (və loor′) ***n., pl.*** **-lours′** (-loorz′, -loor′) ⟦Fr < L *villus,* shaggy hair⟧ a fabric with a soft nap like velvet

ve·lum (vē′ləm) ***n., pl.*** **-la** (-lə) ⟦L, a veil⟧ SOFT PALATE

vel·vet (vel′vət) ***n.*** ⟦< L *villus,* shaggy hair⟧ **1** a rich fabric of silk, rayon, etc. with a soft, thick pile **2** anything like velvet in texture —***adj.*** **1** made of velvet **2** like velvet —**vel′vet·y** ***adj.***

vel′vet·een′ (-və tēn′) ***n.*** a cotton cloth with a short, thick pile like velvet

ve·nal (vē′nəl) ***adj.*** ⟦L *venalis,* for sale⟧ open to, or characterized by, bribery or corruption —**ve·nal·i·ty** (vi nal′ə tē) ***n.***

vend (vend) ***vt., vi.*** ⟦< L *venum dare,* offer for sale⟧ to sell (goods) —**ven′dor** or **vend′er** ***n.***

ven·det·ta (ven det′ə) ***n.*** ⟦It < L *vindicta,* vengeance⟧ a bitter feud, as between families

vending machine a coin-operated machine for selling small articles, refreshments, etc.

ve·neer (və nir′) ***vt.*** ⟦< Fr *fournir,* furnish⟧ to cover with a thin layer of more costly material; esp., to cover (wood) with wood of finer quality —***n.*** **1** a thin surface layer, as of fine wood, laid over a base of common material **2** superficial appearance *[a veneer of culture]*

ven·er·a·ble (ven′ər ə bəl) ***adj.*** worthy of respect because of age, dignity, etc. —**ven′er·a·bil′i·ty** ***n.***

ven·er·ate (ven′ər āt′) ***vt.*** **-at′ed, -at′ing** ⟦< L *venerari,* to worship⟧ to look upon with feelings of deep respect; revere —**ven′er·a′tion** ***n.***

ve·ne·re·al (və nir′ē əl) ***adj.*** ⟦< L *venus,* love⟧ **1** of sexual intercourse **2** transmitted by sexual intercourse *[venereal disease]*

Ve·ne·tian (və nē′shən) ***adj.*** of Venice or its people or culture —***n.*** a person born or living in Venice

Venetian blind [*also* **v- b-**] a window blind of thin, horizontal slats that can be set at any angle

Ven·e·zue·la (ven′ə zwā′lə) country in N South America: 352,143 sq. mi.; pop. 19,405,000 —**Ven′e·zue′lan** ***adj., n.***

venge·ance (ven′jəns) ***n.*** ⟦< L *vindicare,* avenge⟧ the return of an injury for an injury, as in retribution; revenge —**with a vengeance** **1** with great force or fury **2** excessively

venge·ful (venj′fəl) ***adj.*** seeking vengeance; vindictive —**venge′ful·ly** ***adv.***

ve·nial (vēn′yəl, vē′nē əl) ***adj.*** ⟦< L *venia,* a grace⟧ that may be forgiven; pardonable *[a venial sin]*

Ven·ice (ven′is) seaport in N Italy built on more than 100 small islands: pop. 306,000

ve·ni·re·man (və nī′rē mən) ***n., pl.*** **-men** (-mən) ⟦< ML *venire facias,* cause to come⟧ one of a group of people from among whom a jury will be selected

ven·i·son (ven′i sən, -zən) ***n.*** ⟦< L *venari,* to hunt⟧ the flesh of a deer, used as food

ven·om (ven′əm) ***n.*** ⟦< L *venenum,* a poison⟧ **1** the poison secreted by some snakes, spiders, etc. **2** malice

ven′om·ous ***adj.*** **1** full of venom; poisonous **2** spiteful; malicious

ve·nous (vē′nəs) ***adj.*** ⟦L *venosus*⟧ **1** of veins **2** designating blood carried in veins

vent[1] (vent) ***n.*** ⟦< L *ventus,* wind⟧ **1** expression; release *[giving vent to emotion]* **2** a small opening to permit

THESAURUS

veer ***v.*** swerve, bend, deviate; see TURN 1, 2, 3.

vegetable ***a.*** plantlike, herblike, floral, blooming, blossoming, growing, flourishing.

vegetable ***n.*** plant, herbaceous plant, herb, legume, edible root. *Common vegetables include the following:* cabbage, potato, turnip, bean, carrot, pea, celery, lettuce, parsnip, spinach, squash, zucchini, tomato, pumpkin, asparagus, onion, corn, lentil, leek, chicory, kale, garlic, radish, cucumber, artichoke, eggplant, beet, scallion, pepper, okra, kohlrabi, parsley, chard, rhubarb, cauliflower, Brussels sprout, broccoli, endive, Chinese cabbage, watercress, rutabaga.

vegetate ***v.*** **1** [To germinate] bud, sprout, blossom; see BLOOM, GROW 1. **2** [To stagnate] hibernate, stagnate, languish; see WEAKEN 1.

vegetation ***n.*** plants, plant growth, trees, shrubs, saplings, flowers, wildflowers, grasses, herbage, herbs, pasturage, weeds, vegetables, crops.

vehicle ***n.*** *Vehicles include the following:* carriage, buggy, wagon, sleigh, cart, motor car, jeep, bus, automobile, truck, van, motorcycle, taxicab, railroad car, cab, taxi, SUV, limousine, limo*.

veil ***n.*** **1** [A thin fabric] scarf, kerchief, mask; see WEB. **2** [A curtain] screen, cover, shade; see CURTAIN.

vein ***n.*** **1** [A fissure] cleft, aperture, opening, channel, cavity, crack, cranny, rift, chink, break, breach, slit, crevice, flaw, rupture, bed, seam. **2** [A persistent quality] strain, humor, mood, temper, tang, spice, dash; see also CHARACTERISTIC, TEMPERAMENT. **3** [A blood duct leading to the heart] *Important veins include the following:* jugular, pulmonary, subclavian, portal, iliac, hepatic, renal, axillary, femoral, saphenous; vena cava.

velocity ***n.*** quickness, rapidity, swiftness; see SPEED.

velvet ***a.*** silken, shining, plushy; see SOFT 2.

velvet ***n.*** cotton velvet, rayon, corduroy; see GOODS.

venal ***a.*** mercenary, on the take*, dishonest; see CORRUPT, GREEDY.

veneer ***n.*** surface, exterior, covering; see COVER 1.

venerable ***a.*** revered, old, aged, ancient, hoary, reverenced, honored, honorable, noble, august, grand, esteemed, respected, dignified, imposing, grave, serious, sage, wise, philosophical, experienced.—*Ant.* INEXPERIENCED, callow, raw.

venerate ***v.*** revere, reverence, adore; see LOVE 1, WORSHIP.

veneration ***n.*** respect, adoration, awe; see REVERENCE, WORSHIP 1.

vengeance ***n.*** retribution, return, retaliation; see REVENGE 1.

vengeful ***a.*** spiteful, revengeful, rancorous; see CRUEL.

venom ***n.*** poison, virus, toxin, bane, microbe, contagion, infection.

vent[1] ***n.*** ventilator, vent hole, venting hole, smoke hole, flue, aperture, chimney.

vent[1] ***v.*** let out, drive out, discharge; see FREE.

passage or escape, as of a gas —*vt.* **1** to make a vent in or for **2** to express; let out

vent[2] (vent) *n.* ⟦< L *findere,* to split⟧ a vertical slit in a garment

ven·ti·late (vent′'l āt′) *vt.* **-lat′ed, -lat′ing** ⟦< L *ventus,* wind⟧ **1** to circulate fresh air in (a room, etc.) **2** to provide with an opening for the escape of air, gas, etc. —**ven′ti·la′tion** *n.*

ven′ti·la′tor *n.* an opening or a device used to bring in fresh air and drive out foul air

ven·tral (ven′trəl) *adj.* ⟦< L *venter,* belly⟧ of, near, or on the belly

ven·tri·cle (ven′tri kəl) *n.* ⟦see prec.⟧ either of the two lower chambers of the heart —**ven·tric′u·lar** (-trik′yə lər) *adj.*

ven·tril·o·quism (ven tril′ə kwiz′əm) *n.* ⟦< L *venter,* belly + *loqui,* speak⟧ the art of speaking so that the voice seems to come from a source other than the speaker —**ven·tril′o·quist** *n.*

ven·ture (ven′chər) *n.* ⟦see ADVENTURE⟧ **1** a risky undertaking, as in business **2** something on which a risk is taken —*vt.* **-tured, -tur·ing** **1** to expose to danger or chance of loss **2** to express at the risk of criticism *[to venture an opinion]* —*vi.* to do or go at some risk

ven′ture·some (-səm) *adj.* **1** inclined to venture; daring **2** risky; hazardous Also **ven′tur·ous** (-əs)

ven·ue (ven′yo͞o′) *n.* ⟦< L *venire,* come⟧ **1** *Law a)* the locality in which a cause of action or a crime occurs *b)* the locality in which a jury is drawn and a case is tried **2** the scene of a large gathering for some event

Ve·nus (vē′nəs) *n.* **1** the Roman goddess of love and beauty **2** the brightest planet in the solar system: see PLANET

Venus' fly·trap (flī′trap′) a swamp plant with hinged leaves that snap shut, trapping insects

Ve·nu·si·an (vi no͞o′shən) *adj.* of the planet Venus —*n.* an imaginary inhabitant of Venus

ve·ra·cious (və rā′shəs) *adj.* ⟦< L *verus,* true⟧ **1** habitually truthful; honest **2** true; accurate

ve·rac·i·ty (və ras′ə tē) *n.* **1** honesty **2** accuracy **3** truth

Ver·a·cruz (ver′ə kro͞oz′) state of Mexico, on the E coast: 28,114 sq. mi; pop. 6,228,000

ve·ran·da or **ve·ran·dah** (və ran′də) *n.* ⟦< Port *varanda,* balcony⟧ an open porch or portico, usually roofed, along the outside of a building

verb (vurb) *n.* ⟦L *verbum,* a word⟧ a word expressing action, existence, or occurrence

ver·bal (vur′bəl) *adj.* **1** of, in, or by means of words **2** in speech; oral **3** of, like, or derived from a verb —**ver′bal·ly** *adv.*

ver′bal·ize′ *vi.* **-ized′, -iz′ing** to use words for communication —*vt.* to express in words —**ver′ba·li·za′tion** *n.*

verbal noun *Gram.* a noun derived from a verb (Ex.: *swimming* is fun)

ver·ba·tim (vər bāt′əm) *adv., adj.* ⟦< L *verbum,* a word⟧ word for word

ver·be·na (vər bē′nə) *n.* ⟦L, foliage⟧ an ornamental plant with spikes or clusters of showy red, white, or purplish flowers

ver·bi·age (vur′bē ij′) *n.* ⟦Fr < L *verbum,* a word⟧ an excess of words; wordiness

ver·bose (vər bōs′) *adj.* ⟦< L *verbum,* a word⟧ using too many words; wordy —**ver·bos′i·ty** (-bäs′ə tē) *n.*

ver·dant (vur′dənt) *adj.* ⟦prob. VERD(URE) + -ANT⟧ **1** green **2** covered with green vegetation

Ver·di (ver′dē), **Giu·sep·pe** (jo͞o zep′pe) 1813-1901; It. operatic composer

ver·dict (vur′dikt) *n.* ⟦< L *vere,* truly + *dictum,* a thing said⟧ **1** the formal finding of a judge or jury **2** any decision or judgment

ver·di·gris (vur′di grēs′, -gris) *n.* ⟦< OFr *vert de Grece,* lit., green of Greece⟧ a greenish coating that forms on brass, bronze, or copper

ver·dure (vur′jər) *n.* ⟦< OFr *verd,* green⟧ **1** the fresh-green color of growing things **2** green vegetation

verge[1] (vurj) *n.* ⟦< L *virga,* rod⟧ the edge, brink, or margin (*of* something) —*vi.* **verged, verg′ing** to be on the verge: usually with *on* or *upon*

verge[2] (vurj) *vi.* **verged, verg′ing** ⟦L *vergere,* to bend, turn⟧ **1** to tend or incline (*to* or *toward*) **2** to change or pass gradually (*into*)

verg·er (vur′jər) *n.* ⟦ME, ult. < L *virga,* rod⟧ a church caretaker or usher

Ver·gil (vur′jəl) *alt. sp. of* VIRGIL

ver·i·fy (ver′ə fī′) *vt.* **-fied′, -fy′ing** ⟦< L *verus,* true + *-ficare,* -FY⟧ **1** to prove to be true by demonstration, evidence, etc.; confirm **2** to test the accuracy of —**ver′i·fi′a·ble** *adj.* —**ver′i·fi·ca′tion** *n.*

ver·i·ly (ver′ə lē) *adv.* [Archaic] truly

ver·i·si·mil·i·tude (ver′ə si mil′ə to͞od′) *n.* ⟦< L *verus,* true + *similis,* like⟧ the appearance of being true or real

ver·i·ta·ble (ver′i tə bəl) *adj.* ⟦see fol.⟧ true; actual

ver·i·ty (ver′ə tē) *n.* ⟦< L *verus,* true⟧ **1** truth; reality **2** *pl.* **-ties** a principle, belief, etc. taken to be fundamentally true; a truth

ver·mi·cel·li (vur′mə sel′ē, -chel′ē) *n.* ⟦It < L *vermis,* a worm⟧ pasta like thin spaghetti

ver·mic·u·lite (vər mik′yə līt′) *n.* ⟦< L *vermis,* a worm⟧ a hydrous silicate mineral that expands when heated, used as in insulation

ver·mi·form (vur′mə fôrm′) *adj.* ⟦< L *vermis,* a worm + -FORM⟧ shaped like a worm

vermiform appendix the appendix extending from the cecum of the large intestine

ver·mil·ion (vər mil′yən) *n.* ⟦< L *vermis,* a worm⟧ **1** a bright-red pigment **2** a bright red or scarlet

ver·min (vur′mən) *n., pl.* **-min** ⟦< L *vermis,* a worm⟧ **1** [*pl.*] various destructive insects or small animals regarded as pests, as rats **2** a vile person

Ver·mont (vər mänt′) New England state of the U.S.: 9,249 sq. mi.; pop. 563,000; cap. Montpelier: abbrev. *VT* —**Ver·mont′er** *n.*

ver·mouth (vər mo͞oth′) *n.* ⟦< Ger *wermut,* wormwood⟧ a white fortified wine flavored with herbs, used in cocktails and as an aperitif

ver·nac·u·lar (vər nak′yə lər) *adj.* ⟦< L *vernaculus,* indigenous⟧ **1** of, in, or using the native language of a place **2** native to a country —*n.* **1** the native language or dialect of a country or place **2** the common, everyday language of a people **3** the jargon of a profession or trade

ver·nal (vur′nəl) *adj.* ⟦< L *ver,* spring⟧ **1** of or in the spring **2** springlike **3** youthful

ver·ni·er (vur′nē ər) *n.* ⟦after P. *Vernier,* 17th-c. Fr mathematician⟧ a short graduated scale sliding along a longer graduated instrument to indicate parts of divisions: also **vernier scale**

Ver·sailles (vər sī′) city in NC France, near Paris: site of a palace built by Louis XIV: pop. 88,000

ver·sa·tile (vur′sə təl) *adj.* ⟦< L *vertere,* to turn⟧ competent in many things —**ver′sa·til′i·ty** (-til′ə tē) *n.*

verse (vurs) *n.* ⟦< L *vertere,* to turn⟧ **1** a single line of poetry **2** poetry **3** a particular form of poetry **4** a poem

THESAURUS

ventilate *v.* freshen, let in fresh air, circulate fresh air, vent, air cool, air out, free, oxygenate; see also AIR.

ventilated *a.* aired out, having adequate ventilation, not closed up; see AIRED 1, COOL 1, OPEN 1.

ventilation *n.* airing, purifying, oxygenating, freshening, opening windows, changing air, circulating air, air conditioning.

venture *n.* adventure, risk, hazard, peril, stake, chance, speculation, dare, experiment, trial, attempt, test, essay, gamble, undertaking, enterprise, investment, leap in the dark, plunge*, flyer*, crack*, fling*.

venture *v.* attempt, hazard, try out; see TRY 1.

ventured *a.* risked, chanced, dared; see DONE 1.

verb *n. Verbs include the following:* finite, active, passive, transitive, intransitive, modal, auxiliary, linking, copulative, reflexive, strong, weak, regular, irregular, helping, phrasal.

verbal *a.* told, linguistic, lingual; see ORAL, SPOKEN.

verbally *a.* orally, by word of mouth, person-to-person; see SPOKEN.

verbatim *a.* exactly, word for word, to the letter; see LITERALLY.

verdict *n.* judgment, finding, ruling, decision, answer, opinion, sentence, determination, decree, conclusion, deduction, adjudication, arbitrament.

verge[1] *n.* edge, brink, border; see BOUNDARY.

verge[1] *v.* border, edge, touch; see APPROACH 2.

verification *n.* verifying, attestation, affirmation; see CONFIRMATION.

verify *v.* establish, substantiate, authenticate, prove, check, document, test, validate, settle, corroborate, confirm.

vermin *n.* flea, louse, mite; see INSECT.

versatile *a.* many-sided, adaptable, dexterous, varied, ready, clever, handy, talented, gifted, adroit, resourceful, ingenious, accomplished; see also ABLE.

versatility *a.* flexibility, utility, adjustability; see ADAPTABILITY.

verse *n.* **1** [Composition in poetic form] poetry, metrical composition, versification, stanza, rhyme, lyric, sonnet, ode, heroic verse, dramatic

5 a stanza 6 *Bible* any of the short divisions of a chapter

versed (vʉrst) ***adj.*** ⟦< L *versari,* be busy⟧ skilled or learned (*in* a subject)

ver·si·fy (vʉr′sə fī′) ***vi.*** **-fied′, -fy′ing** ⟦< L *versus,* a verse + *facere,* make⟧ to compose verses —***vt.*** **1** to tell about in verse **2** to put into verse form —**ver′si·fi·ca′tion** ***n.*** —**ver′si·fi′er** ***n.***

ver·sion (vʉr′zhən) ***n.*** ⟦see VERSE⟧ **1** a translation, esp. of the Bible **2** an account showing one point of view **3** a particular form of something

ver·sus (vʉr′səs) ***prep.*** ⟦ML < L, toward⟧ **1** against **2** in contrast with

ver·te·bra (vʉr′tə brə) ***n.***, *pl.* **-brae′** (-brē′, -brā′) or **-bras** ⟦L < *vertere,* to turn⟧ any of the single bones of the spinal column —**ver′te·bral** ***adj.***

ver′te·brate (-brit, -brāt′) ***adj.*** **1** having a backbone, or spinal column **2** of the vertebrates —***n.*** any of a large division of animals having a spinal column, as mammals, birds, etc.

ver·tex (vʉr′teks′) ***n.***, *pl.* **-tex′es** or **-ti·ces′** (-tə sēz′) ⟦L⟧ **1** the highest point; top **2** *Geom.* the point of intersection of the two sides of an angle

ver·ti·cal (vʉr′ti kəl) ***adj.*** **1** of or at the vertex **2** upright, straight up or down, etc. —***n.*** a vertical line, plane, etc. —**ver′ti·cal·ly** ***adv.***

ver·tig·i·nous (vər tij′ə nəs) ***adj.*** of, having, or causing vertigo

ver·ti·go (vʉr′ti gō′) ***n.*** ⟦L < *vertere,* to turn⟧ a sensation of dizziness

verve (vʉrv) ***n.*** ⟦Fr < OFr, manner of speech⟧ vigor; energy; enthusiasm

ver·y (ver′ē) ***adj.*** ⟦< L *verus,* true⟧ **1** complete; absolute *[*the *very* opposite*]* **2** same *[*the *very* hat I lost*]* **3** being just what is needed **4** actual *[*caught in the *very* act*]*: often an intensive *[*the *very* rafters shook*]* —***adv.*** **1** extremely **2** truly; really *[*the *very* same man*]*

very high frequency any radio frequency between 30 and 300 megahertz

very low frequency any radio frequency between 10 and 30 kilohertz

ves·i·cant (ves′i kənt) ***adj.*** ⟦< L *vesica,* a blister⟧ causing blisters —***n.*** a vesicant agent, as mustard gas used in warfare to blister skin and lungs

ves′i·cle (-kəl) ***n.*** ⟦< L *vesica,* bladder⟧ a small, membranous cavity, sac, or cyst —**ve·sic·u·lar** (və sik′yə lər) or **ve·sic′u·late** (-lit) ***adj.***

ves·pers (ves′pərz) ***n.*** ⟦ult. < L *vespera,* evening⟧ [*often* **V-**] [*usually with sing v.*] an evening prayer or service

Ves·puc·ci (ves po͞ot′chē), **A·me·ri·go** (ä′me rē′gô) (L. name *Americus Vespucius*) 1454-1512; It. navigator & explorer

ves·sel (ves′əl) ***n.*** ⟦< L *vas*⟧ **1** a utensil for holding something, as a bowl, kettle, etc. **2** a boat or ship **3** a tube or duct of the body, containing a fluid

vest (vest) ***n.*** ⟦< L *vestis,* garment⟧ a short, sleeveless garment, esp. one worn under a suit coat by men —***vt.*** **1** to dress, as in clerical robes **2** to place (authority, etc.) in someone **3** to put (a person) in control of, as power, etc. —***vi.*** to pass to a person; become vested (*in* a person), as property

ves·tal (ves′təl) ***adj.*** ⟦< L *Vesta,* goddess of the hearth⟧ chaste; pure —***n.*** a virgin priestess of the Roman goddess Vesta: in full **vestal virgin**

vest·ed (ves′tid) ***adj.*** ⟦pp. of VEST⟧ *Law* fixed; settled; absolute *[*a *vested* right*]*

vested interest **1** an established right, as to some future benefit **2** [*pl.*] groups pursuing selfish goals and exerting controlling influence

ves·ti·bule (ves′tə byo͞ol′) ***n.*** ⟦L *vestibulum*⟧ a small entrance hall, as to a building

ves·tige (ves′tij) ***n.*** ⟦< L *vestigium,* footprint⟧ **1** a trace, mark, or sign, esp. of something that has passed away **2** *Biol.* a degenerate part, more fully developed in an earlier stage —**ves·tig′i·al** (-tij′ē əl, -tij′əl) ***adj.***

vest′ing ***n.*** the retention by an employee of all or part of pension rights

vest·ment (vest′mənt) ***n.*** ⟦< L *vestire,* clothe⟧ a garment or robe, esp. one worn by a the clergy

vest′-pock′et ***adj.*** very small, or unusually small

ves·try (ves′trē) ***n.***, *pl.* **-tries** ⟦< L *vestis,* garment⟧ **1** a room in a church where vestments, etc. are kept **2** a room in a church, used as a chapel **3** a group of church members managing the temporal affairs of the church

Ve·su·vi·us (və so͞o′vē əs) active volcano in S Italy, near Naples

vet[1] (vet) ***vt.*** to evaluate thoroughly or expertly

vet[2] *abbrev.* **1** veteran **2** veterinarian **3** veterinary

vetch (vech) ***n.*** ⟦< L *vicia*⟧ a leafy, climbing or trailing plant of the pea family, grown for fodder

vet·er·an (vet′ər ən, ve′trən) ***adj.*** ⟦< L *vetus,* old⟧ **1** old and experienced **2** of veterans —***n.*** **1** one who has served in the armed forces **2** one who has served long in some position

Veterans Day a legal holiday in the U.S. honoring all veterans of the armed forces: observed on ARMISTICE DAY

vet·er·i·nar·i·an (vet′ər ə ner′ē ən) ***n.*** one who practices veterinary medicine or surgery

vet′er·i·nar′y (-ē) ***adj.*** ⟦< L *veterina,* beasts of burden⟧ designating or of the branch of medicine dealing with animals —***n.***, *pl.* **-ies** VETERINARIAN

ve·to (vē′tō) ***n.***, *pl.* **-toes** ⟦L, I forbid⟧ **1** *a)* an order prohibiting some act *b)* the power to prohibit action **2** *a)* the power of one branch of government to reject bills passed by another *b)* the exercise of this power —***vt.*** **-toed, -to·ing** **1** to prevent (a bill) from becoming law by a veto **2** to forbid

vex (veks) ***vt.*** ⟦< L *vexare,* agitate⟧ **1** to disturb; annoy, esp. in a petty way **2** to distress; afflict

vex·a·tion (vek sā′shən) ***n.*** **1** a vexing or being vexed **2** something that vexes —**vex·a′tious** ***adj.***

VHF or **vhf** *abbrev.* very high frequency

VHS ⟦*v*(*ideo*) *h*(*ome*) *s*(*ystem*)⟧ *trademark for* an electronic system for recording video and audio information on videocassettes

vi *abbrev.* intransitive verb

VI *abbrev.* Virgin Islands: also **V.I.**

vi·a (vī′ə, vē′ə) ***prep.*** ⟦L, way⟧ by way of

vi·a·ble (vī′ə bəl) ***adj.*** ⟦< L *vita,* life⟧ **1** sufficiently developed to be able to live outside the uterus **2** workable *[viable* ideas*]* —**vi′a·bil′i·ty** ***n.***

vi·a·duct (vī′ə dukt′) ***n.*** ⟦< VIA + (AQUE)DUCT⟧ a bridge

THESAURUS

poetry, blank verse, free verse. **2** [A unit of verse] line, verse, stanza, stave, strophe, antistrophe, hemistich, distich, quatrain.

version ***n.*** **1** [One of various accounts] report, account, tale; see STORY. **2** [A translation] paraphrase, redaction, transcription; see TRANSLATION.

vertebrae ***n.*** spine, spinal column, backbone, chine.

vertical ***a.*** perpendicular, upright, on end; see STRAIGHT 1.

very ***a.*** extremely, exceedingly, greatly, acutely, indispensably, just so, surprisingly, astonishingly, incredibly, wonderfully, particularly, certainly, positively, emphatically, really, truly, pretty, decidedly, pressingly, notably, uncommonly, extraordinarily, prodigiously, highly, substantially, dearly, amply, vastly, extensively, noticeably, conspicuously, largely, considerably, hugely, excessively, imperatively, markedly, enormously, sizably, materially, tremendously, immensely, superlatively, remarkably, unusually, immoderately, quite, indeed, somewhat, rather, simply, intensely, urgently, exceptionally, severely, seriously, in a great measure, to a great degree, beyond compare, on a large scale, ever so, beyond measure, by far, in the extreme, in a marked degree, to a great extent, without restraint, more or less, in part, infinitely, very much, real*, right*, awfully*, good and*, powerful*, powerfully*, hell of a*, precious*, so*, no end*.

vessel ***n.*** **1** [A container] pitcher, urn, kettle; see CONTAINER. **2** [A ship] boat, craft, bark*; see SHIP. **3** [A duct; *especially for blood*] blood vessel, artery, capillary; see VEIN 2.

vest ***n.*** waistcoat, jacket, garment; see CLOTHES.

vestige ***n.*** trace, remains, scrap; see REMAINDER.

veteran ***n.*** **1** [An experienced person] master, one long in service, old hand, one of the old guard, old bird*, old dog*, old timer*.—*Ant.* AMATEUR, rookie*, youngster. **2** [An experienced soldier] ex-soldier, seasoned campaigner, ex-service man, reenlisted man, old soldier, war horse*, ex-G.I.*, vet.

veterinarian ***n.*** animal specialist, vet, animal doctor; see DOCTOR.

veto ***n.*** rejection, prohibition, negative; see DENIAL, REFUSAL.

veto ***v.*** interdict, prohibit, decline; see DENY, REFUSE.

vetoed ***a.*** declined, rejected, disapproved; see NO, REFUSED.

vex ***v.*** provoke, irritate, annoy; see BOTHER 2.

via ***prep.*** by way of, by the route passing through, on the way to, through the medium of; see also BY 2, THROUGH 4.

consisting of a series of short spans, supported on piers or towers

Vi·ag·ra (vī ag′rə) *trademark for* a compound used to treat erectile dysfunction of the penis

vi·al (vī′əl) ***n.*** ⟦< OFr *fiole*⟧ a small vessel or bottle for liquids

vi·and (vī′ənd) ***n.*** ⟦< L *vivere,* to live⟧ an article of food

vibes (vībz) ***pl.n.*** **1** VIBRAPHONE **2** [Slang] qualities thought of as being like vibrations which produce an emotional reaction in others

vi·brant (vī′brənt) ***adj.*** **1** quivering or vibrating **2** produced by vibration **3** vigorous, vivacious, etc. —**vi′bran·cy** ***n.*** —**vi′brant·ly** ***adv.***

vi·bra·phone (vī′brə fōn′) ***n.*** a musical instrument like the marimba, with electrically operated resonators —**vi′bra·phon′ist** ***n.***

vi·brate (vī′brāt′) ***vt.*** **-brat′ed, -brat′ing** ⟦< L *vibrare*⟧ to set in to-and-fro motion —***vi.*** **1** to swing back and forth; oscillate **2** to move rapidly back and forth; quiver **3** to resound **4** to be emotionally stirred —**vi·bra′tion** ***n.*** —**vi′bra′tor** ***n.***

vi·bra·to (vi brät′ō) ***n.***, *pl.* **-tos** ⟦It⟧ a pulsating effect produced by rapid alternation of a given tone with a barely perceptible variation in pitch

vi·bra·to·ry (vī′brə tôr′ē) ***adj.*** **1** of, like, or causing vibration **2** vibrating or capable of vibrating

vi·bur·num (vī bʉr′nəm) ***n.*** ⟦L, wayfaring tree⟧ a shrub or small tree with white flowers

vic·ar (vik′ər) ***n.*** ⟦< L *vicis,* a change⟧ **1** *Anglican Ch.* a parish priest receiving a stipend **2** *R.C.Ch.* a church officer acting as a deputy of a bishop

vic′ar·age ***n.*** **1** the residence of a vicar **2** the position or duties of a vicar

vi·car·i·ous (vī ker′ē əs) ***adj.*** ⟦< L *vicarius,* substituted⟧ **1** endured or performed by one person in place of another **2** shared in by imagined participation in another's experience *[a vicarious* thrill*]* —**vi·car′i·ous·ly** ***adv.***

vice[1] (vīs) ***n.*** ⟦< L *vitium*⟧ **1** *a)* an evil action or habit *b)* evil conduct *c)* prostitution **2** a trivial fault or failing

vi·ce[2] (vī′sē) ***prep.*** ⟦L < *vicis,* a change⟧ in the place of

vice- ⟦see prec.⟧ *prefix* a subordinate; deputy *[vice-*president*]*

vice·ge·rent (vīs′jir′ənt) ***n.*** ⟦< VICE- + L *gerere,* to direct⟧ a deputy

vice′-pres′i·dent ***n.*** an officer next in rank below a president, acting during the president's absence or incapacity: for the U.S. official, usually **Vice President** —**vice′-pres′i·den·cy** ***n.***

vice·roy (vīs′roi′) ***n.*** ⟦MFr < *vice-* (see VICE-) + *roy,* king⟧ a person ruling a region as the deputy of a sovereign

vi·ce ver·sa (vī′sə vʉr′sə, vīs′ vʉr′sə) ⟦L⟧ the relation being reversed

vi·chys·soise (vē′shē swäz′, vish′ē-) ***n.*** a thick, cold soup of potatoes, leeks, and cream

vi·cin·i·ty (və sin′ə tē) ***n.***, *pl.* **-ties** ⟦< L *vicus,* village⟧ **1** nearness; proximity **2** the surrounding area

vi·cious (vish′əs) ***adj.*** ⟦< L *vitium,* vice⟧ **1** characterized by vice; evil or depraved **2** faulty; flawed **3** unruly *[a vicious* horse*]* **4** malicious; spiteful *[a vicious* rumor*]* **5** very intense, forceful, etc. *[a vicious* blow*]* —**vi′cious·ly** ***adv.*** —**vi′cious·ness** ***n.***

vicious circle a situation in which the solution of one problem gives rise to another, eventually bringing back the first problem: also **vicious cycle**

vi·cis·si·tudes (vi sis′ə to͞odz′) ***pl.n.*** ⟦< L *vicis,* a turn⟧ unpredictable changes in life; ups and downs

Vicks·burg (viks′bʉrg′) city in W Mississippi: besieged & captured by Grant in the Civil War (1863): pop. 21,000

vic·tim (vik′təm) ***n.*** ⟦L *victima*⟧ **1** someone or something killed, destroyed, sacrificed, etc. **2** one who suffers some loss, esp. by being swindled

vic′tim·ize′ (-īz′) ***vt.*** **-ized′, -iz′ing** to make a victim of

vic·tor (vik′tər) ***n.*** ⟦< L *vincere,* conquer⟧ the winner in a battle, struggle, etc.

Vic·to·ri·a[1] (vik tôr′ē ə) 1819-1901; queen of Great Britain & Ireland (1837-1901)

Vic·to·ri·a[2] (vik tôr′ē ə) capital of British Columbia, Canada: pop. 74,000

Vic·to′ri·an ***adj.*** **1** of or characteristic of the period of the reign of Queen Victoria **2** showing the respectability, prudery, etc. attributed to the Victorians —***n.*** a person of that time —**Vic·to′ri·an·ism′** ***n.***

vic·to·ri·ous (vik tôr′ē əs) ***adj.*** **1** having won a victory; triumphant **2** of or bringing about victory

vic·to·ry (vik′tər ē, -trē) ***n.***, *pl.* **-ries** ⟦< L *vincere,* conquer⟧ the winning of a battle, war, or any struggle

vict·uals (vit′′lz) ***pl.n.*** ⟦< L *victus,* food⟧ [Inf. or Dial.] articles of food

vi·cu·ña (vī kyo͞o′nyə, -nə) ***n.*** ⟦Sp⟧ **1** a small llama of South America **2** its soft, shaggy wool

vi·de (vī′dē) ***v.*** ⟦L⟧ see; refer to (a certain page, etc.)

vid·e·o (vid′ē ō′) ***adj.*** ⟦L, I see⟧ **1** of television **2** of the picture portion of a telecast **3** of data display on a computer —***n.***, *pl.* **-os′** **1** TELEVISION **2** *short for* VIDEOCASSETTE, VIDEOTAPE, etc.

vid′e·o·cas·sette′ ***n.*** a cassette of videotape

videocassette recorder a device for recording on and playing back videocassettes: also **vid′e·o·re·cord′er** ***n.***

vid′e·o·con′fer·enc·ing ***n.*** the holding of a conference at several locations by TV

vid′e·o·disc′ ***n.*** a disc on which images and sounds can be recorded for reproduction on a TV set: also **vid′e·o·disk′**

video game any of various games involving images, controlled by players, on a TV screen, computer monitor, etc.

vid′e·o·tape′ ***n.*** a magnetic tape on which images and sounds can be recorded for reproduction on TV —***vt.*** **-taped′, -tap′ing** to record on videotape

vie (vī) ***vi.*** **vied, vy′ing** ⟦< L *invitare,* invite⟧ to struggle for superiority (*with* someone); compete

Vi·en·na (vē en′ə) capital of Austria: pop. 1,516,000 —**Vi·en·nese** (vē′ə nēz′), *pl.* **-nese′**, ***adj.***, ***n.***

Vi·et·nam (vē′et näm′, -nam′) country on the E coast of Indochina: partitioned into two republics (**North Vietnam & South Vietnam**) in 1954, and reunified in 1976 as **Socialist Republic of Vietnam**: 127,246 sq. mi.; pop. 64,412,000 —**Vi′et·nam·ese′** (-nə mēz′), *pl.* **-ese′**, ***adj.***, ***n.***

view (vyo͞o) ***n.*** ⟦< L *videre,* to see⟧ **1** a seeing or looking, as in inspection **2** range of vision **3** mental survey *[a* correct *view* of a situation*]* **4** a scene or prospect *[a* room with a *view]* **5** manner of regarding something; opinion —***vt.*** **1** to inspect; scrutinize **2** to see; behold **3** to survey mentally; consider —**in view** **1** in sight **2** under consideration **3** as a goal or hope —**in view of** because of —**on view** displayed publicly —**with a view to** with the purpose or hope of

view′er ***n.*** **1** one who views something **2** an optical device for individual viewing of slides

view′find′er ***n.*** a camera device for viewing what will appear in the photograph

THESAURUS

vibrant ***a.*** energetic, vigorous, lively; see ACTIVE.

vibrate ***v.*** **1** [To quiver] fluctuate, flutter, waver; see WAVE 3. **2** [To sound] echo, resound, reverberate; see SOUND.

vibration ***n.*** quake, wavering, vacillation, fluctuation, oscillation, quiver, shake; see also WAVE 3.

vice[1] ***n.*** corruption, iniquity, wickedness; see EVIL 1.

vice versa ***a.*** conversely, in reverse, the other way round, turn about, about-face, in opposite manner, far from it, on the contrary, in reverse.

vicinity ***n.*** proximity, nearness, neighborhood; see ENVIRONMENT, REGION 1.

vicious ***a.*** wicked, corrupt, bad, debased, base, impious, profligate, demoralized, faulty, vile, foul, impure, lewd, indecent, licentious, libidinous; see also BAD 1.—*Ant.* PURE, noble, virtuous.

vicious circle ***n.*** chain of events, cause and effect, interreliant problems; see DIFFICULTY 1, 2.

viciously ***a.*** cruelly, spitefully, harmfully; see BRUTALLY, WRONGLY.

victim ***n.*** prey, sacrifice, immolation, sufferer, wretch, quarry, game, hunted, offering, scapegoat, martyr.

victimize ***v.*** cheat, swindle, dupe, trick, fool; see also DECEIVE.

victor ***n.*** conqueror, champion, prizewinner; see WINNER.

victorious ***a.*** winning, triumphant, mastering; see SUCCESSFUL.

victory ***n.*** conquest, mastery, subjugation, overcoming, overthrow, master stroke, lucky stroke, winning, success, triumph, gaining, defeating, subduing, destruction, killing*, knockout, pushover*.

vie ***v.*** contend, strive, rival; see COMPETE.

view ***n.*** glimpse, look, sight, panorama, aspect, show, appearance, prospect, distance, opening, stretch, outlook, way, extended view, long view, avenue, contour, outline, scene, spectacle. —**in view** visible, in sight, not out of sight, perceptible, perceivable; see also OBVIOUS 1. —**in view of** in consideration of, because, taking into consideration; see CONSIDERING. —**on view** displayed, on display, exposed; see SHOWN 1. —**with a view to** in order to, so that, anticipating; see TO 4.

view ***v.*** observe, survey, inspect; see SEE 1.

viewer ***n.*** watcher, onlooker, spec-

view′point′ ***n.*** the mental position from which things are viewed and judged; point of view

vig·il (vij′əl) ***n.*** ⟦< L, awake⟧ **1** *a)* a watchful staying awake *b)* a watch kept **2** the eve of a church festival

vig·i·lant (vij′ə lənt) ***adj.*** ⟦< L *vigil,* awake⟧ staying watchful and alert to danger or trouble —**vig′i·lance *n.***

vig·i·lan·te (vij′ə lan′tē) ***n.*** ⟦Sp, watchman⟧ one who acts outside the law to punish or avenge a crime —**vig′i·lan′tism′ *n.*** —**vig′i·lan′tist *adj.***

vi·gnette (vin yet′) ***n.*** ⟦Fr < *vigne*, vine⟧ **1** an ornamental design used on a page of a book, etc. **2** a picture shading off gradually at the edges **3** a short literary sketch, scene in a film, etc.

vig·or (vig′ər) ***n.*** ⟦< L *vigere,* be strong⟧ active force or strength; vitality; energy: Brit. sp. **vig′our** —**vig′or·ous *adj.*** —**vig′or·ous·ly *adv.***

vik·ing (vī′kiŋ) ***n.*** ⟦ON *vikingr*⟧ [*also* **V-**] any of the Scandinavian pirates of the 8th to the 10th c.

vile (vīl) ***adj.*** ⟦< L *vilis,* cheap, base⟧ **1** morally evil; wicked **2** disgusting **3** degrading; mean **4** very bad *[vile* weather*]* —**vile′ness *n.***

vil·i·fy (vil′ə fī′) ***vt.*** **-fied′**, **-fy′ing** ⟦see prec. & -FY⟧ to use abusive language about or of; defame —**vil′i·fi·ca′tion *n.***

vil·la (vil′ə) ***n.*** ⟦It < L, a farm⟧ a country house or estate, esp. a large one

vil·lage (vil′ij) ***n.*** ⟦see prec.⟧ **1** a community smaller than a town **2** the people of a village, collectively —**vil′lag·er *n.***

vil·lain (vil′ən) ***n.*** ⟦< VL *villanus,* a farm servant⟧ a wicked or evil person, or such a character in a play, etc. —**vil′lain·ess *fem.n.*** —**vil′lain·ous *adj.***

vil′lain·y ***n.***, *pl.* **-ies** **1** wickedness; evil **2** a villainous act

vil·lein (vil′ən) ***n.*** ⟦see VILLAIN⟧ a feudal serf who had become a freeman, except to his lord

vim (vim) ***n.*** ⟦prob. echoic⟧ vigor

vin (van; *E* vin) ***n.*** ⟦Fr⟧ wine

vin·ai·grette (vin′ə gret′) ***n.*** ⟦Fr < *vinaigre,* vinegar⟧ a salad dressing of vinegar, oil, etc.

Vinci, Leonardo da *see* DA VINCI, Leonardo

vin·di·cate (vin′də kāt′) ***vt.*** **-cat′ed**, **-cat′ing** ⟦< L *vis*, force + *dicere*, say⟧ **1** to clear from criticism, blame, etc. **2** to defend against opposition **3** to justify —**vin′di·ca′tion *n.*** —**vin′di·ca′tor *n.***

vin·dic·tive (vin dik′tiv) ***adj.*** ⟦see prec.⟧ **1** revengeful in spirit **2** said or done in revenge —**vin·dic′tive·ly *adv.*** —**vin·dic′tive·ness *n.***

vine (vīn) ***n.*** ⟦< L *vinum,* wine⟧ **1** *a)* a plant with a long, thin stem that grows along the ground or climbs a support *b)* the stem of such a plant **2** a grapevine

vin·e·gar (vin′ə gər) ***n.*** ⟦< medieval Fr *vin,* wine + *aigre,* sour⟧ a sour liquid made by fermenting cider, wine, etc. and used as a condiment and preservative —**vin′e·gar·y *adj.***

vine·yard (vin′yərd) ***n.*** land devoted to cultivating grapevines

vi·no (vē′nō) ***n.*** ⟦It & Sp⟧ wine

vin ro·sé (*r*ō zā′; *E* rō zā′) ⟦Fr⟧ ROSÉ

vin·tage (vin′tij) ***n.*** ⟦< L *vinum,* wine + *demere,* remove⟧ **1** the grape crop of a single season **2** the wine of a particular region and year **3** the model of a particular period *[*a car of prewar *vintage]* —***adj.*** **1** of a particular vintage: said of wine **2** representative of the best *[vintage* Hemingway*]* **3** of a past period *[vintage* clothes*]*

vint·ner (vint′nər) ***n.*** ⟦< ME < L *vinum,* wine⟧ one who sells or makes wine

vi·nyl (vī′nəl) ***n.*** ⟦< L *vinum,* wine⟧ any of various compounds polymerized to form resins and plastics (**vinyl plastics**)

vi·ol (vī′əl) ***n.*** ⟦< VL *vitula*, a fiddle⟧ any of an early family of stringed instruments, usually having six strings, frets, and a flat back

vi·o·la (vē ō′lə, vī-) ***n.*** ⟦It⟧ a stringed instrument of the violin family, slightly larger than a violin

vi·o·la·ble (vī′ə lə bəl) ***adj.*** that can be, or is likely to be, violated

vi·o·late (vī′ə lāt′) ***vt.*** **-lat′ed**, **-lat′ing** ⟦< L *violare,* use violence⟧ **1** to fail to obey or keep (a law, etc.) **2** to rape **3** to desecrate (something sacred) **4** to break in upon; disturb —**vi′o·la′tor *n.***

vi′o·la′tion (-lā′shən) ***n.*** a violating or being violated; specif., *a)* infringement, as of a law *b)* rape *c)* desecration of something sacred *d)* disturbance

vi′o·lence (-ləns) ***n.*** ⟦< L *violentus*, violent⟧ **1** physical force used so as to injure **2** powerful force, as of a hurricane **3** harm done by violating rights, etc. **4** a violent act or deed

vi′o·lent ***adj.*** **1** acting with or having great physical force **2** caused by violence **3** furious *[violent* language*]* **4** extreme; intense *[*a *violent* storm*]* —**vi′o·lent·ly *adv.***

vi·o·let (vī′ə lit) ***n.*** ⟦< L *viola*⟧ **1** a plant with white, blue, purple, or yellow flowers **2** a bluish-purple color —***adj.*** bluish-purple

vi·o·lin (vī′ə lin′) ***n.*** ⟦< VIOLA⟧ any of the modern family of four-stringed musical instruments played with a bow; specif., the smallest and highest-pitched one of this family —**vi′o·lin′ist *n.***

vi·ol·ist (vī′əl ist; *for 2* vē ō′list) ***n.*** **1** a viol player **2** a viola player

vi·o·lon·cel·lo (vē′ə län chel′ō, vī′ə lən-) ***n.***, *pl.* **-los** CELLO

VIP (vē′ī′pē′) ***n.*** ⟦*v*(*ery*) *i*(*mportant*) *p*(*erson*)⟧ a high-ranking official or important guest

THESAURUS

tator; see OBSERVER.

viewpoint ***n.*** point of view, perspective, standpoint, angle, slant, position, stand, aspect, light, respect, attitude, point of observation, outlook.

vigilant ***a.*** alert, watchful, on guard; see CAREFUL, OBSERVANT.

vigor ***n.*** **1** [Activity] exercise, action, energy; see VITALITY. **2** [Health] well-being, endurance, vitality; see HEALTH.

vigorous ***a.*** **1** [Done with vigor] energetic, lively, brisk; see ACTIVE. **2** [Forceful] powerful, strong, potent; see EFFECTIVE.

vigorously ***a.*** energetically, alertly, eagerly, quickly, nimbly, agilely, strenuously, resolutely, firmly, forcibly, forcefully, urgently, unfalteringly, purposefully, actively, boldly, adventurously, zealously, lustily, robustly, stoutly, hardily, wholeheartedly, earnestly, warmly, fervidly, fervently, ardently, intensely, passionately, sincerely, devoutly, appreciatively, with heart and soul, healthily, fearlessly, mightily, decidedly, by brute force, like blazes*; see also POWERFULLY.—*Ant.* CALMLY, aimlessly, slowly.

vile ***a.*** sordid, corrupt, debased; see SHAMEFUL 1, 2.

village ***n.*** hamlet, settlement, small town; see TOWN 1.

villain ***n.*** scoundrel, knave, brute; see CRIMINAL.

vindicate ***v.*** **1** [To clear] acquit, free, absolve; see EXCUSE. **2** [To justify] prove, bear out, warrant; see PROVE.

vindication ***n.*** defense, acquittal, clearance; see PROOF 1.

vindictive ***a.*** revengeful, resentful, spiteful; see CRUEL.

vine ***n.*** creeper, climbing plant, creeping plant, trailing plant, stem climber, leaf climber, tendril climber; see also PLANT. *Vines include the following:* grapevine, honeysuckle, trumpet vine, English ivy, Virginia creeper, poison ivy, blackberry, raspberry, briar, rambler, teaberry, dewberry, morning-glory, bougainvillea, jasmine, pea vine, watermelon, cantaloupe, cucumber, wild cucumber, squash, gourd, pumpkin, passionflower.

violate ***v.*** **1** [To transgress] outrage, disrupt, infringe, break, tamper with; see also MEDDLE 1. **2** [To rape] dishonor, molest, defile, ravish.

violation ***n.*** infringement, transgression, negligence, misbehavior, nonobservance, violating, shattering, transgressing, forcible trespass, trespassing, contravention, breach, breaking, rupture, flouting; see also CRIME.

violence ***n.*** **1** [Violent disturbance] rampage, tumult, disorder, clash, onslaught, struggle; see also CONFUSION, DISTURBANCE 2, UPROAR. **2** [Violent conduct] fury, force, vehemence, frenzy, brutality, savagery; see also INTENSITY.

violent ***a.*** strong, powerful, forceful, forcible, rough, mighty, great, potent, coercive, furious, mad, savage, fierce, passionate, vehement, frenzied, demonic, frantic, fuming, enraged, disturbed, agitated, impassioned, impetuous, urgent, maddened, aroused, inflamed, distraught, hysterical, vehement, extreme, unusual, brutal, destructive, murderous, homicidal, rampageous.—*Ant.* CALM, GENTLE, QUIET.

violently ***a.*** destructively, forcibly, forcefully, combatively, powerfully, strongly, coercively, flagrantly, outrageously, overwhelmingly, compellingly, disturbingly, turbulently, stormily, ruinously, stubbornly, with violence, in a violent manner, abruptly, noisily, with a vengeance, like fury, rebelliously, riotously, furiously, angrily, vehemently, fiercely, brutally, frantically, hilariously, hysterically, passionately, urgently, madly, frenziedly, ardently, enthusiastically, impulsively.—*Ant.* MILDLY, gently, undisturbedly.

violet ***a.*** lavender, mauve, purplish; see PURPLE.

violin ***n.*** fiddle, viola, Stradivarius; see MUSICAL INSTRUMENT.

VIP* ***n.*** very important person, notable, important figure; see LEADER

vi·per (vī′pər) ***n.*** ⟦OFr < L *vipera*⟧ **1** a venomous snake **2** a malicious or treacherous person —**vi′per·ous *adj.***

vi·ra·go (vi rä′gō, -rā′-) ***n.***, *pl.* **-goes** or **-gos** ⟦< L *vir,* a man⟧ a shrewish woman; scold

vi·ral (vī′rəl) ***adj.*** of or caused by a virus

vir·e·o (vir′ē ō′) ***n.***, *pl.* **-os′** ⟦L, a type of finch⟧ a small American songbird, with olive-green or gray feathers

Vir·gil (vur′jəl) 70-19 B.C.; Rom. poet: author of the *Aeneid*

vir·gin (vur′jən) ***n.*** ⟦< L *virgo*, a maiden⟧ one, esp. a young woman, who has never had sexual intercourse —***adj.*** **1** being a virgin **2** chaste; modest **3** untouched, unused, pure, etc. *[virgin* land*]* —**the Virgin** Mary, the mother of Jesus

vir′gin·al *adj.* VIRGIN

Vir·gin·ia (vər jin′yə) state of the S U.S.: 39,598 sq. mi.; pop. 6,187,000; cap. Richmond: abbrev. *VA* —**Vir·gin′i·an *adj., n.***

Virginia Beach city in SE Virginia, on the Atlantic: pop. 393,000

Virginia creeper WOODBINE (sense 2)

Virginia reel an American variety of reel danced by couples in two parallel rows

Virgin Islands group of islands in the West Indies, divided between those forming a British territory & those constituting a U.S. territory (**Virgin Islands of the United States**): U.S. part, 134 sq. mi., pop. 102,000

vir·gin·i·ty (vər jin′ə tē) ***n.*** a being a virgin

Virgin Mary Mary, the mother of Jesus

Vir·go (vur′gō′) ***n.*** ⟦L, virgin⟧ the sixth sign of the zodiac

vir·gule (vur′gyo͞ol′) ***n.*** ⟦< L *virgula,* small rod⟧ a diagonal line (/) used in dates or fractions (3/8) and also standing for "or", "per", etc.

vir·ile (vir′əl) ***adj.*** ⟦< L *vir,* a man⟧ **1** of or characteristic of a man; masculine **2** having manly strength or vigor **3** sexually potent —**vi·ril·i·ty** (və ril′ə tē) ***n.***

vi·rol·o·gy (vī räl′ə jē) ***n.*** ⟦< VIR(US) + -O- + -LOGY⟧ the study of viruses and virus diseases —**vi·rol′o·gist *n.***

vir·tu·al (vur′cho͞o əl) ***adj.*** being so in effect, although not in actual fact or name —**vir′tu·al·ly *adv.***

virtual reality computer simulation of three-dimensional images, with which one may seemingly interact using special electronic devices

vir·tue (vur′cho͞o) ***n.*** ⟦< L *virtus,* worth⟧ **1** general moral excellence **2** a specific moral quality regarded as good **3** chastity **4** *a)* excellence in general *b)* a good quality **5** efficacy, as of a medicine —**by** (or **in**) **virtue of** because of

vir·tu·o·so (vur′cho͞o ō′sō) ***n.***, *pl.* **-sos** or **-si** (-sē) ⟦It, skilled⟧ one with great skill in a fine art —**vir′tu·os′i·ty** (-äs′ə tē) ***n.***

vir·tu·ous (vur′cho͞o əs) ***adj.*** **1** having, or characterized by, moral virtue **2** chaste: said of a woman —**vir′tu·ous·ly *adv.***

vir·u·lent (vir′yoo lənt, -oo-) ***adj.*** ⟦see fol.⟧ **1** *a)* extremely poisonous *b)* full of hate **2** *Med. a)* violent and rapid in its course *b)* highly infectious —**vir′u·lence *n.***

vi·rus (vī′rəs) ***n.*** ⟦L, a poison⟧ **1** a microscopic infectious agent causing various diseases **2** any harmful influence **3** unauthorized, disruptive, spreadable computer program instructions

vi·sa (vē′zə, -sə) ***n.*** ⟦< L *videre*, see⟧ an endorsement on a passport, granting entry into a country

vis·age (viz′ij) ***n.*** ⟦see prec.⟧ **1** the face; countenance **2** aspect; look

vis-à-vis (vē′zə vē′) ***adj., adv.*** ⟦Fr⟧ face to face; opposite —***prep.*** **1** opposite to **2** in relation to

vis·cer·a (vis′ər ə) ***pl.n.***, *sing.* **vis′cus** (-kəs) ⟦L⟧ the internal organs of the body, as the heart, lungs, intestines, etc.

vis′cer·al *adj.* **1** of the viscera **2** intuitive, emotional, etc. rather than intellectual

vis·cid (vis′id) ***adj.*** ⟦< LL *viscidus,* sticky⟧ thick, syrupy, and sticky

vis·cose (vis′kōs′) ***n.*** ⟦see VISCID⟧ a syruplike solution of cellulose, used in making rayon and cellophane

vis·cos·i·ty (vis käs′ə tē) ***n.***, *pl.* **-ties** **1** a viscous quality **2** *Physics* the resistance of a fluid to flowing freely

vis·count (vī′kount′) ***n.*** ⟦see VICE- & COUNT[2]⟧ a nobleman next below an earl or count and above a baron —**vis′count′ess *fem.n.***

vis·cous (vis′kəs) ***adj.*** ⟦see VISCID⟧ **1** syrupy; viscid **2** *Physics* having viscosity

vise (vīs) ***n.*** ⟦< L *vitis,* vine, lit., that which winds⟧ a device having two jaws closed by a screw, used for holding firmly an object being worked on

Vish·nu (vish′no͞o) ***n.*** a Hindu god, often in human incarnation

vis·i·bil·i·ty (viz′ə bil′ə tē) ***n.***, *pl.* **-ties** **1** a being visible **2** *a)* the relative possibility of being seen under the prevailing conditions of distance, light, etc. *[*red has good *visibility] b)* range of vision

vis·i·ble (viz′ə bəl) ***adj.*** ⟦< L *videre*, to see⟧ **1** that can be seen **2** apparent —**vis′i·bly *adv.***

vi·sion (vizh′ən) ***n.*** ⟦see prec.⟧ **1** the power of seeing **2** something seen in a dream, trance, etc., or supernaturally revealed **3** a mental image **4** the ability to perceive or foresee something, as through mental acuteness **5** something or someone of great beauty

vi′sion·ar′y (-er′ē) ***adj.*** **1** seen in a vision **2** not realistic; impractical *[*a *visionary* scheme*]* —***n.***, *pl.* **-ies** **1** one who sees visions **2** one whose ideas, etc. are impractical

vis·it (viz′it) ***vt.*** ⟦< L *videre*, to see⟧ **1** to go or come to see **2** to stay with as a guest **3** to afflict or trouble —***vi.*** **1** to make a social call **2** [Inf.] to chat —***n.*** **1** a social call **2** a stay as a guest

vis′it·ant *n.* a visitor

vis·it·a·tion (viz′ə tā′shən) ***n.*** **1** an official visit, as to inspect **2** a reward or punishment, as sent by God **3** the

THESAURUS

2.

virgin ***a.*** **1** [Chaste] pure, modest, virginal; see CHASTE. **2** [Original or natural] undisturbed, new, untamed; see NATURAL 3, ORIGINAL 1, 3.

Virgin ***n.*** Madonna, Blessed Virgin Mary, Queen of Saints, Our Lady, Mother of God, Mary, the Queen of Heaven, Queen of Angels, Star of the Sea, The Virgin Mother, Immaculate Conception, Immaculate Mary; see also SAINT.

virginity ***n.*** maidenhood, girlhood, chastity; see VIRTUE 1.

virile ***a.*** masculine, potent, macho; see MALE, MANLY.

virility ***n.*** potency, masculinity, manliness; see MANHOOD 2.

virtually ***a.*** for all practical purposes, practically, implicitly; see ESSENTIALLY.

virtue ***n.*** **1** [Moral excellence] morality, goodness, righteousness, uprightness, ethical conduct, good thing, respectability, rectitude, honor, honesty, merit, fineness, character, excellence, value, chastity, quality, worth, kindness, innocence, generosity, trustworthiness, faithfulness, consideration, justice, prudence, temperance, fortitude, faith, hope, charity, love.—*Ant.* EVIL, immorality, depravity. **2** [An individual excellence] quality, characteristic, attribute, way, trait, feature, accomplishment, achievement, property, distinction, capacity, power.—*Ant.* LACK, inability, incapacity. **3** [Probity in sexual conduct] virginity, purity, decency; see CHASTITY. **—by virtue of** on the grounds of, because of, looking toward; see BECAUSE.

virtuoso ***n.*** maestro, artiste, expert; see MASTER 3, MUSICIAN.

virtuous ***a.*** good, upright, moral; see HONEST 1, WORTHY.

virus ***n.*** **1** [An infection] sickness, communicability, illness; see ILLNESS 2. **2** [An organism] microorganism, bacillus, bacteriophage; see GERM.

visceral ***a.*** instinctive, intuitive, emotional, gut*.

vise ***n.*** clamp, holder, clasp; see FASTENER.

visibility ***n.*** perceptibility, discernibility, distinctness; see CLARITY.

visible ***a.*** apparent, evident, noticeable; see OBVIOUS 1.

vision ***n.*** **1** [The faculty of sight] sight, perception, perceiving, range of view, optics, eyesight. **2** [Understanding] foresight, discernment, breadth of view, insight, penetration, intuition, divination, astuteness, keenness, foreknowledge, prescience, farsightedness, acumen, wisdom. **3** [Something seen through powers of the mind] imagination, poetic insight, fancy, fantasy, image, concept, conception, inspiration, idea; see also THOUGHT 1, 2. **4** [Something seen by other than normal sight] revelation, trance, ecstasy, fantasy, hallucination, phantom, apparition, ghost, wraith, specter, apocalypse, nightmare, spirit, warlock; see also ILLUSION.

visionary ***a.*** **1** [Impractical] ideal, romantic, utopian; see IMPRACTICAL. **2** [Imaginary] not real, delusory, dreamy; see IMAGINARY.

visit ***n.*** social call, call, appointment, interview, formal call, talk, evening, stay, holiday, visitation, vacation.

visit ***v.*** stay with, dwell with, stop by, call on, call upon, come around, be the guest of, make a visit, sojourn awhile, revisit, look in on, visit with, stop off, stop in, stop over, have an appointment with, pay a visit to, tour, take in, drop in on, hit, look around*, look up*, look in, drop over, pop in, have a date.

legal right to visit one's children, as after divorce **4** the visiting of a family in mourning

vis'i·tor *n.* a person making a visit

vi·sor (vī'zər) *n.* ⟦< OFr *vis,* a face⟧ **1** a part of a helmet that protects the face, often one that can be raised and lowered **2** a projecting brim, as of a cap, for shading the eyes

vis·ta (vis'tə) *n.* ⟦< L *videre,* to see⟧ **1** a view, esp. one seen through a long passage **2** a mental view of events

vis·u·al (vizh'o͞o əl) *adj.* ⟦< L *videre,* to see⟧ **1** of or used in seeing **2** based on the use of sight **3** that can be seen; visible

vis'u·al·ize' *vt., vi.* **-ized', -iz'ing** to form a mental image of (something not present to the sight) —**vis'u·al·i·za'tion** *n.*

vi·ta (vīt'ə, vēt'ə) *n.* ⟦< *curriculum vitae* < L, course of life⟧ a summary of one's personal history and professional qualifications, as that submitted by a job applicant; résumé

vi·tal (vīt''l) *adj.* ⟦< L *vita,* life⟧ **1** of or concerned with life **2** essential to life *[vital organs]* **3** fatal *[a vital wound]* **4** *a)* essential; indispensable *b)* very important **5** full of life; energetic —*n.* [*pl.*] **1** the vital organs, as the heart, brain, etc. **2** any essential parts —**vi'tal·ly** *adv.*

vi·tal·i·ty (vī tal'ə tē) *n., pl.* **-ties 1** power to live **2** power to endure **3** mental or physical vigor

vi·tal·ize (vīt''l īz') *vt.* **-ized', -iz'ing** to make vital; give life or vigor to

vital signs the pulse, respiration, and body temperature

vital statistics data on births, deaths, marriages, etc.

vi·ta·min (vīt'ə min) *n.* ⟦< L *vita,* life⟧ any of certain complex substances found variously in foods and essential to good health

vitamin A a fat-soluble alcohol found in fish-liver oil, egg yolk, carrots, etc.: a deficiency of this results in imperfect vision in the dark

vitamin B (complex) a group of unrelated water-soluble substances including *a)* **vitamin B_1** (see THIAMINE) *b)* **vitamin B_2** (see RIBOFLAVIN) *c)* NICOTINIC ACID *d)* **vitamin B_{12}**, a vitamin containing cobalt, used in treating anemia

vitamin C a compound occurring in citrus fruits, tomatoes, etc.: a deficiency of this results in scurvy

vitamin D any of several fat-soluble vitamins found in fish-liver oils, milk, etc.: a deficiency of this results in rickets

vitamin E a substance occurring in wheat germ, etc., vital to the reproductive processes in some animals

vitamin K a substance occurring in green vegetables, fish meal, etc., that clots blood

vi·ti·ate (vish'ē āt') *vt.* **-at'ed, -at'ing** ⟦< L *vitium,* a vice⟧ **1** to spoil; corrupt; pervert **2** to invalidate (a contract, etc.) —**vi'ti·a'tion** *n.*

vit·re·ous (vi'trē əs) *adj.* ⟦< L *vitrum,* glass⟧ **1** of or like glass **2** derived from or made of glass

vitreous humor (or **body**) the transparent, jellylike substance filling the eyeball between the retina and the lens

vit·ri·fy (vi'trə fī') *vt., vi.* **-fied', -fy'ing** ⟦< L *vitrum,* glass + Fr *-fier,* -FY⟧ to change into glass or a glasslike substance by heat

vit·rine (vi trēn', vi'trēn') *n.* ⟦see VITREOUS⟧ a glass-paneled cabinet or display case

vit·ri·ol (vi'trē ôl') *n.* ⟦< L *vitreus,* glassy⟧ **1** *a)* any of several sulfates of metals, as of copper (*blue vitriol*) or iron (*green vitriol*) *b)* SULFURIC ACID **2** caustic remarks —**vit'ri·ol'ic** (-äl'ik) *adj.*

vi·tu·per·ate (vī to͞o'pər āt', vi-) *vt.* **-at'ed, -at'ing** ⟦< L *vitium,* a fault, + *parare,* prepare⟧ to speak abusively to or about —**vi·tu'per·a'tion** *n.* —**vi·tu'per·a'tive** *adj.*

vi·va (vē'vä) *v.impersonal* ⟦It & Sp⟧ long live (someone specified)!

vi·va·ce (vē vä'chā) *adj., adv.* ⟦It⟧ *Music* in a lively, spirited manner: also written ***vivace***

vi·va·cious (vī vā'shəs, vi-) *adj.* ⟦< L *vivere,* to live⟧ full of animation; lively —**vi·va'cious·ly** *adv.* —**vi·vac'i·ty** (-vas'ə tē) or **vi·va'cious·ness** *n.*

vive (vēv) *v.impersonal* ⟦Fr⟧ long live (someone specified)!

viv·id (viv'id) *adj.* ⟦< L *vivere,* to live⟧ **1** full of life **2** intense: said as of colors **3** active; daring *[a vivid imagination]* —**viv'id·ly** *adv.* —**viv'id·ness** *n.*

viv·i·fy (viv'ə fī') *vt.* **-fied', -fy'ing** ⟦< L *vivus,* alive + *facere,* make⟧ to give life to

vi·vip·a·rous (vī vip'ər əs) *adj.* ⟦< L *vivus,* alive + *parere,* produce⟧ bearing living young, instead of laying eggs

viv·i·sec·tion (viv'ə sek'shən) *n.* ⟦< L *vivus,* alive + SECTION⟧ surgery performed on a living animal in medical research —**viv'i·sec'tion·ist** *n.*

vix·en (vik'sən) *n.* ⟦OE *fyxe,* female fox⟧ **1** a female fox **2** a shrewish or malicious woman

Vi·yel·la (vī yəl'ə) ⟦arbitrary coinage⟧ *trademark for* a fabric like flannel, a blend of lamb's wool and cotton

viz. or **viz** *abbrev.* ⟦< L *videlicet*⟧ that is; namely

vi·zier (vi zir', viz'yər) *n.* ⟦< Ar *wazara,* bear a burden⟧ a high government official in the Turkish empire (*c.* 1300-1918): also sp. **vi·zir'**

viz·or (vī'zər) *n. alt. sp. of* VISOR

VLF or **vlf** *abbrev.* very low frequency

vo·cab·u·lar·y (vō kab'yə ler'ē) *n., pl.* **-ies** ⟦ult. < L *vocare,* to call⟧ **1** a list of words, etc. as in a dictionary or glossary **2** all the words used in a language or by a person, group, etc.

vo·cal (vō'kəl) *adj.* ⟦< L *vox,* voice⟧ **1** of or produced by the voice **2** sung **3** capable of making oral sounds **4** speaking freely —**vo'cal·ly** *adv.*

vocal cords membranous folds in the larynx that vibrate to produce voice sounds

vo·cal·ic (vō kal'ik) *adj.* of, like, or involving a vowel or vowels

vo·cal·ist (vō'kəl ist) *n.* a singer

vo'cal·ize' *vt., vi.* **-ized', -iz'ing** to speak or sing

vo·ca·tion (vō kā'shən) *n.* ⟦< L *vocare,* to call⟧ **1** the career to which one feels one is called **2** any trade or occupation

vo·ca'tion·al *adj.* **1** of a vocation **2** designating or of training, etc. for an occupation or trade

voc·a·tive (väk'ə tiv) *n.* ⟦see VOCATION⟧ *Gram.* a case indicating the person or thing addressed

vo·cif·er·ate (vō sif'ər āt') *vt., vi.* **-at'ed, -at'ing** ⟦< L *vox,* voice + *ferre,* to bear⟧ to shout loudly; clamor —**vo·cif'er·a'tion** *n.*

vo·cif·er·ous (vō sif'ər əs) *adj.* noisy; clamorous

vod·ka (väd'kə) *n.* ⟦Russ < *voda,* water⟧ a colorless alcoholic liquor distilled from rye, wheat, etc.

vo-ed (vō'ed') *adj., n.* [Inf.] (of) vocational education

vogue (vōg) *n.* ⟦Fr⟧ **1** the current fashion **2** popularity —*adj.* in vogue: also **vogu·ish** (vō'gish)

voice (vois) *n.* ⟦< L *vox*⟧ **1** sound made through the mouth, esp. by human beings **2** the ability to make such

THESAURUS

visitor *n.* caller, visitant, official inspector; see GUEST.

visual *a.* seen, optical, of the vision; see OBVIOUS 1.

visualize *v.* see in the mind's eye, picture mentally, conceive; see IMAGINE.

vital *a.* **1** [Necessary] essential, indispensable, requisite; see NECESSARY. **2** [Alive] live, animate, animated; see ALIVE. **3** [Vigorous] lively, energetic, lusty; see ACTIVE.

vitality *n.* life, liveliness, animation, vim, vigor, intensity, continuity, endurance, energy, spirit, ardor, audacity, spunk*, fervor, verve, venturesomeness, pep*, get-up-and-go*.

vitals *n.* organs, entrails, intestines; see INSIDES.

vitamin *n. Types of vitamins include the following:* vitamin A, vitamin B_1 or thiamine, vitamin B_2 or riboflavin, vitamin B_6 or pyridoxine, vitamin B_{12}, nicotinic acid or niacin, pantothenic acid, choline, folic acid, inositol, para-aminobenzoic acid, vitamin C or ascorbic acid, vitamin D, vitamin D_2 or ergocalciferol, vitamin D_3 or cholecalciferol, vitamin E or tocopherol, vitamin H or biotin, vitamin K or menadione; see also MEDICINE 2.

vivid *a.* **1** [Brilliant] shining, glowing, gleaming; see BRIGHT 1. **2** [Distinct] strong, striking, lucid; see CLEAR 2, DEFINITE 2.

vividly *a.* glowingly, strikingly, flamingly; see BRIGHTLY.

vocabulary *n.* wordbook, dictionary, lexicon, thesaurus, stock of words, glossary; scientific, literary, active, passive, etc. vocabulary; see also DICTION.

vocal *a.* **1** [Verbal] expressed, uttered, voiced; see ORAL, SPOKEN. **2** [Produced by the voice; *said especially of music*] sung, scored for voice, vocalized; see MUSICAL 1.

vocalist *n.* chorister, caroler, songster; see MUSICIAN, SINGER.

vocation *n.* calling, mission, pursuit; see PROFESSION 1.

voice *n.* **1** [A vocal sound] speech, sound, call, cry, utterance, tongue, whistle, moan, groan, song, yell, hail, howl, yowl, bark, whine, whimper, mutter, murmur, shout, bleat, bray, neigh, whinny, roar, trumpet, cluck, honk, meow, hiss, quack; see also NOISE 1.—*Ant.* SILENCE, dumbness,

sounds **3** anything regarded as like vocal utterance **4** an expressed wish, opinion, etc. **5** the right to express one's wish, etc.; vote **6** utterance or expression **7** a verb form showing the relation of the subject to the action: see ACTIVE (*adj.* 4), PASSIVE (*adj.* 3) **8** singing ability —*vt.* **voiced, voic'ing** to give utterance or expression to —**with one voice** unanimously —**voice'less** *adj.*

voice box LARYNX

voice mail **1** an electronic system whereby voice messages can be recorded, stored, and then delivered **2** such messages

voice'-o'ver *n.* the voice of an unseen announcer or narrator, as on TV

void (void) *adj.* ⟦< L *vacare,* be empty⟧ **1** containing nothing **2** devoid (*of*) *[void* of common sense*]* **3** ineffective; useless **4** of no legal force —*n.* **1** an empty space **2** a feeling of emptiness —*vt.* **1** to empty **2** to make void; annul —**void'a·ble** *adj.*

voi·là (vwä lä') *interj.* ⟦Fr⟧ behold; there it is

voile (voil) *n.* ⟦Fr, a veil⟧ a thin fabric, as of cotton

vol *abbrev.* volume

vol·a·tile (väl'ə təl) *adj.* ⟦< L *volare,* to fly⟧ **1** evaporating quickly **2** *a*) unstable; explosive *b*) fickle —**vol'a·til'i·ty** (-til'ə tē) *n.* —**vol'a·til·ize'** (-īz'), **-ized', -iz'ing,** *vt., vi.*

vol·can·ic (väl kan'ik, vôl-) *adj.* **1** of or caused by a volcano **2** like a volcano; violently explosive

vol·ca·no (väl kā'nō, vôl-) *n., pl.* **-noes** or **-nos** ⟦< L *Volcanus,* Vulcan⟧ **1** a vent in the earth's crust through which molten rock, ashes, etc. are ejected **2** a cone-shaped mountain of this material built up around the vent

vole (vōl) *n.* ⟦< earlier *vole mouse* < Scand, as in ON *vǫllr,* meadow⟧ any of various small rodents with a stout body and short tail

Vol·ga (väl'gə, vōl'-) river in European Russia, flowing into the Caspian Sea

vo·li·tion (vō lish'ən) *n.* ⟦ult. < L *velle,* be willing⟧ the act or power of using the will —**vo·li'tion·al** *adj.*

vol·ley (väl'ē) *n., pl.* **-leys** ⟦< L *volare,* to fly⟧ **1** *a*) the simultaneous discharge of a number of weapons *b*) the bullets, etc., so discharged **2** a burst of words or acts **3** *Sports a*) a returning of a ball, etc. before it touches the ground *b*) an extended exchange of shots, as in tennis —*vt., vi.* **-leyed, -ley·ing** **1** to discharge or be discharged as in a volley **2** *Sports* to return (the ball, etc.) as a volley

vol'ley·ball' *n.* **1** a team game played by hitting a large, light, inflated ball back and forth over a net with the hands **2** this ball

volt (vōlt) *n.* ⟦after A. *Volta* (1745-1827), It physicist⟧ the basic unit of electromotive force

volt·age (vōl'tij) *n.* electromotive force expressed in volts

vol·ta·ic (väl tā'ik) *adj.* of or by electricity produced by chemical action

Vol·taire (vōl ter') 1694-1778; Fr. writer & philosopher

volt'me'ter *n.* an instrument for measuring voltage

vol·u·ble (väl'yə bəl) *adj.* ⟦< L *volvere,* to roll⟧ characterized by a great flow of words; talkative —**vol'u·bil'i·ty** *n.* —**vol'u·bly** *adv.*

vol·ume (väl'yo͞om) *n.* ⟦< L *volumen,* a scroll⟧ **1** *a*) a book *b*) one of a set of books **2** the amount of space occupied in three dimensions **3** *a*) a quantity, bulk, or amount *b*) a large quantity **4** the loudness of sound

vo·lu·mi·nous (və lo͞om'ə nəs) *adj.* **1** producing or consisting of enough to fill volumes **2** large; bulky; full —**vo·lu'mi·nous·ly** *adv.*

vol·un·ta·rism (väl'ən tər iz'əm) *n.* (system of) voluntary participation in a course of action

vol'un·tar'y (-ter'ē) *adj.* ⟦< L *voluntas,* free will⟧ **1** brought about by one's own free choice **2** acting of one's own accord **3** intentional **4** controlled by one's mind or will —**vol'un·tar'i·ly** *adv.*

vol·un·teer (väl'ən tir') *n.* one who chooses freely to do something, as entering military service —*adj.* **1** serving as a volunteer **2** of a volunteer or volunteers —*vt.* to offer or give of one's own free will —*vi.* to offer to enter into any service of one's own free will

vo·lup·tu·ar·y (və lup'cho͞o er'ē) *n., pl.* **-ar'ies** ⟦< L *voluptas,* pleasure⟧ one devoted to sensual pleasures

vo·lup'tu·ous (-cho͞o əs) *adj.* full of, producing, or fond of sensual pleasures —**vo·lup'tu·ous·ness** *n.*

vo·lute (və lo͞ot') *n.* ⟦< L *volvere,* to roll⟧ a spiral or whorl

vom·it (väm'it) *n.* ⟦< L *vomere,* to vomit⟧ matter ejected from the stomach through the mouth —*vt., vi.* **1** to eject (the contents of the stomach) through the mouth; throw up **2** to discharge or be discharged with force —**vom'i·tous** (-ə təs) *adj.*

voo·doo (vo͞o'do͞o') *n., pl.* **-doos'** ⟦of WAfr orig.⟧ a religion of the West Indies, based on a belief in magic, charms, etc. —*adj.* of or resembling voodoo

vo·ra·cious (vô rā'shəs) *adj.* ⟦< L *vorare,* devour⟧ **1** greedy in eating; ravenous **2** very eager *[a voracious* reader*]* —**vo·rac'i·ty** (-ras'ə tē) *n.*

vor·tex (vôr'teks') *n., pl.* **-tex'es** or **-ti·ces'** (-tə sēz') ⟦< L *vertere,* to turn⟧ **1** a whirlpool **2** a whirlwind **3** anything like a whirlwind, etc. in effect

vo·ta·ry (vōt'ə rē) *n., pl.* **-ries** ⟦< L *vovere,* to vow⟧ **1** one bound by a vow, esp. by religious vows, as a monk or nun **2** one devoted to a cause, study, etc.

vote (vōt) *n.* ⟦< L *votum,* a vow⟧ **1** a decision on a proposal, etc., or a choice between candidates for office **2** *a*) the expression of such a decision or choice *b*) the ballot, etc. by which it is expressed **3** the right to vote **4** votes collectively —*vi.* **vot'ed, vot'ing** to give or cast a vote —*vt.* to decide or enact by vote —**vot'er** *n.*

THESAURUS

stillness. **2** [Approval or opinion] decision, conclusion, assent, negation, approval, recommendation, wish, view; see also CHOICE, OPINION 1. —**with one voice** all together, by unanimous vote, without dissent; see UNANIMOUSLY.

voice *v.* assert, cry, sound; see TALK 1, TELL 1.

voiced *a.* vocal, sonant, sounded; see ORAL, SPOKEN.

void *a.* barren, sterile, fruitless, meaningless, useless, invalid, vain, voided, unconfirmed, unratified, null and void, worthless, unsanctioned, set aside, avoided, forceless, voted out, ineffectual, ineffective, voidable.—*Ant.* VALID, in force, used.

volatile *a.* **1** [Having the qualities of a gas] gaseous, vaporous, buoyant; see LIGHT 5. **2** [Having a sprightly temperament] lively, vivacious, playful; see ACTIVE.

volitional *a.* willing, voluntary, free; see OPTIONAL.

volley *n.* round, discharge, barrage; see FIRE 2.

voltage *n.* electric potential, potential difference, charge; see ENERGY 2.

voluble *a.* talkative, glib, loquacious; see FLUENT.

volume *n.* **1** [Quantity] bulk, mass, amount; see EXTENT, SIZE 2. **2** [Contents] cubical size, space, dimensions; see CAPACITY. **3** [A book] printed document, tome, pamphlet; see BOOK. **4** [Degree of sound] loudness, amplification, strength; see SOUND 2.

voluntarily *a.* by preference, willingly, deliberately, optionally, spontaneously, freely, intentionally, by choice, of one's own choice, on one's own, in one's own sweet way, of one's own free will, to one's heart's content, at one's discretion, on one's own initiative.

voluntary *a.* willing, intentional, spontaneous; see OPTIONAL.

volunteer *n.* enlistee, unpaid worker, charity worker; see CANDIDATE, RECRUIT.

volunteer *v.* come forward, enlist, sign up, submit oneself, take the initiative, offer oneself, do on one's own accord, do of one's own free will, take upon oneself, speak up, stand up and be counted, go in*, chip in*, do on one's own hook*, take the bull by the horns, stand on one's own feet, take the bit between one's teeth, take the plunge; see also JOIN 2.

volunteered *a.* offered, proffered, given freely; see JOINED.

voluptuous *a.* epicurean, sensuous, erotic; see SENSUAL.

vomit *v.* throw up, eject, bring up, spit up, dry heave, be seasick, be sick, hurl forth, retch, ruminate, regurgitate, give forth, discharge, belch forth, spew up, puke*, barf*, toss one's cookies*.

voracious *a.* insatiable, hoggish, ravening; see GREEDY.

vote *n.* **1** [A ballot] tally, ticket, slip of paper, butterfly ballot, punch card, absentee ballot, yes or no, secret ballot. **2** [A decision] referendum, choice, majority; see ELECTION. **3** [The right to vote] suffrage, the franchise, manhood suffrage, universal suffrage, woman suffrage, enfranchisement; see also RIGHT.

vote *v.* ballot, cast a vote, cast a ballot, give a vote, enact, establish, choose, determine, bring about, effect, grant, confer, declare, suggest, propose; see also DECIDE. —**vote down** decide against, refuse, blackball; see DENY. —**vote for** give one's vote to, cast a ballot for, second; see SUPPORT 2. —**vote in** elect, put in, put in office; see CHOOSE. —**vote out** reject, remove from office, vote down; see DEFEAT, DISMISS.

voted *a.* decided, willed, chosen; see NAMED 2.

voter *n.* elector, balloter, registered voter, member of a constituency, member of the electorate, vote caster, native, naturalized citizen, taxpayer, voter by proxy, absentee voter; see also CITIZEN.

vo·tive (vōt′iv) ***adj.*** ⟦see prec.⟧ designed to fulfill a promise, express devotion, etc.
vouch (vouch) ***vi.*** ⟦< L *vocare,* to call⟧ to give, or serve as, assurance, a guarantee, etc. (*for*) *[to vouch* for someone's honesty*]*
vouch′er ***n.*** **1** one who vouches **2** a paper serving as evidence or proof; specif., a receipt
vouch·safe (vouch sāf′) ***vt.*** **-safed′**, **-saf′ing** ⟦< ME *vouchen safe,* vouch as safe⟧ to be kind enough to give or grant
vow (vou) ***n.*** ⟦< L *votum*⟧ **1** a solemn promise, esp. one made to God **2** a promise of love and fidelity *[marriage vows]* —***vt.*** to promise or declare solemnly —***vi.*** to make a vow —**take vows** to enter a religious order
vow·el (vou′əl) ***n.*** ⟦< L *vocalis,* vocal⟧ **1** a speech sound in which the air passes in a continuous stream through the open mouth **2** a letter representing such a sound, as *a, e, i, o,* or *u*
voy·age (voi′ij) ***n.*** ⟦< L *via,* way⟧ a relatively long journey by ship or spacecraft —***vi.*** **-aged**, **-ag·ing** to make a voyage —**voy′ag·er** ***n.***
voy·eur (voi ʉr′, vwä yʉr′) ***n.*** ⟦< L *videre,* see⟧ one who has an exaggerated interest in viewing sexual objects or activities —**voy·eur′ism′** ***n.*** —**voy′eur·is′tic** ***adj.***
VP *abbrev.* Vice-President
vs. or **vs** *abbrev.* versus
vt *abbrev.* transitive verb
VT Vermont
Vul·can (vul′kən) ***n.*** the Roman god of fire and of metalworking
vul·can·ize (vul′kən īz′) ***vt.*** **-ized′**, **-iz′ing** to treat (crude rubber) with sulfur under heat to make it stronger and more elastic —**vul′can·i·za′tion** ***n.***
Vulg *abbrev.* Vulgate
vul·gar (vul′gər) ***adj.*** ⟦< L *vulgus,* common people⟧ **1** of people in general; popular **2** vernacular **3** lacking culture, taste, etc.; crude; boorish **4** indecent or obscene —**vul′gar·ly** ***adv.***
vul·gar′i·an (-ger′ē ən) ***n.*** a rich person with coarse, showy tastes
vul′gar·ism′ (-gər iz′əm) ***n.*** **1** a word, phrase, etc. used widely but regarded as nonstandard, coarse, or obscene **2** vulgarity
vul·gar′i·ty (-ger′ə tē) ***n.*** **1** a being vulgar **2** *pl.* **-ties** a vulgar act, habit, usage in speech, etc.
vul′gar·ize′ (-gər īz′) ***vt.*** **-ized′**, **-iz′ing** **1** to popularize **2** to make vulgar, coarse, obscene, etc. —**vul′gar·i·za′tion** ***n.***
Vulgar Latin the everyday Latin spoken by ancient Romans as distinguished from standard written Latin
Vul·gate (vul′gāt′) ***n.*** ⟦ML *vulgata (editio),* popular (edition)⟧ a Latin version of the Bible, used in the Roman Catholic Church
vul·ner·a·ble (vul′nər ə bəl) ***adj.*** ⟦< L *vulnus,* a wound⟧ **1** that can be wounded or injured **2** open to, or easily hurt by, criticism or attack **3** affected by a specified influence, temptation, etc. —**vul′ner·a·bil′i·ty** ***n.*** —**vul′ner·a·bly** ***adv.***
vul·pine (vul′pīn) ***adj.*** ⟦< L *vulpes,* a fox⟧ of or like a fox; cunning
vul·ture (vul′chər) ***n.*** ⟦< L, akin to *vellere,* to tear⟧ **1** a large bird that lives chiefly on carrion **2** a greedy, ruthless person
vul·va (vul′və) ***n.***, *pl.* **-vae** (-vē) or **-vas** ⟦L, womb⟧ the external genital organs of the female
vy·ing (vī′iŋ) ***adj.*** that vies; competing

THESAURUS

vouch ***v.*** assert, attest, affirm; see ENDORSE 2.

vow ***n.*** pledge, solemn assertion, oath; see PROMISE 1.

vowel ***n.*** nonconsonant, open-voiced sound, vowel sound, diphthong, digraph; see also LETTER 1. *Linguistic terms referring to vowel sounds include the following:* high, mid, low, front, central, back, tense, slack, rounded, unrounded, stressed, unstressed, nasalized, clipped, diphthongized. *In the English alphabet, vowels are represented as follows: a, e, i, o, u,* and sometimes *y.*

voyage ***n.*** tour, trip, excursion; see JOURNEY.

vulgar ***a.*** sordid, ignoble, mean, base, obscene, indecent, gross, filthy, villainous, dishonorable, unworthy, fractious, inferior, disgusting, base-minded, mean-spirited, malicious, ill-tempered, sneaking, deceitful, slippery, loathsome, odious, foulmouthed, brutish, debased, contemptible, profane, abhorrent, nasty, tasteless, low, uncouth.—*Ant.* NOBLE, high-minded, lofty.

vulgarity ***n.*** impudence, discourtesy, crudity; see RUDENESS.

vulnerable ***a.*** woundable, exposed, assailable; see UNSAFE, WEAK 2, 5.

w[1] or **W** (dub′əl yo͞o′) ***n.***, *pl.* **w's, W's** the 23d letter of the English alphabet
w[2] *abbrev.* **1** waist **2** watt(s) **3** week(s) **4** weight **5** west(ern) **6** wide **7** width **8** wife **9** with **10** win(s)
W[1] *abbrev.* **1** watt(s) **2** Wednesday **3** west(ern) **4** win(s)
W[2] ⟦*w*(*olfram*), alt. name of tungsten⟧ *Chem. symbol for* tungsten
WA Washington (state)
Wac (wak) ***n.*** a member of the Women's Army Corps (**WAC**)
wack·o (wak′ō) [Slang] ***adj.*** *var. of* WACKY —***n.***, *pl.* **-os** one who is wacko
wack·y (wak′ē) ***adj.*** **-i·er, -i·est** ⟦< ?⟧ [Slang] erratic, eccentric, or irrational —**wack′i·ness** ***n.***
wad (wäd) ***n.*** ⟦ML *wadda*, wadding⟧ **1** a small, soft mass, as of cotton or paper **2** a lump or small, firm mass —***vt.*** **wad′ded, wad′ding 1** to compress, or roll up, into a wad **2** to plug or stuff with a wad or wadding
wad′ding ***n.*** any soft material for use in padding, packing, etc.
wad·dle (wäd′əl) ***vi.*** **-dled, -dling** ⟦< fol.⟧ to walk with short steps, swaying from side to side, as a duck does —***n.*** a waddling gait
wade (wād) ***vi.*** **wad′ed, wad′ing** ⟦OE *waden*, go⟧ **1** to walk through any resisting substance, as water, mud, etc. **2** to proceed with difficulty *[*to *wade* through a dull book*]* **3** [Inf.] to attack with vigor: with *in* or *into* —***vt.*** to cross by wading
wad′er ***n.*** **1** one that wades **2** [*pl.*] *a*) high waterproof boots *b*) waterproof overalls with bootlike parts for the feet
wa·di (wä′dē) ***n.***, *pl.* **-dis** or **-dies** ⟦Ar *wādī*⟧ in Arabia, N Africa, etc., a ravine or watercourse that is usually dry
wading bird any long-legged bird that wades the shallows and marshes for food
wa·fer (wā′fər) ***n.*** ⟦< MDu *wafel*⟧ **1** a thin, flat, crisp cracker or cookie **2** any disklike thing resembling this
waf·fle[1] (wä′fəl) ***n.*** ⟦see prec.⟧ a crisp batter cake baked in a waffle iron
waf·fle[2] (wä′fəl) ***vi.*** **-fled, -fling** ⟦< echoic *waff*, to yelp⟧ to speak or write in a wordy or vague way
waffle iron a utensil with two flat, studded plates pressed together to bake a waffle
waft (wäft, waft) ***vt., vi.*** ⟦< Du *wachter*, watcher⟧ to carry (sounds, odors, etc.) lightly through the air or over water or to move in this way —***n.*** **1** an odor, sound, etc. carried through the air **2** a gust of wind **3** a wafting movement
wag[1] (wag) ***vt., vi.*** **wagged, wag′ging** ⟦ME *waggen*⟧ to move rapidly back and forth, up and down, etc. —***n.*** a wagging
wag[2] (wag) ***n.*** ⟦prob. < obs. *waghalter*, joker⟧ a comical person; wit —**wag′ger·y**, *pl.* **-ies**, ***n.***
wage (wāj) ***vt.*** **waged, wag′ing** ⟦< OFr *gage*, a pledge⟧ to engage in or carry on (a war, etc.) —***n.*** **1** [*often pl.*] money paid for work done **2** [*usually pl.*] what is given in return
wa·ger (wā′jər) ***n.*** ⟦see prec.⟧ a bet —***vt., vi.*** to bet
wag·gish (wag′ish) ***adj.*** **1** of or like a wag; roguishly merry **2** playful; jesting
wag·gle (wag′əl) ***vt., vi.*** **-gled, -gling** ⟦< WAG[1]⟧ to wag, esp. with short, quick movements —***n.*** a waggling —**wag′gly** ***adj.***
Wag·ner (väg′nər), **Rich·ard** (riH′ärt) 1813-83; Ger. composer
wag·on (wag′ən) ***n.*** ⟦Du *wagen*⟧ **1** a four-wheeled vehicle, esp. one for hauling heavy loads **2** *short for* STATION WAGON —**on** (or **off**) **the wagon** [Slang] no longer (or once again) drinking alcohol
waif (wāf) ***n.*** ⟦< NormFr⟧ a homeless person, esp. a child
wail (wāl) ***vi.*** ⟦< ON *væ*, woe⟧ to make a long, loud, sad cry, as in grief or pain —***n.*** such a cry
wain (wān) ***n.*** ⟦OE *wægn*⟧ [Old Poet.] a wagon
wain·scot (wān′skät′, -skət) ***n.*** ⟦< MDu *wagenschot*⟧ a wood paneling on the walls of a room, sometimes on the lower part only —***vt.*** **-scot′ed** or **-scot′ted, -scot′ing** or **-scot′ting** to line (a wall) with wood, etc.
wain′scot′ing or **wain′scot′ting** ***n.*** **1** WAINSCOT **2** material used to wainscot
wain·wright (wān′rīt′) ***n.*** ⟦WAIN + WRIGHT⟧ one who builds or repairs wagons
waist (wāst) ***n.*** ⟦< OE *weaxan*, grow⟧ **1** the part of the body between the ribs and the hips **2** the part of a garment that covers the body from the shoulders to the waistline **3** the narrow part of any object that is wider at the ends
waist′band′ ***n.*** a band encircling the waist, as on slacks or a skirt
waist·coat (wes′kət, wāst′kōt′) ***n.*** [Brit.] a man's vest
waist′line′ ***n.*** (the circumference of) the narrowest part of the waist
wait (wāt) ***vi.*** ⟦< NormFr *waitier*⟧ **1** to remain (until something expected happens) **2** to be ready **3** to remain undone *[*it can *wait]* **4** to serve food at a meal: with *at* or *on* —***vt.*** **1** to await **2** [Inf.] to delay serving (a meal) —***n.*** an act or period of waiting —**lie in wait (for)** to wait so as to catch after planning a trap *(for)* —**wait on** (or **upon**) **1** to act as a servant to **2** to serve (a customer) —**wait table** to serve food to people at a table —**wait up** to delay going to bed until someone arrives, etc.
wait′er ***n.*** one who waits; esp., a man who waits on tables, as in a restaurant
wait′ing ***adj.*** **1** that waits **2** of or for a wait —***n.*** the act of one that waits —**in waiting** in attendance, as on a king
waiting game a scheme by which one wins out over another by delaying action until one has an advantage
waiting list a list of applicants, in the order of their application
waiting room a room in which people wait, as in a bus station or doctor's office
wait′per′son ***n.*** a waiter or waitress
wait·ress (wā′tris) ***n.*** a woman who waits on tables, as in a restaurant
waive (wāv) ***vt.*** **waived, waiv′ing** ⟦< ON *veifa*, fluctuate⟧ **1** to give up or forgo (a right, etc.) **2** to postpone; defer
waiv·er (wā′vər) ***n.*** *Law* a waiving of a right, claim, etc.
wake[1] (wāk) ***vi.*** **woke** or **waked, waked** or **wok′en, wak′ing** ⟦< OE *wacian*, be awake & *wacan*, arise⟧ **1** to

THESAURUS

wad ***n.*** **1** [A little heap] bundle, pile, clump; see BUNCH. **2** [*A considerable amount of money] fortune, bankroll, mint*; see WEALTH.
wad ***v.*** stuff, pad, cushion; see PACK 2.
wade ***v.*** walk in the surf, paddle, get one's feet wet; see SWIM.
wafer ***n.*** biscuit, cracker, slice; see BREAD.
wag[1] ***v.*** waggle, swing, sway; see WAVE 3.
wage ***v.*** conduct, make, carry on; see DO 1.
wager ***n.*** risk, hazard, challenge; see BET.
wages ***n.*** salary, earnings, payment; see PAY 2.
waggish ***a.*** humorous, playful, jocular; see FUNNY 1.
wagon ***n.*** pushcart, buggy, truck, coach, carriage, caravan, car, covered wagon, prairie schooner, Conestoga wagon, cab.
wail ***v.*** moan, weep, lament; see MOURN.
waist ***n.*** waistline, middle, midriff; see STOMACH.
wait ***n.*** halt, holdup, time wasted; see DELAY, PAUSE.
wait ***v.*** **1** [To await] expect, anticipate, tarry, pause, wait for, look for, watch for, abide, dally, remain, idle, bide one's time, mark time, stay up for, lie in wait for, ambush, lie low, hole up*, hang around*, stick around*, cool one's heels*.—*Ant.* LEAVE, hurry, act. **2** [To serve food at a table] serve, deliver, tend, act as waiter, act as waitress, arrange, set, ready, place on the table, help, portion, bus tables, wait tables. —**wait for** await, expect, stay up for; see WAIT 1. —**wait on** accommodate, serve, attend; see WAIT 2. —**wait up (for)** expect, stay up for, stay awake; see WAIT 1, WORRY 2.
waiter ***n.*** headwaiter, steward, attendant, footman, busboy, servant, innkeeper, host, lackey, counterman, soda jerk*.
waiting ***a.*** standing, languishing, in line, next in turn, expecting, hoping for, marking time, in wait, cooling one's heels*.—*Ant.* MOVING, hurrying, acting.
waiting room ***n.*** restroom, salon, lounge, terminal, reception room, hall, antechamber, foyer, preparation room, depot, station.
waitress ***n.*** female attendant, servant, maidservant, hostess, counter girl, restaurant employee, carhop.
waive ***v.*** forgo, neglect, reject; see ABANDON 1.
wake[1] ***v.*** **1** [To waken another] call, rouse, bring to life, arouse, awaken, wake up, prod, shake, nudge, break into one's slumber. **2** [To become awake] get up, awake, be

come out of sleep; awake: often with *up* **2** to stay awake **3** to become active: often with *up* **4** to become alert (*to* a realization, etc.) —***vt.*** **1** to cause to wake: often with *up* **2** to arouse (passions, etc.) —***n.*** a time set aside for viewing a corpse before burial

wake[2] (wāk) ***n.*** ⟦< ON *vök*, hole⟧ **1** the track left in water by a moving ship **2** the track or course of anything —**in the wake of** following closely

wake'ful ***adj.*** **1** alert; watchful **2** unable to sleep —**wake'ful·ness** ***n.***

wak·en (wā'kən) ***vi.***, ***vt.*** to awake

Wal·dorf salad (wôl'dôrf') ⟦after the old *Waldorf*-Astoria Hotel in New York City⟧ a salad made of diced raw apples, celery, and walnuts, with mayonnaise

wale (wāl) ***n.*** ⟦OE *walu*, weal⟧ **1** a welt raised by a whip, etc. **2** a ridge on the surface of cloth, as corduroy

Wales (wālz) division of the United Kingdom: a peninsula of WC Great Britain: 8,018 sq. mi.; pop. 2,812,000

walk (wôk) ***vi.*** ⟦OE *wealcan*, to roll⟧ **1** to go on foot at a moderate pace **2** to follow a certain course *[walk* in the ways of peace*]* **3** *Baseball* to go to first base after the pitching of four balls (see BALL[1], *n.* 6) —***vt.*** **1** to go over, along, etc. on foot **2** to cause (a dog, etc.) to walk, as for exercise **3** to accompany on a walk or stroll *[*to *walk* a friend home*]* **4** *Baseball* to advance (a batter) to first base by pitching four balls (see BALL[1], *n.* 6) —***n.*** **1** the act of walking **2** a stroll or hike **3** a distance walked *[*an hour's *walk]* **4** a sphere of activity, occupation, etc. *[*people from all *walks* of life*]* **5** a path for walking **6** *Baseball* the walking of a batter —**walk (all) over** [Inf.] to domineer over —**walk away** (or **off**) **with** **1** to steal **2** to win easily —**walk out** to go on strike —**walk out on** [Inf.] to desert; abandon

walk'a·way' ***n.*** an easily won victory

walk'er ***n.*** **1** one that walks **2** a tubular frame with wheels used by babies who are learning to walk **3** a framework used as a support in walking, as by the lame

walk·ie-talk·ie (wôk'ē tôk'ē) ***n.*** a compact, portable radio transmitter and receiver

walking stick a stick for carrying when walking; cane

Walk·man (wôk'mən, -man') *trademark for* a portable, pocket-size radio or tape player with headphones

walk'-on' ***n.*** a minor role in which the actor has few or no lines

walk'out' ***n.*** a labor strike

walk'-up' ***n.*** **1** an upstairs apartment or office in a building without an elevator **2** the building

walk'way' ***n.*** a path, passage, etc. for pedestrians, esp. one that is sheltered

wall (wôl) ***n.*** ⟦< L *vallus*, palisade⟧ **1** an upright structure of wood, stone, etc., serving to enclose, divide, or protect **2** something like a wall in appearance or function —***vt.*** **1** to enclose, divide, etc. with or as with a wall **2** to close up (an opening) with a wall: usually with *up* —**drive** (or **push**) **to the wall** to place in a desperate position —**off the wall** [Slang] **1** insane; crazy **2** very eccentric

wal·la·by (wä'lə bē) ***n.***, *pl.* **-bies** ⟦< Australian native name *wolabā*⟧ a marsupial of Australia, etc., like a small kangaroo

wall·board (wôl'bôrd') ***n.*** fibrous material in thin slabs for making or covering walls and ceilings

wall'cov'er·ing ***n.*** decorative fabric or material, as wallpaper, for covering the walls of a room

wal·let (wô'lit) ***n.*** ⟦ME *walet*⟧ a flat case or folder, as of leather, for carrying money, cards, etc.

wall'eye' ***n.*** ⟦< ON *vagl*, a beam + *eygr*, eye⟧ **1** an eye that turns outward, showing much white **2** a fish with large, glossy eyes, esp. a North American freshwater perch: in full **wall'eyed' pike**

wall'flow'er ***n.*** [Inf.] a person who merely looks on at a dance, etc. as from shyness

Wal·loon (wä lo͞on') ***n.*** ⟦< OHG *walh*, foreigner⟧ **1** a member of a chiefly Celtic people in S Belgium **2** the French dialect of this people

wal·lop (wä'ləp) [Inf.] ***vt.*** ⟦< OFr *galoper*, to gallop⟧ **1** to beat or defeat soundly **2** to strike hard —***n.*** **1** a hard blow **2** a thrill

wal·low (wä'lō) ***vi.*** ⟦OE *wealwian*, roll around⟧ **1** to roll about, as in mud **2** to indulge oneself fully (*in* a specified thing) —***n.*** **1** a wallowing **2** a muddy or dusty place

wall'pa'per ***n.*** decorative paper for covering the walls of a room —***vt.*** to hang wallpaper on or in

Wall Street **1** street in New York City; financial center of the U.S. **2** U.S. financiers and their power, policies, etc. **3** the U.S. securities market

wall'-to-wall' ***adj.*** **1** covering a floor completely **2** [Inf.] *a)* pervasive *b)* comprehensive

wal·nut (wôl'nut') ***n.*** ⟦< OE *wealh*, foreign + *hnutu*, nut⟧ **1** a shade tree valued for its nuts and wood **2** its edible nut **3** its wood

wal·rus (wôl'rəs) ***n.*** ⟦< Dan *hvalros*⟧ a massive arctic sea mammal somewhat like a seal, having two tusks projecting from the upper jaw

waltz (wôlts) ***n.*** ⟦< Ger *walzen*, dance about⟧ **1** a ballroom dance for couples, in 3/4 time **2** music for this —***vi.*** **1** to dance a waltz **2** to move lightly

wam·pum (wäm'pəm) ***n.*** ⟦< AmInd⟧ small beads made of shells and used by North American Indians as money, for ornament, etc.

wan (wän) ***adj.*** **wan'ner**, **wan'nest** ⟦OE *wann*, dark⟧ **1** sickly pale **2** feeble or weak *[*a *wan* smile*]*

wand (wänd) ***n.*** ⟦< ON *vǫndr*⟧ **1** a staff symbolizing authority **2** a rod regarded as having magical powers **3** any of various rod-shaped devices, as one for reading bar codes

wan·der (wän'dər) ***vi.*** ⟦OE *wandrian*⟧ **1** to roam aimlessly; ramble **2** to stray (*from* a path, etc.) **3** to go astray in mind or purpose **4** to meander, as a river —***vt.*** to roam in or over —**wan'der·er** ***n.***

wan'der·lust' ***n.*** ⟦Ger⟧ an urge to wander or travel

wane (wān) ***vi.*** **waned**, **wan'ing** ⟦OE *wanian*, to decrease⟧ **1** to grow gradually less in extent: said of the

THESAURUS

roused, get out of bed, open one's eyes, rise, arise, stir, stretch oneself. —**wake up** rise and shine, arise, get up, awake, get going*, get cracking*.

walk ***n.*** **1** [Manner of walking] gait, tread, stride; see STEP 1. **2** [Course over which one walks] pavement, sidewalk, pathway, footpath, track, trail, driveway, boardwalk, pier, promenade, avenue, road, drive, lane, alley, dock, platform, gangway; see also STREET. **3** [A short walking expedition] stroll, ramble, turn, hike, promenade, airing, saunter, tramp, trek, march, circuit, jaunt, tour.

walk ***v.*** **1** [To move on foot] step, pace, march, tread, amble, stroll, hike, saunter, wander, ramble, go out for an airing, take a walk, promenade, trudge, tramp, trek, tour, take a turn, roam, rove, meander, traipse about, patrol, knock about*, knock around*, hoof it*, toddle along, shuffle, wend one's way, cruise. **2** [To cause to move on foot] lead, drive, exercise, train, order a march, escort, accompany, take for a walk. —**walk (all) over*** subdue, trample on, beat up*; see ABUSE. —**walk away** vanish, depart, split*; see ABANDON 1, 2, LEAVE 1. —**walk off** depart, go one's own way, stalk off; see LEAVE 1. —**walk out on*** desert, leave, walk off from; see ABANDON 2.

walkie-talkie ***n.*** portable transmitter and receiver, field radio, cellular phone; see RADIO 2.

walking ***a.*** strolling, rambling, trudging, hiking, touring, ambling, sauntering, tramping, marching, promenading, passing, roaming, wandering, wayfaring, trekking*.

walkout ***n.*** protest, boycott, demonstration; see STRIKE 1.

wall ***n.*** **1** [A physical barrier] dam, embankment, dike, ditch, bank, levee, stockade, fence, parapet, retainer, rampart, bulwark, palisade, fort, cliff, barricade, floodgate, sluice. **2** [An obstacle; *figurative*] barrier, obstruction, bar, cordon, entanglement, hurdle, resistance, defense, snag, hindrance, impediment, difficulty, limitation, restriction, retardation, knot, hitch, drawback, stumbling block, check, stop, curb, red tape, fly in the ointment, bottleneck, red herring, detour.

wallet ***n.*** billfold, purse, moneybag; see BAG, FOLDER.

wallop ***v.*** thump, thrash, strike; see HIT 1.

wallow ***v.*** grovel, welter, flounder, lie in, roll about in, bathe in, toss, immerse, be immersed in, besmirch oneself.

wall up ***v.*** close up, surround, wall in; see ENCLOSE.

wan ***a.*** colorless, sickly, anemic; see PALE 1.

wander ***v.*** **1** [To stroll] hike, ramble, saunter; see WALK 1. **2** [To speak or think incoherently] stray, maunder, digress; see RAMBLE 2.

wanderer ***n.*** adventurer, voyager, gypsy; see TRAVELER.

wandering ***a.*** **1** [Wandering in space] roving, roaming, nomadic, meandering, restless, traveling, drifting, straying, going off, strolling, ranging, prowling, ambulatory, straggling, on the road, peripatetic, itinerant, roundabout, circuitous.—*Ant.* IDLE, home-loving, sedentary. **2** [Wandering in thought] discursive, digressive, disconnected; see INCOHERENT.

wane ***v.*** decline, subside, fade away; see DECREASE 1, FADE 1.

visible face of the moon **2** to grow dim **3** to decline in power, etc. **4** to approach the end —***n.*** a waning

wan·gle (waŋ′gəl) [Inf.] ***vt., vi.*** **-gled, -gling** ⟦< ? WAGGLE⟧ to get or cause (something) by persuasion, tricks, etc.

wan·na·be (wä′nə bē′) ***n.*** [Slang] one who wants to be like someone else or attain some status: also **wan′na-be′**

want (wänt, wônt) ***vt.*** ⟦< ON *vanta*⟧ **1** to lack **2** to wish for; desire **3** to wish to see or apprehend *[wanted* by the police*]* **4** [Chiefly Brit.] to require —***vi.*** to have a need or lack: usually with *for* —***n.*** **1** a shortage; lack **2** poverty **3** a craving **4** something needed

want ad [Inf.] an advertisement for something wanted, as a job

want′ing ***adj.*** **1** lacking **2** not up to standard —***prep.*** without or minus —**wanting in** deficient in

wan·ton (wänt′'n) ***adj.*** ⟦< OE *wan*, lacking + *teon*, educate⟧ **1** sexually unrestrained **2** [Old Poet.] playful **3** unprovoked or malicious **4** recklessly ignoring justice, decency, etc. —***n.*** a wanton person; esp., a sexually unrestrained woman

wap·i·ti (wä′pə tē) ***n.*** ⟦< AmInd⟧ a large North American deer with widely branching antlers; elk

war (wôr) ***n.*** ⟦< NormFr *werre*⟧ **1** open armed conflict as between nations **2** any active hostility or struggle **3** military operations as a science —***adj.*** of, in, or from war —***vi.*** **warred, war′ring** **1** to carry on war **2** to contend; strive —**at war** in a state of active armed conflict

war·ble (wôr′bəl) ***vt., vi.*** **-bled, -bling** ⟦< NormFr *werbler*⟧ to sing (a song, etc.) melodiously, with trills, quavers, etc., as a bird does —***n.*** a warbling

war·bler (wôr′blər) ***n.*** **1** one that warbles **2** a small, often brightly colored songbird

war crime a violation of laws or norms of humane behavior, committed during war

ward (wôrd) ***vt.*** ⟦OE *weardian*, to guard⟧ to turn aside; fend (*off*) —***n.*** **1** a being under guard **2** one under the care of a guardian or court **3** a division of a jail, hospital, etc. **4** a division of a city or town, for purposes of voting, etc.

-ward (wərd) ⟦OE *-weard*⟧ *suffix* in a (specified) direction *[inward]*: also **-wards** (wərdz)

war·den (wôrd′'n) ***n.*** ⟦< NormFr *wardein*⟧ **1** one who guards, or has charge of, something *[game warden]* **2** the chief official of a prison

ward′er ***n.*** a watchman

ward heeler a follower of a politician, who solicits votes, etc.: often used with mild contempt

ward·robe (wôr′drōb′) ***n.*** **1** a closet, cabinet, etc. for holding clothes **2** one's supply of clothes

ward′room′ ***n.*** in a warship, a room used for eating, etc. by commissioned officers

ware (wer) ***n.*** ⟦OE *waru*⟧ **1** anything for sale: *usually used in pl.* **2** pottery

ware′house′ ***n.*** a building where goods are stored —***vt.*** **-housed′, -hous′ing** to store in a warehouse

war·fare (wôr′fer′) ***n.*** (armed) conflict

war′head′ ***n.*** the front part of a torpedo, etc., containing the explosive

war′horse′ ***n.*** [Inf.] one who has been through many struggles; veteran

war·i·ly (wer′ə lē) ***adv.*** cautiously —**war′i·ness** (-ē nis) ***n.***

war′like′ ***adj.*** **1** fond of or ready for war **2** of war **3** threatening war

war·lock (wôr′läk′) ***n.*** ⟦OE *wærloga*, liar⟧ a man who practices black magic

war′lord′ ***n.*** **1** a high military officer in a warlike nation **2** a local ruler or bandit leader

warm (wôrm) ***adj.*** ⟦OE *wearm*⟧ **1** *a)* having or giving off a moderate degree of heat *b)* hot *[a warm night]* **2** that keeps body heat in *[a warm hat]* **3** ardent; enthusiastic **4** lively, vigorous, etc. **5** quick to anger **6** *a)* genial; cordial *[a warm welcome]* *b)* sympathetic or loving **7** newly made; fresh, as a trail **8** [Inf.] close to discovering something —***vt., vi.*** to make or become warm —**warm up** to practice or exercise, as before going into a game, contest, etc. —**warm′er** ***n.*** —**warm′ish** ***adj.*** —**warm′ly** ***adv.***

warm′blood′ed ***adj.*** having a body temperature that is relatively constant and usually higher than that of the surroundings

warmed′-o′ver ***adj.*** **1** reheated **2** presented again, without significant change, as ideas

warm front the forward edge of a warm air mass advancing into a colder mass

warm′heart′ed ***adj.*** kind, sympathetic, friendly, loving, etc.

war′mon′ger (-muŋ′gər, -mäŋ′-) ***n.*** one who tries to cause war —**war′mon′ger·ing** ***adj., n.***

warmth (wôrmth) ***n.*** **1** *a)* the state of having heat *b)* mild heat **2** *a)* enthusiasm, ardor, etc. *b)* affectionate feelings

warm′-up′ ***n.*** the act of warming up

warn (wôrn) ***vt., vi.*** ⟦OE *wearnian*⟧ **1** to tell of a danger, coming evil, etc. **2** to caution about certain acts **3** to notify in advance; inform

THESAURUS

want ***n.*** **1** [Need] privation, dearth, shortage; see LACK 2. **2** [Desire] wish, craving, demand; see DESIRE 1.

want ***v.*** **1** [To desire] require, aspire, fancy, hanker after, have an urge for, incline toward, covet, crave, long for, lust for, have a fondness for, have a passion for, have ambition, thirst for, hunger for, be greedy for, ache for*, have a yen for*, have an itch for. **2** [To lack] be deficient in, be deprived of, require; see NEED.

wanted ***a.*** needed, necessary, desired, in need of, sought after, in demand, requested, asked for.—*Ant.* SATISFIED, fulfilled, filled.

wanting ***a.*** **1** [Deficient] destitute, poor, in default of, deprived of, bereft of, devoid of, empty of, bankrupt in, cut off, lacking, short, inadequate, defective, remiss, incomplete, missing, substandard, insufficient, absent, needed, unfulfilled, on the short end. **2** [Desiring] desirous of, covetous, longing for; see ENVIOUS, GREEDY.

wanton ***a.*** **1** [Unrestrained] reckless, extravagant, capricious, unreserved, unfettered, free, wayward, fluctuating, changeable, whimsical, fitful, variable, fanciful, inconstant, fickle, frivolous, volatile. **2** [Lewd] wayward, lustful, licentious; see LEWD 2.

war ***n.*** fighting, hostilities, combat. *Types of wars include the following:* air, guerrilla, shooting, ground, sea, jungle, desert, mountain, amphibious, trench, naval, aerial, land, push-button, hot, cold, total, limited, civil, revolutionary, religious, preventive, world, offensive, defensive, biological, bacteriological, germ, chemical, atomic, nuclear, psychological, war to end all wars, war of nerves, war of attrition, war of liberation, campaign, crusade, *Blitzkrieg* (German).

war ***v.*** fight, battle, go to war, wage war on, make war against, engage in combat, take the field against, contend, contest, meet in conflict, march against, attack, bombard, shell, kill, shoot, murder.

ward ***n.*** **1** [A territorial division] district, division, territory; see REGION 1. **2** [A juvenile charge] orphan, foster child, adopted child; see CHILD. **3** [Hospital room] convalescent chamber, infirmary, emergency ward; see HOSPITAL.

warden ***n.*** official, officer, overseer, superintendent, guardian, tutor, keeper, head keeper, jailer, bodyguard, guard, governor, prison head.

wardrobe ***n.*** **1** [A closet] chest, bureau, dresser; see CLOSET. **2** [Clothing] apparel, garments, attire; see CLOTHES.

warehouse ***n.*** wholesale establishment, storehouse, stockroom, storage place, distribution center, repository, depot, shed, stockpile, depository, bin, elevator, storage loft, barn.

wares ***n.*** goods, lines, stock, products, commodities, manufactured articles, merchandise, stuff.

warfare ***n.*** military operations, hostilities, combat; see WAR.

warlike ***a.*** belligerent, hostile, offensive; see AGGRESSIVE.

warm ***a.*** **1** [Moderately heated] heated, sunny, melting, hot, mild, tepid, lukewarm, summery, temperate, clement, pleasant, glowing, perspiring, sweaty, sweating, flushed, warmish, snug as a bug in a rug*.—*Ant.* COOL, chilly, chilling. **2** [Sympathetic] gracious, cordial, compassionate; see FRIENDLY.

warm ***v.*** heat up, warm up, put on the fire; see COOK, HEAT 2.

warmed-over ***a.*** stale, trite, unoriginal; see COMMON 1.

warmth ***n.*** **1** [Fervor] fever, passion, feeling; see EMOTION. **2** [Affection] friendliness, kindness, sympathy; see FRIENDSHIP. **3** [Heat] light, glow, warmness; see HEAT 1, TEMPERATURE.

warn ***v.*** forewarn, give notice, put on guard, give fair warning, signal, advise, prepare, alert, inform, remind, enjoin, hint, prepare for the worst, offer a word of caution, admonish, counsel, exhort, dissuade, reprove, threaten, forbid, predict, remonstrate, deprecate, prescribe, urge, recommend, prompt, suggest, advocate, cry wolf, tip off*, give the high sign, put a bug in one's ear*.

warned ***a.*** informed, admonished, made aware, cautioned, advised, given warning, prepared for the worst, told, forewarned, tipped off*, put on the lookout.

warn′ing ***n.*** **1** the act of one that warns **2** something that serves to warn —***adj.*** that warns

warp (wôrp) ***n.*** ⟦OE *weorpan*, to throw⟧ **1** *a)* a distortion, as a twist or bend, in wood *b)* any similar distortion **2** a mental quirk, bias, etc. **3** *Weaving* the threads running lengthwise in the loom —***vt.*** **1** to bend or twist out of shape **2** to distort, pervert, etc.: said of the mind, character, etc. —***vi.*** to become bent or twisted

war′path′ ***n.*** the path taken by American Indians on a warlike expedition —**on the warpath 1** ready for war **2** actively angry; ready to fight

warp speed ⟦< (TIME) WARP + SPEED⟧ [Slang] in science fiction, a very high rate of speed

war·rant (wôr′ənt, wär′-) ***n.*** ⟦< NormFr *warant*⟧ **1** *a)* authorization, as by law *b)* justification for some act, belief, etc. **2** something serving as a guarantee of some event or result **3** *Law* a writ authorizing an arrest, search, etc. —***vt.*** **1** to authorize **2** to serve as justification for (an act, belief, etc.) **3** to guarantee

warrant officer a military officer ranking above a noncommissioned officer but below a commissioned officer

war·ran·ty (wôr′ən tē, wär′-) ***n.***, *pl.* **-ties** an assurance by a seller that goods will be repaired or replaced if not as represented; guarantee

war·ren (wôr′ən, wär′-) ***n.*** ⟦< NormFr *warir*, to preserve⟧ **1** an area in which rabbits breed or are numerous **2** any crowded building or buildings

war·rior (wôr′yər, -ē ər) ***n.*** ⟦see WAR⟧ a person experienced in conflict, esp. war; soldier

War·saw (wôr′sô′) capital of Poland: pop. 1,651,000

war′ship′ ***n.*** any combat ship, as a battleship

wart (wôrt) ***n.*** ⟦OE *wearte*⟧ **1** a small, usually hard, tumorous growth on the skin, caused by a virus **2** a small protuberance, as on a plant —**wart′y, -i·er, -i·est,** ***adj.***

wart hog a wild African hog with large tusks, and warts below the eyes

war·y (wer′ē) ***adj.*** **-i·er, -i·est** ⟦OE *wær*, aware⟧ on one's guard; cautious —**wary of** careful of

was (wuz, wäz) ***vi.*** ⟦OE *wæs*⟧ *1st & 3d pers. sing., pt., of* BE

wash (wôsh, wäsh) ***vt.*** ⟦OE *wæscan*⟧ **1** to clean with water or other liquid **2** to purify **3** to wet or moisten **4** to flow over, past, or against: said of a sea, waves, etc. **5** to soak (*out*), flush (*off*), or carry (*away*) with water **6** to erode; wear (*out* or *away*) by flowing over *[*the flood *washed* out the road*]* —***vi.*** **1** to wash oneself **2** to wash clothes **3** to undergo washing **4** to be removed by washing: usually with *out* or *away* **5** to be worn or carried (*out* or *away*) by the action of water *[*the bridge had *washed* out*]* **6** [Inf.] to withstand examination *[*that excuse won't *wash]* —***n.*** **1** a washing **2** a quantity of clothes, etc. washed, or to be washed **3** the rush or surge of water **4** the eddy of water or air caused by a propeller, etc. **5** silt, mud, etc. carried and dropped by running water **6** a liquid for cosmetic or medicinal use *[mouthwash]* **7** in the W U.S., the dry bed of a stream **8** [Inf.] a situation in which contrasted elements offset each other —***adj.*** that can be washed without damage; washable —**wash down** to follow (food, etc.) with a drink —**wash′a·ble** ***adj.***, ***n.***

wash′-and-wear′ ***adj.*** of fabrics that need little or no ironing after washing

wash′board′ ***n.*** a ridged board for scrubbing dirt out of clothes

wash′bowl′ ***n.*** a bowl, esp. a bathroom fixture, for use in washing one's hands, etc.: also **wash′ba′sin**

wash′cloth′ ***n.*** a small cloth used in washing the body: also **wash′rag′**

washed′-out′ ***adj.*** **1** faded **2** [Inf.] tired; spiritless; pale and wan

washed′-up′ ***adj.*** **1** [Inf.] tired; exhausted **2** [Slang] finished; done for; having failed

wash′er ***n.*** **1** one who washes **2** a flat ring of metal, rubber, etc., used with a nut, faucet valve, bolt, etc. **3** a machine for washing

wash′er·wom′an ***n.***, *pl.* **-wom′en** a woman whose work is washing clothes

wash′ing ***n.*** clothes, etc. to be washed

washing machine a clothes WASHER (*n.* 3)

Wash·ing·ton[1] (wôsh′iŋ tən, wäsh′-), **George** 1732-99; 1st president of the U.S. (1789-97)

Wash′ing·ton[2] **1** NW coastal state of the U.S.: 66,582 sq. mi.; pop. 4,867,000; cap. Olympia: abbrev. *WA* **2** capital of the U.S., coextensive with the District of Columbia: pop. 607,000: also called **Washington, DC** —**Wash′ing·to′ni·an** (-tō′nē ən) ***adj.***, ***n.***

wash′out′ ***n.*** **1** the washing away of soil, etc. by water **2** [Slang] a failure

wash′room′ ***n.*** **1** a room for washing **2** RESTROOM

wash′stand′ ***n.*** a table or plumbing fixture with a washbowl, etc.

wash′tub′ ***n.*** a tub, often with faucets and a drain, for washing clothes, etc.

wash′y ***adj.*** **-i·er, -i·est** feeble; insipid

wasp (wäsp, wôsp) ***n.*** ⟦OE *wæsp*⟧ a winged insect with a slender body and, in the females and workers, a painful sting

WASP or **Wasp** (wäsp, wôsp) ***n.*** a white Anglo-Saxon Protestant

wasp′ish ***adj.*** bad-tempered; snappish

was·sail (wäs′əl, -āl′) ***n.*** ⟦< ON *ves heill*, be hearty⟧ **1** a toast formerly used to drink to the health of a person **2** the spiced ale, etc. with which such toasts were drunk **3** a drinking party —***vi.***, ***vt.*** to drink a wassail (to)

wast·age (wās′tij) ***n.*** **1** loss by use, decay, etc. **2** anything wasted

waste (wāst) ***vt.*** **wast′ed, wast′ing** ⟦< L *vastare*⟧ **1** to devastate; ruin **2** to wear away **3** to make weak or ema-

THESAURUS

warning ***n.*** caution, admonition, notice, advice, forewarning, alert, intimation, premonition, notification, sign, omen, alarm, indication, token, hint, lesson, information, example, distress signal, prediction, signal, injunction, exhortation, high sign, word to the wise, tip-off, SOS*, handwriting on the wall.

warp ***v.*** curve, twist, pervert; see BEND.

warrant ***n.*** authorization, certificate, credential, official document, license, summons, subpoena, security, pass, testimonial, passport, credentials, permit, permission, verification, authentication.

warrant ***v.*** **1** [To guarantee] assure, insure, vouch for; see GUARANTEE. **2** [To justify] bear out, call for, give grounds for; see EXPLAIN.

warranty ***n.*** written guaranty, guarantee, pledge; see GUARANTY.

warrior ***n.*** battler, fighter, combatant; see SOLDIER.

warship ***n.*** fighting ship, armored vessel, gunboat, man-of-war, frigate, ship-of-the-line; see also BOAT, SHIP. *Warships include the following:* battleship, cruiser, destroyer, destroyer escort, submarine, guided-missile frigate, guided-missile destroyer, missile cruiser, attack submarine, dreadnought, capital ship, landing ship, submarine chaser, aircraft carrier, escort carrier, torpedo boat, PT-boat, raider, flagship.

wart ***n.*** protuberance, spot, mole, projection, blemish, growth, bulge, lesion, tumor.

wary ***a.*** circumspect, cautious, alert; see CAREFUL, SLY.

wash ***n.*** **1** [Laundry] wet wash, washing, linen, family wash, soiled clothing, dirty clothes, clean clothes, washed clothing, flat pieces, finished laundry. **2** [The movement of water] swishing, lapping, roll, swirl, rush, surging, eddy, wave, undulation, surge, heave, flow, murmur, gush, spurt. **3** [A stream bed that is usually dry] arroyo, gulch, canyon; see GAP 3. **4** [A prepared liquid] rinse, swab, fluid; see LIQUID.

wash ***v.*** **1** [To bathe] clean, cleanse, shine, immerse, douse, soak, take a bath, take a shower, soap, rub the dirt off, scour, scrub, rinse, wipe, sponge, dip, freshen up, wash up, clean up. **2** [To launder] clean, starch, scrub, put in a washing machine, boil, soap, send to the laundry, scour, rinse out, soak, drench.—*Ant.* DIRTY, stain, spoil. **3** [To brush with a liquid] swab, whitewash, color; see PAINT 2. **4** [*To be convincing] be plausible, stand up, endure examination; see ENDURE 1, SUCCEED 1.

washable ***a.*** pre-washed, wash-and-wear, unfading, launderable, permanent-press, colorfast, preshrunk.

washed ***a.*** **1** [Laundered] cleaned, scrubbed, bleached, boiled, put through the wash, soaped.—*Ant.* DIRTY, soiled, foul. **2** [Watered] bathed, dipped, drenched, sponged, doused, soaked, cleansed, submerged, showered.—*Ant.* DRY, scorching, desert.

washed-up* ***a.*** finished, defeated, done for*, over the hill*, dead in the water*; see also RUINED 1, 2.

washer ***n.*** dishwasher, washing machine, laundry machine; see APPLIANCE, MACHINE.

washing ***n.*** laundry, soiled clothes, dirty clothes; see WASH 1.

washout* ***n.*** disaster, disappointment, mess; see FAILURE 1, 2.

waste ***a.*** futile, discarded, worthless, valueless, useless, empty, barren, dreary, uninhabited, desolate, profitless, superfluous, unnecessary, functionless, purposeless, pointless, unserviceable.

waste ***n.*** **1** [The state of being

ciated *[wasted* by age*]* **4** to use up needlessly; squander **5** to fail to take advantage of **6** [Slang] to kill —***vi.*** **1** to lose strength, etc., as by disease **2** to be used up or worn down gradually —***adj.*** **1** uncultivated or uninhabited; desolate **2** left over or superfluous **3** excreted from the body **4** used for waste —***n.*** **1** uncultivated or uninhabited land **2** a devastated area **3** a wasting or being wasted **4** discarded material, as ashes **5** excretions from the body, as urine —**go to waste** to be wasted —**lay waste (to)** to destroy —**wast'er** ***n.***

waste'bas'ket ***n.*** a container for wastepaper, etc.: also **wastepaper basket**

wast·ed (wās'təd) ***adj.*** [Slang] **1** intoxicated by a drug **2** drunk

waste'ful ***adj.*** using more than is necessary —**waste'ful·ly** ***adv.*** —**waste'ful·ness** ***n.***

waste'land' ***n.*** **1** barren land **2** an unproductive activity, endeavor, etc.

waste'pa'per ***n.*** paper thrown away after use: also **waste paper**

waste'wa'ter ***n.*** water discharged as sewage

wast·rel (wās'trəl) ***n.*** one who wastes; esp., a spendthrift

watch (wäch, wôch) ***n.*** ⟦OE *wæcce*⟧ **1** a keeping awake, esp. in order to guard **2** close observation for a time **3** a guard, or the period of duty of a guard **4** a small timepiece carried in the pocket or worn on the wrist **5** *a)* any of the periods of duty (usually four hours) on shipboard *b)* the crew on duty during such a period —***vi.*** **1** to stay awake, esp. at night; keep vigil **2** to be on the alert **3** to look or observe **4** to be looking or waiting attentively: with *for* —***vt.*** **1** to guard or tend **2** to observe carefully **3** to wait and look for —**watch oneself** to be careful —**watch out** to be alert or careful —**watch'er** ***n.***

watch'band' ***n.*** a band of leather, metal, etc. to hold a watch on the wrist

watch'dog' ***n.*** **1** a dog kept to guard property **2** one that keeps watch in order to prevent waste, unethical practices, etc.

watch'ful ***adj.*** watching closely; vigilant; alert —**watch'ful·ly** ***adv.*** —**watch'ful·ness** ***n.***

watch'man (-mən) ***n.***, *pl.* **-men** (-mən) a person hired to guard property

watch'tow'er ***n.*** a high tower from which watch is kept, as for forest fires

watch'word' ***n.*** **1** a password **2** a slogan or cry

wa·ter (wôt'ər, wät'-) ***n.*** ⟦OE *wæter*⟧ **1** the colorless liquid of rivers, lakes, etc., which falls as rain **2** water with reference to its depth, surface, or level *[above water]* **3** a body secretion, as urine **4** a wavy, lustrous finish given to linen, silk, metal, etc. —***vt.*** **1** to give (animals) water to drink **2** to supply (crops, etc.) with water **3** to moisten, soak, or dilute with water **4** to give a wavy luster to (silk, etc.) —***vi.*** **1** to fill with tears: said of the eyes **2** to secrete saliva *[his mouth watered]* **3** to take on a supply of water **4** to drink water —***adj.*** of, for, in, on, near, from, or by water —**hold water** to remain sound, logical, etc.

water bed a heavy vinyl bag filled with water and used as a bed or mattress: also **wa'ter·bed'** ***n.***

water buffalo a slow, powerful buffalo of S Asia used as a draft animal

water chestnut **1** a Chinese sedge with a nutlike tuber **2** this tuber

water closet TOILET (*n.* 2)

wa'ter·col'or ***n.*** **1** a pigment mixed with water for use as a paint **2** a painting done with such paints **3** the art of painting with watercolors

wa'ter-cooled' ***adj.*** cooled by water circulated around or through it

wa'ter·course' ***n.*** **1** a stream, river, etc. **2** a channel for water, as a canal

wa'ter·craft' ***n.***, *pl.* **-craft'** a boat, ship, or other water vehicle

wa'ter·cress' ***n.*** a white-flowered water plant: its leaves are used in salads, etc.

wa'ter·fall' ***n.*** a steep fall of water, as of a stream, from a height

wa'ter·fowl' ***n.*** a water bird, esp. one that swims

wa'ter·front' ***n.*** land or docks at the edge of a stream, harbor, etc.

water hole a pond or pool

wa'ter·lil'y ***n.***, *pl.* **-lil'ies** **1** a water plant with large, flat, floating leaves and showy flowers **2** the flower

wa'ter·line' ***n.*** the line to which the surface of the water comes on the side of a ship or boat

THESAURUS

wasted] disuse, misuse, dissipation, consumption, uselessness, devastation, ruin, decay, loss, exhaustion, extravagance, squandering, wear and tear, wrack and ruin; see also WEAR.—*Ant.* USE, PROFIT, VALUE. **2** [Refuse] rubbish, garbage, scrap; see TRASH 1. **3** [Unused land] desert, wilds, wilderness, wasteland, fen, tundra, marsh, marshland, bog, moor, quagmire, dustbowl, badlands, swamp, wash.

waste ***v.*** **1** [To use without result] dissipate, spend, consume, lose, be of no avail, come to nothing, go to waste, misuse, throw away, use up, misapply, misemploy, labor in vain, cast pearls before swine.—*Ant.* PROFIT, use well, get results. **2** [To squander] burn up, lavish, scatter, splurge, spend, be prodigal, indulge, abuse, empty, drain, fatigue, spill, impoverish, misspend, exhaust, fritter away, ruin, be spendthrift, divert, go through, gamble away, throw money away*, run through, hang the expense*, blow*, burn the candle at both ends.—*Ant.* SAVE, be thrifty, manage wisely. **3** [To be consumed gradually] decay, thin out, become thin, wither, dwindle, lose weight, be diseased, run dry, wilt, droop, decrease, disappear, drain, empty, wear out, wear down.—*Ant.* GROW, develop, enrich.

wasted ***a.*** squandered, spent, destroyed, lost, consumed, eaten up, worn down, worn out, thrown away, shriveled, gaunt, emaciated, decayed, depleted, scattered, drained, gone for nothing, missapplied, useless, to no avail, down the drain, unappreciated, of no use, worthless.

wasteful ***a.*** extravagant, profligate, dissipated, prodigal, liberal, immoderate, overgenerous, cavalier, incontinent, thriftless, lavish, squandering, profuse, unthrifty, improvident, careless, reckless, wild, destructive, with money to burn*, easy come easy go.

wastefully ***a.*** extravagantly, carelessly, improvidently, wildly, immoderately, thriftlessly, recklessly, prodigally, destructively, foolishly, lavishly, inconsiderately, openhandedly, imprudently, ruthlessly, profusely, overgenerously, with no thought for tomorrow, without a second thought, without good sense, without consideration, without restraint.

watch ***n.*** **1** [A portable timepiece] wristwatch, pocket watch, stopwatch, digital watch, analog watch, sportsman's watch, fashion watch, ladies' watch, men's watch, children's watch, chronometer; see also CLOCK. **2** [Strict attention] lookout, observation, observance, awareness, attention, vigilance, guard, heed, watchfulness.—*Ant.* NEGLECT, sleepiness, apathy. **3** [A period of duty or vigilance] nightwatch, guard duty, patrol; see GUARD. **4** [Persons or a person standing guard] guard, sentry, sentinel; see GUARDIAN 1.

watch ***v.*** **1** [To be attentive] observe, see, scrutinize, follow, attend, mark, regard, listen, wait, attend, take notice, contemplate, mind, view, pay attention, concentrate, look closely, focus on. **2** [To guard] keep an eye on, patrol, police; see GUARD. —**watch out** take care, heed, be cautious, be careful, proceed carefully, mind, go on tiptoe, take precautions, be on one's guard, make sure of, be doubly sure, keep an eye peeled, handle with kid gloves*, look alive*. —**watch over** protect, look after, attend to; see GUARD.

watched ***a.*** guarded, spied on, followed, held under suspicion, scrutinized, observed, marked, kept under surveillance, noticed, noted, bugged*.

watchful ***a.*** on guard, vigilant, prepared; see CAREFUL.

watchfulness ***n.*** vigilance, alertness, caution; see ATTENTION.

watching ***a.*** vigilant, wary, alert; see CAREFUL.

watchman ***n.*** day watchman, sentinel, scout, spy, ranger, observer, spotter, signalman, flagman, shore patrol, night watchman, security guard, curator, guard, guardian, patrolman, detective, policeman, sentry, keeper, caretaker, lookout.

water ***n.*** **1** [Water as a liquid] rain, rainwater, liquid, drinking water, city water, mineral water, salt water, spa water, distilled water, bottled water, limewater, H_2O. **2** [Water as a body] spring, lake, ocean, sea, gulf, bay, sound, strait, marsh, loch, puddle, pond, basin, pool, river, lagoon, reservoir, brook, stream, creek, waterfall, bayou.

water ***v.*** sprinkle, spray, irrigate; see MOISTEN.

watered ***a.*** **1** [Given water] sprinkled, showered, hosed, sprayed, washed, sluiced, bathed, drenched, wetted, irrigated, flooded, baptized, doused, soused, sodden, slaked, quenched; see also WET 1. **2** [Diluted] thinned, weakened, adulterated, lessened, contaminated, mixed, debased, impure, corrupt, blended, weakened, spread out, inflated, cheapened.

waterfall ***n.*** cataract, cascade, chute, falls.

wa'ter·logged' (-lôgd') ***adj.*** soaked or filled with water so as to be heavy and sluggish

Wa·ter·loo[1] (wôt'ər lo͞o', wät'-) ***n.*** ⟦after fol.⟧ any disastrous or decisive defeat

Wa'ter·loo'[2] town in central Belgium: scene of Napoleon's final defeat (1815)

water main a main pipe in a system of water pipes

wa'ter·mark' ***n.*** **1** a mark showing the limit to which water has risen **2** a mark in paper, produced by pressure of a design, as in the mold —***vt.*** to mark (paper) with a watermark

wa'ter·mel'on ***n.*** a large, green melon with sweet, juicy, red pulp

water moccasin a large, poisonous water snake of the SE U.S.

water pipe **1** a pipe for water **2** a smoking pipe using water, as a hookah

water polo a water game played with a ball by two teams of swimmers

water power the power of running or falling water, used to drive machinery, etc.: also **wa'ter·pow'er** ***n.***

wa'ter·proof' ***adj.*** that keeps out water, as by being treated with rubber, etc. —***vt.*** to make waterproof

water rat any of various rodents living on the banks of streams and ponds

wa'ter-re·pel'lent ***adj.*** that repels water but is not fully waterproof

wa'ter·shed' ***n.*** **1** a ridge dividing the areas drained by different river systems **2** the area drained by a river system

wa'ter·side' ***n.*** land at the edge of a body of water —***adj.*** of, at, or on the waterside

wa'ter-ski' ***vi.*** **-skied', -ski'ing** to be towed on skilike boards (**water skis**) by a line attached to a speedboat —**wa'ter-ski'er** ***n.***

wa'ter·spout' ***n.*** **1** a pipe for spouting water **2** a whirling funnel-shaped column of air full of spray occurring over water in tropical areas

water table the level below which the ground is saturated with water

wa'ter·tight' ***adj.*** **1** so snugly put together that no water can get in or through **2** that cannot be misconstrued, nullified, etc.; flawless

water tower an elevated tank for water storage

wa'ter·way' ***n.*** **1** a channel through which water runs **2** any body of water suitable for boats, ships, etc., as a canal or river

water wheel a wheel turned by running water, as for power

water wings an inflated device to keep one afloat as while learning to swim

wa'ter·works' ***pl.n.*** [*often with sing. v.*] a system of reservoirs, pumps, etc. supplying water to a city

wa'ter·y ***adj.*** **1** of or like water **2** full of water **3** thin; diluted **4** tearful **5** weak —**wa'ter·i·ness** ***n.***

WATS (wäts) ***n.*** ⟦*w*(*ide*) *a*(*rea*) *t*(*elecommunications*) *s*(*ervice*)⟧ a long-distance telephone service using a network at special rates

watt (wät) ***n.*** ⟦after James *Watt* (1736-1819), Scot inventor of steam engine⟧ a unit of electrical power, equal to the power developed in a circuit by a current of one ampere flowing through a potential difference of one volt; $\frac{1}{746}$ horsepower

watt'age ***n.*** amount of electrical power, expressed in watts

wat·tle (wät''l) ***n.*** ⟦OE *watul*⟧ **1** a woven work of sticks intertwined with twigs or branches **2** a fleshy flap of skin hanging from the throat of certain birds or lizards —***vt.*** **-tled, -tling** **1** to intertwine (sticks, twigs, etc.) **2** to build of or with wattle

wave (wāv) ***vi.*** **waved, wav'ing** ⟦OE *wafian*⟧ **1** to move or sway to and fro **2** to signal by moving a hand, arm, etc. to and fro **3** to have the form of a series of curves —***vt.*** **1** to cause to wave **2** to brandish (a weapon) **3** *a*) to move or swing (something) as a signal *b*) to signal (something) to (someone) by doing this **4** to give an undulating form to (hair, etc.) —***n.*** **1** a ridge or swell moving along the surface of the ocean, etc. **2** an undulation or curve, as in the hair **3** a motion to and fro, as with the hand in signaling **4** a thing like a wave in action or effect; specif., an upsurge [*a crime wave*] **5** *Physics* a periodic motion or disturbance, as in the propagation of sound or light

Wave (wāv) ***n.*** ⟦< *W*(*omen*) *A*(*ppointed for*) *V*(*oluntary*) *E*(*mergency*) *S*(*ervice*)⟧ a member of the women's branch of the U.S. Navy (**WAVES**)

wave'length' ***n.*** **1** *Physics* the distance measured along a wave from any given point to the next similar point **2** [Inf.] chiefly in the phrase **on the same wavelength**, in accord

wave'let (-lit) ***n.*** a little wave

wa·ver (wā'vər) ***vi.*** ⟦< ME *waven*, to wave⟧ **1** to sway to and fro **2** to show indecision; vacillate **3** to falter, flicker, tremble, etc. —***n.*** a wavering

wav·y (wā'vē) ***adj.*** **-i·er, -i·est** **1** having or like waves **2** moving in a wavelike motion —**wav'i·ness** ***n.***

wax[1] (waks) ***n.*** ⟦OE *weax*⟧ **1** a plastic, dull-yellow substance secreted by bees; beeswax **2** any plastic substance like this; specif., *a*) paraffin *b*) a substance exuded by the ears —***vt.*** to rub, polish, cover, or treat with wax

wax[2] (waks) ***vi.*** **waxed, wax'ing** ⟦OE *weaxan*, grow⟧ **1** to increase in strength, size, etc. **2** to become gradually full: said of the moon **3** [Literary] to become; grow [*to wax angry*]

wax bean a variety of the common garden bean with long, edible, yellow pods

wax·en (wak'sən) ***adj.*** **1** made of wax **2** pale

wax museum an exhibition of wax figures, as of famous persons

wax myrtle an evergreen shrub with grayish-white, wax-coated berries

wax paper a paper made moisture-proof by a wax coating: also **waxed paper**

wax'wing' ***n.*** a fruit-eating bird with brown or gray silky plumage and scarlet waxlike tips on the wings

wax'works' ***n.*** an exhibition of wax figures

wax'y ***adj.*** **-i·er, -i·est** of, full of, or like wax —**wax'i·ness** ***n.***

way (wā) ***n.*** ⟦ME < OE *weg*⟧ **1** a road, street, path, etc. **2** space for passing **3** a route or course **4** course of life or

THESAURUS

water power ***n.*** hydraulics, waterworks, water pressure, hydroelectric power; see also ENERGY 2.

waterproof ***a.*** impermeable, tight, airtight, vacuum-packed, oiled, rubber-coated, watertight, insulated, impervious, hermetically sealed.

watery ***a.*** moist, damp, humid, soggy, sodden, wet, thin, colorless, washed, waterlike.—*Ant.* DRY, parched, baked.

wave ***n.*** **1** [A wall of water] comber, swell, roller, heave, tidal wave, billow, tide, surge, crest, bore, breaker, whitecap, tsunami. **2** [A movement suggestive of a wave] surge, gush, swell, uprising, onslaught, influx, tide, flow, stream, swarm, drift, rush, crush, fluctuation. **3** [Undulating movement] rocking, bending, winding; see sense 2.

wave ***v.*** **1** [To flutter] stream, pulse, flow, shake, fly, dance, flap, swish, swing, tremble, whirl.—*Ant.* FALL, droop, hang listless. **2** [To give an alternating movement] motion, beckon, call, raise the arm, signal, greet, return a greeting, hail. **3** [To move back and forth] falter, waver, oscillate, vacillate, fluctuate, pulsate, vibrate, shake, wag, waggle, sway, lurch, bend, swing, dangle, seesaw, wobble, reel, quaver, quiver, swing from side to side, palpitate, move to and fro; see also ROCK.

waver ***v.*** fluctuate, vacillate, hesitate, dillydally, seesaw, deliberate, reel, teeter, totter, hem and haw, pause, stagger.

wavy ***a.*** **1** [Sinuous] undulating, bumpy, crinkly; see ROUGH 1, TWISTED 1. **2** [Unsteady] wavering, fluctuating, vibrating; see UNSTABLE 1.

wax[1] ***n.*** *Waxes include the following:* paraffin, resin, spermaceti, beeswax, honeycomb, sealing wax, earwax, cerumen, carnauba wax, automobile wax, floor wax, ski wax, furniture polish.

waxy ***a.*** slick, glistening, polished, slippery, smooth, glazed, sticky, tacky, glassy; see also SMOOTH 1.

way ***n.*** **1** [Road] trail, walk, byway; see HIGHWAY. **2** [Course] alternative, direction, progression, trend, tendency, distance, space, extent, bearing, orbit, approach, passage, gateway, entrance, access, door, gate, channel. **3** [Means] method, mode, plan, technique, design, system, procedure, process, measure, contrivance, stroke, step, move, action, idea, outline, plot, policy, instrument. **4** [Manner] form, fashion, gait, tone, guise, habit, custom, usage, behavior, style. **—by the way** casually, by the by, as a matter of fact; see INCIDENTALLY. **—by way of** routed through, detoured through, utilizing; see THROUGH 4. **—get out of the** (or **one's**) **way** go, remove oneself, retire; see LEAVE 1, REMOVE 1. **—give way** **1** [To collapse] sag, fall, crumble; see GIVE 2. **2** [To concede] yield, accede, grant; see ADMIT 2. **—in the way** bothersome, nagging, obstructing; see DIS-

conduct *[avoid evil ways]* **5** a method of doing something **6** a manner of living, acting, etc. *[the way of the world]* **7** distance *[a long way off]* **8** direction of movement or action **9** movement forward **10** respect; specific point *[right in some ways]* **11** wish; will *[get one's own way]* **12** [Inf.] *a)* a condition *[he's in a bad way]* *b)* a locality *[out our way]* **13** [*pl.*] a timber framework on which a ship is built —***adv.*** [Inf.] away; far *[way behind]* —**by the way** incidentally —**by way of 1** passing through **2** as a method, etc. of —**give way 1** to yield **2** to break down —**lead the way** to be a guide or example —**make way 1** to clear a passage **2** to make progress —**under way** moving; advancing

way'far'er (-fer'ər) ***n.*** a traveler, esp. on foot —**way'far'ing *adj.*, *n.***

way·lay (wā'lā') ***vt.*** **-laid', -lay'ing 1** to lie in wait for and attack **2** to wait for and accost (a person) on the way

way'-out' ***adj.*** [Inf.] very unusual or unconventional

-ways (wāz) ⟦ME < *way* (see WAY)⟧ *suffix* in a (specified) direction, position, or manner *[sideways]*

ways and means methods of raising money; specif., such methods, including legislation, in government

way'side' ***n.*** the edge of a road

way'ward ***adj.*** ⟦see AWAY & -WARD⟧ **1** headstrong, willful, disobedient, etc. **2** unpredictable; erratic —**way'ward·ly *adv.*** —**way'ward·ness *n.***

we (wē) ***pron.***, *sing.* **I** ⟦OE⟧ **1** the persons speaking or writing **2** I: used by a monarch, editor, etc. when speaking for others

weak (wēk) ***adj.*** ⟦< ON *veikr*⟧ **1** lacking physical strength; feeble **2** lacking moral strength or willpower **3** lacking mental power **4** lacking power, authority, force, etc. **5** easily torn, broken, etc. *[a weak railing]* **6** lacking intensity, etc. *[a weak voice]* **7** diluted *[weak tea]* **8** unconvincing *[a weak argument]*

weak'en ***vt.*, *vi.*** to make or become weak or weaker

weak'-kneed' (-nēd') ***adj.*** lacking in courage, determination, resistance, etc.

weak'ling ***n.*** one that is low in physical or moral strength

weak'ly ***adj.*** **-li·er, -li·est** sickly; feeble —***adv.*** in a weak manner

weak'ness ***n.*** **1** state of being weak **2** a weak point **3** an immoderate fondness (*for* something)

weal[1] (wēl) ***n.*** ⟦< WALE⟧ a mark raised on the skin, as by a blow; welt

weal[2] (wēl) ***n.*** ⟦< OE *wela*, wealth, well-being⟧ well-being; welfare *[the public weal]*

wealth (welth) ***n.*** ⟦< prec.⟧ **1** much money or property; riches **2** a large amount *[a wealth of ideas]* **3** valuable products, contents, etc. **4** everything having value in money

wealth·y (wel'thē) ***adj.*** **-i·er, -i·est** having wealth; rich —**wealth'i·ness *n.***

wean (wēn) ***vt.*** ⟦OE *wenian*, to accustom, train⟧ **1** to accustom (a child or young animal) to take food other than by suckling **2** to withdraw (a person) by degrees (*from* a habit, etc.)

weap·on (wep'ən) ***n.*** ⟦OE *wæpen*⟧ **1** any instrument used to injure or kill **2** any means of attack or defense —**weap'on·less *adj.***

weap'on·ry ***n.*** weapons collectively

wear (wer) ***vt.*** **wore, worn, wear'ing** ⟦OE *werian*⟧ **1** to have (clothing, etc.) on the body **2** to show in one's appearance *[to wear a smile]* **3** to impair or diminish by use, friction, etc.: often with *away* **4** to make by rub-

THESAURUS

TURBING. —**make one's way** progress, succeed, do well; see SUCCEED 1. —**make way** draw back, give way, withdraw; see LEAVE 1. —**on the way out** declining, no longer fashionable, going out; see OLD-FASHIONED, UNPOPULAR. —**out of the way 1** [Taken care of] disposed of, attended to, settled; see MANAGED 2. **2** [Secluded] unfrequented, isolated, rural; see REMOTE 1. —**parting of the ways** breakup, agreement to separate, difference of opinion; see FIGHT 1, SEPARATION 1. —**under way** advancing, starting, making headway; see MOVING 1. —**way out** means of escape, salvation, loophole; see ESCAPE.

wayfarer ***n.*** pilgrim, rambler, voyager; see TRAVELER.

way-out* ***a.*** very different, revolutionary, strange; see EXTREME.

ways and means ***n.*** methods, approaches, devices; see MEANS 1.

wayward ***a.*** unruly, disobedient, perverse, headstrong, capricious, delinquent, refractory, willful, unruly, unmanageable, insubordinate, incorrigible, recalcitrant, self-indulgent, changeable, stubborn.—*Ant.* OBEDIENT, stable, resolute.

we ***pron.*** you and I, he and I, she and I, they and I, us.

weak ***a.*** **1** [Lacking physical strength; *said of persons*] delicate, puny, flabby, flaccid, effeminate, frail, sickly, debilitated, senile; see also SICK.—*Ant.* STRONG, healthy, robust. **2** [Lacking physical strength; *said of things*] flimsy, makeshift, brittle, unsubstantial, jerry-built, rickety, tumbledown, sleazy, shaky, unsteady, ramshackle, rotten, wobbly, tottery.—*Ant.* STRONG, shatterproof, sturdy. **3** [Lacking mental firmness or character] weak-minded, fainthearted, irresolute, nervous, spineless, unstrung, palsied, wishy-washy, hesitant, vacillating, frightened, timid, fearful.—*Ant.* BRAVE, courageous, adventurous. **4** [Lacking in volume] thin, low, soft, indistinct, feeble, faint, dim, muffled, whispered, bated, inaudible, light, stifled, dull, pale.—*Ant.* LOUD, strong, forceful. **5** [Lacking in military power] small, paltry, ineffectual, ineffective, inadequate, impotent, ill-equipped, insufficiently armed, limited, unorganized, undisciplined, untrained, vulnerable, exposed, assailable, unprepared. **6** [Lacking in capacity or experience] unsure, untrained, young; see UNSTABLE 2.

weaken ***v.*** **1** [To become weaker] lessen, lose, decrease, relapse, soften, relax, droop, fail, crumble, halt, wane, abate, limp, languish, fade, decline, totter, tremble, flag, faint, wilt, lose spirit, become disheartened, fail in courage, slow down, break up, crack up*, wash out*.—*Ant.* STRENGTHEN, revive, straighten. **2** [To make weaker] reduce, minimize, enervate, debilitate, exhaust, cripple, unman, emasculate, castrate, devitalize, undermine, impair, sap, enfeeble, unnerve, incapacitate, impoverish, thin, dilute, take the wind out of someone's sails, wear down; see also DECREASE 2.—*Ant.* REVIVE, quicken, animate.

weakling ***n.*** puny person, feeble creature, coward, crybaby, milksop, jellyfish*, softy*, sissy*, pushover*, cream puff*, namby-pamby.

weakness ***n.*** **1** [The state of being weak] feebleness, senility, delicacy, invalidity, frailty, faintness, prostration, decrepitude, debility, impotence, enervation, dizziness, infirmity.—*Ant.* STRENGTH, good health, vitality. **2** [An instance or manner of being weak] fault, failing, bad habit, deficiency, defect, disturbance, lapse, vice, sore point, gap, flaw, instability, sin, indecision, inconstancy, vulnerability.—*Ant.* VIRTUE, good, strength. **3** [Inclination] liking, tendency, bent; see HUNGER, INCLINATION 1.

wealth ***n.*** capital, capital stock, economic resources, stock, stocks and bonds, securities, vested interests, land, property, commodities, cash, money in the bank, money, natural resources, assets, means, riches, substance, affluence, belongings, investments, portfolio, fortune, hoard, treasure, resources, revenue, cache, competence, luxury, opulence, prosperity, abundance, money to burn*, dough*.—*Ant.* POVERTY, pauperism, unemployment.

wealthy ***a.*** opulent, moneyed, affluent; see RICH 1.

weapon ***n.*** armament, protection, weaponry, deadly weapon, military hardware, lethal weapon, defense. *Weapons include the following:* club, spear, arrow, knife, catapult, bullet, dart, missile, cruise missile, heat-seeking missile, laser-guided missile, guided missile, ICBM (intercontinental ballistic missile), ABM (antiballistic missile), MIRV (multiple independently-targetable re-entry vehicle), CBW (chemical and biological warfare), bomb, car bomb, truck bomb, letter bomb, smart bomb, stick, ax, firearm, cannon, gun, musket, rifle, blackjack, whip, sword, pistol, handgun, automatic weapon, semiautomatic weapon, weapon of mass destruction, mortar, rocket, bazooka, flamethrower, land mine, mine, napalm, revolver, bayonet, machine gun, warhead, tank.

wear ***n.*** depreciation, damage, loss, erosion, wear and tear, loss by friction, diminution, waste, corrosion, impairment, wearing away, disappearance, result of friction.—*Ant.* GROWTH, accretion, building up.

wear ***v.*** **1** [To use as clothing or personal ornament] bear, carry, effect, put on, don, be clothed, slip on, have on, dress in, attire, cover, wrap, harness, get into*; see also DRESS 2.—*Ant.* UNDRESS, take off, disrobe. **2** [To wear down] use up, use, consume, wear thin, wear out, waste, diminish, cut down, scrape off, exhaust, fatigue, weather down, impair. **3** [To be consumed by wear] fade, go to seed, decay, crumble, dwindle, shrink, decline, deteriorate, decrease, waste, become threadbare. —**wear down** wear out, get thinner, get worn out; see DECREASE 1, WASTE 3. —**wear off** go away, get better, diminish; see STOP 2. —**wear out** become worn, be worthless, get thinner; see WASTE 1, 3.

bing, flowing, etc. [to *wear* a hole in the rug] **5** to tire or exhaust —*vi.* **1** to become impaired or diminished, as by use **2** to hold up in use [that suit *wears* well] **3** to have an irritating effect (*on*) —*n.* **1** a wearing or being worn **2** things worn; clothes [women's *wear*] **3** impairment or loss, as from use, friction, etc. —**wear off** to diminish by degrees —**wear'a·ble** *adj.* —**wear'er** *n.*

wear and tear loss and damage resulting from use

wea·ri·some (wir'i səm) *adj.* causing weariness; tiresome or tedious —**wea'ri·some·ly** *adv.*

wea·ry (wir'ē) *adj.* **-ri·er, -ri·est** ⟦OE *werig*⟧ **1** tired; worn out **2** without further patience, zeal, etc. **3** tiring —*vt., vi.* **-ried, -ry·ing** to make or become weary —**wea'ri·ly** *adv.* —**wea'ri·ness** *n.*

wea·sel (wē'zəl) *n.* ⟦OE *wesle*⟧ **1** an agile flesh-eating mammal with a long, slender body and short legs **2** a sly, cunning person —*vi.* [Inf.] to avoid a commitment: with *out* —**wea'sel·ly** *adj.*

weath·er (weth'ər) *n.* ⟦OE *weder*⟧ **1** the condition of the atmosphere with regard to temperature, moisture, etc. **2** storm, rain, etc. —*vt.* **1** to expose to the action of weather **2** to pass through safely [to *weather* a storm] **3** *Naut.* to pass to the windward of —*vi.* to become worn, etc. by exposure to the weather —**under the weather** [Inf.] ill

weath'er-beat'en *adj.* showing the effect of exposure to sun, rain, etc.

weath'er·cock' *n.* a weather vane in the shape of a rooster

weath'er·ing *n.* the effects of the forces of weather on rock surfaces

weath'er·ize' *vt.* **-ized', -iz'ing** to weatherstrip, insulate, etc. (a building) —**weath'er·i·za'tion** *n.*

weath'er·man' (-man') *n., pl.* **-men'** (-men') one whose work is forecasting the weather, or, esp., reporting it, as on TV

weath'er·proof' *adj.* that can be exposed to wind, snow, etc. without being damaged —*vt.* to make weatherproof

weath'er·strip' *n.* a thin strip of metal, felt, etc. covering the joint between a door or window and the casing, to keep out drafts, etc.: also **weath'er·strip'ping** —*vt.* **-stripped', weath'er·strip'ping** to provide with weatherstrips

weather vane a vane for showing which way the wind is blowing

weave (wēv) *vt.* **wove** or, chiefly for *vt.* 5 & *vi.* 2, **weaved, wo'ven** or **wove** or, chiefly for *vt.* 5 & *vi.* 2, **weaved, weav'ing** ⟦OE *wefan*⟧ **1** to make (a fabric, basket, etc.) by interlacing (threads, straw, etc.), as on a loom **2** to construct in the mind **3** to twist (something) into or through **4** to spin (a web), as spiders do **5** to make (one's way) by moving from side to side or in and out —*vi.* **1** to do weaving **2** to move from side to side or in and out —*n.* a method or pattern of weaving —**weav'er** *n.*

web (web) *n.* ⟦OE *webb*⟧ **1** any woven fabric **2** the network spun by a spider, etc. **3** a carefully woven trap **4** a network **5** a membrane joining the digits of various water birds, etc. **6** [*usually* **W-**] *Comput.* WORLD WIDE WEB: usually with *the* —*vt.* **webbed, web'bing** to join by, or cover as with, a web

web'bing *n.* a strong fabric woven in strips and used for belts, etc.

web'foot' *n., pl.* **-feet'** a foot with the toes webbed —**web'-foot'ed** *adj.*

Web page a single file on the World Wide Web, providing text, pictures, etc.

web'site' *n.* [*occas.* **W-**] a location on the World Wide Web, consisting of one or more Web pages: also **web** (or **Web**) **site**

Web·ster (web'stər), **No·ah** (nō'ə) 1758-1843; U.S. lexicographer

wed (wed) *vt., vi.* **wed'ded, wed'ded** or **wed, wed'ding** ⟦OE *weddian*⟧ **1** to marry **2** to unite or join

Wed *abbrev.* Wednesday

wed·ded (wed'id) *adj.* **1** married **2** of marriage **3** devoted [*wedded* to one's work] **4** joined

wed'ding *n.* **1** the marriage ceremony **2** a marriage anniversary **3** a joining together

wedge (wej) *n.* ⟦OE *wecg*⟧ **1** a piece of wood, metal, etc. tapering to a thin edge: used to split wood, lift a weight, etc. **2** anything shaped like a wedge **3** any act serving to open the way for change, etc. —*vt.* **wedged, wedg'ing** **1** to force apart, or fix in place, with a wedge **2** to crowd together or pack (*in*) —*vi.* to push or be forced as or like a wedge

wedg'ie (-ē) *n.* a shoe having a wedge-shaped piece under the heel, which forms a solid, flat sole

wed'lock' *n.* ⟦OE *wedlac*⟧ the state of being married

Wednes·day (wenz'dā) *n.* ⟦< *Woden*, Germanic god⟧ the fourth day of the week

wee (wē) *adj.* **we'er, we'est** ⟦OE *wege*⟧ **1** very small; tiny **2** very early [*wee* hours of the morning]

weed (wēd) *n.* ⟦OE *weod*⟧ any undesired, uncultivated plant, esp. one that crowds out desired plants —*vt., vi.* **1** to remove weeds from (a garden, etc.) **2** to remove as useless, harmful, etc.: often with *out* —**weed'er** *n.* —**weed'less** *adj.*

weeds (wēdz) *pl.n.* ⟦< OE *wæde*, garment⟧ black mourning clothes, esp. those worn by a widow

weed'y *adj.* **-i·er, -i·est** **1** full of weeds **2** of or like a weed

week (wēk) *n.* ⟦OE *wicu*⟧ **1** a period of seven days, esp. one from Sunday through Saturday **2** the hours or days of work in this period

week'day' *n.* any day of the week except Sunday and, often, Saturday

week'end' or **week'-end'** *n.* the period from Friday night or Saturday to Monday morning: also **week end** —*vi.* to spend the weekend

THESAURUS

wear and tear *n.* depletion, wearing, effect of use; see DAMAGE 1, 2, DESTRUCTION 2.

weariness *n.* tiredness, exhaustion, dullness; see FATIGUE.

weary *a.* exhausted, fatigued, overworked; see TIRED.

weary *v.* **1** [To make weary] annoy, vex, distress, irk, tax, strain, overwork, exhaust, fatigue, tire, harass, bore, disgust, dishearten, dispirit, wear out, leave someone cold, depress, cloy, jade, glut, burden, sicken, nauseate. **2** [To become weary] flag, be worn out, sink, droop, lose interest, fall off, tire, grow tired, drowse, doze, sicken.—*Ant.* ENJOY, excite, be amused.

weather *n.* climate, clime*, atmospheric conditions, air conditions, drought, clear weather, sunny weather, foul weather, tempest, calm, windiness, the elements, cloudiness, heat, cold, warmth, chilliness.

weather *v.* **1** [To expose to the weather] dry, bleach, discolor, blanch, whiten, pulverize, tan, burn, expose, harden, petrify. **2** [To pass through adversity successfully] overcome, stand up against, bear the brunt of; see ENDURE 1, SUCCEED 1.

weather-beaten *a.* decayed, battered, weathered; see OLD 2, 3, WORN 2.

weatherman *n.* weather reporter, weather prophet, weather forecaster, meteorologist, climatologist.

weather report *n.* weather prediction, weathercast, meteorological forecast; see FORECAST.

weave *n.* pattern, design, texture; see WEB.

weave *v.* **1** [To construct by interlacing] knit, sew, interlace, spin, twine, intertwine, crisscross, interlink, wreathe, mesh, net, knot, twill, fold, interfold, ply, reticulate, loop, splice, braid, plait, twist. **2** [To move in and out] dodge, sidle through, make one's way, twist and turn, snake, zigzag, beat one's way, insinuate oneself through, wedge through.

web *n.* cobweb, lacework, netting, plait, mesh, mat, matting, wicker, weft, warp, woof, network, interconnection, reticulation, intermixture, entanglement, tracery, filigree, interweaving, trellis.

wed *v.* espouse, join in wedlock, take in marriage; see MARRY 1, 2.

wedded *a.* married, espoused, in holy matrimony; see MARRIED.

wedding *n.* wedlock, nuptials, matrimony; see MARRIAGE.

wedge *n.* spearhead, shim, chock; see MACHINE, TOOL 1.

weed *n.* **1** [Wild plant] noxious weed, unwanted plant, prolific plant; see PLANT. *Common weeds include the following:* ragweed, clover, chickweed, crab grass, knotgrass, sheep sorrel, speedwell, yarrow, nettle, wild morning glory, pigweed, buckthorn, dandelion, lamb's-quarters, dog fennel, plantain, couch grass, jimson weed, ironweed, wild sunflower, wild hemp, horsemint, foxtail, milkweed, wild barley, wild buckwheat, mullein, Russian thistle, tumbleweed, burdock, wild carrot, wild parsley, vervain, wild mustard. **2** [*Cigarette or cigar] coffin nail*, fag*, smoke; see TOBACCO. **3** [*Marijuana] pot*, Mary Jane*, grass*; see MARIJUANA.

week *n.* wk., seven days, six days, forty-hour week, working week, work week.

weekday *n.* working day, Monday through Friday, workday; see DAY 1.

weekend *n.* end of the week, Saturday to Monday, short vacation, long weekend, holiday weekend.

week'ly *adj.* **1** done, happening, etc. once every week **2** of a week, or of each week —*adv.* once a week; every week —*n., pl.* **-lies** a periodical published once a week
ween (wēn) *vi., vt.* ⟦OE *wenan*⟧ [Archaic] to think
weep (wēp) *vi., vt.* **wept, weep'ing** ⟦OE *wepan*⟧ **1** to shed (tears) **2** to mourn (*for*) **3** to drip or exude (water, etc.) —**weep'er** *n.*
weep'ing *n.* the act of one who weeps —*adj.* **1** that weeps **2** having graceful, drooping branches
weeping willow an ornamental willow tree with drooping branches
weep'y *adj.* **-i·er, -i·est** (inclined to) weeping
wee·vil (wē'vəl) *n.* ⟦OE *wifel*⟧ a beetle whose larvae feed on grain, cotton, etc.
weft (weft) *n.* ⟦< OE *wefan*, to weave⟧ *Weaving* the yarns carried back and forth across the warp
weigh (wā) *vt.* ⟦OE *wegan*, carry⟧ **1** to determine the weight of **2** to have (a specified) weight **3** to consider and choose carefully *[weigh* one's words*]* —*vi.* **1** to have significance, importance, etc. **2** to be a burden —**weigh anchor** to hoist a ship's anchor —**weigh down** to burden or bear down on
weight (wāt) *n.* ⟦OE *wiht*⟧ **1** a quantity weighing a definite amount **2** *a*) heaviness *b*) *Physics* the force of gravity acting on a body **3** amount of heaviness **4** *a*) any unit of heaviness *b*) any system of such units *c*) a piece having a specific amount of heaviness, placed on a balance or scale in weighing **5** any mass of material used for its heaviness *[a paperweight]* **6** a burden, as of sorrow **7** importance or consequence **8** influence; power —*vt.* **1** to add weight to **2** to burden
weight'less *adj.* having little or no apparent weight: said as of an astronaut floating freely in an orbiting space vehicle —**weight'less·ness** *n.*
weight lifting the athletic exercise or sport of lifting barbells —**weight lift'er**
weight'y *adj.* **-i·er, -i·est** **1** very heavy **2** burdensome **3** significant; important —**weight'i·ness** *n.*
weir (wir) *n.* ⟦OE *wer*⟧ **1** a low dam built to back up water, as for a mill **2** a fence, as of brushwood, in a stream, etc., for catching fish
weird (wird) *adj.* ⟦< OE *wyrd*, fate⟧ **1** of or about ghosts, etc.; mysterious, eerie, etc. **2** strange; bizarre —**weird'ly** *adv.* —**weird'ness** *n.*
weird·o (wir'dō) *n., pl.* **-os** [Slang] one that is weird, bizarre, etc.: also **weird'ie** (-dē)
wel·come (wel'kəm) *adj.* ⟦OE *wilcuma*, welcome guest⟧ **1** gladly received *[a welcome* guest*]* **2** freely permitted *[he is welcome* to use my car*]* —*n.* a welcoming —*vt.* **-comed, -com·ing** to greet or receive with pleasure, etc. —**you're welcome** you're under no obligation
weld (weld) *vt.* ⟦< obs. *well*⟧ **1** to unite (pieces of metal, etc.) by heating until fused or until soft enough to hammer together **2** to unite closely —*vi.* to be welded —*n.* **1** a welding **2** a joint formed by welding —**weld'a·ble** *adj.* —**weld'er** *n.*
wel·fare (wel'fer') *n.* ⟦ME: see WELL² & FARE⟧ **1** a condition of health, happiness, prosperity, etc.; well-being **2** *a*) the organized efforts of government agencies granting aid to the poor, the unemployed, etc. *b*) such aid —**on welfare** receiving government aid because of poverty, etc.
wel·kin (wel'kin) *n.* ⟦< OE *wolcen*, a cloud⟧ [Archaic] the vault of the sky
well¹ (wel) *n.* ⟦OE *wella*⟧ **1** a natural spring and pool **2** a hole sunk into the earth to get water, oil, etc. **3** a source of abundant supply **4** a shaft, etc. resembling a well **5** a container for a liquid, as an inkwell —*vi., vt.* to flow or gush from or as from a well
well² (wel) *adv.* **bet'ter, best** ⟦OE *wel*⟧ **1** in a satisfactory, proper, or excellent manner *[treat her well*; you sing *well]* **2** prosperously *[to live well]* **3** with good reason *[one may well ask]* **4** to a considerable degree *[well advanced]* **5** thoroughly *[stir it well]* **6** with certainty; definitely **7** familiarly *[I know her well]* —*adj.* **1** suitable, proper, etc. **2** in good health **3** favorable; comfortable —*interj.* used variously to express surprise, agreement, etc. —**as well** **1** in addition **2** equally —**as well as** in addition to
well-ad·vised (wel'əd vīzd') *adj.* showing or resulting from careful consideration or sound advice; prudent
well'-ap·point'ed *adj.* excellently furnished
well'-bal'anced *adj.* **1** precisely adjusted or regulated **2** sane, sensible, etc.
well'-be·haved' *adj.* displaying good manners
well'-be'ing *n.* the state of being well, happy, or prosperous; welfare
well'-born' *adj.* born into a family of high social position
well'-bred' *adj.* showing good breeding; courteous and considerate
well'-dis·posed' *adj.* friendly (*toward* a person) or receptive (*to* an idea, etc.)
well'-done' *adj.* **1** performed with skill **2** thoroughly cooked: said esp. of meat
well'-fed' *adj.* plump or fat
well'-fixed' *adj.* [Inf.] wealthy
well'-found'ed *adj.* based on facts, good evidence, or sound judgment
well'-groomed' *adj.* clean and neat

THESAURUS

weekly *a.* once every seven days, once a week, occurring every week.
weep *v.* wail, moan, lament; see CRY 1.
weigh *v.* **1** [To measure weight] scale, put on the scales, hold the scales, put in the balance, counterbalance, heft*; see also MEASURE 1. **2** [To have weight] be heavy, carry weight, be important, tell, count, show, register, press, pull, be a load, burden, tip the scales at. **3** [To consider] ponder, contemplate, balance; see CONSIDER. —**weigh down** pull down, burden, oppress; see DEPRESS 2.
weight *n.* **1** [Heaviness] pressure, load, gross weight, net weight, dead weight, molecular weight, specific gravity, burden, mass, density, ponderability, ponderousness, tonnage, ballast, substance, G-force, atomic weight; see also MEASUREMENT 2, PRESSURE 1.—*Ant.* LIGHTNESS, buoyancy, airiness. **2** [An object used for its weight] counterbalance, counterweight, counterpoise, ballast, paperweight, stone, rock, lead weight, sinker, anchor, plumb, sandbag. *Common weights include the following:* grain, dram, ounce, pound, ton, short ton, long ton, troy weight, pennyweight, troy ounce, troy pound, carat, kilogram, centigram, gram, milligram, metric ton, metric carat. **3** [Importance] influence, authority, sway; see IMPORTANCE.
weird *a.* uncanny, ominous, eerie; see MYSTERIOUS 2.
welcome *interj.* greetings, come right in, make yourself at home, how do you do?, glad to see you, won't you come in?.
welcome *a.* gladly received, gladly admitted, desired, appreciated, honored, esteemed, cherished, desirable, agreeable, pleasant, grateful, good, pleasing, delightful.—*Ant.* UNDESIRABLE, disagreeable, unpleasant. —**you're welcome** my pleasure, forget it, think nothing of it, don't mention it, it's nothing.
welcome *n.* greetings, salute, salutation, a hero's welcome, handshake, warm reception, free entrance, entree, hospitality, friendliness, the glad hand*.—*Ant.* rebuke, snub, cool reception. —**wear out one's welcome** bore others, stay too long, make others weary with one; see WEARY 1.
welcome *v.* embrace, hug, take in; see GREET.
welcomed *a.* received, accepted, initiated; see WELCOME.
weld *v.* fuse, unite, seam; see JOIN 1.
welfare *n.* **1** [Personal condition] health, happiness, well-being, prosperity, good, good fortune, progress, state of being. **2** [Social service] poverty program, social insurance, health service; see INSURANCE.
well¹ *n.* **1** [A source of water] spring, fountain, font, spout, geyser, wellspring, mouth, artesian well, reservoir. **2** [A shaft sunk into the earth] pit, hole, depression, chasm, abyss, oil well, gas well, water well, gusher. **3** [Any source] beginning, derivation, fountainhead; see ORIGIN 3.
well² *a.* **1** [In good health] fine, sound, fit, trim, healthy, robust, strong, hearty, high-spirited, vigorous, hardy, hale, blooming, fresh, flourishing, rosy-cheeked, whole, in fine fettle, in shape*, hunky-dory*, great*, fit as a fiddle, chipper*.—*Ant.* SICK, ill, infirm. **2** [Satisfactorily] up to the mark, suitably, adequately, commendably, excellently, thoroughly, admirably, splendidly, favorably, rightly, properly, expertly, strongly, irreproachably, capably, soundly, competently, ably, fine, great*.—*Ant.* BADLY, poorly, unsatisfactorily. **3** [Sufficiently] abundantly, adequately, completely, fully, quite, entirely, considerably, wholly, plentifully, luxuriantly, extremely.—*Ant.* HARDLY, insufficiently, barely. —**as well** in addition, additionally, along with; see ALSO. —**as well as** similarly, alike, as much as; see EQUALLY.
well-balanced *a.* steady, sensible, well-adjusted; see RELIABLE.
well-behaved *a.* mannerly, courteous, civil; see POLITE.
well-being *n.* prosperity, happiness, fortune; see HEALTH, WELFARE 1.
well-fixed* *a.* well-to-do, wealthy, in comfortable circumstances; see RICH 1.

well′-ground′ed *adj.* having a thorough basic knowledge of a subject
well′head′ *n.* **1** a source; fountainhead **2** the top of a well, as an oil or gas well
well′-heeled′ *adj.* [Slang] rich; prosperous
well′-in·formed′ *adj.* having considerable knowledge of a subject or of many subjects
Wel·ling·ton (wel′iŋ tən) capital of New Zealand: pop. 149,000
well′-in·ten′tioned *adj.* having or showing good or kindly intentions
well′-knit′ *adj.* sturdy in body build
well′-known′ *adj.* **1** widely known; famous **2** thoroughly known
well′-made′ *adj.* skillfully and soundly put together
well′-man′nered *adj.* polite; courteous
well′-mean′ing *adj.* **1** having good intentions **2** said or done with good intentions, but often not wisely or effectually: also **well′-meant′**
well′-nigh′ *adv.* very nearly; almost
well′-off′ *adj.* **1** in a fortunate condition **2** prosperous
well′-pre·served′ *adj.* in good condition or looking good, in spite of age
well′-read′ (-red′) *adj.* having read much
well′-round′ed *adj.* **1** well-planned for proper balance **2** showing diverse talents **3** shapely
well′-spo′ken *adj.* **1** speaking easily, graciously, etc. **2** properly or aptly spoken
well′spring′ *n.* **1** the source of a stream, etc. **2** a source of abundant supply
well′-tak′en *adj.* apt and sound or cogent
well′-thought′-of′ *adj.* having a good reputation
well′-timed′ *adj.* timely; opportune
well′-to-do′ *adj.* prosperous; wealthy
well′-turned′ *adj.* **1** gracefully shaped **2** expressed or worded well *[a well-turned* phrase*]*
well′-wish′er *n.* one who wishes well to another or to a cause, etc.
well′-worn′ *adj.* much worn or used
welsh (welsh) *vi.* [Slang] to fail to pay a debt, fulfill an obligation, etc.: often with *on* **—welsh′er** *n.*
Welsh (welsh) *n.* ⟦OE *Wealh,* foreigner⟧ the Celtic language of Wales **—*adj.*** of Wales or its people, language, etc. **—the Welsh** the people of Wales **—Welsh′man** (-mən), *pl.* **-men,** *n.*
Welsh rabbit a dish of melted cheese served on crackers or toast: also **Welsh rarebit**
welt (welt) *n.* ⟦ME *welte*⟧ **1** a strip of leather in the seam between the sole and upper of a shoe **2** a ridge raised on the skin as by a blow
wel·ter (wel′tər) *vi.* ⟦< MDu *welteren*⟧ to roll about or wallow **—*n.*** a confusion; turmoil
wel·ter·weight (wel′tər wāt′) *n.* ⟦prob. < *welt,* to beat⟧ a boxer with a maximum weight of 147 pounds
wen (wen) *n.* ⟦OE *wenn*⟧ a benign skin tumor
wench (wench) *n.* ⟦OE *wencel,* child⟧ a young woman: derogatory or jocular term
wend (wend) *vt.* **wend′ed, wend′ing** ⟦OE *wendan,* to turn⟧ to go on (one's way)
went (went) *vi., vt. pt. of* GO
wept (wept) *vi., vt. pt. & pp. of* WEEP
were (wʉr) *vi.* ⟦OE *wæron*⟧ *pl. & 2d pers. sing., past indic., and the past subjunctive, of* BE
we're (wir) *contr.* we are
were·wolf (wer′woolf′, wir′-) *n., pl.* **-wolves′** ⟦OE *wer,* man + *wulf,* wolf⟧ *Folklore* a person changed into a wolf: also sp. **wer′wolf′,** *pl.* **-wolves′**
Wes·ley (wes′lē, wez′-), **John** 1703-91; Eng. clergyman; founder of Methodism **—Wes′ley·an** *adj., n.*
west (west) *n.* ⟦OE⟧ **1** the direction in which sunset occurs (270° on the compass) **2** a region in or toward this direction **—*adj.*** **1** in, of, toward, or facing the west **2** from the west *[a west* wind*]* **—*adv.*** in or toward the west **—the West 1** the western part of the U.S. **2** Europe and the Western Hemisphere
West Berlin *see* BERLIN
west′er·ly *adj., adv.* **1** toward the west **2** from the west
west′ern *adj.* ⟦OE *westerne*⟧ **1** in, of, or toward the west **2** from the west **3** [W-] of the West **—*n.*** a movie, book, etc. about life in the western U.S., esp. during the frontier period
west′ern·er *n.* a person born or living in the west
Western Hemisphere that half of the earth which includes North & South America
west′ern·ize′ *vt.* **-ized′, -iz′ing** to make Western in habits, ideas, etc.
Western Samoa *former name for* SAMOA
West Germany *see* GERMANY
West In·dies (in′dēz′) large group of islands in the Atlantic between North America & South America **—West Indian**
West Point military reservation in SE New York: site of the U.S. Military Academy
West Virginia state of the E U.S.: 24,232 sq. mi.; pop. 1,793,000; cap. Charleston: abbrev. *WV* **—West Virginian**
west′ward *adv., adj.* toward the west: also **west′wards** *adv.*
wet (wet) *adj.* **wet′ter, wet′test** ⟦OE *wæt*⟧ **1** covered or saturated with water or other liquid **2** rainy; misty **3** not yet dry *[wet* paint*]* **—*n.*** **1** water or other liquid; moisture **2** rain or rainy weather **—*vt., vi.*** **wet** or **wet′ted, wet′ting** to make or become wet **—all wet** [Slang] wrong
wet′back′ *n.* [Inf.] a Mexican who illegally enters the U.S. to work: term of derision or contempt
wet blanket a person or thing whose presence or influence lessens the enthusiasm of others
wet′land′ *n.* [*usually pl.*] **1** swamps or marshes **2** an area of swamps, etc. preserved for wildlife
wet nurse a woman hired to suckle another's child **—wet′-nurse′, -nursed′, -nurs′ing,** *vt.*
wet suit a closefitting suit of rubber worn by skin divers for warmth: also **wet′suit′** *n.*
whack (hwak) *vt., vi.* ⟦echoic⟧ to strike or slap with a sharp, resounding blow **—*n.*** **1** a sharp, resounding blow **2** the sound of this **—have** (or **take**) **a whack at** [Inf.] **1** to aim a blow at **2** to make an attempt at **—out of**

THESAURUS

well-informed *a.* informed, well-read, advised; see LEARNED 1, EDUCATED.

well-known *a.* famous, reputable, recognized, renowned, eminent, illustrious, familiar, widely known, noted, acclaimed, popular, public, celebrated, in the public eye, notorious, infamous.—*Ant.* UNKNOWN, obscure, undiscovered.

well-off *a.* prosperous, well-to-do, wealthy; see RICH 1.

well-read *a.* bookish, scholarly, erudite; see EDUCATED, INTELLIGENT.

well-rounded *a.* well-informed, with broad interests, having a good background; see BALANCED.

well-to-do *a.* wealthy, well-off, prosperous; see RICH 1.

welt *n.* wound, bruise, weal; see INJURY.

west *a.* **1** [Situated to the west] westward, in the west, on the west side of, toward the sunset, west side, western, westerly, westernmost. **2** [Going toward the west] westbound, westward, to the west, headed west, in a westerly direction, out of the east. **3** [Coming from the west] eastbound, eastward, to the east, headed east, in an easterly direction, out of the west.

West *n.* **1** [Western Hemisphere] New World, the Americas, North and South America, America. **2** [European and American Culture] the Occident, Western civilization, Christian society, Europe, European Community, European Union. **3** [Western United States; *especially the cowboy and mining culture*] the range, the prairies, Rocky Mountain country, Far West, Northwest, Southwest, where men are men*, wild-and-woolly country*, the wide open spaces*, buffalo range*, Cow Country*.

western *a.* **1** [Concerning the direction to the west] westerly, westward, on the west side of; see WEST 1. **2** [Concerning the western part of the United States] West, Pacific, Pacific Seaboard, West Coast, Northwestern, Southwestern, cowboy, middle-western, far-western, in the sagebrush country, on the Western plains, in the wide open spaces, in the Wild West, in the Rockies, in God's country, in the wild-and-woolly West*, out where the men are men*. **3** [Concerning Europe and America] American, European, Continental, British, Canadian, Caribbean, Latin American, French, German, Italian, Spanish.

wet *a.* **1** [Covered or soaked with liquid] moist, damp, soaking, soaked, drenched, soggy, muggy, dewy, watery, dank, slimy, dripping, saturated, sodden.—*Ant.* DRY, dried, clean. **2** [Rainy] drizzly, slushy, snowy, slippery, muddy, humid, foggy, damp, clammy, showery, stormy, drizzling, cloudy, misty.—*Ant.* CLEAR, sunny, cloudless.

wet *v.* sprinkle, dampen, splash; see MOISTEN.

whack *n.* stroke, thump, wham; see BLOW. **—out of whack*** out of order, not working, spoiled; see RUINED 1, 2.

whack [Inf.] not in proper working condition —**whack'er** ***n.***

whacked'-out' ***adj.*** [Slang] **1** exhausted **2** STONED **3** wacky, bizarre, etc.

whale[1] (hwāl) ***n.*** ⟦OE *hwæl*⟧ a large, warmblooded sea mammal that breathes air —***vi.*** **whaled, whal'ing** to hunt whales —**a whale of a** [Inf.] an exceptionally large, fine, etc. example of a (class or group)

whale[2] (hwāl) ***vt.*** **whaled, whal'ing** ⟦prob. < WALE⟧ [Inf.] to beat, whip, etc.

whale'bone' ***n.*** BALEEN

whal'er ***n.*** **1** a whaling ship **2** one whose work is whaling

wham (hwam) ***interj.*** used to suggest the sound of a heavy blow, explosion, etc. —***n.*** a heavy blow, etc. —***vt., vi.*** **whammed, wham'ming** to strike, explode, etc. loudly

wham'my ***n.***, *pl.* **-mies** [Slang] a jinx

wharf (hwôrf) ***n.***, *pl.* **wharves** or **wharfs** ⟦OE *hwerf,* a dam⟧ a structure on a shore, at which ships are loaded or unloaded; dock

what (hwut, hwät) ***pron.*** ⟦OE *hwæt,* neuter of *wha,* who⟧ **1** which thing, event, etc. *[what* is that object?*]* **2** that or those which *[*to know *what* one wants*]* —***adj.*** **1** which or which kind of: used interrogatively or relatively **2** as much, or as many, as *[*take *what* men you need*]* **3** how great, surprising, etc. *[what* nonsense!*]* —***adv.*** **1** in what way? how? *[what* does it matter?*]* **2** how greatly, etc. *[what* tragic news!*]* —***interj.*** used to express surprise, anger, etc. —**what about** what do you think, feel, etc. concerning? —**what for?** why? —**what with** because of *[what with* the bad weather, we'll be late*]*

what·ev'er ***pron.*** what: an emphatic variant; specif., *a)* which thing, event, etc.? *b)* anything that *[*say *whatever* you like*]* *c)* no matter what *[whatever* you do, don't hurry*]* —***adj.*** **1** of any kind *[*I have no plans *whatever]* **2** being who it may be *[whatever* man said that, it is not true*]*

what'not' ***n.*** a set of open shelves, as for bric-a-brac

what's (hwuts) *contr.* **1** what is **2** what has **3** [Inf.] what does *[what's* he want?*]*

what·so·ev·er (hwut'sō ev'ər) ***pron., adj.*** whatever: an emphatic form

wheal[1] (hwēl) ***n.*** ⟦ME *whele*⟧ a small, itching elevation of the skin, as from an insect bite

wheal[2] (hwēl) ***n.*** WEAL[1]

wheat (hwēt) ***n.*** ⟦OE *hwæte*⟧ a cereal grass having spikes containing grains used in making flour, cereals, etc.

wheat germ the highly nutritious embryo of the wheat kernel, milled out as a flake

whee·dle (hwēd''l) ***vt., vi.*** **-dled, -dling** ⟦< ?⟧ to influence or persuade (a person), or get (something), by flattery, coaxing, etc.

wheel (hwēl) ***n.*** ⟦OE *hweol*⟧ **1** a circular disk or frame turning on a central axis **2** anything like a wheel in shape, movement, etc. **3** the steering wheel of a motor vehicle **4** [*pl.*] [Slang] an automobile **5** [*usually pl.*] the moving forces *[*the *wheels* of progress*]* **6** a turning movement **7** [Slang] an important person —***vt., vi.*** **1** to move on or in (a wheeled vehicle) **2** to turn, revolve, etc. **3** to turn so as to change direction —**at** (or **behind**) **the wheel** steering a motor vehicle, ship, etc.

wheel'bar'row ***n.*** a kind of cart for carrying small loads, having a wheel in front and two shafts with handles in back for raising the vehicle off its two back legs and moving it

wheel'base' ***n.*** the length of a motor vehicle between the centers of the front and rear wheels

wheel'chair' ***n.*** a chair mounted on large wheels, for persons unable to walk

wheeled (hwēld) ***adj.*** having wheels

wheel·er-deal·er (hwēl'ər dēl'ər) ***n.*** [Slang] one who is aggressive in a showy way, as in arranging business deals

wheel'house' ***n.*** PILOTHOUSE

wheel'wright' ***n.*** one who makes and repairs wheels and wheeled vehicles

wheeze (hwēz) ***vi.*** **wheezed, wheez'ing** ⟦< ON *hvæsa,* to hiss⟧ to breathe hard with a whistling, breathy sound, as in asthma —***n.*** a wheezing —**wheez'y, -i·er, -i·est,** ***adj.***

whelk (hwelk) ***n.*** ⟦OE *wioluc*⟧ a kind of large marine snail

whelm (hwelm) ***vt.*** ⟦ME *welmen*⟧ **1** to submerge **2** to overpower or crush

whelp (hwelp) ***n.*** ⟦OE *hwelp*⟧ a young dog, etc. —***vt., vi.*** to give birth to (young): said of some animals

when (hwen) ***adv.*** ⟦OE *hwænne*⟧ **1** at what time? *[when* did they leave?*]* **2** on what occasion? —***conj.*** **1** at what time *[*tell me *when* to go*]* **2** at the time that *[when* we were young*]* **3** at which *[*a time *when* people must work*]* **4** as soon as *[*we will eat *when* he comes*]* **5** although **6** if —***pron.*** what or which time —***n.*** the time (*of* an event)

whence (hwens) ***adv.*** ⟦ME *whennes*⟧ from what place, cause, etc.? *[whence* do you come?*]*

when·ev'er ***adv.*** [Inf.] when: an emphatic form —***conj.*** at whatever time *[*go *whenever* you can*]*

where (hwer) ***adv.*** ⟦OE *hwær*⟧ **1** in or at what place? *[where* is it?*]* **2** to or toward what place? *[where* did he go?*]* **3** in what respect? *[where* is he to blame?*]* **4** from what place or source? *[where* did he learn it?*]* —***conj.*** **1** at what place *[*I see *where* it is*]* **2** at which place *[*I went home, *where* I ate dinner*]* **3** wherever **4** to the place to which *[*we go *where* you go*]* —***pron.*** **1** the place at which *[*it's a mile to *where* I live*]* **2** what place *[where* are you from?*]* —***n.*** the place (*of* an event)

where'a·bouts' (-ə bouts') ***adv.*** near or at what place? —***n.*** [*now usually with pl. v.*] the place where one is

where·as' ***conj.*** **1** in view of the fact that **2** while on the contrary *[*I'm slim, *whereas* he is fat*]*

where·at' ***conj.*** [Archaic] at which point

where·by' ***conj.*** by which

where'fore' (-fôr') ***adv.*** [Archaic] for what reason? why? —***conj.*** [Archaic] **1** for which **2** because of which —***n.*** the reason; cause

where·in' ***conj.*** in which

where·of' ***adv., conj.*** of what, which, or whom *[*the things *whereof* he spoke*]*

where·on' ***conj.*** [Archaic] on which

where'up·on' ***conj.*** at which

wher·ev·er (hwer ev'ər) ***adv.*** [Inf.] where: an emphatic form —***conj.*** in, at, or to whatever place or situation *[*go *wherever* you like*]*

THESAURUS

wham ***n.*** hit, knock, whack; see BLOW.

wharf ***n.*** boat landing, quay, pier; see DOCK.

what ***pron.*** **1** [An indication of a question] which?, what sort?, what kind?, what thing?, what means?. **2** [Something indefinite] that which, whatever, something, anything, everything, whichever, anything at all. —**and what not** et cetera, and other things too numerous to mention, some more; see ANYTHING, EVERYTHING. —**what about** but what, remember, and then; see BUT 1, 2, 3. —**what for** but why, to what end, for what purpose; see WHY.

whatever ***pron.*** anything, everything, no matter what, whatsoever.

wheat ***n.*** staff of life, breadstuff, wheat flour; see GRAIN 1.

wheel ***n.*** **1** [A thin circular body that turns on an axis] disk, ratchet, ring, hoop, roller, caster, drum, ferris wheel, wheel trolley, flywheel, cogwheel, steering wheel, sprocket wheel, chain wheel, water wheel. **2** [*An important person] personage, VIP, big shot*; see CELEBRITY, EXECUTIVE. —**at** (or **behind**) **the wheel** driving, in control, running things; see RUNNING 1, 2.

wheels* ***n.*** car, vehicle, auto; see AUTOMOBILE.

wheeze ***v.*** breathe heavily, puff, pant; see GASP.

when ***a., conj.*** **1** [At what time?] how soon?, how long ago?, in what period?, just when?, at which instant?. **2** [Whenever] if, at any time, at the moment that, just as soon as, in the event that, on the condition that; see also IF. **3** [During] at the same time that, immediately upon, just as, just after, at, while, meanwhile; see also DURING.

whenever ***conj.*** at any time, at any moment, on any occasion, at the first opportunity, if, when, should.

where ***a., conj.*** **1** [A question as to position] in what place?, at which place?, at what moment?, whither?, in what direction?, toward what?. **2** [An indication of position] wherever, anywhere, in whatever place, at which point, in which, to which, to what end.

whereabouts ***n.*** location, spot, site; see PLACE 3.

whereas ***conj.*** since, inasmuch as, insomuch as, forasmuch as, considering that, when in fact, while, while on the contrary.

whereby ***conj.*** by which, through which, in accordance with which, with the help of which, how.

wherefore ***a.*** why?, for what?, for which reason?, therefore, so, accordingly, thereupon.

whereupon ***conj.*** at which point, thereupon, at the conclusion of which, whereon, upon which, consequently.

wherever ***a., conj.*** where, in whatever place, anywhere, in any place that, wheresoever, regardless of where, in any direction.

where·with′ *conj.* [Archaic] with which
where′with·al′ (-wi*th* ôl′) *n.* the necessary means, esp. money: usually with *the*
wher·ry (hwer′ē) *n., pl.* **-ries** ⟦ME *whery*⟧ a light rowboat
whet (hwet) *vt.* **whet′ted, whet′ting** ⟦< OE *hwæt*, keen⟧ **1** to sharpen by rubbing or grinding (the edge of a knife or tool) **2** to stimulate
wheth·er (hwe*th*′ər) *conj.* ⟦OE *hwæther*⟧ **1** if it be the case that *[ask whether she sings]* **2** in case; in either case that: introducing alternatives *[whether it rains or snows]*
whet·stone (hwet′stōn′) *n.* an abrasive stone for sharpening knives, etc.
whew (hyo͞o) *interj.* ⟦echoic⟧ used to express relief, surprise, dismay, etc.
whey (hwā) *n.* ⟦OE *hwæg*⟧ the watery part of milk, that separates from the curds
which (hwich) *pron.* ⟦OE *hwylc*⟧ **1** what one (or ones) of several? *[which do you want?]* **2** the one (or ones) that *[he knows which he wants]* **3** that *[the boat which sank]* —*adj.* what one or ones *[which man (or men) left?]*
which·ev′er *pron., adj.* **1** any one *[take whichever (desk) you like]* **2** no matter which *[whichever (desk) he chooses, they won't be pleased]*
whiff (hwif) *n.* ⟦echoic⟧ **1** a light puff or gust of air, etc. **2** a slight odor
whif·fle·tree (hwif′əl trē′) *n. var. of* WHIPPLETREE
Whig (hwig) *n.* ⟦< *whiggamore* (derisive term for Scot Presbyterians)⟧ **1** a member of a former English political party that championed reform **2** a supporter of the American Revolution **3** a member of a U.S. political party (*c.* 1834-56)
while (hwīl) *n.* ⟦OE *hwil*⟧ a period of time *[a short while]* —*conj.* **1** during the time that *[I read while I eat]* **2** although; whereas *[while not poor, she's not rich]* —*vt.* **whiled, whil′ing** to spend (time) in a pleasant way: often with *away*
whi·lom (hwī′ləm) *adj.* ⟦< OE⟧ former
whilst (hwīlst) *conj.* [Chiefly Brit.] WHILE
whim (hwim) *n.* a sudden, passing idea or desire
whim·per (hwim′pər) *vi., vt.* ⟦? akin to WHINE⟧ to cry or utter with low, whining, broken sounds —*n.* a whimpering sound or cry
whim·si·cal (hwim′zi kəl) *adj.* **1** full of whims or whimsy **2** oddly out of the ordinary —**whim′si·cal′i·ty** (-kal′ə tē) *n.* —**whim′si·cal·ly** *adv.*
whim·sy (hwim′zē) *n., pl.* **-sies** ⟦< ?⟧ **1** a sudden, odd notion **2** quaint or fanciful humor Also sp. **whim′sey**, *pl.* **-seys**
whine (hwīn) *vi.* **whined, whin′ing** ⟦OE *hwinan*⟧ **1** *a)* to utter a high-pitched, nasal sound, as in complaint *b)* to make a prolonged sound like this **2** to complain in a childish way —*n.* **1** a whining **2** a complaint uttered in a whining tone —**whin′y, -i·er, -i·est,** *adj.*
whin·ny (hwin′ē) *vi.* **-nied, -ny·ing** ⟦prob. echoic⟧ to neigh in a low, gentle way: said of a horse —*n., pl.* **-nies** a whinnying
whip (hwip) *vt.* **whipped** or **whipt, whip′ping** ⟦< MDu *wippen*, to swing⟧ **1** to move, pull, throw, etc. suddenly *[to whip out a knife]* **2** to strike, as with a strap; lash **3** to wind (cord, etc.) around (a rope, etc.) so as to prevent fraying **4** to beat into a froth *[to whip cream]* **5** [Inf.] to defeat —*vi.* **1** to move quickly and suddenly **2** to flap about —*n.* **1** a flexible instrument for striking or flogging **2** a blow, etc. as with a whip **3** an officer of a political party in a legislature who maintains disclipine, etc. **4** a whipping motion —**whip up 1** to rouse (interest, etc.) **2** [Inf.] to prepare quickly
whip′cord′ *n.* **1** a hard, twisted or braided cord **2** a strong, diagonally ribbed worsted cloth
whip hand control or advantage
whip′lash′ *n.* **1** the lash of a whip **2** a sudden, severe jolting of the neck, as in an automobile accident
whip′per·snap′per *n.* an insignificant person who appears presumptuous
whip·pet (hwip′it) *n.* ⟦< WHIP⟧ a swift dog resembling a small greyhound, used in racing
whip·ple·tree (hwip′əl trē′) *n.* ⟦< WHIP + TREE⟧ SINGLETREE
whip·poor·will (hwip′ər wil′) *n.* ⟦echoic⟧ a dark-colored bird of E North America, active at night
whip′py *adj.* springy; flexible
whir or **whirr** (hwʉr) *vi., vt.* **whirred, whir′ring** ⟦ME *quirren*⟧ to fly, revolve, vibrate, etc. with a whizzing or buzzing sound —*n.* such a sound
whirl (hwʉrl) *vi.* ⟦< ON *hvirfla*⟧ **1** to move rapidly in a circle or orbit **2** to rotate or spin fast **3** to seem to spin *[my head is whirling]* —*vt.* to cause to rotate, revolve, or spin rapidly —*n.* **1** a whirling motion **2** a confused or giddy condition —**give it a whirl** [Inf.] to make an attempt
whirl·i·gig (hwʉr′li gig′) *n.* a child's toy that whirls or spins, as a pinwheel
whirl′pool′ *n.* **1** water in violent, whirling motion, tending to draw floating objects into its center **2** a bath in which an agitating device propels a current of warm water with a swirling motion: in full **whirlpool bath**
whirl′wind′ *n.* **1** a forward-moving current of air whirling violently in a vertical spiral **2** anything like a whirlwind —*adj.* impetuous; speedy
whisk (hwisk) *n.* ⟦< ON *visk*, a brush⟧ **1** a brushing with a quick, light, sweeping motion **2** such a motion **3** a kitchen utensil of wire loops in a handle, for whipping cream, etc. —*vt.* to move, carry, brush (*away, off, out,* etc.) with a quick, sweeping motion —*vi.* to move quickly or nimbly
whisk broom a small, short-handled broom for brushing clothes, etc.
whisk·er (hwis′kər) *n.* **1** [*pl.*] the hair growing on a man's face, esp. on the cheeks **2** any of the long, bristly hairs on the upper lip of a cat, rat, etc. **3** a very small amount or margin
whis·key (hwis′kē) *n., pl.* **-keys** or **-kies** ⟦< Ir *uisce*, water + *beathadh*, life⟧ a strong alcoholic liquor distilled from the fermented mash of grain: also sp. **whis·ky**, *pl.* **-kies**: in general, U.S. and Irish usage favors *whiskey*, and Brit. and Cdn. usage favors *whisky*
whis·per (hwis′pər) *vi., vt.* ⟦< OE *hwisprian*⟧ **1** to speak or say very softly, esp. without vibrating the vocal cords

THESAURUS

wherewithal *n.* resources, money, funds; see FUNDS.
whether *conj.* if, either, even if, if it follows that. —**whether or not 1** [Surely] in any case, certainly, positively; see SURELY. **2** [If] whether, yes or no, whichever; see IF.
which *pron., a.* what, whichever, that, whatever, and that, and which, one, who.
whichever *pron., a.* which, whatever, whichsoever, no matter which, whoever.
whiff *n.* scent, puff, fume; see SMELL 1, 2.
while *conj.* **1** [As long as] during, at the same time that, during the time that, whilst, throughout the time that, in the time that. **2** [Although] even though, whereas, though; see ALTHOUGH. —**for a while** for a short time, for a few minutes, briefly; see AWHILE.
whim *n.* notion, vagary, caprice; see INCLINATION 1.
whimper *v.* fuss, weep, snivel; see COMPLAIN, WHINE.
whimsical *a.* playful, capricious, comical; see FUNNY 1.
whine *v.* sing, hum, whistle, whimper, drone, cry, moan, murmur, grumble, complain, gripe*, beef*.
whip *n.* switch, strap, rod, cane, lash, scourge, knotted cord, knout, cat-o-nine-tails, thong, blacksnake, dog whip, ox whip, bullwhip, horsewhip, buggy whip, riding whip, quirt.
whip *v.* thrash, strike, scourge; see BEAT 2, PUNISH.
whipping *n.* beating, thrashing, strapping; see PUNISHMENT.
whir *v.* whiz, swish, vibrate; see HUM.
whirl *n.* **1** [Rapid rotating motion] swirl, turn, flurry, spin, gyration, reel, surge, whir; see also REVOLUTION 1. **2** [Confusion] hurry, flutter, fluster, ferment, agitation, tempest, storm, rush, tumult, turbulence, commotion, hurly-burly, bustle.
whirl *v.* turn around, rotate, spin; see TURN 1.
whirlpool *n.* eddy, vortex, swirl, maelstrom, undertow, undercurrent, rapids.
whiskers *n.* beard, mustache, sideburns, goatee, burnsides, mutton chops, facial hair, bristles, (hogs, etc.), vibrissa (cats, etc.).
whiskey *n.* bourbon whiskey, rye whiskey, corn whiskey, Scotch whiskey, Irish whiskey, Canadian whiskey, hard liquor, spirits, aqua vitae, booze*, firewater*, hooch*, homebrew, moonshine*, mountain dew*; see also DRINK 2.
whisper *n.* **1** [A low, sibilant sound] rustle, noise, murmur, hum, buzz, drone, undertone, hissing. **2** [A guarded utterance] disclosure, divulgence, rumor; see SECRET.
whisper *v.* speak softly, speak in a whisper, speak under one's breath, speak in an undertone, tell, talk low, speak confidentially, mutter, murmur, speak into someone's ear.—*Ant.* YELL, speak aloud, shout.
whispering *a.* rustling, sighing, buzzing, humming, murmuring, droning, hissing.

2 to talk or tell furtively, as in gossiping 3 to make a rustling sound —*n.* 1 a whispering 2 something whispered 3 a soft, rustling sound

whist (hwist) *n.* ⟦< earlier *whisk*⟧ a card game that is the forerunner of bridge

whis·tle (hwis′əl) *vi.* **-tled, -tling** ⟦OE *hwistlian*⟧ 1 to make a clear, shrill sound as by blowing through puckered lips 2 to move with a shrill sound, as the wind does 3 *a*) to blow a whistle *b*) to have its whistle blown *[the train whistled]* —*vt.* 1 to produce (a tune, etc.) by whistling 2 to signal, etc. by whistling —*n.* 1 a device for making whistling sounds 2 a whistling —**whis′tler** *n.*

whis′tle-blow′er *n.* one who informs on a wrongdoer

whis′tle-stop′ *n.* 1 a small town 2 a brief stop in a small town on a tour

whit (hwit) *n.* ⟦< OE *wiht*, wight⟧ the least bit; jot

white (hwīt) *adj.* **whit′er, whit′est** ⟦OE *hwit*⟧ 1 having the color of pure snow or milk; opposite to black 2 of a light or pale color 3 pale; wan 4 lacking color 5 pure; innocent 6 [*sometimes* **W-**] having a light-colored skin; Caucasoid —*n.* 1 *a*) white color *b*) a white pigment 2 a white or light-colored part, as the albumen of an egg or the white part of the eyeball 3 [*sometimes* **W-**] a person with a light-colored skin —**white′ness** *n.*

white blood cell (or **corpuscle**) LEUKOCYTE

white′-bread′ *adj.* [Inf.] 1 of or like the white middle class, its values, etc. 2 bland, conventional, etc.

white′cap′ *n.* a wave with its crest broken into white foam

white′-col′lar *adj.* designating or of office or professional workers

white-collar crime fraud, embezzlement, etc., committed by a person in business, government, or a profession

white elephant 1 an albino elephant 2 something of little use, but expensive to maintain 3 any object no longer wanted by its owner, but possibly useful to another

white′fish′ *n., pl.* **-fish′** or (for different species) **-fish′es** a white or silvery, edible fish, found in cool lakes of the Northern Hemisphere

white flag a white banner or cloth hoisted as a signal of truce or surrender

white gold a gold alloy that looks like platinum

white goods 1 household linens, as sheets and towels 2 large household appliances, as refrigerators and stoves

white heat 1 a temperature at which material glows white 2 a state of intense emotion, excitement, etc. —**white′-hot′** *adj.*

White′horse′ capital of the Yukon Territory, Canada: pop. 19,000

White House, the 1 official residence of the President of the U.S. in Washington, DC 2 the executive branch of the U.S. government

white lead a poisonous, white powder, lead carbonate, used in paint

white lie a lie about a trivial matter, often told to spare someone's feelings

white metal any of various light-colored alloys, esp. one containing much lead or tin, as pewter

whit·en (hwīt′'n) *vt., vi.* to make or become white or whiter —**whit′en·er** *n.* —**whit′en·ing** *n.*

white′-out′ *n.* ⟦< *Wite-Out*, a trademark⟧ a quick-drying, white fluid that is brushed on to cover printed errors and allow for corrections

white paper 1 an official government report 2 any in-depth, authoritative report

white sale a sale of household linens

white slave a woman forced into prostitution for the profit of others —**white slavery**

white′wall′ *adj.* designating or of a tire with a circular white band on the side —*n.* such a tire

white′wash′ *n.* 1 a mixture of lime, chalk, water, etc., as for whitening walls, etc. 2 a concealing of faults in order to exonerate —*vt.* 1 to cover with whitewash 2 to conceal the faults of 3 [Inf.] *Sports* to defeat (an opponent) soundly

white′-wa′ter *adj.* of or having to do with recreational kayaking, rafting, etc. on rivers with rapids, fast currents, etc. (**white water**)

whith·er (hwi*th*′ər) [Now Rare] *adv.* ⟦OE *hwider*⟧ to what place, condition, result, etc.? —*conj.* 1 to which place, result, etc. 2 wherever

whit·ing[1] (hwīt′iŋ) *n.* ⟦< MDu *wit*, white⟧ any of various unrelated food fishes of North America, Europe, etc.

whit·ing[2] (hwīt′iŋ) *n.* ⟦ME *hwiting*⟧ powdered chalk used in paints, etc.

whit′ish *adj.* somewhat white

Whit·man (hwit′mən), **Walt**(**er**) 1819-92; U.S. poet

Whit·ney (hwit′nē), **Mount** mountain in EC California: 14,495 ft.

Whit·sun·day (hwit′sun′dā) *n.* ⟦OE *Hwita Sunnandæg*, lit., white Sunday⟧ PENTECOST

whit·tle (hwit′'l) *vt.* **-tled, -tling** ⟦< OE *thwitan*, to cut⟧ 1 *a*) to cut thin shavings from (wood) with a knife *b*) to carve (an object) thus 2 to reduce gradually —*vi.* to whittle wood

whiz or **whizz** (hwiz) *vi.* **whizzed, whiz′zing** ⟦echoic⟧ 1 to move swiftly with a buzzing or hissing sound 2 to make this sound —*n.* 1 this sound 2 [Slang] an expert *[a whiz at football]*

who (ho͞o) *pron.* ⟦OE *hwa*⟧ 1 what or which person or persons *[who is he? I asked who he was]* 2 the person or persons that, or a person that *[a man who knows]*

WHO *abbrev.* World Health Organization

whoa (hwō) *interj.* stop!: used esp. in directing a horse to stand still

who·dun·it (ho͞o dun′it) *n.* ⟦< WHO + DONE + IT⟧ [Inf.] a mystery novel, play, etc.

who·ev′er *pron.* 1 any person that 2 no matter who *[whoever said it, it's not so]* 3 who?: an emphatic usage *[whoever told you that?]*

whole (hōl) *adj.* ⟦OE *hal*⟧ 1 healthy; not diseased or injured 2 not broken, damaged, etc.; intact 3 containing all the parts; complete 4 not divided up; in a single unit 5 not a fraction —*n.* 1 the entire amount 2 a thing complete in itself —**on the whole** in general —**whole′ness** *n.*

whole′heart′ed *adj.* with all one's energy, enthusiasm, etc.; sincere

THESAURUS

whistle *n.* 1 [A shrill sound] cry, shriek, howl, blast, piping, siren call, fire alarm, birdcall, signal, toot, blare; see also NOISE 1. 2 [An instrument that produces a shrill sound] fife, pipes, pennywhistle; see ALARM.

whistle *v.* 1 [To produce a shrill blast] fife, pipe, flute, trill, hiss, whiz, wheeze, shriek, howl, blare, toot, tootle; see also SOUND. 2 [To call with a whistle] signal, summon, warn; see SUMMON.

white *a.* 1 [The color of fresh snow] ivory, silvery, snow-white, snowy, frosted, milky, milky-white, chalky, pearly, blanched, ashen, pale, wan, albescent.—*Ant.* DARK, black, dirty. 2 [Colorless] clear, transparent, clean, blank, spotless, pure, unalloyed, neutral, achromatic, achromic. 3 [Concerning the white race] fair-skinned, light-complexioned, Caucasian; see EUROPEAN, WESTERN 2. 4 [Pale] ashen, wan, pallid; see PALE 1.

white-collar *a.* professional, office, administrative, skilled.

whiten *v.* 1 [To become white] grow hoary, blanch, turn white, turn gray, grow pale, be covered with snow, be silvered, change color, fade. 2 [To make white] bleach, blanch, silver, paint white, whitewash, apply powder, chalk.—*Ant.* DIRTY, smudge, blacken.

whitewash *v.* gloss over, cover up, play down, minimize, dissemble over, downplay, sweep under the carpet, turn a blind eye to; see also EXCUSE.

whittle *v.* pare, carve, shape, fashion, shave, model, chip off, lessen, diminish, shave, decrease, pare down.

who *pron.* what, that, which, he, she, they, I, you, whoever, whichever.

whoever *pron.* he who, she who, the one who, whatever person, no matter who.

whole *a.* 1 [Entire] all, every, inclusive, full, undivided, integral, complete, total, aggregate, indivisible, inseparable, indissoluble, gross, undiminished, utter.—*Ant.* UNFINISHED, partial, incomplete. 2 [Not broken, damaged, or split up] thorough, mature, developed, unimpaired, unmarred, full, unbroken, undamaged, entire, in one piece, sound, solid, untouched, without a scratch, intact, uninjured, undecayed, completed, preserved, perfect, complete, safe, in A-1 condition*, shipshape, in good order, together, unified, exhaustive, conclusive, unqualified, fulfilled, accomplished, consummate.—*Ant.* BROKEN, mutilated, defective. 3 [Not ill or injured] hale, hearty, sound; see HEALTHY, WELL 1.

whole *n.* unity, totality, everything, oneness, entity, entirety, collectivity, sum, assemblage, aggregate, aggregation, body, lump, gross, length and breadth, generality, mass, amount, bulk, quantity, universality, complex, assembly, gross amount.—*Ant.* PART, portion, fraction. —**as a whole** collectively, altogether, in toto, en masse; see also COMPLETELY.

wholehearted *a.* sincere, earnest, candid; see HEARTY.

whole′-hog′ ***adj., adv.*** [Slang] without reservation; complete(ly)

whole milk milk from which no butterfat, etc. has been removed

whole note *Music* a note having four times the duration of a quarter note

whole′sale′ ***n.*** the selling of goods in large quantities and at lower prices, esp. to retailers —***adj.*** **1** of or having to do with such selling **2** extensive or indiscriminate *[wholesale* criticism*]* —***adv.*** **1** at wholesale prices **2** extensively or indiscriminately —***vt., vi.*** **-saled′, -sal′ing** to sell wholesale —**whole′sal′er** ***n.***

whole′some ***adj.*** ⟦ME *holsom*⟧ **1** promoting good health or well-being; healthful **2** improving the mind or character **3** healthy; sound —**whole′some·ness** ***n.***

whole tone *Music* an interval consisting of two adjacent semitones: also **whole step**

whole′-wheat′ ***adj.*** ground from whole kernels of wheat or made of flour so ground

whol·ly (hōl′lē) ***adv.*** to the whole amount or extent; totally; entirely

whom (ho͞om) ***pron.*** *objective case of* WHO

whom·ev′er (-ev′ər) ***pron.*** *objective case of* WHOEVER

whoop (hwo͞op, wo͞op, ho͞op) ***n.*** ⟦< ? OFr *houper*, cry out⟧ **1** a loud shout, cry, etc., as of joy **2** the convulsive intake of air following a fit of coughing in whooping cough —***vt., vi.*** to utter (with) a whoop or whoops

whoop·ing cough (ho͞o′piŋ, hwo͞o′-) an acute infectious disease, esp. of children, with coughing fits that end in a whoop

whop·per (hwäp′ər, wäp′ər) ***n.*** ⟦< inf. *whop*, to beat⟧ [Inf.] **1** anything extraordinarily large **2** a great lie

whop′ping ***adj.*** [Inf.] extraordinarily large

whore (hôr) ***n.*** ⟦OE *hore*⟧ a prostitute —**whor′ish** ***adj.***

who′re (ho͞o′ər) *contr.* who are

whorl (hwôrl, hwurl) ***n.*** ⟦ME *whorwyl*⟧ anything with a coiled or spiral appearance, as any of the circular ridges that form the patterns of a fingerprint —**whorled** ***adj.***

who's (ho͞oz) *contr.* **1** who is **2** who has

whose (ho͞oz) ***pron.*** ⟦OE *hwæs*⟧ that or those belonging to whom —***poss. pronominal adj.*** of, belonging to, or done by whom or which

who·so·ev·er (ho͞o′sō ev′ər) ***pron.*** whoever

why (hwī, wī) ***adv.*** ⟦OE *hwæt*, what⟧ for what reason, cause, or purpose? *[why* eat?*]* —***conj.*** **1** because of which *[*no reason *why* you shouldn't go*]* **2** the reason for which *[*that is *why* he went*]* —***n.***, *pl.* **whys** the reason; cause —***interj.*** an exclamation of surprise, impatience, etc.

WI Wisconsin

Wich·i·ta (wich′ə tô′) city in S Kansas: pop. 304,000

wick (wik) ***n.*** ⟦OE *weoca*⟧ a piece of cord, etc., as in a candle or oil lamp, that absorbs the fuel and, when lighted, burns

wick·ed (wik′id) ***adj.*** ⟦ME < *wikke*, evil⟧ **1** morally bad; evil **2** generally bad, unpleasant, etc. *[*a *wicked* storm*]* **3** mischievous **4** [Slang] showing great skill —**wick′ed·ly** ***adv.*** —**wick′ed·ness** ***n.***

wick·er (wik′ər) ***n.*** ⟦< Scand⟧ **1** a thin, flexible twig **2** *a)* such twigs or long, woody strips woven together, as in making baskets *b)* WICKERWORK (sense 1) —***adj.*** made of wicker

wick′er·work′ ***n.*** **1** things made of wicker **2** WICKER (*n.* 2*a)*

wick·et (wik′it) ***n.*** ⟦ME *wiket*⟧ **1** a small door or gate, esp. one in or near a larger one **2** a small window, as in a box office **3** *Croquet* any of the small wire arches through which balls are hit

wide (wīd) ***adj.*** **wid′er, wid′est** ⟦OE *wid*⟧ **1** extending over a large area, esp. from side to side **2** of a specified extent from side to side **3** of great extent *[*a *wide* variety*]* **4** open fully *[*eyes *wide* with fear*]* **5** far from the point, etc. aimed at: usually with *of [wide* of the target*]* —***adv.*** **1** over a relatively large area **2** to a large or full extent *[wide* open*]* **3** so as to miss the point, etc. aimed at; astray —**wide′ly** ***adv.*** —**wide′ness** ***n.***

-wide (wīd) *combining form* existing or extending throughout *[statewide]*

wide′-an′gle ***adj.*** designating or of a camera lens having a wider than ordinary angle of view

wide′-a·wake′ ***adj.*** **1** completely awake **2** alert

wide′-eyed′ ***adj.*** **1** with the eyes opened widely, as in surprise or fear **2** naive or unsophisticated

wid·en (wīd′′n) ***vt., vi.*** to make or become wider

wide′-o′pen ***adj.*** **1** opened wide **2** having no or few legal restrictions against prostitution, gambling, etc. *[*a *wide-open* city*]*

wide′spread′ ***adj.*** occurring over a wide area

widg·eon (wij′ən) ***n.*** *alt. sp. of* WIGEON

wid·ow (wid′ō) ***n.*** ⟦OE *widewe*⟧ a woman whose husband has died and who has not remarried —***vt.*** to cause to become a widow —**wid′ow·hood′** ***n.***

wid′ow·er ***n.*** a man whose wife has died and who has not remarried

width (width) ***n.*** **1** distance from side to side **2** a piece of a certain width *[*two *widths* of cloth*]*

wield (wēld) ***vt.*** ⟦OE *wealdan*⟧ **1** to handle (a tool, etc.), esp. with skill **2** to exercise (power, influence, etc.)

wie·ner (wē′nər) ***n.*** ⟦< Ger *Wiener wurst*, Vienna sausage⟧ a smoked link sausage; frankfurter: also [Inf.] **wie′nie** (-nē)

wife (wīf) ***n.***, *pl.* **wives** ⟦OE *wif*, woman⟧ a married woman —**wife′less** ***adj.*** —**wife′ly** ***adj.***

wig (wig) ***n.*** ⟦< PERIWIG⟧ a covering of real or synthetic hair worn as to hide baldness —***vt.*** **wigged, wig′ging** **1** to furnish with a wig **2** [Slang] *a)* to annoy, upset, etc. *b)* to make excited, crazy, etc. (often with *out*) —***vi.***

THESAURUS

wholesale ***a.*** **1** [Dealing in large lots] large-scale, in the mass, quantitative, in bulk, bulk, to the retailer, by the carload, loose, in quantity, in job lots; see also COMMERCIAL. **2** [Indiscriminate] sweeping, widespread, comprehensive; see WHOLE 1.

wholesome ***a.*** nutritive, nourishing, beneficial; see HEALTHFUL.

wholly ***a.*** totally, entirely, fully; see COMPLETELY.

whom ***pron.*** that, her, him; see WHO, WHAT 2.

whopper* ***n.*** great lie, falsehood, fabrication; see LIE, STORY.

whore ***n.*** hooker*, tramp*, slut*; see PROSTITUTE.

whorl ***n.*** twirl, twist, spiral; see COIL.

whose ***poss. pronominal adj.*** to whom, belonging to what person, of the aforementioned one, from these.

why ***a., conj.*** for what reason?, how so?, how?, how is it that?, on whose account?, what is the cause that?, to what end?, for what purpose?, on what foundation?, how do you explain that?, how come?*.

wicked ***a.*** sinful, immoral, corrupt, evil, base, foul, gross, dissolute, wayward, irreligious, blasphemous, profane, evil-minded, vile, bad, naughty, degenerate, depraved, incorrigible, unruly, heartless, shameless, degraded, debauched, hard, toughened, disreputable, infamous, indecent, mean, remorseless, scandalous, atrocious, contemptible, nasty, vicious, fiendish, hellish, villainous, rascally, devilish, malevolent, conspiratorial, flagrant, criminal, heinous, murderous, tricky, sinister, ignoble, monstrous, rotten*, low-down*, good-for-nothing, dirty, felonious, dangerous, cut-throat, ratty*, slippery, crooked.—*Ant.* HONEST, just, kind.

wickedness ***n.*** evil, depravity, immorality; see EVIL 1.

wide ***a.*** **1** [Broad] extended, spacious, deep; see BROAD 1. **2** [Loose] broad, roomy, full; see LOOSE 1. **3** [Extensive] large-scale, all-inclusive, universal; see GENERAL 1.

wide-awake ***a.*** alert, watchful, vigilant; see CAREFUL.

widely ***a.*** extensively, generally, publicly, nationally, internationally, universally, in many places, broadly, comprehensively.

widen ***v.*** **1** [To make wider] add to, broaden, stretch, extend, increase, enlarge, distend, spread out, give more space, augment. **2** [To become wider] unfold, grow, open, stretch, grow larger, increase, swell, multiply.

widespread ***a.*** extensive, general, sweeping, broad, comprehensive, far-reaching, pandemic, widely accepted, boundless, popular, public, unrestricted, unlimited, on a large scale, over-all.—*Ant.* OBSCURE, secret, limited.

widow ***n.*** widow woman, dowager, divorcée, husbandless wife, dead man's wife; see also WIFE.

widower ***n.*** surviving husband, grass widower, widowman*; see HUSBAND.

width ***n.*** breadth, wideness, girth, diameter, distance across, amplitude, cross dimension, cross measurement, expanse.—*Ant.* LENGTH, height, altitude.

wield ***v.*** handle, manipulate, exercise; see HOLD 1.

wiener ***n.*** frankfurter, sausage, hot dog*; see MEAT.

wife ***n.*** married woman, spouse, lady, dame, madam, matron, helpmate, consort, mate, housewife, better half*, the missis*, the little woman*, wifey*, the old lady*.—*Ant.* WIDOW, spinster, old maid.

wig ***n.*** hairpiece, fall, human-hair wig, synthetic wig, toupee, rug*, periwig, peruke; see also HAIR 1.

[Slang] to be or become upset, excited, etc.: often with *out*

wi·geon (wij′ən) ***n.*** ⟦prob. < L *vipio*, small crane⟧ any of certain wild, freshwater ducks

wig·gle (wig′əl) ***vt.***, ***vi.*** **-gled**, **-gling** ⟦ME *wigelen*⟧ to move or cause to move with short, jerky motions from side to side —***n.*** a wiggling —**wig′gler** ***n.*** —**wig′gly**, **-gli·er**, **-gli·est**, ***adj.***

wight (wīt) ***n.*** ⟦OE *wiht*⟧ [Archaic] a human being

wig·let (wig′lit) ***n.*** a small wig

wig·wag (wig′wag′) ***vt.***, ***vi.*** **-wagged′**, **-wag′ging** ⟦< obs. *wig*, to move + WAG[1]⟧ **1** to move back and forth; wag **2** to send (a message) by a visible code —***n.*** the sending of messages in this way

wig·wam (wig′wäm′) ***n.*** ⟦< Algonquian⟧ a North American Indian dwelling of a dome-shaped framework of poles covered with mats or bark

wild (wīld) ***adj.*** ⟦OE *wilde*⟧ **1** living or growing in its original, natural state **2** not lived in or cultivated; waste **3** not civilized; savage **4** not easily controlled *[a wild child]* **5** lacking social or moral restraint; dissolute *[a wild time]* **6** turbulent; stormy **7** enthusiastic *[wild about golf]* **8** fantastically impractical; reckless **9** missing the target *[a wild shot]* **10** *Card Games* having any desired value: said of a card —***adv.*** in a wild manner —***n.*** [*usually pl.*] a wilderness or wasteland —**wild′ly** ***adv.*** —**wild′ness** ***n.***

wild′cat′ ***n.*** **1** any fierce, medium-sized, undomesticated cat, as the bobcat, ocelot, etc. **2** an oil well in a previously unproductive area —***adj.*** **1** unsound or risky **2** illegal or unauthorized *[a wildcat strike]* —***vi.*** **-cat′ted**, **-cat′ting** to drill for oil in a previously unproductive area

wil·de·beest (wil′də bēst′, vil′-) ***n.*** ⟦Afrik⟧ GNU

wil·der·ness (wil′dər nis) ***n.*** ⟦< OE *wilde*, wild + *deor*, animal⟧ an uncultivated region

wild′-eyed′ ***adj.*** **1** staring in a wild or demented way **2** very foolish or impractical

wild′fire′ ***n.*** a fire that spreads widely and rapidly

wild′flow′er ***n.*** **1** any flowering plant growing wild in fields, etc. **2** its flower Also **wild flower**

wild′fowl′ ***n.***, *pl.* **-fowls′** or **-fowl′** a wild bird, esp. a game bird: also **wild fowl**

wild′-goose′ chase a futile search or pursuit

wild′life′ ***n.*** wild animals and birds

wild oats a wild grass common in the W U.S. —**sow one's wild oats** to be promiscuous or dissolute in one's youth

wild rice **1** an aquatic grass of the U.S. and Canada **2** its edible grain

Wild West [*also* **w- W-**] the western U.S. in its early frontier period of lawlessness

wile (wīl) ***n.*** ⟦< OE *wigle*, magic⟧ **1** a sly trick; stratagem **2** a beguiling trick: *usually used in pl.* —***vt.*** **wiled**, **wil′ing** to beguile; lure —**wile away** to while away (time, etc.)

wil·ful (wil′fəl) ***adj.*** *alt. sp. of* WILLFUL

Wilkes-Bar·re (wilks′bar′ē) city in NE Pennsylvania: pop. 48,000

will[1] (wil) ***n.*** ⟦OE *willa*⟧ **1** the power of making a reasoned choice or of controlling one's own actions **2** determination **3** attitude toward others *[a man of good will]* **4** *a)* a particular desire, choice, etc. of someone *b)* mandate *[the will of the people]* **5** a legal document directing the disposal of one's property after death —***vt.*** **1** to desire; want *[to will to live]* **2** to control by the power of the will **3** to bequeath by a will —***vi.*** to wish, desire, or choose —**at will** when one wishes

will[2] (wil) ***v.aux.*** *pt.* **would** ⟦OE *willan*, to desire⟧ **1** used to indicate simple future time *[when will she arrive?]* **2** used to express determination, obligation, etc. *[you will listen to me]* **3** used in polite questions *[will you have some wine?]* **4** used to express habit, expectation, etc. *[they will talk for hours]* **5** used to express possibility ***USAGE***—the distinction between WILL[2] (for second and third person subjects) and SHALL (for the first person) in expressing simple future time or determination, etc. is today virtually nonexistent in North American English; WILL[2] and SHALL and their respective past tenses WOULD and SHOULD are usually interchangeable, with WILL[2] (and WOULD) being the preferred form in all persons

will′ful (-fəl) ***adj.*** **1** said or done deliberately **2** doing as one pleases —**will′ful·ly** ***adv.*** —**will′ful·ness** ***n.***

Wil·liam I (wil′yəm) 1027?-87; duke of Normandy who invaded England: king of England (1066-87): called *William the Conqueror*

Wil·liams·burg (wil′yəmz burg′) city in SE Virginia, restored to its 18th-c. look: pop. 12,000

wil·lies (wil′ēz) ***pl.n.*** ⟦< ?⟧ [Slang] a nervous feeling; jitters: with *the*

will′ing ***adj.*** **1** favorably disposed; consenting *[willing to play]* **2** acting, giving, etc. or done, given, etc. readily and cheerfully —**will′ing·ly** ***adv.*** —**will′ing·ness** ***n.***

wil·li·waw or **wil′ly·waw′** (wil′i wô′) ***n.*** **1** a violent, cold wind blowing from mountain passes toward the coast **2** confusion; turmoil

will-o′-the-wisp (wil′ə *th*ə wisp′) ***n.*** a delusive hope or goal

wil·low (wil′ō) ***n.*** ⟦OE *welig*⟧ **1** a tree with narrow leaves, and flexible twigs used in weaving baskets, etc. **2** its wood

wil′low·y ***adj.*** like a willow; slender, lithe, etc.

will′pow′er ***n.*** strength of will, mind, or determination; self-control

wil·ly-nil·ly (wil′ē nil′ē) ***adv.***, ***adj.*** ⟦contr. < *will I, nill I*: *nill* < OE *nyllan*, be unwilling⟧ **1** (happening) whether one wishes it or not **2** in a disordered way; helter-skelter

Wil·son (wil′sən), **(Thomas) Wood·row** (wood′rō) 1856-1924; 28th president of the U.S. (1913-21)

THESAURUS

wiggle ***v.*** wag, waggle, wriggle, squirm, shimmy, shake, flounce, dance sensually.

wigwam ***n.*** wickiup, tepee, lodge; see SHELTER, TENT.

wild ***a.*** **1** [Not controlled] unrestrained, unmanageable, boisterous; see UNRULY. **2** [Uncivilized] barbarous, savage, undomesticated; see PRIMITIVE. **3** [Not cultivated] luxuriant, lush, exuberant, dense, excessive, desolate, waste, desert, weedy, untrimmed, uninhabited, native, natural, untouched, virgin, overgrown, uncultivated, untilled, overrun, uncared for, neglected, impenetrable, free, rampant. **4** [Inaccurate] erratic, off, unsound; see WRONG 2. **5** [Stormy] disturbed, raging, storming; see TURBULENT. **6** [Very excited] hot, eager, avid; see EXCITED. **7** [Dissolute] loose, licentious, profligate; see LEWD 2. **8** [Imprudent] reckless, foolish, incautious; see CARELESS.

wildcat ***n.*** mountain lion or cougar, bobcat, Canada lynx, caracal.

wilderness ***n.*** wilds, wasteland, back country, the woods, the North woods, primeval forest, uninhabited region; see also DESERT, FOREST.

wildly ***a.*** hastily, rashly, fiercely, violently, ferociously, uncontrollably, carelessly, quixotically, savagely, unwittingly, recklessly, confusedly, pell-mell.—*Ant.* CAREFULLY, prudently, judiciously.

will[1] ***n.*** **1** [Desire] inclination, wish, disposition, pleasure, yearning, craving, longing, hankering. **2** [Conscious power] resolution, volition, intention, preference, will power, mind, determination, self-determination, decisiveness, moral strength, discretion, conviction, willfulness.—*Ant.* DOUBT, vacillation, indecision. **3** [Testament for the disposition of property] bequest, disposition, instructions, last wishes, bestowal, dispensation, last will and testament. —**free will** willingness, volition, intention, purpose, choice, free choice, power of choice, freedom, pleasure, discretion, inclination, desire, wish, intent, option, determination, mind, consent, assent.—*Ant.* RESTRAINT, predestination, unwillingness.

will[1,2] ***v.*** **1** [To exert one's will] decree, order, command, demand, authorize, request, make oneself felt, decide upon, insist, direct, enjoin. **2** [To wish] want, incline to, prefer; see WISH. **3** [An indication of futurity] shall, would, should, expect to, anticipate, look forward to, hope to, await, foresee, propose.

willful ***a.*** intentional, premeditated, contemplated; see DELIBERATE.

willing ***a.*** energetic, prompt, reliable, active, obedient, enthusiastic, zealous, responsible, agreeable, prepared, voluntary, ready, compliant, amenable, tractable, feeling, like, in accord with.—*Ant.* OPPOSED, averse, unwilling.

willingly ***a.*** gladly, readily, obediently, agreeably, voluntarily, with relish, at one's pleasure, on one's own account, of one's own accord, without reservation, without a second thought, with good cheer, freely, with pleasure, cheerfully, with all one's heart, at the drop of a hat*, like a shot*.

willingness ***n.*** zeal, enthusiasm, readiness, earnestness, eagerness, alacrity, cordiality, hospitality, courteousness, compliance, good will, geniality.

will-o'-the-wisp ***n.*** fancy, ephemera, dream, pipe dream, *ignis fatuus* (Latin), shadow, illusion, vision, delusion.

wilt (wilt) ***vi.*** ⟦< obs. *welk*, to wither⟧ **1** to become limp, as from heat or lack of water; droop: said of plants **2** to become weak or faint; lose strength or courage —***vt.*** to cause to wilt

Wil·ton (carpet or **rug)** (wilt′'n) ⟦after *Wilton*, England⟧ a kind of carpet with a velvety pile of cut loops

wi·ly (wī′lē) ***adj.*** **-i·er, -i·est** full of wiles; crafty; sly —**wi′li·ness *n.***

wimp (wimp) ***n.*** ⟦< ?⟧ [Slang] a weak, ineffectual, or insipid person —**wimp′ish *adj.*** —**wimp′y, -i·er, -i·est, *adj.***

wim·ple (wim′pəl) ***n.*** ⟦OE *wimpel*⟧ a nun's head covering that leaves only the face exposed

win (win) ***vi.*** **won, win′ning** ⟦< OE *winnan*, to fight⟧ **1** *a)* to gain a victory *b)* to finish first in a race, etc. **2** to succeed in reaching a specified condition or place; get *[to win back to health]* —***vt.*** **1** to get by labor, struggle, etc. **2** to be victorious in (a contest, etc.) **3** to get to with effort *[they won the camp by noon]* **4** to prevail upon; persuade: often with *over* **5** to gain (the sympathy, favor, etc.) of (someone) **6** to persuade to marry one —***n.*** a victory

wince (wins) ***vi.*** **winced, winc′ing** ⟦< OFr *guenchir*⟧ to shrink or draw back slightly, usually with a grimace, as in pain —***n.*** a wincing

winch (winch) ***n.*** ⟦OE *wince*⟧ **1** a crank with a handle for transmitting motion **2** a machine for hoisting, etc. using a cylinder upon which is wound the rope, etc. attached to an object

Win·ches·ter (win′ches′tər) ⟦after O. F. *Winchester* (1810-80), the manufacturer⟧ *trademark for* a type of repeating rifle

wind[1] (wīnd) ***vt.*** **wound** or [Rare] **wind′ed, wind′ing** ⟦OE *windan*⟧ **1** to turn *[to wind a crank]* **2** to coil into a ball or around something else; twine **3** to cover by entwining **4** *a)* to make (one's way) in a twisting course *b)* to cause to move in a twisting course **5** to tighten the spring of (a clock, etc.) as by turning a stem: often with *up* —***vi.*** **1** to move or go in a curving or sinuous manner **2** to take a devious course **3** to coil (*about* or *around* something) —***n.*** a turn; twist —**wind up** **1** to wind into a ball, etc. **2** to bring to an end; settle **3** to make very tense, excited, etc. **4** *Baseball* to perform a WINDUP (sense 2) —**wind′er *n.***

wind[2] (wind) ***n.*** ⟦OE⟧ **1** air in motion **2** a strong current of air; gale **3** air bearing a scent, as in hunting **4** air regarded as bearing information, etc. *[a rumor in the wind]* **5** breath or the power of breathing **6** empty talk **7** [*pl.*] the wind instruments of an orchestra —***vt.*** **1** to get the scent of **2** to put out of breath —**break wind** to expel gas from the bowels —**get wind of** to hear of —**in the wind** happening or about to happen

wind·bag (wind′bag′) ***n.*** [Inf.] one who talks much but says little of importance

wind′break′ ***n.*** a hedge, fence, etc. serving as a protection from wind

Wind′break′er *trademark for* a warm jacket with close-fitting waistband and cuffs

wind′burn′ ***n.*** a reddened, sore skin condition, caused by overexposure to the wind

wind′chill′ factor an estimated measure of the cooling effect of air and wind on exposed skin

wind chimes (or **bells**) a cluster of small chimes or pendants hung so that they strike one another and tinkle when blown by the wind

wind·ed (win′did) ***adj.*** out of breath

wind·fall (wind′fôl′) ***n.*** an unexpected gain, stroke of good luck, etc.

wind farm a network of modern, high-speed windmills for generating electricity

wind·ing sheet (wīn′diŋ) a shroud

wind instrument (wind) a musical instrument sounded by blowing air through it, as a flute

wind·jam·mer (wind′jam′ər) ***n.*** a large sailing ship or one of its crew

wind·lass (wind′ləs) ***n.*** ⟦< ON *vinda*, to WIND[1] + *ass*, a beam⟧ a winch, esp. one worked by a crank

wind′mill′ ***n.*** **1** a mill operated by the wind's rotation of large vanes radiating from a shaft **2** a device like this, as one to harness wind power

win·dow (win′dō) ***n.*** ⟦< ON *vindr*, WIND[2] + *auga*, an eye⟧ **1** an opening in a building, vehicle, etc. for letting in light, air, etc. usually having a pane of glass in a movable frame **2** a windowpane **3** an opening resembling a window **4** the interval during which something can be done

window box a long, narrow box on or outside a window ledge, for growing plants

window dressing **1** the display of goods in a store window **2** that which is meant to make something seem better than it really is —**win′dow-dress′ *vt.*** —**window dresser**

win′dow·pane′ ***n.*** a pane of glass in a window

win′dow-shop′ ***vi.*** **-shopped′, -shop′ping** to look at goods in store windows without entering to buy

win′dow·sill′ ***n.*** the sill of a window

wind·pipe (wind′pīp′) ***n.*** TRACHEA

wind′row′ (-rō′) ***n.*** a row of hay, etc. raked together to dry

wind shear a sudden change in wind direction, esp., dangerous vertical wind shifts

wind′shield′ ***n.*** in automobiles, etc., a glass screen, in front, to protect from wind, etc.

wind′sock′ ***n.*** a long, cloth cone flown at an airfield to show wind direction: also **wind sleeve**

Wind·sor (win′zər) port in SE Ontario, Canada: pop. 198,000

Windsor knot a double slipknot in a four-in-hand necktie

wind′storm′ ***n.*** a storm with a strong wind but little or no rain, hail, etc.

wind′surf′ ***vi.*** to ride for sport on a kind of surfboard with a pivoting sail —**wind′surf′ing *n.***

wind tunnel a tunnel-like chamber through which air is forced, for testing the effects of wind pressure on aircraft, motor vehicles, etc.

wind·up (wīnd′up′) ***n.*** **1** a conclusion; end **2** *Baseball* the motion of the pitcher leading up to throwing the ball

wind·ward (wind′wərd) ***n.*** the direction from which the wind blows —***adv.*** toward the wind —***adj.*** **1** moving windward **2** on the side from which the wind blows

Windward Islands S group of islands in the West Indies, south of the Leeward Islands

wind·y (win′dē) ***adj.*** **-i·er, -i·est** **1** with much wind *[a windy city]* **2** stormy, blustery, etc. **3** long-winded, pompous, etc. —**wind′i·ness *n.***

wine (wīn) ***n.*** ⟦< L *vinum*⟧ the fermented juice of grapes, etc., used as an alcoholic beverage —***vt., vi.*** **wined,**

THESAURUS

wilt *v.* droop, wither, weaken, shrivel, flag, dry up, fade, become flaccid, lose freshness, faint.—*Ant.* GROW, STAND, stiffen.

win *n.* triumph, conquest, victory; see SUCCESS 1.

win *v.* **1** [To gain a victory] be victorious, prevail, get the best of, come out first, conquer, overcome, come out on top, overwhelm, triumph; see also SUCCEED 1. **2** [To obtain] get, acquire, gain; see GET 1. **3** [To reach] attain, accomplish, effect; see APPROACH 2, 3.

wind[1] ***v.*** **1** [To wrap about] coil, reel in, entwine, wreathe, shroud, fold, cover, bind, tape, bandage. **2** [To twist] convolute, screw, wind up; see BEND. **3** [To meander] zigzag, weave, snake, twist, loop, turn, twine, ramble, swerve, deviate. —**wind up** conclude, be through with, come to the end of; see END 1.

wind[2] ***n.*** draft, air current, breeze, gust, gale, blast, flurry, whisk, whiff, puff, whirlwind, flutter, wafting, zephyr, trade wind, sirocco, northeaster, nor'easter, southwester, sou'wester, tempest, blow, cyclone, typhoon, twister, hurricane, sandstorm, prevailing westerlies, stiff breeze, chinook, Santa Ana. —**get** (or **have**) **wind of*** hear about, have news of, trace; see HEAR 1. —**take the wind out of someone's sails** best, get the better of, overcome; see DEFEAT 2, 3.

windbag* *n.* blowhard*, loudmouth, big talker*; see TALKER.

winded *a.* tired, exhausted, out of breath, breathless, gasping, panting, heaving, fagged.

winding *a.* turning, gyrating, gyring, spiraling, twisting, snaky, serpentine, convoluted.—*Ant.* STRAIGHT, direct, vertical.

window *n.* skylight, porthole, bay window, bow window, picture window, casement, double-hung window, dormer, stained-glass, show window, rose window, transom, jalousie window, peephole.

windowpane *n.* pane, square of glass, glass; see WINDOW.

windpipe *n.* airpipe, bronchus, trachea; see THROAT.

windshield *n.* windscreen, protection against the wind, wraparound; see SCREEN 1.

windy *a.* breezy, blustery, raw, stormy, wind-swept, airy, gusty, blowing, fresh, drafty, wind-shaken, tempestuous, boisterous.—*Ant.* CALM, quiet, still.

wine *n.* *Wines include the following:* still, sparkling, fortified, dry, sweet, red, white, rosé, blush, vintage, nonvintage, varietal, *appellation contrôlée;* blackberry, cherry, currant, gooseberry, dandelion; sac-

win'ing usually in the phrase **wine and dine**, to entertain lavishly
wine'-col'ored *adj.* dark purplish-red
win·er·y (wīn'ər ē) *n.*, *pl.* **-ies** an establishment where wine is made
wing (wiŋ) *n.* ⟦ON *vaengr*⟧ **1** either of the paired organs of flight of a bird, bat, insect, etc. **2** something like a wing in use, position, etc., esp., *a*) a (or the) main lateral supporting surface of an airplane *b*) a subordinate, projecting part of a building *c*) either side of the stage out of sight of the audience **3** the section of an army, fleet, etc. to the right (or left) of the center **4** a section, as of a political party, with reference to its radicalism or conservatism **5** a unit in an air force —*vt.* **1** to provide with wings **2** *a*) to send swiftly as on wings *b*) to make (one's way) by flying *c*) to pass through or over, as by flying **3** to wound in the wing, arm, etc. —*vi.* to fly —**on the wing** (while) flying —**take wing** to fly away —**under one's wing** under one's protection, etc. —**wing it** [Inf.] to improvise in acting, etc. —**winged** (wiŋd; *poet.* wiŋ'id) *adj.* —**wing'less** *adj.*
wing'ding' (-diŋ') *n.* ⟦< ?⟧ [Slang] an event, party, etc. that is very festive, lively, etc.
wing'span' *n.* **1** the distance between the tips of an airplane's wings **2** WINGSPREAD (sense 1)
wing'spread' *n.* **1** the distance between the tips of fully spread wings **2** WINGSPAN
wink (wiŋk) *vi.* ⟦OE *wincian*⟧ **1** to close the eyelids and open them again quickly **2** to close and open one eyelid quickly, as a signal, etc. **3** to twinkle —*vt.* to make (an eye) wink —*n.* **1** a winking **2** an instant **3** a signal given by winking **4** a twinkle —**wink at** to pretend not to see
win·ner (win'ər) *n.* one that wins
win·ning (win'iŋ) *adj.* **1** victorious **2** attractive; charming —*n.* **1** a victory **2** [*pl.*] money won
Win·ni·peg (win'ə peg') capital of Manitoba, Canada: pop. 618,000
win·now (win'ō) *vt.*, *vi.* ⟦< OE *wind*, WIND[2]⟧ **1** to blow (chaff) from (grain) **2** to scatter **3** to sift out
win·o (wī'nō) *n.*, *pl.* **-os** [Slang] an alcoholic who drinks cheap wine
win·some (win'səm) *adj.* ⟦OE *wynsum*, pleasant⟧ sweetly attractive; charming —**win'some·ly** *adv.*
Win·ston-Sa·lem (win'stən sā'ləm) city in NC North Carolina: pop. 143,000
win·ter (win'tər) *n.* ⟦OE⟧ **1** the coldest season of the year, following autumn **2** a period of decline, distress, etc. —*adj.* of, during, or for winter —*vi.* to pass the winter —*vt.* to keep, feed, etc. during winter
win'ter·green' *n.* **1** an evergreen plant with white flowers and red berries **2** an aromatic oil (**oil of wintergreen**) made from its leaves and used as a flavoring **3** the flavor
win'ter·ize' *vt.* **-ized'**, **-iz'ing** to put into condition for winter
win'ter·kill' *vt.*, *vi.* to kill or die by exposure to winter cold or excessive snow and ice —*n.* the process or an instance of winterkilling
win'ter·time' *n.* the winter season
win·try (win'trē) *adj.* **-tri·er**, **-tri·est** of or like winter; cold, bleak, etc. *[a wintry day]*
win'-win' *adj.* designating or of a situation from which all possible outcomes are satisfactory
win·y (wī'nē) *adj.* **-i·er**, **-i·est** like wine in taste, smell, color, etc.
wipe (wīp) *vt.* **wiped**, **wip'ing** ⟦OE *wipian*⟧ **1** to clean or dry by rubbing with a cloth, etc. **2** to rub (a cloth, etc.) over something **3** to apply or remove by wiping —*n.* a wiping —**wipe out 1** to remove; erase **2** to kill off **3** to destroy —**wip'er** *n.*
wiped'-out' *adj.* [Slang] exhausted
wire (wīr) *n.* ⟦OE *wir*⟧ **1** metal drawn into a long thread **2** a length of this **3** a telegram **4** the finish line of a horse race —*adj.* made of wire —*vt.* **wired**, **wir'ing 1** to furnish, connect, etc. with wire **2** to telegraph —*vi.* to telegraph
wired (wīrd) *adj.* [Slang] **1** provided with concealed electronic listening or recording equipment **2** extremely excited, nervous, etc.
wire'hair' *n.* a fox terrier with a wiry coat: also called **wire'-haired' terrier**
wire'less (-lis) *adj.* operating by electromagnetic waves, not with conducting wire —*n.* **1** wireless telegraphy or telephony **2** [Chiefly Brit.] *old-fashioned term for* RADIO
wire service an agency sending news electronically to subscribing newspapers, etc.
wire'tap' *vi.*, *vt.* **-tapped'**, **-tap'ping** to tap (a telephone wire, etc.) to get information secretly —*n.* **1** a wiretapping **2** a device for wiretapping
wir'ing *n.* a system of wires, as to provide a house with electricity
wir·y (wīr'ē) *adj.* **-i·er**, **-i·est 1** of wire **2** like wire; stiff **3** lean and strong —**wir'i·ness** *n.*
Wis·con·sin (wis kän'sən) Midwestern state of the U.S.: 56,154 sq. mi.; pop. 4,892,000; cap. Madison: abbrev. *WI* —**Wis·con'sin·ite'** *n.*
wis·dom (wiz'dəm) *n.* ⟦OE: see WISE[1] & -DOM⟧ **1** the quality of being wise; good judgment **2** learning; knowledge
wisdom tooth the back tooth on each side of each jaw
wise[1] (wīz) *adj.* **wis'er**, **wis'est** ⟦OE *wis*⟧ **1** having or showing good judgment **2** informed *[none the wiser]* **3** learned **4** shrewd; cunning **5** [Slang] conceited, impudent, fresh, etc. —**wise'ly** *adv.*
wise[2] (wīz) *n.* ⟦OE⟧ way; manner

THESAURUS

ramental, dessert, dinner, medicinal, aperitif, cooking; California, New York State, French, Italian, German, Spanish; sherry, Tokay, port, claret, muscatel; Burgundy, Bordeaux, champagne, sauterne, Rhine wine, Chablis, Chianti, Beaujolais, Barolo; retsina, sake, rice wine; cabernet sauvignon, pinot noir, merlot, chardonnay, sauvignon blanc, Gewürztraminer, zinfandel, pinot grigio, Riesling, Concord, catawba; sangria; see also DRINK 2.

wing *n.* **1** [An organ or instrument of flight] appendage, aileron, airfoil; see FEATHER. **2** [An architectural unit or extension] annex, addition, projection, hall, section, division, part. **3** [An organized group of aircraft] flying unit, formation, air squadron; see UNIT. —**take under one's wing** favor, help, protect; see ADOPT 2.

wink *v.* squint, blink, flirt, make eyes at, bat the eyes.

winner *n.* victor, conqueror, prizewinner, champion, winning competitor, hero, successful contestant, leading entrant, Olympic champion, titleholder, champ*, frontrunner.

winning *a.* **1** [Engaging] attractive, appealing, agreeable; see CHARMING. **2** [Victorious] champion, conquering, leading; see SUCCESSFUL.

winsome *a.* engaging, entrancing, fetching; see CHARMING.

winter *n.* cold season, frosty weather, wintertime, Christmastime, Jack Frost.

wintry *a.* chilly, frosty, icy, snowy, frigid, cold, bleak, raw, biting, cutting.—*Ant.* WARM, summery, balmy.

wipe *v.* rub, clean, dry, dust, mop, clear, wash, swab, soak up, obliterate. —**wipe out** slay, annihilate, eradicate; see DESTROY, KILL 1, REMOVE 1.

wire *n.* **1** [A metal strand] line, electric wire, cable, aerial, circuit, wiring, live wire, coil, conductor, filament, musical string, wire tape, wire cord. **2** [A metal net] barbed wire, wire fence, wire cage; see FENCE. **3** [A telegraphic message] cablegram, message, cable; see TELEGRAM. —**down to the wire** to the very end, at the last, eventually; see FINALLY 2. —**get (in) under the wire** just make it, be just in time, squeak through*; see ARRIVE.

wire *v.* **1** [To install wire] set up a circuit, install electricity, lay wires, connect electric cables, prepare for electrical service, pipe*; see also ELECTRIFY. **2** [To send a message by wire] flash, telegraph, notify; see TELL 1.

wiring *n.* wirework, electric line, cable work, cables, electrical installations, facilities for electric power, circuit system, electrical wire distribution, tubing, circuit pattern, circuiting, threading, process, route, line, path, pattern, trail.

wiry *a.* agile, sinewy, tough; see STRONG 1.

wisdom *n.* prudence, astuteness, sense, reason, clear thinking, good judgment, sagacity, understanding, sanity, shrewdness, experience, practical knowledge, carefulness, vigilance, tact, balance, poise, stability, caution, solidity, hardheadedness, brains, common sense, horse sense*, savvy*.—*Ant.* STUPIDITY, irrationality, rashness.

wise[1] *a.* **1** [Judicious] clever, sagacious, witty; see THOUGHTFUL 1. **2** [Shrewd] calculating, cunning, crafty; see SLY. **3** [Prudent] tactful, sensible, wary; see CAREFUL. **4** [Erudite] taught, scholarly, smart; see EDUCATED, LEARNED 1. **5** [Informed] wise to*, on to*, aware of; see FAMILIAR WITH.

wisely *a.* tactfully, prudently, circumspectly, sagaciously, shrewdly, judiciously, discreetly, carefully, admirably, discerningly, sagely, knowingly, reasonably, sensibly, intelligently.—*Ant.* FOOLISHLY, stupidly, unthinkingly.

-wise (wīz) ⟦< prec.⟧ *suffix* **1** in a (specified) direction, position, or manner *[lengthwise]* **2** in a manner characteristic of *[clockwise]* **3** with regard to *[budgetwise]*

wise·a·cre (wīz′ā′kər) ***n.*** ⟦ult. < OHG *wizzago*, prophet⟧ one who makes annoyingly conceited claims to knowledge

wise′crack′ [Slang] ***n.*** a flippant or facetious remark —***vi.*** to make wisecracks

wish (wish) ***vt.*** ⟦OE *wyscan*⟧ **1** to have a longing for; want **2** to express a desire concerning *[I wish you well]* **3** to request *[I wish you to go]* —***vi.*** **1** to long; yearn **2** to make a wish —***n.*** **1** a wishing **2** something wished for **3** a polite request, almost an order **4** [*pl.*] expressed desire for a person's health, etc. *[best wishes]* —**wish′er** ***n.***

wish′bone′ ***n.*** the forked bone in front of a bird's breastbone

wish′ful (-fəl) ***adj.*** having or showing a wish; desirous —**wish′ful·ly** ***adv.***

wish·y-wash·y (wish′ē wôsh′ē) ***adj.*** [Inf.] **1** weak; feeble **2** vacillating; indecisive

wisp (wisp) ***n.*** ⟦prob. < Scand⟧ **1** a small bundle, as of straw **2** a thin or filmy piece, strand, etc. *[a wisp of smoke]* **3** something delicate, frail, etc. —**wisp′y**, **-i·er**, **-i·est**, ***adj.***

wis·te·ri·a (wis tir′ē ə) ***n.*** ⟦after C. *Wistar* (1761-1818), U.S. anatomist⟧ a twining vine with showy clusters of flowers: also **wis·tar′i·a** (-ter′-)

wist·ful (wist′fəl) ***adj.*** ⟦< earlier *wistly*, attentive⟧ showing or expressing vague yearnings —**wist′ful·ly** ***adv.*** —**wist′ful·ness** ***n.***

wit[1] (wit) ***n.*** ⟦OE⟧ **1** [*pl.*] powers of thinking; mental faculties **2** good sense **3** *a)* the ability to make clever remarks in a sharp, amusing way *b)* one characterized by wit

wit[2] (wit) ***vt.***, ***vi.*** **wist** (wist), **wit′ting** ⟦OE *witan*⟧ [Archaic] to know —**to wit** that is to say; namely

witch (wich) ***n.*** ⟦OE *wicce*⟧ **1** a woman thought to have supernatural power as by a compact with evil spirits **2** an ugly, old shrew **3** [Inf.] a fascinating woman or girl

witch′craft′ ***n.*** the power or practices of witches

witch doctor in certain primitive societies, one thought able to cure sickness, ward off evil, etc. by using magic or incantations

witch′er·y (-ər ē) ***n.***, *pl.* **-ies** **1** witchcraft; sorcery **2** bewitching charm

witch hazel ⟦< OE *wice*⟧ **1** a shrub with yellow flowers **2** a lotion made from its leaves and bark, used on inflammations, etc.

witch hunt ⟦so named in allusion to persecutions of persons alleged to be witches⟧ a highly publicized investigation carried out ostensibly to uncover disloyalty, etc., relying upon little evidence

with (with, with) ***prep.*** ⟦OE⟧ **1** in opposition to *[to argue with a friend]* **2** *a)* alongside of; near to *b)* in the company of *c)* into; among *[mix blue with yellow]* **3** as a member of *[to play with a string quartet]* **4** concerning *[happy with his lot]* **5** compared to **6** as well as *[she rides with the best]* **7** in the opinion of *[it's OK with me]* **8** as a result of *[faint with hunger]* **9** by means of **10** having received *[with your consent, I'll go]* **11** having as a possession, attribute, etc. **12** in the keeping, care, etc. of *[leave it with me]* **13** in spite of **14** at the same time as **15** in proportion to *[wages that vary with skill]* **16** to; onto *[join one end with the other]* **17** from *[to part with one's gains]* —**with that** after, or as a consequence of, that

with- *combining form* **1** away, back *[withdraw]* **2** against, from *[withhold]*

with·al (with ôl′, with-) ***adv.*** **1** besides **2** despite that

with·draw′ ***vt.*** **-drew′**, **-drawn′**, **-draw′ing** **1** to take back; remove **2** to retract or recall (a statement, etc.) —***vi.*** **1** to move back; go away; retreat **2** to remove oneself (*from* an organization, activity, etc.)

with·draw′al ***n.*** **1** the act of withdrawing **2** the process of giving up a narcotic drug, typically accompanied by distressing physical and mental effects (**withdrawal symptoms**)

with·drawn′ ***vt.***, ***vi.*** *pp. of* WITHDRAW —***adj.*** shy, reserved, etc.

withe (with, with) ***n.*** ⟦< OE *withthe*⟧ a tough, flexible twig of willow, osier, etc., used for binding

with·er (with′ər) ***vi.*** ⟦< ME *wederen*, to weather⟧ **1** to dry up; wilt, as plants **2** to become wasted or decayed **3** to weaken; languish —***vt.*** **1** to cause to wither **2** to cause to feel abashed

with·ers (with′ərz) ***pl.n.*** ⟦< OE *wither*, against⟧ the part of a horse's back between the shoulder blades

with·hold (with hōld′, with-) ***vt.*** **-held′**, **-hold′ing** **1** *a)* to hold back; restrain *b)* to deduct (taxes, etc.) from wages **2** to refrain from granting

withholding tax the amount of income tax withheld, as payment in advance, from an employee's pay

with·in (with in′, with-) ***adv.*** ⟦OE *withinnan*⟧ **1** on or into the inside **2** indoors **3** inside the body, mind, etc. —***prep.*** **1** in the inner part of **2** not beyond **3** inside the limits of —***n.*** the inside

with′-it (-it) ***adj.*** [Slang] **1** sophisticated, up-to-date, etc. **2** fashionable; stylish

with·out′ ***adv.*** ⟦OE *withutan*⟧ **1** on the outside **2** out-of-doors —***prep.*** **1** [Now Rare] at, on, or to the outside of **2** lacking **3** free from **4** with avoidance of *[to pass by without speaking]*

with·stand′ (-stand′) ***vt.***, ***vi.*** **-stood′**, **-stand′ing** to oppose, resist, or endure, esp. successfully

THESAURUS

wish ***n.*** longing, yearning, hankering, desire, thirst, disposition, request, hope, intention, preference, choice, want, prayer, invocation, liking, pleasure, injunction, command, order.

wish ***v.*** **1** [To desire] covet, crave, envy; see WANT 1. **2** [To express a desire] hope, request, entreat, prefer, want, pray for, invoke, command, order, solicit, beg, look forward to, require; see also NEED.

wishful ***a.*** desirous, longing, eager; see ZEALOUS.

wishy-washy* ***a.*** indecisive, spineless, feeble; see WEAK 3.

wisp ***n.*** tuft, cluster, shred, a few strands, lock, bit, shock, cowlick, stray lock.

wit[1] ***n.*** wittiness, smartness, whimsicality, pleasantry, drollery, banter, burlesque, satire, jocularity, witticism, sally, whimsy, repartee, joke, aphorism, jest, quip, epigram, pun, wisecrack*, gag. —**at one's wits' end** downhearted, desperate, helpless; see TROUBLED. —**have** (or **keep**) **one's wits about one** be ready, take precautions, be on one's guard; see WATCH OUT. —**live by one's wits** use sharp practices, live dangerously, be street-smart*; see TRICK.

witch ***n.*** sorcerer, warlock, magician, enchantress, charmer, hag, crone.

witchcraft ***n.*** sorcery, magic, black magic, necromancy, witchery, divination, devil worship, enchantment, spell, bewitchment, voodooism, shamanism, demonology.

witch hunt ***n.*** persecution, show trial, kangaroo court, miscarriage of justice.

with ***prep.*** by, in association with, in the midst of, among, amidst, along with, in company with, arm in arm, hand in glove, in conjunction with, among other things, beside, alongside of, including.

withdraw ***v.*** **1** [To retire] depart, draw back, take leave; see RETREAT. **2** [To remove from use or circulation] revoke, rescind, abolish, repeal, annul, abrogate, veto, suppress, repress, retire, stamp out, declare illegal, ban, bar, nullify, repudiate, reverse, retract, throw overboard, invalidate, quash, dissolve.

withdrawal ***n.*** removal, retreat, retraction, resignation, alienation, abandonment, recession, revulsion, abdication, relinquishment, departure.—*Ant.* PROGRESS, advance, appearance.

withdrawn ***a.*** retired, secluded, isolated, removed, departed, cloistered, reclusive, drawn back, gone into retirement, taken out, absent, retreated.—*Ant.* ACTIVE, involved, progressing.

wither ***v.*** shrivel, shrink, droop, wilt, decay, die, grow brown, dry up, dry out, fade, lose freshness, deteriorate, fall away.—*Ant.* REVIVE, reawaken, bloom.

withered ***a.*** shriveled, wilted, decayed, deteriorated, shrunken, dead, browned, faded, parched, dried up, drooping, wrinkled.—*Ant.* FRESH, blooming, alive.

withheld ***a.*** concealed, held back, hidden, checked, restrained, interdicted, delayed, denied, kept on leash, on ice*.—*Ant.* FREE, opened, made visible.

withhold ***v.*** hold back, reserve, keep; see DENY.

within ***a.***, ***prep.*** inside, indoors, in, not further than, not beyond, not over, in reach of, in a period of, not outside; see also INSIDE 2.

with-it* ***a.*** up-to-date, well-informed, contemporary, hip*, stylish, in the know*, on the ball*, in the swing of things*; see also MODERN 1.

without ***a.***, ***prep.*** **1** [Outside] out, outdoors, outwardly, externally, on the outside, standing outside, left out. **2** [Lacking] not with, not having, in the absence of, free from, deprived of.

withstand ***v.*** face, oppose, confront, resist, endure, stand up to, hold

wit·less (wit′lis) ***adj.*** lacking wit; foolish —**wit′less·ly** ***adv.***

wit·ness (wit′nis) ***n.*** ⟦< OE *witan*, know⟧ **1** evidence; testimony **2** one who saw, or can give a firsthand account of, something **3** one who testifies in court **4** one who observes, and attests to, a signing, etc. —***vt.*** **1** to testify to **2** to serve as evidence of **3** to act as witness of **4** to be present at —**bear witness** to testify

wit·ti·cism (wit′ə siz′əm) ***n.*** ⟦< WITTY⟧ a witty remark

wit·ting (wit′iŋ) ***adj.*** ⟦ME *wytting*⟧ intentional

wit·ty (wit′ē) ***adj.*** **-ti·er, -ti·est** ⟦OE *wittig*⟧ having or showing wit; cleverly amusing —**wit′ti·ly** ***adv.*** —**wit′ti·ness** ***n.***

wive (wīv) ***vi.***, ***vt.*** **wived, wiv′ing** ⟦OE *wifian*⟧ [Archaic] to marry (a woman)

wives (wīvz) ***n.*** *pl. of* WIFE

wiz·ard (wiz′ərd) ***n.*** ⟦ME *wisard*⟧ **1** a magician; sorcerer **2** [Inf.] one very skilled at a specified activity

wiz′ard·ry ***n.*** magic; sorcery

wiz·ened (wiz′ənd) ***adj.*** ⟦< OE *wisnian*, wither⟧ dried up; withered

wk *abbrev.* **1** week **2** work

wkly. *abbrev.* weekly

w/o *abbrev.* without

wob·ble (wäb′əl) ***vi.*** **-bled, -bling** ⟦prob. < LowG *wabbeln*⟧ **1** to move unsteadily from side to side **2** to shake **3** to vacillate —***vt.*** to cause to wobble —***n.*** wobbling motion —**wob′bly, -bli·er, -bli·est,** ***adj.*** —**wob′bli·ness** ***n.***

woe (wō) ***n.*** ⟦OE *wa*⟧ **1** great sorrow; grief **2** trouble —***interj.*** alas!

woe′be·gone′ (-bē gôn′, -bi-) ***adj.*** of woeful appearance; looking sad or wretched

woe′ful (-fəl) ***adj.*** **1** full of woe; sad **2** causing woe **3** pitiful; wretched —**woe′ful·ly** ***adv.***

wok (wäk, wôk) ***n.*** ⟦Chin⟧ a bowl-shaped cooking pan used for frying, steaming, etc.

woke (wōk) ***vi.***, ***vt.*** *alt. pt. of* WAKE[1]

wok·en (wō′kən) ***vi.***, ***vt.*** *alt. pp. of* WAKE[1]

wolf (woolf) ***n.***, *pl.* **wolves** (woolvz) ⟦OE *wulf*⟧ **1** a wild, flesh-eating, doglike mammal of the Northern Hemisphere **2** *a*) a cruel or greedy person *b*) [Slang] a man who flirts with many women —***vt.*** to eat greedily: often with *down* —**cry wolf** to give a false alarm —**wolf′ish** ***adj.***

wolf′hound′ ***n.*** a breed of large dog, once used for hunting wolves

wol·ver·ine (wool′vər ēn′) ***n.*** ⟦< WOLF⟧ a stocky, flesh-eating mammal of N North America and N Eurasia

wolves (woolvz) ***n.*** *pl. of* WOLF

wom·an (woom′ən) ***n.***, *pl.* **wom·en** (wim′ən) ⟦< OE *wif*, a female + *mann*, human being⟧ **1** *a*) an adult female human being *b*) women collectively **2** a female servant **3** womanly qualities

-wom·an (woom′ən) *combining form* woman of a (specified) kind, in a (specified) activity, etc.: sometimes used to avoid the masculine implications of -MAN

wom′an·hood′ ***n.*** **1** the state of being a woman **2** womanly qualities **3** women collectively

wom′an·ish ***adj.*** like or characteristic of a woman

wom′an·ize′ ***vt.*** **-ized′, -iz′ing** to make effeminate —***vi.*** to be sexually promiscuous with women —**wom′an·iz′er** ***n.***

wom′an·kind′ ***n.*** women in general

wom′an·ly ***adj.*** **1** womanish **2** characteristic of or fit for a woman —**wom′an·li·ness** ***n.***

womb (wo͞om) ***n.*** ⟦OE *wamb*⟧ UTERUS

wom·bat (wäm′bat′) ***n.*** ⟦< native name⟧ a burrowing marsupial resembling a small bear, found in Australia, etc.

wom·en (wim′in) ***n.*** *pl. of* WOMAN

wom′en·folk′ ***pl.n.*** [Inf. or Dial.] women or womankind: also **wom′en·folks′**

won (wun) ***vi.***, ***vt.*** *pt. & pp. of* WIN

won·der (wun′dər) ***n.*** ⟦OE *wundor*⟧ **1** a person, thing, or event causing astonishment and admiration; marvel **2** the feeling aroused by something strange, unexpected, etc. —***vi.*** **1** to be filled with wonder; marvel **2** to have curiosity, sometimes mingled with doubt —***vt.*** to have curiosity or doubt about *[he wondered what happened]*

won′der·ful ***adj.*** **1** that causes wonder; marvelous **2** excellent, fine, etc. —**won′der·ful·ly** ***adv.***

won′der·land′ ***n.*** any place, real or imaginary, full of wonders

won′der·ment ***n.*** amazement

won·drous (wun′drəs) ***adj.*** wonderful: now chiefly literary —***adv.*** [Archaic] surprisingly

wont (wônt, wōnt) ***adj.*** ⟦< OE *wunian*, dwell⟧ accustomed *[she was wont to rise early]* —***n.*** usual practice; habit

won't (wōnt) *contr.* will not

wont·ed (wôn′tid, wōn′-) ***adj.*** customary

won ton (wän′ tän′) ⟦Cantonese⟧ Chinese dumplings of noodle dough filled with chopped meat, etc., often served in a soup (**won′-ton′ soup**)

woo (wo͞o) ***vt.*** ⟦OE *wogian*⟧ **1** to seek the love of, usually in order to propose marriage **2** to seek *[to woo fame]* —***vi.*** to woo a person —**woo′er** ***n.***

wood (wood) ***n.*** ⟦OE *wudu*⟧ **1** [*usually pl., with sing. or pl. v.*] a thick growth of trees; forest **2** the hard, fibrous substance beneath the bark of trees and shrubs **3** lumber or timber **4** *Golf* any of certain clubs, originally with wooden heads —***adj.*** **1** made of wood; wooden **2** grow-

THESAURUS

out.

witness ***n.*** observer, onlooker, eyewitness, bystander, spectator, testifier, beholder, signatory. —**bear witness** affirm, attest, give evidence; see TESTIFY 2.

witness ***v.*** see, observe, be a witness, be on the scene, behold, be present, testify, vouch for, stand for, look on, say under oath, depose, be on hand.

witnessed ***a.*** sworn to, vouched for, alleged, borne out, validated, valid, established, verified, authenticated, substantiated, supported, upheld, endorsed, brought forward.

witty ***a.*** quick-witted, clever, amusing; see INTELLIGENT.

wizard ***n.*** magician, soothsayer, witch, witch doctor, sorcerer, fortuneteller, astrologer, alchemist, medicine man, conjurer, shaman, enchanter, hypnotist, diviner, seer, clairvoyant, augurer, medium, palmist.

wobble ***v.*** shake, quaver, flounder, vacillate, tremble, quiver, move unsteadily, dodder, teeter, totter, be unsteady, waver, quake, stagger, shuffle, waggle.

wobbly ***a.*** wavering, unbalanced, precarious; see UNSTABLE 1.

wolf ***n.*** wild dog, coyote, timber wolf; see DOG.

woman ***n.*** **1** [An adult female] lady, dame, matron, gentlewoman, maid, debutante, nymph, virgin, girl, chick*, doll*, babe*, gal*, broad*. **2** [A wife or mistress] love, lover, wife; see WIFE. **3** [Womankind] femininity, the fair sex, womanhood, the female of the species*.

womanhood ***n.*** adulthood, maturity, majority, womanliness, sexual prime, nubility, marriageable age, maidenhood, matronhood, spinsterhood.

womanizer ***n.*** promiscuous man, playboy, skirtchaser*, tomcat*, Casanova, Lothario, seducer, adulterer.

womanly ***a.*** ladylike, feminine, female, gentle, modest, compassionate, wifely, sisterly, maternal, motherly, protective, womanish, fair.—*Ant.* MANLY, virile, masculine.

womb ***n.*** uterus, female cavity, belly; see STOMACH.

won ***a.*** gained, achieved, conquered, taken, got, triumphed, overwhelmed.—*Ant.* BEATEN, lost, failed.

wonder ***n.*** **1** [Amazement] surprise, awe, stupefaction, admiration, wonderment, astonishment, puzzlement, wondering, stupor, bewilderment, perplexity, fascination, consternation, perturbation, confusion, shock, start, jar, jolt, incredulity. **2** [A marvel] miracle, curiosity, oddity, rarity, freak, phenomenon, sensation, prodigy, act of God, portent, wonderwork, spectacle, prodigious event, something unnatural, the unbelievable.

wonder ***v.*** **1** [To marvel] be surprised, be startled, be fascinated, be amazed, be dumbfounded, be confounded, be dazed, be awestruck, be astonished, be agape, be dazzled, stand aghast, be struck by, be unable to take one's eyes off, admire, gape, be taken aback, stare, be flabbergasted. **2** [To question] be curious, query, hold in doubt; see ASK.

wonderful ***a.*** fine, enjoyable, pleasing; see PLEASANT 2.

wonderfully ***a.*** beautifully, admirably, excellently; see WELL 2.

wonderland ***n.*** paradise, Eden, utopia, Garden of Eden, Land of Milk and Honey, nirvana, best of all worlds, fantasyland.

wood ***n.*** **1** [A forest; *often plural*] grove, woodland, timber; see FOREST. **2** [The portion of trees within the bark] timber, lumber, sapwood, heartwood, pith, knot, growth ring. *Varieties of wood include the following:* oak, chestnut, mahogany, sugar maple, red maple, cherry, cedar, walnut, hickory, butternut, hemlock, spruce, hornbeam, ebony, linden, beech, birch, poplar, tamarack, white pine, yellow pine, gumwood, elm, cypress, redwood, fir, Douglas fir, ash, red oak, live oak, white oak, willow, cottonwood, zebrawood, bamboo.

ing or living in woods —**out of the woods** [Inf.] out of difficulty, danger, etc.

wood alcohol METHANOL

wood'bine' (-bīn') ***n.*** ⟦< OE *wudu,* wood + *binde,* to bind⟧ **1** a climbing honeysuckle **2** a climbing vine with dark-blue berries

wood'carv'ing ***n.*** **1** the art of carving wood by hand **2** an object so made —**wood'carv'er** ***n.***

wood'chuck' ***n.*** ⟦< AmInd name⟧ a burrowing and hibernating marmot of North America

wood'cock' ***n.*** a small game bird with short legs and a long bill

wood'craft' ***n.*** **1** matters relating to the woods, as camping, hunting, etc. **2** WOODWORKING

wood'cut' ***n.*** **1** a wooden block engraved with a design, etc. **2** a print from this

wood'cut'ter ***n.*** one who fells trees, cuts wood, etc. —**wood'cut'ting** ***n.***

wood'ed ***adj.*** covered with trees

wood'en ***adj.*** **1** made of wood **2** stiff, lifeless, etc. **3** dull; insensitive —**wood'en·ly** ***adv.***

wood'land (-lənd, -land') ***n.*** land covered with woods —***adj.*** of the woods

wood'lot' ***n.*** a piece of land where trees are raised, as for firewood, lumber, etc.

wood'peck'er (-pek'ər) ***n.*** a climbing bird with a strong, pointed bill used to peck holes in bark to get insects

wood'pile' ***n.*** a pile of wood, esp. of firewood

wood screw a screw with a sharp point, for use in wood

wood'shed' ***n.*** a shed for storing firewood

woods·man (woodz'mən) ***n.***, *pl.* **-men** (-mən) **1** one who lives or works in the woods **2** one skilled in woodcraft

wood'sy (-zē) ***adj.*** **-si·er, -si·est** of or like the woods —**wood'si·ness** ***n.***

wood·wind (wood'wind') ***n.*** any of a family of wind instruments made, esp. orig., of wood, as the flute, clarinet, or oboe

wood'work' ***n.*** **1** work done in wood **2** the wooden moldings, doors, etc. of a house

wood'work'ing ***n.*** the art or work of making things of wood

wood'y ***adj.*** **-i·er, -i·est** **1** covered with trees **2** consisting of or forming wood **3** like wood —**wood'i·ness** ***n.***

woof[1] (wo͞of) ***n.*** ⟦ult. < OE *wefan,* to weave⟧ WEFT

woof[2] (woof) ***n.*** ⟦echoic⟧ the gruff barking sound of a dog —***vi.*** to make this sound

woof·er (woof'ər) ***n.*** a large, high-fidelity speaker for reproducing low-frequency sounds

wool (wool) ***n.*** ⟦OE *wull*⟧ **1** the soft, curly hair of sheep or of some other animals, as the goat **2** woolen yarn, cloth, clothing, etc. **3** anything that looks or feels like wool

wool'en ***adj.*** **1** made of wool **2** relating to wool or woolen cloth —***n.*** [*pl.*] woolen goods Also [Chiefly Brit.] **wool'len**

Woolf (woolf), **Virginia** 1882-1941; Eng. novelist & critic

wool'gath'er·ing (-ga*th*'ər iŋ) ***n.*** aimless daydreaming or speculation

wool·ly (wool'ē) ***adj.*** **-li·er, -li·est** **1** of or like wool **2** bearing or covered with wool **3** rough and uncivilized: used chiefly in **wild and woolly** **4** confused *[woolly* ideas*]* Also sp. **wool'y**

wooz·y (wo͞o'zē, wooz'ē) ***adj.*** **-i·er, -i·est** [Inf.] dizzy or befuddled, as from drink or a blow —**wooz'i·ness** ***n.***

word (wurd) ***n.*** ⟦OE⟧ **1** *a)* a speech sound, or series of such sounds, having meaning as a unit of language *b)* the written or printed representation of this **2** a brief remark *[a word* of advice*]* **3** a promise or assurance *[he* gave his *word]* **4** news; information **5** *a)* a password *b)* a command, order, etc. **6** [*usually pl.*] *a)* speech *b)* lyrics **7** [*pl.*] a quarrel —***vt.*** to put into words; phrase —**in a word** briefly —**in so many words** exactly and plainly —**the Word** the Bible —**word for word** in precisely the same words

word'age ***n.*** **1** words **2** wordiness

word'ing ***n.*** choice of words; diction

word of honor solemn promise

word of mouth speech, as opposed to writing

word'play' ***n.*** **1** repartee **2** punning

word processor a computerized device consisting of a keyboard, video screen, printer, etc., used to generate, edit, store, or duplicate documents, as letters or reports —**word processing**

Words·worth (wurdz'wərth), **William** 1770-1850; Eng. poet

word·y (wur'dē) ***adj.*** **-i·er, -i·est** containing or using too many words; verbose —**word'i·ness** ***n.***

wore (wôr) ***vt., vi.*** *pt. of* WEAR

work (wurk) ***n.*** ⟦OE *weorc*⟧ **1** effort exerted to do or make something; labor; toil **2** employment; occupation

THESAURUS

wooded ***a.*** timbered, forested, tree-covered, wild, tree-laden, treed, reforested, woody, jungly, having cover, timber-bearing, lumbering, uncut, not lumbered, not cut over, with standing timber, primeval, below the timberline, jungle-covered.

wooden ***a.*** wood, frame, frame-built, long-built, boarded, clapboarded, plank, built of slabs, pine, oak, elm, ash, mahogany.

woodwork ***n.*** molding, fittings, paneling, stairway, wood finishing, doors, window frames, sashes, jambs, wood trim.

woodworking ***n.*** woodcraft, woodcarving, wood turning, cabinetmaking, carpentry, joinery.

wool ***n.*** fleece, lambswool, Angora wool, Shetland wool, tweed, flannel, gabardine, worsted, woolen suiting, serge, broadcloth, frieze, mohair, felt, blanketing, carpeting; see also GOODS 1.

word ***n.*** **1** [A unit of expression] term, name, expression, designation, concept, vocable, utterance, sound, a voicing, form of speech, speech, locution, free morpheme, lexeme. *Classes of words include the following:* common noun, proper noun, personal pronoun, possessive pronoun, demonstrative pronoun, relative pronoun, interrogative pronoun, indefinite pronoun, definite article, indefinite article, transitive verb, intransitive verb, reflexive verb, auxiliary verb, descriptive adjective, quantitative adjective, participial adjective, adverb, coordinating conjunction, subordinating conjunction, preposition, interjection, modifier, subject, predicate, source word, synonym, antonym, homograph, homophone, etymon, cognate word, colloquialism, jargon, slang word, dialect word, provincialism, translation, native word, foreign word, idiom, acronym, compound word, exclamation, greeting, spoken word, written word. **2** [Promise] pledge, commitment, word of honor; see PROMISE 1. **3** [Tidings] report, message, information; see NEWS 1. —**a good word** favorable comment, recommendation, support; see PRAISE 2. —**by word of mouth** orally, verbally, spoken; see ORAL. —**have words with** argue with, differ with, bicker; see ARGUE, FIGHT. —**in so many words** succinctly, cursorily, economically; see BRIEFLY. —**take at one's word** trust in, have confidence in, put one's trust in; see BELIEVE. —**the word** information, the facts, the lowdown*; see KNOWLEDGE 1.

wordiness ***n.*** redundance, redundancy, diffuseness, circumlocution, repetition, verbiage, verbosity, bombast, tautology, indirectness, flow of words, rhetoric, copiousness, tediousness.—*Ant.* SILENCE, conciseness, succinctness.

wording ***n.*** locution, phrasing, turn of phrase, contents, style, expression, way of putting it.

wordy ***a.*** tedious, bombastic, long-winded; see DULL 4.

work ***n.*** **1** [Something to be done] commitment, task, obligation; see JOB 2. **2** [The doing of work] performance, endeavor, employment, production, occupation, practice, activity, manufacture, industry, operation, transaction, toil, labor, exertion, drudgery, functioning, stress, struggle, slavery, trial, push, attempt, effort, pains, elbow grease*, muscle*. **3** [The result of labor; *often plural*] feat, accomplishment, output; see ACHIEVEMENT. **4** [Occupation] profession, craft, business; see JOB 1. —**at work** working, on the job, engaged; see BUSY 1. —**in the works*** prepared for, budgeted, approved; see READY 2. —**make short** (or **quick**) **work of** finish off, deal with, dispose of; see DO 1. —**out of work** not hired, dismissed, looking for a job; see UNEMPLOYED.

work ***v.*** **1** [To labor] toil, slave, sweat, do a day's work, do the chores, exert oneself, apply oneself, do one's best, overexert, overwork, overstrain, get to work, work overtime, work day and night, work one's way up, tax one's energies, pull, plod, tug, struggle, strive, carry on, do the job, punch a time clock*, put in time, pour it on*, work one's fingers to the bone*, buckle down, bear down, work like a horse*, work like a dog, work like a slave, keep at it, stay with it, put one's shoulder to the wheel, burn the candle at both ends, burn the midnight oil. **2** [To be employed] earn a living, have a job, hold a post, occupy a position, report for work, be on the staff, be among the employed, be on the job. **3** [To function] go, run, serve; see OPERATE 2. **4** [To handle successfully] control, accomplish, manage; see ACHIEVE, OPERATE 3. **5** [To fashion] give form to, sculpture, mold; see FORM 1. —**work at** attempt, endeavor, do one's best; see TRY 1. —**work in** introduce, find a place for, squeeze in;

3 something one is making or doing; task **4** something made or done; specif., *a*) an act; deed (*usually used in pl.*) *[*good *works]* *b*) [*pl.*] collected writings *c*) [*pl.*] engineering structures, as bridges, dams, etc. **5** [*pl., with sing. v.*] a place where work is done, as a factory **6** workmanship **—*adj.*** of, for, or used in work **—*vi.*** **worked** or **wrought**, **work'ing** **1** to do work; labor; toil **2** to be employed **3** to function or operate, esp. effectively **4** to ferment **5** to move, proceed, etc. slowly and with difficulty **6** to come or become, as by repeated movement *[*the door *worked* loose*]* **—*vt.*** **1** to cause; bring about *[*his idea *worked* wonders*]* **2** to mold; shape **3** to solve (a mathematical problem, etc.) **4** to manipulate; knead **5** to bring into a specified condition, as by moving back and forth *[*to *work* a nail loose*]* **6** to cultivate (soil) **7** to operate; use **8** to cause to work *[*to *work* a crew hard*]* **9** to make (one's way, etc.) by effort **10** to provoke; rouse *[*to *work* oneself into a rage*]* **11** [Slang] to proceed ingratiatingly through (a crowd, etc.) **—at work** working **—out of work** unemployed **—the works** **1** the working parts (*of* a watch, etc.) **2** [Inf.] everything: also **the whole works** **—work off** to get rid of **—work on** **1** to influence **2** to try to persuade **—work out** **1** to solve **2** to result **3** to develop **4** to have a workout **—work up** **1** to advance **2** to develop **3** to excite

work·a·ble (wʉr'kə bəl) ***adj.*** **1** that can be worked **2** practicable; feasible

work'a·day' (-dā') ***adj.*** **1** of workdays; everyday **2** ordinary

work'a·hol'ic (-hôl'ik) ***n.*** ⟦WORK + -AHOLIC⟧ a person having an irrational need to work

work'bench' ***n.*** a table at which work is done, as by a carpenter

work'book' ***n.*** a book of questions, exercises, etc. for use by students

work'day' ***n.*** **1** a day on which work is ordinarily done **2** the part of a day during which work is done

work'er ***n.*** **1** one who works for a living **2** one who works for a cause, etc. **3** a sterile ant, bee, etc. that does work for the colony

work'fare' (-fer') ***n.*** ⟦WORK + (WEL)FARE⟧ a government program requiring employable recipients of welfare to register for work, training, etc.

work'horse' ***n.*** **1** a horse used for working **2** a reliable worker with a heavy workload

work'house' ***n.*** a prison where petty offenders are confined and made to work

work'ing ***adj.*** **1** that works **2** of, for, or used in work **3** sufficient to get work done **4** on which further work may be based *[*a *working* hypothesis*]* **—*n.*** the act of one that works

working class the social class consisting of industrial and manual workers

work'ing·man' (-man') ***n.***, *pl.* **-men'** (-men') a worker, esp. an industrial worker

work'load' ***n.*** the amount of work assigned for completion within a given time period

work'man (-mən) ***n.***, *pl.* **-men** (-mən) **1** WORKINGMAN **2** a craftsman

work'man·like' ***adj.*** capable; competent

work'man·ship' ***n.*** skill of a workman or the quality of the work done

work'out' ***n.*** a session of physical exercises or any strenuous work

work'place' ***n.*** the office, factory, etc. where one works

work sheet a paper sheet with working notes, etc., or with problems, etc. to be worked on by students

work'shop' ***n.*** **1** a room or building where work is done **2** a seminar for specified intensive study, work, etc.

work'sta'tion ***n.*** **1** a person's work area, including furniture, etc. and, often, a microcomputer **2** a terminal or personal computer connected to a network

work'ta'ble ***n.*** a table at which work is done

work'-up' ***n.*** a complete medical study of a patient, including tests

work'week' ***n.*** the total number of hours or days worked in a week

world (wʉrld) ***n.*** ⟦OE *werold*⟧ **1** *a*) the earth *b*) the universe **2** *a*) mankind *b*) people generally; the public **3** *a*) [*also* **W-**] some part of the earth *[*the Old *World]* *b*) any sphere or domain *[*the animal *world]* **4** individual experience, outlook, etc. *[*her *world* is narrow*]* **5** secular life and interests, or people concerned with these **6** [*often pl.*] a large amount *[*a *world* of good*]* **—for all the world** exactly

world'-class' ***adj.*** of the highest class, as in international competition

world'ly ***adj.*** **-li·er, -li·est** **1** of this world; secular **2** devoted to the affairs, pleasures, etc. of this world **3** worldly-wise **—world'li·ness *n.***

world'ly-wise' ***adj.*** wise in the ways or affairs of the world; sophisticated

world'-shak'ing ***adj.*** of great significance, effect, or influence; momentous

world'view' ***n.*** a comprehensive, esp. personal, philosophy of the world and of human life

World War I the war (1914-18) involving Great Britain, France, Russia, the U.S., etc. on one side and Germany, Austria-Hungary, etc. on the other

World War II the war (1939-45) involving Great Britain, France, the Soviet Union, the U.S., etc. on one side and Germany, Italy, Japan, etc. on the other

world'-wea'ry ***adj.*** bored with living

world'wide' ***adj.***, ***adv.*** (extending) throughout the world

THESAURUS

see INCLUDE 1. **—work on** (or **upon**) try to encourage, use one's influence with, talk to; see INFLUENCE. **—work out** **1** [To solve] come to terms, compromise, reach an agreement; see AGREE. **2** [To satisfy a requirement] finish, do what is necessary, get something done; see ACHIEVE.

workable *a.* useful, practicable, functional; see WORKING 1.

worker *n.* laborer, toiler, mechanic; see WORKMAN.

working *a.* **1** [Functioning] operational, running, in operation, functioning, moving, in process, in working order, humming along*, firing on all cylinders, in gear, in collar. **2** [Employed] laboring, on the job, punching a clock; see BUSY 1.

workman *n.* operator, mechanic, machinist, craftsman, tradesman, artist, artisan, technician, journeyman, master worker, handworker, skilled workman. *Workers include the following:* carpenter, cabinetmaker, upholsterer, paperhanger, plasterer, bricklayer, plumber, electrician, metalworker, locksmith, boilermaker, pipefitter, coppersmith, printer, pressman, prepress technician, compositor, typesetter, linotype operator, glassworker, glazier, tiler, concrete worker, automobile mechanic, punch press operator, shipping clerk, file clerk, packager, assembler, conductor, brakeman, locomotive engineer, switchman, surveyor, fireman, barber, custodian, truck driver, bus driver, carpet installer, carpet cleaner, gardener, tree surgeon, seamstress, tailor, baker, butcher, farm worker, cowboy, dairyman, waiter, waitress, laundry worker, welder, drill operator, hydraulic press operator, diesinker, mason, lathe operator, gear-cutting machine operator, threading machine operator, operator, textile worker, tool-and-die maker, postal clerk, policeman, painter, galvanizer, draftsman, appliance repairman, TV repairman, cameraman, meat cutter, packer, assembly-line worker, maintenance worker, machine operator, patternmaker, foundry worker, road worker, heavy-equipment operator, construction worker, lineman, cook, dishwasher, caterer, janitor, groundskeeper, landscaper, security guard, HVAC technician.

workmanship *n.* craftsmanship, skill, quality of work, performance, handicraft, working ability, handiwork, achievement, manufacture, execution.

workout *n.* exercise, conditioning, gymnastics; see DISCIPLINE 2.

works *n.* **1** [Working parts] cogs, belts, cams, wheels, gears, pistons, springs, coils, chains, rods, pulleys, wires; see also INSIDES. **2** [*Everything; *with "the"*] totality, entirety, the whole; see ALL, EVERYTHING.

workshop *n.* **1** [Place where work is done] plant, works, laboratory, foundry, studio, yards, mill. **2** [Seminar] discussion group, study group, class.

world *n.* **1** [The earth] globe, wide world, planet; see EARTH 1. **2** [The universe] cosmos, nature, creation; see UNIVERSE. **3** [A specific group] realm, division, system; see CLASS 1. **4** [All one's surroundings] environment, atmosphere, childhood, adolescence, adulthood, experience, life, inner life, memory, idealization. **—bring into the world** give birth to, bear, have a baby; see PRODUCE 1. **—on top of the world** feeling fine, exuberant, successful; see HAPPY. **—out of this world** extraordinary, strange, remarkable; see UNUSUAL 1, 2.

worldly *a.* mundane, earthly, ungodly, practical, matter-of-fact, secular, strategic, grubbing, moneymaking, unprincipled, power-loving, self-centered, opportunistic, sophisticated, cosmopolitan, terrestrial, profane, human, natural, temporal.

worldwide *a.* global, universal, extensive; see GENERAL 1.

World Wide Web a group of Internet sources giving access to text, images, sound, etc.

worm (wurm) ***n.*** ⟦< OE *wyrm,* serpent⟧ **1** a long, slender, soft-bodied animal **2** an abject or contemptible person **3** something spiral in shape, etc., as the thread of a screw **4** [*pl.*] any disease caused by parasitic worms in the intestines, etc. —***vi.*** to proceed like a worm, in a winding or devious manner —***vt.*** **1** to bring about, get, make, etc. in a winding or devious manner **2** to purge of intestinal worms —**worm'y, -i·er, -i·est,** ***adj.***

worm gear a gear consisting of a rotating screw meshed with a toothed wheel

worm'wood' (-wood') ***n.*** ⟦< OE *wermod*⟧ a strong-smelling plant that yields a bitter-tasting oil formerly used in making absinthe

worn (wôrn) ***vt.,*** ***vi.*** *pp. of* WEAR —***adj.*** **1** damaged by use or wear **2** showing the effects of worry or anxiety

worn'-out' ***adj.*** **1** used until no longer effective, usable, etc. **2** exhausted; tired out

wor·ri·ment (wur'ē mənt) ***n.*** (a) worry

wor'ri·some (-səm) ***adj.*** causing worry

wor·ry (wur'ē) ***vt.*** **-ried, -ry·ing** ⟦< OE *wyrgan,* to strangle⟧ **1** to treat roughly, as with continual biting [a dog *worrying* a bone] **2** to annoy, bother, etc. **3** to make troubled or uneasy —***vi.*** **1** to bite or tear (*at* an object) **2** to be anxious, troubled, etc. —***n.,*** *pl.* **-ries** **1** a troubled state of mind; anxiety **2** a cause of this —**wor'ri·er** ***n.***

wor'ry·wart' (-wôrt') ***n.*** ⟦prec. + WART⟧ [Inf.] one who tends to worry, esp. over trivial matters

worse (wurs) ***adj.*** ⟦OE *wiersa*⟧ **1** *compar. of* BAD[1] & ILL **2** *a*) bad, evil, harmful, etc. in a greater degree *b*) of inferior quality **3** in poorer health; more ill **4** in a less satisfactory condition —***adv.*** **1** *compar. of* BADLY & ILL **2** in a worse manner **3** to a worse extent —***n.*** that which is worse —**worse off** in worse circumstances

wor·sen (wur'sən) ***vt.,*** ***vi.*** to make or become worse

wor·ship (wur'ship) ***n.*** ⟦< OE *weorthscipe*⟧ **1** a service or rite showing reverence for a deity **2** intense love or admiration **3** [**W-**] [Chiefly Brit.] a title of honor: used in addressing magistrates, etc. —***vt.*** **-shiped** or **-shipped, -ship·ing** or **-ship·ping** **1** to show religious reverence for **2** to have intense love or admiration for —***vi.*** to engage in worship —**wor'ship·er** or **wor'ship·per** ***n.***

wor'ship·ful (-fəl) ***adj.*** feeling or offering great devotion or respect

worst (wurst) ***adj.*** ⟦OE *wyrsta*⟧ **1** *superl. of* BAD[1] & ILL **2** *a*) bad, evil, harmful, etc. in the highest degree *b*) of the lowest quality **3** in the least satisfactory condition —***adv.*** **1** *superl. of* BADLY & ILL **2** in the worst manner **3** to the worst extent —***n.*** that which is worst —***vt.*** to defeat —**at worst** under the worst circumstances —**if (the) worst comes to (the) worst** if the worst possible thing happens —**(in) the worst way** [Slang] very much; greatly

wor·sted (woos'tid, wur'stid) ***n.*** ⟦after *Worstead,* England⟧ **1** a smooth, firmly twisted wool thread or yarn **2** fabric made from this

wort (wurt) ***n.*** ⟦OE *wyrt-*⟧ a liquid, produced from malt, that can be fermented to make beer, etc.

worth (wurth) ***n.*** ⟦OE *weorth*⟧ **1** material value, esp. as expressed in terms of money **2** importance, value, merit, etc. **3** the quantity to be had for a given sum [a dollar's *worth*] —***prep.*** **1** deserving or worthy of **2** equal in value to **3** having wealth amounting to

worth'less ***adj.*** without worth or merit; useless —**worth'less·ness** ***n.***

worth'while' ***adj.*** worth the time or effort spent

wor·thy (wur'thē) ***adj.*** **-thi·er, -thi·est** **1** having worth, value, or merit **2** meriting —***n.,*** *pl.* **-thies** a person of outstanding worth, etc. —**wor'thi·ly** ***adv.*** —**wor'thi·ness** ***n.***

would (wood) ***v.aux.*** ⟦OE *wolde*⟧ **1** *pt. of* WILL[2] **2** used to express a supposition or condition [he *would* write if he knew you *would* answer] **3** used to make a polite request [*would* you please open the window?] —***vt.*** [Old Poet.] I wish [*would* that she were here] See usage note at WILL[2]

would'-be' ***adj.*** **1** wishing or pretending to be **2** intended to be

wound[1] (woond) ***n.*** ⟦OE *wund*⟧ **1** an injury in which tissue is cut, torn, etc. **2** any hurt to the feelings, honor, etc. —***vt.,*** ***vi.*** to inflict a wound (on or upon); injure

wound[2] (wound) ***vt.,*** ***vi.*** *pt. & pp. of* WIND[1]

wove (wōv) ***vt.,*** ***vi.*** *pt. & alt. pp. of* WEAVE

THESAURUS

worm ***n.*** caterpillar, grub, larva, maggot, leech, parasite, helminth. *Common worms include the following:* angleworm, earthworm, threadworm, tapeworm, silkworm, flatworm or platyhelminth, gordian worm, ribbon worm or nemertean, marine worm, hookworm, pinworm, planarian, tubifex worm, horsehair worm, blindworm, slowworm, roundworm or nematode worm, annelid worm, cutworm, army worm, wireworm, measuring worm.

worm ***v.*** inch, creep, slink; see CRAWL, SNEAK.

worn ***a.*** **1** [Used as clothing] carried, put on, donned, displayed, exhibited, used, sported*. **2** [Showing signs of wear] frayed, threadbare, old, secondhand, ragged, shabby, used, consumed, deteriorated, patched, torn, the worse for wear.—*Ant.* FRESH, new, whole.

worn-out ***a.*** used up, gone, destroyed; see RUINED 1, 2, USELESS 1.

worried ***a.*** troubled, bothered, perturbed, vexed, distressed, miserable, annoyed, concerned, nervous, upset, suffering, torn, in conflict, pained, burdened, ill at ease, racking one's brains, uptight*, all hot and bothered*, anxious, hung up*; see also EXCITED.

worrisome ***a.*** troubling, distressing, ominous, foreboding, disturbing, worrying, fear-inducing, anxious, apprehensive.

worry ***n.*** **1** [The state of anxiety] concern, anxiety, misery; see DISTRESS. **2** [A cause of worry] problem, upset, disturbance; see FEAR, TROUBLE 1.

worry ***v.*** **1** [To cause worry] annoy, trouble, bother; see DISTURB. **2** [To indulge in worry] fret, chafe, fear, take to heart, break one's heart, despair, stew, be anxious, worry oneself, have qualms, wince, agonize, writhe, suffer, turn gray with worry, become sick with worry, sweat out*; see also BOTHER 1.

worship ***n.*** **1** [Adoration] prayer, devotion, homage, adulation, benediction, invocation, supplication, beatification, veneration, offering, burnt offering, reverence, honor. **2** [A religious service] Mass, services, devotions; see CHURCH 2.

worship ***v.*** sanctify, pray to, invoke, venerate, glorify, praise, exalt, offer one's prayers to, pay homage to, give thanks, offer thanks to, sing praises to, reverence, celebrate, adore, revere, laud, extol, magnify, chant, sing, bow down; see also PRAY 2.

worshiper ***n.*** churchgoer, communicant, member of the congregation, believer, supplicant, devotee, devotionalist, adorer, pietist, pious person, devout person, celebrant, priest, priestess.—*Ant.* SKEPTIC, atheist, agnostic.

worst ***a.*** most terrible, most harmful, most lethal, poorest, lowest, least, last, most ghastly, most horrible, most pitiful, least meaningful, meanest, least understanding, least effective.

worst ***n.*** lowest point, nadir, bottom; see BOTTOM. —**at worst** under the worst possible circumstances, unluckily, grievously; see BADLY 1, UNFORTUNATELY. —**(in) the worst way** unluckily, disastrously, horribly; see UNFORTUNATELY.

worth ***a.*** deserving, meriting, equal in value to, priced at, exchangeable for, valued at, worth in the open market, pegged at, cashable for, good for, appraised at, having a face value of, reasonably estimated at, bid at, held at. —**for all one is worth** greatly, mightily, hard; see POWERFULLY.

worth ***n.*** goodness, value, quality, character, importance, significance, meaning, estimation, benefit, excellence, merit; see also VALUE 1, 3.

worthless ***a.*** profitless, counterproductive, barren, unprofitable, unproductive, unimportant, insignificant, counterfeit, bogus, cheap, sterile, waste, wasted, no good, trashy, inconsequential, petty, piddling, paltry, trivial, trifling, unessential, beneath notice, empty, good-for-nothing, no-account*, not worth the trouble*, not worth speaking of*, not able to say much for*.

worthlessness ***n.*** uselessness, inefficiency, impracticality; see WASTE 1.

worthwhile ***a.*** good, serviceable, useful, important, profitable, valuable, remunerative, estimable, worthy, helpful, beneficial, meritorious, excellent, rewarding, praiseworthy.

worthy ***a.*** good, true, honest, honorable, reliable, trustworthy, dependable, noble, charitable, dutiful, philanthropic, virtuous, moral, pure, upright, righteous, decent, incorruptible, meritorious, creditable, qualified, fit, deserving, right-minded, worthy of, model, exemplary, sterling, sinless, stainless, blameless.—*Ant.* WORTHLESS, bad, evil.

would-be ***a.*** assuming, supposed, *manqué* (French); see HOPEFUL 1.

wound[1] ***n.*** bruise, hurt, scar; see INJURY.

wound[1] ***v.*** **1** [To hurt the body] gash, scrape, injure; see HURT 1. **2** [To hurt the feelings] trouble, upset, pain; see BOTHER 2, DISTURB.

wound[2] ***a.*** twisted, wrapped,

wo·ven (wō'vən) *vt.*, *vi. alt. pp. of* WEAVE
wow (wou) *interj.* used to express surprise, pleasure, etc. —*vt.* [Slang] to arouse enthusiasm in
wpm *abbrev.* words per minute
wrack (rak) *n.* ⟦< MDu *wrak*, a wreck⟧ *alt. sp. of* RACK²
wraith (rāth) *n.* ⟦Scot⟧ a ghost
wran·gle (raŋ'gəl) *vi.* **-gled**, **-gling** ⟦< OE *wringan*, to press⟧ to argue; quarrel, esp. noisily —*n.* a noisy dispute —**wran'gler** *n.*
wran'gler (-glər) *n.* ⟦< AmSp *caballerango*, a groom⟧ a cowboy who herds livestock, esp. saddle horses —**wran'gle, -gled, -gling,** *vt.*
wrap (rap) *vt.* **wrapped**, **wrap'ping** ⟦ME *wrappen*⟧ **1** to wind or fold (a covering) around something **2** to enclose and fasten in paper, etc. —*vi.* to twine, coil, etc.: usually with *over, around*, etc. —*n.* **1** an outer covering or garment **2** [*pl.*] secrecy; censorship *[to keep plans under wraps]* **3** *Film* the completion of the filming of a scene, etc. —**wrapped up in** engrossed in or involved in —**wrap up** [Inf.] to conclude; settle
wrap'per *n.* **1** one that wraps **2** that in which something is wrapped **3** a woman's dressing gown
wrap'ping *n.* [*often pl.*] the material in which something is wrapped
wrap'-up' *n.* [Inf.] a concluding, summarizing statement, report, etc.
wrath (rath) *n.* ⟦OE, angry⟧ intense anger; rage; fury —**wrath'ful** *adj.*
wreak (rēk) *vt.* ⟦OE *wrecan*, to revenge⟧ **1** to give vent to (one's anger, etc.) **2** to inflict (vengeance, etc.)
wreath (rēth) *n.*, *pl.* **wreaths** (rē*th*z, rēths) ⟦OE *writha*⟧ **1** a twisted ring of leaves, flowers, etc. **2** something like this in shape *[wreaths of smoke]*
wreathe (rē*th*) *vt.* **wreathed**, **wreath'ing** **1** to form into a wreath **2** to coil or twist around; encircle **3** to decorate with wreaths
wreck (rek) *n.* ⟦< ON *vrek*, driftwood⟧ **1** a shipwreck **2** the remains of something destroyed **3** a run-down person **4** a wrecking or being wrecked —*vt.* **1** to destroy or damage badly **2** to tear down (a building, etc.) **3** to overthrow or thwart
wreck'age *n.* **1** a wrecking or being wrecked **2** the remains of something wrecked
wreck'er *n.* **1** one who wrecks **2** one that salvages or removes wrecks
wren (ren) *n.* ⟦OE *wrenna*⟧ a small songbird with a stubby, erect tail
wrench (rench) *n.* ⟦OE *wrenc*, a trick⟧ **1** a sudden, sharp twist or pull **2** an injury caused by a twist, as to the back **3** a sudden feeling of grief, etc. **4** a tool for turning nuts, bolts, pipes, etc. —*vt.* **1** to twist or jerk violently **2** to injure with a twist **3** to distort (a meaning, etc.)
wrest (rest) *vt.* ⟦OE *wræstan*⟧ **1** to pull or force away violently with a twisting motion **2** to take by force; usurp
wres·tle (res'əl; *often* ras'-) *vi.*, *vt.* **-tled**, **-tling** ⟦see prec.⟧ **1** to struggle hand to hand with (an opponent) in an attempt to throw him or her **2** to contend (*with*) —*n.* a wrestling —**wres'tler** *n.*
wres'tling *n.* a sport in which the opponents wrestle, or struggle hand to hand
wretch (rech) *n.* ⟦OE *wrecca*, an outcast⟧ **1** a miserable or unhappy person **2** a despised person
wretch'ed *adj.* **1** very unhappy; miserable **2** distressing; dismal **3** poor in quality **4** contemptible —**wretch'ed·ly** *adv.* —**wretch'ed·ness** *n.*
wrig·gle (rig'əl) *vi.* **-gled**, **-gling** ⟦medieval Low G *wriggeln*⟧ **1** to twist and turn; squirm **2** to move along with a twisting motion **3** to make one's way by shifty means —*n.* a wriggling —**wrig'gler** *n.* —**wrig'gly, -gli·er, -gli·est,** *adj.*
wright (rīt) *n.* ⟦< OE *wyrcan*, to work⟧ one who makes or constructs: chiefly in compounds *[shipwright]*
wring (riŋ) *vt.* **wrung**, **wring'ing** ⟦OE *wringan*⟧ **1** *a)* to squeeze, press, or twist *b)* to force out (water, etc.) by this means (usually with *out*) **2** to clasp and twist (the hands) in distress **3** to clasp (another's hand) forcefully in greeting **4** to extract by force, threats, etc. —*n.* a wringing
wring'er *n.* a machine with rollers to squeeze water from wet clothes
wrin·kle¹ (riŋ'kəl) *n.* ⟦ME *wrinkel*⟧ **1** a small furrow in a normally smooth surface **2** a crease in the skin —*vt.*, *vi.* **-kled**, **-kling** to form wrinkles (in); pucker; crease —**wrin'kly, -kli·er, -kli·est,** *adj.*
wrin·kle² (riŋ'kəl) *n.* ⟦< OE *wrenc*, a trick⟧ [Inf.] a clever trick, idea, or device
wrist (rist) *n.* ⟦OE⟧ the joint between the hand and forearm —**a slap** (or **tap**) **on the wrist** a token punishment
wrist'band' *n.* a band that goes around the wrist, as on a cuff
wrist'watch' *n.* a watch worn on a strap or band around the wrist
writ (rit) *n.* ⟦OE < *writan*, write⟧ a formal legal document ordering or prohibiting some action
write (rīt) *vt.* **wrote**, **writ'ten**, **writ'ing** ⟦OE *writan*⟧ **1** to form (words, letters, etc.) on a surface, as with a pen **2** to compose (literary or musical material) **3** to communicate (with) in writing *[she wrote (me) that she was ill]* **4** to cover with writing *[to write three pages]* **5** to fill in (a bank check, etc.) **6** to show clearly *[anger was written on his face]* **7** *Comput.* to record (information) on a disk, etc. —*vi.* to produce writing —**write off** **1** to remove

THESAURUS

coiled; see WOVEN.
wounded *a.* injured, hurt, disabled, stabbed, cut, shot, scratched, bitten, gashed, hit, beaten, attacked, winged, nicked.
woven *a.* spun, interlinked, netted, netlike, wreathed, sewn, intertwined, united, interlaced, interwoven.
wrap *v.* roll up, swathe, muffle, bind, fold about, encircle, coil, enclose, swaddle, bandage, envelop, enwrap, protect, encase, sheathe, cover up, shelter, clothe, cover with paper, shrink-wrap, enclose in a box.—*Ant.* UNWRAP, unsheathe, open up. —**wrap up*** finish off, bring to an end, polish off*; see COMPLETE.
wrapped *a.* covered, sheathed, swaddled, swathed, enclosed, protected, enveloped, encased, shrouded, concealed, hidden, clothed, done up.—*Ant.* OPEN, unwrapped, uncovered. —**wrapped up in** devoted to, engrossed by, implicated in; see LOVING.
wrapper *n.* envelope, package, shrink-wrap; see COVER 1.
wrath *n.* fury, vengeance, madness; see ANGER.
wreck *n.* **1** [Anything wrecked] junk, ruins, skeleton, hulk, bones, scattered parts, crash, smashup, pileup*, relic, litter, pieces, shreds, waste, wreckage, debris. **2** [A person in poor physical or mental condition] incurable, consumptive, nervous wreck, basket case*, a shadow of one's former self, overworked person, mess*, goner*, washout*, shadow, skin-and-bones*, walking wounded*.
wreck *v.* spoil, ruin, destroy, devastate, demolish, raze, knock down, disfigure, mangle, smash, tear down, break, split, efface, batter, torpedo, tear to pieces, put out of order, impair, injure, bash in, mess up, play hell with*, put out of commission.—*Ant.* REPAIR, restore, rebuild.
wreckage *n.* remains, ruins, hulk, remnants, flotsam and jetsam; see also WRECK 1.
wrecked *a.* demolished, destroyed, broken up, knocked to pieces, ruined, smashed to bits, shipwrecked, stranded, beached, grounded, scuttled, capsized, put out of order, blown to bits, junked, dismantled, shattered, on the rocks, gone to pot, shot to hell*.
wrench *n.* **1** [A violent twist] jerk, strain, sprain, tug, pull, dislodgement, extrication, dislocation. **2** [A spanner] *Wrenches include the following:* monkey, single-head, double-head, pipe, Stillson, crescent, sparkplug, hubcap, flat, S-socket, bearing, connecting-rod; see also TOOL 1.
wrench *v.* twist, strain, distort; see BEND.
wrestle *v.* grapple, struggle with, contend with, perform in a wrestling bout, wrassle*, tangle*, tussle; see also FIGHT.
wrestling *n.* contention, grappling, bout; see FIGHT 1.
wretched *a.* **1** [Afflicted] distressed, woeful, sorrowful; see SAD 1. **2** [Poor in quality] weak, faulty, cheap; see POOR 2.
wring *v.* squeeze out, compress, press; see TWIST.
wrinkle¹ *n.* crease, furrow, crinkle, ridge, fold, corrugation, line, crow's foot, pucker, pleat.
wrinkle¹ *v.* rumple, crease, furrow, pucker, twist, crumple, compress, crinkle.—*Ant.* STRAIGHTEN, smooth out, iron.
wrinkled *a.* creased, rumpled, furrowed, puckered, warped, twisted, crumpled, crinkled, dried up, withered, unironed, unpressed, shriveled.—*Ant.* SMOOTH, ironed, pressed.
write *v.* **1** [To compose in words] set forth, formulate, draft, turn out, crank out*, pen, put in writing, communicate, rewrite, produce fiction; work as an author, journalist, etc. **2** [To set down in writing] inscribe, sign, scrawl, address, print, letter, autograph, transcribe, jot down, scribble, record, dash off, put in black and white, typewrite, typeset, produce hard copy, put down on paper. —**write off** charge off, take a loss on, recognize as a bad debt; see LOSE 2.

from accounts (bad debts, etc.) **2** to drop from consideration **3** to amortize —**write out 1** to put into writing **2** to write in full —**write up** to write an account of

write′-in′ ***n.*** **1** a candidate whose name is not on the ballot, but is written in by a voter **2** a vote of this kind

write′-off′ ***n.*** a cancelled debt, amortized expense, etc.

writ′er ***n.*** one who writes, esp. as an occupation; author

write′-up′ ***n.*** [Inf.] a written report

writhe (rīth) ***vi.*** **writhed, writh′ing** ⟦OE *writhan,* to twist⟧ **1** to twist or turn; squirm *[to writhe in agony]* **2** to suffer great emotional distress

writ·ing (rīt′iŋ) ***n.*** **1** the act of one who writes **2** something written **3** written form **4** *short for* HANDWRITING

writ·ten (rit′'n) ***vt., vi.*** *pp. of* WRITE

wrong (rôŋ) ***adj.*** ⟦< ON *rangr,* twisted⟧ **1** not in accordance with justice, law, morality, etc. **2** not suitable or appropriate **3** *a)* contrary to fact, etc.; incorrect *b)* mistaken **4** not functioning properly **5** not meant to be seen *[the wrong side of a fabric]* —***adv.*** in a wrong manner, direction, etc. —***n.*** an unjust, immoral, or illegal act —***vt.*** to treat badly or unjustly —**in the wrong** not on the side supported by truth, justice, etc. —**wrong′ly** ***adv.*** —**wrong′ness** ***n.***

wrong′do′ing ***n.*** any wrong act or behavior —**wrong′do′er** ***n.***

wrong′ful ***adj.*** **1** unjust or injurious **2** unlawful —**wrong′ful·ly** ***adv.***

wrong′head′ed ***adj.*** stubborn or perverse —**wrong′head′ed·ly** ***adv.*** —**wrong′head′ed·ness** ***n.***

wrote (rōt) ***vt., vi.*** *pt. of* WRITE

wroth (rôth) ***adj.*** ⟦OE *wrath*⟧ angry

wrought (rôt) ***vi., vt.*** *alt. pt. & pp. of* WORK —***adj.*** **1** formed; made **2** shaped by hammering, etc.: said of metals

wrought iron tough, ductile iron containing very little carbon —**wrought′-i′ron** ***adj.***

wrought′-up′ ***adj.*** very disturbed or excited

wrung (ruŋ) ***vt.*** *pt. & pp. of* WRING

wry (rī) ***adj.*** **wri′er** or **wry′er, wri′est** or **wry′est** ⟦< OE *wrigian,* to turn⟧ **1** distorted in a grimace *[a wry face]* **2** ironic, dry, etc. *[wry humor]* —**wry′ly** ***adv.*** —**wry′ness** ***n.***

wt *abbrev.* weight

Wu·han (wōō′hän′) city in EC China: pop. 3,288,000

wuss (woos) ***n.*** [Slang] a person regarded as weak, ineffectual, etc.; wimp: also **wuss′y,** *pl.* **wuss′ies**

WV West Virginia

WWI *abbrev.* World War I

WWII *abbrev.* World War II

WWW or **www** *abbrev.* World Wide Web

Wy·o·ming (wī ō′miŋ) Mountain State of the W U.S.: 97,105 sq. mi.; pop. 454,000; cap. Cheyenne: abbrev. **WY** —**Wy·o′ming·ite′** ***n.***

THESAURUS

writer ***n.*** author, journalist, reporter, newspaperman, magazine writer, contributor, poet, novelist, essayist, biographer, dramatist, playwright, literary critic, foreign correspondent, feature writer, sports writer, fashion writer, shorthand writer, stenographer, anecdotist, amanuensis, ghostwriter, songwriter, copyist, scribe, editor, contributing editor, war correspondent, special writer, freelance writer, technical writer, speechwriter, member of the Fourth Estate, scribbler, pen pusher*, hack, newshound*. *Major writers include the following—British:* Daniel Defoe, Jonathan Swift, Henry Fielding, Samuel Johnson, Lawrence Sterne, Sir Walter Scott, Jane Austen, William Makepeace Thackeray, Charles Dickens, Anthony Trollope, Charlotte Brontë, George Eliot, Matthew Arnold, Thomas Hardy, Joseph Conrad, Rudyard Kipling, James Joyce, Virginia Woolf, D.H. Lawrence, George Orwell, Evelyn Waugh, Samuel Beckett; *American:* James Fenimore Cooper, Ralph Waldo Emerson, Nathaniel Hawthorne, Edgar Allan Poe, Henry David Thoreau, Herman Melville, Samuel Langhorne Clemens (Mark Twain), Henry Adams, Henry James, Edith Wharton, Stephen Crane, Theodore Dreiser, Willa Cather, F. Scott Fitzgerald, William Faulkner, Ernest Hemingway, John Steinbeck, Eudora Welty, Saul Bellow, Flannery O'Connor; *French:* Michel Eyquem de Montaigne, (François-Marie Arouet de) Voltaire, Jean Jacques Rousseau, Stendhal, Honoré de Balzac, Victor Hugo, Alexandre Dumas, Gustave Flaubert, Émile Zola, Guy de Maupassant, Marcel Proust, Albert Camus; *Italian:* Niccolò Machiavelli, Giovanni Boccaccio, Alessandro Manzoni; *German:* Thomas Mann, Franz Kafka, Günter Grass; *Russian:* Nikolai Gogol, Ivan Turgenev, Fyodor Dostoevsky, Leo Tolstoy, Anton Chekhov, Boris Pasternak; *Spanish:* Miguel de Cervantes, Jorge Luis Borges; *Yiddish:* I.B. Singer.

write-up* ***n.*** report, account, publicity; see WRITING 2.

writhe ***v.*** contort, move painfully, squirm, distort, suffer, twist and turn, undergo agony, turn with pain, throw a fit*.—*Ant.* REST, be at ease, move easily.

writing ***n.*** **1** [The practice of writing] transcribing, inscribing, reporting, corresponding, letter-writing, copying, handwriting, typewriting, penmanship, lettering, printing, graphology, signing, autographing, stenography. **2** [Anything written] literature, written matter, document, composition, article, poem, prose, paper, theme, editorial, discourse, essay, thesis, dissertation, book, manuscript, novel, play, literary production, scenario, drama, work, signature, letter, pamphlet, tract, treatise, disquisition, comment, commentary, review, recitation, certificate, record, bill, bit*, item, piece. **3** [The occupation of a writer] journalism, reporting, literature, authorship, freelance writing, professional writing, auctorial pursuits, the pen, the Fourth Estate, creative writing, feature writing, technical writing, speechwriting, newspaper work, the writers' craft, hack writing, ghostwriting.

written ***a.*** **1** [Composed] set forth, authored, penned, drawn up, reported, signed, turned out, fictionalized, arranged, rearranged, adapted, ghostwritten, recorded, dictated. **2** [Inscribed] copied, scriptural, transcribed, printed, lettered, autographed, signed, put in writing, in black and white, in one's hand.

wrong ***a.*** **1** [Immoral] evil, sinful, wicked, naughty, salacious, base, indecent, risqué, blasphemous, ungodly, amoral, dissolute, dissipated, wanton, profane, sacrilegious, depraved, corrupt, profligate, shady*, lowdown*, smutty.—*Ant.* GOOD, righteous, virtuous. **2** [Inaccurate] inexact, erroneous, mistaken, in error, incorrect, fallacious, untrue, erring, astray, amiss, ungrounded, spurious, unsubstantial, unsound, erratic, misguided, self-deluded, in the wrong, under an error, beside the mark, laboring under a false impression, out of line, at fault, to no purpose, not right, awry, faulty, mishandled, miscalculated, misfigured, misconstructed, misconstrued, altered, not precise, perverse, wide of the mark, not according to the facts, badly estimated, a mile off*, all off, crazy*. **3** [Inappropriate] unfitted, disproportionate, ill-fitting; see IMPROPER. —**go wrong** fall apart, take a wrong turn, go astray; see FAIL 1.

wrong ***n.*** vice, sin, misdemeanor, crime, immorality, indecency, transgression, unfairness, imposition, oppression, foul play, prejudice, bias, partiality, unlawful practice, villainy, delinquency, error, miscarriage, mistake, blunder, offense, wrongdoing, violation, tort, hurt, persecution, malevolence, cruelty, libel, abuse, harm, damage, spite, slander, lie, slight, misusage, outrage, inhumanity, malfeasance, misfeasance, dereliction, insult, discourtesy.—*Ant.* KINDNESS, good deed, consideration.

wrong ***v.*** hurt, oppress, defame; see ABUSE.

wrongdoer ***n.*** lawbreaker, tortfeasor, perpetrator; see CRIMINAL.

wrongly ***a.*** unfairly, prejudicially, wrongfully, partially, badly, unjustifiably, illegally, disgracefully, sinfully, unreasonably, unlawfully, criminally, inexcusably, unsuitably, improperly, awkwardly, incongruously, incorrectly, unbecomingly, indecorously, questionably, imprudently, rashly, unnaturally, illogically; see also INADEQUATELY.—*Ant.* APPROPRIATELY, tastefully, prudently.

wrung ***a.*** twisted, squeezed out, pressed; see TWISTED 1.

x[1] or **X** (eks) ***n.***, *pl.* **x's, X's 1** the 24th letter of the English alphabet **2** *Math.* an unknown quantity
x[2] *abbrev.* extra: also **X**
x[3] (eks) *symbol* **1** by (in indicating dimensions) *[*3 ft. *x* 4 ft.*]* **2** *Optics* the power of magnification **3** *Math.* times *[*2 *x* 3 = 6*]*
X (eks) ***n.*** **1** the Roman numeral 10 **2** a film rating meaning that no one under seventeen is to be admitted
X chromosome *see* SEX CHROMOSOME
Xe *Chem. symbol for* xenon
xe·non (zē′nän′) ***n.*** a colorless, nonreactive, gaseous chemical element
xen·o·pho·bi·a (zen′ə fō′bē ə) ***n.*** ⟦< Gr *xenos*, foreign + -PHOBIA⟧ fear or hatred of strangers or foreigners —**xen′o·phobe′** (-fōb′) ***n.*** —**xen′o·pho′bic** (-fō′bik) ***adj.***
xe·rog·ra·phy (zir äg′rə fē) ***n.*** ⟦< Gr *xēros*, dry + -GRAPHY⟧ a process for copying printed material, etc. by the action of light on an electrically charged surface
Xe·rox (zir′äks′) *trademark for* a device for copying by xerography —***vt.***, ***vi.*** [*usually* **x-**] to reproduce by xerography —***n.*** [*usually* **x-**] a copy so made
Xer·xes I (zurk′sēz′) 519?-465 B.C.; king of Persia (486-465)
xi (zī, sī) ***n.*** the 14th letter of the Greek alphabet (Ξ, ξ)
XL *abbrev.* extra large
X·mas (eks′məs) ***n.*** *inf. var. of* CHRISTMAS
X-rat·ed (eks′rāt′əd) ***adj.*** designating or like a film with a rating of X; explicit, obscene, etc.
X-ray (eks′rā′) ***n.*** **1** a type of electromagnetic wave of very short wavelength, that can penetrate solid substances: used to study internal body structures and treat various disorders **2** a photograph made by means of X-rays —***adj.*** of or by X-rays —***vt.*** to examine, treat, or photograph with X-rays Also **X ray, x-ray,** or **x ray**
XS *abbrev.* extra small
xy·lem (zī′ləm) ***n.*** ⟦< Gr *xylon*, wood⟧ the woody vascular tissue of a plant
xy·lo·phone (zī′lə fōn′) ***n.*** ⟦< Gr *xylon*, wood + -PHONE⟧ a musical percussion instrument consisting of a series of graduated wooden bars that are struck with small, wooden mallets —**xy′lo·phon′ist** (-fō′nist, zī läf′ə nist) ***n.***

THESAURUS

x[1] ***n.*** unknown quantity, variable, y; see QUANTITY.

Xmas* ***n.*** the Nativity, Christmas, Christmastime, yule, yuletide; see also CHRISTMAS, HOLIDAY.

X-rays ***n.*** Roentgen rays, radioactivity, radium emanation, actinic rays, actinism, encephalogram, ultraviolet rays, refractometry, radiant energy, cathode rays; see also ENERGY 2, RAY.

xylophone ***n.*** carillon, vibraphone, vibes, vibraharp, mallet instrument, glockenspiel, marimba; see also MUSICAL INSTRUMENT.

Y

y or **Y** (wī) ***n.***, *pl.* **y's, Y's** the 25th letter of the English alphabet

Y *Chem. symbol for* yttrium

-y1 (ē, i) ⟦ME⟧ *suffix* little one, dear *[kitty, daddy]*

-y2 (ē, i) ⟦OE *-ig*⟧ *suffix* **1** full of, like *[dirty]* **2** somewhat *[yellowy]* **3** tending to *[sticky]*

-y3 (ē, i) ⟦< L *-ia*⟧ *suffix* **1** quality or condition *[jealousy]* **2** a (specified) kind of shop, goods, or group *[bakery]*

-y4 (ē, i) ⟦< L *-ium*⟧ *suffix* action of *[inquiry]*

yacht (yät) ***n.*** ⟦Du *jacht*⟧ a small vessel for pleasure cruises, racing, etc.

yacht'ing (-iŋ) ***n.*** the sport of sailing a yacht — **yachts'man** (-mən), *pl.* **-men** (-mən), ***n.***

ya·hoo (yä'ho͞o') ***n.*** ⟦after a race of people in Swift's novel *Gulliver's Travels*⟧ a person regarded as vulgar, uneducated, etc.

Yah·weh or **Yah·we** (yä'we, -wā) ***n.*** ⟦< Heb⟧ God

yak1 (yak) ***n.*** ⟦< Tibet *g-yag*⟧ a long-haired wild ox of Tibet and central Asia

yak2 (yak) [Slang] ***vi.*** **yakked, yak'king** ⟦echoic⟧ to talk much or idly —***n.*** a yakking

yam (yam) ***n.*** ⟦< WAfr native name⟧ **1** the edible, starchy, tuberous root of a tropical climbing plant **2** an orange-colored variety of sweet potato

yam·mer (yam'ər) ***vi.*** ⟦< OE *geomerian,* to lament⟧ **1** to shout, yell, etc. **2** to talk loudly or continuously — **yam'mer·er** ***n.***

yang (yäŋ, yaŋ) ***n.*** ⟦Chin⟧ in Chinese philosophy, the masculine force or principle in the universe: cf. YIN

Yan·gon (yan gôn') capital of Myanmar: pop. 2,513,000

Yang·tze (yaŋk'sē) *a former transliteration of* CHANG

yank (yaŋk) ***n., vt., vi.*** ⟦< ?⟧ [Inf.] jerk

Yank (yaŋk) ***n.*** [Slang] a Yankee; esp., a U.S. soldier in WWI and WWII

Yan·kee (yaŋ'kē) ***n.*** ⟦< ? Du *Jan Kees,* a disparaging nickname⟧ **1** a New Englander **2** a person born or living in the northern U.S. **3** a citizen of the U.S. —***adj.*** of or like Yankees

yap (yap) ***vi.*** **yapped, yap'ping** ⟦echoic⟧ **1** to make a sharp, shrill bark **2** [Slang] to talk noisily and stupidly —***n.*** **1** a sharp, shrill bark **2** [Slang] *a)* jabber *b)* the mouth

yard1 (yärd) ***n.*** ⟦OE *gierd,* rod⟧ **1** a measure of length, 3 feet or 36 inches **2** *Naut.* a slender rod or spar fastened across a mast to support a sail

yard2 (yärd) ***n.*** ⟦OE *geard,* enclosure⟧ **1** the ground around or next to a building **2** an enclosed place for a particular purpose *[shipyard]*

yard'age ***n.*** **1** measurement in yards **2** the extent so measured

yard'arm' ***n.*** *Naut.* either half of a yard supporting a square sail, etc.

yard goods textiles made in standard widths, usually sold by the yard

yard·man (yärd'man', -mən) ***n.***, *pl.* **-men'** (-men', -mən) a person who works in a yard

yard'stick' ***n.*** **1** a graduated measuring stick one yard long **2** any standard used in judging, etc.

yar·mul·ke (yär'məl kə, yä'-) ***n.*** ⟦Yiddish < Pol⟧ a skullcap traditionally worn by Jewish men, as at prayer: also **yar'mel·ke**

yarn (yärn) ***n.*** ⟦OE *gearn*⟧ **1** fibers of wool, cotton, etc. spun into strands for weaving, knitting, etc. **2** [Inf.] a tale or story

yat·ter (yat'ər) [Slang] ***vi.*** ⟦prob. < YA(K)2 + (CHA)TTER⟧ to talk idly about trivial things —***n.*** idle talk; chatter

yaw (yô) ***vi.*** ⟦ON *jaga,* to sway⟧ **1** to swing back and forth across its course, as a ship does when pushed by high waves **2** to rotate or oscillate about the vertical axis: said of a spacecraft, etc. —***n.*** a yawing

yawl (yôl) ***n.*** ⟦< Du *jol*⟧ a small, two-masted sailboat rigged fore-and-aft

yawn (yôn) ***vi.*** ⟦ME *yanen*⟧ **1** to open the mouth wide involuntarily and inhale, as when one is sleepy or bored **2** to open wide —***n.*** a yawning

yaws (yôz) ***n.*** ⟦of WInd origin⟧ an infectious skin disease of the tropics

yay (yā) ***adv.*** **1** YEA (*adv.* 1) **2** [Inf.] this; so: often with a gesture indicating size —***interj.*** YEA

Y chromosome *see* SEX CHROMOSOME

y·clept or **y-clept** (ē klept') ***vt.*** ⟦<OE *clipian,* to call⟧ [Archaic] called; named: also sp. **y·cleped'**

yd *abbrev.* yard(s): also, for the plural, **yds**

ye1 (*thə, thi, thē; now often erroneously or facetiously* yē) ***adj., definite article*** *archaic var. of* THE

ye2 (yē) ***pron.*** ⟦OE *ge*⟧ [Archaic] YOU

yea (yā) ***adv.*** ⟦OE *gea*⟧ **1** yes **2** indeed; truly —***n.*** **1** an affirmative vote **2** a person voting in the affirmative — ***interj.*** [Inf.] hurrah: a shout used in cheering for a team

yeah (ya, ye) ***adv.*** [Inf.] yes

year (yir) ***n.*** ⟦OE *gear*⟧ **1** a period of 365 days (366 days in leap year), divided into 12 months beginning Jan. 1 **2** the period (365 days, 5 hours, 48 minutes, and 46 seconds) of one revolution of the earth around the sun: also **solar year** **3** a period of 12 calendar months reckoned from any date **4** an annual period of less than 365 days *[a school year]* **5** [*pl.*] *a)* age *[old for his years]* *b)* a long time *[years ago]* —**year after year** every year

year'book' ***n.*** an annual book; specif., *a)* a book giving data of the preceding year *b)* a publication of the graduating class of a school or college

year'ling ***n.*** an animal in its second year

year'ly ***adj.*** **1** done, happening, appearing, etc. once a year, or every year *[a yearly event]* **2** of a year, or of each year —***adv.*** every year

yearn (yurn) ***vi.*** ⟦< OE *georn,* eager⟧ to be filled with longing or desire —**yearn'ing** ***n.***

THESAURUS

yacht ***n.*** pleasure boat, sloop, racing boat; see BOAT, SHIP.

yammer ***v.*** nag, whine, whimper; see COMPLAIN.

yank ***n.*** twitch, jerk, wrench; see JERK 1.

yank* ***v.*** haul, tug, drag, jiggle, jerk*, flip, wrench, twitch; see also DRAW 1, PULL 2.

Yankee ***a.*** **1** [Having New England qualities] homespun, individualistic, conservative; see MODERATE 3, 4, 5, PRACTICAL. **2** [Concerning the United States] North American, Western, Americanized; see AMERICAN.

Yankee ***n.*** **1** [A New Englander] Northerner, Easterner, early settler, Abolitionist, Unionist. **2** [A person from the United States] American, American citizen, North American, westerner, Yank*.

yap* ***v.*** jabber, rant, chatter; see BABBLE, TALK 1.

yard1,2 ***n.*** **1** [An enclosure, usually next to a building] court, courtyard, barnyard, backyard, corral, fold, patch, patio, terrace, play area, lawn, grass, garden, clearing, quadrangle, lot; see also PLAYGROUND. **2** [An enclosure for work] brickyard, coalyard, junkyard, navy yard, dockyard, railyard, stockyard, lumberyard. **3** [Tracks for making up trains] railroad yard, switchyard, railway yard, marshalling yard, terminal. **4** [A unit of measurement] three feet, pace, step, arm-span, thirty-six inches; see also MEASURE 1.

yardstick ***n.*** criterion, basis for judgment, standard, index, measuring stick, basis for comparison; see also MEASURE 2.

yarn ***n.*** **1** [Spun fiber] spun wool, twist, flaxen thread, cotton fiber, rug yarn, crochet thread, knitting yarn, alpaca yarn; see also FIBER. **2** [A tale] anecdote, sea story, adventure story, tall tale, fictional account; see also STORY. **3** [A lie] fabrication, tall tale*, alibi, fish story*, cock-and-bull story*; see also LIE.

yaw ***v.*** curve, swerve, bank; see TURN 6.

yawn ***v.*** **1** [To open wide] gape, split open, spread out; see DIVIDE, GROW 1. **2** [To give evidence of drowsiness] gape, be sleepy, make a yawning sound, show weariness; see also SLEEP, TIRE 1.

yea ***a.*** okay, aye, well; see YES.

year ***n.*** twelve months, annual cycle, continuum of days; see AGE 3, TIME 1, 2. *Kinds of years include the following:* civil, legal, calendar, lunar, solar, astronomical, natural, sidereal, tropical, equinoctial, leap, school, fiscal. **—year after year** year by year, annually; year in, year out; see YEARLY.

yearbook ***n.*** annual, almanac, yearly report; see CATALOG, RECORD 1.

yearling ***n.*** suckling, nursling, weanling; see ANIMAL, BABY.

yearly ***a.*** annually, once a year, every winter, every spring, every summer, every autumn, year by year; see also REGULARLY.

yearn ***v.*** want, crave, long for, fret, chafe, grieve, mourn, droop, pine, covet, be eager for, be desirous of, be ardent, be fervent, be passionate, wish for, thirst for, hunger for, aspire to, set one's heart upon, hanker for, have a yen for*; see also TRY 1.—*Ant.* AVOID, be content, be indifferent.

yearning ***n.*** want, longing, craving; see DESIRE 1, WISH.

year′-round′ *adj.* open, in use, operating, etc. throughout the year

yea′say′er *n.* one having a positive attitude toward life

yeast (yēst) *n.* ⟦OE *gist*⟧ **1** a moist, yellowish mass of certain fungi that cause fermentation: used in making beer, etc., and as leavening in baking **2** yeast dried in flakes or granules or compressed into cakes **3** ferment; agitation

yeast′y *adj.* **-i·er, -i·est 1** of, like, or containing yeast **2** in a ferment; restless

yegg (yeg) *n.* ⟦< ?⟧ [Old Slang] a burglar, etc.

yell (yel) *vi., vt.* ⟦OE *giellan*⟧ to cry out loudly; scream —*n.* **1** a loud outcry **2** a rhythmic cheer in unison

yel·low (yel′ō) *adj.* ⟦OE *geolu*⟧ **1** of the color of ripe lemons **2** having a somewhat yellow skin **3** [Inf.] cowardly **4** sensational: said as of a newspaper —*n.* **1** a yellow color **2** an egg yolk —*vi.* to become yellow —**yel′low·ish** *adj.*

yellow fever an infectious tropical disease caused by a virus transmitted by the bite of a certain mosquito

yellow jacket a wasp or hornet having bright-yellow markings

Yel′low·knife′ capital of Northwest Territories, Canada: pop. 17,000

Yellow River HUANG HE

Yellow Sea arm of the East China Sea, between China & Korea

yelp (yelp) *vi.* ⟦OE *gielpan,* to boast⟧ to utter a short, sharp cry or bark, as a dog does —*n.* a short, sharp cry or bark

Yel·tsin (yelt′sin), **Bor·is** (bôr′is) 1931- ; president of Russia (1990-99)

Yem·en (yem′ən) country in S Arabia, formed (1990) by the merger of the **Yemen Arab Republic** and a country directly east of it, the **People's Democratic Republic of Yemen**: 214,287 sq. mi.; pop. 13,000,000 —**Yem′en·ite′** or **Yem′e·ni** (-ə nē) *adj., n.*

yen[1] (yen) *n., pl.* **yen** ⟦Jpn⟧ the monetary unit of Japan

yen[2] (yen) *n.* ⟦prob. < Chin *yan,* opium⟧ [Inf.] a strong longing or desire

yeo·man (yō′mən) *n., pl.* **-men** (-mən) ⟦ME *yeman*⟧ **1** [Brit. Historical] a freeholder of a class below the gentry **2** *U.S. Navy* a petty officer assigned to clerical duty

yeo′man·ry *n.* yeomen collectively

yes (yes) *adv.* ⟦OE *gese*⟧ **1** aye; yea; it is so: expressing agreement, consent, etc. **2** not only that, but more *[*ready, *yes,* eager to help*]* —*n., pl.* **yes′es** an act of saying *yes*; an affirmative reply, vote, etc. —*vt., vi.* **yessed, yes′sing** to say *yes* (to)

ye·shi·va (yə shē′və; *Heb* ye shē vä′) *n., pl.* **-vas** or Heb, **-vot′** (-vōt′) ⟦Heb, lit., act of sitting⟧ a Jewish school combining religious and secular studies

yes man [Slang] one who is always approving what is said by a superior

yes·ter·day (yes′tər dā′) *n.* ⟦OE *geostran,* yesterday + *dæg,* day⟧ **1** the day before today **2** a recent day or time —*adv.* **1** on the day before today **2** recently

yes′ter·year′ (-yir′) *n., adv.* **1** last year **2** (in) past years

yet (yet) *adv.* ⟦OE *giet*⟧ **1** up to now; thus far *[*he hasn't gone *yet]* **2** at the present time; now *[*we can't go just *yet]* **3** still *[*there is *yet* a chance*]* **4** in addition; even *[*he was *yet* more kind*]* **5** nevertheless *[*she's kind, *yet* shy*]* —*conj.* but *[*she seems well, *yet* she is ill*]* —**as yet** up to now

yew (yo͞o) *n.* ⟦OE *iw*⟧ **1** an evergreen tree with flattened needle leaves **2** its wood

Yid·dish (yid′ish) *n.* ⟦< Ger *jüdisch,* < L *Judaeus,* Jew⟧ a language derived from medieval High German, written in the Hebrew alphabet and spoken esp. by East European Jews

yield (yēld) *vt.* ⟦OE *gieldan,* to pay⟧ **1** to produce as a crop, result, profit, etc. **2** to surrender **3** to concede —*vi.* **1** to produce **2** to surrender **3** to give way to physical force **4** to lose precedence, etc.: often with *to* —*n.* the amount yielded

yield′ing *adj.* **1** flexible **2** submissive

yin (yin) *n.* ⟦Chin⟧ in Chinese philosophy, the feminine force or principle in the universe: cf. YANG

yip (yip) *n.* ⟦echoic⟧ [Inf.] a yelp, or bark —*vi.* **yipped, yip′ping** [Inf.] to yelp, or bark

YMCA *abbrev.* Young Men's Christian Association

yo (yō) *interj.* [Inf.] used as to gain attention, greet someone, emphasize a remark, etc.

yo·del (yōd′'l) *vt., vi.* **-deled** or **-delled, -del·ing** or **-del·ling** ⟦Ger *jodeln*⟧ to sing with abrupt alternating changes to the falsetto —*n.* a yodeling

yo·ga (yō′gə) *n.* ⟦Sans, union⟧ a mystic and ascetic Hindu discipline for achieving union with the supreme spirit through meditation, prescribed postures, controlled breathing, etc.

yo·gi (yō′gē) *n., pl.* **-gis** one who practices yoga: also **yo′gin** (-gin)

yo·gurt (yō′gərt) *n.* ⟦Turk *yoğurt*⟧ a thick, somewhat solid food made from fermented milk: also **yo′ghurt**

yoke (yōk) *n.* ⟦OE *geoc*⟧ **1** a wooden frame for harnessing together a pair of oxen, etc. **2** such a pair harnessed together **3** bondage; servitude **4** anything like a yoke, as something that binds or unites, or a part of a garment fitted to the shoulders or hips as a support for the gathered parts below —*vt.* **yoked, yok′ing 1** to harness (an animal) to (a plow, etc.) **2** to join together

yo·kel (yō′kəl) *n.* a person living in a rural area; bumpkin: a contemptuous term

Yo·ko·ha·ma (yō′kə hä′mə) seaport in S Honshu, Japan: pop. 2,774,000

yolk (yōk) *n.* ⟦OE *geolca*⟧ the yellow, principal substance of an egg

THESAURUS

yell *n.* **1** [A shout] bellow, cry, yelp, roar, whoop, howl, screech, shriek, squeal, holler*, hoot, yawp, hubbub, hullabaloo, hue and cry, protest; see also NOISE 1. **2** [Organized cheering] hip-hip-hurray, rooting, cheer; see ENCOURAGEMENT.

yell *v.* bellow, cry out, scream, shout, yelp, yap, bawl, roar, halloo, vociferate, whoop, howl, screech, shriek, squeal, squall, yammer, hoot, cheer, call, yip, give encouragement, call down, raise one's voice, holler, whoop it up; see also SOUND.

yelling *a.* boisterous, clamorous, noisy, bawling, uproarious, turbulent, drunken, aroused, riotous, cantankerous, blatant, vociferous; see also HARSH, LOUD 2.—*Ant.* QUIET, subdued, silent.

yelling *n.* cry, scream, shout, outcry, vociferation, screeching, bawling, yowling, bellowing, howling, yelping; see also NOISE 1, YELL.

yellow *n. Tints and shades of yellow include the following:* cream color, ivory color, old ivory, ivory-yellow, tan, lemon color, orange-yellow, saffron, jasmine, tawny, sand, gold, sallow, buff, brilliant yellow, chrome yellow, Dutch pink-yellow, Dutch yellow, golden yellow, Imperial yellow, platinum yellow, yellow carmine, yellow madder, yellow ocher; see also COLOR, GOLD.

yellow *a.* **1** [Having a yellowish color] yellowish, golden, jaundiced. **2** [*Cowardly] low, cringing, lily-livered, white-livered, craven, treacherous; see also COWARDLY, VULGAR.

yelp *v.* howl, screech, hoot; see CRY 2, SOUND.

yen[2]* *n.* longing, craving, hunger; see DESIRE 1.

yes *a.* surely, of course, certainly, good, fine, aye, true, granted, very well, all right, OK*, okay*, oke*, okey-dokey*, Roger, we copy, over to you, most assuredly, by all means, agreed, oh yes, amen, naturally, without fail, just so, good enough, even so, in the affirmative, you bet*.

yes man* *n.* toady, company man*, brown-noser*, bootlicker*, go-along man*, get-along man*.

yesterday *a.* recently, previously, earlier; see BEFORE.

yesterday *n.* the other day, the day before, recently, last day, not long ago; see also PAST 1.

yet *a.* **1** [Nevertheless] notwithstanding, however, in spite of, despite, still, but, though, although, at any rate, on the other hand. **2** [Thus far] until now, till, hitherto, prior to, still; see also UNTIL. **3** [In addition] besides, additionally, further; see BESIDES. **—as yet** still, not yet, till now; see YET 2.

yield *v.* **1** [To surrender] give up, capitulate, succumb, resign, abdicate, relinquish, quit, cede, bow, lay down arms, cease from, let go, submit, give oneself over, relent, admit defeat, suffer defeat, forgo, humble oneself, waive, throw in the towel*, call it quits*, back down*, holler uncle*, eat crow*; see also ABANDON 1.—*Ant.* RESIST, withstand, repulse. **2** [To produce] bear, bring forth, blossom; see BLOOM, PRODUCE 1, 2. **3** [To grant] accede, concur, acquiesce; see ADMIT 2, AGREE.

yielding *a.* **1** [Producing] green, fruitful, productive; see FERTILE, RICH 3. **2** [Flexible] pliant, plastic, malleable; see FLEXIBLE. **3** [Docile] submissive, pliable, tractable; see HUMBLE 1, OBEDIENT 1.

yogi *n.* mystic, fakir, anchorite, ascetic, practitioner of yoga, guru, devotee.

yoke *v.* couple, link, connect, hitch, harness; see also FASTEN, JOIN 1.

yokel *n.* rustic, bumpkin, hayseed*; see BOOR.

Yom Kip·pur (yäm′ ki po͝or′) the Day of Atonement: a major Jewish holiday and a day of fasting

yon (yän) ***adj., adv.*** ⟦OE *geon*⟧ [Now Chiefly Dial.] yonder

yon·der (yän′dər) ***adj., adv.*** ⟦ME⟧ (being) at or in that (specified or relatively distant) place; over there

Yon·kers (yäŋ′kərz) city in SE New York: pop. 188,000

yoo-hoo (yo͞o′ho͞o′) ***interj., n.*** (a shout or call) used to attract someone's attention

yore (yôr) ***adv.*** ⟦OE *geara*⟧ [Obs.] long ago **—of yore** formerly

you (yo͞o) ***pron.***, *pl.* **you** ⟦OE *eow* < *ge,* YE[2]⟧ **1** the person or persons spoken to **2** a person or people generally; one *[you* can never tell!*]*

young (yuŋ) ***adj.*** **young′er** (-gər), **young′est** (-gəst) ⟦OE *geong*⟧ **1** being in an early period of life or growth **2** youthful; fresh; vigorous **3** in an early stage **4** inexperienced; immature **—*n.*** **1** young people: often with *the* **2** young offspring **—with young** pregnant **—young′ish *adj.***

young adult an age group, from about 12 to about 18 years of age, used as a reader category as in libraries

young blood **1** young people; youth **2** youthful strength, vigor, etc.

young′ster ***n.*** a child or youth

your (yoor; *often* yôr) ***poss. pronominal adj.*** ⟦OE *eower*⟧ of, belonging to, or done by you: also used before some titles *[Your* Honor*]*

you're (yoor, yo͞or) *contr.* you are

yours (yoorz; *often* yôrz) ***pron.*** that or those belonging to you: possessive form of YOU *[*that book is *yours*; *yours* are better*]*

your·self (yoor self′, yər-) ***pron.***, *pl.* **-selves′** (-selvz′) a form of YOU, used as an intensive *[*you said so *yourself]*, as a reflexive *[*you hurt *yourself]*, or with the meaning "your true self" *[*you are not *yourself* today*]*

yours truly **1** a phrase used in ending a letter **2** [Inf.] I or me

youth (yo͞oth) ***n.***, *pl.* **youths** (yo͞o*th*z, yo͞oths) ⟦OE *geoguthe*⟧ **1** the state or quality of being young **2** the period of adolescence **3** an early stage of growth or existence **4** young people collectively **5** a young person; esp., a young man

youth′ful ***adj.*** **1** young; not yet old or mature **2** of, like, or fit for youth **3** fresh; vigorous **4** new; early **—youth′ful·ly *adv.*** **—youth′ful·ness *n.***

yowl (youl) ***vi., n.*** ⟦< ON *gaula*⟧ howl or wail

yo-yo (yō′yō′) ***n.***, *pl.* **yo′-yos′** ⟦< ?⟧ **1** a spool-like toy reeled up and let down by a string **2** [Slang] a person regarded as stupid, inept, etc. **—*vi.*** [Inf.] to move up and down; fluctuate

yr *abbrev.* **1** year(s) **2** your

yrs *abbrev.* **1** years **2** yours

YT Yukon Territory

yt·tri·um (i′trē əm) ***n.*** a rare, silvery, metallic chemical element: used in color TV tubes, etc.

Yu·ca·tán or **Yu·ca·tan** (yo͞o′kə tan′) state of Mexico, on a peninsula separating the Gulf of Mexico from the Caribbean: 15,189 sq. mi.; pop. 1,363,000

yuc·ca (yuk′ə) ***n.*** ⟦< AmSp *yuca*⟧ **1** a desert plant with stiff leaves and white flowers **2** its flower

yuck[1] (yuk) ***n., vi.*** *alt. sp. of* YUK

yuck[2] (yuk) [Slang] ***n.*** something unpleasant, disgusting, etc. **—*interj.*** used to express distaste, disgust, etc. **—yuck′y, -i·er, -i·est, *adj.***

Yu·go·slav·i·a (yo͞o′gō slä′vē ə, -gə-) country in the NW Balkan Peninsula: four republics separated from it in 1991: 39,449 sq. mi.; pop. 10,394,000 **—Yu′go·slav′** or **Yu′go·sla′vi·an *adj., n.***

yuk (yuk) ***n.*** ⟦echoic⟧ [Slang] a loud laugh of amusement, or something causing such a laugh **—*vi.*** **yukked, yuk′king** [Slang] to laugh loudly

Yu·kon (yo͞o′kän′) territory of NW Canada, east of Alaska: 186,661 sq. mi.; pop. 31,000; cap. Whitehorse: abbrev. *YT*: usually used with *the*: in full **Yukon Territory**

yule (yo͞ol) ***n.*** ⟦OE *geol*⟧ [*often* **Y-**] Christmas or the Christmas season

yule′tide′ (-tīd′) ***n.*** [*often* **Y-**] the Christmas season

yum·my (yum′ē) ***adj.*** **-mi·er, -mi·est** [Inf.] very tasty; delectable

yup (yup) ***adv.*** [Slang] yes: an affirmative reply

yup·pie (yup′ē) ***n.*** ⟦< *y*(*oung*) *u*(*rban*) *p*(*rofessional*)⟧ [Inf.] a young professional regarded as affluent, ambitious, materialistic, etc.

YWCA *abbrev.* Young Women's Christian Association

THESAURUS

yonder ***a.*** farther, away, faraway; see DISTANT, REMOTE 1.

you ***pron.*** yourself, you yourself, thee, thou, all of you, you too, you alone, you all*.

young ***a.*** **1** [In the early portion of life] boyish, girlish, adolescent, juvenile, budding, in one's teens, childlike, youthful, pubescent, boylike, girllike, new-fledged, blooming, burgeoning, childish, half-grown, growing, blossoming, at the breast, babe in arms, knee high to a grasshopper*.—*Ant.* OLD, aged, senile. **2** [Inexperienced] callow, green, immature, tender, raw, puerile, untutored, unlearned, junior, subordinate, inferior, unfledged, ignorant, undisciplined, tenderfoot, wet behind the ears*; see also INEXPERIENCED, NAIVE.—*Ant.* EXPERIENCED, veteran, expert. **3** [New] fresh, modern, recent, newborn; see also FASHIONABLE.

youngster ***n.*** child, boy, girl, pupil, kid*, tyke*, young'un*, bambino; see also YOUTH 3.

youth ***n.*** **1** [The state or quality of being young] boyhood, adolescence, girlhood, childhood, early manhood, early adulthood, puberty, tender age, minority, youthfulness, teen age, virginity, bloom, teens, age of ignorance, age of indiscretion, awkward age, salad days.—*Ant.* MATURITY, old age, senility. **2** [Young people] children, the younger generation, the rising generation, the next generation, the young, college youth, working youth. **3** [A young person] boy, junior, teenager, lad, youngster, stripling, minor, young man, miss, girl, maiden, fledgling, juvenile, urchin, adolescent, student, kid*, teen, preteen, gosling, pup*, calf*; see also CHILD.

youthful ***a.*** **1** [Possessing youth] young, childlike, adolescent; see ACTIVE, YOUNG 1, 2. **2** [Suited to youth] keen, enthusiastic, zestful, vigorous, active, buoyant, lighthearted, prankish, fresh, lithe, full-blooded, full of life, spirited, limber, athletic, lightfooted, coltish, bubbling over, full of the devil; see also MODERN 1.—*Ant.* SLOW, cautious, serious.

yowl ***n.*** howl, yelp, wail; see CRY 1, YELL 1.

yule ***n.*** Christmas, Xmas*, Nativity, Christmas season, Christmastide, Christmastime, yuletide, Advent.

Z

z or **Z** (zē; *Brit* zed) ***n.***, *pl.* **z's, Z's** the 26th and last letter of the English alphabet

zaf·tig (zäf′tig) ***adj.*** ⟦< Yiddish *zaft,* juice⟧ [Slang] having a full, shapely figure: said of a woman

Za·ire or **Za·ïre** (zä ir′) **1** CONGO (River) **2** *former name for Democratic Republic of the Congo*: see CONGO

Zam·bi·a (zam′bē ə) country in S Africa: 290,586 sq. mi.; pop. 7,818,000

za·ny (zā′nē) ***n.***, *pl.* **-nies** ⟦< It dial. *zanni,* < *Giovanni,* John⟧ a silly or foolish person —***adj.*** **-ni·er, -ni·est** foolish or crazy —**za′ni·ness** ***n.***

Zan·zi·bar (zan′zə bär′) island off the E coast of Africa: part of Tanzania

zap (zap) ***vt.***, ***vi.*** **zapped, zap′ping** ⟦echoic⟧ [Slang] to move, strike, stun, kill, etc. suddenly and with great speed and force —***interj.*** used to signify sudden, swift action or change

zeal (zēl) ***n.*** ⟦< Gr *zēlos*⟧ strong interest or devotion; intense enthusiasm; fervor

zeal·ot (zel′ət) ***n.*** one who shows zeal, esp. fanatic zeal

zeal·ous (zel′əs) ***adj.*** of or showing zeal; fervent —**zeal′ous·ly** ***adv.*** —**zeal′ous·ness** ***n.***

ze·bra (zē′brə) ***n.*** ⟦Port⟧ an African mammal related to the horse and having dark stripes on a white or tawny body

ze·bu (zē′byōō′) ***n.*** ⟦Fr *zébu* < ?⟧ a domesticated ox of Asia and Africa

zed (zed) ***n.*** ⟦< Gr *zēta*⟧ [Brit.] the letter Z, z

zeit·geist (tsīt′gīst′) ***n.*** ⟦Ger, time spirit⟧ the trend of thought and feeling in a period

Zen (zen) ***n.*** ⟦Jpn ult. < Sans *dhyāna,* thinking⟧ a variety of Buddhism in which enlightenment is sought through introspection and intuition

ze·nith (zē′nith) ***n.*** ⟦ult. < L *semita,* path⟧ **1** the point in the sky directly overhead **2** the highest point

zeph·yr (zef′ər) ***n.*** ⟦< Gr *zephyros*⟧ a breeze

zep·pe·lin (zep′ə lin, zep′lin) ***n.*** ⟦after Count F. von *Zeppelin* (1838-1917), its Ger designer⟧ [*often* **Z-**] a type of rigid airship designed around 1900

ze·ro (zir′ō, zē′rō) ***n.***, *pl.* **-ros** or **-roes** ⟦< Ar *ṣifr,* cipher⟧ **1** the symbol 0, representing the absence of any quantity or magnitude; cipher; naught **2** the point, marked 0, from which quantities are reckoned on a graduated scale **3** nothing **4** the lowest point —***adj.*** of or at zero —**zero in on** to concentrate attention on; focus on

zero hour **1** the time set for beginning an attack, etc. **2** any crucial moment

zero (population) growth a condition of equilibrium in a given population, in which the birthrate equals the death rate

ze′ro-sum′ (-sum′) ***adj.*** of or being a situation in which a gain for one must result in a loss for another or others

zest (zest) ***n.*** ⟦Fr *zeste,* orange peel⟧ **1** a thin piece of orange or lemon peel used as flavoring **2** stimulating quality **3** keen enjoyment [*a zest* for life] —**zest′ful** ***adj.***

ze·ta (zāt′ə) ***n.*** the sixth letter of the Greek alphabet (Z, ζ)

Zeus (zōōs, zyōōs) ***n.*** *Gr. Myth.* the chief deity

zig·gu·rat (zig′oo rat′) ***n.*** ⟦< Assyrian *ziqqurratu*⟧ an ancient Assyrian or Babylonian temple tower in the form of a terraced pyramid

zig·zag (zig′zag′) ***n.*** ⟦Fr⟧ **1** a series of short, sharp angles in alternate directions **2** a design, path, etc. in this form —***adj.*** having the form of a zigzag —***adv.*** in a zigzag course —***vt.***, ***vi.*** **-zagged′, -zag′ging** to form or move in a zigzag

zilch (zilch) ***n.*** ⟦nonsense syllable⟧ [Slang] nothing; zero

zil·lion (zil′yən) ***n.*** ⟦< MILLION⟧ [Inf.] a very large, indefinite number

Zim·ba·bwe (zim bäb′wā′) country in S Africa, north of South Africa: 150,872 sq. mi.; pop. 10,402,000

zinc (ziŋk) ***n.*** ⟦Ger *zink*⟧ a bluish-white, metallic chemical element, used in alloys, as a protective coating for iron, etc.

zinc oxide a white powder used in making rubber articles, cosmetics, ointments, etc.

zin·fan·del (zin′fən del′) ***n.*** ⟦< ?⟧ a dry red wine made chiefly in California

zing (ziŋ) ***n.*** ⟦echoic⟧ [Slang] **1** a shrill, high-pitched sound, as of something moving fast **2** zest, vigor, etc.

zing′er ***n.*** [Slang] **1** a clever, witty remark **2** a sharp, usually critical remark

zin·ni·a (zin′ē ə, zin′yə) ***n.*** ⟦after J. G. *Zinn* (1727-59), Ger botanist⟧ a plant having colorful composite flowers

Zi·on[1] (zī′ən) ***n.*** ⟦< fol.⟧ **1** the Jewish people **2** heaven

Zi·on[2] (zī′ən) **1** a hill in Jerusalem, site of Solomon's Temple **2** Jerusalem **3** Israel

Zi′on·ism′ ***n.*** a movement formerly for reestablishing, now for supporting, the state of Israel —**Zi′on·ist** ***n.***, ***adj.***

zip (zip) ***n.*** ⟦echoic⟧ **1** a short, sharp hissing or whizzing sound **2** [Inf.] energy; vigor —***vi.*** **zipped, zip′ping** **1** to make, or move with, a zip **2** [Inf.] to move with speed —***vt.*** to fasten with a zipper

ZIP Code (zip) ⟦*Z(one) I(mprovement) P(lan)*⟧ *trademark for* a system of code numbers assigned by the postal service: each code designates a delivery area —[*usually* **zip code**] such a code number, containing five or nine digits

zip·per (zip′ər) ***n.*** a device used to fasten and unfasten two edges of material, as on clothing: it consists of two rows of interlocking tabs worked by a sliding part

zip′py ***adj.*** **-pi·er, -pi·est** [Inf.] full of energy; brisk

zir·con (zur′kän′) ***n.*** ⟦ult. < Pers *zar,* gold⟧ a crystalline silicate mineral, used as a gem

zir·co·ni·um (zər kō′nē əm) ***n.*** a ductile, metallic chemical element used in alloys, ceramics, etc.

zit (zit) ***n.*** [Slang] a pimple, esp. one on the face

zith·er (zith′ər, zith′-) ***n.*** ⟦< Gr *kithara,* lute⟧ any of various musical instruments with strings stretched across a flat soundboard and plucked, bowed, struck with mallets, etc., as the dulcimer

zi·ti (zē′tē) ***n.*** ⟦It⟧ pasta in the shape of tubes

Zn *Chem. symbol for* zinc

zo·di·ac (zō′dē ak′) ***n.*** ⟦< Gr *zōdiakos* (*kyklos*), (circle) of animals⟧ **1** an imaginary belt across the sky extending on either side of the apparent path of the sun and divided into twelve equal parts, or signs, named for constellations **2** a diagram representing this —**zo·di′a·cal** (-dī′ə kəl) ***adj.***

THESAURUS

zeal ***n.*** **1** [Enthusiasm] ardor, fervor, eagerness. **2** [Industry] earnestness, hustle, hustling, bustle, bustling, intensity, industry, willingness, inclination, application, determination, promptitude, dispatch, diligence, perseverance, intentness, assiduity, readiness, aptitude, enterprise, initiative, push*, stick-to-itiveness*; see also ATTENTION, CARE 1, COOPERATION.—*Ant.* IDLENESS, slackness, indolence.

zealot ***n.*** partisan, fan, bigot, fanatic, lobbyist, devotee, enthusiast, dogmatist, opinionist, missionary, fighter, cultist, follower, disciple, true believer, propagandist, bitter-ender*, crank*, addict, bug*, faddist, fiend*.

zealous ***a.*** fervent, earnest, intense, fanatical, industrious, diligent, intent, dogmatic, devoted, ardent; see also ENTHUSIASTIC.

zealously ***a.*** with zeal, assiduously, fiercely; see INDUSTRIOUSLY, VIGOROUSLY.

zenith ***n.*** top, pinnacle, summit, acme, apogee, culmination, highest point, apex, tip, crest, cap, crown, peak.

zero ***n.*** **1** [A cipher] naught, nothing, nadir, love, below freezing, the lowest point, goose egg*, nix*, zip*, zilch*, *nada* (Spanish), *bupkes* (Yiddish). **2** [Nothing] nullity, oblivion, void; see BLANK 1.

zest ***n.*** **1** [Relish] gusto, enjoyment, pleasure; see HAPPINESS. **2** [Savor] taste, tang, piquancy, spice, bite, nip, pungency, punch, snap, ginger, kick, guts*, body; see also FLAVOR.

zigzag ***a.*** oblique, inclined, sloping, awry, crooked, sinuous, twisted, askew, transverse, diagonal, curved, bent, crinkled, serrated, jagged, straggling, meandering, devious, erratic, rambling, oscillating, fluctuating, waggling, undulatory, vibratory, indirect, spiral, tortuous; see also ANGULAR, IRREGULAR 4.—*Ant.* STRAIGHT, parallel, undeviating.

zip* ***n.*** energy, vigor, vim; see STRENGTH.

zip* ***v.*** run, dash, rush; see RUN 2, HURRY.

zodiac ***n.*** celestial meridian, signs of the zodiac, sky signs, groups of stars, constellations; see also PLANET, STAR 1. *The twelve signs of the zodiac are as follows:* Aquarius or the Water Bearer, Pisces or the Fish, Aries or the Ram, Taurus or the Bull, Gemini or the Twins, Cancer or the Crab, Leo or the Lion, Virgo or the Virgin, Libra or the Scales, Scorpio or the Scorpion, Sagittarius or the Archer, Capricorn or the Goat.

zom·bie (zäm′bē) ***n.*** ⟦of Afr orig.⟧ **1** in folklore, an animated corpse **2** [Slang] a person who is listless, machine-like, etc. Also **zom′bi**

zone (zōn) ***n.*** ⟦Fr < Gr *zōnē*⟧ **1** an encircling band, stripe, etc. **2** any of the five great latitudinal divisions of the earth's surface: see TORRID ZONE, TEMPERATE ZONE, and FRIGID ZONE **3** any area with reference to a specified use or restriction *[*a canal *zone*, war *zone]* —***vt.*** **zoned**, **zon′ing** to mark off into zones —**in the** (or **a**) **zone** [Inf.] in a state producing high achievement, seemingly beyond explanation —**zon′al** ***adj.***

zonked (zôŋkt, zäŋkt) ***adj.*** [Slang] **1** highly intoxicated or under the influence of a drug **2** exhausted

zoo (zo͞o) ***n.*** ⟦< *zoo(logical garden)*⟧ **1** a place where wild animals are kept for public showing **2** [Slang] a place of confusion, disorder, etc.

zoo- ⟦< Gr *zōion*, animal⟧ *combining form* animal(s) *[zoology]*

zo·ol·o·gy (zō äl′ə jē) ***n.*** ⟦ModL *zoologia*: see ZOO- & -LOGY⟧ the science that deals with animals and animal life —**zo′o·log′i·cal** (-ə läj′i kəl) ***adj.*** —**zo·ol′o·gist** ***n.***

zoom (zo͞om) ***vi.*** ⟦echoic⟧ **1** to make a loud, low-pitched, buzzing sound **2** to climb in an airplane suddenly and sharply **3** to move speedily upward or forward **4** to focus with a zoom lens —***vt.*** to cause to zoom —***n.*** a zooming

zoom lens a system of lenses, as in a film or TV camera, that can be rapidly adjusted for close-up or distant shots while keeping the image in focus

zo·o·phyte (zō′ə fīt′) ***n.*** ⟦ult. < Gr *zōion*, an animal + *phyton*, a plant⟧ any animal, as a coral or sponge, that looks and grows somewhat like a plant —**zo′o·phyt′ic** (-fit′ik) ***adj.***

Zo·ro·as·ter (zō′rō as′tər) *c.* 6th or 7th c. B.C.; Pers. founder of Zoroastrianism

Zo·ro·as·tri·an·ism (zō′rō as′trē ən iz′əm) ***n.*** the religion of the ancient Persians before Islam

Zr *Chem. symbol for* zirconium

zuc·chi·ni (zo͞o kē′nē) ***n.***, *pl.* **-ni** or **-nis** ⟦It⟧ a summer squash that looks like a cucumber

Zu·lu (zo͞o′lo͞o) ***n.*** **1** *pl.* **-lus** or **-lu** a member of a people living in South Africa **2** the language of this people —***adj.*** of the Zulus or their language, etc.

Zu·ni (zo͞o′nē) ***n.*** **1** *pl.* **-nis** or **-ni** a member of a pueblo-dwelling North American Indian people of W New Mexico **2** the language of this people Also, formerly, **Zu·ñi** (zo͞on′yē)

Zur·ich (zoor′ik) city in N Switzerland: pop. 353,000

zwie·back (swē′bak′, swī′-) ***n.*** ⟦Ger < *zwie-*, twice + *backen*, to bake⟧ a kind of biscuit that is sliced and toasted after baking

zy·de·co (zī′də kō′) ***n.*** ⟦< ?⟧ a heavily syncopated dance music of S Louisiana, containing elements of blues, white Cajun music, etc.

zy·gote (zī′gōt′) ***n.*** ⟦< Gr *zygon*, a yoke⟧ a cell formed by the union of male and female gametes

zymo- ⟦< Gr *zymē*, a leaven⟧ *combining form* fermentation: also **zym-**

zy·mur·gy (zī′mər jē) ***n.*** ⟦prec. + -URGY⟧ the chemistry of fermentation, as applied in brewing, etc.

THESAURUS

zone ***n.*** **1** [A band] circuit, meridian, latitude; see BAND 1, STRIPE. **2** [An area] region, district, territory; traffic, building, danger, quiet, school, hospital, parking, etc. zone; Frigid, Temperate, Torrid Zone; see also PLACE 3, POSITION 1.

zoo ***n.*** menagerie, zoological garden, terrarium, aquarium, aviary.

zoological ***a.*** animal, zoologic, marsupial, mammalian, mammalogical, ornithological, herpetological, ichthyological, echinological, conchological, entomological, arachnological, crustaceological; see also ALIVE, BIOLOGICAL.

zoology ***n.*** life science, biological science, natural history; see LIFE 1, SCIENCE.

zoom ***v.*** speed, rush, hum; see CLIMB, HURRY 1, RISE 1.

WEIGHTS AND MEASURES

Linear

12 inches	=	1 foot
3 feet	=	1 yard
5.5 yards	=	1 rod
40 rods	=	1 furlong
8 furlongs	=	1 mile

Liquid

16 ounces	=	1 pint
2 pints	=	1 quart
4 quarts	=	1 gallon
31.5 gallons	=	1 barrel
2 barrels	=	1 hogshead

Metric Equivalents

1 inch	=	2.5400 centimeters
1 foot	=	0.3048 meter
1 yard	=	0.9144 meter
1 mile	=	1.6093 kilometers
1 centimeter	=	0.3937 inch
1 meter	=	39.3701 inches
1 kilometer	=	0.6214 mile
1 quart (dry)	=	1.1012 liters
1 quart (liquid)	=	0.9464 liter
1 gallon	=	3.7854 liters
1 liter	=	0.9081 dry quart
1 liter	=	1.0567 liquid quarts

Square

144 sq. inches	=	1 sq. foot
9 sq. feet	=	1 sq. yard
30.25 sq. yards	=	1 sq. rod
160 sq. rods	=	1 acre
640 acres	=	1 sq. mile

Circular

60 seconds	=	1 minute
60 minutes	=	1 degree
360 degrees	=	1 circle

Metric Equivalents

1 sq. inch	=	6.4516 sq. centimeters
1 sq. foot	=	929.0304 sq. centimeters
1 sq. mile	=	2.590 sq. kilometers
1 sq. centimeter	=	0.155 sq. inch
1 sq. meter	=	1.196 sq. yards
1 sq. kilometer	=	0.3861 sq. mile

Cubic

1,728 cu. inches	=	1 cu. foot
27 cu. feet	=	1 cu. yard
128 cu. feet	=	1 cord (wood)

Dry

2 pints	=	1 quart
8 quarts	=	1 peck
4 pecks	=	1 bushel

Metric Equivalents

1 cu. inch	=	16.3871 cu. centimeters
1 cu. inch	=	16.3871 milliliters
1 cu. foot	=	0.0283 cu. meter
1 cu. foot	=	28.3169 liters
1 cu. meter	=	35.3147 cu. feet
1 ounce (avdp.)	=	28.3495 grams
1 pound	=	0.4536 kilogram
1 gram	=	0.0353 ounce
1 kilogram	=	2.2046 pounds
1 ton (2,000 pounds)	=	907.1847 kilograms

Temperature Conversion Formulas

$$°F = 32 + (1.8 \times °C)$$

$$°C = \frac{°F - 32}{1.8}$$

THE INTERNATIONAL SYSTEM OF UNITS (SI)

Any prefix can be combined with any unit; e.g. milli- + ampere = milliampere (m + A = mA); kilo- + gram = kilogram (k + g = kg); mega- + hertz = megahertz (M + Hz = MHz).

SI base units and prefixes

unit	symbol	quantity
ampere	A	electric current
candela	cd	luminous intensity
kelvin	K	thermodynamic temperature
kilogram	kg	mass
meter	m	length
mole	mol	amount of substance
second	s	time

prefix	symbol	multiplier*
yotta-	Y	$\times 10^{24}$
zetta-	Z	$\times 10^{21}$
exa-	E	$\times 10^{18}$
peta-	P	$\times 10^{15}$
tera-	T	$\times 10^{12}$
giga-	G	$\times 10^{9}$
mega-	M	$\times 10^{6}$
kilo-	k	$\times 10^{3}$
hecto-	h	$\times 10^{2}$
deka-; deca-	da	$\times 10$
deci-	d	$\times 10^{-1}$
centi-	c	$\times 10^{-2}$
milli-	m	$\times 10^{-3}$
micro-	μ	$\times 10^{-6}$
nano-	n	$\times 10^{-9}$
pico-	p	$\times 10^{-12}$
femto-	f	$\times 10^{-15}$
atto-	a	$\times 10^{-18}$
zepto-	z	$\times 10^{-21}$
yocto-	y	$\times 10^{-24}$

Common SI derived units with special names

name	symbol	quantity
coulomb	C	electric charge
degree Celsius	°C	temperature (0°C = 273.16 K)
hertz	Hz	frequency
joule	J	energy; work
newton	N	force
ohm	Ω	electric resistance
pascal	Pa	pressure; stress
volt	V	electric potential; EMF
watt	W	power

Other common units used with the SI

name	symbol	quantity
hectare	ha	area (=10,000 m^2 or 2.471 acres)
knot	kn; kt	speed (navigation) (= 1 NM per hour or 1.1508 mph)
liter	l; L	volume; capacity (= 1,000 cm^3)
metric ton	t	mass (= 1,000 kg)
nautical mile (U.S.)	NM	distance (navigation) (= 1.1508 statute miles)
standard atmosphere	atm	atmospheric pressure (= 101,325 Pa)

* $10^2 = 10 \times 10 = 100$; $10^3 = 10 \times 10 \times 10 = 1{,}000$; $10^{-1} = 1/10^1 = 0.1$; $10^{-2} = 1/10^2 = 0.01$
So, 2 km = 2×10^3 meters = 2,000 meters; 2 mm = 2×10^{-3} meter = 0.002 meter.

THE UNITED STATES

State	Capital	Postal Code
Alabama	Montgomery	AL
Alaska	Juneau	AK
Arizona	Phoenix	AZ
Arkansas	Little Rock	AR
California	Sacramento	CA
Colorado	Denver	CO
Connecticut	Hartford	CT
Delaware	Dover	DE
[District of Columbia	—	DC]
Florida	Tallahassee	FL
Georgia	Atlanta	GA
Hawaii	Honolulu	HI
Idaho	Boise	ID
Illinois	Springfield	IL
Indiana	Indianapolis	IN
Iowa	Des Moines	IA
Kansas	Topeka	KS
Kentucky	Frankfort	KY
Louisiana	Baton Rouge	LA
Maine	Augusta	ME
Maryland	Annapolis	MD
Massachusetts	Boston	MA
Michigan	Lansing	MI
Minnesota	St. Paul	MN
Mississippi	Jackson	MS
Missouri	Jefferson City	MO
Montana	Helena	MT
Nebraska	Lincoln	NE
Nevada	Carson City	NV
New Hampshire	Concord	NH
New Jersey	Trenton	NJ
New Mexico	Santa Fe	NM
New York	Albany	NY
North Carolina	Raleigh	NC
North Dakota	Bismarck	ND
Ohio	Columbus	OH
Oklahoma	Oklahoma City	OK
Oregon	Salem	OR
Pennsylvania	Harrisburg	PA
Rhode Island	Providence	RI
South Carolina	Columbia	SC
South Dakota	Pierre	SD
Tennessee	Nashville	TN
Texas	Austin	TX
Utah	Salt Lake City	UT
Vermont	Montpelier	VT
Virginia	Richmond	VA
Washington	Olympia	WA
West Virginia	Charleston	WV
Wisconsin	Madison	WI
Wyoming	Cheyenne	WY

U.S. CITIES BY POPULATION

Rank	City, State	1990 Census Population*
1.	New York, NY	7,323,000
2.	Los Angeles, CA	3,486,000
3.	Chicago, IL	2,784,000
4.	Houston, TX	1,630,000
5.	Philadelphia, PA	1,586,000
6.	San Diego, CA	1,111,000
7.	Detroit, MI	1,028,000
8.	Dallas, TX	1,008,000
9.	Phoenix, AZ	983,000
10.	San Antonio, TX	935,000
11.	San Jose, CA	782,000
12.	Indianapolis, IN	742,000
13.	Baltimore, MD	736,000
14.	San Francisco, CA	724,000
15.	Jacksonville, FL	673,000
16.	Columbus, OH	633,000
17.	Milwaukee, WI	628,000
18.	Memphis, TN	610,000
19.	Washington, DC	607,000
20.	Boston, MA	574,000
21.	Seattle, WA	516,000
22.	El Paso, TX	515,000
23.	Nashville, TN	511,000
24.	Cleveland, OH	506,000
25.	New Orleans, LA	497,000
26.	Denver, CO	468,000
27.	Austin, TX	466,000
28.	Fort Worth, TX	448,000
29.	Oklahoma City, OK	445,000
30.	Portland, OR	439,000
31.	Kansas City, MO	435,000
32.	Long Beach, CA	429,000
33.	Tucson, AZ	405,000
34.	St. Louis, MO	397,000
35.	Charlotte, NC	396,000
36.	Atlanta, GA	394,000
37.	Virginia Beach, VA	393,000
38.	Albuquerque, NM	385,000
39.	Oakland, CA	372,000
40.	Pittsburgh, PA	370,000
41.	Sacramento, CA	369,000
42.	Minneapolis, MN	368,000
43.	Tulsa, OK	367,000
44.	Honolulu, HI	365,000
45.	Cincinnati, OH	364,000
46.	Miami, FL	359,000
47.	Fresno, CA	354,000
48.	Omaha, NE	336,000
49.	Toledo, OH	333,000
50.	Buffalo, NY	328,000

* *rounded to the nearest thousand*

PRESIDENTS OF THE UNITED STATES

Name	Term	Political Party
George Washington	1789–1797	Federalist
John Adams	1797–1801	Federalist
Thomas Jefferson	1801–1809	Democratic-Republican
James Madison	1809–1817	Democratic-Republican
James Monroe	1817–1825	Democratic-Republican
John Quincy Adams	1825–1829	Democratic-Republican
Andrew Jackson	1829–1837	Democratic
Martin Van Buren	1837–1841	Democratic
William H. Harrison	1841	Whig
John Tyler	1841–1845	Whig
James K. Polk	1845–1849	Democratic
Zachary Taylor	1849–1850	Whig
Millard Fillmore	1850–1853	Whig
Franklin Pierce	1853–1857	Democratic
James Buchanan	1857–1861	Democratic
Abraham Lincoln	1861–1865	Republican
Andrew Johnson	1865–1869	Republican
Ulysses S. Grant	1869–1877	Republican
Rutherford B. Hayes	1877–1881	Republican
James A. Garfield	1881	Republican
Chester A. Arthur	1881–1885	Republican
Grover Cleveland	1885–1889	Democratic
Benjamin Harrison	1889–1893	Republican
Grover Cleveland	1893–1897	Democratic
William McKinley	1897–1901	Republican
Theodore Roosevelt	1901–1909	Republican
William H. Taft	1909–1913	Republican
Woodrow Wilson	1913–1921	Democratic
Warren G. Harding	1921–1923	Republican
Calvin Coolidge	1923–1929	Republican
Herbert Hoover	1929–1933	Republican
Franklin D. Roosevelt	1933–1945	Democratic
Harry S Truman	1945–1953	Democratic
Dwight D. Eisenhower	1953–1961	Republican
John F. Kennedy	1961–1963	Democratic
Lyndon B. Johnson	1963–1969	Democratic
Richard M. Nixon	1969–1974	Republican
Gerald R. Ford	1974–1977	Republican
Jimmy Carter	1977–1981	Democratic
Ronald Reagan	1981–1989	Republican
George Bush	1989–1993	Republican
Bill Clinton	1993–2001	Democratic
George W. Bush	2001–	Republican

CANADA

Province or Territory	Capital	Postal Code
Alberta	Edmonton	AB
British Columbia	Victoria	BC
Manitoba	Winnipeg	MB
New Brunswick	Fredericton	NB
Newfoundland	St. John's	NF
Northwest Territories	Yellowknife	NT
Nova Scotia	Halifax	NS
Nunavut	Iqaluit	NU
Ontario	Toronto	ON
Prince Edward Island	Charlottetown	PE
Quebec	Quebec	QC
Saskatchewan	Regina	SK
Yukon Territory	Whitehorse	YT

NATIONS OF THE WORLD

Nation	Capital	Currency
Afghanistan	Kabul	afghani
Albania	Tirana	lek
Algeria	Algiers	dinar
Andorra	Andorra la Vella	*(Fr.) franc; *(Sp.) peseta
Angola	Luanda	kwanza
Antigua and Barbuda	St. John's	dollar[1]
Argentina	Buenos Aires	peso
Armenia	Yerevan	dram
Australia	Canberra	dollar
Austria	Vienna	schilling[3]
Azerbaijan	Baku	manat
Bahamas	Nassau	dollar
Bahrain	Manama	dinar
Bangladesh	Dhaka	taka
Barbados	Bridgetown	dollar
Belarus	Minsk	ruble
Belgium	Brussels	franc[3]
Belize	Belmopan	dollar
Benin	Porto Novo	franc[2]
Bhutan	Thimphu	ngultrum
Bolivia	La Paz; Sucre	boliviano
Bosnia and Herzegovina	Sarajevo	dinar
Botswana	Gaborone	pula
Brazil	Brasília	real
Brunei	Bandar Seri Begawan	dollar
Bulgaria	Sofia	lev
Burkina Faso	Ouagadougou	franc[2]
Burundi	Bujumbura	franc
Cambodia	Phnom Penh	riel
Cameroon	Yaoundé	franc[2]
Canada	Ottawa	dollar
Cape Verde	Praia	escudo

Nation	Capital	Currency
Central African Republic	Bangui	franc[2]
Chad	N'Djamena	franc[2]
Chile	Santiago	peso
China	Beijing	yuan
Colombia	Bogotá	peso
Comoros	Moroni	franc
Congo, Democratic Republic of the	Kinshasa	franc
Congo, Republic of the	Brazzaville	franc[2]
Costa Rica	San José	colón
Croatia	Zagreb	kuna
Cuba	Havana	peso
Cyprus	Nicosia	pound
Czech Republic	Prague	koruna
Denmark	Copenhagen	krone
Djibouti	Djibouti	franc
Dominica	Roseau	dollar[1]
Dominican Republic	Santo Domingo	peso
Ecuador	Quito	**(U.S.)* dollar
Egypt	Cairo	pound
El Salvador	San Salvador	**(U.S.)* dollar
Equatorial Guinea	Malabo	franc[2]
Eritrea	Asmara	nakfa
Estonia	Tallinn	kroon
Ethiopia	Addis Ababa	birr
Fiji	Suva	dollar
Finland	Helsinki	markka[3]
France	Paris	franc[3]
Gabon	Libreville	franc[2]
Gambia	Banjul	dalasi
Georgia	Tbilisi	lari
Germany	Berlin	deutsche mark[3]
Ghana	Accra	cedi
Greece	Athens	drachma[3]
Grenada	St. George's	dollar[1]
Guatemala	Guatemala City	quetzal
Guinea	Conakry	franc
Guinea-Bissau	Bissau	franc[2]
Guyana	Georgetown	dollar
Haiti	Port-au-Prince	gourde
Honduras	Tegucigalpa	lempira
Hungary	Budapest	forint
Iceland	Reykjavík	króna
India	New Delhi	rupee
Indonesia	Jakarta	rupiah
Iran	Tehran	rial
Iraq	Baghdad	dinar
Ireland	Dublin	punt[3]
Israel	Jerusalem	shekel
Italy	Rome	lira[3]
Ivory Coast	Yamoussoukro	franc[2]
Jamaica	Kingston	dollar
Japan	Tokyo	yen
Jordan	Amman	dinar
Kazakhstan	Astana	tenge
Kenya	Nairobi	shilling
Kiribati	Tarawa	**(Austral.)* dollar
Korea, North	Pyongyang	won

Nation	Capital	Currency
Korea, South	Seoul	won
Kuwait	Kuwait	dinar
Kyrgyzstan	Bishkek	som
Laos	Vientiane	kip
Latvia	Riga	lats
Lebanon	Beirut	pound
Lesotho	Maseru	loti
Liberia	Monrovia	dollar
Libya	Tripoli	dinar
Liechtenstein	Vaduz	*(*Swiss*)* franc
Lithuania	Vilnius	litas
Luxembourg	Luxembourg	franc[3]
Macedonia	Skopje	denar
Madagascar	Antananarivo	franc
Malawi	Lilongwe	kwacha
Malaysia	Kuala Lumpur	ringgit
Maldives	Malé	rufiyaa
Mali	Bamako	franc[2]
Malta	Valletta	lira
Marshall Islands	Dalap-Uliga-Darrit	*(*U.S.*)* dollar
Mauritania	Nouakchott	ouguiya
Mauritius	Port Louis	rupee
Mexico	Mexico City	peso
Micronesia	Palikir	*(*U.S.*)* dollar
Moldova	Chişinau	leu
Monaco	Monaco	*(*Fr.*)* franc
Mongolia	Ulan Bator	tugrik
Morocco	Rabat	dirham
Mozambique	Maputo	metical
Myanmar	Yangon	kyat
Namibia	Windhoek	dollar
Nauru	—	*(*Austral.*)* dollar
Nepal	Katmandu	rupee
Netherlands	Amsterdam	guilder[3]
New Zealand	Wellington	dollar
Nicaragua	Managua	córdoba
Niger	Niamey	franc[2]
Nigeria	Abuja	naira
Norway	Oslo	krone
Oman	Muscat	rial
Pakistan	Islamabad	rupee
Palau	Koror	*(*U.S.*)* dollar
Panama	Panama City	*(*U.S.*)* dollar
Papua New Guinea	Port Moresby	kina
Paraguay	Asunción	guaraní
Peru	Lima	sol
Philippines	Manila	peso
Poland	Warsaw	złoty
Portugal	Lisbon	escudo[3]
Qatar	Doha	riyal
Romania	Bucharest	leu
Russia	Moscow	ruble
Rwanda	Kigali	franc
Samoa	Apia	tala
San Marino	San Marino	*(*It.*)* lira
São Tomé and Príncipe	São Tomé	dobra
Saudi Arabia	Riyadh	riyal

Nation	Capital	Currency
Senegal	Dakar	franc[2]
Seychelles	Victoria	rupee
Sierra Leone	Freetown	leone
Singapore	Singapore	dollar
Slovakia	Bratislava	koruna
Slovenia	Ljubljana	tolar
Solomon Islands	Honiara	dollar
Somalia	Mogadishu	shilling
South Africa	Pretoria	rand
Spain	Madrid	peseta[3]
Sri Lanka	Colombo	rupee
St. Kitts and Nevis	Basseterre	dollar[1]
St. Lucia	Castries	dollar[1]
St. Vincent and the Grenadines	Kingstown	dollar[1]
Sudan	Khartoum	dinar
Suriname	Paramaribo	guilder
Swaziland	Mbabane	lilangeni
Sweden	Stockholm	krona
Switzerland	Bern	franc
Syria	Damascus	pound
Taiwan	Taipei	dollar
Tajikistan	Dushanbe	ruble
Tanzania	Dodoma	shilling
Thailand	Bangkok	baht
Togo	Lomé	franc[2]
Tonga	Nukualofa	pa'anga
Trinidad and Tobago	Port-of-Spain	dollar
Tunisia	Tunis	dinar
Turkey	Ankara	lira
Turkmenistan	Ashgabat	manat
Tuvalu	Fongafale	*(*Austral.*) dollar
Uganda	Kampala	shilling
Ukraine	Kiev	hryvnia
United Arab Emirates	Abu Dhabi	dirham
United Kingdom	London	pound
United States	Washington, D.C.	dollar
Uruguay	Montevideo	peso
Uzbekistan	Tashkent	som
Vanuatu	Vila	vatu
Vatican City	—	*(*It.*) lira
Venezuela	Caracas	bolívar
Vietnam	Hanoi	dong
Yemen	Sana	rial
Yugoslavia	Belgrade	dinar
Zambia	Lusaka	kwacha
Zimbabwe	Harare	dollar

* Indicates the use of the currency of another country, as specified.

1 Indicates the use of the currency of the Organization of Eastern Caribbean States, an organization of nine Caribbean states.

2 Indicates the use of the currency of the African Financial Community, an organization of fourteen African countries.

3 Indicates ongoing phased conversion to the euro, the basic monetary unit of the European Union.